The Encyclopedia of New York City

The Encyclopedia

of New York City

Edited by KENNETH T. JACKSON

YALE UNIVERSITY PRESS *New Haven & London*

THE NEW-YORK HISTORICAL SOCIETY *New York*

Designed by Richard Hendel.
Set in Monotype Garamond by The Composing Room of Michigan, Inc., Grand Rapids, Michigan.
Printed and bound in the United States of America by R. R. Donnelley & Sons Company

Library of Congress Cataloguing-in-Publication Data

The encyclopedia of New York City / edited by Kenneth T. Jackson.
p. cm.
Includes index.
ISBN 0-300-05536-6 (hc : alk. paper)
1. New York (N.Y.)—Encyclopedias. I. Jackson, Kenneth T.
F128.3.E75 1995
974.7′1′003—dc20 95-2811
CIP

A catalogue record of this book is available from the British Library.

The paper in this book meets the guidelines for permanence and durability of the Committee on Production Guidelines for Book Longevity of the Council on Library Resources.

10 9 8 7 6 5 4 3

Major support for
The Encyclopedia of New York City
was provided by

The National Endowment
for the Humanities

McGraw–Hill, Inc.

Frederick P., Daniel, and
Elihu Rose

The Susan and Elihu Rose
Foundation

Additional support was received from

The Lucius N. Littauer Foundation
The Frederick W. Richmond Foundation
The Frances and Benjamin Benenson Foundation
The Charles H. Revson Foundation
The Weiler–Arnow Investment Company
The Josiah Macy, Jr. Foundation
The J. M. Kaplan Fund
The Horace W. Goldsmith Foundation
Citicorp
The Consolidated Edison Company of New York
The Durst Foundation
The J. Aron Charitable Foundation
The New York Times Company Foundation
The Pattee Charitable Lead Trust
The Philip Morris Companies
The Jill and Marshall Rose Foundation
The Robert Schalkenbach Foundation
The Seth Sprague Charitable and Educational Foundation
The Lawrence A. Wien Foundation
Chase Manhattan Bank
The Vincent Astor Foundation
The Young & Rubicam Foundation
Lester Wunderman
The Bernhill Fund
Sidney J. Bernstein
Brooklyn Union Gas
Ann L. and Lawrence B. Buttenwieser
Brown, Harris, Stevens
The Edison Parking Corporation
The Edward S. Gordon Company
Home Life Insurance Company
HRO International
Kenneth T. and Barbara B. Jackson
Lintas: New York
Maidenform Inc.
Marine Midland Bank
The Port Authority of New York and New Jersey
Proskauer Rose Goetz & Mendelsohn
Sheldon H. Solow
Silverstein Properties
J. Walter Thompson USA
The Zeckendorf Company
Abrams Benisch Riker
Tishman Speyer Properties
The Bronx County Historical Society
History of New York City Project, Inc.
Joel and Bonnie Fox Schwartz

PROJECT STAFF

Executive Editor	Fred Kameny	
Sponsoring Editor	Edward Tripp	
Managing Editors	Peter Eisenstadt (1990–92) Deborah S. Gardner (1988–90)	
Deputy Managing Editors	Alana J. Erickson Walter Friedman	
Senior Project Editor	James Bradley	
Project Editors	Eric Wm. Allison Kerry Candaele Eileen K. Cheng Marc Ferris Nancy Flood Janet Frankston Shan Jayakumar Erica Judge Kevin Kenny Laura Lewison Joseph S. Lieber Chad Ludington Melissa M. Merritt	Ruth Morris Becky Nicolaides Edward T. O'Donnell Sandra Opdycke Grai St. Clair Rice Cara Sadownick Allen J. Share Joanna Usher Silver Jeff Sklansky Robert W. Snyder Robert Sanger Steel Naomi Wax
Senior Illustrations Editor	Grai St. Clair Rice	
Illustrations Editors	Deborah S. Gardner Melissa M. Merritt	
Associate Illustrations Editor	Dale L. Neighbors	
Senior Copy Editor	Pamela H. Sturner	
Copy Editors	Amy Balser William J. Moses Shawn Simmons	
Chief Proofreader	Lawrence Kenney	
Production Controller	Cele Syrotiak	

PREFACE

How does one take the measure of New York City? Even casual visitors can see and feel and sense that it is different from other places. Its buildings are bigger, its pace quicker, its streets noisier, and its sidewalks more crowded than those of other communities. It often overwhelms tourists from Europe and Asia, who are typically told that it is the least American of cities and that they must travel far from New York City if they are to understand and know the United States.

In this case the stereotype is correct: New York City is different. For one thing, it is older than virtually every other American city. Boston, Philadelphia, Charleston, Savannah, Newport, and Williamsburg come to mind when one thinks of historic places, yet New York City is older than all of them. As for the settlements that were already established when Dutch traders first landed on Manhattan – St. Augustine, Jamestown, Fort St. George, Hampton, and Santa Fe – Jamestown and Fort St. George disappeared and the other three failed to prosper for the first three centuries of their existence.

New York City is also unusual because of its extreme density. In 1900 the Lower East Side was the most densely inhabited place in the world. As late as 1960 Manhattan contained half of all the world's skyscrapers of fifty stories or more. And the city's midtown office district has more office space per acre than any other central business district on earth; in fact only lower Manhattan and the Chicago Loop are even half as dense. Suburbanization has greatly reduced the worst overcrowding in America, and New York City is now less densely settled than Hong Kong, Tokyo, and Calcutta, among other places. But it remains far and away more crowded than any other city in the United States, with twice the population density of Chicago, and many times the density of Houston and Los Angeles.

Finally, New York City has long been unusual because of its sheer size. Even before 1775, when its population was never more than 25,000, it ranked with Boston, Philadelphia, Charleston, and Newport as one of the five leading cities in the colonies. It surpassed Philadelphia by 1810 to become the largest city in the United States, and Mexico City by 1830 to become the largest in the western hemisphere. By 1900 it was the second-largest city in the world (after London), and by 1930 the largest. It remains the only American municipality ever to exceed four million residents. And in 1990 each of its five boroughs was large enough to have been an important city in its own right, with Queens having more inhabitants than Philadelphia, Brooklyn several times as many as Boston and San Francisco, the Bronx far more than Detroit, and Staten Island more than St. Louis.

Figures for the metropolitan area are even more impressive. When the Regional Plan Association in 1930 defined the metropolitan region as comprising the city and thirty-one adjacent counties in New York, New Jersey, and Connecticut, the region was already the first in the history of the world to exceed ten million residents, and in 1970 it became the first to exceed fifteen million. Although eventually surpassed by Tokyo and Mexico City, the New York metropolitan region still counted 19.3 million persons in 1990, or almost as many as lived in all the cities of the earth combined in 1700.

The very vastness of New York City has discouraged historians and other researchers from trying to encompass it in a single volume. Although well over ten thousand books have already been written about the city, with another hundred or so appearing annually by the 1990s, New York City has not received the scholarly attention of Chicago or Boston. Only a few persons have considered the city in its entirety, notably Robert A. Caro in *The Power Broker: Robert Moses and the Fall of New York* (1974), Robert A. M. Stern in his three volumes on architecture (1983–95), and Wallace S. Sayre and Harold Kaufman in *Governing New York City: Politics in the Metropolis* (1960). Every scholar and every general reader is indebted to I. N. Phelps Stokes. His six-volume work

The Iconography of Manhattan Island, 1498–1909, published between 1915 and 1928, remains a model of careful research and appropriate illustration. Those fortunate few who own the complete set possess what is probably the greatest single reference work about any American city. But Phelps Stokes concentrated on the natural environment. He did not write about neighborhoods or buildings or streets or fires or institutions. Moreover the scope of his achievement did not extend far into the twentieth century.

Indeed there has never been a reference book about New York City comparable to this encyclopedia. There have been guidebooks since the nineteenth century, but none of the same range and depth. There has been no place where the reader could quickly and efficiently answer questions both basic and arcane:

Was William M. Tweed ever mayor of New York City?
Who was Major Deegan?
When did the Tony Awards begin?
When was the nickel fare abandoned?
What and where was Tin Pan Alley?
Where is Dutch Hill?
How has the homicide rate in New York City changed since 1940?
Who were the New York Highlanders, and where did they play?
What was Murder Incorporated?
What was Tammany Hall?
How long is the Brooklyn Bridge?
Where was Swing Street?
Was Seth Low the mayor of New York City, Brooklyn, or both?
Who was called the Father of Greater New York?
How old is Peter Luger's Steak House?
What is the Panorama of New York City?
What were the greatest fires in the history of New York City?
What was the Great Fire?
What were the Draft Riots?
Where is the Hall of Fame for Great Americans?
What is an egg cream?
Where is Hell's Kitchen?

The Encyclopedia of New York City answers these questions and thousands of others. There is an entry on espionage and another on the famous murder in 1836 of a prostitute, Helen Jewett. Other entries recount the tragedy of the *General Slocum*, the story of a once-famous and now defunct restaurant called Lundy's in Sheepshead Bay, and the search for Son of Sam. Not every reader will want to know the name of the borough president of the Bronx in 1937, but the reader who does will now know where to turn.

The need for such an encyclopedia, one that both researchers and general readers would find useful, was first recognized by Edward Robb Ellis, a newspaperman and the author of *The Epic of New York City* (1966), who about 1970 began to compile an encyclopedia of New York City singlehandedly. But the task was too overwhelming for any one person, however talented and diligent, and Ellis had essentially abandoned his goal by 1980. Unaware of Ellis's ambition, or of the *Encyclopedia of Cleveland History* then under preparation by David Van Tassel and a team at Case Western Reserve University, Edward Tripp conceived of this encyclopedia in 1982. A longtime New Yorker who had worked for seventeen years in reference publishing in Manhattan before joining Yale University

Press in 1970, he persuaded John G. Ryden, director of the press, to support the project, and in 1983 he chose its editor. An advisory committee was formed as a result of many meetings held during the ensuing months. Although progress was slow for several years, the enthusiasm of a small group of supporters, notably Caro, Frank Vos, Richard C. Wade, Robert F. Fox Jr., and Ann L. Buttenwieser, reassured both editor and publisher even as early requests for federal funds were denied. Out of these preliminary meetings came the decision to hold the book to one volume and to seek most of the financial support from the private sector. In 1986 the New-York Historical Society agreed to co-publish the encyclopedia with Yale University Press. Nearly a decade later, when some observers are calling into question the relevance of the society, it bears mentioning that without its participation this encyclopedia could never have been realized. The project took a large step forward in 1987, when it received a generous challenge grant from an anonymous donor.

In 1988, after receiving support from the National Endowment for the Humanities, the McGraw–Hill Foundation, and the Rose family, the encyclopedia opened an office in the gallery above the library at the New-York Historical Society. The first tasks were to name a managing editor – a role ably filled by Deborah S. Gardner – and nearly seventy associate editors charged with overseeing individual topics. The project was fortunate in being able to draw on many of the finest scholars in the nation for this purpose, among them David Rosner on health and medicine, Eugenie Ladner Birch on urban planning, Patricia U. Bonomi on the colonial period, Lynn Garafola on dance, Timothy J. Gilfoyle on crime and prostitution, Larry A. Greene on Harlem, Carol Groneman and Virginia Sánchez Korrol on immigration, Jeffrey S. Gurock on Jews, Gary D. Hermalyn on the Bronx, Margaret Latimer on Brooklyn, Richard K. Lieberman and Jon A. Peterson on Queens, Naomi Rosenblum on photography, Charles L. Sachs on Staten Island, Emmanuel Tobier on the economy, Harold Wechsler on education, and Sean Wilentz on labor. In addition to offering expert guidance these editors were able to recruit other leading scholars to write entries, such as Stuart Bruchey on the American Stock Exchange, Edward Countryman on the American Revolution, Henry Feingold on the American Jewish Committee, Raymond D. Horton on the budget, G. Thomas Tanselle on printing, Martin E. Marty on religion, Arnold Rampersad on the Harlem Renaissance, Kathryn Kish Sklar on Catharine Beecher, and Samuel Walker on the American Civil Liberties Union.

The editors made several decisions that guided work on the encyclopedia over the years. First, the encyclopedia would range chronologically from prehistory to the present and would treat the natural environment. Thus there are entries on the earliest human inhabitants of what is now New York City, as well as on geological features, flora, and fauna. Second, it would cover the entire area now making up the five boroughs, most of which did not become part of New York City until 1898. Thus the entry on Brooklyn discusses its history during the eighteenth and nineteenth centuries, when it was successively a separate settlement, village, and city. Third, the editors and contributors would make a concerted effort to include groups that had long been neglected in scholarly and popular writings, namely women, African–Americans, Latinos, and immigrants. Even so the final product includes more white men than any other group, simply because the encyclopedia, like any historical work, must in the end represent its subject as it has been and not as it should have been.

Ultimately the encyclopedia came to include 4300 entries by 680 authors. They range from six thousand words about architecture to twenty-six words about Hallett's Cove. Because of the limitations of space most entries are brief, but still the encyclopedia could not include every important person or building or church or school. Winnowing down lists of suggested entries was a time-consuming and frustrating task.

There were other challenges as well. Originally conceived on a modest scale, the encyclopedia steadily evolved into a more ambitious work, as the addition or expansion of one subject would invariably justify the addition or expansion of others. That this growth could be sustained is a tribute to the many contributors, who worked tirelessly to see the book through to completion. James E. Mooney, former head librarian of the New-York Historical Society, merits special mention for having written 212 entries, considerably more than anyone else. The only point when the encyclopedia showed any sign that it might decrease in scope was when one borough threatened to change the very definition of New York City by seceding.

Although unique among reference works because of its subject, the encyclopedia adheres to principles of reference publishing that have evolved over hundreds of years. Its aim is above all to provide basic information, and it is a place to begin research, not end it: those who seek further information are referred to other sources through bibliographic citations. The interpretations contained in the entries are those of the individual authors rather than the editors, and these interpretations will sometimes differ. (Compare, for example, the entry on Mayor Robert F. Wagner and the entry on government and politics with regard to Wagner's decision not to seek a fourth term.) Like other reference books the encyclopedia is a secondary rather than a primary source, a work that synthesizes rather than extends existing scholarship. But it also includes material that has never before been published or compiled. Vincent Seyfried's organizational charts on railroads, for example, are unprecedented, as are Alana J. Erickson's tables of newspapers and Kenneth R. Cobb's list of ticker-tape parades. Other tables contain information that is a matter of public record but is not easy to find: such is the case with the election table in the entry on government and politics, which gives the local vote for all major candidates in presidential elections from 1836 to 1992.

Whether the entries contain new scholarship or simply summarize what is already known, the aim is that all information be accessible and easy to use, and for this reason the encyclopedia is alphabetically arranged. There have been many attempts to organize reference books along thematic lines, sometimes successfully, but the scale and complexity of this encyclopedia would have made such an arrangement impractical. Some of the entries are overviews of large topics, like commercial banking, filmmaking, and sports; others are on important individuals and institutions. Several hundred of the entries have illustrations, which have been carefully chosen and in many cases have not been previously published. The entries are also supplemented by nearly a hundred tables, which represent a departure from the principle of selectivity that informs the encyclopedia as a whole. Only figures of the first rank are the subject of individual entries, but the tables include the names of all school superintendents, fire commissioners, borough presidents, and mayors, whether their impact was profound or negligible. The index to the encyclopedia includes the name of virtually every person in the book who is not the subject of a separate entry.

New York City has never been a static entity, and neither is the encyclopedia. Future editions are planned to bring the book up to date and, inevitably, enlarge it. And although every one of the 1.3 million words in this book has been read by the editor in chief, the executive editor, and one or more copy editors and fact checkers (and usually by a managing editor and an associate editor as well), the encyclopedia is certain to contain errors. The editor accepts responsibility for them all and asks that corrections and suggestions be sent to him at the Department of History, Columbia University, New York, New York 10027.

ACKNOWLEDGMENTS

Because this encyclopedia involved more than a thousand people over a period of more than ten years, it is obviously impossible to thank everyone whose efforts contributed to its completion. Several individuals, however, were crucial to the enterprise. Edward Tripp conceived this project at Yale University Press in 1982, supported it for many years when progress was slow, and continued to offer invaluable advice after his retirement in 1990. Robert A. Caro, Kenneth Conboy, Robert Fox Jr., Frank Vos, and Richard C. Wade formed the initial support group that encouraged Yale University Press to go forward. Albert L. Key raised the money that allowed the project office to open. My fellow historian Elihu Rose, the first and only head of the advisory board, provided leadership, enthusiasm, knowledge, and friendship for these many years. The National Endowment for the Humanities, McGraw–Hill Inc., and the Rose family made substantial contributions to underwrite the research, as did more than fifty other persons and foundations.

Of the archivists and librarians who helped our staff and contributors, Kenneth R. Cobb deserves special mention. He knows local records better than anyone else, and from his post at the archives of the City of New York he has won deserved praise for his courtesy and judgment. John Tauranac drew most of the maps, based on many hours of research by Frank Vardy of the New York City Planning Department and Gary D. Hermalyn of the Bronx County Historical Society. The Identity Map Company kindly contributed maps of Greenwich Village, lower Manhattan, and Times Square. Arnold Markoe of Brooklyn College generously reviewed hundreds of entries and made many improvements, while Nathan Kantrowitz of the New York City Planning Department painstakingly checked tables and charts for accuracy. We also thank Charlotta DeFillo and Barnett Shepherd of the Staten Island Historical Society; Wayne Forman of the New York Public Library; Judy Walsh of the Brooklyn Public Library; Marguerite Lavan and Tony Pisan of the Museum of the City of New York; Barbara Natanson and staff of the Prints and Photographs Division of the Library of Congress; Norma McCormick of the AT&T Archives; the Schomburg Center for Research in Black Culture; Richard Buck and his staff at the New York Public Library for the Performing Arts at Lincoln Center; Clair Lamers, Irene Tichenor, and David Kahn at the Brooklyn Historical Society; Anita Duquette at the Whitney Museum of American Art; City Lore; the Avery Architectural Library at Columbia University; and Alan C. Solomon, head of reference, and the other reference librarians at Sterling Memorial Library, Yale University. Vincent Seyfried not only wrote several dozen entries but also seemed to know everything about railroads in general and the borough of Queens in particular; he was always willing to share with us his matchless reservoir of information.

At the New-York Historical Society we are particularly indebted to Dale L. Neighbors, curator of photography; Wendy Shadwell, curator of prints; Mary Beth Betts, curator of architecture; and Diana Arecco, coordinator of rights and reproduction. James E. Mooney and Jean Ashton, former directors of the library, went out of their way to help the dozens of encyclopedia researchers who called on their services. We also thank Laird Ogden for technical assistance, Patricia Paladines for curatorial assistance, Gabriela Salazar for technical assistance on architecture, and Glenn Castellano for his help on photographs. Mariam Touba, newspaper librarian; May N. Stone, reference librarian; Annette Blaugrund, senior curator of painting, sculpture, and drawing; and Timothy Anglin Burgard, assistant curator, responded patiently to our requests. Ione Saroyan and the switchboard staff graciously handled thousands of telephone calls to the encyclopedia office. James Bell, Barbara Debs, and Betsy Gotbaum, successive presidents of the New-York Historical Society over the last thirteen years, not only co-sponsored the project but became friends and confidants in the process.

On the encyclopedia staff, special thanks go to Deborah S. Gardner and Peter Eisenstadt, who as managing editors gave shape and coherence to the effort, and to Walter Friedman and Alana J. Erickson, who not only tamed our computers but tackled dozens of sensitive and complicated questions. James Bradley compiled a number of difficult tables as well as the extensive material on elections. Chad Ludington saved us at the end by writing difficult entries at virtually the last minute.

At Yale University Press the reference editor, Fred Kameny, worked tirelessly on this project for five years. He read every word of every entry, often several times, and became the indispensable man as the book moved toward publication. A friend as well as a trusted and respected colleague, he combined professionalism with a genuine affection for the city and an "encyclopedic" knowledge of its past. Several members of his staff, especially Pamela H. Sturner, Amy Balser, William J. Moses, Shawn Simmons, and Melissa M. Merritt, copy edited the entire volume and provided essential help as publication neared. William Stempel, deputy general counsel of Yale University, patiently answered numerous legal questions. John G. Ryden, director of Yale University Press, gave consistent and enthusiastic support at every stage of the process. Only he knows how important his advice and counsel were to me at critical stages of the preparation.

Late in the project, when most of those involved were moving on to other endeavors, the work was only beginning for the design and production staffs. The encyclopedia benefited greatly from Rich Hendel's elegant design, as well as his perceptive editorial suggestions. At the Composing Room of Michigan, Marcia Glass and her staff proved imperturbable in the face of an enormously complex task.

Finally, I want to thank my wife, Barbara, for cheerfully coming with me to New York City from Memphis more than three decades ago and for sharing my enjoyment and love of the city.

Arthur Ashe, Elliott B. Nixon, Harrison Salisbury, and A. M. Sperber have died since writing their entries. The encyclopedia is dedicated to their memory and to the 676 other contributors whose labors made the entire project possible.

KENNETH T. JACKSON, *March 1995*

ABBREVIATIONS

AB	Artium Baccalaureus
A.D.	Anno Domini
AFL–CIO	American Federation of Labor–Congress of Industrial Organizations
AIDS	Acquired Immune Deficiency Syndrome
Ala.	Alabama
AM	amplitude modulation; Artium Magister
a.m.	ante meridiem [before noon]
app.	appendix
Ariz.	Arizona
Ark.	Arkansas
Aug	August
b	born
BA	Baccalaureus Artium / Bachelor of Arts
BArch	Bachelor of Architecture
B.C.	before Christ
B.C.	British Columbia
BD	Bachelor of Divinity
B.P.	before the present [in geological contexts; present reckoned as A.D.1950]
BS	Bachelor of Science
C	centigrade
ca	circa
Calif.	California
CD-ROM	compact disc–read-only memory
chap(s).	chapter(s)
Co.	Company
Colo.	Colorado
comp(s).	compiler(s), compiled by
Conn.	Connecticut
Corp.	Corporation
d	died
d.	denarius, denarii [penny, pence]
DDS	Doctor of Dental Surgery
Dec	December
Del.	Delaware
diss.	dissertation
DPhil	Doctor Philosophiae / Doctor of Philosophy
Dr.	Doctor
ed(s).	editor(s), edited by
EdD	Doctor of Education
edn	edition
Eng.	English
et al.	et alii [and others]
F	Fahrenheit; Federal Reporter [in legal citations]
Feb	February
fl	floruit [he/she flourished]
Fla.	Florida
FM	frequency modulation
Ga.	Georgia
HMS	His/Her Majesty's Ship
Ill.	Illinois
Inc.	Incorporated
Ind.	Indiana
introd.	introduction
Jan	January
JD	Juris Doctor [Doctor of Laws]
Jr.	Junior
kHz	kilohertz
Ky.	Kentucky
£	libra(e) [pound(s) sterling]
La.	Louisiana
LLB	Legum Baccalaureus [Bachelor of Laws]
LLD	Legum Doctor [Doctor of Laws]
LLM	Legum Magister [Master of Laws]
Ltd.	Limited
M.	Monsieur
MA	Magister Artium / Master of Arts
MArch	Master of Architecture
Mass.	Massachusetts
MBA	Master of Business Administration
MD	Medicinae Doctor / Doctor of Medicine
Md.	Maryland
MFA	Master of Fine Arts
MHz	megahertz
Mich.	Michigan
Minn.	Minnesota
Miss.	Mississippi
Mme	Madame
Mo.	Missouri
Mont.	Montana
MPhil	Magister Philosophiae / Master of Philosophy
Mr.	Mister
Mrs.	Mistress
MS	Master of Science
n.	note
N.C.	North Carolina
n.d.	no date
Neb.	Nebraska
N.H.	New Hampshire
N.J.	New Jersey
N.M.	New Mexico
no(s).	number(s)
Nov	November
n.p.	no place
n.pub.	no publisher
N.Y.	New York
N.Y.S.	New York State [in legal citations]
Oct	October
Okla.	Oklahoma
Ont.	Ontario
O.P.	Ordo Praedicatorum [Order of Preachers (Dominicans)]

Ore.	Oregon
orig.	originally
Penn.	Pennsylvania
PhD	Philosophiae Doctor / Doctor of Philosophy
p.m.	post meridiem [after noon]
pop.	population
pubd	published
repr.	reprinted
rev.	revised
Rev.	Reverend
R.I.	Rhode Island
s.	solidus, solidi [shilling(s)]
Sask.	Saskatchewan
S.C.	South Carolina
Sept	September
Sr.	Senior
SSR	Soviet Socialist Republic
St(s).	Saint(s)
Ste.	Sainte
STL	Sacrae Theologiae Licentiatus [Licentiate in Sacred Theology]
STM	Sacrae Theologiae Magister [Master of Sacred Theology]
suppl(s).	supplement(s)
Tenn.	Tennessee
TNT	trinitrotoluene
TV	television
UCLA	University of California, Los Angeles
unpubd	unpublished
U.S.	United States
USS	United States Ship
USSR	Union of Soviet Socialist Republics
v.	versus
Va.	Virginia
Vt.	Vermont
Wash.	Washington
Wis.	Wisconsin
WPAG	*New York City Guide: A Comprehensive Guide to the Five Boroughs of the Metropolis: Manhattan, Brooklyn, the Bronx, Queens, and Richmond* (New York: Random House, 1939; repr. New York: Pantheon, 1982, as *The WPA Guide to New York City: The Federal Writers' Project Guide to 1930s New York*)
W.Va.	West Virginia
Wyo.	Wyoming
YIVO	Yidisher visnshaftlekher institut
YMCA	Young Men's Christian Association
YM-YWHA	Young Men's and Young Women's Hebrew Association
YWCA	Young Women's Christian Association

ABBREVIATIONS USED ON MAPS

AIG	American International Group
Amer	American
Assoc.	Association
Av(s)	Avenue(s)
Bldg.	Building
Blvd	Boulevard
Bway	Broadway
Ctr	Center
E	East
Ex	Exchange
Expwy	Expressway
Ft	Fort
Hgts	Heights
HQ	Headquarters
INS	Immigration and Naturalization Service
IRS	Internal Revenue Service
LIRR	Long Island Rail Road
Mt	Mount
N	North
NJ	New Jersey
NYC	New York City
NYU	New York University
Pct.	Precinct
Pkwy	Parkway
Pl	Place
PO	Post Office
PS	Public School
R.C.	Roman Catholic
Rd	Road
RR	Railroad
Sq	Square
St	Street
Vill	Village
W	West
Wash	Washington

NOTES ON THE USE OF THE ENCYCLOPEDIA

COVERAGE

There is no more difficult and contentious issue facing the editors of a reference work than what to put in and what to leave out. In this encyclopedia the criteria vary according to whether the subject is a person, a neighborhood, an institution, an ethnic or religious group, or a broad, thematic topic, as well as varying from one historical period to another. Such criteria will ease the task of selection, but only to a degree. In the end subjectivity plays a part, as it must in any reference work other than a directory.

The people included in the encyclopedia are those whom the editors judged to have left a permanent mark on the city's history or culture. Most subjects of biographical entries lived in the city for much of their lives, although some were influential visitors (such as Lafayette, Lincoln, and Dickens), and one never so much as set foot in the city (the Duke of York, for whom the city is named). After the mid twentieth century residence is a much more elusive criterion. On the one hand there are figures who had important careers in New York City but lived in the suburbs: they cannot rightly be disqualified. On the other hand are prominent figures in the worlds of film, music, and sports with national and international careers: they may have had a residence in New York City, but they will also have had other residences and their links to the city will be tenuous. A further consideration is that a person is less likely to be the subject of an entry if his or her career is adequately treated elsewhere. Thus only five of the twenty-three men who have conducted the New York Philharmonic in a permanent capacity are the subject of individual entries, but fifteen others are discussed in the entry on the orchestra itself. Finally, the tables and the index are repositories for figures who are not important enough to merit entries but are too important to be neglected altogether. Examples include most of the city's early mayors, who served at a time when the position was appointive and largely ceremonial, and about whom, in several cases, virtually nothing is known.

The more than four hundred entries on neighborhoods include all those generally recognized as extant, as well as the best-known of those that are defunct. In other categories – business firms, restaurants, magazines, radio stations – the choice of subjects is highly selective. National organizations and firms are generally included only if based in New York City. And to keep the encyclopedia to a manageable size, certain categories have been excluded entirely as subjects of entries, notably line agencies of the municipal government and individual creative works such as novels and films.

In every entry the focus is on the connection of the subject to New York City, with careers outside the city compressed or omitted entirely. On this principle the entry on Thomas Jefferson does not discuss his presidency or his writing of the Declaration of Independence: it deals solely with the six months that he spent in New York City in 1790.

The lengths of the entries are in rough proportion to the importance of their subjects, but length is not an exact measure in any reference work: the word "set," subject of the longest entry in the *Oxford English Dictionary*, is hardly the most important word in the English language. The amount of space given to a subject will reflect the amount of scholarly attention it has received, which will in turn reflect other factors – the longevity and recency of the subject's career, the availability and extent of primary materials, and the vicissitudes of scholarship. If the treatment of some important subjects seems inordinately brief, that is often because the materials on which to base an entry are lacking: such is the case with a number of the larger immigrant groups that settled in the city in the 1980s.

USAGE

New York City is an American city, and the encyclopedia is overwhelmingly a work by American editors and authors, for which it would have been inconceivable to adopt anything but American usage. But in the interest of making the encyclopedia comprehensible to as many readers as possible, the editors have striven to employ American usages that are also idiomatic to speakers of English from other parts of the world. This policy lies behind the decision to refer to the numeral 1,000,000,000 as one thousand million, and to give weights and measures in both the imperial and metric forms (except in a few sporting and nautical contexts).

Place-names and institutional names are given in the form that prevailed at the time being discussed. This practice extends to substantive orthographic changes (thus the form Williamsburgh is used in references before 1855, the form Williamsburg thereafter), but not to changes in spacing or hyphenation (the Long Island Rail Road is referred to consistently as such, even though it was known as the Long Island Railroad until 1944). The city is referred to either as New York City or (in exceptional cases) as the City of New York. The form New York is used only in bibliographies, for the colony of New York, and in references to New York State where it is unmistakable that the state is being referred to (otherwise the form New York State is used).

The ampersand in corporate names is generally expanded, although it is used where necessary to avoid confusion (notably with the Ringling Brothers and Barnum & Bailey Circus) and in acronyms (such as AT&T). The en dash (–) is used rather than the hyphen (-) in institutional names like Helmsley–Spear, which are derived from two surnames rather than a single hyphened surname. Idiosyncratic typography is disregarded (for example in the name of the book publisher Harper Collins). Transliteration follows the Pinyin system for Chinese and the YIVO system for Yiddish.

ALPHABETIZATION

The encyclopedia follows a letter-by-letter system, in which a heading of more than one word is treated as if it were spelled solid: spaces, hyphens, diacritical marks, and periods are disregarded, as are elements in brackets and parentheses. In accordance with established cataloguing practice, names beginning with "Mc" and "St." are alphabetized as if beginning with "Mac" and "Saint," and headings beginning with "U.S." are alphabetized as if the abbreviation were spelled out. Corporate and institutional names that begin with a person's forename (such as R. H. Macy and the Solomon R. Guggenheim Museum) are alphabetized under the first letter of the forename, not the surname. The reader who looks for such entries under their latter part (Macy and Guggenheim) will be referred to the appropriate place by a cross-reference.

HEADINGS

The heading of an entry about a person takes this form:

> **Washington, George** (*b* Bridges Creek, near Fredericksburg, Va., 22 Feb 1732; *d* Mount Vernon, Va., 14 Dec 1799).

Parentheses are used to show parts of a name not ordinarily used by a person (or institution or other entity). These parts are in boldface:

> **Ives, Charles (Edward)**
> **Koch, Edward I(rving)**
> **Catholic Medical Center (of Brooklyn and Queens)**

Brackets are used for alternative names. These are in lightface:

> **Ellington, Duke** [Edward Kennedy]
> **Clermont** [North River Steamboat]

A person who has more than one name is entered under the best-known one, with alternative names given in brackets:

> **Twain, Mark** [Clemens, Samuel (Langhorne)]

The formula "née" is used for maiden names:

> **Astor** [née Schermerhorn]**, Caroline Webster**

Where there is more than one bracketed name these are separated by semicolons and the order is that of reverse chronology:

> **Malcolm X** [Shabazz, el-Hajj Malik el-; Little, Malcolm]

Titles of nobility are given in lightface:

> **Bing,** Sir **Rudolph**
> **Hyde, Edward**, Viscount Cornbury
> **Moody** [née Dunch]**, Deborah**, Lady Moody

For a firm or institution, the name appearing in the heading will be the current form if the entity is extant and based in New York City, and the best-known form if the entity is defunct or based elsewhere.

Where two or more entries have an identical heading they are distinguished by lowercase roman numerals:

> **West Brighton (i).** Name by which WEST NEW BRIGHTON is sometimes known.
> **West Brighton (ii).** Neighborhood in southwestern Brooklyn.

When a person, place, institution, or other entity that is the subject of an entry is referred to in running text elsewhere, the form used is that of the boldface heading of the entry (including the lowercase roman numeral if there is one, unless the reference is unmistakable without it); anything in lightface, parentheses, or brackets is disregarded.

DATES

The dates appearing in the heading of an entry about a person provide the fullest information available on that person's birth and death. The following forms are used to indicate uncertain dates:

?1 Jan 1900	day of month is conjectural, month and year are not
1 ?Jan 1900	month is conjectural, day and year are not (date was the first day of some month in 1900 but perhaps not January)
1 Jan ?1900	year is conjectural, day and month are not
1/2 Jan 1900	1 January and 2 January are equally likely
baptized 17 Aug 1653	date of birth unknown
fl 1725–50	flourished between 1725 and 1750, nothing known about dates of birth and death
ca 1750 to *ca* 1760	both dates approximate
ca 1750 to 1760	only first date approximate
?1904 to ?1905	both years conjectural
?1904 to 1905	only first year conjectural

Life dates are given in running text where relevant. All dates are given in new style, according to the Gregorian calendar.

STRUCTURE OF ENTRIES

The text of each entry on a person or institution begins with a verbless definition that describes the subject's principal activity or activities. Definitions of neighborhoods include the latest available population figures (if known) and approximate boundaries. In cases where such boundaries cannot be fixed with any certainty, the definition identifies the center of the neighborhood, the names of surrounding neighborhoods, or the location within the borough.

Nearly all entries are ordered chronologically. The longest are divided into sections, each beginning with a subheading.

CROSS-REFERENCES

A cross-reference directs the reader to another entry (for text, illustration, or bibliography) or to another part of the same entry. If referring to another entry it is printed in small capitals, except for one letter, which is a large capital to show how the entry being referred to is alphabetized.

Cross-references are of three types:

1. The cross-reference from an acronym or alternative name to the main entry:

> **ACLU.** See AMERICAN CIVIL LIBERTIES UNION.
> **North River Steamboat.** See CLERMONT.
> **Clemens, Samuel (Langhorne).** See TWAIN, MARK.

2. The cross-reference from one entry to a second entry, used where the second entry contains a substantial amount of addi-

tional information about the subject of the first. It may appear in text, or at the end of the entry, after any bibliography and before the signature:

> These measures contributed to widespread HOMELESSNESS.
> For further illustration see RIIS, JACOB A.
> See also THEATER, §5.

3. The cross-reference from one part of an entry to another:

> (see also §6, above)

Some restraint has been exercised to avoid besieging the reader with endless lists of entries and transforming the encyclopedia into a concordance to itself. Cross-references are used to direct the reader to substantive discussions, not passing mentions. Entries from thematic entries may cross-refer to other thematic entries, but not to entries on individual persons or institutions: thus the entry on science refers the reader to those on anthropology, biology, geology, physics, and psychology, but not to entries on individual scientists and scientific institutions.

BIBLIOGRAPHIES

The bibliographies are intended to provide suggestions for further research. They are selective and will not necessarily include all the sources consulted by the authors or editors.

The first edition of a book is always cited. For books with more than one edition the most recent is cited as well if it appeared at least ten years after the first edition (a subsequent edition that appeared sooner may be cited if it is bibliographically significant). Only one place of publication is given for each publisher. Places of publication and names of publishers for revisions and subsequent editions are given only if they differ from those of the first edition. The abbreviation "p(p)." is used only where necessary to avoid confusion.

Articles in periodicals are cited thus:

> Ellen G. Landau: "Lee Krasner's Early Career," *Arts Magazine* 56 (1981), no. 2, pp. 110–22; no. 3, pp. 80–89

Fascicle numbers (2 and 3 in the example above) are given only if each fascicle is separately paginated. If the periodical is through-paginated only the volume number is given.

Bibliographic items are ordered chronologically, earliest items first. Two or more items published in the same year are ordered alphabetically by authors' surnames.

SIGNATURES

If an entry has more than one author the names are given in alphabetical order by surname, separated by a comma:

> Carol Groneman, David M. Reimers

The following form is used to distinguish a primary from a secondary author:

> Charles Musser (with David James)

If each author has written different sections of a multi-section entry the following form is used:

> John W. Frick (§§1–6), Martha S. LoMonaco (§§7–8)

In cases such as the preceding one, ordering by section number supersedes alphabetical ordering.

CLOSING DATE

Information in the encyclopedia is believed to have been accurate as of 31 March 1995.

A

A&P. See Great Atlantic and Pacific Tea Company.

Abbott, Berenice (*b* Springfield, Ohio, 17 July 1898; *d* Monson, Maine, 10 Dec 1991). Photographer. During eight years in Europe she learned photography and became a well-known portraitist before returning to New York City in 1929. Fascinated by the contrasts between old buildings awaiting demolition and tall buildings under construction, she embarked on an ambitious project to document the entire city. Most of her photographs were taken in Manhattan, but each of the other boroughs is represented; when she finished the project in 1939 the images became the subject of her book *Changing New York*, still considered the best record of the city made before the Second World War. She next photographed scientific phenomena. A number of portraits of local artists, along with photographs of downtown streets and interiors, were collected in the book *Greenwich Village Today and Yesterday* (1948). Abbott moved to Maine in 1966.

Hank O'Neal: *Berenice Abbott: American Photographer* (New York: McGraw–Hill, 1982)

For illustrations see Automats, Bakeries, Buses, Kosher foods, and Port of New York.

Avis Berman

Abbott, George (Francis) (*b* Forestville, N.Y., 25 June 1887; *d* Miami Beach, 31 Jan 1995). Director, producer, and playwright. He began his career as an actor in 1913–34 and later produced, directed, and wrote more than seventy-five plays and musicals, including *Twentieth Century* (1932), *Boy Meets Girl* (1935), *Where's Charley?* (1948), *The Pajama Game* (1954), and *A Funny Thing Happened on the Way to the Forum* (1962). With Richard Rodgers and Lorenz Hart he wrote the book for *On Your Toes* (1936), directed and wrote *The Boys from Syracuse* (1938), and produced and directed *Pal Joey* (1940). He also worked on the adaptation for the stage of Betty Smith's *A Tree Grows in Brooklyn* (1951), which he produced and directed, and was an author and the director of *Damn Yankees* (1955) and *Fiorello!* (1959). He worked on a revival of *Damn Yankees* in 1994.

Sara J. Steen

Abbott, Lyman (*b* Roxbury [now in Boston], 18 Dec 1835; *d* New York City, 22 Oct 1922). Minister. After a brief period in the Midwest he wrote for *Harper's Magazine* and moved to New York City, where he worked with Henry Ward Beecher on the publication *Christian Union* (later renamed the *Outlook*); he became the editor in 1881, and the journal was soon known as the leading exponent of progressive Christian social thought, especially the Social Gospel. Abbott took part in Henry George's mayoral campaigns, was later active in the Progressive Party, and wrote four books on Christianity and contemporary issues. In 1890 he succeeded Beecher as the pastor of Plymouth Congregational Church in Brooklyn Heights.

Ira V. Brown: *Lyman Abbott, Christian Evolutionist: A Study in Religious Liberalism* (Cambridge: Harvard University Press, 1953)

Eileen W. Lindner

ABC. See American Broadcasting Company.

Abel, Rudolf (Ivanovich) [Golfus, Emil R.; Fisher, William August] (*b* Newcastle upon Tyne, England, 11 July 1903; *d* Moscow, 15 Nov 1971). Spy. He began a career as a Soviet intelligence officer in Moscow in 1927. From 1950 he lived in Brooklyn and coordinated the activities of a number of spies for the Soviet Union, using the alias Emil R. Golfus and working out of an art and photographic studio. Denounced by his partner Lieutenant Colonel Reino Hayhanen, who had also been trained in Moscow, he was arrested by the Federal Bureau of Investigation on 21 July 1957; a search of his home uncovered spy equipment including a shortwave transmitter and receiver. On 25 October 1957 a federal district court in Brooklyn sentenced Abel to thirty years in prison. He was sent to the Soviet Union on 10 February 1962 in an exchange for Francis Gary Powers, the pilot of an American reconnaissance plane who had been shot down over the Soviet Union.

Louise Bernikow: *Abel* (New York: Trident, 1970)

Martin Ebon

Abercrombie and Fitch. Firm of retailers, formed during the late nineteenth century as an outdoor-supply store by David T. Abercrombie, a railroad engineer and prospector. It opened on South Street in Manhattan, where one of the first customers was Ezra H. Fitch, a wealthy lawyer and sportsman who became Abercrombie's partner. In 1908 the store provided President Theodore Roosevelt with equipment for an African safari, including snake-proof sleeping bags. Abercrombie left in 1912, and in 1917 Fitch moved the store to Madison Avenue at 45th Street, where a fly-casting pond was installed on the roof and a shooting range in the basement (closed after a friend of Ernest Hemingway injured his shoulder while firing an elephant gun). Well-known customers in the following years included Admiral Richard Byrd, Charles Lindbergh, and Amelia Earhart, as well as Presidents William Howard Taft and Warren G. Harding, who both bought golf clubs, Woodrow Wilson (riding equipment), Herbert Hoover (fishing tackle), and Dwight D. Eisenhower (boots for weekends at Camp David); King Hussein of Jordan outfitted his yacht there and Katharine Hepburn occasionally rode a bicycle across the main floor. In 1977 the firm, which operated a chain of nine

Sporting equipment at Abercrombie and Fitch, 1912

stores, declared bankruptcy. The name was bought in 1978 by Oshman's Sporting Goods, which opened its first Abercrombie and Fitch store in 1979 in Beverly Hills, California, and another at South Street Seaport in 1984. Abercrombie and Fitch was sold to the Limited in 1988 and in the mid 1990s had forty stores, including two in New York City.

Eric Wm. Allison

ABET. See ACCREDITATION BOARD FOR ENGINEERING AND TECHNOLOGY.

Abigail Adams Smith Museum. Historic house at 421 East 61st Street in Manhattan, built as a carriage house in 1799. Along with twenty-three acres (ten hectares) of surrounding land it was owned by Colonel William S. Smith and Abigail Adams Smith, daughter of John Adams. The building was converted in 1826 and for seven years was a fashionable day resort called the Mount Vernon Hotel. After purchasing the building in 1924 the Colonial Dames of America restored and furnished it and in 1939 opened it as a museum, which now has nine period rooms, a collection of Federal artifacts and furniture, and a garden in eighteenth-century style. The building is one of few in the city constructed of Manhattan schist.

Linda Elsroad

Abingdon Square. Name given to the intersection of West 12th Street, 8th Avenue, and Hudson Street in Manhattan, and by extension to the surrounding neighborhood. Its eponym is Charlotte Warren, by marriage the Countess of Abingdon; she was the daughter of Susannah de Lancey and the English privateer Admiral Peter Warren, whose estate of three hundred acres (121 hectares) encompassed most of what is now the West Village. The neighborhood has a varied architecture that includes nineteenth-century row houses, apartment buildings, tenements, and commercial buildings, as well as factory buildings and warehouses at Westbeth and the Gansevoort Meat Market that have been converted to residences for artists. Its principal commercial thoroughfares are Hudson Street and Bleecker Street, which are lined with furniture shops, antique shops, and restaurants. The population is affluent and predominantly white.

Joyce Mendelsohn

abolitionism. A resolution to abolish slavery in New York State was introduced by Gouverneur Morris at the state constitutional convention in 1777 and approved by a large majority of the delegates. No further action was taken until 1785, when several abolitionist measures were debated in the state legislature. Among them was a plan introduced by Aaron Burr to free all slaves immediately, which won the support of Federalists (who sought to extend civil rights to blacks) but was soundly defeated; another plan calling for gradual emancipation, an approach supported by a majority of the legislature, was defeated because it would also have extended suffrage to blacks. Federalists concentrated on ending the slave trade, and in 1785 a bill was passed banning the sale of slaves in New York State but allowing slaves to be brought into the state and remain there for no longer than nine months. During the same year the New York Manumission Society was formed by such well-known figures as John Jay (its first president), Alexander Hamilton (its second president), Chancellor Livingston, Philip Schuyler, and Hector St. John de Crèvecoeur to encourage public support for abolition. The society mediated indentureship negotiations and provided legal assistance to blacks who were denied their freedom; its efforts to ensure compliance with the law of 1785 were largely unsuccessful, because slaveowners often found loopholes that allowed sales of slaves out of state. The legislature in 1799 passed the Act for the Gradual Emancipation of Negroes and Other Slaves, which declared free the children of slaves born on or after 4 July, granted freedom to slaves born before that date at the age of twenty-four for women and twenty-eight for men, and required the registration of children indentured to their masters until the age of manumission. To end abuses of the law the legislature in 1817 declared all slaves free as of 4 July 1827. Complete abolition was not achieved until 1841, when the state rescinded the provisions allowing nonresidents to hold slaves for as long as nine months.

Abolition did not end discrimination against blacks in New York, who were denied full rights of citizenship. The Democrats controlling the state constitutional convention of 1821 redefined the property requirement for the franchise along racial lines, abolishing it altogether for whites while introducing one of $250 for blacks. Free blacks were also threatened by the continuation of slavery in the South, leading many to join the abolitionist movement, which was also taken up by the first black newspapers in New York City, *Freedom's Journal* (1827–29) and the *Rights of All* (1829). The city became an abolitionist center during the 1830s, and in 1833 the American Anti-Slavery Society was formed there as the first national organization of its kind. Some of its most influential members were leaders of the city's black community, including Samuel E. Cornish and Theodore S. Wright, who were elected to the executive committee at the first meeting. Under the society's auspices Wright and Henry Highland Garnet made speaking tours of the northern and western states and with other black abolitionists from the city became leading spokesmen for the anti-slavery movement: they linked the debasement of free blacks to the perpetuation of slavery in the South, arguing that blacks would not enjoy the full rights of citizenship until slavery was eradicated throughout the country. By demonstrating political acumen and oratorical skills they also sought to destroy myths of inferiority that provided a basis for discriminatory legislation. A movement was formed in the city by blacks, with the support of prominent whites such as Gerritt Smith, Arthur Tappan, and Lewis Tappan, to organize mass protests against slavery and racism.

Interracial tensions mounted during the 1830s. Many white abolitionists were unwilling to challenge racism and some advocated repatriating blacks to Africa, leading blacks to build a separate movement against racism while continuing to work with whites. Such prominent blacks from the city as Philip Bell Cornish and J. W. C. Pennington attended the first National Negro Convention in Philadelphia from 15 to 24 September 1830, the first of several conventions held in the 1830s. At the New York State Negro Convention, held in New York City on 25 January 1831, a number of delegates denounced efforts by the New York Colonization Society to resettle blacks in Africa as a scheme to perpetuate slavery and proclaimed their dedication to abolition and the uplift of free blacks. Abolitionism failed to win much support among whites and even intensified anti-black sentiment among white workers who viewed blacks as competitors in the labor market. During an eight-day rampage in 1834 known as the Journeymen's Riot, white day laborers disrupted a meeting of abolitionists at Chatham Street Chapel and attacked the homes of Lewis Tappan and scores of blacks.

The *Colored American*, launched in 1837, provided coverage of the movement until ceasing publication in 1841. Black churches were among the most important venues for abolitionism. Through astute biblical exegesis, hard-nosed political analysis, and fiery oratory black clergymen inspired their congregations to embrace "moral suasion," a policy of eschewing political action and converting slaveholders to abolitionism through moral argument. In 1840 a number of blacks left the American Anti-Slavery Society after disagreeing with members who favored moral suasion and helped to form the American and Foreign Anti-Slavery Society. Blacks during the 1840s continued to hold state and local conventions, where speakers protested racism, criticized business for maintaining ties to the southern economy, and encouraged blacks to vote for candidates of the Liberty and Free Soil parties, hoping that in return for the support of black voters the parties would oppose limitations on black suffrage in New York State. A more militant stance was adopted by such leaders as Garnet, who at a convention in Buffalo in 1843 urged slaves to fight for their freedom. The abolitionist cause was also taken up by the newspaper the *Ram's Horn* (1847).

Protecting the freedom of blacks also became an abolitionist cause in the city, where slave hunters sought to recapture the many fugitive slaves who settled there and to kidnap free blacks to sell in the South. Concern mounted after the Fugitive Slave Act (1850), which outlawed efforts to help runaway slaves and required officials to cooperate in recapturing them. The case of James Hamlet, a resident of Williamsburgh captured by local authorities and transported to Baltimore, became a *cause célèbre* in the city's black community: the New York Vigilance Committee (1835), an organization dedicated to helping fugitives, raised $800 to buy his freedom, and on 5 October 1850 his return to the city was celebrated with a rally at City Hall Park. In a racially integrated prayer meeting at Shiloh Presbyterian Church, Garnet eulogized John Brown and his followers as heroic freedom fighters. Resentment against blacks reached a peak on 13 July 1863, when a mob of white workers protested the federal draft act by attacking the local draft office and killing several state militiamen who had been called in. During the course of the day they moved north from the Five Points, destroying the homes of blacks and the shops of whites who traded with them, and dragging their occupants into the street. Eventually they reached the Colored Orphan Asylum on 5th Avenue between 43rd and 44th streets, where they murdered an infant. Hundreds of blacks in the city who sought to join the Union Army when the Civil War broke out were turned away by New York State, which began accepting blacks in 1864 to meet a quota imposed by the federal government. Blacks from the city were incorporated into the 20th Regiment by 5 May 1864 and the 31st Regiment by 27 March 1865 and accounted for 877 casualties by the end of the war.

Herbert Aptheker: "Militant Abolitionism," *Journal of Negro History* 26 (1941), 438–84
Benjamin Quarles: *Black Abolitionists* (New York: Oxford University Press, 1969)
C. Peter Ripley: *The Black Abolitionist Papers* (Chapel Hill: University of North Carolina Press, 1985–)

Thelma Foote

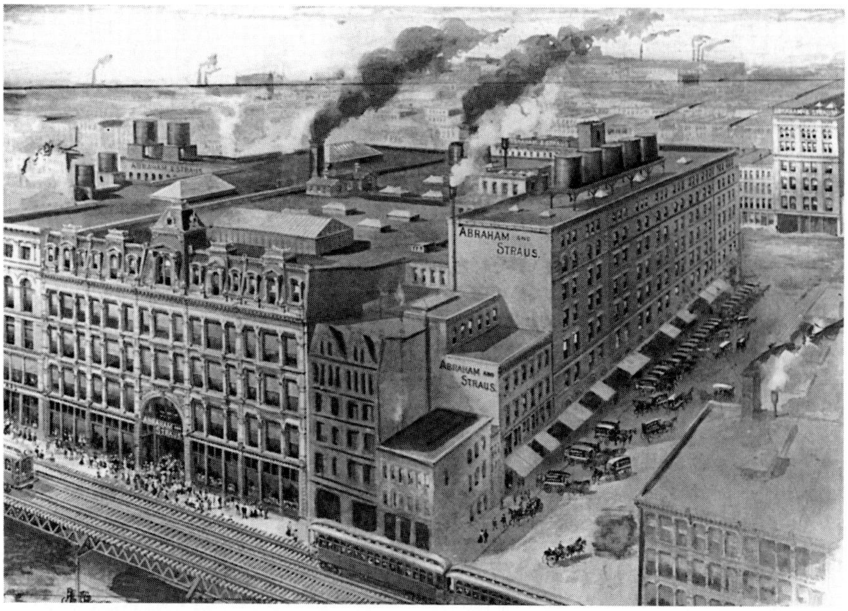

Abraham and Straus, 1904

Abraham and Straus. Firm of retailers, originated in 1865 in Brooklyn as a small dry-goods shop called Wechsler and Abraham by Abraham Abraham, who was twenty-two at the time, and Joseph Wechsler. When the Brooklyn Bridge was completed in 1883 Abraham and Wechsler foresaw that a new shopping district would emerge at its eastern terminus, and they moved the business to a five-story building at 422 Fulton Street that by 1889 was the largest dry-goods store in New York State. In 1893 Abraham joined with Isidor and Nathan Straus to buy out Wechsler's share of the business and gave the store its current name; the new partnership dissolved in 1920. The store was incorporated, joined the American Merchandising Corporation, and in 1925 became publicly owned. It expanded outside of Brooklyn in 1934 when a store opened in Jamaica, and became a division of Federated Department Stores in 1949. With fifteen stores, Abraham and Straus was the second-largest department store chain in the metropolitan area until 1995, when Federated announced plans to discontinue the name.

Leon A. Harris: *Merchant Princes: An Intimate History of Jewish Families Who Built Great Department Stores* (New York: Harper and Row, 1979)
Robert Hendrickson: *The Grand Emporiums: The Illustrated History of America's Great Department Stores* (New York: Stein and Day, 1979)
Joseph Devorkin: *Great Merchants of Early New York: "The Ladies' Mile"* (New York: Society for the Architecture of the City, 1987)

Laura Gwinn

Abrams, Charles (*b* Vilnius [now in Lithuania], 16 Feb 1902; *d* New York City, 22 Feb 1970). Lawyer and public official. After a brief and highly successful career in private practice he helped to draft the Municipal Housing Authorities Law of New York State in 1934 and became the first counsel of the New York City Housing Authority (1934–37). His victory in *New York City Housing Authority v. Muller* (1936) established the authority's right to employ the power of eminent domain for clearing slums. As the chairman of the New York State Commission against Discrimination (1955–59) he challenged broad patterns of discrimination by launching wide-ranging investigations. He also taught at Columbia University, worked as a housing consultant, and traveled on behalf of the United Nations. His published writings include *Revolution in Land* (1939), *The Future of Housing* (1946), *Forbidden Neighbors* (1955), and *The City Is the Frontier* (1965).

Rosalie Genevro

Abrams v. United States. Case decided in 1919 (250 U.S. 616) by the U.S. Supreme Court. It upheld the convictions of five Russians from New York City sentenced to twenty-year terms in prison under the Espionage Act for distributing circulars that criticized capitalism, American intervention in Bolshevik Russia, and President Woodrow Wilson's character. Only Justices Oliver Wendell Holmes and Louis D. Brandeis dissented, arguing that the circulars posed no clear threat to the government and that the convictions violated the defendants' rights under the First Amendment.

George J. Lankevich

Abyssinian Baptist Church. One of the oldest, largest, and most influential Protestant congregations in the United States. It traces its origins to 1808, when a few free black parishioners left the First Baptist Church of New York City because they were unwilling to accept racially segregated seating in a house of worship. Together with a group of Ethiopian merchants they established themselves in a building on Anthony Street (later Worth Street). After meeting in a series of buildings on Anthony, Thompson, and Spring streets the congregation moved to Waverly Place and then to 40th Street. In 1908 Adam Clayton Powell Sr., a young preacher from New Haven, Connecticut, became the pastor. Under his leadership the congregation in 1920 purchased lots on 138th Street between Lenox and 7th avenues in Harlem. After a successful tithing campaign to which two thousand members responded, a cavernous Gothic and Tudor structure, replete with imported stained-glass windows and an Italian marble pulpit, was dedicated on 17 June 1923. In 1937, by which time the congregation had grown to seven thousand members, Powell gave up the pastorate in favor of his only son, Adam Clayton Powell Jr. An intrepid preacher and civil rights leader who also served fourteen terms in the U.S. House of Representatives, the younger Powell made Abyssinian what he called the "church of the masses," combining the Christian message of justice and equality with the militant oratory of liberation. Powell's successors, Samuel DeWitt Proctor and Calvin O. Butts III, continued his tradition of political activism. In the mid 1990s the church continued to serve thousands of communicants each week, many of them attracted by the superb choir and the sixty-seven-rank organ. The New York Philharmonic has performed at the church, as have such internationally acclaimed musicians as Leontyne Price and André Watts.

Kenneth T. Jackson

Abzug [née Savitzky], **Bella** (*b* New York City, 24 July 1920). Congresswoman. She attended Hunter College (BA 1942) and Columbia Law School (LLB 1947) and from 1961 to 1970 was the legislative director of Women Strike for Peace. In 1970 she was elected to Congress as a Democrat, representing the Upper West Side. When her seat was eliminated by redistricting after the census of 1970, she chose to oppose Representative William F. Ryan for the Democratic nomination in 1972, a decision that angered many liberals. Although defeated by Ryan in the primary election, on his death in September she was named to replace him on the ballot, and she then was elected to fill his seat. In 1976 she sought the Democratic nomination for the U.S. Senate, narrowly losing to Daniel P. Moynihan, and in the following year she was an unsuccessful candidate for mayor. In the 1980s she failed in an attempt to win a seat in Congress from Westchester County. Abzug's career was brief but colorful. She was known for her unabashed liberalism and feminism, her advocacy of such campaigns as one to make New York City a fifty-first state, and her brash personality. Her trademark was a wide-brimmed hat that she was seldom seen without.

Academy of American Poets. Organization formed in 1934 to encourage the writing of American poetry. It administers awards (including the Tanning Prize), sponsors readings and workshops, and issues several periodicals. In the mid 1990s the chancellors of the academy included such prominent figures as John Ashbery, John Hollander, Stanley Kunitz, W. S. Merwin, and Richard Wilbur. The offices are at 584 Broadway in Manhattan.

Academy of Arts and Letters. See AMERICAN ACADEMY OF ARTS AND LETTERS.

Academy of Design. See NATIONAL ACADEMY OF DESIGN.

Academy of Holy Infancy. Original name of MANHATTAN COLLEGE.

Academy of Medicine. See NEW YORK ACADEMY OF MEDICINE.

Academy of Mount St. Vincent. Original name of the COLLEGE OF MOUNT ST. VINCENT.

Academy of Music. Opera house opened in 1854 at the northeast corner of 14th Street and Irving Place. It was built with donations from wealthy New Yorkers at a time when the area near Union Square was an affluent neighborhood. The building was lavish and had a stage sufficiently large for grand opera, many private and stage boxes, and about four thousand seats upholstered in crimson velvet; the interior of the hall was painted white and gold and illuminated by thousands of gaslights. Irving Hall, an annex at Irving Place and 15th Street, was the home of the New York Philharmonic in 1861–63. In several seasons during 1856–86 the Philharmonic performed in the main theater, which for thirty years was the principal venue for foreign opera singers visiting the city. The building was destroyed by fire in 1866 but rebuilt by 1868; a more serious blow was the opening in 1883 of the Metropolitan Opera House, which drastically reduced its audience. The Academy of Music was unable to compete and closed in 1886; its manager Colonel James Mapelson lamented his inability to "fight Wall Street." The space continued to be used for several years for labor meetings, plays, vaudeville acts, and motion picture screenings; the site is now occupied by a building of Consolidated Edison.

John Frederick Cone: *First Rival of the Metropolitan Opera* (New York: Columbia University Press, 1983)

Nancy Shear

Academy of Sciences. See NEW YORK ACADEMY OF SCIENCES.

Academy of the Fine Arts. See AMERICAN ACADEMY OF THE FINE ARTS.

accounting. Until the late nineteenth century most accounting was handled by clerks with only basic bookkeeping skills: the pace of business was slow and transactions uncomplicated, and certified financial statements were considered unnecessary (many businessmen based their dealings on informal assessments of character). A demand for new services arose during the 1880s as large corporations were formed: investors required audits to verify financial statements by corporate managers, and the managers sought advice in developing and improving their accounting systems. The number of accountants in the city increased, and in 1882 the Institute of Bookkeepers and Accountants was formed by bookkeepers, businessmen interested in accounting, and accountants who worked primarily for small businesses; it later became the New York Institute of Accounts (NYIA). Among the directors of the organization was Charles Waldo Haskins, who operated one of the city's largest accounting firms, Haskins and Sells (now Deloitte and Touche). Training in accounting was offered through an apprenticeship system based on the British model and in proprietary bookkeeping academies such as that of Silas S. Packard in Manhattan, which was highly successful. Several accounting associations were soon formed in the city. One of the first was the American Association of Public Accountants (AAPA; from 1957 the American Institute of Certified Public Ac-

Second site of the Academy of Music, 14th Street and Irving Place, ca 1910

countants (AICPA)), which began operations in 1887 after an English chartered accountant, Edwin Guthrie, traveled to the city seeking reputable American accountants to engage as correspondents. It attracted an élite membership based mainly in the East that was often called on to devise new accounting methods for transactions of unprecedented complexity. Seeking recognition as specialists, the members promoted auditing as an element of corporate governance that had proved its effectiveness in investment banking; they also set standards for internal regulation based on those adopted by British chartered accountants earlier in the century.

Efforts to set standards for education and licensing were undertaken in the following years. In 1895 the AAPA opened the College of Accounts, which offered a one-year certification course consisting of a thousand hours of instruction; it closed soon after the New York State Board of Regents refused it the right to grant degrees. During the 1890s separate efforts to establish state licensing were pursued by accountants in the NYIA and by the AAPA. The accountants of the NYIA prevailed because they were concentrated in New York City and because they were led by Haskins, who through his connection by marriage to the Havemeyer family was able to win the support of Melvil Dewey, secretary of the Board of Regents (which controlled professional licensing). Haskins's colleagues in the NYIA formed the New York Society of Certified Public Accountants in 1897. Dissatisfied with existing training and apprenticeship programs, Haskins made plans for a university curriculum: he believed that the quantitative nature of accounting made it akin to physical science, and shared the hope of many Progressives that its precision might allow a high degree of control over the affairs of business and government. His enthusiasm and financial guarantees led to the formation of the College of Commerce, Accounts and Finance at New York University in 1899, of which he was the first dean. His ideas were reinforced by his close associate Charles Ezra Sprague, a faculty member whose book *The Philosophy of Accounts* (1908) and other writings were among the first to define a theory of accounting. The college became a model for institutions nationwide, and by 1927 its graduates accounted for fifty-seven of the 179 college-educated members of the American Institute of Certified Public Accountants.

Accounting developed rapidly between 1900 and 1904, owing to a sudden increase in mergers. The demand for audits rose sharply as bankers in the city floated securities in London, where statement certification was common practice. The importance of accounting became firmly established in 1901 when the House of Morgan engaged the firm of Price Waterhouse to certify statements of U.S. Steel, the country's first manufacturing corporation with more than $1000 million in assets. The AICPA set ethical standards prohibiting such practices as using knowledge of accounting contrary to the public interest; these standards proved durable as the profession developed in later years. After the federal income tax was introduced in 1913 accountants were increasingly engaged in preparing tax returns. A uniform certifying examination was introduced by the AAPA in 1917 and later adopted by all state licensing boards nationwide. By the 1920s most firms listed on the New York Stock Exchange presented annual certified statements; they were required to do so after the formation of the Securities and Exchange Commission, which considered such statements vital to restoring public confidence in the country's financial markets. From the 1930s the AAPA set standards for such practices as accounting and auditing, and later tax preparation, consulting, attestations, and reviews. Educational standards rose, largely because of Haskins's efforts, leading New York State in 1940 to require candidates for certification to have a baccalaureate, the first such mandate in the country. Doctoral programs were established by New York University (1944), Columbia University (1954), and Baruch College (1974). During the 1970s the AICPA assumed new responsibilities for review and oversight, through which it sought to protect the public; it also published books and periodicals to promote competence and achieve consensus about matters of practice. By 1993 the AICPA had 300,000 members and was essentially self regulated. New York City remained a leading center for education, and eighteen colleges and universities in the city offered bachelor's and master's degree programs in accounting.

Paul J. Miranti Jr.

Accreditation Board for Engineering and Technology [ABET]. Organization formed in 1932 to monitor, evaluate, and certify the qualifications of engineering education in colleges and universities in the United States. Its founding institutional members were the American Society of Civil Engineers, the American Society of Mechanical Engineers, the American Institute of Electrical Engineers (a predecessor of the Institute of Electrical and Electronics Engineers), the American Institute of Chemical Engineers, and three other organizations. The headquarters are at the United Engineering Center on 47th Street and 1st Avenue.

Trudy E. Bell

Ackerman, Frederick L(ee) (*b* Edmeston, N.Y., 9 July 1878; *d* New York City, 17 March 1950). Architect and urban planner. He was the chief designer of low-rent housing and the town planner for the Fleet Corporation, an organization formed during the First World War to provide emergency housing for shipyard workers. In collaboration with Clarence S. Stein and Henry Wright he developed Sunnyside Gardens in Queens (1924) and led the movement toward building housing units in clusters and constructing apartment buildings with common social space. As the director of the New York City Housing Authority from 1934 to 1938 he advocated low-rise, walk-up apartment buildings within the cost limits of public housing. Later he conducted site studies used by housing authorities during the late 1940s, and with Lafayette Goldstone designed the Lillian Wald Houses (1949) on the Lower East Side. Ackerman wrote *The Housing Famine: How to End It* (1920)

Joel Schwartz

ACLU. See AMERICAN CIVIL LIBERTIES UNION.

Acquired Immune Deficiency Syndrome. See AIDS.

Actors' Equity Association. Labor union of professional actors and stage managers working in the legitimate theater. It was formed in New York City in May 1913 by 112 actors committed to fighting the arbitrary work rules and low wages then prevalent in the American theater. In August 1919 it mounted a strike for recognition, which increased its membership to more than eight thousand and led to a five-year contract between the union and the Producing Managers' Association. The union is affiliated with the AFL–CIO through its parent organization, the Associated Actors and Artistes of America, and has its headquarters in Manhattan. In 1990 Actors' Equity had 35,947 members nationwide, of whom 15,405 resided in metropolitan New York.

Alfred Harding: *The Revolt of the Actors* (New York: William Morrow, 1929)

Martha S. LoMonaco

Actors Studio. School opened in 1947 by Elia Kazan, Robert Lewis, and Cheryl Crawford of the Group Theatre to encourage actors to develop their craft without the demands of public performance. Its artistic director from 1951 was Lee Strasberg, who introduced the Method, a controversial psychological approach to acting that stressed the actor's life experiences. Among the members of the studio was Marlon Brando, whose visceral acting style came to exemplify the Method. After Strasberg's death in 1982 joint leadership was assumed by Ellen Burstyn and Al Pacino. In 1988 Frank Corsaro became the studio's artistic director.

Foster Hirsch: *A Method to Their Madness: The History of the Actors Studio* (New York: W. W. Norton, 1984)

D. S. Moynihan

ACTU. See ASSOCIATION OF CATHOLIC TRADE UNIONISTS.

ACT-UP [AIDS Coalition to Unleash Power]. Organization formed in 1987 by activists in New York City to advocate stronger measures against AIDS and to defend those suffering from it. It offers information on the medical and social consequences of AIDS, pharmaceuticals, and treatments. The group has given rise to dozens of similar groups throughout the United States and the world. ACT-UP is widely known for its confrontational tactics toward government at all levels, the medical profession, and the pharmaceutical industry.

Women, AIDS, and Activism (New York: South End, 1990)

Robert A. Padgug

Adams, Franklin P(ierce) (*b* Chicago, 15 Nov 1881; *d* New York City, 23 March 1960). Columnist. After working for the *Chicago Tribune* he moved to New York City in 1904 and in 1913 joined the *New York Tribune* to write a column called "The Conning Tower," which appeared in various newspapers in the city until 1941; he usually wrote under the pseudonym "F.P.A." He was also a regular guest on the radio quiz program "Information Please" (from 1938) and a member of the Algonquin Round Table. He lived at 124 West 13th Street (1925–28) and 26 West 10th Street (1929 to the mid 1930s). A humorist with a taste for the epigrammatic and the sardonic, Adams was among the most widely read journalists in New York City. His newspaper column was a forum for literary opinion, gossip, and commentary and light verse by him and others (including Ring Lardner, Sinclair Lewis, and Dorothy Parker); to be published in it was considered an honor.

Robert E. Drennan, ed.: *The Algonquin Wits* (New York: Citadel, 1968)

Brenda Wineapple

Adams, Thomas (*b* Corstorphine, near Edinburgh, 10 Sept 1871; *d* Henleys Down, England, 24 March 1940). Architect and planner. He studied garden cities, agriculture, and rural planning in England and worked in Canada before moving to New York City, where he formed the Town Planning Institute and became well known as the director of the Regional Plan of New York between 1923 and 1930. Toward the end of his life he taught at Harvard University and the Massachusetts Institute of Technology. Adams wrote *The Building of the City* (1931), *Recent Advances in Town Planning* (1932), and *Design of Residential Areas* (1934).

Michael Simpson: *Thomas Adams and the Modern Planning Movement* (New York: Mansell, 1985)

James E. Mooney

Addams, Charles (Samuel) (*b* Westfield, N.J., 7 Jan 1912; *d* New York City, 29 Sept 1988). Cartoonist. He attended Colgate University, the University of Pennsylvania, and the Grand Central School of Art and first published cartoons in 1935 in the *New Yorker*, which carried his work for more than half a century. Known for their macabre humor, his cartoons were shown at the Metropolitan Museum of Art, the Museum of the City of New York, and Harvard University, and inspired the television series "The Addams Family" (1964–66). Addams published a dozen books including *Addams and Evil* (1947), *Monster Rally* (1950), and *Favorite Haunts* (1976).

James E. Mooney

Addisleigh Park. Housing development in central Queens, just north of the former site of a golf course in St. Albans later occupied by the Veterans Administration Extended Care Center. It was begun in 1927 when the Addisleigh Homes Company and the Rodman and English Building Company built several blocks of houses in the English style on large plots on 179th and 180th streets between Murdock Avenue (114th Street) and Linden Boulevard. The houses cost $12,000 to $30,000 at a time when prices in Queens typically ranged from $8000 to $12,000. Buyers were drawn by the proximity of the golf course and the train station at St. Albans. Among the residents were such prominent black entertainers as Lena Horne and Count Basie. The Depression and the building up of available land put an end to development in 1939.

Vincent Seyfried

Adler, Felix (*b* Alzey, Germany, 13 Aug 1851; *d* New York City, 24 April 1933). Religious leader. His family emigrated from Germany and settled in New York City in 1857, when his father was invited to assume the rabbinate of Temple Emanu-El. Educated at Columbia College (BA 1870) and in Semitic studies at the University of Heidelberg (PhD 1874), he was influenced by Kantian religious idealism, studied European approaches to the problems of labor and industrial society, and taught Hebrew and Oriental studies at Cornell University for two years. With the support of German businessmen and professionals who were adherents of Reform Judaism he formed the New York Society for Ethical Culture in 1876, which drew on traditional creeds, ritual, and prayer and at the same time emphasized activism, secularism, and universalism. He also helped to train leaders for societies in St. Louis, Philadelphia, Chicago, and London and remained the leader of the society to the end of his life. Active in causes of civic and social improvement in the city between 1876 and 1925, he strongly supported industrial education, kindergartens, settlement houses, good-government clubs, tenement reform, child labor legislation, and the construction of small parks, public baths, and laundries. His interest in labor and his belief in providing young people with training in ethics led to the opening by the society of a kindergarten in 1878 (the first in the eastern United States) and a workingman's school in 1880, the first of several Ethical Culture schools in the city. In his writings and lectures Adler discoursed on the philosophical, ethical, and practical applications of Ethical Culture and his belief that religion should be based on intellectual truth, that the moral development of the individual and of society was paramount, and that morality need not rely on theology.

Howard B. Radest: *Toward Common Ground: The Story of the Ethical Societies in the United States* (New York: Ungar, 1969)

Robert S. Guttchen: *Felix Adler* (New York: Twayne, 1974)

Benny Kraut: *From Reform Judaism to Ethical Culture: The Religious Evolution of Felix Adler* (Cincinnati: Hebrew Union College Press, 1979)

Horace Leland Friess: *Felix Adler and Ethical Culture: Memories and Studies* (New York: Columbia University Press, 1981)

Jane Allen

Adler, Jacob (*b* Odessa, Ukraine, 1855; *d* New York City, 1 April 1926). Actor, father of Stella Adler. In the Ukraine in 1879 he made his début in the Yiddish theater, then a recently developed genre. After performing in eastern Europe he settled in 1882 in London, where he became well known for his performance in the title role of Karl Gutzkow's *Uriel Acosta*. By the time he settled in New York City in 1887 he enjoyed an international reputation. He was most popular in grand emotional roles and was associated with such literary repertory as Jacob Gordon's *Der yidishe kenig Lear*. A glamorous figure, Adler married several prominent actresses, including Sara Heine-Haimovitch and Dina Stettin Feinman. Stella Adler and several other children of his worked in the Yiddish and English-language theater: Celia Adler, Luther Adler, and Frances Adler.

Lulla Rosenfeld: *Bright Star of Exile: Jacob Adler and the Yiddish Theater* (New York: Thomas Y. Crowell, 1977)

Nahma Sandrow

Adler, Samuel (*b* Worms, Germany, 3 Dec 1809; *d* New York City, 9 June 1891). Rabbi. After earning a doctorate in Germany in 1836 he became a leader of the Reform movement in Judaism. In 1857 he moved to New York City to lead the congregation of Temple Emanu-El, where he continued his reform work and sought to raise the level of religious consciousness. His revised version of the Hebrew prayer book became widely used. Adler formed the Hebrew Orphan Asylum of New York, which stressed religious training for children, and worked toward equality for women in religious matters. His published writings include *Leitfaden für den israelitischen Religionsunterricht* (1864).

James E. Mooney

Adler, Stella (*b* New York City, 10 Feb 1901; *d* Los Angeles, 21 Dec 1992). Acting teacher, actress, and director, daughter of Jacob Adler. She first appeared on stage at the Grand Street Theater on the Lower East Side when she was four. In 1925 she began studying the Method, the revolutionary technique created by Konstantin Stanislavsky that focused on the development of an actor's internal sensory, psychological, and emotional abilities. During the Depression she joined the Group Theatre, an experimental union of writers, directors, and actors who promoted socially relevant theater in the United States. With one of the company's founders, Lee Strasberg, she became a leading authority on the application of the Method. Throughout her long career she appeared in nearly two hundred stage productions and won high praise for both her acting and directing talents. She also appeared in three Hollywood films: *Love on Toast* (1938), *Shadow of a Thin Man* (1941), and *My Girl Tisa* (1948). In 1949 she founded the Stella Adler Conservatory of Acting in Manhattan. A highly demanding and impassioned teacher, she shaped the careers of hundreds of notable performers, including Marlon Brando, Warren Beatty, and Robert De Niro. Her book *Stella Adler on Acting* was published in 1988. For many years Adler lived in an apartment on the Upper East Side.

Robert Sanger Steel

Adriance Farmhouse. Historic house in Queens, built in 1772 by Jacob Adriance and now at 75-50 Little Neck Parkway in Floral Park and part of the Queens County Farm Museum. The first farm on the site, built in 1697, was one of many established by colonial settlers who were drawn to the region by the rich soil deposited by glaciers. The farmhouse that stands in its place is built in the Dutch style with a steeply pitched roof and a shingled exterior; it was doubled in size in the 1830s. From 1890 to 1926 the property was a truck farm; it was acquired in 1927 by the Creedmoor State Hospital and until the 1960s patients tilled the soil. Two years after the last members of the hospital staff left the premises the house and farm were opened as a museum in 1975.

Albert W. Ryerson: *The Ryerson Genealogy: Genealogy and History of the Knickerbocker Families of Ryerson, Ryerse, Ryerss, also Adriance and Martense Families, All Descendants of Martin and Adriaen Reyersz (Reyerszen), of Amsterdam, Holland* (Chicago: Privately printed for Edward L. Ryerson, 1916)

Historic Houses in New York City Parks (New York: Department of Parks and Recreation / Historic House Trust of New York City, 1989)

Jonathan Kuhn

adult education. During the colonial period adult education consisted of instruction in English and the Bible. In 1857 the philanthropist and inventor Peter Cooper opened the Union for the Advancement of Science to provide free technical training in the evenings for people who worked during the day, and to sponsor lectures and discussions through the Cooper Union Forum (which remained active into the 1990s). At the turn of the century night schools offered classes in English and civics to immigrants. In 1919 James Robinson and Charles Beard opened the New School for Social Research at 66 West 12th Street as a center for adult education, with emphasis on the social sciences and psychology. Adult education was greatly increased by the passage of the Servicemen's Readjustment Act of 1944 (popularly known as the GI Bill) and the Universal Military Training and Services Act of 1951, which provided thousands of veterans with the opportunity to complete high school and college. Many of those who took advantage of this legislation were the first in their families to receive higher education. As social and economic conditions changed in the 1970s and 1980s a large number of women entered adult education programs.

The public school system in New York City provides a wide range of free courses for adults at more than 250 locations, in which more than 55,000 men and women are enrolled each year. New Chance is a special program for mothers seventeen to twenty-one years old who did not complete high school. Most of the colleges in the city have special programs for older students: at the City University of New York, for example, people at least sixty-five years old may enroll in any course for a minimal charge. The New York City Adult Literacy Initiative prepares adult students for tests in English as a second language and high school equivalency tests; it offers classes free of charge at community organizations, public schools, branches of the City University of New York, and public libraries. In addition to adult education of the conventional sort, New York City also has a thriving industry in profit-making adult education offered by such companies as the Learning Annex, which teach nontraditional and practical subjects ranging from belly dancing to résumé writing.

Huey B. Long: *Adult and Continuing Education: Responding to Change* (New York: Teachers College Press, 1983)

Nell Eurich: *The Learning Industry: Education for Adult Workers* (Princeton, N.J.: Carnegie Foundation for the Advancement of Teaching, 1990)

Rachel Shor

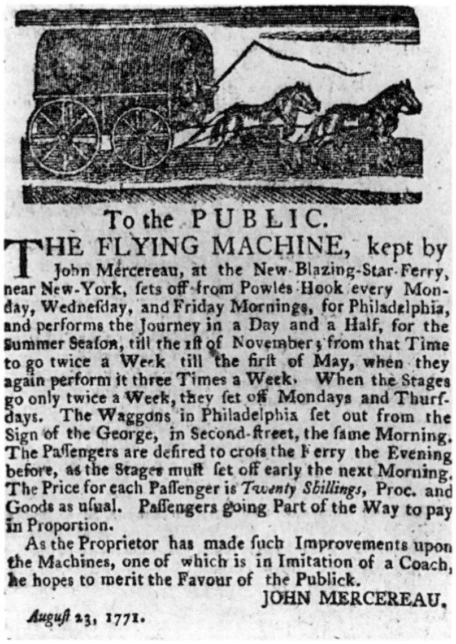

To the PUBLIC.

THE FLYING MACHINE, kept by John Mercereau, at the New-Blazing-Star-Ferry, near New-York, ſets off from Powles Hook every Monday, Wedneſday, and Friday Mornings, for Philadelphia, and performs the Journey in a Day and a Half, for the Summer Seaſon, till the 1ſt of November; from that Time to go twice a Week till the firſt of May, when they again perform it three Times a Week. When the Stages go only twice a Week, they ſet off Mondays and Thurſdays. The Waggons in Philadelphia ſet out from the Sign of the George, in Second-ſtreet, the ſame Morning. The Paſſengers are deſired to croſs the Ferry the Evening before, as the Stages muſt ſet off early the next Morning. The Price for each Paſſenger is *Twenty Shillings*, Proc. and Goods as uſual. Paſſengers going Part of the Way to pay in Proportion.

As the Proprietor has made ſuch Improvements upon the Machines, one of which is in Imitation of a Coach, he hopes to merit the Favour of the Publick.

JOHN MERCEREAU.

Auguſt 23, 1771.

The New York Gazette and Weekly Post-Boy, *1771*

advertising. During the eighteenth century advertising in New York City appeared mainly in newspapers. Classified advertisements took up half or more of the printed page in the *New-York Gazette* (1725), the *New-York Weekly Journal* (1733), and the *New York Daily Advertiser.* By 1800 New York City was beginning to surpass Philadelphia in its number of newspapers, and advertisements became more common and more vivid, often carrying display type and crude illustrations. They also appeared in magazines, which in the first quarter of the nineteenth century numbered more than five hundred. Advertising acquired an unsavory reputation because of extravagant claims for patent medicines and other products, but despite vigorous protests from the public the dependence of publishers on advertising revenues precluded reforms. The first advertising agent in the United States, Volney B. Palmer, opened an office in New York City a few years after he began operations in the early 1840s in Philadelphia: his commission of 25 percent was charged not to the merchants that placed advertisements but to the newspapers that printed them. An early competitor of Palmer, S. M. Pettingill, in 1852 became the first agent to prepare advertisements himself, a practice that gave rise to the modern advertising agency. For some fifty years during the nineteenth century the newspaper that carried the most advertising in New York City was the *New York Herald* (1835) of James Gordon Bennett Sr., the first publisher to recognize that the public saw advertising as a form of news: he required that his advertisers should provide new advertisements every two weeks.

Advertising gained in importance after the Civil War. Magazines became more numerous, and George P. Rowell made several innovations in newspaper advertising: his practice of buying up advertising space in bulk from newspapers and then selling it off piecemeal to advertisers, which he developed in Boston, prompted him to move to New York City. There he issued *Rowell's American Newspaper Directory* (1869), which listed all the newspapers in the country and for the first time gave an accurate estimate of their circulation, a service of great value to advertisers. In

1888 he launched *Printer's Ink*, the first advertising trade magazine. In 1875 N. W. Ayer and Son introduced the "open contract," which made it clear that the agent represented the advertiser rather than the newspaper, and which specified the amount to be spent on the advertising, as well as the commission to be paid by the advertiser to the agent (12 percent, later raised to 15 percent). In 1879 Ayer conducted the first marketing survey. Soon after the Civil War J. Walter Thompson began his career in New York City by placing advertisements in magazines, and in 1880 Cyrus H. K. Curtis conceived magazines that were not primarily literary publications but rather vehicles for advertising. By the end of the century magazines like *Cosmopolitan* could carry as many as a hundred pages of advertising in an issue. One of the great innovators in advertising in nineteenth-century New York City was P. T. Barnum, who astutely promoted a woman who he alleged was the 161-year-old nurse of George Washington, the midget Charles Stratton (advertised as General Tom Thumb), the Swedish soprano Jenny Lind, and a circus advertised as the "Greatest Show on Earth."

The electrification of New York City led to the introduction in the 1890s of enormous illuminated advertising signs, and by 1893 Broadway was already known as the "Great White Way." The first electric signs were on the Hotel Cumberland, at the intersection of Broadway, 5th Avenue, and 23rd Street. The city had twenty-five small advertising agencies by the turn of the century. By this time criticisms that advertising was fraudulent and deceptive had reached a peak, and the business took steps to improve its reputation: in 1911 the vigilance committee of the Advertising Club of New York supported a "truth in advertising" bill in the state legislature that was enacted and soon inspired similar measures in thirty-six other states, and in 1917 the American Association of Advertising Agencies was formed to establish service standards for the industry and encourage ethical practices (it continued in New York City into the 1990s). The image of advertising improved further as a result of the First World War, during which representatives of advertising agencies aided the war effort through the Council of National Defense. From 1918 to 1929 advertising agencies in the city grew along with a rapidly industrializing economy. They sold cigarettes, tires, soaps, toothpaste, mouthwash, liniment, sewing machines, piano lessons, soft drinks, and automobiles. Radio broadcasts began in 1920 and within two years more than two million sets were in use. Radio advertisements began almost at once, and after a few years of great resistance became an important means of selling inexpensive and often-purchased items as well as durable goods like refrigerators.

During the 1920s J. Walter Thompson emerged as the leading advertising agency in the United States, in part through an emphasis on market research that it began in 1923 when it conducted a quantitative study of magazine circulation, and that proved widely influential. Another important agency, Young and Rubicam, began in 1923 in Philadelphia and moved to New York City in 1926. One of its leaders, Raymond Rubicam, was a brilliant copywriter who helped to focus greater attention on the creative side of the business. The agency also engaged George Gallup in 1932 to conduct research into copy testing and marketing. Advertising continued virtually unabated during the Second World War: advertisers prepared to satisfy the pent-up demand that would be released when the war ended, and advertisements showing how a firm's products were helping to win the war were common. At the same time the War Advertising Council helped the government to mobilize the country for war, sell war bonds, recruit soldiers, and conserve scarce resources. After the war the council remained in operation as the Advertising Council and sponsored public service advertisements.

The late 1940s and the 1950s saw an enormous expansion of the advertising business in New York City. Advertising was irrevocably changed when television was introduced in 1948. By 1952 there were eighteen million television sets and 110 commercial transmitters in the United States, and by 1954 the Columbia Broadcasting System was the largest advertising medium in the world. Radio as an advertising medium was hit hard by the introduction of television and struggled for many years to recover. Television advertising became insistent, repetitive, and often tasteless, but it was also effective and by 1957 accounted for $1500 million in spending by advertisers. The advertising business also benefited from the increasing importance of the automobile in the American economy: of the ten largest advertising budgets in the country in 1956, automobiles accounted for nine.

After a decade during which advertising reflected the vigorous and often crass expansion of the postwar American economy, advertising in the 1960s expressed a different concern: to be honest, fresh, and engaging. A new emphasis was placed on the creative side of advertising, in what came to be called the "creative revolution." The most influential exponent of the revolution was William Bernbach, a native of Brooklyn whose work sought drama in the natural, everyday language and expression of ordinary people, for example in his advertisements for Levy's Jewish Rye and his campaign for Volkswagen based on the slogan "Think small." The two other leading figures were Leo Burnett, from Chicago (who conceived the Marlboro man and the Jolly Green Giant), and David Ogilvy, from Great Britain (who conceived the man in the Hathaway Shirt and Commander Whitehead for Schweppes). The creative revolution elevated the copywriter and the art director to central, complementary roles in the production of advertising, displacing the account executive and the researcher. During the 1960s many advertising agencies in New York City were formed with creativity as their guiding principle. At the same time the advertising business was becoming ethnically more heterogeneous: the agency Doyle Dane Bernbach employed Jews, thus breaking with a discriminatory practice long engaged in by most agencies (with the notable exception of Grey Advertising). It also employed many Italian-Americans, as did Benton and Bowles, Grey Advertising, and Wells, Rich, Greene. Gradually other ethnic exclusions were removed, and by the 1980s the advertising business in New York City was essentially open to whoever had sufficient talent to work in it.

The creative revolution faltered during the 1970s, and a renewed emphasis was given to the "hard sell," stressing the product rather than the style of presentation. During the same period a number of the major advertising agencies in the city changed from partnerships to publicly owned corporations, including Doyle Dane Bernbach; Foote, Cone and Belding; Grey Advertising; Ogilvy and Mather; and J. Walter Thompson. Some agencies consolidated through merger and acquisition, including Ted Bates; Interpublic; Ogilvy and Mather; Wells, Rich, Greene; and Young and Rubicam. The trend toward consolidation continued into the 1980s: under the leadership of Martin Sorrell, the WPP Group acquired J. Walter Thompson and the Ogilvy Group, and the Omnicom Group was formed through the merger of BBDO International, Doyle Dane Bernbach, and Needham Harper Worldwide. The number of multinational advertising agencies decreased from twelve in 1978 to eight in 1988, and at the end of the 1980s only four of the fifteen largest agencies in the country had the same ownership and structure as they had had at the beginning of the decade. With the recession of the late 1980s and early 1990s consolidations became less frequent and the advertising business entered a period of retrenchment. These problems notwithstanding, New York City remains the advertising capital of the United States.

James Playsted Wood: *The Story of Advertising* (New York: Ronald, 1958)

Stephen R. Fox: *The Mirror Makers: A History of American Advertising and Its Creators* (New York: William Morrow, 1984)

See also Outdoor advertising.

Chauncey G. Olinger, Jr.

Advertising Women of New York. Association formed in 1912 by Christine Frederick and J. George Frederick in response to discrimination against women at the Men's Advertising League. Initially known as the

League of Advertising Women of New York, it was the first organization of its kind in the country and focused on helping women to advance their careers by offering classes and scholarships, inviting speakers, and holding social events; it also conducted surveys concerning women's progress in advertising and fought for consumer rights. It took its current name in 1934.

Mary Ellen Zuckerman

Afghans. The extent of Afghan immigration to the United States was difficult to measure before 1953, when Afghans first became counted separately by the federal government. Over the following decade seventy-eight Afghans became American citizens, most of whom had arrived on student visas and were members of the Afghan social and economic élite. The number of immigrants increased markedly after Marxists seized control of the Afghan government in 1978. This later group of immigrants represented all classes of Afghan society, and most of its better-educated members found themselves doing work for which they were over-qualified. Some Afghans in New York City practice medicine and engineering; others own bakeries and restaurants (a number specializing in take-out fried chicken) and drive taxicabs and limousines. According to immigration statistics 1868 Afghans entered New York City between 1982 and 1987, a number that excludes those who entered the country illegally. A section of Flushing is sometimes referred to as Little Afghanistan; small Afghan communities have also taken root in Elmhurst, Jackson Heights, Corona, and Midwood (Brooklyn). The great majority of the roughly seven to ten thousand Afghans in New York City are Muslims. The most visible Afghan organization in the country is a group based in Queens known as the Afghan Community in America, which expended considerable effort to dislodge the Soviet Union from Afghanistan and influence American political leaders and public opinion.

Marc Ferris

AFL. See AMERICAN FEDERATION OF LABOR.

African Burial Ground. A burying place for African New Yorkers in use from about 1712 to 1794, occupying five and a half acres (2.2 hectares) and situated one mile (1.6 kilometers) north of the present Wall Street. It was also called the Negro Burial Ground. The origins of the burial ground are believed to be related to the origins of Trinity Church, which received its charter and land title in 1697. In the same year the church declared that Africans would no longer be buried in its churchyard, which had formerly served as a burial ground for paupers. Other restrictions on the burials of enslaved Africans included laws limiting the number of persons in attendance to twelve, and requiring that the burials must take place during daylight, contrary to some African customs. A portion of the burial ground was excavated just north of City Hall in 1991 when the federal government began construction of an office building at Broadway and Duane streets. By the following year 390 human remains were excavated, of which it was estimated that 92 percent were of African origin and nearly 45 percent were of children twelve years old or younger. About six hundred burial artifacts were also excavated, consisting mostly of shroud pins but also including African trade beads, coins, mariners' metals, and copper jewelry. The total number of interments in the burial ground is believed to have been ten to twenty thousand. In response to widespread protests the government altered its original building designs, creating a pavilion area where the two hundred burials yet undisturbed remain underground at Duane and Elk streets. The excavated remains were sent to Howard University in Washington for about five years of study, at the end of which they were to be returned to New York City for reinterment at the pavilion site.

The African Burial Ground has been designated a national historic landmark, and the city has designated the surrounding area the African Burial Ground and Historic Commons District.

John Sharpe: "Proposals for Erecting a School, Library, and a Chapel at New York," New-York Historical Society Collections, Revolutionary Miscellaneous Papers, vol. 3

Sherrill D. Wilson: *New York City's African Slaveowners: A Social and Material Culture History* (New York: Garland, 1994)

Sherrill D. Wilson

African Free Schools. Schools opened by the New York Manumission Society during the late eighteenth century to provide children of African ancestry with moral and practical instruction. The first African Free School, under the instruction of Cornelius Davis, admitted both boys and girls and offered training in reading, penmanship, arithmetic, grammar, geography, and (after 1791) needlework. In 1797 trustees added an evening school for adults taught by William Pirsson and his assistant John Teasman, one of the few early teachers who were black. On Pirsson's retirement Teasman took charge and in 1809 introduced a highly efficient monitorial method of teaching developed in London by Joseph Lancaster. By training a group of student monitors who eventually became teachers themselves, Teasman increased the average attendance at the free school from sixty to more than 350. The first schoolhouse was destroyed by fire in 1814 and the society soon built another one at 245 William Street. A second school was established closer to the city's black population at 135 Mulberry Street in 1820; between 1827 and 1829 the society employed the editor and minister Samuel Cornish to increase enrollment. Five schools opened in 1831–33 under Benjamin H. Hughes and the curriculum of the schools expanded as Charles C. Andrews, the principal instructor, added classes in navigation, business, and skilled trades.

In the early 1830s William Hamilton, Henry Sipkins, and Thomas Downing mounted a successful campaign to remove Andrews because of his support for the African colonization movement. Under increasing local demands for more black teachers the schools appointed John Peterson, Sarah M. Douglass, Ransom F. Wake, and Charles Reason; by 1834 blacks taught in five of the seven schools and held all but one of the assistants' positions. In the same year the Manumission Society transferred control of all seven of its schools to the New York Public School Society, a charity group not belonging to the abolitionist movement. Two of the schools were designated as public schools and the rest at a lower level as public primaries; all became part of the public school system in 1847. During its sixty-year history the African Free Schools prepared many of their students for more advanced education and trained future leaders like the physician James McCune Smith, the abolitionist ministers Samuel Ringgold Ward and Henry Highland Garnet, the Episcopal clergyman and scholar Alexander Crummell, the anti-slavery leader and Liberian government official John B. Russwurm, the businessman Peter Williams, the abolitionist Theodore S. Wright, the engraver Patrick Reason, and the Shakespearean actor Ira Aldridge. Largely denied entry into the skilled trades, other products of the practical curriculum had to settle for work as waiters, coachmen, barbers, servants, shipwrights, and seamen.

Charles C. Andrews: *The History of the New York African Free-schools from Their Establishment in 1787* (New York: Mahlon Day, 1830)

Robert C. Morris

African Methodist Episcopal church. A denomination formed by black members of the St. George Methodist Episcopal Church in Philadelphia, who withdrew in 1787 because of racial discrimination and formed two congregations within the Free African Society, a mutual aid organization in Philadelphia led by Richard Allen, a former slave. Most who withdrew became Episcopalians, but a small group led by Allen formed a congregation named Bethel African Methodist Episcopal Church. Repeated efforts by white Methodists to assert control led Allen to gain autonomy for the congregation in 1807 and to form an independent denomination in 1816, the African Methodist Episcopal Church, of which he became the first bishop. In 1819 Allen sent William Lambert to New York City to hold the first New York Annual Conference; independent congregations in

Brooklyn (1766) and Flushing (1810) were among the first to join the church. During the years before the Civil War the church grew rapidly. In 1918 Reverdy C. Ransom, the pastor of Bethel Church in Manhattan and later a bishop, became the first black to seek election to the U.S. House of Representatives, from the twenty-first congressional district. Floyd H. Flake, the pastor of Allen Church in Jamaica, was elected to the U.S. House of Representatives in 1986 (from the sixth district, in Queens). In the mid 1990s the church had two million members, twenty bishops, and nineteen episcopal districts in North America, South America, the Caribbean, Africa, and Europe; it operated missions and financial agencies, issued publications, and sponsored housing, institutions of higher education, and social service centers.

Daniel A. Payne: *History of the African Methodist Episcopal Church* (Nashville: Publishing House of the A.M.E. Sunday School Union, 1891)

Reverdy C. Ransom: *The Pilgrimage of Harriet Ransom's Son* (Nashville: A.M.E. Sunday School Union, 1949)

George A. Singleton: *The Romance of African Methodism: A Study of the African Methodist Episcopal Church* (New York: Exposition, 1952)

Dennis C. Dickerson

African Methodist Episcopal Zion Church. Church formed by black members of the John Street Church in New York City. Increasing tension with white members led some black members of the John Street Church to ask Bishop Francis Asbury for permission to conduct separate services in 1796. Although officially autonomous, the African Chapel remained within the jurisdiction of the Methodist Episcopal Church until 1820, when a group led by William Stillwell, a supporter of the independent black church movement, broke away. After failing to win independence within the white church, blacks formed the African Methodist Episcopal Zion Church in 1821; congregations were organized in Manhattan, Philadelphia, and New Haven, Connecticut, and on Long Island. James Varick was elected the first superintendent in 1822 and reelected in 1826; Christopher Rush succeeded him in 1828. At the urging of the African Methodist Episcopal Church during preparations for a merger in 1864, the church replaced its superintendency with a lifetime episcopacy. Although the merger failed, the superintendents of the church became bishops in 1868. From 1880 they served without term restrictions. Congregations formed in New England and the Middle Atlantic states, and the church became associated with abolition through the work of such noted members as Sojourner Truth, Harriet Tubman, Jermain Loguen, and Frederick Douglass. After Emancipation missionaries opened churches in the South. Expansion was most rapid in North Carolina and Alabama; many congregations were also formed in other parts of the South, the Midwest, and the West. Membership increased from 13,702 in 1864 to 349,788 in 1890. Well-known members of the church in New York City during these years included T. Thomas Fortune, who between 1881 and 1907 launched the newspapers the *Freeman*, the *Globe*, and the *Age*, and Bishop Alexander Walters, an important black spokesman in the Democratic Party, especially during the presidential election of 1912. In the mid 1990s the church had 1.2 million members in thirteen episcopal districts in the United States, South America, the Caribbean, West Africa, and England and thirteen bishops, who oversaw missions, publications, pension funds, and evangelical efforts. Its principal educational institutions were Livingstone College and Hood Theological Seminary in Salisbury, North Carolina.

David H. Bradley Sr.: *A History of the A.M.E. Zion Church, 1796–1872*, part 1 (Nashville: Parthenon, 1956)

William J. Walls: *The African Methodist Episcopal Zion Church: Reality of the Black Church* (Charlotte, N.C.: A.M.E. Zion Publishing, 1974)

George M. Miller: "This Worldly Mission: The Life and Career of Alexander Walters, 1857–1917" (diss., State University of New York, Stony Brook, 1984)

Dennis C. Dickerson

Africans. The first sub-Saharan African immigrants in New York City apart from those who arrived as slaves were associated with maritime trades such as whaling and shipping and entered the city during the colonial period. They were quite few in number; it is likely that some were temporary residents of the city and that others remained and became part of the extremely small community of free blacks. In the late colonial period and throughout most of the nineteenth century a system of slavery based on African heritage made immigration to New York City of free people of African descent almost impossible (although New York State outlawed slavery relatively early, in 1817). After the Civil War immigration was restricted by racial quotas, which were only somewhat loosened by the immigration acts of 1952 and 1965. Immigration from Africa remained far more restricted than that from Europe into the 1990s. From the 1940s to the 1960s most Africans arrived in New York City to pursue an education. A small number of Nigerians made their way to the city as hands or stowaways on ocean liners. Until the 1970s most African immigrants spent only a short time in New York City before returning to their country of origin. Those who remained were usually guest workers, diplomats, businessmen, academics, and students with more than one degree. Liberians were a majority of the several thousand Africans living in the city during this period. In the 1970s and 1980s Africans in the city numbered more than fifty thousand and included immigrants from Nigeria (about four thousand), Senegal, Mali, the Ivory Coast, Gambia, Chad, and Cameroon. Most West African immigrants entered the city about 1983, when sub-Saharan Africa was ravaged by drought. Severe inflation in Nigeria brought the number of English-speaking Nigerians in the city to more than ten thousand; most of their families were small. Unlike the African immigrants of previous decades the new immigrants were dissuaded from pursuing education by its prohibitively high cost. Young men tended instead to work as taxi drivers, security guards, and street vendors. Christians and Muslims each account for nearly half the Africans in the city; the remaining few are animists. Although most African immigrants return to their country of origin once they have made money, some stay and open restaurants, nightclubs, and import businesses specializing in African textiles sold to street vendors and department stores. Most African immigrants chose to settle in the Bronx, particularly near Yankee Stadium. By the early 1990s a small neighborhood of Liberians and other Africans had taken shape in Clifton in Staten Island; some worshipped at the Faith Christian Center at 20 Park Hill Avenue. Among the more prominent Africans who have lived in New York City is Godfrey L. Binaisa, president of Uganda from June 1979 to May 1980, who joined the city's law department in December 1988.

B. Kimberly Taylor

African Street Festival. Five-day cultural event held annually in Brooklyn, originally known as the Afrikan Street Carnival; it is the largest Afrocentric event of its kind in the United States. Planned as part of commencement exercises by the Uhuru Sasa School (then at 10 Claver Place) and its parent organization, the East, the festival by 1976 was too large for Claver Place and was moved to Boys' and Girls' High School at Fulton Street and Schenectady Avenue. It took its current name in 1986 and became a nonprofit organization. Russell D. Clown, Mama Kuumba, Sun Ra, the Weusi Kuumba Troupe, and the Dinizulu African Drummers, Dancers and Singers became some of the regular performers. The African Street Festival attracts about sixty thousand persons and more than three hundred vendors of African food, clothing, art, crafts, and literature; opening ceremonies are led by the hand drummer Chief Bey.

Sule Greg C. Wilson

AFSCME. See AMERICAN FEDERATION OF STATE, COUNTY AND MUNICIPAL EMPLOYEES.

AFTRA. See AMERICAN FEDERATION OF TELEVISION AND RADIO ARTISTS.

Agee, James (Rufus) (*b* Knoxville, Tenn., 27 Nov 1909; *d* New York City, 16 May 1955).

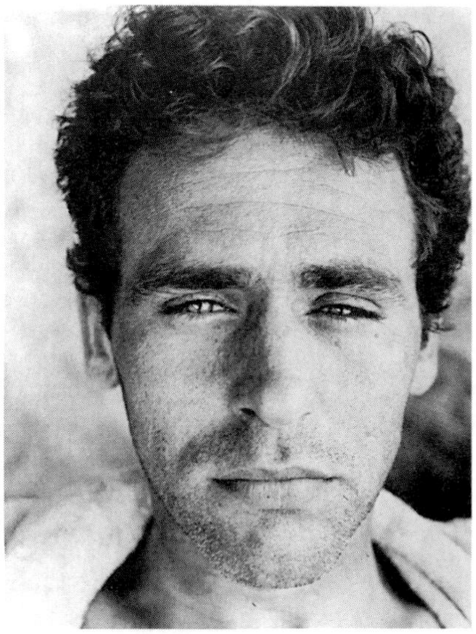

James Agee, 1934

Essayist, poet, and novelist. After graduating from Harvard University in 1932 he moved to New York City to work as a reporter for *Fortune.* He took a basement apartment at 38 Perry Street in Greenwich Village and had an office on the 52nd floor of the Chrysler Building, where he became known for working all night while smoking cigarettes, drinking whiskey, and listening to classical music. He published a volume of poetry, *Permit Me Voyage,* in 1934. In 1936 he received a commission from the magazine to write a series of articles about tenant farming in the South; the result was an impressionistic mixture of prose and poetry that was ten times longer than required. After the magazine relinquished the rights to the story Agee worked alone to complete it, living at times in Brooklyn, as well as in Frenchtown and Stockton, New Jersey; Harper and Brothers provided a small advance but dropped the project after receiving the revised manuscript. Financially ruined and drinking heavily, Agee lived at 322 West 15th Street from 1939 until 1941, when he began working for *Time* and his book was published by Houghton Mifflin as *Let Us Now Praise Famous Men.* He lived at 172 Bleecker Street from the autumn of 1941 until 1951, and in the mid 1940s he worked in a studio at 33 Cornelia Street. His film reviews for *Time* and the *Nation* were among the most influential in the country; he also wrote scripts for a number of films, including (with John Huston) *The African Queen* (1951) and *The Night of the Hunter* (1955), and the novel *The Morning Watch* (1950). He spent the end of his life at 17 King Street in a house built by Aaron Burr. Agee's novel *A Death in the Family* was published in 1957 and won a Pulitzer Prize in 1960; a collection of his essays, *Agee on Film,* was published in 1958–60.

David Madden, ed.: *Remembering James Agee* (Baton Rouge: Louisiana State University Press, 1974)

Lawrence Bergreen: *James Agee: A Life* (New York: E. P. Dutton, 1984)

See also DOCUMENTARY FILMMAKING.

Walter Friedman

AIA. See AMERICAN INSTITUTE OF ARCHITECTS.

AIChE. See AMERICAN INSTITUTE OF CHEMICAL ENGINEERS.

AIDS [Acquired Immune Deficiency Syndrome]. During the decade following the identification of AIDS by public health officials in the early 1980s, New York City was more severely affected by the disease than any other American city. In 1986 epidemiologists estimated that more than half the homosexual men in the city and three fifths of the intravenous drug users were infected with human immunodeficiency virus (HIV), a precursor of AIDS, and by the end of 1987 one in sixty-one women giving birth in the city was infected with AIDS itself. Toward the end of the 1980s AIDS became the leading cause of death in the city among men twenty-five to forty-four years of age and black women fifteen to forty-four years of age, and overwhelmed the city's health care and social welfare system: 13 percent of the in-patient beds in facilities maintained by the Health and Hospitals Corporation were occupied by AIDS patients in 1988. In response the city and private organizations worked to increase in-patient and outpatient services, as well as home health care.

The sudden prevalence of AIDS raised a number of controversial issues of public policy. A debate over whether patients should be tested for infection with HIV, and whether the names of those who tested positive should be kept confidential, was settled when the state legislature passed the Testing Confidentiality Act of 1988, which required informed consent before testing and assured those tested of confidentiality; at the same time the act provided that if patients could not be persuaded to make known their condition to their sex partners and to those who shared intravenous needles with them, health care workers would be empowered to make the disclosure instead. Attempts to interrupt transmission of the virus by distributing condoms and sterile needles also proved controversial; a plan to distribute condoms to high school students was narrowly approved in 1991 by the Board of Education, and a needle-exchange program begun under Mayor Edward I. Koch was discontinued by Mayor David N. Dinkins. Many other measures taken to help those with AIDS were severely impaired by reductions in city and state budgets.

AIDS brought about profound changes among male homosexuals in New York City. Bathhouses and bars closed in the early 1980s, and in the following years there were indications that casual sex was becoming less common and that condoms were being used more widely. The epidemic also inspired activism by such groups as the Gay Men's Health Crisis and the more militant organization ACT-UP (AIDS Coalition to Unleash Power). Artists in the city took part in fund-raising and educational efforts, including an annual event known as the "Day without Art"; works of art inspired by AIDS included Larry Kramer's play *The Normal Heart* and Diamanda Galas's performance piece "Plague Mass." By October 1994 there had been 70,880 cases of AIDS among New Yorkers, and 47,317 persons had died from the disease.

Harlon L. Dalton, ed.: *AIDS and the Law: A Guide for the Public* (New Haven: Yale University Press, 1987)

Charles Perrow: *The AIDS Disaster: The Failure of Organizations in New York and the Nation* (New Haven: Yale University Press, 1990)

David F. Musto

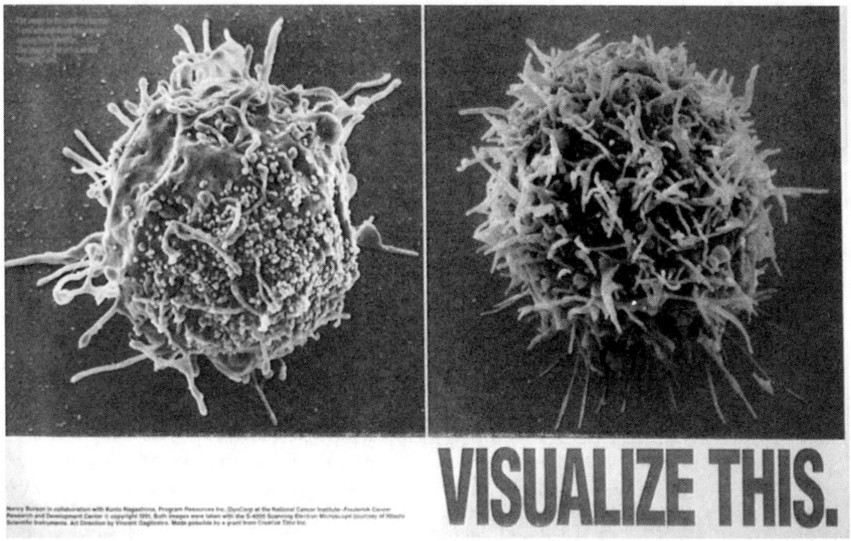

*AIDS awareness poster (1991), showing a normal T-cell (*right*) and one infected by Human Immunodeficiency Virus (HIV) (*left*)*

Deaths from AIDS in New York City by Sex, Race, and Ethnicity, 1982–1992

	Black	Hispanic	White	All Others	Male	Female	Total
1982	N/A	N/A	N/A	N/A	N/A	N/A	30
1983	134	95	182	14	376	49	425
1984	315	236	372	29	826	126	952
1985	533	381	634	45	1,463	200	1,663
1986	876	633	909	232	2,265	385	2,650
1987	1,061	800	986	312	2,651	508	3,159
1988	1,428	1,041	1,092	178	3,086	653	3,739
1989	1,427	1,191	1,299	276	3,488	705	4,193
1990	1,530	1,156	1,396	397	3,663	816	4,479
1991	1,850	1,313	1,417	439	4,060	959	5,019
1992	2,039	1,503	1,550	500	4,433	1,159	5,592

N/A = Not Available
Source: New York City Department of Health, *Summary of Vital Statistics*

AIDS Coalition to Unleash Power. See Act-up.

AIEE. See American Institute of Electrical Engineers.

Ailanthus. The Ailanthus (*Ailanthus altissima*), a tree transported from China to England during the 1750s, was introduced into the United States in 1784 as food for silkworms. Sometimes known as the tree of heaven, it was incorporated into the design of Central Park by Frederick Law Olmsted, who liked its tropical appearance. In the following years it spread to cities, suburbs, and roadsides throughout much of the country.

Steven D. Garber: *The Urban Naturalist* (New York: John Wiley and Sons, 1987)

Steven D. Garber

Ailey, Alvin (*b* Rogers, Texas, 5 Jan 1931; *d* New York City, 1 Dec 1989). Dancer, choreographer, and artistic director. He studied dance with Lester Horton and Martha Graham and moved to New York City in the mid 1950s. In 1958 he formed the Alvin Ailey American Dance Theater with the aim of bringing black dancers into the mainstream of dance. The troupe performed his own dances as well as the work of such established choreographers as Horton, Katherine Dunham, Pearl Primus, Ted Shawn, Talley Beatty, John Butler, and Donald McKayle and such younger ones as Ulysses Dove, Elisa Monte, and Bill T. Jones. A versatile choreographer, Ailey skillfully blended ballet, modern dance, and jazz dance in works set to music by such diverse composers as Ralph Vaughan Williams, John Coltrane, and Duke Ellington, who in 1970 composed *Les trois rois noirs* and *The River* for him. Some of his dances are thematic, often drawing on black culture (including his best-known work, *Revelations*, and *Blues Suite*); others focus on abstract movement and have often been performed by ballet companies (*Streams, The River*, and *The Lark Ascending*). Ailey was among the first modern-dance choreographers to create new ballets for classical dance companies like the American Ballet Theater, the Joffrey Ballet, and the Harkness Ballet, and for opera productions in the United States and abroad.

Susan Cook and Joseph H. Mazo: *The Alvin Ailey American Dance Theater* (New York: William Morrow, 1978)
Elinor Rogosin: *The Dance Makers: Conversations with American Choreographers* (New York: Walker, 1980)

Brenda Dixon Gottschild

Alan Guttmacher Institute. Nonprofit organization in New York City and Washington, formed in 1968 as the Center for Family Planning Program Development, a division of the Planned Parenthood Federation of America. Its founders, Frederick S. Jaffe and the obstetrician and gynecologist Alan F. Guttmacher, then president of the federation, intended that the new organization should protect reproductive rights throughout the world (especially among the young and the poor) and communicate to policymakers and the public the findings of research in the fields of reproductive rights, reproductive health, and population. The institute became independent and separately incorporated in 1977. Jaffe served as its president until his death in 1978. In the mid 1990s the Alan Guttmacher Institute had an annual budget of $5 million and issued several publications, including *Family Planning Perspectives, International Family Planning Perspectives*, and *State Reproductive Health Monitor: Legislative Proposals and Actions.* The offices in New York City, at 120 Wall Street, are the center for all research, publishing, and information activities.

Albanians. Albanian peasants and unskilled workers settled in New York City at the turn of the century; most found work in shoe, glass, and textile factories. Neighborhoods were formed according to religious affiliations: Catholics on South Fordham Road opened the Albanian Catholic Center, Muslims in central Brooklyn the Albanian American Islamic Center, and Eastern Orthodox in Jamaica the St. Nicholas Albanian Church. There was another influx of immigrants after the First World War. Refugees, political exiles, and professionals settled in the city after the Second World War and launched a number of periodicals and organizations. The Free Albania Committee, an alliance of various political groups, promoted freedom and democracy in Albania and in 1957 began publishing *Shqiptari i Lire* (The Free Albanian). The farmers' organization the Agrarian Democratic Party (also known as Balli Kombetar) issued the publication *Shgrbistari* (The Serviceman, 1950–61) for its youth branch and also introduced the newspaper *Zeri i Ballit* (The Voice, 1950–). *Jeta Katholike Shkiptare* (Catholic Albanian Life, 1966–) and the Muslim publication *Perpejka e Jone* (Our Effort, 1974–) were intended to provide religious, social, and political news. The Albanian Kosovar Youth reported on violations of the political rights of Albanians living in Yugoslavia. Small businessmen belonged to the Albanian Owners Association.

In the mid 1990s there were between twenty thousand and 25,000 Albanians in New York City. Many were professionals, office workers, small businessmen, and food-service and maintenance workers; they promoted education and also sought to preserve their customs and ethnic heritage. Well-known Albanians in the city have included the writer and social activist Nemnie Zaimi and the writer and literary scholar Arshi Pipa.

Francis Brown and Joseph S. Roucek, eds.: *One America: The History, Contributions and Present Problems of Our Racial and National Minorities* (Englewood Cliffs, N.J.: Prentice Hall, 1952)

Vladimir Wertsman

Albee, Edward (Franklin) (*b* Washington, 12 March 1928). Playwright. He achieved some notoriety with his early works *The Zoo Story* (1959), which is set in Central Park, and *The American Dream* (1961), and won a Tony Award and a New York Drama Critics Circle award for *Who's Afraid of Virginia Woolf?* in 1962. During his early career he lived in a duplex in Greenwich Village, and in 1978 he began dividing his time between a loft in Tribeca and homes in Long Island and Florida. His later plays include *Tiny Alice* (1965), *A Delicate Balance* (1966), winner of a Pulitzer Prize, and *Three Tall Women* (1994).

Kenneth T. Jackson

Alexander, William, Lord Stirling (*b* New York City, 1726; *d* Albany, N.Y., 15 Jan 1783). General. After receiving his education in New York City he went to England to claim his title, which was refused by the House of Lords; he then returned to the city, where he became a governor of King's College, held several offices after his marriage to Governor William Livingston's sister, and in 1769 recorded the transit of the planet Venus. He opposed the Stamp Act and during the American Revolution captured a British transport, was appointed brigadier general of the Continental Army, and oversaw the construction of fortifications including Forts Lee and Washington. Captured during the Battle of Long Island, he was freed during an exchange of prisoners and fought in the battles of Westchester, Trenton, Brandywine, and Germantown; his attack on British forces on Staten Island was repulsed. By the end of the war Alexander was promoted to the rank of major-general.

Paul David Nelson: *William Alexander, Lord Stirling* (Tuscaloosa: University of Alabama Press, 1987)

James E. Mooney

Alexander Hamilton. Sidewheel steamboat, designed by J. W. Millard and built by the Bethlehem Shipbuilding Corporation of Maryland in 1924. She measured 349 feet (106 meters) by seventy-seven feet (twenty-three meters) and had a triple-expansion inclined engine and feathering sidewheels. From 1924 until 6 September 1971 the ship was operated by the Hudson River Day Line between New York City and other points along the Hudson; her retirement marked the end of the scheduled steam service along the Hudson that had been initiated in 1807. Efforts to preserve the vessel failed: the hulk lies in Sandy Hook Bay, New Jersey.

Arthur G. Adams

Alexander Robertson School. Private elementary school, opened in 1789 in Manhattan by the Second Presbyterian Church and originally situated at Broadway and King's Street (now Pine Street); it is the oldest fully coeducational institution in New York City. The school is named for the principal benefactor of the church, a Scotsman who lived in New York City and raised money to repair the church after Hessian mercenaries used it as a barracks during the American Revolution. The school moved in 1813 to West 14th Street and in 1900 to 95th Street and Central Park West. A Scottish flavor persists despite the diverse populations of both school and church: the emblem of the school is a thistle, bagpipes are played at special events, and each graduation ceremony ends with the singing of "Auld Lang Syne."

Richard Schwartz

Alexander's. Firm of retailers. Its first department store was opened in 1928 at 3rd Avenue and 152nd Street in the Bronx by George Farkas (1902–80) and named after his father. The firm built its reputation by selling fashionable clothes at discount prices and concentrating on lower- to middle-income customers. In 1963 Farkas moved the main store to 59th Street and Lexington Avenue, just across from Bloomingdale's. Alexander's filed for bankruptcy in May 1992 and closed its eleven retail outlets in the city.

Leslie Gourse, Kenneth T. Jackson

Alfred A. Knopf. Firm of book publishers founded in 1915 by Alfred A. Knopf and his wife, Blanche, at 220 West 42nd Street. It published in a variety of areas, emphasizing subjects such as history and music that were of personal interest to the Knopfs, and established a lasting reputation for the quality of both its fiction and nonfiction. In particular the firm became known for introducing the works of foreign writers to American readers and for raising the standards of book design. Sold to Random House in 1960, which was in turn taken over by the Radio Corporation of America in 1966 and by Newhouse Publications in 1980, Alfred A. Knopf continued as a separate imprint. In 1969 it moved to its present location at 201 East 50th Street.
See also Book publishing.

Eileen K. Cheng

Alger, Horatio(, Jr.) (*b* Chelsea, Mass., 13 Jan 1832; *d* Natick, Mass., 18 July 1899). Writer. Born to a patrician family in an area that is now part of Revere, he was educated as a Unitarian minister and in 1866 settled in New York City, where he supported a number of charitable social causes, including the Newsboys Lodging House, and wrote juvenile novels about street boys who eventually became wealthy through luck and hard work. From 1872 to 1876 he lived at 26 West 34th Street. During his career Alger wrote 103 juvenile novels, among them the best-seller *Ragged Dick* (1868); these were modestly received during his lifetime but became popular between the world wars, when they were presented to children as models for achieving success.

Franz Gruber: *Horatio Alger, Jr.: A Biography and Bibliography* (West Los Angeles: Jones Press, 1961)

Michael Joseph

Algerians. The first Algerians to settle in New York City were a few hundred students who traveled there in the early 1970s on government scholarships. During the next decade there was a second group of immigrants, most of whom were middle-class families seeking relief from economic hardship. By the early 1990s a third phase of immigration was under way, consisting mainly of young, single people from France escaping racism toward North Africans. Still the numbers remained small: by the mid 1990s the number of Algerian New Yorkers probably did not exceed six hundred. Most of the students who had been the first immigrants had become professionals in scientific and technical fields by 1990; they maintained cultural solidarity through the Algerian American National Association. Algerian rai music, a mix of Arab, African, and rock music with themes of social commentary and protest, became quite popular in the city through the work of such musicians as Cheba Fadela, Cheb Tati, and Cheb Mami.

Paula Hajar

Algonquin Hotel, ca *1910*

Algonquin Hotel. A hotel opened in 1902 on West 44th Street between 5th and 6th avenues. The name was the inspiration of Frank Case, an employee who later operated the hotel from 1907. The building, designed by Goldwyn Starrett, has a façade of red brick and limestone, and is decorated with eighteenth-century English and American furnishings. In the 1920s and 1930s the hotel was a center of literary and theatrical life: it was closely associated with the *New Yorker* and was the home of the Algonquin Round Table. Alan Jay Lerner wrote the musical *My Fair Lady* in room 908. After Case's death in 1946 control of the hotel passed to Ben Bodne; on his retirement in 1987 it was acquired by Caesar Park Hotels.

Frank Case: *Tales of a Wayward Inn* (New York: Frederick A. Stokes, 1938)

B. Kimberly Taylor

Algonquin Round Table. The name given to a group of lively theatrical and literary figures who met daily for lunch at the Algonquin Hotel on West 44th Street for about a decade beginning in 1919. The group met first in the Pergola Room (now the Oak Room), until Frank Case, manager of the Algonquin, moved it in 1920 to the round table in the larger Rose Room so that the members would be more visible to the public.

The central figure in the group was Alexander Woollcott, drama critic of the *New York Times.* Its other members included the writer Franklin P. Adams, author of the highly popular newspaper column "The Conning Tower" and generally considered the dean of the table; the press agents Murdock Pemberton and John Peter Toohey; the writers Heywood Broun and his wife, Ruth Hale; Jane Grant of the *New York Times* and her husband, Harold Ross, who founded the *New Yorker* and published the work of several members of the table in its pages; Dorothy Parker, Robert E. Sherwood, and the humorist Robert Benchley, all writers for *Vanity Fair*; Art Samuels of *Harper's Bazaar*; the writers Marc Connelly, George S. Kaufman, and Donald Ogden Stewart; and the illustrator Neysa McMein. From time to time others were invited to the table, including the actors Douglas Fairbanks, Harpo Marx, Alfred Lunt and Lynn Fontanne, Tallulah Bankhead, Ina Claire, and Margallo Gilmore, the novelists Edna Ferber, Margaret Leech, and Alice Duer Miller, the playwrights Noël Coward and Charles MacArthur, the screenwriter Herman Mankiewicz, and the young violinist Jascha Heifetz.

The group was celebrated for being at once glamorous, irreverent, acerbic, worldly, and clannish. Its influence stemmed largely from the power that newspaper columnists wielded during the prosperous years of the 1920s, when the public was fascinated with success, talent, and amusement and the commercial success of the theater was near its peak (in 1921 there were seventy-six legitimate theaters in New York City). The members of the round table read, discussed, and quoted each other; they became the people whom other people enjoyed reading about.

By the end of the 1920s the Algonquin Round Table had virtually ceased to exist, and the onset of the Depression made its sophistication and wit painfully outmoded. Even in its heyday such critics as Edmund Wilson found the metropolitan focus of the table provincial and its talents evanescent (apart from those of Parker). But although the individual reputations of the members of the group have for the most part faded, they remain the symbols of a literate humor that is inextricably associated with New York City, and the reminders of a time when urban living and urbanity were often combined.

Margaret Case Harriman: *The Vicious Circle: The Story of the Algonquin Round Table* (New York: Rinehart, 1951)

James R. Gaines: *Wit's End: Days and Nights of the Algonquin Round Table* (New York: Harcourt Brace Jovanovich, 1977)

For illustration see HIRSCHFELD, AL.

Brenda Wineapple

Alice Austen House. Historic house in Staten Island. The first house on the site was built by the Dutch in the 1690s as part of a farm near the Narrows. The property was acquired in 1844 by the grandfather of the photographer Alice Austen, who expanded the house and added peaked windows and a gingerbread trim, giving it the appearance of a Victorian cottage. The family moved into the house shortly after Austen was born in 1866 and she remained there until 1945; the more than seven thousand photographs that she took while living at the house are now at the Staten Island Historical Society. The house and grounds were restored in the 1980s and reopened as a historic museum, with temporary exhibitions.

Ann Novotny: *Alice's World: The Life and Photography of an American Original, Alice Austen, 1866–1952* (Old Greenwich, Conn.: Chatham, 1976)

Historic Houses in New York City Parks (New York: Department of Parks and Recreation / Historic House Trust of New York City, 1989)

Jonathan Kuhn

Allan, Sidney. Pseudonym of SADAKICHI HARTMANN.

Allen, Stephen (*b* New York City, 2 July 1767; *d* southern Westchester County, 28 July 1852). Mayor. He worked as an apprentice for a sail maker during the American Revolution and later formed a partnership with his employer. Soon after starting his own business he amassed a fortune ($100,000 in 1805) by applying his spartan work habits and bypassing ship chandlers to deal directly with wholesalers. A staunch Jeffersonian, he became president of the Mechanics City, a director of the Mechanics Bank, and a city alderman. Allen was elected mayor for three terms (1821–24) and in his later years became a Jacksonian Democrat. He died during the burning of the steamboat *Henry Clay.*

Howard Rock

Allen, Woody [Konigsberg, Allan (Stewart)] (*b* Brooklyn, 1 Dec 1935). Filmmaker, writer, and actor. He grew up in Flatbush and during his first year at Midwood High School wrote material for the columnist Earl Wilson; in 1952 he took his current name. After briefly attending New York University and City College of New York he appeared as a stand-up comedian at the Bitter End and the Blue Angel, on the "Ed Sullivan Show," and on the "Tonight Show," of which he was also a guest host. His play *Don't Drink the Water* (1966) ran for eighteen months on Broadway. In 1965 he wrote and acted in *What's New, Pussycat?* and in 1969 he directed his first complete feature film, *Take the Money and Run.* His later films, which numbered more than twenty by the mid 1990s, are often set in New York City and are largely autobiographical; notable examples include *Manhattan* (1979), *Radio Days* (1987), and *Husbands and Wives* (1992). *Hannah and Her Sisters* (1986), much of which was filmed at the Langham, 135 Central Park West, includes an architectural tour of Manhattan; other films were made at locations ranging from Sutton Place to Coney Island. In 1993 Allen was embroiled in a highly public custody dispute with his estranged companion, the actress Mia Farrow.

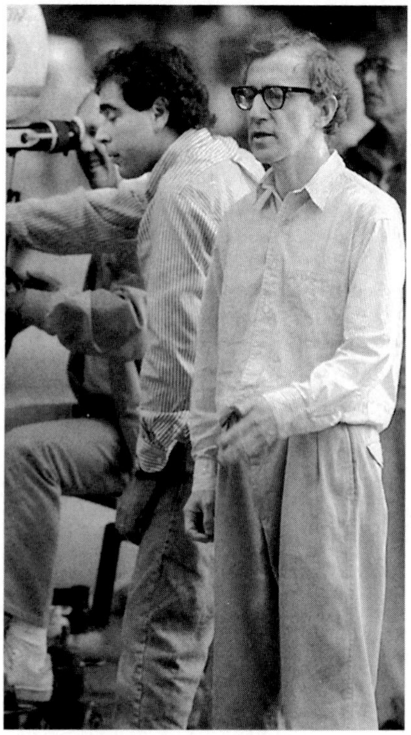

Woody Allen on the set of Alice *(1990)*

Natalie Gittelson: "The Maturing of Woody Allen," *New York Times Magazine*, 22 April 1979, pp. 30–32

Leslie Bennets: "Woody Allen's Selective Vision of New York," *New York Times*, 7 March 1986, §C, p. 1

Caryn James: "Auteur! Auteur!," *New York Times Magazine*, 19 Jan 1986, pp. 18–30

Eric Lax: *Woody Allen* (New York: Alfred A. Knopf, 1991)

Maurice Yacowar: *Loser Take All: The Comic Art of Woody Allen* (New York: Continuum, 1991)

Val Ginter

Alley. Name formerly applied to a neighborhood in northwestern Queens, at the head of Little Neck Bay along a valley 125 feet (thirty-eight meters) deep made by Alley Pond. A royal grant for the land was given in 1673 to Thomas and Christopher Foster, who soon built the first house. By 1691 a grist mill was operated by John and Stephen Hicks just south of what is now Northern Boulevard; Alley Pond was dammed just upstream to provide power for a second mill (1752), to the east of which Thomas Foster built a house in 1758 that survived until the 1930s. In the 1820s a wool mill operated at or alongside the site of this second mill, and from 1821 to 1826 the hamlet of Alley Pond provided a post office for Flushing (the second in Queens County). The mill was bought in 1828 by Benjamin Lowerre of Flushing, who operated it and a country store until 1859. His son-in-law William C. Buhrmann took over the business and repaired and improved the mill machinery as late as 1878; Buhrmann's sons continued to operate the store from his death in 1898 until 1920. The film *Zaza* was made in the neighborhood in 1908. By 1926, when the mill was destroyed by fire, the hamlet of Alley Pond had grown to include about a dozen houses. The store was demolished to make way for the Cross Island Parkway in October 1939; Alley Pond was filled in and the mill was demolished in 1955 during the construction of an embankment for the Long Island Expressway. In the 1970s row houses were built on new streets to the south and a shopping mall opened on the east side of the valley.

Vincent Seyfried

Alley Pond Park. Second-largest public park in Queens, measuring 624.78 acres (253 hectares) and bordered to the north by Little Neck Bay, to the east by Douglaston, to the south by the Union Turnpike, and to the west by Bayside. The park is transected by the Belt Parkway from north to south, by the Long Island Expressway south of Oakland Lake, and by the Grand Central Parkway at its southernmost corner. Most of the park was acquired and cleared by the city in 1927, but the area was moderately augmented in 1936 by small sections south of Grand Central Parkway (on either side of the old Motor Parkway) and around Oakland Lake; meadowlands north of Northern Boulevard were added in 1961–62. In the northern end of the park sits Lake Oakland, which flows into Alley Creek and on to Little Neck Bay. North of the Long Island Expressway there are meadowlands and to the south woodlands. The Alley Pond Environmental center has a library, a museum, animal exhibits, guided nature walks, and trails for horseback riding.

Vincent Seyfried

Allied Chemical. Firm of chemical manufacturers, formed on 17 December 1920 as the Allied Chemical and Dye Corporation, one of two major American holding companies that sought to counter German control of the chemical industry during the First World War. On its formation the firm commanded assets of $282.7 million from five large makers of related products: the Solvay Process Company, maker of alkalis and nitrogen products; the Semet–Solvay Corporation, a pioneer in the production of soda ash, caustic soda, and coke by-products; the Barrett Company, a maker of coal tar products; the General Chemical Company, the first maker of synthetic ammonia and contact acid in the United States; and the National Aniline and Chemical Company, which erected the first integrated dyestuffs plant in the United States. In 1922 Allied Chemical and Dye acquired Heyl Laboratories and began to produce medical products; during the 1940s the original five corporations were liquidated and a large research laboratory was constructed. The firm took the name Allied Chemical Corporation in 1958. In 1971 it moved its corporate headquarters from New York City to a large complex at Morris Township, New Jersey. Later it was renamed the Allied Corporation before merging with the Signal Companies in 1985 to become Allied–Signal.

Williams Hayes, ed.: *American Chemical Industry*, vol. 6, *The Chemical Companies* (New York: D. Van Nostrand, 1949)

David B. Sicilia

The Female Almshouse on Blackwell's Island, ca *1885–90*

almshouses. The first almshouse in what is now New York City was built in 1653 on Beaver Street in New Amsterdam; it was replaced under Dutch and English rule by structures on Broad and Wall streets called deacons' houses, which were privately supported by charitable contributions to churches. A publicly financed almshouse opened in 1736 on the site of the present City Hall and included a range of facilities for the poor: a workhouse for those fit to work, a poorhouse for the unfit, and a house of correction for "unworthy" paupers who were considered criminals. In 1784 the city appointed commissioners of the Alms-House and Bridewell (the prison), and in 1832 it formed the Alms House Department. The commissioners shared the prevailing attitude of the day that the problems of health, housing, and unemployment afflicting the lower classes resulted from moral deficiencies and could be solved by practicing the Christian virtues of hard work, thrift, and temperance. In the almshouse Protestant clergymen preached to predominantly Irish Catholic inmates. Strict rules were prescribed and harsh measures imposed to enforce proper behavior, including physical punishment, solitary confinement on bread and water, and leg irons. Overcrowding was acute, particularly during the years of cholera and yellow fever; as a result larger almshouses were built, such as the one opened in April 1816 at 26th Street near the East River in Bellevue. Over the years separate facilities opened for paupers with contagious diseases, for prostitutes, for criminals, and for mental patients. Children living at the almshouse were moved in 1832 to the Long Island Farms in Queens County and then in 1848 to "nurseries" on Randalls Island. A workhouse was set up on Blackwell's (now Roosevelt) Island in the following year. During the same period almshouses also opened in Brooklyn, Queens, and Staten Island. The commissioners of the almshouses complained that poor immigrants overburdened their facilities; by 1854–60 the almshouse population was on average 86 percent foreign born. Reports of the period abound with descriptions of destitution, disease, and death.

The agency charged with overseeing the almshouses was restructured and renamed several times. After consolidation (1898) the city began to subsidize the care of poor children in private institutions, and in 1902 the board of trustees of the Bellevue and Allied Hospitals assumed responsibility for the public charity hospitals. In 1936 the last of the almshouse facilities was abolished when the penitentiary at Blackwell's Island was moved to Rikers Island. The Almshouse Department became the Department of Welfare in 1936, which in turn became the Department of Social Services in 1967.

Minutes [of the Common Council], 1784–1831, vol. 2, pp. 661–72 (New York: M. B. Brown Printing, 1930)

David M. Schneider: *The History of Public Welfare in New York State*, vol. 1, *1609–1866* (Chicago: University of Chicago Press, 1938)

Raymond A. Mohl: *Poverty in New York, 1783–1825* (New York: Oxford University Press, 1971)

Juliana F. Gilheany

alternate-side-of-the-street parking. A system of regulations imposed in 1950 that limits curbside parking to one side of the street during certain periods. The regulations began as an experiment on the Lower East Side to facilitate street cleaning, which had recently become mechanized, and were soon extended to all of Manhattan, the Bronx, Brooklyn, and Queens. In many areas parking was allowed only on the south side of the street during three-hour periods on Mondays, Wednesdays, and Fridays, and only on the north side during three-hour periods on Tuesdays, Thursdays, and Saturdays. Fines levied against violators were at first nominal but increased as the city began to rely more heavily on parking tickets as a source of revenue: by 1991 the fine for alternate-side-of-the-street violations reached $35 and receipts from parking citations of all kinds exceeded $100 million. More than ten thousand miles (sixteen thousand kilometers) of street fell under alternate-side-of-the-street rules, and motorists ritualistically moved their vehicles each morning from one side of the street to the other, often just ahead of the street cleaners. Over the years the parking system steadily accumulated a list of "suspended" days when the regulations were not in force. At first the regulations were suspended only on Sundays and civic holidays such as Veterans Day, but later the City Council added the Jewish high holy days (1952) and holidays of various Christian sects, including Holy Thursday and Greek Orthodox Holy Thursday (1990), eventually bringing the number of suspended days to thirty-two; the regulations are also routinely suspended after heavy snowfalls. In 1983 Glen Bolofsky began publishing a calendar listing all the suspended days. During a budget crisis in 1991 the city indefinitely suspended street cleaning, and therefore alternate-side-of-the-street parking rules, on Wednesdays and Saturdays.

Edward T. O'Donnell

Days When Alternate-side-of-the-street Parking Is Suspended

New Year's Day
Martin Luther King Jr. Day
Lincoln's Birthday
Washington's Birthday
Holy Thursday
Good Friday
Passover, 1st day
Passover, 2nd day
Greek Orthodox Holy Thursday
Passover, 7th day
Passover, 8th day
Memorial Day
Feast of the Ascension
Shavuot, 1st day
Shavuot, 2nd day
Independence Day
Feast of the Assumption
Labor Day
Rosh Hashanah, 1st day
Rosh Hashanah, 2nd day
Yom Kippur
Sukkot, 1st day
Sukkot, 2nd day
Shemini Atzereth
Simcas Torah
Columbus Day
All Saints' Day
Election Day
Veterans Day
Thanksgiving Day
Feast of the Immaculate Conception
Christmas Day

Compiled by Edward T. O'Donnell

alternative press. A term used for periodicals with a nontraditional content and readership, often combining characteristics of newspapers and magazines and sometimes published irregularly. *Freedom's Journal*, launched in 1827 by and for blacks, was the first newspaper of its kind in the country and remained in operation until 1829. The *Free Enquirer*, published from 1829 to 1830 by the communitarian theorist Robert Dale Owen and the feminist Fanny Wright, supported women's rights and birth control and encouraged frank debates about religion. It influenced George Henry Evans, who published the *Working Man's Advocate* (weekly, 1829–45), the most widely read labor newspaper during the 1830s and 1840s, as well as the *Man* (1834–35), the *Radical* (1841–42), and *Young America* (1844–49); he eventually aligned himself with advocates of land reform who adopted the slogan "vote yourself a farm." During the labor movement of the 1830s advocates of prison reform, broad-based education, and democratic changes in suffrage presented their ideas in alternative publications. Craft unions in the city formed the General Trades Union during the mid 1830s and published the *Union* (1834–36) under the editorship of the labor leader John Commerford. Although efforts to organize workers diminished during a severe depression in 1837, capitalist speculators and their sympathizers in Tammany Hall remained the target of several newspapers, among them the *Subterranean*, published by the politician Mike Walsh from 1845 to 1847. The newspaper *Sybyl* promoted women's rights in the 1840s, and Victoria Woodhull and her sister Tennessee Claflin published *Woodhull and Claflin's Weekly* from 1870 to 1876, which advocated women's rights and also contained articles on marriage (attacked as a form of slavery), extramarital sex, prostitution, abortion, and venereal disease.

After organizing the Socialist Labor Party in 1877 a number of German intellectuals published the first English-language socialist newspaper that became widely read, as well as the *People* (1891–99) and the *Daily People* (1900–14), the most important publications of the party. Such alternative newspapers were crucial to politics in the city; almost every socialist, radical, and anarchist group produced a newspaper to recruit and educate members. As the labor movement grew the city became a national center of the alternative press. In 1883 John Swinton, a former managing editor of the *Sun*, launched a newspaper to encourage workers to engage in politics. Known as *John Swinton's Paper*, it was read by trade unionists throughout the country but ceased operations in 1887 after consuming $40,000 of Swinton's savings. Among the staunchly socialist publications in the city when the Socialist Party was at its peak was the *Masses* (1911–17), a literary and political journal based in Greenwich Village that challenged the cultural status quo. Edited by Max Eastman, it attracted such writers as John Reed and Walter Lippmann but was eventually undermined by tension between the radical intellectuals, artists, and labor leaders whom it sought to bring together. The Bolshevik Revolution divided the socialist movement: the communist ideology of the Soviet Union was embraced by *Class Struggle* (1917–19), *Revolutionary Age* (1918–19), and *Worker's Council* (1921), and rejected by the *Socialist Review* (1919–21), *Labor Age* (1921–33), and the *American Socialist Monthly* (1935–37).

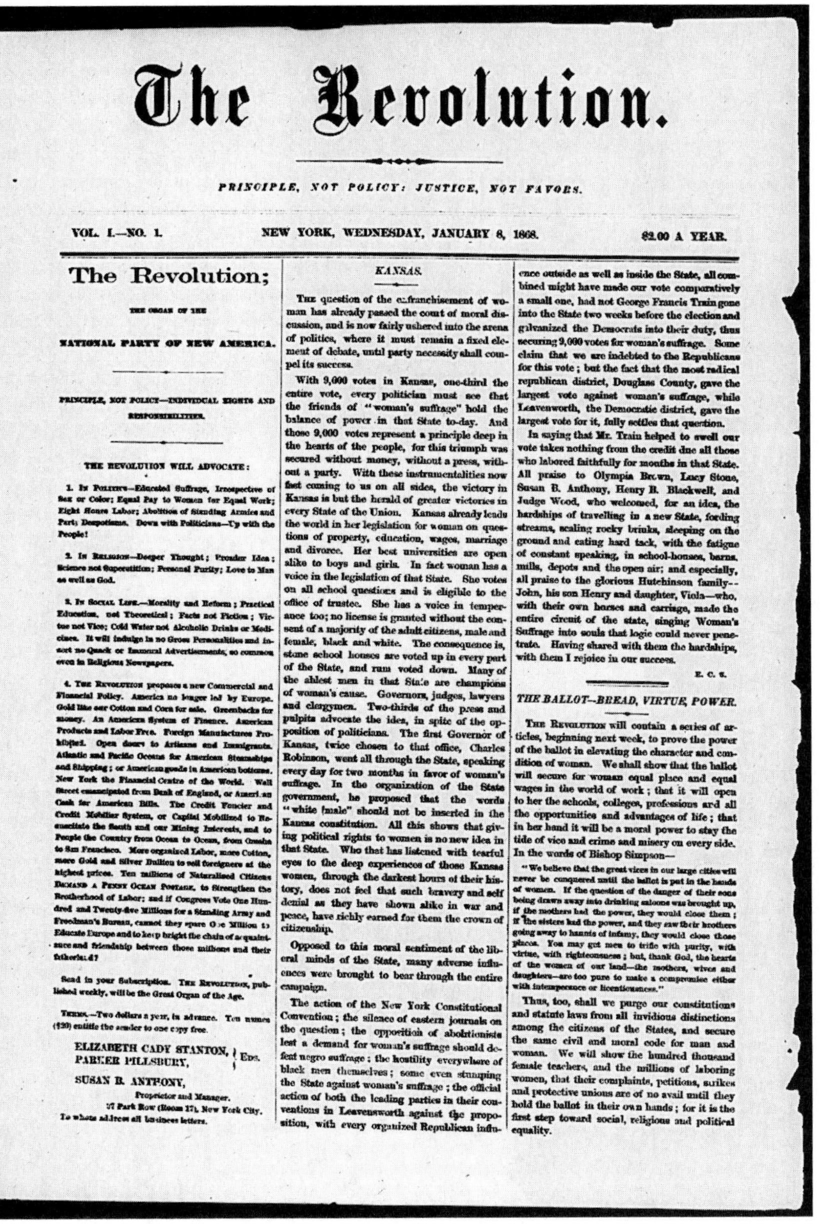

The Revolution.

PRINCIPLE, NOT POLICY: JUSTICE, NOT FAVORS.

VOL. I.—NO. 1. NEW YORK, WEDNESDAY, JANUARY 8, 1868. $2.00 A YEAR.

The Revolution;

THE ORGAN OF THE

NATIONAL PARTY OF NEW AMERICA.

PRINCIPLE, NOT POLICY—INDIVIDUAL RIGHTS AND RESPONSIBILITIES.

THE REVOLUTION WILL ADVOCATE:

1. In Politics—Educated Suffrage, Irrespective of Sex or Color; Equal Pay to Women for Equal Work; Eight Hours Labor; Abolition of Standing Armies and Party Despotisms. Down with Politicians—Up with the People!

2. In Religion—Deeper Thought; Proader Idea; Science not Superstition; Personal Purity; Love to Man as well as God.

3. In Social Life.—Morality and Reform; Practical Education, not Theoretical; Facts not Fiction; Virtue not Vice; Cold Water not Alcoholic Drinks or Medicines. It will indulge in no Gross Personalities and insert no Quack or Immoral Advertisements, so common even in Religious Newspapers.

4. The Revolution proposes a new Commercial and Financial Policy. America no longer led by Europe. Gold like our Cotton and Corn for sale. Greenbacks for money. An American System of Finance. American Products and Labor Free. Foreign Manufactures Prohibited. Open doors to Artisans and Immigrants. Atlantic and Pacific Oceans for American Steamships and Shipping; or American goods in American bottoms. New York the Financial Centre of the World. Wall Street emancipated from Bank of England, or American Cash for American Bills. The Credit Foncier and Credit Mobilier System, or Capital Mobilized to Resuscitate the South and our Mining Interests, and to People the Country from Ocean to Ocean, from Omaha to San Francisco. More organized Labor, more Cotton, more Gold and Silver Bullion to sell foreigners at the highest prices. Ten millions of Naturalized Citizens Demand a Penny Ocean Postage, to Strengthen the Brotherhood of Labor; and if Congress Vote One Hundred and Twenty-five Millions for a Standing Army and Freedman's Bureau, cannot they spare One Million to Educate Europe and to keep bright the chain of acquaintance and friendship between those millions and their fatherland?

Send in your Subscription. The Revolution, published weekly, will be the Great Organ of the Age.

Terms.—Two dollars a year, in advance. Ten names ($20) entitle the sender to one copy free.

ELIZABETH CADY STANTON, }
PARKER PILLSBURY, } Eds.

SUSAN B. ANTHONY,
Proprietor and Manager.
37 Park Row (Room 17), New York City.
To whom address all business letters.

KANSAS.

The question of the enfranchisement of woman has already passed the court of moral discussion, and is now fairly ushered into the arena of politics, where it must remain a fixed element of debate, until party necessity shall compel its success.

With 9,000 votes in Kansas, one-third the entire vote, every politician must see that the friends of "woman's suffrage" hold the balance of power in that State to-day. And those 9,000 votes represent a principle deep in the hearts of the people, for this triumph was secured without money, without a press, without a party. With these instrumentalities now fast coming to us on all sides, the victory in Kansas is but the herald of greater victories in every State of the Union. Kansas already leads the world in her legislation for woman on questions of property, education, wages, marriage and divorce. Her best universities are open alike to boys and girls. In fact woman has a voice in the legislation of that State. She votes on all school questions and is eligible to the office of trustee. She has a voice in temperance too; no license is granted without the consent of a majority of the adult citizens, male and female, black and white. The consequence is, stone school houses are voted up in every part of the State, and rum voted down. Many of the ablest men in that State are champions of woman's cause. Governors, judges, lawyers and clergymen. Two-thirds of the press and pulpits advocate the idea, in spite of the opposition of politicians. The first Governor of Kansas, twice chosen to that office, Charles Robinson, went all through the State, speaking every day for two months in favor of woman's suffrage. In the organization of the State government, he proposed that the words "white male" should not be inserted in the Kansas constitution. All this shows that giving political rights to women is no new idea in that State. Who that has listened with tearful eyes to the deep experiences of those Kansas women, through the darkest hours of their history, does not feel that such bravery and self denial as they have shown alike in war and peace, have richly earned for them the crown of citizenship.

Opposed to this moral sentiment of the liberal minds of the State, many adverse influences were brought to bear through the entire campaign.

The action of the New York Constitutional Convention; the silence of eastern journals on the question; the opposition of abolitionists lest a demand for woman's suffrage should defeat negro suffrage; the hostility everywhere of black men themselves; some even stumping the State against woman's suffrage; the official action of both the leading parties in their conventions in Leavenworth against the proposition, with every organized Republican influence outside as well as inside the State, all combined might have made our vote comparatively a small one, had not George Francis Train gone into the State two weeks before the election and galvanized the Democrats into their duty, thus securing 9,000 votes for woman's suffrage. Some claim that we are indebted to the Republicans for this vote; but the fact that the most radical republican district, Douglass County, gave the largest vote against woman's suffrage, while Leavenworth, the Democratic district, gave the largest vote for it, fully settles that question.

In saying that Mr. Train helped to swell our vote takes nothing from the credit due all those who labored faithfully for months in that State. All praise to Olympia Brown, Lucy Stone, Susan B. Anthony, Henry B. Blackwell, and Judge Wood, who welcomed, for an idea, the hardships of travelling in a new State, fording streams, scaling rocky brinks, sleeping on the ground and eating hard tack, with the fatigue of constant speaking, in school-houses, barns, mills, depots and the open air; and especially, all praise to the glorious Hutchinson family--John, his son Henry and daughter, Viola—who, with their own horses and carriage, made the entire circuit of the state, singing Woman's Suffrage into souls that logic could never penetrate. Having shared with them the hardships, with them I rejoice in our success.

E. C. S.

THE BALLOT--BREAD, VIRTUE, POWER.

The Revolution will contain a series of articles, beginning next week, to prove the power of the ballot in elevating the character and condition of woman. We shall show that the ballot will secure for woman equal place and equal wages in the world of work; that it will open to her the schools, colleges, professions and all the opportunities and advantages of life; that in her hand it will be a moral power to stay the tide of vice and crime and misery on every side. In the words of Bishop Simpson—

"We believe that the great vices in our large cities will never be conquered until the ballot is put in the hands of women. If the question of the danger of their sons being drawn away into drinking saloons was brought up, if the mothers had the power, they would close them; if the sisters had the power, and they saw their brothers going away to haunts of infamy, they would close those places. You may get men to trifle with purity, with virtue, with righteousness; but, thank God, the hearts of the women of our land—the mothers, wives and daughters—are too pure to make a compromise either with intemperance or licentiousness."

Thus, too, shall we purge our constitutions and statute laws from all invidious distinctions among the citizens of the States, and secure the same civil and moral code for man and woman. We will show the hundred thousand female teachers, and the millions of laboring women, that their complaints, petitions, strikes and protective unions are of no avail until they hold the ballot in their own hands; for it is the first step toward social, religious and political equality.

First issue of Revolution *(8 January 1868), launched by Susan B. Anthony*

The relationship of the American left and the Soviet Union remained the most divisive issue in the alternative press during the following decades and led to the formation of several new publications. The editors of the *New Masses* (monthly, 1926–33), Mike Gold and Joseph Freeman, supported strict revolutionary communism, argued for a "proletarian literature," and excluded writers such as Ernest Hemingway, Theodore Dreiser, Langston Hughes, and Richard Wright; strident factionalism gradually abated as the left coalesced in support of the Popular Front in the mid 1930s. At the same time the *Daily Worker* (1924–58), sponsored by the Communist Party, sought a wider audience by adding a sports page and book and film reviews; it was one of the first newspapers in the country to report on racial conflict and also published articles by Wright on politics and culture in Harlem. As a newspaper of the Communist Party it remained closely tied to the interests of the Soviet Union: it did not protest the internment of Japanese–Americans and condemned wartime strikes. Always in debt, it never had more than 38,000 subscriptions and ceased operations after its circulation fell below ten thousand during the 1950s.

A number of young writers who became activists in the 1960s worked in the 1930s and 1940s for newspapers that were not aligned with the Communist Party. The *Catholic Worker*, formed in 1933 by Dorothy Day and the French philosopher Peter Maurin, stressed the virtues of voluntary poverty and nonviolent action and urged readers to take responsibility for achieving social justice. Former Trotskyists including Irving Howe, C. L. R. James, Dwight Macdonald, and James Burnham wrote for the *Militant* (weekly, 1928–) and the *New International* (1934–58); among the political and cultural journals published in the city by former Trotskyists were *Dissent* (1954–) and *Politics* (1944–49). The independent newspaper the *National Guardian*, which began publication in 1948 and was renamed the *Guardian* in 1967, covered national liberation movements in Africa and Southeast Asia long before there was widespread interest in them. The *Daily Worker* resumed publication as the *Daily World* in 1968 and was successively renamed the *People's Daily World* in 1986 and the *People's Weekly World* in 1990.

During the 1960s and early 1970s an "underground" press developed in the city. Several newspapers sought to introduce the politics of the New Left to the counterculture, including the *Village Voice* (1955–, edited by Ed Fancher and Daniel Wolf), the *Realist* (1958–74, Paul Krassner), the *East Village Other* (1965–72, Walter Bowart), and the *New York Rat* (1968–70, Jeff Shero). Oriented toward youth culture and irreverent toward both right and left, these newspapers were known for their psychedelic graphics and sexual frankness. The *East Village Other* called for rent control, safer streets, and investigations of unscrupulous landlords; the *New York Rat* had close links to the antiwar movement. As new, more radical groups were formed the alternative press became increasingly angry and militant: stories appeared under such headlines as "The Year of the Heroic Guerilla," and radical feminists took over the *Rat*, which they renamed *Women's Liberation*. After homosexual patrons of the Stonewall Inn resisted a police raid in June 1969, the periodical *Come Out!* was launched by the Gay Liberation Front. Most publications introduced during these years soon ran out of funds or were abandoned. A few such as the *Village Voice* survived by revamping themselves to reach a wider readership and attract more advertisers.

Alternative Press: A Guide to the Microform Collection (Ann Arbor, Mich.: University Microfilms International, 1990)

Kerry Candaele

Alwyn Court. Apartment building in Manhattan, erected in 1909 at 180 West 58th Street by the architectural firm of Harde and Short. The building is notable for its exuberantly decorated French Renaissance façade of terra cotta, depicting salamanders (symbol of François I of France), flowers, leaves, dragons, and crowns. It has a central courtyard containing an architectural mural by Richard Haas. Designed at the time that large apartment buildings were just beginning to win acceptance as upper-class residences, Alwyn Court originally contained only twenty-two apartments, ranging in size from fourteen rooms to thirty-four. The Depression forced a change, and in 1938 the building was modified to contain seventy-five apartments, each of three to five rooms.

Sandra Opdycke

Amalgamated Bank of New York. Commercial bank opened in 1923 in Union Square by the Amalgamated Clothing Workers Union. It became instrumental in supporting unions by providing low-interest loans and a loan support program for strikers, and was the first bank in New York City to offer unsecured personal loans and free checking with no minimum balance. In the mid 1990s Amalgamated was the only bank in the United States owned entirely by a union. It had assets of more than $1500 million and six branches, which provided pension trust and custodial services, consumer and commercial loans, mortgages, and health care financial services.

The Evolution of Banking: A Story of the Transition from the Medieval Moneylender to the Labor Bank (New York: Amalgamated Bank of New York, 1926)

Laura Gwinn

Amalgamated Clothing Workers of America. Labor union formed in 1914 by men's clothing workers, most of them Jewish and Italian immigrants. It had its roots in a bitter strike at the end of 1912 by workers seeking higher wages and relief from conditions in disease-ridden tenements and dark, poorly ventilated sweatshops. The first enduring institution to defend against employers' abuses in the garment trade, it took an approach that became known as the "new unionism": unlike its affiliate in the American Federation of Labor, the United Garment Workers, which promoted nativism and craft élitism, it sought the membership of immigrants and introduced a method of collective bargaining, sometimes called "industrial democracy," that encouraged workers to help resolve grievances on the shop floor. In the 1930s and 1940s these innovations became the model for industrial labor relations throughout much of American industry. The union also achieved success in a number of social innovations, including unemployment insurance, group health care, affordable credit (through the Amalgamated Bank), and cheap cooperative housing (in Manhattan and the Bronx); these measures prefigured the core reforms of the New Deal and represented a remarkable degree of social conscience at a time when most labor leaders seemed cowed by the corporation.

These gains were threatened by the Depression, and the union survived partly because it organized aggressively and in 1932 rid itself of members with ties to organized crime, an effort carried out with the reluctant help of Mayor James J. Walker. Unable to escape calamity on its own, it sought to strengthen its relations with government and shifted its support from socialism to President Franklin D. Roosevelt, the Democratic Party, and the welfare state. In the city it helped to form the American Labor Party, which delivered the votes of former radicals to Roosevelt, Herbert H. Lehman, and Mayor Fiorello H. La Guardia. After the Second World War the union was compelled to change as blacks from the South, Asians, Latin Americans, and Puerto Ricans became the majority. Membership reached 96,000 in 1952 but declined to 57,000 by 1970, reflecting the decline of garment manufacturing in the city. In the 1970s the union took up the struggle against imports that flooded the American market. Its diminishing fortunes led to its historic merger with the Textile Workers Union of America in 1976, a measure first considered during the early 1920s.

Steve Fraser

Amalgamated Housing Corporation. Organization formed in 1926 by the Amalgamated Clothing Workers (ACW). Its incorporation followed an attempt in the preceding year by Abraham Kazan, manager of the credit union of the ACW, to build reasonably priced cooperative housing for the union's workers by forming the ACW Corporation. With his colleagues he chose a site in the Bronx accessible to the subway, near Van Cortlandt Park and the Jerome Park Reservoir, yet sufficiently distant from the crowded tenements of Manhattan, but he was unable to raise sufficient funds to begin construction. The Amalgamated Housing Corporation was formed by the union as a means of furthering Kazan's project after the state legislature in 1926 passed the Limited Dividend Housing Companies Law to encourage low-cost housing through tax incentives. Kazan was named president of the new corporation by Sidney Hillman, the president of the ACW, and he also remained as president of the ACW Corporation, which became the construction company for the project. In addition to capital raised from cooperative members, the Metropolitan Life Insurance Company and the publishers of the *Jewish Daily Forward* provided a credit fund and a mortgage, enabling groundbreaking to take place in November 1926. In the following year the Amalgamated Cooperative Apartments, designed by the architects George W. Springsteen and Albert Goldhammer, were built north of Sedgwick Street between Saxon and Dickinson avenues. The apartments accommodated 303 families who paid $11 a room a month and $500 a month to buy into the cooperative: because of Kazan's insistence on open membership they were not all associated with the ACW. Among the first tenants was the family of David Dubinsky, president of the International Ladies' Garment Workers' Union (ILGWU). The building was luxurious by the standards of the time, with large rooms and interior garden courtyards. Ice, dental, medical and children's services were provided cooperatively, along with a newspaper (*Community News*) and various cultural activities; house committees oversaw day-to-day functions. In January 1929 construction of an additional 192 apartments began on land adjacent to the original building. In the same year Kazan and the Amalgamated Housing Corporation purchased a block of land on Grand Street, in the center of the crowded tenement district of the Lower East Side, and built the Amalgamated Dwellings (six stories, 236 apartments), designed by Springsteen and Goldhammer. The complex won an award in 1931 from the American Institute of Architects, and a local street was renamed Kazan Street. Another 115 units were added to the original housing in the Bronx in 1931, and a large complex of five- and six-story buildings in a Gothic style was built in 1937. Norman Avenue, which adjoins these extensions, was renamed Hillman Avenue after the union's president. Tenants in the early decades of the Amalgamated projects were primarily Jewish and Italian. In 1950 the three Amalgamated groups along with several cooperatives in the city, labor unions, and neighborhood and fraternal organizations formed the United Housing Foundation to promote cooperative housing, with Kazan as president. In the following year the Hillman Housing Project, comprising three twelve-story buildings, their gardens, and their playgrounds, was constructed at Grand Street between Abraham Kazan Place and Lewis Street, requiring clearance of sixty-five slum tenements in a four-block area; by 1990 the complex contained more than four thousand units. Like the rest of the city the Amalgamated projects became more ethnically diverse in the 1970s and housed an increasing number of black, Latin American, Korean, and other Asian residents. In the mid 1990s more than fourteen hundred apartments operated under the auspices of the Amalgamated Housing Corporation. Both the Amalgamated Houses and the Amalgamated Dwellings were managed by independent cooperative boards composed of local residents, and state law required that residency be open only to those of middle or limited income.

Asher Aschinstein: *Report of the State Board of Housing on the Standard of Living of 400 Families in a Model Housing Project, the Amalgamated Housing Corporation* (?Albany, N.Y.: Burland, 1931)

Thirty Years of Amalgamated Cooperative Housing, 1927–1957 (New York: Warbasse Memorial Library, 1958)

Harold Ostroff: "Labor Co-ops and the Housing Crisis," *AFL–CIO American Federationist*, May 1969, pp. 15–18

Marjorie Harrison

Amato Opera Theater. Opera company formed in 1947 by Anthony Amato and Sally Bellantoni Amato. It initially sponsored performances at unused auditoriums around the city before moving to a site on Bleecker Street now occupied by the Circle in the Square Theatre, and then to a white brick building in the East Village at 319 Bowery at 2nd Street. Although the theater seats only 107 persons and the stage is only twenty feet (six meters) wide, the productions are often ambitious and as many as seventy performers have been on stage at one time. Aspiring singers, who are not paid, hope to be discovered by major companies.

Kenneth T. Jackson

AMAX. Firm of ferrous-metal miners. It was formed in 1887 at 80 Wall Street by a prominent German family as the American Metal Company (Amco), a trader of metals, and moved to 61 Broadway in 1913. Its financial interest in the discovery of molybdenum ore in the Rocky Mountains in 1916 made it internationally known, and it soon developed molybdenum for commercial use and focused increasingly on mining rather than trading. The Climax Molybdenum Company was formed in 1934 with headquarters at 500 5th Avenue and worked closely with Amco until the two companies merged in 1957 to form American Metal Climax, with offices in Rockefeller Center. Renamed AMAX in 1974, it became one of the most successful firms in the city: in 1991 it had sales of more than $3800 million.

James Bradley

Ambassador Hotel. Hotel at 51st Street and Park Avenue, designed by the firm of Warren and Wetmore and erected in 1921. An aristocratic structure, it differed from some of its contemporaries in having individually designed rooms and suites. The furnishings and interior ornamentation, loosely inspired by eighteenth- and nineteenth-century English and French styles, were supplied by John Wanamaker.

Shan Jayakumar

Ambrose, John W(olfe) (*b* Newcastle West, Ireland, 10 Jan 1838; *d* New York City, 15 May 1899). Engineer. After attending New York and Princeton universities he helped to develop docks and channels in New York Harbor and construct elevated railroads. He devoted his last years to seeking funds for enlarging the harbor from Congress, which shortly before his death voted an appropriation for a channel forty-five feet (13.7 meters) deep, two thousand feet (610 meters) wide, and ten miles (sixteen kilometers) long. The Ambrose Channel and Light are named for him.

Elliott B. Nixon

A.M.E. Church. See African Methodist Episcopal Church.

Amerada Hess Corporation. Firm of petroleum distillers formed as the Amerada Corporation in 1920 by Everett de Golyer (1885–1954), with headquarters at 65 Broadway. Initially a small firm that sought new methods for finding petroleum, it became one of the largest independent oil companies in the country after discovering an important oil field in North Dakota in 1952. Through the efforts of Leon Hess (*b* 1914) it merged with the Hess Oil and Chemical Corporation and adopted its current name; the offices were moved in 1973 to Rockefeller Center. In 1989 Amerada Hess had more than $5500 million in sales and was the fourth-largest oil company in New York City and the twelfth-largest in the United States.

James Bradley

American Academy of Arts and Letters. Organization formed in 1904 by élite members of the National Institute of Arts and Letters to honor the country's best writers and artists. Among the first members elected to the academy were Mark Twain, John Hay, William Dean Howells, John La Farge, Edward MacDowell, Augustus Saint-Gaudens, and Edmund Clarence Stedman. In 1976 it merged with the National Institute of Arts and Letters to form the American Academy and Institute of Arts and Letters.

Jeff Finlay

American Academy of the Fine Arts. Organization formed in 1802 as the New York Academy of Arts by Edward Livingston, then the mayor of New York City, and his brother Robert R. Livingston, the American minister to France. During its first year the Livingstons and nearly eighty merchants, physicians, lawyers, and other prominent citizens organized a subscription campaign to purchase casts of antique sculptures in the Louvre. Later the academy was led by De Witt Clinton (1813–16) and by John Trumbull (1817–35), who mounted several exhibitions of heroic paintings and of sculpture inspired by religious themes. The name was changed to the American Academy of the Fine Arts in 1817, and galleries opened at the New York Institution for the Arts in City Hall Park (1816–30) and at 8½ Barclay Street (1831–42). In 1826 members of the academy responded to the contemporary American art exhibits of the National Academy of Design by increasing their display of paintings by old masters and other works that appealed to the city's art patrons. Despite its attempts to compete with other art institutions, the academy found in the mid 1830s that it could not attract support sufficient to maintain its galleries and art collection. Alexander Jackson Davis and other members tried to restore its stability, but officers decided in 1842 to disband the academy and sell its sculpture to the National Academy and paintings to Daniel Wadsworth.

Mary Bartlett Cowdrey: *American Academy of Fine Arts and American Art Union* (New York: New-York Historical Society, 1953)

Carrie Rebora: "The American Academy of the Fine Arts, New York, 1802–1842" (diss., City University of New York, 1990)

Carrie Rebora

The American Anti-Slavery Almanac, *1840*

American Anti-Slavery Society. Abolitionist organization. It was formed in Philadelphia in 1833 by the merger of a group of evangelical reformers in New York City led by Lewis Tappan and a group from Boston favoring immediate abolition and led by William Lloyd Garrison. The society was based in New York City and was dominated by New Yorkers until 1840. Tappan served on the executive committee with such prominent merchants and reformers as John Rankin and William Green, and his brother Arthur Tappan was president of the society. In the 1830s the society experienced its greatest success as it flooded the mails with abolitionist literature and organized a massive petition campaign. It was crippled in 1840 when the faction from New York City led by the Tappans withdrew and formed the American and Foreign Anti-Slavery Society. Control of the American Anti-Slavery Society was assumed by Garrison, who advocated moral suasion, northern secession, and black civil rights. The society disbanded in 1870 after Congress ratified the Fifteenth Amendment.

Commemoration of the Fiftieth Anniversary of the Organization (Philadelphia: T. S. Dando, 1884)

Peter J. Wosh

American Artists' Congress. Art organization formed in the autumn of 1935. It superseded the John Reed Club, which had a more proletarian orientation; its executive secretary was Stuart Davis. The congress attempted to draw a broad spectrum of professional artists to a large conference on the struggle against war and fascism that was held in February 1936 in New York City. The proceedings of the conference were published as *First American Artists' Congress* (1936), an important document of the times. The congress also sponsored exhibitions, primarily in the city. It became divided in early 1940 over the Russian invasion of Finland and later lost its broad influence.

Matthew Baigell and Julia Williams: *Artists against War and Fascism: Papers of the First American Artists' Congress* (New Brunswick, N.J.: Rutgers University Press, 1986)

Cécile Whiting: *Antifascism in American Art* (New Haven: Yale University Press, 1989)

Patricia Hills

American Art-Union. Nonprofit organization formed in 1839 by a group of merchants, bankers, lawyers, and railroad directors in New York City as the Apollo Association for the Promotion of the Fine Arts in the United States; it changed its name in 1844. The stated goals were "cultivating the talent of artists" and "promoting the popular taste." The group bought paintings from American artists such as William Sidney Mount and Thomas Cole and distributed them by lottery to subscribers, who paid an annual membership fee of $5. At the height of its influence in 1849 it distributed 1010 works of art among 18,960 subscribers across the nation. It also published an illustrated periodical (April 1848 to December 1851) and issued one or more engravings to members each year. At a time of growing sectional strife between North and South, the American Art-Union promoted themes of patriotic cohesion. It ceased operations in 1853 as the result of legal actions brought against it because of its lotteries.

Mary Bartlett Cowdrey: *The American Academy of Fine Arts and American Art-Union, 1816–1852* (New York: New-York Historical Society, 1953)

Patricia Hills

American Association of Social Workers. Name of the NATIONAL ASSOCIATION OF SOCIAL WORKERS from 1922 to 1955.

American Ballet Theatre. Dance company formed in 1939 as Ballet Theatre; it gave its first performances in January 1940. The founder was Lucia Chase, who had given financial support to a small company led by the Russian dance teacher Mikhail Mordkin and been encouraged by Richard Pleasant to build a larger company on the European model. Chase and Pleasant assembled a roster of performers that included many Europeans fleeing the hostilities of the Second World War, and engaged Antony Tudor as their resident choreographer. The company's early success came to the attention of the impresario Sol Hurok, who expanded the audience for the company by booking performances at the Metropolitan Opera House but hurt its reputation by disregarding Tudor's seriousness of purpose and seeking to impose his own view that ballet should be frothy, high-spirited entertainment. The company nevertheless gave successful performances of Jerome Robbins's *Fancy Free* (1944) and George Balanchine's *Theme and Variations* (1947). From the late 1940s to the early 1960s the company suffered greatly from its lack of a permanent venue for performances in New York City: after breaking with Hurok it was unable to depend on the Metropolitan Opera House, and when Balanchine's company, the New York City Ballet, became an affiliate of the New York City Center of Music and Drama in 1950 the City Center became unavailable as well. The company was reduced to performing in various theaters on Broadway, an arrangement that proved unsatisfactory. Tours took on an increasingly important role: the company visited small American cities throughout the 1950s and 1960s, Europe in 1956–57 (at which time the company took its current name), and the Soviet Union with the sponsorship of the U.S. Department of State in 1960. These years were marked by such a lack of artistic focus that the tour of the Soviet Union took place only after one early supporter, John Martin of the *New York Times*, failed to dissuade the government from funding it.

Members of the American Ballet Theatre in Fancy Free *(1940; Jerome Robbins, third from left)*

The fortunes of the company revived in 1964 when the New York State Theater opened as part of Lincoln Center for the Performing Arts: by providing a home for the New York City Ballet the theater again freed up the City Center for the American Ballet Theatre, and the New York State Theater was itself available when the New York City Ballet and the City Opera were not in residence there. In 1967 the company gave a well-received performance of the complete *Swan Lake*, staged by David Blair of the Royal Ballet. In the same year Cynthia Gregory emerged as a promising dancer and Eliot Feld made a sensational début as a choreographer. The company continued to emphasize international talent: among those who performed with the company after taking up residence in the United States were the prominent Russian dancers Natalia Makarova (1970) and Mikhail Baryshnikov (1974) and Balanchine's leading ballerina, Gelsey Kirkland. The late 1970s were the company's most successful since its first few seasons.

In a controversial action in 1980 the board of directors seized on Baryshnikov as a new figurehead and forced the retirement of Chase, who was now in her eighties. It was perhaps because of the circumstances surrounding his accession that Baryshnikov, although an artistic director of rare intelligence and vision, was continually subject to critical, popular, and internal criticism. He resigned from the directorship in 1989 and was replaced by Jane Hermann, a former director of the presentations department of the Metropolitan Opera Association. This change also was characterized by bitterness, constant threats of strikes and financial collapse, and fears for the company's financial and artistic survival.

American Ballet Theatre (New York: Alfred A. Knopf, 1977)

Anita Finkel

American Bank Note Company. Firm of engravers formed in 1858 by the merger of seven banknote engraving firms. It was origi-

Stock certificate printed by the American Bank Note Company, ca 1895

nally housed in the Merchants' Exchange Building on Wall Street and soon after its formation became the most renowned financial engraver in the country. In addition to paper money the firm printed stamps and stock certificates. It built headquarters on Broad Street in 1908 and in 1911 opened a large plant in Hunts Point that remained in operation until 1985. When American Bank Note was acquired by the United States Bank Note Corporation in 1990 its offices were moved to Hudson Street.

William H. Griffiths: *The Story of American Bank Note Company* (New York: American Bank Note Company, 1960)

James Bradley

American Bible Society. Interdenominational religious society, formed in New York City in 1816 by delegates representing local bible societies from across the country and having as its aim the circulation of the Bible without doctrinal note or commentary. Despite some early contact with Roman Catholics it remained essentially Protestant until the 1960s. The society first occupied quarters on Nassau Street. During its early years it used new forms of printing technology to produce unprecedented quantities of inexpensive Bibles and testaments, and subsidized missionary translators overseas. From 1836 it set up agencies overseas to coordinate the translation, production, and distribution of Bibles; this trend increased dramatically after the Civil War. The society directed special efforts at urban youths, immigrants, mariners, and American Indians. In 1853 it moved to Bible House on Astor Place, a six-story building that housed its extensive pressroom, bindery, and sales operations while also providing a headquarters for a wide range of Protestant benevolent organizations. Later the offices moved successively to Park Avenue at 57th Street (1936) and Broadway at 61st Street (1966). The society maintained a visible presence in the Near East, the Far East, and Latin America well into the twentieth century. By the middle of the century it began to focus its efforts on distributing not only the Bible in its entirety but also biblical excerpts. At the same time the work of the society was marked by a growing cooperation with Roman Catholics after the Second Vatican Council and by support for the world bible fellowship known as the United Bible Societies, a consortium of national organizations that the society had helped to form in 1946.

Henry Otis Dwight: *The Centennial History of the American Bible Society* (New York: Macmillan, 1916)
Creighton B. Lacy: *The Word-Carrying Giant: The Growth of the American Bible Society* (South Pasadena, Calif.: William Carey Library, 1977)
Peter J. Wosh: *Spreading the Word: The Bible Business in Nineteenth Century America* (Ithaca, N.Y.: Cornell University Press, 1994)

Peter J. Wosh

American Booksellers Association. Trade association for American retail bookstores. Formed in 1900 in New York City, it was originally intended to stabilize book prices and eliminate price cutting. The association offers programs to facilitate book distribution, issues manuals and handbooks, and is a sponsor of the National Book Awards. In 1992 the association moved from New York City to Tarrytown, New York.

Eileen K. Cheng

American Brands. Firm of consumer-product manufacturers, formed as the American Tobacco Company in 1890 by James B. Duke (1856–1925) of North Carolina. Its headquarters were on West 22nd Street off the Hudson River, at one of its many factories in New York City. In 1904 Duke formed the American Tobacco trust by consolidating most of the nation's major tobacco companies, including Liggett and Myers, P. Lorillard, and R. J. Reynolds; headquarters were moved to the Constable Building (5th Avenue and 18th Street). The trust was broken up after the U.S. Supreme Court ruled in 1911 that it violated antitrust laws, but the firm nonetheless remained tremendously successful. At Duke's death it was taken over by George Washington Hill and soon became the leading tobacco company after introducing Lucky Strike, the most popular brand of cigarettes for the next thirty years. In 1955 the firm had 33 percent of the market, more than any competitor, and moved its offices to Lexington Avenue and 42nd Street; it was renamed American Brands in 1968. The firm expanded during the 1980s, when it bought life insurers and manufacturers of office products, hardware, rubber products, and optical goods. In 1989 it had $12,000 million in sales, nearly half from tobacco. American Brands moved its headquarters from New York City in 1986.

John K. Winkler: *Tobacco Tycoon: The Story of James Buchanan Duke* (New York: Random House, 1942)
"Sold American!": The First Fifty Years (New York: American Tobacco Company, 1954)

James Bradley

American Broadcasting Company [ABC]. Television and radio network. It began as the second network of the National Broadcasting Company (NBC), called the Blue Network; put up for sale by a ruling of the Federal Communications Commission in 1943, it was acquired by Edward J. Noble for $8 million and given its current name. Although Noble bought five television stations in major markets in 1946, NBC and the Columbia Broadcasting System (CBS) still had more affiliates and more talent. At first ABC specialized in animated cartoons from Hollywood, and in action and western series such as "Cheyenne" and "Maverick." The news division was run by John (Charles) Daly, also the host of the quiz program "What's My Line?" on CBS. Financial difficulties in 1953 forced a merger with United Paramount Theatres, the president of which, Leonard Goldenson, ran the new company for the next thirty-two years (until he was eighty). ABC was the only network to broadcast the Army–McCarthy hearings live in 1954, but the network was known for the low quality of its news programs, which relied on films supplied by newsreel companies until 1963. During the 1960s it broadcast such popular programs as "77 Sunset Strip" and "Hawaiian Eye," but it did not pose a threat to CBS and NBC until 1975–76, when Elton T. Rule became president and the network overtook both its competitors in the ratings (a position it held for three consecutive years). In 1976 it offered Barbara Walters the unprecedented salary of $1 million a year to become the first woman anchor of a network news program, and it broadcast the series "Roots" (based on the book by Alex Haley), which attracted more viewers than any television program had done before. The network also became known for the sports programs "Wide World of Sports" and "Monday Night Football" and for its coverage of the Olympics; its sports producer Roone Arledge introduced such techniques as slow motion and instant replay. Arledge became president of the news division in 1977. He made an aggressive attempt to improve it by persuading journalists from CBS to join ABC-TV and by developing such highly regarded programs as "Nightline" (with Ted Koppel) and "Sunday Morning with David Brinkley." In the 1980s the evening news program (with Peter Jennings) surpassed those of the other networks in the ratings. Emboldened by its success, the company expanded its facilities on West 66th Street and built more studios in the West 60s. In 1986 ABC was acquired for $3500 million in a friendly takeover by Capital Cities Communications, a firm about one fifth its size led by Thomas Murphy.

Les Brown: *Television: The Business behind the Box* (New York: Harcourt Brace Jovanovich, 1971)
Sterling Quinlan: *Inside ABC: American Broadcasting Company's Rise to Power* (New York: Hastings House, 1979)
Barbara Matusow: *The Evening Stars* (Boston: Houghton Mifflin, 1983)

Judith Adler Hennessee

American Cancer Society. Charitable organization formed in New York City in 1913 as the American Society for the Control of Cancer at a meeting of ten physicians and five laypersons. It sponsors programs of research, diagnosis and treatment, and rehabilitation, as well as education programs focusing on prevention and early detection that are directed at both health care professionals and the general public. The society is the largest source of private cancer research funds in the United States. It has a staff of three hundred and maintains its national headquarters at 90 Park Avenue in Manhattan.

Walter Sanford Ross: *Crusade: The Official History of the American Cancer Society* (New York: Arbor House, 1987)

Montana Katz

American Chicle Company. Firm of chewing gum manufacturers, formed as Adams Sons and Company in 1876 by the glass merchant Thomas Adams (1818–1905) and his two sons. As a result of experiments in a warehouse on Front Street, Adams made chewing gum that had chicle as an ingredient, large quantities of which had been made available to him by General Antonio de Santa Anna of Mexico, who was in exile in Staten Island and at whose instigation Adams had tried to use the chicle to make rubber. Adams sold the gum with the slogan "Adams' New York Gum No. 1 — Snapping and Stretching." The offices and factory were on Vesey Street and were later moved to Murray Street. The firm was the nation's most prosperous chewing gum company by the end of the century: it built a monopoly in 1899 by merging with the six largest and best-known chewing gum manufacturers in the United States and Canada, and achieved great success as the maker of Chiclets. It was renamed the American Chicle Company, with headquarters on 44th Street in Manhattan (moved in 1923 to Thomson Avenue in Long Island City, where the firm had two factories). During the Second World War many of the facilities were used for packing and shipping war rations. The firm merged with the Warner–Lambert Pharmaceutical Company in 1962 and soon left the city; its factories in Long Island City closed in 1981.

Robert Hendrickson: *The Great American Chewing Gum Book* (Radnor, Penn.: Chilton, 1976)

James Bradley

American Civil Liberties Union [ACLU]. Organization devoted to the defense of individual liberties guaranteed by the Bill of Rights of the Constitution of the United States. Its national office is in New York City, as is the office of its affiliate the New York Civil Liberties Union (NYCLU). On its formation in 1920 the ACLU was seen as the successor to the Civil Liberties Bureau (CLB), which had been formed in 1917 to protect freedom of speech, freedom of the press, and the rights of conscientious objectors during the First World War. The leaders of the CLB and of its parent organization, the American Union against Militarism (AUAM), included many social workers and reformers associated with the Henry Street Settlement.

The ACLU is active in the areas of First Amendment rights (freedom of speech, of the press, and of assembly), due process (search and seizure, the right to counsel), equal protection (civil rights for racial minorities and women), and privacy (abortion rights). It is perhaps best known for defending adherents of controversial groups, including communists, American Nazis, and members of the Ku Klux Klan. It has also aroused controversy by advocating a strict separation of church and state that precludes prayer in public schools and religious displays on government property.

During its first decades the national office of the ACLU in New York City handled virtually all the work of the organization, and members of the board of directors and staff lived in the city. Roger Baldwin, the director from 1920 to 1950, was active in many other political and social causes, including pacifism, the labor movement, and civil rights. In the 1950s the ACLU began to develop a network of state affiliates, which now do most of the local and regional work of the organization. The national office coordinates the affiliates, works on special projects in such areas as reproductive freedom, women's rights, and children's rights, and maintains a legislative office in Washington. The NYCLU grew out of the New York Civil Liberties Committee (NCLC) and became a semi-autonomous affiliate with its own professional staff in 1951.

The activities of the ACLU include litigation, lobbying, and public education. At any one time the organization works on about a thousand cases, most of which are handled by volunteer lawyers. Its most notable successes have come about in Supreme Court litigation: by one estimate the organization played a part in four fifths of the important civil liberties and civil rights cases decided by the Supreme Court between the mid 1920s and the mid 1990s. During that time the membership of the ACLU rose from one thousand to nearly 300,000.

Samuel Walker: *In Defense of American Liberties: A History of the ACLU* (New York: Oxford University Press, 1990)

Samuel Walker

American Committee for Cultural Freedom. Organization formed in 1951 by intellectuals in New York City to resist communist influence in cultural and intellectual life. Launched as an affiliate of the International Congress for Cultural Freedom (formed in Berlin in June 1950), it was inspired by a protest led by Sidney Hook against the Cultural and Scientific Conference for World Peace of 1949, which many intellectuals considered a communist propaganda effort aimed at discrediting American foreign policy. The committee attacked such groups as the Emergency Civil Liberties Committee and took a hard line toward the Soviet Union. Because it professed a commitment to free inquiry it opposed a number of campaigns against communists, but it also justified the denial to communists of academic freedom and employment on college faculties. The committee became deeply divided after it sponsored *McCarthy and the Communists* (1954), a book by James Rorty and Moshe Decter criticizing McCarthyism that liberal members considered too mild and conservatives considered too harsh. Even as fear of communism began to subside in the mid 1950s, many in the group remained fervently anticommunist. Faced with declining membership and a lack of funds, the committee ceased operations in 1957.

Christopher Lasch: *The Agony of the American Left* (New York: Alfred A. Knopf, 1969)
Mary Sperling McAuliffe: *Crisis on the Left: Cold War*

Politics and American Liberals, 1947–1954 (Amherst: University of Massachusetts Press, 1978)

Peter Coleman: *The Liberal Conspiracy: The Congress for Cultural Freedom and the Struggle for the Mind of Postwar Europe* (New York: Free Press, 1989)

Terry A. Cooney

American Committee for the Defense of Leon Trotsky. Committee formed by anti-Stalinists to defend Trotsky against charges of conspiracy leveled by Stalin. Its impetus was a series of trials begun in Moscow in 1936 that led a number of socialists, former communists, and Trotskyists to seek asylum for Trotsky and sponsor an inquiry into the charges against him. Under the direction of John Dewey the committee traveled to Coyoacán, Mexico, in April 1937 to meet with Trotsky during his exile; it published *The Case of Leon Trotsky* (1937) and *Not Guilty* (1938).

John Dewey: *"Truth Is on the March": Report and Remarks on the Trotsky Hearings in Mexico* (New York: American Committee for the Defense of Leon Trotsky, n.d. [1937])

Terry A. Cooney

American Council of Learned Societies. Organization of scholarly societies formed in 1919 for the study of the humanities. It has fifty-three organizations as members, among them the American Philosophical Society (formed in 1743 by Benjamin Franklin), the American Dialect Society, the History of Science Society, and the Metaphysical Society of America. The council promotes research, offers fellowships, and sponsors the International Research and Exchanges Board, the Council for International Exchange of Scholars, a program to encourage American studies in Europe and Asia, committees on Chinese civilization, and exchanges with scholars from Russia and eastern Europe. Books published under its auspices include grammars of Azerbaijani, Armenian, Finnish, Mongol, and Bashkir, the papers of Charles Darwin, the census of medieval manuscripts, and such reference works as the *Dictionary of Scientific Biography* (1970–80), the *Dictionary of the Middle Ages* (1982–89), and the *Dictionary of American Biography* (1928–). The council also produces an annual report, a quarterly newsletter, and an occasional papers series. The offices are at 228 East 45th Street.

James E. Mooney

American Craft Museum. Museum opened in 1956 at 40 West 53rd Street by the American Craft Council. It mounts exhibitions of jewelry, textiles, and robots, has a slide collection and an extensive library open to members, and sells exhibition catalogues, crafts, and books.

Paul J. Smith: *Craft Today: Poetry of the Physical* (New York: American Craft Museum, 1986)

James E. Mooney

First traveler's cheque, invented and copyrighted by American Express, 1891

American Cyanamid. Firm of chemical and pharmaceutical manufacturers. It had headquarters in New York City at Rockefeller Center from 1928 to 1962 and a plant on Willoughby Street in Brooklyn where surgical sutures and ligatures were manufactured from 1945 to 1952. When it left the city for suburban Connecticut in 1963 American Cyanamid was a diversified company with more than $750 million in sales.

Kenneth C. Towe: *William Brown Bell, 1879–1950: Quaker, Lawyer, Business Leader* (New York: Newcomen Society, 1953)

James Bradley

American Ethnological Society. Anthropological society formed in New York City in 1842 by a group including Albert Gallatin, who was also its first president. Weakened by factionalism and financial difficulties during the 1850s and 1860s, it nevertheless continued to meet sporadically to the end of the nineteenth century. After 1900 the society was revitalized under the direction of Franz Boas, who drew on the anthropological resources of Columbia University and the American Museum of Natural History. In the mid 1950s the American Ethnological Society became a national organization, with publications issued from the University of Washington in Seattle.

June Helm, ed.: *Social Contexts of American Ethnology, 1840–1984* (Washington: American Ethnological Society, 1985)

Ira Jacknis

American Express. Firm that began in 1850 as a joint stock corporation formed by the merger of three former rivals: Wells and Company; Butterfield, Wasson and Company; and Livingston, Fargo and Company. The new firm constructed a building on Jay and Hudson streets and enjoyed a virtual monopoly on the transport of goods, currency, and securities throughout New York State. In 1874 it moved to 65 Broadway. Soon the firm offered services nationwide by reaching agreements with other express companies (including Wells Fargo), railroads, and steamship companies. It expanded to include financial services by offering money orders from 1882 and introducing the world's first traveler's check in 1891. By the early twentieth century the express companies came under the scrutiny of the Interstate Commerce Commission. The firm discontinued its express business altogether when the government took over the railroads during the First World War. It opened a travel division in 1915, constructed a new building at 65 Broadway (1917), opened branches in several countries, and set up a banking subsidiary with offices throughout the world. During the 1920s the firm offered around-the-world cruises and one of the first air travel arrangements, from London to Zurich. In 1929 Chase Securities Corporation, an affiliate of Chase National Bank, purchased 97 percent of the firm in an attempt to gain access to its extensive international network, but the Depression prevented Chase from acquiring full ownership, and when the government ruled in 1933 that banks could not conduct nonbanking operations Chase divested itself of American Express entirely. After the Second World War the firm increased the number of its foreign offices from fifty to 139 in response to a markedly increased demand for tours and excursions, and in 1958 it introduced its charge card. An attempt by a fraudulent subcontractor to sell large quantities of water as soybean oil in November 1963 left the firm with enormous liabilities (the incident became known as the salad-oil scandal), but creditors' claims were quickly settled. The charge card operation was at first unprofitable, but by 1967 cardholders numbered more than two million and the volume of charges reached $1100 million.

In 1968 American Express acquired the Fireman's Fund Insurance Company, which became one of its largest subsidiaries, and in 1971 it launched the magazine *Travel and Leisure.* It acquired the data processing firm First Data Resources as well as the brokerage house Shearson, Loeb, Rhoades in 1981, and Investors Diversified Services in 1984; in the following year it began selling off the Fireman's Fund Insurance Company, which had proved to be a financial drain because of cyclical losses. It moved its headquarters to the World Financial Center at Battery Park City in 1986. By the mid 1990s American Express had four major divisions: Travel Related Services, Investors Diversified Services, the American Express Bank, and Lehman Brothers Holdings.

Peter Z. Grossman: *American Express: The Unofficial History* (New York: Crown, 1987)

Mary Hedge

American Federation of Labor [AFL]. Trade union organization formed in 1886. Among its forerunners was the Cigar Makers International Union (CMIU), based in New York City, which was organized efficiently along craft lines and offered generous benefits to members in exchange for high dues. Under Adolph Strasser, the international president, and Samuel Gompers, the president of Local 144, the organization responded to a recent depression and the political activism of socialists, greenbackers, and others by joining with Peter McGuire, who had organized carpenters in St. Louis, to form the Federation of Organized Trades and Labor Unions in 1881; this remained smaller than its rival, the Knights of Labor, but played an important role in agitating for the eight-hour day. After a bitter dispute in the city between the CMIU and District 49 of the Knights, labor leaders including Strasser and Gompers called for the formation of a stronger federation, and in December 1886 the American Federation of Labor held its first convention in Columbus, Ohio, electing Gompers its president. The most influential trade unionist in New York City, he held the position until his death in 1924 (except for a year in 1894), his tenure marked by the growth of skilled craft unionism in many industries including the building trades. Under his direction the federation became the most powerful organization of its kind in the United States; during a time when it had little money he made his apartment its headquarters.

Gompers came to believe that moderate political activities and trade unionism could be complementary but must remain separate, and in 1889 he came into bitter conflict with Daniel DeLeon, the socialist leader of the Central Labor Federation (CLF), an organization chartered in the AFL. DeLeon refused to dissociate his Socialist Labor Party from the federation, which from 1894 responded by discouraging the participation of socialists and opposing socialist alternatives to capitalism. The national organization made no effort to organize unskilled workers and became increasingly conservative: Gompers eventually joined the National Civic Association, which was dominated by business and dedicated to rationalizing relations between labor and management. In 1922 Rose Schneiderman of the Women's Trade Union League resigned from the New York City Central Trades and Labor Council, the governing body of the federation in the city, because she was convinced that it would never seriously support women's labor issues.

During the 1920s and early 1930s the AFL suffered nationwide from a fierce campaign against unions waged by corporations, and at the onset of the Depression membership declined from about five million to about three million. During 1933 and 1934 New York City saw a resurgence of organizing in the garment trade. Both Sidney Hillman's Amalgamated Clothing Workers of America (ACWA) and David Dubinsky's International Ladies' Garment Workers Union (ILGWU) won strikes and organizing drives in the city and other industry strongholds. Eventually Hillman took the ACWA into the newly formed Committee of Industrial Organizations (CIO; later renamed the Congress of Industrial Organizations), formed by Hillman and John L. Lewis to organize workers in mass production industries who had been ignored by the AFL. The ILGWU at first also joined the CIO, but it returned to the AFL in 1940. The AFL denounced the CIO for its links to communism even as some of its affiliates, including the teamsters, adopted organizing methods of the CIO. One of the most important trade unionists at the time was George Meany, president of the AFL in New York State, who built alliances with city and state political leaders that ensured the passage of laws requiring unemployment insurance and workers' compensation.

The AFL gained strength by adapting to the anticommunist movement after the Second World War: its unions readily accepted the anticommunist provisions of the Taft–Hartley Act (1947), while the CIO suffered from internal struggles that led to the expulsion of unions with links to communists. A merger of the two organizations took place in 1955 to form the AFL–CIO but was not completed in New York City until 1959, when the Greater New York Central Trades and Labor Council of the CIO was replaced by the New York City Central Labor Council (CLC) as the central body of the AFL–CIO in the city. The first president of the CLC was Harry Van Arsdale, a business agent with the International Brotherhood of Electrical Workers (IBEW); he was largely responsible for persuading Mayor Robert F. Wagner to recognize the right of public workers to organize, and for winning strong encouragement from the CLC for the organizers of Local 1199 of the Hospital Workers' Union, most of whom were black women.

In the mid 1990s the CLC remained one of the largest and most politically influential organizations of its kind in the country, despite severe cutbacks in industrial employment. It played an important role in the election of Mario M. Cuomo as governor of New York in 1982. After Van Arsdale's death in 1986 a rift developed between building-trade unions and municipal unions during the disputed election of Van Arsdale's son Thomas Van Arsdale as the council's president. The younger Van Arsdale charged Victor Gotbaum, his rival and the outgoing president of District Council 37 of the American Federal State, County and Municipal Employees (AFSCME), with supporting communist governments abroad but won the election after a ruling by Lane Kirkland, president of the AFL–CIO.

Stuart Bruce Kaufman: *Samuel Gompers and the Origins of the American Federation of Labor, 1848–1896* (Westport, Conn.: Greenwood, 1973)

John H. M. Laslett: "Samuel Gompers and the Rise of American Business Unionism," *Labor Leaders in America*, ed. Melvyn Dubofsky and Warren Van Tine (Urbana: University of Illinois Press, 1987), 62–89

Leon Fink and Brian Greenberg: *Upheaval in the Quiet Zone: A History of the Hospital Workers' Union, Local 1199* (Urbana: University of Illinois Press, 1989)

Richard Yeselson

American Federation of Radio Artists [AFRA]. Original name of the AMERICAN FEDERATION OF TELEVISION AND RADIO ARTISTS.

American Federation of State, County and Municipal Employees [AFSCME]. Labor union formed in Wisconsin in 1932. Its first local in New York City dates to 1937. In 1944 District Council 37 was chartered to coordinate this and other locals in the city. Several thousand municipal employees joined AFSCME by 1949, but in 1952 its two largest units defected to the International Brotherhood of Teamsters: one, led by John J. DeLury, became the Uniformed Sanitationmen's Association; the other, led by Henry Feinstein, became Local 237. Under the leadership of Jerry Wurf, who began working for AFSCME in 1948, the union slowly recovered, capitalizing on Mayor Robert F. Wagner's commitment to collective bargaining and civil service unions. It also grew through its affiliation with various independent groups. By 1961 District Council 37 had twenty thousand members. After his election in 1964 as international president of AFSCME Wurf was succeeded in 1965 as executive director of District Council 37 by Victor Gotbaum, who like him was college educated and had joined the labor movement through socialist youth groups. Shortly after Gotbaum took office District Council 37 won a recognition election involving twenty thousand hospital workers and became the largest municipal union; its certification as the representative of most employees of mayoral agencies gave it the right to bargain for pensions and benefits for most city workers, including those represented in wage negotiations by other unions. Its strength, organizing campaigns, favorable contracts, and occasional job actions helped to increase its membership to nearly 100,000 by the early 1970s. Growing membership among employees of nonprofit social service agencies led the union to set up District Council 1707 in 1974 to represent them.

During the fiscal crisis of the mid 1970s Gotbaum helped to negotiate agreements among leaders in government, business, and labor that saved the city from bankruptcy. With other unions District Council 37 agreed to wage deferrals, reductions in benefits, and a massive purchase of municipal bonds with pension funds, even as thousands of its members were put out of work. Gotbaum emerged from the crisis as the city's most prominent labor leader, known for his blustering style and close ties to financial and business leaders. AFSCME introduced a wide range of offerings for members, including legal, medical, and social services, educational programs, and cultural activities. It also took part in local and state politics: its financial contributions, phone banks, volunteers, and organizing techniques became important assets for the candidates it supported, usually liberal Democrats. Gotbaum retired in 1987; his successor was Stanley Hill, who worked for the city as a caseworker from 1959 and rose in the union through a series of elected and staff positions. The most prominent black unionist in the city, he played important roles in the presidential campaign of Jesse Jackson in 1988 and the election of Mayor David N. Dinkins in 1989. In the mid 1990s AFSCME remained the city's largest union of public employees.

Jewel Bellush and Bernard Bellush: *Union Power and New York: Victor Gotbaum and District Council 37* (New York: Praeger, 1984)

Joshua B. Freeman

American Federation of Television and Radio Artists [AFTRA]. Labor union formed as the American Federation of Radio Artists (AFRA) in New York City in 1937; its first president was the entertainer Eddie Cantor. In 1952 the union broadened its scope to include television performers and took its current name. During the 1950s the union fined, censured, and expelled members who failed to cooperate with the House Committee on Un-American Activities. The local in New York City had about 25,000 members in 1991, roughly a third of the national membership. AFTRA represents actors, broadcasters, musicians, dancers, disc jockeys, puppeteers, and other performers who work in radio, television, and a few areas unrelated to broadcasting; it has successfully organized performers in public broadcasting but met with some challenges in cable television and video recording. The union establishes minimum salaries and fees through collective bargaining with networks, local stations, advertisers, and other producers. Initiation fees and dues are used primarily to support contract negotiations and enforcement. The union is affiliated with the AFL–CIO.

Gerard Thomas Koeppel

American Geographical Society. Organization formed at 179 Broadway in Manhattan on 9 October 1851 as the American Geographical and Statistical Society; it is the oldest geographical society in the United States. The original membership numbered about one hundred and included some of the most prominent figures in New York City, among them Alexander Isaac Cotheal, Henry Evelyn Pierrepont, Charles A. Dana, Henry J. Raymond, Freeman Hunt, and Judge Alexander Warfield Bradford. Early activities of the society included publication of its *Bulletin* (from 1852) and the reading of papers on such topics as the exploration of South America and the polar regions, construction of a railroad to the Pacific, and the extension of the telegraph. Despite concerns about insufficient funds and membership the society was granted a charter by the state legislature in 1854. It moved its headquarters to Cooper Union in 1866 and took its current name in 1871; it later moved successively to 11 West 29th Street (1876), West 81st Street, 3755 Broadway, at Audubon Terrace (1911), and 156 5th Avenue. In the 1880s the society focused on such concerns as development of the Congo basin and the siting of a ship canal between the Atlantic and the Pacific. Its president between 1903 and 1906 was Commander Robert E. Peary, explorer of the North Pole. In 1912 the society gained international recognition when it sponsored the Transcontinental Excursion, which introduced distinguished European geographers to the American landscape. The *Bulletin* became the *Geographical Review* in 1916.

The society was an important source of strategic information to the American military during both world wars. It launched a quarterly magazine for the general reader called *Focus* in 1950, and in the following year it published the *Millionth Map of Latin America.* It played an important role in preparing the *Columbia Lippincott Gazetteer of the World* (1952) and also assembled an important map collection (now at the University of Wisconsin at Milwaukee). In later years the society reaffirmed its commitment to strengthening geographical education in American schools. A travel program was begun in 1985 to sponsor educational voyages throughout the world. In the mid 1990s the American Geographical Society had about twelve hundred members.

Elizabeth J. Kramer

American Heart Association. Organization for the prevention and cure of heart disease. Among its forerunners was the Society for the Prevention and Relief of Heart Disease, formed by physicians in New York City concerned with the management of heart disease. Organizational meetings were held at the New York Academy of Medicine in 1915, the first annual meeting on 26 January 1916. During the next eight years the society provided information and assistance to physicians in other cities who were organizing similar groups. At the initiative of the society the American Heart Association was formed in 1924 and held its first meeting in February 1925. In the mid 1990s one of the most important affiliates of the association was the New York Heart Association, also known as the American Heart Association, New York City Affiliate.

William Lee Frost

American Home Products. Manufacturer of pharmaceuticals, surgical supplies, personal-care products, veterinary medicines, biotechnology products, and food, formed in 1926. Initially the firm made only nonprescription medicines; it added prescription medicines to its line after buying Wyeth Laboratories in 1932 and in the following years grew steadily by making acquisitions and advertising aggressively. It had sales of $8400 million in 1993. In 1994 the firm had 51,000 employees worldwide, including 22,000 in the United States, and owned such consumer brands as Chef Boyardee, Wheatena, Maypo, Chapstick, Advil, Anacin, Dristan, Preparation H, and Robitussin. For many years the headquarters were at 685 3rd Avenue in Manhattan; in 1993, when the firm had about nine hundred employees in New York City, it moved to Madison, New Jersey.

Gilbert Tauber

American Indians. Indian people have been living in and around what is now New York City for at least 11,500 years. Remains associated with what archaeologists call Paleo-Indians represent the oldest known verifiable physical record of human occupation in the area. The most direct evidence is Clovis points, distinctive lance-shaped chipped-stone projectile points with a long, narrow channel flake (called a "flute") removed from the center; they have been found at North American sites occupied between 11,500 and 10,000 B.P. and have been recovered on Staten Island, notably at Port Mobil. Paleo-Indians and people who lived in the Archaic period (*ca* 10,000 to 3000 B.P.) and the Early and Middle phases of the Woodland period (*ca* 3000 to 1000 B.P.) were hunters and gatherers.

Artifacts made and used by these hunting and gathering people have been found at sites throughout the metropolitan area. Some, like Clovis points, were popular for long periods. Others were used comparatively briefly, such as shallow, lug-handled, oblong soapstone bowls made by people who also used Orient Fishtail chipped stone projectile points. Such artifacts were crafted almost entirely between 3300 and 3000 B.P. from the Late Archaic period to the Early Woodland period. Thousands of stylistically distinct objects, known as diagnostic markers, have also been found in the city, including pottery, which was first introduced into the Northeast during Early Woodland times. Most of these objects have been found in large sites repeatedly reoccupied by different peoples at different times, among them the Ryder's Pond site near Sheepshead Bay in Canarsie, the Bay Terrace site on Little Neck Bay in Queens, and the Ward's Point National Historic Landmark on Staten Island. Others have been discovered in small sites briefly occupied and used for special purposes, such as the rock shelters in Inwood Park at the northern tip of Manhattan Island and the many shell middens (thick garbage heaps of shells discarded by Indians) that formerly lined the local waterways.

Studies of the physical evidence and of living societies that use the same tools suggest that Paleo-Indians and succeeding hunting and gathering peoples in the metropolitan area belonged to small, mobile bands that divided into flexibly organized task groups consisting of family and friends; these groups traveled on foot or in watercraft and used tools, weapons, and ornaments crafted from stone, bone, shell, horn, and wood. Hunters and warriors used spears and darts tipped with antler projectile points or chipped stone, much of which often came from local cobbles and rock outcrops; discoveries of projectile points made from cherts, flints, and other stones quarried in Pennsylvania, New Jersey, Connecticut, and upstate New York suggest contact with people from those areas. At specific times of year members of these groups traveled to particular places to quarry stones, gather such items as wild plants, shellfish, and eggs, and catch fish using spears, nets, or weirs. Gathering together in villages or camping separately, they lived in dome-shaped, sapling-framed houses covered with bark or grass mats, and stored their goods in bark or skin containers, in pits, in wooden-splint or woven grass baskets, and (during Woodland times) in fired clay pots and jars.

Living in Ice Age times, Paleo-Indians hunted such animals as caribou and elk roaming dense spruce and pine forests similar to those now found in northern Canada and Siberia; these conclusions are supported by finds of caribou bones in strata containing Clovis points in the Dutchess Quarry Cave (Orange County, New York) and of spruce and pine pollen in soil cores from Late Pleistocene layers in the Hackensack Meadowlands in New Jersey.

Remains of plants and animals adapted to more temperate environments have been found in deposits post-dating Paleo-Indian times. The presence of deer bones, oyster and clam shells, and pollen from deciduous trees indicates that present-day climatic conditions arose in the region about 8000 B.P. The climate continued to change over the following years. Changes in the kinds and amounts of pollen show shifts in temperature and humidity. The presence of different shells in different layers of shell middens suggests changes in water temperature, salinity, and sea level.

Variations in the types and styles of artifacts and the frequency with which they are found may reflect social responses to environmental changes. Archaeological evidence indicates that direct and indirect contact with people from more interior portions of the continent increasingly influenced the life of Indians in the metropolitan area during Woodland times. Sites have yielded Meadowood and Adena projectile points from the Early Woodland period of a kind most commonly found farther north and west and dated to between 3000 and 2000 B.P. Several of these sites contain the oldest pottery yet found in the Northeast. Middle Woodland sites dating from 2000 to 1000 B.P. have provided evidence of increasing contact with groups in other regions. One group was people from upstate New York of the Kipps Island phase, whose presence within the present city limits became traceable through discoveries at Ward's Point of tools made from jasper stones quarried in Pennsylvania, olivella shells from the southern Atlantic coast, mica from the Carolina highlands, copper from the Great Lakes used in a child's grave, and a platform pipe similar to others usually found in the Ohio Valley. Many archaeologists believe that the arrival of Indians later known as Delawares is confirmed by discoveries at several sites (including Ward's Point) of pottery belonging to the Abbott Farm series, as well as stone projectile points in the Fox Creek style made of argillite quarried from the Delaware Valley.

Evidence of sweeping changes in social organization has been found in deposits dating to the earliest phases of the Late Woodland period, between 1200 and 800 B.P., at Ward's Point and Bowman's Brook on Staten Island, Ryder's Pond in Brooklyn, and Clason's Point in the Bronx. Thick midden layers of occupational debris and dense clusters of hearths and storage or refuse pits at these sites indicate that Late Woodland people spent much of their time in towns of unprecedented size and density. New styles of pottery and small, triangular, chipped stone projectile points used with newly introduced bows and arrows have been found in these towns and smaller campsites like those discovered at the Cold Spring Harbor site in northern Manhattan, the Van Cortlandt site in the Bronx, and the Aqueduct site in Queens.

Other evidence suggests that during these times Indians in the area also began to live in bark- or grass-covered longhouses and to grow or consume cultivated plants including corn, beans, squash, and tobacco. This was the culture encountered by the Florentine navigator Giovanni da Verrazano when he made the first recorded landfall by a European in New York Harbor in 1524. Neither he nor Henry Hudson, who conducted the next documented voyage to the area in 1609, noted the names or identities of the people they met. They were eventually called Delawares, a name given to all linguistically and culturally related Indians living along the Atlantic seaboard between the Delaware and Hudson valleys at the time of initial contact with Europeans; the name was originally applied to those living along the Delaware River, which was named in 1610 after the governor of Virginia, Thomas West, the baron de la Warr.

According to Delaware traditionalists currently living in such places as Oklahoma, Wisconsin, and Ontario, the Indians of the metropolitan area called themselves *Lenape* (people) and their homeland *Lenapehoking* (land of the people). It is widely believed that those living in the northernmost reaches of Lenapehoking spoke variants of a Delaware dialect known as Munsee (stony country). Colonial records documenting relations with Indians indicate that kinship, political ties, and economic ties linked Munsee-speakers into a widespread social network that extended across the lower Hudson and upper Delaware valleys from southeastern New York to northeastern Pennsylvania.

Early European records are unclear about the structure of Munsee society; ethnographic evidence provided later by Delawares indicates that all Munsees belonged to one of several maternally linked clans living together in sapling-framed longhouses and consisting of related women, their children, and husbands from other families. Some communities were evidently dominated by particular family groups, and others contained households belonging to several clans.

Munsees lived near reliable sources of water, well-drained soils, and places favorable for hunting, fishing, and foraging. In the spring they felled trees, burned undergrowth, and planted crops between tree stumps; they also fished for shad, eel, and herring migrating upstream in massive spawning runs, gathered greens, nuts, roots, and berries, and collected eggs from nests of migrating birds. During communal hunts they burned sections of forest to drive game off cliffs or into pens or rivers. In the summer they dispersed to small camps, traded, traveled, made war, undertook vision quests, and held thanksgiving celebrations like the Green Corn ceremony. They gathered together again during the fall to harvest crops, gather nuts, catch fish, collect shellfish, and hunt deer and migrating waterfowl. During the winter they made and repaired tools and weapons, told stories, and held religious festivals.

Munsees belonged to societies lacking institutionalized inequalities. They followed men and women of proven ability who governed by the power of persuasion. Unfettered by coercive governments or authoritarian leaders, Munsees could move to any community willing to accept them. Women usually owned their homes and fields and moved infrequently; men moved more often because of customs such as matrilocal post-marital residence rules (requiring the husband to move into his wife's household). Men retained membership in their original clans throughout their lives, but many shifted their political loyalties when they moved. Such shifts were essential for those who took on leadership responsibilities in new communities. One figure who did was Waumetompack, known in the 1650s as a Rockaway chief in Queens County but later prominent among Matinecocks living farther east along the northern shore of Long Island.

There were a number of Munsee communities documented in the area by European settlers during the seventeenth century. In addition to Rockaway (sandy place) and Matinecock (at the lookout point) there was Maspeth (bad water place) and Jamaica (beaver place) in Queens, as well as five communities in Brooklyn: Marechkawick (sandy place) near Borough Hall, Nayack (point of land), Wichquawanck (sandy bank) at Fort Hamilton, Techkonis (translation unknown) in Gravesend, and Canarsie (grassy place), a village in the marshy Flatlands. Settlers often referred to Indians from what are now the Bronx and Westchester County as Wiechquaesgecks (birch bark or swampy country), the Indian name for what became Dobbs Ferry, New York. Indian communities formed in the Bronx along Long Island Sound at Hunt's Point, Soundview, Throgs Neck, and Pelham Bay, along the Harlem River in Hell Gate, Mosholu, and Marble Hill, and at various places in Manhattan including Cold Spring Harbor. According to two accounts from the early seventeenth century, there was a group in the eastern Bronx called Siwanoys (southerners). Other documents indicate that the Rechgawawancks (sandy hillside), who were believed to have lived in the western Bronx, were more probably the Haverstraws, another Munsee group on the western bank of the Hudson River living in a town bearing their name in Rockland County. Another Munsee village, Aquehonga (sandy hillside), sat on bluffs overlooking Raritan Bay near what is now the Ward's Point National Historic Landmark. Colonists on Staten Island noted other Munsee communities on the banks of the Great Kills, the Narrows, the Kill van Kull, and the Arthur Kill.

Manhattan stood at the center of this world. Its name is derived from the Delaware word *menatay* (island). In 1626 the island was reportedly sold by Indians for sixty guilders' worth of goods to Peter Minuit, the first governor of New Netherland, who established the capital of New Amsterdam at its southern tip. Munsees sold Staten Island to the Dutch in 1630. Both islands soon became important trading centers where visiting Munsees exchanged pelts, food, and cylindrical blue and white shell beads known as wampum for European textiles, glass beads, and implements made of iron, brass, and copper. Many also managed to obtain guns, ammunition, and liquor from colonists who ignored laws prohibiting the sale of such items to Indians. Firearms allowed game to be brought down with unprecedented ease and efficiency and also made raids and warfare more dangerous than ever before.

Alcohol presented a serious threat to Munsee communities, which were disrupted and demoralized by the violence of drunkards. The threats posed by guns and alcohol paled in comparison to the devastation caused by deadly epidemics of smallpox, measles, and malaria, which struck Indian communities every five to ten years throughout the colonial era and may have killed nine out of ten Munsees. Weakened by losses from disease, alcohol abuse, and increasingly lethal warfare, Munsees found themselves caught between powerful rivals desiring control over their lands. Armed with Dutch guns, such powerful interior nations as the Mohawks and Mahicans denied Munsee hunters access to trapping grounds; they also extorted wampum and other commodities from more poorly armed Munsees. Desiring their land, Dutch settlers quickly came to regard the impoverished Munsees as unwanted neighbors, and an increasingly violent struggle ensued in which insults, thefts, and assaults gave way to a series of unpunished murders.

War finally broke out in 1640 when a Dutch detachment was sent to Staten Island by Governor Willem Kieft to investigate the theft of a pig but instead attacked a Raritan Indian community. This set off what became known among Europeans as Governor Kieft's War, part of a wider struggle sparked by the European invasion of the Northeast and often pitting Indians against each other during the seventeenth century. The first phase of the war ended when Munsee warriors from Long Island and the lower Hudson Valley attacked and defeated the Raritans. A Mahican attack on Wiechquaesgecks and Hackensacks during the winter of 1643–44 set the stage for the war's second and more violent phase. Seizing the opportunity to avenge several settlers' murders, Kieft ordered an attack on the more than 120 Wiechquaesgeck and Hackensack refugees sheltering among the Dutch in camps at Pavonia (in what is now Jersey City) and Corlear's Hook (in lower Manhattan); most of the refugees were killed during a surprise attack on the night of 23 February 1643. Munsee warriors united by hatred of the Dutch soon attacked outlying settlements throughout New Netherland, where they killed or captured scores of colonists, among them the well-known Puritan dissenter Anne Hutchinson and most of her family; they also drove colonists from Staten Island and much of the adjacent mainland. The Dutch moved quickly in mounting retaliatory strikes. Led by John Underhill, the ruthless commander of the Mystic Fort massacre on 26 May 1637 during the recent Pequot War in Connecticut, Dutch and English colonists killed hundreds of Munsees in Westchester County and Long Island in 1644. Despite devastation on both sides the struggle remained indecisive, and a peace treaty was signed on 30 August 1645.

The peace proved uneasy. Munsees resentful of Dutch encroachments on their lands attacked settlements in and around Manhattan in 1655. The renewed hostilities became known as the Peach War, after a Dutch settler who was alleged to have murdered an Indian woman for picking peaches in his orchard, and dragged on for several years. The outbreak of war with Esopus Indians living farther upriver in 1658 further weakened the Dutch colony, which was denied adequate support by the Netherlands and fell easily to an English squadron after years of almost continual Indian warfare. Eager to avoid these mistakes, the English quickly signed treaties of friendship with Indian leaders. Although rumors of Indian conspiracies circulated throughout the region for the next hundred years, Munsees never again took up arms against settlers in the metropolitan area. Munsees were soon compelled by English settlers to sell all their remaining lands within what are now the city limits; by 1701 they had put their marks to thirty-nine deeds to lands there. Staten Island was resold in 1657 by Indians who had driven settlers away during Governor Kieft's War and again in 1670 by English colonists eager to secure clear and uncontested title to the land. All lands in Brooklyn were alienated from Indians through twenty-two deeds signed between 1636 and 1684; among the last areas of the county to be handed over was Canarsie.

Dispossessed Indians unwilling to leave their lands lived as tenants on colonial farmsteads or moved to remote or unwanted swamplands. As they lost their land and its resources Munsees grew poorer and subsisted as best they could. Most dressed in English clothes and spoke a trade jargon of mixed English, Dutch, and Delaware words when speaking to colonists; many also sought to master English. Men found work as laborers, farmhands, and seamen; women worked as servants and sold homemade straw brooms, splint baskets, and grass mats. Elderly Munsee herbalists and healers found many patients among both Indians and Europeans.

Most Munsees gradually moved away, often settling in mountainous enclaves in the Hudson Highlands of northern New Jersey and southern New York. Others moved to small

Jacob A. Riis, Mountain Eagle and His Family of Iroquois Indians *(1895)*

tracts of land set aside as reservations in Nassau County at Cow Neck, Matinecock Neck, and Fort Neck. Many of these people ultimately joined other Munsees at the large Minisink towns along the upper Delaware Valley; all were finally forced westward into exile at the end of the Seven Years' War in 1762.

Some Munsees refused to abandon their old homes, among them a number of Matinecock families who continued to live in small communities scattered along the northern shore of Queens and Nassau counties. Other Indians lived quietly in unwanted backlots in Washington Heights and Canarsie and on Staten Island. Increasingly unable to find spouses among the few remaining Indians in the region, most married non-Indians. Children born into these households rarely learned Indian language or customs. The Munsee language finally died out in the city as the last elders fluent in it died during the early nineteenth century.

Indians from elsewhere began moving to New York City in search of work during the nineteenth century. Men found work as longshoremen, factory workers, and laborers, women as artisans, seamstresses, washerwomen, and servants. A number took an active interest in their Indian heritage. A Chibcha artist from Colombia named Emilio Cabral Diaz worked with such local non-Indian historic preservationists as Reginald Pelham Bolton and William L. Calver to establish an "Indian life reservation" in Inwood Park during the 1920s; it was the site of powwows and encampments until the 1950s. Many of those in attendance were Mohawks from reservations in upstate New York and Canada, uniquely skilled in high steel work and readily able to find work in bridge and skyscraper construction. They formed a small community at Gowanus in Brooklyn during the 1920s; most left by the 1960s.

The federal census of 1990 enumerated 27,531 Indian persons in New York City (about 0.4 percent of the total population). Most Indians descended from communities in the metropolitan area call themselves Delawares or Lenapes, and those from Queens are usually known as Matinecocks. An important center of Indian life is the American Indian Community House in Manhattan, which administers cultural programs and service projects.

Edward Manning Ruttenber: *History of the Indian Tribes of Hudson's River* (Albany, N.Y.: J. Munsell, 1872)

Clark Wissler: *The Indians of Greater New York and the Lower Hudson* (New York: American Museum of Natural History, 1909)

Alanson B. Skinner: *The Indians of Manhattan Island and Vicinity* (New York: American Museum of Natural History, 1932)

Reginald Pelham Bolton: *Indian Life of Long Ago in the City of New York* (New York: Joseph Graham, 1934)

Allen W. Trelease: *Indian Affairs in Colonial New York: The Seventeenth Century* (Ithaca, N.Y.: Cornell University Press, 1960)

Robert S. Grumet: *Native American Place Names in New York City* (New York: Museum of the City of New York, 1981)

Herbert C. Kraft: *The Lenape: Archaeology, History, and Ethnography* (Newark, N.J.: New Jersey Historical Society, 1986)

Robert S. Grumet

American Institute of Architects [AIA]. Organization formed on 23 February 1857 by thirteen architects, including Richard Upjohn, Richard M. Upjohn, Jacob Wrey Mould, Richard M. Hunt, and Leopold Eidlitz. These founders invited twelve other architects to become members, of whom at least two, Thomas U. Walter and Alexander Jackson Davis, had belonged to a similar organization in 1836 that quickly disbanded because its membership was small and widely dispersed. The institute stated in its constitution (signed 18 May 1857) that its purpose was "to promote the scientific and practical perfection of its members and to elevate the standing of the profession." It soon focused its attention on the concerns of an emerging profession, including fee schedules, training for students and young practitioners, professional ethics, and fair standards for architecture competitions. The institute inaugurated a system of local chapters when it formed one in New York City in 1867. It admitted its first female member, Louise Bethune, in 1888, merged with the Western Association of Architects in 1889, and in 1898 moved its headquarters from New York City to the historic Octagon House in Washington. The local chapter in the city now works through an extensive structure of volunteer committees; it offers continuing education and formulates positions on public building and planning issues. The *AIA Guide to New York City* (1967; 3rd edn 1988) by Eliot Willensky and Norval White is the standard architectural guide to the city.

Frederick Albert Gutheim: *One Hundred Years of Architecture in America, 1857–1957: Celebrating the Centennial* (New York: Reinhold, 1957)

Rosalie Genevro

American Institute of Chemical Engineers [AIChE]. Organization formed in 1908 to advance the theory and practice of chemical engineering and to serve the profession and its members, who in 1990 numbered 52,000. It was one of the five engineering societies that formed the United Engineering Trust, which operates the United Engineering Center on 47th Street and 1st Avenue.

Larry Resen and N. R. Amundson, eds.: *Diamond Jubilee Historical Review Volume* (New York: American Institute of Chemical Engineers, 1983)

Trudy E. Bell

American Institute of Electrical Engineers [AIEE]. Organization formed in 1884 by inventors seeking to further the telegraph, the electric light, and the generation of electric power. It was one of the five founding societies of the United Engineering Trust, which operates the United Engineering Center at 47th Street and 1st Avenue. The institute merged in 1963 with the Institute of Radio Engineers to form the INSTITUTE OF ELECTRICAL AND ELECTRONICS ENGINEERS.

Trudy E. Bell

American Institute of Physics [AIP]. Organization formed with a grant from the Chemical Foundation in 1931 to foster communication among physicists dispersed through different fields and facing rising costs of publication. It was proposed at a joint committee of physicists at Columbia University and set up quarters in offices owned by the Chemical Foundation; it soon moved into its own office on East 57th Street and then to larger quarters at 335 East 45th Street after the Second World War. In the following years the institute became the largest and most important physical science organization in the country, gaining tens of thousands of members in dozens of chapters nationwide. It opened a publishing facility in Woodbury, Long Island, and in the mid 1990s published more than 90 percent of American physicists' research and 25 percent of that by physicists abroad, including many translations of work from Russian and Chinese. Its office in Manhattan houses the Niels Bohr Library.

Chad Ludington

American International Group. Firm of insurers. It began in 1919 as C. V. Starr and Company of Shanghai, which arranged insurance for the China trade of American businesses. In the 1960s the firm acquired several insurance companies in the United States, including National Union Fire (1968), New Hampshire Insurance Company (1969), and American Home (1969), and established its headquarters on Pine Street in Manhattan. In the mid 1990s the group had affiliates worldwide and was one of the leading insurers in the world, with assets exceeding $28,000 million.

Robert J. Gibbons

American Irish Historical Society. Organization formed in Boston in 1897 and later based in New York City. In 1940 it moved its offices to 991 5th Avenue. The focus of the society on Irish contributions to the history of the United States has inspired the publication of many books and articles, largely about the colonial period.

The American Irish Historical Society, 1897–1972: Seventy-fifth Anniversary (New York: American Irish Historical Society, 1972)

William D. Griffin

American Jewish Committee. Jewish defense agency formed in 1906 in response to pogroms in Russia. It initially drew much of its membership from among wealthy Jews of German descent and had an executive committee of fifteen. Because the organization remained exclusive it was threatened with marginalization as Jews from eastern Europe moved to the city in large numbers. It responded by forming the New York Kehillah in 1908, which became its local chapter. Under its second president, Louis Marshall, the committee fought the Ku Klux Klan and the restrictive Immigration Act of 1924; it also promoted an anti-lynching law in 1924 that was ultimately rejected by the state legislature. Its journal, *Commentary*, began as a publication of a group of Jewish thinkers and writers on political and cultural subjects. Not originally a Zionist organization, the committee became a strong defender of Israel after 1948. In the mid 1990s it was best known for its research on intermarriage, pluralism, ethnicity, and the Jewish family. It has headquarters in New York City.

Naomi Cohen: *Not Free to Desist: The American Jewish Committee, 1906–1966* (Philadelphia: Jewish Publication Society of America, 1972)
Henry L. Feingold: *A Jewish Survival Enigma: The Strange Case of the American Jewish Committee* (New York: American Jewish Committee, 1981)

Henry Feingold

American Jewish Congress. Organization inspired by the Congress movement in New York City and Philadelphia, which sought to make Jewish organizations democratic, and formed to give American Jews a voice at the peace conference in Versailles. It was formally established as a national organization after communal elections were held in June 1917. After the peace conference it made its headquarters in New York City until 1922, when it adjourned. In the following years the congress was reorganized to become the most politically activist Jewish secular organization in the United States. Under Stephen S. Wise it enjoyed success through its Commission on Law and Social Action and offered staunch support to the Zionist movement. Unlike other Jewish defense agencies it took part directly in local and national politics, relying on coalitions with other organizations representing minority groups to accomplish its goals. It focused its efforts on political reform and often used the courts to implement its program of social justice, which pursued improvements in public housing, education, and civil rights. With the advent of Nazism it sought to focus public attention on the issue of rescue by sponsoring protest rallies and boycotts; a rally at Madison Square Garden inspired dozens of others in cities nationwide. After the Second World War the American Jewish Congress shifted its efforts to the civil rights movement and social welfare causes such as public housing and women's rights. It became best known for its staunch support of the Labour Party in Israel.

Morris Frommer: "The American Jewish Congress: A History, 1914–1950" (diss., Ohio State University, 1978)

Henry Feingold

American Jewish Joint Distribution Committee. Organization formed as the Joint Distribution Committee on 27 November 1914 in New York City to help displaced eastern European Jews. It soon merged with the American Jewish Relief Committee, an organization of German Jews, and the Central Relief Committee, an organization of Orthodox Jews; it took its current name in 1915 after merging with the People's Relief Committee, which represented workers. After the war the committee took part in reconstruction and formed loan cooperatives. During the 1930s it aided European Jews; its office in Paris offered vocational training and provided relief for Jews fleeing the Nazis, and the organization played a vital role in rescuing eighty thousand Jews from occupied Europe, guiding them mainly through Spain and Vichy France. Between 1945 and 1952 the committee spent more than $350 million to assist 250,000 displaced persons and from 1949 it cooperated with the Israeli government to form Malben, an organization that helps ill, handicapped, and elderly immigrants. It also maintained medical, educational, and vocational programs in North Africa, Iran, France, and eastern Europe. One of the most effective organizations of its kind, the American Jewish Joint Distribution Committee had helped millions of Jews worldwide by the mid 1990s.

Oscar Handlin: *A Continuing Task: The American Jewish Joint Distribution Committee, 1914–1964* (New York: Random House, 1964)
Yehuda Bauer: *My Brother's Keeper: A History of the American Jewish Joint Distribution Committee, 1929–1939* (Philadelphia: Jewish Publication Society of America, 1974)

Michael N. Dobkowski

American Labor Party. Political party formed in 1936 by leaders of the garment trades unions. It endorsed Democratic and Republican candidates in local, state, and national elections and occasionally sponsored independent candidates for local and state office; many of its votes came from adherents of the Socialist Party who wished to support Franklin D. Roosevelt and other candidates committed to the New Deal but were reluctant to vote for a "bourgeois" party like the Democrats. Despite the anticommunist leanings of its founders David Dubinsky and Alex Rose the American Labor Party quickly came under the influence of communists; its most prominent spokesman was the congressman from East Harlem Vito Marcantonio, a sympathizer with the communists on many issues. In the late 1930s the Labor Party played an important role in the politics of New York City by helping to provide more than one fifth of the votes for the reelection of Mayor Fiorello H. La Guardia in 1937; it also supported Mike Quill, president of the Transport Workers Union, who maintained close ties to the Communist Party and was elected to the City Council as a candidate of the American Labor Party in 1937, 1943, and 1945. When communists gained control of the party in the early years of the Second World War Rose and others left it to form the Liberal Party. The Labor Party received an average of 13 percent of the vote in elections in the city between 1938 and 1949 and was strongest in Jewish, black, and Puerto Rican neighborhoods. As

Rally of the American Labor Party at Madison Square Garden, 1936

the surrogate in New York State for the Progressive Party in 1948 it helped Leo Isacson to win a special election for a seat in Congress as a representative from the southern Bronx, and in November it gave the presidential candidate Henry Wallace more than half the votes that he received nationwide (Isacson failed to win reelection to a regular term in the same election). Marcantonio lost his seat in 1950. Attacked as a communist front, the American Labor Party lost support during the cold war and was dissolved in 1956.

Kenneth Waltzer: "The Party and the Polling Place: American Communism and the American Labor Party in the 1930s," *Radical History Review* 23 (autumn 1980), 104–29

Max Gordon: "A Response," *Radical History Review* 23 (autumn 1980), 130–35

Gerald Meyer: *Vito Marcantonio, Radical Politician, 1902–1954* (Albany: State University of New York Press, 1989)

Gerald Meyer: *The American Labor Party, 1936–1954* (New York: Garland, forthcoming)

Maurice Isserman

American Lung Association. Organization formed in New York City in 1907 as the National Tuberculosis Association to coordinate the activities of various state affiliates, including the NEW YORK LUNG ASSOCIATION.

American Museum of Natural History. One of the largest and most important museums in the world, conceived by the scientist Albert Bickmore in the early 1860s and established in 1868. It opened in 1869 at the New York Arsenal, where several specimen collections were put on display in the following year. The many businessmen and politicians on the museum's board of trustees helped to secure funds from the city and private donations. In 1874 President Ulysses S. Grant took part in the groundbreaking for a new building on Central Park West between 77th and 81st streets. The trustees soon purchased many collections, but the museum lacked a systematic process for acquiring specimens and adequate means for displaying them. Situated well north of the center of the city and closed on Sundays during the 1870s, the museum attracted few visitors and eventually fell into debt.

Important changes were made by Morris K. Jesup, a wealthy railroad securities broker who became the third president of the museum in 1881. He employed a taxidermist to create displays that were attractive and comprehensible and supported Bickmore's plan to inaugurate lectures on nature for schoolteachers. This program and a new policy that kept the museum open on Sundays increased the popularity and visibility of the museum. Jesup had a strong interest in evolution and scientific research. He appointed the zoologist Joel A. Allen as the curator of mammalogy and ornithology, asked Henry Fairfield Osborn to develop a new program in vertebrate paleontology (1891) and Franz Boas to join the department of anthropology (1896), and defined the primary objective of the museum as that of providing a spiritually uplifting place where the public could both learn about nature and find respite from the bustling city.

As the curator of vertebrate paleontology Osborn furthered Jesup's interests by promoting expeditions and publications that illuminated evolutionary biology. A wealthy aristocrat, he formed close ties to the trustees and rose quickly through the ranks of the museum's administration, becoming president in 1908. During a tenure that lasted twenty-five years he sponsored the search for human ancestors in Mongolia led by Roy Chapman Andrews and expeditions to Africa led by Carl Akeley. These dramatic undertakings captured public attention and led to the establishment of new scientific departments and large exhibit halls. Osborn drew considerable philanthropic support for these and other expeditions and tripled contributions made by the city, efforts that allowed the museum to build a new wing in the 1930s. Like Jesup he channeled contributions into disciplines that documented evolution, such as vertebrate paleontology, anthropology, mammalogy, and ornithology. New exhibits such as the Hall of the Age of Man and the Akeley African Hall revealed his interest in protecting nature from encroaching urbanization and his attachment to maintaining the power and prestige of peoples of northwestern European ancestry. A program in astronomy, promoted by Osborn in the 1920s, was given greater attention by the museum in the 1930s with the construction of the Hayden Planetarium (1935).

American Museum of Natural History, 1937

Medal commemorating the tercentenary of the purchase of Manhattan Island, struck for the American Numismatic Society (designed by Hermon A. MacNeil)

In the 1940s and 1950s traditional taxonomic studies continued, while at the same time scientists such as Ernst Mayr and George Gaylord Simpson offered important new interpretations of evolution and Margaret Mead, head of anthropology at the museum, emphasized social and cultural anthropology. G. K. Noble and other scientists conducted research on animal behavior at the department of experimental biology and Albert E. Parr, appointed director of the museum in 1942, replaced many of the displays on evolution with ones that reflected new findings in ecology and physical geography. The importance given to expeditions continued and in the 1950s led to the opening of several new field stations for biological research. In the 1960s civil rights groups attacked the few remaining displays that reflected Osborn's racist beliefs; the Hall of the Age of Man was replaced in 1961 by a Hall of the Biology of Man. Efforts were begun in the 1980s to revamp mammal and dinosaur displays in the light of new knowledge and interpretations. The museum in the mid 1990s had about three million visitors a year, a staff of seven hundred, and a budget of $55 million.

John Michael Kennedy: "Philanthropy and Science in the City: The American Museum of Natural History, 1868–1968" (diss., Yale University, 1968)
Geoffrey T. Hellman: *Bankers, Bones, and Beetles: The First Century of the American Museum of Natural History* (Garden City, N.Y.: Natural History Press, 1969)
Ronald Rainger: *An Agenda for Antiquity: Henry Fairfield Osborn and Vertebrate Paleontology at the American Museum of Natural History, 1890–1935* (Tuscaloosa: University of Alabama Press, 1991)

Ronald Rainger

American Newspaper Guild. Labor union that represents newspaper reporters across the United States. Led in its early years by Heywood Broun, it became affiliated with the American Federation of Labor in 1936. The guild at first focused on obtaining better pay and conditions but became increasingly oriented toward the left as communist members helped it in battles with publishers.

Daniel J. Leab: *A Union of Individuals: The Formation of the American Newspaper Guild, 1933–1936* (New York: Columbia University Press, 1970)

Michael Green

American Numismatic Society. Association formed in 1858 by collectors and others interested in coins, medals, and similar items. It maintains a museum and a library at 155th Street that has seventy thousand volumes; it also sponsors an annual conference on the coinage of the Americas, offers training programs and fellowships for graduate students and museum professionals, and publishes monographs and journals.

Howard L. Adelson: *The American Numismatic Society, 1858–1958* (New York: American Numismatic Society, 1958)

James E. Mooney

American Peace Society. Organization of peace reformers. Its forerunner was the New York Peace Society, formed in 1815 by the devout Presbyterian layman David Low Dodge (1777–1852) and dedicated to the condemnation on biblical principles of all warfare, defensive as well as offensive. This group joined with others of similar beliefs in May 1828 to form the American Peace Society. The society favored negotiation, arbitration, and a "Congress of Christian Nations" to resolve international conflicts. After a period of stagnation in the years following the Civil War the society revived under the influence of pragmatic philanthropists during the progressive movement. In the mid 1990s its national offices were in Washington.

Edson Leone Whitney: *The American Peace Society: A Centennial History* (Washington: American Peace Society, 1928)

Peter J. Wosh

American Research Bureau. Original name of Arbitron ratings.

American Review of Reviews. Monthly magazine of public affairs. It was launched in 1891 by Albert Shaw (1857–1947), who was the owner, editor, and manager and remained associated with the magazine for forty-six years. The magazine began as an offshoot of the *Review of Reviews*, first published in London in 1890 by the English journalist and social reformer William T. Stead. By 1897, having surpassed its parent in quality and circulation (ninety thousand), it took the name the *American Review of Reviews* and became a separate publication. It was known for its book reviews, news, commentary, and editorials on foreign affairs, education, religion, and politics; articles on international issues by distinguished journalists, professors, and writers were especially well regarded. At its peak during the First World War the magazine had 240,000 subscribers. From that time its readership declined, and it merged in 1932 with the *World's Work* and in 1937 with the *Literary Digest*, which became the *Digest* and ceased publication six months later.

Frank Luther Mott: *A History of American Magazines*, vol. 3, *1885–1905* (Cambridge: Harvard University Press, 1957), 657–60
Obituary of Albert Shaw, *New York Times*, 26 June 1947

Jane Allen

American Revolution. New York City in the eighteenth century embodied many of the complexities of revolution and experienced all of its turmoil. It was an important base for the Sons of Liberty but also the capital of Loyalist America, a position solidified by the British conquest of the city in 1776. With the end of the war in 1783 the city rebuilt and prospered.

1. Early Developments, 1764–1774

New York City in the late colonial period was second in importance in British America only to Philadelphia. By the mid eighteenth century it was wealthier and more populous than Boston, and at independence it had about 25,000 inhabitants, who were crowded into the area below what is now City Hall. Well to the north lay the village of Harlem; most of Staten Island and the counties of Queens, Kings, and Westchester (which began at the Harlem River) were farmland. The racial, ethnic, religious, and economic divisions in the city helped to build a tradition of turbulent politics. Some New Yorkers gained tremendous wealth in transatlantic trade and wartime supply contracts: the Loyalist Oliver de Lancey (1718–85) asserted after the revolution that his confiscated estate had been worth £115,000. These wealthy traders had luxuries and maintained connections with people of high social rank in England; they adapted elements of English culture to their colonial environment to create a distinctive cultural life. Their culture was given voice in the *Independent Reflector*, a journal published

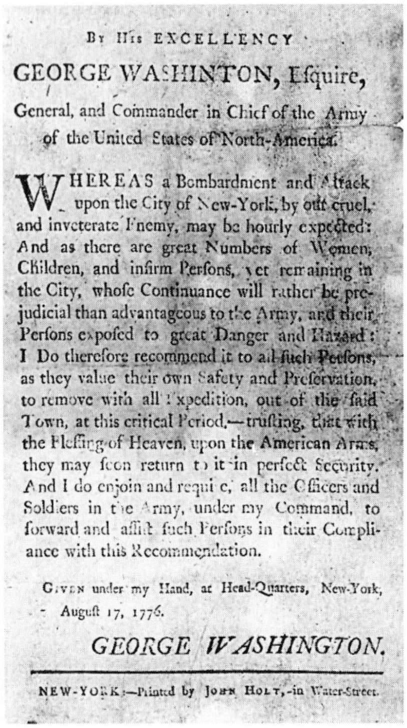
By His EXCELLENCY

GEORGE WASHINTON, Esquire,

General, and Commander in Chief of the Army of the United States of North-America.

WHEREAS a Bombardment and Attack upon the City of New-York, by our cruel, and inveterate Enemy, may be hourly expected: And as there are great Numbers of Women, Children, and infirm Persons, yet remaining in the City, whose Continuance will rather be prejudicial than advantageous to the Army, and their Persons exposed to great Danger and Hazard: I Do therefore recommend it to all such Persons, as they value their own Safety and Preservation, to remove with all Expedition, out of the said Town, at this critical Period,—trusting, that with the Blessing of Heaven, upon the American Arms, they may soon return to it in perfect Security. And I do enjoin and require, all the Officers and Soldiers in the Army, under my Command, to forward and assist such Persons in their Compliance with this Recommendation.

Given under my Hand, at Head-Quarters, New-York, August 17, 1776.

GEORGE WASHINGTON.

NEW-YORK:—Printed by John Holt, in Water-Street.

George Washington's notice to the citizens of New York City, August 1776

Représentation du Feu terrible à Nouvelle Yorck, *by François Xavier Haberman*

from November 1752 to November 1753 that was written by William Livingston, William Smith Jr., and John Morrin Scott and modeled after the *Independent Whig* of London. Artisans and independent craftsmen, another important group, made products that competed with merchants' imports, and to protect their interests they banded together, sometimes instigating riots.

The city prospered while the British made it their headquarters during the Seven Years' War (1756–63) but experienced a depression when the war ended. Spending on relief for the poor tripled, and merchants' turnovers were halved. The growing poverty was denounced in the press, especially in the *New-York Journal*, a militant newspaper operated by John Holt. Merchants were incensed by the Sugar Act of 1764, which imposed British control on the American sugar market, and the provincial assembly in which many had seats inveighed against it. The Stamp Act of 1765, which mandated the use of stamps on all legal and commercial documents, led the colonies to create the Stamp Act Congress, which met in the city. About this time there emerged a group of popular leaders of the revolution who came to be known as the Sons of Liberty. They included both artisans like Holt and small merchants like Isaac Sears and Alexander McDougall, and had a network throughout the colonies. The Sons of Liberty were committed to direct action and in late October 1765 led their first uprising, in which they destroyed carriages and sleighs belonging to Lieutenant Governor Cadwallader Colden, the enforcer of the Stamp Act, and an elegant house rented by Major Thomas James, who had trained the guns of Fort George on the city. One of their last public riots was the sacking in the following May of a new theater that was considered an irresponsible luxury in a time of public distress.

Tensions continued to rise over issues of commerce and military supply. The Quartering Act required the colonial assemblies to appropriate supplies for British troops garrisoned in America. When the assembly in New York refused to grant supplies for the troops stationed in the city, Parliament passed the New York Restraining Act of 1767. This forbade the city to act at all until it appropriated the supplies. By the time news of the act arrived the assembly had in fact complied, but John Dickinson's influential *Letter from a Pennsylvania Farmer* cited the restraining act as a major colonial grievance. During the same year that the act was passed many merchants joined in the nonimportation movement against the Townshend taxes, but their alliances shifted as they quarreled among themselves and with other revolutionaries. The elections of 1768 and 1769 led to a division in the assembly between the Livingstons, who were landholders, and the de Lanceys, merchants who gained the support of the Sons of Liberty by berating the Livingstons for supplying British troops. The presence of these troops in the city led to increased tension. They competed with New Yorkers for work, which they were permitted to seek while off duty; and they made relations worse by tearing down successive liberty poles erected by colonists in the Fields (later City Hall Park). The Sons of Liberty were alarmed by the large garrison at the upper barracks (near the Fields) and lower barracks (near the Battery), and they ended their alliance with the de Lanceys when the assembly controlled by the de Lanceys voted that surrounding British troops should receive supplies. The de Lanceys became Loyalists, and under their control from 1769 to 1775 the assembly ceased to be militant. In his broadside "To the Betrayed Inhabitants of the City and Colony of New-York" McDougall in 1769 lambasted the assembly for voting to supply the British and was imprisoned. In the same year the merchants of New York City joined those of Philadelphia and Boston in a boycott of British commerce to protest the Townshend taxes. In January 1770 tensions between colonists and British troops led to the Battle of Golden Hill and the Nassau Street Riot; although no lives were lost the issues being fought over were the same as those that led to the killing of five civilians in the Boston Massacre two months later. Merchants in the city repealed their boycott of British commerce later that year after Parliament rescinded all the Townshend taxes except the one on tea. Artisans protested the rescission because they had benefited from the boycott and been excluded from the decision to end it, and when rumor arose about a new crisis over the tax on tea they formed their own Committee of Mechanics and purchased a place to hold meetings. The first tea ship headed for the city during this time was turned back at Sandy Hook, New Jersey. When tea was found aboard the *London* in April 1774 revolutionaries began costuming themselves as "Mohawks," as the participants in the Boston Tea Party had done; during their preparations a crowd boarded the ship, dumped the tea, and burned the empty chests at the Fields.

2. Tensions Leading to War, 1774–1776

A month after the *London* was stormed the city elected fifty-one men to its first revolutionary committee, in which moderates outnumbered radicals including McDougall, Sears, and John Lamb. At the meeting that chose the committee the young aristocrat Gouverneur Morris likened members of the city's "mob" who were beginning "to think and to reason" to "poor reptiles" who were casting off "their winter's slough" and would bite "'ere noon."

Eleven radical members resigned from the committee in July 1774 to protest its timid policies. The second revolutionary committee comprised sixty members elected in November to enforce the Continental Association; this was the trade boycott ratified by the Continental Congress in response to measures taken by the British in retaliation for the Boston Tea Party. It was replaced by a Committee of One Hundred, elected in April 1775 after the battles at Lexington and Concord. The province of New York had already chosen the first of its revolutionary congresses, which elected delegates to the Second Continental Congress. At the outset of the war full power was gradually assumed by the congress, which met in the city, and by local committees such as the Committee of One Hundred. Governor William Tryon (1729–88) called an assembly election at the end of 1775 to undercut these revolutionary bodies, but the new assembly never met; he escaped to a British ship in the harbor, and the mayor and aldermen found themselves powerless. Loyalists nevertheless remained strong in the city, and the Sons of Liberty met fierce resistance from merchants engaged in transatlantic trade: fifty-seven members of the Chamber of Commerce became Loyalists, twenty-one remained neutral, and only twenty-six were revolutionaries. The de Lanceys strongly opposed the revolution. Others who did included the printer James Rivington and the Anglican ministers Samuel Seabury and Myles Cooper.

In the rural counties around the city the revolution found virtually no support: the sparsely populated counties of Queens, Kings, and Richmond (Staten Island) were prosperous and shunned the political turmoil of the city, even after resistance had turned to revolution. In January 1776 Queens was captured, its firearms seized, and its leaders arrested by General Charles Lee, one of Washington's most zealous officers. He inspired no support there, and when British troops invaded during the following August, thirteen hundred persons signed a congratulatory address, and eight hundred joined the first militia under the renewed royal government.

Early in 1776 *Common Sense* by Thomas Paine became popular in the city for its condemnation of monarchy and its call for simple republican institutions. After the British commander Sir William Howe (1729–88) evacuated Boston in March, Washington prepared for a British invasion by moving his troops to New York City and its environs, occupying lower Manhattan, Brooklyn Heights, and Bay Ridge. In May the Committee of Mechanics, the largest radical faction that remained, called for the popular acceptance of whichever new constitution the province might adopt to become an independent state. After the Declaration of Independence was signed on 4 July 1776 New Yorkers toppled a statue of George III that had stood at Bowling Green. Although some in the city urged the abolition of the old order, many others, especially the mercantile élite, had to be forced to accept independence and wanted no political experiments.

Howe and his brother, the admiral Lord Richard Howe, met no resistance on Staten Island in July when the first part of their vast fleet approached the city. On 22 August they crossed the Narrows and moved their army of British and Hessian soldiers into Flatbush and Flatlands. Washington had garrisoned the passes along a corridor that is now the portion of Flatbush Avenue bordering and running through Prospect Park; he had defended the road to Jamaica only lightly and the British used it to turn his flank during the Battle of Long Island (26–31 August). His forces were routed and thirteen hundred Americans were captured. The rest of his army retreated to Brooklyn Heights, where it was nearly trapped before Washington organized a nighttime withdrawal across the East River. After another battle on 16 September he retreated to Harlem Heights. In the autumn of 1776 two fires destroyed more than three hundred buildings in the city, including one third of its housing. The British occupying force took control of Manhattan, Long Island, Staten Island, and southern Westchester County. Washington again tried to take New York City on 16 November but was defeated at Fort Washington, where 2800 soldiers in the Continental Army were captured by the British, who now had more American prisoners than Washington had soldiers. He withdrew from the city, which remained under British control.

3. From Center of Loyalism to National Capital, 1776–1789

The British rebuilt quickly; New York City became impregnable, and Loyalists fled there in large numbers, among them slaves who understood that their best chance for freedom lay in adhering to the king. The population rose toward what it had been before independence, and merchants reopened their businesses to serve the British army. Rivington, whose press had been smashed in November 1775 by a group under the leadership of Sears, began publishing the *Royal Gazette*, a Loyalist paper. Tryon returned and Smith, once an advocate of rebellion and later a member of the royal council, was appointed the chief justice. Wealthy Loyalists and officers in the British army and navy entertained one another in style. Real power remained in the hands of the military, and although some talked of restoring civil government no attempt was made to reconvene the provincial assembly. The British commanders Sir William Howe, Sir Henry Clinton (*b* ?1738; *d* 1795), and Sir Guy Carleton (1724–1808) maintained martial rule, and for much of the war the city was governed by the aged major-general James Robertson, who had a reputation for promiscuity and corruption. When commerce with the mainland was almost closed off privation set in, and this worsened when American privateers were successful against British merchant vessels.

In April 1777 the state's "Convention of the People" adopted a relatively conservative state constitution, with a strong governor and state senate. The occupied counties were represented in both the assembly and the senate by appointed members until the British evacuation. In the city itself some 3800 Loyalists organized themselves into a militia to aid the British; this was not much more than a home guard and was never deployed against the American army. Early in 1781 the Associated Loyalists were organized under their own board of directors. The group was led by Loyalist gentlemen, including Oliver de Lancey and Benjamin Franklin's son William, who had been governor of New Jersey, and included in its ranks many refugees from areas under revolutionary control. Until April 1782 they conducted raids across the Hudson and into Westchester and southern New England but were disbanded after one of their captains, Richard Lippincott, incurred the anger of both Americans and British by hanging a prisoner, Joshua Luddy, whom he had agreed to exchange.

New York City became the main site for holding American prisoners of war, who were kept initially in public buildings and warehouses; eleven ships moored in Wallabout Bay later became the most infamous prisons (see Prison ships). As many as eleven hundred men were held on the *Jersey*, where misery was extreme and death rates high. Some prisoners were soldiers, but many were privateers captured at sea. Their conditions did not improve until Carleton became the British commander of the city in 1782. It is estimated that eleven thousand revolutionaries died on the ships, a number unparalleled in American history in an area so small. The suffering of the American prisoners is commemorated by a monument in Fort Greene Park dedicated in 1908.

The surrender of Lord Cornwallis at Yorktown broke the resolve of the British troops to win and created two difficult tasks for Carleton: to evacuate British troops and Loyalists, and to transfer power. Many Loyalists realized that they could not regain their confiscated property or escape punishment under the laws that the independent state had passed to punish them, and they sought refuge in Britain. The large number of black Loyalists knew that returning to their American owners meant reenslavement; some who tried to evacuate were taken off their ships by their owners. The reincorporation of the city and the rest of the southern district by the government of New York State caused other hardships for Loyalists who stayed. Those whose property had not been confiscated had to pay double tax and were denied the protection of the courts, and the entire southern district was made to pay a special tax to share the cost of the war. The Citation Act allowed patriots to bring damage suits against people who had used their property during the occupation.

After Evacuation Day (25 November 1783) the city faced tremendous obstacles to prosperity. Its physical structure was seriously damaged, its currency devalued, its commerce in chaos owing to the dumping of British goods, and its political and economic prospects in doubt. In 1784 the formation of a new city government paved the way for restructuring, and from 1789 to 1790 New York City was the nation's capital. Most of those who had fled the city returned, businesses emerged, and a stable municipal and federal government laid the foundation for a strong city that became the largest and most successful in the nation during the following decades.

Carl L. Becker: *The History of Political Parties in the Province of New York, 1760–1776* (Madison: University of Wisconsin Press, 1909; rev. 1960)

Milton M. Klein: *The Politics of Diversity: Essays in the History of Colonial New York* (Port Washington, N.Y.: Kennikat, 1974)

Gary B. Nash: *The Urban Crucible: Social Change, Political Consciousness, and the Origins of the American Revolution* (Cambridge: Harvard University Press, 1979)

Edward Countryman: *A People in Revolution: The American Revolution and Political Society in New York, 1760–1790* (Baltimore: Johns Hopkins University Press, 1981; repr. New York: W. W. Norton, 1989)

Paul A. Gilje: *The Road to Mobocracy: Popular Disorder in New York City, 1763–1834* (Chapel Hill: University of North Carolina Press, 1989)

See also Hudson river.

Edward Countryman

American Society for the Control of Cancer. Original name of the American cancer society.

American Society for the Prevention of Cruelty to Animals [ASPCA]. Humane society, formed in 1866 by Henry Bergh as the first humane society chartered in the United States. In addition to performing rescue work its agents are empowered by state legislation to issue summonses for violations of animal cruelty and animal control laws. The national headquarters on East 92nd Street in Manhattan house the Bergh Memorial Animal Hospital, an animal shelter open twenty-four hours a day, and an adoption center. The society also maintains a shelter and hospital in Brooklyn, and pet receiving centers in the Bronx, Queens, and Staten Island. The Animalport at Kennedy Airport serves as a hotel for animals in transit and is the only such facility in the world. The concerns of the organization now include education, the treatment of animals used for food, for clothing, and in laboratory research, and the protection of endangered species. Much of this work is sponsored by legislative initiative and conducted through the society's office in Washington, sometimes in conjunction with other humane organizations.

John J. Gallagher

American Society of Civil Engineers [ASCE]. Organization formed on 5 November 1852 to facilitate the exchange of information among engineers responsible for building roads, canals, bridges, and railroads. It is the oldest national engineering society in the United States. In 1990 the society had more than 107,000 members, including ten thousand outside the United States. It was one of the five societies that formed the United Engineering Trust, which operates the United Engineering Center at 47th Street and 1st Avenue.

William H. Wisely: *The American Civil Engineer, 1852–1974: The History, Traditions, and Development of the American Society of Civil Engineers, Founded 1852* (New York: American Society of Civil Engineers, 1974)

Trudy E. Bell

American Society of Mechanical Engineers [ASME]. Organization formed in 1880 to address issues of machine design and construction, power generation, and industrial production processes. It was one of the five societies that formed the United Engineering Trust, which operates the United Engineering Center on 47th Street and 1st Avenue. In 1990 the society had 119,000 members.

Trudy E. Bell

American Standard. Firm of plumbing and building-fixture manufacturers. It was formed in 1929 as the American Radiator and Standard Sanitary Corporation after a merger of the American Radiator Company (formed in the city in 1905) and the Standard Sanitary Corporation, and took its current name in 1967. Between 1968 and 1971 the firm sponsored vocational training, improvements in public transit, and affordable housing. Among its programs was Construction for Progress, which sponsored several low-income housing projects in Harlem and the southern Bronx. During the 1980s the firm sold mostly plumbing and air conditioning supplies. It was taken private in 1988 and moved its executive offices to 1114 6th Avenue in the following year. One of the city's largest industrial firms, it had more than $3500 million in sales in 1990. The American Standard Building on West 40th Street, Raymond M. Hood's first commission in the city, is a municipal landmark. Among the many buildings in the city appointed with the firm's products is the World Trade Center.

James Bradley

American Stock Exchange. Stock exchange in the financial district of New York City. It was originally composed of dealers too poor to become members of the New York Stock and Exchange Board (1817; later the New York Stock Exchange) and was known as the Curb, because members met their clients in the streets and became known as "curbstone brokers" who traded mostly the

American Stock Exchange, ca 1905

stocks of firms smaller, younger, and riskier than those represented on the older exchange. In the 1860s shares were sold in mining companies formed after the discovery of gold in California in 1848. The volume of activity was tremendous: on a busy day, when six thousand shares of stocks might be sold at the New York Stock and Exchange Board, seventy thousand shares might be sold at the Curb, where after the Civil War new securities and stocks in small manufacturing companies were first sold. By tacit agreement the New York Stock and Exchange Board concentrated on established issues and on maintaining high standards for listing and trading. Determined to cleanse the Curb of marginal men and securities, a curbstone broker named Emmanuel S. Mendels Jr. in 1904 published an official Curb directory of 209 reliable brokers and in 1908 organized the New York Curb Market Agency. In 1911 the exchange became known simply as the New York Curb Market and drew up a constitution; it moved indoors to 113–23 Greenwich Street in 1921 and in 1929 was renamed the New York Curb Exchange.

The volume of stocks and bonds traded during the 1920s grew rapidly, especially that of foreign securities. By 1930 the exchange had more foreign issues on its list than all other American securities markets combined. The price of a seat rose from $6800 in 1921 to $254,000 in 1929. As firms became well known they often moved to the New York Stock Exchange, but the Curb continued to attract new firms and foreign ones. It took its current name in 1953 and soon became known as the Amex. During the 1960s and 1970s it introduced a number of innovations, including the listing of stock options, automation, and surveillance of trades. Although the American Stock Exchange is the second-largest securities exchange in the United States it is far smaller than the New York Stock Exchange, and also far smaller than the over-the-counter market: in 1990 the average daily volume was 13,157,780 shares traded.

Stuart Bruchey: *The Modernization of the American Stock Exchange, 1971–1989* (New York: Garland, 1991)

Stuart Bruchey

American Sunday School Union. Interdenominational Protestant philanthropy formed in 1824 as an offshoot of the Sunday and Adult School Union and based in Philadelphia. It organized a national network of Sunday school supporters, developed standardized curricula and pedagogical techniques, and published moral and religious literature for American youths. Chapters in New York City were active throughout the nineteenth century. The union altered its focus toward rural areas after the Civil War and ultimately evolved into the American Missionary Fellowship in 1974.

Peter J. Wosh

American Symphony Orchestra. Orchestra formed in 1962 in New York City by Leopold Stokowski, who announced that his aims were "to afford opportunity to gifted musicians, regardless of age, sex, or racial origin, and to offer concerts of great music within the means of everyone." Carnegie Hall was chosen as the site of its concerts, which initially numbered six each season. In its repertory the orchestra covered a wide range, performing many modern and American works. Perhaps its most notable performance was the world première of Ives's Symphony no. 4 in 1965. The orchestra was reorganized as a co-operative in 1973. In the 1980s it suffered a decline in subscribers, but it regained some visibility under the direction of Leon Botstein, who became its conductor in 1992 and reoriented the programming to emphasize lesser-known works of the nineteenth century.

American Telephone and Telegraph [AT&T]. Telecommunications firm, formed in 1885 in Boston as a subsidiary of the American Bell Telephone Company to develop long-distance communications channels and maintain the parent company's control of telephony in the United States. In 1899 the offices were moved to 195 Broadway in New York City, where AT&T became the parent firm of several regional telephone companies and of the manufacturing subsidiary Western Electric. It briefly acquired control of Western Union in 1909 before the two firms were separated by antitrust action. AT&T kept competitors out of the long-distance market by providing "universal service" at low cost and making constant technological improvements. Its control of telephony was strengthened by passage of the Mann–Elkins Act (1910), the "Kingsbury Commitment" (1913), and subsequent federal regulation, which established the Bell system as the manager of the national telephone network. In 1925 Bell Telephone Laboratories was incorporated as a subsidiary. The firm launched a number of radio stations in the 1920s, and on 7 April 1927 it made the first television broadcast from its laboratory on West Street. In the late 1930s the Federal Communications Commission reaffirmed the firm's position as the dominant carrier of telecommunications, but in 1949 AT&T and Western Electric were sued for antitrust violations and a consent decree prevented AT&T from engaging in business other than telephony. During the following years the firm's monopolies in telephone equipment and long-distance service were gradually weakened by regulators, and in 1982 an antitrust action led to a settlement under which the firm (then the largest in the world) agreed to divest itself of its regional operating companies, though it remained free to enter such new, unregulated fields of business as computer hardware and data transmission. In 1983 AT&T moved its offices to 550 Madison Avenue.

N. R. Danielian: *AT&T: The Story of Industrial Conquest* (New York: Vanguard, 1939)
John Brooks: *Telephone: The First Hundred Years* (New York: Harper and Row, 1976)
Peter Temin: *The Fall of the Bell System: A Study in Prices and Politics* (New York: Cambridge University Press, 1987)

See also WESTERN UNION and TELEPHONY.

George David Smith

American Temperance Union. Temperance group. Formed in 1836 in Saratoga, New York, and based in New York City, it sought to unify, coordinate, and structure the work of hundreds of societies throughout North America favoring complete abstinence from alcohol. Its forerunner was the United States Temperance Union, which had been formed by the National Temperance Convention in 1833, and its first president was Stephen Van Rensselaer. The union relied on moral suasion, religious publications, and legislative action to further its goals and was influential in reformist circles from its founding to the late 1840s. It represented the wealthier, more evangelical, avowedly prohibitionist wing of the temperance movement and in the 1850s supported a state prohibition law in Maine. In 1865 the union was absorbed by the newly formed National Temperance Society and Publication House, also based in New York City.

Permanent Temperance Documents of the American Temperance Union (New York: American Temperance Union, 1846)

Peter J. Wosh

American Tract Society. Protestant organization formed in 1825 by the merger of societies based in New York City and Boston. It became one of the largest publishers in the antebellum United States, producing each year thousands of religious books, pamphlets, tracts, and hymnals that missionary book peddlers circulated throughout the country as they preached salvation. After the Civil War the society increasingly concentrated its efforts on freed slaves, and the focus of its publishing operations shifted away from tracts and toward books and foreign-language publications. In the late 1940s it reaffirmed its traditional emphasis on small, English-language gospel tracts. The society left its landmark building at 150 Nassau Street in 1963 and eventually moved to Garland, Texas.

Stephen Elmer Slocum: "The American Tract Society, 1825–1975: An Evangelical Effort to Influence the Religious and Moral Life of the United States" (diss., New York University, 1975)

Peter J. Wosh

America's Cup. International yachting challenge trophy. It is named after the yacht *America*, which in 1851 achieved one of the first American successes in international sporting competition by winning the Royal Yacht Squadron Cup, a race of sixty miles (ninety-seven kilometers) around the Isle of Wight that was held in conjunction with the Crystal Palace Exposition of the same year; the yacht was owned by a syndicate of six men led by John Cox Stevens, the commodore of the New York Yacht Club. The Hundred Guineas Cup, a silver trophy twenty-seven inches (sixty-nine centimeters) tall weighing eight pounds, six ounces (3.75 kilograms), was taken by the victors to New York City and deeded in 1857 to the New York Yacht Club as a perpetual challenge cup for which organized yacht clubs of any country could compete; it was put on display by the club and given its current name. Challenges for the cup were mounted periodically from 1870. The first thirteen races were held near Sandy Hook, New Jersey, until the competition was moved after the challenge of 1903 to the more neutral waters of Newport, Rhode Island. The New York Yacht Club successfully defended the cup twenty-four times until 1983, when Alan Bond's yacht *Australia II*, sailed by John Bertrand, defeated Dennis Connor's yacht *Liberty* in Newport. In 1987 the America's Cup returned to the United States but its new home was the San Diego Yacht Club.

Melvin L. Adelman: *A Sporting Time: New York City and the Rise of Modern Athletics, 1820–1870* (Urbana: University of Illinois Press, 1986)

Doug Riggs: *Keelhauled: Unsportsmanlike Conduct and the America's Cup* (Newport, R.I.: Seven Seas Press, 1986)

Joseph S. Lieber

Ammann, Othmar H(erman) (*b* Schaffhausen, Switzerland, 26 March 1879; *d* Rye, N.Y., 22 Sept 1965). Engineer. He graduated from the Swiss Polytechnic Institute and left for America in 1904. For several years he worked in engineering firms in Pennsylvania and New York City, where in 1912 he joined the firm of Gustav Lindenthal, serving as the chief assistant on the Hell Gate Bridge (1917). He left the firm in the early 1920s to devote his energies to a plan for a bridge over the Hudson River, and in 1925 the Port of New York Authority adopted his plan and appointed him the chief engineer of what was later named the George Washington Bridge (1931). While working on the bridge he completed another project for the authority, the Bayonne Bridge (1931). For the Triborough Bridge and Tunnel Authority he designed the Triborough Bridge (1936), the Bronx–Whitestone Bridge (1939), the Throgs Neck Bridge (1961), and the Verrazano Narrows Bridge (1964). Ammann was the unrivaled master of the modern steel bridge.

Fritz Stüssi: *Othmar H. Ammann: Sein Beitrag zur Entwicklung des Brückenbaus* (Basel, Switzerland: Birkhauser, 1974)

Rebecca Read Shanor

Office of the Amsterdam News

amphibians and reptiles. At the time of European settlement amphibians and reptiles thrived in the varied estuarine, aquatic, and terrestrial habitats of what is now New York City. In 1927 G. K. Noble, curator of herpetology at the American Museum of Natural History, listed seventy species, including three of lizards, five of marine turtles, eleven of aquatic turtles, fifteen of salamander, fifteen of frogs and toads, and twenty-one of snakes, among them the Copperhead and the Rattlesnake, which were rapidly disappearing. As streams, marshes, and swamps were filled in or drained, critical habitats were lost, severely reducing the number and diversity of amphibians and reptiles. Those that survived tended to be species found in large lakes and small, secretive species with simple requirements and the ability to live in parks, cemeteries, and other green areas. Efforts to restore other species to the landscape were undertaken jointly by the National Park Service, the New York Zoological Society, and the New York City Department of Parks and Recreation.

Among the native species that are still fairly common in New York City are the Spring Peeper, the Grey Treefrog, Fowler's Toad (on Staten Island and Long Island), the American Toad (in the Bronx), the Wood Frog, the Green Frog, the Bullfrog, the Redback and Spotted salamanders, the Red-spotted Newt, the Garter and Brown snakes, the Snapping Turtle, the Painted Turtle, and the Diamondback Terrapin (in Jamaica Bay). Several rarer species are found in the remaining wild areas of the Greenbelt in Staten Island, in Pelham Bay and Van Cortlandt parks in the Bronx, and in Jamaica Bay, Forest Park, and Alley Pond Park in Queens. Aquatic turtles are among the only species in the ponds of such landscaped and heavily trafficked parks as Central Park, Prospect Park, and Flushing Meadows–Corona Park; many exotic pet turtles are also released into these ponds but few survive.

Robert P. Cook

Amsterdam News. Weekly newspaper, first published in 1909 with John Henry Anderson as its managing editor and an editorial focus on issues of interest to blacks; Sadie Warren Davis became its manager and treasurer in 1921. A strike by the Newspaper Guild led to the acquisition of the newspaper in 1935 by C. B. Powell and P. M. H. Savory. From its inception the newspaper was strongly supportive of civil rights and of Democratic candidates for office. Although in the 1940s it contained gossip of the sort found in the daily tabloids, by the 1970s its tone had become more serious and it was one of the largest and most influential black newspapers in the United States. It was purchased in 1971 by a group that included Percy E. Sutton, H. Carl McCall, and Clarence E. Jones, who became the editor and publisher. Sometimes criticized by activists for its conciliatory politics, in the following decades the newspaper became more confrontational: its editor in the late 1980s, Wilbert A. Tatum, was an outspoken leader in the successful effort to deny a fourth mayoral term to Edward I. Koch. The newspaper also broadened its coverage, at first strongly oriented toward Manhattan, by adding sections on national news and on Brooklyn and Queens. Over the years the staff of the *Amsterdam News* has included such notable writers as Dan Burley, T. Thomas Fortune, Roy Wilkins, and Floyd McKissick. Its circulation is more than eighty thousand.

W. Augustus Low and Virgil A. Clift, eds.: *Encyclopedia of Black America* (New York: McGraw–Hill, 1981)

Mario A. Charles

Amtrak [National Railroad Passenger Corporation]. Railroad that operates several passenger routes connecting Pennsylvania Station in New York City with other cities, including routes formerly operated by the New York Central Railroad and the Pennsylvania Railroad. Among the services that it operates is the Metroliner, which runs to Washington in about two and a half hours.

anarchism. New York City became a center of anarchism during the mid nineteenth century, when European anarchists fleeing oppression moved there and joined with libertarians in challenging perceived injustices of capitalism and the state. *Woodhull and Claflin's Weekly* was published from 1870 to 1876 by Victoria Woodhull, who with Stephen Pearl Andrews organized libertarian sections of the International Working Men's Association. Many radicals were inspired by the writings and rousing speeches of Johann Most, who published the newspaper *Freiheit* (1882–1910) and organized German anarchists; the leading advocate of terrorism, he sought to redress class grievances through the strategic use of dynamite. The execution of anarchist leaders in 1886–87 after a riot in Haymarket Square in Chicago incited anarchists in New York City to action, especially among Italian and Jewish immigrants. Jews on the Lower East Side formed the Pioneers of Liberty (1886), protested the Haymarket affair, organized workers' educational clubs, and between 1880 and 1930 launched more than a dozen anarchist publications including the Yiddish-language newspaper *Fraye arbeter shtime* (1890–1977), which became the most prominent and enduring periodical of its kind in the country. Italian anarchists settled in Brooklyn and Paterson, New Jersey. *L'Anarchico*, the first Italian anarchist newspaper in the United States, was launched in 1888. Anarchism was often accompanied by a sweeping rejection of traditional values, especially those of organized religion: some Jews celebrated the solemn fast day of Yom Kippur with feasting, dancing, and atheistic harangues. Holidays and worker picnics commemorated such events as the Haymarket affair, the Commune of Paris, and the birthdays of Peter Kropotkin and Mikhail A. Bakunin.

The assassination of President William McKinley by the anarchist Leon Czolgosz in 1901 led to widespread violence against anarchists in the city: anarchist headquarters were vandalized, immigrants were attacked, and many public figures called for the "lynch law" and the "extermination" of anarchists. Most was arrested and imprisoned for inciting violence, and in 1903 foreigners known to be anarchists were barred by federal legislation from entering the country. Among anarchists McKinley's assassination widened the division between advocates of violence and those who sought change peacefully. Education and aid were emphasized in modern schools, among them one named for the Spanish anarchist and educational reformer Francisco Ferrer: they stressed the history of revolution and of the working class and avoided that of religion and capitalism. In 1907 an anarchist Red Cross was formed in the city to assist political prisoners of the Russian Revolution. After Most's death in 1906 Emma Goldman and Alexander Berkman became leading figures of anarchism in the United States; they published the journal *Mother Earth* (1906–17), addressed May Day rallies in Union Square, protested against the First World War, organized strikes, gave lectures on contraception and "free love," and helped to renew the intellectual vigor of anarchism. Carlo Tresca published the newspaper *L'Avvenire* in New York City from 1913, and also helped to organize a strike by hotel workers that was led by the Industrial Workers of the World.

In 1918 Mollie Steimer, Jacob Abrams, and other anarchists in Harlem affiliated with the journal *Der shturm* were convicted of criticizing American intervention in the Russian Revolution. Their cause was taken up by many liberals determined to protect free speech, among them Louis Brandeis and Oliver Wendell Holmes, who together dissented from a decision by the Supreme Court to uphold the conviction. The anarchist movement was considerably weakened after 1919, when Steimer, Goldman, Berkman, and others were exiled during a "red scare" inspired by fear of the Russian Revolution, and between 1920 and 1960 most anarchist newspapers ceased publication. Although the decline of anarchism was due partly to repression, a more important cause was the rise of communism, which attracted many of those on the fringes of the anarchist movement. Libertarian ideals were preserved by anarchists, liberals, and socialists opposed to fascism; anarchist philosophy was the basis of Dwight Macdonald's periodical *Politics* and of Dorothy Day's newspaper the *Catholic Worker* (1933), and the Libertarian Book Club was formed in the 1940s. The assassination of Tresca in July 1943 marked the end of a period when anarchism was inextricably associated with immigrants.

The civil rights movement and opposition to the Vietnam War revitalized interest in anarchist ideals during the 1960s and 1970s. At the New School for Social Research Herbert Marcuse inveighed against insidious consumerism and political conformity. Ayn Rand praised capitalism in discussions of objectivism broadcast by the radio stations WKCR and WBAI; her books were available at the Objectivist Book Service on 34th Street. Paul Goodman denounced statist policies and "compulsory mis-education" and argued that student protests of the time were anarchic in origin. Sex, violence, and social disruption were glorified by some groups on the Lower East Side including Up against the Wall Motherfuckers, led by Ben Morea and named after a poem by the black nationalist LeRoi Jones; the group published the magazine *Black Mask* and worked with such radical "collectives" as the Liberation News Service and the *Rat*, an underground newspaper. Between 1968 and 1971 Transcendental Students, a group of about forty students at New York University, protested against the Vietnam War by disrupting orientation activities and other events. Many anarchists scorned the radical group Students for a Democratic Society for being too conciliatory toward established society. Abbie Hoffman and other "yippies" organized relief for the poor and in 1967 aided blacks during riots in Newark, New Jersey. In March 1968 six thousand radicals including Hoffman disrupted service at Grand Central Terminal and were violently dispersed by police officers in full riot gear.

During the early 1980s "punk" styles became fashionable as a kind of cultural anarchism in the East Village, and on the Lower East Side self-described anarchists took over abandoned buildings. In the mid 1990s anarchism continued to be supported in the city by the Libertarian Book Club, which organized lectures and provided information about anarchist history as well as contemporary social and political issues.

David E. Apter and James Joll, eds.: *Anarchism Today* (New York: Doubleday, 1971)

William O. Reichert: *Partisans of Freedom: A Study in American Anarchism* (Bowling Green, Ohio: Bowling Green University Press, 1976)

Paul Avrich: *Anarchist Portraits* (Princeton, N.J.: Princeton University Press, 1988)

David A. Balcom

Anastasia, Albert (*b* Calabria, Italy, 1903; *d* New York City, 25 Oct 1957). Organized-crime figure. After growing up in Sicily he moved to New York City, where with his brother "Tough Tony" he took control of the waterfront in Brooklyn in 1920 and gained power in its union. After killing a fellow longshoreman he spent eighteen months on death row at Sing Sing, the state penitentiary at Ossining, New York; he was released after key witnesses disappeared. With Louis "Lepke" Buchalter he became an enforcer for Murder Incorporated, a criminal organization responsible for five hundred deaths and disappearances. Nicknamed the "Mad Hatter," he was protected and controlled by Lucky Luciano (until he was deported) and Frank Costello (until he became preoccupied with his own legal problems). Shortly after threatening Meyer Lansky, Anastasia was murdered by two gunmen in a barber shop at the Park Sheraton Hotel.

Salvatore Anastasia: *Anastasia mio fratello*, ed. Benedetto Mosca (Rome: Novissima, 1967)

James E. Mooney

Anchor Savings Bank. Savings bank formed at the beginning of the twentieth century as the Bay Ridge Savings Bank. Many of its customers were sailors, and the bank adopted an anchor as its symbol. The bank took its current name in 1968 when it merged with the Bushwick Savings Bank. By the mid 1990s it had taken over fifteen savings banks and had $7900 million in total assets and about sixty branches in New York State, New Jersey, and Florida. In 1994 the bank announced plans to merge with the Dime Savings Bank.

Leslie Gourse

Ancient Order of Hibernians. Roman Catholic society formed in Ireland in 1565. Its first branch in the United States was founded as a social and benevolent society in 1836 at St. James Roman Catholic Church in Manhattan. The society is made up of separate men's and women's groups that are largely independent but work in close cooperation. There are about eighty local divisions in New York City, based mainly in neighborhoods that have a large Irish population. The Ancient Order of Hibernians is nonpartisan in American politics but has a strong tradition of support for nationalist movements in Ireland. It organizes dances, concerts, educational programs, and religious celebrations.

Thomas F. McGrath: *History of the Ancient Order of Hibernians* (Cleveland: Thomas F. McGrath, 1898)

John T. Ridge: *Erin's Sons in America: The Ancient Order of Hibernians* (New York: Ancient Order of Hibernians, 1986)

John T. Ridge

Anderson, Alexander (*b* New York City, 21 April 1775; *d* Jersey City, N.J., 17 Jan 1870). Physician and engraver. He worked at Bellevue Hospital during yellow fever epidemics in 1793 and again in 1798, during which the loss of his wife, children, and many other close relatives led him to abandon the medical profession. Inspired by the English illustrator Thomas Bewick, he turned to engraving for his livelihood. The American edition of *A History of Quadrupeds* (1804) included more than three hundred woodcuts after designs by Bewick and brought him wide recognition. In later decades his illustrations appeared in hundreds of children's books and in editions of poetry, Aesop's fables, and the Bible. Anderson was the first American to make prominent use of the woodblock, and his woodcuts were the first important examples of popular American book illustration. A selection of his tools is at the New-York Historical Society; some woodblocks are held by the Free Library of Philadelphia and the Springfield (Massachusetts) Public Library, and in private collections.

Frederic Martin Burr: *Life and Works of Alexander Anderson, M.D.* (New York: Burr Brothers, 1893)

John F. Dingman: *Alexander Anderson, 1775–1870, and the Background of Wood-Engraving in America* (San Marcos, Calif.: J. F. Dingman, 1984)

For illustration see STREET LIFE.

Robert I. Goler

Anderson, Charles W(illiam) (*b* Oxford, Ohio, 28 April 1866; *d* New York City, 28 June 1938). Public official. After moving to New York City in 1886 he became active in Republican politics, and in 1890 he was elected president of the Young Men's Colored Republican Club of New York County. He was a gauger in the district office of the Internal Revenue Service, the private secretary to the treasurer of New York State (1895–98), and the supervisor of accounts for the state racing commission (1898–1905). In 1905 he was appointed by President Theodore Roosevelt as the collector of internal revenue for the second district of New York City (encompassing Wall Street and the major piers), considered one of the most important federal positions in the city. He reportedly received the appointment through the influence of his friend and close political associate Booker T. Washington. Dismissed from office by President Woodrow Wilson in a purge of black Republicans, he later held senior positions in state government and again served as collector of internal revenue from 1923 to 1934.

James S. Kaplan

Andrew W. Mellon Foundation. Charitable organization. It began operations in June 1969 with the merger of the Avalon Foundation, formed in 1940 by Ailsa Mellon Bruce (*d* 25 Aug 1969) and based in New York City, and the Old Dominion Foundation, formed in Virginia in 1941 by Paul Mellon (*b* 11 June 1907). The foundation makes grants in the areas of higher education, cultural affairs and the performing arts, population, conservation and the environment, and public affairs. In 1992 it was the ninth-largest private grant-making organization in the United States, with assets of $2100 million and grants totaling $95.9 million. Its offices are at 140 East 62nd Street.

Kenneth W. Rose

Androvetteville. Name applied in the eighteenth century to CHARLESTON.

Annadale. Neighborhood in southwestern Staten Island, overlooking the Raritan Bay. It was once inhabited by Raritan Indians and was given its current name about 1860 in honor of Anna Seguine, a member of a prominent local family. The first houses in the area were fishing bungalows. There was relatively little development until the opening of the Verrazano Narrows Bridge, and the construction of private houses on a large scale began only about 1975. The neighborhood is the site of Blue Heron Pond Park, to the north of which is a station of Staten Island Rapid Transit. The housing stock in Annadale varies from the modest to the opulent; there is a large Italian population, and the neighborhood is ethnically diverse.

Martha S. Bendix

Ansonia Hotel, 1994

Annexed District. Name applied to the lands annexed by New York City in 1874 (the present neighborhoods of Kingsbridge, Morrisania, and West Farms in the Bronx) and 1895 (the rest of what is now the Bronx).

Gary Hermalyn: "The Bronx at the Turn of the Century," *Bronx County Historical Society Journal* 36 (1989), 92–112

Gary D. Hermalyn

Ansonia. Seventeen-story apartment building on Broadway between 73rd and 74th streets. Designed in a beaux-arts style by the architectural firm of Graves and Duboy, it was built in 1904 by the developer W. E. D. Stokes and soon became well known for attracting such residents as Babe Ruth, Enrico Caruso, Theodore Dreiser, Igor Stravinsky, Arturo Toscanini, Florenz Ziegfeld, Mischa Elman, Sol Hurok, Lauritz Melchior, Ezio Pinza, and Lily Pons. During renovations in the 1980s some portions were converted into studios for voice coaching and space for theater rehearsals. Ornamented façades, balconies, and corner towers make the Ansonia Hotel an outstanding structure on the West Side. It was declared a landmark in 1972.

Thomas E. Bird

Anthology Film Archives. Museum dedicated to avant-garde cinema formed in 1969 by the filmmakers Jonas Mekas and Jerome Hill; it was the first museum of its kind in the United States. From 1970 it mounted exhibitions at Joseph Papp's Public Theater in an "invisible cinema" designed by Peter Kubelka, in which viewers were separated from each other by black partitions and a seat hood that minimized perceptual interference while allowing for a communal sense of viewing. Its collection, the Essential Cinema Repertory, was selected by a committee of theoreticians, filmmakers, and poets to celebrate the aesthetics of cinema and provoke discussion about alternative cinema. It launched its publication program in 1970 with the *Film Culture Reader* (edited by P. Adams Sitney). The archive introduced the Independent Film Preservation program and began its library collection in 1972, introduced video exhibitions in 1974, and maintained a theater at 80 Wooster Street from 1973 to 1980. In 1988 the Anthology Film Archives moved to a former courthouse building at 2nd Avenue and 2nd Street.

P. Adams Sitney, ed.: *The Essential Cinema* (New York: Anthology Film Archives / New York University Press, 1975)

Peter Feinstein, ed.: *The Independent Film Community* (New York: Committee on Film and Television Resources and Services, 1977)

Sidney Peterson: *The Dark of the Screen* (New York: Anthology Film Archives / New York University Press, 1980)

Grai St. Clair Rice

anthropology. New York City became noted for its contributions to the field of anthropology in the early nineteenth century through the work of Albert Gallatin, who conducted research on American Indian languages and helped to organize the American Ethnological Society in 1842. The American Museum of Natural History opened an anthropology department in 1874, but it was not directed by trained curators until 1894, when it was reorganized by Frederic Putnam of Harvard University. Prominent anthropologists in the department included Franz Boas, who was curator from 1895 to 1905, Clark Wissler, Robert Lowie, Herbert Spinden, Harry Shapiro, and Margaret Mead. The New York Academy of Sciences opened an anthropology division in 1896. After 1900 the center of anthropology in New York City gradually shifted toward Columbia University, where Boas began teaching in 1896. Among his first students were Alfred Kroeber (to whom Columbia awarded its first PhD in anthropology in 1901), Lowie, Edward Sapir, Paul Radin, and Alexander Goldenweiser, who all centered their work on salvaging the vanishing culture of the American Indian. In the 1920s Boas's students included Mead, Ruth Benedict, Gladys Reichard, Ruth Bunzel, and Melville Herskovits. Ralph Linton, who like Benedict studied culture and personality, became a professor at Columbia in 1937 after Boas's retirement.

Between the two world wars many schools in the city introduced anthropology into their curricula, including all four public colleges in New York City (City College, Hunter College, Brooklyn College, and Queens College) and the New School for Social Research, where Elsie Clews Parsons and Goldenweiser taught when the school opened in 1919. The French anthropologist Claude Lévi-Strauss taught at the New School from 1942 to 1945 and was the cultural attaché to the French embassy from 1946 to 1947. In 1941 the Viking Fund (later known as the Wenner–Gren Foundation for Anthropological Research), an important source of grants for anthropological study abroad, established its headquarters in the city.

Although the city's preeminence as a center of anthropology declined after the Second World War as the field gained popularity throughout the country, in 1966 doctoral programs in anthropology were launched at New York University, the New School, and City University of New York. Into the 1990s the New York Academy of Sciences was an important center for anthropologists throughout the city.

Sydel Silverman, ed.: *Totems and Teachers: Perspectives on the History of Anthropology* (New York: Columbia University Press, 1981)

Ira Jacknis

Anti-Defamation League. Nonprofit organization formed as an affiliate of B'nai B'rith in 1913 to combat negative portrayals of Jews in books, periodicals, and advertising. Initially the league supported the censorship of texts that it believed would encourage anti-Semitism, including works of Shakespeare and Dickens. In 1946 the organization moved to New York City from Chicago and broadened its mission to include defending the rights of all Americans: it filed a brief in the school desegregation case *Brown v. Board of Education* (1954) and drafted the first anti-discrimination bill, the Ives–Quinn Act. In later years the league supported the Civil Rights Act of 1964 and defended the rights of Jews in the Soviet Union.

Bernard Postal, ed.: *This Is B'nai B'rith: A Manual of Facts* (Washington: B'nai B'rith, 1941)

Edward Grusd: *B'nai B'rith: The Story of a Covenant* (New York: Appleton Century, 1966)

Deborah Dash Moore: *B'nai B'rith and the Challenge of Ethnic Leadership* (Albany: State University of New York Press, 1981)

Jean Ulitz Mensch

Anti-Slavery Society. See AMERICAN ANTI-SLAVERY SOCIETY.

Antonetty, Evelina (*b* Salinas, Puerto Rico, 19 Sept 1922; *d* New York City, 19 Nov 1984). Activist. She moved to the mainland in 1933 and settled in New York City, where in the 1940s she organized unions and worked to improve educational opportunities for Puerto Ricans. In the 1960s and 1970s she led parents and other activists in demonstrations against discriminatory practices in the public schools. She was the founder and executive director of United Bronx Parents, an organization that encouraged parents to take part in the school system and eventually offered social services in the southern Bronx.

Nélida Pérez

Antonini, Luigi (*b* Vallata Irpina, Italy, 11 Sept 1883; *d* New York City, 29 Dec 1968). Labor leader. He joined the International Ladies' Garment Workers' Union as a dress presser in 1913 and became a leader of Italian workers in New York City. In 1919 he organized Italian Dressmakers Local 89, of which he served as general secretary. Elected vice-president of the union in 1934, he joined with its president, David Dubinsky, to form the American Labor Party in New York City in 1936 and the Liberal Party in 1944. Antonini later led the Italian–American Labor Council in opposition to Mussolini and assisted in rebuilding democratic trade unions in Italy after the Second World War.

John Stuart Crawford: *Luigi Antonini: His Influence on Italian–American Relations* (New York: Education Department, Italian Dressmakers' Union, Local 89, International Ladies' Garment Workers' Union, 1950)

Robert D. Parmet

AP. See ASSOCIATED PRESS.

apartments. The first apartment building in New York City was the Stuyvesant Apartments, designed in 1869 by the well-known architect Richard Morris Hunt, the first American to attend the École des Beaux-Arts. The building was also called the "French Flats," a term later used more broadly for any dwellings of the same kind (which were not known as apartments until the 1880s). Early apartment buildings in Manhattan were constructed at a time when most middle-class families in the city lived in row houses. In contrast to the row house and its descendant the brownstone, which had a dark interior and was costly to maintain, the apartment building symbolized modern technology and new ways of family living; it signaled a shift in the cultural ideals of the upper middle class from its colonial Anglo-Saxon origins to the culture of the Continent, especially that of Second Empire Paris. In 1871 Hunt completed the Stevens House, an eight-story building with a passenger elevator and other technological innovations. Dozens of similar apartment buildings were erected in Manhattan in the 1880s, some having as many as twenty rooms: one of the best-known was the Dakota (1884, Henry J. Hardenbergh). To counter the prejudice against apartments that was still common among wealthy residents, many of the new buildings were developed as COOPERATIVES:

this arrangement gave residents a financial interest in their apartment that was tantamount to ownership, and offered services such as catered meals and domestic help.

Not all apartment buildings were luxurious. TENEMENTS provided compact rental housing for poor and working-class immigrants at a monthly rent of $2 to $3 a room. Before the late nineteenth century most tenements in New York City were RAILROAD APARTMENTS, or railroad flats, which contained several rooms in a line, usually without windows, entered one from another and lacking a hallway. The Tenement House Law of 1879 set standards for space, ventilation, and hygiene, and implemented the "dumbbell" design: between the front and back rooms the exterior walls were indented, creating large air shafts between adjacent buildings (see DUMBBELL TENEMENTS). In 1901 the law was amended to mandate a toilet for each dwelling, separate living and sleeping rooms, and adequate light, which brought the tenement closer to the level of other apartment buildings in the city. At the same time the number of luxury apartments increased in Manhattan, especially on the Upper East Side and on the Upper West Side, where three large apartment buildings along Broadway were each briefly promoted as the world's largest: the Ansonia (1904, seventeen stories, Graves and Duboy), the Apthorp (1908, Clinton and Russell), and the Belnord (1908, Hiss and Weeks). In the 1920s a great number of apartments were built, but they were less luxurious than their forerunners: the new large-scale apartment building was the modest domain of the middle class. The gap between tenement and apartment building was further narrowed by the Multiple Dwellings Law (1929), which eliminated the legal distinction between the two types of dwelling and united all categories of housing under a uniform set of design controls. With the onset of the Depression luxury apartments became smaller: in the Century on Central Park West (1931, Jacques Delamarre) each apartment had only one or two bedrooms.

Most innovations in the building of apartments from the late 1920s were made in the outer boroughs, where low-rise "garden apartments" for the expanding middle class were built on cheap land newly accessible by subway. Large developments were constructed in Jackson Heights and later along the Bronx River Parkway, Pelham Parkway in the Bronx, and Eastern Parkway in Brooklyn. Some apartment buildings in Manhattan had small gardens enclosed in courtyards, among them the Hudson View Gardens (1924, George F. Pelham), Tudor City (1928, H. Douglas Ives), and London Terrace (1930, Farrar and Watmaugh). Many of the housing projects built with government sponsorship from the 1930s were garden apartments, including Hillside Homes in the Bronx (1935, Clarence Stein) and Harlem River Houses in Manhattan (1937, Archibald Manning Brown); public funds also subsidized the construction of such large complexes as Parkchester in the Bronx (1940, Richmond H. Shreve) and Stuyvesant Town in Manhattan (1949, Gilmore D. Clarke). After the Second World War pressures to reduce construction costs, and the movement of the middle class to the suburbs, encouraged the development of a design known as "tower in the park," characterized by a large apartment building surrounded by open space. The design was further encouraged by changes in zoning in 1961 and was seen in such developments as the Kips Bay Plaza (1965, I. M. Pei and Partners) and Co-op City (1968–70, Herman J. Jessor), the largest postwar apartment complex in New York City. Among the most innovative apartment complexes of the 1960s and 1970s were Riverbend (1967, Davis, Brody), made up of duplex apartments facing terraces, several projects sponsored by the Urban Development Corporation at Twin Parks in the Bronx, and Battery Park City in lower Manhattan (1979, Alexander Cooper and Associates).

Tax policy and RENT REGULATION encouraged landlords in the 1980s to convert several hundred thousand rental apartments in New York City to cooperatives and condominium units, a process that became known as gentrification. There was considerable new construction in Hell's Kitchen (which became known as Clinton) and along upper Broadway. Trump Tower on 5th Avenue (1983, Sanke, Hayden, Connell) became a symbol of the lavish apartment building of the 1980s. In the outer boroughs many of the spacious apartment buildings of the 1920s were abandoned or destroyed by arson, and the city made plans to replace them not with apartment buildings but rather with owner-occupied houses.

Richard Plunz: *A History of Housing in New York City: Dwelling Type and Social Change in the American Metropolis* (New York: Columbia University Press, 1990)

Richard Plunz

Apgar, Virginia (*b* Westfield, N.J., 7 June 1909; *d* New York City, 7 Aug 1974). Anesthesiologist. She worked for most of her professional life at the Columbia–Presbyterian Medical Center, where in 1938 she became the first woman to lead a department; she was also the first female physician to hold a full professorship at the College of Physicians and Surgeons and in 1949 became the first professor of anesthesiology there, remaining until 1959. She is best known for developing the Apgar Score (1952), a quick method for determining whether newborn infants require special medical attention. Apgar ended her career at the National Foundation–March of Dimes, where she held several prominent positions. With Joan Beck she wrote *Is My Baby All Right?: A Guide to Birth Defects* (1972).

Joseph S. Lieber

Apollo Association for the Promotion of the Fine Arts in the United States. Original name of the AMERICAN ART-UNION.

Apollo Theatre. Theater in Harlem, built in 1914 at 253 West 125th Street. Frank Schiffman and Leo Brecher began presenting stage shows there in 1934. Among those who performed at the Apollo in the 1930s and 1940s were the dance team Buck and Bubbles and the dancer Bill "Bojangles" Robinson, the singers Bessie Smith, Billie Holiday, and Ethel Waters, and the jazz orchestras of Duke Ellington, Jimmie Lunceford, and Charlie Barnet. Chorus girls backed the star performers, and the Apollo sometimes offered revues from such cabarets as the Cotton Club and the Ubangi Club. The Apollo was also a venue for speeches by sports figures and organizers of political causes, including the defense of the "Scottsboro boys." Amateur nights, held on Wednesdays, helped launch the careers of Ella Fitzgerald, Sarah Vaughan, and James Brown. By the 1950s the Apollo had eliminated its chorus line. It was the site of performances by musicians ranging from Nat "King" Cole to Charlie Parker and by actors such as Sidney Poitier, Ossie Davis, and Canada Lee. Rhythm-and-blues and soul musicians including Marvin Gaye, Stevie Wonder, Bo Diddley, and Diana Ross performed there in the 1960s.

The Apollo was converted into a movie theater in 1975, then reopened as a venue for live performances in 1983 after the building was bought by Inner City Broadcasting, a firm led by a former borough president of Manhattan, Percy E. Sutton. In the early 1990s regular concerts were given at the theater and the syndicated television series "Show Time at the Apollo" was broadcast from there. The

Apollo Theater, 1994

Apollo was known for many years as the leading variety theater in Harlem. Performers considered its sophisticated audiences among the most challenging in the country.

Jack Schiffman: *Harlem Heyday: A Pictorial History of Modern Black Show Business and the Apollo Theatre* (New York: Prometheus, 1984)

Kathy J. Ogren

Apple Bank for Savings. Savings bank formed in 1863 as the Harlem Savings Bank. It took its current name in May 1983. In the early 1990s the bank had its headquarters at 205 East 42nd Street and thirty-two branches in the metropolitan area. Its total assets at the end of 1994 were $3809 million.

Leslie Gourse

apprenticeship. During the colonial period apprentices in New York City as elsewhere were trained in crafts through legal attachments to master tradesmen. In return for their labor they received food, clothing, shelter, a rudimentary education, and religious training. Although the standard period of apprenticeship in America was seven years or until the age of twenty-one, terms were often shorter in colonial New York City because of a labor shortage that allowed apprentices to become wage-earning journeymen early. This trend was reinforced by the growth of the marketplace after independence and led semiskilled youths to enter the workshop as journeymen at progressively earlier ages. The authority of the master was considerably undermined by the individualistic emphasis of republican ideology and evangelical religion, and by technological advances that obviated full understanding of a trade. In the early nineteenth century an apprentice would often live apart from his master's household and demand a cash wage. Between six and eight thousand apprentices labored in the city in 1820. With the introduction of heavy machinery in many trades at the time of the Civil War apprentices virtually disappeared from New York City.

W. J. Rorabaugh: *The Craft Apprentice: From Franklin to the Machine Age in America* (New York: Oxford University Press, 1986)

Howard Rock

Apthorp Apartments. Residential building between Broadway and West End Avenue south of 79th Street. It was designed for the Astor estate as luxury rental housing by the firm of Clinton and Russell and completed in 1908. Built in the style of an Italian Renaissance palazzo, it covers 86 percent of the block, is twelve stories high, and has two vaulted carriage ways leading from the street to an interior courtyard with an impressive fountain. At the time the Apthorp was completed its size and full range of concierge services surpassed those of the Ansonia, its rival in luxury hotel housing.

Joel Schwartz

Aquarium. See New York aquarium.

Aqueduct. Neighborhood in southwestern Queens, adjoining the western edge of Aqueduct Racetrack between Rockaway Boulevard and the Southern Parkway. One of the first developments was a cemetery (now nearly obliterated), begun in 1680 at what is now 149th Avenue and Redding Street. In the eighteenth century and the early nineteenth the area was sparsely populated and tilled by families of Dutch descent, including the Ryders, Duryeas, and Rapalyes. The neighborhood was first known as South Woodhaven; the current name became used locally after a conduit for the Brooklyn Water Works was built in 1854–58 south of what is now the parkway, and more widely after the Long Island Rail Road opened a station there in 1880. The Centerville (Eclipse) Race Course stood south of Rockaway Boulevard and east of Cross Bay Boulevard and was popular in the 1850s and 1860s. The Queens County Jockey Club bought land in 1892 and opened a racetrack on 15 September 1894. The railroad station later became the Aqueduct subway station.

Vincent Seyfried

Aqueduct Racetrack. Thoroughbred racetrack in Ozone Park, opened on 27 September 1894 and operated by the Queens County Jockey Club. A minor facility at its inception, it eventually became the site of such famous races as the Carter Handicap on 10 July 1944, which ended in a triple dead heat. In 1959 the New York Racing Association spent $33 million to renovate the track, which opened on 14 September with a capacity of eighty thousand. Thirty minutes by express subway from Times Square, it became the leading betting track in the United States in 1960 when it achieved a daily handle of $2,698,419. In later years attendance, handle, and the number of horses taking part in races declined sharply, and the disastrous winter of 1993–94, during which many racing dates were canceled, called the future of the track into question.

Steven A. Riess

Arabs. The first Arabic-speaking residents of New York City were Syrian and Lebanese, most of them Christian, who emigrated from the Ottoman province known as Greater Syria between 1878 and 1924. By the late nineteenth century the area in lower Manhattan around Rector and Washington streets had become known as Little Syria; other Syrian–Lebanese neighborhoods later took form in Cobble Hill, Park Slope, and Bay Ridge in Brooklyn. Many of the early immigrants worked first as peddlers, then as businessmen and merchants, some becoming quite wealthy in the import–export trade. In the first three decades of the twentieth century New York City developed a vibrant Arabic literary establishment that greatly influenced Arab letters not only in the western hemisphere but also in the Arab world; it included such writers as Khalil Gibran. Because of its size, commercial strength, and vibrant press the city's Arab community was considered the mother colony of all other Arabic-speaking communities in the United States. Until the 1960s it was the most influential in the country. After the immigration restrictions imposed in 1924 were lifted in 1965, a second phase of immigration began, this one spurred by such military and political upheavals as the Arab–Israeli wars of 1948 and 1967 and the resultant loss of Palestine; revolutions in Egypt and Iraq in the 1950s; the civil war in Lebanon from 1975 to 1990; the unfulfilled economic expectations of a newly educated Arab élite; and economic pressures in the poorer Arab countries. Between 1965 and the mid 1990s the number of residents of New York City of Arab origin probably doubled, to an estimated 120,000 Muslims and Christians from Arab countries. In addition to the descendants of the early Syrian and Lebanese immigrants (a group accounting for about half the total), there was a substantial number of new immigrants from Syria and Lebanon, as well as large groups of Palestinians, Jordanians, Yemenis, Egyptians, Moroccans, and Sudanese, and smaller groups of Iraqis, Algerians, Tunisians, Libyans, Saudis, and Kuwaitis. Although perhaps 95 percent of the early immigrants were Christian, after 1965 Muslims accounted for at least half of all immigrants and possibly for much more.

Among Arabs religious affiliation defines to a great extent personal and public identity, a situation fostered by the Ottoman practice of governing subject people according to their membership in a religious community. The Arab world is the birthplace of three major religions — Islam, Christianity, and Judaism — and in a reflection of this varied heritage Arabs in New York City practice nine religions indigenous to the Arab East. These include Sunni and Shiite Islam, the Druze religion, Christianity, including half a dozen eastern Christian sects (Arabs also practice Roman Catholicism and belong to various branches of Protestantism), and Judaism. The diversity of Arab Christianity, which is two thousand years old, stems from the development of local liturgies and theological differences among Christian communities in the early centuries of the church; these were further complicated by the split between the Roman Catholic and Eastern Orthodox churches in 1054, and the succession of alliances and realignments among smaller Christian groups. The Lebanese Maronites and the Iraqi Chaldeans, whose liturgy is partly in Aramaic, are both Catholic; the Maronites worship at Our Lady of Lebanon Cathedral on Remsen Street in Brooklyn Heights (there are too few Chaldeans to maintain a church). The Melkites, who are also Catholic, were aligned with the Antiochian (Arab) Orthodox until 1724 and still share their Byzantine rites and liturgy; they worship at the Church of the Virgin Mary in Park Slope. The Antiochian Orthodox worship at St. Nicholas Orthodox Cathedral on State Street and St. Mary's Orthodox Church in Bay Ridge. Egyptian Copts in New York City, who also are Orthodox, worship at St. George's Coptic Orthodox Church in Brooklyn, St. Mary's and St. Anthony's Coptic Orthodox Church in Queens, and the Coptic Orthodox Church of Archangel Michael and St. Mena in Staten Island. About five hundred families belong to the Druze sect (an offshoot of Islam): although they have no priesthood or church organization they are served by the head of the Druze Council of North America, which is based in New Jersey. The city has from thirty thousand to sixty thousand or more Jews from Arab countries. About half descend from Syrians who immigrated at the beginning of the twentieth century; the rest immigrated later from Syria, Iraq, Yemen, and the countries of North Africa. Arab Jews have much in common linguistically and culturally with other Arab immigrants, and many have retained their Arabic language and cultural values at least as successfully as other Arabs have.

Although second- and third-generation Arabs are for the most part assimilated and middle class and tend to work in business and the professions, the later immigrants have a wider range of experiences and ways of life. Some are drawn to the city's fluid service economy: working at whatever jobs they can find, they resist assimilation and continue as much as possible their traditions in Cobble Hill, Sunset Park, Bay Ridge, and Astoria, hoping to return to their countries when conditions improve. For other immigrants, well educated and with money to invest, immigration is permanent and reflects a decision to begin a new life, despite the personal social costs that some aspects of Americanization may entail.

Although a wide occupational range characterizes every Arab national group, there is a disproportionate number of Yemenis, Moroccans, and Sudanese in low-level occupations and of Syrians and Iraqis in the professions. Arab entrepreneurs work in wholesale and retail trade (food, clothing, furniture, jewelry) and services (automotive repair, food catering, real estate, accounting, and insurance). In the professions and white-collar occupations, law, engineering, academia, and banking are especially important. More than twenty Arab banks have full branches in New York City; ABANA, the Arab Banking Association of North America (formed 1983), links Arab and American bankers and financial institutions in the city and nationwide.

There are a number of Arab–American organizations in the city that bridge national and sectarian interests. Active Arab clubs at Columbia University, Hunter College, New York University, City College of New York, the College of Staten Island, and the Borough of Manhattan Community College offer forums for discussing issues concerning the Middle East. The radio station WNWK has two weekly programs focusing on Arab and Islamic concerns. In 1991 channel 67, a cable television station in Brooklyn, began offering Arabic programming for thirteen hours a day, including films, documentaries, soap operas, and programs of interest to children and immigrants. This programming was scheduled to be available nationwide by the end of 1994. A number of the city's Arab–Americans have become nationally known, including the opera singer Rosalind Elias, the secretary of health and human services Donna Shalala (a former president of Hunter College), the actor F. Murray Abraham, the fashion designers Norma Kamali and Joseph Abboud, the diplomat Philip Habib, and the Broadway stage director A. J. Antoon. Edward Said, a professor of comparative literature at Columbia University and a distinguished cultural critic, is a Palestinian who was born in Jerusalem; he is the most visible and eloquent spokesman in the United States for the Palestinian cause.

Many Arab–American New Yorkers have found that open discussion of Middle Eastern issues is made difficult by widespread support in New York City for the state of Israel, and they feel that they have continually to remind the city's public officials and political candidates that their views are as deserving of a hearing as those of any other group. In the mayoral election of 1989 Democratic campaign workers discouraged Arab–American endorsement and rejected an offer of an Arab–American fund-raising event; in the election of 1993 Arab–American participation was more welcome and more visible in the two major parties. One reason for the increase in participation and visibility was the work over the preceding decade of two national grass-roots organizations: the American Arab Anti-Discrimination Committee (ADC), formed in 1980 to fight stereotyping of Arabs in the press and in public discourse, and the Arab American Institute (AAI), formed in 1985 and intended to help Arab–Americans become integrated into the political process and establishment. Both groups organize activities locally, and both help constituents to voice their concerns to the press and to public officials. The tensions generated by the bombing of the World Trade Center in 1993 seemed to threaten the gains that Arab New Yorkers had made in their battle against negative stereotyping, but the crisis also prompted some constructive discussions in the news media and city government about the community and its needs.

With the dramatic increase in the number of Arabs in New York City after the mid 1960s, new Arab neighborhoods were created and old ones reinvigorated. By the mid 1990s it was no longer unusual to hear Arabic spoken in the city's streets, or to find Arabic newspapers at newsstands in midtown. Despite the negative impact of some events in the news, Arab culture is increasingly becoming a part of the city's cultural mosaic. Arabic food, including Syrian bread ("pita"), hummus, baba ghanouj, tabouleh, and falafel, is now firmly established as part of the city's cuisine, and Arabic music is frequently heard on radio and in the city's concert halls. Simon Shaheen, a Palestinian violinist, oudist, and musicologist who moved to New York City in 1980, frequently performs classical Arab music at Carnegie Hall, Merkin Auditorium, and Alice Tully Hall.

Gregory Orfalea: *Before the Flames: A Quest for the History of Arab Americans* (Austin: University of Texas Press, 1988)

Paula Hajar

Arbeiter Ring. See Workmen's circle.

Arbeiter Union. A central labor council formed to consolidate twenty-six German unions in 1864. Led by Conrad Kuhn, it published the *Arbeiter Union* (edited by Adolf Douai), the first daily German labor newspaper in New York City, which was published weekly between 13 June 1868 and 15 May 1869 and daily between 20 May 1869 and 17 September 1870. The union became the leading labor organization in the city and with affiliated unions led a strike for the eight-hour work day in 1872. Although more than 100,000 persons took part, the strike was crushed and the Arbeiter Union disbanded.

Stanley Nadel

Arbitron Ratings. Broadcast ratings service, formed in 1949 as the American Research Bureau by Jim Seiler. It began by conducting surveys of television viewing in three markets and expanded rapidly during the 1950s. Surveys of viewing in New York City began in 1950 and an office was opened there in 1953. By 1955 the bureau issued television ratings for more than 140 markets and from 1964 it also issued ratings of radio broadcasts. The bureau was acquired in 1961 by the Council for Economic and Industry Research (CEIR), which was in turn acquired in 1967 by the Control Data Corporation. The name was changed to Arbitron in 1973 and took its current form in 1982. In the mid 1990s Arbitron was the largest radio rating service in the United States.

George Winslow

Arbus [née Nemerov], **Diane** (*b* New York City, 14 March 1923; *d* New York City, ?27 July 1971). Photographer. She began her career as a fashion photographer in New York City, studied with Lisette Model from 1958 to 1960, and became known during the 1960s as a photographer of the absurd who often captured her subjects in unflattering poses: her subjects ranged from beauty contestants to nudists. She taught at the Parsons School of Design (1965–66) and Cooper Union (1968–69) and had an exhibition of her work at the Museum of Modern Art in 1967. A posthumous traveling exhibition sponsored by the Museum of Modern Art in 1972 established Arbus as an important figure in photography. She lived at 319 East 72nd Street (1954–58), 71 Washington Place (1958–59), where she also opened a studio, 121½ Charles Street (1959–68), 120 East 10th Street (1968–70), and 463 West Street (from 1970 until her death).

Patricia Bosworth: *Diane Arbus: A Biography* (New York: Alfred A. Knopf, 1987)

Laura Gwinn

archaeology. The first formal, professional archaeological investigations in New York City were undertaken after deposits of seventeenth-century artifacts were discovered during construction at Old Slip and excavations for the World Trade Center. The first excavations began in 1979 at the former site of the Stadt Huys, built as a tavern at Pearl Street and Coenties Alley and used as the town hall of New Netherland and then New York City from 1653 to 1699. This, a site at Broad Street (1983), and another at 60 Wall Street (1984) were dug in the original part of Manhattan. Excavations were also conducted at Hanover Square (1981), the Telco (telephone company) Block (1981), 175 Water Street (1981–82), the site of Barclays Bank (1984), and the site of the Assay office (1984), blocks built on landfill amassed from the seventeenth century onward. The excavations uncovered such architectural remains as the foundations of houses, warehouses, taverns, and shops, as well as hundreds of thousands of artifacts, both whole and fragmentary, including ceramics, bottles, smoking pipes, buttons, coins, gun parts, and toys, large deposits of food, and materials used as ballast in merchant ships, such as English flint, coral from the Caribbean, and yellow bricks from the Netherlands. Smaller deposits from later periods were found before construction of the American Express building at the World Financial Center and of a block at 53rd Street near 3rd Avenue, as well as a site at Sullivan and 3rd streets, which contained important material from a late-eighteenth-century "suburb." The discovery and excavation in 1991 of the African Burial Ground, used for slaves and free New Yorkers of African descent throughout the eighteenth century, provided from the human remains recovered the first direct information on health, disease, and some kinds of physical trauma. The Five Points site, examined at the same time, revealed material from the city's most notorious nineteenth-century slum. Excavations have also taken place at a number of prehistoric sites, including Ryder's Pond in Brooklyn, Clason's Point and several sites in Pelham Bay Park in the Bronx, and Ward's Point in Staten Island; at the site of such historic houses as those of Pieter Claessen Wyckoff (*ca* 1641) in Brooklyn, and Adrian Onderdonck (1731) in Queens, and John Bowne (1661) in Flushing; and in the nineteenth-century free black communities of Weeksville in Brooklyn and Sandy Ground in Staten Island. Many amateur archaeologists and historians worked to preserve information about local sites beginning in the early twentieth century; avocational archaeologists continue to play an important role in protecting resources and recovering data.

The artifacts from these studies have provided stunning insight into the history of New York City, especially during the colonial period. Aspects of community planning have been revealed in a number of sites, especially methods of making land and filling in swampy areas, a procedure controlled by the local legislature throughout colonial times. At Hanover Square archaeologists discovered a wall built shortly after 1687 by six Dutch families to hold fill in place. A similar joint effort was made almost sixty years later at 175 Water Street, where a vessel used in the Caribbean trade until the 1740s (now known as the Ronson Ship, after the developer of the office building on the site) was sunk across several lots, also to hold fill. By the next stage of filling, which occurred after the American Revolution as revealed at the Assay site, the techniques for making land had become much more sophisticated. Most of the excavations were done in what was at the time an affluent neighborhood, and some of the deposits have been linked to important colonial figures, including the merchants Robert Livingston (Hanover Square), Cornelius Van Tienhoven (Broad Street), and Lewis Carre (Stadt Huys), the well-known silversmith and goldsmith Simeon Soumaine (Hanover Square), and the physician Hans Kierstede (Broad Street). Information about colonial social life has been inferred from objects found at such tavern sites as that of the Lovelace Tavern, which stood next to the Stadt Huys and served briefly as the city hall. Taverns were the most important social centers of the early city, and analysis of ceramics and pipes from the Lovelace Tavern reveals not only that its patrons did much more drinking and smoking than eating but also that smuggling from the Netherlands took place during the English trade embargo and that fashions in the city were different from those in surrounding areas. Deposits from later periods have yielded evidence about changing family organization and sex roles and health practices.

Artifacts from many local sites are held by several institutions, including the South Street Seaport Museum, the William Duncan Strong Museum at Columbia University, and New York University. A permanent outdoor exhibition about the Stadt Huys is maintained at the headquarters of Goldman, Sachs at 85 Broad Street, and an indoor exhibit is at the Urban Archaeology Center at 17 State Street.

Nan A. Rothschild and Diana diZerega Rockman: "Method in Urban Archaeology: The Stadt Huys Block," *Archaeology of Urban America*, ed. Roy S. Dickens Jr. (New York: Academic Press, 1982), 3–18

Nan A. Rothschild, Joan H. Geismar, and Diana diZ. Wall, eds.: "Urbanization and Social Change in Historical Archaeology," *American Archeology* 5 (1985), 162–221

Edward Staski: "Living in Cities: Current Research in Urban Archaeology," *Historical Archaeology*, special pubn 5 (1987)

Nan A. Rothschild

Archbishop Molloy High School. Catholic high school for boys at 85-53 Manton Street in Jamaica, opened in 1892 as an elementary and secondary school by the Marist Brothers at 151 East 76th Street in Manhattan. Later named St. Ann's Academy, it drew most of its students from Brooklyn and Queens by the 1950s, when the Marist Brothers decided to replace the aging plant at 76th Street. In 1957 it moved to its new building in Queens and was renamed for Thomas Molloy, the bishop of Brooklyn from 1921 to 1956. In 1992 enrollment was about sixteen hundred.

Gilbert Tauber

Archdiocesan Union of the Holy Name Society. Catholic organization of Holy Name societies, the first of which was formed in 1868 at the Church of St. Vincent Ferrer by Stephen Byrne, a priest who sought to encourage greater religious faith among Catholic men and who modeled the organization after similar ones in Europe. This first society received a charter from the diocese in 1871 and by 1882 inspired the formation of similar societies in the parishes of St. Agnes, St. Anthony, St. John the Evangelist, and the Transfiguration. To enlarge and unify the movement the archdiocese formed the Diocesan Union of Holy Name Societies (1882), which held annual meetings for delegates from each society to elect officers and plan a grand celebration at St. Patrick's Cathedral. In the late nineteenth century the union was the largest and most prominent organization of its kind in the city: within a decade of its formation it had twenty-five affiliates. It received a new constitution from the diocese in 1894, when it took its current name. There were 307 societies with more than 100,000 members in 1925. The annual celebration became increasingly popular and in 1942 was moved to Yankee Stadium to accommodate all participants; it drew crowds of fifty thousand to 100,000 and was sometimes held at the Polo Grounds until 1959, when it was discontinued in favor of smaller celebrations throughout the city. The union began publishing a newsletter in 1947 and formed more than twenty-five vocational branches by the 1960s, including one for employees of the police, fire, sanitation, transit, and public works departments. In their parishes the societies and their Ladies Auxiliaries began to sponsor religious events (special Masses, retreats, and public demonstrations of faith), charities (soup kitchens, shelters for the homeless, and blood banks), and fund-raising activities (bingo games and summer fairs).

After the mid 1960s membership in the societies declined sharply, as it did in most Catholic institutions, and in the 1970s one hundred societies were closed. In 1991 there were 25,000 members in many vocational branches of the union and in twenty societies on Staten Island, thirty in Manhattan, and forty in the Bronx. The union retained headquarters in the New York Catholic Center at 1011 1st Avenue.

Edward T. O'Donnell

Architectural League of New York. Organization formed on 18 January 1881 at a meeting of fifty young architects convened by Cass Gilbert, who sought to promote their artistic development. Most of the architects recognized that their training was inferior to that offered by the École des Beaux-Arts in Paris but doubted whether they could look to the American Institute of Architects for help. At frequent meetings that continued for several years members took turns assigning sketch problems and having their solutions evaluated by prominent architects. After a brief dormant period the league was reconstituted in 1886 by Russell Sturgis, who inaugurated a program of exhibitions, lectures, dinners, and tours that continued into the 1990s. The same year marked the inception of annual exhibitions of the best new work in architecture and the related arts (continued to 1938), and the league soon became influential in defining architectural taste in New York City and nationally. By the early 1930s the league had become staid, and it was overtaken as an aesthetic arbiter by the Museum of Modern Art, newly established and vehemently modernist. It reemerged in the 1960s as an important forum for architectural debate through exhibitions of the work of a new generation of architects, a series of avant-garde installations called "Environments," and a reasserted engagement with the planning and building problems of New York City. It also organized and circulated major exhibitions on women in American architecture, architectural drawing, and architectural competitions, sponsored design studies on issues of concern to New York City, and held an annual competition for young architects. Its presidents have included a number of the city's best-known architects, among them George B. Post, Henry Hardenbergh, Grosvenor Atterbury, Raymond M. Hood, Wallace K. Harrison, Ulrich Franzen, and Robert A. M. Stern.

Robert A. M. Stern, Gregory F. Gilmartin, and Thomas Mellins: *New York 1930: Architecture and Urbanism between the Two World Wars* (New York: Rizzoli, 1987)

Rosalie Genevro

architecture. The history of architecture in New York City has mirrored the rise of the city as the economic and cultural capital of the nation. Rapid growth invigorated architectural work and led to engineering advances and to new styles and building types, many of which influenced architecture worldwide. Continuous redevelopment of sites throughout the city led to increasing densities, especially in Manhattan, the center of large-scale construction from the mid nineteenth century onward.

Little of this could have been foreseen in the colonial period as the city evolved from a Dutch settlement of a few hundred persons in the 1620s to a small town of about 25,000 by the end of the American Revolution in 1783. Structures of wood and earth built by Indians provided models for shelter only during the earliest years. The influence of European building styles extended well past colonial rule: the city's seventeenth-century houses with stepped gables were modeled on the urban rows of Amsterdam, and the low swooping roofs of eighteenth-century farmhouses in Queens and Brooklyn recalled the countryside of the Netherlands. Georgian MANSIONS, churches, and large public buildings such as King's College (later Columbia University) and New York Hospital were modified versions of English buildings. By the time of independence taverns, workshops, stables, and stores intermingled with houses in a compact town where space was already at a premium.

Parts of the colonial street plan survive in lower Manhattan, but in all of New York City fewer than three dozen colonial buildings remain, a small remnant compared to the hundreds found in Boston and Philadelphia, both of which are newer. Most are residences, including several at Historic Richmond Town in Staten Island and others scattered throughout Brooklyn and Queens, but there are religious structures as well: the Friends Meeting House (1694, 1719) in Flushing, St. Paul's Chapel (1768, 1794) in Manhattan, and the Old New Dorp Moravian Church (1764) on Staten Island.

1. Federal and Antebellum New York City, 1784–1860

As New York City expanded from a modest seaport of sixty thousand in 1800 to a metropolis of more than 900,000 on the eve of the Civil War, design and construction were generally handled by local builders. They copied the work of others or relied on pattern books that supplied everything from the detail of a stair bannister to a complete plan. Most buildings erected during the early nineteenth century were small, stood one to three stories tall, and combined several uses. Modest houses of brick or wood often contained retail shops or workshops at street level. Three- and four-story brick buildings near the piers of South Street had merchants' counting-houses on the first story and manufacturing and storage facilities in lofts in the upper stories. Until the mid 1820s the few buildings with any pretense displayed the simple detail of the late Georgian and early Federal styles. A notable exception was the French-inspired City Hall, one of the first important public buildings in the city, designed by the émigré architect Joseph-François Mangin with his American-born colleague John McComb Jr.

During the 1840s and 1850s differentiation in building types increased. Commercial architecture emerged to house the offices of lawyers, merchants, insurance companies, and banks. As land became more costly in the business districts of Manhattan and Brooklyn, houses were demolished or converted to mercantile use. Residential neighborhoods took shape away from the busy downtown but no farther than a long walk, an omnibus ride, or a ferry trip across the East River. In areas such as Brooklyn Heights and Greenwich Village the streets were lined with new ROW HOUSES modeled after the terraces of English cities. Built by speculators for craftsmen and the middle class, these row houses were suited to the city's grid plan, which created narrow lots, and to its market, shaped by high land costs. As a result the wealthy often supplemented their small town houses with large country houses on the outskirts of the city, among them Gracie Mansion (1804, now the mayor's residence), Hamilton Grange and Wave Hill (1802, 1844, now museums), and Litchfield Villa (1857, now borough offices of the city's parks department).

Initially there were few people in New York City who called themselves architects, formally trained in design and engineering beyond simple construction. The first men to take that title in the 1830s were usually trained in England, France, or Germany. They in turn took on American pupils, for there were no architectural schools in the United States; a few Americans were self-taught. Their residential designs included mansions on 5th Avenue and the grander row houses of the 1840s and 1850s surviving around Washington Square, at Colonnade Row on Lafayette Street in Manhattan, and in Brooklyn Heights. The names of the leading architects, Alexander Jackson Davis and his partner Ithiel Town, Minard Lafever, Richard Upjohn, and Detlef Lienau, became better known to New Yorkers through the commissions that they received for religious, institutional, commercial, and government buildings. These public buildings — large, costly structures with complex plans or "programs" — required knowledge of sophisticated construction technology and appropriate style. In 1857 two dozen architects in the city founded the American Institute of Architects (AIA). Their goals were to distinguish architects from carpenters, to improve architectural training, and to educate the public through newspaper and journal articles.

Greek Revival was a popular style for government buildings and others because of its historical association with the ancient Greek republics. It was used by Lafever as early as 1833 for Sailors' Snug Harbor, a home for retired mariners on Staten Island, and as late as 1848 by Gamaliel King for Brooklyn City Hall (now Brooklyn Borough Hall). Several fine examples of the style date to the reconstruction of lower Manhattan after the Great Fire of 1835, including the U.S. Custom House (now Federal Hall) by Town and Davis and the Merchants' Exchange (now Citibank) by Isaiah Rogers, both completed in 1842. Greek Revival details also adorned two innovative commercial buildings. The Astor House (1836) was the city's first modern hotel: it had ornate public rooms, comfortable bedrooms, and running water, facilities far surpassing those of the taverns, inns, and boarding houses then serving travelers to New York City. The most important antebellum store, which revolutionized retail practices and paved the way for the department store, was designed for A. T. Stewart and opened on Broadway in 1846. Both the Astor House and Stewart's store quickly became tourist attractions. Sizable religious buildings also appeared during this period. In the third Trinity Church (1846) Richard Upjohn introduced the Gothic Revival style to American religious architecture. Among the foremost examples in later years was St. Patrick's Cathedral, begun in 1853 and designed by James Renwick Jr. in a style inspired by the German Gothic.

In the decade before the Civil War two technological advances originated in New York City. The use of cast iron for mass-produced structural columns and ornamental façade elements, first promoted in the 1840s by James Bogardus as a means of fireproofing, made it possible to build larger and better-lit commercial buildings (see CAST-IRON ARCHITECTURE). And after the introduction of the passenger elevator, first installed in 1857 in the Haughwout Building at Broadway and Broome streets, space in the upper stories of buildings became more accessible and profitable. These innovations later led to the development of steel cage construction and the skyscraper. Cast-iron architecture flourished from the mid 1850s to the 1880s, and created the streetscape of loft buildings and stores in the neighborhoods of lower Manhattan now called Tribeca and SoHo, and in Williamsburg and the Fulton Ferry district in Brooklyn.

2. From the Civil War to the Depression, 1860–1930

Between 1865 and 1930 the population of New York City increased from one million to almost seven million, and with consolidation in 1898 the city came to occupy an area of 320 square miles (820 square kilometers). A series of bridges and tunnels beginning with the Brooklyn Bridge (1883) linked four of the five boroughs and helped cause a demographic explosion and an enormous, citywide expansion in the housing stock. Although the quality of housing varied depending on the social class for which it was built, one characteristic made New York City unique: by 1920 the majority of its population lived in apartments and were renters. The modern apartment house evolved from two distinct sources: TENEMENTS and luxury suites.

Thousands of tenements, the first multiple dwellings, were built between 1860 and 1900 to accommodate the hundreds of thousands of immigrants who settled in the city. The tenements initially lacked sufficient windows, running water, and indoor toilets, and were so badly built that they posed health and safety hazards, prompting the city to regulate them with increasing stringency. The infamous DUMBBELL TENEMENTS, so-called for their shape in plan, were finally outlawed by the Tenement House Law of 1901. A few prestigious architects, including Ernest Flagg and I. N. Phelps Stokes, continued to prepare model designs to improve housing for the poor. In such projects as the Home and Tower Buildings (1877, 1879, Hicks and Baltic streets, Brooklyn) and the York Avenue Estate (1901–13, 79th Street and York Avenue, Manhattan), investors like Alfred T. White and the limited-dividend housing company City and Suburban Homes sought to create housing that was affordable for the working class yet had basic amenities and returned a small profit. From the heritage of the tenements and the limited-dividend developments emerged the apartment buildings for the working and middle classes, built in upper Manhattan, Queens, Brooklyn, and the Bronx from 1910 to the 1930s.

Luxury apartments became fashionable among the wealthy, with the "French flat" containing the varied living and service spaces (including the private bathroom and toilet facilities lacking in tenements) of the brownstone (see BROWNSTONES). The French flat was introduced in the 1860s and popularized by the Stuyvesant (1869, Richard Morris Hunt) on East 18th Street. More elegantly finished and larger apartments were sold in buildings of the 1880s, such as the Dakota (1884, Henry J. Hardenbergh) on 72nd Street and Central Park West, which also was one of the first apartment buildings to have a large internal courtyard. This feature provided light and air to apartments fronting on the court as well as space for play and ornamental fountains. The courtyard's expansion to half the site was evident at the Apthorp (1908, Clinton and Russell) at Broadway and 79th Street. Plans for studio and duplex arrangements were formulated after 1900. All luxury buildings had rooms for servants. By the 1920s Park and 5th avenues were lined with luxury apartment buildings, and large complexes such as Tudor City and London Terrace occupied full city blocks surrounding courtyard gardens. A small number of architectural firms specialized in apartment buildings, among them Edward and George Blum, Schwartz and Gross, George Pelham, Emory Roth, and J. E. R. Carpenter, which designed many on the East and West sides of Manhattan. Occasionally a socially prominent architect would design apartment buildings for the upper middle class and the wealthy. Delano and Aldrich, for example, designed 925 Park Avenue (1907) and 1040 Park Avenue (1923), while the work of Charles A. Platt ranged from the palazzo-like Studio Building (1906) on East 66th Street to the austere tower at 120 East End Avenue (1929) commissioned by Vincent Astor, which contained apartments ranging from five to twenty-three rooms. As early as the 1880s a number of apartment buildings for the wealthy were set up as cooperatives, a financial arrangement later adopted more broadly. Decorative styles of apartment houses of the 1920s and 1930s were varied: Georgian was fashionable in Manhattan, Tudor in Jackson Heights, and art deco on the Grand Concourse.

Free-standing one-family houses were as diverse as apartment buildings, ranging from modest frame buildings to the more substantial "country estates" built from the 1870s to the 1920s in Staten Island (New Brighton), the Bronx (Riverdale), and Queens (Jamaica Estates). Although successful businessmen built mansions in Brooklyn Heights, Park Slope, and Fort Greene, the most lavish dwellings were constructed in Manhattan. 5th Avenue, nicknamed "millionaire's row," was the site of increasingly expensive houses, beginning with the home of A. T. Stewart (1869), then the châteaux of the Astors and Vanderbilts (built in the 1880s and 1890s), and finally the houses on the Upper East Side of Andrew Carnegie (1901, Babb, Cook and Willard) and Otto H. Kahn (1918, J. A. Stenhouse with C. P. H. Gilbert).

Row houses, often called brownstones because of the color of the sandstone facing used on many of their façades, were built in a uniform design in groups of half a dozen to an entire block front. They proliferated in Manhattan and Brooklyn from the 1870s until the eve of the First World War, when the need for more housing drove up the price of land and dictated the construction of apartment buildings instead. The simplest row houses, intended for tradesmen and factory workers, were usually erected by local builders and consisted of two stories with brick façades. The most elaborate stood four, five, or six stories tall, had libraries, multiple parlors and bedrooms, and servants' quarters, and ornate façades of limestone, brownstone, or combinations of masonry and brick. Brownstones soon lined the streets in such areas as the Upper East Side, Harlem, Park Slope, Carroll Gardens, and Mott Haven. These locales became Historic Districts in the twentieth century as appreciation grew for the architectural features, flexible plans, backyards, and stoops characteristic of the row house. Townhouses – individually designed large row houses – were built in Manhattan for the wealthy, especially on the Upper East Side, where such families as the Roosevelts, the Pratts, and the Morgans resided.

New York City was the site not only of mass production of basic housing types but also of interesting experiments in American urban housing. The planned communities of Forest Hills Gardens (begun 1910, Grosvenor Atterbury and Frederick Law Olmsted Jr.), a garden-like suburb of one-family houses and terraces, and Sunnyside Gardens (1924–28, Clarence S. Stein, Henry Wright, and Frederick Ackerman), a neighborhood of densely developed row houses, were sponsored by groups that favored more rational land use to lower housing costs and create better communities. The apartments built in the Bronx by the Amalgamated Clothing Workers Union (Amalgamated Cooperatives, 1927–37, Springsteen and Goldhammer) allowed working-class residents to be owners instead of tenants, and to enjoy a large number of communal social activities. Arrangements similar to Sunnyside and the Amalgamated were not revived in any serious way for another fifty years.

The development of the city as the nation's commercial, industrial, and financial capital profoundly increased the scale and variety of its buildings, and influenced commensurately the work of its architects. The city attracted talented designers who practiced in firms, contracting their services one job at a time; a few were employed by government agencies supervising public construction projects and sometimes designing buildings. Architects' social class often determined the source of their commissions. Those who belonged to exclusive social clubs gained wealthy and influential clients, while others had to depend on small investors. Patrician firms such as Carrère and Hastings and McKim, Mead and White obtained the majority of large public commissions. Ethnicity played a role too: firms run by Jews and Catholics were usually small and often specialized in particular building types such as churches or apartment houses. Firms varied in size, from one principal employing a single draftsman to large establishments with several prominent partners supported by a large staff. Platt had a medium-sized firm with seventeen employees in 1920. McKim, Mead and White employed 110 persons in 1909 and was the most influential firm in the country from 1885 to 1920. Its staff worked on dozens of projects at once and produced the hundreds of drawings needed for the most important commissions, which included the Municipal Building (1914) and Pennsylvania Station (1911).

Medium-sized and large firms were also important for furthering the training of architects through a studio system brought to New York City in 1857 by Richard Morris Hunt, the first American to graduate from the École des Beaux-Arts in Paris. Dozens of others followed him to France, studying at the École after obtaining a college degree or an architectural degree in the United States. (Although drafting courses had been offered in New York City since the founding of Cooper Union in 1859, the city had no degree program in architecture until one was established in 1881 at Columbia University by William R. Ware.) On their return they welcomed as apprentices talented young men who studied the classical architecture of Greece and Italy, as well as the interpretations of the classics in the Renaissance and seventeenth- and eighteenth-century Europe that were at the heart of the Beaux-Arts curriculum.

Until the 1920s there were almost no women or minority architects practicing in New York City. Marcia Mead (1879–1967) became the first woman to graduate from the Columbia School of Architecture in 1913. She established her own firm in the city but built most of her important commissions elsewhere. The few women working in architecture were limited to designing small houses. The best-known building by a woman before 1930 was the reconstructed Theodore Roosevelt Birthplace (1923); its design was overseen by Theodate Pope Riddle (1868–1946), a wealthy and successful designer of country houses and private schools in Connecticut. There were even fewer black architects. Vertner Tandy (1885–1949) was a graduate of Tuskegee Institute and the designer of a number of buildings in Harlem, including St. Phillip's Church and Rectory (1911, with George W. Foster), Madame C. J. Walker's townhouse (1917), and Smalls' Paradise (1925), a jazz club. Among those who trained with him was John L. Wilson (1898–1989), who became the first black graduate of Columbia in 1928. He worked on the plans for the Harlem River Houses (1936–37, Archibald Manning Brown), then was employed by the parks department and had his own practice. The most prominent building by a black architect in New York City was the James B. Duke Mansion (1912, now the Institute of Fine Arts) at 5th Avenue and 78th Street. It was the design of Julian Abele (1882–1950), the first black graduate of the École des Beaux-Arts and the chief designer for the firm of Horace Trumbauer and Associates in Washington.

Between 1890 and 1920 the city was transformed by the influence of the education that American architects obtained at the École des Beaux-Arts. This training encompassed an ornamental language, a preference for monumental scale, and a method of planning both individual buildings and large complexes that relied on symmetry, axial composition, and grand spatial progressions. Its manifestation in city planning was a movement known as the "City Beautiful." The cosmopolitan style expressed the confident mood of the city's businessmen and government officials. Its classicism appealed to patrons seeking to build or expand symbols of the city's cultural primacy in such institutions as the New York Public Library, the Brooklyn Museum, Audubon Terrace, the Metropolitan Museum of Art, and the American Museum of Natural History. The campuses of Columbia University (planned 1894) in Morningside Heights and New York University (planned 1892–94) in the Bronx, both designed by McKim, Mead and White, were the largest beaux-arts complexes.

The beaux-arts style flourished in both governmental and commercial buildings, including the major portals to the city, Grand Central Terminal (1913, by Reed and Stem, and Warren and Wetmore) and Pennsylvania Station (1911), where skilled engineers worked with the architects to mask the newest technology with ancient splendor. The style also conferred the dignity and solidity required by the buildings of the nation's financial center. The design for the New York Stock Exchange (1903) was influenced by Roman architecture, as were the designs for a number of metropolitan banks (Bowery Savings Bank, Williamsburg Trust Company), which were housed in adaptations of the Pantheon. Among the most important and largest public commissions of these years were the Municipal Building (1913) and the new U.S. Custom House (1907, Cass Gilbert) at Bowling Green. The Custom House and the Hall of Records (1899–1907, John R. Thomas and Horgan and Slattery, also known as the Surrogate's Court) on Chambers Street exemplified another aspect of beaux-arts design: the integration of a full sculptural program on the exterior. Unlike other American cities of the time New York City did not build a full-fledged civic center inspired by the beaux-arts style or the City Beautiful movement. Plans for one were prepared by the New York City Improvement Commission (1904–7) but never fully adopted. Grand Army Plaza in Brooklyn is among the few public spaces that reflect the beaux-arts sensibility.

From the 1890s to the 1920s even the design of utilitarian public buildings was considered important, an idea that was lost for several decades after the Second World War. Leading architects designed bathhouses, precinct stations, firehouses, and public toilets. The city's commitment to an expanded system of public education led to the construction of dozens of new schools, including many impressive high schools with plans, art work, and architecture that were emulated nationwide. The talented architect responsible for their design was Charles B. J. Snyder, who worked for the Board of Education from 1891 to 1923. Another symbol of the city's investment in social services was the innovative design of its public hospital buildings, including Bellevue Hospital (1908, McKim, Mead and White) on 1st Avenue at 25th Street, and Seaview Hospital (1914, Raymond F. Almiral) on Staten Island, the largest municipal tuberculosis hospital. The firm of Heins and LaFarge, which designed the whimsical buildings of the New York Zoological Park, or Bronx Zoo (1899), was responsible for all the stations of Interborough Rapid Transit (1904), the first subway line in Manhattan. The New York Public Library engaged several firms, among them Carrère and Hastings and McKim, Mead and White, to design its branch buildings.

Even though the beaux-arts style was widely influential, the years between the 1870s and the 1920s were marked by a high degree of eclecticism in architecture. Medieval European sources continued to inform religious architecture. The Episcopal Cathedral of St. John the Divine (1892–1911, Heins and LaFarge; 1911–42, Cram and Ferguson) combined Byzantine, Romanesque, and French Gothic elements, and many smaller neighborhood Episcopal churches were influenced by English parish buildings. Large synagogues often drew on sources that were vaguely Middle Eastern, or "Moorish": examples include the Central Synagogue (1871–72, Henry Fernbach) on Lexington Avenue and the Eldridge Street Synagogue (1886–87, Herter Brothers). Wealthy families of long American ancestry favored the Colonial Revival style for the settlement houses that they funded to promote the assimilation of immigrants, such as the University Settlement (1901, Howells and Stokes, 184 Eldridge Street), as well as for their own townhouses and social clubs on the East Side. Styles characterized as Second Empire, Romanesque, Italianate, Renaissance, Victorian Gothic, neo-Grec, and art deco all found favor. Architects of the day were extremely versatile: George B. Post, for example, designed the Long Island (now Brooklyn) Historical Society (1881) in the Queen Anne style, the campus of City College (1897–1908) in Collegiate Gothic, and the New York Stock Exchange (1903) in beaux-arts Roman Revival. Buildings designed in one style were often enlarged or completed in another, such as the former New York County Courthouse (1861–71, John Kellum; also called the Tweed Courthouse), a building in Renaissance style with a medieval wing (1874–77) added by Leopold Eidlitz.

During this period architects sought to strengthen their public image as professionals. In 1881 they formed the Architectural League of New York, the same year Columbia launched its program in architecture. Graduates of the École des Beaux-Arts formed the Society of Beaux-Arts Architects in 1893 and the Beaux-Arts Institute of Design in 1916 to perpetuate its influence in architectural education. Architects secured a position on the Art Commission created by the new municipal charter of 1898, worked to raise state standards for education and licensing, and were influential members of the Improvement Commission and the Committee of the Regional Plan of New York and Its Environs (1922–31).

The city was also the center of the architectural press. Criticism was published in specialized journals as well as newspapers and magazines such as *Harper's*. Mariana Griswold Van Rensselaer published thoughtful essays for the *Century* in the 1880s and was followed in the 1890s by the columnists Russell Sturgis and Montgomery Schuyler. Two of the best-known critics after 1900 were Herbert Croly, who edited and wrote for the *Architectural Record*, and Royal Cortissoz, the art critic of the *New York Tribune* for more than fifty years and the author of monographs and articles on local architects. Lewis Mumford made the *New Yorker* a forum for architectural comment beginning in the 1920s.

From the 1890s to the 1930s the skyline of Manhattan took shape and became world-famous, as church towers were overshadowed by office towers. The development of steel cage construction, along with fast elevators, electric lighting, and sophisticated heating and plumbing systems, made possible the construction of SKYSCRAPERS, which became icons of the city's global importance. Most skyscrapers were office towers planned for thousands of workers; they housed national and international corporations and the businesses that supported them, such as law firms, advertising agencies, and accounting firms. The Singer, Woolworth, and Metropolitan Life Insurance companies built their own corporate headquarters, at once giant advertising symbols and competitors in a relentless contest to build the world's tallest building. This competition culminated in the Empire State Building (1931), reaching the equivalent of 102 stories and setting a record that remained unbroken for more than forty years. From the beginning heated debate surrounded the design of office towers, which drew criticism for their appearance and for blocking light to the streets. The completion of the looming forty-story Equitable Building at 120 Broadway in 1915 helped to ensure the passage in 1916 of the city's first comprehensive zoning code, which regulated land use and limited the height of buildings according to a formula involving their street frontage. As a result the straight tower was replaced by the setback form, some striking examples of which are the Williamsburgh Savings Tower (1929, Halsey, McCormack and Helmer), the only skyscraper built outside Manhattan, the Chrysler Building (1930, William van Alen), the Bank of Manhattan building (1930, H. Craig Severance with Yasuo Masui), and the Cities Service building (1932, Clinton and Russell).

Although the skyscraper was the most famous architectural form in New York City, the city was also renowned for its entertainment industry and the opulence of such performance spaces as Carnegie Hall, the Brooklyn Academy of Music, the Metropolitan Opera, and the Palladium; these had fantastic ornamentation ranging in style from Baroque to Egyptian. During the 1920s and 1930s majestic movie houses were built for the national chains of Loews and Paramount. A few firms specialized in such projects, among them Rapp and Rapp, and Herts and Tallant; their commissions in the city set the standard for the country. Motion-picture production facilities were built in Astoria and in Manhattan before the industry moved west.

Entertainment and cultural institutions attracted tourists from around the world, and numerous luxury hotels competed from the 1890s to attract customers. Their dramatic lobbies and lounges were public living rooms on a grand scale, where afternoon tea might be served in a romantic palm court, as at the Plaza, or in an exotic "peacock alley," as at the Waldorf–Astoria. Splendid restaurants and fancifully decorated bars thrived before Prohibition changed social habits.

The glamour of New York City coexisted with the city's role as an important manufacturing center. The industrial brick vernacular popular from about 1870 to 1900 is well represented by slaughterhouses and markets in Manhattan, the warehouses, breweries, and sugar refining plants along the waterfront in Brooklyn, factories in the Bronx and Staten Island, and armories throughout the city. This style was succeeded by a concrete vernacular in the second and third decades of the twentieth century, exemplified by the buildings of the Brooklyn Army Terminal (1918, Cass Gilbert) and by many factories in Queens. Commissions for such buildings were often handled by local architects whose budgets allowed for little ornamentation other than terra-cotta tile or pressed stone trim.

3. From the New Deal to the 1990s

The stock market crash of 1929 and subsequent hard times initially led to massive unemployment among architects and construction crews. A few large projects already under way were completed, such as the Daily News Building (1930, Howells and Hood) and the McGraw–Hill Building (1931, Raymond M. Hood, Godley and Foulhoux). Yet with the sponsorship of the federal government many interesting projects were designed and built during the 1930s. Under the auspices of the Public Works Administration and later the New York City Housing Authority, the city became the site of the country's first public housing projects: the Harlem River Houses (1937) won a prize for the clarity of their plan, and the Williamsburg Houses (1937) were honored for their modern styling. Among the federally funded projects of the time were the charming buildings of the Central Park and Prospect Park zoos, designed by Aymar Embury. Local architects also designed post offices, hospitals, schools, playgrounds, municipal swimming pools, and beach facilities, as well as the new roads and bridges that reshaped the city. One of the few major private commissions to proceed was Rockefeller Center (designed 1929, built 1932–40), sponsored by John D. Rockefeller Jr., who was also responsible for Riverside Church (1930) and the Cloisters (1934–38), the medieval branch of the Metropolitan Museum of Art. Designed by a consortium of architects, Rockefeller Center became a model for the corporate and retail center that was built in many cities after the Second World War.

The resumption of building construction in the late 1940s brought to public notice a whole new generation of architectural firms, as well as the International style. Based on the sleek lines and modern materials favored in Europe by the 1920s and formally introduced in a major exhibition at the Museum of Modern Art in 1932, the style sought to convey an image of modernity and industrial progress. Elements of it appeared in a few buildings in New York City in the 1930s, notably at the World's Fair of 1939–40, and it came to dominate the design of office buildings from the 1950s to the early 1980s, creating a sharp contrast with the historically based detail characteristic of design predating the Second World War. One element associated with the International style was the glass curtain wall, which became common after it was introduced at the United Nations (1947–53), designed by an international group of architects led by Wallace K. Harrison, and at Lever House (1952), designed by Gordon Bunshaft of Skidmore, Owings and Merrill, a firm that soon exerted its influence nationwide. Two buildings of equal significance were the metal-and-glass Seagram Building (1958, Ludwig Mies van der Rohe with Philip Johnson) and the Chase Manhattan Bank Tower (1955–61, Gordon Bunshaft, Skidmore, Owings and Merrill); these were the first office towers set in plazas, a model that replaced the setback and that was adopted in the zoning code in 1961, to prevail for thirty years.

During the 1950s and 1960s the federal government encouraged new construction with slum clearance and urban renewal programs. Sites of several acres called "superblocks" were cleared and their streets eliminated to make park-like areas suitable for the construction of tall towers. Superblocks were initially used for public housing projects as well as for housing projects sponsored by labor unions,

The Daily News Building, designed by Raymond M. Hood and John M. Howells, 1950

insurance companies, and private developers. These projects contained hundreds to thousands of units of working- and middle-class housing, stores, schools, and other amenities. The largest projects included Stuyvesant Town, Peter Cooper Village, Park West Village, and Washington Square Village and Washington Square South in Manhattan; Parkchester and Co-op City in the Bronx; Lefrak City, Rochdale Village, and Electchester in Queens; and Cadman Plaza and Starrett City in Brooklyn. Although many of these complexes became successful communities, urban renewal also changed neighborhoods and displaced people and small businesses. Jane Jacobs's seminal book *The Life and Death of American Cities* (1961) provoked discussions of the impersonal nature of urban renewal projects and the importance to the city's vitality of small-scale buildings and neighborhoods. Her ideas eventually led to scaled-down housing projects: "scatter-site" building and smaller-scale construction prevailed in the 1970s and 1980s. Promoted by variously sponsored local development corporations such as the church-sponsored Nehemiah Houses and the Housing Partnership, middle-income families were provided with row houses, small apartment buildings, and garden apartments, and in one instance with one-family houses of suburban character (1986, Charlotte Street in the Bronx).

Despite its shortcomings urban renewal provided much needed new housing for New Yorkers, and the city acquired new commercial and cultural complexes such as Lincoln Center, a cultural hub that inspired similar projects elsewhere. Lincoln Center also proved influential in having been designed by a team of architects, an approach taken in designing Roosevelt Island and Battery Park City in the 1970s, Metrotech Center in the 1980s, and Queens West in the 1990s, all sponsored by local development authorities. On these large sites landscape designers and artists took part in the architectural process, adding parks and sculpture to the grounds.

Many of the architectural firms that rose to acclaim from the 1950s to the 1980s had become large, complex business organizations, where designers were supported by technical, legal, and marketing consultants. Among the leading firms of the period were Eggers and Higgins; Davis, Brody; Emery Roth and Sons; Fox and Fowle; Gruzen Sampton Steinglass (originally Kelly and Gruzen); Gwathmey Siegel; Harrison and Abramovitz; Pei Cobb Freed (originally I. M. Pei); Kohn Pedersen Fox; and Skidmore, Owings and Merrill. Architects saw their work reviewed and judged by community planning boards, independent local groups, civic organizations such as the Municipal Art Society, and columnists such as Brendan Gill of the *New Yorker* and Paul Goldberger of the *New York Times*. Designs were also subject to complex environmental and zoning regulations. Bonus space requirements for outdoor plazas and indoor public space and neighborhood zoning for retail street use and new theaters all affected building design. Regardless of these constraints, members of the architectural community energetically debated and wrote about new ideas. The Institute for Architecture and Urban Studies, which thrived from the late 1960s to the 1980s under the leadership of Peter Eisenman, promoted theoretical discussions and exhibitions about architecture, and published *Skyline* and *Oppositions* to bring its ideas to a wider public and to the profession. The Architectural League and the Municipal Art Society sponsored many lively programs, and students in the city's architectural programs at Columbia, Pratt Institute, City College, Cooper Union, and the Parsons School of Design took part in debates about style, design, and social responsibility. From 1972 to the mid 1980s the Alliance of Women in Architecture worked to improve professional opportunities for women, while the Archive of Women in Architecture documented the work of women in the field and sponsored lectures and walking tours.

The profession gradually acquired a more diverse profile. Women architects became involved with the design of all types of buildings from the 1940s onward, and Natalie de Blois was a senior designer on many office buildings at Skidmore, Owings and Merrill from 1944 to 1965. By the 1990s women and minorities still accounted for less than 15 percent of the city's registered practicing architects, but women constituted half the enrolled students in degree programs. Some of the best-known women architects were associated with housing planning and design. Among them was Lynda Simmons, who worked on Riverbend Houses (1967) while at Davis, Brody and then became president of Phipps Houses, the largest nonprofit manager of middle-income housing in New York City. An influential administrator in the field was Kathryn Wilde, president of the innovative Housing Partnership. Other leading women architects of the 1970s and 1980s included Judith Edelman, Frances Halsband (dean of the Pratt School of Architecture), and Susana Torre (head of the architecture department at Parsons). Women also played important roles as critics: notable figures include Catherine Bauer, who condemned public housing design in the 1950s, and Jacobs. In 1963 Ada Louise Huxtable was appointed architectural critic of the *New York Times*, the first national newspaper to create such a position, thus reviving the important role of public commentator.

A few black architectural firms came to prominence in the 1970s and 1980s with practices in the city that drew national and international clients. Perhaps the foremost black architect of the postwar years was J. Max Bond Jr., dean at the City College School of Architecture; from 1969 to 1990 his firm (Bond, Ryder Associates) designed the Schomburg Center for Research in Black Culture in Harlem, and apartment towers in Battery Park City and elsewhere. The firm eventually merged with Davis, Brody, for which Bond worked on several buildings at the Audubon Biomedical Science and Technology Park (Broadway and 165th Street) of Columbia University, site of the assassination of Malcolm X. Other notable black architects included Harry J. Simmons Jr. of Simmons Architects, a founder of the Coalition of Black Architects; Robert Washington, active in the design of the Harlem International Trade Center; and William E. Davis Jr., a member of the New York City Landmarks Preservation Commission and the head of the African Burial Ground Competition Coalition in 1994.

Some of the city's most unusual and notable buildings from the 1950s to the 1980s were clearly outside the aesthetic mainstream. The Guggenheim Museum (1959), a concrete spiral by Frank Lloyd Wright (his only major building in New York City); the Whitney Museum of American Art (1966, Marcel Breuer), a cantilevered, masonry-covered concrete box; the Trans World Airlines Terminal at John F. Kennedy International Airport (1960, Eero Saarinen), singular for its expressionistic curves; and the undulating, aluminum-sheathed buildings of the Bronx Developmental Center (1976, Richard Meier) all attracted widespread comment.

Half a dozen other new buildings were distinctive for breaking the design mold. The twin towers of the World Trade Center (1970, Minoru Yamasaki) became the city's tallest buildings, their abrupt flat-roof profile hovering over lower Manhattan. The Jacob K. Javits Convention Center (1986, James Ingo Freed of I. M. Pei and Partners), a faceted glass box supported by an innovative space frame, recalls the city's first exhibition hall, the Crystal Palace of 1853. The granite facing of the IBM building (1983, Edward Larrabee Barnes) marked the first departure from the ubiquitous glass and metal. The AT&T Building (1984, Johnson/ Burgee) introduced post-modern architecture to New York City in a historically based ornamental pediment in Chippendale style at roof level. The North River Sewage Treatment Plant was designed with a twenty-acre (eight-hectare) state park (1991, Richard Dattner) on its roof overlooking the Hudson, to provide recreational space to a densely populated neighborhood. Citicorp broke with the flat-roofed profile that had become the norm in the 1950s and 1960s when it adopted a steeply slanted roofline for its headquarters building (1978, Hugh Stubbins) in Manhattan. The company also built a tower (1989, Skidmore, Owings and Merrill) of forty-eight stories in Long Island City, the first postwar skyscraper outside Manhattan to compete with its skyline.

As new buildings recast the profile of Manhattan in the 1950s and 1960s, the city's economic revitalization seemed to be wiping out its past, and concerned citizens organized to balance progress with the preservation of history. The destruction of Pennsylvania Station in 1963 lent a sense of urgency to the movement. After the Landmarks Preservation Law was passed in 1965, efforts to preserve historic structures and neighborhoods were undertaken by a wide range of sponsors. Private groups took on the care of individual buildings like the Bowne House (1661) in Flushing, the Old Merchant's House (1832) on East 4th Street, and the Weeksville Houses (*ca* 1830–70) in Brooklyn, while the city's parks department administered more than a dozen historic houses, including the Alice Austen House (*ca* 1695) on Staten Island and King Manor (1733–55) in Queens. A judicious mixture of economic redevelopment and preservation made the area around South Street Seaport thrive as the state, the museum, and a developer worked together. The use of "air rights," a real-estate tool, made it possible to transfer the unused space over low historic buildings for structures elsewhere and provided an economic incentive for preservation.

As a result more architects were commissioned to refurbish and restore prized older buildings, and Columbia University in 1965 introduced a graduate program in historic preservation, the first of its kind, directed by James Marston Fitch. Preservationists promoted "adaptive reuse" projects. One of the first was Giorgio Cavaglieri's conversion into a public library of the Jefferson Market Courthouse, a Victorian Gothic structure in Greenwich Village. There were many other kinds of inventive transformations. Warehouses became artists' housing at Westbeth and market-rate housing at the Eagle Warehouse and the Ansonia Piano Factory in Brooklyn; churches became apartments and discothèques; mansions became libraries, organizational headquarters, and museums. The Carnegie Mansion on 5th Avenue was converted into the Cooper–Hewitt Museum (under the direction of Hardy Holzman Pfeiffer Associates). The sleek displays of the International Design Center in Long Island City belie the origins of the buildings as chewing gum, cracker, and electric battery factories. Artists gained loft space, studios, and galleries from the transformation of P.S. 1, a century-old school building in Long Island City, while an old city asphalt plant became a neighborhood recreation center, Asphalt Green. Unused motion-picture studios in Astoria were converted into the Museum of the Moving Image. Perhaps the largest project of the 1980s was the restoration of the immigration buildings on Ellis Island, managed by Beyer Blinder Belle (one of the leading preservation firms), and resulting in a historic site that draws millions of visitors each year. The gradual renovation of Grand Central Terminal and the New York Public Library in the 1980s and 1990s provided New Yorkers with a new appreciation of their turn-of-the-century heritage. Another imaginative project of the early 1990s was the reconfiguration by Hardy Holzman Pfeiffer of B. Altman's beaux-arts department store (1906, 1914, Trowbridge and Livingston) into an office center and a division of the New York Public Library. The refurbished U.S. Custom House at Bowling Green, a project directed by Ehrenkranz Eckstut and Whitelaw, created space in the 1990s for the Museum of the American Indian as well as federal offices and courts.

Interest in historic preservation and the city's architecture and neighborhoods was popularized from the 1960s by walking tours of historic neighborhoods and house tours sponsored by museums, community associations, professional tour guides, and civic groups like the Friends of Cast Iron Architecture. The publication of guidebooks about the city's architecture also increased. The *AIA Guide to New York City* (1967; 3rd edn 1988) by Elliot Willensky and Norval White proved a comprehensive successor to the *New York City Guide* (1939) prepared by the Federal Writers' Project and inspired a host of imitators in other cities. Dozens of specialized guides were also published, devoted to such topics as cemeteries, synagogues, sculpture, and neighborhoods.

In the mid 1990s issues of policy rather than design seemed to dictate the course of architecture in the city. One of the few individual projects to elicit much comment was Robert Venturi's winning design for a new Staten Island Ferry Terminal, featuring a giant clock facing the harbor; its construction was delayed for financial reasons. Master plans for such areas as Queens West and Riverside South were the subject of extensive public review, and the redevelopment of Times Square focused more on questions of signage and building bulk than design. Many projects sponsored by the public sector or social service agencies were challenged by community groups that sought to halt their construction. The constraints of building codes, zoning, environmental laws, finances, and citizen participation imposed design limitations for architects in the 1990s that were probably more challenging than those of the preceding hundred years. How these would be resolved was certain to determine the city's landscape of the future.

New York City Guide: A Comprehensive Guide to the Five Boroughs of the Metropolis: Manhattan, Brooklyn, the Bronx, Queens, and Richmond (New York: Random House, 1939; repr. Pantheon, 1982, as *The WPA Guide to New York City: The Federal Writers' Project Guide to 1930s New York*)

Charles Lockwood: *Bricks and Brownstones: The New York Row House, 1783–1929* (New York: Abbeville, 1972)

Gerard R. Wolfe: *New York: A Guide to the Metropolis: Walking Tours of Architecture and History* (New York: New York University Press, 1975)

Susana Torre, ed.: *Women in American Architecture: A Historic and Contemporary Perspective* (New York: Whitney Library of Design, 1977)

Robert A. M. Stern, Gregory Gilmartin, and John Massengale: *New York 1900: Metropolitan Architecture and Urbanism, 1890–1915* (New York: Rizzoli, 1983)

Donald Martin Reynolds: *The Architecture of New York City: Histories and Views of Important Structures, Sites, and Symbols* (New York: Macmillan, 1984)

Robert A. M. Stern, Gregory Gilmartin, and Thomas Mellins: *New York 1930: Architecture and Urbanism between the Two World Wars* (New York: Rizzoli, 1987)

Norval White and Elliot Willensky, eds.: *AIA Guide to New York City* (New York: American Institute of Architects, New York Chapter, 1967; 3rd edn San Diego: Harcourt Brace Jovanovich, 1988)

Michele H. Bogart: *Public Sculpture and the Civic Ideal in New York City, 1890–1930* (Chicago: University of Chicago Press, 1989)

Elizabeth Collins Cromley: *Alone Together: A History of New York's Early Apartments* (Ithaca, N.Y.: Cornell University Press, 1990)

Richard Plunz: *A History of Housing in New York City* (New York: Columbia University Press, 1990)

Andrew Alpern: *Luxury Apartment Houses of Manhattan: An Illustrated History* (New York: Dover, 1992)

Andrew Dolkart: *Guide to New York City Landmarks* (Washington: Preservation Press, 1992)

Robert A. M. Stern, Thomas Mellins, and David Fishman: *New York 1960: Architecture and Urbanism between the Second World War and the Bicentennial* (New York: Monacelli, 1995)

See also HOUSING and THEATER ARCHITECTURE.

Deborah S. Gardner

archives. The collections of historical records known as archives are seldom autonomous institutions but rather units of a larger body. This is true whether an archival repository contains the records of one organization (as institutional archives do) or is a collection of original materials amassed from many sources (as are most of the manuscript and archival collections of libraries and historical societies). Archives are found in a wide range of government agencies, nonprofit organizations, and corporations.

The history of archives in New York City mirrors the development of archival management in New York State and the nation. Unlike the countries of Europe the United States for many years lacked an archival tradition. This began to change with the formation in 1934 of the National Archives and Records Service (from 1985 the National Archives and Records Administration), and with the work of the Historical Records Survey of the Works Progress Administration, which between 1936 and 1941 took inventory of hundreds of church and government repositories in New York City. Nevertheless New York was the last state in the country to have a formal archives program, established by legislation in 1971 but not in full operation until the late 1970s.

For many years the quality of archival care in the city varied widely. In the absence of professional standards the preservation of some collections was adequate, that of others haphazard. The most efficiently run collections were part of libraries. The Astor Library, formed in 1848, included among its holdings the records of the U.S. Sanitary Commission, a private relief organization that supported the Union troops in the Civil War; its holdings were supplemented by those of the Lenox Library when the two institutions merged to form the New York Public Library in 1895. By the middle of the twentieth century organizations such as the Carnegie Endowment for International Peace and Citizens Union had transferred their records to the Columbia University Libraries, while the New-York Historical Society collected large numbers of eighteenth- and nineteenth-century account books of merchants from New York City and New York State, the records of the American Fur Company (owned by John Jacob Astor) and the New York Board of Trade and Transportation, and the procedural and business records of the American Art Union. The papers of individuals and families were also collected by these libraries and others, including the Brooklyn Historical Society (formerly the Long Island Historical Society) and the Staten Island Institute of Arts and Sciences. Archives of an informal sort were kept by some cultural and nonprofit organizations (such as the New York Philharmonic) and by some businesses. In 1946 the publishing firm Time Inc. became the first corporation in the city to establish a formal archival program; others followed, though not for nearly a decade.

In the following years archives increased in number and in importance. Because archives are somewhat difficult to define precisely they are also difficult to count, and different sources often give different figures: *A Guide to Archives and Manuscripts in the United States* (1961), edited by Philip M. Hamer, counted fifty-six repositories in New York City; its successor, the *Directory of Archives and Manuscript Repositories in the United States* (1988), counted 168; and according to the Historical Documents Inventory, initially sponsored by Cornell University and later overseen by the New York State Archives, the number of publicly accessible archives in the city in the late 1980s was 285. Notwithstanding this discrepancy the trend from the 1960s to the 1980s was clearly upward. New kinds of archives were established, such as the Lesbian Herstory Archives (1974) and the archives of the Center for Puerto Rican Studies at Hunter College (1981). Archival management emerged as a professional field, owing in part to the growing historical awareness fostered by the bicentennial of the United States in 1976. The history department of New York University in 1976 established a two-year program in archives and documentary editing leading to a master's degree. Later Columbia University, St. John's University, and Pratt Institute increased their offerings in archival management in their graduate library schools. In a reflection of the growing interest in local and ethnic history, a consortium of educational and cultural institutions called the Brooklyn Rediscovery Project began in 1977 to survey archival source materials and promote archival programs. The Archivists Round Table of Metropolitan New York was formed in 1979 and soon had more than two hundred individual members, making it one of the largest regional archival organizations in the nation; in 1990 its members represented 113 institutions in New York City. As the amount of information that could be saved by repositories increased dramatically, archivists at the American Institute of Physics helped to devise an approach to acquiring holdings called documentation strategy, a basic premise of which is that not every document can or should be retained. From 1989 the Archivists Round Table sponsored an annual "archives week" and mounted publicity campaigns to increase the awareness of archives among the public.

There were losses as well. In difficult economic times archives in many corporations and nonprofit institutions were seen as expendable. Chemical Bank, the Bowery Savings Bank, and the YMCA of Greater New York all ended their archival programs; after a corporate merger the archives of J. Walter Thompson were closed and the records given to Duke University. As the cost of real estate in New York City increased in the 1980s some corporations like J. C. Penney and charitable organizations like the Salvation Army left the city, taking their archives with them.

The largest repositories in the city are those of governmental and quasi-governmental agencies, in particular the MUNICIPAL ARCHIVES, which hold the records of municipal government (more than ninety thousand cubic feet, or 2500 cubic meters). This collection is complemented by the holdings of the Office of the New York County Clerk (seventeen thousand cubic feet, or 480 cubic meters). The records of federal agencies with offices in greater New York are in the custody of the National Archives–Northeast Region (63,000 cubic feet, or 1780 cubic meters). The archives of the United Nations contain historical records relating to the organization and its agencies (thirty thousand linear feet, or 9100 linear meters).

Libraries, historical societies, and research institutes account for the next large segment of repositories, which hold personal papers and organizational records from a wide range of sources. The holdings of archival materials in the Research Libraries of the New York Public Library are divided among several locations. The largest of these is the Manuscripts and Archives Section of the Rare Books and Manuscripts Division, which has collections of general historical and literary interest as well as the records of the library itself (27,000 linear feet, or 8200 linear meters); there are important special collections in the theater, dance, music, and recorded sound divisions of the Performing Arts Research Center at Lincoln Center, and at the Schomburg Center for Research in Black Culture. The New-York Historical Society (formed in 1804) holds more than two million items that illuminate the history of New York City and New York State from colonial times to the twentieth century. Its collections include the papers of Rufus King, the Livingston family, Aaron Burr, and James and William Alexander, and extensive military records. Smaller but nonetheless important collections of original records are maintained at the Pierpont Morgan Library, the Brooklyn Historical Society, the Bronx County Historical Society, the Staten Island Historical Society, the Leo Baeck Institute, and the YIVO Institute for Jewish Research.

Among colleges and universities in the city the largest repositories are at Columbia University and New York University. The Rare Book and Manuscript Library at Columbia includes not only extensive general holdings with particular strengths in publishing and political history, but also the distinctive collections of the Herbert Lehman Papers and the Bakhmeteff Archive of Russian and East European History and Culture; Teachers College, an autonomous institution, holds original materials in the history of education and nursing amounting to more than 2700 linear feet (eight hundred linear meters). Notable repositories at New York University include the Wagner Labor Archives in the Tamiment Library, the University Archives, and the Fales Collection of literary manuscripts. University archives and historical collections are also maintained by Pace University, Yeshiva University, the Jewish Theological Seminary, Union Theological Seminary, and City University of New York (as well as by many of its individual colleges).

Other important archives in New York City are maintained by businesses (for example the Chase Manhattan Bank, the New York Stock Exchange, Time Warner, the Shubert Organization); foundations and philanthropies (the United Negro College Fund, the Ford Foundation); religious institutions (the American Bible Society, Trinity Church, the 92nd Street YM-YWHA); museums (the American Museum of Natural History, the Museum of Modern Art, the Metropolitan Museum of Art, the Museum of the City of New York, the Brooklyn Museum); cultural organizations (Carnegie Hall, the New York Philharmonic, the New York Zoological Society); and scientific and medical institutions (the American Institute of Physics, New York Hospital–Cornell Medical Center, the Mount Sinai Medical Center). The status enjoyed by New York City as a center of the arts and the communications industry is reflected by the presence of such diverse repositories as the Anthology Film Archives, the Archive of Contemporary Music, the Bettmann Archive, and archives of film and video at the major television networks.

Phyllis A. Klein: *Our Past before Us: A Five-year Regional Plan for METRO's Archives and Historical Records Program, July 1, 1989–June 30, 1994* (New York: New York Metropolitan Reference and Research Library Agency, 1989), METRO Miscellaneous Publications, no. 40

Mary B. Bowling

Arden, Elizabeth [née Graham, Florence Nightingale] (*b* Woodbridge, Ont., 31 Dec 1878; *d* New York City, 18 Oct 1966). Businesswoman. After moving to New York City in 1908 to work for the chemical firm Squibb she worked as a cashier in Eleanor Adair's beauty salon and in 1910 changed her name and opened the Salon D'Oro at 509 5th Avenue, which offered elaborate and expensive beauty treatments. With $6000 borrowed from her brother she opened other salons and in 1915 developed her first important product, Venetian Cream Amoretta. She later made such preparations as Ardena Skin Tonic and Venetian Cleansing Cream, and was the first person to introduce mascara into the United States and to employ traveling demonstrators as saleswomen. She produced her cosmetics in small quantities, gave them high prices, sold them through exclusive department stores, and attracted customers with innovative packaging and strategically placed advertisements. Her domestic cosmetics line had sales of $4 million in 1929, by which time she had moved her salon to 691 5th Avenue, bought a factory at 212 East 52nd Street and a penthouse at 834 5th Avenue, and become a prominent member of fashionable society in Manhattan. By the mid 1930s she sold 108 products in 595 shapes and sizes. She weathered the Depression partly by developing a line of multi-colored lipsticks designed to match clothing. Her salons numbered twenty-nine in the United States and nineteen abroad and continued to thrive; in 1939 she bought a factory in Long Island City. During the 1940s Arden opened two resort spas. By the time of her death she oversaw an immensely profitable cosmetics conglomerate, which was purchased in 1970 by the pharmaceuticals firm Eli Lilly.

Nancy Shuker: *Elizabeth Arden: Cosmetics Entrepreneur* (Englewood Cliffs, N.J.: Silver Burdett, 1989)

Marc Ferris

Arden Heights. Neighborhood in west central Staten Island. Some houses were built before the Civil War but the area remained mostly rural for many years. The neighborhood was once the site of a resort called the Woods of Arden. Townhouses, schools, and shopping centers were built from the 1960s; a few of the older houses remain. The Village Greens (1972–74) is one of the largest housing sites in the area and one of the more thoughtfully planned developments built on Staten Island in the 1970s. The principal thoroughfare in the neighborhood is Arden Avenue.

Martha S. Bendix

Arendt, Hannah (*b* Hannover, Germany, 14 Oct 1906; *d* New York City, 4 Dec 1975). Philosopher. After studying at the universities of Königsberg (BA 1924) and Heidelberg (PhD 1928) she lived as an exile in Paris (1933–40) and in 1941 moved to New York City, where she lived first on West 95th Street (1941–51) and then at 130 Morningside Drive (from 1951 to the late 1960s). She devoted her intellectual life to exploring the philosophy of Immanuel Kant and the conflicts facing a Jew living in a Christian culture. In *The Origins of Totalitarianism* (1951) she examined the relationship between anti-Semitism, imperialism, and the "phenomenology" of totalitarianism. Her report on the trial of Adolf Eichmann, *Eichmann in Jerusalem* (1963), contrasted Kantian rationalism with the "banality of evil" inherent in Nazism. Arendt joined the graduate faculty of the New School for Social Research in 1967.

Elisabeth Young-Bruehl: *Hannah Arendt, for Love of the World* (New Haven: Yale University Press, 1982)

Peter M. Rutkoff, William B. Scott

Argosy Book Store and Gallery. Retail bookshop opened in 1924 by Louis Cohen, specializing in secondhand books and initially situated on 4th Avenue, then known as Book Row. It moved in 1931 to 114 East 59th Street (near Bloomingdale's department store) and in 1964 to its present location, a curious nineteenth-century structure with an indented façade at 116 East 59th Street. Cohen used the lower stories of the building before acquiring it in the 1950s and expanding to all six stories. In addition to secondhand books Argosy deals in antique prints, first editions, and other rare printed items, many of which are displayed in the store's gallery.

"The Talk of the Town," *New Yorker*, 14 Jan 1991

Thomas M. Hilbink

Arion Gesangverein. A German singing society formed by a group that split from the Deutscher Liederkranz in 1854. The society's comic performances were very popular, especially after 1863 when it adopted the carnival format of the Mainzer Karneval-Verein. It met in Pythagoras Hall in 1863–71, and after absorbing the Teutonia Männerchor bought its own clubhouse in the German neighborhood of Kleindeutschland and brought Leopold Damrosch from Germany to direct its chorus. The club built a lavish new clubhouse in upper Manhattan in 1885 and by 1892 was the leading German social organization in the United States. After the First World War the Arion merged with the Liederkranz.

Arion, New York, von 1854 bis 1904 (New York: Arion Gesangverein, 1904)

Stanley Nadel

Arlen, Harold [Arluck, Hyman] (*b* Buffalo, 15 Feb 1905; *d* New York City, 23 April 1986). Composer. The son of a cantor, he became a singer, pianist, and composer of popular songs for films, stage musicals, and revues (including several at the Cotton Club). Some of his songs are in a jazz and blues idiom, others in the ballad style of Tin Pan Alley. Among his outstanding songs are his first hit, "Get Happy" (1930, lyrics by Ted Koehler), "Over the Rainbow" (1939, lyrics by E. Y. Harburg), and "Blues in the Night" (1941, lyrics by Johnny Mercer). Some of his works were inspired by New York City: "Harlem Holiday" (1932), "Let's Take a Walk around the Block" (1934), "It's a Long Way to Broadway" (1937), and "I Love a New Yorker" (1949).

Edward Jablonski: *Harold Arlen: Happy with the Blues* (Garden City, N.Y.: Doubleday, 1961)

Nicholas E. Tawa

Arlington. Neighborhood in northwestern Staten Island, bounded to the north by Richmond Terrace, to the east by the neighborhood of Mariner's Harbor, to the south by the Staten Island Expressway, and to the west by South Avenue. The area was originally the western part of the town of Northfield and at one time was the site of a station of Staten Island Rapid Transit on the North Shore line (now defunct). To the west of the neighborhood is a rail yard that once belonged to the Chesapeake and Ohio Rail Road. The area consists principally of old Victorian houses, high-rise apartment buildings, and small businesses. Many of the oldest houses belonged to oystermen about 1900. There was considerable growth in Arlington in the 1980s; major developments included Arlington Terrace and Heron Place Apartments.

Martha S. Bendix

Armenian Apostolic Orthodox Church. The first celebration in New York City of the Divine Liturgy of the Armenian church was offered at Grace Episcopal Church on 22 September 1889 by Hovsep Sarajian, a forty-year-old celibate priest from Constantinople and the first missionary of the church in the United States. He requested a scroll of blessing from Archbishop Khoren Ashekian, patriarch of Armenians in Turkey, addressed to Henry C. Potter, Episcopal bishop of New York City, and presented by a delegation in February 1890. After resigning from his missionary assignment in 1894 he briefly left the United States, was consecrated a bishop in Armenia, and then returned to New York City on 7 October 1898; he established his headquarters in Worcester, Massachusetts. By a decision of the diocesan assembly in Boston on 15–16 May 1927 the headquarters were moved to New York City, where they occupied rental facilities from July 1927 to 31 May 1949 and then a complex at St. Vartan Cathedral, at 630 2nd Avenue in Manhattan. Before 1920 an administrative split within the Armenian church in the city resulted in the formation of two parishes each named St. Gregory the Illuminator: the older of the two, at 221 East 27th Street, became known in the early 1920s as St. Illuminator's Cathedral; the other began as a rented house of worship at 337 East 17th Street, made several moves in midtown Manhattan, and from 1950 occupied a purchased property on East 35th Street. St. Vartan Cathedral was eventually demolished to make way for the construction of the diocesan cathedral, during which time the diocesan headquarters were temporarily housed at St. Gregory on East 35th Street; the cathedral absorbed the parish of St. Gregory and was consecrated as St. Vartan on 28 April 1968.

The Holy Cross Church of Armenia (580 West 187th Street), purchased in 1928 and rebuilt in 1952–53, is a well-known landmark. It houses the crypt of the diocesan primate Archbishop Ghevont Tourian, assassinated by political opponents during a liturgy celebrated in the church on 24 December 1933. In Queens the Armenian Church of the Holy Martyrs (209-15 Horace Harding Expressway) was completed on 25 September 1955. The St. Sarkis Church of Bayside, a wooden edifice purchased in 1960, was destroyed by lightning on 21 May 1985; the new St. Sarkis Church was built in Douglaston in 1990. The St. Vartan Cathedral is a fine example of Armenian church architecture. It stands adjacent to the Gulbenkian Cultural Center, which houses the Krikor and Clara Zohrab Information Center. In the mid 1990s the Armenian church had about fifty thousand adherents in New York City.

Arten Ashjian

Armenians. Armenians descend from an ancient ethnic group that inhabited eastern Anatolia (now in Turkey) from 800 B.C. The first Armenian in the United States, a sericulturist known as Martin the Armenian, arrived at the Virginia colony in 1619, and Armenians settled in New York City from the 1830s. From the outset Armenian immigrants displayed a dedication to family, education, thrift, and entrepreneurship and an ability to avoid ethnic bigotry; by 1857 a writer from New York City noted a kinship with Anglo-Saxon Americans and called Armenians the "Yankees of the Near East." The seventy Armenians in the United States before 1870 included several notable figures in the city, such as Khachadur Osganian, president of the New York Press Club, and the pharmacist Kristapor Seropian, who invented the durable green dye used in American currency. During the nineteenth century many Armenians developed successful import–export firms (some dealing in Oriental rugs); others became craftsmen or managers in the photoengraving business. Because women were recognized as equals under Armenian canon law, they were able to obtain an education, have careers, and operate businesses.

Armenians were highly successful in the commercial and artistic life of the Ottoman Empire, but after the empire began its decline in 1890 they were systematically persecuted and expelled by the Turkish authorities, and some 1.5 million were killed between 1915 and 1924. A large number of refugees reached the United States (64,000 by 1914 and 30,771 more between 1919 and 1924), and perhaps twenty thousand remained in New York City. More than 90 percent of the new immigrants in the city already had family there to help them find housing, work, and social support (often with the help of Armenian organizations), and some 80 percent lived in the East 20s in Manhattan and in Washington Heights. In 1915 a group of businessmen led by Cleveland H. Dodge met at 1 Madison Avenue to form the Near East Relief Foundation, to aid Christian victims of the Ottoman Empire, most of whom were Armenians; by 1930 it had sent $110 million overseas, more than any other humanitarian organization. During this period the publication of M. Vartan Malcom's *The Armenians in America* (1919) contributed to a growing awareness among Armenians of their history in the United States. When the Johnson–Reed Immigration Act (1924) limited the number of Armenians who could enter the United States to 150 a year, Malcolm testified as an expert witness in the case of *U.S. v. Cartozian* (1925), which recognized some Asian immigrants as "free white persons" entitled to naturalization in the United States. With the influx of the 1920s many Armenian political parties reestablished themselves in the city, and the continuation of old rivalries resulted in frequent bloodshed. On Christmas Eve 1933 members of the Armenian Revolutionary Federation (known as Dashnags) assassinated the Armenian archbishop of New York, Leon Elisee Tourian, during Mass at the altar of the Holy Cross Church of Armenia, causing a deep schism within the Armenian Apostolic Church of North America (as a result of which the parishes of the original diocese and the new prelacy are now under separate archbishops). The next phase of immigration brought an additional 70,300 Armenians to the United States from the Soviet Union (1948–90) and a somewhat larger number from Eastern Europe and the Muslim countries of the Middle East, but barely 10 percent of these immigrants settled in New York City.

Festivals known as *hantesses* are frequently staged by the Armenian community. Major holidays include Easter, Christmas (celebrated on 6 January in Armenian-language services), St. Vartan's Day (11 February), honoring a martyr who defended Christian domains against a Persian army in 451, Martyrs' Day (24 April), marking the beginning of the massacre of the Armenians in 1915, and Independence Day (28 May), on which Dashnags commemorate the formation of the free Republic of Armenia (1918–21). The Armenian community remains intensely factional, especially in religious affairs. In the United States more than 85 percent of Armenians identify with the Armenian Apostolic Church of North America; about 10 percent are Protestant and 3 percent Roman Catholic. In the mid 1990s there were nine Armenian churches in New York City and fifteen in greater New York, including the Armenian cathedral at 34th Street and 2nd Avenue (headquarters of the Eastern Diocese of the Armenian Apostolic Church of North America), ten Orthodox Apostolic churches (seven under the diocese, of which four in New York City; three under the prelacy, of which two in the city), one Armenian Catholic cathedral (in New York City), and three Protestant churches (one in New York City). Of the three Armenian international political parties still in existence in the early 1990s, the largest was the Armenian Revolutionary Federation (Dashnags), which traditionally supported a free Armenia; the Armenian Democratic Liberal Organization (Ramgavars) included supporters of Soviet Armenia; and the Hunchagian Social Democratic Party (Hunchags) advocated violent revolution to achieve independence in Armenia.

Armenian immigrants have tended to maintain their culture and resist assimilation, and there are about a hundred Armenian institutions in greater New York, including three private schools, two nursing homes, and diverse social organizations. The *Armenian Reporter*, the largest of about a dozen Armenian weekly newspapers in the city, was launched in Queens in 1967; there are also four Armenian-language radio programs. Many Armenians have gained notice in the performing and creative arts of the city, among them the painter Arshile Gorky, the sculptors Reuben Nakian and Khoren Der Harootian, the stage designer Rouben Ter-Arutunian, the Broadway producer Rouben Mamoulian, the television personality Arlene Francis, the composer Alan Hovhaness, the conductor Varoujan Kodjian, the pianist Maro Ajemian, the violinists Anahid Ajemian, Ivan Galamian, and Mihran Kodjian, and the singers Lucine Amara, Lili Chookasian, Edna Garabedian, Armand Tokatyan, Ara Berberian, Michael Kermoyan, Cathy Berberian, and Kay Armen (Manoogian). In the mid 1990s there were eighty thousand to 100,000 Armenians in New York City, the third-largest community in the United States.

M. Vartan Malcom: *The Armenians in America* (Boston: Pilgrim, 1919; repr. San Francisco: R&E, 1969)
Silva Barsumyan and Harold Takooshian: *Armenian Organizations in Metropolitan New York* (New York: Privately printed, 1973)
Arra S. Avakian: *The Armenians in America* (Minneapolis: Lerner, 1977)
Robert Mirak: *Torn between Two Lands: Armenians in America, 1890 to World War I* (Cambridge: Harvard University Press, 1983)
Hamo B. Vassilian, ed.: *Armenian American Almanac: A Guide to Organizations, Churches, Newspapers and Periodicals, Foundations, Television and Radio Programs, Library Collections, Schools and Colleges, Bookstores and Book Publishers, Bibliographies, Scholarships, Armenian Studies Programs, and Special Collections in the U.S.A.* (Glendale, Calif.: Armenian Reference Books, 1985)
David Waldstreicher: *The Armenian Americans* (New York: Chelsea House, 1989)

Harold Takooshian

armories. The armory is a building unique to the United States that houses the drill hall and offices of a local militia unit. Its forerunners included early militia buildings such as the state arsenal in Central Park (1847, later occupied by the Department of Parks and Recreation), which were used primarily to store armaments. The Tompkins Market (1855) on 3rd Avenue also incorporated market stalls, militia company rooms, and a drill hall. A great number of armories were built by the nineteenth century, largely in response to events that took place in New York City after the Civil War and to the fears of social unrest that they provoked among the middle and upper classes; these included increasing numbers of foreign immigrants (many of them unskilled laborers from eastern and southern Europe), the draft riots of 1863, the panic of 1873 and the ensuing six-year depression, and the Tompkins Square Riot of 1874. In response buildings were erected to house the militia in times of siege, like the armory con-

Seventh Regiment Armory, ca *1910*

69th Regiment Armory, ca *1910*

structed for the 23rd Regiment of Brooklyn in 1872 on Bedford Avenue at Pacific Street. From 1880 to 1913 the New York City Armory Board and its counterpart in Brooklyn sponsored the construction of twenty-nine armories at a cost of more than $2.5 million. The city donated a block on Park Avenue between 66th and 67th streets to the élite 7th Regiment of Manhattan, which commissioned the architect Charles Clinton (a member of the troop) to design the Seventh Regiment Armory (1880). Designed much like a Victorian railroad station, the armory was composed of two distinct structures: a single-story drill hall measuring two hundred by three hundred feet (sixty by ninety meters) and roofed with iron trusses, which used technology developed for train sheds to provide an open space for drilling as many as a thousand troops; and a four-story administrative wing ("headhouse") along Park Avenue containing elegant public reception rooms, company headquarters, a gymnasium, and a mess hall. These extensive facilities enabled the regiment to hold frequent dances, teas, and polo matches to attract new members. The exterior of the Seventh Regiment Armory set a precedent for structures built throughout the city and the rest of the country: two armories in Brooklyn nearly identical to it in their general form were the 47th Regiment Armory (later the 17th Corps Artillery Armory) at Harrison Avenue and Lynch Street (1883) and the Second Signal Corps Armory at 793–801 Dean Street (1885). Other armories of this period sought to express their regimental and ethnic identities through flamboyant designs: the Eighth Regiment Armory (1887–89) next door to Squadron A in Manhattan was described as "Scottish baronial," and the Thirteenth Regiment Armory (1891–92) at 357 Sumner Avenue in Brooklyn was modeled after the castle at Chapultepec in Mexico.

By the end of the nineteenth century control over local militia units was assumed by the state and then by the federal government, leading to a new uniformity in the rules governing the militia and in the design of their armory buildings. Still many reflected the work of distinguished architects: the 23rd Regiment Armory (1902) at 1322 Bedford Avenue in Brooklyn was designed by Isaac G. Perry, the architect of the Capitol in Albany, New York, who also supervised the construction of public buildings throughout New York State, and the 17th Separate Company Armory (1904–6) at 137-58 Northern Boulevard in Flushing was built by Perry's successor, George L. Heins. Lewis G. Pilcher, a nationally recognized expert in the architectural design of armories who became a state architect during the Second World War, designed the Troop "C" Armory (1908, later the 42nd Supply and Transport Battalion) at Bedford Avenue and President Street in Brooklyn and the Eighth Regiment Armory.

In a reflection of national trends in architecture, functionalism was the norm in armories at the beginning of the twentieth century. The architectural firm of Hunt and Hunt used overscaled details in the beaux-arts style for the 69th Regiment Armory (1906) on Lexington Avenue and 25th Street in Manhattan, the site in 1913 of the International Exhibition of Modern Art (commonly known as the Armory Show). Details were simplified even in armories designed in the castellated tradition, such as the 22nd Regiment Corps of Engineers Armory (1909–11) at 216 Fort Washington Avenue in Manhattan and the Second Battalion of Field Artillery Armory (1906–8) at 171 Clermont Avenue in Brooklyn. As armory exteriors became standardized, the interiors responded to the changing technology of war. The Second Battalion Naval Militia Armory (1903) at 51st Street and

Eighth Regiment Armory, ca *1900*

Ninth Regiment Armory, ca *1900*

1st Avenue in Sunset Park had a mock bridge and poop deck, and to accommodate huge coastal artillery installations the Kingsbridge Armory (1912) in the Bronx had the largest drill shed in the world (180,000 square feet, or 16,700 square meters). The 369th Regiment Armory (1920–24, home of the "Harlem Hellfighters") at 142nd Street and 5th Avenue, designed in the art deco style, was one of the first complexes built strictly to accommodate motorized transport. During the Depression the Works Progress Administration sponsored the construction of armories throughout the country, such as the Fourth Regiment Armory in Jamaica (1933–36), built in the art moderne style with simple interiors and a relatively small drill shed that was used mainly for storing vehicles. In the 1950s the primary considerations in armory design became proximity to important transport routes and room to accommodate troop outfits with increasingly large and diverse stores of equipment, requirements that few locations in New York City were able to satisfy.

Many armories were decommissioned or demolished after the Second World War. The Second Regiment of Field Artillery Armory and the Fourteenth Regiment Armory (1891–94) in Park Slope were purchased by the city, and the Second Signal Corps Armory was sold to private owners, as was the First Battalion of Field Artillery Armory (1901) at 56 West 66th Street, which was converted into television studios. The Eighth Regiment Armory (1895) on Madison Avenue at 94th Street was partly demolished to make room for a school playground. Armories completely demolished include the Twelfth Regiment Armory at Columbus Avenue and 62nd Street, the Second Battalion Naval Militia Armory, and the Ninth Regiment Armory, on the site of the current 42nd Division Headquarters (1971) on West 14th Street in Manhattan. In 1990 ten armories remained in active use by the National Guard in New York City. They also supported commercial and community activities ranging from high school track meets to film production; in addition all armories except those in Jamaica and Staten Island served as shelters for the homeless.

Robert M. Fogelson: *America's Armories: Architecture, Society and Public Order* (Cambridge: Harvard University Press, 1989)

Pamela W. Hawkes

Armory Show [International Exhibition of Modern Art]. Art exhibition held from 17 February to 15 March 1913 at the 69th Regiment Armory, at Lexington Avenue and 25th Street in Manhattan. It presented modernist trends in European and American art and had an immeasurable influence on the American public. The show was conceived in December 1911 at a meeting of the artists Walt Kuhn, Jerome Myers, Elmer MacRae, and Henry Fitch Taylor, who soon gained the sponsorship of the Association of American Painters and Sculptors; Mabel Dodge, Gertrude Vanderbilt Whitney, and other arts patrons also agreed to contribute funds. Kuhn, the secretary of the association, went to Paris with the painter Arthur B. Davies and met with the critic Walter Pach to secure the loans of European art. The controversial show was both praised and denounced in the press. It consisted of about sixteen hundred works of art, including van Gogh's *Mountains at Saint-Rémy*, Marcel Duchamp's *Nude Descending a Staircase*, Constantin Brancuşi's *Mademoiselle Pogany*, and Francis Picabia's *Dances at the Spring*. Works from abroad accounted for about a third of the total and for 123 of 174 works sold. A smaller version of the show traveled to Boston and Chicago.

Milton W. Brown: *The Story of the Armory Show* (Greenwich, Conn.: New York Graphic Society, 1963; rev. New York: Abbeville, 1988)

Patricia Hills

Armstrong, Edwin H(oward) (*b* New York City, 18 Dec 1890; *d* New York City, 1 Feb 1954). Engineer and inventor. While a student at Columbia University (graduated 1913) his experiments in the basement of Philosophy Hall with Lee De Forest's Audion

Fourteenth Regiment Armory (designed by William A. Mundell), ca *1900*

tube enabled him to amplify radio signals through regenerative circuits (1912). Stationed in France during the First World War, he invented the superheterodyne circuit (1918) for tuning in frequencies of the ignition systems of enemy aircraft. In 1931 he improved the frequency modulation (FM) method of radio broadcasting, which eliminated static while increasing fidelity. A tireless campaigner for his inventions despite opposition from commercial interests, he ran tests from atop the Empire State Building and broadcast the opening of the World's Fair of 1939–40. In 1942 he won the Edison Medal. Legal battles ruined Armstrong financially and contributed to his taking his own life.

Sydney W. Head: *Broadcasting in America* (Boston: Houghton Mifflin, 1956)

Monroe Upton: *Electronics for Everyone* (New York: Signet Science Library, 1957)

Curtis Mitchell: *Cavalcade of Broadcasting* (Chicago: Follett, 1970)

Malcolm W. Browne: "Papers Tell Tragic Story of Man Who Invented FM," *New York Times*, 21 May 1978, p. 13

For illustration see RADIO.

Val Ginter

Armstrong, Louis [Pops; Satchmo] (*b* New Orleans, 4 Aug 1901; *d* New York City, 6 July 1971). Trumpeter and singer. After an apprenticeship in New Orleans he became the second cornetist in King Oliver's Creole Jazz Band in Chicago (1922–24). As a member in New York City of Fletcher Henderson's big band (1924–25) he introduced a conception of tone, technique, improvisation, and swing previously unknown in the city. In Chicago he made recordings with his Hot Five and Hot Seven (1925–28) that document his position as one of the most important figures in jazz. During this period he changed from the cornet to the more brilliant and penetrating trumpet, and developed a technique of improvising delightful nonsense syllables called scat singing. He began working with big bands, often mediocre ones. While appearing in the Broadway revue *Hot Chocolates* (music by Fats Waller) he popularized "Ain't Misbehavin'" and the racial protest song "(What Did I Do to Be So) Black and Blue(?)" (1929). He also appeared in films, including *Pennies from Heaven* (1936). A concert at Town Hall on West 43rd Street in 1947 marked his return to playing with small groups, which he continued to do in performances for the remainder of his career. On record he played with other ensembles as well, and he had several popular hits: "Blueberry Hill" (1949), "Mack the Knife" (1955), "Hello, Dolly!" (1963), and "What a Wonderful World" (1967). His home from 1942 to the end of his life was at 34-56 107th Street in Corona; it is now the Armstrong House National Historic Landmark.

Louis Armstrong

Max Jones and John Chilton: *Louis: The Louis Armstrong Story, 1900–1971* (London: Studio Vista, 1971)

James Lincoln Collier: *Louis Armstrong: An American Genius* (New York: Oxford University Press, 1983)

Gary Giddins: *Satchmo* (New York: Doubleday, 1988)

Barry Kernfeld

Arno, Peter [Peters, Curtis Arnoux] (*b* New York City, 8 Jan 1904; *d* Port Chester, N.Y., 22 Feb 1968). Cartoonist and writer. He graduated from Yale University in 1924 and in the following year joined the staff of the *New Yorker*, where his urbane, satirical cartoons of café society helped to set a breezy tone. He also wrote and produced musical reviews and motion pictures, designed automobiles, painted, and played the piano. A member of the Society of Illustrators, he published several collections of cartoons, including *Whoops Dearie* (1927), *Peter Arno's Parade* (1929), and *Sizzling Platter* (1949). Arno lived at the Dorset Hotel at 30 West 54th Street.

James E. Mooney

Arnold, Pauline (*b* Galesburg, Ill., 1894; *d* 1974). Advertising executive. Trained as a musician at Knox College, she moved to New York City in 1926 and opened one of the first market research firms there, Arnold Research Service. In 1934 she renamed it the Market Research Corporation of America, which her husband, Percival White, joined as a partner; together they reorganized it as White and Arnold in 1952.

Mary Ellen Zuckerman

Arnold Constable. Firm of retailers, one of the oldest in New York City. It was formed in 1825 by Aaron Arnold (1794–1876) and his nephew George Arnold Hearn (1835–1913), who opened a small dry-goods shop at the corner of Mercer and Canal streets; Hearn left the firm in 1837 and was replaced by James Mansell Constable. The firm in 1868 opened a lavish store of five stories on Broadway and 19th Street, in the fashionable shopping district later known as Ladies' Mile. The store became known especially for its mourning clothes and also sold household goods. In addition to retailing the building was used for wholesaling and manufacture. In 1914 the firm followed many other large retailers by moving its store uptown, to 5th Avenue and 39th Street. Although this store closed in 1975 Arnold Constable continued to maintain offices and boutiques in Manhattan.

Leslie Gourse

Arrau, Claudio (*b* Chillán, Chile, 6 Feb 1903; *d* Mürzzuschlag, Austria, 9 June 1991). Pianist. A child prodigy at five, he studied with Martin Krause in Berlin and made his début in 1914 and his American début in 1921. He built a large repertory that included the complete works of Bach (which he eventually decided should not be played on the modern piano) and music by Mozart, Beethoven, Chopin, Liszt, Schumann, and Debussy. In 1941 he settled permanently in Douglaston. He renounced his Chilean citizenship in 1978 to protest the military regime in Chile and in the following year became a citizen of the United States. He moved to Europe shortly before his death.

Richard Kobliner

Arrochar. Neighborhood in northeastern Staten Island, bounded to the north by the Staten Island Expressway, to the east by Fort Wadsworth, and to the west by Hylan Boulevard. The area was apparently inhabited by Lenni Lenape Indians. Its name is derived from that of a sizable estate built in 1840 by the first European settler, W. W. MacFarland, which was named in turn after the village in Scotland from which he originated; his house is now the oldest building on the grounds of St. Joseph Hill Academy. At the turn of the century the area was the gateway to the popular resort areas of South and Midland beaches, and in 1914 the local chamber of commerce described it as the "Riviera of the harbor." In the following decades the neighborhood became settled by Italians and later by members of other ethnic groups. Arrochar is a peaceful enclave of large homes and small businesses.

Martha S. Bendix

art. For discussions of art in New York City see the entries ARCHITECTURE, ART CRITICISM, MURALS, PAINTING, PHOTOGRAPHY, and SCULPTURE, as well as entries on individual figures and institutions.

Art Commission. An appointed group authorized to approve, fund, and oversee public art projects and to regulate the permanent installation on city property of works of art and architecture (including parks and bridges). Modeled after similar commissions in Europe, Boston (1890), and Baltimore (1895), it was established by the charter of 1898 through the efforts of the architect John M. Carrère and art organizations like the Municipal Art Society, the Society of Beaux-Arts Architects, and the Fine Arts Federation. By 1907 the commission approved the plans and designs of all structures proposed for city-owned lands, a mandate that eventually came to encompass fire stations, schools, libraries, hospitals, parks and recreational facilities, bridges, sewage disposal plants, streetlights, and newsstands. The members of the commission, who serve without pay, include the mayor and representatives of the Metropolitan Museum of Art, the New York Public Library, and the Brooklyn Museum; the commission must also include one painter, one sculptor, one architect, one landscape architect, and three laypersons, all seven of whom are nominated by the Fine Arts Federation and appointed by the mayor, and serve staggered three-year terms. The commission meets at City Hall and holds a monthly hearing and confidential ballot on the fine art and urban design proposals of various city agencies. Because its purpose is to rule on the proposals of others the commission is essentially reactive. Its many influential members have included the architects Charles F. McKim, Wallace K. Harrison, and James Ingo Freed; the painters John La Farge, Adolph Gottlieb, and Robert Ryman; and the sculptors Daniel Chester French, Alexander Calder, and Paul Manship. Under the administration of Mayor Edward I. Koch (1978–89) the commission collaborated with various city agencies and assumed a larger and more active role than previously: it took inventory of the art owned by the city, began several conservation programs, and became responsible for the administration of the Tweed Gallery at 52 Chambers Street, which mounts exhibitions in conjunction with other municipal agencies.

John M. Carrère: "The Art Commission of the City of New York and Its Origin," *New York Architect* 2, no. 3 (1908)

Michele H. Bogart: *Public Sculpture and the Civic Ideal in New York City, 1890–1930* (Chicago: University of Chicago Press, 1989), 56–70

Barbara Hager: *The Art Commission of the City of New York* (New York: Art Commission, 1989)

Margot Gayle, Harriet F. Senie

art criticism. Critical writings about art range widely in their aims and methods: from personal appreciations of subject matter and artistic skills, to didactic essays aimed at a popular audience, to highly theoretical treatises. In early-nineteenth-century New York City as in the United States as a whole, the efforts of American painters were measured against the perfection of the Old Masters and the advanced techniques of contemporary European artists. These standards informed William Dunlap's multivolume work *History of the Rise and Progress of the Arts of Design in the United States* (1834). In periodicals such as the *Port Folio*, the *New York Review*, and *Atheneum Magazine*, the highest praise that an artist could be accorded was to be called the "American Hogarth" or the "American Wilkie." As late as 1864 James Jackson Jarves, in his influential book *The Art-Idea*, valued art that strove toward an ideal perfection.

In the 1830s and 1840s excellence in landscape painting meant fidelity to the scenic details of the American countryside and wilderness. Truth to nature, a principle advanced by John Ruskin, was supported by William James Stillman and John Durand, editors of the art journal the *Crayon* (1855–61), which consistently published criticism of a high tone; contributing writers included Charles Eliot Norton of Boston and the painter Asher B. Durand, who advised young artists to study nature before studying pictures. This principle was also followed by the Society for the Advancement of Truth in Art (1863) in its publication the *New Path*. At the same time another critical gauge developed that influenced art by its responsiveness to the needs of a broad democratic audience. To John Neal (1783–1876) of Portland, Maine, the first professional art critic, painting should not be a luxury item for the wealthy but should speak to the needs of the people. The American Art-Union and the Cosmopolitan Art Association called on artists to paint American scenes and patriotic subjects for a democratic patronage, an imperative rooted in western expansionism and unionism. Artists heeded the call with enthusiasm. In his *Book of the Artists* (1867) the critic Henry T. Tuckerman praised genre artists such as Eastman Johnson who met the needs of cultural nationalism while painting pictures with a moral sentiment.

After the Civil War art criticism became increasingly professionalized within newspaper journalism. By the 1880s the influence of Ruskin had decidedly waned. Like their European counterparts, American artists turned from a moralizing and didactic art to one concerned with beauty and art for art's sake. For the new leisure classes the role of art was to bring pleasure not instruction. Critics and artists heeded the growing importance of photography, which called attention to the effects of light and the transience of images, and by the flatness of Japanese *ukiyo-e* (color woodcuts). In the magazine the *Galaxy* (1867) Russel Sturgis Jr. praised the quality of flatness in the drawings of the genre artist W. J. Hennessy, which allowed for subtle effects of light and shading and for brilliant color. Other notable critics open to the new aesthetics included Clarence Cook of the *New York Tribune*, Mariana Griswold Van Rensselaer of the *American Architect and Building News*, S. G. W. Benjamin of the *American Art Review*, and Charles de Kay of the *New York Times*. Henry James occasionally wrote art criticism: his piece on John Singer Sargent for *Harper's Monthly Magazine* in 1887 helped launch Sargent's American career. In the first decade of the twentieth century the criterion of truth moved to the foreground. As defined by the artist Robert Henri, truth was the "spirit of the people." He told the critic Mary Fanton Roberts (who wrote under the name Giles Edgerton) that the future of American art lay in artists' "appreciation of the value of the human quality all about them, which is nothing more or less than seeing the truth, and then expressing it according to their individual understanding of it."

The polarity of truth versus beauty seemed no longer as compelling when the new art — cubism and fauvism — arrived from Europe. To be "modern" now meant to be anti-traditional, anti-academic, and experimental. Among the more sympathetic art critics were Charles Caffin, James Gibbons Huneker of the *Sun*, and the freelance writers Sadakichi Hartmann, Benjamin de Casseres, and Paul Haviland, who with the Mexican artist Marius De Zayas wrote *A Study of the Modern Evolution of Plastic Form* (1913); all were regular contributors to Alfred Stieglitz's journal *Camera Work*. After the Armory Show Willard Huntington Wright wrote *Modern Painting: Its Tendency and Meaning* (1915) and Arthur Jerome Eddy wrote *Cubists and Post-impressionism* (1914), both influential among subsequent generations of critics.

Not all critics embraced the new art. A more traditional view was taken by the academic mural painter Kenyon Cox, who wrote frequently on art, and Royal Cortissoz, art critic for the *New York Tribune* for more than fifty years. Peyton Boswell (1879–1936) of the *New York Herald* called Marcel Duchamp's *Nude Descending a Staircase* (shown at the Armory Show in 1913) a "cyclone in a shingle factory." Boswell later founded the conservative *Art Digest* and during the 1930s campaigned to discredit the social realists. Most art critics during the 1920s and 1930s were more moderate about semi-abstract art and urban realism, including Frank Jewett Mather Jr., an art historian and art critic for the *Nation* and the *New York Evening Post*, Joseph Edgar Chamberlain of the *New York Evening Mail*, who also contributed to *Camera Work*, and Elizabeth Luther Cary of the *New York Times*.

The best serious criticism during the 1920s was written by Henry McBride for the *Sun* and the *Dial* and by Lloyd Goodrich and Forbes Watson, who were partial to American art and also wrote for *Arts*, a magazine launched in 1923 and funded by Gertrude Vanderbilt Whitney. At the same time cultural critics such as Edmund Wilson, Lewis Mumford, and Alain Locke made forays into art criticism. In the 1930s in New York City many artists developed a social realist style critical of capitalism, and many art critics returned to the populist standard, measuring art by its ability to communicate to working people. One of the most respected critics in this school was Elizabeth McCausland (writing as Elizabeth Noble for the leftist publications

Art Front and *New Masses*), who reviewed exhibitions of art that had a social content and consistently praised artists such as Philip Evergood and Jacob Lawrence. The artists Stuart Davis and Louis Lozowick wrote Marxist criticism for *Art Front*, as did the critics Harold Rosenberg and Meyer Schapiro, who denounced Soviet communism at the end of the 1930s. Abstract expressionism, a movement centered in New York City, was championed from the late 1940s by Rosenberg, Schapiro, and especially Clement Greenberg, who inveighed against the idea of art for the masses in *Partisan Review* and the *Nation* and became the city's most theoretically oriented and influential art critic in the 1950s and 1960s. Greenberg was unreceptive to realist painting, pop art, and other experimental forms, unlike such critics as Tom Hess (editor of *Art News*), Dore Ashton and Brian O'Doherty of the *New York Times*, and Robert Coates of the *New Yorker*. The artist Fairfield Porter and the poet Frank O'Hara wrote with a heightened sensitivity toward art of the postwar period without Greenberg's theoretical apparatus, and the art historian Leo Steinberg, who had written art criticism for the magazine *Arts* in the 1950s, was one of the first to challenge Greenberg's theories in public lectures and in his book *Other Criteria* (1972). The early writings of Rosalind Krauss, Michael Fried, and Barbara Rose followed the lead of Greenberg in asserting the primacy of formal purity; all three eventually moved away from what Fried began to see as a "reductionist conception of modernist painting."

By 1970 art criticism had become more diverse. Lawrence Alloway and Lucy R. Lippard wrote favorably on pop art, photorealism, feminist art, and political art. Cindy Nemser launched the *Feminist Art Journal*, and in 1977 a collective of women in the art world published the first issue of *Heresies*, a feminist journal on art and politics, of which Lippard was the major critic. Max Kozloff, an editor at *Artforum*, wrote on photography, which along with video art had become a vanguard art form. In 1976 the post-structuralist critics Annette Michelson and Krauss began the journal *October*, which included features on conceptual art. Gregory Battcock, Carter Ratcliff, John Perreault, Kim Levin, Kay Larsen, Robert Pincus-Witten, Grace Glueck, Thomas McEvilley, Peter Schjeldahl, and Arthur Danto displayed an openness toward different artistic styles and aesthetic approaches. Among the most influential magazines were *Art in America*, *Arts*, *Artnews*, and *Artforum*. More traditional critics included Robert Hughes of *Time*, Douglas Davis of *Newsweek*, and John Canaday and later John Russell of the *New York Times*. As an art critic for the *New York Times* Hilton Kramer emulated the critical aesthetics of Greenberg but more stridently opposed art of social or political comment. In the 1980s he launched the *New Criterion*, which took a purist approach to evaluating art. His successors at the *Times*, Michael Brenson, Roberta Smith, and Michael Kimmelman, were more willing to write about political and feminist artists. At the same time there came to prominence criticism by feminists, gays and lesbians, blacks, American Indians, Latin Americans, and Asian–Americans, which was published primarily in exhibition catalogues and by universities and cooperative galleries. Moreover artists of diverse backgrounds donned critical hats to explicate their own work. The New Museum of Contemporary Art published the writings of Marcia Tucker, Brian Wallis, Craig Owens, Kate Linker, and William Olander, and cultural critics such as Elizabeth Hess, Martha Rosler, and Michele Wallace wrote about the place of art in society.

The diversity that came to characterize art criticism in the 1970s and 1980s is reflected in the wide range of criticism honored by the College Art Association. The many recipients of its annual award for excellence who have been based in New York City represent a wide range of critical schools, including post-structuralism and psychoanalysis (Krauss, 1973; Michelson, 1974; Donald Kuspit, 1983), historicism (Linda Nochlin, 1978; Robert Rosenblum, 1981; Steinberg, 1984), Marxism (Benjamin Buchloh, 1986), feminism and gay criticism (Douglas Crimp, 1989; Martha Gever and Jan Grover, 1990), and criticism focusing on race and sex roles (Lowery Sims, 1991).

John P. Simoni: "Art Critics and Criticism in Nineteenth Century America" (diss., Ohio State University, 1952)

Arlene R. Olson: *Art Critics and the Avant-garde: New York, 1900–1913* (Ann Arbor, Mich.: UMI Research Press, 1980)

Peninah R. Y. Petruck: *American Art Criticism*, 1910–1939 (New York: Garland, 1981)

Francis Frascina, ed.: *Pollock and After: The Critical Debate* (New York: Harper and Row, 1985)

Richard Hertz: *Theories of Contemporary Art* (Englewood Cliffs, N.J.: Prentice–Hall, 1985; 2nd edn 1993)

Susan Noyes Platt: *Modernism in the 1920s: Interpretations of Modern Art in New York from Expressionism to Constructivism* (Ann Arbor, Mich.: UMI Research Press, 1985)

Arlene Raven, Cassandra L. Langer, and Joanna Frueh, eds.: *Feminist Art Criticism: An Anthology* (Ann Arbor, Mich.: UMI Press, 1988)

Patricia Hills

art galleries. The earliest commercial art galleries in New York City were situated on and near 57th Street, largely because of the proximity of the Museum of Modern Art, which opened on West 53rd Street in 1929. Among the most important early galleries were the Julien Levy Gallery and Peggy Guggenheim's Art of This Century on 56th Street, which showed work by Mark Rothko and Jackson Pollock. At the beginning of the pop art movement in the 1950s the district and the area somewhat farther north became the site of the Betty Parsons Gallery, the Sidney Janis Gallery, the Hirschl and Adler Galleries, the Leo Castelli Gallery, and the Ronald Feldman Gallery (now in SoHo). At the same time several new galleries along East 10th Street, largely artists' collectives, showed works by the second generation of abstract expressionists. The next important development occurred in 1969, when Paula Cooper opened on Wooster Street the first art gallery in SoHo, launching the evolution of the neighborhood into an artistic center where artists could take advantage of large, open spaces both for living and for exhibiting their work. The hub of SoHo was the building at 420 West Broadway, housing the Leo Castelli Gallery (which moved downtown in 1971), the Sonnabend Gallery, and the Charles Cowles Gallery. Another important gallery was that of Holly Solomon (1976). In the same area two important alternative spaces, White Columns (1969) and Artists Space, provided exhibition space for socially engaged art that was regarded as unsalable.

A new gallery district took shape in the East Village after the Fun Gallery opened in 1980. Within a few years the area was the site of about fifty galleries, including the Gracie Mansion Gallery, the Civilian Warfare Gallery, and the International with Monument Gallery. These establishments were run for little money (often out of private residences), specialized in work that was highly ironic, and helped bring about the gentrification of the neighborhood. But when the aesthetic represented by virtually all the galleries fell out of favor and the stock market crashed in 1987 the district disappeared almost immediately.

By this time SoHo was enjoying a revival. Its new axis was Broadway, and in place of the storefront galleries that had prevailed in earlier years vertical gallery buildings become more common. Several gallery owners from the East Village attempted to move their operations to SoHo, but because of the much higher costs prevailing there most failed. The continuing search for cheaper rents eventually led to the development of a gallery district on 22nd Street between 10th and 11th avenues, aided by a sense that the former edginess of SoHo had been superseded by an ostentatious consumerism.

In the mid 1990s there were about five hundred galleries in Manhattan and a few more in the other boroughs, as well as about twenty "alternative spaces" (often collectives) that provided an important link between artists and commercial galleries. About half the city's galleries were in SoHo, with a quarter on 57th Street and another quarter elsewhere (such as in Tribeca, in Chelsea, and uptown). Several galleries were widely known: on 57th Street the Marian Goodman Gallery, the Robert Miller Gallery, the Pace/Wildenstein Gallery (also in SoHo), the Sidney Janis Gallery, and the Marlborough Gallery; in SoHo the Leo Castelli Gallery, the Sonnabend Gallery, the Mary Boone Gallery, the Luhring Augustine Gallery, the Barbara Gladstone Gallery, and the Andrea Rosen Gallery; and uptown the Larry Gagosian Gallery (also in SoHo) and the Matthew Marks Gallery (also in Chelsea).

Arthur, Chester A(lan) (*b* Fairfield, Vt., 5 Oct 1829; *d* New York City, 18 Nov 1886). Twenty-first president of the United States. He moved to New York City in 1852 and became a prominent lawyer, taking a special interest in civil rights cases. His success in *Jennings v. Third Avenue Railroad Co.* (1855) helped to make possible the racial integration of passenger railroads in the city. He was active in the Republican Party, which was then newly formed. As the quartermaster general for New York State from 1862 he was responsible for providing care to troops passing through the state. In 1871 his party had him appointed customs collector for the Port of New York, a position long associated with political patronage; he was soon accused of corruption and in 1878 was forced from office. To make up for his lost income the Republicans put him on their national ticket in 1880, and he assumed the presidency in September 1881 on the assassination of President James A. Garfield. The first president since George Washington to take the oath of office in New York City, he was sworn in at his townhouse at 123 Lexington Avenue, near 28th Street. He returned to the city after failing to be renominated for the presidency. In 1899 a seventeen-foot (five-meter) bronze statue of Arthur designed by George Edwin Bissell was erected on the northeast corner of Madison Square Park.

Thomas C. Reeves: *Gentleman Boss: The Life of Chester Alan Arthur* (New York: Alfred A. Knopf, 1975)

Mollie Keller

Arthur Andersen. Accounting firm formed in Chicago in December 1913. It opened headquarters at 17 East 42nd Street in New York City in 1921 and moved them to 67 Wall Street on 1 July 1925; the firm had almost two hundred employees in 1947 and in 1953 moved to 67 Broad Street. Between 1960 and 1969 the staff increased to more than five hundred and offices were moved to 80 Pine Street. In 1992 Arthur Andersen had revenues of $2900 million and was among the country's six largest accounting firms; most of its eleven hundred employees worked in its offices at 1345 6th Avenue.

Janet Frankston

Arthur Kill. A tidal strait about ten miles (sixteen kilometers) long between Staten Island and New Jersey. It opens at its northern end into Newark Bay and at its southern end into Raritan Bay, and is lined with industrial sites (mostly in New Jersey) and salt marshes (in Staten Island). Two islands in the waterway belong to Staten Island: Pralls Island (a bird sanctuary of about thirty acres, or twelve hectares) and the Island of Meadows (about forty acres, or sixteen hectares), situated at the entrance to a deepwater creek known as the Fresh Kills. The Arthur Kill sees considerable marine traffic. It is spanned by the Goethals Bridge, by a lift bridge of Conrail (formerly used by the Baltimore and Ohio Railroad), and by the Outerbridge Crossing.

Gerard R. Wolfe

Arthur Young. Accounting firm formed in Chicago by Arthur Young, a Scottish immigrant, in 1894. An office opened in New York City in 1911 under the direction of R. L. Cuthbert, a Scottish chartered accountant; he was succeeded by Alexander J. Baxter in 1914. This office soon became the firm's headquarters and during the First World War helped to form the Emergency Fleet Corporation (led by General George Washington Goethals). From 1920 to 1943 Luke Nolan was the partner in charge. On 18 August 1989 Arthur Young merged with Ernst and Whinney to form Ernst and Young.

Janet Frankston

Artists and Writers Protest against the War in Vietnam. Organization formed in 1965 in New York City by Rudolf Baranik, Leon Golub, Denise Levertov, Irving Petlin, and May Stevens that held meetings in SoHo. It sponsored a "Peace Tower" in Los Angeles (1966), an "Angry Arts" week in New York City (1967), a collective protest wall called "Collage of Indignation" (1971), a "Leaderless Concert at Midnight" at Town Hall, and "Napalm Poetry Readings."

Lucy R. Lippard: *A Different War: Vietnam in Art* (Seattle: Real Comet, 1990)

Rudolf Baranik

Artkraft Strauss Sign Corporation. Firm of billboard and sign makers formed in 1935 by Jacob Starr, a Russian electrician. In the 1930s Starr was among the first advertisers to use electric signs in promoting motion pictures. Douglas Leigh, a designer for the firm, in the 1950s created such well-known signs as one for Camel cigarettes on the Hotel Claridge that depicted a man blowing smoke rings (with steam provided by Consolidated Edison), and one for Pepsi-Cola atop the Bond Building in which the company's logotype glimmered behind a waterfall that circulated ten thousand gallons (38,000 liters) of water. Artkraft Strauss now controls most of the sign display space in Times Square, where it is also responsible for lowering the "time ball" at midnight on New Year's Eve. The firm employs more than 170 artists, designers, engineers, carpenters, welders, electricians, plumbers, and sign painters to build its signs, which are as large as one thousand square feet (ninety-three square meters). Its main plant is at the corner of 57th Street and 12th Avenue in Manhattan. Artkraft Strauss Sign Corporation remains a family business.

Kathleen Hulser

Art Students League (designed by Henry J. Hardenbergh), ca *1900*

Art Students League. Art school opened in 1875 by members of the National Academy of Design. Strengthened by the addition of William Merritt Chase to the faculty, it developed a close association with the Society of American Artists; together the societies erected a building on West 57th Street that they shared with the Architectural League. By the turn of the century the Art Students League had about a thousand students and occupied the entire building on 57th Street. Classes were taught by Robert Henri (whose students included George Bellows, Rockwell Kent, Guy Pène du Bois, Walter Pach, and Edward Hopper), and later by John Sloan and Thomas Hart Benton. The school's seventy-fifth anniversary was marked by the Metropolitan Museum of Art with an exhibition of the work of seventy-five former students, the hundredth anniversary with an exhibition of the work of a hundred former students. Unlike most schools of its kind the Art Students League has no set curriculum or requirements and is open to students of all ages.

Marchal E. Landgren: *Years of Art: The Story of the Art Students League of New York* (New York: R. M. McBride, 1940)
Art Students League: Selections from the Permanent Collection (New York: Gallery Association, 1987)

James E. Mooney

Art Workers Coalition. Arts organization that emerged in New York City in 1969 out of groups such as Artists and Writers Protest against the War in Vietnam, the Guerrilla Art

Action Group, the Black Emergency Cultural Coalition, and Women Artists in Revolution (WAR). It held meetings in SoHo. In its first public action the coalition presented thirteen demands to the Museum of Modern Art, among them that the museum should appoint artists to its curatorial committees, exhibit regularly the work of black and Latin American artists, and remain open free of charge two evenings a week for workers. It also protested against the Vietnam War, racism, and sexism. Activists in the organization included Carl Andre, Lucy R. Lippard, Benny Andrews, and Rudolf Baranik. The Art Workers Coalition disbanded in 1971.

Lucy R. Lippard: *A Different War: Vietnam in Art* (Seattle: Real Comet, 1990)

Rudolf Baranik

Arverne. Neighborhood in southeastern Queens. It began as a number of streets and villas laid out in April 1882 on Rockaway Peninsula between Beach 47th and Beach 74th streets by the developer Remington Vernam, whose signature on checks, "R. Vernam," inspired the community's name. A fashionable resort between 1888 and 1908, the neighborhood declined in the 1950s and became an area of urban renewal in 1964. In 1990 it was sold by the city to private companies for development as condominiums. The project was intended on its completion to be one of the largest and most innovative housing developments in the city, with ten thousand units in low buildings spread over 278 acres (113 hectares).

Vincent Seyfried

ASCE. See AMERICAN SOCIETY OF CIVIL ENGINEERS.

Ashbery, John (Lawrence) (*b* Rochester, N.Y., 28 July 1927). Poet and art critic. He published poems in a number of well-known literary magazines and anthologies by the late 1940s. After studying at Harvard College (BA in English 1949) and Columbia University (MA 1951) he worked as a copywriter for Oxford University Press (1951–54) and McGraw–Hill (1954–55). During these years he became the most prominent member of the New York School of poets. In 1958 he moved to Paris, and after returning to New York City in the autumn of 1965 he became the executive editor of *Art News*, a position he held until 1972. Ashbery has published about thirty volumes of learned, witty, elliptical poetry informed by a strong visual sense, including *Self-Portrait in a Convex Mirror* (1975, Pulitzer Prize), and half a dozen plays, translated (sometimes under the name Jonas Berry) and edited a dozen other volumes, and taught at Brooklyn College, New York University, and Bard College.

Geoff Ward: *Statutes of Liberty: The New York School of Poets* (New York: St. Martin's, 1993), 83–134

Allen J. Share

Ashcan School. A popular name for the realist artists John Sloan, Stuart Davis, Maurice Becker, Glenn O. Coleman, and Henry Glintenkamp, who drew naturalist depictions of street life for the radical socialist publication the *Masses* in the early twentieth century. The term was coined in March 1916 by the cartoonist Art Young and was intended to be derogatory, but it soon lost its negative connotations and came to be applied to all the early realists, including Robert Henri and George Bellows.

Rebecca Zurier: *Art for the Masses (1911–1917): A Radical Magazine and Its Graphics* (New Haven: Yale University Art Gallery, 1985 / Philadelphia: Temple University Press, 1988)

Patricia Hills

Asia Society. Organization formed in 1957 to improve relations between Asia and the West. In 1960 it opened several art galleries at 725 Park Avenue for the exhibit of painting, sculpture, and graphic art from Japan, China, Korea, Tibet, India, and other Asian nations. Exhibitions are drawn from the society's holdings, including the Mr. and Mrs. John D. Rockefeller III Collection of Asian Art, and those of other institutions. The society also offers films and programs in dance and music, and publishes catalogues, handbooks of its collections, and the annual publication *Archives of Asian Art.*

James E. Mooney

Asimov, Isaac (*b* Petrovichi, Russia, 2 Jan 1920; *d* New York City, 6 April 1992). Writer. He moved to the United States as an infant, learned to read English in the streets of Brooklyn, and taught himself to read Yiddish at the age of seven. He earned his high school diploma at fifteen and sold his first science fiction story at eighteen. After attending Columbia University (BS 1939, MA 1941, PhD in chemistry 1948) he taught biochemistry at Boston University from 1949 to 1958. He then abandoned teaching to write full time, which he did at the rate of ten to twelve books a year for the rest of his life. His published writings include fiction, nonfiction on subjects ranging from the sciences to Shakespeare, four hundred monthly columns and articles for the magazine *Fantasy and Science Fiction*, an immense number of limericks, and several autobiographical works (including *In Memory Yet Green*, 1979).

James E. Mooney

ASME. See AMERICAN SOCIETY OF MECHANICAL ENGINEERS.

ASPCA. See AMERICAN SOCIETY FOR THE PREVENTION OF CRUELTY TO ANIMALS.

Aspinwall, William Henry (*b* New York City, 16 Dec 1807; *d* New York City, 18 Jan 1875). Merchant. After attending public schools he worked as an apprentice in the mercantile firm of his mother's brothers, G. G. and S. Howland, and by the age of thirty was a partner in Howland and Aspinwall, the city's largest mercantile firm. He set up railroads and steamship lines in Latin America in time to profit from the traffic of miners across the Isthmus of Panama during the California gold rush and by the time of the Civil War was among the city's wealthiest men. Aspinwall supported Abraham Lincoln, formed the Union League Club, and amassed an art collection that he opened to the public; he was also a director of the Lenox Library and the Chamber of Commerce.

James E. Mooney

Aspira. Organization formed in 1961 in New York City under the direction of Antonia Pantoja and other Puerto Rican leaders. Its principal aim is to encourage young Puerto Ricans to complete high school and attend college; it also conducts research and engages in advocacy programs. In 1972 the group was represented by the Puerto Rican Legal Defense and Education Fund in a suit against the Board of Education that resulted in a consent decree requiring the board to provide transitional bilingual education programs. Aspira of America was formed in 1968, with offices in New Jersey, Pennsylvania, Illinois, and Puerto Rico as well as New York City.

Virginia Sánchez Korrol

Associated Press [AP]. News service formed in 1848 by six newspapers in New York City: the *Sun*, the *New York Herald*, the *Courier and Enquirer*, the *Journal of Commerce*, the *New York Tribune*, and the *New York Express*. The original members were joined in 1851 by the *New York Times*. The organization faced competition from the Western Associated Press (1865), which criticized it for monopolistic practices in gathering news and setting prices. An investigation in 1891 revealed that several principals of the AP had entered into a secret agreement with a rival organization, a disclosure that led to the complete reformation of the service in 1892 as a nonprofit cooperative called the Associated Press of Illinois. In 1900 the service reincorporated in New York State and took its present name, while retaining its nonprofit cooperative status.

The AP grew rapidly under the direction of Kent Cooper from 1925 to 1948, adding a photographic service in 1927 and a wirephoto network in 1935, and greatly enlarging its overseas distribution. In later years it expanded into radio (1941), television, automated picture reception (1952), and satellite transmission (in the 1980s). In the mid 1990s the Associated Press had 143 domestic bureaus and more than 230 foreign bureaus, and served more than seventeen hundred newspapers in the United States and 8500 news outlets in 110 countries abroad. Its headquarters are at 50 Rockefeller Center in Manhattan.

Shan Jayakumar

Association for Children with Retarded Mental Development. Voluntary, nonprofit, nonsectarian organization formed in 1951 as the Parents Association for Children with Retarded Mental Disabilities by Ida Rappaport, the parent of a retarded child. Its advocacy of special classes for the retarded was prompted by the tendency of the school system in New York City in the early 1950s to ignore the differences among disabilities and to emphasize maintaining order at the expense of instruction. The association also favored recreational programs for the retarded, including summer camps. In the 1970s and 1980s it added services for adults. Some services of the association are privately funded; others are provided under contract to the New York City Department of Mental Health, Mental Retardation and Alcoholism Services. The offices of the association are at 162 5th Avenue.

Sandra Opdycke

Association for Improving the Condition of the Poor. Charity organized in 1843 to morally uplift and help the deserving poor. An offshoot of the New York City Mission Society, it was led by such prominent New Yorkers as the merchant Robert Minturn. Its first general secretary, Robert M. Hartley, supervised more than three hundred upper-class men who volunteered to visit persons in need; his careful records demonstrated a relationship between mortality and filthy, crowded living conditions and became an example for scientific philanthropists in the late nineteenth century. The association constructed public BATHHOUSES in 1852, 1892 (the People's Baths), and 1904 (the Milbank Memorial Bath, donated by Elizabeth Milbank Anderson). In 1855 it sponsored the Working Men's Home for black men at 151 Elizabeth Street, considered by many the country's first model tenement, and it was an important advocate of the Metropolitan Health Act of 1866 and other sanitary reforms. After Hartley's retirement in 1876 the association no longer relied solely on upper-class men as volunteers, and in 1879 it became one of the first organizations of its kind to employ women as visitors. With the Charity Organization Society, the New York City Mission and Tract Society, and the Children's Aid Society the association in 1891 became an owner of the United Charities Building at 105 East 22nd Street, donated by John M. Kennedy. Among the other facilities that it established and supported were medical dispensaries and dental clinics, the Neponsit Beach Hospital at Rockaway Beach for nonpulmonary tuberculosis patients, summer camps for children, families, and the elderly, and Sea Breeze, a vacation home for mothers and children at Coney Island. In 1939 the Association for Improving the Condition of the Poor merged with the Charity Organization Society to form the Community Service Society.

Alana J. Erickson

Association for the Help of Retarded Children. Nonprofit, nonsectarian organization formed in 1949 in New York City by a group of parents led by Ann Greenberg, who became its first secretary. Within two years the association had held its first national convention (in Minneapolis), at which the National Association for Retarded Children was formed, had organized clinics for retarded children at Flower Fifth Avenue Hospital in Manhattan and Jewish Hospital in Brooklyn, and had begun a vigorous program of public education. The association was aided in its efforts by the passage of the Vocational Rehabilitation Act of 1954 (which allowed federal support for its workshops) and of state legislation in 1955 that acknowledged public responsibility for the costs of educating all retarded children. It sponsored scout troops from 1956, and opened its first occupational day center in 1958 and its first adult community residence, Fineson House, in a mansion on Stuyvesant Square in 1970. Thirteen of its classes for the severely handicapped were taken over in 1974 by the Board of Education. During the 1970s and 1980s private sources of support for the association were increasingly augmented by contracts from the New York City Department of Mental Health, Mental Retardation and Alcoholism Services in keeping with the growing emphasis by the state on community-based care for the retarded. In the mid 1990s the association had its headquarters at 200 Park Avenue South; it was one of the largest agencies in New York City serving the mentally retarded, with an annual budget of more than $30 million.

Sandra Opdycke

Association of American Publishers. Trade association for book publishers, formed in 1970 by the merger of the American Book Publishers Council and the American Educational Publishers Institute. In addition to informing its members on such issues as copyright and marketing, it represents the publishing business to both government and the public. The association has offices at 220 East 23rd Street in New York City, as well as in Washington.

Eileen K. Cheng

Association of Catholic Trade Unionists [ACTU]. Labor organization formed in New York City in 1937 by John Cort, Martin Wersing, and John P. Monaghan, who hoped to "make Catholic social principles an effective force for sound unionism and industrial relations." It established "labor schools" where Catholic workers studied religious and social principles, and published the *Labor Leader*, a national newspaper dedicated to Catholic social teaching and workers' rights; it also promoted the organization of unions, mediated labor disputes, supported more than three hundred strikes nationwide, and provided legal defense for striking workers. The association was closely allied with the Congress of Industrial Organizations (CIO). At its peak in 1940 there were ten thousand members drawn from many occupations; non-Catholics were welcomed as associate members and numbered ninety thousand. By the early 1940s the association had its national headquarters in New York City and twenty-four chapters nationwide. It lost support in the following years as it worked with growing intensity to eliminate the influence of communists in the CIO and other labor organizations, and by 1950 its membership declined and many chapters closed. The chapter in New York City lasted until 1973.

Douglas P. Seaton: *Catholics and Radicals: The Association of Catholic Trade Unionists and the American Labor Movement, from Depression to Cold War* (Lewisburg, Penn.: Bucknell University Press, 1981)

Edward T. O'Donnell

Association of Junior Leagues International. Voluntary women's organization formed in New York City in 1901 by Mary Averell Harriman (later Mrs. Charles Rumsey), daughter of the financier Edward H. Harriman. Initially it was called the Junior League for the Promotion of Settlement Movements and was composed of débutantes who were inspired to use their education and position to improve social conditions among the poor. As its first project the league undertook to raise funds for the College Settlement House on Rivington Street. In 1907 it became the Junior League for the Promotion of Neighborhood Work and broadened its scope to include city parks and playgrounds, public schools, and children's health. To provide housing for working girls in New York City the organization opened the Junior League House in 1911. In the mid 1990s there were 285 Junior Leagues throughout the United States, Canada, Mexico, and Great Britain. Members worked in their communities on issues ranging from substance abuse, child welfare, and domestic violence to historic preservation, urban revitalization, and the environment. The headquarters of Junior Leagues International are at 660 1st Avenue.

Anne Lyon Haight: *Banned Books* (New York: R. R. Bowker, 1935)

Marjory Potts

Association of Neighborhood Workers. Nonprofit organization formed in December 1900 by Mary Simkhovitch and John Elliott to "effect cooperation among those who are working for neighborhood and civic improvement, and to promote movements for social progress." It met regularly at neighborhood centers, which provided some financial support. The association accomplished much of its work through committees; it investigated conditions in housing, the workplace, and schools, published pamphlets, organized neighborhood groups, produced exhibitions, and promoted legislative reforms. In 1919 it incorporated as the United Neighborhood Houses at 70 5th Avenue.

Betty Boyd Caroli

Association of the Bar of the City of New York. Association organized on 1 February 1870 to protect the integrity of the legal profession in New York City. It was planned during the late 1860s by lawyers concerned about corruption and judicial malfeasance rampant in William M. "Boss" Tweed's government; a petition circulated in December 1869 was endorsed by more than two hundred lawyers by late January 1870. William Evarts was chosen as the first president on 15 February and remained in office for a decade. Most members were Protestant graduates of élite universities who worked for large firms and took an interest in national politics. The association formed law, grievance, and judiciary committees in November and soon became a model for the bar associations of Brooklyn (1872), New York State (1876), and the nation (1878). It quickly gained power through its battles with Tweed by assuming the authority to discipline members of the profession: it led efforts to establish ethical standards, and by 1884 its responsibility for policing professional conduct was recognized by the appellate division of the state supreme court, which lacked the resources to carry out the task itself. Elegant headquarters were opened on West 26th Street, and elaborate screening procedures and high fees were introduced to ensure that membership remained exclusive: all presidents into the 1920s were listed in the *Social Register.* To preserve its status as the most influential organization of its kind it resisted incorporation into the state bar association. It also led opposition to David Dudley Field's civil codification of legal precedents, preferring to rely on the traditional but arcane system of common-law precedents. Among its members were Joseph Choate and Elihu Root, who together brought about changes in the state constitution in 1894 that established the appellate division and greatly facilitated the process of review. When the association moved in 1896 to a building at 42 West 44th Street designed by Cyrus Eidlitz it had fewer than fourteen hundred members but enjoyed unparalleled influence. Its plan for international arbitration between nations was presented to the Hague Conference of 1899.

From the 1920s the association gradually broadened its interests. It was bitterly split when it condemned the state legislature for expelling five duly elected Socialists in 1920. Well-known members at this time included such national figures as Charles Evans Hughes, Henry L. Stimson, and John W. Davis. As the society's president from 1924 to 1925 Henry Taft sought to expand membership (his efforts were nullified by his successor). Another president, C. C. Burlingham, orchestrated investigations of municipal corruption in 1929 that led to the resignation of Mayor James J. Walker in 1932. The organization first admitted women in 1937. Under Harrison Tweed (1945–48) it established the position of executive secretary and began publishing the *Record.* In later years it led the fight against the Bricker Amendment from 1953 to 1956 (which would have empowered Congress "to regulate all Executive and other agreements with any foreign power or international organization"), opposed the American Bar Association by denouncing federal loyalty oaths, and in 1954–55 published reports that led to the New York State Court Reorganization Act of 1962. It also appointed more Jewish lawyers to important committees than previously and in 1956 elected its first Jewish president, Louis Loeb. During the 1960s the number of members increased after many requirements for membership were dropped and the association became more active in social concerns: it defended the Civil Rights Acts (1964–65), supported the civil rights efforts of Martin Luther King Jr., and sent twelve hundred lawyers to Washington to protest intervention in Cambodia (1969). From the 1970s some positions on the board were reserved for women and members of ethnic and racial minorities. The association ceded authority for disciplining lawyers in 1980 but continued to press for high professional standards, efficiency in the courts, and increasing the number of elective judgeships; it also revised mental health and divorce laws in New York State, endorsed legal services for the poor, encouraged lawyers to work pro bono for charities, and set up committees on the environment, sex and law, and consumer affairs. In 1987 it opposed the nomination of Robert H. Bork to the U.S. Supreme Court, and in 1990 the first black president, Conrad K. Harper, took office. About a third of the city's lawyers were members in 1992. The Association of the Bar of the City of New York maintains a reference library of some 450,000 volumes.

George J. Lankevich

Astaire [Austerlitz], **Fred(erick)** (*b* Omaha, Neb., 10 May 1899; *d* Los Angeles, 22 June 1987). Dancer. With his sister Adele (*b* 18 Sept 1896; *d* 25 Jan 1981) he made his début as a child in a vaudeville act staged by Ned Wayburn; as a pair the two became well known on Broadway for dancing in such musicals as *Over the Top* (1917), *Lady, Be Good* (1924), *Funny Face* (1927), and *The Band Wagon* (1931), performed in London, and in 1919 lived at the Hotel Majestic at 115 Central Park West. After Adele's retirement in 1932 he became known internationally in the theater, in musical films in which he appeared with Ginger Rogers, and on television. Astaire is widely considered the most accomplished and innovative dancer in the musical theater. He wrote *Steps in Time* (1959).

Arlene Croce: *The Fred Astaire and Ginger Rogers Book* (New York: Outerbridge and Lazard, 1972)
John E. Mueller: *Astaire Dancing: The Musical Films* (New York: Alfred A. Knopf, 1985)

Barbara Cohen-Stratyner

Astor [née Russell], **(Roberta) Brooke** (*b* Portsmouth, N.H., 1902). Philanthropist. As a child she lived in Beijing and Shanghai before attending the Miss Madeira School near Washington. After moving to New York City she studied creative writing at Columbia University, ran a writing workshop in her home at 1 Gracie Square, and worked as a feature editor for *House and Garden.* In the 1950s she married Vincent Astor, whom she assisted in philanthropic pursuits, and on his death in 1959 she devoted herself largely to the work of the Vincent Astor Foundation. In this capacity she oversaw the donation of nearly $200 million in grants by the mid 1990s, benefiting the city's cultural and educational organizations, notably the New York Public Library, as well as projects for the poor and the disadvantaged. Astor's published writings include *Patchwork Child* (1962) and *Footprints* (1980).

Chad Ludington

Astor [née Schermerhorn], **Caroline (Webster)** (*b* New York City, 22 Sept 1830; *d* New York City, 3 Oct 1908). Society figure. She was born into an established family and was educated in New York City and in France. Determined to lead the city's élite, she married William Astor and with Ward McAllister chose a group known as the "four hundred," named for the number of guests who could be accommodated in her ballroom; her dinner parties, balls, and musicales became well known. After McAllister's death she chose Harry Lehr, a much more flamboyant figure, as his successor. In 1894 she had a mansion built at 5th Avenue and 65th Street, where she remained until the end of her life.

James E. Mooney

Astor, John Jacob (*b* Waldorf, Germany, 17 July 1763; *d* New York City, 29 March 1848). Entrepreneur. He began his career as a fur trader in the Pacific Northwest and in March 1784 arrived in New York City, where he lived at what are now 362 Pearl Street (1785–90) and 149 Broadway (1794–1803). In the following years he amassed a real-estate empire that included buildings and parcels of land in Manhattan acquired from 1810. Unlike most real-estate investors he did not engage in short-term speculation or develop property for sale: instead he bought land at low prices and waited for the market to change and for urban growth to drive up the value of his properties. While waiting for these long-term increases he collected a large income in rents from his extensive commercial and residential holdings, seldom investing in improvements; he generally sold only if he needed money to buy more property and occasionally when values were increasing quickly. After selling his fur business in 1834 he focused solely on real estate in Manhattan, particularly in what is now midtown. For a time he lived at 223 Broadway in a building that became the Astor House Hotel in 1836 (demolished 1913) and later at 585 Broadway; he also had a summer home known as "Astoria" or "Hell Gate Farm" at what is now East 87th Street between York and East End avenues. During the panic of 1837 he bought many distressed properties and foreclosed on hundreds of others for which he held or obtained mortgages. By 1840 he was the country's wealthiest man and one of the city's best-known businessmen, owning an estate worth more than $20 million; his urban properties were estimated to have increased ten times in value from the time he purchased them. Shortly before his death he declared: "Could I begin life again, knowing what I now know, and had money to invest, I would buy every foot of land on the island of Manhattan."

Astor's vast empire was managed by his heirs and descendants into the twentieth century. A great-grandson, William Waldorf Astor, built luxury hotels and apartment buildings in Manhattan during the 1890s, including the Waldorf Hotel, erected on the site of the family's mansions at 5th Avenue and 34th Street and later merged with the Astoria Hotel (owned by John Jacob Astor IV) to form the Waldorf–Astoria. Astor's great-great-grandson Vincent Astor worked from 1942 with the developer William Zeckendorf to increase the value and returns of the family's holdings, which declined after the Second World War in a changing market.

Marc A. Weiss

Astor House. A five-story hotel on the west side of Broadway between Barclay and Vesey streets. Designed by Isaiah Rogers in the Greek Revival style for John Jacob Astor and erected in 1834–36, it was the first luxury hotel in New York City. There were many fine public rooms and more than three hundred guest rooms, and running water was pumped by steam even to the upper stories before the Croton water system opened in 1842. For several decades the hotel was an internationally renowned meeting place for prominent statesmen and literary figures; it was the site of an impromptu speech by President-elect Lincoln on 19 February 1861. In its later years newer uptown hotels surpassed its services, and in 1913 the Astor House closed to make way for construction of the subway system.

May N. Stone

Astor House, 1899

Astoria. Neighborhood in northwestern Queens (1986 pop. 151,497), constituting the part of Long Island City north of Broadway. It was developed from 1839 by Stephen A. Halsey, a fur merchant who petitioned the state legislature to name it for the prominent fur trader John Jacob Astor. During the 1840s and 1850s it grew slowly inland from the ferry landing at the foot of Astoria Boulevard (where an early settlement was known as Hallett's Cove). Wealthy New Yorkers built mansions on 12th and 14th streets and on 27th Avenue. The German United Cabinet Workers bought four farms in 1869 between 35th and 50th streets and developed a German town. In the following year Schuetzen Park was laid out at Broadway and Steinway Street (this remained a landmark for half a century) and a large tract on both sides of Steinway Street from Astoria Boulevard to the East River was bought by the piano maker William Steinway, who set up factories along the shore and a village to their south. On 4 May of the same year Astoria, Hunter's Point, Steinway, and Ravenswood consolidated to form Long Island City. Treacherous reefs in Hell Gate were dynamited in 1876 and 1885 at the behest of the federal government. Thousands of houses were built during the 1890s and the early twentieth century. The shore of the East River became a park in 1913, and the first rapid transit line, the Astoria elevated, opened on 31st Street on 1 February 1917. Many six-family apartment buildings and housing projects were added during the 1920s and 1930s. The Kaufman Astoria Studios, where Rudolph Valentino, the Marx Brothers, and Paul Robeson made films, were later used by the government for making training and propaganda films. Abandoned in 1971, the studios were eventually restored for television and motion picture production. One of the buildings in the area now houses the Museum of the Moving Image.

The Independent subway extended service along Steinway Street and Broadway on 19 August 1933, and new connections to Manhattan and the Bronx were provided by the Triborough Bridge, which opened on 11 July 1936.

After the Second World War Astoria was largely Italian. Greeks rapidly increased in number after 1965: one third of all Greeks who moved to New York City in the 1980s settled in the neighborhood, and by the mid 1990s they accounted for slightly less than half its population. St. Demetrious, one of eleven Greek Orthodox churches in the area, is probably the largest outside Greece. Greek immigrants who settled in the neighborhood received aid from the Hellenic Americans Neighborhood Action Committee, a locally based social services agency. Other ethnic groups also established communities in the area, including Colombians, Chinese, Guyanese, and Koreans, and to a lesser extent Ecuadorians, Romanians, Indians, Filipinos, and Dominicans.

Vincent Seyfried

Astoria Federal Savings and Loan Association. Thrift institution, formed in 1888 as the Central Permanent Building and Loan Association by residents of Long Island City. Soon one of the chief lenders of home mortgages in Queens, in 1937 it adopted its current name and built headquarters at 37-16 30th Avenue in Long Island City. It opened branches in Ditmars, Forest Hills, and Flushing from the late 1950s, merged with the Metropolitan Federal Savings and Loan of Middle Village (1973), and bought Citizens Savings and Loan of Woodside (1979) and the Whitestone Savings and Loan (1990). The firm's headquarters were moved in 1989 to Bulova Corporate Center in Jackson Heights. In 1991 the Astoria Federal Savings and Loan Association had thirteen branches and assets of more than $3000 million and was the sixth-largest thrift institution in New York City.

James Bradley

Astoria Studio. Motion picture studio opened in 1920 by the Famous Players–Lasky Corporation at 35th Avenue between 34th and 37th streets in Astoria, just across the East River from the company's headquarters in Manhattan. Between 1921 and the time the company became known as Paramount in 1927 about one quarter of its films were made there (the rest were made in Hollywood). Adapted for the production of motion pictures with sound by Western Electric in 1929, the facility was renamed Eastern Studios Inc. The proximity of the studio to Broadway was of benefit to Paramount, which produced such films there as the musical *Heads Up* (1930), by Richard Rodgers and Lorenz Hart. The production of feature films diminished during the mid 1930s and virtually ceased by 1937, though the studio continued to be used for short subjects, "second-unit" work for films made in Hollywood, and Paramount News. In 1942 the U.S. Army took control of the studio, which it renamed the Signal Corps Photographic Center, and began producing and editing wartime films (*A World at War*, 1943; *Autobiography of a Jeep*, 1943); the army continued to use the studio to produce educational and training films until the 1960s. In 1975 the studio reopened for the production of commercial feature films: among the many films made there in the following years were Sidney Lumet's *The Wiz* (1977), Bob Fosse's *All That Jazz* (1979), and Woody Allen's *Radio Days* (1987). In 1988 the studio became the site of the Museum of the Moving Image, while continuing its commercial operations.

Richard Koszarski: *The Astoria Studio and Its Fabulous Films* (New York: Dover, 1983)
Marc Wanamaker: *Encyclopedia of Movie Studios* (forthcoming)

Charles Musser

Astor Place. Neighborhood on the East Side of Manhattan, bounded to the north by 8th Street, to the east by 3rd Avenue, to the south by 4th Street, and to the west by Broadway. On 10 May 1849 the Astor Place Riot broke out at the Astor Place Opera House on a site now occupied by the District 65 Building (1890, George E. Harney), which houses the district offices of the United Auto Workers. For a brief period before the Civil War some of the city's wealthiest families lived there, including the Astors, the Vanderbilts, and the Delanos. By the 1860s manufacturing and warehousing concerns moved into the neighborhood, which fell into disrepair after the turn of the century. It was revitalized in the 1960s and 1970s as a shopping district catering largely to students, and Broadway and 4th Street became lined with shops selling clothes, records, books, and novelties. Notable buildings in the neighborhood include the Astor Place Building at 444 Lafayette Street (1876, Griffith Thomas), an attractive structure of brick and painted cast iron; and 428–34 Lafayette Street, which is all that remains of a once-elegant row of buildings known as Colonnade Row (1833). The Public Theatre, in a building that once housed the Astor Library and from 1921 to 1965 was the headquarters of the Hebrew Immigrant Aid Society, is where the producer Joseph Papp first staged the musicals *Hair* and *A Chorus Line*; it is now a complex of seven performance spaces for plays, concerts, films, and readings, and also houses the headquarters of the New York Shakespeare Festival. A subway station at the corner of 8th and Lafayette streets, restored in 1986, has a cast-iron replica of the original kiosk and bas-relief ceramic plaques depicting beavers, an allusion to the fur trade in which John Jacob Astor made his first fortune. Balanced en point between Lafayette Street and 4th Avenue is Bernard Rosenthal's steel cube *Alamo* (1967). The magnificent Cooper Union Foundation Building (1859) dominates Astor Place between 3rd and 4th avenues.

WPAG

Linda Elsroad

Astor Place Riot. Violence that occurred from 10 to 11 May 1849 at the Astor Place Opera House, triggered by a feud between the English actor William C. Macready and the American actor Edwin Forrest. See Riots.

Astral Apartments. Housing project at 184 Franklin Street between Java and India streets in Greenpoint, Brooklyn, built in 1886 for kerosene refinery workers at Charles Pratt's Astral Oil Company nearby. A Queen Anne structure a block long with many entrances, it became known for its many progressive features. Each of its rooms was light and airy, and there was a settlement house, library, and kindergarten on the premises. Although slightly the worse for wear by the 1990s, the Astral Apartments remained a monument to the hopes of nineteenth-century housing reformers.

Kenneth T. Jackson

AT&T. See American telephone and telegraph.

atheists and freethinkers. Atheism and free thought have never gained a large following in the United States, but many adherents have been attracted to the intellectually tolerant environment of New York City. The earliest movement in free thought and one of the most important was deism, which took hold soon after American independence among élites influenced by the Enlightenment. Many deists asserted that a nonpersonal deity was part of the moral order of the universe; they included such critics and innovators as Benjamin Franklin and Thomas Jefferson. Deism also attracted more radical thinkers, including Thomas Paine, author of *The Age of Reason*; after returning to the United States from Europe in 1802 he spent much time in Greenwich Village and settled there in 1806 at Herring (now Bleecker) Street. Elihu Palmer (1764–1806), one of his lesser-known admirers, established the Deistical Society of New York, hoping to replace conventional churches; his materialist philosophy failed to attract followers, and the society was disbanded. During the presidency of Andrew Jackson a new type of free thought arose that was influenced by agnostics from the British Isles, among them the utopian communalists Robert Owen (1771–1858) and Frances Wright (1795–1858), who moved to New York City in 1824 after a brief visit in 1818. She and Owen's son, Robert Dale Owen (1801–77), lectured in the city and introduced their journal the *Free Inquirer* there in 1829; it antagonized believers without winning adherents and ceased publication in 1835.

In the late nineteenth century the religion of liberal churches annd synagogues no longer satisfied the moralists who had earlier gravitated toward them. One result of this dissatisfaction was the formation in 1876 of the New York Society for Ethical Culture by Felix Adler, a Reform rabbi who was troubled by prayer and ritual and argued that historic Judaism and Christianity stood in the way of human good. The members of the movement emphasized education, moral discourse, and social reform; they sought to transcend the conventions and fetters of piety but eschewed the militant antireligiosity of the Deistical Society of New York and the *Free Inquirer*.

By the twentieth century there were some enclaves of atheism on the Lower East Side in communities of secularized Jews active in the labor movement, but most efforts at organizing movements for free thought and atheism were abandoned as futile: skeptical expression proved too individualized to allow for organization. Although philosophers like Sidney Hook criticized religion and were respected, groups like the American Association for the Advancement of Atheism, formed in the city in 1925, attracted only a few thousand members and had a brief influence. In the late twentieth century free thought and atheism continued in the city but tended to remain unorganized.

Gordon Stein, ed.: *Encyclopedia of Unbelief* (Buffalo: Prometheus, 1985)

Martin E. Marty

Atlantic Mutual Insurance Company. Firm of insurers. Chartered by the state legislature on 11 April 1842, it opened offices at the corner of Wall and William streets and took over the business of a former marine insurer, Atlantic Insurance, a stock company established in 1824. The appeal of the reorganized firm to shipowners and merchants seeking a share of the profits from marine insurance lay in its structure as a mutual firm (owned by policyholders rather than stockholders). A reinsurance agreement with the Insurance Company of North America enabled it to provide larger amounts of insurance for single ships. Under the leadership of Walter Restored Jones, Atlantic Mutual prospered while American clipper ships were in demand: it was the only major American mutual marine insurer to survive the intense competition from British companies at the end of the nineteenth century. Even as the market for marine insurance was declining, the firm expanded by organizing subsidiaries in 1931 to provide fire and casualty insurance. Except during the disastrous year of 1854 it paid a dividend every year for a century and a half. The firm in 1992 had assets of $1500 million, making it one of the largest insurers in the United States, and maintained its home office at 45 Wall Street near its original site.

John N. Cosgrove: *Gray Days and Gold: A Character Sketch of Atlantic Mutual Insurance Company* (New York: Atlantic Companies, 1967)

Robert J. Gibbons

Atterbury, Grosvenor (*b* Detroit, 7 July 1869; *d* Southampton, N.Y., 18 Oct 1956). Architect and planner. He grew up in New York City and after graduating from Yale University studied architecture at Columbia University; he later joined the firm of McKim, Mead and White and received a patent for prefabricated construction materials. Some of his first commissions were for country houses and townhouses of family and friends, followed by model tenements on East 31st Street and Forest Hills Gardens in Queens, a development of prefabricated houses that became a model for garden suburbs. He also helped to design City Hall, a building for the Russell Sage Foundation at Lexington and 22nd Street, the American Wing of the Metropolitan Museum of Art, and the Amsterdam Houses. Atterbury formed the National Housing Association and the National City Planning Institute and was president of the Architectural League of New York.

James E. Mooney

Auburndale. Neighborhood in north central Queens. It was laid out in 1901 by the New England Development and Improvement Company on ninety acres (thirty-six hectares) of farmland previously owned by Thomas Willet and bounded to the north by Crocheron Avenue, to the east by Auburndale Lane, to the south by Northern Boulevard, and to the west by Clearview Expressway. A railroad station was opened in May. The name is derived from that of Auburn, Massachusetts, home town of the president of the company. In the mid 1990s Auburndale was a residential suburb known for its fine homes and well-kept streets.

Vincent Seyfried

Auchincloss, Louis (Stanton) (*b* Lawrence, N.Y., 27 Sept 1917). Writer and lawyer. He grew up in New York City, attended Yale University and the University of Virginia Law School, joined the law firm of Sullivan and Cromwell, and from 1954 until his retirement in 1987 practiced law at the firm of Hawkins, Delafield and Wood. While working as a lawyer he wrote a dozen novels, collections of short stories, and several works of nonfiction. Auchincloss is often regarded as a novelist of manners in the tradition of Henry James and Edith Wharton. His best-known works include *The House of Five Talents* (1960), *The Embezzler* (1966), *The Rector of Justin* (1964), *The House of the Prophet* (1980), a biography of Wharton, and an autobiography, *A Writer's Capital* (1974).

B. Kimberly Taylor

auction system. The auction system of sales dates to the early years of colonial rule, with the first regulatory laws enacted in 1676. The state in 1784 passed a tax of 2½ percent on goods sold at auction. In 1801 the law allowed for twenty-four auctions licenses, a number increased to thirty-six in 1813. Yet auction sales amounted to little until the Jeffersonian Embargo of 1807 and the British blockade during the War of 1812 created the conditions for the vast expansion of auction sales. Denied access to their largest foreign market for almost a decade, British manufacturers were eager to rid themselves of excess inventories, and at the same time Americans were eager for British imports. Auctions allowed British manufacturers to reduce inventories and quickly reestablish their market dominance. Manufacturers' agents based in New York City sold directly to auction houses and offered long credit periods of twelve to eighteen months. In 1817 the city consolidated its dominance of the auction trade by passing laws lowering the tax on auction sales and requiring that all goods put up for auction be sold regardless of the price offered. Opportunities for bargains drew rural retailers and (more importantly) local jobbers who assembled various goods into packages for rural retailers while offering one-year credits. In turn the auction houses made the most of their money by offering six and eight months' credit, called *del credere*, to the large jobbers and shorter credits to rural retailers. The dominance of auction sales was felt in the 1820s when $160 million passed through such important auction houses as John Hone and Sons; Hicks, Lawrence, and Company; and Haggerty and Austin. This figure accounted for 44 percent of the city's imports and a fifth of the nation's.

At first auctions outraged traditional merchants. Having bought quantities of goods in the months immediately following the peace of 1815, merchants were caught with inventories at high and inflexible prices in a quickly glutted market. The dominance of auctioneers produced a futile political backlash among regular merchants, who mounted an unsuccessful slate of candidates in the elections of 1828. The merchants' economic response proved more successful. After 1830 American merchants began sending representatives to Europe, and by offering immediate cash sales to manufacturers they regained control over the import trade. Specializing in one line of business and buying in quantity allowed for more competitive pricing.

After peaking in the late 1820s auction sales stagnated during the 1830s at about $160 million for the decade. This figure, the same as that for the preceding decade, now represented less than 20 percent of the city's vastly expanded trade. Ultimately auction sales were destroyed by the credit crunch of 1836–37 and the subsequent depression: because of their low selling prices, auctioneers' profits accrued from the credit they offered their customers, and they suffered when credit dried up after 1836. Despite its brief history the auction system radically transformed the ways goods were sold throughout the United States.

Robert G. Albion: *The Rise of New York Port, 1815–1860* (New York: 1939)
Ira Cohen: "The Auction System in New York, 1817–1837" (diss., New York University, 1969)

James Ciment

Auden, W(ystan) H(ugh) (*b* York, England, 21 Feb 1907; *d* Vienna, 28 Sept 1973). Poet and novelist. He grew up and was educated in England, where he became well known as a writer before moving to New York City in 1939. During the Second World War he abandoned Marxism and became an Anglican. He lived at 7 Cornelia Street from about 1945 until 1953, when he moved to quarters at 77 St. Mark's Place, remaining there until April 1972. His novel *The Age of Anxiety* (1947), set in a bar and an apartment in the city, won the Pulitzer Prize. Auden also wrote librettos for operas including Igor Stravinsky's *The Rake's Progress* (1951), edited collections of poetry, and taught at Oxford University and a number of colleges in the city.

James E. Mooney

Audrey Cohen College. Private, independent college at 345 Hudson Street in Manhattan, opened in 1964 as the College for Human Services by Audrey C. Cohen, a graduate of the University of Pittsburgh. The college aims to bridge the gap between theoretical and practical education by requiring students to complete a "constructive action" project. With the city's Board of Education in 1983 it developed the College for Human Services Junior High School at Public School 121 (232 East 103rd Street), and by the mid 1990s it had formed similar arrangements with seven public secondary schools in New York City and four others throughout the United States. The college began awarding a master's degree in business administration in 1988. In 1991 thirteen full-time faculty members and several adjuncts taught about eighteen hundred students; the current name dates to 1993. In addition to the main campus there are extension sites in Staten Island and the Bronx.

Marc Ferris

Audubon, John J(ames) (*b* Les Cayes [now in Haiti], 26 April 1785; *d* New York City, 27 Jan 1851). Artist and ornithologist. He worked as an apprentice clerk in New York City in the winter of 1806–7 and practiced taxidermy for Samuel Latham Mitchill. During 1808–26 he engaged in the study of birds, working in various capacities around the United States, and in 1824 he became a member of the Lyceum of Natural History. In 1826 he traveled to England, where he found a publisher for *Birds of America*, a series of his watercolors engraved by Robert Havell Jr.; the series was published in installments between 1827 and 1838 in London, where he sought subscribers and exhibited the original watercolors for the prints in 1839. He settled with his family at 86 White Street in New York City in 1836. The mayor granted him permission in 1841 to shoot rats on the Battery at dawn in order to obtain specimens for the illustration of his *Viviparous Quadrupeds of North America* (1845–48). In the early 1840s he bought a parcel of twenty-four acres (ten hectares) overlooking the Hudson River near what is now 155th Street and Audubon Terrace; he built a mansion there and named the estate Minnie's Land after his wife. He died at Minnie's Land and was buried in Trinity Cemetery. In 1863 the New-York Historical Society purchased from his widow 430 of the 433 original watercolors in *Birds of America* for $4000.

Alice Ford: *John James Audubon* (Norman: University of Oklahoma Press, 1964; rev. New York: Abbeville, 1988)

Susan M. Sivard

Audubon Park. An obsolete name for a hilly plot of land in northern Manhattan, bounded to the north by 156th Street, to the east by Amsterdam Avenue, to the south by 153rd Street, and to the west by the Hudson River. It was the site in 1776 of the Battle of Washington Heights. In 1841 the land was acquired by John J. Audubon, who named it Minnie's Land and built his estate there. In the following year he sold a parcel of twenty-three acres (nine hectares) to Richard F. Carmen; in 1843 this became Trinity Cemetery, where Audubon is buried under a runic cross sixteen feet (five meters) tall. Much of the rest of the land is occupied by the five museums and institutions of Audubon Terrace.

George Bird Grinnell: *Audubon Park: The History of the Site* (New York: Trustees of Audubon Park, 1927)

Rachel Shor

John J. Audubon, American Avocet *(1821)*

Audubon Terrace. Complex on Broadway between 155th and 156th streets, built as an educational and cultural center primarily for students and scholars by Archer Milton Huntington (1870–1955), a railroad magnate, philanthropist, and devotee of Hispanic culture. In 1904 Huntington bought sections of Audubon Park, the former estate and game preserve of the naturalist John James Audubon, and formed the Hispanic Society of America, dedicated primarily to establishing a free public museum and library for the study of Hispanic culture. The nucleus of its holdings consisted of books, paintings, sculptures, architectural fragments, and examples of the decorative arts that he had collected from the Iberian peninsula. The Italianate headquarters of the society were designed by his cousin Charles Pratt Huntington and opened in 1908. Anna Hyatt Huntington, the founder's wife, produced the equestrian statue of El Cid in the courtyard, the lions flanking the doorway of the society, and the bas-reliefs of Don Quixote and Boabdil in its library. During the next few decades Charles Pratt Huntington designed most of the rest of the complex, including the buildings for the American Numismatic Society (built 1906–7), the Church of Our Lady of Esperanza (1909–11, the second Spanish Roman Catholic Church in New York City), the American Geographical Society (1909–11), and the Museum of the American Indian (1916–22). Those for the American Academy of Arts and Letters and the National Institute of Art and Letters (1921–30) were designed in an Italian Renaissance Revival style by William Mitchell Kendall (of McKim, Mead and White) and Cass Gilbert. As the surrounding neighborhood changed, the institutions of Audubon Terrace attracted fewer patrons. The collections of the Museum of the American Indian were eventually taken over by the Smithsonian Institution.

Ella M. Foshay

Audubon Theatre and Ballroom. Building formerly at Broadway and West 165th Street containing a movie theater (seating 2368), offices, and a ballroom on the second story; it was designed by Thomas W. Lamb and built in 1912 by William Fox. One of the first theaters in Fox's chain, it became known for its polychrome terra-cotta façade on Broadway, adorned with a line of three-dimensional fox heads. In February 1965 the ballroom was the site of a rally by the Organization of Afro-American Unity during which Malcolm X was assassinated. The building was later bought by the city and allowed to deteriorate. Plans to demolish it and build a research center were announced by Columbia–Presbyterian Medical Center during the late 1980s and met with opposition from preservation groups; lawsuits to prevent the demolition were unsuccessful. Portions of the façade and ballroom were incorporated into the new complex, Audubon Research Park.

For illustration see LAMB, THOMAS W.

Eric Wm. Allison

Austen, (Elizabeth) Alice (*b* Staten Island, 17 March 1866; *d* Staten Island, 9 June 1952). Photographer. Born to a middle-class family, she learned techniques of photographic processing at an early age. She depicted the life of the middle class in the 1890s by photographing objects and buildings, as well as everyday events and unusual pastimes in her circle of friends; she also photographed scenes in Manhattan, including many that captured the animation and vitality of street

Alice Austen photographing speed trials, ca *1910* (right *Gertrude Tate)*

life. Her photographs of immigrants and street vendors, such as *Hester Street: Egg Stand* (18 April 1895), were taken solely for her own interest and pleasure. Although emotionally more distant than the work of her contemporaries Jacob A. Riis and Lewis Hine, her photographs are elegantly composed and display a fine technique. In her later years Austen supported herself with income from an inheritance, the value of which had been drastically reduced by the stock market crash of 1929. Just before her death her work was acquired by the Staten Island Historical Society. Clear Comfort, her home on bluffs overlooking New York Bay, was preserved as a landmark.

Ann Novotny: *Alice's World: The Life and Photography of an American Original, Alice Austen, 1866–1952* (Old Greenwich, Conn.: Chatham, 1976)

See also Photography. For further illustrations see Buses, Grymes hill, Lower east side, Newsboys, and Taxicabs.

Naomi Rosenblum

automats. Self-service restaurants operated by the Horn and Hardart Company of Philadelphia; the first in New York City opened at 1557 Broadway in Times Square on 2 July 1912. Initially automats offered only buns, beans, fish cakes, and coffee (widely considered the best in the city). Each item cost five cents, was displayed in a compartment behind a glass door, and was bought by dropping a nickel into a slot. By the early 1930s the automats introduced a full range of lunch and dinner entrees. Soon a symbol of life in the city, automats reached the height of their popularity during the 1940s and 1950s, when more than fifty automats in the city served more than 350,000 customers a day. In 1952 Horn and Hardart raised the price of coffee to ten cents, news met with grief by New Yorkers who regarded the nickel coffee of the automats as one of life's great certainties. After fast-food restaurants opened in the early 1970s automats declined in popularity; during the 1970s and 1980s Horn and Hardart replaced many automats with Burger King restaurants. The last automat in the city stood at 42nd Street and 3rd Avenue and closed on 8 April 1991.

Jack Alexander: "The Restaurants That Nickels Built," *Saturday Evening Post,* Dec 1954

James Bradley

automobile racing. New York City and its environs were a leading center of automobile racing from the early years of the sport in the 1890s until about 1919. In 1896 the second automobile race ever run in the United States, the Cosmopolitan Race, covered thirty miles (forty-eight kilometers) through the streets from Kingsbridge to Irvington-on-Hudson north of the city. Races on Long Island for the Vanderbilt Cup (1904–10), sponsored by William K. Vanderbilt, attracted many New Yorkers. At this time there developed a national fad for twenty-four-hour races, the principal venue for which was Brighton Beach (1907–10); other such races were held in Morris Park. The Sheepshead Bay Speedway opened with great fanfare in 1915 and quickly became one of the most popular tracks in the country. Its best-known events were the Harkness Trophy (named for the track's owner Harry S. Harkness) and the Astor Cup. The speedway attracted some of the most prominent figures in international racing until the personal and financial problems of the Harkness family led to its closing in 1919 and its demolition soon after. From the mid 1930s to the mid 1940s "midget races" between small race cars with small engines were highly popular in the city. Races were held in various stadiums; during the winter they were held indoors at such venues as the 105th Field

Berenice Abbott, Automat *(*ca *1935)*

Automobile Racing Sites in New York City

Morris Park (Bronx), from 1907
Brighton Beach (Brooklyn), 1907–10
Sheepshead Bay Speedway (Brooklyn), 1915–19
Dongan Hill Fairgrounds (Staten Island), 1927–28
Maspeth Fairgrounds (Queens), 1927–28
Cross Bay International Speedway (Queens), 1931–39
Holmes Airport Speedway (Queens), 1933–34
Bronx Coliseum (Bronx), 1935–42
Madison Square Garden Bowl (Manhattan), 1936
105th Field Artillery Regiment Armory (Bronx), 1936
106th Regiment Armory (Bronx), 1938
Bay Ridge Oval (Brooklyn), 1938–39
Farmer's Oval Speedway (Queens), 1938–39
Castle Hill Speedway (Queens), 1938–42
Coney Island Velodrome (Brooklyn), 1939–40
Flushing Meadow Park (Queens), 1939–40
Thompson Stadium (Staten Island), 1939–48
Juniper Valley Park (Queens), 1930s to 1940s
Polo Grounds (Manhattan), 1940–59
Kingsbridge Armory Speedrome (Bronx), 1946–52
Dexter Park (Queens), 1951–55
Weissglass Stadium (Staten Island), 1953–72
Madison Square Garden (Manhattan), 1971

Artillery Regiment Armory on Franklin Avenue and 106th Street in the Bronx (1936) and the 106th Regiment Armory at Bedford and Atlantic avenues, also in the Bronx (1938). Bill Shindler was the best-known racer in the city in the heyday of midget racing. In 1940 the World's Fair Grand Prix, staged at the Flushing Meadows Fairgrounds, attracted internationally known drivers. Le Chanteclair (1953–79), a restaurant at 18 East 49th Street, was a gathering place in the city for those connected with racing. Owned by the French racer René Dreyfus and his brother, it was decorated with an auto racing motif. In 1985 a promoter sought to build a racecourse in Flushing Meadows–Corona Park and reintroduce automobile racing in the city on a large scale; although the plan had the backing of both Mayor Edward I. Koch and the borough president of Queens, Donald Manes, it was blocked by strong civic opposition. A number of prominent racing drivers were born in New York City or at one time lived there, including David Bruce Brown, Peter Revson, Joel Thorne, and Ira Vail. Danny Sullivan, winner of the Indianapolis 500 in 1985, drove a taxicab in New York City in the early 1970s.

Peter Helck: *Great Auto Races* (New York: Harry N. Abrams, 1975)

Joseph S. Lieber

automobiles. During the first decade of the twentieth century automobiles were manufactured by thousands of firms throughout the United States and especially in New England, many of which had developed from the carriage and machine industries. New York City was a center for the manufacture of steam and electrically powered vehicles for both passenger and freight transport. In 1900 six factories that together employed nearly five hundred persons manufactured automobiles in the city. The largest producer of electric cars, the Electric Vehicle Company, made cars in factories outside the city limits but was owned by financiers on Wall Street. In 1899 the firm launched a fleet of taxicabs in several major cities, and several hundred ran on the streets of New York City. By 1916 the internal combustion engine had proved itself more powerful, reliable, and cost-effective than its competitors, and the automobile industry shifted to the Midwest, the center for the development of gasoline-powered automobiles that ran on internal combustion engines.

Joanne Abel Goldman

Avedon, Richard (*b* New York City, 15 May 1923). Photographer. After studying at Columbia University (1941–42) and serving in the U.S. Marine Corps (1942–44) he joined *Jr. Bazaar* in 1945, later moving to *Harper's Bazaar*. During these years he worked principally as a fashion photographer. From 1966 his photographs appeared in such varied publications as *Vogue* and *Rolling Stone*. Over the years his work covered a wide range, from portraits to journalistic photographs of the civil rights and antiwar movements. Published collections of Avedon's photographs include *Observations* (1959), *Nothing Personal* (1964), *Portraits* (1976), *Avedon Photographs: 1947–1977* (1978), *In the American West* (1985), and *Evidence, 1944–1994* (1994). His work is also held in the permanent collections of the Metropolitan Museum of Art, the Smithsonian Institution, and the Victoria and Albert Museum. He was the visual consultant for the film version of George Gershwin's musical *Funny Face* (1956).

Shan Jayakumar

aviation. The first "aeronaut" born in the United States, Charles Durant of Jersey City, New Jersey, made a balloon flight on 9 September 1830 of thirty miles (forty-eight kilometers) commencing at Castle Garden before more than thirty thousand spectators. Similar exploits remained popular with New Yorkers throughout the nineteenth century: the first major attempt of the nineteenth century to fly across the Atlantic began at Brooklyn in 1873.

James Gordon Bennett Jr., publisher of the *New York Herald*, in 1906 sponsored the first international aviation races, which were staged in New York City in the following year. By 1910, when the city had more than a dozen firms catering to flyers, the world's largest air meet to date was held at Belmont Park, just outside the city limits. European and American aviators raced inside the park, then ended the meet with a dash across New York City, around the Statue of Liberty, and back to Belmont. Among several bankers who played an important role in promoting aviation in its early days were August Belmont and Cornelius Vanderbilt, who financed the manufacture of the Wright brothers' airplanes after 1909. The first transatlantic flight was launched in 1919 from Rockaway Naval Air Station (later Jacob Riis Park). In New York City as elsewhere one of the first practical uses to which the airplane was put was the delivery of mail. From 1918 the U.S. Army Air Corps delivered mail destined for the city to Belmont Park, but this arrangement proved unsatisfactory. Newark Airport in New Jersey was designated the airmail terminus for the city by the U.S. Post Office after the Kelly Act (1925) allowed the letting of contracts with private carriers.

Colonial Airways established the first regular flights from the metropolitan region on 18 June 1926, with service to Boston. The manufacture of airplanes and related equipment became an important local industry in which thirty-four firms in the city and in nearby communities on Long Island were engaged in 1929, including Curtiss–Wright Aviation Company, Curtiss Airports Corporation, Fairchild Aviation Corporation, and Sikorsky Aircraft; Wright engines were manufactured in Paterson, New Jersey. The New York, Rio, and Buenos Aires line, based in Manhattan and led by Ralph O'Neill, began international seaplane service in 1930. With the connivance of the post office this line was taken over in 1930 by Pan American Airlines, based in Port Washington, Long Island, and led by Juan Trippe. Pan American also used seaplanes, which at the time were both larger and easier to fly into the city than land planes. Daniel Guggenheim's Fund for the Promotion of Aviation sponsored important innovations in the late 1920s and 1930s and in 1929 helped to form the first modern airline in the nation (Western).

By this time it was apparent that the city needed to build a new airport or expand an existing one. Roosevelt Field, the starting point for Charles Lindbergh's transatlantic flight in 1927, was considered too remote from the city's post office, and Mayor James J. Walker believed that there was insufficient space for expansion at Holmes Field (in Jackson Heights) and Glenn H. Curtiss Airport (later North Beach Airport, now La Guardia Airport). Walker favored building an airport on Governors Island, but cost and military considerations foreclosed this plan, as well as one widely backed in 1930 for an artificial island of 783 acres (317 hectares) between Governors Island and Staten Island, complete with subway connections. In 1930 the city decided on Barren Island in Brooklyn. The following year saw the introduction of hourly flights between Newark and Washington by the Ludington Line, and of scheduled sightseeing flights between Newark and North Beach Airport by a flying school based at North Beach. By 1934 the airport at Barren Island was completed. Named for Floyd Bennett, a member of Admiral Richard Byrd's expedition to the North Pole, this field covered 367 acres (149 hectares) and accommodated the first scheduled land plane service in the city (by American Airlines), but poor accessibility to Manhattan precluded airmail service. Some airlines continued to use Newark Airport, which after a major expansion in 1928–29 became the busiest airfield in the world. Several triumphant flights during what is considered the heyday of aviation (1929–39) ended in the city, including the circling of the globe in three and a half days by Howard Hughes in 1937.

The dominant commercial position of the city, its topography, and its large population combined to make it a leader in domestic and international aviation and in related industries in the late 1930s. When La Guardia Airfield opened in 1939 it handled more than 250 flights a day in its first year of operation, giving New York City the heaviest air traffic in the United States. By 1938 the number of manufacturers of airplanes and related equipment in the region had fallen to twelve (reflecting consolidation during the Depression), but among these were such large firms as Fairchild, Grumman Industries, North American Aviation, and Chance–Vought Industries. The Second World War brought prosperity to these manufacturers and others in the area, notably Charles L. Norden and Company (1929–49), which produced the Norden bombsight in both Manhattan and White Plains, New York.

The position of the city as an innovator in regional airport planning and as the dominant force in intercontinental air travel was strengthened by the opening in 1948 of Idlewild International Airport (now John F. Kennedy International Airport) and by the administrative takeover in 1947–48 of Idlewild, La Guardia, Newark, and Teterboro (New Jersey) airports by the Port of New York Authority. American Overseas Airlines (a subsidiary of American Airlines) began transatlantic landplane service from La Guardia Airport on 25 October 1945; it was followed by Trans World Airlines on 5 February 1946 and by Pan American soon after. Commercial jet service began in New York City on 4 October 1958 with flights to London on the Comet IV by British Overseas Airways.

Plans for a fourth large airport in the region foundered in the 1960s, but New York City retained a central role in several new developments in aviation, including the establishment of the first modern air shuttle (by Eastern Airlines in 1961 to Boston and Washington) and the introduction of the Boeing 747 (by Pan American). Military aviation manufacturing continued to prosper on Long Island: North American Aviation produced the F-105 (to 1986) and the A-10, Grumman the F-14 "Tomcat," the A-6A, and the space shuttle. In 1990 the three major airports in greater New York served more than 74 million passengers and accounted for 24 percent of all international departures from the United States.

R. E. G. Davies: *A History of the World's Airlines* (London: Oxford University Press, 1964)
Roger Pineau: *Ballooning, 1782–1972* (Washington: Smithsonian Institution Press, 1973)
Dick Wirth: *Ballooning: The Complete Guide* (New York: Random House, 1980)
Roger E. Bilstein: *Flight in America, 1900–1983: From the Wrights to the Astronauts* (Baltimore: Johns Hopkins University Press, 1984)
Joshua Stoff: *Aerospace Heritage of Long Island* (Interlaken, N.Y.: Heart of the Lakes, 1989)

Paul Barrett

Avon Products. Firm of cosmetics manufacturers, formed in 1886 as the California Perfume Company by David McConnell, a bible salesman. It operated from a warehouse at 126 Chambers Street and maintained a force of door-to-door salesmen that numbered ten thousand by the turn of the century. In 1939 the firm took its current name, purportedly in honor of Shakespeare's place of birth. After the Second World War it grew into the world's largest cosmetics firm, with sales of more than $3000 million in 1983. Although the firm dispersed most of its manufacturing plants and administrative staff across the country in 1986 it maintained its corporate headquarters at Rockefeller Center into the 1990s.

Sonny Kleinfield: *Staying at the Top: The Life of a CEO* (New York: New American Library, 1986)

Marc Ferris

Ayres, Anne (*b* London, 3 Jan 1816; *d* New York City, 9 Feb 1896). Nun. An admirer and associate of William Augustus Muhlenberg, the Episcopal rector of the Church of the Holy Communion, she was inspired by his dedication to philanthropic enterprises to offer herself for celibate religious service. Although no Episcopal sisterhoods existed at the time she was unilaterally consecrated a sister of the Holy Communion by Muhlenberg in 1845. In 1859 she undertook the organization of his most ambitious enterprise, St. Luke's Hospital, on 5th Avenue between 54th and 55th streets. She wrote *Evangelical Sisterhoods* (1867) and after Muhlenberg's death published a collection of his articles and papers as well as a biography, *The Life and Work of William Augustus Muhlenberg* (1880).

Allen C. Guelzo

B

Bacall, Lauren [Perske, Betty Jean] (*b* New York City, 16 Sept 1924). Actress. After working briefly in the theater she made her film début opposite Humphrey Bogart (1899–1957) in *To Have and Have Not* (1944), loosely based on the novel by Ernest Hemingway, in which she spoke the memorable phrase "If you want something, just whistle." She became known for her portrayal of assertive, elegant women and her languid delivery of scathing lines. One of her most celebrated roles was that of the older sister in a motion picture adapted in 1944 from Raymond Chandler's novel *The Big Sleep*, in which she engages in witty exchanges with Bogart. The films she made during the following years were less distinguished: *Key Largo* (1948), *Young Man with a Horn* (1949), *How to Marry a Millionaire* (1953), and *Northwest Frontier* (1959). She married Bogart in 1945 and after settling in New York City continued to appear in plays (*Cactus Flower*, 1966–68), musicals (*Applause!*, 1969–71, winning a Tony Award for her portrayal of a fading actress modeled after Tallulah Bankhead), and films (*Harper*, 1967; *Murder on the Orient Express*, 1974; *Health*, 1980).

S. D. R. Cashman

Bache, Theophylact (*b* Settle, England, 17 Jan 1735; *d* New York City, 30 Oct 1807). Merchant. After moving to New York City in 1751 he formed a business with an uncle by marriage and another partner, eventually becoming the sole proprietor. He became prosperous through trade in the West Indies and helped to form the Marine Society. A Loyalist during the American Revolution, he suffered extensive losses in business after the British evacuation. Bache was president of the Chamber of Commerce, the New York Hospital, and St. George's Society and a vestryman at Trinity Church, where he is buried.

James E. Mooney

Backer and Spielvogel. Advertising agency formed in 1978 by six executives formerly employed by the firm McCann–Erickson. Under the leadership of Carl Spielvogel it became one of the fastest-growing agencies in the United States. It had $500 million in annual revenues at the time of its purchase in 1986 by the firm of Saatchi and Saatchi, which in the following year merged it with another of its subsidiaries, Ted Bates, to form Backer Spielvogel Bates Worldwide.

George Winslow

Badillo, Herman (*b* Caguas, Puerto Rico, 21 Aug 1929). Congressman, borough president, and deputy mayor. He moved in 1941 to Spanish Harlem, lived briefly near Chicago and Los Angeles, then returned to New York City, where he graduated from Haaran High School (1947), City College of New York (1951), and Brooklyn Law School (1954). He soon became one of a few Puerto Rican political leaders in the city to achieve prominence without working as a community organizer. After serving as the commissioner of the city's office of relocation he became the first Puerto Rican borough president of the Bronx (1966–69) and the first Puerto Rican voting member of the U.S. House of Representatives (1971–76). He ran unsuccessfully for the mayoralty in 1969 and 1973 and was a deputy mayor under Mayor Edward I. Koch. From 1970 to 1971 he was a Distinguished Professor of Urban Education at Fordham University and in 1990 he became a trustee of the City University of New York. Badillo in 1993 was part of the fusion ticket formed by the mayoral candidate Rudolph W. Giuliani, remaining a registered Democrat but nominated for the office of comptroller by the Republican and Liberal parties; he lost the election to Alan G. Hevesi.

Virginia Sánchez Korrol

bagels. The bagel became closely associated with New York City in the early twentieth century, when it was made and consumed by the city's large community of eastern European Jews. Made with malt (rather than sugar) and high-gluten processed flour, bagels were boiled and then baked, to give the finished product a crisp outer crust and a chewy inside. The recipe was strictly upheld for many years and the trade was closely guarded, passed from father to son through apprenticeships. Bagel Bakers Local 338, which was based in New York City, had nearly three hundred members between 1910 and 1915. By the 1950s the popularity of bagels extended beyond the city's Jewish neighborhoods, and this trend continued in the 1960s with the development of the bagel-making machine and the frozen bagel. By the 1990s bagels were served in fast-food chains; according to one estimate the number of bagels consumed nationwide increased more than tenfold between 1962 and 1992.

Marilyn Bagel and Tom Bagel: *The Bagel Bible* (Old Saybrook, Conn.: Globe Pequot, 1992)
Molly O'Neill: *New York Cookbook* (New York: Workman, 1992)

Thomas M. Hilbink

Baha'is. The Baha'i community in New York City is a religious community of about five hundred ethnically diverse followers. The religion was founded in 1897 in Persia by followers of Baha'u'llah (1817–92), a Persian man whom adherents of the faith accept as the last messenger of God after Muhammad. Followers are committed to the elimination of prejudice, the equality of women, the achievement of universal education, and tolerance of all religions; the religion is governed through local, self-governing communities. The Baha'i Center on East 11th Street and 1st Avenue in lower Manhattan provides weekly public meetings, worship services, and offices for the local assembly. The World Congress in 1992 was held at the Jacob K. Javits Convention Center and attended by thousands of members.

Robert H. Stockman: *The Baha'i Faith in America* (Wilmette, Ill.: Baha'i Publishing Trust, 1985)

Leyli Shayegan

Baker, Ella Josephine (*b* Norfolk, Va., 13 Dec 1903; *d* New York City, 13 Dec 1986). Civil rights leader. She lived in Littleton, North Carolina, from the age of eight. After graduating from Shaw University she moved to New York City in 1927. During the Depression she taught consumer education in Harlem for the Works Progress Administration and also helped to organize the Young Negroes' Cooperative League and chapters of the National Association for the Advancement of Colored People throughout the South. She directed the branch of the association in the city during the Second World War and in 1953 ran unsuccessfully as a Liberal for a seat in the state assembly. At the request of Martin Luther King Jr. she led the Southern Christian Leadership Conference in 1958. After a meeting of sit-in protesters at Shaw University in 1960 she helped to form the Student Nonviolent Coordinating Committee and became its advisor. In 1964 she attended the Democratic National Convention and helped to organize the Mississippi Freedom Summer and the Mississippi Freedom Democratic Party office in Washington. Baker returned to Harlem after the 1960s.

Sule Greg C. Wilson

Baker, George F(isher) (*b* Troy, N.Y., 27 March 1840; *d* New York City, 2 May 1931). Banker. He began working as a teller for the First National Bank in 1863, the year of its founding, and remained there for his entire career. He quickly achieved positions of progressively greater responsibility and became president of the bank in 1877. He retired from the presidency of the bank in 1909 and became its chairman, a position he retained to the end of his life. When he appeared in 1913 before a committee led by Representative Arsène Pujo he was a director of fifty-eight corporations. Baker typified the conservative banker of the late nineteenth century. He never spoke to the press and ran one of the dominant commercial banks of the period from a single office. In his later years he gave large gifts to educational, cultural, and medical institutions in the city.

Sheridan A. Logan: *George F. Baker and His Bank, 1840–1955: A Double Biography* (New York: George F. Baker Trust, 1981)

Joan L. Silverman

Baker, Josephine (*b* St. Louis, 3 June 1906; *d* Paris, 12 April 1975). Dancer and singer. After a childhood of poverty in St. Louis she moved to New York City and became famous for her performance in the musical *Chocolate Dandies* (1924). She moved to Paris in 1925 and became the most beloved music-hall artist in Europe during the 1920s and 1930s. Although she returned to the city several times she rarely achieved the degree of success that she had enjoyed in Europe, and her stays in the United States were plagued by racism. After accusing the Stork Club of refusing to serve her in 1951 she had a public dispute with the gossip columnist Walter Winchell that left her embittered. Baker was among the first black performers to achieve international renown.

Bryan Hammond and Patrick O'Connor: *Josephine Baker* (Boston: Little, Brown, 1991)

Joan Acocella

bakeries. Although most baking was done at home in the eighteenth century, there were seven retail bakeries in New York City in 1700, which sold mostly bread. Some of the bakers in lower Manhattan were V. J. Cortlandt (Broadway), Coevrad and House (Broad Street), and George Dieterich (Pearl Street). Bakery workers conducted their first strike in the city in 1741. The number of retail bakeries rose to twelve in 1800 and thirty-eight in 1840; after an influx of immigrants there were 476 in 1850. At the time the leading bakers were Robert Spier, Erastus Titus, and C. T. Goodwin; Treadwell and Harris, formed by E. Treadwell in 1825, was one of the most popular establishments until the end of the nineteenth century. By the 1850s bakeries offered not only bread but cakes and other sweets, biscuits, and bagels. Wholesale bakeries, formed during the second half of the nineteenth century, established routes and sales territories, delivering their products by horse and wagon to grocery stores. Among the first successful firms were Holmes and Coutts, the Purssell's Manufacturing Company, and the S. B. Thomas Company, which introduced English muffins. The first large bakers' union in the city, the Journeymen Bakers Union of New York and Brooklyn, was formed in 1880 and had its headquarters alternately in Manhattan and Brooklyn until the turn of the century, when the headquarters were moved to Chicago and the union was renamed the Bakery and Confectionery Workers International Union. There were more than a hundred locals in New York City, most divided along ethnic lines; some of the best-known were those operated by Germans, Italians, Jews, and Bohemians.

By the 1890s mergers and trusts characterized the business. The most important trust was the New York Biscuit Company, an amalgamation of firms from the Northeast. Its plant at 10th Avenue and 14th Street housed its headquarters and the country's

Bread Store *(1937), by Berenice Abbott*

largest baking factory. The National Biscuit Company (formed in 1898), which dominated baking in the Northeast, had headquarters in Chicago and many factories in New York City (including one on 10th Avenue), where it developed Animal Crackers, Lorna Doones, and other well-known products. By 1900 there were nearly 2500 bakeries in New York City.

Antitrust battles exacerbated tension between management and labor. The Ward Baking Company, which made Tip-Top Bread and owned several large factories in Brooklyn and the Bronx, was the dominant baker in the city in the 1920s and continually provoked the antagonism of workers. Innovations were made in baking technology, and many firms became manufacturers of baking ovens and machines; the most prominent was Fowler and Rockwell. Some of the best-known brands of bread and cakes were made in the city. The Continental Baking Company, which was formed by Ward and made Wonder Bread and Hostess cakes, had its headquarters there from 1923 to 1984. Other manufacturers included Dugan Brothers of Queens Village, Silver Cup Bread of Long Island City, Fink Baking, and the General Baking Company.

By the early 1990s there were fewer baking conglomerates in the city but more than a thousand bakeries. Wonder Bread had a factory in Jamaica, the Taystee Baking Company had headquarters in Flushing, and Drake Bakeries and the Stella D'Oro Biscuit Company remained in the Bronx. Brick-oven bread remained tremendously popular, and bakeries of a traditional sort were scattered throughout the city, among them Orwasher's on East 78th Street in Manhattan (1916), Parisi Bakery on Mott Street in Little Italy, and Mosha's Pumpernickel Bakery on Wythe Street in Bay Ridge (1890). Among the leading ethnic bakeries were Patisserie J. Lanciani in Greenwich Village (French), the White Eagle in Greenpoint (Polish), the Franczoz Bakery Shop in Borough Park (kosher), the Damascus Bakery on Atlantic Avenue in Brooklyn (Middle Eastern), and the International Bake Shop in Ridgewood (eastern European). There were also many shops specializing in Caribbean, Latin American, and Asian baked goods.

William G. Panschar: *Baking in America* (Evanston, Ill.: Northwestern University Press, 1956)
Stuart Kaufman: *A Vision of Unity: A History of the Bakery and Confectionery Workers International Union* (Urbana: University of Illinois Press, 1986)

James Bradley

Balanchine, George (*b* St. Petersburg, 22 Jan 1904; *d* New York City, 30 April 1983). Choreographer. He trained in Russia and became a successful choreographer in western Europe with Serge Diaghilev's Ballets Russes. At the invitation of the arts patron Lincoln Kirstein he emigrated to the United States and settled in New York City in 1933, with a vision of creating a permanent ballet company. In 1934 the two opened the School of American Ballet at 637 Madison Avenue. His first ballet in the United States, the group composition *Serenade* (to Tchaikovsky's music), was performed by students in June 1934; the ballet's emphasis on choreography rather than plot, costumes, or star dancers reflected principles that Balanchine followed for the rest of his career. During these years he lived at 11 East 77th Street and 120 East End Avenue in Manhattan. He continued his collaboration with Kirstein in his work for such companies as the American Ballet, which was the resident dance troupe of the Metropolitan Opera (1935–38), and the Ballet Society (1946–48), a chamber company that produced original ballets with newly commissioned music and décor. He also provided choreography for several Broadway shows, notably *On Your Toes* (1936) by Richard Rodgers and Lorenz Hart, which includes the famous ballet "Slaughter on Tenth Avenue." Between 1944 and 1946 he was a choreographer for the touring company Ballet Russe de Monte Carlo.

From the 1940s Balanchine forged a new style of classical dance. In the ballets *Concerto Barocco* (1941), *Ballet Imperial* (1941), and *Symphony in C* (1947) he heightened, quickened, and inverted traditional movements, but unlike other revolutionaries such as Martha Graham and Merce Cunningham he never abandoned classical technique. He further developed this idiom in *The Four Temperaments* (1946). At the invitation of Morton Baum, chairman of the executive committee of the City Center of Music and Drama, he joined with Kirstein in 1948 to form a resident company that became known as the NEW YORK CITY BALLET. With the company he created such reductive masterpieces as *Agon* (1957), *Episodes* (1959), *Movements for Piano and Orchestra* (1963), *Violin Concerto* (1972), and *Symphony in Three Movements* (1972). He also provided choreography for such narrative ballets as *The Nutcracker* (1954) and *Coppélia* (1974), spectacles such as *Vienna Waltzes* (1977) and *Jewels* (1967), and many classical display pieces.

In 1964 the New York Ballet moved to the New York State Theater at Lincoln Center. Balanchine trained many dancers there in a style characterized by sharp, precise, and often large movements. Among the most celebrated dancers with whom he worked were Maria Tallchief, Tanaquil LeClercq, Melissa Hayden, Suzanne Farrell, Patricia McBride, Merrill Ashley, Jacques d'Amboise, Edward Villella, and Peter Martins, who with Jerome Robbins became a ballet master of the company on Balanchine's death. In 1990 a segment of West 63rd Street near the New York State Theater was renamed George Balanchine Way.

Bernard Taper: *Balanchine: A Biography* (New York: Harper and Row, 1963; rev. Times Books, 1984)
Nancy Reynolds: *Repertory in Review: Forty Years of the New York City Ballet* (New York: Dial, 1977)
George Balanchine: A Catalogue of Works (New York: Viking, 1984)

Nancy Reynolds

Baldwin, James (Arthur) (*b* New York City, 2 Aug 1924; *d* St. Paul de Vence, France, 30 Nov 1987). Novelist, playwright, and essayist. The eldest of nine children, he grew up in Harlem and between the ages of fourteen and sixteen was a preacher in a small revivalist church. After leaving high school he worked, studied, and wrote in Greenwich Village. In 1948 he moved to Paris. His experiences as a teenager informed his novel *Go Tell It on the Mountain* (1953), which recasts the story of Ishmael as a young man's struggle to free himself from his family, and his play *The Amen Corner*, about a female evangelist, first performed at Howard University in Washington in 1955. He gained critical acclaim in the United States after publishing a collection of essays, *Notes of a Native Son* (1955). In 1956 he published his second novel, *Giovanni's Room*. After returning to the United States in the following year he published *Nobody Knows My Name* (1961), a collection of essays on race relations, and the novel *Another Country* (1962), which explores the racial and sexual recollections of a sister, a mistress, and various companions of the fictional jazz musician Rufus Brown. An extended essay by Baldwin about the Nation of Islam, black separatism, and integration took up an entire issue of the *New Yorker* in 1962 and was published in the following year as *The Fire Next Time* (1963). His views were unpopular with both radicals and Muslims, who considered his brand of liberalism outmoded. In his next work, the play *Blues for Mr. Charlie*, he treated the themes of racism and oppression somewhat bitterly, and the play received mixed reviews when it opened on Broadway in 1964. *The Amen Corner* was better received when it opened in the city in 1965. Among Baldwin's later works are the collection of essays *Going to Meet the Man* (1965), the novels *Tell Me How Long the Train's Been Gone* (1968), *If Beale Street Could Talk* (1974), and *Just above My Head* (1979), the essay "The Evidence of Things Not Seen" (1985), about murders of children in Atlanta between 1979 and 1981, and the collection of essays *The Price of a Ticket* (1985).

S. D. R. Cashman

Baldwin, Roger (Nash) (*b* Wellesley, Mass., 21 Jan 1884; *d* New York City, 26 Aug 1981). Civil libertarian. After graduating from Harvard University he became a nationally known social worker in St. Louis. In April 1917 he moved to New York City to assist Crystal Eastman and the Civil Liberties Bureau (CLB) in defending conscientious objectors, freedom of speech, and freedom of the

James Baldwin with Nina Simone

press during the First World War. He spent nearly a year in prison (1918–19) for refusing to be inducted into the armed forces. In 1920 he helped reorganize the CLB as the American Civil Liberties Union (ACLU), of which he became the director. He established a national reputation as a leading advocate of civil liberties and was active in many social and political causes. After retiring from the ACLU in 1950 Baldwin devoted himself to international human rights issues. He was awarded the presidential Medal of Liberty in early 1981.

Samuel Walker: *In Defense of American Liberties: A History of the ACLU* (New York: Oxford University Press, 1990)

Samuel Walker

Ball, Thompkins and Black [Ball, Black and Company]. Firm of jewelers that later became Black, starr and frost.

Ballantine Books. Firm of book publishers, formed in 1952 by Ian Ballantine, formerly of the firm Bantam, and his wife, Betty. The firm distinguished itself by publishing paperbound books simultaneously with clothbound editions issued by established houses, and by offering royalties to authors of 7.5 percent, then thrice the going rate. The book trade was aghast but the firm was a success. It published science fiction by Ray Bradbury and others, as well as anthologies based on the magazine *Mad*. After the firm was acquired in 1973 by Random House, Ballantine resigned to form a book packager, Rufus Publications, that had a short life.

James E. Mooney

Ballet Hispanico of New York. Dance company formed in 1970 by the Venezuelan dancer Tina Ramirez. It is the nation's leading modern dance company that draws on Latin American sources. In addition to performing regularly in New York City it operates a school at 167 West 89th Street and several programs in the public schools.

Marc Ferris

Ballet Theatre. Original name of the American ballet theatre.

B. Altman. Firm of clothing retailers, founded in April 1865 by Benjamin Altman as a small dry-goods shop at 39 3rd Avenue between 9th and 10th streets. It moved in the early 1870s to larger quarters on 6th Avenue between 21st and 22nd streets and in 1876 to an elegant six-story building at 627 6th Avenue (at 19th Street). Altman began buying land in the block bounded by 35th Street, Madison Avenue, 34th Street, and 5th Avenue, and in 1905 work began on a twelve-story building in the Italian Renaissance style. Completed in 1914, it was built largely of French limestone and took up the entire block; its elegant interior had broad aisles, high ceilings, parquet floors, and crystal chandeliers. Known as one of the most fashionable department stores in the city, Altman attracted many visitors with its window displays of mechanized tableaux during the winter holidays. The firm was bought in 1987 by L. J. Hooker, a firm owned by the Australian corporate raider George Herscu, and at the end of 1989 it ceased operations.

Robert Hendrickson: *The Grand Emporiums: The Illustrated History of America's Great Department Stores* (New York: Stein and Day, 1979), 159–62

Joseph Devorkin: *Great Merchants of Early New York: "The Ladies Mile"* (New York: Society for the Architecture of the City, 1987), 52–53

Allen J. Share

BAM. See Brooklyn academy of music.

bands. The first military band in New York City was the 11th Regiment Militia Band, led by Thomas Brown and stationed on Bedloe's Island (now Liberty Island). The military tradition inspired a civilian brass band movement in the early to mid nineteenth century. Thomas Dilks's Independent Band, formed in 1825 as the city's first professional wind band, played for several seasons at Castle Garden before dividing into two factions in 1835, one of which was directed from the following year by Allen Dodworth and became the most successful and influential band in the city. Dodworth invented and patented specially designed marching instruments in 1838 and published the highly regarded manual *Brass Band School* in 1853. He managed the group until 1860, when his brother Harvey took charge. In the same year John F. Stratton, a manufacturer based in New York City, began mass production of brass instruments. After the Civil War a number of leading bandmasters were based in the city: Harvey Dodworth led the Dodworth Band and the 13th Regiment Band of the New York National Guard, Claudius Grafulla led the 7th Regiment Band until he was succeeded in 1881 by the trombonist Carlo Cappa, and David L. Downing led the 9th Regiment Band. All three derived prestige and steady financial support from their association with the armed forces, and all were given free artistic rein. In 1873 Patrick S. Gilmore assumed leadership of the 22nd Regiment Band, widely known from then on as Gilmore's Band. Under his direction the 22nd regularly toured the nation with the best-known soloists of the time, and set new standards for performance. After Gilmore's death in 1892 nineteen of his musicians joined a band based in the city and formed by John Philip Sousa that became nationally renowned.

One of the most popular bands in New York City was that formed in 1887 by Frederick Innes, a trombonist and former leader of the 13th Regiment Band in Brooklyn. It often gave summer concerts at Prospect Park and performed regularly throughout the city until Innes moved to Denver in 1913. After ten years as a renowned trombone soloist with Sousa's band, which he also helped to lead, Arthur Pryor in 1903 formed his own ensemble, which in the same year made its début at the Majestic Theatre (3 November) and recorded the first commercial discs issued by the Victor Company; for several seasons it also played at Luna Park in Coney Island. By this time several bands based in New York City maintained regular touring schedules and appeared at such venues as Manhattan Beach, Hamilton Fish Park, and Madison Square Garden. In 1915 Sousa's band gave daily concerts between May and September at the Hippodrome, and Pryor performed during the summers of 1921–25 at Lido Beach in Coney Island. The New York Military Band was formed in 1911 by Edwin Franko Goldman, formerly a cornetist with the Metropolitan Opera Orchestra and an instructor at Columbia University; known from 1918 as the Goldman Band, it performed annual summer concerts at Columbia and the Central Park Mall, commemorated in Goldman's popular march "On the Mall" (1923). Other compositions by Goldman inspired by New York City include "Central Park," "New Yorker," "Hail, Brooklyn," and "On the Hudson." The Goldman Band also played on the first radio broadcast of the National Broadcasting Company on 15 November 1926.

From the 1920s professional concert bands diminished in number, and bands became associated primarily with school, civic, and fraternal organizations. Bands were formed by the fire department (1922), the police department, the Knights of Columbus, City College (1925), Columbia University (1928), and Fordham University (1928). The Goldman Band performed until 1979 under the direction of Goldman's son Edward, who died in the following year; under the direction of Ainslee Cox the group continued as the Goldman Memorial Band and performed throughout the five boroughs into the 1990s, by which time it was the city's longest-lived band and the third-oldest professional musical association of any kind. The city's most visible bands are those of local high schools, which regularly perform at parades throughout the city.

Margaret Hindle Hazen and Robert M. Hazen: *The Music Men: An Illustrated History of Brass Bands in America, 1800–1920* (Washington: Smithsonian Institution Press, 1987)

Marc Ferris

Bangladeshis. The Bangladeshi community in New York City is discussed in the entry South asians.

Bangs, Nathan (*b* Stratford, Conn., 2 May 1778; *d* New York City, 3 May 1862). Minister and editor. A leading exponent of American Methodism in New York City, he saved the Methodist Book Concern as its director from 1820 to 1828. He also edited the important Methodist periodicals *Christian Advocate and Journal and Zion's Herald* and the *Methodist Quarterly Review*, and led the American Methodist

Headquarters of the Bankers Trust Company (designed by Trowbridge and Livingston), 1912

missionary organization. Bangs was later the pastor of three congregations in the city.

Charles Yrigoyen, Jr.

Bankers Trust Company. Firm of commercial bankers, formed in 1903 by Henry P(omeroy) Davison (1867–1922) with J. P. Morgan and his associates in response to stricter regulations of trusts. It was designed not to compete with commercial banks but to perform fiduciary work for commercial banks. The first partners were among the most influential financiers in the city. Davison was respected for his role in assuaging investors' fears during the panic of 1907 and for his close alliance with Morgan; he remained the chairman of the bank until his death. Other officers of the bank in its early years included its president Edmund C. Converse (1849–1921) and its treasurer Thomas W. Lamont (1870–1948), both former directors of the Liberty National Bank. Lamont became the most powerful financier on Wall Street during the 1920s. The first capital stock offering of Bankers Trust yielded some $20 million. The headquarters were first in the Jersey Central Building at 143 Liberty Street and soon moved to 7 Wall Street. In 1909 the firm leased a building of twenty-two stories at 16 Wall Street, to which were added thirteen stories and a pyramid designed by the firm of Trowbridge and Livingston. The bank grew rapidly between 1910 and 1920, primarily by acquiring other firms, including the Mercantile Trust Company in 1911 (its offices at 120 Broadway became the first branch of Bankers Trust) and the Manhattan Trust Company in 1912.

The formation of the Federal Reserve System in 1914 ended the need for most trust services, and the firm pursued commercial banking under the direction of Seward Prosser (1871–1942), its president from 1914 to 1929. It bought the Astor Building on Wall Street and the Astor Trust Company in 1917 (the main office at 5th Avenue and 42nd Street was converted into a branch), the Empire Trust Company Building at 7 Pine Street in 1918, and the former building of the Hanover National Bank at Pine and Nassau streets in 1928; by 1933 a new building of twenty-five stories designed by the firm of Shreve, Lamb and Harmon covered the eastern half of the block bounded by Pine Street, Nassau Street, Wall Street, and Broadway. In 1928 the Bankers Company was formed as a wholly owned subsidiary to underwrite the firm's investment securities; it was dismantled in the autumn of 1931 in anticipation of the Glass–Steagall Act. Many positions were eliminated during the Depression, but despite the economy the firm's assets reached more than $1000 million in 1935. It moved its headquarters to the former site of the Harriman National Bank at the corner of 5th Avenue and 44th Street in 1936.

Under the leadership of S. Sloan Colt (1892–1975) the firm introduced retail banking operations after the Second World War, opening branches at Rockefeller Center in 1946. It moved to larger quarters at Park Avenue and 57th Street in the same year. In 1950 it bought the Lawyers Trust Company, the banking division of the Title Guarantee and Trust Company, and the Flushing National Bank; dozens of branches were also added. Other acquisitions in the 1950s included the Commercial National Bank and Trust Company, the Bayside National Bank, and the Public National Bank and Trust Company. The firm had assets of nearly $2750 million and deposits of more than $2500 million in 1955, making it one of the largest commercial banks in the country. William H. Moore (*b* 1914), chairman and chief executive officer from 1957 to 1974, continued to expand the firm's retail banking operations. Between 1955 and 1965 twenty-two branches were added: ten in Manhattan, three in Queens, three in Staten Island (including the former South Shore Bank in Great Kills), one in Brooklyn, one in the Bronx, and four in Nassau County. In 1962 executive headquarters designed by Henry Dreyfuss were erected at 280 Park Avenue between 48th and 49th streets. In 1974 a new headquarters forty stories tall, Bankers Trust Plaza, opened adjacent to the World Trade Center.

After a period of solid growth in the 1960s and 1970s Bankers Trust transformed its operations to reflect changing financial markets and new technology. In the early 1980s it sold its retail banking network and focused on commercial lending: its net income increased from $114 million in 1979 to $620 million in 1989. The firm in 1990 had operations in more than thirty-five countries and assets of more than $55,000 million. It remained one of the most profitable banks in the nation, as well as the fifth-largest commercial bank in New York City.

Susan Aaronson

Bankhead, Tallulah (Brockman) (*b* Huntsville, Ala., 31 Jan 1902; *d* New York City, 12 Dec 1968). Actress. The daughter of a Speaker of the U.S. House of Representatives, she made her début on Broadway in 1918 and after a number of mixed performances became well known in *Dark Victory* (1934), by George Brewer Jr. and Bertram Bloch, and a revival of W. Somerset Maugham's *Rain*. From 1931 to 1938 she lived at the Hotel Elysée at 56–60 East 54th Street. One of her most memorable roles was that of Regina Giddens in Lillian Hellman's *The Little Foxes* (1939). Her performance in Thornton Wilder's *The Skin of Our Teeth* (1942) was well received, and she toured in a successful revival of Noël Coward's *Private Lives* (1945–50). During the 1940s she had permanent quarters at the Hotel Gotham at 2 West 55th Street. Known for her deep voice, she was the host of the city's last important radio variety program, "The Big Show" (1945–50). Bankhead made a few motion pictures; of these only Hitchcock's *Lifeboat* (1943) conveys her distinctiveness. She bought the building at 230 East 62nd Street in 1956 and lived there until 1962, when she moved to 447 East 57th Street, her home for the last six years of her life.

Lee Israel: *Miss Tallulah Bankhead* (New York: G. P. Putnam's Sons, 1972)

David J. Weiner

banking. For information on banking in New York City see COMMERCIAL BANKING, CREDIT INSTITUTIONS, CREDIT UNIONS, INVESTMENT BANKING, SAVINGS AND LOAN ASSOCIATIONS, and SAVINGS BANKS, as well as entries on individual figures and institutions.

Bank of New York. The first chartered bank in New York City. Its formation followed the placing of a small advertisement in the *New York Packet* on 23 February 1784, only three months after British troops left New York City, calling on the "Gentlemen of this City to establish a Bank on liberal principles." The bank was organized on the following evening during a meeting at the Merchant's Coffee House, with Alexander Hamilton enlisted to write up its constitution, and it opened for business at the Wanton House on 9 June 1784. The charter called for a capital stock of $500,000; shares of $1000, payable in gold or silver, were all bought up immediately. In 1797 the bank erected its headquarters at 48 Wall Street. The center of the city's financial life, it provided financing for importers and helped the federal government to establish a firm financial basis. After four years on the board of directors Hamilton became the secretary of the treasury under President George Washington in 1789 and soon negotiated the government's first loan from the bank, which put up $200,000 against warrants drawn by the U.S. Treasury. In the following years the bank became a major lender to New York City, New York State, and a number of foreign governments. The bank eventually merged with such prominent institutions as the New York Life Insurance and Trust Company (1922), the Fifth Avenue Bank (1948), the Empire Trust Company (1966), Empire National Bank (1980), and the Long Island Trust Company (1987). After acquiring the Irving Bank in 1988 the Bank of New York became the tenth-largest bank holding company in the United States, with assets of about $50,000 million. In the mid 1990s it was the country's oldest bank operating under its original name. It still has its headquarters at 48 Wall Street.

Herbert S. Parmet: *200 Years of Looking Ahead: Commemorating the Bicentennial of the Founding of the Bank of New York, 1784–1984* (Rockville, Md.: History Associates for the Bank of New York, 1984)

Allis Wolfe

Bank of United States. Commercial bank formed in 1913 by Joseph Marcus, formerly a garment manufacturer. It was situated at first on the corner of Orchard and Delancey streets; from 1918 the head office was at 5th Avenue and 32nd Street. The bank catered specifically to a clientele of Jews and recent immigrants. Control of the bank was assumed in 1927 by Bernard Marcus (son of the founder) and his partner Saul Singer, who acquired five other banks at inflated prices and used depositors' money to pursue speculative personal ventures. The bank had 440,000 depositors and fifty-nine branches by the time of its failure on 11 December 1930, then the largest in American history. In the ensuing crisis in the banking system some members of the New York Clearing House were accused of anti-Semitism for having allowed the bank to fail, although even those who made the accusation acknowledged that the bank had engaged in questionable practices. Bernard Marcus and Singer were sent to Sing Sing Prison in March 1931.

M. R. Werner: *Little Napoleons and Dummy Directors: Being the Narrative of the Bank of United States* (New York: Harper and Brothers, 1933)

Joan L. Silverman

Bank Street College of Education. Private institution formed in 1916 as the Bureau of Educational Experiments by Lucy Sprague Mitchell (1878–1967), a former pupil of John Dewey at Teachers College who sought to study the physical, social, and emotional growth of children and to develop environments conducive to learning. With her colleague Harriet Johnson she organized the first all-day nursery schools (1918) and adopted a scientific and creative approach to pedagogy. Under her leadership the bureau funded health and nutrition studies, vocational projects, sex education programs, and schools where educational theories could be tested and students' behavior observed. The bureau received $50,000 a year from Mitchell's cousin Elizabeth Sprague Coolidge. In 1930 the bureau moved from six brownstones on West 12th and 13th streets to 69 Bank Street and organized the Cooperating School for Student Teachers; it was granted a charter by the Regents of the State of New York in 1941 and certified under its current name in 1950. Bank Street College is active in public and private schools in the city and has gained national recognition for its participation in such programs as Head Start, Follow Through, and Right to Read, and for its role in publishing the Little Golden Books and Bank Street Readers for children. Situated at 610 West 112th Street in Manhattan, the college has an enrollment of about seven hundred students, all at the graduate level, and awards the master of science in education and the master of education. It also operates the Bank Street School for children from six months to fourteen years old, which has an enrollment of 450.

Lucy Sprague Mitchell: *Two Lives: The Story of Wesley Clair Mitchell and Myself* (New York: Simon and Schuster, 1953)

Joyce Antler: *Lucy Sprague Mitchell: The Making of a Modern Woman* (New Haven: Yale University Press, 1987)

Linda Elsroad, Alfonso J. Orsini

Bank Street School. Nursery school opened in 1918 by Lucy Sprague Mitchell under the auspices of the Bureau of Educational Experiments (later known as the Bank Street College of Education). Initially situated in her brownstone in Greenwich Village, the school moved with the bureau in 1930 to a disused factory of the Fleischmann Yeast Company on 69 Bank Street, where it expanded into a full elementary school. The educational methods at the school reflected the influence of Mitchell's study with John Dewey at Teachers College and her collaborations with Caroline Pratt at the Play School and Elisabeth Irwin at the Little Red School House. Eventually the school moved to West 112th Street, where it served both as a community school and as an experimental facility for education students and experts. In the mid 1990s it enrolled 450 children from six months to fourteen years old.

Joyce Antler: *Lucy Sprague Mitchell: The Making of a Modern Woman* (New Haven: Yale University Press, 1987)

Alfonso J. Orsini

Bantam Books. Firm of paperback book publishers, formed in 1945 by Ian Ballantine. Headquarters were opened at 1107 Broadway and moved to 25 West 45th Street in 1950. With its parent firm, Grosset and Dunlap, Bantam was sold in 1968 to National General Corporation. Headquarters were moved to 666 5th Avenue in 1970 and the firm was sold in 1974 to IFI International, an Italian conglomerate. In 1977 a controlling interest was bought by the Bertelsmann Publishing Group, which became the sole owner in 1981. In the mid 1990s Bantam was the country's leading publisher of papaerbacks, with 22 percent of the market and $85 million a year in sales.

Clarence Petersen: *The Bantam Story: Twenty-five Years of Paperback Publishing* (New York: Bantam, 1970)

Allen J. Share

Bantam Doubleday Dell. Division of the Bertelsmann Publishing Group formed by the merger of Bantam Books, Doubleday, and Dell Publishing Company. In the mid 1990s Bertelsmann was one of the world's largest media companies and book publishers and Bantam Doubleday Dell had offices at 666 5th Avenue.

Allen J. Share

Baptists. The first notice of Baptist activity in New Netherland is a report from the pastors of the Reformed church in 1657 that "a fomenter of error," a cobbler from Rhode Island named William Wickenden, "began to preach at Flushing, and then went with the people into the river and dipped them," for which he was banished from the province. A congregation was organized in 1724 by Nicholas Ayres, who had been converted to the Baptist position in meetings held in his house. A meeting house was built, and Ayres remained as its pastor until he resigned in 1731. In the following year the property was claimed by one of the trustees and the congregation dissolved. First Baptist Church (1762) was organized by a group that had first met informally and then become members of the Scotch Plains Baptist Church in New Jersey. John Gano was called as pastor, and a meeting house was built on Gold Street. The church was closed during the American Revolution and used for a stable by British troops. Gano served as a chaplain to the Continental Army and returned in 1784, finding only thirty-seven of the two hundred members still in the city. Abyssinian Baptist Church (1808) was organized by "free colored" members of First Baptist. The first Baptist churches in what later became the other boroughs were Baptist Temple (organized as First Baptist Church, 1823) in Brooklyn, Park Baptist Church (1841) in Staten Island, Ridgewood Baptist

Church (organized as First German Baptist Church, 1855) in Queens, and Fulton Avenue Baptist Church (organized as German Bethel Baptist Church of Morrisania, 1857) in the Bronx. The first African–American congregations in Brooklyn, Queens, and the Bronx were respectively the Concord Baptist Church of Christ (1847), Ebenezer Baptist Church of Flushing (1870), and Day Star Baptist Church (organized 1888 in Manhattan). In 1830 Baptists were among the four leading denominations in New York City, with 2931 baptized members. By 1870 this number increased to 11,203 in Manhattan and 6812 in Brooklyn. Successive phases of immigration brought new groups of people to the city from Europe, the Caribbean, Latin America, Asia, and Africa, prompting the formation of many foreign-language Baptist congregations: First German Baptist Church (1846), Trinity Baptist Church (First Swedish Baptist Church, 1853), First Italian Baptist Church (1897), First Norwegian–Danish Baptist Church (1903), First Czechoslovak Baptist Church (Bohemian Baptist Church, 1905), First Latvian Baptist Church (1905), First Hungarian Baptist Church (1906), First Estonian Baptist Church (1919), First Spanish Baptist Church (1919), First Russian Baptist Church (1923), First Chinese Baptist Church (1926), First Polish Baptist Church (1926), Haitian Baptist Church (1965), Korean Baptist Church (1976), First Rumanian Baptist Church (1979), First Portuguese-Speaking Baptist Church (1982), Bronx Bible Church (Filipino, 1986), and First Indonesian Baptist Church (1993).

The first organization of Baptists in greater New York was the New-York Association, formed in 1791 by three churches in the city, three from New Jersey, and one from Long Island. In time this body became the Southern New York and the Long Island Baptist Associations, in fellowship with American Baptist Churches USA. The Baptist Female Missionary Society (1806), Baptist Sunday School Society (1816), and Baptist Widows and Orphans Fund (1839) were also sponsored by churches in New York City. In 1841 they organized the Representative Mission Society of the Baptist Association, incorporated in 1893 as the New York City Baptist Mission Society, which together with the Baptist Church Extension Society of Brooklyn and Queens (1918) conducted mission work throughout the city. Edward S. Judson developed Judson Memorial Baptist Church (1890) as an institutional church serving the Italian community in Greenwich Village. In 1901 the Mission Society conducted five daily vacation Bible schools, the first in the city. Charles Hatch Sears, executive secretary from 1904 to 1943, was an outstanding mission planner and administrator who greatly increased the scope of the society's work in the city to encompass the organization of many new churches, educational work with African–American churches, and Christian Friendliness programs to serve immigrant families. In 1972 the two Baptist associations (Southern New York; Long Island) and the two city mission societies (New York; Brooklyn and Queens) merged to form American Baptist Churches of Metropolitan New York (ABC Metro), which by the mid 1990s had 148 member churches in the five boroughs: because of congregational autonomy many of these also belong to other Baptist bodies.

A strong sense of ethnic identity, as well as theological and political conflicts, led to the formation of other bodies of Baptist churches that also included congregations in the city. Among these were the North American Baptist Conference (1865, now with two churches in the city), founded by German Baptists, and the Baptist General Conference (1879, now with six churches), founded by Swedish Baptists. African–American churches have three national conventions: National Baptist Convention USA (1895, now with 285 member churches in New York City), the parent convention of black Baptists; the National Baptist Convention of America (now with twenty-three churches), which divided from the other body in 1915; and the Progressive National Baptist Convention (1961, now with sixty-three churches), which had as its first president Gardner C. Taylor, then pastor of Concord Baptist Church of Christ in Brooklyn. Theological controversies with American Baptists caused the formation of the General Association of Regular Baptists (1932, three churches in New York City) and the Conservative Baptist Association of American (1947, twenty-seven churches). The Southern Baptist Convention, organized in 1845, began missionary activity in the city in 1957; the Metropolitan New York Baptist Association now includes seventy-five churches in the five boroughs.

New York City has also been a center for national Baptist organizations. The American Baptist Home Mission Society was organized on 27 April 1832 in the Mulberry Street Baptist Church. Some sessions were also held at the Oliver Street Baptist meeting house: its pastor, Spencer H. Cone, was elected the first president. The Northern Baptist Convention, founded in 1907 in Washington with Governor Charles Evans Hughes of New York as its president, was incorporated in the state and established headquarters in the city. In 1911 American Baptists organized the Ministers and Missionaries Benefit Board, which was incorporated with offices in New York City. From 1920 to 1963, when national American Baptist headquarters were moved to Valley Forge, Pennsylvania, the city was the site of the national offices of the American Baptist Foreign Mission Society, the Woman's American Baptist Foreign Mission Society, the American Baptist Home Mission Society, the Woman's American Baptist Home Mission Society, and the Northern Baptist Convention, as well as the Benefit Board, which remain in the city. Many important Baptist national meetings and conferences have been held in the city, but only the National Baptist Convention USA has conducted its national convention there (in 1935 and 1993).

Several leading Baptist leaders and thinkers have lived and worked in New York City. William Colgate, founder of the soap manufacturing company bearing his name, was a Baptist deacon. Walter Rauschenbusch, a leading exponent of the Social Gospel, developed his theological perspective as the pastor of a German congregation near Hell's Kitchen from 1886 to 1902; he joined with his fellow Baptist pastors Samuel Zane Batten, Nathaniel Schmidt, and Leighton Williams to form the Brotherhood of the Kingdom, devoted to social thought and action. The first woman to be ordained by a Baptist congregation was Mabel Lee in 1925: she succeeded her father as minister of the Morningstar Chinese Mission, which became First Chinese Baptist Church. John D. Rockefeller Jr. was a Baptist layman and philanthropist who financed the move of Park Avenue Baptist Church to Morningside Heights, where it became the Riverside Church. Its first pastor was Harry Emerson Fosdick, an advocate in the pulpit of liberal theology and biblical criticism, whose sermon "Shall the Fundamentalists Win?" was bitterly attacked by John Roach Straton, pastor of Calvary Baptist Church. Adam Clayton Powell Jr., who succeeded his father as pastor at Abyssinian Baptist Church, led civil rights demonstrations in Harlem before being elected to Congress in 1944. Bertha Grimmell Judd was president of the Woman's American Baptist Home Mission Society from 1937 to 1942 and wrote the society's fifty-year history. Marguerite Hazzard was its president from 1951 until 1955, when it merged with the American Baptist Home Mission Society.

Because of dual alignment some churches are counted more than once, but if independent congregations are also included there were at least 558 Baptist churches in New York City in 1992. By this time the total number of baptized believers in Baptist congregations in the five boroughs had increased to an estimated 365,855.

Jonathan Greenleaf: *A History of the Churches of All Denominations in the City of New York from the First Settlement to the Year 1846* (New York: E. French, 1846)

William Parkinson: *A Jubilee Sermon, Containing a History of the Origin of the First Baptist Church in the First Fifty Years since Its Constitution, Delivered in the Meeting-House of Said Church, January 1, 1813* (n.p. [?New York]: J. Gray, 1846)

Garland P. Dissowey: *The Earliest Churches of New York and Its Vicinity* (New York: James C. Gregory, 1865)

George D. Younger

Barbadians. Immigrants from Barbados began settling in New York City about 1900, largely for economic reasons. The Sons and Daughters of Barbados Benevolent Society, formed in 1913, was an early center for the community. Several thousand Barbadians, most of them black, arrived during the following decades. Throughout the 1950s racial prejudice confined them almost exclusively to the black neighborhoods of Harlem and Bedford–Stuyvesant, and to menial and unskilled work even though most were literate and skilled. Tens of thousands of Barbadians arrived in New York City after the passage of the Hart–Celler Act in 1965. They settled primarily in the black neighborhoods of Brooklyn and in racially integrated neighborhoods throughout the city.

Barbadians in the city work in crafts, management, business, technical occupations, and the professions, but the unskilled continue to account for a large part of the work force. The city's Barbadians have been active in the Combermere School Alumni Association of New York, the Barbados Nurses' Association of New York, and the Barbados Ex-police Association of New York, as well as in a number of cricket clubs. Prominent Barbadians have included Herbert Bruce (a district leader in Harlem), Mabel Staupers (a local and national leader of black nurses), and Herman Stoute, a criminal judge in the municipal courts in the 1950s and 1960s. In the mid 1990s the number of Barbadians in New York City was estimated at forty to fifty thousand.

Ira DeA. Reid: *The Negro Immigrant: His Background, Characteristics, and Social Adjustment, 1899–1939* (New York: Columbia University Press, 1939)
Calvin B. Holder: "The Causes and Composition of West Indian Immigration to New York City, 1900–1952," *Afro-Americans in New York Life and History* 11 (1987)
Veronica Udeogalanya: *A Comparative Analysis of Caribbean Immigrants Admitted into the United States, 1985–1987* (New York: Medgar Evers College, Caribbean Research Center, 1991)

Calvin B. Holder

Bard, Samuel (*b* Philadelphia, 1 April 1742; *d* Hyde Park, N.Y., 24 May 1821). Physician. The son of the prominent physician John Bard, he moved to New York City as a young man. He studied medicine from 1760 to 1765 in London and Edinburgh and in 1767 helped found at King's College the first medical school in New York City; this was later absorbed by the College of Physicians and Surgeons, of which he became the second president (1811–21). Throughout his career in New York City he maintained an extensive private practice; he was also George Washington's physician. Bard wrote several major works, including *A Compendium of the Theory and Practice of Midwifery* (1808).

John Brett Langstaff: *Doctor Bard of Hyde Park* (New York: E. P. Dutton, 1942)

Joseph S. Lieber

Milbank Hall at Barnard College, 1915

Barent Eylandt. Former name of RANDALLS ISLAND.

Barnard College. Undergraduate college for women within Columbia University, formed on 1 April 1889 with its own buildings, faculty, curriculum, administration, budget, and trustees. It was named for Frederick A. P. Barnard, the president of Columbia from 1864 to 1888, who was unable to persuade the trustees of Columbia to admit women as undergraduates. Annie Nathan Meyer, the young wife of a doctor, was largely responsible for raising the initial funds and assembling the first board of trustees, of which Barnard was a member. The first secular institution in New York City to grant the AB degree to women, it opened with a student body of fourteen and a faculty of six and occupied a brownstone building at 343 Madison Avenue, near the site then occupied by Columbia at Madison Avenue and 49th Street. After Columbia moved to Morningside Heights in 1897 Barnard followed in 1900 to a site of one acre (forty ares) at Broadway and 119th Street where a single building was erected. The college was led by a dean until 1952 and from that time by a president; among those to occupy these positions were Virginia C. Gildersleeve (1911–47) and Millicent Cary McIntosh (1947–62). Most students lived off campus until 1980, but the dormitories were expanded in the following years and by the mid 1990s about 90 percent of the students lived on campus. Despite several proposals to merge with Columbia College, Barnard remained independent, even after Columbia decided to admit women for the first time in 1983. In 1993 the school received a record number of applications for admission. The campus in the mid 1990s occupied four acres (1.6 hectares) and had nine buildings, 270 faculty members, 2100 students, and more than 25,000 alumnae.

A History of Barnard College: Published in Honor of the Seventy-fifth Anniversary of the College (New York: Barnard College, 1964)
Helen Lefkowitz Horowitz: *Alma Mater: Design and Experience in the Women's Colleges from Their Nineteenth-century Beginnings to the 1930s* (New York: Alfred A. Knopf, 1984)

Jane Allen

Barnes, Djuna (*b* Cornwall-on-Hudson, N.Y., 12 June 1892; *d* New York City, 18 June 1982). Novelist and playwright. As a reporter for the *Brooklyn Daily Eagle* shortly before the First World War she wrote about Greenwich Village, where she settled about 1915. Associated with a circle of radical poets and artists who frequented Bruno's Garret on Washington Square South, she wrote innovative plays for the Provincetown Players, experimental verse, and droll vignettes of manners, and at the end of the war moved to Paris, where she wrote her best-known work, the novel *Nightwood* (1936). After returning from Europe in 1940 she lived in Patchin Place. Some of her later novels draw on the eccentric types of Greenwich Village. Toward the end of her life she became regarded as one of the earliest exponents of an avowedly lesbian sensibility in American letters.

Andrew Field: *The Life and Times of Djuna* (New York: G. P. Putnam's Sons, 1983)
Andrew Field: *The Formidable Miss Barnes* (Austin: University of Texas Press, 1985)

Jan Seidler Ramirez

Barnes and Noble. Firm of book publishers and booksellers. It began in 1873 as a firm of wholesale book jobbers operated by William R. Barnes and G. Clifford Noble, who supplied schools, colleges, libraries, and book dealers with new and used books; they opened their first bookstore on 5th Avenue in 1917. The first publishing venture, launched in 1931, was the College Outline Series, which provided summaries of college courses. The firm was bought by Ampel in 1969 and the publishing division was sold to Harper and Row in 1971. During the 1970s Barnes and Noble became one of the country's first discount retail booksellers; it bought the firm of

B. Dalton in 1986 and Doubleday Book Shops, a chain of forty stores, in 1990. In the mid 1990s it operated about eight hundred B. Dalton bookstores nationwide, two hundred Barnes and Noble college stores, and fifty Barnes and Noble retail stores. It has headquarters at 122 5th Avenue. By most measures the bookstore on 5th Avenue is the largest in the world.

Frank L. Schick: *The Paperbound Book in America: The History of Paperbacks and Their European Background* (New York: R. R. Bowker, 1958), 201–5

Allen J. Share

Barnet and Doolittle. Firm of lithographers formed in 1821 by William Armand Barnet and Isaac Doolittle (*b* New Haven, Conn., 13 Oct 1784; *d* Rochester, N.Y., 17 April 1852), both trained in France. Situated at 23 Lumber Street (later Trinity Place), it was the first commercial lithography firm in the United States. The firm was responsible for creating the incunabula of the lithographic art until it ceased operations in mid 1822 because of a shortage of work and an epidemic of yellow fever. It produced the first American book with lithographs (*A Grammar of Botany*, comp. Henry Muhlenberg, 1822, drawings by Arthur J. Stansbury), an untitled view of the Black River falls, bridge, and mill near Brownville, New York, illustrations for the *American Journal of Science* (1822), and other works, some of which are held by the New-York Historical Society.

Harry T. Peters: *America on Stone: The Other Printmakers to the American People* (New York: Doubleday, Doran, 1931)

Wendy Shadwell: "Prized Prints," *Imprint* 11, no. 1 (1986), 14–18

Wendy Shadwell

Barneys New York. Firm of men's clothing retailers, formed in 1923 at 7th Avenue and 17th Street by Barney Pressman (1895–1991). In the early years Pressman angered competitors and manufacturers by purchasing brand-name suits from independent retailers in the South and reselling them at low prices. The firm owed its early success in part to his skill at developing clever promotions and radio and print advertising. By the 1960s Pressman's son Fred shifted the focus from discount toward high-priced retailing, and the store became the first in New York City to sell the work of famous European designers. It added women's apparel and elegant housewares in 1976 and in 1986 opened a separate women's branch in six brownstone buildings adjacent to the main store. An outlet at the World Financial Center opened in 1988, and in the following year three joint venture agreements were reached with the Japanese retailing concern Isetan, which called for the opening of stores across the United States and in Japan and Southeast Asia. In 1993 Barneys opened a large uptown branch at Madison Avenue and 61st Street. The firm is privately held.

Marc Ferris

Barnum, P(hineas) T(aylor) (*b* Bethel, Conn., 5 July 1810; *d* Bridgeport, Conn., 7 April 1891). Impresario. In 1841 he took over the site and contents of Scudder's Museum, a defunct institution at the intersection of Broadway and Ann Street, and opened the American Museum. His astute promotion of appearances there by such performers as the midget Charles Stratton (General Tom Thumb) and the Swedish soprano Jenny Lind made this the most successful of the many dime museums in the city. The museum was destroyed by fire on 13 July 1865, reopened on Broadway at Spring Street, then burned again in 1868. Barnum retired briefly to work on a revised edition of his autobiography (first published 1855, revised 1927), and on 10 April 1871 he opened with William Coup in Brooklyn what is generally acknowledged to have been the first three-ring circus. The various circuses with which he was associated were the first large-scale entertainments to travel by railway; they performed annually in New York City at the Hippodrome on 27th Street and later at the original Madison Square Garden. In 1882 he had the giant elephant Jumbo sent from England and paraded him through the streets of New York City. Often accused of perpetrating hoaxes (he once exhibited a "Fejee mermaid"), Barnum cheerfully capitalized on the gullibility of an amused public. Along with baby contests, melodramas, and poultry shows he exhibited live animals, scientific specimens, and curiosities of the natural world, providing inexpensive entertainment to a wide and varied audience. Although a permanent resident of Bridgeport (where he served as mayor), he maintained homes in Manhattan throughout his career, including one at 52 Frankfort Street from 1835 to 1840 and another at 438 5th Avenue from 1868.

P. T. Barnum and Commander George Washington Nutt, ca *1860*

Neil Harris: *Humbug: The Art of P. T. Barnum* (Boston: Little, Brown, 1973)

A. H. Saxon: *P. T. Barnum: The Legend and the Man* (New York: Columbia University Press, 1989)

See also CIRCUSES.

Jean Ashton

Baron, Salo Wittmayer (*b* Tarnow, Galicia, 26 May 1895; *d* New York City, 25 Nov 1989). Historian. Arguing against what he called the "lachrymose" treatment of Jewish history, he sought to provide a more balanced account that integrated culture, religion, economics, and politics. From 1930 until his retirement in 1963 he taught at Columbia University, where he directed the Center of Israel and Jewish Studies from 1950 to 1968. His apartment on Claremont Avenue was known nationally as a gathering place for scholars. Baron was president of the American Academy for Jewish Research, the Conference on Jewish Social Studies, and the American Jewish Historical Society. He wrote hundreds of articles and thirteen books, including *A Social and Religious History of the Jews* (1937–89), published in eighteen volumes.

Michael N. Dobkowski

Baron de Hirsch Fund. Charitable organization incorporated in February 1891 with $2.4 million from Baron Maurice de Hirsch (1831–96), a German immigrant who also established the Jewish Colonization Association in London. Dedicated to assisting Jewish immigrants, the fund operated solely within the United States until a change in its constitution in 1970 enabled it to begin assisting immigrants in Israel. In 1991 the fund reported assets of $6.5 million and grants totaling $572,500 for work in New York City and Israel.

Samuel Joseph: *History of the Baron de Hirsch Fund: The Americanization of the Jewish Immigrant* (New York: Baron de Hirsch Fund, 1935)

Kenneth W. Rose

Barondess, Joseph (*b* Kamenets-Podolsk [now Kamanets-Podolski], Ukraine, 3 July 1867; *d* New York City, 19 June 1928). Labor leader. He emigrated from England to the United States, where he helped organize a union for cloakmakers in New York City. In 1891 he was unjustly convicted of extortion in a labor dispute, but he was pardoned in the following year. He later helped to organize the International Ladies' Garment Workers' Union, the Hebrew Actors' Union, and the Hebrew–American Typographical Union. A Zionist from 1900, he represented American Jewry at the Paris Peace Conference in 1919;

he also served two terms on the New York City Board of Education. Barondess spent the last years of his life working as an insurance broker.

Robert D. Parmet

"barrel murder." A murder committed in 1903, discovered on 14 April when a man was found stabbed and nearly decapitated in an ash barrel on a corner of East 11th Street. The crime led to widespread panic that an international criminal syndicate based in Sicily was preparing to launch attacks on non-Italian Americans. Public fears diminished after police identified the man as Benedetto Madonia and determined that the crime had been motivated by a matter within the syndicate. Tomasso Petto was suspected of complicity in the crime but never convicted.

Arrigo Petacco: *Joe Petrosino*, trans. Charles Lam Markmann (New York: Macmillan, 1972)

Humbert S. Nelli: *The Business of Crime: Italians and Syndicate Crime in the United States* (New York: Oxford University Press, 1976), 72–74

Mary Elizabeth Brown

Barren Island. An island in Jamaica Bay near the shoreline of Flatlands, lying within the borough of Brooklyn and far from residential areas. In the mid nineteenth century it was the site of the largest dump in New York City. Eventually there were many factories for boiling bones and making fertilizer, glue, and fish oil. In 1930 the island became the site of Floyd Bennett Field after the municipal government filled in marshland to connect it to the mainland. The island's population of four hundred was evicted in 1939 to make way for the Belt Parkway. The U.S. Navy bought the airfield in 1942 and owned it until 1971, when control reverted to the city.

Stephen Weinstein

bars, taverns, and saloons. In 1641 the Stadt Herbergh, or City Tavern, sold wine and beer imported by the Dutch East India Company for the citizens of New Amsterdam, and the tavern became so central to the community that it was later made the town hall. Peter Stuyvesant complained in 1648 that 25 percent of the houses in the city were taverns, and he proceeded to impose strict regulations on their hours of business. The King's Arms at Cedar Street and Broadway became the rendezvous for opponents of Jacob Leisler in the 1680s. After the British captured New Amsterdam the design of the English tavern came to predominate. Elaborately painted signs were mounted in front of such taverns as the Black Horse, the St. George, and the White Lion. At the center of the typical tavern stood a large fireplace that provided heat and cooked food, and around the fireplace were tables and chairs for customers. The bar had a small, secure cabinet to protect liquor from thievery and brawls. Ales and porters were the most widely consumed beverages, though

Steve Brodie's Bowery Saloon, ca *1895*

rum, brandy, and Madeira also were popular. Most taverns offered two meals: a hot dinner at noon and a cold supper in the evening. Visitors from other cities and others in need of accommodations were quartered in small rooms on the second story or given pallets near the fireplace. Taverns were frequented only by men — merchants, lawyers, artisans, and sailors — and ranged in grade from the luxurious Fraunces Tavern (now rebuilt on its original site at 54 Pearl Street) to cheap taverns near the East River. Many were stopping places for stagecoaches, as well as centers for such entertainments as lectures, animal shows, bear baitings, cockfights, and rat killings. They served many other functions as well: in the early eighteenth century sailors seeking employment went to the Sign of the Pine Apple near the docks on the East River; politicians and businessmen often negotiated at the Merchants' Coffee House on Broad Street (from 1754) and the Black Horse Tavern at William Street and Exchange Place; drovers and butchers haggled over the price of cattle at the famous Bulls Head Tavern on the east side of the Bowery north of Canal Street; and early in the nineteenth century the Blue Boar on William Street was a national employment center for carpet weavers.

In the mid nineteenth century the functions of the tavern were assumed by various other establishments: the hotel emerged as a place specifically for lodging, and the barroom or saloon (a term derived from the drinking salon of the 1850s) became a place where a working-class clientele consumed beer and other liquors. As tens of thousands of Irish and German immigrants settled in the city the saloon evolved into a central institution. Usually situated on a street corner, it was a single room dominated by a long, straight bar, usually without any chairs or seats. The change from tavern to saloon was accompanied by a growth in the popularity of lager beer, first brewed in the city in the late 1840s by Frederick and and Maximilian Schaefer. By the 1860s and 1870s "stand-up" barrooms, mostly owned by breweries, were found throughout New York City. Some taverns suffered from the effects of the temperance movement and in particular from a decline in patronage among the middle class, but in tenement neighborhoods barrooms became deeply integrated into the local way of life.

The saloon came to be regarded as the "poor man's club" that provided the many single young men in the city with an appealing alternative to the lodging house and the tenement. Because saloons had no seats they could accommodate the rush of factory workers at midday and after work, and as early as the 1850s they served a free lunch to those purchasing beer. Workers could spend the evening playing shuffleboard, billiards, and cards, or reading newspapers that the saloons provided; some men even received their mail there. Tammany Hall recognized the importance of saloons in working-class life and used them to muster votes from immigrants. Its last great leader, Charles F. Murphy, began his career in politics in the 1880s as the owner of a saloon on 19th Street and Avenue C that sold customers a glass of beer and a bowl of soup for five cents. Toward the end of the century Jacob A. Riis took photographs of customers at "black-and-tans" (underground bars that were dimly lit and often dangerous). By 1885 there were ten thousand drinking places in the city, or one for every 140 residents. The great majority were local stand-up bars, but some were specialized establishments: beer gardens in Little Germany with tables, chairs, and brass bands (see BEER HALLS); elegant saloons in hotels; "sporting saloons" such as Harry Hill's at Crosby and Houston streets, where boxing matches attracted both the wealthy and the working class; CONCERT SALOONS that provided musical and theatrical entertainment before the rise of vaudeville; and sailors' barrooms such as Jimmy the Priest's on Fulton Street (the model for the saloon in Eugene O'Neill's *The Iceman Cometh*).

The period between the 1860s and 1919 saw only modest changes in the function and design of saloons. Although they remained overwhelmingly male, by 1910 women were sometimes admitted with a male escort. During Prohibition drinking moved from legal establishments to illegal speakeasies, which were ubiquitous and well attended despite a common view that they were lacking in ambience. Saloons reopened after the repeal of Prohibition but failed to regain the central position in the life of the city that they had occupied before, in part because improvements in housing conditions made evenings at home more bearable, and in part because restrictions on immigration in the 1920s decreased the city's population of single men. Female customers increased in number after the Second World War and were admitted to most drinking places by about 1960. The few bars that continued to admit only men were gradually forced by the women's movement to relent: the last was McSorley's Old Ale House in 1970, which had long been known by the slogan "good ale, raw onions, and no ladies." In the 1960s and 1970s bars were the backdrop for the city's changing sexual mores: the period saw the opening of many "singles bars," especially on the Upper East Side (the best-known was Maxwell's Plum), and of gay bars such as the Stonewall Inn on Christopher Street (site of the well-known rebellion in June 1969). Both types of bar declined in the 1980s and 1990s with the spread of AIDS and other sexually transmitted diseases, and a worsening economy. At the same time "brew pubs" (which brewed their own beer) and sports bars increased in popularity.

By the mid 1990s the neighborhood bar was an endangered institution in many parts of the city and especially in Manhattan, largely because the income that it generated was not commensurate with the high cost of real estate. In working-class neighborhoods many bars maintained a racial or ethnic character, and in poorer neighborhoods unlicensed bars were common. Among the bars that have become well-known in the history of New York City are the White Horse Tavern in Greenwich Village, Pete's Tavern at Irving Place, the Landmark Tavern at 46th Street and 11th Avenue, and the Ear Inn on Spring Street.

The British Mechanic's and Labourer's Hand Book and True Guide (London: C. Knight, 1840)

W. Harrison Bayles: *Old Taverns of New York* (New York: Frank Allaben Genealogical Company, 1915)

Joseph Mitchell: "McSorley's Wonderful Saloon," *Up in the Old Hotel* (New York: Pantheon, 1992)

Richard Stott

Bartók, Béla (*b* Nagyszentmiklós, Hungary [now Sînnicolau Mare, Romania], 25 March 1881; *d* New York City, 26 Sept 1945). Composer and pianist. After studying in Budapest at the Royal Academy of Music (to 1903) and spending most of his career there, he fled from the Nazis and in October 1940 arrived in New York City, living first at 110-31 73rd Road in Forest Hills. During the same year he was appointed a research assistant in music at Columbia University, where he transcribed and edited a collection of Serbo-Croatian women's songs. For three years he lived at 3242 Cambridge Avenue in Riverdale. He gave concerts with his wife, the pianist Ditta Pásztory, but advancing illness soon prevented him from performing and teaching; he nonetheless composed the Concerto for Orchestra (1943), a commission by Serge Koussevitzky that won him the attention of a wider public and entered the standard orchestral repertory; the Sonata for Solo Violin (1943), commissioned by Yehudi Menuhin, who gave the work its première at Town Hall; and all but the final bars of the Piano Concerto no. 3 (1945). Bartók was a respected musicologist who wrote several books on Hungarian, Slovakian, and Romanian folk music. From 1944 until his death he lived at 309 West 57th Street in Manhattan.

S. D. R. Cashman

Barton, Bruce (*b* Robbins, Tenn., 5 Aug 1886; *d* New York City, 5 July 1967). Congressman. He attended Berea College and in 1907 graduated from Amherst College. After working in publishing in Chicago he moved to New York City, where in 1919 he opened an advertising firm (later known as Batten, Barton, Durstine and Osborn), had a syndicated newspaper column, and wrote several best-sellers about his approach to business as well as hundreds of newspaper and magazine articles. In 1936 he was elected as a Republican to the U.S. House of Representatives from New York; he became known for leading opposition to the New Deal and left office in 1941 after mounting an unsuccessful campaign for the U.S. Senate in 1940.

James E. Mooney

Bartow–Pell Mansion. Historic house in the Bronx. It stands on a tract in Pelham Bay Park bought in 1654 by the English physician Thomas Pell and was built between 1836 and 1842 by Robert Bartow, a publisher and a descendant of Pell. It remained in the family until 1888, when it was acquired by the city. The mansion is an elegant stone building with lavishly decorated Greek Revival interiors and a grand spiral staircase. In 1914 an orangerie was added and the International Garden Club took over the maintenance of the mansion, carriage house, and grounds. The mansion served Mayor Fiorello H. La Guardia as a summer office in 1936 and was opened as a public museum in 1947. The carriage house was restored and then opened to the public in 1993.

Lockwood Barr: *Genealogical Charts and Biographical Notes on the Pell Family, with Special Reference to the Lords of the Manor of Pelham, Westchester County, New York, also the Allied Bartow Family of the Bartow Mansion* (Pelham Manor, N.Y.: n.pub., 1946)

Historic Houses in New York City Parks (New York: Department of Parks and Recreation / Historic House Trust of New York City, 1989)

Jonathan Kuhn

Baruch, Bernard (Mannes) (*b* Camden, S.C., 19 Aug 1870; *d* New York City, 20 June 1965). Financier, son of Simon Baruch. After moving to New York City with his parents and three brothers in 1880 he lived with his family at 144 West 57th Street, later living at 345 West End Avenue and until 1899 at 51 West 70th Street. He graduated from City College in 1889 and then joined the brokerage firm of A. A. Housman as a clerk earning $3 a week; by the time he was thirty he had amassed a fortune of more than $1 million. At thirty-three he was elected to the governing committee of the New York Stock Exchange. A supporter of Mayor William J. Gaynor, he was appointed a trustee of City College in 1910. His most successful investment was in the Gulf Sulphur Company (later Texas Gulf Sulphur) in 1912. He was appointed by President Woodrow Wilson as chairman of the War Industries Board in 1918 and after the war to a senior advisory position with the American peace delegation in Paris. In the 1920s he bought a mansion at 1055 5th Avenue, where he lived until 1946 (the site is now occupied by 1050 5th Avenue). Although he lost money during the stock market crash of 1929 he recovered quickly and his fortune was estimated at $20 million to $25 million during the Depression; in the early 1930s he had the foresight to buy gold. A conservative Democrat, he was a sometimes reluctant ally of President Franklin D. Roosevelt and an adversary of President Harry S. Truman, who named him the American representative to the United Nations Atomic Energy Commission in 1946. As a long-time member of the Committee on Unlisted Securities he worked to advance the acceptance of mining issues by the other governors. His greatest disappointment in business was his inability to gain control of a railroad. In his later years Baruch warned repeatedly against inflation. From the mid 1940s until his death he lived at 4 East 66th Street. He wrote *Baruch: My Own Story* (1957) and *Baruch: The Public Years* (1960).

Jordan A. Schwartz: *The Speculator: Bernard M. Baruch in Washington, 1917–1965* (Chapel Hill: University of North Carolina Press, 1981)

James Grant: *Bernard M. Baruch: The Adventures of a Wall Street Legend* (New York: Simon and Schuster, 1983)

James Grant

Baruch, Simon (*b* Schwersenz [now Swarzedz, near Poznań, Poland], 29 July 1840; *d* New York City, 3 June 1921). Physician, father of Bernard Baruch. He emigrated to the United States as a boy and settled with his family in the South. In 1881 he moved to New York City, where he helped found the Montefiore Home for Chronic Invalids in 1884 at Avenue A and 84th Street; he was the first chief of its medical staff. A leading proponent of hydrotherapy, of which he became a professor at the College of Physicians and Surgeons, in 1901 he helped to open the first public baths in the United States on Rivington Street.

Dorothy Levenson: *Montefiore: The Hospital as Social Instrument, 1884–1984* (New York: Farrar, Straus and Giroux, 1984)

Joseph S. Lieber

Baruch College. College of the City University of New York, formed in 1919 at 17 Lexington Avenue in Manhattan as a branch of City College dedicated to business and civic administration. It was named in 1953 after the financier Bernard Baruch, one of the most successful graduates of City College, and became an independent college of the city university system in 1968. Baruch is the largest business college in the United States and the only public institution in New York City to offer bachelor's and master's degrees in business administration. It also offers undergraduate degrees in liberal arts and education, a master's degree in education, and the doctorate in business. The college houses several research organizations including the New York State Legislative Institute and the Center for the Study of Collective Bargaining in Higher Education. At one time the enrollment at Baruch was predominantly male; the proportion of female students began to increase in the 1970s and reached half by 1990. The college owns or rents space in seven locations between 18th and 26th streets in Gramercy Park. More than 90 percent of the 15,853 undergraduate and graduate students enrolled full or part time in the autumn of 1990 studied business subjects.

Selma C. Berrol: *Getting Down to Business: Baruch College in the City of New York* (Westport, Conn.: Greenwood, 1989)

Selma Berrol

The first home of Baruch College, Lexington Avenue and 23rd Street

Barzini, Luigi (Giorgio), Jr. (*b* Milan, 21 Dec 1908; *d* Rome, 30 March 1984). Writer and social critic. He moved to New York City at sixteen, in 1930 graduated from the Columbia School of Journalism, and worked for the *New York World* and as a correspondent for the prestigious newspaper *Corriere della Sera* in Milan. His first book, *Nuova York*, was published in 1931. An opponent of fascism and Mussolini, he was forced into exile during the Second World War. In 1953 he published his first book in the United States, *The Americans Are Alone in the World*, a translation from the Italian original. He also wrote two best-sellers: *The Europeans* (1957) and *The Italians* (1964), an amusing but critical history of his people (whom he regarded as "self-defeating individualists"). Barzini served in the Italian Parliament from 1958 to 1972.

Obituary, *New York Times*, 1 April 1984

Leslie Gourse

Barzun, Jacques (Martin) (*b* Créteil, France, 30 Nov 1907). Historian. His long association with Columbia University began when he enrolled there as a student at the age of sixteen (AB 1927, MA 1928, PhD 1932); he became a lecturer in 1927, took American citizenship in 1933, and became a full professor in 1945. Later he was dean of the graduate faculties (1955–67) and provost of the university (1958–67). He taught nineteenth- and twentieth-century European history, translated literary works, and wrote on a wide range of topics including the methods of historical research, intellectual history, music, racism, Romanticism, scholarship, and the work of William James. In 1972 he retired from active teaching at Columbia. Barzun's published writings include *Darwin, Marx, Wagner* (1941; 2nd edn 1981), *The Modern Researcher* (1957; 5th edn 1992), *Science: The Glorious Entertainment* (1964), *Berlioz and the Romantic Century* (1950; 3rd edn 1969), and *The Culture We Deserve* (1990).

Mary Elizabeth Brown

baseball. Although the precise date and place of origin of baseball are hotly debated, it is beyond dispute that Manhattan and Brooklyn played an important role in its early development. In 1846 a set of rules defining the "New York game" was issued by a committee led by Alexander J. Cartwright and comprising members of the New York Knickerbocker Club, an organization of white-collar workers from Madison Square and Murray Hill. The rules provided for a diamond-shaped infield with bases separated by a distance of ninety feet (twenty-seven meters); the pitcher stood in the center of the diamond at a distance from home plate of forty-five feet, or fourteen meters (changed in 1893 to sixty feet and six inches, or eighteen meters). The first game played under these rules reportedly took place on 19 June 1846 in Hoboken, New Jersey. When Cartwright later joined the gold rush of 1849 he introduced the New York game in San Francisco. With continuing modifications it eclipsed such rival versions of baseball as "town ball" and the "Massachusetts game" and became standard. During the next fifteen years some sixty organized baseball clubs played matches in and around New York City. In the 1850s the popularity of baseball in eastern cities surpassed that of cricket, and baseball was soon being referred to as the national game. Its acceptance was promoted by the journalist Henry Chadwick, who reported on games for local newspapers and devised a box score for recording each player's achievements. In 1860 organized baseball was most popular in cities in the Northeast. Among the best-known teams in the area were the Knickerbockers, Eagles, Empires, and Gothams of Manhattan, the Eckfords, Atlantics, Putnams, and Excelsiors of Brooklyn, and the Unions

Polo Grounds, New York City.
Home of the New York Giants.

Postcard of the Polo Grounds, home of the New York Giants, ca *1918.* Inset *Johnny McGraw*

of Morrisania. Some clubs like the Knickerbockers and the Excelsiors limited membership to white-collar workers; a few like the Uniques of Brooklyn were composed of black players. During the Civil War soldiers of both armies learned the game and helped to spread it to other areas of the country. At the same time strong amateur teams attracted large crowds.

The National Association of Base Ball Players was formed in 1857 by amateurs seeking to promote the game, and although it never organized a league or a championship schedule more than three hundred clubs belonged to it by 1867. Leading teams erected fenced parks, charged admission, and paid good players for their services. Gamblers openly accepted wagers and sometimes offered bribes to players. The association was unable to curb either these practices or the growth of professionalism. By 1869 the New York Mutuals paid their starting players; the first team to pay all its players, the Cincinnati Red Stockings, were managed by Harry Wright, a former professional cricket player with the St. George Club of Staten Island. The Red Stockings toured the nation and remained unbeaten until losing a game in extra innings to the Atlantics in the summer of 1870 before a large crowd at the Capitoline Grounds in Brooklyn. A meeting at Colliers' Cafe on Broadway and 13th Street on 17 March 1871 led to the formation of the National Association of Professional Base Ball Players, which hastened the demise of the National Association of Base Ball Players. The new association lasted five seasons and is considered the first major league. Its teams in the metropolitan region included the Mutuals (1871–75), the Atlantics (1872–75), and the Eckfords (1872). Between 1872 and 1875 the Boston Red Stockings won the championship of the league in each year; the best effort during this period by a team from New York City was the second-place finish in 1874 by the Mutuals.

The National League of Professional Base-Ball Clubs was formed in 1876 by a group of club owners meeting at the Grand Central Hotel in New York City. The Mutuals were one of the first eight members of the league but were expelled after refusing to play their final games in the first season. From 1877 to 1882 no team from New York City played in the league, although several strong teams played from 1877 to 1879 in a rival one, the International Association. In 1882 the National League admitted a team from the city called the Giants, which won the championship of the league and the World Series in 1888 and 1889 and inspired several other teams in later years to take its name. In the following decade the fortunes of the New York Giants plummeted: they were able only to place second in 1894, and in the following year they came under the ownership of Andrew Freedman, a politician from Tammany Hall whose quixotic and abortive effort to dominate the league stirred dissension among other owners. New York City was also represented in the American Association, which was recognized by the National League as a major league under the National Agreement of 1883. The association lasted to the end of 1891 and fielded two teams in the area. The New York Metropolitans joined in 1883 and in the following season won the championship of the association before losing the first World Series to the champions of the National League (from Providence, Rhode Island). The owner of the Metropolitans, John Day, also owned the Giants of the National League, the team to which he shunted his best players; the Metropolitans were severely weakened as a result and left the American Association in 1887. In the same year the Brooklyn Bridegrooms joined the association. Owned by Charles Byrne, they won the championship of the association in 1889, which had been won for four consecutive seasons by the St. Louis Browns. After losing the World Series to the Giants the Bridegrooms moved in the following year to the National League and won its championship, becoming the only team ever to win consecutive pennants in different major leagues. In the World Series of 1890 the Bridegrooms played to a draw against the champions of the American Association (from Louisville, Kentucky). In 1890 a third major league, the Players National League, was organized by John Ward, the captain of the New York Giants and the head of the Brotherhood of Professional Base Ball Players. The league opposed several practices

New York Black Yankees, 1934

of the owners in the other leagues, including those of selling players, extending their contracts unilaterally, and limiting their salaries. It had teams in Manhattan and Brooklyn and attracted many players from the other leagues but was declared bankrupt after one season. The American Association disbanded in 1891 under pressure from the National League, which absorbed four of its eight teams: the result was a single major league with twelve teams, the National League and American Association of Professional Base Ball Clubs. This operated to the end of 1899, when its championship was won by the team from Brooklyn, then known as the Superbas. The same team won the championship in 1900, when the league reduced the number of its teams to eight.

New York City in the early twentieth century was the home of several important baseball teams as well as the birthplace of some of the best-known baseball traditions: local fans were among the first to eat hot dogs at the ballpark (introduced at the Polo Grounds by Harry M. Stevens after 1900) and the first to hear the song "Take Me Out to the Ball Game" (1908), by Al Von Tilzer and Jack Norworth (who were both from New York City). The American League was formed in the city in 1901 and recognized as a major league under the National Agreement of 1903. Under the new system of two major leagues the World Series was revived and major league baseball began a half-century of unprecedented stability: after a team moved from Baltimore to New York City in 1903 and became the Highlanders no other teams changed their location until 1952. The Highlanders played at a wooden stadium at 165th Street and Broadway called Hilltop Park until 1913, when they became tenants of the New York Giants at the Polo Grounds and were renamed the Yankees; in 1923 they moved to Yankee Stadium at East 161st Street and Jerome Avenue in the Bronx. Between 1903 and 1923 the Giants of the National League emerged as the most powerful and profitable team in the major leagues. During the tenure of their manager John McGraw (1902–32) they won the championship of the league ten times and the World Series three times (their humbling loss of the series in 1908 was brought on by the failure of "Bonehead" Fred Merkle to touch second base). During these years the league championship was won twice by the team from Brooklyn, now renamed the Dodgers. In 1914–15 the Federal League sought unsuccessfully to be recognized as a major league. One of its members was the Brooklyn Federals, a mediocre team owned by Robert Ward, an important financial backer of the league whose death in 1915 soon led to its dissolution.

A far more enduring challenge to the major leagues was mounted by the Negro leagues, the first of which was formed in 1920 by Rube

Major League Ballparks of New York City

NAME	LOCATION	YEAR(S)	TEAM (League)
59th Street Sandlot	59th to 60th streets between 1st Avenue and Sutton Place, Manhattan	1939	Cubans (NNL)
Capitoline Grounds	Halsey Street and Marcy, Putnam, and Nostrand avenues, Brooklyn	1865–76	Excelsiors, Atlantics (NA), Mutuals (NL)
Catholic Protectory Oval	Tremont Avenue and Unionport Road, Bronx	1923–36	Lincoln Giants (ECL), Cubans (NNL)
Dexter Park [Bushwick Park, Sterling Oval]	Bushwick Avenue, Woodhaven, Queens	1923–1940s	Royal Giants (ECL)
Dyckman Oval [Inwood Hill Park Oval]	Inwood Hill Park, 214th and Seaman streets	1922–32	Cuban Stars (NNL, NE–WL), Cuban Stars West Cuban Stars East (ECL, ANL), Bacharach Giants (ECL)
Eastern Park	Eastern Parkway, Belmont Avenue, Sackman Street, and Van Sinderen Avenue, Brooklyn	1890–97	Wonders (PL), Bridegrooms (NL)
Ebbets Field	Bedford Avenue, Montgomery Street, McKeever Place, and Sullivan Place, Brooklyn	1913–57	Dodgers (NL), Eagles (NNL), Brown Dodgers (USL)
Fashion Race Course [National Course]	Willets Point, Queens	1858	New York–Brooklyn series
Hilltop Park	165th to 168th streets between Broadway and Fort Washington Avenue, Manhattan	1903–12	Highlanders/ Yankees (AL), Giants (NL)
Jasper Oval [Hebrew Orphan Asylum Oval]	136th to 138th streets between Convent Avenue and St. Nicholas Terrace, Manhattan	1920s	Bacharach Giants (ECL)
John J. Downing Stadium [Randalls Island Stadium, Triborough Stadium]	Randalls Island, Manhattan	1938	Black Yankees (NNL)
Manhattan Field	155th Street and 8th Avenue, Manhattan	1889–90	Giants (NL), Gladiators (AA)
Maspeth Ball Grounds [Long Island Recreation Grounds]	Maspeth, Queens	1890	Trolley Dodgers (AA)
Metropolitan Park	107th to 109th streets between 1st Avenue and East River, Manhattan	1884	Metropolitans (AA)
Olympic Field	135th to 138th streets between 5th and Madison avenues, Manhattan	1928–29	Lincoln Giants (ECL, ANL)
Polo Grounds (i)	100th to 112th streets between 5th and 6th avenues, Manhattan	1880–88	Gothams (NL), Giants (NL), Metropolitans (AA)

(*continued*)

Major League Ballparks of New York City *(Continued)*

NAME	LOCATION	YEAR(S)	TEAM (League)
Polo Grounds (ii) [Brotherhood Park, Brush Stadium]	155th to 157th streets between 8th Avenue and Harlem River Speedway, Manhattan	1890–1963	Giants (NL), Yankees (AL), Cuban Giants, Mets (NL)
Ridgewood Park [Wallace's Ridgewood Grounds, Horse Market, Meyerrose's Union League Park]	Onderdonk and Elm avenues, Queens	1889–90	Trolley Dodgers (AA)
Satellite Grounds	Brooklyn	1867	Uniques
St. George Cricket Club	Staten Island	1853	Washington Club (later Gotham Club)
St. George Grounds	St. George, Staten Island	1886–89	Metropolitans (AA), Giants (NL)
Shea Stadium [William A. Shea Municipal Stadium]	Flushing Meadows–Corona Park, Queens	1964–	Mets (NL), Yankees (AL)
Union Grounds	Lee Avenue and Rutledge Street, Brooklyn	1871–77	Mutuals (NA), Eckfords (NA), Atlantics (NA)
[name unknown]	near Melrose Station of the Harlem Railroad, Manhattan	1886	Unions
Washington Park (i)	3rd to 5th streets between 4th and 5th avenues, Manhattan	1883–91	Dodgers (AA, NL)
Washington Park (ii)	1st to 3rd streets between 3rd and 4th avenues, Brooklyn	1898–1915	Dodgers (NL), Tip Tops (FL)
Wild West Grounds	Tompkinsville, Staten Island	1887	Metropolitans (AA)
Yankee Stadium	157th to 161st streets between 5th and Madison avenues, Bronx	1923–	Yankees (AL), Black Yankees (NNL)

AA = American Association
AL = American League
ANL = American Negro League
ECL = Eastern Colored League
FL = Federal League
NA = National Association
NE–WL = Negro East–West League
NL = National League
NNL = Negro National League
PL = Players League
USL = United States League
Source: Michael Benson: *Ballparks of North America* (Jefferson, N.C.: McFarland, 1989)

Compiled by Laura Lewison

Foster as the Negro National League and included teams from the Midwest. New York City was represented by the Lincoln Giants and the Brooklyn Giants in the Eastern Colored League, formed in 1923 by Nat Stron. Among the best-known players on these teams were the pitchers Smokey Joe Williams and Cannonball Dick Redding, the shortstop John Henry Lloyd (known as the "black Honus Wagner"), and the catcher Louis Santop. Both the Eastern Colored League and the Negro National League disbanded at the onset of the Depression. By this time the New York Yankees of the American League had begun to overshadow the New York Giants of the National League and during the next four decades were undeniably the best team in baseball. Between 1921 and 1964 they won twenty-nine league pennants and twenty World Series, led by such prominent players as Babe Ruth, Lou Gehrig, Joe DiMaggio, and Mickey Mantle. The Yankees played against the Giants in six World Series (known as "subway series"), of which they lost two (1921, the first series to be broadcast on radio, and 1922) and won four (1923, 1936, 1937, and 1951). Among the best-known players on the Giants in these years were Mel Ott (1926–47) and Carl Hubbell (1928–43). A second Negro National League was formed in 1933, followed by a Negro American League in 1937. The Negro National League in 1935 included the Brooklyn Eagles and the New York Cubans, who won the second of two championships contested during each half of the season. From 1936 both the Cubans and the New York Black Yankees belonged to the league, but after major league baseball at last became racially integrated in 1947 when Jackie Robinson joined the Brooklyn Dodgers, the Negro National League disbanded in the following year. The Cubans and the Black Yankees in 1949 joined the Negro American League, which played its final game in 1950 (by which time the Cubans were its only remaining team from the city).

The audience for baseball expanded rapidly with the introduction of broadcasts on television, the first of which was made from New York City in 1939 by Red Barber. In the 1940s the Dodgers became a formidable team in the National League, owing largely to the accomplishments of Duke Snider, Gil Hodges, and Robinson. The team played seven World Series against the Yankees but won only one (1955) and lost six (1941, 1947, 1949, 1952, 1953, 1956). Competition for the league championships and in the World Series during these years was marked by intense rivalry and several dramatic successes and failures: a missed third strike by the Dodgers' catcher Mickey Owen that helped the Yankees to win the World Series in 1941, a streak by DiMaggio in the same year during which he hit safely in fifty-six consecutive games, a home run by the Giants' outfielder Bobby Thomson that won a playoff against the Dodgers for the championship of the National League in 1951, and a perfect game pitched by Don Larsen of the Yankees against the Dodgers in the World Series of 1956. The popularity of baseball nationwide was encouraged by the status of New York City as the center of print and broadcast journalism: some twenty-five newspapers were published there in 1950.

Baseball in the city was dealt a severe blow in the winter of 1957, when both its teams in the National League announced plans to move to California in the following season: the Giants and their popular outfielder Willie Mays to San Francisco, the Dodgers to Los Angeles. In 1962 the city was awarded one of two new teams in the league, the New York Mets, who performed at a rarely matched level of ineptness in their early seasons before astonishing observers by winning the World Series in 1969; the Mets again won the series in 1986. The Yankees played poorly in the late 1960s

Major League Professional Baseball Teams in New York City

1871–76	New York Mutuals	National Association, 1871–75 National League, 1876
1872	Brooklyn Eckfords	National Association
1872–75	Brooklyn Atlantics	National Association
1883–87	New York Metropolitans	American Association
1883–1957	New York Giants	National League
1884–1957	Brooklyn Dodgers[1]	American Association, 1884–89 National League, 1890–1957
1890	Brooklyn Wonders[2]	Players League
1890	New York Phillies	Players League
1903–	New York Yankees[3]	American League
1914–15	Brooklyn Tip Tops[4]	Federal League
1922	Cuban Stars	Negro National League
1923–29	Lincoln Giants	Eastern Colored League, 1923–26, 1928 American Negro League, 1929
1923–29	Cuban Stars East	Eastern Colored League, 1923–28 American Negro League, 1929
1923–29	Bacharach Giants	Eastern Colored League, 1923–28 American Negro League, 1929
1923–30	Cuban Stars West	Negro National League
1923–27	Brooklyn Royal Giants	Eastern Colored League
1935	Brooklyn Eagles	Negro National League
1935–50	New York Cubans	Negro National League, 1935–48 Negro American League, 1949–50
1936–48	New York Black Yankees	Negro National League
1962–	New York Mets	National League

1. Although primarily known as the Trolley Dodgers from the 1890s and as the Dodgers from 1910, the team had several other names. Official names: Bridegrooms (1884–98), Superbas (1899–1926), Robins (1927–31, for the manager Wilbert Robinson), Dodgers (1932–33), Brooklyns (1934–37), Dodgers (1938–57). Unofficial names: Ward's Wonders (for John M. Ward, who joined the team after the Brooklyn Wonders of the Players League disbanded in 1890), Foutz's Phillies (for Dave Foutz, manager 1893–96), Barney's Boys (for Billy Barney, manager 1897–98), Byrne's Boys (for Charles Byrne, president 1890–98), Infants (about 1910).
2. Also called Ward's Wonders, for the star player John M. Ward.
3. Originally called the Highlanders; the name Yankees first used in 1905, both names used for the next eight years. In 1912 the team moved to its new stadium, the Polo Grounds on East 155th Street, and in 1913 the name was officially changed to the Yankees.
4. The name Brookfeds was introduced but never widely adopted.

Sources: Frank G. Menke: *The Encyclopedia of Sports* (New York: A. S. Barnes, 1953)
Harold Seymour: *Baseball* (New York: Oxford University Press, 1960)
Donn Rogosin: *Invisible Men* (New York, Atheneum, 1983)
Michael Benson: *Ballparks of North America* (Jefferson, N.C.: McFarland, 1989)

Compiled by Laura Lewison

and early 1970s but revived briefly under their controversial owner George Steinbrenner (from 1973), winning the World Series in 1977 and 1978. In the mid 1990s many New Yorkers remained ardent fans of baseball, and the city continued to exert a strong influence on the game.

Harold Seymour: *Baseball* (New York: Oxford University Press, 1960–71; rev. 1989–91)
David Quentin Voigt: *American Baseball*, vols. 1, 2 (Norman: University of Oklahoma Press, 1966–70)
David Quentin Voigt: *American Baseball*, vol. 3 (University Park: Pennsylvania State University Press, 1983)
Melvin L. Adelman: *A Sporting Time: New York City and the Rise of Modern Athletics, 1820–1870* (Urbana: University of Illinois Press, 1986)
George B. Kirsch: *The Creation of American Team Sports: Baseball and Cricket, 1838–1872* (Urbana: University of Illinois Press, 1989)

See also SPORTS. For further illustration see BROOKLYN DODGERS.

David Q. Voigt

Basie, Count [William] (*b* Red Bank, N.J., 21 Aug 1904; *d* New York City, 26 April 1984). Pianist and bandleader. He moved to New York City about 1924; there he learned to play the pipe organ from Fats Waller. In 1927 he left New York City for the Southwest, where he soon became a leading performer of the hard-driving swing that developed in Kansas City. He returned to New York City in 1936 as the leader of the Count Basie Orchestra, which attracted such well-known soloists as the tenor saxophonists Lester Young and Herschel Evans, the trombonist Dicky Wells, the trumpeters Buck Clayton and Harry "Sweets" Edison, and the singers Billie Holiday, Jimmy Rushing, and Helen Humes; he played in the rhythm section with Walter Page, Jo Jones, and Freddie Green. For a while the members of the band lived at the Woodside Hotel in Harlem, inspiring the composition "Jumpin' at the Woodside" (1938). Basie dismantled the big band in 1950 and organized another one in 1951 that had tighter and more polished arrangements and performed around the world. With his wife, Catherine, he moved to St. Albans in 1946. His book *Good Morning Blues: The Autobiography of Count Basie* was published in 1985.

Stanley Dance: *The World of Count Basie* (New York: Charles Scribner's Sons, 1980)

Douglas Henry Daniels

basketball. New York City is widely acknowledged to have become the spiritual home of basketball soon after the sport was invented in Springfield, Massachusetts, in 1891 and to have remained so for the next century. By 1900 basketball was played throughout the metropolitan area at chapters of the YMCA and in settlement houses, school gymnasiums, lofts, armories, and dance halls, and amateur and semiprofessional teams soon flourished. The year 1914 marked the formation of the New York Celtics, who played for three seasons before disbanding when the United States entered the First World War. After the war the promoter Jim Furey and his brothers sought to reorganize the team, which became known as the Original Celtics when the owner of the New York Celtics refused to relinquish his rights to their name. Along with the New York Whirlwinds, which had been organized by the well-known promoter Tex Rickard, the Original Celtics were one of the outstanding teams of the period. Their success and popularity stimulated the interest of the public in professional basketball, and in 1925 the American Basketball League (ABL) was formed with teams in Brooklyn, Washington, Cleveland, Rochester (New York), Fort Wayne (Indiana), Boston, Chicago, Detroit, and Buffalo. The Original Celtics did not at first join the league (the owners believed that they could make more money by barnstorming), but teams that did belong to the league hoped to capitalize on the popularity of the Original Celtics by challenging them to exhibition games, only to be embarrassed by losing decisively and regularly. The Original Celtics finally joined the ABL as a replacement for Brooklyn, which had the poorest record in the league, and in two seasons won seventy-two games and lost only fourteen; in playoffs the team won eight games and lost one. Professional basketball had a precarious existence in New York City in the next two decades, and by 1929 the ABL was defunct.

A number of notable black teams were

formed in the 1920s. The best of these was the New York Renaissance (popularly known as the New York Rens), formed in 1922 by Bob Douglas and named after the Renaissance Casino in Harlem where the team played its home games. By the mid 1930s the Rens were acknowledged to have succeeded the Original Celtics as the leading team in New York City; they continued to play until after the Second World War. The well-known team the Harlem Globetrotters, notwithstanding its name, was based in Chicago.

New York University, St. John's College, and Fordham University all had powerful teams in the 1920s. Between 1928 and 1936 St. John's won 179 games and lost only thirty-two under the coaching of Buck Freeman, probably the greatest exponent of the deliberate style of play associated with the Original Celtics and the Rens. College basketball reached a new level of popularity in 1934, when both City College of New York and New York University finished their seasons undefeated and played against each other in March for the unofficial championship of the city. The game was staged at the 168th Street Armory by Ned Irish (1905–82), a sportswriter who had arranged games to benefit the city relief fund at the behest of Mayor James J. Walker, and drew a crowd of sixteen thousand.

The city and the metropolitan area were the site during these years of the best collegiate basketball in the country. City College and New York University were always competitive, St. John's remained a consistent winner after Joe Lapchick replaced Freeman as the head coach in 1937, and other schools such as Long Island University, St. Francis College, and St. Peter's College and Seton Hall College in New Jersey were emerging as basketball powers. This success in collegiate basketball culminated in 1938 in the first staging of the National Invitation Tournament (NIT), sponsored by the Metropolitan Basketball Writers Association; the success of the NIT inspired the National Collegiate Athletic Association (NCAA) to organize its own tournament in 1939. In its first thirteen years the NIT was won five times by teams from New York City, and in 1950 City College became the first school to win both the NIT and the championship of the NCAA. In the following year college basketball in the city was devastated by the results of an investigation led by the district attorney of Manhattan, Frank Hogan, into allegations of "point shaving" (deliberately reducing the margin of victory in a game to accommodate bettors). Thirty-two players were indicted from seven local schools, including City College, Manhattan College, New York University, and Long Island University. Madison Square Garden soon ceased to be a major venue for college games, the NIT lost some of its glamour, and most local colleges severely reduced their basketball programs or eliminated them entirely. Not until the late 1970s did another local school, St. John's University, field a team that achieved a high national ranking.

Professional basketball began to arouse the interest of fans after the Second World War. The Basketball Association of America, formed in 1946, included as one of its original members the New York Knickerbockers; after two years the association merged with the National Basketball League to form the National Basketball Association (NBA), which had seventeen teams. The Knickerbockers were among the first racially integrated teams in basketball: Nat "Sweetwater" Clifton (*b* 1922), one of the two first black players in the NBA, joined the team in the autumn of 1950. On the court the Knickerbockers achieved little distinction in their first twenty-three years and won only two divisional titles, but after several astute trades and drafts they won the championship of the NBA in 1969–70 and again in 1972–73.

New York City is noted for having outstanding basketball players in its high schools and playgrounds. Hundreds of players each year are recruited in the city by colleges throughout the country, and brokers of high school basketball players, called "street agents," are often seen at high school and playground games. Among local players who have become prominent in college and as professionals are Kareem Abdul-Jabbar (*b* 1947), who played in the city as Lew Alcindor, Connie Hawkins (*b* 1942), Roger Brown (*b* 1942), Julius Erving (*b* 1950), Albert King (*b* 1959), Nate "Tiny" Archibald (*b* 1948), and Nancy Lieberman. The best-known playground players include Hermann "Helicopter" Knowings (1942–80), Joe "the Destroyer" Hammond (*b* 1950), Pablo Robertson (1944–90), Jumpin' Jackie Jackson (*b* 1940), Bobby Hunter (*b* 1942), Ron Jackson (*b* 1943), and Earl "the Goat" Manigault (*b* 1948), considered by his peers to have been as talented as Abdul-Jabbar. The importance of playground basketball in the city is reflected by the presence of weekend tournaments such as the Rucker Pro Tournament (first staged in 1950), played at the Holcombe Rucker Memorial Playground opposite the site of the old Polo Grounds on 155th Street and Frederick Douglass Boulevard (8th Avenue). The tournament attracts the best local players, members of touring teams such as the Globetrotters, and some professionals.

Larry Fox: *Illustrated History of Basketball* (New York: Grosset and Dunlap, 1974)
Neil D. Isaacs: *All the Moves: A History of College Basketball* (Philadelphia: J. B. Lippincott, 1975)
Daniel Rudman, ed.: *Take It to the Hoop: A Basketball Anthology* (Richmond, Calif.: North Atlantic, 1980)

Albert Figone

Bates USA. Advertising agency, formed in 1987 as Backer Spielvogel Bates Worldwide through the merger by the firm of Saatchi and Saatchi of two of its subsidiaries: Ted Bates, and Backer and Spielvogel. In 1990 the agency handled $3700 million in billings and was led by Carl Spielvogel. In June 1994 the firm took its current name. Bates USA is the sixth-largest advertising agency in the United States. Its headquarters are at 405 Lexington Avenue in Manhattan.

George Winslow

Bath Beach. Neighborhood in southeastern Brooklyn (1990 pop. 35,021), bounded to the north by 86th Street, to the east by Bay Parkway, to the south by Gravesend Bay, and to the west by 14th Avenue; it is a section of Bensonhurst. Named for the inland English spa of Bath, it was a resort known for its yacht clubs, fashionable villas, and a restaurant called the Captain's Pier at the foot of 19th Avenue until the Belt Parkway was built in 1939. The housing consists mostly of two-

Bath Beach, 1992

and three-family red brick houses and six-story apartment buildings. The population is mostly Italian, and many residents work in Manhattan.

Stephen Weinstein

Bathgate. Neighborhood in the central Bronx, immediately west of Crotona Park. It is often said to include the neighborhood of Claremont. The name is that of a family that worked the lands of Morris Manor before establishing its own farm in Morrisania in 1841 on a tract of more than 140 acres (fifty-seven hectares), with a farmhouse situated near what is now 3rd Avenue and East 172nd Street. The land was sold to the city about 1883 as part of the Parks Act and became Crotona Park (plans to name it after the Bathgates were forestalled by a dispute between the family and the surveyors). Many Jews from the Lower East Side moved to new five-story apartment buildings in the area after the 3rd Avenue elevated line was extended north in the 1890s. By the mid 1950s there were increasing numbers of blacks and Puerto Ricans, and Bathgate Avenue became a thriving commercial strip known into the 1960s for its ethnic restaurants. The Bathgate Industrial Park occupies eight blocks along Bathgate Avenue between the Cross Bronx Expressway and Claremont Parkway. Built on the site of apartment buildings that were burned and abandoned in the 1970s, it is one of the most successful business zones in the Bronx.

John McNamara: *History in Asphalt: The Origin of Bronx Street and Place Names* (New York: Bronx County Historical Society, 1984)

Gary D. Hermalyn

bathhouses. A quick sponging off was considered adequate for personal cleanliness during colonial times in New York City. Gradually the élite began to enjoy bathing, and in 1792 Nicholas Denise opened a "very convenient Bathing House, having eight rooms, in every one of which Baths may be had with either fresh, salt or warm water . . . prices fixed at 4s per person." The opening of the Croton Aqueduct in 1842 made bathing easier for those who could afford to install running water in their homes; most of the city's population continued to rely on public hydrants. Interest in building public baths in New York City mounted about the mid nineteenth century, when a national movement was organized to promote personal cleanliness in crowded tenements lacking adequate bathing facilities. The movement in New York City achieved its first success in 1849, when the Association for Improving the Condition of the Poor built the People's Bathing and Washing Establishment at 141 Mott Street, the first public bath. Open only during the summer, it provided laundry facilities, a swimming pool, and baths for men and women. The rates were prohibitive for the poor: three cents an hour to use the laundry, and from five to ten cents to take a bath. Initially the bath attracted sixty thousand persons a year and was hailed by the association as a great success, but it closed in 1861 for lack of patronage.

Concern over the cleanliness of the poor intensified after the Civil War as immigrants from southern and eastern Europe crowded into the city's slums. In 1870 the Department of Public Works built its first floating baths, large wooden structures installed in the Hudson and East rivers that formed large pools for bathing free of charge from June to October. By 1888 fifteen such baths attracted about 2.5 million men and 1.5 million women a year. Insisting that the pools were designed for cleanliness and not for recreation, the authorities imposed a twenty-minute limit on their use. On hot days young boys evaded this regulation by moving from pool to pool, dirtying themselves en route. Soon after construction was completed, pollution became a serious problem, and from 1914 the floating baths were required to be watertight and filled with purified water. Spurred by the germ theory of disease, which lent new importance to the battle against dirt, reformers and the press urged the city government to open free baths during the 1880s. The city refused on the grounds that the proposals lacked public support, and the physician Simon Baruch launched a campaign to seek other sponsors. He eventually persuaded the Association for Improving the Condition of the Poor to build a new bathhouse on the Lower East Side. Contributions to the venture included $27,000 from various sources and eighty pounds (thirty-six kilograms) of soap from the firm of Colgate. The People's Baths opened in the early 1890s, its grand arch inscribed with the maxim "Cleanliness Next to Godliness"; this was the first successful indoor bathhouse in the country and was widely imitated. Built of concrete and iron and fitted with showers instead of tubs, it was easy to keep clean and inexpensive to operate. A five-cent fee provided for a towel and soap. In 1898 alone the bathhouse attracted 115,685 patrons. Its success inspired other private charities to build similar facilities, and some businesses introduced baths for their employees.

The city did not begin to build a public bath until 1895, when the state legislature passed a law requiring municipalities with populations of fifty thousand or more to build free bathhouses. During the same year the reform Republican William L. Strong won the mayoral election and endorsed the public bath movement. The first free bath began operation in March 1901 on Rivington Street. By 1914 the city had built sixteen more public baths in Manhattan, seven in Brooklyn, and one each in Queens and the Bronx, most of them in neighborhoods populated by immigrants; the result was the most elaborate and expensive bath system in the country. Men and women entered separate waiting rooms and took a number. Once called, they were given twenty minutes to shower in a small cubicle divided into a changing area and a shower stall. Attendants controlled the timing and the temperature of the water. Most of the baths built after 1904 included gymnasiums and swimming pools to attract more patrons. People generally preferred to bathe at home if they could, and bathing facilities were increasingly provided by landlords after the Tenement House Law of 1901 required tenements to have running water on all stories. Use of the public baths declined even before the last one was completed in 1914. During these years commercial bathhouses thrived. In 1897 there were sixty-two such facilities including Russian (steam) baths, Turkish (hot air) baths, vapor baths, and medicated baths as well as

Asser Levy Recreation Center (foreground, *designed by Arnold W. Brunner and William Martin Aiken*), *1991*

swimming pools. More than half were owned and used by Jews from eastern Europe seeking to uphold religious and social traditions of bathing. The best-known included the Russian Turkish Baths on 10th Street between Avenue A and 1st Avenue.

Many municipal baths were renovated during the 1930s by the Works Progress Administration; most were demolished or converted to other uses after the Second World War (the last one, the Allen Street Baths, was shut down during the 1970s). Commercial bathhouses catering to gays played a central role in the gay liberation movement of the 1970s. A bitter controversy erupted during the 1980s over whether these bathhouses contributed to the spread of AIDS by allowing casual sex on their premises; local health officials were ultimately given the power to close them by the state legislature in 1985. During the same years the growth of homelessness prompted the city to reintroduce free showers, this time in municipal shelters.

In the mid 1990s few of the original municipal baths remained. One, the Asser Levy Bath on East 23rd Street, was designated a landmark and reopened in 1990 as a swimming pool after $8 million in restorations.

David Glassberg: "The Public Bath Movement in America," *American Studies* 20, no. 2 (1979), 5–21

Richard L. Bushman and Claudia L. Bushman: "The Early History of Cleanliness in America," *Journal of American History* 74 (1988), 1213–38

Marilyn Thornton Williams: *Washing "The Great Unwashed": Public Baths in Urban America, 1840–1920* (Columbus: Ohio State University Press, 1991)

Corinne T. Field, Marilyn Thornton Williams

Batten, Barton, Durstine and Osborn [BBDO]. Advertising agency formed in 1928 when the George Batten Company merged with Barton, Durstine and Osborn. Its accounts included General Electric and General Motors and by 1929 its billings reached $32.6 million. In 1940 Alex Osborn, one of the company's founders, coined the term "brainstorming" to describe his technique for devising ideas for advertising campaigns. The agency was the first to set up a radio department and made plans for television advertising as early as 1931. Under the management of Ben Duffy in 1946–57 its work in television increased billings to more than $200 million, and the agency shifted its emphasis from advertising for banks, insurers, electric utilities, and other institutions to advertising for packaged goods. During the 1960s and 1970s it remained among the four largest advertising agencies in the United States, and in 1986 it merged with Doyle Dane Bernbach and Needham Harper to form a new public holding company, the Omnicom group, with total billings of about $5000 million.

James Playsted Wood: *The Story of Advertising* (New York: Ronald, 1958)

Stephen R. Fox: *The Mirror Makers: A History of American Advertising and Its Creators* (New York: William Morrow, 1984)

Chauncey G. Olinger, Jr.

Battery Park. Public park at the southern tip of Manhattan. It occupies a site offering ready access to the harbor and the Hudson River, an advantage recognized by both American Indians and Dutch settlers, who called the area Capske Hook (from an Indian term for rocky ledge). The modern name is derived from the gun batteries once housed by the bulkhead. The park is built on landfill, which is extensive owing to repeated extension of the shoreline in the eighteenth and nineteenth centuries: Fort George nearby (originally called Fort Amsterdam) was demolished in 1788 and its remnants added to the shore filling; Castle Clinton, a circular fort of red sandstone near the western edge of the park, was some one hundred yards (thirty meters) offshore when it was built in 1811. This naval fortification, designed by John McComb Jr. (an architect of City Hall) and Jonathan Williams, was never used for military purposes and was ceded to the city in 1823. As Castle Garden it was the leading entertainment hall in the city for more than thirty years, perhaps best known for a performance there in 1850 by the singer Jenny Lind presented by P. T. Barnum. The building was later used as the federal immigration center for the east coast (1855–90, before the opening of the facility at Ellis Island), and after being reconfigured by Stanford White as the New York Aquarium (1896–1941) was operated by the parks department. From 1940 to 1952 the park was closed while the Brooklyn–Battery Tunnel was built beneath it; on reopening it had new landscaping and an additional two acres (eighty ares) of land. In 1963 President John F. Kennedy dedicated the East Coast Memorial to the 4596 servicemen who lost their lives in the Atlantic during the Second World War, one of many monuments in the park honoring soldiers, explorers, inventors, and immigrants. In 1982 New York State designated Battery Park as part of Harbor Park, a group of historic waterfront sites.

Jonathan Kuhn

Battery Park City. Commercial and residential complex in lower Manhattan, bounded to the north by Chambers Street, to the east by West Street, to the south by Pier A, and to the west by the Hudson River. It is built on an expanse of landfill with an area of ninety-two acres (thirty-seven hectares), of which dredgings from the construction of the World Trade Center account for twenty-five acres (ten hectares). The complex was developed by the Battery Park City Authority, a public-benefit corporation formed in 1968 by the state legislature. The authority used proceeds from the sale of state bonds to deposit the landfill, develop the infrastructure, and build public parks, and then chose private developers for the commercial and residential areas. A portion of the profits was used to finance public amenities as well as to build and rehabilitate low- and middle-income housing elsewhere in New York City. Construction began in 1974 on Gateway Plaza, a residential complex. A master plan drawn up in 1979 by Alexander Cooper and Stanton Eckstut allocated 42 percent of the land for

Battery Park (background *downtown office district*), ca *1935–40*

The esplanade at Battery Park City, 1992

housing, 30 percent for open space (including an esplanade along the river), 19 percent for streets and avenues, and 9 percent for commercial and office space. Olympia and York was the sole developer of the commercial area, the World Financial Center, which is adjacent to the financial district around Wall Street and connected to it by two walkways. Designed by Cesar Pelli Associates, the center includes four office towers ranging in height from thirty-three to fifty-one stories, two octagonal buildings of nine stories each, commercial and retail space, an outdoor plaza (designed with the landscape architects M. Paul Friedberg and Partners), and a marina for twenty-six oceangoing yachts; the Winter Garden, which has ceilings 120 feet (thirty-seven meters) high and contains sixteen palm trees forty feet (twelve meters) tall, is an enclosed glass public space where free performances are sponsored by corporate residents. Among the architects who are represented at the complex are Charles Moore; Cesar Pelli; Davis, Brody and Associates; Skidmore, Owings and Merrill; Menz and Cook; Mitchell/Giurgola; the Gruzen Partnership; Bond Ryder James; Ulrich Franzen; the Vilkas Group; James Stewart Polshek and Partners; Ehrenkrantz, Eckstut and Whitelaw; Costas Kondylis; and Gruzen Samton Steinglass. Artists whose work may be seen at Battery Park City include R. M. Fischer (*Rector Gate*, 1989, a whimsical entryway between park and esplanade), Richard Artschwager (*Sitting/Stance*, 1989, a collection of fanciful street furniture), Ned Smyth (*Upper Room*, 1987, a small park with a variety of decorative architectural motifs), Siah Armajani, Scott Burton, and Mary Miss.

The initial plan for Battery Park City was completed in 1988; a ferry connection to Hoboken, New Jersey, began service in 1989. In 1992 Stuyvesant High School opened its new building at the northern end of the complex, designed by Alexander Cooper and Partners. In the mid 1990s more than five thousand persons lived at the complex and twenty thousand worked there; plans called for these figures to rise eventually to 25,000 and 35,000. Among the additions to the complex in various stages of construction were a waterfront park of eight acres (3.2 hectares) adjacent to the high school, designed by Carr Lynch Associates in conjunction with Oehme, van Sweden and Associates, and a park of three acres (1.2 hectares) at the southern end of the complex, designed by Alexander Cooper, Nicholas Quennell, and the artist Jennifer Bartlett. Further additions being planned included a memorial to the Holocaust and a museum of Jewish heritage, a luxury hotel, a fifth office tower, and more housing.

Nan Ellin

Battista, Vito P(iranesi) (*b* Bari, Italy, 7 Sept 1908; *d* Brooklyn, 24 May 1990). Architect and political leader. With his family he moved to New York City at the age of three and settled in Bushwick. After attending night school he studied architecture at the Carnegie Institute, the Massachusetts Institute of Technology, the École des Beaux-Arts in Paris, and Columbia University. He helped to design structures for the World's Fair of 1939–40 and Cadman Plaza, became president of the Society of Architects in Brooklyn, and organized the Institute of Design and Construction (1947). A Republican in a predominantly Democratic city, he was known as a gadfly with a showman's flair and a perennial candidate for municipal office who spoke for ordinary people while inveighing against taxes, rent control, welfare abuse, and municipal waste. Battista served on the Republican State Committee, attended five Republican National Conventions, and was a state assemblyman from 1965 to 1975.

George J. Lankevich

Bayard, Nicholas (*b* Alphen, Netherlands, 1644; *d* New York City, ?1709). Mayor. A nephew of Peter Stuyvesant, he began his career as a clerk for the provincial secretary of New Amsterdam and held a similar position after the English conquest; he was appointed receiver general when the Dutch returned to power in 1673 but was removed from his offices when the English returned and subsequently imprisoned by Governor Edmond Andros. He was a favorite of Governor Thomas Dongan, who appointed him mayor of New York City in 1685 and a member of the governor's council in 1687. A leading opponent of Jacob Leisler, Bayard was imprisoned by the Leislerians in early 1690. On his release in 1691 he was reappointed to the governor's council and helped to ensure that Leisler was executed on charges of treason later the same year. Bayard was dismissed from office in 1697 and was himself convicted of treason and sentenced to death in 1702, when Leisler's former allies controlled the provincial government, but he was pardoned before the sentence was carried out.

Henry Collins Brown, ed.: "Early Mayors of New York," *Valentine's Manual of Old New York: 1925* (New York: Museum of the City of New York, 1924), 147–203

Robert C. Ritchie: *The Duke's Province: A Study of New York Politics and Society, 1664–1691* (Chapel Hill: University of North Carolina Press, 1977)

David William Voorhees

Bayard, William (*b* New York City, 1761; *d* New York City, 18 Sept 1826). Merchant. The son of Loyalist parents, he remained in New York City after his family moved to England in 1783 and with Herman LeRoy formed an international shipping company that was one of the strongest of its kind for four decades. He also speculated in land upstate, was a privateer in the War of 1812, tried to obtain loans for the Erie Canal, was president of the Morris Canal Company and the Bank of America, and belonged to the Chamber of Commerce. Toward the end of his life Bayard was troubled by accusations that his firm, then managed by his sons, engaged in profiteering during the Greek Revolution. He wrote *An Exposition of the Conduct of the Two Houses* (1826).

James E. Mooney

Bayard–Condict Building. Office building at 65 Bleecker Street between Broadway and Lafayette Street, erected in 1898. It is the only building in New York City designed by Frank Lloyd Wright's teacher Louis H. Sullivan. The building is ornamented with terra cotta. Between the columns and an intricately filigreed cornice are six angels said to have been added over Sullivan's objections. The original capitals from the first-floor columns are now in the sculpture garden of the Brooklyn Museum.

John Voelcker

Baychester. Neighborhood in the northeastern Bronx and the site of Co-op City, bounded to the east by the Hutchinson River and Pelham Bay Park and to the southwest and west by the New England Thruway. The area was a marsh until it became the site of a cucumber farm and pickle factory from the 1870s to 1895; it was then used to farm strawberries and in the 1890s was given its current name by real-estate developers. A few years later the land was sold to the Curtiss–Wright Aviation Company for a municipal airport that was never built; it was also considered a possible site for a racetrack. An amusement park called Freedomland occupied the area from 1960 until the construction in 1968–70 of Co-op City, one of the largest housing developments in the United States. Sixty thousand persons live in 15,372 apartments in the development, which has thirty-five buildings (mostly high rise), movie theaters, eight multistory garages, five shopping centers, a firehouse, a heating plant, and an educational park. Apart from Co-op City the neighborhood consists principally of one- and two-family houses and a large shopping mall. Some residents of the area west of the New England Thruway also consider their neighborhood part of Baychester. By 1990 the population was largely black and Latin American.

John McNamara: *McNamara's Old Bronx* (New York: Bronx County Historical Society, 1989)

Gary D. Hermalyn

Bayonne Bridge. The longest steel arch bridge in the world. It crosses the Kill van Kull between Port Richmond in Staten Island and Bayonne, New Jersey. The bridge was designed by Othmar H. Ammann and the architect Cass Gilbert and completed by the Port of New York Authority in 1931 at a cost of $13 million. It has a dramatic, high arch of 266 feet (81.1 meters) that carries the road bed for 1675 feet (511 meters) without intermediary piers. The total length of the bridge, including approaches, is 8460 feet (2580 meters), and the clearance above water at mid-span is 150 feet (forty-six meters). The original plan called for granite sheathing (designed by Gilbert) to be laid over the steelwork of the arch abutment, but this feature of the project was eliminated to lower costs.

Harold M. Lewis and Charles Herrick: *1930 Report of the City Plan Commission, Bayonne, N.J. including Plans for Development of East Side Waterfront, a System of Rail and Highway Communications, a Civic Center* (Bayonne, N.J.: City Plan Commission, 1930)

Rebecca Read Shanor

View of Bayonne Bridge from Staten Island to New Jersey, 1932

Bay Ridge. Neighborhood in southwestern Brooklyn (1990 pop. 110,708), bounded to the north by 61st Street, to the east by the Gowanus Expressway, to the south by 86th Street, and to the west by Upper New York Bay. The land was part of a tract bought by the Dutch West India Company from the Nyack Indians in 1652. The neighborhood was called Yellow Hook for the color of the clay found in the area; so as not to evoke unpleasant associations with the yellow fever epidemic of 1848–49 this name was abandoned in 1853 in favor of the current one, which recalls the position of the neighborhood by the bay and the glacial ridge that runs along what is now Ridge Boulevard. After the Civil War the area became the suburban retreat of the wealthy, whose mansions lined the bluffs above the Narrows. The Crescent Athletic Club (now Fort Hamilton High School) was the center of fashionable society. After the opening of the 4th Avenue subway in 1915 high-rise apartment buildings replaced most of the earlier houses. The population consisted largely of Italians and Scandinavians, and after the Second World War also of Irish, Greeks, and Arabs. The neighborhood was the setting in 1978 for the film *Saturday Night Fever*, several scenes of which were filmed at a local nightclub. During the 1980s the Chinese community centered at Sunset Park expanded into the neighborhood, and some abandoned factories and warehouses were converted into garment factories run by Chinese entrepreneurs. The Chinese were by far the largest single group of new immigrants settling in Bay Ridge in the 1980s, accounting for more than a quarter of all immigrants; there were also large numbers from Italy, the Soviet Union, Greece, Korea, Lebanon, Egypt, Syria, and Jordan. The neighborhood has an active army installation at Fort Hamilton and is the terminus in Brooklyn of the Verrazano Narrows Bridge. Two mansions remain: the Fontbonne Hall Academy at 9901 Shore Road (now a private school) and the Gingerbread House at 82nd Street and Narrows Avenue (designated a landmark). Bay Ridge is a community of one- and two-family row and frame houses with bay fronts, garages, basements, and lawns. The main shopping streets are 86th Street and 3rd and 5th avenues.

Nanette Rainone, ed.: *The Brooklyn Neighborhood Book* (New York: Fund for the Borough of Brooklyn, 1985)

Elizabeth Reich Rawson

Bay Ridge Savings Bank. Original name of ANCHOR SAVINGS BANK.

Bayside. Neighborhood in northeastern Queens (1988 pop. 113,000), on Little Neck Bay, for which it is named. First inhabited by Matinecock Indians, it was part of the area for which William Lawrence received patents from Charles I in 1644. During the American Revolution it was settled first by John Rodman, a Quaker, and later by Thomas Hicks, a resident of Flushing whose land was included in a parcel of 246 acres (one hundred hectares) bought in 1824 by Abraham Bell. About this time the Lawrence family also settled in Bayside, which grew after the North Shore Railroad was extended in 1866. During the following thirty years many mansions were built on the high ground around the bay by wealthy New Yorkers, including F. N. Lawrence, G. Howland Leavitt, and G. W. Harway; many of their estates were dissolved in the 1920s and 1930s when houses were built by film stars and sportsmen, among them Pearl White, Norma Talmadge, John Golden, and James J. Corbett. Between 1908 and 1928 J. Wilson Dayton and the McKnight Realty Company put up many houses on sidestreets of Bell Boulevard and on new streets built inland from Little Neck Bay. After the Second World War the character of Bayside was altered by highways and bridges built to the east and west, including the Cross Island Parkway, which cut off access to Little Neck Bay, and the Throgs Neck Bridge (1961) and Clearview Expressway (1961–63). Large apartment complexes such as Bay Terrace and Clearview Gardens were built in the late 1960s. Queensboro Community College opened in 1967 on the former site of the Oakland Golf Course. Bayside is a comfortable middle-class, suburban neighborhood, with a growing Chinese, Korean, and Indian population.

Vincent Seyfried

Bayswater. Neighborhood in southwestern Queens, constituting the part of Far Rockaway north of Bayswater Avenue and Mott Avenue. It was developed by William Trist Bailey, who built cottages and a brick hotel called the Bayswater House on land bought in 1878 from J. B. and W. W. Cornell, descendants of Richard Cornell, the first settler in Rockaway. Summer mansions were later built on large lots by many prominent residents of Brooklyn. In June 1905 Trist was declared bankrupt and his tract was sold piecemeal at auction. Bayswater Point, a site of twelve acres (five hectares) on Jamaica Bay, was acquired in 1986 by New York State, which in 1991 designated the area a state park to be administered by the Audubon Society. By this time many older houses in the neighborhood had been demolished and replaced by housing for the middle class.

Vincent Seyfried

Bay Terrace. Neighborhood in east central Staten Island, centered at a station of the same name of Staten Island Rapid Transit and lying within the neighborhood of Oakwood. It consists mainly of modern estates. The tiny chapel of Madonna del Ponte still offers masses in Latin.

Martha S. Bendix

BBDO. See Batten, barton, durstine and osborn.

Beach, Alfred Ely (*b* Springfield, Mass., 1 Sept 1826; *d* New York City, 1 Jan 1896). Newspaper and magazine publisher and inventor. With his brother Moses Sperry Beach he acquired control of the *Sun* in 1848 from their father, the newspaper publisher Moses Yale Beach; in 1852 he relinquished his share of the paper. An owner and editor of *Scientific American*, he helped to transform the magazine into a publication of national stature. He also contributed to the invention of the typewriter, and took out a patent for a model in 1847; he invented a typewriter for the blind in 1857. Among his other inventions were pneumatic tubes for mail and passengers (1865) and a shield used for tunneling under streets and rivers (1868). In 1870 he built a section of pneumatic subway under lower Manhattan that is considered by many to have been the prototype for the subway system that was eventually built.

Steven H. Jaffe

Beach, Moses Yale (*b* Wallingford, Conn., 15 Jan 1800; *d* Wallingford, 19 July 1868). Newspaper publisher and inventor, father of Alfred Ely Beach. After inventing a rag-cutting machine for the manufacture of paper and a combustion engine, in 1834 he became the manager of the mechanical department at the *New York Sun*, which was owned by his brother-in-law Benjamin Day. He bought the *Sun* from Day in 1838 and transformed it into one of the country's most prosperous and widely read "penny papers." A prominent Democrat, he was sent by President James K. Polk on a secret mission to Mexico (1846), where he attempted unsuccessfully to negotiate an end to the Mexican–American War. Between 1842 and 1855 he published a pamphlet, *The Wealth of New York*, in which he included himself on a list of the city's thousand richest citizens. He retired from the *Sun* in 1848 and turned it over to his sons, Alfred Ely Beach and Moses Sperry Beach (*b* Springfield, Mass., 5 Oct 1822; *d* Peekskill, N.Y., 25 July 1892). With five other newspaper publishers in 1848–49 he formed the cooperative news-gathering organization that later became the Associated Press.

Frank M. O'Brien: *The Story of the Sun, New York: 1833–1928* (New York: D. Appleton, 1928)

Frank Luther Mott: *American Journalism: A History of Newspapers in the United States through 260 Years: 1690–1950* (New York: Macmillan, 1941; 3rd edn 1962)

Steven H. Jaffe

Beals, Jessie Tarbox (*b* Hamilton, Ont., 23 Dec 1870; *d* New York City, 31 May 1942). Photographer. She pursued photography as a hobby, in 1897 married her darkroom assistant Alfred Tennyson Beals, and in 1900 became a full-time photojournalist. After traveling widely she settled in New York City in 1905. There she recorded subjects ranging from society figures to the slums of the Lower East Side, and gained regular assignments for leading newspapers and magazines. After separating from her husband in 1917 she opened a tea shop in Sheridan Square that doubled as a photography studio, and in the following years she documented the bohemian milieu of Greenwich Village in a series of memorable print and postcard views. Other favorite photographic subjects were city gardens and cigar-store Indians.

Alexander Alland: *Jessie Tarbox Beals: First Woman Photographer* (New York: Camera / Graphic Press, 1978)

For further illustrations see Parades and Visiting nurse service of new york.

Jan Seidler Ramirez

Beame, Abraham D(avid) (*b* London, 20 March 1906). Mayor. His family emigrated from Warsaw via London to the United States in 1906 and settled in New York City. He earned an accounting degree from City College of New York, taught public school, and at the age of twenty-four joined the Madison Democratic Club in Brooklyn. During his early years in public service he was appointed budget director (1952) and elected comptroller (1961). In 1965 he became the first Jew since the consolidation of New York City (1898) to win the Democratic nomination for mayor, but he lost the general election to John V. Lindsay. After winning reelection as comp-

Jessie Tarbox Beals, "Great Lurid Blobs of Color on a Wooden Box and Bobby Edwards in His Garret 'neath the Stars Creating Eukalalies." Postcard of a painter in his studio in Greenwich Village

troller in 1969 he was elected mayor in 1973. During his term a serious fiscal crisis forced him to spend his time conducting financial negotiations with state and federal officials, banks, and municipal unions. To avert bankruptcy he laid off large numbers of city employees and delayed maintenance and important capital expenditures. He was accused by the Securities and Exchange Commission of using unsound budgeting practices, but defended by others for having made politically difficult decisions in a time of widespread economic difficulty. The formation of the Municipal Assistance Corporation and the emergency financial control board in 1975 severely restricted Beame's ability to exercise the traditional powers of the mayor. Discredited by the fiscal crisis, he sought reelection in 1977 but lost the Democratic primary election and retired from politics.

Ken Auletta: *The Streets Were Paved with Gold* (New York: Random House, 1979)

Chris McNickle

Bear, Stearns. Firm of investment bankers formed as a brokerage in New York City in 1923 by Harold C. Mayer, Joseph Ainslie Bear, and Robert B. Stearns. It initially had offices at 100 Broadway and by 1940 had departments for institutional bonds, risk arbitrage, and municipal bond trading. The firm opened its investment banking division in 1943, and an international department in 1948; several domestic and European offices were opened in the 1950s and 1960s. Under the leadership of Alan C. Greenberg in the 1980s the firm became a leading worldwide investment banking and securities trading firm, with major American and international corporations among its clients. In 1994 the firm had more than seven thousand employees, eight domestic offices, and twelve international offices, including representative offices in Beijing and Shanghai. The headquarters are at 245 Park Avenue.

Mary E. Curry

Beard, Charles A(ustin) (*b* near Knightstown, Ind., 27 Nov 1874; *d* New Haven, Conn., 1 Sept 1948). Historian. In 1902 he enrolled at Columbia University (MA 1903, PhD in political science 1904), where he became a lecturer in history (to 1907) and then taught public law as an adjunct professor, associate professor (from 1910), and professor (from 1915). He became an expert in municipal government, helped to establish public administration as a field of study, and wrote *American City Government: A Survey of Newer Tendencies* (1912). His highly influential work *An Economic Interpretation of the Constitution* (1913) reflected his belief in the primacy of economic forces in history. Several of his later works were written in collaboration with his wife, Mary Ritter Beard. In 1915 he became the director of the Training School for Public Service (the first graduate school of public administration in the United States), a branch of the New York Bureau of Municipal Research (the first research institute in the United States designed to promote efficiency in municipal government), and in 1918 he became the director of the entire bureau. He resigned from Columbia in 1917 (to protest the dismissal of his colleague James McKeen Cattell) and in 1919 he was one of the founders of the New School for Social Research. After leaving the Bureau of Municipal Research (1921) and the New School he moved to New Milford, Connecticut, and spent the rest of his life writing and lecturing. In his later years he appeared to disavow the progressivism of his early career when he became an outspoken critic of President Franklin D. Roosevelt.

Jane S. Dahlberg: *The New York Bureau of Municipal Research: Pioneer in Government Administration* (New York: New York University Press, 1966)
Richard Hofstadter: *The Progressive Historians: Turner, Beard, Parrington* (New York: Alfred A. Knopf, 1968)

Allen J. Share

Beard, James (Andrews) (*b* Portland, Ore., 5 May 1903; *d* New York City, 23 Jan 1985). Chef. After moving to New York City in 1938 he wrote his first book in 1940. He served in the army during the Second World War. In 1955 he launched Beard's Cooking Classes, which were later held in his townhouse in Greenwich Village. A food editor for the *New York Times* for many years, he also wrote a syndicated column for United Press and gave demonstrations on the television program "Elsie Presents." Beard wrote more than two dozen books, including *Fowl and Game Cookery* (1944), *Cook It Outdoors* (1941), and his autobiography, *Delights and Prejudices* (1981).

Evan Jones: *Epicurean Delight: The Life and Times of James Beard* (New York: Alfred A. Knopf, 1990)
Robert Clark: *James Beard: A Biography* (New York: Harper Collins, 1993)

James E. Mooney

Beard, Mary Ritter (*b* Indianapolis, 5 Aug 1876; *d* Scottsdale, Ariz., 14 Aug 1958). Historian and feminist. She moved to New York City in 1902, pursued graduate study in sociology at Columbia University until 1904, and worked with the National Women's Trade Union League in organizing the shirtwaist makers' strike of 1909. In the following year she became active in the Woman Suffrage Party of New York State, serving briefly as the vice-chairman of its branch in Manhattan (1910–11) and as the editor of its official organ, the *Woman Voter* (1911–12). Her interest in municipal reform led to the publication of her book *Women's Work in Municipalities* (1915). She collaborated on several other works with her husband, Charles A. Beard. From 1935 she attempted to establish the World Center for Women's Archives, which incorporated and set up an office in New York City, but disbanded in 1940 for lack of support and funds. At the age of seventy she published her most important and influential book, *Woman as a Force in History* (1946).

Nancy F. Cott, ed.: *A Woman Making History: Mary Ritter Beard through Her Letters* (New Haven: Yale University Press, 1991)

Allen J. Share

Beard, William Holbrook (*b* Painesville, Ohio, 13 April 1824; *d* New York City, 20 Feb 1900). Painter. At about twenty he moved to New York City and became a portrait painter; he later worked in Buffalo and studied in Europe before returning to the city in 1860, where he became known for such paintings as *Bulls and Bears*, *Teddy Bear's Picnic*, and *Deer in a Wood* depicting animals behaving like people. Beard was a member of the National Academy of Design, the Century Association, and the Artists' Fund Society.

William H. Gerdts: *William Holbrook Beard: Animals in Fantasy* (New York: Alexander Gallery, 1981)

James E. Mooney

Bearden, (Fred) Romare (Howard) (*b* Charlotte, N.C., 2 Sept 1911; *d* New York City, 11 March 1988). Painter. The son of a well-known political activist and newspaper editor in Harlem, he became acquainted as a youth with such jazz musicians and writers as Fats Waller and Langston Hughes. He studied in 1936–37 at the Art Students League with George Grosz and then joined the 306 Group of black artists in Harlem; a friendship with Stuart Davis developed in part because of a shared interest in jazz. In the mid 1940s shows devoted exclusively to his work were mounted at the Samuel Kootz Gallery, where Robert Motherwell and Adolph Gottlieb also exhibited. After living in Paris in 1950 he returned to New York City, where he continued to paint, organize exhibitions, and write. From 1963 he created collages for the Spiral Group, initially as part of a collaboration with other black artists on themes drawn from black life, and in the following year he was appointed the art director of the Harlem Cultural Council. He was also an organizer of the Cinque Gallery, which showed the work of young black artists. A retrospective of his work at the Museum of Modern Art entitled "Romare Bearden: The Prevalence of Ritual" (1971) brought him wider recognition. Bearden worked in an improvisatory manner that he likened to that of a jazz musician. His work is characterized by a vivid and often jarring juxtaposition of disparate images from urban life. With the artist Carl Holty he wrote *The Painter's Mind: A Study of Structure and Space in Painting* (1969).

Albert Murray and Dore Ashton: *Romare Bearden: 1970–1980* (Charlotte, N.C.: Mint Museum, 1980)
Avis Berman: "Romare Bearden: 'I Paint out of the

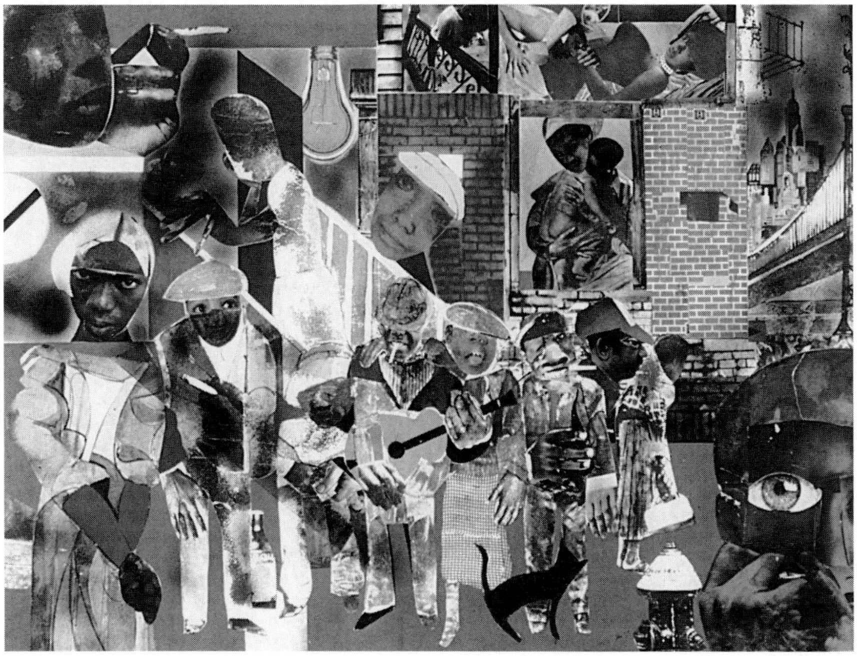

Romare Bearden, The Street *(1975). Collage on board*

Tradition of the Blues,'" *Art News* 79, no. 10 (Dec 1980), 60–67

Mary Schmidt Campbell: "Romare Bearden: Rights and Riffs," *Art in America* 69, no. 10 (Dec 1981), 134–41

Mona Hadler

Beatrice International Holdings. See TLC BEATRICE INTERNATIONAL HOLDINGS.

beats. Members of a literary movement centered from about 1950 to the mid 1960s in lower Manhattan (as well as San Francisco),

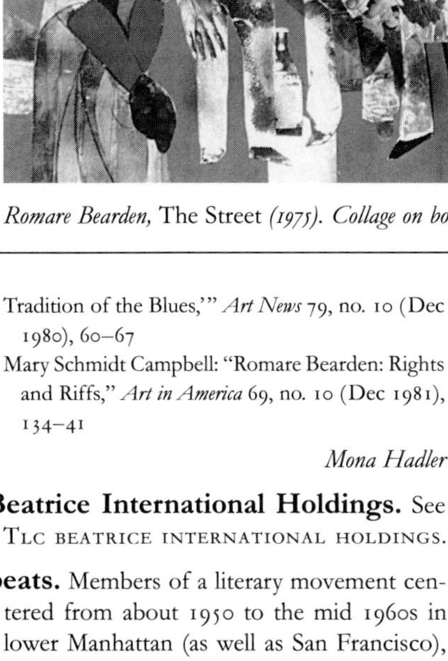

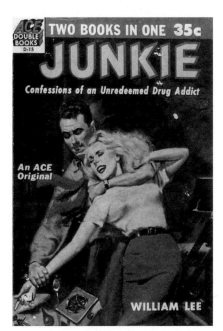

Cover design for William Burroughs's novel Junkie: Confessions of an Unredeemed Drug Addict *(1953)*

characterized by bohemianism, a hostility toward commercialism and conformity, and an enthusiasm for visionary states induced by hallucinogenic drugs. The movement had its roots in informal discussions held in 1944 by Allen Ginsberg and Lucien Carr, both undergraduates at Columbia University, and William Burroughs and Jack Kerouac, all seeking what they called a "new vision" in literature; they often met at the West End Cafe, on Broadway and 113th Street near Columbia.

The most important texts of the beat movement date from the early 1950s: Kerouac's first novel, *The Town and the City* (1950); his most popular work, *On the Road* (1951, published 1957), written in an apartment at 454 West 20th Street in Manhattan; *Go* (1952), by John Clellon Holmes, a vivid description of the beat movement, which by the time the book was published had grown to include many friends and acquaintances of the original members; Burroughs's first novel, *Junkie: Confessions of an Unredeemed Drug Addict* (1953, under the pseudonym William Lee), which depicts the author's early years of drug addiction; and Ginsberg's *Howl and Other Poems* (1956), an influential collection of free verse. The members of what became known as the beat generation gained visibility after *On the Road* was reviewed in the *New York Times* and became a best-seller. In 1957 Norman Mailer analyzed the aesthetics of the movement in his essay "The White Negro" (published in *Dissent*), Norman Podhoretz attacked the beats for "expressing contempt for coherent, rational discourse" in the spring issue of *Partisan Review* (his criticism was rebutted by LeRoi Jones and others), and an unruly symposium on the beats was held at Hunter College. In the same year Ginsberg returned from a visit to Europe to settle on the Lower East Side, where he joined other beat writers including Jones, Gregory Corso, Peter Orlovsky, and Diane Di Prima, poets like Frank O'Hara who did not belong to the movement but were sympathetic toward it, and poets associated with Black Mountain College (such as Robert Creeley) and San Francisco (such as Michael McClure). The work of the beats was circulated by small publishers like the Grove Press, Totem Press, and Corinth Books, and by such bookshop owners as Ted Wilentz of the 8th Street Bookshop, Robert A. Wilson of the Phoenix Bookshop, Andreas Brown of the Gotham Book Mart, and Ed Sanders of the Peace Eye Bookshop. Poetry readings and experimental plays flourished downtown at the Living Theater, the Artist's Studio, and the Gas Light Cafe. In 1959 Ginsberg, Corso, and Orlovsky read their poetry to a receptive audience at Columbia and made a film entitled "Pull My Daisy" with Kerouac, the artist Larry Rivers, the musician David Amram, and the photographer Robert Frank in the studio of the painter Alfred Leslie in Manhattan.

Kerouac described his favorite scenes of New York City in *Lonesome Traveler*, a collection of travel sketches published in 1960. In the same year three popular anthologies of beat writing were published in New York City: *The Beats*, edited by Seymour Krim; *The Beat Scene*, edited by Elias Wilentz with photographs by Fred McDarrah of the *Village Voice*; and *Beat Coast East: An Anthology of Rebellion*, edited by Stanley Fisher, who tried to define the word "beat" by walking the streets of Greenwich Village and asking "an assortment of squalid squares and plastered saints what they thought the word meant" (he was given twenty definitions). In 1961 Ted Joans, a young painter and poet, satirized the "beatniks" of Washington Square and the tendency of the press toward sensational coverage of the beat movement in his witty collage book *The Hipsters*.

The early 1960s saw a proliferation of little magazines in Greenwich Village and on the Lower East Side dedicated to experimental writing, among them *Yugen*, *Floating Bear*, and *Fuck You: A Magazine of the Arts*. This period has been described by Di Prima in *Memoirs of a Beatnik* (1969), Sanders in *Tales of Beatnik Glory* (1975), Joyce Johnson in *Minor Characters* (1983), and Hettie Jones (formerly married to LeRoi Jones) in *How I Became Hettie Jones* (1990).

The beat movement was largely spent by the mid 1960s, but it strongly influenced the hippie movement of the late 1960s and early 1970s, in which some beat figures were active: Sanders and Tuli Kupferberg took part in protests on 5th Avenue against the Vietnam War by performing with their rock group the Fugs, and Kupferberg's book *1001 Ways to Beat the Draft* (1966) enjoyed wide circulation. A new generation of experimental writers carried on the beat traditions of small-press publishing and poetry reading in New York City, perhaps best exemplified by the Poetry Project at St. Mark's Church in the Bowery. Ginsberg became a Distinguished Professor of English at Brooklyn College, continued to live on the Lower East Side, and remained a prominent figure in the literary, musical, and artistic avant-garde.

Ann Charters: "The Beats: Literary Bohemians in Post-war America," *Dictionary of Literary Biography*, vol. 16 (Detroit: Gale Research, 1983)
Barry Miles: *Ginsberg: A Biography* (New York: Simon and Schuster, 1989)

Ann Charters

Beaux-Arts Institute of Design. Institute opened by the Society of Beaux Arts Architects (1894) to promote the classical values of the French school among architects in the United States. It offered free classes to draftsmen and had unparalleled influence in architectural instruction from 1900 until the 1930s. The principal function of the institute was to sponsor juried competitions. Its programs were used by nearly three quarters of the country's architecture students. Headquarters in an art deco style were designed in 1927 by Frederick C. Hirons and built at 304 East 44th Street (now a city landmark). With the rise of modernism the institute lost much of its influence and was reorganized as the National Institute for Architectural Education.

John Frederick Harbeson: *The Study of Architectural Design, with Special Reference to the Program of the Beaux-Arts Institute of Design* (New York: Pencil Points Press, 1927)

Carol Willis

Becker–Rosenthal case. The shooting of Herman Rosenthal on 16 July 1912 in New York City generated much interest because it involved public figures and had political and anti-Semitic overtones. Rosenthal was the operator of a gambling house on the Lower East Side and reputedly a minor figure in organized crime. The police lieutenant Charles Becker (1869–1915), who led a "strong arm squad" to eradicate gambling, was charged with his murder; Rosenthal had accused Becker of graft in a long article in the *New York World* published two days before he was killed. The investigation of the murder was supported by leading citizens dedicated to reforming city government and rooting out police corruption. Becker was weakly and briefly defended in public by Mayor William J. Gaynor, who was denounced by Jewish leaders for his attack on "lawless foreigners" (a group in which he included Rosenthal). The district attorney who successfully prosecuted the case, Charles Whitman, embarked on a career in politics: as governor of New York he approved Becker's execution, which took place at Sing Sing Prison on 7 July 1915. Herbert Bayard Swope, an enterprising reporter for the *World*, became the best-known journalist of his day for his coverage of the case.

Andy Logan: *Against the Evidence: The Becker–Rosenthal Affair* (New York: McCall Publishing, 1970)

Norris Randolph

Bedford Corners. Early name for a part of Brooklyn now lying within BEDFORD-STUYVESANT.

Bedford Park. Neighborhood in the northwestern Bronx, bounded to the northeast by Mosholu Parkway, to the east by the New York Botanical Garden, to the south by 198th Street, and to the west by the Jerome Park Reservoir. It was planned in the 1880s and was named after the town of Bedford, England, which also inspired its design as a suburban park and the Queen Anne architecture of its original houses. With the opening of the Jerome Avenue subway line in 1917 and the 3rd Avenue elevated line in 1920 the area became more accessible and more heavily built up. In spite of the Depression a large number of buildings were erected in the 1930s, including many apartment buildings in the art deco style. Among those who resided in the neighborhood was William Fox, a founder of the film company that later became 20th Century Fox. After the Second World War the neighborhood remained middle class, with a large population of Irish and Jews and later of Latin Americans, blacks, and Koreans. In the 1980s the largest single group of immigrants was Dominican; other groups included Jamaicans, Guyanese, Cambodians, Koreans, Mexicans, and Vietnamese.

Bedford Park's Art Deco Treasures (New York: Bronx County Historical Society, 1981) [exhibition catalogue]

Gary D. Hermalyn

Bedford–Stuyvesant. Neighborhood in north central Brooklyn (1990 pop. 135,000), bounded to the north by Flushing Avenue, to the east by Broadway and Saratoga Avenue, to the south by Atlantic Avenue, and to the west by Classon Avenue. Before 1977 it extended as far south as Eastern Parkway. Its name is derived from those of two middle-class communities in nineteenth-century Brooklyn — Bedford (to the west) and Stuyvesant Heights (to the east) — and is often abbreviated as Bed–Stuy. In the 1630s and 1640s the Dutch West India Company purchased from the Canarsee Indians the woodlands that became Bedford, a community recognized by the English governor Richard Nicolls in 1677. Its central location between the towns of Bushwick, Jamaica, and Flatbush influenced the farmer Thomas Lambertse to build a public inn in 1668. Seventeenth-century Bedford was a farming hamlet inhabited by Dutch families and African slaves. Farmers carted surplus goods, to be sold in neighboring communities, to the Breuklen Ferry down the main road, which was close to Fulton Street, and Hunterfly Road. After the Battle of Long Island the area was invaded by English troops. Later it became gradually transformed as farmland was divided into housing lots and sold to new arrivals. As early as 1790 more than a quarter of the residents were blacks (mostly slaves). The Lefferts family bought land from the Lambertses, who became prominent developers in the area. Leffert Lefferts became a judge and town clerk in Bedford after he graduated from King's College, and his family was among the first to sell land to blacks. In 1835 John Lefferts sold the land that became known as Weeksville to Henry C. Thompson, a free black; Carrsville was built on the land bought in 1832 by another free black, William Thomas. These transactions and others affected the ethnic composition of Bedford, which by 1834 was also referred to as Bedford Corners.

The neighborhood was the site of a station of the Brooklyn and Jamaica Railroad (forerunner of the Long Island Rail Road), which was constructed in 1836 and traversed Atlantic Street (now Atlantic Avenue). Its population reached fourteen thousand in 1873 and included Irish, Germans, Jews, Scots, Dutch, and blacks. The ethnic diversity of the neighborhood was reflected in the names of its institutions: the Jewish Hospital, the Colored Orphans Asylum, St. John's Episcopal Church, and St. Mary's Hospital. The opening of the elevated railway (about 1885) and the Brooklyn Bridge (1903) linked the area more closely with Manhattan and spurred the construction of brownstones and the growth of new neighborhoods called East Brooklyn, New Brooklyn, and St. Marks (all in what is now Bedford–Stuyvesant). At the turn of the century Bedford Corners and particularly Stuyvesant Avenue attracted residents from the middle and upper classes, including the retailing entrepreneurs F. W. Woolworth and Abraham Abraham. More than 45,000 persons lived in the neighborhood in 1920.

As the population continued to grow, brownstones that had formerly housed one family were subdivided into several units. The opening of the municipal subway system in 1936 gave the neighborhood a new link to Manhattan. The neighborhood attracted large numbers of eastern European Jews, Italians, and later blacks from the South and the Caribbean, many of whom settled in the western section. As the population rose the communities of Bedford and Stuyvesant Heights became one large area of black settlement, and the neighborhood acquired its current name. By 1940 it had more than 65,000 black residents, and members of other ethnic groups left. Organizations were established to give financial and social assistance to blacks, among them the Paragon Progressive Federal Credit Union, formed by F. Levi and other

West Indians in 1937. Black churches moved to Stuyvesant Avenue and other parts of the neighborhood and worked with the National Urban League, the National Association for the Advancement of Colored People, and other institutions to fight racial discrimination, segregation, and poverty, but inadequate housing and unemployment persisted and impoverished the neighborhood. At the same time residents began to exert a stronger political influence, and in 1968 they elected Shirley Chisholm to the U.S. Congress, where she was the first black woman to serve. Senator Robert F. Kennedy's visit to the neighborhood in the late 1960s inspired his support for the Bedford Stuyvesant Restoration Corporation. The Society for the Preservation of Weeksville and Bedford–Stuyvesant History was formed in 1971 to commemorate the role that blacks played in developing the neighborhood, and the Bedford–Stuyvesant Restoration Plaza, which includes the Billie Holiday Theater, was completed in 1976. The 1980s saw large-scale settlement of black immigrants from the Caribbean, primarily Guyana, Jamaica, and Barbados, and to a lesser extent Trinidad and Tobago, Haiti, and St. Vincent and the Grenadines.

Bedford–Stuyvesant is the largest black neighborhood in New York City. Although it has considerable poverty and some badly deteriorated housing in the northeastern section, its reputation as a slum is largely undeserved: most of the neighborhood consists of well-maintained brownstone and brickfront housing built in the early twentieth century. Among the historic features of Bedford–Stuyvesant are the Weeksville Historic District, the Stuyvesant Heights Historic District, and the Brooklyn Children's Museum (built in 1899). Boys High School (1891) is an enormous, striking terra-cotta building in a Romanesque Revival style; among those who attended the school were Isaac Asimov and Norman Mailer. The population of Bedford–Stuyvesant is 85 percent black, 13 percent Latin American, and 1 percent white.

Mary H. Manoni: *Bedford–Stuyvesant: The Anatomy of a Central City Community* (New York: Quadrangle / New York Times Books, 1973)

David Ment and Mary S. Donovan: *The People of Brooklyn: A History of Two Neighborhoods* (New York: Brooklyn Educational and Cultural Alliance, 1980)

Mario A. Charles

Bedford Stuyvesant Restoration Corporation. The first nonprofit community development corporation in the United States, formed in 1967. It was founded through the bipartisan efforts of Senators Robert F. Kennedy and Jacob K. Javits, who worked with residents of Bedford–Stuyvesant to improve the quality of life and economy of the neighborhood. Among the buildings that it helped to construct with private and public capital were a commercial center of 300,000 square feet (28,000 square meters) known as Restoration Plaza, a major health care facility (55,000 patients' visits annually), and 2225 residential housing units. The corporation also created a joint venture with Pathmark Stores to develop a supermarket of thirty thousand square feet (2800 square meters), found employment for 25,000 persons, and provided more than $9 million in loans to 134 local businesses. Cultural facilities sponsored by the corporation included the Billie Holiday Theatre (seating 214), the Skylight Gallery at the Center for Art and Culture, and the Restoration Dance Theatre. The corporation is governed by a board of twenty-six community members, assisted by a business advisory board of nine members from the greater metropolitan area. The success of the Bedford Stuyvesant Restoration Corporation prompts a large number of national and international visitors, academic institutions, and foundations to study its methods of community development.

Charles Palms

Formation of the Bedford Stuyvesant Restoration Corporation at City Hall, 1967.
From left: *Mayor John V. Lindsay, Senator Robert F. Kennedy, Franklin A. Thomas, Thomas R. Jones*

Bee, Clair (*b* Grafton, W.Va., 2 March 1900; *d* Cleveland, 20 May 1983). Basketball coach. As the coach of the men's basketball team at Long Island University he won 410 games and lost only eighty-six between 1931 and 1952. The team was undefeated in two seasons (1935–36 and 1938–39) and won the National Invitation Tournament in 1939 and 1941; it also won forty-three consecutive games from February 1935 to December 1936 as well as 139 consecutive home games at the gymnasium of the Brooklyn College of Pharmacy and at Madison Square Garden, where some of its more important games were played. After Long Island University eliminated its basketball program in 1952 in response to the gambling scandal of the preceding year Bee coached professional basketball for a few years, taught at the New York Military Academy, operated basketball camps, wrote fiction, and maintained a farm in upstate New York.

Neil D. Isaacs: *All the Moves: A History of College Basketball* (Philadelphia: J. B. Lippincott, 1975)

Albert Figone

Beecher, Catharine (Esther) (*b* East Hampton, N.Y., 6 Sept 1800; *d* Elmira, N.Y., 12 May 1878). Writer and educator. The daughter of Lyman Beecher and a sister of Harriet Beecher Stowe, Henry Ward Beecher, and Isabella Beecher Hooker, she opened girls' schools in Hartford (Connecticut), Cincinnati, and Milwaukee, and energetically promoted teaching as a profession for women. She lived intermittently in Brooklyn with her brother. Beecher's many published writings include advice books (*Treatise on Domestic Economy*, 1847), political tracts (*An Essay on Slavery and Abolitionism, with Reference to the Duty of American Females*, 1837), and commentaries on domestic life (*The Evils Suffered by American*

Women and American Children: The Causes and the Remedy, 1846).

Kathryn Kish Sklar: *Catharine Beecher: A Study in American Domesticity* (New Haven: Yale University Press, 1973)

Kathryn Kish Sklar

Beecher, Henry Ward (*b* Litchfield, Conn., 24 June 1813; *d* Brooklyn, 8 March 1887). Minister, brother of Catharine Beecher. He studied in Massachusetts and Ohio and for eight years was a pastor in Indianapolis. On 10 October 1847 he took charge of the prosperous Plymouth Congregational Church at 75 Hicks Street in Brooklyn Heights, where he gave sermons that attracted large crowds every Sunday. He lived at 22 Willow Street in 1848, at 176 Columbia Heights from 1851 to 1855, and at 124 Hicks Street from the 1860s. Beecher exerted tremendous influence over public morality in New York City as a lecturer and as the editor of the weekly publications the *Independent* (1861–64) and the *Christian Union* (1870–81). Some of his most enthusiastic supporters were middle-class women who inspired him to endorse the woman suffrage movement. His career suffered after Theodore Tilton, editor of the *Independent* (1864–70), accused him of having committed adultery with his wife and filed suit for damages of $100,000 in 1874. Beecher had indeed visited the Tiltons' household often, and a trial was held that lasted six months; it ended with Beecher's acquittal, and although he continued to lead the Plymouth until the end of his life his public influence was much reduced.

Theodore Tilton vs. Henry Ward Beecher: Action for Crim. Con. (New York: McDivitt, Campbell, 1875)

Clifford E. Clark: *Henry Ward Beecher: Spokesman for a Middle-class America* (Urbana: University of Illinois Press, 1978)

Jeff Finlay

Beechhurst. Neighborhood in northeastern Queens, lying within Whitestone. It began as a tract of 135 acres (fifty-five hectares) bounded to the north by the East River, to the east by 162nd Street, to the south by Cryder's Lane, and to the west by 154th Street and laid out as a residential park in 1906 by the Shore Acres Realty Company. Some lots measured only twenty by one hundred feet (six by thirty meters), but more than half were lots of a quarter-acre (ten ares) designed to encourage the construction of larger houses, especially along the shore and to the east. In the 1920s Beechhurst attracted many people active in the theater, including the producer Arthur Hammerstein, whose house was later made a landmark. The Whitestone branch of the Long Island Rail Road offered convenient commuter service until the Depression. In the 1960s large apartment buildings were erected east of 162nd Street and on the shore of the East River, on land by then considered part of the neighborhood.

Vincent Seyfried

Beekman, Gerard G. (*b* New York City, 29 July 1719; *d* Flushing [now in Queens], 1797). Political and mercantile leader, grandson of Gerardus Beekman. He was active in international trade and engaged in marine insurance underwriting and other legitimate ventures as well as in smuggling. A Loyalist, he chose to remain in New York during its occupation by the British. He moved to Flushing about 1780 and remained there until his death.

William B. Aitken: *Distinguished Families in America, Descended from Wilhelmus Beekman and Jan Thomasse Van Dyke* (New York: G. P. Putnam's Sons, 1912)

Philip L. White: *The Beekmans of New York in Politics and Commerce, 1647–1877* (New York: New-York Historical Society, 1956)

Philip L. White, ed.: *The Beekman Mercantile Papers, 1746–1799* (New York: New-York Historical Society, 1956)

Jacob Judd

Beekman, Gerardus (baptized New Amsterdam, 17 Aug 1653; *d* New York City, 10 Oct 1723). Political and mercantile leader. He was the son of William (Wilhelmus) Beekman (1623–1707), a merchant who after emigrating to New Amsterdam in 1647 with Peter Stuyvesant was active in municipal and provincial politics and acquired extensive properties on Manhattan Island and in the Hudson River Valley. After studying medicine he began a practice in Midwout (Flatbush) about 1677. An adherent of Jacob Leisler, he was arrested by Governor Henry Sloughter, convicted of treason, and sentenced to death in 1691, but his life was spared and he continued to take part in politics. He later acquired additional property in Kings County and lower Manhattan and opened the Beekman Slip on the East River in 1722. The holdings of his family came to encompass three large farms: one between what are now Beekman and William streets, a second bounded by what are now Pearl, Gold, Ann, and Fulton streets, and a third along the East River bounded by what are now 49th Street, 2nd Avenue, and 61st Street; much of this land remains in the family's possession. His brother Henry Beekman (1652–1716) was a provincial legislator who fought for a general assembly strong enough to withstand the powers of the Crown and its appointed governor. His later descendants included Gerard Beekman (1842–1918), a great-great-great-grandson who donated to the New-York Historical Society the family's coach, acquired in 1771, the blue room from its mansion, where the British had their headquarters during the American Revolution, and the bedroom of the mansion, used by Major John André; and the physician Fenwick Beekman (1882–1962), a great-great-great-great-grandson who was a major donor to the New-York Historical Society and its president from 1947 to 1956. Beekman Street, Ann Street, and William Street are all named for members of the family, as are the New York Infirmary Beekman Downtown Hospital at 170 William Street and the R. Livingston Beekman House at 854 5th Avenue (1903–5), now the Yugoslavian Mission to the United Nations.

For bibliography see BEEKMAN, GERARD G.

Jacob Judd

Beekman, Henry, Jr. (*b* New York City, 1688; *d* New York City, 1776). Political and mercantile leader. As the sheriff of the colony of New York he chose the jury for the trial of John Peter Zenger in 1735. Although a staunch advocate of the Dutch Reformed church he voted in 1754 in favor of forming King's College, an institution then dominated by Anglicanism, but insisted on the appointment of a Dutch Reformed professor of divinity. He was the most influential political leader in his family.

For bibliography see BEEKMAN, GERARD G.

Jacob Judd

Beekman Place. Neighborhood on the Upper East Side of Manhattan, bounded to the north by 51st Street, to the east by the East River, to the south by 49th Street, and to the west by 1st Avenue. It is a small residential enclave named after the mansion of the Beekman family, which stood on the site from 1765 to 1874, was used briefly during the American Revolution as a British headquarters, and was the site of the trial and execution of Nathan Hale. The mansion was demolished as the city grew northward, and the property was subdivided and developed. The neighborhood was at first favored by the working class but soon after the successful redevelopment of Sutton Place (1920) its character changed: writers and actors moved into the neighborhood and formed the Beekman Hill Association to oversee its transformation into a quiet and secluded domain of the élite. The first of several luxury apartment buildings along Beekman Place were developed by Joseph G. Thomas and his wife, the muralist Clara Fargo Thomas. The couple was responsible for the construction of Beekman Terrace (1924), the Beekman Mansion (1926), and the Campanile Apartments (1926–30). In addition to a number of lavishly appointed townhouses there are other luxury apartment buildings in the area, including 1 Beekman Place (1930), 2 Beekman Place (1931), and the Beekman Tower (1928), originally a residential hotel for sorority women known as the Panhellenic Tower. It is famous for its rooftop ballroom and cocktail lounge.

Owen D. Gutfreund

Beene, Geoffrey (*b* Haynesville, La., 30 Aug 1927). Fashion designer. After designing clothing for several firms on 7th Avenue, including Harmay and Teal Traina, he formed his own business in 1963. His distinctive juxtaposition of modern fabrics and old-fashioned craftsmanship and techniques has made him one of the most highly acclaimed designers in the United States. Beene often uses embroidery, top-stitching, and appliqué in his work.

Caroline Rennolds Milbank

beer halls. Beer halls were a prominent feature of Kleindeutschland and other German neighborhoods in New York City, which from 1855 to 1880 had the largest German-speaking community in the Americas. Various kinds of establishments lined Avenue A and the Bowery and provided relief from crowded tenements. Basement bars catered to the rough and loose; *Lokale* attracted residents of the same neighborhood, workers in the same trade, immigrants from the same region, and members of churches and political groups, and often contained bars, meeting rooms, ballrooms, and even bowling alleys. Among the well-known halls were Hillenbrands on Hester Street, the Concordia on Avenue A, and Germania on the Bowery. There were also opulent halls where families gathered to drink, eat, sing, dance, and be entertained by music and drama, especially on Sundays; the best-known were the Deutsches Volksgarten, the Atlantic Gardens, Niblo's Saloon, and Magar's Concert Hall. During the summer beer halls of all kinds moved outdoors into the lots behind their buildings to form beer gardens. After 1880 most of the city's German population moved to Yorkville on the Upper East Side. Beer halls there survived until the mid twentieth century.

Zelda Stern: *The Complete Guide to Ethnic New York* (New York: St. Martin's, 1980)

Stanley Nadel: *Little Germany* (Urbana: University of Illinois Press, 1990)

Chad Ludington

Beiderbecke, Bix [Leon Bismarck] (*b* Davenport, Iowa, 10 March 1903; *d* New York City, 6 Aug 1931). Cornetist, pianist, and composer. He first played in New York City in September 1924 with his band the Wolverines while living at 119 West 71st Street. Although he traveled a great deal he played frequently in the city. He performed with a number of orchestras, including those of Jean Goldkette (1924–27) and Paul Whiteman (1927–29), and with the saxophonist Frankie Trumbauer he led an ensemble in 1925 and 1926. In 1930–31 he often stayed in room 605 of the 44th Street Hotel, 120 West 44th Street. Shortly before his death he moved into an apartment at 43-30 46th Street in Sunnyside, where he died of chronic alcoholism. Beiderbecke was one of the most influential jazz musicians of his time; his warm, lyrical, and swinging style contributed to the development of the jazz ballad. He was widely known for his self-destructive way of life.

Richard M. Sudhalter and Phillip R. Evans: *Bix: Man and Legend* (New Rochelle, N.Y.: Arlington House, 1974)

Loren Schoenberg

Belafonte, Harry [Harold George, Jr.] (*b* New York City, 1 March 1927). Singer and actor. Born of Caribbean ancestry, he moved to Jamaica at the age of eight with his family and at thirteen returned to New York City, where he attended George Washington High School, worked as a handyman, and in 1945 enrolled in Erwin Piscator's drama workshop at the New School for Social Research. In 1949 he made his singing début at the Royal Roost. After working with the American Negro Theater and appearing on the television program "John Murray Anderson's Almanac" (1953) he made recordings of calypso songs in 1956 and 1957 that made him widely known. Although his popularity ebbed somewhat in the 1960s he continued to live and perform in the city.

Arnold Shaw: *Belafonte: An Unauthorized Biography* (Radnor, Penn.: Chilton, 1960)

Marc Ferris

Interior of the German Winter-Garden Theatre at 45 Bowery

Belarusans. The first Belarusan settlers moved to New York City in the 1890s during a time of hardship in their country. The number of immigrants peaked between 1910 and 1913; many were from Minsk, Vilna, Grodno, Vitebsk, Gomel, Mogilev, Smolensk, Brest, Białystok, and Pinsk. They were counted by the U.S. Immigration Service as Russians if they were Eastern Orthodox and as Poles if they were Roman Catholic. The first Belarusan organization in New York City was the White Russian National Committee (1921). More Belarusans moved to the city after Belarus was incorporated into the Soviet Union in 1945, including many Jews. During this time several Belarusan churches were formed (most under the jurisdiction of the Belarusan Autocephalous Orthodox Church), as were such organizations as the United Byelorussian–American Relief Committee (1948), the Byelorussian–American Association (1949), the Byelorussian Institute of Arts and Sciences (1951), the Byelorussian–American Relief (1957), and the Byelorussian–American Union (1965). The newspaper *Bielarus* was published from 1950 by the Byelorussian–American Association, which in the early 1990s sponsored youth programs and a supplementary school and was the largest Belarusan organization in the United States. The Byelorussian Institute of Arts and Sciences became one of the most productive publishers of Belarusan scholarship. Most Belarusan organizations have headquarters at the Krecheuski Foundation, a Belarusan philanthropic group in Jamaica. Of the half-million Belarusans who settled in the United States between 1909 and the mid 1990s, between fifty thousand and 75,000 settled in the metropolitan area.

Vitaut Kipel

Belasco, David (*b* San Francisco, 24 July 1853; *d* New York City, 14 May 1931). Producer and playwright. He began working as a stage manager in New York City in 1882 and achieved some renown for the way he adeptly devised and managed stage effects. As a producer he was responsible for 121 productions in New York City (including revivals). He also wrote some seventy plays, many in collaboration with others. In 1902 he broke with the Theatrical Syndicate, after which he became known for the extreme realism of his stage productions. Many of these were mounted at the innovative structure he built in 1907, named the Belasco Theatre and still standing at 111 West 44th Street. He lived from about 1926 at the Hotel Gladstone, 114 East 52nd Street, and retired in 1930. Belasco's most important plays include *The Heart of Maryland* (1895), *Madame Butterfly* (with John Luther Long, 1900), and *The Girl of the Golden West* (1905).

Lise-Lone Marker: *David Belasco: Naturalism in the American Theater* (Princeton, N.J.: Princeton University Press, 1974)

See also STAGE DESIGN.

Don B. Wilmeth

Bel Canto Opera Company. Opera company formed in 1969 by Theodore Sieh to present bel canto works and infrequently performed operas of many periods and styles. It produced more than 120 works during its first twenty seasons in New York City, including Daniel Auber's *Manon Lescaut*, Johann Christian Bach's *Temistocle*, Gaetano Donizetti's *Caterina Cornaro*, Ferencz Erkel's *Bank Ban*, William Henry Fry's *Leonora*, Stanisław Moniuszko's *The Haunted Manor*, and Nikolai Rimsky-Korsakov's *The Snow Maiden*. Several singers who performed with the company became well known, including Claudia Catania, Elizabeth Hynes, and Samuel Ramey. The unusual repertory of the company has attracted such renowned conductors and directors as Cynthia Auerbach, Victoria Bond, Janet Bookspan, Igor Chichagov, Frank Corsaro, Thomas Martin, Frederick Roffman, and Johannes Somary.

Harvey E. Phillips: "New York Is Home for Thirty-seven Opera Companies," *New York Times*, 7 Oct 1973

Thomas E. Bird

Bellaire. Neighborhood in east central Queens, centered on Jamaica Avenue and 211th Street between Hollis and Queens Village. Originally a tract of farmland of forty-two acres (seventeen hectares) owned by the Haubitzer family, it was bought in June 1899 by J. A. H. Drissel, the secretary and treasurer of the National Pigeon Shooters Association, who built a grandstand and casino on the site and named it Interstate Park. Many shooting events were held there from 1900, including the Grand American Handicap in 1901 and 1902. The park was declared bankrupt after the shooting of birds was prohibited in November 1902. In 1907 a realty company demolished the grandstand and developed the land as a suburb named Bellaire Park; Bellaire Gardens was promoted as a development in 1921. Later the area was usually considered part of Queens Village.

Vincent Seyfried

Belle Harbor. Neighborhood in southwestern Queens, lying within Rockaway Beach and bounded to the north by Jamaica Bay, to the east by 129th Street, to the south by the Atlantic Ocean, and to the west by Beach 141st Street. The first sections were developed in 1907 by Frederick J. Lancaster, president of the West Rockaway Land Company; the waterfront between Beach 125th and Beach 128th streets was later added for the Belle Harbor Yacht Club. The company installed sewers, wide streets, sidewalks, and utilities and sold lots measuring twenty by one hundred feet (six by thirty meters) for year-round homes. In 1915 the area was remapped to provide for 234 beach and bayfront lots; trolley service was begun in 1917. In the mid 1990s Belle Harbor was a well-kept, upper-middle-class suburban neighborhood.

Vincent Seyfried

Bellerose. Neighborhood straddling the border between Nassau County and Queens. Its original expanse (now entirely in Nassau), bounded to the north by Jericho Turnpike, to the east by Remsen Lane, to the south by the Long Island Rail Road, and to the west by Colonial Road, was laid out by Helen M. Marsh, a real-estate agent from Lynn, Massachusetts, who about 1897 bought five parcels of land and in 1906 formed the United Holding Company, which supervised development until 1927. Streets were configured in a semicircular pattern with the railroad station at its center; some were given the names of states and of the Great Lakes. A large adjoining area across the city line in Queens was opened to residential development in 1910 and also named Bellerose. Bounded to the north by Grand Central Parkway, to the east by Little Neck Parkway, to the south by Jericho Turnpike, and to the west by the Cross Island Parkway, this section (1980 pop. 22,880) became a densely built up neighborhood of one-family houses shaded by trees. In the mid 1990s the portion of Bellerose lying in Queens was a comfortable neighborhood, largely white and middle class to upper middle class. The neighborhood is the site of the Queens County Farm Museum, which has a working chicken coop and an array of other barnyard animals.

Vincent Seyfried

Bellevue Hospital. Municipal hospital opened in 1736 as a six-bed infirmary by the Public Work House and Home of Correction at lower Broadway, on a site now occupied by City Hall. The city purchased a building in 1794 on five acres (two hectares) at 26th Street and 1st Avenue to house victims of epidemics, and a site for an almshouse in 1811 occupying 150 acres (sixty hectares) bounded by 28th Street, the East River, 23rd Street, and 2nd Avenue; the almshouse was completed in 1816 and became known as the Bellevue Establishment. When the hospital took its current name in 1825 its facilities were used mainly for the victims of epidemics. Filth, neglect, and high mortality rates were rampant until mid century, when the hospital was separated from the almshouse and reorganized by a medical board. The hospital averaged between 550 and 850 beds by the 1850s. It was the first hospital in the United States to use hypodermic syringes (1856) and the first to develop a hospital-based ambulance service (1869), and its services were expanded to include an outpatient dispensary (1867), a reception hospital on Canal Street (1869), and an auxiliary hospital on 95th Street and 10th Avenue for accident cases (1871). Bellevue treated American soldiers during the Civil War and later during the Spanish–American War. Several schools were founded at the hospital, including the Bellevue Hospital Medical College (1861), nursing schools for women (the first Nightingale school of nursing in the United States, 1873) and men (1888), and a school of midwifery (1911). Wards for alcoholics and a pavilion for the insane were added in the late 1870s to accommodate the growing number of patients. New pavilions also opened for the treatment of emergencies (1877), surgical cases (1878), and women and children (1882). At the pavilion specializing in gynecology and obstetrics (1887) doctors performed the first cesarean section in an American hospital in 1887. Bellevue was overseen by various charities and correction boards un-

Bellevue Hospital, ca *1905. The balconies provided fresh air, which was thought to speed patients' recovery*

til the twentieth century, when it came under the jurisdiction of municipal hospital boards. As the hospital gave greater attention to services for outpatients it opened a tuberculosis clinic (1903), a social services department (1906), a psychopathic clinic (1908), a dental clinic (1908), and the nation's first ambulatory cardiac clinic (1911). Until the late twentieth century Bellevue dwarfed all other hospitals in New York City: it had about 1150 beds in the second decade of the century and about 2700 by the 1950s. During the world wars it organized base hospital units to serve overseas. New York University–Bellevue Medical Center, opened in 1947, later became a center for trauma, limb reimplantation, head and spinal cord injury, and cardiac care. Control of the hospital was transferred in 1970 to the New York City Health and Hospitals Corporation. Expansion continued with the opening of a new outpatient facility in 1973, an inpatient facility in 1975, and a psychiatric hospital in 1985. The hospital is affiliated with the New York University School of Medicine.

Page Cooper: *The Bellevue Story* (New York: Thomas Y. Crowell, 1948)

John Starr: *Hospital City* (New York: Crown, 1957)

Don Gold: *Bellevue: A Documentary of a Large Metropolitan Hospital* (New York: Harper and Row, 1975)

Jane E. Mottus: *New York Nightingales: The Emergence of the Nursing Profession at Bellevue and New York Hospital, 1850–1920* (Ann Arbor, Mich.: UMI Research Press, 1981)

Jane E. Mottus

Bellows, George (Wesley) (*b* Columbus, Ohio, 12 Aug 1882; *d* New York City, 8 Jan 1925). Painter and printmaker. The son of an architect, he studied under Robert Henri at the New York School of Art and developed a bold, naturalistic style. In 1909 he became the youngest artist elected to the National Academy of Design. His scenes of everyday city life allied him with the Ashcan School; he also depicted boxing matches, seascapes, and portraits. After rooming with friends at 352 West 58th Street he moved in 1906 to the Lincoln Arcade Building on Broadway. In 1910 he moved to a house at 146 East 19th Street and renovated the third floor for a studio. Many of Bellows's paintings are at the Brooklyn Museum.

Charles H. Morgan: *George Bellows: Painter of America* (New York: Reynal, 1965)

E. A. Carmean Jr. et al.: *Bellows: The Boxing Pictures* (Washington: National Gallery of Art, 1982)

Marianne Doezema: *George Bellows and Urban America* (New Haven: Yale University Press, 1992)

Michael Quick et al.: *The Paintings of George Bellows* (New York: Harry N. Abrams, 1992)

For illustration see Boxing.

Judith Zilczer

Bellows, Henry Whitney (*b* Boston, 11 June 1814; *d* New York City, 30 Jan 1882). Clergyman. After receiving his education at Harvard College and the Harvard Divinity School he became the pastor of the First Congregational Church in New York City (later renamed the Church of All Souls). Known as an orator, he led the U.S. Sanitary Commission during the Civil War and oversaw its efforts to improve sanitation in army camps and to provide ambulances, doctors, and nurses on the battlefield. In an address to the alumni of the Harvard Divinity School in 1859 he deplored the lack of faith in the institution of the church and called for a universal church based on freedom in religious matters and a statement of purpose. In April 1865 he played an important role in forming the National Conference of Unitarian Churches. Bellows presided over All Souls until the end of his life.

Walter Donald Kring: *Henry Whitney Bellows* (Boston: Unitarian Universalist Association, 1979)

Walter Donald Kring

Bell Telephone Laboratories. Research and engineering firm. It was an outgrowth of the engineering department of Western Electric, a manufacturing division of American Telephone and Telegraph (AT&T) that began operations at 463 West Street in 1907. The main purpose of the firm was to develop practical improvements in telephony, but its activities expanded to such an extent that by the time AT&T underwent reorganization in 1913 the laboratories were among the most advanced in the world for research in the electrical sciences. In 1925 the firm was incorporated as a subsidiary owned equally by AT&T and Western Electric. It remained independent of the daily operations of its parent firm, which it provided with a sustained competitive advantage in telephony through such innovations as coaxial cable, microwave radio, and direct long-distance dialing. It also made innovations in fields less directly related to telephony: the first synchronous-sound motion picture system, the negative-feedback amplifier, the electrical-relay digital computer, advances in information theory, and the transistor (1947, for which John Bardeen, William Shockley, and Walter H. Brattain were awarded the Nobel Prize in physics in 1956). In 1947 Bell Laboratories moved to New Jersey.

M. D. Fagan, ed.: *A History of Engineering and Science in the Bell System* (n.p.: Bell Telephone Laboratories, 1975)

Leonard S. Reich: *The Making of American Industrial Research: Science and Business at GE and Bell, 1876–1926* (New York: Cambridge University Press, 1985)

George David Smith: *The Anatomy of a Business Strategy: Bell, Western Electric, and the Origins of the American Telephone Industry* (Baltimore: Johns Hopkins University Press, 1985)

George David Smith

Belmont. Neighborhood in the west central Bronx, bounded to the north by Fordham University, to the east by the Bronx Zoo, to the south by Tremont, and to the west by the Grand Concourse. It was originally the easternmost part of the manor of Fordham, which was eventually donated to the Dutch Reformed church in New York City as a source of income to pay its ministers. The church leased the land to farmers before selling it in 1755. The area remained farmland into the early nineteenth century, when a privately owned Episcopal boys' boarding school operated by William Powell opened on part of the property. Later most of the farms were included in Jacob Lorillard's estate, called Belmont. After the Civil War the Lorillards bequeathed their mansion to the Home for Incurables (now St. Barnabas Hospital). From the 1880s the City of New York cut streets through the farms and real-estate

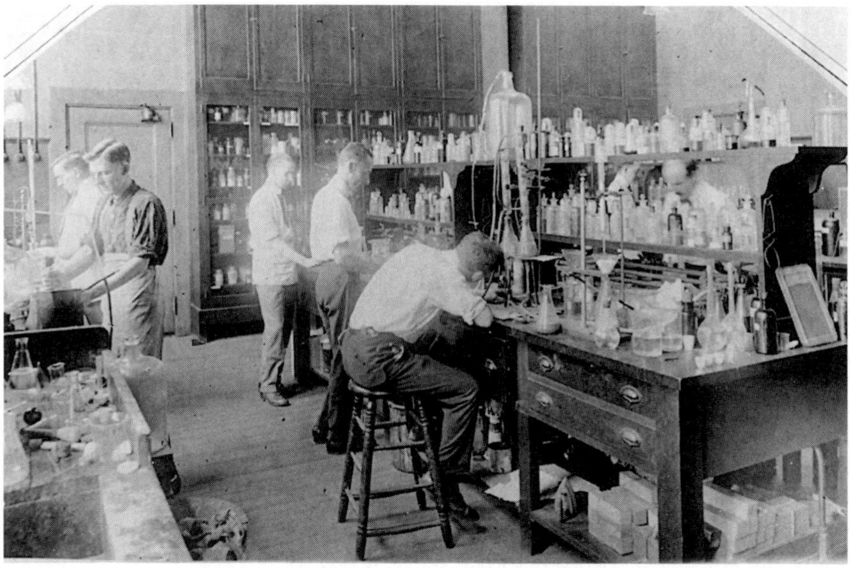

Chemical Analytical Laboratory at 463 West Street, Bell Telephone Laboratories, 1922

developers built housing on the land. The great spur to development in the 1890s was the extension to Fordham Road of the elevated line along 3rd Avenue at the western edge of the neighborhood. At the same time the New York Zoological Society was developing the Bronx Zoo in Bronx Park to the east, a project that required many workers to landscape the grounds and construct the buildings that would house the animals. These were types of work that had already drawn millions of Italian immigrants to the United States, and real-estate interests openly appealed to Italians to settle in Belmont. By the beginning of the twentieth century the neighborhood had become densely populated. It eventually became known as the Little Italy of the Bronx, and its ethnic character is still reflected in the presence of the Enrico Fermi Cultural Center and of a large market and many Italian food shops along Arthur Avenue. Until 1940 there were also pushcarts, but these were removed to the New York Retail Market building on the avenue by Mayor Fiorello H. La Guardia. In the 1980s a large number of Catholic Albanian immigrants from Yugoslavia also settled in the neighborhood. The housing stock includes one-family frame and brick houses, two-family houses, four-story brick walkup apartment buildings dating from the early twentieth century, five-story apartment buildings from the 1920s, and a few tall apartment towers from the mid 1970s. In 1986 Fordham Plaza was built at the northwest corner of the neighborhood, the first new office building in the Bronx in decades. Most of the northern section of Belmont along Fordham Road consists of automobile showrooms.

Lloyd Ultan

Belmont [Vanderbilt; née Smith], **Alva (Ertskin)** (*b* Mobile, Ala., 17 Jan 1853; *d* Paris, 26 Jan 1933). Suffragist and society figure. Educated in France, she moved to New York City in the early 1870s, married William K. Vanderbilt in 1875, and persuaded her husband to commission the architect Richard Morris Hunt to build a château at 5th Avenue and 52nd street costing $3 million; this was the site in 1883 of a famous and extravagant costume ball. After her scandalous divorce from Vanderbilt in 1895 and her remarriage to Oliver Belmont she devoted her time and considerable resources to woman suffrage: she formed and presided over the New York Political Equality League, in 1909 rented an entire floor of a building on 5th Avenue for the National American Woman Suffrage Association, and in 1921 was elected president of the National Woman's Party. Belmont later moved to France, where she spent the rest of her life.

Thea Arnold, James E. Mooney

Belmont, August (*b* Alzey, Germany, 8 Dec 1816; *d* New York City, 24 Nov 1890). Banker and diplomat. Of German Jewish background, he was the American agent for the Rothschilds of Frankfurt am Main. He settled in New York City in 1837 and formed his own firm on Wall Street, which engaged in arbitrage, commodity speculation, private lending, foreign exchange, and corporate, real-estate, and railroad investment. The rapid success of the firm made him a prominent figure in society, well known for his lavish parties. In 1849 he married Caroline Perry, a daughter of Commodore Matthew C. Perry, at the Church of the Ascension; their children were brought up as Episcopalians. An active Democrat, he was rewarded in 1853 for supporting Franklin Pierce's presidential campaign with a diplomatic post in the Netherlands, to which he was later appointed minister (1855–57); he was also chairman of the Democratic National Committee (1860–72) and a founder of the Manhattan Club (1865). Belmont owned one of the finest stables of thoroughbred horses in the country: he was a founder in 1866 of the American Jockey Club and in 1867 he inaugurated the Belmont Stakes, first held at Jerome Park in the Bronx.

Irving Katz: *August Belmont: A Political Biography* (New York: Columbia University Press, 1968)
Vincent P. Carosso: *Investment Banking in America: A History* (Cambridge: Harvard University Press, 1970)
Daniel Black: *The King of New York: The Fortunes of August Belmont* (New York: Dial, 1981)

See also AVIATION.

Theresa Collins

Belmont Island. Former name of U THANT ISLAND.

Belmont Stakes. Thoroughbred horse race for three-year-olds, first run in 1867 and now one of the oldest races in the United States. Held each June, it is the third event in the Triple Crown, after the Kentucky Derby and the Preakness Stakes. The race was first run at Jerome Park in the Bronx before being moved east of the Bronx River in 1890 to the Morris Park Racecourse, where it remained until moving again in 1905 to Belmont Park in Elmont, Long Island, just outside New York City. The length of the race, one and a half miles (2.4 kilometers), is the same as that of the Epsom Derby in Britain and the greatest of any major horse race in the United States. Perhaps the most memorable running of the Belmont Stakes was in 1973, when Secretariat won the race by thirty-one lengths and set a track record for the distance, becoming the first horse in twenty-five years to win the Triple Crown. In the mid 1990s only eleven horses had won the Triple Crown, the last being Affirmed in 1978.

Ashbel Green

Belnord Apartments. Residential building occupying the entire block between Broadway and Amsterdam avenues on the north side of 86th Street. Designed in an eclectic Renaissance style by the architectural firm of Hiss and Weeks and opened in 1908, it is a twelve-story palazzo with an interior court entered by carriage vaults on 86th Street; a delivery entry on 87th Street leads underground, thus insulating the building's residents from tradesmen. The Belnord has 175 apartments arranged in suites of eight to fourteen rooms; at one time it had full concierge services and pneumatic mail delivery. It maintains a standard of luxury beyond that of the smaller Ansonia and Apthorp apartment buildings.

Joel Schwartz

Belter, John Henry [Heinrich, Johann] (*b* Ulm, Württemberg, 1804; *d* New York City, 23 Sept 1863). Cabinetmaker and furniture manufacturer. He was first listed as a cabinetmaker at 40½ Chatham Street in directories in New York City in 1844. Within two years he moved to more fashionable quarters on Broadway. In 1853 he exhibited an ebony and ivory center-table at the New York Crystal Palace (now part of the Manney Collection). John H. Belter and Company opened a factory on 3rd Avenue at 76th Street in 1854 and showrooms at 552 Broadway in 1856, moving them to 772 Broadway in 1861. In mid 1847 Belter secured his first patent, which covered machinery for sawing "Arabesque" chairs; he later received others for an improved bedstead (1856), a technique for laminating and molding gilded layers of veneer into a cylinder from which multiple chair backs were cut (1858), and improvements to a bureau drawer and its locking device (1860). In his work he used from five to sixteen layers of veneer and carved decorations ranging from scrolls to complex patterns of flowers, fruit, and animals. His partners continued the business until they were forced to declare bankruptcy in 1867. In later years Belter's name became a generic term for ornate Rococo Revival furniture of laminated construction.

Marvin D. Schwartz, Edward J. Stanek, and Douglas K. True: *The Furniture of John Henry Belter and the Rococo Revival* (New York: E. P. Dutton, 1981)

Deborah Dependahl Waters

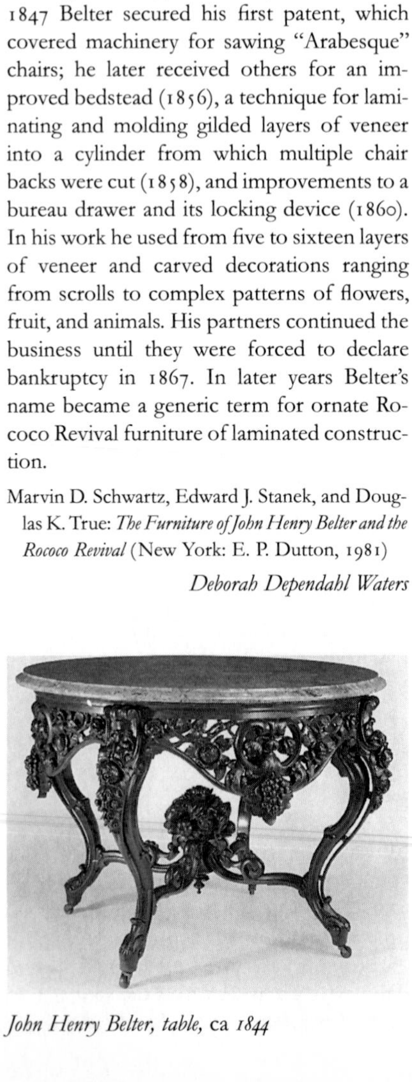

John Henry Belter, table, ca *1844*

Benchley, Robert (Charles) (*b* Worcester, Mass., 15 Sept 1889; *d* New York City, 21 Nov 1945). Essayist, humorist, and actor. After graduating from Harvard University in 1912 he moved to New York City to write. Initially he had little success, publishing his work only occasionally. His first humorous piece appeared in *Vanity Fair* in October 1914, and in 1916 he was engaged by Franklin P. Adams as an associate editor of the Sunday magazine of the *New York Tribune*. As the managing editor of *Vanity Fair* he met Dorothy Parker and Robert E. Sherwood. A member of the Algonquin Round Table, he was well known for such quips as "I'd like to get out of this wet suit and into a dry martini." He lived at the Algonquin Hotel in 1919 and later moved to the Royalton Hotel at 44 West 44th Street, where he kept a suite for twenty-four years. After leaving *Vanity Fair* he took an office with Parker and turned to freelance writing, producing the column "Books and Other Things" for the *New York World* and working as a drama critic for *Life* and the *New Yorker*. At the same time he became a popular comedian, best known for the monologue "The Treasurer's Report," which he performed in many stage revues and in a film made at the Fox studios in Astoria in 1928; he later made more than forty other films. Often self-deprecating in his humor, Benchley wrote of his own career: "It took me fifteen years to discover I had no talent, but I couldn't give it all up because by that time I was too famous."

Babette Rosmond: *Robert Benchley: His Life and Good Times* (Garden City, N.Y.: Doubleday, 1970)

Walter Friedman

Benedict [née Fulton], **Ruth** (*b* New York City, 5 June 1887; *d* New York City, 17 Sept 1948). Anthropologist, feminist, and poet. After graduating from Vassar College in 1909 she married and settled near New York City in 1914 and in 1919 became a student of the anthropologists Alexander Goldenweiser and Elsie Clews Parsons at the New School for Social Research. She transferred to Columbia University in 1921 to study with Franz Boas and earned her PhD there in 1923. She was also influenced by the linguist Edward Sapir and Margaret Mead, a former pupil who became her close friend. During the 1920s she wrote poetry under the name Anne Singleton. At Columbia she worked closely with Boas and rose from the rank of lecturer (1923) to that of full professor (1948). Instrumental in popularizing the field of anthropology, she was credited with making New York City a center for its study in the 1930s and 1940s. Benedict carried out fieldwork among several American Indian peoples, notably the Zuni of the southwestern United States, focusing on the relationship between individual personality and culture. She wrote two popular and influential works: *Patterns of Culture* (1934) and *The Chrysanthemum and the Sword: Patterns of Japanese Culture* (1946). After the Second World War she directed the project known as Research in Contemporary Cultures at Columbia.

Judith Schachter Modell: *Ruth Benedict: Patterns of a Life* (Philadelphia: University of Pennsylvania Press, 1983)

Margaret M. Caffrey: *Ruth Benedict: Stranger in This Land* (Austin: University of Texas Press, 1989)

Ira Jacknis

Benét, Stephen Vincent (*b* Bethlehem, Penn., 22 July 1898; *d* New York City, 13 March 1943). Writer, brother of William Rose Benét. He was educated at Yale University (BA 1919, MA 1920), where he was a writer and editor for the *Yale Literary Magazine* and the *Yale Record*. New York City figured prominently in his work. *Heavens and Earth* (1920) included a section of poems entitled "The Tall Town" that depicted everyday experiences there. Of two minds about the city's literary life, he spent much of his time in Paris. In 1929 he won a Pulitzer Prize for *John Brown's Body* (1928), an epic poem depicting the Civil War through sketches of historical and fictional characters set in rhymed verse. In the same year he was elected to the National Institute of Arts and Letters, later becoming its vice-president. He lived at 326 East 57th Street during the late 1920s and at 220 East 69th Street during the 1930s before moving in 1939 to 215 East 68th Street, where he remained for the rest of his life. Inspired by the collapse of the American economy, the rise of fascism in Europe, and his own financial and physical difficulties, he turned to apocalyptic themes in such works as "Metropolitan Nightmare," a poem published in *Burning City* (1936) about tropical heat and a fictional steel-eating termite in New York City. Benét lectured widely, wrote book reviews for the *New York Herald Tribune* and the *Saturday Review of Literature*, and was elected to the American Academy of Arts and Letters (1938). His written works include operettas, short stories such as "The Devil and Daniel Webster" (1936), and *Western Star* (1943, Pulitzer Prize 1944), the first volume in what was to have been a series about a pioneer's experiences.

Charles Andrews Fenton: *Stephen Vincent Benét: The Life and Times of an American Man of Letters, 1898–1943* (New Haven: Yale University Press, 1958)

Naomi Wax

Benét, William Rose (*b* Brooklyn, 2 Feb 1886; *d* New York City, 4 May 1950). Writer, brother of Stephen Vincent Benét. He attended the U.S. Military Academy before graduating from Yale University in 1907. In a collection of colorful, romantic poems entitled *The Falconer of God and Other Poems* (1914) he juxtaposed images of the streets of New York City with others of visionary dreamlands. After working as an assistant editor at *Century Magazine* he joined with Henry Seidel Canby, Amy Loveman, and Christopher Morley to launch the *Literary Review* of the *New York Evening Post* in 1920, where he was chief contributor, and the *Saturday Review of Literature* in 1924, where he was the poetry critic, author of the column "The Phoenix Nest" (1924–50), and an editor until the end of his life. For a time he lived in a studio at 37 West 10th Street before moving with his wife, the poet Elinor Wylie, to 142 East 18th Street (1923–26). Benét also worked as a translator and children's storyteller. His published writings include verse and prose for children, short stories, textbooks, the verse novel *Rip Tide* (1932), and *The Dust Which Is God*, a fictionalized autobiographical narrative in verse that won a Pulitzer Prize in 1942.

Laura Benét: *When William Rose, Stephen Benét, and I Were Young* (New York: Dodd, Mead, 1976)

Naomi Wax

Benjamin, Park (*b* British Guiana [now Guyana], 14 Aug 1809; *d* New York City, 12 Sept 1864). Writer and editor. Born to slaveowners, he settled in New England as a young man and joined a literary circle that included Oliver Wendell Holmes and Henry Wadsworth Longfellow. After moving to New York City he became the literary editor of the *New Yorker* under Horace Greeley. In 1839 he began publishing the *New World*, a weekly literary journal that soon had a national circulation and was dedicated to promoting distinguished American and European literature. As the editor of the daily newspaper the *Evening Signal* he engaged in frenzied controversies of public life. Benjamin spent his last years as one of the most popular lecturers on the American Lyceum circuit, where he presented satirical and humorous verse and often appeared with Greeley and Henry Ward Beecher.

Merle M. Hoover: *Park Benjamin, Poet and Editor* (New York: Columbia University Press, 1948)

Andrew Wiese

Bennett, James Gordon, Jr. (*b* New York City, 10 May 1841; *d* Beaulieu, France, 14 May 1918). Newspaper publisher. He took control of the *New York Herald* when his father, the publisher, retired in 1867, and he continued the newspaper's tradition of sparing no expense to collect news. In 1896 he sent the reporter Henry Morton Stanley to Africa to find the missionary David Livingstone. An eccentric society figure and commodore of the New York Yacht Club, he lived off the newspaper's profits while supervising operations from his home in Paris. In 1887 he launched the Paris edition of the *Herald*, which later became the *International Herald Tribune*. Perhaps better known as a sportsman than as a journalist, Bennett sponsored many regattas and horse, automobile, and airplane races.

Don C. Seitz: *The James Gordon Bennetts: Father and Son* (Indianapolis: Bobbs–Merrill, 1928)

Steven H. Jaffe

Bennett, James Gordon, Sr. (*b* Keith, Scotland, 1 Sept 1795; *d* New York City, 1 June 1872). Newspaper publisher and editor. In 1829 he became the associate editor of the *Courier and Enquirer*, and in May 1835 he launched the *New York Herald* from a basement on Wall Street with $500; its financial reportage, coverage of crime and scandal, and enterprise in collecting national and international news soon made it one of the most successful "penny papers" in the United States. Bennett's editorial attacks on his competitors and iconoclastic contempt for religious norms made him arguably the most controversial American newspaperman of his day. Outraged subjects of his articles physically assaulted him at least six times, and he was excluded from polite society in New York City. The *Herald* had the highest circulation of any American daily newspaper. Although it initially disavowed party politics, Bennett editorialized regularly against abolition and for American territorial expansion, and after 1840 he tended to support Democratic presidents. Although initially critical of Lincoln, the *Herald* became supportive of him after 1864, presumably because Lincoln offered Bennett the mission to France (which he declined). Bennett is considered one of the inventors of American popular journalism.

Don C. Seitz: *The James Gordon Bennetts: Father and Son* (Indianapolis: Bobbs–Merrill, 1928)

Frank Luther Mott: *American Journalism: A History of Newspapers in the United States through 260 Years, 1690–1950* (New York: Macmillan, 1941; 3rd edn 1962)

James L. Crouthamel: *Bennett's New York Herald and the Rise of the Popular Press* (Syracuse, N.Y.: Syracuse University Press, 1989)

See also ADVERTISING.

Steven H. Jaffe

Bennett [DiFighlia], Michael (*b* Buffalo, 8 April 1943; *d* Tucson, Ariz., 2 July 1987). Director and choreographer. After growing up in Buffalo he made his début on Broadway as a dancer in *Subways Are for Sleeping* (1961) and as a choreographer in *A Joyful Noise* (1966). He provided choreography for television variety programs taped in New York City, including "Hullabaloo" and "The Ed Sullivan Show" in the late 1960s. His first major success was the musical *Promises, Promises* (1968), and he won his first Tony Award for the musical *Follies* (1971). He became widely known when he directed the musical *A Chorus Line* (1975) and with Bob Avian provided its choreography; the show won many awards and remained on Broadway for fifteen years. Bennett also directed *Ballroom* (1978) and *Dreamgirls* (1981).

Denny Martin Flinn: *What They Did for Love: The Untold Story behind the Making of A Chorus Line* (New York: Bantam, 1989)

Ken Mandelbaum: *A Chorus Line and the Musicals of Michael Bennett* (New York: St. Martin's, 1989)

Barbara Cohen-Stratyner

Benny, Jack [Kubelsky, Benjamin] (*b* Chicago, 14 Feb 1894; *d* Beverly Hills, Calif., 27 Dec 1974). Comedian. He grew up in Waukegan, Illinois, where he learned to play the violin and began a career in vaudeville theater; he spent the First World War in the navy and after 1927 lived for a few years at the Hotel Edison (228 West 47th Street). After making his début on Ed Sullivan's radio program in 1931 he began his own program in New York City in the following year and moved it to the West Coast in 1935. He led the national ratings, launched a television series, and competed with Bob Hope until his last radio broadcast in 1954. After his television program was canceled in 1964 he began a series of annual television specials. With his daughter he wrote an autobiography, *Sunday Nights at Seven* (1990).

James E. Mooney

Benson, Egbert (*b* New York City, 21 June 1746; *d* Jamaica [now in Queens], 24 Aug 1833). Statesman. He graduated from King's College in 1765 and during the American Revolution became a patriot; he was later active in state government and in the provincial congress, was a delegate to the Congress of the Confederation and the Annapolis Convention of 1786, and served two consecutive terms in the U.S. Congress. Benson was appointed to the state supreme court in 1794 and to the chief judgeship of the U.S. Circuit Court, a position he left to return to Congress. He was also a trustee of Columbia College and helped to form the New-York Historical Society.

Wythe Holt: *Egbert Benson, First Chief Judge of the Second Circuit* (New York: Second Circuit Committee, 1987)

James E. Mooney

Bensonhurst. Neighborhood in southwestern Brooklyn (1990 pop. 150,000), adjoining Bay Ridge, Borough Park, and Coney Island and bounded to the north by 61st Street, to the east by McDonald Avenue, to the south by Gravesend Bay, and to the west by 14th Avenue. Once a small section of New Utrecht, it was covered by farms and had fewer than four thousand inhabitants before the construction of steam railroads in the 1870s. In the late 1880s the developer James Lynch bought large parcels of land from several members of the Benson family and built the suburb of Bensonhurst-by-the-Sea on a plot of 350 acres (142 hectares) bounded to the north by 78th Street, to the east by 23rd Avenue, to the south by Gravesend Bay, and to the west by 20th Avenue. He planted five thousand shade trees and designed villas for a thousand families. The area was six miles (ten kilometers) from City Hall in Brooklyn, and middle-class families were attracted by its rural character and its proximity to Manhattan; 22nd Avenue was replaced by Bay Parkway, built by the City of Brooklyn as part of a tree-lined route from Prospect Park to the sea. Along Gravesend Bay the Bensonhurst Yacht Club, the Atlantic Yacht Club, and the Crescent Athletic Club catered to the affluent sporting population of Brooklyn. When the town was annexed to Brooklyn in 1894 the population was less than ten thousand.

The area became heavily populated soon after being linked to Manhattan in 1915 by the 4th Avenue subway along a route formerly used by the Sea Beach and West End steam railways. Brick houses for two to three families and apartment buildings of four to six stories built in the 1920s were occupied mostly by Italians and Jews from the Lower

Loading hay in Bensonhurst, 1900

Backyards in Bensonhurst, 1977

East Side. The population increased dramatically during the first quarter of the twentieth century, to nearly 150,000 by 1930. An increasing number of Jews turned to local institutions for education and recreation, including the Jewish Community House, which opened in 1927 at Bay Parkway and 78th Street.

Residential growth continued after the Second World War. In 1949 the Shore Haven Apartments complex was built by Fred Trump at 21st Avenue off the Belt Parkway; with five thousand apartments this was then the largest private housing development in Brooklyn. The 1950s saw an influx of immigrants from southern Italy (primarily Sicily and Naples). Several local residents became well known, among them the opera singer Robert Merrill, the actor Elliott Gould, the comedian Buddy Hackett, and the baseball pitcher Sandy Koufax. The neighborhood also became famous through the popular television series "The Honeymooners" as the home of Ralph Kramden, a boisterous bus driver portrayed by Jackie Gleason. For many years the neighborhood was one of the most homogeneous in the city. In 1980 the population was 93 percent white and about 80 percent Italian; more than 70 percent of the residents occupied one- and two-family houses. In the 1980s immigrants from Asia and the Soviet Union moved into the neighborhood; Chinese immigrants settled mostly in one- to three-family houses between Bay 25th and Bay 50th streets, Russians in the many apartment buildings lining Bay Parkway. Other ethnic groups that moved into the neighborhood in the 1980s included Greeks, Koreans, Israelis, Poles, and Arabs, especially from Egypt, Lebanon, Syria, and Jordan. Tensions between whites and blacks in the neighborhood erupted in August 1989 when a black teenager was murdered by a gang of whites.

The population of Bensonhurst is mostly lower middle class and tightly knit. Family and church are central in many residents' lives, and several generations of a family are likely to live on the same block. The Regina Pacis Roman Catholic Church stands on 65th Street. Blacks live mostly in the Marlboro public housing project, which lies at the eastern edge of the neighborhood. The Jewish Community House offers social service programs for senior citizens and Russian immigrants. Most Italians live along 18th Avenue between 63rd and 86th streets and along 86th Street between 14th Avenue and Bay Parkway. In September a feast is held for Santa Rosalia, the patron saint of Sicily. Well-known restaurants include Tommaso's (86th Street near Bay 8th), Gino's Focacceria (18th Avenue and 71st Street), and L&B Spumoni Gardens (86th Street; opened 1939).

Stephen Weinstein

Benton, Thomas Hart (*b* Neosho, Mo., 15 April 1889; *d* Kansas City, 19 Jan 1975). Painter and muralist. A grand-nephew of the senator of the same name from Missouri, he studied in Paris (1908–11), where he befriended Morgan Russell and Stanton Macdonald-Wright, and worked in New York City from 1912. There he experimented with synchromist color abstraction and took part in exhibitions of the Peoples Art Guild and the Forum Exhibition (1916). After 1918 he developed a monumental figurative style that celebrated the folk culture of the United States. His first mural commission was a nine-part cycle for the New School for Social Research called *America Today* (1931, now at the Equitable Life Assurance Society of the United States), which depicts industry and city life before the Depression. Later murals, such as those for the Whitney Museum of American Art (1932), focused on native, rural, and folk themes central to the Regionalist movement. Benton left New York City in 1935. He wrote *An American in Art: A Professional and Technical Autobiography* (1969).

Henry A. LaFarge: *Thomas Hart Benton* (New York: Graham Gallery, 1968)

Emily Braun and Thomas Branchick: *Thomas Hart Benton: The "America Today" Murals* (Williamstown, Mass.: Williams College Museum of Art, 1985)

Thomas Hart Benton, City Activities with Dance Hall *(1931). Mural in a series entitled* America Today *commissioned by the New School for Social Research*

Henry Adams: *Thomas Hart Benton: An American Original* (New York: Alfred A. Knopf, 1989)

Judith Zilczer

Benton and Bowles. Advertising agency and market research firm formed several months before the stock market crash of 1929 by William Benton and Chester Bowles, both graduates of Yale University who met while working at the George Batten Company, an advertising firm in New York City. Benton was president of the new firm and Bowles took charge of the creative side. The firm began with capital of $1800 and occupied a two-room office in the Chanin building at 122 East 42nd Street at Lexington Avenue before moving in 1930 to 5 East 45th Street. To research the public's opinion of a gelatin product made by the General Foods Corporation, their first important account, Benton and Bowles surveyed housewives door to door for four months. The success of the ensuing advertising campaign led General Foods to award an additional six accounts to the firm in 1932, which allowed it to survive the Depression and to emerge as one of the leading advertising agencies in the country. Other major accounts included Procter and Gamble, and Bristol–Myers. In 1932 the agency moved to 444 Madison Avenue. It was one of the first agencies to use radio for advertising purposes, and also produced the radio programs "Beauty Box" (for Palmolive), "Showboat" (for Maxwell House), Fred Allen's "Town Hall Tonight," and "Gang Busters." Benton became chairman of the board in 1935 but resigned in the following year, and Bowles left the firm in 1941; each later served in several high-ranking government positions. The firm moved to 666 5th Avenue in 1957 and to 909 3rd Avenue in 1969. In 1986 Benton and Bowles merged with the Midwestern advertising firm D'Arcy MacManus Masius to form D'Arcy Masius Benton and Bowles, with headquarters in New York City.

Sidney Hyman: *The Lives of William Benton* (Chicago: University of Chicago Press, 1969)

Chester Bowles: *Promises to Keep: My Years in Public Life* (New York: Harper and Row, 1971)

Marjorie Harrison

Berg, Gertrude Edelstein (*b* New York City, 3 Oct 1899; *d* New York City, 14 Sept 1966). Actress and writer. A graduate of public school and Columbia University, she played the role of Mollie Goldberg on the radio program "The Rise of the Goldbergs" from 1929 to 1950 and acted on television (1949–54), in motion pictures, and on the stage in such plays as *Molly and Me* (1948), *Majority of One* (1959–62), and *Dear Me the Sky Is Falling*. She also wrote and produced plays. Her memoirs, *Molly and Me*, were published in 1961.

James E. Mooney

Bergdorf Goodman. Firm of clothing retailers. Formed in 1894 as Bergdorf and Voight by Herman Bergdorf and Herman Voight, it first operated a small ladies' tailoring and fur shop at 125 5th Avenue. A tailor in the shop, Edwin Goodman (1878–1953), bought a share of the business and a few years later Bergdorf retired to France. The firm specialized in high fashion and catered to an élite clientele. Its success made necessary a move to new quarters: a small shop was built in 1928 at 5th Avenue and 58th Street, which eventually extended as far as 57th Street. In 1987 the store was acquired by the Neiman–Marcus Group, and in 1990 the men's department was moved across the street, to 745 5th Avenue.

Booton Herndon: *Bergdorf's on the Plaza: The Story of Bergdorf Goodman and a Half-century of American Fashion* (New York: Alfred A. Knopf, 1956)

Leslie Gourse

Bergen Beach. Neighborhood in southeastern Brooklyn, bounded to the north by Paerdegat Basin and Canarsie, to the east by Jamaica Bay, to the south by Mill Basin, and to the west by Flatlands. A family descended from Hans Hansen Bergen, a Dutch settler of the seventeenth century, owned the land and eventually sold it to Percy Williams, an entrepreneur who developed it as a summer resort. His enterprise thrived in the 1890s and the early twentieth century but became unable to compete with Coney Island and Rockaway Beach, and by 1926 the last section had been sold for a development of one-family houses. Some houses were built and picnic groves were run through with streets, but most of the area remained undeveloped into the 1990s.

Ellen Marie Snyder-Grenier

Berkman, Alexander (*b* Vilnius [now in Lithuania], 21 Nov 1870; *d* Nice, France, 28 June 1936). Anarchist. He moved in 1888 to the Lower East Side, where he joined the Pioneers of Liberty. During a steelworkers' strike in 1892 in Homestead, Pennsylvania, he tried to assassinate Henry Clay Frick and was subsequently imprisoned for fourteen years; he remained one of the best-known anarchists in the United States from 1906 to 1919. In New York City he edited *Mother Earth* (a publication launched by Emma Goldman), organized opposition to the First World War, and helped to form the Ferrer School, which was devoted to libertarian causes and the working class. Exiled in 1919, Berkman moved to Paris, where he wrote for the Jewish Anarchist Federation of New York.

David A. Balcom

Berkshire. Steamboat built by the New York Shipbuilding Company of Camden, New Jersey, in 1913. The largest steamboat on the Hudson River, she registered 4500 tons, measured 422 feet (128 meters) by fifty feet (fifteen meters), had feathering wheels, and was powered by a vertical-beam engine that had an eighty-five inch (212-centimeter) cylinder and a twelve-foot (four-meter) stroke. The ship was known for her classic interior and was operated as a night boat by the Hudson Navigation Company between New York City and Albany, New York, until being retired in 1937.

Arthur G. Adams

Berle, A(dolf) A(ugustus), Jr. (*b* Boston, 29 Jan 1895; *d* New York City, 17 Feb 1971). Public official. He earned a degree from Harvard Law School at twenty-one and worked for the firm of Louis D. Brandeis before volunteering for the army in 1917; he later moved to New York City, where he taught law at Columbia University, provided financial advice to Mayor Fiorello H. La Guardia, and directed the Planning Commission and the Housing Authority while also serving as chamberlain of New York City between 1934 and 1938. As an advisor to President Franklin D. Roosevelt he promoted central planning, and he worked as a Latin American expert and diplomat for him and for presidents Harry S. Truman and John F. Kennedy. He also helped to organize the Liberal Party and wrote a number of books on law and politics, including *The Modern Corporation and Private Property* (1932).

Jordan A. Schwarz: *Liberal: Adolf A. Berle and the Vision of an American Era* (New York: Free Press, 1987)

James E. Mooney

Berle [Berlinger], **Milton** (*b* New York City, 12 July 1908). Actor. After years in vaudeville he made his début on Broadway in Earl Carroll's *Vanities* (1932) and Ziegfeld's *Follies* (1936, 1943). Never wholly successful in film or on radio, he became well known in "Texaco Star Theater" (1948–56), a television program produced in New York City by the Columbia Broadcasting System. His broad humor and antics came across well on television and were important in spurring sales of television sets. Known often as "Uncle Miltie" or "Mr. Television," Berle was one of the best-known television actors of his time.

David J. Weiner

Berlin. Former name of a section of northwestern Queens at the eastern edge of Laurel Hill, bounded to the north by the Long Island Expressway, to the east by 50th Street, to the south by Newtown Creek, and to the west by 48th Street. It was promoted as Berlinville in 1871 and developed to draw German immigrants; all the streets were named after German cities. By the 1990s the area had been given over almost entirely to industry.

Vincent Seyfried

Berlin, Irving [Baline, Israel] (*b* Tyumen, Russia, 11 May 1888; *d* New York City, 22 Sept 1989). Composer, songwriter, and producer. The son of a cantor, he moved to New York City from Russia in 1893 and without formal musical instruction began his career on the Lower East Side as a street singer and singing waiter, and in Tin Pan Alley as a song plugger. He performed in vaudeville and Broadway revues and achieved his first great success with the song "Alexander's Ragtime Band" (1911). In 1919 he formed Irving Berlin Music and with Sam Harris in 1921 he opened the Music Box Theatre, at 239 West 45th Street, where he introduced his newest songs. He lived for most of his life on the Upper East Side of Manhattan and spent his last years as a recluse in a mansion on Beekman Place.

Berlin usually wrote the lyrics to his own songs. Because he was a self-taught pianist able to play in only one key, he was able to write songs in other keys only by having his piano equipped with a unique keyboard-shifting device. His songs are remarkable for their unforced melodies and rhythms and their forthright sentiments; they captured the public fancy and were eagerly sought after by musicians in Tin Pan Alley and elsewhere. The best-known include "God Bless America" (1918), "White Christmas" (1942), and many songs inspired by New York City, among them "Where Is My Little Old New York" (1924), "Puttin' on the Ritz" (1929), "Manhattan Madness" (1932), "Harlem on My Mind" (1933), "Easter Parade" (1933), "Slumming on Park Avenue" (1937), and "Washington Square Dance" (1950). Berlin's successful Broadway shows *Annie Get Your Gun* (1946) and *Call Me Madam* (1950) both featured Ethel Merman; his last Broadway production was *Mr. President* (1962).

Laurence Bergreen: *As Thousands Cheer: The Life of Irving Berlin* (New York: Viking, 1990)

Nicholas E. Tawa

Bernays, Edward L. (*b* Vienna, 22 Nov 1891; *d* Cambridge, Mass., 9 March 1995). Public relations executive. He emigrated to the United States and settled in New York City at the age of one with his father and his mother, the sister of Sigmund Freud. Before the First World War he was a press agent on Broadway and during the war he worked for the Committee of Public Information. In 1919 he formed a publicity agency with Doris E. Fleischman (1892–1980), who later became his wife. In addition to offering publicity for sales promotion, proxy fights, and lobbying efforts, Bernays wrote several books on public relations, including *Biography of an Idea: Memoirs of Public Relations Counsel Edward L. Bernays* (1965), and taught the first course on the subject in 1923 at New York University.

Alan R. Raucher

Bernstein, Leonard [Louis] (*b* Lawrence, Mass., 25 Aug 1918; *d* New York City, 13 Oct 1990). Conductor, composer, and educator. In 1943 he was named assistant conductor of the New York Philharmonic and soon after gave a dramatic performance leading the orchestra as a substitute for Bruno Walter, who had been taken ill. He conducted the New York City Symphony from 1945 to 1948

Leonard Bernstein

and in 1957 returned to the New York Philharmonic as its co-conductor (with Dimitri Mitropoulos). In the following year he became the first music director of the orchestra both born and trained in the United States, and remained in this position until he was named its laureate conductor in 1969. A committed and enthusiastic advocate of modern works, he projected an image strikingly different from that of the stern, foreign-born conductor to which American audiences were accustomed. He performed more concerts with the orchestra than any other conductor in its history, giving thirty-six world premières and fourteen American premières. He was the first conductor to understand and master television as a medium for music education: after making several programs in 1954 for the television series "Omnibus" he began two series with the New York Philharmonic in 1958: Young People's Concerts, which continued for fifteen years, and a series geared toward adults that continued until 1962.

In addition to being the focus of much of Bernstein's career as a conductor, New York City provided the inspiration for a great many of his compositions. His first ballet, *Fancy Free* (1944, choreography by Jerome Robbins), was so well received at its première by the Ballet Theatre at the Metropolitan Opera House that it was soon transformed into the full-length Broadway musical *On the Town* (1944). His other works for the stage include *Wonderful Town* (1953), *Candide* (1956), *West Side Story* (1957), and *Mass* (1971), and two operas, *Trouble in Tahiti* (1952) and *A Quiet Place* (1984). He also wrote three symphonies (*Jeremiah*, 1942; *The Age of Anxiety*, 1949; and *Kaddish*, 1963), the orchestral works *Facsimile* (1946) and *Serenade* (1954), and chamber and vocal music. Bernstein wrote *West Side Story* while living at the Osborne on West 57th Street; for many years until the end of his life he lived in the Dakota on West 72nd Street.

John Briggs: *Leonard Bernstein: The Man, His Work and His World* (New York: World, 1961)

Humphrey Burton: *Leonard Bernstein* (New York: Doubleday, 1994)

For further illustration see MUSICAL THEATER.

Barbara Haws

Berra, Yogi [Lawrence Peter] (*b* St. Louis, 12 May 1925). Baseball player. Born to parents from northern Italy, he spent his entire playing career as a catcher for teams in New York City. From 1946 to 1963 he was a central figure with the New York Yankees. During this period the team won ten World Series and he set many World Series records, including those for most series played (fourteen), most series games played (seventy-five), most hits (seventy-one), and most times at bat (259). He was named "most valuable player" in the American League three times (1951, 1954, and 1955), a record. After leaving the Yankees he remained active in professional baseball as a manager of the Yankees (in 1964, when they won the American League pennant, in 1984, and for the first sixteen games of the season in 1985) and of the New York Mets (1972–75, winning the National League pennant in 1973). He also played briefly for the Mets in 1965 and worked as a coach. Berra is perhaps the most often quoted figure in baseball. His aphoristic, colorful malapropisms have entered the American vernacular: an extensive selection is included in the first chapter of his autobiography *Yogi: It Ain't Over* (1989). He was inducted into the Baseball Hall of Fame in 1972.

Gene Schoor: *The Story of Yogi Berra* (New York: Doubleday, 1976)

Joseph S. Lieber

Best. Firm of women's and girls' clothing retailers. Formed in 1879 by Albert Best and James A. Smith, its first establishment was a children's store at 315 6th Avenue. On the death of Smith his share in the business was bought by Thomas Hall; after the death of Best the president of the firm, Philip LeBoutillier, introduced bonuses for employees and innovations in buying. The firm moved its retail operations to a twelve-story building at 5th Avenue and 51st Street in 1947 and later opened several branches. At its peak it operated fourteen stores, of which three alone reportedly had $10 million worth of inventory. The firm ceased operations in 1970; its main store was replaced by Olympic Tower, an office and residential building.

Leslie Gourse

Bethany Baptist Church. Church at 460 Sumner Avenue in Brooklyn, founded in 1883. It is notable for having been the first black congregation to move into the heart of Bedford–Stuyvesant. It moved to its present site in 1924 during the height of white resistance to black migration.

Kenneth T. Jackson

Bethel Tabernacle African Methodist Episcopal Church. Church in Weeksville, Brooklyn. Founded in 1847, it continued to thrive past the 1870s, when the predominantly black community of Weeksville was slowly overwhelmed by the larger white community around it. In 1978 the church moved to 1630 Dean Street, directly across the street from its original home. The new building had earlier been Public School 83, an all-white school that had been integrated in 1864 by students from Colored School no. 2, which had itself been founded a few years earlier by some of the leading citizens of Weeksville.

Kenneth T. Jackson

Beth Israel Medical Center. General-care hospital in Stuyvesant Square, opened in May 1891 as a facility for Orthodox Jews by the Beth Israel Hospital Association, which in 1889 had opened a dispensary at 97 Henry Street. It began with twenty beds at 196 East Broadway and later occupied quarters at 206 East Broadway and 195 Division Street. The hospital served kosher food and had a Yiddish-speaking staff. It relied heavily on donations from wealthy Jews and from 1894 also received support from the Saturday and Sunday Association; as late as 1915 about 93 percent of the patients received medical treatment free of charge. In 1917 the hospital became a member of the Federation of Jewish Philanthropic Societies. The annual number of outpatients exceeded 100,000 in 1918. In 1929 the hospital moved to a facility with 115 beds at Jefferson and Cherry streets and opened the Beth Israel Training School for Nurses (now the Phillips Beth Israel School of Nursing); by this time it had acquired a reputation for medical services of high quality and no longer served only the poor. In 1945 it became a teaching hospital of the New York University School of Medicine. Beth Israel purchased Manhattan General Hospital in 1964. During the next two years it opened the Linsky Pavillion, the Bernstein Institute, Fierman Hall, and Gilman Hall, and formed an affiliation with the New York Eye and Ear Infirmary. It set up the nation's largest methadone program in 1977, was named a center for AIDS care by New York State in 1987, and in 1988 acquired a nursing home with 230 beds in White Plains, New York, and an inpatient unit with twelve beds for AIDS patients. In the early 1990s the medical center had 949 beds. Among the institutions associated with it were Doctors Hospital (229 beds), the Beth Israel Nursing Home (230), and the ambulatory care facility New York Health Care.

Tina Levitan: *Islands of Compassion: A History of the Jewish Hospitals of New York* (New York: Twayne, 1964)

Bernadette McCauley

Bethune [née Graham], **Joanna** (*b* Fort Niagara [now in N.Y.], 1 Feb 1770; *d* New York City, 28 July 1860). Philanthropist. She helped to form the Orphan Asylum Society (1806), which built an orphanage to accommodate two hundred children, and the Female Union Society for the Promotion of Sabbath Schools, which during its first year opened twenty-two schools with 250 teachers and more than three thousand students. After the Female Union Society became an auxiliary in 1827 of the American Sunday School Union, which was dominated by males, she formed the Infant School Society: its religiously oriented day-care center in the basement of the Canal Street Presbyterian Church had about 180 students.

George W. Bethune: *Memoirs of Mrs. Joanna Bethune* (New York: Harper and Brothers, 1863)

Page Putnam Miller

Bettmann Archive. Photographic archive formed in 1935 in New York City by Otto L. Bettmann, a refugee from the Nazis who began the business with a few prints and negatives that he had taken with him from Germany. The archive began at just the time when large picture magazines such as *Life* and *Look* were beginning publication, and these magazines became its first important customers. The archive moved in 1961 from two crowded basement rooms at 215 East 57th Street to a suite at 136 East 57th Street. In 1984 the archive took over the photographic library of United Press International, thus increasing the number of its images from about three million to more than sixteen million, and in the following year it became the photographic library for Reuters. These two transactions changed the business from an almost exclusively historical archive into a news archive as well. By 1990 the Bettmann Archive / Bettmann Newsphotos contained seventeen million images and was the world's largest commercial repository of prints and photographs. Bettmann sold the business to the Kraus–Thompson organization in 1981. In 1989 the family of H. P. Kraus became the sole owners and the archive moved to larger quarters at 902 Broadway.

Otto Bettmann: *Bettmann: The Picture Man* (Gainesville: University Press of Florida, 1992)

Allen J. Share

Betts, Samuel Rossiter (*b* Richmond, Mass., 8 June 1786; *d* New Haven, Conn., 3 Nov 1868). Judge. He attended Lenox Academy and Williams College (graduated 1806), studied law in Hudson, New York, and began a practice in Monticello, New York. During the War of 1812 he served in the army as a major and helped to defend New York Harbor. After representing Orange and Sullivan counties in the U.S. Congress (1816–18) he moved to Newburgh, New York, became district attorney of Orange County, and was appointed circuit judge of the New York State Supreme Court in 1823. Appointed to the U.S. District Court for the Southern District of New York by President John Quincy Adams, he served from 1827 to 1867. In this capacity he heard mostly maritime cases, some of which during the Civil War concerned the blockade, the rights of neutral ships, and prize law; during these years he lived at 16 St. Mark's Place. After retiring from the bench he moved to New Haven. Betts wrote *Admiralty Practice* (1838), a standard text, and is credited with having established an American practice distinct from English precedents.

Jeffrey A. Kroessler

Biaggi, Mario (*b* New York City, 26 Oct 1917). Congressman. After becoming the most decorated police officer in the history of New York City he won election to the House of Representatives in 1968 as a Democrat from the tenth district (Astoria and parts of the Bronx). He remained in office for ten years, eventually representing the nineteenth district (part of the Bronx and Yonkers). An important member of the Democratic machine in the Bronx and a champion of Irish and Jewish causes, he sought the mayoralty in 1973, ultimately withdrawing when it was revealed that he had invoked the Fifth Amendment before a federal grand jury. In 1987 he was convicted of having accepted bribes from Coastal Dry Dock, a firm that received nearly $500 million in navy ship rebuilding contracts during the 1980s and gave nearly $2 million a year in insurance business to a company owned by Meade Esposito, leader of the Democratic machine in Brooklyn; the bribes came in the form of free vacations that Biaggi took with his mistress while his wife was fatally ill. In 1988 he was defeated for reelection by Eliot Engel in a primary and later was convicted of illegally helping Wedtech, a defense contractor based in the Bronx, to obtain city-owned property. After spending twenty-one months in federal prison in Fort Worth, Texas, he was released in early 1991 for reasons of health. In 1992 Biaggi ran for his old seat in Congress, losing to Engel.

Jesse Drucker

Bible Teachers Training School [Biblical Seminary in New York]. Institution that later became the NEW YORK THEOLOGICAL SEMINARY (ii).

bicycling. Although bicycling in New York City is something of a challenge, the challenge is braved by a large number of New Yorkers who bicycle for recreation and as a means of

Mercury Wheel Club, Flushing Race Track, June 1894

transport. An early bicycle with a large front wheel called the velocipede was introduced at the New York Athletic Games in November 1868. Like much of the United States, the city experienced a bicycle craze during the 1890s. Riding schools proliferated, and some recruited fashionably dressed women known as "bicyclettes" to ride around the city promoting bicycling and bicycling instruction. By 1894 bicycle exhibitions were being held annually at Madison Square Garden. An especially notable one in 1896 attracted some 120,000 persons, including a number of the city's most socially prominent residents. By 1899 there were fifty-three bicycle clubs in New York City.

The Depression brought about a renewed interest in bicycling, and bicycles appeared on 5th Avenue for the first time since the 1890s. The New York Cycle Club was formed in 1937 and became an important proponent of bicycle racing; by 1990 it had nearly one thousand members and was one of the largest organizations of its kind in the United States. One of the first American bicycle touring companies, Country Cycling Tours (now Brooks Country Cycling and Hiking), was formed in New York City in the 1970s to offer bicycle tours ranging from one day in the metropolitan region to two weeks overseas. About this time recreational cycling gained great popularity, especially in Central Park and Prospect Park, where the city provided paved bicycle paths. There were occasional skirmishes between cyclists on the one hand and runners, joggers, and pedestrians on the other, who nevertheless reached an uneasy accommodation. The Five-Boro Bicycle Tour, held each May and covering about forty miles (sixty-four kilometers), was inaugurated by American Youth Hostels in the late 1970s; later renamed Bike New York, it has drawn more than 23,000 participants and inspired similar tours in San Francisco and other cities. Recreational bicycling continued to flourish into the 1990s as a number of specialty cycling clubs were formed.

Bicycle commuting became popular for a number of reasons: a growing concern for fitness and the environment, a sharp increase in gasoline prices in the 1970s, the maddeningly slow pace of automotive traffic, shortcomings in public transit and public transit strikes, and the development in the 1980s of heavy "mountain" bicycles that many riders found better suited than lightweight, narrow-tire racing bicycles to the uneven surfaces of city streets. As elsewhere in the United States commuting cyclists in New York City were outspoken in demanding better conditions: showers and lockers in new office buildings, more bicycle racks outside existing buildings, and protected bicycle lanes on major thoroughfares. In response to their demands the city designated bicycle lanes on Broadway and across the Brooklyn Bridge and laid down concrete dividers along 6th Avenue in 1980, but then quickly removed the dividers after concluding that they were ineffective. One problem that continued to plague commuting cyclists was a high rate of theft, of which the city became an unofficial capital: bicycle thieves managed to defeat even the sturdiest locks and chains with freon, heavy-duty cable cutters stolen from the telephone company, and in some cases plastic explosives, and proved so adept that one well-known manufacturer of bicycle locks specifically exempted New York City from the guarantee that it offered with its products. Despite these hardships the number of commuting cyclists in the city was estimated at seventy thousand in the early 1990s.

A large number of bicycle-messenger services were formed in the 1970s and 1980s, as entrepreneurs recognized that increasingly heavy vehicular traffic was making it difficult for businesses in Manhattan to deliver and receive packages and documents. Because the messengers were generally paid in proportion to the number of packages they delivered, they had an incentive to ride quickly and sometimes recklessly, and near misses and even collisions with automobiles and pedestrians were common. Some companies dispatching the messengers disclaimed responsibility for any injuries and damages resulting from these accidents on the grounds that the messengers were not their employees but rather independent contractors. By about 1990 the number of messenger services had been sharply reduced by the growth of facsimile transmission and overnight package services. One bicycle messenger who achieved prominence in competitive cycling was Nelson Vails, who won a silver medal in the match sprints in the Olympic games of 1984. There were about five thousand bicycle messengers working in the city in the early 1990s.

Trudy E. Bell

Big Allis. A nickname for one of the three generating units at Ravenswood Generating Station in Long Island City, the largest power plant operated by Consolidated Edison. It derives from the name of the manufacturer, the Allis Chalmers Corporation. When the generator was put on line in 1965 its potential output of one million kilowatts made it the largest electric generator in the world. At Ravenswood alone Consolidated Edison produces enough electricity to supply nearly two million residences in New York City.

Elizabeth J. Kramer

Big Apple. Nickname for New York City, first popularized in the 1920s by John J. Fitz Gerald, a reporter for the *Morning Telegraph*, who used the term to refer to the city's racetracks; he had heard it used by black stablehands in New Orleans in 1921. Black jazz musicians in the 1930s used the name to refer to the city (and especially Harlem) as the jazz capital of the world. The nickname was largely unknown by the 1950s. It was revived in 1971 as part of a publicity campaign by Charles Gillett, president of the New York Convention and Visitors Bureau.

Gerald Leonard Cohen: *Origin of New York City's Nickname "The Big Apple"* (Frankfurt am Main: Peter Lang, 1991)

Gerald Leonard Cohen

Bigelow, John (*b* Bristol [now Malden-on-Hudson], near Saugerties, N.Y., 25 Nov 1817; *d* New York City, 19 Dec 1911). Editor and diplomat. He attended Union College in Schenectady, New York, moved to New York City at seventeen, and at twenty was admitted to the bar. In 1848 he became an owner and editor with William Cullen Bryant of the *New York Post.* As American consul general in Paris during the Civil War he helped to persuade Napoleon III not to grant diplomatic recognition to the Confederacy. While in Paris he unearthed Benjamin Franklin's manuscript autobiography, which he edited and published. After the death of his close friend Samuel J. Tilden he helped to unite his trust with the Astor and Lenox libraries to form the New York Public Library. Bigelow was long resident at 21 Gramercy Park in Manhattan.

Margaret A. Clapp: *Forgotten First Citizen: John Bigelow* (Boston: Little, Brown, 1947)

Ormonde de Kay

Biggs, Hermann M(ichael) (*b* Trumansburg, N.Y., 29 Sept 1859; *d* New York City, 28 June 1923). Physician and bacteriologist. A pioneer in discovering and addressing the bacterial causes of contagious diseases, he held several important posts at Bellevue Hospital from 1883 to 1912. In 1892 he began his long association with the health department of New York City, where he was placed in charge of a new bacteriology laboratory. He introduced the diphtheria antitoxin to the United States in 1894 and helped to establish a system of clinics for the treatment of tuberculosis. Biggs was the commissioner of health of New York State from 1914 to 1923.

Charles-Edward A. Winslow: *The Life of Hermann M. Biggs, M.D., D.Sc., LL.D., Physician and Statesman of the Public Health* (Philadelphia: Lea and Febiger, 1929)

Joseph S. Lieber

Big Manuel (*b* Africa; *d* New Amsterdam, *ca* 1680). Landowner. He was one of the first Africans in New Amsterdam and may have been one of the eleven Angolan men brought to the colony by the Dutch West India Company in 1626. Soon after this group became part of the colony one of the Africans was found murdered; when questioned the rest confessed in solidarity, and Big Manuel was chosen by the company to be hanged. He was spared when the noose snapped and the hangman, Black Peter, complied with the spectators' demand that he not be hanged again. In 1644, after nearly twenty years of service, he and ten other Africans petitioned successfully for their freedom. They were given title to land north of the city, where many already tilled plots. Big Manuel received swampy land just north of Minetta Brook that is now Washington Square.

Sule Greg C. Wilson

bilingual education. In New York City the presence of a culturally diverse population has led to repeated calls for curricula taught wholly or partly in languages other than English. The use of students' native languages for instruction began in 1968, when Spanish was introduced into the public school curriculum. At Public School 25 in the southeastern Bronx nine hundred pupils took part in a voluntary, experimental bilingual program funded by the school district; half the students spoke mostly English and the other half mostly Spanish (of these, 86 percent were Puerto Rican and most of the rest were black). At Public School 155 a bilingual program prepared students for full English instruction by the third grade. Both programs received the support of local, state, and national community organizations, policy groups, and legislators. In 1970 there were federally funded programs in thirty-two schools serving 2332 students of Spanish-speaking background. The city's Office of Bilingual Education was formed in 1972 with a budget of $1 million. A lawsuit filed by various Puerto Rican community organizations led by Aspira resulted in a consent decree in 1974 that established standards for entitlement programs; these standards dealt with instructional, organizational, personnel, and other matters. In 1992–93 there were 143,029 students in the city who were entitled to special language services, and eleven language groups that received some form of bilingual instruction: Spanish, Chinese, Haitian–Creole, Russian, Korean, Arabic, Vietnamese, French, Bengali, Urdu, and Greek.

Francesco Cordasco, ed.: *Bilingual Education in New York City* (Salem, N.H.: Ayer, 1978)
Bilingual Education Student Information Survey (New York: Board of Education, 1989–90)

Maria E. Torres-Guzman

Languages Spoken by 100 or More Public School Students in New York City, 1989–90

Spanish 70,259
Chinese 11,058
Haitian–Creole 6,468
Russian 3,048
Korean 3,033
Arabic 1,480
Urdu 952
French 918
Italian 889
Vietnamese 872
Hindi 736
Bengali 625
Dari–Farsi 561
Khmer 519
Hebrew 514
Polish 482
Albanian 405
Portugese 361
Serbo-Croatian 312
Filipino 299
Romanian 285
Gujarati 237
Malayalam 229
Punjabi 190
Japanese 189
Turkish 153
Thai 135
Pashto 113
All other languages 1,654

Source: Suzanne DeCamp: *The Linguistic Minorities of New York City* (New York: Community Service Society, 1991)

Compiled by James Bradley

Billboard. Weekly trade magazine. Originally a journal for publishers of sheet music when it began publication in New York City in 1894, it became best known for its "charts," which measure the sales of recorded music and are highly influential in the popular-music business. From its inception the magazine was owned by the Littleford family, which sold it to private investors in 1984 for an estimated $40 million. The magazine was sold again in 1987 for about $100 million to Affiliated Publications.

Galen Gart: *First Pressings: Rock History as Chronicled in Billboard* (Milford, N.H.: Big Nickel, 1986–)

Owen D. Gutfreund

billboards. See Outdoor advertising.

billiards. Various forms of billiards and pocket billiards became popular pastimes for New Yorkers in the 1730s. Billiard tables were found chiefly in hotels and coffee houses until billiards gained favor with the general public about 1840. By the time Tobias O'Connor and Hugh W. Collender manufactured the first billiard tables in the city in 1850, about sixty billiard saloons thrived in lower Manhattan, and the game was strongly associated with gambling, drinking, and Irish immigrants. The person who did the most to popularize billiards in New York City was Michael Phelan (*b ca* 1814; *d* 1871), a player, manufacturer, and owner of billiard parlors who wrote *Billiards without a Master* (1850) and *The Game of Billiards* (1857) and published *The Billiard Cue*, the nation's first periodical devoted exclusively to the game. An aggressive promoter who attracted large crowds to well-publicized matches where players competed for generous purses, he helped make billiards one of the most popular pastimes in nineteenth-century America among both spectators and participants, and also made New York City the billiards capital of the United States. With Collender he operated a table factory and showroom at the corner of Crosby and Spring streets from 1854. Phelan's most lasting contribution to billiards was his invention of a sharp-edged cushion made of India rubber, perfected in 1854 and still in use. Phelan's chief competitors, Dudley Kavanagh and Levi Decker, introduced a catgut cushion in the following year that did not prove popular with the city's billiards enthusiasts. By 1858 four firms in the city turned out billiard tables in a business characterized by bitter rivalries. Manufacturers published magazines in which they disparaged their competition, and after Phelan formed the American Billiard Players Association in September 1865 he was accused of engaging in monopolistic practices by Kavanagh, who in 1866 formed the National American Billiards Association and began manufacturing his own tables with Decker at a five-story factory on the corner of Centre and Canal streets.

In spite of these differences it was generally agreed that the image of billiards was in need of improvement. Kavanagh and Phelan defended the game as one enjoyed by George Washington and Thomas Jefferson, beneficial to mind and body, and open to women as well as men. In 1856 the firm of Griffith and Decker published the first issue of the *Ladies Billiard Messenger*, a magazine devoted to "billiards and literature," and in *The Game of Billiards* Phelan made a special appeal to the "wives and sisters of America." Billiards benefited from an explosion of popularity in the city during the last three decades of the nineteenth century, and by 1900 New Yorkers supported at least 130 "public rooms" and thirteen manufacturers of billiard tables that sold almost $700,000 worth of tables and accessories. Billiard parlors, or pool halls, increased in number during the following decades, although they continued to be associated in the public mind with drinking, prostitution, and gambling (they were the first places where off-track wagering on horse races was conducted systematically). By the 1920s it was estimated that four thousand pool halls in the city attracted a steady business. Billiards declined in popularity after the Second World War, owing to its persistently low status and the dispersal of urban men across the metropolitan area. Only 257 pool halls were left in the city in 1961. In the 1980s and early 1990s billiard tables were still found in many bars, and a few fashionable new pool halls catered to young professionals.

Willie Hoppe: *Thirty Years of Billiards* (New York: G. P. Putnam's Sons, 1925; repr. Dover, 1975)

Marc Ferris

Billings, John S(haw) (*b* Switzerland County, Ind., 12 April 1838; *d* New York City, 11 March 1913). Librarian. He was trained as a surgeon, then distinguished himself as an innovative organizer at the Surgeon General's Library in Washington from 1864 to 1895. After winning the contest to design the Johns Hopkins Hospital in Baltimore he moved to New York City in 1895 to oversee the consolidation of the libraries of the Astor, Lenox, and Tilden foundations and the ensuing formation of the New York Public Library. He sketched the original design for a building to house the new library on 5th Avenue, and during the years of its construction supervised the process by which the holdings of the New York Public Library were catalogued and its branch libraries formed from existing free libraries. He was the director of the library until his death.

Harry Miller Lydenberg: *John Shaw Billings: Creator of the National Medical Library and Its Catalogue, First Director of the New York Public Library* (Chicago: American Library Association, 1924)

Joseph S. Lieber

Billopp's Point. Former estate at the southern tip of Staten Island, bounded to the north and east by Tottenville, to the south by Raritan Bay, and to the west by the Arthur Kill. The area is named for Christopher Billopp, an English naval officer and a favorite of the Crown who in 1675 was granted thirteen hundred acres (527 hectares) of land to establish a colonial presence on the island; he built a stone manor house (later known as the Conference House) and in 1709 opened ferry service to Perth Amboy, New Jersey. During the nineteenth century the area was called Ward's Point after its owner, Caleb T. Ward. In the mid 1990s it remained largely undeveloped and was part of Conference House Park.

Barnett Shepherd

Biltmore Hotel. A twenty-six-story hotel between 43rd and 44th streets and Madison and Vanderbilt avenues. Designed by the firm of Warren and Wetmore as part of a grand plan for Terminal City (a proposed complex of seven hotels), it was built in 1913 by the New York Central Railroad and opened with a gala dinner on New Year's Eve. The cornice of the building was uniform with that of Grand Central Terminal, and its lower floors were in the neo-palazzo style. Above the cornice the façade was of brick and terra cotta in a modernized Italian Renaissance style. A floor plan in the shape of the letter H allowed for one thousand outside rooms, of which nine hundred had private baths; the stairs and elevators of the building were linked to the pedestrian passageways of the terminal. The hotel was the national campaign headquarters for the Democratic Party in 1936–52, and in the 1940s it became famous for offering reduced rates to college students and even high school students to attract weekend business; the hotel is referred to in J. D. Salinger's *The Catcher in the Rye.* The hotel closed in 1981, and there were plans to strip the building down to its steel frame and rebuild it as the Bank of America. Preservationists sought to protect at least the Palm Court, but developers moved in a wrecking crew on a Friday night. A large clock from the Biltmore is now in the atrium of the building occupying the site of the hotel.

John Tauranac

Biltmore Program. Declaration issued by members of the Zionist movement during a conference at the Biltmore Hotel in New York City between 6 and 11 May 1942, urging the transformation of Palestine into a Jewish commonwealth and the replacement of the British mandate there by the Jewish Agency.

Michael N. Dobkowski

Bing, Alexander S(imon) (*b* New York City, 1905; *d* New York City, 12 Nov 1969). Community planner. With his brother Leo Bing he built a number of successful luxury apartment buildings in Manhattan in the early twentieth century. While working for the U.S. Housing Corporation he became interested in public service, affordable housing, and developing low-income communities. In the early 1920s he formed the City Housing Corporation of New York (CHC) to build a development in Queens, Sunnyside Gardens, based on the English garden city concept of Ebenezer Howard. For this he engaged the architects Clarence Stein and Henry Wright and sought help from such reformers as Eleanor Roosevelt, Richard Ely, Lewis Mumford, and Catherine Bauer. The success of the project enabled him to buy a large parcel of land in Fair Lawn, New Jersey, through the CHC; there he built Radburn in 1928, a "town for the motor age" within commuting distance of New York City. Construction ceased during the Depression and the CHC encountered serious problems with its cash flow, eventually declaring bankruptcy. Radburn remains one of the country's best-known experiments in community planning by a private developer.

Daniel Schaffer: *Garden Cities for America: The Radburn Experience* (Philadelphia: Temple University Press, 1982)

Marc A. Weiss

Bing, Sir **Rudolf** (*b* Vienna, 9 Jan 1902). Opera manager. The son of a Viennese industrialist, he worked in a bookshop before serving as an assistant to Carl Ebert at the Hessian State Theater, Darmstadt (1928–30), and as an assistant manager of the Charlottenburg Opera, Berlin (1930–33). In 1933 he emigrated to England, where he managed the Glyndebourne Opera during the war, as well as Harrod's department store in London. A British subject from 1946, he was a founder of the Edinburgh Festival and its manager in 1947–49. As the general manager of the Metropolitan Opera in New York City from 1950 to 1972 he undertook important revivals of Verdi and Mozart, for which he engaged stage directors from the legitimate theater (among them Margaret Webster, Alfred Lunt, and Tyrone Guthrie), and oversaw the company's move into its new theater at Lincoln Center in 1966. He was knighted by the British Crown in 1971. Brusque and intransigent, Bing sometimes clashed with singers, notably Maria Callas, but he maintained high production standards. In 1972 he unwillingly left the Metropolitan after a tenure second in length only to that of Giulio Gatti-Casazza. He became a consultant in the following year to Columbia

Artists Management. Bing wrote a memoir, *A Knight at the Opera* (1981).

Gerald Fitzgerald, ed.: *Annals of the Metropolitan Opera Guild: The Complete Chronicle of Performances and Artists: Chronology, 1883–1985* (New York: Metropolitan Opera Guild / Boston: G. K. Hall, 1989)

John W. Freeman

Binkerd, Robert S(tudebaker) (*b* Dayton, Ohio, 7 Nov 1882; *d* New York City, 28 Oct 1969). Reformer. Concerned about municipal corruption, he became the secretary of Citizens Union (1908–9), which owing to his efforts was transformed into a civic organization immune from political control. He was the secretary of the Fusion Committee of 1909 during its unsuccessful campaign to defeat Tammany Hall in the mayoral election, and as secretary of the City Club of New York (1909–13) he was the city's unofficial representative in Albany, New York. In 1911 he helped to defeat a proposal backed by Tammany Hall to revise the city charter. He wrote *Home Rule for Cities* (1912).

Bernard Hirschhorn

Biograph Company. Film studio formed early in 1896 as the American Mutoscope Company, with offices at 841 Broadway in Manhattan. It soon produced short comedies with somewhat risqué scenes on the roof of the building, which by early March 1897 was covered with an elaborate open-air stage that could be turned to catch the rays of the sun. After its name was changed to the American Mutoscope and Biograph Company in 1899, the firm opened a new, indoor studio at 11 East 14th Street in May 1903: this was the first motion picture studio in the world to rely exclusively on electric lights for illumination of the stage. Many films were directed there by Wallace McCutcheon (*A Search for Evidence*, 1903) and D. W. Griffith (*The Lonely Villa*, 1909). The company was renamed the Biograph Company in 1908, and in early 1913 it completed construction on a third and much larger studio at 175th Street and Prospect Avenue in the Bronx, which Griffith did not have a chance to use before he joined a rival organization. Biograph made films at the facility to the end of 1916, when it ceased production. The space became a rental studio in 1917 and was used by most of the major production companies during the silent period, including Metro Film Corporation, Fox Film Corporation, Warner Brothers, Selznick Pictures, and First National. It was leased by the U.S. Signal Corps during the First World War, closed in 1927, and in 1933 was converted to sound and rented by various independent producers. After being used by the Army Signal Corp during the Second World War the building fell into disrepair. It was revamped in the 1950s, when as Gold Medal Studios it was employed for such films as Elia Kazan's *A Face in the Crowd* (1957), Sidney Lumet's *The Fugitive Kind* (1959), Daniel Mann's *Butterfield 8* (1960), and Peter Yates's *John and Mary* (1969), as well as for television series such as "Car 54 Where Are You?" and "Naked City." By the mid 1970s it had been abandoned to vandals.

Charles Musser: *The Emergence of Cinema: The American Screen to 1907* (New York: Charles Scribner's Sons, 1990)
Marc Wanamaker: *Encyclopedia of Movie Studios* (forthcoming)

Charles Musser

biology. The first graduate program in biology in New York City was set up at Columbia University in the early 1890s by Henry Fairfield Osborn. In its early years the program emphasized evolutionary biology and became affiliated with the American Museum of Natural History, where Osborn laid the foundation for a research program in vertebrate paleontology. He and his students used the large collection of specimens at the museum to help answer a wide range of questions about morphology and evolution. Edmund Beecher Wilson helped to make the university a center of research in cellular biology and embryology, and made careful microscopical studies that he summed up in his classic text *The Cell in Development and Heredity* (1896). Important research in genetics was conducted at Columbia during the first two decades of the twentieth century by Wilson and Nettie M. Stevens, who in 1905 discovered the chromosomal pairings that determine sex. Thomas Hunt Morgan conducted important experiments with fruit flies, which provided additional evidence that genes on chromosomes influence the inheritance of particular traits and formed the basis for classical transmission genetics. Theodosius Dobzhansky and L. C. Dunn, who joined Columbia respectively in 1927 and 1928, made additional contributions to the field. Dobzhansky documented the role of genetic mutations in evolution, and his work, along with studies done by Ernst Mayr and George Gaylord Simpson of the American Museum of Natural History, helped lead the way to the evolutionary synthesis of the 1940s.

The Rockefeller Institute for Medical Research also made important advances in the field of biology. In 1910 Jacques Loeb, a biochemist at the institute who was well known for his work on artificial parthenogenesis, began a research project with his assistant John Howard Northrup on nucleoproteins. Another biologist at the institute, Alexis Carrel, improved techniques for cultivating tissues outside the body. In 1935 Wendell M. Stanley confirmed the crystalline structure of the tobacco mosaic virus, a discovery that won him the Nobel Prize in chemistry in 1946. Experiments by Oswald T. Avery, Colin MacLeod, and Maclyn McCarty in 1944 suggesting the role played by DNA (deoxyribonucleic acid) in transforming benign bacteria into virulent strains promoted the development of molecular biology, particularly molecular genetics.

George W. Corner: *History of the Rockefeller Institute, 1901–1953: Origins and Growth* (New York: Rockefeller Institute Press, 1964)
Garland E. Allen: *Thomas Hunt Morgan: The Man and His Science* (Princeton, N.J.: Princeton University Press, 1978)
Philip J. Pauly: *Controlling Life: Jacques Loeb and the Engineering Ideal in Biology* (New York: Oxford University Press, 1987)

Ronald Rainger

Birdland. Jazz club, opened on 15 December 1949 in a basement at 1678 Broadway, just north of 52nd Street. Named by its owners Morris and Irving Levy for the alto saxophonist Charlie Parker (known as "Bird"), who performed there, it seated four hundred and was the site of performances by other leading musicians such as Dizzy Gillespie, Bud Powell, and Count Basie. The impresario Symphony Sid broadcast some of his radio programs from the club. In 1965 the club closed because of increased rents; it reopened for one night in 1979. Birdland inspired George Shearing's song "Lullaby of Birdland" (1952), and the name was later appropriated by an unrelated jazz club at 2745 Broadway, near 106th Street.

Peter Eisenstadt, Marc Ferris

birds. Pollution from pesticides and the loss of habitat to development drove several species of birds to extinction in New York City. Others were threatened, especially harriers like the Osprey and the Peregrine Falcon, which absorbed large quantities of pesticide in the fish they ate and produced thin-shelled eggs that usually broke before reaching maturity. Their numbers and those of Grasshopper Sparrows, Piping Plovers, and Roseate Terns increased after endangered species laws were passed, pesticides banned, and nesting poles erected. To compensate for the loss of farmlands in the metropolitan area more than eighteen nesting boxes for Barn Owls were installed in the Jamaica Bay Wildlife Refuge, where the first recorded nest of a Peregrine Falcon was discovered in 1993. At Floyd Bennett Field in Brooklyn one Barn Owl box began producing four to six young a year in the early 1980s. Proximity to the Hudson–Raritan estuary makes New York City along the Atlantic Flyway a potentially ideal habitat for birds: 10 percent of the species identified in the continental United States have been observed in and around Jamaica Bay. Birds remain an important means of monitoring the city's environmental quality.

One of the best locations for observing land birds in New York City is Central Park, where fifteen species are common. Mourning Doves, Downy Woodpeckers, Blue Jays, American Crows, Black-capped Chickadees, Northern Mockingbirds, Cardinals, and House Finches are seen year round. American Robins, Common Yellowthroats, Red-winged Blackbirds, Common Grackles, American Goldfinches, and Rufous-sided Towhees are often seen during warmer months; Dark-eyed Juncos are seen in winter. Well over one hundred species may be observed during the spring migration in April and May. More than 320 species of birds have been observed breeding, migrating, or roosting in the Jamaica Bay Wildlife Refuge. Situated along the Atlantic Flyway, this major bird migratory area provides a year-round opportunity to see a diversity of species. Five species of water birds are seen in the bay, ponds, and marshes at the refuge: the Double-crested Cormorant, the Glossy Ibis, the Canada Goose, the Mallard, and the Herring Gull. During spring, summer, and autumn Egrets are easily identified by their startling white plumage, Glossy Ibises by their long, decurved bills. Each September and October the autumn migration of Marsh Hawks, Sharp-shinned Hawks, Kestrels, and Red-tailed Hawks is a spectacular event over Jamaica Bay and Breezy Point. More than fifteen hundred hawks were once counted in a single season at Fort Tilden, an abandoned Nike missile defense base that is now part of the Gateway National Recreation Area.

John Bull: *Birds of the New York Area* (New York: Harper and Row, 1964)

John Bull: *Birds of New York State* (New York: Doubleday / Natural History Press, 1974)

Macmillan Field Guide to the Birds of North America: Eastern Region (New York: Macmillan, 1985)

John Bull: *Birds of New York State, including the 1976 Supplement* (Ithaca, N.Y.: Cornell University Press, 1985)

John Bull, John T. Tanacredi

Bishop McDonnell Memorial High School. Catholic high school for girls, opened in 1926 at 260 Eastern Parkway in Brooklyn. At its height it had more than two thousand students drawn from the entire diocese of Brooklyn, which until 1957 included all of Long Island. In later years enrollment was limited to girls from Brooklyn and Queens. The school closed in 1973; its building was taken over by the St. Francis de Sales School for the Deaf.

Gilbert Tauber

Bitter, Karl (Theodore Francis) (*b* near Vienna, 6 Dec 1867; *d* New York City, 9 April 1915). Sculptor. After studying architectural sculpture in Vienna he emigrated to the United States in 1889 and settled in New York City, later establishing a home and studio in Weehawken, New Jersey. Through the patronage of the prominent architect Richard Morris Hunt he quickly gained recognition in the fields of public and architectural sculpture, and he executed several fine works of sculpture at the appellate court, the customs house, and the Metropolitan Museum of Art. A founding member of the National Sculpture Society in 1893, he was its president in 1906–7 and again in 1914. He was also the director of sculpture for the world's fairs of 1901 (Buffalo), 1904 (St. Louis), and 1915 (San Francisco). The collaborative planning of the fairs instilled in him a vision of urban improvement and provided the early inspiration of the "city beautiful" movement. At a time of increasing hostility toward Germans and Austrians before the First World War he executed a large monument of the German-American statesman and reformer Carl Schurz at Morningside Drive and 116th Street (1909–13). Appointed to the New York City Art Commission in 1912, he oversaw the development of Grand Army Plaza on 5th Avenue, to which he contributed the Pulitzer Fountain. Bitter died after being struck by an automobile while crossing the plaza.

James M. Dennis: *Karl Bitter, Architectural Sculptor, 1867–1915* (Madison: University of Wisconsin Press, 1967)

Susan Rather

B. Kreischer and Sons. Firm of firebrick makers. Formed in 1845 as Kreischer and Mumpeton by Balthazar Kreischer (*b* 13 March 1813; *d* 25 Aug 1886), an immigrant from Bavaria, it became one of the leading manufacturers in the metropolitan area of firebricks, gas retorts, and molded decorative clay building materials (briefly including terra cotta). It operated the New York Fire-Brick Manufactory at Delancey and Goerck streets in Manhattan from 1845 to 1876 and from 1854 to 1927 managed clay mines and an extensive factory complex in Staten Island called Kreischerville (now known as Charleston) that resemble a company village. Its administrative headquarters were at Goerck and Mangin streets in Manhattan. The company owned additional clay mines in New Jersey and Pennsylvania and during the 1860s and 1870s also had a factory in Philadelphia. During the 1890s the plant in Staten Island employed more than three hundred persons. The factory closed just before the Depression and was destroyed by fire in 1936. Several prominent architects based in New York City used the firm's products: terra cotta by Kreischer decorates Barnard College, St. Luke's Hospital, and other buildings. Remains of the enterprise at Charleston include the Charles Kreischer Mansion and a row of workers' housing (both designated landmarks by the city), and the Clay Pit Ponds State Park Preserve. Product samples and documents are preserved at the Staten Island Historical Society, the Staten Island Institute of Arts and Sciences, and the New-York Historical Society.

Asher and Adams' Pictorial Album of American Industry (New York: Asher and Adams, 1876; repr. New York: Routledge, 1976), 82

Moses King, ed.: *King's Handbook of New York: An Outline, History and Description of the American Metropolis* (Boston: Moses King, 1892), 880–81, 886–87

Mabel Abbott: "Kreischerville: A Forgotten Chapter in Staten Island History," *Proceedings of the Staten Island Institute of Arts and Sciences* 11, no. 2 (Jan 1949), 31–43

Shirley Zavin and Elsa Gilbertson: *Staten Island Walking Tours* (New York: Preservation League of Staten Island, 1986)

Charles L. Sachs: *Made on Staten Island: Agriculture, Industry, and Suburban Living in the City* (New York: Staten Island Historical Society, 1988)

Charles L. Sachs

Black, Starr and Frost. The oldest firm of jewelers in the United States. Formed in 1801 in Savannah, Georgia, as Marquand and Paulding, it was moved in 1810 to New York City by Isaac Marquand, who in 1813 bought out the jewelry shop of James H. Hyde at 166 Broadway. In 1819 he merged his business with that of Erastus Barton, whom he bought out in 1823; his son Frederick then took over the business and changed the name first to F. Marquand and in 1833 to Marquand and Company. Henry Ball and William Black entered the firm and opened a new shop at 181 Broadway. When the Marquands withdrew from the business in 1839 Erastus O. Thompkins became a partner and the firm was renamed Ball, Thompkins and Black, in new quarters at 247 Broadway; on the death of Thompkins in 1852 it became Ball, Black and Company. The firm offered household and gift items such as porcelain, silver, paintings, and bronze statuary, as well as gemstone jewelry and precious objects. It was one of few American retailers to display its wares in London at the Crystal Palace Exposition of 1851. Shops were opened at Broadway and Prince Street in 1860 and at several locations along 5th Avenue: at 28th Street in 1876, when Cortlandt Starr and Aaron V. Frost became partners and the name became Black, Starr and Frost; at 39th Street in 1898; and at 48th Street in 1912. In 1929 the firm merged with Gorham and was called Black, Starr, Frost–Gorham, becoming Black, Starr and Gorham in 1940. After a merger with Marcus and Company in 1962 the name reverted to Black, Starr and Frost. The firm was purchased in 1972 by Kay Jewelers and in 1990 by the firm of Sterling.

Through One Hundred Years: The Hundredth Anniversary of the Oldest Retail Jewelry House in New York, together with Some Facts as to its Different Departments (New York: Black, Starr and Frost, 1910)

At the Sign of the Golden Eagle, 1810–1912 (New York: Black, Starr and Frost, 1912)

Penny Proddow and Debra Healy: *American Jewelry: Glamour and Tradition* (New York: Rizzoli, 1987)

Janet Zapata

blackouts. Electric power blackouts occurred nearly every year in New York City after the Brush arc lighting system failed on 10 June 1881. The blizzard of 1888 toppled overhead power lines and shut off lights for three hours, during the first of many blackouts in the city caused by unusual weather. In 1936 an by Marcus Garvey, who argued that blacks in the New World should be repatriated to Africa and that Africa should be liberated from European colonial rule. The core of Garvey's support was the large West Indian population of Harlem, but the group recruited members from all over the city through parades and conventions in Madison Square Garden, and it soon became an unprecedentedly large black organization. The UNIA disintegrated in the mid 1920s after Garvey was convicted of mail fraud, sentenced to a term in federal prison in Atlanta, and later deported. Although other militant black organizations such as the Marxist nationalist African Blood Brotherhood had large followings, as did radicals like Cyril Briggs, Hubert Henry Harrison, and William Bridges, who were all active in New York City, they failed to capture the imagination of blacks in the city as Garvey had.

In the 1920s writers and artists traveled to Harlem from all over the United States to be part of the literary and artistic movement known as the Harlem Renaissance. Charles S. Johnson, editor of the magazine *Opportunity* (published by the National Urban League), held a meeting of leading black writers and white publishers at the Civic Club in March 1924 that helped to launch the careers of such talented black writers as Langston Hughes, Claude McKay, Zora Neale Hurston, Countee Cullen, Jean Toomer, and Rudolph Fisher. The painters Aaron Douglas, William H. Johnson, Palmer Hayden, and Malvin Gray Johnson and the sculptor Augusta Savage strove to invent a black American art by studying African art and emulating its styles and themes. Plays with black themes and actors enjoyed great success, notably Eugene O'Neill's *The Emperor Jones* (1920) and *All God's Chillun Got Wings* (1924), and Marc Connelly's *The Green Pastures* (1930).

During the Depression 50 percent of blacks in New York City were unemployed, double the unemployment rate of whites. In 1929 the Republican Charles W. Fillmore was elected the city's first black district leader, but many blacks soon shifted their support from the Republicans to the Democrats, who for the first time received a majority of the black vote in elections for the presidency (1932), mayoralty (1933), and governorship (1934). By the mid 1930s the first effective black political organization in Brooklyn had developed among the Democrats of Bedford–Stuyvesant. At the same time white merchants on 125th Street in Harlem refused to employ black sales clerks, and a boycott against them was organized in 1934 by Sufi Abdul Hamid. The Citizens League for Fair Play, a middle-class black organization led by John H. Johnson, became a powerful force in the boycott. The boycott ultimately failed when a court order prohibited the picketing of white merchants and the groups became riven by disagreements. A rumor that the police had killed an adolescent boy, Lino Rivera, for stealing a penknife sparked a riot in Harlem in 1935. In 1938 a second boycott of the white merchants on 125th Street, led by Adam Clayton Powell Jr. and the Greater New York Coordinating Committee, was more successful in ending employment discrimination. Additional boycotts were launched against the bus and telephone companies, which also refused to employ blacks. The Communist Party received much publicity by protesting police brutality against blacks, racial bias in the city's public schools, and inadequate services and discrimination at Harlem Hospital.

The outbreak of the Second World War and the American military buildup did not benefit blacks in the city to the same extent that it did whites: 40 percent of the city's black population in 1940 remained on relief or dependent on federal funds for temporary work relief. A survey of seventy-two defense plants in Brooklyn taken by the Urban League in 1941 revealed that they employed only 234 blacks in a total work force of 13,840, and almost half the plants excluded blacks entirely. In the same year A. Philip Randolph formed the March on Washington Committee in New York City to prevail on the federal government to end the political disfranchisement of blacks in the South, desegregate the army, and prohibit discriminatory employment practices by defense contractors. Fearful of a potential threat to national unity, President Franklin D. Roosevelt asked Eleanor Roosevelt and Mayor Fiorello H. La Guardia to persuade Randolph to call off the protest march. Randolph agreed, provided that the government ban discrimination in companies with defense contracts; in response Roosevelt on 25 June 1941 issued an executive order banning discrimination in defense industries. Even then blacks were relegated to less lucrative forms of work: they tended not to work in defense industries but rather to take the place of whites who did, as well as whites who had gone to war.

The Second World War saw the emergence of Powell as an important political figure in the city and the nation. After serving as the pastor of Abyssinian Baptist Church he won a seat on the City Council in 1941. Although La Guardia had supported his candidacy the two men were soon at odds over Powell's charges of racial discrimination and police brutality in New York City. In 1942 Powell protested the refusal of City College to reappoint a black leftist professor, Max Yergan, at a time when the school did not have any full-time tenured black professors. He also criticized La Guardia for allowing the U.S. Navy to use Hunter College and Walton High School as training facilities for the Women's Reserve, which practiced racial segregation, and for contracting with the Metropolitan Life Insurance Company to build Stuyvesant Town, a tax-exempt, quasi-public housing project on the Lower East Side that excluded blacks from its properties. The city eventually agreed to prohibit the discriminatory selection of tenants in all its future projects.

The shooting of a black military policeman by a white policeman in mysterious circumstances at a hotel in Harlem on 1 August 1943 led to a riot in which five persons were killed and 307 were injured. Plate-glass windows of stores along 125th Street were smashed and the total damage exceeded $5 million. The anger of the community was evident that autumn when the communist Benjamin Davis was elected to the City Council because of his strong sponsorship of civil rights. Davis replaced Powell, who had resigned from the council and won a seat in Congress as a Democrat in 1944. In 1953 Assemblyman Walter Gladwin became the first black elected official in the Bronx, and Hulan E. Jack, a seasoned Democratic politician, became the first black borough president of Manhattan. Brooklyn elected its first black city councilman, J. Daniel Diggs, in 1957.

The unemployment rate of blacks in New York City in the 1950s remained double that of whites. Of the students who entered academic high schools in Harlem in 1959, about 53 percent failed to graduate, as did 61 percent of those entering vocational schools. By the mid 1960s only about half the children in Harlem lived with their parents, compared with 83 percent in New York City as a whole. As the population of Harlem declined and the black population of the other boroughs increased, poverty and unemployment remained. In 1961 the Congress of Racial Equality (CORE) demanded that a milk plant operated by Sealtest–Sheffield Farms in Bedford–Stuyvesant increase its black labor force, which then consisted of seven out of 367 employees, and in 1963 it demanded that more blacks work on the construction of the Downstate Medical Center. Constance Baker Motley served as the borough president of Manhattan (1965–66), as did Percy Sutton. In 1964 J. Raymond Jones, known as the "Harlem Fox," became the first black leader of Tammany Hall and Kenneth Brown became the first black elected to the state assembly from Queens. In the same year Milton Galamison and the City-Wide Committee for Integrated Schools led two student boycotts of classes to demand integration of the city's schools and the removal of the president of the Board of Education, and Jesse Gray organized rent strikes in Harlem by black tenants to obtain affordable housing. The killing of a black youth by a white police lieutenant in the summer of 1964 led to a riot in Harlem that lasted three nights; one person was killed, 141 were seriously injured (including forty-eight policemen), and 519 were arrested. Amid this unrest militant black leaders like Malcolm X and organizations like the Nation of Islam gained increasing popularity in Harlem. After the riot Mayor Robert F. Wagner invited Martin Luther King Jr. to New York City to obtain his advice on racial matters, and charges of police brutality led to the formation of a civilian police review board. Mayor John V. Lindsay's efforts to promote better race relations in the city contributed to its escape from the massive rioting that besieged Los Angeles, Detroit, Newark (New Jersey), and other cities in the late 1960s.

In 1968 Shirley Chisholm of Brooklyn became the first black woman to be elected to the U.S. Congress by defeating James Farmer, a nationally known civil rights leader and former head of the Congress of Racial Equality. Despite his troubles with the Congress stemming from charges of conflict of interest, Powell was repeatedly reelected until he lost his seat to Charles B. Rangel in 1970. During the administration of President Lyndon B. Johnson the Bedford Stuyvesant Restoration Corporation, an anti-poverty agency in Brooklyn, obtained about $50 million from government and foundation sources, an impressive sum that nevertheless amounted to only $125 for each resident of the area over a seven-year period. With the deescalation of the war on poverty and the shift from manufacturing to a service economy that relied on a more highly educated and technically skilled labor force, employment prospects for many lower-income blacks diminished: in New York City between 1970 and 1984 industrial employment requiring only a minimum of education fell from 492,000 to 239,000. The city's black population increased from 458,000 in 1940 to 1,668,000 in 1970, while suburbanization reduced the white population from 6,977,000 to 6,048,000. Many blacks left Manhattan to live in less crowded areas, and consequently the number of blacks living in the outer boroughs increased sharply.

In November 1989 David N. Dinkins was elected the first black mayor of New York City after asking residents to vote their hopes, not their fears. He made strenuous efforts to manage the city, which he frequently referred to as a "gorgeous mosaic" of racial, ethnic, and religious groups, but he was unable to stem the tide of economic decay and ethnic factionalism abetted by years of official neglect. This lack of success led to his narrow defeat in 1993 by Rudolph W. Giuliani, although his record was consistent with that of other mayors of large American cities in the early 1990s.

According to the federal census the non-Hispanic black population of New York City in 1990 stood at 1,847,049 (including 417,506 foreign-born), accounting for 25.2 percent of the total population and representing an increase of 9 percent over the preceding decade.

James Weldon Johnson: *Black Manhattan* (New York: Alfred A. Knopf, 1930)

Seth M. Scheiner: *Negro Mecca: A History of the Negro in New York City, 1865–1920* (New York: New York University Press, 1965)

Gilbert Osofsky: *Harlem: The Making of a Ghetto, 1890–1930* (New York: Harper and Row, 1966)

Harold X. Connolly: *A Ghetto Grows in Brooklyn* (New York: New York University Press, 1977)

Jervis Anderson: *This Was Harlem: A Cultural Portrait, 1900–1950* (New York: Farrar, Straus and Giroux, 1981)

Sherrill D. Wilson (§1), Larry A. Greene (§2)

black theater. Black actors, playwrights, and producers have taken part in the rich theatrical history of New York City, and themes drawn from African–American life have been the subject of numerous productions. Black theater in the city probably began in 1821, when William A. Brown opened the African Theatre off lower Broadway. The company produced Shakespeare, musical comedies, pantomimes, and Brown's own play *The Drama of King Shotoway* (1823), the first by a black American. Although city authorities closed the African Theatre in 1823, from its ranks emerged the celebrated actor Ira Aldridge (1807–67), a native of the city who left the United States in 1825 and earned international recognition as a tragedian.

The most popular "black" performers of the antebellum period were not blacks at all but white minstrels in blackface. New York City was where blackface MINSTRELSY was born, with a performance in 1843 at the Bowery Amphitheatre by four white entertainers calling themselves the Virginia Minstrels, whose comic song-and-dance routines were intended to depict black life on southern plantations. Minstrel shows dominated the musical stage for decades and fixed Negro stereotypes that inhibited the acceptance of black actors on the legitimate stage. After the Civil War minstrel shows more often included African–American performers; some who excelled in the genre included Ernest Hogan, Sam Lucas, and James Bland, composer of "Carry Me Back to Ol' Virginny."

A break in the minstrel tradition occurred in 1898, when the vaudeville performers Bob Cole and Billy Johnson produced the first black musical comedy, *A Trip to Coontown*, in which Cole performed out of blackface. Cole then joined J. Rosamond Johnson to write and produce two other shows. Another pair of vaudevillians, Bert Williams and George Walker, joined with the writer Jesse Shipp and the composer Will Marion Cook to produce elaborate musicals. They achieved great success with *In Dahomey* (1903): the show was staged in London, where a royal command performance was given. On the dramatic stage openings for black actors came first with black companies in plays written by whites. In 1884 J. A. Arneaux organized the Astor Place Company of Colored Tragedians, which produced *Othello*, *Richard III*, and John Banim's *Damon and Pythias* (1821). From 1915 black companies appeared regularly at the Lafayette Theatre in Harlem (for illustration see LAFAYETTE THEATRE). Although still absent from Broadway black performers also worked downtown, in productions of Ridgely Torrence's *Three Plays for a Negro Theatre* (1917) and of Eugene O'Neill's *The Emperor Jones* (1920), in which Charles Gilpin played the leading role. Paul Robeson began his career on Broadway in 1925 in a revival of *The Emperor Jones*; he later appeared in *Stevedore* (1935), by Paul Peters and George Sklar. After a somewhat fallow period the 1920s saw several new black musicals, including *Shuffle Along* (1921), by Eubie Blake and Noble Sissle, which had a run of 504 performances. Other important musicals of the decade included *Runnin' Wild* (1926), by James P. Johnson and Cecil Mack after a book by Flourney Miller and Aubrey Lyles, and *Hot Chocolates* (1929), by Fats Waller and Andy Razaf. For several decades after 1930 blacks wrote relatively few Broadway musicals. After the call for a new Negro theater "about, by, for, and near" blacks by W. E. B. Du Bois, editor of the *Crisis*, repeated attempts were made to establish a viable African–American theater that would present plays in Harlem by blacks. The Krigwa Players (1926), the New Negro Art Theatre (1927), and the Harlem Experimental Theatre (1928) were organized, none lasting more than a few years. The late 1920s and 1930s saw the production of a number of plays on aspects of black life in America, many of them by white authors. Perhaps the trend can be dated to *Show Boat* (1927), by Jerome Kern and Oscar Hammerstein II, and its memorable songs on black themes such as "Ol' Man River"; Robeson appeared in a revival of the work in 1932. Marc Connelly's *The Green Pastures* (1930), an evocation of black conceptions of Heaven, led to a vogue for Broadway shows with white authors and all-black casts. Two memorable American operas of the 1930s were staged with black casts: *Four Saints in Three Acts* (1933), by Virgil Thomson and Gertrude Stein, and *Porgy and Bess* (1936), by George Gershwin. In 1935 Langston Hughes's melodrama *Mulatto*, dealing with racial tensions in a household in Georgia, opened at the Vanderbilt Theatre and won praise for the actress Rose McClendon. Hughes also wrote *Don't You Want to Be Free?* (1937), a music drama about working-class solidarity that played in his Harlem Suitcase Theatre (1937) and ran for 135 weekend performances. His collaboration with Zora Neale Hurston, *Mule-bone*, had its belated première in New York City in 1991.

As orphanages and other institutions for children became more crowded during the 1880s contagious eye diseases spread rapidly. A survey conducted by the city Board of Health and the New York Academy of Medicine in 1885 found that one quarter of the children in city institutions had some kind of eye disease. These findings helped to bring about a state law requiring more rigorous annual medical examinations of institutionalized children, as well as the isolation of those infected; the law helped to reduce the rate of blindness among children. Services for blind adults in New York City expanded toward the end of the nineteenth century, as the depression of 1893 and the arrival of thousands of immigrants made it increasingly difficult for the blind to obtain regular employment. One new institution was the Industrial Home for the Blind, which began with a small workshop in Brooklyn in 1893 and soon added a home for blind mechanics. St. Joseph's Asylum for Blind Girls in Pleasant Plains opened in 1897. In response to a survey showing that nearly one fifth of the city's schoolchildren had eye diseases, the health department in 1902 opened an eye hospital and clinic at Gouverneur Hospital; New York City thus became the first city in the country to set up a hospital unit in support of its school medical inspections. At the same time the fear of eye disease helped keep many prospective immigrants out of the city. The third doctor encountered by every new arrival during the medical inspection at Ellis Island was the dreaded "eye man," who rapidly checked inside each person's eyelids for signs of conjunctivitis or of trachoma, which accounted for half of all medical detentions (for illustration see Ellis Island); many of those detained were eventually sent back to Europe.

The city steadily improved its vision services for those who already lived there. Many private agencies for blind children were formed in the early years of the century, including the Sunshine Home, Nursery, Hospital, and Kindergarten for Blind Babies (1904) in Dyker Heights, and the Catholic Institute for the Blind, a child-care facility on Eastchester Road in the Bronx. Organizations that served adults as well as children also began operations during these years, notably the libraries for the blind of the New York Public Library (1905), the New York Association for the Blind (1905; now known as the Lighthouse), and the New York Guild for the Jewish Blind (1914; now the Jewish Guild for the Blind). Other new agencies included the American Jewish Association for the Blind (a residence for Orthodox Jews) and the Catholic Center for the Blind (a boarding home for blind working girls in Manhattan). Initially children with trachoma and other communicable eye diseases were denied entrance to the school system, but in 1912 the Board of Education opened its first "vision" school for these children. New York State also began to provide services and advocacy for blind city residents through the New York State Commission for the Blind (1913). In 1921 the American Foundation for the Blind was formed in the city to represent the interests of the blind nationally. The organization developed a library that gained worldwide recognition, the leading professional journal in the field, extensive facilities for training and research, and a talking-book program; for forty-seven years Helen Keller was a member of its board.

During the Depression the federal government came to play a larger role in services for the blind. Some employment for the blind was provided by work relief projects, and the Social Security Act in 1935 brought the federal government into partnership with the states in offering assistance. In 1954 workers disabled by blindness (and their dependents) were brought under the social security pension system, and in 1974 the establishment of Supplemental Security Income gave the federal government full responsibility for assisting the needy blind. Legislation for the physically handicapped also brought growing federal support to many public and private programs for the blind in the city. In later decades a number of these programs also extended services to the multiply handicapped, particularly those with an orthopedic, psychiatric, or developmental disability in addition to blindness. In 1985 there were an estimated 112,000 persons in New York with severe visual impairment; this figure included 23,000 who were legally blind, of whom two thirds were sixty-five or older.

David M. Schneider: *The History of Public Welfare in New York State, 1867–1940* (Chicago: University of Chicago Press, 1938–41)

Paul A. Zahl: *Blindness: Modern Approaches to the Unseen Environment* (Princeton, N.J.: Princeton University Press, 1950)

Gabriel Farrell: *The Story of Blindness* (Cambridge: Harvard University Press, 1956)

John Duffy: *A History of Public Health in New York City* (New York: Russell Sage Foundation, 1968, 1974)

Berthold Lowenfeld: *The Changing Status of the Blind: From Separation to Integration* (Springfield, Ill.: Charles C. Thomas, 1975)

Aliki Coudroglou and Dennis L. Poole: *Disability, Work, and Social Policy* (New York: Springer, 1984)

Sandra Opdycke

Bliss, Lillie P(lummer) (*b* Boston, 11 April 1864; *d* New York City, 12 March 1931). Music and arts patron. She was one of the three founders of the Museum of Modern Art and as a vice-president of the museum helped to establish its international reputation. In 1934 she gave to the museum 122 works by European and American artists, including Arthur B. Davies, Walt Kuhn, Renoir, Degas, Gauguin, Seurat, Toulouse-Lautrec, Matisse, Cézanne, Modigliani, and Picasso. Bliss also founded the Kneisel Quartet.

Linda Elsroad

Blissville. Neighborhood in northwestern Queens, lying within Long Island City just north of Newtown Creek between Dutch Kills Creek and Greenpoint Avenue. It was named after Neziah Bliss, who with Eliphalet Nott in 1837 bought the Hunter farm, which included all of Hunter's Point. Monument works, hotels, and saloons opened after Calvary Cemetery was laid out in 1848 on the eastern edge. Borden Avenue was extended through Blissville in 1870 and a horse car line began operations in 1874. Distilleries and oil refineries were built along Newtown Creek; many who worked in industry and in the cemetery lived in plain frame houses along Bradley, Starr, and Review avenues. In the mid 1990s the neighborhood remained heavily industrial.

Vincent Seyfried

blizzard of 1888. A major snowstorm that began just after midnight on Monday 12 March 1888 and lasted until just before midnight on Tuesday 13 March. It was caused by the collision of a cold-weather front from Canada and an unusually warm front from the South by way of New Jersey. When the fronts collided over New York City the dry and intensely cold air chilled the moisture of the warm front and caused a blinding snowfall, and by 7:00 a.m. on Monday all the roads and highways of the city were blocked. The snowfall was made worse by powerful northern gales of as much as sixty miles (ninety-six kilometers) an hour, which in some places blew the streets clear and in others piled up drifts to the second story of buildings. Hopes of clearing the streets quickly were ruined when the temperature sank to 5°F (−15°C). The blizzard was the worst in New York City since 1857: the total accumulation of snow was twenty-one inches (fifty-three centimeters), property damage was estimated at $20 to $25 million, and the city did not fully recover for ten to fourteen days. One consequence of the blizzard was a directive by Mayor Hugh J. Grant in January 1889 that all overhead wires should be placed underground.

Mary Cable: *The Blizzard of '88* (New York: Atheneum, 1988)

Vincent Seyfried

Block, Adriaen (*fl* 1610–24). Navigator. He explored the waterways around what is now New York City on behalf of Dutch merchants seeking to establish a fur trade. In 1613 his ship was destroyed by fire off Manhattan, forcing him and his crew to camp on the island for the winter. The rude huts that they built made up the first European settlement on Manhattan. With the help of Indians he

Woodbine Street between Broadway and Bushwick Avenue in Bushwick two days after the blizzard of 1888

and the crew built a new ship, the *Restless*, that was the first Dutch sailing vessel made of North American timber. In 1614 Block navigated the straits off Wards Island, naming the passage Hellegat (Hell Gate). He also named Long Island and Block Island.

William Martin Williamson: *Adriaen Block: Navigator, Fur Trader, Explorer, New York's First Shipbuilder, 1611–1614* (New York: Marine Museum of the City of New York / Museum of the City of New York, 1959)

Michael G. Kammen: *Colonial New York: A History* (New York: Charles Scribner's Sons, 1975)

Henri A. van der Zee and Barbara van der Zee: *A Sweet and Alien Land: The Story of Dutch New York* (New York: Viking, 1978)

Matthew Kachur

bloodsports. In colonial New York City bloodsports included such traditional English recreations as cockfighting, dogfighting, bear and bull baiting, and ratting (contests pitting men or dogs against rats), as well as gander pulling, in which a greased gander was hung by the neck between horizontal sticks and men rode by and tried to pull the gander from its head. Bloodsports were popular among all classes before the nineteenth century, but with increased social stratification they became restricted largely to working-class culture in antebellum New York City, where young and usually unmarried men spent their leisure time enjoying the rough camaraderie of saloons, pool halls, volunteer fire houses, and gambling parlors. The height of popularity for bloodsports was reached during the 1860s and 1870s, when contests took place in saloons like Kit Burns's Sportsman's Hall (273 Water Street) and Harry Hill's (22–34 East Houston Street). Although bloodsports were illegal and frequently resulted in prosecutions they remained popular to the end of the century. Cockfighting enjoyed widespread support, especially among immigrants from the Mediterranean and the Caribbean. Breeders in the rural South supplied many of the birds used in the city. The rise of such spectator sports as baseball and football after the turn of the century caused the popularity of bloodsports to decline, and cockfighting was made a felony under the state agricultural and markets law. Some Latin American immigrants continued to engage in the sport in the late twentieth century: in 1988 seventy-seven spectators at a cockfighting festival in Bushwick were arrested, and an illegal Cuban social club in Morrisania where cockfights were staged was raided in 1989.

Elliott J. Gorn: *The Manly Art: Bare-knuckle Prize Fighting in America* (Ithaca, N.Y.: Cornell University Press, 1986)

Elliott J. Gorn

Bloomfield. Neighborhood in northwestern Staten Island; it lies southwest of Old Place and is bisected by the West Shore Expressway. Known during the seventeenth century as Daniell's Neck, it was later called Merrell Town (after a local farmer) and Watchogue. Merrill Avenue, which ran straight for a mile (1.6 kilometers), was once called "the long, long lane that has no turning." The western section was sometimes called "Beulah Land." For many years the area was sandy and rural. In 1973 a tank of liquefied natural gas owned by the firm of Texas Eastern exploded as it was being repaired, killing forty workers. Many houses were built during a flurry of development in the 1970s and 1980s. To the north lies Gulfport, the shipping complex of the Gulf Oil Corporation. The neighborhood is largely residential.

Martha S. Bendix

Bloomingdale. Name used until the mid nineteenth century for the UPPER WEST SIDE of Manhattan; it is a corruption of the Dutch name Bloemendael, or Bloomendal (vale of flowers). The area was named for a town near Haarlem in the Netherlands and was largely rural, with a few farmhouses and villages. The Bloomingdale Road, opened in 1703, ran between what are now 23rd and 147th streets and followed roughly the same route of the present Broadway. The name Bloomingdale became obsolete as farms and country estates gave way to urban development, but it is still used by the Bloomingdale House of Music and a local branch of the New York Public Library.

Michele Herman

Bloomingdale Insane Asylum. The first mental hospital in New York State, opened in 1821 in Morningside Heights at the behest of Thomas Eddy as a branch of New York Hospital (1791). It combined traditional medical interventions with a form of reeducation known as "moral treatment." During its first two decades the asylum received a subsidy from the state and cared for a heterogeneous population that included members of the lower classes. The number of poor patients declined after the opening of a municipal institution in 1839 and a state hospital in 1843, and the subsequent elimination of state support. The asylum grew more slowly than public mental hospitals: between 1830 and 1875 the average number of patients increased only from 136 to 182. The resident physicians who directed the institution included James Macdonald (1825–37), Pliny Earle (1844–49), Charles F. Nichols (1849–52, 1877–89), and D. Tilden Brown (1852–77). By the 1880s real-estate promoters seeking to develop the Upper West Side put increasing pressure on the governors of New York Hospital to move the asylum, and in 1891 the governors approved plans to move it to a site in White Plains, New York, acquired in 1868. The move was completed by the end of 1894 and the site of the asylum became part of the campus of Columbia University.

William Logie Russell: *The New York Hospital: A History of the Psychiatric Service, 1771–1936* (New York: Columbia University Press, 1945)

Gerald N. Grob

Bloomingdale Asylum, ca *1890*

Nellie Bly. Halftone printed in a supplement of the New York World, *2 February 1890*

Bloomingdale Road. Early road in Manhattan, the precursor of Broadway. It opened in 1703 and ran from what is now 23rd Street to the northern end of Bloomingdale Village, near what is now 114th Street. In 1795 the road was extended north to 147th Street and linked to the old Kingsbridge Road. In 1869 the Western Boulevard was built over it north of 59th Street; this road later became known simply as the Boulevard, and in 1899 the name Broadway was adopted for the entire route north and south of 59th Street.

WPAG

Moses King, ed.: *King's Handbook of New York City: An Outline, History and Description of the American Metropolis* (Boston: Moses King, 1892)

Andrew Sparberg

Bloomingdale's. Firm of retailers. It began as a dry-goods store opened on 17 April 1872 by Lyman Bloomingdale and his brother Joseph Bloomingdale and known as the "great East Side bazaar." Initially it occupied a building at 938 3rd Avenue near 56th Street (well north of the fashionable shopping district) with a large beehive decoration on the roof; sales for the first day of business amounted to $3.68. The store attracted customers from miles away after the 3rd Avenue elevated line was built in 1879, leading the store eventually to adopt the slogan "all cars transfer to Bloomingdale's." It soon became highly successful and moved on 5 October 1886 to larger quarters at 3rd Avenue and 49th Street. By 1927 it occupied the entire block bounded by 60th Street, 3rd Avenue, 59th Street, and Lexington Avenue, where a building was completed in 1931 at a cost of $3 million. The store catered to the middle class, offering "the best possible value for the least possible price." When in 1929 it became part of Federated Department Stores, the largest chain of department stores in the country, it had annual sales of $25 million. In the late 1940s the store improved the quality of its merchandise, increased prices, and adopted new advertising strategies to appeal to chic customers worldwide. After the 3rd Avenue line was razed in 1954 the surrounding neighborhood was revitalized. As part of a reorganization the firm opened a series of boutiques within its stores during the 1970s and 1980s. Its survival became uncertain when Federated was taken over in 1988 by the Canadian developer Robert Campeau; after his corporation experienced financial troubles the chain of seventeen Bloomingdale's stores was put up for sale in September 1989, but it was not sold. Unlike many of its competitors Bloomingdale's has remained popular and held its own against discount chains, specialty shops, and mail-order concerns.

Robert Hendrickson: *The Grand Emporiums: The Illustrated History of America's Great Department Stores* (New York: Stein and Day, 1979), 104–10
Maxine Brady: *Bloomingdale's* (New York: Harcourt Brace Jovanovich, 1980)
Marvin Traub and Tom Teicholz: *Like No Other Store . . . : The Bloomingdale's Legend and the Revolution in American Marketing* (New York: Times Books / Random House, 1993)

Allen J. Share

Bloomingview. Former name of Huguenot.

Blue Cross Blue Shield. See Empire Blue Cross and Blue Shield.

Bly, Nellie [Seaman [née Cochrane], Elizabeth] (*b* Cochrane's Mills, near Ford City, Penn., 5 May 1867; *d* New York City, 27 Jan 1922). Journalist. She began her career at the *Dispatch* in Pittsburgh. As a "stunt" journalist for the *New York World* in New York City in the late 1880s she became well known for making an undersea descent in a diving bell and an ascent in a hot-air balloon, for exposing the horrors of an asylum by feigning insanity, and for circling the globe in seventy-two days. After marrying the industrialist Robert Seaman in 1895 she interrupted her career. On his death in 1915 Bly joined the *New York Journal*, where she worked for the rest of her life. She wrote *Nellie Bly's Book: Around the World in Seventy-two Days* (1890).

Kathy Lynn Emerson: *Making Headlines: A Biography of Nellie Bly* (New York: Dillan, 1989)

Julian S. Rammelkamp

Blytheborne. Former neighborhood in Brooklyn, bounded by Couvenhouven Lane (now defunct), New Utrecht Avenue, and the railroad tracks along 61st Street. There were old Dutch houses in the area when the developer Electus B. Litchfield built a number of cottages in 1887. The population was mostly Protestant, and several schools and churches were built; many residents left about 1910, when there was an influx of Russian Jews. Elevated trains spanned New Utrecht Avenue, and apartment buildings replaced estates. Eventually the area became part of the adjacent neighborhood of Borough Park. By the mid 1920s the name was essentially obsolete, though it continues to be used by the main post office in Borough Park.

Norman Litchfield: "Blythebourne: A Community That Was Swallowed Up," *Journal of Long Island History* 4 (1964), summer, 28–39

James Bradley

BMT. See BROOKLYN–MANHATTAN TRANSIT CORPORATION.

B'nai B'rith International. Secular Jewish fraternal order formed in 1843 by a group of German-speaking immigrants who met at Sinsheimer's saloon on Essex Street in Manhattan. Initially a mutual aid society, the order devoted itself to philanthropy as its members achieved a measure of financial security. The order sponsored orphanages, hospitals, and old-age homes during its early years and by 1882 formed chapters in thirty countries. The influx of eastern European Jews to the United States during the late nineteenth century prompted the organization to establish employment bureaus; one of these, the Industrial Removal Office, sought to secure employment for recent immigrants outside New York City. To promote rapid acculturation B'nai B'rith also sponsored "Americanization" programs. A women's auxiliary became the independent B'nai B'rith Women's Organization in the early twentieth century, and the ANTI-DEFAMATION LEAGUE was formed as an affiliate in 1913 to combat negative portrayals of Jews in books, periodicals, and advertising. The 1920s saw the emergence of youth groups and of Hillel, a service agency for Jewish college students. During the Second World War B'nai B'rith helped Jews to obtain visas and provided religious and recreational programs for a government refugee encampment in Oswego, New York. Like many other American Jewish agencies it did not fight immigration quotas during the Holocaust. The organization moved its headquarters to Washington in 1957.

Bernard Postal, ed.: *This Is B'nai B'rith: A Manual of Facts* (Washington: B'nai B'rith, 1941)
Deborah Dash Moore: *B'nai B'rith and the Challenge of Ethnic Leadership* (Albany: State University of New York Press, 1981)

Jean Ulitz Mensch

B'nai Jeshurun. Conservative synagogue formed in 1825 by a faction that seceded from Shearith Israel after a dispute regarding the distribution of communal honors; it was the second synagogue in New York City. Initially it occupied a former church on Elm Street and had a largely English congregation. During the 1870s it sought to replace segregated seating with family pews, a plan that met with opposition and led to a heated civil trial. The congregation moved northward and during the 1920s built a lavish temple in a Moorish style on West 88th Street. B'nai Jeshurun is the city's oldest Ashkenazic congregation and the oldest Conservative synagogue in continuous operation.

Jenna Weissman Joselit

Board of Education. The chief governing body of the public school system in New York City. It was formed in 1842 to resolve religious and political controversies over the role of the Public School Society, which had managed the city's schools until then. At the time it was recognized that the schools in the city could not be effectively governed like those in most school districts in New York State, where the popular election of school boards and the financing and management of schools all occurred at the district level: in New York City a single board chosen at large would have been unrepresentative, and dividing the city into districts would have been inequitable. The system of governance that was chosen as a compromise provided for the election of school commissioners, trustees, and inspectors in each ward and for the representation of each ward committee on a central board of education. After 1871 these ward trustees were appointed, but they continued to provide an important element of local influence to the system. Having the responsibility to appoint teachers and contract for school repairs, trustees helped to bridge the gap between city leadership and neighborhood interests.

Ward trustees continued to function until 1896, when reformers effectively pointed out the failure of the localized system to satisfy the educational needs generated by immigration and economic development. A movement to entrust the management of the schools to educational experts resulted in the elimination of ward trustees in Manhattan and the Bronx; a somewhat parallel "local committee" system in Brooklyn was replaced in 1901. The reformers' model was fully implemented in 1902, with the city's schools centralized under a single board, and management of the schools delegated to the superintendent of schools and his associate superintendents.

The centralized board retained primary authority over the school system until the 1960s, when it was challenged by advocates of more effective education for black and Spanish-speaking children and other children in poor neighborhoods. Experiments with various forms of shared power included "community control" in three demonstration districts and the decentralization of authority under the community school board system adopted in 1970. Tension over the selection, operation, and relative powers of the central board, the community boards, and other officials continued during the 1970s and 1980s. In the mid 1990s the Board of Education consisted of seven members who served four-year terms, two appointed by the mayor and one appointed by each of the five borough presidents.

David Ment

Board of Elections. The creation of the Board of Elections of New York City in 1901

Changes in the Board of Education

1842	First Board of Education for New York City: 34 commissioners popularly elected, 2 from each of 17 wards (later increased to 2 from each of 22 wards). Board of 5 trustees popularly elected in each ward to appoint teachers and manage most affairs of the schools; 2 inspectors elected in each ward to inspect schools and certify teachers' qualifications.
1853	Board of Education acquires schools of the Public School Society. Board has 59 members: 44 commissioners popularly elected (2 from each of 22 wards) and 15 members transferred from the former board of the Public School Society for a transition period until 1855.
1855	Board has 44 members: 2 commissioners from each ward. Ward trustees and inspectors as in 1842.
1864	Board has 21 members: 3 commissioners elected from each of 7 school districts. Districts contain from 2 to 7 wards to produce roughly equal number of pupils in each district. Board of 5 trustees elected in each ward. Trustees retain major role in appointing teachers and managing schools. Each school district has 3 inspectors appointed by the mayor with responsibilities for inspecting schools and certifying teachers' qualifications.
1869	Board has 12 members, appointed by the mayor to serve to the end of 1871. Ward trustees and inspectors continue, locally elected.
1871	Board of Education replaced by a municipal Department of Public Instruction under direct authority of the mayor, who appoints its 12 members. Ward trustees and inspectors also appointed by the mayor.
1873	Board of Education reestablished with 21 members appointed by the mayor, 3 from each of 7 school districts; 5 ward trustees in each ward, appointed by the Board of Education; 3 inspectors in each school district, appointed by the mayor.
1896	Ward trustees abolished. Most direct powers of appointment and management of schools transferred to a board of superintendents composed of professional educational managers. Board of Education has 21 members appointed by the mayor; 5 inspectors in each of 15 inspection districts also appointed by the mayor.
1898	Consolidation of greater New York and confederation of school boards.

(continued)

Board of Education (*Continued*)

Borough school boards retain powers of appointment and school management. New York City Board of Education (21 members) is retained and becomes School Board for the Boroughs of Manhattan and the Bronx, future appointments to be made by the mayor. Brooklyn Board of Education (45 members) is retained and becomes School Board for the Borough of Brooklyn, future appointments to be made by the mayor. School Board of the Borough of Queens (9 members) and School Board of the Borough of Richmond (9 members) also appointed by the mayor. Board of Education of the City of New York ("Central Board") comprises 19 representatives chosen by the borough boards (11 from Manhattan and the Bronx, 6 from Brooklyn, 1 each from Queens and Richmond).

1901 Full powers transferred to citywide Board of Education and superintendent of schools. Borough boards abolished. Board has 46 members appointed by the mayor (22 from Manhattan, 14 from Brooklyn, 4 from the Bronx, 4 from Queens, 2 from Richmond); executive committee has 15 members; 46 local school boards that are largely advisory each have 7 members (5 appointed by the borough president, 1 each by the Board of Education and the district superintendent).

1917 Smaller Board of Education reflects trend toward streamlining urban school systems. Board has 7 members appointed by the mayor (2 from Manhattan and Brooklyn, 1 from each of the other boroughs).

1948 Board enlarged to reflect shifts in population: 9 members appointed by the mayor (2 each from Manhattan, the Bronx, Brooklyn, and Queens, 1 from Richmond).

1961 Former board removed during scandal; 9 members now appointed by the mayor from names submitted by a screening panel.

1968 Decentralization: board acquires authority to delegate powers to local boards and expands to 13 members appointed by the mayor; 25 local school boards appointed by the Board of Education have 9 members each.

1969 Further decentralization: community school boards acquire powers of appointment and management in elementary and junior high schools. Interim Board of Education has 5 members, 1 appointed by each borough

(continued)

Board of Education (*Continued*)

president; 32 school districts each have 1 community school board with 9 members, to be popularly elected in special school elections from 1970.

1973 Expansion of central board to 7 members (2 appointed by the mayor, 1 by each of the borough presidents).

City of Brooklyn

1835 Separate school districts with citywide control: 3 trustees in each school district appointed by the Brooklyn Common Council, 3 citywide inspectors and 3 citywide commissioners also appointed by the Common Council.

1843 First Brooklyn Board of Education: 2 members from each school district (initially numbering 14), appointed by the Common Council.

1850 Central Board of Education with substantial powers of appointment and school management delegated to local committees. Board has 33 members, at least 1 from each school district, appointed by the Common Council. Committees of the board formed for each school with extensive powers of oversight.

1854 Expansion reflects incorporation of Williamsburgh and Bushwick. Board has 45 members, 13 from the new Eastern District, appointed by the Common Council.

1862 Mayor given power to appoint members, subject to confirmation by the Common Council.

1882 Mayor's appointments no longer subject to approval by Common Council.

1898 Consolidation of greater New York. Brooklyn Board of Education becomes School Board of the Borough of Brooklyn.

was a major political reform intended to eliminate corruption of the city's elections. It replaced the Bureau of Elections, which worked under the police department, but had more sweeping powers, including the preparation of ballots for primary, special, and general elections, the enforcement of election laws, and the counting of votes. In the mayoral election of 1925 the board introduced mechanical voting machines to replace the paper ballots previously used. Originally the board consisted of four commissioners of elections, two Democrats and two Republicans from Brooklyn and Manhattan selected by the party leaders and confirmed by the City Council. By the early 1970s this arrangement was under attack from reformers, who believed that it was unrepresentative and encouraged

Superintendents of the New York City Board of Education

William H. Maxwell 1898–1918
William L. Ettinger 1918–24
William J. O'Shea 1924–34
Harold G. Campbell 1934–42
John E. Wade 1942–47
William Jansen 1947–58
John J. Theobald 1958–62
Bernard E. Donovan 1962–63, 1965–69
Calvin E. Gross 1963–65
Nathan Brown 1969–70
Irving Anker 1970, 1973–78
Harvey B. Scribner 1970–73
Frank J. Macchiarola 1978–83
Richard F. Halverson 1983
Anthony J. Alvarado 1983–84
Nathan Quinones 1984–87
Charles I. Schonhaut 1988
Richard R. Green 1988–89
Bernard Mecklowitz 1989
Joseph A. Fernandez 1990–93
Ramon C. Cortines 1993–

political cronyism. These criticisms intensified after a court in 1972 reversed the victory in a primary election of Representative John J. Rooney over Allard K. Lowenstein because of vote fraud. In the following year the board was reconfigured to consist of one Democrat and one Republican from each borough, with terms fixed at four years. At the time the president of the Board of Elections was David N. Dinkins, the future mayor, who resigned in 1973 because of the board's failure to enact voter registration reforms. Throughout the 1980s the board struggled with modernizing its voting and registration systems.

James Bradley

Board of Estimate. A formerly existing governing body for New York City, formed in 1901 with the authority to set the city's budget and exercise "residual powers." It rivaled the mayoralty in power by the time of the administration of Mayor William J. Gaynor (1910–13). The board comprised the mayor, the president of the City Council, the comptroller, and the presidents of the five boroughs; it was dominated by the comptroller and often the borough presidents, and tended to reflect the desires of the local Democratic organizations. Each citywide official had four votes and each borough president two, and for many years voting was conducted privately with the understanding that there would be public unanimity on resolutions. The board deliberated on information and proposals prepared by subordinate agencies such as the Bureau of Engineering and the Bureau of Franchises, which advised on which companies should receive permits for building and operating railways, buses, and utility lines. The Board of Estimate was abolished in 1990 after the U.S. Supreme Court ruled unconstitutional its system of giving equal representation to boroughs as disparate in size and racial composition as Staten Island (small and predominantly white) and Brooklyn (large and heavily nonwhite).

Wallace S. Sayre and Herbert Kaufman: *Governing New York City: Politics in the Metropolis* (New York: Russell Sage Foundation, 1960)

Martin Shefter

Board of Estimate v. Morris. Case decided in 1989 (489 U.S. 688) by the U.S. Supreme Court, which invalidated the voting structure of the Board of Estimate. The board at the time consisted of the three citywide elected officials (the mayor, the president of the City Council, and the comptroller), who each cast two votes, and the five borough presidents, who each cast one vote. Because of the wide disparity of population among the five boroughs, the Supreme Court unanimously held that giving equal voting power to each borough violated the constitutional requirement of "one person, one vote." The decision led to a revision of the city charter that abolished the Board of Estimate and redistributed its powers.

Richard Briffault

Board of Examiners. An agency responsible for creating and administering licensing examinations for employees of the Board of Education. Formed in 1897 by the charter that took effect on consolidation, it initially comprised four examiners appointed by the Board of Education for four-year terms. Its formation was one of several steps taken by the public schools to phase in the "merit," or civil service, system. Although the board's licensing system largely eliminated patronage, its examinations were often criticized for favoring members of ethnic groups already working in the schools. In 1969 much of the board's power was undermined by a decentralization law permitting the 45 percent of schools scoring lowest in reading to appoint teachers on the basis of the National Teachers Examination. The board was further weakened in 1971 when a federal district court ruled that the examination for the position of principal was unconstitutional because it lacked proven validity and produced eligibility lists containing disproportionately few black candidates; the ruling authorized community school boards to appoint acting principals without regard to the eligibility lists. The Board of Examiners remained a target of reformers until it was eliminated in 1990 by legislation proposed by Chancellor Joseph A. Fernandez.

David Ment

Board of Standards and Appeals. Municipal agency formed in 1916 in conjunction with the zoning regulations of the same year. It is empowered to modify zoning and construction laws for builders and developers. The board is composed of five commissioners, appointed by the mayor to six-year terms. One must be a registered architect, one a professional planner, and one a professional engineer, and each of these three must have at least ten years of experience. No more than two members of the board may be residents of any one borough. Because of its broad powers to exempt developers from the city's zoning laws, the board has frequently been an object of controversy. Mayor James J. Walker was charged with receiving payoffs in return for zoning variances. During the administration of Mayor Edward I. Koch the board came under repeated criticism, sometimes from the mayor himself, for permitting the conversion of lofts in manufacturing areas to residential use, and for contributing to overdevelopment and a glut of office space by being too eager to award variances to developers.

James Bradley

Board of Trade. An administrative body with jurisdiction over the North American colonies during English rule. It was formed in 1696 by the Crown after the Lords of Trade and Plantations had proven themselves unable to administer the colonies adequately, and was intended to forestall an effort by Parliament to form a committee not under the Crown's jurisdiction. The members of the board were politicians familiar with the colonies who had broad powers of oversight: they monitored the ever-expanding system of colonial trade established by the Navigation Acts, gave advice to the Crown concerning the appointment of colonial governors, examined colonial laws and recommended which ones should be vetoed, wrote instructions for new governors, and proposed legislation on colonial matters to Parliament. Despite its broad authority the board rarely provided vigorous leadership in colonial affairs: the secretary of state for the Southern Department had sufficient latitude in administering the colonies that he could ignore the board altogether, and the more powerful politicians on the board had other means of influencing government policy. As a result colonists circumvented the board and instead availed themselves of personal contacts. By the time of the American Revolution the Board of Trade had very little influence in colonial affairs.

Charles McLean Andrews: *British Committees, Commissions and Councils of Trade and Plantations, 1622–1675* (Baltimore: Johns Hopkins University Press, 1908)

George Louis Beer: *The Old Colonial System, 1660–1754* (New York: Macmillan, 1913)

I. K. Steele: *Politics of Colonial Policy: The Board of Trade in Colonial Administration, 1696–1720* (Oxford: Oxford University Press, 1968)

Peter D. G. Thomas: *The Townshend Duties Crisis: The Second Phase of the American Revolution, 1767–1773* (Oxford: Oxford University Press, 1987)

Robert Ritchie

Boas, Franz (*b* Minden [now in Germany], 9 July 1858; *d* New York City, 21 Dec 1942). Anthropologist. After obtaining a doctorate in physics from the University of Kiel in 1881 he turned first to geography, then to anthropology, undertaking fieldwork among the Baffinland Eskimos from 1883 to 1884. He spent three months with the Indians of the Northwest Coast before settling in New York City in January 1887, where he became the geography editor for the magazine *Science* (1887–88) and married his Austrian–American fiancée Marie Krackowizer. In 1896 he was appointed assistant curator of ethnology at the American Museum of Natural History; in the same year he became a lecturer in anthropology at Columbia University, and from 1897 to 1902 he led Morris K. Jesup's expedition to the northern Pacific coast. A full professor at Columbia from 1899, he resigned his position at the museum in June 1905 to devote himself to teaching full time. After his retirement in 1936 he continued to teach and often spoke out against racism. Boas is credited with making New York City the center of American anthropology during the first half of the twentieth century. His research challenged the existing emphasis in anthropological theory on biological heredity, replacing it with a culturally based environmentalism that had a profound influence on the field.

George W. Stocking Jr.: *The Shaping of American Anthropology, 1883–1911: A Franz Boas Reader* (New York: Basic Books, 1974)

Aldona Jonaitis: *From the Land of the Totem Poles: The Northwest Coast Indian Art Collection at the American Museum of Natural History* (New York: American Museum of Natural History / Seattle: University of Washington Press, 1988)

Marshall Hyatt: *Franz Boas, Social Activist: The Dynamics of Ethnicity* (Westport, Conn.: Greenwood, 1990)

See also AMERICAN ETHNOLOGICAL SOCIETY.

Ira Jacknis

Boerum Hill. Neighborhood in northwestern Brooklyn (1990 pop. 8299), covering thirty-six blocks and bounded to the north by State Street, to the east by 4th Avenue, to the south by Warren Street, and to the west by Court Street. It is named for the colonial farm of the Boerum family that once stood in the area. Most of the housing consists of three-story row houses built between 1840 and 1870. In 1973 an area of six blocks around Dean Street was designated a Historic District by the Landmarks Preservation Commission. The population is middle and upper middle class. There are shops nearby on Fulton, Smith, and Court streets and Atlantic Avenue.

John J. Gallagher

Bogardus, James (*b* Catskill, N.Y., 14 March 1800; *d* New York City, 13 April 1874). Inventor. After fulfilling an apprenticeship to a watchmaker he moved to New York City, where in 1820 he was awarded the Gold Medal of the American Institute for a clock design; he later patented a complex clock mechanism and invented machinery for cotton spinning, sugar grinding, and metal engraving. He is best known for developing construction methods that allowed entire buildings to be made of cast iron (see CAST-IRON ARCHITECTURE); he first used these methods in constructing a façade at 183 Broadway (1848) and a row of five stores at the corner of Murray and Washington streets (1849). A few of his buildings remain at an intersection named for him in SoHo.

James E. Mooney

Bogart, Humphrey (DeForest) (*b* New York City, 25 Dec 1899; *d* Beverly Hills, Calif., 14 Jan 1951). Actor. He was born in a four-story row house at 245 West 103rd Street in Manhattan and attended Trinity School from 1913 to 1917. After working as an office boy from 1920 to 1922 he became a road manager and assistant stage manager for a theater company owned by the producer William S. Brady; he also performed a variety of chores at World Film Corporation, Brady's film studio in the city. In 1920 he took a two-line walk-on part in a play entitled *Experience* that he was managing, and he was then able to find steady work in a wide range of roles as a stage actor. He moved from his family's house to 43 East 25th Street and in 1930 secured his first role in a motion picture, a ten-minute short entitled *Broadway's Like That.* His role as the gangster Duke Mantee in *The Petrified Forest* (1935) marked the height of his career on the stage and helped him to become well known; the motion picture version in 1936 made him a star, and he soon moved to Hollywood. In the following years he often played big-city hoodlums in such films as *The Racket Busters* (1938), in which he played a gang leader trying to muscle his way into the trucking business in Manhattan. He is best known for his role as Rick Blaine, the witty, jaded café owner in *Casablanca* (1942), who on mentioning that he was born in New York City is asked by Major Heinrich Strasser whether he can imagine the Germans in his home town, to which he replies: "Well, there are certain sections of New York, Major, that I wouldn't advise you to try to invade." In 1945 he married Lauren Bacall. Bogart appeared in more than seventy-five films, including John Huston's *The African Queen* (1951, Academy Award for best actor).

Alan G. Barbour: *Humphrey Bogart* (New York: Galahad, 1973)

Robert Sklar: *City Boys: Cagney, Bogart, Garfield* (Princeton, N.J.: Princeton University Press, 1992)

Allen J. Share

Boissevain, Inez Milholland (*b* Brooklyn, 6 Aug 1886; *d* Los Angeles, 25 Nov 1916). Suffragist. As an undergraduate at Vassar College (graduated 1909) she earned notoriety for advocating socialism and woman suffrage. She earned a law degree at New York University, married Eugen Boissevain, and became prominent in the women's rights and radical labor movements by writing for *McClure's Magazine* and taking part in the "shirtwaist strike" of 1909, the Women's Trade Union League, the Women's Political Union, and the National Woman's Party. Her death from pernicious anemia followed an exhausting national tour in which she campaigned for woman suffrage.

Jan Seidler Ramirez

Boni and Liveright. Firm of book publishers formed by Horace Liveright and Albert Boni in 1917 to produce books of standard format. It attracted such writers as Eugene O'Neill, Ben Hecht, Sherwood Anderson, and Ernest Hemingway and was often a target of censors and the Society for the Suppression of Vice; in 1924 it waged a successful campaign against the "clean books bill" proposed by Justice John Ford in the state legislature. In July 1918 the partners resolved a disagreement by deciding to toss a coin, with the winner to get the firm and the loser to leave; Boni lost. Liveright wrote many articles on censorship and other issues relevant to publishing.

Gilmer Walker: *Horace Liveright: Publisher of the Twenties* (New York: D. Lewis, 1970)

See also BOOK PUBLISHING.

James E. Mooney

Bonwit Teller. Firm of clothing retailers. It was formed in 1905 by Paul J. Bonwit (1862–1939) and Edmund D. Teller, who first opened a store at 6th Avenue and 18th Street; they later moved their operations to 23rd Street near 6th Avenue in 1897 and to 5th Avenue and 56th Street in 1930. The firm specialized in high fashion and achieved great success. After Bonwit retired in 1934 the company was sold successively to the Atlas Corporation, the Hoving Corporation (1946), Genesco (1956), the Allied Stores Corporation (1979), and the Hooker Corporation (1987). The managers of Bonwit Teller seemed interested principally in the value of their stores as real estate. After the developer Donald Trump demolished the main building of Bonwit Teller on 5th Avenue to make way for Trump Tower, the firm ceased operations in May 1990.

Hortense M. Odlum: *A Woman's Place: The Autobiography* (New York: Charles Scribner's Sons, 1939; repr. Arno, 1980)

Leslie Gourse, Kenneth T. Jackson

book publishing. Book publishing is a vital part of the culture and economy of New York City, which has the largest concentration of publishers and book-related enterprises in the United States.

Display window designed by Salvador Dali, 1936. Dali was reportedly displeased with the results and drove an automobile through one of the windows facing 5th Avenue.

Books were first produced in the city by William Bradford, a printer trained in London. He worked in Philadelphia before moving in 1693 to New York City, where he was active for fifty years. Among important printer–publishers who followed was Hugh Gaine, who after 1752 printed almanacs, books for children, and classics in addition to a newspaper. The bookseller James Rivington published poetry and sermons from 1773, imported music and lawbooks, and was one of the earliest publishers to "pirate" (reprint without payment) British editions of popular works. Thomas Swords and James Swords (1785) produced literary works, college and religious texts, and children's books. During the early nineteenth century the city surpassed Boston and Philadelphia as the country's most important publishing center. John Wiley (1807, later John Wiley and Sons) initially issued literary works and later became a major publisher of technical, scientific, college, professional, and medical books. Harper and Brothers (1817) bought stereotype platemaking machinery, roller presses for high-speed mass production, and a steam press; it was among the first to use electrotyping in producing illustrations, and probably introduced cloth-over-board covers to the United States. The firm continually sought new markets and was a leading publisher of series, or "libraries," of literary works. The American Bible Society (1816) aimed to circulate the Bible without doctrinal note or commentary: it eventually published or sold most English-language editions of the Bible and distributed editions in many languages worldwide.

Initially most publishers offered broad lists. The firm of D. Appleton, formed in 1830 by Daniel Appleton, published religious books, children's books, travel books, textbooks such as Noah Webster's *Elementary Spelling Book*, science books such as Darwin's *The Origin of Species*, and Spanish-language materials. Later renamed Appleton, Century, Crofts, it became an important producer of encyclopedias and dictionaries. Dodd, Mead (1839) was known for serious religious and general trade books, but also the "Elsie Dinsmore" series for girls (for seventy years from 1867) and the Red Badge detective mystery series (from 1931). George Palmer Putnam, a former partner of Wiley, in 1847 launched the firm that later became G. P. Putnam's Sons. He assembled a strong list, in part through regular meetings with publishers in London. He opposed piracy and sought to extend international copyright laws. His firm was later directed by his son George Haven Putnam, who continued his father's work with copyrights. After graduating from Princeton University, Charles Scribner opened a firm in 1848 that soon issued three best-sellers. It later published religious books and secondary school textbooks and offered imported books; it was renamed Charles Scribner's Sons in 1871. The city's first important specialized publisher was David Van Nostrand, who from 1848 published and imported works of military history, science, and technology. Picture books and storybooks for children were offered at low prices from the late 1840s, notably by the firm of McLoughlin. From the mid nineteenth century cheap paperback editions of literary works became widely available, in part through distribution at railroad stations. In 1866 Frederick W. Leypoldt and Henry Holt opened a firm specializing in foreign-language books and translations, including German pocket-sized paperbacks known as Tauchnitz Editions. After the partnership dissolved in 1872 Leypoldt and Richard Rogers Bowker launched *Publishers Weekly* and in 1876 the *Library Journal*; their firm took the name R. R. Bowker and became known for directories, bibliographies, and reference works for the book trade. E. P. Dutton (1858) moved from Boston to New York City in 1869 and specialized in Episcopalian and other religious books. The British firm of Macmillan, eager to exploit new markets and combat piracy, opened a branch in the city under George Edward Brett that became an important general publisher in its own right. Leypoldt's and Holt's firm evolved into Henry Holt and Company in 1873 and maintained a solid, comprehensive list.

About the turn of the century publishers focused on expanding both output and markets. The first two of several university presses in the city were established: Columbia University Press (1893) and the American branch of Oxford University Press (1896). Grosset and Dunlap was formed in 1898 by Alexander Grosset and George Dunlap and a few years later became the leading publisher of inexpensive hardcover reprints and popular children's books, selling especially through retail outlets in department stores and variety stores. During the same year the firm of Doubleday began operations and the *New York Times Book Review* was launched as the first publication of its kind in the city. To take advantage of growing markets, Frank Nelson Doubleday joined briefly with the magazine publisher J. S. McClure to form Doubleday, McClure; in 1899 Walter Hines Page replaced McClure, and the firm became Doubleday, Page. The reputation of Harper and Brothers in the realm of collected works was enhanced in 1903 when Mark Twain named the firm his "authorized" publisher. In 1904 the Teachers College Press was formed independently of Columbia University Press. George H. Doran began his distinguished literary imprint in 1908, and in the same year Yale University Press (now of New Haven, Connecticut) opened at an office desk in Manhattan; New York University Press followed in 1916. The demand for technical books increased: McGraw–Hill (1909) became one of the largest publishers of college textbooks, business magazines, and economics, engineering, and professional books, and Prentice Hall, formed in 1913 by E. P. Ettinger, published business books, financial information services, and some trade titles. By 1915 Alfred A. Knopf left Doubleday to form a company with his wife, Blanche, which in the following decades stressed high quality in its offerings of fiction and nonfiction, scholarly works, and children's books. The firm introduced the works of foreign writers to the United States, and set new standards in typography and book design. Among the scores of writers whom it attracted were Dashiell Hammett, H. L. Mencken, John Hersey, Thomas Mann, and John Updike.

Innovations accelerated after the First World War. Horace Liveright and Albert and Charles Boni in 1917 founded the Modern Library of reprinted classics, providing funds for more controversial new literature. In 1919 the Bonis broke away but Liveright continued (as Horace Liveright and Company), becoming a groundbreaking publisher in the literary renaissance of the 1920s. Alfred Harcourt and Donald Brace, both previously with Holt, established Harcourt, Brace in 1919 and within eighteen months had initiated an important general list, including children's and educational books. In 1921 George Delacorte founded the Delacorte Press. At this firm, and at its descendant Dell Books, Helen Meyer exerted a strong influence on the trade from the 1920s to the 1950s. New approaches in children's book publishing were introduced in 1919 by Louise Seaman (Bechtel) at Macmillan and in 1922 by May Massee at Doubleday, stressing excellence in writing, illustration, and design. Other publishers followed suit. The movement created new openings for talented women editors and artists. From the 1920s editors of children's literature took advantage of improvements in color printing, illustration, and typography. At the mass-market retail level children's books at affordable prices were also offered by many publishers, among them Grosset and Dunlap, McLoughlin, and Platt and Munk (1920). In the adult nonfiction and college fields the firm of W(arder) W. Norton (1923) announced as its motto "Books That Live." It maintained an unusually large, selective backlist, later including many trade paperbacks. Book reviewing was increasingly important: in 1924, competing with the *New York Times Book Review*, *New York Herald Tribune Books* began publication, as did the *Saturday Review of Literature*, an outgrowth of a weekly review section in the *New York Post*. During the same year Simon and Schuster was formed by Richard L. Simon and M. Lincoln Schuster, who enlivened book publishing and advertising. The firm was scorned by its more traditional competitors but consistently had best-sellers; some of its most successful ideas were provided by Leon Shimkin, the financial advisor and later the owner. In 1925 Bennett A. Cerf, an editor for Liveright, and Donald S. Klopfer took over the Modern Library. They adopted the corporate name Random House in 1927, and earned early fame for issuing Joyce's *Ulysses.* Another former editor at Liveright, Saxe Commins, brought luster to the firm as the editor of Eugene O'Neill and William Faulkner among others.

A number of publishing ventures begun in 1926 became highly successful. William Morrow began operations. Viking Press did as well, under Harold K. Guinzburg and George S. Oppenheimer, who chose a Viking ship as their logotype because it was a symbol of adventure and enterprise. Viking soon acquired the firm of Ben W. Huebsch, an editor with a distinguished list of American and foreign writers, and became known for literary excellence, distinctive design, and children's books. The firm of John Day was formed by Richard Walsh, and later specialized in books about Asia under the direction of Pearl S. Buck. Vanguard Press, led by James Henle, was supported by several foundations and issued politically progressive, well-designed books at low cost (it ceased operations in the 1960s). The year 1926 also saw the acquisition of the Literary Guild from Guinzburg by Doubleday, Page and the launching of the Book-of-the-Month Club by Harry Scherman. These clubs enjoyed a success that inspired the formation of other clubs, including many that were specialized. The club movement greatly changed the way books were sold.

Doubleday merged with Doran in 1927 to form Doubleday, Doran, which was known after 1935 as Doubleday and Company and expanded its line of book clubs, developed a large children's book department, opened a chain of bookstores, and introduced hardcover reprints, trade and general paperbacks, and religious books. About this time a number of publishers began producing fine books for collectors. The longest-lived and most systematic effort was that of George Macy, whose Limited Editions Club (1929) attracted some of the leading designers and illustrators. During this same period Charles Scribner's Sons reached its peak as a literary publisher, largely owing to the efforts of the editor Maxwell Perkins, who attracted important writers of fiction, including Thomas Wolfe, F. Scott Fitzgerald, and Ernest Hemingway.

Many publishers flourished during the 1930s in spite of the Depression. Farrar and Rinehart, founded in 1929 by the editors John Farrar, Stanley Rinehart, and Frederick Rinehart, became highly successful. Under Cass Canfield from 1931 Harper and Brothers published such well-known writers as J. B. Priestley, J. B. S. Haldane, Robert E. Sherwood, Eleanor Roosevelt, and Jacques Cousteau. Probably the city's first specialized publisher of art books was Studio Books, which moved from London in 1932 and set high standards in art printing (it later became known as Viking Studio). Harper and Brothers continued as a major publisher of bible and general religious titles, as did Oxford. Crown Publishers (1936) grew out of Outlet Books, a remainder bookselling company bought by Nat Wartels and Robert Simon in 1934. They developed an increasingly broad list of popular titles, largely nonfiction. New Directions Press, formed in 1936 by James Loughlin to publish works of the avant-garde, became known for its list of modern prose and poetry, including the work of William Carlos Williams, Ezra Pound, and E. E. Cummings. After the 1930s Holt became known for its editions of works by contemporary writers, including Robert Frost, Bernard Baruch, and Albert Schweitzer. Meanwhile the paperback industry was developing. In 1932 paperback production in pocket-sized (later "rack-size") format began with the release of the first ten Pocket Book titles by Robert De Graff. The successful Penguin Books (of Britain) began production in 1940. And the nonprofit Armed Services Editions, given to thousands of enlisted personnel during the Second World War, helped to create a prospective audience for cheap paperbacks. Mass circulation of inexpensive books became possible by linking the popular paperbacks with the nation's wholesale magazine distributors. Early competitors included Avon Books (1941), of the Hearst Corporation; George Delacorte's Dell Books (1942); and Popular Library (1942). Dover Publications, formed by Hayward Cirker in 1941, put its own stamp on the trade by issuing facsimiles and reprints of out-of-print titles in a variety of sizes and selling them cheaply in stores and through the mail; it carried books on a wide range of subjects. Ian Ballantine left Penguin to help form Bantam Books in 1945. Competition intensified among paperback publishers, who vied for display space, aided by eye-catching cover designs.

Publishers explored new avenues during the 1940s and 1950s. In 1942 Simon and Schuster introduced a line of children's storybooks called Golden Books. Produced by leading writers and artists under the direction of Albert Rice Leventhal and sold for twenty-five cents each, the books attained a popularity during and after the war that led to the introduction of Golden lines for all ages. Many distinguished books were produced at Doubleday by Kenneth D. McCormick, an editor there from the 1940s. German wartime and postwar émigré publishers also appeared in New York City: Helen and Kurt Wolff, respected literary editors, founded Pantheon Books in 1942; Salman Schocken established Schocken Books in 1946, issuing books of Jewish and general interest. Farrar left Farrar and Rinehart in 1944 and in 1946 joined Roger Straus to form Farrar, Straus (later Farrar, Straus and Giroux), which became highly regarded for the literary works of many writers, among them T. S. Eliot and Edmund Wilson; Rinehart later was absorbed by Holt. In 1947 Victor Weybright and Kurt Enoch, editors at Penguin, launched the New American Library of World Literature, applying mass-market manufacturing techniques to serious nonfiction, sold largely through college and major general bookstores. And Cambridge University Press opened an office in New York City in 1949. Advances in color lithography and offset printing in the 1950s greatly changed the appearance of books. New technology in color separation and multi-colored printing, which allowed for spectacular fine arts reproductions, were exploited by Harry N. Abrams, who established a firm under his own name in 1950 (and later the Abbeville Press, 1977). Art publishers and such specialized photography publishers as Aperture (1952) applied refined techniques of reproducing black-and-white photographs. A bold direction in literature was taken by Barnet Rosset, who in 1951 acquired the Grove Press and published work by unknown writers (much of it in translation) and writers associated with the beat movement; he also successfully defended himself against censorship in publishing D. H. Lawrence's *Lady Chatterley's Lover* and Henry Miller's *Tropic of Cancer.* In 1952 Macmillan of London set up a branch known as St. Martin's Press in New York City, and Ian Ballantine formed Ballantine Books, publishing original and reprint paperbacks, and some titles in simultaneous hardcover and paperback editions.

In the early 1950s Jason Epstein developed the idea of high-quality paperback editions of literary and scholarly works to be sold in general and college bookstores. Accordingly, at Doubleday he successfully initiated the first titles in the Anchor Books line in 1953. "Quality paperbacks" (later known as "trade paperbacks") were soon produced by other publishers such as Knopf, which added the paperback division Vintage Books in 1954 and later engaged Epstein to expand it. In 1955 William Jovanovich gained control of Harcourt, Brace. In 1957 Alfred A. (Pat) Knopf Jr. left his father's firm, joining Simon Michael Bessie, who left Harper, and Hiram Haydn, who left Random House, to form Atheneum Publishers. It built a respected list and in 1961 added a children's book department. Knopf assumed control after Bessie and Haydn left in 1963. Harper and Brothers introduced Harper Torchbooks and took the name Harper and Row after buying the textbook publisher Row, Peterson. The publishers of *Time* set up Time–Life Books in 1959: its heavily illustrated series on world cultural history and the sciences sold in large quantities, primarily through the mail. Doubleday developed a line of religious books, both general and scholarly, some of them issued as paperbacks. Yeshiva University Press was begun in 1960 to publish books of religious scholarship.

The 1960s saw a rash of mergers, takeovers, and reorganizations among many of the city's publishers. In 1960 Harcourt, Brace bought the World Book Company and became Harcourt, Brace and World (in 1970 the name changed to Harcourt Brace Jovanovich). The Columbia Broadcasting System (CBS) bought Holt, Rinehart and Winston, and Knopf became an autonomous division of Random House, retaining its identity during later acquisitions. The encyclopedia publisher Crowell–Collier took control of the Macmillan Company from George P. Brett and other stockholders in 1961. The *New York Review of Books* began operations in 1963. In 1966 Prentice Hall moved to Englewood Cliffs, New Jersey. *New York Herald Tribune Books* ceased publication. Time–Life Books bought the Book-of-the-Month Club in 1966 and the firm of Little, Brown (Boston) in 1968. In the same year R. R. Bowker sold itself to the Xerox Corporation. Holt sold its educational line to Harcourt Brace Jovanovich and its trade list to the German firm Verlagsgruppe Georg van Holtzbrinck, which retained the name Henry Holt. D. Van Nostrand, bought by Litton Industries during the same year, became Van Nostrand Reinhold after another acquisition and was later bought by International Thomson Publishing. McGraw–Hill was strengthened during the 1960s and 1970s by Curtis Benjamin, who found markets for exports, and by Harold W. McGraw Jr., who worked to improve relations with the retail book trade.

Mergers continued to reshape publishing in the 1970s and 1980s. Warner Publishing (1972), which merged the film and communications divisions of Warner, became a force in the mass-market book trade. Led by Thomas J. MacCormick from 1972, St. Martin's Press expanded its programs in publishing original as well as imported titles. After buying Jove Publications (from Harcourt Brace Jovanovich), the Berkley Publishing Corporation, and Coward McCann, G. P. Putnam's Sons was itself bought in 1975 by MCA, an entertainment and media conglomerate, to form the Putnam Berkley Group, later led by Phyllis Grann. It acquired Grosset and Dunlap in 1982. Simon and Schuster, led by Richard Snyder and highly regarded for its excellence, was bought in 1975 by Gulf and Western (later Paramount Communications). In the same year Viking Press merged with the American subsidiary of Penguin to form Viking Penguin. Doubleday acquired the Dell Publishing Company in 1976. In 1977 the German publishing conglomerate Bertelsmann bought Bantam. Harper and Row acquired Thomas Y. Crowell (1977) and J. B. Lippincott of Philadelphia (1978), and Atheneum became a subsidiary of Scribner's (1979). After Morrow's death his firm continued under Thayer Hobson, sustaining its reputation as a publisher of children's books and good commercial fiction. It was bought in 1981 by the Hearst Corporation (which already owned Avon Books) but continued to operate independently. The merger by Werner Mark Linz in 1980 of several firms including Crossroads, Herder and Herder, and Frederick Ungar resulted in the Crossroad/Continuum Publishing Group, publishers of scholarly and general religious works.

By the mid 1990s scores of publishers were owned by about twelve conglomerates. In 1980 Advance Publications, owned by S. I. Newhouse and Donald Newhouse, took over Random House, including Knopf, Pantheon, and the trade paperback line Vintage. By the 1990s the Newhouses had also acquired Times Books (1984), Schocken Books (1988), and Crown Publishers (1988) with its affiliates, notably Clarkson N. Potter. Prentice Hall in 1984 became a division of Simon and Schuster (under Paramount) and was reorganized into departments devoted to trade, educational, professional, and electronic publishing. The British firm of Reed Holdings bought R. R. Bowker from Xerox in 1985, later placing the Bowker magazines under its subsidiary Cahners, in New York City; Bowker became a division of Reed Reference (New Providence, New Jersey). In 1986 Bertelsmann bought Doubleday (which had previously acquired Dell) and formed the Bantam Doubleday Dell Publishing Group. In the same year Viking Penguin bought E. P. Dutton and New American Library, which became operations of the parent company, Penguin USA. Warner Communications and Time–Life Books merged in 1987 to form Time Warner, and the newspaper magnate Rupert Murdoch bought Harper and Row and merged it with William Collins to form Harper Collins Publishers. Harcourt Brace Jovanovich was sold in 1991 to General Cinema, which then changed its corporate name to Harcourt General; the name of the publisher was changed back to Harcourt Brace after Jovanovich retired. The firm of Crowell Collier Macmillan was taken over in 1988 by the British entrepreneur Robert Maxwell and became part of a conglomerate that in 1992 owned the Macmillan Publishing Company, Charles Scribner's Sons, Atheneum Publishers, Audel Technical Books, and Schirmer music books. In the breakup of Maxwell's properties that followed his death, Macmillan school books went to McGraw–Hill in 1993, and in 1994 Paramount Communications bought the rest of Macmillan. Also in 1994 Paramount was bought by Viacom, a multimedia conglomerate.

See also CHILDREN'S BOOK PUBLISHING, LITERATURE, and SCIENTIFIC PUBLISHING.

Chandler B. Grannis, Martha W. Grannis

Book Row. An area of secondhand bookstores concentrated from the late nineteenth century in seven blocks along 4th Avenue between Union Square and Astor Place. It contained about a dozen stores during the 1920s and 1930s and about twenty-five in the years after the Second World War, among them the Arcadia Bookshop, Biblo and Tannen, the Fourth Avenue Bookstore, the Green Bookshop, the Pageant Bookshop, the Raven Bookshop, Stammer's Bookstore, the Strand Book Store, and the Samuel Weiser Bookstore. As rents increased and buildings were demolished during the mid 1950s a number of the shops moved nearby to Broadway. The secondhand book business declined and in 1991 only the Pageant, Strand, Samuel Weiser, and University Place bookshops remained in the area.

Robert Egan: *The Bookstore Book: A Guide to Manhattan Booksellers* (New York: Avon, 1979)
Marvin Mondlin: *Book Row America: An Anecdotal and Pictorial History of the Fourth Avenue Antiquarian Book Trade* (forthcoming)

Allen J. Share

booksellers. The first bookshop in New York City began operations in 1693 and was run by William Bradford, the official printer for the colony who also issued its first newspaper (the *Gazette*, 1725–44). For two years beginning in 1694 one of his apprentices was John Peter Zenger, whose wife, Catherine, in 1742 opened the second bookshop in the colony, specializing in pamphlets and stationery. Apprenticeships continued to lead to new establishments throughout the colonial period and helped to build a network among printers. By 1751 Hugh Gaine opened the Bible and Crown at Hanover Square; although controversial during the American Revolution for his Loyalist views he remained in business in 1800. Colonial bookstores also functioned as post offices and listening posts and often sold stationery and dry goods. Many booksellers engaged in printing as well, a practice that continued well into the nineteenth century. The growth of the fiction market after the revolution led to a growth in bookshops. By 1802 booksellers and publishers in the city held their first Literary Fair, during which half a million books were sold in five days. The first secondhand bookshop in the city was that of Samuel Wood on Pearl Street (1804). Charles Wiley set up a shop in 1807 at 6 Reade Street and moved it by the 1820s to 167 Broadway, in a newly developing booksellers' neighborhood; there his back room became known as the Den, a meeting place for such intellectuals as William Cullen Bryant, James Fenimore Cooper, Fitz-Greene Halleck, and Samuel F. B. Morse. Among those who began their careers by working for Wiley was George Palmer Putnam, who later founded his own bookshop and publishing house. Daniel Appleton, a dealer in dry goods, began selling books in his shop on Exchange Place in 1825 and became a publisher in 1831: his shop was the most popular bookselling establishment in New York City until it closed in 1881. Isaac Baker and Charles Scribner opened a bookshop in 1846 on Nassau Street and a publishing firm in the 1850s. Nassau Street was the center of secondhand bookstores: William Gowon, who had 300,000 volumes at his shop there, was a prominent secondhand dealer in the 1830s. After the Astor Library opened on Lafayette Street, fashionable bookstores moved in the 1850s to Astor Place and secondhand dealers moved to 4th Avenue, which between Astor Place and 14th Street became known as "booksellers' row."

August Brentano, an Austrian immigrant, from 1853 had a newsstand on lower Broadway specializing in foreign and hard-to-find materials. By the 1870s Brentano's Literary Emporium on Union Square was a meeting place for writers like Henry Ward Beecher, Edwin Booth, and Artemus Ward. Booksellers became more specialized in the 1880s as department stores began to sell discounted books as "loss leaders." By the turn of the century several fashionable booksellers had moved near Madison Square, including those of Brentano, Putnam, Scribner, and E. P. Dutton; at the same time 4th Avenue became the province of secondhand dealers. In 1913 Scribner moved into the company building at 597 5th Avenue. Brentano followed on the opposite side of the avenue in 1924.

A number of shops were established in the early years of the twentieth century by booksellers whose names later became associated with large retail chains. These included Womrath's (1902), the first in a network of bookshops that operated rental libraries; Doubleday and Page (1910, Pennsylvania Station); and Barnes and Noble (1917; store at 105 5th Avenue opened in 1932). Smaller shops specialized in books on women (the Woman's Book-Shop at Lexington Avenue and 52nd Street, 1916), modern literature (the Gotham Book Mart, 1920, frequented by W. H. Auden, Marianne Moore, and Delmore Schwartz), the theater (the Drama Bookstore at 723 7th Avenue, 1923), used and rare books (the Argosy Book Store at 116 East 59th Street, 1924; the Strand at 828 Broadway, 1928), the occult (Samuel Weiser at 132 East 24th Street, 1926), black and African subjects (Lewis H. Michaux's National Memorial African Bookstore on 125th Street, 1930–74; the University Place Bookshop at 821 Broadway, 1932), and beat poetry (Elias Wilentz's Eighth Street Bookstore, 1947–79).

The decades following the Second World War saw a marked growth in bookstores operated by such chains as Barnes and Noble, Doubleday, B. Dalton, and Waldenbooks. By the 1980s few booksellers remained on 4th Avenue. Books were increasingly sold by sidewalk vendors in areas of high pedestrian traffic: some specialized in remainders of road atlases, dictionaries, and children's books, and others sold a variety of new titles. These street vendors encountered considerable opposition from conventional booksellers who found it difficult to match their low prices.

Henry Walcott Boynton: *Annals of American Bookselling, 1638–1850* (New York: John Wiley and Sons, 1932)

Edwin D. Hoffman: "The Bookshops of New York City, 1743–1948," *New York State Historical Association Quarterly* 30 (1949), Jan

Manuel B. Tarshish: "The Fourth Avenue Book Trade," *Publishers Weekly*, 20 Oct 1969, 27 Oct 1969, 3 Nov 1969

Marc H. Aronson

Booth, Edwin (Thomas) (*b* Bel Air, Md., 13 Nov 1833; *d* New York City, 7 June 1893). Actor. The son of the actor Junius Brutus Booth (1796–1852), he spent much of his career in New York City although he traveled widely in the United States and abroad. His first major appearance in the city was at Burton's Theatre in May 1857. During 1864–65 he set a record by giving a hundred performances as Hamlet, arguably his greatest role. On 25 November 1864 he appeared in *Julius Caesar* at the Winter Garden in his only performance with his brothers John Wilkes Booth (1839–65), better known as the assassin of Abraham Lincoln, and Junius Brutus Booth Jr. (1821–83). He also excelled as Iago, as Sir Giles Overreach in Philip Massinger's *A New Way to Pay Old Debts* (1625), and as Betruccio in Tom Taylor's *The Fool's Revenge* (1859). He managed successively the Winter Garden (1864–67) and Booth's Theatre (1869–74), at the southeast corner of 6th Avenue and 23rd Street. In 1888 he donated his home at 16 Gramercy Park South to the Players, then newly established, while retaining an apartment where he remained to the end of his life. He gave his last performance, as Hamlet, at the Brooklyn Academy of Music in 1891. A statue of Booth erected in 1918 in Gramercy Park stands opposite the Players.

Stanley P. Kimmel: *The Mad Booths of Maryland* (Indianapolis: Bobbs–Merrill, 1940; rev. and enlarged New York: Dover, 1969)

Eleanor Ruggles: *Prince of Players: Edwin Booth* (New York: W. W. Norton, 1953)

Charles H. Shattuck: *The Hamlet of Edwin Booth* (Urbana: University of Illinois Press, 1969)

Don B. Wilmeth

Booth Memorial Hospital and Medical Center. Nonprofit general-care hospital in Flushing, opened in 1955 by the Salvation Army. It began as a rescue home for women, opened in 1892 by the Salvation Army, that offered shelter and medical care to all comers, especially mothers and women addicted to alcohol and drugs. After moving to several sites on the East Side it was given more permanent quarters on East 15th Street, and in 1914 the name was changed to Booth Memorial Hospital; in 1918 the facility was licensed as a general hospital. The rapid growth of Queens led to pressure for more medical facilities in the borough, and in 1957 the hospital moved to Flushing, where it had 210 beds and provided general and maternity care. It eventually expanded to 487 beds, treated more than 150,000 patients annually, and became an important teaching hospital affiliated with the New York University School of Medicine.

Edward H. McKinley: *Marching to Glory: The History of the Salvation Army in the United States of America, 1880–1980* (New York: Harper and Row, 1980)

Jane Allen

boots. The manufacture of boots is discussed in the entry SHOES, BOOTS, AND LEATHER.

Borden. Firm of food processors, the descendant of a dairy business formed in 1856 by Gail Borden, who operated a milk depot on Canal Street and a factory in Wollcottsville, Connecticut. The business sold sanitary, condensed milk produced with a patented vacuum evaporation method. It failed twice, owing to a wariness on the part of New Yorkers toward milk that was not fresh from the dairy, bad economic times, and a lack of financial backing. In 1858 Borden met Jeremiah Milbank, a wholesale grocer on Front Street who promised to provide adequate capital. Renamed the New York Condensed Milk Company, the business was helped by reports in *Frank Leslie's Illustrated Newspaper* that exposed the filthy conditions at dairies in New York City and suggested that they were responsible for the city's high infant mortality rate. Demand soared after Borden took out an advertisement in Leslie's newspaper in May 1858 vaunting his product's "purity, durability, and economy." Delivery routes were established between lower Manhattan and 51st Street, with additional offices at 53 South Street and in Brooklyn at Fulton and Front streets. With the onset of the Civil War, Borden supplied a steady supply of his canned milk to soldiers, who were often too far from a dairy to get fresh milk. Soldiers returned home telling of the miraculous product from New York City, pushing production yet higher. In 1861 the factory moved from Connecticut to Wassaic, New York, fifty-five miles (ninety kilometers) from New York City, to which the milk was transported by train. Borden bought from local farmers virtually all the milk they could provide, freeing them from the task of finding retail customers and from the risk of losing excess supplies to spoilage. In return the firm required that farmers follow strict sanitary guidelines.

Despite varying fortunes after the Civil War the firm continued to expand, and its success helped to create the modern dairy industry. Incorporated in 1899 as the Borden Condensed Milk Company, it remained in the dairy business almost exclusively during the first quarter of the twentieth century, buying other dairies and ice cream companies. In 1928 massive diversification began, with entities purchased in Europe and Canada, and in 1932 the firm introduced Elmer's Glue-All, which eventually became the largest-selling household glue in the United States. During the Second World War the firm supplied dairy products to American forces and also manufactured synthetic adhesives for military purposes. It expanded into plastics and chemicals in the 1950s and into rubber in the 1960s, when sales reached $1000 million. In the 1980s Borden further expanded its food business. By 1994, when the firm was bought out by Kohlberg, Kravis, Roberts and Company (a food conglomerate with holdings that included RJR Nabisco), it had moved its corporate headquarters to Columbus, Ohio, and shut down its factories in New York City.

Joe B. Frantz: *Gail Borden, Dairyman to a Nation* (Norman: University of Oklahoma Press, 1951)

Thomas M. Hilbink

Boricua College. A private, nonprofit college opened in 1974. The main campus is at 3755 Broadway at Audubon Terrace in Manhattan (the former site of the American Geographical Society), and there are also campuses in Brooklyn at 9 Graham Avenue and 186 North 6th Street. The students live off campus and the curriculum is oriented toward the interests of Puerto Ricans and other Latin Americans in New York City. The college was the first in the United States to offer bilingual education in Spanish and English. Fully accredited in 1980, Boricua offers associate and bachelor's degrees in liberal arts, elementary education, business administration, human services, inter-American studies, and other subjects, as well as programs in Latin American caseworker training and Puerto Rican documentary. There were about eleven hundred students in 1990, of whom almost three quarters were Puerto Rican and four fifths were women. The school maintains the Hispanic Collection of materials relating to Puerto Ricans in New York City, the Congressman Herman Badillo Collection, and the Hispanic Music Collection.

Marc Ferris, Rachel Shor

Borough of Manhattan Community College. Junior college of the City University of New York, opened in 1964. It operated from several locations in midtown Manhattan until 1983, when it moved to a new complex four blocks long at 199 Chambers Street. The college concentrates on training graduates for business careers and offers liberal arts courses for students planning to transfer to four-year colleges. In spring 1991 it had 7839 full-time and 7139 part-time students.

Marc Ferris

Borough Park. Neighborhood in southwestern Brooklyn (1990 pop. 109,624), lying within New Utrecht southeast of Green-Wood Cemetery and covering two hundred blocks bounded to the north by 37th Street, to the east by McDonald Avenue, to the south by 64th Street, and to the west by 8th Avenue. The area was the site of commercial nurseries in the early nineteenth century and was developed in the 1880s as Blythebourne by Edwin C. Litchfield. Initially the residents were mostly Irish immigrants. There was an influx of Jews from Williamsburg in the 1920s and of Italians from the Lower East Side of Manhattan in the 1930s. From the 1960s many Jewish residents moved to the suburbs; other Jews who moved in from Williamsburg and Crown Heights were for the most part Orthodox. The population continued to grow as Jews moved to the neighborhood from other parts of Brooklyn, Israel, central Europe, and the Soviet Union and as the birth rate rose (bringing the average number of children in a family to seven). Among the organizations that were formed were the Council of Jewish Organizations, a consortium of 170 educational, religious, and service institutions, and the Jewish Youth Library, offering education in the Orthodox tradition. Orthodox Jews account for 80 percent of the population; there are about two hundred temples, fifty yeshivas (including those in the Bais Yakov school system, which enrolls more than twenty thousand students), and more than twenty Hasidic sects, including the Belts, the Bobov, the Ger, the Satmar, and the Spinka. Many residents work in Manhattan or in northern Brooklyn, often riding to work on the buses of locally organized lines. The most important event is the celebration of Purim every spring, which draws crowds from throughout the metropolitan area. Borough Park has many immigrants from Israel and the Soviet Union, and to a lesser extent from India, Romania, Poland, Guyana, and Italy. The neighborhood is densely populated and mostly residential; the housing consists of one- and two-family houses. There are no parks.

Rita Seiden Miller, ed.: *Brooklyn USA* (New York: Brooklyn College Press, 1979)

John J. Gallagher

borough presidents. The offices of borough president were established by charter in 1898 to preserve "local pride and affection for the old municipalities" after consolidation. When the charter was revised in 1901 the five borough presidents became members of the Board of Estimate and gained considerable administrative power, especially over the physical development of the city. Their influence on the board was enhanced by an agreement to vote as a bloc on certain local issues, and they often helped to resolve conflicts between neighborhoods and City Hall. All charters written after 1901 tended to centralize financial functions (such as assessment) and services (such as building inspection), thus

Borough Presidents in New York City

BRONX

Louis F. Haffen 1898–1909
John F. Murray 1909
Cyrus C. Miller 1910–13
Douglas Mathewson 1914–17
Henry Bruckner 1918–33
James J. Lyons 1934–61
Joseph Periconi 1962–65
Herman Badillo 1966–69
Robert Abrams 1970–77
Stanley Simon 1978–87
Fernando Ferrer 1987–

BROOKLYN

Edward M. Grout 1898–1901
J. Edward Swanstrom 1902–3
Martin W. Littleton 1904–6
Bird S. Coler 1906–9
Alfred Steers 1910–13
Lewis H. Pounds 1913–17
Edward J. Riegelman 1918–24
Joseph A. Guider 1925–26
James J. Byrne 1926–30
Henry Hesterberg 1930–33
Raymond V. Ingersoll 1934–40
John Cashmore 1940–61
John F. Hayes 1961
Abe Stark 1961–70
Sebastian Leone 1970–76
Howard Golden 1976–

MANHATTAN

Augustus W. Peters 1898–99
James J. Coogan 1899–1901
Jacob A. Cantor 1902–3
John F. Ahearn 1904–9
J. Cloughin 1909
George McAneny 1910–13
Marcus A. Marks 1914–17
Frank L. Dowling 1918–19
Henry H. Curran 1920–21
Julius Miller 1922–30
Samuel Levy 1931–37
Stanley M. Isaacs 1938–41
Edgar J. Nathan 1942–45
Hugot Rogers 1946–50
Robert F. Wagner Jr. 1950–53
Hulan E. Jack 1954–61
Louis Cioffi (acting) 1961
Edward R. Dudley 1961–64
Constance Baker Motley 1965–66
Percy Sutton 1966–77
Andrew J. Stein 1978–85
David N. Dinkins 1986–89
Ruth Messinger 1990–

QUEENS

Frederick Bowley 1898–1901
Joseph Cassidy 1902–5
Joseph Bermel 1906–8
Lawrence Gresser 1909–11
Maurice E. Connolly 1911–28
Bernard M. Patten 1928
George U. Harvey 1929–41

(*continued*)

Borough Presidents in New York City *(Continued)*

James A. Burke 1942–49
Maurice A. Fitzgerald 1950–51
James J. Lundy 1952–57
James J. Crisona 1958–59
John T. Clancy 1959–62
Mario J. Cariello 1963–68
Sidney Leviss 1969–71
Donald Manes 1971–86
Claire Shulman 1986–

STATEN ISLAND

George Cromwell 1898–13
Charles J. McCormack 1914–15
Calvin VanName 1915–21
Matthew J. Cahill 1922
John A. Lynch 1922–33
Joseph A. Palma 1934–45
Cornelius A. Hall 1946–53
Edward G. Baker 1953–65
Albert V. Maniscalco 1955–65
Robert T. Connor 1966–77
Anthony R. Gaeta 1977–84
Ralph J. Lamberti 1984–89
Guy Molinari 1990–

reducing the borough presidents' authority. This movement culminated in the outright elimination of the Board of Estimate in 1990. Although the borough presidents lost many powers they gained new ones, including the authority to appoint the members of community boards, the Board of Education, and the City Planning Commission. The borough presidents serve four-year terms that are coterminous with those of the mayor. Although the borough presidency does not usually lead to higher office, Robert F. Wagner (ii) and David N. Dinkins did proceed from the office of borough president of Manhattan to that of mayor.

Nora L. Mandel

boroughs. The five administrative divisions of New York City, created by consolidation in 1898. Each borough elects a borough president and is coextensive with one county: Manhattan with New York County, the Bronx with Bronx County, Brooklyn with Kings County, Queens with Queens County, and Staten Island with Richmond County.

Boston Post Road. One of the earliest major thoroughfares in New York City, also known as the King's Highway and the Great Road. The road followed the course of an American Indian trail that existed before the time of European settlement. During the colonial period it was the main overland link between Boston and New York City, and at the behest of Charles II it became the first official post road in North America in 1673. Regularly improved to facilitate efficient travel and postal service, it promoted the growth of several roadside towns in New York, Connecticut, and Massachusetts. During the American Revolution it was used by retreating American soldiers after their defeat in the Battle of New York. In 1789 it was chosen for President Washington's inaugural tour of New England. It continued to carry post riders until the advent of the railroad in the 1840s. The road originated near the Battery at the southern tip of Manhattan, headed north along what is now the Bowery past what is now Union Square, then roughly followed the present Park Avenue. It continued north past Harlem, crossed over to the mainland at Kingsbridge (near the present Broadway and 228th Street), and cut diagonally from southwest to northeast through the Bronx. Although the Boston Post Road eventually became engulfed by the growing metropolis, vestiges remain in the form of the Bowery in Manhattan, Boston Road in the Bronx, and U.S. Highway 1 in New England.

Stewart H. Holbrook: *The Old Post Road* (New York: McGraw–Hill, 1962)

For illustration see West farms.

Robert Sanger Steel

botanical gardens. The Elgin Botanic Garden in New York City was established in 1801 by David Hosack, a professor of botany and materia medica at Columbia College, to provide plant materials for study by medical students. The first public botanical garden in the United States, it covered twenty acres (eight hectares) of land then considered remote from the center of the city and later occupied by Rockefeller Center. Hosack's own finances were insufficient to continue maintaining the garden, and in 1810 he sold it at a loss to the state; the land was granted in 1814 to Columbia College and was held by Columbia University until 1985. John Torrey (1796–1873), a pupil of Hosack, in 1817 published a catalogue of plants growing within thirty miles (forty-eight kilometers) of the city; his work established the approach to fieldwork that distinguished botanists in New York City in the nineteenth century. In 1856 Torrey became a trustee of Columbia, where he was given a house in exchange for opening his library and herbarium to the university. By 1867 he had formed the Torrey Botanical Club, which in 1870 began publishing the first American periodical on botany, the *Bulletin of the Torrey Botanical Club.* Members of the club, notably Nathaniel Lord Britton (1859–1934), a professor of botany at Columbia, and his wife, Elizabeth Knight Britton (1858–1934), an expert on lichens, campaigned for the establishment of a major American botanical garden, and on 28 April 1891 the New York Botanical Garden was created by an act of the state legislature. The site chosen was at the northern end of Bronx Park along East Fordham Road and designed by a committee on plans that included Calvert Vaux and Calvert Parsons Jr. Some earlier structures from the Lorillard estate were retained, including a stone snuff mill, built on the present site in 1840. The city would not aid the establishment of the garden before sufficient funds were raised from private sources: this was accomplished through the public philanthropy of such businessmen as Cornelius Vanderbilt, Andrew Carnegie, and J. P. Morgan, all of whom later served on the board of managers. In 1896 Nathaniel Britton became the first director of the garden; he soon began a program of scientific publication and initiated a research program in plant exploration and field collection that emphasized systematic botany and taxonomy. He consolidated the libraries and herbaria of Hosack and Torrey to form the research collections of the New York Botanical Garden, and in 1900 organized public lectures, the beginning of an education program that came to include botanical and horticultural education at all levels, from children's gardening classes to advanced degree programs. Tropical and economic plants were first housed indoors at the garden in 1902, in a conservatory modeled after the Palm House at the Royal Botanic Gardens in Kew, England, and built of glass and iron by Lord and Burnham. A rose garden designed by the noted landscape gardener Beatrix Farrand was begun in 1916 and became an important specialty garden. T. H. Everett by 1932 established a formal program for the training of gardeners, which was continued by the School of Horticulture. The rock garden was initially designed in 1934 by Everett. The Institute for Economic Botany was set up in 1981 to apply botanical science to ecological problems, as was the Institute for Ecosystems Studies (now a separate institution based in Millbrook, New York).

Enid A. Haupt Conservatory, New York Botanical Garden

The Brooklyn Botanic Garden, originally

part of the Brooklyn Institute of Arts and Sciences, was built in 1910 next to the Brooklyn Museum along Washington and Flatbush avenues, on rough meadow land previously used by the parks department as an ash dump. Under its first director, C. Stuart Gager (1872–1943), the garden became known for its emphasis on plant physiology and genetics and for its efforts in public education: the world's first children's gardening program was established there in 1914. Gager oversaw the making of a Japanese hill-and-pond garden that incorporated four styles (designed by Takeo Shiota in 1915), the Cranford Memorial Rose Garden (opened in June 1927), and the grove collection of flowering Japanese cherry trees. A popular series of handbooks began publication in 1945. The Steinhardt Conservatory (completed in 1988) was designed by Davis, Brooks and Associates to house the Trail of Evolution and several habitat groups, as well as the outstanding bonsai collections begun in 1925.

The Queens Botanic Garden was initially a horticultural display called "Gardens on Parade," built on five acres (two hectares) on a reclaimed ash dump for the World's Fair of 1939–40. It was enlarged in 1941 to twenty-six acres (eleven hectares) and managed by the Queens Botanical Garden Society as a public garden. When this land was needed for the World's Fair of 1964–65 the garden was moved to a site adjoining Flushing Meadow Park. In 1991 its specialty gardens included a rose garden, a bird garden, and a Victorian wedding garden. Flushing was the site of the Prince family nurseries, the first commercial nursery in America (from 1737 to the 1870s).

The Staten Island Arboretum (later the Staten Island Botanic Garden) was founded in 1960 and moved to Snug Harbor Cultural Center in 1977. Designed to match its setting, a community established in 1831 along Richmond Terrace for retired seamen, it lies on eighty acres (thirty-two hectares) and includes Victorian plantings, a perennial border, a butterfly garden, and special collections of Siberian iris, orchids, and rhododendrons.

Edward Hyams: *Great Botanical Gardens of the World* (New York: Macmillan, 1969)

See also HORTICULTURE.

Bernadette G. Callery

Boucicault, Dion (*b* Dublin, 26 Dec 1820; *d* New York City, 18 Sept 1890). Actor and playwright. After achieving success in London he arrived in New York City in 1853 and found work writing and acting for Lester Wallack and Laura Keene. He made his local acting début on 10 November 1854 and on 8 December 1857 at Wallack's produced his first play, *The Poor of New York*, which was immediately successful. Known for melodrama, comedy, and sensational special effects, his later works were also tremendously popular, among them *The Octoroon* (1857) and *The Colleen Bawn* (1860), which was his first play on an Irish theme and one that was enthusiastically received by Irish audiences in the city. *The Shaughraun* (1874) ran for four months at Wallack's and earned gross receipts of $220,000. Boucicault produced thirty-three plays in New York City. He is buried in Mount Hope Cemetery.

Townsend Walsh: *The Career of Dion Boucicault* (New York: Dunlap Society, 1915)
Robert G. Hogan: *Dion Boucicault* (Boston: Twayne, 1969)
Richard Fawkes: *Dion Boucicault: A Biography* (London: Quartet, 1979)

Marion R. Casey

Boudin, Leonard (B.) (*b* Brooklyn, 20 July 1912; *d* New York City, 24 Nov 1989). Lawyer. He graduated from St. John's Law School in 1936 and practiced labor law before forming a partnership in the late 1940s with Victor Rabinowitz. In 1958 he won the case of *Kent v. Dulles*, in which the U.S. Supreme Court ruled that the U.S. Department of State could not refuse to issue passports for political reasons. During the 1960s he represented several clients in cases related to the Vietnam War, among them Julian Bond, a young state legislator from Georgia denied his seat for opposing the war, Benjamin Spock, who with others was charged with conspiracy to violate the Selective Service Act, and Daniel Ellsberg, charged with disclosing the Pentagon Papers, a classified account of the war.

Obituary, *New York Times*, 26 Nov 1989

Jonathan D. Bloom

Bourne, Randolph (Silliman) (*b* Bloomfield, N.J., 30 May 1886; *d* New York City, 23 Dec 1918). Critic. At Columbia University (graduated 1913) he came under the influence of John Dewey, Franz Boas, and Charles Beard. Deformed by spinal tuberculosis, he wrote anonymously of his disability in the *Atlantic*. In *Youth and Life* (1913) he argued for an American cultural revolution and a regenerated American democracy. In his writings Bourne drew a distinction between a "beloved community" arrived at through democratic association and the coercive cohesion of the nation state. At the end of his life he was developing ideas about the value of intellectuals as an oppositional force.

Alexander Bloom

Bowery. A street in lower Manhattan that stretches for about one mile (1.6 kilometers) from Chatham Square to Cooper Square. Following the route of an Indian path from the southern tip of the island to Harlem, it derives its name from *bowerij*, the Dutch word for farm, because in the seventeenth century it was a farming area north of the city. Governor Peter Stuyvesant bought much of the land there in 1651. The Bowery remained on the outer fringe of the city until about 1800, and it was most important as part of the main route to Boston. As the city's exploding population moved northward the Bowery became broad and elegant, the home of such diverse personages as the philanthropist Peter Cooper and the songwriter Stephen Foster. It was especially important for entertainment, and its sidewalks were lined with taverns, oyster bars, and minstrel theaters. The largest auditorium on the continent, the Great Bowery Theater, was dedicated on 23 October 1826. Damaged and rebuilt on several occasions as a result of disastrous fires, it was one of several theaters in the area that dominated the theatrical life of the city between 1850 and 1875. After the Civil War the Bowery ceased to compete with Broadway as a commercial thoroughfare and with 5th Avenue as an elegant residential address. Its specialty became nickel museums featuring mermaids, snakes, sword swallowers, lions, dwarfs, and women in various states of undress. At the same time that the Bowery became more closely associated with cheap entertainment it was dealt a blow by the transportation system from which it never recovered, when the 3rd Avenue elevated line was placed over it. After 26 August 1878 little steam engines showered pedestrians below with oil drippings and hot coals. Middle-class men and women could easily avoid such nuisances by walking along other streets, such as Broadway, that were not degraded by the ugly elevated lines. Meanwhile the Bowery became synonymous with homeless derelicts and tramps. It was the site of cheap lodging houses, missions, and late-night saloons, and its brothels were so numerous that it became a veritable magnet for visiting sailors. In 1892 the Bowery was the butt of a popular song by Charles M. Hoyt:

> The Bowery, the Bowery!
> They say such things and they do such things
> On the Bowery, the Bowery!
> I'll never go there any more!

Early in the twentieth century the Bowery was even more infamous as a place of squalor, alcoholism, and wretchedness. Even prostitutes gravitated to other neighborhoods. In 1907 the street had 115 clothing stores for men, none for women. In the same year the nightly population of the "flop houses," missions, and hotels on the Bowery was estimated at 25,000. No other skid row in the United States attracted so many vagrants or so much notoriety. At the same time many stores along the street developed successful specialties in lighting fixtures and secondhand restaurant equipment.

After 1970 the homeless population of the Bowery sharply declined, as New York City dispersed its indigent to other neighborhoods. Efforts at gentrification also had some effect, and in the mid 1990s the street seemed almost empty, with scarcely a vagrant in sight. But the Bowery seemed likely to remain the sanctuary

Reginald Marsh, Tattoo–Shave–Haircut *(1932). Etching. Collection of the Whitney Museum of American Art*

for the forgotten in American society, in reputation if not in fact. Detractors should remember that behind its sullied face was a benevolent character often overlooked.

Kenneth T. Jackson

Bowery Bay Beach. Original name of NORTH BEACH.

Bowery Savings Bank. Savings bank, formed on 2 June 1834 by a group of local businessmen that included Hamilton Fish (1808–93), Peter C. Stuyvesant (1778–1847), and Anson G. Phelps (1781–1853). It initially attracted depositors of low and middle income and occupied rent-free quarters in the Butchers' and Drovers' Bank (later a rival) on Bowery Street. Within two years the bank bought a building on 130 Bowery Street that wrapped around the Butchers' and Drovers' Bank and had entrances on Bowery and Grand streets; this was redesigned in 1894 by the firm of McKim, Mead and White and declared a city landmark in 1966. Despite several financial panics the bank expanded steadily and became one of the city's leading banks by 1860, when it had almost 42,000 depositors and assets of more than $10 million; at the turn of the century its assets reached $75 million. An important lender of home mortgages, the bank also granted loans for the construction of subways and a number of large buildings in the city. It merged with the Universal Savings Bank in 1920 and in the following year built executive offices on 42nd Street near Park Avenue (a branch was moved into the building at 130 Bowery Street). A branch opened at 34th Street and 5th Avenue in 1931, the first of many during the following decades. The bank had assets of more than $1000 million in 1950 and funded such projects as Fordham Plaza, housing sponsored by the Bedford Stuyvesant Restoration Corporation, the Albee Square Shopping Mall, many apartment buildings and offices, and the renovation of Times Square. In 1990 the Bowery Savings Bank had twenty branches and more than $6000 million in assets. It was acquired in 1992 by Home Savings of America.

Oscar Schisgall: *The Bowery Savings Bank of New York: A Social and Financial History of the Bowery Savings Bank* (New York: American Management Association, 1984)

James Bradley

Bowery Theatre. Theater in Manhattan, opened in 1826 at the corner of Canal Street and the Bowery. In its early years it was in competition with the Park Theatre on Park Row and offered a similar repertory, but by the 1830s it specialized in the melodrama and spectacle sought after by the residents of its immigrant neighborhood; foreign-language productions were mounted from 1879. The theater burned in 1828, 1830, 1836, 1838, and 1845 and was rebuilt each time. It burned for the last time in 1929.

Don B. Wilmeth

Bowes, Edward (*b* San Francisco, 14 June 1874; *d* Rumson, N.J., 13 June 1946). Radio entertainer and real-estate entrepreneur. Brought up in San Francisco, he went to work at an early age to help support his widowed mother and his sisters. He did well in real estate and the earthquake of 1906 proved only a temporary setback. After moving to New York City in 1918 he bought and built several theaters including the Capitol, which he promoted on the radio. By 1935 he was the host of "Major Bowes' Amateur Hour," broadcast first by the National Broadcasting Company and then by the Columbia Broadcasting System (his military title was from a reserve commission given to him as an entertainment specialist during the First World War). The program's remarkable popularity led to road shows, a magazine, a staff of sixty-five, and great wealth, which he used to support his interests in sailing, book and wine collecting, and philanthropy. Bowes is buried in Sleepy Hollow Cemetery in Tarrytown, New York.

James E. Mooney

Bowling Green. Public park in Manhattan, the oldest existing one in New York City. Situated opposite the old fort at the foot of Broadway, it was a parade and cattle market during the seventeenth century and the early eighteenth. The local government laid out a bowling green in 1733 and offered it for rent to three local residents for one peppercorn a year. The British in 1770 erected a gilded statue of George III, which was toppled by irate citizens in 1776. Elegant townhouses were built around the park, and during the early nineteenth century the park was largely the private domain of their occupants. The public did not gain full access to the park until about 1850, when the northward movement of residential Manhattan had led to the conversion of the townhouses to shipping offices. Eventually such nonresidential structures as the Produce Exchange and the U.S. Custom House replaced the townhouses, and the park suffered from neglect until the mid 1970s, when it was restored by the city.

Spencer Trask: *Bowling Green* (New York: G. P. Putnam's Sons, 1898)
Margaret Latimer: "A Stroll through Old New York," *The Department of Cultural Affairs [and Other Institutions and Agencies] Invite You to Celebrate July 4th in Old New York* (New York: Department of Cultural Affairs, n.d. [?1973])

Margaret Latimer

Bowman, Patricia (*b* Washington, 12 Dec 1904). Dancer and teacher. She moved to

*Bowling Green at Broadway, ca 1925–30, flanked by the Standard Office Building (*right*) and the Cunard Building (*left*)*

New York City in 1919 to study ballet with Michel Fokine and made her début on Broadway in George White's *Scandals* of 1919. During the next thirty years she danced in Broadway musicals, vaudeville, and operetta. She also appeared at the Roxy Theatre and at Radio City Music Hall and was a founding member of Ballet Theatre. Bowman made her final appearance in the city in 1955 in *Les Sylphides* at the Metropolitan Opera House.

Walter Ware: *Ballet Is Magic: A Triple Monograph: Harriet Hoctor, Paul Haakon, Patricia Bowman* (New York: Ihra, 1936)

Barbara Barker

Bowne, John (*b* Matlock, England, 1628; *d* ?Flushing, 1695). Religious dissenter. Dissatisfied with the Congregational town church in Boston, he moved from New England to Flushing, where in 1657 he converted to Quakerism. In 1662 he was arrested, imprisoned, and fined for holding Quaker meetings in his home. He sought an appeal from the directors of the Dutch West India Company, who instructed Governor Peter Stuyvesant not to persecute dissenters as long as they were not socially disruptive. His house at Bowne Street and 37th Avenue in Flushing still stands.

Arthur J. Worrall

Bowne and Company. Firm of stationers and printers. Formed in 1775 at what is now 149 Pearl Street in Manhattan by Robert Bowne, it is one of the oldest continuously operating businesses in the United States. Initially it sold various goods that included stationery, cloth, cutlery, and furs. John Jacob Astor was an employee before he began his own fur-trading business. By the late 1820s the firm had narrowed its focus to stationery and commercial printing; later it became a leading financial printer. Bowne and Company became publicly owned in 1968 and is traded on the New York Stock Exchange. Its principal location is 345 Hudson Street, and there is also a retail branch at the South Street Seaport.

Bowne and Co., 1775–1952 (New York: Bowne and Company, 1952)

Nineteenth-century Job Printing Display: The Poster (New York: Bowne and Company, 1991)

Owen D. Gutfreund

Bowne House. Historic house in Queens. It was built in 1661 by John Bowne and stands at Bowne Street and 37th Avenue in Flushing. The house is a wood-frame English colonial saltbox, notable for its steeply pitched roof with three dormers. It was altered and expanded several times in the late seventeenth century and the early eighteenth. Nine generations of Bowne's descendants lived in the house until 1945, when the Bowne Historical Society assumed control of it. The house has original architectural details as well as seventeenth- and eighteenth-century documents, furniture, and artifacts that belonged to the family.

Thomas Allen Glenn: *Some Colonial Mansions and Those Who Lived in Them* (Philadelphia: H. T. Coates, 1898–1900)

Trebor Haynes: *Bowne House: A Shrine to Religious Freedom* (New York: Flushing Savings Bank, n.d. [?1952])

Jonathan Kuhn

boxing. The first noted American fighter was a former slave from Staten Island, Bill Richmond (*b* 1763), who had a distinguished career in England, and the first recognized boxing match in the United States was that between Jacob Hyer and Tom Bealey in New York City in 1816. The city was the national center of boxing when the sport became popular in the 1840s, albeit illegally. Combatants were mainly Irish and English professionals or tough Americans associated with rival ethnic and political gangs. The first national championship was won by Tom Hyer of New York City (son of Jacob Hyer) over Yankee Sullivan in 1849. Sullivan claimed the title after Hyer's retirement but lost it to John Morrissey of New York City in thirty-seven rounds in 1853. The sport declined in the 1860s and had little following. Matches were either impromptu or arranged in sporting taverns like Harry Hill's Dance Hall. The world heavyweight champion John L. Sullivan defended his title in New York City in 1883, but because of interference by the police there were no important matches from 1885 until the early 1890s, when boxing was revived at Coney Island under the protection of political bosses. In 1896 the state legislature liberalized the restrictions on boxing by passing the Horton Act, and New York City again became the national boxing capital. Notable bouts included Jim Jeffries's defeat in twenty-two rounds of James J. Corbett for the world heavyweight championship on 11 May 1900. The Horton Act was repealed in the same year, and from that time bouts were held in

George Bellows, Dempsey and Firpo *(1924). Oil on canvas.*
Collection of the Whitney Museum of American Art. Gift of Gertrude Vanderbilt Whitney

secret on barges, in the backrooms of saloons, or at ostensibly private clubs where restrictions on boxing went unenforced. In 1911 the state legislature, controlled by the Democrats, passed the Frawley Act, which permitted ten-round "no decision" bouts under the supervision of an athletic commission. Venues ranged from small neighborhood firetraps like the Sharkey Athletic Club to Madison Square Garden and Ebbets Field. In 1913 alone there were forty-nine licensed clubs. The Frawley Act was repealed in 1917 by Republican reformers opposed to corruption, violence, and socially unredeeming sports.

Boxing under a supervisory athletic commission was reestablished in 1920 by the Walker Act. Madison Square Garden became the leading venue for boxing in the nation, and major bouts were important social affairs. Control of the ring passed from politicians to members of organized crime, like Waxey Gordon, Dutch Schultz, and Owney Madden. Poor neighborhoods continued to produce a disproportionate share of fighters, including the Irish heavyweight champions Gene Tunney (1926–29) and Jimmy Braddock (1935–37). Among the many famous bouts of the interwar years were several for the heavyweight championship, including victories by Jack Dempsey over Luis Firpo on 14 September 1923 (drawing 82,000 spectators at the Polo Grounds), by Joe Louis over Max Schmeling on 19 June 1936, in 2:04 of the first round (drawing 75,000 at Yankee Stadium), and by Louis over Billy Conn on 18 June 1941 (drawing 54,487 at the Polo Grounds). Louis was associated with the nation's dominant promoter, Mike Jacobs, who staged three eighths of all championships in the United States between 1937 and 1949. After Jacobs retired, the main promoter was the International Boxing Club: run by James Norris and closely tied to the organized-crime figure Frankie Carbo, it arranged four fifths of all championship fights from 1949 to 1953. Prominent local fighters during these years included the middleweight champions Rocky Graziano (1947–48) and Jake La Motta (1949–51), who deliberately lost a fight to gain a chance at the title. The enormously popular sport declined in the late 1950s from overexposure on television (audience shares fell from 31 percent to 10.6 percent), investigations of its corruption, the death of fighters on television (such as that of Benny Paret at the hands of Emile Griffith in a fight for the welterweight championship on 26 March 1962), and competition from other sports. In 1956 Floyd Patterson, a native of New York City, won the world heavyweight championship at the age of twenty-one; he held it for three years, until being knocked out in an upset by Ingemar Johansson at Yankee Stadium. Only 18,215 attended the fight and net receipts were only $407,000, but media income, which included closed-circuit television, exceeded $900,000. Patterson in 1960 became the first heavyweight to regain the title, which he lost again in 1962 to Sonny Liston. On 8 March 1971 the city was the site of a historic fight between Joe Frazier and Muhammad Ali at Madison Square Garden, before 29,445 spectators and a closed-circuit audience of 1.3 million. The fight was advertised as the only one ever held between two undefeated heavyweights, each of whom had a legitimate claim to the world championship. Frazier won by a unanimous decision in what is regarded as the third-greatest fight in history. In 1987 Mike Tyson, originally from Brooklyn, became the first world heavyweight champion from New York City in a quarter-century; in 1990 he lost the title, which in the following years was held by two more fighters from Brooklyn, Riddick Bowe (1992–93) and Michael Moorer (1994).

By this time New York City was no longer the site of major bouts. There were virtually no neighborhood gymnasiums for novices to learn their craft, and the emergence of cable and pay-for-view television lessened the importance of gate receipts for promoters. Most glamorous fights were staged in Las Vegas and Atlantic City, New Jersey, by gambling casinos. In 1993 Madison Square Garden ended its role as a venue for boxing.

Steven A. Riess: "In the Ring and Out: Professional Boxing in New York, 1896–1920," *Sport in America: New Historical Perspectives*, ed. Donald Spivey (Westport, Conn.: Greenwood, 1985), 95–128

Melvin L. Adelman: *A Sporting Time: New York City and the Rise of Modern Athletics, 1820–1870* (Urbana: University of Illinois Press, 1986)

Steven A. Riess: *City Games: The Evolution of American Urban Society and the Rise of Sports* (Urbana: University of Illinois Press, 1989)

Steven A. Riess

Boys and Girls Clubs of America. Nonprofit organization formed in 1860 in Hartford, Connecticut, as the Boys' Club Federation of America. It moved successively to Boston and in 1930 to New York City, where it occupied offices near Grand Central Terminal. Herbert Hoover was its chairman from 1936 until his death in 1964. In 1960 the organization dedicated a national headquarters at 771 1st Avenue, across the street from the United Nations. The headquarters were moved out of New York City in March 1994, but twelve local clubs in the city remained.

James Bradley

Boys and Girls High School. Secondary school opened in 1878 as the Central Grammar School at Court and Livingston streets in Brooklyn; it is the oldest high school in New York City that began as a public school. The girls' division moved in 1886 to a new building designed by James W. Naughton at Nostrand Avenue between Macon and Halsey streets, and in 1891 the two divisions were formally established as separate institutions: Boys High School and Girls High School. Boys High School moved in the following year to a new building designed by Naughton in the Romanesque Revival style on Madison Street between Marcy and Putnam avenues. Girls High School closed in 1964. In 1976 Boys High

School moved to 1700 Fulton Street, began admitting girls, and was again named Boys and Girls High School; its former building was designated a city landmark in 1975 and now houses the Street Academy, an alternative high school. In 1991 Boys and Girls High School had 3409 students. Well-known alumni of Boys High School include Aaron Copland, Isaac Asimov, and Norman Mailer; alumnae of Girls High School include Lena Horne and Shirley Chisholm.

Erica Judge

Boys' Club of New York. Organization founded in 1876 by Edward H. Harriman, a Wall Street tycoon and railroad magnate who gave the organization about $500,000 over the next thirty-three years. It began operations in the basement of the Wilson Mission School at Avenue A and 8th Street near Tompkins Square in lower Manhattan. From the beginning the club welcomed any boy between the ages of six and seventeen and sought especially to serve the needs of the immigrant poor. In 1901 it moved to a new six-story brick and sandstone building at Avenue A and 10th Street. A seven-story addition, replete with an indoor pool, a gymnasium, and a library, opened in 1917. In 1927 the club added a branch at 321 East 111th Street in Jefferson Park, a heavily Italian section of East Harlem. E. Roland Harriman, son of the founder, became president in 1934 at the age of thirty-eight. He served the club for fifty-seven years, successively as a trustee, president, and chairman. The building at Tompkins Square was renamed the Harriman clubhouse in 1988. By the mid 1990s the organization had tens of thousands of alumni throughout the United States.

Sharon Zane: *The Boys' Club of New York: A History* (New York: Boys' Club, 1990)

Kenneth T. Jackson

Boys' High School. Original name of DE WITT CLINTON HIGH SCHOOL.

Brace, Charles Loring (*b* Litchfield, Conn., 19 June 1826; *d* Switzerland, 11 Aug 1890). Philanthropist. He graduated from Yale University in 1846 and later studied theology at the Yale Divinity School and Union Theological Seminary. In the early 1850s he began working with homeless, unschooled, immigrant boys in New York City. With the assistance of several prominent New Yorkers he formed the Children's Aid Society in 1853, of which he was the executive officer for the next thirty-seven years. A staunch believer in self-help, he opposed all charitable aid that might encourage dependence. He acquired an international reputation as a practitioner of the "new philanthropy" by explaining the basic principles of the society and movingly describing its assistance to poor children in books and articles such as *The Dangerous Classes of New York and Twenty Years' Work among Them* (1872). At his death his son Charles Loring Brace Jr. (1855–1938) succeeded him as executive secretary of the society. His memoir *The Life of Charles Loring Brace, Chiefly Told in His Own Letters, Edited by His Daughter* was published in 1894.

Jane Allen

Brady, Diamond Jim [James Buchanan] (*b* New York City, 12 Aug 1856; *d* Atlantic City, N.J., 13 April 1917). Businessman. The son of a saloon keeper on the West Side, he was born at 90 West Street and lived there until the age of eleven. After working as a bellboy and messenger and for the New York Central Railroad he began selling portable rail-cutting saws in 1879, beginning a successful career as a salesman of railroad equipment during which he earned as much as $1 million a year. He frequented well-known restaurants, nightclubs, and theaters, and became known for his voracious appetite, lavish attire (he owned thirty complete sets of jewelry with a total value of more than $1 million), sweet and sympathetic nature, willingness to spend money on himself and others, and partiality toward attractive women. His friendship with Lillian Russell was the subject of much speculation. From about 1900 Brady's home was at 7 West 86th Street.

Parker Morrell: *Diamond Jim: The Life and Times of James Buchanan Brady* (New York: Simon and Schuster, 1934)

George A. Thompson, Jr.

Brady, Mathew B. (*b* Warren County, N.Y., *ca* 1823; *d* New York City, 15 Jan 1896). Photographer. He mastered the daguerreotype process from the photographic pioneer Samuel F. B. Morse and foresaw a role for photography in preserving historical record. In 1844 he opened the Daguerrian Miniature Gallery, a studio and portrait gallery on Broadway at Fulton Street. This proved successful both artistically and commercially, and from 1845 to 1850 he photographed the most important figures of his time. *A Gallery of Illustrious Americans* (1850), published with the lithographer Francis D'Avignon, includes portraits from Brady's daguerreotypes of Andrew Jackson, Daniel Webster, and John J. Audubon. In 1853 Brady built a larger and more lavish studio at 359 Broadway, near Franklin Street. A third studio stood at 643 Broadway, and his last and most lavish studio opened in the summer of 1860 at 785 Broadway, at 10th Street. His profits rose as thousands of customers returned to be photographed with the new collodian wet-plate process, which allowed multiple prints from a single negative. Brady seldom operated the camera himself and instead employed "operators," many of whom later established their own careers as photographers, including Timothy O'Sullivan (*b ca* 1840; *d* 1882) and Alexander Gardner (1821–82). He was forced to declare bankruptcy in 1871 after incurring debts from his best-known and most ambitious project, the documentation of the Civil War. He never regained the popularity he had enjoyed earlier but remained one of the most influential American photographers of the nineteenth century. His last residence was at 127 East 10th Street.

James D. Horan: *Mathew Brady: Historian with a Camera* (New York: Crown, 1955)
Roy Meredith: *Mathew Brady's Portrait of an Era* (New York: W. W. Norton, 1982)

Dale L. Neighbors

Brady, William V(ermilye) (*b* New York City, 1811; *d* New York City, 31 March 1870). Mayor. A fiscally conservative Whig, he served as mayor of New York City from 1847 to 1848. During his tenure his proposal to eliminate the newly created police department was rejected by the Common Council. He later served as the city's postmaster.

Howard Kaplan

Brearley School. Private girls' secondary school opened in 1884 in Manhattan by Samuel Brearly Jr., who had intended to teach at a boys' school but was persuaded by Mrs. Joseph H. Choate to remedy the shortage of good schools for young women. To fund its operations he borrowed several thousand dollars from a classmate at Harvard, Charles Bonaparte (a great-nephew of Napoleon). The school was so successful that by the second year it had to turn away students. After occupying many locations Brearley moved to 610 East 83rd Street in 1930.

Richard Schwartz

Breezy Point. Neighborhood in southwestern Queens, lying at the western tip of the Rockaway Peninsula; it includes Rockaway Point and Roxbury. The area remained undeveloped until the early twentieth century, when the Rockaway Point Company rented tent sites for about $20 a summer to visitors, most of whom were Irish. By the 1920s a colony of residents owned bungalows on rented land. In 1961 the firm of Northern Properties bought for $17.5 million all the land west of Jacob Riis Park (except Fort Tilden) to erect a high-rise development for a population of 220,000. Residents formed the Breezy Point Cooperative and paid $11.5 million for the land. Construction began on two fourteen-story apartment buildings but ceased when the city announced plans to acquire the peninsula for parkland in 1963; the unfinished apartments were demolished in 1978. The city's plans to condemn the entire neighborhood were opposed with particular vehemence by residents who had taken pains to make their cottages habitable year round, and a compromise permitted all to remain: land owned by the city was incorporated into the Gateway National Recreation Area in 1972, and property of the Breezy Point Cooperative was excluded from it. In the mid 1990s the community had about 2800 houses, with an estimated population of five thousand year round and twelve thousand during the summer.

Jeffrey A. Kroessler

Bretons. The Bretons began emigrating to the United States from Brittany in the early twentieth century. They were distinguished from other French citizens by their Celtic origin, and about 40 percent of those who emigrated spoke a Celtic language closely related to Welsh. Although most entered the United States through the Port of New York and settled in central New Jersey, during the late 1940s New York City became the center of Breton–American life. Soon after their arrival Bretons were widely distributed in the work force: of the many types of businesses they owned and managed their crêpe restaurants were particularly well known. In New York City Bretons formed a sporting association, the Stade Breton, and the Breton Association of the United States, a sponsor of cultural and social events. In the mid 1990s an estimated ninety thousand Breton emigrants and their descendants lived in New York City.

Paul Robert Magocsi

Brevoort, James Renwick (*b* Yonkers, N.Y., 20 July 1832; *d* Yonkers, 15 Dec 1918). Landscape painter. He grew up in Williamsbridge and Fordham and in 1850 began to study architecture, working as an assistant to his cousin James Renwick Jr., whom he helped to prepare designs for St. Patrick's Cathedral. In 1854 he earned a certificate in architecture from the School of Design at New York University, and he soon enrolled at the National Academy of Design, where he mounted exhibitions from 1856 to 1901. His work was also shown at the Brooklyn Art Association between 1861 and 1881. He lived on 10th Street from 1858 to 1861 and at 212 5th Avenue from 1863 to 1872. During the 1870s and 1880s he often traveled and worked in Europe, primarily in England, Italy, and the Netherlands; he returned to Yonkers in 1890, built a house at 390 North Broadway, and between 1898 and 1906 also maintained a residence at 52 East 23rd Street. Brevoort's paintings are leading examples of a phase in American landscape painting known as "Native Impressionism" and "American Luminism."

Sutherland McColley, comp.: *The Works of James Renwick Brevoort, 1832–1918: American Landscape Painter* (Yonkers, N.Y.: Hudson River Museum, 1972) [exhibition catalogue]

Allen J. Share

brewing and distilling. Brewing was a small-scale industry in New York City during the seventeenth century. English techniques and a top-floating yeast were used to produce beer, ale, and porter, which did not require cooling, were sold in local markets, and were consumed at warm temperatures. Distilling was a separate undertaking confined mostly to the production of rum, using sugar cane transported from the West Indies by colonial merchants. By 1770 there were four distilleries in Manhattan and twelve others nearby that produced rum for sale locally and abroad. When whiskey displaced rum as the most popular liquor during the early nineteenth century, the distilling industry gradually moved west to Peoria, Illinois. Both industries were transformed by industrial technology. Spirits were bought by wholesale firms in the city that colored, flavored, and bottled them and sent them to retailers, often saloons. German brewers who settled in the city during the 1840s introduced yeasts that required cool temperatures and produced "lager," or stored beer, which became especially popular in the summer heat. Brewing flourished for a time after water of good quality became widely available. The Hell Gate Brewery, opened by the German immigrant George Ehret in 1866, was the country's largest in 1877, and that of Jacob Ruppert was the eighth-largest. In 1879 the number of breweries reached seventy-eight in Manhattan and forty-three in Brooklyn; it declined after 1880, when cheap rail transportation and mechanical refrigeration allowed entrepreneurs in Milwaukee, St. Louis, and Cincinnati to make inroads into local markets. Successful breweries made larger investments in production and distribution facilities, and small firms disappeared. In 1895 the Hell Gate Brewery was the country's fourth-largest, Ruppert the twelfth-largest. By 1910 there were only thirty-nine breweries in the city; they usually sold their beverages in kegs through saloons under their control. Formed by western suppliers in 1899, the Distilling Company of America made its headquarters in New York City and sought unsuccessfully to dominate the spirits trade. It was reorganized as National Distillers Products in 1932.

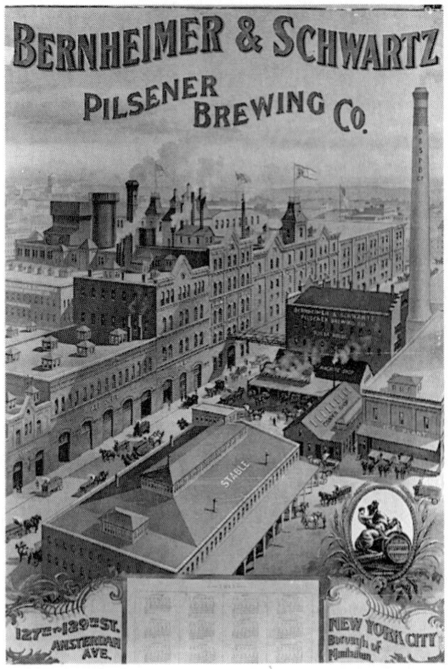

Advertisement for Bernheimer and Schwartz Pilsner Brewing Company, 1911

Under the Eighteenth Amendment the manufacture, transportation, and sale of alcoholic beverages became forbidden in 1920. Some breweries declared bankruptcy, while others reorganized to make such products as soft drinks and ice cream. Many New Yorkers defied Prohibition, and illegal factories opened locally to supply their needs. Such efforts became known nationally through news media based in the city, and led much of the country to conclude that Prohibition had failed to reduce liquor consumption effectively. After the Eighteenth Amendment was repealed in 1933 twenty-three of the city's brewers resumed business, most aiming their products only at the large local market. Stores displaced saloons as the most important retail outlets, and brewers expanded their sales of bottled beer and during the 1930s introduced canned beer. Only the firm of F and M Schaefer Brewing sought to compete in national markets. After 1937 the firm of Seagram's had its headquarters in the city and was the world's largest distiller. National Distillers Products became National Distillers and Chemical after 1948 and was one of four large companies that dominated the American distilling industry to the end of the 1960s. Between the late 1940s and the mid 1970s brewing in the city declined, as small firms were forced out of business by large ones with national distribution. The country's four largest firms (none in the city) increased their share of the national market from 21 percent to 59 percent. By 1950 only five local firms brewed beer, and brewers blamed the city's high electricity and water rates for their inability to compete. The country's second-largest brewer, Joseph Schlitz, bought the Hell Gate Brewery in 1949 and maintained operations there until 1973, when it withdrew to escape the city's high labor costs and invest in newer facilities. The city's last brewery closed in 1976. Expensive beers were produced in small quantities for exclusive markets by "micro-breweries" that opened during the 1980s. In 1987 National Distillers and Chemical sold its liquor division to American Brands.

Stanley Wade Baron: *Brewed in America: A History of Beer and Ale in the United States* (Boston: Little, Brown, 1962)

K. Austin Kerr

Briarwood. Neighborhood in east central Queens (1980 pop. 25,800), bounded to the north by Union Turnpike, to the east by Parsons Boulevard, to the south by Hillside Avenue, and to the west by the Van Wyck Expressway. The area was first developed about 1905 by Herbert A. O'Brien; the name was suggested by his wife, Adeline, for the thick woods and briars covering the land. The Briarwood Land Company later declared bankruptcy and the area remained largely undeveloped until the mid 1920s, when it was divided into lots that were sold at auction. With the New York Life Insurance Company the United Nations built Parkway Village in 1947 to provide housing for its staff members. The development became a cooperative in 1983 and had residents of many nationalities, although by this time few worked for the United Nations. Several apartment buildings rise above the surrounding one- and two-family houses; many of the streets are winding. Well-known residents have included the diplomat Ralph Bunche, the feminist and social activist Betty Friedan, and the civil rights leader Roy Wilkins.

Plan for New York City, 1969: A Proposal, vol. 5 (Cambridge: MIT Press, 1969)

Patricia A. Doyal

Brice, Fanny [Borach, Fannie] (*b* New York City, 29 Oct 1891; *d* Los Angeles, 29 May 1951). Comedian. She became known for performing songs and parodies of the arts and society in such revues on Broadway as Florenz Ziegfeld's *Follies* between 1910 and 1920. She lived from 1914 to 1918 at 8 West 58th Street and from 1918 to 1921 at 230 Central Park West. In the early 1920s she bought a house at 306 West 76th Street, where she lived with Nicky Arnstein until their divorce in 1927, and she then had an apartment at 15 East 69th Street (now the Westbury Hotel) and lived there with Billy Rose after they were married in February 1929. She became well known in Rose's musical revues *Sweet and Low* (1930) and *Crazy Quilt* (1931). During the 1930s and 1940s she performed as "Baby Snooks" on the radio. Brice was the subject of the musical *Funny Girl* (1964, film version 1968) and the motion picture *Funny Lady* (1975). She was the first female Yiddish comedian to work successfully in musical comedy and radio in the commercial mainstream.

Barbara Wallace Grossman: *Funny Woman: The Life and Times of Fanny Brice* (Bloomington: Indiana University Press, 1991)

Barbara Cohen-Stratyner

Brick Presbyterian Church. Church formed as the First Presbyterian Church by John Rodgers in 1768. It occupied a building erected on Beekman Street in Manhattan and remained under Rodgers's ministry until 1809, when it took its current name. Under the pastorate of Gardner Spring from 1810 to 1873 the church moved to 5th Avenue and 37th Street (1858), and in 1937 it moved to Park Avenue and 85th Street before Paul Austin Wolfe became its pastor (1938–64). Noted members of the church have included Edmund H. Morgan, former governor of New York, John Foster Dulles, secretary of state under President Dwight D. Eisenhower, Mrs. Andrew Carnegie, and Thomas J. Watson, founder of International Business Machines. Clarence Dickinson, the church organist and choirmaster from 1909 to 1965, founded the School of Sacred Music, the Union Theological Seminary, and the American Guild of Organists.

A Quarter Century of Brick Church History, 1911–1936 (New York: Brick Presbyterian Church, 1936)

David Meerse

Bridewell. A name once used to refer to certain prisons in New York City. The first Bridewell in the city was built in 1734, the second in 1775 at City Hall, near where the Sons of Liberty fought to maintain the liberty pole. The site became a rallying point for protests against the British and the jail was first used to imprison and punish patriots and revolutionary soldiers. After the war it was used as a city jail.

William Jackson Davis: *Reminiscences of the City of New York and Its Vicinity* (New York: Privately printed, 1855)

Joseph P. Viteritti

bridge. The game of bridge was introduced to New York City in 1893 by Henry I. Barbey, a banker and yachtsman who lived in Europe for many years and wrote the first book of rules for the game. Initially called auction bridge, it became popular in clubs, schools, and hotels but was supplanted in the mid 1920s by a new version known as contract bridge, for which rules were set and published by the Whist Club of New York. The Cavendish Club was formed in 1925 by Wilbur F. Whitehead and for the next eight years met at the Mayfair Hotel, which became the most important gathering place for bridge players and sponsored the Cavendish Trophy from 1928. The club itself met in a succession of hotels that included the Ritz Tower and Carlton House, and in 1941 became a nonprofit membership corporation. The city was made the site of the Eastern States Regionals, first held in 1929. Local newspapers published bridge columns edited by such experts as Albert H. Morehead, who worked for the *New York Times* from 1935 until 1963, when he was succeeded by Alan F. Truscott. New York City lies in the twenty-fourth district of the American Contract Bridge League and is the site of the Fun City Regionals, launched in 1970.

James E. Mooney

bridges. There are 2027 bridges serving New York City, of which seventy-six are over water, 329 are used by railroads, 1011 are over land, and the rest are in parks, serve subways, or are private pedestrian bridges. Because the city is virtually an archipelago (only the Bronx is connected to the mainland) bridges are heavily used by motor vehicles, trains, subways, and to a lesser extent pedestrians. The first bridge in the city was the King's Bridge (1693; demolished and buried in 1917), a small structure of stone and timber that spanned Spuyten Duyvil Creek between Manhattan and what is now the Bronx. It was built by the Philipse family and a toll was required to cross it until 1759, when the Farmer's Free Bridge (demolished 1911) opened over the Harlem River and forced the King's Bridge to become free as well. Other bridges over the Harlem River included Dyckman's Bridge (1756), Coles Bridge (1795, also known as the Harlem Bridge), a toll timber drawbridge at East 129th Street with a span of three hundred feet (91.5 meters) and a width of twenty-four feet (7.3 meters), and Macombs Dam Bridge (1813), a low stationary toll bridge at 155th Street, built to furnish power for milling, that allowed the tide to flow in but not out. The dam was destroyed in 1838 in a raid by more than a hundred angry citizens who believed that it illegally blocked a navigable stream. An unsuccessful suit by the owners of the bridge against those who had destroyed the dam established the precedent that the right to free passage to "an arm of the sea" can be limited only by the U.S. Congress. The High Bridge was built in 1837–48 to carry the large water pipes of the Croton Aqueduct system over the Harlem River. The early vehicular bridges provided access to the post roads leading to Albany (New York) and Boston but were of lesser use to most New Yorkers, who were concentrated in lower Manhattan and surrounded on two sides by water that could be crossed only by sloop, raft, canoe, or dinghy, and later by steam-powered ferry. In 1869 the parks department of New York City was given authority over the bridges spanning the Harlem River and their approach streets, thus extending the city's direct jurisdiction beyond its northern border before it annexed what later became the Bronx.

The city's economy and way of life depended on a system of waterborne transport that was frequently interrupted by ice and fog, prompting demands for more reliable links, especially between Manhattan and Brooklyn. In the 1850s builders of suspension bridges became confident of their ability to span the East River, and in 1883 John Augustus Roebling completed construction of the Brooklyn Bridge, the first modern vehicular crossing over water in the region. A period of extensive bridge building followed: the Williamsburg (1903), Manhattan (1905), and Queensboro (1909) bridges were constructed over the East River, as were eight over the Harlem River, including the Spuyten Duyvil railroad bridge (in the 1880s), the Washington Bridge (1889), the Third Avenue Bridge (1899, the third structure on the site originally occupied by Coles Bridge; for illustration see HARLEM RIVER), and the Willis Avenue Bridge (1901). A respected bridge engineer of the time was Alfred Pancoast Boller, who designed the Park Avenue Railroad Bridge (1891), the second Macombs Dam Bridge (1895), the 145th Street Bridge (1905), the Broadway Bridge (1908, replacing a bridge dating from 1895 that was floated downstream to become the University Heights Bridge at West Fordham Road), and the second Madison Avenue Bridge (1910). By 1910 bridges also spanned Dutch Kills, Newtown Creek, and the Gowanus Canal. The Hell Gate Bridge (1917), at one time the world's longest steel bridge, carried trains of the Pennsylvania Railroad over the Hell Gate Channel into Manhattan. Traversing the formidably wide Hudson River took several attempts. Two train tunnels and two vehicular tunnels were built beneath before the construction of the George Washington Bridge (1931), a graceful structure designed by Othmar H. Ammann. Unlike the Brooklyn Bridge and other suspension bridges before it, the George Washington Bridge was built of bare steel, without granite cladding or architectural ornament. Ammann adhered to the same principle in his later bridges: the Triborough Bridge (1936), the Bronx–Whitestone Bridge (1939), the Throgs Neck Bridge (1961), and the Verrazano Narrows Bridge (1964). Severe cutbacks in bridge maintenance and repair in the 1970s and 1980s led to structural problems and occasional closings. In the 1990s plans were under way to spend $3000 million on rehabilitating many of the city's aging bridges, including four over the East River: the Williamsburg, the Manhattan, the Brooklyn, and the Queensboro. The city's oldest surviving bridge is the High Bridge, rehabilitated after being declared a national landmark.

I. N. Phelps Stokes: *The Iconography of Manhattan Island, 1498–1909, Compiled from Original Sources and Illustrated by Photo Intaglio Reproductions of Important Maps, Plans, Views and Documents in Public and Private Collections* (New York: Robert H. Dodd, 1915–28; repr. Arno, 1967)

Norval White and Elliot Willensky, eds.: *AIA Guide to New York City* (New York: American Institute of Architects, New York Chapter, 1967; 3rd edn San Diego: Harcourt Brace Jovanovich, 1988)

Carl W. Condit: *American Building: Materials and Techniques from the First Colonial Settlements to the Present* (Chicago: University of Chicago Press, 1968)

Sharon Reier: *The Bridges of New York* (New York: Quadrant, 1977)

Gary D. Hermalyn, Rebecca Read Shanor

Bridge Street African Wesleyan Methodist Episcopal Church.

Church formed in Brooklyn in 1766. The first congregation included whites and blacks and was led by a British army officer. After racial discord erupted, black members withdrew and formed the African Wesleyan Methodist Episcopal Church (1818), which became part of the African Methodist Episcopal Church in 1820. Richard H. Cain, the pastor between 1861 and 1863 and later a bishop, was elected to the U.S. House of Representatives from South Carolina in 1873. Susan Smith McKinney-Steward, the first black woman physician in New York State, was the organist

Bridges of New York City

High Bridge	1848	Harlem River	Manhattan–Bronx
Brooklyn	1883	East River	Manhattan–Brooklyn
Washington	1888	Harlem River	Manhattan–Bronx
Carroll Street	1889	Gowanus Canal	Brooklyn
Third Avenue	1889	Gowanus Canal	Brooklyn
Macombs Dam	1895	Harlem River	Manhattan–Bronx
Third Avenue	1899	Harlem River	Manhattan–Bronx
City Island	1901	Pelham Bay Narrows	Bronx
Willis Avenue	1901	Harlem River	Manhattan–Bronx
Grand Street	1903	Newtown Creek	Queens–Brooklyn
Williamsburg	1903	East River	Manhattan–Brooklyn
Ninth Street	1905	Gowanus Canal	Brooklyn
145th Street	1905	Harlem River	Manhattan–Bronx
Third Street	1905	Gowanus Canal	Brooklyn
Union Street	1905	Gowanus Canal	Brooklyn
Borden Avenue	1908	Dutch Kills	Queens
Pelham	1908	Eastchester Bay	Bronx
University Heights	1908	Harlem River	Manhattan–Bronx
Manhattan	1909	East River	Manhattan–Brooklyn
Queensboro	1909	East River	Manhattan–Queens
Hunters Point Avenue	1910	Dutch Kills	Queens
Madison Avenue	1910	Harlem River	Manhattan–Bronx
Hell Gate	1917	East River	Queens–Wards Island
Ocean Avenue (pedestrian)	1917	Sheepshead Bay	Brooklyn
Eastchester	1922	Eastchester Creek	Bronx
North Channel	1925	North Channel	Queens
Roosevelt Avenue	1925	Flushing River	Queens
B&O Railroad	1928	Arthur Kill	Staten Island–New Jersey
East 174th Street	1928	Bronx River	Bronx
Goethals	1928	Arthur Kill	Staten Island–New Jersey
Outerbridge Crossing	1928	Arthur Kill	Staten Island–New Jersey
Greenpoint Avenue	1929	Newtown Creek	Queens–Brooklyn
Stillwell Avenue	1929	Coney Island Creek	Brooklyn
George Washington	1931	Hudson River	Manhattan–New Jersey
Bayonne	1931	Kill van Kull	Staten Island–New Jersey
Cropsey Avenue	1931	Coney Island Creek	Brooklyn
Fresh Kills	1931	Richmond Creek	Staten Island
Hook Creek	1931	Hook Creek	Queens–Nassau
Little Neck	1931	Alley Creek	Queens
Metropolitan Avenue	1933	English Kills	Brooklyn
Henry Hudson	1936	Harlem River	Manhattan–Bronx
Triborough	1936	East River, Harlem River, Bronx Kills	Queens–Wards Island, Manhattan–Randalls Island
Marine Parkway–Gil Hodges	1937	Rockaway Inlet	Brooklyn–Queens
Westchester Avenue	1938	Bronx River	Bronx
Bronx–Whitestone	1939	East River	Bronx–Queens
Cross Bay–Veterans' Memorial	1939	Jamaica Bay	Queens
Flushing (Northern Boulevard)	1939	Flushing River	Queens
Kosciuszko	1939	Newtown Creek	Queens–Brooklyn
Whitestone Expressway	1939	Flushing River	Queens
Midtown Highway	1940	Dutch Kills	Queens
Mill Basin	1940	Mill Basin	Brooklyn

(continued)

Bridges of New York City (*Continued*)

Hutchinson River Park Extension	1941	Eastchester Creek	Bronx
Hamilton Avenue	1942	Gowanus Canal	Brooklyn
Wards Island (pedestrian)	1951	East River	Manhattan–Wards Island
Bruckner Boulevard	1953	Bronx River	Bronx
Unionport	1953	Westchester Creek	Bronx
Pulaski	1954	Newtown Creek	Queens–Brooklyn
Roosevelt Island	1955	East River	Queens–Roosevelt Island
Lemon Creek	1958	Lemon Creek	Staten Island
Throgs Neck	1961	East River	Bronx–Queens
Broadway	1962	Harlem River	Manhattan–Bronx
Alexander Hamilton	1963	Harlem River	Manhattan–Bronx
Hawtree Basin (pedestrian)	1963	Hawtree Basin	Queens
Verrazano Narrows	1964	Narrows	Brooklyn–Staten Island
Rikers Island	1966	Bowery Bay	Queens–Rikers Island

Source: Norval White and Elliot Willensky, eds.: *AIA Guide to New York City* (New York: American Institute of Architects, New York Chapter, 1967; 3rd edn San Diego: Harcourt Brace Jovanovich, 1988)

Compiled by James Bradley

during the 1890s. There were 506 members in 1906 and four thousand in the mid 1990s.

Amos M. Jordan, Christine A. Powell, and Andy M. Smith: *African Wesleyan Methodist Episcopal Church* (Brooklyn: Privately printed, 1890)
Daniel A. Payne: *History of the African Methodist Episcopal Church* (Nashville: Publishing House of the A.M.E. Sunday School Union, 1891)

Dennis C. Dickerson

Briggs, Charles A(ugustus) (*b* New York City, 15 Jan 1841; *d* New York City, 8 June 1913). Minister and theologian. The son of a cooper, he was educated in Virginia and Germany. In 1874 he became a professor at Union Theological Seminary, where he eventually became known as an exponent of historical, critical methods of biblical scholarship. His joint editorship of *Presbyterian Review* (1880–88) brought him into conflict with Presbyterians who insisted on biblical inerrancy and scrupulous adherence to the doctrines of the Westminster Confession of 1647 and the Westminster Standards of Christian Behavior. His controversial inaugural lecture as the Robinson Professor of Biblical Theology at Union had two important consequences: in 1892 the General Assembly of the Presbyterian Church attempted to exercise its previously unused right to veto seminary appointments, which led Union to renounce its formal ties with the Presbyterian church; and in 1893 the General Assembly in Washington began a series of heresy trials that culminated in Briggs's conviction and his suspension from his ministerial office. He remained a faculty member at Union during the last two decades of his life, during which his scholarly interests shifted toward ecumenical matters. Briggs withdrew from the Presbyterian church in 1898 and in the following year became an Episcopal priest.

Lefferts A. Loetscher: *The Broadening Church: A Study of Theological Issues in the Presbyterian Church since 1869* (Philadelphia: University of Pennsylvania Press, 1954)
George H. Shriver, ed.: *American Religious Heretics: Formal and Informal Trials* (Nashville: Abingdon, 1966)
Robert T. Handy: *A History of Union Theological Seminary in New York* (New York: Columbia University Press, 1987)

David Meerse

Briggs, Cyril (*b* Nevis, 28 May 1887; *d* ?Los Angeles, 18 Oct 1966). Political activist. He became one of the earliest and most articulate advocates of black nationalism in Harlem as a writer for the *Colored American Review* (1915) and the *Amsterdam News* (1914–19). In 1919 he launched his own journal, the *Crusader*, and founded the African Blood Brotherhood, a paramilitary group intended to further black nationalism in the United States and Africa. He wrote favorably about the Bolshevik Revolution by 1920 and called for alliances between blacks and progressive whites; he probably joined the Communist Party at this time. Over the next two years he sought to join the black nationalist group the Universal Improvement Association, but was rebuffed by its leader Marcus Garvey because of his socialist connections. Under his leadership the African Blood Brotherhood formed an affiliation with the Communist Party (1925) and thus became the first black communist group in New York City. In the late 1920s and 1930s he edited the communist newspaper the *Harlem Liberator* but clashed frequently with the party's leadership over black nationalism, and was expelled from the party in 1942. Briggs moved to California in 1944.

Harold Cruse: *The Crisis of the Negro Intellectual* (New York: William Morrow, 1967)
Mark Naison: *Communists in Harlem during the Depression* (Urbana: University of Illinois Press, 1983)

Calvin B. Holder

Brighton Beach. Neighborhood in southwestern Brooklyn (1990 pop. 26,784), lying between Manhattan Beach and Coney Island and bounded to the north by Neptune Avenue, to the east by Corbin Place, to the south by the Atlantic Ocean, and to the west by

Boardwalk at Brighton Beach, Coney Island, ca *1905*

Boardwalk at Brighton Beach, 1991

Ocean Parkway. Initially developed by William A. Engeman in 1868, the area was named for the resort in England in 1878 by Henry C. Murphy and a group of businessmen who bought a large parcel to build the elegant Hotel Brighton. North of Brighton Beach Avenue Engeman built the Brighton Beach Racetrack, which made the area an important center of thoroughbred horse racing. In 1907 the Brighton Beach Baths opened on the site of a former amusement park to provide swimming, tennis, and entertainment (in the mid 1990s the baths were threatened by residential development). To meet the increased demand for housing in the 1920s developers built more than thirty six-story apartment buildings with elevators south of Brighton Beach Avenue between Coney Island Avenue and Ocean Parkway. The population consisted mostly of Jews from Brownsville, East New York, and the Lower East Side. Convenient transportation to Manhattan was provided by an express subway route with four tracks. On the former site of the racetrack wood-frame houses and bungalows predominated but by 1970 had deteriorated severely. After the Soviet Union relaxed emigration policies during the 1970s about thirty thousand Jews settled in the neighborhood and its environs; many were from Odessa in the Ukraine and were attracted by the proximity of the neighborhood to the ocean. Of the immigrants who settled in Brighton Beach during the 1980s the great majority were from the Soviet Union; many of the rest were from China, India, Pakistan, and Vietnam. In the mid 1990s much of the population was elderly and the housing consisted mostly of dense rows of apartment buildings. Along Brighton Beach Avenue Russian restaurants, nightclubs, fruit stands, and bookstores owned by immigrants stand in the shadow of the elevated train.

Stephen Weinstein: "The Nickel Empire: Coney Island and the Creation of Urban Seaside Resorts in the United States" (diss., Columbia University, 1984)

Annelise Orleck: "The Soviet Jews: Life in Brighton Beach, Brooklyn," *New Immigrants in New York*, ed. Nancy Foner (New York: Columbia University Press, 1987), 273–304

Stephen Weinstein

Brighton Beach Bath and Racquet Club. Private athletic club at 3205 Coney Island Avenue in Brooklyn, founded in 1907 and occupying fifteen acres (six hectares) on the Atlantic Ocean. Once advertised as the world's largest beach resort, it had more than thirteen thousand members by the 1960s. The club featured knish-eating contests, ferocious mah-jongg and one-wall handball games, three swimming pools, a miniature-golf course, steam rooms, a solarium, and an area reserved for card playing. On weekends the bandshell was the site of performances by Milton Berle, Lionel Hampton, Herman's Hermits, and Tallulah Bankhead. By the early 1990s the neighborhood had been transformed and the club had declined. In 1994 a court gave the owners the right to close the complex and replace it with 1489 apartments.

Kenneth T. Jackson

Brighton Heights. Neighborhood in northeastern Staten Island, lying between Silver Lake Park and Randall Manor and bounded to the north by Castleton Avenue, to the south by Forest Avenue, and to the west by Brighton Avenue. Once part of the Village of New Brighton, it consists primarily of small houses and businesses. The most prominent building is Morris Intermediate School, which stands at the corner of Castleton and Brighton avenues and is named for William Morris, a prominent black businessman who lived in the area in the early twentieth century; some of his descendants still live on Staten Island.

Martha S. Bendix

Brill, A(braham) A(rden) (*b* Kanczuga [now in Poland], 12 Oct 1874; *d* New York City, 2 March 1948). Psychoanalyst. A native of Galicia, he moved alone to New York City at fifteen. After several years of training in Europe, where he became a disciple of Freud, he returned to the city in 1908 and became the first practicing psychoanalyst in the United States. He taught at New York University (1913–20), New York Post-Graduate Medical School (1914–18), and the College of Physicians and Surgeons (1927) and was also affiliated at various times with many other institutions, including Bellevue Hospital, Bronx Hospital and Dispensary, and the Vanderbilt Clinic. Best known as the translator into English of Freud's works, Brill was also the leading spokesman in the United States for the new science of psychoanalysis. His published writings include *Basic Principles of Psychoanalysis* (1949). In 1947 the New York Psychoanalytic Institute and Society dedicated the Abraham A. Brill Library.

Joseph S. Lieber

Brisbane, Arthur (*b* Buffalo, 12 Dec 1864; *d* New York City, 25 Dec 1936). Newspaper executive. The son of the utopian socialist Albert Brisbane, he began his career as the editor of Charles A. Dana's newspaper the *Sun*. In 1896 he was named the editor of the Sunday edition of the *New York World* by Joseph Pulitzer. He became the circulation director of the *World* during a period of intense competition with William Randolph Hearst's *New York Journal*. As an assistant to Hearst he became well known for his unrestrained editorials and for encouraging the frenzied newspaper war.

Oliver Carlson: *Brisbane: A Candid Biography* (New York: Stackpole and Sons, 1937)

John E. Drewry, ed.: *Post Biographies of Famous Journalists* (Athens: University of Georgia Press, 1942)

Julian S. Rammelkamp

Bristol–Myers Squibb. Firm of pharmaceutical manufacturers, incorporated in New York City as Bristol–Myers in 1900. Its forerunner was the Clinton Pharmaceutical Company, formed in 1887 in Clinton, New York, by William McLaren Bristol and John R. Myers. By 1928 the firm manufactured proprietary drugs at plants in New Jersey and had markets in twenty-six countries. It was taken over and operated by Drug Inc. from 1928 to 1933 but later grew by acquiring other firms, including Harris Laboratories in 1942 and Cheplin Biological Laboratories in 1943. It merged in 1989 with the Squibb Corporation and took its present name. The new firm was large enough to finance modern pharmaceutical research and development. In its first year it had 34,100 employees and sales of $5400 million. The headquarters are at 345 Park Avenue.

David J. S. King

Broad Channel. Neighborhood in southeastern Queens (1991 pop. 2500) on the only inhabited island in Jamaica Bay, which occupies one and a half acres (sixty ares) west of a waterway also called Broad Channel. It consisted at first of a few fishermen's shacks and could be reached only by boat. In 1880 it was made the site of one of four fishing platforms built alongside a railroad trestle five miles (eight kilometers) long across the bay from southern Queens to the Rockaway Peninsula. A hotel and a saloon were opened in the following year; visitors rented rowboats and baymen continued to fish and to dig for clams. The Board of Health in 1916 declared Jamaica Bay polluted and prohibited fishing. Cross Bay Boulevard was opened through the center of Broad Channel in 1924 and a large residential community took shape within five years; nine inlets were dredged along the western shore and about fifteen short streets were laid out. The city retained title to the land, giving the householders renewable ten-year leases. Because of the marshy ground many of the houses were built on stilts. Between 1950 and 1955 the city realigned the railroad route and radically changed the shape of the islands in the bay. A subway station opened on 28 June 1956. In 1982 the city permitted local residents to buy their houses, the average value of which rose rapidly from $10,000 to $100,000. For many years most houses used septic tanks and there was no sewage system: one was slowly being installed in the early 1990s. Broad Channel is a largely Irish lower-middle-class community with a reputation for being insular and suspicious of city government.

Vincent Seyfried

Broadway. Street beginning at the Battery and extending for seventeen miles (twenty-seven kilometers) through Manhattan and four miles (six kilometers) through the Bronx. It was originally a trail built atop a natural ridge by American Indians and became an important trade route linking the harbor with upstate New York. Named Heere Straat (High street) by the Dutch, it was one of two main roads leading north from a fort at the tip of lower Manhattan. During the American Revolution British and American troops traveled and fought along it. Broadway is perhaps most often associated with entertainment. One of the first theaters in New York City was the Playhouse on Broadway (in the early 1730s), between Beaver Street and Exchange Place. Later hundreds of playhouses, music halls, opera houses, and movie theaters lined Broadway and its sidestreets. By the early twentieth century the theater district had moved up Broadway to Times Square; because of its abundant electric signs used for advertising the street became known as the "great white way." Broadway leaves the city at 262nd Street and continues north through Yonkers and Westchester County to Albany and beyond.

Lloyd Morris: *Incredible New York* (New York: Random House, 1951)

Mary C. Henderson: *The City and the Theatre: New York Playhouses from Bowling Green to Times Square* (Clifton, N.J.: James T. White, 1973)

Carin Drechsler-Marx and Richard F. Shepard: *Broadway* (New York: Harry N. Abrams, 1988)

Linda Elsroad

Broadway Junction. Neighborhood in northeastern Brooklyn (1990 pop. 2273), bounded to the north by Broadway, to the east by Van Sinderen Avenue, to the south by Atlantic Avenue, and to the west by Rockaway Avenue. Known as Jamaica Pass during colonial times, it was used during the Battle of Long Island in August 1776 by British troops as a passage to Gowanus, where they trapped and defeated colonial troops. It is residential, has light industry, and is the transfer point for the Fulton Street "A," the Canarsie "L," and the Broadway "J" elevated rapid transit lines. The neighborhoods of East New York and Stuyvesant Heights meet at the intersection of Jamaica Avenue, Broadway, and Fulton Street. Highland Park and the Cemetery of the Evergreens are nearby.

Stephen Weinstein

Broadway United Church of Christ. Congregational church organized in 1836 as the Broadway Tabernacle Church with funds from the reformers Lewis and Arthur Tappan, partly in an attempt to attract to New York City the evangelist Charles Grandison, who served as pastor for the first year. The abolitionist preacher Joseph P. Thompson was pastor from 1845 to 1871. Over the years the church underwent several changes of location and name. The congregation worshipped until 1857 in the Broadway Tabernacle (1836) on Broadway between Leonard and Worth streets, from 1859 in a new building at 6th Avenue and 34th Street, and from 1905 in a new building on Broadway and 56th Street (demolished 1970). The name was changed in the early 1950s to Broadway Congregational Church, and after the merger in 1957 of the Congregational church with the Evangelical and Reformed church to Broadway United Church of Christ. Later the church shared space: from 1970 with the Church of St. Paul the Apostle (Roman Catholic) at 59th Street and 9th Avenue, from 1980 with Rutgers Presbyterian Church on 73rd Street and Broadway, and from 1985 with St. Michael's Church (Episcopal) on 99th Street between Broadway and Amsterdam Avenue.

History of Broadway Tabernacle Church (New York: S. W. Benedict, 1846)

Kevin Kenny

Broadway United Church of Christ, ca *1910*

Bronck, Jonas (*b* Komstad, Småland, Sweden, 1600; *d* Westchester County, 1643). Colonist. He lived on his father's farm in Sweden before moving to Amsterdam, then taught himself navigation and became a sea captain. With his wife and indentured servants he settled in New Netherland in 1639. His stone house contained the largest library in the colony and was the site of a peace conference with the Weckquasgeek Indians in 1642. The Bronx River and by extension the borough of the Bronx are named for him.

Lloyd Ultan: *The Bronx in the Frontier Era: From the Beginning to 1696* (New York: Bronx County Historical Society, 1993)

Lloyd Ultan

Population of Selected Towns within the Present Boundaries of the Bronx, 1790–1890

	Eastchester	Morrisania	Pelham	Westchester
1790	N/A	133	199	1,141
1800	1,581	258	N/A	992
1820	1,021	N/A	283	2,162
1830	1,030	N/A	334	2,362
1840	1,502	N/A	789	4,154
1850	1,679	N/A	577	2,492
1860	5,582	9,245	1,025	4,250
1870	7,491	19,609[1]	1,790	6,015
1880	8,737		2,540	6,789
1890	15,442		3,941	10,029

1. Incorporated into New York City in 1874.
N/A = Not Available
Note: Population figures for towns were not included in the census of population of 1810.
Compiled by James Bradley

Bronx. The northernmost borough of New York City. It encompasses forty-two square miles (109 square kilometers) and is the only section of New York City that belongs to the North American mainland. Undulating hills and valleys mark the western half; east of the Bronx River the land slopes gently toward Long Island Sound. The borough has a population of about 1.2 million (federal census of 1990) and by the late 1980s its bridges, highways, and railroads were more heavily traveled than those of any other part of the United States. There are eleven colleges and universities in the borough: Fordham University, the Maritime College of the State University of New York, three branches of the City University of New York (Lehman College, Bronx Community College, and Hostos Community College), the Albert Einstein College of Medicine of Yeshiva University, the College of Mount St. Vincent, Manhattan College, Mercy College, the College of New Rochelle, and Monroe Junior College. About 24 percent of the land area is parkland (more than in any other borough); this includes the Bronx Zoo and the New York Botanical Garden, which is the site of the last remnant of a hemlock forest that once covered the city and contains such artifacts as the earliest known petrograph in the area, a turtle drawn by Weckquasgeek Indians, Algonquin-speakers who inhabited the land thousands of years before European exploration.

1. From 1609 to the 1890s

Henry Hudson, probably the first European to see the shoreline, in 1609 sought cover from a storm for his vessel the *Halve Maen* in Spuyten Duyvil Creek. The eastern shore was described by Adriaen Block, the first European to navigate the East River (1614). The mainland was settled in 1639 by Jonas Bronck, a Swedish sea captain from the Netherlands who eventually built a farmstead at what became 132nd Street and Lincoln Avenue; a small group of Dutch, German, and Danish servants settled with him. In 1642 a peace treaty ending a war between the Dutch and the Weckquasgeeks was negotiated in Bronck's home. During the same year two settlements were established by colonists from Rhode Island: one by Ann Hutchinson near the river that was later named for her, another by John Throckmorton in what is now Throgs Neck; both settlements were destroyed in a war between the Dutch and the Weckquasgeeks. Bronck's servants scattered after his death in 1643. In 1646 a patroonship was formed by Adriaen van der Donck in an area that now includes Riverdale and a part of Westchester County (he was given an enormous land grant in return for attracting fifty families to it) and Thomas Cornell, a colonist from Rhode Island, built a farm in what became Clason Point. In 1655 both settlements were destroyed during another conflict between the Dutch and the Weckquasgeeks. Most of the eastern half of the area was bought in 1654 by Thomas Pell of Connecticut, who invited sixteen families to form the village of Westchester near what is now Westchester Square. Westchester was between 1683 and 1714 the seat of Westchester County (which included the Bronx until the second half of the nineteenth century) and as a chartered borough was the only town in the colony with an elected mayor. It was the first town without a property qualification for suffrage: settlers chose a representative to the provincial assembly and had their own municipal court. Horses, cattle, sheep, and wheat were the main agricultural products and a cottage industry in cloth making thrived. A semiannual fair was held to promote manufacturing and commerce. St. Peter's Church on Westchester Avenue organized the first parish in 1693. In the same year Frederick Philipse, a wealthy merchant of New York City, obtained from Governor Benjamin Fletcher the hereditary right to build and operate a toll bridge (the King's Bridge) across Spuyten Duyvil Creek to Manhattan.

During English rule most inhabitants were English, of English descent, or Dutch. Anglicanism was the religion sanctioned by colonial law, but Presbyterians, Quakers, and members of the Dutch Reformed church were in the majority. The first blacks, slaves from the West Indies, soon made up 10 to 15 percent of the population; in most households there were one or two who worked as farmhands or housemaids. In 1698 the first free black, a cooper, was recorded. Indians left the area soon after 1700. At this time the Bronx was composed of two towns and all or part of four huge manors (feudal grants allowing the proprietor exclusive rights to build grain mills and establish courts to try tenants): lying entirely within the present Bronx was the town of Westchester; to the north and including part of the present Westchester County was the town of Eastchester; to the northeast and including another part of the present Westchester County was the manor of Pelham, owned by the Pell family; to the southwest was the manor of the Morris family, Morrisania; in most of the western section was the manor of Fordham, settled in 1671 by John Archer (later owned by the Dutch Reformed church of New York City, then absorbed by Westchester in 1755); and to the northwest and including much of the present Westchester County was the manor of Philipsburgh, owned by the Philipse family. Catholics first moved to the area about 1750, the first Jewish family about ten years later. The King's Bridge fell into disuse and the toll was eliminated in 1759, after a parallel bridge (the Farmers' Free Bridge) was built by farmers under the leadership of Benjamin Palmer, who planned eventually to build a city to rival New York City. Hoping to lure the commercial traffic of Long Island Sound he formed a consortium to buy an island in Pelham Manor that he named City Island, but the project failed.

The area saw constant conflict during the American Revolution. Fortifications erected by General George Washington to protect the

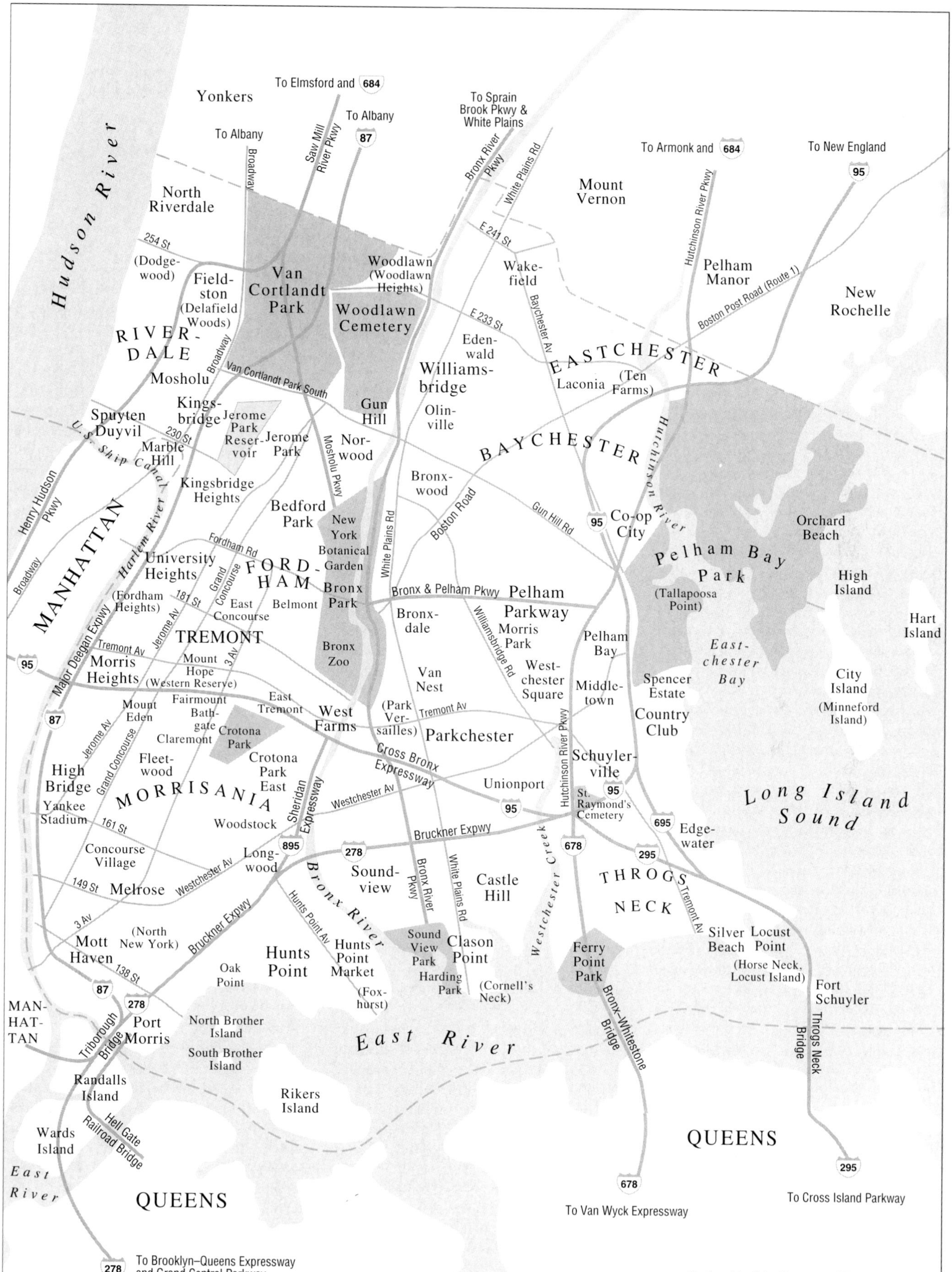
Yonkers
To Elmsford and 684
To Albany
To Albany 87
Saw Mill River Pkwy
To Sprain Brook Pkwy & White Plains
Bronx River Pkwy
White Plains Rd
To Armonk and 684
To New England 95
Hudson River
North Riverdale
Mount Vernon
Hutchinson River Pkwy
Broadway
254 St
(Dodge-wood)
Field-ston (Delafield Woods)
Van Cortlandt Park
Woodlawn (Woodlawn Heights)
Woodlawn Cemetery
E 241 St
Wake-field
Pelham Manor
New Rochelle
Boston Post Road (Route 1)
E 233 St
Baychester Av
RIVER-DALE
Eden-wald
EASTCHESTER
Mosholu
Van Cortlandt Park South
Williams-bridge
Laconia
(Ten Farms)
Spuyten Duyvil
Kings-bridge
Jerome Park Reser-voir
Gun Hill
Olin-ville
U.S. Ship Canal
230 St
Marble Hill
Jerome Park
Mosholu Pkwy
Nor-wood
BAYCHESTER
Hutchinson River
Henry Hudson Pkwy
Kingsbridge Heights
Bronx-wood
Boston Road
Gun Hill Rd
Bedford Park
New York Botanical Garden
White Plains Rd
95
Co-op City
Orchard Beach
MANHATTAN
Harlem River
Fordham Rd
University Heights
FORD-HAM
Pelham Bay Park
(Tallapoosa Point)
High Island
Broadway
Grand Concourse
181 St
Bronx Park
Bronx & Pelham Pkwy
Pelham Parkway
(Fordham Heights)
East Concourse
Belmont
Bronx-dale
Williamsbridge Rd
Morris Park
Hart Island
Major Deegan Expwy
Jerome Av
TREMONT
Pelham Bay
East-chester Bay
Tremont Av
Bronx Zoo
West-chester Square
95
Morris Heights
Mount Hope (Western Reserve)
3 Av
Van Nest
Middle-town
Spencer Estate
City Island
Fairmount
East Tremont
Mount Eden
Bath-gate
West Farms
(Park Ver-sailles)
Tremont Av
Country Club
(Minneford Island)
87
Jerome Av
Claremont
Crotona Park
Parkchester
Hutchinson River Pkwy
High Bridge
Grand Concourse
Fleet-wood
Crotona Park East
Cross Bronx Expressway
Schuyler-ville
95
Long Island Sound
MORRISANIA
Sheridan Expressway
Westchester Av
Unionport
St. Raymond's Cemetery
Yankee Stadium
161 St
95
695
Edge-water
Woodstock
Bruckner Expwy
Concourse Village
Westchester Av
895
Long-wood
278
678
295
Bronx River
Sound-view
Bronx River Pkwy
White Plains Rd
Castle Hill
Westchester Creek
THROGS NECK
149 St
Melrose
Hunts Point Av
Tremont Av
3 Av
(North New York)
Bruckner Expwy
Mott Haven
Hunts Point
Hunts Point Market
Sound View Park
Clason Point
Harding Park
(Cornell's Neck)
Ferry Point Park
Silver Beach
Locust Point
(Horse Neck, Locust Island)
138 St
Oak Point
(Fox-hurst)
Fort Schuyler
87
278
MAN-HAT-TAN
Port Morris
Triborough Bridge
North Brother Island
South Brother Island
East River
Bronx–Whitestone Bridge
Throgs Neck Bridge
Randalls Island
Rikers Island
Hell Gate Railroad Bridge
Wards Island
QUEENS
East River
QUEENS
678
To Van Wyck Expressway
295
To Cross Island Parkway
278
To Brooklyn–Queens Expressway and Grand Central Parkway

Designed by John Tauranac, of Tauranac, Ltd.

Harlem River valley proved ineffective on 12 October 1776 when British troops outflanked the Continental Army by landing at Throgs Neck. During the Battle of Pell's Point on 18 October about 750 men led by Colonel John Glover of Marblehead, Massachusetts, stayed the march of four thousand British and Hessians, enabling Washington to evacuate his army to White Plains in Westchester. For much of the rest of the war the Bronx remained in British hands and was subjected to raids by rebels that caused widespread destruction. In November 1783 Washington and Governor George Clinton began a march from the Van Cortlandt Mansion (now in Van Cortlandt Park) to take possession of New York City from the departing British. A recommendation in 1783 by Lewis Morris that Morrisania be the capital of the United States was rejected, but during an epidemic of yellow fever in Philadelphia in October 1797 President John Adams governed from the farmhouse of his daughter and son-in-law in what is now Eastchester.

The chief occupations of lower Westchester County were growing wheat and raising livestock in the early nineteenth century; between 1800 and 1830 the population rose from 1755 to 3023. Severe famine in Ireland and the growth of industry and commerce in the city drew thousands of Irish to the Bronx as laborers. There was a brief period of industrial growth during the War of 1812, when paint, glass, pottery, and bleaching factories opened in West Farms. Many Irish immigrants were employed in the construction of the High Bridge over the Harlem River, the New York and Harlem Railroad (1841; the first railroad in the area), and the Croton Aqueduct (1842), and also in the first iron foundry and industrial village at Mott Haven (1841), developed by Jordan L. Mott. Much of the area consisted of fertile lands that yielded fruits, vegetables, and dairy products for sale in the city. The first railroad tracks were laid over these lands, and rural stations eventually became the centers of new villages such as Melrose, Morrisania, Tremont, Fordham, Williamsbridge, Wakefield, Highbridge, Morris Heights, Kingsbridge, and Riverdale; the campus of St. John's College (later Fordham University) was built near a station in 1841. Increasing numbers of New Yorkers chose to live in the country and work in the city. Summer homes were built along waterways in the Bronx by industrialists and financiers, among them Richard M. Hoe, William E. Dodge, and Collis P. Huntington. As the railroad was extended, the center of population shifted west from the area east of the Bronx River, and the towns of West Farms (1846) and Morrisania (1855) were established.

Economic opportunity in the United States and a failed revolution in Germany in 1848 led thousands of Germans to move to the Bronx. Many settled in Melrose and Morrisania and became shopkeepers, brewers, and saloon owners. They also organized choral societies, *Turnvereine* (athletic clubs), and social clubs such as the Tallapoosa Club and the Schnorer Club, which became social centers for businessmen. In 1863 the Janes and Beebe ironworks at 149th Street and Brook Avenue produced the dome for the Capitol in Washington. The Johnson Iron Foundry on Spuyten Duyvil Creek made munitions during the Civil War and the Spanish–American War. Many Irish immigrants settled near new factories and in areas where construction work could be found. Several developments were intended largely for wealthy residents of upper Manhattan and other sections, from Woodlawn Cemetery (1863) to the Jerome Park Racetrack (1867). By this time it was generally assumed that towns on the mainland would be annexed by New York City as it expanded northward. In 1868 Morrisania numbered its streets to make them conform to those of the city, and in the following year the municipal parks department was given control of the bridges over the Harlem River and the streets leading to them. In 1874 the towns of Morrisania, West Farms, and Kingsbridge (all of which lay west of the Bronx River) were annexed to the city; known as the Annexed District, they were placed under the jurisdiction of the parks department and became the city's twenty-third and twenty-fourth wards. The journalist John Mullaly organized a movement urging the city to buy huge tracts and set them aside for parks while land in the Bronx was still cheap, and in 1888 a commission purchased what later became Van Cortlandt, Crotona, Claremont, St. Mary's, Bronx, and Pelham Bay parks and the Mosholu, Pelham, and Crotona parkways. In 1888 the 3rd Avenue elevated line was extended to 132nd Street, precipitating the most rapid growth that the Bronx had ever seen.

A commissioner of street improvements was elected from 1890 in response to complaints by inhabitants of the Annexed District that the parks department did not repair or build roads. Under the direction of the commissioner (and later of the borough president) the Grand Concourse was designed and built. A wide avenue modeled after the Champs-Élysées, it was lined with trees and had an innovative design based on the use of underpasses at major street crossings. The Belmont Stakes was run at Jerome Park from 1867 before being moved east of the Bronx River in 1890 to the Morris Park Racecourse, where it remained until moving again to Belmont Park in Nassau County in 1905. In the northern section of Bronx Park the New York Botanical Garden opened in 1891 and soon became known worldwide; the Bronx Zoo, in the southern section, displayed and bred many species (the American Bison Society used a herd at the zoo to restock western ranges). During the late nineteenth century New York University opened a campus in University Heights; the principal buildings were designed by Stanford White and included a colonnade that became the Hall of Fame for Great Americans, the first hall of fame in the world.

2. From the 1890s to the 1990s

By the 1890s there was strong support in parts of Eastchester, Pelham, and the village of Wakefield for consolidating with New York City the area east of the Bronx River, along with Brooklyn, Queens, and Staten Island. Most people assumed that high real-estate values in Manhattan would cover the public debt already incurred by the towns and pay for further public improvements being planned, such as a sewer system in Wakefield. In 1894 a nonbinding referendum on consolidation was passed by voters in New York City and its outlying areas but defeated overwhelmingly in the city of Mount Vernon and by one vote in the town of Westchester. The state legislature defeated a bill inspired by the referendum but in 1895 passed another bill annexing to the city the area east of the Bronx River, parts of the towns of Pelham and Eastchester, the village of Wakefield, and the town of Westchester, which because of its central location was included despite its negative vote in 1894. The newly annexed area became part of the twenty-fourth ward and was placed under the jurisdiction of the commissioner of street improvements (the office eventually became the model for that of borough president).

After consolidation in 1898 the twenty-third and twenty-fourth wards became the borough of the Bronx, which with Manhattan remained part of New York County (the other boroughs were already separate counties). But the journey from the Bronx to the courts in southern Manhattan was so long that inhabitants of the Bronx soon petitioned for county designation. Morris High School, the first public high school in the Bronx, opened in 1897. Many of the Italian immigrants who moved to the city about the turn of the century settled in the Bronx, often near the factories of Melrose or in Belmont, where they found work in the building trades or in landscaping the New York Botanical Garden and the Bronx Zoo nearby. Others helped to build the Jerome Park Reservoir and some bought farms in the rural northeastern Bronx. A studio was opened on 142nd Street between Brook and Willis avenues by the Piccirilli brothers of Pisa, who carved the statue of Abraham Lincoln for the Lincoln Memorial from a design by Daniel Chester French, and a statue of George Washington for the World's Fair of 1939–40. In 1904 the first subway connecting the Bronx to Manhattan was built under 149th Street, providing cheap rapid transit that with the 3rd Avenue elevated line persuaded hundreds of thousands during the first third of the twentieth century to leave tenements in Manhattan for spacious new apartments in the Bronx. Yugoslavians, Armenians, and Italians were among those who made the move, but the largest group was Jews from central and eastern Europe. In 1912 the state legislature established the County of Bronx as the sixty-second county in the state, effective 1 January 1914.

With the influx of population in the first third of the century the economy of the Bronx grew rapidly. The 3rd Avenue elevated line was gradually extended northward and in the process trolley lines were connected to it, forming a rapid transit line that provided access from lower Manhattan to expanses of undeveloped land. Many apartment buildings and commercial buildings were soon erected along the corridor of the elevated line, which reached its northern terminus at Gun Hill Road in 1920. In 1923 Yankee Stadium was opened at 161st Street and River Avenue as the home of the New York Yankees, who became known as the "Bronx Bombers" because of the large number of home runs hit in the following decades by such players as Babe Ruth, Lou Gehrig, Joe DiMaggio, Mickey Mantle, Roger Maris, and Reggie Jackson. Eventually the stadium was also used for football games, championship boxing matches, and religious gatherings. Grocery stores, restaurants, vegetable and fruit markets, tailors, and hardware stores became common characteristics of neighborhood shopping districts. Inhabitants throughout the borough shopped in department stores and boutiques at 149th Street and 3rd Avenue, an area known as the Hub that also had movie palaces and vaudeville theaters. Alexander's opened a department store there in 1928 and a branch on Fordham Road in 1938, where it soon made more sales per square foot than any other department store in the nation. Eventually a section of Fordham Road eclipsed the Hub as the main shopping district. In 1929 Loew's theater syndicate built the Paradise Theatre for $4 million on the Grand Concourse immediately south of Fordham Road; it had four thousand seats and a baroque décor that included a ceiling painted dark blue to resemble a nighttime sky, with small light bulbs added to resemble stars and simulated clouds blown across the ceiling by machine.

The onset of the Depression ended the period of tremendous growth that had begun in 1888, but privately financed apartment buildings continued to be constructed (most in the predominant style of the time, art deco). This was especially true of the area of the Grand Concourse, which became a symbol of social and economic success and had many apartment buildings of five or six stories with wide entrance courtyards bordered with grass and shrubs. About 49 percent of the inhabitants in 1930 were Jews, most of whom worked in Manhattan. By 1934 the housing in the borough had many more amenities than that of the other boroughs: almost 99 percent of residences had private bathrooms, about 95 percent central heating, more than 97 percent hot water, and more than 48 percent mechanical refrigeration. The largest housing development of the time, Parkchester, was undertaken by the Metropolitan Life Insurance Company. Completed in 1942, it housed forty thousand residents and had parks, playgrounds, sculptures, convenience stores, and movie theaters. Edward J. Flynn, the Democratic leader of Bronx County and an early supporter of the New Deal, secured public funds to repair streets and build the county jail and the central post office, as well as neighborhood parks. The borough became known for its colleges and universities and its growing number of public high schools, among them the Bronx High School of Science for gifted students (which by the mid 1990s had a higher number of graduates who had gone on to receive doctorates than any other high school in the country). The first important meetings of the United Nations Security Council were held at Hunter College in the Bronx (later renamed Lehman College).

After the Second World War new housing was built and the makeup of the population changed. Construction ranged from luxury apartment buildings in Riverdale to public housing in the southern Bronx. Long-time residents and former servicemen moved from older housing in the southern neighborhoods of Hunts Point, Morrisania, and Mott Haven into privately built housing in the northern Bronx, to the other boroughs, and to the suburbs. About 170,000 persons displaced by slum clearing in Manhattan, mostly black and Puerto Rican, moved to Hunts Point and Morrisania, as well as to Melrose, Tremont, and Highbridge. In 1950 social workers reported enduring poverty in a section of the southern Bronx. Systematic rent control was introduced during the Second World War to prevent rents from skyrocketing as empty apartments became scarce; it soon prevented conscientious landlords from paying for repairs to their aging buildings. Buildings were often set afire, at some times by unscrupulous landlords hoping to collect insurance, and at others by unscrupulous tenants taking advantage of the city's policy that burned-out tenants should be given priority for public housing and receive money for new furnishings. A period of rampant arson in the late 1960s and early 1970s ended only after this policy was changed and a limit was imposed on insurance payments for reconstructing burned-out apartment buildings. From that time one-family houses and row houses were built, hundreds of apartment buildings restored, and several apartments converted to cooperatives and condominium units, permitting more residents of the southern Bronx to own their homes.

After Flynn's death in 1953 Charles A. Buckley succeeded him as the Democratic leader of Bronx County and gained federal funds for the construction in the 1950s and 1960s of housing and a network of highways linking the Bronx with the rest of the city, among them the Major Deegan Expressway, the Cross Bronx Expressway, and the Bruckner Expressway. As commuting by automobile became more convenient, high-rise apartment buildings were erected in southern and eastern neighborhoods along the new roads, including Soundview, Castle Hill, Spuyten Duyvil, and Riverdale. Co-op City, a complex of 15,372 units built in the northeastern Bronx between 1968 and 1970, housed sixty thousand persons and was among the largest housing developments in the world. The distribution of products to the metropolitan area and the rest of the east coast became easier for industries occupying new industrial parks in the Bronx, such as those along Bathgate and Zerega avenues, and for fruit and vegetable dealers in the Hunts Point Food Market (1965). Puerto Ricans accounted for a growing share of the population (20 percent in 1970) and became more active in politics: Herman Badillo was the first Puerto Rican to be elected to the borough presidency (1965) and later to the U.S. Congress; Robert Garcia was elected to Congress in 1978; Fernando Ferrer was elected borough president in 1987; and Jose Serrano succeeded Garcia in 1990. The campus of New York University at University Heights was taken over by Bronx Community College in 1974. Condominiums were built on City Island and elsewhere along Long Island Sound, but at the same time the southern Bronx by 1977 was known nationally as a symbol of urban blight.

By the mid 1990s the population of the Bronx was increasing. It was about a third black, a third Latin American, and a third Asian and white. Some musicologists maintain that salsa music and break dancing originated in the Bronx. Puerto Ricans accounted for more than a quarter of the population by 1990, and there were also growing numbers of Koreans, Vietnamese, Indians, Pakistanis, Cubans, Dominicans, Jamaicans, Greeks, and Russians. Many Albanians settled in Belmont, many Cambodians in Fordham. Co-op City remained a successful development, luxury apartments built in Riverdale in the 1950s became cooperatives, and the housing stock continued to include the world's largest concentration of buildings in the art deco style. Entrepreneurs formed new businesses, and the borough's public schools were overcrowded with new immigrants.

Stephen Jenkins: *The Story of the Bronx* (New York: G. P. Putnam's Sons, 1912)

Lloyd Ultan: *The Beautiful Bronx, 1920–1950* (New Rochelle, N.Y.: Arlington House, 1979)

Lloyd Ultan and Gary D. Hermalyn: *The Bronx in the Innocent Years, 1890–1925* (New York: Harper and Row, 1985)

Lloyd Ultan: *The Bronx in the Frontier Era* (New York: Bronx County Historical Society, 1993)
Lloyd Ultan and Gary Hermalyn: *The Bronx: It Was Only Yesterday, 1935–1965* (New York: Bronx County Historical Society, 1993)

Gary D. Hermalyn, Lloyd Ultan

Bronx Community College. Junior college of the City University of New York, opened in 1957 at the former site of the Bronx High School of Science on 184th Street and Creston Avenue. In 1973 it moved to a disused campus of New York University at University Avenue and 181st Street. The college offers career training, courses in liberal arts, and adult education. In the spring of 1991 it enrolled 4171 full-time and 2561 part-time students. The campus is the site of the Hall of Fame for Great Americans.

Marc Ferris

Bronx County Historical Society. A private, nonprofit cultural and educational institution opened in 1955 to document and interpret the social and economic history of the Bronx from the seventeenth century to the present. It has a research library and extensive collections (including more than eighteen thousand photographs and slides), and also runs Poe Cottage (*ca* 1812), the writer's last home and now a historic museum, and the Valentine–Varian House (*ca* 1758), now the Museum of Bronx History. The society publishes the *Journal of Bronx History*. Its offices and collections are at 3309 Bainbridge Avenue.

Gary D. Hermalyn

Bronxdale. Neighborhood in the central Bronx, bounded to the north by Pelham Parkway, to the east by Morris Park, to the south by Van Nest, and to the west by Bronx Park. It was settled in the nineteenth century as a village on the eastern bank of the Bronx River. Cloth-tape and cloth-print mills and bleacheries built in the mid nineteenth century were forced to move when Bronx Park was laid out in 1888. Jews moved to the neighborhood in large numbers after the opening in 1917 of the White Plains Road branch of Interborough Rapid Transit. In the mid 1990s there remained factories and warehouses on Bronxdale Avenue and the Bronx headquarters of the parks department in Bronx Park.

Lloyd Ultan

Bronx High School of Science. One of the most distinguished secondary schools in the United States, opened in 1938 at 184th Street and Creston Avenue for gifted students interested in science and mathematics. In its first year it admitted three hundred boys on the basis of a written examination, and in 1946 it began to admit girls. The school moved in 1958 to a building at 205th Street and Jerome Avenue, north of Lehman College. The curriculum includes advanced college placement courses in science and mathematics, as well as independent research programs. Students at the Bronx High School of Science have won many city, state, and national academic honors, and nearly all go on to attend engineering, technical, or liberal arts colleges. In 1991 the school had an enrollment of about 2700 and was one of three specialized high schools in the city's public education system. Distinguished alumni of the Bronx High School of Science include four Nobel laureates in physics: Leon Cooper (1972), Sheldon Glashow (1979), Steven Weinberg (1979), and Melvin Schwartz (1988). Other notable graduates of the school include the former secretary of defense Harold Brown, the journalist William Safire, the novelist E. L. Doctorow, the electrical sound engineer Robert Moog, the singer Bobby Darin, and the activist Stokely Carmichael.

Gerard Thomas Koeppel

Bronx Home News. Newspaper launched by James O'Flaherty (1874–1939), published weekly from 1907 and daily from 1922 from offices at East 148th Street and 3rd Avenue. It focused on local news, and always named as many residents of the Bronx as possible. Perhaps its most famous headline was "Bronx Man Leads Russian Revolution," a reference to Leon Trotsky, who had lived in the Bronx in 1917. In 1939 the newspaper had a circulation of 110,000 (with a heavy reliance on home delivery) and published neighborhood editions in upper Manhattan, but it soon went into decline and was sold to the owners of the *New York Post* on 30 May 1945. The *Bronx Home News* ceased publication on 18 February 1948.

Stephen A. Stertz

Bronx Hospital. Private hospital in the Bronx. It opened in 1911 with only six beds but quickly expanded; originally it served Jewish immigrants. In 1918 the hospital moved to the Eichler estate at 169th and Fulton Avenues. A new building was completed in 1932, and the old hospital became a nursing home. The hospital merged in 1962 with Lebanon Hospital to form BRONX-LEBANON HOSPITAL CENTER.

Tina Levitan: *Islands of Compassion* (New York: Twayne, 1964)

Andrea Balis

Bronx–Lebanon Hospital Center. Private hospital in the Bronx, the largest serving the southern part of the borough. Its two major divisions are one mile (1.6 kilometers) apart on the Grand Concourse and on Fulton Avenue. The hospital was formed in 1962 by the merger of Lebanon Hospital and Bronx Hospital. In 1971 it became a teaching hospital of the Albert Einstein College of Medicine. Bronx–Lebanon has two in-patient facilities, extensive outpatient facilities, and a center for the treatment of AIDS, and maintains housing, nutrition, and food distribution programs.

Tina Levitan: *Islands of Compassion* (New York: Twayne, 1964)

Andrea Balis

Bronx Municipal Hospital Center. Largest municipal hospital complex in the Bronx, administered by the New York City Health and Hospitals Corporation. A teaching affiliate of the Albert Einstein College of Medicine of Yeshiva University, it is composed of two hospitals on the same campus, on Pelham Parkway and Eastchester Road. One hospital, opened on 15 September 1954, is named for Nathan B(ristol) Van Etten (1866–1954), who maintained a family practice in the Bronx for more than sixty years, in 1911 became one of the few general practitioners to be elected president of the American Medical Association, and later became known for his work with communicable diseases after the influenza and typhoid epidemics of the First World War. This hospital was intended originally for tuberculosis patients but was later converted to general care. The second hospital, opened on 1 November 1955, is named for Abraham Jacobi (1836–1919), an internationally renowned professor of pediatrics in New York City who also was a president of the American Medical Association. The facility was primarily the work of Marcus Kogel, who as the city's commissioner of hospitals oversaw its design and construction. Bronx Municipal Hospital Center has periodically suffered from the same financial constraints as the rest of the municipal system, but it has also won distinction for its burn unit, trauma center, and day care center for children with AIDS (the first in the nation), and its departments of neurology, newborn intensive care, and acute psychiatry. The hospital had 774 beds in 1994.

Jesse Drucker, Sandra Opdycke

Bronx Park. Public park in the north central Bronx, covering 662 acres (268 hectares) and bounded to the north by Gun Hill Road, to the east by Bronx Park East and Unionport Road, to the south by East 180th Street, Boston Road, and Bronx Park South, to the west by Southern Boulevard and Dr. Theodore Kazimiroff Boulevard, and to the northwest by Webster Avenue; it is bisected by Fordham Road and within its borders the Bronx River Parkway runs roughly parallel to the Bronx River. The park was laid out during the 1880s as part of a plan to reserve parkland in undeveloped areas annexed or soon to be annexed to New York City. During the 1890s it was chosen as the site for the city's zoological and botanical gardens. The area south of Fordham Road was to be used by the New York Zoological Society, and what later became known as the Bronx Zoo opened to the public in 1899. In the mid 1990s this was the largest urban zoo in the United States, covering 261 acres (105 hectares) and housing more than four thousand animals representing 650 species. Most of the area north of Fordham Road (about 250 acres, or a hundred hectares) became the site of the New York Botanical Garden (1891), which was modeled on the Royal Gardens in Kew, England, and became one of the finest gardens of its kind in the world. An acre (forty ares) of gardens was planted in the Enid A. Haupt Conservatory, which opened in 1902 and was restored during the 1970s. The garden contains the Hemlock Forest, which covers forty acres (sixteen hectares) and is the only virgin forest in the city. At the edges of the park are playgrounds and a bicycle path.

Ann Schmitz and Robert Loeb: "'More Public Parks': The First New York Environmental Movement," *Bronx County Historical Society Journal* 21, no. 2 (1984), 51–66

Timothy Rub: "The Institutional Presence in the Bronx," *Building a Borough: Architecture and Planning in the Bronx, 1890–1940*, ed. Evelyn Gonzalez (New York: Bronx Museum of the Arts, 1986)

Peter Derrick

Bronx River. A meandering, scenic waterway partly in the Bronx. Its source is in the hills of Westchester County near the Kensico Dam. The river drains a valley fifteen miles (twenty-four kilometers) long and flows south through the middle of the Bronx into the East River between Hunt's Point and Clason Point. It is especially picturesque at the Bronx River Gorge in the New York Botanical Garden; the rocky shores and outcroppings show clearly the glacial action of the retreating Wisconsin Ice Sheet. The Bronx River is navigable only for 2.6 miles (4.2 kilometers), to East 172nd Street. A dredging project by the U.S. Army Corps of Engineers begun in 1913 was about 80 percent complete by the mid 1990s, with the depth averaging ten to twelve feet (three to four meters). It is said that at the outbreak of the American Revolution the British War Office was so ignorant of the topography of the Bronx that it ordered Admiral Richard Howe to sail his fleet up the river and attack "whatever American ships he found there."

Gerard R. Wolfe

Bronx Symphony Orchestra. Community orchestra formed in 1940. It gave one concert during its first season before disbanding, and then was re-formed in 1947 under the leadership of Irwin Hoffman, conductor, and Edward I. Cohen, orchestra manager. Rehearsals and performances took place at Walton High School in the Bronx. Hoffman was succeeded in 1952 by Leon Hyman; later the orchestra was led by Paul Wolfe (*ca* 1959–62), Saul Schectman and Moshe Budmore (*ca* 1962–63), Louis F. Simon (*ca* 1964–68), Michael Spierman (1968–81), Joseph Delli Carri (1981–84), Robert Black (1986–89), Spierman (1989–91), George Rothman (1991–93), and Gheorghe Costinescu (1993–94). In 1980 the orchestra moved to the Performing Arts Center at Lehman College, where it gives four to six concerts a year.

Mark Laiosa: "History of the Bronx Symphony Orchestra," *Bronx County Historical Society Journal* 19, no. 2 (1982), 51–55

Mark Laiosa

Bronx Terminal Market. Indoor market complex covering thirty-two acres (thirteen hectares) along the Harlem River between 149th and 152nd streets in Mott Haven. Construction on a cold-storage warehouse began under Mayor John F. Hylan in 1917 and was completed in the 1920s, when other buildings were added to form an indoor market. The market was not successful until the 1930s, when Mayor Fiorello H. La Guardia expanded it as part of his program to eliminate pushcarts. Ten buildings were added to the south of the original warehouse, and the market became the city's main wholesale distribution center for ethnic foods. In December 1935 Mayor La Guardia prohibited the sale and possession of artichokes there to end the inflation of their price by organized crime; in the following year the price declined and the ban was lifted. The complex was leased to the firm of Arol Development under Mayor John V. Lindsay in 1972. This arrangement came into conflict with the rebuilding of Yankee Stadium during the 1970s, which called for the construction of a parking area on land already leased to Arol. In 1993 about 75 percent of the market lay empty, and Mayor David N. Dinkins condemned the lease with Arol after George Steinbrenner, owner of the New York Yankees, threatened to move the team out of the Bronx. During the same year plans were made to refurbish the Bronx Terminal Market by demolishing certain buildings, erecting new ones, and improving public access.

Melissa M. Merritt

Image of the Bronx River, 1905

Bronx–Whitestone Bridge. Suspension bridge that spans the East River, connecting the Hutchinson River Parkway and Ferry Point Park in the Bronx to Whitestone in Queens. Designed by the engineer Othmar H. Ammann and the architectural firm Cass Gilbert and Company, it was constructed in twenty-three months at a cost of $17,785,000 and opened on 30 April 1939; at the time it was the fourth-longest suspension bridge in the world. The bridge reaches a maximum clearance above mean high water of 150 feet (forty-six meters), and the total length of its main span (excluding approach drives) is 2300 feet (701 meters). It has four traffic lanes, each thirty feet (nine meters) wide. Connected a few years after its completion to the parkways of the Bronx and Queens, it greatly improved access between Long Island and Westchester and points north and east, and spurred a housing boom in the adjacent areas of Queens that was interrupted only by the Second World War. The Bronx–Whitestone Bridge is operated by the Triborough Bridge and Tunnel Authority.

Stephen A. Stertz

Bronxwood Park. Name formerly applied to a development built in 1880 in the north central Bronx and bounded to the north by North Oak Drive, to the east by Bronxwood Avenue, to the south by South Oak Drive, and to the west by White Plains Road; all the streets were named for trees. The area later became a residential section of Williamsbridge. In the mid 1990s most of the housing consisted of small one-family houses and apartment buildings.

John McNamara: *History in Asphalt: The Origin of Bronx Street and Place Names* (New York: Bronx County Historical Society, 1984)

Gary D. Hermalyn

Bronx Zoo. One of the best-known zoos in the world, opened in 1899. For more information see Zoos.

Brook. Social club formed in 1903. It was intended to offer uninterrupted service day and night, and was named for Tennyson's poem (the last two lines of which read: "For men may come and men may go, / But I go on forever"). Among the founding members was Stanford White, who designed the first clubhouse (at 6 East 35th Street) and the second (at 7 East 40th Street), a brownstone with an added classical façade to which the club moved after one year. These buildings were furnished with libraries, antique furniture, fine china, and paintings by Benjamin West and Gilbert Stuart. Later the club moved to a building at 111 East 54th Street designed by another member, William Adams Delano.

James E. Mooney

Tollgate at Jamaica Avenue and Van Wyck Boulevard in Brooklyn, 1897 (demolished 1897)

Brooklyn. The most populous borough in New York City (1990 pop. 2,300,664), occupying eighty-one square miles (210 square kilometers) on the southwestern tip of Long Island and situated on New York Harbor across the East River from Manhattan. Once an independent municipality, it was the nation's third-largest city for nearly half a century. Although it became a borough of New York City in 1898 it still retains the qualities of a large urban complex, with a strong, independent central business district and government center, remnants of a sizable industrial base, educational and cultural institutions, many varied and clearly identifiable neighborhoods, about sixty-five miles (105 kilometers) of natural shoreline, including some seven miles (eleven kilometers) of sandy beaches, 5959 acres (2413 hectares) of parkland, and about a quarter of the Gateway National Recreation Area.

1. From Settlement to Consolidation

At the time of European settlement the territory was the home of Munsee-speaking Indians known as the Lenapes or Delawareans. Some two thousand Lenape Indians inhabited several villages in the southwestern section of Long Island, among them Keschaechquereren, Marechkawieck, and Canarsie. Until the arrival of Europeans the Indians lived harmoniously and subsisted on fish, shellfish, wild animals, and harvested produce. The first European ship to sight what became Brooklyn was probably that of Giovanni da Verrazano in 1524, but the first contact was most likely made by the crew of Henry Hudson's *Halve Maen* in 1609. Basing its claim on Hudson's voyage, the Dutch West India Company settled what is now Brooklyn as part of the Dutch colony of New Netherland about 1635, or about a decade after New Amsterdam (Manhattan). The company found the natural harbor, fertile lands, forests, and wetlands an ideal locale. The earliest recorded European land purchases were made in 1636 in what became Flatlands and Flatbush by a director of New Netherland, Wouter van Twiller, and his associates. Over the next several years other purchases were made in the areas of Gowanus and Wallabout Bay for which the next director, Willem Kieft, issued patents. Regular ferry service to Manhattan began in the early 1640s, primarily to serve the needs of local farmers.

Antagonism between the Indians and Europeans emerged almost immediately in Brooklyn as well as other parts of New Netherland, owing partly to differing concepts of land ownership and efforts by the director to collect taxes from the Indians. A conflict in the mid 1640s, referred to as Governor Kieft's War, resulted not only in a marked decrease of the Indian population but also in a weakening of the Dutch colony's economy. For both political and economic reasons the Dutch West India Company encouraged the formation of towns. Within about a decade the company formally and informally chartered the original six towns of what is now Brooklyn. Five of these were Dutch settlements: Breuckelen (Brooklyn) in 1646, directly across the East River from New Amsterdam and most likely named for the community in the Netherlands south of Amsterdam; New Amersfoort (Flatlands) in 1647; Midwout (Flatbush) in 1652; New Utrecht in 1657; and Boswick (Bushwick) in 1661. The sixth town was the English town of Gravesend, founded by a group of followers of the Anabaptist Lady Deborah Moody and chartered in 1645. The original towns tended to be situated on existing Indian paths: Breuckelen was settled along a path leading from Marechkawieck, which became known as the "road from the ferry," and later formally named Fulton Street. Only Gravesend adapted a formal layout. Its four-square plan of 1646, constituting one of the country's first planned communities, survives at an angle to the surrounding grid.

The director of New Netherland appointed magistrates for most of the towns, but they

1 Willoughby Street, 1916

Population of Selected Towns in Brooklyn, 1790–1890

	Brooklyn	Bushwick	Flatbush	Flatlands	Gravesend	New Utrecht	Williamsburgh
1790	1,603	540	941	423	426	562	N/A
1800	2,378	656	946	493	489	778	N/A
1820	7,175	930	1,027	512	534	1,009	N/A
1830	15,396	1,620[1]	1,143	596	565	1,217	N/A
1840	36,233	1,295	2,099	810	799	1,283	5,094
1850	96,838	3,739	3,177	1,155	1,064	2,129	30,780
1860	266,661	N/A	3,471	1,652	1,286	2,781	N/A
1870	396,099	N/A	6,309	2,286	2,131	3,296	N/A
1880	566,663	N/A	7,634	3,127	3,674	4,742	N/A
1890	806,343	N/A	12,338	4,075	6,937	8,854	N/A

1. Includes Williamsburgh.
NA = Not Available
Note: Williamsburgh and Bushwick were annexed by Brooklyn in 1855. Population figures for towns were not included in the census of population of 1810.

Compiled by James Bradley

held minimal authority. Except in Gravesend the major town institution was the Dutch Reformed church. Town settlers maintained their affiliations with the Dutch church in New Amsterdam until 1655, when a church was constructed in Flatbush. Soon the other towns erected their own churches, but with only one minister to serve them all for the first several years. With the church came schools, which were supported by compulsory taxation, and modest town centers took shape. The colony exhibited a degree of religious tolerance, and in addition to the English settlers early residents included Walloons (generally Huguenots from what are now southeastern Belgium and nearby France), French, and immigrants from elsewhere in Europe.

The six farming towns grew slowly, and the takeover of the colony in 1664 by the English under the Duke of York affected them little. In 1683 Kings County was established as an administrative entity of the province of New York. Over the next several decades county administration evolved from simple colonial courts and a county clerk to a board of supervisors, with representatives from each town. Elected town officials, usually chosen from among the community's more prosperous farmers, were concerned primarily with regulations governing the collection of taxes, the use and subdivision of land, and the laying out of roads. Intertown highways were the responsibility of the Board of Supervisors. Farming remained the chief occupation, with surplus produce brought to market in the town of Brooklyn across the river from Manhattan, or directly to Manhattan by the ferry, which was adjacent to the market. By the 1680s the remaining Indian population of Brooklyn was virtually annihilated, its ability to subsist eroded by the relinquishing of virtually all Indian land, and its health ravaged by diseases imported from Europe. The European settlers increasingly relied on African slaves to provide an assured labor force, supplemented by indentured servants. At the end of the seventeenth century the county's population was about two thousand.

The quiet life of the towns continued for much of the eighteenth century, and the population less than tripled over the next hundred years. Although the residents on the whole remained passive in the drive for independence that pervaded the colonies in mid century, Kings County was the site of the Battle of Long Island (August 1776), the first major contest of the American Revolution and a disaster for the Continental Army, after which the British controlled both Manhattan and Kings County. After seven years of British occupation, marked by the notorious retention of thousands of prisoners in British ships moored in Wallabout Bay, the county resumed its docile, rural existence.

Only one area of Kings County exhibited strong growth. As New York City evolved into a major urban center, the town of Brooklyn close to the ferry experienced gradual commercial development. Ropewalks, breweries, distilleries, slaughterhouses, and shops began to appear, and in a clear sign that the area around the ferry was losing its rural character, the town officials in the late 1780s demarcated it as a separate fire district. In 1799 the county's first newspaper, the *Long Island Courier*, began publication there. The growth of business encouraged a growth in population; within the next two decades the population of the town of Brooklyn tripled while the other five towns grew by less than a third.

With the introduction of Robert Fulton's steam ferry in 1814, farsighted entrepreneurs began to transform Brooklyn into one of the world's first commuter suburbs. Brooklyn Heights, on the hill above the ferry, was promoted as the ideal residence for affluent businessmen from Manhattan. In 1816 the town's built-up area was incorporated as the Village of Brooklyn, with its own elected trustees. The first urban street improvement project began in the village in 1819 with a survey and formal mapping of streets, followed by the grading and graveling of major roads and the introduction of sidewalks on Fulton Street. In 1834, overcoming the opposition of New York City, the entire town of Brooklyn was chartered as the City of Brooklyn; at the time Brooklyn had fewer than sixteen thousand residents, and all of Kings County fewer than 25,000, compared with more than 200,000 in New York City. A second area of growth was emerging farther up the East River, also in response to the progress of New York City: in 1801 the U.S. Navy purchased a small shipyard on Wallabout Bay between the ferry district and the Town of Bushwick, just north of the yard another ferry to Manhattan had begun operation, and in 1827 this part of Bushwick was incorporated as the Village of Williamsburgh.

After the establishment of the City of Brooklyn local officials asked the state legislature to appoint a commission to map streets and public squares. The resulting plan of 1839 consisted of a rectangular grid of streets, overlaid by several wider diagonal avenues and interspersed with several small parks. The subsequent development of Brooklyn generally followed this plan. In 1869 the state established the Town Survey Commission to map the towns of Flatbush, Flatlands, New Utrecht, and Gravesend; its plan of 1874 ex-

Mayors of the City of Brooklyn, 1834–1898

George Hall 1834
Jonathan Trotter 1835–36
Jeremiah Johnson 1837–38
Cyrus P. Smith 1839–41
Henry C. Murphy 1842
J. Sprague 1843–44
Thomas G. Talmage 1845
Francis B. Stryker 1846–48
E. Copland 1849
Samuel Smith 1850
Conklin Brush 1851–52
Edward A. Lambert 1853–54
George Hall 1855–56
Samuel S. Powell 1857–60
Martin Kalbfleisch 1861–63
Alfred M. Wood 1864–65
Samuel Booth 1866–67
Martin Kalbfleisch 1868–71
Samuel S. Powell 1872–73
John W. Hunter 1874–75
F. A. Schroeder 1876–77
James Howell 1878–81
Seth Low 1882–85
Daniel D. Whitney 1886–87
Alfred C. Chapin 1888–91
David A. Boody 1892–93
Charles A. Schiern 1894–95
Frederick W. Wurster 1896–98

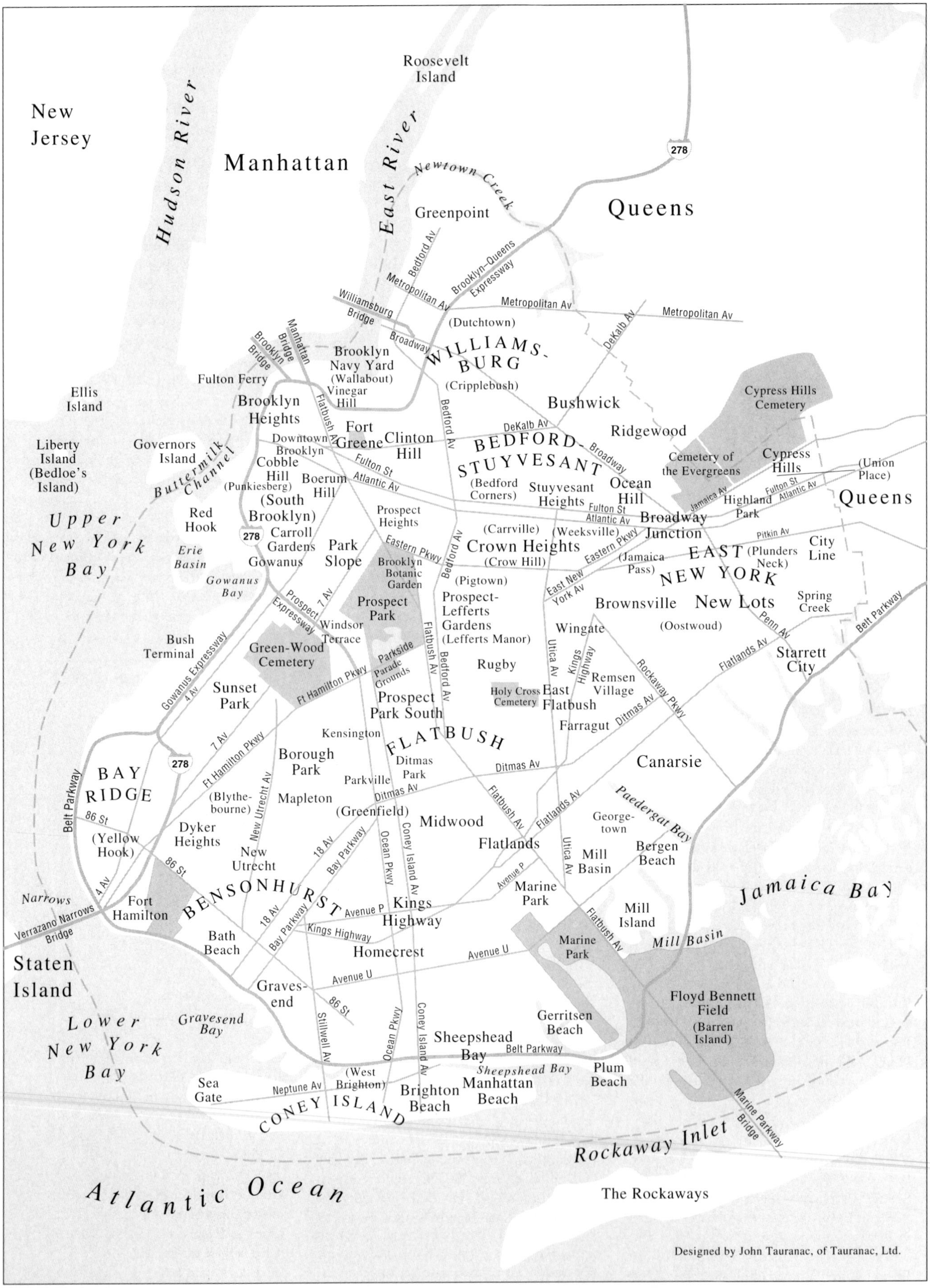

Roosevelt Island
New Jersey
Hudson River
Manhattan
East River
Newtown Creek
Greenpoint
Queens
278
Bedford Av
Brooklyn–Queens Expressway
Metropolitan Av
Williamsburg Bridge
(Dutchtown)
DeKalb Av
Manhattan Bridge
Brooklyn Bridge
Broadway
WILLIAMSBURG
Brooklyn Navy Yard (Wallabout)
Vinegar Hill
Fulton Ferry
(Cripplebush)
Ellis Island
Brooklyn Heights
Bushwick
Cypress Hills Cemetery
Flatbush Av
Fort Greene
Clinton Hill
Ridgewood
Liberty Island (Bedloe's Island)
Governors Island
Downtown Brooklyn
BEDFORD-STUYVESANT
Cemetery of the Evergreens
Cypress Hills
Buttermilk Channel
Cobble Hill
Fulton St
Atlantic Av
(Union Place)
(Punkiesberg)
Boerum Hill
(Bedford Corners)
Stuyvesant Heights
Ocean Hill
Jamaica Av
Highland Park
Upper New York Bay
(South Brooklyn)
Prospect Heights
Broadway Junction
Red Hook
Carroll Gardens
Park Slope
(Carrville)
(Weeksville)
Crown Heights
Pitkin Av
City Line
Erie Basin
Gowanus
Eastern Pkwy
(Crow Hill)
(Jamaica Pass)
EAST NEW YORK
(Plunders Neck)
Gowanus Bay
Brooklyn Botanic Garden
(Pigtown)
East New York Av
Prospect Expressway
7 Av
Prospect Park
Prospect-Lefferts Gardens (Lefferts Manor)
Brownsville
New Lots
Spring Creek
Windsor Terrace
Wingate
(Oostwoud)
Penn Av
Belt Parkway
Bush Terminal
Green-Wood Cemetery
Parkside
Parade Grounds
Utica Av
Kings Highway
Rugby
Rockaway Pkwy
Flatlands Av
Starrett City
Gowanus Expressway
4 Av
Sunset Park
Ft Hamilton Pkwy
Prospect Park South
Holy Cross Cemetery
East Flatbush
Remsen Village
Kensington
Farragut
Ditmas Av
FLATBUSH
Borough Park
Ditmas Park
Canarsie
BAY RIDGE
Parkville
Mapleton
(Blythebourne)
New Utrecht Av
(Greenfield)
Midwood
Paedergat Bay
Georgetown
86 St
(Yellow Hook)
Dyker Heights
18 Av
Bay Parkway
Ocean Pkwy
Coney Island Av
Flatlands
Bergen Beach
New Utrecht
Mill Basin
Avenue P
Marine Park
Jamaica Bay
Narrows
BENSONHURST
Kings Highway
Fort Hamilton
Verrazano Narrows Bridge
Avenue P
Mill Island
Bath Beach
Homecrest
Marine Park
Staten Island
Avenue U
Graves-end
Floyd Bennett Field (Barren Island)
Lower New York Bay
Gravesend Bay
Stillwell Av
Gerritsen Beach
Sheepshead Bay
Sea Gate
Neptune Av
(West Brighton)
Brighton Beach
Manhattan Beach
Plum Beach
CONEY ISLAND
Marine Parkway Bridge
Rockaway Inlet
Atlantic Ocean
The Rockaways
Designed by John Tauranac, of Tauranac, Ltd.

tended the street grid as far as Jamaica Bay. The grid changed angles slightly at town boundaries and shifts in topography. As the steam railway and the elevated railway reached the outlying towns, each town was annexed by Brooklyn.

The remainder of Kings County continued its measured growth, enjoying considerable agricultural prosperity as a result of the development of both Brooklyn and New York City. Even with the adoption of laws requiring gradual emancipation, slaveholders in Kings County seemed more reluctant than those of the state's other counties to abandon slavery. In 1800 more than a quarter of the county's residents were slaves, and not until mandatory emancipation in New York State in 1827 were they all freed. Many former slaves remained in Kings County, securing employment as farm workers or fishermen. In the 1830s and 1840s they founded several communities in central Brooklyn such as Weeksville and Carrville.

Brooklyn continued to grow as New York City became the dominant city in the United States. After the opening of the Erie Canal in 1825 new waterfront warehouses, tanneries, and factories manufacturing such commodities as paint, glass, and glue began operations along the East River. These new enterprises generated the need for artisans such as wheelwrights and coopers as well as the obligatory retail businesses, banks, and insurance companies, along with schools, churches, newspapers, libraries, and benevolent organizations. New ferry routes were initiated in the 1830s, and a steam railroad from the harbor to Jamaica began running in 1836.

For cultural enlightenment residents of Brooklyn depended largely on theaters and concert halls in Manhattan until the mid nineteenth century. The origins of most major cultural institutions in Brooklyn may be traced to the Apprentices Library (1823), which was intended to provide apprentices and others with training in industry and intellectual subjects. After two unsettled decades its founders formed a new corporation, the Brooklyn Institute, which included an art gallery, a public hall for lectures and readings, and space for classes and natural history exhibits. By the 1850s the institute had become the center of the borough's cultural life. The Brooklyn Academy of Music was organized in 1859 by wealthy citizens to encourage an interest in music and literature and to lessen reliance on institutions in Manhattan. Its original building was completed in 1861 one block from Brooklyn City Hall, and from time to time housed programs of the Brooklyn Institute. Other cultural institutions included the Mercantile Library, erected across the street several years later, and the Long Island Historical Society (1863; now the Brooklyn Historical Society).

Brooklyn at mid century experienced tremendous growth. The Village of Williamsburgh became a city in 1851, and in 1854 Brooklyn annexed both Williamsburgh and the Town of Bushwick. By 1855 nearly half the 205,000 residents of Brooklyn were foreign born; of these more than half were Irish, and slightly less than a quarter each were German and English. The immigrant growth led to a proliferation of churches and ethnic social service organizations, and Brooklyn became known as both the "city of homes" and the "city of churches."

City Hall (now Brooklyn Borough Hall), a Greek Revival structure completed in 1849 on Fulton Street uphill from the ferry landing, became the center of the downtown civic, business, shopping, and entertainment district. Municipal services — water supply, fire and police protection, and street lighting — and school systems expanded. Gaslights were introduced in Brooklyn in 1848, and the first horse-drawn street railways began operating in 1854. In the mid 1850s a board of water commissioners was established, and soon water was being pumped through Brooklyn from a new supply system.

By 1860 Brooklyn had 266,661 inhabitants, a figure exceeded only by New York City and Philadelphia. The remaining towns of Kings County were still largely rural, with a combined population of less than 12,500. Gradually those nearest Brooklyn began to be influenced by the city's phenomenal growth: a part of Flatbush was chartered as the Town of New Lots, farms gave way to row houses, and ferry lines, street grids, and transportation systems emerged. Meanwhile the working class and immigrants began living in neighborhoods different from those inhabited by the middle class. The annexed area (called the Eastern District), for example, was heavily German, and its many German breweries helped give the community a distinctive character.

As the center of population moved east away from the harbor, cultural institutions followed. The Brooklyn Institute reorganized in 1890 as the Brooklyn Institute of Arts and Sciences. Its directors decided to build a grand museum on land adjacent to Prospect Park, the great landscaped green space designed by Frederick Law Olmsted and Calvert Vaux and completed in the early 1870s. Although the museum's imposing plans by McKim, Mead and White were never fully realized, the Brooklyn Museum, renowned for an outstanding permanent collection of Egyptian, American, and African materials, became one of the major institutions of art in the country.

As the port in Manhattan became so overdeveloped that virtually no vacant space remained in its industrial districts or along its shorelines, more firms moved to Brooklyn. And as the original waterfront district in Brooklyn filled up, shipbuilding and other heavy industries became concentrated along the waterfront of the Eastern District to the north. By 1865 manufacturing employment in the city of Brooklyn reached almost fourteen thousand, with many more thousands working in transportation, warehousing, and related industries. Manufacturers found the waterfront of Brooklyn ideal for the region's heavy and bulky industries, including grain storage, sugar refining, and glass manufacturing. Some seven miles (eleven kilometers) of docks, warehouses, basins, grain elevators, drydocks, and freight terminals lined the shore from Red Hook in South Brooklyn to Newtown Creek in Greenpoint at the city's northern boundary.

Growth continued unabated during the last years of the nineteenth century, and steady migration from Europe and rural America transformed the social and political life of the community. A number of leading Republicans were found among the Germans of the Eastern District, as were some of the leading Democrats among the Irish of South Brooklyn. New industries moved into Williamsburgh and Greenpoint, including printing firms (D. Appleton and A. S. Barnes both moved their operations from Manhattan), oil refineries (Pratt Astral Oil Works being the largest), and iron foundries (such as the Hecla Architectural Iron Works and the firm of Cheney and Hewlett). By the 1880s Brooklyn was handling more waterborne tonnage than New York City, making it the nation's fourth-largest industrial city.

Transportation advances also influenced growth. Horesecar lines were supplanted by steam railroads, which were built out to the beach resorts of Coney Island in Gravesend and Canarsie in Flatlands in the 1860s and 1870s. In 1885 the first elevated railroad in Brooklyn was completed, and within a few years more elevated lines began to extend into the county's outlying areas. These lines, along with the simultaneous conversion of the street railways from horse power to electricity, hastened the urbanization of the nearer suburbs and signaled the imminent development of the rural outer regions. Working conditions on the electrified railways, or trolleys, deteriorated as the companies recoiled from the costs of electrification and frequent reorganization, and in 1895 Brooklyn experienced an explosive trolley strike. The completion of the Brooklyn Bridge in 1883, the first physical link between the country's largest and third-largest cities, symbolized both their economic interdependence and their impending political union. Brooklyn was growing not only in population and commerce but also in physical size. In 1886 it annexed the Town of New Lots, and between 1894 and 1896 it annexed the remaining four original towns of Kings County. By the turn of the century the amusement parks and grand hotels of Coney Island, Brighton Beach, and Manhattan Beach provided new entertainment forms for thousands of visitors from Brooklyn and Manhattan.

Having nearly reached its allowable state debt limit and nearly exhausted its ability to issue bonds, the governmental apparatus in Brooklyn could no longer support its impressive development. For some decades the Democratic machine, led by Hugh McLoughlin, controlled the city's government, with an occasional interruption by Republican reformers such as Seth Low. After years of contention the Democratic machine, supported by the working class and immigrants, lost out to the reformers, who joined their counterparts in New York City and New York State to move toward consolidation. On 1 January 1898 the City of Brooklyn became the Borough of Brooklyn.

2. From Consolidation to the Late Twentieth Century

The loss of political independence did nothing to hinder growth. By 1900 the population of Brooklyn exceeded one million. The expansion of existing transit lines, the arrival of subways, and the extension of public utilities made possible widespread residential and commercial development. During the first decades of the twentieth century the outlying towns of Flatbush, Gravesend, New Utrecht, and Flatlands began to urbanize. The first subway into Brooklyn, which opened in 1908, and two additional bridges crossing the East River from Manhattan, completed by 1909, contributed to rapid residential and industrial development. The electrification of the elevated railways and steam railways by 1900 and the takeover of many of the existing lines by the Brooklyn Rapid Transit Company enabled the connection of various routes.

Industry in Brooklyn was still expanding, with more than 100,000 factory workers by 1905 and more than 165,000 by the 1920s. Industrial complexes such as Bush Terminal (1902) that fused docking, factory, warehousing, and transportation functions continued to draw large manufacturers, and industrial and business expansion brought more population. Until the passage of the national immigration laws, culminating in the Immigration Act of 1924, Brooklyn attracted hundreds of thousands of immigrants, many of them from eastern and southern Europe. Rural Americans, now including many blacks from the South, were also arriving, particularly during the Depression. The cultural institutions moved from the older downtown area farther into central Brooklyn, following the movement of population. Schools and libraries multiplied. And with the arrival of the automobile, suburban developments, attached houses, and apartment buildings began filling in the street grids in outlying areas. By the 1920s the Brooklyn Dodgers were becoming a symbol of fortitude for masses of local residents. Brooklyn had more than 2.5 million residents by 1930, making it the most populous borough in New York City. The new modes of transportation were rendering the old obsolete. In 1924 the Fulton Ferry was discontinued. and the first airport in New York City, Floyd Bennett Field, was dedicated in 1931. In 1936 the Independent subway (IND) opened in Brooklyn, and in 1940 elevated service ceased operation on Fulton Street downtown.

As outlying residential areas developed, neighborhoods closer to downtown were transformed. Older one-family houses and row houses were converted into rental apartments and rooming houses, and already congested working-class communities became more so. Decline and deterioration, the arrival of the "slum," seemed inevitable. The New Deal brought several public housing projects and other public improvements, such as community swimming pools. And the Second World War brought new jobs: the Brooklyn Navy Yard, which alone produced more warships than all of Japan between 1942 and 1945, employed some seventy thousand men and women in continuous shifts. The postwar years brought general prosperity to Brooklyn, and its population peaked in 1950 at 2.7 million. In the 1950s a renewal project of the borough's civic center eliminated a substantial amount of older housing and businesses, but the resulting housing, parks, and wide thoroughfares left the district devoid of its former cosmopolitan vitality.

Postwar prosperity did not last, as the borough fell into a decline symbolized by the demise in 1955 of its one nationally known daily newspaper, the *Brooklyn Eagle*, and the departure in 1957 of its fabled baseball team, the Dodgers. The same automobile that had stimulated development of the borough's suburban areas now took residents beyond its borders to yet newer suburbs. Spurred by new federal housing mortgage and highway construction programs and the completion of the Verrazano Narrows Bridge in 1964, hundreds of thousands of white, middle-class residents abandoned Brooklyn for Long Island, Staten Island, and New Jersey, to be replaced largely by minority populations.

Brooklyn experienced a severe loss in jobs at the same time. Total manufacturing employment fell from more than 235,000 in 1954 to less than 200,000 by 1970, as companies looked beyond the borough for vacant land on which to build more efficient facilities, as well as cheaper labor and utilities, and lower taxes. Taking advantage of federal tax credits for new capital investment, whole industries such as shipping and brewing abandoned the borough outright. In 1956 the Port of New York Authority purchased and renovated two miles (three kilometers) of deteriorating waterfront, but in less than two decades, after failing to provide the requisite facilities for containerization, the piers were all but abandoned. In 1966 the federal government shut down the Brooklyn Navy Yard, leaving the waterfront almost totally inactive. By 1970 entire industrial and residential districts had taken on the appearance of bombed-out communities of wartime.

After 1970 Brooklyn experienced hardship as well as revitalization. Once-vigorous working-class and immigrant communities became desolate wastelands. Even where the city made some efforts to build subsidized housing, as in Coney Island, the new projects often failed to revive the community. In other neighborhoods efforts by long-time residents and new arrivals were more successful. Using public and private funds, organizations such as the Bedford Stuyvesant Restoration Corporation and the Pratt Center for Community and Environmental Development and businesses such as the Brooklyn Union Gas Company and Consolidated Edison improved housing conditions and created new amenities. At the same time local initiatives began to supply new low- and moderate-cost housing, notably in Brownsville and East New York, where the Nehemiah Plan produced new residences. The landmarks preservation movement inspired the revitalization of many historic neighborhoods, including Boerum Hill, Brooklyn Heights (the first Historic District approved by the city's Landmarks Preservation Commission), Carroll Gardens, Clinton Hill, Cobble Hill, Ditmas Park, Fort Greene, Greenpoint, Park Slope, Prospect Heights, Stuyvesant Heights, and Sunset Park.

Through government and private intervention Brooklyn strove to revitalize its economic core. In the early 1970s the City of New York, in cooperation with local nonprofit groups, began to transform the disused Brooklyn Navy Yard into an industrial park. This met with some success, as did several maritime projects in South Brooklyn. A number of national companies such as International Business Machines (IBM) collaborated on economic development with the Bedford Stuyvesant Restoration Corporation. The downtown business district, which during the 1970s declined from third-largest in the United States to sixth-largest, still employed some forty thousand workers. In efforts to stem its decline, a public–private partnership built the Fulton Mall in 1977, transforming the district's major street into a pedestrian artery. Although manufacturing employment fell below 100,000 by the early 1980s, there was a slight increase in later years, and service employment increased as well. And by the mid 1990s MetroTech, a large academic and high-technology office and research complex, was adding thousands of workers and a new vitality to downtown.

The borough remains widely known for its cultural institutions. The Brooklyn Public Library (formed in 1896, merged in 1903 with the Mercantile Library) occupies a headquarters erected in the 1930s near Prospect Park, and also administers some fifty-eight branches and a business library. The Brooklyn Botanic Garden, opened in 1911 next to Prospect Park, is one of the world's great public horticultural institutions and was the first botanical garden to establish a garden specifically for children. Other notable institutions include the Brooklyn Children's Museum (1899), the first museum of its kind in the world; the Brooklyn Academy of Music, one of the nation's premier avant-garde performing arts centers; the Brooklyn Historical Society, which features a permanent exhibition on the history of Brooklyn in addition to an extraordinary library and numerous public programs; the New York Aquarium (moved to Brooklyn in 1957); the federally administered Harbor Defense Museum; and many educational institutions, including Brooklyn College, Pratt Institute, Long Island University, and Polytechnic University.

Periods of phenomenal growth and devastating declines have both contributed to the richness of Brooklyn. While the growth has allowed the borough to prosper, the declines have resulted inadvertently in the survival of of aspects of local history that might have disappeared had the prosperity been constant — street names, houses, factory buildings, cultural institutions, whole neighborhoods, and even remnants of the original town centers. The combination of these vestiges of the past with the energy of the present gives Brooklyn its promise for the future.

Henry R. Stiles, ed.: *History of the City of Brooklyn* (Brooklyn: Published by subscription, 1867–70)
Henry R. Stiles, ed.: *The Civil, Political, Professional and Ecclesiastical History and Commercial and Industrial Record of the County of Kings and the City of Brooklyn, New York, from 1683–1884* (New York: W. W. Munsell, 1884)
David Ment: *The Shaping of a City: A Brief History of Brooklyn* (New York: Brooklyn Educational and Cultural Alliance, 1979)
Margaret Latimer: *Brooklyn Almanac: Illustrations, Facts, Figures, People, Buildings, Books* (New York: Brooklyn Educational and Cultural Alliance, 1984)

Margaret Latimer

Brooklyn, Bath and West End Railroad. The successor to the Brooklyn, Bath and Coney Island horsecar line, founded in 1862, that connected 25th Street and 5th Avenue in Brooklyn and the ferry slip at 39th Street in Brooklyn with the Tivoli Hotel and Amusement Park in Coney Island. The line was completed in 1867, and in 1870 steam power replaced the horses. In 1885 the line was renamed the Brooklyn, Bath and West End when it was acquired by the Atlantic Avenue Railroad. It merged in 1898 with the Nassau Electric Railroad and in the following year became part of the Brooklyn Rapid Transit Company. Electric trolley service began in 1901 and an elevated line was completed in 1917 (it is now part of the "B" line). The trolley service continued on the original grade until 1947.

James C. Greller and Edward C. Watson: *Brooklyn Elevated* (Hicksville, N.Y.: N.J. International, 1987)

John Fink

Brooklyn, Canarsie and Rockaway Beach Rail Road. Railroad opened on 21 October 1865 as a subsidiary of the Long Island Rail Road. It connected East New York with Canarsie Landing by rail, with a ferry from the Canarsie Landing to Rockaway Beach. The line was electrified in 1906, when its road was leased to the Brooklyn Union Elevated Railroad (a subsidiary of Brooklyn Rapid Transit). During the early years of the twentieth century the line offered the most popular route for New Yorkers seeking to visit the amusement park at Canarsie Beach. Service between Canarsie Landing and Rockaway Avenue was provided from October 1917 by a trolley shuttle and from 1951 by buses. In 1928 the elevated tracks of the railroad were connected to the subway line of Brooklyn Manhattan Transit running to 14th Street in Manhattan.

James C. Greller and Edward C. Watson: *Brooklyn Elevated* (Hicksville, N.Y.: N.J. International, 1987)

John Fink

Brooklyn, Flatbush and Coney Island Railway. Railroad that began service on 2 July 1878. It began as a steam railroad connecting the Brighton Hotel near Coney Island with the Long Island Rail Road at Atlantic and Franklin avenues. In 1887 the line merged with the Brooklyn Union Elevated Railroad (a subsidiary of Brooklyn Rapid Transit) and was renamed the Brooklyn and Brighton Beach Railway. An extension was then built between Prospect Park and Fulton Street (now known as the "S" line, or Franklin Avenue Shuttle) to provide direct access between Brighton and downtown Brooklyn. In 1905 electric power replaced steam and the line was rebuilt, with an "open cut" between Prospect Park and Avenue H and an elevated structure south of Avenue H. The company extended the elevated line in 1917 to Stillwell Avenue on Coney Island, thus forming a double-level structure that became strongly associated in the popular mind with Coney Island. Direct service between Brighton Beach and midtown Manhattan was established in 1920 when the subway between Prospect Park and DeKalb Avenue was completed. The railroad was the forerunner of the "D" and "Q" subway lines in Brooklyn.

James C. Greller and Edward C. Watson: *Brooklyn Elevated* (Hicksville, N.Y.: N.J. International, 1987)

John Fink

Brooklyn Academy of Music [BAM]. Performing arts center on Lafayette Avenue in downtown Brooklyn. The present building was erected by the firm of Herts and Tallant in 1908, and replaces one at Montague and Clinton streets opened on 15 January 1861 and destroyed by fire on 30 November 1903. The academy is a stately, cream-colored brick building in the neo-Italianate style that includes three major performance spaces: the Opera House (seating 2121), the Playhouse, a former music hall (seating 1078), and Leperq Space, a former ballroom (seating five hundred); there are also many offices, meeting rooms, dressing rooms, and an impressive lobby of five thousand square feet (465 square meters). From 1935 to 1970 BAM was one of several organizations in the borough affiliated with the Brooklyn Institute of Arts and Sciences. At the initiative of Harvey Lichtenstein, president and executive producer, the academy expanded its offerings in 1967 to encompass ethnic music, dance, and theater. The Next Wave Festival, an avant-garde series, was launched in 1981. In the same year the academy formed a local development corporation that purchased and refurbished several performing sites nearby. The academy emphasizes new and unusual repertory and draws audiences from throughout the metropolitan area. The Brooklyn Philharmonic is the resident orchestra.

"Formal Opening of the Academy of Music in Brooklyn," *Musical Courier*, 23 Sept 1908, pp. 12–13
Ruth Robinson: "Brooklyn Academy of Music Reawakens from Its Cultural Limbo," *New York Times*, 8 Feb 1971, p. 29
Brendan Gill: "BAM Grows in Brooklyn," *New York Times Magazine*, 24 Oct 1976, pp. 68–72
Martha McGowan: *Growing Up in Brooklyn: The Brooklyn Academy of Music: Mirror of a Changing Borough* (New York: Brooklyn Union Gas, 1983)
Irving Kolodin et al.: "New York," *The New Grove Dictionary of American Music*, ed. H. Wiley Hitchcock and Stanley Sadie (London: Macmillan, 1986)
Cathleen McGuigan: "The Avant-Garde Courts Corporations: The Brooklyn Academy of Music Raises Millions for Its Performance Arts Festival," *New York Times Magazine*, 2 Nov 1986, pp. 34–37, 58, 64–65

Bruce C. MacIntyre

Brooklyn Apprentices Library. Forerunner of the BROOKLYN MUSEUM.

Brooklyn Army Terminal. Military ocean supply facility situated in Sunset Park along 2nd Avenue from 58th to 65th streets. It was designed by Cass Gilbert and completed in 1919. The terminal covered ninety-seven acres (thirty-nine hectares) and consisted of nineteen structures, including two eight-story warehouses of reinforced concrete, one of which was the largest warehouse in the world. A unique interior well permitted direct loading and unloading to any level of the building, and three enclosed two-story piers permitted the simultaneous loading of twenty oceangoing vessels. During the Second World War many of the three million troops and sixty-three million tons (fifty-seven million metric tons) of supplies sent overseas by the New York Port of Embarkation passed through it. In 1984 the New York Public Development Corporation bought the facility, which was converted to manufacturing space for many small businesses.

"United States Army Supply Base, New York," *American Architect*, 26 Nov 1919, pp. 651–58, plates 179–85

Herbert S. Crocker: *Army Supply Base Brooklyn, N.Y. Completion Report* (Washington: U.S. Department of War, Department of the Army, Construction Division, 1919)

Andrew L. Yarrow: "Garment Makers Find New Home in Brooklyn," *New York Times*, 27 Oct 1991, §1, p. 26

Joseph F. Meany Jr.

Right *Brooklyn Borough Hall,* ca *1896,* center *Kings County Courthouse (both designed by Gamaliel King),* left *Kings County Elevated Railroad along Fulton Street*

Brooklyn Atlantics. Baseball team. Formed in August 1856 in Bedford, Brooklyn, it was one of the dominant teams of the early years of baseball. The social club that sponsored the team had as members many butchers and others from the food trades, and enjoyed close ties with local political factions. The team had a large working-class following and won several unofficial championships during the 1860s. Originally an amateur organization, it fielded a few paid players after the Civil War. Perhaps its greatest achievement was its defeat in 1870 of the first entirely professional baseball team, the Cincinnati Red Stockings, which until then had won eighty-four consecutive games. Reorganized as an all-professional team, the Atlantics competed in the National Association of Professional Base Ball Players from 1872 to 1875.

George B. Kirsch

Brooklyn–Battery Tunnel. The longest continuous underwater tunnel for motor vehicles in North America, spanning Upper New York Bay between the southern tip of Manhattan and the Brooklyn–Queens Expressway in Brooklyn. The tunnel was designed by Ole Singstad. Construction began in 1940 and was suspended during the Second World War; the tunnel opened to traffic on 25 May 1950. Two tubes lined in cast iron and measuring 31 feet (9.5 meters) in diameter span 9117 feet (2781 meters). Air is circulated through the tunnel by four ventilating towers, including one situated near Governors Island. The Brooklyn–Battery Tunnel is used by 59,000 vehicles a day.

Rebecca Read Shanor

Brooklyn Borough Hall. Building at 209 Joralemon Street, opened in 1848 as the city hall of Brooklyn. Plans were laid in 1835, a year after Brooklyn was granted its city charter. The winning entry in a design competition was submitted by the architect Calvin Pollard, who proposed a majestic building in a Greek Revival style. Construction began in 1836 but was halted after the foundation was completed owing to the city's precarious financial condition and the panic of 1837. Interest in resuming construction revived in the early 1840s. In 1845 a bond issue of $50,000 was authorized by the state legislature and Gamaliel King, an architect from Brooklyn, was commissioned to design a building for the existing foundation. His design, a simplified version of Pollard's, called for a structure of Tuckahoe marble with an Ionic portico and a wooden cupola. In 1895 the cupola and sections of the interior were destroyed by fire; in 1898 Vincent Griffith and the firm of Stoughton and Stoughton designed and installed a cupola of cast iron. On the consolidation of New York City in 1898 the building became the borough hall. The room formerly used by the Common Council was converted into a courtroom in a beaux-arts style by the architect Axel Hedman in 1902. Brooklyn Borough Hall deteriorated steadily until its restoration was completed in 1989 under the direction of the firm of Conklin Rossant.

William J. Conklin and Jeffrey Simpson: *Brooklyn's City Hall* (New York: Department of General Services, 1983)

Andrew S. Dolkart: *Borough Hall, 1848–1949* (New York: Fund for the Borough of Brooklyn, 1989)

Andrew S. Dolkart

Brooklyn Bridge. Steel suspension bridge across the East River between Brooklyn and Manhattan, opened on 24 May 1883. Its span of 1595.5 feet (486.3 meters) between towers was for a time the longest in the world. The bridge was the inspiration of the engineer John Augustus Roebling, the inventor of wire cable and an accomplished bridge builder who in 1867 put forth a plan to William C. Kingsley, publisher of the *Brooklyn Eagle.* He envisioned two massive stone towers, a network of steel cables suspended from the towers and embedded in anchorages at either end, vertical wires connecting the roadbed to the cables and reinforced by diagonal stays running down from the towers, and iron trusses underpinning the suspended floor from tower to tower to stiffen the roadbed. The unprecedented use of steel in a suspension bridge was intended to provide unmatched strength and stability. A bill to incorporate the New York Bridge Company, introduced in the state legislature at the behest of Kingsley by Henry Murphy, a state senator and former mayor of Brooklyn, was passed in April 1867 after an unusually cold winter that emphasized the vulnerability of ferry service to the elements. The project suffered a severe setback in June 1869, when just as the necessary approvals had been secured Roebling was fatally injured by a ferry that toppled him from a waterfront piling. His place was taken by his son Washington Roebling, who solved many structural problems in what remained a difficult and dangerous project. So that the towers of the bridge would sit firmly on bedrock, the riverbed was excavated by men working in huge, bottomless wooden boxes called caissons. The risk of fire was ever present and the men were susceptible to the bends (then called caisson disease and poorly understood). Roebling himself fell victim to the bends while working alongside the men sinking the western caisson in the summer of 1872, and was an invalid to the end of his life. He continued nevertheless to supervise operations through a telescope from his room on

View of the Brooklyn Bridge from Manhattan, ca *1883*

Columbia Heights while his wife, Emily Warren Roebling, relayed his instructions to workers and managers. The project continued to be plagued with difficulties: in 1878 Washington Roebling found that defective wire rope had been woven into the bridge cables, the result of graft on the part of the suppliers (he used sound wire to reinforce the cables), and soon afterward the project ran short of money (new appropriations were made in 1879). On its completion the bridge was widely acclaimed as the "new eighth wonder of the world." Its lavish dedication was attended by the mayors of Brooklyn and New York City, Governor Grover Cleveland, and President Chester A. Arthur, but not by Roebling, whose relations with the bridge company for the last four years of the project had been deeply strained. The opening of the bridge to the public a week later was marred by the deaths of twelve pedestrians, who were trampled during a panic set off by a shouted warning, anonymous and groundless, that the bridge was in danger of imminent collapse.

The Brooklyn Bridge became a highly recognizable landmark and an important cultural icon, and many artists and writers saw it as a symbol of American urbanization and industrialization. To Walt Whitman it was the work of engineering that completed Columbus's mission and helped to create a more closely linked world; to Hart Crane in the 1920s it was an affirmation of love, beauty, and the divine wholeness and unity of all history. The early-twentieth-century painters John Marin and Joseph Stella saw the bridge and the skyscrapers nearby as the embodiment of the evolving new world. Henry James detested the bridge, which he characterized as a mechanical monster and a soulless loom across which the "electric bobbins" of trains wove together two cities and by extension the world. But the critic Lewis Mumford believed that the Brooklyn Bridge had become "a source of joy and inspiration to the artist, perhaps the most completely satisfying structure of any kind that [has] appeared in America." No other bridge has ever been so richly woven into American culture.

Alan Trachtenberg: *Brooklyn Bridge: Fact and Symbol* (New York: Oxford University Press, 1965)
David G. McCullough: *The Great Bridge* (New York: Simon and Schuster, 1972)

For further illustration see FULTON FERRY.

Ellen Fletcher

Brooklyn Children's Museum. Museum opened in 1899 in two Victorian mansions at 5 Brooklyn Avenue and St. Mark's Avenue as the first children's museum in the United States. In 1976 a spacious new building was erected on the same site. The museum was the first to use interactive, "hands-on" exhibits to help children understand the physical and cultural world. Most of the museum is underground and not visible from the street.

Laura J. Lewison

Brooklyn College. College of the City University of New York, opened in 1910 as an extension division of City College for Teachers. It was enlarged in 1917 to offer evening classes at the freshman level open to all male high school graduates. In 1926 the state's Board of Higher Education (then newly formed) opened the Brooklyn Collegiate Center of City College, a two-year college for men in an office building at Willoughby and Bridge streets. The formation of a new four-year college for men and women in Brooklyn was authorized by the Board of Higher Education in 1930 and came to fruition in 1937 with the opening of a newly constructed neo-Georgian campus on Avenue H in Flatbush. Harry D. Gideonse, the president from 1939 to 1966, built a college faculty and bureaucracy amid severe tensions between students and administration in the years surrounding the Second World War. The college had a reputation as a center of left-wing sentiment and was sometimes referred to as the "little red schoolhouse," although in reality the number of radicals on the campus was never very large (see COMMUNISM). After the war the college expanded its campus and programs but often suffered from a lack of space. During the 1960s and 1970s it was convulsed by demonstrations and takeovers of buildings led by black and Puerto Rican students demanding more power, peace protesters, and advocates of open admissions. The college suffered from high attrition rates and several critics asserted that open admissions had damaged its standards. In 1990 Brooklyn College had 16,603 full- and part-time students, taught by a distinguished faculty that included the poet Allen Ginsberg and the violinist Itzhak Perlman.

Murray M. Horowitz: *Brooklyn College: The First Half Century* (New York: Brooklyn College Press, 1981)

Selma Berrol

Brooklyn Collegiate and Polytechnic Institute. Original name of POLYTECHNIC UNIVERSITY.

Brooklyn Daily Times. Name from 1855 to 1932 of the BROOKLYN TIMES–UNION.

Brooklyn Dodgers. Baseball team, formed in 1883 when the Interstate Minor League granted a franchise in Brooklyn to Charles Byrne and Joseph Doyle, both businessmen from New York City, and Ferdinand Abell, a casino owner from Rhode Island. The team joined the major leagues in 1884 when it moved to the American Association; in 1890 it moved to the National League. The name derived from the reputed skill of residents of Brooklyn at evading the streetcars of the burgeoning trolley system; other names applied to the team in its early years included the Bridegrooms (inspired by a series of marriages by team members in 1889), the Superbas (because the manager at the turn of the century was Ned Hanlon, and a popular theatrical group at the time was called Hanlon's Superbas), and the Robins (after the manager from 1914 to 1931, Wilbert Robinson). The team played at two stadiums in South Brooklyn, each called Washington Park, and at Eastern Park in Brownsville near Broadway Junction before moving to Ebbets Field in 1913. The strong pitching of Jeff Pfeffer and Burleigh Grimes and the consistent batting and fielding of the left fielder Zach Wheat helped the team to win the National League pennant in 1916 and 1920, but it lost the World Series to the Boston Red Sox and the Cleveland Indians. In 1920 it played a twenty-

Ticket for the Brooklyn Dodgers' opening day at Ebbets Field, 1941

six-inning game at Boston that ended with the score tied at 1, and it also suffered the embarrassment of hitting into an unassisted triple play at Cleveland in the World Series. From 1909 to 1925 Wheat established team records for games played, hits, doubles, triples, and total bases. The first member of the Dodgers other than a pitcher to be elected to the Baseball Hall of Fame, Wheat was highly popular with fans throughout his career.

From 1925 to 1938 the Dodgers played an inept and unintentionally comic brand of baseball that earned them the nickname the Daffiness Boys. Their fortunes changed after Larry MacPhail became the general manager in 1938: he named Leo Durocher the manager, acquired young players like Pee Wee Reese and Pete Reiser, and engaged as the team's radio broadcaster Red Barber, whose relaxed Southern manner and knowledge of the game along with the Dodgers' improved play greatly increased the team's following. The fans in Brooklyn became widely known for their eccentricity. During the 1930s and 1940s Hilda Chester sat in the bleachers in center field bellowing at players and ringing a cowbell, and the Sym-Phony Band paraded through the stands serenading opposing players and umpires. The unofficial symbol of the team was a depiction by the cartoonist Willard Mullin of a Dodger player as an amiable bum. During the war years Branch Rickey assumed control of the team and in 1945 he signed Jackie Robinson to a contract with the Dodgers' minor league affiliate in Montreal. Robinson joined the team in 1947 as the first black player in the modern major leagues. His strength of character in withstanding severe racial bigotry united the team, and his outstanding play brought it wide acclaim. Between 1947 and 1957 the Dodgers benefited from a powerful offense led by Reese, Robinson, Duke Snider, Gil Hodges, Roy Campanella, and Carl Furillo that enabled them to win six National League pennants; opposed each time in the World Series by the New York Yankees, they were able to win only in 1955, largely because apart from Don Newcombe and Carl Erskine they were lacking in strong pitchers. After the 1957 season the Dodgers' president Walter O'Malley moved the team to Los Angeles.

Roger Kahn: *The Boys of Summer* (New York: Harper and Row, 1971)

Jules Tygiel: *Baseball's Great Experiment: Jackie Robinson and His Legacy* (New York: Random House, 1983)

Richard Goldstein: *Superstars and Screwballs* (New York: E. P. Dutton, 1991)

See also Sports, §§3, 4.

Stephen Weinstein

Brooklyn Eagle. Weekly newspaper. It began in 1841 as an organ of the Democratic Party called the *Brooklyn Eagle and King's County Democrat* and published daily. For two years its chief editor was Walt Whitman, who in 1846 articulated the principle that partisanship should not prevent the newspaper from speaking to all the people of Brooklyn. Although it focused for many years on promoting Brooklyn, by the time of the Civil War it was the most widely read afternoon newspaper in the United States, and during the war it was one of several publications that the federal government threatened to suspend. It remained the largest daily and Sunday newspaper in Brooklyn, and in 1937 absorbed its last major competitor, the *Brooklyn Times–Union.* Over the years the newspaper won the Pulitzer Prize four times, once for exposing corruption in the police department during the administration of Mayor William O'Dwyer. After a decline in daily circulation to 125,000, a long-running dispute with the New York Newspaper Guild, and a lengthy strike it ceased publication in 1955. For a few months in 1960 it resumed publication as a weekly newspaper, and it was published daily for a year ending in mid 1963. Among those who wrote for the *Brooklyn Eagle* were St. Clair McKelway, Hans von Kaltenborn, Edward Bok, Nunnally Johnson, and Winston Burdett. Until 1955 the offices were on Johnson Street (now Cadman Park East).

Raymond A. Schroth: *The Eagle and Brooklyn* (Westport, Conn.: Greenwood, 1974)

John J. Gallagher

Brooklyn Female Academy. Original name of Packer Collegiate Institute.

Brooklyn Ferry. Former name of Brooklyn Heights.

Brooklyn Friends School. Coeducational elementary and secondary school opened in 1867 in the basement of the Quaker Meeting House on Schermerhorn Street. In 1972 it moved to 375 Pearl Street in Brooklyn Heights (the former site of the Brooklyn Law School). The school adheres to Quaker educational principles and emphasizes academic excellence, tolerance, compassion, equality, community service, and pacifism. It was among the earliest schools in New York City to promote ethnic and racial diversity in its student body. The school sponsors a chorus consisting of students and the elderly that was the subject of the documentary film *Close Harmony*, which won an Academy Award.

Edgerton Grant North: *Seventy-five Years of Brooklyn Friends School* (New York: Brooklyn Friends School, 1942)

Richard Schwartz

Brooklyn Gas Light Company. Utility chartered in 1825. It failed but was revived in 1847 after receiving a contract to light streets. From 1849 it delivered gas manufactured from coal in a plant beside the Brooklyn Navy Yard. In 1895 it was one of seven firms that merged to form the Brooklyn Union Gas Company.

William J. Hausman

Brooklyn Heights. Neighborhood in northwestern Brooklyn (1992 pop. 19,874), bounded to the west and north by Columbia Heights and the Brooklyn–Queens Expressway, to the east by Court Street and Cadman Plaza West, and to the south by Atlantic Avenue. Canarsee Indians lived on the bluffs above the East River and called the place Ihpetonga. By 1642 farms in the area were served by ferries, the most important of which was run by Cornelis Dircksen from the foot of what is now Fulton Street to Peck Slip in Manhattan. The village of Brooklyn thrived around the ferry landing and along Fulton Street, but until the second decade of the nineteenth century the high ground overlooking the river was sparsely settled with a few good-sized farms; there were some factories along the wharves at water level. General Israel Putnam withdrew his troops to the area after the American defeat in the Battle of Long Island, during which Washington maintained his headquarters in a house at the foot of what is now Montague Street. Washington evacuated the troops across the river under cover of fog on 27 August 1776.

Speculative development in the area began soon after Robert Fulton's steam ferry began its dependable schedule of crossings of the East River in 1814. Streets were laid out and graded after Brooklyn was incorporated as a village in 1816, and from 1823 the merchant Hezekiah Pierpont advertised his property as

Brooklyn Heights, ca *1904.* Foreground *docks along the shore of Manhattan*

"the nearest country retreat" convenient for businessmen working in lower Manhattan. Soon other landowners including John Hicks, Jacob Middagh Hicks, John Middagh, Henry Remsen, and Teunis Joralemon divided their farms into lots measuring twenty-five by one hundred feet (eight by thirty meters) that are still the common unit of property in the neighborhood. The building boom of the 1820s began at the northern end of the district, on Hicks Street and the adjacent cross streets. Frame and brick buildings two and a half stories high in a late Federal style with pitched and gambrel roofs were standard; many belonged to tradespeople, seamen, and waterfront workers and a number still stand. By the 1830s and 1840s more substantial houses of brick and brownstone with Greek Revival details were being built farther south. In the following decades the houses grew larger, exhibiting the entire range of revival styles that swept American architecture: Italianate, Second Empire, Victorian Gothic, Romanesque, neo-Grec, and Classical Revival. Some of the houses belonged to merchants whose ships docked at the wharves below. Throughout the nineteenth century the neighborhood had an unmatched elegance. Warehouses along Furman Street below the bluff had trees and grass planted on their roofs: these were the back gardens of the houses of Columbia Heights.

In 1908 Interborough Rapid Transit opened its subway, breaking the seclusion of Brooklyn Heights and making it easier to live there and work elsewhere. Many of the patricians fled, and their mansions were partitioned into apartments and boarding houses. Artists and writers were attracted by the character of the neighborhood. Several large hotels were built, including the St. George on Clark Street, once the largest in New York City. By the time of the Depression much of the middle class was gone. The boarding houses had deteriorated into low-grade rooming houses, and social planners were describing parts of the neighborhood as slums. A section of the neighborhood was later designated for clearance and redeveloped under the Cadman Plaza Project. During the 1940s and 1950s the neighborhood suffered some stunning blows, notably the loss of its entire northwest corner for the construction of the Brooklyn–Queens Expressway in 1953. Many brownstone rows were felled to make way for large apartment buildings and institutional dormitories. An important step in redeveloping the neighborhood was taken when local civic groups such as the Brooklyn Heights Association cooperated with Robert Moses in planning the Esplanade, a park along the East River completed in 1950. In 1958 a group of residents formed the Community Conservation and Improvement Council (later absorbed by the Brooklyn Heights Association), which in 1965 succeeded in having the neighborhood listed on the National Register of Historic Places and designated the first Historic District in New York City. In the 1970s and 1980s gentrification transformed boarding houses into middle-class residences and multifamily condominiums. One of the more prominent structures in the neighborhood is the world headquarters of the Jehovah's Witnesses at 124 Columbia Heights.

Brooklyn Heights, 1992

WPAG

Clay Lancaster: *Old Brooklyn Heights: New York's First Suburb* (New York: C. E. Tuttle, 1961; repr. Dover, 1979)

David Ment: *The Shaping of a City: A Brief History of Brooklyn* (New York: Brooklyn Educational and Cultural Alliance, 1979)

Ellen Fletcher

Brooklyn Historical Society. Organization formed in 1863 as the Long Island Historical Society. It is one of the oldest historical societies in the country. The society first occupied quarters in the Hamilton Building at Court and Joralemon streets near Borough Hall and later moved to a building at 128 Pierrepont Street in Brooklyn (where it remained into the 1990s). Designed and built by George B. Post and completed in 1880, the new building originally housed an auditorium, offices, a museum on the fourth story, and a research library on the second story with black ash woodwork and stained glass windows. It was the first major structure in greater New York to use extensive terra-cotta ornament and in 1991 was declared a National Historic Landmark; the library is one of few interior landmarks in Brooklyn. In the early twentieth century the society suffered a decline in membership and income, the auditorium was converted into commercial space, and the museum closed. Renewed growth in the early 1980s enabled the society to expand its public programs and mount changing exhibitions; in 1985 it took its current name. Brooklyn's History Museum, a permanent exhibition on the history of Brooklyn, opened in the renovated former auditorium in 1989. The society continues to operate a research library and sponsors exhibitions and educational programs for schoolchildren and adults. Its collection of materials related to Brooklyn, the largest in existence, includes paintings, sculptures, and other works of fine art and decorative art, archaeological artifacts, books, photographs, manuscripts, and ephemera.

Ellen Marie Snyder-Grenier

Brooklyn Howard Orphan Asylum. The first orphanage and philanthropic institution controlled and operated by blacks in greater New York. It was opened in 1866 at the corner of Dean Street and Troy Avenue by Sarah A. Tillman, a black minister's widow who took in twenty children of emancipated slaves when they could not be accommodated at the Colored Orphan Asylum. She was assisted in her efforts by General Oliver Otis Howard, later a founder of Howard University. Black control of the asylum was maintained for more than fifty years, much of that time under the leadership of the preacher William F. Johnson. Under increasing financial pressure, the all-female, all-black board of managers was replaced in 1913 by an all-male board with a white majority and a white president. Wartime shortages and the deterioration of its physical plant forced the orphanage to close in 1918. It was then transformed into the Howard Memorial Fund, which provided scholarships for needy children into the 1990s.

Seth M. Scheiner: *Negro Mecca: A History of the Negro in New York City, 1865–1920* (New York: New York University Press, 1965)

Carleton Mabee: "Charity in Travail: Two Orphan Asylums for Blacks," *New York History* 55 (1974), 55–77

Mike Sappol

Brooklyn Jewish Center. Conservative synagogue on Eastern Parkway, designed in a neoclassical style in 1919 by Louis Abramson. The building had an enormous sanctuary, a gymnasium, a swimming pool, and a kosher restaurant. The congregation, which in the 1940s included more than two thousand families, was presided over for half a century by Israel H. Levinthal. The Brooklyn Jewish Center offered a wide range of classes, lectures, and publications and helped to enlarge the role of the American synagogue.

Jenna Weissman Joselit

Brooklyn Law School. Private law school in downtown Brooklyn near several federal and state courthouses, opened in 1901 by William Payne Richardson (1864–1945). Its merger with St. Lawrence University (Canton, New York) in 1903 and its return to independent status in 1943 were both overseen by Richardson, who remained the dean until his death. Situated in its early years at various buildings in Brooklyn Heights and then at 305 Washington Street (from 1904) and 375 Pearl Street (from 1928), the school in 1968 built a ten-story facility at 250 Joralemon Street, to which it later added an annex. In the mid 1990s Brooklyn Law School had about fourteen hundred full- and part-time students.

Brooklyn Law School (New York: Brooklyn Law School, 1940)

Marc Ferris

Brooklyn–Manhattan Transit Corporation [BMT]. One of two privately operated subway companies in New York City in the late nineteenth century and the early twentieth. Formed in 1896 as the Brooklyn Rapid Transit Company (BRT), a securities holding firm, it was greatly enlarged over the next five years through a series of mergers and leases that combined such previously independent entities as the Brooklyn Union, Kings County, and Seaside and Brooklyn Bridge elevated lines; the Sea Beach, Brighton, and West End steam surface railroads; and a number of electric and horse railways. In 1899 the company concluded an important traffic-sharing agreement with the Long Island Rail Road: the railroad was allowed to develop transit lines in Queens, and the BRT took over some of its routes in Brooklyn, such as the Culver and South Brooklyn lines.

The Brooklyn Rapid Transit Company controlled nearly all the street and elevated lines in Brooklyn by 1901. Yet its multiple, overlapping routes had never been combined into a coherent network, and although the company served many passengers who commuted to the financial district in downtown Manhattan its elevated lines ended at ferry terminals at the edge of the East River in Brooklyn (except for one short shuttle line across the Brooklyn Bridge). These shortcomings and the extension of service to Brooklyn by Interborough Rapid Transit (IRT) in January 1908 prompted the company to build its own subways. In March 1913 the BRT signed a contract with the New York Public Service Commission known as Contract no. 4, which

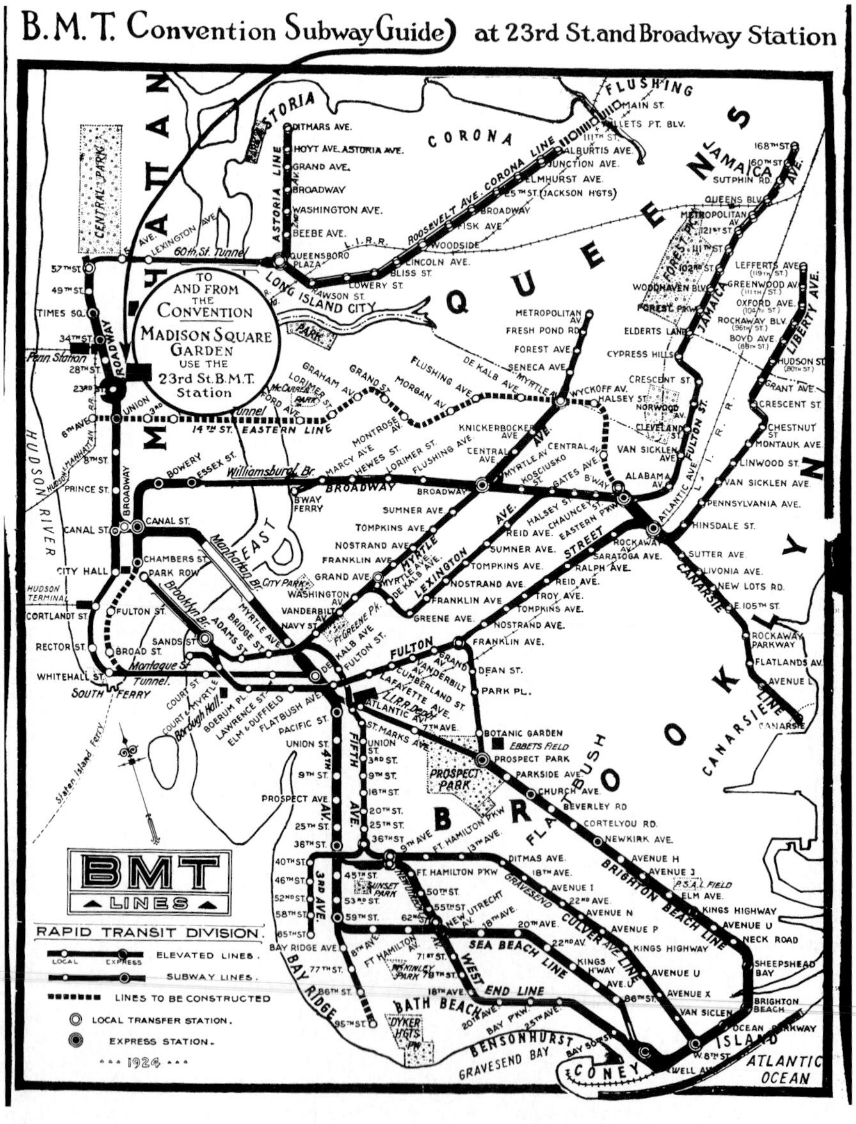

Map of the Brooklyn–Manhattan Transit system issued for the Democratic National Convention at Madison Square Garden, June 1924

provided for the construction of 111 miles (179 kilometers) of new rapid transit routes in Brooklyn, Manhattan, and the Bronx. These new lines unified the company's sprawling system and allowed its riders to travel directly from Manhattan to Brooklyn. Contract no. 4 and a complementary agreement between the Public Service Commission and the IRT effected the single largest expansion of the subway system in the city's history.

Inflation after the First World War affected the Brooklyn Rapid Transit Company severely. The price of materials like coal and iron escalated, but Contract no. 4 limited the fare that the company could charge to five cents. On 1 November 1918 the BRT experienced the single worst accident in the history of American mass transit when a train derailed at Malbone Street in Brooklyn, killing 102 passengers. This accident and continuing financial problems forced the company to declare bankruptcy on 31 December 1918. When it emerged from bankruptcy on 15 March 1923 the company changed its name, largely in an attempt to erase the stigma of the crash. The Depression ruined the BMT: its receipts declined 12 percent from 1928 to 1937, its earnings from $6.6 million in 1928 to $601,800 in 1939. On 1 June 1940 the City of New York under Mayor Fiorello H. La Guardia acquired the assets of the Brooklyn–Manhattan Transit Corporation, and its rapid transit lines became a division of the city's transit system.

The Rapid Transit Situation in Greater New York (New York: Brooklyn–Manhattan Transit Corporation, 1927)

Clifton Hood

Brooklyn Manor. Section of Woodhaven in southwestern Queens, lying on both sides of the abandoned Rockaway branch of the Long Island Rail Road. It was once the Vanderveer farm between Woodhaven Boulevard and 96th Street, from which 603 building lots were made in 1892 north of Jamaica Avenue. Brooklyn Hills was developed in 1905 from the former estate of the Napier family and extended from Forest Park to Atlantic Avenue between 100th and 104th streets.

Vincent Seyfried

Brooklyn Museum, 1994

Brooklyn Museum. Museum at 200 Eastern Parkway. Its forerunner was the Brooklyn Apprentices Library, formed in 1823 by the local merchant William Wood for the moral education of apprentices; modeled after the Apprentice's Library opened by Benjamin Franklin in Philadelphia, it occupied a number of sites successively before being moved into the Brooklyn Lyceum on Washington Street, which housed a small natural history collection and offered public lectures and classes. Under the auspices of the manufacturer Augustus Graham the lyceum and the library merged to form the Brooklyn Institute in 1843, which soon offered small exhibitions and more extensive educational programs; Graham endowed a library and a fine arts gallery. In 1890 the Citizens' Committee on Museums of Art and Science publicly advocated continued support of the institute to accommodate the growing population of Brooklyn. During the following decade the institute was expanded and renamed the Brooklyn Institute of Arts and Sciences. Loosely modeled on the Metropolitan Museum of Art and the Museum of Natural History, it was intended to attract a wider audience and house larger collections. Such institutions as the Brooklyn Academy of Music, the Brooklyn Botanic Garden, and the Brooklyn Children's Museum now became part of the Brooklyn Museum. The first director, Franklin W. Hooper, reorganized the existing collections and amassed new ones and oversaw the construction of a new building designed in 1893 by the architecture firm of McKim, Mead and White to be the largest of its kind in the world. Based on a design by the French theorist J. N. L. Durand, the plans called for a series of beaux-arts quadrant pavilions (square buildings with a glass-enclosed central court), linked together to represent an encyclopedia of human culture; only one quadrant was completed (1927).

The collections expanded and the museum reorganized again during the second and third decades of the twentieth century under William Henry Fox, and under Philip Youtz, the director from 1933. The natural history and science collections were given to other institutions and the art collections made available for study by designers. Controversy erupted in 1934 when Youtz had the grand staircase at the entrance removed to make the building symbolically more accessible and less imposing. In later years the collections were refined as the museum attracted a larger group of patrons, including the Havemeyers, the Friedsams, and the Kevorkians. The collections of Egyptian and African art at the Brooklyn Museum are among the finest in the United States; in 1993 the museum unveiled its newly organized Egyptian galleries, designed by Arata Isozaki.

Joan Darragh, Leland Roth, et al.: *A New Brooklyn Museum: The Master Plan Competition* (New York: Brooklyn Museum, 1988)

Linda Ferber: "History of the Collections," *Masterpieces in the Brooklyn Museum* (New York: Harry N. Abrams, 1988)

Peter L. Donhauser

Brooklyn Navy Yard. The popular name of a shipyard on the East River at Wallabout Bay, officially known as the New York Naval Shipyard. The purchase of land was authorized in 1800 by Secretary of the Navy Benjamin Stoddart; the commandant's house, designed by Charles Bulfinch and completed in 1806, is now on the National Register of Historic Places. In its early years the shipyard fitted out ships for ventures against Caribbean and Barbary pirates and during the War of 1812 readied more than a hundred vessels for raids on British merchant shipping. In the first half of the nineteenth century it benefited from the growth of the Port of New York and from developments in steam propulsion at private shipyards on the East River. Among the ships launched were the *Fulton*, the first oceangoing steamship in the U.S. Navy, and the steam frigate *Niagara*, which helped lay the first transatlantic cable. The United States Naval Lyceum was formed at the shipyard in 1833: a professional and cultural organization, it included among its members James Fenimore Cooper and Matthew C. Perry. During the Civil War more than six thousand workers

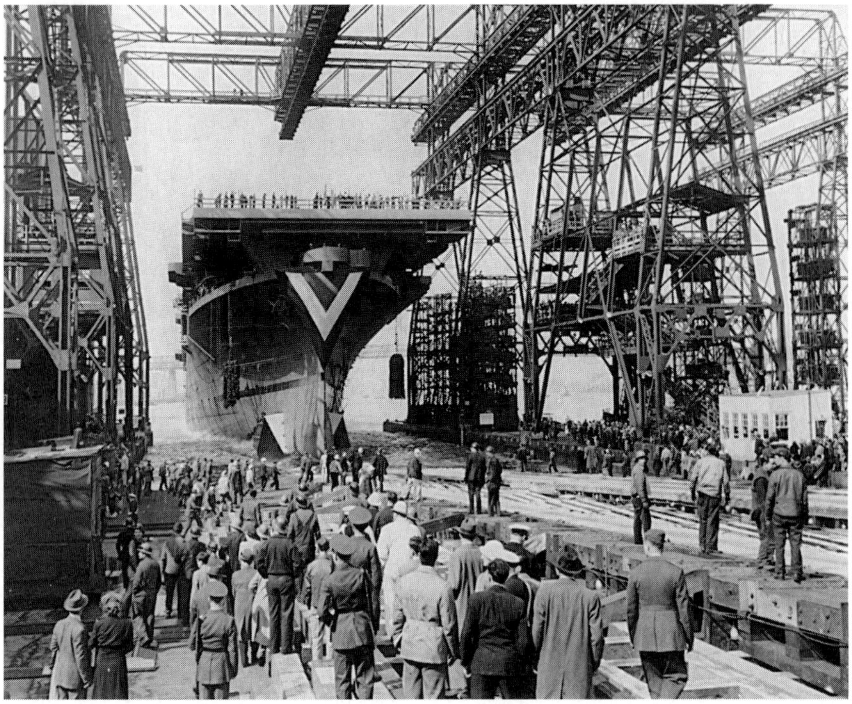

Launching of the USS Bon Homme Richard *at the Brooklyn Navy Yard, 29 April 1944*

built sixteen vessels, converted more than four hundred merchant and private ships to naval service, and fitted out the ironclad *Monitor.* The shipyard was the central base for ship repair and for distributing supplies to the Union fleet. During a worldwide race toward larger warships the battleship *Maine* (6682 tons) was launched in 1895, and the shipyard became the navy's principal supply depot during the Spanish–American War. The *Arizona* and six other battleships were built between 1906 and 1926, and in 1918 employment reached eighteen thousand.

During the Second World War the Brooklyn Navy Yard was the largest naval construction facility in the United States. Among the vessels completed there were the *Missouri* (45,000 tons), on the decks of which the Second World War officially ended on 2 September 1945. More than 71,000 men and women worked in shifts around the clock by 1944; in addition to battleships they built aircraft carriers and auxiliary vessels, repaired more than five thousand ships, and converted another 250. The shipyard by then included six drydocks, two building ways, eight piers, 270 buildings, nineteen miles (thirty kilometers) of streets, and thirty miles (forty-eight kilometers) of railroad track. It was the largest industrial center in the navy, as well as the largest in New York State. Naval construction declined in the late 1940s but revived during the cold war. In December 1960 fifty persons were killed when the aircraft carrier *Constellation* was ravaged by fire. From that time only six ships were built, as shipbuilding operations shifted to such southern ports as Newport News (Virginia) and Pascagoula (Mississippi). By 1965 fewer then seven thousand persons worked at the shipyard, and the navy closed the facility in 1966. The city then purchased 255 acres (103 hectares) of land on the site for an industrial park.

Adolph Wittemann: *U.S. Navy Yard, Brooklyn* (New York: Albertype, 1904)

Arnold Markoe

Brooklyn Public Library. Library system formed in Brooklyn in 1897. Its organizers envisioned a network of small libraries throughout Brooklyn rather than a system dependent on a large central library; construction nonetheless began for such a library in 1912 at Grand Army Plaza. Because funds were raised in stages the building was not completed until 1941, when it was named Ingersoll Memorial Library after the borough president at the time. Its modern architecture was praised in 1940 by the critic Lewis Mumford in the *New Yorker.* The first director was Mary E. Craigee, who oversaw the development of the system from its inception until 1898. The first branch, opened at Brooklyn Public School 3 in Bedford, had separate reading rooms for men and women and was one of the first libraries that allowed readers to browse. Between 1901 and 1923 Brooklyn received $1.6 million from the philanthropist Andrew Carnegie and built twenty-one branch libraries, most of which remained in use into the 1990s. A children's branch opened in Brownsville in 1914, equipped with child-sized furniture and fancifully decorated with scenes and figures from well-known stories (it is now the Stone Avenue Branch). The business library, opened in 1943 at 280 Cadman Plaza West, amassed a large collection and introduced a telephone reference service that in 1989 answered 115,700 queries. By 1990 the Brooklyn Public Library had fifty-eight branches. Among the services offered by the Brooklyn Public Library are programs for the elderly and the homebound, instruction in reading and writing for adults, a telephone reference service, and telecommunications devices for the deaf and hearing-impaired. The Central Library maintains a collection of books, sheet music, films, records, compact discs, and videocassettes. It has materials in sixty-four languages, including traveling collections in Russian, Vietnamese, Chinese, and Spanish. The Education and Job Information Center has study guides and college catalogues and a staff that assists in career counseling and résumé preparation, and a youth services department sponsors term paper workshops.

GraceAnne A. DeCandido

Brooklyn Rapid Transit Company [BRT]. A precursor of the BROOKLYN–MANHATTAN TRANSIT CORPORATION, formed in 1896.

Brooklyn Surface Railroad Riots. Violence that erupted throughout Brooklyn between 14 January and 2 February 1895 among striking surface railroad workers. See RIOTS.

Brooklyn Technical High School. A specialized high school at 29 Fort Greene Place. Plans for a science high school were promoted at the end of the First World War by Albert L. Colston, chairman of the mathematics department at Manual Training High School, who recognized the need for an advanced science, mathematics, and engineering curriculum in the city. Under his direction the technical program at Manual Training High School was overhauled, and an innovative engineering program was introduced that won approval from the Board of Superintendents in November 1918 and attracted more than twelve hundred students in the following year. The need for a modern facility was soon apparent, and in May 1922 the Board of Education announced plans for a technical high school. A renovated factory loft building at 49 Flatbush Avenue Extension (near the Manhattan Bridge) was the first site of Brooklyn Technical High School, which opened on 11 September 1922 with nearly 2500 students; Colston was named its principal. Mayor James J. Walker broke ground in 1930 for the present nine-story building on the block between South Elliot Place and Fort Greene Place, built at a cost of $5 million (unprecedented in the United States) and opened in September 1933. Students were admitted only after passing a demanding entrance examination. From November 1938 the school had a radio station, WNYE, that was used by the Board of Education. There were six thousand students from throughout the city by 1960; in 1970 the school became coeducational. Facilities for high-technology programs were added as part of $13 million in renovations begun in 1984. Enrollment stood at nearly five thousand in the mid 1990s. Among the graduates of Brooklyn Tech are the Nobel laureates George Wald (class of 1923, prize in physiology or medicine 1967) and Arno Penzias (class of 1951, prize in physics 1978).

Elliot Willensky: *When Brooklyn Was the World, 1920–1957* (New York: Harmony, 1986)

Allen J. Share

Brooklyn theater fire. Fire on 5 December 1876 in an elegant theater at 313 Washington Street, where a thousand spectators saw Miss Kate Claxton perform in *The Two Orphans*; the fire broke out backstage shortly before the end of the play. Although there was enough time for all to evacuate the building, the stairs became blocked when five hundred patrons in the balcony rushed for the exits, and 295 persons were killed. The fire consumed the entire theater: more than a hundred victims were so badly burned that they were buried in a common grave in Green-Wood Cemetery. The disaster became internationally known and compelled Brooklyn and New York City to impose stricter standards for fire inspections in theaters. In its number of casualties the fire was exceeded only by that at the Iroquois Theater in Chicago in 1903.

Report of the Executive Committee (Brooklyn: Brooklyn Theatre Fire Relief Association, 1879)

Edward T. O'Donnell

Brooklyn Times–Union. Daily newspaper. Launched in 1848 as the *Williamsburgh Daily Times*, it became the *Brooklyn Daily Times* on the unification of Brooklyn and Williamsburgh in 1855. The newspaper supported the anti-slavery movement and the presidential candidacy of Abraham Lincoln. Walt Whitman was a reporter and later the managing editor after he left the *Brooklyn Eagle*. Published seven days a week, the newspaper at one point had a circulation area that included all of Brooklyn and parts of Long Island. It became known as the *Brooklyn Times–Union* after buying the *Standard Union* in 1932. In 1937 it was bought by the *Brooklyn Eagle*.

Raymond A. Schroth: *The Eagle and Brooklyn* (Westport, Conn.: Greenwood, 1974)

John J. Gallagher

Brooklyn Union Gas Company. Utility formed in 1895 by the merger of the Brooklyn Gas Light Company (1825), Fulton Municipal Gas, Citizens Gas Light, Metropolitan Gas Light, Williamsburg Gas Light, People's Gas Light, and Nassau Gas Light. It later purchased several smaller companies and expanded into Queens. The company manufactured gas for several decades. It began to convert to natural gas after New York City was connected by the transcontinental pipeline in 1950 to the gas fields of the southwestern United States, and by August 1952 the conversion was complete. Later it acquired the New York and Richmond Gas Company (1957), which served Staten Island, the Kings County Lighting Company, and the Brooklyn Borough Gas Company (1959). After the energy crisis of the mid 1970s it purchased subsidiaries engaged in exploration and production. Brooklyn Union Gas in 1989 was the ninth-largest gas transmission and distribution company in the United States. In addition to natural gas it sold methane, propane, and gas appliances.

Elwin S. Larson: *Brooklyn Union Gas: Fueling Growth and Change in New York City* (New York: Newcomen Society, 1987)

William J. Hausman

Brooks Brothers. Firm of men's clothing retailers, opened in 1818 by Henry Sands Brooks at Catherine and Cherry streets, the center of the wholesale clothing trade. It became known for fine quality and was among the first stores to offer both custom- and ready-made clothing. After Brooks's death in 1833 the business was taken over by his sons Henry, Daniel, John, Elisha, and Edward. They gave the firm its current name in 1850 and opened a store at Broadway and Grand Street in 1858. The firm supplied uniforms for Union soldiers during the Civil War, efforts that made its original store a target of mob violence during the draft riots in 1863; it remained a military outfitter for many years. The years after the war were marked by several important developments. The store on Cherry Street closed in 1874 and the remaining one moved with the retail district to successive sites uptown until finally settling at Madison Avenue and 44th Street in 1915. In 1900 the firm became the first in the country to offer shirts with button-down collars. Partners were increasingly drawn from outside the Brooks family, and in 1903 the firm was transformed from a partnership into a corporation. In the following years stores were opened in Boston, San Francisco, Los Angeles, and Newport, Rhode Island. From the mid 1920s Brooks Brothers faced increasing financial difficulties. Its earnings dropped steadily during the 1930s, and by the end of 1935 it had an operating deficit of more than $1 million. In 1946 it was taken over by Julius Garfinckel, a retail firm in Washington, ending control by the Brooks family. Under the new management unprecedented sales and profits were achieved during the mid 1950s. Between 1955 and 1988, when the business was bought by the retail chain of Marks and Spencer, Brooks Brothers expanded its operations from six to forty-seven stores in the United States and twenty-one in Japan. It nonetheless suffered during an economic recession in the late 1980s as it was forced to compete with more stylish designers and stores. To attract younger customers it brought its conservative "Ivy League" styling up to date and adjusted its standards to produce more affordable clothing.

Eileen K. Cheng

Broun, (Matthew) Heywood (Campbell) (*b* Brooklyn, 7 Dec 1888; *d* Stamford, Conn., 18 Dec 1939). Columnist. He worked in New York City for the *New York Tribune* and the *New York World* (1921–28), where he wrote a column called "It Seems to Me" that later appeared in the *New York World–Telegram* and the *New York Post*; he also contributed to the *Nation* and the *New Republic*. He was nominated by the Socialist Party for Congress in the seventeenth district in Manhattan in 1930 and helped to found the American Newspaper Guild, of which he also served as president. His passionate defense of Sacco and Vanzetti eventually cost him his position as a columnist with the *World*. Broun was known for his opinionated and humorous writing and for his acumen, compassion, and wide-ranging interests. He lived from 1921 to 1928 at 333 West 85th Street and from 1933 at 1 West 67th Street.

Dale Kramer: *Heywood Broun: A Biographical Portrait* (New York: Current, 1949)

Brenda Wineapple

Brown, Charles Brockden (*b* Philadelphia, 17 Jan 1771; *d* Philadelphia, 22 Feb 1810). Novelist and journalist. A lawyer by profession, he visited New York City frequently from 1794 and lived there from October 1796 to March 1797 and from July 1798 to 1800. While in the city he published several novels, including *Ormond* (1799) and *Wieland* (1799), and edited and wrote for the literary and cultural journal *Monthly Magazine, and American Review*, which between April 1799 and December 1800 published eighteen issues containing American fiction and poetry, historical and scientific studies, reviews of American books, and essays extolling American culture. The gothic element in Brown's fiction was an important influence on Poe.

George A. Thompson, Jr.

Brown, Elmer E(llsworth) (*b* Kiantone, near Jamestown, N.Y., 28 Aug 1861; *d* New York City, 3 Nov 1934). Educator. He graduated from the State Normal College in Illinois in 1881, became a superintendent in Belvidere County (Illinois) later that year, and earned an AB at the University of Michigan (1889) and the PhD at the University of Halle–Wittenberg in Germany (1890). After working as a high school principal and teaching at the University of Michigan and the University of California at Berkeley he was appointed commissioner of education by President Theodore Roosevelt in 1906. During his tenure he became noted for his attention to Progressive reforms like rural education, the expansion of high schools, the teaching of home economics, and international education. In 1911 he resigned to become the seventh chancellor of New York University. There he continued the expansion begun by his predecessor, Henry Mitchell MacCracken, by developing a coeducational facility called Washington Square College (1914), improving the professional schools, establishing New York University Press (1916), enlarging the library system, and renovating buildings and property (including the School of Education in 1929). On his retirement in 1933 the university had more than forty thousand students and was the largest private university in the United States. Brown's published writings include *The Making of Our Middle Schools* (1903).

Theodore F. Jones: *New York University, 1832–1932* (New York: New York University Press, 1933)

Paul H. Mattingly

Brown, William Adams (*b* New York City, 29 Dec 1865; *d* New York City, 15 Dec 1943). Minister and educator. He graduated from Union Theological Seminary in 1890 and became a professor there in 1898. He was influenced in his commitment to church unity by the trial for heresy of Charles A. Briggs, and in his devotion to Christian social witness by the writings of William James. Elected to the national Board of Home Missions (1910), he championed the work of Charles Telzle and the Labor Temple. In 1927 and 1937 he was a delegate to the world conferences on church union, and he played an important role in developing the World Council of Churches (1938). He made many efforts to improve seminary education as the chairman of the Department of Research and Education of the Federal Council of Churches (1924) and as the president of the Religious Education Association (1928–31). Brown wrote the concluding volume of *The Education of American Ministers* (1934).

The Church through Half a Century: Essays in Honor of William Adams Brown (New York: Charles Scribner's Sons, 1936)

David Meerse

Brown Brothers Harriman. Firm of commercial bankers. It was formed by Alexander Brown in Philadelphia in 1818 as the firm of John A. Brown, an offshoot of a firm of Irish linen importers. In 1825 a branch called Brown Brothers was opened in New York City by James Brown, a son of Alexander Brown; with the firm of William and James Brown of Liverpool, it became an important commission house and merchant bank. The branch moved its offices to 59 Wall Street in 1843. Brown Brothers was known as a conservative house that helped to reorganize railroads during the late nineteenth century, and it was a leading provider of letters of credit throughout the world. In 1907 seven of the fourteen partners were members of the Brown family. After becoming independent of the firm in England in 1918 the American operation expanded during the 1920s and opened a large bond department. On 1 January 1931 it received its current name after merging with the private banks of W. Averell Harriman (formed in 1919) and the Harriman brothers (formed in 1927 by Harriman and his brother E. Roland Harriman). With the passage of the Banking Act of 1933 the firm ceased underwriting corporate securities and became a commercial bank. By 1994 it had sixteen offices worldwide, thirty-six general partners, and four limited partners. Brown Brothers Harriman is the oldest and largest private commercial bank in the United States.

John A. Kouwenhoven: *Partners in Banking: An Historical Portrait of a Great Private Bank* (Garden City, N.Y.: Doubleday, 1968; repr. 1983)

Mary E. Curry

Brownson, Orestes A(ugustus) (*b* Stockbridge, Vt., 16 Sept 1803; *d* Detroit, 17 April 1876). Philosopher and writer. He lived in New York City from 1826 to 1831. In 1838 he launched the *Boston Quarterly Review* as a radical publication. His indictment of capitalism in his essay "The Laboring Classes" was seized on by the Whigs in 1840 as a means of tarring President Martin Van Buren, whom he supported. The demagoguery of the election led Brownson to doubt the possibilities of democratic reform. He discontinued the *Review* in 1842 to write for the *U.S. Democratic Review*, published in New York City by John L. O'Sullivan. After exploring several faiths and organizing his own church in 1836 he caused a sensation by converting to Catholicism in 1844. As the editor and principal writer of *Brownson's Quarterly Review* (1844–64, 1873–75) he became an important critic of developments in literature, philosophy, science, religion, and government. Among the topics he explored were the relationship between church and state and the nature of civil and religious liberties. He moved the *Review* to New York City in 1855 and to Elizabeth, New Jersey, after a quarrel with Archbishop Hughes. Brownson wrote an autobiography, *The Convert* (1857), and *The American Republic* (1866), a philosophical essay on the indissolubility of the Union.

Arthur M. Schlesinger Jr.: *Orestes A. Brownson: A Pilgrim's Progress* (Boston: Little, Brown, 1939)
Thomas R. Ryan: *Orestes A. Brownson: A Definitive Biography* (Huntington, Ind.: Our Sunday Visitor Press, 1975)

Robert Emmett Curran

brownstones. Residential, sandstone row houses of two and three stories built throughout New York City during the nineteenth century. They evolved when the rising price of property in Manhattan during the 1840s and 1850s caused developers to modify the design of the traditional Federal or Greek Revival row house: a front setback was carved out to provide a feeling of spaciousness; the basement was raised to admit light, so that it could be used as a scullery and servants' work area; a large staircase with rails of wrought iron was installed, leading to a high stoop with a balustrade; and the entire building was extended into the rear yard to enlarge the space for family and servants. Brownstones were built in blocks of several at a time, and their flat cornices, continuous string-coursing, and regular stoops gave them an imposing regularity. Italianate windows and door hoods above the entrances accentuated the façades with striking shadows. "Jersey freestone," a reddish-brown sandstone of varying hues, was quarried in Passaic County, New Jersey, sawed by modern steam machinery into sheets four or six inches (ten or fifteen centimeters) thick, and mounted over a brick structural frame. Weathering eventually changed the stone to a chocolate brown and darkened the mortar to give the buildings a somber veneer. Although wealthy families at first resisted the new structures they came to appreciate their stolid private space, and during the social turbulence of the 1850s many families moved to the areas of major brownstone development, such as Gramercy Park and Brooklyn Heights. In the 1880s and 1890s creative and eclectic stylistic innovations appeared: heavy arched windows in the Richardsonian Romanesque style, asymmetrical features in the Queen Anne style, and the triangular roof lines, gabled niches, and three-paneled window bays of Charles Eastlake. The trim of some buildings was decorated with red, yellow, and tan brick and terra cotta, and several blocks of brownstones on the Upper West Side displayed a stunning variety of color.

The interior of a brownstone was cramped. One entered the front door into a vestibule about five feet (1.5 meters) square. Straight ahead were an ascending staircase and a hallway leading to the rear of the building; to the side of the vestibule lay a front parlor, at the rear of which overlooking the backyard lay a nearly identical dining room, where most entertaining took place. The parlor and the dining room could be united by opening a set of double doors surrounded by a decorative molding. Brownstones were often sufficiently deep that between the front and back rooms a third room could be interposed, usually a formal dining hall with a marbleized fireplace and gilt mirror. In a typical brownstone the family quarters were on the second story and the servants' quarters on the third, which sometimes contained interior rooms ventilated by air shafts.

The confining and expensive brownstones could not compete with the sprawling luxury apartments of the Dakota and the Ansonia or the suburban homes that became popular at the turn of the century, and in the early 1930s blocks of brownstones were leveled to allow for the construction of offices, notably around Rockefeller Center. Of those brownstones that remained many in midtown were subdivided before the Second World War into cheap rental apartments and rooming houses. Further demolition of brownstones funded by Title I of the Housing Act of 1949 and overseen by Robert Moses angered many residents and inspired them to political action. A renewal of interest in historic preservation led to the renovation of brownstones in Greenwich Village, on the Upper West Side, in Chelsea, and later in Park Slope. The Landmarks Preservation Commission, formed in 1965, protected the brownstone heritage of areas such as the Metropolitan Museum Historic District, Riverside Drive, and West 80th and 81st streets.

Charles Lockwood: *Bricks and Brownstones: The New York Row House, 1783–1929: An Architectural and Social History* (New York: McGraw–Hill, 1972)

For illustration see PARK SLOPE.

Joel Schwartz

Brownsville. Neighborhood in southeastern Brooklyn (1990 pop. 84,451), bounded to the north by Eastern Parkway, to the east by Van Sinderen Avenue, to the south by Linden Boulevard, and to the west by Rockaway Boulevard. It is named for Charles S. Brown, who built 250 frame houses there from 1865. Development remained slow until Aaron Kaplan in 1887 purchased land, built tenements, and enticed to the area several Jewish garment makers from the Lower East Side. Further settlement was spurred by the opening of the Fulton Street elevated railway in 1889. As the neighborhood became more accessible two-family homes and small tenements with storefronts at street level replaced earlier houses, and by 1910 large multi-family buildings made for crowded conditions. The area was a largely Jewish slum, with sweatshops and pushcarts and no sewers or paved streets. Living conditions improved after 1920, as did rapid transit connections to Manhattan with the completion in 1922 of the New Lots branch of Interborough Rapid Transit. The neighborhood prospered from the 1920s to the 1940s but nevertheless remained a center of labor radicalism: it elected socialists to the state assembly between 1915 and 1921 and a candidate of the American Labor Party in 1936. Margaret Sanger opened the first birth control clinic in the United States at 46 Amboy Street on 16 October 1916 (closed nine days later by the vice squad). During these years the neighborhood inspired some of the most evocative accounts of the Jewish experience in New York City, including Henry Roth's novel *Call It Sleep* (1934) and Alfred Kazin's memoir *A Walker in the City* (1951). Some local residents who later became prominent include the composer Aaron Copland, the actor Danny Kaye, and the impresario Sol Hurok.

Brownsville declined after the Second World War when many of its residents moved to the suburbs. Blacks who moved into the neighborhood faced discrimination, reduced services, and poor prospects for employment. There followed a cycle of decay, abandonment, vandalism, and arson, which high-rise public housing projects built during the 1950s and 1960s did little to alleviate. Later housing renewal efforts were more successful, notably those sponsored by the Council of East Brooklyn Churches to provide affordable one-family houses at Marcus Garvey Village and Nehemiah Housing. Pitkin Avenue, the main commercial thoroughfare, is lined with small businesses, shoe and clothing outlets, and restaurants. Loew's Pitkin Theater, a lavish movie theater built in 1930 by Thomas W. Lamb, stands at the corner of East New York Avenue and Pitkin Avenue and is now a retail store. The heavyweight boxing champions Mike Tyson and Riddick Bowe both grew up in the neighborhood, which attracted many immigrants from the Caribbean during the 1980s, especially from Jamaica (accounting for 30 percent of all immigrants), Guyana and Haiti (each about 15 percent), Grenada, Barbados, and Trinidad and Tobago.

David W. McCullough: *Brooklyn — and How It Got That Way* (New York: Dial, 1983)

Nanette Rainone, ed.: *The Brooklyn Neighborhood Book* (New York: Fund for the Borough of Brooklyn, 1985)

Elizabeth Reich Rawson

Bruckner, Henry (*b* Bronx, 17 June 1871; *d* Bronx, 14 April 1942). Public official. After representing the Bronx as a state legislator (1900) he was a commissioner of public works (1901–12), a member of the U.S. Congress (1912–17), and a borough president (1918–33). His loyal adherence to Tammany Hall enabled him to win elections consistently. At the same time he developed Bruckner Beverages, the city's largest bottler of soda water. Bruckner's political career ended when in an investigation of Tammany Hall his removal from the borough presidency was recommended by Judge Samuel Seabury. Although Bruckner declined to resign, Edward J. Flynn, Democratic leader of Bronx County, did not designate him for reelection.

Jill Jonnes: *We're Still Here: The Rise, Fall, and Resurrection of the South Bronx* (New York: Atlantic Monthly Press, 1986)

Neal C. Garelik

Bruère, Henry (Jaromir) (*b* St. Charles, Mo., 15 Jan 1882; *d* Winter Park, Fla., 17 Feb 1958). Reformer. After moving in 1905 to New York City he formed the New York Bureau of Municipal Research in 1907, which studied the structure of the city government and its administration of social services. He became city chamberlain during the administration of Mayor John Purroy Mitchel in 1914 and chairman of the Committee for Better Housing under Mayor Robert F. Wagner. Bruère wrote *The New City Government: A Discussion of Municipal Administration, Based on a Survey of Ten Commission-governed Cities* (1912).

Bernard Hirschhorn

Bruno, Guido [Kisch, Curt Joseph] (*b* Mladá Boleslav, Bohemia, 15 Oct 1884; *d* Bala

Brownsville, ca *1910*

Cynwyd, Penn., 31 Dec 1942). Book dealer and printer. He grew up near Prague, emigrated to the United States in 1907, and from 1914 to 1916 was the proprietor of Bruno's Garret on Washington Square South, which functioned as an art gallery, lecture hall, talent agency, and print shop specializing in the offbeat. He published local news gazettes, literary chapbooks, and whimsically illustrated pamphlets, as well as *Fragments from Greenwich Village* (1921). He was also a partner in the short-lived Thimble Theater at 10 5th Avenue. In his later years Bruno was a dealer in rare American manuscripts and autographs.

Arnold I. Kisch: *The Romantic Ghost of Greenwich Village: Guido Bruno in His Garret* (Frankfurt am Main: Peter Lang, 1976)

Jan Seidler Ramirez

Brushville. Former name of Queens Village. It was taken from that of Thomas Brush, who established a wheelwright and blacksmith shop there in 1824. Later he built a tavern, a general store, and a tobacco-curing warehouse. In 1865 residents voted to adopt the name Queens despite the risk of confusing the village with the county; the word Village was added in 1924 by the Long Island Rail Road when it erected an elevated station.

Vincent Seyfried

Bryant, William Cullen (*b* Cummington, Mass., 3 Nov 1794; *d* New York City, 12 June 1878). Poet, editor, and civic leader. He was initially a staunch Federalist. After moving to New York City in 1825 he succeeded E. L. Godkin as the editor of the *New York Review* and the *Evening Post.* In 1829 he bought the *Post*, where he continued to work until nearly the end of his life. Initially revered as a poet, he became the city's most influential resident through his public work, and he abandoned Federalism for liberal positions on a number of issues, including abolition and free soil; he also supported Abraham Lincoln. In 1867 he bought his last home, a house at 24 West 16th Street. An influential advocate of public parks, public health, and other civic causes, Bryant was among those who created the Century Association in 1846, Central Park in the 1850s, and the Metropolitan Museum of Art in 1870, and he was the first president of the board of trustees of New York Medical College. Bryant Park was named in his memory.

Charles Henry Brown: *William Cullen Bryant* (New York: Charles Scribner's Sons, 1971)

Jeff Finlay

Bryant High School. Former name of WILLIAM CULLEN BRYANT HIGH SCHOOL.

Bryant Park. Public park in Manhattan, at the corner of 6th Avenue and 42nd Street. It was laid out as a potter's field in 1823 and became a public park in 1847, when it was named Reservoir Square after the reservoir adjacent to it (on the site now occupied by the New York Public Library). The Crystal Palace, a grand exposition hall of glass and steel, occupied the site from 1853 until its destruction by fire in 1858. The park was given its current name in 1884 in honor of the poet and newspaper editor William Cullen Bryant, an early advocate of public parks. It did not undergo substantial improvements until the reservoir was drained in 1899 to make way for the New York Public Library, completed in 1911. A temporary, full-scale replica of Federal Hall was erected behind the library in 1932 to honor the bicentenary of Washington's birth. In the following year a privately sponsored competition for the redesign of the park was won by Lusby Simpson. Formal landscaping designed in 1934 by Gilmore Clarke, in large part inspired by Simpson, added a sunken central lawn, side promenades lined with London planes, a granite balustrade around the perimeter, and reshaped entrances on 6th Avenue. In the 1970s the park became the site of open drug dealing and was often used as a refuge by the homeless. Restorations in the late 1980s and early 1990s under the auspices of the Bryant Park Restoration Corporation provided for underground library storage, improved public access and landscaping, and a restaurant kiosk. There are six monuments in the park, including a niche statue of Bryant, a bust of Goethe, and a bronze statue of Gertrude Stein (by Jo Davidson).

Jonathan Kuhn

Buchalter, Louis "Lepke" (*b* New York City, 1897; *d* Ossining, N.Y., 4 March 1944). Organized-crime figure. He grew up on the Lower East Side and worked in extortion, protection rackets, loan sharking, and various illegal enterprises for both labor and management. Known for his violent tactics and his quiet but luxurious style of life, he was soon a target of the district attorney of Manhattan, Thomas E. Dewey. After violating narcotics and antitrust laws he went into hiding in 1937, spending most of his time on 3rd Street in Brooklyn. Outwitted by Walter Winchell and J. Edgar Hoover, he surrendered in 1939. While in prison he was convicted of masterminding the murder of a store owner in Brooklyn, and he was executed at Sing Sing State Prison.

Meyer Berger: "Lepke's Reign of Crime Lasted over 12 Murder-strewn Years," *New York Times*, 5 March 1944, p. 30

Margaret Latimer

bucket shops. Fraudulent businesses that ostensibly buy and sell stocks, bonds, and commodities on behalf of customers but in fact use their money to engage in deceptive and speculative practices. During the nineteenth century bucket shops had little effect on stock prices because they failed to execute most orders that their customers placed. In other cases they would bilk their customers by freezing orders to buy when a downward trend was expected in the market and then pocketed the difference. Bucket shops were forced to discontinue their practices after an investigation by Charles Evans Hughes in 1909. The long bear market of 1919–21 saw new firms open that executed orders and then reversed them through dummy accounts; rising stock prices after 1922 forced these operations out of business. In March 1923 an investigation by the district attorney Joab Banton was joined by the attorney general of New York State. By this time it was estimated that scores of customers had been cheated out of $800 million since November 1918. The New York Stock Exchange barred its members from dealing with bucket shops, and in 1924 a "padlock" injunction closed the National Stock, Cotton and Grain Exchange. Despite this success Banton estimated in June that fraud still exceeded $1000 million a year. It was not until October 1934 that a federal law was passed to outlaw bucket-shop techniques and the Securities and Exchange Commission declared all such operations illegal.

George J. Lankevich

Buckley, Charles A(nthony) (*b* New York City, 23 June 1890; *d* New York City, 22 Jan 1967). Congressman. As a young man he worked as a construction laborer and was an active member of the North End Democratic Club. Elected to Congress in 1934, he became the chairman of the public works committee, which oversaw federal construction contracts. In 1953 he became the Democratic leader of Bronx County. Buckley's political influence in the city weakened after he opposed Mayor Robert F. Wagner's successful reelection campaign in 1961, and he lost his congressional seat to the reformer Jonathan Bingham in a Democratic primary in 1964. He nonetheless remained in charge of the Democratic Party in the Bronx to the end of his life. He lived at 21 West 192nd Street.

Jill Jonnes: *We're Still Here: The Rise, Fall, and Resurrection of the South Bronx* (New York: Atlantic Monthly Press, 1986)

Chris McNickle

Buckley, William F(rank), Jr. (*b* New York City, 24 Nov 1925). Writer, publisher, and commentator. Born into a wealthy family, he served in the U.S. Army during the Second World War and graduated with honors from Yale University in 1950. He was the founder in 1955 in New York City and the editor-in-chief until 1990 of *National Review*, generally regarded as the leading journal of conservative opinion in the United States. As the candidate of the Conservative Party for mayor of New York City in 1965 he attacked the city's liberal social policies and advocated fiscal responsibility and law and order. Although he finished third behind the Republican candidate John V. Lindsay and the Democratic candidate Abraham D. Beame, he exceeded the expectations of many observers by winning

341,226 votes (13 percent of all votes cast). In the following year he became the host of "Firing Line," an interview program taped weekly in New York City and broadcast nationwide on public television. Buckley maintains a residence at Park Avenue in Manhattan.

John B. Judis: *William F. Buckley, Jr.: Patron Saint of the Conservatives* (New York: Simon and Schuster, 1988)

Edward T. O'Donnell

Buddhists. New York City is an important center of American Buddhism, in part because its residents include immigrants from most countries that have a strong Buddhist tradition, among them China, Japan, Thailand, Korea, Tibet, Burma, Vietnam, Cambodia, Laos, and Sri Lanka. The first Buddhists in the city were Chinese who settled there in the mid to late nineteenth century. It is not known where they established their first temple, because they often worshipped in nondescript rooms at the headquarters of secular Chinese associations. Buddhism became a subject of wide interest after the Theosophical Society was formed in the city in September 1875 by Helena Blavatsky. Japanese Buddhism established a presence in the city in 1930 when the artist and writer Sokei-an Sasaki, an adherent of Rinzai Zen, formed the Buddhist Society of America (renamed the first Zen Institute of America in 1945). Later led by Mary Farkas and situated at 113 East 30th Street, this organization began publishing *Zen Notes* in 1954. Another important Japanese sect, Jodo Shinshu, was represented by the New York Buddhist Church, formed in 1938 at 331 Riverside Drive as an affiliate of Buddhist Churches of America. The church held separate Sunday services in Japanese and English and in 1948 began supporting the American Buddhist Academy, which ordains priests and offers a master's degree in Buddhist studies. During the 1960s Buddhism was popularized by such beat poets as Allen Ginsberg and Jack Kerouac and other figures in the counterculture. The Zen Studies Society was formed in 1968 at 223 East 67th Street, and the Chinese (Ch'an) Institute of Chung-Hwa, Buddhist Culture Meditation Center, opened in 1979 in Elmhurst.

Tibetan Vajrayana Buddhism also gained a large following, with institutions ranging from such formal ones as the Tibet Center (Gelugpa school) and the Dharmadhatu of New York (Kagyu school) to less formal ones like the Buddhist Center (Sakya school), led by the guru Lama Pema Wang Rak. The New York Buddhist Vihara, an enclave of monks formed in 1980 in Kew Gardens and directed by a Sri Lankan spiritual leader, represented Heravada Buddhism, an ascetic tradition most closely associated with Thailand and Southeast Asia. American-born Buddhists in the city took an early interest in efforts to modernize the religion, to make its hierarchy more democratic and open to women, and to encourage dialogue between its sects. The American Buddhist Movement, formed at 301 West 45th Street in 1980 by Kevin O'Neil, published the *American Buddhist* between 1980 and 1988 and in the mid 1990s had more than five hundred members, mostly middle class and American born. By this time there were eleven Buddhist temples in Chinatown and several more in Flushing, and the Buddhist Association of the United States, which was primarily Chinese, supported the Temple of Enlightenment at 3070 Albany Crescent in the Bronx. Most Buddhist organizations in the city maintain rural retreats in upstate New York.

Charles S. Prebich: *American Buddhism* (North Scituate, Mass.: Duxbury, 1979)

Marc Ferris

budget. Municipal spending was relatively low in seventeenth- and eighteenth-century New York City, when efforts at social betterment were conducted largely by private charities and religious organizations, and the city's taxing power was strictly circumscribed. The city's total budget in 1850 was $3,368,163, or $6.53 per inhabitant. Spending increased after the city established a system for the comprehensive collection and assessment of property taxes in 1859.

After consolidation in 1898 the government of the newly enlarged New York City spent $78 million in its first year and $94 million in its second. But in 1900 municipal spending declined to slightly less than $91 million, the first of only ten declines in spending between the turn of the century and 1995 (including two during the period after the Second World War). Nearly continuous growth between 1898 and 1933 raised the municipal budget to $578 million. Its expansion during this period reflected the substantial infrastructure investments required to tie the new city together (particularly the cost of building subways), as well as the demand for improved services in the 1920s. During this thirty-five-year period municipal expenditures rose at an average annual rate of 6 percent.

Many things that rose in the 1920s declined during the 1930s, but not the municipal budget. Municipal spending did not decline until 1933, four years after the collapse of the New York Stock Exchange, because of a fiscal crisis in 1932 that halted the city's ability to borrow. Spending declined again in 1936 before resuming its normal course. Although the rate of growth in the 1930s was slower than in the 1920s, the Second World War had a more profound impact on the municipal budget than the Depression. The war forced advocates of the New Deal to redirect federal resources toward defending the nation and away from economic "pump-priming" (an activity that included federal aid to cities like New York City). Municipal spending declined in fiscal years 1941, 1942, 1944, and 1945, though a large increase in 1943 made for an increase during the war years as a whole. During the period from 1933 to 1945 municipal spending rose to $737 million, an average of 2 percent a year.

After the war the budget resumed a pattern of steady growth that lasted until the mid 1960s. Pent-up demand for the expansion of the municipal government was financed primarily by the growth of revenues from municipal taxes on real property and sales, though by this time transfers from the State of New York and the federal government were beginning to make substantial contributions as well. Between the end of the Second World War and 1965 the budget grew an average of 8 percent a year, reaching $3349 million.

From the mid 1960s municipal spending grew at unprecedented rates. It surpassed $4000 million in 1967, $5000 million in 1968, $6000 million in 1969, $7000 million in 1971, $8000 million in 1972, $9000 million in 1973, and $10,000 million in 1974, reaching $11,654 million in 1975. In the period 1965–75 the budget grew by an average of 13 percent a year, driven by three forces over which municipal officials had relatively little control. First, in 1965 the federal government and the State of New York required the city to help finance public assistance and Medicaid for poor New Yorkers. Under the federal mandate the state paid half of the program's costs, and the state in turn compelled the city to pay half of that. This requirement that the city pay for 25 percent of welfare and Medicaid costs from municipal revenues, coupled with socioeconomic changes that were increasing the number of dependent poor, drove municipal spending up by $3300 million between 1965 and 1975. Second, the municipal government expanded the municipal bureaucracy by sixty thousand positions, partly to provide the mandated welfare and health services. In addition the expansion of a collective bargaining program introduced in the 1950s provided the leaders of municipal unions with a new forum for winning higher wages and benefits for their members. The expansion in the number and compensation of municipal employees added $3600 million to the municipal budget between 1965 and 1975. Third, debt service, or payments of principal and interest to the holders of municipal bonds and notes, rose by nearly $1500 million. Such payments were not uncontrollable in a strictly legal sense, as were the payments made pursuant to federal mandates and collective bargaining contracts, but the prospect of being unable to borrow money was sufficient to ensure that creditors were paid.

The rapid growth of expenditures that municipal officials were unable to control required that they find new revenue sources, notwithstanding the boom in revenues that accompanied the expansionary economy of the 1960s. During the second half of the 1960s

The Growth of the Budget of New York City, 1830–1990

	1830	1840	1850	1860	1869	1880	1890
Fire	$ 23,462	$ 76,788	$ 44,969	$ 167,573	$ 907,940	$ 1,387,991	$ 2,123,367
Police	99,521	271,709	487,541	1,395,122	2,901,133	3,227,069	4,587,599
Health	1,252	4,677	7,229	161,070	194,936	256,425	390,434
Streets, Sewers, and Public Health	50,378	160,840	287,188	914,784	1,333,210	1,005,129	1,656,458
Education	25,995	94,411	374,553	1,278,781	3,150,000	3,422,307	4,149,563
Charities and Correction	131,021	254,000	400,000	746,199	953,000	1,318,793	2,124,750
Asylums and Related Institutions	4,000	6,921	9,863	109,661	939,219	930,399	1,154,644
Other	340,989	736,396	1,756,820	5,012,866	16,153,323	18,206,420	18,798,865
Total Budget	$676,618	$1,605,742	$3,368,163	$9,786,056	$26,532,761	$29,754,533	$34,985,680

	1900	1910	1920	1930	1940	1950
Debt service	$18,033,269	$ 46,443,695	$ 76,486,538	$175,405,957	$153,620,293	$ 189,076,993
Police	11,992,503	15,110,797	24,595,186	50,137,369	58,873,297	101,964,808
Fire	4,840,767	8,153,542	13,186,753	20,676,528	33,119,278	58,087,070
Education	17,160,097	28,578,432	50,831,347	100,637,912	103,180,322	288,646,779
Charities	2,857,084	4,734,252	8,149,387	9,855,150	15,275,502	197,036,034
Street cleaning	5,031,282	7,531,362	13,163,523	28,252,188	28,466,356	52,069,339
Health	1,055,515	2,747,723	7,565,455	23,478,454	34,141,500	91,715,932
Corrections	762,775	1,271,351	2,445,551	3,222,207	3,976,475	7,040,504
Other	29,045,680	48,559,116	77,265,745	153,104,063	156,856,816	201,230,072
Total Budget	$90,778,972	$163,130,270	$273,689,485	$564,769,828	$587,509,839	$1,186,867,531

	1960	1970	1980	1990
Debt service	$ 294,389,265	$ 724,598,084	$ 1,720,434,679	$ 2,098,847,435
Police	208,258,278	616,358,752	674,037,283	1,627,487,683
Fire	109,476,530	273,230,862	321,290,820	690,242,803
Education	578,124,929	1,750,635,119	2,808,791,726	6,669,264,270
Social services	327,596,170	1,562,911,121	3,099,814,418	5,530,878,823
Sanitation	88,931,612	280,001,882	629,371,133	629,371,133
Health	162,324,383	671,392,699	508,344,450	1,529,579,049
Corrections	15,840,800	61,224,999	139,067,231	708,882,488
Other	390,004,990	939,532,696	2,938,015,937	7,142,662,776
Total Budget	$2,174,946,957	$6,879,886,214	$12,839,167,677	$26,627,216,450

Note: Charities includes the city's payments to private charitable instutitions. Health includes Department of Health and Department of Hospitals, and in 1980 and 1990 also includes Health and Hospitals Corporation and Department of Mental Health. Education includes Board of Education and Board of Higher Education.
Source: Edward D. Durand: *The Finances of New York City* (New York: Macmillan, 1898)
Annual budget, City of New York

Compiled by James Bradley and Edward T. O'Donnell

the city raised rates on existing sales and property taxes and also introduced new taxes on business and personal income. After 1969, when the local economy began to experience what turned out to be a long and severe recession, municipal officials stopped raising taxes and began using proceeds from note and bond sales to pay day-to-day operating expenses. These practices contributed to a steep rise in debt service costs in the first half of the 1970s. By 1975 the city had accumulated a budget deficit of more than $3000 million, and needed to borrow $7000 million simply to pay off notes that were coming due.

The second of the city's twentieth-century fiscal crises began in May 1975, when the financial institutions that had been underwriting municipal bond and note sales ceased doing so. In the face of municipal default the state created the Municipal Assistance Corporation (MAC) in June. The corporation was to issue long-term bonds, backed by municipal revenues, in order to pay off municipal creditors. In September, after it became clear that a refinancing strategy would not be sufficient, the state also created the Emergency Financial Control Board to control municipal spending. Not until 1981 was the budget balanced. This enabled the city to regain access to credit markets, which set the stage for the end of state control of the municipal budget in 1982. During the control period expenditure growth was limited by freezing welfare benefits to the poor and wages of municipal employees, and eliminating sixty thousand municipal positions. Capital spending was also halted, except for projects supported by intergovernmental funds. The state also helped limit the growth of expenditures by assuming the cost of certain services previously funded by the city, including higher education. Between 1975 and 1982 municipal spending fell only once (in 1980), but for the period as a whole average annual spending rose only 4 percent. The end of the control period was also facilitated by a recovery of the local economy beginning in 1977, which pushed up municipal revenues and provided the foundation for renewed expansion of the budget.

During the 1980s economic growth and the desire to make up for the effects of the fiscal crisis led to another expansionary period in municipal budgeting. Between 1982 and 1990 the budget grew an average of 7 percent a year, to $26,627 million. The greater part of the increase, $7800 million, reflected an attempt to restore the size and wages of the municipal work force to the levels that had prevailed before the fiscal crisis. Some fifty thousand workers were added to the payroll. Between 1990 and 1994 the budget grew to an all-time high of $31,768 million, but at a slower average rate of increase, 5 percent, than in the 1980s.

Increasing fiscal stress resulted from the expansion of municipal employment and higher debt service, reflecting the refinancings during the fiscal crisis and the resumption of capital spending in the 1980s. In 1989 the local economy experienced another sharp downturn. The number of municipal workers began to fall again by the mid 1990s, presaging even harder fiscal times. In 1995 the city's adopted budget called for a reduction in spending for the first time since 1980.

Martin Shefter: *Political Crisis, Fiscal Crisis: The Collapse and Revival of New York City* (New York: Basic Books, 1985)

Gerald Benjamin and Charles Brecher, eds.: *The Two New Yorks: State–City Relations in the Changing Federal System* (New York: Russell Sage Foundation, 1988)

Charles Brecher and Raymond D. Horton: *Power Failure: New York City Politics and Policy since 1960* (New York: Oxford University Press, 1993)

Raymond D. Horton

building trades. Most builders in colonial New York City worked for "masters" and were part of an amorphous group known as "mechanics" that led resistance efforts against the British. Many also belonged to the resistance group the Sons of Liberty. By 1774 they formed the General Committee of Mechanics, a group subdivided into committees of resistance and influenced by the writings of Thomas Paine; it opposed the importation of British manufactured goods and supported the First Continental Congress. As the market economy grew after the American Revolution, such groups were transformed into trade societies and unions, among them the New York Society of Journeymen House Carpenters. Builders were organized citywide in the New York General Trades' Union, which under the leadership of John Commerford aligned itself with the National Trade Union and fought for the ten-hour day. With middle-class intellectuals tradesmen helped to form the New York Workingmen's Party, which sometimes cooperated with Tammany Hall and achieved such important goals as reforming education and converting appointive municipal offices into elective ones. In the nineteenth century builders came into competition with immigrants and suffered during several economic depressions. During a severe depression in the 1870s the Committee of Safety was formed to demand more public works projects. Skirmishes between workmen and the police at a number of rallies and demonstrations culminated in the Tompkins Square Riot on 13 January 1874.

In response to growing pressures the building trades unions adopted restrictive entry requirements, including steep initiation fees and stringent rules of apprenticeship, and closely monitored the number of men entering the trades. To ensure that contractors employed only union members the unions organized joint actions and sympathy strikes, which were nearly always successful. Conflicts between contractors and unions were common until the turn of the century, when contractors gradually came to regard the union hiring hall as a convenient source of highly skilled workers, and union labor as providing some measure of protection against claims of poor workmanship. Many unions strengthened their hand, including those representing carpenters, bricklayers, derrickmen, hod carriers, pavers, masons, millwrights, stone cutters and stone setters, roofers, plasterers, and painters and paperhangers. Although unions provided some stability, workers continued to face hardship during the winter and competition from immigrants. When Jewish and Italian immigrants were refused membership in the Painters' Union, which had about eight thousand members, they formed the Alteration Painters and Paper Hangers Union of New York, which by 1913 had three thousand members and became affiliated with the International Brotherhood of Painters in 1914. Other unions including the Painters' Union formed locals to accommodate various ethnic groups.

As more skyscrapers were built, unions were formed by boilermakers, steamfitters, structural ironworkers, plumbers, electricians, floor coverers, cement workers, glaziers, lathers, marble cutters, upholsterers, and bridge painters. Union officials often extorted bribes from contractors, and such figures as Sam Parks, Philip Zausner, and Bob Brindell demanded illegal payments to guarantee workers' cooperation. The ease with which union officials obtained bribes attracted the interest of organized crime, which began by protecting picket lines and quickly became embedded in powerful locals that it continued to control into the 1990s.

The political conservatism of the building trades in New York City was highlighted during the "hard hat" demonstration of May 1970. Coordinated by their leaders, two hundred construction workers attacked a rally against the Vietnam War, chanting "All the way with the USA" and other slogans. The event provided an enduring stereotype of the reactionary working-class man.

Walter Hugins: *Jacksonian Democracy and the Working Class: A Study of the New York Workingman's Movement, 1829–1837* (Stanford, Calif.: Stanford University Press, 1960)

Staughton Lynd: "The Mechanics in New York Politics, 1774–1788," *Labor History* 5 (1964), 225–46

Herbert Gutman: "The Tompkins Square 'Riot' in New York City on January 13, 1874: A Re-examination of Its Causes and Its Aftermath," *Labor History* 6 (1965), 44–70

Howard B. Rock: *Artisans of the New Republic: The Tradesmen of New York City in the Age of Jefferson* (New York: New York University Press, 1979)

Corruption and Racketeering in the New York City Construction Industry: Final Report to Governor Mario M. Cuomo from the New York State Organized Crime Task Force (New York: New York University Press, 1990)

Colin J. Davis

Bulgarians. Bulgarians settled in New York City about 1900, along avenues B and C at 3rd and 4th streets on the Lower East Side. The Bulgarian American Mutual Aid Society, formed in 1906, was the first organization of its kind in the United States. It was soon followed by the Bulgarian Subsidiary Committee (1915–17), which helped immigrants and orphans of the First World War. Promoting Bulgarian culture was the goal of the Bulgarian Students Association (1924–27), the Bulgarian Society (1929), and the Bulgarian Institute (1935). Political organizations were formed by refugees and political exiles who settled in the city after the Second World War. The Bulgarian National Committee (1946–) was a coordinating organization that eventually moved its headquarters to New Jersey. Through its publication *American–Bulgarian Review* the American Bulgarian League (1947–68) sought to unite anticommunist groups in fighting for democracy in Bulgaria; a similar goal was later pursued by the Bulgarian National Front (1958–67) through its publication *Borba* (Fight). The Bulgarian Social Democrats (1955–57) published *Svoboden Narod* (Free People) before moving their organization to Austria. During the 1950s and 1960s most of the city's Bulgarian population moved to neighborhoods throughout Manhattan and to the Bronx (especially Tremont Avenue and Fordham Road) and suburbs in New York, New Jersey, and Connecticut. There was also a Bulgarian National Council (1960–65) that served as an umbrella organization for all political entities.

In the mid 1990s there were between fifteen hundred and two thousand Bulgarians in the city, including teachers, writers, artists, small businessmen, food-service and maintenance workers, and painters. Many were Eastern Orthodox and belonged to the church of Sts. Cyril and Methodius in Manhattan and St. Apostol Andrew in the Bronx, a popular site for social gatherings and cultural events and a center for the study of the Bulgarian language. Well-known Bulgarians in the city have included the journalist Kristo Konovsky.

Francis J. Brown and Joseph S. Roucek, eds.: *Our Racial and National Minorities* (New York: Prentice Hall, 1937; rev. Englewood Cliffs, N.J.: Prentice Hall, 1960, as *One America: The History, Contributions and Present Problems of Our Racial and National Minorities*), 179–83

Nikolay G. Altankov: *The Bulgarian–Americans* (Palo Alto, Calif.: Ragusan, 1979)

Vladimir Wertsman

Bull's Head. Neighborhood in central Staten Island, centered at the intersection of Victory Boulevard and Richmond Avenue. The area was named for a ferocious bull with large eyes and short horns that adorned the sign of a tavern said to be a gathering place for Tories. After the tavern was destroyed by fire the town was known as Phoenixville and later as London Bridge. Residents in 1849 formed the Asbury Methodist Episcopal Church (now the Son-Rise Charismatic Interfaith Church), named after the American Methodist preacher Francis Asbury, who visited Staten Island as early as 1771. In the graveyard lies Ichabod Crane, whose name was borrowed by his friend Washington Irving for the short story "The Legend of Sleepy Hollow." A number of farmers who settled in the neighborhood in the 1920s were the first members of a sizable Greek community that built Holy Trinity Greek Orthodox Church on Victory Boulevard. Until the mid 1960s Richmond Avenue was lined with truck farms. In later years the area became more ethnically diverse, with a large influx during the 1980s of immigrants from India, Korea, and the Philippines. A Hellenic cultural center was being built in the early 1990s with the support of about eight hundred families. Bull's Head is commercial and residential.

Martha S. Bendix

Bulova. Firm of watchmakers. Formed as the J. Bulova Company in 1875, it was incorporated in 1911 and reincorporated under its current name in 1923. It achieved immense commercial success in the mid twentieth century, especially under the leadership of Arde Bulova (1889–1958). At its operations in Woodside and Flushing it made innovations in watchmaking and developed a number of watchmaking tools. Foreign competition and outmoded technology brought on its decline during the late 1960s and 1970s. In 1979 the firm was bought by the Loews Corporation, which reversed its decline by improving quality control, introducing many new styles of watches, and advertising extensively. The firm returned to profitability in 1986.

Peter A. Coclanis

Bunshaft, Gordon (*b* Buffalo, 8 May 1909; *d* New York City, 6 Aug 1990). Architect. He attended the Massachusetts Institute of Technology (BArch 1933, MArch 1935), worked briefly in Buffalo, and was introduced to modern architecture while visiting Europe on a traveling fellowship. On his return he worked at intervals in New York City in the offices of Edward Durell Stone and Raymond Loewy before joining the firm of Skidmore, Owings and Merrill, where he became a full partner in 1949 and remained until 1979. Bunshaft's precise, refined architecture was influenced by Le Corbusier and Ludwig Mies van der Rohe, while displaying a sensitivity to local, technological, and financial constraints. His best-known works are commercial buildings for which he was a design partner: Lever House (1952), the first glass-walled private office building, which introduced the idea of a plaza beside a high structure and helped to inspire the zoning revisions of 1961; the Veterans Administration Hospital in Brooklyn (1951); Chase Manhattan Plaza (1961), a catalyst for the renewal of Wall Street; and the controversial but powerful 9 West 57th Street (1974), which slopes to fit into the zoning "envelope." An art collector, Bunshaft placed works by important artists in most of his buildings.

Carol H. Krinsky: *Gordon Bunshaft of Skidmore, Owings and Merrill* (New York: Architectural History Foundation / Cambridge: MIT Press, 1988)

Carol Krinsky

Bureau of City Betterment. Civic organization, a forerunner of the INSTITUTE OF PUBLIC ADMINISTRATION.

Bureau of Educational Experiments. Original name of the BANK STREET COLLEGE OF EDUCATION.

Bureau of Municipal Research. Civic organization, a forerunner of the INSTITUTE OF PUBLIC ADMINISTRATION.

burlesque. The evolution of theatrical burlesque in New York City at first paralleled its evolution elsewhere: traditional parodies of standard theatrical works, exemplified by John Gay's *The Beggar's Opera* (performed in New York City in 1750 by the English company of Walter Murray and Thomas Kean), gradually gave way to more unsophisticated forms of entertainment less concerned with lampooning works of literature than with displaying female bodies.

The beginnings of this trend may be traced to the early nineteenth century, when female stage performers began to appear in tights. The first of these was Francisque Hutin at the Thalia Theatre in New York City in 1827. Adah Isaacs Menken (1835–68) wore beige tights for her role in *Mazeppa* at the Broadway Theatre in April 1866, thus giving an illusion of nudity and causing a sensation. Tights were worn by an entire female chorus when *The Black Crook* opened in September of the same year at Niblo's Garden (an event that also marked the first performance in New York City of the cancan), and by the English troupe the "British Blondes," which in September 1868 performed a burlesque of Greek mythology, *Ixion*, under the direction of Lydia Thompson at Wood's Theatre. By May 1869 fourteen of the sixteen theaters in New York City were offering "naked drama." The person perhaps most responsible for Americanizing the burlesque show was Michael B. Leavitt (1843–1935), the producer of the Rentz–Santley shows. He combined ideas borrowed from the productions of Thompson with elements of minstrelsy, variety shows, and theatrical extravaganzas, all performed in an unvarying sequence: musical numbers and comedy, a series of specialty acts (the olio), and an after-piece and finale. Dancing figured prominently in Leavitt's produc-

Reginald Marsh, Minsky's Chorus *(1935). Collection of the Whitney Museum of American Art*

tions, which drew large audiences in New York City and elsewhere in the 1870s and 1880s. One of the first women from his troupe to gain recognition as a performer in her own right was May Howard (*b* ?1870; *d* 1935), who by 1888 appeared at variety houses in Manhattan as the leader of a company that bore her name and that later achieved great prominence. Another important troupe in this period was the Rose Sydell Burlesque Company, better known as the "London Belles." One of the first theater owners in New York City to offer burlesque entertainment was Henry Clay Miner, first at the Bowery and then at the Eighth Avenue Theatre (built 1881). Weber and Fields did so as well at their Broadway Music Hall (opened September 1896).

By the turn of the century the characteristics of the modern burlesque show had become fixed: chorus girls in tights, bare-bellied solo cooch dancers (female dancers whose routines were derived from belly dancing and featured erotic movements), and comedians. The years 1900 to 1914 were the heyday of burlesque in New York City. The best-known performers included Billy Watson (1866–1945), who appeared with a "beef trust" of chorines each weighing as much as two hundred pounds (ninety kilograms), "Sliding Billy" Watson, Bozo Snyder, Leon Errol, and Alexander Carr, and in later years Al Jolson, Jack Pearl, Fanny Brice, Eddie Cantor, Joe Cook, Bud Abbott and Lou Costello, Phil Silvers, and Joey Faye. The importance of New York City as a center of burlesque grew with the establishment of national burlesque chains, called wheels. The first of these, the Columbia wheel, was formed in 1905 by Samuel Scribner and Lawrence Weber and devoted to "clean" burlesque, or burlesque suitable for families. Its flagship theater, the Columbia, opened in New York City in January 1910 at 7th Avenue and 47th Street; in Brooklyn Columbia controlled the Star Theater on Jay Street. Many other theaters were controlled by the Minsky family. Among those that were not were the Olympic and Irving Place, both near 14th Street, and the Eltinge on 42nd Street. As the burlesque of the wheels became increasingly hard to distinguish from vaudeville, the burlesque of resident stock companies, most closely identified with the Minskys, became increasingly risqué. The character of burlesque changed markedly with the introduction about 1927 of the striptease, which began as an encore and in the following years grew in explicitness and prominence; by 1930 the Irving Place Theater was known specifically for this brand of entertainment. Among the best-known strippers were Ann Corio, Margie Hart, Gypsy Rose Lee, and Georgia Sothern. When Fiorello H. La Guardia became mayor in 1934 he began a crusade against burlesque, which by now had acquired an unsavory reputation. Although burlesque was allowed in 1937 to continue in modified form, it was banned in May 1942.

Bernard Sobel: *Burleycue: An Underground History of Burlesque* (New York: Farrar and Rinehart, 1931)
Irving Zeidman: *The American Burlesque Show* (New York: Hawthorn, 1967)
Morton Minsky and Milt Machlin: *Minsky's Burlesque* (New York: Arbor House, 1986)

William Green

Burlingham, Charles C(ulp) (*b* Plainfield, N.J., 31 Aug 1858; *d* New York City, 6 June 1959). Admiralty lawyer and civic reformer. Known as "New York's first citizen," he served two terms as president of the Association of the Bar of the City of New York and was later a confidential advisor to Mayor Fiorello H. La Guardia. For half a century Burlingham remained highly influential in judicial appointments and politics.

"C. C. B." As We Knew Him: Charles Culp Burlingham, August 31, 1858–June 6, 1959 (New York: St. George's Church, 1959)

Frank Vos

Burr, Aaron (*b* Newark, N.J., 6 Feb 1756; *d* Port Richmond [now in Staten Island], 14 Sept 1836). Vice president of the United States. After a distinguished military career he arrived in New York City in 1783 as a colonel when British forces evacuated, settling at 3 Wall Street (1783–84). He established a thriving legal practice, emerged as a leader of the Republican Party, and served in the state assembly (1784–85, 1797–99), as the attorney general of New York State (1789–91), and in the U.S. Senate (1791–99). During these years he lived at 10 Maiden Lane (1784–90), 4 Broadway (1790–94), and Mortier House in Greenwich Village (most of the time from 1794 to 1804). In 1799 he was instrumental in chartering the Manhattan Company, which was the second bank in New York City, and in the following year his efforts at ensuring the election of a Republican state legislature enabled him to mount a successful candidacy for the vice presidency. From the 1780s he was a political rival of Alexander Hamilton, whom he blamed for his own loss of the presidency in 1800 and of the governorship of New York in 1804. He eventually challenged Hamilton to a duel that took place on 11 July 1804, at Weehawken, New Jersey, in which Hamilton was killed. The duel ended Burr's political career. Enmeshed in political intrigues in the West, he stood trial for treason (of which he was acquitted), spent several years in Europe, and returned to New York City in 1812 to resume the practice of law. Houses at 127 and 131 MacDougal Street were built for him in 1829. In 1833 he married Eliza Jumel, with whom he lived for several months in a house at Edgecombe Avenue near West 160th Street (now known as the Morris–Jumel Mansion). He spent the end of his life in genteel poverty and his last weeks at Winant's Inn at 2040

Portrait of Aaron Burr by John Vanderlyn, 1802

Richmond Terrace in Port Richmond (later named the St. James Hotel and the Port Richmond Hotel).

James Parton: *The Life and Times of Aaron Burr* (New York: Mason Brothers, 1858)
Milton Lomask: *Aaron Burr* (New York: Farrar, Straus and Giroux, 1979–82)
Mary-Jo Kline and Joanne W. Ryan, eds.: *Political Correspondence and Private Papers of Aaron Burr* (Princeton, N.J.: Princeton University Press, 1982)

See also Abolitionism.

Barbara A. Chernow

Burson–Marsteller. Public relations firm, formed in 1953 by Harold Burson and Bill Marsteller, the head of an advertising agency based in Chicago. The firm was a pioneer in the branch of public relations that came to be known as "crisis communication," successfully allaying the concerns of consumers over contaminated products for its clients Tylenol and Perrier in the 1980s. By the mid 1990s it was the largest public relations firm in the world, with offices in many cities, including Moscow and Beijing. In 1994 the headquarters were at 230 Park Avenue South in Gramercy Park, and Harold Burson was still prominent within the firm.

James Bradley

Burton, Scott (*b* Greensboro, Ala., 23 June 1939; *d* New York City, 29 Dec 1989). Sculptor. He studied literature at Columbia University and New York University and worked as a freelance critic and editor for *Artnews* and *Art in America.* In his early sculptures, which took the form of furniture, he attacked what he saw as the artificial boundary between art and design. He had his first solo exhibition at Artists Space in Manhattan in 1975. His public pieces include the lobby of the Equitable Center (1985–86, 787 7th Avenue), street furniture along 51st and 52nd streets, and a project done in collaboration with Cesar Pelli, Siah Armajani, and M. Paul Friedberg at the World Financial Center Plaza (1988) in Battery Park City. Burton's work invites the public to use it and has proved highly influential.

Brenda Richardson and Trish Waters: *Scott Burton* (Baltimore: Baltimore Museum of Art, 1986)

Harriet F. Senie

buses. The first person to operate horse-drawn omnibuses in New York City was Abraham Brower in 1831. The Fifth Avenue Coach Company operated horse-drawn buses from 1885 and motorbuses from 1905, and established single- and double-decker buses as durable mass transit vehicles. In 1908 all horse-drawn buses were retired. Mayor John F. Hylan provided bus franchises to private operators from 1920. Bus service began in Staten Island in 1921 after the local streetcar company discontinued its operations. By 1925 Fifth Avenue Coach had developed a large network in Manhattan, where in the following year it acquired the leading streetcar operator, New York Railways. Fifth Avenue Coach operated two bus routes along the Grand Concourse from 1924 to 1928. It then yielded the franchise to the Third Avenue Railway, which operated a far-reaching streetcar network in the Bronx and received an exclusive bus franchise; many of its routes entered upper Manhattan by means of the bridges across the Harlem River. In Queens fledgling bus operators emerged in the 1920s and developed a large network, and from 1931 the Brooklyn–Manhattan Transit Corporation (BMT) ran buses that provided access to its streetcars and subways. Trolley buses, which were hybrid vehicles combining features of motor buses and streetcars, were introduced in 1932 and again in 1948 before being eliminated in 1960.

Mayor Fiorello H. La Guardia set out in 1934 to establish a coherent, citywide policy on surface transit: he eliminated some streetcar lines and granted franchises to strong private bus operators in each borough. In Queens the eastern part of the borough was served by North Shore Bus, the southwestern part by Green Bus, and the northwestern part by Triboro Coach; there were also three smaller operators, Jamaica Bus, Queens Transit, and Steinway Omnibus. In 1935–50 Fifth Avenue Coach and Third Avenue Railway introduced large, diesel-powered buses on heavily traveled routes. The only streetcar routes left in Manhattan by 1936 were those of Third Avenue Railway, which operated along Broadway, 3rd Avenue, and Amsterdam Avenue, and across 42nd, 59th, and 125th streets. Between February 1935 and August 1936 Fifth Avenue Coach formed the subsidiary New York City Omnibus and converted all the routes formerly operated by New York Railways to bus routes. In Staten Island La Guardia granted franchises to two companies, the more powerful of which, Staten Island

Alice Austen, Fifth Avenue Auto Stage *(ca 1910)*

Coach, took over all the routes in the borough in 1937. Queens Transit and Steinway Omnibus came under common ownership in 1939. In the following year the city bought the BMT and inherited the huge streetcar network in Brooklyn. Between 1941 and 1956 this entire network was converted to bus service. Third Avenue Railway and the city signed a new franchise agreement in 1940 that provided for complete conversion of its streetcar lines in Manhattan and the Bronx to bus service by 1960. The conversion took place between March 1941 and August 1948, after which Third Avenue Railway became the Surface Transportation Corporation.

In Staten Island the bus franchise of Staten Island Coach was sold in March 1946 to Isle Transportation, which abandoned the operation in February 1947 and sold it to the city's Board of Transportation, preserving important services to the Staten Island Ferry at St. George. In March 1947 the core of the Queens Bus Division of the New York City Transit Authority (NYCTA) was formed when North Shore Bus returned its franchise to the city, forcing the Board of Transportation again to rescue a local bus operation. Green Bus continued to operate independently and obtained ownership of Triboro Coach (1947), Jamaica Bus (1949), and Command Bus (1979). In 1948 the city acquired two small bus companies in Manhattan with five routes, including ones along 1st and 2nd avenues and across 49th and 50th streets. Fifth Avenue Coach and New York City Omnibus merged in 1954, and in 1956 they acquired Surface Transportation. In April 1957 surface transit routes became converted entirely to buses with the replacement of the last streetcar route, crossing the Queensboro Bridge. Between 1948 and 1962 the bus routes of New York City were controlled entirely by the city in Brooklyn and Staten Island, by the city and five private companies in Queens, and largely by the combined operation of Fifth Avenue Coach and Surface Transportation in Manhattan and the Bronx. Transfers were eliminated in Manhattan and the Bronx in 1962, after which the NYCTA and private companies in every borough except the Bronx allowed selective transfers between their own routes only. Early in the same year an investment group led by Harry Weinberg purchased Fifth Avenue Coach, prompting a strike by drivers on 1 March when the new management sought to discharge some unionized employees as a cost-cutting measure. The city quickly intervened and took over the entire system, creating a subsidiary of the NYCTA, the Manhattan and Bronx Surface Transit Operating Authority (MABSTOA); from this time MABSTOA and the NYCTA operated virtually all local routes except for those of private companies in Queens (Green, Triboro, Jamaica, and Queens–Steinway).

Express buses that transported passengers from the outer boroughs to Manhattan for a premium fare began about 1968. These routes are now operated by the NYCTA and nine private companies, including Domenico Bus (which serves Staten Island), Command Bus and Metro Apple Express (which serve Brooklyn), and New York Bus Service and Liberty Lines (which serve Riverdale, Co-op

Berenice Abbott, Greyhound Bus Terminal, *244–48 West 34th Street, 14 July 1936*

City, Williamsbridge, and other outlying sections of the Bronx). In 1980 the NYCTA discovered major structural problems with its newly purchased fleet of Flxible buses, manufactured by Grumman. Used buses were borrowed from the local system in Washington while the buses were being repaired, but the repairs were unsuccessful and the Flxible buses were permanently taken out of service in 1984. Small, private bus lines continued to be acquired by larger lines and by the city, which in 1980 took over Avenue B and East Broadway Transit of Manhattan. Queens Transit and Steinway Omnibus were sold in 1986 and then merged as the Queens Surface Corporation.

The NYCTA and MABSTOA operate virtually all local bus routes in Manhattan, the Bronx, Brooklyn, and Staten Island. Routes in Queens are divided between the NYCTA and four publicly subsidized private operators, all of which run important express routes to Manhattan. The system as a whole comprises three hundred routes and carries 500 million passengers a year on 4200 buses. The largest fleet is that of the NYCTA in Brooklyn (seventy routes, more than 150 million riders a year, one thousand buses). In Manhattan buses carry far fewer passengers than subways do: they are perhaps most useful to passengers traveling crosstown (who cannot easily do so by subway) and to the elderly and handicapped (half fares for passengers older than sixty-five were introduced in 1969, "kneeling buses" in 1976, wheelchair lifts in 1980). The disadvantages of buses include slowness and the need to pay with subway tokens or large amounts of coin (bus drivers stopped making change on 31 August 1969 and the fareboxes do not accept bills). For most of the history of mass transit in New York City the bus fare and subway fare have been the same, differing only from 1 July 1948 to 1 July 1950 when subways cost ten cents and buses seven cents.

Intercity buses first served New York City in 1924. With the construction of the Holland and Lincoln tunnels intercity services expanded, and many small, independent terminals were built in the western part of midtown. Plans by the city to develop a single, off-street bus terminal with ramps leading directly to the Lincoln Tunnel took shape in 1945 and led to the construction in 1947–50 of the Port Authority Bus Terminal, where all intercity buses now depart and arrive.

Andrew Sparberg

Bush Terminal. Industrial park in northwestern Brooklyn, bounded to the north by Upper New York Bay, Gowanus Bay, and 32nd Street, to the east by 3rd Avenue, to the south by 41st Street, and to the west by Upper New York Bay. The first facility of its kind in New York City to have many tenants, it was planned as a center of manufacturing and distribution by Irving T. Bush, who hoped to make of it "an industrial city within a city." It consisted of one warehouse in 1890 but later had its own rail system, fire and police forces, steam and power plants, deep-water piers, and access to the highway. New buildings were erected from 1902. At its greatest extent the facility occupied about two hundred acres (eighty-one hectares) between 27th and 50th streets, handled fifty thousand railroad freight cars, and had eighteen piers that were the port of call for twenty-five steamship lines. By the 1960s it was called Industry City and had 150 tenants employing 25,000 workers, most of whom lived nearby in Sunset Park. It was bought by a group led by Harry B. Helmsley in 1965. In the early 1990s Bush Terminal had 6.5 million square feet (600,000 square meters) of floor space in sixteen buildings of six to twelve stories each, and was managed by the firm of Helmsley–Spear. Most of the occupants are manufacturers and distributors of garments, printed products, women's fashion accessories, processed food, plastics, electronics, and toys.

Irving T. Bush: *Working with the World* (Garden City, N.Y.: Doubleday, Doran, 1928)

John J. Gallagher

Bushwick. Neighborhood in northeastern Brooklyn (1990 pop. 102,572), bounded to the north by Flushing Avenue, to the east by Queens County, to the south by the Cemetery of the Evergreens and Conway Street, and to the west by Broadway. One of the original six towns of Brooklyn during Dutch rule, it was established as Boswijck (heavy woods) in 1660 between Bushwick Creek and Newtown Creek and remained a farming community well into the nineteenth century. There was a large influx of German immigrants after 1840, and between 1850 and 1880 at least eleven breweries were operating within a fourteen-block area known as "brewer's row." Peter Cooper's first factory was one that made glue in Bushwick in the 1840s. With Williamsburgh the town became part of the City of Brooklyn in 1854. In 1869 Adrian Martenses Suydam developed the family farm for housing, and the land was the site of 125 residences by 1884. Development increased after the opening in 1888 of an elevated line to Manhattan. In later years the ethnic composition of the neighborhood changed several times: after the Depression the German population declined, in the 1930s and 1940s there developed one of the largest concentrations of Italians in Brooklyn, and after the Second World War many Italians moved to Queens and the suburbs while blacks and Puerto Ricans moved in. The neighborhood entered a period of decline marked by reduced city services and the closing of factories. Of the seven local breweries remaining after the Second World War the last two, Rheingold and F and M Schaefer, ceased operations in 1976. Arson and looting during the blackout of 1977 further damaged the neighborhood. In the 1980s some sections were revitalized by new housing and the refurbishing of existing housing. About a third of the new immigrants who settled in Bushwick in the 1980s were from the Dominican Republic. Smaller numbers were from Guyana, Ecuador, Jamaica, India, and China. Notable buildings in the neighborhood include the Reformed Church of South Bushwick at 15

Himrod Street (1853) and St. Mark's Lutheran Church and School at 626 Bushwick Avenue (1892). Knickerbocker Avenue and Broadway are the main commercial streets. The population is primarily Latin American and black, with some Italians and Asians.

Bushwick South and Bushwick Avenue (New York: New York City Landmarks Commission, n.d.) [report on proposed Historic District]

Tony Sanchez: *Bushwick Neighborhood Profile* (New York: Brooklyn in Touch Information Center, 1988)

Elizabeth Reich Rawson

Bushwick Savings Bank. Bank that merged with the Bay Ridge Savings Bank to form ANCHOR SAVINGS BANK.

Business Week. Weekly magazine launched in 1929 by the McGraw–Hill Publishing Company. It grew into the nation's largest business publication: from 1975 it carried more advertising pages annually than any magazine in the United States, and in the mid 1990s its circulation was more than one million worldwide. *Business Week* publishes an international edition in English, as well as editions in Chinese, Russian, Hungarian, and Polish.

The Business Week Almanac (New York: McGraw–Hill, 1982)

Donald S. Rubin

Butler, Nicholas Murray (*b* Elizabeth, N.J., 2 April 1862; *d* New York City, 7 Dec 1947). Educator. At Columbia College he was a student (AB 1882, PhD in philosophy 1884) and a teacher of philosophy (1885–90). In 1889 he founded the New York College for the Training of Teachers (now Teachers College), of which he was president until 1891. As the dean of the faculty of philosophy at Columbia (from 1890) he opposed a curriculum narrowly based on the classics and worked to ease admission and graduation requirements for undergraduates. During the same period he launched the *Educational Review* (which he edited from 1891 to 1919), was active in efforts to reform the public schools in New Jersey and centralize those in New York City, as well as in the movement for municipal consolidation, and was president of the National Education Association (1893–94) and an initiator of its Committee of Ten (1892–94), which advocated a liberalization of the high school curriculum; he also helped to form the College Entrance Examination Board in 1900 and was its first chairman (to 1914). In 1902 he became the president of COLUMBIA UNIVERSITY after the incumbent, Seth Low, was elected mayor of New York City. During his tenure (to 1945) he greatly increased the size and standing of the university as well as the power of his office, enabling Columbia to add five divisions (including a summer school, an extension division, and a school of journalism), thirty buildings, 2800 faculty members, and more than 23,000 students. He also continued to be active in other fields, and was instrumental in forming the Carnegie Foundation for the Advancement of Teaching (1905), which sponsored an influential report on reforming medical education by Abraham Flexner, and the Carnegie Corporation (1911), of which he was later chairman (1937–45). In 1912 he was nominated by the Republicans as their vice-presidential candidate after the death of Vice President James S. Sherman, and he unsuccessfully sought the Republican presidential nomination in 1920. A staunch advocate of international peace through conciliation, he was chairman of the Lake Mohonk Conferences on International Arbitration, president of the Carnegie Endowment for International Peace (1925–45), and a sponsor of the Kellogg–Briand treaty (1929). For these efforts he shared the Nobel Peace Prize with Jane Addams in 1931. Butler's published writings include *Across the Busy Years: Recollections and Reflections* (1939–40).

William Summerscales: *Affirmation and Dissent: Columbia's Response to the Crisis of World War I* (New York: Teachers College Press, 1970)

Richard Whittemore: *Nicholas Murray Butler and Public Education, 1862–1911* (New York: Teachers College Press, 1970)

Albert Marrin: *Nicholas Murray Butler* (Boston: Twayne, 1976)

David C. Hammack: *Power and Society: Greater New York at the Turn of the Century* (New York: Russell Sage Foundation, 1982)

Harold Wechsler

Butter and Cheese Exchange. Original name of the NEW YORK MERCANTILE EXCHANGE.

butterflies. Butterflies thrive in New York City, where they are supported by a variety of habitats including fields, shrub thickets, developing woodlands, shaded trails and glades, wet meadows, and salt marshes. The most abundant species are Swallowtails, Whites, Sulphurs, Gossamer Wings (*Lycaenidae*), Brushfoots (*Nymphalidae*), Skippers, and Milkweed Butterflies. In the autumn the Viceroy, a common orange and black butterfly that "mimics" the Monarch, may be seen throughout the city during its migration to Mexico; it is especially common on Staten Island, where large stands of Seaside Goldenrod provide food for its larval caterpillar. Alkaloids from the plant make both the caterpillar and its metamorphosed adult distasteful to predators.

Don Reipe, Jim Ingraham, and Guy Tudor: *Butterflies of the Jamaica Bay Wildlife Refuge* (Washington: National Park Service, U.S. Department of the Interior, 1993)

John T. Tanacredi

Butterick, Ebenezer (*b* Sterling, Mass., 29 May 1826; *d* Brooklyn, 31 March 1903). Businessman. He worked as a tailor and in 1863 entered the business of making clothing patterns, which he was the first to produce in a variety of sizes. In 1864 he moved from Fitchburg, Massachusetts, to New York City, where with two partners he formed E. Butterick and Company at 589 Broadway. By 1871

E. Butterick's Report of New York Fashions, *summer 1873*

E. Butterick's Report of New York Fashions, *autumn and winter 1872–73*

his firm made patterns in more than 12,500 styles and had sales of $4 million a year. Through Butterick's patterns fashionable, closely fitting apparel was made available to women who could not afford the services of dressmakers.

Claudia B. Kidwell: *Cutting a Fashionable Fit: Dressmakers' Drafting Systems in the United States* (Washington: Smithsonian Institution Press, 1979)

Margaret Walsh: "The Democratization of Fashion: The Emergence of the Women's Dress Pattern Industry," *Journal of American History* 66 (Sept 1979), 299–313

Nancy Page Fernandez: "'If a Woman Had Taste . . .': Home Sewing and the Making of Fashion, 1850–1910" (diss., University of California, Irvine, 1987)

Wendy Gamber

Buttermilk Channel. A body of water separating Governors Island from the southeastern tip of Red Hook in Brooklyn. Its name may have been inspired by the white water of its shallow rapids. Over the years the channel was dredged to at least forty feet (twelve meters). In Brooklyn it adjoins the entrance to the Atlantic Basin and Docks (built in the 1840s), now the site of the Red Hook container port. The channel is used primarily by the U.S. Coast Guard.

Elizabeth Reich Rawson

Butts, Calvin O(tis), III (*b* New York City, 19 July 1949). Pastor and activist. A graduate of Morehouse College, Union Theological Seminary, and Drew University, he became the pastor of Abyssinian Baptist Church in Harlem. Active in efforts to improve African-American life in New York City and elsewhere, he led campaigns against police brutality, billboard advertisements (especially those of liquor and tobacco companies aiming their products at the inner city), and rap lyrics that demean women and advocate violence.

Sherrill D. Wilson

Byrnes, Thomas F. (*b* Dublin, 15 June 1842; *d* 7 May 1910). Detective and superintendent of police. He became widely known in the 1880s when he solved the robbery of $3 million from the Manhattan Bank. In 1883 he persuaded the state legislature to place under the command of his headquarters all precinct detectives, whose primary activity until then had been to collect payoffs for the precinct captain. He advanced to the rank of chief inspector in 1888 and became superintendent of the force in 1892. A brutal man who purportedly invented the "third degree," Byrne enjoyed cooperative relations with the underworld and on his retirement was said to have amassed a fortune of $350,000.

Joseph P. Viteritti

teacher's seminary in Vilnius, where he was introduced to the radical ideas of the Narodnaya Volya (People's Will Party), which was responsible for assassinating Tsar Alexander II in March 1881. After evading the Russian police he moved to New York City in June 1882, where he soon became active in politics: he gave his first socialist lecture in Yiddish on 18 August 1882. A leader of Yiddish-speaking radical unionists, he helped to launch the *Jewish Daily Forward* in 1897; as its editor from 1901 until his death he made it a forum for immigrants seeking to organize industrial unions. He also edited *Tsukunft*, wrote for the *Naye Zeit* and the *Arbeiter Tsaytung*, and published articles, stories, and literary criticism in the *Sun*, the *New York World*, the *Evening Post*, the *Workman's Advocate*, and the *Atlantic Monthly*. Cahan also worked on Lincoln Steffens's *Commercial Advertiser* for four years. His published writings include *Yekl: A Tale of the New York Ghetto* (1896), which William Dean Howells called the "vanguard of New York," *Imported Bridegroom* (1898), *The White Terror and the Red* (1905), and *The Rise of David Levinsky* (1917), his well-known novel about an immigrant's experience in New York City. Cahan lived for many years at 224 East 11th Street.

Moses Rischin: *The Promised City: New York's Jews, 1870–1914* (Cambridge: Harvard University Press, 1962)

Seth Kamil: "The Formative Years of Jewish Trade Unions in Turn-of-the-Century New York City" (thesis, University of Massachusetts, Amherst, 1989)

Seth Kamil

Cahill Gordon and Reindel. Law firm. It was formed in 1919 by George Franklin and Joseph P. Cotton, who held positions in President Woodrow Wilson's government during the First World War. William G. McAdoo, Wilson's treasury secretary and son-in-law, soon joined as a partner. The current name was taken in 1973. The firm defended the Grumman Corporation and the Great Atlantic and Pacific Tea Company against hostile takeovers and represented the U.S. Treasury when loan guarantees for the Chrysler Corporation were granted in 1980. One of the partners, Floyd Abrams (*b* 1936), represented the *New York Times* in the Pentagon Papers case and the television networks in a case concerning the release of videotapes related to the "Abscam" scandal in 1980. Cahill Gordon and Reindel has worked pro bono for inmates on death row in Mississippi and for homeless AIDS patients; its litigation on behalf of the Municipal Art Society in connection with the preservation of Grand Central Terminal culminated in a decision by the U.S. Supreme Court in 1978 that upheld the city's landmarks preservation law.

Gilbert Tauber

Calkins, Earnest Elmo (*b* Genesco, Ill., 25 March 1868; *d* New York City, 4 Oct 1964). Editor and publisher. As a child he became deaf after contracting measles; he educated himself, took up the printing trade, and worked for a local newspaper before moving to New York City, where he edited the *Butchers' Gazette and Sausage Journal*. Initially unsuccessful, he moved back to Illinois but returned to the city to open his own firm, Calkins and Holden, which published the book *Modern Advertising*. In 1908 he organized the first exhibition of advertising materials at the National Arts Club. Calkins published a book of memoirs, *And Hearing Not: Annals of an Adman* (1946).

James E. Mooney

Calloway, Cab(ell) (*b* Rochester, N.Y., 25 Dec 1907; *d* Hosckessin, Del., 18 Nov 1994). Singer and bandleader. After growing up in Baltimore and Chicago he briefly played the drums and worked as a master of ceremonies. For a time he led the band the Alabamians before taking over another one known as the Missourians, which he renamed Cab Calloway and His Orchestra. Within a few years of his début at the Cotton Club in 1931 he became a sensation known for his dancing and his white suits as well as his singing. His band attracted such musicians as Milt Hinton and Dizzy Gillespie and remained one of the most successful bands of the swing era until it was dismantled in 1948. Many of his songs such as "Minnie the Moocher" (1931) celebrate the drug culture and disreputable aspects of nightlife in New York City. He performed and recorded music for various entertainments, including animated films, the motion pictures *Stormy Weather* (1943) and *The Blues Brothers* (1980), the opera *Porgy and Bess* (1952), and the musical *Hello, Dolly!* (1968). Calloway wrote an autobiography, *Of Minnie the Moocher and Me* (1976).

For illustration see Horne, Lena.

Douglas Henry Daniels

Calvary Cemetery. Roman Catholic cemetery in Queens. It comprises Old Calvary Cemetery (one parcel, bounded to the north by the Long Island Expressway, to the east by Laurel Hill Boulevard, to the south by review Avenue, and to the west by Greenpoint Avenue) and New Calvary Cemetery (three parcels, bounded to the north by Queens Boulevard, to the east by 58th Street, to the south by the Long Island Expressway, and to the west by 48th and 49th streets). Owned by the Archdiocese of New York, it is the largest cemetery in the United States (in interments). The original tract of land occupied eighty acres (thirty-two hectares) of the Alsop farm on the northern bank of Newtown Creek on Laurel Hill and was purchased by the trustees of St. Patrick's Cathedral in 1846 for $18,000. The first body was interred on 31 July 1848. Initially most burials were of children and poor Irish immigrants from the tenements of lower Manhattan. By 1867 the original tract was full and church authorities began to annex neighboring farms; this continued until 1888, when the northern edge of the cemetery reached Queens Boulevard. Early burial parties arrived by ferry across Newtown Creek, but in 1870 Borden Avenue was opened, providing overland access. Tracts were later added south and then north of what is now the Brooklyn–Queens Expressway (1879), and south of what is now the Long Island Expressway between 50th and 58th streets (1900). For many years there were more burials at the cemetery than at any other in the city. In the early 1990s the cemetery had nearly three million graves, a number greater than the population of Queens, and the only burials conducted were in reused lots and family plots.

Calvary Cemetery, 1984

The Visitor's Guide to Calvary Cemetery, with Map and Illustrations (New York: J. J. Foster, 1876)

Vincent Seyfried

Calvary Church. Episcopal church formed in 1835 on 4th Avenue at 21st Street. Under the rectorship of Samuel Shoemaker (1893–1963) it had extensive outreach activities, including programs for alcoholics and evangelistic efforts aimed at local office workers. The church was also a center of the Oxford Group Movement, which emphasized personal transformation, and helped to found Alcoholics Anonymous. In the mid 1970s it formed a united parish with the Church of the Holy Communion and St. George's Episcopal Church; the building continued to be used for worship services.

Robert Bruce Mullin

Calyo, Nicolino (*b* Naples, 1799; *d* New York City, 9 Dec 1884). Painter. He studied at the Academy in Naples, left Italy as a political refugee and traveled through Europe for eight

Nicolino Calyo, The Soap-Locks, ca *1847*

years, and about 1834 emigrated to the United States, where he worked in Philadelphia and Baltimore and then settled in New York City in 1835. He is best known for a series that he painted in gouache of the Great Fire (16–17 December 1835), which was engraved by William James Bennett (1787–1844) and enjoyed wide circulation. Between 1839 and 1846 he depicted street vendors in two series called "The Cries of New York." He made dioramas, panoramas, and theatrical set designs with his sons John Calyo (1829–93) and Hannibal Calyo (1835–83) and also painted portraits, miniatures, and landscapes.

For further illustrations see Great fire and Markets.

Annette Blaugrund

Cambreleng, Churchill C(aldom) (*b* Washington, N.C., 24 Oct 1786; *d* Huntington, N.Y., 30 April 1862). Congressman. He grew up in North Carolina and in 1802 moved to New York City, where he later became a close associate of John Jacob Astor. Elected to the U.S. House of Representatives in 1820, he was the first congressman from the city to earn national recognition as a Jacksonian, and he led the powerful Committee on Ways and Means during the bank war of 1836. He remained in office for eighteen years, a record that went unbroken in the city for almost a century. After leaving Congress he remained active in Democratic politics. Cambreleng is buried in Green-Wood Cemetery.

James Bradley

Cambria Heights. Neighborhood in southeastern Queens, lying within St. Albans and bounded to the north by 115th Avenue, to the east by Nassau County, to the south by 120th Avenue, and to the west by Springfield Boulevard. The origin of the name is unknown. The area was developed in 1923 on 163 acres (sixty-six hectares) of farmland formerly owned by the Buck, Fausner, and Hartmann families and acquired by Oliver B. LaFreniere, a real-estate agent from East New York. After the Second World War it became a largely black middle-class suburb. Many blacks from the Caribbean settled in the neighborhood in the 1980s, half of them from Jamaica and many others from Haiti, Guyana, Trinidad and Tobago, and Barbados.

Vincent Seyfried

campaign finance. The New York City Campaign Finance Act, enacted in 1988 pursuant to a charter amendment, provides for partial public funding in primary, runoff, and general elections for qualifying candidates for mayor, other citywide offices, borough president, and City Council. The city's campaign finance program is one of a very few operated by an American city, and in its coverage of offices and elections it is one of the most extensive in the United States at any level of government — local, state, or federal.

Participation in the campaign finance program is voluntary. Candidates who wish to qualify for public funds must limit contributions and expenditures and abide by reporting and disclosure rules. Those who raise a minimum amount of private contributions (the amount varying according to the office sought) are eligible for a dollar-for-dollar match of public funds, to a maximum of $500 per private contribution. The program is administered by a five-member Campaign Finance Board, which also publishes an annual voter's guide that it distributes to every household having at least one registered voter.

Richard Briffault

Canadians. Canada forged a link with New York City soon after the American Revolution, when more than 28,000 Loyalists from the city sought refuge there. Among those who did were David Mathews, a former mayor of the city, and the well-known lawyer William Smith Jr., the first historian of New York State and later a chief justice of the Province of Quebec. The flow was reversed in the nineteenth century, when Canada was often a way station for European emigrants traveling to the United States. In 1855 there were 4612 Canadians in the area now making up New York City and by 1890 there were 14,451. Canadians who emigrated to the United States were predominantly farmers, laborers, lumbermen, and fishermen from rural Cape Breton, Nova Scotia, New Brunswick, and Prince Edward Island. In Prospect Park West in the 1930s there lived a small colony of Newfoundlanders who worked on fishing smacks that sailed from Sheepshead Bay. The number of Canadians in the city reached 40,345 in 1940 and 42,823 in 1960 before declining to 15,874 in 1980.

Most Canadians assimilated very quickly and did not form a distinct group. Among those who became prominent for their accomplishments in New York City were the political scientist, philanthropist, and urban reformer Elgin R. L. Gould (*b* Oshawa, Ont.; *d* 1915), author of *The Housing of the Working People* (1895) and a leading figure in the city's housing reform movement in the 1890s; the historian James T. Shotwell (*b* Strathroy, Ont., 1874; *d* 1965), who received the PhD from Columbia University in 1902 and was Bryce Professor of History and International Relations at Columbia from 1908 to 1942; and the entrepreneur Elizabeth Arden, originally of Woodbridge, Ontario, who settled in New York City in 1908 and proceeded to build one of the largest cosmetics firms in the United States. In later years well-known Canadians who lived in the city included two television journalists — Peter Jennings (*b* Toronto, 1938), who moved to New York City in 1964 to work as a correspondent for the American Broadcasting Company and became the anchorman of "World News Tonight" in 1983, and Robert MacNeil (*b* Montreal, 1931), who worked for the National Broadcasting Company after his arrival in the city in 1965 and in 1976 became a host of "The MacNeil–Lehrer Report" on public television — the real-estate developer Mortimer B. Zuckerman, also the owner of the *Daily News*, and the actors Mary Pickford (*b* Toronto, 1893; *d* 1979), Walter Huston (*b* Toronto, 1894; *d* 1950), Norma Shearer (*b* Montreal, 1900; *d* 1983), Raymond Burr (*b* New Westminster, B.C., 1917; *d* 1993), Leslie Nielsen (*b* Regina, Sask., 1926), and Michael Sarrazin (*b* Montreal, 1940). Guy Lombardo, from London, Ontario, and his band the Royal Canadians led celebrations every New Year's Eve from 1929 to 1962 at the Roosevelt Grill.

Andrew Carnegie's mansion (designed by Babb, Cook and Willard), ca 1910. The house with its gardens and conservatory occupied half a block between 90th and 91st streets on 5th Avenue; it became the Cooper–Hewitt Museum in 1977.

Carnegie, Andrew (*b* Dunfermline, Scotland, 25 Nov 1835; *d* Shadowbrook, Mass., 11 Aug 1919). Industrialist. He moved to the United States with his parents in 1848 and settled in western Pennsylvania. His pluck and business acumen earned him work as a private secretary to the superintendent of the Pennsylvania Railroad in Pittsburgh, a position he held for about twelve years before becoming superintendent himself. After the Civil War he entered the iron and steel business, prospering within a few years. He considered the accumulation of wealth a form of idolatry and gave away much of his fortune. In 1882 the first of thousands of Carnegie libraries was given to the town of his birth. In 1901 he moved to 2 East 91st Street and sold his firm, the Carnegie Steel Corporation, to U.S. Steel; his share in the profits amounted to about $25 million a year. His bequests often reflected his interest in nature, learning, peace, books, and music. By the end of his life he had given away about $350 million, including $280 million in the United States. In New York City he used $125 million to form the Carnegie Corporation of New York, which became his residuary legatee, and also endowed Carnegie Hall on 57th Street and 7th Avenue, the Carnegie–Mellon Museum, the Teachers Insurance and Annuity Association, and a number of libraries.

Joseph Frazier Wall: *Andrew Carnegie* (New York: Oxford University Press, 1970)

James E. Mooney

Carnegie [Carnagey], **Dale** (*b* Harmony Church, near Maryville, Mo., 24 Nov 1888; *d* Queens, 1 Nov 1955). Public speaker and writer. After moving to New York City he opened an office in Carnegie Hall, which led him to change his surname. He employed a staff to research the habits of successful people, and devised a method of public-speaking instruction that combined acting, writing, and sales techniques and that he outlined in his book *How to Win Friends and Influence People* (1936). The book sold thirty million copies and was translated into twenty languages, and his motivational principles were adopted by figures ranging from Norman Vincent Peale to Pope John Paul I. In the mid 1990s there were 142 licensed sponsors and eleven "centers of excellence" teaching his principles worldwide. Carnegie lived in Forest Hills Gardens toward the end of his life.

Giles Kemp: *Dale Carnegie: The Man Who Influenced Millions* (New York: St. Martin's, 1989)

Val Ginter

Carnegie, Hattie [Kanengeiser, Henrietta] (*b* Vienna, 14 March 1886; *d* New York City, 22 Feb 1956). Fashion designer. Her adopted surname was apparently inspired by that of the industrialist Andrew Carnegie. In the 1930s and 1940s she was the best-known designer in the United States. She employed more than a thousand persons at her couture house on East 49th Street and in businesses that made ready-to-wear clothing as well as perfume and accessories. Among the designers who worked for her were Jean Louis, Norman Norell, Claire McCardell, and Pauline Potter (later known as Pauline de Rothschild).

Caroline Rennolds Milbank

Carnegie Corporation of New York. Philanthropic organization formed in 1911 by Andrew Carnegie and endowed with $135 million to "promote the advancement and diffusion of knowledge and understanding among the people of the United States and the British dominions and colonies." It was the largest single foundation established by Carnegie, who was its first president and served until his death in 1919. Under Carnegie's stewardship the corporation reflected his interests in libraries and pipe organs. Its first major effort was to fund the construction of the Carnegie Free Public Libraries throughout the English-speaking world; by the time the program ended in 1917 it had constructed 2509 library buildings at a cost of $56 million. After Carnegie's death the corporation broadened its scope, and between 1919 and 1923 it created the National Research Council, the American Law Institute, and the National Bureau of Economic Research. Frederick P. Keppel, the corporation's president from 1923 to 1942, emphasized cultural philanthropy and in particular programs in adult education and the arts. During his tenure the corporation provided funds for promoting arts societies and the study of art in public schools to the American Federation of Arts (founded by Carnegie's associate Elihu Root in 1909 in opposition to the Ashcan School). It also helped the People's Institute to sponsor lectures by philosophers and social scientists like Morris Raphael Cohen and Lewis Mumford, and funded classes for workers at the Workers' Education Bureau of America (formed in 1921 by Charles A. Beard and others).

After the 1940s the influence on public policy of the Carnegie Corporation lessened as that of newer and larger foundations like the Ford Foundation increased, and as the federal government formed new agencies and markedly increased its role in education with the passage of the Elementary and Secondary Education Act of 1965. The corporation continued nonetheless to finance research and writing projects, including Gunnar Myrdal's study of race problems *An American Dilemma* (1944) and David Riesman's study of alienation *The Lonely Crowd* (1950), as well as such educational projects as the Children's Television Workshop and "Sesame Street," first broadcast in 1969. By the early 1990s the Carnegie Corporation had donated more than $500 million to universities, libraries, and research institutes to further the goals of individualism, liberty, equal opportunity, internationalism, and peace.

Ellen C. Lagemann: *The Politics of Knowledge: The Carnegie Corporation, Philanthropy and Public Policy* (Middletown, Conn.: Wesleyan University Press, 1989)

Stephen Weinstein

Carnegie Hall. The most famous concert hall in the United States, situated at the southeast corner of 57th Street and 7th Avenue. It was built between 1889 and 1891 and known until 1894 as the Music Hall. The construction

Carnegie Hall, 1899

of the hall cost $1 million and was paid for by Andrew Carnegie, to whom the conductor Walter Damrosch had suggested that a home was needed for the Oratorio Society and the New York Symphony Society. The building was designed in a neo-Renaissance style by the architect William B. Tuthill and built by the firm of Isaac A. Hopper and Company entirely of terra cotta and brick, with an iron framework on a natural foundation of solid granite. Originally the building comprised four public spaces: the Main Hall, now seating 2804; the Chamber Music Hall (renamed Carnegie Recital Hall in 1898 and Weill Recital Hall in 1986), seating 268; Chapter Hall, used for lectures, meetings, and religious services until its renovation in 1985, when it was renamed the Kaplan Space and became used primarily for rehearsals and recordings; and the Recital Hall, which became the home of the Carnegie Lyceum in 1898, the Carnegie Playhouse in 1960, and the Carnegie Hall Cinema in 1970. In 1894 and 1896 two towers housing 150 studios were constructed around and atop the original building as a means of providing supplemental income. These residential and working spaces, designed by the architect Henry J. Hardenbergh, later housed such tenants as Charles Dana Gibson, the Authors' Club, Isadora Duncan, the American Academy of Dramatic Arts, Agnes de Mille, and the studios of the Victor Talking Machine Company, where Enrico Caruso made his first American recordings in 1904.

Carnegie Hall officially opened on 5 May 1891 and was widely praised for its acoustical excellence, favorable sightlines, and intimate ambience. The inaugural music festival lasted five days and was highlighted by an appearance by Tchaikovsky, who conducted several of his own works. The American début of the Polish pianist Jan Ignace Paderewski at the hall on 17 November 1891 was followed by the début of virtually every important classical musician of the next hundred years.

In its first century more than fifty thousand musical and nonmusical events took place at Carnegie Hall. From 1892 the principal tenant was the Philharmonic Society of New York (from 1928 the Philharmonic-Symphony Society of New York, later known generally as the New York Philharmonic), which remained there until 1961. Between 1891 and 1990 more than thirteen hundred compositions received their world première or American première at the hall, among them Antonín Dvořák's symphony *From the New World* (world première, 16 December 1893), George Gershwin's *Concerto in F* (1928), and Duke Ellington's *Black, Brown and Beige* (1943). Many well-known composers took part in performances of their own works, including Camille Saint-Saëns, Gustav Mahler, Sergei Prokofiev, Maurice Ravel, Ottorino Respighi, Aaron Copland, Igor Stravinsky, Virgil Thomson, William Schuman, John Cage, and Philip Glass. The hall was the site of performances by leading orchestras, chamber ensembles, and soloists from throughout the world, and by performers of jazz, folk music, popular music, and rock, among them James Reese Europe and his Clef Club (1912), Fats Waller (1928), Benny Goodman (1938), Dizzy Gillespie (1947), Woody Guthrie (1946), Pete Seeger (1946), Miles Davis (1957), Edith Piaf (1957), Judy Garland (1961), Frank Sinatra (1964), the Beatles (1964), and the Rolling Stones (1964). The acoustics of the hall also made it a forum for public speakers, including explorers, authors, politicians, and religious leaders.

Carnegie retained ownership of the hall until his death in 1919. His wife, Louise Whitfield Carnegie, sold the building in 1924 to the real-estate developer Robert E. Simon; on his death in 1935 ownership passed to his son Robert E. Simon Jr., who maintained the building until 1960. Scheduled for demolition as the New York Philharmonic prepared to move to a new home in Lincoln Center, Carnegie Hall was saved by a coalition of musicians, politicians, and civic figures led by the violinist Isaac Stern. It was bought by the City of New York in 1960 and registered as a National Historic Landmark in 1964.

On 18 May 1986 Carnegie Hall closed for the most comprehensive renovation and restoration in its history. In seven months at a cost of $60 million the firm of James Stewart Polshek and Partners restored much of the building to the way it had appeared in 1891, while improving its technical features. At the same time steps were taken to help ensure the financial stability of the hall: an adjacent lot on 57th Street (which had been acquired by Andrew Carnegie in 1903) was subleased by the Rockrose Development Corporation from the Carnegie Hall Corporation to allow for the construction of a sixty-story building, Carnegie Hall Tower.

Ethel Peyser: *The House That Music Built: Carnegie Hall* (New York: Robert M. McBride, 1936)

Richard Schickel: *The World of Carnegie Hall* (New York: Julian Messner, 1960)

Theodore O. Cron and Burt Goldblatt: *Portrait of Carnegie Hall: A Nostalgic Portrait in Pictures and Words* (New York: Macmillan, 1966)

Richard Schickel and Michael Walsh: *Carnegie Hall: The First One Hundred Years* (New York: Harry N. Abrams, 1987)

Gino Francesconi

Carnegie Hill. Neighborhood on the Upper East Side of Manhattan, bounded to the north by 96th Street, to the east by 3rd Avenue, to the south by 86th Street, and to the west by 5th Avenue. The area was the rural site of a few charitable institutions, modest houses, and squatters' shacks when the steel magnate Andrew Carnegie built an imposing neo-Georgian mansion at 91st Street and 5th Avenue in 1902. An affluent residential neighborhood took shape after he sold nearby lots to such wealthy businessmen as Otto H. Kahn, James Burden, and John Henry Hammond. Along with their mansions, gracious townhouses and luxury apartment buildings were built until the Depression. Elegant shops and restaurants now line Madison Avenue, the main commercial street. Much of the housing in Carnegie Hill consists of mansions, townhouses, and luxury apartment buildings; there are also private schools and cultural institutions, among them the Cooper–Hewitt Museum, the Guggenheim Museum, and the Jewish Museum.

Kate Simon: *Fifth Avenue: A Very Social History* (New York: Harcourt Brace Jovanovich, 1978)
Carnegie Hill: An Architectural Guide (New York: Carnegie Hill Neighbors, 1989)

Joyce Mendelsohn

carousel manufacturing. Brooklyn was a center of carousel manufacturing between 1875 and 1918, when animal carvers such as Charles I. D. Looff, M. C. Illions, Charles Carmel, Solomon Stein, and Harry Goldstein developed a wildly exuberant "Coney Island style." The style is exemplified in horses by Carmel at Prospect Park, Coney Island, and Playland Park (Rye, New York), by Illions at Flushing Meadows, and by Stein and Goldstein at Central Park.

Stephen Weinstein

Carpatho-Rusyns. The Carpatho-Rusyns are a Slavic people. They and their branches are also known variously as Rusyns, Ruthenians, Carpatho-Russians, Carpatho-Ukrainians, and Lemkos. During the 1880s they began emigrating to the United States from the north central ranges of the Carpathian Mountains, until 1918 part of the Austro-Hungarian Empire. Most of the Carpatho-Rusyns in New York City are descendants of immigrants who arrived between 1880 and 1914. They settled primarily on the Lower East Side and in Brooklyn, working as laborers in the garment industry, in small factories, and in the service trades. When most of their homeland became part of Poland and Czechoslovakia after the First World War a few thousand more Carpatho-Rusyns emigrated; many were Lemkos from the Polish province of Galicia. In New York City Lemkos formed the League for the Liberation of Carpatho-Russia (1917), which published a newspaper and strove to unify the Carpathian homeland with a democratic Russia. During the 1930s Carpatho-Rusyns settled in Yorkville alongside Czechs and Hungarians, and their numbers increased by several hundred after the Second World War, when Carpatho-Rusyns fled the communist regimes of Eastern Europe – the Ukrainian SSR, Czechoslovakia, and Poland.

Carpatho-Rusyns have sometimes aligned themselves with other ethnic groups, such as Russians, Slovaks, Ukrainians, and Czechs, but have also maintained their own religious and secular organizations. Their political organizations in New York City have supported a range of solutions for the Carpatho-Rusyn homeland: unity with the Soviet Union (Carpatho-Russian National Committee, 1939), unity with an independent Ukraine (Organization for the Defense of the Lemko Land, 1940), and unity with Czechoslovakia (Council of Free Carpatho-Ruthenia in Exile, 1951). These groups have issued their own publications in Russian, Ukrainian, and the Carpatho-Rusyn vernacular. The predominant faith of Carpatho-Rusyns is Eastern Christianity, and New York City has several parishes belonging to the Byzantine Ruthenian Catholic Church and the American Carpatho-Russian Orthodox Greek Catholic Church. The most architecturally striking church is the Byzantine Ruthenian Church of St. Mary, built in 1963 on the corner of East 15th Street and 2nd Avenue in Manhattan. Many Carpatho-Rusyns also belong to parishes of the Orthodox Church in America, which is oriented toward Russian Orthodoxy. Carpatho-Rusyn Jews include a community of Hasidim in Borough Park led by the grandson of the renowned rabbi of Mukachevo (Ukraine). Several Carpatho-Rusyn cultural organizations have their headquarters in New York City: the Carpathian Research Center (1958), for two decades led by the former parliamentarian and minister of the Carpatho-Ukraine, Julian Revay (1899–1979); the Lemko Research Foundation (1978), which promotes knowledge of the Lemkos living in Poland; and the Carpatho-Rusyn Research Center (1978). Perhaps the best-known Carpatho-Rusyn in the cultural history of the city is the painter and filmmaker Andy Warhol.

Walter C. Warzeski: *Byzantine Rite Rusyns in Carpatho-Ruthenia and America* (Pittsburgh: Byzantine Seminary Press, 1971)
Paul Robert Magocsi: *Our People: Carpatho-Rusyns and Their Descendants in North America* (Toronto: Multicultural History Society of Ontario, 1984)
Paul Robert Magocsi: *The Carpatho-Rusyn Americans* (New York: Chelsea House, 1989)

Paul Robert Magocsi

Carpenter and Vermilye. Original name of the investment banking firm DILLON, READ.

Carrère and Hastings. Firm of architects formed in 1884 by John M(erven) Carrère (1858–1911) and Thomas Hastings (1860–1929), former students at the École des Beaux-Arts in Paris who had worked as draftsmen in the offices of McKim, Mead and White. The partners were successful from the outset, receiving commissions for large country estates, churches, and hotels, including the Ponce de León Hotel (1888) in St. Augustine, Florida. In 1897 the firm achieved national prominence after winning the design competition for the New York Public Library with a plan that combined a majestic façade, rich yet functional interior spaces, terraces, and gardens (for illustration see NEW YORK PUBLIC LIBRARY). Later the firm completed the First Christian Science Church (1903) at Central Park West and 96th Street, the triumphal arch and colonnade at the approach to the Manhattan Bridge (1905), Richmond Borough Hall (1906; for illustration see STATEN ISLAND), Grand Army Plaza (1912) in Manhattan, the Frick mansion (1914), and Richmond County Courthouse (1919). After Carrère's death Hastings continued to practice under the firm's name. In association with other architects he designed several notable office buildings, including the Cunard Building (1921) and the Standard Oil Building (1922). Two marble busts of Carrère and Hastings may be seen on the first landing of the main staircase at the New York Public Library.

Rebecca Read Shanor

Carroll, Earl (*b* Pittsburgh, 16 Sept 1893; *d* Mount Carmel, Penn., 17 June 1948). Theater producer. In 1923–32 he produced the revue *Vanities*, which along with Florenz Ziegfeld's *Follies* and George White's *Scandals* was one of the best-known Broadway shows of the jazz age. Critical reaction was mixed; a critic from the *Brooklyn Eagle* once remarked that "Carroll's showmanship consisted in selling gutter humor and naked female flesh to morons," but often reviews in the *New York Times* were not unkind. In 1927 Carroll was found guilty of perjury for denying that the champagne in which a nude showgirl bathed at one of his late-night parties contained alcohol, and he was sent to Atlanta Penitentiary. After his release he had an inconsequential career in Hollywood.

Ken Murray: *The Body Merchant: The Story of Earl Carroll* (New York: W. Ritchie, 1976)

George A. Thompson, Jr.

Carroll Gardens. Neighborhood in northwestern Brooklyn, occupying forty blocks and bounded to the north by Degraw Street, to the east by Hoyt Street, to the south by 9th Street, and to the west by the Gowanus and Brooklyn–Queens expressways. It was originally considered part of Red Hook. The current name was adopted in the 1960s by real-estate agents; the eponym of the neighborhood is Charles Carroll, an immigrant from Ireland and a signer of the Declaration of Independence. The area was settled by Irish in the early nineteenth century. From the late nineteenth century to the 1950s it attracted many Italians, and between 1920 and 1950 most of the Irish left for more affluent communities. The Carroll Gardens Association was formed in 1964 to discuss community issues and gradually succeeded in improving the image of the neighborhood and in breaking a political machine that had dominated since the 1930s. In the 1960s many young, middle-class professionals moved to the area, drawn by its safety, tranquility, and proximity to Manhattan. Carroll Gardens is distinguished by its brownstones and its exceptionally large front yards, a feature resulting from a plan drawn up in 1846 by the land surveyor Richard Butts. These yards may be seen on 1st to 4th places between Henry and Smith streets and on President, Carroll, and

Lounge of the Earl Carroll Theatre, 755 7th Avenue

2nd streets between Smith and Hoyt streets. Part of this area was designated a Historic District in 1973 (President and Carroll streets between Smith and Hoyt streets and Hoyt Street between President and 1st streets). Carroll Gardens remains an Italian enclave where several dialects of Italian are spoken. There are a number of fraternal and benevolent societies representing towns in Italy, frequent bocce games, a procession on Good Friday, extravagant fireworks displays on Independence Day, and a large number of Italian restaurants, delicatessens, bakeries, and pastry shops.

Nan Ellin

Carrville. Former neighborhood in west central Brooklyn, lying in Bedford next to Weeksville. Along with Weeksville it was settled in the 1830s by free black farmers, laborers, and craftsmen. The name is of unknown origin but may be a corruption of Crow Hill, a name applied to the surrounding area. A church opened in 1839 but soon closed. An African free school was established about the same time, but in 1841 white trustees of school district no. 3 took over its management and renamed it Colored School no. 2; it later moved to Weeksville. A racially integrated organization laid out Citizens Union Cemetery in the area in 1851 (black burials were often prohibited in white cemeteries). In the 1850s Carrville and Weeksville became demographically one large black community, of which large sections were destroyed along with the cemetery when a road that became Eastern Parkway was cut through the area in 1869–70. Carrville was all but obliterated when streets were laid out from 1870 to 1875.

Robert J. Swan: "The Origin of Black Bedford–Stuyvesant," *An Introduction to the Black Contribution to the Development of Brooklyn* (New York: New Muse Community Museum of Brooklyn, 1977)

Ellen Marie Snyder-Grenier

Carter, Henry. Given name of FRANK LESLIE.

Carter, James C(oolidge) (*b* Lancaster, Mass., 14 Oct 1827; *d* New York City, 14 Feb 1905). Lawyer. He left Harvard Law School in 1853 and became well known as a litigator. Among the cases in which he took part was the prosecution of William M. "Boss" Tweed. A founder of Carter, Ledyard and Milburn and a leading figure of the bar during the late nineteenth century, he argued many cases before the U.S. Supreme Court. He was a devotee of the common law and led the forces that defeated the Field Civil Code. Carter helped to organize the Association of the Bar of the City of New York and belonged to many civic reform groups.

James A. Wooten

Cartier. Firm of jewelers formed in Paris in 1847. It opened its first American branch on 1 November 1909 at 712 5th Avenue under the direction of Pierre Cartier (1878–1965). In exchange for a pearl necklace the firm in 1917 acquired the Renaissance palace of the banker Morton F. Plant at 653 5th Avenue, which became its new location. The branch in New York City offered jewels from the main shop in Paris before setting up its own workshop, where art deco jewelry was produced based on Egyptian and Oriental models as well as on modern designs. Cartier's nephew Claude Cartier (1925–75) took over the branch in 1948 and remained president until 1962, when the company was taken over by outside interests. Robert Hocq, Joseph Kanoui, and Alain-Dominique Perrin assumed control of the firm in 1972 and of the branch in New York City in February 1976. The result was the formation of Cartier International, again bringing the management of all the houses under one hand.

Gilberte Gautier: *Cartier, the Legend* (London: Arlington, 1983)
Hans Nadelhoffer: *Cartier: Jewelers Extraordinary* (New York: Harry N. Abrams, 1984)

Janet Zapata

carting. During the first two centuries of the history of New York City, cartmen dominated all intracity transport. They pledged to obey municipal ordinances derived from English and Dutch law, in consideration of which they were given a monopoly on licenses. The cartmen refused employment to blacks, juveniles, and nonresidents of the city, and held strikes in 1677 and 1684 to protect their monopoly and resist further municipal regulation of their trade. In 1691 the city set fees for cartage and rules for the ownership of carts, standardized the measurement of loads, and required that cartmen serve any orderly person seeking their assistance; these laws remained in effect with little change until 1844. By the colonial period there were about four hundred cartmen in the city, some of whom specialized in the transport of furniture, mercantile goods, firewood, hay, or food. The typical cartman was easily recognizable by his white frock, farmer's hat, and clay pipe. After the American Revolution cartmen helped to rebuild the city's economy. A political controversy arose when Mayor Richard Varick in 1789 ended the custom of awarding freemanships to licensed carters, a loss that denied the suffrage to many impoverished carters. In an effort to have the custom reinstated the cartmen aligned themselves with the emerging Democratic Republican Party and in 1795 helped to elect the cartman Alexander Lamb to the state assembly.

In the first decades of the nineteenth century cartmen defended their monopoly against an increasing number of Irish immigrants looking for work. After a bitter dispute in 1818 Mayor Marinus Willett divided the business between general carting, to be performed by citizens, and dirt carting, to be performed by the Irish. In 1825 a new law restricted general carting licenses to citizens. Despite the protests of black residents of New York City the business remained rigidly segregated. Throughout the nineteenth century cartmen evoked the anger of the middle class because of their reckless driving, surly

Bud Fisher, "Sixty Seconds Make One Minute," published in the New York World, *24 May 1922*

behavior, cruelty to horses, and rate gouging during plagues and fires and each year on 1 May (when the city's residents traditionally moved into new dwellings). Their monopoly was again attacked during the Workingman's Movement of 1829 and remained a political controversy throughout the 1830s, when 3500 cartmen sided with the Whig Party against the Democrats, who favored the elimination of restrictive licensing. In 1844 the Board of Aldermen abolished licensing restrictions and the requirement that each driver own his cart, partly because more cartmen were needed in the expanding city. The business began to collapse in the 1850s as the carters' monopoly became unenforceable in the growing metropolis and larger express wagons replaced small carts.

Howard B. Rock: *Artisans of the New Republic: The Tradesmen of New York in the Age of Thomas Jefferson* (New York: New York University Press, 1979)

Graham Hodges: *New York City Cartmen, 1676–1850* (New York: New York University Press, 1986)

Graham Hodges

cartooning. During the last quarter of the nineteenth century cartoons emerged as a medium that captured the dynamism and adventure of New York City. As a cartoonist for *Harper's Weekly* Thomas Nast lambasted William M. "Boss" Tweed and popularized such characters as the Democratic donkey and the Tammany Hall tiger. *Puck*, launched in 1876, provided a forum for such cartoonists as Joseph Keppler and Bernard Gillam, and the *Judge* followed in the same vein from 1881. Charles Dana Gibson contributed caricatures of social and political figures to *Harper's* and other magazines, and in 1895 R. F. Outcault introduced "Hogan's Alley" in Joseph Pulitzer's newspaper the *New York World*. In a single, crowded panel, each installment depicted the pathos, tumult, and squalor of life in the Irish slums through the experiences of a baby-faced urchin in a yellow nightshirt. The harsh, mischievous humor of the strip became so popular that Outcault was persuaded by William Randolph Hearst to move to the *New York Journal*, where the series was renamed "The Yellow Kid." Outcault portrayed a childhood robbed of its innocence by ugliness, menace, and delinquency. In a typical panel from 1897 a chaotic dog show takes place in an alley while a parrot sagely advises in the customary slang of the strip: "Children if you want to live tro dis stay on yer perch." The yellow ink used to print the cartoon gave rise to the term "yellow journalism."

Outcault's success inspired the first comic strips, so named because they included several panels: the "Katzenjammer Kids" (1897) by Rudolph Dirks, based on the German strip "Max und Moritz" by Wilhelm Busch; "Happy Hooligan" (1899) by Frederick Burr Opper; "Buster Brown" (1902) by Outcault; and "Mutt and Jeff" (1907) by Bud Fisher, the first strip to appear daily. From 1913 the *New York American* printed the first strip in which each installment was an episode in a continuing story: "Bringing Up Father," by the Irish immigrant George McManus (1884–1954), satirized wealthy New Yorkers and romanticized the Irish working class through the adventures of Jiggs and Maggie, an Irish working-class couple who struck it rich and were suddenly thrust into a life of leisure. Jiggs constantly sought to slip away from his elegant surroundings and return to the corner saloon and the corned beef and cabbage of his old neighborhood, but whenever his ambitious and showy wife Maggie discovered his escapades she pummeled him with "fisticuffs" and kitchenware. McManus contrasted the haughty silliness of the rich and vacuous with the earthy charm, wisdom, and good humor of the slums. Although he showed respect for a society that allowed a hod carrier and a washerwoman to acquire great wealth, he suggested that no one could ever fully leave poverty behind and questioned whether anyone should want to. The strip became hugely popular, appeared in about five hundred newspapers, and at its height reached eighty million readers in forty-six countries, running for forty-one years. Rube Goldberg's comic strip recounting the adventures of Boob McNutt was popular for twenty years. Other cartoons served political ends or were aimed at a more sophisticated readership: in 1911–17 the leftist magazine the *Masses* published cartoons by such artists as French Sloan, George Bellows, Boardman Robinson, and Art Young; and cartoons by James Thurber, Peter Arno, and Charles Addams appeared in the *New Yorker*.

From the 1920s newspapers and pulp magazines printed comic strips based on detectives and adventure characters. *Famous Funnies* (1934) began by reprinting comic strips from newspapers and then introduced strips of its own, many with humorous animal characters. Other early comic books included *Tip Top Comics* and *King Comics*. The first "superhero," Superman, was created by Jerry Siegel and Joe Shuster and first appeared in *Action Comics* (1938), published by Detective Comics (later known as DC Comics), which soon after introduced Batman (by Bob Kane and Bill Finger, first featured in *Detective Comics* in 1939). In 1941 Marvel Comics introduced Captain America (by Joe Simon and Jack Kirby). From 1940 to 1952 Will Eisner (*b* New York City, 1917) produced his influential weekly strip "The Spirit," chronicling the adventures of a masked crime fighter in a seamy version of New York City called Central City. O'Sullivan has described the city as at once the Spirit's "adversary and amour," which "is blighted but possesses a cunning life of its own . . . Unlike the Spirit itself, the city is vigorously aggressive, asserting itself immediately in the strip's first frame." The Spirit was the product in part of the Yiddish theater, an insecure, confused, lower-middle-class New Yorker given to self-deprecating monologues. One of the many cartoonists influenced by Eisner was Jules Feiffer, whose weekly comic strip popularized a distinctive brand of humor infused with neurosis, angst, and the absurdities of urban life. A rather more sophomoric approach was taken by William M. Gaines: in April 1955 he launched the satirical magazine *Mad*, in which cartoons and comic strips parodied advertisements and popular culture. Gaines began the magazine after spending part of his earlier career publishing comic books devoted to crime and horror, a type of publication that provoked a strong reaction from the political right. In the face of growing pressure and hearings by subcommittees of the U.S. Senate, comic book publishers in the 1950s adopted a form of self-censorship called the Comics Code of America. Among the less controversial comics of the period was "Apartment 3-G" (1961), a conventional soap opera in the form of a comic strip by Nick Dallis and Alex Kotzky, in which three young women share an apartment in Manhattan next door to a bearded sage who offers them paternal guidance. After assuming control of Marvel Comics, Kirby and Stan Lee in 1962 introduced Spider-Man, an anguished teenager turned crime fighter. The company later published a large number of comic strips set in New York City and helped to revitalize the comic book business. Although in the 1970s and 1980s both Superman and Batman gained new life in big-budget motion pictures, by the 1990s New York City was no longer the undisputed center of comic book publishing.

Comic strips continue to be published in newspapers ranging from the *Daily News* (which also prints cartoons in its sports section) to the *Village Voice* (which publishes Feiffer, the politically oriented comic strips of Mark Alan Stamaty, and the "Real Life Funnies" of Stan Mack). Caricatures of literary and political figures by David Levine appear regularly in the *New York Review of Books.* Courses in cartooning are offered at the School of Visual Arts, known as the School of Cartoonists and Illustrators when it opened in 1947.

Ron Goulart, ed.: *The Encyclopedia of American Comics* (New York: Facts on File, 1990)

Judith O'Sullivan: *The Great American Comic Strip: One Hundred Years of Cartoon Art* (Boston: Little, Brown, 1990)

Jeff Sklansky

Caruso, Enrico [Errico] (*b* Naples, 27 Feb 1873; *d* Naples, 2 Aug 1921). Singer. He sang opera in Italy before traveling to the United States, where he gave his first performance at the Metropolitan Opera in November 1903, in Verdi's *Rigoletto.* His performances over the next few years made him the best-known operatic tenor of his generation. With the Metropolitan Opera he sang thirty-seven roles in 626 performances in New York City and 235 on tour. He also made more recordings than any other singer of his time (for Victor) and many concert appearances, some to promote Liberty Bonds during the First World War. On 11 December 1920 he suffered a throat hemorrhage while performing at the Brooklyn Academy of Music; he gave his last performance on 24 December 1920 in New York City. Caruso was known for a robust yet warm, mellow voice, and reissues of his recordings remain popular. He lived from 1908 to 1920 at the Hotel Knickerbocker (42nd Street and Broadway) and from 1920 to the end of his life at the Vanderbilt Hotel (34th Street and Park Avenue).

Enrico Caruso as the Duke of Mantua in Verdi's Rigoletto

Howard Greenfield: *Caruso* (New York: G. P. Putnam's Sons, 1983)

Gerald Fitzgerald, ed.: *Annals of the Metropolitan Opera Guild: The Complete Chronicle of Performances and Artists: Chronology, 1883–1985* (New York: Metropolitan Opera Guild / Boston: G. K. Hall, 1989)

See also CARNEGIE HALL.

John W. Freeman

Cascade Linen and Uniform Service. Firm of laundry and linen suppliers in Brooklyn, formed in 1898 as General Linen Supply and Laundry by Charles Bonoff, a Russian immigrant. It eventually became the largest firm of its kind in the world. The main plant at Myrtle and Marcy avenues in Brooklyn incorporates the original building. In the mid 1990s the firm employed five hundred persons and used the oldest operating electric generating facility in New York City.

Kenneth T. Jackson

Casey, William (Joseph) (*b* Elmhurst, N.Y., 13 March 1913; *d* Glen Cove, N.Y., 6 May 1987). Businessman and political leader. After earning a BA at Fordham University (1934) and a law degree at St. John's University (1937) he worked during the Second World War in the Office of Strategic Services, where he developed a passion for espionage and politics. In the late 1940s he returned to the city to give lectures on tax law at New York University. Soon considered an expert, he gained immense wealth and power through his extensive knowledge of financial markets and in 1957 joined the law firm of Hall, Casey, Dickler and Howley, where he remained until 1971. He was a powerful insider in both the city and Washington and gained several government posts while maintaining strong ties to businesses and law firms in the city. In 1978 he formed the Manhattan Institute, a nonprofit education and research institute. He was appointed director of the Central Intelligence Agency in 1981 by President Ronald Reagan. Casey's tenure was marked by controversy and suggestions that he had taken part in an illegal scheme to sell arms to Iran and finance an insurgent movement in Nicaragua with the proceeds; subpoenaed by a congressional committee, he died shortly before he was scheduled to testify.

Joseph E. Persico: *Casey: From the OSS to the CIA* (New York: Viking, 1990)

James Bradley

Cashmore, John (*b* Brooklyn, 7 June 1895; *d* Brooklyn, 7 May 1961). Borough president. He grew up in Brooklyn and attended the local public schools. After graduating from New York University he was elected in 1923 to the state assembly from the fifth district (Stuyvesant Heights) and in 1925 to the city's Board of Aldermen (renamed the City Council in 1928). He remained on the council until 1940, when as its majority leader he was chosen to fill the vacated borough presidency of Brooklyn. During twenty-one years in this office he oversaw the construction of Coney Island General Hospital, of a civic center in downtown Brooklyn consisting of ten buildings (built for $100 million on the site of several deteriorating blocks), and of public parks and housing. He was also instrumental in gaining $115 million to build schools in the 1950s. His proposal in 1955 for a new baseball stadium to keep the Dodgers in Brooklyn was not acted on, and in 1957 the team left for California. From 1945 to 1950 Cashmore was active in the Democratic Party as a leader in the fifth assembly district and in Kings County. He ran unsuccessfully for the U.S. Senate in 1952 against the Republican incumbent, Irving M. Ives.

Edward T. O'Donnell

casitas. Wood-framed buildings of one story and one or two rooms built on vacant, city-owned lots by Puerto Rican residents of the southern Bronx, East Harlem, and the Lower East Side. Once a common form of housing among the poor of the Puerto Rican rural highlands, coastal regions, and urban shantytowns, the casita first appeared in New York City in the late 1970s, where it became used variously as a shelter and meeting place for various community organizations: social clubs, block associations, cultural centers, and horticultural groups. Constructed from recycled scrap lumber and store-bought materials, it is characterized by a pitched roof, an entrance at the gabled end, and a porch (or "balcón"), the railings of which are commonly fashioned with decorative X's, and is often painted in the vibrant colors of the Caribbean. A casita may have a working kitchen with a refrigerator, stove, and running water, and is frequently surrounded by a landscaped, dooryard garden and a nonvegetated, clean-swept yard (or "batey"), which simulates the rural, preindustrial Caribbean topography. The casita and its surrounding property are protected from vandals by a chain-link fence. A number of casita builders lease property from the city as participants in the Green Thumb community garden program. Members of neighborhoods often construct a casita in an attempt to keep neglected city property from being used for dumping, drug abuse, "chop shops," and prostitution, yet the city considers casitas "illegal structures" and routinely demolishes them.

Joseph Sciorra: "'I Feel Like I'm in My Country': Puerto Rican Casitas in New York City," *Drama Review* 34 (1990), 156–68

Joseph Sciorra

Castelli, Leo (*b* Trieste, Italy, 4 Sept 1907). Art dealer. He moved to the United States in 1941, studied at Columbia University, and in 1957 opened the Leo Castelli Gallery at 4 East 77th Street. In the following decades the gallery displayed the work of some of the leading figures in contemporary American art, including Jasper Johns and Robert Rauschenberg (mounting their first exhibitions in 1958), Frank Stella (1959), Roy Lichtenstein (1961), John Chamberlain, Dan Flavin, Donald Judd, Ellsworth Kelly, Claes Oldenburg, James Rosenquist, Richard Serra, Cy Twombly, and Andy Warhol. In 1971 the gallery moved to 420 West Broadway, where it helped to fuel the development of SoHo as an art district.

Ann Heindry, ed.: *Claude Berri Meets Leo Castelli* (Paris: Renn, 1990)

Avis Berman

Poster for D. D. Badger's Architectural Iron Works

cast-iron architecture. The versatile high-carbon ferrous alloy known as cast iron was made available in quantity and at an affordable price by British technological advances toward the end of the eighteenth century. American inventors, engineers, and architects soon adapted the medium to the emerging needs of rapidly growing cities. Although cast iron was first used only for small exterior decoration of the sort still seen on Greek Revival and Federal houses in Greenwich Village and Brooklyn Heights, because of its great strength in compression it was later cast into slender columns to lend structural support in building interiors (for example to hold up balconies in the Park Theatre, rebuilt in 1822). Cast iron was increasingly adapted to urban uses: in 1823 New York City specified iron for gas mains and in 1828 the Manhattan Company replaced its wooden water supply pipes with cast-iron ones.

Cast iron held major advantages for builders: inexpensive, versatile, and lighter than stone, it required far less hand labor than brickwork and no hand carving, because ornamental detailing could be achieved in the casting process. Construction was rapid because the parts were prefabricated and bolted together at the building site to form a frame that was raised into place, and although not fireproof cast iron was quite fire-resistant. Behind almost every iron front was a conventional interior made of timber with brick walls, but the front itself was a feat of engineering: supported by cast-iron columns that were often highly ornate, it could contain hundreds of parts and hold large glass panes. The Italianate designs of repeating arches and panels were well suited to mass production and to the enlargement of existing cast-iron buildings.

New York City became the center of cast-iron architecture in the United States in the early nineteenth century. By the end of the 1820s shop fronts with cast-iron columns and glass show windows were introduced, an idea probably imported from Paris. These occupied the ground floors of otherwise conventional brick or stone commercial buildings, allowing display of merchandise and more light and floor space. One of the first iron shop-fronts was advertised for rent in 1825 on John Street near the East River. In 1837 a complete iron storefront was offered commercially by the inventor and foundryman Jordan L. Mott. When iron fronts became widespread in the 1850s architects turned to established foundries, which made stock parts sold through catalogues and also did custom work. The modest foundries that produced cast iron were mostly scattered along waterways in Manhattan and Brooklyn so that pig iron, coal, and special sand for molding could be brought in by water, and finished products readily shipped out. The first foundry in the city to offer architectural iron was that of James L. Jackson on East 28th Street near the present site of Bellevue Hospital, a firm that functioned from 1840 well into the period of large steel construction. In 1846 the ironsmith Daniel D. Badger moved his operations from Boston to Manhattan, establishing a small foundry at 42 Duane Street. He was known for a patented iron storefront design that combined cast-iron columns with rolling shutters made of iron, giving strong protection against burglars and above all against fire. He later set up a foundry on East 14th Street that shipped iron building elements all over the country and was one of the largest foundries in the city. Other important ironworks in the city included the Aetna, the Excelsior, the Atlantic, the Hecla (established by Neil Poulsen in 1876 in Greenpoint, and unmatched for its large-scale ornamental ironwork for what were then called elevator buildings), and the foundries of the brothers J. B. and W. W. Cornell (on the Hudson River near 26th Street) and Jordan L. Mott (established in 1828 on the shore of the Harlem River in the southern Bronx, where Mott built a village for his workers called Mott Haven).

In the 1840s James Bogardus began an impassioned campaign for buildings made entirely of cast iron, inside and out. During a stay in England and on the Continent in 1836–40 he had learned about Italian Renaissance architecture and the British use of cast iron not only for bridges and aqueducts but also for interiors of market halls and libraries. Scoffed at in New York City and eager to demonstrate the advantages of cast iron, he used the material to build a factory for producing one of his own inventions, a universal grinding mill. Designs for the iron building parts, to be cast in multiples, were contracted out to several small foundries in the city. Soon there were two customers: in 1848 the prescient French pharmacist John Milhau ordered a façade entirely of iron to modernize his small brick building at 183 Broadway, and in 1849 the merchant Edgar Laing had a row of five stores with iron fronts erected on his empty coal yard at the corner of Murray and Washington streets. Bogardus filled both orders from the supply of parts cast for his own factory, so that all three buildings were created from the same few basic iron elements. He also constructed a large, five-story building with two iron façades in 1850–51 for A. S. Abell, publisher of the *Baltimore Sun*. To replace the buildings of the publishing house Harper and Brothers at 333 Pearl Street, which had been destroyed by fire on 10 December 1853, he drew heavily on his work for the *Sun*, even using the patterns from it so that he could rapidly produce statues of Franklin, Washington, and Jefferson. To achieve fire-resistant construction he used an interior frame of cast-iron columns and exposed bowstring trusses, with wrought-iron beams and brick jack arches.

From the 1850s architects made good use of the strength and relative lightness of cast iron to produce other innovative structures, often very tall or very large. Bogardus built four high, free-standing cast-iron towers in Manhattan: two were open-frame firewatch towers for the fire department, one a hundred feet (thirty meters) tall on 9th Avenue (1851) and another 125 feet (thirty-eight meters) tall on Spring Street (1853). In 1855 he built a tower 175 feet (fifty-three meters) tall on Centre Street for a manufacturer of gunshot, followed in 1856 by a second 217 feet (sixty-six meters) tall on Beekman Street. The gunshot was produced by dropping molten metal through a sieve from a great height into a vat of cold water below. To prevent hot pellets from being blown into the street, Bogardus's iron-frame shot towers had an infill of brick walls that were not load-bearing. This use of a brick wall in a self-supporting iron frame is often cited as a precursor of skyscraper curtain-wall construction. Another innovation was the use of glass walls supported by an iron framework, creating vast spaces flooded with light: this technique was employed for the Crystal Palace (1853), a huge pavilion of iron and glass designed by the firm of Carstensen and Gildemeister and built in Bryant Park to house the first American world's fair. The heyday of cast-iron architecture in New York City began in the mid 1850s and lasted for more than three decades. Scores of large, handsome structures were built with cast-iron fronts, notably the Haughwout Building (1856) on Broadway at Broome Street. Other important buildings are the Cary Building (1856) on Chambers Street, and a restrained classical building by Bogardus on Canal Street at Lafayette Street (1857). None was grander or caught the public fancy more than the train shed at Cornelius Vanderbilt's Grand Central Depot (1869). Its soaring, filigreed iron arches and glass roofs made it a tourist attraction second only to the U.S. Capitol. In the same year as the depot was constructed Peter Gilsey used a lavish Second Empire style for his eight-story hotel on Broadway, a structure with large iron fronts on both Broadway and 29th Street that was a favorite of theatergoers and railwaymen. Cast iron also had more mundane uses: for public market buildings such as the Tompkins Market at 3rd Avenue at 6th Street (1860) and the Manhattan Market at 34th Street and the Hudson River (1877), for large ferry terminals such as the Brooklyn Ferry at Fulton Street (1863), and for modest iron-front buildings of no more than five stories throughout the commercial districts of lower Manhattan and downtown Brooklyn, built on lots twenty-five feet (eight meters) wide.

Retailers who catered to the carriage trade built some of the most stylish cast-iron fronts along the Ladies' Mile: among the best-known are those of A. T. Stewart (1862; later known as Wanamaker's), which gradually expanded to fill an entire city block and became one of the largest iron structures in the world; James McCreery (1868); Lord and Taylor on Broadway (1869), perhaps the exemplar of the retail emporium; Arnold Constable on 5th Avenue (1876); B. Altman on 6th Avenue at 18th Street (1876); and Stern Brothers on West 23rd Street (1878). Fabric merchants and other wholesale firms that drew buyers from around the country occupied imposing iron-front headquarters, particularly in the areas now known as SoHo and Tribeca. Most are in the Italianate or Second Empire style and are intended to resemble stone, such as the Gunther Building (1871) at the corner of Broome Street, 72 Greene Street (1872, known as the "king of Greene Street"), which has many columns and a pedimented entrance, and 30 Greene Street (1872). Richard Morris Hunt was critically acclaimed for the Roosevelt Building at 478 Broadway (1874), a highly original neo-Grec structure, and for a building next door done in a brightly painted Moorish style (1876; demolished). By the 1880s the expanse of glass windows in cast-iron buildings was remarkable, for example in 1 Bond Street (1880) and 361 Broadway (1881). Cast iron continued to be used for interior structural columns, often in combination with timber and rolled-iron beams, in brick and stone commercial buildings that became progressively taller after the safety elevator gained acceptance.

Cast iron was used less often for building purposes when steel became available in the mid 1880s, but it continued to serve many needs, and small foundries remained in the city into the twentieth century. In 1904 the Hecla Iron Works provided 133 ornamented kiosks of cast iron and glass for the new subway entrances of Interborough Rapid Transit. Cast iron was also used in decorative window enframements, such as the elegant glass and iron front of Charles Scribner's Bookstore on 5th Avenue at 48th Street (1913), and the front of 181 Madison Avenue, a nineteen-story art deco building at the corner of 34th Street (1928). The ubiquitous, simple, one-story storefront continued to be made of cast-iron elements into the 1920s, but by this time the use of cast iron for architecture was practically at an end. From the time of the Depression cast-iron buildings were endangered by neglect, changing patterns of commerce, and demolition. Whole cast-iron districts were threatened by urban renewal after the Second World War. These dangers stimulated a new interest in iron architecture and efforts at preservation. Several iron-front buildings received landmark designation, and an area of SoHo encompassing 139 iron-front buildings on twenty-six city blocks was designated a

Historic District by the city in August 1973 and a National Historical Landmark in June 1978.

Daniel D. Badger: *Badger's Illustrated Catalogue of Cast-Iron Architecture* (New York: Baker and Godwin, 1865; repr. Dover, 1981)
A History of Real Estate, Building and Architecture in New York City during the Last Quarter of a Century (New York: Real Estate Record Association, 1898; repr. Arno, 1967)
Turpin C. Bannister: "Bogardus Revisited," *Journal of the Society of Architectural Historians* vol. 15 (1956), no. 4; vol. 16 (1957), no. 1
SoHo: Cast Iron District Designation Report (New York: New York City Landmarks Preservation Commission, 1973)
Margot Gayle and Edmund V. Gillon: *Cast-Iron Architecture in New York: A Photographic Survey* (New York: Dover, 1974)

Margot Gayle

Castle [née Foote], **Irene** (*b* New Rochelle, N.Y., 7 April 1893; *d* Eureka Springs, Ark., 25 Jan 1969). Dancer. In 1911 she married the English dancer Vernon (Castle) Blythe (*b* 2 May 1877; *d* Texas, 15 Feb 1918), a member of Lew Fields's comedy troupe. The two performed with Fields in his popular musical comedy *The Summer Widowers* (1911) before beginning their career in Paris as the dance team Vernon and Irene Castle. For the next five years they were the most popular team of ballroom dancers in the world, appearing mostly in cabarets and at their salon at the Castle House, 26 East 46th Street; they also made a number of films, performed in musicals on Broadway (including Irving Berlin's *Watch Your Step*, 1914), commissioned dance music from such composers as Berlin and James Reese Europe, and wrote the book *Modern Dancing* (1914). After her husband's death in an airplane crash in 1917 Irene Castle continued to act in films before retiring in 1924. She wrote *My Husband* (1919) and *Castles in the Air* (1958). Vernon and Irene Castle were portrayed in a film biography made in 1938 by Fred Astaire and Ginger Rogers.

Barbara Cohen-Stratyner

Castle Clinton. Fort built between 1808 and 1811 on an artificial stone island one hundred yards (ninety meters) off the Battery. Originally known as the West Battery, it was one of seven forts proposed in 1807 by Lieutenant Colonel Jonathan Williams to protect New York Harbor from invasion by the British. The current name dates to 1815. Although the design has traditionally been attributed to John McComb Jr., it was probably the work of Williams, with McComb designing only the entranceway to the fort and serving as the building contractor. The original plan called for many tiers of massive brownstone blocks, but because of financial constraints only one tier with twenty-eight gun mountings was built. The fort was never used in combat, and after the War of 1812 it ceased to be an important military facility; it was given to the city in 1823 and converted by entrepreneurs into Castle Garden, a center for popular entertainment. It was the starting point on 9 September 1830 of a balloon flight of thirty miles (forty-eight kilometers) made by the "aeronaut" Charles Durant, and the site in 1850 of a performance by the singer Jenny Lind presented by P. T. Barnum. The fort was reclaimed by the city in 1855 and used as an immigration station until 1890; it was converted in 1896 into the New York Aquarium by the firm of McKim, Mead and White. Robert Moses forced the aquarium to move in 1941 and sought to demolish the fort to accommodate a bridge between Brooklyn and the Battery and later a ventilation unit for the Brooklyn–Battery Tunnel. After the aquarium was demolished a conflict ensued over preserving the remaining walls of the fort. In 1950 the fort was ceded to the U.S. Department of Interior and designated a national monument. Restored during the 1970s, Castle Clinton houses ticket booths for the ferries to the Statue of Liberty and Ellis Island.

Thomas M. Pitkin: *Historic Structures Report: Castle Clinton National Monument* (Washington: U.S. Department of the Interior, 1960)
Charles B. Hosmer Jr.: *Preservation Comes of Age: From Williamsburg to the National Trust, 1926–1949* (Charlottesville: University of Virginia Press, 1981)

Andrew S. Dolkart

Castle Hill. Neighborhood in the southeastern Bronx lying on a peninsula bounded to the north and east by Westchester Creek, to the south by the East River, and to the west by Pugsley's Creek. Its most striking topographical feature is a small hill that led Captain Adriaen Block, the first European observer, to characterize the land as a castle; later it was owned by the Wilkins family and named after their estate. By the 1920s there were a few one-family houses scattered among truck farms that gradually diminished in number

Castle Clinton (left), ca *1900*. Right *Fireboat station at the edge of Battery Park*

Jenny Lind at Castle Garden, 1850

before disappearing in the 1940s. Low-income housing projects were built on empty lots in the 1960s. In the mid 1990s the YMCA and the Elias Karmon Gymnasium occupied Castle Hill Point.

Gary D. Hermalyn

Castleton. Former town in northern Staten Island, covering about 3880 acres (1570 hectares) of land and bounded to the north by the Kill van Kull and to the east by Upper New York Bay. Its area encompasses the neighborhoods of New Brighton, Brighton Heights, Randall Manor, Silver Lake, Castleton Corners, St. George, Tompkinsville, Four Corners, and West New Brighton. One of the original four subdivisions of the County of Richmond, it was the governor's manor and was named for Governor Thomas Dongan's manor of Cassiltowne in County Kildare, Ireland. The manor house, which stood on a lot bounded to the north by Richmond Terrace, to the east by Dongan Street, to the south by Castleton Avenue, and to the west by Bodin Street, was reportedly a place for assembly and celebration by local Indians before being destroyed by fire on 25 December 1878.

Martha S. Bendix

Castleton Corners. Neighborhood in northern Staten Island, bounded to the east by Manor Road and to the south by Victory Boulevard. Once called Centreville, the neighborhood lay at a corner of Governor Thomas Dongan's land grant and was the site of a brewery during the nineteenth century. After the Verrazano Narrows Bridge was completed the Staten Island Expressway was extended to the area, spurring the construction of many houses. In the 1980s there were modest levels of immigration to the area from India, Korea, the Philippines, China, Israel, and Egypt. Castleton Corners in the mid 1990s was largely a white, middle-class residential area, with a growing number of Asians and some commercial sections.

Martha S. Bendix

Castle Williams. A fort on Governors Island, begun in 1807 and completed in 1811 according to the designs of Jonathan Williams. It was popularly known as the "cheese box" because of its circular shape. Two hundred feet (sixty meters) in diameter, with ivied red sandstone walls forty feet (twelve meters) high and eight feet (2.5 meters) thick, it housed three tiers of guns and was intended to blast away at any enemy ships that managed to force their way past Forts Wadsworth and Hamilton at the southern entrance to the harbor. During the Civil War Castle Williams housed Confederate prisoners of war; in the first half of the twentieth century it was a disciplinary barracks for the U.S. Army, and later it was operated by the U.S. Coast Guard.

Kenneth T. Jackson

Castro, Bernard (*b* Palermo, Sicily, 11 Aug 1904; *d* Ocala, Fla., 24 Aug 1991). Businessman. He moved to New York City in 1919, worked as an apprentice upholsterer, and learned English at night school. In 1931 he invented the fold-out sofabed, or convertible, and in the same year opened a retail store at 5th Avenue between 14th and 15th streets. Sales were sluggish until he began running advertisements on local television in 1948 that featured his daughter Bernadette. He eventually opened forty-eight stores in twelve states and maintained a conspicuous billboard in Times Square for about thirty years until September 1983. Under his daughter's management the firm operated five stores in the city in 1991.

Marc Ferris

Caswell–Massey. Pharmacy established in 1752 by William Hunter in Newport, Rhode Island, and later moved to New York City, where it was acquired by John Caswell and William Massey. Situated successively at 5th Avenue and 25th Street and at 48th Street and Lexington Avenue, it is reportedly the oldest pharmacy in the city. The business was taken over in 1906 by the brothers Ralph and Milton Taylor and remained in their family until it was sold in 1989 to a holding company based in Hong Kong. Under the name Caswell–Massey the company operates more than two dozen outlets and distributes nationwide an array of specialty soaps, colognes, and beauty care products.

Owen D. Gutfreund

Cathedral College. Private college, opened in Brooklyn in 1914 as the Cathedral College of the Immaculate Conception. In 1967 it moved to a campus designed by John O'Malley in Douglaston, where it provided undergraduate education to candidates for the Catholic priesthood. After the school closed in 1989 the building became a pastoral center and a house for seminarians attending local colleges and for retired priests.

Christina Plattner

Cathedral of St. John the Divine. The largest church in the United States, situated at Amsterdam Avenue and West 112th Street in Morningside Heights, and incorporated in 1873; it is the principal church of the Episcopal Diocese of New York. The firm of Heins and LaFarge drew up plans in 1891 and the first stone was laid in 1892. In 1911 the commission for the design was transferred to the firm of Cram and Ferguson, and the east end and the crossing were completed. The sanctuary and choir were built in a Romanesque style; the nave was designed in a French Gothic style by Ralph Adams Cram, its main vault built to a height of 124 feet (thirty-eight meters). After the entire length of 601 feet (183 meters) was finished in 1941 construction halted until 1979. Stained-glass windows depicting biblical characters and modern personages were installed and the traditional décor was embellished with modern themes. During the 1980s and early 1990s the Cathedral of St. John the Divine became known for its attention to the arts, the community, youth, the elderly, ecumenism, the environmental movement, and international issues. It is reportedly the world's largest cathedral and the third-largest church, after Our Lady at Yamasoukro in the Ivory Coast and St. Peter's in Rome.

Cathedral of St. John the Divine, 1994

Howard E. Quirk: *The Living Cathedral of St. John the Divine: A History and Guide* (New York: Crossroad, 1993)

J. Robert Wright

Cathedral School. An Episcopal elementary and secondary school for children of all faiths, occupying thirteen acres (five hectares) on the grounds of the Cathedral of St. John the Divine at Amsterdam Avenue and 112th Street in Manhattan. It opened in 1901 as a boarding school for forty boys, originally to provide the cathedral with its choir. The choir earned a long-standing reputation as one of the finest in the United States. The school became coeducational in 1974 and now enrolls about 240 children from diverse ethnic and religious backgrounds in kindergarten to the eighth grade.

Richard Schwartz

Cather, Willa (Sibert) (*b* Winchester, Va., 7 Dec 1873; *d* New York City, 24 April 1947). Novelist. At nine she moved with her family to Nebraska, where she grew up among European pioneers who inspired much of her writing. She graduated from the University of Nebraska at Lincoln in 1895 and moved to Pittsburgh, where she worked as a journalist.

After publishing her first collection of poems and short stories she was invited to join the editorial staff of *McClure's* in New York City in 1906. From 1908 to 1913 she lived at 82 Washington Place. On the success of her novel *O Pioneers!* (1913) she left her editorial position and moved to 5 Bank Street, where she remained until 1927. Her portrayals of simple, courageous men and women living on the prairie in such novels as *My Ántonia* (1917) reflected her nostalgia for the American West, a feeling intensified by her increasing awareness of materialism in the city during the early twentieth century. She won a Pulitzer Prize for the novel *One of Ours* (1922). Cather lived at the Grosvenor Hotel at 35 5th Avenue from 1927 until 1932, when she moved to 570 Park Avenue.

James Leslie Woodress: *Willa Cather: A Literary Life* (Lincoln: University of Nebraska Press, 1987)

James E. Mooney

Catholic Charities of the Archdiocese of New York. Charitable organization formed in 1920 by Archbishop Patrick Hayes to centralize and coordinate Catholic charities and reduce waste and duplication in staffing and services revealed by a diocesan survey in 1919. At the outset it was responsible for thirty-two charitable institutions including hospitals, orphanages, nurseries, and homes for the aged, as well as benevolent associations and various other groups. It set up divisions responsible for families, health, children, protective care, social action, and finance. In 1990 the organization distributed $16.6 million to eighteen family service centers, eleven health care facilities for the elderly, sixteen nursing homes, sixteen child welfare agencies, fourteen day-care centers, fourteen general hospitals, twenty-two facilities for the homeless, twelve mental health centers and homes, various youth organizations, "big brother" and "big sister" programs, visiting-nurse services, and maternity services for unwed mothers.

Florence D. Cohalan: *A Popular History of the Archdiocese of New York* (Yonkers, N.Y.: U.S. Catholic Historical Society, 1983)

Bernadette McCauley

Catholic Club of the City of New York. Organization formed in March 1871 to promote Catholic service and the study of Catholic history, literature, science, and art. Initially known as the Xavier Union, it was an offshoot of the Xavier Alumni Sodality (1863), an organization of graduates of St. Francis Xavier College. The club was incorporated in 1873 and renamed the Catholic Club on 22 November 1888. Members included professionals and most of the prominent Catholic businessmen in New York City; they were often called on to represent the city's Catholics in civic ceremonies. The club was a lay organization with its own administration but had the approval of the Roman Catholic Archdiocese of New York. It operated a building at 120 Central Park South from March 1892 and published a bulletin from 1891 to 1930. In 1925 it had a reference library of thirty thousand volumes, the largest of its kind in the country open to the public. The club declined after 1930 and ceased operations in 1958.

Marion R. Casey

Catholic Medical Center (of Brooklyn and Queens). Hospital system formed in 1967 by the Catholic Diocese of Brooklyn to reduce costs through centralized management; it was the first network hospital system approved by New York State. The center comprises Holy Family Nursing Home (1879) and St. Mary's Hospital (1882) in Brooklyn, and St. John's Hospital (1891), Mary Immaculate Hospital (1902), St. Joseph's Hospital (1962), and the Monsignor Fitzpatrick Skilled Nursing Pavillion (1987) in Queens, as well as two occupational medical centers and twelve clinics. It also operates three home health care agencies as part of the largest hospital-based home care program in the country and is a major teaching affiliate of Cornell University Medical College and New York Hospital. In 1991 the center had 1334 beds, six thousand employees, and more than twelve hundred attending physicians.

Bernadette McCauley

Catholics. At the end of the Revolutionary era Catholics in New York City numbered no more than two hundred, but they became the city's largest religious denomination by the mid nineteenth century and remained so 150 years later. The city's Catholic community has been noteworthy for both the rapidity of its growth in the nineteenth century and its ethnic diversity in the twentieth. In many respects Catholicism in New York City re-

Roman Catholic Bishops, Archbishops, and Cardinals of the Archdiocese of New York

Richard Luke Concanen, O.P.	Bishop	1808–10
(*b* 27 Dec 1747; *d* 19 June 1810)		(never arrived)
John Connolly, O.P.	Bishop	1815–25
(*b* 5 Oct 1799; *d* 6 Feb 1825)		
John DuBois	Bishop	1826–42
(*b* 24 Aug 1764; *d* 20 Dec 1842)		
John Hughes	Bishop	1842–50
(*b* 24 June 1797; *b* 3 Jan 1864)	Archbishop	1850–64
John Cardinal McCloskey	Archbishop	1864–75
(*b* 10 March 1810; *d* 10 Oct 1885)	Cardinal	1875–85
Michael Corrigan	Archbishop	1885–1902
(*b* 13 Aug 1839; *d* 5 May 1902)		
John Cardinal Farley	Archbishop	1902–11
(*b* 20 April 1842; *d* 17 Sept 1918)	Cardinal	1911–18
Patrick Cardinal Hayes	Archbishop	1919–24
(*b* 20 Nov 1867; *d* 4 Sept 1938)	Cardinal	1924–38
Francis Cardinal Spellman	Archbishop	1939–46
(*b* 4 May 1889; *d* 2 Dec 1967)	Cardinal	1946–67
Terence Cardinal Cooke	Archbishop	1968–69
(*b* 1 March 1921; *d* 6 Oct 1983)	Cardinal	1969–83
John Cardinal O'Connor	Archbishop	1983–85
(*b* 15 Jan 1920)	Cardinal	1985–

Compiled by Edward T. O'Donnell

Roman Catholic Bishops of the Diocese of Brooklyn

John Loughlin	1853–91
(*b* 20 Dec 1817; *d* 29 Dec 1891)	
Charles Edward McDonnell	1891–1921
(*b* 1 Feb 1854; *d* 8 Aug 1921)	
Thomas Edmund Malloy	1922–56
(*b* 4 Sept 1884; *d* 26 Nov 1956)	
Brian J. McEntegart	1957–68
(*b* 5 Jan 1893; *d* 30 Sept 1968)	
Francis J. Mugavero	1968–90
(*b* 8 June 1914; *d* 12 July 1991)	
Thomas V. Daily	1990–
(*b* 23 Sept 1927)	

Compiled by Edward T. O'Donnell

mains what it has always been: the immigrant church.

1. Colonial and Early Federal Periods, 1640–1815

For most of the colonial period Roman Catholic worship in New York City was clandestine or nonexistent, because the Protestant Dutch and then the English enforced laws prohibiting the organization and maintenance of Roman Catholic churches. In 1643 the French Jesuit missionary Isaac Jogues visited New Amsterdam and found only two Catholic inhabitants, and under English rule they remained few in number. With the restoration of the Stuarts in 1660 a period of greater toleration for Catholics began in England and the colonies, and in New York Catholics were able to practice their religion without fear of prosecution from 1674 to 1688. Under the guidance of Governor Thomas Dongan (1682–88), an Irish Catholic, the colonial assembly passed the "Charter of Liberties and Privileges" (1683), which granted religious freedom to all Christians. Dongan also admitted to the colony three English Jesuits who opened a school and on 30 October 1683 celebrated the first Mass in the city, near the site of the old Customs House. The Glorious Revolution in England in 1688–89 and Leisler's Rebellion in New York City in 1689–91 brought an end to religious toleration in the city; by 1696 there were only nine professed Catholics, and in 1700 a law barred Catholic priests from entering the colony under penalty of life imprisonment. As hostility toward Catholics revived, rhetoric and diatribes against "papists" became a regular feature of political and popular commentary. Each year on 5 November New Yorkers celebrated Guy Fawkes Day (or Pope's Day) with drinking, parading, and anti-Catholic speeches, culminating in the burning of the pope in effigy. Violently anti-Catholic and anti-black hysteria swept the city during the "Negro plot" of 1741, when rumors circulated that Catholic conspirators had encouraged a slave revolt. Among the victims executed for treason was John Ury, an Anglican clergyman who was mistaken for a Catholic priest.

From 1756 the German-born Jesuit Ferdinand Steinmeyer of Pennsylvania (also known as Father Farmer) visited the city occasionally to celebrate Mass for a tiny Catholic community. The repeal of the anti-priest law in 1784 and the arrival of the Irish Capuchin friar Charles Whelan led to the organization of the first permanent Catholic parish in the city. Whelan found a largely poor community of about two hundred Catholics of at least five nationalities: Irish, French, German, Spanish, and Portuguese. A parish was formed at the initiative of a group of Catholic laymen under the leadership of the French consul Hector St. John de Crèvecoeur, and on 10 June 1785 the Roman Catholic Church in the City of New York was incorporated. In little more than a year a simple frame church was erected at the corner of Barclay and Church streets on three lots purchased from Trinity Church, and the building was formally dedicated as St. Peter's Church on 4 November 1786. Distinguished early members of St. Peter's parish included Elizabeth Ann Seton from 1805 to 1808 and Pierre Toussaint from 1787 to 1853. In 1808 Pope Pius VII established the Diocese of New York, which contained all of New York State and northern New Jersey. The first bishop, Richard Luke Concanen, O.P., died in Italy in 1810, unable to reach his diocese because of the Napoleonic Wars. The initial development of the see was instead conducted by the Alsatian Jesuit Anthony Kohlmann in 1808–15. He supervised the construction of the second Catholic church, the original St. Patrick's Cathedral (1815) on Mulberry Street, and opened the New York Literary Institute, a short-lived Jesuit college that closed in 1813 so that the Jesuits could concentrate their limited manpower at Georgetown College.

2. Immigration and the Development of Hierarchy and Parish

The bishop in 1815–25 was John Connolly, O.P., another Irish Dominican and the first bishop to reach New York City. On his arrival in 1815 he found that he had only three churches and four priests in the whole diocese. Between 1815 and 1842 the number of Catholics increased from about fifteen thousand to 200,000, causing a severe shortage of priests and increasing the membership of several parishes in Manhattan to nearly ten thousand. Most of the new Catholics were poor Irish immigrants, but many were German, and a few were French. The massive influx revived anti-Catholic bigotry and ethnic rivalry within the Catholic community. Despite these problems the Catholic church in New York City became larger, stronger, and more diverse in the decades before the Civil War. The Sisters of Charity opened a Catholic orphanage in 1817. Father John Power, the pastor of St. Peter's Church in 1819–49, in 1825 launched the *Truth Teller*, the first Catholic newspaper in the city, and in the following year helped to establish the predominantly Irish parish of St. Mary on Grand Street, which was the third Catholic church in the city. The equally popular Cuban-born priest Felix Varela founded Christ Church (1827), which served a diverse parish and was divided into the parishes of St. James and Transfiguration in 1833. Chronic debt plagued many of the parishes. Priests and parishioners tried numerous schemes to refinance the mounting debt, among them soliciting public donations, renting out pews, and holding church fairs, and a few wealthy lay Catholics like Cornelius Heeney (a business partner of John Jacob Astor) were generous benefactors, but the threat of insolvency persisted for many parishes throughout the early nineteenth century.

During the 1840s John Hughes became the most influential Catholic prelate in the United States. Born in Ireland and a priest of the Diocese of Philadelphia before moving to New York City, he became the coadjutor bishop to Bishop John DuBois in 1838 and successfully eliminated "trusteeism" by shifting the control of parish property from local lay trustees to the pastors and the bishop. In 1840 he criticized the Public School Society (a government-subsidized private organization that operated the city's public schools) for its openly anti-Catholic curriculum and its mandatory use of the Protestant King James Bible; he also demanded that state and municipal authorities grant the same funds to Catholic schools as they did to other private and sectarian schools. As a result the state legislature in 1842 replaced the Public School Society with locally elected school boards that gradually removed the Bible from the curriculum, and Hughes built his own system of parochial schools within the diocese. Hughes alarmed many Protestants who believed that his attack on the school system violated the separation of church and state and was an effort to drive the Bible from the public schools. Hughes's success with the state legislature did lead to the eventual secularization of the public schools, a result that he neither intended nor desired.

Hughes became the fourth bishop of New York in 1842 and continued to attract national attention by his vigorous response to anti-Catholic bigotry. In 1844 a nativist mob killed thirteen Irish Catholics and destroyed three churches in Kensington, a suburb of Philadelphia. When similar attacks were threatened in New York City, Hughes posted armed guards around his churches and warned the nativist mayor James Harper that if any harm should come to his churches or his people, he would transform the city into "a second Moscow" (a reference to the tactics of Tsar Alexander I against Napoleon). His firm leadership maintained peace and prevented the sort of bloodshed that occurred elsewhere. To alleviate the chronic shortages of priests and sisters, Hughes invited ten religious communities to the diocese. The Society of Jesus arrived in 1845 and was entrusted with administering St. John's College, which was then newly established (it later became known as Fordham University). The largest of the new communities was the Sisters of Charity, which staffed many of the new parochial schools; in 1846 the sisters formed their own diocesan community, the Sisters of Charity of Mount St. Vincent, and during the cholera epidemic of 1849 they founded St. Vincent's Hospital. Hughes also encouraged the formation of the Paulist Fathers, an American religious community founded by the convert Isaac Hecker in 1858. The Paulist periodical the *Catholic*

World was launched in 1865. The enormous growth of the diocese led the Holy See to restructure it as an archdiocese in 1850. The creation of new sees in Buffalo and Albany, New York (1847), and in Brooklyn and Newark, New Jersey (1853), reduced the area of the archdiocese to one tenth its former size. In 1850 Hughes became the first archbishop of New York.

During the massive immigration of 1840–65 the number of Catholics in the diocese reached almost 400,000, making them the single largest denomination in the city. Most Catholics in New York City were Irish. "National parishes," which were ethnic rather than territorial, were formed to meet the pastoral needs of German- and French-speaking Catholics. The same practice was followed later for Italian and Slavic immigrants. At the close of the Civil War in 1865 there were thirty-two parishes in Manhattan, of which twenty-three were territorial (and mainly Irish), eight were German, and one was French. A few parishes such as St. Alphonsus on Thompson Street were ethnically mixed, catering to both Irish and German Catholics. In all Hughes was responsible for the establishment of sixty-one new parishes in the Archdiocese of New York and for the construction of the new St. Patrick's Cathedral on 5th Avenue (begun 1859, consecrated 1879). On his death in 1864 probably one of every two New Yorkers was a Catholic, and the parochial schools educated 16 percent of the 100,000 children in the city.

John McCloskey was the first native-born archbishop of New York (1864–85) and the first American cardinal (1875–85) during a period when Irish Catholics continued to increase their political power. Catholic charitable institutions continued to provide health and social services; one of the most important was the New York Foundling Hospital, opened in 1870 by Sister Irene Fitzgibbon of the Sisters of Charity. In 1872 John Kelly replaced William M. "Boss" Tweed as the head of Tammany Hall and inaugurated a period of Catholic domination (his wife was a niece of McCloskey). William R. Grace, a successful businessman and sometime opponent of Tammany Hall, was elected the city's first Catholic mayor in 1880, and in the following year Father John Drumgoole opened the Mission of the Immaculate Virgin for the Protection of Homeless and Destitute Children, one of the largest orphanages in the country. Situated first at the corner of Lafayette and Great Jones streets, in 1883 it added a much larger facility at Mount Loretto on Staten Island. The first black Catholic church, St. Benedict the Moor, opened in 1883 in a former Protestant church on Bleecker Street in Greenwich Village to serve the tiny black Catholic community and later moved to the new black neighborhood around West 53rd Street.

In 1885–1902 the archbishop was Michael A. Corrigan, a leading figure in the conservative wing of the American Catholic hierarchy and a conscientious administrator who added ninety-nine parishes to the archdiocese. Despite his administrative abilities Corrigan was widely regarded as an uninspiring leader, and he was the only archbishop of New York during a period extending from McCloskey's tenure into the 1990s who did not become a cardinal.

As the conservative Catholic laity gained control of the local Democratic Party, a group of diocesan priests known as the Accademia began to advocate radical reforms in both church and society, including the adoption of a vernacular liturgy, the abolition of religious orders, and the passage of social welfare legislation. The most widely known of these priests was Edward McGlynn, pastor of St. Stephen's Church on East 28th Street. His activity in municipal politics and notably in the mayoral campaign of Henry George (1886) led to his temporary excommunication (1887–92), during which he remained a popular public figure as the head of the Anti-Poverty Society, and a thorn in the side of Archbishop Corrigan.

3. Changing Structure and Composition of the Church

The consolidation of New York City in 1898 meant that ecclesiastically the city was now divided between the Archdiocese of New York (comprising Manhattan, the Bronx, Staten Island, and seven upstate counties) and the Diocese of Brooklyn (comprising Brooklyn, Queens, and the rest of Long Island). Both dioceses grew rapidly in the early twentieth century. In the Diocese of Brooklyn the Catholic population increased from 500,000 in 1900 to 800,000 in 1920; in the Archdiocese of New York the Catholic population increased from 825,000 in 1900 to 1,325,000 in 1920, with much of the growth occurring in the Bronx, Westchester, and Staten Island. Many of the new Catholics were Italian immigrants who arrived in large numbers between 1880 and 1910. Corrigan responded to this pastoral challenge by recruiting priests from Italy, especially from the Pious Society of the Missionaries of St. Charles, better known as the Scalabrinians. Another community active in the Italian Apostolate was the Missionary Sisters of the Sacred Heart of Jesus, formed by Mother Frances Xavier Cabrini, who later opened Columbus Hospital (1892; now Cabrini Medical Center). In 1902–18 the archbishop of New York was John M. Cardinal Farley, the last in a long line of Irish-born prelates to lead the archdiocese. During his last years a series of highly critical state and city investigations into Catholic charitable institutions caused a crisis in the church's social apostolate, but both the Archdiocese of New York and the Diocese of Brooklyn continued to grow at an impressive rate. By 1920 the Diocese of Brooklyn had 223 parishes and 117 parochial schools with 74,000 students, while the Archdiocese of New York had 391 parishes, 188 parochial schools, and 93,000 students. In the same year fifty-one of the 113 parishes in Manhattan were "national parishes," serving eighteen ethnic groups.

The archbishop in 1919–38 was Patrick Cardinal Hayes, a first-generation Irish–American from the Lower East Side. Under his leadership Irish domination of the local church continued even as the Irish population of the city declined. Largely in response to the scandals that occurred under Farley, Hayes in 1920 reorganized the several hundred charitable institutions and agencies of the archdiocese as the Catholic Charities of the Archdiocese of New York, a super-organization that set new standards of professionalism for Catholic social work around the country. Dorothy Day, Peter Maurin, and others launched a movement on 1 May 1933 that combined orthodox theology with radical social activism, and from the same year published the *Catholic Worker*. Another influential group included "labor priests" such as Philip Carey of the Society of Jesus (the founder of the Xavier School of Industrial Relations in 1934) and Monsignor John P. Monaghan (an influential proponent of the Social Gospel among the diocesan clergy). The Catholic Interracial Council first met in 1934 under John LaFarge of the Society of Jesus to address the concerns of black Catholics, and the Association of Catholic Trade Unionists was formed in 1937 under the inspiration of Monaghan with the goal of educating industrial workers in the principles of the papal social encyclicals.

In April 1939 Francis J. Spellman, auxiliary bishop of Boston and a close friend of the new pope, Pius XII, was named archbishop of New York. The appointment surprised many who had expected the appointment of a New Yorker. Spellman refinanced the debt of $28 million that the archdiocese had incurred during the Depression under Hayes, and placed the archdiocese on a sound financial basis. He then launched the largest expansion program in diocesan history and increased the number of parishes by forty-five. During his twenty-eight-year tenure Spellman spent almost $600 million to build and renovate Catholic educational and charitable facilities, and also centralized the financial and administrative operations of the archdiocese.

In the late 1940s the Catholic population of the Archdiocese of New York increased markedly after a decade of decline. The increase was due almost entirely to a huge influx of Latin American Catholics, first from Puerto Rico and then from Cuba, the Dominican Republic, and other countries. Spellman's response was timely and effective. He established an archdiocesan office for Latin American Catholics, sent a large number of diocesan priests to learn Spanish, and welcomed the new parishioners into existing territorial parishes rather than establish new national parishes for them. In June 1953 more than 4500 Puerto Ricans attended the first annual Spanish Mass at St. Patrick's Cathedral in celebration of the *fiesta* of St. John the Baptist, the patron saint of Puerto Rico. Spellman also desegregated Catholic charitable and educational institutions and welcomed black candidates for the priesthood into St. Joseph's Seminary at Dunwoodie.

At the Second Vatican Council (1962–65) Spellman was responsible for the presence of Father John Courtney Murray, an American Jesuit whose progressive views on church and state were suspect to many conservative theologians. Spellman worked for the passage of the council's *Declaration on Religious Liberty*, and he won the gratitude of the Jewish community of New York City by vigorously supporting *Nostra Aetate*, the council's conciliatory decree on non-Christian religions. Under Spellman New York City remained an important center of American Catholicism. It was the place of publication of both major Catholic weeklies, *America* (owned by Jesuits) and *Commonweal* (lay-controlled), and of the older Paulist periodical the *Catholic World*. Under the editorship of the ultra-conservative Patrick J. Scanlan, the *Brooklyn Tablet* attracted a national following among right-wing Catholics.

Spellman became the best-known member of the American hierarchy since the death of James Cardinal Gibbons in 1921. His support of Senator Joseph R. McCarthy in the 1950s and of the Vietnam War in the 1960s drew both praise and criticism and placed him at the forefront of American Catholic conservatism. In 1957 the Diocese of Brooklyn was reduced in size when Nassau and Suffolk counties were made into a separate diocese with its seat in Rockville Centre. Brooklyn became the only totally urban diocese in the United States and the smallest in area, though it remained one of the largest in population, with more than one million Catholics. On 4 October 1965 Pope Paul VI visited New York City; he addressed the United Nations and celebrated an outdoor Mass at Yankee Stadium. As a result of the immigration reforms of 1965 the church had to provide for the pastoral needs of new Catholic immigrants from Asia, Africa, and the Caribbean. The civil rights movement of the 1960s also led Catholics to take a more active position on the rights of minorities, especially blacks. In 1968 the Diocese of Brooklyn and the Archdiocese of New York established Project Equality, to encourage parishes to support businesses that advanced affirmative action and equal opportunity in the workplace.

Terence Cardinal Cooke, whom Spellman chose as his successor, assumed his post in 1968 amid major changes in the church as a result of the Second Vatican Council. During his administration the total Catholic population of the Archdiocese of New York remained at about 1.8 million, but only because Latin American and Asian immigrants replaced the dwindling number of older middle-class Catholics. The number of parishes remained stable at about 410, but the number of diocesan priests declined from 1108 to 777, and parochial schools lost 75 percent of their teaching sisters. During this period of retrenchment Cooke used his financial expertise to establish a cooperative system under which wealthy parishes were taxed to support poorer ones. Thus only thirty-one of the 305 parochial schools closed, despite a decline in enrollment from 167,000 to 88,000 students. In October 1979 Pope John Paul II visited the city. John Cardinal O'Connor succeeded Cooke in January 1984 and soon assumed a higher profile, clashing with local and state officials on the issue of abortion. By the early 1990s the Archdiocese of New York had 2.2 million members and 411 parishes (of which 122 in Manhattan, thirty-six in Staten Island, and seventy-one in the Bronx). The church remained predominantly an immigrant church: in the Archdiocese of New York almost half the parishioners were now Latin American, and national parishes were formed for new immigrant groups such as Arabs, Portuguese, Koreans, and Albanians. On Sundays Mass was offered in twenty-three languages. In 1991 a three-year campaign began to raise funds for financially ailing parishes. Education remained central to the work of the church: in 1993 its 243 elementary schools and fifty-five secondary schools were attended by 102,685 students, many of whom were poor, non-Catholic, and members of minority groups. In the Diocese of Brooklyn 217 parishes served more than 1.5 million Catholics, Mass was celebrated in seventeen languages, and there were 181 elementary and secondary schools attended by 74,133 children. Both dioceses sought to adapt their numerous charitable programs to meet the changing conditions of life in New York City, and in particular to address the problems of AIDS, drugs, and homelessness.

John Talbot Smith: *The Catholic Church in New York* (New York: Hall and Locke, 1905)

John Cardinal Farley: *The Life of John, Cardinal McCloskey, First Prince of the Church in America, 1810–1885* (New York: Longmans, Green, 1918)

John K. Sharp: *Priests and Parishes of the Diocese of Brooklyn, 1820–1944* (Manhasset, N.Y.: John K. Sharp, 1944)

John K. Sharp: *History of the Diocese of Brooklyn, 1853–1953* (New York: Fordham University Press, 1954)

Robert D. Cross: *The Emergence of Liberal Catholicism in America* (Cambridge: Harvard University Press, 1958)

Robert I. Gannon: *The Cardinal Spellman Story* (Garden City, N.Y.: Doubleday, 1962)

Jay P. Dolan: *The Immigrant Church: New York's Irish and German Catholics, 1815–1865* (Baltimore: Johns Hopkins University Press, 1975)

Richard Shaw: *Dagger John: The Unquiet Life and Times of Archbishop John Hughes of New York* (New York: Paulist Press, 1977)

Robert Emmett Curran: *Michael Augustine Corrigan and the Shaping of Conservative Catholicism in America, 1878–1902* (New York: Arno, 1978)

Hispanics in New York: Religious, Cultural and Social Experiences: A Study of Hispanics in the Archdiocese of New York (New York: Office of Pastoral Research, Archdiocese of New York, 1982)

Florence D. Cohalan: *A Popular History of the Archdiocese of New York* (Yonkers, N.Y.: United States Catholic Historical Society, 1983)

Margaret Carthy: *A Cathedral of Suitable Magnificence: St. Patrick's Cathedral, New York* (Wilmington, Del.: Michael Glazier, 1984)

Jay P. Dolan: *The American Catholic Experience: A History from Colonial Times to the Present* (Garden City, N.Y.: Doubleday, 1985)

One Faith, One Lord, One Baptism: The Hopes and Experiences of the Black Community in the Archdiocese of New York (New York: Archdiocese of New York, 1988)

Thomas J. Shelley: *Dunwoodie: The History of St. Joseph's Seminary* (Westminster, Md.: Christian Classics, 1993)

T. J. Shelley

Catholic schools. The first Roman Catholic school in New York City opened in 1800 at St. Peter's Church in lower Manhattan. It remained the only Catholic school until 1817, when a "free school" was set up in the basement of St. Patrick's Old Cathedral under the leadership of Bishop John Connolly. Both schools were characterized by poor conditions because their parishes could not afford to maintain them. During the tenure of John DuBois, appointed Connolly's successor in 1826, the first school building in the Diocese of New York was erected at St. Patrick's Cathedral in 1837 and a second school was built in the following year at St. Peter's. DuBois also helped to establish Catholic secondary education in New York City, opening St. Joseph's Select School for girls in 1833 (which became Mount St. Vincent's Academy in 1847) and St. Mary's Academy in 1835. While DuBois was indisposed his duties as the diocesan administrator were assumed by John J. Hughes, who in 1840 oversaw the opening of St. Joseph's Seminary in the Bronx, staffed successively by Italian Vincentians and French Jesuits before the Diocese of New York took charge. Hughes was appointed bishop in 1842, at a time when anti-Catholic sentiment in the public schools was strong. Children were not allowed to read from the Catholic version of the Bible, and with the passing of the Maclay Bill in 1842 religious instruction was prohibited in the public schools. In response Hughes announced that the archdiocese would give high priority to building Catholic schools, a task that until then had been handled primarily by

First graduating class of St. Rita's School, 1915

individual parishes. Hughes in effect committed himself and other leaders of the church to establishing a Catholic parochial school system in New York City. By 1858 the assets of the Catholic educational system of New York City were valued at about $2 million. At the time of Hughes's death in 1864 there were about fifteen thousand children attending the twelve select schools and thirty-one free schools in the Archdiocese of New York.

Parochial schools served the city's growing immigrant population. German parochial elementary schools and high schools began opening in the city in the 1860s. Not all Catholics supported parochial education: some feared that it would further separate Catholics from the mainstream of society and others believed that Catholic leaders should focus on churches, not schools. Most Catholics were concerned about the tremendous financial burden schools placed on their parishes. By a decree of the Third Plenary Council of American bishops, held in 1884 in Baltimore, each pastor was required to build a parochial school in his parish within two years; anyone who failed to do so was subject to removal from his pastorate. A strong advocate of the council's decrees concerning Catholic education was Michael A. Corrigan, under whose leadership the Archdiocese of New York opened seventy-five schools and three academies by the time of his death in 1902 (although it fell short of the goal of a school in every parish). Under Corrigan's successor, John Cardinal Farley, the Cathedral Girl's High School, a free parochial school, opened in 1905. By 1908 there were 3736 girls attending Catholic secondary schools in the Archdiocese of New York. St. Peter's, a Catholic high school opened in 1915 on Staten Island, attracted many Catholic students who could not afford the tuition of a private high school. The Jesuits established Regis High School in 1914 exclusively for scholarship students; other religious orders ran Catholic secondary schools and met their operating expenses by charging tuition. The Sisters of Charity, who maintained ten academies, were the main order providing secondary education for girls; the Jesuits and the De La Salle Brothers directed most of the secondary schools for boys. Farley invited a number of other communities into the archdiocese to help support secondary education, including the Christian Brothers of Ireland and the Religious of the Sacred Heart of Mary. By the time of his death in 1918 he had opened fifty schools with about 28,000 students. Most parish churches in New York City that did not have a school had plans to build one by the time Francis Spellman was appointed archbishop in 1939. He expanded parochial education for boys, opening Cardinal Hayes High School (1941) in the Bronx, the first secondary school to be administered by diocesan clergy. During his tenure a controversial bill was introduced in Congress by Representative Graham Barden that would have required the federal government to pay the states $50 for each child enrolled in public primary and secondary schools. The Catholic church fought passage of the bill because parochial schools would not receive any of the money. This led Spellman to disagree publicly with Eleanor Roosevelt and others who did not support state aid for parochial education.

The number of parochial schools grew between 1940 and 1965 (the peak year for Catholic parochial school attendance in the United States). In Manhattan, the Bronx, and Staten Island the number of schools increased from 146 to 183. Despite this growth most Catholic schoolchildren were not enrolled in parochial schools, which in 1966 enrolled about 40 percent of all Catholic students and 27 percent of Catholic high school students. The 1970s saw the opening of parochial schools at each of the seven black parishes; many of the students attending these schools were non-Catholics. The staffs of Catholic schools, historically composed of members of male and female religious orders, gradually changed after about 1965. By the mid 1990s the great majority of Catholic schoolteachers were laypersons.

Jay P. Dolan: *The Immigrant Church: New York's Irish and German Catholics, 1815–1865* (Baltimore: John Hopkins University Press, 1975)

Florence D. Cohalan: *A Popular History of the Archdiocese of New York* (New York: United States Catholic Historical Society, 1983)

Margaret M. McGuinness

Catholic Worker. Weekly newspaper launched in 1933 by DOROTHY DAY.

cat shows. Madison Square Garden was the site of the first cat show in North America, sponsored by the Englishman James T. Hyde on 8 May 1895. The Atlantic Cat Club held its first show at Madison Square Garden in 1903 and about ten more in later years; in 1906 the club became affiliated with the Cat Fanciers Association. Another affiliate of the association, the Empire Cat Club, was formed in 1913 and in 1917 began staging annual shows in New York City, until 1984 usually at Madison Square Garden and occasionally at hotels in Manhattan. Later venues included the New York Passenger Ship Terminal at Pier 90 in Manhattan (1985), the Jacob K. Javits Convention Center (1986), the Borough of Manhattan Community College (1988), and the Seaview Home on Staten Island (from 1989). Madison Square Garden was also the site of shows held by the Knickerbocker Cat Club (in the 1970s) and the International Cat Association (annually from 1985). In 1971 the Brooklyn Cat Fanciers, a club affiliated with the Cat Fancier's Federation, began holding an annual show at the Hall of St. Finbar's, at Bay 20th Street and Bath Avenue.

Joseph S. Lieber, Kayla Soyer Stein

Catt [Chapman; née Lane], **Carrie (Clinton)** (*b* Ripon, Wis., 9 Jan 1859; *d* New Rochelle, N.Y., 9 March 1947). Suffragist. After serving briefly as the president of the National American Woman Suffrage Association she shifted her attention to New York City, where in 1909 she organized the New York City Woman Suffrage Party to unify local suffragists. She organized efforts to hold a referendum in 1915 on giving women the vote by amending the state constitution; after this failed she regained the presidency of the national suffrage association, a post she held until the Nineteenth Amendment to the U.S.

Carrie Chapman Catt welcomed back to New York City by the former governor Alfred E. Smith in August 1920, after returning from Tennessee, the last state to ratify the Nineteenth Amendment

Constitution was passed. She reorganized the association after 1920 as the League of Women Voters but concentrated her energies on pacifism and international feminism. With Nettie Rogers Shuler she wrote *Woman Suffrage and Politics: The Inner Story* (1923).

Ellen Carol DuBois

Cattell, James McKeen (*b* Easton, Penn., 25 May 1860; *d* Lancaster, Penn., 20 Jan 1944). Psychologist. After graduating from Lafayette College he studied at Johns Hopkins University and Göttingen before earning a PhD in 1886 in Leipzig under Wilhelm Wundt, one of the first experimental psychologists. He became the first professor of psychology in the world in 1889 at the University of Pennsylvania and in 1891 was appointed the first professor of psychology at Columbia University, where he was the head of the psychology department and during the next two decades helped to establish psychology as a discipline and an independent experimental science. He shared the functionalists' interest in measuring intelligence and developed the first tests based on pain thresholds and reaction times. The results that these tests produced were found in the early twentieth century to have little correlation to subjects' academic performance and his work was eventually supplanted by Alfred Binet's. Nevertheless his contributions to studies of intelligence testing and individual differences continued to be widely acknowledged, and many of his students became well known. He helped to form the American Psychological Association in 1892 and was its president in 1895. With J. M. Baldwin he launched *Psychological Review*, of which he remained the owner and editor until 1903, and *Psychological Monographs* (now *Psychological Abstracts*). He also assumed control of several other periodicals: the weekly journal *Science*, which he acquired from Alexander Graham Bell in 1895 and converted into the journal of the American Association for the Advancement of Science, *Popular Science Monthly* (1900), which he renamed *Scientific Monthly*, and the magazine *American Naturalist* (1908). He also published the biographical directories *American Men of Science* (1906) and *Leaders in Education* (1932). In 1915 he began publishing *School and Society* and helped to form the American Association of University Professors. A tireless advocate of academic freedom, he was known for his outspokenness on controversial issues and his contentious relationship with the president of Columbia, Nicholas Murray Butler, and he was nearly dismissed in 1910 for criticizing the university's pension plan and again in 1913 when he published *University Control*, a collection of essays and letters by himself and others that attacked Wall Street for its influence on American colleges. He was finally dismissed in October 1917 after the trustees charged him with treason and sedition for defending the rights of conscientious objectors in the First World War (the historian Charles A. Beard resigned to protest their decision). Cattell never returned to teaching but continued to conduct research, write, and work as a science editor. He also helped to form the Psychological Corporation, a firm that provided psychological services to businesses (1921), and Science Press, and was president of the American Association for the Advancement of Science (1924), the International Congress on Psychology (1929), and the Science Service in Washington (1930–34). He was the first psychologist elected to the National Academy of Sciences (1890) and the American Academy of Science (1901).

A. T. Poffenberger, ed.: *James McKeen Cattell, 1860–1944: Man of Science* (Lancaster, Penn.: Science Press, 1947)

See also SCIENCE.

Kevin Kenny, Sandra Opdycke

CBGB (& OMFUG) [Country, Bluegrass, Blues and Other Music for Uplifting Gourmandizers]. A rock club at 315 Bowery near Bleecker Street in lower Manhattan, opened in 1973 by Holly Kristal. After a brief, undistinguished existence as a venue for country music it began featuring rock groups in 1974. Among those who appeared there were such punk rock and new wave performers as the B-52s, Deborah Harry, David Byrne, Joan Jett, Ric Ocasek, and Joey Ramone. In 1994 the owners made plans to open a franchise in Miami Beach. By the mid 1990s CBGB was the best-known rock club in the United States and possibly the world.

Kenneth T. Jackson

CBS. See COLUMBIA BROADCASTING SYSTEM.

Cedar Grove. Neighborhood in east central Staten Island. Once known as Cedar Grove Beach, it was first shown on maps in 1850 as a small colony of summer houses for sport fishermen. The Cedar Grove Beach Club was formed in 1938. The sixty-seven bungalows in the area were condemned by the City of New York in 1962 for a highway that was never built; the occupants of the bungalows still rent them from the city.

Martha S. Bendix

Celler, Emmanuel (*b* New York City, 6 May 1888; *d* New York City, 15 Jan 1981). Congressman. After graduating from Columbia College and Columbia Law School he was admitted to the bar in 1912. In 1922 he was elected as a Democrat to the U.S. House of Representatives, where he remained for fifty years. He also organized the Madison State Bank and Brooklyn National Bank and in 1936 became a partner in the firm of Weisman, Celler, Quinn, Allan, and Spett. He supported Zionism and civil liberties, opposed Senator Joseph R. McCarthy, and played an important role in the passage of the civil rights acts of 1957, 1960, and 1964. In 1972 he was defeated for reelection by Elizabeth Holtzman. His autobiography is entitled *You Never Leave Brooklyn* (1953).

James E. Mooney

cemeteries. In 1656 Governor Peter Stuyvesant granted Congregation Shearith Israel land for a cemetery outside the city (on a site north of what is now Wall Street); the site was

Lutheran Cemetery, Middle Village, Queens

eventually redeveloped and from 1682 to 1828 the congregation used another cemetery that is now at 55 St. James Place. Prospect Cemetery was opened in Jamaica in the 1660s. In colonial times some outlying churches had their own cemeteries, including St. Ann's (Episcopal) Church in the Bronx and the Dutch Reformed Church in Flatbush. There were also cemeteries on private estates, including Pelham Manor and the estate of the Ferris family. The Old West Farms Soldiers' Cemetery was opened in 1815. Stuyvesant was buried in the chapel on his farm, which eventually became the site of St. Mark's Church in the Bowery (2nd Avenue and 10th Street). A cemetery for blacks once occupied the site of City Hall Park; cemeteries on Frankfort and lower Nassau streets, in Maiden Lane, next to the John Street Methodist Church, and near Burling Slip became disused and were used for building lots. In some cases buildings were erected over cemeteries; in others the dead were exhumed and then reinterred elsewhere.

Shearith Israel had a cemetery at 76 West 11th Street from 1805 to 1829 and another at 98–110 West 21st Street from 1829 until 1851, when it consecrated ground in Newtown on Long Island. In Manhattan an ordinance passed in 1830 forbade burials south of Canal Street. A private group built the city's first nonsectarian cemetery, the New York Marble Cemetery, on a site of half an acre (twenty ares) bounded by 3rd Street, 2nd Avenue, 2nd Street, and the Bowery. Investors built 156 underground vaults and sold them to upper-class residents of nearby neighborhoods; in 1832 they built the New York City Marble Cemetery at 52–74 East 2nd Street. Several other private cemeteries were built in the area in the 1840s and 1850s (none survive). Green-Wood (1838) and Woodlawn (1865) cemeteries opened as nonsectarian, nonprofit corporations. In 1846 Trinity Church built a cemetery at Broadway and 155th Street (in the mid 1990s it was the only cemetery in Manhattan that still accommodated burials, in community and family mausoleums). The State Rural Cemeteries Act (1847) encouraged the construction of suburban cemeteries, which in keeping with Romantic ideals were designed as retreats from the crowding and pressures of the city. It was also believed that air made unhealthful by human remains would be purified by trees.

The theft of A. T. Stewart's body from the burial ground of St. Mark's Church in the Bowery in 1878 inspired the wealthy to build fortress-like mausoleums in outlying cemeteries. W. H. Vanderbilt commissioned Frederick Law Olmsted to lay out a private cemetery on a site of twenty-one acres (nine hectares) adjacent to the Moravian Cemetery on Staten Island; a mausoleum was designed by Richard Morris Hunt in 1886. The greatest concentration of cemeteries took shape in Newtown, which lay on the border between Brooklyn and Queens and was sometimes called "the city of the dead": by 1893 it had twenty-four cemeteries covering two thousand acres (eight hundred hectares) and containing a million and a half interments. Christian cemeteries there include Calvary, Evergreen, Cypress Hills, Maple Grove, Linden, Mount Olivet, St. John's, St. Michael's, and Holy Cross; Jewish cemeteries include Salem Field, Ahawath Chesed, Washington, Machpelah, Mount Nebo, and Union. Many cemeteries in the outer boroughs still offer space, usually in community mausoleums or columbariums. Others are being restored and maintained as historic sites, providing green retreats within the city. Styles vary enormously, from the simplicity of the Quaker cemetery in Prospect Park and the African Methodist Episcopal Zion Church Cemetery on Staten Island to the grandeur of Woodlawn Cemetery. A few churchyard burial grounds survive in Manhattan, including those of Trinity Church, St. Paul's Chapel, and St. Patrick's Old Cathedral on Mott Street, where the city's earliest bishops are buried. In 1863 the church began interring bishops in the crypt of St. Patrick's Cathedral uptown, on 5th Avenue.

Judi Culbertson and Tom Randall: *Permanent New Yorkers: A Biographical Guide to the Cemeteries of New York* (Chelsea, Vt.: Chelsea Green, 1987)

See also Potter's fields.

Edward F. Bergman

censorship. Many struggles over the censorship of speech and the press have been waged in New York City, long the national center of publishing and broadcasting. One of the earliest cases in the United States occurred in the city in 1735, when John Peter Zenger, a German immigrant, was charged with seditious libel for printing in his *Weekly Journal* that William Cosby, the royal governor of New York, was among other things a "rogue"; Zenger's lawyer persuaded the jury to acquit him by arguing that the truth was sufficient to defend against a charge of libel, an argument contrary to the prevailing doctrine of English law. No major cases arose during the eighteenth and nineteenth centuries, although conflicts over freedom of the press were common. In 1873 Anthony Comstock, perhaps the best-known censor in the history of the city, formed the New York Society for the Suppression of Vice and became its secretary. The organization was later renamed the New York Society for the Improvement of Morals by John S. Sumner, who became its director. Comstock was largely responsible for the passage of the federal statute on obscenity of 1873, which was popularly known as the Comstock Act and barred from the mails any "obscene, lewd, and lascivious" publications. He and others were influential in censoring many works, including those of Ovid, Boccaccio, Rabelais, Rousseau, Fielding, Flaubert, and André Gide; they also condemned *The Genius* by Theodore Dreiser (1916) and *God's Little Acre* by Erskine Caldwell (1933). In response to the Comstock Act many publishers practiced informal censorship by urging authors to change the words and tone of their books before publication. The publishing house of D. Appleton pressured Stephen Crane to make such changes when it agreed to issue his novel *Maggie: A Girl of the Streets* in 1896. Section 211 of the Comstock Act barred from the mails devices used for birth control and was invoked to suppress Margaret Sanger's newspaper the *Woman Rebel* in 1914 and to close her birth control clinic in Brownsville in 1916.

Sections of the police department regulations known as the "New York cabaret laws" set the precedent for the censorship of artistic expression by the city. Section 20 of the regulations reads as follows: "no person shall be permitted to appear in any scene, sketch or act with breasts or lower part of torso uncovered or so thinly covered or draped as to appear uncovered." In 1947 the police commissioner denied Helen Gould Beck (Sally Rand) the identification card that she needed to perform legally because he believed that her performance would violate section 20. Beck received her permit when the judge who heard her case ruled that this denial was a prior restraint on free expression and symbolic speech (*Beck v. Wallender*, 71 N.Y.S. 2d 237 (1947)). The regulations also banned obscene language in public performances, which led to the prosecution of many performers including the comedian Lenny Bruce in 1964, and prevented performers with police records from working in the city, among them the musicians Billie Holiday and Thelonious Monk.

Many precedents for federal standards of censorship have been set in New York City, especially those defining obscenity and PORNOGRAPHY. In 1934 the national statute defining obscenity was overruled in federal court in New York City in a case concerning *Ulysses* by James Joyce (*United States v. One Book Entitled Ulysses*, 72 F. 2d 705 (1934)); it was held that obscenity should be determined by the effect that a book read in its entirety would have on a person of average sexual instincts. This definition became known as the "Ulysses standard" and was refined and made more specific by subsequent decisions. The rule that prevailed before the Ulysses standard was nonetheless applied in New York City as late as 1952, when a city magistrate determined that magazines containing pictures of nude and seminude women were obscene. The case of *New York Times Company v. Sullivan* (1964), heard in a county court in Alabama, helped to set guidelines for freedom of the press: it concerned an advertisement placed in the *New York Times* containing some false statements about the civil rights record of the City of Montgomery. The *Times* was fined $500,000 by the court in Alabama, but the U.S. Supreme Court reversed the verdict by ruling that a public official suing for libel must prove that the material in question was published with knowledge of its falsity or with reckless disregard for its truth or falsity. The standard set by the court, which became known as the "Sullivan rule," continued to be tested in courts in the city; two of the most prominent cases were *General William Westmoreland v. CBS* (1985) and *General Ariel Sharon v. Time Magazine* (1985).

A furor was created in 1989 when homoerotic photographs by Robert Mapplethorpe were included in federally funded exhibitions. The National Endowment for the Arts responded to the controversy by requiring the recipients of its grants to eschew obscenity. Opposition to the new rules was led by a number of performers and arts administrators in the city, including Karen Finley and Joseph Papp.

Censorship: 500 Years of Conflict (New York: Oxford University Press, 1984)

Leon Hurwitz: *Historical Dictionary of Censorship in the United States* (Westport, Conn.: Greenwood, 1985)

Leon Hurwitz

Currier and Ives, Central Park *(1862)*

Central Grammar School. Original name of BOYS AND GIRLS HIGH SCHOOL.

Central Park. Public park in Manhattan, covering 843 acres (340 hectares) bounded to the north by 110th Street, to the east by 5th Avenue, to the south by 59th Street (Central Park South), and to the west by Central Park West. It was the first landscaped public park in the United States. Advocates of its construction were mostly wealthy merchants and landowners who admired the public grounds of London and Paris and argued that comparable facilities would give New York City an international reputation; they also believed that a public park would offer their families an attractive setting for carriage rides and provide workers with a healthful alternative to the saloon. After three years of debating the size and cost of the park, the state legislature in 1853 authorized the city to use the power of eminent domain to acquire a parcel of more than seven hundred acres (285 hectares) in the middle of Manhattan. A site bounded by 106th Street, 5th Avenue, 59th Street, and 8th Avenue was chosen, where an irregular terrain of swamps, bluffs, and rocky outcroppings made the land undesirable for private development.

The question of control over the park was initially settled by the state legislature, which was predominantly Republican: by appointing

Bethesda Terrace (designed by Calvert Vaux and Jacob Wrey Mould) on Central Park Lake, with fountain "Angel of the Waters" (designed by Emma Stebbins), 1991

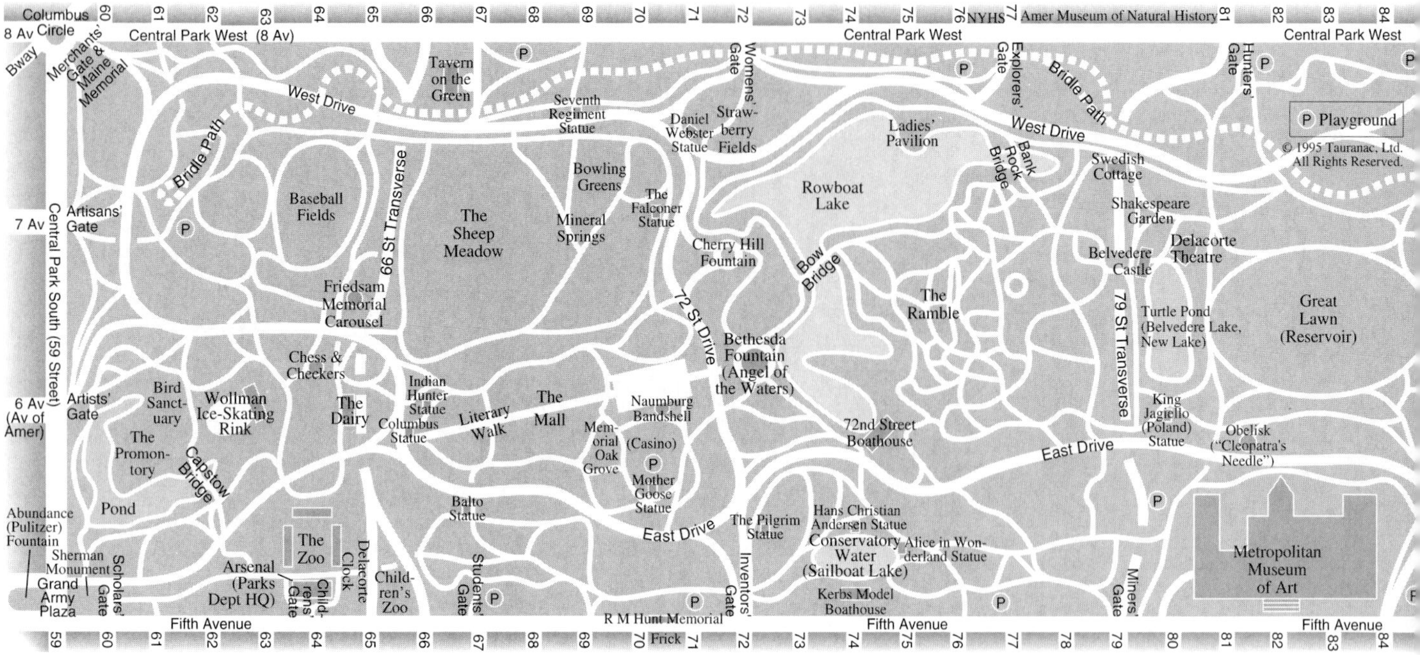

the Central Park Commission in 1857 it abandoned the principle of "home rule" to keep control of the park from local officials, who were mostly Democrats. The commission was the city's first planning agency and under the leadership of Andrew Haswell Green oversaw the planning of uptown Manhattan as well as management of the park itself. In 1857 it held a contest to design the park, the first such contest in the country: the winning entry was the "Greensward plan," which called for a pastoral landscape in the English romantic tradition and was submitted by Frederick Law Olmsted, the superintendent of the park, and Calvert Vaux, a former partner of Andrew Jackson Downing. Their plan called for a combination of the pastoral (open, rolling meadows), the picturesque (the Ramble), and the formal (the dress grounds of the Mall, or Promenade, and Bethesda Terrace). An impression of uninterrupted expanse was maintained by building four transverse roads eight feet (two and a half meters) below the park's surface to carry crosstown traffic. Pressure from local critics soon led Olmsted and Vaux to separate carriage drives, pedestrian walks, and equestrian paths from each other. Assisted by Jacob Wrey Mould, Vaux designed more than forty bridges to eliminate grade crossings between the various routes.

The construction of the park was one of the most extensive public works projects undertaken in the city during the nineteenth century. About sixteen hundred residents of shantytowns in the area were displaced, including Irish pig farmers and German gardeners. Seneca Village, a black settlement at 8th Avenue and 82nd Street that had three churches and a school, was also demolished. About twenty thousand workers were engaged, including native-born stonecutters, engineers from New England, Irish laborers, and German gardeners. They blasted out ridges with gunpowder (more than was used in the Battle of Gettysburg), removed nearly three million cubic yards (2.3 million cubic meters) of soil, planted more than 270,000 trees and shrubs, and built a curvilinear reservoir just north of an existing rectangular one. The park opened to the public in the winter of 1859, when thousands skated on lakes built over former swamps. In 1863 the northern boundary was extended to 110th Street.

In the decade after the opening more than half of those visiting the park arrived in carriages (which less than 5 percent of the city's population could afford to own) and each day there were elaborate carriage parades in the late afternoon. Middle-class residents went skating in winter and attended concerts on Saturday afternoons in summer. Many Irish and Germans were discouraged from going to the park by stringent rules, especially a ban on group picnics. Small tradesmen were not allowed to use commercial wagons for family drives, and only schoolboys with a note from their principal could play ball on the meadows. These rules were repeatedly contested. By 1865 there were more than seven million visitors to the park a year, and during the late nineteenth century the park was opened to a wider range of uses. Under a new city charter (1870) the park came under local control and the mayor appointed park commissioners, who gradually authorized new facilities, including a carousel, goat rides, tennis on the lawns, and bicycling on the drives. The zoo moved into permanent quarters in 1871 and soon became the most popular feature. In the 1880s workers successfully campaigned for concerts on Sunday, their only day of rest.

In the early twentieth century neighborhoods populated mostly by immigrants developed at the park's borders and the number of visitors to the park reached a peak. Progressive reformers joined with workers in advocating facilities for active recreation. In 1927 August Heckscher donated the first equipped playground, which was built on the southeastern meadow. When plans were announced to drain the rectangular reservoir, Progressives urged that a sports arena, a swimming pool, and playing fields be built over it. Others, inspired by the "city beautiful" movement, proposed a formal civic plaza and promenade to connect the museums at the eastern and western borders. Landscape architects and preservationists campaigned against these suggestions and the site was made into the Great Lawn. Mayor Fiorello H. La Guardia gave control of a new centralized park system in 1934 to Robert Moses, who during his twenty-six years in office provided many of the facilities requested by Progressive reformers. During the Depression he used federal money to build twenty playgrounds on the periphery of the park, renovate the zoo, realign the drives to accommodate automobiles, build athletic fields in the North Meadow, and expand recreational programs. He later added permanent ballfields to the Great Lawn for corporate softball teams and neighborhood little league teams. In the early 1950s and early 1960s private benefactors

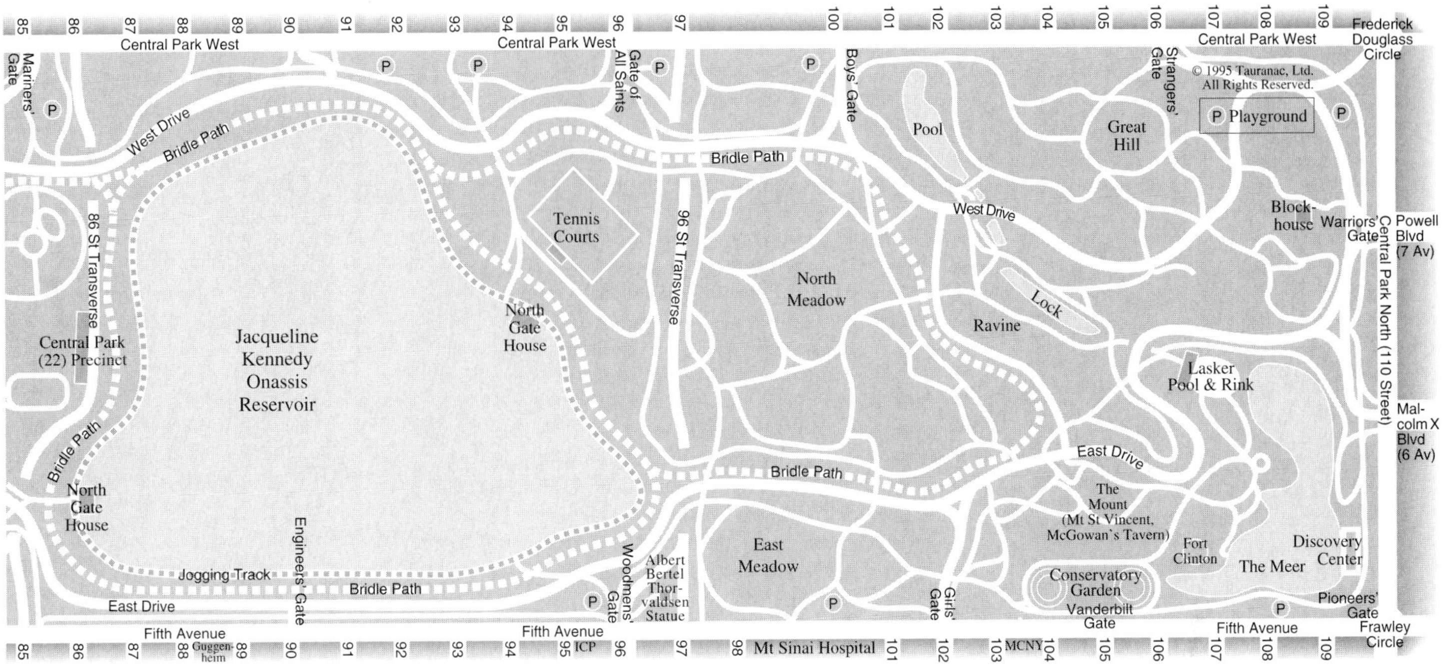

contributed the Wollman Skating Rink, the Lasker Rink and Pool, new boathouses, and a chess and checkers house. The park became the site of summer performances by the New York Shakespeare Festival in 1957 and by the New York Philharmonic in 1965.

Thomas Hoving and August Heckscher (grandson of the philanthropist), the parks commissioners appointed by Mayor John V. Lindsay, encouraged such events as rock concerts and "be-ins" during the 1960s, making the park a symbol of both urban revival and the counterculture. During the 1970s severe budget cuts, a steady decline in maintenance, and the revival of the preservation movement prompted a new approach to managing the park. A private fund-raising body known as the Central Park Conservancy took charge of restoring features of the Greensward plan in 1980, including Sheep Meadow, Bethesda Terrace, and Belvedere Castle (designed by Vaux and Mould); by 1990 the group contributed more than half the budget for the park and greatly influenced decisions about its future. Debates over use of the park and modifications to the Greensward plan persist, and Central Park continues to be shaped by those who use it, including bicyclists, joggers, rollerskaters, softball players, birdwatchers, and nature lovers.

Henry Hope Reed and Sophia Duckworth: *Central Park: A History and a Guide* (New York: Clarkson N. Potter, 1967)

Frederick Law Olmsted Jr. and Theodora Kimball, eds.: *Forty Years of Landscape Architecture: Central Park* (Cambridge: MIT Press, 1973)

Charles Capen McLaughlin, Charles Beveridge, and David Schuyler, eds.: *The Papers of Frederick Law Olmsted* (Baltimore: Johns Hopkins University Press, 1977)

Galen Cranz: *The Politics of Park Design: A History of Urban Parks in America* (Cambridge: MIT Press, 1982)

David Schuyler: *The New Urban Landscape: The Redefinition of City Form in Nineteenth-century America* (Baltimore: Johns Hopkins University Press, 1986)

Roy Rosenzweig and Elizabeth Blackmar: *The Park and the People: A History of Central Park* (Ithaca, N.Y.: Cornell University Press, 1992)

Elizabeth Blackmar, Roy Rosenzweig

Central Park Casino. Nightclub in Central Park near East 66th Street, designed in 1864 by Calvert Vaux. Under the name Ladies Refreshment Salon it was used as a small nightclub in the early 1920s. After James J. Walker was elected mayor it was leased to his friend the restaurateur Sidney Solomon and lavishly redesigned by Joseph Urban. From 1926 to 1934 the club was a high-priced establishment that became widely known as the center of the mayor's active social life. After he resigned in 1932 there were plans to have the structure serve a wider public, but the parks commissioner Robert Moses, a political rival of Walker, insisted that it be demolished and replaced by a playground.

Sandra Opdycke

Central Park jogger. The name popularly applied to a twenty-eight-year-old investment banker who was raped and assaulted by a gang of youths near in the middle of the park 102nd Street on the evening of 19 April 1989. The crime gained notoriety because of its randomness and brutality, as well as its racial overtones (the victim was white and her attackers black). In 1990 five of the assailants were convicted of various charges in two trials; the victim returned to work after eight months but suffered permanent injuries.

Central Synagogue. Reform temple at the corner of 55th Street and Lexington Avenue in Manhattan. The building is a twin-towered structure erected in 1870–72 as the fifth house of worship of Ahawath Chesed (formed in 1846 by Bohemian Jews on the Lower East Side); the congregation merged in 1898 with the members of Shaar Hasomayim and took its current name in 1920. Designed by Henry Fernbach, one of the first Jewish architects in the United States, the building was erected of sandstone with limestone trim in a Moorish Revival style, and modeled after the Dohany Street Synagogue in Budapest. The synagogue is the oldest in continuous use in New York City; it has been designated a city landmark (1966) and is the only synagogue in the state to have been designated a National Historic Landmark (1975). Across 55th Street is the Phyllis and Lee Coffey Community House (1965–68, designed by Kahn and Jacobs), built as a memorial to Jonah B. Wise, one of the congregation's distinguished rabbis.

Herbert Maier Schwarz: *Your Temple: A Unique Story of Devotion* (New York: Central Synagogue, 1958)

Stella F. Fuld, ed., with Janet Stone and Mildred Ross: *Central Synagogue, 140 Years* (New York: Harry N. Abrams, 1979)

Cissy Grossman: *The Jewish Family's Book of Days* (New York: Abbeville, 1989)

Joy M. Kestenbaum

Centreville. Name formerly applied to CASTLETON CORNERS.

Century Association. One of the oldest and most prestigious social clubs in the United States, formed in 1846 by William Cullen Bryant and others to promote interest in literature and the fine arts. It was an outgrowth of the Sketch Club and was to be limited in its membership to a hundred authors and artists and their supporters. During its early years the club occupied a number of buildings. It had about eight hundred members by the time it moved to a new one in 1891 at 7 West 43rd Street designed by Stanford White. Despite problems with contractors, budgets, and schedules the new building was a remarkable achievement, notable in particular for a façade resembling that of a Renaissance palace. During the 1980s the Century was the subject of a great deal of attention for its refusal to admit women as members, a policy that eventually changed.

James E. Mooney

Century Illustrated Monthly Magazine. Periodical launched in 1870 as *Scribner's Monthly*, edited by the poet and essayist Josiah Gilbert Holland. In 1881 it became independent of Charles Scribner's Sons and was renamed. An engraving process developed by Alexander W. Drake and the printing of Theodore Low De Vinne made the magazine the most visually appealing publication of its day. Edited by Richard Watson Gilder, it sought to inspire, uplift, and unite the nation. "The War Series," which consisted of memoirs of Union and Confederate veterans and ran for three years, raised circulation to 250,000 in the 1880s. *Century* declined in the face of competition from mass-market magazines like *McClure's* and ceased publication in 1930.

Arthur John: *The Best Years of the Century: Richard Watson Gilder, Scribner's Monthly and Century Magazine, 1870–1909* (Urbana: University of Illinois Press, 1981)

Marc H. Aronson

ceramics. The production of pottery in New Amsterdam began after the necessary raw materials were discovered there in abundance. The first documented potter in the settlement was Dirck Claesen, who worked in Manhattan during the 1650s. During the seventeenth century most potters in the city produced simple household containers and roof tile of an unrefined red earthenware. In later years suitable clay was found for making stoneware, which unlike redware could be made hard and watertight. Stoneware was produced by Dutch, German, and English potters in New York City as early as the 1730s, long before it was made elsewhere in the colonies in comparable quantities. In 1718 a stoneware pottery was opened on Pottbaker's Hill between Reade and Duane streets by William Crolius, a potter from Neuwied. It became one of the most enduring potteries of its kind in the city, carried on by his sons William Crolius and John Crolius; by John's four sons, including Clarkson Crolius, who was also city collector, an assemblyman, and a member of the Common Council; and later by Clarkson Crolius Jr., a civic leader and the last member of the family to run the pottery, from which he retired in 1850. A small porcelain factory staffed by skilled French workers was opened about 1813 by Henry Mead. After it failed in 1824 another factory was opened in the following year on the same site by two Frenchmen, Louis François Decasse and Nicolas Louis Édouard Chanou. It was known for producing products of high quality before being destroyed by fire in 1828.

Toward the mid nineteenth century the demand for stoneware declined, in part because of the invention of glass canning jars. The city's prosperity as a marketing center pushed ceramics manufacturers to the outskirts, especially Brooklyn, Staten Island, and New Jersey. At the same time the demand for porcelain and white earthenware manufacture increased. During the 1840s and 1850s handwork and small shops in the porcelain industry were gradually replaced by mechanized production in larger factories that could produce goods at lower cost, making porcelain available to the middle class for the first time. Between 1840 and 1860 many porcelain workers were skilled German and English immigrants, and Brooklyn became one of the country's leading ceramic centers, along with Trenton, New Jersey, and East Liverpool, Ohio. Hotels, boardinghouses, and saloons proliferated and required dinnerware, bar vessels, and toilet accessories. At the Crystal Palace Exhibition of the Industry of All Nations in 1853, the country's first international exposition, the firms of Charles Cartlidge and William Boch and Brothers exhibited their wares. Both had factories in Greenpoint and produced heavy porcelain tableware and a wide range of house trimmings, including name plates, keyhole covers, and knobs for doors, drawers, and shutters. Cartlidge's firm closed in 1854. In 1867 Thomas C. Smith joined Boch, which was renamed the Union Porcelain Company and later the Union Porcelain Works. Soon the largest and most successful ceramics manufacturer in the area, it had a sizable factory complex that in 1884 employed two hundred workers and made an average of $250,000 in annual sales. It designed artwares that were exhibited nationally and remained in operation until about 1922.

From the time of the First World War traditional ceramic forms were often rejected for more sculptural ones. In the following decades New York City became an international center for ceramic art, where many artists, especially European and Asian immigrants, settled near the universities where they worked and taught.

William C. Ketchum Jr.: *Potters and Potteries of New York State, 1650–1900* (Syracuse, N.Y.: Syracuse University Press, 1987)

Alice Cooney Frelinghuysen

Cerf, Bennett (Alfred) (*b* New York City, 25 May 1898; *d* Mount Kisco, N.Y., 27 Aug 1971). Publisher and writer. After earning a bachelor's degree and a degree in journalism from Columbia University he joined the publishing firm Boni and Liveright, where he became a vice-president; he left in 1925 to found the Modern Library and in 1927 Random House. As the director of both houses for the next forty years he published such writers as Franz Kafka, Eugene O'Neill, and William Faulkner. In 1933 he won a drawn-out court case permitting him to publish Joyce's *Ulysses*. During the 1940s he lived at the Navarro Hotel at 112 Central Park South. Cerf wrote two dozen books, among them *Laughing Stock* (1945), *Try and Stop Me* (1945), and *At Random: The Reminiscences* (1977).

James E. Mooney

Chadbourne, Thomas L(incoln) (*b* Houghton, Mich., 1871; *d* New York City, 15 June 1938). Lawyer. He was a large stockholder in both Brooklyn–Manhattan Transit and Interborough Rapid Transit and an important fund raiser for the national Democratic Party. Between 1923 and 1928 he secretly gave Governor Alfred E. Smith about $400,000 in cash and stocks to supplement his official salary.

David Margolick: "Deleted from Book: Gifts to Alfred E. Smith," *New York Times*, 22 May 1985, §A, p. 1

Frank Vos

Chadbourne and Parke. Law firm established in 1902 by Thomas Chadbourne. Known for reorganizing corporations, it grew rapidly in the 1920s, gaining Eastern Airbus and Trans World Airlines as clients, to which it later added Sperry Gyroscope and Rockwell. Chadbourne himself drew up an international plan to restore the stability of sugar prices in 1930. During the 1970s the firm structured leveraged buyouts and defended manufacturers in important product liability cases; in later years it planned the recapitalization of the Bowery Savings Bank and oversaw the takeover of the Manhattan Savings Bank. In the mid 1990s it had more than three hundred lawyers, with offices at 30 Rockefeller Center and in the United Arab Emirates and Moscow. Its clients in the city included the Vivian Beaumont Theatre, the Sachler Institute, and the State Council of the Arts.

George J. Lankevich

Chadwick, Henry (*b* Exeter, England, 5 Oct 1824; *d* Brooklyn, 20 April 1908). Sportswriter. He moved to New York City with his family in 1837, settling in Brooklyn. In 1856 he filed cricket reports for the *New*

York Times and later that year became a cricket and baseball editor for the *Brooklyn Daily Eagle*, a position he held until 1894. He was the best-known promoter of "New York," or "Brooklyn," baseball and helped to make it more popular than both "Massachusetts" baseball and cricket. While writing about baseball for the *New York World* and the *Sun* he developed the box score, a method of compiling game statistics. From 1881 to 1908 he edited the *Spalding Baseball Guide*, the leading publication of its kind. Throughout his career he promoted baseball as an outlet for competitive energies and an alternative to drinking and fighting; he devoted much of his time to combating gambling, which threatened the wholesome reputation of what he called "America's game." In 1896 the National League voted to give him a lifetime pension. Known to many as the "father of baseball," Chadwick worked in baseball journalism to the end of his life. He is buried in Green-Wood Cemetery.

James A. Vlasick: *A Legend for the Legendary: The Origin of the Baseball Hall of Fame* (Bowling Green, Ohio: State University Popular Press, 1990)

Edward T. O'Donnell

chamberlain. The office of chamberlain was established in 1868 to maintain financial records, deposit public moneys, and compile quarterly financial reports. Appointed by the mayor, the chamberlain received a commission on the accounts that he supervised. The establishment of the comptroller's office in 1802 diminished the chamberlain's powers. The office of the chamberlain became a part of the department of finance in 1916 and was abolished in 1938.

Rebecca B. Rankin: *The Treasurer, Chamberlain and the Comptroller of the City of New York* (New York: New York Municipal Reference Library, 1949)

Thelma E. Smith: *Guide to the Municipal Government of the City of New York* (New York: Meilen, 1973)

Neal C. Garelik

Chamber of Commerce. See NEW YORK CHAMBER OF COMMERCE AND INDUSTRY.

Chambers, (Jay David) Whittaker (*b* Philadelphia, 1 April 1901; *d* Westminster, Md., 9 July 1961). Journalist and spy. He graduated from Columbia University and worked as a freelance journalist. After joining the Communist Party in 1931 he was a spy courier for the Soviet Union until the Nazi–Soviet pact of 1939 led him to abjure communism. From 1939 to 1948 he enjoyed a prominent career as a senior editor at *Time*, specializing in cultural and world affairs. He achieved notoriety in 1948 when in testimony before the House Un-American Activities Committee he accused Alger Hiss, then president of the Carnegie Endowment for International Peace in New York City, of having removed and copied classified documents while working at the state department. Hiss professed his innocence but in 1950 was convicted of perjury and served four years in prison. Chambers spent his later years issuing apocalyptic warnings of the Soviet threat and became something of a hero for American conservatives. He wrote a memoir, *Witness* (1952).

Allen Weinstein: *Perjury: The Hiss–Chambers Case* (New York: Alfred A. Knopf, 1978)

Martin Ebon

Champion, Gower (*b* Geneva, Ill., 22 June 1919; *d* New York City, 25 Aug 1980). Choreographer, director, and dancer. The year of his birth is often given incorrectly as 1921. He grew up in Los Angeles, and at the age of fifteen began a career as a dancer when he won a contest at the Coconut Grove with Jeanne Tyler. While serving in the U.S. Coast Guard (from 1942) he met Sid Caesar, and after leaving the service he became reacquainted with Marjorie Belcher (now known professionally as Marjorie Bell), with whom he had attended high school and whose father, Ernest, owned the dance school he had attended. The two formed a dance team, married on 5 October 1947, and appeared on Milton Berle's television program and at the Persian Room of the Plaza Hotel. With Caesar and Imogene Coca they worked on the "Admiral Broadway Review" (1947–48), an important early television program that was a forerunner of "Your Show of Shows." In the following years Champion worked as a choreographer, winning the first of his seven Tony awards for the Broadway show *Lend an Ear* (1948). He conceived of and directed the musical revue *Three for Tonight* (1955) at the Plymouth Theatre in New York City, and also directed *Bye Bye Birdie* (1960), *Carnival* (1961), *Hello, Dolly!* (1964), *I Do! I Do!* (1966), and *Sugar* (1972). In 1980 he directed David Merrick's production of *42nd Street*; he died hours before the curtain rose on opening night.

Alana J. Erickson

Chanin, Irwin (*b* New York City, 29 Oct 1891; *d* New York City, 24 Feb 1988). Real-estate developer. With his brother Henry Chanin (1894–1973) he opened a firm to build houses in Brooklyn, the Bronx, Queens, and Staten Island; the two eventually expanded their operations to Manhattan, where they erected apartment buildings and many theaters and hotels on Broadway, and became leading developers in the 1920s. Irwin worked with the firm of Sloan and Robertson to design the Chanin Building, a dramatic structure of fifty-six stories with a terra cotta façade on 42nd Street and Lexington Avenue near Grand Central Terminal; completed in 1929, it was the Chanins' most ambitious project, containing more commercial space than the Woolworth Building and known as the tallest building north of Wall Street until the Chrysler Building was completed in 1930. With the onset of the Depression the Chanins experienced financial difficulties and eventually lost most of their properties.

Marc A. Weiss

Chapin, Alfred C(lark) (*b* South Hadley, Mass., 8 March 1848; *d* 2 Oct 1936). Mayor of Brooklyn. He practiced law and belonged to the Democratic Party. As mayor from 1888 to 1891 he advocated civic improvements: his tenure brought improved police protection, an increased water supply, a growth in park acreage, and the construction of the monumental arch at the entrance to Prospect Park.

Ellen Fletcher

Chapin School. Private elementary and secondary school opened in 1901 in two brownstones on East 57th Street as Miss Chapin's School for Girls by Maria Bowen Chapin, who had earlier run a preparatory school for the Brearley School and the Spence School. The school was incorporated in 1925 and moved in 1928 to a building on East End Avenue at 84th Street. Chapin retired in 1932 from active management of the school, which took its current name in February 1934. In 1994 the school had 574 students.

Richard Schwartz

Charity Hospital. Hospital on Blackwell's Island, a forerunner of ELMHURST HOSPITAL CENTER.

Charity Organization Society [COS]. Society organized in 1882 in New York City by the reformer Josephine Shaw Lowell to evaluate and refer applicants for charity. It kept extensive records about living conditions in the city and concentrated on preventing poverty, an approach that led other groups to shift their focus from charity and moral correction to social welfare. Known for taking active interest in those with whom they worked, the society's "friendly visitors" later became a model for social case workers. Among the directors was the reformer Edward T. Devine. With the Association for Improving the Condition of the Poor, and the Children's Aid Society, the society in 1891 became an owner of the United Charities Building at 105 East 22nd Street, which was donated by John M. Kennedy. During the same year the society formed a national publication committee that launched the journal *Charities Review*, which after several changes of name eventually became the *Survey*, the most influential publication of its kind in the country. The society also sponsored Laurence Veiller's tenement exhibition in 1900 and his work in drafting the city's Tenement House Law of 1901. In 1939 the Charity Organization Society merged with the Association for Improving the Condition of the Poor to form the Community Service Society.

Grace Florence Marcus: *Some Aspects of Relief in Family Casework* (New York: Charity Organization Society, 1929)

Alana J. Erickson

Charles H. Revson Foundation. Charitable organization formed in 1956 by Charles H. Revson (*b* 11 Oct 1906; *d* 24 Aug 1975), a founder of the cosmetics firm Revlon. During his lifetime the foundation donated $10 million to medical, educational, and Jewish organizations in New York City: these gifts funded a diagnostic center at the Albert Einstein College of Medicine and an institute of ophthalmology at New York Medical Center. Enlarged by an endowment after Revson's death, the foundation in 1978 took on a full-time staff and defined four areas of activity: urban affairs, education, biomedical research policy, and Jewish philanthropy and education. Contributions are aimed in particular at projects relating to the future of New York City, the changing role of women in society, government accountability, and the impact of modern communications on education. In the decade after 1978 the foundation made 352 grants totaling $63 million to 135 organizations for 185 projects. Of this amount $19 million was given to projects pertaining to the future of New York City, among them neighborhood revitalization programs, a fellowship at City College to train lawyers for service in low-income communities, and fellowships at Columbia University. In 1990 the foundation had assets of $82.7 million and made grants totaling $5.2 million.

Kenneth W. Rose

Charles Scribner's Sons. Firm of book publishers formed in 1846 by the booksellers Charles Scribner and Isaac Baker, who specialized in didactic material. It was led from 1871 to 1930 by Charles Scribner and employed William Crary Brownell as its literary advisor from 1888 to 1928; it also published *Scribner's Magazine* (1886–1914), edited by Edward I. Burlingame, and operated a bookstore at 597 5th Avenue (now a landmark) designed by Ernest Flagg, whose sister Louise married Charles Scribner Jr. From 1910 to 1947 Maxwell Perkins redefined the image of the editor and championed such authors as F. Scott Fitzgerald, Ernest Hemingway, and Thomas Wolfe. Owned and managed for many years by the same family, Scribner's was long highly regarded as a publishing house. In 1984 it was acquired by Macmillan and the bookstore was sold.

Roger Burlingame: *Of Making Many Books: A Hundred Years of Reading, Writing, and Publishing* (New York: Charles Scribner's Sons, 1946)

Charles Scribner Jr.: *In the Company of Writers: A Life in Publishing* (New York: Charles Scribner's Sons, 1990)

Marc H. Aronson

Charleston. Neighborhood in southwestern Staten Island (1990 pop. 17,500), bounded to the north by Clay Pit Ponds, to the east by Sandy Ground, to the south by Tottenville, and to the west by the Arthur Kill. It was known as Androvetteville in the eighteenth century. The area is rich in the type of clay needed for making bricks, and in 1854 a Bavarian immigrant named Balthazar Kreischer opened a factory where heat-resistant bricks were made by German and Irish workers. By the 1890s these workers numbered more than three hundred. A company town called Kreischerville took shape that consisted of Kreischer's Italianate mansion, the residences of two of his sons, an inn, a hotel, a grocery store, and housing for workers. The family also built St. Peter's Evangelical Reformed Church (1883), now known as the Free Hungarian Reformed Church. After the factory closed in 1927 the neighborhood was given its current name. The mixed-use zoning prevailing in the neighborhood has been a concern of homeowners seeking to protect a tranquil residential environment from the traffic, noise, and debris generated by local businesses. In the 1970s there were discussions about using the municipally owned land for an amusement park and about including Charleston in various development schemes, one of which, for a new town, was advanced by James Rouse. Some of the old clay pits may be seen at Clay Pit Ponds State Park.

Mabel Abbot: "Kreischerville," *Proceedings of the Staten Island Institute of Arts and Sciences* 11, no. 2 (Jan 1949), 31–43

"Lifestyle: Charleston," *Staten Island Advance*, 5 June 1989, §B, pp. 1–2

Howard Weiner

Charlotte Gardens. Urban renewal project in the southern Bronx, bounded to the north by East 174th Street, to the east by Southern Boulevard, to the south by Jennings Street, and to the west by Corona Park. In October 1977 President Jimmy Carter visited the area and pledged federal aid for the removal of its abandoned "new law" tenements and for its redevelopment. Ronald Reagan also expressed concern about the area during his presidential campaign in 1980. The South Bronx Development Organization received $3 million in federal aid, and in the summer of 1983 a complex of ninety-four ranch houses was completed, each house selling for a subsidized price of $54,000. The project was the most successful attempt to redevelop the southern Bronx in the 1980s, but in the mid 1990s Charlotte Gardens remained an incongruous presence amid the surrounding burned-out tenements.

Joel Schwartz

Charlotteville. Neighborhood in northwestern Queens, lying within Woodside and bounded to the north by 31st Avenue, to the east by 68th Street, to the south by Northern Boulevard, and to the west by Hobart Street. Development was begun by John A. Mecke but interrupted by his death in May 1867. In June and August 1868 his heir auctioned off lots, and in 1880 the area was annexed to Woodside. A large unsold portion was redeveloped in the 1890s as North Woodside. The name gradually fell into disuse as Woodside expanded after consolidation.

Vincent Seyfried

charter. New Amsterdam was incorporated by a charter of the Dutch West India Company in 1653. Under English rule a corporation that became known as "the Mayor Aldermen and Commonality of the city of New York" was formed in response to local petition, as required by English law. According to the charters of Governors Richard Nicolls (1665), Thomas Dongan (1686), Lord Cornbury (1708), and John Montgomerie (1731) the mayor and other officials were appointed by the provincial governor and council. Until the late eighteenth century charters of incorporation for New York City were not custom arily changed without due process of law and

Charlotte Street, 1987

Changes to the City Charter, 1653–1989

	LEGISLATIVE	EXECUTIVE	COURTS AND BOARDS
1653	New Amsterdam receives its first charter from the Dutch West India Company, establishing the offices of schout, two burgomasters, and five schepens, all of whom are appointed by the director general. Together these office holders form a court of inferior jurisdiction as well as a legislative body.	The burgomasters are responsible for nominating church wardens, fire inspectors, and surveyors, subject to the approval of the colony's director general.	
1665	Under English rule the Dutch form of government is continued briefly until replaced by a mayor, five aldermen, and one sheriff, together serving as the city's governing body. All are appointed by the governor.	The mayor is empowered to grant tavern licenses.	
1686	The charter of Governor Thomas Dongan calls for the freemen in each of the city's six wards to elect one alderman and one assistant, who together with the mayor and recorder form the Common Council. This body possesses most of the power for governing the city, including the power to regulate markets, transportation of goods, and access to docks, and to levy fines and penalties on offenders. All legislation passed expires after three months unless confirmed by the governor and council.	The mayor is appointed annually by the governor. He is a justice of the peace and judge of the court of common pleas, and has the power to award tavern licenses, appoint the city's high constable, and (with the Common Council) grant citizenship.	The mayor, recorder, and aldermen are justices of the peace. The mayor, recorder, and any two aldermen constitute a court of sessions of peace. The mayor or recorder and any two others qualify as a court of common pleas.
1689	Leisler's Rebellion results in the overthrow of the colonial government established by Dongan's charter. A provincewide convention calls for elections in the autumn of 1689.	Peter Delanoy becomes the city's first elected mayor. He is overthrown in early 1691.	
1730	The charter of Governor Thomas Montgomerie leaves the function of the city's government virtually unchanged, though it does create a seventh ward (called the Montgomerie Ward) and thus raises the number of aldermen and assistant aldermen to seven each. Laws passed by the Common Council expire after one year unless confirmed by the governor and council.	The mayor is still appointed annually by the governor. His powers over commerce and business done in the city are enhanced as he is made clerk of the market. All fees and fines from these offices go to the mayor.	The mayor, recorder, and aldermen are *ex officiis* justices of the peace. The mayor or recorder and any three others may hold general courts of session of peace. The mayor or recorder and three or more aldermen constitute a court of record to hear civil cases.
1777		The mayor is appointed by the governor of the state, on advice from the council of state, to a one-year term.	
1791	The city eliminates the names of wards in favor of numbers.		
1813	The state legislature declares that the Common Council will now perform the same duties required of supervisors of other state counties.	The powers of clerk of the market are transferred from the mayor to the Common Council.	
1821		An amendment to the state constitution authorizes the Common Council to select the mayor, a power formerly exercised by the state legislature and governor.	
1830	A new charter separates the Board of Aldermen and Board of Assistant Aldermen into distinct bodies, which together form the Common Council. Each ward elects one alderman and one assistant alderman for one-year terms. Legislation may originate in either chamber, but must be approved by both before being sent to the mayor.	The mayor is removed from the Common Council and gains power of veto over ordinances and resolutions passed by it. This veto may be overridden if a majority of both boards repasses the legislation. The office of deputy mayor (since 1675 a position held by an alderman chosen by the mayor to act in his absence) is transferred to the president of	

(*continued*)

Changes to the City Charter, 1653–1989 *(Continued)*

LEGISLATIVE	EXECUTIVE	COURTS AND BOARDS
Restraints are placed on the fiscal powers of the Common Council: it may not draw money from the treasury except for purposes previously specified by legislation and may not borrow against the credit of the corporation except in anticipation of future revenues. The council does however possess the important power to appoint the heads of the executive departments.	the Board of Aldermen. No city departments fall under the direct control of the executive.	
1834	An amendment to the state constitution calls for annual public mayoral elections.	
1849 The term for aldermen, but not assistants, is increased to two years. Assistants are granted the sole power to impeach city officials. The Common Council loses the power to appoint the heads of executive departments and to perform executive business, but retains the crucial powers to tax and spend and administer municipally owned lands. Although heads of executive departments are now elected, the council wields influence over them because their appointments must be approved.	The mayor is strengthened by an increase in his term of office from one to two years and by being made head of the police department (but not chief). He does not yet possess full executive powers, as the ten executive department heads are elected rather than named by the mayor, and most are empowered to appoint their subordinates.	
1853 A Board of Councilmen replaces the Board of Assistant Aldermen and together with the Board of Aldermen constitues the Common Council. The Board of Councilmen is made up of sixty men elected annually from as many newly drawn districts of roughly equal population. The councilmen are placed in charge of all legislation concerning expenditures, to which the Board of Aldermen may only suggest amendments. The powers of the Common Council are weakened as members are denied the right to sit as judges in municipal courts and to appoint policemen. The council loses control of the police department, which is placed under a Board of Commissioners. All contracts, leases, and sales in excess of $250 must be open to public bidding.	The mayor's power is enhanced as the Common Council now needs a two-thirds majority in each chamber to override his veto. Because of their elective status the heads of executive departments remain largely independent of the mayor. A Board of Commissioners, comprising the mayor, recorder, and city judge, presides over the police department.	Removal of councilmen as judges in municipal courts leads to a more independent judiciary.
1857 The city's aldermen are no longer elected by ward, but rather one each from seventeen larger districts. The Board of Councilmen is made up of six members elected from each senate district in the city for one-year terms. The Common Council loses powers to the comptroller, who is made administrator of the city's real estate and auditor of its accounts, overseer of disbursements, and collector of taxes. Aldermen are no longer members of the Board of Supervisors of New York County. Aldermen are empowered to remove department heads by a two-thirds vote, without the mayor's approval.	The mayor gains greater control over the executive branch as he is empowered to appoint and remove most heads of executive departments, although with the consent of the aldermen. At the same time the state replaces the Municipal Police with its own Metropolitan Police, combining New York, Kings, Richmond, and Westchester counties and supervised by a commission of five state-appointed overseers and the mayors of New York City and Brooklyn as *ex officiis* members.	A separate New York County Board of Supervisors is created as a check on city government. A board of six elected and six appointed (by the mayor) supervisors replaces the mayor, recorder, and aldermen as the members of the board.

(continued)

Changes to the City Charter, 1653–1989 *(Continued)*

COUNCIL	MAYOR	BOARD OF ESTIMATE
1864		The Board of Estimate and Apportionment is established. It includes the commissioners of the Metropolitan Police and the comptrollers of New York City and Brooklyn. It is to estimate the annual cost of operating the Metropolitan Police.
1868 An amendment to the city charter abolishes the Board of Councilmen and replaces it with the Board of Assistant Aldermen. One assistant and one alderman are elected from each assembly district, each to a two-year term.		
1870 The charter of William M. "Boss" Tweed, and its amendments of 1871, modify the Board of Aldermen to consist of fifteen men elected from the city at large. The Board of Assistant Aldermen consists of one man elected from each assembly district. Members of each board serve one-year terms. All legislation involving expenditures requires a three-fourths vote of approval from each board. The comptroller, corporation counsel, commissioner of public works, and heads of the various municipal departments are granted non-voting seats on the Board of Aldermen.	The mayor's powers increase as he is given the right to appoint officials in executive departments (except those of finance and law) without approval from the Common Council. Most departments are to be led by groups of commisioners with terms of four to eight years, thus allowing a mayor's influence in city government to extend well beyond his two-year term. His veto is enhanced as a three-fourths majority vote of each board of the Common Council is required to override. Significantly, authority over the police department is returned to the mayor after thirteen years of state control.	The Board of Supervisors of New York County is terminated as a distinct body and its powers are returned to the former supervisors (see 1813), the aldermen, the mayor, and the recorder. A Board of Apportionment is created, comprising the mayor, comptroller, commissioner of public works, and president of the department of public parks. The board is empowered to estimate and apportion money sufficient to run each department of city government for the coming year. It must send this budget for certification to the county supervisors (the mayor, recorder, and aldermen). By taxes on real and personal estate the supervisors then raise the funds necessary to meet these expenditures and the interest due on the city's bonds.
1873 The "Reform Charter" eliminates the Board of Assistant Aldermen, making the Board of Aldermen alone the Common Council. Three aldermen are elected from each senate district and six others as at-large candidates for a total of twenty-one members. To prevent one-party domination of the council, voters are limited to voting for no more than two aldermen from their senate district and four at large. The term of office for aldermen is reduced from two years to one. These changes do not take effect until 1875.	Pending approval by the Board of Aldermen, the mayor appoints all department heads and commissioners, except the commissioners of public instruction, the comptroller, the corporation counsel, the president of the department of police, and the commissioner and president of public works.	The Board of Apportionment becomes the Board of Estimate and Apportionment and its membership is reorganized to include the mayor, comptroller, president of the Board of Aldermen, and president of the Department of Taxes and Assessment. Based on requests from individual departments, it estimates the cost of government operations, apportions a sum to each department, and establishes a tax rate. This budget is sent to the aldermen for non-binding recommendations and then must be certified by the comptroller. The board is also empowered to issue stocks and bonds.
1874 The number of aldermen making up the Common Council is set at twenty-two. Six alderman are elected at large and sixteen others as representatives of as many aldermanic districts.		The mayor and recorder are removed as supervisors of the County of New York, thus making the Board of Supervisors and the Board of Aldermen equivalent.
1884 The president of the Board of Aldermen is no longer elected by the aldermen from among their number, but rather by the general electorate as an at-large candidate.		
1888 The Board of Aldermen is now composed of one representative from each of the city's twenty-five assembly districts and a president elected at large. All serve one-year terms (increased to two years in 1892).		
1898 The Common Council is replaced by a Municipal Assembly consisting of a Council	The term of the mayor is increased to four years, though he may not seek reelection. His	The offices of borough president are created. Elected like the mayor to four-year terms, the

(continued)

Changes to the City Charter, 1653–1989 (*Continued*)

COUNCIL	MAYOR	BOARD OF ESTIMATE
and a Board of Aldermen. The Council includes twenty-eight members elected to four-year terms from ten council districts (four in Manhattan, three in Brooklyn, and one each in the Bronx, Queens, and Staten Island). All districts elect three members each except for that in Staten Island, which elects only one. The twenty-ninth member is the president, elected at large. The Board of Aldermen is made up of one member from each of the sixty assembly districts, elected for a term of two years. Board members elect a president from among their number. All the heads of the various municipal departments are allowed to attend these meetings, but may not vote. This marks the end of the Common Council.	appointments must take place within the first six months of his term, but they do not require confirmation by the Municipal Assembly. The mayor's hand in financial and franchise issues is strengthened by a clause requiring a five-sixths majority in the Municipal Assembly to override his veto. The office of comptroller remains elective.	borough presidents are responsible for local administration and public works (streets and sewers). The members of the Board of Estimate are the mayor, comptroller, corporation counsel, council president, and president of the Department of Taxes and Assessments. The board submits an annual city budget to the Municipal Assembly, which may only vote to decrease individual apportionments. The Mayor is empowered to veto such decreases.
1901 The city charter is amended to terminate the Municipal Assembly in favor of a single Board of Aldermen. Seventy-three aldermen are elected from as many districts to two-year terms. The president of the board is again elected at large. Vacancies are filled by majority vote of the board, and a person who fills a vacancy must be a member of the same party as the previous office holder.	The term of the mayor is reduced to two years, though he is again eligible for reelection.	The Board of Estimate and Apportionment is now made up of the mayor, the comptroller, and the president of the Board of Aldermen (who each have three votes), and the five borough presidents (who each have one vote). The borough presidents' term of office is reduced to two years but they gain new powers, including those formerly assigned to the Board of Public Improvements and the power to regulate buildings, sewers, and highways. In 1902 the duties and powers of the Board of Public Improvements are transferred to the Board of Estimate and Apportionment.
1905	The term of the mayor is increased to four years.	The power to grant franchises is transferred from the Board of Aldermen to the Board of Estimate and Apportionment.
1911		The Board of Estimate and Apportionate is empowered to authorize public improvements and determine the tax revenue needed to pay for them.
1917		The Board of Estimate and Apportionment is empowered to regulate buildings and zoning.
1924 An amendment to the state constitution grants the city home rule: its legislature is free from virtually all state interference in the governing of the city, and pending approval by public referendum it is empowered to amend the city charter. A new Municipal Assembly is established with the Board of Aldermen constituting the lower chamber and the Board of Estimate and Apportionment the upper. The Board of Aldermen is composed of one president elected at large, five borough presidents, and sixty-five men elected from as many districts for two-year terms.		The Board of Estimate and Apportionment is composed of the mayor, the comptroller, the president of the Board of Aldermen, and the five borough presidents.
1938 The sixty-five-member Municipal Assembly is eliminated in favor of a smaller City Council. Members of the council are elected by a system of proportional	The office of deputy mayor is created. It is eliminated in 1939.	The Board of Estimate and Apportionment is renamed the Board of Estimate and is empowered to veto any legislation of the City Council. The powers of the Commissioners

(*continued*)

Changes to the City Charter, 1653–1989 (*Continued*)

	COUNCIL	MAYOR	BOARD OF ESTIMATE
	representation, with each borough electing one councilman for every 75,000 voters. Coucilmen serve two-year terms.		of the Sinking Fund over municipally owned land are transferred to the board, which is now the most powerful governing body in the city.
1945	The term for councilmen is increased to four years, the same as the mayor.		
1946		The office of deputy mayor is restored as a full-time position.	
1949	Proportional representation is abolished and henceforth one councilor is elected from each state senate district within the city.		
1958			The voting powers within the Board of Estimate are changed. The mayor, comptroller, and president of the City Council each have four votes, and the five borough presidents each have two votes.
1963	A new charter provides for the election of one councilman from each state senate district within the city and two councilmen-at-large from each borough.	The mayor is empowered to appoint additional deputy mayors and to estimate general fund revenues for budget purposes, a function formerly performed by the comptroller. The mayor also has the power to estimate the maximum debt that the city may incur for capital projects.	
1975			Six amendments to the city charter are passed by referendum. Together they represent an attempt to improve government efficiency and the oversight of individual agencies, especially in fiscal matters. No substantive changes are made to the powers of the City Council, the Board of Estimate, and the office of the mayor.
1978			The number of votes on the Board of Estimate is changed, giving two each to the mayor, the comptroller, and the president of the City Council, and one to each borough presidents. Because the proportions remain the same the change is not substantive.
1989	The City Council is expanded from thirty-five to fifty-one seats to improve the chances of candidates who are members of racial and ethnic minorities. The council is granted full power over the municipal budget and authority over zoning, land use, and franchises.	The mayor controls municipal agencies and approves contracts through them, proposes an annual budget and estimate of revenues, and is empowered to appoint seven members to the newly created City Planning Commission.	The Board of Estimate is eliminated. A new City Planning Commission is created, to consist of thirteen members: seven appointed by the mayor, one by the president of the City Council, and one by each of the borough presidents. The commission is empowered to recommend zoning changes, grant special land-use permits, and vote on sites chosen for city projects.

Compiled by Edward T. O'Donnell

the consent of all parties, which gave the city a measure of autonomy. By the early nineteenth century the city requested powers from the state beyond those given in Montgomerie's charter. Pressures for greater democratic participation led to popular election of the mayor (1834) and some department heads (1849). Legal precedent expanded the power of private corporations and restricted the power of public ones. At the city's request and because of public pressure and new interpretations of the law, the state government took more active part in the city's affairs, which it virtually controlled by the mid 1850s. For many years changes to the municipal charter were made only by the state legislature, which was usually Republican (the city government was usually Democratic).

The charter of 1870, which restored power to local government, was said to have been bought by William M. "Boss" Tweed in the legislature for $600,000. The reform charter of 1873 strengthened the powers of the comptroller. In 1881 the state legislature granted a charter to Brooklyn that became a model for other American cities. The Charter of Greater New York (1898) set the present boundaries of the city and provided for central governing institutions. A new charter in 1901 decentralized city government by strengthening the borough presidents and establishing a powerful board of estimate. During the twenty-five years after consolidation several unsuccessful attempts were made to change the city's charter. The legislature in 1914 gave all cities in the state except New York City a role in defining their charters, a right that was extended to New York City in 1924; in the same year all city councils were granted the right to initiate revisions to their charters, which then required approval by referendum (as did all revisions to municipal charters, whether initiated by state or local government). A referendum in 1935 on the proposals of a commission led by Thomas Day Thacher, the first charter referendum in the city since 1853, brought about a change to proportional representation in city council elections. From the 1960s changes to the charter were introduced not in the City Council, but usually by local charter commissions formed by the mayor under powers granted by state law in 1961. A commission led by John T. Cahill (1961) established an electoral system for the City Council that assured representation for minority parties, strengthened the mayor's budgetary powers, and weakened the borough presidents and the comptroller. A commission formed by the state legislature and led by State Senator Roy Goodman (1973–75) urged that city government be decentralized.

Federal lawsuits over equal representation had several consequences for the charter in the 1980s. In response to one suit, a charter commission led by Michael I. Sovern (1983) eliminated council seats filled by at-large (boroughwide) elections and introduced a reapportionment scheme for the council. A second suit challenging the system of representation used by the Board of Estimate, *Morris v. Board of Estimate* (1989), inspired the formation of commissions led by Richard Ravitch (1986–88) and F. A. O. Schwarz Jr. (1988–89), which recommended abolishing the Board of Estimate and redistributing its powers, changing procedures for budgeting, land use, elections, and administration, devising safeguards of governmental integrity, and transforming the City Council from a body widely considered incompetent and corrupt into an effective legislature that balanced the mayor's power. The changes recommended by the charter commissions were adopted and the Board of Estimate was abolished.

James Kent: *Charter of the City of New York, with Notes thereon; Also a Treatise on the Powers and Duties of the Mayor, Aldermen, and Assistant Aldermen, and the Journal of the City Convention* (New York: Childs and Devoe, 1836)

Mark Ash: *The Greater New York Charter* (New York: Baker, Voorhis, 1898; 5th edn 1925)

Frank J. Mauro and Gerald Benjamin, eds.: *Restructuring the New York City Government: The Reemergence of Municipal Reform* (New York: Academy of Political Science, 1989)

Gerald Benjamin

Chase, Edna Woolman (*b* Asbury Park, N.J., 14 March 1877; *d* Sarasota, Fla., 20 March 1957). Magazine editor. She began working for the fashion magazine *Vogue* in 1895 and was appointed editor-in-chief in 1914 by its owner, Condé Nast. In the same year she staged a fashion show in New York City, the first in the United States. Throughout her career she made innovations in graphic design and photography, adhered to high standards in fashion, and encouraged American fashion designers. She was put in charge of all editions of the magazine in 1948 and retired in 1952. With Ilka Chase she wrote *Always in Vogue* (1954).

Mary Ellen Zuckerman

Chase, William Merritt (*b* Williamsburg, Ind., 1 Nov 1849; *d* New York City, 25 Oct 1916). Painter. After studying art in Indiana he moved to New York City in 1869, where he attended the National Academy of Design and worked in a studio at the YMCA for several years. He lived briefly in Europe but returned to the city to teach at the Art Students League and set up a number of studios, including one at 51 West 10th Street and another in the Tiffany Building. In 1893 he moved to Stuyvesant Square. He taught many students not only in the city but also at his schools on Long Island and in California and Europe, and was a president of the Society of American Artists and a prominent member of the Tile Club. Chase is best known for his still lifes.

Keith L. Bryant: *William Merritt Chase: A Genteel Bohemian* (Columbia: University of Missouri Press, 1991)

James E. Mooney

Chase Manhattan. Commercial bank formed in 1955 through the merger of the Manhattan Company and Chase National Bank. Its total resources of $7600 million made it the largest bank in New York City and the second-largest in the United States. Although the new bank was nominally governed by the charter of the Manhattan Company (written in 1799), in practice operations were managed by Chase National. A sixty-story building was designed by the firm of Skidmore, Owings and Merrill as a headquarters for the new bank; built in 1955–61 at a cost of $121 million at 1 Chase Manhattan Plaza, near Pine Street and Liberty Street, it spurred a revival of office building construction in the city's financial district. Chase Manhattan became a national bank in 1965. David Rockefeller, son of John D. Rockefeller Jr., was president of the bank from 1961 to 1969 and chairman from 1969 to 1981. One of the most influential corporate leaders of his time, he introduced electronic automation and expanded the bank's international activities. Chase helped to bring about several major projects in Manhattan during the late 1960s and early 1970s, including Madison Square Garden, New York Plaza, South Street Seaport, the World Trade Center, and Lincoln Center. In the mid 1970s inflation, the oil embargo, poor real-estate investments, and loans to developing countries caused the most severe crisis for the bank since the Depression. Although the bank recovered in the 1980s it was then overshadowed by the city's investment banks. The bank greatly expanded its global operations in these years, opening thirty international branches, eleven representative offices, and sixty-five subsidiaries in more than fifty countries. By 1990 Chase had nearly $100,000 million in assets and 231 branches in New York City, making it the fourth-largest commercial bank in the United States. At the same time a recession in the city's banking sector led to rumors of a possible consolidation with another large bank in New York City.

John Donald Wilson: *The Chase: The Chase Manhattan Bank, N.A., 1945–1985* (Boston: Harvard Business School Press, 1986)

Ann C. Gibson

Chase National Bank. Commercial bank founded in 1877 at 104 Broadway by John Thompson and named after Salmon P. Chase, secretary of the treasury under President Abraham Lincoln. After Henry W. Cannon became chairman in 1887 it moved its offices to Nassau Street and became an established correspondent bank, providing capital through short-term loans to other banks. Its growth continued under the leadership of A. Barton Hepburn, president from 1904 to 1911 and chairman from 1911 to 1917. The Chase Securities Corporation, formed in 1918, underwrote and managed large securities, which it sold to individuals and institutions from 1927; it was liquidated after the passage of the Glass–Steagall Act (1933), which prohibited commercial banks from underwriting securities. During the 1920s Chase also merged with several important banks in the city, such as the Metropolitan Bank (1851) in 1921, the Mechanics National Bank (1810) in 1926, and Equitable Trust (1902) in 1930. The merger with Equitable Trust made Chase the largest bank in the world and established its connection with the Rockefeller family: John D. Rockefeller Jr., the largest shareholder in Equitable, eventually owned nearly 4 percent of the stock in Chase. These mergers were largely the work of Albert H. Wiggin, chairman of the bank from 1911 to 1933. His reputation was sullied when investigations by the Senate Banking and Currency Committee in 1933 revealed that he and his colleagues at Chase had made a profit of $10 million during the stock market crash of 1929 by short-selling shares in their own bank. Wiggin was succeeded in 1933 by Rockefeller's brother-in-law Winthrop W. Aldrich. By 1946 Chase had more than $6000 million in assets. John J. McCloy, a businessman and government official who became chairman in 1953, introduced retail banking and engineered the formation in 1955 of Chase Manhattan Bank through a merger with the Manhattan Company, a bank with more than fifty branches in New York City.

Ann C. Gibson

Chase School of Art. Original name of the PARSONS SCHOOL OF DESIGN.

Chayefsky, Paddy [Sidney] (*b* New York City, 29 Jan 1923; *d* New York City, 1 Aug 1981). Playwright. Brought up in the Bronx, he graduated from City College and wrote realistic, intimate dramas for television. The best known of these early works was *Marty* (1953), the story of a lonely butcher in the Bronx who typified the urban working class in the 1950s. His screen adaptation of *Marty* (1955) and his scathing social satires *The Hospital* (1971) and *Network* (1975) won Academy awards for best screenplay. His stage plays *The Tenth Man* (1959), *Gideon* (1961), and *The Passion of Josef D* (1964) were all produced on Broadway.

Shaun Considine: *Mad as Hell: The Life and Work of Paddy Chayefsky* (New York: Random House, 1994)

For illustration see FILMMAKING

Sara J. Steen

Chebra Ansche Chesed. Original name of TEMPLE ANSCHE CHESED.

Chelsea (i). Neighborhood on the West Side of Manhattan (1990 pop. 41,000), bounded to the south by West 14th Street and to the west by the Hudson River. The northern and eastern boundaries are difficult to define but correspond roughly to 30th Street and 6th Avenue. A farm owned by Jacob Somerindyck and his wife covered a parcel bounded by what became 24th Street, 8th Avenue, and 21st Street, and by the Hudson River, the eastern bank of which lay along what is now 10th Avenue. The farm was bought on 16 August 1750 and named Chelsea by Thomas Clarke, a retired British army captain. It was extended to what is now 19th Street by his daughter Charity and her husband, Benjamin Moore. They opposed a plan of 1807–11 to add streets north of 14th Street and in 1813 deeded the property to their son, Clement Clarke Moore. He eventually became a developer and a faculty member of General Theological Seminary, which in 1825 accepted a site that he donated on 9th Avenue; he also donated land on 20th Street for St. Peter's Episcopal Church (1836–38). As the area was extended with landfill, leveled, and graded he sought the assistance of the builder James N. Wells in shaping the development. Deed covenants specified architectural details, lot front coverage, and setbacks, and also forbade stables, trade, and manufacturing. For the next thirty years one-family houses were built by speculators and residents, among them faculty of the seminary, building tradesmen, and merchants. A mansion was built on 9th Avenue facing the seminary by the merchant and banker Don Alonzo Cushman, who developed other properties including a row on 20th Street that was named for him. The neighborhood expanded beyond its original boundaries to include adjacent properties that had been owned by Robert Ray and Henry Eckford, and an industrial area took form along the Hudson. Ray donated land at 9th Avenue and 28th Street for the Church of the Holy Apostles (consecrated 1848), which grew out of services to immigrant children held at various locations from 1836.

In the 1820s Scottish weavers formed Paisley Place east of 7th Avenue and south of what is now 17th Street; there were also German, Italian, and British enclaves. Several Baptist, Methodist, and Presbyterian churches were formed, as were the Church of St. Vincent de Paul (by French Catholics in 1840), St. Columba Roman Catholic Church (by Irish Catholics in 1845), and Congregation Emunath Israel (1851). By 1869 a theater district extended along 23rd Street from 6th Avenue to 8th Avenue and Samuel Pike opened an opera house west of 8th Avenue. This was soon acquired by Jay Gould and Jim Fisk and renamed the Grand Opera House (Fisk's funeral was held there in 1872). About fifty persons were killed during a riot between Irish Catholics and Irish Protestants on 12 July 1871 at 8th Avenue and 24th Street. Freight handling and warehousing became important industries in the area, and the area west of 10th Avenue became the site of lumberyards, breweries, factories, rail yards, and piers. Tenements were built to accommodate workers and some houses were converted into apartments or rooming houses. In 1895 John Lovejoy Elliott formed the Hudson Guild to address the social problems of working-class residents.

About 1900 the population peaked at 85,000. Greeks developed the fur business on 7th Avenue and by 1950 were the largest group of white immigrants in the neighborhood. The theater flourished into the early twentieth century, and many performers stayed at the Chelsea Hotel. Several motion picture studios opened in the neighborhood after 1907, the most productive of which was Adolph Zukor's Famous Players (1912). The Hellenic Orthodox Community of St. Eleftherios Church (1918) was the site in 1931 of Athenagoras's enthronement as the archbishop of North and South America; later destroyed by fire, the church was rebuilt in 1976. In 1930 a block dating from the time of Clement Clarke Moore was replaced by London Terrace, a high-rise apartment complex bounded by 24th Street, 9th Avenue, 23rd Street, and 10th Avenue. A few other high-rise structures were also built, but additional plans for development were abandoned during the Depression. The announcement of the Elliott Housing Project in 1939 marked the beginning of urban renewal: although construction was delayed during the Second World War when the site was used to house a thousand members of the U.S. Coast Guard, after the war it became the first public housing project built in the city. The number of Puerto Rican immigrants increased dramatically and parts of the neighborhood became crowded. Some one-family houses remained and many townhouses were divided into apartments. The West 400 (21st–23rd) Block Association was formed in 1952 (in the mid 1990s it was the oldest continuously operating block association in the city). About 1960 the Chelsea Houses were built on a parcel bounded by 27th Street, 9th Avenue, 25th Street, and 10th Avenue, and the Robert Fulton Houses were built on 9th Avenue between 16th and 19th streets. Penn South (1962), a housing cooperative circumscribed by 29th Street, 8th Avenue, 23rd Street, and 9th Avenue, was sponsored by the International Ladies' Garment Workers' Union. The Chelsea Residence was established to allow retarded adults to live independently.

Several piers dating from the 1960s were obsolete at completion because they could not handle containerized cargo. At the same time townhouses were refurbished and the neighborhood became newly fashionable. In 1973 twenty-two rooming houses (on 22nd and 23rd streets west of 9th Avenue) were sold by Louise Gard, a major holder of such accommodations, and eventually became the Fitzroy Place cooperative apartments. Most of Moore's remaining developments were declared landmarks, but some high-rises were built in the 1980s. The neighborhood also became a center for television production. Warehouses were converted into nightclubs and restaurants replaced bodegas. Two residences for the mentally disabled were opened (St. Francis Residence II and St. Francis Residence III), as was Holy Apostles Soup Kitchen in 1982. Humanities High School was renamed in 1990 for the civil rights activist and local resident Bayard Rustin.

Samuel White Patterson: *Old Chelsea and Saint Peter's Church: The Centennial History of a New York Parish* (New York: Friebele, 1935)

Rhetta M. Arter: *Living in Chelsea: A Study of Human Relations* (New York: New York University Center for Human Relations Studies, 1954)

Robert Baral: *Turn West on 23rd: A Toast to New York's Old Chelsea* (New York: Fleet, 1965)

Hilda Regier

Chelsea (ii). Neighborhood in northwestern Staten Island, bounded to the north by South Avenue, to the east by the William T. Davis Wildlife Refuge, to the south by Meredith Avenue and Victory Boulevard, and to the west by the Arthur Kill. The area was sometimes called Prallstown after the Prall family that was granted the land in 1675, and during the American Revolution it was facetiously known as Peanutville because the villagers stored nuts for those who rode the ferries between New York and New Brunswick, New Jersey. It consists mostly of open marshland and is little developed apart from a few businesses, among them the large communications complex known as the Teleport. There are also several small pockets of older, one-family houses.

Richard M. Bayles: *History of Richmond County, Staten Island, New York* (New York: L. E. Preston, 1887)
William T. Davis: "Staten Island Names: Ye Olde Names and Nicknames," *Proceedings of the Natural Science Association of Staten Island* 5, no. 5 (1896), 20–76
Charles W. Leng and William T. Davis: *Staten Island and Its People* (New York: Lewis Historical Publishing, 1930)

John-Paul Richiuso

Chelsea Hotel. Hotel at 222 West 23rd Street in Manhattan, designed by Hubert, Pirsson and Company and opened in 1884 as an apartment building with forty units that was one of the first residential cooperatives in New York City. The building is a twelve-story brick structure with iron balconies in an eclectic Victorian style that has French and British influences. Early residents included several artists, among them Charles Melville Dewey (from 1885). The building became a hotel in 1905 and was visited by the actresses Sarah Bernhardt and Lillian Russell and the writers Mark Twain and O. Henry. In the 1930s Thomas Wolfe wrote *You Can't Go Home Again* at the hotel, and the artist John Sloan lived there. After a bankruptcy the hotel was purchased in 1939 by a group led by David Bard. It continued to attract well-known residents, including the writers James T. Farrell, Dylan Thomas, Brendan Behan, and Arthur Miller, and the composer Virgil Thomson (from 1940 until his death in 1989). Andy Warhol's film *The Chelsea Girls* (1966) was made there. The hotel now contains about 250 units ranging in size from one room to five and a half, of which at least 75 percent are occupied by permanent residents. In the lobby are displayed works by artists associated with the hotel, including Larry Rivers, André François, and Patrick Hughes. In the mid 1990s the Chelsea was managed by Stanley Bard.

Chelsea Hotel, 1994

Robert Baral: *Turn West on 23rd: A Toast to New York's Old Chelsea* (New York: Fleet, 1965)
Florence Turner: *At the Chelsea* (New York: Harcourt Brace Jovanovich, 1987)

Hilda Regier

Chemical Bank. A commercial bank formed in 1824 as a subsidiary of the New York Chemical Manufacturing Company, a maker of drugs and chemicals in Greenwich Village. It was situated first at 216 Broadway opposite St. Paul's Church, well north of most of the twelve banks then operating in the city, which were clustered around Wall Street. Chemical owed much of its early success to its second president, John Mason, a leading merchant and a founder of the New York and Harlem Railroad who served from 1831 until his death in 1839 and reduced the bank's reliance on chemical manufacturing. After Mason's death the bank was run successively until 1878 by his cousins by marriage, Isaac Jones and John Jones, who disbanded the chemical works and renewed the bank's charter in 1844. Chemical maintained a small capitalization of $300,000 and successfully built a large surplus, as a result of which it declared its first annual dividend at 6 percent in 1849. In the following year the bank moved to large headquarters at 270 Broadway at Chambers Street. Its annual dividend grew to 18 percent in 1855 and to 24 percent in 1856. The bank was instrumental in 1853 in forming the New York Clearing House, the first such organization in the United States. During the panic of 1857 it acquired the nickname "old bullion" for its policy of paying specie on demand. As the bank's reputation grew during the nineteenth century the value of its stock reached $425 a share in 1860 and $1500 a share in 1875, the highest of any bank based in New York City. The annual dividend peaked at 150 percent in 1888, a level that was maintained until 1907.

During the early twentieth century Chemical Bank continued to expand. It bought the Citizens National Bank in 1920 and opened its first branch office in 1923, at 5th Avenue and 29th Street. The first international office opened in London in 1929, and in the same year the bank converted to a state charter that enabled it to merge with the United States Mortgage Trust Company. Later Chemical acquired more than a dozen banks in New York City, including the Corn Exchange Bank Trust Company in 1954, from which it gained many additional branches, the New York Trust in 1959, operator of an extensive wholesale banking network, and Security National Bank in 1975, a leading bank on Long Island. It was one of the founding members in 1985 of the New York Cash Exchange (NYCE), an automated teller network that radically transformed consumer banking, and in 1991 it merged with Manufacturers Hanover Trust to create the second-largest bank in the United States. In the mid 1990s Chemical Bank was a multinational financial institution with more than twenty thousand employees. It was the bank of about 40 percent of all the American firms that had annual sales of $250 million or less.

History of the Chemical Bank, 1823–1913 (New York: Privately printed, 1913)

Stephen Weinstein

chemicals. As early as 1626 the chief commercial agent of the Dutch West India Company remarked on the potential in New Amsterdam for processing lime, used in the manufacture of mortar and glass. Although before 1700 most chemicals were produced and used within private households, businessmen continued to explore opportunities for commercial mineral refinement. Large naval stores used tar oil and pitch, and a number of small firms tanned hides (see Boots, shoes, and leather), produced Paints, dyes, and varnishes, refined sugar, made soap and candles (see Soap and toiletries), and operated breweries and distilleries. The noxious odors and chemical dangers that accompanied the development of the industry drove out many residents, and others demanded regulation within the city limits: tar pits were banned in 1676, as were lime-burning pits and rum distilleries in 1703. By the early eighteenth century factories produced glass, dyes, paper, potash, and linseed oil, and the city became a leading center of sugar refining, with large factories owned by John van Courtlandt, William Rhinelander, Peter Livingston, and Nicholas Bayard (who in 1730 opened a multi-story refinery on Wall Street between William and Nassau streets). Tanning was centered on "Beekman's Swamp"; tanneries as well as starch factories, breweries, tar houses, furnaces, and potteries were on the shores of the Collect. In 1744 tanning and water pits for the dressing of leather were banned from the city. The Society for the Promotion of Arts, Agriculture, and Economy was formed in 1766, and professorships in chemistry were established at King's College in 1767 and 1792.

The manufacture of fine chemicals dates to 1793, when the Schieffelin family began to mix drugs at their shop on Pearl Street; the firm remained an important manufacturer of Pharmaceuticals into the twentieth century. In 1797 restrictions were placed on the manufacture of glue, soap, and tallow. With the development of coal and petroleum destructive distillation (slow cooking in homemade ground kilns or in kettles) the production of heavy chemicals increased markedly. From 1823 alums and acids were manufactured by the New York Chemical Manufacturing Company (a forerunner of Chemical Bank); Martin Kalbfleisch opened a color works in Harlem in 1835 and later diversified into sulfuric acid, sulfates, mineral acids, and salt production at factories in Harlem and Brooklyn. New York City had 3387 chemical factories in 1850, and at the end of the century it was a leading center of production, especially of heavy industrial chemicals such as acids, bleaches, soda, potashes, alums, coal-tar products, fertilizers, wood products, and cyanide; one of few areas in which it could not compete was dyemaking, which was dominated by German concerns. Chemical and paint factories were clustered along the East River in Brooklyn and its tributary Newtown Creek, and near abattoirs, metal refineries, and other nuisance industries. But the industry was soon compelled to expand outward, first to upper Manhattan and then to outlying areas such as Hunts Point and Hudson County, New Jersey, where costs were low, restrictions on industry few, waterways deeper than Newtown Creek, riverbanks less crowded than those of the East River, and settlements sparser than those of lower Manhattan.

By the early twentieth century Manhattan had 1350 chemical plants that produced a quarter of the nation's heavy chemicals; the average plant employed fifty-two workers, and eleven plants employed more than a thousand. Rapid growth occurred in the production of such heavy chemicals as soda acids, ammonia, potash bleaching compounds, and compressed and liquified gases. Procter and Gamble erected a large facility at Port Ivory in 1907. Most of the fertilizer manufacturers moved out of Manhattan and into New Jersey. In 1922 only one in ten chemical workers in the city worked below 59th Street in twenty-nine small plants; Brooklyn and Queens had forty-three large plants. After the Second World War many chemical manufacturers set up facilities around Newark Bay and Raritan Bay, and along their linking waterways. At the same time petrochemical plastics became a major product for giant firms like Union Carbide and the Allied Chemical and Dye Corporation. In 1947 thirty-seven factories produced plastics, and it was partly because of plastics manufacturing that even as the number of chemical firms based in the city continued to decline, their total output increased: there were 1696 manufacturers in the metropolitan area in 1947 with a total value added of $88.9 million, 986 in 1963 with a value added of $794.3 million, and 685 in 1977 with a value added of $1600 million.

Several leading chemical firms retained corporate headquarters in Manhattan during the 1970s, including makers of industrial products (Air Reduction, Allied Chemical, Celanese, National Distillers and Chemical, NL Industries, Texas Gulf Sulphur, and W. R. Grace) and of consumer products (American Home Products, Bristol–Myers, Colgate–Palmolive, and Pfizer). But only four chemical firms among the five hundred largest industrial corporations in the United States remained in the city in 1990: W. R. Grace, with sales of $6100 million (food and agricultural products, industrial chemicals, videotapes, sealing compounds, plastic adhesives, paper, oil and gas field machinery, business research, and software), Quantum Chemical, with sales of $2600 million (propane, butane, and other gases, soaps and detergents, plastics and resins, polypropylene sheet and film, polyethylene and polypropylene resins, and industrial inorganic materials), Witco Chemical, with sales of $1600 million (cleaning and polishing preparations, organic plasticizers, plastics and resins, petroleum products, rubberized fabrics, filtering clays, and oils and greases), and Inspiration Resources, with sales of $1400 million (fertilizers and agricultural chemicals, herbicides and insecticides, and anhydrous ammonia).

William T. Bonner: *New York: The World's Metropolis* (New York: R. L. Polk, 1924)

C. A. Browne: "The Story of Chemistry in Old New York," (New York: American Chemical Society, 1935)

Williams Haynes: *American Chemical Industry* (New York: D. Van Nostrand, 1945–54)

David B. Sicilia

Chemists' Club. Organization formed on 29 November 1898 to promote the interests of chemists and chemistry. The first offices were at 108 West 55th Street. Under the leadership of its first president, C. F. Chandler, the club began assembling a large library. By 1901 there were 140 resident and 119 nonresident members. With financial assistance from its president Morris Loeb the club purchased new quarters at 50–54 East 41st Street in 1909 and moved there in 1911. As chemical firms after the First World War moved to midtown the club's membership greatly expanded, and came to include businessmen as well as scientists. In the mid 1990s the Chemists' Club had 2500 members and a staff of ninety.

Elizabeth J. Kramer

Chesebrough–Pond's. Firm of cosmetics manufacturers. It was formed on Sullivan Street in Brooklyn in 1870 as the Chesebrough Manufacturing Company by Robert A. Chesebrough (1837–1933), who developed Vaseline petroleum jelly in the early 1850s in his oil refinery on Delevan Street. The firm was immediately successful and in the early 1880s became part of the Standard Oil trust, opened several branches in Europe, and built headquarters on State Street in Manhattan that it retained for the next seventy-five years. After the breakup of Standard Oil in 1911 it became independent again. In 1955 it merged with Pond's Extract Company and was given its current name. Headquarters were opened on Lexington Avenue, and during the following decades the firm bought many cosmetics, perfume, and toiletry companies. Although its main offices were moved out of the city in 1972 many of its subsidiaries remained there. Chesebrough–Pond's was bought by Unilever United States in 1987.

James Bradley

chess. The first national chess tournament in the United States was the First American Chess Congress, held in New York City in 1857. The tournament was won by Paul Morphy, a twenty-year-old prodigy from New Orleans who in the following year proved himself the best player in the world by defeating European masters during a Continental tour (in Paris he played blindfolded against eight players, winning against six and drawing with two). His stunning victories greatly popularized the game in the United States and he was acclaimed on his return to New York City in 1859, but he later showed an antipathy toward the game, and after returning to New Orleans in 1860 he never again played in public. Morphy's passage through New York City invigorated a chess community that became the center of American chess for a century, attracting the nation's strongest players and many prominent émigrés, among them the next three world champions. Wilhelm Steinitz (*b* Prague, 1836), Emmanuel Lasker (*b* Berlinchen, Germany [now Barlinek, Poland], 1868) and José (Raúl) Capablanca (*b* Havana, 1888) all took up residence in New York City, although Lasker did so late in life (1937) and Capablanca did so unofficially, first as a student at Columbia University and later when

Chess players in Washington Square Park, 1991

he held a nominal position in the Cuban diplomatic service. Steinitz, recognized as the world's best player when he moved to New York City in 1883, became the first official world champion in 1886 by defeating Johannes Zukertort of Germany in a match played in New York City, St. Louis, and New Orleans.

Tournaments held in New York City in 1924 (won by Lasker) and 1927 (won by Capablanca) were probably the most important international competitions ever held in the United States. The high point of American chess was the 1930s, during which the United States won the world team championships known as the Chess Olympiads four consecutive times (1931, 1933, 1935, and 1937). Competition in the United States at the time was organized primarily through chess clubs, the most influential of which were in New York City and belonged to the Metropolitan Chess League. An annual match between the Manhattan Chess Club (uptown) and the Marshall Chess Club (downtown) in which the strongest players in the country took part was the last and most important event of the season. All the members of the four teams that won the Chess Olympiads were drawn from these two clubs: Reuben Fine, Samuel Reshevsky, Frank J. Marshall, Arthur Dake, Isaac Kashdan, Israel Horowitz, and Herman Steiner. After the Second World War the United States no longer dominated international chess, but the clubs in New York City continued to produce such prominent players as Larry Evans, William Lombardy, Robert Byrne, Donald Byrne, and most notably Bobby Fischer. After winning the World Championship in 1972 and greatly popularizing the game Fischer withdrew from public competition for two decades, eerily recalling the example of Morphy a century earlier. The 1960s and 1970s saw the development of a strong national chess federation sanctioning open tournaments throughout the country. The chess clubs lost their role as the leading organizers of the game, although the Manhattan and Marshall clubs remained exceptionally active and the city continued to attract leading players, both Americans and émigrés (especially from Russia and eastern Europe). The World Chess Federation chose New York City as the site for the first half of the World Championship Match of 1990, making it the fifth such event held there (more than in any other city except Moscow). Chess in New York City flourishes not only at the grandmaster level but also in informal settings out of doors, particularly in Washington Square Park. Matches there are often accompanied by wagering, and a few enterprising players are able to make a living at their game.

David Lawson: *Paul Morphy, the Pride and Sorrow of Chess* (New York: McKay, 1976)

Edward G. Winter, ed.: *World Chess Champions* (Elmsford, N.Y.: Pergamon, 1981)

David Hooper and Kenneth Whyld: *The Oxford Companion to Chess* (New York: Oxford University Press, 1984)

James Glass

Chickering Hall. Concert hall opened by the piano makers of the same name in November 1875 at the northwest corner of 5th Avenue and 18th Street. It was intended to compete with Steinway Hall on East 14th Street, and became well known in 1875 when Hans von Bülow played a series of piano recitals there. As fashionable society moved uptown the hall suffered from its location and in 1893 the building was remodeled into retail stores.

Marc Ferris

child labor. Child labor reformers organized on a large scale during the late nineteenth century. In 1902–3 the New York Child Labor Committee was formed by settlement house workers and reformers such as George Alger. Backed by wealthy business leaders and soon also by organized labor, scholars, and the clergy, the organization had on its staff such reformers as George Hall and Jeanie Minor. To gain the support of the public, reformers needed to destroy the prevailing notions that children required only a simple education and could build a lifetime career on work done in childhood. Another large obstacle was the esteem held for children who supported poor or ailing parents. The committee employed innovative techniques in attacking these attitudes. It conducted investigations establishing the detriment of work to children and then presented its findings to the public in flyers, leaflets, and photographs showing that child workers were defenseless, exploited, robbed of their childhood and often their lives, and limited in adulthood. Eventually persuaded of the moral and economic evil of child labor, the public supported legislative campaigns that focused on changing the law, and the child labor movement became one of the most sustained and widely supported in the city. Although far from complete, reform efforts had considerable success between 1903 and the 1930s. The age at which children could leave school was raised from fourteen to sixteen in 1935, the number of hours they could work daily and weekly was steadily reduced, and children were barred from working at night and under dangerous conditions. The laws also broadened in scope to include work not only in factories but also in stores, canneries, the home, and the street.

Adequate enforcement was difficult to achieve, and with regard to homework it was nearly impossible. There were not enough inspectors, the laws were often vague and contained loopholes, and enforcement was resisted by parents, employers, and even some public school officials seeking to reduce class size and remove disruptive students. The situation gradually improved. Machines designed for semiskilled adults took over the work previously assigned to children, and during the Depression many children lost their jobs to adults. Enforcement of existing laws became more stringent. In the late 1930s homework was reduced after it was barred in many industries by the federal government, which also banned child labor under the age of sixteen and established a minimum wage. Child labor was increasingly discouraged, as societal pres-

Jacob A. Riis, In a Sweatshop *(ca 1890), showing a twelve-year-old boy pulling basting threads*

sure mounted to educate children for individual success and a more sophisticated labor market. Violations of child labor laws in New York City increased after federal restrictions on homework were eased (while continued in the garment industry). Many of the children employed are illegal immigrants.

Jeremy Felt: *Hostages of Fortune: Child Labor Reform in New York State* (Syracuse, N.Y.: Syracuse University Press, 1965)

Irwin Yellowitz

Children's Aid Society. Philanthropic organization formed in 1853 by Charles Loring Brace. It was one of the first agencies of its kind in the United States and became well known for opening lodging houses (five for boys and one for girls) in the poorest and most populous districts of New York City. A night's lodging cost ten cents, a meal seven. The society also operated twenty-one industrial schools (six of them associated with lodging houses) where carpentry, woodworking, printing, dressmaking, laundry work, and typewriting were taught at no charge. Eventually it opened kindergartens, free reading rooms, night schools, baths, gymnasiums, and seaside vacation houses, as well as a convalescent home for sick children. It also found foster homes for about ninety thousand children in the Midwest, mainly in Michigan, Iowa, Illinois, and Wisconsin. Although a few of the children were bound to trades, most were placed with farm families, on the assumption that farmers' homes were the best place to bring up homeless orphans or outcast children (most were eventually adopted by their foster families). In the 1890s the society organized a farm school in Westchester to give older boys training in agriculture before they were sent to the farms. At his death in 1890 Brace was succeeded by his son Charles Loring Brace Jr.; together their tenures amounted to seventy-five years, during which they raised $25 million for the society.

Charles Loring Brace: *The Dangerous Classes of New York and Twenty Years' Work among Them* (New York: Wynkoop and Hallenbeck, 1872)
Children's Aid Society of New York: Its History, Plan and Results (New York: Children's Aid Society, 1893)
Emma Brace: *The Life of Charles Loring Brace, Chiefly Told in His Own Letters, Edited by His Daughter* (New York: Charles Scribner's Sons, 1894)
Charles Loring Brace Jr.: *Country Homes for Dependent Children: A Review of the Placing Out Work* (New York: Wynkoop, Hallenbeck, Crawford, 1898)
The Crusade for Children: A Review of Child Life in New York during 75 Years, 1853–1928 (New York: Children's Aid Society, 1928)

For further illustration see Riis, Jacob A.

Jane Allen

Jacob A. Riis, Children's Aid Society: Going West *(ca 1890). The last group of boys sponsored by Mrs. John Jacob Astor, posing in front of the offices of the Children's Aid Society at 24 St. Mark's Place*

children's book publishing. Until the early nineteenth century the only children's books produced in New York City were reprints of English works drawn from the popular publications of John Newbery. Amusing but moralistic fare devised from the educational precepts of John Locke was issued for a liberal Anglican audience by Hugh Gaine of Hanover Square, and William Durell of Queen Street, his chief successor. The first publisher in the city to specialize in children's books was Samuel Wood, who began operations on Pearl Street in 1806 and published *Cries of New York* (1808), which gave children a glimpse of city life. About this time engraving techniques were introduced by Alexander Anderson: these replaced clumsy woodcut and copper-plate engraving as the primary means of producing illustrations and transformed the design of children's books. Other technological advances also fostered the growth of children's literature. The country's first stereotyping plant was opened in the city by David Bruce, allowing publishers to reissue popular works without maintaining extensive supplies of type. In 1839 Joseph A. Adams, a pupil of Alexander Anderson employed by Harper and Brothers, invented a process to render multiple copies from a copper plate using engraved woodblocks. This process proved invaluable in augmenting a publisher's stock of illustrations.

During the 1840s New York City became the center of the book trade. A distinctly American style emerged in the work of F. O. C. Darley, who abandoned the custom of copying English conventions and based his style on observations of American life. Some of his best-known illustrations were those for Clement Clarke Moore's "The Night before Christmas" (1862) depicting Santa Claus in a rural landscape like those described by Washington Irving; his work became a model for other American illustrators. About the time of the Civil War the firm of R. Hoe in the city introduced the power-driven press, which greatly increased the profitability of longer prose works. The firms of Harper, Charles Scribner, G. P. Putnam, and D. Appleton soon took advantage of this form of technology to

"A Misunderstanding," by Margaret Johnson, in St. Nicholas's Baby World, *1884*

publish children's stories by distinguished writers of mature fiction, often after the stories had been serialized in such popular children's periodicals as *St. Nicholas Magazine.* Unable to compete, many small specialty publishers suffered. One such publisher, McLoughlin Brothers on Beekman Street, made important advances in illustration by adapting several color printing processes. Between 1860 and 1900 the firm introduced chromoxylography, chromolithography, and photo-engraving and helped to make popular a kind of picture book that led to other innovations in the early twentieth century. Another important publisher of children's books about the turn of the century was Grosset and Dunlap, formed in 1898.

Between 1916 and 1955 publishers in the city produced about 74 percent of the country's children's books, and their offerings often reflected a local bias. By 1926 children's departments had been set up by Harper and Brothers, Macmillan, Doubleday, Longman, E. P. Dutton, and Harcourt, Brace. More children's books were produced than in previous years, and illustrations became more sophisticated. The photo-offset process simplified color printing and refined its palette. Advanced technology and the artistic guidance of such astute editors as Louise Seaman (Bechtel) and May Massee allowed the publication of stunning picture books by Macmillan and Doubleday. In 1942 Simon and Schuster introduced a line of storybooks called Golden Books. Produced by leading writers and artists under the direction of Albert Rice Leventhal and sold for twenty-five cents each, the books attained great popularity.

Children's book publishing in the city continued to flourish after the Second World War. The partiality toward New York City characteristic of earlier children's books eventually gave way to a broader outlook. A number of leading writers and illustrators of children's books have been associated with the city, including Theodor Seuss Geisel, who contributed cartoons to the magazine *Judge* before achieving renown as Dr. Seuss, and Maurice Sendak.

Jane Bingham and Grayce Scholt: *Fifteen Centuries of Children's Literature: An Annotated Chronology of British and American Works* (Westport, Conn.: Greenwood, 1980)

Michael Joseph

Children's Museum. See Brooklyn Children's Museum.

Children's Television Workshop. Nonprofit corporation formed in 1968 by Joan Ganz Cooney and Lloyd Morrisett to develop educational television programs for children. It became especially well known for "Sesame Street," a program for two- to five-year-olds that eventually won more than fifty Emmy awards and was shown in ninety countries. The workshop also developed other television series, launched *Sesame Street Magazine*, and expanded into print and electronic educational materials, home video, and software. The offices are at 1 Lincoln Plaza in Manhattan.

Gladys Chen

Childs. Restaurant chain founded in 1889 by William and Samuel Childs. Their original self-service restaurant, on Cortlandt Street, catered mainly to office workers. The early expansion of the chain was aided by the pressure of the temperance movement against taverns. By 1916 there were more than forty outlets, typically with white tile walls to emphasize cleanliness and discourage loitering, a décor that was imitated by competitors. Childs later operated more expensive restaurants with waitress service. The flagship of the

Snuffleupagus and Big Bird with Maria (Sonia Manzano), 1991

chain, opened in 1925, was at 604 5th Avenue. In 1961 the chain was acquired by the Riese Organization, which converted the remaining Childs restaurants into fast-food outlets.

Gilbert Tauber

Childs, Richard S(pencer) (*b* Manchester, Conn., 24 May 1882; *d* Ottawa, Ont., 26 Sept 1978). Businessman and reformer. The son of William Hamlin Childs, a wealthy businessman who founded the Bon Ami Company, he moved with his family to 226 Clinton Avenue in Brooklyn in 1892, to 880 Carroll Street near Prospect Park in 1896, and to a house at 53 Prospect Park West in Park Slope in 1900. In 1912 he married Grace Pauline Hatch and moved to 8 West 9th Street in Man-

Childs, 1899

hattan. In 1909–10 he formed the Short Ballot Organization (offices at 383 4th Avenue), which sought to reduce the number of elective offices at the state, county, and municipal levels. Largely in response to his efforts toward reducing corruption in local government, the city appointed a citywide medical examiner in 1918 and a citywide sheriff and register in 1942. Childs was the president of the City Club of New York (1926–38) and chairman of Citizens Union (1941–50). He failed in 1947 to retain proportional representation for the City Council, but his advocacy of the council (or city manager) plan, which called for an appointed municipal chief executive, led Mayor Robert F. Wagner to appoint a chief administrator in 1954. In the 1960s he worked unsuccessfully to abolish the marshal system and to have local judges appointed rather than elected. He wrote *Short Ballot Principles* (1911) and *Civic Victories: The Story of an Unfinished Revolution* (1952).

Alva W. Stewart: *Richard S. Childs: His Contribution to American Local and State Government* (Monticello, Ill.: Council of Planning Librarians, 1977)

Bernard Hirschhorn

child welfare. During the eighteenth and nineteenth centuries New York City made innovative efforts to alleviate the problems of neglected and delinquent children. The New York Poorhouse, opened in 1736, was the first public institution in the city to provide care for children, who at the time constituted a large number of those living in ALMSHOUSES. In 1797 concern for the quality of care in poorhouses led to the formation of the New York City Ladies' Society for the Relief of Poor Widows with Small Children, a volunteer child-care agency. Reorganized as the Orphan Asylum Society, it established the New York Orphan Asylum (1807–19), where children received shelter until they were old enough to be apprenticed. In 1825 efforts to separate juvenile offenders from adult criminals in Bellevue Prison led to the opening of the nation's first and best-known juvenile reformatory, the House of Refuge. Although its founders John H. Griscom and Thomas Eddy envisioned a progressive, rehabilitative institution, a harsh penal attitude was soon assumed toward the juvenile inmates. Other institutions for needy children that were supported by private citizens in New York City included the Catholic Orphan Asylum, the Leake and Watts Orphan Asylum (opened in 1830–31), and the Colored Orphan Asylum (1836–63). Children and adults were housed together until nurseries opened on Randalls Island in 1848.

Having led the movement toward placing children in institutions, New York City was also a leader in removing them from congregate care and placing them in foster homes. The New York Juvenile Asylum (1851–60) sheltered children for as long as five years before placing them with families. The most important large-scale attempt to remove children from congregate institutions was that of the Children's Aid Society (1853) under the direction of Charles Loring Brace, which rescued impoverished children from the streets and placed them in foster homes in the western United States. Although the society and other groups like it were nonsectarian, their work was perceived by some as a Protestant attempt to convert young Catholic and Jewish children. It was partly in response to this perception that a number of child-care institutions were incorporated in the city under religious auspices, including the Hebrew Benevolent Society (1860) and the New York Catholic Protectory (1863). The New York Society for the Prevention of Cruelty to Children (1874) also protected children from homes that it deemed improper. Although private, it enjoyed the status of a law-enforcement agency and came to exercise a powerful influence over child welfare in New York City, and especially over the protection of neglected and abandoned children. Efforts to remove children from the almshouse altogether culminated in the Children's Law (1875), which prohibited the retention of children between three and sixteen years of age in almshouses throughout the state. The first law of its kind in the country, it led to the abolition of the nurseries on Randalls Island and contributed to the proliferation of private child-care agencies in the late nineteenth century. A direct outgrowth of the child protection movement was the establishment in New York City of the first children's court in the state (1900); reorganized as an independent tribunal by the New York City Children's Court Act (1924), it had the power to place neglected and delinquent children on probation and to refer them to diagnostic and treatment facilities.

In the early twentieth century New York City established a system under which child care services were performed by private child care agencies under contract to the city. The city also experimented with its own foster home and adoption service, the Children's Home Bureau (1916), under the auspices of the Department of Public Charities. This service failed to take hold and was discontinued in 1917 because of a prevailing belief that children were better served by private organizations. The government again took on a role in institutional and foster care when private efforts diminished during the Depression and the Second World War: the Works Progress Administration opened twenty-seven nursery schools in New York City from 1933 to 1943, which later came under the control of local child welfare agencies. The Racial Discrimination Amendment (1942) and the more stringent Brown–Isaacs Law (1952) forbade racial discrimination in agencies receiving municipal funds.

New York City continued to strengthen its child-care system during the mid twentieth century. The Citizen's Committee for Children of New York was organized in 1944 to investigate inadequate care for children whose mothers worked in war industries, and day care in the city continued to be characterized by effectiveness and activism. Although state aid to day care in the city ceased in 1947, ninety-seven centers were opened by the Day Care Council of New York City (1948), a nationally recognized body that helped to focus attention on day care and in 1961 gained the support of President John F. Kennedy. In the mid 1990s New York City was a nationally acknowledged leader in such early childhood education programs as Project Giant Step.

David M. Schneider and Albert Deutsch: *The History of Public Welfare in New York State*, vol. 2, *1867–1940* (Chicago: University of Chicago Press, 1941)

Robert H. Bremner, ed.: *Children and Youth in America: A Documentary History* (Cambridge: Harvard University Press, 1970–74)

Merril Sobie: *The Creation of Juvenile Justice: A History of New York's Children's Laws* (Albany: New York Bar Foundation, 1987)

Mary McDonald

Chinatown. Neighborhood on the Lower East Side of Manhattan (1985 pop. 70,000), covering about thirty-five blocks and bounded to the north by Kenmare and Delancey streets, to the east by Allen Street, to the south by East and Worth streets, and to the west by Broadway. The first Chinese in New York City were mostly sailors and merchants working in trade between China and the United States from 1784 to 1850; usually they remained only briefly in the city, but some took English names and married local women, and by 1850 there was a Chinese–American enclave. According to the state census of 1855 the first documented Chinese immigrant in New York City was a man who had taken the name William Brown and married an Irishwoman after moving to the city in 1825. By 1859 the *New York Times* estimated that there were 150 Chinese men living in lower Manhattan, many of whom found work as sailors, cooks, candy and cigar vendors, and operators of boarding houses catering to Asian sailors. In the 1870s the population of the neighborhood grew to more than two thousand, spurred by a violent anti-Chinese movement in the West and the completion of the transcontinental railroad (1862–69).

Prospective Chinese immigrants were prevented from settling in the United States and becoming American citizens by the Chinese Exclusion Act (1882). Chinatown began as a tiny enclave bounded by Pell and Doyer streets and including the lower portion of Mott Street. Immigration laws prevented most men from having their wives and families join them; the neighborhood became known as the "bachelor society," and the population remained below four thousand until the Second World War. Chinese immigrants

Mott Street in Chinatown, 1994

Tenements at 7–11 Mott Street in the heart of Chinatown, ca *1900*

could engage in only a few kinds of business including hand laundries, which required a small initial investment and minimal knowledge of English and in which there was no competition from other groups. About the 1890s entrepreneurs opened restaurants in the neighborhood to attract tourists; soon there were also gift shops and "temples." For aid and the resolution of disputes residents turned to traditional Chinese organizations, many of which were respectable; some fraternal ones known as tongs became embroiled in disputes over membership and gambling that sometimes became violent. In the early years of the twentieth century a series of battles between tongs became known by outsiders as the tong wars, the last of which occurred in 1924.

After China and the United States became allies in the Second World War President Franklin D. Roosevelt signed a measure in 1943 repealing the Chinese Exclusion Act, and Chinese immigrants were granted the right to become citizens. At the same time a quota for Chinese immigration was set at 105 persons a year, and Chinatown continued to grow slowly. The neighborhood was seen as a community of hard-working people who respected law and family, and outsiders called it the "gilded ghetto" and its population the "model minority." Nonetheless residents found opportunities restricted to the neighborhood, which by 1965 occupied seven blocks and had a population of twenty thousand that was still disproportionately male. During the same year legislation was introduced to abolish the system of immigration quotas based on national origin, and after 1 July 1968 twenty thousand Chinese immigrants a year were allowed to enter the United States. With the rapid growth of the Chinese community after 1965 and the easing of prejudices that had kept its housing patterns limited, Chinatown expanded beyond its traditional boundaries, absorbing much of Little Italy and parts of the Lower East Side, and becoming the most populous Chinese community in the western hemisphere. The neighborhood lost its status as the only center of the Chinese population in New York City, as Chinese settlements took root in Elmhurst, Flushing, Sunset Park, and Bay Ridge. By the 1980s only about 30 percent of all Chinese in the city lived in Chinatown. At the same time the neighborhood became ethnically more diverse: although more than three quarters of all immigrants who settled in Chinatown in the 1980s were Chinese, there were also enclaves of immigrants from other Asian countries, including Bangladesh, Burma, Vietnam, the Philippines, and Malaysia, as well as a Latin American population that was largely Dominican and Puerto Rican.

Food market in Chinatown, 1992

Peter Kwong: *The New Chinatown* (New York: Hill and Wang, 1987)

Charlie Chin

Chinese. Chinese sailors and peddlers lived in New York City as early as 1820s and 1830s, and in the 1850s about 150 sailors lived in lower Manhattan. Most planned to return to China after making a fortune, but some sought to remain in the United States. In 1868 at least ten Chinese in Manhattan had American citizenship. Although welcomed initially, Chinese by the 1860s and 1870s became targets of racism promoted by some politicians and union organizers. Mutual aid and protection societies known as *fang*, or *fong* ("house"), were organized according to kinship and geographical origin; they provided temporary lodging and financial assistance and sponsored social events, cultural festivals, and funerals. One of the first was Gongsi Fang, which remained an important institution well into the 1940s. During the 1870s many miners and railroad workers moved east to escape anti-Chinese agitation in the West, and the neighborhood in the city grew as they settled along Pell, Mott, Bayard, Doyer, and Canal streets and later on Chatham Square; the area was soon known as Chinatown. The first grocery in the neighborhood was probably the Wo Kee store, opened in 1872 at 34 Mott Street and soon followed by other groceries and by vegetable stands and fish markets. About three hundred Chinese were sent from San Francisco by James B. Harvey to replace militant Irish women employed in his Passaic Steam Laundry in Belleville, New Jersey. By the early 1880s all the Chinese workers were discharged, and many of them moved to the city to open hand laundries. Relatives joined them from the Far West, Hong Kong, and China. Chinese lived scattered throughout the city, often in quarters attached to hand laundries, and Chinatown became the headquarters for a wide range of organizations.

According to the federal census of 1890 there were 2048 Chinese in the city in the 1880s; the true figure was probably between eight and ten thousand, as immigrants often remained there only temporarily. Before the 1940s most Chinese immigrants in the city were from Guangdong (Canton) and largely preserved their customs and ethnic identity. The community adhered to traditional ethical principles, among them Confucian ideals of piety, loyalty, righteousness, and reciprocity. All important festivals were celebrated, including the lunar New Year, Qing Ming (Tomb-sweeping Day), and Mid-autumn. Dragon and lion dancing took place on every proper occasion. Chinese deities were worshipped in temples, or "joss houses" (two were built in the 1880s), and ancestor shrines were erected. A Cantonese theater opened and newsstands sold Chinese-language newspapers that provided news from China. Anti-Chinese sentiment intensified, forcing Chinese to move to Chinatown to escape discrimination. Tourism nonetheless became an important source of income for the community by the 1880s. Excluded from most occupations except those requiring cheap unskilled labor, many Chinese instead ran "chop suey" restaurants, which like laundries required little capital or knowledge of English. The Chinese also exploited American curiosity about Chinese culture aroused by the visit to New York City in 1896 of a high-ranking Chinese official, Li Hung-Chang, to promote the chop suey business. The restaurants and laundries were supplied by stores in

Stafford M. Northcote, Hi Hee Chinese Theater *(1900)*

Chinatown that imported food, clothing, and other goods from China. Souvenir shops offered items made with Chinese silk and porcelain.

Under the Chinese Exclusion acts passed by the U.S. Congress during the late nineteenth century and the early twentieth, Chinese immigrants were barred from naturalization, becoming the first ethnic group to be excluded from the United States. Many subsequently had ambiguous status and were subject to intimidation and political, social, and economic exploitation, especially if they had entered the country illegally. Clan associations of persons bearing the same surnames sponsored welfare programs and were usually dominated by wealthy merchants. Several dating from 1887 became some of the largest: Ng's Association, Loong Kung Kong Saw (formed by Liu, Guan, and Zhang), and Lee's Family Association. Organizations known as *hui guan*, or *gong suo* ("meeting halls"), were larger than clan associations and fang and were organized by persons from the same district in China. They provided medical services, cared for the elderly and the poor, built cemeteries, shipped the remains of deceased members to China, and built temples in which members performed sacrificial rites. The New York Ning Yang Hui Guan (Ning Yung Association), formed in 1890 by immigrants from Taishan (Toishan) in Guangdong, became the most powerful. Fang, clan associations, and hui guan belonged to an umbrella organization called Zhonghua Gong Suo (1883), or New York Chinese Consolidated Benevolent Association (CCBA). For many years the association was an informal local government: it acted as a liaison to other segments of American society, settled disputes among Chinese organizations, collected funds for legal expenses incurred defending the community's interests, and sponsored various social welfare programs. Its leaders were chosen by the merchant élite from the largest hui guan, alternately the Ning Yang Hui Guan and the Liancheng Gong Suo. Until the 1950s all Chinese in the metropolitan area were automatically members of the CCBA. Other influential organizations included the Chinese–American Citizens Alliance (organized by American-born Chinese), the Chinese Chamber of Commerce, and the Chinese Restaurants Association.

Chinese women were barred from joining their husbands in the United States, leading to a severe imbalance: for every Chinese fifteen-year-old girl in New York City there were forty boys in 1910, sixteen in 1920, fourteen in 1930, and nine in 1940. Many men turned to fang, which served as substitute families, and others to gambling, prostitutes, and opium, which were controlled by secret societies known as *tang*, or *tong*. During the early twentieth century the most powerful of these organizations in the city were Hip Sing and On Leong, which often fought bloody battles to exact revenge and defend their spheres of business. The "tong wars" did not end until the mid 1930s, after American authorities threatened to deport the tong leaders. Attributing their situation in American society to weakness and backwardness in China, many immigrants became active in Chinese politics. The community in New York City supported Sun Yat-sen in overthrowing the Manchu

Qing Dynasty, donating money and even returning to China to take part in the revolution, which dominated Chinese-language newspapers in the city and often split the community. The number of social organizations increased. In response to the Ning Yang Hui Guan, non-Taishan Cantonese organized the Liancheng (Lun Sing) Gong Suo in 1900, which did not admit non-Cantonese organizations until after the 1970s and even then remained predominantly Cantonese. Prominent clan associations of the early twentieth century included the Wing Chun Tong of Chan's Family Association, known as Sam Yip Gung Saw (1900), Shao Lum Gung Saw (1911), and Wong Kong Har Tong (1911). The New York Chinese Public School (Niuyue Huaqiao Gongli Xuexiao) opened in 1908 to teach children the rudiments of Chinese language and culture. Supported by tuition and donations from associations and individuals, it operated after school and on weekends and survived frequent financial crises, continuing to operate into the 1990s. The quality of its offerings was criticized, and before the 1940s wealthy merchants often sent their children to China for middle school.

Chinese in the city became increasingly active in politics. In the 1920s Chinatown became a base for Chinese seamen, who formed organizations there and sought support in their struggle for equal treatment. Fang were especially vital during the Depression and saved many Chinese from starvation. In response to the Japanese invasion of China during the 1930s Chinese in the city banded together to form the New York Overseas Chinese Anti-Japanese Salvation General Committee for Military Funds (1937), an organization of the Popular Front that cut across all clan, district, and political lines to coordinate patriotic activities. It collected money for relief and the military in China, sponsored programs exposing Japanese atrocities against the Chinese, and also sought to arouse American sympathy for the Chinese cause. A leading organization, the Chinese Hand Laundry Alliance, adopted the slogan "To Save China, to Save Ourselves" and linked the struggle against exploitation and discrimination in the United States to patriotic support for China. This campaign won the support of many Americans and helped to improve the status of the Chinese community. During the Second World War many Chinese joined the American armed forces. Thousands of Chinese seamen worked for shipping companies of the Allied countries, many losing their lives. They formed a number of organizations in the city, among them the Chinese Seamen's Patriotic Association, the Chinese Seamen's Union, and the Chinese section of the National Maritime Union. A labor shortage and an improvement in their public image also allowed many Chinese to find work in war-related industries, and in 1943 the Chinese Exclusion acts were repealed.

After the war Chinese veterans were granted legal residency and many took advantage of the GI Bill to advance their education and careers. With the passage of the War Bride Act (1945) and the GI Fiancées Act (1946) women were allowed to join their husbands, and the ratio of men to women in the Chinese community gradually stabilized. Most of the women did not speak English and provided cheap labor for garment factories, where they worked in sweatshop conditions. Many sailors settled in the city, and the population grew to include northern and eastern Chinese, among them speakers of Mandarin and Fukienese. Hand laundries declined as washers and dryers became widely available, but restaurants remained an economic mainstay, many of them specializing in the cuisines of Beijing, Hunan, Szechuan, and Shanghai. The establishment of the People's Republic of China in 1949 left thousands of Chinese students stranded in the United States. Many later settled in the metropolitan area and some later became known internationally for their professional achievements, among them T. D. Lee (*b* 1926) of Columbia University and C. N. Yang (*b* 1922) of the State University of New York at Stony Brook, who together won the Nobel Prize for physics in 1957. The American-born children of immigrants often became professionals and moved out of Chinatown.

From the mid 1960s the population grew rapidly. Immigration accelerated and families were reunited after the Immigration Act of 1965 abolished restrictions on immigration according to race. New York City became the most popular destination for Chinese immigrants because of its employment opportunities, especially in garment factories, which from the 1960s accounted for an increasing portion of the economy in Chinatown. Social agencies staffed by Chinese–Americans and financed with private, federal, state, and city funds were established to help immigrants and poor families. These facilitated integration into American society and weakened the influence of traditional organizations, which could not offer comparable services. The largest social welfare agency, the Chinatown Planning Council, provided English classes, vocational training and placement, legal assistance, and mental health services and sponsored day-care centers, youth facilities, low-income housing projects, and a senior citizens' center. Other important social agencies formed during the 1960s and 1970s included the Chinatown Manpower Project, Asian Americans for Equality, and the Asian American Legal Defense and Education Fund. As its influence declined the CCBA was criticized, especially for its policy of appointing rather than electing officials, and during the 1980s demands were made for structural reforms. English replaced Chinese as the primary language in many families and the number of interracial marriages increased.

By 1980 the Chinese community in New York City was the largest in the country, surpassing the one in San Francisco. Immigrants who settled in the city during the 1960s and 1970s were often professionals from cities but had to take unskilled jobs because they did not speak English. Chinatown in lower Manhattan expanded and other neighborhoods grew in Brooklyn and Flushing; Cantonese immigrants remained in the majority. Fashion, food, and ideas from throughout Asia were introduced, and from the late 1970s wealthy immigrants from Taiwan, Hong Kong, and Southeast Asia invested large amounts of capital in real estate and various businesses (by the mid 1990s Chinatown had twelve banks). With the influx of immigrants, overcrowding, unemployment, and crime worsened. Teenagers alienated by American culture were often recruited by the tong into gangs that fought each other and engaged in legal and illegal business and violent crime. Chinese-language newspapers and radio and cable television stations proliferated, encouraging integration while also strengthening ties to China. By the mid 1990s residents of the city read nine Chinese newspapers published daily, several more published weekly and monthly, and dozens of publications from Hong Kong, Singapore, Taiwan, and the People's Republic of China. Half a dozen movie theaters offered motion pictures from China, Taiwan, and Hong Kong. Leading cultural organizations included Chen and Dancers, the Four Seas Players, the Asian American Dance Theater, and the New York Chinatown History Project.

Renqiu Yu: *To Save China, to Save Ourselves: The Chinese Hand Laundry Alliance* (Philadelphia: Temple University Press, 1992)

Min Zhou: *Chinatown: The Socioeconomic Potential of an Urban Enclave* (Philadelphia: Temple University Press, 1992)

Renqiu Yu

Chinese Hand Laundry Alliance of New York [CHLA]. Organization formed on 23 April 1933 to protest an ordinance forcing Chinese hand laundries in New York City to cease operations. It defeated the ordinance and became the foremost agency in the struggle for the economic, political, and civil rights of Chinese laundry workers; it also helped to launch the Chinese-language newspaper *China Daily News* (1940–89). At its peak the organization had 3200 members. During the 1950s it was harassed by the Federal Bureau of Investigation for alleged ties to communism, and several members were deported. The alliance took part in the civil rights movement of the 1960s and remained in operation into the 1990s.

Renqiu Yu: *To Save China, to Save Ourselves: The Chinese Hand Laundry Alliance* (Philadelphia: Temple University Press, 1992)

Renqiu Yu

Chisholm [née St. Hill], **Shirley (Anita)** (*b* New York City, 30 Nov 1924). Congresswoman. The daughter of Quakers, she moved with her family at the age of two from Brooklyn to Barbados, her mother's native country, and remained there until the age of ten. She received her BA from Brooklyn College and an MA from Columbia University and in 1964 was elected to the state assembly as a Democrat from Bushwick and Bedford–Stuyvesant. In 1968 she became the first black woman elected to the U.S. House of Representatives. During her seven terms in office she supported legislation promoting education, employment, and the rights of Haitian refugees, served on the House Rules Committee, and was the secretary of the House Democratic Caucus. She sought the Democratic presidential nomination in 1972. Chisholm retired from Congress in 1982, owing partly to discouragement over the policies of President Ronald Reagan, and in the same year was appointed to the Purington Chair at Mount Holyoke College. She later led the National Political Congress of Black Women and was the keynote speaker at the National Women's Political Caucus. She wrote *Unbought and Unbossed* (1970) and *The Good Fight* (1973).

Barbara A. Reynolds: *And Still We Rise: Interviews with 50 Black Role Models* (Washington: USA Today Books, 1988)

Sule Greg C. Wilson

Choate, Joseph (Hodges) (*b* Salem, Mass., 24 Jan 1832; *d* New York City, 14 May 1917). Lawyer. He moved to New York City in 1855 and was a clerk for the law firm of William Evarts, where he soon became a partner. At the height of his career in the last decades of the nineteenth century he was the counsel for Standard Oil and the American Tobacco Company, and he also played a central role in the struggle by the Bell System to protect its telephone patent rights. In *Pollock v. Farmer's Trust* (1895) his emotional argument against the federal income tax persuaded the Supreme Court to void it. He was one of the most popular "club men" in the city and a favorite after-dinner speaker. He was also a founding trustee of the American Museum of Natural History and the Metropolitan Museum of Art. Known for his charm and keen intellect, Choate was for many years one of the best corporate lawyers in the nation.

Theron G. Strong: *Joseph H. Choate* (New York: Dodd, Mead, 1917)

Frederick S. Voss

Chock Full O'Nuts. Firm of coffee importers formed in 1922 by William Black (1903–83) and incorporated in 1932. It began as a retailer of coffee beans and opened a restaurant in 1933 that soon expanded into one of the first fast-food chains in the city, well known for its simple menu, low prices, and takeout counters; its headquarters were at 425 Lexington Avenue. In 1953 the firm owned twenty-five restaurants in Manhattan and two in Brooklyn and introduced a commercial brand of coffee, which became a great success in part because of a catchy advertising jingle. At the height of its growth in the 1960s and 1970s the firm owned more than 150 restaurants in the city. It concentrated increasingly on coffee in the late 1970s and in 1983 sold its remaining restaurants. It had sales of more than $250 million in 1990. In May 1994 the firm capitalized on the growing popularity of cafés in New York City by opening one on Madison Avenue. Chock Full O'Nuts has its headquarters at 370 Lexington Avenue; one of its main coffee plants is on Butler Street in Brooklyn.

James Bradley

cholera. Cholera was probably the most feared epidemic disease of the nineteenth century. It was a relative stranger to American shores until the 1830s. From that time the barrier created by the Atlantic Ocean against the spread of epidemic diseases became steadily less protective, as transatlantic steamship travel and immigration from impoverished regions of the world to the United States increased. The most serious cholera epidemics in New York City occurred in 1832 (3513 deaths), 1849 (5071 deaths), 1854 (2509 deaths), and 1866 (1137 deaths). The blame for the epidemics during these years rested too often on its victims: "intemperate" and impoverished New Yorkers in the 1830s, Irish immigrants in the 1840s and 1860s, and Jewish immigrants from eastern Europe at the close of the nineteenth century. After Robert Koch's discovery in 1883 of the etiologic agent *Vibrio cholerae*, the means by which the cholera bacterium is transmitted became better understood. The first use of cholera culture methods to prevent entry of the disease at a seaport was performed by Hermann M. Biggs and T. Mitchell Prudden on behalf of the New York City Department of Health and the New York Quarantine Station in 1887. The last cholera epidemic in New York City, in 1892, was contained to fewer than 120 deaths despite a number of political skirmishes.

Charles Rosenberg: *The Cholera Years: The United States in 1832, 1849, and 1866* (Chicago: University of Chicago Press, 1962)

John Duffy: *A History of Public Health in New York City* (New York: Russell Sage Foundation, 1968, 1974)

Howard Markel: "Layers of Separation: Epidemics and the Quarantining of East European Jewish Immigrants in New York City during 1892" (diss., Johns Hopkins University, 1994)

Howard Markel

choruses. The first choruses in New York City sang in Anglican and Episcopal churches in the late eighteenth century. The nineteenth century saw the rise of men's chamber choruses like the Mendelssohn Glee Club (1866, professional) and the University Glee Club (1894, amateur) and of such large, independent choral societies as the Oratorio Society: formed in 1873 by Leopold Damrosch, this group gave the first of many annual performances of Handel's *Messiah* at Christmas of the following year and in 1891 performed Berlioz's *Te Deum* for the opening of Carnegie Hall. Important choruses begun in the early twentieth century include the St. Cecilia Chorus (1906); the Schola Cantorum (1909–71), conducted from 1926 to 1971 by Hugh Ross; the Dessoff Choirs (1930), led from 1983 by Amy Kaiser, which originally specialized in music of the fourteenth to seventeenth centuries but later branched out into music of all periods; the Cantata Singers, formed in 1934 by Paul Boepple and active into the late 1960s; and the Collegiate Chorale, formed in 1941 by Robert Shaw at the Marble Collegiate Church. The All-City High School Chorus was organized in 1936 by P. J. Wilhousky. By mid century there were choruses ranging in size from sixteen members to two hundred, including school choruses, glee clubs, and chamber choirs, as well as professional choruses and opera choruses. The New York Choral Society was formed as an amateur chorus in 1959 by Robert DeCormier. Several chamber choruses were established from the 1960s, including amateur ensembles like the Canby Singers (led by Edward T. Canby, 1960), the Sine Nomine Singers (Harry Saltzman, 1968), the Canticum Novum Singers (Harold Rosenbaum, 1973), and the New York City Gay Men's Chorus (Gary Miller, 1980) and such professional ones as the Amor Artis Chorale (Johannes Somary, 1961), the Gregg Smith Singers (1961), the National Chorale (Martin Josman, 1969), Musica Sacra (Richard Westenburg, 1970), Melodious Accord (Alice Parker, 1984), and the New York Concert Singers (Judith Clurman, 1988). The National Choral Council was formed in 1968 by Martin Josman and others to encourage and strengthen choral singing in the city and elsewhere through performance, community service, and education; it became the sponsor of a "Messiah Sing-In" each December at Lincoln Center.

Among the notable church choirs in the city are those of St. Bartholomew's Church, the Church of the Ascension, Riverside Church, St. Patrick's Cathedral, St. Peter's Episcopal Church, St. Ignatius Loyola Church, St. Thomas Church (5th Avenue and 53rd Street), the Church of Our Saviour, First Presbyterian Church, Fifth Avenue Presbyterian Church, Church of the Incarnation (Episcopal), Marble Collegiate Church, and the Church of St. Mary the Virgin. Several churches in Manhattan have boys' choirs, including St. Thomas Church, the Church of the Transfiguration, Grace Church, and the Church of St. Luke-in-the-Fields. The Boys Choir of Harlem, formed in 1968 by Walter Turnbull, has toured throughout the world. Some churches offer concert series: "Eve-

Concert by the Choral Society at Madison Square Garden, 1883

nings with J. S. Bach" at Holy Trinity Lutheran Church, "Music for a Great Space" at the Cathedral of St. John the Divine, and "Music before 1800" at Corpus Christi Catholic Church. In addition to the permanent choruses of the Metropolitan Opera and the New York City Opera, choruses are often engaged by opera and musical theater companies in New York City through the American Guild of Musical Artists, an organization of professional choristers that includes graduates of the Juilliard School, the Manhattan School of Music, the Mannes College of Music, and Westminster Choir College (Princeton, New Jersey). Among the best-known choruses in the city are the Oratorio Society (led by Lyndon Woodside), which has about 180 members, the St. Cecilia Chorus (David Randolph, director emeritus), the New York Choral Society (John Daly Goodwin), and the Collegiate Chorale (Robert Bass). The All-City High School Chorus performs regularly under John L. Motley. In the outer boroughs most choruses are affiliated with educational institutions (for example the Brooklyn College Chorus, the Queens College Glee Club, and the Richmond Choral Society). Special events and festivals sponsored by local choruses include "Summer Sings" of the New York Choral Society, the "Messiah Sing-In" of the National Choral Council, and the "Basically Bach Festival" of Musica Sacra. Of the many performances by visiting choruses perhaps the most popular are those of the Vienna Boys Choir at Carnegie Hall.

Henry E. Krehbiel: *Notes on the Cultivation of Choral Music, and the Oratorio Society of New York* (New York: Edward Schuberth, 1884)

Henry E. Krehbiel: "American Choral Societies and Conductors," *Harper's Weekly*, 1 Feb 1890, suppl., 93–96

Arthur H. Messiter: *A History of the Choir and Music of Trinity Church* (New York: E. S. Gorham, 1906)

Anton Paul Allwardt: "Sacred Music in New York City, 1800–1850" (diss., Union Theological Seminary, 1950)

Irving Kolodin et al.: "New York," *The New Grove Dictionary of American Music*, ed. H. Wiley Hitchcock and Stanley Sadie (London: Macmillan, 1986)

Bruce C. MacIntyre

Christ Church. Episcopal church in the Bronx, built in 1866 along what is now the Henry Hudson Parkway. Its members have included the baseball player Lou Gehrig, whose funeral was held there, and Fiorello H. La Guardia, in whose honor stained-glass windows were installed.

Thomas M. Hilbink

Christian Scientists. The Christian Science Society in New York City held its first meeting on 27 November 1887. It was incorporated as the Church of Christ, Scientist, in 1888 and renamed the First Church of Christ, Scientist, in 1896. The congregation met successively in a number of buildings before moving in 1903 to a church at 96th Street and Central Park West, designed by the firm of Carrère and Hastings, that remains one of the city's finest examples of beaux-arts architecture. In 1991 the Church of Christ, Scientist, had twenty-two churches in the city.

Hugh A. S. Kennedy: *Christian Science and Organized Religion* (Los Gatos, Calif.: Farallon Foundation, 1961)

Kevin Kenny

Christie's. Auction house formed in London in 1766 by James Christie. The success of its first salesroom in New York City, opened at 520 Park Avenue in 1977, led to the addition of a second, Christie's East, at 219 East 67th Street in 1979. Several records were set at its operations in the city: the Tremaine Collection of Contemporary Art sold for $25,824,700 in 1988, the largest sum paid for the modern collection of a single owner, and in 1990 Vincent van Gogh's *Portrait of Dr. Gachet* sold for $82.5 million, the largest sum paid for any lot at auction. The salesrooms in New York City are the only ones in the United States and serve as an anchor for Christie's operations in thirteen other American cities and thirty countries.

Janet Frankston

Christodora House. Settlement house in the East Village. Founded in 1897 by the philanthropists Sara Libby Carson and Christina MacColl, it originally occupied the basement and ground floor of a tenement at 1637 Avenue B. As Russian, Polish, and Ukrainian immigrants settled in New York City in increasing numbers after the turn of the century, the settlement provided food, shelter, education, and health services to nearly five thousand residents of the area each week. In 1928 funds donated by the railroad magnate Arthur Curtis James facilitated the construction of the present building, a seventeen-story edifice at 147 Avenue B on the corner of East 9th Street. Because this was the world's tallest structure dedicated to social service, it became known as the "sky-scraper settlement house." In addition to its remarkable size it had a music school, a poet's guild, a playhouse, a gymnasium, a swimming pool, and a dining hall with a river view. George Gershwin, whose brother led the poet's guild, gave his first public performance at a recital on the third floor. Christodora House continued to serve as a social settlement until shortly after the Second World War, when it fell into disrepair. It was taken over by the city soon after. Occupied by community groups in the 1960s, it was sealed after a fire destroyed its electrical system. In 1975 it was sold at public auction for $62,500. Renovated in 1986–87 and converted into luxury condominiums, the building ironically became the target of opposition by local activists who denounced the structure as a symbol of unwanted gentrification in the neighborhood.

"A New Centre on the East Side," *New York Times*, 28 Dec 1928

Harry P. Kraus: *The Settlement House Movement in New York City, 1886–1914* (New York: Arno, 1980)

Carol von Pressentin Wright: *Blue Guide New York* (New York: W. W. Norton, 1991)

Robert Sanger Steel

Christ the King Regional High School. Catholic high school at 68-02 Metropolitan Avenue in Queens, occupying a four-story building completed in 1964 as the last of six high schools built by the diocese of Brooklyn to accommodate children born after the Second World War; it is thought to be the largest Catholic high school building in the world. Planned for three thousand students, the school originally consisted of a boys' school run by the Marist Brothers and a girls' school run by the Daughters of Wisdom. These were separated by a central block housing the library and other shared facilities. The school became coeducational in 1973 and eventually had a predominantly lay faculty. In 1992 it had about eighteen hundred students.

Gilbert Tauber

Christy, Howard Chandler (*b* Morgan County, Ohio, 10 Jan 1873; *d* New York City, 3 March 1952). Illustrator. Trained as a painter, he became known for his drawings, which appeared in periodicals such as *Harper's* and *Scribner's* and in books by James W. Riley and others. He was also the creator of an ideal female type known as the "Christy Girl" that was featured in several books of drawings, including *The American Girl as Seen and Portrayed by Howard Chandler Christy* (1906) and *The Christy Girl: Drawings by Howard Chandler Christy* (1906). About 1920 he resumed painting, executing portraits, figure subjects, and *plein air* landscapes, as well as murals for the Park Lane Hotel and the Café des Artistes. His last studio was in the Hotel des Artistes at 1 West 67th Street. Christy is recognized as one of the foremost illustrators in New York City of the early twentieth century.

Ronald G. Pisano: *The Students of William Merritt Chase* (Huntington, N.Y.: Heckscher Museum, 1973) [exhibition catalogue]

Norris F. Schneider: *Howard Chandler Christy* (Zanesville, Ohio: n.pub. [N. F. Schneider], 1975)

Howard Chandler Christy: Artist/Illustrator of Style (Allentown, Penn.: Allentown Art Museum, 1977) [exhibition catalogue]

Carol Lowrey

Chrysler Building. Art deco skyscraper at 405 Lexington Avenue, standing 1046 feet (319 meters) tall and designed by William Van Alen (1882–1954). It began as a speculative venture by William H. Reynolds, the developer of Dreamland at Coney Island. In 1927 the entire project, including leases and architectural plans, was bought by the automobile magnate Walter P. Chrysler, for whom were added such details as the decorative stainless-steel eagle heads and Chrysler radiator caps and the helmet-like top, known as the vertex. Inside the pinnacle was a private executive dining hall known as the Cloud Club; the seventy-first story, which also afforded stunning views, was set aside for a visitors' center that displayed Chrysler's first tool kit. On completion in 1930 the building was the tallest in the world (surpassed a few months later by the Empire State Building). Tube lighting illuminating the vertex at night was included in the original plans but not installed until 1981. The façade was designated a landmark in 1978, as was the lobby, known for its splendid ceiling mural and marble veneers, and the marquetry on its elevator doors.

Chrysler Building, ca 1940

Carol Willis

Church, Frederic(k) E(dwin) (*b* Hartford, Conn., 4 May 1826; *d* New York City, 7 April 1900). Painter. He studied painting in Catskill, New York, from 1844 to 1846 with Thomas Cole, who taught him to consider landscape painting as a means for expressing noble ideas. In 1847 he moved to New York City, where he worked in studios in the American Art Union building (1847–58) and in the Tenth Street Studio (1858–89); he was elected to the National Academy of Design in 1849 and to the Century Association in 1850. His aesthetic was shaped in part by the writings of John Ruskin, which encouraged artists to depict nature as a reflection of divine creation, and by the works of J. M. W. Turner, whose spectacular lighting effects he emulated. Soon he was known internationally as the foremost painter of the Hudson River School. Inspired by the German scientist Alexander von Humboldt, who urged artists to evoke cosmic truths by synthesizing art and science in depictions of nature, he traveled to South America (1853, 1857), Labrador and Newfoundland (1859), Jamaica (1865), and Europe and the Middle East (1867–68). His greatest rival was Albert Bierstadt (1830–1902), known for his detailed panoramic paintings of Western scenes, especially the Rocky Mountains. Church's reputation declined after the Civil War. Between 1867 and 1872 he designed a farmhouse in a Persian style with Calvert Vaux for Olana, a farm overlooking the Hudson River near Hudson, New York, to which he retired in 1889. Among Church's best-known paintings are *Niagara* (1857) and *Heart of the Andes* (1859). His studio is at Olana, with two thousand books, several thousand manuscripts, and more than seven hundred art works.

David C. Huntington: *The Landscapes of Frederic Edwin Church: Vision of an American Era* (New York: George Braziller, 1966)

Franklin Kelly et al.: *Frederick Edwin Church* (Washington: National Gallery of Art, 1990)

Timothy Anglin Burgard

Church Club of New York. A club formed in 1887 in Manhattan by laymen of the Episcopal Diocese of New York. Among its aims were to promote interest in the history and theology of the church and to engage in good works for the benefit of the poor in New York City. Early members included such prominent figures as Nicholas Murray Butler, J. P. Morgan, and Cornelius Vanderbilt. Membership was at first limited to white males; racial restrictions were removed in 1954 and women were admitted from 1975. Over time the club became an important meeting place, independent of clerical influence, for active Episcopal laymen from many of the churches in the city and the surrounding dioceses. It also made contributions to Episcopal theological seminaries. Although the Church Club has occasionally organized to pursue a particular aspect of church policy, more often its influence has been exerted by individual members acting in their local parishes and on diocesan committees.

James Elliott Lindsley: *The Church Club of New York: The First Hundred Years* (New York: Church Club of New York, 1994)

Chauncey G. Olinger, Jr.

churches. The first congregation in what is now New York City was the Collegiate Dutch

Reformed Church in Manhattan, formed in 1628. It eventually included Middle, Marble, West End, and Fort Washington Collegiate churches. The first house of worship, the Friends Meeting House in Flushing, was built in 1694. In 1766 the John Street Methodist Church in Manhattan was established as the first Methodist church in the United States. One of its sextons, Peter Williams, later left to form the African Methodist Episcopal church. St. Peter's, the first Roman Catholic parish, was organized in Manhattan in 1785. By 1786 the city had seventeen Protestant churches serving Presbyterians, members of the Dutch Reformed church, Episcopalians, German Lutherans, Quakers, Baptists, Methodists, and Moravians. The Abyssinian Baptist Church (1808) was the first black church in the city and became one of the most influential, later providing a political base for Adam Clayton Powell Sr. and Adam Clayton Powell Jr. After the formation of the Roman Catholic Diocese of New York in 1808 plans were made to build a cathedral on the Lower East Side. Now known as St. Patrick's Old Cathedral, this was completed in 1815 and was the bishop's see until 1879, when a new St. Patrick's Cathedral came into use (1858–77, designed by James Renwick Jr.). St. Phillip's Episcopal Church (1818) bought scores of apartments in Harlem, playing a critical role in the development of the area and becoming the country's wealthiest black congregation.

During the mid nineteenth century Gothic styles dominated church architecture, owing largely to the influence of Richard Upjohn. He designed the Church of the Ascension in Manhattan (1841, Episcopal); Christ Church in Cobble Hill (1841–42, Episcopal); the Congregational Church of Pilgrims (1844, now the Maronite Rite Roman Catholic Church of Our Lady of Lebanon), which has a piece of Plymouth Rock jutting from one wall and was the first church in the country built in a Romanesque style; the Church of the Holy Communion in Manhattan (1844–46, Catholic; now a nightclub); Trinity Church in Manhattan (1846, Episcopal); Grace Church in Brooklyn (1847, Episcopal); Trinity Chapel in Manhattan (1850–55, Episcopal; now the Serbian Orthodox Cathedral of St. Sava); St. George's Church in Flushing (1853, Episcopal); and Christ Church in the Bronx (1866, Episcopal). His most important rival was Renwick, who worked principally in the Gothic style and designed Grace Church in Manhattan (1843–45, Episcopal), Calvary Church, also in Manhattan (1847, Episcopal), the Riverdale Presbyterian Church (1863), and St. Ann's Church (1869, Episcopal). Using Gothic, Greek Revival, and Italianate styles Minard Lafever designed St. James Church in Chinatown (1835–37, Roman Catholic), the Mariner's Temple on the Lower East Side (1842, Baptist), the Church of the Savior in Brooklyn Heights (1844, now First Unitarian Church), Holy Trinity Church, also in Brooklyn Heights (1847, Episcopal), the Church of the Holy Apostles in Manhattan (1848, Episcopal), and the Strong Place Baptist Church in Cobble Hill (early 1850s, now St. Francis Cabrini Chapel).

Several churches were centers of movements for temperance, Sabbatarianism, and abolitionism. One of the best-known was the Plymouth Church in Brooklyn Heights, which under Henry Ward Beecher led campaigns against slavery from 1847. Several Eastern Orthodox congregations of Greeks, Russians, and eastern Europeans built churches from the late nineteenth century. By 1890 the city directory listed 450 churches of many denominations, including Congregationalists, Evangelicals, African Methodist Episcopalians, Reformed Presbyterians, United Presbyterians, Unitarians, Universalists, Disciples of Christ, Swedenborgians, and members of the Salvation Army. There were also churches formed by such ethnic groups as Germans, Swedes, French, French Canadians, Chinese, Italians, Latin Americans, Poles, and Irish. Storefront churches became common in some neighborhoods, often opened by charismatic preachers and belonging to no larger denomination. During the first decades of the twentieth century Bertram Grosvenor Goodhue introduced a new level of sophistication to the Gothic style in his designs for St. Thomas Church in midtown Manhattan (1909–14, Episcopal), the Church of the Intercession in Harlem (1911–14, Episcopal), the Church of St. Vincent Ferrer in Manhattan (1916–18, Roman Catholic), and St. Bartholomew's Church in midtown Manhattan (1917–19, Episcopal), which incorporated Byzantine elements.

In the mid 1990s there were about 2200 Protestant and Orthodox churches and 351 Roman Catholic churches in the city. With 40,200 members the Church of the Incarnation in Inwood was the largest Roman Catholic parish in the city; St. Patrick's Cathedral had the largest Sunday attendance, with 6900 communicants. The Concord Baptist Church of Christ in Bedford–Stuyvesant, with twelve thousand members, was the largest black congregation in the country and probably the largest Christian congregation in the city. In some neighborhoods Anglican immigrants from the West Indies enlarged Episcopal congregations that had long declined; St. Mark's Church in Crown Heights had three thousand members and was the city's largest Episcopal congregation. The largest Presbyterian church was the Fifth Avenue Presbyterian Church (2715 members). Among the few that remained devoted to a single ethnic or national group were congregations of Swedes, Norwegians, Finns, Czechs, and Hungarians. The number of Roman Catholic churches offering services in Spanish increased, and Chinese and Korean Protestant congregations were formed as well: one of the largest was the Korean Presbyterian Church of Queens in Flushing, which had eighteen hundred members. The Cathedral of St. John the Divine, the see of the Episcopal Bishop of New York, remained the largest church in the country and probably the largest cathedral in the world. Among the city's newest churches were Grace Methodist Church on West 86th Street in Manhattan and the Norwegian Seaman's Church on East 52nd Street.

Susanna A. Jones

Church of Our Lady of Mount Carmel. Roman Catholic church on East 115th Street in East Harlem. The parish was organized by Pallottine missionaries in 1884 at the behest of the Archdiocese of New York after the feast of Our Lady of Mount Carmel was celebrated by immigrants from Polla, Salerno. The basement chapel of the Romanesque church opened for baptisms on 29 November; the feast statue was placed in the main sanctuary on 23 June 1923. The church sponsors an annual celebration of the Feast of Our Lady of Mount Carmel on 16 July, which draws among its celebrants immigrants from Latin America and the Caribbean.

Robert Anthony Orsi: *The Madonna of 115th Street: Faith and Community in Italian Harlem, 1880–1930* (New Haven: Yale University Press, 1985)

Mary Elizabeth Brown

Church of Our Lady of Pompeii. Roman Catholic church at 25 Carmine Street in Manhattan. A chapel was opened for a new parish on 8 May 1892 by Pietro Bandini, chaplain of the Society of St. Raphael for the Protection of Italian Immigrants. From 1897 to 1926 the congregation met at the Church of St. Benedict the Moor, which was demolished during the widening of 6th Avenue. The current building, modeled after southern Italian churches, contains a church (dedicated 27 October 1928), a school (opened 1930), and a convent. The plaza in front honors Antonio Demo, pastor from 1899 to 1933.

Constantino Sassi: *Parrochia della Madonna di Pompei in New York: Notizie storiche dei primi cinquant' anni dalla sua fondazione, 1892–1942* (Rome: Santa Lucia, 1946)

Michael Consenza: *Church of Our Lady of Pompeii in Greenwich Village: History of the Parish, 1892–1967* (New York: Parish of Our Lady of Pompeii, 1967)

Mary Elizabeth Brown: *From Italian Villages to Greenwich Village: Our Lady of Pompei, 1892–1992* (New York: Center for Migration Studies, 1992)

Mary Elizabeth Brown

Church of St. Ann and the Holy Trinity. Episcopal church in Brooklyn, incorporated in 1787. In the nineteenth century it became a national center of the Low Church movement in American Episcopalianism, and it supported missionary work, Sunday schools, bible classes, an orphanage, and societies to help educate poor children. In 1869 it moved to a Gothic Revival church (Clinton and Livingston streets), designed by the firm of Renwick and Sands, which was sold by the congregation in 1969 to the Packer Collegiate Institute after St. Ann's merged with the Church of the Holy Trinity. From that time the congregation met in the neo-Gothic Church of the Holy Trinity (1847) at Montague and Clinton streets. It established a school and a performing arts center that became known nationally. In the mid 1990s it continued to support both institutions and had organized the restoration of the Church of the Holy Trinity.

Peter J. Wosh

Church of St. Anthony of Padua. Roman Catholic church at 153–57 Sullivan Street in Manhattan. The first efforts to form a parish for Italians in the area were made in 1858, and in 1866 Franciscans of the Province of the Immaculate Conception were invited to the archdiocese by John McCloskey and reorganized the parish. The current Romanesque church was dedicated on 10 June 1888. The church sponsors a feast honoring its patron saint on 13 June. Father Fagan Park on 6th Avenue is named for a member of its clergy who died while leading others to safety during a fire at a monastery on 4 November 1938.

Souvenir of the Golden Jubilee: Saint Anthony of Padua School, 1874–1924 (New York: Parish of St. Anthony of Padua, 1924)

Mary Elizabeth Brown

Church of St. Benedict the Moor. Roman Catholic church. It was formed by black parishioners in 1883 at the former Third Universalist Church, a building in a Greek Revival style on Bleecker and Dowling streets that closed on 1 May 1898. The building was demolished in 1927 to widen 6th Avenue. The parish reconvened on 20 November 1898 at the former Second Evangelical Church, a Corinthian building at 320 West 53rd Street. On 28 February 1954 members of the clergy from the Franciscan Third Order Regular opened a ministry for Latin Americans at St. Benedict's. A number of black nuns from the community of the Handmaids of the Most Pure Heart of Mary formed a convent and day nursery of St. Benedict uptown, which eventually moved to 34 West 134th Street.

Jorge Coll: *Una iglesia pionera: Ensayo histórico sobre la parroquia de San Benito de Palermo, en la ciudad de Nueva York, EE.UU. de America* (New York: Privately printed, 1989)

Mary Elizabeth Brown

Church of St. Luke-in-the-Fields. Episcopal parish church on Hudson Street in the West Village, between Christopher and Barrow streets. It occupies the third-oldest church building still in use in Manhattan. The congregation was formed in 1820 by a group including Clement Clarke Moore, who served as the first warden and helped design the building, a simple, rectangular, late Federal brick version of an English village church with a tower at the eastern end. The building opened in 1822; extensions in Gothic style were added on the south side in 1859 and the north side in 1875. Throughout its history the church has emphasized service to a changing community and the liturgical piety of the Anglican High Church tradition. In the 1840s its rector John Murray Forbes helped to introduce the principles of the Oxford Movement in New York City, and in 1847 it was the site of one of the first professions of monastic vows in the Episcopal church. From 1911 until the Second World War Edward Schlueter, serving a working-class neighborhood dependent on the docks of the Hudson River, redesigned the sanctuary in high medieval style and developed programs and summer camps for local children. Under the leadership of Ledlie Laughlin the parish became independent in 1976 and expanded its community programs. A fire in 1981 gutted the building; rebuilt after a fund-raising campaign, the church reopened in 1985. The interior design by Hardy, Holtzman, Pfeiffer Associates restored much of the lost simplicity of the original Federal style while evoking other features of the old church with graceful restraint.

H. Crosswell Tuttle: *History of Saint Luke's Church in the City of New York, 1820–1920* (New York: Appeal Printing Company, 1926)

Donald F. M. Gerardi

Church of St. Mary the Virgin. Episcopal parish church at 145 West 46th Street, near Times Square. The congregation was formed in 1868 by Thomas McKee Brown under a state law allowing religious organizations to incorporate and remain self-governing. Affiliated from the outset with the Episcopal Diocese of New York, it emphasized the Catholic tradition of rituals and music in Anglicanism. Its church building became known as the "Mother Church of Anglo-Catholicism" and informally as "Smokey Mary's" because incense was often used during services. The congregation moved into its present building in 1895. During the 1970s the church took part in the liturgical renewal that inspired a revision of the Book of Common Prayer in 1979. St. Mary's also became known for its neighborhood ministries in the 1980s and early 1990s.

Newbury Frost Read: *The Story of St. Mary's* (New York: Privately printed, 1931)

J. Robert Wright

Church of St. Peter. Roman Catholic church organized in 1785. Its first parishioners included Elizabeth Ann Bayley Seton, Pierre Toussaint, and representatives of the Spanish Crown. The current church, dedicated in February 1838, stands at 18 Barclay Street. The parish was one of those touched by the antebellum trustee controversies, and from 1800 to 1940 it operated the nation's first free parochial school. The congregation was largely Irish in the 1880s, Polish and Ruthenian in the 1920s; eventually many parishioners worked in the area but did not live there. The congregation was almost nonexistent in the 1960s but grew as it attracted new members among residents of Battery Park City.

Leo Raymond Ryan: *Old Saint Peter's: The Mother Church of Catholic New York (1785–1935)* (New York: United States Catholic Historical Society, 1935)

St. Peter's Church: The Oldest Catholic Parish in New York State (New York: Parish of St. Peter, n.d. [?1985])

Mary Elizabeth Brown

Church of St. Vincent Ferrer. Roman Catholic church at Lexington Avenue and 66th Street. The parish was formed in 1867; the third church to house it was designed in a French Gothic Revival style by Bertram Grosvenor Goodhue, who considered it his best work. Its dedication on 5 May 1918 was the occasion for performances by the New York Symphony Orchestra and a chorus of the Metropolitan Opera. Oil paintings by Telford Paullin and Ethel Paullin depict the Stations of the Cross. There is also a statue of the Fatima Madonna by Thomas McGlynn, which became the prototype for a well-known statue in Portugal.

Richard Oliver: *Bertram Grosvenor Goodhue* (New York: Architectural History Foundation, 1982)

Thomas E. Bird

Church of the Holy Apostles. Episcopal parish church formed in 1844 at 9th Avenue and 28th Street in Manhattan. In 1848 it moved into its current building, designed in an Italian Tuscanate style by William Maynard LeFevre and soon known for its stained-glass windows by William Jay Bolton and John Bolton, brothers widely considered the first stained-glass makers in the United States. Extensions designed by Richard Upjohn in the 1850s were added to the transepts and sanctuary. A stronghold of abolitionism, the church became a station on the Underground Railroad before the Civil War. It opened a soup kitchen in 1982 that by the end of 1990 had served 1,535,754 meals and was the largest facility of its kind in the city: the day after a devastating fire destroyed much of the church on 9 April 1990, the kitchen served 943 cold meals by candlelight.

Lucius A. Edelblute: *The History of the Church of the Holy Apostles (Protestant Episcopal), 1844–1944* (New York: Privately printed, 1944)

J. Robert Wright

Church of the Holy Communion. Episcopal church at 6th Avenue and 20th

Street, formed by W. A. Muhlenberg in 1844 as a "free" church, or one in which pew rents were abolished. It was noted both for its service to the community and for practices in worship that were unusual for the Episcopal church in the nineteenth century: daily prayer, weekly Eucharist, lighted candles, antiphonal chanting, and altar flowers. In the mid 1970s it formed a united parish with Calvary Church and St. George's Episcopal Church; the building is now used for nonreligious purposes.

Robert Bruce Mullin

Church of the Most Holy Redeemer. Roman Catholic church at 173 East 3rd Street in Manhattan. It was founded in 1844 on 3rd Avenue as a German national parish by the Redemptorists. A school staffed by the School Sisters of Notre Dame opened in the same year and Gabriel Rumpler was appointed the first pastor by Archbishop John Hughes. A new church was dedicated in 1851. As a result of the changing ethnic composition of the area in which it is situated, the church by the mid 1990s ministered principally to Latin American Catholics.

Margaret M. McGuinness

Church of the Most Holy Trinity. German Catholic Church founded in 1841 on Montrose Avenue in Williamsburgh. The parish was formed by John Stephen Raffeiner to serve the area's growing German population, and the first church building was erected in 1841. In 1853 a larger church was built on an adjacent lot to house the growing congregation and to provide a parish for the Sisters of St. Dominic (from Regensburg, Germany). Parishioners and clergymen formed the Orphan Home Society (1861) and St. Catherine's Hospital (1868) on Bushwick Avenue. A third church, a large Gothic cathedral, was built in 1885. Membership declined along with the German population of the neighborhood after the turn of the century. Many Latin Americans joined the church in the 1960s, and in 1981 the Franciscan Friars took over the administration of the parish.

Bernadette McCauley

Church of the Transfiguration (i). Roman Catholic church at 29 Mott Street in Manhattan, known as the English Lutheran First Church of Zion when it was built in 1801. It was purchased in 1853 for $30,000 by John McClellan and his congregation, who at the time occupied a church at 45 Chambers Street formerly known as the Dutch Reformed Presbyterian Church. Profits from the sale of their old church helped to retire the debts incurred by the parish, which consisted mainly of poor Irish immigrants from the Five Points. More than a thousand students attended a girls' school run by St. Elizabeth Seton's Sisters of Charity that opened at the church in 1856 (where one of the teachers was Mother Cabrini), and a boys' school run by the Christian Brothers that opened in 1857 (where one of the students was Patrick Hayes, later a cardinal). In the 1890s the Irish leaders in the parish relegated the more than eight thousand Italian immigrants to a basement congregation. Tensions between the Irish and the Italians in the parish remained strong until 1902, when Ernest Coppo arrived from Italy with a group of Salesian priests, took over as pastor, and moved the Italians upstairs.

Coppo also established a Chinese mission at the church to minister to the more than two thousand Chinese who lived nearby. From the 1920s to the 1950s the parish thrived as a central institution in Little Italy and Chinatown; Jimmy Durante belonged to the church as a youth and the opera singer Enrico Caruso was known to attend services. In the 1940s Francis Cardinal Spellman assigned the church to the Maryknoll Fathers, an order that had served in China, and in the 1950s the parish added masses with sermons in Cantonese. The archdiocese took over the administration of the church in 1975 and in 1976 named Mark Cheung as its first Chinese pastor. In the mid 1990s the Church of the Transfiguration remained an important institution in Chinatown.

Edward T. O'Donnell

Lich Gate (designed by Frederick Clarke Withers), Church of the Transfiguration (ii)

Church of the Transfiguration (ii). Church on 29th Street near 5th Avenue, and one of the first Anglo-Catholic parishes of the Episcopal church. Formed in 1848, it became known as the Little Church around the Corner. The church was a station of the Underground Railroad and a refuge for blacks during the Civil War. Well-known members who took part in the abolitionist movement were the mother of Theodore Roosevelt and G. H. Houghton, a rector who in 1863 repelled white lynch mobs by brandishing a cross. The outline of the present neo-Gothic building was completed by 1864; notable features include the Lich Gate (1896) and the Mortuary Chapel (1908). In 1988 the interior was refurbished and a new organ was built by the firm of C. B. Fisk. The Church of the Transfiguration is the headquarters of the Episcopal Actors' Guild and has the oldest boys' choir in the city, formed in 1881. It is also a popular site for weddings.

J. H. Randolph Ray: *My Little Church around the Corner* (New York: Simon and Schuster, 1957)

J. Robert Wright

Cigar Makers' International Union. Labor union organized in 1864 by Czech, German, and Hungarian immigrants in New York City who sought to protect their cigar shops from sweeping industrial changes. The United Cigarmakers joined the union as Local 144 in 1875, at a time when innovations such as molds, bunching machines, and suction tables threatened the hand-rolled cigar industry. Weakened by a series of costly strikes in its formative years (1869, 1873, and 1877), the union was reorganized by Samuel Gompers and Adolph Strasser (both from Local 144), who introduced financial and administrative reforms associated with the "new model" unions of Great Britain. Its longtime rivalry with the Progressive Cigarmakers culminated in the formation of the American Federation of Labor; it absorbed the Progressive Cigarmakers in 1886, the year its membership in New York City reached eight thousand (almost one third of the union's total). In 1900 continued technological innovation caused fears of job displacement and triggered many strikes. Women in the industry gained recognition during the strikes and were encouraged with lowered initiation fees to join the union in 1915. Cigar makers during the interwar years began to move from union enclaves such as New York City to other parts of the United States, and national membership in the union fell from forty thousand in 1919 to seven thousand in 1940. The union left New York City after the Second World War.

Norman Ware: *The Labor Movement in the United States, 1860–1895: A Study in Democracy* (New York: D. Appleton, 1929)
Willis Nissley Baer: *Economic Development of the Cigar Industry in the United States* (Lancaster, Penn.: Art Printing, 1933)
Patricia Cooper: *Once a Cigar Maker: Men, Women and Work Culture in American Cigar Factories, 1900–1919* (Urbana: University of Illinois Press, 1987)

See also KNIGHTS OF LABOR, DISTRICT ASSEMBLY 49.

Ronald Mendel

CIO. See CONGRESS OF INDUSTRIAL ORGANIZATIONS.

Circle in the Square. Theater company formed by the producer and director Theodore Mann and the director José Quintero in 1951. Early on it was known for its acclaimed productions of such commercially unsuccessful plays as Tennessee Williams's *Summer and Smoke* (1952) and Eugene O'Neill's *The Iceman Cometh* (1956). Among the many prominent actors who launched their careers at the theater are Geraldine Page, Jason Robards, George C. Scott, and Colleen Dewhurst. In 1972 Circle in the Square moved from Bleecker Street to a theater seating 682 on West 50th Street and became the first nonprofit theater on Broadway.

Robert Hatch: *Circle in the Square* (New York: Horizon, 1960)

See also THEATER, §6.

D. S. Moynihan

Circle Line. Excursion boat line formed in 1945 by Francis J. Barry (1906–86) through the merger of several earlier lines. From a pier at West 43rd Street its boats originally circled Manhattan Island clockwise; the direction was later changed to counterclockwise. Tour guides point out historic and architectural landmarks and the residences of well-known figures. In 1962 the Circle Line acquired the Hudson River Day Line. The Circle Line runs from mid March until the end of December and carries about 590,000 passengers a year.

George A. Thompson, Jr.

circuses. New York City became a favored destination of circus acts during colonial times because of its large population. A live lion was exhibited there as early as May 1728. In the decades after the American Revolution the city was one of few cities in the United States where leisure pursuits were not prohibited for moral reasons. The first circus was probably that of the Englishman John Bill Ricketts, which ran from 7 August 1793 until 4 November and returned five more times by 1799. An elephant, the first in the country, was shown in 1796. Exhibitions were mounted several times by the team of Victor Pépin and John Breschard between 1808 and 1813 and by the Englishman James West between 1817 and 1822. Seeking to eliminate competition from him, two theater producers bought out West and engaged the first bareback rider, James Hunter, who made his début in New York City in 1823. These circuses and a few others, most of them managed by Europeans, performed for weeks or months in temporary buildings and at such pleasure gardens as Vauxhall, Niblo's Garden, and one at Richmond Hill (as early as 1823). By the late 1820s there were a dozen or more circuses and many traveling shows, most operated by Americans. The introduction of tents made circuses less dependent on long engagements in cities. Several menageries toured the country, and in the 1830s they became able to move wagonloads of caged animals and tenting equipment daily, leading to important changes in the circus business. In late 1834 there were nine such menageries in the country, and these merged to form the Zoological Institute, which made its headquarters at 37 Bowery. An exhibition hall fifty by 225 feet (fifteen by seventy meters) was built there and saw many performances by Isaac Van Amburgh, one of the country's first wild-animal trainers. In 1835 the institute controlled all thirteen American touring menageries and merged several with circuses, leaving only five touring circuses still independent. In a rigged stock sale the institute raised $329,325 from 123 investors but

Aerial performers in the Big Apple Circus, 1990

Ringling Brothers and Barnum & Bailey Circus at Madison Square Garden, 1933

was forced to declare bankruptcy during the panic of 1837.

Various theaters, exhibition halls, and vacant lots were sites of one-ring circuses that competed with each other annually in the city until after the Civil War. From the winter of 1838–39 the hall at 37 Bowery was known as the Bowery Amphitheatre, a major venue for circuses and exhibitions until it was refitted as the Stadt Theatre in 1854. Franconi's Hippodrome, an impressive canvas-covered building modeled after the Hippodrome in Paris by Aldridge Winham Jr., occupied two acres (eighty ares) at Broadway and 23rd Street. For two seasons in 1853 and 1854 circus acts and opulent spectacles competed with races of chariots, ostriches, and ponies ridden by monkeys; several acts were imported from Europe by American showmen. On 8 February 1864 an iron structure known as the Hippotheatron opened on 14th Street between 3rd and 4th avenues, opposite the Academy of Music; it was 110 feet (thirty-four meters) in diameter with a dome seventy-five feet (twenty-three meters) high and had steam heat. The facility was taken over in the autumn of 1865 by Lewis B. Lent, manager of the New York Circus. During the following summer he added a large false front to the building and covered it with pictures of circus entertainments. He also made space under the tiered seats to exhibit animals and curiosities. From 1866 to 1876 he ran Lent's New York Circus, one of the first to travel cross country by rail. The building was bought in 1872 by P. T. Barnum, who moved his circus there in November, and was destroyed by fire on 24 December, as was the entire circus except for two elephants.

The following years saw the mergers of several large circuses. In the autumn of 1873 Barnum leased land formerly used by the New York and Harlem Railroad between Madison and 4th avenues at 26th and 27th streets. There he erected the New York Hippodrome, which measured two hundred by 425 feet (sixty by 130 meters), and presented his circus from 27 April 1874 to 1 August, 2 November to 27 February 1875, and 29 March to 10 April. Known as Gilmore's Garden during the late 1870s, the building was also used by other circuses including that of James Cooper and James A. Bailey, and renamed Madison Square Garden in May 1879 by the new owner, Cornelius Vanderbilt. Barnum's circus was sometimes held at the American Institute at 63rd Street and 3rd Avenue. In 1881 it merged with Bailey's circus to form a three-ring circus that was introduced at Madison Square Garden and in the following years dominated the circus business in the city. The building was replaced in 1890 with another of the same name that was the venue of the Adam Forepaugh–Sells Brothers Circus (owned by Bailey) while Barnum and Bailey toured Europe from 1898 to 1902; the new building was demolished in 1925. In 1905 another structure called the New York Hippodrome was erected at 6th Avenue between 43rd and 44th streets. After Bailey's death from an insect bite at Madison Square Garden in 1906, Barnum and Bailey was sold to the Ringling brothers in 1907; in 1909 it opened in Chicago and the Ringling circus was moved to Madison Square Garden. The shows combined in 1919 to form the Ringling Brothers and Barnum & Bailey Circus, the performances of which in New York City became associated with the arrival of spring.

Ringling Brothers enjoyed a virtual monopoly in the city. Cole Brothers, which featured the animal trainer Clyde Beatty, opened for only one season in New York City, appearing for three weeks at the New York Hippodrome in 1937. As the Clyde Beatty–Cole Brothers Circus it opened at the New York Coliseum in late 1962, an unsuccessful engagement that coincided with a 114-day strike of newspaper workers. After that time it usually held its spring opening at the Commack Arena on Long Island. After abandoning the canvas big top in 1956 in favor of arenas, Ringling Brothers no longer opened its season at Madison Square Garden, but its springtime engagement in the city still remained the longest of the season, averaging six weeks or more. As part of a Soviet–American exchange program the Moscow Circus performed at the Felt Forum in September 1963 and in later years. An important innovation in the style of American circuses was the Big Apple Circus. Conceived by Paul Binder as the nonprofit New York School for Circus Arts, it was modeled on European one-ring circuses and supported mostly by local philanthropists. It opened under canvas at Battery Park on 20 July 1977 and in the following years toured the city and other sites in the Northeast; it appeared under canvas on 4 December 1981 at Damrosch Park near Lincoln Center, which became the site of an annual engagement that gradually lengthened to more than two months during the holiday season. By the 1980s Ringling Brothers and Barnum & Bailey shortened its engagement at Madison Square Garden in favor of appearances at several suburban arenas in the metropolitan area.

George C. D. Odell: *Annals of the New York Stage* (New York: Columbia University Press, 1927–49)

George Speaight: *The History of the Circus* (San Diego: A. S. Barnes, 1980)

Richard W. Flint

Citibank. The largest commercial bank in the United States, formed by a group of merchants in New York City on 14 September 1812 as a state-chartered institution called the City Bank of New York. Its name was changed successively to National City Bank of New York (1865, after the bank joined the national banking system), First National City Bank of New York (1955, after a merger with the First National Bank of the City of New York), First National City Bank (1962), and Citibank (1976). A holding company, First National City Corporation, was formed in 1968 with the bank as its principal subsidiary; it became known as Citicorp in 1974. The headquarters of the bank remained for almost a century at 52 Wall Street before moving in 1908 to 55 Wall Street (previously the Merchants' Exchange and the U.S. Custom House), then in 1961 to 399 Park Avenue. Citicorp Center, containing additional offices, opened in 1977 at Lexington Avenue and 53rd Street.

The first president of the bank, Colonel Samuel Osgood (1812–13), had been the first postmaster general of the United States, a naval officer of the Port of New York, and a director of the Bank of the Manhattan Company. Isaac Wright, the fifth president (1827–32), was the founder of the Black Ball Shipping Line, which provided the first regularly scheduled sailing routes between New York City and Liverpool. After the panic of 1837 control of the bank passed to Moses Taylor, who as a director and then as the president of the bank (1856–82) took a comprehensive approach to finance, offering a full range of commercial and investment banking services, and stressed liquidity, or "ready money," for commodity merchants. Under the leadership of James Stillman (1891–1918) the bank grew from a small commercial institution into the largest bank in the United States. During the panic of 1893 its reputation for safety attracted the deposits of leading corporations, and the bank also became a major underwriter of securities for American business. Frank A. Vanderlip (1909–19), whom Stillman had chosen as his successor, formed the National City Company, which sold foreign and domestic bonds to retail customers. As president of the bank from 1921 to 1933 Charles E. Mitchell expanded on Vanderlip's strategy of diversification. He increased the number of local branches, offered compound interest, and extended personal loans to small depositors. From 1927 the National City Company sold common stocks to its customers, using the world's largest private telegraph line, and in 1929 the Farmers Loan and Trust Company became part of the bank, which now offered trust services nationwide.

The Depression led to a drastic reversal of the bank's fortunes. A planned merger with the Corn Exchange Bank collapsed. The bank also had political problems: the chief counsel of the Senate Banking Committee, Ferdinand Pecora, blamed the bank and Mitchell in particular for the stock market crash, and Mitchell resigned on 26 February 1933. The Glass–Steagall Act separated commercial and investment banking and forced the liquidation of the National City Company. A need for funds in the late 1950s led to the development in 1961 by Walter B. Wriston of the negotiable certificate of deposit, a financial instrument that allowed the bank to enter a highly competitive market for funds and expand its assets. As its president (1967–70) and then chairman (1970–84) Wriston transformed the bank into a global financial services institution. The bank expanded its businesses across state lines and emphasized consumer products as regulatory barriers fell. It was the first bank to introduce automatic teller machines (1978) and became a national leader in credit cards, student loans, and home mortgages. In response to the oil shocks of the 1970s it led other banks to "recycle" petrodollars (using excess funds deposited by Arab oil-producing nations by extending loans to the third world, primarily Latin America), and after the government of Mexico defaulted on its loans in August 1982 it organized an effort to restructure these loans. Wriston was succeeded as the chairman of Citibank by John S. Reed, who had streamlined the back office of bank and led its consumer bank to profitability. In the early 1990s Citibank remained by far the largest American banking institution, with operations in thirty-two states and the District of Columbia and ninety-two countries, and assets of well over $210,000 million.

Harold van B. Cleveland and Thomas F. Huertas: *Citibank, 1812–1970* (Cambridge: Harvard University Press, 1985)

Joan L. Silverman

Citicorp Building. A forty-eight-story skyscraper, 663 feet (202.2 meters) tall, at 44th Drive and 45th Avenue in Hunter's Point, Queens. Designed by the firm of Skidmore, Owings and Merrill and built in 1989, it provides backup office space for the Citicorp Center across the East River, which is one subway stop away. The Citicorp Building is taller than any other building in Queens, Brooklyn, or Long Island.

Citicorp Center. A skyscraper between 53rd and 54th streets on the east side of Lexington Avenue; at the northern end the base of the building extends as far east as 3rd Avenue. Designed by Hugh Stubbins with Emery Roth and Sons and completed in 1977, it has a height of 915 feet (279 meters) and is the third-tallest building in midtown Manhattan. The building is a sleekly modern aluminum and glass tower in the shape of a square column, entirely supported at its base by four stilt-like pillars 127 feet (38.7 meters) tall that are centered on each side. The asymmetrical roof is stepped and steeply sloped on its southern face; a sunken plaza functions as an entrance to the lower level and to the subway. Originally the building was intended to have apartments on the upper stories, each with a southern terrace, but the plan was abandoned when a request for a zoning variance was denied. A later proposal that the slanted face of the roof be used for solar energy collectors went unrealized into the 1990s. The Citicorp Center is arguably the most dramatic skyscraper built after the Second World War.

John Tauranac

Citicorp Center, Lexington Avenue and 53rd Street, 1994

Citizens Budget Commission. Civic association formed during the fiscal crisis of 1932 to advocate low taxes, efficiency, and tight controls over the finances of New York City. It was sponsored by such large taxpayers as real-estate owners in Manhattan, banks, and large retail and wholesale businesses, but sought to appeal to all citizens, especially homeowners. The commission's staff publishes information about the city's revenues, borrowing, expenditures, and operations, testifies at city hearings, and often advises municipal officials. Among the best-known leaders of the Citizens Budget Commission have been the real-estate attorney Peter Grimm, the Republican leader Harold Riegelman, the budget analyst Herbert J. Ranschberg, and the professor of business Raymond Horton, who was its president in the early 1990s.

Wallace S. Sayre and Herbert Kaufman: *Governing New York City* (New York: Russell Sage Foundation, 1960), 505–8

David C. Hammack

Citizens Committee for Children. Nonprofit membership organization devoted to child advocacy. It was formed in New York City in 1944 by a group of citizens that included Eleanor Roosevelt, who were prompted to act after investigating day-care facilities in the city for children whose mothers worked in war industries. The group now works to reinforce child services offered by public and private agencies.

Mary McDonald

Citizens' Housing and Planning Council. An organization formed as the Citizens' Housing Council in 1937 by Harold S. Buttenheim, editor of the *American City*, to unite the many constituencies for housing reform and development in New York City, formulate and analyze housing policy, and support housing legislation. Its members included bankers, representatives of construction, real-estate, and other businesses, architects, engineers, labor and tenant leaders, and social workers. The council's early studies of how housing was affected by tax policy and rent control filled gaps in existing research and were published as a report called *Housing the Metropolis* in 1938. From 1941 it published a *Legislative Information Bulletin* that tracked and evaluated bills related to housing and community development. *A Housing Program for New York City* (1945) forecast the supply of housing that the city would need after the war and proposed financing and administrative means to achieve it. The council assumed its current name in 1948. In the following decades it analyzed public housing management (1958), offered an approach to neighborhood conservation (1962), gave an overview of the property market in the city (1975), and predicted financial difficulties in Mitchell–Lama housing (1977). In the report *On Its Own: New York City Approaches Affordable Housing* (1985) the council evaluated the effects of the federal government's virtual withdrawal from the production of subsidized housing, and outlined actions that the city might undertake to address its still-urgent need for affordable dwellings. Its later reports included *The Challenge and the Change* (1989) and *Preserving New York's Low-Income Housing Stock* (1992). The council relies heavily on the technical and political expertise of its board of directors, which in 1989 consisted largely of development executives (from both profit-making and nonprofit ventures), lawyers, and bankers.

Rosalie Genevro

Citizens Union. Civic association. It began as a political party formed on 22 February 1897 by Elihu Root and 164 other prominent citizens to oppose Tammany Hall in the first municipal election after consolidation; R. Fulton Cutting was its first chairman (to 1908). The organization was committed to separating municipal elections from those at the state and national levels. Forming clubs in various districts in the city, it declined to join with local Republicans to nominate fusion candidates in the mayoral election of 1897, naming instead an independent ticket led by Seth Low, then the president of Columbia University. Low lost the election but won in 1901 after the union agreed to a slate of fusion candidates. By 1908 patronage seekers were infiltrating the party, and it became a nonpartisan civic organization. Now at 198 Broadway, Citizens Union evaluates candidates for local office, publishes an annual voters' directory, and monitors city legislation, as well as state legislation affecting New York City. It advocates the selection of judges based on merit, reforms in campaign finance and election law, and other legislative reforms to improve governmental efficiency and integrity. Among those who have served as its chairman are William Jay Schieffelin (1909–41), Richard S. Childs (1941–50), Milton M. Bergerman (1950–70), and Robert B. McKay (1971–77), Terence H. Benbow (1977–83), Malcolm MacKay (1983–86), and Robert F. Wagner (1986–93).

"The Citizens Union, 1897–1919," *Searchlight* 9, no. 6 (1919), 10–13, 16

Walter Tallmadge Arndt: "A Quarter Century of the Citizens Union: A Chapter in the Political History of New York City," *Searchlight* 12, no. 4 (1922), 3–22, 24

Richard S. Childs: "75 Years of Citizens Union," *Across from City Hall: Citizens Union News* 27, no. 6 (1973), 1–7

Bernard Hirschhorn

City and Suburban Homes. Firm of real-estate developers formed in 1896, specializing in limited-profit housing projects for low-income workers. It built model apartments on West 68th and 69th streets (now demolished), using a design by Ernest Flagg that had won a competition in 1896. In 1898 it engaged James E. Ware to adapt his own design, which had won second prize in the same competition, as the plan for a housing project in Manhattan, the First Avenue Estate, which eventually occupied sites at 1168–90 1st Avenue, 1194–1200 1st Avenue, 401–29 East 64th Street, and 402–30 East 65th Street. Refinements were later made by Phillip H. Ohm, who with Percy Griffin and the firm of Harde and Short was engaged to design the Avenue A Estate at 1470–92 Avenue A, 501–31 East 78th Street, and 502–28 East 79th Street; this was the largest housing project of its kind from its completion in 1913 until the 1930s. City and Suburban Homes continued to build model apartments in the city until shortly after the Second World War. Its most successful ventures became the basis for many other housing developments, including those built by the federal government from the 1930s. The First Avenue Estate and the Avenue A Estate were designated city landmarks in 1990. A portion of the estates was later stripped of its landmark designation by the Board of Estimate at the request of Peter Kalikow, who owned the site and wished to build luxury apartment buildings there. In 1993 the courts overturned the action of the Board of Estimate, restoring landmark designation to the entire complex.

Eric Wm. Allison

City Bank of New York. Bank formed in 1812 that eventually became known as Citibank.

City Center of Music and Drama. A concert hall at 131 West 55th Street in Manhattan, dedicated in 1924 as the Mecca Temple by the Ancient and Accepted Order of Nobles of the Mystic Shrine, or Shriners. After a foreclosure on the hall Mayor Fiorello H. La Guardia and the producer Jean Dalrymple saved it from demolition in 1943 and purchased it for the city; it reopened on 11 December with a concert by the New York Philharmonic. City Center was the first performing arts center in the United States that could legitimately claim to be a people's arts center. It offered dramatic, musical, and dance performances at ticket prices of no more than $2. In its early years the hall was the home of the City Center Opera Company (later the New York City Opera) and the New York City Ballet, both of which encouraged American performers, composers, and choreographers. The City Center Orchestra was conducted by such figures as Leopold Stokowski and Leonard Bernstein during its relatively brief existence, and actors such as Gertrude Lawrence and Orson Welles appeared at the hall in theatrical productions. After the opening of the New York State Theater at Lincoln Center in 1966 the New York City Opera and the New York City Ballet left the City Center, which continued to stage various cultural events.

Martin Sokol: *The New York City Opera: An American Adventure* (New York: Macmillan, 1981)

Barbara L. Tischler

City Club. An organization formed in 1892 to promote social interaction among men interested in efficient city government and the election of "fit persons" to municipal office. The management of the affairs of the club and the political campaigns that it sponsored were traditionally in different hands. The club publishes an annual report as well as books and pamphlets on such diverse subjects as rapid transit, bridges, public charities, the water supply, the school calendar, the police department, and the city charter.

James E. Mooney

City College of New York. College of the City University of New York, formed in 1847 by citywide referendum as the Free Academy. First housed in a building at 17 Lexington Avenue, the school offered a pre-freshman year and four years of liberal arts instruction by five faculty members, and was administered by a president. It conferred its first baccalaureate degrees in 1853 and took its current name in 1866. In addition to offering higher education the college administered the élite Townshend Harris High School. The student body consisted in the early years largely of German Jews and by the turn of the century of Russian Jews, and attendance at the college soon came to be regarded as a means of escaping the poverty of the Lower East Side. Jews accounted for three fourths of the students by 1903 and for at least four fifths during the 1920s and 1930s. In 1907 construction was completed on a new campus of thirty-five acres (fourteen hectares) at 138th Street and Convent Avenue, designed in a neo-Gothic style and built of Manhattan schist excavated during the digging of subway tunnels, with a trim of white terra cotta. An amphitheater carved into the slopes of upper Manhattan was given to the college in 1915 by the mining magnate Adolph Lewisohn and named Lewisohn Stadium (demolished 1973).

City College became known for academic excellence after the First World War, and enrollment increased sharply, reaching the unprecedented level of 32,030 in October 1929. To ease the strain on facilities, campuses were set up in Brooklyn and Queens that later became Brooklyn College and Queens College. In the early 1930s the college emerged as a leader in collegiate basketball, and in 1950 it became the first school to win both the National Invitational Tournament and the championship of the National Collegiate Athletic Association; these achievements were tarnished in the following year when several players were found to have been guilty of "point shaving" (deliberately reducing the margin of victory in a game to accommodate bettors). Between the 1930s and the 1950s the student body also became known for its leftist sympathies, and many socialist, communist, and Trotskyist groups were formed on the campus (see Communism). As the school improved its reputation it increased the minimum high school average required for admission, from sixty in 1928 to eighty-eight in 1941. In 1961 the school became a part of the

City College (designed by George B. Post), ca *1910.* Right *assembly hall*

City University of New York, which in 1970 instituted a controversial policy of open admissions that guaranteed a place in the university system to every graduate of a high school in New York City. In 1976 the city imposed tuition fees for the first time.

After decades of expansion the school added five professional schools: the School of Architecture, the School of Nursing, the School of Engineering, the School of Education, and the Sophie Davis School of Biomedical Education. It completed a performing arts center called Aaron Davis Hall in 1979 and the North Academic Center in 1984, a facility costing $125 million and housing laboratories, classrooms, and the largest library in the university system. In part because of open admissions the college's student body by the 1980s began to the reflect the city's ethnic diversity: in 1992 blacks accounted for almost 38.7 percent of the undergraduate student body, Latin Americans for 25.5 percent, Asians for 16 percent, whites for 12.7 percent, and American Indians for less than 0.4 percent (6.7 percent did not respond). In the spring of 1991 the college enrolled 10,124 degree and nondegree undergraduate students and 2322 degree and nondegree graduate students. It was the center of controversy in the early 1990s, when the administration removed from the chairmanship of its black studies department the professor Leonard Jeffries, who had espoused bizarre racial theories in the classroom and in an interview made remarks about Jews and Italians that were regarded as disparaging. The removal was later overturned in court and Jeffries was awarded damages. Well-known alumni of City College include the financier Bernard Baruch (1889), the novelist Upton Sinclair (1897), Senator Robert F. Wagner (1898), Justice Felix Frankfurter (1902), the actor Edward G. Robinson (1914), the lyricist Ira Gershwin (1918), the historian Lewis Mumford (1918), the labor leader A. Philip Randolph (1919), the physician Jonas E. Salk (1934), the politicians Edward I. Koch (1945) and Herman Badillo (1951), General Colin L. Powell (1958), and eight Nobel laureates, the most from any public college.

Solomon Willis Rudy: *The College of the City of New York: A History, 1847–1947* (New York: City College Press, 1949; repr. Arno, 1977)

Louis G. Heller: *Death of the American University, with Special Reference to the Collapse of City College* (New Rochelle, N.Y.: Arlington House, 1973)

Marc Ferris

City Council. The legislative branch of municipal government. The first charter after consolidation provided for a bicameral legislature called the Municipal Assembly, but this was abandoned in 1901 in favor of a Board of Aldermen that initially had one member from each of seventy-three districts who served two-year terms. The number of districts was reduced to sixty-seven in 1916 and sixty-five in 1921. Several charter reforms were undertaken to strengthen the council, which in 1936 was reshaped into a single house based on proportional representation. Between the elections of 1937 and 1945 the size of the membership varied from twenty-six in 1937 and 1941 to seventeen in 1943. Proportional representation was abandoned in 1949, when the council became a body of twenty-five members, elected one to a district by majority vote. Charter revisions effective in 1963 called for ten more members, two elected at large from each borough: to promote pluralism in a body that was overwhelmingly Democratic, it was stipulated that in each borough the at-large members must not be drawn from the same party. For many years City Council districts were coextensive with state assembly districts and later with state senate districts: when the boundaries of assembly districts were redrawn in the early 1960s in compliance with a decision by the U.S. Supreme Court to apply the doctrine of "one man, one vote" to state legislatures, the city increased the number of council districts to twenty-seven in time for the municipal elections of 1965.

After a state law established the New York City Health and Hospitals Corporation, the council was required to appoint five of the sixteen members of the board. Council seats were reapportioned after the federal census of 1970, and in 1973 elections were held for thirty-three districts. The amended boundaries were successfully challenged in court, leading to federally mandated elections using a new set of boundaries in 1974. In the following year the council was required to approve several appointments that had previously been made at the mayor's discretion. The elections scheduled for 1981 required redistricting based on figures from the census of 1980. The boundaries drawn by the council were found to violate the Voting Rights Act (1966) because they reduced the representation of racial minorities, and the elections were postponed until 1982 while new boundaries were drawn: the number of districts was increased to thirty-five, benefiting racial minorities and incumbents. The ten at-large seats were ruled

Presidents of the Board of Aldermen (1898–1937) and City Council (1938–93)

Randolph Guggenheimer 1898–1901
Charles V. Fornes 1902–5
Patrick McGowan 1906–9
John Purroy Mitchel 1910–13
George McAneny 1914–16
Frank L. Dowling 1917
Alfred E. Smith 1918
Robert L. Moran 1919
Fiorello H. La Guardia 1920–21
Murray Hulbert 1922–24
William T. Collins 1925
Joseph V. McKee 1926–33
Bernard S. Deutsch 1934–35
Timothy J. Sullivan 1936
William F. Brunner 1937
Newbold Morris 1938–45
Vincent R. Impellitteri 1946–49
Joseph T. Sharkey 1950
Rudolph Halley 1951–53
Abe Stark 1954–61
Paul R. Screvane 1962–65
Frank D. O'Connor 1966–70
Sanford D. Garelik 1971–73
Paul O'Dwyer 1974–77
Carol Bellamy 1978–85
Andrew J. Stein 1986–93

Compiled by James Bradley

unconstitutional because they violated the principle of "one man, one vote," and no new at-large members were elected in 1981 or 1982; the seats were abolished by referendum in 1983. Elections were held for all thirty-five district seats in 1985 and 1989. Charter reforms passed in 1989 increased the size of the council to fifty-one in 1992 and abolished the Board of Estimate, leaving the council with sole legislative authority over the operating and capital budgets; authority over zoning and land use also was transferred to the council, from the Board of Estimate.

Elections for the fifty-one district seats were held in November 1991 based on district boundaries drawn using data from the census of 1990. In 1993 council members were first elected to four-year terms. Despite reforms the council remained weak in the mid 1990s. Its authority was limited because it shared power with the mayor, who could veto most local laws, and because state laws took precedence over local ones. Only the council's oversight and investigative powers were extensive: it could appoint special committees with full investigative powers, and its standing committees could investigate the operations of the executive branch related to their jurisdiction. But few investigations were undertaken, despite repeated charges of inefficiency and corruption. The council attracted few capable members because of its limited powers, and its lackluster record prevented reformers from granting it more powers. The choice of candidates was strongly influenced by party leaders (especially Democrats, who dominated the council), and the mayor easily obtained the council's approval for various measures by using patronage and executive powers.

The president of the City Council was elected citywide and stood next in the line of succession to the mayor's office until 1993–94, when as a result of the charter revisions of 1989 the office was replaced by that of the public advocate. The public advocate also was given the responsibility of presiding over the council and serving as a member ex officio of all its committees, but with greatly reduced powers because of the newly enlarged role of the council's speaker.

Wallace Sayre and Herbert Kaufman: *Governing New York City: Politics in the Metropolis* (New York: Russell Sage Foundation, 1960)

Frank J. Mauro and Gerald Benjamin, eds.: *Restructuring the New York City Government: The Reemergence of Municipal Reform* (New York: Academy of Political Science, 1989)

Charles Brecher

city directories. City and business directories served an important function for consumers and commercial establishments before the advent of the telephone, and they remain valuable tools for research. In 1786 David C. Franks published the first list of heads of households, homemakers, and businesses in New York City, a slim volume containing 856 entries. Franks issued only one more directory; others were issued by the printing firm of Hodge, Allen, and Campbell between 1789 and 1792 and by William Duncan between 1792 and 1795. When Duncan left the directory business David Longworth and his son Thomas published the first of forty-five editions of their *American Almanac, New-York Register, and City Directory*. Although not a formal census, the almanac was intended to provide a comprehensive listing of the primary consumer in each household. Each issue included an alphabetical listing of the names, occupations, and addresses of the city's "heads of households" (mostly men), "homemakers" (mostly widows and women who owned their own businesses), and business partnerships, as well as lists of judges, politicians, ministers, and fraternal organizations. Canvassing and cataloguing began each year on 1 May, the date traditionally known as Moving Day. After several rival printers attempted to enter the trade David Longworth increased his revenues in 1813 by inserting a small advertising section in the front of his directory. He complained ceaselessly about the difficulties of the directory business, and in particular about those who borrowed copies of the book without paying for them, swindlers who pocketed advertising revenues by masquerading as his agents, allegedly plagiarized editions published in 1811, 1812, and 1813 by the firm of Elliot and Chrissy, and residents who refused to give their names accurately to avoid tax collectors, military service, or jury duty (he once likened the task of canvassing to "pulling teeth without the use of ether"). After Thomas Longworth retired in 1841 directories were published until 1849 by John Doggett Jr., the first printer to interleave pages of advertising with those containing listings. During the 1850s three companies competed for the market; John F. Trow emerged dominant in 1860.

The *Brooklyn City Directory* was first issued in 1822 by Alden Spooner, who continued as its publisher for seven years; between 1832 and 1860 seven firms published the directory, along with a separate street guide and business directory. Later directories of Brooklyn were published by J. Lain and Company (from 1861), the Lain and Healy Company (from 1892), and George Uppington (from 1900). Trow introduced a number of changes in the format of the city directory. When advertising revenues fell during the Civil War he responded by selling advertisements on the borders of pages. Directory publishing became the principal focus of his firm, which he renamed the Trow City Directory Company in 1871. He also published a street guide, a directory of partnerships, and *Wilson's Business Directory*, which was organized according to occupation or service and was less important as a guide than as an outlet for advertising.

The spread of telephones about the turn of the century slowly rendered city and business directories redundant. In 1898 the publishers of the nation's directories organized into the American Association of Directory Publishers in an effort to stem the decline. By 1900 Trow branched into the package delivery and message business, and he published his last directory of Manhattan in 1913. Ralph L. Polk, a directory magnate from Detroit, bought out Trow's publishing interests in 1915 and continued to issue directories under Trow's name after consolidating the city directory, the street guide, and the directories of businesses and partnerships into one volume. The city directory of Manhattan appeared sporadically during the 1920s. The last was published in 1932 by the Emergency Unemployment Relief Committee.

City Directories of the United States, 1860–1901 (Woodbridge, Conn.: Research Publications, 1984)

Marc Ferris

city halls. A tavern facing Coenties Slip on Pearl Street was the center of colonial administration for New Amsterdam and became the first city hall on 6 February 1653. Administrative offices were moved on 14 October 1703 to a building on Wall Street, which saw the trial of John Peter Zenger for libel (1735) and meetings of the Stamp Act Congress (1765) and the Continental Congress (1785); it was

Entrance to City Hall facing City Hall Park, ca *1905*

remodeled in 1788 by Pierre L'Enfant (for illustrations see FEDERAL HALL). On 4 October 1802 the city announced plans for a new building near what is now the intersection of Broadway and Park Row designed by John McComb Jr. and Joseph François Mangin. One of the most prominent structures of its time, it was set in a park and had a marble exterior, a dome, a rotunda, and a cupola affording spectacular views of the surrounding countryside. At its completion in 1812 offices and legislative and judicial chambers were moved there and the former city hall on Wall Street was demolished. During festivities in 1858 celebrating a demonstration of a transatlantic cable, the cupola, dome, and rotunda were set on fire by fireworks launched from the roof; reconstruction was supervised by Leopold Eidlitz. The body of President Lincoln lay in state there for a few days during the funeral procession from Washington to Illinois. All judicial offices were moved elsewhere by the time of consolidation in 1898, and from that time the building was used by the mayor and the city legislature solely for offices and legislative chambers. The interior was restored between 1907 and 1918 by Grosvenor Atterbury: the Governor's Room, among his most representative works, has furniture from the Federal period and a portrait collection that includes many works by John Trumbull.

William L. Lebovich: *America's City Halls* (Washington: Preservation Press, 1984)

Mary Beth Betts

City Hospital (Center at Elmhurst). Hospital that later became ELMHURST MEDICAL HOSPITAL.

City Housing Corporation. Limited-profit corporation formed in 1924 by members of the Regional Planning Association of America to put into practice their theories of planning and housing design. It sponsored the construction between 1924 and 1928 of Sunnyside Gardens in Queens, which spanned twelve contiguous city blocks and provided affordable housing for 1202 families. The innovative features of Sunnyside Gardens included common ownership of shared courtyards and the mixing in the same development of different types of buildings and apartments and different forms of ownership. The corporation also sponsored the building of Radburn Garden City in New Jersey.

Clarence S. Stein: *Toward New Towns for America* (Cambridge: MIT Press, 1951)
Carl Sussman, ed.: *Planning the Fourth Migration: The Neglected Vision of the Regional Planning Association of America* (Cambridge: MIT Press, 1976)

Michael Kwartler

City Island. An island in the northeastern Bronx and the site of a neighborhood of the same name. Nearly a mile and three quarters (three kilometers) long at its longest point, the island is connected at its northern end by a bridge to the mainland but is separated from the nearest residential area there by the expanse of Pelham Bay Park, and because of its isolation the neighborhood has retained much the feel of a village in New England. At the northeastern tip is a causeway connecting the island to High Island, an uninhabited island of three acres (1.2 hectares). The island was called Minnewits by the local Indians and Minneford Island by the British, and received its current name only after it was purchased on behalf of a syndicate in 1761 by Benjamin Palmer, who saw the island as a potential commercial rival to New York City. Although his plans were thwarted with the onset of the American Revolution, local residents earned an income from fishing and clamming, and from 1830 the Solar Salt Works retrieved salt from evaporated seawater. In the late nineteenth century and the early twentieth many marine pilots lived on the island, boarding steamships from New England to guide them through the treacherous waters of Hell Gate to Manhattan. The island also became a center for building yachts, and several financiers and industrialists anchored their boats there. In the twentieth century City Island became a center for boat building and sailmaking. Landing craft were manufactured during the Second World War, and after the war five yachts designed at the island won the America's Cup. The island also became a summer resort of rented cottages and summer homes. Minneford Shipyard, the last boatyard on the island, closed in 1982, but sailmakers and other maritime businesses continued to flourish. City Island Avenue, the main street, has seafood restaurants and marinas along with antique shops, boutiques, and the North Wind Undersea Institute, a marine museum. Most residents live in one-family houses, although there are also some condominiums.

Lloyd Ultan: *The Beautiful Bronx, 1920–1950* (New Rochelle, N.Y.: Arlington House, 1979)
John McNamara: *McNamara's Old Bronx* (New York: Bronx County Historical Society, 1989)

Lloyd Ultan

City Line. Neighborhood in east central Brooklyn, bounded to the north by Atlantic Avenue, to the east by the border with Queens County, and to the south and west by North Conduit Boulevard. It was named before Brooklyn was incorporated into New York City. In 1943 residents erected a war memorial by private subscription at Liberty Avenue and Eldert Lane. Once Italian and Irish, the population became predominantly Latin American, with some residents from the Caribbean and Guyana. Just north of the area at Grant and McKinley avenues stands St. Sylvester's Roman Catholic Church, where services are given in both Spanish and English; it is an important community center. Liberty Avenue is the main commercial district (the City Line Cinema once stood there). One- and two-family houses predominate but there are also several small apartment buildings.

Ellen Marie Snyder-Grenier

Citymeals-on-Wheels. Charitable program launched in 1981 in New York City by the writers Gael Greene, James Beard, and Barbara Kafka to supplement Meals-on-Wheels, a federal program offering five hot meals a week to the homebound elderly. It raises more than $4 million a year to provide hot meals on weekends and holidays and in emergencies for about nine thousand homebound elderly residents. The program is funded privately and overseen by the city's department for the aging.

Alana J. Erickson

City of New York v. State of New York. Case decided in 1990 (76 N.Y. 2d 479) by the New York State Court of Appeals, which sustained a state law authorizing a referendum of voters in Staten Island to determine whether they wished to create a commission to draft a charter making Staten Island an independent city. Noting that the referendum would not actually authorize secession or commit the state to support secession, the court held that the referendum would not violate the city's home rule. In the referendum, conducted in November 1990, the charter commission proposal was supported by 82 percent of the borough's voters.

Richard Briffault

city planning. City planning in colonial New York City consisted of little more than satisfying such needs as providing for defense, regulating port activities, and isolating noxious industry. A more comprehensive approach was taken during the nineteenth century to accommodate rapid growth of the population (from sixty thousand to half a million during the first half of the century) and commerce. The government devised a visionary plan based on efficient transport and on uniform, easily marketable parcels of property: it laid out a comprehensive street grid, installed a citywide water system, built Central Park, and passed legislation regulating tenements and allowing the city to build a rapid transit system. Calls to increase the role of government followed from tremendous growth of the population and economy during the late nineteenth century, and on consolidation in 1898 responsibility for city planning was divided among the borough presidents, the municipal legislature (consisting of the Board of Aldermen and the Board of Estimate and Apportionment), and the mayor. Among the most important jurisdictions was street mapping and park planning (only about 40 percent of the city was mapped at the time); this was overseen by the borough presidents and subject to approval by the Board of Estimate. The legislature was granted authority over investments in the infrastructure, purchases of land for public use, and such matters as building and housing codes; the mayor supervised the agencies responsible for delivering services and enforcing codes.

By the turn of the century progressives led by George McAneny identified planning as a vital element of municipal reform. Inspired by the architecture of the World's Columbian Exposition in Chicago in 1893, they urged that the downtown should be modernized under the direction of a nonpartisan, expert municipal commission responsible for developing a master plan and a capital budget. They persuaded the Board of Aldermen to appoint a citizens' advisory group that would draft a plan to beautify streets and parks, and secured the passage of state legislation that gave the city jurisdiction over local planning and zoning.

At the same time, pressure mounted to regulate land use more strictly, owing to the proliferation of enormous skyscrapers in lower Manhattan and to conflicts between the garment industry in midtown and exclusive stores nearby on 5th Avenue. At McAneny's urging the Board of Estimate formed two committees to deal with these matters. Each was directed by McAneney and composed of the borough presidents, had a paid staff, and established citizens' advisory commissions. The first, the Commission on the Heights of Buildings, submitted its *Report of the Heights of Buildings Commission to the Committee on Heights, Size and Arrangement of Buildings* to the Board of Estimate within a year and disbanded. It described serious problems caused by uncontrolled growth and recommended expanding the police power for ZONING, an idea inspired by legislation limiting the height of buildings in other American cities and by the German practice of restricting land use. The second group, the Committee on the City Plan, addressed the issues of zoning, transit, ports and terminals, recreation, civic architecture, and the city map. In its report to the Board of Estimate in 1914, *Development and Present Status of City Planning in New York*, it called for a permanent planning commission patterned on those in twenty other cities including Baltimore and Hartford, Connecticut. Under the committee's supervision the Commission on Building Districts and Restrictions was formed to draft a zoning code for the city. Based on a broad legal framework conceived by Edward M. Bassett, the code divided the city into districts for residential, commercial, and unrestricted use and regulated building density to provide for adequate light and air; the code was adopted as law by the Board of Estimate in 1916. The requirement that skyscrapers be built with setbacks soon altered the skyline of Manhattan, as needle-like towers such as the Chrysler and Empire State buildings defined the prevailing style in commercial architecture. The Committee on the City Plan reviewed almost fifty subjects for the Board of Estimate, functioning essentially as a planning commission. It nonetheless failed to become a separate agency for lack of political support, especially among the borough presidents, who feared that their power would be usurped.

Several other public and private agencies carried out their own planning efforts. The Russell Sage Foundation sponsored a model housing community known as Forest Hills Gardens in 1911; this was followed by Sunnyside Gardens, a similar but smaller community built by the City Housing Corporation, a limited-dividend company. In 1921 the Port of New York Authority was formed to plan and operate regional transportation. During the 1920s the Russell Sage Foundation funded an ambitious initiative for the city and the twenty-two counties around it. Published as *The Regional Plan for New York and Its Environs*, the plan focused on transportation, open space, and the relations between the city and its suburbs. Many of its recommendations, especially for highways and regional parks, were implemented in the following decades.

In the wake of the *Regional Plan* the campaign to establish a permanent planning commission resumed, and at the insistence of such advocates as McAneny and Bassett, Mayor James J. Walker formed the City Committee on Plan and Survey. Noting that Chicago had allotted more than $300 million to carry out its plan of 1909, the committee made recommendations that led in 1930 to the appointment of a planning commissioner supported by a planning department and a nine-member citizens' advisory board. One of the commissioner's first tasks was to draw up a master plan for reviewing capital programs (his own power in this regard was weak). In 1932 both the commissioner's position and the department were eliminated as the city descended into fiscal crisis.

At the urging of planning advocates, Mayor Fiorello H. La Guardia in 1934 formed the Mayor's Committee on City Planning. With funds from the Works Progress Administration the group conducted real-estate surveys, amended the zoning ordinance, drafted a new street plan, and mounted a large exhibition on city planning at the Russell Sage Foundation. More important, it made certain that city planning was a central issue in the charter revision of 1935. Under the new charter, approved in 1936, a permanent planning commission was formed to draw up a master plan and the capital budget, maintain the official map, and oversee the zoning ordinance. The commission had seven members (six appointed by the mayor in addition to the chief engineer of the Board of Estimate, who served ex officio) and several mandates, and its chairman oversaw a city planning department of twenty-seven members. Each borough president was given the power to appoint a citizens' advisory board on land use. Mayor La Guardia appointed as the first chairman Rexford Tugwell, an advisor to President Franklin D. Roosevelt. Among the other commissioners were Vernon Moon, chief engineer of the Board of Estimate; Cleveland Rogers, editor of the *Brooklyn Daily Eagle*; the architect Edwin A. Salmon; Arthur V. Sheridan, chief engineer of the Bronx; and Lawrence Orton, secretary of the Regional Plan Association, who served for four terms until 1969. Initially the commission focused on the zoning ordinance of 1916, which it brought up to date by strengthening protection for districts with one-family housing and reclassifying unrestricted areas for retail, business, or manufacturing. In response to pressure for development and new ideas about providing affordable housing, the commission revamped sections of the street system. One result was that the grid was eliminated in the layout of the area in the Bronx that became Parkchester, a housing development built by the Metropolitan Life Insurance Company.

During these years the commission began to draw up a master plan, and by 1941 it announced plans for slum clearance, low-cost housing, parks, transportation, and education. The most controversial element was the land use scheme, which addressed the flight of the middle class to the suburbs. Relying heavily on contemporary theories and methods and on census data, it assumed that the population would stay virtually unchanged at 7.3 million and focused on placing residents near their places of work. To accomplish this it recommended reclaiming blighted areas for residential use, building high-density housing developments near parks and riverfronts and low-density ones beyond transit lines, and establishing business districts at transport hubs; it also sought to increase the amount of open space from 29,000 to 76,000 acres (11,745 to 30,780 hectares), allowing for "greenbelts" separating incompatible districts and for a reserve surrounding Jamaica Bay.

The plan was unveiled in 1940 before an audience of five hundred civic and political leaders at Hunter College and met almost immediately with criticism. The most outspoken opponent was the city's parks commissioner, Robert Moses, who according to the *New York Times* dismissed the plan as "ivory tower, theoretical planning" that was "silly, fantastic and irresponsible" and its architects as "itinerant carpetbag experts." Despite approval from other quarters the commission never adopted the plan and within months Tugwell resigned. Moses promptly arranged for his own appointment to the commission, where he remained a dominant figure for eighteen years. During his tenure he blocked the notion of comprehensive planning and led the commission to focus instead on specific projects and the zoning ordinance. As the city's construction coordinator and the head of the Mayor's Committee on Slum Clearance he also directed the city's efforts in public building, slum clearance, and urban renewal, thus performing a highly personal and unorthodox brand of planning, totally unimagined by its original promoters.

The years after the Second World War saw the scope of city planning expand rapidly. By the late 1940s the zoning ordinance had become unworkable: it had three maps for each district, allowing hundreds of combinations, carried fourteen hundred amendments, and made provision for a population of seventy million. The architectural firm of Harrison, Ballard and Allen conducted a two-year study that ended with the publication of the *Plan for Rezoning the City of New York* by the planning commission under Wagner. The report recommended a zoning ordinance based on a single map, eighteen categories of land use, and thirty-eight districts. It also sought to regulate building density according to the floor area ratio (a measure expressing the "total permitted floor area as a multiple of the area of the lot, for all lots regardless of use"), defined an acceptable angle of light obstruction known as the sky exposure plane, and introduced requirements for open space, yards, and parking.

Little effort was made to implement these measures until the real-estate magnate James Felt was appointed chairman in 1956 by Wagner, who won election as mayor in 1953. Felt soon engaged the firm of Voorhees, Walker, Smith and Smith to prepare the text and maps for a new ordinance. These were completed in less than two years and published as *Zoning New York City: A Proposal for a Zoning Resolution for the City of New York*. By 1961 the new ordinance was in place: providing for a population of eleven million (while assuming a population of eight million for 1975), it designated half the city's area for infrastructure (streets, open space, and airports), reserved almost a third for residential development, and divided a fifth evenly between commercial development and manufacturing.

Another central element of planning after the war was a massive rebuilding program stimulated by such federal legislation as the Housing Act of 1937, the Housing and Slum Clearance Act of 1949, and successive amendments encouraging urban renewal. Seeking to preserve the city's stature in commerce, culture, education, and health care, the commission planned to replace factories and tenements with structures supporting the service sector, modern apartment buildings, and middle-income housing; it approved such projects as Lincoln Center, the Brooklyn Civic Center, the expansion of Pratt Institute and New York University, and the development of enormous residential districts like the West Side Urban Renewal Area, Washington Market, and Kips Bay. With federal money the city eventually built more than 100,000 units of public housing, mostly in large developments on slum-cleared land.

These efforts met with anger from community activists, who protested the destruction of their neighborhoods and the massive displacement of population. Some of the best-known leaders of the movement were Charles Abrams and Jane Jacobs, residents of Greenwich Village who fought a plan to extend 5th Avenue through Washington Square Park, and who became increasingly outspoken in their criticism. Jacobs's book *The Death and Life of Great American Cities* (1961) transformed planning throughout the United States, and Abrams later led the planning program at Columbia University, which along with Hunter College and Pratt Institute developed advocacy planning, an approach that strengthened the role of local communities. Such measures helped to increase popular activism, and after a charter revision in 1963 mandated the establishment of community districts, fifty-nine planning areas with community boards were formed. In 1961 Elinor Guggenheimer became the first woman appointed to the city planning commission.

Both public and private concerns undertook ambitious projects. Under David Rockefeller's leadership during the 1950s, the Downtown Lower Manhattan Association sponsored a plan for the redevelopment of 564 acres (228 hectares) in lower Manhattan. This called for improved transportation and redevelopment of Washington Market and South Street Seaport as well as rezoning, all of which was accomplished in succeeding years, triggered by the decision of Chase Manhattan Bank to build new headquarters in the area. In the 1960s the planning commission oversaw new initiatives and the staff of the planning department expanded to more than four hundred. After his appointment by Mayor John V. Lindsay, Donald H. Elliott formed the Urban Design Group to sponsor innovative approaches to urban problems, opened borough branches, and oversaw the creation of fifty-nine community planning districts, an idea promoted by a predecessor, Robert F. Wagner Jr. Concern about the waterfront became a persistent issue, although a general waterfront plan was achieved only in the early 1990s under Richard Schaffer. New York State also took a larger role in city planning at this time.

During these years planners focused on redefining development in the city. In 1969 the planning commission published its long-awaited master plan as the six-volume *Plan for New York City*, which was immediately controversial and never adopted. Many, including the professional planning association, considered it little more than an inventory because it lacked conventional components. Others objected to the cost (more than $1.5 million) and found the plan inaccessible to all but experts, and many discredited the plan because the public had not been consulted. At various times the commission amended the zoning ordinance of 1961 to promote specific types of development and preservation: it protected unique features by providing for special districts, offered incentives to achieve such aims as adding open public spaces to densely built-up areas, and introduced contextual zoning to make new construction visually compatible with its surroundings. Among the most important changes resulted from charter revisions in 1975 and 1989. The first of these revisions guaranteed the public a larger voice in project reviews, and both revisions perfected the uniform land use review process to assess zoning and planning matters, under which community boards and borough presidents hold public hearings and review planning issues before their consideration by the planning commission and City Council. The charter of 1989 enlarged the planning commission to thirteen members appointed by the mayor, the borough presidents, and the public advocate, and assigned it a new set of functions.

Although the planning commission continues to oversee the zoning ordinance and the uniform land use review process, the charter no longer mandates that it develop a single master plan. Instead it issues a quadrennial planning and zoning report, reviews and adopts local plans (known as 197a plans), and uses its Fair Share criteria to regulate the distribution of locally unwanted land uses. The department of city planning continues to perform staff functions for the commission, and works with other municipal agencies to maintain a citywide geographic information system and prepare a series of planning reports mandated by the charter: an annual statement of needs, an annual report on social and economic indicators, and a ten-year capital strategy.

Eugenie Ladner Birch

City University of New York

[CUNY]. The first step toward a municipal college system in New York City was taken in 1926, when the state legislature of New York created the Board of Higher Education to administer City College and Hunter College, the first institutions of higher learning in the city, and two extensions in Brooklyn and Queens (later Brooklyn College and Queens College). After the Second World War a rising birth rate and the ensuing demand for higher education led to a period of modest expansion, culminating in the formation in 1961 of the City University of New York. This consisted of four four-year colleges (City College, Hunter College, Brooklyn College, and Queens College) and four community colleges (Bronx Community College, Queensborough Community College, Staten Island Community College, and New York City Community College, renamed New York Technical College in 1980), all funded by the city. Over the following decades a graduate school (1961), a law school at Queens College (1983), and a medical school were added, as were several other two-year and four-year colleges. The system grew rapidly after its second chancellor, Albert Bowker, instituted a policy of open admissions in 1970 that guaranteed a place in the university to every high school graduate in the city, the student's precise location to be determined by high school grades and class rank. The cost of this expansion contributed to a fiscal crisis in 1975 and 1976: beset by its own financial problems, the city for the first time imposed tuition on students at the university, while mitigating the effects somewhat with an assistance program. In 1979 the state assumed financial responsibility for the four-year colleges and agreed to share in the costs of the community colleges.

There were many critics of the policy of open admissions, which led several colleges to offer remedial programs for a student body that was often ill prepared. Other changes also occurred: single-sex colleges were eliminated, women came to outnumber men in most colleges, older students abounded, and it took longer for most students to earn a degree, partly because most needed to work while attending classes. The most dramatic change was in ethnicity. Because they were limited by quotas at several private colleges in the city, Jewish students predominated in all the municipal four-year colleges from the 1890s to the mid 1950s, when Italians and Irish became numerous. In later years the student body included an increasing number of blacks, Latin Americans, and Asians. By 1988 whites constituted a minority in all but three of the four-year colleges, a pattern even more evident in the community colleges.

Although CUNY toward the end of the twentieth century was very different from the municipal college system of a hundred years earlier, it remained the largest urban educational institution in the United States, with an operating budget of a $1000 million, 7500 unionized faculty members, a diverse student body of 188,000, and twenty schools and colleges (the graduate school, the medical school, the law school, Bernard M. Baruch College, Brooklyn College, City College, the College of Staten Island, Herbert H. Lehman College, Hunter College, the John Jay College of Criminal Justice, New York City Technical College, Queens College, York College, Borough of Manhattan Community College, Bronx Community College, Medgar Evers College, Hostos Community College, Kingsborough Community College, Fiorello H. La Guardia Community College, and Queensborough Community College).

A Long-Range Plan for the City University (New York: Board of Education, 1962)

A New College Student: The Challenge to City University Libraries (Rockaway Park, N.Y.: Scientific Book Service, n.d. [?1969])

Sheila Gordon: "The Transformation of the City University of New York" (diss., City University of New York, 1975)

Florence Neumann: "Access to Free Public Higher Education in New York City, 1847–1961" (diss., City University of New York, 1988)

Selma Berrol

Branches of the City University of New York

GRADUATE SCHOOL	
Graduate School and University Center (1961)	33 West 42nd Street, Manhattan
FOUR-YEAR COLLEGES	
Baruch College (1919)	17 Lexington Avenue, Manhattan
Brooklyn College (1910)	2900 Bedford Avenue
City College (1847)	Convent Avenue and 138th Street, Manhattan
Hunter College (1869)	695 Park Avenue, Manhattan
John Jay College of Criminal Justice (1967)	444 West 56th Street, Manhattan
Lehman College (1968)	Bedford Park Boulevard West, Bronx
Medgar Evers College (1969)	1650 Bedford Avenue, Brooklyn
Queens College (1937)	65-30 Kissena Boulevard
College of Staten Island (1976)	2800 Victory Boulevard
York College (1966)	94-20 Guy R. Brewer Boulevard, Jamaica
COMMUNITY COLLEGES	
Borough of Manhattan Community College (1964)	199 Chambers Street
Bronx Community College (1957)	University Avenue and 181st Street
Eugenio Maria de Hostos Community College (1968)	475 Grand Concourse, Bronx
Kingsborough Community College (1963)	2001 Oriental Boulevard, Brooklyn
La Guardia Community College (1971)	31-10 Thompson Avenue, Long Island City
Queensborough Community College (1958)	22-05 56th Avenue, Bayside
PROFESSIONAL COLLEGES	
New York City Technical College (1946)	300 Jay Street, Brooklyn
CUNY Law School (1983)	Queens College
Mount Sinai School of Medicine (1968)	1 Gustave Levy Place, Manhattan

civic associations. Organizations that work outside the political party system to further the public interest and nonpartisan government, as these purposes are defined by their

Chamber of Commerce of the State of New York, ca *1905*

members. The Chamber of Commerce of the State of New York, arguably the first civic association, was formed in 1768 as part of the campaign against the Townshend Acts and was chiefly active in New York City. Other early civic associations such as the New York Hospital (1791), the Free School Society (1805), the Society for Prevention of Pauperism (1818), and the Association for Improving the Condition of the Poor (1843) offered medical, educational, and social services. Most civic associations sought municipal regulations and subsidies to advance their work, and for many years their requests were received favorably by city officials, who were often drawn from the same wealthy social circles as the associations' leaders. Universal suffrage for white males increased the diversity of the City Council after 1850; wealthy merchants responded by creating the Citizens' Association (1863), a self-styled nonpolitical advocate of good government that sponsored studies of sanitary and housing conditions throughout the city, successfully demanded stricter regulations to improve them, and evaluated the departments and officials of the city government. Like the Chamber of Commerce of the State of New York, the association was a sort of unofficial or private government until it ventured directly into politics at the behest of Peter Cooper and others. It was active in municipal affairs well into the 1870s, when some of its most prominent members formed the New York County Democracy, an overtly partisan group opposed to Tammany Hall. Civic associations allied with the Republican Party of the period included the Union League Club (1863), the New York Civil Service Reform Association (1877), and the City Reform Club (1882), in which Theodore Roosevelt briefly played a leading role. Efforts by the People's Municipal League (1890), the City Club (1892) and its Committee of Seventy (1894), and Citizens Union (1897) to encourage the participation of "independent" Democrats and Republicans in mayoral campaigns brought civic associations to their high point. The vast, diverse electorate created by consolidation in 1898 made it more difficult for civic associations to compete against Democratic and Republican organizations that had strong alliances at the state and national levels and sophisticated leadership (such as that provided the Democrats by Charles F. Murphy).

With the expansion of municipal government at the end of the nineteenth century, most civic associations became pressure groups with a narrow focus. Women led many of the new groups, including the Charity Organization Society, the New York State Charities Aid Association, the Women's Health Protective Association, the Kindergarten Association, and the Public Education Association. Organizations concerned specifically with women's issues included the Women's City Club, the New York City Federation of Women's Clubs, several woman suffrage organizations, and the League of Women Voters (1920). Citizens Union alone continued to enjoy considerable electoral success with "fusion" mayoral candidates such as Seth Low and John Purroy Mitchel and ultimately Fiorello H. La Guardia. After the Second World War the Regional Plan Association of New York and the Citizens Budget Commission sought to play a broad role in policy planning comparable to that of the "private governments" of the nineteenth century. Notable associations with sharply defined purposes include the United Parents Association, the Citizens Committee on Children, the Citizens Housing and Planning Council, and the Friends of Central Park. Citywide and neighborhood chambers of commerce and block associations are also civic associations, as are ethnic associations such as B'nai B'rith, the National Association for the Advancement of Colored People, and the Italian–American Defense Fund.

Albert Shaw: "The Higher Life of New York City," *Outlook,* 25 Jan 1896, pp. 132–39

Everett P. Wheeler: "The Unofficial Government of Cities," *Atlantic Monthly* 86 (1900), 370–76

Wallace S. Sayre and Herbert Kaufman: *Governing New York City: Politics in the Metropolis* (New York: Russell Sage Foundation, 1960)

Richard Skolnik: "Civic Group Progressivism in New York City," *New York History* 51 (1970), 411–39

M. J. Heale: "From City Fathers to Social Critics: Humanitarianism and Government in New York, 1790–1860," *Journal of American History* 58 (June 1976), 21–41

David C. Hammack: *Power and Society: Greater New York at the Turn of the Century* (New York: Russell Sage Foundation, 1982)

David C. Hammack

civil defense. There was little fear of foreign military attack in New York City during the First World War, despite rumors of sabotage, but the Second World War brought a different perception and a very different reality. Early in the war German U-boats sank thousands of

"Our City, Defeat of Slander" (1909, designed by Robert L. Bracklow), erected in Long Acre Square by the Association for New York

tons of shipping near the entrance of New York Harbor. New Yorkers were reminded that "loose lips sink ships." After the Allies bombed Berlin in 1942 German radio vowed retribution against New York City, and blackout drills took on an understandable urgency. Mayor Fiorello H. La Guardia warned that the city was the "world's number one target."

Rejected for a commission in the military, Mayor La Guardia in May 1941 was named the unpaid head of the U.S. Office of Civilian Defense, a position that he vigorously discharged but held only until early 1942. In the following year he appointed Grover A. Whalen, the guiding spirit behind the World's Fair of 1939–40, to lead the city's Civilian Defense Volunteers Office. During the war more than 400,000 New Yorkers enrolled. Organized at the local level by block leaders, about half the volunteers were assigned to "civilian protective groups," which included aircraft spotters, air raid wardens, and auxiliary firemen and policemen. Blackout drills were held at three-month intervals, and sirens were tested each Saturday at noon. The other volunteer programs, designated "community war services," involved activities such as child care, nutrition education, housing information, carpooling, and rationing. The rationing of gasoline, rubber, sugar, coffee, meat, and processed food by the U.S. Office of Price Administration (OPA) was supervised in New York City by fifteen local offices. Regulations were so specific that they differentiated between hard and soft salami. Barrels to collect rubber, rags, and metal were placed in the lobbies of apartment buildings and public buildings. Schoolchildren collected tin foil. Colleges provided training for military units, Columbia University offered courses to improve the efficiency of defense plants, and students at Brooklyn College went upstate to help bring in the crops. The city's branch of the American Association of University Women sponsored lectures on the psychological effects of war.

Near the war's end plans were made to sell the air raid sirens and close the city's civil defense offices. But the cold war strategy of nuclear deterrence assumed an atomic survival plan, and the U.S. Civil Defense Act of 1950 "assigned the main responsibility for action to state and local authorities with appointed local volunteer staffs." The New York City Office of Civil Defense, at 135 East 55th Street in Manhattan, coordinated all matters affecting civil defense and natural disasters, and had the power to mobilize civil defense forces and direct other municipal agencies. Schools held "duck and cover" drills; newspapers printed air raid instructions; shelter sites were designated in basements and subways; sirens were placed in firehouses; dehydrated foods, medicines, and supplies, including postcards to be mailed to relatives, were stockpiled throughout the city; buses were designed for conversion into ambulances; and documentary films as well as a thirty-four-page pamphlet entitled "You and the Atomic Bomb" were widely distributed. There was however little support from the legislature, implementation was haphazard, with few dollars and fewer volunteers, and the public was essentially apathetic. The military editor of the *New York Times*, Hansen Baldwin, described the city's civil defense effort as "non-existent."

In 1955 Mayor Robert F. Wagner and Governor W. Averell Harriman argued that civil defense was a federal responsibility. Although the city was seen as a prime target of Soviet missiles, many New Yorkers questioned the value of shelters to protect against the immense destruction of a hydrogen bomb. Ulster and Sullivan counties were examined as evacuation sites despite widespread doubt that evacuation from a missile attack was possible. One county executive in Westchester said that in the event of an attack he would close the boundaries with New York City. In the early 1960s Governor Nelson A. Rockefeller promoted shelters, notwithstanding continued debate about their worth, and sought to stock them with federal agricultural surpluses.

For illustration see WARS.

Arnold Markoe

Civilian Review Board. A panel formed in 1966 during the administration of Mayor John V. Lindsay to hear complaints of misconduct by the police. The original plan to have the board consist entirely of private citizens provoked bitter opposition from the Patrolmen's Benevolent Association, which failed to defeat the plan in court but then succeeded in doing so by an overwhelming margin in a referendum. The board was then put in place with a membership consisting solely of employees of the police department (under the name Civilian Complaint Review Board). There was little public discussion or controversy in 1986 when Mayor Edward I. Koch signed a bill changing the composition of the board so that half its members would be private citizens. In the late 1980s the board heard allegations of police brutality in connection with several incidents, including a riot involving the police and advocates for the homeless in Tompkins Square Park in 1988. At the urging of Mayor David N. Dinkins, the City Council in 1993 passed a bill requiring all members of the board to be civilians (five selected by the mayor, five by the City Council, three by the police commissioner).

Joseph P. Viteritti

civil service. Political loyalties were openly considered when public offices were filled in New York City during colonial times and after independence. In the late eighteenth century there were three appointed offices in the city for every eight persons in the electorate. Not all appointments were desirable, and the charter of Governor John Montgomerie stipulated a penalty for appointees who refused to serve. Among the positions filled by the state council of appointment was the mayoralty, which commanded such control over patronage that to accept it De Witt Clinton resigned in 1803 from the U.S. Senate. During the 1830s the electorate expanded, the mayoralty and other municipal offices became elected positions, and municipal appointments came to be used to build and sustain broadly based local party organizations, or political machines. In some cases appointees collected salaries as city employees but were engaged only in political work. During the mid nineteenth century control of municipal appointments was an important issue in conflicts over local government between Democrats in the city and Republicans in state government. An important role in dispensing patronage was played by Tammany Hall, and especially by its leaders William M. "Boss" Tweed and John Kelly.

The first civil service reform association in the United States was formed in the city in 1877, and in 1883 New York City and Brooklyn became the first cities in the nation to adopt civil service regulations (these inspired a national civil service movement). During the same year a law established the state civil service commission, the first such agency in the nation, and also permitted mayors to apply civil service regulations in cities with at least fifty thousand inhabitants. The application of the regulations in these cities was made mandatory for certain groups of employees by a state law passed in 1884. In 1894 the new state constitution stipulated that state and local employees should be appointed and promoted according to "merit and fitness" determined in competitive examinations.

In the decades after consolidation, civil service reformers and party leaders struggled for control of municipal appointments. Initially the conflict was marked by issues of ethnicity and class: most reformers were Protestant and middle or upper middle class, and most members of party organizations were immigrants and Irish Catholics. The parties lost influence but quickly embraced the notion of merit and fitness, which had become extremely popular: they incorporated it into their platforms but simultaneously worked to constrain its reach by excluding certain positions from civil service requirements, establishing temporary appointments, and manipulating civil service rules and procedures.

Although intended as a reform, civil service was sometimes an obstacle to reform. It was a potent political weapon for Mayors John Purroy Mitchel, Fiorello H. La Guardia, and John V. Lindsay: often accused by their opponents of bypassing the civil service, they exploited the system to deny resources to adversaries and to build a political base among ethnic groups lacking influence with the dominant county organizations. Civil service rules also prevented reformers from employing outside experts in city government. The efforts of Mayor Robert F. Wagner led to a state law establishing a personnel department for city government (1954), collective bargaining with municipal employees' labor unions (1958), and a reduced role for the municipal civil service commission in policy making. After it was disclosed in 1989 that Mayor Edward I. Koch maintained a "talent bank" of supporters seeking municipal appointments, the State Commission on Government Integrity (led by John Feerick) argued that to make municipal employment more widely accessible the number of posts requiring special qualifications should be limited. The Civil Service Commission remained an important safeguard of the standard of merit and fitness in the face of mounting pressure to consider race, sex, and ethnicity in making municipal appointments.

William L. Riordon: *Plunkitt of Tammany Hall* (New York: McClure, Phillips, 1905)

Wallace S. Sayre and Herbert Kaufman: *Personnel Administration in the Government of New York City* (New York: Mayor's Committee on Management Survey of the City of New York, 1952)

Theodore J. Lowi: *At the Pleasure of the Mayor: Patronage and Power in New York City, 1898–1958* (New York: Free Press, 1964)

Gerald Benjamin

civil service unions. Some of the first municipal workers who organized in New York City were street cleaners; they joined the Knights of Labor and the International Brotherhood of Teamsters but ceased their efforts after an unsuccessful strike in 1911. The New York Teachers' Union (1916) was succeeded by the United Federation of Teachers, which did not sign its first contract until mid century. A number of organizations were formed that provided mutual aid and fought for better conditions but did not engage in collective bargaining, among them the Patrolmen's Benevolent Association (PBA), the Firemen's Mutual Benefit Association, and the Civil Service Forum. Interest in unions among city employees increased during the 1930s as the Civil Service Forum declined, the national labor movement revived, and the political left grew in importance (many municipal unions were led by socialists and communists). By the time of the Second World War unions had a foothold in the public welfare, hospital, and sanitation departments and the boards of transportation and education. Mayor Fiorello H. La Guardia allowed employees to join unions but barred them from striking and the city from engaging in collective bargaining. His stand was tested in 1940 during the takeover of the Interborough Rapid Transit Company (IRT) and the Brooklyn–Manhattan Transit Corporation (BMT), which employed unionized workers. After a series of clashes with the Transport Workers Union, La Guardia entered into negotiations about wages and other issues but refused to allow formal bargaining. In 1947 the state's Condon–Wadlin Act outlawed strikes by public employees and made the dismissal of strikers automatic.

Municipal unions made some of their most important gains under Mayor Robert F. Wagner. Seeking the support of labor during the mayoral election of 1953, Wagner pledged to institute reforms such as collective bargaining. In 1954 he established employee grievance procedures and guaranteed the right of city workers to organize without reprisal. The city in 1956 allowed unions to collect dues from employees by means of voluntary withholding from paychecks, and in the same year it held its first union recognition election. Executive Order 49, issued by Wagner in 1958, granted many workers the right to bargain with the city through exclusively recognized unions of their choice. Blue-collar employees were among the first to take advantage of these gains. Some were represented by unions within single agencies, such as the Uniformed Sanitationmen's Association. Employees scattered throughout city government were sought out by Teamsters Local 237 and District Council 37 of the American Federation of State, County and Municipal Employees, which soon became the largest municipal union. During the mid 1960s professional and clerical workers, many of whom were women, joined unions in large numbers, and several police officers' and firefighters' benevolent associations became collective bargaining agents. There were few strikes during Wagner's term, and those that occurred had little impact on the public, except for one by welfare workers in 1965 that lasted for twenty-eight days. Under Mayor John V. Lindsay strikes were frequent and disruptive. The moment he took office in January 1966 transit workers began a twelve-day strike that virtually paralyzed the city. During the next three years doctors, nurses, teachers, social workers, and sanitation workers went on strike, and the PBA held a five-day "sick-out." The unions' militancy brought about dramatic improvements in wages, benefits, and pensions and led to the replacement of the Condon–Wadlin Act in 1967 by the Taylor Law, which upheld the ban on strikes but placed greater emphasis on resolving disputes.

Civil service unions became increasingly important in politics and civic life. At a time when unionized employment in private industry was declining, the public unions grew rapidly, gaining many black and Latin American members and bolstering the labor movement in the city, which remained one of the country's strongest centers of unionization. Most civil service unions supported the civil rights movement and the liberal wing of the Democratic Party, but police unions generally followed a more conservative path. By 1970 civil service unions had more than 250,000 members and represented more than 90 percent of the city work force in collective bargaining. During the fiscal crisis of the mid 1970s civil service unions helped the city to avoid bankruptcy by agreeing to wage deferrals, benefit reductions, large-scale dismissals, and the use of pension funds to buy $2500 million in municipal bonds. Union backing was also crucial in the election of Governor Mario M. Cuomo in 1982 and Mayor David N. Dinkins in 1989.

In the mid 1990s civil service unions had well over 300,000 members and remained influential in the routine operations and long-term development of municipal government.

Raymond D. Horton: *Municipal Labor Relations in New York City: Lessons of the Lindsay–Wagner Years* (New York: Praeger, 1973)

Jewel Bellush and Bernard Bellush: *Union Power and New York: Victor Gotbaum and District Council 37* (New York: Praeger, 1984)

Mark H. Maier: *City Unions: Managing Discontent in New York City* (New Brunswick, N.J.: Rutgers University Press, 1987)

Joshua B. Freeman

Claflin, Horace B(righam) (*b* Milford, Mass., 18 Dec 1811; *d* New York City, 14 Nov 1885). Merchant. He moved to New York City in 1843 and opened a dry-goods wholesale firm, H. B. Claflin's, that provided wares to retail merchants throughout the country and became one of the city's first department stores. During the Civil War he had sales of more than $70 million in one year, and he weathered the panic of 1873. Claflin was a trustee of Plymouth Church during Henry Ward Beecher's tenure as pastor.

John D. Claflin: *Horace B. Claflin* (New York: Atlantic Publishing, 1885)

James E. Mooney

Claiborne, Liz [Ortenberg, Elisabeth Claiborne] (*b* Brussels, 31 March 1929). Fashion designer. She emigrated to the United States in 1939, at the age of twenty won the Jacques Heim National Design Contest (sponsored by *Harper's Bazaar*), and in 1949 moved to New York City to work as a sketch artist at the sportswear house Tina Leser. She worked as a designer for Dan Keller and Youth Group Inc. before forming a business under her own name in 1976. By focusing on affordable clothes for working women she achieved $23 million in sales within two years and $391 million by 1984, by which time she had broadened her line to include accessories, men's and children's clothes, and fragrances.

Anne E. Kornblut

Clare, Ada (McElhenney) (*b* Charleston, S.C., July 1834; *d* New York City, 4 March 1874). Actress, feminist, and writer. Born to an aristocratic Southern family, she moved to New York City in 1854, took up acting, engaged in a widely publicized liaison with the pianist and composer Louis Moreau Gottschalk, and bore a son out of wedlock. During the height of her acting career she frequented Pfaff's Cellar, where she became known as the "queen of Bohemia"; she also wrote for the *Saturday Press*, an iconoclastic weekly magazine of the arts. Her only novel, *Only a Woman's Heart* (1866), was so poorly received by reviewers that she abandoned writing and spent the rest of her career acting in a provincial stock company. A dog bite suffered in the office of her theatrical agent resulted in her death from rabies.

Gloria Goldblatt: "The Queen of Bohemia Grew Up in Charleston," *Carologue*, autumn 1988, pp. 10–11, 28

Jan Seidler Ramirez

Claremont. Neighborhood in the southwestern Bronx (1990 pop. 14,007), lying in the northernmost section of Morrisania and bounded to the north by the Cross Bronx Expressway, to the east by Crotona Park, to the south by East 169th Street, and to the west by Claremont Park. It is often considered part of Bathgate. The name Claremont was first applied to the estate of the Zborowski family, which occupied a triangular parcel of thirty-eight acres (15.4 hectares) west of Webster Avenue; it was separated from the neighboring estate of the Bathgate family (later Crotona Park) by a carriage road that became Claremont Parkway. The Zborowski and Bathgate estates were bought for parkland by New York City in 1888 and later became Claremont Park and Crotona Park. The neighborhood developed in between the parks on lower ground, becoming populous in the 1920s and 1930s. It was predominantly Jewish until the 1950s, when the population became increasingly black and Spanish-speaking. By the early 1990s crime, drugs, abandoned housing, and demolished blocks left Claremont one of the most deteriorated sections of the southern Bronx.

Evelyn Gonzalez, Gary D. Hermalyn

Claremont Riding Academy. A riding school housed in an equestrian stable at 175 West 89th Street in Manhattan. It is the oldest continuously operated equestrian stable in New York City and perhaps the oldest in the United States. The building (now a landmark), designed by Frank A. Rooke in Romanesque Revival style and completed in 1892, was a common structure for its time and housed a succession of livery businesses. The academy was formed in 1927, at a time when many stables in the city had been razed or converted into parking garages. The academy offers riding instruction at all levels; students use its indoor ring as well as the nearby bridle paths in Central Park.

Clarissa L. Bushman

Clarenceville. An obsolete name for a small section of Richmond Hill in central Queens. It began as a development in January 1853 when a group led by the prominent lawyer W. T. B. Milliken bought a farm on the south side of Jamaica Avenue, extending from one hundred feet (thirty meters) west of 110th Street to one hundred feet east of 112th Street. A post office and a railroad station opened in July 1869. By August 1872 the community had essentially become absorbed by the surrounding development of Richmond Hill, and it abandoned its own name. The Long Island Rail Road nevertheless continued to use the name Clarenceville for a station at 111th Street until service there ceased in 1940.

Vincent Seyfried

Clarendon Hotel. An eight-story hotel at the corner of Broadway at 38th Street in Manhattan, designed by William Hume and constructed in 1850 by the businessman and hotel operator Joseph Fisher at a cost of $300,000. Based on the European plan of hotel design and service, the hotel was an elegant establishment frequented by foreigners, particularly diplomats. A newspaper account in 1873 called the Clarendon one of the few first-class hotels in New York City still retaining the table d'hôte system of meals.

Shan Jayakumar

Clark, Aaron (*b* Northampton, Mass., 1784; *d* New York City, 3 Aug 1861). Mayor. A lawyer and wealthy landowner, he became a Whig alderman and won a three-way election during the panic of 1837 to become the second popularly elected mayor of New York City. In 1838 he was reelected by a margin of five hundred votes; he narrowly lost the election in the following year.

James E. Mooney

Clark, Kenneth (Bancroft) (*b* Canal Zone, 24 July 1914). Psychologist. He moved to Harlem, attended public schools, and earned a BA and an MA from Howard University. After he completed his PhD in psychology at Columbia University he became the first black member of the faculty at City College of New York. His work with Mamie Phipps Clark on racial awareness in children played a critical role in the decision *Brown v. Board of Education* (1954), in which the U.S. Supreme Court ruled racial segregation in public schools unconstitutional. Clark formed the organization Haryou and began several experimental programs in education. His published writings include *Dark Ghetto*, a discussion of the problems of blacks during the 1960s.

David Rosner

Clark [née Phipps], **Mamie (Katherine)** (*b* Hot Springs, Ark., 1917; *d* Hastings-on-Hudson, N.Y., 11 Aug 1983). Psychologist. She spent her youth in Hot Springs, attended Howard University, and earned the PhD in psychology from Columbia University. Her research on racial awareness in young children was furthered by her husband, Kenneth Clark, and played a critical role in the decision *Brown v. Board of Education* (1954), in which the U.S. Supreme Court ruled racial segregation in public schools unconstitutional. Clark was the director of the Northside Center for Child Development from 1946 to 1979.

David Rosner

Clason Point. Neighborhood in the south central Bronx, bounded to the north by White Plains Road and the Bruckner Expressway, to the east by Pugsley's Creek, to the south by the East River, and to the west by the Bronx River. The first inhabitants were Siwanoys, whose village, Snakapin, was one of the largest Indian villages along the shoreline of the Bronx. Known as Cornell's Neck by European settlers (for Thomas Cornell, a farmer who settled there in 1654), it was later named for Isaac Clason, a wealthy merchant of the nineteenth century, and became the site of the Clason Military Academy. The view and proximity to the East River and the mouth of the Bronx River led to the development of resorts that included dance halls, bathing piers, and restaurants. During the Second World War the last pedestrian ferry from Clason Point to College Point in Queens ended service; after the war Kane's Casino became the site of Shorehaven Beach Club, which was later the site of a housing development planned for a thousand units. In the 1980s more than a quarter of new immigrants settling in Clason Point and its environs were Dominican. There were also large numbers of immigrants from Ecuador, Honduras, Colombia, Jamaica, Guyana, and China.

John McNamara: *History in Asphalt: The Origin of Bronx Street and Place Names* (New York: Bronx County Historical Society, 1984)

John McNamara: *McNamara's Old Bronx* (New York: Bronx County Historical Society, 1989)

Gary D. Hermalyn

Beach party at Clason Point, ca *1922*

classical music. New York City established itself as the national musical capital in the mid nineteenth century. Its continued dominance during the next century was ensured by its orchestras, opera companies, concert halls, and conservatories, and by its role in music publishing and recording.

1. Beginnings to 1890

The Dutch sang psalms in their own language long after the English captured the colony (1664) and formed Trinity Church (1697). Musical life in eighteenth-century New York City was undistinguished. The earliest documented public performance, advertised in the *New-York Gazette* as a "consort of musick, vocal and instrumental," was held in 1736 at the home of the vintner Robert Todd. The first concert hall in the city was the Nassau Street Theatre at 64–66 Nassau Street, where operas were staged from about 1750. A singing school opened in 1753 by William Tuckey, a clerk at Trinity Church, offered biweekly classes and helped the church to develop an accomplished choir. Music dealers and instrument makers often supplemented their income by giving music lessons; two of the best-known were W. C. Hulett (a violin teacher and dancing master from 1759 to 1799) and Alexander Reinagle (who gave keyboard lessons to George Washington's adopted daughter, Nellie Custis). About 1760 Francis Hopkinson, later a signer of the Declaration of Independence, provided translations in English for the psalter. The New Theatre opened in 1798 on Park Row facing City Hall Park and later became known as the Park Theatre. During these years musical life remained dominated by England: the theater in New York City was in effect a provincial branch of the theater in London, and many English immigrants were musicians and singing actors, some of whom also worked as teachers, publishers, composers, and entrepreneurs. Among the most important were James Hewitt (1770–1827), who moved to the city in 1792 and wrote the music for the play *Tammany; or, the Indian Chief* (1794), Benjamin Carr (1769–1831), composer of the opera *The Archers; or, The Mountaineers of Switzerland* (1796), and Victor Pelissier (*b ca* 1740; *d ca* 1820), composer of the opera *Edwin and Angelina* (1796). John Jacob Astor, who later made a fortune in the fur trade and in real estate in Manhattan, opened a music shop in the city in 1786 and within a decade found himself competing with Hewitt and Carr in importing and distributing music and instruments, principally from England.

Music in New York City developed with great rapidity during the nineteenth century, as the number of inhabitants and especially of immigrants steadily increased. Traveling theatrical companies presented a variety of English, French, and Italian works in newly constructed theaters, and after the War of 1812 several notable European musicians arrived in the city. At the Park Theatre in 1825 Manuel García's troupe mounted a production of Rossini's *Il Barbiere di Siviglia* (the first Italian opera performed in the city in its entirety) and another of Mozart's *Don Giovanni* that was attended by the author of the libretto, Lorenzo Da Ponte, a resident of New York City since 1805. Da Ponte was a leading backer of the Italian Opera House at Church and Leonard streets (opened in 1833, closed in 1835, reopened in 1836 as the National Theatre), a highly successful opera and entertainment hall that was destroyed by fire in 1841. Washington Irving, the city's leading literary figure, an amateur flutist, and the author of another English version of *Der Freischütz*, took part in the negotiations surrounding the production of *Il Barbiere* (an effort also supported by Astor). He also joined with other literary figures to help bring about the first complete American production in 1839 of Beethoven's *Fidelio*, which attracted full houses to the Park Theatre for fourteen consecutive nights.

One of the most important concert venues in the nineteenth century was Niblo's Garden at Broadway and Prince streets (built by William Niblo in 1829, destroyed by fire in 1846, rebuilt in 1849, again destroyed by fire in 1895). There Gaetano Donizetti's *Lucia di Lammermoor* received its first staging in New York City in 1843. Italian opera also established a strong following at the Richmond Hill Theatre at Charlton and Varick streets, where Vincenzo Bellini's *Il Pirata* was given its American première; the theater was also known as Tivoli Garden and changed its name successively to the New Greenwich Theatre and the New York Opera House before closing in 1849. The American première of Bellini's *I Puritani* in 1844 was the opening production of Palmo's Opera House, the most distinguished opera house in early-nineteenth-century New York City, which also staged the first opera by Verdi in the United States (*I Lombardi* in 1847); after a change in ownership in 1848 the repertory changed from music to theater. In 1847 a group of wealthy patrons opened the Astor Place Opera House. The riot that took place nearby in 1849 tarnished its reputation irretrievably, and in 1854 the owners sold the opera house to the Mercantile Library Association, which converted the building to Clinton Hall. The same year marked the opening of the Academy of Music, the first permanent opera house in New York City. Concerts were given from 1859 at the Great Hall at Cooper Union (still in operation in the 1990s) and from 1861 at the Brooklyn Academy of Music on Montague Street (destroyed by fire in 1903).

Although New York City at mid century did not have a school of composers equal to the Knickerbocker poets or the painters of the Hudson River School, a number of resident composers wrote music of lasting merit. One was Anthony Philip Heinrich (1781–1861), composer of fanciful orchestral pieces such as *The Ornithological Combat of Kings; or, The Condor of the Andes and the Eagle of the Cordilleras* (1836), who lived in New York City from 1837 until his death. Another important composer who flourished in the city was William Henry Fry (1813–64), an ebullient lecturer and a writer for Horace Greeley's *New York Tribune* whose works include *Leonora* (1845), the first American bel canto opera in English, and the symphony *Santa Claus* (1853). The popular composer Stephen Foster spent some of the most important years of his songwriting career in the city and died at Bellevue Hospital. The first internationally recognized American keyboard virtuoso, Louis Moreau Gottschalk (1829–69), made New York City his home during much of his peripatetic later career. His piano compositions, based on Caribbean music, influenced later developments in popular music that led to ragtime and jazz, and his two-movement symphony *A Night in the Tropics* (1858) foreshadows by almost a century the style of much twentieth-century American music. George F(rederick) Bristow (1825–98), a native of Brooklyn, became the best-known American composer in England when the Andante from his Symphony no. 2 was performed there in 1854 by the Jullien Orchestra, and his *Rip Van Winkle* (1855), the first American opera on an American subject, ran for four weeks at Niblo's Garden. Lesser-known composers included Caryl Florio (the pseudonym of William Robjohn, 1843–1920) and Horace Nicholl (1848–1922). Musical life in New York City at mid century was so active that the prominent diarist George Templeton Strong could attend a concert almost every night of the week. The city was also the most important center for organ builders, piano makers, and music publishers, especially on lower Broadway. Leading music publishers included the firms of William Hall; Firth, Pond and Company; and Charles H. Ditson. The first foreign music publisher to establish a branch in the city was the German firm of André and Company, which offered among other items a complete inventory of music by Mozart; it was followed shortly by the British firm of Novello, which sold sacred music from its shop at 389 Broadway. Many of the hymn-books distributed throughout the United States were published in Manhattan, and the *Jubilee Songs*, the first published sheet music of blacks that eschewed caricature, were issued from East 9th Street. The firm Steinway and Sons was formed in 1853 and opened a large factory at 53rd Street and 4th Avenue in 1860.

Music education at mid century was increasingly the domain of such small academies as the New York Conservatorio at 417 Houston Street (opened in 1836 by Elam Ives Jr.), where classes were held during the day for women and in the evening for men, John Watson's Musical Academy at 385 Broadway (from 1839), which offered lessons in singing, organ, piano, harmony, and composition, and the American Musical Institute at 466 Broadway (1846–48), which during its final year had on its faculty the acclaimed pianist Henri Herz (he taught at the neighboring offices of André and Company, 477 Broadway). Amateur singing societies proliferated as German-speaking immigrants increased in number and formed social organizations; the more notable included the Deutsche Liederkranz (which performed its first concert in 1847 with Thomas L. Damas conducting) and its offshoot the Männergesangverein Arion (1854).

Religious music also flourished. A widespread interest in congregational singing spurred mass education in vocal music. Lowell Mason (1792–1872), originally from Boston, formed the New York Musical Normal Institute for training music teachers in 1853 along with other such influential musicians as Thomas Hastings (1784–1872), George James Webb (1803–87), William S. Bradbury (1816–68), and George F. Root (1820–95). Their novel teaching methods and instructional hymn-books influenced generations of amateur American singers, as did their large repertory of new tunes, many of which became classics; the school moved to Massachusetts in 1856. From 1846 to 1859 the organist at Trinity Church was Edward Hodges (1798–1867), born and trained in England, who helped to revitalize church music through his performances of organ masterworks, founding of a male choir, and composition of services and anthems. His efforts culminated in the founding of such secular and non-denominational organizations as the Church Choral Society (1869) and the Oratorio Society (1873). A breach widened about this time between on the one hand the populist tradition of vocal hymnody and on the other a movement for higher aesthetic standards that saw music as a morally efficacious force. The extent of the division was made clear when the award by New York University of honorary doctorates in music to Mason (1853) and Hastings (1855), the first granted by a major institution of higher learning in the United States, was criticized by such leading professional composers as Fry and Bristow. By 1880 there were about 370 houses of worship in the city, most of which required the services of organists, choir directors, and professional singers.

Such advocates of the Episcopal liturgical revival as Hodges and W. A. King, aided by enlightened vestry members such as P. A. Schermerhorn and H. C. DeRham of Grace Church, were active in 1842 in forming the Philharmonic Society of New York (later known as the New York Philharmonic), the first permanent symphonic ensemble in the United States. The orchestra gave its first concert on 7 December at the Apollo Rooms, which stood on the site formerly occupied by the Broadway Theatre at Canal and Walker streets; it later was based at Niblo's Garden (1854–56, 1858–59), the Academy of Music, built in 1854 at 14th Street and Irving Place (at intervals, 1856–86), Irving Hall, an annex of the academy at Irving Place and 15th Street (1861–63), and Steinway Hall at 73–77 East 14th Street (1866), an important concert hall until it closed in 1890. Strong was president of the society from 1870 to 1874. Opera and especially Italian opera continued to flourish in the city in the second half of the nineteenth century. Built in 1868 as (Samuel) Pike's Opera House, the Grand Opera House at 8th Avenue and 23rd Street presented the American première of Leoncavallo's *Pagliacci*. The New York Stadt Theatre at 45 Broadway opened in 1868 and presented the first American performance of Wagner's *Lohengrin* in 1871.

By mid century New York City had become the focal point of international concert tours, and many artists made extended stays. Among the operatic singers to appear in the city were García's daughter Maria Malibran (1808–36), who married a French merchant while living in New York City, Jenny Lind (1820–87), whose concert appearances at Castle Garden in 1850 (promoted by P. T. Barnum) were enthusiastically received, and Adelina Patti (1843–1919), who at the age of seven made her operatic début in the city in a charity concert in 1850 at Tripler's Hall, 667–77 Broadway, an important venue that was damaged by a series of fires in the following years, reopened in 1854, and took several other names before closing in 1867. Other popular visitors included Jullien (at the Crystal Palace, 1853), the eccentric Norwegian violinist Ole Bull (1810–80), the pianist Hans von Bülow (1830–94), and the composer Arthur Sullivan (1842–1900).

Professional schools of music began in earnest after the Civil War. Among the best-known were the Grand Conservatory (1874), the New York College of Music (1878, absorbed in 1920 by New York University), and the National Conservatory of Music (opened in 1885 at 128 East 17th Street, closed in the 1920s). Under the directorship of Jeannette Thurber the National Conservatory had on its faculty the pianist Rafael Joseffy and the composer and cellist Victor Herbert; its director from 1892 to 1895 was Antonín Dvořák, who during his tenure wrote his symphony "From the New World." The Metropolitan Conservatory opened in 1886. During these years the city's primacy in music was reinforced by its growing number of music publishers, including G. Schirmer (1861) and Carl Fischer (1872), and by the formation in 1883 of the Metropolitan Opera, which staged its first performances at Broadway between 39th and 40th streets.

Music in New York City in the late nineteenth century was heavily central European. Germans both Jewish and Christian dominated the city's musical life and German music was ubiquitous: Wagner was performed not only at the Metropolitan Opera but by brass bands. At the centenary in 1889 of Washington's inauguration as president, massed German singing societies supplied most of the music. Some émigré musicians distinguished themselves as impresarios, notably Max Maretzek (1821–97), Bernard Ullman (1817–85), and the brothers Maurice Strakosch (1825–87) and Max Strakosch (1834–92). Prominent German-born conductors included Leopold Damrosch, who formed the New York Symphony Society in 1878 and excelled as a conductor of German opera, and Theodore Thomas, leader of the Thomas Orchestra (1867–91), the Philharmonic Society (1871–91), and later the Chicago Symphony, who set a high standard of orchestral performance, encouraged a generation of American composers by programming their works, and conducted young people's concerts as early as 1883. Among the leading musicians who were not of German origin the most famous was the composer Edward MacDowell, an accomplished pianist and inventive harmonist who early achieved wide recognition for his two concertos for piano and orchestra, four epic keyboard sonatas, and many elegant character pieces. In his last works he adapted the tuneful manner of Anglo-Celtic melody to his sophisticated harmonic style, and made a point of exclusively employing English rather than Italian terms as tempo indications and marks of expression. Among MacDowell's friends was George Templeton Strong Jr. (1856–1948), who on deciding to pursue a career in music was nearly disowned by his father. Schooled abroad and an expatriate for most of his life, he composed several large-scale symphonic works, of which the most accomplished was the symphony *Sintram* (1888).

2. From the Opening of the Music Hall to the Second World War

The opening concerts on 5 May 1891 of the Music Hall (now Carnegie Hall) at 57th Street and 7th Avenue were conducted by Tchaikovsky and reinforced the emergence of New York City as one of the world's major musical centers. The city was soon visited by the pianists Jan Ignace Paderewski (1860–1941) and Teresa Carreño (1853–1917). The Church Choral Society and the Oratorio Society gave the first performances of such important American works as *Phoenix Expirans* (1892) by George W. Chadwick (1854–1931), *Hora Novissima* (1893) by Horatio Parker (1861–1919), and *Vexilla Regis* (1894) by Harry Rowe Shelley (1858–1947). Toward the end of the century the first settlement schools provided music instruction to poor children, among them the Henry Street Settlement (1892), which later opened a music wing (1927). Emilie Wagner and David Mannes in 1894 opened the Music School Settlement, which later moved successively to 3rd Street (where it took the name Third Street Musical School Settlement) and East 11th Street and eventually became the nation's oldest community arts school. Columbia University formed a department of music in 1896 under MacDowell. New York City was one of the last major American cities to include music in the standard public school curriculum. In 1898 the Symphony Society began a regular series of children's concerts under Leopold Damrosch's son Frank Damrosch, later succeeded by his brother Walter Damrosch.

After the turn of the century the city was changed markedly by the immigration of thousands of Italians, Germans, Russian Jews, and Irish. Anton Seidl's thirteen years in the city with the Metropolitan Opera Orchestra and the New York Philharmonic bolstered the performance of the German repertory, as did Gustav Mahler's years as the conductor of the Metropolitan Opera and the Philharmonic (1908–11). Walter Damrosch conducted the Metropolitan Opera, the New York Symphony, and the Philharmonic, composed operas (*The Scarlet Letter*, 1896; *The Man without a Country*, 1937), and at the end of his long career was a popular radio personality. Frank Damrosch became a leading choral director with the Metropolitan Opera and the Oratorio Society (founded by his father), and in 1905 formed the Institute for Musical Art (later renamed the Juilliard School). In 1903 the Metropolitan Opera gave the first staged performance outside Bayreuth of Wagner's last opera, *Parsifal.* Italian music was also well represented. In his almost twenty years in New York City Enrico Caruso became the most famous operatic singer who had ever lived, and through the city's fledgling recording industry the first international recording artist.

Efforts to strengthen a largely ineffectual system of copyright protection led to the formation in the city in 1914 of the American Association of Composers, Authors and Publishers (ASCAP), which included among its founding members Herbert, Irving Berlin, and John Philip Sousa (whose works were the focus of several early lawsuits won by the association). At first licensing fees were payable to ASCAP only for live performances of music by its members; eventually the association also monitored broadcasts and recordings.

In time the operatic and symphonic repertory broadened, as the Philharmonic and the New York Symphony performed less music by German, Austrian, and Hungarian composers and enabled French, Russian, and American works to enter the repertory. At the same time classical music continued to reach a wider audience. The mining magnate Adolph Lewisohn endowed Lewisohn Stadium (1915) at City College, between 136th and 138th streets and Amsterdam and Convent avenues, with the stipulation that inexpensive concerts be given there during the summer (an annual feature that lasted until 1966). Two important music schools opened about the same time: the David Mannes School (1916, later the Mannes College of Music) and the Neighborhood Music School (1917, later the Manhattan School of Music). In 1923 New York University introduced its baccalaureate music degree, and the School of Sacred Music opened at Union Theological Seminary (this lasted until 1973, when it moved to Yale University). Major concert halls opened during these years included Town Hall at 123 West 43rd Street, built by suffragists in 1921 as a site for public meetings, and the Mecca Temple, constructed at 131 West 55th Street in 1923 by the Ancient and Accepted Order of Nobles of the Mystic Shrine, or Shriners (now known as City Center). The Philharmonic Symphony

Society of New York and the New York Symphony merged in 1928, by which time the city was regularly visited by orchestras from throughout the country and the world. Smaller orchestras were also based in New York City, such as the American National Orchestra (to 1923), the State Symphony Orchestra (to 1926), and the City Symphony (1940–47). In 1924 the Philharmonic began a series of children's concerts under the direction of Ernest Schelling.

As concert life became more active, American composers broke with European models and forged distinctive styles. Charles Ives, a prosperous partner in a life insurance business whose independent means freed him from the constraints imposed by a conservative public, wrote works that were often dissonant and modern for their time. He moved to New York City soon after his graduation from Yale University in 1898 and remained there until 1911, during which time he wrote his piano trio, first piano sonata, first two violin sonatas, second and third symphonies, and various smaller pieces. Prominent modernist composers based in New York City during the early twentieth century included Edgar Varèse, who moved to the city in 1915, Carl Ruggles, who moved there in 1917, and Henry Cowell. Among composers in a more conservative vein were Daniel Gregory Mason (professor at Columbia) and the opera composer Deems Taylor. A number of organizations promoted the performance of modern music, such as the International Composers' Guild, formed in 1921 partly through the efforts of Varèse, the League of Composers and the American section of the International Society for Contemporary Music (both formed in 1923, merged in 1954), the Pan-American Association of Composers, in which Cowell played a leading role, and later Composers' Forum (active 1935–40, revived 1947).

During the years surrounding the First World War the concert tradition and the vernacular influenced each other considerably. Ragtime composers often worked in classical forms, and many classical composers looked to ragtime for inspiration. The bandmaster James Reese Europe led a concert by the Clef Club at Carnegie Hall in 1912 that displayed a number of hybrid ragtime and classical pieces; George Gershwin wrote his *Rhapsody in Blue*, given its première in 1924 by Paul Whiteman and his orchestra, and his *Concerto in F* (1925) for piano and orchestra; the Harlem stride pianist James P. Johnson composed several works of "symphonic jazz," notably *Yamekraw* (1928, orchestrated by William Grant Still); Scott Joplin during the last years of his life made a desperate and largely unsuccessful attempt to interest backers in producing his opera *Treemonisha* (which was widely acclaimed when it was finally staged long after his death, in 1976); and the early output of Aaron Copland included several works strongly informed by jazz, among them *Music for the Theater* (1925) and *Four Piano Blues* (1926). Copland was also an influential member of the League of Composers and a contributor to its journal *Modern Music.* Another composer well known for his critical writings was Virgil Thomson, who with Gertrude Stein wrote the operas *Four Saints in Three Acts* (1928) and *The Mother of Us All* (1947, about Susan B. Anthony) and from 1940 to 1954 was the principal music critic at the *New York Herald Tribune.* A number of modernist composers were active in leftist politics, particularly those associated with the Composers' Collective, who contributed to two workers' songbooks published by the Workers Music League. Workers' rounds were written by Elie Siegmeister (1909–91), who used the pseudonym L. E. Swift, and Charles Seeger (1886–1979), who wrote as Carl Sands. Copland in 1934 won a song competition sponsored by the *New Masses* with his composition "Into the Streets of May," and Marc Blitzstein's opera *The Cradle Will Rock* (1937) was imbued with the ideology of the Popular Front. At the same time the phonograph achieved greater commercial viability. In New York City the recording firms Victor and Columbia Talking Machine were among early leaders of the field, which they continued to dominate after electric recording was introduced in 1925. During the 1920s both firms evolved into conglomerates active in such areas as broadcasting and theater management. They also expanded beyond New York City, especially after the 1930s when the advent of radio and the Depression prompted the industry to move most of its popular-music divisions to the west coast. Long an important center for music management, the city about 1920 became the base of operations for the impresario Sol Hurok, who remained in the forefront of the business for five decades.

The rise of Nazism brought a number of distinguished émigré musicians to the city, including the conductors Bruno Walter and Erich Leinsdorf, the pianists Rudolf Serkin and Claudio Arrau, the singers Lauritz Melchior (1890–1973), Lotte Lehmann, Elizabeth Schumann, Friedrich Schorr, and Alexander Kipnis, and the composers Stefan Wolpe, Béla Bartók (who worked at Columbia), and Paul Hindemith (who taught at Yale). New symphony orchestras were formed, notably the NBC Symphony Orchestra, conducted by Arturo Toscanini from 1937 to 1954, principally on the radio. The New York Philharmonic broadcast over the Columbia Broadcasting System (CBS) from 1930, and from 1931 Texaco sponsored nationwide radio broadcasts by the Metropolitan Opera, which staged French, German, Italian, American, English, and Russian works performed by such singers as Rosa Ponselle (1897–1981), often in spectacular productions. Walter Damrosch gave radio broadcasts for schoolchildren in the 1930s, and the pianist Olga Samaroff-Stokowski offered "audience development" courses from the mid 1930s to 1948, first at the David Mannes School and later at Town Hall. The New Friends of Music presented concerts of chamber music between 1936 and 1953. The dominance of ASCAP in licensing was challenged when it failed to reach a contract agreement with radio broadcasters in 1939, and a consortium of six hundred broadcasters then formed a competing organization, Broadcast Music Inc. (BMI), which specialized in popular genres such as folk music and blues. The radio station WQXR began broadcasting in 1936 as the first full-time classical music station in the United States; the municipal station WNYC also broadcast a large amount of classical music, especially during the administration of Mayor Fiorello H. La Guardia. From 1935 to 1943 the Music Project of the Works Progress Administration provided free concerts, educational programs, and music instruction to New Yorkers, and in 1935 Composers' Forum began a series of lecture–performances at which a featured composer took questions and comments from the audience.

From the 1920s to the 1940s many composers wrote works celebrating American history, the city, and the American West. These works were usually programmatic and often patriotic: well-known examples include Copland's *A Lincoln Portrait* (1942), Earl Robinson's *Ballad for Americans* (1938), Blitzstein's *Airborne Symphony* (1943–46), composed during the Second World War for the 8th Air Force, John Alden Carpenter's *Skyscrapers* (1926), Adolph Weiss's *American Life: Scherzo Jazzoso* (1928), and Duke Ellington's symphonic jazz piece *Harlem Air Shaft* (1940). For the centenary of the New York Philharmonic in 1942–43 nine conductors programmed twenty-two compositions by Americans, and between October 1943 and January 1945 the Philharmonic played nine pieces commissioned by the League of Composers and CBS, some of which had been inspired by the war; these reached a large audience when broadcast by CBS over the radio. After a foreclosure on the Mecca Temple Mayor La Guardia saved it from demolition in 1943 and purchased it for the city. Renamed City Center, the building became the home in the following year of the City Center Opera Company (later the New York City Opera), which featured young American singers in productions of high quality at low prices. In its early years the company presented a short season devoted to the music of Gilbert and Sullivan, and later its offerings were often more adventurous than those of the Metropolitan Opera.

3. After the Second World War

New chamber ensembles were formed in New York City after the war, among them the Juilliard String Quartet (1946), and in 1948 the

Metropolitan Opera began broadcasting performances on television. Composers living in the city worked in diverse styles. The art songs of Ned Rorem (*b* 1923), on texts by American poets as disparate as Walt Whitman and Sylvia Plath, were indebted to Ravel and Debussy. Copland exerted an influence on a large group of composers, including David Diamond (*b* 1915), William Schuman, composer of the opera *The Mighty Casey* (1951–53), Peter Mennin (*b* 1923), and Siegmeister, who based his cantata *I Have a Dream* (1967) on the life of Martin Luther King Jr. and also wrote such works as *A Sunday in Brooklyn* (1946). In addition to composing, Siegmeister was a tireless advocate of modern music, and both Schuman and Mennin were presidents of the Juilliard School. Ellington continued to write quasi-symphonic works, notably *Harlem (A Tone Parallel to Harlem)* (1950). The most influential and most difficult to categorize among composers in the city was Leonard Bernstein, who wrote compositions ranging from successful Broadway musicals to operas, ballets, and symphonic pieces composed in an eclectic, accessible style, and who was also the music director of the New York Philharmonic from 1957 to 1969. From 1958 he led the orchestra in forty-seven young people's concerts broadcast on television. Composers of electronic music worked at the Columbia–Princeton Electronic Music Center, formed in the city in 1959 by Milton Babbitt (*b* 1916), Otto Luening (*b* 1900), Vladimir Ussachevsky (1911–90), and Roger Sessions (1896–1985). John Cage, a resident of the city from 1943, wrote several compositions based on chance methods, a notorious, completely silent work called *4′33″* (1952), and music for "prepared piano" (the sound of which was altered by having nuts, bolts, and other objects inserted between its strings). He collaborated frequently with Merce Cunningham's dance company. The dense, rhythmically intricate, and often daunting music of Elliott Carter, perhaps more successful among critics than with audiences, constituted one of the most impressive bodies of work written by an American. Not all composers were tolerant of the stylistic diversity that characterized classical music in the city. Some of them, especially those affiliated with universities and with such organizations and ensembles as the League of Composers/ ISCM, the Group for Contemporary Music, Speculum Musicae, and the New York New Music Ensemble, espoused an orthodox view of composition that accepted as legitimate only the twelve-tone techniques of Arnold Schoenberg and Anton Webern and their disciples.

Concert life in the city continued to be centered at Carnegie Hall, the home of the New York Philharmonic until the opening at Lincoln Center on 24 September 1962 of Philharmonic Hall (eventually renamed Avery Fisher Hall). Carnegie Hall later survived efforts by real-estate developers to have it razed. Lincoln Center was also the site of the New York State Theater, which became the home of the New York City Opera in 1966. In the same year the New York Philharmonic and the Metropolitan Opera began presenting regular seasons of outdoor concerts on the Great Lawn in Central Park and at other parks throughout the five boroughs. The Chamber Music Society of Lincoln Center, formed in 1969, presented concerts in Alice Tully Hall at Lincoln Center by a resident ensemble supplemented by guest soloists.

Far from the mainstream of classical music there developed schools of composition that flourished in the lofts, art galleries, and nightclubs of lower Manhattan. Inspired by the work of Cage, "minimalists" such as La Monte Young (*b* 1935), Meredith Monk (*b* 1943), Steve Reich, and Philip Glass repudiated the complexity of modern composition and built extended works by frequently repeating simple rhythmic and melodic fragments. Groups such as Experiments in Art and Technology (EAT), which was associated with Bell Laboratories in New Jersey, explored novel combinations of technology and art. Composers such as Laurie Anderson (*b* 1947) and John Zorn attempted a fusion of classical music and avant-garde rock. The festival New Music/New York of 1979 led to the formation of the New Music Alliance, a group dedicated to promoting performances of new music throughout the United States.

In the mid 1990s a large number of performing ensembles were based in New York City, ranging from symphony orchestras (which numbered more than forty in the metropolitan area) to groups specializing in early music (the Waverly Consort, the New York Cornet and Sackbut Ensemble), founded by graduate students and inspired by the study of pre-Baroque music at universities, to groups specializing in modern music (the Contemporary Chamber Ensemble, the Group for Contemporary Music, Speculum Musicae). Operas were staged by the Metropolitan Opera and the New York City Opera, as well as by such smaller companies as the New York Grand Opera (which in 1994 launched a seven-year festival of all of Verdi's operas, the first such project ever), the Amato Opera Company, the Opera Orchestra of New York, the Brooklyn Academy of Music, and the opera companies of the Juilliard School, the Manhattan School of Music, and the Mannes College of Music. Although music programs in the public schools had suffered greatly from budgetary reductions (there were fewer than a thousand licensed music teachers in the system in the mid 1990s, compared with three thousand in the 1960s), musical training of high quality was offered at Fiorello H. La Guardia High School of Music and Art and Performing Arts (opened in 1936). In addition to its well-known conservatories the city had several notable community music schools, including the Greenwich House Music School, the Turtle Bay Music School, the Bloomingdale House of Music, and the Harlem School of the Arts.

The city's many concert venues cover a wide range. Carnegie Hall remains the favored auditorium for many visiting orchestras, chamber ensembles, and recitalists; others perform at Avery Fisher Hall, Alice Tully Hall, and the Walter Reade Theatre (all at Lincoln Center). Kaufman Concert Hall at the 92nd Street YM-YWHA (1929, seating 916) supports resident orchestras and presents renowned guest orchestras and soloists. In 1978 the Hebrew Arts School added a concert hall seating 457 to its building at 129 West 67th Street, renamed Merkin Concert Hall in 1981. Classical music is also performed at several schools and universities, including Columbia (at the Kathryn Bache Miller Theatre), Hunter College (at the Sylvia and Danny Kaye Playhouse), City College (Aaron Davis Hall), Lehman College (the Lehman Center for the Performing Arts), and Queens College (the Colden Center), and at such museums as the Metropolitan Museum of Art, the Guggenheim Museum, the Asia Society, the Museum of Modern Art, and the Whitney Museum of American Art. Many churches offer performances of classical music at Christmas and Easter. Performance spaces specializing in the avant-garde include PS 122 (1st Avenue and 9th Street), the Clocktower Gallery (108 Leonard Street), Franklin Furnace (112 Franklin Street), and the Kitchen (512 West 19th Street), which became a leading venue for performance art and experimental music soon after its opening in SoHo in 1971. Bargemusic, a floating concert hall moored in Brooklyn beneath the Brooklyn Bridge, began presenting a notable chamber music series in 1977. Symphony Space, at 95th Street and Broadway, is a disused movie theater that was converted into a concert hall in 1978.

Although much of the music business left New York City for California after the 1930s, the large record companies Polygram, BMG, and Sony have their headquarters in the city, as do such specialized labels as Composers Recordings, Inc. (CRI), New World, and Nonesuch (now part of Elektra/Warner). The Recording Industries Association of America (RIAA), a trade organization formed in 1952, is also based in the city. Along 57th Street, near Carnegie Hall, are most of the country's large music management agencies, many of which were established by former associates of Hurok: Columbia Artists Management, ICM Artists, Thea Dispeker, and Harold Shaw. ASCAP has offices on Broadway across from Lincoln Center, and BMI is on 57th Street.

The study of music history in general and American music in particular owes much to the work of scholars based in New York City, such as Frederic Louis Ritter in the late nineteenth century and especially John Tasker Howard (author of *Our American Music*, 1931). The American Musicological Society was organized in 1939 in a townhouse on Washington Square. Otto Kinkeldey, Gustave Reese, Curt Sachs, Paul Henry Lang, Eric Werner, and Oscar Sonneck established the city as a center for musicology through their activities as university professors, writers on music history, and librarians. Two institutions of great importance are the *Musical Quarterly* (1915–) and the music division of the New York Public Library for the Performing Arts, which has a unique collection of Americana and remains unsurpassed in the metropolitan region for the breadth of its holdings.

Gilbert Chase: *America's Music: From the Pilgrims to the Present* (New York: McGraw–Hill, 1966; 3rd edn Urbana: University of Illinois Press, 1987)
George Whitney Martin: *The Damrosch Dynasty: America's First Family of Music* (Boston: Houghton Mifflin, 1983)
John Rockwell: *All American Music: Composition in the Late Twentieth Century* (New York: Alfred A. Knopf, 1983)
Barbara L. Tischler: *An American Music: The Search for an American Musical Identity* (New York: Oxford University Press, 1986)
Vera Brodsky Lawrence: *Strong on Music: The New York Music Scene in the Days of George Templeton Strong, 1836–1875*, vol. 1, *Resonances* (New York: Oxford University Press, 1988)

James M. Keller, Nancy Shear, Barbara L. Tischler, Victor Fell Yellin

Clearing House Association. See New York Clearing House Association.

Clearwater. Sloop used for teaching about the ecology of the Hudson River. Designed like the sloops used for trade on the Hudson River during the nineteenth century, the ship was built during a campaign led by the folk singer Pete Seeger to clean up the Hudson and first sailed in New York Harbor in the summer of 1970.

Cleary Gottlieb Steen and Hamilton. Law firm that began as a partnership formed on 1 January 1946 by George Cleary and Leo Gottlieb. Its first client was the entertainer Bing Crosby and it later represented the Beatles; the firm also became known for financial expertise through its work with the investment banking firm of Salomon Brothers and gained clients internationally after opening an office in Washington under George Ball. During the 1980s it specialized in corporate debt and equity exchanges and handled the restructuring of debt in Brazil, Chile, and Mexico. In 1990 the firm had seven offices worldwide (including headquarters at 1 Liberty Plaza), 103 partners, and 342 associates. Among its clients were the radio station WNYC, Macy's department store, and the publishing firm of Macmillan, as well as influential concerns in Africa and the Middle East. It organized the Lehman Foundation, donated funds for the children's zoo in Central Park and the Lehman Suite at Columbia University, and launched a program through which it paid associates to volunteer for four months with the Community Action for Legal Services.

George J. Lankevich

Clemens, Samuel (Langhorne). See Twain, Mark.

Cleopatra's Needle [Obelisk]. Red granite shaft sixty-nine feet (twenty-one meters) tall and weighing two hundred tons (181 metric tons) that stands in Central Park near the Metropolitan Museum of Art. It was erected in Heliopolis about 1475 B.C. by Pharaoh Thutmose III. Roman soldiers moved it in 12 B.C. to Alexandria, where it remained until it was shipped to New York City in 1880 as a gift to the United States from the khedive of Egypt. Unloaded at Staten Island, it was sent on pontoons up the Hudson River, then rolled on cannonballs to its present site. Another obelisk known as Cleopatra's Needle, also a gift of the khedive, stands in London. Despite their name neither is known to have any connection with Cleopatra.

Ernest Alfred Wallis Budge: *Cleopatra's Needles and Other Egyptian Obelisks* (London: Religious Tract Society, 1926)

Sandra Opdycke

Cleopatra's Needle, ca *1900*

Clermont [North River Steamboat]. The first commercially successful steamboat in America. Designed by Robert Fulton and built by Charles Brown(e) in New York City, she measured about 140 feet (42.6 meters) by sixteen feet (4.9 meters), although the size was modified several times; the side paddle-wheels were powered by an engine made by the English firm Boulton and Watt. The first demonstration trip of the steamboat, between New York City and Albany, New York (17–19 August 1807), was quickly followed by commercial service on this route beginning on 4 September. The steamboat was retired in 1814, replaced by others that were larger and more technically advanced. She was known during Fulton's life as the *North River Steamboat*, and came to be called the *Clermont* only after his death in 1815.

Cynthia Owen Philip: *Robert Fulton: A Biography* (New York: F. Watts, 1985)

Arthur G. Adams

Cleveland, (Stephen) Grover (*b* Caldwell, N.J., 18 March 1837; *d* Princeton, N.J., 24 June 1908). Twenty-second and twenty-fourth president of the United States. He was a mayor of Buffalo and a governor of New York before being elected president as a Democrat in 1884. After failing to win reelection in 1888 he moved with his wife, Frances, to New York City, where they lived in an elegant, four-story townhouse of red brick and brownstone at 816 Madison Avenue (near 68th Street). He was of counsel to the law firm of Bangs, Stetson, Tracy and MacVeagh (15 Broad Street), where he formed close alliances with many financiers on Wall Street including J. P. Morgan. After he regained the presidency in 1892 the family sold the house on Madison Avenue and lived briefly at 12 West 51st Street before returning to the White House. Cleveland returned to the city in 1893 for an operation for throat cancer: this was performed aboard a yacht at Pier A in the East River and kept secret for fear that news of it would exacerbate a severe financial crisis, which was ended in 1895 when Cleveland enlisted Morgan's help.

Allan Nevins: *Grover Cleveland: A Study in Courage* (New York: Dodd, Mead, 1932)

James Bradley

Clews, Henry (*b* Straffordshire, England, 14 Aug 1834; *d* New York City, 31 Jan 1923). Financier. After emigrating in 1850 to the United States he opened the securities firm of Stout, Clews and Mason in 1859, which became the second-largest underwriter of American government bonds during the Civil War and continued to prosper after the war ended. He was active in Republican politics and helped to form the Committee of Seventy, a reform group that forced William M. "Boss" Tweed from office. Renamed Henry Clews and Company in 1877, the firm by the 1890s was the largest negotiator of railroad loans in America or Europe. Clews wrote *Wall Street Point of View* (1900) and *Fifty Years in Wall Street* (1908), an important source of information on Wall Street in the last half of the nineteenth century.

George Winslow

Clifton. Neighborhood in northeastern Staten Island (1990 pop. 3000), bounded to the north by Stapleton, to the east by Upper New York Bay, to the south by Rosebank, and to the west by Van Duzer Street. A town of the same name laid out in 1837 occupied a somewhat larger area; its early history was closely tied to that of the Vanderbilts. As a young man Cornelius Vanderbilt ran a ferry service to Manhattan from the foot of the avenue that now bears his name. The neighborhood is the site of Bayley Seton Hospital, formerly the U.S. Public Health Service Hospital, a sprawling complex that houses the original headquarters and laboratories of the National Institutes of Health (now in Bethesda, Maryland). By the early 1990s a neighborhood of Liberians and other West Africans took shape around Targee Street; many of the African residents worshipped at Faith Christian Center at 20 Park Hill Avenue. Most residents of Clifton live in one-family houses, and some live in apartment complexes. The principal thoroughfares are Tompkins Avenue and Bay Street. There is also a station of Staten Island Rapid Transit.

Charles W. Leng and William T. Davis: *Staten Island and Its People* (New York: Lewis Historical Publishing, 1930)

Henry G. Steinmeyer: *Staten Island, 1524–1898* (New York: Staten Island Historical Society, 1950; repr. 1987)

John-Paul Richiuso

Clinton. The name given in 1959 to a neighborhood on the West Side of Manhattan bounded to the north by 59th Street, to the east by 8th Avenue, to the south by 42nd Street, and to the west by the Hudson River. It occupies most of the area formerly known as HELL'S KITCHEN.

Clinton, De Witt (*b* Little Britain, N.Y., 2 March 1769; *d* Albany, N.Y., 11 Feb 1828). Mayor and governor. The son of the Revolutionary general James Clinton, he entered élite circles of government and society in New York State after being employed as a private secretary by his uncle Governor George Clinton about 1790. Within a decade one of the most powerful politicians in the state, he was appointed to the U.S. Senate in 1802 and returned to the city in 1803 after being appointed mayor; he was reappointed every year until 1815, except in 1807 and 1810 when political opponents controlled the state's Council of Appointment. While in office he helped to form the Free School Society, the New-York Historical Society, the Literary and Philosophical Society, and the Orphan Asylum, improved sanitation, administered public markets, guided plans to expand the city northward, and strengthened the defenses of New York Harbor to prepare for war with Britain. In the presidential election of 1812 he ran against James Madison, seeking the support of both Federalists who opposed the war and Republicans who wished to wage it more successfully; he won eighty-nine electoral votes to Madison's 128.

After his defeat Clinton was overshadowed in popularity by Governor Daniel D. Tompkins (whose election he had engineered in 1807) and by 1815 no longer held public office. He soon returned to politics to promote the plan for the Erie Canal, for which he managed to secure the legislature's approval despite opposition from the Bucktails of Tammany Hall. When Tompkins resigned in 1817 to become vice president he was elected to replace him as governor, winning 43,310 votes to his opponent's 1479. As mayor and governor Clinton had a vision of the city's future as a great commercial center, and by means of commercial success he hoped to raise the city to cultural eminence as well. To this end he sponsored many measures to aid education and cultural institutions, although a good number were weakened or blocked by political opponents. His plans for the city, like the plan for the Erie Canal, called for the active participation of government. He won reelection in 1820 against Tompkins but did not seek another term in 1822 because of strong opposition from the Bucktails, led by Martin Van Buren. In 1824 he was again elected governor, with the support of voters outraged that the Bucktails had dismissed him from his position as an unsalaried canal commissioner. Clinton presided over the opening ceremonies of the canal in 1825 and remained in office until his death. Two neighborhoods, a high school, and several parks in the city are named for him.

De Witt Clinton

Jabez D. Hammond: *Political Parties in the State of New York, from the Ratification of the Federal Constitution to December 1840* (Albany, N.Y.: C. Van Benthuysen, 1842)

Dixon Ryan Fox: *The Decline of Aristocracy in the Politics of New York, 1801–1840* (New York: Columbia University Press, 1919; repr. Harper and Row, 1965)

Evan Cornog

Clinton Hill. Neighborhood in northwestern Brooklyn. Overlooking Wallabout Bay and centered at Pratt Institute, it is bounded to the north by the Brooklyn–Queens Expressway, to the east by Classon Avenue, to the south by Atlantic Avenue, and to the west by Vanderbilt Avenue. The neighborhood is named for De Witt Clinton and occupies the highest ground in the area. In 1832 Clinton Avenue was laid out as a tree-lined boulevard along the crest of the hill, and some grand villas had been built by the 1840s. The area was considered a rural retreat until the speculative development in the 1860s of row houses, which by 1880 lined most of the streets and attracted affluent professionals. Between 1880 and 1915 the wealthiest industrialists of Brooklyn built mansions on Clinton and Washington avenues. Development was spurred by the decision of the oil executive Charles Pratt to build a house at 232 Clinton Avenue in 1874: this magnificent residence, now part of St. Joseph's College, is surrounded by three of the four other houses that Pratt gave to his sons as wedding gifts. In 1887 Pratt founded Pratt Institute at 200 Willoughby Street, an art and industrial school that became the focus of the neighborhood and remained so for more than a century. Apartment buildings were constructed from about 1900, and during the 1920s and 1940s largely replaced the mansions along Clinton and Washington avenues. During the 1950s and 1960s one-family houses became rooming houses. Robert Moses in 1954 cleared a five-block area south of Pratt Institute for renewal, and in the 1970s many of the fine brownstones of the neighborhood were restored.

Clinton Hill is a neighborhood of shingled, clapboard, brick, limestone, and brownstone houses, interspersed with frame houses and mansions predating the Civil War and apartment buildings. It is inhabited by a large number of artists, architects, photographers, and craftsmen and is racially diverse (45 percent black, 55 percent white and Asian), with many Italians and a number of black immigrants from the Caribbean. There is a wide range in the quality and price of housing, from elegant brownstones and mansions to inexpensive apartments for students. Designated a Historic District in 1981, the neighborhood includes such city landmarks as the Emmanuel Baptist Church (1887) and the Steele–Skinner House (1812), both on Lafayette Avenue, and the Church of St. Luke and St. Matthew (1889) and the Royal Castle Apartments (1910), both on Clinton Avenue. The main buildings of the Pratt campus on Hall Street are all landmarks, as are the Mechanics Temple (1889, formerly the Lincoln Club) at 67 Putnam Avenue and St. Mary's Episcopal Church (1859) at 230 Classon Avenue. DeKalb Avenue is the main thoroughfare.

Clinton Hill Brooklyn (New York: Society for Clinton Hill, n.d.)

Nanette Rainone, ed.: *The Brooklyn Neighborhood Book* (New York: Fund for the Borough of Brooklyn, 1985)

Elizabeth Reich Rawson

Clio Award. An annual award for excellence in advertising, inaugurated in 1959 by Wallace Ross, David Ogilvy, and John P. Cunningham. The organization that grants the awards was acquired in 1971 by Ross for $150,000. In later years mismanagement of funds drove the organization to bankruptcy, and the trademark for the Clio Award was purchased in 1991 from Bill Evans by Ruth Ratney. The offices of the Clio Award are at 276 5th Avenue in Manhattan.

B. Kimberly Taylor

Cloisters. Museum in Manhattan at Fort Tryon Park that houses a collection of medieval art and architecture chiefly assembled by the sculptor George Grey Barnard in Europe. It was known as the Barnard Cloisters until its purchase in 1925 with a donation from John D. Rockefeller Jr. by the Metropolitan Museum of Art, which expanded and remodeled the building and opened it as a branch in 1938. The museum incorporates architectural monuments from the cloisters of five French monasteries. Its chapels and exhibition halls contain fine works of Romanesque and Gothic art, the most notable of which are the Unicorn Tapestries.

Bonnie Young: *A Walk through the Cloisters* (New York: Metropolitan Museum of Art, 1977)

Elliot S. Meadows

The Cloisters, ca 1938

Clove Lakes Park. Public park in Staten Island, occupying two hundred acres (eighty hectares) in West New Brighton. It contains several freshwater lakes, adjoined by a brook that extends through the park from Victory Boulevard to the Kill van Kull. From the seventeenth to the nineteenth centuries several dams were built in the brook that created water pressure for local mills as well as many ponds, most of which no longer exist. Brooks Pond provided the island's water supply in the late nineteenth century and the early twentieth. In 1926 the area was taken over by the city's parks department and given its current name. Clove Lakes Park in the mid 1990s was the most popular park in Staten Island, offering facilities for boating, fishing, hiking, and horseback riding. It was also the site of local offices of the parks department.

James Bradley

clubs. For information on clubs see Political clubs, Social clubs, University clubs, and Women's clubs.

Clurman, Harold (*b* New York City, 18 Sept 1901; *d* New York City, 9 Sept 1980). Drama critic, director, teacher, and actor. He became interested in the theater after seeing the Yiddish actor Jacob Adler in *Uriel Acosta* at the Grand Street Theatre in 1907. After studying at Columbia University and the Sorbonne, where he lived with Aaron Copland, he settled in New York City. There he made his acting début as a walk-on in Stark Young's play *The Saint* at the Greenwich Village Theatre in 1924. As a reader for the Theatre Guild he met Cheryl Crawford and Lee Strasberg and with them formed the Group Theatre (1931–41) to produce plays with both aesthetic and social relevance. He later directed such important premières as those for Carson McCullers's *A Member of the Wedding* (1950, Empire Theatre) and William Inge's *Bus Stop* (1955, Music Box Theatre), wrote influential reviews for the *New Republic* (1949–52), the *Nation* (1953–80), and the *Observer* (1955–63), and taught directing at Hunter College (1964–80). Clurman's published writings include *The Fervent Years* (1945), a history of the Group Theatre; three volumes of criticism, *Lies like Truths* (1958), *The Naked Image* (1966), and *The Divine Pastime* (1974); and *On Directing* (1972), a widely read text among theater students.

Cobble Hill. Neighborhood in northwestern Brooklyn (1980 pop. 6900), bounded to the north by Atlantic Avenue, to the east by Court Street, to the south by Degraw Street, and to the west by the Brooklyn–Queens Expressway; it is one of several small neighborhoods that once made up South Brooklyn and lies between Brooklyn Heights and Carroll Gardens. The area was settled in the mid seventeenth century by Dutch farmers who called it Punkiesberg. A hill at what is now the corner of Atlantic Avenue and Court Street was known as Cobbleshill at the time of the American Revolution, but the name became disused during the nineteenth century. The area remained rural until 1836, when ferry service to Atlantic Avenue spurred suburban development. Between 1840 and 1880 many brownstone and brick row houses were built in the Greek Revival and Romanesque styles; the population was upper middle class. In the 1870s the philanthropist Alfred T. White built two experimental housing projects in the area: the Towers (439–45 Hicks Street), a Romanesque Revival apartment building intended for working-class tenants, and Warren Place, a mews of tiny one-family experimental housing developments built around a private courtyard for middle-class tenants; both remained standing into the 1990s. In the early twentieth century there was an influx of lower-middle-class immigrants from Ireland, Italy, and the Middle East. The neighborhood contains many churches predating the Civil War and one of the city's finest collections of nineteenth-century houses, including the birthplace of Winston Churchill's mother, Jennie Jerome, at 154 Amity Street. Long Island College Hospital (1848) occupies several buildings on Henry Street and Amity Place. The Israel Ashei Emes Synagogue, in an early Romanesque former church building on Kane Street, is the home of the oldest Jewish congregation in Brooklyn. Brownstone enthusiasts moved in during the late 1950s and revived the name Cobble Hill; they organized a successful effort to resist public housing and were instrumental in having the neighborhood designated a Historic District in 1969. Housing prices rose steadily during the 1970s and 1980s, and by the early 1990s Cobble Hill was again affluent.

Philip Kasinitz

Cocclestown. Original name of RICHMONDTOWN.

cockroaches. In New York City the cockroach (or roach) has a notorious reputation and an almost ubiquitous presence. The city's roach population was inadvertently introduced by trade. Such species as the American, Oriental, Australian, German, and brown-banded cockroaches are all found in the city. Most species measure about 0.1 to 0.2 inches (two and a half to five millimeters) in length, but some reach 1.75 inches (four and a half centimeters). The color varies from tawny gray to brown or black to reddish brown, and the structure varies as well: for example, female Oriental roaches are almost wingless as adults, and American roaches have well-developed wings. Roaches are also variable with respect to food preference. Many are scavengers that feed on garbage, dead insects, and human food, and some species invade human habitats. In nature, species live under logs, stones, and bark, and in ant and termite nests; but in the city certain species have become common household pests and are found almost everywhere, from the subways to fine restaurants. Cockroaches are especially visible in poorly maintained buildings, because wall voids and accumulations of debris provide good shelter. Cracks around windows, doorways, and plumbing provide easy access to sources of food, but the insects easily enter new apartments as well, often by riding in on the clothing or shopping bags of residents, or by flying and crawling in from other buildings. They often seek the water around pipes and sinks, and are known to be attracted to toothpaste. Evidence that cockroaches spread disease is conclusive: their unsightly appearance, putrid odor (when in large numbers), and ability to contaminate food with feces have encouraged the development of insecticides, which contributes to the large number of exterminators doing business in New York City. Although extermination by chemical control has sometimes proven effective, often it merely forces roaches into a neighboring apartment or building, and in some places roaches have become resistant to the most widely used substances. Research into more effective roach control focuses on growth regulators, pheromones, and molting hormones to disrupt the life processes of roaches and cause the populations to fall.

William J. Bell and K. G. Adiyodi: *The American Cockroach* (New York: Chapman and Hall, 1981)

Louis N. Sorkin

coffee. In the nineteenth century New York City was the world's leading port for the importation and processing of coffee. A coffee district emerged along several blocks of Old Slip and Front, Water, and Wall streets, where longshoremen unloaded coffee beans in jute bags weighing 160 pounds (seventy-three kilograms). In 1860 almost half the coffee imported nationwide entered through the Port of New York, and the proportion exceeded 80 percent by the 1890s. Initially consumers did their own roasting and grinding of coffee beans. Coffee that was already roasted and ground by the dealer was introduced to the American market by such entrepreneurs as James P. "Handsome Jim" Bennett (1845–1908), who operated out of a five-story building at 10 Fulton Street and used traveling salesmen to sell his Trademark Royal Java to retail grocers far beyond Manhattan. By 1878 a trade journal in New York City noted that the era "when every household performed the roasting for itself was passing." In the mid 1990s Americans remained the world's leading coffee consumers, and New York City was (with New Orleans) one of the nation's principal coffee importing centers. The Coffee, Sugar, and Cocoa Exchange in the World Trade Center and the Green Coffee Association of New York City on John Street testified to the area's continuing centrality in the international coffee trade. But the coffee district near Front Street was largely gone, and most buyers and roasters of green coffee had dispersed to other parts of the metropolitan area and other regions of the United States.

Steven H. Jaffe: "A Trader in Brown Gold," *Seaport Magazine*, summer 1994, pp. 44–46

Kenneth T. Jackson

Coffee, Sugar and Cocoa Exchange. A commodities market incorporated as the Coffee Exchange of the City of New York in 1885. It was relatively small, sustained by connections to producers in Latin America and banks, as well as by daily reports from local business newspapers and other commodity exchanges and by monthly estimates of crop conditions and other harvest news from government agencies in provinces and shipping centers. The name was changed to the New York Coffee and Sugar Exchange in 1916, when the sugar markets in Europe were closed by the First World War and trade shifted to New York City. Coffee futures trading was plagued with difficulties caused by grading standards that could allow substitution of one variety for another, so that the need for arbitration of disputes between buyers and sellers increased. Importers complained in the 1950s to the Federal Trade Commission that the narrow definitions of grades excluded them from hedging opportunities. After an investigation the exchange entered into a consent decree that broadened its standard contract to cover about 70 percent of the world's coffee. The exchange in the 1960s had 350 members and controlled much of the world spot and futures business in sugar. In 1979 it absorbed the New York Cocoa Exchange (opened 1925), which was an important center of trading in Latin American cocoa, an increasingly important commodity as supplies from Africa diminished. Trading volume in the 1980s quintupled for cocoa (largely because lower output worldwide led to a sextupling of prices) and more than doubled for coffee. The Federal Trade Commission responded with more rigorous scrutiny of traders and efforts to bring about better self-governance. In the mid 1990s the exchange shared trading facilities with three other major exchanges in the World Trade Center.

New York Coffee and Sugar Exchange, Inc.: Its Role in the Marketing of Sugar (New York: Hobbs, Dorman, 1965)

Martin J. Pring, ed.: *The McGraw–Hill Handbook of Commodities and Futures* (New York: McGraw–Hill, 1985)

Morton Rothstein

coffee houses. During the colonial period coffee houses were important meeting places for politicians, merchants, and military officers in New York City. Like their English counterparts these coffee houses sold alcohol and were centrally situated. In 1696 John Hutchins opened the King's Arms, also known as the Coffee House, on the west side of Broadway just north of the cemetery of Trinity Church. A focal point for opponents of Jacob Leisler, it was frequented by a genteel clientele. By 1747 new owners referred to the King's Arms as the Exchange Coffee House to reflect its function as a marketplace for many commodities, including slaves, ships, horses, and real estate. Another important center of commerce and conviviality was the Merchants' Coffee House, opened about 1737 at the southeast corner of Wall and Water streets. Along with George Burns' Coffee House, which supplanted the old King's Arms, the Merchants' was an important meeting place for the Sons of Liberty; there Isaac Low, Alexander MacDougall, James Duane, and John Jay on 23 May 1774 drafted the famous letter of the New York Committee of Correspondence protesting against the Intolerable Acts and supporting the formation of the Continental Congress. In later years the Merchants' Coffee House was the site of meetings that led to the formation of the Chamber of Commerce (1768), the Bank of New York (1784), the New York Hospital Society (1785), the Society of the Cincinnati (1786), and the Manhattan Company (1799). The Merchants' also oversaw the first public auction of stock in 1790 and remained in operation until the building was destroyed by fire on 18 December 1804. The Tontine Coffee House, opened in 1794 on the northwest corner of Wall and Water streets, was perhaps the best-known establishment of its kind in New York City and an important institution until 1826. Coffee houses diminished in number by the 1830s, as the city's boundaries expanded and various populist movements created a hostile climate that persuaded the rich and powerful to take their business to exclusive private clubs and other institutions.

Frederic De Peyster: *History of the Tontine Building* (New York: Nesbitt, 1855)

Elizabeth Brown Cutting: *Old Taverns and Posting Inns* (New York: G. P. Putnam's Sons, 1898)

Marc Ferris

Coffin, Henry Sloane (*b* New York City, 5 Jan 1877; *d* Lakeville, Conn., 25 Nov 1954). Minister. He was brought up in Manhattan at 13 West 57th Street and attended Yale University and the Union Theological Seminary. While serving at the Bedford Park Presbyterian Church in the Bronx and the Madison Avenue Presbyterian Church (1905–26) he became known for his impassioned preaching style and his writings on the Social Gospel movement. He rallied immigrants in support of educational programs, Bible classes, and missionary work in China, and helped to increase the size of the congregation at Madison Avenue Presbyterian Church from six hundred to 2500. During his tenure as the president of Union Theological Seminary (1926–45) the seminary occupied new buildings, appointed the first women to its faculty (1927), added a School of Sacred Music (1928), and absorbed Auburn Seminary from upstate New York (1939). Among the notable faculty that he drew to the school were the eminent theologians Reinhold Niebuhr and Paul Tillich and the biblical translator James Moffatt. In addition he expanded seminary opportunities for blacks and helped students to reconcile religious pacifism with American involvement in the Second World War. As a leader of the local presbytery's Board of Church Extension he helped to support new congregations. He was also a member of the Board of Home Missions (1903) of the American Presbyterian church and a charter member of the Board of National Missions (1923). Elected moderator of the General Assembly (1943), the highest post in the Presbyterian church, he advocated ecumenism after the Second World War and committed himself to unifying the northern and southern branches of the Presbyterian church, an objective that was achieved forty years later. Coffin's published writings include *Social Aspects of the Cross* (1908), *A More Christian Industrial Order* (1920), and *A Half-century of Union Theological Seminary, 1896–1945: An Informal History* (1954).

Morgan Phelps Noyes: *Henry Sloane Coffin: The Man and His Ministry* (New York: Charles Scribner's Sons, 1964)

Robert T. Handy: *A History of Union Theological Seminary in New York* (New York: Columbia University Press, 1987)

David Meerse

Cohalan, Daniel Florence (*b* Middletown, N.Y., 1865; *d* 1946). Judge and political leader. Educated at Manhattan College, he became active in politics in New York City in 1890 and by 1900 was the chief advisor to Charles F. Murphy, leader of Tammany Hall. He was a justice of the New York State Supreme Court (1911–24) and a leading member from 1916 to 1932 of the nationalist group the Friends of Irish Freedom.

William D. Griffin

Cohan, George M(ichael) (*b* Providence, R.I., ?4 July 1878; *d* New York City, 5 Nov 1942). Singer, actor, playwright, composer, and producer. As a child he toured with his family in vaudeville. During the first decades of the twentieth century he wrote and often performed in fast-paced musical melodramas and revues notable for their unabashed flag-waving, settings in New York City, slang, and widely popular songs. For some years he lived in the Hotel Knickerbocker at 142 West 42nd Street. Cohan wrote and produced Broadway plays and musicals throughout the 1920s, often appearing in them. From the 1930s he lived in an apartment at 993 5th Avenue. Toward the end of his career he received critical acclaim for his performances in *Ah, Wilderness!* (1933) by Eugene O'Neill and *I'd Rather Be Right* (1937) by Richard Rodgers and Lorenz Hart. Cohan wrote "Give My Regards to Broadway" and "I'm a Yankee Doodle Dandy." A statue of him stands in Duffy Square in midtown Manhattan.

Patrick McGilligan: *Yankee Doodle Dandy* (Madison: University of Wisconsin Press, 1981)

Cohen, Morris Raphael (*b* Minsk, Ukraine, 25 July 1880; *d* Washington, 28 Jan 1947). Philosopher. He moved with his parents to New York City in 1892, where he attended public schools and City College of New York (BS 1900). While an undergraduate he became active in the Educational Alliance, and with Thomas Davidson he opened a night school for workers where he taught philosophy and history; he later taught at Townshend Harris Hall (1902–4, 1906–12) and City College (1912–38). After beginning graduate work at Columbia he transferred to Harvard University (PhD 1906). A philosophic naturalist, he favored the use of rational methods in pursuing knowledge. He made critical reflections on social morals and laws in much of his work and adhered to a social philosophy calling for government intervention to eliminate social inequities. Cohen also helped to organize conferences on legal and social philosophy (1913) and Jewish relations (1933–41) and was president of the American Philosophical Association (1928). Among his published writings are *Reason and Nature: An Essay on the Meaning of Scientific Method* (1931), *Law and the Social Order* (1933), *Preface to Logic* (1944), *The Faith of a Liberal* (1945), *The Meaning of Human History* (1947), *A Dreamer's Journey: The Autobiography* (1949), and *American Thought: A Critical Sketch* (1954). The Cohen Library at City College is named for him.

Leonora Cohen Rosenfield: *Portrait of a Philosopher* (New York: Harcourt, Brace and World, 1962)

Walter Friedman

Cohn, Roy (Marcus) (*b* New York City, 20 Feb 1927; *d* New York City, 2 Aug 1986). Lawyer. He graduated from Columbia Law School, worked in Manhattan for the U.S. Attorney, whom he assisted in the celebrated espionage trial of Julius and Ethel Rosenberg, and became known for his combative style in the courtroom. In Washington in 1953–54 he was the chief counsel to the committee led by Senator Joseph R. McCarthy that held hearings on purported communist influence in the army; he then returned to New York City and joined the law firm that became Saxe, Bacon and Bolan. During the following decades he acquired a reputation as one of the most powerful, flamboyant, and controversial lawyers in the city. He defended a number of organized-crime figures and was associated with conservative causes. Acquitted on federal charges of conspiracy, bribery, and fraud, Cohn was disbarred in New York State for misuse of his clients' funds only weeks before his death from AIDS.

Nicholas Von Hoffman: *Citizen Cohn* (New York: Doubleday, 1988)

Lisa Gitelman

Cohnheim, Max (*fl* 1848–61). Humorist, playwright, and political activist. In Germany he was associated with the humor magazine *Kladderadatsch* in Berlin. After the revolution of 1848 he emigrated to the United States and settled in New York City. He wrote comic songs for the Arion Gesangverein, edited the *New Yorker Humorist* in 1858–60, and became one of the leading German playwrights in the city. One of his plays, about a triumphant German revolution, was partly set in the Shakespeare Hotel in New York City. He worked briefly for the Republican Party in 1856 before joining with other German–American radicals in 1857 to form the Kommunisten Klub. He later served as a captain of artillery in the Civil War.

Stanley Nadel

coin dealers. For information on coin dealers see Stamp and coin dealers.

Colby, Bainbridge (*b* St. Louis, 22 Dec 1869; *d* Bemus Point, N.Y., 11 April 1950). Secretary of state. A Wall Street lawyer active in local, state, and national politics, he was elected to the state assembly in 1902 as a Republican from the twenty-ninth district and became known as a partisan progressive. In 1912 he helped to form the Progressive Party, serving as a delegate at its first convention and supporting Theodore Roosevelt's presidential candidacy. He unsuccessfully sought a seat in the U.S. Senate in 1914 and again in 1916, when he campaigned for the reelection of President Woodrow Wilson. As Wilson's secretary of state from February 1920 to March 1921 he refused to recognize the government of the Soviet Union, a policy not reversed until 1933 (by President Franklin D. Roosevelt) and one that made for early conflicts leading to the cold war.

Daniel Malloy Smith: *Aftermath of War: Bainbridge Colby and Wilsonian Diplomacy, 1920–1921* (Philadelphia: American Philosophical Society, 1970)

Andrew Wiese

Colden, Cadwallader (*b* Duns, Scotland, 7 Feb 1688; *d* Spring Hill, Long Island, N.Y., 28 Sept 1776). Lieutenant governor and scientist. The son of Scottish parents, he was trained as a doctor in Edinburgh and London and practiced medicine in Philadelphia until 1718, when he moved to New York City to become surveyor general. In 1721 he was appointed to the governor's council. An avid scholar, he was a correspondent of Charles Linnaeus, Benjamin Franklin, Samuel Johnson, Peter Collinson, and Alexander Garden. His first well-known publication was *The History of the Five Indian Nations Depending on the Province of New York* (1727). After learning the Linnaean system he completed a classification of local flora that was published in 1749 in Sweden; he also studied yellow fever and throat distemper, and wrote two papers on cancer and several on light and colors, gravitation, astronomy, mathematics, and philosophy. He was appointed lieutenant governor in 1761 and governed the colony of New York for fourteen years, his tenure interrupted only by the brief terms of several governors. During the years before the American Revolution he became unpopular for his stance on such issues as the Stamp Act and smuggling, and he was burned in effigy by a mob in New York City. Colden was the father of the botanist Jane Colden (*b* 27 March 1724; *d* 10 March 1766).

Alice Mapelsden Keys: *Cadwallader Colden: A Representative Eighteenth-century Official* (New York: Columbia University Press, 1906)

See also Courts, §2.

James E. Mooney

Colden, Charles S(enff) (*b* Whitestone [now in Queens], 3 June 1885; *d* Queens, 14 Sept 1960). Judge. A descendant of Mayor Cadwallader D. Colden, he was appointed district attorney of Queens by Governor Franklin D. Roosevelt in 1932 and a justice of the state supreme court by Governor Herbert H. Lehman in 1943; he left the court in 1956. He helped to endow Queens College, where the Colden Center for the Performing Arts is named for him.

Thomas E. Bird

Cole, Thomas (*b* Bolton-le-Moors, England, 1 Feb 1801; *d* Catskill, N.Y., 11 Feb 1848). Painter. He moved to the United States in 1818 and worked as an engraver and portrait painter in Philadelphia, Pittsburgh, and Steubenville, Ohio. In 1825 he moved to New York City and made his first sketching tour up the Hudson River to the Catskill Mountains. He became well known during the same year after three of his landscapes were bought by John Trumbull, William Dunlap, and Asher B. Durand, an event considered to have marked the beginning of the Hudson River School. He traveled to Europe (1829–32, 1841–42) and around New York State and New England. The first painter to treat landscape as a metaphor for the new nation, he argued in his "Essay on American Scenery" (1835) that the United States was a new Eden where the landscape revealed the presence of God and a future of promise. The allegorical series "The Course of Empire" (1833–36, painted for Luman Reed) and "The Voyage of Life" (1839–40, painted for Samuel Ward) were based on his conception that landscape painters should combine morality and imagination with observations of nature. Among his pupils was Frederic E. Church; he also encouraged Durand to become a landscape painter. In 1836 he left the city and settled in Catskill. Considered the most influential member of the Hudson River School, Cole helped to form the National Academy of Design (1826) and the Sketch Club (1827).

Ellwood C. Parry III: *The Art of Thomas Cole: Ambition and Imagination* (Newark: University of Delaware Press, 1988)

William H. Truettner and Alan Wallach, eds.: *Thomas Cole: Landscape into History* (New Haven: Yale University Press, 1994)

Timothy Anglin Burgard

Coleman, Ornette (*b* Fort Worth, Texas, 9 March 1930). Saxophonist and composer. He made his début in New York City in November 1959 at the Five Spot Café, where his group was so well received that the engagement was extended for six months. In the following year he recorded the album *Free Jazz*, the title of which came to refer to a genre that he played a large role in developing. His performances and recordings in the 1960s and early 1970s were characterized by jagged rhythms, harmonies that were at least outwardly atonal, and the sequential repetition of short melodic motifs, and helped to earn him a reputation as one of the most radical innovators in the history of jazz. He often performed with the trumpeter Don Cherry, the double bass player Charlie Haden, and the drummer Ed Blackwell. In 1971 he opened a performance space called Artist's House at 131 Prince Street in SoHo and in 1976 he formed the band Prime Time, which blends free jazz, funk, and soul.

Thomas Cole, The Course of Empire: The Consummation of Empire *(1835–36)*

Nat Hentoff: *The Jazz Life* (New York: Dial, 1961)
A. B. Spellman: *Four Lives in the Bebop Business* (New York: Pantheon, 1966)
Barry McRae: *Ornette Coleman* (London: Apollo, 1991)

Ira Berger

Coler, Bird S(im) (*b* Champaign, Ill., 9 Oct 1867; *d* Brooklyn, 12 June 1941). Public official. He worked in his father's private bank and as a young man amassed a fortune trading securities. He then turned to politics and with the backing of Tammany Hall was elected in 1898 as the first comptroller of the consolidated city. Defeated in the gubernatorial election of 1902, he won public office in 1906 as the borough president of Brooklyn. He was the commissioner of charities under Mayors John F. Hylan and James J. Walker. In 1929 he broke with the Democrats to seek the presidency of the Board of Aldermen on Fiorello H. La Guardia's unsuccessful mayoral ticket. Coler wrote widely on municipal government and finance. A hospital on Roosevelt Island is named in his honor.

See also WATER, §2.

Frank Vos

Coles, Honi [Charles] (*b* Philadelphia, 1911; *d* Queens, 12 Nov 1992). Dancer. He began tap dancing on the streets of Philadelphia at twelve years of age and later became famous and influential for his elegant style and sustained involvement in the dance world of Harlem and throughout New York City. During the 1930s he performed at the Harlem Opera House and the Apollo Theatre (both in Harlem), and by 1940 he was a soloist with Cab Calloway. With Charles "Cholly" Atkins he formed the team of Coles and Atkins: their specialty was synchronized, identical-step dance routines, and in 1949 they began a two-year engagement on Broadway in the cast of the show *Gentlemen Prefer Blondes.* Although the public's interest in tap dancing subsided during the 1950s, their team was one of the longest-lived. Coles became the production manager of the Apollo in 1960, continued to perform occasionally, and worked with younger dancers. In 1988 he received the Capezio Award for providing an "inspiration to a new generation of tap dancers." He lived in East Elmhurst.

Robert Seder

Colgate, William (*b* Hollingbourne, England, 25 Jan 1783; *d* New York City, 25 March 1857). Soap maker. In 1795 he moved to the United States with his family to escape public hostility toward his father, who had supported the French Revolution. After settling in New York City in 1804 he became a manager of Slidell and Company, the city's largest tallow chandler. In 1806 he opened his own firm, Colgate and Company, which operated a soap factory on Dutch Street in Manhattan that remained the firm's headquarters until 1908; manufacturing operations were moved to Jersey City, New Jersey, in 1847 and the firm was renamed Colgate–Palmolive–Peet in 1922. A leading philanthropist, Colgate was active in the American Bible Society and helped to found Colgate College.

Howard D. Williams: *A History of Colgate University, 1819–1969* (New York: Van Nostrand Reinhold, 1969)
David R. Foster: *The Story of Colgate–Palmolive: One Hundred and Sixty-nine Years of Progress* (New York: Newcomen Society, 1975)

James Bradley

Colgate–Palmolive. Firm of soap and toiletry manufacturers, formed in 1806 on Dutch Street in New York City by William Colgate as a starch, soap, and candle enterprise called Colgate and Company. Its first advertisement for "Soap Mold and Dipt Candles" appeared in 1817. After the factory was moved to New Jersey in 1847 the business office remained in the city. The main products were toilet essence, soap, and pearl starch. The firm merged with Palmolive Peet Company of Chicago in 1922, and the present name was adopted in 1953. The domestic and international headquarters were established at 300 Park Avenue in New York City in 1956. Colgate–Palmolive manufactures a wide range of consumer products, including toothpaste, detergents, hospital supplies, soaps, pet foods, crystal and giftware, wood cleaner, mouthwash, antiperspirants, and liquid bleach.

Richard Kobliner

Coliseum. See NEW YORK COLISEUM.

Collect. A large pond sixty feet (eighteen meters) deep formerly in lower Manhattan, just north of the present City Hall Park; it was also called Fresh Water Pond. Fed by an underground spring, its overflow ran through the marshes of Lispenard Meadows to the Hudson River. The name is a corruption of the Dutch word *kolch* (a small body of water), erroneously written as *kalch* (lime) by some nineteenth-century writers, probably in reference to the lime from the heaps of oyster shells left around the pond by Indians. During the eighteenth century the pond was a favored spot for picnics in the summer and ice skating in the winter, and in 1796 the first experimental steamboat was launched on its waters. It also provided drinking water at the Tea Water Pump in Chatham Street and water for the tanneries, breweries, ropewalks, and slaughterhouses that were built on its southern and eastern banks; by the late eighteenth century the pond was already considered "a very sink and common sewer." Several proposals for new uses of the pond were submitted to the Common Council, including one for a park designed by Pierre L'Enfant and another for a canal between the Hudson and the East River, but the pond was instead filled in between 1803 and 1811 by earth from the surrounding hill. By 1813 the pond was virtually covered as Centre Street was extended northward.

Carol Groneman

College Board. Nonprofit educational association formed to develop standardized college admission tests for secondary-school students. Its first meeting was held on 17 November 1900 in the library of Columbia University. The board was conceived by Charles William Eliot, president of Harvard University, as a means of simplifying the college admission process by eliminating the separate entrance examinations administered by each college. The idea was energetically taken up by Nicholas Murray Butler, soon the president of Columbia, who was the first secretary of the board and later its president. Initially the board offered essay examinations in history, mathematics, physics, chemistry, and ancient and modern languages. In 1926 it introduced the Scholastic Aptitude Test, a multiple-choice examination divided into verbal and mathematical sections that completely displaced the essay examinations by 1940. In 1947 the board joined with the Carnegie Foundation and the American Council on Education to form the Educational Testing Service, which took over many of the board's testing services and other services. The board reintroduced examinations in 1955 not unlike the early essay examinations as part of the Advanced Placement Program, which allowed high school students to enroll in college-level courses. The College Scholarship Service also was introduced in the 1950s: it provided a common application form for financial aid and promoted scholarships based on financial need. The board was chartered in 1957 by the University of the State of New York as a nonprofit educational association governed by a board of trustees.

For many years the College Board was housed in offices provided by Columbia University. It moved into the Interchurch Center on Riverside Drive in 1960 and then to 888 7th Avenue before purchasing the nine lowest floors of the Sofia Building at 45 Columbus Avenue in 1985.

Claude M. Fuess: *The College Board: Its First Fifty Years* (New York: College Entrance Examination Board, 1967)
John A. Valentine: *The College Board and the School Curriculum: A History of the College Board's Influence on the Substance and Standards of American Education, 1900–1980* (New York: College Entrance Examination Board, 1987)

John C. Aubry

College for Human Services. Name until 1993 of AUDREY COHEN COLLEGE.

College of Mount St. Vincent. Independent liberal arts college, formed in 1847 by the Sisters of Charity of Mount St. Vincent as a secondary school for women called the Academy of Mount St. Vincent. The first site was at

Mount St. Vincent at McGowan's Pass in what is now Central Park; the school moved to its current site in Riverdale in 1857, when the Sisters of Charity purchased Fonthill, the estate of the actor Edwin Forrest. The curriculum was expanded to include post-secondary education in 1910, and in the following year the school took its current name and opened with twenty-eight students enrolled as freshmen and sophomores; degrees were awarded from 1913. The first president was the archbishop of New York, John Cardinal Farley, and the first dean was Mary Ambrose Dunphy of the Sisters of Charity. In 1964 the college initiated a cooperative program with Manhattan College. Male students were first admitted in 1974. The college received authorization from the New York State Board of Regents in 1988 to confer a master of science in nursing. It also added a master's program in business. In the mid 1990s Mount St. Vincent had an enrollment of 3293.

Marie De Lourdes Walsh: *The Sisters of Charity of New York, 1809–1959* (New York: Fordham University Press, 1960)

Mary Oates, ed.: *Higher Education for Catholic Women: An Historical Anthology* (New York: Garland, 1987)

Bernadette McCauley

College of Staten Island. College of the City University of New York. It was formed in 1976 by the merger of Staten Island Community College (1955) in Sunnyside and Richmond College (1965) in St. George, at a time when both institutions were threatened by a citywide fiscal crisis. The president of Richmond, Edmond Volpe, became the first head of the new institution, which continued to operate on both campuses until 1993, when a new campus opened at Willowbrook on a site of 204 acres (eighty-three hectares). This campus, the largest of any college in New York City, incorporates buildings from the former campus as well as new library, performing arts, science, athletic, and student activities facilities. The college offers two-year and four-year undergraduate degrees and master's degrees. In the mid 1990s it had about eleven thousand full-time and part-time students and 370 full-time faculty members. Marlene Springer was named president of the college in 1994.

The College of Staten Island at Willowbrook (New York: City University of New York, 1985)

Howard Weiner

College Point. Neighborhood in north central Queens (1985 pop. 25,000), northwest of Flushing along the East River and Flushing Bay. It was built in 1854 by Conrad Poppenhusen to accommodate the workers at his hard-rubber factory, and he alone guided the development of its streets, houses, businesses, and schools. In 1870 it became a village incorporating the neighborhoods of Flammersburg and Strattonport. As breweries, silk mills, and paint works were built the area grew rapidly in the 1880s and 1890s and attracted mostly a German population. Its beer halls and amusement parks, especially Point View Island, made it popular for outings, steamboat excursions, and political clubs. During Prohibition the resorts declined and were eventually replaced by aircraft and aviation parts factories built by Sikorsky Aircraft, the LWF Company, and the Edo Corporation. College Point in the mid 1990s remained predominantly residential, with condominiums along the waterfront and light industry along the main streets.

Vincent Seyfried

colleges and universities. The first institution of higher learning in New York City was King's College, opened at Trinity Church on Wall Street in 1754 by Anglicans allied with members of the Dutch Reformed church and offering a traditional curriculum of Greek, Latin, and mathematics. Closed during the American Revolution, it reopened in 1784 as Columbia College. General Theological Seminary was formed in 1822, followed by Union Theological Seminary (Presbyterian) in 1836. The University of the City of New York (1831, later renamed New York University) was established in response to the conservative curriculum and dominance of Episcopalians at Columbia but nonetheless offered a curriculum of Greek, Latin, and mathematics for much of the nineteenth century; a law school was added in 1835. The first college for women was Rutgers Female Institute (1838); renamed Rutgers Female College in 1867, it ceased operations in 1895. St. John's College (1841) in what is now the Bronx was the first Catholic college in the metropolitan area. It was turned over to the Jesuits in 1846 by Bishop John Hughes and later became Fordham University. Institutions for women included Packer Collegiate Institute (1845) and the Academy of the Sacred Heart (1846, renamed Manhattanville College in 1917 and eventually moved to Purchase, New York). The Academy of Holy Infancy, established by Brothers of the Christian Schools in 1853, later became known as Manhattan College and moved from Manhattanville to Riverdale in 1923. Public higher education was first offered at the Free Academy (1848), which in 1866 changed its name to City College of New York and introduced college-level courses. The Polytechnic Institute of Brooklyn, founded in 1854 as an academy called the Brooklyn Collegiate and Polytechnic Institute, was chartered as a college in 1890 and later became Polytechnic University.

During the second half of the nineteenth century New York University Law School and the Columbia School of Law (1858) dominated legal education in the city. Cooper Union for the Advancement of Science and Art (1859), endowed by Peter Cooper, distinguished itself by offering training in architecture, engineering, and the fine arts without cost to students. St. Francis Academy (1859), organized by the Franciscan Brothers in Brooklyn, was taken over by Jesuits in 1884. The Homoeopathic Medical College of New York opened in 1860, as did the Long Island College Hospital Medical School in Brooklyn (later renamed Downstate Medical Center and in 1950 the Health Science Center at Brooklyn). At the invitation of John D. Loughlin, archbishop of Brooklyn, St. John's College, founded by the Vincentian Fathers in Brooklyn in 1870, later moved its main campus to Jamaica. In 1971 it assumed control of Notre Dame College in Staten Island. Most colleges continued to exclude women; among the exceptions was the Normal College for Women (1870, later renamed for its founder Thomas Hunter), which trained many of the

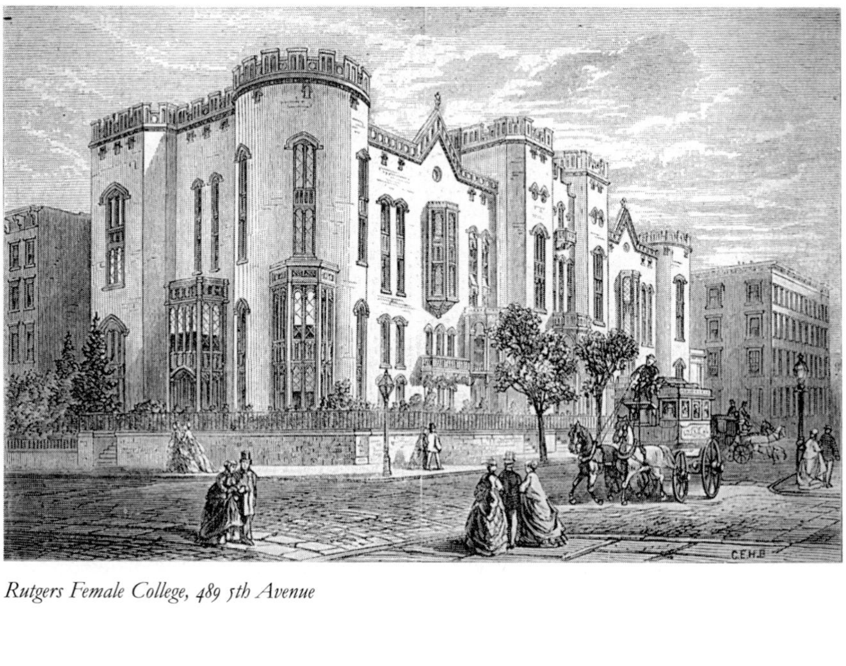

Rutgers Female College, 489 5th Avenue

teachers in the city's public schools. The Jewish Theological Seminary of America opened in 1886 to train Conservative rabbis and eventually had five divisions at its campus in Morningside Heights. The same year saw the opening of the Isaac Elchanan Seminary, an Orthodox institution that eventually became Yeshiva University (first based on the Lower East Side, moved in 1929 to Washington Heights). Pratt Institute (1887) began as a technical secondary school in Brooklyn and then expanded into a university with six divisions. Barnard College (1889), an undergraduate college for women, developed a close affiliation with Columbia during its first century but retained its own faculty and administration. In Fordham Heights specialized instruction was offered at the Webb Institute of Naval Architecture, which moved to Glen Cove, Long Island, in 1949.

At the end of the nineteenth century the metropolitan region became a center for professional education. Three of the best-known institutions were medical schools: New York University School of Medicine (1841), the College of Physicians and Surgeons (part of Columbia from 1860), and Cornell University Medical College (1898). Others were schools of law, including New York Law School (1891), formed by Theodore Dwight, who had resigned his position as dean of Columbia Law School after a dispute with the university's president Seth Low; Brooklyn Law School (1901); and law schools at St. John's and Fordham. Other schools opened during these years included Teachers College (1886, a part of Columbia from 1898); a school of pedagogy at New York University (1890); Adelphi College (1896), which began in Brooklyn and later moved to Garden City on Long Island; the Juilliard School (1905), a conservatory that later became known as well for dance and drama; Pace University (1906), which began as a school of accounting on a site near City Hall; and the New York College for Podiatric Medicine (1911), now the site of the largest foot clinic in the United States. Cathedral College of the Immaculate Conception opened in Brooklyn in 1914 to train Catholic priests and later moved to Douglaston. St. Joseph's College, formed in 1916 as a college for Catholic women in Brooklyn, eventually admitted men and added a branch campus in Suffolk County. The Bureau of Educational Experiments (1916) became known for such innovative projects as the country's first nursery school (1918): as the Bank Street College of Education (1950) it was responsible in the 1960s for the Bank Street readers, a series of primers that were among the first to depict characters of different races. The Mannes College of Music (1916) provided instruction at the undergraduate and graduate levels and also introduced high school and extension programs. The New York School of Interior Design (1916) first granted degrees

Colleges, Universities, and Religious Seminaries in New York City Granting Baccalaureate or Graduate Degrees
(excludes colleges of the City University of New York)

BRONX	
College of Mount St. Vincent (1847)	Riverdale Avenue and West 263rd Street
Fordham University (1841), College at Rose Hill	East Fordham Road
Manhattan College (1849)	Manhattan College Parkway, Riverdale
Maritime College (1874), State University of New York	Fort Schuyler[1]
BROOKLYN	
Boricua College:	
Greenpoint Extension (1974)	186 North 6th Street
Williamsburg Extension (1980)	9 Graham Avenue
Brooklyn Law School (1901)	250 Joralemon Street
Empire State College, State University of New York (1974), Bedford–Stuyvesant Unit	20 New York Avenue
Long Island University (1926), Brooklyn Campus	1 University Plaza
Polytechnic University (1854)	333 Jay Street
Pratt Institute (1887)	200 Willoughby Avenue
St. Francis College (1884)	180 Remsen Street
St. Joseph's College (1916)	
Brooklyn Campus	245 Clinton Avenue
Health Science Center at Brooklyn (1860), State University of New York[2]	450 Clarkson Avenue
MANHATTAN	
Bank Street College of Education (1916)	610 West 112th Street
Barnard College (1889)	Broadway and 116th Street
Boricua College (1974)	3755 Broadway
College for Human Services (1964)	345 Hudson Street
College of Insurance (1962)	1 Insurance Plaza 101 Murray Street
Columbia University (1754)	Broadway and 116th Street
Cooper Union for the Advancement of Science and Art (1859)	41 Cooper Square
Cornell University Medical College (1898)	1300 York Avenue
Empire State College, State University of New York:	
Metropolitan Center (1971)	666 Broadway
Harry Van Arsdale Jr. School for Labor Studies (1971)	330 West 42nd Street
Lower East Side Unit (1977)	107 Suffolk Street
Fashion Institute of Technology (1944), State University of New York	227 West 27th Street
Fordham University:	
College at Lincoln Center	113 West 60th Street
Fordham University Law School (1961)	140 West 62nd Street
General Theological Seminary (1817)	175 9th Avenue
Hebrew Union College (1875)[3]	1 West 4th Street
Jewish Theological Seminary of America (1887)	3080 Broadway
Juilliard School (1905)	144 West 66th Street
Laboratory Institute of Merchandising (1939)	12 East 53rd Street
Manhattan School of Music (1917)	120 Claremont Avenue
Mannes College of Music (1916)	150 West 85th Street
Marymount Manhattan College (1936)[4]	221 East 71st Street

(continued)

Colleges, Universities, and Religious Seminaries in New York City Granting Baccalaureate or Graduate Degrees *(Continued)*

New School for Social Research (1919)	66 West 12th Street
New York College for Podiatric Medicine (1911)	53 East 124th Street
New York Institute of Technology (1955)	1855 Broadway
New York Law School (1981)	57 Worth Street
New York School of Interior Design (1916)	155 East 56th Street
New York Theological Seminary (1900)	5 West 29th Street
New York University (1834)	22 Washington Square North
Pace University (1906)	1 Pace Plaza
Parsons School of Design (1896)	66 5th Avenue
Rockefeller University (1901)	1230 York Avenue
School of Visual Arts (1947)	209 East 23rd Street
State University of New York, College of Optometry (1971)	100 East 24th Street
Touro College (1971)	240 East 123rd Street 844 6th Avenue
Union Theological Seminary (1836)	3041 Broadway
Yeshiva University (1886)	500 West 185th Street
QUEENS	
Rabbinical Seminary of America (1933)	92-15 69th Avenue, Forest Hills
St. John's University (1870)	Grand Central and Utopia parkways, Jamaica
STATEN ISLAND	
Wagner College (1883)[5]	631 Howard Avenue
St. John's University, Staten Island Campus (1970)	300 Howard Avenue, Grymes Hill

Compiled by Marc Ferris

1. Occupied various sites before moving to Fort Schyuler in 1938.
2. Known as Long Island College of Medicine before joining the state university system in 1950.
3. Formed in 1875 in Cincinnati; in 1950 merged with the Jewish Institute of Religion (1922) and opened a branch in New York City.
4. Opened in 1936 as a branch of Marymount College of Tarrytown, New York; became independent in 1961.
5. Formed in 1883 in Rochester, New York, before moving to Staten Island in 1918.

in 1976. The Manhattan School of Music, opened in 1917–18, awarding bachelor's degrees from 1943 and doctorates from 1973; it moved to Morningside Heights in 1969. Wagner College (1883), an institution for the training of Lutheran clergymen, moved in 1918 from Rochester, New York, to Staten Island, where it became coeducational and introduced a comprehensive undergraduate program (it remains affiliated with the Lutheran Church of America).

After the First World War the number of institutions in the city increased. The New School for Social Research (1919) was organized by Charles A. Beard, John Dewey, Alvin Johnson, James Harvey Robinson, and Thorstein Veblen as the country's first university for adults; its University in Exile and its École Libre des Hautes Études became a haven for a number of European intellectuals in exile during the Second World War. Adult divisions and weekend programs were introduced by other colleges and attracted workers and parents. City College opened a school of business and civic administration (1919), a school of technology (1919), and a school of education (1921). The Jewish Institute of Religion, a Reform rabbinical college founded by Stephen S. Wise in 1922, merged in 1950 with Hebrew Union College of Cincinnati to become Hebrew Union College–Jewish Institute of Religion, which in 1979 moved to a site near New York University. Long Island University, opened in Brooklyn in 1926, expanded to Southampton and Greenvale, Long Island, and added a college of pharmacy and health sciences. To meet an increasing demand for public higher education the state legislature in 1926 replaced the City College Board of Trustees with the Board of Higher Education, which soon opened a branch of City College in downtown Brooklyn (1926) that was absorbed by Brooklyn College (1930); Queens College (1937); and a division of Hunter College in the Bronx (1931) that became Herbert H. Lehman College (1968).

The first two-year independent colleges offered programs that permitted students to transfer to four-year colleges as well as terminal vocational programs. From 1928 to 1936 Seth Low Junior College operated as an affiliate of Columbia, accepting Jewish and Catholic students who transferred to professional schools requiring less than four years of college for admission. Hofstra University opened on Long Island in 1935 as a branch of New York University. A two-year women's college formed in 1936 by the Religious of the Sacred Heart of Mary was renamed Marymount Manhattan College and became a four-year college after being chartered as a branch of Marymount College (1946) in Tarrytown, New York; it became independent in 1961.

The demand for higher education after the Second World War rose sharply. The New York Institute of Technology (1945) moved from Brooklyn to Manhattan in 1958. Jurisdiction over New York City Community College (1946, now New York City Technical College) was transferred from the state education department to the Board of Higher Education. The School for Cartoonists and Illustrators (1947, later the School of Visual Arts) offered degrees in fine arts, film, media arts, and photography. To make college education more generally accessible, the state legislature established the State University of New York (1948), which eventually took over the Fashion Institute of Technology (1944), Downstate Medical Center (1950, later the Health Science Center at Brooklyn), a maritime academy at Fort Schuyler, a regional center of Empire State College (1971), and the State College of Optometry (1971). In 1954 the Rockefeller Institute for Medical Research became a degree-granting institution called Rockefeller University. Yeshiva University opened Stern College for Women in 1954 in midtown Manhattan and the Albert Einstein College of Medicine in 1955 at its campus in the Bronx. Polytechnic Institute of New York opened a graduate center in Farmingdale, Long Island, in 1954 and absorbed the New York University School of Engineering and Science in 1973. The first public community college of the City University of New York was Staten Island Community College (1955); other community colleges opened by the Board of Higher Education specialized in programs for adults and immigrants, including Bronx Community College (1957), which moved to the former campus of New York University in University Heights in 1973, Queensborough Community College (1958), Manhattan Community College (1964), and Kingsborough Community College (Brooklyn, 1963). The board also oversaw the founding of the John Jay College of Criminal Justice (1967) and took over Baruch College (1919).

Rising enrollments in the 1960s led to a rapid expansion of higher education, both public and private. In 1968 the Malcolm–King Harlem College Extension Center was established by Marymount Manhattan College with the sponsorship of Fordham University and the College of Mount St. Vincent. The Mount Sinai School of Medicine opened in 1968 on the Upper East Side. Several public colleges were built, among them York College in Jamaica (1966, four-year), Eugenio Maria de Hostos College in the Bronx (1968, two-year), Medgar Evers College in Brooklyn (1969, four-year), and Fiorello H. La Guardia College in Long Island City (1971, two-year). Touro College (1970), a private liberal arts college in Manhattan, emphasized Jewish history and culture in its curriculum. Efforts by the City University of New York to build new facilities accelerated after 1970, when it adopted a policy of open admissions (guaranteeing a place at the university to every graduate of the city's public high schools). Boricua College (1974), a private institution, offered an undergraduate curriculum taught in English and Spanish.

The city's fiscal crisis of the mid 1970s caused a severe retrenchment. City University discontinued its policy of open admissions and began charging tuition for the first time. Richmond College (1965) and Staten Island Community College were forced to merge in 1976, to form the College of Staten Island. Among the institutions that abandoned the city during the 1960s and 1970s were St. Vladimir's Orthodox Theological Seminary, which moved from Manhattan to Crestwood, New York, in 1962, and New York Medical College, which moved to Valhalla, New York, in 1978 after becoming affiliated with Pace University in 1973.

Sidney Sherwood: *The University of the State of New York: History of Higher Education in the State of New York* (Washington: Government Printing Office, 1900)
Frank C. Abbott: *Government Policy and Higher Education: A Study of the Regents of the University of the State of New York, 1784–1949* (Ithaca, N.Y.: Cornell University Press, 1958)
Harold S. Wechsler: *The Qualified Student: Selective College Admission in America, 1870–1970* (New York: Wiley–Interscience, 1977)
Douglas Sloan: "Science in New York City, 1867–1907," *Isis* 71 (1980), 35–76
Thomas Bender: *New York Intellect: A History of Intellectual Life in New York City from 1750 to the Beginnings of Our Own Time* (New York: Oxford University Press, 1987)
Thomas Bender, ed.: *The University and the City: From Medieval Origins to the Present* (New York: Oxford University Press, 1988)
Lawrence A. Cremin: *American Education: The Metropolitan Experience, 1876–1980* (New York: Harper and Row, 1988)

Harold Wechsler

College Settlement. First college settlement in the United States, opened in 1889 at 95 Rivington Street as an educational exchange for educated and underprivileged women. Initially there were seven full-time residents who were recent graduates of Smith, Vassar, and Wellesley colleges; they organized clubs focusing on one interest for the neighborhood's children and adults, most of whom were German (eventually there were also Russian and Polish Jews). The organization soon expanded: by 1895 it had a kindergarten, a circulating library, a Penny Provident Fund, and a vacation home, and provided instruction in sewing, cooking, woodcarving, basketwork, singing, literature, politics, history, and debating. The first head residents included Jean Fine Spahr (1889–92), Jane E. Robbins (1893–97), Mary Kingsbury Simkhovitch (1898), and Elizabeth Sprague Williams (1899–1915). Encouraged by the success of the organization, a group of alumnae from several eastern women's colleges formed the College Settlements Association in 1890, which through membership subscriptions and the recruitment of resident staff opened additional college settlements in Philadelphia, Boston, and Baltimore. As the neighborhood changed, the settlement decided to focus on teaching arts and dramatics and organizing leisure activities, and in 1930 it closed and reopened uptown as an arts workshop.

William H. Tolman and William I. Hull: *Handbook of Sociological Information, with Especial Reference to New York City* (New York: G. P. Putnam's Sons, 1894)
Lilian W. Betts: "New York's Social Settlements," *Outlook*, 27 April 1895, pp. 683–86
Robert A. Woods et al.: *The Poor in Great Cities: Their Problems and What Is Doing to Solve Them* (New York: Charles Scribner's Sons, 1895)
Jane E. Robbins: "Charity That Helps and Other Charity," *Forum* 18 (Dec 1897), 502–7
Elizabeth Sprague Williams: "New York College Settlement," *Harper's Bazaar*, 19 May 1900, pp. 152–55
William H. Tolman and Charles Hemstreet: *The Better New York* (New York: Baker and Taylor, 1904)
Robert A. Woods and Albert J. Kennedy: *Handbook of Settlements* (New York: Russell Sage Foundation, 1911)
Jane E. Robbins: "The First Year at the College Settlement," *Survey*, 24 Feb 1912, pp. 1800–2

Jane Allen

Collegiate School. Independent day school for boys, the oldest school in New York City. Efforts to provide education in the Dutch Reformed church were first made in 1628 by Jonas Michaëlius, the first Dutch Reformed minister in New Netherland. The school opened in 1687 at the first of its seventeen successive sites, on Beaver Street between Broadway and Broad Street; it closed from 1776 to 1783 during the British occupation of New York City. Eventually the school settled on West End Avenue between 77th and 78th streets in 1892. Collegiate became an independent corporation in 1940 but maintained close ties to the Reformed Protestant Dutch church. In 1993–94 the school had 545 students.

Henry W. Dunshee: *History of the School of the Reformed Protestant Dutch Church in the City of New York from 1633 to the Present Time* (New York: J. A. Gray, 1853; rev. New York: Aldine, 1883)
William H. Kilpatrick: *The Dutch Schools of New Netherland and New York* (Washington: Government Printing Office, 1912)
Jean Parker Waterbury: *A History of Collegiate School, 1638–1963* (New York: C. N. Potter, 1965)
Charles T. Gehring and Nancy A. M. Zeller, eds.: *Education in New Netherland and the Middle Colonies: Papers of the 7th Rensselaerswyck Seminar of the New Netherland Project* (Albany, N.Y.: New Netherland Project, New York State Library, 1985)

William Lee Frost

Colles, Christopher (*b* Dublin, 9 May 1739; *d* New York City, 4 Oct 1816). Civil engineer and inventor. After moving to New York City he built the city's first public waterworks (1774–76), which employed a steam engine of his own design; destroyed before its completion during the British occupation, the system was later adapted by the Manhattan Company. His plan to link the Hudson River with the Great Lakes by way of the Mohawk River (1785) is regarded as having inspired the Erie Canal. He drew the routes leading north and south from New York City in *A Survey of the Roads of the United States of America* (1789), the first comprehensive mapping of the nation's highways. He was also the first superintendent of the New York Institution (1816). Although he achieved success during his life Colles died impoverished. His friend John Pintard arranged for him to be buried at St. Paul's Episcopal Church.

Neil Longley York: *Mechanical Metamorphosis: Technological Change in Revolutionary America* (Westport, Conn.: Greenwood, 1985)

Gerard Thomas Koeppel

Collier's. Weekly magazine. Launched in 1888 by Peter Collier in New York City, it soon became a leading popular magazine, specializing in muckraking and in the work of such writers as Henry James and Richard Harding Davis and of such artists as Frederic Remington and Charles Dana Gibson. The magazine was commended for its reportage of the Second World War, notably that of Ernest Hemingway and Quentin Reynolds. Members of the editorial staff included Theodore H. White and George J. W. Goodman (who later wrote under the pseudonym Adam Smith). After the war the magazine declined under ineffective management. In the early 1950s it lost 40 percent of its advertising, and although circulation reached a peak of four million *Collier's* ceased publication in December 1956. It was perhaps the first major casualty of the growing influence of advertising on magazines.

Ashbel Green

Collins, Ellen (*b* ?31 Dec 1828; *d* New York City, 8 July 1912). Housing reformer. She came from a Protestant background and was a member of the New York Mission Society and the Association for Improving the Condition of the Poor. During the 1880s she bought and repaired four "rookeries" on Water Street on the Lower East Side and organized model tenements; these were rented to working-class tenants who were held to a strict code of moral behavior. She limited her profit to 6 percent in this venture, and along with Olivia Dow and Edith Miles introduced tenement reforms that were adopted by the more systematic limited-dividend housing programs of corporate philanthropists in the 1890s.

Joel Schwartz

Collins Line. Passenger ship line. It was formed in 1850 by Edward Knight Collins (1802–78), an operator of sailing ships, and had five luxury liners. One of these, the *Baltic*, won a prize in 1852 for her speed in crossing the Atlantic. Two other ships were lost: the *Arctic* sank in a collision off Newfoundland that cost many lives, including those of Collins's wife and two children, and the *Pacific* vanished en route from Liverpool to New York City. The Collins Line ceased operations soon after the federal subsidy for transporting mail was withdrawn in 1857 owing to Southern opposition.

Warren Armstrong: *The Collins Story* (London: R. Hale, 1957)

Frank O. Braynard

Collyer brothers. Collectors and recluses. Langley Collyer (1886–1947), a concert pianist, and his brother Homer (1883–1947), a former admiralty lawyer who had been blinded and paralyzed by a stroke in the early 1930s, spent their retirement barricaded in a dilapidated brownstone at 5th Avenue and 128th Street in Harlem. They had no gas, water, electricity, or sewer connection, admitted no one to the house, had only an old crystal set radio for contact with the outside world, and never disposed of anything. Langley explained to an acquaintance that he kept thousands of old newspapers in the house because Homer would want to read them when he regained his sight, and that he had fourteen grand pianos because Homer liked to hear him play. On 21 March 1947 the police received a mysterious telephone call reporting that Homer had died in the house. Officers were dispatched to the scene, only to find that all the doors and windows were blocked. After many attempts they were able to break through an upper-story window; they found the house filled with rats and honeycombed with passages between piles of junk. Homer's body was found in an upstairs room, but there was no sign of Langley, and rumors circulated that he was still inside the house hiding. The investigation received extensive coverage in the local press, and crowds gathered to catch a glimpse of Langley Collyer or at least his fantastic collections. After clearing out the house for several weeks the police discovered the body of Langley, who had apparently triggered one of many booby traps he had set for thieves who he believed were plotting to break in; he had died of heart failure after a suitcase, three breadboxes, and several bundles of newspapers fell on him, and Homer had died of starvation several days later. In addition to the fourteen pianos the police found tons of newspapers, several old chandeliers, many cats, and the chassis of an old automobile in the basement.

Jonathan Aspell

Colonnade Row. A row of nine attached Greek Revival mansions constructed in 1833 by Seth Geer in Manhattan, on the west side of Lafayette Place (now Lafayette Street), just below Astor Place. Originally named La Grange Terrace after the Marquis de Lafayette's country home in France, the row was distinguished by its marble façade, which consisted of twenty-seven Corinthian columns rising from a rustic base. All the stone work was done by inmates of the state penitentiary at Sing Sing. The houses were occupied by several prominent figures, including John Jacob Astor, before it became fashionable to move uptown. In 1902 the five southernmost houses were demolished to make way for an annex to Wanamaker's department store. Four houses remained in the mid 1990s, in dilapidated condition.

Elliott B. Nixon

Colony Club. Social club for women, the first of its kind in New York City. It was formed in 1903 by Florence "Daisy" Jaffray (Mrs. J. Borden) Harriman (1870–1967), who modeled it on clubs for prominent men. With other wealthy women including Anne Tracy Morgan (1873–1952), a daughter of J. P. Morgan, she raised half a million dollars and commissioned Stanford White to build a luxurious facility at 120 Madison Avenue near 30th Street: it was decorated by Elsie de Wolfe and had a swimming pool, a roof garden, a gymnasium, a squash court, a library, a card room, a cocktail bar, a smoking room, dining facilities, reception areas with a musician's gallery, and ten bedrooms. There were about a thousand members, who attended lectures, entertained, secured support for charitable causes, and held their daughters' débutante balls at the club. By 1913 more space was needed and the firm of Delano and Aldrich was engaged to build a new facility at 564 Park Avenue at 62nd Street: this one was more elaborate, containing in its twelve levels more bedrooms than the first, as well as a floor of servants' quarters and a room for pets.

Anne O'Hagan: "A Beautiful Club for Women: The Colony Club of New York," *Century*, Dec 1910, pp. 216–24
"Colony Club Builds an Elaborate Home," *New York Times*, 8 Aug 1915, §2, p. 13

Karen J. Blair

Colored American. Weekly newspaper launched in New York City in March 1837 by Samuel Cornish and Philip Bell, a prominent black journalist. It was financially supported by abolitionists and dedicated to the advancement of black Americans. Cornish resigned as the editor in 1839 and was replaced by Charles Bennett Ray, pastor of the Bethesda Congregational Church and an active supporter of the Underground Railroad in New York City. Bell continued his association with the newspaper until it ceased publication in 1842.

Martin E. Dann: *The Black Press, 1827–1890: The Quest for National Identity* (New York: G. P. Putnam's Sons, 1971)
Roland E. Wolseley: *The Black Press, U.S.A.* (Ames: Iowa State University Press, 1971)

Sandra Roff

Colonnade Row, ca 1910

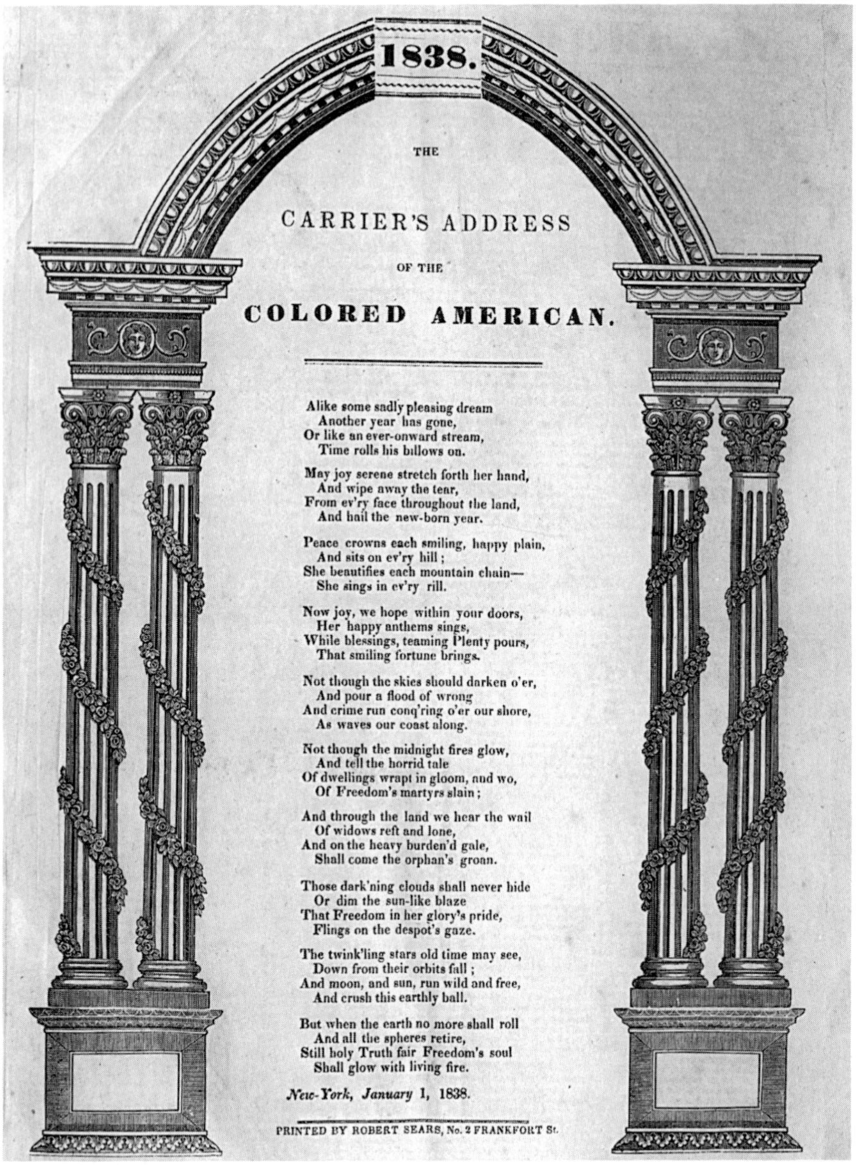

1838.

THE

CARRIER'S ADDRESS

OF THE

COLORED AMERICAN.

Alike some sadly pleasing dream
Another year has gone,
Or like an ever-onward stream,
Time rolls his billows on.

May joy serene stretch forth her hand,
And wipe away the tear,
From ev'ry face throughout the land,
And hail the new-born year.

Peace crowns each smiling, happy plain,
And sits on ev'ry hill;
She beautifies each mountain chain—
She sings in ev'ry rill.

Now joy, we hope within your doors,
Her happy anthems sings,
While blessings, teaming Plenty pours,
That smiling fortune brings.

Not though the skies should darken o'er,
And pour a flood of wrong
And crime run conq'ring o'er our shore,
As waves our coast along.

Not though the midnight fires glow,
And tell the horrid tale
Of dwellings wrapt in gloom, and wo,
Of Freedom's martyrs slain;

And through the land we hear the wail
Of widows reft and lone,
And on the heavy burden'd gale,
Shall come the orphan's groan.

Those dark'ning clouds shall never hide
Or dim the sun-like blaze
That Freedom in her glory's pride,
Flings on the despot's gaze.

The twink'ling stars old time may see,
Down from their orbits fall;
And moon, and sun, run wild and free,
And crush this earthly ball.

But when the earth no more shall roll
And all the spheres retire,
Still holy Truth fair Freedom's soul
Shall glow with living fire.

New-York, January 1, 1838.

PRINTED BY ROBERT SEARS, No. 2 FRANKFORT St.

"The Carrier's Address of the Colored American," poem for the New Year, 1838

Colored Home and Hospital for the Sick, Aged and Indigent. A charitable institution for blacks founded in 1839 by the Society for the Relief of Worthy Aged Colored Persons (a Quaker women's organization). Initially it was called the Colored Home and housed "respectable, worn out colored servants." In the mid 1840s it was authorized to shelter all the sick and destitute blacks in the city by the commissioner of almshouses, and a facility was constructed at 1st Avenue between 64th and 65th streets with a grant of $10,000 from the state legislature; this included a home for the aged and infirm, a men's hospital, a women's hospital, a lying-in hospital, a nursery, a "house of industry," a chapel, and a school. Children, the sick, and the destitute of all ages were received, excluding only the insane and those afflicted with smallpox. Among the first occupants were a number of retired black sailors who had been denied admission to the city almshouse and Sailors' Snug Harbor despite having contributed to the mariners' fund. During the 1850s there were two hundred beds, enough to house virtually all the city's sick black population. By paying the weekly fee of sixty cents charged to each resident the city contributed 80 percent of all revenues. In 1872 the name was changed to the Colored Home and Hospital for the Sick, Aged and Indigent. The institution expanded its capacity in the 1890s to three hundred beds; it began charging fees to patients and accepting voluntary contributions, and eventually public funds accounted for only about 30 percent of annual income. In 1898 the home and hospital moved to 141st Street and Southern Boulevard in the Bronx; outpatient dispensary services were added, and the Training School for Colored Nurses opened as the first formal nursing school for black women in the country. Because the Bronx was then predominantly white (most residents were recent immigrants) the move meant that the institution became distanced from the blacks whom it was originally intended to serve, and in 1902 it began to admit white patients and was renamed the Lincoln Hospital and Home. The old-age home continued to operate as an institution for blacks (until 1927), as did the nursing school (until the early 1970s).

Mary W. Thompson: *Broken Gloom: Sketches of the History, Character, and Dying Testimony of Beneficiaries of the Colored Home, in the City of New-York* (New York: J. F. Trow, 1851)

Seth M. Scheiner: *Negro Mecca: A History of the Negro in New York City, 1865–1920* (New York: New York University Press, 1965)

Rhoda G. Freeman: "The Free Negro in New York City in the Era before the Civil War" (diss., Columbia University, 1966)

Leonard P. Curry: *The Free Black in Urban America, 1800–1850* (Chicago: University of Chicago Press, 1981)

Mike Sappol

Colored Orphan Asylum. School and shelter for black children opened in 1836 by Mary Murray and Anna Shotwell. It was managed solely by women for more than a century and attained celebrity before the Civil War as a model institution. Fewer than a third of the asylum's inmates were orphans, and about the age of twelve most were returned to their parents or placed in positions as farm laborers or domestic servants. After its building at 43rd Street and 5th Avenue was destroyed by a mob during the draft riots (1863) the asylum was rebuilt in 1867 at 143rd Street and Amsterdam Avenue. In 1907 facilities were constructed in Riverdale according to the "cottage plan," a reform of the Progressive era that reorganized large, dehumanizing philanthropic institutions into campuses of smaller, home-like "cottages." The first black member of the board of directors was appointed in 1939, the first man in 1940. In 1944 the asylum was renamed the Riverdale Children's Association. After a controversy over conditions in the orphanage was aired in the press, it was decided in 1946 to discontinue institutional care and concentrate on foster care and dispersed small-group settings. The campus in Riverdale was sold to the Jewish Home for the Aged, and the offices of the association moved with medical and dental clinics to East 79th Street. In 1968 the association launched a program to preserve families by providing referrals, counseling, and other services rather than place children in foster care. It moved to Riverside Drive and 168th Street, changing its name to the Westside Center for Family Services. In March 1988 the Westside Center merged with Harlem–Dowling Children's Services.

From Cherry Street to Green Pastures: A History of the Colored Orphan Asylum at Riverdale-on-Hudson,

Colored Orphan Asylum, 1861

1836–1936 (New York: Riverdale Children's Association, 1936)
120th Anniversary, 1836–1956 (New York: Riverdale Children's Association, 1956)
Carleton Mabee: "Charity in Travail: Two Orphan Asylums for Blacks," *New York History* 55 (1974), 55–77
Mike Sappol: "The Uses of Philanthropy: The Colored Orphan Asylum and Its Clients" (thesis, Columbia University, 1990)

Mike Sappol

Coltrane, John (William) (*b* Hamlet, N.C., 23 Sept 1926; *d* New York City, 17 July 1967). Saxophonist and composer. He grew up in Philadelphia and played in various groups before moving to New York City in 1955. During the next four years he became prominent as the tenor saxophonist in the small groups of Miles Davis and Thelonious Monk. He lived from 1957 to 1959 in an apartment on the second floor of 203 West 103rd Street in Manhattan and from 1959 to 1963 at 116-60 Mexico Street in Queens. He recorded the album *Giant Steps* (1959), his first important album as a leader, and then formed a quartet with the pianist McCoy Tyner, the double bass player Jimmy Garrison, and the drummer Elvin Jones. In the following years his music grew increasingly dissonant. He became the leading figure of the jazz avant-garde, a circle of musicians based principally in the city who were seeking to overcome what they considered the limitations of bop and its offshoots. He was also the key figure in the resurgence of the soprano saxophone, which had been an obscure instrument in jazz for several years until he took it up in 1960. In his later career he obliterated the boundaries of jazz harmony and often performed solos of unprecedented length. Coltrane's important recordings include *My Favorite Things* (1960), *A Love Supreme* (1964), *Ascension* (1965), and three albums recorded at clubs in New York City — *Live at the Village Vanguard* (1961), *Live at Birdland* (1963), and *Live at the Village Vanguard Again* (1966). More than any other jazz musician of his time he enjoyed a reputation well beyond the usual audience of aficionados.

Cuthbert Ormond Simpkins: *Coltrane: A Biography* (New York: Herndon House, 1975)

Peter Keepnews

Columbia Broadcasting System [CBS]. Television and radio network formed in January 1927 as United Independent Broadcasters, comprising sixteen radio stations and operating from the Paramount Building. It was financially unsuccessful until it was bought in September 1927 for $503,000 by William S. Paley, the twenty-six-year-old heir to a cigar fortune, who gave the network its current name. He engaged Lowell Thomas in 1930 as the newscaster of the first daily network news broadcast on radio, and Frank Stanton in 1935 to develop methods of surveying audiences. In 1938 he acquired the American Record Company and renamed it CBS Records. Stanton took charge of corporate matters and became president of the network in 1946, a position he held until 1972; Paley continued to make the decisions about programming. Initially CBS had fewer and weaker affiliates than the National Broadcasting Company, because it lacked radio personalities. Paley persuaded Jack Benny, Edgar Bergen, and others to leave NBC and join his network. He also had success with Ed Sullivan, Jackie Gleason, and Lucille Ball. Having less capital than his competitors, he decided to focus on news programs that were relatively cheap to produce. The network is considered to have originated broadcast journalism. Its leading newscaster was Edward R. Murrow, who during the Second World War broadcast a series of reports called "This Is London" and assembled a team of reporters that included Charles Collingwood, Eric Sevareid, Howard K. Smith, and Richard C. Hottelet. In New York City he and his producer Fred W. Friendly broadcast the first news documentary series on television, "See It Now" (1951–58). The best-known program was a strongly negative report on the activities of Senator Joseph R. McCarthy aired in 1954. During the 1950s, which were regarded as the "golden age" of television, New York City was the center for entertainment programming as well as news. CBS produced "Studio One" and "Playhouse 90" (live broadcasts of dramas and comedies in which well-known actors from the Broadway theater appeared) and soon had the highest ratings of the three networks. The anchor of the network's evening news program, Douglas Edwards, was replaced in 1962 by Walter Cronkite, who held the position for almost twenty years. In 1965 the company moved its corporate headquarters from 485 Madison Avenue to a new building designed by Eero Saarinen at 51 West 52nd Street; its news division worked out of a renovated dairy at 524 West 57th Street. In 1968 the network first broadcast the news-magazine program "60 Minutes," which became the longest-running television program of its kind.

Between 1962 and 1979 the net annual income of CBS rose from $41.8 million to $200 million, and by 1977 the network was a conglomerate with holdings of $2500 million. Its diverse holdings included the baseball team the New York Yankees, the piano maker Steinway and Sons, the toy maker Creative Playthings, and the book publisher Holt, Rinehart and Winston. In 1981 CBS launched a cable television service focused on the performing arts. These businesses proved hugely unprofitable and the company divested itself of most of them. With the rise of the American Broadcasting Company and the Cable News Network in the 1980s, profits fell and

Ford Symphony Control Room at the Columbia Broadcasting System, ca 1937

CBS was no longer the most successful network in television. It was taken over in 1985 by Laurence Tisch, president of Loews Corporation, who closed or sold off its remaining subsidiary businesses (including CBS Records, sold to Sony in 1988 for $200 million).

A. M. Sperber: *Murrow: His Life and Times* (New York: Freundlich, 1986)

Peter J. Boyer: *Who Killed CBS?: The Undoing of America's Number One News Network* (New York: Random House, 1988)

Sally Bedell Smith: *In All His Glory: The Life of William S. Paley* (New York: Simon and Schuster, 1990)

For further illustration see RADIO.

Judith Adler Hennessee

Columbia Grammar and Preparatory School. Coeducational high school opened in 1764 in Manhattan as the preparatory school for King's College (now Columbia University). It was advocated by Samuel Johnson, the first president of the college, because of his conviction that before entering college a student should be well trained in grammar. The school was affiliated with the university until 1864. It moved several times to various locations throughout the city and now occupies three buildings on West 93rd and 94th streets, including a high school building completed in 1985.

Ross Dixon and McDonald Sullivan, eds.: *Columbia Grammar School, 1764–1964: A Historical Log* (New York: Columbia Grammar School, 1965)

Richard Schwartz

Columbia Journalism Review. Bimonthly magazine published under the auspices of the Graduate School of Journalism at Columbia University. It was launched in 1961 by Edward W. Barrett as a quarterly publication that monitored print and broadcast news in the United States and published bimonthly after ten years. *Columbia Journalism Review* is the largest, oldest, and most widely respected magazine of its kind. It is known for the popular features "The Lower Case" and "Darts and Laurels." In 1991 it was published by Joan Konner and edited by Suzanne Braun Levine, and had a circulation of 31,000.

Alfred Balk and James Boylan, eds.: *Our Troubled Press: Ten Years of the Columbia Journalism Review* (Boston: Little, Brown, 1971)

Laura Gwinn

Columbia–Presbyterian Medical Center. One of the most prestigious medical centers in the United States, opened in 1928 as the result of an affiliation between Presbyterian Hospital and the College of Physicians and Surgeons of Columbia University. It is situated in Washington Heights between 165th and 168th streets and between Broadway and Fort Washington Avenue. On its completion the hospital moved into a facility with 694 beds that included the Harkness Pavilion (150 private rooms) and the Squier Urological Clinic. In 1933 the center opened the Institute of Ophthalmology, which was integrated with the Herman Knapp Memorial Eye Hospital in 1939. After negotiating with the city for a cancer hospital in 1940 the center opened the Francis Delafield Hospital (1950). The New York Orthopaedic Hospital, affiliated with Presbyterian Hospital from 1945, moved to the center in 1950. In the mid 1990s Columbia–Presbyterian Medical Center was the largest hospital in New York City, with 1548 beds. As many as 35 percent of its patients were from outside the city. The hospital is a leading organ transplant center in the Northeast and a federally designated comprehensive cancer center. The center is also renowned for its neonatal care and its work with patients suffering from Parkinson's disease.

David Bryson Delavan: *Early Days of the Presbyterian Hospital in the City of New York* (East Orange, N.J.: Abbey Printshop, 1926)

The "Rinso" program with Ken Murray on Radio Theater

Albert R. Lamb: *The Presbyterian Hospital and the Columbia–Presbyterian Medical Center, 1868–1943: A History of a Great Medical Adventure* (New York: Columbia University Press, 1955)
Ina L. Yalof: *Life and Death: The Story of a Hospital* (New York: Fawcett Crest, 1990)

Jane E. Mottus

Columbia University. The oldest and most famous education institution in New York City, situated principally on a campus of thirty-six acres (14.5 hectares) in Morningside Heights in Manhattan. Chartered on 31 October 1754 as King's College, it opened with eight students in the vestry room of Trinity Church and moved to its own building in 1760. The first president was Samuel Johnson (to 1763), a convert from the Congregational church to the Anglican church and the first in a line of Anglican and Episcopalian presidents that lasted for nearly two hundred years. His successor was Myles Cooper (to 1775), a Loyalist under whom the college nevertheless attracted as students such revolutionaries as Alexander Hamilton (1773–75), John Jay (AB 1764), Robert Livingston (AB 1765), and Gouverneur Morris (AB 1768). A medical department was added in 1767. The college building was a military hospital during the American Revolution, when classes were suspended. After the war the school was rechartered in 1784 as Columbia College by the state legislature, which envisioned the college as part of a projected state university; the legislature returned control of the college to locally based trustees in 1787. Columbia divested itself of its medical department by allowing it to merge in 1813 with the New York College of Physicians and Surgeons. This college itself became a division of Columbia in 1860 during the presidency of Charles King (1849–64), who also oversaw a move in 1857 to a campus at Madison Avenue and 49th Street, as well as the opening of the School of Law (1858) and the School of Mines (1864, now part of the School of Engineering and Applied Sciences). Other professional schools were added during the following decades: under Frederick A. P. Barnard (1864–89) the School of Architecture, Planning, and Preservation (1881) and the School of Library Service (1887), led by Melvil Dewey, and under Seth Low (1890–1901) the School of Nursing (1892) and Teachers College (opened in 1889, affiliated from 1898). The brand of professional education favored by Columbia was broad and "scientific" rather than narrow and practical, an emphasis that caused some controversy: Theodore Dwight, who dominated the law school for thirty years, resigned as its dean in 1891 after a dispute with Low and founded New York Law School. Graduate faculties were established in political science (1880), philosophy (1890), and pure science (1892), and the name of the institution was changed to Columbia University in 1896 (changed again to Columbia University in the City of New York in 1912). In 1897 the university moved to its current location, a rectangular campus with buildings designed in an Italian Renaissance style by the firm of McKim, Mead and White. The centerpiece of the new campus was Low Memorial Library, a classical Roman building with Grecian detail. The rest of the campus was marked by the harmonious design of its undergraduate, graduate, and professional buildings, a symbol of the continuity of liberal and professional education.

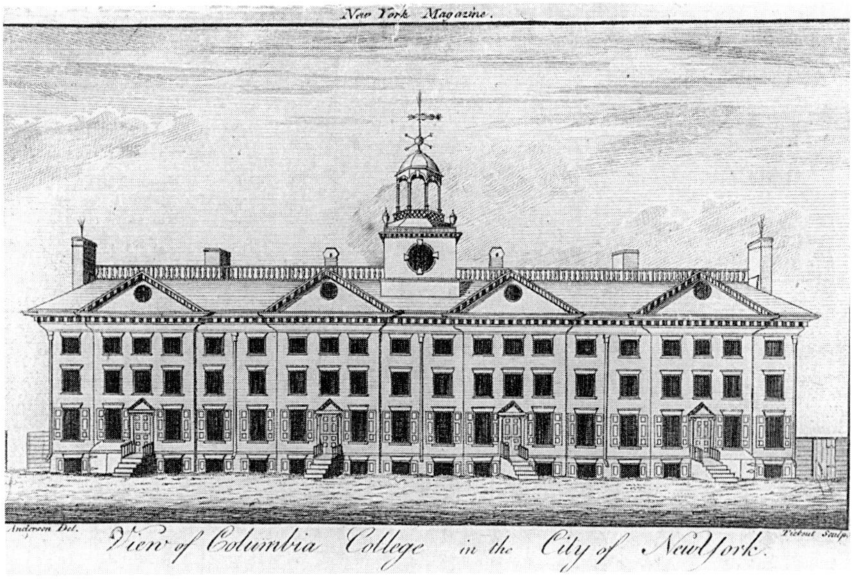

Original building of Columbia College, 1790

As New York City evolved into a major international city in the early twentieth century, the efforts begun by Barnard and Low to shift the focus from an undergraduate curriculum dominated by the classics and toward the graduate and professional schools was continued by such professors as the political scientist John W. Burgess and especially by Nicholas Murray Butler, president of the university from 1902 to 1945. A prominent figure in local and national politics who had influence with Presidents Theodore Roosevelt, William Howard Taft, and Warren G. Harding, Butler oversaw the absorption in 1904 of the New York College of Pharmacy (founded 1831, closed 1976) and in 1905 of the School of Philanthropy (founded 1898, in 1963 renamed the School of Social Work), and the opening of the Graduate School of Journalism (1912), the Business School (1916), the School of Dental and Oral Surgery (1917, merged in 1923 with the New York College of Dental and Oral Surgery), the School of Optometry (1910–56), University Extension (1920, renamed the School of General Studies in 1947), and the School of Public Health (1921). He also liberalized admission and graduation requirements for undergraduates (increasing the number of permissible electives), and made it easier for them to pursue liberal arts and professional degrees simultaneously (an option exercised by more than 60 percent of all students at Columbia College in 1939). During these same years Columbia became known for a distinctive approach to the social sciences. A belief that events were determined by social forces rather than *a priori* laws and that conclusions about human behavior emerged from induction rather than deduction informed the work of John Dewey in education, psychology, and philosophy, James McKeen Cattell in psychology, James Harvey Robinson in history, E. R. A. Seligman in economics, Franz Boas in anthropology, and Charles A. Beard in political science and history. Tensions beset the university during the First World War: the Student Army Training Corps was active on campus and many faculty members worked on military research and propaganda, while at the same time Dewey helped to form the American Association of University Professors to protect the academic freedom of faculty members, and Cattell defended the rights of conscientious objectors, for which he was dismissed in 1917 by Butler (prompting the resignation of Beard, who then joined with Dewey and Robinson to form the New School for Social Research in 1919). One indirect result of the war and its propaganda efforts was the introduction in 1919 of a compulsory survey course for undergraduates called Contemporary Civilization, which traced the development of Western thought from Plato to the present. A complementary course in the humanities was introduced in 1937. In 1921 the College of Physicians and Surgeons moved from midtown to Washington Heights and formed an affiliation with Presbyterian Hospital.

During the interwar years Columbia College remained in the university's shadow, although its course in contemporary civilization be-

Columbia University, 1898. Center *Low Library*

came widely known and imitated. Several members of the faculty were active in local, national, and international affairs: the philologist John D. Prince served in the New Jersey state legislature and was an ambassador to Denmark (1921–26) and Yugoslavia (1926–33); the law professor A. A. Berle was a member of President Franklin D. Roosevelt's "brain trust," as was the economist Rexford Guy Tugwell (who later led the New York City Planning Commission from 1938 to 1940); the economists Seligman and Robert Haig worked for the League of Nations; and the historian Carlton Hayes was ambassador to Spain (1942–45). The school was also a power in collegiate football, and won a decisive upset over Stanford University in the Rose Bowl in 1934. Left-wing students demonstrated on campus during the Depression. Butler worked toward the Kellogg–Briand treaty and for international reconciliation, and was awarded the Nobel Peace Prize in 1931. The physicist Michael Pupin advocated electrification with direct current rather than alternating current, which led to clashes with local utility companies. Many refugees from Nazism found their way to the university in the 1930s, including the sociologist Paul Lazarsfeld, who founded the Bureau of Applied Social Research at Columbia and undertook important work with Robert Merton, and the members of the Institute of Social Research, which moved from Frankfurt am Main to a brownstone owned by the university. A number of physicists connected with the Manhattan Project studied nuclear fission at Columbia until the project moved to the University of Chicago in 1942, among them I. I. Rabi, Enrico Fermi, John R. Dunning, Harold Urey, and George B. Pegram (later head of the university's Division of War Research). Literary and cultural critics who became prominent during these years included the art historian Meyer Schapiro, the literary scholars Lionel Trilling, Gilbert Highet, Mark Van Doren, and Rufus Mathewson, the sociologists Daniel Bell and C. Wright Mills, and the historians Jacques Barzun, Allan Nevins, and Richard Hofstadter. After the Second World War the university introduced area studies programs and in 1946 opened the School of International Affairs (later renamed the School of International and Public Affairs). By the early 1950s the university was the center of a group of cultural iconoclasts and bohemians known as the beats, whose most important members were Allen Ginsberg and Jack Kerouac. The continued dominance of the professional schools was signaled by the completion of five buildings with designs strikingly at odds with those of McKim, Mead and White. Dwight D. Eisenhower, who was president of the university from 1948 until he left for the White House in 1953, was the first head of the university since its founding who was not Anglican or Episcopalian. During the administration of his successor, Grayson Kirk (1953–68), Columbia opened the School of the Arts (1965).

The growing national and international reputation of Columbia stood in contrast to the university's strained relations with its neighbors. Increasingly selective admissions policies militated against applicants from New York City, and as the largest owner of real estate in Morningside Heights the university was accused of excluding working-class and minority tenants from its residential housing. The same criticisms were leveled by many students, who also objected to the role of some professors in secret defense research during the Vietnam War and to a mode of governance at the university that they considered autocratic. These tensions culminated in April 1968 in violent demonstrations by students against the construction of a new gymnasium in Morningside Park. Demonstrators occupied five buildings, the university called in the police, and many students were arrested. One consequence of the demonstrations was the formation of the University Senate, a deliberative body in which the administration, students, faculty, staff, and alumni are represented. Columbia College in 1983 became the last division of the university to admit women. (Barnard College, for women only, is adjacent to Columbia and has many affiliations with it but has its own administration, governing board, and faculty.) Among the members of the faculty at Columbia who played prominent roles in the federal government between the 1960s and the 1980s were the law professor William Cary (head of the Securities and Exchange Commission, 1961–64), the economist Arthur Burns (head of the Federal Reserve, 1970–78, and ambassador to Germany, 1981–85), and the political scientist Zbigniew Brzezinski (national security advisor to President Jimmy Carter). In 1993 George Rupp became the president of the university and resolved to increase its commitment to undergraduate education.

In addition to sixty-three buildings on its main campus the university comprehends the Columbia–Presbyterian Medical Center in Washington Heights, the Lamont–Doherty Geological Observatory in Palisades, New York, Nevis Laboratories in Irvington, New York, Arden House in Harriman, New York, and a fifty-story office tower at 570 Lexington Avenue, the former headquarters of General Electric. The university is also the site of seventy-one centers and institutes for specialized research. Its endowment on 30 June 1993 was $1,882,795,000, the sixth-largest among universities in the United States. In the autumn of 1993 the sixteen schools at Columbia enrolled 19,800 students (10,400 men and 9400 women); with its affiliates Barnard College and Teachers College the total stood at 26,000. Columbia College had about 3447 students (the smallest undergraduate enrollment in the Ivy League) and 35,697 living alumni. The university's library system held 6.4 million volumes, 4.7 microform units, and 25 million manuscript items, making the system the seventh-largest among members of the Association of Research Libraries (an organization that does not include public libraries). As of 1993 a total of fifty-four Nobel Laureates had studied or taught at Columbia, including Rabi, Polykarp Kusch, Willis E. Lamb, Tsung-Dao Lee, James Rainwater, Charles H. Townes, André F. Cournand, and Dickenson W. Richards.

Sidney Sherwood: *The University of the State of New York: History of Higher Education in the State of New York* (Washington: Government Printing Office, 1900)

A History of Columbia University, 1754–1904 (New York: Columbia University Press, 1904)

John William Robson: *A Guide to Columbia University* (New York: Columbia University Press, 1937)

Dwight C. Miner, ed.: *A History of Columbia College on Morningside* (New York: Columbia University Press, 1954)

David C. Humphrey: *From King's College to Columbia, 1746–1800* (New York: Columbia University Press, 1976)

Harold S. Wechsler: *The Qualified Student: Selective College Admission in America, 1870–1970* (New York: Wiley–Interscience, 1977)

Thomas Bender: *New York Intellect: A History of Intellectual Life in New York City from 1750 to the Beginnings of Our Own Time* (New York: Oxford University Press, 1987)

Harold Wechsler

Columbia University Press. University press formed in 1893 by ten trustees of Columbia University. It was the first university press in New York City and one of the first in the United States. The press publishes both scholarly works in a wide range of fields and books of general interest. Its best-known publications are *Granger's Index to Poetry* (1904–, first published by Columbia in 1945) and the *Columbia Encyclopedia* (first published 1935; 5th edn 1993). Columbia University Press is at 562 West 113th Street in Manhattan.

Eileen K. Cheng

Columbus Circle. The area in Manhattan surrounding the intersection of Broadway, Central Park West, 8th Avenue, and 59th Street. It was named after becoming the site of a memorial to Columbus consisting of a rostral column of Carrera marble eighty feet (twenty-four meters) high, which was donated by Italians in the city and unveiled on 12 October 1892. A statue of Columbus by Gaetano Russo was added in 1894. Plans to develop the area as a public space were never realized, largely because of the volume of traffic on the surrounding streets. Nearby at the Merchant's Gate into Central Park a monument was erected to those killed in the explosion of the *Maine* (Harold Von Magonigle, 1913; sculptures by Attilio Piccirilli). A neighborhood west of the circle was known for several years as San Juan Hill. Nightclubs in the area included Reisenweber's Café, where in 1917 the Original Dixieland Jazz Band made its début in the city. Such landmarks as the Colonnade building and the Park Theatre were later replaced by the New York Coliseum (Leon Levy and Lionel Levy, 1965), the Gulf and Western Tower (Thomas Stanley, 1970; later occupied by Paramount Communications), and the Huntington Hartford Gallery (Edward Stone, 1965; now used by the city's Department of Cultural Affairs). Plans to replace the Coliseum with office towers met with resistance in part because the towers would cast long shadows over the circle. The memorial to the *Maine* and Columbus's statue were refurbished for the five hundredth anniversary of Columbus's landing in the New World. In 1994 the city canceled its nine-year development agreement with Mortimer B. Zuckerman and seized his $33.8 million deposit, leaving the future of the site unclear.

George J. Lankevich

Columbus Circle, ca 1910

Columbus Hospital. Original name of CABRINI MEDICAL CENTER.

Columbusville. Name formerly applied to a section of Maspeth in northwestern Queens. It was developed by Edward Dunn in 1854–55 on 69th Place (old 5th Avenue) between Grand and Caldwell avenues and was soon absorbed by Maspeth, which lay a few blocks away. The name fell into disuse in the 1890s.

Vincent Seyfried

Comden and Green. Team of lyricists. Its members, Betty Comden (*b* Brooklyn, 3 May 1918) and Adolph Green (*b* New York City, 2 Dec 1915), met in the 1930s and formed a nightclub act called the Revuers that also included Judy Tuvim (later known as Judy Holliday) and Alvin Hammer, and that wrote its own material because it could not afford to pay copyright fees. The two wrote the lyrics for Leonard Bernstein's musicals *On the Town* (1944) and *Wonderful Town* (1952), which won a Tony Award. They also won the award for *Hallelujah, Baby* (1969), *Applause* (1970), and *On the Twentieth Century* (1978). Their work is noted for its elegance, enthusiasm, and wit.

Robert Seder

Commentary. Monthly journal launched by the American Jewish Committee in November 1945. It was edited by Elliot E. Cohen from 1945 to 1959, and the art critic Clement Greenberg was its associate editor from 1945 to 1957. Early contributors included such prominent intellectuals as Harold Rosenberg, George Orwell, Reinhold Niebuhr, Hannah Arendt, Arthur M. Schlesinger Jr., Martin Buber, John Dewey, Daniel J. Boorstin, Philip Roth, Lionel Trilling, and Albert Camus. At first known for its liberalism, the journal pursued an increasingly conservative bent under Norman Podhoretz, a contributor from 1953 who became the editor in 1960. *Commentary* has its editorial offices at 165 East 56th Street.

Melissa M. Merritt

commercial banking. Commercial banking began in New York City less than seven months after the British evacuation. Favorable legislation encouraged expansion, and by the mid twentieth century the city was the largest commercial banking center in the world.

1. To 1900

The first commercial bank in New York State, the Bank of New York, began operations on 9 June 1784 with $500,000 in capital. It opened an office at Wall and William streets in the spring of 1798 and granted the federal government its first loan (an advance of $200,000 in 1789) before receiving its corporate charter from New York State on 21 March 1791. Already in 1791 the bank had deposits worth 50 percent more than its bank note liabilities. A branch of the First Bank of the United States (1791–1811) opened on Wall Street in 1792, followed by what may have been the first private bank, organized by Nathaniel Ward in 1796. The Manhattan Company, which was chartered to provide the city with wholesome water, opened a bank on 1 September 1799 with $2 million in capital; it was supported by Republicans who saw it as a counterweight to the Bank of New York, which was dominated by Federalists. Merchants Bank began operations on 2 June 1803 with $1.25 million in capital but because of strong opposition from other banks was not granted a corporate charter until March 1805. In 1810 a benevolent society for poor members of more than thirty trades known as the General Society of Mechanics and Tradesmen was granted a charter for the Mechanics' Bank, which had capital of $1.5 million. Union Bank was formed in 1811 by the directors of Jersey Bank in Jersey City, New Jersey, with $800,000 in capital. The role of banks in the national economy became the subject of intense and increasingly fractious political debate. The First Bank of the United States was viewed by most banks in the city as unwanted competition, and its closing in 1811 led to the formation of three banks in mid 1812: the Bank of America ($6 million in capital), City Bank ($2 million), and the bank of the New York Manufacturing Company ($700,000). Eventually the New York Manufacturing Company, a maker of ironware, brassware, and cotton and wool carding equipment, was

Interior of National Park Bank at 214 Broadway, ca *1910*

allowed to discontinue its manufactures by the state legislature, owing to "the embarrassments attending the manufactures of the country"; it changed its name to Phoenix in July 1817. By 1812 there were eight chartered banks in the city, all on Wall Street.

Commercial banks performed a number of functions during the early nineteenth century. They could receive deposits, lend capital to businesses, and facilitate trades between businesses through discounted notes and bills of exchange. Merchants could undertake similar transactions, but only chartered commercial banks were allowed to issue bank notes, which served as currency for the first half of the century. Banks without corporate charters (known as private banks) performed many functions of incorporated banks: they received deposits, discounted notes, sold bills of exchange, and dealt in coin and bullion. Private bankers had unlimited liability; shareholders of chartered banks were liable for double the par value of their shares. During the early nineteenth century private banks dominated foreign exchange. As the city's economy expanded, new banks opened. The authorized capital held by the city's banks rose from $5.4 million in 1805 to $13.5 million in 1815 and $25.1 million in 1825. Almost a third of the loans to the U.S. Treasury during the War of 1812 were made by local banks. Jacob Barker's Exchange Bank (1815) accommodated borrowers unable to secure loans from incorporated banks and issued notes that were widely accepted; it was forced to close after a run in June 1819. A branch of the Second Bank of the United States opened at 65 Broadway in 1817 and was resented by local banks because it offered competition, receiving large deposits from the U.S. Treasury that were earned through customs collections. The branch eventually moved to Wall Street, where it remained until it was closed after the bank's federal charter expired in 1836. For more than a century after the collapse of the Second Bank in 1841 the country's largest bank was in New York City. Franklin Bank (1818) was named after Benjamin Franklin, as were two other banks in later years. The city's first trust company was formed in 1822 as the Farmer's Fire Insurance and Loan Company (renamed Farmers' Loan and Trust Company in 1836). This and the city's second trust company, New York Life Insurance and Trust Company (1830), focused on executing and supervising trusts but increasingly encroached on the business of commercial banks.

Eight banks were formed during the 1820s. The North River Bank was chartered in 1821. In 1824 charters were granted to Fulton Bank and the Chemical Manufacturing Company, a producer of medicines and dyes that was authorized to form the Chemical Bank with capital of $500,000; it opened offices on Broadway opposite City Hall Park. During the same year the Delaware and Hudson Canal Company received a charter for twenty years and began operations with capital of $500,000. In 1825 the Bank of the New York Dry Dock Company received a perpetual charter, and the firms of Samuel Ward and James G. King merged with Prime to form Prime, Ward and King, an important private bank until its dissolution in the 1840s. The firm of James G. Brown began operations in 1826 as an offshoot of a private bank in Baltimore and Philadelphia (the name was changed to Brown Brothers Harriman in 1931). In 1827 Phoenix built headquarters resembling a Greek temple, a style soon imitated by other banks. Banks chartered under the Safety Fund Law (1829) were required to contribute to an emergency fund for insolvent institutions; the Manhattan, Chemical, Dry Dock, North River, and Fulton banks were exempt. Between 1829 and 1838 only ten banks were formed, beginning with Merchants' Exchange Bank and National Bank in April 1829. Initially the city's existing banks refused to take out charters, but eight incorporated before 1829 were rechartered under the law in 1831.

By the 1830s New York City was the country's largest banking center. Balances were kept there by banks in upstate New York and the Midwest, which sent in deposits during the spring and summer and withdrew money to move crops in autumn. Banks in the city also provided advice about banking operations and collected and cleared bank notes and checks for banks elsewhere. Call loans were introduced during the 1830s and became a fixture of the city's money market by the 1850s. Several safety-fund banks were organized in the early 1830s, including the Butchers and Drovers' Bank, Mechanics and Traders' Bank, and Greenwich Bank (1830), the Leather Manufacturers Bank (1832, $600,000), the Commercial Bank in the City of New York (1834), and La Fayette Bank (1834). During the formation of the Seventh Ward Bank in 1833 only forty of the 3710 shares offered were sold to the public: a third were reserved for friends of the commissioners distributing the shares and the rest for state officials. After years of controversy over the price and quality of water from the Manhattan Water Company, voters in 1835 approved the Croton Aqueduct, completed in 1842. In 1837 nine of the city's twenty-three banks held 78 percent of all bankers' deposits in New York City. Toward the end of the decade banks in the city had $20 million in capital. Obtaining a charter often entailed lengthy negotiations and a good deal of political bargaining, until the state legislature in April 1838 passed the General Banking Law, which encouraged free competition and made it far easier for banks to receive charters. The first charter under the new law was granted on 16 July to the North American Banking and Trust Company, followed by fifteen others in only two years. Within a decade thirteen "free banks" had suspended operations, most by 1843. The Bank of Commerce (1839) opened with $5 million in capital, more than any other bank in the city to that time, and soon expanded into investment banking. In 1839 deposits in the city's banks were worth 2.4 times the value of their bank note liabilities.

On several occasions depositors were prevented from exchanging their credit balances for specie. The banks suspended payments in specie from May 1837 to April 1838 and again for two months beginning on 13 October 1857; this policy was denounced by merchants as "selfish, discordant, imbecile, and suicidal." In 1846 there were twenty-five banks in the city, and eight of them held 82 percent of all bankers' deposits in New York City. By this time there were thirteen banks on Wall Street, two on Pearl Street, two on Greenwich Avenue, and one each on Chatham Street, William Street, Grand Street, Hudson Street, Avenue D, and the Bowery. Total capital of the city's banks reached $24 million in 1848 and nearly $50 million in 1855. In 1850 the city had 5.1 percent of the country's banks and 11.2 percent of its bank resources. Its strength lay in reserves kept by out-of-town banks known as correspondents, which included about six hundred of the seven hundred banks in the nation. The Bank of Commerce ceased issuing bank notes in November 1849, as did City Bank in 1851. State bank notes were taxed out of existence in 1866. The city's national banks issued relatively few notes from 1863 to 1935. Imposing headquarters were built by such banks as Hanover Bank (1851), which occupied a stately Italianate building (now occupied by the India House). Washington Irving allowed a bank to be named after him in 1851; this became an important institution, and in later years four banks were named for Alexander Hamilton, three for John Jacob Astor, two for Abraham Lincoln, and one each for George Washington, Thomas Jefferson, and James Monroe.

Between early 1851 and August 1853 twenty-eight banks were opened, many of them led by inexperienced men. To ensure that business went smoothly, especially collections between local banks, fifty-two banks formed the New York Clearing House, which opened on 11 October 1853; First National Bank of Brooklyn (1853) was the sole member outside Manhattan. Only five small banks refused to join: Dry Dock, New York Exchange, Island City, Suffolk, and Central. The Bank of the Union (1853) withdrew after a formal constitution was adopted by the other members on 6 June 1854; a month later it closed, and it was soon followed by Suffolk (December), Central (January 1855), and Island City (October 1857). The utility of the clearing house was demonstrated in the panic of 1857, and during panics in later years when loan certificates were issued. The United States Trust Company (1853) became a leading firm. The city's banks cleared just under $6000 million in 1854. Bankers pursued a conservative course, discouraging speculation and fostering "legitimate" commerce, and the city's prosperity became closely tied to the credit of its banks. The capital held by the Bank of Commerce doubled to $10 million during the late 1850s, and in 1859 bank deposits in the city were 10.7 times its bank note liabilities. In 1860 only 27 percent of New York State bank notes in circulation were issued by the city's banks, which held 62 percent of the bank capital in the state. By 1860 eighty-two banks had been chartered.

The Civil War brought a number of changes to banking. In August 1861 bankers in New York City, Boston, and Philadelphia agreed to lend $150 million to the Union cause. Restrictions on cash payments went into effect in December and were not lifted until April 1862. Payments in specie were suspended on 30 December and not resumed until 1 January 1879. Gold was traded as a commodity, and in the autumn of 1864 the Bank of New York took charge of examining, bagging, and sealing gold coins on behalf of the Board of Gold Dealers. The private bank of J. P. Morgan and Company opened in 1862. A few banks were associated with certain trades and industries, among them Central National Bank (1863) at Broadway and Pearl Street, which catered to dry-goods firms. In February 1863 the National Currency Act enabled banks to obtain national rather than state charters, and eleven national banks were established in New York City: First, Second, Third, Fourth, Fifth, Sixth, Eighth, Ninth, Tenth, and Central national banks and the National Currency Bank. In addition to commercial banking First National Bank (at Wall Street and Broadway) also engaged in investment banking and was initially denied admission to the Clearing House, which refused to exchange its notes. The New York National Exchange Bank (formerly the New York Exchange Bank) was the only state bank to convert, in March 1864. During the same year the New York Guaranty and Indemnity Company and the New York Gold Exchange Bank were chartered by the state.

Seeking to attract all state-chartered banks to the national system, Congress amended the National Currency Act in mid 1864 to make

Ladies' department at the New Amsterdam National Bank, 1906. To encourage genteel women to do business in what was essentially a male institution, banks provided separate areas to make them feel more comfortable.

New York City the only central reserve city where national banks throughout the country could redeposit a portion of their required reserves. (It remained the most important center even after Chicago and St. Louis became reserve cities in 1887.) The Bank of Commerce, the country's largest, became a national bank on 13 January 1865; it was followed by Seventh Ward Bank in April (later renamed Seventh National Bank) and eventually forty-three others. (Peoples, Oriental, Bank of Manhattan Company, and Corn Exchange were the only state banks opened before the war that never took out national charters.) By the autumn of 1866 eleven state banks remained; of these only the Bank of America, the Bank of Manhattan Company, Nassau Bank, and Corn Exchange had more than $1 million in capital. In 1867 the state chartered Stuyvesant Bank and the Eleventh Ward Bank, which absorbed Dry Dock. A state law enabled national banks to convert easily to a New York charter. In 1869 the first three conversions were made and five new state banks were chartered. The next few years saw the formation of several new state institutions: Germania Bank (1869), German American Bank (1870), Equitable Trust Company (1871), Bank of the Metropolis (1871; at Union Square), the Loaners Bank (1871), which lent on "collateral in hand" until suspending operations in 1876, and German Exchange Bank (1872). During the early 1870s the city's dozen trust companies first offered serious competition to commercial banks: they were not subject to the reserve requirements of commercial banks and paid interest on deposits. By 1872 seven of the city's fifty banks had 72 percent of all bankers' deposits in New York City. Cash payments were suspended again in September–October 1873.

By 1876 fifteen banks lined Wall Street and fifty-five others had offices in Manhattan, one as far north as 123rd Street and 3rd Avenue. A national organization of commercial banks known as the American Bankers Association was formed in 1876 and made its headquarters in the city. In 1877 the National Bank of Commerce reduced its capital to $5 million owing to taxes that made it difficult to earn adequate dividends on capital of $10 million. The city's banks served 486 counties nationwide in 1881, and in 1882 the city was called the "clearing house of the western world" by the comptroller of currency, John Jay Knox. Importers and Traders National Bank opened the first credit department in the city. In 1883 the city had 506 private banks. After Marine National Bank closed in May 1884 a panic in the stock market nearly resulted in the suspension of cash payments. In 1885 the capital of the Bank of America reached $8 million, the largest of any bank in the city. Commercial banks organized during this period included Southern National Bank (1885), Market and Fulton National Bank (December 1887, the result of the first merger in the city, by Market and Fulton), Empire State Bank (1888), Twenty-third Ward Bank (1888, the first commercial bank in the Bronx), the Bank of Harlem (1888), and Hamilton Bank (1888). By the late 1880s there were more state banks and trust companies in the city than national banks. The Jarvis–Conklin Mortgage Trust Company opened an office in London in 1887, the first foreign office of an institution based in New York City (later taken over by the Equitable Trust Company). A few Canadian banks opened branches in the city during the late nineteenth century. Market National Bank focused on shipping and the metal and stoves trade, and the Shoe and Leather Bank focused on hardware and other "conservative" trades.

As early as 1891 the Knickerbocker Trust Company (234 5th Avenue) opened a branch at 18 Wall Street, which may have been the first bank branch in the city. In 1891 Hide and Leather National Bank and the Astor Place Bank opened, and the New York Guaranty and Indemnity Company expanded its business before taking the name Guaranty Trust Company in 1896; it later became the largest trust company in the country. The Bank of Harlem and Hamilton Bank merged in 1892. Most of the city's banks suspended cash payments in August–September 1893, bringing the premium on currency to 4 percent. The first foreign exchange department in the city was opened by the Bank of New York in 1893; National City opened one in 1897 and in 1902 advertised that it could pay out any sum of money in any city of the world within twenty-four hours. In 1896 Southern National Bank was taken over by Market and Fulton and the Astor Place Bank absorbed the Empire State Bank after a fire. National City Bank surpassed National Park Bank as the largest commercial bank in the nation. Trust companies offered increasingly stiff competition to commercial banks: between 1897 and 1902 their deposits increased 150 percent, those of commercial banks only 40 percent. A law enacted in 1898 allowed banks to open branches throughout the five boroughs that now composed the city, and branch banking grew during the first decades of the twentieth century, leading to 148 mergers between 1899 and 1925. About this time bank clearings in the city exceeded those in London. Banks increasingly lent on single-name paper (signed only by the borrower) and emphasized analysis of financial statements. By 1899 there were fewer than ten credit departments in the country — all in New York City. The influence of the city's banks on American business grew steadily: by 1900 banks in the city held 25.4 percent of the country's resources and had as correspondents 80 percent of the country's banks, although they themselves accounted for only 1.2 percent of the country's banks.

2. After 1900

Commercial banks expanded in the following years. Barred from offering trust services, national banks formed the Bankers Trust Company (1903) to provide trust services without offering competition to commercial banks. In 1904 Coal and Iron National Bank was formed. By this time bank clearings in the city totaled $60,000 million, representing 58 percent of the country's total. Fifteen banks and nine trust companies had opened in the outer boroughs by 1905, including the Bank of Long Island in Brooklyn (1824), the Brooklyn Bank (1832), the Staten Island Bank (1838, in operation for only four years), Flushing and Queens County Bank (1873, the first bank in Queens), the Bank of Staten Island (1886), First National Bank of Staten Island (1886), Flushing Bank (1888), the Bank of Jamaica (1889), and Citizens Trust Company of Brooklyn (1905). Banks established affiliates that allowed them to underwrite securities directly. First National Bank organized the first such firm, First Security Corporation, in 1907. During the same year the failure of the Knickerbocker Trust Company led to a major financial panic and renewed calls for the establishment of a central bank. The premium on currency rose to 3 percent after cash payments were suspended on 28 October. European investors' concern over these and other problems on Wall Street prevented the city from placing some of its obligations abroad. A $30 million rescue fund was raised by J. P. Morgan, who insisted on forming a bankers' committee to oversee the city's bookkeeping practices. National Copper Bank was formed in 1907 and in 1910 merged with Mechanics Bank to form Mechanics and Metals National Bank. In 1910 the city's banks served 943 counties nationwide. By then national banks in the city accounted for 15 percent of the loans made by all national banks, and their single-name paper loans surpassed those on double-name paper (signed by the borrower and another endorser). In 1911 National City opened a securities affiliate, the National City Company, which became the leading firm of its kind by the end of the 1920s. Neighborhood banks served small businesses and other community concerns.

During the first decades of the twentieth century a number of the city's banks consolidated. Citizens Trust Company of Brooklyn acquired Manufacturers National Bank of Brooklyn in 1914, becoming Manufacturers Trust Company in 1915. This bank moved its headquarters to Broadway and Cedar Street, and it merged with twelve banks in the following years. In April 1912 three of the city's banks each had more than $200 million in resources, and National City had balances from more than four hundred foreign banks. By 1913 Hanover National had more than four thousand correspondent accounts with out-of-town banks, Chase National more than three thousand, and National Park Bank more than 2400. Correspondent balances were lent in the call-loan market on the security of stock exchange collateral. Banks in the city often stepped in to supply such funds when other sources could not. In 1914 a third of all call funds came from the city's national banks.

The Federal Reserve Act of 1913 aimed to diminish the power and influence of the city's banks, leading to the organization of twelve district federal reserve banks. The Federal Reserve Bank of New York, which opened on 16 November 1914, initially counted among its members only the city's thirty-three national banks. The first state-chartered member bank, the Broadway Trust Company, joined in the summer of 1915; the next were Corn Exchange (1916) and Guaranty Trust (October 1917), and others followed in the spirit of wartime patriotism. Under Benjamin Strong the Federal Reserve Bank of New York dominated national monetary policy making. After 1913 the city's banks, including National City, sought customers among smaller corporations nationwide. Trust companies and banks increasingly resembled each other, and in 1914 national banks were allowed to offer trust services; a few trust companies remained that did not accept deposits.

Banks helped to finance the First World War and prospered: they bought Treasury securities and promoted them to the public. In 1914 four of the city's banks had branches overseas. During the summer of 1914 wartime exchange restrictions complicated the city's repayment of $80 million owed to foreign investors; all but three of the city's 127 banks joined in a gold-export program and helped to lend $100 million. Restrictions on foreign exchange and the movement of gold also helped the city to become the main source of financing for American foreign trade and most European trade with Asia and Latin America. Deposits continued to accumulate from foreign investors, including some governments, and by 1917 dollar banker's acceptances reached $1000 million (to that time London had been the main source). National City had thirty-five overseas branches, which grew to eighty-three in 1930. By 1917 interbank balances no longer counted as part of member banks' required reserves. The city's banks nonetheless continued to hold large deposits from members of the Federal Reserve while serving nonmember correspondents ineligible to use the facilities of the Federal Reserve. One of the first subsidiaries opened by a foreign bank was the French–American Banking Corporation (1919).

The city was the world's leading financial center from the end of the war until 1925, when it was surpassed by London. Many foreign banks opened subsidiaries in the city during the 1920s, among them the Anglo-South American Trust Company and the J. Henry Schroder Banking Corporation, both in 1923. Such securities affiliates as Chase Securities (1917), the Guaranty Company (1920), and the Bankers Company of New York (1928) enjoyed tremendous success during the height of the securities flotation boom. During a depression in 1920–21 the Federal Reserve Bank provided local members with resources to lend to correspondents nationwide. In 1922 the New York Life Insurance and Trust Company merged with the Bank of New York. The city had thirty-one of the hundred largest American banks in 1923, and in 1926 forty of the ninety-three banks based in Manhattan had their headquarters south of Fulton Street. Between 1926 and 1930 there were ninety-seven mergers, including twelve in 1926 and twenty-nine in 1929. Most involved small neighborhood banks; among the larger ones were the acquisition of the National Bank of Commerce by the Guaranty Trust Company in 1929 and that of Equitable Trust by Chase National Bank in 1930, which resulted in the largest bank in the world. In 1928 National City Bank became the first major commercial bank to offer consumer loans. By 1929 there were 630 branches in the five boroughs. Corn Exchange Bank had sixty-seven branches, the Bank of Manhattan sixty-four, Bank of United States fifty-eight, Manufacturers Trust forty-five, National City thirty-seven, the Bank of America thirty-four, and Public National thirty-three. In 1929 Farmers' Loan and Trust became an affiliate of National City Bank and the Bank of Manhattan completed its skyscraper at 40 Wall Street, which at 927 feet (283 meters) was briefly the tallest building in the world. The city was the nation's predominant money market. In 1929 the city's banks had just under 23 percent of the assets held by all the banks in the nation.

The Depression brought important changes. By 1930 seventy-nine of the country's one hundred largest banks were outside the city. Bank of United States was forced to close in December 1930, in the largest American bank failure before 1974. Call loans ceased to be important. In 1931 the Federal Reserve Bank provided funds for members to lend to their correspondents. A few projects were completed in 1931: a tower of fifty-seven stories at 22 William Street by City Bank Farmers Trust Company, and one of fifty stories at 1 Wall Street by Irving Trust. National City took over the Bank of America. The acquisition by Manufacturers of Chatham and Phenix National Bank in early 1932 was the last large merger for the next twenty years. As banks sought to economize, the number of branches in the city declined to 552 in 1932. Cash payments were suspended from 4 March to 13 March 1933, for the first time under order from Washington. In October the city signed a bankers' agreement with Bankers Trust, Chase, Guaranty, Morgan, and National City to avoid defaulting on its floating debt and restore its credit. Congressional hearings after the stock market crash of 1929 uncovered questionable actions by securities affiliates, especially those of National City and Chase, leading some banks to dissolve their affiliates even before all member banks were ordered to do so by the Banking Act of 1933 (commonly known as Glass–Steagall).

The Second World War marked the ascent of the United States as a global financial leader. During the war the city's commercial banks were again important buyers and promoters of Treasury securities. At the same time competition among banks in the city intensified, especially as they lost the business of customers who moved to the suburbs. They had more than 30 percent of the country's deposits by 1940 but less than 21 percent in 1946, when Bank of America in California became the nation's largest. After the war major banks offered personal and small business loans and increasingly sought business overseas. The banking district remained south of Chambers Street, where in 1947 thirty-seven of fifty-one banks in Manhattan had their headquarters. Chase National Bank was the largest in the city until 1948, when it was surpassed by National City. The amount of American bank assets held in the city dropped below 19 percent in 1949, and during the 1940s and 1950s interbank balances there declined relative to those in other cities. In 1954–55 leading Wall Street banks combined with other commercial banks known for their large neighborhood networks. Manufacturers Trust led with 112 offices; Chemical merged with Corn Exchange to form Chemical Corn Exchange, which had ninety-eight; Chase and the Bank of the Manhattan Company formed Chase Manhattan Bank, which had ninety-six offices and became the city's largest bank in total deposits; First National City, formed by combining First National Bank and National City in March 1955, had seventy-three offices; and after merging with Public National, Bankers Trust had forty-two. At this time half of the commercial loans made by the city's banks went to borrowers outside the metropolitan area. Chase Manhattan introduced a consumer charge plan in the city in 1958 but abandoned it after a few years. Ties to foreign banks were strengthened: at the end of 1958 twenty-six foreign banks had agencies and forty-one had representative offices in the city. National City, Chase Manhattan, Morgan Guaranty, Bankers Trust, and Hanover had among them sixty-four foreign branches in 1959. New York City ceased to be the most important international financial center with the development of the Eurodollar from the late 1950s, and in 1959 it had fewer than 17 percent of the deposits in American banks.

The 1960s saw renewed expansion. Banks in the city were permitted to open branches in adjacent Nassau and Westchester counties in 1960, and in 1961 foreign and Puerto Rican banks were allowed to open deposit-taking branches. The city's financial center moved from lower Manhattan to midtown as Citibank moved its headquarters to 399 Park Avenue (at 53rd Street) in 1961 and other important banks like Chemical, Manufacturers Hanover, and Bankers Trust opened offices nearby. In February 1961 First National City became the first major bank to pay interest to large business depositors, offering negotiable certificates of deposit at a rate competitive with those of Treasury bills. Others soon followed, but in mid 1965 banks in the city had fewer than 15 percent of the country's deposits. Chase Manhattan formed the first small business investment company in 1962 and in 1965 became a national bank, relinquishing the perpetual charter granted to the Manhattan Company. The city's banks were hurt by a federal tax on long-term bank loans to foreigners and other restraints on foreign credit extensions introduced in 1965; from this time they also underwrote the city's growing debt. During the late 1960s they introduced bank credit cards: the Everything card (First National City, August 1967), Master Charge, later renamed Master Card (Manufacturers Hanover, Chemical, and Marine Midland, 1968; First National City, 1969), Unicard (Chase Manhattan, 1969), and Bank Americard, later renamed Visa (Chase Manhattan, 1972). The first automated teller machine (ATM) in the city was opened by Chemical Bank in 1969; by the late 1980s almost every bank in the city offered ATM facilities.

As financial markets became increasingly deregulated from the late 1960s, commercial banks faced stiff competition from other financial institutions. The Bank Holding Company Act enabled bank holding companies to operate subsidiaries devoted to such services as mortgages and consumer lending anywhere in the country. In October 1968 the owners of First National City Bank exchanged their stock for shares in a bank holding company, First National City Corporation (now Citicorp). Shareholders of Chase became the owner of Chase Corporation in June 1969, and within a few years all large banks turned themselves into subsidiaries of bank holding companies. The goal of First National City was to become the leading global financial services institution. By the early 1990s it had 1947 subsidiaries and affiliates in ninety-two countries.

In 1975 the city's banks held $1200 million in municipal securities, about 10 percent of the outstanding amount. At the height of the city's fiscal crisis during the summer of 1975, leading banks exchanged short-term notes for bonds issued by the Municipal Assistance Corporation. When the city again faced default in the autumn, Ellmore Patterson of Morgan, Walter Wriston of Citibank, and David Rockefeller of Chase sought a federal loan or loan guarantee; Congress extended to the city an unprecedented $2300 million line of credit. Statewide branches were allowed in 1976. During the late 1970s all the major banks in the city except Citibank formed an ATM consortium known as the New York Cash Exchange (NYCE).

Commercial banks focused increasingly on foreign markets, where they were permitted to engage in all aspects of investment banking. In 1977 Chase extended more credit abroad than in the United States. To enable American financial institutions to compete in overseas Eurocurrency markets, the New York Clearing House proposed international banking facilities (IBFs); these were approved in December 1981, and by 1989 they numbered 527. Half of these were in New York City and belonged to 150 American banks, forty-nine Edge Act corporations (subsidiaries of American banks engaged exclusively in international banking), and thirty-seven foreign banks and agencies. Although IBFs had little effect on employment, they helped to stem the growth of offshore shell branches in the Caribbean. Interest in foreign lending slackened after 1982, when third world countries were unable to repay borrowings. Employment in commercial banking increased from 5.2 percent of total employment in the private sector in 1982 to 5.7 percent in 1987 but declined soon after. Chase Manhattan had 331 branches in every major market in New York State by 1984 and operated in seventy-one countries by 1985, deriving half its deposits and loans overseas. Citicorp became the country's largest bank and its holding company the ninth-largest in the world; it and Chase, Morgan, and Bankers Trust had more than half their assets overseas in 1987. The Bank of New York merged with Irving Trust in 1989, the largest local merger to that time. Between 1975 and 1989 the number of foreign banking facilities increased from sixty-eight to 255; these held 74 percent of total facilities' assets in the United States.

The city's commercial banks ceased to lead in international lending as Europe and Japan prospered during the 1980s. Tarnished by bad loans to the third world, poor real-estate investments, and leveraged-buyout financing, they were less competitive than more diversified foreign institutions because of their high overhead. In mid 1989 the city's commercial banks had fewer than 9 percent of the country's deposits; by 1990 only seven of the largest fifteen were in the city, and as a recession set in, loans declined and workers were dismissed. Major banks lost business in commercial loans to the "junk-bond" market and the banks petitioned to reverse the ban on securities underwriting imposed by the Glass–Steagall Act. They also expanded to the extent permitted by federal regulation: in 1990 Morgan Guaranty became the first bank holding company allowed to underwrite a limited amount of corporate stock. Leading institutions also set up out-of-state subsidiaries to process credit card transactions and consumer loans; many of these were in Delaware and South Dakota, where state banking laws and taxation were especially favorable. By 1991 foreign banks had 463 offices in New York City, far more than in any other American city. Chemical Bank and Manufacturers Hanover merged in July 1991 to form the country's third-largest banking organization, and other major banks were said to be considering similar action. A quarter of the city's bank workers were employed by its 366 foreign banks. In the mid 1990s there were more than one thousand offices and almost seventy commercial banks with headquarters in New York City. Of these only Brown Brothers Harriman remained private.

Benjamin J. Klebaner: *Commercial Banking in the United States: A History* (Hinsdale, Ill.: Dryden, 1974; rev. Boston: Twayne, 1990, as *American Commercial Banking: A History*)

Benjamin J. Klebaner: "The Manufacturers Hanover Decision and New York City Banking since 1945," *International Review of the History of Banking* 32–33 (1986), 86–109

Benjamin J. Klebaner

commercial fishing. Cod, mackerel, bluefish, and striped bass were once plentiful in the waters off New York City, as were shad, sturgeon, and eels in nearby bays and the Hudson River; there were also lobsters and oysters. For decades a fish known as menhaden and valued for its oil rather than its meat was also caught in the metropolitan area. Although most whaling was done off Nantucket and New Bedford, Massachusetts, whaling vessels sailed from the Port of New York as early as 1768, and between 1792 and 1877 at least forty-nine whaling ships were based there, making extended voyages to grounds in the Pacific and Indian oceans. During the colonial period shallow water off Communipaw (now in Jersey City, New Jersey) was the local center for oystering and Upper New York Bay was the center for fishing, but both areas ceased to be used in the early nineteenth century because of depleted stocks and increasing pollution. About this time the Fulton Fish Market on the East River in lower Manhattan became the regional distribution center for seafood. From March to June mackerel was brought there by a large fleet of schooners from New England that operated between North Carolina and eastern Long Island. Farmers living near the shore supplemented their income by fishing and delivered their catch to the market themselves or loaded it on steamboats that operated between local landings and Manhattan. A number of styles of net were used: seine nets hauled ashore by teams of men or horses; moored, cylindrical "fyke" nets and pound nets hundreds of feet long erected on poles offshore that trapped fish in a pocket at one end; and gill nets, which were attached to poles or allowed to drift and entangled the gills of fish (these were outlawed in much of the area during the 1940s because they depleted the stock too rapidly).

Raritan Bay became a vital area for fishing, clamming, and oystering during the nineteenth century. Along with oysters harvested in Long Island Sound those harvested in Raritan Bay were sold late in the century in the oyster markets of Manhattan, which consisted of distinctive barges moored in groups along the waterfront; they were the headquarters of various wholesalers and received their catch directly from oyster sloops. On each barge stood a two-story structure with doors and windows facing the shore: the first story was used for packing and distribution, the second for offices. Oystering and clamming were greatly reduced in the twentieth century by pollution and the depletion of stocks in the Sound and Raritan Bay. In the mid 1990s a few lobstermen operated in the bay and the Atlantic, and in Lower New York Bay a few crews set pound nets and harvested blue crabs and hard clams; in the spring shad fishermen based in Edgewater, New Jersey, set moored gill nets in shallows near the towers of the George Washington Bridge.

Norman J. Brouwer

Commercial High School for Girls. Original name of WASHINGTON IRVING HIGH SCHOOL.

commodity exchanges. Merchants handling commodities in New York City first gathered in the 1750s in small quarters on Broad Street and in 1768 moved to an area outside the New York Chamber of Commerce. The completion of the Erie Canal in 1825 and increased business activity led to the construction of the Merchants' Exchange (1827) on William Street, destroyed by fire in 1835 and rebuilt on Wall Street. New York City led the nation in handling goods such as sugar, coffee, and cocoa from Latin America and in conducting export business in cotton, breadstuffs, tobacco, and other farm produce. The New York Mercantile Exchange extended futures trading to perishable commodities in 1872 with limited effect. The informal, unregulated methods in commodity trading gave way in the 1860s and 1870s to organized exchanges in major American and European ports, where most trading was in a limited number of nonperishable commodities and in futures contracts. It was rare for contracts to be settled by delivery of the commodity in question; instead the difference between a contracted price and a market price was usually paid in cash. This practice led to the development of "hedging" facilities, where prices were more stable and the risk of price changes was shifted from merchants and processors to speculators. Gradually this system spread to a range of commodities during the late nineteenth century and the early twentieth, surviving a period of stagnation during the Depression.

The federal government first imposed regulations on commodities exchanges in the 1920s. The Commodity Exchange Act and laws governing grains and cotton required exchanges to make accurate reports of their transactions and to improve their self-governance. Greater pressure was later placed on exchanges when investigations exposed instances of insider trading and manipulation of reported transactions (mostly in Chicago). A major target of these regulations was the Commodity Exchange (COMEX), formed in 1933 by the merger of the New York Rubber, National Silk, National Metal, and New York Hide exchanges. During the Second World War the New York Mercantile Exchange opened a successful futures market in potatoes, eggs, butter, and rice. During the 1950s and 1960s most trading on the COMEX was in gold, silver, and copper. It grew steadily by offering trading in government securities futures, foreign exchange, and stock index futures; aluminum futures met with less success. In the 1960s and 1970s the formal trading system that developed in the late nineteenth century was extended to precious metals, raw materials, and a range of financial instruments. This system required exchanges to adhere to complex rules, use clearing house functions to settle differences in gains and losses, and accept limits on the number of their members, who alone were entitled to serve as brokers.

The New York Mercantile Exchange, the chief rival of the COMEX, became an important market during the energy crisis of 1973 because of its contracts for crude oil, heating oil, and unleaded gasoline. The Commodity Futures Trading Commission, formed in 1974, provided much broader, stricter regulation of futures trading in commodities than its predecessor, established under the relatively weak Commodities Exchange Act of the 1930s. The New York Mercantile Exchange revived its potato trading in 1981, in addition to expanding into platinum and palladium. By 1990 it was the fastest-growing and most prosperous commodity exchange in New York City. Four major commodity exchanges shared trading facilities in the World Trade Center in the mid 1990s: the New York Mercantile Exchange, the New York Cotton Exchange, the Commodity Exchange, and the New York Coffee, Sugar, and Cocoa Exchange.

Sonny Kleinfield: *The Traders* (New York: Holt, Rinehart and Winston, 1983)

Michael Atkin: *Agricultural Commodity Markets: A Guide to Futures Trading* (London: Routledge, 1989)

Martin Mayer: *Markets* (New York: W. W. Norton, 1989)

Morton Rothstein

Commodore Hotel. Hotel in Manhattan that later became the GRAND HYATT.

Common Council. Legislative branch of the government of New York City, established by the charter of Governor Thomas Dongan of 1686. In addition to the mayor and the recorder it included one alderman and one assistant alderman elected to one-year terms from each of the city's six wards. Although the council had the power to regulate virtually all aspects of commerce and public safety, from monitoring strangers to setting the price of bread, drawing up the rules of the city market, and controlling the ever-present hogs, its actions could be vetoed by the governor and his council or simply allowed to become null if they were not approved within three months. The city's government lacked a clear separation of powers: the mayor presided over the council and both the mayor and aldermen served as justices of the peace and as justices in the court of common pleas. In 1813 the state legislature empowered the council to act as a Board of County Supervisors for New York County and in 1821 the council gained the power to appoint the mayor.

The charter of 1830 divided the council into a board of aldermen and a board of assistant aldermen and removed the mayor from the council. Legislation could originate in either board, but required the approval of both before being forwarded to the mayor. The council could override a mayoral veto by majority vote of both boards and retained the power to appoint the heads of executive departments. The nature of the council was again altered when the charter of 1849 increased the terms for aldermen (but not assistant aldermen) to two years, took away the council's power to appoint executive department heads, and required the council to muster a two-thirds majority in each board to override the mayor's veto.

In 1853 further changes in the charter eliminated the board of assistants in favor of a sixty-member board of councilmen in charge of all legislation concerning expenditures. Members of the Common Council lost the right to sit in city courts and their control over the police department. The comptroller assumed power over city finances in 1857 and the council no longer acted as the board of supervisors for the county. The board of assistant aldermen was reinstated in 1868 and eliminated for the last time by the "reform charter" of 1873, which vested all legislative power in a board of aldermen with twenty-one members elected annually. The board was empowered to approve or reject the mayor's appointments to executive offices; the powers of finance and taxation were increasingly the province of the Board of Estimate and Apportionment. With consolidation in 1898 the Common Council ceased to exist and the city gained a bicameral legislature, which lasted

Presidents of the Board of Aldermen, Board of Assistant Aldermen, and Board of Councilmen, 1831–1897

BOARD OF ALDERMEN		BOARD OF ASSISTANT ALDERMEN	
1831–32	Samuel Stevens	1831–32	James B. Murray
1832–33	Henry Meigs	1832–34	William Van Wyck
1833–34	John Y. Cebra		
1834–35	James Monroe	1834–35	George W. Bruen
1835–36	Isaac L. Varian (1 July 1835 to 28 Dec 1836)	1835–36	James R. Whiting
1836–39	Egbert Benson (from 28 Dec 1836)	1837–39	Caleb S. Woodhull
1839–40	A. V. Williams	1839–40	Nathaniel Jarvis Jr.
1840–42	Elijah F. Purdy	1840–41	Frederick R. Lee
		1841–42	Thomas R. Lee
1842–43	Caleb S. Woodhull	1842–43	William Adams
		1843–44	Charles P. Brown
1844–45	Richard L. Schieffelin	1844–45	William Everdell
1845–46	Oliver Charlick	1845–46	Nathaniel Pierce
1846–47	David S. Jackson	1846–47	Neil Gray
1847–49	Morris Franklin	1847–48	Linus W. Stevens
		1848–49	Wilson Small
1849–50	James Kelly (8 May 1849 to 7 Jan 1850)	1849–50	Edwin D. Morgan (8 May to 7 Jan)
1850–51	Morgan Morgans	1850	Oscar W. Sturtevant
		1851	Alonzo A. Alvord
1852–53	Richard T. Compton	1852–53	Jonathan Trotter
		BOARD OF COUNCILMEN	
1854	Nathan C. Ely	1854	Edwin J. Brown
1855–56	Isaac O. Barker	1855	Daniel D. Conover
		1856	Benjamin F. Pinckney
1857–58	John Clancy	1857	Jonas N. Phillips
		1858	Charles H. Haswell
1859	Thomas McSpedon	1859	Charles G. Cornell
1860	William J. Peck	1860–61	Morgan Jones
1861	Henry W. Genet		
1862	John T. Henry	1862	Charles T. Pinckney
1863	William Walsh	1863	Morgan Jones
1864	John T. Henry	1864–65	James Hayes
1865	Morgan Jones		
1866	John Brice	1866	J. Wilson Green
1867	Joseph Shannon	1867	James G. Brinkman
1868–71	Thomas Coman	1868	John Stacom
		1869	James A. Monaghan
		1870	John Riley (Jan–June)
		BOARD OF ASSISTANT ALDERMEN	
		1870–71	John Galvin (June–Jan)
1872	John Cochrane	1872	Otis T. Hall
1873–74	Samuel B. H. Vance	1873	William Wade
1875–76	Samuel Lewis	1874	Joseph P. Strack
1877	Henry D. Purroy		
1878	William R. Roberts		
1879	Jordan L. Mott		
1880	John J. Morris		
1881	Patrick Kiernan		
1882	William Sauer		
1883	John Reilly		
1884	William P. Kirk		
1885	Adolph A. Sanger		
1886	Robert B. Nooney		
1887	Henry R. Beekman		
1888	George H. Forster (*d* 8 Nov)		
1889–92	John H. V. Arnold		
1893–94	George B. McClellan		
1895–97	John Jeroloman		

Compiled by Edward T. O'Donnell

until 1901. From that time the legislative branch of city government was a unicameral body called successively the Municipal Assembly, the Board of Aldermen, and the City Council.

Edward O'Donnell

Common Starling. A chunky bird about eight inches (twenty centimeters) long with a short tail, mostly black but having some iridescent green and purple feathers; it has white spots and a dark bill in autumn and winter and a yellow bill in spring and summer. Introduced to Central Park in 1890 from Europe, it was well established by the early 1920s. It begins breeding in early spring and builds nests in nearly all available bird boxes and dead trees, thus excluding such species as woodpeckers, Tree Swallows, Purple Martins, and Eastern Bluebirds. The bird is noisy and dirty and is considered a nuisance.

John Bull: *Birds of the New York Area* (New York: Harper and Row, 1964)

John Bull: *Birds of New York State* (New York: Doubleday / Natural History Press, 1974)

John Bull: *Birds of New York State, including the 1976 Supplement* (Ithaca, N.Y.: Cornell University Press, 1985)

John Bull

Commonwealth Fund. Charitable organization formed in 1918 with an endowment of $10 million from Anna M. Harkness for "benevolent, religious, educational and like purposes." In its early years the fund supported projects related to the welfare of women and children, and medical education; it also contributed to war relief. Later the fund made contributions in the fields of public health (including mental hygiene), community health, and medical research. In New York City the fund has contributed to Columbia University, Union Theological Seminary, the New York Red Cross, public television, and many settlement houses. Additional gifts to the endowment were made by Harkness, her son Edward S. Harkness (1874–1940), and his wife, Mary S. Harkness (1874–1950). In 1993 the Commonwealth Fund had assets of $365.1 million and made grants totaling $11.3 million.

A. McGehee and Susan L. Abrams: *For the Welfare of Mankind: The Commonwealth Fund and American Medicine* (Baltimore: Johns Hopkins University Press, 1986)

Erwin Levold

communism. The role played by communism in New York City was at one time so large that the drama critic Lionel Abel, a former Trotskyist sympathizer, remarked in his memoirs that in the 1930s the city "went to Russia and spent most of the decade there." In the city many former socialists joined the communist movement after the founding of the Communist International in 1919. New York City was the place of publication of two daily newspapers issued by the Communist

Headquarters of the Communist Party on Union Square East, 1941. Right *offices of the* Daily Worker; left *offices of* Freiheit

Party USA, *Morgen Freiheit* (in Yiddish, 1922) and the *Daily Worker* (1924), as well as its influential literary magazine the *New Masses* (1926). The party also established its publishing house International Publishers in New York City, and a number of schools, cultural groups, immigrant fraternal organizations, and political auxiliaries. Throughout the 1920s factional disputes among American communists mirrored those taking place in the Soviet Union. In the middle of the decade the party found strong support among workers in the garment trades, including many members of Local 25 of the International Ladies' Garment Workers' Union (ILGWU), with which the party lost influence after leading an unsuccessful six-month strike in 1926. In the early years of the movement most communists in the city were of foreign origin; as late as 1931 the foreign-born made up more than four fifths of the membership in the metropolitan district.

In 1927 the party moved its national headquarters to New York City from Chicago. For the next two decades its activities were directed from the ninth floor of a building that it owned at 35 East 12th Street, one block south of Union Square. The party came close to developing a mass following in the city: at the height of its strength it drew tens of thousands to march in its annual parade on May Day and filled Madison Square Garden with twenty thousand cheering spectators. On 6 March 1930, four months after the crash of the stock market, the Communist Party in the city called for a demonstration of the unemployed in Union Square; the number of participants was estimated as more than 100,000 by the *Daily Worker* and as 35,000 by the *New York Times*. Like many other communist gatherings in the early 1930s this one ended violently, when mounted police swinging clubs rode into the crowd to prevent it from marching on City Hall. Later that year and in the years that followed, communists throughout the city organized councils of the unemployed, led protest marches on city relief offices, and gathered crowds to resist evictions. Some neighborhoods were likened to the "red belt" surrounding Paris: cooperative apartments organized by the Communist Party on Allerton Avenue in the Bronx were a stronghold of party support, as were parts of Harlem, East Harlem, Brooklyn, the Lower East Side, and the waterfront.

The party grew in the mid 1930s, as it became more adept at attracting American-born adherents. In accord with the policies of the Popular Front approved in Moscow, American communists eschewed the revolutionary rhetoric of earlier years in favor of uniting people in a coalition against fascism. The party leader Earl Browder described communism as "twentieth-century Americanism." Communists now agreed to endorse liberal politicians they had once despised, including Fiorello H. La Guardia. Increasingly the party was made up of the native-born children of immigrant parents; it also developed a large following among blacks. Many young members had taken part in radical student politics at City College of New York and Brooklyn College.

After the formation in the 1930s of the Committee for Industrial Organization (CIO; later renamed the Congress of Industrial Organizations) communists gained unprecedented influence within the union movement. In the city they were instrumental in organizing the Transport Workers Union, led by their close ally Mike Quill. They were also influential in the National Maritime Union, the United Electrical Workers (UE), District 65 of the United Retail and Wholesale Employees, and the American Newspaper Guild. Ben Gold, president of the Fur Workers Union, was one of few labor leaders in the United States who openly avowed his affiliation with the party. Although their greatest strength was in the new unions of the CIO the communists also retained a following in locals of the American Federation of Labor, such as the Painters Union, the Hotel and Restaurant Workers Union, and the American Federation of Teachers. Communism was popular among writers, intellectuals, and artists in the city. The John Reed Clubs were formed in the 1930s, as was the League of American Writers, which sponsored congresses in the city in 1935, 1937 and 1939 that were well attended. Many who were not communists but were concerned by the spread of fascism in Europe were drawn to support anti-fascist groups controlled by the Communist Party, including the American League against War and Fascism, which had as its chairman in the late 1930s Harry F. Ward, a professor at Union Theological Seminary.

By 1938 the Communist Party had 38,000 members in New York State, about half its national membership, and most of these lived in New York City. A Communist candidate for the presidency of the city's Board of Aldermen received nearly 100,000 votes in 1938, and during the Second World War two avowed communists, Peter V. Cacchione of Brooklyn and Benjamin Davis of Harlem, held seats on the City Council. The loyalty of the party to the Soviet Union did not hinder its growth so long as Moscow advocated international collective security against the Nazis. Despite such events as the Moscow trials of the late 1930s the faith of most communists in the virtues of the "workers' fatherland" remained unshaken. The nonaggression pact between Germany and the Soviet Union in August 1939 ended the respectability of the Popular Front in the United States: former allies dropped away and right-wing opponents of communism went on the attack. The Rapp–Coudert investigations (1940–41) by the state legislature into communist influence in the municipal colleges led to the dismissal or resignation of about sixty faculty members from City College and Brooklyn College. The party briefly regained strength during the "grand alliance" that followed the Nazi invasion of the Soviet Union in June 1941, but after the Nazis were defeated communists came under sustained attack. The trial of eleven communist leaders in 1949 for conspiring to overthrow the government and the trial of Julius and Ethel Rosenberg in 1951 for espionage were both held in New York City, and both ended in convictions. In 1956, by which time membership had fallen to about twenty thousand, the party was further weakened by Khrushchev's denunciation of Stalin and the suppression of the Hungarian revolution by the Soviet Union; by the end of the 1950s the party was a small sectarian group. Leadership of the party was assumed in 1959 by Gus Hall (*b* Iron, Minn., 8 Oct 1910), a frequent candidate for the presidency of the United States. When communism collapsed in the Soviet Union in the early 1990s the party lost many long-time members, but it remained loyal to its Leninist ideology. Its national headquarters remained open at 235 West 23rd Street in Manhattan.

Irving Howe and Lewis Coser: *The American Communist Party: A Critical History* (Boston: Beacon, 1957)
Maurice Isserman: *Which Side Were You On?: The American Communist Party during the Second World War* (Middletown, Conn.: Wesleyan University Press, 1982)
Mark Naison: *Communists in Harlem during the Depression* (Urbana: University of Illinois Press, 1983)
Harvey Klehr: *The Heyday of American Communism: The Depression Decade* (New York: Basic Books, 1984)

Maurice Isserman

community gardens. Organized communal growing spaces with individually worked plots first appeared in the United States in Detroit, as part of a plan to relieve social and economic problems caused by the panic of 1893. The idea spread quickly to other American cities including New York City. Community gardens reappeared briefly in the city during the First World War as part of the program known as Liberty Gardens, but did not become widespread until city-owned land was made available for gardens during the Depression. The program expanded during the Second World War when the government encouraged the cultivation of Victory Gardens. These gardens were uprooted shortly after the surrender of Japan and community gardens did not reappear in New York City until the early 1970s, when individuals and community groups across the city transformed garbage-strewn lots into thriving community spaces. A highly successful and visible garden planted at the Bowery and Houston Street in lower Manhattan in 1972 by a volunteer activist group called the Green Guerrillas attracted much attention and encouraged others to begin similar projects in their neighborhoods. In 1978 New York City launched Operation Green Thumb to make city-owned vacant lots available for gardens for $1 a year. At first strictly a leasing program, this eventually took on a more active role in helping to develop and maintain gardens and provide equipment and technical assistance to community groups. By 1991 the program had led to the planting of more than five hundred gardens in New York City.

Mark Francis, Lisa Cashdan, and Lynn Paxson: *Community Open Space: Greening Neighborhoods through Community Action and Land Conservation* (Washington: Island, 1984)
Tom Fox, Ian Koeppel, and Susan Kellam: *Struggle for Space: The Greening of New York City, 1970–1984* (New York: Neighborhood Open Space Coalition, 1985)
Diana Balmori and Margaret Morton: *Transitory Gardens, Uprooted Lives* (New Haven: Yale University Press, 1993)

Craig D. Bida

Community Service Society. Organization formed in 1939 by the merger of the Association for Improving the Condition of the Poor and the Charity Organization Society, two of the most influential private charities in New York City. Initially it concentrated on family casework, fresh air programs, and community health but gradually closed its clinics and summer camps. Influenced by the poverty programs of the 1960s, it shifted its focus to legislative work and pilot antipoverty programs. During the early 1970s it gradually eliminated its social casework and sought instead to empower the poor in their own communities by helping eligible persons to obtain welfare, encouraging the formation of tenants' councils in public housing, and sponsoring local programs for the elderly. In the mid 1990s it provided short-term rent grants to those facing eviction and emergency funds for public benefits applicants, coordinated the ten thousand members of its Retired Senior Volunteer Program, sought to develop permanent housing for the homeless, and conducted studies on poverty. It also launched a voter registration program for the poor and remained one of their most important advocates in health care, education, and housing.

Marilyn Thornton Williams

Composers Collective. A musical association that grew out of a workshop offered in New York City in 1931 by the John Reed Club. Its leading members included the composers Henry Cowell, Charles Seeger, Aaron Copland, Elie Siegmeister, and Marc Blitzstein, who met weekly in an apartment on West 14th Street. Influenced by the *New Masses* and the proletarian musical perspectives of Hanns Eisler, Kurt Weill, and Bertolt Brecht, the collective published the *Workers Song Book* (1934), which included the song "May Day" as well as Copland's "Into the Streets of May." The Composers Collective disbanded in 1935 when many of its members became associated with the American Music League.

Barbara Tischler: *An American Music: The Search for an American Musical Identity* (New York: Oxford University Press, 1986)

Peter M. Rutkoff, William B. Scott

Comptrollers of New York City after Consolidation

Bird S. Coler 1898–1901
Edward M. Grout 1902–5
Herman Metz 1906–8
W.A. Pendergast 1910–17
Charles L. Craig 1918–25
Charles W. Berry 1926–32
George McAneny 1933
Arthur Cunningham 1934
Joseph D. McGoldrick 1935
Frank J. Taylor 1936–37
Joseph D. McGoldrick 1938–45
Lazarus Joseph 1946–53
Lawrence E. Gerosa 1954–61
Abraham D. Beame 1962–65
Mario Procaccino 1966–69
Abraham D. Beame 1970–73
Harrison J. Goldin 1974–89
Elizabeth Holtzman 1990–93
Alan G. Hevesi 1994–

comptroller. The chief financial officer of New York City. The position was established in 1801 to countersign all warrants drawn on the chamberlain and was initially filled by appointment. The comptroller became the head of the department of finance in 1831, an elected official in 1884, and the head of a separate office in 1938. Elected citywide to a four-year term and second in the line of succession should the mayor's office fall vacant, the comptroller issues an annual report advising the mayor and City Council and audits all financial transactions. The abolition in 1989 of the Board of Estimate, of which the comptroller had been a member ex officio since 1874, significantly reduced the comptroller's power.

Rebecca B. Rankin: *The Treasurer, Chamberlain and the Comptroller of the City of New York* (New York: New York Municipal Reference Library, 1949)
Thelma E. Smith: *Guide to the Municipal Government of the City of New York* (New York: Meilen, 1973)

Neal C. Garelik

computers. New York City has an important history as a center of innovations in computing technology. The Computing–Recording–Tabulating Company, formed in the city by Thomas J. Watson, was an early leader in data processing and later became well known as International Business Machines (IBM). The Columbia Statistical Bureau, a laboratory for educational test scores, was opened at Columbia University in 1928 by Ben D. Wood with equipment borrowed from Watson; in 1930 IBM developed for the bureau the "Columbia machine," an electromechanical calculator that could interpolate tables, calculate correlation coefficients, and automatically shift numbers between its ten registers (allowing it to handle both ten-digit numbers and ten numbers at one time). The bureau did important work in scientific computing for the astronomy department at Columbia, and its experiments also proved useful in demographic studies and led to machines such as the IBM 600-series calculating punches. Further advances in computer technology were made during the 1930s at Columbia when the astronomer Wallace J. Eckert opened a laboratory in Pupin Hall with IBM accounting machines and other equipment: this made possible a rudimentary program for complex calculations, an important step toward the first computer. In 1939 IBM experimented with the vacuum tube, a relatively new device, with the aim of using it in computing. Research at the firm's headquarters in New York City and at its engineering laboratory in Endicott, New York, led to the development of multipliers a thousand times faster than electromechanical calculators.

After the outbreak of the Second World War some work in computing in New York City continued. Work on the transistor, the first generation of a silicon-based semiconductor that had a profound effect on computing technology, was conducted in the city in 1947. Fortran (formula translation), the first widely used programming language, was developed in the mid 1950s at the IBM Watson Scientific Computing Laboratory near Columbia and at the corporate headquarters of IBM (590 Madison Avenue) by a team of scientists led by the mathematician John Backus; they also designed a compiler, a set of 28,000 programming instructions for translating Fortran into machine code. Based on algebra and containing grammar and syntax rules, Fortran was an efficient language that enabled programmers to communicate with the computer by means of straightforward mathematical instructions rather than in long strings of binary code. Because Fortran was markedly easier to learn than earlier languages, programming was no longer the exclusive domain of the computer specialist. During the 1960s Fortran was standardized, and it remains the most widely used scientific programming language.

After the 1960s the west coast eclipsed New York City as a center of computer innovation and development. IBM moved its corporate headquarters to suburban Westchester in 1964 and was soon followed by other firms, many of which nonetheless kept branches in New York City. Computer operations related to banking and financial services for the most part remained in the city, which as a result became an important center for the sale of new and used computer equipment.

J. Mack Adams and Douglas H. Haden: *Social Effects of Computer Use and Misuse* (London: John Wiley and Sons, 1976)

Stan Augarten: *Bit by Bit: An Illustrated History of Computers* (New York: Ticknor and Fields, 1984)

John Case: *Digital Future: The Personal Computer Explosion: Why It's Happening and What It Means* (New York: William Morrow, 1985)

Elliot S. Meadows

Comstock, Anthony (*b* New Canaan, Conn., 7 March 1844; *d* Summit, N.J., 21 Sept 1915). Reformer. Brought up in a devout Congregationalist household, he moved to New York City after the Civil War, married, and worked in a dry-goods establishment. In 1872 he helped to form the New York Society for the Suppression of Vice, a private agency given limited powers by the police to regulate and monitor sexual behavior, and in the following year he successfully sought a federal anti-obscenity statute known as the "Comstock Law." He enforced the law as a special agent of the Post Office Department, arresting more than 3600 persons from 1872 to 1915 for selling obscene pictures, contraception articles, abortifacients, and gambling materials. He achieved his best-known exploit in 1878, when after posing as an impoverished father unable to support another child he arrested the prominent abortionist Ann Lohman, known as Madame Restell; she took her own life in prison. In 1906 he raided the Art Students League and confiscated paintings of nudes. By this time George Bernard Shaw had introduced the word "comstockery" to describe the American obsession with regulating morality and suppressing sexuality. Although Comstock's activities in New York City inspired groups around the nation, his indiscriminate raids on art galleries, newspapers, and businesses eventually called into question his campaign against obscenity. He also wrote several books about urban dangers: *Frauds Exposed* (1880), *Traps for the Young* (1883), and *Morals versus Art* (1887). From 1871 he lived at 354 Grand Avenue in Williamsburg.

Heywood Broun and Margaret Leech: *Anthony Comstock: Roundsman of the Lord* (New York: A. and C. Boni, 1927)

Timothy J. Gilfoyle

concert saloons. Bars offering alcohol and entertainment in New York City from the 1840s until the turn of the century. They ranged from the palatial to the seedy and were

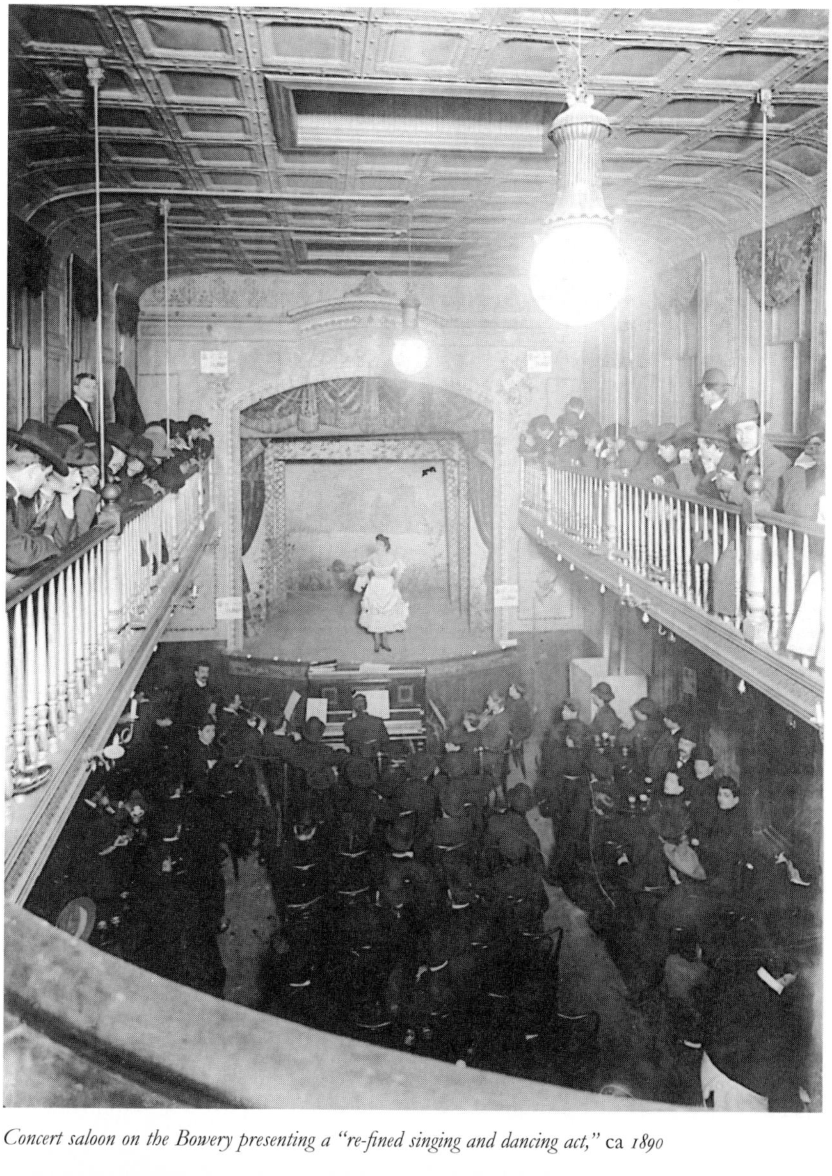

Concert saloon on the Bowery presenting a "re-fined singing and dancing act," ca 1890

initially clustered in lower Manhattan along Broadway and the Bowery, where they drew a male clientele from the working class and a few from the slumming middle class. Those women who appeared in the saloons were usually waitresses or prostitutes, and sometimes both. One of the best-known establishments was Harry Hill's on Houston Street. At the beginning of the Civil War concert saloons became popular among soldiers and war contractors stationed in the city, and in 1861 forty of the saloons advertised in local newspapers. Increased patronage caught the attention of moral reformers, who attacked the saloons for promoting drunkenness and prostitution. In April 1862 the state legislature banned the sale of alcohol and the employment of waitresses in saloons and required all places of amusement to obtain a license, with the fees used to support the Society for the Reformation of Juvenile Delinquents; saloon owners soon became adept at obtaining political protection and circumventing the law. The saloons became central to the culture of sporting men and eventually moved north to midtown and the Tenderloin. With the decline of prostitution in the early twentieth century they were replaced by cabarets, nightclubs, and vaudeville theaters, which offered forms of entertainment developed by such saloon performers as Tony Pastor.

Lewis A. Erenberg: *Steppin' Out: New York Nightlife and the Transformation of American Culture* (Westport, Conn.: Greenwood, 1981)

Robert W. Snyder: *The Voice of the City: Vaudeville and Popular Culture in New York* (New York: Oxford University Press, 1989)

Timothy J. Gilfoyle: *City of Eros: New York City, Prostitution, and the Commercialization of Sex, 1790–1920* (New York: W. W. Norton, 1992)

Robert W. Snyder

Concord. Neighborhood in northeastern Staten Island (1990 pop. 3500), bounded to the north by Cypress Hill, to the east by Grasmere, to the south by Dongan Hills, and to the west by Emerson Hill. The area was called Dutch Farms until about 1845, when having been visited by Ralph Waldo Emerson and Henry David Thoreau it was renamed after their home in Massachusetts. In the early nineteenth century it was inhabited chiefly by German immigrants. The neighborhood now consists of one-family houses, small apartment buildings, and new condominiums. The center of the neighborhood is traversed by some of the most heavily traveled roads in Staten Island, among them Clove Road, Richmond Road, Targee Street, and the Staten Island Expressway. The population is ethnically diverse.

William T. Davis: "Staten Island Names: Ye Olde Names and Nicknames," *Proceedings of the Natural Science Association of Staten Island* 5, no. 5 (1896), 20–76

Charles W. Leng and William T. Davis: *Staten Island and Its People* (New York: Lewis Historical Publishing, 1930)

John-Paul Richiuso

Concord Baptist Church. Church at 833 Marcy Avenue in Bedford–Stuyvesant, formed in 1848 by members of the Abyssinian Baptist Church of Manhattan. One of the first black churches in Brooklyn, it was initially led by the noted abolitionist Sampson White and took an active role in the anti-slavery movement. Over the years the church became noted for its commitment to education, adding a director of religious education in 1919, a preschool nursery in 1948, and the Concord Elementary School in 1960. It also sponsored a nursing home, a clothing exchange, a credit union, and various other enterprises. From 1942 to 1990 the church was led by Gardner Taylor, known as the dean of black pastors in the United States.

Aileen Laura Love

Condé Nast Publications. Firm of magazine publishers formed in 1909 by Condé Nast through his purchase of *Vogue* (1892), a magazine of high fashion that gained in influence under the editorship of Edna Woolman Chase. The company's reputation grew with the launching of *Dress and Vanity Fair* (September 1913, renamed *Vanity Fair* in 1914), which was edited by Frank Crowninshield and featured the art of Pablo Picasso, the photographs of Edward Steichen, and the writing of Dorothy Parker, Robert Benchley, and Colette. Nast took over *House and Garden* (1901) in 1915 and *American Golfer* in 1928. His operations were severely affected by the Depression, as a result of which *Vanity Fair* and *American Golfer* ceased publication in 1935. In 1939 he introduced the magazine *Glamour*. After his death in 1942 the firm was owned and operated by a British publisher until it was purchased in 1959 by S. I. Newhouse, who remained chairman of the board into the 1990s. In 1993 the firm announced that it would acquire Knapp Communications, the publishers of *Architectural Digest* and *Bon Appétit*. Condé Nast continues to publish *Vogue*, *House and Garden*, and *Vanity Fair* (reintroduced in 1983), *Mademoiselle* (1935), *Gourmet* (1940), *Gentleman's Quarterly* (1957), *Brides* (1934), and *Self* (1978). The offices are at 350 Madison Avenue.

Caroline Seebohm: *The Man Who Was Vogue: The Life and Times of Condé Nast* (New York: Viking, 1982)

Laura Gwinn

Coney Island. Neighborhood in southwestern Brooklyn (1990 pop. 48,124), bounded to the north by Coney Island Creek and the Belt Parkway, to the east by Ocean Parkway, to the south by the Atlantic Ocean, and to the west by Norton's Point; until 1878 it included the expanse of land stretching five miles (eight kilometers) from Norton's Point to Manhattan Beach. The area was named by the Dutch for the wild rabbits (*konijn*) that abounded there during the seventeenth century. In 1824 the Terhune brothers opened the Coney Island House near what is now Shell Road, which was soon visited by such personages as P. T. Barnum and Daniel Webster. After the Civil War development accelerated: five railroads were built connecting the area to the rest of Brooklyn, more than at any other resort (the subway system later took over the Brighton, Culver, Sea Beach, and West End lines). Local government was placed in the hands of John Y. McKane, whose policies enabled many immigrant businessmen to operate concessions. Several of their innovations became popular, including frankfurters (introduced about 1870 by Charles Feltman), carousels, roller coasters (1884), and mixed

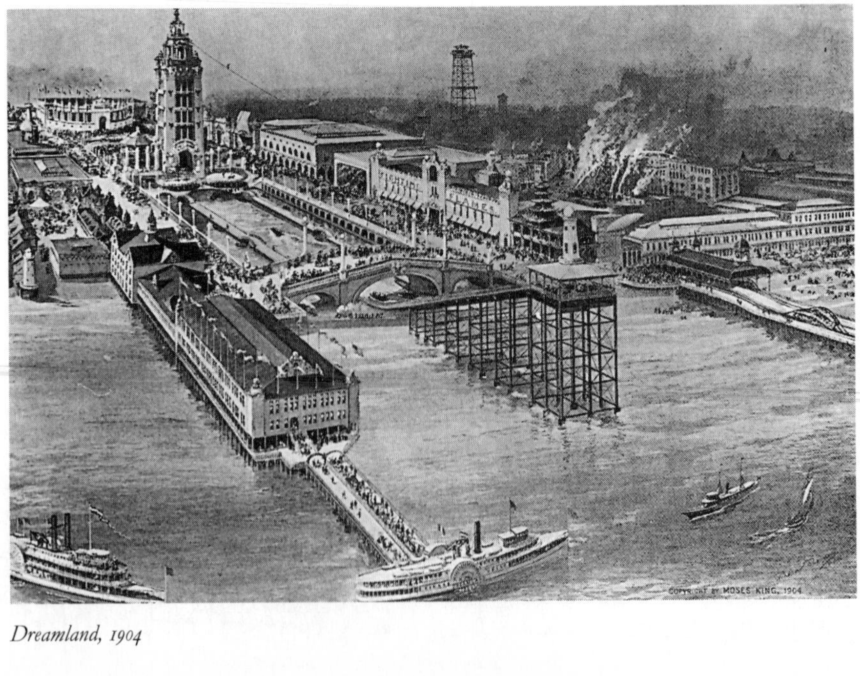

Dreamland, 1904

Coney Island Beach, ca *1898. Ropes strung above the water helped bathers to keep their footing*

public bathing. The Futurity and Suburban stakes drew thousands of spectators to thoroughbred racetracks at Brighton Beach, Sheepshead Bay, and Gravesend (the races continue to be run at Belmont Park). Heavyweight championship boxing matches were held in an arena on Surf Avenue and West 8th Street, including one in 1899 between Jim Jeffries and Tom Sharkey. Gambling dens, dance halls, and brothels operated in an area adjacent to Ocean Parkway known as the Gut. After Manhattan Beach and Brighton Beach were developed as fashionable resorts in the late nineteenth century they became separate from the neighborhood, as visitors and local entrepreneurs tried to dissociate their facilities from other local amusements.

Between 1897 and 1904 three amusement parks opened along Surf Avenue: Steeplechase Park at West 17th Street (George C. Tilyou, 1897), Luna Park at West 10th Street (Frederick Thompson and Elmer Dundy, 1903), and Dreamland at West 5th Street (William H. Reynolds, 1904). These establishments soon replaced the concessions of small businessmen who lacked the foresight and the capital to undertake commercial development on a large scale. The new parks had several features that transformed the amusement industry: they charged admission, banned alcohol, and offered mechanical rides that awed the public by combining speed with a hint of danger. On an average weekend in 1907 visitors mailed about 250,000 postcards from the area, spreading the reputation of the parks nationwide. Visitors to Steeplechase Park were greeted by the Funny Face, a cartoon figure with an enormous, toothy smile. A main attraction was the Steeplechase Race, in which customers raced around the Pavillion of Fun on mechanical horses attached to iron rails as high as thirty-five feet (10.6 meters). At the end of the race clowns from the Blowhole Theater whacked them with paddles or prodded them with electric rods while others who had already run the gantlet howled with laughter. On the Human Roulette Wheel riders held on to a spinning wooden disc and tried to avoid being thrown off, often without success. Throughout the park jets of air shot up from beneath iron grates and sent women's dresses skyward, and full-size mirrors distorted the reflections of passers-by. Elsewhere people tried to walk upright through a series of large revolving wooden barrels.

Luna Park was designed to have an ambience of fantasy by Thompson, who disdained the classical structures of the World's Columbian Exposition in Chicago (1893) and the "city beautiful" movement and instead used spires, minarets, and elliptical shapes, with colorful half-moons adorning the entrances. In 1904 he moved the immensely popular show Trip to the Moon to the park from Buffalo; in a darkened theater visitors watched as passengers embarked on an imaginary trip through outer space. At night the park was lit with more than a million incandescent bulbs that outlined the façade of every structure. In 1904 the average daily attendance was ninety thousand, at a time when crowds of twenty thousand at major league baseball games were considered large. Thompson accommodated them all by shortening rides to one minute and theatrical shows to less than twenty minutes.

Dreamland was built at a cost of $3.5 million. Reynolds, a politician and the developer of Borough Park and Long Beach (Long Island), intended that it should appeal to popular tastes and promote civic improvement. Designed for those made uneasy by a recent influx of immigrants, it offered a sharp contrast to the congested city. It was quiet and had spacious grounds: advertisements promised "avenues wide and imposing— no crowding." Architecturally it adhered to the principles of the city beautiful movement: it had a graceful replica of the Tower of Seville and buildings with painted murals depicting Switzerland, the canals of Venice, and the fall of Pompeii. Attractions included the Leap-Frog Railway, in which two electric railroad cars hurtled toward each other on a single track; the Fighting Flames show, in which firemen rescued women and children from a block-long line of buildings set on fire; and daily chariot races held on the hippodrome track that circled a lagoon. The park never achieved the popularity of Luna Park and could not be maintained profitably as an exclusive facility. Before opening day in May 1911 it was destroyed by fire.

There was almost no year-round population until the first decade of the twentieth century, when Italians settled on West 15th, 16th, and 17th streets between Surf and Neptune avenues and formed Our Lady of Solace Roman Catholic Church on West 17th Street; Jews settled farther west along Mermaid Avenue. Until the Second World War the population remained virtually unchanged, and most of the housing consisted of two-story stucco houses and four- to six-story brick apartment buildings. After the subways reached the area in 1920 there were a million visitors a day during the summer. The amusement parks became unable to grow as more apartments were filled with year-round residents. To alleviate increasing congestion the city in 1923 built a boardwalk that stretched four miles (6.4 kilometers) from Brighton Beach to Sea Gate.

The neighborhood changed dramatically between 1934 and 1960, when the city parks department was led by Robert Moses, an opponent of commercial amusements. Small businessmen who owned mechanical rides suffered after he rebuilt the boardwalk and widened the beach by 15 percent. More crowds were drawn away from the amusement parks by Jones Beach, which was built in 1929 under his auspices. He later added parkways, and increasingly families with automobiles preferred Jones Beach to the dirtier and more crowded beaches of the neighborhood. In 1944 Luna Park was destroyed by fire. During the Second World War investment in the amusement area became negligible and the number of visitors declined further after 1945, when many residents of Brooklyn moved to Long Island. Urban renewal programs of the 1950s and 1960s transformed the residential sections, to which city agencies moved poor blacks and Latin Americans, including many welfare recipients. Steeplechase Park and its parachute jump closed in 1964.

In the mid 1990s the residents of Sea Gate

Luna Park, 1911

(West 37th Street to Norton's Point) and West Brighton (Ocean Parkway to West 8th Street), who were mostly white, considered their neighborhoods separate from Coney Island, which local organizations and the city worked to revitalize. More than four hundred one-family houses were built in the western section, and the suburban Saltaire Gardens, sponsored by the city, were a success. Restaurants like the Carolina on Mermaid Avenue, Gargiulo's on West 15th Street, and Nathan's remained popular (for illustration see NATHAN'S). A small amusement district remained in a few blocks between West 8th and West 15th streets. The Wonder Wheel (a massive ferris wheel), the Cyclone roller coaster at Surf Avenue and West 10th Street, and the B&B Carousel (the last in the neighborhood) continued to operate.

Edo McCullough: *Good Old Coney Island: A Sentimental Journey into the Past* (New York: Charles Scribner's Sons, 1957)
John F. Kasson: *Amusing the Million: Coney Island at the Turn of the Century* (New York: Hill and Wang, 1978)
Stephen Weinstein: "The Nickel Empire: Coney Island and the Creation of Urban Seaside Resorts in the United States" (diss., Columbia University, 1984)

Stephen Weinstein

confectioners. Some of the first confectioners in the colonies were Dutch bakers in New Amsterdam in the mid seventeenth century. Confections of the sort that they made (including sugar wafers, sugar plums, and macaroons) were bought mostly by the élite until the early nineteenth century. Some of the largest firms were those of Ridley and Company (1806) on Hudson Street, R. L. Stuart, which had a factory on Greenwich Street (Stuart himself later became a prominent sugar refiner), John Stryker, James Thompson and Sons, and the Delmonico brothers. By the 1850s production increased owing to new technology such as the revolving steam pan, and the manufacture of confections became important in the city, where the sugar industry was concentrated and there was a large market. A candy shop was opened on Canal Street in 1860 by William Loft and his wife; the firm, which remained in the city for almost 130 years, eventually produced more than 350 kinds of candy and operated one of the largest chains of candy stores in the country. Henry Heide, an immigrant, formed a business under his own name in 1869, which sold a variety of chocolates and hard candies including Jujyfruits, Jujubes, and Red Hot Dollars. Milton S. Hershey had a candy firm in the city in the late nineteenth century before building a chocolate empire in Pennsylvania. Tootsie Rolls were introduced by Leo Hirschfield in 1896 and for a time were made in the city by the Sweets Company of America.

The number of confection factories in the city increased from 108 in 1900 to more than eleven hundred in 1922, but they did not gain a larger share in the national industry: many were small and sold their products directly to druggists and cigar shops. Most candy workers were immigrant women who worked in squalor for long hours and little pay. An investigation of their condition led to the passage of the New York State Fair Wage Bill in 1928. The chocolate bar known as Chunky was introduced in the mid 1930s by the confectioner Philip Silverstein and named after his granddaughter (who had been plump as an infant). Many popular candies were made in the city: Bonomo's Turkish Taffy by the Gold Medal Candy Corporation of Brooklyn, Mike and Ikes and Hot Tamales in Brooklyn in the 1920s by the firm of Just Born, Hopalongs by the Ryan Candy Company, and Now and Laters during the 1950s and 1960s by the Phoenix Company. Eventually the industry became automated, the demand for workers diminished, and the confection industry became highly consolidated. As the cost of factory maintenance rose and the sugar industry declined, most confection firms left the city or were forced out of business. Among the few candy companies remaining in the city in 1990 were Cella's Confections (known for its chocolate-covered cherries) in Manhattan and several companies in Brooklyn, including the Cocoline Chocolate Company, Barton's Bonbonniere, and the Joyva Corporation (makers of halvah). In the mid 1990s retail sales of candy remained high, particularly those of "premium" chocolates, exquisite candies sold by department stores and mail-order firms.

Ray Broeckel: *The Great American Candy Bar Book* (Boston: Houghton Mifflin, 1982)

James Bradley

Conference Board. Organization formed in 1916 in Bronxville, New York, as the National Industrial Conference Board. It represented employers' associations and was intended to combat a perceived antipathy toward business among the public. During the

First World War it made recommendations that led to the formation of the National War Labor Board as an adjudicator of labor disputes. In its early years it also helped businesses to improve relations with their employees and took stands on legislative and regulatory issues. Eventually it withdrew from its role as a partisan advocate of business interests, and in 1924 it was reconstituted in New York City as a nonprofit organization with open membership and the support of labor, which earlier had been an opponent. During the following decades the focus gradually shifted away from industrial relations and government regulation and toward broader economic concerns. Among other activities the board was responsible for beginning the scientific measurement of the cost of living. The board took its current name in 1970. Its offices are at 845 3rd Avenue.

David Schorr

Congregationalist Church on Forest Avenue, 1903

Conference House. Historic house in Staten Island at 7455 Hylan Boulevard, beside the Raritan Bay near the southernmost point of New York City and New York State. It was built as a stone farmhouse about 1680 by Christopher Billopp, a captain of the British navy. A rear lean-to added in 1720 created the present saltbox structure. The house is named after a peace conference held on 11 September 1776 between Admiral Richard Howe of the British forces and a group of American patriots including Benjamin Franklin and John Adams, the failure of which led to the continuation of hostilities for seven more years. Later the house served variously as a hotel and a small-scale factory. The Conference House Association was formed in 1925 and deeded the property to the city in the following year; it restored the house and dedicated it as a museum in 1937. The house is situated among large shade trees and has a large colonial kitchen and several period rooms.

William Thompson Davis: *The Conference or Billopp House* (Lancaster, Penn.: Science Press, 1926)
Historic Houses in New York City Parks (New York: Department of Parks and Recreation / Historic House Trust of New York City, 1989)

Jonathan Kuhn

Congregationalists. The origins of Congregationalism in New York City date to 1643, when English settlers from New England and Virginia formed a church in New Amsterdam. Congregationalists were given considerable freedom by the Dutch, who found no theological objections to their beliefs. A few more churches were established during the second stage of the Great Awakening (1740–60), but Congregationalists remained few in number and often sought the fellowship of Presbyterians until the early nineteenth century. Congregationalism remained largely concentrated in New England, and the General Association of New York was not formed until 1824. The oldest churches moved north as the city expanded, among them the Worth Street congregation, which was formed in 1840 and moved to 34th Street in 1857. The New Congregational Church was organized in Brooklyn Heights by twenty congregants who engaged as their first pastor Henry Ward Beecher, a nationally known proponent of progressive liberal Christianity. Soon renamed Plymouth Church, the congregation became the city's most influential Congregational church largely through his efforts. Beecher was succeeded in 1890 by Lyman Abbott, whose writings also circulated nationally. The congregation left the General Association in 1882. Important contributions were also made by the revivalist Charles G. Finney, who as pastor of the Chatham Street Chapel stressed warm personal piety and moral conduct with attention to social improvement. Others also linked spiritual and social renewal, among them Samuel Cochran, pastor of the Sullivan Street Congregational Church. Liberal evangelical ideas about the relation of religious faith to society were explored in the *Independent*, a noted Congregational journal published in the city.

From about 1900 Congregationalists in the city focused on mission work and drew attention to the needs of immigrants and the poor. In 1902 the Worth Street congregation ceased to exist, but its ministry was continued by the Broadway Tabernacle Church at 56th Street and Broadway, which formed a mission congregation known as Bethany Church at 10th Avenue and 35th Street that extended ministries to the poor. During the first decades of the twentieth century some of the most influential work was done by college students from New England. Settlement houses were opened on the Lower East Side and in Hell's Kitchen by a number of institutions, including Yale University, Wellesley College, and Smith College, often with the help of pastors active in the Social Gospel movement. Through such measures Congregationalists gained influence disproportionate to their small number.

In 1957 the Congregational Christian churches merged with the Evangelical and Reformed church to form the United Church of Christ. In the following decades social responsibility and enlivened spirituality remained the fundamental concerns of several parishes of the new organization. In an enduring expression of congregationalism Riverside Church retains its affiliations to both the United Church of Christ and the American Baptist Church.

J. William T. Youngs: *The Congregationalists* (Westport, Conn.: Greenwood, 1990)

Eileen W. Lindner

Congregation Ansche Chesed. Former name of TEMPLE ANSCHE CHESED.

Congregation Baith Israel Anshei Emeth. Former name of the KANE STREET SYNAGOGUE.

Congregation Kehilath Jeshurun. Orthodox synagogue, formed by immigrants as Anshe Jeshurun in Yorkville in 1872. The congregation built a large Romanesque temple on East 85th Street between Park and Lexington avenues in 1902. Before the First World War many of the members were Russian Jews; under the direction of Joseph H. Lookstein for more than fifty years the congregation set standards for American Orthodox Judaism.

Jenna Weissman Joselit

Congress. New York City was the seat of the national legislature, and the nation's capital, from January 1785 to 1790. For most of this time the national government operated under the Articles of Confederation (in effect from 2 March 1781). This document vested authority in a unicameral legislature, the Continental Congress, in which each state had one vote and appointed from two to seven delegates. A vote of the Continental Congress on 23 December 1784 designated New York City as its tenth meeting place, pending the construction of a federal district on the banks of the Delaware River near Philadelphia. Because no existing structure was suitable for housing the congress, a state lottery was conducted to raise funds and Pierre Charles L'Enfant (1755–1825) redesigned the Old City Hall (later Federal Hall) at the intersection of Broad and Wall streets.

The congress was overseen by a president who was given the impressive title of "President of the United States in Congress Assembled" but nevertheless wielded little power. While the congress met in New York City the presidency was held by Richard Henry Lee (11 January 1785 to 12 November 1785), John Hancock (23 November 1785 to 6 June 1786), Nathaniel Gorham (6 June 1786 to 2 February 1787), Arthur St. Clair (2 February 1787 to 22 January 1788), and Cyrus Griffin (22 January 1788 to 21 October 1788). Increasingly power was exercised by the heads of executive departments appointed by the congress, including the postmaster general (Ebenezer Hazard, 1782–89), the secretary of foreign affairs (Robert Livingston, 1781 to July 1784; John Jay, July 1784 to 1789), the superintendent of finance (Robert Morris, who resigned under pressure on 1 November 1784), the members of the Board of Treasury, which replaced the superintendent of finance (Arthur Lee, Samuel Osgood, and Walter Livingston), and the secretary of war (Henry Knox, elected 8 March 1785). Jay conducted much of his business from Fraunces Tavern and from his home at 11 Broadway, at the corner of what later became Exchange Place. In April 1785 the tavern was leased to the Department of Foreign Affairs, which made the structure its virtual headquarters. Until 1788 the war and treasury departments also occupied space in the building.

The first session of the congress in New York City began on 11 January 1785, by which time the limits on its power and effectiveness had fueled growing demands for a new government; absenteeism was rampant, long adjournments were common, and so many congressional delegates attended the Constitutional Convention in Philadelphia in 1787 that the congress was virtually shut down. Nonetheless several important pieces of legislation were ratified by the Continental Congress, notably the Northwest Ordinance of 13 July 1787, which provided the framework for the expansion of the United States.

New York State approved the Constitution of the United States on 26 July 1788, amid much rejoicing in the city. At the first session of the new congress under the U.S. Constitution (4 March 1789) the organization of the national government was the first order of business. George Washington was inaugurated president of the United States at Federal Hall on 30 April. The executive departments were organized within a year, with the Department of Foreign Affairs renamed the Department of State on 15 September 1789. The Federal Judiciary Act (24 September 1789) organized the structure of the federal judiciary and the Supreme Court, and the Department of Justice was formed on 26 September. Other important legislation included the first Tariff Act (4 July 1789), the Census Act (1 March 1790), and the Naturalization Act (26 March 1790), measures establishing the coast guard (4 April 1790) and putting into effect Alexander Hamilton's refunding plan (26 July 1790), under which the federal government assumed debts incurred by the states during the American Revolution, and the Treaty of New York (signed in Federal Hall on 7 August 1790), whereby the Creek Indians recognized the sovereignty of the United States. The crowning legislative achievement of the federal congress in New York City was the formal submission to the states on 25 September 1789 of twelve proposed amendments to the Constitution, the first ten of which were ratified in 1791 as the Bill of Rights. On 10 July 1790 the House of Representatives voted to begin construction of a national capital on the Potomac River and to move the capital in the interim to Philadelphia. The final session of Congress in New York City concluded on 12 August 1790.

Charlene Bickford Bangs and Kenneth R. Bowling: *Birth of the Nation: The First Federal Congress, 1789–1791* (New York: Second Circuit Committee, 1989)

Robert I. Goler

Congress of Industrial Organizations

Organizations [CIO]. Council of industrial unions formed in New York City. Its forerunner was the Committee for Industrial Organization, an association formed in Washington in November 1935 by union presidents, including John L. Lewis of the United Mine Workers, who were frustrated by the refusal of the American Federation of Labor (AFL) to organize unskilled workers in mass production. Directed by Lewis, it did not formally break with the AFL and received crucial support from labor leaders in New York City, especially David Dubinsky of the International Ladies' Garment Workers' Union (ILGWU) and Sidney Hillman of the Amalgamated Clothing Workers of America (ACWA). From the 1930s the Communist Party provided many organizers who were welcomed by Lewis, largely out of expediency, but not by Hillman, who led a faction opposed to communism. After victories at U.S. Steel and General Motors in 1936 and 1937 that set American unionism in a new direction, the committee held its first convention in 1938, where it took the name Congress of Industrial Organizations and became independent, leading Dubinsky to transfer his allegiance back to the AFL in 1940. Hillman's influence steadily increased. A supporter of state intervention to rationalize relations between labor and management, he sought to align the CIO with the Democratic Party. After a number of setbacks he formed the CIO Political Action Committee in 1943 to accept money and provide support for political candidates (usually Democrats) who were sympathetic toward unions. It won a large following in heavily unionized areas and played an important role in the reelection of President Franklin D. Roosevelt in 1944, cementing the relationship between organized labor and the Democratic Party and dashing the hopes of activists who sought to form an independent labor party.

Tensions within the CIO between communists and anticommunists mounted during the 1940s. The Greater New York Industrial Council, formed in 1940 as the central body of the CIO in the city, was controlled by a powerful leftist faction that Hillman opposed. The conflict grew increasingly bitter after he withdrew the ACW from the council, but a number of leaders with ties to the Communist Party nonetheless became highly influential, among them Mike Quill, president of the Transport Workers' Union, and Lee Pressman, Lewis's chief aide and the counsel to the CIO. In 1948 disagreements erupted over whether to support Harry S. Truman, the presidential nominee of the Democratic Party, or Henry Wallace, the nominee of the Progressive Party, which was dominated by communists. Pressman resigned to work for Wallace, Quill renounced the Communist Party at a convention of the TWU, and in 1949–50 the CIO expelled eleven unions with communist ties, ending its internal struggles. The decline of its influence was nonetheless signaled by the election of Dwight D. Eisenhower as president in 1952. Except for a few powerful unions such as the United Auto Workers and the United Steelworkers of America its affiliates were small and financially weak compared to their counterparts in the AFL. As the country moved increasingly toward the right the leadership decided that organized labor might best close ranks, and in 1955 the CIO merged with the AFL to form the AFL–CIO. The election as its first president of George Meany, president of the AFL, indicated that the social concerns of the CIO would be subordinated to the administrative ones of the AFL.

Irving Bernstein: *The Turbulent Years: A History of the American Worker, 1933–1941* (Boston: Houghton Mifflin, 1969)

Joshua B. Freeman: *In Transit: The Transport Workers Union in New York City, 1933–1966* (New York: Oxford University Press, 1989)

Steven Fraser: *Labor Will Rule: Sidney Hillman and the Rise of American Labor* (New York: Free Press, 1991)

Richard Yeselson

Connolly, James (*b* Edinburgh, 5 June 1868; *d* Dublin, 12 May 1916). Political activist. He visited New York City in 1902 and moved to the United States in the following year. Disillusioned with the Socialist Labor Party under Daniel DeLeon, he turned to the Industrial Workers of the World (IWW), which offered him a position as a union organizer in the city. He lived in Newark, New Jersey, before moving to Elton Avenue in the Bronx at the end of 1907. From his office at 60 Cooper Square in Greenwich Village he launched the Propaganda League of the IWW and organized workers, focusing his efforts in the building trades. With a number of Irish labor leaders including Elizabeth Gurley Flynn he formed the Irish Socialist Federation in March 1907 at 79 MacDougal Street; to report and promote its work he launched a monthly newspaper in January 1908, the *Harp*, which had a circulation of three thousand by 1909 and ceased publication in 1910. His work with the federation led him away from the IWW and toward the brand of socialism advocated by Eugene V. Debs. In 1909 Connolly was appointed organizer of the Socialist Party of America and on its behalf embarked on an eleven-month national tour in May. He was given a farewell dinner by the Irish Socialist Federation in New York City on 14 July 1910 and left for Dublin on 16 July. Later the same year he published *Labor in Irish History*, much of which he had written while in New York City. After signing the Irish declaration of independence in 1916 Connolly commanded Republican forces in the Easter insurrection of the same year and was executed by the British.

Austen Morgan: *James Connolly: A Political Biography* (Manchester, England: Manchester University Press, 1988)

Kevin Kenny

Connolly, John (*b* Slane, Ireland, 1750; *d* New York City, 6 Feb 1825). Roman Catholic bishop. He joined the Dominican order, was ordained about 1774, and from 1775 to 1814 lived at San Clemente in Rome, where he was the librarian of the Casanate Library, an agent for several Irish bishops, and a prior (1782–96). After his appointment as bishop of the Diocese of New York on 4 October 1814 he moved to New York City on 25 November 1815. He approved new parishes, welcomed the Sisters of Charity, opened an orphanage, and dealt with conflict over the ownership by lay trustees of church property. Connolly is buried beneath St. Patrick's Old Cathedral.

Mary Elizabeth Brown

Connolly, Maurice E. (*b* Queens, 22 June 1880; *d* Queens, 24 Nov 1935). Borough president. He earned a BA from St. Johns College and a law degree from Columbia University, and after working as an attorney was appointed a city magistrate. He became well known in 1911 for criticizing the administration of the borough president of Queens, Lawrence Gresser, who was soon removed from office by Governor John A. Dix for corruption. Amid calls for reform the Board of Aldermen selected Connolly as his successor. From 1911 Connolly oversaw the construction of streets, sewers, and subways costing millions of dollars. Eventually homeowners protested high assessments for sewer construction, and in December 1927 charges of fraud were filed with Governor Alfred E. Smith against Connolly, who resigned only days before public hearings were to begin. In June 1928 he was indicted by a grand jury along with the sewer contractor John M. Phillips and two engineers; testimony revealed that Phillips had illegally received millions of dollars from sewer contracts issued by Connolly's administration, and a jury of the state supreme court found both men guilty of conspiracy to defraud the city. Connolly was sentenced to a year in prison, which he served on Welfare Island from 9 May 1930 to 4 March 1931.

Edward T. O'Donnell

Conservative Party. Statewide political party formed in 1961 in New York City by the lawyers J. Daniel Mahoney and Kieran O'Doherty to free the Republican Party in New York State from the influence of liberals such as Jacob K. Javits and Nelson A. Rockefeller. It opposed civil rights legislation and favored a strongly anticommunist foreign policy; its manifesto, the Declaration of Principles, expressed concern about inflation, the quality of education, taxation, the power of corrupt labor unions, and laxness in prosecuting crime. First sponsoring candidates for office in 1962, the party sometimes nominated its own candidates and at other times endorsed Republicans or (less often) Democrats for local, state, and national office. It became widely known in 1965 during the mayoral campaign of William F. Buckley Jr., which was intended as a protest against John V. Lindsay's liberal Republicanism. Buckley won 13 percent of the vote, an unexpectedly high total drawn mostly from middle-class homeowners in the outer boroughs. The party outpolled the Liberal Party in the city in the gubernatorial election in 1966 and during the same year was instrumental in defeating a referendum proposing a civilian review board to oversee the police department. It reached the peak of its influence in 1970, when Buckley's brother James Buckley was elected to the U.S. Senate as its nominee, defeating the liberal Republican incumbent Charles E. Goodell and the Democratic nominee Richard Ottinger; Buckley failed to win reelection in 1976. In the 1980s and early 1990s the party lost some of its adherents to the Right-to-Life Party. In early 1994 there were 26,803 registered Conservatives in New York City, representing 0.8 percent of all registered voters.

J. Daniel Mahoney: *Actions Speak Louder* (New Rochelle, N.Y.: Arlington House, 1968)
Charles Lam Markmann: *The Buckleys: A Family Examined* (New York: William Morrow, 1973)

Lawson Bowling

Consolidated Edison. The electric utility that provides gas and electricity to most of New York City, formed on 10 November 1884 as the Consolidated Gas Company of New York by six gaslight companies. It absorbed United Electric Light and Power in 1890 and two gas companies in 1899, giving it complete control of the gas business in Manhattan and much of the rest of the city (except Brooklyn). In the early decades of the twentieth century it continued to expand and acquire other companies, and in 1936 it took its present name, which is commonly shortened to Con Edison. In the mid 1990s Consolidated Edison had more than $10,000 million in assets and nineteen thousand employees, and sold nearly 40,000 million kilowatt-hours of electricity to about three million customers. See also BIG ALLIS and LIGHT AND POWER. For illustrations see LIGHT AND POWER.

Consolidated (Stock and Petroleum) Exchange [CSE]. Stock exchange formed in 1885 by the merger of four smaller exchanges to handle odd lots, which brokers belonging to the New York Stock Exchange (NYSE) discouraged because of the low commissions that they generated. Four hundred brokers who began to sell odd lots contrary to the rules of the NYSE attended the formation of the Consolidated Exchange, which soon became known as the "Little Board." The new exchange printed the transactions of the New York Stock Exchange with Western Union tickers and drew away some of its business. Although its issues and brokers were marginal the Consolidated Exchange was one of the city's first workable clearing houses and made innovations in recruiting small investors. It eventually became the second-largest stock exchange in the city and for a time was the only major rival of the NYSE, which sought to destroy it. The exchange suffered from poor leadership, and in 1903 a series of government investigations began. The Consolidated Exchange had only a marginal role in securities trading by the early 1920s and ceased operations in 1928.

Jonathan Aspell

consolidation. The incorporation on 1 January 1898 of New York City within its present boundaries. It grew out of efforts by the city's merchant élite, led by ANDREW HASWELL GREEN, to improve New York Harbor and promote the development of shipping, railroads, and utilities by substituting centralized municipal government for the existing system, which was highly fragmented because control was shared by forty local governments. During its first two centuries New York City was coextensive with Manhattan; Kingsbridge, Morrisania, and West Farms, then in Westchester County, were annexed in 1874. Green advanced a plan to annex all the territory now making up the Bronx, Brooklyn, Queens, and Staten Island in 1868, endorsed by the Chamber of Commerce of the State of New York and Mayor Abram S. Hewitt in 1888, and seen through the state legislature by Thomas C. Platt, the "easy boss" of the state Republican Party, who saw consolidation as politically advantageous. Many residents of Brooklyn and outlying districts objected to consolidation, which they feared would deprive them of local control over taxes, expenditures, development policies, and even the racial and ethnic composition of their neighborhoods: the Loyal League of Brooklyn and the *Brooklyn Eagle* argued outspokenly that consolidation would destroy the homogeneously Protestant character of their community. The City of Brooklyn was however so deeply in debt that it could not build desperately needed water mains, sewer lines, or schools. Property owners there and in northern Manhattan and the Bronx favored consolidation so that their communities could draw on revenues from real-estate taxes in central Manhattan. Consolidation was voted on in a nonbinding referendum in all areas to be affected in 1894 and was approved everywhere except in two villages in eastern Queens, with a total vote of 176,170 in favor and 131,706 opposed; the governor approved the plan in 1896. In 1895 the city annexed the rest of the territory now making up the Bronx. A charter of the greater city was issued by a state commission under the direction of Seth Low and approved in 1897, and the new city's first elections were held in the same year. The consolidated city was known as greater New York, a term that later became popularly applied to a larger area including parts of Westchester, Long Island, New Jersey, and Connecticut.

Consolidation made New York City the most extensive and populous city in the United States (its population increased instantaneously from two million to 3.4 million), brought property tax rates and assessments under a consolidated system, and gave the city jurisdiction over nearly all areas to be developed as suburbs during the next fifty years (with the significant exception of northern New Jersey). But the new city's bicameral legislature was unwieldy and procedures for planning and making public improvements were complicated. As a result a commission appointed by the state legislature drafted a new charter, which provided for an elected mayor and comptroller, a powerful Board of Estimate that included the five borough presidents, and a single Board of Aldermen composed of members from seventy-three districts; the new charter took effect in 1901.

David C. Hammack: *Power and Society: Greater New York at the Turn of the Century* (New York: Russell Sage Foundation, 1982), chap. 7

David C. Hammack

consulates. The first consulates in New York City were set up by France, Spain, and the Netherlands shortly after the American Revolution. The city now has more than eighty-five consulates, most of which are on the Upper East Side. Established by foreign governments to promote their interests abroad, consulates enhance the city's status as an international center and contribute an estimated $1000 million a year to the local economy. The city strives to maintain good relations with diplomats: the Commission for the United Nations and Consular Corps (1962) meets newly appointed consuls general, provides information about diplomatic immunities and privileges, advises on housing, schools, and cultural events in New York City, sponsors outings and seminars, and mediates disputes between diplomats and the city's government, businesses, and private citizens. Strained relations between consular employees and citizens of New York City often arise over the privileges given to diplomats: consular property is exempt from real-estate taxes and zoning laws, diplomats do not pay the municipal sales tax or income tax, and according to international law diplomats are exempt from prosecution under the laws of the host country. Parking violations in particular are a contentious issue in New York City: the Parking Violations Bureau issues thousands of parking tickets to diplomats annually, but the charges are automatically dismissed. The security of the consular corps is the responsibility of the New York Police Department. Local precincts assign regular patrols to consulates, and the department assigns extraordinary security concerns to the dignitary protection unit of its intelligence division. The city absorbs the cost of all security services except for crowd control, guard duty, and the protection of visiting dignitaries, all of which are reimbursable by the federal government. About one third of the consular employees in the city change each year; new members must be accredited by their embassy in Washington and by the U.S. Department of State. Some members of the consular community live in the suburbs, but most prefer to spend their few years in the United States within New York City itself. About one thousand children of consular employees attend the city's public schools. The diplomatic community in New York City numbers about 35,000, which includes employees of both consulates and missions to the United Nations.

Lauren Markoe

Consumers' League. See NATIONAL CONSUMERS' LEAGUE.

Continental Corporation. A holding company based in New York City for a group of insurers active principally in commercial and personal property insurance, and casualty insurance. Its origins may be traced to 1853, when a group of twelve prominent businessmen from New York City set up the Continental Insurance Company, a fire insurance firm with capital of $500,000. The first president was William V. Brady, a former mayor of the city, and the first office was in the basement of 6 Wall Street. In 1860 the offices were moved to Broadway, where many other insurers soon followed. During the Civil War the sympathies of the firm lay squarely on the Union side, and leaves of absence with full pay were granted to employees who volunteered for the Union Army. The firm also donated $500 to establish a local guard for the city's financial institutions while the militia was at war; this guard served during the draft riots in July 1863. In 1864 the firm contributed another $500 to set up a full-time, professional fire department in New York City. An office opened in Brooklyn in 1868, but during the next forty years most of the company's capital was spent outside the metropolitan area on claims that followed devastating fires in Chicago, Boston, Baltimore, and San Francisco. Rapid growth occurred after 1911, when the firm began issuing automobile and later aviation insurance. By 1918 it owned other smaller insurers that formed a corporation called the America Fore Group. This weathered the Depression and the Second World War, prospered during the 1950s, and later evolved into the Continental Insurance Companies (1962) and the Continental Corporation (1968). In the mid 1990s Continental was a publicly owned, multinational firm with more than $13,000 million in assets.

Chad Ludington

Continental Grain. Firm of commodity traders, formed and incorporated in New York City in 1944 by the Fribourg family of Belgium. Its headquarters were originally at 2 Broadway and were moved in 1974 to Park Avenue and 43rd Street. During the 1980s the firm entered the international agribusiness market while continuing to trade commodities. Continental Grain was the most profitable privately held company in the city by the mid 1980s, with sales in 1990 of more than $15,000 million.

James Bradley

Convent of the Sacred Heart. Catholic school for girls spanning all grades from kindergarten to high school. It was opened in 1881 at 533 Madison Avenue and run by the Society of the Sacred Heart, an order formed in France in 1801 by Ste. Madeleine Sophie Barat (1779–1865). The school moved in 1934 to the former mansion of Otto H. Kahn at 1 East 91st Street (1918, designed by J. Armstrong Stenhouse with C. P. H. Gilbert) and expanded in 1966

Convent of the Sacred Heart, ca *1900*

into the adjacent Burden house (1905, designed by Warren and Wetmore); both buildings are designated city landmarks. From 1976 the board of trustees was composed predominantly of laity. In 1992 the student enrollment was 470.

Convent of the Sacred Heart: A History, 1881–1981 (New York: Alumnae Association of the Convent of the Sacred Heart, 1981)

Gilbert Tauber

Coody, Abimelech. Pseudonym of GULIAN C. VERPLANCK.

Coogan's Bluff. Neighborhood in northern Manhattan, bounded to the north by 160th Street, to the east by the Harlem River, to the south by 155th Street, and to the west by the Harlem River Drive. The area is known for a steep escarpment that descends 175 feet (fifty-three meters) below sea level. It is named for James Jay Coogan (1845–1915), a real-estate merchant who served as borough president of Manhattan (1899–1901), was twice an unsuccessful mayoral candidate, and owned much property in the area, including the Polo Grounds (built in 1890 as Brotherhood Park), a stadium that was the home of the baseball New York Giants and the New York Mets, among other teams. After the Giants moved to California the city took over the stadium, which it demolished in 1965 to make way for a public housing project. From that time the name Coogan's Bluff fell into disuse.

John Kieran: *A Natural History of New York City* (Boston: Houghton Mifflin, 1959)

James Bradley

Cooke, Terence (*b* New York City, 1 March 1921; *d* New York City, 6 Oct 1983). Archbishop. The son of Irish immigrants, he was born on the Upper West Side and grew up in Throgs Neck, where he attended Catholic schools. He received his BA from Cathedral College in New York City and was ordained a priest in 1945; his first parish was that of St. Athanasius in the southern Bronx (1946–47). After receiving his PhD in social work from Catholic University (1949) he worked as an assistant director of the Catholic Youth Organization, taught at Fordham University (1949–54), and was the procurator at St. Joseph's Seminary in Yonkers (1954–57). In 1957 he was appointed a secretary to John Cardinal Spellman, archbishop of New York, and later became a vice chancellor (1958–61), chancellor (1961–65), and vicar general and titular bishop (1965–67). After Spellman's death in 1967 he assumed the position of archbishop (1968) and then cardinal (1969). Although theologically conservative and often criticized for not taking a bold public stand on social issues, Cooke was responsive to the initiatives of the Second Vatican Council (1965). He caused controversy at the St. Patrick's Day Parade in 1983 when he broke with tradition by refusing to greet the grand marshal, who was associated with the Irish Republican Army.

Florence D. Cohalan: *A Popular History of the Archdiocese of New York* (New York: United States Catholic Historical Society, 1983)
Benedict J. Groeschel and Terrence L. Weber: *Thy Will Be Done: A Spiritual Portrait of Terence Cardinal Cooke* (New York: Alba House, 1990)

Bernadette McCauley

Co-op City. A large housing development in BAYCHESTER, consisting of 15,372 apartments and constructed in the late 1960s.

Cooper, Edward (*b* New York City, 26 Oct 1824; *d* New York City, 25 Feb 1905). Mayor and industrialist, son of Peter Cooper. He graduated from Columbia College and with Abram S. Hewitt opened a firm of iron manufacturers. During the 1870s he investigated William M. "Boss" Tweed's bank accounts and promoted sanitation reform; he won the mayoral election of 1879 as a fusion candidate supported by Republicans and by fellow Democrats opposed to Tammany Hall. An earnest reformer, Cooper helped to enact the Tenement House Law of 1879.

James E. Mooney

Cooper, Peter (*b* New York City, 12 Feb 1791; *d* New York City, 4 April 1883). Inventor, manufacturer, and philanthropist. He had almost no formal education but was trained in business by his father and demonstrated unusual talents as an inventor and entrepreneur. During the War of 1812 he prospered by making equipment for cutting cloth. He then became a grocer and by his early twenties was a wealthy glue manufacturer. In 1828 he opened the Canton Iron Works in Baltimore, where he built the country's first functional steam engine, the "Tom Thumb," and greatly enlarged his fortune. Among his later ventures were rolling-mills and wire factories; eventually he controlled more than half the telegraph lines in the United States. He also manufactured the first structural beams for fire-retardant buildings, introduced the Bessemer process to the United States, invented a number of mining devices, and helped to finance the first transatlantic telegraph cable. An adherent of Jacksonian principles, he was elected to the Common Council with the backing of Tammany Hall (1828–31) and the Civic Reform Party (1840–41). As a member of the council and the Citizens' Association he sought to free the police and fire departments from political interference, ensure an adequate water supply and better sanitation, provide public education for the poor, and improve prison conditions. In 1857–59 he formed Cooper Union for the Advancement of Science and Art to provide a free education to gifted students from the working class. Cooper unsuccessfully sought the presidency as a Greenback in 1876: the campaign of his Democratic opponent, Samuel J. Tilden, was led by his son-in-law Abram S. Hewitt, who served in Congress and later was elected mayor, as was Cooper's son Edward

Poster from Peter Cooper's presidential campaign, 1876

Cooper. Cooper is buried in Green-Wood Cemetery.

Allan Nevins: *Abram S. Hewitt, with Some Account of Peter Cooper* (New York: Harper and Brothers, 1935)

Edward C. Mack: *Peter Cooper, Citizen of New York* (New York: Duell, Sloan and Pearce, 1949)

Evan Cornog, Jerome Mushkat

cooperage. The barrel was once a unit of measurement, and cooperage played such a large role in the development of commerce in New York City that two casks are prominently depicted on the city's official seal. In the late seventeenth century the city's vital flour trade depended on barrels, as did the city's sugar refineries after 1730, as well as local distilleries, breweries, taverns, and coffee merchants. Until the Civil War most barrel wood was floated down the Hudson from upstate and stored at docks in Brooklyn and Manhattan. Coopers worked in small artisanal shops near the wharves, and traditional methods of production were employed for far longer than in most other trades. In 1855 there were 1018 coopers in the city, almost three quarters of whom were immigrants. Anson T. Briggs of Brooklyn in 1860 became one of the first coopers in the United States to employ mechanical production. When the Brooklyn Cooperage Company of Lowell M. Palmer began manufacturing staves by machine in 1865 employees staged a four-month strike in protest; by 1895 the firm was sufficiently prosperous to expand nationwide. There were ninety coopering firms in Manhattan and thirty-six in Brooklyn in 1900. In the following decades coopering plants left the city for locations closer to large forests, and by 1922 they employed only 1258 unskilled employees citywide, most of them at adjuncts to the sugar refineries in Brooklyn. There were only twenty-one coopering shops in the city by 1930. Pre-packaging of goods formerly sold in barrels and the use of plastic, fiberboard, and steel containers virtually eliminated commercial coopering from New York City, except for a few firms that built the wooden water tanks seen on the roofs of apartment buildings.

Franklin E. Coyne: *Development of the Cooperage Industry in the United States, 1620–1940* (Chicago: Lumberers Publishing, 1940)

Marc Ferris

Cooper and Hewitt. Firm of iron manufacturers, opened about 1850 by Edward Cooper and Abram S. Hewitt, the son of an engineer, after they were given the Trenton Iron Works by Peter Cooper. It had the country's first open-hearth furnace and produced some of the first iron beams and girders, at one time employing three thousand men. During the Civil War it provided steel for gun barrels.

James E. Mooney

cooperatives. Apartment buildings with ownership arranged on a corporate basis first became popular in the late nineteenth century. Cooperatives differ from condominiums in that they provide for ownership of shares in a corporation rather than outright ownership of an individual residential unit. Residents of a cooperative may usually sell their shares at any price, provided that the board of directors approves of the prospective buyer. The first cooperative in New York City was probably the Rembrandt, a nine-story building on West 57th Street designed by Philip Hubert in 1881 (later demolished). Buildings with a similar form of ownership were soon erected, including the Gramercy at 34 Gramercy Park East (1883, George da Cunha) and the Chelsea at 222 West 23rd Street (1884, Hubert, Pirsson and Company; later converted into the Chelsea Hotel). All these buildings had spacious apartments planned for prosperous upper-middle-class families. The Central Park Apartments at Central Park South and 7th Avenue (1883, Hubert, Pirsson and Company; often called the Navarro) failed in 1888. This ended the construction of cooperatives until 1901, when a group of artists began the 67th Street Studios at 23 West 67th Street (1903, Sturgis and Simonson), which had large units con-

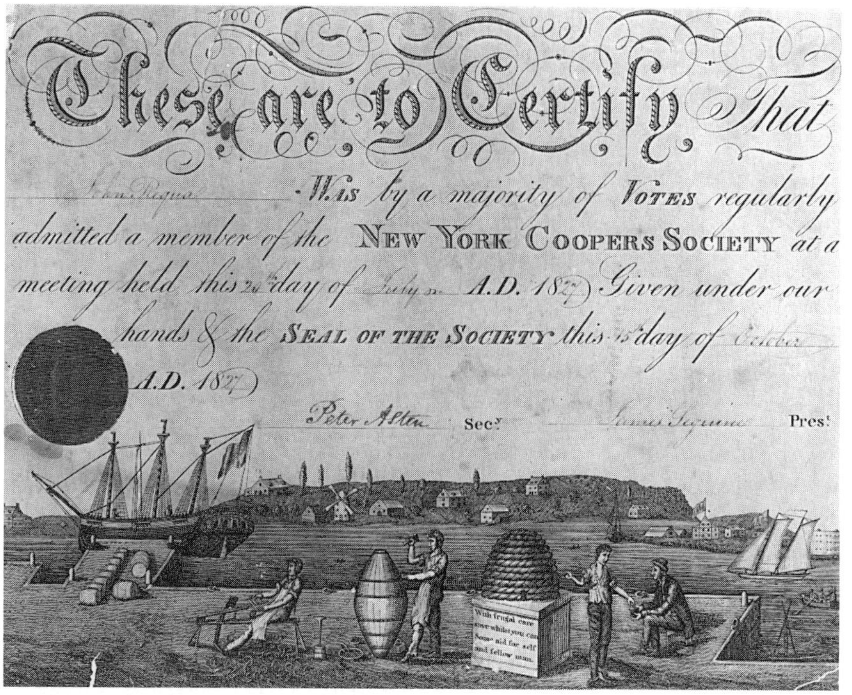

Certificate of membership in the New York Coopers Society, 1827

taining studios two stories tall and adjacent duplex living spaces. Their success led to a wave of cooperative construction during the first two decades of the twentieth century. Duplexes planned for artists or those who wished to live in an artistic milieu were especially popular, among them the Hotel des Artistes on West 67th Street (1918, George Mort Pollard). The Bryant Park Studios on West 40th Street (1901, Charles A. Rich) and the Gainsborough Studios on Central Park South (1908, Charles Buckham) were erected on sites with unobstructed northern exposure. Cooperatives were also built on Gramercy Park and the Upper East Side, most of them by syndicates or clubs of prospective tenants rather than by firms of developers. Generally not all the units were individually owned: some were rented for income.

By the 1920s cooperatives were so popular in New York City, especially on the Upper East Side, that speculators became active in their construction. At the same time middle-class cooperatives became common: the first was Linden Court (1919, Andrew J. Thomas) in Jackson Heights, built by the Queensborough Corporation as a complex of ten buildings and interior gardens on one city block. Many similar developments were built in Jackson Heights, including a number designed by Thomas and others by Thomas Wells and George Wells. Elsewhere in the city the most important middle-class cooperative was Hudson View Gardens in Washington Heights (1924, George Pelham), a picturesque complex in a Tudor style built around a semicircular drive and a large garden.

The first nonprofit, or limited-dividend, cooperative was the Alku at 816 43rd Street in Sunset Park (1916, Maxwell Cantor), one of several cooperatives built by Finnish immigrants. In these cooperatives residents usually owned a single share and shareholders could not sell at a profit: the idea was to create housing of high quality rather than profit-making housing. The number of nonprofit cooperatives increased in the 1920s, many built by labor unions and other groups seeking to provide comfortable housing for workers. The largest such complexes were in the Bronx and were known for their high quality, among them the Amalgamated Houses on Van Cortlandt Park South and the United Workers Houses (known as the "coops") on Allerton Avenue.

Many cooperatives failed during the Depression and were converted into rental housing. After the Second World War government programs such as Mitchell–Lama and section 13 (overseen by the Federal Housing Administration) provided incentives to build nonprofit cooperatives for working- and middle-class families. Cooperatives regained their popularity during the 1970s, leading to new construction (generally at the luxury level) and the conversion of thousands of rental apartments.

Christopher Gray: "The 'Revolution' of 1881 Is Now in Its 2d Century," *New York Times,* 28 Oct 1984, §12, pp. 57–64

Richard Plunz: "Reading Bronx Housing, 1890–1940," *Building a Borough: Architecture and Planning in the Bronx, 1890–1940* (New York: Bronx Museum of the Arts, 1986)

Andrew S. Dolkart: "Hudson View Gardens: A Home in the City," *SITES* 20 (1988), 34–44

Andrew S. Dolkart: "Homes for People: Nonprofit Cooperatives in New York City, 1916–1929," *SITES* 21–22 (1989), 30–42

Andrew S. Dolkart

Cooper–Hewitt Museum. Art museum opened at Cooper Union in 1897 as the Cooper Union Museum of Art and Decoration. A small museum for instruction in the applied arts at Cooper Union was planned by Peter Cooper but did not open until his granddaughters Eleanor Hewitt and Sarah Hewitt raised sufficient funds to form and maintain a collection. Modeled after the Musée des Arts Décoratifs in Paris, it contained scrapbooks, patterns, drawings, prints, and decorative art objects, and was intended to instruct professional designers and workers. With the help of such well-known patrons as the merchant George A. Hearn the Hewitts amassed holdings during the first decades of the twentieth century that included several important collections of textiles given by J. P. Morgan, more than three hundred drawings and small paintings from the estate of Winslow Homer, and two thousand sketches by Frederic E. Church given by Church's son. The museum became part of the Smithsonian Institution in 1969 and moved in 1976 to the former Carnegie mansion at 5th Avenue and 91st Street (for illustration see Carnegie, Andrew). The museum expanded its exhibitions and programs for the public, and introduced a graduate curriculum in decorative arts.

Eleanor G. Hewitt: *The Making of a Modern Museum* (New York: Wednesday Afternoon Club, 1919; repr. Cooper Union Museum for the Arts of Decoration, 1941)

Russell Lynes: *More Than Meets the Eye: The History and Collections of the Cooper–Hewitt Museum* (New York: Smithsonian Institution, 1981)

Peter L. Donhauser

Coopers and Lybrand. Accounting firm formed as Lybrand, Ross Brothers and Montgomery on 1 January 1898 in Philadelphia by William Lybrand, T. Edward Ross, Adam A. Ross, and Robert H. Montgomery. It opened an office at 25 Broad Street on 1 June 1902 that became influential in local and national affairs. From 1916 it often handled funding reports and party records during presidential campaigns. The office donated its services to the city through the Emergency Unemployment Relief Committee in 1930, and several partners acted as comptrollers from 14 September 1931 to 8 February 1932. In 1947 one of the partners, Prior Sinclair, led opposition to a bill that would have allowed accountants to become licensed without passing the state examination for certification. In the mid 1990s Coopers and Lybrand was one of the country's six largest accounting firms.

Janet Frankston

Cooper Union (for the Advancement of Science and Art). Private, tuition-free college at 41 Cooper Square offering degrees in engineering, architecture, and art. Formed by Peter Cooper to provide higher education for workers, it opened at Astor Place in 1859 and initially had a free reading room, classrooms, and exhibitions of art and technology. It also absorbed the Female School of Design, formed in 1846 to provide women with an alternative to menial employment. Public debates, lectures, and speeches were held in the Great Hall (Abraham Lincoln spoke there in 1860). Under the direction of Cooper's son-in-law Abram S. Hewitt the school gradually became more like a traditional college after the Civil War, offering degrees in engineering from 1886. Its practical curriculum and nonsectarian, coeducational approach were emulated by other institutions such as Rice University and the Tuskegee Institute. Hewitt and the department store owner George Hearn encouraged a plan by Cooper's daughters to form the Museum for the Arts of Decoration, which opened in 1896 and was later renamed the Cooper–Hewitt Museum. An autonomous school of architecture opened in the same year. At the turn of the century the School of Art became less of a philanthropic venture and more of a professional school. Between 1898 and 1933 the People's Institute directed public programs in the Great Hall, where Felix Frankfurter, Samuel Gompers, and Jacob A. Riis were among those introduced to political activism and higher learning. Programs in the Great Hall led to the formation of the National Woman Suffrage Association, the International Ladies' Garment Workers' Union, and the National Association for the Advancement of Colored People. In the mid 1990s Cooper Union had about one thousand students. Among its divisions is the Herb Lubalin Study Center of Design and Typography (founded in 1985), which maintains an archive of twentieth-century design history and sponsors publications and exhibitions on contemporary design theory.

Allan Nevins: *Abram S. Hewitt, with Some Account of Peter Cooper* (New York: Harper and Brothers, 1935)

Edward C. Mack: *Peter Cooper, Citizen of New York* (New York: Duell, Sloan and Pearce, 1949)

Peter G. Buckley

Copacabana. Nightclub at 10 East 60th Street in Manhattan, opened in 1940. Until the late 1950s it was a glamorous venue for performances by such entertainers as Frank Sinatra, Ella Fitzgerald, Nat King Cole, and Jimmy Durante. It then declined in popularity and closed in 1973. In the mid 1990s the space was used as a discothèque and as a facility for various functions.

James E. Mooney

Copland, Aaron (*b* New York City, 14 Nov 1900; *d* North Tarrytown, N.Y., 2 Dec 1990). Composer. The son of Russian Jewish immigrants, he studied composition with Rubin Goldmark at 140 West 87th Street from 1917 to 1921. From 1921 to 1924 he was one of the first of the many young American composers who studied with Nadia Boulanger in Paris. After his return to the United States he provoked controversy with dissonant, angular compositions influenced by jazz, such as *Music for the Theater* (1925). He also wrote for the journal *Modern Music*, spoke on musical topics at the New School for Social Research, and with Roger Sessions organized concerts in 1928 to introduce new compositions; during the Depression he was allied with the Composers Collective and took an interest in writing music with an overtly political content. Copland's compositional style became less astringent in the 1930s and 1940s: he frequently evoked American legend and folklore, especially in his well-known ballet scores for Agnes de Mille (*Billy the Kid*, 1938; *Rodeo*, 1942) and Martha Graham (*Appalachian Spring*, 1944). In the 1950s and 1960s his compositions again became less accessible. His *Connotations* (1962), commissioned for the opening of Philharmonic Hall in 1962, was written in a densely serial style. He lived at the Empire Hotel, just across from Lincoln Center, until 1961, when he moved to Peekskill in Westchester County. After a rich and varied compositional life his output ebbed after 1970. Copland was the most influential American composer of the twentieth century. Although best remembered for his celebrations of rural America, he proved equally adept at portraying the urban pastoral in such works as *Quiet City* (1940) and *Music for a Great City* (1963). In 1982 Queens College of the City University of New York named its music school in his honor. With Vivian Perlis he wrote two volumes of memoirs (1984, 1989).

Barbara L. Tischler

Copperheads. A name applied to Confederate sympathizers in the North during the Civil War, first used in print in the *New York Tribune* in July 1861. Sympathy for the South in New York City was fueled by racism, ties to the southern economy, and resentment of the extraordinary powers exercised by the federal government during the Civil War. The city's most prominent Copperhead was Mayor Fernando Wood, a Democrat who sought to advance his political career by exploiting the public's displeasure with the war: unlike Tammany Hall his organization, Mozart Hall, supported the efforts of the Peace Democrats. In May 1863 meetings were held in the city to denounce the arrest of the Copperhead Clement Vallandigham in Ohio, and riots broke out on 13 July when attempts were made to implement the first federal conscription act. The Copperheads lost much support after their role in the riots became known, and in highly publicized cases a number were prosecuted by such members of Tammany Hall as A. Oakey Hall and John T. Hoffman. After Copperheads helped Confederates to commit acts of sabotage in the city, Union forces were dispatched there by President Abraham Lincoln for fear of a riot on Election Day in 1864. A plot by Confederate agents, with Copperhead assistance, to set fire to the city's hotels was carried out on 25 November and resulted in minor damage to several sites, including nineteen hotels and Barnum's museum.

Sidney David Brumer: *Political History of New York State during the Period of the Civil War* (New York: Columbia University Press, 1911)

Jerome Mushkat: *Tammany: The Evolution of a Political Machine, 1789–1865* (Syracuse, N.Y.: Syracuse University Press, 1971)

Iver Bernstein: *The New York City Draft Riots: Their Significance for American Society and Politics in the Age of the Civil War* (New York: Oxford University Press, 1990)

Evan Cornog

Corbett, Harvey Wiley (*b* San Francisco, 8 Jan 1873; *d* New York City, 24 April 1954). Architect. After studying at the University of California, Berkeley, and the École des Beaux-Arts he moved to New York City in 1901, where he worked in several firms before forming a partnership with F. Livinston Pell in 1903. The two were known for their designs in revival styles, among them the neoclassical New York School of Applied Design for Women at 160 Lexington Avenue (1909). In 1912 Corbett became a partner of Frank J. Helmle, who had a practice in Brooklyn. He became known in the 1920s as a leading defender of skyscrapers and increased urban density. He wrote extensively on the impact of the zoning law of 1916 and offered futuristic proposals for multilevel traffic separation and pedestrian bridges. Among the many skyscrapers that he designed was the Bush Tower at 132 West 42nd Street (1918), which was widely acclaimed and housed his offices in its two top stories. The firm was renamed Corbett, Harrison, and MacMurray after Helmle's retirement in 1928 and later became Harvey Wiley Corbett Associates. Other commissions included the Master Apartments at 310 Riverside Drive (1929), the National Title Guaranty Building of Metropolitan Life Insurance on Madison Square (1932, with D. Everett Wald), and the Criminal Courts Building at 100 Centre Street (1939).

Carol Willis

Corbett, James J(ohn) (*b* San Francisco, 1 Sept 1866; *d* Queens, 18 Feb 1933). Boxer. The son of Irish immigrants, he fought as an amateur in gentlemen's clubs in San Francisco while working in a bank. After turning professional he defeated Joe Choynski in June 1889, fought sixty-one rounds with Peter Jackson, and in September 1892 won the world heavyweight championship from John L. Sullivan (by a knockout in the twenty-first round). Known as "Gentleman Jim," he was popular among fans for his speed and finesse in the ring and for his style, grace, and refinement. He lost the world title to Bob Fitzsimmons in March 1897 (in fourteen rounds) and was knocked out during attempts to regain it from Jim Jeffries in 1900 and 1903. After retiring from boxing in 1903 he became a promoter, lecturer, and actor, making programs for radio and performing in the theater and in ten motion pictures. He also wrote a book, *The Roar of the Crowd: The True Tale of the Rise and Fall of a Champion* (1925).

John J. Concannon

Corbin, Austin (*b* Newport, N.H, 11 July 1827; *d* Newport, 4 June 1896). Real-estate developer. He formed the Corbin Banking Company in New York City in 1865, and while on vacation in Coney Island in 1873 made plans to develop a lavish summer resort at its eastern tip called Manhattan Beach, which eventually included the Manhattan Beach Hotel and the Oriental Hotel. The resort soon lost much of its exclusiveness, as customers from all classes were drawn to Coney Island by vaudeville shows and other popular amusements. Corbin was also the owner of the Long Island Rail Road from 1880 until his death.

Paul Zunz: *The Crisis: A Celebrated Case at Manhattan Beach* (New York: Paul Zunz, 1879)

Stephen Weinstein

Corcoran's Roost. Neighborhood in the East 40s of Manhattan during the late nineteenth century. The area was rocky and covered by small shacks when the Irish immigrant John Corcoran settled there in the 1850s; through his activities and those of his family the area became known for lawlessness. For many years his tenement at 317 East 40th Street was the headquarters of the gang Corcoran's Roosters, which declined after the turn of the century. The character of the neighborhood improved markedly after the elegant apartment village Tudor City was built in the 1920s.

James Bradley

Cordero, Angel (Thomas, Jr.) (*b* Santurce, Puerto Rico, 8 Nov 1942). Jockey. He was born into a family of jockeys and trainers, grew up in Puerto Rico, and became an apprentice jockey in 1959. Penniless and unable to speak English, he arrived in New York City in 1965 and attracted attention for his aggressive riding style. In 1967 he became the leading jockey in New York City, and in the following year he was the leading jockey in North America with 345 victories. As his career rapidly advanced he angered many riders who objected to his combativeness, and he was suspended on several occasions; he also had many accidents and injuries. On 12 January 1992 he was forced to retire after he suffered serious internal injuries in a fall at Aqueduct Racetrack. During his outstanding career he won 7057 races (third on the all-time career list), earned nearly $165 million in purses, and twice won the Eclipse Award, given to the leading jockey in the United States. His greatest triumphs include three victories in the Kentucky Derby, two in the Preakness, one in the Belmont Stakes, and four in the Breeders Cup. He was especially successful in New York City, where he once won six races in a single day (on 17 March 1975 at Aqueduct). In 1988 he was inducted into the Thoroughbred Racing Hall of Fame. While recuperating from the accident that ended his career as a rider he began working as a thoroughbred trainer. He won his first victory as a trainer in June 1992.

Ira Berkow: "The Rise and Fall of an Emperor Named Cordero," *New York Times*, 24 Feb 1992

Robert Sanger Steel

Corlear's Hook. Former neighborhood in lower Manhattan, covering fifty acres (twenty hectares) and bounded to the north by Delancey Street, to the east by the East River, to the south by Montgomery Street, and to the west by east Broadway. In the early twentieth century activists from the Henry Street, University, and Grand Street settlements advocated the removal of the area's "old law" tenements and decaying piers so that low-income housing could be constructed. The Amalgamated Dwellings (1930) and the Vladeck Houses (1940) were developed through municipal and federal financing and built by the city housing authority; and the Hillman Houses (1949) and Corlear's Hook project (1955), conducted under Title I of the Housing Act of 1949, were sponsored by the United Housing Foundation, with the intention of transforming slums into middle-income developments.

Joel Schwartz

Cornbury, Lord. See HYDE, EDWARD.

Cornell, Joseph (*b* Nyack, N.Y., 24 Dec 1903; *d* Queens, 29 Dec 1972). Sculptor. In 1929 he took up residence in an ordinary house on Utopia Parkway in Flushing, where he lived and worked to the end of his life. During the 1930s he was associated with a circle of surrealists at the Julien Levy Gallery. He became well known for his assemblages, which were usually small, sectioned wooden boxes filled with photographs, maps, and found objects. An avid collector, Cornell frequented the secondhand book dealers on 4th Avenue in search of old books, engravings, and souvenirs. He characterized his work as "a natural outcome of love for the city."

Diane Waldman: *Joseph Cornell* (New York: George Braziller, 1976)

Harriet F. Senie

Cornell, Katharine (*b* Berlin, 16 Feb 1893; *d* Vineyard Haven, Mass., 9 June 1974). Actress. Made independent by a legacy, she moved to New York City in 1916 to become

Katharine Cornell

an actress. She joined the Washington Square Players, performed her first important roles with Jessie Boustelle's stock company, and in 1924 appeared on Broadway as the star of Shaw's *Candida.* She later acted in such classics as *Romeo and Juliet*, *St. Joan*, and *Three Sisters*, and a number of inferior plays that she sustained by her talent. Her greatest roles were Candida and Elizabeth Barrett in Rudolf Besier's *The Barretts of Wimpole Street.* In 1921 she married Guthrie McClintic, with whom she formed Cornell and McClintic Productions in 1930; with Cornell in starring roles and McClintic as the director the two mounted shows on Broadway and toured the country. She lived from 1921 to 1952 at 23 Beekman Place and from 1961 on East 51st Street.

George A. Thompson, Jr.

Cornell University Medical College. Medical school opened in New York City on 14 April 1898 on the grounds of Bellevue Hospital by the board of trustees of Cornell University; in 1900 it moved to a new building at 1st Avenue and 28th Street. The first graduating class of fifty-eight students included ten women. In 1912 the college became affiliated with New York Hospital; the two institutions agreed on 14 June 1927 to build the New York Hospital–Cornell Medical Center on York Avenue between 67th and 68th streets, which began receiving patients on 1 September 1932. In the mid 1990s the school had four hundred students who received clinical training at New York Hospital and other affiliated hospitals.

Comprehensive Medical Care and Teaching: A Report on the New York Hospital–Cornell Medical Center Program (Ithaca, N.Y.: Cornell University Press, 1967)

Adele A. Lerner

corners and panics. Financial crises brought on by speculation have played an important role in the history of New York City.

"The Great Financial Panic —Closing the Doors of the Stock Exchange on Its Members, Saturday, Sept. 20th," Frank Leslie's Newspaper, *4 October 1873*

During the early Federal period an increase in trading in government bonds helped to bring about the formation in 1790 of the New York Stock Exchange, and eventually rampant speculation that one writer characterized as "scriptomania" caused a panic in 1792. Alexander Hamilton, the secretary of the treasury, was criticized for his handling of the crisis, which ultimately had little impact on the city's economy. As finance and industry took on a larger role in the city's economy, panics assumed larger proportions. In the 1830s Jacob Little and other speculators made huge profits by organizing pools of investors and manipulating stock prices. A period of speculation in railroads, canals, cotton, and real estate ended in 1837 when a financial panic ruined many banks and speculators. The depression that followed constrained Wall Street until the 1850s, when economic growth and easy credit ignited another round of speculation, primarily in railroads. The market collapsed in August 1857, and by December the streets of New York City were filled with rioters and unemployed workers, who blamed the banks and speculators for their troubles. The panic of 1857 effected a generational change on Wall Street, and a new breed of speculator dominated the market after the Civil War, at a time when the markets had gained such a powerful influence on the American economy that financial panics frequently led to severe economic dislocation. One of the most profitable schemes of the speculators during these years was known as executing a corner: buying all available supplies of a stock or commodity to drive up the price. This speculative maneuver created a financial panic in 1869 when Jay Gould made $40 million by attempting to corner the market for gold. Speculators like Daniel Drew and Cornelius Vanderbilt also manipulated share prices during their takeover battles for the Erie Railroad and other firms. A major financial scandal resulted from the bankruptcy in 1873 of Crédit Mobilier, which had bribed scores of politicians to obtain government subsidies for the building of the Union Pacific Railroad. The scandal caused stock prices to plunge, producing the worst depression of the nineteenth century, and ruined Jay Cooke, then the most powerful man on Wall Street. The failure of a brokerage house owned by Ulysses S. Grant after his presidency produced a minor panic in 1884, and the federal government nearly became bankrupt between 1893 and 1895: it recovered only when J. P. Morgan bought several bond issues on the condition that Washington return to the gold standard. Panics were caused by attempted corners in 1901 (by James Hill and Edward H. Harriman for control of the Northern Pacific Railroad), and 1907 (by Frederick Heinze and Charles Morse for control of United Copper), when Morgan again played an important, stabilizing role: after several banks closed and the stock market fell sharply he joined with the U.S. Department of the Treasury to shore up the banking system with fresh capital.

After the turn of the century it became more difficult to manipulate prices, because of the creation of the Federal Reserve in 1913 and because more shares were traded. Even so Allan Ryan in 1920 was able to increase the price of shares in the Stutz Motor Company by buying all the stock, and Jesse Livermore, working at the behest of Clarence Saunders, was able to corner the stock in the grocery firm Piggly-Wiggly. The New York Stock Exchange forced Ryan and Saunders to give up their shares, but throughout the 1920s easy credit fueled widespread speculation by allowing corporations to go heavily into debt and encouraging speculators to buy stocks on credit. In 1928 a pool of speculators organized by William Durant cornered the stock in the Radio Corporation of America (RCA), which increased in price by sixty points a share in just four days. The market finally stalled in September 1929 and crashed in October, the economy slipped into the worst depression of the twentieth century, and the stock market lost 80 percent of its value by 1933. By this time it was clear that the nation's financial markets suffered from enormous structural weaknesses, which the reforms of the New Deal were intended to remedy: the federal government formed the Securities and Exchange Commission in 1934, outlawed manipulation of the stock market, and strengthened regulations. These reforms made panics and corners considerably rarer but did not eliminate them completely. Prices dropped 27 percent in a panic between December 1961 and June 1962 known as the Kennedy slide, and the Dow Jones Industrial Average lost 37 percent of its value between 1968 and 1970. As late as 1979 the brothers Nelson Bunker Hunt and W(illiam) H(erbert) Hunt unsuccessfully attempted to corner the market in silver, but federal regulators intervened to prevent a financial crisis and the Hunts lost more than $4000 million (they eventually declared bankruptcy). On 19 October 1987 the Dow Jones Industrial Average underwent a decline of 508 points, or 23 percent, the largest in its history.

Robert Sobel: *Panic on Wall Street: A History of America's Financial Disasters* (New York: Collier, 1972)

George Winslow

Cornish, Samuel Eli (*b* New York City, 1793; *d* New York City, 6 Nov 1858). Civil rights leader. He formed the First Colored Presbyterian Church (later renamed Shiloh Presbyterian Church) in 1821 and was its pastor until 1827, when with John B. Russwurm, a proponent of the "back to Africa" movement, he launched *Freedom's Journal*, the first black newspaper in the United States, from an office at 150 Church Street. After the journal ceased publication in 1829 he edited several others devoted to abolition and civil rights, including *Rights for All* (1829) and the *Colored American* (1837–41). He attended the first National Negro Convention, held in Philadelphia in 1830, as a delegate from New York City and became a prominent figure in the Negro convention movement. An advocate of practical education, he promoted literacy among blacks in the North and with philanthropists raised money to build schools dedicated to preparing black youths for industrial work. He was appointed to the executive committee of the American Anti-Slavery Society in 1833.

Lawrence D. Reddick: "Samuel E. Cornish," *Negro History Bulletin* 5 (Nov 1941), 38

Thelma Foote

Corona. Neighborhood in north central Queens (1980 pop. 67,402), adjoining Flushing Bay and Flushing Meadow Park. It was developed in 1854 by a group of speculators from New York City and named West Flushing. The same year marked the beginning of service by the Long Island Rail Road and the opening of the National Race Course (later Fashion Race Course), which continued to operate until the Civil War. Developers planned the streets according to the route of the railroad and settlement increased. In 1872 the village changed its name to Corona (the "crown" of villages on Long Island). Early factories made china, portable houses, and from 1893 into the 1930s Tiffany glass. The population reached 2500 by 1898 and 6200 by 1910, and it continued to grow after the introduction of rapid transit in 1917. The commercial center shifted in the 1920s from near the railroad station to Northern Boulevard. From 1943 to 1971 the great jazz trumpeter Louis Armstrong lived in the neighborhood, which was then largely Italian and Jewish. The area attracted a large Latin American community after the Second World War, at first Puerto Rican and after 1965 increasingly Dominican. The movement of immigrants to the neighborhood in the 1980s was heavy: the Dominican Republic accounted for almost half of all immigrants who settled there, China and Colombia for about a tenth each. Other countries that were well represented included Korea, India, the Philippines, Ecuador, Pakistan, Peru, and Guyana. In the early 1970s the neighborhood was the site of heated conflicts between middle-class homeowners and advocates of low-income housing. Corona was the fictional home of Archie Bunker in the popular television series "All in the Family" (1971–83).

Vincent Seyfried

coroner. See MEDICAL EXAMINER.

corporation counsel. The lawyer appointed to defend the legal interests of New York City. A similar office was held first by James Graham, the city's recorder from 1683 to 1701, and in the following century by such distinguished men as Robert R. Livingston and Richard Varick. It was merged into a new position known as attorney of the corporation in 1801. After the offices became separate again on 14 May 1839 Peter A. Cowdrey was named counsel, Samuel J. Tilden attorney. In April 1849 the counsel became an elected official in charge of the new municipal law department approved by the state legislature; the election held soon after was won by Henry Davies. The position became appointive again under William M. "Boss" Tweed's charter of 1870, and the corporation counsel now exercised nearly complete control over litigation involving the city. While in office William C. Whitney (1875–82) introduced divisional specialization. The city's counsel was used by Mayor John F. Hylan to block proposals for increasing transit fares and utility fees, and by Mayor Fiorello H. La Guardia to prepare a new administrative code. By the mid 1970s the office performed so poorly that it was denounced by Judge Bentley Kassal, leading Allen Schwartz to carry out reforms and secure agreements from major law firms to provide lawyers to the city free of charge. In the mid 1990s the corporation counsel had nineteen divisions dealing with such areas as zoning, homelessness, the federal census, contracts, accidents, and redevelopment. The offices are at 100 Church Street.

George J. Lankevich

Corporation of the City of New York. In addition to wielding government powers the city is a corporation, a status giving it the legal capacity to own property, sue and be sued, and exercise other functions. New Amsterdam was granted a limited municipal government in 1653. The charter promulgated by Governor Richard Nicolls (1665) changed the "Forme and Ceremony" of government to conform with British practice but recognized the city as a "body Politick and Corporate." Under the laws of that time the Corporation, although having governmental powers, was treated as a private institution. Successive colonial charters, especially that of Governor John Montgomerie (1731), defined its rights and privileges, and gave it an endowment of "private" land that included most of Manhattan Island north of the present Canal Street as well as the underwater land adjacent to the shoreline in lower Manhattan. Voting and the holding of municipal office were limited to freemen (Dutch burghers) who were required to meet certain property and residence qualifications and were the only people allowed to engage in trade or skilled occupations in the city. The freemanship was gradually expanded, but it persisted as a distinct class even after American independence. The early Corporation of the City of New York did not have the authority to levy direct taxes. Its revenue derived mainly from regulatory and licensing fees, franchises, and income from its property. Throughout the eighteenth century the corporation made numerous grants of underwater land to be filled in. The grantee typically paid a modest quit rent in cash, but was also required to build specific public improvements such as streets, piers, and bulkheads. In this way the city was able to manage its expansion and provide improved facilities for its growing maritime trade. The growth of population in the late eighteenth century and the early nineteenth created a need for additional public services and facilities. The corporation became increasingly dependent on the state legislature for the authority to levy taxes and do other things not contemplated in the colonial charters. Through a series of court decision and charter revisions, the Corporation of the City of New York by the 1860s had lost nearly all its former autonomy, and like other municipal corporations was an instrumentality of the State of New York. By this time the corporation had also divested itself of most of its former landholdings or turned them over to public purposes such as parks.

Murray Hoffman: *A Treatise upon the Estate and Rights of the Corporation of the City of New York, as Proprietors* (New York: McSpedon and Baker, 1853)

George W. Edwards and Arthur E. Peterson: *New York as an Eighteenth-century Municipality* (Port Washington, N.Y.: I. J. Friedman, 1917)

Hendrik Hartog: *Public Property and Private Power: The Corporation of the City of New York in American Law, 1730–1870* (Ithaca, N.Y.: Cornell University Press, 1989)

Gilbert Tauber

Michael A. Corrigan, 1888

Corrigan, Michael A(ugustine) (*b* Newark, N.J., 13 Aug 1839; *d* New York City, 2 May 1902). Archbishop. He was a coadjutor bishop to Cardinal John McCloskey from 1880 until being appointed archbishop of New York City in 1885. Responding to the needs of Catholic immigrants, he opened seventy-five parochial schools, centralized the parochial system, and built St. Joseph's Seminary in Yonkers, New York. He also formed a number of charitable institutions (consolidated in 1902 as the Association of Catholic Charities), which he staffed by attracting twenty-four religious orders to the archdiocese, including the Scalabrinians and the Missionary Sisters of the Sacred Heart. He emerged as a conservative leader and drew sharp criticism from many Catholics after excommunicating the priest Edward McGlynn for supporting Henry George in the mayoral campaign of 1886 (over Corrigan's protests McGlynn was reinstated by the Vatican in 1892). Corrigan's anti-progressive position was nonetheless supported by papal encyclicals culminating in *Testem Benevolentiae* (1899).

Robert Emmett Curran: *Michael Augustine Corrigan and the Shaping of Conservative Catholicism in America, 1878–1902* (New York: Arno, 1978)

Robert Emmett Curran

Cortelyou, Jacques (*b* Utrecht, Netherlands, *ca* 1625; *d* ?New Utrecht, New Netherland, between 28 Feb and 27 July 1693). Landowner and surveyor. Of French parentage, he attended the University of Utrecht and worked as a tutor and land surveyor in America. In 1652 he settled in New Netherland, where he tutored the children of Cornelis Van Werckhoven, a member of the Dutch West India Company. After Van Werckhoven's death he secured a patent in 1657 for land that is now the site of Fort Hamilton; he divided this land into twenty lots and established the town of New Utrecht. As the surveyor general of New Netherland he drew the first map of New Amsterdam in 1661. He lived at Fort Hamilton and traveled daily to his office on Whitehall Street. Cortelyou's descendants include Isaac Cortelyou, a fence viewer and overseer of the poor in the 1770s who lived in a stone house in Gowanus (eventually known as the Vechte–Cortelyou House) that was the scene of fierce fighting during the Battle of Long Island (August 1776), and George B. Cortelyou, a prominent Republican politician who was chairman of the Republican National Committee (1904), postmaster general (1905), and secretary of the treasury (1907).

Mrs. Bleecker Bangs: *Reminiscences of Old New Utrecht and Gowanus* (New York: Brooklyn Daily Eagle Press, 1912)

Henry R. Stiles, ed.: *The Civil, Political, Professional and Ecclesiastical History, and Commercial and Industrial Record of the County of Kings and the City of Brooklyn, N.Y., from 1683 to 1884* (New York: W. W. Munsell, 1884)

Stephen Weinstein

cosmetics. Wigs, rouge, and face powder were used by both men and women in colonial New York City. After the American Revolution most face and hair powder, toilet waters, and lotions were made at home; chemists prepared more complex products such as oils, creams, pomades, perfumes, and dyes; and such prominent merchants in New York City as Nicholas Low and James Rivington imported cosmetics from England and France. The nineteenth century saw a decline in the use of cosmetics, but the city remained the site of many cosmetics firms and of several innovations in the industry, as well as the central receiving point for English and French cosmetics bound for the United States. The English chemist Robert Bach, who set up shop at 128 Pearl Street in 1798, imported most of his preparations. His business evolved by 1872 into the prosperous firm of Dodge and Olcott, which distilled raw materials for export and operated from 88 William Street until it moved to New Jersey in 1904. Two cosmetics firms in the city during the early nineteenth century later evolved into multinational conglomerates: those of Robert Chesebrough and the chemist Theron Pond (whose enterprises merged to form Chesebrough–Pond in 1955), and of the candle and fancy soap maker William Colgate at 6 Dutch Street (1806), which eventually became the Colgate–Palmolive Company. Both businesses also had operations in Brooklyn: Pond bottled his immensely popular witch hazel there from 1846, and Chesebrough manufactured petroleum jelly at 24 State Street from 1870. Pond later manufactured cold cream, for which he became widely known.

The period between 1880 and 1900 is regarded as a low point in the use of cosmetics nationwide, but in New York City there were nonetheless ninety hairdressers operating in 1890, most of whom visited customers in their homes. Commercial beauty salons and makers of hair-care products gradually increased in number. Manuel Besosa manufactured a brand of hair dye called Orija at 66 West 125th Street, and forty-four perfumers and seven importers did a thriving business. In a brochure in 1882 Simonson's Human Hair Emporium at 34 East 14th Street advertised not only its usual supply of wigs, toupees, and human hair but also cosmetics imported from France, including the cream Fountaine de la Beauté, the hair color Fluide Magique, and Velontine Face Powder. Simonson's helped to establish the practices of associating cosmetics with foreign exoticism, maintaining a fashionable address, and charging high prices: at a dollar a bottle few wage earners could afford Simonson's imported makeup. Another successful beautician who profited during the last two decades of the nineteenth century was Mary E. Cobb, who first offered complete beauty treatments in 1886 at her salon at 66 West 23rd Street and remained in business until 1906. The nation's largest cosmetics firm, Avon, began inauspiciously in 1886 when David McConnell, a bible salesman based in the city, offered customers a bottle of perfume free of charge as an incentive. By 1897 McConnell's California Perfume Company employed one hundred salesmen and operated from a warehouse at 126 Chambers Street; the firm manufactured its perfume in Suffern, New York.

The beginning of the twentieth century marked a turning point for the American cosmetics industry. Having long been associated with aristocratic extravagance or prostitution, cosmetics were now regarded as a symbol of freedom by women eager to liberate themselves from the constraints of Victorian morality. Magazines and motion pictures helped to define cultural standards of beauty and stimulated consumers' demand for cosmetics and glamour. Several developments in the first decades of the century solidified the city's position as the center of the world's cosmetics industry. Manufacturers, importers, and marketers believed that an address on 5th Avenue would lend their products an aura of elegance and gentility, and as they relied increasingly on bold advertising, highly developed transportation, and distribution through department stores, the need to locate in New York City became more pressing. Beauty products, salons, and exclusive sales outlets multiplied rapidly in the early twentieth century, spurred primarily by such locally based pioneers as Elizabeth Arden and Helena Rubinstein.

Born Florence Nightingale Graham in Woodbridge, Ontario, Arden moved to the city in 1908 to work for the chemical firm Squibb and soon took a cashier's position in Eleanor Adair's beauty salon. After falling out with Adair (who remained a fierce competitor over the years) she opened the Salon D'Oro at 509 5th Avenue and changed her name in 1910. With $6000 borrowed from her brother she opened salons across the country and in Europe, and in 1915 she developed her first important product, Venetian Cream Amoretta. She later made other preparations, including Ardena Skin Tonic and Venetian Cleansing Cream, and was the first to introduce mascara into the United States and to employ traveling demonstrators as saleswomen. Arden produced her cosmetics in small quantities, gave them high prices, sold them through exclusive department stores, and attracted customers with innovative packaging and strategically placed advertisements. Her domestic cosmetics line had sales of $4 million in 1929, by which time she had moved her salon to 691 5th Avenue, bought a factory at 212 East 52nd Street and a penthouse at 834 5th Avenue, and become a prominent member of fashionable society in Manhattan. She weathered the Depression by developing a line of multi-colored lipsticks designed to match clothing.

Arden's chief rival in business and society was Helena Rubinstein, a Polish Jew who moved to New York City in 1914 and in the following year opened the Maison de Beauté de Valaze at 14 East 49th Street, which featured her Crème Valaze. Factory-made but narrowly marketed, her products quickly became successful among fashion-conscious New Yorkers, and she soon expanded her salons and her product line to exclusive outlets in several European and American cities. Rubinstein was responsible for many innovations in the cosmetics industry. Depicted in advertisements wearing a white laboratory coat and inspecting her products, she was the first to link her products with a scientifically designed beauty program, a marketing strategy that became widely imitated. She also offered the first line of cosmetics for oily, dry, and normal skin, and introduced a mascara applicator that remained in use into the 1990s. Her Valaze Skin Food and other products became the target of federal regulators after the passage of the Pure Food and Drug Act of 1936, but in the long run her profits were scarcely affected. Among Rubinstein's successful competitors was Dorothy Gray, who began her career as a custom cosmetician for Elizabeth Arden in 1915 and in the following year opened her own salon at 57th Street and Madison Avenue (moved in 1926 to 753 5th Avenue); her business was eventually acquired by the firm of Lehn and Fink.

During these years the metropolitan region gained in importance as a market for hair products, especially those intended for blacks. As early as the 1880s the Lyon Manufacturing Company in Brooklyn made a hair straightener called Kaitharon that was sold nationwide. Other beauticians who catered specifically to blacks included Madame Jennie L. Crawford at 454 Lenox Avenue, Anna Malone's Poro Beauty School at 2525 7th Avenue, Madame Estella's Salon de Beauty at 3671 Broadway. The hair care magnate Madame C. J. Walker moved to the city in 1914 and bought a townhouse at 108–10 West 136th Street where she lived and operated a beauty salon. The first permanent hair wave was performed in the city in 1906 by Charles Nestle, who opened a parlor in 1916 at Aeolian Hall (33–35 West 42nd Street).

The Manufacturers' Perfumers Association of the United States was formed in New York City in 1894. In 1920 the group, now known as the Toilet Goods Association, published a comprehensive register of wholesalers, manufacturers, and importers of cosmetics and raw materials that listed 480 cosmetics firms operating in Manhattan, forty-eight in Brooklyn, three in Long Island City, and one in Flushing. Among these were a number of large chemical firms that supplied raw materials for cosmetics, including Pfizer, Squibb, Burroughs–Wellcome, Merck, Schmid, and Schieffin, as well as the firm of Maurice Levy, who invented the lipstick case. In 1937 the catalogue listed 506 cosmetics businesses in Manhattan, of which many were branches of foreign firms like Chanel, Fabergé, and Jean Naté; others were chemical factories like the Adams Chemical Laboratories at 561 West 147th Street. One of the smaller firms in the catalogue was Revlon, a five-year-old business led by Charles Revson and based at 125 West 45th Street. Revson saw an untapped market in the large number of women unable to afford the products of Rubinstein and Arden. He sold his nail polish in drugstores, in 1940 introduced the first color-coordinated nail polish and lipstick ("matching lips and fingertips") and the first pink nail polish, and by 1941 achieved a near-monopoly for his products in beauty salons. Borrowing some of the techniques used to sell automobiles, he introduced new color lines each spring and autumn, devised advertisements that associated his products with heightened sexuality (an advertising campaign in 1952 based on the slogan "fire and ice" caused a sensation and was highly influential), and was the first cosmetics manufacturer to sponsor a television program ("The $64,000 Question"). He also led a trend in the cosmetics industry toward diversification by expanding into vitamins, toilet bowl cleaners, and shoe polish in the 1950s and eye shadow in the 1960s. By the time of his death in 1975 Revson had built his firm into the second-largest cosmetics manufacturer in the world.

One of the city's most important cosmetics manufacturers from the 1950s was Estée Lauder, born Josephine Esther Mentzer and brought up on Hillside Avenue in Corona, who entered the business soon after her uncle developed a facial cream. Beginning with a modest line of fragrances, skin cream, cleansing oil, lipstick, face powder, and turquoise eye shadow, she sold her products at Bonwit Teller and eventually Saks Fifth Avenue and aimed specifically at affluent Jewish women. Lauder incorporated in 1947 and kept her company privately held. In 1953 she introduced a bath oil called Youth Dew, which was manufactured at two small plants in upper Manhattan and became successful. She introduced the practice of offering promotional gifts with purchases and was the first cosmetics maker to feature a single fashion model throughout a series of advertisements. In contrast to the autocratic Revson she was well liked and during the 1960s became part of the city's social circles. By 1965 Lauder's firm had gross sales of $14 million and was encroaching on Revlon's market, and a strong rivalry ensued. Lauder in 1965 introduced a line of twenty-one products for men under the marque Aramis; Revlon in the following year introduced a line of men's cosmetics called Braggi. Revlon maintained its offices in the General Motors building at 767 5th Avenue; Lauder moved her corporate headquarters there in 1968.

During the 1960s many cosmetics firms expanded into skin-care products with which they rarely associated themselves, a strategy intended to make the number of choices available to consumers seem larger than it actually was. This path was followed by Lauder in promoting a line of skin-care products under the name Clinique, which Revlon quickly countered with a line called Ultima II. The continuing rivalry between Lauder and Revlon transformed the industry: tremendous advertising budgets made fashion magazines into bloated promotional vehicles in which editorial matter was secondary; cosmetics firms expanded into ancillary products such as men's cosmetics, fragrances, clothing, and cleansers; and Revson and Lauder sponsored foundations that extended their competition into the realm of philanthropy.

Very little cosmetics manufacturing remained in the city after the Second World War. Although the largest firms maintained their headquarters there, high land costs, wages, and taxes made it more economical for them to operate their factories elsewhere. The industry also experienced a trend toward consolidation, exemplified by the acquisition of Almay, a small firm based in Brooklyn, by the conglomerate TLC Beatrice. From the 1960s cosmetics firms faced criticism from feminists, animal-rights activists, and consumers skeptical of products with artificial ingredients. Many responded by associating their products with purity and scientific certitude: Revlon was the first cosmetics maker to describe its products as hypo-allergenic. In the mid 1990s virtually every major cosmetics firm in the world maintained at least an office in the city, including such French firms as Lancôme, L'Oréal, and Chanel, and the giant Japanese firm Shiseido. The cosmetics industry remained a linchpin for magazine publishers, television stations, department stores, chemical firms, and the fashion business.

Maggie Angeloglou: *A History of Make-up* (New York: Macmillan, 1970)
Margaret Allen: *Selling Dreams: Inside the Beauty Business* (New York: Simon and Schuster, 1981)

Marc Ferris

Cosmopolitan. Monthly magazine. It was launched in Rochester, New York, in 1887 and moved to New York City, where in 1888 it was purchased and developed into a magazine of domestic and foreign policy by John Brisben Walker, a former newspaperman who had made a fortune in iron and real estate. During the Spanish–American War two reporters covered the front while Theodore Dreiser wrote a story on a munitions factory, and Stephen Crane reported on the Boer War. Walker was not averse to influencing public policy: in 1895 he used the magazine to offer Spain $100 million in exchange for Cuban independence; in 1902 he proposed a world congress of nations; and he advocated nationalizing the railway system. He was also an early proponent of aviation, and in 1892 he used the magazine to provide one of the first forums for articles on "aerial navigation." In 1905 Walker sold the magazine for $400,000 to William Randolph Hearst, who was more assertive than Walker had been in using the magazine as a vehicle for venting his opinions. A story published in 1905 called "The Treason of the Senate," about the alliance between big business and several senators, led Theodore Roosevelt to coin the term "muckraking" to describe what he saw as sensationalistic but incisive reporting. From 1912 the magazine emphasized fiction: a serial by Robert W. Chambers entitled "The Common Law" and illustrated by Charles Dana Gibson increased circulation by 70 percent. Fiction continued to be published for the next thirty years. By 1965 the magazine's circulation was foundering and the Hearst Corporation appointed as its editor Helen Gurley Brown, the author of *Sex and the Single Girl*, who sought out a readership of single working women by celebrating a hedonistic, materialistic way of life: she briefly published centerfold photographs of male nudes and introduced various changes in format that eventually increased circulation from 700,000 to two million.

John Tebbel: *The American Magazine: A Compact History* (New York: Hawthorn, 1969)
William H. Taft: *American Magazines for the 1980s* (New York: Hastings House, 1982)

Rachel Sawyer

Costello, Frank [Castiglia, Francesco] (*b* Laurapoli, Calabria, Italy, 1891; *d* New York City, 18 Feb 1973). Organized-crime figure. As an infant he moved to New York City with

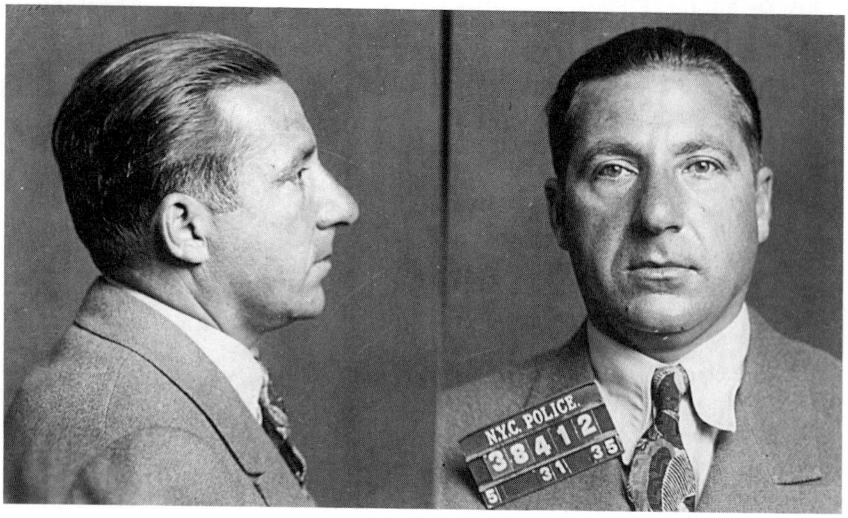

Frank Costello, May 1935

his family. After being imprisoned in 1924 for carrying a gun he became an organized-crime leader in the city during the 1920s and 1930s. His main work was buying favors from political leaders, judges, and the police, which he reportedly accomplished with support from Lucky Luciano and Meyer Lansky and $20,000 a week to dispense. For many years he had a penthouse in the Majestic Apartments at 115 Central Park West. He was forced to end his activities after they were discovered during an investigation led by Senator Estes Kefauver in the 1950s. After serving a short term at the federal penitentiary in Atlanta in 1959, Costello retired to his estate on Long Island, where he remained until the end of his life.

George Walsh: *Public Enemies: The Mayor, the Mob, and the Crime That Was* (New York: W. W. Norton, 1980)

See also ORGANIZED CRIME.

James E. Mooney

Costikyan, Edward N(azar) (*b* Weehawken, N.J., 14 Sept 1924). Lawyer. He graduated first in his class from Columbia Law School and at the age of thirty became the youngest Democratic district leader in the history of the city. From 1960 he was a partner in the law firm of Paul, Weiss, Rifkind, Wharton and Garrison. As the leader from 1962 to 1964 of the Democratic County Committee of New York County, he worked to eliminate the influence of Tammany Hall over municipal government and judicial appointments. From 1969 he led a task force that drafted revisions to the city charter (implemented in 1975). Costikyan wrote *Behind Closed Doors: Politics in the Public Interest* (1966) and *How to Win Votes: The Politics of 1980* (1980).

Harold Takooshian

Cotton Club. Nightclub. It opened in 1922 at 142nd Street and Lenox Avenue in quarters formerly occupied by the Douglas Casino and the Club Deluxe. Under the management of Owney Madden, reputedly an underworld figure, it became one of the leading cabarets in Harlem. It was noted for its elegant interior and could seat seven hundred. Although the Cotton Club generally did not admit blacks as customers it did engage them as musicians and entertainers: Duke Ellington opened there in early July 1927 (the primitivist décor of the club may have contributed to the development of his "jungle sound"), and his orchestra recorded "Black and Tan Fantasy" and "Creole Love Call" while performing at the club. Other prominent performers who appeared at the club included the dancers Ed "Snakehips" Tucker, Evelyn Welch, Bill Robinson, and Buck and Bubbles; the comedian Stepin Fetchit; jazz orchestras led by Cab Calloway, Andrew Preer, Louis Armstrong, and Jimmie Lunceford; the songwriter Harold Arlen; and the singers Lena Horne, Ethel Waters, and Ivie Anderson. In 1936 the club moved to Broadway and 48th Street, where it continued to offer elaborate revues until 1940. A cabaret of the same name opened at 666 West 125th Street in the mid 1980s.

Jim Haskins: *The Cotton Club* (New York: Random House, 1977)

Kathy J. Ogren

Cotton Exchange. See NEW YORK COTTON EXCHANGE.

Coudert Brothers. Law firm formed in 1854 by three brothers from France, including Frédéric René Coudert (1832–1903), a president of the city's bar association and a liberal Democrat partly responsible for having the Statue of Liberty donated to the United States. It was the first firm in the city to have a branch in Paris (1879) and soon developed a relationship with Chemical Bank that helped it to place foreign investments in the city. In 1979 it opened an office in the People's Republic of China, the first law firm in the city to

do so. Under Sol Linowitz its office in Washington became known for negotiating international settlements in Panama and the Middle East. In 1990 the firm had ninety-nine partners and 333 associates. It has headquarters at 200 Park Avenue.

Allan Nevins: *A Half Century of International Problems: A Lawyer's Views* (New York: Columbia University Press, 1954)

George J. Lankevich

Council of Jewish Women. Volunteer organization formed in 1893. A local chapter formed in New York City in the following year was led by Rebekah Kohut and Sadie American, who developed programs to aid Jewish immigrants, especially women and children. It sent volunteers to the docks to help women traveling alone, founded the Lakeview Home for Girls, and maintained recreation rooms on the Lower East Side. It also served refugees from both world wars, set up programs to aid the blind, handicapped, and hospitalized, and worked with other civic groups to pass social legislation.

Elisabeth Israels Perry

Council of Learned Societies. See AMERICAN COUNCIL OF LEARNED SOCIETIES.

Council on Foreign Relations. Nonprofit organization formed in 1921 to bring together leading figures in academia, business, law, and journalism to study issues of foreign policy; it occupied offices at 45 East 65th Street, next door to Franklin D. Roosevelt's townhouse, before moving in 1945 to the Harold Pratt House, a five-story mansion on the southeast corner of 68th Street and Park Avenue, across from Hunter College. The building was given to the council by the widow of Harold Pratt, one of the original directors of the Standard Oil Company; John D. Rockefeller donated a fund for its maintenance. The leadership of the council reflected its strong ties to the Morgan family of bankers until the early 1950s, when David Rockefeller and other members of his family became prominent among its senior officers and directors. The council played an important role in both Democratic and Republican presidential administrations after the Second World War and was an early supporter of the presidential candidacy of Dwight D. Eisenhower, who while serving as president of Columbia University led a group at the council in 1949–50 that studied aid to Europe. The council publishes the influential quarterly journal *Foreign Affairs*, sponsors meetings and conferences at Pratt House and occasionally on Wall Street, and produces a program for the city's radio station (WNYC). The members of the council join by invitation; the by-laws require that between a third and a half of them live or work near the city. Membership stood at 2670 in June 1990. More than fifty persons work at

the offices in New York City; another office is in Washington, and there are thirty-eight affiliate committees throughout the United States.

Robert D. Schulzinger: *The Wise Men of Foreign Affairs: The History of the Council on Foreign Relations* (New York: Columbia University Press, 1984)

Marjorie Harrison

Couney, Martin A. (*b* Alsace, 30 Dec 1870; *d* Brooklyn, 1 March 1950). Pediatrician. He studied in Paris under the pediatrician P. C. Budin, and in 1896 at an international exposition in Berlin he demonstrated an incubator for infants modeled after a device used in poultry breeding. The invention proved a medical and financial success and was demonstrated in London, Paris, Omaha (Nebraska), and Buffalo between 1897 and 1901. In 1903 he opened a nursery on Coney Island where he was able to offer free treatment for premature infants by charging an admission fee of twenty-five cents to sightseers. His work was exhibited in New York City at the World's Fair of 1939–40 and at Luna Park and Dreamland until 1943, about which time the Cornell Medical Center opened a central hospital ward for premature infants. Couney lived at 3728 Surf Avenue in Sea Gate.

A. J. Liebling: "Patron of the Preemies," *New Yorker,* 3 June 1939, pp. 20–24

William A. Silverman: "Incubator-baby Side Shows," *Pediatrics* 64, no. 2 (1979), 127–41

George A. Thompson, Jr.

counterfeiting. In colonial New York City the counterfeiting of paper money was widespread even though it was a capital offense. Counterfeiters also produced coins, especially British and Irish halfpence. When a bag of coppers from the city was examined in 1753 a third were found to be counterfeit, many having been cast in sand, and when the halfpenny was devalued, to fourteen to the New York shilling, a riot ensued. During the American Revolution Continental currency and notes of the New York City Waterworks were counterfeited by the British on a warship in New York Harbor. In the 1780s many counterfeit halfpence were struck at Machin's Mills in Newburgh, New York, which according to hoard evidence were put into circulation in New York City. Virtually all the gold coins countermarked by the goldsmith Ephraim Brasher in New York City in the 1780s were counterfeit. As the private banknotes of state-chartered banks went into circulation, counterfeiters forged the notes of good banks, printed up others for nonexistent banks, and raised denominations of small notes. Owners of fruitstands who sold produce near the ferries in lower Manhattan passed off counterfeit coins in the fading light of winter dusk. Counterfeiting became riskier during the Civil War, when uniform banknotes were introduced and the Secret Service was formed, but it revived during the Depression, when counterfeiters made lead nickels and quarters, and paper money.

Kenneth Scott: *Counterfeiting in Colonial New York* (New York: Oxford University Press, 1953)

Eric P. Newman: "Counterfeit Continental Currency Goes to War," *Numismatist* 70 (1957), 5–16, 137–47

John M. Kleeberg

counties. There are five counties within New York City, each one coextensive with one of the five boroughs: New York County with Manhattan, Bronx County with the Bronx, Kings County with Brooklyn, Queens County with Queens, and Richmond County with Staten Island.

Country Club. Neighborhood in the northeastern Bronx, bounded to the north by Pelham Bay Park, to the east by Long Island Sound, to the south by Throgs Neck, and to the west by Bruckner Boulevard. The land was owned by the Ferris family during the eighteenth century and most of the nineteenth. Country Club Road once led to the Westchester Country Club, which was patronized by yachtsmen and polo players during the nineteenth century. A development called the Country Club Land Association was mapped in 1892, and in the 1920s more lots were added after the adjoining estate of the Spencer family was dissolved. The area is known for its stately homes and quiet streets.

John McNamara: *History in Asphalt: The Origin of Bronx Street and Place Names* (New York: Bronx County Historical Society, 1984)

John McNamara: *McNamara's Old Bronx* (New York: Bronx County Historical Society, 1989)

Gary D. Hermalyn

courthouses. There were courts of law in New Amsterdam by the 1650s, which were usually housed in buildings also used for other government offices. In 1802 the city sponsored a competition to design a new city hall, specifying that the building must include chambers for both the local legislature and the judiciary. The winning entry, designed by John McComb Jr. and Joseph François Mangin, was completed in 1812 and had a broad flight of exterior stairs, an entrance portico, classical details, and a cupola adorned with John Dixey's statue *Justice.* During the early nineteenth century courts that became too large for their quarters were usually moved from there into the Rotunda, the almshouse, and other buildings in City Hall Park. The Richmondtown Courthouse (1837–39), the third courthouse of Richmond County, was built in a Greek Revival style that incorporated severe classical details, an exterior flight of stairs, an entrance portico, and a cupola. It housed all judicial offices of the county until consolidation in 1898; it became part of Richmondtown Restoration in the early 1990s and is now the oldest courthouse in the city.

The city's rapid growth during the late 1840s and the 1850s led to the construction of several buildings to house police courts, among them the Jefferson Market Courthouse. These did not provide all the courtrooms and gov-

Foley Square, ca 1940. Diagonally from lower left: *New York County Courthouse;* left *New York City Department of Health,* right *Department of Motor Vehicles; New York City Criminal Courts Building and Men's House of Detention*

ernment offices needed, and in 1861 construction began on a county court building in City Hall Park. Often called the Tweed Courthouse, it was designed by John Kellum and was one of the first courthouses in an eclectic style (called Anglo-Italianate by some). Kellum used such traditional features as a broad flight of exterior stairs, a portico, and classical details; the southern wing, designed by Leopold Eidlitz after Kellum's death, has Romanesque details. The city paid for materials more expensive than those actually used and for labor that was never performed, and the money generated by these practices lined the pockets of William M. "Boss" Tweed and his cronies. The courthouse was not completed until 1880 and the scandals surrounding it eventually led to Tweed's imprisonment. Eclecticism also marked the courthouse of the state supreme court in Long Island City, built in a beaux-arts style (1876, George Hathorne; rebuilt in 1908 by Peter Coco), and a courthouse in Harlem in a Romanesque style (1893, Thom and Wilson).

In the early twentieth century several majestic courthouses were built according to principles of the "city beautiful" movement as elements in well-designed clusters of buildings. A courthouse at 26th Street and Madison Square for the appellate division of the state supreme court (1900, James Lord Brown) was widely praised for its stylistic coherence. Its park setting and marble colonnades on Madison Avenue and 26th Street gave it an urban grandeur; judicial themes were depicted in allegorical sculptures on the exterior by such sculptors as Daniel Chester French and Karl Bitter and in elaborate interior murals completed under the supervision of John La Farge. Similar principles guided the design of the borough courthouse at East 161st Street and Brook Avenue in the Bronx (1906, Michael Garvin) and the county courthouse on Richmond Terrace in Staten Island (1913–19, Carrère and Hastings).

In 1912 Guy Lowell won a competition to design a county courthouse to replace Tweed. His entry called for a monumental scale, austere details, and a circular plan with traditional elements such as exterior stairs, classical porticos, and allegorical sculptures. The proposed site at City Hall Park was opposed by many who feared that the new building would detract from City Hall, and in 1915 Lowell and the city chose the area now known as Foley Square. Concerns about expense forced Lowell to make his design smaller and hexagonal, though he retained the stairs, portico, sculpture, and austerity of the first design. The rotunda and interior balcony were decorated with a cycle of frescos, *Law through the Ages* (1936–38, Attilo Pusterla). After the courthouse was completed in 1926 a cluster of others were built in Foley Square; Lowell's innovations inspired the plans for several. Cass Gilbert integrated a skyscraper with a base similar to that of the county courthouse in his design for the federal courthouse (1936). In planning the state criminal courts building (1939; also known as "the Tombs") Harvey Wiley Corbett rejected traditional styles for a setback shape and a simplicity typical of American skyscrapers of the 1920s. He also included a huge granite base that made an abstract portico at the entrance. For the appellate court building on Monroe Place and Pierrepont Street in Brooklyn (1937) the firm of Slee and Bryson adopted pared down versions of traditional elements, including a short stairway leading to a door flanked by two Doric columns, and sculptural medallions across the attic depicting figures associated with the judiciary. Foley Square was extended by the civil courthouse (1960, William Lescaze), in which a modern metal-and-glass, non-load-bearing "curtain wall" made up the exterior; the development of the square continued to the end of the 1980s.

Robert A. M. Stern, Gregory Gilmartin, and John Montague Massengale: *New York 1900: Metropolitan Architecture and Urbanism, 1890–1915* (New York: Rizzoli, 1983)

Robert A. M. Stern, Gregory F. Gilmartin, and Thomas Mellins: *New York 1930: Architecture and Urbanism between the Two World Wars* (New York: Rizzoli, 1987)

Mary Beth Betts

courts. New York City was the site of municipal courts early in its history and of the principal state courts until Albany became the state capital in 1797. A number of important federal cases have been heard in the city, notably by the U.S. District Court for the Southern District of New York.

1. Municipal

On the orders of the Dutch government a court was organized in New Amsterdam in 1653, despite the objections of the colonial director, Peter Stuyvesant. This consisted of a schout, who prosecuted cases and executed the court's orders and judgments, two burgomasters, and five schepens (aldermen), all appointed by the colonial director. Similar courts were soon set up in Harlem and the five Dutch towns in what is now Brooklyn. In 1665 Governor Richard Nicolls replaced the Dutch magistrates with a mayor, five aldermen, and a sheriff, who together formed the mayor's court. From 1684 the mayor and aldermen and a recorder held a court of sessions to try felonies, misdemeanors, and ordinance violations. The charter promulgated by Governor Thomas Dongan (1686) designated the mayor's court a court of common pleas with common-law jurisdiction over contract, tort, and property disputes; it consisted of the mayor and recorder (one presided) and at least two of the aldermen. Under the charter of Governor Richard Montgomerie (1730) the court was retained, but magistrates also were empowered to try civil cases where the plaintiff sued for less than 40*s*. Through acts in 1732 and 1744 the assembly empowered magistrates to hold a special court of sessions to try minor offenders who were unable to post bail within two days of arrest (persons convicted were publicly flogged).

The city courts were suspended between 1776 and 1783, when the civilian population of the city and Long Island was subject to courts-martial by the occupying British forces. Soon after it resumed in early 1784 the mayor's court tried the case of *Rutgers v. Waddington*, in which Alexander Hamilton defended the wartime tenant of a brewery against a suit by its previous owner for back rent. Mayor James Duane's ruling to award only partial damages weakened the state's Trespass Act (aimed at Loyalists) and helped

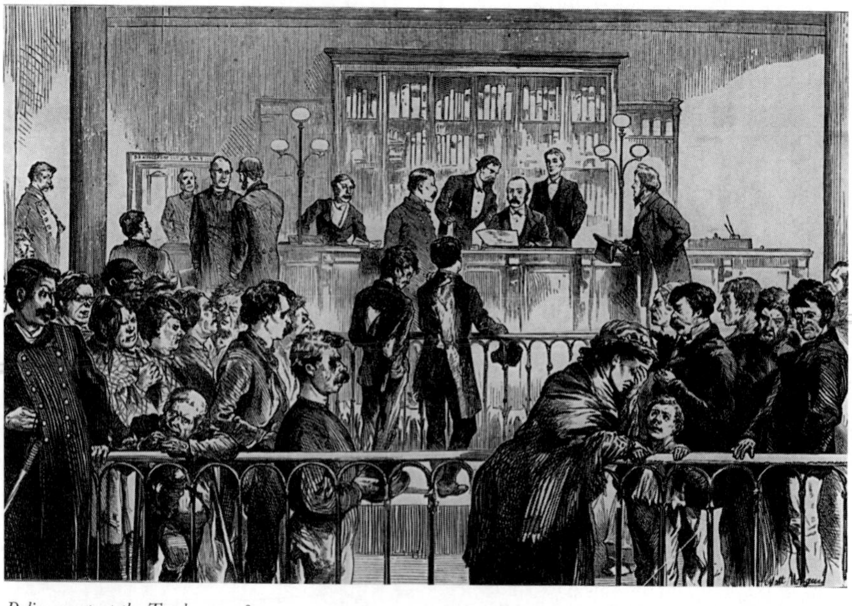

Police court at the Tombs, ca *1870*

to establish the principle of judicial review of legislation. The city's rapid growth led to the formation of lower civil courts. Under a statute of 1782 magistrates were permitted to try lawsuits involving claims of less than £10. From 1787 courts for such cases were presided over by assistant justices, who in 1800 were granted jurisdiction over lawsuits between seamen and ship captains or owners. Reorganized as a justice's court in 1807, the assistant justice's court was renamed the marine court in 1819; in this court seamen could have a jury trial and plead their cases orally instead of filing written pleadings. Its civil jurisdiction was increased at intervals, reaching $2000 by 1875. Assistant justices' courts established in 1807 were the lowest civil courts, organized initially by wards and later by districts; from 1822 the assistant justices were appointed by the Common Council, and in 1852 the courts were renamed the district courts. The lowest criminal tribunal, the police court, was formally named the police office in 1798 and was overseen by "police justices" who issued warrants, arraigned suspects, granted bail, and in lieu of bail committed arrested individuals to jail pending trial; they were appointed by the Common Council from 1797. Corporal punishment for misdemeanors was limited by statutes in 1785 and 1789 and abolished in 1801 (hard labor or fines were substituted).

The city's court system continued to grow during the nineteenth century. In 1821 the mayor's court was renamed the court of common pleas, and the mayor had long since ceased to preside over it. A chief judge and associate judges were appointed instead (Charles P. Daly served variously in both capacities for forty-one years), and aldermen were removed in 1847. The Village of Brooklyn had justices of the peace and in 1827 received a municipal court to handle civil cases. In 1828 a superior court began operation in New York City to handle a backlog of civil cases from the court of common pleas and the supreme court. After 1847 its jurisdiction and that of the court of common pleas were the same, giving the city three higher civil courts (common pleas, superior, and supreme), each with its own judges, clerks, trial and appellate terms, and case reports. They sometimes handed down conflicting decisions, and under the state constitution of 1894 the superior and common pleas courts were merged into the supreme court, effective in 1896. There were three levels of criminal courts. The court of general sessions tried felony cases: the recorder presided and any two of the common pleas judges, the mayor, and the aldermen completed the bench. The court of special sessions tried misdemeanors and ordinance violations and unlike its equivalents in the rest of the state had no juries but rather a panel of three judges. This consisted of the recorder and two common pleas judges from

Court System in New York City

NAME OF COURT	JURISDICTION	APPEALS TO
Civil Courts (arranged chronologically)		
Mayor's Court, 1665–73, 1674–1821[1] (also known as Court of Common Pleas after 1686)	Civil and Criminal	Court of Assizes, 1665–73, 1674–84; Court of Oyer and Terminer, 1683–91; Supreme Court after 1691
Court of Common Pleas, 1821–95 (merged into Supreme Court)	Civil	Court of Common Pleas (General Term), 1848–95; Supreme Court (General Term), 1828–48, 1877–95; Court of Appeals, 1848–77
Superior Court, 1828–95 (merged into Supreme Court)	Civil (commercial)	Superior Court (General Term), 1848–95; Supreme Court (General Term), 1828–48, 1877–95; Court of Appeals, 1848–77
Assistant Justices' Courts, 1787–97 (succeeded by Justices' Courts)	Limited civil	Supreme Court
Justices' Courts, 1797–1819	Limited civil; marine after 1800	Supreme Court
Marine Court, 1819–83 (succeeded by City Court)	Intermediate[2] civil; marine	Supreme Court, 1819–28; Superior Court, 1828–53; Marine Court (General Term),[3] 1853–83; Court of Common Pleas (General Term), 1853–83
City Court, 1883–1962 (succeeded by Civil Court)	Intermediate civil; marine	City Court (General Term), 1883–1902; Court of Common Pleas (General Term), 1883–95; Supreme Court (Appellate Division), 1896– 1902/14; Supreme Court (Appellate Term), 1902–62 (New York, Bronx[4] counties), 1914–62 (Kings, Queens, Richmond counties)
Assistant Justices' Courts, 1807–52 (succeeded by District Courts)	Limited civil	Supreme Court, 1807–18; Court of Common Pleas, 1818–28; Superior Court, 1828–52
District Courts, 1852–98 (succeeded by Municipal Court)	Limited civil	Superior Court (General Term), 1852–77; Court of Common Pleas (General Term), 1877–95; Supreme Court (Appellate Division), 1896–98
Municipal Court, 1898–1962 (succeeded by Civil Court)	Limited civil; small claims after 1934	Supreme Court (Appellate Division), 1898–1902/11; Supreme Court (Appellate Term), 1902–62 (New York, Bronx counties), 1911–62 (Kings, Queens, Richmond counties)
Civil Court, 1962–	Limited civil; small claims	Supreme Court (Appellate Term)
Criminal Courts (arranged chronologically)		
Court of Special Sessions, 1732–1962 (succeeded by Criminal Court)	Limited criminal	Court of General Sessions to 1895; Supreme Court (General Term), 1895; Supreme Court (Appellate Division)
"Police Court," 1798–1895 (succeeded by Magistrates' Court)	Limited criminal	Court of General Sessions
Magistrates' Courts, 1895–1962 (succeeded by Criminal Court)	Limited criminal	Court of General Sessions, or (outside New York county) County Court, 1895–1922; Court of Special Sessions (Appellate Part), 1922–62

(continued)

Court System in New York City (*Continued*)

NAME OF COURT	JURISDICTION	APPEALS TO
Criminal Court, 1962–	Limited criminal	Supreme Court (Appellate Term)
Family Court (branch of Magistrates' Court), 1918–33 (merged into Domestic Relations Court)	Family	Same as Magistrates' Court
Children's Court, 1924–33 (formerly branch of Court of Special Sessions; merged into Domestic Relations Court)	Juvenile	Supreme Court (Appellate Division)
Domestic Relations Court, 1933–62 (succeeded by Family Court: see table of New York State courts)	Family and Juvenile	Supreme Court (Appellate Division)

1. The Mayor's Court was also known as the Court of Common Pleas from 1868. In 1821 the name was legally changed to Court of Common Pleas, as the mayor no longer presided.
2. Intermediate and limited civil jurisdiction were defined in terms of the value of cases heard by each court.
3. General Term courts were appellate panels, in this case selected from the Marine Court and in others selected from other courts. For clarity the General Terms of the Marine Court, Superior Court, and Court of Common Pleas have been omitted from this table.
4. Bronx County existed legally from 1898, although it was not organized until 1914.

Compiled by James D. Folts with the assistance of Kevin Kenny

1830 until 1858, when they were replaced by the police justices. In 1849 the courts in Brooklyn were reorganized so that justices of the peace tried small civil cases, and police justices held preliminary hearings and courts of special sessions. A city court with higher civil and criminal local jurisdiction equivalent to that of the supreme court was also formed and in 1896 was merged into the supreme court.

The selection of judges became a highly contentious issue during the mid nineteenth century. Until that time magistrates in New York City were not locally elected or appointed. The recorder and the judges of the common pleas, superior, and marine courts were appointed by the governor with the consent of the state senate, until statutes between 1847 and 1850 made these and the police justices elective. From 1848 the police justices were assigned to districts, and in 1860 a board of police justices was formed to supervise the system. By the 1860s Tammany Hall controlled the judicial nominations for the police and district courts and filled court jobs at all levels with party hacks and no-shows. Many cases were dismissed by the recorder John Hackett and the superior court judge John McCunn, both chosen by the Tweed Ring, in exchange for political favors and bribes. The police courts were especially lax and corrupt, and after the fall of the Tweed Ring in 1873 the police justices ceased to be elected and were instead appointed by the mayor, who remained the city's chief magistrate; aldermen were barred from becoming police justices.

Efforts at reorganization and reform began during the last decades of the nineteenth century. In 1883 the marine court was renamed the city court. Problems in the police courts recurred, leading to an investigation of them (and the police force) during the 1890s by Senator Clarence Lexow that began a municipal reform movement. In 1895 the police courts were replaced by magistrates' courts and a separate court of special sessions was also established, its justices appointed by the mayor. After 1892 state law required that children under sixteen charged with crimes be detained and tried separately from adults, and between 1902 and 1910 children's courts opened in each borough as divisions of the court of special sessions. After consolidation in 1898 the city court replaced the district and justice's courts in Brooklyn and Long Island City, and the magistrates' and special sessions courts of New York City were extended to Brooklyn, Queens, and Staten Island, which continued to have their own county courts. Specialized magistrates' courts were set up after 1900, among them a women's court (1910) in Manhattan and the Bronx to handle prostitution cases; night, felony, and homicide courts for arraignments; and traffic, probation, gambler's, and commercial-frauds courts to relieve the caseloads of the district magistrates' courts. Despite these structural changes ethical problems remained. A legislative commission under Alfred R. Page in 1910 criticized the treatment of women and children in magistrates' courts and recommended improvements in decorum and facilities; legislative acts during the same year and in 1915 provided for better administration. The children's court became a separate division with its own probation department in 1915, and a family court opened in 1918 as a division of the magistrates' court to handle spousal and child-support cases.

Reorganization efforts continued during the following decades. After 1914 the Bronx had its own county court. During state constitutional conventions in 1915 and 1921 proposals were made to combine the city's lower civil courts and abolish the four county courts; these were voted down by the public, but under a constitutional amendment in 1925 the civil jurisdiction of the county courts was transferred to the city court, effective in 1927. The children's court became independent in 1924 and was given jurisdiction over juvenile criminals and delinquents, as well as cases of child neglect. From this time the courts of general and special sessions tried criminal defendants between the ages of sixteen and nineteen as "youthful offenders," with probation the usual outcome. Public policy increasingly directed the court to rehabilitate young offenders rather than punish them, and after 1932 the children's court ceased to follow the procedure and use the standards of proof that prevailed in criminal courts. In 1932 Judge Samuel Seabury issued a report on the magistrates' courts and found that bribery, extortion, and the use of political influence were widespread. A domestic relations court was set up to administer the family and children's courts in 1933. Branches of the magistrates' courts known as adolescent courts opened in Brooklyn and Queens in the 1930s and later in the other boroughs to try youths between the ages of sixteen and eighteen as "wayward minors"; these were intended to separate minors from older and more hardened offenders but failed to stem the rise in juvenile crime after the Second World War. In 1934 a small-claims division of the municipal court was formed to clear a backlog of small suits. During the same year the women's court was extended citywide.

After the war the city's caseload increased rapidly, first in automobile accident claims and later in criminal and family cases. From 1951 jurisdiction over delinquent girls between the ages of sixteen and twenty was given to a girls' term. The city courts were hampered by overlapping jurisdictions and uncoordinated administration, and in 1955 a state commission under Harrison Tweed recommended the consolidation of all the city's lower civil and criminal courts into one court. The plan failed, largely because of opposition from politicians who relied on the courts to distribute patronage, but reorganization was finally mandated under a constitutional amendment in 1961. From September 1962 the Court of Special Sessions and the magistrates' courts were merged into a criminal court responsible for trying misdemeanors and ordinance violations, and for preliminary felony hearings; the mayor was empowered to appoint the judges to serve for ten years. The court of general sessions of New York County and the four other county courts were abolished, their criminal business transferred to the supreme court, and the domestic relations court was replaced by a statewide family court. The city court and the municipal court were merged in 1962 into a civil court responsible for lawsuits as great as $25,000 and overseen by judges elected to ten-year terms. The women's court was abolished in 1967. Cases involving minor traffic and housing codes were removed from the criminal courts: from 1970 moving violations were handled by the state department of motor vehicles, and in 1972 a housing section of the civil court was formed to handle housing code and rent cases. The development of a statewide judicial administration during the 1970s helped to unify the city's court system. A deputy administrative judge supervised all state and local courts in the city after 1974 and assigned judges wherever needed; after 1977 the state assumed all operating costs for the city courts.

2. State

New York City was the seat of the major colonial and state courts until 1797, when the capital was moved to Albany. The "Duke's Laws" of 1665, issued under authority of the Duke of York, set up a court of assizes composed of the governor, his council, and other officials that met yearly in the city to try important cases. It was replaced in 1683 with county courts of oyer and terminer empowered by the first colonial assembly to "hear and determine" major criminal and civil cases; they were composed of two provincial judges and designated local magistrates. A court of chancery handled matters of equity including injunction, the foreclosure of mortgages, the discovery of evidence, and the appointment and supervision of trustees. It held its sessions in New York City from 1683 and had the royal governor as its chancellor. Probate jurisdiction was vested in the colonial governor and (after 1691) his delegate or "surrogate."

An act of the assembly in 1691 replaced the courts of oyer and terminer with a supreme court of judicature possessing all the civil, criminal, and appellate jurisdictions of English common-law courts; court terms were held in the city by an appointed chief justice and two associates. The act also established courts of common pleas (civil) and sessions (criminal) in each county. In 1692 the assembly empowered a supreme court justice to preside over circuit courts in each county and try major civil and criminal cases. The governor objected to the assembly's attempts to reenact the judiciary act of 1691, and after 1698 ordinances of the governor were the legal basis for the supreme and chancery courts. English court procedure was introduced rapidly, allowing the city's merchants to use the courts to collect debts more easily.

Court System in New York State, 1777–1847

COURT	JURISDICTION	APPEALS TO
Court for the Correction of Errors	Final Appeals and Impeachment	
Supreme Court, General Term	Intermediate Appeals	Court for the Correction of Errors
Supreme Court		
Circuit Courts	Civil	Supreme Court, General Term
Courts of Oyer and Terminer	Criminal	Supreme Court, General Term
Court of Exchequer (to 1823)	Fines and Penalties	Supreme Court, General Term
Court of Chancery	Civil (Equity)	Court for the Correction of Errors
Court of Probates (to 1823)	Probate	Court of Chancery
Surrogate Courts (after 1787)	Probate	Court of Probates (to 1823); Court of Chancery (1823–47)
Courts of Common Pleas	Civil	Supreme Court, General Term
Courts of Sessions	Criminal	Supreme Court, General Term
Justices of the Peace Courts (to 1824) Courts of Common Pleas (after 1824)	Limited Civil	Supreme Court, General Term
Courts of Special Sessions (to 1824) Courts of Common Pleas (after 1824)	Limited Criminal	Supreme Court, General Term
City and Village Courts	Limited Civil and Criminal	Various

Court System in New York State, after 1847

COURT	JURISDICTION	APPEALS TO
Court of Appeals	Final Appeals	
Court of Appeals, Second Division (1888–96)	Appeals	Court of Appeals
Court for the Trial of Impeachments	Impeachment	Court of Appeals
Supreme Court, General Term (to 1896) Supreme Court, Appellate Division (after 1896)	Intermediate Appeals	Court of Appeals
Supreme Court, Appellate Term (after 1896)	Intermediate Appeals	Supreme Court, Appellate Division (civil matters) Court of Appeals (criminal matters)
Supreme Court		
Circuit Courts (to 1896) Trial Term, Civil (after 1896)	Civil	Supreme Court, General Term or Appellate Division
Courts of Oyer and Terminer (to 1896) Trial Term, Criminal (after 1896)	Criminal	Supreme Court, General Term or Appellate Division
Special Term (to 1958)	Civil (Equity)	Supreme Court, General Term or Appellate Division
County Courts Supreme Court, Appellate Term, for certain criminal matters, Long Island	Civil and Criminal	Supreme Court, General Term or Appellate Division
Courts of Sessions (absorbed by county courts, 1896)	Criminal	Supreme Court, General Term
Children's Court (1922–62)	Juvenile and Family	Supreme Court, Appellate Division
Family Court (after 1962)	Juvenile and Family	Supreme Court, Appellate Division

(*continued*)

Court System in New York State, 1777–1847 *(Continued)*

COURT	JURISDICTION	APPEALS TO
Surrogate Courts	Probate	Supreme Court, General Term or Appellate Division or Appellate Term
City Courts	Limited Civil and Criminal	County Courts; Supreme Court, Appellate Term, Long Island
Town and Village Justice Courts	Limited Civil and Criminal	County Courts; Supreme Court, Appellate Term, Long Island
District Courts (Long Island only, after 1973)	Limited Civil and Criminal	Supreme Court, Appellate Term

Compiled by James D. Folts with the assistance of Kevin Kenny

Political trials were often given much attention. One of the most divisive began in 1733, when the incoming governor, William Cosby, sued the acting governor, Rip Van Dam, for back salary. He ordered the Supreme Court to sit as a court of exchequer so that the case could be tried without a jury. The chief justice, Lewis Morris, challenged the legality of this arrangement and was dismissed (James de Lancey replaced him), prompting him and his supporters to launch the *New-York Weekly Journal*, a publication dedicated to attacking Cosby. Cosby bypassed the grand jury in having the editor, Peter Zenger, charged with seditious libel. In the trial that followed, Zenger was defended by Andrew Hamilton, a lawyer from Philadelphia who won the case by arguing brilliantly for freedom of the press and for the jury's right to decide not only the fact of publication but also the truth of the libel. The supreme court was at the center of controversy again during the 1760s, when a political faction led by the Livingston family opposed the plan of Cadwallader Colden, the acting governor, to appoint supreme court justices to serve at pleasure rather than for life. Colden stubbornly sought to review on appeal the facts as well as the law in *Forsey v. Cunningham*, a case argued before the Supreme Court, but failed and was denounced by the provincial élite for undermining the right of juries to determine facts.

Under the state constitution of 1777 the trial court system was retained unchanged and a court was added for the correction of errors, replacing the governor and council as the highest appellate court. During the colonial period the governor had served as chancellor and set up the court of chancery without legislative consent. After 1778 there was an appointive chancellor. In 1787 the court of chancery was given jurisdiction over divorce cases and a surrogate's court was established in each county. Until 1823 a court of probates heard appeals from the county surrogates' courts and supervised the settlement of estates of persons who had died out of state. The office of public administrator opened in 1799 to settle estates of city residents without heirs. The constitution of 1822 authorized the appointment of circuit judges in eight circuits; these judges visited each county to try civil cases originating in the supreme court and to hold courts of oyer and terminer for felonies, including all capital crimes (New York City was in the first circuit). The supreme court heard appeals from the lower courts and ruled on points of law raised in the circuit courts. From 1823 equity powers were divided between the court of chancery and a supreme court circuit judge or a vice-chancellor assigned to New York.

During the 1820s William Sampson and Henry D. Sedgwick, prominent lawyers in the city, called for a reform of the state's antiquated common-law court procedure; a code of civil procedure became law in 1848. Under the constitution of 1846 the state courts were reorganized, and from 1847 an elective court of appeals replaced the court of errors as the highest appellate court. An elective supreme court was established in 1847 to combine law and equity jurisdictions. A second division of the court of appeals was established in the city to handle a large backlog of cases between 1889 and 1892. Supreme court justices appointed to hear appeals in a general term took appeals from higher trial courts, while appeals from the superior and common pleas courts in New York County and from the city court in Brooklyn went directly to the court of appeals. Circuit courts and courts of oyer and terminer remained the county-level trial terms of the supreme court until 1896, from which time the supreme court justices continued to preside over trial terms of the supreme court in each county.

The state constitution of 1894 established a supreme court appellate division, which began operation in 1896 and had in its first department New York County (and later Bronx County as well) and in its second Kings, Queens, and Richmond counties. A court of claims was formed in 1897 to handle claims against the state, holding sessions in New York City.

The early twentieth century saw the construction of several court buildings, among them the ornate courthouse of the supreme court appellate division (first department) at 27 Madison Avenue in 1900, the Queens County courthouse in Long Island City (1908), and the Hall of Records on Chambers Street (1911), erected to house the many books and files of the surrogate's court of New York County, the busiest in the state. Special terms were added in the first and second departments to hear appeals from the city and municipal courts in 1914 and later from the court of special sessions as well. A number of courts moved to new quarters during the following decades: the Richmond County courthouse (1919) replaced a courthouse erected in Richmondtown in 1839; the New York County supreme court building on Foley Square (1927) took over the functions of the courthouse built under William M. "Boss" Tweed from 1861 to 1872; and new quarters were assumed by the Bronx County civil courts (in the county building, opened in 1934), the Bronx County appellate division, second department (in a building at 45 Monroe Place in Brooklyn, 1938), the supreme court of Queens County (in a building completed in Jamaica in 1939), and the supreme court of Kings County (in the civic center, 1957). In response to a report prepared by James A. Foley, the New York County surrogate, practice of the surrogate's court and the law of estates was reformed during the 1930s.

Justices are elected to the state supreme court by district to fourteen-year terms. The districts in New York City are nos. 1 (New York County), 2 (Kings and Richmond counties), 11 (Queens County, established 1963), and 12 (the Bronx, established 1983).

3. Federal

The most important federal court in New York City is that for the Southern District of New York State. Its precursor, the U.S. District Court of New York, was established under the Judiciary Act of 1789 as the first federal court to meet under the Constitution (the Supreme Court did not meet until February 1790). It convened on 3 November 1789, in the Exchange Building on Broad Street, across from Fraunces Tavern. Like the Admiralty Court in Britain the court had jurisdiction over cases arising under the Constitution and federal statutes, admiralty and maritime cases, disputes between citizens of different states and between states and the federal government, and all "Controversies to which the United States shall be a Party." President Washington appointed the distinguished lawyer James Duane as the court's first justice; among the attorneys admitted to practice in the court on its first day were Alexander Hamilton and Aaron Burr. The number of cases was at first small but grew so rapidly that on 9 April 1814 Congress divided the court into the Northern and Southern districts of New York State. The earliest cases dealt with admiralty and maritime law, and in both precedent and practice the court followed the tradition of the British Admiralty Court in the Province of New York. The court inherited the records of the British court as well, and these cases involved piracy and privateers (such as letters of marque from the French and Indian War), the treatment of seamen (who often had to sue ships' owners and captains for their wages), and smuggling or other violations of the Navigation, Townshend, Sugar, and Tea acts. Many cases involved American ships trading with French and Dutch ports in the Caribbean. When the British confiscated a ship and its cargo on charges of smuggling, officials responsible for enforcing the law often acquired the goods at auction, a blatant conflict of interest that fed the growing discontent of colonial merchants in the years before the American Revolution. Precedents established in the admiralty court remained in force after independence. During the undeclared naval war with France, the USS *Constitution* brought a captured merchantman into New York Harbor and asked the court to declare it a legitimate prize of war, the proceeds from its sale to be distributed among the officers and crew. This traditional law of the sea remained in practice as late as the Civil War, when ships of the U.S. Navy brought in captured Confederate blockade runners as prizes. Other maritime cases involved accidents at sea. The court was the venue for lawsuits against owners of the *Titanic*, the *Lusitania*, and the *Andrea Doria*, and for a number of obscenity cases: under federal law the court was responsible for determining whether materials imported into the United States were obscene or indecent. In the nineteenth century the articles in question included books, photographs, playing cards, and drugs, articles, and medicines "used for the prevention of conception or for causing unlawful abortion." The court ruled in 1932 that D. H. Lawrence's *Lady Chatterley's Lover* was obscene and in 1939 that James Joyce's *Ulysses* was not. During the First World War John Reed was among many who were indicted on charges of sedition. In 1919 Emma Goldman was deported to Russia as an "alien anarchist" after her writ of habeas corpus was denied in the court. Her lawyer had unsuccessfully argued that an individual could not be deported for an "attitude of mind or the holding of political, social or economic views, or the expression thereof." The court was the venue during the Second World War for the prosecution of Fritz Kuhn, leader of the German American Bund, and during the "red scare" after the war for the perjury trial of Alger Hiss and the espionage trial of Julius and Ethel Rosenberg. It also heard a large number of cases in corporate law, antitrust law (including the landmark prosecution of the American Tobacco Company), and bankruptcy (including those of Mathew Brady and the City Housing Corporation). During Prohibition there were prosecutions under the Volstead Act, ranging from those for the sale of a single glass of beer to the tax evasion trial of Dutch Schultz. In the area of patent law and copyright infringement Thomas Edison, Rudyard Kipling, Irving Berlin, and the creators of the Lone Ranger, Mickey Mouse, and Batman have all at one time or another asked the court to protect their copyrights.

Congress created the U.S. District Court for the Eastern District of New York in 1865, splitting Long Island and Staten Island from the Southern District of New York, but both courts held jurisdiction over the harbor. The first judge appointed to the bench of the new court was Charles Linnaeus Benedict; the number of judgeships was later increased to two in 1910, six in 1940 (after Prohibition and the Depression had swelled the caseload), and eight in 1960. The courthouse is in downtown Brooklyn. A second courthouse that opened in Westbury (Nassau County) in 1971 moved in 1981 to Uniondale, and a third courthouse opened in Hauppauge (Suffolk County) in 1987. Major cases tried in the Eastern District of New York include *Schechter Poultry Corp. v. United States* (1935), which resulted in a ruling that the National Industrial Recovery Act was unconstitutional; a case concerning the deplorable conditions for the severely retarded at the Willowbrook State Development Center on Staten Island (1975); the successful challenge to the constitutionality of the Board of Estimate; the bribery trials of Meade Esposito (Democratic leader in Brooklyn) and Representative Mario Biaggi; the mail fraud and extortion trial of Joseph Margiotta (Republican leader of Nassau County); the bribery trial of Judge William Brennan of the New York State Supreme Court; the prosecutions in the "Abscam" case (a "sting" operation by the Federal Bureau of Investigation in which federal officials took bribes); *Beekman v. City of New York* (1979), which challenged the physical examination administered by the Fire Department of New York on the grounds that it discriminated against women; *Arthur v. Starrett City*, over the use of quotas to maintain racial balance in a housing complex; and the prosecution of the Puerto Rican terrorist organization Fuerzas Armadas de Liberación Nacional (FALN) for as many as thirty bombings in New York City.

David McAdam, ed.: *History of the Bench and Bar of New York* (New York: New York History Company, 1897)
Alden Chester: *Courts and Lawyers of New York: A History, 1609–1925* (New York: American Historical Society, 1925)
Richard B. Morris, ed.: *Select Cases of the Mayor's Court of New York City, 1674–1784* (Washington: American Historical Association, 1935)
Anna M. Kross: "Magistrates' Courts of the City of New York," *Brooklyn Law Review* 7 (1937–38), 133–79, 295–341
Alfred J. Kahn: *A Court for Children: A Study of the New York City Children's Court* (New York: Columbia University Press, 1953)
Bad Housekeeping: The Administration of the New York Courts (New York: Association of the Bar of the City of New York, n.d. [?1955])
Joseph H. Smith and Leo Hershkowitz: "Courts of Equity in the Province of New York: The Cosby Controversy, 1732–1736," *American Journal of Legal History* 16 (1972), 1–50

James D. Folts (§§1–2), Jeffrey A. Kroessler (§3)

Covello, Leonard (*b* Avigliano, Italy, 26 Nov 1887; *d* Italy, 19 Aug 1982). Teacher and principal. At nine he moved to East Harlem, where he found schools indifferent or hostile to Italians. He became a high school language teacher in 1913 and in 1922 persuaded officials to make Italian an elective language; he also advocated academic rather than vocational education for Italians. In 1934 he was appointed the first principal of Benjamin Franklin High School, which he made an inclusive school despite racial tensions in East Harlem. On his retirement in 1956 he became the educational consultant to the Puerto Rican Migration Division and continued to write about education. He returned to Italy in 1972. Covello wrote a memoir, *The Heart Is the Teacher* (1958).

Mary Elizabeth Brown

Covenant House. A nonprofit charitable organization that operates shelters for homeless and runaway youths. The first was opened in 1968 by Bruce Ritter, a Franciscan friar, in two abandoned tenements in the East Village. The organization opened several shelters throughout New York City, including one on 41st Street near Times Square kept open twenty-four hours a day, and an outreach center on West 44th Street. In 1990 Ritter was forced to resign amid allegations of sexual and financial misconduct, which he vigorously denied. Covenant House is the largest organization in the world devoted to helping teenage runaways, of whom it serves some 25,000 a year through its shelters in the United States, Canada, and Latin America.

Mary Rose McGeady: *God's Lost Children: Letters from Covenant House* (New York: Covenant House, 1991)

Frank Morrow

Cowley, (David) Malcolm (*b* Belsano, Penn., 24 Aug 1898; *d* New Milford, Conn., 27 March 1989). Writer, editor, and literary historian. In 1934 he published *Exile's Return*, which came to be regarded as the definitive chronicle of the 1920s. He helped to organize the first American Writer's Congress in 1935 and was active in its offshoot the League of American Writers. From the early 1930s to November 1935 he lived in an apartment at 360 West 22nd Street. Cowley was largely responsible for bringing critical recognition to Faulkner by editing a collection of his works in 1946.

B. Kimberly Taylor

Craft Museum. See AMERICAN CRAFT MUSEUM.

Crane, Stephen (*b* Newark, N.J., 1 Nov 1871; *d* Badenweiler, Germany, 5 June 1900). Novelist. He attended Lafayette College and Syracuse University but left college at his mother's death in 1890. He soon moved to New York City, where as a writer for such newspapers as the *New York Herald* and the *New York Tribune* he lived on East 23rd Street and became acquainted with life in the streets and saloons. His first novel, *Maggie: A Girl of the Streets*, was printed in 1892 with money borrowed from his brother and was poorly received; his next, *The Red Badge of Courage*, was serialized by a newspaper in Philadelphia, widely praised, and published by D. Appleton in 1895. He published a volume of poems, *The Black Riders*, during the same year and made trips to the American West and to Cuba that inspired a number of short stories. At this time he lived at 165 West 23rd Street. A stint as a correspondent for the *New York World* during the Spanish–American War provided material for *Wounds in the Rain* (1900), a collection of war sketches. Crane returned to the city in broken health and in 1899 moved to England. He died of tuberculosis.

James B. Colvert: *Stephen Crane* (New York: Harcourt Brace Jovanovich, 1984)

See also LITERATURE, §1.

James E. Mooney

Crater, Joseph F(orce) (*b* Easton, Penn., 1889; *d* ?1930). Judge. He earned a law degree at Columbia Law School, opened a private practice that became successful, and took up quarters at 40 5th Avenue; he also became politically active and was made president of the Cayuga Democratic Club, an organization closely associated with Tammany Hall. In April 1930 he was appointed to the state supreme court by Governor Franklin D. Roosevelt. After dinner at a restaurant in Manhattan on 6 August he stepped into a taxicab with about $5000 in his wallet, waved goodbye to a friend, and disappeared. An investigation by a grand jury hinted at corruption in the Cayuga Club; Crater was never found.

James E. Mooney

Cravath, Swaine and Moore. Law firm established in New York City as Blatchford, Seward and Griswold in 1854 by the merger of the practices of Richard M. Blatchford (formed in New York City in 1819) and Judge Elijah Miller and William H. Seward (formed in Auburn, New York, in 1823). The firm settled patent, real estate, trust, and estate matters, conducted litigation, and represented the Bank of England in the United States. After the Civil War its major clients included express companies, and from the 1880s it enlarged its reputation for expertise in finance and corporate law. In 1899 Paul D. Cravath (1861–1940), a graduate of Oberlin College in 1882 and Columbia Law School in 1886, developed a new corporate structure and training system, and in 1906 the firm became Cravath, Henderson and de Gersdorff. During the 1920s and 1930s litigation, tax work, antitrust cases, and securities matters were emphasized. The firm represented Westinghouse, Bethlehem Steel, the Royal Dutch–Shell Group, and Kuhn, Loeb and Company. After being reorganized in 1944 under its current name the firm greatly increased its litigation practice and in the 1970s and 1980s entered the field of mergers and acquisitions. In the mid 1990s Cravath, Swaine and Moore remained one of the oldest and largest law firms in the city, with 343 lawyers and a clientele that included blue-chip corporations, financial organizations, and government agencies.

Robert T. Swaine: *The Cravath Firm and Its Predecessors, 1819–1948* (New York: Ad Press, 1946–48)

Marilyn Tobias

Crazy Eddie. Chain of retail electronics stores opened by Eddie Antar, an entrepreneur from Brooklyn and the grandson of Syrian immigrants. It began as a store that Antar opened in Brooklyn in 1969, which sold a large volume of electronic equipment (mainly televisions and stereos) nearly at cost. The firm prospered during the early 1980s with the rising popularity of video cassette recorders; more stores were opened throughout the metropolitan area, and a number of television commercials were made featuring Jerry Carroll, who waved his arms and frantically screamed: "Crazy Eddie's prices are insane!" At its peak the chain consisted of forty-three stores and had $350 million in assets. Sales declined from late 1986 and the firm filed for bankruptcy protection in 1989. Antar was arrested in Israel in June 1992 on suspicion of having passports under three names and of carrying millions of dollars stolen from the stockholders of Crazy Eddie; he was later sentenced to twelve and a half years in prison for fraud and ordered to repay $121 million in restitution.

Melissa M. Merritt

credit institutions. Credit institutions other than banks were very common in New York City in the eighteenth and nineteenth centuries. They usually charged higher interest than banks, but unlike banks they did not require borrowers to renew notes every sixty days. Among the many loan societies that offered this service were the Friendly Club (1770), the Friendly Brothers of St. Patrick (1774), and the Mutual Benefit Society (1805). The managers of the Society for the Prevention of Pauperism opened a Saving Fuel Fund Society in 1818 to encourage the poor to invest their money in benefit societies. Many ethnic mutual aid societies were formed to assist immigrants, including the German Society of the City of New York (1804) and the New York Irish Emigrant Association (1817); the Native American Association (1835) catered to anyone except immigrants. Many insurance companies also functioned as creditors. The Atlantic Mutual Insurance Company (1824) provided marine insurance, advanced money on stocks, and made loans on mortgages; a second firm of the same name was formed in 1829 and became the Atlantic Mutual Insurance Company in 1842. In the 1830s the New York Life Insurance and Trust Company made loans on stocks and bonds and offered mortgages to farmers. The stocks were assigned as collateral and the borrower's note was made payable on demand; if the stock depreciated, the company reduced the amount of the loan or sold the stock. The Provident Loan Society offered credit from 1894, when it was formed in New York City by the Charity Organization Society. In the commercial sector most importing and exporting was based on credit: the Merchants Association of New York, incorporated in 1897, aided merchants in their transactions.

Robert Greenhalgh Albion: *The Rise of New York Port, 1815–1860* (New York: Charles Scribner's Sons, 1939; repr. Newton Abbot, England: David and Charles, 1970)

J. Carroll Moody and Gilbert C. Fite: *The Credit Union Movement: Origins and Development, 1850–1970* (Lincoln: University of Nebraska Press, 1971; 2nd edn Dubuque, Iowa: Kendall/Hunt, 1984)

Mary Ann Romano

credit unions. The first credit union in New York City was organized in 1914 by the employees of Bing and Bing after the Russell Sage Foundation had prevailed on New York State to make credit unions legal. In the following year there were nineteen credit unions in the state, eleven of which were in New York City. Mayor John Purroy Mitchel organized a credit union in 1916 for municipal workers to end the practice of garnishing their salaries, and during the 1920s credit unions increased in number and size, though many failed during the Depression. Those that survived benefited from a loss of faith in commercial banks and other financial institutions, which were perceived as impersonal. After the growth of credit unions slowed in the 1940s rapid expansion resumed, and by the late 1960s the municipal credit union was one of the largest in the country. Federal insurance of deposits in credit unions did not prevent rumors and a suspension of dividends from causing a run on the municipal credit union in 1977. Deregulation in 1980 and 1982 freed credit unions from restrictions on their interest rates and portfolios, allowed them to offer checking accounts, and imposed uniform reserve requirements.

J. Carroll Moody and Gilbert C. Fite: *The Credit Union Movement: Origins and Development, 1850–1970* (Lincoln: University of Nebraska Press, 1971; 2nd edn Dubuque, Iowa: Kendall/Hunt, 1984)

Dean F. Amel: "Trends in Banking Structure since the Mid 1970s," *Federal Reserve Bulletin*, March 1989, pp. 120–33

Bernard Shull

Creedmoor. A tract of land in east central Queens, one mile (1.6 kilometers) north of Queens Village and centered on Braddock Avenue and old Rocky Hill Road (now Braddock Avenue). The name is used only locally and does not refer to any village or settlement, past or present. Conrad Poppenhusen of College Point ran a railroad through the area parallel to Braddock Avenue in 1871 and donated some of the surplus land to the National Rifle Association for use by the state National Guard, which opened firing ranges in 1873. The growth of Queens Village from the 1890s and the hazards connected with the firing ranges led to the eviction of the National Guard in 1908. In 1910 the tract became the site of a large state hospital.

Vincent Seyfried

Creedmoor Psychiatric Center. State mental hospital on Winchester Boulevard near Queens Village, built on land originally owned by the Creed family. It opened in 1912 as a "farm colony" for the Brooklyn Psychiatric Center in facilities formerly used as barracks for the National Guard. With the construction of new buildings in 1926, 1929, and 1933 Creedmoor became a separate state hospital. Although its nominal capacity was 3300 there were six thousand patients by the 1940s, and the problems of overcrowding were exacerbated by staff shortages and limited funds. During these years various new treatments for mental illness were introduced at Creedmoor, including hydrotherapy, insulin therapy, electroshock therapy, and in a few cases lobotomy. A more important innovation was the introduction of antidepressant and tranquilizing drugs, which became widely used in the state mental health system in 1955. At Creedmoor the new drugs meant quieter wards, fewer injuries to staff and patients, and a dramatic increase in the number of patients who could manage daily life in the community. As a result the number of in-patients at the hospital declined to eleven hundred by 1991, while outpatient services and residential placements were expanded in keeping with the new policy of deinstitutionalization. As it became clear in the late 1980s that many of the homeless in New York City had urgent psychiatric needs, Creedmoor established a special in-patient program of psychiatric rehabilitation intended specifically for the homeless.

Susan Sheehan: *Is There No Place on Earth for Me?* (Boston: Houghton Mifflin, 1982)

Sandra Opdycke

Creelman, James (*b* Montreal, 12 Nov 1859; *d* Berlin, 12 Feb 1915). News correspondent. In his youth he emigrated to the United States and settled in New York City, where from 1878 he worked as a reporter for the *New York Herald.* He was assigned by James Gordon Bennett Sr., the founder of the newspaper, to interview Sitting Bull, and he later edited the European edition of the *Herald* (from 1889). His vivid coverage of the Sino-Japanese War for the *New York World* attracted the attention of William Randolph Hearst, who offered him an assignment at the *New York Journal* covering the Greco-Turkish War in 1897 and then the Spanish–American War in the following year; he also reported on the Filipino uprising against American occupation. Creelman died while covering the First World War. He wrote *On the Great Highway: The Wanderings and Adventures of a Special Correspondent* (1901).

F. Lauriston Bullard: *Famous War Correspondents* (Boston: Little, Brown, 1914)

Julian S. Rammelkamp

Cremin, Lawrence A(rthur) (*b* New York City, 31 Oct 1925; *d* New York City, 4 Sept 1990). Educator and historian. After graduating from Townsend Harris High School and City College he took his master's and doctoral degrees at Columbia University. He served as president of Teachers College at Columbia (1974–84), the Spencer Foundation (1985–90), the National Academy of Education (1969–73), the History of Education Society (1959–60), and the National Society of College Teachers of Education (1961–62). Among his many honors were the Pulitzer Prize, the Bancroft Prize, a Guggenheim Fellowship, and the award of the American Education Research Association (1969). He wrote more than a dozen major books and was writing a biography of the educator John Dewey at the time of his death. A lifelong resident of Manhattan, Cremin was the foremost historian of education in the United States.

Kenneth T. Jackson

cricket. Organized cricket in New York City began in 1838 with the founding of the St. George Cricket Club; in 1844 John Richards and William T. Porter formed the New York Cricket Club. English-born merchants, professionals, diplomats, and military officers dominated these clubs, but some native-born Americans also joined. From the mid nineteenth century until the early twentieth, teams representing these and other organizations from Manhattan, Brooklyn, and Staten Island competed against teams from Boston, Philadelphia, and Newark, New Jersey. Several of the clubs from Manhattan established playing grounds in Staten Island and in or near Hoboken, New Jersey. The St. George Cricket Club arranged international contests that matched select teams from the United States against teams from Canada and England. Cricket was eclipsed in popularity first as a team sport by baseball in the 1860s, then as a pastime for the élite by tennis and golf in the early twentieth century. After the First World War immigrants from Great Britain and its colonies kept cricket alive. In the late twentieth century several thousand West Indians and other immigrants continued to pitch their wickets in public parks throughout the city.

Melvin Adelman: *A Sporting Time: New York City and the Rise of Modern Athletics, 1820–1870* (Urbana: University of Illinois Press, 1986)
George B. Kirsch: *The Creation of American Team Sports: Baseball and Cricket, 1838–1872* (Urbana: University of Illinois Press, 1989)

George B. Kirsch

crime. The history of crime in New York City is closely related to the city's most enduring qualities: wealth and human diversity. Its riches have long made it a fertile ground for criminals, from petty thieves to racketeers. And the city's vast array of people has long made it a place of divergent moral codes, where it is difficult to maintain a single standard of order.

A growth in crime during the eighteenth century paralleled the growth of New York City as a cosmopolitan center. Crime surged with the population and economic fluctuations of the 1730s and 1760s. The number of thefts and assaults rose as the city became more crowded: maritime trade brought more sailors to the city and more prostitution (often prosecuted as "keeping a disorderly house"). In general the legal system could not control crime, especially theft. Riots were tolerated as expressions of political discontent.

Homicides per 100,000 Residents in New York City, 1866–1990

1866–70	4.0
1871–75	6.5
1876–80	4.8
1881–85	4.9
1886–90	4.5
1891–95	3.5
1896–1900	2.5
1901–5	3.8
1906–10	5.5
1911–15	5.8
1916–20	4.9
1921–25	5.4
1926–30	6.0
1931–35	7.4
1936–40	4.5
1941–45	3.5
1946–48	4.7
1949–51	4.0
1952–55	4.3
1956–60	4.7
1961–65	7.6
1966–70	12.6
1971–75	21.7
1976–80	23.5
1981–85	24.9
1986–90	26.7

Number of Offenses Reported to Police in New York City, 1945–1988

	Total	Murder	Rape	Robbery	Assault	Burglary	Theft	Automobile Theft
1945	32,843	292	N/A	1,417	2,579	4,348	11,981	12,226
1955	137,254	306	N/A	7,133	8,679	38,963	69,790	12,383
1960	164,188	435	841	6,597	11,021	36,049	88,176	21,069
1965	187,795	681	1,154	8,904	16,325	51,072	115,782	34,726
1966	323,107	734	1,761	23,539	23,205	120,903	163,683	44,914
1967	396,421	809	1,905	35,934	24,828	150,245	182,151	58,169
1968	482,990	976	1,840	54,405	28,515	173,559	216,245	77,448
1969	478,990	1,116	2,120	59,152	29,717	171,393	190,540	85,796
1970	517,716	1,201	2,141	74,102	31,255	181,694	193,005	94,835
1971	529,447	1,513	2,415	88,994	33,865	181,331	187,232	96,624
1972	434,303	1,757	3,271	78,202	37,130	148,046	134,664	75,865
1973	475,855	1,740	3,735	72,750	38,148	149,311	127,500	82,731
1974	519,825	1,607	4,054	77,940	41,068	158,321	163,157	73,731
1975	581,247	1,690	3,866	83,190	43,481	177,032	188,832	83,201
1976	658,147	1,647	3,400	86,183	42,948	195,243	232,069	96,682
1977	610,077	1,553	3,899	74,404	42,056	178,907	214,838	94,420
1978	570,354	1,503	3,882	74,028	43,271	164,447	200,110	83,112
1979	621,110	1,733	3,875	82,572	44,203	178,162	220,813	89,748
1980	710,151	1,812	3,711	100,550	43,476	210,703	249,421	100,478
1981	725,846	1,826	3,862	107,475	43,783	205,825	258,369	104,706
1982	688,567	1,668	3,547	95,944	42,784	172,794	264,400	107,430
1983	622,877	1,622	3,662	84,243	43,326	143,698	253,801	92,725
1984	600,216	1,450	3,829	79,540	47,472	128,687	250,759	88,478
1985	601,467	1,384	3,880	79,532	50,356	124,838	262,051	79,426
1986	635,199	1,582	3,536	80,827	57,306	124,382	281,713	85,853
1987	656,505	1,672	3,507	78,890	64,244	123,412	289,126	95,654
1988	718,483	1,896	3,412	86,578	71,030	127,148	308,479	119,940

N/A = Not Available

The crime rate remained low during the first two decades of the nineteenth century but rose rapidly from the 1820s, when immigration and the growth of manufacturing and trade gave rise to ethnic and class tensions. Recent immigrants often fell prey to swindlers and were also blamed for disorderliness, public drunkenness, and more serious crimes; Irish immigrants who moved to the city in the 1840s were especially singled out. Temperance advocates tried to close saloons frequented by immigrants, especially the Irish, whose gangs often fought against nativist gangs. The number of murders per 100,000 inhabitants increased from 2.5 in the late 1840s and early 1850s to 4.4 in the 1850s and 1860s. In the middle of the century ethnic and racial hostility and economic inequities led to racist assaults on blacks and made riots more common and more dangerous. The worst riots in the history of the city were the draft riots of 1863, which began as a protest against the conscription policies of the Union and degenerated into a race riot. During the second half of the century violent crime decreased owing to the ministrations of political machines, improved policing, and residents' adaptations to the strains and discipline of urban life, but vices such as prostitution and gambling flourished, often with the cooperation of the political machines. Most criminal operations were run by successive members of immigrant groups: at mid century the Irish, and at the turn of the century Jews and Italians. Eventually moral reformers pressured government to control saloons, brothels, and gambling dens, which turned for protection to Tammany Hall and other political organizations. The red-light district in the city, the Tenderloin, became a national symbol of urban depravity that was widely depicted in novels and tabloid newspapers.

The number of murders declined by the turn of the century. Widely differing murder rates among whites and blacks continued to reflect economic disparities: the rates per 100,000 inhabitants for whites and blacks were 3.7 and 9.8 in 1900, 5.1 and 21.7 in 1910, 5.0 and 23.0 in 1920, and 5.8 and 28.7 in 1930. Murders reached a peak during Prohibition, when violence worsened as crime gangs were reorganized. As the gangs imported liquor and distributed it throughout the nation they adopted conventional business techniques and redefined their relations with government, and they continued to do so after the repeal of Prohibition in 1933. At the same time ORGANIZED CRIME in the city focused increasingly on narcotics, gambling, and waterfront racketeering. In 1935 acute economic trouble in black neighborhoods caused the murder rate among blacks to reach 35.1 citywide (compared with 4.3 per 100,000 for whites citywide). Harlem was beset by riots in 1935 and 1943. Other parts of the city had a fairly low incidence of crime from the 1930s to the 1960s: there were fewer than three hundred murders in 1945 and 435 in 1960.

In the 1960s New York City, like most American cities, witnessed a dramatic increase in violent crime. Riots in minority neighborhoods and the over-representation of blacks among criminals and victims inevitably linked discussions of crime and race, much as nineteenth-century New Yorkers had linked their crime problem to the Irish. Law and order became a volatile issue: for some a code word for racism, for others a cry for safety in a dangerous city. The referendum in 1966 on the Civilian Review Board charged with overseeing the police, and other debates over crime and policing, led to divisive arguments that undermined the reputation of the city for tolerance. The number of murders reached 1116 in 1969, after which the number remained above a thousand into the 1990s. People felt unsafe and routines of life changed. Many businesses retained private security guards, and features intended to thwart criminals became incorporated into the design of buildings. Signs reading "no radio" were routinely placed in the windows of automobiles to ward off thieves. Despite some fluctuations crime continued to increase in the 1970s and 1980s, virtually overwhelming the municipal justice system. The number of reported incidents of rape nearly doubled, from 2141 in 1970 to 3875 in 1979 (perhaps in part because it became a crime that women were more willing to report). Other American cities had proportionately more crime, but New York City became a symbol of urban lawlessness because of its size and prominence. On average more than fifteen hundred murders a year were committed during the 1970s and 1980s. The increase in the number of assaults, automobile thefts, and other thefts was linked to the abuse of drugs, especially heroin, cocaine, and crack cocaine, which became enduring features of urban life. Aided by the Racketeer Influenced and Corrupt Organizations (RICO) laws, federal law enforcement agencies continued to fight organized crime but could not extinguish it. Frustration with crime undermined the city's reputation for liberalism. No event symbolized this more than the mayoral victory in 1977 of Edward I. Koch. A congressman from the East Side with a liberal voting record, Koch shed his old image and was elected on a platform emphasizing law enforcement and the death penalty.

Developments in the 1980s and 1990s showed that the city's mixture of wealth and diversity continued to provide a fertile ground for crime. The boom on Wall Street in the 1980s created opportunities for corrupt practices like insider trading that led to prosecutions of prominent financial figures like Ivan Boesky. Felonies remained a major concern of voters and politicians, but racial and ethnic divisions among New Yorkers prevented the formation of a united front against crime. Investigations of racial bias among police officers, and the racially motivated killings of black men in Howard Beach and Bensonhurst and of a Hasidic Jew in Crown Heights, all tore at the city's fabric. In 1989 David N. Dinkins, a liberal black Democrat, was elected mayor after promising to be firm with criminals. His victory suggested that a stern attitude toward crime was now widely shared by New Yorkers of all races. In 1993 he was defeated for reelection by Rudolph W. Giuliani, a former prosecutor who made fighting crime a major theme of his campaign.

Despite its reputation as a dangerous place, New York City by the mid 1990s was no longer among the twenty-five cities with the highest homicide rates.

Douglas Greenberg: *Crime and Law Enforcement in the Colony of New York* (Ithaca, N.Y.: Cornell University Press, 1976)

Charles E. Silberman: *Criminal Violence, Criminal Justice* (New York: Random House, 1978)

Ted Robert Gurr: *Violence in America*, vol. 1, *The History of Crime* (Newbury Park, Calif.: Sage, 1989)

Robert W. Snyder

Crimmins, John D(aniel) (*b* New York City, 18 May 1844; *d* New York City, 9 Nov 1917). Businessman and art collector. He was a partner in his family's contracting firm, the Crimmins Company. One of the city's largest employers, the firm made a fortune in the construction of municipal and state public works projects, including the Croton Aqueduct, the extended waterfront, sewers, gas mains, electric duct lines, streets, and elevated railways. From 1883 to 1887 he was the president of the Board of Commissioners of Public Parks of New York City, and he belonged to the Greater New York Charter Revision Commission of 1901; he was also on the boards of many financial institutions, including the New York Title and Mortgage Company, of which he was president from 1901 to 1914. A trustee of several cultural and charitable organizations, he also held positions on the executive committee of St. Patrick's Cathedral. He built the cathedral's Chapel of St. Anne and in 1888 dedicated it to his late wife, Lily Lalor Crimmins. Crimmins had the most complete collection of maps and pictures of old New York City (about five thousand items), as well as a large collection of Gaelic manuscripts and books on Irish subjects. He wrote two books, *St. Patrick's Day: Its Celebration in New York and Other American Places, 1737–1845* (1902) and *Irish American Historical Miscellany* (1905).

Marion R. Casey

Cripplebush. Name applied to WILLIAMSBURG until the 1820s. The area was named for the thickets of scrub oak that proliferated until the American Revolution, when British troops harvested most of the wood for fuel. Farms were built after the war; the area remained sparsely populated.

James Bradley

Crisis. Monthly periodical. Launched in 1910 in New York City by W. E. B. Du Bois, it became the official publication of the National Association for the Advancement of Colored People (NAACP). As the first editor Du Bois covered activities of the association as well as incidents of anti-black discrimination; he also published articles by young black authors. Although Du Bois built a sizable circulation, his independent way of operating and certain of his views prompted criticism that led to his resignation in 1934. The NAACP continued to publish the *Crisis* into the 1990s, focusing predominantly on issues of political and legal discrimination.

Elliott Rudwick: *W. E. B. Du Bois: Propagandist of the Negro Protest* (New York: Atheneum, 1968)

Seth M. Scheiner

Croatians. A Croatian community formed in New York City about 1888 and consisted mostly of young Dalmatian men who lived on the West Side in the area bounded by 48th Street, 10th Avenue, 34th Street, and 11th Avenue. Many were peasants or sailors who deserted their ships. Poor economic conditions, compulsory military service, and political unrest due to an increased Magyarization policy in Croatia also led men to move to the city, where they found work as stevedores, longshoremen, tugboat crewmen, freight handlers, and railroad employees, often with the New York Central Railroad. They frequently lived as boarders with relatives or fellow villagers, or in cooperative households known as *društvo*. The weekly newspaper *Narodni List* (National Gazette) was launched by 1898 and published daily from 1902. Its editor, Frank Zotti, was a leading Croatian entrepreneur at the beginning of the twentieth century. A number of other newspapers were published at the time, including *Hrvatski Svijet* (Croatian World) and *Domovina* (The Homeland); they provided news of developments in Croatia and the United States, and their nationalistic editorial policies divided the community. Fraternal societies provided cohesion and gained many members. Men often gathered at Croatian groceries, barber shops, and steamship agencies; Croatian saloons were the center of their social life, and saloonkeepers acted as bankers, steamship agents, and subscription agents for Croatian newspapers. About a third of the population was illiterate.

Before the First World War, Croatian immigrants were listed in immigration records as Austrians, Hungarians, Slovenians, or members of southern Slavic groups. In 1912 the population in Manhattan was estimated at between 2500 and three thousand and included few women and children and only 150 to two hundred families; most were men between the ages of seventeen and forty-five, 60 percent were from Dalmatia, few became American citizens, and nearly 50 percent returned to Croatia after saving money for their families. The war and the southern Slav unification movement in Croatia intensified nationalistic sentiments and led many Croatians to understand the importance of American citizenship and the vote. The Croatian Roman Catholic Church, Sts. Cyril and Methodius, was formed in 1913 by the Franciscan Fathers to offer religious services in Croatian. At the end of the war rates of immigration and repatriation increased as news of American prosperity spread. The incorporation of Croatia into a kingdom dominated by Serbs led many Croatian immigrants to remain in the United States. In the following years immigration decreased after quotas were imposed and the economy declined. A few Croatians were drawn to the city for the World's Fair of 1939–40 and remained after the outbreak of the Second World War. The community in New York City became divided over the issue of support for the fascist Ustasha government of Ante Pavelic but reunited against the communist dictatorship of Josip Broz Tito after receiving reports of atrocities in Yugoslavia.

The political refugees who settled in the city after the war were usually educated and led opposition to the Yugoslavian government. An educational organization known as the Croatian Academy of America was formed in 1953 to focus on Croatian history and culture and by 1960 published the *Journal of Croatian Studies*. The *Croatian Press* moved to the city in 1956 and became a leading proponent of Croatian independence. Croatians held liberation parades along 5th Avenue, raised funds to repair churches and establish ambulatory services in Croatia, and also sent food, clothing, and medical supplies. At the same time a number of Croatian doctors settled in the city. Other immigrants found employment as kitchen workers, waiters, longshoremen, construction workers, and painters and often held two jobs; women worked in factories, cleaned offices, and took clerical positions. In many families both husband and wife worked, one during the day and the other at night if there were children, allowing them to buy homes in Brooklyn and Queens. Immigrants who moved to the city after 1970 were more militant. After a failed attempt to separate from Yugoslavia in 1971, Croatian nationalists sought refuge in the United States, especially New York City: according to the federal census 22,000 Yugoslavs lived there in 1980. During the following decade the number who settled in the city declined to a few hundred a year.

In the mid 1990s fifteen to twenty thousand Croatians lived in New York City, most of them American citizens; the largest concentration was in Queens. Well-known Croatians in the city have included the artist Ivan Mestrovic, the opera singers Zinka Kunc-Milanov and Milka Trnina, and the conductor Ivan Cerovac.

Gerald Gilbert Govorchin: *Americans from Yugoslavia* (Gainesville: University of Florida Press, 1961)
Frances Kraljic: *Croatian Migration to and from the United States, 1900–1914* (Palo Alto, Calif.: Ragusan, 1978)
George J. Prpic: *South Slavic Immigration in America* (Boston: Twayne, 1978)

Frances Kraljic

Croker, Richard (*b* Blackrock, near Dublin, 24 Nov 1841; *d* Dublin, 29 April 1922). Political leader. In his youth he was a machine-tool worker, earned a reputation as a tough amateur boxer, and became the leader of the Fourth Avenue Tunnel Gang, which he used as a political base. He was elected an alderman in 1869 and held a series of appointed and elected city government offices until 1886, when he became the leader of the Democratic organization in New York County, known as Tammany Hall. His tenure was marked by frequent but unsuccessful challenges to his rule mounted by Democratic district leaders, and by widespread disclosures of political corruption that hurt his candidates. Revelations in 1894 by a state investigating committee that Tammany Hall had abused the police department cost it the mayoralty in 1895. An investigation in 1900 led to the election of the fusion candidate Seth Low as mayor in 1901 and destroyed Croker's credibility. By then a wealthy man, Croker retired to Ireland to breed horses and engage in philanthropy.

Alfred Henry Lewis: *Richard Croker* (New York: Life Publishing, 1901)
M. R. Werner: *Tammany Hall* (New York: Doubleday, Doran, 1928)
Theodore Lothrop Stoddard: *Master of Manhattan: The Life of Richard Croker* (New York: Longmans, Green, 1931)
Mark Hirsch: "An Interim Report on the Early Career of a 'Boss' of Tammany Hall," *Essays in the History of New York*, ed. Irwin Yellowitz (Port Washington, N.Y.: Kennikat, 1978)

Chris McNickle

Croly, Herbert (David) (*b* New York City, 23 Jan 1869; *d* Santa Barbara, Calif., 17 May 1930). Writer and magazine editor. Born to a middle-class family of journalists, he learned the value of education and expertise as the foundation of social improvement. He promoted big government and labor unions, considering them an inevitable result of industrialization, and supported an interventionist foreign policy despite his disillusionment with the outcome of the First World War. In 1914 he helped to launch the magazine the *New Republic.* Croly wrote *The Promise of American Life* (1909), in which he took issue with what he perceived as a Jeffersonian bias toward small-scale organization among American reformers.

David W. Levy: *Herbert Croly of the New Republic: The Life and Thought of an American Progressive* (Princeton, N.J.: Princeton University Press, 1985)

Lawson Bowling

Croly, Jane Cunningham [June, Jenny] (*b* Market Harborough, Leicestershire, England, 19 Dec 1829; *d* New York City, 23 Dec 1901). Journalist. She moved to New York State as a child and to New York City in 1855, where she remained for most of her life. Through her work for several newspapers she became well known as one of the first female syndicated columnists in the country; she also contributed regularly to the *New York World* and several popular periodicals. She formed Sorosis in 1868, one of the first women's clubs in the nation, and the General Federation of Women's Clubs in 1890, a national network of volunteer organizations. Croly compiled *The History of the Woman's Club Movement in America* (1898). *Memories of Jane Cunningham Croly, "Jenny June"* (1904) was compiled by friends after her death.

Elizabeth Bancroft Schlesinger: "Nineteenth-century Woman's Dilemma and Jennie June," *New York History* 42 (1961), 365–79
Elizabeth Bancroft Schlesinger: "Jane Cunningham Croly," *Notable American Women*, ed. Edward T. James et al. (Cambridge: Harvard University Press, 1971)
Karen J. Blair: "Jane Cunningham Croly," *American Women Writers: A Critical Reference Guide*, ed. Lina Mainiero (New York: Frederick Ungar, 1979–82), 422–24

Karen J. Blair

Cromwell, George (*b* New York City, 3 July 1860; *d* New York City, 17 Sept 1934). Borough president. A graduate of Brooklyn Polytechnic Institute, Yale College, and Columbia Law School, he practiced law and was elected to the state assembly and senate as a Republican before serving for fifteen years as president of the borough of Staten Island. He was also a member of several commissions, including ones dealing with taxation and charter revision, and a prominent trustee of the Staten Island Institute of Arts and Sciences.

James E. Mooney

Cross Land Savings Bank. Bank formed as the East Brooklyn Savings Bank by Samuel C. Barnes. It opened at Myrtle Avenue in Bedford (now Bedford–Stuyvesant) in 1860 and served primarily customers in the neighborhood. Its headquarters were moved to Bedford Avenue in 1922 and to Montague Street in Brooklyn Heights in 1962. The firm was renamed the Metropolitan Savings Bank in 1969 and acquired the Fulton Savings Bank in 1978 before merging with Brooklyn Savings Bank and Greenwich Savings Bank in 1981; when it became a federal mutual savings bank in 1985 it took its current name. By 1988 the bank had assets of more than $15,000 million and was the city's largest savings bank, as well as a major lender in the city's commercial and residential real-estate market. It was severely weakened by its large-scale investments in "junk bonds," leveraged buyouts, and real estate during the 1980s. The federal government seized control of the bank in January 1992 and renamed it the Crossland Federal Savings Bank. Many of the bank's housing projects were subsequently sold.

James Bradley

Crotona Park East. Neighborhood lying north of Hunts Point and east of Morrisania in the west central Bronx (1990 pop. 22,645), bounded to the north by the Cross Bronx Expressway, to the east by the Bronx River, to the south by Westchester and Prospect avenues, and to the west by Crotona Park; it has variously been considered part of Hunts Point and Morrisania. The area was the site of large estates in the town of West Farms in Westchester County until it was annexed to New York City in 1874. Some sections were developed in the 1890s after trolley connections were built to the 3rd Avenue elevated line; the rest became densely covered by apartment buildings after the subway was extended in 1904. The population became predominantly Jewish but there were also a few German, Irish, and Italian immigrants. During the 1950s many white residents moved to the suburbs and an increasing number of blacks and Puerto Ricans moved in. Poverty, misguided public policy, and the availability of drugs led to an increase in arson and other crimes in the following decades. The burnt-out apartment buildings of the neighborhood gave an impression of urban devastation and became a national symbol of inner-city decay in the 1970s. Charlotte Street was visited by two presidential candidates: Jimmy Carter in 1976 and Ronald Reagan in 1980. With funds from public programs one-family houses were built on Charlotte Street in the early 1980s, put up for sale in 1983, and first occupied in the summer of 1984. Other new housing was also built during the 1980s with funds from community groups and public programs. In the mid 1990s a few vacant, rubble-strewn blocks remained, but large parts of the neighborhood had a suburban character.

"Improving the Tiffany and Vyse Estates," *Real Estate Record and Builders Guide*, 5 June 1915
Ira Rosen: "The Glory That Was Charlotte Street," *New York Times Magazine*, 7 Oct 1979

Evelyn Gonzalez

Croton Aqueduct. A large water conduit that in 1842 began to provide the first dependable water supply for New York City, by then the largest city in the United States. Designed by the engineer John B. Jervis and approved by referendum in April 1835, it consisted of iron pipes protected by brick masonry, and covered a distance of forty-one miles (sixty-five kilometers), from the Croton Dam in up-

Croton Aqueduct, 1893

state New York, over the High Bridge across the Harlem River, to a receiving reservoir between 79th and 86th streets in what is now Central Park, to the distributing reservoir, an imposing fortress-like structure at 42nd Street and 5th Avenue, the current site of the New York Public Library and Bryant Park. Construction of the aqueduct cost $11.5 million and was one of the great engineering achievements of the nineteenth century. The aqueduct opened to great fanfare on 4 July 1842 and served the city well into the twentieth century. In 1890 the substantially larger New Croton Aqueduct was placed in service, and what had been the Croton Aqueduct became known as the Old Croton Aqueduct. Parts of the Old Croton Aqueduct may still be seen along University Avenue above West Tremont Avenue in the Bronx. Much of its route is now a walking path, designated a Scenic and Historic Corridor by the state legislature in 1976.

Charles H. Weidner: *Water for a City* (New Brunswick, N.J.: Rutgers University Press, 1974)

The Old Croton Aqueduct: Rural Resources Meet Urban Needs (Yonkers, N.Y.: Hudson River Museum, 1992)

James Bradley, David Major

Crouch and Fitzgerald. Firm of luggage and leatherware retailers, formed in 1839 by George Crouch as a harness and luggage maker. The firm achieved early success by supplying wood-framed leather trunks to traveling salesmen. By 1892 it had a factory on West 41st Street, three retail outlets in Manhattan, and two hundred employees. In 1988 the firm was bought by Lenox Inc., a division of the Brown–Forman Corporation.

Kenneth T. Jackson

Crow Hill. Former neighborhood in northeastern Brooklyn, stretching from the hills east of Prospect Park to East New York. According to folklore it was named for the largest hill in the area, which was infested with crows; the *Brooklyn Eagle* in 1873 suggested that the area was named for a settlement begun in the 1830s by blacks, who were called "crows" by whites. Many residents worked in the fish and meat markets in Manhattan and lived in shanties on the hill. As the city limits were extended and whites bought property in the area blacks were forced out. The Kings County Penitentiary was built on the crest of Crow Hill after a land purchase in 1846; eventually considered a blight, it was demolished in 1907 and the land became the site of Brooklyn Preparatory School and the Church of St. Ignatius Loyola. By a slight change of orthography the area was renamed Crown Heights in the early twentieth century.

Ellen Marie Snyder-Grenier

Crown Heights. Neighborhood in west central Brooklyn, bounded to the north by Atlantic Avenue, to the east by Ralph Avenue, to the south by Empire Boulevard, and to the west by Flatbush Avenue. The first settlements in the area, Weeksville and Carrville, were formed by free blacks in the 1830s. After mid century, development accelerated. Mansions were built on former farmland in the northern section and were eventually followed by limestone row houses. The southern section was developed about 1900, when mansions, one- and two-family row houses, and semidetached houses were built; blocks of detached houses and apartment buildings (some with elevators) were later built in the same area and along Eastern Parkway. In the early twentieth century the neighborhood was given its current name and many black immigrants from the Caribbean settled in it. The 1920s saw an influx of Germans, Scandinavians, Irish, Italians, and Jews, who by the early 1940s accounted for much of the population; many were Lubavitch Hasidim from the Soviet Union. A number of white residents moved to the suburbs after the Second World War, and many black immigrants from the Caribbean moved in after 1965. During the 1960s the abandonment of apartment buildings led to a cycle of decay and arson that was halted in the 1970s and 1980s by efforts at preservation, many focused on the brownstones in the neighborhood. Ebbets Field, long the home of the Brooklyn Dodgers, stood at Bedford Avenue and Sullivan Place until it was demolished in the 1960s (the site is now occupied by an apartment complex). In August 1991 racial tensions rose after a black child was accidentally killed by an automobile driven by a Lubavitch Hasid. Riots ensued in which a Hasid visiting the city was killed in retaliation.

In the 1980s and early 1990s black immigrants from the Caribbean continued to settle in Crown Heights. About a quarter were Jamaican and almost as many Haitian, with large numbers from Guyana, Trinidad and Tobago, Barbados, Grenada, Panama, the Dominican Republic, and St. Vincent and the Grenadines. The principal thoroughfare is Eastern Parkway; the main commercial districts lie on Kingston, Franklin, Nostrand, and Utica avenues. The neighborhood has several important institutions and landmarks: Prospect Park, Eastern Parkway, the Brooklyn Museum, the Brooklyn Children's Museum, the Botanic Gardens, the central branch of the Brooklyn Public Library, the Society for the Preservation of Weeksville and Bedford–Stuyvesant History, and Medgar Evers College (1650 Bedford Avenue). A West Indian parade held every Labor Day attracts more than a million spectators. The Lubavitch world headquarters are at 770 Eastern Parkway.

Ellen Marie Snyder-Grenier

Cruger, John (*b* Germany, *ca* 1680; *d* New York City, 13 Aug 1744). Mayor, father of John Cruger Jr. He moved to New York City from Bristol, England, in 1698. After becoming successful as a shipper and slave trader he won election as an alderman from the dock ward in 1712, a position he retained until 1735. Appointed mayor in 1739, he remained in office for five consecutive one-year terms. Cruger is remembered for having ruthlessly suppressed the "Negro plot" of 1741.

Henry Collins Brown, ed.: "Early Mayors of New York," *Valentine's Manual of Old New York: 1925* (New York: Museum of the City of New York, 1924), 198–201

Thomas J. Davis: *A Rumor of Revolt: The "Great Negro Plot" in Colonial New York* (New York: Macmillan, 1985)

David William Voorhees

Cruger, John, Jr. (*b* New York City, 18 July 1710; *d* New York City, 27 Dec 1791). Mayor. A son of Mayor John Cruger, he was an alderman of New York City from 1754 until 1756, when he was appointed mayor. In 1765, the last year of his tenure, he saw the city through the Stamp Act protests. Cruger was the last speaker of the provincial assembly, where he held a seat from 1759 to 1775. In 1768 he helped to organize the New York Chamber of

Commerce, of which he was the first president.

Joseph Bucklin Bishop: *A Chronicle of One Hundred and Fifty Years: The Chamber of Commerce of the State of New York, 1768–1918* (New York: Charles Scribner's Sons, 1918)

Malcolm Decker: *Brink of Revolution: New York in Crisis, 1765–1776* (New York: Argosy Antiquarian, 1964)

David William Voorhees

Crummell, Alexander (*b* New York City, 3 March 1819; *d* Point Pleasant, N.J., 10 Sept 1898). Abolitionist and clergyman. A descendant of African royalty, he graduated from the African Free Schools in New York City and as a young man was the secretary of the New York State Anti-Slavery Society. He was denied admission to the General Theological Seminary in 1839 because of his race but was accepted at the diocese of Massachusetts, where he was ordained an Episcopal priest in 1844. After completing his religious study at Queens College, Cambridge, he became a missionary in Liberia. He returned to the United States in 1872 after disputes in Liberia forced him to leave, and he settled in Washington, where he established St. Luke's Church and taught at Howard University after retiring from the priesthood in 1894. Crummell was instrumental in 1897 in forming the American Negro Academy, an organization dedicated to promoting art, literature, and science among African-Americans.

Benjamin Quarles: *Black Abolitionist* (New York: Da Capo, 1969)

Virgil A. Clift and W. Augustus Low, eds.: *Encyclopedia of Black America* (New York: Da Capo, 1981)

Sherrill D. Wilson

Crystal Palace, ca 1853

Crystal Palace. A cast-iron and glass building completed in 1853 on a site bounded to the north by 42nd Street, to the east by the Croton distributing reservoir, to the south by 40th Street, and to the west by 6th Avenue. Designed by the architects Georg J. B. Carstensen and Charles Gildemeister, it was built in the shape of a Greek cross with a dome at its center and reputed to be fireproof. The building opened on 14 July 1853 as the site of the first world's fair in the United States, an event entitled "Exhibition of the Industry of All Nations" that was inspired by the Great Exhibition at the Crystal Palace in London of 1851. The fair had more than four thousand exhibitors from around the world, of which those from the United States were the most numerous. Like its predecessors in London and Dublin (1852) the fair in New York City exhibited the products of agriculture and industry, and housed a collection of sculpture; it was also the first world's fair to exhibit paintings in a picture gallery. Although paid attendance at the exhibition exceeded one million, the sponsors were left with $300,000 in debt when the exhibition closed on 1 November 1854. In the following years space was leased out to various organizations for events such as one celebrating the laying of the transatlantic telegraph cable. The Crystal Palace caught fire on 5 October 1858 and was completely destroyed, purportedly within fifteen minutes. Bryant Park was later developed on the site.

Charles Hirschfield: "America on Exhibition: The New York Crystal Palace," *American Quarterly* 9 (1957), 101–16

Ivan D. Steen: "The New York Crystal Palace Exhibition" (thesis, New York University, 1959)

Ivan D. Steen: "America's First World's Fair: The Exhibition of the Industry of All Nations at New York's Crystal Palace, 1853–54," *New-York Historical Society Quarterly* 47 (1963), 257–87

I. Steen

CS First Boston. Firm of investment bankers. It was formed in New York City as the First Boston Corporation in June 1934 by a merger of the investment banking divisions of First National Bank of Boston and Chase National Bank after the Glass–Steagall Act required the separation of commercial and investment banks. In the 1930s and 1940s it was the only large publicly owned firm of its kind and underwrote securities for many corporations and public utilities, including electric and oil companies. It also underwrote securities for commercial banks and for securities firms. After the stock market crash of October 1987 the firm sought to refinance temporary loans that it had made during the 1980s; it received capital from Credit Suisse and was restructured in December 1988, becoming a privately held subsidiary of an international investment bank controlled by CS Holding, the parent company of Credit Suisse. The firm took its current name in September 1993. CS Holding eventually increased its share in CS First Boston from 44.5 percent to 69 percent. In the mid 1990s CS First Boston had headquarters at Park Avenue Plaza and thirty-five offices in twenty-one countries.

Roy C. Smith: *The Global Bankers* (New York: E. P. Dutton, 1989)

Mary E. Curry

Cuban Giants. Baseball team. Formed in the summer of 1885, it was the first black ballclub to play professionally. Its amateur forerunners included the Brooklyn Uniques (in the late 1860s) and other teams that often played against white teams with support from wealthy sponsors, until a growing prohibition against interracial games took hold after Reconstruction. The founder of the Cuban Giants was Frank Thompson, the headwaiter at the Argyle Hotel in Babylon, Long Island, and the players included a number of his fellow waiters. The name of the team was taken in the belief that the players would encounter less racial discrimination if they were thought to be foreigners, and for this reason they also spoke gibberish on the field. Bought by John L. Lang, who was white, soon after it was formed, the team achieved a record in 1885 of six wins, two losses, and one tie. George Williams, Abe Harrison, and Shep Trusty were signed by Lang from the Philadelphia Orions and helped the Cuban Giants to become the best black team before 1890. Lang then sold the team to another white man, Walter Cook, who engaged a black manager, S. K. Govern. Salaries typically ranged from $10 a week for pitchers and catchers to $12 a week for outfielders; white major leaguers earned about $50 a week at the time. In the first Colored Championships of America in New York City in 1888 the Cuban Giants finished first and the New York Gorhams third. After the Cuban Giants moved to Pennsylvania and became the York Monarchs there emerged a new team called the Cuban Giants (later the Genuine Cuban Giants); another team with a similar name, the Cuban X Giants, was formed by E. B. Lamar and won the Colored Championships in 1895 against the Page Fence Giants.

Solomon White: *Sol. White's Official [Negro] Base Ball Guide* (Philadelphia: n.pub. [Camden House], 1907)

Robert Peterson: *Only the Ball Was White* (Englewood Cliffs, N.J.: Prentice Hall, 1970)

Arthur Ashe: *A Hard Road to Glory* (New York: Amistad/Warner, 1988)

Arthur Ashe

Cubans. A few Cuban immigrants settled in New York City during the 1870s and 1880s. Most had fled the Cuban struggle for independence from Spain, were Catholic, and worked in cigar factories opened by fellow immigrants. The most important member of this community was José Martí, a writer, politician, and leader of the Cuban independence movement who escaped prison in Spain and moved to the city in 1880. Living among tobacco workers, he continued to lead the independence movement, formed the Partido Revolucionario Cubano in 1892, gave the order to resume hostilities against Spain in 1895, and left the city to join the battle. During the 1940s and 1950s such musicians as Machito, his wife, Graciella, and her brother Mario Bauzá introduced Afro-Cuban jazz to the city, which profoundly influenced such jazz musicians as Dizzy Gillespie. Immigration from Cuba reached a peak between 1959 and 1962, when 155,000 members of the Cuban élite fled Fidel Castro's communist government. The metropolitan area was the second-most popular destination (after southern Florida), a pattern that held during an influx of white-collar and unskilled workers between 1962 and 1973. During the early 1970s between 12 and 13 percent of the Cuban immigrants who moved to the United States settled in the city. After declining in the mid 1970s Cuban immigration increased during the 1980s and early 1990s, when more than five thousand Cubans settled in New York City, about 4 percent of all those who moved to the United States. The cigar factories eventually closed and unemployment among Cubans rose above the national average, but many family businesses were highly successful, among them restaurants popular for their fish, pork, and chicken dishes accompanied by rice and black beans. In the mid 1990s the city had a Cuban newspaper, radio station, and cable television station. The largest Cuban neighborhoods were in Washington Heights, Astoria, Elmhurst, and Jackson Heights in Queens. Although known to be sometimes divided by racial antagonism, the Cuban community in New York City is conspicuously tight knit and politically conservative.

Chad Ludington

Cullen, Countee (Porter) (*b* New York City, 30 May 1903; *d* New York City, 9 Jan 1946). Poet and novelist. After graduating from De Witt Clinton High School he earned his bachelor's degree from New York University and a master's degree from Harvard University in 1926. He worked briefly as an assistant editor of *Opportunity: A Journal of Negro Life* before winning a Guggenheim fellowship to travel in France, where he wrote *Black Christ and Other Poems* (1929) and the novel *One Way to Heaven* (1932). In 1934 he returned to New York City, where he taught at Frederick Douglass Junior High School and wrote until the end of his life. A branch library and a school in Harlem are named for him.

Margaret Perry: *A Bio-bibliography of Countee P. Cullen* (Westport, Conn.: Greenwood, 1971)

See also HARLEM RENAISSANCE.

James E. Mooney

Cullen, Michael J(oseph) (*b* Newark, N.J., 10 April 1884; *d* Queens, 24 April 1936). Businessman. He worked as a clerk in an A&P store in Newark from 1902 until 1919, when he moved to the Midwest to work for other grocery chains. He developed a plan for selling food on a large scale, but his attempts to have it put into effect were rebuffed in 1929 by Kroger (a grocery chain for which he worked as a manager in Illinois) and then by A&P. In August 1930 he opened King Kullen, the country's first supermarket, in a disused garage at 171-06 Jamaica Avenue in Queens. The store became tremendously successful: it attracted customers by offering ample parking and large amounts of merchandise in convenient displays, and controlled expenses by keeping furnishings to a minimum and emphasizing self-service. Cullen called himself the "world's greatest price wrecker," advertised in newspapers, and distributed circulars that read "Save, Save, Save . . . Low, Low, Low Prices." By 1932 he had eight supermarkets that earned $6 million a year in sales.

John J. Concannon

Culver Line. Railway incorporated in 1869 as the Prospect Park and Coney Island Railroad by the lawyer Andrew R. Culver, to whom the state legislature granted permission to build a line along McDonald Avenue from 9th Avenue and 20th Street in Park Slope to Gravesend. Culver proceeded to consolidate a route to the beachfront at Coney Island by successively leasing Gravesend Road, buying out the Coney Island Bridge Company, and then buying out a horse-car line on Vanderbilt Avenue (1871) to gain access to downtown Brooklyn. In June 1875 he opened a steam line that popularized the day excursion to Coney Island and transported as many as twenty thousand passengers each Sunday. The line was extended to Norton's Point in 1879, and during the 1880s patrons were attracted by the addition of parlor cars and a newly constructed pier and observatory at Coney Island. In 1885 the Long Island Rail Road (LIRR) permitted Culver to run trains from Parkville to the 65th Street ferry terminal over its tracks in Bay Ridge, and in 1889 the Brooklyn Union Elevated Railroad permitted the connection of the line to the elevated terminus at 5th Avenue and 36th Street; to make this connection the Culver Extension was built over the West End line from McDonald Avenue to 5th Avenue and 37th Street. Service began in June 1890, and the extension was soon the most heavily used section of the line. In January 1893 Culver sold the line to the LIRR, and in August 1895 its president, Austin Corbin, arranged with Brooklyn Union Elevated to run elevated trains on both the Culver Line and the Culver Extension, making the entire system a continuous rapid transit line. Despite these developments the line lost money in the 1890s. In 1899 it was electrified: elevated trains on 5th Avenue ran to 36th Street on power from a third rail, and then to Coney Island on trolley wire. In 1902 the line was leased and then sold to the Brooklyn Rapid Transit system. It was completely integrated into the rapid transit system in 1919 when the entire line from 9th Avenue to Coney Island was elevated and converted to operate with 4th Avenue subway trains. In 1954 a connection was built between Church and Ditmas avenues, integrating the Culver Line into the Independent subway system.

Vincent Seyfried

Cummings, E(dward) E(stlin) (*b* Cambridge, Mass., 14 Oct 1894; *d* North Conway, N.H., 3 Sept 1962). Poet. Educated at Cambridge University, he drove an ambulance in France during the First World War and later moved to New York City, settling in Greenwich Village; he made extended trips to Paris and to New Hampshire, where he wrote and painted. After returning from travels in Europe in 1923 he moved to quarters at 4 Patchin Place in Greenwich Village that he retained for the rest of his life. Cummings's poetry was highly personal: he saw conventional capitalization and punctuation as impediments to expression, and he generally eschewed them in his poems (he also omitted capital letters from his name). Because his work was often rejected by publishers he used family money to produce his first collections — *W* (1931), *no thanks* (1935), and *5* (1926) — and the play *Him* (1927). He received the Dial Award in 1925 and became well known during the 1950s, when he was elected to the National Institute of Arts and Letters and published *95 Poems* (1958).

Norman Friedman: *E. E. Cummings: The Growth of a Writer* (Carbondale: Southern Illinois University Press, 1964)

James E. Mooney

Cunard Line. First transatlantic passenger line. An English company formed in 1840 by Samuel Cunard (1787–1865), of Nova Scotia, its first scheduled trips connected England with Halifax, Nova Scotia, and with Boston. The company chose New York City in 1847 as its western terminal port and later occupied offices at the Cunard Building, 25 Broadway (built 1921). The steamers of the Cunard Line were at first recognizable by their assonant names: the *Britannia* (its first steamer), the *Mauritania* (built in 1907 and long known as the "speed queen" of the Atlantic), and the *Lusitania* (sunk by a German U-boat in 1915 off the coast of Ireland). Perhaps its best-known ships were the *Queen Mary*, the *Queen Elizabeth*, and the *Queen Elizabeth II*. The *Queen Mary* arrived in New York City in 1936 and gained an enduring popularity for her speed, service, and beautiful interiors. She carried troops between New York City and the United Kingdom during the Second World War and later resumed commercial service from New York City. The flagship of Cunard in the mid 1990s was the superliner *Queen Elizabeth II*, which sailed between New York City and the Caribbean during the winter and across the Atlantic during the summer.

Francis Edwin Hyde: *Cunard and the North Atlantic, 1840–1973: A History of Shipping and Financial Management* (London: Macmillan, 1975)

Frank O. Braynard

Cunningham, Merce (*b* Centralia, Wash., 16 April 1919). Dancer and choreographer. After moving to New York City he was a principal dancer in Martha Graham's company from 1939 to 1945. In 1942 he began a collaboration with the composer John Cage that lasted until Cage's death in 1992: the two performed together in the city in 1944; were commissioned by Lincoln Kirstein in 1947 to create *The Seasons* (set designs by Isamu Noguchi), performed by Ballet Society (forerunner of the New York City Ballet); and in the early 1950s undertook radical, influential experiments in which random methods such as tossing coins were used to determine musical pitch, duration, and dynamics, as well as choreographic elements like speed, sequence, and location in space. The Merce Cunningham Dance Company, formed in the summer of 1953 at Black Mountain College in North Carolina, was based in New York City from 1953. The original members included Carolyn Brown, Viola Farber, Remy Charlip, and Paul Taylor (dancers), Cage (music director), and David Tudor (composer and pianist); later members included the painters Robert Rauschenberg (designer, 1954–64), Jasper Johns (artistic advisor, 1967–84), and Mark Lancaster (artistic advisor, 1980–85). Cunningham also collaborated with a number of other painters, including Frank Stella, Andy Warhol, Robert Morris, and Bruce Nauman, as well as with the composers Morton Feldman, Earle Brown, Christian Wolff, David Behrman, and Takehisa Kosugi. In the early 1970s he began providing choreography for film and videotape in conjunction with the company's resident filmmakers, Charles Atlas and later Elliot Caplan. Most of these works were later adapted for the stage, notably *Channels/Inserts* (1981) and *Points in Space* (1986). Cunningham's notebooks have been collected and edited in *Changes: Notes on Choreography* (1968), and a series of interviews with him was published as *Le danseur et la danse* (1980; Eng. trans. 1985).

Merce Cunningham, Sixteen Dances for Soloist and Company of Three *(1946, music by John Cage)*

James Klosty, ed.: *Merce Cunningham* (New York: Saturday Review Press, 1975; rev. Limelight, 1986)

David Vaughan

CUNY. See City university of new york.

Cuomo, Mario M(atthew) (*b* Queens, 15 June 1932). Governor. The son of Italian immigrants, he attended St. John's University Law School and was admitted to the bar in 1956. He worked for liberal causes, defended community groups, and proved an adept mediator during a dispute over low-income housing in Forest Hills in the 1960s. Appointed secretary of state of New York by Governor Hugh L. Carey in 1975, he investigated abuses in nursing homes and negotiated solutions to various disputes on the governor's behalf. In 1977 he was persuaded by Carey to seek the mayoralty of New York City but lost the Democratic primary to Edward I. Koch, whom Carey supported in the general election even though Cuomo remained on the ballot as the candidate of the Liberal Party. During Carey's second term (1979–83) he served as lieutenant governor. He himself sought the governorship when Carey declined to seek reelection in 1982, defeating Koch in the Democratic primary and the Republican businessman Lewis Lehrman in the general election. As governor Cuomo established himself as an effective negotiator and budget planner, a champion of bipartisan politics, and an independent thinker and eloquent speaker who differed with his own church by favoring abortion rights and with a large segment of the electorate by opposing the death penalty. He was reelected to the governorship by overwhelming margins in 1986 and 1990. Widely regarded as a prospective candidate for the presidency, he spent a good deal of time in 1991 considering whether to mount a campaign before deciding to remain in Albany. In 1994 he was defeated in his attempt to win a fourth consecutive term.

Robert S. McElvaine: *Mario Cuomo: A Biography* (New York: Charles Scribner's Sons, 1988)

For illustration see Dinkins, David N.

Leslie Gourse

Curling, 1870

Curb. Original name of the American stock exchange.

curling. Game of Scottish origin in which a disc of stone or iron is slid toward a target by two teams of four players each. It became popular in New York City during the late nineteenth century. Among the many clubs formed the best-known was the New York Caledonian Curling Club, which had headquarters on Sullivan Street; others included the St. Andrew's Curling Club, the New York Thistle Curling Club, and the Brooklyn Caledonian Curling Club. Matches were often held on Central Park Lake, and the Grand National Curling Club championships attracted crowds from throughout the Northeast. In Brooklyn matches were at Prospect Park Lake. Curling was eventually eclipsed in popularity by baseball and other sports.

James Bradley

Currier and Ives. Firm of lithographers, formed in New York City in 1857. Its elder partner was Nathaniel Currier (*b* Roxbury [now in Boston], 27 March 1813; *d* New York City, 20 Nov 1888), who served an apprenticeship in Boston with the lithography firm of William and John Pendleton before settling in New York City, where he was in business as N. Currier by 1835. Originally he was a job printer who produced tickets, billheads, flyers,

Currier and Ives, "The Age of Brass" (1869; also known as "The Triumph of Woman's Rights")

and certificates commissioned by others; one highly successful image was *Awful Conflagration of the Steam Boat Lexington*, a dramatic scene of the disaster of January 1840 that appeared in editions of the *Sun*. About 1840 Currier put into effect a plan to produce and market works by his own firm. Among the decorative and timely lithographs that he offered were *City Hotel: Broadway, New York*, *Jenny Lind: Als Tochter des Regiments*, and a temperance caricature, *The Drunkards Progress*. In 1852 Currier engaged as his bookkeeper James Merritt Ives (*b* New York City, 5 March 1824; *d* Rye, N.Y., 3 Jan 1895), who proved an indispensable businessman and became a partner. The firm of Currier and Ives had two main locations in lower Manhattan, at Nassau Street and 33 Spruce Street, near Gold Street.

During the following decades Currier and Ives virtually abandoned job printing and focused on providing reasonably priced decorative images to the general public nationwide and in Europe. Their work displayed little if any artistic or technical superiority over that of their competitors, but their skill at marketing enabled them to become the most successful lithography firm in the United States. The firm's huge inventory of about seven thousand titles included sporting prints (such as *The Yacht Dauntless of N.Y.* and *Mr. William H. Vanderbilt's Celebrated Team Small Hopes and Lady Mac: Driven by their Owner*), views (*Great East River Suspension Bridge*, *Central Park, the Drive*, *The Narrows from Staten Island*, and *New York and Brooklyn*), comic series (*Life in New York*) and fashion prints (*The Grecian Bend: Fifth Avenue Style*), romantic images (*The Belle of New York*), and political portraits (*Hon. Wm. A. Wheeler: of New York*). Among the artists whose works they reproduced were Louis Maurer, James Buttersworth (who specialized in depicting ships), George Henry Durrie (country scenes, especially seasonal ones), and Fanny Palmer (still lifes and rural views). The best-known lithographers employed by the firm were James Cameron and Napoleon Sarony.

Currier retired in 1880, and under Ives's direction the firm worked in chromolithography until his death. Both men are buried in Green-Wood Cemetery. Two sons of the founders were unsuccessful in their attempts to run the business, which closed in 1907. After the First World War major collections of the work of Currier and Ives were formed by businessmen in New York City such as Harry Peters: his collection is now held by the Museum of the City of New York. Other important holdings are at the Library of Congress and the New-York Historical Society.

Harry T. Peters: *Currier and Ives: Printmakers to the American People* (Garden City, N.Y.: Doubleday, Doran, 1929)

Bernard F. Reilly Jr.: Introd., *Currier and Ives: A Catalogue Raisonné* (Detroit: Gale Research, 1984)

James Brust and Wendy Shadwell: "The Many Versions and States of The . . . Lexington," *Imprint* 15, no. 2 (1990), 2–13

For illustration see CENTRAL PARK.

Wendy Shadwell

Curry, John F(rancis) (*b* Ireland, 2 Nov 1873; *d* Coral Gables, Fla., 25 April 1957). Political leader. After election to the state assembly (1902) he became the leader of his district on the West Side (1905) and commissioner of records (1911–29). Long at odds with the "new Tammany," he was elected by his colleagues to lead Tammany Hall in 1929, with the backing of Mayor James J. Walker and James J. Hines. In 1931 he refused to waive immunity during the investigation of municipal government led by Samuel Seabury. His fatal mistake was to try to block the nominations of Franklin D. Roosevelt for president and Herbert H. Lehman for governor in 1932. In the following year the mayoral candidate whom he backed, John P. O'Brien, was defeated, and he was himself ousted from the leadership of Tammany Hall in 1934.

Frank Vos

Curtis, George William (*b* New York City, 24 Feb 1824; *d* New York City, 31 Aug 1892). Writer, editor, and reformer. After a youth spent in New England and abroad he returned in 1850 to New York City and began a career in book publishing and journalism at a time when the city's firms were increasingly dominating the field. He first gained recognition for a series of popular travel narratives and social satires, including *Nile Notes of a Howadji* (1851), *The Potiphar Papers* (1853), and *Prue and I* (1856). During the mid 1850s he edited the short-lived but influential *Putnam's Monthly* with his friend Frederick Law Olmsted and began an association with the leading publishing house Harper and Brothers that lasted for thirty-five years. From his office in the Harper building on Franklin Square and more often from his suburban villa on Staten

Currier and Ives, "The Age of Iron" (1869)

Island he composed monthly essays for *Harper's Monthly Magazine* under the rubric "Editor's Easy Chair" (1854–92), a series of moral and social sketches entitled "Manners upon the Road" for *Harper's Bazar* (1867–73), and the editorial columns for *Harper's Weekly* (from 1863 until his death). In his writings he advocated woman suffrage and attacked high tariffs and patronage politics; he also led the campaign for a professional civil service and was the president of the National Civil Service Reform League in 1881–92. With E. L. Godkin at the *Nation* Curtis was a powerful shaper of élite public opinion during the Gilded Age. His career exemplified the close links between professional journalism, literary culture, commerce, and public activism among upper-class intellectuals in the late nineteenth century.

Edward Cary: *George William Curtis* (Boston: Houghton Mifflin, 1894)

Gordon Milne: *George William Curtis and the Genteel Tradition* (Bloomington: Indiana University Press, 1956)

See also INTELLECTUALS.

David Scobey

Curtis High School. Secondary school opened in 1904 at Hamilton Avenue and St. Mark's Place in St. George. Named after the editor, writer, and reformer George William Curtis, it was the first public high school on Staten Island. In 1991 it had sixteen hundred students and offered programs in fashion design, theater arts, computer science, and international service as well as an international baccalaureate degree. Some of its students take part in the Naval Junior Reserve Officer Training Corps.

Erica Judge

Cushman, Charlotte (Saunders) (*b* Boston, 23 July 1816; *d* Boston, 18 Feb 1876). Actress. She made her début in New York City as Lady Macbeth (1836) and in several appearances abroad became the first American-born actress to earn an international reputation. She gave successful performances in several roles in 1871 at Booth's Theatre, where she also gave her farewell performance as Lady Macbeth on 7 November 1874.

Don B. Wilmeth

Cushman, Don Alonzo (*b* Coventry, Conn., 1 Oct 1792; *d* New York City, 1 May 1875). Businessman. He moved to New York City at eighteen, was a clerk in the dry-goods trade, and by the age of twenty-one owned his own firm. In 1830 he purchased a sizable piece of land at what is now 172 9th Avenue in Chelsea and built a house that still stands; he later became a principal developer of the area. Cushman was a leading member of both Trinity Church and St. Peter's Church, a founder of the Greenwich Savings Bank, a director of the Erie Railway Company, and an alderman for the sixteenth ward. Cushman Row (406–18 West 20th Street) is named for him, as are the DONAC apartment building (402 West 20th Street) and the Cushman–Wakefield Realty Company.

Val Ginter

Cutter, Bloodgood H(aviland) (*b* Little Neck [now in Queens], 5 Aug 1817; *d* Queens, 26 Sept 1906). Poet. Born to a family long established in Flushing, he was the master of a coastal schooner before inheriting his grandfather's estate, after which he settled into the life of a gentleman farmer; in 1840 he married Emmaline Allen, daughter of a prosperous farmer from Little Neck. Several of his poems refer to incidents of the Civil War. His best-known include "On Laying the Corner Stone of the Town Hall at Flushing, Long Island," "To the Health Authorities of Naples," "On Tobacco Smoking in Queens County Court House," and "Spare That Cottage." *The Long Island Farmer's Poems*, a five-hundred-page collection of his works, was published in 1886. Cutter was the "poet lariat" in *Innocents Abroad* by Mark Twain, who described his verse as "barberous rhyme." He is buried in Zion Episcopal Church in Douglaston.

Jeffrey A. Kroessler

CYO. See CATHOLIC YOUTH ORGANIZATION.

Cypress Hills. Neighborhood in northeastern Brooklyn (1990 pop. 7797), lying on a terminal moraine and bounded to the north by the Queens county line, to the east by Eldert Lane, to the south by Atlantic Avenue, and to the west by Pennsylvania Avenue. It was called Union Place after a local racecourse during the 1820s before being renamed for the trees growing on hills in the area. To the north lie Highland Park and eighteen cemeteries that contain the graves of twenty thousand veterans from the Civil War and later wars, as well as those of Harry Houdini, Mae West, Edward G. Robinson, and Sholem Aleichem. Cypress Hills is working class and the housing consists of one-, two-, and three-family houses; Fulton Street is the main commercial thoroughfare.

Monro MacCloskey: *Hallowed Ground: Our National Cemeteries* (New York: Richard Rosen, 1968)

Alter Landesman: *A History of New Lots, Brooklyn to 1887* (Port Washington, N.Y.: Kennikat, 1977)

John J. Gallagher

Cypriots. Cypriots first emigrated to the United States during the early twentieth century; they entered through Ellis Island and the great majority settled in New York City. Large numbers followed in the 1950s, and many Greek Cypriots arrived after the Turkish invasion of Cyprus in 1974. Greek Cypriots initially settled in Manhattan and later moved to Queens, New Jersey, and Long Island. They formed many cultural organizations under the auspices of the Cyprus Federation of America (1951), as well as three Greek Cypriot community centers in Astoria. Their high level of education enabled Greek Cypriots to rise socially and economically along with other Greek–Americans. Turkish Cypriots settled at first in the Bronx and formed the Turkish–Cypriot Aid Society (1931) and the Inonou School (1979) to teach Turkish language and culture to children. In later years a number of Turkish Cypriots moved to Queens, upstate New York, and New Jersey. In the mid 1990s it was estimated that there were thirty thousand Greek Cypriots in New York City and five thousand Turkish Cypriots.

Antonia S. Mattheou

D

Daché, Lilly (*b* Beigles, France, ?1892; *d* Louvecienne, France, 31 Dec 1989). Milliner. At the age of fourteen she left school to assist her aunt, a milliner, and after an apprenticeship in Paris she moved to the United States in 1924. She began by selling hats at R. H. Macy and soon was able to open her own shop, where she introduced one of her signature designs, a hat molded snugly to the head. In 1937 she moved into a building on East 57th Street that served as her work studio, sales floor, and home. She created custom hats for fashionable customers, including many film stars, and also began selling ready-to-wear hats through department stores. Her turban, snood, and war worker's hats were among her most famous designs. As her store became more successful she expanded her design repertory to include gloves, lingerie, dresses, perfumes, and men's shirts and ties. When she retired in 1968 her daughter Suzanne pursued millinery in her stead. Daché wrote *Talking through My Hats* (1946) and *Glamour Book* (1956).

Anne E. Kornblut

D'Agostino. Firm of food retailers, formed by a family that moved to New York City from Abruzzi in 1921. Nicola D'Agostino became a pushcart peddler along with his brother Pasquale (Patsy), who later worked in a butcher shop. In 1932 the brothers combined several specialized food shops in one emporium at Lexington Avenue and 83rd Street that was a forerunner of the modern supermarket. Patsy D'Agostino was also active in retail food distribution. After the death of Pasquale D'Agostino in 1960 Nicola D'Agostino retired in 1964 in favor of his sons. In 1986 Nicholas D'Agostino Jr. became chairman of the board of what was now a chain of twenty-four supermarkets with headquarters in New Rochelle, New York.

Mary Elizabeth Brown

Dahl-Wolfe, Louise (*b* San Francisco, 19 Nov 1895; *d* Allendale, N.J., 11 Dec 1989). Photographer. She studied at the San Francisco Institute of Art and used her background in fine art to create vibrant photographs, portraits, and pictorials, with subjects ranging from well-known personages and fashion models to women living in the mountains of Tennessee. Between 1936 and 1958 she produced eighty-six covers and more than sixteen hundred photographs for *Harper's Bazaar*, which remain her best-known work. The Museum of Modern Art and many galleries in New York City and elsewhere have exhibited her photographs. She wrote *Louise Dahl-Wolfe: A Photographer's Scrapbook*.

Linda Elsroad

Daily Mirror. Daily newspaper launched in 1924 in New York City by William Randolph Hearst. It began as a tabloid indistinguishable from its competitor, the heavily illustrated *Daily News*, but later developed a more sensational style characterized by manufactured stories and heavy use of doctored photographs and "picture snatching" (the taking of unauthorized photographs). Its writers included the gossip columnist Walter Winchell and the political commentator Drew Pearson. Although the newspaper drew many advertisers it was second in both advertising and circulation to the *Daily News* for many years and in the 1950s experienced declining profits. A newspaper strike that lasted 114 days in 1962 further weakened the *Daily Mirror*, which on 16 October 1963 printed its final edition.

Simon Michael Bessie: *Jazz Journalism: The Story of the Tabloid Newspapers* (New York: E. P. Dutton, 1938)

Lindsay Chaney and Michael Cieply: *The Hearsts: Family and Empire: The Later Years* (New York: Simon and Schuster, 1981)

Madeline Rogers

Daily News. Newspaper first published on 26 June 1919 as the *Illustrated Daily News* by Joseph Medill Patterson; the name changed to its current form during the first year. Inspired by Lord Northcliffe's *Daily Mirror* of London, Patterson intended to publish the first successful American tabloid by satisfying the tastes of a mass audience. The newspaper became noted for its use of newly developed illustration techniques, especially halftone photographs, and its focus on popular feature stories, local news, and personality profiles. The offices were situated first in the Evening Mail building at 25 City Hall Place and moved after two years to 25 Park Place. During the early years Patterson oversaw operations from Chicago, the center of his wealthy family's newspaper dynasty. The earliest editions were cheaply printed on rented presses and circulation was disappointing, but by late 1920 the newspaper began to show a small profit as New Yorkers responded to its convenient size and gritty sensationalism. In 1922 circulation reached 400,000 and a Sunday edition was introduced, and in 1924 circulation reached 750,000, making the *Daily News* the most widely read newspaper in the United States.

The immense popularity of the *News* during the 1920s was due to its inclusion of numerous photographs, illustrations, comic strips, contests, and coupons, as well as its sensationalist coverage of local news stories, scandals, fires, and crime. A famous front-page photograph in January 1928 of the execution of the murderess Ruth Snyder, taken surreptitiously by a photographer who had strapped a camera to his leg, sold thousands of extra copies of the newspaper. Techniques were developed to include sex and violence in otherwise mundane articles, and great effort was taken to make reading the newspaper a participatory experience, for example by including the full names and addresses of those interviewed. The most popular items were the "Inquiring Photographer" (a feature widely imitated) and a section of letters called "Voice of the People." In the spring of 1926 circulation exceeded one million on weekdays and 1.25 million on Sundays. In 1930 the newspaper moved to a thirty-seven-story art deco skyscraper at 220 East 42nd Street, designed by John Mead Howells and Raymond M. Hood and erected at a cost of more than $10 million.

Patterson tempered the newspaper's more extreme sensationalisms during the 1930s and began to address the more serious issues brought on by the Depression and by the New Deal, which the newspaper solidly supported for most of the decade. But it continued to exemplify tabloid journalism, as it inaugurated a "beautiful baby" contest, sponsored dance marathons, and defended itself against libel suits by Lou Gehrig and others. By 1939 the Sunday edition was the most widely read newspaper in the world, selling more than three million copies. Notwithstanding its history of support for Roosevelt, the *News* took a staunchly isolationist stand toward Nazi aggression in Europe, opposing the Lend-Lease bill in 1940 and gasoline rationing in 1941, and eventually likening Roosevelt to Napoleon and Mussolini. On Patterson's death in 1946 control of the newspaper passed to Roy Hollis, a member of the board of directors who died in an automobile accident three months later. Richard Clarke was then named executive editor, reporting to the new head of the News Syndicate Company, Eleanor "Cissy" Patterson (sister of the founder).

After the Second World War the newspaper became markedly more conservative in its politics. It continued to be identified with a lively writing style characterized by breeziness, puns, and aphorisms: a front-page headline that appeared when the federal government refused to extend help to the city during its fiscal crisis in 1975, "Ford to City: Drop Dead," became a classic of tabloid journalism. In the meantime readership steadily declined as the newspaper lost much of its traditional base — blue-collar workers, immigrants, and members of racial minorities — to the suburbs, television, and to a lesser extent the foreign-language press. The *News* lost $11 million in 1981 and the owners made an unsuccessful attempt to sell the newspaper in the following year. By this time circulation stood at 1.5 million on weekdays and 2.1 million on Sunday.

A crippling strike by deliverers begun in October 1990 threatened the newspaper's survival and led to profound changes. The owners continued to publish by urging em-

Daily News Building (designed by Howells and Hood), housing both offices and printing plant, ca *1935*

ployees to cross picket lines and securing replacement workers, and the union urged boycotts by advertisers and newsdealers. In March 1991 negotiations collapsed, and it was announced that the newspaper would cease publication unless a buyer was found. Robert Maxwell, a successful newspaper publisher from Britain, then purchased the *News* when the union agreed to drastic staff reductions. Maxwell drowned under mysterious circumstances in November; in the following year control was assumed by Mortimer B. Zuckerman, a successful real-estate developer. In 1994 the newspaper announced plans to move to a sixteen-story office building at 450 West 33rd Street.

By the mid 1990s the *Daily News* had recovered much of the circulation that it had lost during the strike, but its future remained uncertain in view of a widespread perception that New York City could not long support four daily newspapers, including three tabloids.

Jack Alexander: "Vox Populi," *New Yorker,* 6 Aug 1938, 13 Aug 1938, 20 Aug 1938

Frank Luther Mott: *American Journalism: A History of Newspapers in the United States through 250 Years, 1690 to 1940* (New York: Macmillan, 1941)

John Tebbel: *An American Dynasty* (New York: Greenwood, 1968)

Leo E. McGivena et al.: *The News: The First Fifty Years of New York's Picture Newspaper* (New York: News Syndicate, 1969)

Steve Rivo

Daily Worker. Newspaper of the American Communist Party, later known as the PEOPLE'S WEEKLY WORLD.

dairying. Cattle were introduced to New Amsterdam in 1625, including a few milk cows. According to a report by Jonas Michaëlius in 1628, dairy products were sought after but scarce in Manhattan. Local herds proliferated and in 1644 colonists built a wall near what is now Wall Street to prevent cattle from leaving pastures in Battery Park. Larger grounds near City Hall were used for summer pastures from 1653, and meadows in northern Manhattan were used into the nineteenth century. Each morning summer herdsmen employed by the city blew horns to move the cattle to fresh pasture; in the evening they returned each animal to its owner, ready to be milked and bedded down. Winter fodder was mostly corn or wild marsh-hay from Long Island. Throughout the seventeenth and eighteenth centuries dairying remained a practice of general farming, and milk, butter, and cheese (which was especially scarce) were sometimes bartered to neighbors or traded to local retailers. Ice cream made by skilled confectioners became popular in the city during the American Revolution, and by 1779 it was made for home delivery by Joseph Corree in his shop at 17 Hanover Square; it soon became known as "everyman's dessert." In 1806 the cheese maker Ephraim Perkins urged wheat farmers of Herkimer County, New York, to shift to dairying and produce cheese for the city market. He himself opened a dairy farm in Herkimer County that by 1828 had seventy-eight cows and shipped as much as sixteen tons (14.5 metric tons) of cheddar cheese a year to the city, and farms in the surrounding counties soon also became suppliers. The merchant and geographer John Melish wrote in 1807 that the first milkmen walked around the city carrying two buckets of tepid milk suspended from a yoke.

As the city grew during the nineteenth century, farmland and cattle became scarce in Manhattan and dairy farmers moved to Williamsburgh, other parts of Brooklyn, and Queens County. Haphazard breeding practices and poor management left dairying primarily in the hands of farmers who sought large profits and followed advice given in newspapers and agricultural tracts by Zadock Pratt, Silas L. Loomis, and Xerxes A. Willard.

Meadow Brook Dairy, 100 Canal Street, Stapleton

Local dairies were unable to satisfy demand and in the 1820s swill milk was first offered, produced by cows fed a mixture of mash, warm slop from stills, and brewer's grain, and kept in sheds attached to breweries and distilleries. Swill milk producers rented stalls to cattle owners in Manhattan for $5 a year and sold their milk (labeled "pure country milk") for four or five cents a quart (or liter); the largest firm was that of William M. Johnson and Son on 16th Street. The cows were often unhealthy, tied in stalls three feet (one meter) wide and fed thirty-two gallons (120 liters) of slop and three pounds (1.4 kilograms) of hay daily. As early as 1826 some farmers who sold milk and butter in the city used as middlemen such captains on the Hudson River as Joel D. Hunter, who opened the firm of Hunter Walton. One enterprising farmer, Thomas W. Decker, used flatboats to transport milk from his farm in Fordham to markets on the East Side, where he had a thriving business; he later joined with other milkmen to form Sheffield Farms, which became one of the largest milk producers in the Northeast. By 1830 large-scale producers used horse-drawn carts for home delivery, and in the 1840s "hokey-pokey men" first sold homemade, hand-dipped ice cream from small wagons pulled by goats; after 1848 they used small freezers.

Milk was first shipped to the city regularly in special ice-cooled cars in 1842 by the New York and Erie Railroad, which by 1850 shipped 13,428,311 gallons (56,758,785 liters) a year. As demand rose, farms in Queens, Orange, and Westchester counties supplied milk to the city. Such improved breeds as the Ayrshire, Holstein–Frisian, and Simmetal were imported about this time. The New York and Harlem Railroad shipped four million gallons (17.1 million liters) in 1847 and double that quantity by 1852, when there were twenty-five milk companies in the city, with twelve hundred employees and nearly eight hundred horses. Even after they were connected to the city by rail, farms in outlying areas faced stiff competition from factories in the city: in the 1850s two thirds of the city's milk was supplied by cows fed distillery grains. From 1842 the reformer Robert M. Hartley contended that New Yorkers' health was deteriorating because of swill milk, which had a bluish tint and uneven consistency that prompted retailers to add borax, chalk, starch, flour, sugar, calves' brains, or water, an especially dangerous additive because the city's supply was often impure. Other reformers joined Hartley in fighting horrendous conditions in swill milk factories in northern Manhattan and Brooklyn. In the 1850s Hartley's findings were published in *Frank Leslie's Illustrated Newspaper*, which with John Mullaly's pamphlet *The Milk Trade of New York and Vicinity* (1853) argued that swill milk caused the deaths of thousands of children in the city. Swill milk maintained its hold on the fluid market until legislation in 1862 reduced its market share; legislation in 1864 prohibited retailers from diluting milk with water.

Jacob Fussell, the first ice cream wholesaler, sold his product for twenty-five cents a quart in 1864 (confectioners charged $1.25). Butter from Goshen and other towns in Orange County, New York, dominated the city's market until 1873, when the Oleo-Margarine Manufacturing Company opened in Manhattan and produced oleomargarine that tasted like butter and cost less. Children continued to suffer from the effects of adulterated and spoiled milk. Harvey D. Thatcher developed the "Common Sense Milk Bottle" (patented in 1884), a glass bottle fitted with a rubber O-ring, as well as a complex system of packing, shipping, and reusing bottles that allowed milk to be delivered under more sanitary conditions. In 1889 Henry Koplik opened the first milk depot that pasteurized milk for poor infants. "Certified" milk, which was approved by physicians and supposedly sold only to children, was introduced by Henry L. Coit in the 1890s. Milk depots became popular after Nathan Straus's laboratory on the East 3rd Street Pier offered "sterilized milk" at four cents a quart. In 1912 Ernest J. Lederle, the health commissioner, made pasteurization mandatory for all milk for children despite opposition from dealers seeking to avoid the expense; nonetheless 10 percent of the milk consumed in the city was still unpasteurized in 1920. Cottage cheese, cream cheese, and sour cream were made by the firm of Breakstone Foods on the Lower East Side from 1882, and in 1900 the Constantinople-on-the-Pike, or Cornucopia (ice cream in a cone), was served in stores that flourished on Chatham Street. After the turn of the century parmesan and mozzarella cheese also became popular as restaurants increasingly catered to a diverse population.

After 1913 bowls of ice cream were offered for five cents by Horn and Hardart's Automat; Cho-Cho novelty bars, Cherio-bars, and Sidewalk Sundaes were introduced in the 1920s but were overshadowed by the Mel-O-Rol, a specialty at the World's Fair of 1939–40. Such local producers as the J. M. Horton Ice Cream Company in Manhattan and the Reid and Union Dairy and the Blue Ribbon Ice Cream Company in Brooklyn became unable to compete. By 1930 they were bought by the Pioneer Ice Cream Division of Borden, which in 1932 became the first ice cream plant in the metropolitan area to abandon metal cans for paper cartons. As the city grew, dairy producers could no longer offer personal service, and cooperative marketing associations were formed to run processing plants and sell dairy products in retail stores and along home delivery routes in the city. New Deal policies in the 1930s set strict government guidelines for quality control, and in 1933 New York State enacted milk control laws to stabilize prices and protect small, independent dealers, a practice that inspired similar efforts by other states and soon had the effect of restricting entry into the market. In 1942 Daniel Carasso and Juan Metzger began making Dannon Yogurt in the Bronx, a product that became highly successful after the firm changed from whole milk to skim milk in the 1970s.

Dairying in New York City and its environs declined sharply during the following decades, in the face of increasing urbanization, rising taxes and land costs, and improved technology for storing milk and transporting it over long distances. As late as 1940 the federal census of agriculture counted six farms with 328 cows in Brooklyn, nine farms with 563 cows in Queens, and nine farms with 127 cows in Staten Island. By 1978 there remained only one farm in Queens and one in Staten Island. Local ice cream brands including Borden and Sealtest lost a large portion of the market during the 1970s and 1980s to "premium" and "super premium" brands. In an effort to balance the needs of producers, middlemen, and consumers, New York State continued to regulate the production and sale of milk: the Milk Control and Milk Producers Security Reform Act of 1987 effectively eliminated both intrastate and interstate competition.

Robert M. Hartley: *An Historical, Scientific and Practical Essay on Milk* (New York: Jonathan Leavitt, 1842)

John Mullaly: *The Milk Trade of New York and Vicinity* (New York: n.pub., 1853)

Eric E. Lampard: *The Rise of the Dairy Industry in Wisconsin* (Madison: State Historical Society of Wisconsin, 1963)

Ralph Selitzer: *The Dairy Industry in America* (New York: Dairy and Ice Cream Field, 1976)

Thomas D. Beal

Daitch–Shopwell. A chain of supermarkets formed in New York City in December 1955 from the merger of Daitch Crystal Dairies and Shopwell Foods. By 1962 it had grown to include 103 stores, but it declined during the 1960s and 1970s. Most of the stores had been renamed Shopwell or Food Emporium by 1986, when the chain was acquired by the Great Atlantic and Pacific Tea Company.

Howard Kaplan

Dakota. Apartment building at 1 West 72nd Street in Manhattan. It was built between 1882 and 27 October 1884 by Henry J. Hardenbergh, later the designer of the Plaza Hotel, at the initiative of Edward Clark, president of the Singer Manufacturing Company. The name of the building reflects its remoteness at the time it was built, on a site so far north of the fashionable parts of the city that a friend of Clark once likened it to the Dakota Territory. Despite its inconvenient location and a feeling on the part of many wealthy New Yorkers that apartments were no better than tenement housing, the building was fully

The Dakota, ca *1890.* Foreground *ice skating in Central Park*

rented by the time of its completion, without benefit of paid advertising. The new building had eighty-five apartments of four to twenty rooms each, with drawing rooms as large as twenty-five by forty feet (eight by twelve meters), ceilings ranging in height from fifteen feet (4.5 meters) on the second floor to twelve feet (3.6 meters) on the seventh floor, and interior walls paneled in fine woods. The roof was steeply gabled, and decorative patterns were etched on an exterior of yellow brick, rose marble, and dark brownstone (over time these darkened to various shades of brown). The tenants were served by a staff of 150. A ten-room apartment in the building cost $250 a month, an extravagant sum by the standards of the day. Over the years the Dakota became perhaps the most recognizable apartment building in the city. It was the setting for Roman Polanski's film *Rosemary's Baby* (1968) and the home of many figures in the arts and entertainment, including Leonard Bernstein, Boris Karloff, Judy Garland, and Judy Holliday. One of the best-known residents, John Lennon, was fatally shot in front of the building in December 1980.

Stephen Birmingham: *Life at the Dakota: New York's Most Unusual Address* (New York: Random House, 1979)

Clarissa L. Bushman

Dalton School. Private elementary and secondary school at 108 East 89th Street in Manhattan, opened in 1919 by Helen Parkhurst, who was active in the progressive education movement. Originally called the Children's University School and situated at West 74th Street, it moved in 1922 to another building on the same street and in 1929 to its current location. As the school's headmaster Parkhurst implemented the Laboratory Plan, which stressed cooperation between students and teachers to set individualized goals. The school used no tests or grades and virtually no discipline. It remained true to Parkhurst's principles after she retired in 1942 and continued operating into the 1990s. Its enrollment in the mid 1990s was 1290, including students from kindergarten to the twelfth grade.

Diane Lager: "Helen Parkhurst and the Dalton Plan" (diss., University of Connecticut, 1983)

Alfonso J. Orsini

Daly, (John) Augustin (*b* Plymouth, N.C., 20 July 1838; *d* Paris, 7 June 1899). Playwright. As a young man he moved to New York City and worked as a theater critic for several newspapers including the *Sunday Courier*, the *Sun*, and the *New York Times*. His plays *Under the Gaslight* (1867), *Horizon* (1871), and *Divorce* (1871) were well received, and in 1869 he formed his own company at the Fifth Avenue Theatre. After the theater was destroyed by fire in 1873 he leased another one and named it Daly's Fifth Avenue Theatre. He also ran the Grand Opera House, where his *Roughing It* was a tremendous success and where he presented adaptations of English and European works. From 1884 he led companies on tours of Europe. By the end of his life Daly had written and adapted more than ninety plays.

Joseph Francis Daly: *The Life of Augustin Daly* (New York: Macmillan, 1917)

Marvin Felheim: *The Theater of Augustin Daly: An Account of the Late Nineteenth-century American Stage* (Cambridge: Harvard University Press, 1956)

James E. Mooney

Damrosch, Frank (Heino) (*b* Breslau, Germany [now Wrocław, Poland], 22 June 1859; *d* New York City, 22 Oct 1937). Educator and conductor, son of Leopold Damrosch. He attended City College, lived in Denver for several years, and returned to the city to become the choirmaster of the Metropolitan Opera in 1885–91. He founded the People's Choral Union (which performed until 1909), conducted a small a cappella chorus called the Musical Art Society (1893–1920), supervised music education in the public schools (1897–1905), and conducted the Oratorio Society (1898–1912). In 1905 he opened the Institute of Musical Art; he directed the institute until 1926, when it and the Juilliard Graduate School (1924) became branches of the Juilliard School of Music, of which he was the dean until 1933.

George Whitney Martin: *The Damrosch Dynasty: America's First Family of Music* (Boston: Houghton Mifflin, 1983)

Nancy Shear

Damrosch, Leopold (*b* Posen, Germany [now Poznań, Poland], 22 Oct 1832; *d* New York City, 15 Feb 1885). Violinist, conductor, and composer, father of Frank and Walter Damrosch. After taking a degree in medicine he became the first violinist in the ducal orchestra at Weimar and a friend of Liszt and Wagner. In 1871 he took his family to New York City, and until 1883 he led the Männergesangverein Arion. He founded the Oratorio Society (1873) and the Symphony Society (1878) and conducted the Metropolitan Opera, and remained associated with each institution until his death. Committed to the German repertory, he gave the American première of Brahms's Symphony no. 1, conducted at the first large-scale music festival in the city in 1881 (with an orchestra of 250 and a chorus of twelve hundred), and in 1884–85 gave the American premières of Wagner's *Der Ring des Nibelungen* and *Tristan und Isolde*. Damrosch and his sons determined the shape of opera in New York City. The outdoor musical amphitheater just south of the Metropolitan Opera House at Lincoln Center is named for his family.

George Whitney Martin: *The Damrosch Dynasty: America's First Family of Music* (Boston: Houghton Mifflin, 1983)

Nancy Shear

Damrosch, Walter (Johannes) (*b* Breslau, Germany [now Wrocław, Poland], 30 Jan 1862; *d* New York City, 22 Dec 1950). Conductor and educator, son of Leopold Damrosch. He became a director of the Metropolitan Opera with Anton Seidl on the death of his father in 1885, and remained with the company until 1891. In 1885–98 he conducted the New York Oratorio Society, and in 1894 he formed the Damrosch Opera Company, which introduced opera in many cities across the United States. Between 1885 and 1928 he periodically conducted the New York Philharmonic, and in 1899 he returned to the Metropolitan for two seasons of German opera. He produced a European tour by the New York Symphony Society in 1920, the first by an American orchestra, and in 1925 he conducted the first orchestral concert broadcast nationally on radio. Damrosch was the host of a weekly music appreciation program with the NBC Symphony in 1928–42, and for many years he presented lectures, recitals, and children's concerts.

George Whitney Martin: *The Damrosch Dynasty: America's First Family of Music* (Boston: Houghton Mifflin, 1983)

Nancy Shear

Dana, Charles A(nderson) (*b* Hinsdale, N.H., 8 Aug 1819; *d* Glen Cove, N.Y., 17 Oct 1897). Newspaper editor and publisher. After a sojourn at the utopian colony Brook Farm, he joined the *New York Tribune* in 1847, becoming Horace Greeley's assistant and arguably the first American newspaperman to hold the position of managing editor. In 1867–68 he bought and became the chief editor of the *Sun*, which under his direction became noted for its independence from both political parties and its opposition to civil service reform and the labor movement. Dana was among the most influential newspapermen of the century, and his emphasis on colorful human interest stories and eye-catching headlines prefigured the practices of yellow journalism.

Candace Stone: *Dana and the Sun* (New York: Dodd, Mead, 1938)

Steven H. Jaffe

dance. The first well-documented dance performance in New York City was "The Adventures of Harlequin and Scaramouch, or the Spaniard Trick'd," a pantomime performed by the English dancer Henry Holt in February 1739. From the eighteenth century to the early nineteenth acrobats (or "posture-makers"), harlequins, jugglers, hornpipe dancers, and rope dancers were common entertainers; some dances performed on stage were based on social dances such as the minuet. Dance until the early nineteenth century was usually part of variety programs that often included plays, operas, burlesques, pantomimes (harlequinades), short recitations, singing, and acrobatics, but there were also a few one-act ballets. By 1750 the Nassau Street Theatre offered regular seasons of variety programs in which dance was included. John Gay's *The Beggar's Opera* was presented for the benefit of the actor Thomas Kean on 15 January 1751, and the dance at the end of each act was performed by "a Gentleman lately from London," possibly Robert Upton. From the early 1750s performances were given by William Hulett, a dancing-master and expert in hornpipes and harlequin dances. Lewis Hallam's American Company presented the pantomime "Harlequin Collector" at the John Street Theatre in April 1768; afterward a group of Cherokee chiefs and warriors in the audience performed a war dance on stage. One of the first known black impersonations was a "Negro dance" performed at the John Street Theatre in 1767 by Mr. Tea. Performances of this sort eventually became a genre that formed the basis of minstrelsy in the nineteenth century.

Madame Taglioni performing in La Gitana

A resolution against public amusements was passed by the Continental Congress in 1774, and theaters closed during the American Revolution before reopening somewhat cautiously in the 1780s. New York City became part of a tour circuit that included Philadelphia and Charleston, South Carolina. Because of the prevailing sentiment that theater was too frivolous an amusement for a new nation emerging from war, some theater companies disguised their entertainments as edifying recitations. John Durang, the first well-known American dancer, performed the hornpipe and patriotic dances in the city from 1784 to 1796 with the Old American Company. In 1794 he performed in "Tammany; or, the Indian Chief," the first American production incorporating opera and ballet. During the early 1790s dance flourished in the city as many French dancers settled there after escaping the French Revolution. Among them was Alexandre Placide, an acrobat, mime, and dancer who sometimes performed on a tightrope; he moved to the city in 1792 and with his common-law wife, Suzanne Vaillande, produced fifteen European ballets and pantomimes, many of which became popular. His ballets were also staged in the city by Durang, who presented his own dancers and worked with the Dutch dancer William Francis, the English ballet-master James Byrne, and M. Francisquy, a dancer in the Paris opera who introduced pantomimes based on American themes. Durang was a partner of Mme Gardie, a talented Dominican-born dancer who performed in *Sophia of Brabant* (1794), the first classical ballet given in the city.

The 1820s saw an influx of European dancers who introduced classical French ballet technique, among them Claude Labasse, Francisque Hutin, M. and Mme Achille, and Charles and Marietta Ronzi Vestris. By the 1830s and 1840s romantic ballets were regularly presented by Europeans. *La Sylphide* was first performed in part by Mlle Céleste in 1835 and in its entirety by Paul and Amalie Taglioni in 1839, the same year that marked the début of Jean Petipa and his son Marius Petipa (later the choreographer of the Russian Imperial ballet). With James Sylvain as her partner the well-known Fanny Elssler of the Paris opera performed *La Tarentule*, *La Sylphide*, and several character dances in 1840 before embarking on a two-year national tour during which she trained local dancers to augment her casts; her performances inspired an American balletomania. Several American-born ballet dancers became successful, among them Augusta Maywood, who in 1838 at thirteen made her début in the city in *Le Dieu et la bayadère* (she moved to Europe in 1839), and Mary Ann Lee, who also made her début in the city (at sixteen), studied with Jean Coralli in Paris, and returned to the United States to introduce such classics from the French repertory as *Giselle*. One of her regular partners was George Washington Smith, who also toured in Elssler's American company in 1840, studied with Sylvain, and was later the partner of Julia Turnbull, Giovanna Ciocca, Giuseppina Morlacchi, and Pepita Soto. He became the ballet-master of the Bowery Theatre in 1847 and of the Lyceum Theatre in 1850; he also arranged dances for Lola Montez during her tour in 1851 and at times was her partner. Ballets and pantomimes were often performed at the Park Theatre and Vauxhall Gardens. Audiences were generally white and of mixed social class.

Competitive Tap dancing, a blend of Irish clogging and African syncopated rhythms, was first performed in saloons and dance halls in the Five Points. By the end of the nineteenth century black minstrel shows were performed in theaters and there was also a black vaudeville circuit. Some black entertainers such as Bert Williams performed in white vaudeville shows. The extravagant ballet *The Black Crook* opened in 1866 at Niblo's Garden on Broadway and soon became one of the most popular productions of its kind in the city. The leading parts were danced by Marie Bonfanti and Rita Sangalli; the production lasted nearly six hours and incorporated dazzling fairyland transformations, a troupe of child precision dancers, and female dancers with their legs bared below mid thigh. It became a model for musical theater, vaudeville, music hall productions, and variety spectacles such as *America*, a lavish celebration of technological invention produced by Imre Kiralfy for the World's Columbian Exposition in Chicago in 1893 and performed in the same year at the Metropolitan Opera. About this time modern dance was developed in the city by Loie Fuller, Isadora Duncan, Ruth St. Denis, and others, some of whom had studied with Italian ballet dancers. They were also influenced by vaudeville skirt dancing, the expressive techniques of François Delsarte, acting, and Hindu and Japanese dances presented by international expositions and amusement parks. In their work they explored the theme of rugged American individualism, recasting elements of popular entertainment and genteel parlor dances. Fuller and Duncan began their careers in the city in the 1890s and after becoming well known in Europe returned to the United States. After her début in the city in 1906 and a successful European tour St. Denis made the city her headquarters, as she performed her mystical Orientalist dances on the national vaudeville circuit. She married Ted Shawn and with him in 1915 in Los Angeles organized the Ruth St. Denis and Ted Shawn School of Dancing and Related Arts, known as Denishawn; it had branches in several cities, including New York City.

There was no American school of ballet until 1909, when the Metropolitan Opera engaged Malvina Cavallazzi as a teacher for its company. Interest in ballet was revived in the city by Anna Pavlova and Mikhail Mordkin, former dancers in Serge Diaghilev's Ballets Russes. In 1910 they danced in *Coppélia*, *Aziade*, and such *divertissements* as *The Dying Swan*, which was performed at the Metropolitan Opera for two years. In 1911 Theodore Kosloff danced with Gertrude Hoffman at the Winter Garden Theatre in works from the repertory of the Ballets Russes, of which he had been a member. The Ballets Russes made two tours of the country in 1916–17, reproducing ballets that had enjoyed tremendous success in Paris, including *Petrouchka*, *Schéhérazade*, *Les Sylphides*, and *Afternoon of a Faun*. During the second tour Vaslav Nijinsky presented his last ballet, *Till Eulenspiegel*, based on the story of the medieval Flemish trickster and set to music by Richard Strauss.

From the end of the nineteenth century until the 1940s many of the ballets in the city were offered by the Metropolitan Opera, which presented its own company and touring companies. Versions of Diaghilev's works were performed by the Ballets Russes and others. The engagement of Rosina Galli, a graduate of the La Scala school in Milan, as the lead dancer in 1914 and as the ballet-master in 1919 gave luster to the opera's company, which until the Depression presented full-scale ballets as part of operas or on their own. Several small ballet companies performed elsewhere. For a season at the Booth Theatre in 1917 Adolph Bolm's Ballet Intime performed Bolm's restagings of Michel Fokine's ballets and presented such guest performers as Roshanara, Ratan Devi, and Michio Ito in Asian dances. Fokine worked at the Hippodrome and performed in Florenz Ziegfeld's *Follies* during the 1920s, and in 1924 he organized a small company to perform his works. In 1926 Mordkin formed the Mordkin Ballet Company, which performed in the Greenwich *Follies* and toured briefly. Martha Graham, Doris Humphrey, Charles Weidman, and Louis Horst, the music director of St. Denis's company, left the Denishawn school during the 1920s for New York City. Dissatisfied with the fin-de-siècle decorativeness of her training, Graham worked to extrapolate a specifically American form of dance from the rhythms of city life. Horst became her mentor and an influential composition teacher to successive groups of modern dancers. Humphrey and Weidman formed their own school and company in 1928, basing their technique on Humphrey's principles of fall and recovery. Weidman's gift was for comedy; Humphrey combined principles of musical visualization that she had explored with St. Denis and embodiments of social utopias and social conflicts.

In the 1920s many black entertainers found work in the Cotton Club and other nightclubs where the owners and the audiences were white. Blacks first became concert dancers during the Harlem Renaissance, when they gained access to theaters, financing, and work as dancers, composers, musicians, and writers for the stage. A number of musicals intended for black audiences and produced entirely by blacks were introduced, often based on racial stereotypes traditional in minstrel shows. Among these were *Shuffle Along* (1921, Flourney Miller and Aubrey Lyles; Noble Sissle and Eubie Blake), *Plantation Revue*, *From Dixie to Broadway*, *Runnin' Wild*, and *Chocolate Dandies*. Many performers found employment in these productions and a number became internationally known, including Josephine Baker and Bill "Bojangles" Robinson. Initially presented in Harlem, the musicals eventually moved to Broadway and were performed for white audiences, after which the charleston became a social dance and tap dancing was incorporated into many white musical comedies. At the same time a number of black dancers sought to develop forms of concert dancing shaped by black history. In 1931 Hemsley Winfield formed the Negro Art Theater Dance Group, which in its first concert presented dances based on African themes and set to black spirituals by Edna Guy, who had studied at the Denishawn school. As the witch doctor in *The Emperor Jones* in 1933 Winfield became the first black dancer to perform at the Metropolitan Opera. Asadata Dafora, a musician born in Sierra

Leone and trained in Europe, moved to the city in 1929 and in 1934 produced *Kykunkor*, a program of African music and dance elegantly arranged for the theater and performed by a cast of Africans and black Americans; it met with success and became a model for others.

By the 1930s the city had become the world's foremost center for dance, especially modern dance. Mary Wigman sent one of her pupils, Hanya Holm, to open a branch of her school of German modern dance there in 1931, and by the late 1930s it was the Hanya Holm Studio. Holm worked with Graham, Humphrey, and Weidman to help shape the modern dance movement. Her critique of capitalism through dance influenced many younger dancers, some of whom belonged to Graham's and Humphrey's companies, took part in the unionization movement, and were allied with cultural organizations of the Communist Party. With the support of the Workers' Dance League they formed political dance troupes like the Red Dancers, the New Duncan Dancers, the Modern Negro Dance Group, the New Dance Group, and the Theater Union Dance Group. They treated such themes as the Spanish Civil War, German fascism, and American racism. While the Popular Front was active the league softened its treatment of class conflict and renamed itself the New Dance League, which celebrated American folk themes and invited less politically radical dancers to take part in its performances. Helen Tamiris, a leftist choreographer, directed the city's branch of the Federal Dance Project of the Works Progress Administration from 1936 to 1939 and wrote her first choreographies for Broadway musicals in the 1940s. Several modern dance groups included black dancers and choreographers by 1937, when an evening of the works of Guy, Dafora, Katherine Dunham, and Talley Beatty was presented at the 92nd Street YMHA, a central venue for modern dance. During the same year Eugene von Grona organized the American Negro Ballet, which after its début at the Lafayette Theatre in Harlem received criticism that reflected long-standing prejudices about dance and race. Dunham moved to the city in 1939 to direct the Labor Stage, for which she provided choreography for a production of *Pins and Needles* before embarking on a long career of synthesizing Caribbean, African, and European styles. Several of her pupils became well known, including Beatty, Janet Collins, Lavinia Williams, Jean-Léon Destine, and Charles Moore, and she remained an important influence in black concert dance into the 1990s.

Regular ballet seasons were introduced in the city in the 1930s. Managed by Wassily de Basil, the Ballet Russe de Monte Carlo had several successful seasons from 1933 during which Léonide Massine was its ballet-master; it presented Diaghilev's repertory as well as comedies and new symphonic ballets by Massine, including *Les Présages*, *Choreartium*, and *Symphonie fantastique*. In 1938 Sergei Denham became its impresario and it presented *Gaîté parisienne*, a new character ballet by Massine that became one of the company's staples. The Original Ballet Russe was formed by de Basil in 1938, and the two companies became rivals. From 1935 Sol Hurok and other impresarios regularly sponsored visiting dance companies at the Metropolitan Opera before and after the resident company's season. On Galli's retirement the resident company became the American Ballet, led by George Balanchine (1935–38). Although the new director of the Metropolitan Opera, Edward Johnson, had promised artistic reforms, Balanchine's dances were considered too nontraditional and overpowering, and in 1938 Boris Romanov, a member of the Ballets Russes, became the resident choreographer, a position he held until 1941. The Mordkin Ballet was revived in 1937; several of its members formed the Ballet Theatre in 1939.

New York City became an international center of ballet during the 1940s. The Ballet Theatre committed itself to preserving traditional ballet and encouraging new work, and was soon one of the most important companies in the city. Its first choreographer was Jerome Robbins, who produced *Fancy Free* in 1944 and with the English choreographer Antony Tudor trained such dancers as Nora Kaye, Harold Lang, Michael Kidd, Alicia Alonso, and Hugh Laing. The Ballet Russe de Monte Carlo became the most popular touring company in the country during and after the Second World War. From 1938 it engaged such renowned dancers as Alexandra Danilova, Alicia Markova, Mia Slavenska, Igor Youskevitch, Mary Ellen Moylan, Leon Danielian, and Maria Tallchief, and many of its dancers became influential teachers. In 1942 Massine left the company, which produced several ballets by Balanchine as well as Agnes de Mille's *Rodeo*, and in 1944 Frederick Franklin became the ballet-master. At times the company competed for audiences with the Original Ballet Russe, and in 1950 it ceased to offer regular seasons in New York City; it was dissolved in 1962. For a few seasons a number of companies organized by Balanchine and Lincoln Kirstein joined forces as the Ballet Society, a subscription organization that performed at the New York City Center for Music and Dance. The group changed its name to the New York City Ballet when it became the resident company there in 1948 and was quickly embraced by the city's intelligentsia for incorporating classical values in abstract works set to music by modern composers like Stravinsky and Paul Hindemith. In 1964 it became the resident company of the New York State Theater in Lincoln Center.

After the Second World War a new group of modern dancers emerged. Humphrey's humanist themes and balanced orchestration of weighted movements were adopted by one of her pupils, José Limón, in such works as *The Moor's Pavane* (1949). The political and mythical themes of the 1920s and 1930s were abandoned for an abstract approach by Alwin Nikolais, who had studied at the Holm school, and by Merce Cunningham, who danced with Graham and worked from the premise that music and dance are independent partners in time and space. Paul Taylor, who danced with both Graham and Cunningham, initially embraced minimalism in his choreography but during the early 1960s became more accessible and eclectic, often using symphonic music. Pearl Primus, born in Trinidad and trained as an anthropologist, studied at the New Dance Group and in 1943 made her début in *African Ceremonial*, an "anthropological" modern dance. After a research trip to the South in 1944 she provided choreography for dances like *Strange Fruit* (about a lynching) and *Hard Times Blues* (about sharecropping). She specialized in African dances and in 1948 made the first of many trips to Africa, where she found material that inspired her later work. With such choreographers as Anna Sokolow, Jane Dudley, Sophie Maslow, William Bales, and Daniel Nagrin she took part in group concerts throughout the 1940s and early 1950s at the studio of the New Dance Group, which also sponsored a performing group and offered dance classes at rates affordable to working people (a policy that it maintained in the mid 1990s). Donald McKayle, a pupil of Primus who had also been trained in ballet, formed a company in 1951. Among his dances are *Games* (1951), about city children, *Rainbow 'round My Shoulder* (1959), about a chain gang, and *District Storyville* (1962), set to New Orleans jazz. In the 1960s he began providing choreography for Broadway productions, television, and films.

Choreographers for the Metropolitan Opera in these years included Tudor (1950–51, 1956–61) and Markova (1963–69). Several small troupes assembled by Robert Joffrey in the 1950s together formed the Joffrey Ballet in 1960, which became one of the major companies in the city. It was disbanded in 1964 but reorganized in the following year when Gerald Arpino became its principal choreographer, and it was soon renowned for its youthfulness. Alvin Ailey formed a company in 1958 that presented dances set to black music and based on themes of the civil rights movement (including *Revelations*, 1960, set to spirituals). In the early 1960s a number of choreographers called themselves postmodernists to distinguish themselves from others who became prominent in the years between the world wars. Influenced by visual art and "happenings," a genre of live art produced in the late 1950s and 1960s, many postmodernists were pupils of Cunningham. Robert Dunn, a composer and a pupil of John Cage, taught a choreography workshop from 1960 to 1962 that led to the formation of a cooperative group known as the Judson Dance Theater, which flourished from 1962 to 1964 and continued into the late 1960s. Among its choreographers were Yvonne Rainer, Steve Paxton, Trisha Brown, David Gordon, Judith Dunn, Deborah Hay, and Lucinda Childs; there were also composers, filmmakers, and visual artists such as Robert Rauschenberg and Robert Morris. Although the group was never aesthetically united its members shared an interest in nontraditional physical techniques, chance juxtapositions, cooperative production, and the incorporation of untrained dancers into their works. Intimate performances were given at Judson Church in Greenwich Village and in unconventional venues like lofts and the outdoors.

In the 1970s some members of the Judson group formed companies and in their own work explored reductive structures such as repetition and mathematics; they often performed in silence and used uninflected phrasing. Some of their best-known works include *Trio A* by Rainer (1966), *Structured Pieces* by Brown (1973), and *Calico Mingling* by Childs (1973). Several choreographers formed the Grand Union, an improvisation group. Meredith Monk and Kenneth King experimented with theater that incorporated several media. Hay and Simone Forti explored natural movement and the meanings of non-Western physical disciplines like Tai Chi Chuan. In the 1970s the experimental dancer Twyla Tharp formed the Twyla Tharp Dance Company and joined the artistic mainstream. Her intellectually rigorous works, often set to popular music, blended elements of black social dancing, jazz dancing, and ballet. Many touring ballet companies visited the city and the Harkness and Feld ballets were formed. Prejudices about dance and race lingered into the late 1960s, when the Dance Theatre of Harlem began operations (1969). In the 1970s a number of young black choreographers became prominent, among them Rod Rogers, Eleo Pomare, Garth Fagan, and Dianne McIntyre.

Choreographers well-known during the 1960s and 1970s collaborated on large-scale productions with visual artists and composers during the 1980s, often making use of refined movements and performing before large audiences. They and some younger dancers like Jim Self and Susan Marshall also received commissions to write ballets. Under the leadership of Mikhail Baryshnikov the American Ballet Theatre encouraged adventurous new works, including some by Gordon, Karole Armitage, and Mark Morris, a major choreographer of the 1980s who directed the Mark Morris Dance Group and became known for his musicality and his experiments with sex roles. Venues for postmodern dance included the Dance Theater Workshop, the Kitchen, P.S. 122, and the Next Wave Festival at the Brooklyn Academy of Music. Many dancers prominent in the 1980s and early 1990s linked postmodern dance with contemporary movements in art and architecture. They shifted frames of meaning and in pastiches such as *Snow Queen* (1986), by the group Kinematic, alluded to and sometimes criticized popular culture. Works concerned with questions of identity were produced by Self, Bill T. Jones, Arnie Zane, Tim Miller, Ishmael Houston-Jones, Fred Holland, Viveca Vazquez, Dancenoise, and the Urban Bush Women, a group led by Jawole Willa Jo Zollar that drew on black culture in Africa and the United States to explore themes of black women's identity.

An early attempt to establish a dance archive in the Museum of Modern Art ended in 1948, and most of the materials were eventually transferred to the New York Public Library. The museum nevertheless retained a collection of stage and costume designs to which it continued to add into the 1990s, as well as materials on dance in its motion-picture archive. The New York Public Library for the Performing Arts at Lincoln Center contains the world's largest dance archive, which traces the early days of classical ballet in the United States and the development of modern dance. Documents in the archive include the papers of the American Ballet Theatre and of the Ballet Russe de Monte Carlo, photographic scrapbooks of St. Denis and Shawn, Duncan's correspondence with Gordon Craig, and the manuscripts of the choreography of Balanchine, donated by Kirstein. Also available are videotaped performances by such choreographers as Cunningham and Tharp, and videotapes from the Brooklyn Academy of Music, the Dance Theater Workshop, and the Dance Theatre of Harlem. There are also dance collections at the Asia Society, the Kitchen, the Museum of Television and Radio, the Shubert Archives, and the Anthology Film Archives, as well as archives maintained by dance companies.

Paul Magriel, ed.: *Chronicles of the American Dance from the Shakers to Martha Graham* (New York: Dance Index, 1948; repr. Da Capo, 1978)

Lynn Fauley Emery: *Black Dance in the United States from 1619 to 1970* (Palo Alto, Calif.: National, 1972)

Deborah Jowitt: *Time and the Dancing Image* (New York: William Morrow, 1988)

See also Folk and ethnic dancing.

Sally Banes

dance criticism. Dance writing in New York City began during the mid nineteenth century and consisted mainly of short, unimaginative reviews. Most writers discussed dance as a social event or as a costume spectacle; not surprisingly dance reviews were frequently placed on the society page of local newspapers. When Carl Van Vechten began writing about dance for the *New York Times* (1906–13) dance reviews became a respected form of criticism. By explaining technical terms and defending innovative performances he expanded public awareness of dance. From early in his writing career his tastes were cosmopolitan and egalitarian: he became a champion of both Russian ballet and tap dancing. While working for the *Times* and the *Press* (1913–14) he wrote about crucial events in the history of dance in New York City, including the débuts of Anna Pavlova, Mikhail Mordkin, Maud Allan, and Loie Fuller. In *Interpreters and Interpretations* (1917) and other books he introduced the work of Isadora Duncan and Vaslav Nijinsky to a wider audience. Although he virtually retired by 1920 his vivid, uncondescending, and personal accounts helped to establish dance as a recognized art form. Several of his pieces are collected in *The Dance Writings of Carl Van Vechten* (1974). The first full-time dance critic in the city was John Martin (1893–1985), engaged in June 1927 by the *New York Times* in response to petitions from readers inspired by Denishawn, the company of Ruth St. Denis and Ted Shawn. An advocate of modern dance, he was known for his controversial treatment of ballet; he also explained and justified modern dance in classes at the New School for Social Research (1930–34) and in several books. His close association with Martha Graham, Doris Humphrey, and other pioneers of modern dance made him the most influential dance writer in the United States until his retirement from the *Times* in 1962. Martin's judgments were strongly opposed by Lincoln Kirstein, founder of the New York City Ballet and the School of the American Ballet, who campaigned tirelessly for traditional dance in his book *Blast at Ballet: A Corrective for Americans* (1938), his magazine *Dance Index*, and many articles.

Walter Terry (1913–82), dance critic for the *New York Herald Tribune* from 1936 until 1966, was a well-trained dancer who reviewed performances more as a friend of dance than as an aesthetic judge. Edwin Denby (1903–83), who wrote successively for the bimonthly magazine *Modern Music* (1936–43), for the *Herald Tribune* while Terry was fulfilling military service (1942–45), and for the periodicals *Dance* and *Center*, was the most widely respected and influential critic in the history of American dance. There are several collections of his published writings: *Looking at the Dance* (1949), which includes among other early pieces his reviews of *Apollo* and other classic dances by George Balanchine; *Dancers, Buildings and People in the Streets* (1965), which includes an essay of the same name and one on Balanchine's *Agon* (1959); and *Dance Writings* (1987). Arlene Croce (*b* 1934), who founded the quarterly journal *Ballet Review* in 1965 and was its editor for fourteen years, is the writer most frequently cited as having continued the tradition established by Denby. She became the dance critic for the *New Yorker* in 1973. Her highly detailed articles, many of which were collected in *Sightlines* (1987), are sympathetic toward the works of Balanchine, Mark Morris, and David Gordon. Martin's successor at the *Times*, Allen Hughes, was in turn succeeded in 1965 by Clive Barnes (*b* 1927), who from 1967 also wrote theater criticism; shortly after losing his position as theater critic he left the *Times* in 1977 to become a critic and assistant editor for the *New York Post* and was succeeded at the *Times* by Anna Kisselgoff. Other prominent dance critics include Jill Johnston and Deborah Jowitt of the *Village Voice*, Tobi Tobias of *New York*, and Marcia Siegel of the *Hudson Review*. Important publications in addition to *Dance* and *Ballet Review* include *Dance Perspectives* (1959–76) and *Dance Scope* (1965–80).

William C. MacKay

dance halls and discothèques. Dance halls for members of the working class were present in New York City by the middle of the nineteenth century and soon acquired an unsavory reputation. John Allen, known as the "wickedest man in New York," ran a dance hall during the 1860s at 304 Water Street that was also a bordello. Local residents commonly referred to Harry Hill's famous dance hall at 26 East Houston Street (1868–90) as the city's "most respectable disreputable house" and to the Black and Tan Concert Hall at 153 Bleecker Street as the "Chemise and Drawers." At the same time members of fashionable society danced waltzes, polkas, and the lancers in stylish dress and sumptuous surroundings. Allen Dodworth, a bandmaster and a violinist with the New York Philharmonic, opened a dancing school at 402 Broadway in 1842 and became so closely associated with the city's social élite that one of the studios he opened later, at 681 5th Avenue, was a temporary site for the Metropolitan Museum of Art. One of the nation's preeminent dancing masters, Dodworth published *Dancing, and Its Relation to Education and Social Life* in 1885 and retired in the following year, leaving control of the school to his nephew George, who bought a building at 12 East 49th Street where he taught the daughters of such prominent families as the Astors, the Gallatins, the Hones, the Belmonts, the Vanderbilts, and the Dwights. The Dodworths were more than simply dance teachers: they hoped to bring good manners to the dance floor and believed that proper dance technique and etiquette could help to refine society.

The growing influence of ragtime music and dance between 1890 and the First World War complicated the Dodworths' mission. Rental halls that were the primary venues for dancing between 1890 and 1910 gained in popularity in neighborhoods inhabited by immigrants and the working class. By one estimate there were 130 dance halls in the city in 1895 (most on the Lower East Side) and 195 by 1910. Social dancing peaked between 1911 and 1915, and venues ranging from cabarets in Times Square and elegant hotels to large, nondescript dance halls struggled to keep pace with a rapidly increasing demand. Two types of dance hall played the largest role. The first were dance palaces that accommodated from five hundred to three thousand patrons and included Grand Central Palace, the city's first (opened in 1911 at 488 Lexington Avenue), the Manhattan Casino (2926 8th Avenue), and the Harlem Casino (100 West 116th Street). Such halls catered mostly to teenagers and featured professional musicians and promotional events. Other dance halls such as Tangoland on East 86th Street, known as "closed" or "taxi" dance halls, were situated above street level, had amateurish bands, and were sparsely decorated; patronized solely by single males (and therefore popularly associated with prostitution), they offered female dancing partners for hire at a fixed price for each dance, which the dancer split equally with the owner of the hall. This practice was commemorated in the song "Ten Cents a Dance" (1930) by Richard Rodgers and Lorenz Hart.

The proliferation of dance halls raised the ire of reformers. They joined such groups as the Committee of Fourteen (1905–32) and the Committee on Amusement Resources of Working Girls (1909–15), which prevailed on the state legislature to amend the city charter in 1910 to provide for the licensing of dance halls, and then helped to refine the state law by securing passage at the municipal level of the Dance Hall Law of 1911. To ensure propriety on the city's dance floors George Dodworth and other concerned dance teachers organized the New York Society of Teachers of Dancing in 1914. These groups were less influential than Vernon and Irene Castle, whose refined versions of the latest dance steps met with huge success on the floors of cabarets and hotels. To counter the reformers many owners of dance halls renamed their establishments academies and schools, and some opened large dance spaces that offered refined surroundings, among them Roseland, opened by Louis J. Brecker on New Year's Eve 1919, and the Savoy Ballroom in Harlem, which opened in 1925. During the 1920s and 1930s Arthur Murray ran a chain of studios in the city to teach social dancing. In 1925 there were 786 licensed dance spaces in the five boroughs, of which 238 were in Manhattan. The Advisory Dance Hall Committee calculated that about 14 percent of the city's males and 10 percent of its females aged seventeen to forty frequented at least one dance hall a week and spent more than $3.5 million on dancing each year.

Dance halls remained popular during the 1930s. At the Savoy Ballroom in Harlem a racially mixed crowd numbering as many as five thousand danced the Lindy hop to the accompaniment of the country's leading jazz bands. Fashionable hotels such as the Pennsylvania, the Lincoln, and the New Yorker opened ballrooms that featured swing and "sweet society" bands such as that of Eddy Duchin. Many dance palaces closed during the Depression, but taxi dance halls continued to draw customers and criticism. In 1936 the police raided twenty such establishments around Sands Street near the Brooklyn Navy Yard, and as late as 1964 Bernard J. O'Connell, the city's license commissioner, revoked the permits of six dance halls in Times Square for offending public decency. Developers razed the Savoy Ballroom to make way for a housing project in 1958, and eventually taxi dancing disappeared from New York City.

The decline of the dance hall coincided with the rise of the discothèque. The Peppermint Lounge, opened on West 45th Street in 1959, was associated from the following year with the dance called the twist and remained a popular venue for celebrities until it closed in December 1965. Other early discothèques that attracted a fashionable clientele included Ondine (308 East 59th Street), the private discothèques Le Club (416 East 55th Street) and L'Interdit (in the Gotham Hotel), and Arthur (154 East 54th Street, 1965–69), which was owned by several stage and film performers and was known for the bold dress of its patrons. Cheetah, opened at Broadway and 53rd Street in April 1966 and owned by Borden Stevenson (a son of Adlai Stevenson), featured rock dancing and was frequented by teenagers. By the mid 1960s several large dance clubs were situated in the theater district and in Greenwich Village. The Electric Circus, at 23 St. Mark's Place, presented an opening gala on 27 June 1967 that attracted celebrities, hippies, and the curious, who were entertained by trapeze acts and performance artists, as well as dizzying lights and a deafening sound system that required the laying of a special cable in St. Mark's Place by Consolidated Edison. Dom, directly downstairs from the Electric Circus, was the primary dance club for blacks in Greenwich Village during the late 1960s.

Those who patronized discothèques in the 1970s danced not to rock but to the four-square rhythms of disco. The most exclusive clubs admitted only the prominent and fashionably dressed and were written about relentlessly by gossip columnists. Lighting and sound systems were increasingly elaborate, and illegal drugs widely used. The best-known club of the period was Studio 54, owned by Stephen Rubell and Ian Schrager, which opened on 26 April 1977 at 254 West 54th Street in the shell of the abandoned Gallo

Theater. Its chief competitor was Xenon, also in a former theater, at 124 West 43rd Street. Other discothèques catered to the working class, especially in the outer boroughs; a club of this sort is vividly depicted in the film *Saturday Night Fever* (1977). The decadent excesses of the more lavish clubs ended about 1980, when the owners of Studio 54 were sentenced to three and a half years in prison for tax evasion. At the same time other venues opened in disused warehouses in Chelsea, lower Manhattan, and the meatpacking district; at these clubs racially mixed crowds danced to rap, "house," and other forms of music on enormous dance floors. Among the few clubs of this kind to last more than a year or two were the Palladium at 126 East 14th Street (1984), an ultramodern club opened by Rubell and Schrager; the Limelight (1985), in a disused church at 47 West 20th Street; and Area at 157 Hudson Street (1983–87), which redesigned its interior every season and drew huge crowds. Other notable establishments included the Tunnel (a former railroad station at 12th Avenue and 28th Street) and Mars (a warehouse at 28 10th Avenue), both frequented by fashionable young people and residents of the suburbs; 12 West at 491 West Street, opened in 1975 by Michael Fesco as the city's first discothèque with an overtly homosexual clientele; the Mudd Club at 77 White Street (during the late 1970s and early 1980s); and Nell's, an intimate club at 246 West 14th Street (opened in 1986).

Ballroom dancing retained its appeal. By the time Murray retired from dance instruction in 1964 he oversaw an empire that included a thriving mail-order business and more than three hundred franchised dance studios with annual revenues exceeding $25 million. In the same year there were at least twenty-five other ballroom dance schools and studios in Manhattan. Refined social dancing continued to be practiced at Roseland and at the Red Parrot (617 West 57th Street). Latin American dances and rhythms, which first gained popularity during the 1940s and 1950s, became more prevalent as the number of Spanish-speaking immigrants increased. At the Palladium (Broadway and 53rd Street) Frank "Killer Joe" Piro taught such Latin dances as the samba, the mambo, and the conga. The city's Spanish-speaking population also frequented illegal social clubs, a practice that was usually ignored by other residents of the city until it was brought to their attention by such tragic incidents as the Happy Land fire of 1990, in which eighty-seven persons died. During the 1980s influential Latin dance clubs included the Corso (205 East 86th Street) and the Copacabana (10 East 60th Street).

Marc Ferris

Augustus Van Heerden and Judy Tyrus in Firebird *(choreography by John Taras) at the Dance Theatre of Harlem, 1989*

Dance Theater Workshop. Organization for modern dancers. Formed in 1965 as a cooperative for choreographers, it grew under the directorship of David White after 1975 and came to offer comprehensive support for experimental dancers in New York City. It introduced the New York Dance and Performance Awards, or "Bessie" Awards, in 1984 and formed the National Performance Network in 1985, a program to support experimental dance outside the city. Its headquarters above a tire factory at 219 West 19th Street contain a theater of a hundred seats where about fifty choreographers present their work each year. The Dance Theater Workshop also helps members with publicity and other practical aspects of presentation.

Joan Acocella

Dance Theatre of Harlem. Dance company formed in New York City in 1969. Its artistic director, Arthur Mitchell (*b* New York City, 27 March 1934), had been the first full-time black member of the New York City Ballet (1955–68) and one of its most popular soloists, creating many roles in ballets by George Balanchine; its ballet-master was Karel Shook. The company made its début at the Guggenheim Museum in 1971, gave successful performances in the United States and abroad, and became known for flouting racial stereotypes and what Mitchell called "the myth that ballet has something to do with race, creed, and class." It assembled a large, varied repertory that included nineteenth-century Russian classics, many ballets by Balanchine, and works by such contemporary choreographers as Glen Tetley and Garth Fagan. In the 1980s it revisited *Giselle* in a Creole setting. Among those who have been associated with the company are Ronald Perry, Mel Tomlinson, and Paul Russell. Its school at West 152nd Street in Manhattan continues to train hundreds of students.

Tobi Tobias: *Arthur Mitchell* (New York: Thomas Y. Crowell, 1975)

Brenda Dixon Gottschild

Danes. Danish sailors were among the crew of Henry Hudson's ship the *Halve Maen*, which sailed into New York Harbor in 1609. Among the many Danish settlers who lived in New Amsterdam was Jonas Bronck, who moved there in 1629 and bought large tracts of land just north of Manhattan that became known as the Bronx (probably after him). At least a hundred Danes lived in New York City by 1675, and in 1704 they joined with Norwegians to build a small Lutheran chapel near the intersection of Broadway and Rector Street. Immigration from Denmark reached a peak during a period of political unrest there between 1850 and 1900, and most Danes passed through the city on their way west; those who remained usually lived in the Scandinavian section of Bay Ridge in Brooklyn. Danish men were often mechanics, seamen, carpenters, and bricklayers. Many of them belonged to unions, and some were prominent musicians and professionals. Most Danish immigrants were Lutheran but many married members of other ethnic groups. Dania, a health insurance organization for Scandinavian immigrants, opened a branch in Brooklyn in 1886. A Danish-language paper, *Nordlyset* (The Northern Light), was published in the city from 1891 to 1953, and in 1903 seventeen Danish organizations were listed, none with more than a hundred members. By 1930 the Danish-born accounted for less than 1 percent of the population of New York City, but about 200,000 persons were of Danish descent. One of the best-known Danes in the city was Jacob A. Riis, a photographer, reformer, and writer whose book *How the Other Half Lives* (1890) exposed the destitution of the city's slums; he was called "New York's most useful citizen" by President Theodore Roosevelt, and his work led to many reforms in tenement regulations.

Chad Ludington

Danilova, Alexandra (*b* Peterhof [now Petrodvorets], Russia, 20 Nov 1903). Dancer. She was trained in St. Petersburg and in 1924 left Russia with her schoolmate George Balanchine. She danced first with Serge Diaghilev's Ballets Russes and during the peak of her career (1938–51) with the Ballet Russe de Monte Carlo. From 1964 to 1989 she taught at Balanchine's School of American Ballet in New York City. Through her dancing and teaching Danilova helped to incorporate the charm and glamour of late-nineteenth-century Russian classical ballet into the sleek classical styles developed in the United States during the late twentieth century, especially by the New York City Ballet under Balanchine's direction. She wrote *Choura: The Memoirs of Alexandra Danilova* (1986).

Joan Acocella

Dannon Yogurt. Firm of yogurt makers formed in 1942 in the Bronx by Daniel Carasso, the son of a Spanish yogurt maker. It moved in the following year to Long Island City and was acquired in 1959 by Beatrice Foods and in 1981 by the French firm BSN Groupe. By 1993 it sold six types of yogurt in twenty-two flavors and was the largest firm in the business in the United States. It moved its main office to suburban White Plains, New York, in 1986.

Leslie Gourse

Da Ponte, Lorenzo [Conegliano, Emanuele] (*b* Ceneda [now Vittorio Veneto], Italy, 10 March 1749; *d* New York City, 17 Aug 1838). Librettist, bookseller, impresario, and teacher. After writing the librettos of many celebrated operas, notably Mozart's *Don Giovanni* and *Le nozze di Figaro*, he moved to New York City in 1805 with the intention of spreading Italian culture. Soon after arriving he was befriended by Clement Clarke Moore, who helped him to establish a school where he taught students the language and literature of Italy, France, and Spain. After seven years in an unsuccessful foray into commerce in Sunbury, Pennsylvania, he returned to New York City and with his brother Carlo began importing Italian books to the United States. First operating out of his home on Broadway and later from a store, he wrote a widely read annotated catalogue for his customers that contained a history of Italian literature. He continued to write and speak on Italian literature and from 1825 taught Italian at Columbia College, to which he sold his library of Italian books. In November 1825 he helped to bring about productions by a visiting opera company of Rossini's *Il barbiere di Siviglia* and of *Don Giovanni.* Convinced of the need for a full-fledged professional opera company in New York City, he pursued patrons and in 1833 proposed, commenced, and completed construction of the Italian Opera House. The neoclassical building was considered the most sumptuous theater ever built in the United States, and displaced the Park Theatre as the leading theater in the city. Da Ponte succeeded in firmly establishing opera as an art form in New York City by the time the theater was destroyed by fire in 1841.

Sheila Hodges: *Lorenzo DaPonte* (London: Granada, 1985)

Lorenzo DaPonte: A Vision of Italy from Columbia College (New York: Columbia University, 1991)

Thomas M. Hilbink

D. Appleton. Firm of publishers formed by Daniel Appleton, the owner of a general store at 16 Exchange Place. Appleton published his first book, an inspirational volume of biblical texts, in 1831 and during the next few years became known for publishing devotional and theological books as well as reprints of British fiction. He made his son William Henry Appleton a partner in 1838, and together they produced Spanish-language and children's books, ventures that proved shrewd and profitable. After his father's death in 1849 William Henry Appleton took over the firm and engaged his brothers as partners; his association with Edward L. Youmans led to the publication of many important scientific works by such writers as Darwin and Herbert Spencer. Known for its varied list, the firm also produced sentimental fiction, medical books, the novels of Edith Wharton, *Alice's Adventures in Wonderland*, General William T. Sherman's memoirs, and such reference works as the *New American Cyclopaedia*, a work in sixteen

Advertisement for D. Appleton Stereoscopic Views, ca *1870*

volumes. D. Appleton remained in the Appleton family until a business failure in 1900. In 1933 it merged with the firm of Century to become D. Appleton–Century.

Charles A. Madison: *Book Publishing in America* (New York: McGraw–Hill, 1966)

John Tebbel: *Between Covers: The Rise and Transformation of Book Publishing in America* (New York: Oxford University Press, 1987)

Alice Fahs

D'Arcy Masius Benton and Bowles. Advertising agency formed in 1986 by the merger of Benton and Bowles, formed in New York City in 1929, and D'Arcy MacManus Masius of Detroit; initially it occupied the former offices of Benton and Bowles at 909 3rd Avenue. It acquired Medicus Intercon International, the largest health-care advertising agency in the country, and Manning Selvage and Lee, a public relations firm with offices at 79 Madison Avenue, and produced three soap operas for Procter and Gamble: "Guiding Light," "As the World Turns," and "Another World." It won important accounts with Burger King and Maxwell House in 1989, at which point it represented forty "number one" brand-name products. The parent firm, its branch in New York City (DMB&B/New York), and Medicus Intercon International moved to a building at 1675 Broadway in November 1989. Other accounts of DMB&B/New York include Richardson–Vicks, Kraft General Foods, M&M/Mars, Corning, and Norelco. In 1991 D'Arcy Masius Benton and Bowles was the fourth-largest advertising agency in the United States and had ninety-three offices in thirty-one countries with about 5500 employees, one thousand of whom worked in New York City.

Walecia Konrad: "The 'Bridesmaid' Ad Agency Finally Catches the Bouquet," *Business Week*, 12 June 1989, pp. 27–28

Marjorie Harrison

Darley, F(elix) O(ctavius) C(arr) (*b* Philadelphia, 23 June 1822; *d* Claymont, Del., 27 March 1888). Illustrator. He moved to New York City in 1848 and became one of the most popular and influential illustrators of his time. During the late 1840s and 1850s he illustrated works by Washington Irving and James Fenimore Cooper and a collection of comic essays by William Evans Burton, *The Yankee among the Mermaids* (1854–58). His style was one of the first with a distinctively American point of view and brand of humor; he had a talent for satire and subtle overstatement, and his work encouraged other illustrators to develop their own styles rather than imitate English ones. He was best known for his engravings for *Rip Van Winkle* (1848) and *The Legend of Sleepy Hollow* (1849). Darley helped to form the American Society of Painters in Water Colors and also belonged to the Artists' Fund Society of New York and the National Academy of Design.

Ethel M. King: *Darley, the Most Popular Illustrator of His Time* (New York: T. Gaus' Sons, 1964)

Michael Joseph

David Mannes Music School. Original name of the MANNES COLLEGE OF MUSIC.

Davies, J. Clarence (*b* 1868; *d* 13 April 1934). Real-estate developer. Born to middle-class German Jewish parents and educated at City College, he opened a real-estate office in the Bronx in 1889 with funds borrowed from his family and soon became successful. He was one of the organizers of the Bronx Board of Trade, had important local political connections, and became known for his collection of historical memorabilia connected with New York City, including more than fifteen thousand items that he willed to the Museum of the City of New York. He was also a longtime trustee of the Association for the Improvement of the Education of the Deaf. Davies called himself the "king of the Bronx" because of his prominent role in the development of real estate in the area.

Stephen A. Stertz

Davis, Alexander Jackson (*b* New York City, 24 July 1803; *d* West Orange, N.J., 14 Jan 1892). Architect. With Ithiel Town he designed the U.S. Custom House on Wall Street (1833–42, now Federal Hall) in the Greek Revival style. In buildings such as the chapel of New York University (1835–37, formerly at Washington Square), designed in the Gothic Revival style, he introduced an irregular picturesque style that reached its height in the villas of Grace Hill in Prospect Park (1854–56, commissioned by Edwin Litchfield) and Lyndhurst in Tarrytown, New York (1838–42, enlarged 1864–67). With the landscape architect Andrew Jackson Downing he promoted these as an ideal form of domestic architecture. A member of the short-lived American Institution of Architects (1836–37) and later of the American Institute of Architects, he actively took part in attempts to professionalize American architecture by forming organizations to promote standards of education and practice. Considered a leading architect of his time, Davis introduced many of the revival styles that became popular during the mid to late nineteenth century. He is also known for his design of the nation's first planned suburb, Llewellyn Park in New Jersey, a model of picturesque design that he laid out in 1853.

Roger Hale Newton: *Town and Davis, Architects: Pioneers in American Revivalist Architecture, 1812–1870* (New York: Columbia University Press, 1942)

Amelia Peck, ed.: *Alexander Jackson Davis, American Architect, 1803–1892* (New York: Rizzoli, 1992)

Mary Beth Betts

Davis, Benjamin Jefferson (*b* Dawson, Ga., 8 Sept 1903; *d* New York City, 22 Aug 1964). Civil rights leader. He was elected as a Communist to the City Council from Harlem, replacing Adam Clayton Powell Jr. after his election to the U.S. Congress in 1944.

Gerald Horne: *Black Liberation / Red Scare: Ben Davis of the Communist Party* (Newark: University of Delaware Press, 1994)

Janet Frankston

Davis, John W(illiam) (*b* Clarksburg, W.Va., 13 April 1873; *d* Charleston, S.C., 24 March 1955). Lawyer, diplomat, and presidential candidate. He attended Washington and Lee University (BA 1892, LLB 1895) and was elected to the U.S. Congress as a Democrat in 1910 and 1912, later serving as solicitor general of the United States (from 1913) and ambassador to Great Britain (1918–21). After settling in New York City he formed the law firm that later became Davis Polk and Wardwell. At the Democratic National Convention in New York City in 1924 he received the presidential nomination on the 103rd ballot, but he campaigned ineffectively against Calvin Coolidge and lost the general election by a wide margin. He then resumed his legal career, during which he argued 141 cases before the U.S. Supreme Court.

William H. Harbaugh: *Lawyer's Lawyer: The Life of John W. Davis* (New York: Oxford University Press, 1973; repr. Charlottesville: University Press of Virginia, 1990)

Davis, Miles (Dewey, III) (*b* Alton, Ill., 25 May 1926; *d* Santa Monica, Calif., 28 Sept 1991). Trumpeter and bandleader. The son of a dentist and a musician, he grew up in East St. Louis (Illinois) and at thirteen learned to play the trumpet from one of his father's patients, Elwood Buchanan, who taught him to play cleanly and without vibrato. He was taken to bars around St. Louis by his next teacher, Clark Terry. Known for his sensitive and somewhat fragile sound, he soon joined the rhythm-and-blues band the Blue Devils and became its music director. After graduating from high school he moved to New York

Miles Davis

City to enroll at the Juilliard School in 1945; within a month he was well known in jazz clubs across the city that were introducing bebop. He moved into an apartment with the saxophonist Charlie Parker, with whom he made his first recordings, "Now's the Time," "Billie's Blues," and "Ko Ko." He used short grace notes before longer notes and was one of few players who could slide evenly between pitches without producing a break in the sound. In 1948 he organized a nonet with the trumpeter Johnny Carisi, the saxophonists Gerry Mulligan (*b* 1927) and Lee Konitz (*b* 1927), the pianist John Lewis (*b* 1920), and the arranger Gil Evans (1912–88) that performed at the Royal Roost and other clubs. Its first recording, *Birth of the Cool*, was made in 1949 for Capitol Records and included the compositions "Boplicity," "Israel," and "Jeru." While attending the International Jazz Festival in Paris during the same year he became addicted to heroin. His work suffered, Capitol terminated his contract, and he moved to Chicago, where he took only enough work to finance his drug habit; he decided to seek a cure while working in a second-rate club in Detroit.

Between 1954 and 1958 Davis played in a quintet with John Coltrane, Red Garland, Philly Joe Jones, and Paul Chambers. He became known for rendering ballads with a unique emotional intensity, for his improvisations on such standards as "Bye, Bye Blackbird," "Surrey with the Fringe on Top," and "My Funny Valentine," for his own compositions such as "Four," and for an aggressive, unembellished blues style on "Walkin'" and "Bags' Groove." He engaged Cannonball Adderley to play with the group, signed a recording contract with Columbia Records, and by the late 1950s was considered an originator of "hard bop." His best-known albums of the period were *'Round about Midnight* (1956), *Miles Ahead* (1957), *Milestones* (1958), and *Straight, No Chaser* (1958). His band shifted its focus to modal improvising and recorded the album *Kind of Blue* (1959), then developed a more impressionistic style during the 1960s after Bill Evans joined. By this time Davis's sound was large and expressive. He formed a group in 1963 with Ron Carter, Herbie Hancock, and Tony Williams, joined in the following year by Wayne Shorter, that played mostly original material and lasted until 1968, when Davis began to experiment with rhythm-and-blues, rock, and electronic instrumentation. Until 1971 he worked mostly in his own "fusion" style with the pianists Chick Corea and Joe Zawinul, the electric guitarist John McLaughlin, and others, producing the best-selling albums *In a Silent Way* (1969) and *Bitches Brew* (1969). Plagued by ill health, he played fewer solos in the 1970s. After breaking both legs in an automobile accident in 1972 he retired in 1974 but resumed performing in 1981. In all he recorded about thirty-five albums. Throughout his career Davis made New York City his base, and he lived in a series of hotel rooms and apartments before purchasing a brownstone at 312 West 77th Street in 1961. Later he moved to 5th Avenue and 79th Street, where he spent much of his time until the end of his life.

Ian Carr: *Miles Davis: A Biography* (New York: William Morrow, 1982)

S. D. R. Cashman, Peter Eisenstadt, Marc Ferris

Davis, Richard Harding (*b* Philadelphia, 18 April 1864; *d* Mount Kisco, N.Y., 11 April 1916). Journalist. He entered journalism in Philadelphia as a young man, encouraged by his father, a journalist, and his mother, a novelist. After reporting on the Johnstown Flood in 1889 he joined the *Sun*, and he later became the editor of *Harper's Weekly*. As a war correspondent for several journals he covered the Greco-Turkish, Boer, Spanish–American, Russo-Japanese, and Balkan wars, and the First World War, often in sensational prose. Davis also wrote and published fiction, plays, and a popular musical comedy.

F. Lauriston Bullard: *Famous War Correspondents* (Boston: Little, Brown, 1914)

Gerald Langford: *Richard Harding Davis Years: A Biography of a Mother and Son* (New York: Henry Holt, 1961)

Julian S. Rammelkamp

Davis, Stuart (*b* Philadelphia, 7 Dec 1892; *d* New York City, 24 June 1964). Painter. The son of two artists, he moved to New York City in 1909 to study with Robert Henri. His work was exhibited at the Armory Show in 1913, and in the same year he joined the staff of the independent socialist magazine the *Masses* as a protégé of the realist artist John Sloan; he left the magazine in 1916 over a dispute with the editors. Exhibitions of his work at the Newark Museum in New Jersey and at the Whitney Studio Club sponsored by Gertrude Vanderbilt Whitney encouraged his new interest in experimenting with formal problems, and in 1928 he spent a year in Paris. Seeking to create an unsentimental, uniquely American art and influenced by jazz, he developed a cubist style that used flat, overlapping, brightly colored shapes and motifs from everyday life, such as gasoline pumps, commercial logotypes, and billboard advertisements. Many consider his images, such as *Lucky Strike* (1921), prototypes for pop art. During the 1930s he sought to develop an art with social content through his abstract style. He also belonged to the Artists' Union and edited its publication *Art Front*, and was the executive secretary of the American Artists' Congress (1936–40). Under the auspices of the Federal Art Project he painted murals for the Williamsburg Housing Project and for the radio station WNYC. In 1991 the Metropolitan Museum of Art held a major retrospective of his work.

Patricia Hills: *Stuart Davis* (New York: Harry N. Abrams, forthcoming)

Patricia Hills

Davis Polk and Wardwell. Law firm, founded in 1849 by Francis N. Bangs (1828–85), a noted trial lawyer. It became preeminent in the area of corporate law under Francis Lynde Stetson (1846–1921). As counsel to J. P. Morgan from 1887, Stetson worked on industrial and railroad reorganizations with such authority that he became known as "J. P.

Stuart Davis, Two Figures and El *(1931). Lithograph. Collection of the Whitney Museum of American Art*

Morgan's attorney general." His associates in the firm included Grover Cleveland, the former president, and his successor as the head of the firm was John W. Davis, the country's best-known appellate lawyer and the Democratic presidential nominee in 1924. Davis reorganized the firm in 1925 with Frank L. Polk (1871–1943), leader of the American delegation to the peace conference ending the First World War, and Allen Wardwell (1873–1953), head of the wartime mission to Russia of the American Red Cross. The firm has been involved in several major cases, defending the steel industry against a government takeover in 1952 and representing clients in large asbestos, nuclear power, and drug product liability suits between 1964 and 1990. In addition to litigation its main practice areas include corporate finance, banking, taxation, and bankruptcy. Noted partners have included two special counsels who have investigated presidents, Lawrence E. Walsh and Robert B. Fiske Jr.

John Rousmaniere

Day, Benjamin (Henry) (*b* West Springfield, Mass., 10 April 1810; *d* New York City, 21 Dec 1889). Newspaper publisher and editor. After beginning his career as a printer he launched the *Sun* in September 1833, which under his direction attained the highest circulation of any daily newspaper in the United States. His innovations included using newsboys to sell newspapers in the streets, eschewing party journalism, and emphasizing crime reportage and sensational hoaxes. In 1838 Day sold the *Sun* to Moses Yale Beach, and in 1842 he assumed management of the illustrated literary periodical *Brother Jonathan.*

Francis Beacham Whitlock: *Two New Yorkers, Editor and Sea Captain, 1833* (New York: Newcomen Society, 1945)

Steven H. Jaffe

Day, Dorothy (May) (*b* Brooklyn, 8 Nov 1897; *d* New York City, 29 Nov 1980). Social activist. She became interested in the socialist movement while attending the University of Illinois and on her return to New York City worked as a reporter for the *New York Call*, a socialist daily newspaper. During the 1920s she married and divorced, published a novel, and bore a daughter out of wedlock. After converting to Catholicism she founded the weekly newspaper the *Catholic Worker* in 1933 with the French religious mystic and social critic Peter Maurin. The paper sold for one cent and had a circulation that reached 185,000 in 1940; it explored pacifism, anarchist utopianism, and Catholic social thought through spiritual essays and radical reporting. In 1933 the newspaper inspired a social movement when Day and her followers opened a soup kitchen on the Lower East Side. By 1938 twelve hundred persons were fed there every day, and other "houses of responsibility" opened in dozens of other cities by the end of the decade. The *Catholic Worker* lost many supporters when its opposition to violence provoked hostility during the Second World War, but it influenced later generations of Catholic social activists and maintained editorial offices in the city into the 1990s. After Day's death St. Joseph House on East 1st Street and Maryhouse on East 3rd Street continued to operate. She wrote *The Long Loneliness: The Autobiography* (1952).

Mel Piehl: *Breaking Bread: The "Catholic Worker" and the Origin of Catholic Radicalism in America* (Philadelphia: Temple University Press, 1982)

Maurice Isserman

DC Comics. Firm of comic book publishers formed in 1935 in New York City as National Allied Publications. In the year of its founding it introduced *New Fun Comics*, a comic book containing adventure stories. In 1936 the firm became Detective Comics, a name that it also used as the title for a comic book of crime and suspense published in the following year. It introduced Superman, its first "superhero," in *Action Comics* in 1938. Batman, who first appeared in *Detective Comics* in 1940, fought crime in Gotham City, a fictitious version of New York City. The company soon developed many other characters, including the Flash (1940), the Green Lantern (1941), and Wonder Woman (1942), who together formed the Justice Society of America. Although interest in superheroes declined after 1945 the firm revived its fortunes by revamping its characters in 1956. In 1977 it took its current name. DC Comics published a twelve-issue series called *Crisis on Infinite Earth* in 1985 and an acclaimed "graphic novel" featuring Batman called *The Dark Knight Returns* in 1986.

Reinhold Reitberger and Wolfgang Fuchs: *Comics: Anatomie eines Massenmediums* (Munich: H. Moss, 1971; Eng. trans. Boston: Little, Brown, n.d. [1972])
Will Jacobs and Gerard Jones: *The Comic Book Heroes: From the Silver Age to the Present* (New York: Crown, 1985)
Mike Benton: *The Comic Book in America: An Illustrated History* (Dallas: Taylor, 1989)

Patricia A. Perito

DDB Needham Worldwide. Advertising agency formed in 1986 through a merger of Needham Harper Worldwide and the Doyle Dane Bernbach Group. Needham Harper was founded in 1925 in Chicago by Maurice H. Needham and opened its first office in New York City in 1939. Doyle Dane Bernbach was formed in 1949 in New York City by Ned Doyle, Maxwell Dane, and the well-known copywriter William Bernbach, who in the 1960s was the most influential figure in the "creative revolution" in advertising that aimed for a union of art, copy, and personal style. In 1992 the firm had nearly $2000 million in billings.

Stephen R. Fox: *The Mirror Makers: A History of American Advertising and Its Creators* (New York: William Morrow, 1984)

Chauncey G. Olinger, Jr.

Dead End. Name sometimes applied in the early twentieth century to a small neighborhood in the East 50s along the East River, so named because of the extreme poverty of the area and because the streets "dead-ended" there at the edge of the river. A play about the neighborhood, Sidney Kingsley's *Dead End*, was produced in 1935; it inspired several films in which the street gang the Dead End Kids appeared.

Irving Lewis Allen

Dead Man's Curve. A nickname for a sharp curve on the Broadway cable car line at Union Square just north of 14th Street. It came into use after 1891, when the horses that had drawn cars between South Ferry and Central Park were replaced by cables. Gripmen knew that if they applied the brakes in the middle of the curve the cars would become stranded, and as a result the cars were driven quickly around the curve with no concession for other vehicles or pedestrians, causing many accidents. The danger persisted until electric streetcars were introduced after the turn of the century.

Frank Rowsome: *Trolley Car Treasury: A Century of American Streetcars, Horsecars, Cable Cars, Interurbans, and Trolleys* (New York: McGraw–Hill, 1956)

Andrew Sparberg

Dead Rabbits. Irish gang in the sixth ward; the term "dead rabbit" was a slang term for a rowdy. The gang supported Mayor Fernando Wood and was apparently known as the Mulberry Street Boys until a riot with the rival nativist gang the Bowery Boys in the Five Points on 4 July 1857, which was prompted by the formation of a new state police force and the enactment of liquor laws intended partly to undermine Wood's power. The Metropolitan Police were driven from the neighborhood by the Mulberry Street Boys and were then replaced by the Bowery Boys. The violence of the riot (twelve persons were killed) prompted the renaming of the Mulberry Street Boys by the press and the police. Although little is known about the gang apart from hearsay, later chroniclers considered the Dead Rabbits the most violent gang of the mid nineteenth century.

Joshua Brown: "The 'Dead Rabbit'–Bowery Boy Riot: An Analysis of the Antebellum New York Gang" (thesis, Columbia University, 1976)

Joshua Brown

deafness. One of the first of several important institutions for deaf New Yorkers was the New York School for the Deaf, opened in 1818 in the city almshouse as the second institution of its kind in the United States. In 1829

Dead Man's Curve, ca *1900*

a building was dedicated on 50th Street between 4th and 5th avenues. The school floundered until 1831, when Harvey Pringle Peet became the principal; he developed a vocational program that became standard in residential schools for deaf children (1831), replaced a weak staff with several of the school's finest graduates and college-educated hearing teachers (including F. A. P. Barnard, later president of Columbia University), and introduced home instruction of deaf children, who by law were not permitted to attend the school until the age of twelve. Recognized as one of the finest schools of its kind in the country, it used the French method of instruction, which relied on sign language as the primary mode of communication. The school was the site of the first Convention of American Instructors of the Deaf in 1850 and in 1852 introduced a "high class" for its most promising students, who received three years of college preparatory work after completing the regular course. Their success led to the formation in 1864 of the world's first collegiate institution for deaf students, now known as Gallaudet University. In 1852 Thomas Gallaudet, the hearing son of a deaf woman, formed St. Ann's Church, the first church in the country designed for a deaf congregation: afternoon services were signed, and morning services were spoken for the family and friends of deaf parishioners. The popularity of the church led to the introduction of deaf services nationwide and to the ordination of deaf ministers in the Episcopal church and other denominations. In 1856 the New York School for the Deaf moved to a property in Washington Heights known as Fanwood, which became its popular name.

In 1867 the New York Institution for the Improved Instruction of Deaf-mutes opened on Lexington Avenue between 67th and 68th streets as a private school for the deaf children of German-speaking immigrants; it later became known as the Lexington School. The director was Bernhard Engelsman, who had taught deaf children in Vienna according to the German tradition of teaching deaf students without sign language, relying instead on speech and speechreading. He was the first in the United States to make successful use of this method, which was also adopted by his successors. In 1870 Fanwood became the world's largest school of its kind with 616 pupils, and Lexington secured state support on the same basis as Fanwood, guaranteeing its survival. The Manhattan Literary Society for the Deaf was formed by the deaf artist and intellectual John Carlin. It was followed by the Deaf-mutes' Union League, which was organized in 1887 by graduates of Lexington and united deaf professionals around common goals, especially philanthropic activities; the league was unusual in its acceptance of oral education. The country's most important publication during this period was the *Deaf-mutes' Journal,* launched in Mexico, New York, by Henry Rider, a graduate of Fanwood. It eventually became affiliated with the school and under the direction of Edwin Hodgson during the 1890s and early twentieth century became a fierce advocate of educational, professional, and personal rights. The success of the Lexington School lent strength to the growing popular support of the oral method. German-speakers established similar institutions in Milwaukee, Detroit, and Baltimore, and by 1920 the oral method was in virtually universal use in the United States. Fanwood moved to White Plains, New York, in 1938; enrollment declined to about three hundred by 1970.

The deaf community in New York City has had a number of prominent members, especially in the arts. Helen Keller lived in Forest Hills from 1917 to 1938. The poet James Nack lived in the city, as did the photographer Alexander Pach. In 1934 Emerson Romero, a graduate of the Wright Oral School, set up a theater guild in the city for deaf actors unwelcome in Hollywood after the advent of "talkies." From 1937 to 1963 Ernest Marshall, a graduate of Fanwood, made motion pictures in sign language. Bernard Bragg, also a graduate of Fanwood, helped to form the National Theatre of the Deaf, which presented productions with deaf actors for hearing audiences. Such efforts were instrumental in the success that deaf actors began to achieve by the early 1990s.

St. Ann's ceased operations as a separate church in 1949 but in the mid 1990s remained a mission affiliated with the Episcopal Diocese of New York. The American Professional Society was organized in 1966 by the engineer Albert Hilbok, the psychologist Barbara Brauer, and the microsurgeon Donald Ballantyne. Some of the most important political activists were Hodgson and Thomas Fox, teachers at the New York School for the Deaf who later led the National Association of the Deaf, and Fred Schreiber, a graduate of Lexington and Fanwood who during the 1960s transformed the association into a powerful advocacy organization.

Edward Allen Fay, ed.: *Histories of American Schools for the Deaf, 1817–1893* (Washington: Volta Bureau, 1893)

Jack R. Gannon: *Deaf Heritage: A Narrative History of Deaf America* (Silver Spring, Md.: National Association of the Deaf, 1981)

John Vickrey Van Cleve and Barry A. Crouch: *A Place of Their Own: Creating the Deaf Community in America* (Washington: Gallaudet University Press, 1989)

John Vickrey Van Cleve

Dean Witter Reynolds. Firm of securities brokers formed in 1978 by merger of Dean Witter and Company (1924) and Reynolds Securities (1931). At the time the merger was the largest in the history of the securities business. In 1981 the firm was acquired by Sears, Roebuck and Company and became the nucleus of its financial services network. It launched the Discover credit card in 1986. In the mid 1990s Dean Witter Reynolds was one of the largest investment firms in the United States, with headquarters at 2 World Trade

Center and more than four hundred other offices.

Chad Ludington

Debevoise and Plimpton. Law firm formed on 1 October 1931 as Debevoise and Stevenson by Eli Whitney Debevoise (a great-great-grandson of Eli Whitney) and William Edwards Stevenson. The name was changed to Debevoise, Stevenson and Plimpton after Francis T. P. Plimpton, a classmate of Debevoise at Harvard Law School, became a partner in 1933. The firm took its current name on 1 October 1981. In the mid 1990s Debevoise and Plimpton had 369 lawyers, including eighty-three partners, and offices at 875 3rd Avenue in Manhattan.

Janet Frankston

debtor's prison. The attic of the old city hall served as a debtor's prison in colonial New York City until the New Gaol, with three stories and a basement, was built on Chambers Street in 1755. Under colonial and early state law, debtors could often be imprisoned on a creditor's unproven suspicion that they were hiding assets. Once in prison debtors were forced to rely on family, friends, and private charity for their upkeep. Most prisoners were desperately poor workers who fell victim to the panics of the time: in some years half owed less than $10 and several owed less than $1. There were also some merchants, among them William Duer, the largest financial speculator of the 1790s. In later years, especially after 1810, debtors were often allowed to post bond and live on the "limits," an area that eventually extended south of 14th Street to the tip of Manhattan. In 1784 the state legislature permitted insolvent debtors to be freed from future obligations if consent was obtained from the creditors representing three fourths of their debt; the quota was changed to two thirds in 1813. From 1801 to 1803 state insolvency law was superseded by federal bankruptcy law allowing for voluntary (debtor-initiated) declarations, but this was for merchants and traders only. Women with debts of less than $50 were exempted from prison in 1811; debtors who were not freeholders and had less than $25 in assets were exempted in 1817 (the amount was increased to $50 in 1824). Eventually reformers like Joseph Fay helped to convince the public that in the credit-driven economy insolvency was a consequence of misfortune rather than moral failure, and that imprisoning non-fraudulent debtors was impractical and unjust. In 1831 New York became the second state (after Kentucky) to forbid imprisonment for insolvency.

George Philip Bauer: "The Movement against Imprisonment for Debt in the United States" (diss., Harvard University, 1935)

Peter J. Coleman: *Debtors and Creditors in America: Insolvency, Imprisonment for Debt, and Bankruptcy, 1607–1900* (Madison: State Historical Society of Wisconsin, 1974)

James Ciment: "In the Light of Failure: Bankruptcy, Insolvency and Financial Failure in New York City, 1790–1860" (diss., City University of New York, 1992)

James Ciment

Deckertown. Obsolete name of TRAVIS.

decorative arts. New York City became a center for the production and importation of stylish furnishings during colonial times. Distinctive regional furniture forms developed, such as *kasten* — large, freestanding wooden cupboards or wardrobes, generally with two doors. Kasten were made in Dutch cultural areas from the mid seventeenth century until the first quarter of the nineteenth, when they were supplanted by more fashionable design clothes presses. Design traditions and patterns of workmanship that complemented those of existing shops were brought to New York City by the cyclical influx of artisans trained in Europe, many of whom moved to the city to escape political and religious persecution and economic depression in their countries, such as Huguenot silversmiths in the late seventeenth century. As an international port and commercial center the city had access to raw materials like mahogany and rosewood from the Caribbean and South America, Italian and native marble, English and French furniture mounts and hardware, and textiles from Europe and Asia, giving local firms advantages over those of other regions well into the late nineteenth century. By the late eighteenth century the city's craftsmen were known nationally for the quality of their products. A prominent figure of the time was the cabinet and chair maker Thomas Burling (*fl* 1769–1802), who served his apprenticeship with Samuel Prince (*d* 1778). Burling was commissioned by George Washington to make a writing desk (Historical Society of Pennsylvania) and two armchairs (Smithsonian Institution). One figure possibly associated with Burling (and later his son's partner in a looking-glass shop from 1796 to 1798) was Robert Carter (*fl* 1783–1801), who led the cabinetmakers' contingent in the New York Federal Procession in 1788 to promote ratification of the Constitution.

In 1805 *Longworth's American Almanack* listed sixty-six cabinetmakers (including Duncan Phyfe), nineteen chairmakers, fifteen carvers and gilders, ten turners, and twenty-three upholsterers with shops in the city. The early nineteenth century saw the influx of such French ébenistes as Charles-Honoré Lannuier (*fl* 1803–19) and Joseph Brauwers (*fl* after 1814). Upholsterers traditionally performed a range of services, such as making curtains and hanging wall coverings. According to the federal census of 1840 furniture manufacturers employed 793 workers in seven of the city's seventeen wards; among these were the French-born cabinetmaker Alexander Roux (1813–86) and J. and J. W. Meeks (*fl* 1836–60).

A new profession emerged in the nineteenth century: that of the interior decorator, who completed interiors after construction was finished. Some architects including Alexander Jackson Davis designed furniture to complement specific commissions, such as his Gothic Revival designs for William Paulding's mansion Lyndhurst, in Tarrytown, New York. One mid-century specialist was George Platt (1812–73), who was praised by Andrew Jackson Downing. After the Civil War furniture manufacturers such as Pottier and Stymus, Leon Marcotte and Company, and Herter Brothers expanded their services and product lines to provide complete interiors. These firms were joined by others, including Sypher and Company, which also dealt in interiors, antiques, and decorative accessories, and the influential but short-lived firm of Associated Artists, formed by Louis Comfort Tiffany and three colleagues in 1879. These leading exponents of artful interiors gained patrons among the prominent and wealthy nationwide.

Two influential publications by New Yorkers further promoted interior design reform in the twentieth century. *The Decoration of Houses* (1897) by Edith Wharton and the architect Ogden Codman and *The House in Good Taste* by Elsie de Wolfe called for simple classical interiors, eschewing Victorian clutter. In the years surrounding the First World War such recently immigrated architects and designers as Paul T. Frankl (1887–1958), Joseph Urban (1872–1933), Eugene Schoen, and William Lescaze introduced modern, functional European designs. The International Style received its most concentrated publicity in an exhibition at the Museum of Modern Art in 1932 for which the curators were the critic Lewis Mumford, the architectural historian Henry Russell Hitchcock, and the architect Philip Johnson. Industrial designers based in the city adapted streamlined functionalism to appliances and furnishing manufactured for national markets; among the best-known were Raymond Loewy, Norman Bel Geddes, Walter Dorwin Teague (1883–1960), and Russel Wright (1904–76). The interior designer Donald Deskey (1894–1989) employed the "moderne" style in commissions for interiors such as those of Radio City Music Hall. Knoll International (formed 1937) became a leading American and international manufacturer and distributor of furniture in modern and post-modern styles for the contract and residential markets.

The use of historic American styles paralleled the modern trend in twentieth-century interior design. The opening of the American Wing of the Metropolitan Museum of Art in 1924 stimulated the manufacture of reproductions of museum-quality antiques, as well as an interest in traditional interiors. Such interior designers and design firms as McMillen Inc., Mrs. Henry ("Sister") Parish II of

Parish–Hadley Associates, and Mark Hampton (*b* 1940) successfully applied traditional schemes to residential, civic, and commercial projects. For a broader market the fashion designer Ralph Lauren branched out from designing sporty, traditional clothing for men to designing environments for his customers. In the mid 1990s the city's showrooms, trade shows, and custom workrooms continued to display a broad spectrum of design for metropolitan homes.

See also Furniture and Interior design.

Deborah Dependahl Waters

Deegan, William F. (*b* New York City, 29 Dec 1882; *d* New York City, 3 April 1932). Architect and political leader. He was educated at Cooper Union and served as a major in the First World War under General George W. Goethals. After the war he became active in the American Legion and in 1921 was named commander of New York State. A Democrat, he spent his political career in the Bronx. As an architect he worked for many important firms, including McKim, Mead and White; Post, Magnicke and Franke; and Starrett and Van Vieck. He was the president of the Bronx Chamber of Commerce, from which he resigned when the organization became critical of Mayor James J. Walker. Appointed commissioner of tenement housing in June 1928, he remained in office until his death. In 1930 Walker put him in charge of the Mayor's Committee on Receptions to Distinguished Guests. The Major Deegan Expressway in the Bronx, completed in 1956, is named for him.

Andrew Sparberg

De Forest, Lee (*b* Council Bluffs, Iowa, 26 Aug 1873; *d* Los Angeles, 30 June 1961). Engineer and inventor. He received his PhD from Yale University in 1899 and moved to New York City in 1902. In 1906 he invented the Audion, a three-element vacuum tube consisting of a diode with an added grid that not only controlled the flow of electrons but also oscillated wireless waves. This invention enabled him to make some of the earliest radio broadcasts, from a transmitter at Coney Island. With an arc transmitter, a more conventional device, he engineered the broadcast of a performance by Enrico Caruso at the Metropolitan Opera in 1910. De Forest remained in New York City until 1925, residing on the Upper West Side and in the Bronx. He wrote an autobiography, *Father of Radio* (1950).

Curtis Mitchell: *Cavalcade of Broadcasting* (Chicago: Follett, 1970)

Thomas S. W. Lewis: *Empire of the Air: The Men Who Made Radio* (New York: Edward Burlingame, 1991)

Val Ginter

De Forest, Robert (Weeks) (*b* New York City, 25 April 1848; *d* New York City, 6 May 1931). Philanthropist and housing reformer. A graduate of Yale College and Columbia Law School, he built a successful law practice and for fifty years was general counsel for the Central Railroad of New Jersey, becoming one of the wealthiest men in the United States. In 1882 he helped to found the Charity Organization Society, and in 1900 Governor Theodore Roosevelt named him chairman of the New York State Tenement Housing Commission, which then drafted and sponsored the important housing law of 1901. He was then appointed the first commissioner of the city's Tenement House Department by Mayor Seth Low. De Forest served as president of the Russell Sage Foundation, the Welfare Council of New York City, Survey Associates, the National Housing Association, and the Metropolitan Museum of Art, to which he donated the American wing. He lived at 7 Washington Square in Greenwich Village.

Kenneth T. Jackson

De Hueck, Catherine (*b* Russia, 15 Aug 1900; *d* 1985). Humanitarian. Born into a Roman Catholic family, she married Baron Boris De Hueck in 1915 and after the Bolshevik Revolution fled with him to Toronto. She moved to New York City and in 1938 opened Friendship House in Harlem to provide direct assistance to the needy and promote racial justice through education and social action. Her published writings include *Friendship House* (1947) and *Fragments of My Life* (1979).

Bernadette McCauley

de Kooning, Willem (*b* Rotterdam, Netherlands, 24 April 1904). Painter. He moved to New York City in 1927, settled into a studio in Manhattan, and became acquainted with the artists John Graham, David Smith, and Arshile Gorky and the art student Elaine Fried, whom he later married. From 1935 he worked briefly in the mural division of the Federal Art Project sponsored by the Works Progress Administration. He later received other mural commissions in the city, including one for the Hall of Pharmacy at the World's Fair of 1939–40. His early paintings depict male figures during the Depression in ambiguous surroundings. At his first solo show (at the Egan Gallery in 1948) his black-and-white abstractions, swiftly reversing and intermixing form and space, firmly established his reputation. A central figure among the abstract expressionists, de Kooning continued to live and work in the city until 1963, when he moved to Springs, Long Island.

Thomas B. Hess: *Willem de Kooning* (New York: Museum of Modern Art, 1968)

Paul Cummings, Jörn Merkert, and Claire Stoullig: *Willem de Kooning: Drawings, Paintings, Sculpture* (New York: Whitney Museum of American Art, 1983)

Mona Hadler

Delacorte, George (Thomas, Jr.) (*b* New York City, 20 June 1894; *d* New York City, 4 May 1991). Publisher and philanthropist. He attended Harvard University and then Columbia University (BA 1913) and formed Delacorte Press in 1921, which became successful as a publisher of popular magazines and comic books. In 1942 he introduced Dell Books, pocket-size paperbacks selling for twenty-five cents; between seven and eleven million were sold a year, despite

Willem de Kooning, 1937

shortages of materials during the Second World War. By 1945 Delacorte owned more than two hundred magazines. He remained the chairman of Dell until he sold it to Doubleday for $35 million in 1976. With some of the proceeds from the sale he set up the Delacorte Fund to maintain and build public monuments in the city. He also built Delacorte Theatre in Central Park and renovated City Hall Park.

James E. Mooney

Delafield, Edward (*b* New York City, 7 May 1794; *d* New York City, 13 Feb 1875). Ophthalmologist. Born into a prominent family, he became one of the first ophthalmologists in the United States. He studied at the London Infirmary and modeled after it the New York Eye Infirmary, which he established with his colleague John Kearney Rodgers in 1820 and with which he remained associated throughout his career; he was also a founder and a president of the American Ophthalmological Society (formed 1864). From 1825 to 1838 he taught at the College of Physicians and Surgeons, where he was president from 1858 to 1875. He was the father of the pathologist Francis Delafield.

Sullivan H. Weston: *Memorial Sermon [on the Brothers Delafield]* (New York: Evening Post Steam Presses, 1875)

Joseph S. Lieber

de Lancey, James (*b* New York City, 27 Nov 1703; *d* New York City, 30 July 1760). Statesman, eldest son of Stephen de Lancey. He studied in England before practicing law in New York City. Appointed to the state supreme court as a judge and later its chief justice, he became unpopular when he took the side of the government in the trial of John Peter Zenger. After a political contest with Governor George Clinton between 1744 and 1753 over the control of the provincial judicial and legislative branches, he emerged as the victor with the post of lieutenant governor. He presided over the Albany convention in 1754 and signed the charter for King's College, an occasion that his family and the Livingstons exploited to form opposing political factions. At his death de Lancey was succeeded as lieutenant governor by his political rival Cadwallader Colden.

James E. Mooney

de Lancey, Stephen [de Lancy, Étienne] (*b* France, 24 Oct 1663; *d* New York City, 18 Nov 1741). Merchant. The son of a wealthy family, he moved to New York City in 1685 after the Edict of Nantes was revoked and set up a mercantile business, which prospered in part because of his connection through marriage to the Van Cortlandt family. De Lancey was also an alderman and a member of the state senate; his house at the corner of Queen (now Pearl) Street and Canal (now Broad) Street later became well known as Fraunces Tavern.

George Lockhart Rives: *Genealogical Notes* (New York: Knickerbocker, 1914)

James E. Mooney

Delanoy, Abraham, Jr. (*b* New York City, 1742; *d* Westchester County, N.Y., 1795). Painter. After working for the painter Benjamin West in London he returned to New York City in 1767 to become a portrait painter; he was unsuccessful and by the 1780s found work painting signs. Toward the end of his life Delanoy received commissions for portraits in New Haven, Connecticut. A few of his paintings are held by the New-York Historical Society.

James E. Mooney

DeLeon, Daniel (*b* Curaçao, 14 Dec 1852; *d* New York City, 11 May 1914). Activist and political leader. He worked for Henry George's mayoral campaign in New York City in 1886 and in 1890 joined the Socialist Labor Party (SLP); named the editor of the party's newspaper the *People* in the early 1890s, he dominated the party from the mid 1890s until the end of his life. He joined the Industrial Workers of the World in 1905 but was expelled in 1908 because he refused to repudiate political action as a primary strategy for working-class action. DeLeon's disputes with union leaders and fellow socialists caused a split within the branch of the SLP in the city and led to the formation of the Socialist Party of America.

Glen Seretan: *Daniel DeLeon: The Odyssey of an American Marxist* (Cambridge: Harvard University Press, 1979)

See also AMERICAN FEDERATION OF LABOR.

Melvyn Dubofsky

delicatessens. The first food stores in New York City selling such specialties as cured meats, pickled vegetables, flavored sodas, and seeded breads opened during the mid nineteenth century and offered ethnic specialties from central Europe, especially Germany. By the early twentieth century many delicatessens specialized in eastern European Jewish cuisine, and more than sixty were opened on the Lower East Side alone. "Appetizing stores" provided fish delicacies, in many instances prepared according to kosher laws, including lox, pickled herring, and whitefish, as well as salads, cheeses, bagels, and bialys. Such well-known enterprises as Zabar's, Barney Greengrass ("the Sturgeon King"), and Russ and Daughters helped to make bagels and lox a favorite Sunday breakfast. In 1936 there were more than four hundred appetizing stores in the city, including thirty-six on the Lower East Side. Delicatessens remained popular after the Second World War and attracted customers from many ethnic backgrounds. There were about six thousand delicatessens in the city in the mid 1990s; among the best-known were Katz's Delicatessen on Houston Street, the Second Avenue Kosher Delicatessen, the Carnegie Delicatessen, and the Stage Deli.

Jenna Weissman Joselit

Delineator. Magazine launched in New York City in January 1873 by the firm of E. Butterick. It initially contained only dressmaking patterns but by the 1890s also included fiction, nonfiction articles, and homemaking advice. Under the editorial direction of Theodore Dreiser (1907–10), Honore Willsie Morrow (1914–20), and Marie Mattingly Meloney (1921–26) it exposed women's inequities be-

Katz's Delicatessen, 205 East Houston Street, 1991. The owners retain advertisements from the Second World War that read "Send a Salami to Your Boy in the Army."

fore the law and the plight of poor children, and called for educational reforms. The most successful of Butterick's publications, it was merged with another, the *Designer*, in 1928. In 1937 it merged with the *Pictorial Review*, put out by Hearst Publications until January 1939.

Henry L. K. Shaw et al., eds.: *The Happy Child* (New York: Dodd, Mead, 1925)

Mary Ellen Zuckerman

Dell Publishing Company. Firm of book and magazine publishers formed in New York City in 1920 by George T. Delacorte Jr. It published "pulp" magazines exclusively for two decades and during the 1930s was the world's leading publisher of comic books. In 1942 it introduced Dell Books, a line of small paperbacks that sold for twenty-five cents. It eventually opened Dial Press and Delacorte Press to publish hardcover books. In 1976 Dell Publishing Company was bought by Doubleday, reportedly for $35 million.

William H. Lyles: *Putting Dell on the Map: A History of the Dell Paperbacks* (Westport, Conn.: Greenwood, 1983)

Allen J. Share

Delmonico's. Restaurant opened in 1827 by the Swiss brothers Giovanni and Pietro Delmonico at 21–25 William Street. Taken over in 1831 by their nephew Lorenzo, it became the best-known restaurant in the United States in the nineteenth century. After the original location was destroyed by fire in 1835 the restaurant moved to a second one at 76 Broad Street; this too was destroyed by fire, in 1845. The restaurant then reopened as a five-story hotel and restaurant at 23–25 Broadway before moving successively to 5th Avenue at 14th Street (1861) and 26th Street (1876) as the city expanded northward. The restaurant popularized the leisurely lunch and dinner and drew its clientele from the city's élite. It became known for the elegant presentation of fresh foods supplied by its farm in Brooklyn as well as for such culinary innovations as baked Alaska and lobster Newburg. A number of social events were held there, including the first débutante ball in the city held outside a private home (1870). Closed in 1923 because of Prohibition and competition from other restaurants, Delmonico's was reopened in the late 1920s by Oscar Tucci, who managed it until July 1977, and again in 1982 at 56 Beaver Street by the Huber family. Famous patrons of the restaurant have included several presidents, Charles Dickens, Diamond Jim Brady (who reportedly sat five inches (thirteen centimeters) from the table and stopped eating only when his stomach touched it), and Claus von Bülow.

Michael Batterbury: *On the Town in New York, from 1776 to the Present* (New York: Charles Scribner's Sons, 1973)

Betty Kaplan Gubert

Deloitte, Haskins and Sells. Accounting firm, formed in Manhattan by Charles Waldo Haskins in 1886. Elijah Watt Sells became a partner in 1893, and on 4 March 1895 offices were opened at 2 Nassau Street. Haskins was highly influential in setting professional standards for accountants in New York State. The firm eventually became one of the largest accounting firms in the United States before merging with Touche Ross in 1989 to form Deloitte and Touche.

Janet Frankston

Deloitte and Touche. Accounting firm, formed in 1989 by the merger of Deloitte, Haskins and Sells with Touche Ross. In the mid 1990s it was the third-largest accounting firm in New York City, with about 2200 professionals at its offices at 1 World Trade Center in Manhattan.

de Mille, Agnes (*b* New York City, 24 Sept 1909; *d* New York City, 7 Oct 1993). Dancer and choreographer. She began her performing career as a concert dancer in the 1930s; her dramatic solos and duets led to her work for the popular stage and for ballet companies. Her innovative choreography for the dream ballet in the musical *Oklahoma!* (1943) was highly influential. She later worked on more than a dozen other Broadway musicals, was the first woman to direct on Broadway (*110 in the Shade*, 1963), and the first American woman to lead a labor union (the Society of Stage Directors and Choreographers, 1965). De Mille's work reflects her belief that movement is as important as music and dialogue to the development of plot.

Barbara Barker

de Miranda, Francisco (*b* Caracas, 28 March 1750; *d* Cádiz, Spain, 14 July 1816). Revolutionary. During the American Revolution he fought as a captain with the Spanish forces against the British, whom he helped to defeat at Fort Pensacola, Louisiana, on 9 May 1781 and in the Caribbean. Inspired to seek freedom for South America from Spanish rule, in January 1784 he moved to New York City, where he met with Thomas Paine and several statesmen including Governor George Clinton of New York, Robert Livingston, and Alexander Hamilton to discuss plans for a revolt in Venezuela. He moved in July 1784 to Europe, where he spent the next twenty years in exile. He left London in October 1805 and returned to New York City in November, where he called on several friends, among them Rufus King, whom he had known in London; he also visited Philadelphia and Washington, where he met with Aaron Burr, James Madison, and Thomas Jefferson. After winning the tacit approval of the British and American governments for an expedition to Caracas he returned to New York City on 23 December 1805, assembled a motley crew of two hundred men, and set sail on the *Leander* on 2 February 1806 to meet other ships off Hispaniola. Their attacks on Venezuela were easily repulsed and de Miranda soon returned to exile in Europe. While leading a rebellion in Venezuela in 1812 he was captured by the Spanish and taken to Spain, where he died in prison. He was the only man to take part in the American Revolution, the French Revolution, and the liberation of South America from Spanish rule.

Joseph F. Thorning: *Miranda: World Citizen* (Gainesville: University of Florida Press, 1952)

Kevin Kenny

Democratic Party. Political party formed in the early nineteenth century. After the first party system ended with the disintegration of the Federalist Party and the triumph of the Jeffersonian Republicans, a second national party system emerged in the 1820s and 1830s. Profiting from the political skills of Martin Van Buren, the Democratic Party in New York City and New York State became an important component of the second party system. It was challenged from the left by the Workingmen's Party in the 1820s and 1830s and from the right by the Whig Party after 1834. The most influential Democratic organization in the city was TAMMANY HALL, which predated the party itself (it was formed in the 1780s). The organization was challenged by a faction known as the Locofocos in 1835, leading to a re-formation of the party in 1837. As the city grew, the party became powerful by encouraging immigrants to become members. In the years before the Civil War its candidates lost several elections to the Whigs, who were often supported by nativists; a few Democratic leaders embraced nativism, but in general the Democratic Party remained sympathetic to immigrants, and its base of support among workers eventually allowed it to win most elections. During the 1850s and 1860s Fernando Wood was elected mayor with the support of Mozart Hall, an influential organization that he led. Differences of ethnicity, class, and religion led factions to develop within the party, among them Hunkers, Barnburners, Softs, Hards, and Swallowtails (a wealthy faction). The Democratic National Convention of 1868 was held at the new Tammany Hall on 14th Street near 3rd Avenue. Bitter battles erupted over Reconstruction and economic policy, and it was only after considerable debate that Governor Horatio Seymour of New York was nominated for the presidency; Seymour garnered many votes in the general election but lost to Ulysses S. Grant. Between 1872 and 1886 the mayoralty was controlled by the Swallowtails. The party survived a serious division in 1886 when the radical economist Henry George gained wide support in his mayoral campaign.

Consolidation in 1898 brought a number of new Democratic organizations into city politics, in particular the political "machines" of Hugh McLaughlin in Brooklyn, Patrick J.

Gleason in Long Island City, and John Y. McKane in Gravesend. From the 1920s the Pondiac Club, led by Edward J. Flynn, dominated politics in the Bronx for several decades, and in Queens during the interwar years Maurice Connolly controlled a powerful political machine that was riddled with scandal. The most important Democratic organization in the city remained Tammany Hall, which extended its reach to the outer boroughs under the astute guidance of Charles F. Murphy, its leader from 1902 until his death in 1924. Democratic politics during these years was almost exclusively dominated by the Irish. In the early twentieth century Tammany Hall gradually embraced reforms and sponsored such nationally known progressives as Alfred E. Smith and Robert F. Wagner (i), but corruption remained widespread, and the investigations led by Judge Samuel Seabury that ended the administration of Mayor James J. Walker sent the party into a decline that proved exceedingly difficult to reverse.

The Democrats in the 1930s were on the defensive, largely because of the brilliant success of Fiorello H. La Guardia. His election in 1933 to the first of three mayoral terms as a Republican with strong backing from Jews and Italians signaled a decline in the strength of the Irish, the most strongly Democratic ethnic group in the city. In 1949 Carmine DeSapio became the first non-Irish leader of Tammany Hall since William M. "Boss" Tweed, and La Guardia's supporters initiated civil service reforms that diminished the Democrats' powers of patronage. The indifference of Tammany Hall toward the New Deal enabled La Guardia and other Democratic organizations in the city, notably that of Flynn, to garner the largest share of federal support and largesse. Despite these difficulties the Democrats returned to power in 1945 and controlled the mayor's office for the next twenty years. Black democrats such as Adam Clayton Powell Jr., Hulan E. Jack, and J. Raymond Jones became powerful figures in the party.

Tammany Hall was dealt a severe blow when Mayor Robert F. Wagner sided with a reform movement that forced DeSapio's removal from office in 1961. The importance of political parties declined as the importance of television increased, a shift that was clearly evident during the mayoral campaign of 1965, won by the Republican John V. Lindsay. The Democratic machine nevertheless retained considerable power in the outer boroughs, where strong organizations were developed by Meade Esposito in Brooklyn, Donald Manes in Queens, and Stanley Friedman in the Bronx. The most prominent Democrat in New York City in the 1980s was Mayor Edward I. Koch, who began his career as a reformer opposed to DeSapio. After his election in 1977 Koch became markedly more conservative and reached an accommodation with the city's political machines, one result of which was a scandal that engulfed the Parking Violations Bureau during his third term. Many of his strongest critics were black Democrats; among them was David N. Dinkins, a liberal long associated with the Democratic organization in Manhattan who defeated Koch in the Democratic mayoral primary in 1989. The election of 1993, in which Rudolph W. Giuliani defeated Dinkins to become the first Republican mayor in a generation, marked a serious defeat for the Democrats, but the party retained an overwhelming majority on the City Council and in the city's delegation in Congress.

In early 1994 there were 2,272,613 registered Democrats in New York City, representing 68.9 percent of all registered voters.

Jerome Mushkat: *Tammany: The Evolution of a Political Machine, 1789–1865* (Syracuse, N.Y.: Syracuse University Press, 1971)

David Hammack: *Power and Society: Greater New York at the Turn of the Century* (New York: Russell Sage Foundation, 1982)

Amy Bridges: *A City in the Republic: Antebellum New York and the Origins of Machine Politics* (New York: Cambridge University Press, 1984)

Evan Cornog, Peter Eisenstadt

Democratic Republicans. In New York State the political coalition that formed in opposition to the ideals of Alexander Hamilton found its early support in the political organization of the former governor George Clinton, the wealthy landowner Robert Livingston, and upstate farmers. Although in the presidential election of 1789 the party won only 373 votes to the Federalists' 2342 in New York City, it gained a strong majority of the city's voters in the next decade, largely by appealing to artisans. Party leaders invited aspiring tradesmen to seek office as their candidates, and effectively advocated egalitarianism, tariff assistance to needy crafts, support of the French Revolution, and assistance to immigrants and the poor. The plurality that the Democratic Republicans won in the city in the presidential election of 1800 helped to elect Thomas Jefferson, and in the following years the party eclipsed the Federalists, who lost their majority on the Common Council. The Democratic Republicans then splintered: Aaron Burr, an important ally of Clinton and Livingston in 1800, formed his own ticket for the governorship in 1804; infighting occurred after the Embargo of 1808 between followers of De Witt Clinton and of James Madison, whose headquarters were at Tammany Hall; and Clinton waged an independent campaign for the presidency in 1812 but continued to support the party. By the 1820s most members of the party were divided into two camps, one led by Andrew Jackson (who attracted supporters of Clinton), the other by John Quincy Adams (who attracted supporters of Madison).

Alfred Fabian Young: *The Democratic-Republicans of New York: The Origins, 1763–1797* (Chapel Hill: University of North Carolina Press, 1967)

Howard Rock

Democratic Union of Women. Political organization formed by women in Manhattan in 1922 to oppose the gubernatorial candidacy of William Randolph Hearst and support that of Alfred E. Smith. Its leaders included Belle Moskowitz, Emily Newell Blair, Frances Perkins, Eleanor Roosevelt, and Caroline O'Day. After its first campaign succeeded, the union organized "National Schools of Democracy," a series of workshops aimed at increasing political awareness among women. The organization remained active in local campaigns for Smith and candidates not affiliated with Tammany Hall. In 1932 it was absorbed by the women's division of the Democratic National Committee.

Elisabeth Israels Perry

Demorest, Madame [née Curtis, Ellen Louise] (*b* Schuylerville, N.Y., 15 Nov 1824; *d* New York City, 10 Aug 1898). Businesswoman and philanthropist. She worked as a milliner and with her husband, William Jennings Demorest, built a fashion empire in New York City that included Madame Demorest's Fashion Emporium, Demorest's paper patterns, and the publications *Demorest's Illustrated Monthly Magazine* and *Mme. Demorest's Mirror of Fashions*. From 1860 to 1887 she operated an emporium successively at 473 Broadway, 838 Broadway, and 17 East 14th Street; it housed a dressmaking firm and from 1872 a pattern factory. Demorest turned her attention to philanthropy after 1876. She was a founding member of Sorosis, the first women's club in the nation. By the time of her retirement Demorest's patterns had been largely supplanted by those of E. Butterick and Company.

Ishbel Ross: *Crusades and Crinolines: The Life and Times of Ellen Curtis Demorest and William Jennings Demorest* (New York: Harper and Row, 1963)

Wendy Gamber

Dempsey, Jack [William Harrison] (*b* Manassa, Colo., 24 June 1895; *d* New York City, 31 May 1983). Boxer. He first boxed in New York City in 1916. In 1919 he won the world heavyweight championship, which he twice defended in the city. On 14 December 1920 he knocked out Bill Brennan at Madison Square Garden in the twelfth round, when he was well behind in scoring; and on 24 September 1923 he knocked out Luis Firpo at the Polo Grounds in the second round, after having been knocked out of the ring in the first. After losing the heavyweight title to Gene Tunney in 1926 he earned a rematch by knocking out Jack Sharkey at Yankee Stadium on 21 July 1927. On his retirement from the ring he operated a well-known restaurant at 50th Street and 8th Avenue. In 1934–35 he lived at the Ritz–Carlton at 112 Central Park

South, and for a number of years he had an apartment at 145–46 Central Park West.

Randy Roberts: *Jack Dempsey: The Manassa Mauler* (Baton Rouge: Louisiana State University Press, 1979)

For illustration see BOXING.

Steven A. Riess

De Niro, Robert (*b* New York City, 17 Aug 1943). Actor, director, and producer. Trained at the Actors Studio, he made his film début in *Greetings* in 1968 and became widely known for his intense, riveting performances in *The Godfather, Part 2* (1974, Academy Award for best supporting actor) and in two films set and shot in New York City, *Taxi Driver* (1976) and *Raging Bull* (1980, Academy Award for best actor), a biography of the prizefighter Jake La Motta. In the following years he appeared in *Once upon a Time in America* (1984), *The Mission* (1986), *The Untouchables* (1987), and *Cape Fear* (1991), and directed *A Bronx Tale* (1993). In addition to appearing in films De Niro has played an important part in revitalizing film-making in the city. In 1988 he formed the company Tribeca Productions to produce films in New York City both independently and for the major studios. It is based at the Tribeca Film Center in a former coffee factory at 375 Greenwich Street.

Peter W. Kaplan: "Tribeca Tycoon," *Manhattan Inc.*, Sept 1989

Rohit T. Aggarwala

department stores. New York City became a mercantile center during the colonial period, and by the nineteenth century the city was the largest concentrated urban market in the nation: it was the major seaport and financial center, had the largest population, and by mid century was the center of the needle trades and the garment industry. Merchants and wholesalers from out of town went to New York City to purchase dry goods for distribution across the country, and women went there to shop. Whether of home manufacture or imported from Europe, consumer goods made the city a hub of retailing. A tourist guide informed prospective visitors in 1892 that "all America goes to New York for its shopping."

The forerunner of the department store was the dry-goods emporium, which sold fabrics and sheetings and a modest assortment of notions and ready-made items for women and children. In the decades after the Civil War merchants such as Rowland Macy, John Wanamaker in Philadelphia, A. T. Stewart in New York City, and Marshall Field in Chicago transformed the dry-goods emporium by taking advantage of the new speed and regularity of transport and communication, which facilitated production and distribution. The modern urban establishments that they created were known as department stores by the 1890s and continued to bear the names of their founders more than a century later. Initially little more than wholesalers or enlarged, departmentalized dry-goods stores offering a limited assortment of merchandise, these establishments evolved into large mercantile palaces designed expressly for retailing. The department stores became mass-market distributors of goods ranging from furniture, jewelry, and glassware to books, toys, shoes, foodstuffs, and especially clothing; they also became the late-nineteenth-century symbol of every aspiring city.

The first generation of prominent American merchants was succeeded by a new one that included many German Jews: such entrepreneurs as Adam Gimbel, Herbert Marcus, Morris Rich, Abraham Abraham, Samuel and Jacob Lit, Isidor and Nathan Straus, and Fred and Ralph Lazarus moved the department store on to its modern foundations.

With minor variations dry-goods merchants in the late nineteenth century adopted similar business strategies to withstand the feverish growth of the department stores. In moving from a form of entrepreneurial capitalism, in which owners managed their stores, to an elaborate administrative structure modeled after that of large corporations, merchants were at the forefront of a new business culture that reorganized work along more efficient and bureaucratic lines. They sought to maintain a high volume of sales and rapid turnover of stock by keeping both prices and profit margins low. A one-price policy that prevented bargaining became a standard feature, as did a money-back guarantee. The heart of the store was the shopgirl: like the male clerk in the traditional dry-goods store, the female salesclerk became the typical employee of the modern department store. By the 1890s the largest stores in New York City, such as R. H. Macy and Siegel–Cooper, employed thousands of young, single, primarily working-class women. Mature women achieved a modicum of prestige as skilled sales personnel and were visible in management as buyers, floorwalkers, and cashiers.

The story of retail trade in New York City is one of constant geographical change. As New Yorkers moved uptown, shopkeepers followed. In the eighteenth century and the early nineteenth the city's many small specialty shops and general merchandise stores were clustered in the port area around Hanover Square, Exchange Place, and Pearl Street. By the mid nineteenth century a burgeoning population had outgrown lower Manhattan, and the important commercial houses were centered at Broome, Grand, and Canal streets and near City Hall Park, just south of what was the finest residential section of the city. Broadway, which had an array of stores, hotels, restaurants, and theaters, became the principal thoroughfare for fashionable shopping and display. Macy, a newcomer to New York City, unwittingly brought about the next round of moves in 1858 when he opened a small dry-goods store on 6th Avenue between 13th and 14th streets, well uptown from convenient shopping. In 1862 Stewart, the well-known merchant and proprietor of a uniquely successful dry-goods establishment on Broadway and Rector Street, followed Macy to the area above Washington Square and erected a store on an entire block front on Broadway between 9th and 10th streets. Stewart's gleaming, white, cast-iron palace was a spectacle in itself, which unlike his "Marble Palace" on lower Broadway was built expressly for retailing. Standing five stories tall, it had large display windows of French plate glass, a gaslit interior, and a vast assortment of domestic and imported goods. Stewart's and the streets around it were reportedly filled with throngs of carriages and fashionable women taking part in a new, exciting consumer culture. For a short time A. T. Stewart was the largest, most innovative, and best-known dry-goods store in the United States.

By the late 1880s, as residents moved gradually farther uptown, virtually all the stores that made New York City the nation's shopping and fashion capital moved to the former residential area bounded by Broadway and 6th Avenue between 10th and 23rd streets. The best-known included Arnold Constable; B. Altman; the Adams Company; Best and Company; Bonwit Teller; Brooks Brothers; Ehrich Brothers; Greenhut; Herns; Lord and Taylor; James McCreery; McCutcheon; R. H. Macy and Company; O'Neill's; Simpson, Crawford and Simpson; Stern Brothers; Tiffany and Company; and W. and J. Sloane. At the end of the century Siegel–Cooper (which began in Chicago) rounded out this series of moves when it opened the largest and most flamboyant retail store in New York City on the block front between 18th and 19th streets on 6th Avenue. On the avenue between 14th and 23rd streets, a section eventually known as the Ladies' Mile, the architecture was so spectacular and the mercantile display so extravagant that the area became the central location for retail trade for a generation of New Yorkers. The crowds attracted to the big stores were huge. At the opening in 1895 of James McCreery and Company, on the southwest corner of 23rd Street and 6th Avenue, the owners boasted that ten thousand persons could move comfortably within the store at one time. In the following year Siegel–Cooper, which called itself the "Big Store," attracted a crowd on opening day estimated at 150,000. The heyday of the large American department store was at hand and reflected a permanent change in American consumer habits. Shopping became a pastime that needed no justification: it provided the context for diverse forms of public and even cultural life, and dwarfed all other activities, particularly for women. The department stores were for and about women, and merchants catered to them with service, magnificent displays, and low prices. Wealthy women mingled with the working class as almost everyone seemed to pour into the stores, if not to buy then at least to look.

The supremacy of the Ladies' Mile as a shopping district was short-lived. R. H. Macy, the first store to move uptown just before the Civil War, was the first to move farther uptown in the early twentieth century. Pushed northward by changes on 14th Street and pulled by the developing subway and commuter rail service at 34th Street, it moved to Herald Square in 1904. In 1909 Gimbel Brothers, a firm that began in Philadelphia, followed Macy and opened a large retail establishment on Broadway between 32nd and 33rd streets. Over the years 5th Avenue came to be the principal thoroughfare for department stores and elegant shopping: in the years following Macy's move to Herald Square every major department store and specialty shop moved from 6th Avenue, most to 5th Avenue between 34th and 57th streets. By 1915 Lord and Taylor, B. Altman, and Arnold Constable had opened major stores on the avenue and anchored the new shopping district. Not all the major department stores followed the movement of population up Manhattan Island, and other retail districts took shape throughout the city: Bloomingdale's opened at 59th Street and 3rd Avenue in 1887, expanded the store west to Lexington Avenue, and remained in business at this original location into the 1990s; 116th and 125th streets became shopping thoroughfares in Harlem; Abraham and Straus on Fulton Street in Brooklyn became the retail flagship of the borough, for many residents second in importance only to the Dodgers; in the Bronx local shopping was centered at Fordham Road (the site of Loehmann's and Alexander's) and in the area commonly known as the Hub (around 149th Street and 3rd Avenue); and in Queens retail districts took form along Jamaica Avenue (by the 1920s) and Queens Boulevard (in the 1960s), where both Macy's and Abraham and Straus opened stores.

In the 1970s many of the best-known retail institutions in New York City went out of business. The future of 5th Avenue as the nation's premier shopping street became unclear, as it became pressed on the one hand by boutiques and specialty shops on Madison Avenue and by discount chains and suburban shopping malls, and on the other hand by a changing retail economy in which department stores became part of large conglomerates and retained little individuality. Among the more promising signs were the expansion of Bergdorf Goodman and Saks Fifth Avenue and the removal in the spring of 1991 of Henri Bendel from 57th Street to 5th Avenue, which remains a preeminent location for shops and shopping in New York City.

Elaine Abelson

Depew, Chauncey M(itchell) (*b* Peekskill, N.Y., 23 April 1834; *d* New York City, 5 April 1928). Lawyer and statesman. After graduating from Yale University he became a lawyer and a leader in the Republican Party, serving as secretary of New York State during the Civil War. He worked as a lawyer for the New York Central Railroad before being appointed the firm's president, a position he retained until he became a member of the U.S. Senate in 1899. Depew was a delegate to every Republican National Convention for four decades. He wrote an autobiography, *My Memories of Eighty Years* (1922).

James E. Mooney

De Peyster, Abraham (baptized New Amsterdam, 8 July 1657; *d* New York City, 3 Aug 1728). Mayor. The son of a mercantile family from Amsterdam, he went to the Netherlands in 1675 to work in his family's firm, then returned to New Amsterdam in 1684 and was appointed to the city's board of aldermen the following year. A supporter of Jacob Leisler in 1689, he later joined the anti-Leislerians and was widely respected for his moderation in the bitter factional disputes of the day. Appointed mayor in 1691 by Governor Henry Sloughter, he remained in office until 1693, was appointed in 1696 to the council of Governor Richard Coote, the earl of Bellomont, and served briefly as acting governor in 1700. At the end of his life De Peyster was one of the city's wealthiest merchants.

David William Voorhees

Deren [Derenkowsky], **Maya (Eleanora)** (*b* Kiev, Ukraine, 1917; *d* New York City, 13 Oct 1961). Filmmaker and writer. After emigrating to the United States through Ellis Island in 1922 she lived in Syracuse, New York, and took an interest in union organizing and political writing. She settled in Manhattan in 1935. In 1940 she moved to Los Angeles with the Katherine Dunham Dance Company as a literary collaborator and assistant. After completing the film *Meshes of the Afternoon* with Alexander Hammid she returned to New York City in 1943. The first film that she made by herself was *Witch's Cradle* (unfinished), shot during late summer with Marcel Duchamp in the surrealist gallery Art of This Century. Her studio on Morton Street became a magnet for the burgeoning intellectual and artistic life of New York City, which became an integral element in her subjective films *At Land* (1944), *A Study in Choreography for the Camera: Pas de Deux* (1945), and *Ritual in Transfigured Time* (1946). Deren focused public interest on personal, independent cinema through her writings, including *An Anagram of Ideas on Art, Form and Film* (1946), and popularized alternative exhibitions by renting the Provincetown Playhouse to screen films. She was awarded the first Guggenheim grant for creative work in motion pictures in 1946, and began traveling to Haiti in 1947, where she continued her avant-garde film work with poetic experience, form, and ritual. Her other films include *Meditation on Violence* (1948), *The Very Eye of Night* (1959), and *Divine Horseman: The Living Gods of Haiti* (completed posthumously, 1977).

VeVe A. Clark, Millicent Hodson, and Catrina Neiman: *The Legend of Maya Deren: A Documentary Biography and Collected Works*, vol. 1, part 1, *Signatures (1917–1942)* (New York: Anthology Film Archives / Film Culture, 1984)

Lauren Rabinovitz: *Points of Resistance: Women, Power and Politics in the New York Avant-garde Cinema, 1943–1971* (Urbana: University of Illinois Press, 1991)

Grai St. Clair Rice

DeSapio, Carmine (Gerard) (*b* New York City, 10 Dec 1908). Party leader. Born in Greenwich Village, he became the first Italian to be named the head of the Democratic organization of New York County in 1949. He played a critical role in the elections of Mayor Robert F. Wagner (1953) and Governor W. Averell Harriman (1954), and attempted to run the Democratic Party more openly than Tammany Hall traditionally had done. After his candidates for the governorship, the office of state attorney general, and the U.S. Senate lost elections in 1958, a reform movement led by Herbert H. Lehman, Eleanor Roosevelt, and Wagner forced his removal from office in 1961. DeSapio's efforts to return to politics failed when he was defeated by Edward I. Koch in primary elections for Democratic district leaderships in 1963 and 1965.

Warren Moscow: *The Last of the Big-time Bosses: The Life and Times of Carmine DeSapio* (New York: Stein and Day, 1976)

See also Law schools.

Chris McNickle

detective agencies. About the middle of the nineteenth century private detective agencies arose in New York City, where rapid growth was accompanied by an increase in criminal activity. The first agency in the United States was opened by George Relyea and two partners at 48 Centre Street; in the *National Police Gazette* (16 October 1845) the firm offered to conduct "both Criminal and Civil business [to find] all kinds of property . . . obtained by False Pretenses, Forgery, Burglary, or by any other dishonest means," with assurance that its agents were "always ready, at a moment's warning, to travel to any part of the United States." Relyea's offer to apprehend criminals in other cities and the frontier reflected a limitation of public law enforcement: although New York City was the only major city with a police force, the jurisdiction of the force ended at the city limits, and criminals from other cities who fled there were not generally pursued. From the beginning some of the real and rumored activities of detective agencies met with widespread distrust: it was believed that detectives colluded with thieves to retrieve stolen property, a dim view was taken of their investigations on behalf of wealthy families into the backgrounds of suitors, and some critics blamed marital investigations for an epidemic of "sudden explosions in domestic life."

A branch of the Pinkerton National Detective Agency was formed in New York City in 1865. It distinguished itself and reassured its customers by refusing to work for rewards and by seeking the arrest and prosecution of those whom it apprehended, and soon it was the leading agency in the nation. Private detectives continued to be held in low repute, especially as agencies began to conduct espionage in the workplace (for example using "spotters" on streetcars to catch conductors who kept, or "knocked down," the nickel fare). Employers regularly used private detectives to investigate the private lives of their workers, and it was reported that detectives sometimes rose to positions of leadership within unions to subvert their activities and facilitate strike breaking. Detectives were also criticized for operating spurious voluntary societies such as the Association for the Suppression of Gambling (1851) and the Society for the Prevention of Crime (1880), which observed places of criminal activity, gathered the names of customers, and in some cases reported these names to employers. Pinkerton detectives sometimes assisted district attorneys and the police and at other times competed with them. In 1880 Inspector Thomas F. Byrnes opened a branch of the police department's detective bureau on Wall Street and announced in a letter to the businessmen of the financial district that he intended to offer services similar to those of Pinkerton. By the 1880s Pinkerton had branches in all the major cities along with extensive files of photographs and records on criminals; the word Pinkerton became a generic term for a private detective. Notable successes of Pinkertons included a raid led by Robert Pinkerton in 1882 on the office in New York City of the Kentucky State Lottery (recounted in the *New York Times* under the headline "The Police Not Needed"), the apprehending of Marm Mandelbaum in 1884, and the unexpected arrest in 1904 of the gang leader Monk Eastman, who attempted to rob a drunken, wealthy young man being guarded by Pinkerton agents.

With the development of federal and state law enforcement agencies in the early decades of the twentieth century the role of the private detective in crime investigation decreased. Pinkerton and its competitors were replaced in strike-breaking work in New York City by the agencies of Pearl L. Bergoff and others, which were nominally private detective agencies but seem to have done nothing but organize squadrons of thugs. After the New Deal curtailed this sort of activity detective agencies increasingly focused on marital investigations; as early as 1912 the tracing of children hidden during custody disputes was mentioned as customary work. Private detectives remained active in business espionage. They also worked on corporate takeovers, often looking for incriminating information about a business or principal, or for hints that a firm was willing to negotiate or back down, and sometimes simply investigating the real worth of a business. Landlords in New York City used private detectives to determine whether rent-controlled apartments were in fact their tenants' principal domiciles.

Frank Morn: *"The Eye That Never Sleeps": A History of the Pinkerton National Detective Agency* (Bloomington: Indiana University Press, 1982)

William Parkhurst: *True Detectives: The Inside Stories of Today's Top Private Investigators* (New York: Jove, 1989; repr. with suppls., 1993)

Deutscher Liederkranz. German singing society formed in New York City in 1847. It was led after mid century by Oswald Ottendorfer and the piano maker William Steinway, who in 1867 raised the initiation fee to $50 and the annual dues to $24. The society nevertheless continued to grow and by 1869 had more than a thousand members. It built its own quarters on 4th Street in 1863; when the city's wealthier German–Americans later moved uptown it built a new and far more sumptuous Liederkranz Halle on East 58th Street in 1881.

History of the Liederkranz of the City of New York, 1847 to 1947, and of the Arion (New York: Drechsel, 1948)

Stanley Nadel

Deutschlandle. Alternative name of KLEINDEUTSCHLAND.

de Valera, Eamon [Edward] (*b* New York City, 14 Oct 1882; *d* Dublin, 29 Aug 1975). Political activist. The son of an Irish mother and a Spanish father, he was born on East 43rd Street and christened at St. Agnes's Roman Catholic Church. He lived for two years in the city before moving to Ireland, where during the insurrection of 1916 he led Irish forces and was saved from execution because he held both British and American citizenship. After escaping from a British prison in 1919 he traveled as a stowaway from Liverpool to New York City, where he began a tour of the United States to raise support for Irish independence. Dissatisfied with the terms of the Anglo-Irish Treaty, he led forces against those of the Irish parliament in the Irish Civil War (1922–23). Between 1932 and 1937 he led the Irish government. After drafting the constitution in 1937 de Valera served three terms as *taoiseach* (prime minister) and two as president of the Irish Republic.

T. Ryle Dwyer: *De Valera's Darkest Hour: In Search of National Independence, 1919–1932* (Dublin: Mercier, 1982)

John Bowman: *De Valera and the Ulster Question, 1917–1973* (New York: Oxford University Press, 1989)

Kevin Kenny

developmental disabilities. During the seventeenth and eighteenth centuries few services in New York City were available to people suffering from mental retardation, epilepsy, cerebral palsy, and other developmental disabilities. Those who lacked the support of family were cared for at the city's almshouse, where they lived with paupers, alcoholics, and the insane until a new, separate facility for the insane was built in the early nineteenth century. During one of the periodic efforts to reform the overcrowded almshouses (1866) an asylum opened on Randalls Island for children considered "feeble-minded," a term that included the physically disabled as well as the mentally retarded. The asylum operated the School for the Mental and Physical Improvement of Idiot Children, which was intended to screen children for the state facility at Syracuse and to care for the very young and the severely retarded. As it turned out, Syracuse rapidly reached capacity and most of the city's developmentally disabled children remained on Randalls Island and in other local institutions.

Organizations in New York City first offered services to the disabled who were not institutionalized during the early twentieth century. The People's University Extension Society of New York City at 111 5th Avenue provided free training in manual and domestic skills for the crippled, the blind, and the mentally retarded. From 1905 the Board of Education offered special "ungraded" classes in neighborhood schools, taught by teachers who were required to take an eight-hour examination. The ungraded classes, which numbered more than a hundred by 1912, were largely custodial rather than educational: they mixed together all children who were seen as unfit for the regular school program, including the retarded, the disturbed, epileptics, truants, and delinquents. The Progressive era saw the expansion of the complex at Randalls Island and the large-scale involuntary commitment of the mentally disabled. A body of seriously flawed research linked mental deficiency and crime. In a report for the city's Public Education Association entitled *The Feeble-Minded in New York* (1911) Anne Moore observed that the limited capacity at Randalls Island left many of the mentally disabled "a menace to themselves and others." In 1912 New York State passed a law authorizing sterilization of the mentally retarded, and in 1919 it replaced the term "feeble-minded" with "mental defective." Eugenic practices ended as organizations like the New York Committee on Feeble-Mindedness (1916) and the Vocational Adjustment Bureau of New York City (1919) placed greater emphasis on early care and training instead of segregation. Parents of developmentally disabled children launched a number of voluntary services in the 1940s that became leaders in advocacy. Public support also increased, and in 1945 the city's health department established the nation's first facility that provided both medical care and education for children with cerebral palsy. In 1975 the public school system strengthened its programs for developmentally disabled children in accordance with state legislation. At the same time national legislation was passed that guaranteed federal support for specialized programs.

The first state institution for the developmentally disabled in New York City, Willowbrook State School, opened on Staten Island in 1947. It was built for 3500 patients, but by 1971 it housed more than five thousand and was severely criticized for its overcrowding and substandard custodial care. A television exposé on the conditions there and a class action lawsuit initiated by the Association for the Help of Retarded Children led to a consent decree in 1975 that profoundly altered services for the developmentally disabled. Health officials placed a new emphasis on community care for all but the most severely disabled and ensured that newly constructed facilities in Manhattan, Brooklyn, Queens, and the Bronx were much smaller than Willowbrook (about three hundred beds each). Willowbrook itself (renamed Staten Island Developmental Center in 1980) was steadily reduced in size and closed in 1987. Some of the patients at Willowbrook were assigned to other institutions, but most were placed in the growing network of community residences licensed by the New York Office of Mental Retardation and Developmental Disabilities; by 1991 there were about four hundred such homes in New York City, with more than four thousand beds. The four remaining developmental centers in the city were scheduled to close during the 1990s as residential alternatives became available. In 1991 state officials estimated that there were about 150,000 developmentally disabled persons in the city (2 percent of the total population), of whom about three quarters were mentally retarded.

David M. Schneider and Albert Deutsch: *The History of Public Welfare in New York State, 1867–1940* (Chicago: University of Chicago Press, 1941)

Stanley Powell Davies: *The Mentally Retarded in Society* (New York: Columbia University Press, 1959)

John Duffy: *A History of Public Health in New York City* (New York: Russell Sage Foundation, 1968, 1974)

Michael J. Begab and Stephen A. Richardson, eds.: *The Mentally Retarded and Society: A Social Science Perspective* (Baltimore: University Park Press, 1975)

R. C. Scheerenberger: *A History of Mental Retardation* (Baltimore: Paul H. Brookes, 1983)

Sandra Opdycke

Devery, William S. "Big Bill" (*b* New York City, *ca* 1855; *d* Queens, 20 June 1919). Chief of police. He worked as a bartender on the Bowery and then paid a bribe to Tammany Hall to become a policeman in 1878. Promoted to sergeant in 1884 and to captain in 1891, he soon obtained one of the most lucrative police jobs in the city, running the Eldridge Street Station in a well-known red-light district. Reportedly he told his men during his inaugural address: "If there's any gratin' to be done, I'll do it. Leave it to me!" Shamelessly corrupt, he had his aides approach saloon owners just before an election, promising protection if the ticket backed by Tammany Hall were elected. In addition to getting rich he won promotion, becoming chief of police in 1898. Although frequently exposed by Lincoln Steffens and other reformers, Devery was resilient. He never fined a policeman for breach of duty, only for getting caught. He lost his position when Seth Low defeated Mayor Robert A. Van Wyck in 1901, but he was still a rich man, dividing his time between a mansion on West End Avenue and a profitable real-estate operation in Rockaway.

Kenneth T. Jackson

Devine, Edward T(homas) (*b* Union, Iowa, 6 May 1867; *d* Oak Park, Ill., 27 Feb 1948). Reformer, educator, and writer. In 1896 he became general secretary of the New York Charity Organization Society, a position he held until 1917. He also launched *Charities* (later called the *Survey*), a leading journal of social work. Under his guidance the society formed committees for tenement house reform and the prevention of tuberculosis and opened the New York Summer School of Philanthropy (1898, later the Columbia University School of Social Work). Devine directed the school from 1904 to 1907 and again from 1912 to 1917, and taught social economy at Columbia University at intervals from 1905 to 1919. His published writings include *When Social Work Was Young* (1939).

Sandra Sidford Cornelius: "Edward T. Devine, 1867–1948: A Pivotal Figure in the Transition from Practical Philanthropy to Social Work" (diss., Bryn Mawr College, 1976)

Sarah Henry Lederman

De Vinne, Theodore Low (*b* Stamford, Conn., 25 Dec 1828; *d* New York City, 16 Feb 1914). Typographer and publisher of fine editions. He moved to New York City in 1848 and in 1850 became an apprentice to Francis Hart, who engaged him as a partner in 1858. Under their direction the firm began printing Charles Scribner's periodical for children, *St. Nicholas Magazine*, in 1872 and in 1876 took on *Scribner's Monthly*. After Hart's death in 1877 De Vinne bought his share of the firm in 1883 and renamed the press for himself. An aesthetic conservative among Victorian printers, he argued forcefully for the simplification of title pages and condemned such fussy details as deckled edges. During a lecture at the Yale Club of New York he said: "I have given the best part of my life to the making of books that have been sold and read, and not rated as pieces of typographic bric-a-brac." De Vinne wrote many books on printing, including *The Invention of Printing* (1876), *Historic Printing Types* (1886), *The Practice of Typography* (1901–4; 4 vols., among them *A Treatise on Title-Pages*), and *Notable Printers of Italy in the Fifteenth Century* (1910).

Michael Edward Davison Koenig: "Theodore Low De Vinne: His Contributions to the Art of Printing" (thesis, University of Chicago, 1968)

Melissa M. Merritt

Devoe and Raynolds. Firm of chemical manufacturers. Its origins date to 1754, when William Post began mixing, grinding, and importing pigments in a shop at his residence on Fletcher Street. Offices remained on the site for a hundred years, and in 1798 the firm of Post and Sons was formed. It grew rapidly under two former clerks, F. W. Devoe and Charles T. Raynolds, and was reorganized several times during the 1850s. The offices were moved in 1855 to 106 and 108 Fulton Street, a factory was built on Horatio Street, and other retail shops opened on Fulton, William, and Ann streets. For several decades the firm was the leading producer of paint in the United States, and by 1917 it had undergone a series of mergers. The factory on Horatio Street was moved to Brooklyn in the 1920s, and the firm's headquarters moved to 44th Street and 1st Avenue in the 1930s. The firm made five major acquisitions by 1948, and in 1976 it was acquired by Grow Chemical (later the Grow Group), also based in New York City. Devoe and Raynolds continues to produce Devoe paints, which are popular in the metropolitan area, as well as protective coatings and art materials.

The Colorful Years, 1754–1942: The Story of a Colonial Venture That Became an American Institution (New York: Devoe and Raynolds, 1942)

David B. Sicilia

Devoy, John (*b* Kill, County Kildare, Ireland, 3 Sept 1842; *d* Atlantic City, N.J., 29 Sept 1928). Irish nationalist. He was arrested and imprisoned for his revolutionary activities in Dublin in 1866. On his release in 1871 he emigrated to the United States and settled in New York City, where he became one of the principal leaders of Clan na Gael, a secret Irish–American society dedicated to the militant republican cause in Ireland. He later launched two weekly newspapers in New York City, the *Irish Nation* (1881–85) and the influential *Gaelic–American* (1903–28): its headquarters at 165 William Street were a frequent rendezvous for revolutionary exiles. It was largely through his fund-raising and organizational efforts in the United States that the militant nationalists were able to carry out the

Easter Monday Rebellion (1916) in Ireland. Devoy wrote *Recollections of an Irish Rebel* (1929).

Desmond Ryan: *The Phoenix Flame: A Study of Fenianism and John Devoy* (London: A. Barker, 1937)

William O'Brien and Desmond Ryan, eds.: *Devoy's Post Bag, 1871–1928* (Dublin: C. J. Fallon, 1948, n.d. [1953])

John T. Ridge

Dewey, Ballantine. Law firm formed in 1909 as Root, Clark and Bird. Among its partners was Arthur Ballantine, the under secretary of the treasury in the administration of President Herbert Hoover; other members included Elihu Root and John Marshall Harlan, later a justice of the U.S. Supreme Court. As New York City became an international center of commerce and banking the firm represented a number of large corporations. Its name was changed to Dewey, Ballantine, Bushby, Palmer and Wood when Thomas E. Dewey became a partner after retiring from the governorship of New York State. The firm assumed its current name in September 1990. Its offices are at 1301 6th Avenue.

Bull 71, no. 33 (4 Sept 1990)

Emery E. Adoradio

Dewey, John (*b* Burlington, Vt., 20 Oct 1859; *d* New York City, 1 June 1952). Philosopher. He grew up in Burlington and after graduating from the University of Vermont earned a doctorate from Johns Hopkins University in 1884. After teaching philosophy and psychology at the University of Michigan he went to the University of Chicago to teach philosophy and become the head of the department of philosophy, psychology, and pedagogy. In 1904 he resigned after disagreeing with the university president about the administration of the education program; he soon accepted a position at Columbia University, and lived in New York City for the rest of his life, moving to 2880 Broadway in 1913, 125 East 62nd Street in 1927, 1 West 89th Street in 1939, and 1158 5th Avenue in 1945. One of his most important contributions to scholarship was his theory of instrumentalism, which posited that the worth of any idea or moral value should be determined by its practical consequences rather than by reference to any transcendental source or standard. In keeping with these ideas he was concerned with the problems of daily life and took active interest in many educational, social, and political issues throughout his career: he helped to form the New York Teachers Union in 1916, the New School for Social Research in 1919, and the American Civil Liberties Union in 1920, took part in the woman suffrage movement, worked with the Henry Street Settlement, and continued to develop his ideas about progressive democratic education. Criticized in some quarters for condoning the infringement of dissenters' civil rights during the First World War, he supported many liberal causes during the next forty years. In such books as *The Public and Its Problems* (1927) and *Liberalism and Social Action* (1935) he provided a model of social policy for educators, bureaucrats, reformers, and social workers. Dewey denounced the New Deal for being too conservative and called for the formation of a third party but opposed communism and all forms of political extremism. He retired in 1939 but remained intellectually active to the end of his life. On his ninetieth birthday fifteen hundred dignitaries, colleagues, and friends gathered for a celebration at the Commodore Hotel. Among his most important works are *The Influence of Darwin on Philosophy* (1910), *Democracy and Education* (1916), and *Experience and Nature* (1925).

Kevin Kenny

Dewey, Melvil(le Louis Kossuth) (*b* Adams Center, N.Y., 10 Dec 1851; *d* Lake Placid, Fla., 26 Dec 1931). Librarian. After attending Amherst College he worked as a librarian there and in Boston, at the same time devising the decimal system of library classification that bears his name. He moved to New York City to become the librarian of Columbia College in 1883, and in 1887 he established at Columbia the School of Library Economy (later the School of Library Service), the first of its kind in the country and the first at the university to admit women. He became the director in 1888 of the New York State Library in Albany. An advocate of simplified spelling, Dewey altered the spelling of his own first name.

Sarah K. Vann, ed.: *Melvil Dewey: His Enduring Presence in Librarianship* (Englewood, Colo.: Libraries Unlimited, 1978)

Mary B. Bowling

Dewey, Thomas E(dmund) (*b* Owosso, Mich., 24 March 1902; *d* Miami, 16 March 1971). Prosecutor, governor of New York, and presidential candidate. After receiving his law degree from Columbia University he spent a few years in private practice before joining the U.S. attorney's office in 1931. Although a Republican he was appointed special prosecutor in charge of the Investigation of Organized Crime in New York City by Governor Herbert H. Lehman, a Democrat. He earned national renown for successfully prosecuting the notorious crime syndicate Murder Incorporated and many racketeers; his work and his colorful image inspired such films as *The Racket Busters.* He was elected district attorney of New York County in 1937 and on the strength of his national reputation as a prosecutor sought the Republican presidential nomination in 1940. This effort was unsuccessful, but in 1942 he was elected governor of New York State, an office he held for three consecutive terms. He received the Republican presidential nomination in 1944 but lost the election to President Franklin D. Roosevelt; he received the nomination again in 1948 but lost to Harry S. Truman. After his third term as governor he resumed private law practice in 1955, becoming a partner of a venerable law firm on Wall Street that changed its name to Dewey, Ballantine, Bushby, Palmer, and Wood. Dewey lived from 1934 to 1935 at 1148 5th Avenue and from 1955 until the end of his life at 141 East 72nd Street.

Richard Norton Smith: *Thomas E. Dewey and His Times* (New York: Simon and Schuster, 1982)

See also LAWYERS.

Emery E. Adoradio

Dewey Arch [Dewey Triumphal Arch and Colonnade]. A planned monument in a pseudo-rococo style favored by some architects of the American renaissance of 1876–1917. Designed by the architect Charles R. Lamb and the sculptor Frederic W. Ruckstall (1853–1942), it was to be installed in Madison Square to commemorate the victory of Commodore George Dewey (1837–1917) over Spanish forces at Manila Bay on 1 May 1898. A full-scale model of plaster and wood was erected on the site to attract subscribers and provide a focus for Dewey's triumphal procession through New York City in 1899, and casts of sculptures intended to decorate the arch were made by Daniel Chester French, Philip Martiny (1858–1927), Henry K. Bush-Brown (1857–1935), and Roland H. Perry (1870–1941). During 1900 Dewey was eclipsed in popularity by Theodore Roosevelt, and subscriptions decreased after he failed to win the Democratic presidential nomination. The plaster model deteriorated and became a dangerous nuisance. It was carried off to the city dump in December 1900 after plans to build a permanent arch were abandoned.

S. D. R. Cashman

Dewhurst, Colleen (*b* Montreal, 3 June 1924; *d* South Salem Village, N.Y., 22 Aug 1991). Actress. She moved to New York City in 1946 to study acting at the American Academy of Dramatic Arts and in 1952 made her début on Broadway as a dancer in a revival of Eugene O'Neill's play *Desire under the Elms.* In 1954 she met Joseph Papp while he was organizing the New York Shakespeare Festival. The two often collaborated in the following years, beginning with her portrayal of Katherine in his production of *The Taming of the Shrew* in Central Park in 1956. She also worked with the director José Quintero in a number of O'Neill's plays, earning critical acclaim for her portrayals of his powerful, tragic female characters. Unable to find satisfying roles on the stage late in her career, she turned to television and motion pictures. Dewhurst was the president of Actors' Equity Association for two terms (from 1985) and won two Emmy awards (one posthumous) for her role in the television series "Murphy Brown" as the main character's mother.

Barbara Lee Horn: *Colleen Dewhurst: A Bio-bibliography* (Westport, Conn.: Greenwood, 1993)

Amanda Aaron

Dewey Arch, 1899. Background *Madison Square Garden*

De Witt Clinton High School. Secondary school opened in 1897 as Boys' High School at 60 West 13th Street; it was the first public high school for boys in Manhattan. In 1900 it took its current name, and in 1929 it moved to Mosholu Parkway and 205th Street in the Bronx. The last public high school in the city to admit only boys, it became coeducational in 1983. In 1991 De Witt Clinton High School had 3800 students, some of whom took part in the Air Force Junior Reserve Officer Training Corps and an exchange program with Middlebury College in Vermont. Well-known alumni of the school include Lionel Trilling, James Baldwin, Burt Lancaster, Neil Simon, and Charles B. Rangel.

Frank Bergen Kelley, ed.: *The DeWitt Clinton Book* (New York: Clinton Memorabilia Society, 1906)

Erica Judge

DeWitt Wallace–Reader's Digest Fund. Charitable organization formed in 1987 by the reorganization of the DeWitt Wallace Fund (1965) and the Lakeview Fund (1966), both established by DeWitt Wallace (*b* 12 Nov 1889; *d* 30 March 1981), a founder of *Reader's Digest.* It supports educational programs for the disadvantaged. In 1992 the fund reported assets of $1130 million and made grants totaling $72.3 million.

Kenneth W. Rose

de Wolfe, Elsie [Ella Anderson] (*b* New York City, 20 Dec 1865; *d* Versailles, France, 12 July 1950). Actress and decorator. She spent her childhood in the British Isles and was presented at the English royal court. In 1884 she returned to New York City and took up acting. A professional actress by 1890, she left the stage in 1905 to become a decorator, her reputation assured by her imaginative interior design at the Colony Club. She marched in a parade along 5th Avenue for woman suffrage in 1912 and published the book *The House in Good Taste* in 1913, which helped her to become nationally known. From about this time she lived mostly in France, where she restored the Villa Trianon at Versailles and was widely considered one of the most influential arbiters of design. De Wolfe lived in the United States during the Second World War but later returned to France. She wrote an autobiography, *After All* (1935).

James E. Mooney

Dewson, Molly [Mary Williams] (*b* Quincy, Mass., 18 Feb 1874; *d* Castine, Maine, 21 Oct 1962). Reformer. As the research secretary of the National Consumers' League from 1919 to 1924 she focused her efforts on the minimum wage. While serving as the civic secretary of the Women's City Club in 1924–25 she met Eleanor Roosevelt, who inspired her to take part in women's Democratic politics, first in the presidential campaign of Alfred E. Smith in 1928 and then in that of Franklin D. Roosevelt in 1932. From 1927 to 1932 she was the president of the New York Consumers' League, where she fought for better labor standards for women workers, a task that became more urgent with the onset of the Depression. Through the professional and personal relationships that she forged in the city she made a number of contributions to the New Deal. From 1933 to 1937 she ran the Women's Division of the Democratic National Committee out of headquarters in New York City. Dewson remained active in political circles in the city until 1952, when she retired to Maine.

Susan Ware: *Partner and I: Molly Dewson, Feminism, and New Deal Politics* (New Haven: Yale University Press, 1987)

Susan Ware

DFS Dorland Worldwide. Advertising agency formed by the merger in 1986 of Dorland Advertising and Dancer Fitzgerald Sample. Dorland Advertising was formed in 1886 by John M. Dorland in Atlantic City, New Jersey. In its early years it set up successful operations in Europe and after the First World War closed its offices in the United States; it later became one of the largest advertising agencies in the United Kingdom. Dancer Fitzgerald Sample had its origins in the agency Blackett–Sample–Hummert, in business from 1923 in Chicago; it specialized in producing radio programs and advertising and in 1948 moved to New York City to be close to the growing television industry.

Chauncey G. Olinger, Jr.

Dial. Literary journal launched in 1880 and inspired by a transcendentalist journal of the same name published in Boston. Considered among the finest publications of its kind in the country, in 1898 it absorbed the *Chap-book*, a literary review based in Chicago. During the 1920s it published work by such members of the "lost generation" as Ezra Pound, Edna St. Vincent Millay, E. E. Cummings, and John Dos Passos, as well as by John Dewey, Jean Cocteau, and Bertrand Russell. Marianne Moore edited the *Dial* from 1925 until 1929, when it ceased publication.

William Wasserstrom: *The Time of the Dial* (Syracuse, N.Y.: Syracuse University Press, 1963)

David A. Balcom

Diamond District. A section of midtown Manhattan near 47th Street between 5th and 6th avenues. It became the center of the retail and wholesale diamond trade in New York City when dealers moved north from an earlier district near Canal Street and the Bowery that took shape in the 1920s, and from the area surrounding the corner of Nassau and Fulton streets, the first site of the Diamond Dealers Club (formed 1931). The district grew in importance when Hitler invaded the Low Countries: thousands of Jews fleeing the diamond centers of Antwerp (Belgium) and Amsterdam settled in New York City, and soon the diamond trade there was dominated by Orthodox Jews. The Diamond Dealers Club moved to 47th Street in 1941. The diamond trade depends on frequent personal contacts, and all transactions in the district are closed with a handshake and the Yiddish

"Diamond and Jewelry Way," 47th Street between 5th and 6th avenues, 1991

words *mazel und brucha* (luck and blessing). Any disputes between dealers are settled by the Diamond Dealers Club, which handles 80 percent of all the diamonds entering the United States. The Diamond District has retail stores, jewelry exchanges, offices, and workshops where diamonds and other stones are cut, set, and prepared for sale.

Murray Schumach: *The Diamond People* (New York: W. W. Norton, 1981)

Janet Zapata

Dickens, Charles (John Huffam) (*b* Portsmouth, England, 7 Feb 1812; *d* Kent, England, 9 June 1870). Novelist. He made the first of his two visits to New York City in 1842 to give lectures, raise support for copyright laws, and record his impressions of the growing nation. He toured the city for a month, during which time he delivered impassioned readings and met with literary luminaries such as Washington Irving and William Cullen Bryant. On 14 February the Boz Ball (named after his pseudonym) was held in his honor at the Park Theatre and attended by three thousand members of the city's élite. Among the sites he visited were the Five Points, Wall Street, the Bowery, and the Tombs. He also marveled at the tirelessness of the city's fire brigade. On his return to England he wrote *American Notes* (1842) and *Martin Chuzzlewit* (1844), which criticized the city's dirty streets, cultural crudeness, and materialistic ideals. Part of this antagonism stemmed from his indignation over the lack of copyright laws and the pirating of his books in the United States. His description of New York City as a place where "a vast amount of good and evil is intermixed and jumbled up together" alienated many of his American readers. He returned to New York City in 1867 and read to several large audiences at Steinway Hall on Broadway (on twenty-two occasions between 9 December and 20 April) and Plymouth Congregational Church in Brooklyn (four times between 16 and 21 January 1868). Commenting on the changes that had occurred in the city since his last visit, he declared: "Everything in it looks as if the order of nature were reversed, and everything grew newer every day, instead of older." At a banquet at Delmonico's on 18 April he promised that he would never again denounce America. Five days later he boarded a ship in New York Harbor and slipped out of the country, barely escaping capture by federal tax agents seeking a share of the proceeds from his lecture tour.

Sidney P. Moss: *Charles Dickens' Quarrel with America* (New York: Whitson, 1984)
Fred Kaplan: *Dickens: A Biography* (New York: William Morrow, 1988)
Jerome Meckier: *Innocent Abroad: Charles Dickens's American Engagements* (Lexington: University Press of Kentucky, 1990)

Robert Sanger Steel

Dickinson, Robert L(atou) (*b* Jersey City, N.J., 21 Feb 1861; *d* Amherst, Mass., 29 Nov 1950). Gynecologist and birth control advocate. Educated at the Long Island College Hospital (MD 1883), he was an early champion of feminist causes including birth control, sex education, and the reform of women's dress. He achieved wide renown at the World's Fair in 1939–40 when he displayed innovative, life-size models showing the development of a fetus from conception to birth. He was also an influential surgeon at King's County Hospital, Brooklyn Hospital, and Methodist Episcopal Hospital and developed a number of surgical techniques. He wrote obstetric guides that were widely used, including the *Birth Atlas* (1941).

Joseph S. Lieber

Dietrich, Marlene [Marie Magdalene] (*b* Berlin, 27 Dec 1901; *d* Paris, 6 May 1992). Actress. Brought up in an upper-middle-class Prussian home, she shortened her name and embarked on an acting career at the age of eighteen. During the 1920s she played increasingly important roles in German stage and film productions. She became an international star after the director Josef von Sternberg chose her for the lead role in *The Blue Angel* (1930), in which she played a seductive cabaret singer named Lola Lola. During the 1930s she cultivated her image as a sultry, sophisticated femme fatale, known for her smokey voice and given to wearing men's clothing. She became an American citizen in 1939. During the Second World War she joined the United Service Organizations and tirelessly entertained Allied troops across Europe and North Africa. In 1947 she was awarded the Medal of Freedom, the highest civilian honor attainable in the United States. She moved in 1951 into an apartment at 933 Park Avenue. In 1967 she made her début on Broadway, appearing in sold-out one-woman shows at the Lunt Fontanne and Mark Hellinger theaters. Her performance earned her a Tony Award. In 1972 she moved to Paris and retired from the public eye. Dietrich made thirty-seven films, including von Sternberg's *Morocco* (1930), *Blonde Venus* (1932), and *The Devil Is a Woman* (1935), Billy Wilder's *Foreign Affair* (1948) and *Witness for the Prosecution* (1958), Alfred Hitchcock's *Stage Fright* (1950), Fritz Lang's *Rancho Notorious* (1952), Orson Welles's *Touch of Evil* (1958), and Stanley Kramer's *Judgment at Nuremberg* (1961).

Donald Spoto: *The Blue Angel: The Life of Marlene Dietrich* (New York: Doubleday, 1992)

Robert Sanger Steel

Dillon, Read. Firm of investment bankers formed in New York City in 1832 as a partnership called Carpenter and Vermilye; it became Vermilye and Company in the 1860s. The sale of Civil War bonds established the reputation of the firm, which in 1905 was renamed after its principal partner, William A. Read. It had offices in four American cities and London, and was known for underwriting bonds issued by New York City, as well as stocks and bonds of railroads and other industries. Clarence Dillon became the leading partner after the First World War; in 1921 the firm took its current name. The firm gained an international reputation through its reorganization of the Goodyear Tire and Rubber Company (1921), its acquisition and refinancing of Dodge Brothers, and its underwriting of foreign bonds. From the 1930s the financing of petroleum and gas pipelines accounted for a large part of its business, as did the underwriting of state and municipal bonds (including those to finance the Triborough Bridge in 1937). The firm was a subsidiary of the Travelers Corporation from 1986 to 1991, when the Travelers sold its interest for $122 million to Baring Brothers and Company, of London; this firm became the owner of 40 percent of Dillon, Read, with management retaining ownership of 60 percent.

In 1994 Dillon, Read had about seven hundred employees and offered a full range of investment banking services to many of the largest firms and municipalities in the United States, as well as international firms. It has headquarters at 535 Madison Avenue and offices in Dallas, San Francisco, Tokyo, Paris, and London.

Robert Sobel: *The Life and Times of Dillon Read* (New York: Truman Talley/Dutton, 1991)

Mary E. Curry

Dime Savings Bank. Savings bank formed in 1859 as the Dime Savings Bank of Brooklyn. It focused on small, individual depositors rather than large depositors and businesses. The bank took its current name in the 1970s, converted from a state to a federal charter in 1983, and became publicly owned in August 1986. In the early 1990s it had headquarters at 589 5th Avenue, about forty-five branches in New York State, and $8300 million in total assets (as of 30 September 1993). The bank announced plans in 1994 to merge with Anchor Savings Bank.

Leslie Gourse

Dinizulu, Nana (Yao Opare) (*b* Augusta, Ga., 20 Nov 1930; *d* Camden, N.J., 10 Feb 1991). Musician, dancer, and Akan priest. During the 1940s he formed Dinizulu and His African Dancers, Drummers and Singers, a troupe devoted to the music and dance of western and southern Africa. The group performed at the World's Fair of 1964–65 and annually at Cooper Union. In 1967 Dinizulu established Bosum-Dzemawodzi, a traditional African religious organization based on the Akan tradition, and in the following year in Queens he opened Aims of Modzawe, an African cultural center. Ordained in traditional shrines in Ghana, Dinizulu was the chief priest of the traditional Akan religion in the United States.

Sule Greg C. Wilson

Dinkins, David N(orman) (*b* Trenton, N.J., 10 Oct 1927). Mayor. A graduate of Howard University and Brooklyn Law School, he fought with the U.S. Marine Corps in Korea and entered private law practice on his return to the United States. He was elected a state assemblyman from Harlem in 1966, was the head of the Board of Elections (1972–73) and the city clerk (1975–85), and in 1985 was elected borough president of Manhattan. In 1989 he defeated Mayor Edward I. Koch in the Democratic mayoral primary, and in the general election narrowly defeated Rudolph W. Giuliani with substantial backing from racial minorities and liberal whites to become the city's first black mayor. Although during the campaign he had supported wage increases for municipal employees and aid to the homeless, during the early years of his administration he was forced by fiscal constraints to modify some of his proposals. His term was also marked by racial and ethnic tension: the boycott of a Korean grocer by blacks in Flatbush, tensions between Hasidim and blacks in Crown Heights, tensions between Dominicans and the police in Washington Heights, a racially charged protest by the police in Manhattan in 1992, and a dispute between sponsors of the St. Patrick's Day Parade and homosexual activists. In 1993 he was defeated by Giuliani in his attempt to win a second term.

See also Police and Poverty.

Martin Shefter

Mayoral inauguration of David N. Dinkins, January 1990. At rear: *Governor Mario M. Cuomo*

Diocesan Union of Holy Name Societies. Name used from 1882 to 1894 by the Archdiocesan union of the holy name society.

diphtheria. Epidemics of diphtheria, typically a disease of childhood once referred to as throat distemper, were reported in New York City as early as 1745. Because diphtheria blocks the upper airway with pseudomembranous tissue resulting from the body's inflammatory process, victims frequently suffocated until methods of intubation were developed in the late 1880s. More vexing to physicians was the ability of diphtheria to create a toxin that circulates throughout the body, worsens the inflammation in the throat, blocks normal heart function, and often causes death four to six weeks after the initial attack. The discovery of the diphtheria anti-toxin in 1890 provided an antidote to the long-term deadly effects of diphtheria bacilli. The New York City Department of Health was instrumental in developing municipal public health laboratories that both produced reliable, standardized quantities of anti-toxin and performed culture diagnoses for physicians in the city beginning in 1893. This work was largely the result of the famed bacteriologist and public health official Hermann M. Biggs and his assistant William H. Park. Although the incidence of diphtheria among schoolchildren in New York City began to fall with these and other public health efforts that continued into the 1930s, it was the development of the diphtheria vaccine in 1936, and its subsequent widespread and safe use among children, that led to the rapid demise of diphtheria. This dreaded disease is now completely avoided by children in the city who are properly immunized against it.

John Duffy: *A History of Public Health in New York City* (New York: Russell Sage Foundation, 1968, 1974)

Howard Markel and F. A. Oski: *The H. L. Mencken Baby Book* (Philadelphia: Hanley and Belfus, 1990), 133–44

Howard Markel

directories. For a discussion of residential and business directories in New York City see City directories.

Disciples of Christ. The first congregation of the Disciples of Christ in New York City was formed after members of the First Baptist Church and the Ebenezer Baptist Church merged in 1810; they became affiliated with the Disciples of Christ after its formation in 1832 by members of the Christian Churches (1804) and the Churches of Christ (1809) who favored a return to primitive, apostolic Christianity. After merging with another congregation of Disciples of Christ the congregation in the city was renamed the Central Christian Church. It occupied a building at 142 West 81st Street from 1910 until 1945, when it moved to a neo-Gothic church (erected 1909) at 1010 Park Avenue near 85th Street and changed its name to Park Avenue Christian

Church; in the mid 1990s it was the oldest continuous Disciples of Christ congregation. After many organizational changes and a schism in 1906 members of the Disciples of Christ were registered in either the Christian Church (Disciples of Christ), which was overseen by a central organization and had 7918 members in thirty-six churches in the city in 1990, or the Church of Christ (Disciples of Christ), which was decentralized and had twenty-five churches in the city in 1990.

Winfred Ernest Garrison: *Religion Follows the Frontier: A History of the Disciples of Christ* (New York: Harper and Brothers, 1931)

N. Eugene Tester: "Schisms within the Disciples of Christ, 1809–1909" (thesis, Northern Illinois University, 1969)

Kevin Kenny

discothèques. For a discussion of discothèques see DANCE HALLS AND DISCOTHÈQUES.

distilling. The history of distilling in New York City is discussed in the entry BREWING AND DISTILLING.

district attorneys. The officials responsible for prosecuting street crimes and other offenses in New York City according to state laws. Each of the city's five counties has one district attorney and a staff of appointed assistants, who present evidence on behalf of the state before grand juries, the principal vehicle for bringing serious charges against a suspect. During colonial times the prosecution of crimes was chiefly the responsibility of appointed lawyers; there was also a grand jury modeled on an English institution intended to check the zealousness of lawyers engaged as prosecutors by the king. The prosecutorial power of the state was limited in 1735 by a jury in the colony of New York that refused to indict John Peter Zenger on charges of seditious libel. During the nineteenth century a state penal code was developed that provided a framework for prosecution. A lavish courthouse built as a public project by William M. "Boss" Tweed became known for expenditures far beyond its budget and for cases argued there in the late nineteenth century by such figures as William Travers Jerome. Until the 1930s the district attorney's office was mainly the preserve of a few politicians and their patrons: district attorneys were elected with the support of local political machines, and they chose assistants not so much for their legal skills as for their political loyalties. Women worked as "confidential secretaries," or "C-girls," who were valued for their ability to "file and forget"; the highest position open to women law graduates was that of paralegal.

In 1936 the district attorney's office in Manhattan prosecuted Lucky Luciano, who was eventually convicted for operating a citywide prostitution ring, largely on the testimony of seventy-seven prostitutes held as material witnesses pursuant to a court order. After Thomas E. Dewey was elected district attorney of New York County in 1938 he did away with cronyism in his office and aggressively prosecuted racketeers, criminal syndicates, and street gangs. Public fascination with the activities of the office reached a peak in the late 1930s: Dewey's handsome figure and dramatic encounters with organized-crime figures inspired such films as *The Racket Busters* and *Smashing the Rackets* (1938). Dewey's successor, Frank Hogan, pursued reforms that made his office a model for prosecutors throughout the country. Under his direction the Criminal Courts Building opened at 100 Centre Street in 1941. Its design was widely seen as a reflection of the rational and ordered approach to law enforcement of the late 1940s: covering two blocks, the building was designed by Harvey Wiley Corbett to house the courts, the city jail, and the offices of the district attorney; its soundproof walls and many entrances and office suites were intended to prevent unethical dealings. Women were employed as prosecutors from the late 1960s, and in 1981 Elizabeth Holtzman became the first woman in the city to be elected district attorney (in Kings County).

By the early 1990s almost five hundred prosecutors worked for the district attorney of New York County and the jail was overcrowded. Although much of the work of the district attorneys is routine they have also prosecuted racketeering in the construction industry (in the late 1980s and 1991), "point shaving" in basketball (1951), the rigging of the television game show "The $64,000 Question" (1955), the theft of jewels from the American Museum of Natural History (1964), the fatal shooting of John Lennon (1981), the death of the graffiti artist Michael Stewart in police custody (1984), the shooting of teenagers in the subway by Bernhard Goetz (1987), and various charges that led to the conviction of the organized-crime figure John Gotti (1991).

Emery E. Adoradio

Ditmars. Neighborhood in northwestern Queens (1990 pop. 188,549), lying within Astoria and bounded to the north by Bowery Bay, to the east by La Guardia Airport, to the south by 23rd Avenue, and to the west by the East River. Older residents refer to the neighborhood as Steinway, after the piano maker Steinway and Sons, which bought a tract of four hundred acres (160 hectares) along the northwestern shore of Queens between 1870 and 1873 and during the next decade built a spacious factory and a town with a church, a library, a kindergarten, and a public trolley line. Unlike other factory towns Steinway was not exclusively for workers: the firm treated it as a real-estate investment, selling land and houses to the highest bidder, and eventually employees counted for fewer than one third of the inhabitants. Nevertheless the town set its clocks by the factory whistle. After the Interborough Rapid Transit line was extended to Ditmars Avenue in 1917 the area attracted many people who worked in Manhattan, as well as newlyweds (mostly Italians and Greeks) seeking their own apartments. Much of the main street, Astoria Boulevard, was destroyed to make way for the Grand Central Parkway, which provided an approach to the Triborough Bridge (1936).

Many Greeks moved to the area after the Second World War, and by the 1980s they made up the largest Greek community outside Athens. As automobile travel became more common the Steinway factory lost its connection to the surrounding community: most of the workers moved farther out on Long Island.

Richard K. Lieberman and Janet E. Lieberman: *City Limits: A Social History of Queens* (Dubuque, Iowa: Kendall/Hunt, 1983)

Richard K. Lieberman

Ditmarsen, Jan Jansen van (*b* ?Ditmarsen, Schleswig–Holstein; *fl ca* 1647). Farmer. In 1647 he settled at Dutch Kills in what is now Long Island City. His descendants included Johannes Ditmarse, town supervisor in Flatbush; Henry Suydam Ditmas, president of Erasmus Hall High School and a resident of what is now Ditmas Park; John Ditmas, a founder of the Flatbush Trust Company; and the genealogist and historian Charles A. Ditmas, founder of the Kings County Historical Society and president of the Brooklyn Sunday School Union.

Charles A. Ditmas: *Historic Homesteads of Kings County* (New York: Privately printed, 1909)

Maude Dillard: *Old Dutch Houses of Brooklyn* (New York: Richard R. Smith, 1945)

Stephen Weinstein

Ditmas Park. Neighborhood in west central Brooklyn (1990 pop. 12,179), bounded to the north by Dorchester Road, to the east by Ocean Avenue, to the south by Newkirk Avenue, and to the west by East 16th Street. It was modeled after the adjacent neighborhood of Prospect Park South by Lewis Pounds, who developed it in the early twentieth century. The Ditmas Park Association was formed in 1908 and enacted special zoning provisions to preserve the character of the neighborhood, which in 1987 was designated a Historic District. Ditmas Park is a middle-class neighborhood of about 175 large, detached frame houses on tree-lined streets. Among its notable buildings are the parish house of the Flatbush Tompkins Congregational Church, the former Brown house (1000 Ocean Avenue), and the Community Temple Beth Ohr (1010 Ocean Avenue).

Stephen Weinstein

Argyle Road in Ditmas Park

Dock, Lavinia Lloyd (*b* Harrisburg, Penn., 26 Feb 1858; *d* Chambersburg, Penn., 17 April 1956). Nurse. She moved to New York City to attend the Bellevue Hospital School of Nursing in 1884 and in 1896 took up residence at the Henry Street Settlement. In the city she helped to shape the profession of nursing and was the first historian of the field, and in addition was a determined crusader against venereal disease and an outspoken suffragist, feminist, and social reformer. A vocal supporter of the labor movement, she was an early member of the New York Women's Trade Union League. She returned to Pennsylvania in 1922. Dock was the author of the first textbook of pharmacology for nurses, *Materia Medica for Nurses* (1890), an author of *A Short History of Nursing* (1907–12), and a contributing editor of the *American Journal of Nursing*.

Janet W. James: *A Lavinia Dock Reader* (New York: Garland, 1985)

Karen Buhler-Wilkerson

Doctorow, E(dgar) L(aurence) (*b* New York City, 6 Jan 1931). Novelist. He grew up near the Grand Concourse, attended the Bronx High School of Science and Kenyon College (BA 1952), and worked as an editor for the New American Library and Dial Press (editor-in-chief 1964–69). His early writings include the satirical science fiction novel *Big as Life* (1966), in which two gigantic naked figures cause pandemonium in Manhattan as they loom over the Pan Am Building. He achieved greater recognition for his novels *The Book of Daniel* (1971), based on the trial of Julius and Ethel Rosenberg, and especially *Ragtime* (1975), which is set in New York City in the early twentieth century and includes fictional as well as historical characters. One of the characters in his novel *Billy Bathgate* (1989) is the organized-crime figure Dutch Schultz. Among Doctorow's other works set in New York City are the play *Drinks before Dinner* (1978) and the novel *World's Fair* (1985).

Carol C. Harter and James R. Thompson: *E. L. Doctorow* (Boston: Twayne, 1990)

B. Kimberly Taylor, Naomi Wax

Doctors' Riot. A violent disturbance from 13 to 14 April 1788 in which five thousand rioters ransacked New York Hospital because they believed that medical students were stealing cadavers from cemeteries. See RIOTS.

documentary filmmaking. Documentary is the term used for various kinds of nonfiction film and video. It was coined by John Grierson in the late 1920s and applied retrospectively to such nonfiction films as *Nanook of the North* (Robert Flaherty, 1922). The documentary film was in fact a continuation of the nineteenth-century illustrated lecture, which used projected lantern slides. Jacob A. Riis's illustrated lecture on immigrant life in the poorest neighborhoods of New York City, "How the Other Half Live and Die" (1888), may thus be seen as one of the first social-issue documentaries in the United States.

New York City became the hub of documentary activity in the United States during the late nineteenth century. After the Edison Manufacturing Company shot the film *Herald Square* with its new portable camera in May 1896, single-shot films of the city's street life were taken frequently by the Edison company, the American Mutoscope Company, and the American Vitagraph Company. During 1896–97 Alexander Black and Henry Evans Northrop of the Brooklyn Institute of Arts and Sciences began to integrate short films into their lantern-slide lectures — the first instances of this innovation in the United States. By 1903 George Kleine was selling a standardized illustrated lecture in the style of Riis, "Lights and Shadows of a Great City, New York," which included sixty-one lantern slides and nine films. Such programs routinely contained a reformist message about the dangers and corruption of city living. On the other hand there were numerous short travelogues of the city: one early example, *Around New York in 15 Minutes*, was released early in 1905 by the firm of Paley and Steiner, which was based in New York City, and showed various views of Manhattan and Brooklyn.

Although most fiction film production moved to Los Angeles and its environs during the second decade of the twentieth century, New York City remained the principal center for nonfiction filmmaking. Paul Strand and Charles Sheeler, young artist–photographers associated with Alfred Stieglitz and his gallery, completed *Manhatta* in 1921. In this eight-

Still photograph from Paul Strand's documentary film The City *(1939)*

minute documentary with intertitles drawn from Walt Whitman's poetry, the filmmakers went beyond the simple depiction of New York City and sought to convey the dynamism of metropolitan living—the ways in which the city alters our sense of space and time—and to express the grandeur of "the proud and passionate city." Through distribution abroad the film helped to initiate a cycle of "city symphony" films, including Walther Ruttmann's *Berlin: Symphony of a Great City* (1927) and several short subjects about New York City, including Jay Leyda's *A Bronx Morning* (1930) and Irving Browning's *City of Contrasts* (1931).

With the onset of the Depression documentary filmmakers became increasingly concerned about the social and economic conditions that burdened life in the city and nation. A generation of documentary filmmakers sympathetic to the political left soon gathered around the local branch of the Film and Photo League, including Leyda, Tom Brandon, Sam Brody, Robert Del Duca, Leo Hurwitz, Leo Seltzer, Lewis Jacobs, Ralph Steiner, and Sidney Meyers. The group began by making newsreels and short documentaries such as *May Day in New York, 1931* (1931), *New York Hoovervilles* (1932), and *Workers Struggle in New York* (1932–33), focusing on aspects of American life that were neglected by Hollywood. Most of these filmmakers, joined by new recruits such as Strand, Ben Maddow, and Herbert Kline, made increasingly ambitious documentaries as the decade progressed. Many were associated with Frontier Films, which produced *Heart of Spain* (1937), *People of the Cumberland* (1938), and *Native Land* (1942). Pare Lorentz, a film critic and advocate of the New Deal based in the city, made his classic documentaries *The Plow That Broke the Plains* (1936) and *The River* (1937) from offices and editing rooms in Manhattan. Only one major film from this period dealt more generally with the problems of New York City and urban life: *The City* (1939), directed by Steiner and Willard Van Dyke, with a commentary written by Lewis Mumford. Shown at the World's Fair of 1939–40 to rave reviews, *The City* painted a grim picture of metropolitan life and advocated the development of greenbelt villages inspired by small towns in preindustrial New England.

During the Second World War documentaries were an important propaganda arm for the U.S. War Department. In March 1942 the Army Signal Corps took over the Astoria studio and used it to produce its many training and propaganda films. At Mason General Hospital nearby John Huston filmed *Let There Be Light* (1946), about the treatment of soldiers who suffered severe psychological disorders during combat. This controversial film was banned by the U.S. Army and not released until 1980. Some films of the Office of War Information were meant to portray ordinary Americans: *Window Cleaner* (Jules Bucher, 1945) follows the activities of a man who cleans the windows of the Empire State Building.

After the war the city's documentary filmmakers generally survived by producing films for industry and nonprofit organizations, and when the opportunity arose they often returned to making films about the urban experience. James Agee, Helen Levitt, and Janice Loeb made *The Quiet One* (1949) and *In the Street* (1952), each about youths struggling to find their way in the city. For *On the Bowery* (1956) Lionel Rogosin had local alcoholics convey the despair of their daily lives. Stan Brakhage's *The Wonder Ring* (1956), Shirley Clarke's *Bridges Go Round* (1958), and D. A. Pennebaker's *Day Break Express* (1958) were more experimental and more celebratory of the city's potential.

The postwar rise of television meant the development of a new type of documentary, made for broadcast; much was produced in New York City by the news divisions of the Columbia Broadcasting System and the National Broadcasting Company. Television stations needed portable 16-millimeter equipment that could shoot news footage with sound synchronized to image. The resulting technology also helped to inaugurate the *cinéma vérité* revolution in documentary of the early 1960s, the exponents of which followed and recorded people going about their daily lives. Drew Associates at Time–Life, led by Robert Drew and including Richard Leacock, Pennebaker, Albert and David Maysles, and Jim Lipscomb, made ground-breaking public affairs films such as *Primary* (1960), *The Chair* (1962), and *Crisis: Behind a Presidential Commitment* (1963). Many were portraits of people under pressure. By mid decade the cameramen had left to form their own companies. The rich relationship between the city's *cinéma vérité* filmmakers and the theater community yielded several unusual documentaries, including Clarke's *The Connection* (1960) and Jonas Mekas's *The Brig* (1964), both of which captured performances by the Living Theater. Even a historical, stock-footage documentary such as Emile de Antonio's *Point of Order* (1964), about the Army–McCarthy hearings, showed a strong *cinéma vérité* influence.

In New York City as elsewhere, documentary was the virtually exclusive province of whites and men until it became increasingly pluralistic in the late 1960s, in part through the influence of funding organizations such as the New York State Council on the Arts and the National Endowment of the Arts. William Greaves, a black actor and aspiring filmmaker who had left New York City in 1952 to learn filmmaking in Canada, returned to the city in 1963 to make documentaries for the United Nations and then the United States Information Agency (USIA). His *Still a Brother: Inside the Negro Middle Class* (1968), made for National Education Television (NET), explored the changing consciousness and increasing militancy of black Americans. He soon became the executive producer of *Black Journal* (1968–70), a monthly news and public affairs program on public television that gave opportunities to a generation of young black documentary filmmakers such as Charles Hobson and St. Claire Bourne. A similar program called *Realidades*, launched in 1972 on WNET and aimed at the city's Latin American community, was overseen by the documentary filmmaker Jose Garcia (*The Ox-Cart*, 1972).

Newsreel, a filmmaking group loosely affiliated with Students for a Democratic Society, was formed in 1967 by politically committed leftists. In some respects modeled after the Film and Photo League, it had a branch in New York City that made documentaries such as *Columbia Revolt* (1968), about the student strike, and *Community Control* (1968), on efforts to decentralize the city school system in Ocean Hill and Brownsville. After a bitter and protracted struggle the whites who had dominated the organization left in 1972, and the remaining members took charge. The renamed Third World Newsreel, under the persevering leadership of Christine Choy, made a series of important films including *From Strikes to Spindles* (1975), about the city's Chinese community, and *Who Killed Vincent Chin?* (1989), with Rene Tajima. Other minority filmmakers, for example Bill Miles (*I Remember Harlem*, 1981), Warrington Hudlin (*Street Corner Stories*, 1977), Carlos DeJesus (*The Devil Is a Condition*, 1972), and Bienvenida Matias (*In the Heart of Loisida*, 1979, with Marci Reaven), also made films about the communities in which they lived. At the same time women gained unprecedented prominence as documentarists. Such New Yorkers as Barbara Kopple (*Harlan County, U.S.A.*, 1975), Mirra Bank (*Yudie*, 1974), Deborah Shaffer (*Chris and Bernie*, 1974, with Bonnie Freedman), Claudia Weil (*Joyce at 34*, 1973, with Joyce Copra), and Mira Nair (*So Far from India*, 1982) were among those making films reflecting feminist concerns. Several were associated with New Day Films, a filmmaker's cooperative that distributed its own work. Other filmmakers who produced important work during these years included Peter Davis (*Hearts and Minds*, 1974), George Stoney (*The Shepherd on the Night Flock*, 1978, with James Brown), George Bulter (*Pumping Iron*, 1977), Lance Burt (*The World of Tomorrow*), Stewart Bird (*The Wobblies*, 1980, with Deborah Shaffer), Steven Fischler and Joel Sucher (*Free Voice of Labor: The Jewish Anarchists*, 1980), and Ken Burns (*Brooklyn Bridge*, 1982; *The Civil War*, 1990).

By the late 1970s and 1980s documentarists increasingly turned to videotape to make their documentaries. Examples include *Third Avenue: Only the Strong Survive* (1979), by Keiko Tsuno and Jon Alpert of Downtown Community Television; the work of Paper Tiger Television, founded by Dee Dee Halleck and others, which trained a critical focus on the social and political roles of the news media in American society; and numerous documentaries about health care and the AIDS crisis in New York City. Even documentaries shot on film were increasingly distributed, often exclusively, on videotape.

Lewis Jacobs, ed.: *The Documentary Tradition: From Nanook to Woodstock* (New York: Hopkinson and Blake, 1971)
Erik Barnouw: *Documentary: A History of the Nonfiction Film* (New York: Oxford University Press, 1974)
Stephen Mamber: *Cinema Verite in America: Studies in Uncontrolled Documentary Film* (Cambridge: MIT Press, 1974)
William Alexander: *Film on the Left: American Documentary Film from 1931 to 1942* (Princeton, N.J.: Princeton University Press, 1981)

Charles Musser

documentary photography. Some of the first documentary photographs from New York City were produced between 1885 and 1902 by the newspaper reporter Jacob A. Riis, who photographed dark alleys and rear tenement interiors on the Lower East Side to supplement his report on the problems of the poor and win support for his efforts to improve urban housing, education, health, and recreation. Lewis Hine soon used photography to examine many of the same issues. His studies of child labor led to nationwide reform and his poignant portraits of immigrants at Ellis Island helped to erode cultural prejudices. In the 1920s the first documentary film, *New York the Magnificent* (1921; later known as *Manhatta*), was made by the photographers Paul Strand and Charles Sheeler. Documentary photography developed more fully during the 1930s, when many photographers were employed by the Federal Art Project and other agencies of the Works Progress Administration to document social displacement and economic struggle across the nation. Under the auspices of the project Berenice Abbott in 1935 began the series "Changing New York" to document the changing character of the city; she adopted a straightforward, unsentimental approach to recording urban contrasts. Other photographers engaged to document buildings and inhabitants of the city included Ben Shahn (1935–38) and Walker Evans (summer 1938). From 1936 to 1951 the Photo League offered classes and lectures by masters in the techniques of documentary photography, including Hine and Abbott. Some members, including Sid Grossman (1913–55), Sol Libsohn (*b* 1914), Dan Weiner (1919–59), and Ruth Orkin (1921–85), made detailed studies of Harlem, Chelsea, and Park Avenue north and south.

In the 1960s and 1970s the role of photojournalism in social documentary expanded. Some photojournalists including Bruce Davidson (*b* 1931) and Danny Lyon (*b* 1942) tried to understand their subjects thoroughly before photographing them. Davidson's photographic essay "East 100th Street" (1970) depicted the difficulty and isolation of life in Spanish Harlem. Others used their work less to influence social reform than to promote self-examination. Through seemingly careless, fragmentary images of daily life, Garry Winogrand (1928–84) and Lee Friedlander (*b* 1934) encouraged viewers to interpret for themselves the needs of urban residents. Diane Arbus's portraits of people usually considered abnormal were without the compassion traditionally expected of a social documentary and introduced a nonhumanistic approach to documentary photography. In the 1980s and early 1990s Larry Clark (*b* 1943) and Nan Goldin (*b* 1953) exulted in the banality of contemporary urban life and also examined sexual and psychological relationships. The methods of Riis, Hine, and others continued to influence documentary photography.

David Featherstone, ed.: *Observations: Essays on Documentary Photography* (Carmel, Calif.: Friends of Photography, 1984)
Peter Bacon Hales: *Silver Cities: The Photography of American Urbanization, 1839–1915* (Philadelphia: Temple University Press, 1984)

See also PHOTOJOURNALISM.

Dale L. Neighbors

Dodd, Mead. Firm of book publishers that began as Taylor and Dodd in 1839 when the former minister Moses Woodruff Dodd purchased a share in the business of John S. Taylor, a publisher of religious books in New York City. After one year Dodd bought out Taylor and opened the firm of M. W. Dodd in the annex of the Brick Church Chapel on Park Row, publishing mostly religious volumes and British titles. Dodd's son Frank joined the firm in 1859 at the age of fifteen and published Martha Finley's *Elsie Dinsmore* (1867), the first in a successful series of books for young readers. With his cousin Edward S. Mead he assumed control of the firm in 1870, now renamed Dodd and Mead. Frank Dodd expanded the scope of the firm and emphasized popular fiction. In 1895 the firm launched the *Bookman*, which became one of the most renowned literary journals of the day (despite which it never enjoyed financial success and was sold off in 1918). It also published Leo Tolstoy, Maurice Maeterlinck, and a number of distinguished English writers including Joseph Conrad, Anthony Trollope, H. G. Wells, G. K. Chesterton, Jerome K. Jerome, Max Beerbohm, and Agatha Christie. Between 1902 and 1904 it published the *New International Encyclopedia*, a seventeen-volume work to which it made various revisions and additions until 1931, when the encyclopedia was sold to Funk and Wagnalls. It also helped launch the career of the poet Paul Lawrence Dunbar and published works of Anatole France. It began publishing Allan Nevins's acclaimed series *American Political Leaders* in 1930, and in 1933 it acquired the American rights to the works of George Bernard Shaw. The firm took over several publishing houses in 1934 and published Winston Churchill's *History of the English-Speaking Peoples* from 1956 to 1958.

Dodd, Mead and Company was purchased in 1981 by Thomas Nelson Publishers of Nashville, the largest publisher of bibles in the United States; Jonathan Dodd became its vice-president. In 1986 a majority interest in the firm was acquired by the Gamut Publishing Company, a partnership of the publishing entrepreneurs Lynne A. Lumsden and Jon B. Harden. In December 1988 Dodd, Mead and Company was liquidated. During its years of operation the firm occupied offices at 59 Chambers Street (from 1855), 506 Broadway (1856), 762 Broadway (1870), the corner of 5th Avenue and 35th Street (1900), 449 4th Avenue at 13th Street (1910), 432 4th Avenue (1941), and 79 Madison Avenue (1967).

Edward Howard Dodd: *The First Hundred Years: A History of the House of Dodd, Mead, 1839–1939* (New York: Dodd, Mead, 1939)
David Dempsey: "Looking Backwards with Dodd, Mead," *Saturday Review*, 12 Dec 1964, pp. 36–37
"The Story of Dodd, Mead and Co., Inc.," *Book Production Magazine* 81 (1965), Jan, 30–33
"Conniff Sues Dodd, Mead, Thomas Nelson," *Publishers Weekly*, 6 Jan 1984, p. 16

Marjorie Harrison

Dodge, Grace H(oadley) (*b* New York City, 21 May 1856; *d* Bronx, 27 Dec 1914). Reformer. Born into a prominent family, she was educated primarily at home and attended finishing school in Connecticut in 1872–74. After returning to New York City she became active in several charities, including the industrial schools of the Children's Aid Society, and began working to make social reform more systematic and efficient. Her friend Louisa Lee Schuyler, who influenced many of her later efforts, encouraged her to join the State Charities Aid Association. In 1881 she formed a club for young women that by 1885 grew into the Association of Working Girls' Societies. She also helped to organize the Industrial Education Association in 1884 and was appointed by Mayor William R. Grace in 1886 as one of the first two women to the Board of Education. Instrumental in founding Teachers College in 1889, she served as its treasurer from 1892 to 1911.

Dodge was also active in the YWCA. A unifying figure at a time when the organization was torn by competing factions, she was active in 1906 in re-forming it as the YWCA of the USA, and she was the first president of the national board, which was based in New York City. She took an interest in moral education and helped to form the New York Travelers Aid Society (1907) and the American Social Hygiene Association (1912). Dodge never married; she lived with her parents and cared for them until the end of their lives.

Abbie Graham: *Grace H. Dodge: Merchant of Dreams* (New York: Woman's Press, 1926)

Ellen Condliffe Lagemann: *A Generation of Women: Education in the Lives of Progressive Reformers* (Cambridge: Harvard University Press, 1979)

Esther Katz: "Grace Hoadley Dodge: Women and the Emerging Metropolis, 1856–1914" (diss., New York University, 1980)

Nancy Marie Robertson

Dodge [née Mapes], **Mary (Elizabeth)** (*b* New York City, 26 Jan 1830; *d* Onteora Park, near Tannersville, N.Y., 21 Aug 1905). Writer and editor. She was deeply influenced by her father, James J. Mapes, who emphasized literature in her upbringing. She enjoyed the friendship of such men of letters as William Cullen Bryant and Horace Greeley, whose home in lower Manhattan was often the site of informal literary gatherings. In 1866 she published the children's story *Hans Brinker; or, the Silver Skates*. As the editor of *St. Nicholas Magazine* (a title she suggested) from 1873 until the end of her life she helped to influence the development of American juvenile literature. During her tenure the magazine published important work by Kipling, Louisa May Alcott, and Mark Twain and became the most popular magazine of its kind in the country.

Alice B. Howard: *Mary Mapes Dodge of St. Nicholas* (New York: J. Messner, 1943)

Michael Joseph

Dodgewood. A section of the northwestern Bronx bounded to the north by West 245th Street, to the east by Arlington Avenue, to the south by West 243rd Street, and to the west by Palisades Avenue. The land was once owned by William E. Dodge, whose holdings extended as far north as Westchester County and as far west as the Hudson River. Two mansions owned by his family still stand. The neighborhood is an exclusive area of winding lanes and fine homes.

John McNamara: *History in Asphalt: The Origin of Bronx Street and Place Names* (New York: Bronx County Historical Society, 1984)

John McNamara: *McNamara's Old Bronx* (New York: Bronx County Historical Society, 1989)

John McNamara

Dollar Dry Dock Savings Bank. Savings bank formed on 5 February 1983 by the merger of the Dry Dock Savings Bank and the Dollar Savings Bank. Its forerunner, the Dry Dock Savings Institution, formed in 1848 by leading shipbuilders for their workers and originally at the corner of 4th Street and Avenue C, attracted mostly local, working-class customers until 1932, when it merged with the U.S. Savings Bank and opened branches throughout the city. The Dollar Savings Bank opened in 1890 at 2771 3rd Avenue in Mott Haven. It merged with the Fordham Savings Bank in 1932 and expanded throughout the Bronx in the 1930s and 1940s, opening branches in Fordham and Parkchester. In 1951 it erected a ten-story building for its headquarters on the Grand Concourse at Fordham Road. Among the many projects that it funded was Co-op City. After merging with the New York Federal Savings and Loan Association in 1976 Dry Dock Savings was renamed Dry Dock Savings Bank; its merger with Dollar Savings Bank created the fifth-largest mutual savings bank in the country. One of the most successful savings banks in the metropolitan area, Dollar Dry Dock moved its headquarters from the city in 1983 but maintained twenty-one branches there in 1991.

Andrew Mills: *The Story of Dry Dock Savings Institution, 1848–1948* (New York: Dry Dock Savings Institution, 1948)

James Bradley

Dolphy, Eric (*b* Los Angeles, 20 June 1928; *d* Berlin, 29 June 1964). Saxophonist, flutist, and bass clarinetist. After moving to New York City in 1959 he played avant-garde jazz as a sideman with Ornette Coleman, John Coltrane, and Charles Mingus. He played piercing, angular solos on three instruments with equal facility, and became known for an uncompromising, complex style characterized by the use of quarter-tones and other devices not usually associated with jazz. His recordings include *Out to Lunch* (1964) and *Last Date* (1964).

Vladimir Simosko and Barry Tepperman: *Eric Dolphy: A Musical Biography and Discography* (Washington: Smithsonian Institution Press, 1971)

Marc Ferris

Domestic Pigeon. See Rock pigeon.

domestic servants. Most servants in New Amsterdam were household slaves allowed to live independently in exchange for work and a fee. Conditions changed after the American Revolution, when workers from the country and free blacks moved to the city and sought employment in domestic service. Between 1790 and 1810 most free black women in the city were servants; a third of free black men, presumably servants as well, lived in white households. A shortage of domestic help also led free blacks to move to the city during the 1820s, and servants' quarters became a regular feature of residences about this time. Women worked as ladies' maids, parlormaids, kitchen maids, cooks, laundresses, and governesses, and men as chauffeurs, gardeners, butlers, and valets; days began with lighting the fires and preparing breakfast and ended with shutting the house for the night, usually after the employers had gone to bed. The work was highly undesirable owing to the long hours, low wages, and isolation associated with it, and many servants left their households abruptly, engaged in petty thievery, and were incompetent. Employers considered satisfactory servants difficult to find, and in 1825 a group of wealthy women established the New York Society for the Encouragement of Faithful Domestic Servants. Young women were often sexually abused by their employers and then dismissed if the abuse came to light: former servants accounted for a quarter of the city's prostitutes in 1839 and almost half in 1859. Irish immigrants competed increasingly with blacks for domestic work after 1845. In 1855 about 40 percent of blacks in the city, 26 percent of Irish immigrants, and 9 percent of all other immigrant groups worked as servants, who numbered 34,302 in Manhattan (including laundry workers) and 4441 in Brooklyn. Women found a more appealing alternative in factory work, which in 1860 paid $2 to $6 a week, as opposed to $3 to $4 a month for domestic service. In 1870 servants (including laundry workers) accounted for 55,044 workers in the city, or 16 percent of the working population, and for more than half of working women. The children of immigrants who worked as servants often found other kinds of employment; children of black servants had fewer opportunities and often became servants themselves.

In 1920 there were by some estimates about 115,000 servants in the city (excluding laundry workers), or 6 percent of the working population. Since many failed to report their income and occupation, the number may have been twice as large. As electric appliances were introduced during the 1920s housework became easier. The number of servants from southern and eastern Europe declined after the National Origins Act of 1924 imposed strict immigration quotas. As wages plummeted during the Depression the demand for domestic help grew and the number of servants rose to 262,469 in 1930. Maids stood waiting for work on more than two hundred street corners in the city known as "slave markets" and were often engaged by the day and paid by the hour. The writers Ella Baker and Marvel Cooke posed as maids and published an exposé called "The Bronx Slave Market" for the *Crisis* in November 1935. In 1937 the Domestic Workers' Union became Local 149 of the Congress of Industrial Organizations; it had few members, made little impact on wages and working conditions, and ceased operations in 1968. At the beginning of the Second World War blacks from the South sought domestic work in the city and retained the custom of living apart from their employers; this arrangement became so common that apartment buildings ceased to be built with maids' quarters in the 1950s. When other kinds of work became abundant during the war the number of domestic workers decreased, especially among men. In 1940 there were about 140,000 – more than 90 percent were women and most were black. The number fell in 1950 to 79,533, or slightly more than 2 percent of the work force. Employment agencies arranged for maids from Great Britain and the South to work in the city, and the Amsterdam Employment Agency (opened in 1947) at Amsterdam Avenue and 149th Street found employment for blacks. During the 1950s a laundry known as the Budge–Wood Service first offered maid service by the hour.

After the Hart–Celler immigration act took effect in 1968 women from the Caribbean and Latin America accounted for most domestic workers in the city. They often obtained visas through employers and domestic service agencies but increasingly worked in the city illegally, resulting in artificially low estimates of the number of domestic workers. In 1980 only 25,500 persons, mostly women and more than 70 percent nonwhite, reported themselves as private household workers. The demand for domestic workers was high during the following decade, owing in part to the number of women working outside the home. Wealthy families had live-in help; many middle-class families engaged part-time housecleaners. Employment agencies that provided foreign workers flourished, among them the Finnish Agency (opened in 1933), the Asian–American Placement Agency, which arranged employment for Filipinos, and several Polish agencies. The Amsterdam Employment Agency closed about 1984. In the mid 1990s child care workers, home attendants, and nurses' aides accounted for most full-time household employees.

Ruth Sergel, ed.: *The Woman in the House: Stories of Household Employment* (New York: Woman's Press, 1938)
George Joseph Stigler: *Domestic Servants in the United States, 1900–1940* (New York: National Bureau of Economic Research, 1946)

Alana J. Erickson

Domingo, W(ilfred) A(dolphus) (*b* Kingston, Jamaica, 1889; *d* New York City, 14 Feb 1968). Writer and political reformer. He moved to New York City in 1913. From 1917 to the early 1920s he wrote articles for the radical black publications the *Messenger*, the *Crusader*, the *Emancipator*, and the *Negro World* (which was aligned with Marcus Garvey), and he maintained close ties to such radical groups as the Socialist Party, the Universal Negro Improvement Association, and the African Blood Brotherhood. He helped to mobilize fellow immigrants from the English-speaking Caribbean in the 1930s in support of political reforms there and assisted the Jamaican socialist organization the People's National Party. After returning to Jamaica at the onset of the Second World War he was arrested by the colonial regime and accused of being an agent provocateur. On his release from prison in 1943 he returned to New York City, where he promoted Jamaican and Caribbean independence.

Harold Cruse: *The Crisis of the Negro Intellectual* (New York: William Morrow, 1967)
Robert A. Hill, ed.: *The Marcus Garvey and Universal Negro Improvement Association Papers*, vol. 1, app. 1 (Berkeley: University of California Press, 1983)
Mark Naison: *Communists in Harlem during the Depression* (Urbana: University of Illinois Press, 1983)

Calvin B. Holder

Dominicans. Although it is difficult to assess the precise number of Dominicans in New York City because of undercounting by the census bureau and the presence of undocumented immigrants, it is generally acknowledged that Dominicans constitute the largest immigrant group to settle in New York City after the mid 1960s, and the second-largest of all Latin American groups in the city (after Puerto Ricans). Estimates of their numbers range from 300,000 to more than one million, and the Dominican community in greater New York accounts for about three quarters of all the Dominicans in the United States. Dominicans are among the most residentially concentrated of the city's new immigrant groups. More than half live in Manhattan, forming distinctive neighborhoods in Washington Heights and to a lesser extent on the Lower East Side and in Manhattan Valley; other Dominicans live in Jackson Heights, the southern Bronx, and Greenpoint. Dominicans who live in Hoboken and Jersey City in New Jersey continue to work and socialize in New York City. Most Dominican immigrants intend to remain in the United States only temporarily and hope to improve their social and economic standing in the Dominican Republic, though an important minority have left the Dominican Republic for political reasons. Before 1961 the number of Dominicans emigrating to the United States was relatively small, owing in large part to severe restrictions imposed from 1930 by the repressive regime of Rafael Trujillo. Political exiles sometimes managed to flee to New York City, along with others who had connections with Trujillo. Between 1950 and 1960 some ten thousand Dominicans emigrated to the United States. The assassination of Trujillo in 1961 and the subsequent removal of restrictions led to a surge of immigration, as did the defeat of a popular revolt in 1965 and the ensuing occupation of the Dominican Republic by the United States. The economic and political uncertainty surrounding elections there after the mid 1960s and later the drastic deterioration of the economy also led a large number of Dominicans to leave their country. The number of Dominicans emigrating to the United States each year increased from fourteen thousand in the 1970s to more than 22,000 in the 1980s; it is likely that undocumented immigration increased as well.

In the earliest years of immigration Dominicans were seldom recognized as a distinct cultural group and tended to be conflated with Puerto Ricans. Initially Dominicans in New York City were politically oriented toward the Dominican Republic. The earliest leaders of the community were members of the economic and social élite. By the mid 1980s Dominicans had become more active in the political life of New York City and began to run for elective office, notably in Washington Heights. A new leadership arose out of community efforts to promote economic development, to work with government agencies, and to combat discrimination. At the same time Dominican culture began to exert a presence in New York City after years of near-invisibility. The music and dance of the merengue came to rival salsa in popularity, and some merengue groups based in the city depicted immigrant life in their work and reached a wide audience in the Dominican Republic. A number of Dominican writers living in the city gained recognition, among them Daisy Cocco de Filippis, Franklin Gutiérrez, José Carvajal, and Alexis Gómez. Casa Dominicana, formed with support from the Dominican government in 1985, organized literary conferences, exhibitions, and poetry and theater workshops until lack of funds forced it to close in 1990.

Dominicans in New York City are on the whole a young group. Many marry in the city, usually with other Dominicans, but a sizable minority intermarry with non-Dominicans, particularly Puerto Ricans. Most Dominicans are Roman Catholic. Few are priests, but Catholic churches in Dominican neighborhoods offer masses in Spanish. A number of Dominicans have converted to evangelical Protestantism. Dominican women in New York City are as likely to work outside the home as other women in the city, and they are more likely to do so than women in the Dominican Republic. They usually work in manufacturing, especially the garment industry. Dominican men also work in manufacturing, as well as in hotels, restaurants, and hospitals. Many Dominicans also own and operate bodegas, garment shops, and nonmedallion, or "gypsy," taxicabs that serve immigrant neighborhoods. Despite growing numbers of professionals, average earnings for Dominicans are among the lowest in the city. Some work more than full time to earn subsistence wages or to save money for the eventual return to the Dominican Republic to which many aspire.

The best-known event associated with Dominicans is Dominican Day Parade, begun in 1981 and held each August on or about Dominican Restoration Day, which commemorates the restoration of the republic after its reannexation by Spain. Modeled on its Puerto Rican counterpart, the parade was first staged in Washington Heights and later moved to Manhattan. The parade is a politically charged event and control over it is hotly contested by various factions. Dominicans are engaged in efforts to improve the quality of education in New York City, especially in Washington

Heights, where they have been elected to the local community school board and on occasion have directed it. Dominican student organizations at the City University of New York have expressed support for a program in Dominican studies, which in the mid 1990s was in the process of being organized.

Only a few distinctively Dominican publications have been launched in New York City, perhaps because newspapers from the Dominican Republic are readily available (and are paying increasing attention to the Dominican community in New York City) and because locally published Spanish-language daily newspapers such as *El Diario–La Prensa* are well established. Magazines such as *Alcance* and *Punto 7* have published poetry, fiction, and essays by Dominican authors who live in New York City.

Glenn Hendricks: *The Dominican Diaspora: From the Dominican Republic to New York, Villagers in Transition* (New York: Teachers College Press, 1974)
Patricia Pessar: "The Dominicans: Women in the Household and in the Garment Industry," *New Immigrants in New York*, ed. Nancy Foner (New York: Columbia University Press, 1987), 103–29
Sherri Grasmuck and Patricia Pessar: *Between Two Islands: Dominican International Migration* (Berkeley: University of California Press, 1991)

Eugenia Georges

Donaldson, Lufkin and Jenrette. Firm of investment bankers formed in New York City in 1959 by William Donaldson, Dan Lufkin, and Richard Jenrette. It was devoted to researching small growth companies before entering investment banking, merchant banking, institutional trading and research, investment management, and brokerage. The firm was bought by the Equitable Life Assurance Society for $440 million in January 1985, and revenues continued to increase after the stock market crash of October 1987. Donaldson, Lufkin and Jenrette has its headquarters at 140 Broadway and offices in London, Paris, Geneva, Lugano (Switzerland), Hong Kong, and Beijing.

Mary E. Curry

Dongan, Thomas (*b* Castletown, Ireland, 1634; *d* London, 14 Dec 1715). Colonial governor. He served in the French and English military forces before his appointment as governor of New York by James, Duke of York, in 1682. During his tenure he encouraged religious toleration, sought to set up postal services between Nova Scotia and the Carolinas, and assessed the strength of the French in Iroquois country. He also approved the "Charter of Liberties" establishing representative government in the colony; this was nullified by James, and in 1688 he was replaced as governor by Sir Edmund Andros. Despite anti-Catholic feelings after the English revolution of 1689, Dongan remained in New York until 1691, when he returned to England. He later became the second Earl of Limerick.

Thomas Patrick Phelan: *Thomas Dongan, Colonial Governor of New York, 1683–1688* (New York: P. J. Kenedy and Sons, 1933)

James E. Mooney

Dongan Hills. Neighborhood in east central Staten Island (1990 pop. 12,000). It is one of the largest neighborhoods in the city in area, extending as far as Todt Hill to the north, Grasmere and South Beach to the east, Ocean Breeze and South Beach Psychiatric Center to the south, and the Richmond County Country Club to the west. It is named for Thomas Dongan, an Irish aristocrat who was appointed governor of the province of New York in 1682 by the Duke of York. As part of the appointment he was granted 5100 acres (2064 hectares) on the northern shore of the island, which he eventually enlarged to 25,000 acres (10,100 hectares), including all of the present neighborhood. The well-known architect Ernest Flagg moved to the area in 1889, purchased twelve acres (five hectares) of land, and built a summer retreat called Stone Court that became St. Charles Seminary after his death in 1947. He built many structures on Staten Island, often using the serpentine stone common to its hills. In the 1890s a number of large firms were purchased to form a real-estate venture called Linden Park. The housing stock of the neighborhood is varied. The Billiou–Stillwell–Perrine House (1661) at 1476 Richmond Road is the third-oldest building in the city. There are also old and new mansions near the country club, blocks of one-family and multi-family houses, a successful city housing project called Berry House, and newly developed townhouses and condominiums. The principal commercial thoroughfares are Richmond Road and Hylan Boulevard. Dongan Hills is a station of Staten Island Rapid Transit.

Charles W. Leng and William T. Davis: *Staten Island and Its People* (New York: Lewis Historical Publishing, 1929–33)
John E. Hurley: "Dongan Hills: An Oasis despite Development," *Staten Island Advance*, 13 Nov 1989, §B, p. 1

John-Paul Richiuso

Donovan, William J(oseph) (*b* Buffalo, 1 Jan 1883; *d* Washington, 8 Feb 1959). Lawyer and government official. He graduated from Columbia Law School (LLB 1907), practiced law in Buffalo and New York City, and served in the First World War. In 1924 he became an assistant attorney general of New York State. He mounted an unsuccessful campaign for the lieutenant governorship of the state as a Republican, and was a senior partner of the law firm Donovan, Leisure, Newton and Lombard. He is best known for having led the Office of Strategic Services (OSS) from 1942 to 1945. Later he resumed his law practice in the city and from 1952 to 1954 was the American ambassador to Thailand. He was often known by the nickname Wild Bill Donovan.

Richard Dunlop: *Donovan: America's Master Spy* (Chicago: Rand McNally, 1982)

Martin Ebon

Dorflinger, Christian (*b* Rosteig, Alsace, 16 March 1828; *d* White Mills, Penn., 11 Aug 1915). Glassmaker. After receiving his training in Alsace he opened a small operation known as the Concord Street Flint Glass Works (later the Long Island Flint Glass Works) in Brooklyn in 1850, where initially he made chimneys for oil lamps and druggists' bottles. He introduced cutting operations by 1854 and changed his specialty to fine cut tableware. He opened a large factory on Plymouth Street (1858) and the Greenpoint Flint Glass Works (1860) before retiring in January 1863 because of ill health. Dorflinger later built a factory in White Mills, where he became known for producing some of the country's finest brilliant cut glass.

John Quentin Feller: *Dorflinger: America's Finest Glass, 1852–1921* (Marietta, Ohio: Antique Publications, 1988)

Alice Cooney Frelinghuysen

Dorr, Rheta Childe [Child, Reta Louise] (*b* Omaha, Neb., 2 Nov 1866; *d* New Britain, Penn., 8 Aug 1948). Journalist and suffragist. She moved to New York City in 1890 to attend the Art Students League but soon devoted herself to journalism and women's rights: for the *Evening Post* she reported on the activities of women's clubs and working women's problems. Later she became well known as a freelance foreign correspondent and war correspondent. Many of her accounts were collected in anthologies and in an autobiography, *A Woman of Fifty* (1924). She edited the *Suffragist*, the publication of a militant suffrage association called the Congressional Union of which she was a member.

Louis Filler: "Rheta Childe Dorr," *Notable American Women*, ed. Edward T. James et al. (Cambridge: Harvard University Press, 1971)

Karen J. Blair

Dorsey, Tommy [Thomas] (*b* Shenandoah, Penn., 19 Nov 1905; *d* Greenwich, Conn., 26 Nov 1956). Bandleader. He played the trombone and in 1924 moved to New York City with his brother Jimmy (*b* Shenandoah, 29 Feb 1904; *d* New York City, 12 June 1957), a saxophonist; the brothers took part in many recording sessions with Bix Beiderbecke, Adrian Rollini, and Red Nichols, played with the orchestras of Jean Goldkette and Paul Whiteman, and formed a band in 1934 that achieved some success. In the following year their public quarrels led them to pursue separate careers. The Tommy Dorsey Orchestra, formed with twelve members of the Joe Haymes Orchestra, became one of the most popular bands of its time; it engaged such well-known soloists as the trumpeter Bunny Berigan and the drummer Buddy Rich but is perhaps best remembered for its performances with Frank Sinatra between 1940 and 1942. The Jimmy Dorsey Orchestra also enjoyed widespread popularity and had sidemen such as Ray McKinley, Lee Castle, and Bobby Byrne. The brothers reunited as the Fabulous Dorseys in September 1953 and played together until Tommy's death. The Dorseys are best known for having popularized a brand of dance music that was influenced by jazz.

George T. Simon: *The Big Bands* (New York: Macmillan, 1967; 4th edn G. Schirmer, 1981)

Loren Schoenberg

Dos Passos, John (Roderigo) (*b* Chicago, 14 Jan 1896; *d* Baltimore, 28 Sept 1970). Novelist. He rented a studio apartment at 14A Washington Mews in 1922 and in 1924 lived briefly at 106–10 Columbia Heights and in Brooklyn Heights. A figure in bohemian literary circles, he wrote the novel *Manhattan Transfer* (1925), which linked the chaos of the city with the aimlessness and confusion of modern life. In 1932 he lived at 214 Riverside Drive. He became increasingly disillusioned with communism after the Spanish Civil War and turned to patriotism and conservatism: some of his later writings were published in the *National Review*.

Virginia Spencer Carr: *Dos Passos: A Life* (New York: Doubleday, 1984)

Lawson Bowling

Douai, (Karl Daniel) Adolf (*b* Saxe-Altenburg, 22 Feb 1819; *d* Brooklyn, 21 Jan 1888). Political activist and writer. He fled Germany for Texas after the revolution of 1848, but was driven out of the state for abolitionist agitation and made his way to New York City, where he organized a school, became the editor of the *New Yorker Demokrat*, and was an early leader of the kindergarten movement in the United States. In 1858 his work *Fata Morgana* won a prize as the best German–American novel and he became a leader of the German Freethinkers' League. After taking over the German labor newspaper the *Arbeiter Union* (1868) he helped to launch the *Volks-Zeitung* (1878), a leading socialist newspaper that he also edited. He wrote a memoir, *Better Times* (1877).

Stanley Nadel

Doubleday. Firm of book publishers formed in 1897 as Doubleday and McClure by the magazine publisher S. S. McClure and Frank Nelson Doubleday, a vice-president of his firm. Initially it operated from McClure's headquarters at 142 East 25th Street. In 1900 Doubleday formed a partnership with Walter Hines Page that became known as the firm of Doubleday, Page, with offices at 34 Union Square East. Pennsylvania Station was the site of the firm's first bookstore (1910) and within twenty years there were more than twenty-five, one of the largest retail book operations in the country. After a merger with the firm of George H. Doran in 1927 the name was changed to Doubleday, Doran and offices were moved to the Doran building at 244 Madison Avenue. In 1938 the administrative, editorial, and sales departments were consolidated and moved to offices at 14 West 49th Street in Rockefeller Center. During the next few years the firm concentrated on inexpensive books for a wide audience. When it was renamed Doubleday and Company in 1946 it was the largest book publisher in the United States. By the mid 1970s the firm operated more than fifteen book clubs, including the highly successful Literary Guild, and in 1980 it bought the New York Mets. In 1986 Doubleday was bought by the Bertelsmann Publishing Group for $475 million.

John Tebbel: *A History of Book Publishing in the United States* (New York: R. R. Bowker, 1972–81), vol. 2, pp. 318–31; vol. 3, pp. 107–13, 527–33; vol. 4, pp. 105–17

See also Book publishing.

Allen J. Share

Douglas, Aaron (*b* Topeka, Kansas, 26 May 1899; *d* Nashville, 2 Feb 1979). Painter. After studying at the University of Nebraska he moved to New York City in 1924 at the urging of Charles Johnson (editor of the magazine *Opportunity*). He fell under the influence of the German painter Winold Reiss, emulating the simplified black-and-white designs and flat patterns in his work, and became associated with the other artists of the Harlem Renaissance. In 1924 he was the only black visual artist to attend the conference in New York City of publishers, editors, and black intellectuals that resulted in the publication of *Harlem: Mecca of the New Negro*. His illustrations appeared in Alain Locke's *The New Negro* (1925), Eugene O'Neill's *The Emperor Jones* (1926), and James Weldon Johnson's *God's Trombones: Seven Negro Sermons in Verse* (1927), and on the covers of *Opportunity*, the *Crisis*, and the radical arts journal *Fire!!: A Quarterly Devoted to the Younger Negro Artists* (1926). He also painted *Aspects of Negro Life* (1934) for the Countee Cullen branch of the New York Public Library (now the Schomburg Center for Research in Black Culture), a modernistic mural with several panels that was intended to symbolize the strength of the "new Negro." Douglas later studied at Columbia University and the Académie Scandinave in Paris and settled in Nashville, where he was the chairman of the art department at Fisk University until his retirement.

Edmund Gaither

Douglaston. Neighborhood in northeastern Queens (1990 pop. 30,000), near the border with Nassau County. It was settled in 1656 by Thomas Hicks on a peninsula first called Little Madman's Neck. In 1796 his estate passed to Thomas Wickes and later to Wynant Van Zandt, who in 1819 built an imposing white mansion (now the Douglaston Yacht Club). Much of the land was bought in 1835 by George Douglas, a Scot, whose son William P. Douglas, a vice-commodore of the New York Yacht Club, donated a right of way in 1866 to the railroad, which named the station for him. The Douglas Manor Company promoted part of the area as a residential area from 1906. Among the well-known residents of the neighborhood were Ginger Rogers, Richard Dix, and Clifton Webb in the mid 1920s, and later the tennis player John McEnroe (who learned to play at the Douglaston Club) and the Chilean pianist Claudio Arrau. In the mid 1990s Douglaston was the wealthiest community in Queens.

Lester Leake Riley: *The Chronicle of Little Neck and Douglaston* (New York: Ledger Printing, 1936)

Vincent Seyfried

Dover. Name briefly applied to Old town by the British.

Dow, Arthur Wesley (*b* Ipswich, Mass., 1857; *d* New York City, 13 Dec 1922). Painter. After studying in Ipswich and Paris he worked from 1895 to 1904 as an instructor at the Pratt Institute and a composition teacher at the Art Students League. He became a professor of fine arts at Teachers College in 1904 and opened the Ipswich Summer School of Art. Through his teaching and a number of books, including one on composition that became widely used, Dow influenced many students, among them Max Weber and Georgia O'Keeffe.

Frederick C. Moffat: *Arthur Wesley Dow* (Washington: Smithsonian Institution Press, 1977)

James E. Mooney

Dow Jones. Firm of financial publishers. Its origins may be traced to the launching in 1882 of a stock bulletin by Charles Dow, Edward Jones, and Charles Bergtresser, who in 1884 published an index of eleven major stocks that eventually evolved into Dow Jones Industrial Average and in 1889 began publishing the *Wall Street Journal*. In 1899 Jones sold his interest in the firm, and in 1902 the two remaining partners sold the firm to Clarence Barron, who launched *Barron's Weekly* in 1921. The firm underwent rapid expansion after the Second World War: the circulation of the *Journal* increased sharply, other newspapers were acquired, and the firm expanded into electronic retrieval services such as Telerate (acquired between 1985 and 1990), which eventually provided stock market quotations to more than sixty countries. In the mid 1990s heirs of Clarence Barron owned about two thirds of the voting stock of Dow Jones, which had come to derive less than half its revenues from business publications.

Jerry Martin Rosenberg: *Inside the Wall Street Journal: The History and the Power of Dow Jones and Company and America's Most Influential Newspaper* (New York: Macmillan, 1982)

Lloyd Wendt: *The Wall Street Journal: The Story of Dow Jones and the Nation's Business Newspaper* (Chicago: Rand McNally, 1982)

George Winslow

Downing, Andrew Jackson (*b* Newburgh, N.Y., 31 Oct 1815; *d* southern Westchester County, 28 July 1852). Nurseryman, landscape gardener, and writer. His work *A Treatise on the Theory and Practice of Landscape Gardening* (1841) established him as an authority in the field. In the *Horticulturist* in August 1851 he outlined the advantages of a large, centrally situated park in New York City. His partner on several projects was Calvert Vaux. Downing's only known work in New York City was his design for the Cemetery of the Evergreens on the border between Brooklyn and Queens, a collaboration with the architect Alexander Jackson Davis. He also prepared an unexecuted design for the New York Crystal Palace. He lost his life when the steamboat *Henry Clay* burned on the Hudson River.

George B. Tatum and Elisabeth B. MacDougall: *Prophet with Honor: The Career of Andrew Jackson Downing, 1815–1852* (Washington: Dumbarton Oaks / Philadelphia: Athenaeum of Philadelphia, 1989)

David Schuyler

Downing, Thomas (*b* Chincoteague, Va., Jan 1791; *d* New York City, 10 April 1866). Restaurateur. Born free in a slave-holding state, he arrived in New York City in 1819 and began to sell oysters. At the time eating oysters was one of the city's most popular pastimes, and the business was conducted primarily by free black men. By 1830 Downing's Oyster House at the corner of Broad and Wall streets was well-known for its famous patrons, including Charles Dickens and leading politicians of the day. Downing sent "very choice" oysters to Queen Victoria, who in return sent him a gold chronometer. In 1848 he became a founding trustee of the New York Society for the Promotion of Education among Colored Children. He campaigned for black suffrage in New York State, sponsored rallies against the Fugitive Slave Law, and protested the custom of segregation in public transit. He was also a friend and occasional traveling companion of Frederick Douglass. On his retirement his son George took over the restaurant and continued the business until at least 1871, but by then the heyday of the oyster house in the city was already passing. Downing is buried in the St. Philip's Church section of Cypress Hills Cemetery in Brooklyn.

John H. Hewitt: "Mr. Downing and His Oyster House: The Life and Good Works of an African-American Entrepreneur," *New York History*, July 1993, pp. 229–52

Kenneth T. Jackson

Down Town Association. A luncheon club opened in 1860 to provide a meeting place for businessmen in the financial district. It occupies a five-story Romanesque Revival building designed in 1887 by Charles C. Haight, a prominent architect who later became a member of the club. Past members include the lawyers William M. Evarts and John W. Davis, the statesman Henry L. Stimson, and President Franklin D. Roosevelt.

Sixty Years of the Down Town Association, 1860–1920 (New York: R. A. Haag, 1920)

Elliott B. Nixon

Downtown Athletic Club. Private club organized on 10 September 1926 in New York City. On 1 October 1930 it moved into a thirty-five-story building at 19 West Street. The club is perhaps best known as the body that awards the Heisman Trophy each year to the outstanding college football player in the United States. First given in 1935, the trophy is named for John W. Heisman, the club's first athletic director. The club began admitting women as members in 1978. In the mid 1990s the total membership was about 2500.

downtown Brooklyn. Neighborhood in northwestern Brooklyn, encompassing the Fulton Mall, Borough Hall and the civic center, Brooklyn Heights, and the area around Fulton Ferry, and bounded to the north by the Brooklyn–Queens Expressway, to the east by Flatbush Avenue and Flatbush Avenue Extension, to the south by Atlantic Avenue, and to the west by Cadman Plaza. The first European settlers in the area were Dutch farmers and tradesmen who occupied land near the East River in the seventeenth century and soon formed a village called Breuckelen near Fulton Ferry. The introduction of reliable steam ferry service between Brooklyn and Manhattan in the second decade of the nineteenth century spurred the construction of mansions and blocks of row houses and apartment buildings. City Hall was designed in the Classical Revival style and completed in 1849 (it was renamed Brooklyn Borough Hall in 1898). By mid century several private academies had opened in the area, including the Brooklyn Female Academy (1844), which was succeeded by the Packer Collegiate Institute (170 Joralemon Street). Later schools included the Brooklyn Collegiate and Polytechnic Institute (now in Bay Ridge), the Polytechnic Institute of New York (Jay Street), St. Francis College, which first offered classes in 1859 and later moved to Remsen Street, Brooklyn Law School (1901), Long Island University, and New York City Technical College (Jay Street). The building at 311 Bridge Street, formerly the First Free Congregational Church, became the home of the Bridge Street African Methodist Episcopal Church in 1854. The oldest black congregation in the borough, it remained on Bridge Street for eighty-four years before moving to Bedford–Stuyvesant. When the Brooklyn Bridge opened in 1883 traffic was rerouted to the area around Brooklyn City Hall and hotels, theaters, businesses, and newspaper offices opened nearby; department stores and other businesses moved to Fulton Street, which became a prosperous commercial center. Office towers were built on Court Street in the 1920s. Public buildings including headquarters for the Board of Education (Livingston Street) and for the Transit Authority accounted for most construction in the years surrounding the Second World War. Retailing suffered during social and economic upheaval in the 1950s and 1960s. In 1977 ground was broken for the Fulton Mall, which became the site of more than one hundred retail stores (including a branch of Abraham and Straus at 420 Fulton Street) and one of the largest urban shopping districts in the United States. An office tower was erected at Pierrepont and Court streets in the 1980s for the investment banking firm Morgan Stanley.

In the early 1990s downtown Brooklyn became attractive to businesses seeking larger quarters and lower rents than those found in Manhattan. Construction began on Metro Tech, an office park for research and technology bounded by Johnson Street, Flatbush Avenue, and Willoughby and Jay streets. Several local businesses are well known: Junior's (near the mall, at 386 Flatbush Extension on the corner of De Kalb Street) is famous for its cheesecake, and Gage and Tollner's (372 Fulton Street; building 1870, interior 1892) is the only restaurant in Brooklyn with an interior designated a landmark. The area around Borough Hall is a bustling center of transportation and government offices. Stores along the Fulton Mall, Atlantic Avenue, and Court, Livingston, and Montague streets attract many shoppers.

Ellen Marie Snyder-Grenier

Doyle Dane Bernbach. A forerunner of the advertising agency DDB NEEDHAM WORLDWIDE.

draft riots. Riots from 13 to 16 July 1863 in New York City, fueled by attempts to enforce the first federal conscription act and by the wartime hardships of poor Irish immigrants. After President Lincoln delivered the Emancipation Proclamation the orations of Fernando Wood and other members of the Peace Democracy in the city inflamed Irish workers' fears of competition from black workers. Hostility toward Lincoln and black laborers was particularly keen among Irish longshoremen, whose strike in June 1863 had been opposed by federal troops summoned to protect black strikebreakers. The first draft lottery in the city was conducted quietly on a Saturday, 11 July; the next was scheduled for 13 July. On 12 July there were discussions of the draft and especially of a controversial clause in the federal act allowing drafted men to buy a waiver for $300. After dawn on 13 July laborers beat several police officers and proceeded to a draft

Lynching on Clarkson Street during the draft riots of 1863

office uptown, which they stormed about midmorning after selection resumed, smashing the selection wheel and setting the building on fire. The riot quickly swept through many sections of the city and the rioters sought various targets. Throughout the riots they attacked leaders of the Republican Party and their property (the office of the abolitionist editor Horace Greeley was attacked twice). Stores were ransacked, among them Brooks Brothers. Blacks were increasingly sought out after the Colored Orphan Asylum was set on fire on the afternoon of 13 July: during the next three days at least eleven black men were murdered with horrible brutality.

Entreaties by Archbishop John Hughes and other Catholic clergymen to stop the violence were heeded by some of the Irish Catholic workingmen who dominated the crowds. Order was restored on 15–16 July by five regiments of the Union Army rushed north from the battlefield at Gettysburg, Pennsylvania: there were at least 105 dead in all. Rather than impose martial law Lincoln relied on William M. "Boss" Tweed and the Democrats of Tammany Hall to conduct a draft in mid August. Although this was carried out peacefully the memory of the riots lingered, especially for blacks and the governing élite. The riots remain the bloodiest urban disturbance in American history.

Iver Bernstein: *The New York City Draft Riots: Their Significance for American Society and Politics in the Age of the Civil War* (New York: Oxford University Press, 1990)

Iver Bernstein

Drake, Joseph Rodman (*b* New York City, 7 Aug 1795; *d* New York City, 21 Sept 1820). Poet and physician. A descendant of an established New England family, he lived in Hunts Point as a child. While studying medicine in New York City he met Fitz-Greene Halleck, with whom he published in the *New York Post* from March to July 1819 the "Croaker Papers," which lampooned prominent local figures and constituted his only work published during his lifetime. Although he practiced medicine in New York City he is better known for his poems, especially "The Culprit Fay" (an extended romantic fable set in the Hudson Highlands) and "The American Flag," both included in the collection *The Culprit Fay and Other Poems*, published by his daughter in 1835. His poem "Bronx" (1835), a paean to his childhood home, includes the following lines: "Yet I will look upon thy face again, / My own romantic Bronx, and it well be / A face more pleasant than the face of men." Drake's early death from tuberculosis inspired Halleck's elegy "Green be the turf above thee." The cemetery on Hunts Point Avenue in the southern Bronx containing his remains was taken over by the City of New York in 1910; declared a public park, it was dedicated as Joseph Rodman Drake Park in 1915.

Frank Lester Pleadwell: *The Life and Works of Joseph Rodman Drake* (Boston: Merrymount, 1935)

James Bradley, Ormonde de Kay

Dreier, Ethel Eyre Valentine (*b* Brooklyn, 21 Aug 1874; *d* Fort Salonga, N.Y., 15 Dec 1958). Reformer, sister of Katherine Dreier and Mary E. Dreier. Shortly after graduating from the Packer Collegiate Institute she became president of the Asacog Club (later the United Neighborhood Guild), one of the first settlement houses in Brooklyn. A local leader of the suffrage movement, she led the Women's Suffrage Party of Brooklyn from 1913 to 1917. She also was president of the New York Women's City Club (1924–30, 1932–36), actively promoted low-cost housing, and helped to organize the Brooklyn Garden Apartments. Her wide-ranging reform interests extended to good government movements and education. Dreier lived in Brooklyn until 1941, when she moved to Long Island.

Eileen K. Cheng

Dreier, Katherine (Sophie) (*b* Brooklyn, 10 Sept 1877; *d* Milford, Conn., 29 March 1952). Reformer and arts patron, sister of Ethel Eyre Valentine Dreier and Mary E. Dreier. She helped to establish the Little Italy Neighborhood House in Brooklyn and the Manhattan Trade School for Girls in 1903. In 1920 she formed the Société Anonyme to provide an exhibition space for work by Dadaists and other modern artists, which she also promoted through lectures and writings. She wrote *Western Art and the New Era* (1923).

Linda Elsroad

Dreier, Mary E(lizabeth) (*b* New York City, 26 Sept 1875; *d* Bar Harbor, Maine, 15 Aug 1963). Labor activist, sister of Ethel Eyre Valentine Dreier and Katherine Dreier. Born to a middle-class German family, she was drawn into the New York Women's Trade Union League in 1899 by Leonora O'Reilly, one of its most influential members, and in 1906 was elected its president. During her tenure she was arrested for drawing public attention to police brutality against striking women workers in New York City. Although she built a reputation as one of the few middle-class reformers trusted by the working women in the league, she resigned in 1914 because of her belief that the league should be led by a worker. From 1911 to 1915 she served with Robert F. Wagner (i) and Alfred E. Smith on the New York State Factory Investigating Commission, formed after the Triangle Shirtwaist fire of 1911 to investigate conditions in factories and to frame laws regulating occupational safety and health. Dreier also led the city's Woman Suffrage Party during the second decade of the twentieth century. In her later years she worked for labor reform and improving relations with the Soviet Union, and protested against nuclear proliferation.

Annelise Orleck

Dreiser, Theodore (Herman Albert) (*b* Terre Haute, Ind., 27 Aug 1871; *d* Hollywood, 27 Dec 1945). Novelist. The twelfth of thirteen children born to a poverty-stricken family, he spent a year at Indiana University (1889–90) and became a newspaper reporter in Chicago in 1892. In 1894 he read the philosophy of Herbert Spencer and came to believe that human beings are the helpless victims of instinct and social forces, a theme that underlies his writing. He moved to New York City in the same year and stayed at the Mills Hotel (now the Greenwich Hotel) at 160 Bleecker Street, but financial limitations forced him to move to East End Avenue. He married Sara White in 1898 (from whom he was permanently separated in 1912 because of his infidelities) and moved to 6 West 102nd Street in 1913. His first novel, *Sister Carrie* (1900), about a kept woman who despite her immorality becomes a successful actress, caused public controversy and was suppressed by its publisher, Frank Doubleday, which led Dreiser to suffer a nervous collapse. In the nine years after his recovery in a sanitarium he became financially successful as the editor of several women's magazines, which enabled him to write his second novel, *Jennie Gerhardt* (1911). He followed this critical success with *The Financier* (1912) and *The Titan* (1914), two parts of a trilogy based on the life of the financier Charles T. Yerkes; *The Genius* (1915), a semi-autobiographical novel; *The Color of a Great City* (1923), a rhapsodic tribute to New York City; and *An American Tragedy* (1925), the story of a man driven by his social ambitions and passion to commit murder, which became his most critically and commercially successful work. During this period he lived at 439 West 123rd Street (1906–14), 165 West 10th Street (1914–20), 16 St. Luke's Place (1922–23), 118 West 11th Street (1923), and 1799 Bedford Avenue in Bedford–Stuyvesant (1925). In January 1925 he rented an office at 201 Park Avenue South to finish writing *An American Tragedy*, the success of which allowed him to move to 200 West 57th Street. After a trip to Soviet Russia in 1927 he became a social reformer, writing pro-communist works such as *Tragic America* (1932). He lived in Suite 1454 of the Ansonia Hotel at 2101–19 Broadway from 1931 to 1935, moved to Los Angeles in 1938, married his mistress Helen Richardson in 1944, and joined the Communist Party in the following year. Dreiser was the leading figure in the American Naturalist movement, known for his powerfully realistic descriptions of daily life and his exploration of social problems.

W. A. Swanberg: *Dreiser* (New York: Charles Scribner's Sons, 1965)
Richard Lingeman: *Theodore Dreiser: At the Gates of the City, 1871–1907* (New York: G. P. Putnam's Sons, 1986)

See also Cosmopolitan.

Anthony Gronowicz

Drew, Daniel (*b* Carmel, N.Y., 29 July 1797; *d* New York City, 18 Sept 1879). Industrialist. He worked in the cattle business before moving to New York City in 1829. In 1834 he launched steamboats intended to compete with those of Cornelius Vanderbilt, and in 1844 he formed Drew, Robinson and Company, a banking and brokerage house on Wall Street that did a large amount of business for a decade. He began an association in 1853 with the Erie Railroad, of which he was named a director in 1857. As the railroad's treasurer and controlling agent he proceeded to manipulate its stock, and with his confederates Jay Gould and Jim Fisk he engaged Vanderbilt in the notorious "Erie War" between 1866 and 1868. In 1870 he was undone by his own methods when Gould and Fisk turned on him, and he lost the remainder of his fortune after the panic of 1873. He filed for bankruptcy in 1876 and spent his declining years at 3 East 42nd Street. Unscrupulous, shrewd, bold, and illiterate, Drew practiced the sort of flamboyant chicanery that became the hallmark of the "robber barons" of the mid nineteenth century.

Clifford Browder: *The Money Game in Old New York: Daniel Drew and His Times* (Lexington: University Press of Kentucky, 1986)

Allen J. Share

Drexel Burnham Lambert. Firm of investment bankers formed in 1838 in Philadelphia as a brokerage firm by Francis M. Drexel. Renamed Drexel, Morgan after merging with the firm of J. P. Morgan in New York City in 1871, it became the most influential investment banking firm in the United States. By 1894 the firm was known as J. P. Morgan and the branch office in Philadelphia was Drexel. In response to the Glass–Steagall Act of 1933 Drexel ceased its investment banking activities. A new investment bank named Drexel was formed in Philadelphia in 1940, composed of partners from the earlier firm; its customers included some of the city's largest industrial firms. The name changed to Drexel Harriman Ripley in 1966, when the firm moved to New York City; to Drexel Firestone in 1970; to Drexel Burnham in 1973 after a merger with the firm of Burnham (a successful brokerage formed in 1935 by I. W. Burnham); and to its present form in 1976 after a merger with the Compagnie Bruxelles Lambert. Through the efforts of Michael R. Milken in the 1980s the firm controlled the market in "junk bonds" and grew rapidly, eventually having more than five thousand employees. After the stock market crash of 1987 the firm dismissed Milken for his role in an insider trading scheme, and in 1990 it filed for bankruptcy protection after pleading guilty to mail and securities fraud and agreeing to pay $650 million in fines. Its plans to emerge from bankruptcy as a much smaller firm went unrealized.

Connie Bruck: *The Predators' Ball: The Junk Bond Raiders and the Man Who Staked Them* (New York: Simon and Schuster, 1988)
Christopher Byron: "Drexel's Fall: The Final Days," *New York*, 19 March 1990, pp. 32–38

Mary E. Curry

Drug, Hospital and Health Care Employees Union. Labor union. An affiliate was formed in New York City in 1932 as Local 1199.

drug abuse. Efforts to prohibit the sale and use of drugs in New York City began in the late nineteenth century, when in an effort to control an alarming level of opium and morphine addiction the state enacted laws prohibiting the sale of these drugs without a physician's prescription. Small quantities could nevertheless still be included in patent medicines, which were not controlled by law, and opium and morphine, as well as heroin and cocaine, could be obtained from out-of-state mail-order houses until the federal government passed the Pure Food and Drug Act (1906). Early attempts to control the use of cocaine were more successful than efforts to control opiates. Introduced in the United States during the mid 1880s, cocaine was a popular tonic often taken in a wine solution: it was also eaten, injected, sniffed in powder form, and sprayed into the nostrils. Some deaths and a much larger number of chronic users resulting from the uncontrolled, legal use of cocaine eventually gave it a reputation as a deadly, habit-forming drug. In 1907 a state law sponsored by Assemblyman Alfred E. Smith made cocaine obtainable only through a physician, marking the beginning of an attempt at control that culminated in the federal Harrison Act (1914). Gradually cocaine declined to the degree that the Mayor's Committee on Drug Addiction reported in 1930 that cocaine addiction was no longer a serious problem in the city.

Drug treatment programs were developed partly in response to the growing use of heroin, which became popular among opiate users before the First World War and by 1915 was responsible for more admissions to Bellevue Hospital than morphine was. The best-known treatment program was administered at the Towns Hospital, opened by Charles B. Towns, an insurance salesman from the South who moved to New York City in 1907; the hospital treated addiction by administering powerful doses of drugs over three to four days, purging the body and thereby supposedly detoxifying and ending drug craving. In the second decade of the century the work of Ernest Bishop led to a form of treatment in which heroin addicts were given long-term, stable doses of opium. This treatment proved controversial because of an increasing sentiment that drugs should not be used for any purpose, which culminated in a decision by the U.S. Supreme Court in 1919 that prohibited treatment programs relying on indefinite drug maintenance. Despite the disfavor in which drug maintenance was held, New York State had established a network of morphine-maintenance clinics in 1918. One such clinic opened in New York City, but the city's health department opposed maintenance and also concluded that these drug treatment programs were ineffective. The goal of drug abstinence remained the standard until after the Second World War, when Vincent Dole and Marie Nyswander of Rockefeller University persuasively argued that some opiate addicts require indefinite, stable doses of drugs: in their studies a number of habitual addicts

Crack vials on a rooftop, 1989

were successfully treated with methadone, a synthetic opiate.

As drug use became more widespread during the 1960s residential drug treatment programs operated by Daytop, Odyssey House, and Phoenix House relied on drug-free techniques, among them intensive group therapy and efforts to instill individual responsibility; like methadone maintenance this approach suffered from a sharp fall-off in the number of participants in the early stages of treatment. During the 1970s the first attempts were made to end the sale and use of drugs through law enforcement. Laws introduced by Governor Nelson A. Rockefeller and enacted in 1973 mandated minimum prison terms for offenses that earlier had been punishable only by probation. The law increased the number of drug offenders in prison but did not diminish the use of drugs. After cocaine regained popularity during the 1970s its possession and sale became among the most frequently prosecuted offenses. Eventually cocaine came again to be perceived not as a recreational drug but as a dangerous one linked to violence, paranoia, and dependency, especially when a smokable form of cocaine known as "crack" surfaced in the mid 1980s. Crack had a much stronger effect on the body than cocaine ingested by sniffing and was available at lower cost. Fear of the effects of crack led to an increased emphasis on law enforcement that filled the courts and prisons with drug offenders. Attention shifted to intravenous drug users in the 1980s when it became clear that AIDS was being spread rapidly by shared hypodermic needles. The casual use of drugs declined in the early 1990s, although the number of habitual users remained high: in the mid 1990s it was estimated that there were 500,000 drug addicts in New York City, including 200,000 heroin addicts.

David F. Musto

Drumgoole, John Christopher (*b* Granard, Ireland, 15 Aug 1816; *d* New York City, 28 March 1888). Priest. He moved to New York City as a child and was apprenticed to a cobbler. He later taught Sunday school, became a sexton, and helped to run a small bookstore. When he was nearly fifty he began studying for the priesthood at St. Francis Xavier College and St. John's College in Fordham, and after his ordination in 1869 he was assigned to St. Mary's Church, where he had been a sexton. He soon focused on helping homeless boys, building the Mission of the Immaculate Virgin to provide a home for two thousand at a cost of about $1 million, which he raised in charitable contributions.

Katherine Kurz Burton: *Children's Shepherd: The Story of John Christopher Drumgoole* (New York: P. J. Kenedy and Sons, 1954)

James E. Mooney

Dry Dock District. Former neighborhood in lower Manhattan, bounded to the north by 12th Street, to the east by the East River, to the south by Houston Street, and to the west by Avenue B. The area was the site of many ship fitters and iron works during the mid nineteenth century: in 1855 the Novelty Iron Works, the Secor Iron Works, Young and Cutter, and Cornelius H. Delameter (builder of the *Monitor*) were among the largest of these firms and employed more than two thousand workers between them. In 1848 the Dry Dock Savings Bank opened at 619 4th Street to serve dockworkers, seamen, and mechanics; it was liquidated in 1992. The district is now the location of the northern third of the East River Park and of the Jacob Riis Houses, public housing built in 1949.

Kenneth A. Scherzer

Duane, James (*b* New York City, 6 Feb 1733; *d* Schenectady, N.Y., 1 Feb 1797). Mayor. The son of an Irish-born merchant, he was a clerk in the law office of James Alexander before gaining admission to the New York bar in 1754. He was named attorney general of New York in 1767 and was a member of the de Lancey political faction until his marriage to Maria Livingston in 1759, when he joined the Livingston faction. Despite his reservations about independence he served in the Continental Congress from 1774 to 1784. A staunch Federalist, he was appointed mayor by Governor George Clinton in 1784, becoming the first to hold the office after the British evacuation. During his tenure, which lasted until 1789, he was instrumental in the city's rapid recovery from the war but was unsuccessful in his efforts to keep the national capital in the city. From 1789 to 1794 Duane was the U.S. district judge for New York State. A street in lower Manhattan is named for him.

E. Wilder Spaulding: *New York in the Critical Period, 1783–1789* (New York: Columbia University Press, 1932)

Edward P. Alexander: *A Revolutionary Conservative: James Duane of New York* (New York: Columbia University Press, 1938)

Sidney I. Pomerantz: *New York: An American City, 1783–1803: A Study of Urban Life* (New York: Columbia University Press, 1938; 2nd edn Port Washington, N.Y.: I. J. Friedman, 1965)

See also Courts, §§1, 3; and Coffee houses.

David William Voorhees

Dubinsky, David (*b* Brest-Litovsk, Poland, 22 Feb 1892; *d* New York City, 17 Sept 1982). Labor leader. He emigrated to the United States in 1911 and began working as a garment cutter. In 1921 he became the general manager of the Amalgamated Cutters' Union, Local 10 of the International Ladies' Garment Workers' Union. After being elected vice-president of the union in 1922 he helped it to avoid bankruptcy and defeat a strong communist bid for control. When he became president in 1932 the union had more than $1 million in liabilities and fewer than forty thousand members; with loans and frugal management, supported by the National Industrial Relations Act, he greatly improved the union's finances and increased its membership. He secured many benefits for union members, including a thirty-five-hour week, expanded union health centers, retirement pensions, death benefits, and two large cooperative housing developments. Dubinsky later organized the Jewish Labor Committee, in 1934 became vice-president of the American Federation of Labor (AFL), in the following year formed the Committee for Industrial Organization (CIO; later the Congress of Industrial Organizations) within the AFL, and raised funds for anti-fascists during the Spanish Civil War.

Dubinsky resigned from the executive council of the AFL in 1936 when it denounced the CIO as illicit and suspended its member unions, including the ILGWU. He kept the ILGWU independent of both federations until 1940, when it rejoined the AFL. With other labor leaders in New York City he formed the American Labor Party to give Franklin D. Roosevelt an additional ballot line in the presidential election of 1936. In 1944 he abandoned the party, which he believed had become too leftist, and organized the Liberal Party. During the Second World War he foresaw a communist threat to labor unions in western Europe and formed the Free Trade Union Committee within the AFL. He also helped to rescue Jewish labor leaders from Nazism in Poland and formed the International Confederation of Free Trade Unions (1949). His long campaign for action against labor racketeering finally achieved success in 1957 when the AFL–CIO established a code of ethics. With Alex Rose of the United Hatters, Cap and Millinery Workers International Union he guided Liberals and helped to elect John F. Kennedy president of the United States (1960) and John V. Lindsay mayor of New York City (1965). Dubinsky retired in 1966. With A. H. Raskin he wrote *David Dubinsky: A Life with Labor* (1977).

Max D. Danish: *The World of David Dubinsky* (Cleveland: World, 1957)

Robert D. Parmet

DuBois, John (*b* Paris, 24 Aug 1764; *d* New York City, 20 Dec 1842). Bishop. After being educated in Paris he was ordained on 22 September 1787. During the French Revolution he became a refugee and in August 1791 he moved to Norfolk, Virginia; he opened the first Catholic church in Frederick, Maryland, in 1794. Near Emmitsburg, Maryland, he built a chapel in November 1805 where he eventually opened Mount St. Mary's Seminary, and he was made the director of Elizabeth Ann Seton's first convent when it opened in Emmitsburg in June 1809. He also rode circuit from Pennsylvania to Virginia and was affiliated with the Society of St. Sulpice from 1808 to 1826. His appointment as bishop on 29 October 1826 was soon contested by parishioners, who asserted that he had obtained it through undue influence, and he was forced to refute their charges in 1827. With contributions that he collected in Europe (1829–31) he built a seminary; this was uninsured and in 1834 was destroyed by fire. During the same year lay trustees at St. Patrick's Cathedral on Mott Street refused to pay a priest whom he had appointed, and eventually they refused to pay him as well. In February 1838 he suffered a stroke that left him unable to continue the administration of the diocese. DuBois is buried beneath the doorstep of St. Patrick's Old Cathedral on Mott Street, apparently at his request so that people might walk on him in death as they had wished to do in life.

Richard Shaw: *John DuBois, Founding Father: The Life and Times of the Founder of Mount St. Mary's College, Emmitsburg, Superior of the Sisters of Charity, and Third Bishop of New York* (Yonkers, N.Y.: United States Catholic Historical Society / Emmitsburg, Md.: Mount Saint Mary's, 1983)

Mary Elizabeth Brown

Du Bois, W(illiam) E(dward) B(urghardt) (*b* Great Barrington, Mass., 23 Feb 1868; *d* Accra, Ghana, 27 Aug 1963). Writer, poet, and civil rights leader. After teaching at Wilberforce and Atlanta universities he formed the Niagara Movement with other black activists in 1905 to protest against racial oppression. This failed to win a large following and adequate funds and was superseded in 1909 by the National Association for the Advancement of Colored People (NAACP), which appointed him its director of publicity and research in New York City, and the editor of its monthly publication the *Crisis*. Du Bois organized the first Pan-African Congress in 1919 and three subsequent meetings to foster African development and self-determination. His advocacy of "voluntary segregation" as a means of achieving economic development for blacks during the Depression was widely opposed within the NAACP and led to his resignation in 1934. He then returned to Atlanta University but rejoined the association in 1944 to study the global black population. In the following year he was elected international president of the fifth Pan-African Congress (organized by George Padmore). A dispute with Walter White, executive secretary of the NAACP, led to his permanent resignation from the organization in 1948. He became vice-chairman of the Council on African Affairs, led by Paul Robeson, and chairman of the Peace Information Center in 1949, and in 1950 unsuccessfully ran for the U.S. Senate in New York as the candidate of the American Labor Party. During the campaign he was indicted along with other officers of the Peace Information Center for his failure to register as an agent of a foreign government (the center was circulating an appeal to ban nuclear weapons, which the U.S. Department of State considered Soviet propaganda); he was later tried and acquitted. Because he refused to sign an affidavit stating that he was not a communist, the state department forbade him to travel abroad until 1958, when the U.S. Supreme Court ruled that his civil and political rights were being violated. In 1961 he joined the American Communist Party and moved to Ghana. Du Bois published nineteen books (including five novels), edited almost two dozen works, and wrote poetry and plays as well as hundreds of articles. In his well-known collection of essays *The Souls of Black Folk* (1903) he declares that "the problem of the Twentieth Century is the problem of the color line" and criticizes the influential black leader Booker T. Washington for acquiescing in racial oppression while stifling black dissent. His residences in New York City included 650 Greene Avenue (before 1920), the Paul Lawrence Dunbar Apartments at 2594 7th Avenue (until 1934), 409 Edgecomb Avenue (1944–51), and 31 Grace Court in Brooklyn Heights (until 1962).

David Levering Lewis: *W. E. B. DuBois: Biography of a Race, 1868–1919* (New York: Henry Holt, 1993)

R. L. Harris, Jr.

W. E. B Du Bois

Dubos, René (Jules) (*b* St. Brice, France, 20 Feb 1901; *d* New York City, 20 Feb 1982). Microbiologist and environmentalist. From 1927 to the end of his life he worked at the Rockefeller Institute for Medical Research (later known as Rockefeller University), where his discovery in 1939 of the soil-borne antibiotic microbe gramicidin paved the way for the commercial development of antibiotics. He also examined the impact of pollutants on the environment and successfully led an effort to clean up Jamaica Bay, dedicated in 1987 as the René Dubos Wildlife Preserve. His published writings include *So Human an Animal* (1968), winner of the Pulitzer Prize.

Carol L. Moberg and Zanvil A. Cohn: *Launching the Antibiotic Era: Personal Accounts of the Discovery and Use of the First Antibiotics* (New York: Rockefeller University Press, 1990)

Renee D. Mastrocco

Duchamp, Marcel (*b* Blainville, France, 28 July 1887; *d* Neuilly-sur-Seine, France, 2 Oct 1968). Painter and sculptor. After his painting *Nude Descending a Staircase* (1912) provoked a controversy at the Armory Show (1913) he moved in June 1915 to New York City, where he was associated with the collectors Louise and Walter Arensberg, with whom he lived for several months at 33 West 67th Street, and took part in the Dada movement; he remained in the city until 1918. He soon abandoned conventional painting and created sculpture from diverse found objects: a bicycle wheel, a snow shovel, a urinal. Between 1915 and 1923 he completed his most important work, *The Bride Stripped Bare by Her Bachelors, Even*, also known as *The Large Glass*. He returned permanently to New York City in 1942 and helped to mount the exhibition "First Papers of Surrealism." Duchamp is regarded as the founder of conceptual art. The Museum of Modern Art owns examples of his work.

Anne d'Harnoncourt and Kynaston McShine, eds.: *Marcel Duchamp* (New York: Museum of Modern Art / Philadelphia: Philadelphia Museum of Art, 1973)

Judith Zilczer

Duchin, Eddy [Edwin Frank] (*b* Cambridge, Mass., 1 April 1909; *d* New York City, 9 Feb 1951). Bandleader and pianist. He moved to New York City in 1928 to play with Leo Reisman's group at the Waldorf–Astoria. After three years he left to form his own orchestra, which performed regularly for members of fashionable society at the Central Park Casino. His radio program "Hour of Charm" was broadcast locally, and he played at many hotels. Duchin was known for his elegant image and sophisticated piano improvisations.

Marc Ferris

Duer, William (*b* Devonshire, England, 18 March 1747; *d* New York City, 7 May 1799). Financier and statesman. After settling in New York City in 1768 he set up a lumber firm north of Saratoga, New York. A delegate to the Provincial Congress in 1775 and the Continental Congress, he was deputy adjutant general of Continental troops from New York and signed the Articles of Confederation. During the American Revolution he won contracts from the army that allowed him to become wealthy. Duer helped to form the Bank of New York in 1784, was an assistant secretary of the U.S. Treasury, and speculated in land and stocks. His imprisonment for debt in 1792 set off the first financial panic in New York City.

Joseph Stancliffe Davis: *Essays in the Earlier History of American Corporations* (Cambridge: Harvard University Press, 1917)

Robert Francis James: *"The King of the Alley": William Duer: Politician, Entrepreneur, and Speculator, 1768–1799* (Philadelphia: American Philosophical Society, 1992)

James E. Mooney

Duffy, Francis P(atrick) (*b* Ontario, 2 May 1871; *d* New York City, 26 June 1932). Priest. After receiving his education in Ontario he was ordained on 6 September 1896 and became an American citizen on 7 June 1902. He taught at St. Joseph's Seminary from 1898 to 1912, edited the *New York Review* (1905–7), and moved to New York City to form the Church of Our Savior in the Bronx (1912–16). Appointed chaplain of the 69th Regiment in 1914, he served at the Mexican border (1916–17) and in France (1917–18). From 1920 to 1932 he was the pastor of Holy Cross, near which a statue of him was built in Times Square. Duffy is best known for his military assignments during the First World War.

Jim Bishop and Virginia Lee Bishop: *Fighting Father Duffy* (New York: Vision, 1956)

See also Irish.

Mary Elizabeth Brown

Dulles, John Foster (*b* Washington, 25 Feb 1888; *d* Washington, 24 May 1959). Statesman. The son of a distinguished Presbyterian pastor, he graduated from Princeton University in 1908 and attended the Sorbonne and later George Washington University. In 1911 he joined the law firm of Sullivan and Cromwell in Manhattan. Paid only $50 a week at the outset because he lacked a law degree, by 1920 he was a partner in the firm. He became its chief operating partner in 1927 and eventually was reported to be the highest-paid lawyer in the city. From the 1920s he lived at 72 East 91st Street. A specialist in international finance, he settled bondholders' claims against the Kreuger match empire. He also was an advisor to the American delegation at the conference in San Francisco regarding the establishment of the United Nations, advised Thomas E. Dewey on foreign policy, and was the main architect of the peace treaty with Japan after the Second World War. As secretary of state under President Dwight D. Eisenhower, Dulles pursued policies of brinkmanship and massive retaliation that intensified tension during the cold war.

George J. Lankevich

dumbbell tenements. The predominant tenements erected for workers between 1879 and 1901, named for their shape and based on a design by James E. Ware calling for two tenements connected one behind the other by a hallway. Ware's design won a competition in 1878 (sponsored by the journal *Plumber and Sanitary Engineer*) to design a tenement for a lot measuring twenty-five by a hundred feet (eight by thirty meters); it was widely adopted after New York State passed the Tenement House Law of 1879 requiring a window in every tenement bedroom. Dumbbell tenements were usually five to seven stories tall and had fourteen rooms on each floor, seven on each side from front to back, divided into two four-room apartments in front and two three-room apartments in back. The four apartments shared two toilets, and the windows in ten of the fourteen rooms opened onto an air shaft less than five feet (1.5 meters) wide formed by the indented hallway sections of abutting tenements; enclosure on all sides made the shaft dark and airless, and it often became a garbage dump and a fire hazard. From the start the design was criticized for sacrificing the interests of tenants to those of landlords, builders, and real-estate agents. Dumbbell tenements housed about two thirds of the city's population, or 2.3 million persons, by the time their construction was outlawed by the Tenement House Law of 1901. Existing dumbbell tenements continued to house tens of thousands of New Yorkers into the 1990s.

Roy Lubove: *The Progressives and the Slums: Tenement House Reform in New York City, 1890–1917* (Pittsburgh: University of Pittsburgh Press, 1962)

Moses Rischin: *The Promised City: New York's Jews, 1870–1914* (Cambridge: Harvard University Press, 1962)

Allen J. Share

Dun and Bradstreet. Financial rating service. Its precursor was formed in 1841 by Lewis Tappan to provide the credit ratings of retailers to wholesale merchants in New York City. In 1849 Tappan sold his interest in the agency to his brother Arthur Tappan and to Benjamin Douglass (1816–1900), who in 1854 purchased Tappan's interest, changed the name of the firm to B. Douglass and Company, and expanded it to a national scale. In 1855 John M. Bradstreet (1815–63), the agency's strongest competitor, moved his headquarters from Cincinnati to New York City and began publishing credit ratings in a book that he made available by subscription. The service proved popular and easily imitated, by among others Robert Graham Dun (1826–1900), who purchased Douglass's busi-

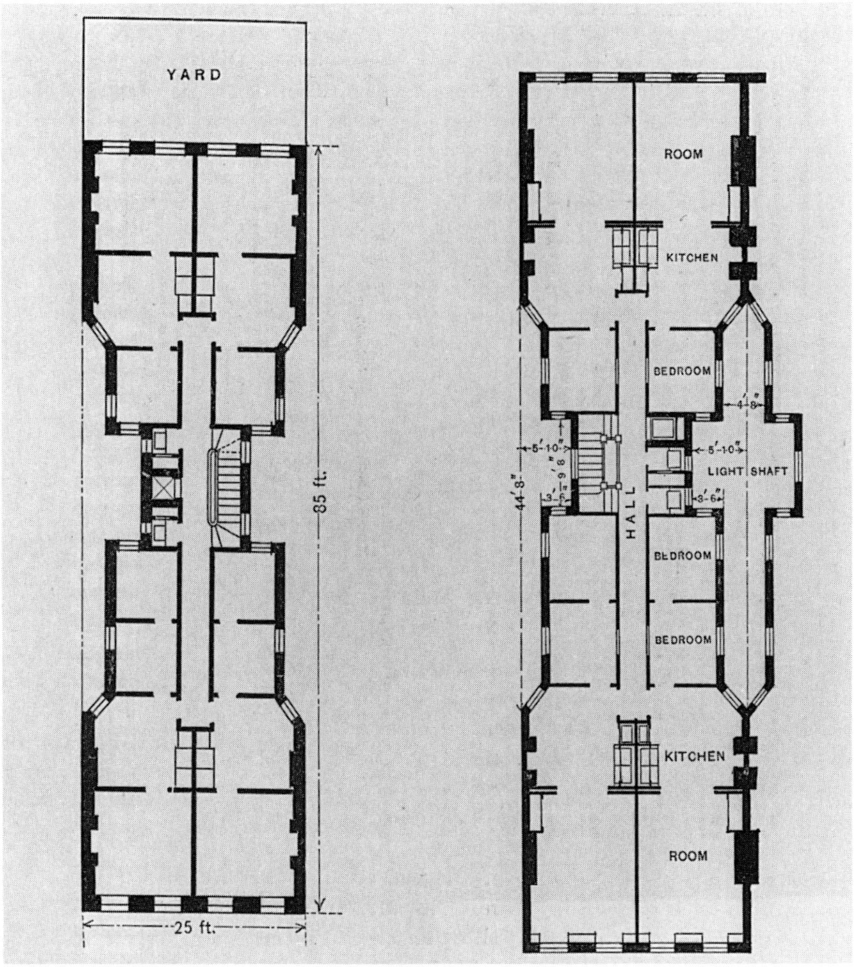

Floor plan for dumbbell tenements, 1887

ness in 1858 and in the same year began publishing the *Mercantile Agency's Reference Book*. In 1930 Dun's firm absorbed the National Credit Office and in 1933 it merged with Bradstreet's firm. Dun and Bradstreet now includes the Reuben H. Donnelly Corporation, the Corinthian Broadcasting Corporation, Moody's Investor Service, the Dun–Donnelly Publishing Corporation, and a management consulting division. The corporate headquarters are at 299 Park Avenue in Manhattan.

Edward N. Vose: *Seventy-five Years of the Mercantile Agency: R. G. Dun and Co., 1841–1916* (New York: R. G. Dun, 1916)

Roy Anderson Foulke: *The Sinews of American Commerce: 100th Anniversary, 1841–1941* (New York: Dun and Bradstreet, 1941)

James H. Madison: "The Evolution of Commercial Credit Reporting Agencies in Nineteenth-century America," *Business History Review* 48 (summer 1974), 164–86

James D. Norris: *R. G. Dun and Co., 1841–1900: The Development of Credit-Reporting in the Nineteenth Century* (Westport, Conn.: Greenwood, 1978)

James D. Norris

Dunbar, Paul Lawrence (*b* Dayton, Ohio, 27 June 1872; *d* Dayton, 9 Feb 1906). Poet and novelist. He first visited New York City in 1896 to give a series of poetry readings and resided briefly at 131 West 3rd Street in May and June 1899. His earliest works were poems, some in Afro-American dialect and others in standard English. He also wrote four novels, of which the first three dealt with white characters and the last with black characters and themes, like most of his short stories. Although Dunbar lived most of his adult life in Washington, he used New York City in such works as his short stories "Finding of Zach," "One Christmas at Shiloh," and "The Trustfulness of Polly," and the novel *The Strength of Gideon* (1900). Episodes from the novel *The Sport of the Gods* (1902) are set in the Banner Cafe in the Tenderloin. Central themes of his work were the false ideals of blacks and the adversities of northward migration and adaptation to the urban environment. Dunbar also wrote lyrics to the musicals of Will Marion Cook, including *In Dahomey* (1902). He was the first black writer to achieve national fame and a major influence on the writers of the Harlem Renaissance.

Tony Gentry: *Paul Lawrence Dunbar* (New York: Chelsea House, 1989)

George A. Thompson, Jr.

Dunbar Apartments. Cooperative apartment complex in Manhattan, financed by John D. Rockefeller Jr., designed by Andrew J. Thomas, and consisting of six garden apartment buildings arranged in the shape of a horseshoe around a courtyard; it was built between 1926 and 1928 on a site bounded by 150th Street, Adam Clayton Powell Jr. Boulevard, 149th Street, and Frederick Douglass Boulevard. Named for the poet Paul Lawrence Dunbar, it was the first development of its kind built for blacks. Units of four, five, and six rooms were offered for a down payment of $150 and $50 a room. Among the amenities were a nursery and kindergarten, a playground, a clubroom for older boys, an athletic field, men's and women's clubs, vocational guidance for tenants, stores, and the Dunbar National Bank, the first large bank in Harlem to have a black manager and staff. Many tenants defaulted on mortgage and maintenance payments during the Depression, forcing Rockefeller to foreclose on the mortgage in 1936; he returned the equity to the tenants, who were allowed to remain as renters. Well-known residents included the poet Countee Cullen, the writer W. E. B. Du Bois, the actor Paul Robeson, the tap dancer Bill "Bojangles" Robinson, the labor leader A. Philip Randolph, and the explorer Matthew A. Henson. The Dunbar Apartments were designated a city landmark in 1970.

Eric Wm. Allison

Duncan, Isadora (*b* San Francisco, 27 May 1878; *d* Nice, France, 14 Sept 1927). Dancer and choreographer. At the age of ten she left school to conduct her own dance classes, and in 1896 she moved to New York City with her mother to pursue a stage career. She left for London in 1900 and developed an infatuation with Europe that lasted throughout her life. Inspired by Greek antiquity, she rejected ballet and introduced a distinctive style characterized by flowing movements and the use of translucent gowns. In 1914–15 she lived at 303 4th Avenue, where she also ran a studio. Duncan became widely known during the First World War for her sexually provocative dancing, her publicly noted liaisons, and her frequent criticism of conventional marriage. She lived at 118 West 57th Street in 1922–23.

Fredrika Blair: *Isadora: Portrait of the Artist as a Woman* (New York: McGraw–Hill, 1986)

Peter M. Rutkoff, William B. Scott

Duncan, John H(emenway) (*b* New Orleans, 1854; *d* Highland Beach, N.J., 18 Oct 1929). Architect. He grew up in Binghamton, New York, and in 1879 moved to New York City to begin his practice. He gained prominence by winning competitions for the Brooklyn Soldiers' and Sailors' Memorial Arch (1892) and for Grant's Tomb (1897; for illustration see GRANT'S TOMB), and later designed the Knox Building at 452 5th Avenue (1902), private houses at 7 West 54th Street

(1900) and 16 East 67th Street (1905), and the twin structures at 16 and 18 East 71st Street (1911). Duncan's adherence to principles of classical architecture put him at odds with the styles prevailing after the First World War.

Elliott B. Nixon

Dunham, Katherine (*b* Chicago, 22 June 1910). Dancer, choreographer, and artistic director. She studied modern dance and ballet, attended the University of Chicago (MA in anthropology), and undertook fieldwork in Haiti and Jamaica. In New York City she formed a dance company in 1939 for which she did her own choreography, effecting an innovative fusion of Afro-Caribbean and European forms; the company was acclaimed worldwide and trained several hundred dancers. In the 1940s and 1950s she worked on Broadway and in Hollywood, and from 1945 to the mid 1950s she taught at the Dunham School of Dance in the city. After her company disbanded in 1967 Dunham moved to East St. Louis, Illinois, where she opened a dance school.

Ruth Beckford: *Katherine Dunham: A Biography* (New York: Marcel Dekker, 1979)

Brenda Dixon Gottschild

Dunlap, William (*b* Perth Amboy, N.J., 19 Feb 1766; *d* New York City, 28 Sept 1839). Painter and playwright. He began painting portraits in New York City when he was about twenty and in 1784 went abroad to study with Benjamin West. Captivated by theater in London, he soon returned to New York City to write plays, many of which were later produced. From 1796 to 1805 he managed the Old American Company, a position that gave him virtual control of the theater in New York City but after several years left him bankrupt and fatigued. Although he remained a prolific writer he derived most of his income after about 1810 from painting miniatures, portraits, and religious pictures such as *Christ Rejected* (1822) and *Death on the Pale Horse* (1824). An active member of the American Academy of the Fine Arts, he joined with Samuel F. B. Morse to found the National Academy of Design in 1826. Dunlap wrote *History of the American Theatre* (1832) and *History of the Rise and Progress of the Arts of Design in the United States* (1834), a chronicle of American artists' lives that remains among the most valuable publications on art in the nineteenth century; he was working on a history of New York City at the time of his death.

Robert H. Canary: *William Dunlap* (Boston: Twayne, 1970)

Carrie Rebora

Dunne, Finley Peter (*b* Chicago, 19 July 1867; *d* New York City, 24 April 1936). Satirist. After working as an editor in Chicago he wrote commentaries in Irish dialect from 1893 as the reformist "Mr. Dooley." He moved to New York City in 1901, where his column appeared in several newspapers and magazines, including the *New York Times*, the *American Magazine*, and *Collier's*, which he also edited. In perhaps his best-known piece he had Mr. Dooley describe his friend "Prisidint Tiddy Rosenfelt" and coined the line: "no matther whether th' constitution follows th' flag or not, th' Supreme Court follows th' iliction returns."

Elmer Ellis: *Mr. Dooley's America: A Life of Finley Peter Dunne* (New York: Alfred A. Knopf, 1941)

Michael Green

Dunton. Name formerly applied to a section of north central Queens south of the Long Island Rail Road between 127th Street and the Van Wyck Expressway. It was developed from 1889 as West Jamaica on the land of several farms acquired by Frederick W. Dunton, a nephew of Austin Corbin who was active in real estate. The name Dunton was adopted in 1890 by a vote of local residents, soon after which Dunton Park opened between Liberty and 109th avenues. Eventually the area became a model community of one-family houses. After the First World War it was absorbed into Jamaica.

Vincent Seyfried

The Katherine Dunham Company performing Tropical Revue

Durand, Asher B(rown) (*b* Jefferson Village [now Maplewood], N.J., 21 Aug 1796; *d* Jefferson Village, 17 Sept 1886). Painter. He was apprenticed to the engraver Peter Maverick (1780–1831) in 1812 near Newark, New Jersey, and in 1817 became Maverick's partner and moved to New York City. His reputation was secured by an engraving (1820–23) after John Trumbull's painting *The Declaration of Independence*. A member of the New-York Historical Society (1821) and the Bread and Cheese Club (1825), he helped to form the New-York Drawing Association (1825), the National Academy of Design (1826), of which he was the second president (1845–61), the Sketch Club (1827), and the Century Association (1847). After receiving a commission for a series of presidential portraits from Luman Reed in 1835 he was able to devote himself entirely to painting. A trip with Thomas Cole to the Adirondack Mountains in 1837 led him to turn to landscape painting; scenes of New York State and New England were his preferred subjects. He traveled to Europe (1840–41) and after Cole's death became the acknowledged leader of the Hudson River School. Inspired by writings of the English critic John Ruskin (1819–1900), he modified his picturesque style in the early 1850s with elements derived from studies of nature. In his "Letters on Landscape Painting" (1855), nine essays published in the periodical the *Crayon* that stated the theories of the Hudson River School, he argued that the faithful de-

Asher B. Durand, Self-portrait *(ca 1830–33). Pencil on paper*

piction of nature could reveal the presence of God. Durand retired to the village of his birth in 1869.

David B. Lawall: *Asher Brown Durand: His Art and Art Theory in Relation to His Times* (New York: Garland, 1977)

Timothy Anglin Burgard

Duryea House. Historic house in Brooklyn. It was built about 1740 as a gabled, Dutch colonial farm cottage in the village of New Lots (now the neighborhood of East New York) soon after its site of one hundred acres (forty hectares) was acquired by Christian Duryea, a Huguenot. His descendants retained ownership of the house until 1886. The last owner of the house, Frederick Eversley, died in 1982; at the time there were only about a dozen eighteenth-century farmhouses remaining in the city and preservationists hoped to maintain the Duryea House by moving it to a public park nearby, but before its transfer to the city could be negotiated the house was destroyed by fire in November 1989.

Jonathan Kuhn

Dutch. The first Dutch expedition to what is now New York City was commissioned by the Dutch East India Company and led in 1609 by the English explorer Henry Hudson, who sailed into the harbor on 3 September and explored the river that was named for him after the English took control of the region in 1664. His report on the possibilities for agriculture, lumbering, and especially fur trading led the Dutch East India Company to sponsor several additional expeditions. A colony called New Netherland was formed in 1614 in the area between the Delaware and Connecticut rivers. Commercial activity was initially centered at Fort Orange (near what is now Albany) and unrestricted except between 1614 and 1617, when the New Netherland Company had a monopoly. In 1621 the Dutch West India Company was created by the States General of the Netherlands; its charter provided for nineteen directors, minimal supervision by the States General, and a monopoly on Dutch trade in a large area extending as far east as West Africa and as far north as Newfoundland. Because its domain was so vast the company virtually ignored New Netherland until 1624, when it sent about thirty families and some single men, mostly Protestant Walloons from the Spanish Netherlands, to set up farms. Most of the colonists were settled at Fort Orange; a few were settled near the mouth of the Delaware River and on Nutten Island (now Governors Island), but of these some were moved in 1625 to Manhattan Island, where they were joined in the following year by settlers fleeing attacks by Indians at Fort Orange. In 1626 Peter Minuit, the company's leading official, bought Manhattan from local Indians for blankets, cloth, metal goods, and trinkets then worth sixty guilders. The colonists near the Delaware were moved to Manhattan in June 1627.

Because of its harbor and strategic location Manhattan soon became the main settlement of the colony. A temporary stockade at its southern tip was replaced by a permanent one of earth and stone that was named Fort Amsterdam by the company, and the settlement became known as New Amsterdam. Makeshift houses around the fort were gradually replaced by more substantial ones. Many were tall and narrow and designed in a traditional Dutch style with stepped gables, and some were built of brick that had been carried to the colony as ballast. The main streets included Tuyn Straet (Garden Street) and Hoogh Straet (High Street). Two canals were built at what are now Beaver and Broad streets, and swampland was drained, filled, and converted into farmland. The main occupations were farming, producing ships' stores, lumbering, and fur trading. A *ziekentrooster* (comforter of the sick) was sent to the colony in 1624 as a lay preacher, followed by another in 1626 and the ordained minister Jonas Michaëlius in 1628, who organized the Reformed church there, a forerunner of the Collegiate church. Religious services were initially on the second story of an old mill until a crude wooden church was built; this was replaced in 1642 by a stone church that stood inside the fort and was named St. Nicholas Church after the patron saint of the Netherlands. Children were educated by the church until 1638, when the schoolmaster Adam Roelantsen was sent to the colony and opened a school that eventually became the Collegiate School. There were two hundred colonists and about thirty houses by the end of 1626 and 270 colonists by 1628.

During the 1630s colonists built settlements on land that eventually became part of Staten Island, Brooklyn, Queens, and the Bronx. A temporary settlement on Staten Island took form as early as the 1630s. By the mid 1630s a few settlers lived in Breuckelen (the forerunner of Brooklyn, named after a village in the Netherlands); informal ferry service soon connected the settlement with New Amsterdam, and as farmland became available for settlement a number of villages were built, including Midwout (Flatbush) and Amersfoort (Flatlands). In 1639 land north of the Harlem River was settled by the Danish captain Jonas Bronck. Land in Queens was bought from Indians during the same year and later became the site of an English settlement called Flushing, after the port city of Vlissingen in the Netherlands. The colonial governors, later called directors general, were appointed by the West India Company and ruled solely according to its wishes. The governors' oppressive policies toward the Indians promoted discontent in the colony. This was especially true of the policies of Willem Kieft (1637–47), which led to several bloody encounters between Indians and settlers. Occasionally the colonists became sufficiently disgruntled that remonstrances and delegations were sent to the company's directors, and the States General requested that the basis of the colonial government be broadened. Such measures were largely ignored in New Amsterdam until the administration of Peter Stuyvesant (1647–64) as governor general, who in April 1652 was instructed to form a municipal government modeled on those in the Netherlands. Early in the following year appointments were made for five *schepens* (aldermen), a *schout* (sheriff and city attorney), and two *burgomasters*; these officials met weekly, and objections to their decisions could be raised with the company's directors. Despite additional reforms the government was never truly representative: Stuyvesant, generally considered the most capable director general, continued to exercise broad powers and chose his associates from among the heads of élite families.

New Amsterdam continued to be developed but attracted few settlers. In 1653 a fortified wall was built between the Hudson and East rivers along the northern end of the town; a wagon road running alongside it later became known as Wall Street. A census taken in 1656 showed that the town had only 120 houses and about a thousand inhabitants. To increase the population orphans and children from poorhouses were sent from the Netherlands in 1655 and 1659, and indentured servants were also sought. In addition to the Dutch there were Germans, English, Scandinavians, Walloons, French Huguenots, and African slaves. Among the religious groups in the town were Lutherans, Quakers, English Independents, Anabaptists, Catholics, and Jews. The official denomination was the Calvinism of the Reformed church, but there were few incidents of hostility toward non-Calvinists, in part because the company urged tolerance for fear that bigotry might threaten trade and discourage immigration. Sephardim fleeing persecution in Brazil first moved to the colony in 1654. Permission was given on 4 March 1658 to form a village called Nieue Haarlem north of New Amsterdam. The first permanent settlement on Staten Island, Oude Dorp (Old town), was formed in 1661.

The English soon considered New Netherland an impediment to English settlements to the north and south, and conflicts with the Dutch over boundaries and trade, especially on Long Island and in what is now Connecticut, led Charles II to grant the colony to his brother James, Duke of York, in March 1664. Colonel Richard Nicolls was then sent to seize the colony, accompanied by four warships and several hundred soldiers. On 28 August his force sailed into New Amsterdam and set up a blockade. The city was virtually defenseless: the walls of the fort were never intended to withstand attack by a fleet and lay in disrepair, less than a third of the supply of gunpowder was usable, and enthusiasm for fighting was so low that only about 150 soldiers could be deployed. Although Stuyvesant was determined to resist, cooler heads prevailed and New Amsterdam formally surrendered on 8 September without a shot fired. The rest of New Netherland soon did the same. Fort Amsterdam and New Amsterdam were respectively renamed Fort James and New York City, and the English conquest was recognized by the Treaty of Breda (July 1667), which ended the Second Anglo-Dutch War.

Life changed little for the Dutch under English rule. By the terms of surrender they were given the same rights as English citizens. Dutch and English members of the upper class shared almost equally in the city's administration, and Dutch culture and institutions remained dominant. As there were few unmarried English women, intermarriage between the English and Dutch became common. Families often attended the Reformed church, which continued to conduct services in the Dutch language. Dutch families, particularly wealthy ones, learned English, and merchants and traders were among the first to adopt English customs. English rule was interrupted briefly in August 1673, when a Dutch naval force commanded by Cornelis Evertsen and Antony Colve entered the harbor and forced the English garrison to surrender within a few days; the victors renamed the city New Orange after the Dutch royal family and soon recaptured other former Dutch settlements. The colony reverted to England by the treaty of Westminster (February 1674), ending the Third Anglo-Dutch War, and the name New York City was restored.

The relationship between the Dutch and the English in the colony remained complex. The ascension of William of Orange to the English throne in February 1689 fostered greater cooperation between them, but divisions surfaced later that year, when the Dutch masses, resentful of English rule, supported Leisler's Rebellion, which was opposed by virtually all the English (as well as by Dutch merchants, officials, and clergymen). The rebellion was put down in 1691 but remained a divisive political issue in the city for years afterward. In 1749 the Swedish botanist Peter Kalm wrote that the Dutch remained the largest segment of the population in both the city and the colony. The clergy of the Reformed church supported the patriots, whom families such as the Van Cortlandts, the Frelinghuysens, the Rutgers, and the Schuylers aided during the American Revolution (Washington referred to New York and New Jersey as his "loyal Dutch belt"). The first federal census (1790) showed that eighty thousand Dutch immigrants and descendants of Dutch settlers lived within fifty miles (eighty kilometers) of the city.

The number of Dutch immigrants decreased steadily after the surrender of New Netherland until the mid nineteenth century, and the importance of Dutch culture gradually eroded as the city became more heterogeneous. The Dutch language was nonetheless common in the city until the end of the nineteenth century, and during legislative debates about a new state constitution in 1846 it was suggested that literacy in both English and Dutch be a requirement to vote. A number of Dutch families settled in the area and became leaders of the city's political and mercantile élite: the Van Cortlandts, Stuyvesants, Vanderbilts, and Van Rensselaers, and later the Roosevelts and Van Wycks. About twenty thousand Dutch immigrants moved to the United States between 1840 and 1861, about fifty thousand during the two decades after the Civil War, and about 75,000 in the early years of the twentieth century; most entered the country at Ellis Island but later settled near the Great Lakes. No Dutch residential quarter was ever formed in the city, but Dutch customs were preserved in the work of such writers as James Fenimore Cooper, Harold Frederic, Charles Fenno Hoffman, David Murdoch, James Kirke Paulding, and Washington Irving, whose mock epic *A History of New York* was supposedly written by Diedrich Knickerbocker, an eccentric antiquarian whose name was adopted by a school of writers, a hospital in Manhattan, a magazine, a hotel, a baseball team and a basketball team, and a brand of beer. The St. Nicholas Society was formed in 1853 and the Holland Society in 1885, which from 1922 published a historical quarterly, *De Halve Maen* (The Half Moon). From 1903 the Netherland Club of New York was a private association for professionals and executives, and the Queen Wilhelmina Chair in the history, language, and literature of the Netherlands was inaugurated in 1913 at Columbia University. Between 1945 and 1965 eighty thousand Dutch immigrants moved to the United States, where many settled in New York City and Los Angeles.

In the mid 1990s New York City was known for its well-preserved examples of Dutch colonial architecture, including Dyckman House in Inwood (the only farmhouse of its kind remaining in Manhattan), Voorlezer House (at Richmondtown Restoration), the Lefferts Homestead in Flatbush, the Wyckoff–Bennett House in Sheepshead Bay, the Lent farmhouse in Steinway, and the Cornelius Van Wyck house in Douglaston Manor.

Arnold Mulder: *Americans from Holland* (Philadelphia: J. P. Lippincott, 1947)
Harry S. Lucas: *Netherlands in America: Dutch Immigration to the United States and Canada, 1789–1950* (Ann Arbor: University of Michigan Press, 1955)
Gerald F. De Jong: *The Dutch in America, 1609–1974* (Boston: Twayne, 1975)
Alice P. Kenney: *Stubborn for Liberty: The Dutch in New York* (Syracuse, N.Y.: Syracuse University Press, 1975)
Henri A. van der Zee and Barbara van der Zee: *A Sweet and Alien Land: The Story of Dutch New York* (New York: Viking, 1978)
Robert P. Swierenga, ed.: *The Dutch in America: Immigration, Settlement, and Cultural Change* (New Brunswick, N.J.: Rutgers University Press, 1985)

Thomas E. Bird, Gerald F. De Jong

Dutch Farms. Name used until about 1845 by CONCORD.

Dutch Hill. A shantytown on the East Side of Manhattan in the mid nineteenth century, near the intersection of 39th Street and 1st Avenue. Like most squatter settlements of the time it was situated north of the built-up area of the city. By the end of the Civil War the growth and northward movement of population made real estate in the area valuable, and the squatters were displaced.

Kenneth T. Jackson

Dutch Kills. Neighborhood in northwestern Queens, lying within Long Island City and largely occupied by Queens Plaza at the western end of the Queensborough Bridge. The area was an important road junction in the American Revolution and the British set up camps there during their occupation of the city from 1776 to 1783. There were scattered farms during the nineteenth century. The hamlet joined Hunter's Point, Ravenswood, Astoria, and Steinway to form Long Island City in 1870. The name is still used locally, and there is a Dutch Kills Community Association.

Vincent Seyfried

Dutch Reformed church. Original name of the REFORMED CHURCH IN AMERICA.

Dutchtown (i). Alternative name of KLEINDEUTSCHLAND.

Dutchtown (ii). Former neighborhood in northwestern Brooklyn, lying east of Williamsburg and mostly along Scholes Avenue,

Meserole Street, and Montrose Avenue. It was settled in the early 1840s by German immigrants who were unwelcome in Williamsburgh, which was mostly Irish and English. The German Savings Bank opened in 1866 on Montrose Avenue, and St. John the Evangelist Lutheran Church was formed on Ten Eyck Street. There was also a local newspaper, the *Triangel.* Germans were eventually accepted in Williamsburgh and by the end of the nineteenth century were its dominant ethnic group.

James Bradley

Duyckink, Evert A(ugustus) (*b* New York City, 23 Nov 1816; *d* New York City, 13 Aug 1878). Writer and editor. He was the son of Harriet June Duyckink (1793–1837) and Evert Duyckink (1765–1833), a successful publisher and bookseller on Water Street in Manhattan who was in turn a descendant of Everett Duÿckink, a painter and glazier who sailed to America from the Netherlands with the Dutch West India Company. In 1835 he graduated from Columbia College; like his brother George L(ong) Duyckink (*b* New York City, 17 Oct 1823; *d* New York City, 30 March 1863) a graduate of Geneva Academy (now Hobart College), he studied law and was admitted to the bar but never practiced. The careers of the two brothers were closely linked: they belonged to the group known as "young America," which espoused literary nationalism and campaigned for fairness in international copyright laws; and together they undertook a number of publications, notably the periodical *Literary World* (1847–53) and the *Cyclopaedia of American Literature* (1856, rev. 1866). Through these activities they became acquainted with many of the great writers of the nineteenth century, including Melville, Poe, Washington Irving, and James Fenimore Cooper. Evert A. Duyckink also published works by Hawthorne and William G. Simms as the editor of the Library of American Books (1845–47) and by Dickens, Carlyle, and Goethe as the editor of the Library of Choice Reading.

Mary B. Bowling

Dvořák, Antonín (Leopold) (*b* Nelahozeves, near Kralupy, Bohemia, 8 Sept 1841; *d* Prague, 1 May 1904). Composer. In June 1891 he was invited to assume the directorship of the National Conservatory of Music in New York City by its founder Jeannette Thurber, and after accepting a two-year appointment he arrived in the city in September 1892. He lived with his family in a four-story building at 327 East 17th Street. In addition to teaching at the conservatory he composed several works while living in the city, including his symphony *From the New World* (given its première at Carnegie Hall on 16 December 1893) and his Cello Concerto (November 1894 to February 1895). He also wrote articles for the *New York Herald* ("Real Value of Negro Melodies," 21 May 1893) and *Harpers New Monthly Magazine* ("Music in America," vol. 110 (1895), 428). After signing a two-year extension of his contract on 28 April 1894 he submitted his resignation to Thurber on 17 August 1895 and returned to Prague in November.

Dyckman House. Historic house in Manhattan, at 204th Street and Broadway in Inwood. It was built about 1785 by William Dyckman, a grandson of the Westphalian immigrant Jan Dyckman, who settled the area in 1661. The house was sold in 1868 but reacquired by the family in 1915, restored, and given to the city. It is made of fieldstone, brick, and white clapboard and has a typically Dutch gambrel roof. The summer kitchen at the south end may predate the rest of the house; the front and back porches were added in 1825. There are period rooms including parlors and a colonial kitchen, as well as exhibits of artifacts from the area. Dyckman House is the last remaining farmhouse in Manhattan.

Bashford Dean and A. M. Welch: *The Dyckman House* (New York: Gilliss, 1916)
Historic Houses in New York City Parks (New York: Department of Parks and Recreation / Historic House Trust of New York City, 1989)

Jonathan Kuhn

dyes. The manufacture of dyes is discussed in the entry PAINTS, DYES, AND VARNISHES.

Dyker Heights. Neighborhood in southwestern Brooklyn, bounded to the north by 8th Avenue and 62nd Street, to the east by New Utrecht and 18th avenues, to the south by Gravesend Bay and Fort Hamilton, and to the west by 8th Avenue and Fort Hamilton Parkway; it encompasses Dyker Beach Park on Gravesend Bay and the huge Dyker Beach Golf Course to its north. Once part of the town of New Utrecht, the area is often considered a section of Bay Ridge. It may have been named for two Van Dykes who helped to divide the land in 1719 or for the dikes used to drain and reclaim marshland that once covered most of the area. It remained largely rural into the early twentieth century, when developers built a number of one- and two-family houses. Mansions along 11th Avenue afforded magnificent views of the Narrows and Gravesend Bay. A business district developed along 13th Avenue. In the mid 1990s the neighborhood was chiefly residential. Most of the housing consisted of one-family detached houses, and the population was predominantly Italian; many families had lived there for four or five generations and put up elaborate, brightly lit lawn displays at Christmastime.

Ellen Marie Snyder-Grenier

Dylan, Bob [Zimmerman, Robert] (*b* Duluth, Minn., 24 May 1941). Singer and songwriter. He taught himself the guitar and harmonica and played in rock bands as a teenager. In January 1961 he moved to New York City, where he began performing at nightclubs and coffee houses in Greenwich Village under his new surname, taken in honor of Dylan Thomas (he made the change legally in August 1962). His performances of traditional folk songs and original compositions, his unique "talkin' blues" singing style, and his witty monologues earned him a devoted following. In April 1961 he was the opening act for John Lee Hooker at Gerde's Folk City on MacDougal Street. A favorable review in the *New York Times* by Robert Shelton soon led to a contract with Columbia Records, for which he recorded such influential protest songs as "Blowing in the Wind," "A Hard Rain's A-Gonna Fall," and "Like a Rolling Stone." In the 1960s he rented a small apartment at 161 West 4th Street and frequently performed in Greenwich Village. He also resided at 94 MacDougal Street and the Chelsea Hotel before moving to Malibu, California, in 1973.

Robert Shelton: *No Direction Home: The Life and Times of Bob Dylan* (New York: Ballantine, 1986)
Clinton Heylin: *Bob Dylan behind the Shades* (New York: Simon and Schuster, 1991)

Robert Sanger Steel

E

Eagle Insurance Company. Firm of fire insurers, the first in New York City organized as a stock company. Incorporated on 4 April 1806 with capital stock of $500,000, it assumed the fire insurance portfolio of the Union Insurance Company of New Jersey in 1813 (this was the first known reinsurance agreement in the United States). Later in the century the firm was acquired by the Norwich Union Fire Insurance Society of Britain. In 1962 it became a subsidiary of Continental Insurance Companies, which acquired all the American business of Norwich Union; the firm was renamed the National Reinsurance Company to reflect its focus on property and casualty reinsurance. In 1980 it moved its headquarters to Stamford, Connecticut. It is now an independent company.

Robert J. Gibbons

Eames, Charles (*b* St. Louis, 17 June 1907; *d* St. Louis, 21 Aug 1978). Designer. He studied architecture in Missouri and at the Cranbrook Academy of Art in Bloomfield, Michigan, where he led the design department. In 1941 his entry of a molded plywood chair won a design competition at the Museum of Modern Art; after the Second World War the museum presented an exhibition of furniture that he designed with his wife, the painter Ray Kaiser Eames, with whom he won a number of awards including the first Kaufman International Design Award. The two were also innovative filmmakers who were engaged as consultants by such leading corporations as International Business Machines and Westinghouse.

Connections: The Work of Charles and Ray Eames (Los Angeles: UCLA Art Council, 1976)

James E. Mooney

Earle [née Beavers], **Genevieve** (*b* New York City, 1883; *d* Bellport, N.Y., 6 March 1956). Councilwoman. She graduated from Adelphi College in 1907 and was employed at the Bureau of Municipal Research from 1908 to 1913. A leader of the suffrage movement, she was a founder of the Women's City Club, supported Mayor John Purroy Mitchel's campaign for reelection, and belonged to the League of Women Voters. In 1935 she was the only woman on the Charter Revision Commission and from 1937 she won five elections to the City Council as a fusion candidate from Brooklyn, becoming the minority leader of the council in 1939. She drew much attention in 1944 when she opposed censorship of Noël Coward's book *Middle East Diary*, which allegedly slurred soldiers from Brooklyn. Earle's published writings include *Pandora Buys a Book* (1933).

Elisabeth Israels Perry

earthquakes and faults. Many geological faults transect the New York metropolitan region, and in New York City the faults tend to run from northwest to southeast. The major faults in New York City are often quite distinctive because the fault zones are characterized by shattered rock that has weathered, disintegrated, and been washed away by water, leaving valleys where the faults are. In northern Manhattan the Dyckman Street fault valley is readily apparent where it transects the Fort Washington Ridge. There is another distinctive fault valley paralleling 155th Street. One of the most conspicuous fault valleys in the area is paralleled by 125th Street. Where this fault zone bisects the Manhattan Ridge, erosion has created the Manhattanville Valley, which has a depth of about two hundred feet (sixty meters) below sea level but is filled with glacial deposits to just slightly above sea level. There is also a fault zone running southeast from about 110th Street and 5th Avenue to about 96th Street and the East River. The present course of the Bronx River appears to be partly controlled by a fault in the northern Bronx. This is particularly apparent in the New York Botanical Garden near the Snuff Mill Restaurant, where the river cuts through soft, highly metamorphosed mica schist of the Manhattan formation to create a beautiful gorge. This is thought to have been created about 20 to 30 million B.P.

It has been postulated that the ground beneath metropolitan New York could be a major shear zone where land masses slide past one another at the rate of about half an inch (thirteen millimeters) a year, with a strain similar to that along the San Andreas fault in California (although California is positioned on the boundary between two plates, whereas New York City rests near the middle of one plate). Records of the U.S. Geological Survey show that there is considerable seismic activity in western Long Island, Westchester County, and southwestern Connecticut. Most earthquakes in New York City have been barely perceptible (although the most severe, in 1737, in 1783, and on 10 August 1884, are retrospectively estimated to have measured 5.0 on the Richter scale), but the strain that builds up along the shear zone is likely to be relieved by a stronger earthquake at some point.

Steven D. Garber

Eastchester. Neighborhood in the northeastern Bronx, bounded to the north by the city of Mount Vernon, to the east by Co-op City, to the south by Edenwald, and to the west by Wakefield. Anne Hutchinson built a house there in 1642 after fleeing Puritans in New England and was killed in the same year by Wiechquaesgeck Indians (the Hutchinson River is named for her). Thomas Pell claimed the area in 1654 as part of a purchase from the Siwanoy Indians and in 1665 sold a large part of it to ten farmers of English stock. This was called at first the Ten Farms and then the town of Eastchester, the center of which was just across the current city limit in what is now Mount Vernon. Colonial farmers raised livestock and then grew wheat; a miller, blacksmith, cobbler, and tailor also worked in the area, and boats delivered goods to and from Manhattan by way of the Hutchinson River once a week. During most of the American Revolution the area was occupied by British and Hessian forces and subjected to raids by irregular American troops. In 1797, when the Boston Road connected the town directly to the Harlem Bridge (now the 3rd Avenue Bridge), President John Adams temporarily governed the nation from the farmhouse of his daughter and son-in-law when an epidemic of yellow fever prevented him from traveling to a meeting of the Congress in Philadelphia.

Farmers in the nineteenth century provided fruit, vegetables, and dairy products for the local market. By the middle of the century the grandchildren of Elizabeth Ann Seton purchased an estate of fifty-one acres (twenty-one hectares), part of which later became Seton Falls Park. In 1877 the town built on Dyre Avenue the Village of Eastchester School, later known as the Little Red Schoolhouse (now a city landmark). The 1890s saw the incorporation of Wakefield as a village and of Mount Vernon as a city, thus bisecting the town: the need for a modern sewer system led residents of the southern part to favor annexation by New York City, which was accomplished in 1895. In 1912 the New York, Westchester and Boston Railway built a high-speed commuter line with a station at Dyre Avenue, and in 1937 the city purchased the right of way south of the border with Westchester County for the Dyre Avenue line of Interborough Rapid Transit. This and the construction in the 1950s of the New England Thruway and Bruckner Expressway drew people and business to the area. In the mid 1990s the neighborhood remained industrial, with one- and two-family houses predominating. The population is ethnically diverse, with blacks, Italians, and Germans in the majority.

Stephen Jenkins: *The Story of the Bronx* (New York: G. P. Putnam's Sons, 1912)

Lloyd Ultan: *The Beautiful Bronx, 1920–1950* (New Rochelle, N.Y.: Arlington House, 1979)

John McNamara: *History in Asphalt: The Origin of Bronx Street and Place Names* (New York: Bronx County Historical Society, 1984)

Lloyd Ultan

East Concourse. Neighborhood in the west central Bronx, bounded to the north by Tremont Avenue, to the east by Webster Avenue, to the south by East 149th Street, and to the west by the Grand Concourse. Its name dates to the formation in 1969 of the East Concourse Neighborhood Action Committee and was later adopted by the city planning commission, but it is still not widely used. The development of the area coincided with the construction of the railroads in the late nineteenth century; much of the housing stock consists of apartment buildings erected at the time the subways were built between the world wars. The population is heavily Latin American and black.

Stephen A. Stertz

East Elmhurst. Neighborhood in north central Queens (1985 pop. 16,500), bounded to the north by La Guardia Airport, to the east by Flushing Bay, to the south by Northern Boulevard, and to the west by 85th Street. It was developed in 1905 as a neighborhood of frame houses on lots measuring forty by one hundred feet (twelve by thirty meters); those on the bluff overlooking the bay had private beaches. Before the Second World War the area was wholly residential, but proximity to the airport brought commercial development to Ditmars Boulevard.

Vincent Seyfried

Eastern Orthodox. New York City has many Eastern Orthodox churches where people from eastern Europe, the Balkans, and the Middle East worship in different languages according to the customs of their homelands. These various Orthodox groups are not denominations but belong to one undivided Eastern Orthodox Church: all acknowledge the primacy of the Ecumenical Patriarch of Constantinople and adhere to the canons defined by the seven ecumenical councils under the Byzantine empire (330–1453). Their differences in the United States are jurisdictional and derive from historical circumstances related to their foundation in North America, and to the impact of political events in Europe. The two largest Eastern Orthodox groups in the United States are the Greek Orthodox Archdiocese of North and South America, which on its formation in 1921 established headquarters in New York City and continues to maintain them there, and the Orthodox Church of America, which had its headquarters in the city until the 1970s. Other Orthodox jurisdictions with national headquarters in New York City include the Bulgarian Eastern Orthodox Church Diocese of New York, the Patriarchal Parishes of the Russian Orthodox Church in the United States and Canada, and the Ukrainian Orthodox Church of America and Canada. Major Orthodox groups with churches in the city include the Serbian Orthodox Church, the Antiochian Orthodox Christian Archdiocese of North America, the Ukrainian Orthodox Church of the USA, the Romanian Orthodox Episcopate of America, the American Carpatho-Russian Orthodox Greek Catholic Diocese of the USA, and the Albanian Orthodox Archdiocese of America.

Eastern Orthodoxy was established in New York City by immigrants from eastern and southern Europe. In 1870 an Orthodox parish was organized by Nicholas Bjerring, a convert from Roman Catholicism who had been ordained in Russia. Under state legislation enacted in the following year the church was incorporated into the Russian consulate and its diplomatic representatives. Bjerring held services in English in his home at 951 2nd Avenue in Manhattan, where he set up a chapel with a sign above the entrance reading "Greek–Russian Church." The chapel was used by Russians, Greeks, Serbs, and Syrians until 1883, when the Russian government withdrew its financial support and the chapel was forced to close. During the next ten years Greek immigrants in New York City formed their own churches outside the Russian Orthodox hierarchy in the United States.

With the encouragement of Prince George of Greece, who visited the city in 1891, about five hundred Greek immigrants later in the year formed the Hellenic Brotherhood of Athena to collect donations for a Greek church, which would allow immigrants to worship in their own language and help them to preserve their ethnic identity. Archimandrite Paisios Pherentinos was sent to New York City by the Holy Synod of Greece to celebrate the first divine liturgy of the Church of the Holy Trinity in January 1892. Regular church services were held in a Protestant church on West 53rd Street near 8th Avenue in Manhattan; Pherentinos also performed services for Greek families residing in Coney Island and other parts of Brooklyn. In 1904 the church purchased its own building at 151–53 East 72nd Street. Disagreement within the church led to the establishment in 1893 of the Annunciation Church, presided over by Archimandrite Callinikos Dilvelis, who had been sent to New York City by the Ecumenical Patriarch in Constantinople. After several shifts the church purchased a building at 310 West 50th Street in 1915. St. Nicholas Chapel, a Russian church formed in the early 1890s, flourished from 1896 under the leadership of Alexander Hotovitsky. In 1902 he succeeded in obtaining financial support from Russia for the establishment of St. Nicholas Cathedral at 15 East 97th Street, which became the center of the Russian Mission Diocese for North America. A Syro-Arabian Mission was formed by the Russian Orthodox Church in 1892 for Arabic-speaking Orthodox Christians in the city, and in 1895 a group of Syrian immigrants formed the Syrian Orthodox Benevolent Society; in the following year Archimandrite Raphael Hawaweeny formed the first Syrian Orthodox parish in the United States at 77 Washington Street in lower Manhattan, the center of the Syrian immigrant community. By 1900 about three thousand Syrian immigrants had settled in Brooklyn and in 1902 Hawaweeny purchased a building at Pacific Street in Brooklyn and formed St. Nicholas Cathedral, now considered the mother parish of the United Stated Antiochian Archdiocese.

The headquarters of the Russian Church in the Americas were transferred from San Francisco to New York City in 1903. In the following year its bishop, Tikhon, attempted unsuccessfully to assert Russian ecclesiastic authority over the Greek Orthodox churches in New York City. The city's Arabic-speaking Orthodox Christians continued to acknowledge Russian jurisdiction, and there was a Serbian mission within the Russian Church. In 1904 Tikhon received permission from the Russian Holy Synod to raise Hawaweeny to the rank of bishop of Brooklyn, and in the following year he himself became the first Eastern Orthodox archbishop in the United States. The Greeks did not recognize the jurisdiction of the Russian hierarchy in New York City and remained without a bishop of their own until 1918.

The number of members of Greek and other Orthodox congregations in New York City was estimated at 3500 by a Greek newspaper in 1895 (and at more than a thousand by the *New York Times* in January of the following year). These numbers increased markedly during the first decades of the twentieth century as more immigrants from Russia, the Balkans, and the Middle East settled in New York City. A census in 1916 reported that the Greeks alone had four parishes and 22,000 communicants. The First World War led to an increase in the number of Eastern Orthodox immigrants who settled in New York City and caused jurisdictional divisions that persisted into the 1990s. In Russia the Bolshevik Revolution led the Russian Church in the United States (the Metropolia) to declare itself autonomous in 1918. In the following year Ukrainian refugees also established an autonomous church in the United States. Although the successor to the Metropolia, the autonomous Orthodox Church of America, was recognized by Moscow in 1970, jurisdictional divisions persisted among other Russian Orthodox groups in the United States over relations with the patriarchate in Moscow. Similar jurisdictional divisions occurred within the Serbian, Bulgarian, Albanian, and Romanian churches after the Second World War when the Soviet Union occupied most of Eastern Europe. These divisions were further complicated with the breakup of the Soviet bloc in the late 1980s.

Constance Tarasar, ed.: *Orthodox America, 1794–1976: Development of the Orthodox Church in America* (Syosset, N.Y.: Orthodox Church in America, 1975)

George Papaioannou: *From Mars Hill to Manhattan: The Greek Orthodox in America under Patriarch Athenagoras I* (Minneapolis: Light and Life, 1976)

Miltiades B. Efthimiou and George A. Christopoulos, eds.: *History of the Greek Orthodox Church in America* (New York: Greek Orthodox Archdiocese, 1984)

Constantine G. Hatzidimitriou

Eastern Parkway. A grand boulevard and scenic landmark in Brooklyn, designed in 1866 by Frederick Law Olmsted and Calvert Vaux. Stretching from Grand Army Plaza through Crown Heights to Ralph Avenue, it was the first six-lane parkway in the world. The broad median strips were built as promenades and equestrian paths, the side lanes as service roads for carriages. Some of the most spectacular nineteenth-century houses in Brooklyn, many on what has long been known as "Doctors' Row," line the thoroughfare. A large Tudor building at 770 Eastern Parkway is the world headquarters of the Lubavitch movement.

Kenneth T. Jackson

Easter Parade. An informal procession held on 5th Avenue on Easter. Begun after the Civil War as a fashion promenade, it was an extension of the weekly "church parade" and drew on European traditions of displaying new clothes, symbolic of new life, during an Easter Sunday walk, one of few activities considered acceptable under strict Sabbath laws. It took its current form in the 1880s. The parade began when the élite stepped out of such grand churches as St. Thomas Episcopal Church, the Fifth Avenue Presbyterian Church, and St. Patrick's Cathedral after the Easter Sunday service and strolled along "millionaire row" (5th Avenue in the 50s) before visiting friends and having lunch at lavish hotels nearby. Milliners and dressmakers from all over the country, especially the Lower East Side, flocked to watch and make sketches of the participants' outfits; department stores produced copies for sale within weeks. At the turn of the century extravagant hats for women became the focus of the parade. Often broad-brimmed and trimmed with ostrich feathers, flowers, and stuffed birds, these made for a "mushroom" silhouette when worn with tube dresses and may have inspired homemade paper bonnets popular at Easter cotillions during the following decade. Smaller Easter parades were held in other parts of the city, including Grand Street in Harlem, but the one on 5th Avenue was the best known and became the subject of songs by George M. Cohan (1927) and Irving Berlin (1933). In later years it attracted demonstrators promoting peace, church attendance, and animal rights, protesting unemployment and the commercialization of Holy Week, and appealing for amnesty for refugees and political prisoners. In the mid 1990s the Easter Parade was known for elegance blended with such whimsical touches as full costumes, fanciful performing ensembles, and exuberant bonnets covered with Easter eggs, bunnies, flowers, and other emblems of spring, usually made and worn by women. A popular tourist event, it extends along 5th Avenue from Rockefeller Center to Central Park from about noon to 2:30 p.m.

William S. Walsh: *Curiosities of Popular Customs and of Rites, Ceremonies, Observances, and Miscellaneous Antiquities* (Philadelphia: J. B. Lippincott, 1898)
Lillian Eichler: *The Customs of Mankind with Notes on Modern Etiquette and the Newest Trend in Entertainment* (Garden City, N.Y.: Doubleday, 1925)

Barbara Kirshenblatt-Gimblett

East Flatbush. Neighborhood in northeastern Brooklyn (1990 pop. 114,898), bounded to the north by East New York Avenue, to the east and south by Kings Highway, and to the west by Nostrand Avenue; it was once called Rugby. Development began in the 1920s after Interborough Rapid Transit extended its subway to Utica Avenue and to Flatbush Avenue along Nostrand Avenue. Modest one- and two-family attached brick houses were built and most of the residents were middle-class Jews and Italians. During the late 1960s many whites left and were replaced by blacks and immigrants from the Caribbean, who continued to settle in the neighborhood during the following decades. East Flatbush in the 1980s drew immigrants from Jamaica (accounting for about 30 percent of the total), Haiti (about 20 percent), Guyana, Trinidad and Tobago, Grenada, Barbados, St. Vincent and the Grenadines, and Panama. A medical complex stands on Clarkson Avenue that includes the Kings County Hospital (1831), Brooklyn State Hospital, and the New York Downstate Medical Center.

Stephen Weinstein

East Harlem. Neighborhood in northern Manhattan (1990 pop. 105,508). The boundaries are imprecise but correspond roughly to East 142nd Street, the East River, East 96th Street, and Park Avenue. The area was rural for much of the nineteenth century. By the 1860s a residential settlement developed north and east of 110th Street and 3rd Avenue. The extension of elevated railways to the area in 1879 and 1880 and the construction of the Lexington Avenue subway in 1919 transformed the neighborhood. By the mid 1880s most streets were lined with bleak tenements, which initially housed poor German, Irish, and Jewish immigrants. About 1917 the Jewish population was ninety thousand, a community that along with that of Harlem (eighty thousand) constituted the second-largest Jewish community in the United States, after the Lower East Side. From the 1880s there was an influx of Italians, who numbered eighty thousand by 1930. Many lived in an enclave bounded by East 119th Street, the East River, East 99th Street, and 3rd Avenue. A central institution was a brand of Catholicism that incorporated folk traditions into popular religious festivals such as that of Our Lady of Mount Carmel. Mutual aid societies and similar organizations abounded. Puerto Ricans first moved to the neighborhood in the 1920s, and by 1930 most of the city's Puerto Rican residents lived there. Among local leaders were Leonard Covello, a principal of Benjamin Franklin High School widely respected for his openness and his skill at resolving conflicts, and Fiorello H. La Guardia, who represented the area in the U.S. Congress from 1923 to 1933; he called Lexington Avenue and 116th Street his "lucky corner" and always held rallies there on the eve of an election. This tradition was continued by his protégé, Vito Marcantonio, a radical who lived in the neighborhood all his life and achieved success by maintaining close relations with Italian and Puerto Rican constituents.

During the 1940s and 1950s Italians moved to less crowded areas and Puerto Ricans became the dominant group, numbering 63,000 in 1950 after an influx during the late 1940s. They formed an enclave where they opened bodegas and botánicas (stores selling herbs and other items used in religious ceremonies), some of which stood in an area known as La Marqueta, an enclosed street market beneath the elevated railroad on Park Avenue between 111th and 116th streets. Many religious institutions were formed: some residents belonged to Catholic churches, others joined revivalist Protestant churches opened in storefronts. Musical traditions were preserved by small record companies and dance halls that provided a source of social cohesion. Although many Puerto Ricans moved to other parts of the city during the 1950s they maintained ties to the neighborhood, which continued to be known as EL BARRIO. During a period of urban renewal in the 1950s the construction of public housing projects forced many residents to leave.

In the mid 1990s East Harlem was a racially diverse neighborhood in which more than a third of the population was Puerto Rican and the rest included blacks, Italians, and other groups. Residents continued to be besieged by persistent poverty, high unemployment, and poor housing. Among the institutions that have demonstrated the community's vitality and its struggle to overcome social ills are Central Park East (a nationally known group of alternative public schools) and the Museo del Barrio, which exhibits the art of Puerto Rican and other Latin American artists.

Virginia Sánchez Korrol: *From Colonia to Community: The History of Puerto Ricans in New York City, 1917–1948* (Westport, Conn.: Greenwood, 1983)
Gerald Meyer: *Vito Marcantonio: Radical Politician, 1902–1954* (Albany: State University of New York Press, 1989)

Michael Lapp

East Jamaica. Former name of HILLSIDE.

Eastman, Crystal (*b* Marlborough, N.Y., 25 June 1881; *d* New York City, 8 July 1928). Reformer, sister of Max Eastman. A graduate of New York University Law School (1907), she became involved in labor, peace, civil liberties, and women's issues and in 1910 drafted the first workers' compensation law in New York State. As the secretary of the American Union against Militarism she campaigned against the entry of the United States into the First World War. To defend conscientious objectors she formed the Civil Liberties Bureau with Roger Baldwin in April 1917, which eventually became the American Civil Liberties Union. Eastman withdrew because of poor health in mid 1917 and worked occasionally on peace and women's rights issues until the end of her life. She wrote *Work Accidents and the Law* (1910). About 1910 she lived with her brother at 118 Waverly Place.

Blanche Wiesen Cook, ed.: *Crystal Eastman on Women and Revolution* (New York: Oxford University Press, 1978)

Samuel Walker

Eastman, Max (Forrester) (*b* Canandaigua, N.Y., 4 Jan 1883; *d* Barbados, 25 March 1969). Writer and editor, brother of Crystal Eastman. A pupil of John Dewey at Columbia University, in 1912 he took over the periodical the *Masses*, which he transformed into the most important radical magazine of the age by recruiting the writers John Reed, Sherwood Anderson, and Carl Sandburg and the artists John Sloan and Art Young, whose political cartoons helped make the magazine widely known. After the *Masses* was suppressed by the federal government because of its opposition to the First World War he joined with his sister in 1918 to launch the *Liberator*, which was more overtly supportive of the Soviet Union. During a visit there in 1922 he allied himself with Leon Trotsky, and he became his leading American sponsor after returning to the United States in 1927, which made him a pariah among the American left. Over the years he expressed growing disenchantment with the Soviet Union, to the point where he had mixed feelings about supporting it during the Second World War. His writings appeared in increasingly conservative publications (including *Reader's Digest* and after the war the *National Review*), and he defended Senator Joseph R. McCarthy. He remained a contributing editor of *Reader's Digest* to the end of his life. Eastman's residences in New York City included 118 Waverly Place (from 1909 to 1911 and again from 1916), 27 West 11th Street (from 1912), 12 East 8th Street (from 1917), and 8 West 13th Street (for the last twenty-five years of his life).

Alexander Bloom

Eastman, Monk [Delaney, William; Osterman, Edward] (*b* Brooklyn, 1873; *d* New York City, 26 Dec 1920). Gang leader. He first worked as a "bouncer" at New Irving Hall, a dance hall, and later became powerful in gambling and prostitution. From the late nineteenth century to the early twentieth he led the Eastmans, a predominately Jewish gang based at 3rd Avenue and 14th Street; his greatest rival was the Five Points Gang, a predominantly Italian gang led by Paul Kelly. Like others before him he skillfully used his connections to Tammany Hall. He was sentenced to ten years in prison for a robbery he committed in 1904. After being freed he fought bravely in the First World War and was pardoned by Governor Alfred E. Smith, who restored his citizenship. Eastman was shot dead at 14th Street and 4th Avenue by a Prohibition agent with whom he had engaged in bootlegging and drug dealing.

Robert W. Snyder

East New York. Neighborhood lying east of Brownsville and Canarsie on the eastern edge of central Brooklyn, bounded to the north by Atlantic Avenue, to the east by South Conduit Boulevard, to the south by Linden Boulevard, and to the west by Pennsylvania Avenue; it overlaps New Lots and is sometimes said to include the neighborhoods of Highland Park, Cypress Hills, Spring Creek, and City Line. Once part of the town of New Lots, the area remained largely rural until 1835, when a merchant from Connecticut named John Pitkin bought up land north of what is now New Lots Avenue; he named the area to suggest that it was the eastern end of New York City and built a shoe factory at Williams Street and Pitkin Avenue, but the panic of 1837 forestalled his plans for development. There was an influx of German immigrants at mid century and the Deutsche Evangelische St. Johannes Kirche (now Grace Baptist Church) was built in 1885 at 223 New Jersey Avenue. Growth accelerated after the opening of the Williamsburg Bridge in 1903 and the completion of a subway line to New Lots by Interborough Rapid Transit in 1922. By 1940 the northern section was densely populated with German, Italian, Russian, Polish, and Lithuanian immigrants. Urban renewal in Brownsville in the 1950s and 1960s led a large number of blacks to settle in East New York. Many whites left; decay set in as buildings were abandoned and absentee landlords neglected their properties. These problems worsened after corruption in the U.S. Department of Housing and Urban Development resulted in foreclosures on housing by the federal government, leaving vacant buildings that were eventually destroyed by arson. Unemployment was high and the area deteriorated. One of the first revitalization projects was the East Brooklyn Industrial Park (1980). Private houses were built under the auspices of the Council of East Brooklyn Churches, including "Nehemiah" houses, one-family row houses of two stories that are especially common along Blake Avenue. Other housing includes two-story detached and semidetached houses, a few apartment buildings, and multistory public housing. In the 1980s East New York attracted immigrants from the Dominican Republic (accounting for a quarter of the total), Jamaica (accounting for somewhat fewer), Guyana, Haiti, Honduras, Ecuador, Trinidad and Tobago, and Panama. The neighborhood in the mid 1990s was mostly black and Latin American, with a small but growing number of Asians. The main commercial thoroughfares are Pitkin Avenue, New Lots Avenue, and Pennsylvania Avenue.

Ellen Marie Snyder-Grenier

East River. A saltwater estuary, or strait, that separates Manhattan Island and the Bronx from the western end of Long Island (Brooklyn and Queens) and connects Upper New York Bay with Long Island Sound. It joins the Harlem River about eight and a half miles (fourteen kilometers) north of the Battery. One of its tributaries is a short commercial waterway called Newtown Creek that forms the natural boundary between Brooklyn and Queens. Although the river is navigable for its entire length of sixteen miles (twenty-six kilometers), its varying depth and narrowness

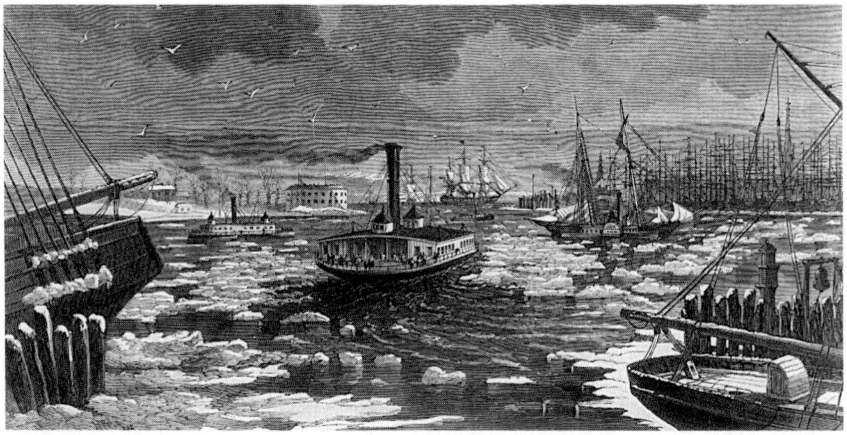

"Breaking Up of the Ice at New York: A View from the East River," Harper's Weekly, *8 February 1862*

subject it to strong tidal fluctuations. The river is spanned by six bridges, of which the most notable is the Brooklyn Bridge (1883), the first bridge linking Long Island with Manhattan. The piers along the East River near South Street in Manhattan were the city's major center of shipping until the beginning of the twentieth century.

Gerard R. Wolfe

East Village. Neighborhood in lower Manhattan, bounded to the north by 14th Street, to the east by Avenue D, to the south by Houston Street, and to the west by the Bowery and 3rd Avenue. It was considered a part of the Lower East Side until the early 1960s, when many intellectuals, artists, musicians, and writers seeking cheap housing moved to the area from Greenwich Village. Soon the population consisted of whites, blacks, Latin Americans, and Asians. Radicalism in politics and art flourished, and the area became known for its poetry houses, coffee houses, and bookshops (the Nuyorican Café, the Peace Eye Bookstore), saloons and bars (Phoebe's, Stanley's), theaters (the Fillmore East), jazz clubs (Slug's, the Five Spot), and restaurants (Paradox Macrobiotics, Orchidia Ukrainian Pizza). The neighborhood was also the home of the Annex Tavern, the Negro Ensemble Company, and several newspapers, including the *East Village Other* and *Rat.* During the 1970s drugs led to decline and social chaos, and neighborhood groups demanded police protection against heroin and crack dealers. Several important figures in punk rock, jazz, painting, and poetry nevertheless continued to live in the area, as did a large community of Ukrainians, which after a period of immigration in the 1970s grew in number to about twenty thousand. Conditions improved during the 1980s, when many art galleries exhibited the work of young artists like Keith Haring and Jean-Michel Basquiat, and the eastern part of the neighborhood (Avenues A to D) attracted recent immigrants from the Dominican Republic, China, the Philippines, the United Kingdom, Poland, and Japan. As gentrification led to a rapid increase in rents, squatters occupied and renovated buildings abandoned by the city; a squatters' movement emerged and riots occurred toward the end of the 1980s. Residents were also active in other political movements such as those on behalf of gay rights and the homeless. Principal thoroughfares include St. Mark's Place (8th Street), 2nd Avenue, and Avenue A; the heart of the neighborhood is Tompkins Square Park. In 1990 the police responded to complaints about drug dealing and filthy conditions by evicting the homeless and closing the park, giving rise to a new round of marches and riots. The park reopened in 1992. Well-known landmarks include St. Mark's Church in the Bowery and Cooper Union (1859), a free institution of higher learning that contains the oldest auditorium in New York City.

Graham Hodges

East Village Other. An "underground" newspaper launched in October 1965 by Allen Katzman, later a leader with Abbie Hoffman and Jerry Rubin of the movement known as the Yippies. Published at first monthly, then semimonthly, then (from 1968) weekly, the newspaper chronicled the counterculture of the 1960s, which in New York City was largely centered at St. Mark's Place. Its reporters, who made no pretense of objectivity, wrote extensively about the drug culture and about radical groups such as the Weathermen. Among those who were the subject of stories and interviews were the poet Allen Ginsberg, the artist Andy Warhol, and the comedian Dick Gregory. The newspaper was also known for running sexually explicit personal advertisements long before they became a feature of mainstream journalism. The *Other* ceased publication in February 1972.

Allen Katzman, ed.: *Our Time* (New York: Dial, 1972)

Thomas M. Hilbink

East Williamsburgh. An obsolete name for a part of west central Queens lying south of Metropolitan Avenue and west of Fresh Pond Road, within Ridgewood and abutting Brooklyn. The area was farmland for most of the nineteenth century; development followed the opening of an important trolley depot in 1881 and of the terminus of the Myrtle Avenue elevated line in 1888. The name fell into disuse during the First World War.

Vincent Seyfried

Ebbets Field. A ballpark in Brooklyn, opened on 9 April 1913 as the fourth home of the Brooklyn Dodgers. Charles Ebbets acquired the land for about $100,000, and the team spent $650,000 to construct an edifice of concrete and steel seating 18,000 (later 31,497) on only 4.5 acres (1.8 hectares). The result was very short foul lines: 297 feet (90.5 meters) to left field, 315 feet (ninety-six meters) to right field. The single largest gate was 41,209 for a doubleheader against the Giants on 30 May 1934, and the highest gate recorded in a single season was 1,807,526 (in 1947). The site of eight World Series, the field closed on 24 September 1957. The land is now occupied by the Jackie Robinson Apartments.

Steven A. Riess

Echo z Polski. Weekly newspaper launched in New York City in 1863 as the first Polish-language periodical in the United States. A political organ of immigrants, it supported the Polish insurrection against Russia that began in January 1863. It ceased publication in 1865.

James S. Pula

Ecker, Frederick H(udson) (*b* Phoenicia, N.Y., 30 Aug 1867; *d* New York City, 20 March 1964). Real-estate developer. During the first half of the twentieth century he led the Metropolitan Life Insurance Company in expanding into real-estate development. Under his direction the company in 1924 built Sunnyside, a residential development in Long Island City consisting of 2125 apartment units in fifty-four low-rise buildings; the development was exempt from property taxes for ten years. Appointed the company's president in 1929 and its chairman in 1936, Ecker in 1940 oversaw the construction of Parkchester, a complex of more than twelve thousand apartments for 35,000 residents in the northern Bronx; completed in 1941, it was the largest development of its kind undertaken by the company and served as a prototype for similar projects in San Francisco, Los Angeles, and Arlington, Virginia. He also promoted urban redevelopment in the 1940s with two major projects on the East Side of Manhattan – Stuyvesant Town and Peter Cooper Village – and with Riverton in Harlem.

Marquis James: *The Metropolitan Life: A Study in Business Growth* (New York: Viking, 1947)

Marc A. Weiss

economy. Settled as a trading post by the Dutch, New York City evolved into an important center of maritime trade and later of manufacturing. After the Second World War it became one of the world's largest financial capitals.

1. Colonial Period

During the early seventeenth century the Dutch West India Company acquired the Hudson Valley and established a trading post, New Amsterdam, at the southern end of Manhattan, which had an excellent port ac-

Occupations of Citizens of New York City, 1855

Blacksmiths 2,611	Laundresses 2,563
Butchers 2,643	Lawyers 1,112
Cabinet makers 2,606	Machinists 1,714
Carters and draymen 5,338	Masons and bricklayers 3,634
Clerks and accountants 13,807	Merchants 6,001
Coopers 1,018	Milliners 1,585
Confectioners 704	Peddlers 1,889
Dealers 1,025	Porters 3,052
Dressmakers 7,436	Sailors and mariners 4,717
Drivers 1,741	Servants 31,749
Engineers 867	Shipbuilding 1,146
Farmers 193	Shoemakers 6,745
Firemen 270	Stone cutters 1,755
Grocers 4,079	Tailors 12,609
Hat makers 1,422	Teachers 1,268
Jewelers 1,099	Tobacconists 1,996
Laborers 19,748	Wine and liquor dealers 619

cessible to Europe and the West Indies and to a deep hinterland free of waterfalls and replete with furs and grain for export. Stockholders were granted land with sixteen miles (twenty-six kilometers) of frontage on the Hudson River if they arranged for the passage and settlement of fifty persons. Under this policy Dutch fiefdoms were soon established on both sides of the river to Albany; one of the largest was that of the Rensselaer family, which lay along both sides and covered more than eleven hundred square miles (2816 square kilometers). The Dutch West India Company was interested primarily in commerce, not settlement, and established a policy of tolerance that benefited a number of groups, including Jewish refugees from Brazil. The company also brought African slaves to the colony. When the English took control the population was about fifteen hundred. In the following years English, Huguenot, and German communities took shape in the port and the number of black slaves increased. In 1734 the population was about nine thousand and 18 percent black. Trade, primarily with the Caribbean, remained the principal economic activity, and competition from other colonial settlements was stiff: the volume of the city's trade was less than half that of Charleston, South Carolina.

During the early seventeenth century many farmers and craftsmen in New Netherland were lured by the abundant resources of the Hudson Valley into the fur trade. As private traders they competed with the Dutch West India Company, which held a monopoly over the trade until 1638. At that time the fur trade became concentrated in the hands of a few exporters in the colony and four large firms in Amsterdam that set high export duties. Those who identified their occupation as peltry exporting during the mid seventeenth century were the wealthiest men in New Amsterdam. These wealthy merchants were hurt by the entry into the fur trade in the 1650s of the French and the English, who bought peltry from American Indians with specie, clothing, and agricultural implements, thus causing a devaluation of wampum. The English further disrupted the Dutch trade by passing the Act of Trade and Navigation of 1651, intended to keep colonial trade tied to England. Increased competition for a diminishing supply of peltry caused the Dutch to reduce their investments in the fur trade in New Amsterdam, and by the time of English conquest in 1664 they had begun to redirect the export trade from peltry to grain, and to expand the reach of their market from Amsterdam and New England to the West Indies and southern Europe. The growing emphasis on exporting grain by the 1680s met with resistance from farmers who wanted flexible selling prices and consumers who were afraid the practice would drive up grain prices in the city; in response merchants in New York City supported a bolting mo-

Leading Manufacturing Industries in New York City and Kings County in Selected Years, 1810–1987

New York City, 1810	Number of Establishments	Value of Products	
Sugar refining	1	$ 420,706	
Rope walks	6	387,200	
Spirits	11	301,838	
Breweries	15	259,908	
Tanneries	9	113,285	
Tobacco and snuff	1	36,500	
Moroccan skins	—	17,500	
Naileries	4	16,732	
Hatteries	5	12,750	
Chocolate	1	8,500	
All other industries	11	4,553	
Total	64	$1,579,472	
Kings County, 1810	Number of Establishments	Value of Products	
Rope walks	4	$108,000	
Spirits	2	80,000	
Tanneries	6	18,811	
Flaxen goods	—	12,087	
Woolen goods	—	3,763	
Cloths	—	1,375	
Moroccan skins	—	700	
Total	12	$224,736	
New York City, 1860	Number of Establishments	Number of Employees	Value of Products
Garments	398	26,857	$ 22,320,769
Sugar refining	14	1,494	19,312,500
Printing and publishing	154	4,025	10,179,155
Furniture	223	3,570	3,947,500
Boots and shoes	491	4,084	3,869,058
Gas	2	2,020	3,784,500
Provisions[1]	29	326	3,676,305
Bread, bakery products	264	1,099	3,325,993
Flour and meal	6	193	2,612,500
Iron castings	42	1,924	2,606,490
All other industries	2,752	44,612	83,472,599
Total	4,375	90,204	$159,107,369
Kings County, 1860	Number of Establishments	Number of Employees	Value of Products
Sugar refining	4	295	$ 3,794,000
Liquors	40	464	3,360,943
Oil	16	312	2,246,964
White lead	8	356	2,129,500
Hats and caps	19	787	1,632,456
Cordage	12	492	1,390,196
Machinery[2]	20	921	1,298,300
Ship and boat building	15	514	1,263,475
Bread, bakery products	122	412	1,139,845
Soaps and candles	5	47	858,200
All other industries	771	8,158	15,127,641
Total	1,032	12,758	$34,241,520
New York City, 1900	Number of Establishments	Number of Employees	Value of Products
Garments	8,266	90,950	$ 239,879,414
Sugar refining	12	3,075	88,598,113
Printing and publishing	1,431	22,960	78,736,099
Masonry, brick, and stone	383	10,236	43,353,473
Slaughtering, meat packing	52	1,932	42,879,218

(continued)

Leading Manufacturing Industries in New York City and Kings County in Selected Years, 1810–1987 *(Continued)*

Foundry, machine products	589	19,560	41,089,475
Malt liquors	89	200	39,105,837
Tobacco	1,841	20,519	37,998,261
Bread, bakery products	1,966	10,915	32,239,307
Carpentering	1,491	8,660	26,061,584
All other industries	23,656	273,756	701,408,000
Total	39,776	462,763	$1,371,358,468

New York City, 1940	Number of Establishments	Number of Employees	Value of Products
Garments	5,542	138,491	$ 962,274,953
Printing and publishing	689	10,544	300,745,053
Furs	1,832	10,872	150,682,842
Bread, bakery products	1,868	20,500	139,833,679
Meat packing, wholesaling	39	3,960	119,291,496
Commercial printing	1,415	13,268	80,131,125
Millinery	682	12,098	61,568,375
Malt liquors	22	1,403	58,703,356
Lithographing	174	5,622	36,236,137
Paints and varnishes	142	2,248	42,294,445
All other industries	14,246	293,660	2,156,898,814
Total	26,651	512,666	$4,108,750,275

New York City, 1967	Number of Establishments	Number of Employees	Value of Products
Printing and publishing	4,251	136,400	$ 2,615,400,000
Garments	10,026	243,300	2,544,600,000
Electronic equipment	772	46,400	566,700,000
Chemical products	654	20,300	479,100,000
Fabricated metal products	1,602	37,300	406,500,000
Textile mill products	1,252	33,800	347,000,000
Machinery	1,120	23,000	313,500,000
Beverages	134	10,900	255,700,000
Leather products	840	30,400	248,700,000
Paper products	544	21,200	234,400,000
All other industries	7,926	292,300	2,234,000,000
Total	29,121	895,300	$10,245,600,000

New York City, 1987	Number of Establishments	Number of Employees	Value of Products
Printing and publishing	3,060	102,000	$11,524,900,000
Garments	3,119	78,400	3,458,900,000
Chemicals	250	6,900	913,300,000
Electronic equipment	309	15,600	898,600,000
Jewelry, silverware	781	11,900	720,600,000
Fabricated metal products	771	16,700	705,900,000
Textile mill products	626	17,000	502,300,000
Industrial machinery	514	10,800	483,400,000
Paper products	245	10,700	410,100,000
Furniture and fixtures	493	10,100	395,100,000
All other industries	4,427	156,000	4,529,700,000
Total	14,595	436,100	$24,542,800,000

1. Pork, beef, preserved fruits and pickles.
2. Steam engines, hay and cotton presses.
Dash denotes zero.
Source: U.S. Bureau of the Census, Census of Manufactures

Compiled by James Bradley

nopoly to channel exportation and control distribution and sales of flour.

Trade with Amsterdam nevertheless remained lucrative for a few English and Dutch merchants, including Cornelis Steenwyck, Oloff Van Cortlandt, Jacques Cousseau, Nicholas de Meyer, Margareta Philipse, Thomas Lovelace, Nicholas Gouverneur, Francis Hooghlandt, Isaac Bedloo, Eagiduis Luyck, Cornelius van Huyven, Jacob Kip, William Beekman, Nicholas Bayard, and Johannes Van Brugh. By the 1680s firm connections were also forged with London by such English immigrant merchants as John Robinson, William Pinhorne, and Edward Antill, who vied with the Dutch for control of the agricultural hinterlands of New Jersey, Connecticut, and the Hudson Valley. Some merchants such as Adolphe Philipse and Abraham dePeyster began by trading with the Netherlands and eventually expanded into worldwide trade in timber, slaves, logwood from the West Indies, tobacco from Virginia, wines from southern Europe, and rice from South Carolina.

By the end of the seventeenth century the population of the colony was eighteen thousand and the number of importers and exporters had grown to about 150. Governors Henry Sloughter and Benjamin Fletcher sought to tie colonial commerce more closely to English firms and capital, but two international wars disrupted the local economy and made expansion difficult, and Fletcher's well-known collaboration with pirate traders tarnished his credibility. Smuggling was widespread in New York City and its surrounding ports after the colony's notorious experience with piracy in the East Indies and Madagascar in the 1680s and 1690s. Merchants actively smuggled in the West Indies, and many traded with forbidden areas or evaded payment of duties. Fletcher's successors Richard Coote, Lord Cornbury, and Robert Hunter established policies that were consistent with the mercantilism of London and discouraged smuggling; shifting groups of merchants experimented with interest-rate manipulations, government loans, shared risk taking in large partnerships, and diversification of both the import and export trades. During this period dry-goods wholesalers who traded primarily with English firms for manufactured goods consistently prospered; grain exporters who traded with Lisbon and Madeira dealt with an unstable market that brought either great fortune or great loss; and traders in the West Indies were subject both to the volatility of Caribbean sugar, molasses, and bills of exchange, and to the difficulty of predicting the size of exportable surpluses in grain, flour, and timber. The West Indies were the fastest-growing market for New York City: the Cortlandt, Schuyler, de Lancey, and de Vries families branched out to cover almost every port in the

Caribbean, and many traders' sons began trading there.

In 1760 the city's merchant community numbered about 450. Included in this group were transatlantic wholesalers, coastal traders, rising lesser merchants, and exporters who had elaborate networks of credit and debt in the colonies. The city's population also supported a great number of peddlers, small shopkeepers, independent craftsmen, tavern and inn keepers, and unskilled laborers. Fortunes rose and fell over the entire century, but by the 1760s about fifty merchant families were wealthy enough to endure periodic economic crises. These families enlarged their fortunes by using their close connections with international correspondents to take advantage of lowered interest rates on shipping, and by cornering markets in valuable commodities such as flaxseed, snuff, and sugar. During the Seven Years' War they profited from privateering, offered high-interest loans to the government, speculated in marine insurance underwriting, and traded with enemy nations in the Caribbean. Consumers enjoyed a widening array of new commodities and greater quantities of items once considered luxuries, and by the 1770s there were signs of an emerging middle class. An increased emphasis on flaxseed, potash, pearl ash, and other "infant industries" (small manufacturers situated outside the city) led to public discussions about future prosperity. Many inhabitants of the city prospered during the Seven Years' War, but in the postwar depression a large number of the newer fortunes were vulnerable to specie shortages, glutted markets for grain in the transatlantic markets, and competition from Philadelphia and New England.

British occupation during the American Revolution put a halt to the early manufactures and disrupted commerce and retailing. Although many of the wealthiest merchants were Loyalists the greatest number of them left the city, which provided opportunities for rising lesser merchants in the 1770s and for new immigrants in the 1780s. New Yorkers in the countryside, mostly patriots, developed economic liaisons with these merchants during the war. The two groups benefited from their alliance in the postwar reconstruction of the city, but the old antagonism between farmer and merchant arose in the debates over ratification of the Constitution, and economic quarrels about prices, embargoes, and paper money reasserted themselves.

Estimated Labor Force Participation in New York City by Sex, Race, and Hispanic Origin, 1930–1990

	Female				Male			
	Hispanic	White	Black	Other	Hispanic	White	Black	Other
1930	N/A	30.8	57.8	25.9	N/A	86.6	92.1	94.6
1940	N/A	32.5	50.7	27.3	N/A	81.1	80.8	86.5
1950	N/A	33.0	47.5	N/A	N/A	79.0	76.0	N/A
1960	38.0[1]	38.3	49.0	N/A	78.7[1]	78.2	78.5	N/A
1970	35.7	42.2	46.1	50.5[2]	74.7	73.9	71.4	70.9[2]
1980	40.7	46.6	51.3	59.3	70.1	70.2	64.5	76.0
1990	48.6	52.2	59.6	61.0	71.8	71.1	67.3	76.5

1. Puerto Rican birth or parentage.
2. Chinese only. Male and female participation rates are 80.6 and 37.3 for Japanese, 75.8 and 74.2 for Filipinos.

N/A = Not Available

Note: Figures are based on civilian labor force (from 1950 exclusive of armed forces), both employed and unemployed, aged 14 and older in 1930–60 and aged 16 and older in 1970–90. Figures for 1930 are estimates based on the category Gainful Workers, defined as persons who usually have an occupation.

Sources: U.S. Bureau of the Census, Census of Population 1930, 1940, 1950, 1960, 1970, 1980, 1990
Evelyn Mann and Joseph Salvo: *New York City's Labor Force,* 1970–1990 (New York: New York City Department of Planning, 1986)

Compiled by Nathan Kantrowitz

2. After 1776

By the eve of the American Revolution the population reached 22,000 and the volume of trade in New York City had increased markedly; it was not yet as large as that of Charleston, which in turn was smaller than those of Boston and Philadelphia. The city was overshadowed primarily by southern ports, which handled tobacco, rice, and indigo, the most important colonial exports. Bread, flour, dried fish, and wheat, the secondary exports, were shipped from ports in New England and the Middle Atlantic, including Baltimore and Philadelphia. New York and New Jersey had a mostly rural population that was only half as large as that of New England and about a third as large as that of Virginia and Maryland (including slaves). The Port of New York handled only 10 percent of the colonies' foreign trade in 1780 but quickly grew in importance during the American Revolution: while trade ceased in most other cities, it thrived in New York City, owing largely to the British occupation. In 1800 the city surpassed Philadelphia as the country's largest. Further disruptions in trade during the War of 1812 left New York City the country's dominant port.

In 1800 ten of the eleven largest cities in the United States lay on the East Coast, and the only exception, Albany, had access to the Atlantic by means of the Hudson River. The early nineteenth century marked the rise of interior waterways as the cheapest means to transport goods to market. New Orleans emerged as a rival to New York City after the Louisiana Purchase and the rapid settlement of Ohio, Indiana, and Illinois; its links to these areas along inland rivers helped to make its volume of foreign trade second only to that of New York City. The Erie Canal, which opened in 1825, linked the Hudson River to Lake Erie, providing a route between the entire Great Lakes region and the city, which by 1830 handled 40 percent of the country's foreign trade. The city's dominance was assured during these years by its ready access to markets and the interior and its concentration of mercantile and financial institutions. These features made it the only one of the nation's five largest cities suited for handling both imports and exports, and it soon determined the flow of imports, exports, and credit to and from the interior. During the two decades before the Civil War the use of interior waterways declined as railroads were built, leading to shifts within the hierarchy of American cities. Cincinnati, St. Louis, Pittsburgh, Louisville (Kentucky), and Buffalo grew rapidly and by 1850 were among the country's twelve largest cities. Chicago, which had a population of less than five thousand in the 1840s, was connected to New York City by rail in 1850, and by 1860 its population reached 100,000. The railroads were extended to the western plains, and a link built to New Orleans in 1859 threatened to draw bulk exports from the West and Midwest away from New York City to the South. This was forestalled by the Civil War, which suspended trade between Chicago and New Orleans.

Shortly before the war, manufactured goods accounted for only 10 percent of the country's exports, foodstuffs and raw materials for most of the rest. The second half of the nineteenth century saw the rise of manufacturing based primarily on coal and steel. Buffalo, Pittsburgh, Cleveland, Detroit, and Milwaukee became metropolitan centers serving as transport points between the coal fields in Appalachia and the iron ore mines at the western end of Lake Superior. Accumulations of capital and labor and proximity to markets, port facilities, and rail links helped older cities to become manufacturing centers as well, among them New York City, Chicago, Philadelphia, and Baltimore. Unlike the new manufacturing centers, these cities focused on goods tied to mass markets rather than sources of raw materials. In New York City manufacturers specialized in finished and semifinished nondurable consumer goods such as clothing, printed materials, textiles, leather goods, and tobacco products, rather than durable producer goods such as primary metals, machinery, and transportation equipment. The expansion of low-wage factory work led to a rise in immigration, and in 1900 factory workers in the city accounted for 11 percent of the national total. After the First World War immigration was sharply restricted and employment in manufacturing drew workers from the South and rural Puerto Rico. For many years New York City offered far more manufacturing jobs than any other American city.

New York City nevertheless remained more economically diversified than other cities. Factory work consistently accounted for a smaller share of the employment there than in such manufacturing centers as Cleveland, Pittsburgh, Detroit, and Buffalo. The city remained the country's leading port and center of commerce, finance, and business services; these assets attracted major corporations seeking to establish headquarters. At mid century the city remained the largest in the United States: by this time manufactured goods accounted for 60 percent of the country's exports, foodstuffs and raw materials for less than 25 percent. American manufacturing reached its peak during the Second World War, when it accounted for more than 41 percent of employment nationwide, and at the end of the war 140 of the country's five hundred largest industrial corporations had their headquarters in New York City, where the manufacturing era peaked earlier and passed more rapidly than elsewhere. The city's attractiveness as a manufacturing site was diminished by its congestion, aging physical plants, and rising costs of land and labor. As the real costs of transporting goods declined, manufacturers became able to supply the city's large market without being based there. Manufacturing employment in the city accounted for nearly 7 percent of the national total in 1950 and only 2 percent in 1990; during the same period the number of manufacturing jobs in the city declined from one million to 338,000, and manufacturing as a share of the city's total employment fell from 30 percent to 12 percent. In these years many corporations moved their headquarters to suburbs and smaller cities.

Manufacturing declined further in the following years, owing primarily to improvements in technology as well as a rise in real income that decreased spending for goods and increased that for services. The average output per worker grew faster than the demand for manufactured goods, the relative number of workers declined, and factory work accounted for less than 25 percent of the

Occupations of the Labor Force of New York City in Major Industry Groups

EMPLOYED PERSONS 16 YEARS AND OLDER, 1900–1930

	1900	1910	1920	1930
Agriculture	10,134	10,836	7,709	7,574
Clerical	N/A	234,860	402,414	535,315
Domestic and personal service	206,215	333,954	306,290	448,838
Manufacturing	419,594	873,497	952,312	1,021,199
Professional service	60,853	127,395	168,037	254,852
Public service	N/A	40,913	60,875	68,149
Trade and transportation	405,675	530,887	1,097,064	851,532
Total	1,102,471	2,152,342	2,994,701	3,187,459

EMPLOYED PERSONS 16 YEARS AND OLDER, 1940–90

	1940	1950	1960	1970	1980	1990
Agriculture, forestry, fisheries, mining	4,434	6,316	5,291	9,537	6,458	8,830
Construction	131,599	144,342	124,337	111,077	78,904	133,954
Manufacturing	746,466	916,911	869,354	657,054	507,103	371,843
Transportation	61,126	213,056	213,823	187,636	201,046	216,862
Communications, public utilities	67,604	96,505	92,448	128,607	90,625	87,396
Wholesale trade	233,400	318,184	172,119	161,064	139,689	131,538
Retail trade	388,357	437,633	453,674	457,212	387,437	428,960
Finance, insurance, real estate	224,460	242,566	272,019	340,199	349,043	401,765
Business and repair services	74,133	111,667	129,233	169,829	192,836	212,276
Personal, entertainment, recreation	336,883	281,809	195,383	187,218	150,374	181,047
Professional and related services	247,816	292,112	334,134	600,679	673,270	925,056
Public administration	126,733	158,147	148,352	181,258	141,398	158,110
Not reported	73,639	57,276	181,023	—	—	—
Total	2,716,650	3,276,524	3,191,190	3,191,370	2,918,183	3,257,637

Occupations of the Labor Force of New York City in Occupation Groups

EMPLOYED PERSONS 16 YEARS AND OLDER, 1940–90

	1940	1950	1960	1970	1980	1990
Professional, technical, and kindred workers	217,032	338,060	378,400	456,304	492,342	656,286
Managers, officials, and proprietors	288,152	380,496[1]	294,525	307,592	333,259	440,090
Clerical and kindred workers	770,804[2]	629,906	726,674	836,171	727,624	672,434
Sales workers	N/A	253,305	239,702	260,648	261,811	335,477
Craftsmen, foremen, and kindred workers	329,479	399,119	358,102	318,288	246,350	244,817
Operatives and kindred workers	580,053	686,249	686,434	323,501	224,233	158,981
Private household workers	123,202	79,533	67,850	39,979	25,525	24,211
Protective service	N/A	N/A	N/A	61,667	65,645	89,619
Service workers (except private household)	346,264	341,593	352,433	326,586	335,188	407,144

(continued)

Occupations of the Labor Force of New York City in Occupation Groups (*Continued*)

EMPLOYED PERSONS 16 YEARS AND OLDER, 1940–90

	1940	1950	1960	1970	1980	1990
Laborers (except farm and mine)	114,168	130,066	138,954	126,048	97,589	99,584
Farming, forestry, and fishing	1,578	N/A	1,906	9,057	8,033	8,352
Transportation and material moving	N/A	N/A	N/A	125,561	100,584	120,642
Others	68,634	38,297	234,494	N/A	N/A	N/A
Total	2,839,366	3,276,624	3,479,474	3,191,402	2,918,183	3,257,637

1. Includes farm managers.
2. Includes sales workers.
Dash denotes zero.
N/A = Not Available
Source: U.S. Bureau of the Census, Census of Population 1900, 1910, 1920, 1930, 1940, 1950, 1960, 1970, 1980, 1990

Compiled by James Bradley

country's employment in the 1970s and less than 20 percent in 1990. In the decades after the Second World War New York City became the site of a "corporate headquarters complex," a cluster of corporate administrative offices supported by firms in such service industries as commercial and investment banking, law, advertising, accounting, communications, security and commodity trading, computer programming, management consulting, engineering, architecture, and public relations. This complex, especially its business service components, grew rapidly as mergers and acquisitions produced multinational conglomerates, as new forms of financing developed (relying to a greater extent than previously on debt), and as the economy became increasingly regulated by government, requiring large corporations to depend more heavily on lawyers and accountants.

The 1980s saw New York City surpassed by Los Angeles as the country's leading manufacturing center. Only fifty-five of the five hundred largest industrial corporations had their headquarters in the city by 1992. In 1993 the economic activities associated with the port during the nineteenth century (the production, transport, and wholesale of goods) accounted for less than 15 percent of the city's employment, while those associated with the corporate headquarters complex accounted for 28 percent and for more than a third of the Gross City Product. By the mid 1990s New York City was a post-industrial city. It remained the only American city that had not declined in rank since the United States became a nation. Its future strength remained closely tied to the fortunes of the corporate headquarters complex, particularly corporate service firms, which thrived in an international market increasingly dominated by large corporations tied together by trade and investment. London, Los Angeles, Tokyo, and Hong Kong emerged as the greatest challengers to its position as a national and international economic force.

Robert A. East: *Business Enterprise in the American Revolutionary Era* (New York: Columbia University Press, 1938)
Beverly Duncan and Stanley Lieberson: *Metropolis and Region in Transition* (Beverly Hills, Calif: Sage, 1970)
Matthew Drennan et al.: *The Corporate Headquarters Complex in New York City* (New York: Conservation of Human Resources, 1977)
Joseph R. Frese and Jacob Judd, eds.: *Business Enterprise in Early New York* (Tarrytown, N.Y.: Sleepy Hollow, 1979)

Matthew Drennan, Cathy Matson (§1), Matthew Drennan (§2)

Ecuadorians. Very few Ecuadorians lived in New York City until the early 1960s, when a steady influx began. The number of Ecuadorians reached 39,000 in 1980, according to the federal census. As the economy of Ecuador deteriorated during the Latin debt crisis of the 1980s the number increased to 72,000, making Ecuadorians one of the largest South American groups in the city. By the estimate of city planners, which took into account undocumented immigrants, there were about 150,000 in the city; according to Ecuadorian civic organizations there were 300,000 in the metropolitan area, including fifty thousand naturalized citizens of the United States. Many immigrants arrived unmarried, and although some were professionals most worked in service trades, manufacturing, and domestic service; a few owned small businesses. Workers were often exploited because they lacked permanent resident status and because immigration laws passed in 1986 called for sanctions against employers of undocumented workers. In the mid 1990s there were large Ecuadorian populations in every borough. Perhaps a quarter to a third of the community lived in Jackson Heights, Elmhurst, Corona, and Flushing in areas dominated by immigrants from other South American countries and the Dominican Republic. Ecuadorian restaurants, clubs, and civic associations are concentrated in Jackson Heights, where the Comité Cívico Ecuatoriano, a nonpolitical association of humanitarian, athletic, and cultural groups, also has its headquarters. Many Ecuadorians, especially those from Guayaquil and other coastal areas, belong to groups affiliated with their home towns and provinces in Ecuador. The monthly publications *Amazonas* and *Equinoccio* cater to Ecuadorians, as do sections of Spanish-language weekly and daily newspapers and radio programs on WADO (1280 kHz) and WNWK (105.9 MHz). Each year about a hundred thousand Ecuadorians take part in the "Semana Ecuatoriana," a weeklong festival in August at Flushing Meadow Park.

Graciela M. Castex

Edenwald. Neighborhood in the north central Bronx, bounded to the east by Seton Falls Park. It is named for an estate owned from 1900 to 1913 by John H. Eden near Boston Road, Light Street, and Connor Street. The land was the site of the Hebrew Orphan Asylum until it was acquired by New York City after the Second World War for a public housing project of 2039 units called the Edenwald Houses, centered at 229th Street and Laconia Avenue. The population of the project and of the surrounding one-family houses was predominantly black in the mid 1990s.

Lloyd Ultan

Ederle, Gertrude (Caroline) (*b* New York City, 23 Oct 1906). Swimmer. At twelve she broke the world record for the women's 880-yard freestyle event; she broke many others during the early 1920s, including some held by men. A member of the New York Women's Swimming Association, in 1926 she became the first woman to swim across the English Channel, cutting nearly two hours from the previous record. When in New York City she lived on Amsterdam Avenue.

James E. Mooney

Edgemere. Neighborhood in southwestern Queens on the Rockaway Peninsula, lying roughly between Beach 32nd and Beach 56th streets. It was acquired in 1892 by Frederick J. Lancaster, who formed the Sea Beach Improvement Company in 1894 to sell beach and meadow property. The area was first called New Venice; the current name means edge of the sea in Anglo-Saxon. Lancaster built the Hotel Edgemere in 1895, which he operated until 1919, as well as several cottages. Edgemere declined in the 1960s and 1970s and became part of the Arverne Urban Renewal area. In 1990 it was approved for middle-class and luxury apartments.

Vincent Seyfried

Edgewater. Neighborhood in the eastern Bronx, lying on the northern shore of the Throgs Neck Peninsula and bounded to the north by Weir Creek, to the east by Eastchester Bay, and to the south and west by the Throgs Neck Expressway. Before European settlement the area was the site of a Siwanoy fishing village. By 1792 it was part of the property of Edward Stephenson, whose farm and woodlands accounted for most of Throgs Neck; in 1851 it was bought and developed as an estate by George Adee and named by his wife. The family sold the land in 1910 to Richard Shaw, who operated a stock farm and rented out parcels as campgrounds. Eventually the tents were replaced with year-round homes, in the 1930s still on rented land. The neighborhood in the mid 1990s was sometimes known as the Park of Edgewater and had a few hundred small houses along its narrow lanes.

John McNamara: *History in Asphalt: The Origin of Bronx Street and Place Names* (New York: Bronx County Historical Society, 1984)

Gary D. Hermalyn

Edison, Thomas (Alva) (*b* Milan, Ohio, 11 Feb 1847; *d* West Orange, N.J., 18 Oct 1931). Inventor. In April 1869 he left his position as a telegraph operator in Boston for the Western Union Telegraph Company to pursue a career as an inventor in New York City. He lived in Newark, New Jersey, and invented products under contract for a number of telegraph companies in New York City, including Western Union and the Gold and Stock Telegraph Company. Among his contributions to telegraphy were improvements to stock tickers and methods of sending multiple messages over a single wire. Early in 1876 he used the wealth he had acquired in telegraphy to build an independent laboratory in Menlo Park, New Jersey, where he moved at the end of March 1876 with many of the men who had assisted him earlier. In his five years there he invented the phonograph, which was manufactured by the Edison Phonograph Company and made him internationally known; the carbon-button telephone transmitter, for which Western Union controlled patents that allowed it to compete with the Bell Telephone Company; and the first incandescent electric light and power system. He formed the Edison Machine Works to manufacture generators and Bergmann and Company to produce lamp fixtures and other components; lamps were made at the Edison Lamp Company in Harrison, New Jersey. The Edison Company for Isolated Lighting marketed small power plants for individual buildings, and the Edison Illuminating Company of New York City operated the first permanent commercial incandescent light and power station, which began operation around Wall Street in September 1882. The Edison Electric Light Company, formed by several investors in Western Union including J. P. Morgan, was the parent company that supported Edison's inventive work. From the summer of 1881 Edison lived for two years at 24 Gramercy Park South in Manhattan, and he later purchased a large house in West Orange, where he worked to the end of his life. In 1892 his electric and power companies were merged with the General Electric Company. Among his later inventions were storage batteries, improvements to the phonograph, motion pictures, and technology for the milling of ore and the production of cement.

Frank L. Dyer and Thomas C. Martin with William H. Meadowcroft: *Edison: His Life and Inventions* (New York: Harper and Brothers, 1910)

Matthew Josephson: *Edison: A Biography* (New York: McGraw-Hill, 1959)

Andre Millard: *Edison and the Business of Invention* (Baltimore: Johns Hopkins University Press, 1990)

See also Light and power and Technology.

Paul Israel

Edison Manufacturing Company. The first indoor motion picture studio in the United States, opened in February 1901 at 41 East 21st Street. It was a glass-enclosed structure that relied on sunlight for filming but allowed for year-round production. From its convenient location at the edge of the city's entertainment district, the studio manager Edwin S. Porter made such films as *How They Do Things on the Bowery* (1902) and *The Miller's Daughter* (1905). Actors often worked in films during the day and on stage at night. The company began preparations in 1905 for a larger production facility at 2826 Decatur Avenue (near Bronx Park), which began operation in 1907 and was itself enlarged in 1909 to give Edison four production units in continuous operation. Films made in the Bronx include Porter's *Rescued from an Eagle's Nest* (1908), with D. W. Griffith, and *Vanity Fair* (1915), with Minnie Maddern Fiske. When Edison ceased film production in 1918 the studios were sold to the Lincoln and Parker Film Company; later they were operated by a number of small, short-lived companies. Converted to sound in 1930, the facility was occasionally used to make animated films, industrial films, and short subjects into the 1960s, when it was demolished.

Charles Musser: *Before the Nickelodeon: Edwin S. Porter and the Edison Manufacturing Company* (Berkeley: University of California Press, 1991)

Marc Wanamaker: *Encyclopedia of the Movie Studios* (forthcoming)

Charles Musser

Ed Sullivan Theater. Theater on Broadway and 53rd Street in Manhattan, built by Arthur Hammerstein and opened in 1927 as Hammerstein's. The theater experienced financial hardship in its early years and in 1934 was converted into a casino and nightclub named Billy Rose's Music Hall. In 1949 the Columbia Broadcasting System (CBS) converted the building into a television studio, and as the set for the immensely popular "Ed Sullivan Show" it became the site of performances by Elvis Presley, the Beatles, and other musicians. In 1967 the theater took its current name. After Sullivan's program ended, the theater remained idle for many years until 1993, when it was renovated by CBS and became the venue for David Letterman's "Late Show."

James Bradley

Still photograph from It Happened on 23rd Street *(1901), Edison Studios*

education. For discussions of education in New York City see the entries ADULT EDUCATION, BILINGUAL EDUCATION, CATHOLIC SCHOOLS, COLLEGES AND UNIVERSITIES, INDEPENDENT SCHOOLS, JEWISH EDUCATION, LAW SCHOOLS, MEDICAL SCHOOLS, PROGRESSIVE EDUCATION, and PUBLIC SCHOOLS, as well as entries on individual institutions and educators.

Educational Alliance. Settlement formed in 1889 at 197 East Broadway, funded and led by German Jews in New York City with the aim of educating eastern European Jewish immigrants on the Lower East Side and helping them to adapt to life in the United States. It soon operated a kindergarten and offered vocational and religious training as well as classes in theater, art, music, English, and citizenship. Many of the foreign-born students enrolled at the settlement later became prominent in the commercial, intellectual, and artistic life of the city, among them the broadcasting executive David Sarnoff, the philosopher Morris Raphael Cohen, the municipal official Anna M. Kross, the comedian Eddie Cantor, and the sculptor Chaim Gross. One of the leading members of the board of trustees was Julia Richman (1855–1912), the first woman and the first Jew to be appointed a district superintendent in the city school system. The public schools eventually adopted many of the programs of the settlement, notably its classes in English for foreigners and its "Peoples University," a series of free evening lectures presided over by a trustee of the alliance, Henry Leipziger (1854–1917), who also founded the Hebrew Technical Institute and was an associate superintendent of the evening schools of the city. The Educational Alliance later expanded its facilities and programs to include a senior citizens' apartment building, two camps in upstate New York, a day care center, a program for handicapped students at Public School 35 in Manhattan, and a branch on the West Side of Manhattan. It continued to operate into the 1990s.

Selma Berrol

Egbertville. Neighborhood in central Staten Island (1990 pop. 1500), near the junction of Rockland Avenue and Richmond Road and surrounded by the Greenbelt. The area was called Morgan's Corner in 1838 and because of its predominantly Irish population was later known as Tipperary Corners, New Dublin, and Young Ireland. It is now named for the Egberts, a family that farmed the area in the eighteenth century. The neighborhood attracted many Italian families during the 1930s and 1940s. It is a bucolic village of one-family houses and some townhouses.

William T. Davis: "Staten Island Names: Ye Olde Names and Nicknames," *Proceedings of the Natural Science Association of Staten Island* 5, no. 5 (1896), 20–76

Charles W. Leng and William T. Davis: *Staten Island and Its People* (New York: Lewis Historical Publishing, 1930)

John-Paul Richiuso

egg cream. A confection made with chocolate syrup, milk, and seltzer water (but neither eggs nor cream), originally served in candy stores on the Lower East Side in the 1920s. According to one account the Yiddish actor Boris Thomashevsky originated it after sampling *chocolat et crème* during a tour of Paris; according to another the drink was first sold by Louis Auster (*d* 1955) in his candy stores at 92 Cannon Street and on 3rd Avenue and Avenue D, who was said to have sold more than three thousand egg creams a day before his stores closed in the 1950s.

Jeffrey Kisselhoff: *You Must Remember This: An Oral History of Manhattan from the 1890s to World War II* (New York: Harcourt Brace Jovanovich, 1989)

Rachel Sawyer

Egyptians. Egyptian emigration to the Americas began when Egypt still belonged to the Ottoman Empire, possibly as early as the 1820s and certainly by the 1860s. Twenty to thirty Egyptians a year emigrated to the United States in the 1880s and 1890s, a period when the Ottoman ban on emigration was unofficially relaxed, British intervention in Egyptian affairs was on the rise, and opportunities for economic advancement in the United States were becoming widely known. The annual number of emigrants diminished to ten or fewer in the early decades of the twentieth century. Probably most of the Egyptian immigrants settled in New York City and worked as craftsmen, petty traders, and laborers. Almost all the immigrants were men and many eventually returned to Egypt. Immigration increased markedly in the 1960s owing to growing discrimination in Egypt against the Christian minority, President Gamal Abdel Nasser's policy of forced nationalization and his encouragement of emigration as a means of controlling overpopulation, and a change in American laws in 1965 that eased the immigration of educated professionals. Most of the new immigrants were young, unmarried men with university degrees (often earned in the United States or Europe), whose adjustment to their new country was relatively smooth, although some were unable to find work commensurate with their education. According to Egyptian estimates most of these emigrants were Christians (Coptic, Armenian, and Greek); about 30 to 40 percent were Muslims and a very small number were Jews. The federal census of 1970 found that 7642 Egyptians lived in New York City, of whom 5587 were foreign born. By some estimates the figures should have been considerably higher: the city's Coptic Christians alone, the world's largest community outside Egypt, were estimated in 1976 to number about six thousand and in 1980 as many as ten thousand. During the years 1982–87 there were 3004 immigrants from Egypt who settled in the city, more than from any other Arab nation.

In the mid 1990s the number of Egyptians in New York City was estimated at twenty to thirty thousand. Most lived in the Arab neighborhood surrounding Atlantic Avenue in Brooklyn, and there was a distinct Egyptian enclave along 18th Avenue. Their educational level was fairly high (about 25 percent had completed college, 70 percent had completed high school or attended some college), and many worked in remunerative fields: 23 percent as managers or supervisors, 20 percent in clerical, technical, and similar positions, 14 percent in sales, 5 percent as engineers or scientists, 3 percent as teachers, and 3 percent in health fields (of which 1.5 percent as physicians).

Egyptian social life revolves around religion. New York City has two Coptic Christian Churches: St. Mary and St. Antonios Coptic Orthodox Church at 606 Woodward Avenue in Ridgewood, and St. George's Coptic Church at 108 St. Edward Street in Fort Greene. Muslim Egyptians worship in mosques throughout the city. The Islamic Anjumar Mosque at 36-07 30th Street in Long Island City was built with support from about three hundred Egyptian New Yorkers. The Egyptian American Association offers support to new immigrants and organizes social events, and the American Egyptian Cooperation Foundation promotes trade between Egypt and the United States.

Erica Judge, John Lowe

Eidlitz, Cyrus L(azelle) W(arner) (*b* New York City, 27 July 1853; *d* New York City, 5 Oct 1921). Architect, son of Leopold Eidlitz. He entered his father's office as a draftsman in 1871 and developed a reputation as an architect of commercial buildings. In 1903 he designed the New York Times tower on Times Square.

Marjorie Pearson

Eidlitz, Leopold (*b* Prague, 29 March 1823; *d* New York City, 22 March 1908). Architect, brother of Marc Eidlitz and father of Cyrus L. W. Eidlitz. He settled in New York City in 1843 and designed St. George's Church in Stuyvesant Square (1846–48, with Otto Blesch) and the southern wing of the Tweed Courthouse (1876–78; for illustration see TWEED COURTHOUSE). His religious and commercial work as well as his theoretical writings strongly influenced his contemporaries. Eidlitz wrote *The Nature and Function of Art, More Especially of Architecture* (1881).

Marjorie Pearson

Eidlitz, Marc (*b* Prague, 31 Jan 1826; *d* New York City, 15 April 1892). Building contractor, bother of Leopold Eidlitz. He moved to New York City in 1847, where he soon became the most prominent building contractor. His commissions, most of which were from the "four hundred," the city's wealthiest residents, included the Metropolitan Opera House, the Broadway Tabernacle, Eden Musée, a portion of the Astor Library, Steinway Hall, the mansions of J. P. Morgan, Otto Goelet, and Robert L. Stuart, and St. Vincent's, St. Francis, and Presbyterian hospitals.

Andrew Wiese

Eight, The. A stylistically diverse group of artists formed in New York City in 1907; its members were the urban realists Robert Henri, John Sloan, George Luks, William Glackens, and Everett Shinn, the romantic symbolist Arthur B. Davies, the impressionist Ernest Lawson, and the post-impressionist Maurice Prendergast. The group was formed after the hanging committee of the National Academy of Design rejected paintings by Shinn, Glackens, and Luks; Henri then resigned his membership in the academy and announced that he and seven other artists would hold an exhibition of their own in protest. The group was named The Eight by James Gibbons Huneker, a sympathetic critic; others less sympathetic called them "the revolutionary black gang" and "the apostles of ugliness." The Eight exhibited only once: sixty-three works were on view at the Macbeth Galleries (450 5th Avenue) from 3 to 15 February 1908 and were then sent on a tour of nine cities. Although only seven paintings were sold, The Eight surpassed their initial goal of deflating the National Academy by broadening the opportunities for other artists to exhibit their work: their success led to the 1910 Exhibition of Independent Artists and the Armory Show of 1913.

Bennard B. Perlman: *The Immortal Eight: American Painting from Eakins to the Armory Show, 1870–1913* (Westport, Conn.: North Light, 1979)

Avis Berman

8th Street Bookshop. Bookstore opened in 1947 by the brothers Elias and Ted Wilentz. It became well known during the 1950s and 1960s as a literary gathering place in Greenwich Village and had close ties to the beat writers and artists. In 1965 the shop moved from 32 West 8th Street to larger quarters at 17 West 8th Street, where under Elias Wilentz it became one of the nation's foremost bookstores. It closed in 1979 on Wilentz's retirement.

Sean Wilentz

Eisenhower, Dwight D(avid) (*b* Denison, Texas, 14 Oct 1890; *d* Washington, 28 March 1969). Thirty-fourth president of the United States. After commanding the Allied forces during the Second World War, he returned to the United States in 1945 and was honored on 19 June with a ticker-tape parade along Broadway in lower Manhattan. In 1948 he declined offers from both the Democrats and the Republicans to seek the presidency of the United States in favor of one to become the president of Columbia University. He lived in the presidential mansion at 60 Morningside Drive during his tenure, and retained his title after becoming the first supreme commander of the North Atlantic Treaty Organization in 1950. In 1952 he attended a rally in his honor at Madison Square Garden, and after much prodding from friends and Republican officials became a candidate for the presidency; after his election he left Columbia in 1953.

Stephen E. Ambrose: *Eisenhower* (New York: Simon and Schuster, 1983–84)

Edward T. O'Donnell

Eisenstaedt, Alfred (*b* Dirschau, Germany [now Tczew, Poland], 6 Dec 1898). Photographer. He studied in Berlin and in 1935 settled in the United States. In the following year the new magazine *Life* published the first of his photographs, beginning an association that extended into the 1990s, when he continued to work at his studio in Rockefeller Center. Eisenstaedt's candid, naturalistic style is typified by his best-known photograph, of a sailor and a nurse embracing in Times Square on V-J Day in 1945. His work has been published in several collections, among them *Eisenstaedt: Remembrances* (1990). He is a longtime resident of Jackson Heights.

Lisa Gitelman

E. J. Korvette. Firm of retailers formed in 1948 by Eugene Ferkauf (*b* 1920). Its name was derived from the first initials of Ferkauf and his associate Joseph Zwillenberg and from the name of a Canadian submarine chaser known as the Corvette used during the Second World War. The firm began operations when Ferkauf opened a luggage shop with backing from his father on the second story of a building on East 46th Street in Manhattan. He sold his goods at a markup of 20 percent (half of what was customary) and later added to his inventory household appliances and jewelry, also sold at low prices. Loss leaders, sold at a discount of 35 percent, drew crowds and lawsuits from competitors, which Ferkauf viewed as free advertising. He maintained an uncomplicated, informal style of work and eschewed neckties, offices, secretaries, and advisors. Under his direction the firm achieved great success and helped to launch a revolution in discount retailing in the 1950s and 1960s; it registered $20 million in annual sales by 1952 from five stores, and over the next twelve years $622 million in total sales from eight stores. Efforts by other retailers to pressure manufacturers into refraining from doing business with Korvette were successfully countered by means of middlemen. After opening a new store on 5th Avenue and another in Herald Square the firm experienced organizational problems that probably stemmed from its rapid, enormous growth. In 1966 Ferkauf merged it with Spartan Industries, an apparel manufacturer, to increase sales and profits. He severed all ties with his stores in 1968 and left the firm entirely in the control of Charles Bassine, the chairman of Spartan. The new managers sought to change the emphasis of Korvette by selling goods of higher quality at higher prices, but a confused marketing strategy failed and the firm began selling its stores in 1980, filed for bankruptcy the next year, and soon discontinued its operations.

Isadore Barmash: *More Than They Bargained for: The Rise and Fall of Korvettes* (New York: Lebhar–Friedman, 1981)

Leslie Gourse, Kenneth T. Jackson

El Barrio. Neighborhood on the East Side of Manhattan, lying within East Harlem and

Teatro Latino, 110th Street and 5th Avenue, 1938

bounded to the north by 120th Street, to the east by 3rd Avenue, to the south by 96th Street, and to the west by 5th Avenue. The population of the neighborhood was predominantly Italian until Puerto Ricans began moving there in the 1920s; their number increased after the Second World War, as did that of Latin Americans from other countries. There are many churches, bodegas, substandard tenements, and large public housing projects. Several community organizations and settlement houses are active in local affairs, as are the Protestant, Evangelical, and Roman Catholic denominations: their activities include organizing demonstrations and influencing legislation to bring about social reform in this generally depressed area. The main shopping thoroughfare is 116th Street, known as Luis Muñoz Marín Boulevard east of Lexington Avenue (for the first elected governor of Puerto Rico). The Museo del Barrio on 5th Avenue and 104th Street is a center of Latin American culture.

Donald Stewart: *A Short History of East Harlem* (New York: Museum of the City of New York, 1972)

Joyce Mendelsohn

Population of New York City 65 Years and Older by Race and Hispanic Origin, 1970–1990 (in Thousands)

		Non-Hispanic			
	Hispanic	White	Black	Other	Total
1970*	35	817	85	11	948
1980	62	750	121	18	952
1990	109	651	159	34	953

Asterisk denotes estimate.
Figures may not add because of rounding.
Source: U.S. Bureau of the Census, Census of Population 1970, 1980, 1990

Compiled by Nathan Kantrowitz

elderly. Most elderly persons in colonial New York City were cared for at home. Public care was first offered by the "deacons house" in New Amsterdam. The city's first almshouse, built in 1736 under English rule, had a number of elderly inmates. When a new almshouse was built in 1796 more than half of its 622 inmates were placed there because they were old, and the same was true of an almshouse opened in larger quarters in 1816 at Bellevue (26th Street and the East River). The first private institutions for the elderly included the Association for the Relief of Respectable Aged Indigent Females, which was organized in 1815 to prepare its residents for death and built a home on 20th Street in 1839. At mid century the elderly population increased, leading many to believe that it was inappropriate to house the elderly with children, vagrants, the insane, and the retarded. In 1849 the city moved its public charities to Blackwell's Island (later Welfare Island, now Roosevelt Island); near its center elderly public charges lived in two stone buildings, one for men and the other for women, and worked at tailoring, broom making, and shoemaking if they were able. By 1855 people older than sixty accounted for almost 3 percent of the city's population. Almshouses were built in Brooklyn by 1870 and in Staten Island and Queens; the last one, completed in 1888 in Queens, had forty-nine elderly persons among its fifty-six inmates. Paupers received public care at the lowest possible cost: they lived in dormitories with little privacy, were fed a bland diet of rice, oatmeal, beef, potatoes, cabbage, and turnips, and were severely punished for breaking rules. Residents of such private homes as the Presbyterian Home (1869), the Baptist Home of Brooklyn (1875), and the nonsectarian Isabella Heimath Home had slightly more privacy but could still be treated harshly or indifferently. By 1890 the Association for the Relief of Respectable Aged Indigent Females moved to 104th Street and concentrated on making the lives of its residents more pleasant.

Increasingly considered a public burden, the elderly poor were suspected of improvidence by such reformers as Josephine Shaw Lowell, director of the Charity Organization Society, who believed that the responsibility for care should fall on relatives and friends. Her views set off a debate about the relative merits of indoor relief (provided in an institution) and outdoor relief (provided in the home) that continued to the end of the century. Most residents of almshouses were foreign born, and in 1904 Charles C. Weisz of the city's department of charities sought to restrict immigration for those older than fifty, arguing that they would become public charges. Between 1910 and 1920 public attitudes softened. More private institutions opened and the belief strengthened that the state should provide special care for the elderly. When the New York State Old Age Security Act was passed in 1930 there were more than 300,000 elderly residents in the city, accounting for 5.5 percent of its population. In 1938 the almshouse department was renamed the Department of Welfare, and the hospitals department took control of the facility on Welfare Island and another in Dongan Hills. The Bureau for the Aged of the Welfare Council of New York City reported in 1940 that these facilities and eighty-eight private homes provided residential care for twelve thousand persons, were filled to capacity, and had waiting lists, and that the Department of Welfare provided financial aid to about 55,000 persons. The Department of Welfare was renamed the Department of Social Services in 1967; its office of aging became independent in 1975. In 1968 the city ceased to operate a home for the elderly and instead provided referrals to private homes.

The population of New York City aged in the 1970s and 1980s. In 1990 those sixty-five years old and older accounted for 13 percent of the total population citywide (14.8 percent in Queens, 13.3 percent in Manhattan, 12.4 percent in Brooklyn, 11.5 percent in the Bronx, and 11.2 percent in Staten Island). In the same year about 18 percent of the city's elderly had incomes below the poverty line.

Alana J. Erickson

Eldridge, Roy [Little Jazz] (*b* Pittsburgh, 30 Jan 1911; *d* New York City, 26 Feb 1989). Trumpeter. He moved in 1930 to New York City, where he soon developed an innovative style influenced by saxophonists and characterized by rapid playing, long phrases, a wide range, and exuberance. From 1941 to 1943 he played with the Gene Krupa Orchestra, becoming one of the first black trumpeters to play with a white band. The preeminent trumpeter of the swing era, he had long engagements at the Arcadia Ballroom, Kelly's Stables, Birdland, the Metropole, and Jimmy Ryan's. Eldridge lived in Hollis from 1956 until the end of his life.

Ira Berger

Eldridge Street Synagogue. Orthodox synagogue, occupying the first large-scale building constructed by eastern Europeans. It opened on the Lower East Side as Kahal Adas Jeshurun Anshe Lubz. Designed in 1887 by the firm of Herter Brothers and built at a cost of $100,000, it became known for its rich woodwork, dozens of stained-glass windows, and the bright frescoes on its walls, contrasting sharply with the unornamented tenements of the surrounding neighborhood. In the years before the First World War the congregation had eight hundred members, including the banker Sender Jarmulowsky and Isaac Gellis, the city's foremost distributor for delicatessens. As the neighborhood changed, the congregation fell on hard times and the building decayed. The synagogue was designated a city landmark in the 1980s and in the mid 1990s was being restored by the Eldridge Street Project.

Jenna Weissman Joselit

Eldridge Street Synagogue, 1991

Electric Bond and Share. An electric utility holding company formed by the General Electric Company in 1905 under the leadership of Sidney Z. Mitchell. Situated at 2 Rector Street, the firm became the largest in the United States during the mid 1920s, generating 14 percent of the country's electricity in 1929. Its subsidiaries eventually operated in more than half the states and several Latin American countries. Dismantled under the Public Utility Holding Company Act of 1935, it became a diversified investment firm and merged with Boise Cascade in 1969. Ebasco Services, the service division and a leading utility consulting firm, became a subsidiary of Enserch.

Sidney Alexander Mitchell: *S. Z. Mitchell and the Electrical Industry* (New York: Farrar, Straus and Cudahy, 1960)

John L. Neufeld

electricity. The electrification of New York City is discussed in the entry LIGHT AND POWER.

elevated railways [els]. The earliest form of rapid transit in the United States, developed in New York City in the last half of the nineteenth century. The need to move large numbers of people between southern Manhattan and the developing northern reaches of the city encouraged a search for a faster alternative to the streetcar. The first elevated line was constructed in 1867–70 by Charles Harvey and his West Side and Yonkers Patent Railway company along Greenwich Street and 9th Avenue between Dey and 29th streets. Tracks were laid atop iron (and later steel) superstructures about thirty feet (nine meters) above the ground, and cars were pulled by a cable connected to a steam-powered generator at the terminus. The service was at first inconvenient, as cables often broke and brought the service to a complete halt, requiring passengers to descend from the tracks by ladder. Such problems kept ridership low, and in 1871 the firm failed. In the following year the firm was reorganized as the New York Elevated Railroad Company, and a number of productive innovations were introduced: steam locomotives (or "dummies") were employed to haul the wooden cars, stations were added, and the line was extended south to South Ferry and north to 9th Street and then 30th Street; by 1878 the line ran up 9th Avenue to 61st Street.

The success of the line encouraged the development of new lines. The Gilbert Elevated Railway, reorganized as the Metropolitan Elevated Railway, opened a line on Trinity Place, Church Street, West Broadway, and 6th Avenue between Rector Place and Central Park in June 1878. The New York Elevated Railway Company built a line on 3rd Avenue that opened in August 1878, and by the end of the year it had track running from South Ferry to 129th Street. In 1879 the Manhattan Railway Company gained control of all the elevated lines in Manhattan and completed construction of the 2nd Avenue line, and on 1 March 1880 it opened the 2nd Avenue line between Chatham Square and 65th Street (extending it to 129th Street by 16 August). By 1880 the 3rd Avenue line was connected to Grand Central Depot and to the ferry terminal of the Long Island Rail Road on the East River at 34th Street. By 1881 the original 9th Avenue line had been almost entirely rebuilt as a double-track line, extended north to 155th Street, and connected to the 6th Avenue line by a track along 53rd Street and by another at Battery Place. The final phase of construction of elevated lines in Manhattan connected the 2nd Avenue and 3rd Avenue lines at Chatham Square (1882) and 129th Street (1891). The elevated trains were noisy, made buildings shake, and placed those below in constant danger of being hit by falling ash, oil, or cinder, but the necessity of the system assured its continuance.

All further construction of elevated lines took place in the Bronx and Brooklyn, where most of the city's expansion about the turn of the century took place. Several steam elevated lines to northern Brooklyn beginning with the Lexington Avenue line (1885) fanned out from downtown and the waterfront, where passengers could connect with ferries to Manhattan. The Suburban Rapid Transit Company was formed in March 1880, and between 1886 and 1902 it constructed a route in stages that connected Manhattan (129th Street and 3rd Avenue) with the Bronx at Bronx Park, just north of Fordham Road. This line crossed the Harlem River on an iron drawbridge, ran on private right of way to 145th Street, and followed 3rd Avenue northward. Separate fares were required for passengers traveling

Elevated railroad at 9th Avenue and 100th Street. Stereograph by E. and H. T. Anthony and Company

between Manhattan and the Bronx. In 1891 the Manhattan Railway Company acquired control of Suburban and took over its operation. Through-service between the Bronx and Manhattan began in 1896 with a single five-cent fare, using the Suburban route north of 129th Street and the 2nd and 3rd Avenue lines south of it. Transfers between all four els in Manhattan were possible at South Ferry, and by using through-routing one could travel between lower Manhattan and the Bronx for five cents.

In Brooklyn by 1893 there were elevated lines along Myrtle Avenue, Lexington Avenue, Fulton Street, Broadway, and 5th Avenue. From 1883 the New York and Brooklyn Bridge Railway operated cable-powered trains from Park Row in Manhattan to Sands Street in Brooklyn. By 1898 the various elevated companies in Brooklyn acquired trackage rights over the bridge and began through-service between boroughs. Large terminals were constructed at Park Row and Sands Street. In the suburban, semirural, and resort communities south of the city of Brooklyn steam railroads originally built in the 1860s were incorporated into the elevated system in 1893–1900; these lines continued to run on the surface using trolley wire, and were the precursors of the Brighton, Culver, Sea Beach, and West End lines. In 1899–1906 the Brooklyn Rapid Transit Company (BRT), which already ran streetcars, unified the various elevated companies of Brooklyn within a single network and replaced steam trains with multiple-unit electric trains (which used Frank J. Sprague's innovative system of electrification). Between 1900 and 1904 the Manhattan Railway instituted a number of changes: steam engines were retired in 1902–3, the 3rd Avenue line was extended to Fordham Road by 1901, and all lines were electrified. The Interborough Rapid Transit Company (IRT) constructed the first subway system from 1900 to 1904; in 1903 it acquired the Manhattan Railway Company to coordinate service on both systems. The first coordinated service between elevated railway and subway began in 1904, when the Westchester Avenue elevated from 149th Street to Bronx Park (180th Street) was constructed; both the 2nd Avenue elevated and the IRT subway used this route. In 1908 the BRT opened a line over the Williamsburg Bridge as an alternative to the Brooklyn Bridge crossing.

Under the "dual contracts" of 1913 the IRT and the BRT agreed to equip and operate new rapid transit lines built by the city and to rebuild many of the old lines to increase service and reduce running times. Within the IRT system, the 2nd Avenue, 3rd Avenue, and 9th Avenue lines were equipped with center express tracks and many "hump" stations with two levels, one for local trains and the other for express trains. Two new drawbridges over the Harlem River connected these lines to the Bronx lines and enabled trains to reach Woodlawn (via Jerome Avenue, 1918) and Gun Hill Road and White Plains Road (via Webster Avenue, 1920). Tracks were also constructed over the Queensboro Bridge, providing access for 2nd Avenue trains to Astoria and Corona (1915–17). Most of the elevated and surface lines belonging to the BRT and built before 1900 were now rebuilt with heavy-duty track to accommodate steel subway cars, per-

Engraving from Frank Leslie's Illustrated Newspaper, *29 April 1878, showing the first train on the Gilbert elevated railway on 6th Avenue, near the Jefferson Market police court*

Elevated Railways of Manhattan

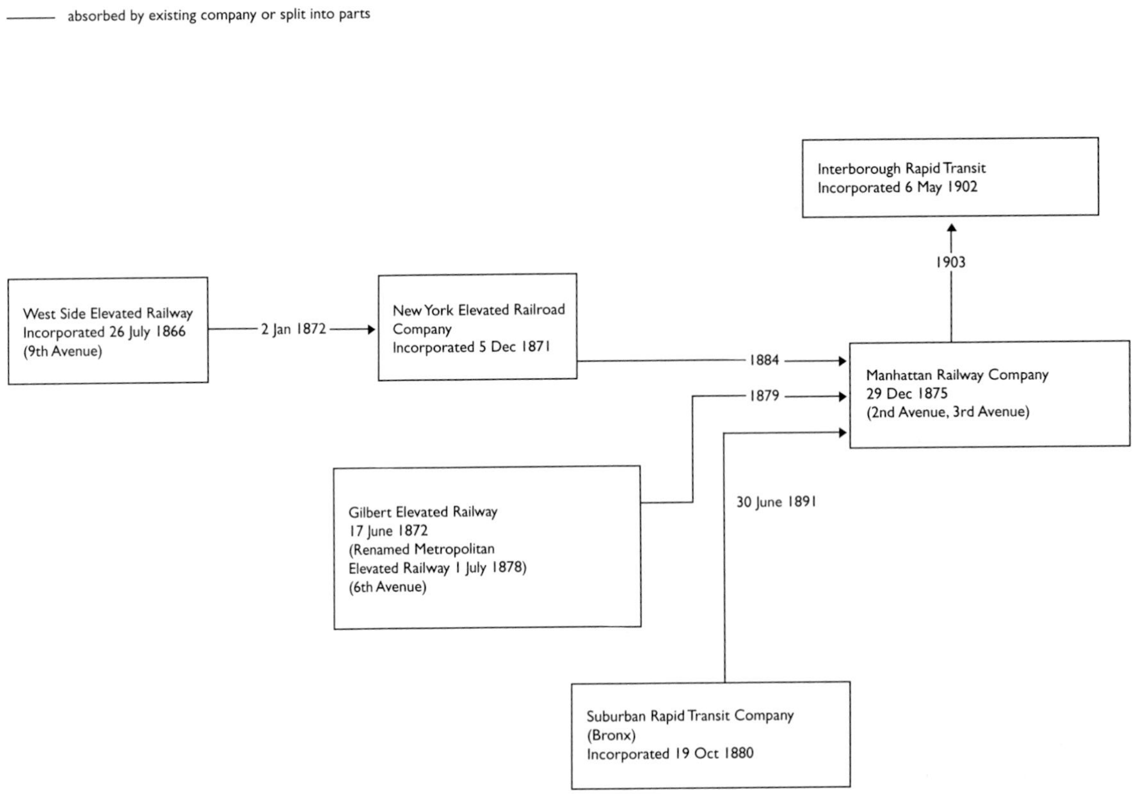

Compiled by Vincent Seyfried with the assistance of Laura Lewison

mitting connections with new subways to be built along 4th and Flatbush avenues in Brooklyn and along Broadway and Nassau Street in Manhattan; service was also extended in Queens. The elevated system reached its greatest level of use in 1921, when it carried 384 million passengers. In 1923 the BRT was reorganized as the Brooklyn–Manhattan Transit Company (BMT). After 1923 a number of elevated lines were abandoned amid a growing perception that they were noisy, unsightly, and obsolete given that subways were being built parallel to them: the 42nd Street spur to Grand Central Terminal was closed in 1923, as were the 6th Avenue el spur between 53rd and 59th streets in 1924, and the East 34th Street spur in 1930.

The Depression sharply decreased ridership, and under Mayor Fiorello H. La Guardia els were eliminated to raise property values along the tracks. The 6th Avenue line was abandoned on 4 December 1938 and razed in 1939, and in June 1940 the city acquired the IRT and the BMT to facilitate the further removal of elevated lines, which during the following decades were abandoned along 9th Avenue (11 June 1940), 2nd Avenue (north of 57th Street on 11 June 1940, south of 57th Street on 13 June 1942), 5th Avenue in Brooklyn (1 June 1940), 3rd Avenue in Brooklyn (1 June 1940), Fulton Street (1 June 1940 and 29 April 1956), the Brooklyn Bridge (5 March 1944), Lexington Avenue (14 Oct 1950), 3rd Avenue between Chatham Square and 149th Street (12 May 1955), and Myrtle Avenue (4 Oct 1969). The portion of the 3rd Avenue line in the Bronx, from 149th Street to Gun Hill Road along 3rd and Webster avenues, closed on 29 April 1973. In the mid 1990s two unrebuilt elevated routes from before 1904 remained standing and in use, both in Brooklyn: the "J" route (built in 1893), along Fulton Street in East New York between Alabama Avenue and Crescent Street, and the Franklin Avenue shuttle (built in 1896), between Prospect Park and Fulton Street.

William Fullerton Reeves: *The First Elevated Railroads in Manhattan and the Bronx* (New York: New-York Historical Society, 1936)

Alan Paul Kahn and Jack May: *The Tracks of New York,* vols. 2, 3 (New York: Electric Railroaders' Association, 1975, 1977)

Robert Reed: *The New York Elevated* (South Brunswick, N.J.: A. S. Barnes, 1978)

James Greller and Edward Watson: *The Brooklyn Elevated* (Hicksville, N.Y.: N.J. International, n.d. [?1985])

For further illustration see SLOAN, JOHN.

Erica Judge, Vincent Seyfried, Andrew Sparberg

elevators. Systems of brackets, pulleys, and ropes provided access to the upper stories of buildings in New Amsterdam. The safety elevator was developed in 1853 in Yonkers, New York, by Elisha Graves Otis, who invented a spring mechanism designed to break the fall of an elevator if the ropes supporting it broke. He demonstrated this device in 1854 in New York City at the Crystal Palace Exhibition by riding an elevator loaded with boxes and having an assistant cut the hoisting rope. The first safety elevator was installed in a factory in Manhattan after a serious elevator accident. Initially freight elevators were open platforms, usually operated by a worker who cranked a windlass or engaged a steam engine to move the platform, although animal power was sometimes used; instructions were shouted by another worker through a series of open hatches that formed the hoistway. In 1857 the first passenger elevator was installed in a store in a cast-iron building on Broadway. Early passenger elevators required the hoistway and platform to be partly enclosed, and a trained mechanic rode the car to maneuver the platform, greet passengers, and work the doors. After elevators were installed in hotels, rooms in the upper stories lost their stigma and commanded high rates; soon apartments in upper stories also became much sought-after. About the time of the Civil War heavy-duty outdoor elevators and cranes became widely used at construction sites, allowing materials and equipment to be moved with greater speed and safety.

Improved elevators allowed the development of skyscrapers. Geared rods, hydraulic

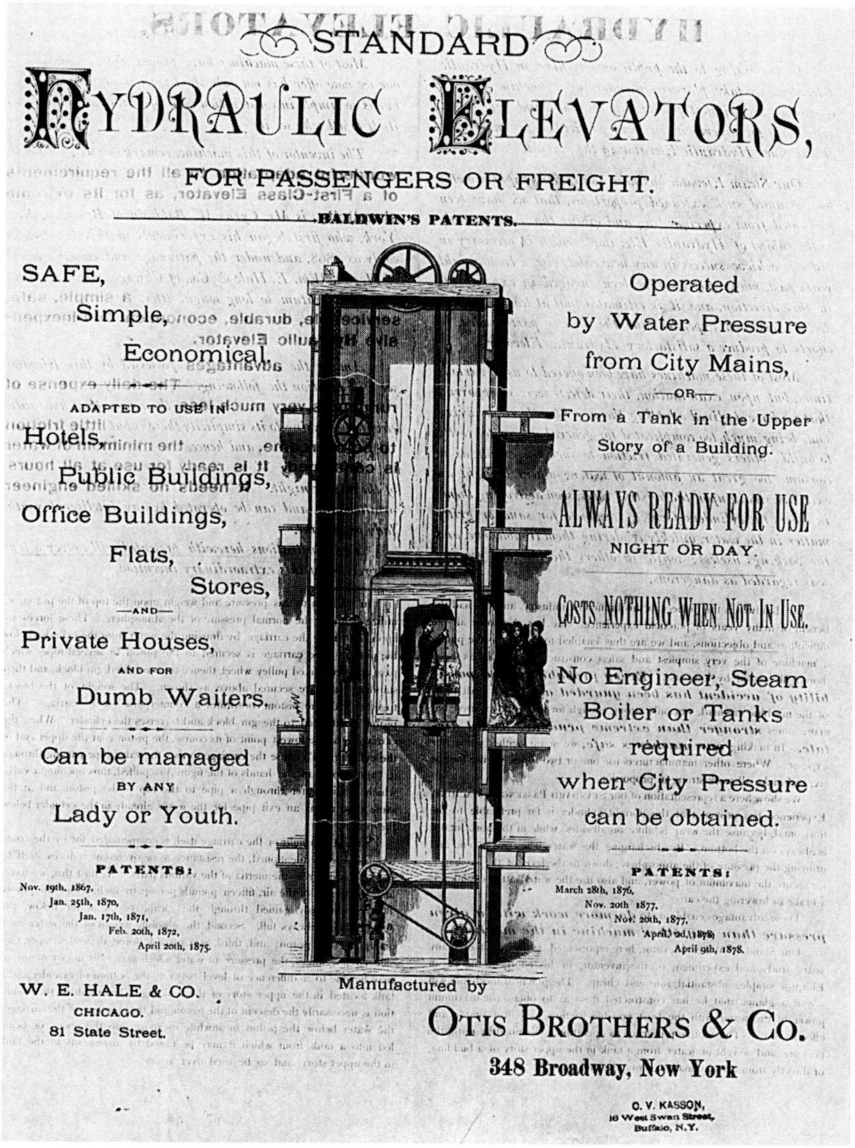

Advertising brochure for Otis Brothers, 1878

cylinders, and counterweights filled with water were some of the innovations introduced in new motors. In many high buildings passenger traffic was managed efficiently by a "starter" who stood in the lobby and gave orders to the operators. Speed increased and control improved after vacuum tubes and electric motors were introduced, elevator operators became largely obsolete, and electric lighting replaced oil lamps. In 1945 an elevator in the Empire State Building fell to a hydraulic bumper at the bottom of its shaft after a B-25 bomber collided with the building; the operator was alone in the car and survived. After the Second World War concerns about security led to the installation of intercoms and surveillance cameras. Most accidents occurred as passengers entered and exited, although in a few cases victims fell to their deaths through broken doors. Many injuries and fatalities resulted from a dangerous game practiced by inner-city youths called "elevator surfing," which involved jumping from the roof of one moving elevator to another.

Elevators in the city are taller and faster than those in many other parts of the country. At least six cables are used where one would be sufficient, and safety inspections are made at least three times every two years by the elevator division of the New York City Department of Buildings.

Fred Eisenstadt

Ellington, Duke [Edward Kennedy] (*b* Washington, 29 April 1899; *d* New York City, 24 May 1974). Bandleader, composer, and pianist. After a failed attempt to break into jazz in New York City in 1922, he returned in the following year to join the Washingtonians, led by the banjoist Elmer Snowden. A fellow sideman was the cornetist Bubber Miley, first among the highly individual soloists with whom he became associated. Later in 1923 the band began working at the Hollywood Club, on West 49th Street at Broadway. After Snowden left in 1924 Ellington took over as its leader, and until 1927 it continued working regularly at the Hollywood (renamed the Kentucky Club in 1925). During this time the trombonist Tricky Sam Nanton joined the band, and Ellington recorded his first masterpiece, *Black and Tan Fantasy* (1927), written with Miley and featuring his growling, wa-wa melody. The trumpeter Cootie Williams (who replaced Miley), the clarinetist Barney Bigard, and the saxophonists Johnny Hodges and Harry Carney brought new solo voices into the orchestra during its engagement from 1927 to 1931 at the Cotton Club (on Lenox Avenue at West 142nd Street). The setting was perverse – a pseudo-African "jungle" revue – but it stimulated Ellington, who brought forth jazz of a wide emotional and sonic palette and supplanted Fletcher Henderson as the foremost big-band leader in jazz.

In 1931 Ellington embarked on a lifetime of international touring, but he maintained his permanent residence in New York City and his band often recorded and occasionally held engagements there, including brief returns to the Cotton Club in 1933 and 1937. Throughout his life he drew inspiration from the vitality of the city, a debt that he acknowledged most directly in the program notes to his composition *Harlem Air Shaft* (recorded in 1940). It was not Ellington but his protégé Billy Strayhorn who composed the well-known celebration of the city's transit system, *Take the "A" Train* (recorded in 1941), which became the band's theme song and was thus closely identified with its leader. In 1943 the orchestra broadcast on radio during its residency at the Hurricane Club (on Broadway and West 51st Street), and it performed at the Zanzibar (Broadway and West 49th Street) in 1945. CARNEGIE HALL was the venue for the première of several of Ellington's ambitious extended works in concerts given periodically between 1943 and 1951, and he first performed his *Second Sacred Concert* at the Cathedral of St. John the Divine in 1968. Ellington's addresses in the city included 381 Edgecomb Avenue (in the 1930s), apartment 4A at 935 St. Nicholas Avenue (1939–61), 400 Central Park West, his sister Ruth's apartment at 333 Riverside Drive (from 1961 until his death), and the Lincoln Towers, 140 West End Avenue.

Stanley Dance: *The World of Duke Ellington* (New York: Charles Scribner's Sons, 1970; repr. Da Capo, 1981)

James Lincoln Collier: *Duke Ellington* (New York: Oxford University Press, 1987)

Mark Tucker: *Ellington: The Early Years* (Urbana: University of Illinois Press, 1991)

Barry Kernfeld

Duke Ellington and His Orchestra at the Kentucky Club, 1923. Front, left to right: *Bubber Miley, Duke Ellington.* Back, left to right: *Sonny Greer, Charlie Ervis, Elmer Snowden, Toby Hardwick*

Elliott, Charles Loring (*b* Scipio, near Auburn, N.Y., 12 Oct 1812; *d* Albany, N.Y., 25 Aug 1868). Painter. He studied art at an academy in Onondaga Hollow, New York, before moving to New York City in 1829. After training under John Quidor he worked as an itinerant portraitist for ten years and returned to the city in 1839. The work of Henry Inman inspired him to further develop his skills as a painter and by 1845 he gained a considerable reputation for fashionable portraiture. He painted hundreds of portraits over the next twenty years, was a founder of the Century Association, and belonged to the National Academy of Design. On Elliott's death his self-portrait at the National Academy of Design was draped in black and surrounded with more than thirty of his works.

Theodore Bolton: "Charles Loring Elliott: An Account of His Life and Work," *Art Quarterly* 5 (1942), 58–96

Carrie Rebora

Ellis, Perry (Edwin) (*b* Portsmouth, Va., 30 March 1940; *d* New York City, 30 May 1986). Fashion designer. He displayed an interest in fashion as a child. After attending the College of William and Mary (BA in business 1961) and the School of Retailing at New York University (master's degree in retailing 1963) he returned to Virginia, where he began his fashion career as a buyer for the department store Miller and Rhodes and then as a merchandiser for John Meyer. Singled out for his ability to predict which clothes would sell, he was recruited by the Vera Companies of Manhattan Industries in 1974. By 1976 his talent at redesigning clothes to boost sales had earned him a chance to create his own line. The "slouchy," oversized look and offbeat sportswear designs that he produced were immediately successful and proved highly influential during the 1970s and 1980s. Ellis's innovative approach earned him dozens of fashion awards and distinguished his work from the more conservative designs of Ralph Lauren and Calvin Klein. Although renowned for creating boxy, baggy casual wear, he also designed products ranging from gloves to fragrances. His studio in New York City, staffed mostly by graduates of the Parsons School of Design, was famous for the creative freedom that it allowed younger designers. At the time of his death Ellis's fashion empire reached $760 million in annual sales.

Anne E. Kornblut

Ellis Island. An island in Upper New York Bay, near the coast of New Jersey. Named for Samuel Ellis, who acquired the island in 1785, it was purchased from his heirs in 1808 by the State of New York and turned over to the federal government. For a time its fort and arsenal were used to defend the harbor. It is best known as the site of a federal immigration center, which between its opening on 1 January 1892 and 1924 was the point of entry for sixteen million immigrants, or 71 percent of all immigrants to the United States. The wooden buildings first used to house the immigration center were destroyed by fire in 1897; a fireproof replacement, designed in a French Renaissance style and trimmed with brick and limestone, was built by the local firm of Boring and Tilton and opened on 17 December 1900. Designed to accommodate as many as half a million immigrants a year, the new building soon became inadequate when the actual volume of immigrants each year was sometimes double this number. The government enlarged the island with landfill, from its original three acres (1.2 hectares) to 27.5 acres (eleven hectares), added new wings and a third floor to the main building, and eventually erected thirty-three additional buildings. The heart of the center was a huge registry room, where officials and health inspectors sought to deny entry to paupers, polygamists, mental defectives, contract laborers, criminals, and people suffering from debilitating and contagious illnesses. More than 98 percent of the prospective immigrants gained entry, and 80 percent did so in less than eight hours. Once cleared, immigrants took a

Immigrants leaving the ferry for the main hall at Ellis Island, 1902

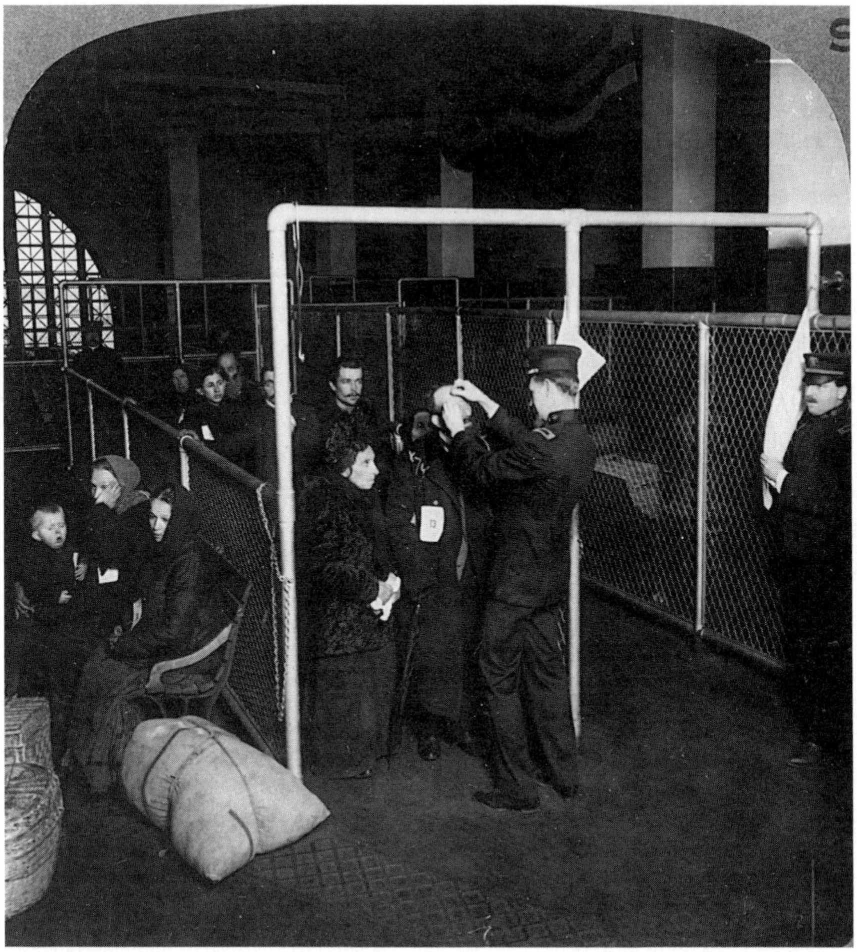

Eye examination at Ellis Island, 1913

ferry to the Battery (one third of them settled in or near New York City) or a train to destinations throughout the country.

Congress in 1924 curtailed mass immigration and provided that those seeking entry would be screened in their countries of origin. This diminished the role of Ellis Island as an immigration center, and from that time it was used primarily to detain deportees. In 1954 the Immigration and Naturalization Service moved its offices to Manhattan, and Ellis Island was declared surplus property. The government attempted to sell the island in the late 1950s, but lack of an adequate bid and public protest saved it from passing into private hands. In 1965 President Lyndon B. Johnson proclaimed the island a national monument to be run in conjunction with the Statue of Liberty by the National Park Service. The Congress however declined to act on his request to appropriate funds for restoring the disused immigration facility as a historic site, and the facility deteriorated in the following years. In 1982 a commission formed by President Ronald Reagan set up a private foundation to collect corporate and individual donations for the repair and restoration of both Ellis Island and the Statue of Liberty. The project to restore Ellis Island began in 1984 with a budget of $160 million. The main building, restored to look as it did between 1918 and 1924 and housing a new museum of immigration, opened to the public in September 1990. At that time plans had not yet been completed for restoring or reusing the remaining buildings on the island.

Thomas M. Pitkin: *Keepers of the Gate: A History of Ellis Island* (New York: New York University Press, 1975)

Harlan D. Unrau: *Ellis Island: Statue of Liberty National Monument, Historic Resource Study* (Denver: U.S. Department of the Interior, National Park Service, 1984)

Barbara Blumberg: *Celebrating the Immigrant: An Administrative History of the Statue of Liberty National Monument, 1952–1982* (Boston: U.S. Department of the Interior, National Park Service, North Atlantic Regional Office, 1985)

Barbara Blumberg

Ellison, Ralph (Waldo) (*b* Oklahoma City, 11 March 1914; *d* New York City, 16 April 1994). Novelist. After working as a bootblack, jazz musician, and photographer he attended Tuskegee Industrial Institute in Alabama (1933–36) and then joined the Federal Writers' Project in New York City. He became widely known for *Invisible Man* (1952), a novel in the tradition of the picaresque slave narrative that recounts the journey of an unnamed protagonist through life and from the Deep South to Harlem; each of the characters, including that of the hero himself, is intended as an archetype, stereotype, or parody of the forms that black Americans have been obliged to assume. The themes of the novel – understanding instead of oppression, consciousness instead of apathy and ignorance, and identity made visible – captured the imagination of a wide readership, partly because they prophesied something of the quest of black Americans for full citizenship. Ellison's other works include two collections of essays: *Shadow and Act* (1964) and *Going to the Territory* (1986).

See also LITERATURE, §2.

S. D. R. Cashman

Elmhurst. Neighborhood in northwestern Queens (1985 pop. 75,764), bounded to the north by Roosevelt Avenue, to the east by Junction Boulevard, to the south by the Long Island Expressway, and to the west by railroad tracks (Conrail). Established in 1652 as Newtown, it was the administrative seat of the town of Newtown from 1683 to 1898, and was renamed in 1896 to avoid any association with the foul smells of Newtown Creek. The neighborhood became known for a fashionable housing development built between 1896 and 1910 by the Cord Meyer Development Company north of the railroad station. Developments were added between 1905 and 1930 in adjoining areas, including Elmhurst Square, Elmhurst South, Elmhurst Heights, and New Elmhurst. After the Second World War Elmhurst evolved from an almost exclusively white, middle-class suburban community with a large Jewish and Italian population to the most ethnically diverse neighborhood in the city. In the 1980s immigrants from 112 countries settled there. Chinese immigrants accounted for one fifth of the total, and there were large numbers as well from Colombia, Korea, India, the Philippines, the Dominican Republic, Ecuador, Pakistan, Peru, and Guyana. There were also many construction projects, including the first enclosed shopping mall in Queens (1973) and several residential developments. Three colonial churches are still used, two of which are known for their historic graveyards. The local subway station is Grand Avenue–Newtown.

Howard Arlington Northacker: *History of the First Presbyterian Church of Newtown at Elmhurst, New York* (New York: First Presbyterian Church of Newtown, 1927)

Vincent Seyfried

Elmhurst Hospital Center. Medical center and teaching hospital, the second-oldest institution in the municipal hospital system. It traces its origins to the establishment on the southern end of Blackwell's Island (now Roosevelt Island) of Island Hospital, which began as an infirmary for a prison nearby and grew into a general-care hospital for patients who could not be accommodated at Bellevue Hospital; the two hospitals were administratively separated in 1847. After a fire destroyed Island Hospital in 1858 prisoners confined on the island quarried granite there and erected a new structure. A stone from these years bearing the name of Island Hospital is now part of the southern façade of the hospital in Elmhurst. After a public outcry over filthy wards and poor care the institution was renamed Charity Hospital in 1870 and its first medical superintendent was appointed. The hospital in 1875 opened a maternity ward, where its use of the new techniques of antisepsis made great progress against puerperal fever. In the same year the hospital opened a school of nursing, the fourth in the United States. Between 1910 and the 1930s the facility (now renamed City Hospital) grew from 742 beds to more than one thousand. It was however impossible to reach by land until 1920, when an elevator connected Blackwell's Island to the Queensboro Bridge.

The need for expansion to serve the growing population of Queens led to the removal of City Hospital to 79-01 Broadway in 1957, at which time it was renamed City Hospital Center at Elmhurst. It became affiliated with the Mount Sinai School of Medicine in 1964 and took its current name in 1988. The first major modernization program since the opening of the facility in Elmhurst was begun in 1989 and scheduled to be completed in 1995. In the mid 1990s the center had 615 beds and a wide range of outpatient services. It offered primary and specialty care to more than one million persons in western Queens and was particularly well known for its emergency department, department of rehabilitation medicine, emergency psychiatric services, programs for patients with AIDS, and women's health services, and for being the only municipal acute care hospital with a skilled nursing unit.

Sandra Opdycke

El Morocco. Nightclub opened as a speakeasy in 1931 at 154 East 54th Street by John Perona. After the repeal of Prohibition it became one of the most popular establishments in New York City. Known for its zebra-striped banquettes and glittering dark blue ceiling, it attracted members of fashionable society, politicians, and entertainers. It moved to 307 East 54th Street in 1960. After Perona's death in 1961 a number of different owners closed and reopened the club several times. Although no longer an establishment of repute, in the mid 1990s it retained much of its original décor and ambience.

Robert Sylvester: *No Cover Charge: A Backward Look at the Night Clubs* (New York: Dial, 1956)

Danton Walker: *Danton Walker's Guide to New York Nitelife* (New York: G. P. Putnam's Sons, 1958)

Michael Batterberry and Ariane Batterberry: *On the Town in New York from 1776 to the Present* (New York: Charles Scribner's Sons, 1973)

Matthew Kachur

Elm Park. Neighborhood in north central Staten Island (1990 pop. 1400), near the Bayonne Bridge and bounded to the north by the Kill van Kull, to the east by Port Richmond, to the south by Forest Avenue, and to the west by Mariner's Harbor. John T. Harrison, a doctor who moved to the area in 1805, had an estate covered with elm trees that gave the area its name. In the nineteenth century it was the site of clay works, brickyards, and chalk manufacture. The neighborhood is now commercial and residential as well as industrial, with most manufacturing concentrated along Richmond Terrace. Elm Park is a blue-collar neighborhood and most residents are of Polish and Italian extraction. Morningstar Road is the main thoroughfare.

Henry G. Steinmeyer: *Staten Island, 1524–1898* (New York: Staten Island Historical Society, 1950; repr. 1987)

For illustration see PAINTS, DYES, AND VARNISHES.

John-Paul Richiuso

els. See ELEVATED RAILWAYS.

Eltingville. Neighborhood in southwestern Staten Island (1990 pop. 20,000), bounded to the north by Greenridge, to the east by Great Kills, to the south by Lower New York Bay, and to the west by Annadale. The area was successively called South Side and Sea Side (1873), both after the name of its post office, before taking its current name, which recalls a family that settled the area in the early nineteenth century. The neighborhood was a wooded area where a largely Scandinavian population lived in small clusters of one-family houses until the completion in 1964 of the Verrazano Narrows Bridge, which led to an influx from the Italian areas in Brooklyn, a sharp increase in the construction of one-family and multi-family houses and townhouses, and a growth in commercial development along such streets as Hylan Boulevard. The population of Eltingville is ethnically diverse. The intersection of Richmond Avenue and Amboy Road is the oldest and most active commercial area and the site of a station of Staten Island Rapid Transit.

Charles W. Leng and William T. Davis: *Staten Island and Its People* (New York: Lewis Historical Publishing, 1929–33)

John E. Hurley: "Eltingville: It's a Boom Town with Attendant Growing Pains," *Staten Island Advance*, 25 Sept 1989, §B, p. 1

John-Paul Richiuso

Ely, Smith(, Jr.) (*b* Hanover, Morris County, N.J., 17 April 1825; *d* Livingston, N.J., 1 July 1911). Mayor. A prosperous merchant in New York City, he was elected as a Democrat to the state senate and twice to the U.S. House of Representatives during the 1870s, resigning after his appointment as mayor in 1877. He was reappointed in 1878 and was the commissioner of Central Park in 1897 and 1898.

Moses Sperry Beach: *The Ely Ancestry* (New York: Calumet, 1902), 219

James E. Mooney

Emerald societies. Irish–American fraternal societies organized according to occupation. In the mid 1990s there were forty societies with more than forty thousand members in the metropolitan area, overseen by the Grand Council of United Emerald Societies (1975). There are societies for employees of federal, state, and city agencies (including the police and fire departments) and of Consolidated Edison and New York Telephone. The Emerald societies sponsor health insurance and dental plans, cruises and charter flights, scholarships, and Irish bagpipe bands.

Francis E. Cull: *History of the Emerald Societies* (New York: Irish Directory Press, 1983)

John J. Concannon

Emergency Medical Service. The principal provider of emergency medical care outside the hospital in New York City. It was formed in 1970 by the same legislation that established the New York City Health and Hospitals Corporation. From 1972 all employees dealing with patients were required to be eligible for state certification as emergency medical technicians, with training in first aid, cardiopulmonary resuscitation, and emergency childbirth. The service inaugurated its own training program for emergency medical technicians in 1973, the first teams of emergency medical technicians began working in city ambulances in 1975, and the service was designated the coordinating agency for emergency medical care in New York City in 1977, with the authority to dispatch ambulances from municipal hospitals as well as private hospitals. The service introduced a training program in 1984 for paramedics, who in addition to the training given to emergency medical technicians learn such procedures as reading electrocardiographs. Calls to the Emergency Medical Service are transmitted to the "911" system of the police department; in response it dispatches basic life-support ambulances, staffed by two emergency technicians, and advanced life-support ambulances, staffed by two paramedics.

Andrea Balis

Emerson, Haven (*b* New York City, 19 Oct 1874; *d* New York City, 21 May 1957). Physician and public health official. As the commissioner of the Metropolitan Board of Health from 1915 to 1917 he expanded the health district plan to Queens and dealt effectively with the polio epidemic of 1916. From 1922 to 1940 he was the director of the DeLamar Institute of Public Health at Columbia University. He was among the first to advocate treating alcoholism as a disease and helped to form the American Heart Association. As the chairman for the American Public Health Association of the Committee on Control of Communicable Diseases he produced several influential reports, among them "Control of Communicable Diseases in Man" (1917). He lived for many years on the East Side of Manhattan.

Joseph S. Lieber

Emerson Hill. Neighborhood in northeastern Staten Island, bounded to the north by the Staten Island Expressway, to the east by Richmond Road, to the south by Dongan Hills, and to the west by Ocean Terrace. It occupies a site with one of the highest elevations in the city (three hundred feet, or ninety meters) and affords a magnificent view of the Narrows and New York Harbor. The history of the area is closely linked to the New England transcendentalists. From 1837 to 1864 it was the home of William Emerson, a judge of Richmond County from 1841 to 1843 whose house at the foot of the hill, called the Snuggery, was visited occasionally by his brother Ralph Waldo Emerson and from May to October 1843 by Henry David Thoreau, who worked as a tutor to Emerson's children. When the Snuggery was destroyed by fire in 1855 Emerson built a house on the hill that later became known as the Unger House. Iron was mined on the hill sometime after the middle of the nineteenth century, but only briefly owing to the decline by the 1870s of the local iron industry. The hill was made into a private community about 1930 by the real-estate developer Cornelius G. Kolff, who gave it its current name. Only two roads lead to the enclave, Emerson Drive to the north and Douglas Road to the east. Emerson Hill remains a small, private community of fine one-family houses.

Charles W. Leng and William T. Davis: *Staten Island and Its People* (New York: Lewis Historical Publishing, 1930)

John E. Hurley: "Emerson Hill: Where Privacy Is a Treasured Value," *Staten Island Advance*, 15 May 1989, §B, p. 1

John-Paul Richiuso

Emery Roth and Sons. Architectural firm. Its founder Emery Roth Sr. (1871–1948) emigrated alone from Hungary at the age of thirteen; in 1893 he settled in New York City, where he worked as a draftsman until he bought an existing practice in 1898. The firm specialized in large residential buildings, particularly hotels and luxury apartments, among them the Ritz Tower (1926), the Beresford (1929), and the San Remo (1930). Roth's sons Julian and Richard were partners by the 1930s and after the Second World War became leading designers of office towers with highly functional, economical interiors. By the 1990s the firm, which included more than three generations of the founder's family, had constructed more than four hundred buildings. In both longevity and volume Emery Roth and Sons ranks among the premier architects in New York City.

Steven Ruttenbaum: *Mansions in the Sky: The Skyscraper Palazzi of Emery Roth* (New York: Balsam, 1986)

For illustration see METROPOLITAN LIFE INSURANCE COMPANY.

Carol Willis

Emigrant Savings Bank. Savings bank, formed in 1850 as an offshoot of the Irish Emigrant Society (1817) to protect immigrants' savings from exploiters. It was organized at the urging of Archbishop John Hughes as the Emigrant Industrial Savings Bank by eighteen businessmen, many of whom were members of the Irish Emigrant Society. The founders rented a building at 51 Chambers Street and assessed themselves $200 each for furniture and supplies. On opening day, 30 September, the bank took in $3009 from twenty depositors. The name was changed to its current form in 1967. In 1993 the Emigrant Savings Bank had headquarters at 5 East 42nd Street in Manhattan, thirty-seven branches (including a number in Manhattan, Brooklyn, and Queens), assets of $6500 million, and 303,000 depositors.

John J. Concannon

Emmet, Thomas Addis (*b* Cork, Ireland, 24 April 1764; *d* New York City, 14 Nov 1827). Lawyer. He moved to New York City in 1804. Although he had extensive schooling and experience his prominence in the Irish rebellion against British rule in 1798 raised the suspicions of conservative Federalists in the city, who initially opposed his admission to the bar. Once accepted he quickly became what the jurist Joseph Story called "the favorite counsellor of New York." His most notable case was *Gibbons v. Ogden* (1824), in which he unsuccessfully defended before the U.S. Supreme Court the legality of the steamboat monopoly of New York State.

Horace H. Hagan: *Eight Great American Lawyers* (Oklahoma City: Harlow, 1923)

Frederick S. Voss

Emmett, Dan(iel Decatur) (*b* Mount Vernon, Ohio, 29 Oct 1815; *d* Mount Vernon, 28 June 1904). Minstrel. With three other unemployed musicians he formed the Virginia Minstrels in February 1843 and presented the first American minstrel show in New York City, which inspired a nationwide obsession with the genre. Between 1858 and 1866 he composed and performed songs for Bryant's Minstrels. His best-known song was "Dixie" ("Dixie's Land"), written for the minstrel stage in New York City in 1859 and adopted by the Confederacy as its unofficial anthem.

Hans Nathan: *Dan Emmett and the Rise of Early Negro Minstrelsy* (Norman: University of Oklahoma Press, 1962; repr. 1977)

Robert B. Winans

Empire Blue Cross and Blue Shield. A private, nonprofit firm that provides health insurance in New York State, formed in 1973 by the merger of the Associated Hospital Service, or Blue Cross (1935), and the United Medical Service, or Blue Shield (1945). Soon after its formation it set up a health maintenance organization (Health Net) and implemented a hospital reimbursement system mandated by the state to contain the cost of in-patient care. During the mid 1990s the firm was one of few remaining nonprofit insurers in the United States to use "community rating," a system under which small group and individual customers with the same policy are charged the same premium regardless of how frequently they use medical services. It also continued to offer open enrollment, or guaranteed acceptance to all applicants able to pay premiums, regardless of their medical status; state regulations helped to support this practice by controlling the rate of increase in hospital rates, thus reducing the gap between reimbursements paid by Blue Cross and Blue Shield and those paid by competing, profit-making insurers. During the mid 1990s Empire Blue Cross and Blue Shield provided insurance to nearly ten million customers, most of them in New York City and its surrounding counties. In May 1993 the head of Empire Blue Cross and Blue Shield was forced to resign after mismanagement had been uncovered by an internal investigation.

Robert A. Padgug

Empire Insurance Company. Firm of insurers. It was formed on 1 March 1925 as the Red Cab Mutual Casualty Company and renamed Empire Mutual Casualty in 1937. The firm took the name Empire Mutual Insurance Company in 1954, when its charter was broadened to permit underwriting property insurance as well as casualty insurance. It ceased underwriting in February 1977 when a financial examination by the state department of insurance showed its financial condition to be unsound. Under the control of the department Empire was reorganized as a stock company on 1 January 1988 with offices at 122 5th Avenue.

Robert J. Gibbons

Empire State Building. The most famous skyscraper in the world, on a site of two acres (eighty ares) on 5th Avenue between 33rd and 34th streets. At 1250 feet (381 meters) in height, it culminated the commercial real-estate boom of the 1920s and remained the world's tallest building until the 1970s. The project was a purely speculative venture for which construction costs were initially estimated at $50 million. The chief investors were

Empire State Building, ca *1930*

the self-made millionaire John J. Raskob and the industrialist Pierre S. du Pont; Alfred E. Smith was the head of the corporation. Contracts for the project were signed in September 1929, only weeks before the stock market crash. The architectural firm of Shreve, Lamb and Harmon collaborated with structural and mechanical engineers and the general contractors Starrett Brothers and Eken to develop the design, guided throughout by the principle of maximum return on investment. Breaking records not only for height but for speed of construction, the entire operation was a spectacular demonstration of modern engineering and managerial efficiency. Demolition of the existing building on the site, the Waldorf–Astoria, began on 1 October 1929, and the first structural steel columns were set on 7 April 1930. At the peak of operations 3500 persons were employed on construction, and in one ten-day period fourteen stories were added to the frame. The job was completed forty-five days ahead of schedule and $5 million under budget. Opening ceremonies were held on 1 May 1931 to wide acclaim, but leasing was slow during the Depression and the building remained only half rented until after the Second World War, prompting some to call it the "Empty State." On the foggy Saturday morning of 28 July 1945, a B-25 bomber crashed into the seventy-ninth story, killing fourteen persons but causing only minor damage to the structure. In 1953 a television antenna two hundred feet (sixty meters) tall was placed atop the structure; floodlighting of the upper stories was introduced in 1964.

Usually described as 102 stories tall, the tower includes eighty-five stories of commercial and office space (2,158,000 square feet, or 200,665 square meters) and an observation deck. A metal-and-glass "mooring mast" for dirigibles (used successfully only once, but immortalized by the film *King Kong*) added the equivalent of sixteen stories. Admired for its majesty and fine proportions, the Empire State Building is visible from many parts of the city and dominates the skyline of midtown Manhattan.

See also UNBUILT PROJECTS. For further illustration see HINE, LEWIS.

Carol Willis

Empire State College. College of the State University of New York, opened in 1971 at 56 Lexington Avenue and intended for working adults and nontraditional students. In 1974 the Harry Van Arsdale Jr. School of Labor Studies was formed as an affiliate at 330 West 42nd Street, and in the following year the main campus, the Metropolitan Center, was moved to 300 Park Avenue South. Branches opened in 1974 at 20 New York Avenue in Bedford–Stuyvesant and in 1977 at 107 Suffolk Street on the Lower East Side. The Metropolitan Center moved to 666 Broadway in 1985. The four campuses of the college enrolled about 2700 students in 1991.

Marc Ferris

Encyclopedia of the Social Sciences. Encyclopedia in fifteen volumes published in 1930–35 by Macmillan in New York City, sponsored by the Social Science Research Council under the editorship of E. R. A. Seligman of Columbia University and Alvin Johnson of the New School for Social Research. The work was influential in legitimating a school of American social science premised on scientific rationalism, cultural pluralism, and democratic social reform. Contributors to the *Encyclopedia of the Social Sciences* included the philosophers John Dewey and Morris Raphael Cohen, the anthropologist Franz Boas, the economist Wesley Mitchell, the political scientist Harold Laski, and the historian Charles A. Beard.

Peter Rutkoff and William B. Scott: *New School: A History of the New School for Social Research* (New York: Free Press, 1986)

Peter M. Rutkoff, William B. Scott

Endicott and Company. Firm of lithographers. Formed in Baltimore as Endicott and Swett, it was moved to New York City in 1831 by George Endicott (1802–48), who by 1840 was joined by his brother William (*b* ?1817; *d* 1851); in 1845 the firm was renamed G. and W. Endicott. The offices were at various locations in its early years, and then successively at 59 Beekman Street (from 1846), 57 Beekman Street (1870–86), and 51 Cedar Street. The firm produced portraits, sheet music, membership certificates, views, and book illustrations, and frequently worked for Currier and Ives. It became a leader in the industry in the mid nineteenth century by engaging versatile painters and printers in an environment that encouraged work of high quality. The firm's artists included George T. Sanford (1815–48), John Penniman (1817–50), Francis D'Avignon (*b* 1813; *d* after 1860), and Charles Parsons (1821–1910), a maritime specialist who began as an apprentice printer for the Endicotts and later became the head of the art department at Harper and Brothers. After the death of the brothers, George's widow, Sarah, and their son Francis took control of the business. Operations and products were standardized in 1851, and in the following year the firm was renamed Endicott and Company and began to cater to a mass market with prints of whaling, equine subjects, and later Civil War scenes. From 1886 to 1896 the firm was run by the second George Endicott, who renamed the firm after himself. Prints of New York City by Endicott and Company include "Park Hotel" (1834), "St. Thomas Chapel, Ravenswood (Queens)" (1839–40), two interior views of the U.S. Post Office on lower Broadway (1845), "View of the Ruins of the Great Fire" (1845), and "Harlem Bridge" (n.d.). The firm won awards for excellence in 1835, 1836, 1846, 1848, and 1856 at the annual American Institute Fair of New York City.

Georgia Brady Bumgardner: "George and William Endicott: Commercial Lithography in New York, 1831–51," *Prints and Printmakers of New York State, 1825–1940*, ed. David Tatham (Syracuse, N.Y.: Syracuse University Press, 1986), 43–65

Wendy Shadwell

Engeman, William A. (*b* New York City, 1838; *d* Brooklyn, 11 Jan 1884). Businessman. As a young man he became wealthy by selling provisions to the Union Army. After the Civil war he moved to Brooklyn, where he purchased undeveloped lots in Duck Hill, a section of Coney Island now known as Brighton Beach. By 1868 he owned two hundred acres (eighty hectares) of land on which he built the Ocean Hotel. He later sold much of his property and used the proceeds to introduce thoroughbred racing at Coney Island in 1879.

Stephen Weinstein

engineering. New York State was the birthplace of professional engineering in the United States. Civil engineering was first offered as an academic subject by the U.S. Military Academy at West Point in 1801, and de-

Footbridge suspended over construction on the Brooklyn Bridge, 1881

grees in the subject were first granted by Rensselaer Polytechnic Institute in 1835. On 5 November 1852 the first professional national engineering society, the Association of Civil Engineers (ASCE), was formed in New York City by twelve engineers led by Alfred W. Craven, chief engineer of the Croton Aqueduct Department. Often civil engineers engaged in public works met with conflict in the municipal bureaucracy: Craven argued that the authority for developing public works should rest with the experts in his office rather than with politicians, and in 1860 he was removed from office for insubordination by Mayor Fernando Wood. In 1865 the state legislature supported Craven by authorizing him to plan and manage the sewage system in Manhattan. The membership of the ASCE remained at twelve in 1867 but increased to 212 in 1871 and to 1090 in 1891. About the turn of the century several other engineering societies were formed in New York City: the American Society of Mechanical Engineers (1880), the American Institute of Electrical Engineers (1884), and the Institute of Radio Engineers (1912). During these years the engineering profession became divided into factions, as the mining, mechanical, and electrical branches forged alliances with business and industry while civil engineers continued to work on public projects. In 1894 Colonel George E. Waring Jr. was appointed the street cleaning commissioner of New York City. A staunch environmentalist, he implemented changes relating not only to street cleaning but also to the water supply, sewerage, drainage, street paving, and household sanitation. The successful efforts of Craven and Waring to unify the administration of the city's public works were furthered during the first two decades of the twentieth century by Nelson P. Lewis, chief engineer of the Board of Estimate and Apportionment from 1902, who saw public works as the foundation of a comprehensive city plan that also provided for transportation and the street system, recreation facilities and public buildings, and a coordinated sanitary system. His efforts to unify engineering and planning culminated in 1921 in his work on the Regional Plan of New York and its Environs, sponsored by the Russell Sage Foundation, which addressed the development of parts of New Jersey and Connecticut in addition to that of the city.

The trend toward integrating municipal services was reversed during the New Deal, when engineering efforts became administered by public authorities with specialized areas of jurisdiction: these included in the field of transportation the Triborough Bridge and Tunnel Authority, the New York City Transit Authority, and the Port of New York Authority, and in sanitation the Interstate Sanitation Commission. These divisions reflected the continued specialization of engineering in general, which persisted despite the efforts of some engineers in the city to unify the profession.

Engineering is taught at several institutions of higher learning in New York City, including the School of Engineering at Columbia University (formed in 1864 as the School of Mines, given its current name in 1926), Cooper Union, and Polytechnic University.

Raymond H. Merritt: *Engineering in American Society, 1850–1875* (Lexington: University Press of Kentucky, 1969)

Edwin T. Layton: *The Revolt of the Engineers: Social Responsibility and the American Engineering Profession* (Cleveland: Case Western Reserve University Press, 1971)

Eugene P. Moehring: *Public Works and the Patterns of Urban Real Estate Growth in Manhattan, 1835–1894* (New York: Arno, 1981)

Joanne Abel Goldman

English. An English fleet took possession of New Netherland in 1664, sent by James, the duke of York (the future King James II, 1685–88). At the time New Amsterdam, the colonial capital, was inhabited by about fifteen hundred persons of Flemish, Walloon, French Huguenot, German, Danish, and Swedish background, most of whom spoke Dutch. A small but significant number of English or Scottish families served as intermediaries between the conquerors and the Dutch: the Bridges (Van Brugges) and Edsalls of New Amsterdam, the Lawrences of Long Island, the Waldrons of Harlem, the Chamberses of Esopus on the Hudson, and the Prettys, Glens, and Sanderses of Schenectady and Fort Orange (later Albany). Although the duke of York's patent for New York included Long Island and land east to the Connecticut River, eastern Long Island remained outside his jurisdiction until it was ceded by Connecticut (under an agreement reached by the first English governor, Richard Nicolls), in return for the Connecticut Valley towns and the mainland towns of what had been New Haven Colony. The patent also extended west and south to the Delaware River and included what is now New Jersey, then occupied by a small number of Swedish and Dutch families. Nicolls, who considered the region the key to rapid cultural transformation of the colony, persuaded Puritans who lived on Long Island to settle there, and offered land on generous terms by issuing the Elizabethtown and Monmouth patents. The governor's plans were upset when the duke granted the region to two courtiers, who promptly began to organize it in 1665 as a distinct colony called New Jersey. It was hoped that the new territory would help to Anglicize New York, but as the English began moving to Jersey most Dutch settlers remained in the Hudson Valley.

The concentration of Dutch in New Amsterdam posed a threat to the new regime that few Englishmen could ignore. When a Dutch fleet attacked the colony in 1673 the Dutch population welcomed the invaders and for fifteen months supported a restoration of New Netherland. At the end of the war the states general again surrendered the colony to England, which restored its institutions for local and provincial government, including an elective assembly (briefly from 1683 to 1685, permanently after 1691). The city charter of 1686, granted by Governor Thomas Dongan, created a municipal government patterned after those of England, with an appointive mayor and an elective board of aldermen and common council.

The English population grew slowly and the shortage of single English women in New York at the time led many unmarried English men to seek brides among the Dutch and the French. For a generation after the conquest the children of Englishmen who intermarried were often brought up in the Dutch Reformed church, which was better organized in New York than the Church of England. Between 1677 and 1703, when about five thousand persons lived in New York, the English share of the city's European population grew only from 20 to 25 percent, but at the same time the English assumed a disproportionate share of the highest offices and wealthiest occupations. Along with the French, the English dominated the Dock Ward near the East River, the city's richest neighborhood. Anglicans formed the tax-supported parish of Trinity Church and installed William Vesey as its first rector on Christmas Day in 1697. Dutch families, particularly the wealthier ones, began learning English and taking other steps to help assimilate into the culture of the conquerors.

The high social price paid by the English for their success was evident in uprisings such as Leisler's Rebellion in May 1689 (a counterpart to the Glorious Revolution of 1688 in

England). Although most Englishmen condemned Jacob Leisler's ethnic and religious reaction against the English government of New York, the Dutch were divided into two groups: merchants, officeholders, and clergy who supported the old order, and laborers and farmers who supported Leisler and feared that the old ruling élite was loyal to James II, a Roman Catholic. In the spring of 1691 William III appointed a governor aligned with exiled opponents of Leisler, who was arrested, tried for treason, and hanged on 16 May. This act of vengeance embittered politics in the city for more than a decade and led the opponents of Leisler to call themselves the English Party, a term flexible enough to include such élite Dutch families as the Bayards, the Philipses, and the Van Cortlandts. The anti-Leislerians also won the loyalty of French Huguenots who had entered the colony since 1685, and who along with earlier French settlers constituted about 12 percent of the city's European population. As Leislerian issues lost their saliency after 1702 with the acquittal of Nicholas Bayard for treason, the control of public life passed almost completely to families that had been loyal to the English Party in the 1690s.

During the eighteenth century the English built cultural institutions to sustain their increasingly dominant position. William Bradford's weekly newspaper the *New York Gazette* became the first newspaper in the city in 1725, soon joined by John Peter Zenger's much more contentious *New York Weekly Journal*. English-speaking religious denominations continued to grow and acquired greater autonomy; a Quaker meeting was formed in 1681, as were Baptist and Presbyterian congregations in 1716. From 1741 to 1758 a New Side (revivalist) Presbyterian Synod made New York City its headquarters. Among Anglicans Trinity Church erected St. George's Chapel in 1752 and St. Paul's Chapel in 1766 (now the oldest public building in Manhattan). It also opened a grammar school and joined in the successful campaign to found King's College in 1754. With the Anglican minister Samuel Johnson as its first president, King's graduated its first class in 1758; it was reorganized as Columbia College after the American Revolution, which left it badly compromised by Loyalism.

The Dutch long remained an ethnic majority within the city but increasingly struggled to preserve their language and customs. In 1730 Dutch settlers accounted for 39.4 percent of the population and probably still outnumbered the English, but they were themselves outnumbered by settlers from all parts of the British Isles (who accounted for 49.5 percent). Outsiders still thought the city was Dutch. Alexander Hamilton, who visited New York City in 1744 from Annapolis, Maryland, noted that the "houses are more compact and regular and, in general, higher built, most of them after the Dutch modell with their gavell ends fronting the street," but that the Dutch "language and customs begin pritty much to wear out and would very soon die were it not for a parcell of Dutch domines here who, in the education of their children, endeavour to preserve the Dutch customs as much as possible." In 1748 Peter Kalm, a naturalist visiting from Sweden, observed that among the Dutch the older people spoke their mother tongue whereas the younger ones spoke English, attended the English church, and even preferred to be called Englishmen. These changes caused more discord among the Dutch settlers than between them and the English. A requirement that all court proceedings be held in English generated no resistance, but the use of the English language in the Dutch church divided the Dutch along lines that closely forecast allegiances during the American Revolution, when Britain was supported by those favoring the Dutch language, the colonies by those favoring English.

By the time of the American Revolution the city had 21,000 inhabitants and the English were the dominant ethnic group in both numbers and influence. At the first federal census in 1790 the total population of the city was more than 33,000, exceeded in the United States only by Philadelphia; 74.2 percent of the total was of British origin, including the English (41.6 percent), Scots-Irish (14.9 percent), Irish (7.9 percent), Scots (7.5 percent), and Welsh (2.3 percent). The Dutch population had fallen to 16.5 percent of the total. In southern New York the Dutch constituted a majority (59 percent) only in Kings County, and there the English share of the population had risen to 31.5 percent.

The victory of the United States in the war made New York City and its surrounding communities more densely British than they had ever been. English immigration resumed soon after the war ended. Although most English immigrants assimilated easily, they encountered some of the same problems faced by other ethnic groups in New York City, as well as many of their own. During the War of 1812 the federal government imposed legal and physical restrictions on British citizens, and English merchants engaged in international trade were interned in an unprovisioned camp at Fishkill, New York. In a reference to the troubles faced by English and Irish immigrants Mayor Philip Hone wrote in his diary on 20 September 1832: "A large proportion of the lower classes find their way into the United States destitute and friendless. They have brought the cholera this year and will always bring wretchedness and want." From 1834 to 1858 English immigrants accounted for a disproportionate share of the residents in Blackwell's Island Penitentiary and City Prison, Bellevue Hospital, the almshouse, and the lunatic asylum, sometimes twice as high as in the city as a whole. The St. George's Society, a club for upper-class professionals and merchants formed in 1770, attempted to aid English immigrants. Religious organizations formed by the British, such as the Salvation Army and the YMCA, also took root in the city and made efforts to assist the needy.

Throughout the nineteenth century many skilled workers and craftsmen emigrated from Great Britain. Textile workers, carpenters, and stonecutters were highly valued in the United States and often received better pay than they did at home. As passage across the Atlantic became cheaper and easier, the number of seasonal workers in New York City increased. At mid century an estimated eight hundred English and Scottish bricklayers sailed to the city to work during the summer months. Prominent among English immigrants were architects such as Richard M. Upjohn and Thomas Adams, and landscapers such as Calvert Vaux, who designed much of Central Park. Women found work primarily as domestic servants and dressmakers.

Workers were assisted by groups such as the General Society of Mechanics and Tradesmen (1785), which in 1820 established a free school for the sons and daughters of deceased and indigent members and in the following year added an apprentices' library. The society in 1833 began what were probably the first free lecture courses in New York City. In the 1820s and 1830s the English joined unions of carpenters, ship carpenters, typographers, printers, and bakers. The membership list of the New York Union Society of Journeymen House Carpenters in 1833–36 consists largely of English, Scottish, and Irish names. Fanny Wright, Robert Dale Owen, Thomas Skidmore, and George Henry Evans all helped to form the New York Workingmen's Party in 1829. In the 1830s several wealthy Englishmen formed a social club on Park Place, where they gathered for meals and games such as billiards, whist, chess, and checkers. The English in the city celebrated national holidays such as St. George's Day and (later) Queen Victoria's jubilees (1887, 1897). Two well-known cricket clubs in the city were the St. George Cricket Club (1838) and the New York Cricket Club (1844). The city also had a number of pubs that served whiskey and porter, like the Richard the Third House, the Brown Jug Tavern, Luke Shaw's Eagle Porter House, and the Albion Hotel.

Most of those who emigrated from England in the nineteenth century were young and either Anglican or Methodist. They initially attended churches already existing in the city and later joined those built to sustain interest in Anglicanism, such as the Free Church of St. George the Martyr, founded in the 1840s. During the first half of the nineteenth century most of the English in New York City read American newspapers, only a few of which were devoted to English interests. Among those published in New York City were *The Albion; or, British, Colonial, and Foreign Weekly Gazette*, which catered to an educated readership and was published from the 1820s to the 1870s, and the *Anglo-American*, which focused on literary articles and news from England, and lasted only a few years in the 1840s. The *Old Countryman*, a newspaper aimed at the less educated and the working man, merged with another newspaper, the *Emigrant*, which ceased publication in the 1840s.

In 1855 the English were the third-largest ethnic group in the city (after the Irish and the Germans), and were represented in all city wards. The sixteenth ward, which extended along the Hudson River from 14th Street to 26th Street, had 1957 English immigrants, more than any other ward. The wealthy tended to live in Greenwich Village; laborers commonly lived in the northwestern wards of the city, or on the Lower East Side between Peck Slip and Catherine Street. The number of English immigrants in the city increased from 22,714 in 1885 to 35,907 by 1890, during which time they nevertheless declined as a proportion of the foreign-born from 7 percent to 5.5 percent and as a proportion of the total population from 3.6 percent to 2.4 percent. In Brooklyn the number of English immigrants also increased absolutely (from 12,611 in 1855 to 27,754 in 1890) and declined relatively. During the depression of 1893–97 and into the twentieth century the number of English immigrants settling in New York City dropped sharply, and by 1920 they represented only 1.3 percent of the total population. English social institutions weakened, schools and churches opened their doors to other ethnic and religious groups, immigrants intermarried, and the group lost much of its distinctive character.

After 1920 women who emigrated to the United States from Britain outnumbered men. The War Brides Act of 1946 increased the number of English women entering New York City, and of the 58,259 English immigrants in the city in 1960 women accounted for 57 percent. Immigration laws increasingly favored the highly skilled and educated. In the 1970s many scientists, engineers, and especially physicians left England for the better opportunities and lower taxes available to them in New York City. In 1990 the city had 28,740 immigrants from the United Kingdom and 172,709 persons of English ancestry; the few organizations that catered to the city's English community included the British–American Chamber of Commerce and the St. George's Society, which began accepting women as members in 1989.

Robert Ernst: *Immigrant Life in New York City, 1825–63* (Port Washington, N.Y.: Ira J. Friedman, 1949)

Thomas J. Archdeacon: *New York City, 1664–1710: Conquest and Change* (Ithaca, N.Y.: Cornell University Press, 1976)

David C. Humphrey: *From King's College to Columbia, 1746–1800* (New York: Columbia University Press, 1976)

Robert C. Ritchie: *The Duke's Province: A Study of New York Politics and Society, 1664–1691* (Chapel Hill: University of North Carolina Press, 1977)

Thomas L. Purvis: "The National Origins of New Yorkers in 1790," *New York History* 67 (1986), 133–53

John M. Murrin: "English Rights as Ethnic Aggression: The English Conquest, the Charter of Liberties of 1683, and Leisler's Rebellion in New York," *Authority and Resistance in Early New York*, ed. William Pencak and Conrad Edick Wright (New York: New-York Historical Society, 1988), 56–94

Randall H. Balmer: *A Perfect Babel of Confusion: Dutch Religion and English Culture in the Middle Colonies* (New York: Oxford University Press, 1989)

Juliana F. Gilheany: "Subjects of History: English, Scottish, and Welsh Immigrants in New York City, 1820–1860" (diss., New York University, 1989)

Joyce D. Goodfriend: *Before the Melting Pot: Society and Culture in Colonial New York City, 1664–1730* (Princeton, N.J.: Princeton University Press, 1992)

Juliana F. Gilheany, John M. Murrin

E. P. Dutton. Firm of book publishers. It began in Boston in 1852 as Ide and Dutton, a shop selling schoolbooks and maps opened by Lemuel Ide and Edward Payson Dutton. By 1855 it expanded into publishing, with an emphasis on religious titles. Dutton bought out Ide's share in the business in 1858 and formed E. P. Dutton and Company, and in 1864 Charles Clapp was made a junior partner. The shop moved in the same year to the Old Corner Bookstore in Boston, which remained its headquarters when Dutton opened a branch office at 726 Broadway in New York City in 1868, and closed in the following year when he moved the entire firm to 713 Broadway at Washington Place. E. C. Swayne, head salesman and European representative for the firm, made a profitable arrangement with the German printer Louis Nister, whose fine color illustrations increased the sales of Dutton's children's books, cards, calendars, and gift books; Swayne became a partner in 1878. With seven hundred titles in its religious and juvenile lines alone the firm moved in 1882 to 31 West 23rd Street, and also opened a shop near its competitors Brentano's, Scribner's, and Putnam's. John Macrae joined the firm in 1884 and became a partner on Swayne's death in 1900. He began a policy of backing unknown writers, and carried on Swayne's successful association of Dutton with British publishers and writers. In 1906 he facilitated an agreement that moved the firm into mass-market publishing when it became the American publisher of Everyman's Library. The company moved to 681 5th Avenue in 1911, occupying three floors and a basement, and in 1913 expanded into educational publishing by acquiring the Thompson–Brown Company, a textbook publisher. Dutton died in 1923, leaving Macrae and Henry Clapp Smith as trustees. In 1928 the two divided the firm, with Macrae remaining in publishing and Smith taking over the retail shop, which he renamed Dutton's. Macrae soon moved his operation back downtown to 300 Park Avenue South, near its former location. Three generations of the Macrae family were active in the firm.

Dutton published such authors as Van Wyck Brooks, Gore Vidal (who was briefly an editor in 1946), Maurice Herzog (whose *Annapurna* became a best-seller in 1953), Françoise Sagan, Alexander Solzhenitsyn and other writers from the Soviet Union, and Jorge Luis Borges. Children's books by such authors as A. A. Milne and Judy Blume were a mainstay. In 1962 the firm moved to 201 Park Avenue South. Under the direction of John (Jack) Macrae III in the 1970s the firm changed owners several times; in 1975 it was sold to the Elsevier Publishing Company. Dutton made several acquisitions in the late 1970s and published such authors as Mickey Spillane, John Irving, Joyce Carol Oates, Lawrence Durrell, and Gail Sheehy. In 1978 it moved to 2 Park Avenue, and in 1981 was purchased from Elsevier by the Dyson–Kissner–Moran Corporation, which had no publishing background, with the new owner John S. Dyson as chairman of the board. It was then purchased in 1985 by the New American Library (NAL), a leading paperback publisher that was acquired in 1989 by Penguin, itself a subsidiary of the British firm Pearson. Many editors were laid off by Penguin in October 1989. Dutton and Penguin moved in 1990 to 375 Hudson Street.

Seventy-five Years; or, The Joys and Sorrows of Publishing and Selling Books at Duttons from 1852 to 1927 (New York: E. P. Dutton, 1927)

Ernest Bevan Jr.: "E. P. Dutton and Company," *American Library Publishing Houses, 1638–1899*, ed. Peter Dzwonkoski (Detroit: Gale Research, 1986)

Marjorie Harrison

Episcopalians. The Episcopal church in America began as part of the Church of England and was therefore known as Anglican. In 1674 the first ministerial stipend was paid for Anglican services in New York City, and by 1686 the bishop of London probably had jurisdiction over Anglican churches in the colony of New York. In 1686 Governor Edmund Andros decreed that services according to the Book of Common Prayer should be held every Sunday and holy day, and that Communion should be administered regularly; he also provided for the licensing of clergymen and schoolmasters by the archbishop of Canterbury. Students preparing for ordination were tutored privately by senior clergymen. In 1692 there were about ninety Anglican families in New York City, and two Anglican congregations in the entire province. Trinity Church

Episcopal Bishops of New York

Samual Provoost (*b* 26 Feb 1742; *d* 6 Sept 1815)	Bishop 1787–1801 (resigned)
Benjamin Moore (*b* 5 Nov 1748; *d* 29 Feb 1816)	Acting Bishop 1801–15 Bishop 1815–16
John Henry Hobart (*b* 14 Sept 1775; *d* 12 Sept 1830)	Assistant Bishop 1811–16 Bishop 1816–30
Benjamin Treadwell Onderdonk (*b* 15 July 1791; *d* 30 April 1861)	Bishop 1830–60 (suspended 1845–61)
Jonathan Mayhew Wainwright (*b* 24 Feb 1792; *d* 21 Sept 1854)	Provisional Bishop 1852–54
Horatio Potter (*b* 9 Feb 1802; *d* 2 Jan 1887)	Provisional Bishop 1854–61 Bishop 1861–87
Henry Codman Potter (*b* 25 May 1834; *d* 21 July 1908)	Acting Bishop 1883–87 Bishop 1887–1908
David Hummell Greer (*b* 20 March 1844; *d* 19 May 1919)	Assistant Bishop 1903–8 Bishop 1908–19
Charles Sumner Burch (*b* 30 June 1855; *d* 20 Dec 1920)	Assistant Bishop 1911–19 Bishop 1919–20
William Thomas Manning (*b* 12 May 1866; *d* 18 Nov 1949)	Bishop 1921–46
Charles Kendall Gilbert (*b* 6 Aug 1878; *d* 19 Nov 1959)	Assistant Bishop 1930–47 Bishop 1947–50
Horace William Baden Donegan (*b* 17 May 1900; *d* 11 Nov 1991)	Assistant Bishop 1947–49 Bishop Coadjutor 1949–50 Bishop 1950–72
Paul Moore Jr. (*b* 15 Nov 1919)	Bishop Coadjutor 1970–72 Bishop 1972–89
Richard F. Grein (*b* 29 Nov 1932)	Bishop Coadjutor 1989 Bishop 1989–

Compiled by Edward T. O'Donnell

was formed by royal charter on 6 May 1697. Its first rector was William Vesey, an Anglican deacon and priest, and until 1700 its congregation met in the only Anglican church building in the province. In 1705 it received a farm of sixty-two acres (twenty-five hectares) from the governor. Ten congregations were formed in the province between 1700 and 1710, all supported by the Church of England. Anglican texts including the Book of Common Prayer were published in New York City as early as 1724. King's College was chartered under Anglican auspices in 1754 with the provisions that its presiding officer be an Anglican and that its chapel conform to the Anglican prayer book. Its first president was Samuel Johnson, a conservative Anglophile and a former Congregationalist minister associated with Yale University. By 1770 St. Paul's Chapel and St. George's Chapel also opened. Many Anglicans remained loyal to the Crown and fled the city after the American Revolution, among them Charles Inglis, the rector of Trinity Church from 1777 (he later became the first bishop of Nova Scotia). His successor was Benjamin Moore, an American-born Tory; in response to Whig opposition the vestry replaced him early in 1778 with Samuel Provoost, a patriot and Latitudinarian (Moore remained as an assistant minister). A dull preacher but an intelligent and prominent man of classical learning, Provoost focused on conserving the church and regaining public trust lost during the war. The first Anglican services in Brooklyn were held on Fulton Street in 1784. One of the church's most prominent members in the city was John Jay, later the first chief justice of the United States and the first president of the New York Society for the Promoting of the Manumission of Slaves (formed in 1785).

The church hierarchy expanded during the following years. At a convention in 1785 the New York Episcopal diocese was formed, and at another in 1786 Provoost was recommended for consecration as its first bishop, the ceremony taking place at Lambeth Palace Chapel in London in 1787. Provoost resigned as the rector of Trinity Church in 1800, arranging for Moore to succeed him and for John Henry Hobart to become assistant minister. At this time the Episcopal church in New York had six clergymen and about twenty-six parishes. Among its well-known laymen was James Duane, the first mayor after the war and a member of the vestry of Trinity Church. There were about fifty churches and thirty-five clergymen in New York State when Provoost retired in 1801. He was succeeded by Moore, who was himself replaced by Hobart in 1811. An advocate of orthodox doctrine, given to controversy and known for his fine sermons, Hobart was influential in founding General Theological Seminary (1817), which was eventually built on land donated by Moore's son Clement Clarke Moore. A black congregation, St. Phillip's, was established in 1809. Hobart's successor, elected in 1830, was Benjamin T. Onderdonk, an assistant minister at Trinity Church and a professor at General Theological Seminary. The Seamen's Church Institute, a chapel aboard a ship moored on the East River near Pike Street, opened during his tenure. A supporter of the Oxford Movement, which called for a revival of High Anglican traditions, Onderdonk encountered resistance to the ordination of Arthur Carey, a student at General Theological Seminary and an enthusiastic supporter of the movement; he waved aside complaints at Carey's ordination on 2 July 1843 on the grounds that they had already been heard and dismissed. Onderdonk was soon charged with licentiousness and immorality by his opponents, and after a trial on 2 January 1845 he was suspended by the presiding bishop; he was not replaced until 1852, when Jonathan Mayhew Wainwright, a supporter of Low Church traditions, was elected provisional bishop with right of succession. The diocese of western New York split off in 1838. About this time the painter Thomas Cole became active in the church and diocese, in part through his efforts to tie the work of the Hudson River School to noble moral and religious purpose.

The number of parishes increased at mid century. The Oxford Movement inspired the formation of the churches of the Transfiguration, St. Mary the Virgin, and St. Ignatius, and a revival of the Gothic style by such architects as Richard Upjohn (Trinity, Holy Communion, and Ascension churches) and James Renwick (Grace, Calvary, and St. James churches). The concept of a total community was introduced by William Augustus Muhlenberg, who formed the Church of the Holy Communion in 1844; the congregation moved into a distinctive building at 6th Avenue and 20th Street (consecrated 1846; sold and converted into a discothèque in the mid 1980s) and sponsored a sisterhood of deaconesses (1852) that expanded the scope of women's social ministries. St. Luke's Hospital, opened in 1850 on 5th Avenue at 54th Street by Muhlenberg, was built around a three-story chapel. Most Episcopalians in the city remained neutral on the issue of slavery before the Civil War. An exception was William Jay, who challenged the rule that blacks could be approved for ordination but not admitted to the diocesan convention. His son John Jay Jr. persuaded the diocese to admit St. Phillip's into full membership in 1853. A women's ministry, the House of Mercy, was established at 86th Street and the Hudson River by Mrs. William Richmond as a home for abandoned girls. It was taken over in 1863 by the Sisters of St. Catherine, who were allied with Muhlenberg and took lifetime vows, a habit, and monastic rule of life; they later became known as the Community of St. Mary. At Wainwright's death in 1854 Horatio Potter, the rector of St. Peter's in Albany, New York, was elected provisional bishop of New York. He reconciled the factions divided during Onderdonk's tenure and proposed to build a cathedral in the city. About 1871 Edward A. Washburn, the rector at Calvary Church, and his assistant, William Graham Sumner, organized the Club, an association of the city's prominent Episcopal clergymen. A number of women's orders were also formed, among them those of St. John the Baptist and St. Margaret. In 1881 the Order of the Holy Cross was established on the Lower East Side by James Otis Sargent Huntington. During the 1880s there were about fifty Episcopal churches in Manhattan. An élite organization for laity, the Church Club of New York (1887), sponsored a library, club rooms, and good works for the benefit of the poor. Seth Low, the president of Columbia University and a well-known reformer who later became mayor of New York City, led opposition to the governance of black congregations under a separate jurisdiction. Henry Codman Potter became the bishop of New York in 1887.

At the turn of the century Sunday services were usually held at 10:30 a.m. and consisted of morning prayer, ante-communion, a litany, and a sermon; baptisms were held immediately afterward, Sunday school in the afternoon (marriages and funerals were generally held in homes). An evening prayer service that incorporated a sermon and music by a choir was common until the 1920s. Most churches had an altar made of wood, but with no cross upon it. Pews were usually subject to annual rental assessments, having been first sold at auction during construction. Music was provided by organists and small paid choirs. In 1903 David H. Greer, the rector of St. Bartholomew's, became the first regular bishop coadjutor. He became bishop of New York in 1908 on the death of Henry Codman Potter (bishop since 1887). The synod house, the bishop's house, the deanery (Ogilvie House), and a school were added to the Cathedral of St. John the Divine. Prominent Episcopalians in the city included the financier J. P. Morgan and Nicholas Murray Butler, president of Columbia. By 1913 the Seamen's Church Institute moved to a new building at 25 South Street, where each night it housed about 411 men for fifteen cents each. Trinity parish built the Chapel of the Intercession at 155th Street and Broadway in 1915. The diocesan conventions of 1917 and 1920 endorsed Prohibition; the one in 1920 proposed selecting women as delegates to diocesan conventions and candidates for vestries. Charles Sumner Burch was chosen to succeed Greer as bishop in 1919; during the same year the national headquarters of the Episcopal church opened at 281 4th Avenue (they were later moved to 815 2nd Avenue). Burch was succeeded in 1921 by the rector of Trinity Church, William Thomas Manning, who was rigidly orthodox and forbade the barefoot liturgical dance at St. Mark's Church in the Bowery, the use of communion cups, and remarriage after divorce. In a sermon at the Cathedral of St. John the Divine in 1930 he attacked Judge Ben Lindsay's stance on divorce, prompting Lindsay to defend himself before the congregation of three thousand. Initially Manning devoted himself to building the Cathedral of St. John the Divine, but he was forced to suspend his efforts in the face of financial difficulty and the Second World War (even the steel scaffolding was given over to the war effort). A strong supporter of women and blacks in the church, he escorted a locksmith to open a parish church closed in a dispute over segregation. He also had an apartment in a slum dismantled and then reassembled in the cathedral for the congregation to see.

As membership waned, the church adapted to meet the changing needs of its parishioners. The membership of St. Bartholomew's, the largest congregation in the city, declined from fourteen thousand in 1926 to two thousand in 1930; that of Trinity, the smallest, declined from eleven hundred to 150. Under the episcopate of Horace William Baden Donegan from 1950 the diocese allowed women to serve on vestries (1957) and to be elected to diocesan convention (1958). Donegan also emphasized social work and with the sports announcer Red Barber erected a building to house the Episcopal City Mission Society. Other prominent Episcopalians at the time included Fiorello H. La Guardia, Franklin D. Roosevelt, and Thomas E. Dewey. James Albert Pike, a former Roman Catholic and agnostic, was a popular speaker and apologist for the Christian faith and the Episcopal church as the chaplain of Columbia and dean of St. John the Divine. Samuel Shoemaker, the rector of Calvary Church, was known for his evangelism and helped to form Alcoholics Anonymous. The Community of the Holy Spirit, established during the late 1940s by Ruth Younger as a religious teaching order for women, opened St. Hilda's and St. Hugh's, a school at 619 West 114th Street. Paul Moore Jr., bishop of New York from 1972, emphasized human rights, social action, and urban problems. Although he could not ordain them, he allowed five women deacons to take part in an ordination service on 15 December 1974; the ordination of women was allowed by the church in 1976. Moore also resumed construction of the cathedral in 1979. Harold L. Wright was elected the first black assistant bishop in 1974. Richard Frank Grein, bishop of New York from October 1989, focused on community programs, evangelism, education, administrative restructuring, and relations with the Orthodox church in Russia.

James Elliott Lindsley: *This Planted Vine: A Narrative History of the Episcopal Diocese of New York* (New York: Harper and Row, 1984)

J. Robert Wright

Equality League of Self Supporting Women. Woman suffrage organization formed in 1907 in New York City by Harriot Stanton Blatch. In contrast to the genteel methods of other suffragist groups it recruited wage-earning women and sought publicity through such tactics as street parades. It developed the militant, agitational style that led to votes for women in New York State in 1917. In 1910 the organization changed its focus to legislative lobbying and was renamed the Women's Political Union. Its strategies influenced the formation of the National Woman's Party.

Ellen Carol DuBois

Equal Rights Party. See Locofocos.

Equitable Life Assurance Society of the United States. Firm of insurers formed on 26 July 1859 by Henry Baldwin Hyde, a twenty-five-year-old entrepreneur who made the firm a leader in the industry and was its president from 1874 to 1899. The firm rapidly expanded its domestic market by using innovations such as tontines (deferred dividend policies), intensive and imaginative marketing, and a large and enterprising sales force trained and motivated by Hyde, an originator of the sales convention. Overseas the firm sold insurance from the 1860s, with such success that it built office buildings in Paris, Berlin, Vienna, Madrid, Sydney, and Melbourne. The first home-office building, constructed in 1870 at 120 Broadway by the firm of Gilman and Kendall and the consulting architect George B. Post, was among the first buildings to use elevators. The firm was the largest insurer in the world by 1886. It did one third of its business in foreign countries by 1894, was the first insurer to extend $1000 million in coverage (in 1899), and became a major source of capital investment in the United States. Shares were held by stockholders until the capital stock was retired (a process begun in 1905 and completed by 1925), and in 1912 the firm designed an innovative group life insurance policy for Montgomery Ward. The home-office building was destroyed by fire on 9 January 1912; a replacement designed by Ernest R. Graham was erected on the same site in 1915 (designated a landmark in 1980; for illustration see Zoning). An increasing number of obstacles to doing business abroad caused the firm to limit itself to the United States and its territories in 1919.

In 1933 Equitable purchased New York State unemployment relief bonds. The firm helped to encourage a renaissance on 6th Ave-other revolutionaries, including many sailors. *Eesti Amerika Postimees* (Estonian American Courier, 1897–1911), the first Estonian publication in the United States, was issued by Hans Rebane from the Lutheran Pilgrimage House on State Street. The American Estonian Benefit Society was formed in 1898 to help immigrants and after merging with the Lotus/Hope organization (1905) was renamed the New York Estonian Society (1910). It later survived internal conflicts, including a failed takeover by communists, to become the Estonian Educational Society (1929), which issued the publication *Meie Teie* (Our Path, 1931–77). Socialists formed an association in 1906 that issued the publication *Uus Ilm* (New Path, 1909–89), sponsored from 1924 by the progressive Kir (Ray) Society. In 1918 many of the socialists joined the Communist Party of America. Estonians in the city campaigned vigorously for Estonian independence after the First World War. During the 1920s and 1930s socialists organized workers' clubs that offered programs for teenagers and women and others devoted to music and sports. Estonian Baptists established a church on East 83rd Street in Manhattan and sought to limit the influence of the political left by offering educational programs; they also issued several publications that became popular, among them *Amerika Tekaija* (American Journeyer, 1918–23) and *Amerska Randor* (American Wanderer, 1930–32).

Efforts to promote independence intensified after Estonia was annexed by the Soviet Union in 1940, and a number of international congresses, organizations, and publications were formed in the city. Refugees and political exiles settled in the city after the Second World War, including many professionals. The Estonian House (1947–) on East 34th Street became the headquarters of the Nordic Press, which published the weekly newspaper *Vaba Eesti Sona* (Free Estonian World, 1949–), and of several organizations formed in the 1950s and 1960s, among them the Estonian American Council, which worked toward political goals, the Estonian Aid Society, which helped immigrants, the Estonian Learned Society, the Estonian Women's League, the Estonian Students' Association, the Estonian Students' Fund, the Estonian Music Center, the Estonian World Association, boy scout and girl scout troops, and philatelic and chess societies.

The 1960s and 1970s saw many Estonian families move to Long Island and New Jersey. In the mid 1990s there were between two thousand and 2500 Estonians in the city: many worked in business and were bankers, musicians, teachers, writers, architects, and military officers. About 80 percent were Evangelical Lutherans and belonged to the Immanuel Lutheran Church and Gustaves Adolphus Church in Manhattan. The rest were Baptists, Pentecostalists, Seventh Day Adventists, and Eastern Orthodox. The Estonian Educational Society remains an important organization in the preservation of Estonian culture. It is the headquarters for various political groups, offers programs in language, art, music, and sports, and maintains a library of more than three thousand Estonian books. Well-known Estonians in the city have included the sculptor Adele Augustas, the engineer and writer Valter Rand, and the graphic artist Agaate Veeber.

Jaan Pennar, Tonu Pamming, and Peter P. Rebane, eds.: *The Estonians in America, 1625–1975: A Chronology and Fact Book* (Dobbs Ferry, N.Y.: Oceana, 1975)

Vladimir Wertsman

Ethical Culture Fieldston Schools. Independent coeducational elementary and secondary day schools in Manhattan and the Bronx. Their origins may be traced to the opening by Felix Adler in 1878 of a free kindergarten sponsored by the Ethical Culture Society. The school added elementary grades in 1880, and tuition-paying students were admitted in 1890. Originally called the Workingman's School, the school took the name Ethical Culture School in 1895. It expanded to include a high school by 1900, graduating its first class in 1905. The school's reputation for innovation in curriculum and pedagogy led to an expanding student body, and in 1928 the Fieldston School, newly constructed on an eighteen-acre (seven-hectare) campus in Riverdale, opened for students in grades seven to twelve. The Fieldston Lower School was built in 1933 on the campus to offer progressive education from preschool to the sixth grade. The name Ethical Culture Fieldston Schools now refers to the Ethical Culture School at 33 Central Park West in Manhattan, Fieldston Lower School, and Fieldston School on Fieldston Road in the Bronx.

Richard Schwartz

Ethical Culture Society of New York. Religious humanist association formed in 1876 by Felix Adler, the rabbi of Temple Emanu-El in New York City and a leading exponent of Reform Judaism. The association was based on his philosophy of ethical idealism, a blend of Kantian ideas and social and pedagogical reform. It soon became a leading advocate of radical political and social reforms, including those aimed at workers, women, and the poor. Some of its first leaders opened the first settlement house in the country, the University Settlement (1886), as well as the Hudson Guild (1895) and the first Workingmen's School (1877), which became the Ethical Culture School. In the mid 1990s the society had 520 members and belonged to the American Ethical Culture Union, which was recognized as a religion but supported no one theology, doctrine, or creed, instead upholding the philosophy that human life is of the utmost value and that improved social, interpersonal, and ecological relations are possible through dedication to the potential and betterment of human beings.

Horace L. Friess: *Felix Adler and Ethical Culture: Memories and Studies*, ed. Fannia Weingartner (New York: Columbia University Press, 1981)

Amie Klempnauer

Eugene M. Lang Foundation. Charitable organization formed in 1968 by Eugene M. Lang (*b* 16 March 1919), a native of New York City and the founder of the Refac Technology Development Corporation. The foundation focuses its efforts on educational institutions, in particular Eugene Lang College at the New School for Social Research. It also supports medical care and research and makes grants to about seventy-five educational, cultural, and social service organizations in the city. During the 1980s Lang offered to pay the college tuition of every member of a sixth-grade class at Public School 121 in East Harlem who completed high school, and he later paid for tutoring and other assistance to the students. By January 1989 his example inspired twenty-one other New Yorkers to make similar commitments to disadvantaged elementary school students. The foundation had assets of about $27.4 million in 1991 and made average annual contributions of $2 million.

Kenneth W. Rose

Eugenio Maria de Hostos Community College. Junior college of the City University of New York, opened in 1968 at 475 Grand Concourse in the Bronx as the first branch of the university deliberately placed in an economically depressed area. The school was a pioneer in bilingual education and developed a strong health sciences program in affiliation with several hospitals in New York City. It offers day care free of charge to its students, who were about 80 percent Latin American during the 1980s. Enrollment consisted of 3875 full-time and 440 part-time students in 1990.

Marc Ferris

Europe, James Reese (*b* Mobile, Ala., 22 Feb 1881; *d* Boston, 10 May 1919). Music director. He moved to New York City in 1903, where he made his reputation as a music director in black musical theater. In 1910 he formed the Clef Club, both a booking agency and an informal union for black musicians in New York City. He led a hundred-piece orchestra drawn from the Clef Club at Carnegie Hall in 1912 in the first of several concerts of music by black composers, emphasizing art music to counteract the prevailing opinion that blacks could produce only ragtime. In 1914 he became the music director for the internationally famous white dance team of Vernon and Irene Castle, which brought him national prominence and engagements from members of fashionable society in New York

City. In the same year he left the Clef Club to form a competing organization, the Tempo Club. During the First World War he led the 369th Infantry military band, which was all black. He was at the height of his career when he was killed by a deranged member of his band.

Robert Kimball and William Bolcom: *Reminiscing with Sissle and Blake* (New York: Viking, 1973)

R. Reid Badger: "James Reese Europe and the Prehistory of Jazz," *American Music* 7, no. 1 (spring 1989), 48–67

Edward A. Berlin

Evacuation Day. The date of final departure of British military forces from the United States, 25 November 1783. The signing of the Treaty of Paris on 3 September signaled the end of the American Revolution. New York City was the last official post held by the British, and after a delay of several days they evacuated the city under the direction of General Guy Carleton at one o'clock in the afternoon of 25 November, ending more than seven years of occupation. Within the hour American forces commanded by Generals George Washington and George Clinton marched the length of Manhattan from McGowan's Pass to the Battery. At Fort George the American flag replaced the British flag. Boisterous celebrations continued for the next ten days, culminating in Washington's poignant farewell to his officers on 4 December at Fraunces Tavern; the last British warship left for England the next day from Staten Island. For more than a century Evacuation Day was marked by martial parades, patriotic oratory, and banquets; its one hundredth anniversary was one of the great civic events of the nineteenth century in New York City. The holiday ceased to be observed after the First World War because of its proximity to Thanksgiving and the decline of anti-English sentiment, except for a brief revival on the occasion of its bicentenary in 1983.

James Raker: *"Evacuation Day," 1783: Its Many Stirring Events* (New York: Privately printed, 1883)

Robert I. Goler

Evans, George Henry (*b* Bromyard, England, 25 May 1805; *d* Granville, N.J., 2 Feb 1856). Editor and land reformer. He moved to the United States with his father and brother in 1820 and worked as a printer's apprentice in Ithaca, New York. He soon became an admirer of Thomas Paine's writings on free thought and moved to New York City, where he joined an intellectual circle of craftsmen sympathetic to Paine's ideas. Allied with Frances Wright and Robert Dale Owen, he became a spokesman for an important faction of the Working Man's Party in 1829 and during the next decade edited several newspapers devoted to labor issues (including the *Working Man's Advocate*), defended the city's union movement, and took part in the Locofoco revolt within the Democratic Party. After 1840 he concentrated on land reform, which by then he considered the only practicable solution to class injustice. Supported by such prominent labor leaders as Mike Walsh and John Commerford, he formed the National Reform Association in 1844, appealing to workers with the slogan "Vote Yourself a Farm," but gained only a small following. Undeterred, he promoted the cause until the end of his life. Evans's ideas later influenced such diverse political efforts as those culminating in the Homestead Act of 1862 and Henry George's campaign for a single tax during the 1880s.

Sean Wilentz

Evans, Walker (*b* St. Louis, 3 Nov 1903; *d* Old Lyme, Conn., 10 April 1975). Photographer. He lived in New York City in the late 1920s, and his career began there in 1930 when his photographs were published in *The Bridge*, an anthology of poems by Hart Crane. In 1932 his work was exhibited at the Julien Ley Gallery, and in 1938 a major exhibition of his photographs for the Farm Security Administration was mounted at the Museum of Modern Art. A later exhibition at the museum (1966) featured photographs he had taken of subway riders in New York City in 1938 and 1941. Evans was a contributing editor at *Time* (1943–45) and an associate editor at *Fortune* (1945–65). A retrospective of his work appeared at the Museum of Modern Art in 1971.

Laura Gwinn

Evarts, William M(axwell) (*b* Boston, 6 Feb 1818; *d* New York City, 28 Feb 1901). Lawyer and statesman. He graduated from Yale College and attended Harvard Law School, and in 1841 he began practicing law in New York City, where he became one of the best-known members of the bar. A staunch Republican, he successfully represented President Andrew Johnson in his impeachment proceedings in 1868 and was rewarded by being appointed attorney general. He was president of the New York Law Institute and a founder and first president of the Association of the Bar of the City of New York. At the Geneva arbitration in 1871–72 he represented the United States in its claims against England for having plundered the *Alabama* during the Civil War. He provided legal counsel for the Republican Party in the disputed presidential election of 1876, and was appointed secretary of state by the eventual winner, President Rutherford B. Hayes (1877–81). In 1885 he was elected by the New York State legislature to the U.S. Senate; he was largely responsible for the passage of the Evarts Act of 1891, which created the federal court of appeals.

Chester L. Barrows: *William M. Evarts: Lawyer, Diplomat, Statesman* (Chapel Hill: University of North Carolina Press, 1941)

Elliott B. Nixon

Everett's Hotel. A hotel at 212 4th Avenue near Union Square, opened in 1854. Named for the statesman Edward Everett, who spoke at Gettysburg along with Lincoln, it was an imposing, classically designed brick structure with large, elegant rooms and antique furniture. Everett's Hotel was considered one of the finest hotels of its time.

Shan Jayakumar

Evergood, Philip (*b* New York City, 26 Oct 1901; *d* Bridgewater, Conn., 11 March 1973). Painter. The son of the Australian painter Meyer Blashki, he was sent to school in England when he was eight years old and received his art training there. He returned to New York City in 1923 and studied at the Art Students League and the Educational Alliance. During the 1930s he worked for the Public Works of Art Project and the mural division of the Federal Art Project of the Works Progress Administration, for which he completed a mural at the Richmond Hill Library in Queens. As the president of the Artists' Union (elected in 1937) he worked for artists' rights and for permanent government sponsorship of the arts. Evergood painted in an expressionist style characterized by an agitated line, distortions of human anatomy, and bold primary colors; his acerbic social comment, often based on his own experiences of protest, mellowed with the years, giving way to an imaginative fantasy. The Whitney Museum of American Art owns a large collection of his works, including *Lily and the Sparrows* (1939).

John I. H. Baur: *Philip Evergood* (New York: Harry N. Abrams, 1975)

Patricia Hills

Everlast Sports Manufacturing. Firm of sporting goods manufacturers formed in 1917 by Jacob Golomb (1893–1951), who named it for a durable men's bathing suit that he invented in 1910 and sold on the Lower East Side. In 1919 Jack Dempsey wore gloves bearing the name of the firm when he won the world heavyweight championship, and in 1921 it began mass-producing boxing equipment, which earned a reputation for reliability and durability. In 1938 the firm moved to a large facility at 750 East 132nd Street in the southern Bronx. It began producing swimwear, T-shirts, and other apparel in 1983, a venture that it soon abandoned in favor of licensing its logotype to other manufacturers; in 1989 licensing fees exceeded $2 million. Everlast was able to endure a decline in the popularity of boxing because of its high name recognition and steady sales in large department stores in New York City. Under the leadership of Daniel Golomb, son of the founder, the firm had sales of about $20 million in 1990.

Elizabeth J. Kramer, Stephen A. Stertz

excursion boats. Recreational waterborne travel for residents of New York City began in the early nineteenth century on sailing

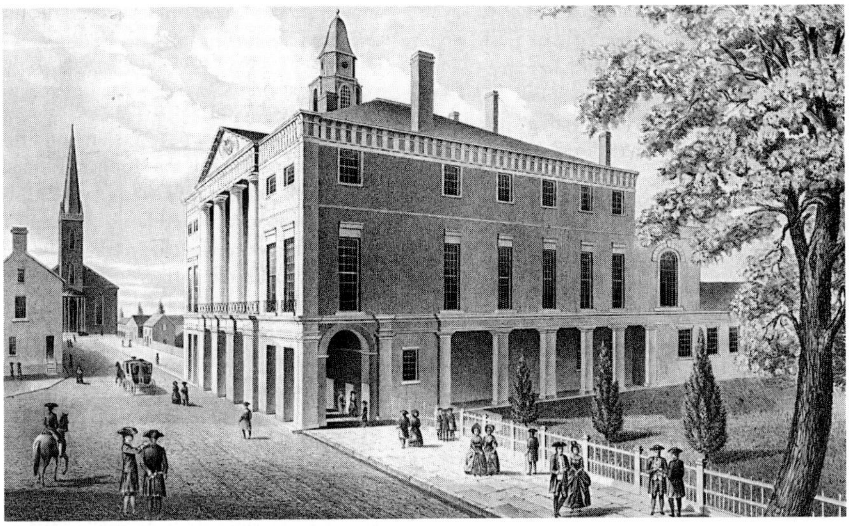

The first Federal Hall, 1789

The second Federal Hall, 1918

filled rotunda; the walls of the building are five feet (one and a half meters) thick.

The building was used successively as the Custom House for the Port of New York (1842–62), as a subtreasury after the Customs Service moved to larger quarters at 55 Wall Street, as a branch of the Federal Reserve Bank (1920–25), for various federal offices (1925–55), and as a museum of the National Park Service (from 1955).

Mollie Keller

Federalist. A series of eighty-five essays advocating ratification of the Constitution of the United States. Seventy-seven of the essays were published in the newspapers the *Independent Journal* and the *New York Packet* between October 1787 and August 1788; these and eight others were included in a book entitled *The Federalist* published in New York City in 1788 by J. and A. M'Lean. The essays were written by Alexander Hamilton (nos. 1, 6–9, 11–13, 15–17, 21–36, 59–61, and 65–85) and John Jay (nos. 2–5 and 64), both natives of New York City, and James Madison (nos. 10, 14, 18–20, 37–58, and 62–63), a Virginian then living in the city, and were all signed with the pseudonym "Publius." The authors addressed the essays to "the People and State of New York," whose support for the Constitution they considered indispensable to the success of the new federal union. The essays were widely read and discussed and have been reprinted many times. They are regarded not only as an important federalist document but as a great work of political philosophy.

Edward Millican: *One United People: The Federalist Papers and the National Idea* (Lexington: University Press of Kentucky, 1990)

Edward T. O'Donnell

Federalist Party. Political party of the late eighteenth century and the early nineteenth. Taking coherent shape between the ratification of the U.S. Constitution in 1788 and the presidential election of 1792, it sought to maintain close ties with Great Britain and was sympathetic to commercial and manufacturing interests. The party became powerful in New York City during the 1790s, owing to the prominence of its leaders Alexander Hamilton and John Jay, property restrictions on voting, and the strength of the party in other parts of the country; it declined because of Thomas Jefferson's success in the election of 1800, the souring of relations with Britain after 1805, the expansion of suffrage, and the arrogance and insensitivity of its leaders, who too often tried to command the deference rather than win the support of the city's voters. Defeats prompted some Federalist candidates to adopt Republican campaign strategies, an approach that proved successful. The party lost control of the Common Council when voting laws were made more liberal in 1804, but regained control briefly in 1806 and again in 1809 as the city suffered the effects of Jefferson's Embargo. Bolstered by the unpopularity of the War of 1812, it retained the majority until 1815, except in 1813 when the council was evenly divided between Federalists and Republicans. The party nominated Rufus King of New York for vice president in 1808 and for president in 1816, and supported De Witt Clinton in 1812. It eventually disintegrated nationwide and ceased to exist in the city by 1820.

Sidney I. Pomerantz: *New York: An American City, 1783–1803: A Study of Urban Life* (New York: Columbia University Press, 1938; 2nd edn Port Washington, N.Y.: I. J. Friedman, 1965)

Howard B. Rock: *Artisans of the New Republic: The Tradesmen of New York City in the Age of Jefferson* (New York: New York University Press, 1979)

Evan Cornog

Federal Reserve Bank of New York. One of twelve banks formed under the Federal Reserve Act to regulate currency, discount commercial credit, and supervise banks belonging to the Federal Reserve System; it opened on 16 November 1914 in temporary quarters at 62 Cedar Street as the keystone of the Federal Reserve System, its main purpose being to dominate a group of private bankers in the East that largely controlled the country's finances. During its first day of business it received $99,611,670 in deposits from 479 commercial banks, thus helping to secure its own supremacy and the success of the system. Its first governor was Benjamin Strong, a president of Bankers Trust who consolidated the bank's position as the heart of the Federal Reserve System by manipulating the regulatory authority of the Congress, drawing on his own knowledge of international finance, and availing himself of the city's strength as a fi-

Gold vault of the Federal Reserve Bank of New York. Courtesy of the Federal Reserve Bank of New York

nancial center (especially its access to foreign money markets, national banks, and deposit reserves). The bank soon dominated the Federal Reserve Board and acted as an agent for the eleven other federal reserve banks in purchasing government securities. Under Strong it introduced a national check collection system, extended its domain to northern New Jersey and Fairfield County in Connecticut (1916), and began accepting and holding the gold of foreign nations (1916). In 1922 construction began on permanent headquarters at 33 Library Street, designed by Phillip Sawyer in a Florentine Renaissance style (the building became a city landmark in 1965). During the 1920s Strong used credit policy to keep interest rates low, thus encouraging expansion in the United States and investment abroad. When speculative fever grew after 1928 he nonetheless raised the discount rate three times, to 5 percent. At his death in October 1928 he was succeeded by George Harrison, who permitted the money supply to shrink and in 1930 failed to win approval from the Open Market Committee of the Federal Reserve to intervene in the bond market. The Federal Reserve Bank of New York lost some of its influence in 1935, when the Federal Reserve was restructured to shift the focus of its operation to Washington. After 1940 presidents of the Federal Reserve Bank of New York included Allan Sproul (1941–56), Alfred Hayes (1956–75), Paul Volcker (1975–79), Anthony Solomon (1980–84), E. Gerald Corrigan (1985–93), and William J. McDonough (1993–). The bank remains a vital element of federal monetary policy, conducting domestic open market operations and all foreign exchange trading on behalf of the Federal Reserve System. The largest and most active federal reserve bank, it handles transactions worth more than $2,000,000 million a day, holds 40 percent of the world's gold for eighty countries in its vast underground vaults, and has three thousand employees.

George J. Lankevich

Federation of Jewish Philanthropies. An agency formed in 1917 by fifty-four Jewish charitable organizations to consolidate their fund raising. During its first campaign it collected $200,000 more than its individual member organizations had done in 1915. To avoid conflicts the agency excluded religious educational organizations; in 1942 it absorbed a parallel organization in Brooklyn. By the late 1960s funds raised for Jewish agencies in Queens, Nassau, Suffolk, and Westchester reached $22 million. In 1974 the Federation combined its fund-raising activities with those of the United Jewish Appeal.

Boris Bogen: *Jewish Philanthropy* (New York: Macmillan, 1917)
Encyclopedia Judaica (New York: Macmillan, 1971)

Jean Ulitz Mensch

Feiffer, Jules (*b* Bronx, 26 Jan 1929). Cartoonist and writer. As a child in the Bronx during the Depression he was influenced by comics and radio programs; he soon imitated master cartoonists' work and at an early age produced his own comic books. From 1946 he worked as an assistant to the syndicated cartoonist Will Eisner, with whom he produced "The Spirit" from 1949 to 1952, a popular cartoon carried by the *New York Daily Compass*, the newspaper of the Progressive Party. He wrote the book *Munro* while serving in the army from 1951 to 1953, followed by *Passionella* and *Sick, Sick, Sick*, none of which he was able to publish. Seeking to arouse interest in these works, he offered his services gratis to the *Village Voice*, which published his weekly comic strip of social and political satire. This became nationally syndicated in 1959; *Sick, Sick, Sick* was published during the same year and *Passionella* in 1960, and *Munro* was eventually made into an animated film by Al Kouzel and Gene Deitch that won an Academy Award. His play *Little Murders* had its première on Broadway in 1967 but closed after seven performances; it reopened in 1969 under the direction of Alan Arkin at the Circle in the Square and won an Obie Award and an Outer Circle Drama Critics award. In 1971 he adapted *Little Murders* for the screen and wrote the screenplay for *Carnal Knowledge* (directed by Mike Nichols). He next completed a dramatization of "Hold Me," a comic strip he had produced in 1962, for the American Place Theater in 1977 and the screenplay for Robert Altman's *Popeye* in 1980. In 1985 he won a Pulitzer Prize for editorial cartooning. Feiffer's many books include *The Great Comic Book Heroes* (1965, edited by E. L. Doctorow), the cartoon novel *Feiffer on Nixon: The Cartoon Presidency* (1974), *Tantrum* (1979), and *Ronald Reagan in Movie-America* (1988). In addition to politics he also bases his work on the struggles of individuals in modern urban society.

Grai St. Clair Rice

Feld Ballet. Ballet company. Formed in 1974 by Eliot Feld, it gave the premières of his own ballets and performed others by George Balanchine, Bronislava Nijinska, and David Parsons. Efforts begun in 1982 with the Board of Original Ballets Foundation to raise funds for a permanent home led to the renovation of an old movie theater, renamed the Joyce Theater. The company made its European début at the Festival International de Danse in Paris and was featured on the public television series "Dance in America." The New Ballet School, opened by Feld in 1978 to offer free training to talented students in the public schools, had given auditions to more than seventy thousand students by 1992.

Peter Maguire

Fellowship of Reconciliation. A pacifist organization formed in 1915 in Garden City, Long Island, and later based in New York City. During the First World War it worked to obtain conscientious objector status for members of the armed forces who had been inducted in spite of their opposition to war, and it attracted as members such prominent New Yorkers as Roger Baldwin, Paul Jones, John Haynes Holmes, and Norman Thomas. In the following decades it continued to advocate pacifism, racial equality, and social change, which it sought to further through union organizing and other nonviolent action.

Its members were instrumental in forming other progressive groups, including the American Civil Liberties Union, and a local chapter of the organization in Chicago evolved into the Congress of Racial Equality in 1943. During the McCarthy period two of its leaders, Thomas and A. J. Muste, debated two communist leaders at Carnegie Hall. In 1957 the Fellowship of Reconciliation left the city for Upper Nyack, New York.

Richard Deats: "The Rebel Passion," *Fellowship*, Jan–Feb 1990

Thomas M. Hilbink

Felt, James (*b* New York City, 29 June 1903; *d* New York City, 4 March 1971). Real-estate developer and public official. He graduated from the Wharton School in 1924, worked in real estate for his father, Abraham Felt, and in 1932 established his own firm, which dealt primarily in building management, tenant relocations, and the assembly of land packages for large development projects. As the chairman of the City Planning Commission from 1 January 1956 to 22 December 1962 he devised a master plan for the rezoning of New York City and conducted a major urban renewal study that called for the rehabilitation of older buildings, despite strong opposition from Robert Moses. In 1961 he urged Mayor Robert F. Wagner to form the Mayor's Committee for the Preservation of Structures of Historic and Esthetic Importance, the predecessor to the Landmarks Preservation Commission. His projects as a developer included Stuyvesant Town and Peter Cooper Village.

Brooke J. Barr

Feltman, Charles (*b* Verden, Germany, 8 Nov 1841; *d* Kassel, Germany, 20 Sept 1910). Businessman. He emigrated to the United States while in his teens and in 1874 opened a shorefront shanty where he sold "Frankfort sausages" encased in oblong rolls. The venture proved so successful that in the following year he opened the Ocean Pavilion, a mammoth restaurant in Coney Island that stretched from Surf Avenue to the shore along West 10th Street (where it remained for more than seventy-five years); he also offered a variety of entertainments ranging from Tyrolean singers to magnificent carousels. Inspired by his example, by 1882 more than eighty immigrant vendors sold frankfurters at Coney Island for five cents each.

Stephen Weinstein

feminism. New York City became a center of feminist activism after the Civil War. The women's club Sorosis was formed in 1868 by the writer Jane Cunningham Croly in response to the decision of the New York Press Club to bar women; it provided an intellectual and social forum for women and was one of the first organizations of its kind in the country. During the same year Elizabeth Cady Stanton and Susan B. Anthony organized the National Woman Suffrage Association (see WOMAN SUFFRAGE), which held conventions during the 1870s that provided platforms for advocates of women's rights, including the radical orator Victoria Woodhull. During the Progressive era the number of women's associations in the city increased rapidly. Among those formed were the Consumer's League (1891), the National Consumer's League (1899), the New York Federation of Women's Clubs (1895), the New York Women's City Club (1915), and a branch of the Woman's Peace Party (1915). The New York Women's Trade Union League (1903) took part in the shirtwaist strike of 1909–10 and protested the Triangle Shirtwaist fire of 1911. Women established many of the eighty-two settlement houses open in the city in 1911, including the College Settlement (1889) and the Henry Street Settlement (1893), which was directed by Lillian Wald. The issue of woman suffrage led to the formation of several local societies: the Woman Suffrage Party, the Equality League of Self Supporting Women, the New York City Equal Suffrage League, the New York Collegiate Suffrage League, and the Progressive Union for Woman Suffrage, which organized the first suffrage parade in 1908. Heterodoxy, a feminist discussion group, was formed by twenty-five women in 1912. Margaret Sanger published the magazine *Woman Rebel* in 1914 and in 1916 opened the country's first birth control clinic, in Brownsville. The pacifist Crystal Eastman and the anarchist Emma Goldman were also prominent figures in the struggle for feminist goals.

During the 1920s such national organizations as the League of Women Voters (1920) and the National Federation of Business and Professional Women's Clubs (1919) opened branches in the city. In 1935 Mary McLeod Bethune organized the National Council of Negro Women at a YWCA in Harlem. Even as feminism declined nationally between the 1920s and the 1950s, the city remained a center for professional women in such fields as publishing, journalism, advertising, and retailing, and attracted women college graduates seeking employment.

During the feminist revival of the 1960s the city became known as a stronghold for women's liberation. Such groups as New York Radical Women, New York Radical Feminists, and Redstockings were formed late in the decade and grew rapidly. The news media covered feminist demonstrations, among them the invasion of McSorley's Old Ale House (which refused admission to women for many years) and protests at the offices of national publications. Feuds within the local branch of the National Organization for Women (1966) also received widespread publicity. On 26 August 1970 thousands of women joined the Strike for Equality, a march to celebrate the fiftieth anniversary of woman suffrage. *Ms.* magazine was launched in the city in 1972. Local feminist leaders included Betty Friedan, president of the National Organization for Women from 1966 to 1970, Gloria Steinem, editor of *Ms.*, and the writers Kate Millett, Robin Morgan, and Susan Brownmiller. In the 1980s and early 1990s feminists in the city were involved in reproductive rights, economic equality, sexual harassment, and violence against women, and a number of local colleges and universities introduced women's studies programs and research centers.

Nancy Woloch

Rally for reproductive freedom at Lexington Avenue and 43rd Street, May 1990, sponsored by the National Organization for Women to protest the agreement by Hill and Knowlton to develop an anti-abortion advertising campaign for the Catholic church

fencing. New York City is the site of the oldest club devoted exclusively to fencing in the United States, the New York Fencers Club (1883), as well as many other clubs involved in fencing to a lesser degree, such as the New York Athletic Club (which added fencing to its activities in the 1880s). The Amateur Fencer's League of America, formed in the city in 1894, eventually became the United States Fencing Association and moved to Olympic training facilities in Colorado Springs. During the same year the Intercollegiate Fencing Association was organized in the city and presented its first trophy, which became known as the "little iron man"; the association later presided over the championships of the Eastern Collegiate Athletic Conference and continued to award its trophy into the 1990s, by which time it was the oldest trophy in American intercollegiate athletics. An important figure in the history of fencing in the city was Giorgio Santelli: after emigrating in the 1920s from Hungary, a country that his father established as a major force in saber fencing, he founded the Salle Santelli in 1939 and taught many national champions in the city before moving his school and fencing equipment business to New Jersey in 1982. One of his coaches continued to operate a school in New York City, with his permission, as Salle Santelli of New York. Fencing programs at City College, Columbia University, Hunter College, St. John's University, and New York University have been some of the most successful in the United States. Between 1986 and 1993 Columbia won the championship of the National Collegiate Athletic Association five times and placed second three times. In 1990 more than 60 percent of the U.S. Olympic Fencing Team was drawn from the city's schools and clubs. One of the best-known fencers from the city is Peter Westbrook, who competed in the Olympics five times beginning in 1976, winning a bronze medal in saber competition in 1984.

Eric Wm. Allison

Ferber, Edna (*b* Kalamazoo, Mich., 15 Aug 1885; *d* New York City, 7 April 1968). Novelist and playwright. She achieved early success with her short stories about Emma McChesney, a traveling saleswoman who sells petticoats in the Midwest, and also worked as a reporter. On the advice of her publisher she moved in 1912 to Manhattan. With George V. Hobart she adapted her stories about McChesney for the stage; their dramatization opened on Broadway in 1915 and ran for 151 performances. She became an occasional member of the Algonquin Round Table and an increasingly prolific writer. In general her work was not critically successful, but she did receive the Pulitzer Prize for her novel *So Big* (1924). Her novel *Show Boat* (1926) was the basis for the musical of the same name by Jerome Kern. Ferber's sentimental realism, strong female characters, and wit are most effective in the plays she wrote with George S. Kaufman, especially those like *Dinner at Eight* (1932) and *Stage Door* (1936) that satirize metropolitan life. She wrote two memoirs, including *A Peculiar Treasure* (1939). She lived in the 1920s at 50 Central Park West, in the early 1930s at the Hotel Lombardy (111 East 56th Street), until 1938 at 791 Park Avenue, and from about 1950 to the end of her life at 730 Park Avenue.

Brenda Wineapple

Fermi, Enrico (*b* Rome, 29 Sept 1901; *d* Chicago, 28 Nov 1954). Physicist. In 1933 he formulated a theory of beta decay based on the neutrino. After winning the Nobel Prize for physics in 1938 he moved to New York City and joined the physics department at Columbia University, where he worked with H. L. Anderson on nuclear fission. He remained at Columbia until 1945. Fermi was an important figure in the Manhattan Project, which developed the atomic bomb.

James E. Mooney

Ferraro, Geraldine A(nne) (*b* Newburgh, N.Y., 26 Aug 1935). Congresswoman and vice-presidential candidate. She taught in public schools while attending law school at Fordham University, practiced law (1961–74), and was an assistant district attorney in Queens County (1974–78). In 1978 she was elected to the House of Representatives as a Democrat from the ninth congressional district of New York. She became the first woman to be nominated for national office by a major party when in 1984 the Democratic presidential nominee, Walter F. Mondale, chose her as his vice-presidential candidate. In 1992 she unsuccessfully sought the Democratic nomination for the U.S. Senate. Ferraro is a long-time resident of Forest Hills Gardens. She wrote a memoir, *Ferraro: My Story* (1985).

Rosemary Breslin and Joshua Hammer: *Gerry!: A Woman Making History* (New York: Pinnacle, 1984)

Mary Elizabeth Brown

ferries. Because it is built largely on islands, New York City depended on ferries before it had bridges and tunnels. American Indians had been crossing local waterways with rafts and canoes for centuries when European settlers first made organized crossings of the East River in 1642. In 1661 the Netherlands Council granted a ferry charter to William Jansen for a route from Manhattan to Communipaw (now in Jersey City), New Jersey. Charters for other routes soon followed.

Early vessels were scows propelled by oars and sails, until small sloops and a distinctive sailing vessel called a "periauger" became dominant in the eighteenth century. The first steam ferry, the *Juliana*, began service in 1811 from Hoboken to Vesey Street under the direction of Colonel John Stevens. In the following year Robert Fulton and Robert R. Livingston established another service across the Hudson River, between Cortlandt Street and Powles Hook, with the *Jersey* and the *York*. Routes from Manhattan to Brooklyn across the East River were inaugurated successively by Fulton and William Cutting (from Beekman's Slip, 1814), by the South Ferry (from Whitehall Street to Atlantic Street, 1836), and by the Hamilton Ferry (from the Battery to Hamilton Avenue, 1846). By 1854 the Union Ferry Company had consolidated a dozen competing lines and was making 1250 crossings a day at a standard fare of two cents. Williamsburgh, for example, was served by six steam ferries leaving Peck Slip every ten minutes during the working day and Grand Street

South Ferry, Brooklyn

for New York State was enacted after many alterations in 1881.

Daun Van Ee: *David Dudley Field and the Reconstruction of the Law* (New York: Garland, 1986)

See also LAWYERS.

James D. Folts

Fieldston. A privately owned neighborhood in the northwestern Bronx, bounded to the north by 250th Street, to the east by Manhattan College, to the south by Manhattan College Parkway, and to the west by the Henry Hudson Parkway. The land was once an estate of 250 acres (one hundred hectares) purchased in 1829 by Major Joseph Delafield, who named it after his family seat in England. At the beginning of the twentieth century it was developed for housing by the Delafield family. Lots were laid out along the contours of the rugged terrain rather than according to the grid adopted in other parts of the city. The name Delafield Woods was used for a while in the first quarter of the twentieth century; game was abundant and deer were seen until 1908. After the Broadway subway was extended to 242nd Street the first house was completed in 1911. In the 1920s houses in a Tudor style were built, many designed by Dwight J. Baum, a local resident. Manhattan College, run by the Christian Brothers, moved to the area from Manhattanville after a land purchase in 1922. Several private schools also established themselves in the area, including the Fieldston School, Horace Mann Preparatory School, and the Riverdale Country Day School. Known for its trees, large houses, and rural ambience, Fieldston was one of the wealthiest neighborhoods in the city in the mid 1990s.

Lloyd Ultan and Gary Hermalyn: *The Bronx in the Innocent Years, 1890–1925* (New York: Harper and Row, 1985)

Gary D. Hermalyn

246th Street and Delafield Road in Fieldston, 1992

Fierstein, Harvey (Forbes) (*b* New York City, 6 June 1954). Playwright. The son of a handkerchief manufacturer, he grew up in Brooklyn and attended high school and studied art in Manhattan. He performed in cabarets on the Lower East Side, often as a female impersonator, and was well known for his portrayal of Ethel Merman. At twenty-two he wrote an autobiographical one-act play that was produced off Broadway; he played the leading role of Arnold Beckoff. This play and two others completed in 1981 became *Torch Song Trilogy*, which ran on Broadway for three years and in 1983 won Tony Awards for best actor and best play. His musical *La Cage aux Folles* (1983), which he wrote while riding the subway to work, also won a Tony Award. In later years Fierstein undertook a number of film and television projects.

Janet Frankston

Fifth Avenue Coach Lines. Firm of bus operators. Formed in 1885, it ran horse-drawn buses on 5th Avenue between Washington Square and 89th Street, and in 1905 it began the first successful motorbus operation in the United States, retiring all its horse-drawn buses in 1908. The firm demonstrated that single- and double-decker buses could be durable, urban mass transit vehicles. As New York City grew in 1900–30 it extended its routes northward to Harlem and Washington Heights along Riverside Drive, upper 7th Avenue, St. Nicholas Avenue, and Broadway, and eastward over the Queensboro Bridge to Jackson Heights. After forming the New York City Omnibus Corporation as a subsidiary in 1926 the firm purchased New York Railways, the dominant streetcar operator in Manhattan, and converted the streetcars to buses between February 1935 and August 1936. Double-decker bus service ceased in 1953. The firm acquired the Surface Transportation Corporation in 1956, assuming its five bus routes in Manhattan and its entire system in the Bronx. In 1962 Fifth Avenue was purchased by a group of investors led by Harry Weinberg, whose efforts to discharge some unionized employees to reduce costs promptly caused a strike on 1 March. As a result of the strike the city acquired the firm's buses and garages by legal condemnation on 22 March, and the routes were taken over by the Manhattan and Bronx Surface Transit Operating Authority, itself now part of the New York City Transit Authority.

Andrew Sparberg

Fifth Avenue Hotel. Hotel on 5th Avenue between 23rd and 24th streets (opposite Madison Square), built by the developer Amos Eno from 1856 to 1858. Initially far from the hotel district, it was known as "Eno's folly" but soon became popular for its luxuriousness. It occupied a six-story building with a colonnade at the entrance and had fireplaces in every bedroom, private bathrooms, and elegant public rooms; it was also the first hotel in the city with elevators, which were steam-operated and known as the "vertical railroad." The hotel could accommodate eight hundred guests, and a staff of four hundred provided some of the best service in the city. Within a few years most of the city's grand hotels moved into the surrounding blocks. The hotel was the headquarters of the state Republican Party and contained an office of the Republican boss Thomas C. Platt, an architect of consolidation; a corridor off the lobby where he met petitioners seeking favors became known as the "amen corner." By the turn of the century fashionable neighborhoods moved north, and in 1908 the Fifth Avenue Hotel was closed and demolished. It is commemorated by a plaque on its former site.

Harold Foote Gosnell: *Boss Platt and His New York Machine* (Chicago: University of Chicago Press, 1924)

Nathan Silver: *Lost New York* (Boston: Houghton Mifflin, 1967)

Oliver E. Allen: *New York, New York* (New York: Atheneum, 1985)

Eric Wm. Allison

Fifth Avenue Presbyterian Church. Church at 5th Avenue and 55th Street, formed in 1875 by a congregation organized in 1808 on Cedar Street. Its first minister, John Brodhead Romeyn (1808–25), a moderator of the Presbyterian General Assembly, gave the church its reputation as the "cathedral church of Presbyterianism." Later ministers at the church included John Hall (1867–96), John Sutherland Bonnell (1935–62), and Bryant Kirkland (1962–87). Among the institutions formed under their leadership were the Duane Street Mission (1836–1913), the Romeyn Chapel on East 14th Street (1858–1904), which enrolled more than eight hundred children in its Sunday school, and a Chinese Sunday school (to 1909). The church's 2715 members made it the largest Presbyterian church in the city in 1991.

A Noble Landmark of New York: The Fifth Avenue Presbyterian Church, 1808–1958 (New York: Fifth Avenue Presbyterian Church, 1960)

David Meerse

52nd Street. A street known for its jazz clubs during the 1930s and 1940s, also called Swing Street. Between 5th and 6th avenues it was lined with Victorian brownstones that were used as speakeasies during Prohibition and converted to restaurants and nightclubs after its repeal in 1933. Clubs such as the Onyx, the Famous Door, Jimmy Ryan's, the Three Deuces, the Downbeat, Hickory House, and Kelly's Stable featured the big bands of Count Basie and Woody Herman and such soloists as the pianists Art Tatum and Fats Waller, the singer Billie Holiday, the trumpeter Roy Eldridge, and the violinist Stuff Smith. The clubs attracted racially mixed audiences and provided a fertile environment for improvisation. By 1943 such innovative bebop players as Charlie Parker, Miles Davis, Bud Powell, and Dizzy Gillespie shifted their attention from Harlem to 52nd Street because of its greater opportunities for money and exposure, and after riots erupted in Harlem in the same year white customers increasingly favored clubs in midtown. The clubs of 52nd Street eventually lost popularity because of the unscrupulous practices of some owners, the association of jazz with drugs, harassment by the police, and an increase in real-estate values as skyscrapers began to crowd midtown Manhattan. Jazz districts took shape around Times Square in the late 1940s and later in Greenwich Village. Several clubs opened on Broadway, among them the Royal Roost (1674 Broadway, 1946), Bop City (1619 Broadway at 49th Street, 1948), and Birdland (on Broadway just north of 52nd Street, December 1949). By January 1950 Jimmy Ryan's was the only club offering live music on 52nd Street itself. During the following years the street was dominated by striptease houses, and in the 1960s large office buildings replaced the brownstones.

Arnold Shaw: *The Street That Never Slept: New York's Fabled 52d Street* (New York: Coward, McCann and Geoghegan, 1971)

Ira Berger, Marc Ferris

Filipinos. Very few people from the Philippines settled in New York City before the 1920s. Most Filipinos in the area were either servicemen assigned to local military installations such as Governors Island or farm workers who moved from the western United States to seek employment. The first known Filipino organization in the city, the Filipino Social Club of Brooklyn, was formed in 1928. More Filipinos moved to New York City after the Second World War, but their numbers remained insignificant; this group included the children of earlier immigrants, students, and tourists who decided to stay in the United States. The third and largest phase of Filipino immigration to New York City began during the American economic boom of the 1960s, as local hospitals actively recruited Filipino doctors and nurses, and Filipino accountants, engineers, and teachers were in demand. Many people fled the Philippines during the dictatorship of Ferdinand Marcos (1971–81), some as political refugees and others for economic reasons. Filipinos during these years assimilated so easily into the American mainstream that they were not as visible as other immigrant groups in New York City. Most were familiar with American culture because of the former status of the Philippines as an American colony (1898–1946), and spoke English in addition to their native language (Tagalog). The federal census of 1990 enumerated 43,229 persons of Filipino origin in New York City. The most common occupation among Filipinos in the city was nursing, and in many local hospitals Filipino nurses came to constitute the majority of the nursing staff.

The largest concentration of Filipinos in New York City is in Woodside, where several Filipino grocery stores and restaurants line Roosevelt Avenue. Filipinos also live in Flushing, Hollis, and Queens Village, and near 1st Avenue and 14th Street in Manhattan. Smaller numbers live in Staten Island and Brooklyn. More than 90 percent of the Filipinos in New York City are Roman Catholic. Our Lady of Pompeii Church in Greenwich Village offers programs for its Filipino parishioners and has a Filipino associate pastor. In addition to the Filipino Mass, Filipino Catholics in New York City practice religious rituals such as the Flores de Mayo (also called the Santa Cruzan) and the block rosary (or Santo Niño). Other Catholic churches that offer services for Filipinos include St. Francis de Sales Church, Holy Innocents Roman Catholic Church, the Church of St. Agnes, and the Church of the Blessed Sacrament in Manhattan; and St. Sebastian's Roman Catholic Church, St. Michael's Church, and Immaculate Conception Church in Queens. Iglesia ni Cristo, a Christian sect formed in the Philippines, has a church in Long Island City. Three weekly Filipino newspapers circulate in New York City: the *Filipino Reporter* (published in the city), the *Filipino Express* (Jersey City, New Jersey), and *Philippine News* (San Francisco), which maintains a news bureau in New York City.

Carlos Bulosan: *America Is in the Heart: A Personal History* (Harcourt, Brace, 1946; repr. Seattle: University of Washington Press, 1981)
Manuel Buaken: *I Have Lived with the American People* (Caldwell, Idaho: Caxton, 1948)
Caridad C. Guidote: "Filipinos in the United States," *Pacific Historical Review* 43 (1974), 521–67
Ronald T. Takaki: *Strangers from a Different Shore: A History of Asian Americans* (Boston: Little, Brown, 1989)

Chibu Lagman, Noël Shaw

Fillmore East. Theater on 2nd Avenue between 6th and 7th streets, opened in an old building about 1968 as a venue for rock concerts. It was operated by Bill Graham, a rock impresario who had also opened the Fillmore in San Francisco. Among the musicians who performed there were Joe Cocker, Jimi Hendrix, and Janis Joplin, and the members of the Grateful Dead, the Incredible String Band, the Jefferson Airplane, Country Joe and the Fish, and Procul Harum. Elaborate "light shows" were mounted by a production company called the Joshua Light Show. The audiences at the Fillmore East were well known for their rowdiness. The theater closed in the late 1970s.

Leslie Gourse

filmmaking. Filmmaking had its origins just outside New York City, when Thomas Edison worked in Orange, New Jersey, from 1888 to 1893 with his staff of experimenters, notably William Kennedy Laurie Dickson. In early 1894 Dickson and the cameraman William Heise initiated regular commercial production at the Black Maria studio next to Edison's laboratory. They made 35-millimeter films, ranging in length from fifty to 150 feet (fifteen to forty-five meters), that were meant for exhibition in the peephole kinetoscope. Charles E. Chinnock, a former employee of Edison, probably made the first motion picture film in what became New York City itself, in November 1894; he built a camera and made films for exhibition in his own, somewhat larger version of the kinetoscope. His first film, shot on the rooftop of 1729 St. Marks Avenue in Brooklyn, was of a boxing match between Robert T. Moore and James W. Lahey. Short films of dancing girls, a cockfight, and other subjects followed, all made in imitation of Edison's work. Early filmmaking in New York City was also pursued by other former associates of Edison: from May 1895 Woodville Latham and his sons Otway and Gray produced pictures for their eidoloscope projector at 35 Frankfort Street in Manhattan; Dickson by the spring of 1896 had become a part owner and the chief cameraman for the American Mutoscope Company; and Charles Webster and Edmund Kuhn formed the International Film Company and were in production by October 1896. After the Edison company completed the construction of a portable camera in May 1896, its staff members were frequently in Manhattan and at Coney Island shooting scenes of everyday life (*Central Park*, *Elevated Railway Station*, *23rd Street*, and *Shooting the Chutes*). Within a short time they were using a makeshift studio on the rooftop of 43 West 28th Street.

New York City quickly became the center of the American film industry, a position it retained until the time of the First World War. Many early film companies were short-lived; the three principal producers before 1906 were the Edison Manufacturing Company, the American Mutoscope Company (later renamed the American Mutoscope and Biograph Company), and the American Vitagraph

The first kinetoscope parlor, opened on 14 April 1894 at 1155 Broadway, where customers used Thomas Edison's Peep-hole Kinetoscope to view a single film loop shot with a kinetograph

D. W. Griffith's The Musketeers of Pig Alley *(1912)*. From left: *Lillian Gish, Dorothy Gish, Adolph Lestina*

Company (its production entity was known from 1905 as the Vitagraph Company of America). After a proliferation of storefront theaters from late 1905 to 1906, film production expanded rapidly. The Kalem Company was formed in early 1907 with offices at 31 West 24th Street. Kalem along with Edison, Biograph, Vitagraph, two European producers with offices in New York City (Pathé and Méliès), and three producers from Chicago and Philadelphia formed the Motion Picture Patents Company in New York City in late 1908. The company intended to control all film production in the United States, but these plans failed. Carl Laemmle's Independent Moving Picture Company (IMP) and the New York Motion Picture Company were making films in New York City and vicinity by 1909. They were followed in 1910–11 by the Yankee Film Company, the Champion Film Company, Reliance, Solax, Rex, Atlas, Thanhouser, Powers, and Nestor. All had offices in New York City, though many had studios in the outer boroughs, in Yonkers and New Rochelle in Westchester, and in Coytesville, Jersey City, and Fort Lee in New Jersey. Several united to form the Universal Film Manufacturing Company in 1912.

In the same year Adolph Zukor, Edwin S. Porter, and Daniel Frohman formed the Famous Players Film Company, with offices on West 26th Street, to make feature films of three or more reels (one hour or more in length). These initially featured well-known theatrical stars in filmed adaptations of their stage hits: James O'Neill in *The Count of Monte Cristo* (1912), James Hackett in *The Prisoner of Zenda* (1913), Mrs. Fiske in *Tess of the D'Urbervilles* (1913). William Fox expanded into filmmaking in 1914, producing *A Fool There Was* (1914) with Theda Bera and *Regeneration* (1915), directed by Raoul Walsh: both offered exterior scenes shot in New York City. In 1913 the vaudeville impresario Jesse Lasky, Samuel Goldfish (later known as Samuel Goldwyn), and Cecil B. DeMille formed the Jesse L. Lasky Feature Play Company. All New Yorkers, the three followed a growing trend by establishing their production studio in Hollywood. They acquired some of David Belasco's employees (notably the lighting designer Wilfred Buckland) and film rights to his plays, which resulted in such productions as *The Girl of the Golden West* (1914) and *The Warrens of Virginia* (1915).

Film producers in New York City seeking better weather and new locales began sending small companies of actors and staff to California, Florida, and Cuba for winter shooting. Biograph, for example, sent a company to Los Angeles in January 1910. By 1912 Bison and Keystone (both owned by the New York Motion Picture Company), Nestor, Selig, Kalem, and Pathé had permanent production units based in Los Angeles, and Hollywood was the dominant production center by 1915, though executive offices remained in New York City. Production in the city continued, but a coal shortage in the winter of 1918–19 forced most remaining production units to move to the west coast and encouraged the further consolidation of operations.

Some production then returned to New York City, where creative personnel sometimes felt more at home. Norma Talmadge returned from the west coast in 1917 and with her husband and producer, Joseph Schenck, opened a studio at 320 East 48th Street where *The Song of Love* was filmed in 1924. By 1920 William Randolph Hearst had converted Sulzer's Harlem River Park and Casino at 127th Street and 2nd Avenue into the Cosmopolitan studio, which turned out pictures featuring his mistress, the comedian Marion Davies (*The*

Restless Sex, 1920; *When Knighthood Was in Flower*, 1922), and *Humoresque*, 1920, set on the Lower East Side. Fox opened a studio in May 1920 on West 55th Street in Manhattan, where Pearl White and Allan Dwan worked briefly. In September of the same year Famous Players–Lasky (forerunner of Paramount) opened a new studio in Astoria where Gloria Swanson made nine films, including *Manhandled* (1924). In 1922 the city's share of American production stood at 12 percent, compared with 84 percent for Hollywood. Hearst and Davies shifted operations to the west coast in 1924; in 1927 the Astoria studio temporarily closed, as did the Biograph studio (which had been operated for several years by First National); and Talmadge retired soon after the arrival of sound. Independent filmmakers producing pictures for specific ethnic or racial groups remained. The Lower East Side nurtured the production of Yiddish films (for example *Broken Hearts*, 1926, directed by Maurice Schwartz), and Harlem became a center for the production of black films. Oscar Micheaux had a business office in the city by 1922, while he shot much of *Body and Soul* (1924, with Paul Robeson) and *The Exile* (1930) in Fort Lee. Avant-garde films were also made occasionally, beginning with *Manhatta* (1921), inspired by Whitman and directed by Charles Sheeler and Paul Strand.

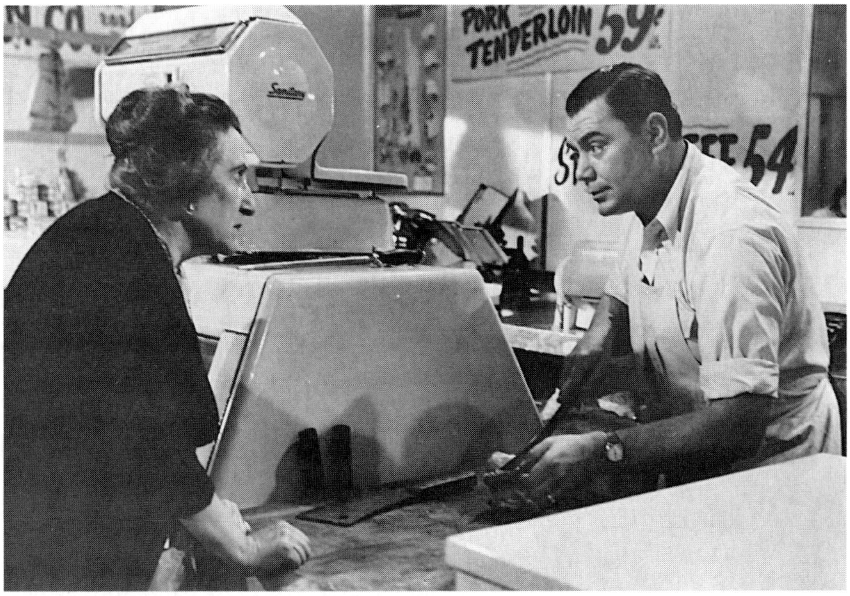

Ernest Borgnine in Marty *(1955, screenplay by Paddy Chayefsky), about a butcher in the Bronx*

Sound at least temporarily revived filmmaking in New York City. By 1926 the Fox Film Corporation was conducting sound experiments at its studio in New York City, which was also the base of Fox Movietone News (begun in 1927). The heavy dependence of feature filmmaking on sound stages reduced some of the advantages of Hollywood (notably its weather), and New York City was much closer to actors and directors who worked on Broadway. Paramount converted the Astoria studio to sound; its first talking feature appeared in 1929. Most films were adaptations of Broadway plays and musicals or vehicles that tested young talent from the stage. Perhaps this was one reason why the critic Harry Potamkin called for a "New York school" of filmmaking in December 1929: *Applause* (1929), made by Rouben Mamoulian, director of the Theater Guild, and two experimental films were somewhat wistfully offered as evidence. Feature filmmaking in New York City had virtually ceased by 1937, a year in which not a single feature was shot there in its entirety, according to the *Film Daily Year Book*. Astoria was producing only shorts and inserts for Hollywood pictures. Even an independent Yiddish production of the late 1930s such as *Dem Khazns Zundl* (The Cantor's Son, 1937) could not be counted, because extensive exteriors were shot in Pennsylvania, New Jersey, and Long Island. Among the very few films of the period made entirely in New York City were films with black casts such as *Moon over Harlem* (1939, directed by Edgar G. Ulmer) and *Murder on Lenox Avenue* (1941). By the late 1930s experienced, adept technicians had all moved to Hollywood. Although Mayor Fiorello H. La Guardia tried to induce makers of fiction films to return east in 1939, the war ended his efforts before any noticeable success.

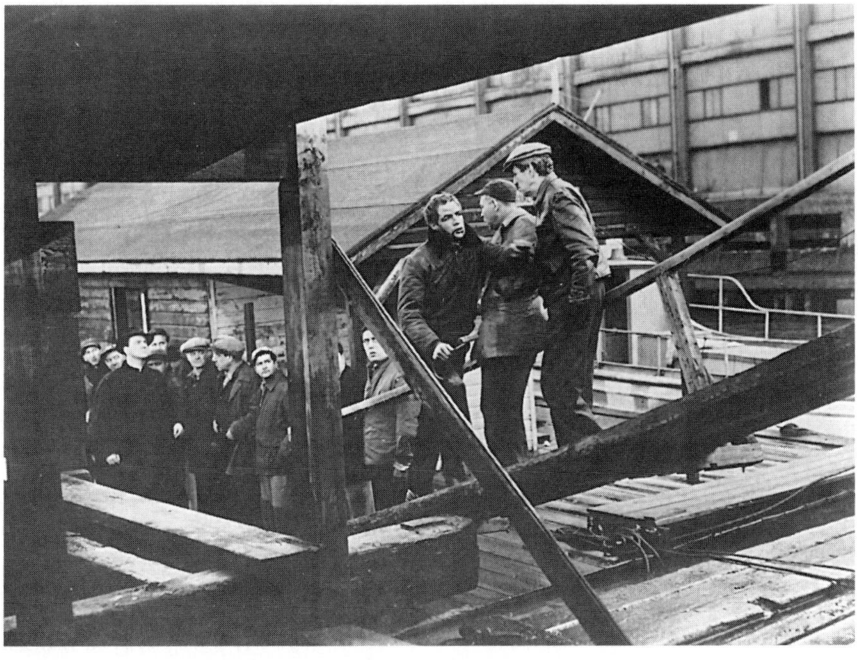

Marlon Brando in Elia Kazan's On the Waterfront *(1954)*

New York City nonetheless remained a center of documentary activity (see Documentary filmmaking), a strength that was reinforced during the war when the Army Signal Corps took over Astoria studio and made it the headquarters for its extensive filmmaking operations. Many Hollywood film people did return to New York City — in uniform. Meanwhile important structural changes were occurring in the industry that ensured a different future for American filmmaking. In 1938 the federal government sued Paramount Pictures for monopolistic practices, among them the exclusion from their theaters of independently produced films. The case broke up the vertically integrated film industry and facilitated independent production. With tax laws further encouraging this trend, the number of independent producers increased rapidly after 1945. The production of feature films that were relatively close to the mainstream re-

Martin Scorsese and Robert De Niro in Times Square during the filming of Taxi Driver *(Columbia Pictures, 1976). Collection of the American Museum of the Moving Image*

turned to the city with such pictures as *The House on 92nd Street* (1945), *Miracle on 34th Street* (1947), and *Naked City* (1948). Radio–Keith–Orpheum (RKO) built a studio on 134th Street and Park Avenue just after the war, used by the Hollywood producer David O. Selznick for *Portrait of Jeannie* (1948). At the same time the city after the Second World War became the most important center of avant-garde filmmaking in the world. The arrival of Hans Richter and other Europeans contributed to this prominence, as did the activities of Maya Deren, who made her own films (beginning with *Meshes of the Afternoon*, 1943) and was associated with the Film Artists Society (1953, renamed the Independent Film Makers Association in 1955), the Creative Film Foundation (1955), and the film society Cinema 16 (1947–63), which educated several generations of cinéastes in experimental and art film.

The rise of television and the continued strength of the theater supported the revival of filmmaking in New York City, providing training for technicians as well as early opportunities for such directors as Elia Kazan and Sidney Lumet. Kazan moved back and forth between filmmaking in Hollywood and theatrical directing in New York City, until *On the Waterfront* (1954), which was shot in Hoboken and on a small stage at the old Vitagraph studio in Brooklyn. Lumet's first film, *Twelve Angry Men* (1957, with Henry Fonda), was shot at the old Famous Players studio on West 26th Street. Both were the work of the cinematographer Boris Kaufman, who helped train a generation of cinematographers in the city.

In the early 1950s the tradition of social realism associated with documentary film gave way to underground films — bizarre sexual extravaganzas by Ron Rice, Ken Jacob, George and Mike Kuchar, and especially Jack Smith. The movement was brought to public prominence by the success of Andy Warhol's *The Chelsea Girls* (1966) and fragmented amid the political activism of the late 1960s: the members of New York Newsreel made agitational political films (such as *Columbia Revolt*, 1968), while other filmmakers forged a school of severely aestheticist "structural" films (beginning with Michael Snow's *Wavelength*, 1967) that bore a kinship with minimalist painting and sculpture. This independent film culture was sustained by many institutions, of which four were especially important: the journal *Film Culture* (first appearing in January 1955), which initially emphasized the European art cinema but by the end of the decade had committed itself to the American avant-garde; the New American Cinema Group, an organization formed to promote independent film production; the Filmmakers' Cooperative, a nondiscriminatory distribution agency run by and for filmmakers; and the Anthology Film Archives, a permanent collection of the "monuments of cinematic art" opened in 1970. A central role in all of these was played by Jonas Mekas, an émigré from Lithuania who also made a series of "diary films" (beginning with *Diaries, Notes and Sketches (Walden)*, 1968).

In the 1950s and 1960s old studios were refurbished: the Biograph Studio in the Bronx became the Gold Medal Studio, where Kazan shot *A Face in the Crowd* (1957). The Famous Players' Studio, renamed the Production Center Studios, was used for such films as Lumet's *Long Day's Journey Into Night* (1961) and Mel Brooks's *The Producers* (1967). A garage across from the old Cosmopolitan Studio was converted into the Filmways Studio, used for shooting Burt Balaban's and Stuart Rosenberg's *Murder Incorporated* (1960), Francis Ford Coppola's *The Godfather* (1971), and Woody Allen's *Annie Hall* (1977). These small and in many ways outdated facilities closed in the late 1970s and were essentially replaced by the newly renovated Astoria studio, reopened in November 1975 and renamed the Kaufman Astoria Studios in 1982. Elsewhere unexpected structures were converted to provide sound stages: the Silver Cup Studios in Long Island City, for example, were an old bakery converted into thirteen stages that opened in 1983; and the Chelsea Piers studio was built in 1988 on an abandoned pier at 23rd Street and the Hudson River.

As a growing number of television series were made on the west coast, feature filmmaking in New York City was to an extent sustained by Madison Avenue, which was creating increasingly sophisticated television advertisements in the 1960s and 1970s. Television commercials provided technical expertise, temporary work for those working in films, and a chance to break into the business for others. The Mayor's Office of Film, Theater and Broadcasting was set up by Mayor John V. Lindsay in May 1966 to facilitate citywide production. It offered greater police cooperation while centralizing and simplifying the issuing of permits for location shooting.

Independent features continued to be made by New Yorkers such as Robert Frank (*Pull My Daisy*, 1959), Shirley Clarke (*Cool World*, 1965), Robert Downey (*Putney Swope*, 1969), and John Cassavetes (*Husbands*, 1970). In the late 1960s and early 1970s there emerged a new generation of filmmakers closer to the commercial mainstream and fiercely committed to New York City: Allen (*Take the Money and Run*, 1969; *Hannah and Her Sisters*, 1986; *Shadows and Fog*, 1992; *Bullets over Broadway*, 1994), Martin Scorsese (*Mean Streets*, 1973; *Taxi Driver*, 1976; *King of Comedy*, 1982), Paul Mazursky (*Next Stop, Greenwich Village*, 1976). Others such as Milos Forman (*Ragtime*, 1981) also worked extensively in the city, as did younger filmmakers such as Spike Lee (*She's Gotta Have It*, 1986; *Do the Right Thing*, 1989). In the 1970s the avant-garde was revitalized by feminists, notably Yvonne Rainer, and members of racial minorities. Production was also pursued by a band of small-time but determined independents such as John Sayles (*The Brother from Another Planet*, 1984), Jim Jarmusch (*Stranger Than Paradise*, 1984), Amos Poe (*Alphabet City*, 1982), Raul Ruiz (*The Golden Boat*, 1990), Charles Lane (*Sidewalk Stories*, 1991), Tod Haynes (*Poison*, 1991), and Hal Hartley (*Trust*, 1991). Filmmakers often engaged issues of particular urgency to the city, notably the politics of race, violence, and American identity. The late 1980s saw something of a revival of the avant-garde, with super-8 film and video figuring prominently.

Many productions spend a few days location shooting in the city while shooting studio scenes in Los Angeles or Europe. According to the Mayor's Office of Film, Theater and Broadcasting, each year during the 1980s from sixty-one to more than a hundred feature films were shot at least in part in the city. Between November 1990 and May 1991 the Hollywood studios boycotted New York City in a labor dispute with local unions. This along with a weak economy and overproduction opened the 1990s on a note of uncertainty, but by mid decade feature filmmaking was returning to the city, with films by Ang Lee (*The Wedding Banquet*, 1993), Brian De Palma (*Carlito's Way*, 1993), and Wayne Wang (*Smoke*, 1995).

Gordon Hendricks: *The Kinetoscope: America's First Commercially Successful Motion Picture Exhibitor* (New York: Beginnings of the American Film, 1966)

P. Adams Sitney: *Visionary Film: The American Avant-garde, 1942–78* (New York: Oxford University Press, 1979)

Richard Koszarski: *The Astoria Studio and Its Fabulous Films: A Picture History with 227 Stills and Photographs* (New York: Dover, 1983)

Richard Alleman: *The Movie Lover's Guide to New York* (New York: Harper and Row, 1988)

David E. James: *Allegories of Cinema: American Film in the Sixties* (Princeton, N.J.: Princeton University Press, 1989)

Eileen Bowser: *The Transformation of Cinema, 1907–1915* (New York: Charles Scribner's Sons, 1990)
Richard Koszarski: *An Evening's Entertainment: The Age of the Silent Feature Picture, 1915–1928* (New York: Charles Scribner's Sons, 1990)
Charles Musser: *The Emergence of Cinema: The American Screen to 1907* (New York: Charles Scribner's Sons, 1990)
J. Hoberman: *Bridge of Light: Yiddish Film between Two Worlds* (New York: Museum of Modern Art, 1991)
Lauren Rabinovitz: *Points of Resistance: Women, Power and Politics in the New York Avant-garde Cinema, 1943–71* (Chicago: University of Illinois Press, 1991)
David E. James, ed.: *To Free the Cinema: Jonas Mekas and the New York Underground* (Princeton, N.J.: Princeton University Press, 1992)
Marc Wanamaker: *Encylopedia of Movie Studios* (forthcoming)

For further illustrations see ALLEN, WOODY, and LUMET, SIDNEY.

Charles Musser (with David James)

financial printing. The printing of prospectuses, annual reports, proxies, registration statements, public-offering circulars, and state and federal disclosure forms has long required a special expertise. The first printers catering to the needs of the financial community were established in the colonial period, among them Bowne and Company, formed in 1775 (which remained in business in the 1990s). In the nineteenth century and the early twentieth the demand for financial printing services was stable and predictable, and the business was a quiet one dominated by a few major firms: Sorg Printing (1820), Charles P. Young and Company (1902), Pandick Press (1923), Emory Fitch and Company, and Packard Press. Mergers and acquisitions in the 1980s markedly increased the demand for the services of financial printers, drawing into the field the large, established firm of R. R. Donnelley as well as many new firms. Financial printers built new plants and replaced hot-lead Linotypes with computer typesetting equipment. To accommodate customers requiring overnight production, they built lavish suites that included conference rooms, banks of telephones, beds, kitchens, and showers. Annual sales volume reached nearly $1000 million by 1987. By August 1989 heavy debt, reduced demand, and aggressive price cutting forced Packard, Sorg, and Charles P. Young into bankruptcy, leaving Bowne, Pandick, and R. R. Donnelley with about two thirds of the market.

Owen D. Gutfreund

Finch College. Women's college in Manhattan. It began in 1900 as a finishing school for young women run from a small apartment on 635 Madison Avenue by Jessica Garetson Cosgrave (1871–1949), a writer, feminist, and editor of the Sunday supplement of the *New York World.* In 1904 she opened the Finch School for Girls at 61 East 77th Street, naming it for her first husband, William Finch. She opened an elementary school in 1916 at 170 East 70th Street called the Lenox School to prepare students for Finch, which in the same year moved to 52 East 78th Street. Eventually the college occupied five brownstone row houses on the same street. By the time the school received a state charter in 1937 and became Finch Junior College it was one of the most famous finishing schools in the nation; in 1952 it became a four-year college offering bachelor's degrees in arts and sciences. It suffered financially in the mid 1970s and closed in 1976, the buildings razed to make way for an Orthodox Jewish school. Notable alumnae of Finch College included Tricia Nixon, daughter of the president, the actresses Suzanne Pleshette and Arlene Francis, and the rock star Grace Slick.

James Bradley

Fine, Reuben (*b* Bronx, 11 Oct 1914; *d* New York City, 26 March 1993). Psychoanalyst and chess player. Born into a poor family, he graduated from City College in 1932 and won the world chess championship in the Netherlands in 1938. One of the most feared players at the Marshall and Manhattan chess clubs in New York City, he was the finest "speed" player in the United States. He won eight of the thirteen international competitions in which he took part and tied for second in most of the others, and also won U.S. Open tournaments seven times between 1932 and 1941. During the Second World War he withdrew from competitive play, earned a doctorate in psychology, and set up a successful practice as a lay analyst in New York City, where he lived for most of his life. He was director of the New York Center for Psychoanalytic Training and the founder and first president of the Division of Psychotherapy and the Division of Psychoanalysis of the American Psychological Association. Fine's published writings include *The Psychology of the Chess Player* (1967) and *The Healing of the Mind: The Technique of Psychoanalytic Psychotherapy* (1971; 2nd edn 1982).

Kenneth T. Jackson

Fine Arts Federation. Arts council formed on 18 April 1895 by the American Institute of Architects, the Municipal Art Society, the National Sculpture Society, the Society of Beaux-Arts Architects, and five other organizations of artists and civic reformers, and incorporated in October 1897. The stated purpose of its founders was to "ensure united action by the Art Societies of New York in all matters affecting their common interests, and to foster and protect the artistic interests of the community." The first president was the noted architect, critic, and writer Russell Sturgis. With other organizations and the architect John M. Carrère the federation was instrumental in establishing the Art Commission of the City of New York in 1898, and it later assumed responsibility for submitting the names of prospective members to the mayor. By the early 1990s the federation had twenty-three member organizations.

Review of City Development, New York City, 1935–1938 (New York: Fine Arts Federation, 1938)
Michele H. Bogart: *Public Sculpture and the Civic Ideal in New York City, 1890–1930* (Chicago: University of Chicago Press, 1989)

Margot Gayle

Finley, John H(uston) (*b* Grand Ridge, Ill., 19 Oct 1863; *d* New York City, 7 March 1940). Educator and journalist. After earning a BA from Knox College (Galesburg, Illinois) he did graduate work in social science at Johns Hopkins University and moved to New York City, where he worked for the State Charities Aid Association in the 1890s. He was president of Knox College until 1900 and taught at Princeton University from 1900 to 1903, when he became president of City College of New York. During his decade in office the college became a major institution dedicated principally to educating male students from the lower middle class. Many of the students were the sons of recent immigrants, and a large number were Jews, whom he welcomed in spite of the rampant anti-Semitism of the time. In 1905 he oversaw the moving of the main campus to a complex of Gothic Revival buildings in upper Manhattan designed by George B. Post. He left New York City in 1913 to become the state education commissioner but returned in 1920 to join the *New York Times*: for two decades he composed many of the lighter items on the editorial page and became a minor celebrity in the city's cultural life.

Marvin E. Gettleman: *An Elusive Presence: The Discovery of John H. Finley and His America* (Chicago: Nelson–Hall, 1979)

Marvin E. Gettleman

Finney, Charles G(randison) (*b* Warren, Conn., 29 Aug 1792; *d* Oberlin, Ohio, 16 Aug 1875). Evangelist, theologian, and pastor. He grew up in upstate New York and taught himself theology, mixing Calvinist and Wesleyan themes into a system of personal conversion, ethical perfectionism, and social reform that was adopted by many antebellum evangelists. He adapted revivalism to suit congregations in New York City during a campaign in the city from the autumn of 1829 to the summer of 1830; during his pastorate at the Second Free Presbyterian Church from 1832 to 1835 he began his publication career with *Lectures on Revivals of Religion* (1835). After a brief pastorate at the Broadway Tabernacle (Congregational) he left the city to teach theology at Oberlin College.

Keith Hardman: *Charles Grandison Finney: Revivalist and Reformer* (Syracuse, N.Y.: Syracuse University Press, 1987)

James D. Bratt

Finns. Until the late nineteenth century most of the Finns who settled in New York City were sailors. The Finnish Seamen's Mission, the first Finnish religious organization in the city, was formed in 1887 by Emil Panelius. According to the federal census the city had 9845 inhabitants of Finnish extraction in the city in 1900. Finns established communities in Bay Ridge on and around 5th Avenue between 115th and 136th streets and along 8th Avenue near Sunset Park, a neighborhood that was named Pukin Maki (Goat hill) by its residents and came to be known as Finntown. Men worked as tailors, goldsmiths, silversmiths, watchmakers, carpenters, and masons, and many women as domestic servants. The Finnish Aid Society Imatra, formed in 1890 with the aim of furthering Finnish culture in the city, built its own hall at 740 40th Street in Brooklyn. In the same year the socialist political organization the Workers' Club Imatra (no. 15) was formed in Manhattan and set up headquarters at 2056 5th Avenue in a building known as Fifth Avenue Hall (where the Socialist Party nominated Eugene V. Debs for the presidency in 1920). The club joined in 1906 with other Finnish socialist groups in the United States to form the Finnish Federation of the Socialist Party and later became more heavily involved in the American labor movement. The newspaper *New Yorkin Uutiset*, launched in 1906, came to play an important role in uniting the local Finnish community. Finns also established athletic clubs, choral groups, temperance societies, libraries, and social and cultural clubs.

In 1916 sixteen Finnish families built a four-story cooperative apartment building in Brooklyn and named it Alku I (Beginning I). It was soon followed by two cooperative garages and a cooperative shopping complex containing a pool room, a restaurant, a meat market, a bakery, and a grocery. The success of this project helped to further the acceptance of the cooperative movement throughout the United States. The number of Finns living in New York City reached 20,043 in 1930, after which time Finnish immigration to the United States slowed markedly. Fifth Avenue Hall was sold in 1955 for financial reasons; the proceeds were used to support the newspaper *Raivaaja* (Pioneer). In 1970 only 6954 persons of Finnish extraction lived in New York City. The Workers' Club Imatra, which after several changes came to be known as the Finnish American League for Democracy, closed in 1974. In the mid 1990s important Finnish churches in New York City included the New York Finnish Evangelical Lutheran Church and the New York Finnish Betania Evangelical Lutheran National Congregation in Manhattan, and the Gloria Dei Evangelical Lutheran Church in Brooklyn. The *New Yorkin Uutiset*, which had a circulation of about 2500 in 1991, was one of only five Finnish-language newspapers in the United States.

Katri Ekman, Corrine Olli, and John B. Olli: *A History of Finnish American Organizations in Greater New York, 1891–1976* (New York: Greater New York Finnish Bicentennial Planning Committee, 1976)

Erica Judge

Fiorello H. La Guardia High School of Music and Art and Performing Arts. Public high school opened in 1936 in upper Manhattan as the High School of Music and Art by Mayor Fiorello H. La Guardia. Admission was based on competitive auditions and the evaluation of portfolios. The enrollment was at first 250 students, admitted semiannually, and eventually grew to about two thousand. Benjamin M. Steigman was the first principal (1936–59). In 1961 the school absorbed the High School of Performing Arts (an annex of the Metropolitan Vocational High School, opened in 1947 on West 46th Street in the theater district). Through efforts begun by the city planning commissioner Robert Moses the school moved in 1984 to a new building behind Lincoln Center, directly across the street from the Library and Museum of the Performing Arts; it took its current name in 1989. The school is considered a model for other high schools of the arts throughout the United States. The High School of Performing Arts on 46th Street was the setting for the film and the television series *Fame*.

Franklin J. Keller: *Principles of Vocational Education: The Primacy of the Person* (Boston: D. C. Heath, 1948)

Benjamin M. Steigman: *Accent on Talent: New York's High School of Music and Art* (Detroit: Wayne State University Press, 1964)

Bernard Hirschhorn

fireboats. The first fireboat in New York Harbor was put into service as early as 1800 and consisted of a hand pumper mounted on a barge manned by twelve volunteers. Between 1867 and 1875 a privately owned steam-propelled "floating engine," the *John Fuller*, was rented by the fire department, which obtained its own vessel, the *William Havemeyer*, in 1875. Fireboats helped land-based units to fight fires aboard ships at dock, including the *North German Lloyd* (1900), the *Normandie* (1942), and the *Constellation* (1960), and also helped to fight a fire at warehouses on Furman Pier in 1935. They were the first units of the fire department to be equipped with two-way radios (1937). The most powerful fireboat in the world, the *Firefighter*, was put into service by the department in 1938. A highly dangerous mission undertaken by fireboats was the scuttling of the freighter *El Estero*, which was loaded with live ammunition and exploded amid other ships carrying high-octane aviation fuel at a pier in Jersey City, New Jersey, on 14 April 1943; the *Firefighter* and the *John B. Harvey* were lashed to the freighter, which they towed away from the populated shore into deep water. The oil tankers *Alva Cape* and *Texaco Massachusetts* were separated by fireboats after colliding and catching fire in 1966, as were the tankers *Sea Witch* and *Esso Brussels* in 1974. Although dozens of piers were abandoned and destroyed by fire after 1945, the fireboat fleet was reduced from ten to five units in 1975. Some of the most pressing concerns in the mid 1990s were the deterioration of aging oil refineries and storage tanks, toxic waste dumps along the shoreline, increasing numbers of liquefied natural gas tankers unloading in the harbor, and the use of Staten Island as a home port by the navy. The only fire protection on the water for the entire port, fireboats are directed by officers trained both as firefighters and marine engineers and often fight fires involving highly volatile cargo that have the potential for massive damage and loss of life. The city's fireboats are frequently asked to respond to alarms in Westchester along the shore of Long Island Sound and along the western bank of the Hudson River as far south as Perth Amboy, New Jersey; they are also used in public celebrations and to greet ships.

Donald J. Cannon

firefighting. In colonial times all able-bodied men were required to help extinguish fires. Fire wardens were paid by the Dutch from 1648 to find poorly maintained chimneys, the principal fire hazard in the city. In 1658 the "rattle watch" was established, in which men patrolled the city with loud rattles that they sounded in the event of fire. The English established strict codes for the design and maintenance of chimneys and required every house and business to have fire buckets. Throughout the seventeenth century fires were quite uncommon in the city owing to the slow rate of development and the predominance of brick in construction. As the city grew larger and more populous after 1700, brick and stone proved too costly for most residents, and the risk of serious fires vastly increased as wood became the favored material for construction. The Common Council recognized the increased danger of fire and imported two Newsham hand pumpers from London in 1731. A volunteer force of thirty "strong, able, discreet, honest, and sober men" was formed in 1737 by the general assembly. The slightly greater efficiency of this force proved crucial in controlling several fires during the "Negro plot" of 1741, including the burning of Fort George. By 1770 the city had eight engines and a force of 170 men. As the city's population declined during the American Revolution, firefighting became a chaotic, improvised affair undertaken by members of the Royal Navy and local residents. Two major fires occurred during the war: the first, actu-

Hook-and-ladder company outside its headquarters in lower Manhattan, 1891

ally a series of fires probably caused by arson, destroyed 493 houses in 1776 (more than one third of the city), the second sixty-four houses near Cruger's Wharf along the East River in 1778.

After a volunteer force of a captain and five men was organized in Brooklyn in 1785, residents voted for volunteers annually in a town meeting. There were few fires in the decades after the American Revolution: only five

Last surviving fire tower in New York City, Mount Morris Park, ca 1905

broke out in 1795 and the annual total never exceeded ten, although there was a large fire in the "coffeehouse district" in 1796. On 20 March 1778 the Fire Department of the City of New York was formed by a special act of the state legislature, which appropriated funds for a chief engineer and six subordinates, to be appointed by the Common Council. In 1799 the Manhattan Company became the first of several private companies authorized to provide a steady supply of water to supplement existing supplies, which were drawn from rivers, cisterns, wells, natural springs, and primitive pumps. A makeshift fireboat, a barge with a hand pumper manned by twelve volunteers, was first used in New York Harbor in 1800 to protect the increasingly vital waterfront. Although there were only six fires during that year there were many more as development intensified and the number of wooden buildings increased. Some fires did great damage, like one in Front Street in 1804. Volunteer companies were established to fill the growing need for greater protection, and by 1810 three hook-and-ladder companies and thirty-four engine companies were staffed by 1005 volunteers. Riveted hose was introduced in 1808 and soon replaced leaky stitched hoses. The reservoir on Chambers Street near City Hall (authorized in 1811) and another on the corner of the Bowery and 13th Street (completed in 1831), which supplied water through hollowed-out logs, soon failed to keep pace with the needs of the growing city. Eventually the demands for a permanent and inexhaustible supply of water led to the design and completion of the Croton water project.

Number of Firefighters in New York City, 1737–1990

1737	30
1742	44
1761	75
1786	300
1793	367
1796	383
1800	600
1810	1,005
1823	1,215
1835	1,500
1840	1,300
1850	1,898
1855	2,925
1860	4,227
1865	3,421
1870	599
1875	748
1880	748
1885	943
1890	1,028
1895	1,113
1900	1,386
1905	2,157
1910	4,332
1915	5,026
1920	6,767
1925	6,969
1930	7,587
1935	7,452
1940	11,631
1946	10,357
1950	11,348
1955	12,226
1960	13,280
1965	13,991
1970	14,855
1975	14,773
1980	12,832
1985	13,017
1990	12,769

Compiled by Edward T. O'Donnell

The fire department during these years was poorly organized: the authority of the chief engineer was not clearly defined, and for a time members of the Common Council were empowered to direct men and equipment during fires. Volunteers lacked discipline and many were accused of drunkenness, theft, and failure to answer alarms. They had inadequate equipment and insufficient water, which usually froze in winter. Firefighting methods were crude and often consisted of tearing down surrounding buildings. The early years of the nineteenth century saw several damaging fires, which destroyed forty houses in 1804, killed five persons in 1808, destroyed more than twenty-five buildings in a poor district in 1809, and severely injured more than twenty firemen in 1816. The largest fire since 1776 occurred in Chatham Square in 1811 as more than a hundred buildings burned. Between

1811 and 1835 there were many small fires, but none on a very large scale. Shortly after its incorporation in 1816, the village of Brooklyn elected its first chief engineer to lead thirty-five firemen assigned to manning three hand pumper companies. During the same year the Common Council in New York City encouraged enlistment in fire companies by exempting firemen from jury duty and service in the militia. After a serious fire at Crane's Wharf and an outbreak of yellow fever, between 1822 and 1835 the city built an enormous reservoir at 14th Street and the Bowery and fifty cisterns. In the 1820s the fire insurance business grew rapidly and fire insurers demanded better fire protection.

From the 1830s to the mid 1860s volunteer companies played a central role in city politics. Although some men joined companies to prove their courage and skill, others recognized that membership in a fire company was often the first step in a political career (as it was for seven mayors elected after 1835). Foremen gained recognition, status, and financial rewards, legal and illegal. One of the best-known foremen was William M. Tweed (later known as Boss Tweed), who formed Americus Engine Company no. 33 in 1848 and became the first boss of Tammany Hall, with which many companies as well as saloons owned by foremen became associated. The companies celebrated their affiliations in poems, plays, and songs. As the fire department became more deeply enmeshed in the intense ethnic, religious, and class divisions that marked the development of the city in the 1840s, rivalries between companies grew so violent as to seriously impair firefighting in the city: companies often ignored their duty and brawled at the scene of fires, and many were allied with local gangs that harassed rival companies and sabotaged their equipment. The names of those suspended or expelled from the force filled the minutes of the Common Council between 1830 and 1865. During these years embezzlement also became a serious problem. Of more than $240,000 approved by the council between 1835 and 1861 for the purchase of new equipment, only about $100,000 was spent as intended: the rest made its way to Tammany Hall or was pocketed by corrupt foremen.

Some New Yorkers attributed the severity of the fire of 1835 to the negligence of the volunteer companies and called for a force of paid professionals. The chief engineer James Gulick was removed from office by the Common Council, which was dominated by Tammany Hall. More than a third of the firemen in the city resigned in protest but rejoined about a year later after Gulick's successor was removed by the council (which had become predominantly Whig) to curtail the influence of the fire department in politics. Tammany Hall nonetheless found ways to assert its interests, and the controversy surrounding Gulick's re-

Major Fires within the Current Boundaries of New York City

Fort George, 18 March 1741. Governor's house, barracks, and chapel destroyed.

Great Fire of 1776, 21 September. One third of city affected, 493 houses destroyed.

Cruger's Wharf, 3 August 1778. Sixty-four houses destroyed.

Coffee House Slip below Front Street between Murray Wharf and the Fly Market, 9 December 1796. Fifty houses destroyed.

Second Coffee House Fire, 18 December 1804, in area surrounding Wall and Pearl streets. Forty houses destroyed.

Great Fire of 1811, 19 May, in area surrounding Chatham Street. One fireman killed, 102 houses destroyed.

Crane's Wharf, Front Street, 24 January 1821. Thirty-one houses destroyed.

Bowery Theater, 18 May 1828, at Bayard Street. Two persons killed, twenty-five to thirty buildings destroyed.

Greenwich Village, 30 April 1833, in area surrounding Hudson and Greenwich streets. Ninety to one hundred buildings destroyed.

Fulton, Nassau, and Ann streets, 12 August 1835. Five persons killed, thirty-five houses destroyed.

Great Fire of 1835, 16 December, at Wall, Broad, and South streets. 674 buildings destroyed.

National Theater, Leonard and Church streets, 23 September 1839. The theater, a school, and three churches destroyed.

Water, Pearl, and Fletcher streets, 5 October 1839. Entire blocks affected, probably more than one hundred buildings destroyed.

Great Fire of 1845, 19 July, at Broad Street, Exchange Place, and William Street. Thirty persons killed, three hundred buildings destroyed.

Henry, Pineapple, Sands, and Washington streets, Brooklyn, 9 September 1848. Seven blocks of buildings destroyed, including three churches, two newspapers, and a post office.

5–7 Hague Street, Queens, 5 February 1850. Explosion kills sixty-four persons.

Offices of Harper and Brothers, Franklin Square, 10 December 1853. Sixteen buildings destroyed.

Jennings, 231 Broadway, 25 April 1854. Eleven firemen killed.

Crystal Palace, 42nd Street and 5th Avenue, 5 October 1858. Building destroyed.

Tenement on Elm Street, 2 February 1860. Twenty persons killed.

Draft riots, 13–16 July 1863. Fires citywide, forty-three buildings destroyed.

Brooklyn Theater, 313 Washington Street, 5 December 1876. 295 persons killed.

World Building, Park Row and Nassau Street, 31 January 1882. Twelve persons killed.

Taylor Building, Park Row, 22 August 1891. Sixty-one persons killed.

Hotel Royal, 6th Avenue and 40th Street, 6 February 1892. Twenty-eight persons killed.

Windsor Hotel, 565 5th Avenue, 17 March 1899. Thirty-three persons killed.

Madison Square Garden, 4 November 1902. Fifteen persons killed.

Burning of the *General Slocum*, 15 June 1904. 1021 persons killed.

Triangle Shirtwaist factory, Washington Place and Greene Street, 25 March 1911. 146 persons killed.

Equitable Life Assurance building, 120 Broadway, 6 January 1912. Six persons killed.

66 North 6th Street and 285–87 North 6th Street, Williamsburg, 2 and 6 November 1915. Twenty-five persons killed.

Twenty acres (eight hectares) lying within the area bounded by Sutton, Norman, and Greenpoint avenues in Greenpoint, 13 September 1919. Thirty oil tanks destroyed.

Sherry Netherland Hotel, 1927. Building razed.

Lincoln Arcade, Broadway between 65th and 66th streets, 29 January 1931.

Coney Island, July 1932.

Ritz Tower Hotel, August 1932. Seven firemen killed.

SS *Panuco*, Pier 27, Brooklyn, 18 August 1941. Forty-one persons killed.

SS *Normandie*, 9 February 1942. One person killed, 128 injured, ship destroyed.

Lodging house at 437–39 West 42nd Street, 24 December 1943. Eighteen persons killed.

Knickerbocker Ice Plant, 184th Street and Amsterdam Avenue, 11 December 1946. Thirty-seven persons killed.

Staten Island Ferry, Battery, 17 January 1946. Three persons killed, many injured, ferry house destroyed.

Luckenbach Steamship Lines, 1956. Nine persons killed.

Wanamaker Building, 16 July 1956. 187 firemen injured, building razed.

Artificial-flower factory at 4065 3rd Avenue, Bronx, 4 April 1956. Six firemen killed.

Elkins Company, 137 Wooster Street, 14 February 1958. Two firemen and four members of a fire patrol killed.

SGS Textile Printing Company, 623 Broadway, 19 March 1958. Twenty-four persons killed.

(continued)

Major Fires within the Current Boundaries of New York City (*Continued*)

USS *Constellation*, Brooklyn Navy Yard, 19 December 1960. Fifty persons killed.
Sefu Soap and Fat Company, 44-15 56th Road, Queens, 26 October 1962. Six firemen killed.
Mill Basin, 10 May 1962. Largest quantity of oil ignited since fire in Greenpoint in 1919.
Telephone company, 3 October 1962. Twenty-three persons killed.
6 East 23rd Street, 17 October 1966. Twelve firemen killed.
Explosion in Queens, January 1967. Four city blocks destroyed.
232–36 Johnson Street, Brooklyn, 8 January 1968. Thirteen persons killed.
115–55 Mexico Street, Queens, 18 July 1968. Eleven persons killed.
595 5th Avenue, February 1969. Eleven persons killed.
31 Covert Street, Brooklyn, December 1969. Eleven persons killed.
Gas tank explosion in Staten Island, 10 February 1973. Forty persons killed.
Social club in the Bronx, 24 October 1973. Twenty-five persons killed.
Happy Land social club, 1959 Southern Boulevard off East Tremont Avenue, Bronx, 25 March 1990. Eighty-seven persons killed.

Compiled by Edward T. O'Donnell

moval lingered for years and became a motive for brawling. In 1838 and 1841 the Common Council tried again to remove the fire department from politics by reorganizing it, but the department continued to be manipulated by Tammany Hall and was increasingly wracked by violence, rioting, and sabotage. The number of suspensions and expulsions grew every year, and Tweed's engine company was one of the most notorious. Despite all the negative publicity, the volunteer fire department enjoyed the support of the working class. At the same time several technological improvements were made: horses were used more often than men to pull engines after 1840, the Croton Aqueduct system completed in 1842 greatly increased the supply of water, a primitive telegraphic fire alarm system was authorized in December 1847, and by the summer of 1851 the city's fire headquarters were unreliably linked to the city's fire bell towers.

The threat of large fires and the disorganization of the volunteer force led to efforts for reform. In the 1850s the chief engineer Alfred Carson railed against the Common Council for failing to treat the problems of the department, noting that the council had reinstated men and companies that he had suspended for brawling and theft (including Tweed's). As long as the council was dominated by Tammany Hall, Carson's criticisms were ignored, except by those who sought to remove him. In February 1857 Carson was narrowly defeated by Harry Howard, who was supported by Tammany Hall and those who opposed any structural or technological reform of the volunteer system. Private fire companies formed by businessmen included the Fire Insurance Patrol, a paid salvage company established in 1854 by insurance companies in the city to rush to fires and save whatever property it could. The first steam-powered engines were used in 1858.

Fire companies in the city were instrumental in both exacerbating and controlling the draft riots of July 1863. On 13 July Black Joke Engine Company no. 33 set fire to the office of the marshall for the ninth district on 3rd Avenue and 47th Street after the names of about fifty conscripts had been drawn, and prevented anyone from extinguishing it; this was the first of many fires that spread through the city. By the following day most companies in the city including the Black Joke were patrolling their neighborhoods, fighting rioters, and protecting property. That evening Hook and Ladder Company no. 12 cut through barricades to extinguish a fire at a police station on 22nd Street. During the night the company extinguished another in a lumberyard on 14th Street and fought rioters until dawn. In letters to local newspapers businessmen and railroad owners praised the fire companies for their vigilance. A few companies noted pointedly that their opposition to the riot did not amount to support for the draft.

By the mid 1860s the close ties between Tammany Hall and the volunteer companies and increasing losses from fires led to renewed demands for a paid professional fire department. In the spring of 1865 the state legislature, dominated by Republicans and representatives from rural areas, replaced the volunteer companies with the Metropolitan Fire Department (MFD), a paid force of seven hundred in Manhattan and Brooklyn exclusively under the direction of a Republican board of commissioners. The shift to a professional department led to improvements in firefighting techniques. By early 1866 steam engines, horses, and a somewhat reliable telegraph system were in service in downtown Manhattan. During the same year efficiency improved after General Alexander T. Shaler, president of the board of fire commissioners (1867–70), reorganized the department according to a military model in which specialization, discipline, and merit were encouraged by a system of daily advisory orders, trials for disobedience, and ranks (the ranks of captain and lieutenant remained in use into the 1990s, as did such terms as "battalion"). Between 1867 and 1875 a private steam-propelled "floating engine," the *John Fuller*, was leased to the department. Instructional classes began in 1869, and a school for foremen (company officers) opened in 1878. By 1870 the MFD had extended service to the "suburban districts" north of 86th Street and won the praise of businesses, newspaper editors, and the public as losses due to fire plummeted. In the same year locked-door fire alarm boxes were set up in the streets and Tweed's "home rule" charter replaced the MFD with a second Fire Department of the City of New York (FDNY), which retained most of Shaler's structural innovations. The new department served a greater area than its immediate predecessor after the city absorbed parts of the Bronx in 1874. New techniques and equipment for fighting fires were gradually introduced, including taller ladders, steam engines with greater pumping pressure, the first fireboat (the *William Havemeyer*, commissioned in 1875), keyless boxes (1881), and telephones (1882). After a fire at the offices of the *New York World* in 1882 a training academy was set up in the following year. Despite attempts by some politicians to interfere with funding and appointments, the introduction of the civil service in 1884 helped to increase professionalism and keep the department out of politics.

After more than 350 persons were killed in

Fire Commissioners of New York City

John J. Scannell 1898–1901
Thomas Sturgis 1902–3
Nicholas J. Hayes 1904–5
John H. O'Brien 1906
Francis J. Lantry 1906–8
Hugh Bonner 1908
Nicholas J. Hayes 1908–9
Rhinelander Waldo 1910–11
Joseph Johnson 1911–13
Robert Adamson 1914–17
Thomas J. Drennan 1918–26
John J. Dorman 1926–33
John J. McElligott 1934–41
Patrick J. Walsh 1941–45
Frank J. Quayle 1946–50
George P. Monaghan 1951
Jacob Grumet 1951–54
Edward F. Cavanagh 1954–62
Edward Thompson 1962–65
Martin Scott 1964–65
Robert O. Lowery 1966–73
John T. O'Hagan 1973–78
Augustus Beekman 1978–80
Charles J. Hynes 1981–82
Joseph E. Spinnato 1982–87
Joseph F. Bruno 1987–90
Carlos M. Rivera 1990–93
Howard Safir 1994–

tenement fires in the 1890s, the FDNY joined the movement for reform. John J. Bresnan, chief officer of a battalion, gave advice to the Tenement House Committee in its revision of the building code in 1894 but died fighting a fire on the Lower East Side before the hearings concluded. In 1895 more of the Bronx was annexed to the city and by the time of consolidation in 1898 the area served by the FDNY had doubled, after the fire departments of the City of Brooklyn and several communities in Queens had been absorbed. When a fire at the Triangle Shirtwaist Company in 1911 killed 146 persons the department helped to draft legislation to improve the safety of factories. A fire at the headquarters of Equitable Insurance in 1912 demonstrated the continuing need for better methods of fighting fires in buildings of more than ten stories. Engines with motors were introduced in 1907 and replaced all others by 1922. Until 1919 firemen were required by the department to be on continuous duty. They remained in their firehouses throughout the week but were given time off twice a day for meals; officers received fourteen days of vacation annually, firemen ten days. After the Uniformed Firefighters Association (UFA) was formed in 1919 two platoons worked in split shifts, allowing firemen to spend more time at home. During that year the department fought 13,429 fires that destroyed property valued at more than $12 million. A fire alarm system was installed with a headquarters in Central Park and 1831 keyless boxes. Volunteer fire departments continued to operate in outlying sections of Brooklyn, Queens, and Staten Island until the 1920s, when many were taken over by the paid department; a few were in operation into the 1990s, including one in Breezy Point.

Fires in the city increased in number into the late twentieth century. The fireboat fleet was modernized in the 1930s and used in 1935 to fight a fire at a warehouse on Furman pier. In 1937 the first two-way radios in the department were installed in fireboats, and in 1938 the most powerful fireboat in the world, the *Firefighter*, went into operation (remaining in service in the mid 1990s). A fire aboard the docked *Normandie* was controlled with fireboats, and the *Firefighter* and the *John B. Harvey* towed the freighter *El Estero* out to sea after its cargo of live ammunition exploded amid several ships loaded with high-octane aviation fuel at a pier in Jersey City, New Jersey, on 14 April 1943. After major brush fires swept Staten Island in the spring of 1963 the department assigned more companies there and installed larger mains. Twelve firemen were killed in October 1966 when the floor of a building on 23rd Street in Manhattan collapsed in the worst disaster in the history of the department. During that year fireboats separated two tankers, the *Alva Cape* and the *Texaco Massachusetts*, after they collided and caught fire. Fireboats were also used to fight a fire aboard a docked ship, the *Constellation*, in 1960 and helped to fight fires in Westchester on the shores of Long Island Sound, on the western bank of the Hudson, and as far south as Perth Amboy, New Jersey. The voice-activated street alarm boxes of the Emergency Reporting Service (ERS) replaced older pull boxes beginning in 1971.

The fire department faced severe challenges in the 1970s. After unsuccessful negotiations for higher salaries the firefighters' union called a strike on 6 November 1973. This lasted only five and a half hours and all participants were fined after the courts ruled that the strike had violated the Taylor Law. Budget cuts reduced the department by thirty-two fire companies in 1975. The fireboat fleet was reduced from ten units to five, even as dozens of piers on both sides of the Hudson were abandoned and burned after 1945. During the 1960s and 1970s thousands of buildings in the southern Bronx, East New York and Brownsville in Brooklyn, and southern Queens were destroyed by fire. The number of alarms increased sharply and inexorably, from 62,021 in 1950, to 128,409 in 1964, to 261,131 in 1970, to 398,867 in 1975. To distribute the workload more equitably between the busiest areas (as many as seven thousand runs a year) and the slowest (about fifteen hundred a year), the department introduced reassignments, interchanges, and supplementary squads. At the same time the department used new technology to improve its efficiency. The ERS was supplemented by computer-assisted dispatching in 1977. Hazardous materials units were formed after the traditional tactics of "surround and drown" were found not only ineffective but dangerous in fighting chemical fires and fires in buildings made of new materials. Tower ladders, more efficient engines, and a superpumper unit were purchased. In the 1980s the number of alarms peaked and began to decline. The average elapsed time between an incoming alarm and the arrival of the first unit on the scene was reduced by 1992 to less than six minutes citywide, as the FDNY responded to 373,923 calls. By comparison, the number of structural and nonstructural fires in the city in 1990 was 96,089. Firefighting remained a dangerous occupation: at least 754 firefighters in the FDNY had been killed in the line of duty by 1989. In the mid 1990s the fireboats eliminated by budget cuts had not been reinstated, raising concern about deteriorating oil refineries, storage tanks, and hazardous waste dumps along the shoreline, increasing numbers of liquid natural gas tankers unloading in the harbor, and a growing naval port on Staten Island.

Affirmative action laws have mandated that some entry-level positions and opportunities for promotion in the fire department be available to blacks, Latin Americans, and women. Forty-two women joined the force in 1980 after a successful class-action suit. In 1990 the FDNY had a force of 9138 firefighters (not including officers), of whom 398 were black, 254 Latin American, twelve Asian, and thirty-five female. The James Gordon Bennett medal and other awards are given each June for acts of bravery.

George W. Sheldon: *The Story of the Volunteer Fire Department of the City of New York* (New York: Harper and Brothers, 1882)

J. Frank Kernan: *Reminiscences of the Old Fire Laddies and Volunteer Fire Departments of New York and Brooklyn, together with a Complete History of the Paid Departments of Both Cities* (New York: M. Crane, 1885)

Augustine E. Costello: *Our Firemen: A History of the New York Fire Departments, Volunteer and Paid* (New York: A. E. Costello, 1887)

Lowell M. Limpus: *History of the New York Fire Department* (New York: E. P. Dutton, 1940)

Stephen Ginsberg: "History of Fire Protection in New York City, 1800–1842" (diss., New York University, 1968)

Dennis Smith: *Report from Engine Co. 82* (New York: McCall, 1972)

Richard B. Calhoun: "From Community to Metropolis: Fire Protection in New York City, 1790–1875" (diss., Columbia University, 1973)

Donald J. Cannon: "The Fire Department of the City of New York, 1835–1898: A Study in Institutional Adaptability" (diss., Fordham University, 1975)

Donald J. Cannon, ed.: *Heritage of Flames: The Illustrated History of Early American Firefighting* (Garden City, N.Y.: Doubleday, 1977)

Gus Johnson: *F.D.N.Y.: The Fire Buff's Handbook of the New York Fire Department, 1900–1975* (Belmont, Mass.: Western Islands, 1977)

Miriam Lee Kaprow: "Magical Work: Firefighters in New York," *Human Organization* 50 (1991), 97

Donald J. Cannon

First Bank of the United States. Federal bank. Proposed by Alexander Hamilton, it was formed with capital assets of $4.7 million in Philadelphia in 1791 as a fiscal agent of the federal government and a commercial bank. It had eight branches, including one on what is now Pearl Street in Manhattan that opened on 1 April 1792 with assets of $1.8 million. The greater allotment of capital to Philadelphia was greatly resented by the branch in New York City, which was often unable to meet customers' demands, and the bank's deflationary policy of demanding the redemption of state notes was fiercely opposed by other banks in the city, including the Bank of New York. One of the most avid foes of the First Bank was John Jacob Astor, who offered to lend his own money to the federal government as an incentive not to renew the bank's charter, which was rescinded by Congress in 1811.

John T. Holdsworth: *First Bank of the United States* (Philadelphia: University of Pennsylvania Press, 1910)

James Bradley

First Baptist Church. Church at 265 West 79th Street in Manhattan, near Broadway. It began as a branch of the New Jersey Scotch Plains Baptist Church before incorporating under its own name in 1762. The church was situated in lower Manhattan until it moved to 39th Street and Park Avenue during the pastorship of Thomas Anderson (1862–78). The current building, designed by George Keister, was constructed in 1894 on a diagonal to the street, breaking the regularity of the city's grid plan. The structure has a unique stained-glass roof and two unequal towers rising on either side of the entrance, the taller one representing Christ as the head of the church and light of the world and the smaller deliberately left incomplete, a symbol of the wait for the return of Christ. The First Baptist Church offers weekly services and community programs, gives aid to eleven missionaries in eight countries, and has a radio program, "The Voice from Broadway."

Aileen Laura Love

First Houses. Complex of eight four- and five-story buildings, each containing 123 apartments, on 3rd Street and Avenue A in Manhattan. It opened for tenants in December 1935 as the first completed project of the New York City Housing Authority and the first municipally built public housing project in the United States. The project began when the chairman of the housing authority, Langdon Post, sought to hasten the transfer of funds promised by the head of the U.S. Public Works Administration, Secretary of the Interior Harold Ickes, by accepting Vincent Astor's offer of a long-term, low-interest mortgage on a group of deteriorated "old law" tenements on the Lower East Side. Bernard Baruch provided a loan that allowed the authority to buy other buildings on the block. A refusal by the owner of the buildings, Andrew Muller, to sell prompted the authority to sue; the decision that slum clearance was a public purpose for which the authority could use eminent domain was reaffirmed in an important opinion by the New York State Court of Appeals, *New York City Housing Authority v. Muller* (1936). Workers funded by the Works Progress Administration built the First Houses from designs by Frederick Ackerman, technical director of the housing authority. They demolished every third building on the block, thus making room for landscaped courtyards that allowed for cross-ventilation in the apartments, and substantially renovated the remaining structures; playgrounds, indoor recreation rooms, laundry rooms, and a health clinic were also built. The First Houses remained one of the authority's most exemplary developments and were designated a landmark by the city in 1974.

"New York City Housing Authority: A Legislative and Fiscal History" (New York: n.pub., n.d.) [photocopy]

Robert A. M. Stern, Gregory F. Gilmartin, and Thomas Mellins: *New York 1930: Architecture and Urbanism between the Two World Wars* (New York: Rizzoli, 1987)

Rosalie Genevro

First National City Bank (of New York). Commercial bank later known as CITIBANK.

First New York Bank for Business. Commercial bank formed in 1975 as the First Women's Bank to provide women with credit and opportunities for careers in banking. It opened a children's bank at the toy store F. A. O. Schwarz in 1988 and in the following year took its current name. By the early 1990s the bank had five branches in New York City and was no longer oriented primarily toward women. It ceased to exist on 13 November 1992 when its deposits were acquired by the Merchants Bank of New York.

Ann C. Gibson

First Presbyterian Church, Brooklyn. Church formed in 1822 on Cranberry Street. It was the site of a celebration when Brooklyn was incorporated as a city in 1834. The church moved in 1846 to 124 Henry Street, where its congregation actively supported abolitionists. Important contributions to church music were made by its pastor Charles S. Robinson (1860–76), author of fifteen collections of hymns, and its organist and choirmaster Raymond H. Woodman (1880–1941). Under Philip Elliott (1931–61) the congregation initiated the Heights Fellowship (1949–52) to promote internationalism, ecumenism, and racial harmony, an effort that continued under Paul Smith (1986–).

David Meerse

First Presbyterian Church in Jamaica. Church at 89-60 164th Street in Queens, formed in 1662 by the oldest continuous Presbyterian congregation in the United States. The congregation first met in a stone building erected in 1699 at Jamaica Avenue and Union Hall Street (used by the British as a military prison during the American Revolution). The second church building was completed in 1813 and moved to 164th Street in 1920. In honor of Andrew Magill, who served as pastor for thirty-four years, the Magill Memorial building was built in 1923 to provide Sunday school rooms and church offices. In 1991 the church had 496 members representing thirty-one nationalities.

David Meerse

Fischer, Bobby [Robert James] (*b* Chicago, 9 March 1943). Chess player. He moved to Brooklyn in 1948, attended Erasmus Hall High School, and came to prominence as a childhood prodigy, winning the U.S. Open at the age of thirteen and becoming a grandmaster at fifteen. After leaving school to pursue a career in chess he won a string of matches in the late 1960s with unprecedented ease, and in 1972 he defeated Boris Spassky for the world championship in Reykjavík, Iceland. A moody and temperamental player, he then retired suddenly from tournament chess and led a reclusive life in Los Angeles. In 1992 he reemerged to defeat Spassky in a tournament in Montenegro and Serbia. Fischer is widely regarded as the greatest American chess player in history.

Frank Robert Brady: *Profile of a Prodigy: The Life and Games of Bobby Fischer* (New York: D. McKay, 1965)

Marc Ferris

Fish, Nicholas (*b* New York City, 28 Aug 1758; *d* New York City, 20 June 1833). Banker. A son of Jonathan and Elizabeth Sackett Fish and a member of a wealthy mercantile family, he became a close friend and political ally of Alexander Hamilton. In 1793 he was appointed revenue supervisor for the district of New York by President Washington, a position that he held until 1801. He married Elizabeth Stuyvesant in 1803. As a Federalist alderman he led the opposition to Tammany Hall on the Common Council in 1806–17. He also invested in real estate and bank stocks and was president of the Butchers' and Drovers' Bank (elected 1831), chairman of the board of trustees of Columbia University (1824–32), and an active member of St. Mark's Episcopal Church in the Bowery. Fish's home on Stuyvesant Street was a favorite haven for Federalist leaders. His eldest son was the governor, senator, and secretary of state Hamilton Fish.

Richard A. Harrison: *Princetonians, 1776–1783: A Biographical Dictionary* (Princeton, N.J.: Princeton University Press, 1981)

Elaine Weber Pascu

Fish, Preserved (*b* Portsmouth, R.I., 3 July 1766; *d* New York City, 23 July 1846). Whaling captain and merchant. He worked as a merchant in New Bedford, Massachusetts, before

Preserved Fish, ca *1830*

moving to New York City. There he formed a partnership in 1815 with his cousin Joseph Grinnell, also a merchant from New Bedford, with whom he sold whale oil and then acquired ships and organized packet lines to Liverpool and London. He retired from the firm in 1826 and succeeded Stephan Allen as president of the Tradesmen's Bank in 1829. Active in politics, he was a leader of the free trade movement in New York City and a prominent Jacksonian Democrat who joined the Whig Party during the specie crisis of 1837. Born a Quaker, Fish became an Episcopalian during the last years of his life.

Robert Greenhalgh Albion: *The Rise of New York Port, 1815–60* (New York: Charles Scribner's Sons, 1939)

Elaine Weber Pascu

Fisher, Avery (*b* Brooklyn, 4 March 1906; *d* New Milford, Conn., 26 Feb 1994). Executive and philanthropist. An amateur violinist, he graduated from New York University in 1929 and then worked in the publishing business for almost fifteen years, while in his spare time building his own radio sets, amplifiers, tuners, and speakers. In 1937 he formed his first company, Philharmonic Radio, which he sold in 1945. He then formed a second, Fisher Radio, which entered the high-fidelity market with a line of premium components and remained at the forefront through its technical innovations. In 1956 it offered the first transistorized amplifier, and in 1958 it brought out the first stereo radio–phonograph. Fisher counted many musicians among his friends and frequently invited groups of them to his apartment on Park Avenue for evenings of chamber music. In 1969 he sold his company to devote himself to philanthropy. His most public gift was an endowment fund to Lincoln Center that supports the Avery Fisher Prize, a gift of $25,000 to an American instrumentalist. Philharmonic Hall was renamed Avery Fisher Hall in 1973 after he donated $10.5 million to Lincoln Center for the Performing Arts.

Kenneth T. Jackson

Fisher, William August. See ABEL, RUDOLF.

fishing. For a discussion of the fishing industry in New York City see COMMERCIAL FISHING; on recreational fishing see SPORT FISHING.

Fisk, Jim [James, Jr.] (*b* Bennington, Vt., 1 April 1834; *d* New York City, 7 Jan 1872). Financier. He opened a brokerage house on Broad Street in 1865 that was promptly driven into bankruptcy by the deflation that followed the Civil War. In 1866 he regained prosperity by serving as the agent in the sale of Daniel Drew's Stonington Steamboat Line. With Drew's help during the same year he formed the brokerage firm of Fisk and Belden on Wall Street, which enabled him to develop close ties to Jay Gould. Both he and Gould were brought onto the board of directors of the Erie Railroad in 1867 by Drew, and in March 1868 the three began their struggle with Cornelius Vanderbilt for control of the railroad. In July Fisk became the general manager and controller, Gould the president and treasurer; within three months they issued $23 million in watered stock. When Drew and other stockholders obtained an injunction against them, William M. "Boss" Tweed interceded and influenced the judge to place the railroad under Fisk's and Gould's receivership. In the autumn of 1869 the two conspired with Abel R. Corbin, President Ulysses S. Grant's brother-in-law, to corner the gold market. After Grant released the federal gold reserves on 24 September (known as "Black Friday") Fisk lost money but Gould sold short and made a fortune. Together they bought Pike's Opera House at 8th Avenue and 23rd Street, where they built plush offices for the Erie; Fisk also mounted stage productions there and at Brougham's Theater (on West 24th Street) and the Academy of Music (on 14th Street), and launched the largest ferry on the Hudson River, which he named for himself. A notorious mountebank, he was well known for his flamboyant style. On 6 January 1872 he was fatally shot by Edward S. "Ned" Stokes in the Grand Central Hotel in a dispute over the actress Helen Josephine "Josie" Mansfield. His funeral was appropriately spectacular. Henry Ward Beecher declared that Fisk was "as absolutely devoid of shame as the desert of Sahara is of grass."

W. A. Swanberg: *Jim Fisk: The Career of an Improbable Rascal* (New York: Charles Scribner's Sons, 1959)
Kenneth D. Ackerman: *The Gold Ring: Jim Fisk, Jay Gould, and Black Friday, 1869* (New York: Dodd, Mead, 1988)
John Steele Gordon: *The Scarlet Woman of Wall Street: Jay Gould, Jim Fisk, Cornelius Vanderbilt, the Erie Railway Wars, and the Birth of Wall Street* (New York: Weidenfeld and Nicolson, 1988)

Allen J. Share

Fiske, Mrs. [Maddern, Minnie; née Davey, Mary Augusta] (*b* New Orleans, 19 Dec 1865; *d* Queens, 15 Feb 1932). Actress. She worked as an actress from the age of three, became widely popular as an adult, and married the playwright and theatrical manager Harrison Grey Fiske. A champion of new works, she appeared in thirteen premières and became known as an exponent of Ibsen for her performances of Nora in *A Doll's House* (1894) and in *Ghosts*, *Rosmersholm*, and *Hedda Gabler*. Fiske also ran a respected repertory company in which she trained young actors.

Sara J. Steen

FIT. See FASHION INSTITUTE OF TECHNOLOGY.

Fitch, John (*b* Windsor, Conn., 21 Jan 1743; *d* Bardstown, Ky., 2 July 1798). Inventor. He worked unsuccessfully in a number of trades and moved many times before settling in Philadelphia in 1785 to design steamboats. With the backing of several states he made a number of workable prototypes but failed to elicit financial support for their commercial development. In 1796 he tested his last prototype, a vessel with a screw propeller, in New York City on the Collect (near the present site of City Hall). After becoming discouraged he moved to Kentucky, where he spent the rest of his life.

Thomas Boyd: *Poor John Fitch: Inventor of the Steamboat* (New York: G. P. Putnam's Sons, 1935)

James E. Mooney

Fitzgerald, F(rancis) Scott (Key) (*b* St. Paul, Minn., 24 Sept 1896; *d* Hollywood, 27 Dec 1940). Novelist and short-story writer. Named after his great-granduncle, the author of the "Star-Spangled Banner," he left Princeton University to serve as an army officer in the First World War but was discharged before seeing action overseas. He moved to New York City in 1919, took a dingy, one-room apartment at 200 Claremont Avenue, and worked for an advertising agency in order to save enough money to marry Zelda Sayre. The novel *This Side of Paradise*, which articulated the new morality of the "flaming youth" of the Jazz Age, was published in March 1920 and quickly became a success. In the same year he moved with his wife into the Biltmore Hotel on East 43rd Street. The couple soon became known for their drunken antics at scandalous parties in such luxury hotels as the Algonquin, the Knickerbocker, and the Plaza, a mirror of the excess that Fitzgerald both romanticized and bitterly criticized in his novels *The Beautiful and the Damned* (1922) and *The Great Gatsby* (1925), about the conflict between the search for the American dream of material success and the moral collapse that accompanies it. In 1924 the couple moved to Paris and the French Riviera, where they became part of the "lost generation" of disillusioned American expatriates that included Ernest Hemingway and Gertrude Stein. After Zelda was institutionalized with incurable schizophrenia (1930) her husband's career declined: his novel *Tender Is the Night* (1934) was poorly received, and in 1937 his attempt at a screenwriting career in Hollywood failed. He left uncompleted *The Last Tycoon*, which was published posthumously (1941). Among his short stories is "The Diamond as Big as the Ritz," a colorful evocation of materialists in the 1920s who lacked any social or personal responsibility.

Matthew J. Bruccoli: *Some Sort of Epic Grandeur: The Life of F. Scott Fitzgerald* (New York: Harcourt Brace Jovanovich, 1981)

Anthony Gronowicz

Five Points. Former neighborhood in Manhattan, lying in the sixth ward near Mulberry Bend. It was named for the intersection of five streets: Mulberry Street, Anthony (now

Five Points, 1827 (from Valentine's Manual, *1855)*

Worth) Street, Cross (now Park) Street, Orange (now Baxter) Street, and Little Water Street (now defunct). The area was swampy and abutted a large pond known as the Collect (now Foley Square); the pond was filled in as a public works project in 1808, and for a few years it was the site of a well-kept neighborhood surrounding Paradise Square. About 1820 the fill began to sink and the area became foul-smelling. Buildings sank and crumbled, and prosperous residents left. Decaying houses, taverns catering to sailors, and shacks remained along the narrow, unpaved streets. A brewery built in 1792 and once known throughout the Northeast for its Coulter beer became run-down and was soon the most squalid and dangerous establishment in the neighborhood. The building was subdivided in the 1830s, and parts of it earned such nicknames as "murderers' alley" and "den of thieves." Some of the residents were freed blacks; destitute Irish immigrants moved in, and soon the neighborhood had an Irish population that was exceeded in size only by that of Dublin.

Filthy conditions left the population vulnerable during the epidemics of the nineteenth century. During an outbreak of cholera in 1832 a third of all the cases reported in the city occurred in the sixth ward. The neighborhood was so disreputable that it attracted the interest of many personages from abroad, including Charles Dickens, who visited in 1842 and wrote in his *American Notes* (1842) of the conditions that he saw: alleys filled with mud knee deep, free-roaming pigs, rotting houses, women sleeping on the floor. By mid century the neighborhood was ruled by infamous Irish gangs, each several hundred strong: among these were the Plug Uglies, the Dead Rabbits, and the Roach Guards. Abraham Lincoln visited the area in 1860, and the city tried unsuccessfully to improve it. In the 1880s the journalist and reformer Jacob A. Riis called attention to its wretched conditions, prompting a largely successful campaign by the city to eliminate the neighborhood. The city acquired and condemned most of the tenements between 1887 and 1894 and later built Mulberry Bend Park (renamed Columbus Park in 1911). Eventually courthouses covered the area, part of which now lies in Chinatown.

Jacob Riis: *How the Other Half Lives* (New York: Charles Scribner's Sons, 1922)

Carol Groneman Pernicone: "'Bloody Ould Sixth': A Social History of a Nineteenth-Century New York City Working-Class Community" (diss., University of Rochester, 1973)

Michele Herman

Five Points Gang. Street gang formed in the 1890s. It was led by the former prizefighter Paul Kelly (Paolo Antonini Vaccarelli) and was predominantly Italian; a subgroup called the James Street Gang was led by Johnny "the Brain" Torrio. By some estimates there were fifteen hundred members. Like earlier nineteenth-century gangs the Five Points Gang used force on behalf of corrupt politicians and businessmen. Involved mostly in illegal enterprises in lower Manhattan, it had as its major rival the Eastmans, a gang led by Monk Eastman that was predominantly Jewish. Kelly made his headquarters at the New Brighton Dance Hall on Great Jones Street. By 1915 business had slowed and the influence of the gang was diminished. Several members later became prominent in organized crime during Prohibition, including Torrio, Al Capone, Lucky Luciano, and Frankie Yale.

Robert W. Snyder

Five Points Mission. Mission formed in 1848 by the Ladies Home Missionary Society of the Methodist Episcopal Church. Given financial support by the Methodist church and wealthy businessmen, by 1850 the society sponsored temperance meetings, a charity day school, and a mission chapel. At first the mission was based in a former saloon at the corner of Cross and Little Water streets. In 1852 the need for larger quarters led to the purchase and demolition of the "old brewery," an infamous tenement on Cross Street (now Park Street), and to the construction in its place of a chapel, a parsonage, a schoolhouse, a bathing room, and dwellings for poor families. The Five Points House of Industry at 155 Worth Street, run by the minister Lewis M. Pease, separated from the mission in 1854. Both institutions were moved out of the area after the city condemned most of it in the 1890s.

Peter J. Wosh

Flagg, Ernest (*b* Brooklyn, 6 Feb 1857; *d* New York City, 10 April 1947). Architect. At the age of fifteen he left school to become an office boy. In 1882–83 he designed the floor plans for cooperative apartment buildings at 121 Madison Avenue and 245 5th Avenue (the Knickerbocker), on which he collaborated with the architect Philip K. Hubert. He was then retained to work on the mansion of Cornelius Vanderbilt, a cousin by marriage whom he so favorably impressed with his work that Vanderbilt sponsored his architectural studies at the École des Beaux-Arts in Paris from 1888 to 1889. On his return to New York City in 1891 he set up an architecture practice and promptly won competitions to design St. Luke's Hospital (at Amsterdam Avenue at 113th Street) and the Corcoran Gallery in Washington. He also designed the U.S. Naval Academy in Annapolis, Maryland (1899–1907), and the Széchenyi Palace in Budapest but made his greatest mark in New York City. In his article "The New York Tenement House Evil and Its Cure" (published in *Scribner's* in 1893) he ascribed the dark, airless quality of tenements to the small size of the lots on which they were built (twenty-five by one hundred feet, or eight by thirty meters), and advocated combining lots to allow for buildings at least one hundred feet square; this became a standard with the passage of the Tenement House Law of 1901. He himself designed model tenements for the City and Suburban Homes Company (at 68th and 69th streets on Amsterdam Avenue) and model workingmen's hotels for Darius Ogden Mills. He also built the Singer Building (1908) at Broadway and Liberty Street; at 612 feet (186.5 meters) this structure was the tallest building in the world, and its construction set off a debate about the effects of skyscrapers and the availability of light and air in New York City. Later he advocated setbacks and the use of only one quarter of a lot for tall towers. Among his other notable buildings in New York City were Oliver G. Jennings's mansarded residence at 7 East 72nd Street and his own country house, Stone Court, in

Singer Tower from Liberty Street, ca *1905–10*

Dongan Hills. Flagg's offices were at 35 Wall Street until 1912, when he moved to 109 Broad Street. About 1906 he built a residence for himself at 109 East 40th Street, and he moved his office to 111 East 40th Street in 1918. His published writings include *Small Houses: Their Economic Design and Construction* (1922).

Alana J. Erickson

Flammersburg. Former name of a neighborhood in north central Queens, lying in the southern half of College Point and bounded to the north by 15th Avenue, to the east by 130th Street, to the south by 23rd Avenue, and to the west by 119th Street. It was originally a parcel of 141 acres (fifty-seven hectares) bought from the Stratton family in 1851 by John A. Flammer, who divided it into eight hundred lots. In 1870 the neighborhood became part of College Point.

Vincent Seyfried

Flatbush. Neighborhood in central Brooklyn (1990 pop. 186,577), bounded to the north by Parkside Avenue, to the east by Nostrand Avenue, to the south by Avenue H, and to the west by Coney Island Avenue. Settled in 1652 as one of the six original towns of Brooklyn, it was situated in the center of the area known as Midwout (middle woods). Its name derives from the Dutch word *vlackebos* (wooded plain). The area remained rural until the 1880s, when it was made ripe for development by the opening of the Brooklyn, Flatbush and Coney Island Railroad (2 July 1878) and the impending annexation by the City of Brooklyn (1894). Henry A. Meyer, a local grocer, was the first to initiate large-scale construction. In 1892 his Germania Land and Improvement Company laid a grid across sixty-five acres (twenty-six hectares) of land formerly occupied by the potato farm of the Vanderveers and built rows of Queen Anne cottages. Acres of farmland quickly became well-planned communities, and by 1910 the area had been transformed into a fashionable suburb that comprised such developments as Vanderveer Park, Ditmas Park, Fiske Terrace, Albermarle–Kenmore Terrace, Manhattan Terrace, Matthews Park, Slocum Park, and Yale Park. After the opening in 1920 of the Brighton Beach subway line, large apartment buildings were erected along Ocean Avenue as far south as Kings Highway. Many of these new buildings were occupied by Jews from Williamsburg, Brownsville, and the Lower East Side. In these years the neighborhood was the site of Ebbets Field, where the Brooklyn Dodgers played from 1915 to 1957. The attention that the team drew helped to make Flatbush an exemplar of the city in the popular mind, and the characteristic patois of its white, middle-class residents became widely known as Brooklynese (a distinction also ascribed to Greenpoint). In the decades following the Second World War the Jewish population was largely supplanted by a Caribbean one, and by immigrants from Pakistan, Afghanistan, Cambodia, Korea, Central America, and the Soviet Union. The number of black immigrants from the Caribbean rose sharply in the 1980s. Haitians accounted for about one third of all immigrants settling in the neighborhood, which attracted about one quarter of all Haitians who moved to the city. There were also a large number of immigrants from Jamaica, Guyana, Trinidad and Tobago, Grenada, Panama, Barbados, St. Vincent and the Grenadines, China, and the Dominican Republic. On the whole Flatbush adapted well to its growing ethnic diversity, but it also had its share of difficulties: in 1990 it was the site of an acrimonious boycott of a Korean grocery by a coalition of black and Caribbean groups who maintained that they had been mistreated by the shopkeepers.

Flatbush has 3500 one- and two-family houses and more than thirty thousand apartments. Notable buildings in the neighborhood include the Flatbush Reformed Dutch Church, at Flatbush and Church avenues (the present structure is the third on the site and was built in 1798; the first was built by order of Peter Stuyvesant); the Erasmus Hall Museum, in the courtyard of Erasmus High School opposite the church (originally Erasmus Hall Academy, opened in 1786 by the Flatbush Reformed Dutch Church and made a public school in 1896); Flatbush Town Hall at 35 Snyder Avenue (1875); and Loew's King on Flatbush Avenue near Beverly Road (1929), a grand movie theater. Newkirk Plaza, between Newkirk and Foster avenues, was one of the city's first commercial revitalization projects in 1977. Prominent residents of the neighborhood have included the entertainer Barbra Streisand and the chess champion Bobby Fischer. The main thoroughfare is Flatbush Avenue.

Nanette Rainone, ed.: *The Brooklyn Neighborhood Book* (New York: Fund for the Borough of Brooklyn, 1985)

Elizabeth Reich Rawson: *Brooklyn Neighborhoods and How They Grew* (New York: Brooklyn Historical Society, 1987) [exhibition catalogue]

"No Need to Leave to Find Better Things," *New York Newsday*, 24 March 1991

Elizabeth Reich Rawson

Albemarle Road in Flatbush, 1991

Flatiron Building, ca 1905

Flatiron Building. Office building at the intersection of Broadway and 5th Avenue at 23rd Street. It was erected in 1902 by Daniel H. Burnham, and conforms to the triangular plot of land from which it acquired its name. Standing twenty stories tall with a rusticated limestone façade on a steel frame, the building quickly became a symbol of the skyscraper era. Early sightseers remarked that when viewed from the north it resembled a ship sailing up the avenue, and despite the far taller buildings that were later built the Flatiron Building remains a striking architectural composition.

"Flat Iron Building," *Architectural Record* 12 (1902), 528–36

Seth M. Scheiner

Flatiron District. Neighborhood in Manhattan (1990 pop. 6000), lying between Chelsea and Gramercy Park and bounded to the north by 23rd Street, to the east by Park Avenue, to the south by 14th Street, and to the west by 6th Avenue. Named for the Flatiron Building on 23rd Street, the area was a flourishing commercial district during the late nineteenth century and the early twentieth. It was known especially for an area of elegant hotels, shops, and restaurants along Broadway between 14th and 23rd streets, later called the Ladies' Mile (designated a Historic District in 1989). The neighborhood became a popular place to live in the late 1960s, when artists, especially photographers, moved into its many inexpensive lofts. During the 1980s the Flatiron District acquired a reputation for its fashionable cafés, restaurants, and nightclubs, its varied housing, and its thriving business center.

James Bradley

Flatlands. Neighborhood in southeastern Brooklyn (1990 pop. 24,517), bounded to the north by Flatlands Avenue, to the east by Paedergat Basin, to the south by Avenue U, and to the west by Flatbush Avenue. The name is also applied to the larger area that made up the seventeenth-century town called New Amersfoort by the Dutch and Flatlands by the British, and that includes the present neighborhoods of Marine Park, Mill Basin, Bergen Beach, Georgetown, Canarsie, East Flatbush, and Starrett City. In this vicinity the terminal moraine of Long Island meets the marshes of Jamaica Bay; the rich soil in the area attracted Canarsee Indians, who called the land Keskachauge. In 1636 the land was bought by Jacob van Corlear, Andries Hudde, Wolfert Gerritsen van Couwenhoven, and Wouter van Twiller, the governor of New Netherland. Under their auspices settlements were built near what became Beverly Road and Utica Avenue and near Kings Highway and Flatlands Avenue. The settlements together formed New Amersfoort in 1647, named after a city on the River Eem in the province of Utrecht. Couwenhoven built a plantation, near the site on Kings Highway where the Flatlands Dutch Reformed Church was later built. By 1651 Governor Peter Stuyvesant had acquired a large plot in the town, and he granted residents local rule in 1661. Farming was the primary occupation. Colonists grew corn, squash, beans, and tobacco and fed their cattle salt hay; fishermen harvested clams in Jamaica Bay. Slaves accounted for about 20 percent of the population and were an important part of the economy until New York State abolished slavery in 1827. In the 1830s the population was about seven hundred, making Flatlands one of the two smallest towns in the county.

The area grew rapidly after the Brooklyn City Railroad Company initiated horsecar service in 1875 to Kings Highway along the recently opened Flatbush Avenue, providing transportation to shops and businesses in downtown Brooklyn. After the Flatbush Avenue streetcars were electrified in 1893, modern suburban houses were built and attracted a more diverse population. In 1896 the town was one of the last in the county to be annexed by the City of Brooklyn. Growth continued between 1900 and the Second World War. Interborough Rapid Transit was extended to the junction of Flatbush and Nostrand avenues, providing service to Manhattan in less than an hour. But the neighborhood was not served by the many transit lines leading to Coney Island and was only transformed by the automobile. Kings Highway, the major east–west artery in southern Brooklyn, stretched be-

House and barn built in Dutch colonial style in Flatlands, 1900

yond Flatbush Avenue in the early 1920s, and two-family brick row houses with garages soon covered fields throughout the town.

After the Second World War much of the remaining open land in southeastern Brooklyn was covered by the neighborhoods of Mill Basin, Bergen Beach, and Georgetown, which were some of the last in Brooklyn to be developed according to a suburban model. The only industrial section was developed in the late 1960s on the northeastern edge of the neighborhood near Canarsie. During the 1980s the neighborhood and its environs attracted immigrants from Jamaica, Haiti, and Guyana, but for the most part the population remained Jewish, Italian, and Irish. From the Dutch colonial period there remain the Flatlands Reformed Dutch Church on King's Highway and several eighteenth-century farmhouses, among them the Stoothoff–Baxter–Kouwenhoven house on East 48th Street and the Coe house on East 34th Street.

Maud Dillard: *Old Dutch Houses of Brooklyn* (New York: Richard R. Smith, 1945)

David Ment: *Building Blocks of Brooklyn: A Study of Urban Growth* (New York: Brooklyn Educational and Cultural Alliance, 1979)

Stephen Weinstein

Flatlands Dutch Reformed Church. Church formed on 9 February 1654 by order of Peter Stuyvesant in New Amersfoort, on a site now at the intersection of King's Highway and East 40th Street. The original building was an octagonal structure covered with spruce shingles that stood until 1794. The site is now occupied by the third church erected there, a building in the Greek Revival style constructed in 1848. The church is surrounded by maple trees and a seventeenth-century cemetery. Designated a landmark by the city in 1973, it was badly damaged by fire in 1977 and rebuilt in the following year.

Stephen Weinstein

Fleetwood. Neighborhood in the southwestern Bronx, centered at Morris Avenue and 165th Street. From 1870 to 1899 it was the site of Fleetwood Park Racetrack, a trotting track with a circumference of one mile (sixteen hundred meters) that was attended by such personages as Ulysses S. Grant, John D. Rockefeller, and the newspaper publisher Robert Bonner. After the track was closed streets were cut through, row houses and apartment buildings erected, and shops opened. The population was at first Irish and Jewish and in the 1960s became largely black and Latin American.

Lloyd Ultan

Fleischer, Nat(haniel S.) (*b* New York City, 3 Nov 1887; *d* New York City, 25 June 1972). Sportswriter and publisher. He graduated from City College of New York in 1908 and went to work as a teacher in the public schools. Between 1912 and 1929 he worked for several different newspapers in New York City, including the *Press*, the *Sun*, and the *Telegram*, and in 1922 he launched a boxing magazine called the *Ring*. As the editor of the publication he improved the image of boxing and advocated equal rights for blacks who practiced the sport. Fleischer continued to publish the *Ring* until the end of his life. He wrote *50 Years at Ringside* (1958).

Randy Roberts

Fleischmann Yeast Company. A company formed in 1868 by Charles and Maximilian Fleischmann, two brothers from Vienna. They skillfully promoted German compressed yeast at the Centennial Exposition in Philadelphia. Their showcase outlet, a bakery and café on Broadway at 10th Street, became a fashionable stop for shoppers along the Ladies' Mile. Raoul H. Fleischmann (1885–1969) worked in the Fleischmann family bakery (1907–11) and its successor, the General Baking Company (1911–25), before joining the F-R Publishing Company (1925–69), publishers of the *New Yorker*. The firm's compressed yeast revolutionized home breadmaking in the United States. In 1979 Fleischmann Yeast was acquired by Standard Brands.

Bradford Garnett

Flexner, Abraham (*b* Louisville, Ky., 13 Nov 1866; *d* Falls Church, Va., 21 Sept 1959). Medical educator, brother of Simon Flexner. From 1908 to 1912 he worked for the Carnegie Foundation for the Advancement of Teaching. In 1910 the foundation published his report *Medical Education in the United States and Canada*, which proved influential in modernizing medical education in North America. In 1913 he joined the staff of the General Education Board of the Rockefeller Foundation, where he was successively assistant secretary (1913–17), secretary (1917–25), and director of the Division of Studies and Medical Education (1925–28). In these positions Flexner secured tens of millions of dollars for the advancement of scientific medical education.

Steven C. Wheatley: *The Politics of Philanthropy: Abraham Flexner and Medical Education* (Madison: University of Wisconsin Press, 1988)

Allen J. Share

Flexner, Simon (*b* Louisville, Ky., 25 March 1863; *d* New York City, 2 May 1946). Physician, pathologist, and microbiologist, brother of Abraham Flexner. A graduate of Dartmouth College, he lectured around the world. At the Rockefeller Institute for Medical Research (later Rockefeller University) he was a member of the board of scientific directors and the director of laboratories, as well as the unofficial head of the institute (1901–24) and its director (1924–35). He assembled a distinguished group of scientists and helped the institute to achieve international prominence. Flexner was also a charter member of the board of trustees of the Rockefeller Foundation and a trustee of the Carnegie Foundation for the Advancement of Teaching.

George W. Corner: *A History of the Rockefeller Institute, 1901–1953: Origins and Growth* (New York: Rockefeller Institute Press, 1964)

Allen J. Share

Floating Hospital. A waterborne hospital established in 1866. It operated only during the warmer months until it began year-round service in 1975. The hospital cruises the Hudson River and provides preventive care, health education, and other services to the city's medically underserved groups, especially children and the elderly. During the summer the ship is berthed at 44th Street and 12th Avenue; during the winter a smaller staff treats patients at South Street Seaport. The ship now used by the hospital, the *Lila Acheson Wallace*, entered service in 1977.

Andrea Balis

flora. The grasses, flowers, shrubs, and trees growing throughout New York City only remotely resemble the varieties that grew there before European settlement. Many species were brought to the area by colonists, some purposely and others accidentally. A number spread to surrounding areas, sometimes crowding out native species, and a few carried diseases that proved devastating, among them the Dutch elm disease and the chestnut blight, which was introduced by a tree from Europe planted in Central Park. A dominant characteristic of plants in the city is their ability to survive highly acidic rain, a high degree of salinity, and air polluted by ozone, sulfur dioxide, and carbon monoxide; many of those from outside the region are also immune to local viruses and bacteria. Like the ecosystems in other cities, those of New York City are rapidly growing and changing. Many of its plants are found in other cities nearby, including Philadelphia, Newark (New Jersey), and New Haven and Hartford (Connecticut). The Autumn Olive (*Elaeagnus unbellata*), a species native to Asia, is used for reclamation planting because it grows profusely and can withstand extreme drought, salinity, and temperature. Its tart red berries provide food for Bobwhite Quail, Cedar Waxwings, robins, starlings, White-throated Sparrows, and Hermit Thrushes throughout the autumn and early winter. Birches such as the Gray Birch (*Betula populifolia*) are among the first to grow in cleared areas. Another species that thrives in sunny areas is the Black Cherry (*Prunus serotina*), which produces clusters of fragrant white flowers in May and berries that provide food for songbirds in late summer; mature trees range in height from forty to one hundred feet (twelve to thirty meters) and have dark, rough outer bark. These trees are soon outgrown by others more tolerant of shade. Other common species in the metropolitan area are the Eastern Red Cedar (*Juniperus virginiana*), the Cottonwood (*Populus deltoides*), the American Holly (*Ilex opaca*), and the Red Maple (*Acer rubrum*). The Salt-spray Rose (*Rosa rugosa*) produces beautiful blossoms from May to October. Its rosehips are a rich source of vitamin C and were eaten in preserves by colonists to prevent scurvy in winter. Mugwort and Sweet Clover grow in salt marshes, often in the wake of construction, as does Reedgrass (*Phragmites australis*), which forces out other marsh grasses but provides a source of food and cover for some wildlife.

Steven D. Garber: *The Urban Naturalist* (New York: John Wiley and Sons, 1987)

Steven D. Garber, John T. Tanacredi

Floral Park. Neighborhood straddling the line between Queens and Nassau County near the intersection of Jamaica Avenue and Little Neck Parkway. It was established about 1870 between Tulip and Carnation avenues in Nassau County and originally named Hinsdale after the chief counsel of the Long Island Rail Road, Elizur B. Hinsdale. The name was changed in 1890 to honor John Lewis Childs, who had opened a large commercial nursery in the area during the 1880s. The neighborhood extended northward into Queens after the Second World War, when the extension of Hillside Avenue as far east as the county line stimulated housing development between the county line and Little Neck Parkway, on land that had long been used for farming. Floral Park remains a community of one-family houses shaded by trees.

Vincent Seyfried

Flower Fifth Avenue Hospital. Teaching hospital in Manhattan. It was formed in 1890 as the Flower Free Surgical Hospital at 450 East 64th Street by administrators of the Homoeopathic Medical College of New York (later New York Medical College), who sought greater training opportunities for their students. The hospital had financial support from a prominent businessman and Democratic politician, Roswell P. Flower. Later the hospital and the college together were known as the New York Homoeopathic Medical College and Flower Hospital (1908) and as the New York Medical College and Flower Hospital (1936); a merger in 1938 with the Fifth Avenue Hospital at 105th Street formed an institution known as the New York Medical College, Flower and Fifth Avenue Hospitals. The hospital remained in the city after the college moved to Westchester County in 1972, but financial reverses in the late 1970s brought it near bankruptcy. In 1978 the Roman Catholic archdiocese of New York took over both the college and the hospital, which was converted in the following year from an acute-care facility into the Terence Cardinal Cooke Nursing Home.

Sandra Opdycke

Floyd Bennett Field. First municipal airport in New York City. Built on fifteen hundred acres (six hundred hectares) of reclaimed marshland in Jamaica Bay and dedicated in 1930 by Mayor James J. Walker, it was named for the pilot who flew Admiral Richard Byrd over the North Pole in 1926. Enlarged in 1936 by the Works Progress Administration, it was used by such aviators as Howard Hughes, Laura Ingalls, and John Glenn, but because it was one hour distant from central Manhattan it never attracted more than one commercial airline flight a day, and its importance was so diminished after La Guardia Airfield opened at a more convenient location in 1939 that in 1942 it was sold to the navy. As Naval Air Station New York it performed a vital function during the U-boat offensive of 1942 by providing air cover for convoys embarking from the Port of New York; the Naval Ferry Squadron based there delivered thousands of aircraft to the fleet from factories on Long Island. In 1972 the field was taken over by the National Park Service. Plans were made to preserve it as the first urban national park and to include in it a museum of aviation, an arboretum, a marina, and shops. The project was slowed by a lack of federal funds but progress toward its fulfillment intensified in April 1991.

Joseph F. Meany Jr.

Flushing. Neighborhood in north central Queens, bounded to the north by Bayside Avenue, to the east by the Clearview Expressway, to the south by Union Turnpike, and to the west by Flushing Meadows–Corona Park. Along with College Point and Whitestone it was established by English settlers who received patents for it from Governor Peter Stuyvesant in 1654. The name is a corruption of Vlissingen, a village in the Netherlands. The area was desirable for its woodlands, freshwater, and salt hay. After the arrival of English Quakers in 1657 Stuyvesant sought to renege on earlier promises of religious toleration, prompting freeholders in the area led by John Bowne to issue the Flushing Remonstrance, considered one of the earliest documents proclaiming religious freedom in America. Quakers bought land in 1692 for a meeting house, which was built in 1694–95 and now stands on Northern Boulevard. One of the first nurseries in the country, the Linnaean Gardens, opened in 1737 just north of Northern Boulevard. After the Battle of Long Island Flushing was occupied by British troops until 1783. The tolerance of the Quakers attracted a number of blacks in the early nineteenth century, of whom the best-known was Lewis Latimer, an electrical inventor who worked with Thomas Edison. The year 1843 saw the publication of a newspaper and the opening of the Flushing Institute, a secondary school for boys that eventually enrolled students from the southern United States, Central and South America, and Europe. Fast, direct rail service to New York City was provided from 1854. Development accelerated after the Civil War as many wealthy New Yorkers built elegant houses. From the 1890s until the First World War the neighborhood expanded to the east and south and new sections opened up to residential development, including Ingleside, Murray Hill, Broadway–Flushing, Bowne Park, Kissena, and Queensborough Hill. Flushing became a

Trustees of Flushing Village, 1887

commuter suburb after trolley lines were extended (1888–99) and the Long Island Rail Road was electrified.

Apartments were built in the 1920s, and the character of the area changed after subway service was introduced with a fare of only five cents in 1928; the neighborhood was the site of the World's Fair of 1939–40. After the Second World War apartments displaced entire blocks of houses, and during the 1960s many Japanese, Chinese, and Koreans settled in the neighborhood. With the World's Fair of 1964–65 Flushing lost the characteristics of a small town and acquired those of a densely populated urban center. It attracted many immigrants during the 1980s, of whom about 20 percent were Chinese (primarily from Taiwan) and 20 percent Korean, with others from India, Colombia, Afghanistan, Guyana, the Dominican Republic, Pakistan, the Philippines, and El Salvador. In the mid 1990s the downtown was heavily commercial and had parking garages near the subway terminal. In the outskirts one-family houses were interspersed with schools, churches, and well-kept cemeteries and parks. Historic buildings include the Bowne House (1661) at 37-01 Bowne Street, the oldest surviving house in Queens; and the Kingsland House on 37th Avenue, built about 1785, a rare example of English architecture. In the heart of the neighborhood at Roosevelt Avenue and Main Street is an extensive network of Asian banks and businesses. There are several large Buddhist houses of worship and a large and ornate Hindu temple. The many nurseries that once flourished in the area are gone, but some of the trees raised in them survive: a well-known example is the "weeping beech tree" on 37th Avenue west of Parsons Boulevard, a city landmark.

Vincent Seyfried

Flushing Meadows–Corona Park. Public park in north central Queens, bounded to the northeast and east by Flushing, to the south by Kew Gardens and Forest Hills, to the west by Elmhurst, and to the northwest by Corona. It is the second-largest park in the city, with an area of 1255 acres (508 hectares). Both the geographical center of the city and its center of population are nearby. The area was once inhabited by the Matinecocks. European settlers harvested the seafood and marsh grasses there, but the area remained largely natural. After the city was consolidated in 1898 and rail lines were extended into the area, landfill was deposited in the tidal wetland to the north and a river from Flushing Bay was blocked. The area was given over to industrial use and waste dumping: one ash heap reached a height of nearly a hundred feet (thirty meters) and became popularly known as Mount Corona. Known originally as Flushing Meadow Park, the park became the site of two world's fairs (1939–40, 1964–65). Both were largely the inspiration of Robert Moses and caused several features to be added to the landscape that were retained: these included from the first fair a lake, a boathouse, paths, plantings, and the New York City Building (the temporary headquarters of the United Nations from 1946 to 1950 and later the Queens Museum); and from the second fair the Unisphere (a large steel globe and the centerpiece of the fair), Shea Stadium (1964, the home stadium of the New York Mets), a public marina at Flushing Bay (1964), Space Park (later the New York Hall of Science), the Singer Bowl (from 1976 Louis Armstrong Stadium at the National Tennis Center), and the Winston Churchill Pavilion (a geodesic structure designed by R. Buckminster Fuller, from 1968 an aviary at the Queens Zoo). In 1967 the World's Fair Corporation returned the park to the city. The Queens Zoo was later redesigned and rebuilt by the New York Zoological Society, and reopened in 1992. In December 1993 an agreement was signed to expand the National Tennis Center, and plans to renovate various other sections of the park were under way. Flushing Meadows–Corona Park is frequently used by immigrants who have settled in the area, and it is the site of many organized soccer games.

The Flushing Meadow Improvement: Official Publication of the City and State (New York: Department of Parks, 1936–39)

Jonathan Kuhn

Flushing Remonstrance. A declaration of religious liberty, drawn up and approved at a town meeting in Flushing and dated 27 December 1657. The document was a reminder to Governor Peter Stuyvesant that the Patent of Flushing (1645) offered "liberty of conscience" to settlers. It was inspired by an order from Stuyvesant, a strict Calvinist, forbidding all colonists to allow Quakers into their homes and imposing a large fine of fifty guilders, with half the money going to any informer. The Flushing Remonstrance is sometimes regarded as the "first declaration of independence" and as a forerunner of the First Amendment. The document itself is now held by the New York State Library in Albany.

Jeanne Field Spallone

Flynn, Edward J(oseph) (*b* Bronx, 22 Sept 1891; *d* Ireland, 18 Aug 1953). Party leader. He earned a bachelor's degree and a law degree at Fordham University and was elected a state assemblyman (1918–21) and sheriff of Bronx County (1922–25). As the leader of the Democratic organization in Bronx County from 1922 he maintained a reputation for honesty and a commitment to liberal policies. He was also an advisor to Franklin D. Roosevelt during his tenure as governor of New York and later as president. While serving as city chamberlain (1925–28), secretary of state of New York State (1929–40), and chairman of the Democratic National Committee (1940–44) he was one of the most influential politicians in New York City. Flynn wrote a memoir, *You're the Boss* (1947).

Jill Jonnes: *We're Still Here: The Rise, Fall, and Resurrection of the South Bronx* (New York: Atlantic Monthly Press, 1986)

See also Bronx, §2.

Chris McNickle

Elizabeth Gurley Flynn speaking in Washington Square to gain support for the Garibaldi Battalion of the International Brigade fighting fascism in Spain, 1937

Flynn, Elizabeth Gurley (*b* Concord, N.H., 7 Aug 1890; *d* Moscow, 5 Sept 1964). Activist and political leader. After moving with her family to New York City in 1900 she attended Public School 9 in the southern Bronx and Morris High School, leaving before graduation to become an organizer for the Industrial Workers of the World. One of its few women organizers, she quickly became known as a strike leader, civil rights advocate, and extraordinary orator. She helped to form the American Civil Liberties Union in 1920; in 1940 she was expelled from its board of directors for her membership in the Communist Party. Convicted of sedition under the Smith Act in 1952, she served three years in federal prison before being released in 1957. At her death she was the leader of the Communist Party.

Martha Foley

F. Marquand. Former name of BLACK, STARR AND FROST.

Fokine, Michel [Mikhail (Mikhailovich)] (*b* St. Petersburg, 23 April 1880; *d* New York City, 22 Aug 1942). Dancer and choreographer. He received his early ballet training at the Imperial School of Ballet in St. Petersburg. Dissatisfied with the management and policies of the Imperial Theatre, he joined Diaghilev's Ballet Russes in Paris in 1909. He taught in New York City from 1919 and in 1923 settled there with his family, where he taught a generation of American dancers and restaged the better known of his more than sixty ballets. Fokine's influential choreographic principles helped to make ballet be taken seriously as a theatrical form rather than as mere entertainment. His book *Fokine: Memoirs of a Ballet Master* was published in 1961.

Dawn Lille Horwitz: *Michel Fokine* (Boston: Twayne, 1985)

Barbara Barker

Foley, James A. (*b* 1888; *d* New York City, 11 Feb 1946). Legislator and surrogate. He served in the state legislature (1907–19), where with Alfred E. Smith and Robert F. Wagner (i) he guided the effort of the "new Tammany" to rewrite the state's labor laws after the Triangle Shirtwaist fire. In 1919 he was chosen Democratic leader of the state senate, which he left to become a surrogate in Manhattan (1920–46). After the death in 1946 of his father-in-law, the Democratic boss Charles F. Murphy, he was elected to lead Tammany Hall but resigned immediately, pleading ill health. Later he was urged to run for mayor and the U.S. Senate, but he declined to leave the probate bench. Foley was a nationally respected authority on the law of estates and an influential delegate to the state constitutional conventions of 1915 and 1938.

Frank Vos

Foley Square. The intersection of Duane, Lafayette, Center, and Pearl streets north of City Hall in Manhattan, and by extension the surrounding area. Much of the land once lay beneath the waters of the Collect, a pond that was drained and completely covered over by 1811; the area soon after became the site of one of the city's most notorious slums. In later years a number of municipal, state, and federal buildings were built around the square, including the New York County Court House (1926) and the U.S. Court House (1936). The square is named for Thomas F. Foley (1852–1925), a saloon keeper and politician associated with Tammany Hall.

Linda Elsroad

folk and ethnic dancing. At the beginning of the twentieth century officials in New York City promoted European folk dancing as a "wholesome" alternative to increasingly popular ragtime dances. The city's most evangelistic supporter of European folk dances was Elizabeth Burchenal (*d* 1959), an employee of the Board of Education who worked with the Playground Association of America and set up after-school programs for girls from 1911. The English Folk Song and Dance Society opened a branch in New York City in 1915 and sent May Gadd (*d* 1979) there in 1927. She became the director of the society in 1937 and remained in office for forty-six years. During her tenure the society, which she renamed the Country Dance and Song Society of America to reflect her interest in Appalachian dances, sponsored seasonal festivals that regularly attracted hundreds of dancers and established folk dance clubs at local high schools and colleges, including Brooklyn College, Barnard College, and the Juilliard School; she also worked with the choreographer Agnes de Mille on the dance steps for the musicals *Oklahoma!* and *Brigadoon.* The New York Folk Festival Council, formed in 1931 and based at 222 4th Avenue, presented annual events in public parks, including a festival in May 1934 in Prospect Park that attracted twenty thousand participants and spectators, and during the Depression it sponsored a course entitled "Folk Songs and Dances of Many Peoples," which met at the New School for Social Research and at International House.

A leader in ethnic dance in the city was Asadata Dafora (*d* 1965), who moved to New York City from Freetown, Sierra Leone, in 1929, formed Shogola Olobo in 1932 and the African Dance Troupe in 1935, and wrote the dance opera *Kykunkor,* which opened at the Unity Theatre on East 23rd Street in April 1934. Dafora also provided choreography for *Bassa Moona,* given its première in 1937 at the Majestic Theatre in Brooklyn and staged at the Daly Theatre in Manhattan, and until 1939 she toured the country with the Federal Theatre Project of the Works Progress Administration. Mary Ann and Michael Herman, who were active in promoting folk dancing in the 1930s, achieved great success after they gave demonstrations of folk dancing at the American Commons of the World's Fair of 1939–40. In 1940 they formed the Community Folk Dance Center, which inspired so many imitators that John Martin, dance critic for the *New York Times,* discontinued his weekly listing of folk dance events for lack of space. The Hermans had several changes of residence before moving in 1951 to 108 West 16th Street. There they opened Folk Dance House, maintained a costume collection and reference library, and conducted classes full time. Although the building was demolished in 1969 they continued to teach and to present traditional folk dance programs at St. Vartan's Armenian Church at 630 2nd Avenue. In 1980 they moved to Long Island. Their contemporary La Meri (*d* 1988) also helped to draw public attention to ethnic dancing during the 1940s. As a young woman she toured the world and studied the dances of Asia, Spain, Mexico, India, and Polynesia. After settling in New York City in 1939 she formed a partnership with the dancer and choreographer Ruth St. Denis, with whom in May 1940 she opened the School of Natya at 66 5th Avenue. She also led the Ethnologic Dance Center, which she moved in 1943 to 110 East 59th Street; there she gave lecture–recitals, trained dance teachers, and presented ethnic dances for twenty-three years. She also provided choreography for a version of *Swan Lake* influenced by Hindu dancing, and for such works as the *Bach–Bharata Suite*, which adapted classical Hindu movement to musical excerpts by Bach.

Several dancers overcame cultural prejudice, racism, and censorship in working to gain acceptance for the folk dances of the southern hemisphere. Katherine Dunham, a figure most closely associated with modern dance, launched the "anthropological" dance movement. After her local début at a "Negro Dance Evening" at the 92nd Street Y in 1937 she moved her troupe to the city in 1939 and accepted the directorship of the New York Labor Stage. In 1945 she opened the Dunham School of Dance and Theater on West 43rd Street, which specialized in Afro-Caribbean dance; the school became well known and lasted until the mid 1950s. The Trinidadian anthropologist and dancer Pearl Primus also invigorated ethnic dance in the city during the 1940s. After a ten-month engagement at Café Society in 1943 she made her début at the Belasco Theater in the following year. Throughout her career she traveled frequently but maintained a connection to the city through her School of Primal Dance (1961) at 17 West 24th Street and her teaching position at Hunter College. The Haitian dancer Jean-Léon Destine presented traditional Afro-Haitian dances in the 1940s and specialized in *vodun* dance. Perhaps best known for his short film *Witch Doctor*, he taught in Manhattan into the 1990s. The Philippine Dance Company of New York was formed in 1943 by Bruna Seril; led from 1969 by Reynaldo Alejandro and benefiting from grants by the Performing Arts Foundation, it achieved great popularity and undertook national and international tours while maintaining a regular performance schedule in the city.

In the mid 1990s ethnic dance troupes representing every region of the globe were based in New York City, including Kanikapila from the Pacific Islands, the Chinese Folk Dance Company (1973), the Tachibana Dance Company (1958), which presented traditional Japanese dances, the Balasaraswati Institute of Indian Music and Dance, Dance Brazil, the Armenian Folk Dance Society, and the West African dance troupe the Djoniba Ensemble. Institutions that supported folk dancing included the McBurney YMCA at 215 West 23rd Street, a provider for more than half a century of rehearsal and administrative space to such organizations as the Scottish Country Dance Society, the Philippine Dance Company, and the Folk Festival Council; the Ethnic Folk Arts Center (1966) at 131 Varick Street; Country Dance New York, an organization distantly related to the Country Dance and Song Society of America that sponsored contra-dances at Metropolitan Duane Hall, 201 West 13th Street; and the 92nd Street Y, which offered instruction in Israeli dancing.

"Profiles: May Gadd," *New Yorker*, 7 Feb 1953, pp. 36–55

Betty Casey: *International Folk Dancing U.S.A.* (New York: Doubleday, 1981)

Simon J. Bronner: *Old-time Music Makers of New York State* (Syracuse, N.Y.: Syracuse University Press, 1987)

Marc Ferris

folk music. Songs from England, Ireland, Scotland, and Africa were sung during the colonial period in public gatherings, homes, and workshops in New York City. Mariners at South Street in the first half of the nineteenth century devised many kinds of ballads and sea chanteys from songs of British and African origin. At mid century Irish, English, and Scottish balladeers performed regularly on the stage and their songs became popular through sing-alongs in homes and taverns. Songs were often published as broadsides to assure wide distribution. At the end of the century German, Swedish, and other immigrants organized choral societies that preserved their folk songs, some of which were later adapted for the vaudeville stage. In the early twentieth century blues songs were introduced in the city by blacks from the rural South.

The Industrial Workers of the World often sang as they picketed during the first two decades of the twentieth century, and folk music became an important vehicle for political expression during the 1930s. The Popular Front, a movement formed during the decade and loosely associated with the Communist Party, spread its ideas through folk music. At the same time many folk musicians took up residence in New York City, including Leadbelly (Huddie Ledbetter; 1885–1949), a singer, songwriter, and blues guitarist from Louisiana who moved to the city in 1935 after his work came to the attention of John A. Lomax and his son Alan Lomax, folklorists at the Library of Congress; Woodie Guthrie, a singer, songwriter, and guitarist who sang about farmers displaced during the Dustbowl; and Pete Seeger, a member of an established family from New England who adopted the ballads and banjo styles of the southern Appalachian mountains. All three performed traditional songs and their own material, were associated with the radical and bohemian culture of Greenwich Village, and helped to make the city a center for a new kind of folk music.

Between 1941 and 1942 the Almanac Singers were organized by Seeger, Guthrie, Lee Hays, and Millard Lampell. Its members lived in a loft known as Almanac House at 130 West 10th Street and performed for drives by the Congress of Industrial Organizations and anti-fascist functions sponsored by the Popular Front. The group included several musicians who later became well-known soloists: Burl Ives, Cisco Houston, Bess Lomax, and Earl Robinson. In the years after the Second World War Greenwich Village remained a center of folk music, and sing-alongs were often held in Washington Square despite the objections of city authorities. The radical group People's Songs was formed about this time, but it was less influential than earlier groups owing to the conservative political climate after the war. From the late 1940s to the early 1950s the Weavers became immensely successful for their arrangements of topical folk songs from around the world, and their song "Good Night Irene" (1950) sold two million copies, an unprecedented number for a folk song. After being blacklisted for alleged ties to the Communist Party the group was unable to secure concert engagements and eventually disbanded.

During the 1950s and 1960s a folk revival was given impetus by Seeger, some of his contemporaries, and a new generation of singers, many of whom had been influenced by the civil rights movement and the student left. Two of the best-known were from Brooklyn: Dave Van Ronk played the blues; Elliot Charles Adnopoz, who took the name Ramblin' Jack Elliott, played in Guthrie's style and traveled west. The most influential folk singer was Bob Dylan, an admirer of Guthrie who performed traditional songs as well as songs of his own composition and usually accompanied himself on acoustic guitar and harmonica; by the mid 1960s he turned to an electric style influenced by rock-and-roll. Judy Collins and the members of the group Peter, Paul and Mary were among many folk singers who lived in the city during the 1960s and sang about the civil rights and antiwar movements. They first performed for small audiences at clubs in Greenwich Village such as Gerde's Folk City on West 3rd Street, and their records were later sold internationally. Irish folk music was revived in Ireland and the United States by a group called the Clancy Brothers and Tommy Makem. The Pennywhistlers performed folk songs from eastern Europe and the Balkans.

As radicalism declined in the 1970s so did the political importance of folk music, but solo folk singers accompanied by guitar continued to be popular in New York City. Indian folk music was performed in such celebrations as the Divali festival, as was *taiko* drumming during Japanese cherry blossom festivals. The rhumba, popular in Latin American neighborhoods, was introduced in nightclubs by well-known performers like Tito Puente and Celia Cruz. In the 1980s the Ethnic Arts Center and the World Music Institute supported performances by a range of international folk artists, and the Eagle Tavern on West 14th Street in Manhattan became a center for Irish folk music. In Greenwich Village musicians established Speakeasy's, a cooperative café on MacDougal Street where singers and songwriters performed topical songs and traditional folk music.

R. Serge Denisoff: *Great Day Coming: Folk Music and the American Left* (Urbana: University of Illinois Press, 1971)
Jerome L. Rodnitzky: *Minstrels of the Dawn: The Folk-protest Singer as Cultural Hero* (Chicago: University of Chicago Press, 1976)
David K. Dunaway: "A Selected Bibliography: Protest Song in the United States," *Folklore Forum* 2 (1977)

Barbara L. Tischler

Folks, Homer (*b* Hanover, Mich., 18 Feb 1867; *d* New York City, 13 Feb 1963). Reformer. He was appointed in 1893 by Louisa Lee Schuyler as the secretary of the State Charities Aid Association, a private organization that monitored public welfare institutions. In 1898–99 he served on the first Board of Aldermen of New York City and worked to reform municipal building codes. As the city's commissioner of public charities (1902–3) he opened the first municipal hospital for tuberculosis, on Blackwell's Island. He also prevailed on the state legislature to pass the Public Health Law (1913) and the Public Welfare Law (1929). In 1921 he was instrumental in opening the East Harlem Health Center, the first neighborhood health center in New York City; its success led the city's public health department to take charge of it, and by 1944 the department operated fourteen other centers in the city and had plans to open eleven more. Folks resigned from the State Charities Aid Association in 1947.

Walter I. Trattner: *Homer Folks: Pioneer in Social Welfare* (New York: Cambridge University Press, 1968)

Sarah Henry Lederman

Follin, Miriam. See Leslie, miriam.

food. New Yorkers enjoy a greater variety of food and drink than most other Americans, because of the city's huge size, its status as a port, and its many immigrant groups. Manhattan was a center of the rum trade during the colonial period, and had four rum distilleries in 1770 (see Brewing and distilling). During the nineteenth century seafood was so abundant that lobsters were an everyday item, oysters were common at large fish houses, and caviar from the Hudson was served without charge by saloons (see Commercial fishing). Much of the seafood destined for American markets passed first through Fulton Market in New York City, enabling local retailers and restaurant owners to take the freshest fish. Even salmon caught in the Pacific Northwest was typically shipped to New York City for sale, then back again to Portland (Oregon) and Seattle. With the arrival of large numbers of German immigrants in the 1840s New York City became an important center of brewing. In 1877 the Hell Gate brewery, established by the German immigrant George Ehret, was the largest brewer in the United States, and by 1879 there were seventy-eight breweries in Manhattan and forty-three in Brooklyn. Much of the demand for seafood and other products resulted from the fondness of New Yorkers for dining out. The grand dining Restaurants of the late nineteenth century and the hotel restaurants of the early twentieth served native fish with a European flair. Among the dishes created or popularized in the city were lobster Newburg, sole Marguery, and baked Alaska (served at Delmonico's), crabmeat Remick (at the Plaza Hotel), clams Casino (by Julius Keller at Narragansett Pier), vichyssoise (at the rooftop garden of the Ritz–Carlton Hotel by Louis Diat), and chicken Divan (at Divan Parisien on East 45th Street). A number of popular mixed cocktails also originated in New York City, including the Bloody Mary (first served at the King Cole Bar in the St. Regis Hotel by the Parisian bartender Ferdinand "Pete" Petiot and known as the "red snapper"), the Manhattan (at the Manhattan Club in 1874 to honor the election of Governor Samuel J. Tilden), the Bronx, made up of gin, sweet vermouth, and orange juice (at the Waldorf Hotel in 1906 by the bartender Johnnie Solon), the Christy girl, made with peach brandy, gin, and grenadine (at the Sherry–Netherland Hotel), the gibson, named for the illustrator Charles Dana Gibson (at the Players), sangria (at the Spanish Pavilion during the World's Fair of 1964–65), and the kamikaze, a drink of lemon juice, lime juice, cointreau, and vodka (at Les Pyrénées by Tony Lauriano in 1972).

In most neighborhoods of New York City elegant French and Italian restaurants are found alongside Korean grocers, pizzerias, Greek diners, soda shops, delicatessens, and Chinese markets. Many popular foods were created by immigrants who adapted their traditional recipes according to what was available in the United States. Italian dishes made in this fashion included veal parmigiana, clams Posillipo, spaghetti and meatballs, veal Marsala, Italian cheesecake, and spaghetti alla Caruso (all adaptations of Neapolitan or Sicilian dishes), pizza (originally poor people's food in Naples), pasta primavera (made with fettucini noodles and vegetables by Sirio Maccioni, the owner of Le Cirque), and the hero sandwich. A large number of the foods associated with American Jews originated in New York City and were at first unknown to Jews in Europe and the Middle East, including bagels, blintzes, knishes, lox, Danish pastries, cheesecake, the Reuben sandwich, and egg creams, a confection sold at candy stores made with chocolate syrup, milk, and seltzer (but neither eggs nor cream). American Jews also popularized seltzer (called "belchwasser" or "Jewish champagne" and drunk as a remedy for dyspepsia), the bottled chocolate drink Yoo-Hoo, and the coffee-flavored soda Manhattan Special. Other ethnic foods originated or popularized in the city include the hot dog (by Nathan Handwerker of Nathan's at Coney Island), the English muffin (by Samuel Bath Thomas sometime after 1880), London broil (in restaurants throughout Manhattan), chocolate fondue (at the Chalet Suisse in 1956 by Konrad Egli), negimaki, a dish of beef rolls and scallions with soy sauce (at the restaurant Nippon by its owner Nobuyoshi Kuraoka in 1959), and eggs Benedict. Although most of these foods were well liked, immigrants also created a market for such exotic items as squid, mussels, salt cod, tripe, brains, heart, kidneys, chilies, cilantro, broccoli, and leeks.

Many of the most popular American candies and confections were first made in New York City (see Confectioners), including Tootsie Roll (named by Leo Hirschfield for his daughter) and Chunky (named by Philip Silverstein for his granddaughter). The German immigrant Henry Heide sold more than 350 brands of candy from his shop in the city, among them Jujubes, Jujyfruits, Red Hot Dollars, Chocolate Sponge, Mexican Hats, Parlay bars, and Turkish Taffy. Yogurt became popular throughout the United States after Daniel Carasso and Juan Metzger began producing it under the name Dannon at a small factory in the Bronx. The ice-cream sandwich and a soft ice cream called frozen custard were introduced in the city, which was also the headquarters of two important makers of "premium" ice cream, Häagen Dazs and Sedutto's.

The principal wholesale food market for the city, at Hunts Point in the Bronx, is the largest produce market in the world. It sells more than $1000 million worth of produce yearly and handles 50 to 60 percent of the nearly 4000 million pounds (1800 million kilograms) of fruit and vegetables consumed annually in greater New York.

Peter Benes, ed.: *Foodways in the Northeast* (Boston: Boston University Press, 1984)
Peggy Katalinich: *Foods of Long Island* (New York: Harry N. Abrams, 1985)

See also Bakeries, Dairying, Meatpacking, Kosher foods, and Soft Drinks.

John F. Mariani

football. Organized football in New York City began in 1870, when Rutgers defeated Columbia University by a score of 6 goals to 3. New York University first played organized football in 1873. From the earliest days games between local colleges were overshadowed by those between colleges from out of town that chose to play in New York City to attract more fans. As early as the 1880s Princeton and Yale played annually in the city on Thanksgiving Day, and in the 1890s crowds of more than thirty thousand attended their games at the Polo Grounds; by the turn of the century these games had ceased owing to pressure from those who found their commercialism incompatible with the needs of college students. During the second decade of the twentieth century there were other games in New York City between colleges. Those between

Professional Football Teams in New York City

Brickley's Giants, NFL, 1921
New York Giants, NFL, 1925–
Brooklyn Horsemen, AFL (i), 1926 (merged with Brooklyn Lions to form Brooklion Horsemen)
Brooklyn Lions, NFL, 1926 (merged with Brooklyn Horsemen to form Brooklion Horsemen)
New York Yankees, AFL (i), 1926
New York Yankees, NFL, 1927–28
Staten Island Stapletons, NFL, 1929–32
Brooklyn Dodgers, NFL, 1930–44
Brooklyn Tigers, AFL (ii), 1936
New York Yankees, AFL (ii), 1936–37
New York Yankees, AFL (iii), 1940
New York Americans, AFL (iii), 1941
Brooklyn Dodgers, AAFC, 1946–48
New York Yankees, AAFC, 1946–49
New York Bulldogs, 1949 / New York Yanks, 1950–51, NFL
New York Titans, 1960–62, AFL (iv) / New York Jets, 1963–69, AFL (iv) / New York Jets, NFL, 1970–
New York Stars, WFL, 1974

NFL = National Football League
AFL = American Football League
AAFC = All-America Football Conference
WFL = World Football League

Army (the team of the U.S. Military Academy in West Point) and Notre Dame drew the largest crowds and created the most excitement, especially among the large Catholic population in the city.

The first team in New York City belonging to the National Football League (NFL) was Brickley's Giants, which played only two games in 1921 before disbanding. A new team called the New York Giants was formed in 1925 when Tim Mara purchased a franchise for the city from the NFL. In the following year Red Grange, who had just finished his career as a player for the University of Illinois, and his agent, Charles Pyle, asked permission from Mara and the NFL to form another team in New York City. When the request was denied they formed the first of four organizations known as the American Football League (AFL). Among the teams in the new league was the first of five teams called the New York Yankees, which played in Yankee Stadium, and another called the Brooklyn Horsemen that played four games before merging with the Brooklyn Lions of the NFL (the new team finished the season as the Brooklion Horsemen); the AFL ceased operations after one year. The NFL soon established several teams in the city, including the New York Yankees (1927–28), the Staten Island Stapletons (1929–32), and the Brooklyn Dodgers (1930–44), owned first by Dan Topping (who in 1939 acquired a controlling interest in the baseball Yankees and in 1946–48 owned the New York Yankees of the All-America Football Conference). Other attempts over the next twenty years to challenge the NFL were all based on the assumption that a successful franchise in New York City was a necessity, and each new league sought to put a team in Yankee Stadium that would be identified with the baseball Yankees.

College football in New York City had its heyday during the interwar years, although it never drew the crowds or generated the enthusiasm that it did elsewhere. New York University played its best football from 1926 to 1928. Led by Ken Strong, a versatile player who could run, pass, and kick, the team lost only four games in three seasons. In 1934 Columbia won a remarkable and unexpected victory over Stanford by a score of 7 to 0 in the Rose Bowl. The team used a play called the KF-79 in which the quarterback, Cliff Montgomery, made a series of handoffs and fake handoffs to the halfbacks. From 1935 to 1937 the Fordham University Rams had a defensive line known as the "seven blocks of granite," which included Vince Lombardi (to 1936) and Alex Wojciechowicz, and played a number of memorable, scoreless games against the powerful University of Pittsburgh. In 1936 Fordham did not surrender a touchdown until the last game of the season, when its loss to New York University by a score of 7 to 0 ended its chances of playing in the Rose Bowl. On 25 October 1947 Columbia won another remarkable upset when it defeated Army, until then undefeated in thirty-two consecutive games.

The late 1930s to the early 1950s were a period marked by a proliferation of professional football teams, many of them short-lived: in the second AFL the Brooklyn Tigers (1936) and the New York Yankees (1936–37); in the third AFL the New York Yankees (1940) and the New York Americans (1941); in the All-America Football Conference the New York Yankees (1946–49) and the Brooklyn Dodgers (1946–48), which were absorbed by the Yankees after three losing seasons; and in the NFL a team called successively the New York Bulldogs (1949) and the New York Yanks (1950–51). The New York Titans, an original member of the fourth AFL (formed 1960), became the New York Jets in 1963 and joined the NFL in 1970 when the two leagues merged. The New York Stars of the World Football League played only six home games at Downing Stadium on Randalls Island in 1974 before disbanding.

New York City has had several enduring rivalries between high school teams, such as those between De Witt Clinton High School and the High School of Commerce (now Louis D. Brandeis High School) and in Brooklyn between Erasmus Hall and Manual Training High School (now John Jay High School). Sid Luckman played for Erasmus Hall before his career at Columbia and with the Chicago Bears, and the baseball player Lou Gehrig played football for Commerce.

Harold Claassen: *Football's Unforgettable Games* (New York: Ronald, 1963)
Richard Whittingham: *Saturday Afternoon: College Football and the Men Who Made the Day* (New York: Workman, 1985)

Joseph A. Horrigan

Foote, Cone and Belding. Advertising and public relations firm, formed in 1943 by three executives formerly associated with Albert Lasker's firm Lord and Thomas. By 1960 it was one of the ten largest firms of its kind in the United States, and in 1963 it became publicly owned. In 1986 the firm took over Leber Katz of New York City, and by 1990 it had some $3600 million in billings and more than one hundred offices worldwide. Its headquarters are at 101 Park Avenue in Manhattan.

James Playsted Wood: *The Story of Advertising* (New York: Ronald, 1958)
Stephen R. Fox: *The Mirror Makers: A History of American Advertising and Its Creators* (New York: William Morrow, 1984)

Chauncey G. Olinger, Jr.

Forbes, Malcolm (Stevenson) (*b* Brooklyn, 19 Aug 1919; *d* Far Hills, N.J., 24 Sept 1990). Publisher. He grew up in Englewood, New Jersey, and attended Princeton University (AB 1941). In 1946 he joined the staff of *Forbes*, a fortnightly business magazine launched by his father, and from the mid 1960s he was its publisher, president, editor-in-chief, and sole owner. He was also a Republican state senator in New Jersey (1952–58) and the unsuccessful Republican gubernatorial candidate in New Jersey in 1957. In his later career he became increasingly well known as a devotee of such hobbies as motorcycle riding and hot-air ballooning, as a collector of Fabergé eggs and historical artifacts and memorabilia, and as the host of lavish parties (several aboard his yacht and one in Morocco). For all his flamboyance and flair for publicity, Forbes was a shrewd businessman whose publishing concerns flourished under his management.

Christopher Winans: *Malcolm Forbes: The Man Who Had Everything* (New York: St. Martin's, 1990)

B. Kimberly Taylor

Ford, Patrick (*b* Galway, Ireland, 12 April 1837; *d* New York City, 23 Sept 1913). Journalist. In 1846 he moved to Boston with his parents, and after working in the printing office of William Lloyd Garrison's journal the *Liberator* he enlisted in the Union Army. He later settled in Charleston, South Carolina, before moving to New York City, where in 1870 he launched the weekly newspaper *Irish World* (renamed *Irish World and American Industrial Liberator* in 1878), soon the most important publication of its kind in the city. Ford supported Irish nationalism, the right to strike, woman suffrage, the eight-hour day, the income tax, abolishing monopolies, insuring federal greenbacks, and nationalizing land in the United States and in Ireland, where he hoped that such a program would become a means for gaining independence. After the Land League was formed in Ireland in 1879 he oversaw the formation of 2500 similar organizations throughout the United States. A powerful voice in city politics, he supported such figures as Edward McGlynn and Henry George, a mayoral candidate in 1886. Ford lived at 350 Clermont Avenue in Brooklyn.

Kevin Kenny

Ford Foundation. The nation's largest philanthropic organization, with assets in 1993 of $6800 million. It was chartered in Detroit in 1936 to further charitable ends and to save the Ford family from having to sell the Ford Motor Company to pay the taxes on the estates of Henry Ford and his son Edsel. Until 1950 the foundation granted about $1 million a year to charities in greater Detroit. In that year the foundation's assets increased markedly when it was bequeathed 88 percent of the company's stock. A five-member study committee was then appointed by Henry Ford II to make plans for expanding the foundation; entities soon formed as a result included the Fund for the Advancement of Education, the Fund for Adult Education (a pioneer in educational television), and the Fund for the Republic. The foundation also set up research and policy organizations such as Resources for the Future and the Council on Library Resources. From 1951 to 1953 the foundation had its headquarters in Pasadena, California, home of its first president, Paul G. Hoffman, former head of the Marshall Plan. When Hoffman was succeeded by H. Rowan Gaither, a lawyer from San Francisco, offices were consolidated in New York City and the foundation put up its own building near the United Nations. In 1955 the foundation sold most of its stock and granted $642.6 million in proceeds to private colleges and universities, hospitals, and medical schools. For nine years the foundation was led by Henry T. Heald, a former president of New York University; during his tenure the foundation continued to support higher education (especially business and engineering) and expanded its arts program (it granted $80 million to symphony orchestras). Along with other foundations it was a target of congressional investigations in the 1950s (prompted by allegations of support for subversive activities, financial self-dealing, and undue accumulation of assets) and of inquiries in the 1960s that led to the Tax Reform Act. Its support of civil rights, minority voter registration, and other liberal causes led to boycotts of products of the Ford Motor Company. The foundation was criticized by the teachers' unions for its role in assisting school decentralization in New York City in 1967, which touched off a bitter strike.

In New York City the foundation supported educational, arts, and social service institutions ranging from Lincoln Center to the Vera Institute of Justice. In 1968 it established the Fund for the City of New York to improve the city's public services. McGeorge Bundy, a former national security advisor, was president of the foundation for thirteen years from 1965, during which the foundation played a prominent role in civil rights, community development in inner cities, and environmental research and advocacy. In 1977 the foundation severed its ties to the Ford company and family. Franklin A. Thomas, a foundation trustee who became president of the foundation in 1979, focused on domestic poverty, problems of refugees and immigrants, and leadership in state government. In the early 1990s the foundation had made grants of $1036 million.

The Ford Foundation occupies a brick-and-glass structure at 321 East 42nd Street, designed by Kevin Roche and John Dinkeloo. Completed in 1967, the building has an enclosed courtyard with trees and greenery and is among the most elegant works of architecture in the city.

Rowan H. Gaither, ed.: *Report of the Study for the Ford Foundation on Policy and Program, November 1949* (Detroit: Ford Foundation, 1950)

Dwight MacDonald: *The Ford Foundation: The Men and the Millions* (New York: Reynal, 1956; rev. New Brunswick, N.J.: Transaction, 1989)

Richard Magat: *The Ford Foundation at Work: Philanthropic Choices, Methods, and Styles* (New York: Plenum, 1979)

Francis X. Sutton: "The Ford Foundation: The Early Years," *Daedalus* 116, no. 1 (winter 1987), 41–91

Richard Magat

Fordham. Neighborhood in the northwestern Bronx, centered at the intersection of Fordham Road and the Grand Concourse and bounded to the north by Kingsbridge Road and East 174th Street, to the east by Fordham University and Webster Avenue, to the south by 183rd Street, and to the west by the Harlem River; to the north is Herbert H. Lehman College and to the south Bronx Community College, which occupies the former uptown campus of New York University. During the

Tiebout Avenue steps in Fordham

seventeenth century a few houses stood near what is now the intersection of Bailey Avenue and Kingsbridge Road, and a nearby ford across the Harlem River was the only direct crossing to the Bronx from Manhattan. A parcel of 3900 acres (1580 hectares) extending from the ford to the eventual site of the High Bridge and lying between the Harlem and Bronx rivers was granted in 1671 by Governor Francis Lovelace to the Dutch settler Jon Arcer (John Archer), who named it Fordham manor after Saxon words meaning "houses by the ford (or wading place)." The first bridge from the Bronx to Manhattan, the King's Bridge, opened in 1693 a short distance from the ford. After Archer's death the manor was divided up into small farms. Claimed mostly by the British but raided by both sides during the American Revolution, the area was the site of many skirmishes between British and Continental troops that devastated local farms. It remained rural until the mid nineteenth century. In 1841 the New York and Harlem Railroad was extended to Webster Avenue and what later became Fordham Road, and near one of its stations was built St. John's College, a Roman Catholic college that later became Fordham University. Edgar Allan Poe moved in 1846 to a small cottage, his last home, near what became Poe Park.

The neighborhood grew tremendously after rapid transit was extended from Manhattan. The 3rd Avenue elevated line was extended to Fordham Plaza in 1900; the Jerome Avenue elevated line opened in 1918, the Grand Concourse subway in 1933. Between 1900 and 1950 a shopping district developed on Fordham Road that included Alexander's department store. Many five-story walk-up apartment buildings and six-story buildings with elevators were erected, a large number of which remained standing in the mid 1990s. Most residents were middle-class and working-class Jews, Irish, and Italians who had moved from crowded sections of Manhattan, and often they were the children and grandchildren of immigrants. The neighborhood became known for its outstanding schools, including the Bronx High School of Science. From the 1950s many residents moved to the suburbs, and by 1980 much of the population consisted of Puerto Ricans, other Latin Americans, and blacks, many from the southern Bronx. In the following years large-scale housing abandonment of the sort that had occurred in the southern Bronx was forestalled, in part through the efforts of the Northwest Bronx Community and Clergy Coalition. In the 1980s about a quarter of new immigrants settling in Fordham and its environs were Dominican. There was also a large population of Jamaicans, Guyanese, Cambodians, Koreans, and Vietnamese. Although the neighborhood has many problems its apartment buildings are for the most part well maintained, as are its few one- and two-family houses. Fordham remains a vital area, best known for its shopping district and as the site of Fordham University.

Harry C. W. Melick: *The Manor of Fordham and Its Founder* (New York: Fordham University Press, 1950)

Peter Derrick

Fordham Preparatory School. Jesuit high school for boys on East Fordham Road in the Bronx, opened in 1841 as part of St. John's College (now Fordham University). Initially a boarding school, it lacked its own principal until 1921 and in the following years it became a day school. In 1970 it formed its own board of trustees and split off from the university, moving to a building on the east side of the university campus in 1972. The student enrollment in 1990 was 1025.

Gilbert Tauber

Fordham University. Roman Catholic university opened in 1841 as St. John's College by Bishop John Hughes in Fordham Manor. The first president was John McCloskey, later archbishop of New York. Unable to staff the school or support it financially, Hughes transferred control to the Society of Jesus in 1846, the year in which the first bachelor's degree was awarded; Augustus J. Thebaud was the first Jesuit president. Until 1855 the Jesuits maintained a seminary for the diocese at the school. The college opened a medical school and a law school in 1905 and in 1907 took its current name and established Fordham University Press. Later it opened the School of Pharmacy (1912), the School of Sociology and Social Service (1916), the School of Business Administration (1920), and the School of Education (1938). The law school moved successively to 42 Broadway in lower Manhattan, 20 Vesey Street, 140 Nassau Street, the Woolworth Building (where it remained for thirty years), and 302 Broadway (1943). The university became widely known for its athletic program in baseball (1859), football (1883), track (1900), and basketball (1902); from 1935 to 1937 the football team achieved great success with a defensive line known as the "seven blocks of granite" that included Vince Lombardi. In 1955 the university became part of the project to develop Lincoln Center, and in the early 1960s several divisions including the law school moved to a new campus near the center bounded by 62nd Street, Amsterdam Avenue, 60th Street, and Columbus Avenue. In 1962 the university inaugurated a chapter of Phi Beta Kappa. When the university merged with St. Thomas More College in 1964 it became coeducational; in 1969 it came under the control of a lay board of trustees. Fordham in the mid 1990s had more than thirteen thousand undergraduate and graduate students in more than seventy academic programs at ten schools and colleges. Two archbishops of New York graduated from Fordham: John Cardinal Farley (1867) and John Cardinal Spellman (1911).

Robert I. Gannon: *Up to the Present: The Story of Fordham* (Garden City, N.Y.: Doubleday, 1967)

Bernadette McCauley

Foreign Policy Association. Organization formed in 1918 in support of efforts to establish a League of Nations. After these efforts failed it remained in operation as a nonpartisan organization dedicated to the study of foreign policy. It sponsors discussion groups as well as an annual survey with more than eight thousand respondents. The offices are at 729 7th Avenue in Manhattan.

Paul Underwood Kellogg: *Ten Years of the F.P.A.* (New York: Foreign Policy Association, 1929)

B. Kimberly Taylor

Forest Hills. Neighborhood in central Queens, bounded to the north by the Long Island Expressway, to the east by Flushing Meadows–Corona Park, to the south by Union Turnpike, and to the west by Junction Boulevard and disused track of the Long Island Rail Road (the former Rockaway Beach line). It occupies what was once farmland owned by Frederick D. Backus, George Backus, and Horatio N. Squires, of which six hundred acres (243 hectares) in the area then known as Whitepot were bought in 1906 by the Cord Meyer Development Company. The area was named Forest Hills for its proximity to Forest Park, and its streets were assigned names arranged in alphabetical order from Atom (75th Avenue) to Zuni (63rd Drive). The company installed utilities and under the direction of George C. Meyer engaged architects like Robert Tappan and William Patterson to design elegant one-family houses, which were built from 108th Street to 112th Street and between Queens Boulevard and 67th Road; some lots were donated for schools and churches. The Long Island Rail Road opened a station in Forest Hills on 5 August 1911, enabling residents to commute to Manhattan in thirty minutes. The trolley along Queens Boulevard inaugurated service on 27 August 1913 from 71st Avenue to 2nd Avenue in Manhattan, and Queens Boulevard was gradually widened during the early 1920s. Development hastened after these improvements were made: in 1922 the Queens Valley Golf Club was laid out on 17.5 acres (seven hectares) of land, and by the end of 1924 there were 340 houses. Construction began on apartments along Queens Boulevard, including the Kelvin (1928) and the Livingston, Georgian, and Portsmouth (all 1929), and between 1927 and 1930 the population increased from 9500 to 18,207. Land along Queens Boulevard was excavated by the city in 1931 for the Independent subway, which opened to Union Turnpike on 31 December 1936 and transformed the part of Forest Hills northeast of Queens Boulevard. Additional apartment buildings were constructed and many stores opened to accommodate the growing population (32,500 in 1940). In the four decades after

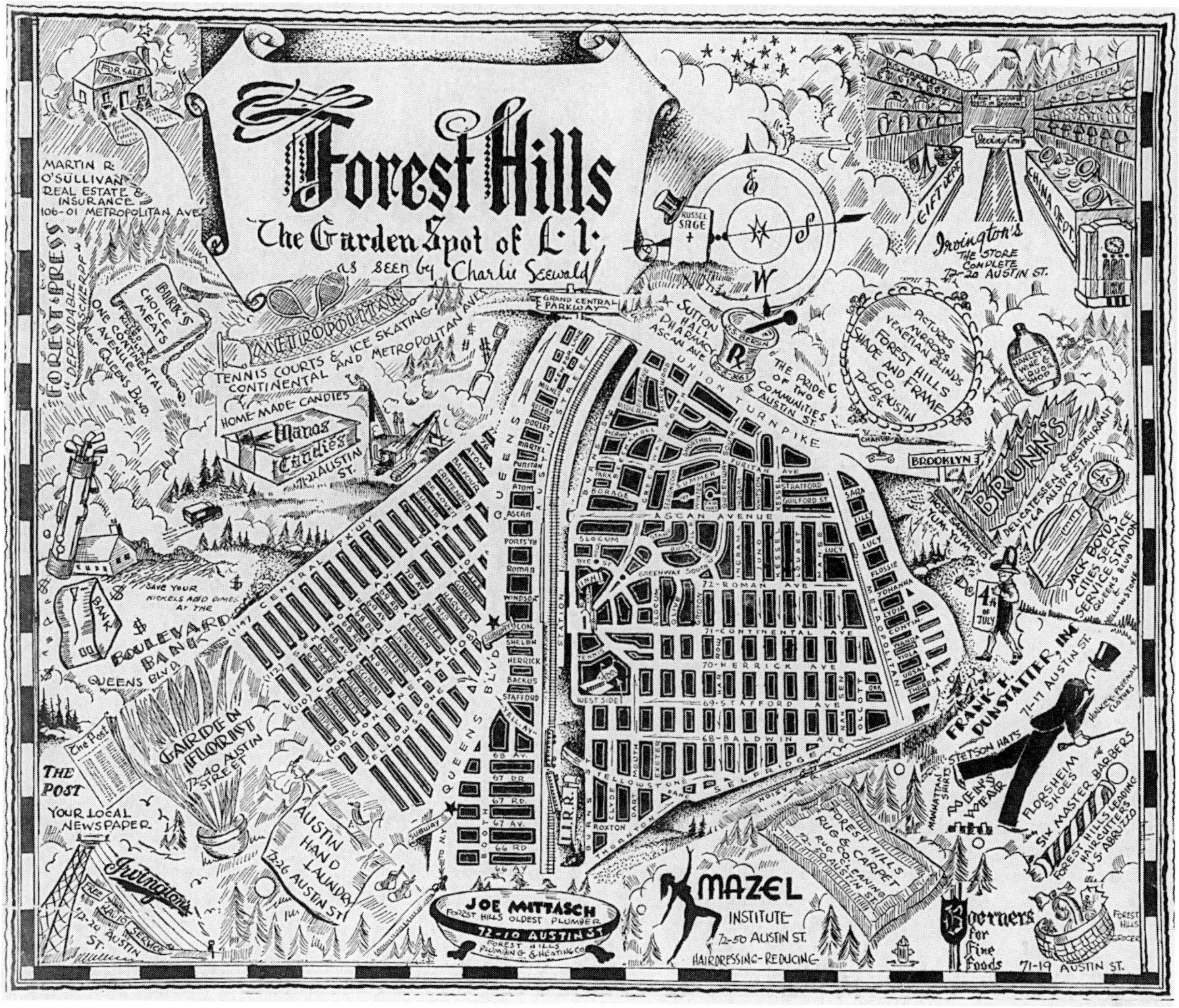

Map of Forest Hills, drawn by Charlie Seewald

the Second World War some private houses were razed to build apartments, and the neighborhood became largely middle class, Jewish, and Italian.

Forest Hills in the early 1970s was the scene of a bitter dispute between middle-class homeowners and advocates of low-income housing. The controversy received national attention and helped to launch the political career of Mario M. Cuomo, a local lawyer who negotiated a compromise that largely defused the tensions. No open land remained in the mid 1990s, and only northern Forest Hills and sections near Queens Boulevard retained one-family houses on individual lots rather than large apartment buildings. Many new immigrants settled in Forest Hills during the 1980s, especially Jews from Europe and Asia. The single largest group was from Iran, followed by China, India, the Soviet Union, Israel, Colombia, Korea, Romania, Pakistan, and Poland.

Vincent Seyfried

Forest Hills Gardens. Housing development in central Queens, bounded to the northeast by Burns Street and to the southeast by Union Turnpike; the southwestern boundary is irregular and runs roughly parallel to Burns Street. The land was originally part of an area formerly known as Whitepot and was later included in a parcel of six hundred acres (243 hectares) bought in 1906 by Cord Meyer, who in 1908 sold a section below Queens Boulevard to Margaret Slocum Sage, the benefactor of the Russell Sage Foundation. On 142 acres (fifty-seven hectares) the landscape architect Frederick Law Olmsted Jr. planned a development in the style of an English village, with a green, a railroad station, an inn, and fifteen hundred houses designed by the architect Grosvenor Atterbury. A brick-paved square shaded by trees was built in front of the railroad station, with a town clock, arched passageways, and garden apartments built to resemble a row of country inns. Narrow, winding roads discouraged through-traffic and provided room for large front gardens. Between February and May 1910 streets were laid out between Continental and Ascan avenues, and during the summer of the same year houses of varied height and design were erected using the new techniques of steel framing and concrete construction. The high price of land and construction drove the rents to $12 a month in 1910, a prohibitive amount for those with moderate incomes. Many elegant brick houses were built between 1910 and 1917, and in 1916–17 luxury houses were built in Greenway Terrace that sold for about $20,000; the Russell Sage Foundation built others by private contract. In 1912 the inn, a garage, and a country club were opened. The post office began service in 1914, and ten acres (four hectares) of land were sold to the West Side Tennis Club, where the U.S. Open tennis championship was contested in August (the well-known tennis stadium opened on 10 August 1923). The Church-in-the-Gardens was built in 1915, followed by the Church of

Our Lady Queen of Martyrs (dedicated on 28 May 1916). Several well-known figures lived in Forest Hills Gardens during these years, including Helen Keller, Dale Carnegie, John F. Hylan, the entertainer Fred Stone, and the sculptor Adolph A. Weinman. Development ceased with the entry of the United States into the First World War. In 1922 the Forest Hills Gardens Corporation, an organization of property owners, bought the common areas. The first apartment building, the Forest Arms, was erected in 1924. In the years following the Second World War only about twenty-five houses were built and by 1964 only two vacant lots remained. There were about 4500 inhabitants in 1970. Streets, parks, sewers, distinctive streetlights, and traffic lights are owned and maintained by the corporation, which preserves the residential character of the neighborhood. In the 1980s a number of new immigrants settled in Forest Hills Gardens and its environs, mostly from Iran, India, the Soviet Union, and Israel.

John R. Stilgoe: *Borderland: Origins of the American Suburb, 1820–1939* (New Haven: Yale University Press, 1988)

Vincent Seyfried

Forest Park. Public park in Queens, bounded to the north by Myrtle Avenue and Union Turnpike, to the east by Park Lane, to the south by Park Lane South, and to the west by Cypress Hills Cemetery. It occupies 535 acres (217 hectares) of hilly terrain and was once known as the Brooklyn Forest because of its acquisition in 1895 by the City of Brooklyn. In 1896 the firm of landscape architects Olmsted, Olmsted and Eliot designed a plan for the park, which was executed about the turn of the century. A golf course, originally of nine holes, opened in 1901; the clubhouse (1905), designed in a Dutch Colonial Revival style by the firm of Helmle, Huberty and Hudswell (which also designed the Williamsburgh Savings Bank), now houses the offices of the park's administrator. Popular carousels by the highly regarded designer Daniel Muller were added in 1918 (destroyed by fire in 1966) and 1972. The park was ravaged in 1912 by a chestnut blight and for a time was used for lumbering; about the same time greenhouses were set up to grow plants for parks throughout the city. Jackson Pond was used for fishing and ice skating before being filled in. The Interborough Parkway between Brooklyn and Queens was built through the park in 1935. Within Forest Park are ballfields, tennis courts, a bandshell (on the site of an earlier bandstand and concert grove), a memorial field called Victory Field, a monument to the First World War known variously as the "Richmond Hill Doughboy" and "My Buddy," and an enclosed area in which model airplanes may be flown.

Jonathan Kuhn

Forrest, Edwin (*b* Philadelphia, 9 March 1806; *d* Philadelphia, 12 Dec 1872). Actor. He made his début in New York as Othello in July 1826, then performed often in the Park and Bowery theaters. From 1839 to 1850 he owned and lived in a townhouse at 436 West 22nd Street. In 1849 his rivalry with the English actor William Charles Macready culminated in the bloody Astor Place Riot. After his bitter divorce in 1851 he returned to his home in Philadelphia but continued to act in New York City. In 1853 he appeared as Macbeth at the Broadway Theatre; the engagement lasted four weeks, an unprecedented run. He played Hamlet at Niblo's Garden in 1860 and gave his final performance in New York City in February 1871. Known for his commanding physique and powerful voice, Forrest was the first American-born actor to achieve an international reputation.

Don B. Wilmeth

Fort Amsterdam. The name of a fort erected by the Dutch in lower Manhattan, and by extension one of several names sometimes applied to the entire settlement of New Amsterdam. The fort was a four-sided structure at the foot of Broadway, opposite Marketfield, Stone, and Bridge streets, near the eventual site of the U.S. Custom House. Unimpressive even by the standards of the seventeenth century, it was unable to protect the Dutch against a British fleet that appeared in the harbor in the late summer of 1664. On 2 September, without loss of life, Governor Peter Stuyvesant surrendered both fort and city.

Kenneth T. Jackson

Fort Apache. Nickname for the forty-first police precinct of New York City, which has its station at Simpson Avenue south of 167th Street in the southern Bronx and covers the neighborhoods of Hunts Point and Crotona Park East. The nickname became used when drugs, crime, and arson severely damaged the surrounding area during the 1960s and 1970s. The crime rate had declined sharply by the 1990s.

Evelyn Gonzalez

Fort Greene. Neighborhood lying at the foot of the Manhattan Bridge in northwestern Brooklyn (1990 pop. 40,000), bounded to the north by the East River, to the east by Vanderbilt Avenue, to the south by Atlantic Avenue, and to the west by Flatbush Avenue. The first European settler (and the first Italian in Brooklyn) was Peter Caesar Alberti, who from 1639 operated a tobacco plantation near Wallabout Bay. The area is named for Nathaniel Greene, a colonial general who oversaw the construction of Fort Putnam in 1776 on a hill overlooking the bay (the fort survived the Battle of Long Island but was abandoned during Washington's retreat). During the American Revolution colonial prisoners were held in cattle and supply ships moored in the bay by the British army, which had too little space in conventional jails for the thousands captured. Overcrowding, contaminated water, starvation, and disease led to the deaths of almost 11,500 men, whose corpses were dumped in trenches along the riverbank. Their remains periodically washed ashore until they were reinterred elsewhere in 1792; several efforts were made to erect a permanent monument and crypt. On the site of the tobacco plantation a shipyard opened in 1791, followed by the Brooklyn Navy Yard in 1801. During the 1840s a growing number of free blacks settled and found skilled work in shipbuilding, and by 1870 more than half the black population of Brooklyn lived in the area; there were also many Irish, German, and

Prison Ship Martyr's Monument in Fort Greene Park (designed by McKim, Mead and White, sculpture by A. A. Weinman), 1991

John Vandergaw's carriage factory

English immigrants. In 1848 Frederick Law Olmsted and Calvert Vaux designed Washington Park, which covered thirty acres (twelve hectares) of land and had cobblestone walks meandering under chestnut trees; it was later renamed Fort Greene Park. An austere Doric column called the Prison Ship Martyrs' Monument was erected in the park in 1908. Shipbuilding remained the economic mainstay of the neighborhood until the navy yard closed in 1966. The population became ethnically and economically mixed, and several housing projects were built by the New York City Housing Authority for tenants of low and middle income. The neighborhood came to have many types of building, including Second Empire brownstones and neo-Grec, Romanesque Revival, Queen Anne, and nineteenth-century Italianate townhouses; in 1978 it was designated a Historic District. Buildings that themselves became landmarks include the original Hanson Place Baptist Church (1860), which served the Underground Railroad, the Lafayette Avenue Presbyterian Church (1862), the Brooklyn Academy of Music (1908), and the Williamsburgh Savings Bank, the tallest building in Brooklyn (1929). The 1980s saw an influx of black and white professionals who were attracted by the proximity of the neighborhood to Manhattan and by brownstones that cost less than in other parts of the city. In the mid 1990s several well-known black artists and musicians lived in the neighborhood, and the population was about two thirds black, a quarter white, and a tenth Latin American.

Barbara Habenstreit: *Fort Greene, U.S.A.* (Indianapolis: Bobbs–Merrill, 1974)

Judith Berck

Fort Hamilton. A fort in Bay Ridge, one of the oldest continuously garrisoned federal posts in the United States. Named for Alexander Hamilton, it stands on the site of an early Dutch blockhouse and of Fort Lewis, an earth and timber work that helped to deter British attack during the War of 1812. The fort was built between 1825 and 1831 as the first granite fort in the harbor. A decade after its construction the post engineer Captain Robert E. Lee supervised expansion of the gun platform and improvements to the water battery, Fort Lafayette. During the Civil War volunteer regiments trained at Fort Hamilton, and Fort Lafayette became a high-ranking federal prison for Confederates. The post commander in the first months of the war was Abner Doubleday (called by some the inventor of baseball), who was later a hero at Gettysburg. A ship barrier across the Narrows assisted Fort Hamilton and its sister forts on Staten Island in protecting the harbor against Confederate raiders. Fort Hamilton also provided troops to help put down the draft riots of July 1863.

Rifled cannon made vertical-walled masonry fortifications obsolete during the Civil War, and in the last decades of the nineteenth century great advances in military technology brought a new generation of long-range guns mounted in inconspicuous emplacements. The guns, in turn made obsolete by air power, were removed from Fort Hamilton in the years surrounding the Second World War. Anti-ship artillery was replaced by anti-aircraft artillery, itself removed in 1954 when Nike missiles began twenty years of protecting New York City. Harbor mines, submarine nets, and other defenses served at the Narrows; all were eventually removed. Fort Hamilton was a major embarkation and separation center during the two world wars. In the mid 1990s it was the home of a recruiting command and the Military Entrance and Processing Station for New York City. Fort Hamilton supports more than two hundred reserve and National Guard units. As the only active army post in the metropolitan area, it does work once performed by several installations.

The name Fort Hamilton sometimes refers to the immediately surrounding civilian community as well, although less so than formerly. During most of the nineteenth century the fort had no chapel and depended on nearby churches that integrated it into the community. St. John's Episcopal Church, known as the "church of the generals," baptized Lieutenant Thomas Jackson (later to achieve fame as Stonewall Jackson), and Lee was one of its vestrymen. Although soldiers were marched to St. John's, many were Irish or German Catholics whose volunteer labor helped put up the first building for nearby St. Patrick's Church. The neighborhood also had several cheap saloons just off post that catered to soldiers. What remained of the civilian neighborhood in the early 1960s was further diminished by the construction of approaches for the Verrazano Narrows Bridge.

Asa R. Runyon: "History of Fort Hamilton" (1928) [unpubd, New York Public Library]

For illustration see Hotels.

Russell S. Gilmore

Fort Hill. Neighborhood in northeastern Staten Island, lying within and near the center of New Brighton at an elevation of 210 feet (sixty-four meters). The name recalls the earthen redoubts built by the British at the time of the American Revolution. During the second half of the nineteenth century the estate of Daniel Low occupied the hill. Eventually the estate was divided up and sold. Fort Hill in later years underwent a resurgence, as many young families purchased houses and restored them to their former condition. It is now a residential area of fine, one-family houses.

Charles W. Leng and William T. Davis: *Staten Island and Its People* (New York: Lewis Historical Publishing, 1930)

John-Paul Richiuso

fortifications. The defense of New York Harbor began with the city's founding. One of the first actions taken by the Dutch settlers was to erect Fort Amsterdam on a site now occupied by the former U.S. Customs House at the foot of Broadway in Manhattan. Soon after, they built small blockhouses at strategic points such as the Narrows. When the colony changed hands in 1664 England altered little in the city's defenses except the name of Fort Amsterdam (which became successively Fort James, Fort William, Fort Anne, and Fort George), but during the first half of the eighteenth century additional guns at the shore near the old fort created a redoubtable defense in the area still called the Battery. Effective anti-ship fortifications spread beyond Manhattan during the American Revolution, and at the same time American engineers threw up the city's only important non-maritime forts. In preparation for the Battle of Long Island they built earthworks at various points on Manhattan, Governors Island, and eastern Long Island. The line of defenses behind which the defeated patriots took refuge, to include Fort Greene, Fort Putnam, and Fort Box, was imposing enough to deter General William Howe from immediate attack and permit Washington's retreat across the East River. The triumphant British returned to maritime concerns and during their seven-year occupation of the city built the first defenses at the Narrows capable of stopping ships.

In the nineteenth century improved technology made it possible and necessary to engage an enemy ever farther out on the water. Later defenses therefore lay in rings progressively more distant from the original settlement. The first half of the century was a time of massive masonry forts, only one of which remains in Manhattan. The rapid expansion of New York City destroyed the early-nineteenth-century Red Fort (or North Fort) within a generation; the White Fort (Fort Gansevoort) did not last much longer. The State of New York built Castle Clinton, which survives, between 1807 and 1811, as tension with England appeared to be building toward another war. (Militarily unneeded by 1823, the fort became Castle Garden in 1823–55, the immigrant station in 1855-90, and the New York Aquarium in 1896–1941, before being returned to its appearance as a fort by the National Park Service.) Governors Island nearby still bears defenses of the same period: Fort Jay (called Fort Columbus, 1806–1904), Castle Williams, and South Battery. Fort Wood, which is now the sub-base of the

Fort Weed, Staten Island, ca *1980. Construction of the massive walls of Fort Weed began in 1841 and was completed in 1860. The structure became known as Battery Weed in 1861 and is now part of the Fort Wadsworth Military Reservation, just south of the Verrazano Narrows Bridge.*

Military Forts in New Amsterdam and New York City

Fort George at the Battery [Fort Amsterdam, Fort James, Fort Willem Hendrick, Fort William Henry, Fort Anne, Queen's Fort] (1626), Whitehall, State, and Bridge streets and Bowling Green, Manhattan
Amersfort Blockhouse (*ca* 1630), Flatlands, Brooklyn
Wall Street Palisade (*ca* 1640), Wall Street, Hudson River to East River, Manhattan
Bushwich (Boswyck) Blockhouses (*ca* 1662), Bushwick, Brooklyn
Fort Wadsworth [Fort Richmond, Battery Weed] (1663), Signal Hill, Staten Island [extant]
Turtle Bay Depot (*ca* 1775), Turtle Bay, East River, 47th Street, Manhattan
Fort Box (1776), Bergen's (Boerum's) Street, Brooklyn
Fort Bunker Hill [Independent Battery, Bayard's Hill Redoubt] (1776), Centre, Broome, Mott, and Grand streets, Manhattan
Citizen's Redoubt [Badlam's Redoubt] (1776), Rutgers Hill at Market and Madison streets, Manhattan
Fort Cock Hill (1776), Inwood Hill, 207th Street, Manhattan
Fort Corkscrew [Fort Cobble Hill, Spiral Fort, Fort Swift] (1776), Atlantic Avenue, Court, Pacific, and Clinton streets, Brooklyn
Decker's Ferry Fort (*ca* 1776), Port Richmond on Kill van Kull
Fort Defiance (1776), Dwight and Beard streets, Brooklyn
Flagstaff Fort (1776), Signal Hill, Staten Island
Fort George at Laurel Hill (*ca* 1776), Hudson River at 192nd Street and Audubon Avenue, Manhattan [extant]
Fort Greene [Fort Sutherland, Fort Masonic] (1776), State and Schermerhorn streets, Brooklyn
Grenadier's Battery (*ca* 1776), Hudson River, Washington and Harrison streets, Manhattan
Fort Hill (*ca* 1776), New Brighton, Staten Island
Horn's Hook Fort (*ca* 1776), Horn's Hook, 89th Street and East End Avenue, Manhattan
Hospital Redoubt (1776), West Broadway and Writh Street, Manhattan
Fort Independence (*ca* 1776), Giles Place between Old Boston and Albany Post roads
Jersey Battery (*ca* 1776), Reade Street, Manhattan
Jones Hill Fort (*ca* 1776), Broome and Pitt streets, Manhattan
King's Bridge Redoubt (*ca* 1776), Spuyten Duyvil Creek at Old Post Road, Manhattan
Lispenard's Redoubt (*ca* 1776), Varick and Laight streets, Manhattan
Mcgown's Pass Redoubt (*ca* 1776), 5th Avenue and East 107th Street, Manhattan
Montresor's Island (1776), Montresor's (Randalls) Island, Manhattan
Narrows Fort (1776), Brooklyn side of Narrows, Bronx
Fort no. 1 (1776), West 230th Street and Sycamore Avenue, Bronx
Fort no. 2 (1776), West 230th Street and Arlington Avenue, Bronx
Fort no. 3 (1776), Netherland Avenue between West 227th and 231st streets, Bronx

(*continued*)

Military Forts in New Amsterdam and New York City *(Continued)*

Fort no. 4 (*ca* 1776), Jerome Park Reservoir, Bronx
Fort no. 7 (1776), Fordham Road and Sedgwick Avenue, Bronx
Fort no. 8 (1776), University Heights, Fordham, Bronx
Oblong Redoubt (1776), Dekalb and Hudson avenues, Brooklyn
Oyster Battery [Mcdougall's Battery] (*ca* 1776), behind Trinity Church, Manhattan
Fort Prince Charles (1776), Fort Charles Place and Kingsbridge Avenue, Bronx
Fort Putnam [Fort Greene] (1776), Fort Greene Park, Brooklyn
Fort Richmond (1776), La Tourette Country Club, Staten Island
Fort Stirling [Half-moon Fort] (1776), Columbia Street between Clark and Orange streets, Brooklyn
Fort Tryon [Forest Hill Redoubt] (1776), Fort Tryon Park, Manhattan [extant]
Fort Washington [Fort Knyphausen] (1776), Fort Washington Avenue between 181st and 186th streets, Manhattan
Waterbury's Battery (1776), Catherine and Cherry streets, Manhattan
Watering Place Redoubts (*ca* 1776), Pavillion Hill, Staten Island
Whitehall Battery (*ca* 1776), South Ferry, Manhattan
Fort no. 5 (1777), Kingsbridge Road, Bronx
Fort no. 6 (1777), Kingsbridge Road and Sedgwick Avenue, Bronx
Fort Brooklyn [the Citadel] (1781), Pierrepont and Henry streets, Brooklyn Heights, Brooklyn
Fort Jay [Fort Columbus] (1800), Governors Island, Manhattan [extant]
Fort Hudson (*ca* 1808), Signal Hill, Staten Island
Fort Morton (*ca* 1808), Signal Hill, Staten Island
Fort Tompkins (*ca* 1808), Signal Hill, Staten Island
Castle Clinton [West Battery, City Battery] (1811), southwest point of Manhattan [extant]
Red Fort [North Battery] (1811), Hudson River at Hubert Street, Manhattan
Castle Williams (1811), Governors Island, Manhattan [extant]
Corlear's Hook Fort (1812), Corlear's Hook, Manhattan
Fort Gansevoort [White Fort] (1812), Hudson River between West 12th and Gansevoort streets, Manhattan
Fort Gibson [Battery Gibson] (1812), Ellis Island, Manhattan
Bath Beach Blockhouse (1813), Bath Beach, Brooklyn
Castle Bogardus (*ca* 1813), Lawrence Hill, Queens
Benson's Point Redoubt (1814), 106th Street between 2nd and 3rd avenues, Manhattan
Blockhouse no.1 (1814), 110th Street and 7th Avenue, Manhattan [extant]
Blockhouse no.2 (1814), 114th Street and Morningside Avenue, Manhattan
Blockhouse no.3 (1814), 121st Street and Morningside Avenue, Manhattan
Blockhouse no.4 (1814), 123rd Street and 10th Avenue, Manhattan
Fort Cummings (1814), between Putnam and Green avenues, Brooklyn
Fort Fish (1814), Central Park near East 107th Street, Manhattan
Fort Horn (1814), Morningside Park at 123rd Street, Manhattan
Fort Lafayette [Brooklyn Bastille, Fort Diamond] (1814), Hendricks Reef, the Narrows, Brooklyn
Fort Laight (1814), West 125th Street and 11th Avenue, Manhattan
Fort Lawrence (1814), Degraw and Bond streets, Brooklyn
Fort Masonic (1814), Nevins and Bond streets, Brooklyn
Mill Rock Blockhouse (1814), Mill Rock, East River, Manhattan
Fort Stevens (1814), Hell Gate on Hallett's Point, Queens
Fort Wood (1814), Bedloe's (Liberty) Island, Manhattan [extant]
Fort Hamilton [Fort Lewis] (1831), Brooklyn side of Narrows, Brooklyn [extant]
Fort Marcy (*ca* 1846), location unknown
Fort Schuyler (1856), Throgs Neck, Bronx [extant]
Camp Scott (*ca* 1861), Old Town, Staten Island
Smith's Cantonment (*ca* 1861), Signal Hill, Staten Island
Camp Sprague (1861), New Dorp, Staten Island
Camp Tompkinsville [Camp McClellan] (*ca* 1861), Staten Island
Camp Arthur (1862), Staten Island
Fort Totten [Fort at Willets Point] (1862), Willets Point, Queens [extant]
Fort Tilden [Camp Rockaway Beach] (1917), Rockaway Beach, Queens [extant]

Source: Robert J. Roberts: *Encyclopedia of Historic Forts: The Military, Pioneer and Trading Posts of the United States* (New York: Macmillan, 1988)

Compiled By Laura Lewison

Statue of Liberty, also stood ready for the War of 1812. The federal government began Fort Hamilton at the Narrows in 1825 and the earliest surviving defense on Fort Wadsworth in Staten Island in 1847. At mid century the federal government also undertook a never-completed granite work ten miles (sixteen kilometers) south at Sandy Hook, New Jersey, to replace Fort Gates, which dated from the War of 1812. Fort Hancock later rose on the same sand spit, which was too important a site to ignore. Until the dredging of the Ambrose Channel early in the twentieth century, Hancock offered the best first shot at an enemy ship nearing the main entrance to New York Harbor.

At the East River entrance to the harbor, army engineers in 1856 completed Fort Schuyler (now the home of the State University of New York Maritime College). Later they began Fort Totten across Long Island Sound at Willets Point. The treacherous waters of Hell Gate provided a great deal of natural protection against an enemy fleet under sail; the paired forts were intended to deal with steamships. The granite work at Willets Point, like the one at Sandy Hook, became obsolete before it was finished. At the turn of the century, however, when equipped with new long-range guns, Fort Totten emerged as the chief protector of the back entrance to New York Harbor, with reinforcement from Fort Schuyler, and Fort Slocum, just south of New Rochelle on Long Island Sound.

Similar long-range guns armed Fort Hancock, rearmed Forts Hamilton and Wadsworth, and pushed first-line defenses to dots of land beyond the eastern tip of Long Island, a hundred miles (160 kilometers) from the city. Battleships also had been improved, but new batteries were more than a match for them. By the mid 1920s Fort Tilden in the Rockaways covered a thirty-mile (fifty-kilometer) fan of ocean with two of the most powerful coast artillery guns ever made, sixteen-inch rifles firing a projectile as heavy as a small automobile. Later interlocking fire was provided by a similar battery completed during the Second World War on the Navesink Highlands near Fort Hancock.

In the 1920s the development of aircraft brought another dimension to the defense of New York City, with bases at both Fort Hamilton and Miller Field, just south of Fort Wadsworth. The navy built Rockaway Naval Air Station (now Jacob Riis Park), from which the first airplane to fly the Atlantic took off in 1919. After a decade as the city's first municipal airport Floyd Bennett Field became a naval air station in 1941. Warplanes brought a new defensive mission to the harbor forts. In 1922 the 62nd Coast Artillery at Fort Totten set up the prototype anti-aircraft installation. During the Second World War Fort Totten served as the anti-aircraft headquarters for the Eastern Defense Command, coordinating guns throughout New York and New Jersey for the city's protection. Nike anti-aircraft missiles replaced anti-aircraft guns in 1954 and stood guard for the next twenty years. In 1990 the navy began construction of its controversial homeport at Stapleton on Staten Island. Many believed that busy and congested New York Harbor was no place for nuclear-armed vessels, but the argument soon became moot, since with the end of the cold war the homeport closed in August 1994. Although no longer based in New York City, the navy, along with the air force, continues to provide for its security; both services would expect to detect enemies and engage them far at sea.

Henry M. Allen: *Historic Forts of New York State* (Auburn, N.Y.: n.pub., 1957)

Emanuel Raymond Lewis: *Seacoast Fortifications of the United States: An Introductory History* (Washington: Smithsonian Institution Press, 1970; repr. Annapolis, Md.: Naval Institute Press, 1993)

Russell S. Gilmore: *Guarding America's Front Door: Harbor Forts in the Defense of New York City* (New York: Publishing Center for Cultural Resources, 1983)

Russell S. Gilmore

Fort Schuyler. A fort in the Bronx, almost directly beneath the Throgs Neck Bridge at the eastern end of Pennyfield Avenue. It was built between 1833 and 1838 to defend New York City against a possible naval attack from Long Island Sound, complementing Fort Totten on Willets Point in Queens on the opposite shore. Never used in battle and all but abandoned between 1878 and 1934, the fort remains an outstanding example of nineteenth-century military architecture: the interior court, known as St. Mary's Pentagon, is particularly impressive. The fort is now part of the campus of the Maritime College of the State University of New York. Visitors may visit a maritime museum within the fort or walk along the ramparts and enjoy a fine view of the northern shore of Long Island.

Kenneth T. Jackson

Fort Totten. A fort at Willets Point in Bayside. Begun in 1862, it was intended to be the highest in the nation's system of seacoast fortifications, with five tiers of heavy guns. Work ceased in 1864 when fighting during the Civil War made it plain that vertical-walled masonry forts were obsolete. The post saw use as a training ground for volunteer units from New York City during the war and afterward was the site of the Grant military hospital, a major facility with five thousand beds. After the Civil War the fort housed the Engineer School of Application, and it later became the maritime mine center for the U.S. Army. Engineers also did important developmental work with searchlights and other technical coast defense equipment. Many distinguished engineer officers served at the fort, as well as the young medical officer Walter Reed, later famous for his work on yellow fever. In 1898 the fort was given its current name, after General Joseph Totten (1788–1864). By the turn of the century a new generation of anti-ship guns in small dispersed batteries, along with the electric mines perfected at Fort Totten, made for a powerful seacoast defense. The fort lost some of this equipment during the First World War when guns were shifted to less secure portions of the American coast and to Europe. The mission after the First World War became largely one of air defense, which had been assigned to coast artillery as a new specialty. As the Second World War neared, the fort became the site of the first anti-aircraft radar installation on the east coast. After the war it continued as an administrative and training center for anti-aircraft artillery, and when Nike missiles replaced the large sky-sweeping cannon in 1954 it became a nerve center for anti-aircraft missiles for several years. In 1963 the secretary of defense announced the end of active service for the fort, and in 1967 it became a subinstallation of Fort Hamilton. Five reserve units based at Fort Totten were activated in Vietnam, twenty-nine during the Gulf War. In the mid 1990s the fort continued to provide military housing, and the huge 77th Reserve Command kept it involved in the nation's military efforts.

Russell S. Gilmore

Fort Tryon Park. Public park in Manhattan, bounded to the east by Broadway, to the south by several streets including West 190th, and to the west and north by Riverside Drive. It contains high, wooded ground once inhabited by the Wiechquaesgecks; until the late seventeenth century it was called Lange Bergh (Long Hill) by Dutch settlers. During the American Revolution a colonial outpost there was seized by Hessian and British troops who named the battlements after Sir William Tryon, the last English governor of the colony of New York. Several mansions were built on the heights by prominent citizens in the nineteenth century, the most impressive one by C. K. G. Billings, a noted horseman from a wealthy family in Chicago. His mansion was bought in 1917 by John D. Rockefeller Jr. and destroyed by fire in 1925. In 1927 Rockefeller sought to build a park on the property and engaged as its designer Frederick Law Olmsted Jr. (son of a designer of Central Park), whose plan retained the entrance arch and several other rustic features of the estate. The city accepted the park as a gift in 1931 and the plan was completed in 1935. In 1938 the Cloisters opened in the park as a showcase for the medieval art collection of the Metropolitan Museum of Art. The promenades of the Cloisters facing the Palisades in New Jersey and the Hudson River provide some of the most striking views in Manhattan.

Jonathan Kuhn

Fortune. Business magazine launched by the publisher Henry R. Luce in February 1930 and at first published monthly. It devoted an entire issue in July 1939 to New York City, the only city to receive such extensive coverage. In July 1955 it published a listing of the largest industrial corporations in the United States called the "Fortune 500," which became a regular feature; it devoted a second issue to New York City in February 1960. The magazine began biweekly publication in January 1978. Among the distinguished literary and political figures who have written for the magazine are Ernest Hemingway, Carl Sandburg, James Thurber, Bernard Baruch, Sidney Hook, Felix Frankfurter, and Adlai Stevenson. In the early 1990s *Fortune* had a circulation of nearly 783,000 and offices in the Time–Life Building at Rockefeller Center, 1271 6th Avenue. The magazine continues to devote attention to the local politics of New York City.

"Excerpts: A Tour through *Fortune*'s Past," *Fortune*, 26 March 1990, pp. 188–94

Marjorie Harrison

Fortune, T(imothy) Thomas (*b* Marianna, Fla., 3 Oct 1856; *d* Philadelphia, 2 June 1928). Journalist. He moved in 1881 to New York City and worked as a printer for the *Weekly Witness*. Later that year he helped to publish the *Rumor*, a weekly newspaper that soon became the *New York Globe*, later working as an editor for the *Freeman* (1884–87) and as a reporter and editorial writer for the *Sun*. As an editor he consistently attacked racism and bigotry and advocated militant radicalism to secure civil rights, and in 1887 he initiated a movement to organize the National Afro-American League. As the editor of the *New York Age* in 1889–1907 he offered a position to Ida Bell Wells Barnett, who had been forced to flee Memphis for denouncing lynchings in the *Memphis Free Speech*. He was eventually influenced by his friend Booker T. Washington to assume a more conservative view of race relations. In 1907 financial and personal problems forced him to sell his interest in the *New York Age* to Fred R. Moore; Washington became a silent partner. Fortune struggled during his remaining years as a writer for various black publications.

Emma Lou Thornbrough: *T. Thomas Fortune: Militant Journalist* (Chicago: University of Chicago Press, 1972)

Sandra Roff

Fortune Society. Association formed in November 1967 to promote prison reform. The name was inspired by John Herbert's *Fortune and Men's Eyes*, a play about prison life staged at the Actor's Playhouse in Greenwich Village. Through a newsletter, a radio program, and public engagements the society publicized prison conditions and urged the penal system to shift its focus from punishment to rehabilitation. It later provided ex-convicts with clothing, food, and advice, as well as employment in a store that the society opened in August 1969 on Sheridan Square in Greenwich Village. Many staff members wore their old prison uniforms to work at the store, which sold goods made by ex-convicts as well as informational materials. The society grew to include members throughout the United States.

Jonathan Aspell

Fortunoff. Firm of jewelry and silverware retailers, formed in 1922 at 561 Livonia Avenue in Brooklyn by the Russian immigrant Max Fortunoff (1896–1987) and his wife, Clara (1902–86). The firm built its reputation by underselling its competitors. Although the main store was moved in 1964 to Westbury, Long Island, outlets were opened in Manhattan at 154 East 57th Street in 1969 and at 681 5th Avenue in 1979.

Leslie Gourse, Kenneth T. Jackson

Fort Wadsworth. The oldest continually staffed military reservation in the United States, beneath the Verrazano Narrows Bridge at Bay Street and Wadsworth Avenue on Staten Island. Along with Fort Hamilton in Brooklyn it commands the Atlantic approaches to New York Harbor. A fortification occupied the site as early as 1663, and the British controlled the installation throughout the American Revolution. On Evacuation Day in 1783 the captain of a warship of the Royal Navy, angered by the jeers of onlooking rebels, fired a shot at the fort that was probably the last of the war. New York State built a fort on the same site during the War of 1812; this was replaced by the present structure in 1847. The installation was renamed in honor of Brigadier General James S. Wadsworth in 1865, soon after he was killed in action during the Battle of the Wilderness. Decommissioned in the early 1990s, Fort Wadsworth is now part of the Gateway National Recreation Area.

Kenneth T. Jackson

Forty Thieves. A corrupt group of members of the Board of Aldermen who extorted money from city contracts, franchises, and legislation at a time of expansive development in the early 1850s. One of its members was William M. Tweed, who learned methods of corruption that he later perfected as Boss Tweed.

M. R. Werner: *Tammany Hall* (New York: Doubleday, Doran, 1928)

Alexander B. Callow: *The Tweed Ring* (New York: Oxford University Press, 1966)

Neal C. Garelik

Forverts. Yiddish-language daily newspaper launched in 1897, published at 173–75 East Broadway by the Forward Association, and known variously as the *Jewish Daily Forward.* At its peak it was among the most widely read newspapers in the country, with a circulation of more than 200,000 in 1924. Under Abraham Cahan from 1901 to 1951 it espoused the cause of democratic socialism, supported the Jewish labor movement, especially trade unions, and published stories and serialized works by such writers as Sholem Asch, Abraham Reisin, Isaac Bashevis Singer, and Zalman Shneor. One of its most popular columns, the "Bintel Brief" (Bundle of letters), offered advice on a variety of topics. The ten-story Forverts building was completed in 1911 and stood at the center of "Yiddish Newspaper Row" along East Broadway. During the 1920s the Forward Association financed the Yiddish-language radio station WEVD. The newspaper moved north in 1972; the building on the Lower East Side was designated a city landmark. *Forverts* became a weekly newspaper in the 1980s and introduced an English-language edition in 1990.

Mordecai Soltes: *The Yiddish Press: An Americanizing Agency* (New York: Teachers College, Columbia University, 1924; repr. 1950)

Charles A. Madison: *Jewish Publishing in America: The Impact of Jewish Writing on American Culture* (New York: Sanhedrin, 1976)

Seth Kamil

Fosdick, Harry Emerson (*b* Buffalo, 24 May 1878; *d* Bronxville, N.Y., 5 Oct 1969). Minister and writer. He first gained fame as the pastor of the First Presbyterian Church in New York City from 1918. His status as a Baptist and as a liberal in the conflict between fundamentalists and modernists in the 1920s, as well as his much publicized sermon "Shall the Fundamentalists Win?" (1922), led to an effort by William Jennings Bryan and others to oust him from his pulpit for heresy. The issue twice went before the national Baptist assembly before Fosdick resigned in 1925. Soon after, John D. Rockefeller Jr. offered to finance a new interdenominational church where Fosdick's thousands of followers could hear him preach each Sunday. The result was the construction of Riverside Church between 120th and 122nd streets in Morningside Heights. The church was dedicated in 1931 and was intended to provide a forum for nonsectarian, interracial, and international ideals. Fosdick remained there until his retirement in 1946. An early supporter of birth control and of Alcoholics Anonymous, he was also a professor at Union Theological Seminary from 1915 to 1946.

Kenneth T. Jackson

Fosse, Bob [Robert Louis] (*b* Chicago, 23 June 1927; *d* Washington, 23 Sept 1987). Choreographer and director. He danced in musical comedies and after serving in the military moved to New York City, where he studied at the American Theater Wing. He won Tony awards for *The Pajama Game* (1954) and *Damn Yankees* (1955), as well as *Redhead* (1959) and *Sweet Charity* (1966), in which his wife, Gwen Verdon, played the leading roles. Fosse received an Academy Award for *Cabaret* (1972) and directed other stage productions, including *How to Succeed in Business without Really Trying* (1961), *Pippin* (1972), and *Chicago* (1975), and the films *Lenny* (1974) and *All That Jazz* (1979).

Kevin Boyd Grubb: *Razzle Dazzle: The Life and Work of Bob Fosse* (New York: St. Martin's, 1989)

James E. Mooney

Foster, George G. (*b ca* 1814; *d* Philadelphia, 16 April 1856). Reporter and satirist. He became one of the first professional city reporters while working for the *New York Tribune* in the 1840s under the direction of Horace Greeley. His experiences at the newspaper led him to write urban sketches that were collected and published as *New York in Slices* (1849) and *New York by Gas-light* (1850); these were widely read and with the collections *Fifteen Minutes around New York* (1853) and *New York Naked* (1854) provide a rather sensational but insightful portrait of the city. Foster also wrote a novel, *Celio; or, New York Above-ground and Under-ground* (1850).

Stuart M. Blumin

Foster, Stephen (Collins) (*b* Lawrenceville [now in Pittsburgh], 4 July 1826; *d* New York City, 13 Jan 1864). Songwriter. After publishing his first song in 1844 he wrote "Oh Susanna!," which became extremely popular, and negotiated one of the first composer's royalty contracts from the publishing firm of Firth and Pond in New York City. He lived at 97 Greene Street in 1860–61 and for some time at 6 Greenwich Street. Many of his songs were introduced by E. P. Christy's Minstrels, including "Camptown Races" and "Old Folks at Home (Swanee River)." Among his later compositions were "My Old Kentucky Home" and "Jeannie with the Light Brown Hair"; his last was "Beautiful Dreamer." Foster suffered from alcoholism and died penniless at Bellevue Hospital.

Catherine Owens Peare: *Stephen Foster: His Life* (New York: Henry Holt, 1952)

David J. Weiner

Foundation Center. Nonprofit membership organization formed in 1956 as the Foundation Library Center with grants from the Carnegie Corporation and the Ford Foundation. It gathers comprehensive information about foundations, which it makes available to foundations, corporations, organizations and individuals seeking grants and employment, and members of the public. In 1989 the center had a budget of more than $7 million; it receives contributions from five hundred sponsoring members, which include corporate, private, and community foundations. The Foundation Center publishes the *Foundation Directory* as well as indexes of foundation grants, foundation profiles and other guides, and a newsletter; it also organizes seminars and maintains a network of 180 affiliates in the United States and abroad.

Jane Allen

foundations. New York City has 3700 of the 32,000 philanthropic foundations in the United States, including eleven of the fifty largest. Foundations based in the city account for 22 percent of the assets of all American foundations ($32,429 million of $151,181 million) and 23 percent of annual grants ($1927 million of $8394 million). Before 1900 the legal climate was hostile toward foundations: the courts often overturned bequests, such as one by Samuel J. Tilden that eventually led to the formation of the New York Public Library. The climate for foundations improved when the city's political leaders recognized that foundations could be used as instruments for influencing public policy and alleviating social ills, and during the first three decades of the twentieth century many of the foundations in the city were formed.

Among the foundations in New York City are such large, well-known independent ones as the Ford Foundation, the Carnegie Foundation, the Rockefeller Foundation, the Commonwealth Funds, the Andrew W. Mellon Foundation, the Surdna Foundation, the Vincent Astor Foundation, the New York Foundation, and the J. M. Kaplan Fund. They have full-time professional staffs and governing boards with many members unconnected to the families that established the foundations. The most common type of foundation in New York City as elsewhere is the smaller independent foundation, which generally does not have a full-time staff and is governed by a board consisting of family members and friends; an example is the Albert Kunstadter Family Foundation, run by a couple working from an apartment on 5th Avenue, which has assets of $2.6 million and supports programs in education, the arts, and international affairs. Corporate foundations in New York City range from those on the scale of the AT&T (American Telephone and Telegraph) Foundation (assets $100.9 million) and the Hasbro Children's Foundation ($51 million), which gives to health, special education, literacy, and homelessness programs for children under twelve, to such small ones as the DLJ (Donaldson, Lufkin, Jenrette) Foundation ($317,113), the Foote Mineral Charitable Trust ($3773), and the Robert Bowne Foundation, funded by the oldest continuously operating business in the city and specializing in literacy. Operating foundations fund their own programs but make few or no grants to other organizations; prominent examples include the Twentieth Century Fund, which publishes studies in communications, economics, and international affairs, the Russell Sage Foundation, which focuses on social research, the Frick Collection, which operates the museum of the same name, the Brooklyn Section Community Senior Citizen Center, and That's the Spirit Productions. Another type, community foundations, receive their funds from many donors rather than a single founder, family, or corporation and grant funds for a wide range of cultural, charitable, and civic activities in one geographic area; the New York Community Trust is the largest such foundation in the United States. Some foundations are intended at the outset to last only a certain number of years because of their donors' belief that the funds will do the most good if expended over a fixed period: the Field Foundation, a leader in support of civil rights, discontinued operations in 1989 after forty-nine years; the Aaron Diamond Foundation (assets in 1991 of $80 million) was set up in 1955 and is due to expire in 1996.

Because of intermittent congressional scrutiny beginning in the 1950s, foundations began to work together more closely to foster public accountability. The New York Regional Association of Grantmakers (1979) has 185 members and an annual budget of $730,000. The Foundation Center maintains a large reference library in Manhattan, has affiliated collections in the Bronx, Brooklyn, and Queens, and publishes directories and other materials on philanthropic giving. Other organizations group together foundations with similar interests, among them Grantmakers in Health, Women in Foundations / Corporate Philanthropy, Funders Concerned about AIDS, and the Agenda for Children Tomorrow, a project of the New York Community Trust, the Foundation for Child Development, and the United Way. About 37 percent of the money granted by foundations in New York City goes to recipients in the city. In 1991 the 293 largest foundations in New York City gave $1464 million in grants. Of this figure nearly 30 percent was given by the three largest foundations (Ford Foundation $263.6 million, Rockefeller Foundation $93.1 million, Andrew W. Mellon Foundation $95.9 million) and more than half by the nine largest. The proportion of foundations based in New York City has declined as huge foundations have been formed in other parts of the country, such as the John D. and Catherine T. MacArthur Foundation in Chicago, the J. Paul Getty Trust in California, and the Annie E. Casey Foundation in Connecticut.

Robert H. Bremner: *American Philanthropy* (Chicago: University of Chicago Press, 1960; rev. 1988)

Waldemar A. Nielsen: *The Big Foundations* (New York: Columbia University Press, 1972)

Stanley N. Katz, Barry Sullivan, and Paul C. Beach: "Legal Change and Legal Autonomy: Charitable Trusts in New York, 1777–1893," *Law and History Review* 3, no. 1 (spring 1985), 51–89

Waldemar A. Nielsen: *The Golden Donors: A New Anatomy of the Great Foundations* (New York: E. P. Dutton, 1985)

See also PHILANTHROPY.

Richard Magat

foundlings. The abandonment of infants was a growing problem in New York City during the nineteenth century. Motivated by

New York Foundling Society. Jacob A. Riis, Sister Irene and Her Foundlings *(1888)*

poverty or shame, parents left their infants in public places or took them to city officials, who placed them in foster care if they were nursing and otherwise in almshouses. Some children were taken in by private arrangement at "baby farms" usually run by women: because these operations could turn a profit only by severely limiting children's care, they eventually became notorious for infanticide. By the 1850s institutions were organized for children under two who could not be cared for in existing orphanages or adopted through the "orphan train" method of the Children's Aid Society (by being sent west). Wet nurses could leave their own infants at Nursery and Child Hospital (1854) while they worked. The Sisters of Charity ran the New York Foundling Hospital (1869) to receive illegitimate infants and thus preserve the reputation of women and families. The New York Infant Asylum (1865, reorganized 1872) accepted pregnant women as well as women nursing their own infants (these were also required to nurse foundlings). The Randall's Island Infant Hospital opened in 1869 as a publicly supported institution for the care of foundlings; by 1896 a controversy over high death rates there led reformers to develop a system of supervised foster care. The last infants were removed from Randalls Island in 1905, and the hospital was later demolished to make way for the Triborough Bridge.

Elsie Essmuller Vignec: *Children of Hope: Some Stories of the New York Foundling Hospital* (New York: Dodd, Mead, 1964)

Mary Elizabeth Brown

foundries. For a discussion of metal foundries see METAL FOUNDING AND METALWORKING.

Four Corners. Neighborhood in north central Staten Island. The area was known as Centreville until the 1870s, when a post office was built and named Castleton–Four Corners for the crossing of Manor Road, running north to south, and Victory Boulevard, running east to west (now the site of the main post office of the borough). In the mid nineteenth century the Constanz Brewery was built on Manor Road just south of Victory Boulevard; it is now a shopping center. The intersection retained the name Four Corners; the surrounding area gradually became known as Castleton Corners. Businesses line both sides of Victory Boulevard.

Marjorie Johnson

Four Seasons. Restaurant in the Seagram Building at 99 East 52nd Street and Park Avenue in Manhattan, opened on 20 July 1959. The elegant interior was designed by Philip Johnson and seats four hundred. The restaurant is among the most fashionable and expensive in New York City; its décor and cuisine change with the seasons. In 1989 the Four Seasons became only the second restaurant designated by the Landmarks Preservation Commission (after Gage and Tollner in Brooklyn).

B. Kimberly Taylor

1466 Broadway. A textile showroom building in Manhattan, standing fifteen stories high on the southeast corner of Broadway and 42nd Street. Opened in 1906 as the Hotel Knickerbocker, it was designed in the French Renaissance style by the architects Martin and Davis, Bruce Price, and Trowbridge and Livingston. The hotel became known for its many publicly displayed works of art: in the main barroom hung Maxfield Parrish's mural *Old King Cole*, later moved to the St. Regis Hotel. The building was converted to office space in 1920, was known as the Newsweek Building from 1940 to 1959, and was renovated on the interior as a textile showroom building in 1980.

May N. Stone

Fox, George L(afayette) (*b* Boston, 3 July 1825; *d* 24 Oct 1877). Actor. He made his début at the National Theatre in New York City in 1850 and quickly became a success. He managed a theater and enjoyed long runs in the pantomimes *Humpty Dumpty* (1868) and *Wee Willie Winkie* (1870).

D. S. Moynihan

Fox, Margaret (*b* Bath, Ont., ?1833; *d* New York City, 1893). Spiritualist. With her sisters (Ann) Leah Fox (*b* Rockland County, N.Y., ?1814; *d* New York City, 1890) and Kate (Catherine) Fox (*b* Ontario, ?1839; *d* New York City, 1892) she became the focus of the spiritualist movement after "rappings" heard at their farmhouse near Rochester, New York, in 1848 were attributed to spirits. Amid intense publicity the sisters were presented in 1850 in New York City, where they settled and became mediums. Unprepared for the pressure of public scrutiny, they were plagued by controversy and distress. Margaret confessed in 1888 that the rappings had been a hoax but later retracted her confession; she and Kate became alcoholic and ended their lives in poverty.

Robert Ellwood

Fox, Richard Kyle (*b* Belfast, 12 Aug 1846; *d* Red Bank, N.J., 14 Nov 1922). Journalist. He settled in New York City in 1874 and within one year became the managing editor of the *National Police Gazette*, which he purchased in 1877. For forty-five years he published the *Gazette* as a lurid sixteen-page magazine that included news of sports, crime, and the stage, as well as sensational columns such as "Noose Notes," detailing executions, and "Crimes of the Clergy." Fox printed extensive news about prizefighting and helped to popularize pit and combat sports. He wrote *Prize Ring Champions of England from 1719 to 1889* (1889).

Randy Roberts

Fox and Fowle. Firm of architects formed in 1978 by Bruce S. Fowle and Robert Fox. It won the Office Building of the Year Award in 1989 for its design for a building at 150 East 52nd Street; in 1990 it won an award from the American Institute of Architects for its designs for the Spence School and a thirty-five-story building at 1675 Broadway supported by cantilevers over the Broadway Theater. Other buildings designed by the firm include the American Craft Museum, the headquarters of the United States Trust Company, offices of National Westminster Bank on Water Street, Christie's East, 767 3rd Avenue (built of wood and brick), 1 Exchange Place, Embassy Suites Times Square, Broad Financial Center, and Le Grand Palais. In the mid 1990s it designed a sixteen-story building for Republic National Bank. Fox and Fowle has offices at 22 West 19th Street.

James E. Mooney

Fox Hills. Neighborhood in northeastern Staten Island, bounded to the west and north by Vanderbilt Avenue, to the east by Tompkins Avenue and the tracks of Staten Island Rapid Transit, and to the south by Steuben Street. The name was first used in the 1870s by Henry Meyer for his estate, but in the 1890s the area was known as Park Hill. The first eighteen-hole golf course in Staten Island was opened there in 1900 and was the site of championships until 1935. During the First World War the largest army hospital in the country was built in four months; the buildings were used during the Second World War as an army training base and as a camp for prisoners of war. Many houses were built after the war. There was some immigration to the area in the 1980s from India, Liberia, China, and Jamaica. The Park Hill Apartments on Vanderbilt Avenue dominate Fox Hills, and the population is largely middle class and white.

Harlow McMillen

fox hunting. Fox hunts were first held in the metropolitan area in colonial times. Large packs of hounds were owned in the 1760s by James de Lancey and Lewis Morris; these were combined soon after de Lancey returned from a trip to England with horses and foxhounds. A hunt that became known as the Riding Hunt was organized by John Evers, de Lancey's hunting manager, and held weekly in what are now the Bronx, Brooklyn, and Queens. A few small packs of hounds were used in hunts on Manhattan, and in 1781 the proprietor of the King's Head Tavern in Brooklyn advertised a hunt in order to assemble a festive gathering of drinkers. In 1812 Cato's Tavern, which stood at what is now 3rd Avenue and 52nd Street, was the headquarters for the Belvidere Hunt. By 1822 all the hunts in Manhattan had been moved to Long Island and Westchester. An effort to revive fox hunting was made in 1856, when the Brooklyn Hunt was launched, but it was discontinued at the outbreak of the Civil War. The last fox hunt in the area was the Queens County Hunt, sponsored in 1877 by Frank Griswold, who imported a pack of Irish hounds for the event.

James E. Mooney

Foxhurst. A nineteenth-century estate in what is now the south central Bronx, on the Hunts Point Peninsula and bordering the Bronx River between what are now Farragut Street and East Bay Avenue. The estate was on a triangular parcel owned by H. D. Tiffany, a son-in-law of William Fox. George Fox, founder of the Quakers, apparently preached there in 1672. Revolutionary records describe the thick forest of Fox Woods. By 1900 Foxhurst had become a groomed estate surrounded by several dairy farms. The land is now occupied by the Hunts Point Terminal Market.

John McNamara: *History in Asphalt: The Origin of Bronx Street and Place Names* (New York: Bronx County Historical Society, 1984)

John McNamara: *McNamara's Old Bronx* (New York: Bronx County Historical Society, 1989)

John McNamara

F.P.A. Pseudonym of the writer FRANKLIN P. ADAMS.

Frank, Jerome N(ew) (*b* New York City, 10 Sept 1889; *d* New Haven, Conn., 13 Jan 1957). Judge. Of German Jewish background, he graduated from the University of Chicago (1909) and University of Chicago Law School (1912) and practiced law in Chicago before moving to New York City in 1928 to join the firm of Chadbourne, Stanchfield and Levy. He was an early supporter of the New Deal, and with the backing of Felix Frankfurter he became counsel for the Agricultural Adjustment Administration (1933–35), counsel to Secretary of the Interior Harold Ickes, and a member of the Securities and Exchange Commission (1937), of which he eventually succeeded William O. Douglas as chairman (1939). Appointed by President Franklin D. Roosevelt to the U.S. Court of Appeals for the Second Circuit, he served from 1941 until his death; during his tenure he upheld the contempt conviction of defense lawyers for eleven communists tried under the Smith Act in 1950 (*U.S. v. Sacher*), as well as the conviction of Julius and Ethel Rosenberg. He was also a visiting lecturer at the Yale Law School (from 1951) and the New School for Social Research. Frank expounded his theory of "legal realism" in *Law and the Modern Mind* (1930); his other published writings include *Save America First* (1938), *Confessions of an Ex-isolationist* (1941), *If Men Were Angels* (1942), *Fate and Freedom* (1945), *Courts on Trial* (1949), and *Not Guilty* (1957). In New York City he lived at Riverside Drive and 84th Street.

Jeffrey A. Kroessler

Frank, Waldo (David) (*b* Long Branch, N.J., 25 Aug 1889; *d* White Plains, N.Y., 9 Jan 1967). Novelist and critic. After graduating from Yale University with a BA and an MA in 1911 he worked for the *New York Post* and the *New York Times*. He launched the literary magazine *Seven Arts* in 1916 and edited it until 1917, when he left to devote himself entirely to writing. Frank wrote about twenty works of fiction, essays, criticism, and travel writing, including *Virgin Spain* (1926) and the novel *The Death and Birth of David Markand* (1934).

Casey Nelson Blake: *Beloved Community: The Cultural Criticism of Randolph Bourne, Van Wyck Brooks, Waldo Frank, and Lewis Mumford* (Chapel Hill: University of North Carolina Press, 1990)

James E. Mooney

Frankenthaler, Helen (*b* New York City, 12 Dec 1928). Painter. She studied with Rufino Tamayo while attending the Dalton School. After graduating from Bennington College in 1949 she returned to New York City and belonged to a circle of artists and poets that included Larry Rivers and John Ashbery. In 1952 she painted her acknowledged masterpiece, *Mountains and Sea*. She married the painter Robert Motherwell in 1958 (they later divorced). A member of the second generation of abstract expressionists, Frankenthaler invented the "soak-stain" technique of paint application and in 1963 abandoned oil paints in favor of acrylics. In 1969 the Whitney Museum of American Art held a major retrospective of her work that solidified her reputation.

Stephen Weinstein

Frank Leslie's Illustrated Newspaper. Publication launched in 1855 by Frank Leslie as the first weekly news magazine in the United States. It covered international, national, and local news, the arts, and sports, often taking a sensational approach to stories of murder and disaster. A folio format provided ample room for both factual and fictional treatments of the lives of the wealthy (and occasionally the poor), often illustrated by lavish wood engravings. The magazine was especially noted for its pictures of the Civil War and Spanish–American War. Sold by Leslie's widow in 1889, it continued under various names until 1922.

Bud Leslie Gambee: *Frank Leslie and His Illustrated Newspaper, 1855–1860* (Ann Arbor: University of Michigan, Department of Library Science, 1964)

Robert Stinson

Franklin D. Roosevelt Boardwalk. Boardwalk in Staten Island bordering South and Midland beaches.

Franklin Furnace. An archive and exhibition space at 112 Franklin Street in Tribeca, founded in 1976 by the performance artist Martha Wilson. It houses the nation's largest collection of publications produced by artists, encompassing more than twelve thousand items dating from 1960 to the present. Among its holdings are early works by Red Grooms, Claes Oldenburg, Jim Dine, and Gilbert and George, as well as publications submitted by artists worldwide whose work is suppressed for political reasons.

Carol V. Wright

Franklin Simon. Firm of women's clothing retailers, formed in 1902 by Franklin Simon (*b ca* 1864; *d* 1934), who had worked for the retail firm of Stern Brothers since 1878. It operated a store at 5th Avenue and 38th Street and then at 33 West 34th Street, where it remained prominent for decades. Simon enabled his employees to attend classes in his store and offered scholarships at New York University. After his death the firm was sold in 1936 to the Atlas Corporation, which in turn sold it to the City Stores Company in 1947. When this company filed for bankruptcy in 1979 Franklin Simon went into liquidation and its stores in twelve states ceased to operate.

Leslie Gourse, Kenneth T. Jackson

Franks, David (*b* New York City, 23 Sept 1720; *d* England, 1794). Merchant, son of Jacob Franks. In 1743 he married Margaret Evans, a member of a leading family in colonial Philadelphia. He was a signatory to the Non-Importation Agreement of 1765, a provisioner for the British troops, and a deputy commissioner of British prisoners before his capture and brief imprisonment by the patriots. His daughter Rebecca (1758/60–1823) and sister Phila (the wife of General Oliver de Lancey) were staunch Loyalists.

The Lee Max Friedman Collection of American Jewish Colonial Correspondence: Letters of the Franks Family (Waltham, Mass.: American Jewish Historical Society, 1968)

Robert I. Goler

Franks, Jacob (*b* London, 1688; *d* New York City, 16 Jan 1769). Merchant, father of David Franks. Of Ashkenazi ancestry, he emigrated to America and settled in New York City in 1708 or 1709 and was declared a freeman by 1710. His marriage in 1712 to Abigail Levy, a daughter of Moses Levy, produced nine children. He eventually became the king's sole agent for the northern colonies and prospered during the French and Indian Wars.

The Lee Max Friedman Collection of American Jewish Colonial Correspondence: Letters of the Franks Family (Waltham, Mass.: American Jewish Historical Society, 1968)

Robert I. Goler

fraternal organizations. In New York City during the eighteenth and nineteenth centuries fraternal organizations both secret and open were formed along geographic, ethnic, religious, and political lines. These organizations provided not only an outlet for social activity but often disability and death benefits for members and their families. The city's oldest and most influential fraternal group was the Freemasons, formally organized in 1730 and often an object of mistrust and hostility: a challenge to the Masons appeared on 26 November 1737 as a letter to the editor of the *New York Gazette*, and the famous Antimasonic social and political movement that spread to the city in 1827 drove the order underground for ten years. Several offshoots of Masonry had their beginnings in the city, and some became nationwide organizations: these included the Ancient Arabic Order of Nobles of the Mystic Shrine, formed in 1870 by two Freemasons, Walter Fleming and the actor Billy Florence; the Order of the Amaranth, formed in June 1873 by James B. Taylor as a recreational, less ritualistic organization for members of the Order of the Eastern Star, or female Masons; and the Independent Order of Odd Fellows, often regarded as the "poor man's Masons," which opened a lodge in Brooklyn in 1822. Orders based on national, ethnic, and religious origins were organized by Scotsmen (the St. Andrews Society, 1756), Germans (the German Society, 1756; and a secret society known as the German Order of Harugari, 1847), Irishmen (the Friendly Sons of St. Patrick, 1784; and the secret society the Ancient Order of Hibernians, 1836, intended to safeguard Catholic churches from hostile mobs), Englishmen (the St. George's Society, 1786), and free blacks (the African Society, 1795), who were barred from other orders. It has been estimated that fifty black organizations emerged between 1800 and 1860, including the New York African Society for Mutual Relief (1810), the Brooklyn African Woolman Benevolent Society (1831, named after John Woolman, a Quaker from New Jersey), the Abyssinian Daughters of Esther Association (1839), and the Boyer Lodge of Prince Hall Freemasonry (1842). The first racially integrated lodge was the Philomethan Lodge of the Odd Fellows, formed in 1843 by members of the Philomethan Literary Society (itself formed in 1829 by Henry Simpkins and Eli Hazzard and based at its own hall on Duane Street) and chartered by the Odd Fellows' governing body in Britain. Another integrated group, the Independent Order of Good Samaritans and Daughters of Samaria (1847), promoted abstinence from alcohol. In 1848 the twenty-four black Odd Fellows groups in Brooklyn and Manhattan counted almost two thousand members. Jewish fraternal organizations formed during these years included B'nai B'rith (1843), intended to promote education and improve the image of Jews, the Free Sons of Israel (1849), B'rith Abraham (1859), and the United Order of True Sisters (1846), formed by Henrietta Bruckman. In opposition to the fraternal orders of immigrants stood a virulently nativistic organization called the American Brotherhood (1844).

The period between the Civil War and the Depression marked the heyday of the city's fraternal organizations, which at any one time numbered at least three hundred. Among the secret societies with branches in the city were the Knights of Pythias (1868) and the National Grange, which had forty-five wholesale merchants and sewing machine manufacturers as members. In 1866 Charles S. Vivian and a group of actors organized the Benevolent and Protective Order of Elks in the city to circumvent the state's Sunday dry law; the group was chartered in 1868 and gained chapters nationwide. During the last quarter of the nineteenth century and the first quarter of the twentieth many mutual aid societies were formed by immigrants, especially by Jews (such as Ahvas Israel, 1890; and the Workmen's Circle, 1900, which in 1918 had 250 branches and 25,000 members). Hundreds of smaller groups known as LANDSMANSHAFTN were organized according to the European and Russian villages from which their members originated: examples include the Independent Grodno Sick Support Society and the Independent Kurlander Benevolent Society, which served perhaps a million New Yorkers before the First World War. Greek fraternal organizations in the city included the Brotherhood of Athena (1891), which at its peak had 450 members, and a long-lasting group called the Panhellenic Union, organized in the basement of Holy Trinity Church at 152½ East 72nd Street in 1907. Nativist groups such as the Order of the American Union (1873) continued to flourish, and the Ku Klux Klan formed a chapter in the city that held regular meetings at the Chelsea Hotel; the hotel was near the Masonic Temple at 71 West 23rd Street and the Klan may have infiltrated the Masons, a charge that was heatedly denied at the time. Among the city's other fraternal organizations were the Daughters of the American Revolution (1890), the predominately Catholic groups the Knights of Columbus (1891) and the Order of Sons of Italy (1905), and the Knights of Liberty (1923), a group opposed to the Ku Klux Klan and led by Andrew J. Padon. In 1929 the city had 351 Masonic lodges.

The Depression was a watershed for the city's fraternal organizations, as the New Deal made the benefits offered by most voluntary associations superfluous. Many organizations established hospitals and foundations as a means of maintaining their sense of purpose. Most of the smaller groups disappeared and those that lasted had difficulty recruiting new members. In 1930 the Masons lost ownership of their lavishly ornamented Level Club at 253 West 73rd Street, completed in 1927 at a cost of $4.3 million and celebrated by a huge parade up 5th Avenue; the club was converted into condominiums in 1983. In 1937 the Shriners foreclosed on Mecca Temple, built in 1924 at 131 West 55th Street (later saved from demolition by the city and renamed the City Center of Music and Drama). Fraternal organizations suffered further after the Second World War, by which time many New Yorkers viewed the rituals practiced by secret societies as hopelessly old-fashioned and even ridiculous. Membership in the Masons declined from its peak of 134,786 in 1957 to 34,765 in 1990 (in 186 lodges), and the Knights of Pythias fared little better: although membership increased briefly when veterans joined after the war, it soon began a rapid decline as many residents of the city moved to the suburbs, and the Pythians were forced to relinquish what was once an elaborate symbol of their power, the ornate Pythian building at 135 West 70th Street (built in 1926, remodeled into condominiums in the 1980s). The Boyer Lodge of Prince Hall Freemasonry took part in civil rights struggles in the 1960s and had as members such prominent figures as Adam Clayton Powell Sr., Adam Clayton Powell Jr., Arthur Schomburg, Julius A. Archibald, and Percy E. Sutton, but it too lost members in the following decades. In the mid 1990s service groups such as the New York Rotary Club (1909) and the Lions Club (1928) remained active, but the enthusiasm of old had ebbed considerably.

Daniel Perlman: "Organizations of the Free Negro in New York City, 1800–1860," *Journal of Negro History* 3 (1971), 181–99

Michael R. Weisser: *A Brotherhood of Memory: Jewish Landsmanschaftn in the New World* (New York: Basic Books, 1985)

Marc Ferris

Fraunces, Samuel (*b* ?West Indies, *ca* 1722; *d* Philadelphia, 1795). Innkeeper. He moved to New York City in the early 1750s, was granted a tavern license in 1756, and operated taverns there and in Philadelphia over the next thirty years. A member of Trinity Parish, he married Elizabeth Dalley and had eight children. He is most often associated with Fraunces Tavern in New York City. First known as the Queen Charlotte (after the young bride of George III), it assumed its proprietor's name after the outbreak of the American Revolution. Fraunces prepared meals in the English style and was renowned for his elegant desserts. He remained in New York City during most of the revolution and after independence was cited for his efforts to aid American prisoners of war by the Congress, which awarded him $2000. After the American Revolution he belonged with his son Andrew to the Columbian Order, or Tammany Society. Appointed steward of President Washington's household in New York City, he followed the president to Philadelphia in 1790. He left him in 1794 to assume the ownership of the renowned Tun Tavern in Philadelphia but died the next year; he was buried in Philadelphia at Christ Church. The suggestion by some historians that Fraunces was black is contradicted by primary sources indicating that he was a free white who owned both black and Indian slaves.

Robert I. Goler

Fraunces Tavern. Meeting hall and inn built in 1719 at the corner of Queen Street (now Pearl Street) and Canal Street (now Broad Street). The building was used first as a private home and then as a public house for several decades before being purchased in 1762 by Samuel Fraunces, who had moved to New York City from the Caribbean in the early 1750s. First known as the Queen Charlotte (after the young bride of George III), it assumed its proprietor's name after the outbreak of the American Revolution. The tavern was strongly associated with the cause of American independence: it was the site of the initial meeting in 1768 of the New York Chamber of Commerce, and also of meetings of the Sons of Liberty and the provincial congress. George Washington bade farewell to his officers there in 1783, and in 1785 the building became one of the first to be occupied by offices of the federal government when New York City was the national capital: it housed the Department of Foreign Affairs, the Department of the Treasury, and the Department of War. The tavern increasingly catered to a working-class clientele in the nineteenth century, although the New York Yacht Club did meet there after being organized in 1844. Run down and damaged by fire, the building was purchased in 1904 by the Sons of the Revolution, who rebuilt and restored it in the Colonial Revival style. It reopened in 1907 with a restaurant and the Fraunces Tavern Museum. The museum now occupies four connecting buildings and focuses on the history of New York City in the eighteenth century. The entire block housing the museum is listed on the National Register of Historic Places. In 1975 Fraunces Tavern was the target of a bomb attack that killed four persons, for which responsibility was claimed by the Fuerzas Armadas de Liberación Nacional (FALN).

Kym S. Rice: *Early American Taverns: For the Entertainment of Friends and Strangers* (Chicago: Regnery Gateway, 1983)

Robert I. Goler

Fraye Arbeter Shtime. Yiddish-language anarchist newspaper, launched in 1890 by the Pioneers of Liberty. It was published on the Lower East Side and chronicled anarchism in the United States and abroad. During Saul Yanovsky's editorship (1899–1919) it ceased to focus on insurgency and instead advocated libertarian schools, unions, and workers' cooperatives. It held annual conferences on anarchism in the city and with *Mother Earth*,

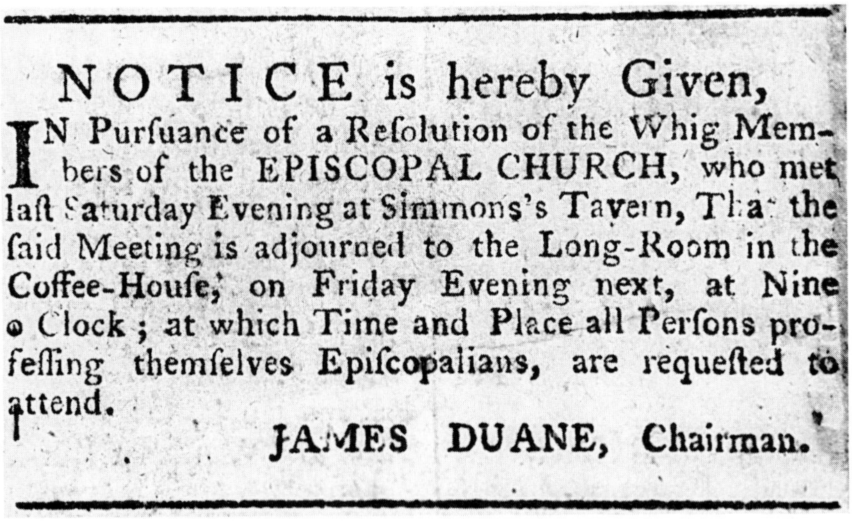
NOTICE is hereby Given,
IN Purſuance of a Reſolution of the Whig Members of the EPISCOPAL CHURCH, who met laſt Saturday Evening at Simmons's Tavern, That the ſaid Meeting is adjourned to the Long-Room in the Coffee-Houſe, on Friday Evening next, at Nine o Clock; at which Time and Place all Perſons profeſſing themſelves Epiſcopalians, are requeſted to attend.
JAMES DUANE, Chairman.

Announcement of a meeting of Whig Episcopalians at Simmons's Tavern (later Fraunces Tavern)

a journal published by Emma Goldman, sponsored a celebration at Carnegie Hall of Peter Kropotkin's seventieth birthday in 1912. Eventually it consisted mostly of historical essays and tributes to anarchist heroes, although it continued to provide commentary on contemporary issues. *Fraye Arbeter Shtime* was the longest-lived publication of its kind in the country when it ceased publication in 1977.

David A. Balcom

Fredericksz, Cryn (*fl* 1625–35). Engineer and surveyor. He was engaged by the Dutch West India Company to lay out the settlement of New Amsterdam and moved there in 1625 with diagrams for fortifications, houses, streets, a mill, a church, a school, and a hospital that had been drawn up in the Netherlands. Across from Bowling Green at the southern end of Manhattan he staked out a site for what became Fort Amsterdam, which was completed in 1635 in a style typical of the period; it was flanked by four bastions and had walls made of brick on the inside and battered earth and sod on the outside. His plan called for about a dozen streets stretching about a mile (1.6 kilometers) in total length. The first to be laid out was the Broad Way, which ran about a quarter of a mile (four hundred meters) to the northern edge of the settlement at Wall Street; Pearl Street marked the eastern boundary, Greenwich Street the western boundary. These streets are nearly all that remains of Fredericksz's plan.

Jonathan Aspell

Freedomland. Amusement park opened in July 1960 on 205 acres (eighty-three hectares) in the eastern Bronx between the Hutchinson River Parkway and the New England Thruway. Advertised as the world's largest outdoor entertainment center and as the city's answer to Disneyland, it cost $65 million to build. It was constructed in the shape of the United States and contained representations of important American cities as well as sixteen theme attractions, including the Great Chicago Fire, the Old West, and Olde New York. Transportation was provided by a monorail system, a paddle-wheel boat, and skyrides. The venture was an enormous failure: attendance fell dramatically when the World's Fair opened in Queens in 1964, and the park was forced to close in the same year. The site is now occupied by Co-op City and shopping centers.

Gary D. Hermalyn

Freedom National Bank. Commercial bank formed in Harlem by the businessman Dunbar McLaurin in 1964. The first deposits were solicited door to door by McLaurin, who appointed the baseball player Jackie Robinson to the board of directors. The bank sought to end redlining by providing capital to black entrepreneurs. It had $1.5 million in capital in 1964 but had made $900,000 in bad loans by 1969. Between 1977 and 1981 assets grew 234 percent, from $38 million to $127 million. Debts and infighting among the directors led federal regulators to close Freedom National Bank in November 1990.

James O. Drummond

Freedom's Journal. Weekly newspaper launched in March 1827 by John B. Russwurm and the Presbyterian clergyman Samuel E. Cornish as the first black publication in the United States. Originally it served as a vehicle for answering the attacks on blacks made by the *New York Enquirer.* Disagreements with Cornish over the issue of colonization led Russwurm to move to Liberia, where he remained for the rest of his life. Cornish continued to publish the newspaper until 1830 as the *Rights of All.*

Sandra Roff

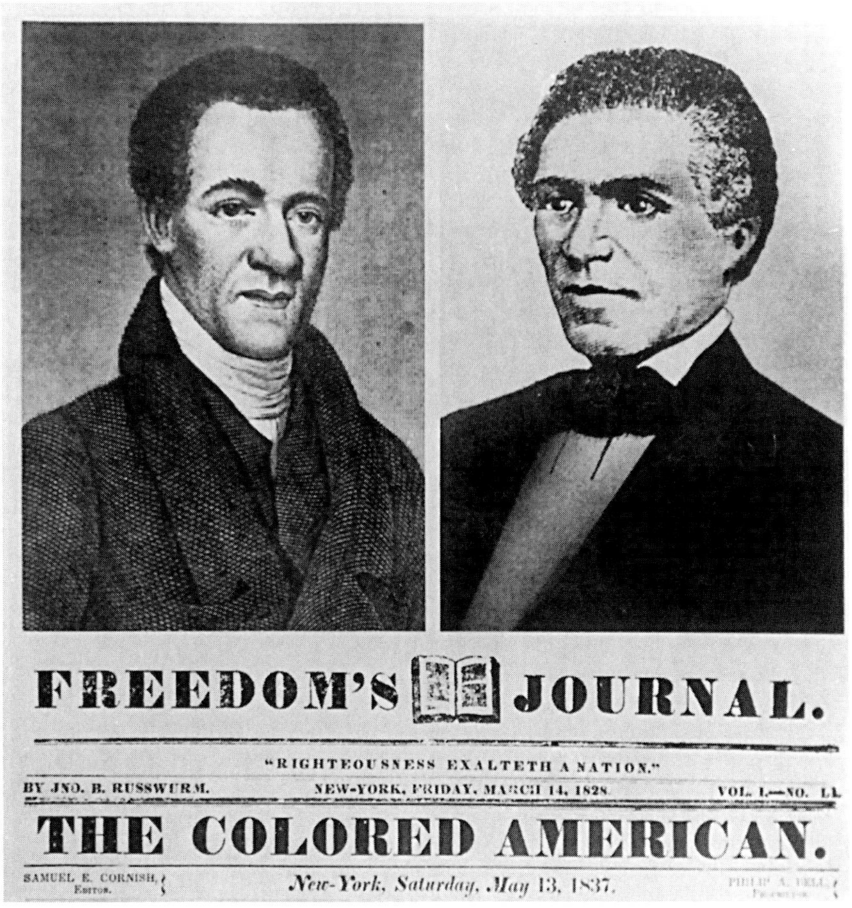

Left *John B. Russwurm,* right *Samuel B. Cornish, and mastheads of* Freedom's Journal *("Righteousness Exalteth a Nation"), 14 March 1828, and the* Colored American, *13 May 1837*

Freeman, Frank (*b* Hamilton, Ont., 1861; *d* Montclair, N.J., 13 Oct 1949). Architect. He lived in Brooklyn and designed a variety of buildings there in the Romanesque Revival tradition during the last decade of the nineteenth century. His skill and versatility were displayed in the Hotel Margaret in Columbia Heights (1889, demolished), the Behr House, 82 Pierrepont Street (1890), the Bushwick Democratic Club (1892, demolished), the Brooklyn Fire Headquarters on Jay Street (1892), the Eagle Warehouse and Storage Company on Cadman Plaza East (1893–94), and the Brooklyn Savings Bank at Pierrepont and Clinton streets (1893–94, demolished).

Marjorie Pearson

Freeman's Journal. Weekly newspaper launched in 1840 by James White and John White and named after a moderate nationalist newspaper in Ireland. It emphasized the rights of Irish Catholics on both sides of the Atlantic and in 1841 was renamed the *Freeman's Journal and Catholic Register.* Bought in 1842 by Bishop John Hughes, it was the official publication of the Catholic church in New York City until it was sold in 1844 to James A. McMaster. Its circulation rose from 4500 in 1846 to sixteen thousand by 1854. The editors supported the brand of nationalism promoted by Daniel O'Connell but firmly opposed such extreme nationalist movements as Young Ireland and Fenianism as well as most American reform movements, especially abolitionism. The *Freeman's Journal* ceased publication in 1918.

Kevin Kenny

Freemasons [Masons]. Members of a secret male fraternal organization formed in the seventeenth century by English stonemasons' guilds. They use an elaborate system of visual symbols evoking items associated with stonemasonry, including aprons and compasses. The organization gained wide acceptance throughout the British colonies; the English Grand Lodge appointed Daniel Coxe the first provincial grand master of New York, New Jersey, and Pennsylvania in 1730, and a Masonic branch was formed in New York City in 1739. In 1787 the lodges in New York City and New York State declared themselves independent of their obligations to the British. Robert R. Livingston, grand master of New York State between 1784 and 1801, administered the first presidential oath at Federal Hall on 30 April 1789 to George Washington, a Mason from 1752 who used for the occasion the Bible of the St. John's Lodge no. 1. There were ten lodges in the city by the end of the eighteenth century, and in 1802 the members began construction of their own building. A wide range of artifacts and prints from the early decades of the Republic bearing Masonic images may have contributed to the Classical Revival in the nineteenth-century United States. Suspicions that freemasonry was a mysterious sect and that it considered itself above the law were intensified by the abduction and murder in upstate New York in 1826 of William Morgan, who was preparing to publish a report disclosing the secrets of masonry, and led to the formation of the Anti-Masonic Party in 1828 in Utica, New York. Although membership in Masonic lodges in the city declined by 85 percent in the decade following Morgan's disappearance, Masons continued to occupy powerful positions in politics and society. In 1930 the Masons lost ownership of their lavishly ornamented Level Club at 253 West 73rd Street, completed in 1927 at a cost of $4.3 million and celebrated by a huge parade up 5th Avenue; the club was converted into condominiums in 1983. Membership in the Masons declined sharply after the Second World War, from a peak of 134,786 in 1957 to 34,765 in 1990 (in 186 lodges). Well-known masons in New York City have included De Witt Clinton, John Jacob Astor, Theodore Roosevelt, Irving Berlin, George M. Cohan, Fiorello H. La Guardia, Al Jolson, Harry Houdini, and Paul Whiteman.

Herbert T. Singer and Ossian Lang: *New York Freemasonry: A Bicentennial History, 1781–1981* (New York: Grand Lodge, 1981)

Marc Ferris, Robert I. Goler

freethinkers. For a discussion of freethinkers see ATHEISTS AND FREETHINKERS.

Frémont, John C(harles) (*b* Savannah, Ga., 21 Jan 1813; *d* New York City, 13 July 1890). Explorer, senator, and businessman. After exploring the West and representing California in the U.S. Senate (1850–51) he moved in 1855 to New York City with his wife, Jessie; they settled at 56 East 9th Street in the following year when he became interested in seeking the presidency of the United States. As the first presidential nominee of the Republican Party in 1856 he was soundly defeated in the general election by James Buchanan. After the Civil War Frémont bought a brownstone mansion at what is now 21 West 19th Street and invested heavily in railroads: poor decisions resulted in the loss of his fortune within a few years. He moved in 1873 to a cottage on Staten Island called the Esplanade, where he wrote his memoirs. From 1878 to 1883 he was governor of the Arizona Territory. Always seeking to regain his fortune, Frémont maintained a residence at 49 West 29th Street in Manhattan until the end of his life.

Allan Nevins: *Frémont, Pathmarker of the West* (New York: Appleton–Century, 1939)

James Bradley

French. The French presence in New York City dates to the 1620s. In 1621 Jean de Forrest, a French Huguenot who settled in the Netherlands after fleeing religious persecution in France, sent a petition to the Dutch West India Company requesting permission to establish a settlement in America. The grant was authorized in 1624, and in May a group of French Huguenots arrived in Manhattan, where they reinforced a garrison built by the Dutch. The colony attracted many more Huguenots from the Netherlands, including the first colonial governor, Peter Minuit. Over time an increasing number of French merchants and skilled craftsmen settled in New Amsterdam. Steven de Lancey (born Étienne deLancy), one of the most successful merchants, acquired enough wealth to build a large home and trading house, now known as Fraunces Tavern; he also presented the city with its first clock. Early progress in the colony was disrupted by conflict between the Dutch, English, and French nations, and by the 1740s the English defeated the French and took their holdings in North America. The English governors of Manhattan nonetheless continued to welcome religious dissenters from France. Although the French settlers and their descendants prospered under British rule, many joined the growing movement against it, among them John Jay, Henry Laurens, Elisam Boudinot, Paul Revere, and James Bowdoin. During the American Revolution France supported the American colonists and contributed crucial engineering and military expertise, soldiers, and money; French–Americans throughout the colonies also contributed strongly to the effort.

Many of those who fled France after its own revolution broke out in 1789 emigrated to the United States. Joseph Bonaparte bought extensive acreage in New York State in 1814 and planned a residence for his brother, the emperor Napoleon. Between 1816 and 1818 the emperor's nephew Joseph Napoleon built several large houses in New York City to hold his art collection and to provide a possible refuge for his uncle. In 1839 these holdings, now part of the property of Bishop John DuBois, became the endowment of Fordham University. Unlike their counterparts in upstate New York (in New Paltz and other towns), New England, and Louisiana, French–Americans in New York City in the early nineteenth century became assimilated into American society and gave up their language, churches, and schools. Few groups and institutions worked to preserve French culture, and new arrivals from France and Americans who had lived and worked there became the main source of French ideas and influence.

In New York City the French influence was most evident in architecture. French architects designed several buildings during the nineteenth century that helped to establish the character of Manhattan. Joseph François Mangin collaborated in the design of City Hall (1802) and designed several other buildings including the original St. Patrick's Cathedral on Mott Street (1809); Jenika de Feriet built a lavish home in 1824, the Hermitage, just outside New York City in what is now the Bronx. The French architectural influence became even more pronounced during the late nineteenth century, when Richard Morris Hunt returned to the city after studying at the École des Beaux-Arts. His ideas of design were reflected in the exuberant Renaissance style of such public buildings as the New York Public Library (begun in 1895) and Grand Central Terminal (begun in 1903), both designed by the French–American architect John M. Carrère. The principles of the École des Beaux-Arts were also visible in private châteaux built in a wide range of styles: François I (the Rhinelander–Waldo mansion, 1895, 72nd Street and Madison Avenue), belle époque (the Burden Mansion, 1902, 5th Avenue at 91st Street), neo-French classical (the Duke mansion, 1911, 5th Avenue and 78th Street), Louis XVI (the Frick mansion, 1910, 5th Avenue at 70th Street), and French Renaissance (the Arts Institute, 1891, 57th Street). The best-known example of belle époque sculpture is the Statue of Liberty, presented to the United States by France in 1883 in honor of the one hundredth anniversary of the ending of the American Revolution, designed by Frédéric Auguste Bartholdi, built by French engineers and artists, and installed in 1886. French ideas and styles also had a strong impact on painting and lithography, in part because many studios were led by Americans who had studied in Paris (John Vanderlyn and Samuel F. B. Morse in the 1820s, and later John Singer Sargent and William Morris Hunt, brother of the architect), and in part because several gifted painters from France and French territories settled in the United States (among them John James Audubon, who landed in New York City in 1804, and Antoine Imbert, who in 1824 opened the first lithography studio in the city). During the early twentieth century the techniques of French post-impressionists, Fauvists, and cubists were learned by many American painters and received wide exposure at the Armory Show (1913). A large number of French artists taught in the United States during the world wars at such institutions as the New School for Social Research; among those who taught in the city were Marcel Duchamp, Fernand Léger, and Marc Chagall. French musicians, writers, philosophers, and art historians also contributed to the direction of American art during these years.

Authentic French cuisine was introduced in the United States at the French pavilion of the World's Fair of 1939–40. Soon after, Henri Soulé, maître d' at the restaurant of the pavilion, opened a lavish French restaurant called Le Pavillon on East 55th Street that inspired many others in the city to open French restaurants as well as cooking schools, notably the French Culinary Institute. Several well-known French–Americans have shaped American fashion and especially haute couture, including Coco Chanel, Lilly Daché, and Pauline Trièrge.

The French-speaking community is served by a number of cultural and educational institutions. Two of long standing, the Alliance Française (1898) and the French Institute (1911), merged in 1971: the combined organization later dedicated Florence Gould Hall, an auditorium where French works are often featured. The city is also the place of publication of the weekly newspaper *France–Amérique.* Among those of French origin who have lived for extended periods in New York City are the historian Jacques Barzun, the philosopher Jean-Paul Sartre, and the anthropologist Claude Lévi-Strauss. The federal census of 1990 reported 38,238 inhabitants of French ancestry in New York City.

France in New York (New York: French Cultural Services, n.d. [?1957])

Abigail Mellen

French, Daniel Chester (*b* Exeter, N.H., 20 April 1850; *d* Stockbridge, Mass., 7 Oct 1931). Sculptor. After achieving national acclaim as a sculptor he became a central figure from 1900 to 1917 in the cultural affairs of New York City, where he made many public sculptures: *Peace* for the temporary Dewey Arch (1899, destroyed), the Richard Morris Hunt Memorial (1901, 5th Avenue at 70th Street), *Justice, Power, and Study* for the appellate courthouse (1900, Madison Avenue at 24th Street), *DeWitt Clinton*, *Alexander Hamilton*, and *John Jay* for the U.S. Chamber of Commerce (1902, removed), *Alma Mater* (1906, Columbia University), *Four Continents* for the U.S. Custom House (1907, Bowling Green),

Daniel Chester French's sculpture at the U.S. Custom House

Greek Epic, *Lyric Poetry*, and *Religion* for the Brooklyn Institute of Arts and Sciences, where he also supervised the entire sculptural program (1908, Eastern Parkway), *Manhattan* and *Brooklyn* for the Manhattan Bridge (1916, Brooklyn Museum), and *Power and Wisdom* for his memorial to the First World War (1919, destroyed). The first sculptor on the City's Art Commission, he was also a delegate to the Fine Arts Federation, a member of the New York City Improvement Commission formed by Mayor George B. McClellan in 1904, and a trustee and director of the department of sculpture at the Metropolitan Museum of Art. For much of his life he lived in New Hampshire and in a house that he bought in 1888 at 125 West 11th Street. Known as the "dean of American sculptors," French expressed the civic aspirations of the élite in blandly earnest public works.

Michael Richman: *Daniel Chester French: An American Sculptor* (New York: Metropolitan Museum of Art, 1977)

Michele H. Bogart: *Public Sculpture and the Civic Ideal in New York City, 1890–1930* (Chicago: University of Chicago Press, 1989)

Michele H. Bogart

French, Eleanor Clark (*b* Germantown, Penn., 29 June 1908; *d* Paoli, Penn., 25 June 1990). Political leader and editor. She taught school briefly and served in France as an administrator of rest homes for war refugees before being named women's news editor for the *New York Times* (1949–55). In 1957 she was appointed vice-chairman of the Democratic State Committee, a position to which she was elected in the following year. Appointed the city's first commissioner to the United Nations by Mayor Robert F. Wagner in 1962, she resigned in 1964 to seek election to the U.S. Congress from the seventeenth district; she was defeated by the incumbent, John V. Lindsay. French also served on the New York City Commission on Human Rights (1961–76) and on the boards of many civic organizations, including the Women's City Club.

Elisabeth Israels Perry

French, Fred(erick) F. (*b* New York City, 1883; *d* Hammersly Hills, N.Y., 30 Aug 1936). Real-estate developer. Using investment capital from individual investors who purchased equity shares in his projects, he built several apartment buildings and office towers in Manhattan. In 1925 he began work on Tudor City, a complex of twelve buildings containing three thousand apartments and six hundred hotel rooms (for illustration see TUDOR CITY). Situated at 42nd Street near the East River and surrounded by slaughterhouses, electricity generators, and tenement buildings, this was the largest development of its kind in the city at its completion in 1928. In 1934 he built Knickerbocker Village, a housing complex for more than sixteen hundred families financed as a limited-dividend project by the federal Reconstruction Finance Corporation and built on a site cleared of tenement buildings on the Lower East Side; this was one of the country's first urban redevelopment projects subsidized publicly and built and owned privately. French was one of the city's most innovative developers of the 1920s and early 1930s.

Marc A. Weiss

French flats. Name for five- and six-story apartment buildings without elevators erected in New York City from the 1860s, such as the Stuyvesant Apartments on East 19th Street (1869). The style of building was a French innovation. By the 1880s the term was applied to buildings of eight to ten stories with elevators; the city's building department used it for all "first-class" apartment buildings. The name went out of fashion in the 1890s as apartments became common.

Alana J. Erickson

Fresh Air Fund. Charitable organization that provides two-week summer vacations for children from New York City. It was formed in June 1877 by the clergyman Willard Parsons, who placed sixty children from the city in homes in Sherman, Pennsylvania, for the summer. Later the same year he turned management over to the *New York Tribune*, which relinquished control on facing bankruptcy in 1962. The fund became independent in 1967 and introduced a farm training program for teenagers in 1976. By the mid 1990s the Fresh Air Fund had provided vacations for more than 1.6 million children between the ages of five and sixteen. It has headquarters in midtown Manhattan and operates four camps on Sharpe Reservation, a facility of three thousand acres (twelve hundred hectares) in Fishkill, New York.

Alana J. Erickson

A child sponsored by the Fresh Air Fund awaiting a bus to the country at the Port Authority Bus Terminal, 1991

Fresh Kills Landfill. A waste disposal facility in Staten Island, the largest in the world. Operated by the Department of Sanitation, it opened in 1948 when the practice of dumping raw garbage and ash into the Atlantic Ocean was discontinued. The site occupies about 2100 acres (850 hectares) and receives the city's raw household waste in addition to ash from the three municipal incinerators. Refuse is transported to the landfill from nine transfer points throughout the city, mostly by barge (carrying about twelve thousand tons, or eleven thousand metric tons, a day) and truck (about one thousand tons, or nine hundred metric tons, a day), and then by trucks or "pay haulers." The working face of the landfill is sealed with several layers of cover to prevent rainwater from seeping in and gas from seeping out, and later topped with soil and seeded with grasses or other plants. Some methane gas is extracted and used as fuel for heating and cooking on Staten Island. Fresh Kills is expected to reach its official capacity by the year 2005, with one mound surpassing five hundred feet (150 meters) in height, making it the highest point on the eastern seaboard.

Gerard R. Wolfe

Fresh Meadows. A housing development in central Queens (1990 pop. 35,000). In 1923 the area became the site of a golf course at the intersection of Fresh Meadow Lane and Nassau Boulevard, planned by Benjamin C. Ribman of Brooklyn, that eventually became the site of major tournaments. On 1 April 1946 land near the intersection of Horace Harding Boulevard and 188th Street was bought by the New York Life Insurance Company for a residential development; Voorhees, Walker, Foley and Smith was the architectural firm and the George A. Fuller Company the general contractor. Construction began on 3 July 1946 and was completed in 1949. Called by many a "model urban community," the development was praised by the critic Lewis Mumford as "perhaps the most positive and exhilarating example of community planning in the country." New York Life sold it in 1972 to Harry B. Helmsley for $53 million, and soon afterward a tenants' association maintained that Helmsley had reduced services and was planning to develop the remaining open spaces. Tenants and owners reached a settlement in 1982 and relations became largely amicable. At first the population was almost exclusively white, prompting a discrimination suit in 1983 by the NAACP Legal Defense Fund that was successful. The area gradually become more diverse, with a growing population of blacks and a large number of Chinese, Japanese, Koreans, and Indians. Fresh Meadows has 6100 privately owned houses and 7750 rental units, and remains a small town within the city.

The Japanese School of New York opened in the neighborhood in 1975 as the city's first Japanese-language day school.

Vincent Seyfried: *Queens: A Pictorial History* (Norfolk, Va.: Donning, 1982)

Patricia A. Doyal

Friars Club. Social club. Formed in 1904 by press agents in New York City, it attracted vaudeville, burlesque, and later film and television performers, many of whom could not gain admittance to more élite clubs such as the Players and the Lambs. The club adopted monastic terms for its officers, including its president (the abbot) and vice-president (the dean), as well as for its clubhouse (the monastery). It undertook philanthropic works and staged social gatherings, including "frolics," "roasts," man-of-the-year awards, and testimonial dinners. The frolics, held yearly between 1908 and 1929 and featuring performances by such figures as Al Jolson and George M. Cohan, were held in New York City and then taken on tour. The roasts, which began as strictly private affairs, were filmed from the 1970s and broadcast on Dean Martin's television program. On 26 April 1960 Mayor Robert F. Wagner renamed Times Square "Friars Square" for a week to honor the humanitarian and civic efforts of the club; Duffy Square was similarly renamed for a week in 1974 on the occasion of the club's seventieth anniversary. In June 1988 the club voted to admit women as members. In the mid 1990s it was based at 57 East 55th Street and had about fifteen hundred members.

Tina Margolis: "A History of Theatrical Social Clubs in New York City" (diss., New York University, 1990)

Tina Margolis

Garden court of the Frick Collection

Frick, Henry Clay (*b* West Overton, Penn., 19 Dec 1849; *d* New York City, 2 Dec 1919). Industrialist. While still in his twenties he recognized that the Bessemer steelmaking process would greatly increase the demand for coke, and with several associates he began to purchase soft coal lands in western Pennsylvania and to build coke ovens. By the time he was thirty he had become a millionaire. In 1881 he benefited from an exchange of shares in his mines and coke ovens for shares in the iron and steel mills owned by Andrew Carnegie, and by 1889 he was in charge of the operations of Carnegie Brothers and Company. As president and then chairman of the board of Carnegie Steel (1889–1900) he oversaw the growth of the concern into the largest producer of steel in the world. He moved in 1900 to New York City, where he began building a magnificent mansion at 1 East 70th Street at 5th Avenue (completed in 1914). In the following year he became a member of the board of directors of the U.S. Steel Corporation, formed by J. P. Morgan. An avid collector of painting and sculpture, particularly of the Italian Renaissance, Frick bequeathed his mansion, his art collection, and an endowment of $15 million to the City of New York. The mansion is now known as the Frick Collection.

George Harvey: *Henry Clay Frick, the Man* (New York: Charles Scribner's Sons, 1928)

Allen J. Share

Frick Collection. Museum on the Upper East Side of Manhattan. Opened in 1935, it contains the collections of the industrialist Henry Clay Frick and is housed in his former mansion at 1 East 70th Street, designed by Thomas Hastings. The museum contains European paintings, mainly from the Renaissance to the end of the nineteenth century, and important collections of small, classically inspired bronzes, Renaissance and eighteenth-century French furniture, Limoges enamels, prints and drawings, and Chinese and French porcelains. It has paintings by El Greco, Vermeer, Rembrandt, Ingres, Renoir, Titian, Giovanni Bellini, John Constable, Jean Fragonard, Thomas Gainsborough, Frans Hals, William Hogarth, Hans Holbein the Younger, Piero della Francesca, J. M. W. Turner, Jan van Eyck, and James McNeill Whistler. A reference library contains some 750,000 photographs and slides and 174,000 books and catalogues.

George B. M. Harvey: *Henry Clay Frick: The Man* (New York: Charles Scribner's Sons, 1928)
The Frick Collection: An Illustrated Catalogue (Princeton, N.J.: Princeton University Press, 1968–82)
Bernice Davidson, Edgar Munhall, and Nadia Tscherny, eds.: *Paintings from the Frick Collection* (New York: Harry N. Abrams, 1990)

Carol V. Wright

Fried Frank Harris Shriver and Jacobson. Law firm. It originated with the practice of Charles A. Riegelman (1879–1950) and took its current name in 1971 after R. Sargent Shriver (*b* 1915), a former director of the Peace Corps and ambassador to France, became a partner at its office in Washington. The firm specializes in corporate mergers and acquisitions, counsel to foreign companies in the United States, and Indian claims (through the office in Washington). In 1993 it had 339 lawyers (including seventy-five partners), of whom 235 were based at its headquarters at 1 New York Plaza in lower Manhattan.

Gilbert Tauber

Friend, Charlotte (*b* New York City, 11 March 1921; *d* New York City, 13 Jan 1987). Medical researcher. She earned a bachelor's degree at Hunter College in 1944 and a PhD in bacteriology at Yale University in 1950. While working at the Sloan–Kettering Institute in 1956 she discovered a virus that causes leukemia in mice, a breakthrough in cancer research. She continued her research at the Mount Sinai School of Medicine from 1966 and in 1971 published an important paper on a technique to make cancer cells revert to normal development patterns. A member of the National Academy of Science, Friend received many awards and worked to further the interests of women in science.

Barbara J. Niss

Friendship House. Catholic settlement house, formed in 1938 at 34 West 135th Street in Manhattan by the Russian émigrée Catherine De Hueck, who had formed an organization of the same name in Toronto in 1930. It was dedicated to providing aid and education for blacks, and all funding was from donations. The house offered instruction in reading, writing, religion, sports, and art, as well as employment referrals, lecture series, and religious instruction, and when possible it paid college tuition for black students. Across the street from its building it rented four stores where it collected donations, distributed clothing, and provided space for various activities. It also supported a youth organization, a Catholic lending library, and a reading room. In 1949 Friendship Houses opened in Washington, Chicago, Portland (Oregon), and Shreveport (Louisiana). Friendship House in New York City closed in 1957.

Bernadette McCauley

Friends Seminary. Elementary and secondary coeducational private school. Opened in 1786 on Pearl Street in lower Manhattan as the Friends Institute by the New York Monthly Meeting of the Religious Society of Friends, it moved in 1826 to Elizabeth Street and in 1860 to Stuyvesant Square. In 1964 a new building was added on 16th Street adjacent to the school and the Friends Meeting House. The educational outlook of Friends Seminary reflects its Quaker heritage: although Quakers account for only about 3 percent of the student body and faculty, the school requires four years of community service and has a meetinghouse among its facilities.

Richard Schwartz

Fugazy, Luigi V. (*b* ?Liguria, Italy, *ca* 1839; *d* New York City, 6 Aug 1930). Businessman and community leader. He moved to New York City in 1869 and was well established by the time a large number of Italians settled in the city in the late nineteenth century; he became wealthy and powerful through padrone services, a bank, a steamship agency, and an employment office and also organized mutual benefit societies, urged Italians to take part in American politics, and developed ties with Tammany Hall. His son Humbert and grandson William were well-known locally as promoters of sporting events.

Gli Italiani negli Stati Uniti (New York: Italian American Directory Company, 1906), 446
Victor R. Greene: *American Immigrant Leaders, 1800–1910: Marginality and Identity* (Baltimore: Johns Hopkins University Press, 1987), 126–30

Mary Elizabeth Brown

Fuller, (Sarah) Margaret (*b* Cambridge, Mass., 23 May 1810; *d* near Fire Island, N.Y., 19 July 1850). Journalist. In her youth she was influenced by the New England transcendentalists. From 1844 she lived in New York City with the family of Horace Greeley and wrote for his newspaper the *New York Tribune*. Her articles covered a wide range of subjects, including prison reform, immigration, prostitution, slavery, and literature. The newspaper sent her to Europe in 1846, where she became the first American woman to be a foreign correspondent. She lost her life aboard the steamer *Elizabeth* on her return voyage.

Paula Blanchard: *Margaret Fuller: From Transcendentalism to Revolution* (New York: Delacorte, 1978)
Charles Capper: *Margaret Fuller: An American Romantic Life* (New York: Oxford University Press, 1992)

See also LITERATURE, §1.

Thea Arnold

Fulton, Robert (*b* Little Britain [now Fulton Township], Lancaster County, Penn., 14 Nov 1765; *d* New York City, 24 Feb 1815). Inventor, engineer, and painter. He grew up in Lancaster and briefly attended school there before turning to drawing, painting, and mechanics and becoming an accomplished gunsmith. At the age of seventeen he went to Philadelphia, where he spent four years painting portraits and landscapes. After studying painting in England he became engrossed in the principles of undersea warfare, mechanically propelled ships, and canals. He designed and tested naval weaponry for the French and the British before meeting the American minister to France, Robert R. Livingston of New York City, who agreed to finance his experiments in steamboat technology and contracted with him to construct a steamboat to ply the Hudson River between New York City and Albany, New York. After landing in New York City in December 1806 he constructed the *North River Steamboat* at the shipyard of Charles Brown(e) in Manhattan. On 17 August 1807 the vessel, powered by a Watt steam engine, began service on the Hudson as the first commercially successful passenger steamboat in the world. Eventually he secured a monopoly on steamboat operations in New York State. Fulton also designed a steam naval vessel for the defense of New York Harbor during the War of 1812, as well as other ships and ferryboats. His last home was at 1 State Street. The *North River Steamboat* became known by its popular name the *Clermont* only after his death.

Self-portrait of Robert Fulton after Elizabeth Emmet, ca *1815. Fulton copied Emmet's portrait but added the exploding boat in the background, a reference to the destruction of the brig* Dorothea *by his diving boat off Deal, England, on 15 October 1805.*

Elaine Landau: *Robert Fulton* (New York: F. Watts, 1991)

See also PORT OF NEW YORK.

James E. Mooney, Darwin H. Stapleton

Fulton Ferry [Fulton Landing]. A Historic District in northwestern Brooklyn, lying at the bottom of the bluffs of Brooklyn Heights at the foot of Fulton Street, and bounded to the north by the East River, to the east by Main Street, to the south by Front and Doughty streets, and to the west by Furman Street. Transport from the area to Manhattan was offered as early as 1642 by sailboats and rowboats for hire. Steam ferries began regular service in 1814 and by 1872 made twelve hundred crossings daily. During the nineteenth century the waterfront around the ferry dock became a bustling mercantile center, and in the surrounding streets huge warehouses were built to accommodate commercial transport;

Fulton Ferry and South Street, ca *1898.* Lower right *terminal of the Fulton Ferry (designed by John Kellum);* center *Fulton Fish Market;* background *Brooklyn Bridge*

there was also industry and a residential section. After the Brooklyn Bridge was completed in 1883 the number of ferry passengers declined and in 1924 service was discontinued. Most of Fulton Street was renamed Cadman Plaza West. Many industrial buildings were later converted to housing: the Eagle Warehouse and Storage Company (28 Fulton Street; 1893) is a residential condominium; the building of the Brooklyn City Railroad Company (8 Cadman Plaza West; 1861) houses the Old Fulton Street apartments; and the Empire Stores (53–83 Water Street; built in sections in 1870 and 1885) and the Tobacco Inspection Warehouse (25–39 Water Street) are part of the Empire Fulton Ferry State Park. A converted barge moored at the Fulton Ferry pier is the site of a chamber music series called Bargemusic and offers superb views of the river. The River Café at 1 Water Street is a popular gourmet restaurant.

Elizabeth Reich Rawson

Fulton Fish Market. Wholesale fish market on the shore of the East River two blocks south of the Brooklyn Bridge. It originally consisted of a number of stalls in a corner of the Fulton Market (1822) that were used until fish dealers moved across South Street to a shed along the river in 1831; a permanent building was erected in 1869. Initially most fish sold there was delivered by fishing schooners and sloops. By the late nineteenth century the use of refrigeration and express railroads allowed fish to be delivered from all parts of the United States and Canada and sometimes from abroad. A freshwater fish market developed near Peck Slip, catering primarily to Jewish customers. The market became the largest in the country and one of the largest in the world, and remained so into the 1990s. Fishing boats ceased to land their catch at the market in the late 1970s but occasionally tied up there to wait out bad weather. One of the last working areas of the waterfront in Manhattan and the last important vestige of outdoor wholesale markets, the Fulton Fish Market is busy from midnight until about 9 a.m., its streets choked with refrigerator trucks from all over the continent and the vans of local retailers.

Norman J. Brouwer

Fun City. A mildly derisive nickname for New York City, coined and popularized by the newspaper columnist Dick Schaap, who was inspired by a remark made by Mayor John V. Lindsay during a severe transit strike in 1966: "I still think it's a fun city."

Gerald Leonard Cohen: *Origin of New York City's Nickname "The Big Apple"* (Frankfurt am Main: Peter Lang, 1991), 70–72

Gerald Leonard Cohen

Fund for the City of New York. Charitable organization formed in 1968 by the Ford Foundation. Its major program is a management information program, under which staff members work with government agencies to improve accountability and assess performance. It also makes grants to advocacy groups and cash-flow loans to nonprofit recipients of government contracts. In 1990 the fund reported assets of $9.5 million and made grants of $430,000.

Kenneth W. Rose

Fulton Fish Market, ca *1937*

furniture. Roughly hewn furniture of cheap construction was made in New Amsterdam. In the second half of the eighteenth century the market for furniture expanded from a regional to an international scope. Artisans made chairs, tables, sideboards, and other furniture, largely in the American Chippendale style. Outstanding makers of furniture such as Andrew Gautier, Gilbert Ash, and Thomas Burling enabled the city to surpass Philadelphia in the quality of furniture produced, and probably also in quantity. As early as 1795 cabinetmakers shipped five thousand Windsor chairs from the city to the West Indies, and by the 1820s furniture was also being shipped to the southern United States and South America. The growing demand for furniture led to the demise of the traditional system of manufacture, in which a master cabinetmaker engaged in all aspects of production and trade, and to increased specialization: about this time there emerged independent firms engaged in chairmaking and upholstering. Growth also led to conflicts between master cabinetmakers and journeymen. In 1802 an organization of masters attempted to issue a new list of rates for piecework, leading to a strike by angry journeymen.

Furniture making reached its height in the city during the first half of the nineteenth century. Shops for the élite produced elaborately carved mahogany pieces that English visitors conceded were superior to the best found in London. The famous shops of Duncan Phyfe and Honoré Lannuier at the beginning of the century attracted skilled workmen with high wages, as did that of John Henry Belter in the 1850s. At the same time more than four thousand poorly trained workmen known as "botches" assembled cheaply made furniture in auction, or "slaughter," shops. In Little Germany such shops used an extensive division of labor to produce furniture for the rural and working-class mass markets. The predominantly German employees of these shops earned $5 to $6 a week, about one third what workers earned in shops of the first rank.

In the two decades before the Civil War about 85 percent of all furniture made in New York City was sold outside the city, and an increasing amount was sent to the West and California. Few economies of scale existed among manufacturers of either cheap or high-quality furniture: eighty to one hundred men were employed in the best shops, which in the 1860s included those of Edward Hutchings on Broome Street and Alexander Roux nearby on Mercer Street, but often fewer than fifty men were employed in the many auction shops. In the 1870s workers in auction shops began organized protests against low wages, and by 1873 the German Cabinetmakers' Association had four thousand members, making it the largest German union in the city and enabling it to stand in the forefront of the movement for an eight-hour day. The slow decline of the furniture industry in New York City began in the 1870s, when Cincinnati and later Grand Rapids, Michigan, became major manufacturing centers, depriving the city of its western trade. Although the city gradually lost the market for cheap furniture, it continued to lead the nation in the manufacture of custom-made and high-grade "imperial" furniture. Small shops remained concentrated in what is now SoHo, where they produced fashionable artistic pieces and employed highly skilled Italian workmen who in 1919 could make $4.80 a day, twice the wage of the average workman in the trade. By 1925 the 384 furniture shops in the city employed only 10,402 workers, fewer than in Chicago or Grand Rapids, but the value of furniture produced exceeded that of all other cities at $71.8 million. Despite its tenacity the industry faced increasing handicaps throughout the twentieth century, especially in the form of rising rents. High-grade work began to leave the city for factories in Grand Rapids and North Carolina (although showrooms were often maintained in Manhattan), and the firms that remained tended to rely on repair work to stay in business. Employment in furniture declined steadily as a proportion of the city's work force from the 1920s into the 1990s. The census of manufactures in 1982 counted 518 shops with eleven thousand employees.

The Furniture Industry (New York: Merchant's Association of New York, 1919)

Nancy McClelland: *Duncan Phyfe and the English Regency, 1795–1830* (New York: William R. Scott, 1939)

See also DECORATIVE ARTS and INTERIOR DESIGN.

Richard Stott

furs. The fur trade in New Netherland was conducted by private Dutch merchants until 1615, when a charter guaranteed to the New Netherland Company exclusive fur trading rights in the colony. The Dutch West India Company acquired these rights in 1621, during a period when settlers from many backgrounds were joining the fur trade. Peltry at the time was a source of quick profits and a substitute for scarce currency. Although beaver dominated the trade, large numbers of otter, mink, and muskrat skins were also exported. By the time the monopoly of the West India Company ended in 1638 the fur trade was concentrated in the hands of a few exporters in the colony and about four large firms in Amsterdam. The trade required a delicate balance among many different peoples and markets: producers and distributors of wampum, Indian suppliers, and merchants on both sides of the Atlantic. During the 1650s French and English competition for peltry forced Dutch traders to diversify into other exports; payment to merchants in New Amsterdam took the form of specie, which resulted in the devaluation of wampum, the "mother of the beaver trade," and led to bidding wars between Indian suppliers and private traders. The fur trade was again hurt in the late 1660s when a shift in fashion preferences in England and Europe away from beaver hats and collars resulted in a glut of peltry. English merchants responded to these trends by attempting to regulate factoring, shipping, and correspondence between Albany (New York) and New York City. Although a rival group of merchants argued that the fur trade should be left open to competition, regulations were intermittently imposed on the trade: an export duty of 1*s.* 3*d.* on each beaver hide was imposed in 1674, increased to 9*s.* on each hide in 1683. In 1701 a Treaty of Neutrality with French Canada and the Iroquois in the peltry-gathering areas made it possible to reestablish an open trade policy. Merchants in New York City who supported regulation fought the new policy and blamed it for weakening exports, which they reported to have fallen by 50 percent between the 1690s and the early 1720s. During the administration of Governor William Burnet (1720–28) English mercantilists tried to dominate the fur trade by steering exports through their port so that they could set prices. English merchants who arrived after the 1660s, such as Charles Lodwick, James Graham, Edward Griffith, Caleb Heathcote, and Samuel Winder, could never compete viably with Cornelius Cuyler, Evertt Wendell Jr., and Robert Livingston Jr., or with the great peltry exporters, such as Stephen de Lancey, Frederick Philipse, and Philip Livingston. When peltry exports concentrated in fewer hands during the early eighteenth century ambitious lesser merchants diversified their shipments; some like Benjamin Aske, Ouzeel Van Sweeten, Brandt Schuyler, Ebenezer Wilson, and Walter Thong became prominent provincial mercantile leaders. Jacob Wendell and Henry Beekman sold peltry to English factors in New York City after 1720 rather than give up the trade entirely.

Disputes in the colony over the fur trade continued over the next few decades, as English merchants further dominated the peltry market. A factoring system led by Cornelius Cuyler in New York City and the firm of Storke and Gainsborough in London bypassed many traders in New York City by establishing direct ties with merchants in and around Albany. Many other traders defied the British factoring system to the end of the colonial period by trading independently along the Hudson River and smuggling peltry across the Canadian border. These offenders were regularly mentioned as a menace to the imperial government in New York City throughout the 1750s and 1760s, even though the number of merchants and skins in this trade had long since become insignificant to the economy of the colony.

By the early nineteenth century New York City was again the site of a thriving wholesale fur market, in which most operations were small. A key figure in the fur business during the following decades was John Jacob Astor, a resident of New York City who made attempts beginning in 1808 to control the fur trade in the Far West. He remained active as a trader until 1834. Both the city's wholesale trade and a lively retail trade were on the Lower East Side by the end of the century, reflecting the heavy concentration there of German and eastern European Jewish merchants and fur workers.

The fur market had moved to a compact area at the perimeter of Chelsea by 1922, occupying the blocks between 25th and 31st streets and between 6th and 8th avenues. This district became the locus both for a skilled, highly differentiated, and labor-intensive business and for a culture: special restaurants, a synagogue, and steam baths in the old Pennsylvania Hotel were as much a part of the district as the racks of skins that moved through the streets. The business was also characterized by militant unionism, and after the Second World War charges of communist affiliation nearly destroyed the Fur and Leather Workers Union, an offshoot of the Fur Workers' Union (formed in 1849).

The fur business reached its peak in the city in the 1940s and 1950s. Later decentralization and foreign manufacturing, notably in Korea and China, caused a sharp decline in the number of shops and workers in the city. In response fur retailers during the 1970s and 1980s sought to broaden its market, seeking in particular to appeal to young working women by emphasizing relatively low-priced fur coats that were ready made rather than custom made. The effort met with some success, and from 1977 to 1986 retail sales of furs in the United States rose from $612.5 million to $1800 million. By the late 1980s the fur business suffered from a worsening economy, increasing competition from foreign companies, the highly visible tactics of the animal-rights movement, and the growing popularity of synthetic furs. Between 1979 and 1989 the number of fur manufacturers in New York City declined from eight hundred to about three hundred, and employment declined from 3600 to nineteen hundred.

The city nevertheless remained the center of the American fur business into the 1990s. Trade organizations such as the Fur Retailers Information Council and the American Fur Industry maintained offices in the city, and a number of trade periodicals were published there. The business was no longer dominated by eastern Europeans but rather by Greeks and especially Koreans.

Philip S. Foner: *Fur and Leather Workers Union: A Story of Dramatic Struggles and Achievements* (Newark, N.J.: Nordan, 1950)

Edgar M. Hoover and Raymond Vernon: *Anatomy of a Metropolis: The Changing Distribution of People and Jobs within the New York Metropolitan Region* (Cambridge: Harvard University Press, 1959)

Thomas Elliot Norton: *The Fur Trade in Colonial New York, 1686–1776* (Madison: University of Wisconsin Press, 1974)

Elaine Abelson, Cathy Matson

fusionism. Coalitions of parties and factions became a means of circumventing political machines during the 1840s in New York City, and after the Civil War fusionism became the principal strategy for those who sought political reform, as Republicans, reform Democrats, and nonpartisan civic organizations repeatedly united to defeat mainstream candidates (almost always Democrats). Municipal reforms successfully backed by fusion movements included the introduction of the secret ballot, the rescheduling of city elections to odd-numbered years (so as not to coincide with state and national elections), and changes in the civil service. Fusion campaigns elected reform candidates such as Seth Low (1901), Fiorello H. La Guardia (1933), and John V. Lindsay (1965), but fusionists suffered from their rejection of the "spoils system," an inability to maintain party structures, a tendency for lawyers and other professionals within their administrations to tire quickly of governance, the Democratic practice of painting fusionists as élitists hostile to the working class, and the splintering of fusion coalitions by national elections.

Restore the City to the People (New York: Brown, 1917)

For illustration see GOVERNMENT AND POLITICS.

Peter Field

F. W. Woolworth. Firm of retailers, formed as a five-and-ten-cent store in 1879 by Frank Winfield Woolworth. In 1912 it merged with chain stores set up by a number of Woolworth's friends and family members, many of whom had initially worked for him. It became highly successful by selling necessary articles cheaply, and when it moved into the Woolworth Building, the tallest building in the world at the time, it had more than a thousand stores in North America. In 1918 the firm had more than $100 million in sales. Woolworth remained in business into the 1990s, by which time it had lost much of its market share to other chain retailers.

James E. Mooney

G

Gaelic Athletic Association of New York [GAA]. Athletic association formed in 1914; it draws representatives from sixty-two clubs that compete in traditional sports. The association arranges and oversees championship matches in Gaelic football, hurling, and camogie (women's hurling), which together are known as the "Games of the Gael," and also offers instruction in these games to Irish–American youths.

Joseph Murphy: "The Gaels in America Cling to Their Games," *Irish Echo*, 17 Nov 1978

Patrick Hennessy: "Gaelic Athletic Association," *Irish–American Voluntary Organizations*, ed. Michael Funchion (Westport, Conn.: Greenwood, 1983)

John J. Concannon

Gaelic Park. Public park in the Bronx, at 240th Street and Broadway. The land was acquired in 1926 by two members of the Gaelic Athletic Association of Greater New York, which in 1928 began using the site for Irish football and hurling events. In the late 1930s the owners became bankrupt and the land was taken over by the city (it eventually passed to the Metropolitan Transit Authority). John O'Donnell leased the park in behalf of the Gaelic Athletic Association from 1941, and with his family he maintained the park's stadium, playing field, bar, and ballroom. After a series of disputes with the association the family ended its involvement with the park, and in 1991 the land was leased to Manhattan College. Gaelic Park and its games played an important role in the social life of several generations of Irish immigrants.

George Winslow

Gage and Tollner. Restaurant in downtown Brooklyn, opened in 1879 on Fulton Street by Charles Gage. In the following year Eugene Tollner became a partner and in 1882 the restaurant moved to its present location at 372 Fulton Street. The restaurant is well known for its varied preparations of oysters, clams, scallops, and lobster and for its interior: the main dining room is one hundred feet (thirty meters) long and has mahogany tables (seating 220), walled mirrors, brocaded velvet, and gaslit chandeliers of cut glass. Both the interior and exterior have been designated landmarks by the city. Gage and Tollner was owned by the Dewey family for sixty-eight years until its sale in 1988 to Peter Aschkenasy.

Stephen Weinstein

Gaine, Hugh (*b* Belfast, Ireland, 1726/27; *d* New York City, 25 April 1807). Newspaper publisher. Although penniless when he arrived in New York City in 1745, he founded and published the *New York Mercury* in 1752 (later called the *New York Gazette*) and became the most successful newspaper publisher in the city before the American Revolution; he also worked as a merchant in cosmetics. A founding member of the Friendly Sons of St. Patrick, he was its treasurer for twelve years. Gaine was an original trustee of the New York Society Library, the first lending library in the city.

Alfred Lawrence Lorenz: *Hugh Gaine: A Colonial Printer–Editor's Odyssey to Loyalism* (Carbondale: Southern Illinois University Press, 1972)

See also Book publishing, Booksellers, and Printing.

William McGimpsey

Gallatin, (Abraham Alfonse) Albert (*b* Geneva, 29 Jan 1761; *d* Astoria [now in Queens], 12 Aug 1849). Diplomat and banker. He married Hannah Nicholson, daughter of Commodore James Nicholson, in 1793 and was secretary of the treasury in 1801–14 under Presidents Thomas Jefferson and James Madison. About 1810 he formed a close association with the financier and fur trader John Jacob Astor, and after retiring from service as a diplomat to France (1816–23) and Great Britain (1826–27) and moving to New York City (1827) he was persuaded by Astor to become the first president (1831) of the National Bank of New York City, a predecessor of Manufacturers Hanover. Although the bank remained small, Gallatin exercised great influence in banking in the 1830s, and was instrumental in encouraging banks in New York City to resume specie payments during the banking crisis of 1837. He maintained a series of residences in the city until 1837, when he settled permanently at 57 Bleecker Street. In several published writings in the 1830s and 1840s he stressed that only gold and silver could serve as an acceptable national currency and that issues of banknotes must be strictly limited. Active in the political, intellectual, and cultural life of the city, he was a founding trustee of New York University (1827), a founder and the first president of the American Ethnological Society (1842), and a president of the New-York Historical Society (1843). He also published extensively on American Indian languages. During the last years of his life Gallatin denounced American participation in the Mexican–American War and urged reconciliation with Great Britain regarding competing claims over the Oregon Territory. He died at the home of his daughter Frances Stevens and was buried at Trinity Church Yard in lower Manhattan.

Henry Adams: *The Life of Albert Gallatin* (Philadelphia: J. B. Lippincott, 1879)

Raymond Walters Jr.: *Albert Gallatin: Jeffersonian Financier and Diplomat* (New York: Macmillan, 1957)

G. Kurt Piehler

Gallico, Paul (William) (*b* New York City, 26 July 1897; *d* Monaco, 15 July 1976). Journalist. He graduated from Columbia University in 1921 and for the next fifteen years worked as a film critic, sportswriter, and editor for the *Daily News*. In 1927 he organized the first Golden Gloves boxing competition. During the Second World War he was a correspondent for *Cosmopolitan*. Gallico wrote forty

Gage and Tollner, 372–74 Fulton Street, Brooklyn

books, among them the Mrs. Arris series, *Snow Goose* (1941), and *Confessions of a Story Writer* (1946).

James E. Mooney

gambling. Betting on shuffleboard, billiards, cards, and other games was common in all social classes in colonial New York City, as it was in Boston, Philadelphia, and Charleston, South Carolina. Often it enlivened gatherings in taverns, coffee houses, and private homes where people sought diversion from the day's work. In the mid eighteenth century lotteries were introduced from England and used by churches, public corporations, and the city government to raise money for charitable causes and public works. In the 1790s most forms of securities trading were considered gambling. At this time "policy" became widespread, especially among the poor, who wagered on one to four numbers from a list of twelve in a lottery drawing.

Gambling in New York City changed little until the 1830s, when the city became the largest in the nation, and its rapidly growing and affluent population sought new diversions. The demand for gambling increased despite concerns about public morality heightened by many scandals in lotteries during the first two decades of the nineteenth century, and bans by the state legislature on lotteries in the 1830s and gambling halls and other public gambling places in the 1840s. Professional gamblers availed themselves of the opportunity to build businesses that were soon linked to city politics and popular entertainment, thus creating the basis for organized crime. New card games were developed and became immensely popular. One of the first was faro, introduced in the city in the 1840s: by placing chips or money on a cloth embossed with a suit of cards, players bet on which card would appear next from a deck turned face down in a dealing box. Faro was the most popular card game of chance in the city during the nineteenth century because of its speed and because the odds were more favorable to the bettor than in any other card game, even though operators cheated in many ways. Professional gamblers were attracted by the enormous profits to be made in faro, and from 1835 they opened posh "hells," forerunners of modern casinos, in choice locations along Broadway from 24th Street to the Battery. By the 1860s there were about one hundred hells; wealth and connections to government allowed the proprietors to operate quite openly.

The introduction of horse racing, baseball, boxing, and other spectator sports provided opportunities for gamblers, who built racetracks, helped to arrange matches, and offered betting services. John Morrissey, a boxer popular among Irish workers, helped to build the first major racetrack in the United States at Saratoga Springs, New York (1864), and became the most important gambler in the city.

Three-card monte on the beach at Coney Island, 1866

Shortly after the Civil War he developed the first off-track betting system in the city, in which results from Saratoga were relayed by telegraph to a partner's "poolroom"; eventually fans could bet on sporting events anywhere in the country and receive the results almost immediately. Off-track betting and bookmaking were developed in the 1870s and soon controlled by professional gamblers, who by the end of the century had a monopoly on the betting services that sustained most spectator sports.

Although gambling was illegal the city's gamblers conducted their business openly, shielded from arrest by their money, political influence, and tight organization. Some professional gamblers formed ties with the heads of political machines, such as Big Tim Sullivan, a leader of Tammany Hall who was elected to the U.S. Congress and the state senate; others held political office in the wards where they maintained their operations. Many exerted influence privately, and gamblers remained powerful in local politics well into the twentieth century. The acceptance of gambling by the public made it possible to earn large profits and encouraged shrewd entrepreneurs. Between 1909 and 1920 Arnold

Mayor Fiorello H. La Guardia destroying a slot machine, ca *1935*

Rothstein exploited his protection by Sullivan and his talent for public relations to build a gambling empire, and he became nationally known after allegedly rigging the outcome of the World Series of 1919. About this time some of the first prominent black gamblers in the city made their careers during the transformation of Harlem into a predominantly black neighborhood. Jose Enrique Miro, William Brunder, Big Joe Ison, and others introduced numbers games there in the 1920s, in which players bet on a single number between 1 and 999. Black numbers operators became wealthy and rose to positions of social and political prominence. Several whites including Dutch Schultz also made money in Harlem by forcing themselves on these black operators as partners.

In the mid twentieth century gambling was changed by the introduction of the telephone and the legalization of some forms of betting. By taking bets over the telephone, gamblers made betting more convenient and obviated poolrooms and other public venues where they risked arrest, and they no longer had to corrupt the police to protect their enterprises. Bookmaking thus became decentralized, and by the 1960s it was beyond the control of any one group or individual. In 1939 voters ratified an amendment to the state constitution to legalize parimutuel betting at racetracks, which was taxed by the state. The revenues were so great that the city also levied a tax on track betting after the Second World War. The state legislature gradually undercut the municipal tax, prompting the city to seek other ways of earning income from gambling. After a decade of debate Off-Track Betting (OTB) was introduced in 1971 but failed to produce as much revenue as expected; surcharges on winnings imposed later decreased payoffs and led bettors to seek out illegal bookmakers. In 1966 the legislature introduced the state lottery, which initially drew few participants because drawings were held only rarely and the payoffs were low. The lottery became one of the largest in the nation only when the state made drawings more frequent, introduced a range of games, and increased the value of prizes.

Despite the legalization of some forms of gambling the illegal forms remained important in the city in the mid 1990s. In fair weather three-card monte dealers set up folding tables on the sidewalks of midtown and downtown Manhattan. Shills lured passers-by and lookouts watched for the police, who would confiscate the dealers' equipment. Churches and other nonprofit groups continued to raise money by holding large-scale bingo games and raffles, which although illegal were tolerated by the authorities.

Herbert Asbury: *Sucker's Progress: An Informal History of Gambling in America from the Colonies to Canfield* (New York: Dodd, Mead, 1938)

David R. Johnson: "A Sinful Business: The Origins of Gambling Syndicates in the United States, 1840–1887," *Police and Society*, ed. David H. Bayley (Beverly Hills, Calif.: Sage, 1977), 17–48

Mark H. Haller: "The Changing Structure of American Gambling in the Twentieth Century," *Journal of Social Issues* 35, no. 3 (summer 1979), 87–114

Peter Reuter: *Disorganized Crime: The Economics of the Visible Hand* (Cambridge: MIT Press, 1983)

Vicki Abt, James F. Smith, and Eugene M. Christiansen: *The Business of Risk: Commercial Gambling in Mainstream America* (Lawrence: University of Kansas Press, 1985)

David R. Johnson

gangs. The first street gangs in New York City were formed at the end of the eighteenth century by journeymen and apprentices free of their masters' control outside the workshop. These single young men organized loosely structured gangs associated with neighborhoods, streets, and trades. Gangs harassed pedestrians and sometimes fought with each other over territory. By the Jacksonian period there were many gangs, attracting members from the trades least affected by industrialization and sometimes from volunteer fire companies. Such groups as the Chichesters, composed mainly of apprentice and journeymen butchers, survived for many years and maintained a hierarchical membership of older leaders and young followers. Gangs were especially popular among young men in the Bowery, where gang members built self-esteem by taking part in pursuits outside the workplace such as brawling, carousing, going to the theater, and target shooting. Many wore long sideburns (called soap locks) and distinctive clothing, emblems of the male culture of the Bowery that became widely known through stories about the "B'hoy," a character depicted in the penny press and the popular theater. As neighborhoods in the city became divided along class lines, gangs congregated in saloons that increasingly became political as well as social institutions. During elections their allegiance was highly sought after by saloon keepers, who often held office: in return for patronage they stole ballot boxes, intimidated supporters of rival candidates, and voted "early and often." Violence escalated in the 1840s as economic depression and an influx of Irish immigrants spurred a power struggle between native-born and immigrant groups within Tammany Hall. Gangs such as the Spartan Association, led by the radical Democrat Mike Walsh, fought pitched battles using fists, clubs, and guns.

Jacob A. Riis, Bandit's Roost *(1888)*

Irish immigrants changed the structure of gangs. When they moved to the city they often transferred to the gangs their allegiance to factions and secret societies in Ireland. In Irish working-class wards such gangs as the Dead Rabbits defended their neighborhood and customs against outside forces ranging from temperance advocates to rival gangs like the nativist Bowery Boys. But gangs also fed conflict within communities, and during the mid nineteenth century neighborhoods were often divided according to unstable alliances that sometimes erupted into violence. After the Civil War the ward gangs were united by Tammany Hall into political clubs run by district leaders. At the same time gangs became increasingly segregated by age, as district leaders sponsored "social clubs" for teenagers. Gangs remained tied to their ethnic groups but also became efficient political tools, frequently providing a link between politicians and criminal enterprises such as gambling and prostitution. By the turn of the century adult gang members were often small-time organized-crime figures engaged in citywide racketeering. Increasingly gangs exacerbated class conflict within ethnic communities: during strikes over unionizing the garment trades on the Lower East Side, local *shtarkes* (sluggers) were hired by both Jewish manufacturers and union organizers.

During the Progressive era reformers identified gang membership as a form of juvenile delinquency. Similar analyses were made in the 1950s, when wars between white, black, and Latin American gangs aroused widespread concern, and the popularity of gangs was attributed to economic deprivation, psychological disorders, and a breakdown of social institutions. Widespread violence between gangs in black and Latin American neighborhoods declined rapidly in the 1960s, a decline variously attributed to youth politics, the military draft, and drug addiction. Gang violence resumed after the early 1970s, when it spread from the southern Bronx to the other boroughs. By 1975 the police in New York City knew of 275 gangs with eleven thousand members; estimates varied widely by the mid 1980s, from four hundred gangs with eight to forty thousand members, to eighty-six gangs with 4300 members. Into the 1990s local news reports were dominated by episodes of violence, as federal funds for social programs were cut and an epidemic of drug abuse consumed poor urban neighborhoods.

Herbert Asbury: *The Gangs of New York* (New York: Alfred A. Knopf, 1928)
Joshua Brown: "The 'Dead Rabbit'–Bowery Boy Riot: An Analysis of the Antebellum New York Gang" (thesis, Columbia University, 1976)
Jenna Weissman Joselit: *Our Crowd: Jewish Crime and the New York Jewish Community, 1900–1914* (Bloomington: Indiana University Press, 1983)
Anne Campbell: *The Girls in the Gang: A Report from New York City* (New York: Basil Blackwell, 1984)
Peter Kwong: *The New Chinatown* (New York: Hill and Wang, 1987)

Joshua Brown

Gansevoort Market. Open-air farmers' market opened in 1882, covering a little more than two acres (eighty ares) and bounded to the north by Little West 12th Street, to the east by Washington Street, to the south by Gansevoort Street, and to the west by West Street. Its use was restricted by law to farmers and gardeners, most from Long Island and New Jersey, who drove to the city daily to sell their own produce to peddlers and retailers; they usually arrived in the evening, stabled their horses, and began working at 3 a.m. or 4 a.m., without protection from the weather until a one-story building was erected in 1914 (demolished in 1957). The area became a wholesale meat district in 1949.

Suzanne R. Wasserman

garbage. For a discussion of garbage and its disposal see Pollution, Recycling, and Sanitation.

Garbo [Gustafson], **Greta (Lovisa)** (*b* Stockholm, 18 Sept 1905; *d* New York City, 15 April 1990). Actress. While studying acting in Stockholm she met the Swedish director Maurice Stiller, who took her to Hollywood in 1925; there she signed a contract with Metro–Goldwyn–Mayer. After appearing in silent films she gave memorable performances in the film version of Eugene O'Neill's *Anna Christie* (1930), *Ninotchka* (1930, her first comedy), *Grand Hotel* (1932), and *Camille* (1936), for which she won the New York Film Critics Award. After retiring in 1941 she remained largely in seclusion and assiduously avoided the press. In New York City she lived at 2 Beekman Place (in the 1930s), the Ritz Tower, and the Campanile, 450 East 52nd Street. Garbo was known for her glamorous appearance and for what one critic described as a "deep, husky, throaty contralto."

Leslie Gourse

Garcia Rivera, Oscar (*b* Mayaguez, Puerto Rico, 6 Nov 1900; *d* Mayaguez, 1969). Political and civic leader. He moved to New York City in 1925 and earned an undergraduate degree from Columbia University and a law degree from St. John's College. With the backing of the American Labor Party, the Republican Party, and the City Fusion Party he challenged Tammany Hall and was elected a state assemblyman from Manhattan in 1937, thus becoming the first Puerto Rican ever elected to public office in the continental United States. In the assembly he supported civil rights legislation, civil service reform, and hot meals in the public schools. He also worked in the Puerto Rican neighborhoods for voter registration, educational programs, and labor reform.

René Torres Delgado: *El primer legislador puertorriqueño en Nueva York: Oscar García Rivera* (San Juan: Colección Hipatia, 1979)

Virginia Sánchez Korrol

Garden Bay Manor. Neighborhood in northwestern Queens, bounded to the north by 19th Avenue, to the east by 81st and 82nd streets, to the south by Grand Central Parkway; it is the easternmost part of Ditmars and abuts the Marine Air Terminal. The name was coined by the original developers. Most of the apartments are in the garden style.

Vincent Seyfried

Garibaldi Memorial, ca *1900*

Garibaldi, Giuseppe (*b* Nice, 4 July 1807; *d* Caprera, Italy, 2 June 1882). Soldier and political leader. After fighting for Giuseppe Mazzini and the Roman republic in 1849 he was denied asylum by the king of Sardinia and moved to the United States on 30 July 1850. To avoid the hero's welcome that awaited him in Manhattan he entered the country at Staten Island, where he was housed by the inventor Antonio Meucci. While living there he avoided political activity and spent most of his time trying unsuccessfully to support himself. Friends finally arranged for him to return to his trade, seafaring. He embarked on a two-year voyage in April 1851 and left the city permanently in November 1853. Italians in the city erected a statue of him by Giovanni Turini in Washington Square Park in 1888. The Garibaldi–Meucci Memorial Museum is at 420 Tompkins Avenue in Rosebank, Staten Island.

Jasper Godwin Ridley: *Garibaldi* (New York: Viking, 1974)

Mary Elizabeth Brown

Garment District. Section of Manhattan dominated by the garment industry, in the 30s between Madison and 8th avenues. It took shape during the late nineteenth century and soon became the country's leading center of garment production. Initially concentrated in tenements on the Lower East Side, the garment business gradually moved north and west as garment manufacturers were driven by law from residential buildings into lofts and increasingly required fancy showrooms for marketing. The district centered on Madison Square by 1910, but the garment trades were forced out by the Fifth Avenue Association during the following decade as the area became fashionable for shopping. In 1920 two sites along 7th Avenue between 36th and 38th streets were developed by the Garment Center Realty Company, an association of thirty-eight large manufacturers of women's clothing, which soon revitalized an area formerly known as the Tenderloin. By 1931 the Garment District had the largest concentration of apparel manufacturers in the world and lay in the heart of Manhattan near hotels, the main retail district, and important railroad terminals in an area bounded by 42nd Street, 6th Avenue, 30th Street, and 9th Avenue. Traffic crowded 6th, 7th, and 8th avenues, and along the sidestreets trucks delivered material and loaded finished garments carted through the traffic on handtrucks by "push boys." At noon thousands of workers, mostly immigrants from eastern and southern Europe, made their way through the streets to local cafeterias and lingered to smoke and listen to pitchmen before resuming work at one o'clock.

After the Second World War the Garment District remained essentially in place, expect that by the 1980s a large amount of production had returned to lower Manhattan, especially Chinatown and the Lower East Side.

Roy B. Helfgott: "Women's and Children's Apparel," *Made in New York: Case Studies in Metropolitan Manufacturing*, ed. Max Hall (Cambridge: Harvard University Press, 1959), 19–134, 329–39

Allen J. Share

garments. The shift from custom-made to ready-made clothing in the United States during the Industrial Revolution was stimulated by the growth of the middle class and a large increase in foreign-born labor. As the chief port of entry for immigrants in America, New York City became the nation's leading center of garment production by the mid nineteenth century. Irish and German workers, who were refugees of famine and economic depression, entered the garment trade in the 1840s; Germans introduced the practice of home manufacturing to the garment industry in New York City and eventually displaced their better-paid Irish and American counterparts. Aided by Elias Howe's invention of the sewing machine in 1846, apparel was the fastest-growing industry in New York City in 1830–60. It was valued in 1858 at $27 million and employed 32,000 workers, who produced clothing for the American South, the West Indies, and South America.

Most German Jewish immigrants who settled in New York City in the mid nineteenth century went to work in the thriving second-hand clothing trade of Chatham Street in an area popularly called Jerusalem. They were less common in the prestigious ready-made trade of the Bowery and lower Broadway than many other immigrant groups. Women predominated in the ready-made trade, men (who were usually paid more) in the custom trade. By the 1870s technology and immigration brought about the displacement of both women and skilled men: unskilled male newcomers readily learned to use the foot-powered sewing machine, and men were more adept than women at handling a newly invented heavy cutting knife (1875) that supplanted conventional shears. Women were further displaced in the 1870s by Jewish men from Germany and Austria–Hungary who worked for substandard wages. Those who remained in the late nineteenth century worked in three kinds of shop: the inside shop, operated by a manufacturer using his own employees; the home-shop, where workers assisted by family members assembled goods brought home from the factory; and the outside shop, operated by a contractor who received an assignment from a manufacturer and used either factory or home labor.

Unregulated industrial homework in unsanitary conditions became characteristic of immigrant labor in lower Manhattan, among not only Germans but also Irish and Italians. Contractors enjoyed a competitive advantage because the cost of home labor was minimal. Despite the long hours, filth, and low pay, newcomers from Europe continued to accept work at home and in sweatshops, often working additional hours so that they could afford to send for family members still in Europe. Economic distress and religious persecution in Russia in the early 1880s led to a flood of Jewish immigrants in New York City. Most of these immigrants were townspeople without specific trades called *luftmenschen*, who worked in the garment trade soon after their arrival and were sympathetic toward unionism and socialism.

The first immigrants from southern Italy, known as *contadini*, or peasants, emigrated to the United States in the 1880s. Italian men with experience in the garment trades frequently found work in the custom tailoring shops in New York City; those without expe-

Handcarts and clothing racks on 7th Avenue, early 1990s

Salesmen ready to assist customers in the retail store of Moe Levy and Company, Clothiers, at Walker and Baxter streets, 1911

rience became sewing-machine operators and pressers. Italian women who were experienced home manufacturers monopolized home garment finishing in New York City by 1900, making four to five cents an hour; single Italian women were more likely to work outside the home than those who were married. The Italian sewing-machine operators and pressers were non-unionized and charged very little; this enabled them to undercut the more expensive Jewish workers, who were simultaneously advancing into higher-paid pursuits, and become the leading ethnic group in the needle trades by the 1930s.

Jews from Russia and Poland who immigrated in 1903 and 1905 to escape government-supported pogroms were more highly skilled than their predecessors. Many were members of the Jewish Labor Bund, formed in 1897 to promote socialism and cultural nationalism. Working conditions worsened with the development of the "task system": under this system teams of workers employed by a contractor were paid not by the hour but for a set amount of work, which nevertheless was to be completed within a specified time. Contractors often added to the daily workload, and the work day could last as long as eighteen hours. The influx of immigrants spurred marked growth between 1880 and 1900, particularly in women's apparel: employment rose from 11,696 to 83,739, and capital invested from $8.2 million to $48.4 million. In the 1880s alone makers of women's apparel increased in number by 226.2 percent, makers of men's apparel by 117.8 percent.

Led by cutters of ladies' garments, Jewish garment workers in New York City began to organize unions in the 1880s. Socialist intellectuals formed the United Hebrew Trades to promote unionism, and by 1900 representatives of seven unions formed the International Ladies' Garment Workers' Union (ILGWU). In the following year the United Cloth Hat and Cap Makers of North America was formed at a convention. During its first decade the ILGWU struggled for survival, but in 1909–10 it was revitalized by successful strikes of shirtwaist workers and cloakmakers; the cloakmakers' walkout revolutionized the garment industry by ensuring the adoption of the "Protocol of Peace," which provided for the resolution of disputes between labor and management and the protection of workers' health. In 1911 a tragic fire at the Triangle Shirtwaist Company in Greenwich Village took 146 lives, shocking the public and persuading the state legislature to enact thirty-six new labor laws within three years. The victory of the cloakmakers in 1910 encouraged fur workers to organize a strike in 1912 that led to the founding in the following year of the International Fur Workers' Union of the United States and Canada. In 1914 Jewish and Italian workers in the men's clothing trade withdrew from the United Garment Workers of America because of its corrupt leaders and formed the Amalgamated Clothing Workers of America.

The garment workers' unions were riven by intense conflicts in the 1920s, as communists challenged socialists for control of the needle trades. By the 1930s the communists' appeal to militant class struggle helped them to win over the furriers, though they failed to attract the Cloth Hat, Cap and Millinery Workers' International Union, the Amalgamated Clothing Workers, or the ILGWU. Extortion and racketeering were widespread in the garment industry during the first half of the twentieth century, and organized-crime figures worked for both labor and management. Among the best-known were Benjamin "Dopey Benny" Fein, Jacob "Little Augie" Orgen, Arnold Rothstein, Louis "Lepke" Buchalter, and Jacob "Gurrah" Shapiro. Neither the special prosecutor Thomas E. Dewey during the 1930s nor other prosecutors in later years were able to eliminate the criminal element.

In addition to enjoying a ready pool of immigrant workers, the garment industry in

Garment workers' strike, 1912

New York City benefited from the proximity of textile mills in Massachusetts, New Jersey, and upstate New York. The industry prospered and moved uptown, following the growth of the city and new transportation patterns; gradually a new garment center took shape on the West Side, extending north from 34th to 40th streets and west from 6th to 9th avenues. Apparel manufacturers moved into buildings with showrooms. In the 1920s women began wearing dresses rather than skirts and blouses, a change that increased the importance of merchandising and gave rise to the jobber, who designed garments to be manufactured under contract and later sold them to retailers. In the knit outerwear trade jobbers were sometimes called converters, a term that in the industry as a whole usually referred to those who arranged to obtain raw fabric for conversion into finished products. Apparel firms also depended on credit, especially to produce seasonal lines; among the more important lenders were factors, or "textile bankers," who used accounts receivable as security to finance manufacturing. Although merchandise continued to be sold in Manhattan, the availability of highways and trucks made it feasible to move production to cheaper locations such as Brooklyn, New Jersey, and Connecticut, all beyond the reach of unions such as the ILGWU (which waged highly successful organizing campaigns in the 1930s). The city's share of the nation's employment in women's apparel declined from 62 percent in 1914 to 41 percent in 1939. The federal government banned industrial homework in 1942.

After the Second World War new production sites were set up across the United States, in the South, Southwest, and West. Unskilled labor in these areas manufactured low- and medium-priced garments and new lines of casual wear. Easy-care finishes and improved cotton fabrics revolutionized the industry. Garment firms consolidated, making the small firm an anachronism. From the 1950s the quest for cheap labor moved much garment production to Hong Kong, South Korea, Taiwan, mainland China, and Japan (which itself eventually became too costly), and later Africa, eastern Europe, and Latin America. Meanwhile Jews and Italians in the industry were displaced by blacks and Latin Americans, primarily Puerto Ricans. After the Immigration Act of 1965 ended quotas based on national origin, the apparel trade attracted large numbers of Dominicans and Chinese: manufacturing expanded greatly in Chinatown, and by 1985 more than 16 percent of the city's garment workers were Chinese.

A large pool of exploitable, undocumented immigrants, stiff competition from imports, and lax enforcement of labor standards because of budget cuts brought about a return of the sweatshop in the 1970s and 1980s. In 1984 the U.S. Department of Labor rescinded its ban on homework in six of the nation's seven apparel-related industries. Women's clothing was the exception. In 1987 there were an estimated three thousand sweatshops and thirty thousand home apparel workers in New York State. By 1990 low-priced imports controlled 60 percent of the domestic market. Although apparel remained a leading manufacturing industry in New York City, in 1993 it employed only 86,000 workers, 53,600 fewer than in 1980.

The Garment Industry Development Corporation, established in 1984 by labor and management with municipal and state funds, assists garment manufacturers in New York City with marketing, management education, and training programs. It sometimes works in cooperation with the Fashion Institute of Technology, opened in 1944 to train workers and managers. The continued vitality of this enterprise is borne out by the presence in the city of several prominent fashion designers, such as Liz Claiborne, Leslie Fay, Nicole Miller, Calvin Klein, Norma Kamali, and Donna Karan.

Roger D. Waldinger: *Through the Eye of the Needle: Immigrants and Enterprise in New York's Garment Trades* (New York: New York University Press, 1986)

Steven Fraser: *Labor Will Rule: Sidney Hillman and the Rise of American Labor* (New York: Free Press, 1991)

Robert D. Parmet

Garnet, Henry Highland (*b* New Market, Md., 23 Dec 1815; *d* Monrovia, Liberia, 13 Feb 1882). At nine he fled his owner's plantation with his father, mother, and older sister by means of the Underground Railroad. After staying briefly in New Hope, Pennsylvania, the family settled in New York City, where he found work as a cabin attendant aboard a ship. During his absence on a short voyage to Washington in 1829 his sister was captured by slave hunters, and then detained by local authorities and tried as a fugitive slave (she was released after several days). To avoid capture he hid at a friend's home on Long Island, where he remained for two years as an indentured farm laborer. He later studied at African Free School no. 1 on Mulberry Street and at the High School for Colored Youth, and with the encouragement of Theodore S. Wright enrolled with several other students at a school in Canaan, New Hampshire, that sought to become racially integrated. The school building was destroyed by a mob that also fired on Garnet's boardinghouse, and he and his classmates were eventually driven from the town. After completing his education in 1840 at the Oneida Institute in Whitesboro, New York, he became a minister and political activist. At the Negro Convention of 1843 in Buffalo he delivered a speech addressed to slaves in the South, declaring: "Let your motto be resistance! resistance! resistance!" His words were suppressed by delegates committed to "moral suasion," a plan to convert slaveowners to abolitionism through moral argument. Soon the most important and most militant black abolitionist in the city, he was known internationally by 1850, made speeches throughout the northern and western states, and traveled to Europe as a representative of the abolitionist movement. After joining the United Presbyterian Church of Scotland he worked as a missionary to Jamaica from 1852 to 1855 and in 1856 became pastor of the Shiloh Presbyterian Church in New York City, where he eulogized such abolitionist martyrs as John Brown, held anti-slavery meetings, and urged blacks to support the Liberty and Free Soil parties, stressing in his sermons that slavery would not be ended by moral suasion alone. His strong support for the Civil War inspired hundreds of blacks from the city to enlist in the Union Army; he himself recruited blacks for the army and became a chaplain for black troops. At President Abraham Lincoln's invitation he delivered a speech before the U.S. House of Representatives on 22 September 1864, the second anniversary of the Emancipation Proclamation. Garnet returned to Shiloh Presbyterian Church after the war and in 1881 accepted an appointment as the diplomatic minister of the United States to Liberia.

William M. Brewer: "Henry Highland Garnet," *Journal of Negro History* 13 (Jan 1928), 36–52

Thelma Foote

Garth, David (Lawrence) (*b* Brooklyn, 5 March 1930). Political consultant. He worked in television in the late 1950s as a sports reporter and in 1960 worked with Eleanor Roosevelt on Adlai Stevenson's unsuccessful candidacy for the Democratic presidential nomination. In 1965 he was the principal advisor to John V. Lindsay's successful mayoral campaign, in which he used television, radio, and other media to great effect: his techniques in the election are widely regarded as having inaugurated the modern era of political campaigning in New York City. He then became one of the city's most successful and sought-after political media strategists, leading Lindsay's successful reelection campaign (1969) and then the mayoral campaigns of Edward I. Koch (1977, 1981, 1985) and Rudolph W. Giuliani (1989, 1993). He was also the media strategist in Governor Mario M. Cuomo's unsuccessful campaign for a fourth term in 1994. His firm, the Garth Group, is at 505 Park Avenue in Manhattan.

James Bradley

Garvey, Marcus (Mosiah) (*b* St. Ann's Bay, Jamaica, 17 Aug 1887; *d* London, 10 June 1940). Black nationalist. After travel in Central America and a year in England he settled in 1914 in Kingston, Jamaica, where he formed the Universal Negro Improvement Association (UNIA). A devout Catholic and a disciple of Booker T. Washington, he sought to instill black pride through industrial training of the sort offered by the Tuskegee Institute and through Christian missionary work in Africa.

Marcus Garvey at Liberty Hall in Harlem, 1920

He moved to the United States in 1916 and in the following year settled in Harlem, where he formed a branch of the UNIA that proved short-lived; in June he gave a fiery speech at a rally for the Colored Liberty League that gained him prominence. Over the next two years the emphasis of his politics changed from racial accommodation to black pride and Africanism, and the UNIA became a powerful group with hundreds of chapters in the United States and Africa. To finance his movement and encourage black enterprise he formed a shipping firm, the Black Star Line, which launched its flagship, the *Frederick Douglass*, in November 1919 and in 1920 acquired two other ships. In the same year he undertook a plan to have black Americans colonize Africa when he began negotiations with the government of Liberia, and in the following years he sent funds there as well as equipment and engineers. By 1922 the UNIA was foundering, the Black Star Line was mismanaged and soon to be bankrupt, and the Liberian government withdrew its colonization agreement. Garvey was then sent to prison on federal charges of mail fraud that were undeniably motivated by politics. After his release in 1927 he was deported to Jamaica.

Edmund David Cronon: *Black Moses: The Story of Marcus Garvey and the United Negro Improvement Association* (Madison: University of Wisconsin Press, 1955)

Greg Robinson

Gashouse District. Neighborhood on the East Side of Manhattan, bounded to the north by 27th Street, to the east by the East River, to the south by 14th Street, and to the west by Park Avenue South. A number of gas tanks were built near the East River in 1842; they became leaky and emitted a foul stench that pervaded the area, which was initially populated mostly by poor Irish workers. A group of young toughs known as the Gashouse Gang terrorized the neighborhood until order was imposed by a police officer known as Clubber Williams. Germans and Jews moved in after the Civil War, Italians during the late nineteenth century. The popular culture of the district and the sashaying antics of its young women inspired Stafford Water's tremendously popular song *The Belle of Avenoo A* (1895). Several hospitals were built in the area: the Lying-In Hospital for indigent women (1822; later converted into luxury housing but maintaining a small museum), Columbus Hospital on 19th Street (1892; initially patronized by Italian immigrants and now known as the Cabrini Medical Center), Willard Parker Hospital for Contagious Diseases, the New York Post Graduate Medical School and Hospital, and the New York Skin and Cancer Hospital. Most of these facilities were later replaced by the Beth Israel Hospital complex. During and after the First World War Slovaks moved to the neighborhood, which was considered part of the Lower East Side. Most residents lived in "old law" tenements; public baths on 23rd Street and Avenue A were the only bathing facilities for many. There were some new buildings and older ones were renovated. Lodging sponsored by the city for homeless men stood on 25th Street, and the first building of the American Society for the Prevention of Cruelty to Animals opened on 24th Street. The northern end of the neighborhood was the site of the largest enclave of Armenians in the city. Some gas tanks remained in operation until after the Second World War. After 1947 the tenements along the streets east of 1st Avenue, along with the remaining gashouses, were replaced by Stuyvesant Town and Peter Cooper Village. The working-class character of the neighborhood disappeared as the housing was renovated for wealthy tenants during the 1970s and 1980s. The northern section of the area became largely Indian in the late 1980s.

WPAG

Herbert Asbury: *The Gangs of New York* (New York: Alfred A. Knopf, 1928)

Edward K. Spann: *The New Metropolis: New York City, 1840–1857* (New York: Columbia University Press, 1981)

Harriet Davis-Kram

Gates, Frederick Taylor (*b* Maine, N.Y., 2 July 1853; *d* Phoenix, 6 Feb 1929). Philanthropic administrator and businessman. As the administrator of John D. Rockefeller's philanthropic endeavors he helped to advance medical research and strengthen colleges of medicine in the United States during the opening decades of the twentieth century. He envisioned, planned, and organized the Rockefeller Institute for Medical Research, and was president of the board of trustees from 1901 until his death. Gates was also the chairman of the General Education Board of the Rockefeller Foundation (1905–12) and director of the foundation (1907–17).

Raymond B. Fosdick: *Adventure in Giving: The Story of the General Education Board, a Foundation Established by John D. Rockefeller* (New York: Harper and Row, 1962)

Allen J. Share

Gates, Horatio (*b* Essex, England, 26 July 1727; *d* New York City, 10 Jan 1806). General. After serving as an officer in the British army for twenty-five years he found his prospects for advancement hindered and moved to Virginia in 1772. Asked by George Washington to serve as an officer in the Continental Army at the outbreak of the American Revolution, he was the commanding officer at the Battle of Saratoga in upstate New York. There his stunning defeat of ten thousand British troops under the command of General John Burgoyne marked the turning point in the war and made him a national hero; some members of the Continental Congress wanted him to succeed Washington as the head of the entire American army. In 1790 he moved to New York City from his estate in Virginia and married the daughter of a wealthy merchant. He lived on an estate of ninety acres (thirty-six hectares) with a house at what is now 24th Street and 2nd Avenue. At the end of the 1790s he opposed the Federalist hold on local politics, and in 1800 he won a seat in the state assembly as a Democratic Republican with the backing of the Tammany Society. Gates is buried in an unmarked grave at Trinity Church.

James S. Kaplan

Gates, John Warne (*b* near Turner Junction, Ill., 8 May 1855; *d* Paris, 9 Aug 1911). Financier and speculator. In the 1880s he made a fortune in the manufacture of barbed wire, and through various mergers he formed the American Steel and Wire Company (later Republic Steel), which was eventually sold to J. P. Morgan and the U.S. Steel Trust. Known to New Yorkers as "Bet a Million" Gates, he won and lost millions of dollars in the stock market and the commodity exchanges. In these financial ventures he generally attempted to rig deals in his own favor but did not always succeed. He also wagered thousands of dollars on horse races and card games, and in casinos; purportedly he once bet on which raindrop would be the first to trickle down a windowpane. When in New York City Gates lived in a lavish suite at the Waldorf–Astoria.

George A. Thompson, Jr.

Gateway National Recreation Area. Recreation area created in 1972 under the auspices of the National Park Service, and one of the first areas of its kind designated in a large metropolitan region. It is constituted of 26,000 acres (10,530 hectares) distributed among three units: Jamaica Bay and Breezy Point in southeastern Brooklyn and southern Queens (to the edge of Kennedy Airport), the shoreline of eastern Staten Island, and Sandy Hook in New Jersey. In its eastern section lies the Jamaica Bay Wildlife Refuge, accessible by Cross Bay Boulevard. Opened in 1953 by Robert Moses and Herbert Johnson, the recreation area attracts more than three hundred species of nesting and migrating birds to 9155 acres (3708 hectares) of protected wetlands; the site also sustains a butterfly garden. In Brooklyn the area includes Floyd Bennett Field, the first municipal airfield in the city; in Breezy Point, south of Jamaica Bay across Rockaway Inlet, are Fort Tilden, the Rockaway Naval Air Station, and the playing fields and oceanfront beach of Jacob Riis Park. The section of the recreation area in Staten Island overlooks Lower New York and Raritan bays and encompasses Great Kills Park (originally an Algonquin site, now a recreational fishing area), Crookes Point (a habitat for plants and small animals), and Miller Field (formerly a hydroplane airport for the U.S. Air Corps). At Sandy Hook are Fort Hancock and the oldest operating lighthouse in the United States (originally built to protect the outer harbor and regulate the shipping lanes), as well as ocean dunes and a rare holly forest. Programs in historical and environmental education are conducted throughout the recreation area.

Rachel Shor

Gay Men's Health Crisis. Social service organization devoted to assisting AIDS patients. It was formed in 1982 by the writer Larry Kramer as an offshoot of an AIDS research group that he directed. The organization provides social services and legal assistance to those infected with AIDS and human immunodeficiency virus (HIV). It also offers information on issues surrounding AIDS, such as the rights of racial minorities and drug abuse.

David F. Musto

Gaynor, John P(lant) (*b* Ireland, 1826; *d* San Francisco, 1889). Architect. He moved to the United States in 1849, opened an office in Brooklyn in 1851, and established himself as a designer of commercial buildings with cast-iron façades in New York City in 1856–62. The best-known of these, for the retailer E. V. Haughwout, was erected at 490 Broadway in 1856. Like the Halsey Building (1856, demolished) on Fulton Street in downtown Brooklyn, it was patterned after Andrea Sansovino's library in Venice. The iron components of Haughwout's and Halsey's buildings were cast by Daniel Badger's Architectural Iron Works and illustrated in its catalogue.

Marjorie Pearson

Gaynor, William J(ay) (*b* Oriskany, N.Y., 2 Feb 1848; *d* on shipboard, 12 Sept 1913). Mayor and judge. Born to farmers of English and Irish ancestry, he was educated in Catholic schools and in 1873 settled in Brooklyn, where he worked as a journalist before becoming a lawyer and entering public affairs. Known as a reformer, he won election as a justice of the state supreme court in 1893 and reelection in 1907. During his terms he made contributions to libel and slander law and won respect for his protection of individual rights. In 1909 he won the Democratic mayoral nomination with the support of Charles F. Murphy, the boss of Tammany Hall, in response to citywide calls for reform. After winning a three-way election he formed a moderately progressive government. Soon after gaining office he appointed a number of officials without connections to Tammany Hall, eliminated useless and "no-show" positions, and instituted other fiscal reforms. After barely escaping from an assassination attempt in August 1910 he became irascible and engaged in serious feuds; the rest of his term was marked by corruption in the police department and unsuccessful efforts to obtain a new city charter and win municipal ownership of the subways. Denied renomination by Tammany Hall in 1913, Gaynor declared his candidacy for reelection with support from reform groups but soon fell ill and died. He is remembered as one of the city's most independent mayors.

Mortimer B. Smith: *William Jay Gaynor: Mayor of New York* (Chicago: Henry Regnery, 1951)
Lately Thomas: *The Mayor Who Mastered New York: The Life and Opinions of William J. Gaynor* (New York: William Morrow, 1969)

Robert F. Wesser

Gay Rights Bill. A bill amending the city's Human Rights Law that prohibits discrimination in housing, employment, and public accommodations on the basis of sexual orientation. A similar bill introduced before the City Council on 6 January 1971 by Councilmen Carter Burden and Eldon Clingan was the first of its kind proposed in the United States. Before its eventual passage the bill was defeated in committee every year except 1974, when it became the first bill in the history of the City Council to pass out of committee and be defeated by a full vote of the council. The measure was reintroduced each year before being passed on 20 March 1986 by a vote of 21 to 15; it was signed into law on 2 April by Mayor Edward I. Koch.

Lee Hudson, Joan Nestle

gays. Because of its size and the volume of traffic in its port, New York City in the late nineteenth century provided a degree of anonymity that allowed a gay subculture to develop, chiefly within a large population of transient, unmarried men who often lived in unsupervised rooming houses and maintained few ties to their families. By the 1890s gay life was centered on the Bowery, the city's largest working-class entertainment district; several saloons and dance halls popular among gays there were called "degenerate resorts." By the 1920s there were a number of gay enclaves. The best-known was in Greenwich Village, where speakeasies and tearooms attracted gays from Brooklyn, the Bronx, Queens, and Staten Island and from the rural United States, as well as heterosexuals wishing to observe gay culture. Among the most popular gathering places in the mid 1920s were Paul and Joe's restaurant on 6th Avenue and the Black Rabbit, a speakeasy on MacDougal Street run by Eva Kotchever, a lesbian from Poland; these closed after attacks by neighbors and the police.

Harlem was also an important center of gay life, especially during Prohibition. Such clubs as Smalls' Paradise and the Clam House were popular, as were smaller speakeasies unknown to heterosexuals. Gay black social clubs organized the city's largest drag (transvestite) balls, some of them held in the Savoy Ballroom and the Rockland Palace. Several figures of the Harlem Renaissance were prominent in the community. There was also an enclave in Times Square, little known by heterosexuals, where gay theater workers met in tearooms, restaurants, and streets, and by the time of the Second World War the men's bar at the Astor Hotel (Broadway and 47th Street) was known nationally by gay sailors as a place to meet civilians while passing through the city. Many composers, poets, and playwrights drawn to the city by its cultural offerings became central figures in the gay world.

During the war men on their way to Europe discovered gay culture in New York City, and afterward many returned to the city to settle. Gay bars were opened, and enclaves formed on the East Side and West Side and in Brooklyn Heights and Jackson Heights; an especially large one developed along the 3rd Avenue elevated line, near the "bird circuit," a strip of bars that included the Golden Pheasant and the White Swan. As gays became more numerous and visible they also came under more frequent attack by political leaders and the police: during the decade after the war thousands of men were arrested on homosexual charges each year, and most gay bars remained in operation only a short time before being closed by the police or the state liquor authority, which prohibited bars and restaurants from serving homosexuals. Resistance to such measures was organized by a few gays and lesbians during the 1950s. A local chapter of the Mattachine Society formed in 1955 was the largest gay-rights organization in the United States by 1960. Under the leadership of Dick Leitsch, its president from 1965, the group adopted a militant stance: it defended men who had been arrested on morals charges by maintaining that they had been entrapped, and protested against the policing of gay bars. With the support of favorable court rulings, the group achieved considerable success by 1967.

Gay bars continued nonetheless to be raided by the police. After a riot broke out in June 1969 when patrons and passers-by resisted a raid on the Stonewall Inn on Christopher

Street, the Gay Liberation Front was organized by young activists. The group was soon superseded by the Gay Activists Alliance and Radicalesbians, which led demonstrations against Mayor John V. Lindsay and institutions considered hostile to gays, including the American Psychological Association (which classified homosexuality as a psychological disorder). The Lambda Legal Defense Fund and the National Gay Task Force were formed in 1973 in New York City to promote gay rights and became prominent nationwide. Groups in the city fought for a municipal gay-rights bill to protect against discrimination in housing and employment; bills were introduced annually from 1971 but one was not passed until 1986. Gay institutions prospered during the 1970s as the threat of police harassment diminished. Bars, discothèques, and bathhouses increased in number and were operated openly, and choruses, athletic leagues, political associations, theater companies, and other organizations were formed. The gay press also flourished in the 1970s and 1980s: periodicals issued in the city included *Come Out!* (1969), *Christopher Street* (1976), and *New York Native*. The New York City Lesbian and Gay Community Services Center, opened in a renovated school building on West 13th Street in 1984, provided offices for several major organizations and meeting facilities for more than two hundred others.

During these years the gay community was ravaged by Acquired Immune Deficiency Syndrome (AIDS), a lethal illness identified in the early 1980s. At first most victims were gay men and the disease was largely ignored, but as the number of deaths rose the country panicked. In response to discrimination against people with AIDS, gays turned increasingly to activism. When the city was slow to allocate funds for such services as AIDS education, a group of men that included the playwright Larry Kramer formed the Gay Men's Health Crisis (GMHC) in 1981 to press for more government services, support men stricken by the disease, and distribute condoms and educational materials in bars. The crisis exacerbated violence against gays, whom many blamed for the epidemic. In response to several vicious attacks in 1980 the New York City Gay and Lesbian Anti-Violence Project was formed by a group in Chelsea. Under the leadership of David Wertheimer (1985–89) it expanded its staff, organized programs to help the police and social workers respond to assaults against gays, and made "queer bashing" a public issue for the first time. At the same time older organizations including the Lambda Legal Defense Fund grew rapidly. Virulent attacks by the press (particularly the *New York Post*) on gays and people with AIDS in the mid 1980s led to the formation of the Gay and Lesbian Alliance against Defamation (GLAAD) in 1985.

The AIDS crisis, the conservative policies of President Ronald Reagan, and the decision of the U.S. Supreme Court to uphold antisodomy laws in *Hardwick v. Bowers* (1986) inspired increased activism and widespread support for organizations devoted to AIDS and gay issues. After the Gay Rights Bill was passed gays demanded rights commensurate with those accorded to heterosexuals, including joint health insurance, visitation rights, and housing rights. Although the rate of infection with AIDS decreased in the late 1980s as gays became educated about preventive measures, the disease continued to ravage the community: ten thousand New Yorkers had died of it by 1987 and twenty thousand by 1991. The crisis led to a resurgence of militant gay organizations, among them the AIDS Coalition to Unleash Power (ACT-UP), formed by Kramer in 1987, and several of its offshoots, such as Queer Nation, which organized "kiss-ins" and "queer nights" at clubs frequented by heterosexuals, led marches on the homes of accused gay bashers, and distributed militant gay literature throughout the city.

A few successes were achieved in the early 1990s. The New York State Court of Appeals ruled in *Braschi v. Stahl Associates* (1989) that the right of succession to a rent-controlled apartment accrued to the longtime partner of a gay man who had died, as it would have to a legal spouse; at the urging of activists the state then extended similar rights regarding rent-stabilized apartments. In 1993 gay couples were granted the right to register with the city as domestic partners, but demands for domestic partnership benefits for municipal employees met with less success. Gay voters played a crucial role in David N. Dinkins's narrow victory in the mayoral election in 1989 and also helped to elect a number of sympathetic judges and other public officials. Deborah Glick, the first openly lesbian state legislator, was elected from a district that included Chelsea and Greenwich Village in 1990, and Tom Duane, a well-known activist, became the first openly gay candidate elected to the City Council in 1991. In the mid 1990s the GHMC was the largest organization of its kind in the country, with a staff of 150, more than two thousand volunteers, a budget of $27.5 million, and a program of services that reached a large population (of which about a quarter was heterosexual).

Eric Garber: "A Spectacle in Color: The Lesbian and Gay Subculture of Jazz Age Harlem," *Hidden from History*, ed. Martin Bauml Duberman et al. (New York: New American Library, 1989)

George Chauncey: *Gay New York: Gender, Urban Culture, and the Makings of the Gay Male World, 1890–1940* (New York: Basic Books, 1994)

See also Lesbians.

George Chauncey Jr.

GE. See General electric.

Geddes, Norman Bel [Geddes, Norman] (*b* Adrian, Mich., 27 April 1893; *d* New York City, 8 May 1958). Designer. After moving to New York City he supervised the design of costumes and scenery for about a hundred productions at the Metropolitan Opera and became known for his innovative stage lighting. About 1927 he focused his efforts on designing vacuum cleaners, yachts, automobiles, and trains; he also received commissions for the Futurama exhibit of General Motors at the World's Fair of 1939–40, the Hayden Planetarium (1935), and about thirty theaters worldwide. Geddes wrote an autobiography, *Horizons* (1932).

Jennifer Davis Roberts: *Norman Bel Geddes: An Exhibition* (Austin: University of Texas, 1979)

James E. Mooney

Gehrig, (Henry) Lou(is) (*b* New York City, 19 June 1903; *d* New York City, 2 June 1941). Baseball player. He was born of German descent at 309 East 94th Street in Yorkville and attended the High School of Commerce and Columbia College. For the New York Yankees he played briefly in 1923 and 1924 and for 2130 consecutive games beginning on 1 June 1925 (a major league record); his durability as a player earned him the nickname the "Iron Horse." His career ended in 1939 when he was found to have an incurable degenerative disease, amyotrophic lateral sclerosis (now often called Lou Gehrig's disease). After a moving speech to his fans at Yankee Stadium on 4 July 1939 he retired from baseball. Later he was appointed to the New York City Parole Commission and served on it during the last months of his life. His last home was at 5204 Delafield Avenue in Fieldston. Gehrig's skill at making extra-base hits rivaled that of his teammate Babe Ruth. Most observers agree that he was the greatest first baseman in the history of baseball. His funeral was at Grace Episcopal Church in Riverdale; he is buried at Kensico Cemetery in Westchester.

Eleanor Gehrig and Joseph Durso: *My Luke and I* (New York: Thomas Y. Crowell, 1976)

Ray Robinson: *Iron Horse* (New York: W. W. Norton, 1990)

Lawrence S. Ritter

Geneen, Harold (Sydney) (*b* Bournemouth, England, 22 Jan 1910). Executive. He moved to the United States in 1911, took American citizenship in 1918, and graduated from New York University (1934). After serving in executive positions at Raytheon, Bell and Howell, and Jones and Laughlin, he became president in 1959 of International Telephone and Telegraph. For the next two decades he oversaw an aggressive policy of diversification that transformed what had been a quiet telecommunications company into a wide-ranging conglomerate: among the firms that it acquired were Avis (automobile rentals), Sheraton Hotels, and Hartford Insurance. One of his most controversial initiatives was an attempted takeover in 1965 of the American Broadcasting Company, which was blocked by the federal government. Geneen retired in 1980.

Robert Schoenberg: *Geneen* (New York: W. W. Norton, 1985)

Owen D. Gutfreund

General Electric. Industrial and financial conglomerate. Initially known as the Edison Electric Light Company, it was formed in 1878 in Menlo Park, New Jersey, by Thomas Edison to support research on incandescent lighting and funded by J. P. Morgan. It opened a power station on Pearl Street in 1882, the first functional one in the country, and enjoyed tremendous success producing lamps and other electrical supplies. In 1892 it ceased to be controlled by Edison, whose bankers arranged a merger with a competitor, the Thomson–Houston Company of Lynn, Massachusetts. Renamed the General Electric Company, the firm became the largest of its kind; its most important rival was the Westinghouse Electric Company. General Electric opened the first industrial research laboratory in the country in 1900 and diversified by developing new products and buying other firms (it eventually made aerospace products and sold real estate). In 1956 it moved its headquarters from Schenectady, New York, to a famous art deco skyscraper at 50th Street and Lexington Avenue that bears its name. The firm maintained its headquarters in New York City until August 1974, when it moved its corporate offices to Fairfield, Connecticut. Under the direction of John F. Welch in the 1980s it concentrated its efforts in technology, services, and manufacturing. In 1986 it bought RCA (including the National Broadcasting Company, the leading television network at the time) and 80 percent of the firm of Kidder, Peabody. In 1991 General Electric was the eighth-largest industrial firm in the world.

Peter A. Coclanis

General Slocum. An excursion vessel that burned on 15 June 1904, resulting in the worst single disaster in the history of New York City and one of the worst in all of maritime history. Named for a Civil War general, the ship was launched in Brooklyn in 1891. Built of wood, she could accommodate 2500 passengers on three open decks. Her coal-fired boilers, built in Hoboken, New Jersey, turned two side paddle-wheels. On the day of the fire she had been chartered to take the congregation of St. Mark's German Lutheran Church on its annual picnic outing to the northern shore of Long Island. The church, on East 6th Street just east of 2nd Avenue, was in the thriving community known as Kleindeutschland, which surrounded Tompkins Square on the Lower East Side. The *General Slocum* departed from the East 3rd Street pier at 9:40 a.m. and began moving up the East River past Blackwell's (now Roosevelt) Island. At about 9:56 a.m. fire was discovered under the door of a forward cabin. Captain William Van Schaick, sixty-eight years old, who in the preceding year had been given an award for safely transporting 35 million passengers, did not learn of the fire for at least seven minutes. By that time the ship had entered the treacherous waters of Hell Gate: because of a strong tide under her stern, a stiff breeze over her bow, and rocks on either side, there was no room to maneuver. Flames enveloped the forward part of the ship, and the half-rotted canvas fire hoses burst under the force of water. Most of the 1331 passengers on board were women and children unable to swim. The captain realized that he would need to beach the vessel to save passengers, but because of the racing current and the rocks below he decided to continue northward for another mile and a half (two and a half kilometers) to North Brother Island.

Although the ship was equipped with more than 2500 life jackets, they proved useless because the canvas had rotted and the cork filler had crumbled. Meanwhile the intense heat kept dozens of nearby vessels from getting sufficiently close to assist. Less than fifteen minutes after smoke was first seen, the *General Slocum* lay a smoldering wreck on North Brother Island, and at least 1021 people were dead. The funerals lasted more than a week, and one of the processions from St. Mark's Church to the Lutheran Cemetery in Queens involved 156 hearses and stretched for almost a mile.

An investigation revealed that the Knickerbocker Steamboat Company, owner of the *General Slocum*, had never replaced the original lifebelts and hoses, and that the first mate had not trained the crew in emergency procedures. The exact cause of the fire was not determined. Captain Van Schaick was convicted of neglect of duty and sentenced to ten years in prison. Pardoned after three and a half years at Sing Sing by President William Howard Taft, he died at the age of ninety. Kleindeutschland did not recover. Partly as a result of the tragedy, its German residents moved uptown to Yorkville on the Upper East Side, Jewish families replaced them, and St. Mark's Church became an Orthodox synagogue. An organization of survivors of the *General Slocum* inaugurated an annual commemoration at the Lutheran Cemetery in Queens.

Kenneth T. Jackson

General Society of Mechanics and Tradesmen. Organization formed in 1785 in New York City by twenty-two artisans to promote the political and financial interests of craftsmen in America. Its members fought for protective tariffs and formed the Mechanics Bank to help meet the credit needs of artisans. It also built a series of impressive meeting halls and established a reputable school and a widely used apprentices' library. To ambitious craftsmen such as Stephen Allen the organization offered opportunities for public service that led to political careers. The General Society of Mechanics and Tradesmen remained active into the 1990s.

Howard Rock

General Theological Seminary. Episcopal seminary at 175 9th Avenue (near 21st Street) in Manhattan, formed by John Henry Hobart, Theodore Dehon, and William White and sponsored by the church's general convention, founded in 1817; it is the oldest

Quadrangle of General Theological Seminary, 1889 (from Harper's Weekly*)*

Front building of General Theological Seminary, 1889 (demolished 1959), from Harper's Weekly

Episcopal seminary in the United States. Classes began with two professors teaching six students at St. Paul's Chapel in the spring of 1819. In 1820 the classes were moved to New Haven, Connecticut, and St. Mark's Library was opened by John Pintard. The first graduation was held in 1822 and the seminary then moved back to New York City.

The first professor of biblical languages at the seminary was Clement Clarke Moore, who taught from 1821 to 1850 and donated the current site, known as Chelsea Square, that became the campus by 1827; the first building, now known as the West Building, was erected in a Gothic Revival style between 1832 and 1836. During the 1830s and 1840s the campus was the American center of the Oxford Movement, which called for the revival of High Anglican traditions. A number of graduates of the seminary formed churches west of the Mississippi River. The seminary received permission to grant degrees in 1869 and conferred the Bachelor of Sacred Theology degree from 1876. Under Eugene Augustus Hoffman, a dean (1879–1902) and major benefactor, it expanded rapidly, adding the quadrangle, most of the grounds, and the library and other buildings, and establishing professorships and endowments. It awarded the doctorate from 1881 and honorary degrees from 1885. By the end of Hoffman's tenure there were nearly 150 students and thirteen full-time faculty members. The Chapel of the Good Shepherd (1885–88), a monument to the Hoffman family, was built in an English collegiate Gothic style with a bell tower 161 feet (fifty meters) tall and bronze doors designed by J. Massey Rhind; it was consecrated by the presiding bishop John Williams on 31 October 1888.

The seminary continued to expand after the turn of the century. In 1926 it introduced a tutorial system to supplement classroom instruction. From the 1950s into the 1990s the average enrollment ranged from 140 to 160. The main front building was added in 1960. Women were admitted as full-time students in the Master of Divinity program in the autumn of 1971. Student marriages during the academic year were allowed from the autumn of 1972; in the same year the faculty issued a statement supporting the ordination of women, the first by an Episcopal seminary in the United States. Over faculty objections the trustees voted in 1978 to sell a Gutenberg Bible donated by Hoffman. After considering several alternatives they voted in 1982 not to move the seminary to a new site, and extensive renovations were undertaken in the 1990s. By the mid 1990s there had been about seven thousand students.

In addition to the three-year Master of Divinity program General Theological Seminary offers a two-year Master of Arts program, the Master of Sacred Theology, and the Doctor of Theology (with a specialty in Anglican studies); it also operates the Center for Christian Spirituality, the Center for Jewish–Christian Studies and Relations, and a summer school. St. Mark's Library has nearly 230,000 volumes (about 2500 are added each year). Its rare-book vault was damaged by fire in September 1993, but the library is still known as the finest theological library in the Episcopal church.

Powel Mills Dawley: *The Story of the General Theological Seminary: A Sesquicentennial History, 1817–1967* (New York: Oxford University Press, 1969)

J. Robert Wright

General Trades' Union. Citywide organization formed in 1833 by delegates from nine trades. It was responsible for a surge of militancy in labor between 1833 and 1836. The union espoused first the moderate criticisms of corrupt, greedy aristocrats by Ely Moore, a politician connected with Tammany Hall, then by 1835 the more pointed attacks of the chairmaker John Commerford on "capital," which by his definition included not only aristocrats but also master artisans. Commerford's views were shared by many journeymen delegates, and even sympathetic small masters were denied membership in the council. Delegates were elected by the many craft unions formed in the mid 1830s, which also set up complex procedures and ad hoc committees to approve and govern strikes, ensure democratic debate and participation, handle grievances, and collect funds. One of the union's achievements was sponsoring parades and lively public celebrations of Independence Day. Despite their record of militancy women craftworkers were not accepted as equals by many members, who hoped that their own efforts against exploitation would allow women to return to domestic life; nonetheless some journeymen pledged support to women on strike. Although the union shared with the Locofoco Democrats a hostility to the Second Bank of the United States, it abstained from formal endorsements and maintained political independence, to avoid the kind of demise suffered by the Working Men's Party in 1829–30. The General Trades' Union reached the height of its influence during a wave of strikes in 1836 but disbanded when the trade union movement was ravaged by the panic of 1837 and the subsequent depression.

John R. Commons et al.: *History of Labour in the United States* (New York: Macmillan, 1918), vol. 1
Walter Hugins: *Jacksonian Democracy and the Working Class: A Study of the New York Workingmen's Movement, 1829–1837* (Stanford, Calif.: Stanford University Press, 1960)
Sean Wilentz: *Chants Democratic: New York City and the Rise of the American Working Class, 1788–1850* (New York: Oxford University Press, 1984)

Iver Bernstein

Genovese murder. A controversial incident that occurred in Kew Gardens in the early morning of 13 March 1964, when Kitty Genovese (*b* 1935), the manager of a bar, was stabbed to death after her repeated screams for help were ignored by thirty-eight witnesses. Winston Moseley, a business machine operator, was convicted of the murder and received the death penalty, which was later commuted to life imprisonment. The case led to many discussions of urban anonymity and of inaction in the face of violent crime.

A. M. Rosenthal: *Thirty-eight Witnesses* (New York: McGraw–Hill, 1964)
Parviz Saney: *Crime and Culture in America: A Comparative Perspective* (Westport, Conn.: Greenwood, 1986)

Robert W. Snyder

geology. The geology of New York City presents an unrivaled picture of the evolutionary processes of the Earth.

1. Features

The Manhattan prong, a narrow projection extending down the east side of the Hudson Valley to the southern tip of Manhattan, dates to the time of the Grenville Orogeny (1000 million B.P.). Most of the rocks of New York

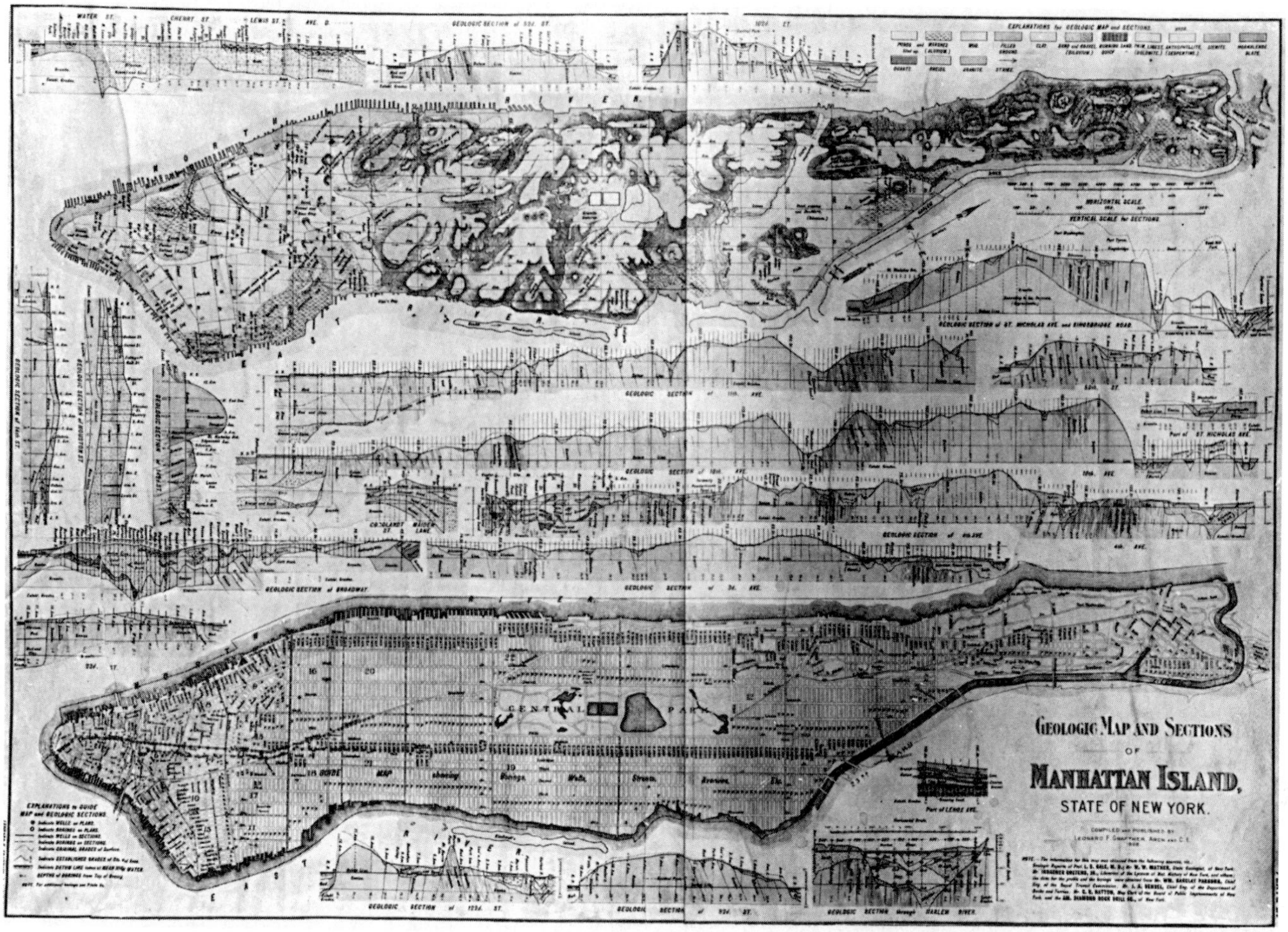

Geological map and sections of Manhattan, 1898

City are generally believed to date from two later mountain-building events, the Taconian Orogeny of the Ordovician period (500 million to 430 million B.P.) and the Acadian Orogeny of the Devonian period (395 million to 345 million B.P.). During these events great compressive force bearing on accumulated sediments caused deep strata of rock to be tilted, folded, and raised; the result in the metropolitan area was a bedrock of igneous and highly metamorphosed rocks that now supports the skyscrapers of Manhattan. Before metamorphosis there was successive accumulation of sedimentary layers of such materials as graywacke sandstone, chert, dolomitic limestone, and sandy shale. Although the original sediments are buried so deep that they are inaccessible, their age could be determined if they were "matched with a recognizable assemblage of rocks from another, nearby locality whose ages are known" (Schuberth).

The topography of New York City results primarily from the different rates of erosion of rock formations that differ in hardness, and secondarily from the effect of the glaciers on what are now Brooklyn and Queens. There remain in New York City three basic formations of rock from the ancestral mountains, arranged in layers overlying the sediments presumed to date from before the Grenville Orogeny, and tilted to the southwest along an axis roughly parallel to Long Island. The oldest formation in the region is Fordham gneiss, named for its prominent distribution in Fordham. It is composed largely of quartz, orthoclase feldspar (in which quartz is found in distinct bands, sometimes with bands of hornblende), and biotite mica. Fordham gneiss is readily recognizable by its light to very dark gray color, displaying folded and distorted bands of foliation planes (layering). It is believed that the gneiss dates from the Precambrian period (more than 1000 million to 570 million B.P.). The second formation is known as Inwood marble, sometimes called Inwood dolomite, for the area at the northern tip of Manhattan where it has many prominent outcrops. It overlies the Fordham gneiss and may therefore be assumed to be a younger formation. Composed primarily of calcium and magnesium carbonate, the marble is almost white and coarsely grained, but prolonged weathering often causes it to disintegrate. Unlike the gneiss it is unfoliated. Before metamorphosis Inwood marble was probably a dolomitic sandstone. Because Inwood marble is much less hard than gneiss it is more vulnerable to erosion and appears only in low-lying areas, its height having been reduced far more quickly; it is visible at ground level in the flat plain of Harlem and as far north as Spuyten Duyvil. The third formation, and the youngest, is the predominant one on Manhattan Island: the ubiquitous mica schist of the Manhattan formation. Light gray in color but weathering to a blackish brown, it is easily recognizable by its tiny, glistening flakes of muscovite mica, as well as widely distributed bands of foliation. It is composed almost entirely of quartz and plagioclase feldspar. Mica schist is highly durable and has long been a favored building material, as may be seen from such structures as the older buildings of City College of New York. Outcrops of the schist are widely distributed in Central Park, along Riverside Drive, at Coogan's Bluff (overlooking the site of the former Polo Grounds), in the Fort George and Fort Tryon ridges, in Inwood Hill Park (where schist and Inwood marble are interlayered with bands of hornblende schist), and along the Cross Bronx Expressway near the Harlem River and Alexander Hamilton Bridge.

Where the Fort George and Fort Tryon ridges merge at about 181st Street to form the Manhattan Ridge, the spine of mica schist continues south, past St. Nicholas Heights to about 125th Street, where it makes a sudden dip under the Manhattan Valley and rises again as Morningside Heights. The ridge then slopes gently down to the surface at 96th Street; on its west side outcrops are evident in Riverside Park as far south as 72nd Street. No further exposures of mica schist occur south of Central Park, although the formation is not far beneath the surface except at Washington Square, where it plunges several hundred feet before rising again near Chambers Street to about forty feet (twelve meters) below the surface; there it provides a solid underpinning for skyscrapers. Above this bedrock is a conglomeration of loose boulders, gravel, sand, clay, soil, and former vegetation called regolith, much of it left behind by the later glaciers.

During the late Paleozoic Period (250 million B.P.) the topography of what is now New York City was undergoing dramatic changes, as the Earth's crust drifted slowly but constantly across the surface of the planet. In the Mesozoic era (225 million to 65 million B.P.) the Atlantic continents drifted together to form a gigantic land mass named Pangaea in 1915 by the German meteorologist Alfred Wegner, who based his theory on the complementarity of the coastlines of the Atlantic continents and the similarity of rock formations on either side of the ocean (to the extent of containing some of the same fossils). When the continents again pulled apart, the Earth's crust was uplifted, while other tectonic plates sank beneath the sea to create deep ocean trenches. The uplifted sediments slowly eroded, and over time were steadily deposited to form the backbone of what are now the shoreline beaches. The beaches of Brooklyn, Queens, and the rest of Long Island well illustrate the deposition of sands and gravel of beaches eroded upland, as well as the effects of wave action and glaciation.

In Van Cortlandt Park in the northern Bronx there is yet another rock formation, the Yonkers granite, an igneous rock that was formed below the surface by intense heat. It intruded into the Fordham gneiss as superhot magma and slowly cooled without being exposed to the atmosphere, until erosion did its work. Resembling gneiss and frequently called granitic gneiss, it is composed of quartz, mica, and a pink feldspar called microcline. Another small formation that intruded into the Fordham gneiss is Ravenswood grandiorite. Of varying shades of gray, it contains quartz, feldspar, and hornblende, with garnets giving it a mottled appearance. It is found in an area of six square miles (15.5 square kilometers) of Ravenswood in northwestern Queens, along the East River.

One of the more unusual rock formations distributed widely on Staten Island is serpentinite, a rock that when exposed to the atmosphere has a reddish-brown hue caused by iron oxide. This colorful rock was much favored by the Indians, who used it to carve the bowls of their pipes. A dramatic light green outcrop of serpentinite, directly across the Hudson from midtown at a bluff called Castle Point on the campus of the Stevens Institute of Technology in Hoboken, was described in 1609 in the journal of Henry Hudson's first mate, Robert Juet, as a "mountain that resembled a silver myne"; there is a small, similar outcrop along 11th Avenue in the West 50s of Manhattan.

Manhattan is marked by a series of faults, which are fractures caused by the movement of one mass of rock against another. The fault lines are easily recognizable as valleys that cut across the ridges of mica schist and form deep depressions or hollows. Examples include a fault at Dyckman Street that bisects the Manhattan Ridge, and another that runs parallel to 155th Street. The most prominent fault is near the Lorillard snuff mill in the New York Botanical Gardens, where the Bronx River once carved its way through the faulted rocks to create a narrow gorge.

The topography of New York City underwent important changes in late geological times, during the Ice Age. Beginning about 1.5 million B.P., during the Pleistocene epoch, the Earth's climate underwent a long period of cooling. The snows that usually melted by spring remained, and as the snow accumulated it turned to ice, growing each year until from its own weight and internal forces it began to move. Gradually the newly formed glaciers covered much of the northern hemisphere. On the North American continent the ice sheet extended across all of Canada and as far south as the lower Midwest, covering northern Pennsylvania and New Jersey and reaching the Atlantic seacoast at what is now New York City. Four ice sheets advanced and retreated during the Pleistocene epoch, each named for the area that marked its farthest point of advance: the Nebraskan, the Kansan, the Illinoian, and the Wisconsin, the most extensive, which moved in a series of brief advances and retreats called secondary fluctuations and for about sixty thousand years imprisoned in its frigid grasp all the area now making up New York City. The Wisconsin had a thickness of two thousand feet (six hundred meters), as great as that of any glacier, and carried with it giant boulders, rocks, gravel, sand, and particles of clay, which it left in a deposit called till. So immense were the powers of the glacier that it deposited huge rocks from the New England Upland on Long Island. In Central Park the force of the glacial advance is evident from the many boulders scattered throughout, some weighing many tens of tons; these boulders, called erratics, remained after the ice withdrew. The action of the glacier also affected the huge outcrops of mica schist, which were gouged by other rocks dragged by the glacial ice and worn smooth by fine particles of sand. Schuberth draws attention to a huge outcrop of mica schist adjacent to the carousel in Central Park: its broad, rounded surface was altered by the grinding effect of the overriding ice mass, giving it a steep, rough "down-glacier," or lee, side, and a smoothly polished and striated "up-glacier," or stoss, side. Other vestiges of the ice sheet are deep, steep-sided indentations called kettles that were formed when enormous chunks of ice broke off from the glacier, became buried by the till, and then melted; occasionally the kettles would fill with runoff or rainwater and become ponds. In Queens many kettles varying in depth from a few feet to more than a hundred are prominent features of Alley Pond Park, Forest Park, and Highland Park.

Of the many remnants of the last Ice Age, about 12,000 to 14,000 B.P., the most visible is the Harbor Hill moraine, a continuous ridge of boulders, gravel, and sand marking the southernmost limit, or terminal, of the advance of the Wisconsin Ice Sheet. It extends the entire length of Long Island, forming a line of prominent bluffs and hilly terrain from Orient Point along the northern shore through Nassau and Queens counties, where the moraine forms the heads of Hempstead Harbor, Manhasset Bay, Little Neck Bay, and Flushing Bay. The moraine derives its name from the highest elevation on Long Island (391 feet, or 120 meters), at Harbor Hill, near Roslyn. The ridge, or terminal moraine, then marks the route of the Grand Central Parkway and passes through Alley Pond, Cunningham, and Forest parks. It forms a very visible escarpment in Highland Park, near the border of Brooklyn and Queens, providing a commanding view of its outwash plain as far as Jamaica Bay, five miles (eight kilometers) to the east. This level stretch of coastal lowland was formed by rushing streams of melting ice pouring forth from the glacier, which deposited a thick layer of stratified and sorted sediments. In Brooklyn the moraine follows Bushwick Avenue, Eastern Parkway, Crown Heights, Prospect Park, Park Slope, and Bay Ridge; near the Verrazano Narrows Bridge it crosses into Staten Island, where it rises 410 feet (127 meters) at Todt Hill, the highest point on the Atlantic coast between Maine and Florida, before crossing into New Jersey and then northern Pennsylvania. One dynamic event caused by the terminal moraine during the Late Pleistocene blocked the Narrows as well as the exit flows of many rivers, causing extensive parts of Manhattan and Queens to be submerged under two new lakes. Lake Hudson, which was situated approximately along the present Hudson River as far north as Haverstraw and may have been joined to Lake Hackensack near Elizabeth, New Jersey, completely inundated the lowland sections of Manhattan Island. Connected to it was Lake Flushing, which engulfed broad areas of northern Queens and Nassau County. According to Schuberth these lakes remained for thousands of years, long enough for about eight feet (two and a half meters) of glacial clay to accumulate in sections of Manhattan Island, where extensive clay deposits now overlay strata of unconsolidated sand and gravel in the Harlem and Inwood lowlands. Peat beds also were deposited in the postglacial sands of lower Manhattan. The postglacial climate created a marshy, swampy environment that supported many varieties of flora and fauna. Among the evidence unearthed by paleontologists are the trunks of several common juniper trees from the late Pleistocene epoch in lower Manhattan, the skeletons of wooly mammoths, giant bison, saber-tooth tigers, hairy tapirs, a ground sloth, a giant mastodon, and a prehistoric horse (discovered in 1926 during excavations for the Independent subway at 134th Street and St. Nicholas Avenue), and human remains and artifacts radiocarbon-dated to 3690 B.P.

In the postglacial period the North Atlantic coastline became tilted downward, with the shoreline southeast of New York City uplifting and the shoreline northeast subsiding. As a result the sea submerged the valleys of many coastal rivers, which became known as drowned valleys; among these were the valleys of the Delaware, the Connecticut, and the Hudson, which once extended eastward into the Atlantic Ocean, 120 miles (193 kilometers) to the edge of the Continental Shelf. The Hudson, a fjord or estuary rather than a river, remains tidal as far as Troy, 140 miles (225 kilometers) north of New York City. As a result of the glaciers many of the city's other waterways are also estuaries, including the East River, the Harlem River, Spuyten Duyvil, the Kill van Kull, and the Arthur Kill, as is Long Island Sound, which was once a river flowing easterly.

The many miles of shoreline in New York City are continually altered by the ocean, in a recurring cycle of erosion and deposition. Because the downward slope of the coastal plain is quite gradual, the sands build up quickly to form an underwater bar parallel to the shoreline. Over time the bar rises above the surface, forming a barrier beach or barrier island. Behind this barrier the trapped seawater becomes a lagoon, which water flows into and out of through tidal inlets. An example of such a lagoon is Jamaica Bay, which over the years became for the most part a saltwater marsh that is now a refuge for sea birds. The bay contains a number of marshy islands called hassocks, formed by the build-up of sand, and its tides are governed by Rockaway Inlet; Rockaway Peninsula and Atlantic Beach nearby are barrier beaches developed over many years.

Annual weather cycles strongly affect the build-up and erosion of the barrier beaches. Violent winter storms and occasional autumn hurricanes attack the shore and erode the beach, interrupting the normal cycle in which beach sands are deposited and washed away, and at times even breaching the barrier beaches and carving new tidal inlets into the lagoon. Because the line of breakers runs from northeast to southwest and therefore approaches the beach obliquely, sand picked up by the backwash of the surf is moved southwest when it is redeposited. This action, called beach drifting, accounts for the yearly movement of hundreds of thousands of cubic yards of sand toward the western end of each barrier beach, and has been only partially stemmed by the construction of huge rock jetties along the Rockaway and Coney Island beaches.

2. Scholarship

A number of scientific institutions in New York City have made important contributions to the study of geology. Research in geology at Columbia University began in its School of Mines, where the faculty included the noted paleontologist John Strong Newberry. After the department of geology dissociated from the School of Mines, Columbia continued to produce many eminent geologists, including the structural geologist Walter Bucher, the geomorphologists Armand Lobeck and Arthur Strahler, the igneous petrologist S. J. Shand, and Rhodes Fairbridge, widely known for his study of changes in sea level. The Lamont–Doherty Earth Observatory in Palisades, New York, affiliated with Columbia, was important in developing the theory of plate tectonics and assembling distinguished scientists such as Bruce Heezen and Marie Tharp, topographers of the ocean floors; Maurice Ewing, a geophysicist and the director of Lamont during the development of plate tectonics; and Lynn Sykes, a geophysicist and seismologist whose work on transform faults helped to validate the theory of plate tectonics. Another important institution in the city is the American Museum of Natural History, known for its resources in mineralogy, meteoritics, and paleontology. Among those associated with the museum is Niles Eldredge, a paleontologist who with Stephen J. Gould developed the theory of punctuated evolution. The Geological Section of the New York Academy of Science, established in 1827, remains an important forum for professional geologists.

J. G. Broughton, D. W. Fisher, Y. W. Isachsen, and L. V. Rickard: *Geology of New York: A Short Account*, Educational Leaflet no. 20, New York State Museum and Science Service (Albany: State Department of Education / University of the State of New York, 1966)

Christopher J. Schuberth: *The Geology of New York City and Environs* (New York: American Museum of Natural History, 1968)

Geological Highway Map, National Bicentennial Edition, Northeastern Region (Tulsa, Okla.: American Association of Petroleum Geologists, 1976)

Chet Raymo and Maureen E. Raymo: *Written in Stone* (Chester, Conn.: Globe Pequot, 1985)

Bradford D. Van Diver: *Roadside Geology of New York* (Missoula, Mont.: Mountain, 1985)

William L. Neuman: *Geologic Time* (Denver: U.S. Geological Survey / U.S. Government Printing Office, 1991)

Gerard R. Wolfe (§1), *Frank Morrow* (§2)

George, Henry (*b* Philadelphia, 2 Sept 1839; *d* New York City, 29 Oct 1897). Economist and reformer. After leaving school in Philadelphia at fourteen he learned typesetting and moved to San Francisco in 1858, where he worked as a reporter and writer and at times lived in poverty. In his book *Progress and Poverty* (1879) he posited that tragic human deprivation was widespread because a few rich landowners were reaping an ever-increasing profit from the natural bounty of the land, the fruits of human labor, and invested capital, a situation that he believed was contrary to natural law. The book was the most influential American economic treatise of the nineteenth century and made him internationally known. His single-tax movement sought the "abolition of all taxes on industry and the products of industry" and consumers, and the financing of government by a heavy tax on land. At the time the prospect of relying on a land tax alone was not unfeasible: spending by localities and states was already financed overwhelmingly by property taxes, and the system could have been restructured to shift the tax burden from buildings and other man-made assets to land. George also wished to abolish the tariff as an obstacle to free trade. In 1880 he moved to New York City because of its importance in national affairs. A charismatic speaker, he lectured in Ireland, England, Scotland, and Australia, where he championed human freedom and condemned oppressive government, socialism, monopoly, corruption, and the misery caused by industrialization in American cities. His *Protection or Free Trade* (1886) articulated powerfully his view of the benefits of international free trade for human well-being. At the urging of labor leaders he waged an independent campaign for the mayoralty of New York City in 1886. His candidacy was opposed by Tammany Hall and by Catholic leaders (Edward McGlynn, a priest who outspokenly supported him, was directed to remain silent and later excommunicated for disobeying), but he enjoyed considerable support among the Irish, who were impressed by his support of the Irish Land League and of American labor rights. After a bitter campaign during which George's views were often misrepresented, the Democratic candidate Abram S. Hewitt received 90,552 votes, George 68,110, and the Republican candidate Theodore Roosevelt 60,435 in what is often considered the most dramatic mayoral election of the nineteenth century in New York City. Although George's followers believed that the election was rigged, fraud could not have accounted for the large differences in the votes tallied.

In 1887 George launched a weekly newspaper called the *Standard* (published at 25 Ann Street) and with several labor unions formed the United Labor Party. After abandoning plans to build a national labor party he helped to form local clubs in support of the single-tax movement. During the presidential campaigns of 1884, 1888, and 1892 he supported Democratic candidates and had some success in spreading his views about the benefits of free trade. He also advocated that churches take a more active role in reducing poverty. Although his health was poor and his book *The Science of Political Economy* unfinished, in 1897 he agreed again to seek the mayoralty of New York City. The campaign proved exhausting, and he died four days before the election; the funeral procession was the longest since that of Abraham Lincoln. Most academic economists of George's day disagreed with him and he spoke disparagingly of them, but in the late twentieth century there was a renewed interest among economists in his views. George lived at 231 East 18th Street (from November 1882), 143 West 14th Street (January to July 1883), 70 Hancock Street in Brooklyn (from July 1883), 8 East 10th Street (from May 1884), 267 Macon Street in Brooklyn (from 14 September 1884), 392 Pleasant Avenue, between 120th and 121st streets (from 10 May 1886), and 323 East 19th Street (from 1887), and maintained an office at 16 Astor Place (from May 1886).

Charles A. Barker: *Henry George* (New York: Oxford University Press, 1955)

Jacob Oser: *Henry George* (Boston: Twayne, 1974)

C. Lowell Harriss

Georgetown. Neighborhood in southeastern Brooklyn, lying north of Mill Basin and bounded to the north by Avenue K and Bergen Avenue, to the east and south by Avenue N, and to the west by Ralph Avenue. It was developed in the mid 1960s as Georgetowne Greens, a suburban community with a shopping center and other amenities. Initially it covered a large tract of landfill at Ralph Avenue and Avenue L; the streets were paved and had curbs and sidewalks, and the housing consisted of two-family houses with brick fronts standing on large landscaped lots with driveways. Developers lost interest in the venture after the administration of Mayor John V. Lindsay proposed to build Harborville, a Mitchell–Lama housing project of nine hundred units on an adjacent lot of thirty-two acres (thirteen hectares) owned by the city. The proposal was defeated after intense local protest but nonetheless forestalled further development of Georgetowne Greens, where the existing houses were sold. Developers bought the remaining land and built attached and semidetached three- and four-family houses. The neighborhood is middle class and most of the population is Italian and Jewish. The main commercial district is the Georgetown Shopping Center on Ralph Avenue between avenues K and L.

Elizabeth Reich Rawson

George Washington Bridge. Steel cable, double-decked bridge spanning the Hudson River between 179th Street in Manhattan and Fort Lee, New Jersey. Designed by Othmar H. Ammann and built and operated by the Port of New York Authority, it opened in 1931 as the longest suspension bridge in the world. Ammann intended for its two towers to be sheathed in granite according to plans drawn up by the architect Cass Gilbert, but with the onset of the Depression he decided to leave the steelwork of the towers exposed. The graceful silhouette of the George Washington Bridge belies its enormous weight. Designed to carry light rail and vehicular traffic, the bridge has a main span of 3500 feet (1068 meters); it contains 113,000 tons (102,500 metric tons) of steel, 28,000 tons (26,300 metric tons) of cable wire, and 200,000 cubic yards (153,900 cubic meters) of masonry. The deck of the bridge is suspended 212 feet (64.6 meters) above the Hudson River from four cables, each four feet (1.2 meters) in diameter; the cables are strung through the tops of the towers and fastened to huge anchorages in Fort Washington Park in New York City and the Palisades in New Jersey. The lower level of the bridge, also designed by Ammann, was added in 1962 to accommodate the rise in traffic across the Hudson. The George Washington Bridge provides access between Long Island, New England, Westchester County, and points beyond and is the only bridge across the Hudson in New York City. Le Corbusier described the bridge as the most beautiful in the world.

WPAG

Carl W. Condit: *American Building: Materials and Techniques from the First Colonial Settlements to the Present* (Chicago: University of Chicago Press, 1968)

David P. Billington: *The Tower and the Bridge: The New Art of Structural Engineering* (New York: Basic Books, 1983)

Rebecca Read Shanor

George Washington Bridge Bus Station. Bus station at Broadway and 178th Street in Manhattan, opened in January 1963 by the Port of New York Authority to replace several small terminals near 168th Street and Broadway. Its construction coincided with the addition of a lower deck on the George Washington Bridge and of several new expressway connections to the bridge, to which the station is connected by ramps. The station is used primarily by commuters from Bergen, Passaic, and Rockland counties, but it is not convenient to most commuters who work in midtown and lower Manhattan and has never been as popular as the Port Authority Bus Terminal. In 1990 about 4.8 million passengers used the facility, which was the point of departure or arrival for 222,000 bus trips.

Andrew Sparberg

German American Bund. Anti-Semitic organization that flourished between 1936 and 1939 with about eight to ten thousand members, most of them immigrants. It distributed anti-Semitic tracts, held rallies and parliamentary exercises throughout the Northeast, and opened a compound, Camp Nordland, in Sussex County, New Jersey. Its leader, Fritz Kuhn (1896–1951), was a devotee of Hitler who encouraged German–Americans to protect themselves against the sort of discrimination they had experienced during the First World War by embracing anti-Semitism,

George Washington Bridge, ca *1937*

German ethnic supremacy, and American patriotism. The efforts of the group were endorsed by the foreign office of the German government until they threatened diplomatic relations with the United States. Investigations by government officials led the city commissioner to issue subpoenas in 1939 to the entire membership, including Kuhn and all known local leaders, as well as two tailors who had supplied the group's military uniforms. The German American Bund ceased operations after Kuhn was imprisoned for embezzlement and its headquarters in New York City were shut down by the federal government on 16 December 1941.

Glen Jeansonne: "America's Nazis: A Democratic Dilemma: A History of the German American Bund," *Journal of Southern History* 58 (1992), 172

Jacqueline Lalley

German Assembly Rooms. A building complex that housed saloons, bowling alleys, and assembly rooms in Manhattan, at 291–93 Bowery. It began as the Steuben House in the 1850s and by the late 1860s was a popular meeting place for German unions and other organizations. For the rest of the century the complex continued to operate as a social center and as a venue for meetings and balls with several thousand participants. Bowling alleys were still in existence in the basement during the mid 1990s.

Stanley Nadel

Germania Life Insurance Company. Original name of the GUARDIAN LIFE INSURANCE COMPANY.

Germans. German immigrants were present in New Amsterdam during its earliest years of settlement. Peter Minuit, who established the colony in 1626, was himself a native of the German town of Wesel am Rhein. Among those who followed him were Johann Ernst Gutwasser, the settlement's first Lutheran minister (1656–59), and the merchant Jacob Leisler, who arrived in 1660. In 1710 about 150 of the nearly 2150 Palatine Germans who fled to America during the War of the Spanish Succession settled in the city; one of those who stayed was the young John Peter Zenger, who later became well known as a printer and publisher. By the time of the census of 1790 Germans numbered about 2500, and there were two German Lutheran churches as well as a German Reformed church, a Moravian church, and a German Society. The first German neighborhood and commercial center in New York City took shape during the 1820s southeast of City Hall, in the area extending from Pearl Street to Pine Street.

By 1840 more than 24,000 Germans lived in the city, and in the following twenty years the mass transatlantic migration brought another hundred thousand Germans fleeing land shortages, unemployment, famine, and political and religious oppression (more than one million other Germans passed through the city). To accommodate this growth a new and much larger German neighborhood developed in the 1840s east of the Bowery and north of Division Street in the tenth and seventeenth wards. It extended to within sight of the East River along Avenue D in the eleventh ward and reached the river in the thirteenth. Known variously as Kleindeutschland, Dutchtown, Little Germany, and Deutschlandle, the neighborhood was the major German–American center in the United States for the rest of the century, with more than a third of the city's German–American residents. Other German–American neighborhoods took form directly across the East River in Williamsburg (connected to Kleindeutschland by ferries at Houston Street and Grand Street) and across the Hudson in Hoboken, New Jersey. In 1860 Germans in New York City numbered more than two hundred thousand, accounting for one quarter of the city's total population, and made up the first large immigrant community in American history that spoke a foreign language. Natural increase and the arrival of seventy thousand immigrants who were politically and economically dislocated by the coalescing German Empire expanded the city's German population to more than 370,000 by 1880 (about one third of the city's total). New German settlements were established in Yorkville around 3rd Avenue and 86th Street and across the East River in Queens, where Steinway and Sons built a piano factory and company town in the 1870s. The southern part of Kleindeutschland, which had older buildings and was more crowded, was abandoned to more recent Jewish immigrants from central Europe by the 1880s and became known as the Lower East Side.

Germans were more religiously diverse than most immigrant groups. The early German settlers, who were predominately Calvinists, were later joined by Lutherans and in the nineteenth century by Catholics from southwestern Germany. Catholics and Jews formed their own subcommunities within the city's German neighborhoods. Adherents of free thought, an outgrowth of the German Enlightenment, ranged from crusading atheists to members of small congregations with beliefs similar to those of Unitarians; freethinkers had their own churches, Sunday schools, "anti-revivals," and holidays, and were well known for the social events they organized for nonreligious Germans in New York City. Germans were also active in the New York Society for Ethical Culture, formed in 1876 by Felix Adler, which continued the German tradition of free thought into the 1990s. Religious intolerance was strong among the city's German Protestants during the 1840s and 1850s, when some of them joined American nativist movements that agitated against immigrants and Catholics. Some German–American Catholics were equally fervent, denouncing Luther and the Protestant "heresy" on the four hundredth anniversary of his birth (1883). The struggle between the German Reformation and Counter-Reformation was however less intense in New York City than in Germany, because of the secularism of the city's artisans, intellectuals, and merchants. Many of the more religiously inclined Germans either fled the city for the churches of Brooklyn or headed for more congenial settlements in the Midwest. This secularism also tended to mute anti-Semitism among Germans: although some Germans in Brooklyn attacked a Jewish funeral procession in 1849, other recorded instances of anti-Semitism in New York City were rare until the 1930s. German Jews were in fact integrated into German society on all social levels, from the criminal gangs to the leadership of the German Society, and from the labor movement to the financial élite.

Particularism rather than religion was a source of division. Those who emigrated from the fragmenting German states during the mid nineteenth century often arrived in the city with little sense of belonging to a German nation. Differences in dialect, politics, cuisine, and other aspects of regional culture left many unable to identify with immigrants who were from other parts of Germany. Kleindeutschland was broken up into smaller neighborhoods of Swabians, Bavarians, Hessians, Westphalians, Hanoverians, and Prussians, and immigrants generally married within them. Voluntary associations were often organized around home-town loyalties, sometimes unintentionally but in most cases purposefully (as Landsmannschaften). In 1862 the Swabians held a regional festival known as the Cannstätter Volksfestverein, an event that gave rise to other ethnic institutions such as a weekly newspaper in the Swabian dialect and *Volksfestvereine* organized by Bavarians (1874), Plattdeutschen (1875), and even Liechtensteiners. These regionally based networks promoted ethnic identities that competed with a larger German–American identity well into the 1920s.

Regional ties were the basis of many associations, but they could not account for the multitude of businesses, sickness- and death-benefit societies, social clubs, political organizations, and other groups that formed when Germans banded together. Fraternal orders such as the Freemasons, the Druids, the Independent Order of Odd Fellows, the Foresters, and the Redmen were joined by German–American orders like the Hermannssöhne, the Harugari, the Vereinigte Deutscher Bruder, and B'nai B'rith. By the early 1870s the Harugari alone had sixty-two lodges with almost seven thousand members in the metropolitan area. Among the most conspicuous German associations in New York City were singing societies, which held concerts and sponsored large choral festivals. The Deutscher Liederkranz and the Arion Gesangverein became élite clubs after the Civil War; other German choral groups continued to be identified with middle- and working-class Germans in the city. German musicians predominated in the New York Philharmonic and provided it with most of its directors, including Leopold Damrosch, an early director of the Arion Gesangverein. Damrosch soon founded the Oratorio Society, became the director of the Philharmonic, and rescued the failing Metropolitan Opera by introducing a full season of German repertory. Under the direction of his son Walter Damrosch and the management of Heinrich Conried, the Metropolitan was built into one of the world's great opera companies, with a staple of German operas and a largely German audience. Many of the cultural organizations received support from German businessmen, notably Otto H. Kahn, one of the leading philanthropists of the period.

The large influx of German immigrants to the city led to the establishment of many breweries. George Ehret, a German immigrant who opened the Hell Gate brewery in 1866, was the largest brewer in the United States in 1879; the eighth-largest was Jacob Ruppert, also of New York City. In 1877 Manhattan had seventy-eight breweries and Brooklyn had forty-three. Germans in New York City often congregated at beer halls, beer gardens, saloons, and other places where beer was sold. Some of the halls had stages where German theater was performed, and many had meeting rooms that were used by singing societies, lodges, clubs, unions, and political organizations. The large and often elaborately decorated German beer halls were the pride of the German neighborhoods. When the city grew too hot for indoor entertainment during the summer, many Germans enjoyed picnics and festivals near Hoboken, New Jersey, and at the elaborate beer garden in Jones's Wood. May festivals as well as music, gymnastic, and sharpshooting festivals attracted tens of thousands of celebrants during the mid nineteenth century. The most prominent sponsor was Turngeminde, an organization formed by radical artisans. Strengthened and radicalized by an influx of exiles after the failed revolution of 1848, the group organized the New York Socialist Turnverein to promote physical conditioning, German culture, nationalism, and the abolition of slavery.

In the nineteenth century Germans in New York City formed numerous socialist political associations, including the Workers' League, the Kommunisten Klub, the First International, and the Socialist Labor Party. Germans were also prominent in the labor movement, and under their leadership in 1872 the New York Eight Hour League organized a strike of more than 100,000 workers. Germans later helped to form the American Federation of Labor, in which Adolph Strasser and Samuel Gompers were prominent, and the Knights of Labor. Although thousands of the city's German workers joined radical unions and socialist organizations, in electoral politics they remained firmly in the Democratic Party. German–American politicians like Anton Dugro, Philipp Merkle, and Magnus Gross formed their own organizations within the party, at first allied with Captain Isahia Rynders's faction in support of Mayor Fernando Wood. When Wood fell out with Tammany Hall and set up his own organization, the Germans remained loyal to him and were the key to his electoral victory in 1858. The abolitionist cause did draw some members of the Turnverein and other radicals into the Republican Party in the late 1850s, and a few remained in the party until the end of the century, but an anti-German riot in 1857 by the Metropolitan Police, sponsored by Republicans, weakened German ties to the party.

The undisputed leader of the German Democrats by the early 1860s was Oswald Ottendorfer, owner of the popular German newspaper the *Staats-Zeitung*. During the next thirty years he led a number of coalitions dedicated to reform and opposed to Tammany Hall. His German Democratic Union Party helped to elect Mayor Charles Godfrey Gunther in 1863. After the organization of William M. "Boss" Tweed eclipsed the German Democrats in the late 1860s Ottendorfer formed a German independent citizens' organization to unite German Democrats and Republicans in the campaign against the Tweed Ring in 1871. Although he helped William F. Havemeyer to win the mayoralty in 1872, Ottendorfer was defeated when he himself sought it in 1874 and his German reform party collapsed.

The German population in New York City reached a peak of 748,882 in 1900, partly as a result of consolidation. There were also 133,689 Austrians in the city, most of whom were of German ethnicity. Although many German institutions remained in Kleindeutschland into the early twentieth century, Yorkville surpassed the old neighborhood in importance, and Astoria and New Jersey grew increasingly popular as suburban settlements, especially among the American-born and the prosperous. Deaths among German-born immigrants and the migration of their children to the suburbs reduced the population of German–Americans in New York City to 584,838 by 1920, but the numbers again increased when about 98,500 Germans fled the economic and political disorder of their country between the end of the First World War and 1930.

Despite their relative decline in importance in New York City in the early twentieth century, Germans continued to shape the city's ethnic politics for many years. A local chapter of the National German–American Alliance (1901) was especially influential. The strength of the German–American community in the city was undermined during the First World War as George Sylvester Viereck and other Germans in the city who advocated neutrality were labeled enemy agents and subjected to governmental repression. German-language courses were eliminated from the public schools and German-language works from the Metropolitan Opera; hamburgers became "liberty sandwiches" and sauerkraut became "liberty cabbage." German immigrants sought to restore their sense of ethnic pride in the interwar years, but these efforts were soon disrupted by the Nazi movement and another round of wartime hostility. German–Americans were forced to make their activities less conspicuous; associations still met and Steuben Day parades were still sponsored, but active assertions of German culture and attempts at collective political action were stifled. The Turneverein became a meeting place for American Nazi activists in the 1930s and was affiliated with a front organization of the German American Bund. The close ties among Germans between Jews and Christians was ruptured by an anti-German boycott organized by Jewish war veterans and by an anti-Jewish boycott that followed.

In the mid twentieth century many refugees of the Second World War settled in the metropolitan area, especially in Washington Heights, but they increasingly chose to live outside the city. The end of mass migration and a move to the suburbs of Long Island and New Jersey helped bring about the rapid decline of Yorkville as a German–American center in the 1960s and 1970s, leaving Astoria as the only neighborhood in New York City with an identifiable German presence in the 1980s. A total of 301,993 New Yorkers claimed German or Austrian ancestry in 1990.

Sander A. Diamond: *The Nazi Movement in the United States, 1924–1941* (Ithaca, N.Y.: Cornell University Press, 1974)

Helmut F. Pfanner: *Exile in New York: German and Austrian Writers after 1933* (Detroit: Wayne State University Press, 1983)

Stanley Nadel: *Little Germany: Ethnicity, Religion and Class in New York City, 1845–1880* (Urbana: University of Illinois Press, 1990)

Stanley Nadel

German Society of New York. Immigrant aid society formed in 1784 as a social organization and led by Baron von Steuben in 1785–94. It began to assist German immigrants in the 1830s and from 1843 arranged free medical care, helped to find friends and relatives, and provided employment services; it also published the pamphlet *Ratgeber für Auswanderer* (1833) and fought for equitable immigration laws. The president of the society became a member of the state Board of Commissioners of Emigration in 1847. During the mid 1990s the society continued to provide services for German immigrants.

Stanley Nadel

Gerritsen Beach. Neighborhood in southeastern Brooklyn, lying near Marine Park on a peninsula and bounded to the north by Avenue U, to the east by Gerritsen Avenue, to the south by Plum Beach Channel, and to the west by Shell Bank Creek and Knapp Street; it is bisected from west to east by the Gotham Avenue Canal. The neighborhood was named for Wolfert Gerrittsen, who in the early seventeenth century built a house and mill on Gerritsen Creek (now part of Marine Park); the mill was destroyed by fire about 1931. Until the early twentieth century the area remained undeveloped except for a few squatters' bungalows at the foot of Gerritsen Avenue. The firm of Realty Associates began building a middle-class summer resort there in 1920, and the southwest corner of Gerritsen's Meadow was soon covered by one-story bungalows with peaked roofs and no backyards. The popularity of this first venture spurred further growth. Some bungalows were made suitable for year-round habitation, two-story houses with backyards were built, and within a decade there were fifteen hundred houses. Gerritsen Avenue is the main thoroughfare and the population is mostly of Irish, German, and Italian descent. The area north of the canal, called New Gerritsen by local residents, is lined with stores and brick houses. The area south of the canal retains the character of a small fishing village and is a popular station for party boats. The volunteer fire department, which began operation in 1921 when the population began to grow, has headquarters at 32 Seba Avenue and may be the only remaining organization of its kind in Brooklyn.

"Mulevehill Heads Fire Volunteers," *New York Times*, 1 July 1936

"A Small Town Holds Its Own in Brooklyn," *New York Post*, 3 April 1972

"Gerrittsen Beach Volunteers Keep Lid on Fires in Area," *New York Times*, 15 Oct 1972

Elizabeth Reich Rawson

Gershwin, George [Gershvin, Jacob] (*b* Brooklyn, 26 Sept 1898; *d* Beverly Hills, Calif., 11 July 1937). Composer, brother of Ira Gershwin. He was the son of Jewish immigrants from Russia. Despite only rudimentary training in music he found work at sixteen as a song plugger in Tin Pan Alley and as a rehearsal pianist on Broadway; later he began writing songs for revues. When he was nineteen he wrote his first successful song, "Swanee" (1919) (lyrics by Irving Caesar). His next song, "I'll Build a Staircase to Paradise" (included in George White's *Scandals* of 1922), was his first collaboration with his brother, who wrote the lyrics with Buddy DeSylva. The shows that he then wrote with his brother are notable for their musical inventiveness and sophisticated lyrics: *Lady, Be Good!* (1924), which includes the songs "Fascinating Rhythm" and "Oh, Lady, Be Good"; and *Strike Up the Band* (1930) and *Of Thee I Sing* (1931), with scripts by George S. Kaufman and Morrie Ryskind, and lyrics by Ira Gershwin. He also achieved success with his concert works, among them *Rhapsody in Blue* (1924), commissioned and given its première by Paul Whiteman, *Concerto in F* (1925) for piano and orchestra, *An American in Paris* (1928), and the opera *Porgy and Bess* (1935). Gershwin's reputation rests on his skillful melding of popular and classical genres. He drew on the conventions of European concert music, the Jewish folk tradition, the music of Tin Pan Alley and Broadway, and elements of ragtime, jazz, and blues; his works are marked by syncopated rhythms, chromatic harmonies, and singable melodies. New York City inspired several of his works, including a one-act opera, *121st Street* (1925), and the songs "I'm Something on Avenue A" (1925), "Harlem River Chanty" (1925), "New York Serenade" (1928), "Harlem Serenade" (1929), "New York Rhapsody" (1931), "Union Square" (1933), and "There's a Boat Dat's Leaving Soon for Old New York" (1935).

Edward Jablonski: *George Gershwin* (New York: G. P. Putnam's Sons, 1962)

Robert Kimball and Alfred Simon: *The Gershwins* (New York: Atheneum, 1973)

Charles Schwartz: *Gershwin: His Life and Music* (Indianapolis: Bobbs–Merrill, 1973)

See also CARNEGIE HALL.

Nicholas E. Tawa

Gershwin, Ira [Gershvin, Israel] (*b* New York City, 6 Dec 1896; *d* Beverly Hills, Calif., 17 Aug 1983). Lyricist, brother of George Gershwin. Born at the corner of Hester and Eldridge streets, he attended Townsend Harris High School and City College. His first successful musical was *Lady, Be Good!* (1924), a collaboration with his brother that opened at the Liberty Theatre on 1 December 1924. He wrote lyrics for many other songwriters, among them Harold Arlen ("Let's Take a Walk around the Block," 1934) and Vernon Duke ("I Can't Get Started," included in Florenz Ziegfeld's *Follies* of 1936). With Kurt Weill he collaborated on *Lady in the Dark* (1941), which played for 467 performances at the Alvin Theatre, and on *The Firebrand of Florence* (1945), Weill's only failure on Broadway. He moved to California in 1936 but retained strong ties to New York City and wrote several works set there, including the play *Park Avenue* (1946), as well as lyrics for the film *The Barkleys of Broadway* (1949), with Fred Astaire and Ginger Rogers. Among Gershwin's residences in the city were 91 2nd Avenue (in 1910), 316 West 103rd Street (from 1926), 125 East 72nd Street, and 33 Riverside Drive.

Robert Kimball and Alfred Simon: *The Gershwins* (New York: Atheneum, 1973)

Marc Ferris

Gertz. Firm of retailers. It was formed by Benjamin and Ida Gerts, who from 1911 sold candy and newspapers from a small shop at 162-10 Jamaica Avenue in Jamaica that became successful during the First World War. In the 1920s the Gertses began to sell stationery and desk equipment for offices. They expanded their business into a chain of stores known as B. Gertz and in 1933 built a five-story building on the site of the original store. After Benjamin Gerts's death in 1933 his four sons and a son-in-law took over the business, which grew during the Depression until it was sold in 1941 to the Allied Corporation by the brothers, the last of whom died in 1957. No members of the family took part in operating the seven stores that remained. The one in Jamaica closed in 1981; Gertz was renamed Stern's in the last step of a merger of two divisions of the Allied Stores Corporation on 1 March 1983.

Leslie Gourse

Gibbons v. Ogden. Case decided in 1824 by the U.S. Supreme Court (9 Wheaton 1), which voted unanimously to void a steamship monopoly granted by the state legislature of New York to Republican politicians in 1798. In his ruling Chief Justice John Marshall made state laws subordinate to those passed by the U.S. Congress. The decision interpreted the "commerce clause" in section 8 of article I of the U.S. Constitution, establishing the right of the federal government to regulate navigation and trade, thus enhancing federal power, undercutting the business élite, and providing impetus for the development of the Port of New York.

Maurice G. Baxter: *The Steamboat Monopoly: Gibbons v. Ogden, 1824* (New York: Alfred A. Knopf, 1972)

George J. Lankevich

Gibran, (Gibran) Kahlil [Khalil] (*b* Bcharre, Lebanon, 6 Jan 1883; *d* New York City, 10 April 1931). Poet and painter. He settled in Boston with his mother and siblings in 1895 and moved in 1911 to New York City, where he took up residence in the Studio Building at 51 West 10th Street. In 1914 he had his first exhibition of paintings at the Montross Galleries, and he became known for his portraits of Sarah Bernhardt, William Butler Yeats, and John Masefield. He wrote in both Arabic and English for the city's flourishing Syrian press. In 1920 he joined with ten other Syrian-Lebanese émigré writers to form the literary circle al-Rabitah al-Qalamiyya (the Pen League), which greatly influenced Arabic poetry. His first book was *The Madman: Parables and Poems* (1918); he is best known for *The Prophet* (1923), which in three editions had sold more than 8.5 million copies by 1990. Gibran wrote of love, beauty, and the problems of life with a mystical, philosophic vision that proved immensely appealing. He lived in the Studio Building until his death.

Barbara Young: *This Man from Lebanon: A Study of Kahlil Gibran* (New York: Alfred A. Knopf, 1945)

Kahlil Gibran and Jean Gibran: *Kahlil Gibran: His Life and World* (New York: New York Graphic Society, 1974)

Ashbel Green, Paula Hajar

Gibson, Althea (*b* Silver, Clarendon County, S.C., 25 Aug 1927). Tennis player. She grew up in New York City, learned to play tennis at public courts on 155th Street, and began playing amateur tennis in the 1940s. A leading amateur player between 1950 and 1955, she was the first black player to be generally recognized as a world champion. In 1957 and 1958 she won both the American singles championship at Forest Hills and the English championship at Wimbledon, and played on the team that won the Whiteman Cup. During these years she lived on Central Park West; later she became a professional golfer and moved to East Orange, New Jersey.

Leslie Gourse

Gibson, Charles Dana (*b* Roxbury [now in Boston], 14 Sept 1867; *d* New York City, 23 Dec 1944). Illustrator. He entered the Art Students League at sixteen and studied there for two years. Initially unsuccessful in finding employment, he was engaged by the editor John Ames Mitchell to work for *Life*, for which in 1890 he developed a character known as the "Gibson Girl," a chic young woman representing a late-nineteenth-century ideal of American womanhood; he introduced a companion for her, Mr. Pipp, in 1898. Many of his drawings for the magazine were published in elegant collections, and in 1903 he charged $1000 for each drawing. Gibson had quarters in the Carnegie Studios and was president of the Society of Illustrators.

Charles Dana Gibson's poster for naval recruitment, ca *1916*

Fairfax Davis Downey: *Portrait of an Era as Drawn by C. D. Gibson: A Biography* (New York: Charles Scribner's Sons, 1936)

James E. Mooney

giglio. A tapering, multi-tiered tower, lifted and carried through the streets by about 125 men as part of four related feasts celebrated by Italian Catholics in greater New York. The name is Italian for lily. The feast has its roots in written texts and oral legends about St. Paulinus (354–431), which relate the story of his imprisonment for the sake of the people of Nola in Campania, Italy, and his welcome with lilies when he returned. The giglio is derivative of the gigantic, ephemeral structures paraded in the civic and religious pageants and spectacles of Europe during the Renaissance and the Counter-Reformation. Immigrants from Nola introduced the feast in New York City in 1903 in Williamsburg. The feast in East Harlem to St. Anthony of Padua was begun in 1918 by immigrants from Brusciano, near Nola. Similar ones for St. Paulinus were begun in Astoria and Fairview–Cliffside, New Jersey, in the 1930s. The feast in Harlem was last held in 1971 and later moved to Pelham Bay. The giglio is constructed of brightly painted papier-mâché attached to a wooden lattice frame. In 1966 an aluminum frame was introduced in Brooklyn. Romualdo Martello (1903–88) was considered the preeminent giglio builder in New York City because of his

Charles Dana Gibson, "The Social Ladder" (1902)

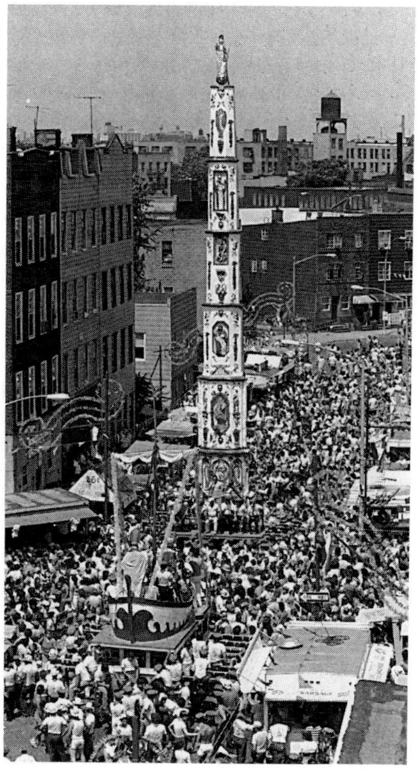

Giglio tower and boat at the feast of St. Paulinus in Williamsburg

technical innovations and the sheer beauty of his designs.

I. Sheldon Posen and Joseph Sciorra: "Brooklyn's Dancing Tower," *Natural History*, June 1983, 31–37

Joseph Sciorra

Gilbert, Cass (*b* Zanesville, Ohio, 24 Nov 1859; *d* Brockenhurst, England, 17 May 1934). Architect. He studied at the Massachusetts Institute of Technology for a year and traveled in Europe before moving to New York City, where he worked as a draftsman for McKim, Mead and White for a year; he then moved to Minnesota and after becoming successful there opened an office in New York City. He won a competition to design the U.S. Custom House at Bowling Green (1907). Among his next commissions were the Union Club and the Woolworth Building on Broadway (for illustration see WOOLWORTH BUILDING), which incorporated terra-cotta facing in a neo-Gothic style over a steel frame and attracted public attention that helped to secure his election as president of the American Institute of Architects in 1908. His appointment to the National Commission of Fine Arts in 1910 led to a number of commissions in Washington, among them the Treasury Annex, the Chamber of Commerce building, and the Supreme Court building. In New York City he later designed the U.S. Court House and the New York Life Insurance building (for illustration see NEW YORK LIFE INSURANCE); his design for the George Washington Memorial Bridge called for masonry covering steel piers and was rejected because of its expense. A president of the National Academy of Design and the National Institute of Arts and Letters and a founder of the Architectural League of New York, Gilbert worked without partners throughout his career. The largest collection of his materials is held by the New-York Historical Society. His memoirs were published as *Cass Gilbert: Reminiscences and Addresses* in 1935.

Sharon Lee Irish: "Cass Gilbert's Career in New York, 1899–1905" (diss., Northwestern University, 1985)

James E. Mooney

Gilbert, C(harles) P(ierrepont) H. (*b* New York City, ?1861; *d* Pelham Manor, N.Y., 25 Oct 1952). Architect. He designed many opulent residences for wealthy New Yorkers and popularized the château-like François I style and the mansarded beaux-arts style from the 1890s to the 1920s. Among his clients were Isaac Fletcher (2 East 79th Street, 1897–99), F. W. Woolworth (5th Avenue and 80th Street, 1899, demolished), Joseph R. Delamar (233 Madison Avenue, 1902–5), Felix Warburg (1109 5th Avenue, 1906–8). With the architect J. A. Stenhouse he designed a house for Otto H. Kahn (1 East 91st Street, 1913–18). Gilbert also designed a group of opulent houses at Riverside Drive and 72nd Street (1899–1901).

Marjorie Pearson

Gilder, Richard Watson (*b* Bordentown, N.J., 8 Feb 1844; *d* New York City, 18 Nov 1909). Editor. Brought up in Flushing, he was an associate editor of *Scribner's Monthly Magazine* in 1870–81 and the editor of *Century Illustrated Monthly Magazine* in 1881–1909. He published Mark Twain, Henry James, and William Dean Howells, along with many other important but lesser-known figures. His reputation for being overly Victorian and priggish, due partly to his having rejected Stephen Crane's *Maggie: A Girl of the Streets* on the grounds that it was not in good taste, is belied by his longtime editorial and personal support of Walt Whitman. Gilder was the secretary of a committee to raise funds for construction of the Washington Square Arch. As the chairman of the New York Tenement House Commission in 1894 he revealed that Trinity Church owned slums. His first home at 103 East 15th Street was a popular meeting place for artists, writers, and intellectuals; in 1888 he moved to 13 East 8th Street. Between 1875 and 1885 Gilder also published sixteen volumes of poetry.

Herbert Franklin Smith: *Richard Watson Gilder* (Boston: Twayne, 1970)

Arthur John: *The Best Years of the Century: Richard Watson Gilder, Scribner's Magazine, and the Century Magazine, 1870–1909* (Urbana: University of Illinois Press, 1981)

George A. Thompson, Jr.

Gillespie, Dizzy [John Birks] (*b* Cheraw, S.C., 21 Oct 1917; *d* Englewood, N.J., 6 Jan 1993). Trumpeter, composer, and bandleader. While working in Cab Calloway's big band (1939–41) he was at the vanguard of the development of a new style, bop, in informal sessions at Minton's Playhouse on West 118th Street. He led a small group at the Onyx on 52nd Street in 1943–44, and then toured with the singer Billy Eckstine's bop big band. The band included the alto saxophonist Charlie Parker, with whom he made the first mature bop recordings (1945). Although not as spectacularly accomplished a musician as Parker, he made important contributions by redefining the speed and harmonic sophistication of jazz trumpeting and by composing several definitive bop themes. He also became known for his antic appearance (usually sporting sunglasses, a beret, and a goatee) and behavior (though he avoided drugs, the downfall of Parker and many other boppers). After an unsuccessful attempt to form a big band he resumed leading small groups. His second big band (1946–50) established Afro-Cuban jazz, a blend of big-band orchestration, bop improvisation, and three rhythmic streams: swing, bop, and Afro-Cuban. Later he mainly led small groups, but he also toured with the Giants of Jazz, which included the pianist Thelonious Monk (1971–72), and when finances allowed he worked again with big bands, such as the United Nations Superband (from 1988). With Al Fraser he wrote *To Be, or Not . . . to Bop: Memoirs* (1979).

Barry Kernfeld

Gilmer, Elizabeth Perkins. See DIX, DOROTHY.

Gilmore, Patrick S(arsfield) (*b* Ballygar, Ireland, 25 Dec 1829; *d* St. Louis, 24 Sept 1892). Bandmaster. After a successful career in Boston he moved to New York City in 1873 to assume leadership of the 22nd Regiment Band of the New York National Guard, a sixty-five-piece ensemble that he transformed during the next twenty years into the nation's only touring brass band. He began a series of concerts on Saturday evenings at the 22nd Regiment Armory on 14th Street, and in May 1875 he leased and remodeled the Hippodrome, where he conducted celebrated daily concerts in spring and autumn that occasionally attracted ten thousand spectators; the venue became popularly known as Gilmore's Concert Garden. He became known for presenting concerts that incorporated church bells, anvils, cannon, and hundreds of musicians. Toward the end of his career he gave regular performances at Manhattan Beach; his last concert in the city was on 30 May 1892. Gilmore lived at 61 West 12th Street in Manhattan. Among his best-known compositions is "When Johnny Comes Marching Home Again."

Marwood Darlington: *Irish Orpheus: The Life of Patrick S. Gilmore, Bandmaster Extraordinary* (Philadelphia: Olivier–Maney–Klein, 1950)

Marc Ferris

Gilpin's Gold Room. Original name of the NEW YORK GOLD EXCHANGE.

Gilroy, Thomas F(rancis) (*b* Sligo, Ireland, 3 June 1839; *d* Queens, 1 Dec 1911). Mayor. Educated in the public schools of New York City, he played a central role in the revival of Tammany Hall under John Kelly, Hugh Grant, and Richard Croker in the years after William M. "Boss" Tweed fell from power. In 1892 he was elected mayor in an agreement with Democratic merchants who favored the presidential candidacy of Grover Cleveland. Like other leaders of Tammany Hall of the time he advocated limited city government, low taxes, and investment in street paving and other public improvements. In 1894 Gilroy declined to seek reelection when the merchants who had supported him two years earlier turned against him. After watching Croker consolidate his control over Tammany Hall he retired from politics in 1897 to concentrate on his real-estate and banking concerns in uptown Manhattan and Far Rockaway.

David C. Hammack: "Thomas F. Gilroy," *Biographical Dictionary of American Mayors, 1820–1980*, ed. Melvin G. Holli and Peter d'A. Jones (Westport, Conn.: Greenwood, 1981), 134

David C. Hammack

Gilsey House. Hotel opened in April 1871 on Broadway at 29th Street. An elaborate structure of seven stories designed in a Second Empire style by Stephen Hatch for the developer Peter Gilsey, it was built of marble and cast iron from Daniel D. Badger's foundry. The hotel closed in 1911 and the building became used for light manufacturing; it was converted into a luxury cooperative apartment building in 1980 and is now a city landmark.

Leslie Dorsey and Janice Devine: *Fare Thee Well: A Backward Look at Two Centuries of Historic American Hostelries* (New York: Crown, 1964)

Margot Gayle and Edmund V. Gillon Jr.: *Cast Iron Architecture in New York* (New York: Dover, 1974)

Christopher Gray: "Nomination to the National Register of Historic Places" (New York: Office of Metropolitan History, 1977)

Margot Gayle

Gimbel's. Firm of retailers. It was operated in New York City from 1909 by two sons of Adam Gimbel, a peddler from Bavaria who in 1842 had opened a store in the frontier territory of Vincennes, Indiana; the brothers opened stores in Milwaukee (1887) and Philadelphia (1894) before building a lavish store in 1910 in Herald Square, one block from Macy's. Under the direction of Bernard Gimbel (1885–1966), a grandson of the founder, the firm became well known for its forceful advertising and promotion and particularly for its fierce competition with Macy's. Discounters eventually made Gimbel's unprofitable, and in 1986 its outlets at 86th Street and Lexington Avenue and at 33rd Street and 6th Avenue were sold to real-estate developers by BAT Industries, the British parent company of the firm.

Leslie Gourse, Kenneth T. Jackson

Ginkgo. The Ginkgo (*Ginkgo biloba*) is a tree belonging to the gymnosperms and related to the cycads and the conifers; it is the only living member of the class Ginkgoae and one of the oldest living species of tree, its fossil record virtually unchanged over 100 million years. The tree was imported to Japan from China and later introduced in the United States. About 1900 it became popular in New York City and Washington for its beauty and its ability to survive gamma radiation, sulfur dioxide, and ozone pollution; it was soon planted in cities across the country. Ginkgos are almost unknown in the wild.

Steven D. Garber: *The Urban Naturalist* (New York: John Wiley and Sons, 1987)

Steven D. Garber

Ginsberg, (Irwin) Allen (*b* Newark, N.J., 3 June 1926). Poet and activist. A student at Columbia University from 1943, he was expelled in 1945 for writing anti-Semitic graffiti but later readmitted, graduating in 1948. In 1956 he published *Howl and Other Poems*, the first of more than forty books of poetry that made him a central figure in the beat movement in New York City, along with Jack Kerouac, William S. Burroughs, and Herbert Huncke (see BEATS). A dedicated antiwar activist and spokesman for the counterculture in the 1960s, he campaigned for homosexual rights in the 1970s. His book *Fall of America* won the National Book Award in 1972, and in the same year he was elected to the American Academy and the Institute of Arts and Letters. In 1986 he joined the faculty of Brooklyn College.

Jane Kramer: *Ginsberg in America* (New York: Random House, 1969)

Barry Miles: *Ginsberg: A Biography* (New York: Simon and Schuster, 1989)

Graham Hodges

Giovannitti, Arturo (*b* Campobasso, Italy, 7 Jan 1884; *d* Bronx, 31 Dec 1959). Writer and political leader. After moving to the United States at seventeen he studied theology, traveled throughout the country, and later preached the "propaganda of the deed" for the Italian Socialist Federation and the Industrial Workers of the World; he was also the editor of *Il Proletario* from 1911. After taking part in the mill strike in Lawrence, Massachusetts, he was charged with murder in the death of a striker but was acquitted in November 1912. While awaiting trial he wrote the book *Arrows in the Gale*, which included "The Walker," his best-known poem. A charismatic figure, he formed the Anti-Fascist Alliance (1923) and was an organizer for the International Ladies' Garment Workers' Union and a member of the Italian Labor Education Bureau. A collection of his poetry was published in 1962.

George J. Lankevich

Girl Scouts of the U.S.A. Organization formed in 1912 in Savannah, Georgia, by Juliette Gordon Low (1860–1927). The first troop was formed in New York City in the following year, and the entire organization moved its headquarters to 17 West 42nd Street in Manhattan in April 1916. A local chapter, the Girl Scout Council of Greater New York, was established in 1940. In the mid 1990s this chapter had some 23,000 members and more than seventeen hundred community-based troops, along with a Girl Scout Service Center in each borough. The national headquarters of the Girl Scouts are at 420 5th Avenue.

James Bradley

Girls' High School. Original name of WADLEIGH HIGH SCHOOL.

Gish, Lillian (*b* Springfield, Ohio, 14 Oct 1893; *d* New York City, 27 Feb 1993). Actress. She won a small part in the stage production of *Convict's Stripes* in Ohio (1902) before moving to New York City, where she danced in a production featuring Sarah Bernhardt in 1910. She appeared in silent films directed by D. W. Griffith, among them *Birth of a Nation* (1915), *Broken Blossoms* (1919), and *Orphans in the Storm* (1922). Renowned for her delicate beauty, she agreed to make six motion pictures for $1 million, a record for the time; she also had a distinguished career on Broadway in such productions as Chekhov's *Uncle Vanya* (1930), *Hamlet* (1936), and Ted Mosel's *All the Way Home* (1960). Among her last films was Robert Altman's *A Wedding* (1978). For many years she lived at 430 East 57th Street. Gish made more than a hundred films.

For illustration see FILMMAKING.

Janet Frankston

Giuliani, Rudolph W(illiam) (*b* Brooklyn, 28 May 1944). Mayor. He attended Catholic schools and graduated from New York University Law School in 1968. After working as a law clerk and an assistant U.S. attorney, he was appointed to a position in the U.S. Justice Department that he held from 1975 to 1977. He then returned to New York City to practice law with the firm of Patterson, Belknap, Webb and Tyler. After President Ronald Reagan took office in 1981 he was named an associate attorney general of the United States. In 1989 he won the Republican mayoral nomination in New York City but narrowly lost the general election to David N. Dinkins. Nominated again by the Republicans in 1993, he waged a vigorous campaign in which he criticized Dinkins for an indifferent approach to managing the city and pledged to reduce business taxes, assume a tougher stance on crime, and privatize some city services. In November he defeated Dinkins to become the city's first Republican mayor in twenty-eight years.

Corinne T. Field

Glackens, William James (*b* Philadelphia, 13 March 1870; *d* Westport, Conn., 22 May 1938). Painter. He was trained in drawing in Philadelphia before moving to New York City, where he worked as an artist for *McClure's*, the *New York World*, and the *New York Herald*. From 1905 he concentrated on painting, becoming a member of The Eight in 1908 and the selection chairman for the Armory Show in 1913.

James E. Mooney

Glad Tidings Tabernacle. Pentecostal church at 416 West 42nd Street, formed in 1907 by Marie Burgess (1880–1971). One of the first Pentecostal churches in New York City, it was led by Burgess until 1909, when she was joined by her husband, Robert Brown (1872–1948). The tabernacle affiliated with the Assemblies of God Church in 1916 and in 1921 moved to 325 West 33rd Street, where it became a Pentecostalist center for the Northeast. It sponsored missions throughout the city, evangelical rallies, and a radio ministry. Brown remained the pastor until her death.

William C. Kostlevy

Glass, Philip (*b* Baltimore, 31 Jan 1937). Composer. He studied at the Juilliard School in the late 1950s and worked in Paris and India with Ravi Shankar and Allah Rakha in the mid 1960s. Soon he composed his first musical productions for the theater. When he returned to New York City in 1966 he moved into a loft on Bleecker Street and formed the Philip Glass Ensemble, a group of instrumentalists and singers that performed at art galleries and museums. In 1974 he gave his first major concert of his own works in the United States at Town Hall. *Einstein on the Beach*, a collaboration with the performance artist Robert Wilson, startled audiences at the Metropolitan Opera in 1976; the première of *Akhnaten* was given at the New York City Opera in 1984. Glass has won a wide audience for his music, often considered minimalist, which is repetitive, harmonically static, and highly rhythmic. He has also been a successful rock producer.

Wim Mertens: *American Minimal Music: La Monte Young, Terry Riley, Steve Reich, Philip Glass* (New York: Broude, 1983)

John Rockwell: "The Orient, the Visual Arts, and the Evolution of Minimalism: Philip Glass," *All-American Music: Composition in the Late Twentieth Century* (New York: Alfred A. Knopf, 1983)

Barbara L. Tischler

glassmaking. The first glassmaking operation in what is now greater New York was that of Everett Duÿcking, which opened as early as the mid seventeenth century and probably manufactured window glass. The few other glasshouses during colonial times opened for the same purpose and to make bottles. Fine glass tableware was made from 1820 by Richard and John Fisher and John L. Gilliland, who opened the Bloomingdale Flint Glass Works (also called the New York Glass Works), a factory known for its plain and cut flint and colored glass until it closed in 1840. Brooklyn became the local center for fine glass production after Gilliland in 1823 formed his own firm, the Brooklyn Glass Works (later the Brooklyn Flint Glass Works), which specialized in richly cut and colored glass, lamps, and chandeliers as well as pressed glass after 1830; it also made the globes for the city's gaslights. With Boston and Pittsburgh, New York City was one of the country's primary centers for glassmaking by the 1830s. The first important stained-glass studio was that of William Jay and John Bolton in Pelham, New York: its windows for St. Ann and the Holy Trinity Church (1843–48) in Brooklyn were one of the first extensive programs of stained glass in the country. The Brooklyn Glass Works became known internationally after winning a medal for wares displayed in London at the Crystal Palace Exposition of 1851. From about 1860 the number of factories in the city declined as glassmaking factories were opened elsewhere, especially west of the Allegheny Mountains near abundant sources of coal. Christian Dorflinger, one of the city's best-known glassmakers, opened a factory in White Mills, Pennsylvania. The Brooklyn Glass Works was taken over by Amory Houghton and his son and moved to Corning, New York, in 1868.

After 1865 glass factories in Brooklyn turned to the manufacture of decorative globes and shades for lamps. After Dorflinger retired, his works in Greenpoint, which employed immigrants and stressed handwork, changed ownership several times. It remained in operation until the 1940s as part of the Gleason Tiebout Company and was known for the innovative etching techniques used for its light fixtures. During the second half of the nineteenth century the city's stained-glass makers became the foremost in the country. As the demand rose for stained glass in churches, public buildings, and private homes the number of studios increased, many of them opened by German and English craftsmen, among them Charles Booth. Most made windows from sheets of colored glass that were painted with enamels and fired to achieve shading and modeling. About the late 1870s Louis Comfort Tiffany invented marbleized glass with gradations of color, texture, and density that could be used to achieve details with little or no paint. He bought sheets of colored and opalescent glass from various sources in and near the city, including the Thill and Heidt glasshouses in Brooklyn, until he built his own factory in Corona in 1893; there he developed vessels blown from his marbleized glass known as Favrile that made him internationally known. The glass industry became increasingly mechanized owing to a number of technological advances and was centered in enormous factories requiring large amounts of capital. Their size alone made them unsuitable for the densely popu-

The Bloomingdale Flint Glass Works of John and Richard Fisher near the Hudson River on West 47th Street, ca *1837*

lated city, and the number of glassmaking firms in Brooklyn declined from twelve in 1880 to six in 1909 and four in 1919.

After a period of decline, interest in glassmaking revived in 1962, when technology was introduced to allow the production of glass in small studios. In 1977 the New York Experimental Glass Workshop opened in Manhattan as the city's first studio devoted to glassmaking; it eventually moved to Brooklyn, where in the mid 1990s artists continued to work and teach.

Joshua Brown and David Ment: *Factories, Foundries, and Refineries: A History of Five Brooklyn Industries* (New York: Brooklyn Educational and Cultural Alliance, 1980)

Alice Cooney Frelinghuysen

Glatshteyn, Yankev (*b* Lublin, Poland, 20 Aug 1896; *d* New York City, 19 Nov 1971). Writer and critic. He arrived in New York City in 1914 and joined with his fellow students Aaron Glanz (A. Leyeles) and N. B. Minkoff in establishing the Inzikhistn (Introspectivists), a modernist literary circle that dominated the American Yiddish avant-garde during the 1920s and 1930s. Best known as a poet, he was celebrated for his linguistic virtuosity, formal daring, and vivid imagery. Glatshteyn wrote ten volumes of poetry over five decades in addition to several novels and many essays on Yiddish and world literature.

Janet Hadda: *Yankev Glatshteyn* (Boston: Twayne, 1980)

Jeffrey Shandler

Gleason, Jackie [Herbert John] (*b* New York City, 26 Feb 1916; *d* Fort Lauderdale, Fla., 24 June 1987). Actor. He performed on the stage as a young man and began a film career with a part in *Navy Blues* (1941); he later won awards for his roles in the motion pictures *The Hustler* (1961) and *Gigot* (1962). On television he became well known for portraying comic characters in such series as "The Life of Riley" and "Cavalcade of Stars"; his best-known role is that of Ralph Kramden, a bus driver from Bensonhurst in the series "The Honeymooners" during the 1950s. Gleason won a Tony Award in 1959 as best actor for his performance in *Take Me Along.*

James Bacon: *How Sweet It Is: The Jackie Gleason Story* (New York: St. Martin's, 1985)

James E. Mooney

Gleason, Patrick J(erome) (*b* Parish of Drum and Inch, County Tipperary, Ireland, 25 April 1844; *d* Queens, 20 May 1901). Mayor of Long Island City. He emigrated to the United States in May 1862, served in the Union Army during the Civil War, and had several unsuccessful business ventures before making a small fortune in alcohol distilling in California. In 1873 he returned to New York City and invested his money in a street railway that served Calvary Cemetery. He began a political career in Long Island City in 1881 as a Democrat. Twice elected to the Board of Aldermen, he was elected mayor in 1884 and again in 1888, failed to win reelection in 1892 because of his corrupt record, and successfully regained the mayoralty in 1896. A member of the charter commission that conceived the consolidation of New York City, he failed to secure the provisions he sought and the charter took effect without his approval. The incorporation of Long Island City by New York City in 1898 eliminated his office and ended his political career. In the late 1890s he lost money on his streetcar line, and he died bankrupt and in obscurity. A tall, burly, rough-mannered man, Gleason was a colorful, autocratic political boss who rewarded his supporters with lucrative contracts and patronage and punished his opponents, whom he sometimes assaulted physically. He was nevertheless fond of posing as the champion of the oppressed and the common people.

Vincent Seyfried

"The Honeymooners," 1954. From left: *Jackie Gleason, Art Carney, Audrey Meadows, Joyce Randolph*

Glendale. Neighborhood in west central Queens, bounded to the north by railroad tracks (Montauk division, Long Island Rail Road), to the east by Woodhaven Boulevard, to the south by a number of cemeteries, and to the west by Fresh Pond Road. It originally consisted of farms and was developed in 1869 by John C. Schooley, a real-estate agent from Jamaica, who reportedly named it after his birthplace in Ohio. He laid out streets and sold lots priced at $300 and measuring twenty-five by one hundred feet (eight by thirty meters). The South Side Railroad was extended to the area in 1867 and opened a station at 73rd Place. Development increased after Myrtle Avenue on 23 May 1893 was given service by steam dummy (a horse car or trolley car powered by a small steam engine); until the First World War many farms were sold and laid out in blocks of row houses and one-family houses. Family shops opened along Myrtle Avenue, which from the 1890s until Prohibition was enjoyed for its picnic parks. After 1905 silk ribbons, matches, and airplanes were manufactured, and in the 1920s there were studios for producing silent films. A large German population was attracted in the 1930s by work available in local breweries and textile factories. The largest employer in the 1940s was Atlas Terminal. In the 1980s the neighborhood attracted a number of immigrants from Romania, Yugoslavia, and Poland, as well as China and the Dominican Republic.

Vincent Seyfried

Glenn L. Curtiss Airport. Original name of La Guardia Airport.

Glen Oaks. Neighborhood in eastern Queens (1991 pop. 12,000), bounded to the north by Grand Central Parkway, to the north and east by Nassau County, to the south by Hillside Avenue, and to the west by Grand Central Parkway and the Creedmoor Psychiatric Center. The area was once part of Flushing and was the site of William K. Vanderbilt's estate, of which 167 acres (sixty-seven hectares) were bought in 1923 by the recently formed Glen Oaks golf club; the clubhouse stood on the highest point in Queens. In 1944 the Gross–Morton Company bought 175 acres (seventy hectares) of land along Union Turnpike and with a loan of $24 million from the Federal Housing Authority built Glen Oaks Village, a garden apartment complex consisting of 2864 units in two-story buildings in the colonial style; among the original residents were many veterans of the Second World War. On an adjacent lot a shopping center was erected in the same style, as were most of the one- and two-family houses nearby between 1947 and 1960. North Shore Towers, a development of three apartment buildings of thirty-three stories each, was built between 1971 and 1974 on the remaining portion of the golf course. In addition to Creedmoor the neighborhood is the site of Long Island Jewish Hospital and Hillside Hospital.

Jeffrey A. Kroessler

Globe and Commercial Advertiser. Daily evening newspaper. It was launched on 9 December 1793 by Alexander Hamilton and others as a Federalist organ called the *American Minerva*, with Noah Webster as its editor. On 2 October 1797 it changed its name to the *Commercial Advertiser*, becoming a muckraker in the late nineteenth century and the early twentieth under the editor Henry J. Wright. It was renamed the *Globe and Commercial Advertiser* on 1 February 1904 and was commonly known and sold by newsboys as the *Globe*. In 1923 it was bought by the newspaper magnate Frank Munsey, who merged it a week later (on 4 June) with the *Sun*.

America's Oldest Daily Newspaper: The New York Globe (New York: New York Globe, 1918)

George Britt: *Forty Years, Forty Millions: The Career of Frank A. Munsey* (New York: Farrar and Rinehart, 1935)

Michael Green

Goddard, Paulette [Levy [Levee], Pauline Marion Goddard] (*b* Queens, 3 June 1911; *d* Ronco, Switzerland, 23 April 1990). Actress. After beginning her career in New York City with a part in the revue *No Foolin'* (1926) she moved to Hollywood in 1931 and played bit parts in various films until Charlie Chaplin cast her in *Modern Times* (1936). She became one of the most popular film stars of the 1940s and appeared in more than forty films, including *The Cat and the Canary* (1939), *The Great Dictator* (1940), and *Hold Back the Dawn* (1941). In the 1950s her popularity waned and she performed only rarely. Goddard bequeathed her entire estate of more than $20 million to New York University.

Sara J. Steen

Goddard Institute for Space Studies. Government institute at 112th Street and Broadway, founded in 1961 by Robert Jastrow; it is affiliated with the National Aeronautics and Space Administration (NASA). The institute is based in New York City because of its close links to local colleges and universities (notably Columbia University and the City University of New York), as well as to four high schools. Its research emphasis is on atmospheric science, especially global warming. In the mid 1990s there were about 150 employees.

Godfrey, Arthur (*b* New York City, 31 Aug 1903; *d* New York City, 16 March 1983). Entertainer. He grew up in New Jersey and after leaving high school in his second year took correspondence courses in radio broadcasting. In 1920 he joined the navy, where he continued his training. At the end of four years' service he returned to civilian life before joining the coast guard in 1927. During the next few years he both served in the military and worked as a radio announcer. In 1945 he captured a national audience on the radio network of the Columbia Broadcasting System with his banter and homespun jokes at the expense of his sponsors. From 1948 he had a talent show on television where he presented such entertainers as Rosemary Clooney. Forced to retire in 1959 because of lung cancer, he later returned but never regained his popularity.

James E. Mooney

Godkin, E(dwin) L(awrence) (*b* Moyne, Ireland, 2 Oct 1831; *d* Brixham, England, 21 May 1902). Writer and editor. After receiving his education in Ireland and England he worked for two years from 1853 as a war correspondent in the Crimea. He then moved to New York City, where he became the editor of the weekly journal the *Nation* and made it one of the most respected publications of its kind. With Carl Schurz he edited the *New York Evening Post* from 1881, becoming the editor-in-chief when Schurz withdrew. He was sympathetic to the Mugwumps, Republicans who opposed political machines and mistrusted organized labor. In a style marked by a keen sense of humor he wrote on Tammany Hall and many other subjects, and was highly influential in the press. Godkin retired in 1900. Among his published writings are *Problems of Modern Democracy* (1896) and *Tendencies of Democracy* (1898).

William M. Armstrong: *E. L. Godkin: A Biography* (Albany: State University of New York Press, 1978)

See also INTELLECTUALS and PARTISAN PRESS.

James E. Mooney

Goethals Bridge. Steel cantilevered bridge spanning the Arthur Kill between Howland Hook in Staten Island and Elizabeth, New Jersey. Designed by the engineer Alexander Waddell and named for the chief engineer of the Panama Canal, General George W. Goethals, the bridge opened to traffic on 29 June 1928 at the same time as the larger Outerbridge Crossing (built downstream and also designed by Waddell), the two providing the first crossings for motor vehicles between Staten Island and the mainland. The structure has a span of 672 feet (205 meters), a total length of 7109 feet (2168 meters), and a clearance above water of 135 feet (41.1 meters).

Rebecca Read Shanor

Goetz shootings. A widely publicized act of vigilantism that occurred on 22 December 1984. The incident involved Bernhard (Hugo) Goetz, a thirty-seven-year-old white electronics engineer, and four black youths who precipitated the incident by asking him for money aboard the no. 2 subway near the Chambers Street station. Goetz drew a handgun, for which he did not have a license, and fired at the youths, hitting all four. Indicted for attempted murder, he became the focus of an international debate over self-defense and public safety. While many observers believed that he was a hero who had fought back against urban crime, others saw him as a depraved vigilante, possibly motivated by racism, whose use of force was disproportionate to the danger that he faced. At a celebrated trial in June 1987 Goetz was acquitted of attempted murder, found guilty only of illegal possession of a handgun, and sentenced to a year in prison and five years' probation. He served eight months at Rikers Island, was released in August 1989, and then returned to his apartment and resumed his career. One of the four youths, Darrel Cabey, was paralyzed and brain-damaged as a result of the shooting. In 1990 he filed a civil suit against Goetz, who counter-sued.

Lillian B. Rubin: *Quiet Rage: Bernie Goetz in a Time of Madness* (New York: Farrar, Straus and Giroux, 1986)

George P. Fletcher: *A Crime of Self-Defense: Bernard Goetz and the Law on Trial* (New York: Free Press, 1988)

Robert Sanger Steel

Goff, John William (*b* County Wexford, Ireland, 1 Jan 1848; *d* New York City, 9 Nov 1924). Judge. Taken to New York City as a child, he was largely self-educated and gained admission to the bar in 1870. He was prominent in Irish nationalist activities and built a large practice among fellow immigrants. His service as counsel to a committee led by State Senator Clarence Lexow that investigated police corruption (1894–95) won him election as recorder of New York City in 1894; he was the last to hold this office. Elected a justice of the New York State Supreme Court in 1906, he served until his retirement in 1919.

William D. Griffin

Gold, Michael [Granich, Itzok] (*b* New York City, 12 April 1893; *d* San Francisco, 14 May 1967). Journalist and essayist. The son of poor Jewish immigrants, he grew up on the Lower East Side and attended New York University and Harvard University briefly before working for the *Masses*, a magazine published by Max Eastman. Between 1914 and 1917 he published his first articles in the *Masses* and was also associated with the Provincetown Players. To protect himself during the "red scare" of 1919–20 he adopted the name Michael Gold, after a Civil War veteran whom he admired. In 1920 he became an editor of the *Liberator*, which was formed after the *Masses* was suppressed by the federal government. He was the editor from 1928 to 1933 of the *New Masses*, a publication devoted to proletarian literature, which he defined as literature written by workers and dealing with workers' issues (he considered most other kinds of literature to be crippled by bourgeois idealism). From 1933 Gold was a columnist for the newspaper the *Daily Worker* (1924–57). His best-known work was *Jews without Money* (1930), an account of life on the Lower East Side.

James D. Bloom: *Left Letters: The Culture Wars of Mike Gold and Joseph Freeman* (New York: Columbia University Press, 1992)

Kevin Kenny

Gold and Stock Telegraph Company. Firm incorporated in August 1867 at 18 New Street to promote the first stock ticker, adapted from the printing telegraph invented by Edward Calahan and installed in 1868 at the New York Stock Exchange. Initially the firm served only brokers from the New York Stock Exchange, but it soon expanded its business to other exchanges throughout the United States. The Western Union Telegraph Company acquired the firm in May 1871 and continued to operate it as a subsidiary. It controlled most of the important printing telegraph patents and well into the twentieth century was the leading supplier of market reports and private-line printing telegraphs, which provided communication banks, linkages between courthouses and lawyers' offices, and private lines connecting homes, offices, and factories. Gold and Stock Telegraph ceased operations in 1962.

Merchants' Telephone Exchange: List of Subscribers (New York: Gold and Stock Telegraph Company, 1880)

Paul Israel

Goldberg, Rube [Reuben Lucius] (*b* San Francisco, 3 July 1883; *d* New York City, 7 Dec 1970). Cartoonist. Born into a prosperous family, he moved to New York City in 1907 to work as a sports cartoonist for the *Evening Mail.* He produced widely syndicated single-frame cartoons and comic strips, and his strip "Boob McNutt" ran for twenty years. When his popularity diminished in the 1930s he turned to political cartooning with a conservative slant. Goldberg's best-known cartoons depict machines that use absurdly complicated means to accomplish simple tasks; his contraptions incorporate dripping water, falling coconuts, bursting balloons, and startled monkeys. He won the Pulitzer Prize for editorial cartooning in 1948, and the National Cartoonists Society gives an award called the "Reuben" in his honor. Goldberg lived in the Brentmore at 88 Central Park West until 1963; his last home was at 169 East 69th Street.

Peter C. Marzio: *Rube Goldberg: His Life and Work* (New York: Harper and Row, 1973)

George A. Thompson, Jr.

Goldman, Emma (*b* Kaunas, Lithuania, 27 June 1869; *d* Toronto, 14 May 1940). Anarchist. She joined the radical movement in New York City in 1890 and dominated it until her deportation in 1919. From 1903 to 1913 she lived at 210 East 13th Street, where from 1906 she published *Mother Earth*, a journal of political and cultural articles far ahead of their time. A feminist who believed in the emancipation of women physically and intellectually, she was perhaps best known as an advocate of birth control and sexual relations outside marriage. She was arrested for criticizing militarism and opposing the entry of the United States into the First World War, and imprisoned on Ellis Island. With hundreds of other immigrants deemed "dangerous radicals" she was deported to the Soviet Union. A critic of the Bolshevik regime, she wandered through Europe for the rest of her life. In exile she continued to speak out for anarchist causes. Her work in behalf of victims of the Spanish Civil War alerted the world to the atrocities wrought by total war on civilian populations.

Martha Foley

Goldman, Sachs. Firm of investment bankers. It began as a firm of dealers in commercial paper formed in New York City in 1869 by Marcus Goldman, a German immigrant. Samuel Sachs became a partner in 1882 and by 1885 the firm was given its current name. A brokerage was added in the 1890s and after 1900 the firm underwrote securities, primarily in consumer goods. Sidney J. Weinberg became a partner in 1927 and a senior partner in 1930. Under the direction of Gustave L. Levy, who joined the firm in the 1930s, the trading department undertook risk arbitrage. There were thirteen partners by the mid 1940s. The firm remained a private partnership; in 1995 there were 173 general partners and the Sumitomo Bank owned a share of 12.5 percent. One of the most successful firms of its kind, Goldman, Sachs has headquarters at 85 Broad Street and more than thirty offices around the world. Its divisions specialize in investment banking, fixed-income and equities securities sales, trading and arbitrage, investment management, currency and commodities, and a broad range of other financing and investment services.

Vincent P. Carosso: *Investment Banking in America: A History* (Cambridge: Harvard University Press, 1970)

Mary E. Curry

Goldmark, Josephine (*b* Brooklyn, 13 Oct 1877; *d* White Plains, N.Y., 15 Dec 1950). Activist. Born into an affluent Jewish family, she graduated from Bryn Mawr College and became an assistant at the headquarters of the National Consumers' League to Florence Kelley, of whom she wrote a biography. She led a committee of the league concerned with the rights of workers and assisted her brother-in-law Louis D. Brandeis (later a justice of the U.S. Supreme Court) in preparing the "Brandeis Brief" (1908), which first intro-

Emma Goldman speaking in Union Square about birth control, 1916

duced sociological evidence into American jurisprudence. As the publications secretary of the league she compiled many important studies on exploitative working conditions, including *Fatigue and Efficiency* (1912).

Kathryn Kish Sklar

Goldwater, S(igismund) S(chultz) (*b* New York City, 7 Feb 1873; *d* New York City, 22 Oct 1942). Hospital and public health official. One of the first hospital directors in the United States with medical training, he administered Mount Sinai Hospital from 1904 to 1928. There he established the second department of social services in the nation (1906), expanded outpatient facilities, and was an early advocate of preventive medicine. His tenure as the city's health commissioner from 1914 to 1915 was marked by broad reform. A trained architect, he became widely known for his work in the planning and building of 156 hospitals worldwide. He was the commissioner of hospitals from 1934 to 1940 under Mayor Fiorello H. La Guardia and the president of the Associated Hospital Service of New York from 1940 to the end of his life; he was also instrumental in 1939 in founding the Welfare Hospital for Chronic Disease on Welfare Island, later renamed Goldwater Memorial Hospital.

Joseph S. Lieber

Goldwater Memorial Hospital. Municipal hospital specializing in rehabilitation and chronic care, administered by the New York Health and Hospitals Corporation. It was built on Welfare Island on the site of a city prison that had been demolished during the 1930s, and opened in July 1939 as the Welfare Hospital for Chronic Disease; it was renamed in 1942 for S. S. Goldwater. An initial focus on the research and treatment of chronic illness was broadened in the 1950s to include comprehensive rehabilitation for the disabled. A skilled nursing facility was established in the 1970s. Goldwater is affiliated with New York University Medical Center.

Sandra Opdycke

golf courses. There are sixteen golf courses in New York City (thirteen municipal, one military, and two private), of which fourteen have eighteen holes and two have nine holes. The first municipal golf course in the United States, at Van Cortlandt Park, was designed by Tom Bendelow in 1895. Another of his designs, Forest Park Golf Course, opened in the following year in Queens and became known for its rugged terrain. In the Bronx, Mosholu Golf Course (1914) opened in Van Cortlandt Park and Pelham Bay Golf Course (1921) and Split Rock Golf Course (1928) opened at Pelham Bay Park, where they shared an art deco clubhouse. Originally private clubs, Clearview Golf Course (1925) and Douglaston Golf Course (1927) were developed in Queens by Willie Tucker and a Spanish-style clubhouse at Douglaston was designed by Clifford Wendehack, the well-known clubhouse architect of the 1920s. The three public courses in Staten Island are Silver Lake Golf Course (1927), La Tourette Golf Course (1928), which has a par of 72 and is considered the city's most challenging course, and South Shore Golf Course (1929); the clubhouse at La Tourette, once a residence, is a municipal landmark. La Tourette, Silver Lake, Split Rock, Dyker Beach Golf Course in Brooklyn (1928), and Kissena Park Golf Course in Queens (1933, the city's shortest course at 4642 yards, with a par of 64), were developed by the architect John R. Van Kleek. The city's longest course, Marine Park Golf Course (6736 yards), was designed in Brooklyn in 1962 by Robert Trent Jones. The city's three non-municipal courses are the Towers (open only to residents of the North Shore Towers in Queens), a nine-hole course on Governors Island for military personnel, and Richmond County Country Club on Staten Island (private). There are also two "pitch and putt" courses (in Flushing Meadows–Corona Park and Gateway National Park). In 1990 golfers played more than 810,000 rounds on the city's public courses.

William Quirin: "Who Did Yours?," *Met Golfer*, March 1991, pp. 14–27

Christina Plattner

Golfus, Emil R. See ABEL, RUDOLF.

Gompers, Samuel (*b* London, 27 Jan 1850; *d* San Antonio, 3 Dec 1924). Labor leader. Of Dutch Jewish origin, he emigrated to the United States in 1863 and settled in New York City, where he worked as a cigar maker. In 1873 he organized the United Cigarmakers, which joined the CIGAR MAKERS' INTERNATIONAL UNION as Local 144 in 1875. As the head of the union's constitutional committee during the 1880s he introduced several measures that helped revitalize the union. Conflicts between the Cigar Makers' International Union and the Progressive Cigarmakers arose in the 1880s and culminated in the formation of the AMERICAN FEDERATION OF LABOR. Elected president of the federation, Gompers endorsed the mayoral candidacy of Henry George, launched by a coalition of unions in 1886, and was an advisor to the Social Reform Club, which promoted workers' compensation, union labels, and collective bargaining. While testifying at state assembly hearings on production in tenements and conditions in sweatshops he urged legislators to enact stricter factory codes. In his later years he spoke at several rallies organized by garment workers and helped to settle disputes involving teamsters (1910), furriers (1912), and transit workers (1916). Gompers wrote *Seventy Years of Life and Labor: An Autobiography* (1925).

Melvin Dubofsky: *When Workers Organize: New York City in the Progressive Era* (Amherst: University of Massachusetts Press, 1968)
Stuart Bruce Kaufman: *Samuel Gompers and the Origins of the American Federation of Labor, 1848–1896* (Westport, Conn.: Greenwood, 1973)
Harold Livesay: *Samuel Gompers and Organized Labor in America* (Boston: Little, Brown, 1978)

Ronald Mendel

Good Government Clubs. Organizations formed in the 1890s by the City Club of New York at the behest of the reformers Edmond Kelly and R. Fulton Cutting. Their aim was to mobilize the city's business and professional communities against Tammany Hall, which derided their members as "goo-goos." There were twenty-four clubs by 1894, when they were influential in securing the election of the fusion mayoral candidate William L. Strong.

Richard Skolnick: "The Crystallization of Reform in New York City, 1890–1917" (diss., Yale University, 1964)
David Israel Aronson: "The City Club of New York, 1892–1912" (diss., New York University, 1975)

Bernard Hirschhorn

Goodhue, Bertram Grosvenor (*b* Pomfret, Conn., 28 April 1869; *d* New York City, 23 April 1924). Architect. He moved to New York City in 1884 from his family's home in Pomfret, Connecticut, to work in the firm of Renwick, Aspinwald and Tucker. He formed a partnership with Ralph Adams Cram and Frank W. Ferguson, moving with them to Boston in 1891 and returning to New York City to run the firm's office there from 1903 to 1913. With Cram and Ferguson he designed St. Thomas Church on 5th Avenue and 53rd Street (1905–13), his best-known neo-Gothic work. He also oversaw the design of the Church of the Intercession at the Trinity Cemetery on Broadway (1910–14). Tension within the firm, especially with Cram over the construction of the Cathedral of St. John the Divine, led Goodhue to open his own firm in 1914 in the Jackson Building on 47th Street, which he ran as an atelier where apprentices including Clarence Stein, Raymond Hood, and Wallace K. Harrison helped to design such distinctive churches as St. Vincent Ferrer on Lexington Avenue (1914–18). A member of the Century Club from 1911, he won the commission for St. Bartholomew's Church on Park Avenue (1917–19), which incorporated a memorial portal commissioned by the Vanderbilts and designed by Stanford White. Goodhue blended neoclassical and modern styles in later designs such as that for Convocation Tower, an office tower and religious complex planned for Madison Square; presentation drawings by Hugh Ferriss were shown at the 36th Annual Exhibition of the Architectural League of New York in 1921.

Richard Oliver: *Bertram Grosvenor Goodhue* (Cambridge: MIT Press, 1983)

Edward A. Eigen

Goodhue, Jonathan (*b* Salem, Mass., 21 June 1783; *d* New York City, 24 Nov 1848). Commission merchant. He arrived in New York City in 1807 and organized Goodhue and Company, a commission house on South Street. In 1813 he married Catharine Rutherford Clarkson, daughter of Matthew Clarkson, and moved to 33 Whitehall Street in Manhattan. With Pelatiah Perit, who joined the firm in 1819, he used his commercial connections to the British banking house of Baring Brothers to gain control of the famous Black Ball Line of packets to Liverpool in 1834. Goodhue was an adherent of the Whig Party and a leader of the free trade movement. Like other prominent merchants he was a director of several banks and insurance companies and a supporter of humanitarian causes.

Robert Greenhalgh Albion: *Square-Riggers on Schedule: The New York Sailing Packets* (Princeton, N.J.: Princeton University Press, 1938)

Elaine Weber Pascu

Goodman, Benny [Benjamin David] (*b* Chicago, 30 May 1909; *d* New York City, 13 June 1986). Clarinetist and bandleader. He first played in New York City in 1928 with Ben Pollack at the Park Central Hotel and with Red Nichols and His Five Pennies. As a studio musician he took part in recording sessions, radio broadcasts, and other performances, including productions on Broadway of *Strike Up the Band* and *Girl Crazy* by George Gershwin (1930). He formed a big band in 1934 that soon attracted a wide audience and helped to broaden the popularity of jazz. He used some arrangements by other bandleaders including Fletcher Henderson and engaged such well-known players as the trumpeters Bunny Berigan and Harry James, the drummer Gene Krupa, and the pianist Jess Stacy; with the addition in 1936 of the pianist Teddy Wilson and the vibraphonist Lionel Hampton his quartet became the first racially mixed group in popular music. He often performed in the Manhattan Room of the Hotel Pennsylvania for audiences of enthusiastic young fans. An appearance at the Paramount Theater in March 1937 led to such chaos that the event became known as the Paramount Riot. Goodman's performance at Carnegie Hall on 16 January 1938 demonstrated the adaptability of dance music to the concert hall. With the Budapest Quartet in 1938 he recorded the Clarinet Quintet by Mozart, and he commissioned Béla Bartók to write *Contrasts* in 1938 and Aaron Copland and Paul Hindemith to write clarinet concertos in 1947. Designated an unofficial "jazz ambassador" of the United States by the Department of State, he toured the Far East in 1956 and the Soviet Union in 1962. For many years he maintained an apartment at 200 East 66th Street. A peerless clarinetist and perhaps the most popular bandleader of the 1930s, Goodman played an important role in shaping the swing era.

D. R. Connor: *Benny Goodman: Listen to His Legacy* (Metuchen, N.J.: Scarecrow, 1988)

Loren Schoenberg

Left *Charles Goodyear's rubber goods store near the intersection of Grand Street and East Broadway, ca 1878*

Goodyear, Charles (*b* New Haven, Conn., 29 Dec 1800; *d* New York City, 1 July 1860). Inventor. Best known for inventing vulcanized rubber, he carried out some of his most important experiments in New York City. After encountering rubber for the first time in 1834, he soon moved to New York City to conduct experiments, working at various times on Bank Street and in Staten Island. After a number of failures he left in 1837 but returned in 1840 for about a year to refine his successful sulfur-and-heat process later known as vulcanization. Goodyear spent little time in the city thereafter.

Robert M. Quackenbush: *Oh, What an Awful Mess: A Story of Charles Goodyear* (Englewood Cliffs, N.J.: Prentice Hall, 1980)

Robert Friedel

Goose Creek. Former fishing colony in southwestern Queens, lying along the cross-bay railroad line on the northernmost island in Jamaica Bay. It began as a few fishermen's shacks built on piles along the shore and was first served by the railroad in 1888. About this time it became known for its weakfish, and in 1899 there were six clubhouses, two saloons, and a hotel. By 1903 there were more row-boats for hire than at any other fishing station in the bay, and Goose Creek was frequented by anglers from other parts of the city who traveled there by train to spend the day. Fishing and the harvesting of shellfish were halted by the gradual pollution of Jamaica Bay, especially after a sewage treatment plant opened in Jamaica in 1914; angling was banned by the city in 1916. Although the fishing stations ceased to operate, the railroad continued to stop on schedule until the end of the summer of 1932.

Vincent Seyfried

Goosepatch. Name formerly applied to New Brighton.

Gorham Manufacturing. Firm of silversmiths, formed in 1865. Its predecessor was a silver manufactory opened in 1831 by Jabez Gorham (1792–1869). Based in Providence, Rhode Island, the firm opened wholesale showrooms in Maiden Lane in Manhattan in 1859 and adopted the English sterling standard of .925 fine silver in 1868. It aggressively marketed its sterling and electroplated wares, ecclesiastical goods, and bronzes through trade catalogues, retail and wholesale showrooms in the city, and exclusive retail distributors nationwide. The firm moved its salesrooms to Broadway and 19th Street in 1883. Later it commissioned the firm of McKim, Mead and White to design a building at 390 5th Avenue for its retail operation, which moved there in 1905. In 1929 the retail store merged with Black, Starr and Frost to become Black, Starr and Frost–Gorham (from 1940 Black, Starr and Gorham). The combined shop operated at various addresses until 1962.

Charles H. Carpenter Jr.: *Gorham Silver, 1831–1981* (New York: Dodd, Mead, 1982)

Deborah Dependahl Waters

Gorky, Arshile [Adoian, Vosdanig] (*b* Khorkom, Vari Hayotz Dzore, Armenia, 15 April 1904; *d* Sherman, Conn., 21 July 1948). Painter. A refugee from the massacre of the Armenians during the First World War, he settled in New York City in 1925 and be-

Arshile Gorky, Painting *(1936–37). Collection of the Whitney Museum of American Art*

came an instructor at the Grand Central School of Art in 1926. His masterly early work *The Artist and His Mother* (Whitney Museum of American Art), painted in the city between 1926 and 1936, is based on a photograph taken in Armenia. Originally influenced by Cézanne and Picasso, he later became involved with the surrealists; the rich fluidity of line and complexity of association in his mature works is in part due to their influence. In 1935 he joined the mural division of the Federal Art Project of the Works Progress Administration. In addition to works executed for the project he painted the mural *Man's Conquest of the Air*, installed at the World's Fair of 1939–40 and now lost. In 1945 he had a show at the Julien Levy Gallery in New York City, for which the surrealist André Breton wrote an essay entitled "The Eye Spring: Arshile Gorky." Under stress from medical and emotional problems, Gorky took his own life.

Ethel K. Schwabacher: *Arshile Gorky* (New York: Macmillan, 1957)

Diane Waldman: *Arshile Gorky, 1904–1948: Retrospective* (New York: Harry N. Abrams / Solomon R. Guggenheim Foundation, 1981)

Jim M. Jordan and Robert Goldwater: *The Paintings of Arshile Gorky: A Critical Catalogue* (New York: New York University Press, 1982)

Mona Hadler

gospel music. A style of vocal music having its roots in the expressive singing and impassioned call-and-response of the Sanctified and Spiritualist black Pentecostal churches. Its earliest exponents came to prominence in Chicago and Philadelphia in the 1930s. During these years a number of gospel groups performed regularly in New York City, including three from Virginia: the Selah Jubilee Singers, the Norfolk Jubilee Singers, and the Golden Gate Jubilee Quartet, who cultivated a secular following and performed at such venues as Barney Josephson's Café Society. Sister Rosetta Tharpe introduced gospel at the Cotton Club in 1939. By the 1940s several leading gospel soloists had moved to New York City, of whom one of the best-known was the Georgia Peach, a powerful contralto who originally performed with male quartets; unlike most female vocal soloists, who were Pentecostal, she was a Baptist. As the Church of God in Christ became the largest black Pentecostal denomination its local branches became the leading venues for gospel concerts. The best-known was Washington Temple in Brooklyn; the wife of its pastor, Bishop F. D. Washington, was the gospel singer Madame Ernestine B. Washington, known as "the Songbird of the East." A forceful performer with a gritty voice, she exemplified the spiritual power of the Sanctified church. Other soloists who performed at Washington Temple were two evangelists from Texas, Madame Emily Bram and Sister Jessie Mae Renfro. Another important figure, Madame Marie Knight, came to prominence at a Spiritualist church and performed for ten years in a duo with Tharpe.

Gospel soloists such as Madame Washington were eclipsed in popularity during the 1950s by male and female gospel groups, who usually wore choir robes and were accompanied by pianos and organs. The outstanding groups in the city included the Daniels Singers (led by Becky Moss Burroughs), Professor Charles Taylor and the Gospel All Stars (led by Ella Mitchell), and the Herman Stevens Singers (led by Dorothy McLeod). In later decades choirs of fifty and more became the major performing ensembles. Several were based in Manhattan and Brooklyn, among them the Washington Temple Choir, led by Timothy Wright.

The city also became known for elaborate gospel concerts staged in local churches. In 1951 Mahalia Jackson sang gospel at Carnegie Hall, and in 1961 Langston Hughes's *Black Nativity*, with Marion Williams and Professor Alex Bradford, became the first gospel musical to be presented off Broadway. Later ones included *Your Arms Too Short to Box with God* (1976) and *Mama I Want to Sing* (1980).

Between 1954 and 1969 the Apollo Theater frequently presented gospel "caravans," concert series a week long that became legendary. The enthusiastic audiences at the Apollo effectively transformed it into a church: programs sometimes ran so long that the intervening films had to be canceled, and nurses were on hand to minister to overwrought members of the audience. Among the performers who evoked the strongest responses were the Clara Ward Singers (led by Williams), the Soul Stirrers (led by Sam Cooke), the Davis Sisters (led by Ruth Davis), the Pilgrim Travelers (Kylo Turner), the Caravans (Inez Andrews and Shirley Caesar), the Nightingales (Julius Cheeks), the Raspberry Singers (Carl Hall), and the Swan Silvertones (Claude Jeter), as well as Bradford and the Rev. James Cleveland.

Anthony Heilbut: *The Gospel Sound: Good News and Bad Times* (New York: Simon and Schuster, 1971)

Irene V. Jackson: *Afro-American Religious Music: A Bibliography and a Catalogue* (Westport, Conn.: Greenwood, 1979)

Anthony Heilbut

Gotham. Anglo-Saxon name meaning "goat town" and popularly applied to New York City. It came into use after 1807, when Washington Irving used it satirically in several essays published as part of the series *Salmagundi: or, the Whim-whams and Opinions of Launcelot Langstaff and Others.* Residents of the original Gotham, near Nottingham, England, were reportedly called "wise fools" in the Middle Ages for avoiding King John's taxes by acting insane. Although Irving seems to have used the name sardonically to suggest a city of self-important but foolish people, the pejorative connotations were gradually lost.

Grosvenor Clarkson: *Why Gotham?: The Story of a Name* (New York: Gotham National Bank, 1915)

"Gotham," *New Yorker,* 7 Aug 1965, pp. 19–20

Irving Lewis Allen

Gotham Book Mart. Bookshop in Manhattan, opened by Frances Steloff on 3 January 1920 at 128 West 45th Street. It moved in 1923 to 51 West 47th Street and in 1946 to 41

West 47th Street, where it remained into the 1990s. From its beginnings the shop emphasized twentieth-century literature. A famous cast-iron sign at the entrance bears the inscription "Wise Men Fish Here." By 1990 the shop contained a quarter-million new, used, and out-of-print books and some fifty thousand magazines. The Gotham has been singled out for its uniqueness by such figures as Arthur Miller and John Updike, and in 1988 it was called the most celebrated bookshop in New York City by the *New Yorker.*

W. G. Rogers: *Wise Men Fish Here: The Story of Frances Steloff and the Gotham Book Mart* (New York: Harcourt, Brace and World, 1965)

Allen J. Share

Gotham Court. A "model tenement" opened in 1850 by the Quaker philanthropist Silas Wood to provide housing for the poor. Situated in Manhattan on the block bounded to the north by Oak Street, to the east by Roosevelt Street, to the south by Cherry Street, and to the west by New Bowery (now St. James Place) and Franklin Square, the complex consisted of two rows of six tenements, each of five stories, standing back to back and facing two mews at 34 and 38 Cherry Street. Each of the 144 apartments in the complex was divided into a living room of fourteen by ten feet (four by three meters) and a bedroom of fourteen by seven feet (four by two meters). Shortly after it was occupied the complex became notorious for overcrowding, filth, and crime. During the 1890s it was criticized by such reformers as Jacob A. Riis, and in 1895 Gotham Court was demolished under the Tenement House Law. The Governor Alfred E. Smith Houses now occupy the site.

Kenneth A. Scherzer

Gotti, John (*b* Bronx, 27 Oct 1940). Organized-crime leader. He joined the Gambino crime family and worked regularly from the Ravenite social club on Mulberry Street in Manhattan and the Bergin Hunt and Fish Club in Queens. Known as the "dapper don," he became the head of the Gambino crime family in 1985 after ordering the assassination of its leader, Paul Castellano, in front of Sparks Steak House on 46th Street in Manhattan. The murder made Gotti the best-known organized-crime figure in the United States. Acquitted of serious charges three times between 1987 and 1990, he was finally convicted in 1992 on a number of charges, among them ordering Castellano's assassination, and sentenced to life in federal prison.

Jesse Drucker

38 Cherry Street in Gotham Court, ca 1885–90. Photograph by Richard Hoe Lawrence

Gottlieb, Adolph (*b* New York City, 14 March 1903; *d* New York City, 4 March 1974). Painter. He grew up in New York City and during the early 1920s studied at the Parsons School of Design and the Art Students League. In 1935 he helped to form The Ten, a group dedicated to expressionist and abstract art. He was a leading figure in the abstract expressionist movement, also called the New York School, especially in its early stages during the 1940s; with Mark Rothko and Barnett Newman he publicly articulated its major themes in 1943 in a letter to Edward Alden Jewell, a critic for the *New York Times.* Gottlieb lived mainly in Brooklyn until 1956 and did not associate closely with other abstract expressionists. His best-known works are *Pictographs* (1941–51), *Grids and Imaginary Landscapes* (1951–57), and *Bursts* (1957–74).

Eileen K. Cheng

Gould, Jay [Jason] (*b* Roxbury, N.Y., 27 May 1836; *d* New York City, 2 Dec 1892). Financier and speculator. After moving to New York City he worked briefly as a leather merchant at 39 Spruce Street in 1859–60. He speculated and invested in railroads, and in 1860 he formed the brokerage house of Smith, Gould and Martin on Wall Street. With Daniel Drew and Jim Fisk he battled Cornelius Vanderbilt during the late 1860s in a struggle to gain control of the Erie Railroad, which he pillaged with the connivance of the railroad directors Peter B. Sweeny and William M. Tweed (later known as Boss Tweed). After the death of Fisk and the overthrow of the Tweed Ring he lost control of the railroad in 1872, and he then used a fortune estimated at $25 million to invest in railroads in the West. He later owned the newspaper the *New York World* (1879–83) and became a part owner of the New York Elevated Railroad Company in 1881, of which he assumed virtually full ownership in 1886. On his death his fortune was estimated at $77 million. Despite his great wealth Gould had a reputation as an unscrupulous scoundrel, which caused him to be shunned by fashionable society in New York City: he was blackballed by the New York Yacht Club, and Mrs. William Astor excluded him from her celebrated "four hundred." With Drew and Fisk he was among the leading "robber barons" of the nineteenth century.

Maury Klein: *The Life and Legend of Jay Gould* (Baltimore: Johns Hopkins University Press, 1986)

John Steele Gordon: *The Scarlet Woman of Wall Street: Jay Gould, Jim Fisk, Cornelius Vanderbilt, the Erie Railway Wars, and the Birth of Wall Street* (New York: Weidenfeld and Nicolson, 1988)

See also WESTERN UNION.

Allen J. Share

government and politics. The government of New York City is far older than that of the United States and of most other American jurisdictions. Its political history has been spirited, contentious, and convoluted, encompassing such diverse figures as De Witt Clinton, William M. "Boss" Tweed, Theodore Roosevelt, Fiorello H. La Guardia, and Nelson A. Rockefeller.

1. Colonial Period

The Dutch granted municipal autonomy to New Amsterdam in 1653, establishing the city's first local government. The city remained the capital of the colony of New York after the defeat of the Dutch by the English in 1664. The first English governor of the colony was Richard Nicolls (1664–68), a colonel who in 1665 issued the Duke's Laws, the first legal and governmental codes promulgated by the Duke of York, the proprietor of the colony. No provision was made for an elected assembly, which would have been dominated by the Dutch (the English were yet a minority in the colony). Municipal government consisted of a mayor, four aldermen, and a sheriff appointed by Nicolls to administer the city. Governor Thomas Dongan (1683–88) granted a revised charter in 1686 that divided the city into six wards: the North, East, West, South, and Dock wards, and an Out ward of farms to the north. The charter also called for a common council, made up of a mayor and a recorder appointed by the governor, as well as an alderman and an assistant alderman elected from each ward and included on the Mayor's Court, an advisory body chosen by the mayor. The recorder provided legal counsel to the Mayor's Court as well as to the council, over which he presided when the mayor was absent. The colony of New York was divided into twelve counties in 1683, of which four counties and part of a fifth accounted for the land now making up New York City: New York (the present Manhattan), Kings (Brooklyn), Richmond (Staten Island), Queens, and southern Westchester (the Bronx).

After the Duke of York ascended to the throne as James II in 1685, New York became a royal colony with a governor and an advisory council of twelve men appointed by the king. The governor worked and lived in a fort at the southern tip of Manhattan (named successively Fort James, Fort William, Fort Anne, and Fort George), where British regulars were stationed to provide for the city's defense. In addition to the king the Admiralty, the Treasury, and the War Office had some jurisdiction over the city. As a major port it was vulnerable to attacks by the French and the Spanish, and cannon were mounted in the area now known as the Battery. In 1696 the city's commerce came more directly under the jurisdiction of the Board of Trade and the Treasury, which were empowered to enforce the Navigation Acts.

After the revolution of 1688–89 in England New Yorkers were divided into supporters

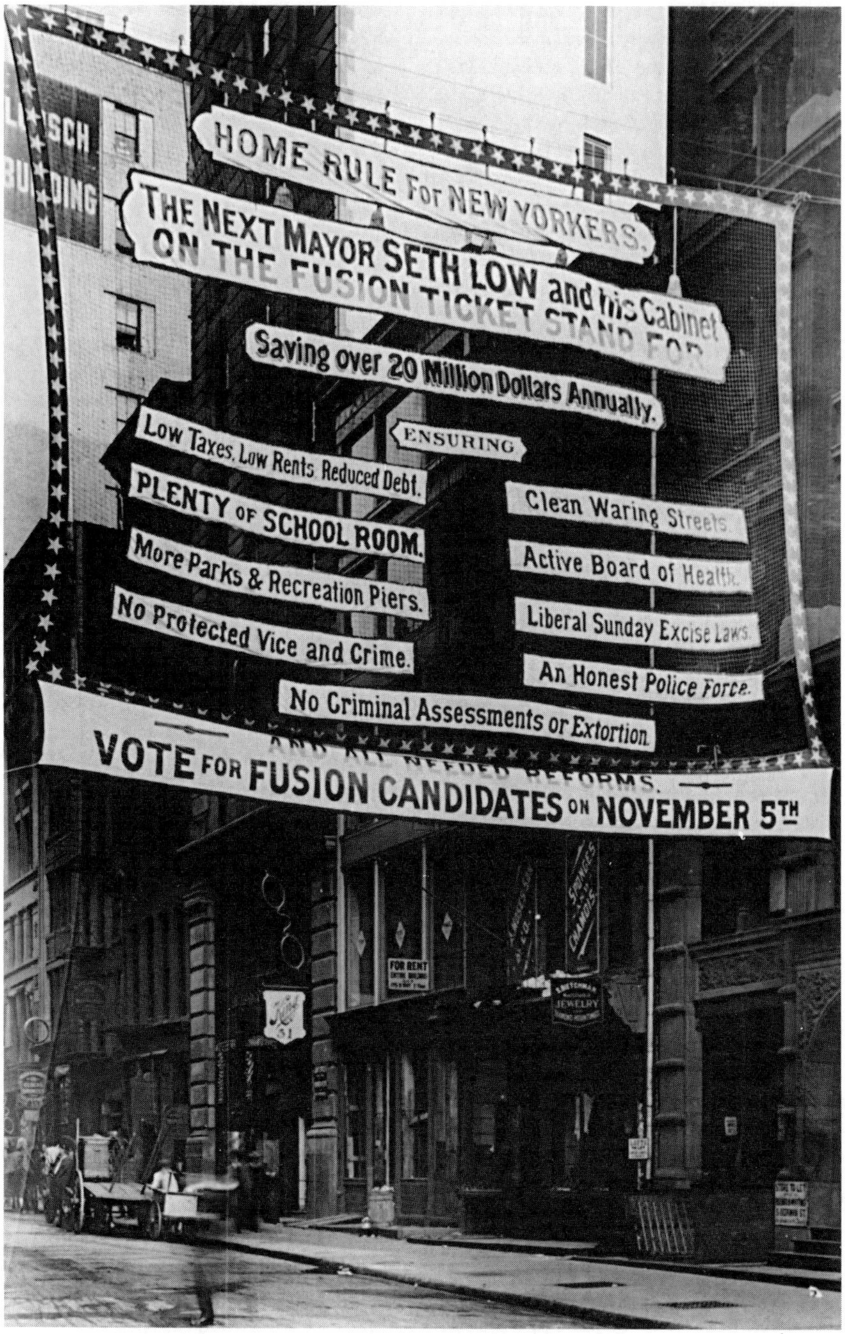

Campaign banner for Seth Low in Maiden Lane, 1891

and opponents of Jacob Leisler, who seized control of the colony in 1689 during an absence of the lieutenant governor, Francis Nicholson. In 1691 King William and Queen Mary named Colonel Henry Sloughter governor and instructed him to hold elections for a permanent general assembly. Eighteen men were elected to the assembly in 1691, meeting at a tavern before acquiring a chamber at City Hall in 1704. Throughout the colonial period New York County always sent four representatives, whereas each of the other counties sent no more than two. Politics were highly partisan: temporary alliances formed around factions, economic and religious groups, and leading families. About one third of the assemblymen belonged to patrician families and one third to the upper middle class; the rest were small farmers, shopkeepers, and artisans. Only merchants were elected to the assembly from the city during the colonial period. They used their influence to control legislative standards for the quality and packing of flour, beef, pork, wood products, and skins produced upriver. Assemblymen customarily resided in their own districts. They were expected to be men of property and standing, but because land was available and status fluid they were socially more diverse than their counterparts in England. The vote was extended to men twenty-one years of age and older whose land was valued at £40 or was capable of producing 40*s.* in annual income, or who held freemen's status in New York City or Albany. Electoral turnouts of more than 50 percent were rare until the 1760s, because many voters lived far from polling places, candidates often ran unopposed, and important issues were rarely addressed.

The king in 1696 created the Lords Commissioners of Trade and Plantations, also called the Board of Trade, a small group of politicians and experts on the colonies that had broad powers: it monitored the system of trade and other affairs in the expanding empire, advised the king on the appointment of colonial governors, examined provincial laws and sometimes recommended vetoes, wrote instructions for incoming governors, and proposed legislation for the colony. Merchants in the city sent representatives to England and encouraged merchants in London and Bristol to protest decrees harmful to trade in the greater Atlantic; colonists also worked with friends in England to circumvent decisions of the board. Although its more powerful members found ways to influence policy, the board was often ignored by the secretary of state for the Southern Department, who had great latitude to administer the colony. The board rarely provided vigorous leadership and by the time of the American Revolution had very little influence.

The eighteenth century saw the governor and the assembly vie for power. Some governors, including Benjamin Fletcher (1692–98), Edward Hyde, Viscount Cornbury (1702–8), William Cosby (1732–36), and George Clinton (1743–53), deemed the colonies lesser branches of the empire ("twigs belonging to the main Tree," according to Cornbury). They firmly enforced the trade laws and pressed the assembly for defense appropriations. Like the Whig governors Richard Coote, earl of Bellomont (1698–?1701), Robert Hunter (1710–19), and Henry Moore (1765–69) they also cultivated the support of a local "court party" to which they awarded patronage, land grants, judicial positions, and contracts; they did this to counteract the challenge posed to their power by the assembly, which increasingly controlled funds (it refused appropriations to Hunter until he agreed in 1714 to accord it greater control over officials' salaries and government expenses). At the same time the governor's council demanded greater autonomy and gradually expanded its role to that of an upper house of the legislature.

Leaders in the city were often members of prominent families, including the de Lanceys, Morrises, Beekmans, Livingstons, and Van Cortlandts. After 1730 elections were frequently contested by members of rival families, inspiring popular participation as ordinary voters found themselves in a position to choose between élite candidates. Merchants

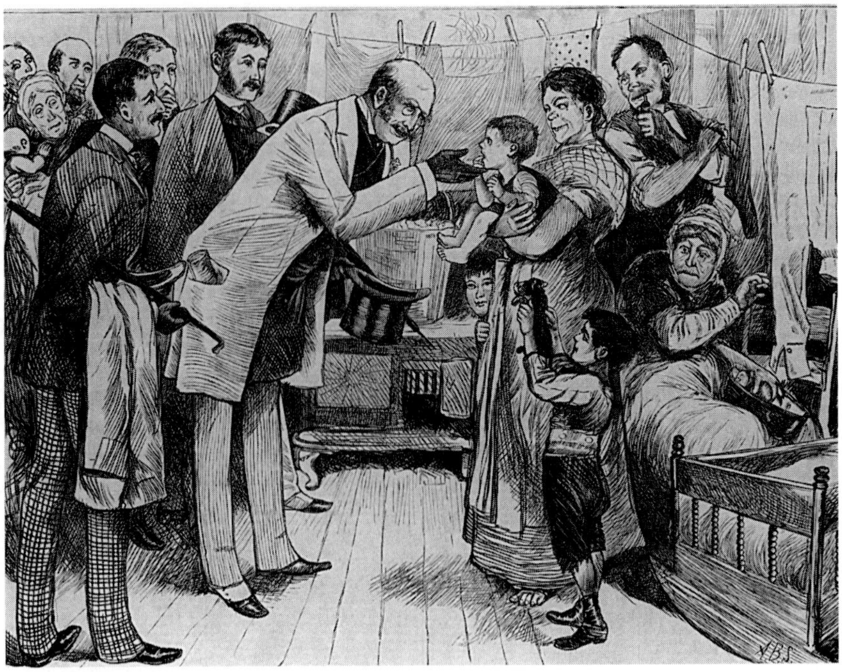

"The Canvass of a 'Swell' Candidate for Political Honors in a Tenement District," from Frank Leslie's Illustrated Newspaper, *19 November 1881*

English Governors of New York, 1664–1775

	Appointed
Richard Nicolls (*b* 1624; *d* 28 May 1672)	8 Sept 1664
Colonel Francis Lovelace (*b ca* 1621; *d* 10 May 1686)	17 Aug 1667
Major Edmund Andros, Knight (*b* 6 Dec 1637; *d* Feb 1714)	10 Nov 1674
Anthony Brockholles, Commander in Chief (*d* 1723)	16 Nov 1677
Sir Edmund Andros	7 Aug 1678
Anthony Brockholles, Commander in Chief	13 Jan 1681
Colonel Thomas Dongan (*b* 1634; *d* 14 Dec 1715)	27 Aug 1682
Sir Edmund Andros	11 Aug 1688
Francis Nicholson, Lieutenant Governor (*b* 12 Nov 1655; *d* 5 March 1728)	9 Oct 1688
Jacob Leisler (*b* 1640; *d* 16 May 1691)	3 June 1689
Colonel Henry Sloughter (*d* 23 July 1691)	19 March 1691
Major Richard Ingoldsby, Commander in Chief	26 July 1691
Colonel Benjamin Fletcher (*b* ?1640; *d* 1703)	30 Aug 1692
Richard Coote, Earl of Bellomont (*b* 1636; *d* 5 March 1701)	13 April 1698
John Nanfan, Lieutenant Governor (*d* 1706)	17 May 1699
Earl of Bellomont	24 July 1700
William Smith, as eldest Councilor present (*b* 2 Feb 1655; *d* 18 Feb 1705)	5 March 1701
John Nanfan, Lieutenant Governor	19 May 1701
Edward Hyde, Viscount Cornbury (*b* 1661; *d* 1 April 1723)	3 May 1702
John, Lord Lovelace (*d* 6 May 1709)	18 Dec 1708

(*continued*)

English Governors of New York, 1664–1775 *(Continued)*

	Appointed
Peter Schuyler, President of Council (*b* 17 Sept 1657; *d* 19 Feb 1724)	6 May 1709
Richard Ingoldsby, Lieutenant Governor	9 May 1709
Peter Schuyler, President of Council	25 May 1709
Richard Ingoldsby, Lieutenant Governor	1 June 1709
Gerardus Beekman, President of the Council (*b* 1653; *d* 10 Oct 1723)	10 April 1710
Brigadier Robert Hunter (*d* March 1734)	14 June 1710
Peter Schuyler, President of Council	21 July 1719
William Burnet (*b* March 1688; *d* 7 Sept 1729)	17 Sept 1720
John Montgomerie (*d* 30 June 1731)	15 April 1728
Rip van Dam, President of the Council (*b ca* 1660; *d* 10 June 1749)	1 July 1731
Colonel William Cosby (*b ca* 1690; *d* 10 March 1736)	1 Aug 1732
George Clarke, President of the Council (*b* 1676; *d* 12 Jan 1760)	10 March 1736
Admiral George Clinton (*b ca* 1686; *d* 10 July 1761)	2 Sept 1743
Sir Danvers Osborne, Baronet (*b* 17 Nov 1715; *d* 12 Oct 1753)	10 Oct 1753
James de Lancey, Lieutenant Governor (*b* 27 Nov 1703; *d* 30 July 1760)	12 Oct 1753
Sir Charles Hardy, Knight (*b ca* 1716; *d* 18 May 1780)	3 Sept 1755
James de Lancey, Lieutenant Governor	3 June 1757
Cadwallader Colden, President of the Council (*b* 17 Feb 1688; *d* 28 Sept 1776)	4 Aug 1760
Major General Robert Monckton (*b* 24 June 1726; *d* 21 May 1782)	26 Oct 1761
Cadwallader Colden, President of the Council	18 Nov 1761
Major General Robert Monckton	14 June 1762
Cadwallader Colden, Lieutenant Governor	28 June 1763
Sir Henry Moore, Baronet (*b* 7 Feb 1713; *d* 11 Sept 1769)	13 Nov 1765
Cadwallader Colden, Lieutenant Governor	12 Sept 1769
John Murray, Earl of Dunmore (*b* 1732; *d* 5 March 1809)	19 Oct 1770
William Tryon (*b* 1729; *d* 27 Jan 1788)	9 July 1771
Cadwallader Colden, Lieutenant Governor	7 April 1774
William Tryon	28 June 1775

Compiled by Edward T. O'Donnell

and the wealthy during the colonial period dominated both the mayoralty and the Common Council, which monitored the movement of visitors, regulated markets and set the price of bread, and sought to control the persistent problem of free-roaming and voracious hogs. The council also included many artisans and shopkeepers, whose presence made the process more democratic and spurred public interest in elections.

In 1731 Governor John Montgomerie put into effect the last city charter of the colonial period, which provided for a seventh ward, Montgomerie, to the northeast. The charter prescribed few other changes and remained in effect until George Washington abandoned the city in 1776.

2. Federal Period to the Second World War

At the end of the American Revolution municipal authority was centered in the Common Council, which represented a small electorate of property owners. For several years the state appointed and removed mayors whenever party control changed: Major Richard Varick was removed after twelve years in office when control changed in Albany in 1803; De Witt Clinton was removed from office in 1809 and returned the next year. The city's growth and complexity stimulated efforts to create a system more responsive to popular will and freer from interference by the state legislature. In 1804 members of Tammany Hall persuaded the legislature to enfranchise men who rented property and to adopt the paper ballot; by the 1820s the legislature removed all property qualifications for white men. The Common Council gained authorization to select its own mayor in 1821, ending the removal of mayors at the whim of the legislature. In 1830 the state fundamentally altered Montgomerie's charter by dividing the Common Council into a board of aldermen and a board of assistant aldermen, and by making the mayor a distinct official with the power to veto actions of the council. A state constitutional amendment enhanced the mayor's independence in 1833 by providing for his direct popular election. When the first mayoral election was held in 1834, more than 35,000 voters took part.

In the 1840s the Common Council organized professional firefighting and police forces, improved the paving and lighting of streets, completed the Croton water system, and expanded social services. To administer these and other municipal functions ten city departments were formed in 1849 that were eventually subdivided into bureaus, of which all except for the police department were led by elected officials. Voters chose from an overwhelming number of candidates because the amended charter rescheduled city elections to the same time as state and national elections. This confusion benefited ward caucuses, which elected delegates for party conventions. Ward meetings were small and easily manipulated by ambitious politicians, a point later emphasized by Theodore Roosevelt when he charged that two thirds of the ward meetings were held in saloons and discouraged the involvement of respectable men. In 1853, after the corruption of the council had earned it the nickname the "Forty Thieves," the state enacted a new charter that restructured the municipal legislature into two distinct boards of aldermen and councilmen. Twenty-two aldermen were elected from the wards and sixty councilmen were elected by districts drawn to counter the influence of wards. The new charter further restrained the aldermen by giving the mayor a veto over legislation, eliminating the aldermen's role as city judges, and transferring the council's control of the police to the mayor and two other elected officials.

A charter was issued by the state legislature in 1857 to separate municipal and state elections by moving those for municipal offices from November to December. The charter empowered the mayor to appoint city inspectors and the heads of the street department and the Croton Aqueduct; the finance and law departments remained under the comptroller and corporation counsel, both elected. Other

Members of the U.S. House of Representatives Elected from Districts All or Partly within the Current Boundaries of New York City

William Floyd (Democratic Republican) 1789–91 (Brooklyn, Queens, Staten Island)
John Laurence (Federalist) 1789–93 (Manhattan, Westchester)
Thomas Tredwell (Federalist) 1791–95 (Brooklyn, Queens, Staten Island)
Philip Van Cortlandt (Democratic Republican) 1793–1809 (Westchester)
John Watts (Federalist) 1793–95 (Manhattan)
Jonathan N. Havens (Democratic Republican) 1795–99 (Brooklyn, Queens)
Edward Livingston (Democratic Republican) 1795–1801 (Manhattan)
John Smith (Democratic Republican) 1800–4 (Brooklyn, Queens, Staten Island)
Samuel L. Mitchell (Democratic Republican) 1801–4 (Manhattan), 1810–13 (Manhattan, Staten Island)
Joshua Sands (Federalist) 1803–5 (Brooklyn, Staten Island), 1825–27 (Brooklyn)
George Clinton Jr. (Democratic Republican) 1804–9 (Manhattan, Brooklyn, Staten Island)
Samuel Riker (Democratic Republican) 1804–5, 1807–9 (Queens)
Gurdon Mumford (Democratic Republican) 1805–11 (Manhattan, Brooklyn, Staten Island)
Eliphalet Wickes (Democratic Republican) 1805–7 (Queens)
William Denning (Democratic Republican) 1809–10 (Manhattan, Staten Island)
Jonathan Fisk (Democratic Republican) 1809–11 (Westchester)
Ebenezer Sage (Democratic Republican) 1809–15, 1819–20 (Queens, Staten Island)
William Paulding Jr. (Democratic Republican) 1811–13 (Manhattan, Staten Island)
Pierre Van Cortlandt (Democratic Republican) 1811–13 (Westchester)
Egbert Benson (Federalist) 1813 (Manhattan)
Pierre Denoyelles (Democratic Republican) 1813–15 (Westchester)
John Lefferts (Democratic Republican) 1813–15 (Brooklyn, Staten Island)
Jotham Post Jr. (Federalist) 1813–15 (Manhattan)
William Iving (Democratic Republican) 1814–19 (Manhattan)
Henry Crocheron (Democratic Republican) 1815–17 (Staten Island)
George Townsend (Democratic Republican) 1815–19 (Queens, Brooklyn, Staten Island)
Jonathan Ward (Democratic Republican) 1815–17 (Westchester)
Peter H. Wendover (Democratic Republican) 1815–21 (Manhattan)
Caleb Tompkins (Democratic Republican) 1817–21 (Westchester)
Henry Meigs (Democratic Republican) 1819–21 (Manhattan)
Silas Wood (Democratic Republican) 1819–29 (Queens, Brooklyn, Staten Island)
James Guyon Jr. (Democratic Republican) 1820–21 (Staten Island)
Churchill C. Cambreleng (Democrat) 1821–39 (Manhattan)
Cadwallader D. Colden (Federalist) 1821–23 (Manhattan)
John J. Morgan (Democratic Republican) 1821–25, 1834–35 (Manhattan)
Jeremiah H. Pierson (Democratic Republican) 1821–23 (Westchester)
Joel Frost (Crawford Republican) 1823–25 (Westchester)
Peter Sharpe (Adams–Clay Republican) 1823–25 (Manhattan)
Jacob Tyson (Crawford Republican) 1823–25 (Brooklyn, Staten Island)
Jeromus Johnson (Jacksonian) 1825–29 (Manhattan)
Gulian C. Verplanck (Jacksonian) 1825–33 (Manhattan)
Aaron Ward (Democrat) 1825–29, 1831–37, 1841–43 (Westchester)
John J. Wood (Jacksonian) 1827–29 (Brooklyn, Staten Island)
Henry B. Cowles (Adams Republican) 1829–31 (Westchester)
Jacob Crocheron (Democrat) 1829–31 (Brooklyn, Staten Island)
James Lent (Democrat) 1829–33 (Queens)
Campbell P. White (Democrat) 1829–35 (Manhattan)
John T. Bergen (Democrat) 1831–33 (Brooklyn, Staten Island)
Abel Huntington (Democratic) 1833–37 (Queens)
Cornelius W. Lawrence (Democrat) 1833–35 (Manhattan)
Dudley Selden (Democrat) 1833–34 (Brooklyn, Staten Island)
Isaac B. Van Houten (Democrat) 1833–35 (Manhattan)
Charles G. Ferris (Democrat) 1834–35 (Manhattan)
Samuel Barton (Democrat) 1835–37 (Manhattan)
Gideon Lee (Democrat) 1835–37 (Manhattan)
John McKeon (Democrat) 1835–37 (Manhattan)
Ely Moore (Democrat) 1835–39 (Queens)
Edward Curtis (Whig) 1837–41 (Westchester)
Josiah Ogden Hoffman (Whig) 1837–41 (Brooklyn, Staten Island)
Thomas B. Jackson (Democrat) 1837–41 (Brooklyn, Staten Island)
Gouverneur Kemble (Democrat) 1837–41 (Manhattan)
Abraham Vanderveer (Democrat) 1837–39 (Manhattan)
James De La Montanya (Democrat) 1839–41 (Brooklyn, Staten Island)
Moses H. Grinnell (Whig) 1839–41 (Manhattan)
James Monroe (Whig) 1839–41 (Queens)
Joseph Egbert (Democrat) 1841–43 (Manhattan)
Charles G. Ferris (Democrat) 1841–43 (Manhattan)
Charles A. Floyd (Democrat) 1841–43
James I. Roosevelt (Democrat) 1841–43 (Westchester)
Fernando Wood (Democrat) 1841–43, 1863–65, 1867–81 (Manhattan)
Joseph H. Anderson (Democrat) 1843–47 (Westchester)
Hamilton Fish (Whig) 1843–45 (Brooklyn, Staten Island)
Moses G. Leonard (Democrat) 1843–45 (Manhattan)
William B. Maclay (Democrat) 1843–49, 1857–61 (Queens)
Henry C. Murphy (Democrat) 1843–45, 1847–49 (Manhattan)
J. Phillips Phoenix (Whig) 1843–45 (Queens)
Selah B. Strong (Democrat) 1843–45 (Manhattan)
William W. Campbell (American) 1845–47 (Brooklyn, Staten Island)
John W. Lawrence (Democrat) 1845–47 (Manhattan)
William S. Miller (American) 1845–47 (Manhattan)
Henry Seaman (American) 1845–47 (Manhattan)
Thomas Woodruff (American) 1845–47 (Queens)
David S. Jackson (Democrat) 1847–48 (Westchester)
Frederick W. Lord (Democrat) 1847–49 (Manhattan)
William Nelson (Whig) 1847–51 (Westchester)
Henry Nicoll (Democrat) 1847–49 (Manhattan)
Frederick A. Tallmadge (Whig) 1847–49 (Manhattan)
Horace Greeley (Whig) 1848–49 (Manhattan)
David A. Bokee (Whig) 1849–51 (Manhattan)
George Briggs (Whig) 1849–53, 1859–61 (Queens, Manhattan)
James Brooks (Whig) 1849–53, 1863–66, 1867–73 (Manhattan)
John A. King (Whig) 1849–51 (Brooklyn, Staten Island)
J. Phillips Phoenix (Whig) 1849–51 (Manhattan)
Walter Underhill (Whig) 1849–51 (Queens)
Obadiah Bowne (Whig) 1851–53 (Brooklyn)

(*continued*)

Members of the U.S. House of Representatives Elected from Districts All or Partly within the Current Boundaries of New York City *(Continued)*

John G. Floyd (Democrat) 1851–53 (Manhattan)
J. H. Hobart Haws (Whig) 1851–53 (Queens, Brooklyn, Staten Island)
Abraham P. Stephens (Democrat) 1851–53 (Westchester)
Thomas W. Cumming (Democrat) 1853–55 (Westchester)
Francis B. Cutting (Democrat) 1853–55 (Manhattan)
James Maurice (Democrat) 1853–55 (Queens, Brooklyn, Staten Island)
Jared V. Peck (Democrat) 1853–55 (Westchester)
William M. Tweed (Democrat) 1853–55 (Manhattan, Brooklyn)
Hiram Walbridge (Democrat) 1853–55 (Manhattan)
William Walker (Democrat) 1853–55 (Manhattan)
Michael Walsh (Democrat) 1853–55 (Manhattan)
John Wheeler (Democrat) 1853–57 (Manhattan)
Thomas Child Jr. (Whig) 1855–57 (Manhattan)
Bayard Clarke (Whig) 1855–57 (Westchester)
John Kelly (Democrat) 1855–58 (Manhattan)
Guy R. Pelton (Whig) 1855–57 (Manhattan)
James S. T. Stranahan (Whig) 1855–57 (Brooklyn)
William W. Valk (American) 1855–57 (Queens, Brooklyn, Staten Island)
Abram Wakeman (Whig) 1855–57 (Manhattan)
Thomas R. Whitney (American) 1855–57 (Manhattan, Brooklyn)
Horace F. Clark (Democrat) 1857–61 (Manhattan)
John Cochrane (Democrat) 1857–61 (Manhattan)
John B. Haskin (Democrat) 1857–61 (Westchester)
John A. Searing (Democrat) 1857–59 (Queens, Brooklyn, Staten Island)
Daniel Sickles (Democrat) 1857–61, 1893–95 (Manhattan)
George Taylor (Democrat) 1857–59 (Brooklyn)
Elijah Ward (Democrat) 1857–59, 1861–65, 1875–77 (Manhattan)
Thomas J. Barr (Democrat) 1858–61 (Manhattan)
Luther C. Carter (Republican) 1859–61 (Queens, Brooklyn, Staten Island)
James Humphrey (Republican) 1859–61 (Brooklyn)
Frederick A. Conkling (Republican) 1861–63 (Manhattan)
Isaac C. Delaplaine (Democrat) 1861–63 (Manhattan)
Edward Haight (Democrat) 1861–63 (Westchester)
James E. Kerrigan (Democrat) 1861–63 (Manhattan)
Moses F. Odell (Democrat) 1861–65 (Brooklyn)
Edward H. Smith (Democrat) 1861–63 (Queens, Brooklyn, Staten Island)
William Wall (Republican) 1861–63 (Manhattan)
Benjamin Wood (Democrat) 1861–65, 1881–83 (Manhattan)
John W. Chanler (Democrat) 1863–69 (Manhattan)
Anson Herrick (Democrat) 1863–65 (Manhattan)
Martin Kalbfleisch (Democrat) 1863–65 (Brooklyn)
William Radford (Democrat) 1863–67 (Westchester)
Henry J. Stebbins (Democrat) 1863–64 (Queens, Staten Island)
Dwight Townsend (Democrat) 1864–65 (Queens, Staten Island)
Teunis G. Bergen (Democrat) 1865–67 (Brooklyn)
William A. Darling (Republican) 1865–67 (Manhattan)
James Morgan Humphrey (Democrat) 1865–66 (Brooklyn)
Morgan Jones (Democrat) 1865–67 (Manhattan)
Henry J. Raymond (Republican) 1865–67 (Manhattan)
Stephen Taber (Democrat) 1865–69 (Queens, Staten Island)
Nelson Taylor (Democrat) 1865–67 (Manhattan)
William E. Dodge (Republican) 1866–67 (Manhattan)
John W. Hunter (Democrat) 1866–67 (Brooklyn)
Demas Barnes (Democrat) 1867–69 (Brooklyn)
John Fox (Democrat) 1867–71 (Manhattan)
John Morrissey (Democrat) 1867–71 (Manhattan)
William H. Robertson (Republican) 1867–69 (Westchester)
William E. Robinson (Democrat) 1867–69, 1881–85 (Brooklyn)
Thomas E. Stewart (Republican) 1867–69 (Manhattan)
Hervey C. Calkin (Democrat) 1869–71 (Manhattan)
Samuel S. Cox (Democrat) 1869–73, 1873–85, 1886–89 (Manhattan)
Clarkson N. Potter (Democrat) 1869–75, 1877–79 (Westchester)
Henry A. Reeves (Democrat) 1869–71 (Queens, Staten Island)
John G. Schumaker (Democrat) 1869–71, 1873–77 (Brooklyn)
Henry W. Slocum (Democrat) 1869–73 (Brooklyn)
Smith Ely Jr. (Democrat) 1871–73 (Manhattan)
Thomas Kinsella (Democrat) 1871–73 (Brooklyn)
William R. Roberts (Democrat) 1871–75 (Manhattan)
Robert B. Roosevelt (Democrat) 1871–73 (Manhattan)
Dwight Townsend (Democrat) 1871–73 (Queens, Staten Island)
Samuel S. Cox (Democrat) 1873–85, 1886–89 (Manhattan)
Thomas Creamer (Democrat) 1873–75, 1901–3 (Manhattan)
Philip S. Crooke (Republican) 1873–75 (Brooklyn)
John D. Lawson (Republican) 1873–75 (Manhattan)
David B. Mellish (Republican) 1873–74 (Manhattan)
Henry J. Scudder (Republican) 1873–75 (Queens, Staten Island)
Stewart L. Woodford (Republican) 1873–74 (Brooklyn)
Simeon B. Chittenden (Republican) 1874–81 (Brooklyn)
Richard Schell (Democrat) 1874–75 (Manhattan)
Archibald M. Bliss (Democrat) 1875–83, 1885–89 (Brooklyn)
Abram S. Hewitt (Democrat) 1875–79 (Manhattan)
Edwin Meade (Democrat) 1875–77 (Manhattan)
Henry B. Metcalfe (Democrat) 1875–77 (Queens, Staten Island)
N. Holmes Odell (Democrat) 1875–77 (Westchester)
Benjamin Willis (Democrat) 1875–79 (Manhattan)
James Covert (Democrat) 1877–81, 1889–95 (Queens, Staten Island)
David Dudley Field (Democrat) 1877 (Manhattan)
Anthony Eckhoff (Democrat) 1877–79 (Manhattan)
Anson G. McCook (Republican) 1877–83 (Manhattan)
Nicholas Muller (Democrat) 1877–81, 1883–87, 1899–1902 (Manhattan)
Alexander Smith (Democrat) 1877 (Westchester)
William Vedeer (Democrat) 1877–79 (Brooklyn)
Edwin Einstein (Republican) 1879–81 (Brooklyn)
Waldo Hutchins (Democrat) 1879–85 (Westchester)
Levi P. Morton (Republican) 1879–81 (Manhattan)

(continued)

Members of the U.S. House of Representatives Elected from Districts All or Partly within the Current Boundaries of New York City *(Continued)*

James O'Brien (Democrat) 1879–81 (Manhattan)
Daniel O'Reilly (Democrat) 1879–81 (Brooklyn)
Perry Belmont (Democrat) 1881–88 (Queens, Staten Island)
P. Henry Dugro (Democrat) 1881–83 (Manhattan)
Peter P. Mahoney (Democrat) 1885–89 (Brooklyn)
Truman A. Merriman (Democrat) 1885–89 (Brooklyn)
Joseph Pulitzer (Democrat) 1885–86 (Manhattan)
William G. Stahlnecker (Democrat) 1885–93 (Westchester)
Egbert L. Viele (Democrat) 1885–87 (Manhattan)
Lloyd S. Bryce (Democrat) 1887–89 (Manhattan)
W. Bourke Cockran (Democrat) 1887–89 (Manhattan)
Amos J. Cummings (Democrat) 1887–89, 1889–94, 1895–1902 (Manhattan)
Ashbel P. Fitch (Democrat) 1887–93 (Manhattan)
Francis B. Spinola (Democrat) 1887–91 (Manhattan)
Steven V. White (Republican) 1887–89 (Brooklyn)
John M. Clancy (Democrat) 1889–95 (Brooklyn)
Edward J. Dunphy (Democrat) 1889–95 (Manhattan)
Frank T. Fitzgerald (Democrat) 1889 (Manhattan)
John H. McCarthy (Democrat) 1889–91 (Manhattan)
Thomas F. Magner (Democrat) 1889–95 (Brooklyn)
John Quinn (Democrat) 1889–91 (Manhattan)
Charles H. Turner (Democrat) 1889–91 (Manhattan)
William C. Wallace (Republican) 1889–91 (Manhattan)
David A. Boody (Democrat) 1891 (Brooklyn)
Alfred C. Chapin (Democrat) 1891–92 (Brooklyn)
W. Bourke Cockran (Democrat) 1891–95, 1904–9, 1921–23 (Manhattan)
John R. Fellows (Democrat) 1891–94 (Manhattan)
Joseph J. Little (Democrat) 1891–93 (Manhattan)
Franklin Bartlett (Democrat) 1893–97 (Staten Island, Manhattan)
John H. Graham (Democrat) 1893–95 (Brooklyn)
Joseph C. Hendrix (Democrat) 1893–95 (Brooklyn)
William Ryan (Democrat) 1893–95 (Westchester)
Lemuel E. Quigg (Republican) 1894–95 (Manhattan)
Isidor Straus (Democrat) 1894–95 (Manhattan)
Charles G. Bennett (Republican) 1895–99 (Brooklyn)
Benjamin Fairchild (Republican) 1895–97, 1917–19, 1921–23, 1923–27 (Bronx)
Israel F. Fischer (Republican) 1895–99 (Brooklyn)
James R. Howe (Republican) 1895–99 (Brooklyn)
Denis M. Hurley (Democrat) 1895–99 (Brooklyn)
Philip B. Low (Democrat) 1895–99 (Manhattan)
George B. McClellan (Democrat) 1895–1903 (Manhattan)
Richard C. McCormick (Republican) 1895–97 (Queens, Staten Island)
Henry Clay Miner (Democrat) 1895–97 (Manhattan)
Richard C. Shannon (Republican) 1895–99 (Manhattan)
William Sulzer (Democrat) 1895–12 (Manhattan)
James J. Walsh (Democrat) 1895–96 (Manhattan)
Francis H. Wilson (Democrat) 1895–97 (Brooklyn)
John M. Mitchell (Democrat) 1896–99 (Manhattan)
Joseph M. Belford (Republican) 1897–99 (Queens, Staten Island)
Thomas J. Bradley (Democrat) 1897–1901 (Manhattan)
Edmund H. Driggs (Democrat) 1897–1901 (Brooklyn)
John H. G. Vehslage (Democrat) 1897–99 (Staten Island, Manhattan)
William L. Ward (Republican) 1897–99 (Westchester)
William A. Chanler (Democrat) 1899–1901 (Manhattan)
Bertram T. Clayton (Democrat) 1899–1901 (Brooklyn)
John J. Fitzgerald (Democrat) 1899–1917 (Brooklyn)
Jefferson M. Levy (Democrat) 1899–1901, 1911–15 (Manhattan)
Mitchell May (Democrat) 1899–1901 (Brooklyn)
Daniel J. Riordan (Democrat) 1899–1901 (Manhattan), 1906–23 (Staten Island, Manhattan)
Jacob Ruppert Jr. (Democrat) 1899–1907 (Manhattan)
Townsend Scudder (Democrat) 1899–1901, 1903–5 (Queens, Staten Island)
John Q. Underhill (Democrat) 1899–1901 (Bronx)
Frank E. Wilson (Democrat) 1899–1905, 1911–15 (Brooklyn)
Oliver H. P. Belmont (Democrat) 1901–3 (Manhattan)
Henry Bristow (Republican) 1901–3 (Brooklyn)
William H. Douglas (Republican) 1901–3 (Manhattan)
Henry M. Goldfogle (Democrat) 1901–15, 1919–21 (Manhattan)
Harry A. Hanbury (Republican) 1901–3 (Brooklyn)
George H. Lindsay (Democrat) 1901–13 (Brooklyn)
Cornelius A. Pugsley (Democrat) 1901–3 (Bronx)
Frederic Storm (Republican) 1901–3 (Queens, Staten Island)
Montague Lessler (Republican) 1902–3 (Staten Island, Manhattan)
Edward Swann (Democrat) 1902–3 (Manhattan)
Robert Baker (Democrat) 1903–5 (Brooklyn)
Edward M. Bassett (Democrat) 1903–5 (Brooklyn)
Charles T. Dunwell (Republican) 1903–8 (Brooklyn)
Joseph A. Goulden (Democrat) 1903–11 (Manhattan, Bronx)
Francis B. Harrison (Democrat) 1903–5, 1907–13 (Manhattan)
William Randolph Hearst (Democrat) 1903–7 (Manhattan)
Ira E. Rider (Democrat) 1903–5 (Manhattan)
Francis E. Shober (Democrat) 1903–5 (Manhattan)
Timothy D. Sullivan (Democrat) 1903–6 (Staten Island, Manhattan)
William S. Bennet (Republican) 1905–11, 1915–17 (Manhattan)
William M. Calder (Republican) 1905–15 (Brooklyn)
William W. Cocks (Republican) 1905–11 (Queens, Staten Island)
Charles B. Law (Republican) 1905–11 (Brooklyn)
J. Van Vechten Olcott (Republican) 1905–11 (Manhattan)
Herbert Parsons (Republican) 1905–11 (Manhattan)
Charles A. Towne (Democrat) 1905–7 (Manhattan)
George E. Waldo (Republican) 1905–9 (Brooklyn)
Charles V. Fornes (Democrat) 1907–13 (Manhattan)
William Willett (Democrat) 1907–11 (Manhattan)
Otto G. Foelker (Republican) 1908–11 (Brooklyn)

(continued)

Members of the U.S. House of Representatives Elected from Districts All or Partly within the Current Boundaries of New York City *(Continued)*

Michael F. Conry (Democrat) 1909–17 (Manhattan)
Steven B. Ayres (Democrat) 1911–13 (Manhattan, Bronx)
Henry George Jr. (Democrat) 1911–15 (Manhattan)
John J. Kindred (Democrat) 1911–13 (Manhattan)
Martin W. Littleton (Democrat) 1911–13 (Queens, Staten Island)
John P. Maher (Democrat) 1911–21 (Brooklyn)
Thomas G. Patten (Democrat) 1911–17 (Manhattan)
William C. Redfield (Democrat) 1911–13 (Brooklyn)
Richard Young (Republican) 1911–13 (Brooklyn)
Lathrop Brown (Democrat) 1913–15 (Queens, Staten Island)
Henry Bruckner (Democrat) 1913–17 (Manhattan, Bronx)
Jacob A. Cantor (Democrat) 1913–15 (Manhattan)
John F. Carew (Democrat) 1913–29 (Manhattan)
Walter M. Chandler (Republican) 1913–19, 1921–23 (Manhattan)
Harry H. Dale (Democrat) 1913–19 (Brooklyn)
Peter J. Dooling (Democrat) 1913–21 (Manhattan)
Daniel J. Griffin (Democrat) 1913–17 (Brooklyn)
George W. Loft (Democrat) 1913–17 (Manhattan)
Herman A. Metz (Democrat) 1913–15 (Brooklyn)
James H. O'Brien (Democrat) 1913–15 (Brooklyn, Queens, Staten Island)
Woodson R. Oglesby (Democrat) 1913–17 (Bronx)
Denis O'Leary (Democrat) 1913–14 (Queens, Staten Island)
Charles P. Caldwell (Democrat) 1915–21 (Queens, Staten Island)
Michael F. Farley (Democrat) 1915–21 (Manhattan)
Joseph V. Flynn (Democrat) 1915–19 (Brooklyn)
Reuben L. Haskell (Republican) 1915–19 (Brooklyn)
Frederick C. Hicks (Republican) 1915–23 (Queens, Staten Island)
G. Murray Hulbert (Democrat) 1915–18 (Manhattan, Bronx)
Meyer London (Socialist) 1915–19, 1921–23 (Manhattan)
Frederick W. Rowe (Republican) 1915–21 (Brooklyn)
Isaac Siegel (Republican) 1915–23 (Manhattan)
Oscar W. Swift (Republican) 1915–19 (Brooklyn, Queens, Staten Island)
George B. Francis (Republican) 1917–19 (Manhattan)
Fiorello H. La Guardia (Republican) 1917–19, 1923–33 (Manhattan)
Daniel C. Oliver (Democrat) 1917–19 (Manhattan, Bronx)
Thomas F. Smith (Democrat) 1917–21 (Manhattan)
Christopher Sullivan (Democrat) 1917–41 (Manhattan)
William E. Cleary (Democrat) 1918–21, 1923–27 (Brooklyn)
John J. Delaney (Democrat) 1918–19, 1931–48 (Brooklyn)
Jerome F. Donovan (Democrat) 1918–21 (Manhattan, Bronx)
Anthony J. Griffin (Democrat) 1918–35 (Manhattan, Bronx)
Thomas H. Cullen (Democrat) 1919–44 (Brooklyn)
James V. Ganly (Democrat) 1919–21 (Bronx)
John B. Johnston (Democrat) 1919–21 (Brooklyn)
John MacCrate (Republican) 1919–20 (Brooklyn)
Richard F. McKiniry (Democrat) 1919–21 (Manhattan, Bronx)
David J. O'Connell (Democrat) 1919–21, 1923–30 (Brooklyn, Queens, Staten Island)
Herbert C. Pell (Democrat) 1919–21 (Manhattan)
Joseph Rowan (Democrat) 1919–21 (Manhattan)
Nathan D. Perlman (Republican) 1920–27 (Manhattan)
Lester D. Volk (Republican) 1920–23 (Brooklyn)
Martin C. Ansorge (Republican) 1921–23 (Manhattan, Bronx)
Charles G. Bond (Republican) 1921–23 (Brooklyn)
Michael J. Hogan (Republican) 1921–23 (Brooklyn)
John Kissel (Republican) 1921–23 (Brooklyn)
Ardolph L. Kline (Republican) 1921–23 (Brooklyn)
Warren I. Lee (Republican) 1921–23 (Brooklyn)
Ogden L. Mills (Republican) 1921–27 (Manhattan)
Andrew N. Peterson (Republican) 1921–23 (Brooklyn, Queens, Staten Island)
Albert B. Rossdale (Republican) 1921–23 (Manhattan, Bronx)
Thomas J. Ryan (Republican) 1921–23 (Manhattan)
Robert L. Bacon (Republican) 1923–38 (Queens, Staten Island)
Loring M. Black (Democrat) 1923–35 (Brooklyn)
Sol Bloom (Democrat) 1923–49 (Manhattan)
John J. Boylan (Democrat) 1923–38 (Manhattan)
Emmanuel Celler (Democrat) 1923–73 (Brooklyn)
Samuel Dickstein (Democrat) 1923–45 (Manhattan)
George W. Lindsay (Democrat) 1923–35 (Brooklyn)
John J. O'Connor (Democrat) 1923–39 (Manhattan)
Frank Oliver (Democrat) 1923–34 (Bronx)
Anning S. Prall (Democrat) 1923–35 (Staten Island, Manhattan)
John F. Quayle (Democrat) 1923–30 (Brooklyn)
Charles I. Stengle (Democrat) 1923–25 (Brooklyn)
Royal H. Weller (Democrat) 1923–29 (Manhattan, Bronx)
Andrew l. Somers (Democrat) 1925–49 (Brooklyn)
Patrick J. Carley (Democrat) 1927–35 (Brooklyn)
William W. Cohen (Democrat) 1927–29 (Manhattan)
James M. Fitzpatrick (Democrat) 1927–49 (Bronx)
William I. Sirovich (Democrat) 1927–39 (Manhattan)
William F. Brunner (Democrat) 1929–35 Queens, Staten Island)
Joseph A. Gavagan (Democrat) 1929–43 (Manhattan, Bronx)
Ruth S. B. Pratt (Republican) 1929–33 (Manhattan)
Martin J. Kennedy (Democrat) 1930–45 (Manhattan)
Matthew V. O'Malley (Democrat) 1931 (Brooklyn, Queens, Staten Island)
Stephen A. Rudd (Democrat) 1931–36 (Brooklyn, Queens, Staten Island)
James J. Lanzetta (Democrat) 1933–35, 1937–39 (Manhattan)
Theodore A. Peyser (Democrat) 1933–37 (Manhattan)
William B. Barry (Democrat) 1935–46 (Queens, Staten Island)
Charles A. Buckley (Democrat) 1935–65 (Bronx)
Edward W. Curley (Democrat) 1935–40 (Manhattan, Bronx)
Marcellus H. Evans (Democrat) 1935–41 (Brooklyn)
Vito Marcantonio (Republican, American Labor) 1935–37, 1939–51 (Manhattan)
James A. O'Leary (Democrat) 1935–44 (Staten Island, Manhattan)
Joseph L. Pfeifer (Democrat) 1935–51 (Brooklyn)

(continued)

Members of the U.S. House of Representatives Elected from Districts All or Partly within the Current Boundaries of New York City *(Continued)*

Richard J. Tonry (Democrat) 1935–37 (Brooklyn)
Bruce Barton (Republican) 1937–41 (Manhattan)
Eugene J. Keogh (Democrat) 1937–67 (Brooklyn, Queens, Staten Island)
Donald L. O'Toole (Democrat) 1937–53 (Brooklyn)
James H. Fay (Democrat) 1939–41, 1943–45 (Manhattan)
Leonard W. Hall (Republican) 1939–51 (Queens, Staten Island)
M. Michael Edelstein (Democrat) 1940–41 (Manhattan)
Walter A. Lynch (Democrat) 1940–41 (Manhattan, Bronx)
Joseph C. Baldwin (Republican) 1941–47 (Manhattan)
Louis J. Capozzoli (Democrat) 1941–45 (Manhattan)
James J. Heffernan (Democrat) 1941–53 (Brooklyn)
Arthur G. Klein (Democrat) 1941–45 (Manhattan)
William T. Pheiffer (Republican) 1941–43 (Manhattan)
Kenneth F. Simpson (Republican) 1941 (Manhattan)
Thomas F. Burchill (Democrat) 1943–45 (Manhattan)
Ellsworth B. Buck (Republican) 1944–49 (Staten Island, Manhattan)
John J. Rooney (Democrat) 1944–74 (Brooklyn)
James H. Torrens (Democrat) 1944–47 (Manhattan, Bronx)
James J. Delaney (Democrat) 1945–47, 1949–78 (Queens, Staten Island)
Henry J. Latham (Republican) 1945–58 (Queens, Staten Island)
Adam Clayton Powell (Democrat) 1945–67, 1969–71 (Manhattan)
Peter A. Quinn (Democrat) 1945–47 (Bronx)
Benjamin J. Rabin (Democrat) 1945–47 (Bronx)
Leo F. Rayfiel (Democrat) 1945–47 (Brooklyn)
James A. Roe (Democrat) 1945–47 (Queens, Staten Island)
Frederic R. Coudert (Republican) 1947–59 (Manhattan)
Jacob K. Javits (Republican) 1947–54 (Manhattan)
Gregory McMahon (Republican) 1947–49 (Queens, Staten Island)
Abraham J. Multer (Democrat) 1947–67 (Brooklyn)
Robert J. Nodar Jr. (Republican) 1947–49 (Queens, Staten Island)
David M. Potts (Republican) 1947–49 (Bronx)
Robert Tripp Ross (Republican) 1947–49 (Queens, Staten Island)
Leo Isacson (American Labor) 1948–49 (Bronx)
L. Gary Clemente (Democrat) 1949–53 (Queens, Staten Island)
Isidore Dollinger (Democrat) 1949–59 (Bronx)
Louis B. Heller (Democrat) 1949–54 (Brooklyn)
Edna F. Kelly (Democrat) 1949–69 (Brooklyn)
Christopher C. McGrath (Democrat) 1949–53 (Bronx)
James J. Murphy (Democrat) 1949–53 (Staten Island, Manhattan)
T. Vincent Quinn (Democrat) 1949–51 (Queens, Staten Island)
Franklin D. Roosevelt Jr. (Democrat) 1949–55 (Manhattan)
Victor L. Anfuso (Democrat) 1951–53, 1955–63 (Brooklyn)
Sidney A. Fine (Democrat) 1951–56 (Bronx)
Albert H. Bosch (Republican) 1953–60 (Queens)
Francis Dorn (Republican) 1953–61 (Brooklyn)
Paul A. Fino (Republican) 1953–68 (Bronx)
Lester Holtzman (Democrat) 1953–61 (Queens)
John H. Ray (Republican) 1953–63 (Staten Island, Brooklyn)
Irwin Davidson (Democrat) 1955–56 (Manhattan)
Herbert Zelenko (Democrat) 1955–63 (Manhattan)
James C. Healey (Democrat) 1956–65 (Bronx)
Leonard Farbstein (Democrat) 1957–71 (Manhattan)
Alfred E. Santangelo (Democrat) 1957–63 (Manhattan)
Ludwig Teller (Democrat) 1957–61 (Manhattan)
Seymour Halpern (Republican) 1959–73 (Queens)
John V. Lindsay (Republican) 1959–65 (Manhattan)
Jacob H. Gilbert (Democrat) 1960–71 (Bronx)
Joseph P. Addabbo (Democrat) 1961–86 (Queens)
Hugh L. Carey (Democrat) 1961–74 (Brooklyn)
William F. Ryan (Democrat) 1961–72 (Manhattan)
Benjamin S. Rosenthal (Democrat) 1962–83 (Queens)
John M. Murphy (Democrat) 1963–81 (Staten Island, Brooklyn; Staten Island, Manhattan)
Jonathan B. Bingham (Democrat) 1965–83 (Bronx)
James H. Scheuer (Democrat) 1965–73 (Bronx)
Lester L. Wolff (Democrat) 1965–81 (Queens)
Theodore R. Kupferman (Republican) 1966–69 (Manhattan)
Frank J. Brasco (Democrat) 1967–75 (Brooklyn)
Bertram L. Podell (Democrat) 1968–75 (Brooklyn)
Mario Biaggi (Democrat) 1969–88 (Bronx)
Shirley B. Chisholm (Democrat) 1969–83 (Brooklyn)
Edward I. Koch (Democrat) 1969–77 (Manhattan)
Bella Abzug (Democrat) 1971–77 (Manhattan)
Herman Badillo (Democrat) 1971–77 (Bronx)
Elizabeth Holtzman (Democrat) 1973–81 (Brooklyn)
Charles B. Rangel (Democrat) 1973– (Manhattan)
Frederick W. Richmond (Democrat) 1975–82 (Brooklyn)
Stephen J. Solarz (Democrat) 1975–93 (Brooklyn)
Leo C. Zeferetti (Democrat) 1975–83 (Brooklyn)
Robert Garcia (Democrat) 1977–89 (Bronx)
S. William Green (Republican) 1977–93 (Manhattan)
Ted Weiss (Democrat) 1977–92 (Manhattan)
Geraldine A. Ferraro (Democrat) 1979–85 (Queens, Staten Island)
John LeBoutillier (Republican) 1981–83 (Queens, Staten Island)
Guy V. Molinari (Republican) 1981–90 (Staten Island, Manhattan; Staten Island, Brooklyn)
Gary L. Ackerman (Democrat) 1983– (Queens, Staten Island)
Major R. Owens (Democrat) 1983– (Brooklyn)
Edolphus Towns (Democrat) 1983– (Brooklyn)
Thomas J. Manton (Democrat) 1985– (Queens, Staten Island)
Charles E. Schumer (Democrat) 1985– (Brooklyn)
Alton R. Waldon Jr. (Democrat) 1986–87 (Queens, Staten Island)
Floyd H. Flake (Democrat) 1987– (Queens, Staten Island)
Nita M. Lowey (Democrat) 1988– (Bronx, Queens)
Eliot Engel (Democrat) 1989– (Bronx)
Susan Molinari (Republican) 1989– (Staten Island, Brooklyn)
José Serrano (Democrat) 1989– (Bronx)
Carolyn B. Maloney (Democrat) 1993– (Manhattan, Queens, Brooklyn)
Jerrold L. Nadler (Democrat) 1993– (Manhattan, Brooklyn)
Nydia M. Velazquez (Democrat) 1993– (Brooklyn, Manhattan, Queens, Staten Island)

Source: Kenneth C. Martis: *The Historical Atlas of United States Congressional Districts, 1789–1983* (New York: Free Press, 1982)
Compiled by James Bradley

measures in the charter of 1857 exposed the long partisan conflict between the strong Democratic forces of the city and the Republicans in the state legislature. As a check on the city the state transformed the county board of supervisors, which consisted of the mayor and city officials, into an independently elected body made up of an equal number of Republicans and Democrats. The charter also merged the police forces of New York City, Brooklyn, and their suburbs into one department to be appointed by a state commission. These measures encouraged Mayor Fernando Wood in 1861 to propose that New York City secede from the state and establish itself as a "free city." Subsequent mayors protested the state's tendency to meddle in city affairs through state-appointed commissions for fire, park, and public health. To resist interference by the state, Tammany Hall consolidated its influence over the city's immigrant population, especially the Irish, who were once excluded from the organization. Politicians aligned with Tammany Hall began to establish power bases in elected posts such as those of county sheriff and city chamberlain, an office created in 1832 to oversee the city's surplus funds. By the late 1860s Tammany Hall, led by William M. "Boss" Tweed, induced the legislature by means of bribes to enact a new charter that abolished the state commissions and returned police and other municipal functions to the city. Despite its tainted origins the charter brought about a favorable reorganization of city government by establishing ten executive departments to manage parks, public health, buildings, the police force, and other services, and gave the mayor the power to appoint the heads of these departments. The charter strengthened the mayor's veto power, which could now be overridden only by a three-quarters vote of the council; at the same time his authority was limited by the terms of the council offices, which were longer than his own. In the charter the legislature also unified the government of the city and county by abolishing the New York County Board of Supervisors, on which Tweed himself had sat since its formation in 1857.

After the fall of the Tweed Ring the legislature signed a new charter in 1873 that replaced the bicameral council with a board of aldermen: six of its twenty-one members were elected. In addition the charter created the Board of Estimate and Apportionment, consisting of the mayor, the president of the Board of Aldermen, and two other officials. Responsible for reviewing the budgets of city departments, the board eventually became a powerful influence in both the executive and the legislative branches of government. The charter was amended in 1884 when the state extended its civil service law to the city, eroding the control of Tammany Hall over patronage. These changes did not prevent the return to power of Tammany Hall, first under John Kelly (a former sheriff) and then under Richard Croker. To win important elections Tammany Hall often aimed to satisfy an influential minority of reform-minded Democrats sympathetic toward business. Threatened by a coalition of Republicans, reformers, and angry workers in 1886, it engineered the election of Abram S. Hewitt, a wealthy businessman and reformer. In the 1880s the legislature passed 390 acts concerning the city, a number that was sharply reduced after a constitutional amendment in 1894 gave the mayor the power to veto such acts.

In 1896 the legislature responded to the demands of businessmen and reformers to consolidate Manhattan, Brooklyn, Queens, the Bronx, and Staten Island into greater New York. When the new charter took effect in 1898 each of the five counties became a borough of the new city: the population of New York City more than doubled, to nearly three and a half million, in large part because Brooklyn had grown into the fourth-largest city in the United States since its incorporation in 1834. Although much of the middle class in Brooklyn was resistant to consolidation its businessmen believed that the change would promote development and reduce taxes. Seth Low, the Republican mayor of Brooklyn in the early 1880s, was eventually elected mayor of the consolidated city. The charter of 1897 preserved the power of the boroughs by allowing each of them to elect a president responsible for local administration of streets and other public works. Although officials such as sheriffs, judges, clerks, and registrars continued to work for the county, most positions were taken over by the new city government. Legislative power was centered in a two-house municipal assembly and judicial functions in a municipal court of twenty-three districts. The mayor (whose term was extended from two years to four) retained a strong veto, which could be overridden only by a five-sixths vote of the assembly; he also retained control over the executive departments except for the finance department, which continued to be led by an independently elected comptroller. The charter weakened the mayor by barring him from a second consecutive term. The Board of Estimate and Apportionment, which prepared an annual budget for the city that could be decreased but not increased by the municipal assembly, acquired the power to control the granting of franchises to public services. Reformers hoped that consolidation would make the government more efficient and dilute the power of Tammany Hall. Greater efficiency was at least partly realized, but the influence of Tammany Hall persisted: the very first mayor elected after consolidation was Robert A. Van Wyck, a tool of Tammany Hall who led one of the most corrupt administrations in the city's history. The legislature amended the charter in 1901 to reduce the mayor's term from four years to two and to increase the power of the borough presidents by giving them a prominent place on the Board of Estimate. Another amendment at this time transformed the bicameral assembly into a single board of aldermen with seventy-three members (reduced to sixty-seven in 1916 and sixty-five in 1921). The first mayor to be affected by the shortened term was Low, a reformer who led one of the city's most effective administrations. He was defeated when he sought reelection in 1903 by George B. McClellan, who enjoyed the backing of Charles F. Murphy (the new leader of Tammany Hall) and Big Tim Sullivan (a powerful figure in the entertainment and vice district centered on the Bowery). Under McClellan civil service was extended to most city employees.

Tammany Hall during the Progressive era nominated reform Democrats for important offices, including Mayors William J. Gaynor and John Purroy Mitchel (1910–17). By the 1920s it was led by Mayor James J. Walker, who with the district leaders of Tammany Hall forged what they called a "practical democracy" dedicated to aiding the poor and the common people. An indirect result of his efforts was state legislation supported by Governor Alfred E. Smith and Senator Robert F. Wagner that improved housing and working conditions, and in the process laid the foundation for a partnership between the state and the city. The charter of 1901 survived for more than thirty years with only one major change: an amendment to the state constitution in 1923 that formed a new, two-house municipal assembly, consisting of the Board of Aldermen and the borough presidents. Among the assembly's expanded powers was that of making amendments to the city charter that were not in conflict with the state constitution. The Fusion Party candidate Fiorello H. La Guardia defeated Tammany Hall in 1933 and as mayor from 1934 to 1945 initiated profound changes in the politics and government of the city. Backed by federal money provided under the New Deal, La Guardia carried through an ambitious program of public works that won him as much support from business and labor as Tammany Hall had commanded earlier. His "little New Deal" assigned many of the functions of government to permanent entities staffed by professionals, such as new college campuses (which later became the City University of New York) and municipal hospitals. In 1936 reformers crafted a new charter, which was notably clearer and shorter than that of 1901. It further augmented the power of the mayor, who was now allowed to appoint a deputy mayor in charge of routine executive duties. The charter abolished the office of city chamberlain and replaced the Board of Aldermen with a smaller, unicameral council. It also established a city planning commission charged with drafting a master plan for the city, preparing public works programs, and issuing

Presidential Election Returns for New York City, 1836–1992 (by County 1836–1896, Including Kings, Queens, Richmond, and Westchester; by Borough 1900–1992)

(Excludes some minor-party candidates; name and party of winning candidate are in boldface.)

1836	**Martin Van Buren (Democrat)**	William H. Harrison (Whig)
New York	17,469	16,348
Kings	2,321	1,868
Queens	1,654	1,399
Richmond	649	649
Westchester	3,009	1,749
Totals	25,102	22,013

1840	Martin Van Buren (Democrat)	**William H. Harrison (Whig)**
New York	21,936	20,959
Kings	3,157	3,293
Queens	2,550	2,522
Richmond	861	903
Westchester	4,354	4,083
Totals	32,858	31,760

1844	**James K. Polk (Democrat)**	Henry Clay (Whig)
New York	28,296	26,385
Kings	4,648	5,107
Queens	2,751	2,547
Richmond	1,063	1,049
Westchester	4,412	4,258
Totals	41,170	39,346

1848	Lewis Cass (Democrat)	**Zachary Taylor (Whig)**
New York	18,975	29,070
Kings	4,881	7,511
Queens	1,310	2,444
Richmond	860	1,099
Westchester	2,146	4,112
Totals	28,172	44,236

1852	**Franklin Pierce (Democrat)**	Winfield Scott (Whig)
New York	34,280	23,122
Kings	10,624	8,491
Queens	2,903	2,209
Richmond	1,324	1,147
Westchester	5,283	4,033
Totals	54,414	39,002

1856	**James Buchanan (Democrat)**	John C. Frémont (Republican)	Millard Fillmore (American)
New York	41,913	17,771	19,924
Kings	14,174	7,846	8,651
Queens	2,394	1,886	2,523
Richmond	1,550	736	947
Westchester	4,600	4,450	3,641
Totals	64,631	32,689	35,686

1860	Stephen Douglas (Democrat)	**Abraham Lincoln (Republican)**
New York	62,482	33,290
Kings	20,599	15,883
Queens	4,391	3,749

(*continued*)

Presidential Election Returns for New York City, 1836–1992 (by County 1836–1896, Including Kings, Queens, Richmond, and Westchester; by Borough 1900–1992) (*Continued*)

Richmond	2,370	1,408
Westchester	8,126	6,771
Totals	97,968	61,101
1864	George B. McClellan (Democrat)	**Abraham Lincoln (Republican)**
New York	73,709	36,681
Kings	25,726	20,838
Queens	5,400	4,284
Richmond	2,874	1,564
Westchester	9,355	7,607
Totals	117,064	70,974
1868	Horatio Seymour (Democrat)	**Ulysses S. Grant (Republican)**
New York	108,316	47,748
Kings	39,838	27,711
Queens	6,388	4,973
Richmond	3,019	2,221
Westchester	11,667	9,642
Totals	169,228	92,295
1872	Horace Greeley (Democrat)	**Ulysses S. Grant (Republican)**
New York	77,814	54,676
Kings	38,108	33,368
Queens	5,655	6,082
Richmond	2,541	2,728
Westchester	11,112	10,233
Totals	135,230	107,087
1876	Samuel J. Tilden (Democrat)	**Rutherford B. Hayes (Republican)**
New York	112,621	58,776
Kings	57,557	39,125
Queens	9,994	6,971
Richmond	4,338	2,884
Westchester	12,054	9,574
Totals	196,564	117,330
1880	Winfield Hancock (Democrat)	**James A. Garfield (Republican)**
New York	123,015	58,776
Kings	61,062	51,751
Queens	10,391	8,151
Richmond	4,815	3,291
Westchester	11,858	11,367
Totals	211,141	133,336
1884	**Grover Cleveland (Democrat)**	James G. Blaine (Republican)
New York	133,222	90,095
Kings	69,264	53,516
Queens	10,367	8,445
Richmond	5,135	3,164
Westchester	12,525	11,286
Totals	230,513	166,506
1888	Grover Cleveland (Democrat)	**Benjamin Harrison (Republican)**
New York	162,735	106,922

(*continued*)

Presidential Election Returns for New York City, 1836–1992 (by County 1836–1896, Including Kings, Queens, Richmond, and Westchester; by Borough 1900–1992) (*Continued*)

Kings	82,507	70,052	
Queens	12,683	11,017	
Richmond	5,764	4,100	
Westchester	14,948	13,799	
Totals	278,637	205,890	
1892	**Grover Cleveland (Democrat)**	Benjamin Harrison (Republican)	
New York	175,267	98,967	
Kings	100,160	70,505	
Queens	15,195	11,704	
Richmond	6,122	4,091	
Westchester	16,088	13,436	
Totals	312,832	198,703	
1896	William Jennings Bryan (Democrat)	**William McKinley (Republican)**	
New York (includes present Bronx)	135,624	156,359	
Kings	76,882	109,135	
Queens	11,980	18,694	
Richmond	4,452	6,170	
Totals	228,938	290,358	
1900	William Jennings Bryan (Democrat)	**William McKinley (Republican)**	
Manhattan and Bronx	181,786	153,001	
Brooklyn	106,232	108,977	
Queens	14,747	12,323	
Staten Island	6,759	6,042	
Totals	309,524	280,343	
1904	Alton B. Parker (Democrat)	**Theodore Roosevelt (Republican)**	
Manhattan and Bronx	189,712	155,003	
Brooklyn	111,855	113,246	
Queens	18,151	14,096	
Staten Island	7,182	7,000	
Totals	326,900	289,345	
1908	William Jennings Bryan (Democrat)	**William H. Taft (Republican)**	
Manhattan and Bronx	160,261	154,958	
Brooklyn	96,756	119,789	
Queens	20,342	19,420	
Staten Island	6,831	7,401	
Totals	284,190	301,568	
1912	**Woodrow Wilson (Democrat)**	William H. Taft (Republican)	Theodore Roosevelt (Progressive)
Manhattan and Bronx	166,157	63,107	98,985
Brooklyn	109,748	51,239	71,167
Queens	28,044	9,201	14,951
Staten Island	8,437	3,035	3,771
Totals	312,386	126,582	188,874
1916	**Woodrow Wilson (Democrat)**	Charles E. Hughes (Republican)	
Manhattan	139,547	111,926	
Brooklyn	125,625	119,675	

(*continued*)

Presidential Election Returns for New York City, 1836–1992 (by County 1836–1896, Including Kings, Queens, Richmond, and Westchester; by Borough 1900–1992) *(Continued)*

Bronx	47,870	40,338	
Queens	31,350	34,670	
Staten Island	8,843	7,204	
Totals	353,235	313,813	
1920	James Cox (Democrat)	**Warren G. Harding (Republican)**	Eugene V. Debs (Socialist)
Manhattan	135,249	275,013	46,049
Brooklyn	119,612	292,692	45,100
Bronx	45,471	106,038	32,823
Queens	35,296	94,360	6,143
Staten Island	9,373	17,844	712
Totals	345,001	785,947	130,827
1924	John W. Davis (Democrat)	**Calvin Coolidge (Republican)**	Robert LaFollette (Progressive)
Manhattan	183,249	190,871	86,625
Brooklyn	158,907	236,877	100,721
Bronx	72,840	79,583	62,212
Queens	58,402	100,793	28,210
Staten Island	15,801	18,007	3,702
Totals	489,199	626,131	281,470
1928	Alfred E. Smith (Democrat)	**Herbert Hoover (Republican)**	
Manhattan	317,227	186,396	
Brooklyn	404,393	245,622	
Bronx	232,766	98,636	
Queens	184,640	158,505	
Staten Island	28,945	24,985	
Totals	1,167,971	714,144	
1932	**Franklin D. Roosevelt (Democrat)**	Herbert Hoover (Republican)	Norman Thomas (Socialist)
Manhattan	378,077	157,014	23,946
Brooklyn	514,172	192,536	50,509
Bronx	281,330	76,587	31,247
Queens	244,740	136,641	14,854
Staten Island	36,857	21,278	2,009
Totals	1,455,176	584,056	122,565
1936	**Franklin D. Roosevelt (Democrat)**	Alfred Landon (Republican)	
Manhattan	517,134	174,299	
Brooklyn	738,306	212,852	
Bronx	419,625	93,151	
Queens	320,053	162,797	
Staten Island	46,229	22,852	
Totals	2,041,347	665,951	
1940	**Franklin D. Roosevelt (Democrat)**	Wendell Willkie (Republican)	
Manhattan	478,153	292,480	
Brooklyn	742,668	394,534	
Bronx	418,931	198,293	
Queens	288,024	323,406	
Staten Island	38,307	38,911	
Totals	1,966,083	1,247,624	

(continued)

Presidential Election Returns for New York City, 1836–1992 (by County 1836–1896, Including Kings, Queens, Richmond, and Westchester; by Borough 1900–1992) *(Continued)*

1944	**Franklin D. Roosevelt (Democrat)**	Thomas E. Dewey (Republican)	
Manhattan	509,263	258,650	
Brooklyn	758,270	393,926	
Bronx	450,525	211,158	
Queens	292,940	365,365	
Staten Island	31,502	42,188	
Totals	2,042,500	1,271,287	
1948	**Harry S. Truman (Democrat)**	Thomas E. Dewey (Republican)	Henry A. Wallace (Progressive)
Manhattan	380,310	241,752	106,509
Brooklyn	579,922	330,494	163,896
Bronx	337,129	173,044	106,762
Queens	268,742	323,459	42,409
Staten Island	30,442	39,539	2,779
Totals	1,596,545	1,108,288	422,355
1952	Adlai Stevenson (Democrat)	**Dwight D. Eisenhower (Republican)**	
Manhattan	446,727	300,284	
Brooklyn	656,229	446,708	
Bronx	399,477	241,898	
Queens	331,217	450,610	
Staten Island	28,280	55,993	
Totals	1,861,930	1,495,493	
1956	Adlai Stevenson (Democrat)	**Dwight D. Eisenhower (Republican)**	
Manhattan	377,856	300,004	
Brooklyn	557,655	460,456	
Bronx	343,823	257,382	
Queens	318,723	466,057	
Staten Island	19,644	64,233	
Totals	1,617,701	1,548,132	
1960	**John F. Kennedy (Democrat)**	Richard M. Nixon (Republican)	
Manhattan	414,902	217,271	
Brooklyn	646,582	327,497	
Bronx	389,818	182,393	
Queens	446,348	367,688	
Staten Island	38,673	50,356	
Totals	1,936,323	1,145,205	
1964	**Lyndon B. Johnson (Democrat)**	Barry Goldwater (Republican)	
Manhattan	503,848	120,125	
Brooklyn	684,839	229,291	
Bronx	403,014	135,780	
Queens	541,418	274,351	
Staten Island	50,524	42,330	
Totals	2,183,643	801,877	
1968	Hubert H. Humphrey (Democrat)	**Richard M. Nixon (Republican)**	George Wallace (American Independent)
Manhattan	370,806	135,458	12,958
Brooklyn	489,174	247,936	33,563
Bronx	277,385	142,314	21,950
Queens	410,546	306,620	44,198
Staten Island	34,770	54,631	9,112

(continued)

Presidential Election Returns for New York City, 1836–1992 (by County 1836–1896, Including Kings, Queens, Richmond, and Westchester; by Borough 1900–1992) *(Continued)*

Totals	1,582,681	886,959	121,781
1972	George McGovern (Democrat)	**Richard M. Nixon (Republican)**	
Manhattan	354,326	178,515	
Brooklyn	387,768	373,903	
Bronx	243,345	196,754	
Queens	328,316	426,015	
Staten Island	29,241	84,686	
Totals	1,342,996	1,259,873	
1976	**Jimmy Carter (Democrat)**	Gerald R. Ford (Republican)	
Manhattan	337,438	117,702	
Brooklyn	419,382	190,728	
Bronx	238,786	96,842	
Queens	379,907	244,396	
Staten Island	47,867	56,995	
Totals	1,423,380	706,663	
1980	Jimmy Carter (Democrat)	**Ronald Reagan (Republican)**	John Anderson (Independent)
Manhattan	275,742	115,911	38,597
Brooklyn	288,893	200,298	24,341
Bronx	181,090	86,843	11,286
Queens	269,147	251,333	32,566
Staten Island	37,306	64,885	7,055
Totals	1,052,178	719,270	113,845
1984	Walter F. Mondale (Democrat)	**Ronald Reagan (Republican)**	
Manhattan	379,521	144,281	
Brooklyn	368,518	230,064	
Bronx	223,112	109,308	
Queens	328,379	285,477	
Staten Island	44,345	83,187	
Totals	1,343,875	852,317	
1988	Michael S. Dukakis (Democrat)	**George Bush (Republican)**	
Manhattan	385,675	115,927	
Brooklyn	363,916	178,961	
Bronx	218,245	76,043	
Queens	325,147	217,049	
Staten Island	47,812	77,427	
Totals	1,340,795	665,407	
1992	**Bill Clinton (Democrat)**	George Bush (Republican)	H. Ross Perot (Independent)
Manhattan	416,142	84,501	27,689
Brooklyn	411,183	133,344	33,014
Bronx	225,038	63,310	15,115
Queens	349,520	157,561	46,014
Staten Island	56,901	70,707	19,678
Totals	1,458,784	509,423	141,510

zoning guidelines. Amendments to the charter could be made by petition of fifty thousand qualified voters. Tammany Hall was weakened considerably by these measures, as well as by the adoption of proportional representation in the City Council in 1937 (which benefited minority parties at the expense of the Democrats), and by the further growth of the merit system. The length of the mayor's term reverted again to four years with the adoption of the charter of 1936.

3. After the Second World War

After 1945 the Democratic organizations in the Bronx and Brooklyn played an increasingly important role in the political process. The mayoral election in that year was won by William O'Dwyer, a former judge and district attorney in Brooklyn. Formed at a time when Tammany Hall was under the sway of the organized-crime figure Frank Costello, his administration was marked by graft and corruption. When O'Dwyer resigned in the first year of his second term to become ambassador to Mexico, Vincent R. Impellitteri succeeded him as acting mayor. In a special election held in 1951 Impellitteri failed to win the support of the Democratic organization, which regarded him as incompetent, but won election as an independent. He was unable to win the organization's support for a full term in 1953: the head of Tammany Hall, Carmine DeSapio, designated instead Robert F. Wagner (ii), the borough president of Manhattan. Wagner's victories in 1953 and again in 1957 strengthened the Democratic organization. During his tenure he recognized and negotiated with municipal employees' unions, and with Robert Moses he used federally funded urban renewal and public housing programs to reshape the city. Wagner perceived the growing importance of black voters and the strength of the reform movement in the Democratic Party, and he repudiated DeSapio when he sought reelection in 1961. County leaders who believed that Wagner's indecisiveness and a number of minor scandals made him a liability supported Arthur Levitt in the Democratic primary, but Wagner won a bitter primary with support from the municipal employees' unions and political advice from Alex Rose (head of the Liberal Party) and J. Raymond Jones (the black district leader from Harlem whom he later helped to defeat DeSapio); after defeating the Republican candidate Louis Lefkowitz in the general election he replaced all the Democratic county leaders except Charles A. Buckley of the Bronx. Despite his accomplishments Wagner failed to build a political base beyond the regular Democratic organizations, in part because he concentrated on consolidating support from the public employees' unions and securing federal funds for constituencies who had traditionally supported him; the increasing militancy of the civil rights movement and protest in the neighborhoods also undermined his power. In 1965 expenditures driven to some extent by the wage demands of municipal employees rose faster than revenues, and caused the first of several increasingly difficult fiscal crises in the city. Wagner announced that he would not seek a fourth term when private polls showed that he could not win.

In Wagner's place the Democrats nominated the city comptroller Abraham Beame; the Republicans tried to revive the alliance of liberal Republicans and reform Democrats that had elected La Guardia by nominating Representative John V. Lindsay; angered by the nomination of Lindsay, William F. Buckley Jr. offered himself as the nominee of the Conservative Party. With support from Governor Nelson A. Rockefeller, Rose, and the garment unions, Lindsay won the election with 43.3 percent of the vote. In office he employed policy analysis and modern management tools, supported the decentralization of government, and expanded the budget with state and federal aid, but he was buffeted by community protests, strikes by public employees, and chronic fiscal difficulty. In attempting to win reelection in 1969 he lost the Republican nomination to a conservative, John J. Marchi; in the general election Marchi competed for the same votes with the Democratic candidate, Mario Procaccino, also a conservative, and Lindsay won by a narrow margin as the nominee of the Liberal Party with support from city employees (who had received generous wage settlements), liberal Democrats, Jews, blacks, and Puerto Ricans. The election of 1969 marked the decline of the political club and the increasing importance of the candidate, and was among the first elections in which a dominant role was played by television and political consultants.

In the early 1970s New York City faced a large budget deficit that was aggravated by increased borrowing. Lindsay declined to run for a third term in 1973 and was succeeded by Beame, the city's first Jewish mayor. By 1975 the financial crises finally led bankers in the city to refuse to extend further credit. The state formed two new agencies, the Municipal Assistance Corporation and the Emergency Financial Control Board, to restructure the city's debt and exert control over budgets and wage settlements. To stabilize finances the state agencies caused the city to reduce its payroll by sixty thousand employees, obtained increased aid from the state, secured loan guarantees from the federal government, and persuaded the custodians of public employees' pension funds to invest in municipal bonds. Charter reform in 1975 gave formal status to community boards (developed by Wagner in the 1950s when he was borough president of Manhattan). In 1977 Beame was viewed as a weak candidate for reelection even though he retained backing from the county Democratic organizations, and in the primary election he drew many opponents, including Representative Herman Badillo, Percy Sutton (former borough president of Manhattan), Mario M. Cuomo, and Representative Edward I. Koch, a reform Democrat from Greenwich Village who advocated fiscal discipline and emphasized his support for the death penalty and his opposition to public unions. Koch narrowly finished first, won a runoff election against Cuomo, and won the general election by soliciting support from minority leaders and from the county Democratic organizations.

In his reelection victories in 1981 and 1985 Koch redefined the Democratic political base along more conservative lines by assembling a coalition of white Catholics and Jews as well as some Latin Americans and blacks. A steady improvement in the city's economy also strengthened his position. During his third term he was politically damaged by corruption in city agencies uncovered by U.S. Attorney Rudolph W. Giuliani, and racial antagonism, which many observers thought he worsened with undiplomatic and sometimes hostile comments about various black leaders. The economic downturn of 1989 also threatened the city's budget, which had doubled since the beginning of his tenure. The success of the Democratic presidential candidate Jesse Jackson in New York City during a primary election in 1988 enabled Koch's opponents to coalesce around David N. Dinkins, borough president of Manhattan, who had close ties to both black regular Democrats and the white reform movement. Dinkins defeated Koch in the Democratic mayoral primary in 1989 with nearly unanimous support from black voters (who had replaced Jews as the largest component of the Democratic electorate), the municipal employees' unions, and white reform Democrats. The Republican and Liberal candidate, Giuliani, attracted many defectors among Democratic voters, but Dinkins narrowly won the general election with support from black voters, Latin Americans, white liberals, and a minority of white ethnic Democrats to become the first black mayor in the city's history. The election took place at a time when the charter was being amended yet again, in response to a decision by the U.S. Supreme Court that effectively abolished the Board of Estimate. The new charter transferred some of the board's powers to the mayor (such as that of granting contracts) and others to the City Council (such as those concerned with land use). Dinkins's success as a candidate was quickly overshadowed by a renewed fiscal crisis, conflict between blacks and Koreans in Flatbush and between blacks and Orthodox Jews in Crown Heights, and a perception of increasing street crime. In 1993 Giuliani again challenged Dinkins for the mayoralty, this time narrowly prevailing.

Herbert L. Osgood et al., eds.: *Minutes of the Common Council of the City of New York, 1675–1776* (New York: Dodd, Mead, 1905)

Charles McLean Andrews: *British Committees, Commissions and Councils of Trade and Plantations, 1622–1675* (Baltimore: Johns Hopkins University Press, 1908)

George Louis Beer: *The Old Colonial System, 1660–1754* (New York: Macmillan, 1912)

I. N. Phelps Stokes: *The Iconography of Manhattan Island, 1498–1909, Compiled from Original Sources and Illustrated by Photo Intaglio Reproductions of Important Maps, Plans, Views and Documents in Public and Private Collections* (New York: Robert H. Dodd, 1915–28; repr. Arno, 1967)

George W. Edwards: *New York as an Eighteenth Century Municipality, 1731–1776* (New York: Columbia University Press, 1917)

Sidney I. Pomerantz: *New York: An American City,*

1783–1803: A Study of Urban Life (New York: Columbia University Press, 1938; 2nd edn Port Washington, N.Y.: I. J. Friedman, 1965)
Wallace S. Sayre and Herbert Kaufman: *Governing New York City: Politics in the Metropolis* (New York: Russell Sage Foundation, 1960)
Charles Garrett: *The La Guardia Years: Machine and Reform Politics in New York City* (New Brunswick, N.J.: Rutgers University Press, 1961)
Theodore J. Lowi: *At the Pleasure of the Mayor: Patronage and Power in New York City, 1898–1958* (New York: Free Press, 1964)
Alexander B. Callow Jr.: *The Tweed Ring: Machine and Reform Politics in New York City* (New York: Oxford University Press, 1966)
I. K. Steele: *Politics of Colonial Policy: The Board of Trade in Colonial Administration, 1696–1720* (Oxford: Oxford University Press, 1968)
Jewel Lubiz Bellush and Stephen M. David, eds.: *Race and Politics in New York City: Five Studies in Policy Making* (New York: Praeger, 1971)
Patricia U. Bonomi: *A Factious People: Politics and Society in Colonial New York* (New York: Columbia University Press, 1971)
Jerome Mushkat: *Tammany: The Evolution of a Political Machine, 1789–1865* (Syracuse, N.Y.: University Press, 1971)
Robert A. Caro: *The Power Broker: Robert Moses and the Fall of New York* (New York: Alfred A. Knopf, 1975)
Ira Katznelson: *City Trenches: Urban Politics and the Patterning of Class in the United States* (New York: Pantheon, 1981)
Edward K. Spann: *The New Metropolis: New York City, 1840–1857* (New York: Columbia University Press, 1981)
Hendrik Hartog: *Public Property and Private Power: The Corporation of the City of New York in American Law, 1730–1870* (Chapel Hill: University of North Carolina Press, 1983)
Martin Shefter: *Political Crisis, Fiscal Crisis: The Collapse and Revival of New York City* (New York: Basic Books, 1985)
Mark Maier: *City Unions: Managing Discontent in New York City* (New Brunswick, N.J.: Rutgers University Press, 1987)
Peter D. G. Thomas: *The Townshend Duties Crisis: The Second Phase of the American Revolution, 1767–1773* (Oxford: Oxford University Press, 1987)
Charles Brecher and Raymond D. Horton, eds.: *Setting Municipal Priorities, 1990* (New York: New York University Press, 1989)
Joyce D. Goodfriend: *Before the Melting Pot: Society and Culture in Colonial New York City, 1664–1730* (Princeton, N.J.: Princeton University Press, 1992)
John Mollenkopf: *A Phoenix in the Ashes: The Conservative Politics of Economic Boom in New York, 1977–1989* (Princeton, N.J.: Princeton University Press, 1992)

Patricia U. Bonomi (§1), Edward K. Spann (§2), John Mollenkopf (§3)

Governors Island. An island in Upper New York Bay (1990 pop. 3400), half a mile (one kilometer) southeast of Manhattan and across Buttermilk Channel from Brooklyn; it covers about 175 acres (seventy hectares) of land. Known as Pagganck by local Canarsee Indians, it was sighted by Giovanni da Verrazano in 1524 and later settled by the Dutch. In 1637 Wouter van Twiller, the second governor general of the Dutch West India Company, reportedly bought it from the Indians for two axe heads, a string of beads, and some iron nails. The name was changed to Nooten Eylandt and in 1664 to Nutten Island by the British. In 1698 the legislature set the island aside "for the benefit and accommodation of His Majesty's governors," whereupon Lord Cornbury had a villa in the Georgian style built there as his official residence. At the outbreak of the American Revolution patriots led by General Israel Putnam held the island until it was bombarded by Admiral Richard Howe's naval forces in 1776, and it remained in British hands until 1783. Construction begun on Fort Jay after peace was restored in 1794 was completed in 1808. In anticipation of another war with England, an imposing semicircular fort of red sandstone called Castle Williams was built from 1807 to 1811 under the direction of Colonel Jonathan Williams, chief of the Army Corps of Engineers; no shot was ever fired at an enemy from its three tiers of cannons. During the Civil War the island became a recruiting depot and Castle Williams a prison for Confederate officers. A headquarters and an administrative center for the U.S. Army were installed after the war. Over time dredgings from the 4th Avenue subway (now the Lexington Avenue line) and the Brooklyn–Battery Tunnel were used to enlarge the island, from which Wilbur Wright took off in the *Flyer* on 20 September 1909 for a flight around the Statue of Liberty and Grant's Tomb. In the following year Glenn Curtis landed on the island after a flight of three segments from Albany, New York, to win a prize of $10,000 offered by Joseph Pulitzer, publisher of the *New York World*. The island had several crucial functions during the First World War: as a training center for pilots, as the post that carried out the seizure of all German ships in the harbor (the first overt American action of the war), and as a supply depot and major point of embarkation for troops bound for France. On 30 June 1966 it was turned over by the U.S. Army to the U.S. Coast Guard for use as the headquarters of the eastern area and of the 3rd Coast Guard District. The island now serves as a training center and base for search and rescue operations, aid to navigation, safety inspection, ice breaking, and drug interdiction. The population consists of about sixteen hundred members of the U.S. Coast Guard and their families. Six buildings are landmarks designated by the city: the Governor's House (completed 1708; now the post commander's house), Fort Jay, Castle Williams, South Battery (1812; now the officers' club), the Admiral's House (1840; formerly the commanding general's house, now the district commander's), and the Blockhouse (1843; now a residence). It is the oldest continuously operated military post in the United States.

Edmund Banks Smith: *Governors Island: Its Military History under Three Flags, 1637–1922* (New York: Valentine's Manual, 1923)
Gerard R. Wolfe: "The Guardian in the Harbor," *New York Chronicle* 3, no. 1 (1990)

Gerard R. Wolfe

Gowanus. Neighborhood in northwestern Brooklyn (1990 pop. 12,500), bounded to the north by Baltic Street, to the east by 4th Avenue, to the south by 14th Street, and to the west by Smith Street. The area was settled by

Gowanus Canal from Hamilton Street Bridge, 1947

the Dutch about 1640. The population increased sharply with the construction in the 1840s of the Gowanus Canal, which provided most residents with the source of their livelihood. A reputation for rowdiness earned the neighborhood the nickname the Gashouse District by the late nineteenth century: in a section twelve blocks long on Smith Street were twenty-three taverns and many rooming houses catering to transients, mostly seamen and laborers. In the twentieth century the neighborhood became quieter. Smith Street, the principal commercial thoroughfare, is lined with family shops and large furniture outlets, notably J. Michaels (founded 1886). A small Italian enclave lies to the east of the canal around Carroll Street, centered at Our Lady of Peace Roman Catholic Church and known until 1993 for Monte's Venetian Room, an Italian restaurant. Landmarks in the neighborhood include the tallest subway viaduct in New York City (on the "F" line at Smith and 9th streets, with a clearance above the canal of 87.5 feet, or 26.7 meters) and the Carroll Street Rail Bridge (1889), one of the few retractile bridges remaining in the United States.

Georgia Fraser: *The Stone House at Gowanus* (New York: Witten and Knitner, 1909)

John J. Gallagher

Gowanus Canal. Artificial waterway in Brooklyn, extending from Hamilton Avenue to Douglass Street. A creek running roughly the same course, named for Gouwane, sachem of the Canarsees, was enlarged in the late 1840s by Edwin C. Litchfield. By 1884 the creek had been transformed into an industrial watercourse 5700 feet (1870 meters) long and one hundred feet (thirty meters) wide, with a depth in high water to fifteen feet (4.5 meters). The canal greatly aided the commercial and residential development of Red Hook. By late century the canal was lined with industrial enterprises, including coal, lumber, brick, and stone yards, foundries, paint and ink factories, electroplating shops, flour, plaster, and paper mills, and an early purveyor of household heating and cooking gas (groups of young hoodlums who preyed on the many sailors and other transients in the area became known as the gas house gangs). The canal was called an open cesspool by the *Daily Eagle* (14 July 1893) and later became one of the city's most polluted waterways. Because tides were ineffective in ridding the northern end of the channel of pollutants, a flushing tunnel 6250 feet (1905 meters) long was built connecting it to Buttermilk Channel. The canal declined in the early 1960s with the move toward containerized shipping. The flushing tunnel was inactive for several years and then restored to operation in 1989, at which time the canal was only a partly used waterway lined with stone, gravel, and concrete yards, some foundries, and petroleum storage facilities.

John J. Gallagher, Matthew Kachur

Goya Foods. Firm of food importers formed in 1936 on Duane Street on the Lower East Side by Don Prudencio Unanue and his wife, Doña Carolina Casal, Spanish immigrants from Puerto Rico. Initially it imported only Spanish olives, olive oil, and canned sardines for sale in bodegas throughout the city but soon offered dozens of other products including beans, rice, coffee, condiments, spices, and frozen foods. Its foods became popular outside the Latin American community and were introduced in supermarkets and specialty stores. As competition increased the firm undertook aggressive advertising campaigns, adopting the motto "Si es Goya, tiene que ser bueno." In the mid 1990s Goya Foods offered more than eight hundred products, distributed from centers in Seville, Chicago, Miami, Tampa (Florida), Secaucus (New Jersey), and Bayamón (Puerto Rico). Owned and operated entirely by the Unanue family, the firm in 1990 had sales of more than $300 million, employed more than eighteen hundred workers, and had its headquarters in Secaucus.

James O. Drummond

G. P. Putnam's Sons. Firm of book publishers. Its origins may be traced to a partnership between John Wiley and George Palmer Putnam; when the two partners separated in 1848 Putnam took over the literary titles and established a firm under his own name at 155 Broadway. After nearing bankruptcy Putnam reopened the firm with his son George Haven Putnam in 1866 as G. P. Putnam and Son, which became G. P. Putnam's Sons in 1872 after two more of Putnam's sons joined the firm and Putnam himself died. Highly regarded during Putnam's lifetime, the firm declined in prestige under his twentieth-century successors but continued to play an important role in publishing. In 1961 it moved to 200 Madison Avenue. With the purchase of Berkley Publishing in 1966 the firm acquired a mass-market paperback subsidiary. G. P. Putnam's Sons was itself taken over by MCA in 1975 and is now part of the Putnam Publishing Group.

See also Book publishing.

Eileen K. Cheng

Grace, William R(ussell) (*b* Cove of Cork [now Cóbh], Ireland, 10 May 1831; *d* New York City, 20 March 1904). Businessman and mayor. Soon after moving to Peru in 1851 he entered the guano trade with the firm of Bryce Brothers, in which he was a partner by 1854. He moved his headquarters to 110 Wall Street in Manhattan in 1866 and founded his own firm, W. R. Grace and Company. In the following years he built a fortune from trade between North America and the western coast of South America. He soon joined with other Democrats in challenging Tammany Hall and reforming local politics. Grace became the first Irish-born Catholic mayor in 1880 and was reelected in 1884.

Lawrence A. Clayton

Grace Church. Episcopal church on Broadway and 10th Street, occupied from 1846 by a congregation organized in 1808 at Broadway and Rector Street. The building is a graceful structure of white limestone, designed by James Renwick Jr. in a decorated Gothic style. Its entrance is framed by a handsome memorial porch and its eastern chancel window filled with English stained glass. The rectors of the church have been highly influential leaders of the branch of American Episcopalianism known as the Low Church. Under the rector Henry Codman Potter (1868–83) a magnificent marble spire was added to the church, and Grace Memorial House was built as a nursery. In keeping with Potter's desire to minister to the poor, Grace Chapel at 132 East 14th Street was rebuilt in 1876 and used as a community center offering language classes and other educational programs for immigrants. His successor as the rector of Grace Church, William R. Huntington (1883–1909), retained Potter's emphasis on community work by running a mission house on the Lower East Side and expanding the operation on 14th Street into what became known as Grace Chapel Settlement. In the mid 1990s Grace Church continued its charitable tradition: it maintained a shelter for homeless men on the side of the church facing 4th Avenue as well as several missions overseas.

Peter J. Wosh

Gracie, Archibald (*b* Dumfries, Scotland, 25 June 1755; *d* New York City, 11 April 1829). Merchant. He arrived in New York City in 1784 and in the following year married Esther (Hetitia) Rogers, sister of the prominent merchants Moses, Nehemiah, and Henry Rogers. He established a firm in Virginia before settling permanently in New York City in 1793. A leading commission merchant and shipowner, he served on the directing boards of banks and insurance companies and was a close associate of the Federalists Alexander Hamilton and Rufus King. He was also a vice-president of the Chamber of Commerce (1800–25) and president of St. Andrew's Society (1818–23). In 1798 he purchased property at Horn's Hook, near what is now East 88th Street, where he constructed his summer home Gracie Mansion. Delays in collecting spoliation claims for shipping losses incurred during the Napoleonic wars led to his financial ruin and the sale of the mansion in 1823.

Elaine Weber Pascu

Gracie Mansion. The mayor's official residence, overlooking the East River at 88th Street and East End Avenue in Carl Schurz Park. Built in 1799–1804 at Horn's Hook as the country home of Archibald Gracie, probably by the carpenter Ezra Weeks, it was one of several residences in upper Manhattan that afforded refuge from the noise and disease of the city. Among the many visitors were Washington Irving and the Marquis de Lafayette.

Gracie Mansion, 1988

Gracie sold the house in 1823 after experiencing severe financial difficulties during the War of 1812. The neighborhood was gradually developed and in 1853 land adjacent to the house was subdivided into lots; the land surrounding the house was designated a city park after Avenue B (now York Avenue) was extended northward to East 83rd Street in 1876. The house remained a private residence until it was taken over by the parks department in 1896, which used it sporadically until 1923. It later housed the Museum of the City of New York, which opened to the public on 7 November 1924 and moved out in 1932. After being restored by the city the house reopened as a museum in 1936. At the urging of the parks commissioner Robert Moses it was made the official mayoral residence in 1942 by Mayor Fiorello H. La Guardia. Furnished in a Federal style, the mansion is open to the public two days a week.

Mary C. Black: *New York City's Gracie Mansion: A History of the Mayor's House* (New York: J. M. Kaplan Fund, 1984)

Mary Beth Betts

Gracie Square. Neighborhood on the Upper East Side of Manhattan (1990 pop. 27,000), lying along East End Avenue in Yorkville and bounded to the north by 92nd Street, to the east by the East River, to the south by 79th Street, and to the west by York Avenue. It was once the site of the country estates of the Astor, Gracie, and Schermerhorn families. Except for a few small developments such as Henderson Place (1882) and City and Suburban Homes (1901–13) the area was covered by brownstones and tenements until luxury apartment buildings were erected in the 1920s; the Chapin and Brearley schools also opened about this time. Construction began on Carl Schurz Park in 1876. The John H. Finley Walk was built over the FDR Drive in 1941. After 1942 the mansion of Archibald Gracie (1799) was used as the mayor's residence. The Municipal Asphalt Plant (1944), which stands at the northern edge of the neighborhood, was converted to a recreational facility. The population is affluent. Well-known residents have included Vincent Astor, Robert Moses, and Gloria Vanderbilt.

Mary C. Black: *New York City's Gracie Mansion: A History of the Mayor's House* (New York: J. M. Kaplan Fund, 1984)

Lee Solon: "If You're Thinking of Living in East End Avenue," *New York Times*, 2 Sept 1990, §10, p. 5

Val Ginter

graffiti. There was little attention paid to graffiti written in New York City until 1970, when a Greek–American teenager from Brooklyn named Demetrius (last name unknown) wrote "Taki 183," his nickname and street address, or "tag," on hundreds of subway cars and walls throughout the city. Although not the first such display, his tag was seen by thousands of persons and was soon imitated by scores of other teenagers. By 1972 there was a flourishing subculture based on graffiti, with its own jargon, informal organizations, and rules of conduct, and the budget of the Transit Authority for removing graffiti had risen from $250,000 in 1970 to more than $1 million. In May 1972 the president of the City Council, Sanford Garelik, proposed a monthly "Anti-Graffiti Day" during which New Yorkers could volunteer to clean up graffiti. During the same month RCA Records and Tapes canceled a full-page advertisement for an album by Lou Reed in the *Village Voice*, which had drawn complaints from the MTA and the Parks, Recreation, and Cultural Affairs Administration for its depiction of a man spray-painting Reed's name on a subway car. The MTA experimented with several cleaning solvents such as DWR (Dirty Word Remover) and Klout; they either proved ineffective or were so corrosive that subway car manufacturers threatened to void their warranties unless use of the solvents was discontinued. For a short time monuments, public facilities, and subway cars (at a cost of about $6000 a car) were coated with Hydron 300, a substance similar to Teflon that was designed to wipe clean easily with soap and water. It deteriorated quickly, proved prohibitively expensive, and was abandoned in November by the transit authority after four months. In October Mayor John V. Lindsay formed an anti-graffiti task force, and the City Council passed a bill that banned the carrying of open spray paint in public facilities without a permit and severely increased the penalty for adult graffiti offenders, raising the maximum fine from $25 to $500 and the maximum prison term from ten days to three months. The bill was signed into law by Mayor Lindsay in November, by which time graffiti could be seen on nearly all seven thousand cars in the subway system.

Not everyone considered graffiti a scourge. In November 1972 Hugo Martinez, a sociology student at City College, formed United Graffiti Artists (UGA) to promote graffiti as an art form. The first exhibition of members' work was held in December at Eisner Hall at City College, and by early 1973 many of the city's intellectuals considered such work "radical chic." Members of the UGA showed twenty canvases at the Razor Gallery in SoHo and won commissions from Twyla Tharp to paint backdrops during performances of her production *Deuce Coupe*. In autumn of the same year the movement was further legitimated when the Museum of Modern Art held a slide show of murals painted on buildings (with their landlords' permission). To the disgust of many, Norman Mailer published a meditative essay on the creative power of graffiti, "The Faith of Graffiti," in 1974. At the height of the graffiti art movement such members of the UGA as "Phase2," "T-Rex 131," and "Bama" commanded as much as $3000 a canvas. The National Organization of Graffiti Artists was formed in July 1974 by Jack Peslinger, a director of Off Broadway theater, but its members never achieved the financial success of their counterparts in the UGA. Interest in graffiti art declined after 1975, when the art season opened with an exhibition of such work at the Artist Space in SoHo. In October 1977 the Transit Authority erected an enormous subway car wash in the Coney Island yard that for an annual cost of

$400,000 drenched cars in a solution of petroleum hydroxide. Known by graffiti artists as the "final solution," the "buff," and the "orange crush" (for the defoliant Agent Orange), the wash was highly effective in quickly removing graffiti from the cars but soon caused controversy when fumes from the yard caused the nearby John Dewey High School to close for a day in November 1977. After two weeks of testing, the fumes were declared safe by the Transit Authority, but workers exposed to them continued to complain of respiratory and neurological problems for years. In 1980 newspapers reported that toxic waste from the wash was being dumped into the sewer system through unauthorized connections; the Transit Authority agreed to take action after at first disclaiming knowledge that the waste was toxic and the hookups illegal.

Interest in graffiti art renewed during the early 1980s. In 1980 an exhibition was held in Times Square by a group of aspiring artists and writers including Keith Haring and Jean-Michel Basquiat (then known as Samo), who became widely known in the following decade. Similar exhibitions were mounted at other galleries, among them the Fun Gallery. Several films explored ties between graffiti art, hip-hop music, and inner-city culture. David Ahearn's film *Wild Style*, featuring the graffiti artist Lee Quinones and the musician and artist Fred Brathwaite (also known as Fab Five Freddy and later as Freddy Love), opened to critical acclaim in March 1983 as part of the New Directors / New Film Series at Lincoln Center. In 1984 Henry Chalfant, long a supporter of graffiti art, helped to produce the documentary *Style Wars* for the Public Broadcasting System. Timothy Hutton played the lead role in *Turk182* (1985), a commercial motion picture about a graffiti artist. The amount of graffiti on buildings and subway cars also increased, and in 1980 the Transit Authority launched its "graffiti enhancement program," which was granted a budget of $5 million a year. Under the program more than two hundred painters were employed to cover graffiti on subway cars with quick-drying white paint; graffiti artists simply painted over the white surfaces, and the program was declared a failure in the autumn of 1980. While speaking with reporters in October Mayor Edward I. Koch, one of the city's most outspoken opponents of graffiti, suggested placing wolves in the subway yards to deter vandals. He was sharply criticized for this remark but nonetheless introduced a $1.5 million program to build fences and provide guard dogs for the Corona yard in September 1981. Three cars painted white were stored in the yard and remained clean, leading Mayor Koch to declare the program a success after three months. In 1982 the MTA was given $22.4 million to fence in all train yards. Razor wire atop the fencing replaced the use of guard dogs, which had drawn criticism for being excessive and brutal.

The city's anti-graffiti policies were called into question by the arrest on 15 September 1983 and subsequent death of Michael Stewart, an alleged graffiti artist. While being taken into custody by the transit police in the subway station at 1st Avenue and 14th Street, Stewart was placed in a choke hold; he lapsed into a coma on the way to the police station and died at Bellevue Hospital on 28 September. The incident generated heated debate and accusations of police brutality, negligence, and racism (Stewart was black, the arresting officers white). In 1984 David Gunn was named chairman of the Transit Authority. He focused his attention on graffiti, employing hundreds of new cleaners and depriving graffiti artists of their audience by immediately removing from service any car that had been defaced. During his tenure the amount of graffiti in the subways decreased quickly, and Gunn was admired by many as the "man who saved the subways." In July 1985 Mayor Koch signed a law banning sales of spray paint and broad-tipped markers to minors, and requiring merchants to display these items in areas inaccessible to minors or face a maximum fine of $500. During the same year $6.3 million was awarded to transit workers with health problems stemming from exposure to fumes from cleaning solvents, and the Stewart case was brought to trial. Elliot M. Gross, the chief medical examiner, initially found no physical injury to Stewart but changed his testimony several times during the proceedings. Eventually six of the arresting officers in the case were acquitted by an all-white jury of charges ranging from criminally negligent homicide and assault to perjury. Gross was dismissed by Mayor Koch in 1987 and in August 1990 Stewart's family won $1.7 million in a suit against defendants that included the city and the Transit Authority.

The late 1980s saw a decline in graffiti. The Transit Authority declared the subways free of graffiti in May 1989 and in February 1990 Gunn resigned. During these years Haring enjoyed tremendous popularity, commanding as much as $350,000 for his canvases of barking dogs, crawling infants, and dancing figures. By 1991 the Transit Authority reported an increase in the amount of graffiti on its trains, the number of "hits" having doubled in 1990 to 46,000, and the anti-graffiti task force was reconvened after a hiatus of eighteen months. The authority spent $1.4 million replacing scratched plastic windows between January 1990 and June 1992, and in 1992 it announced a plan to spend $24.3 million to equip all buses and subway cars with scratch-resistant glass. It also explored such strategies as issuing night-vision goggles to the transit police, and community groups used video cameras to catch graffiti artists in the act.

Craig Castleman: *Getting Up: Subway Graffiti in New York* (Cambridge: MIT Press, 1982)
Steven Hager: *Hip-Hop: The Illustrated History of Break Dancing, Rap Music, and Graffiti* (New York: St. Martin's, 1984)
Richard Levine: "MTA Is Still Seeking an Ideal Grime Grabber," *New York Times*, 8 May 1987, §B, p.3
William G. Blair: "Family Gets $1.7 Million for Stewart's Death," *New York Times*, 19 Aug 1990, §B, pp. 1–2
Jim Dwyer: *Subway Lives: 24 Hours in the Life of the New York City Subway* (New York: Crown, 1991)

Brenda Edmands

Graham, Martha (*b* Allegheny, Penn., 11 May 1894; *d* New York City, 1 April 1991). Dancer and choreographer. She grew up in southern California and from 1916 trained under Ruth St. Denis and Ted Shawn. In 1923 she moved to New York City, where she initially danced in the exotic dance tradition of her mentors but quickly developed an independent style stripped of ornamentation. During the early 1930s she founded a dance company for women and formalized her dance techniques of contraction and release to classical themes. Her early works of choreography, *Lamentations* (1930) and *Primitive Mysteries* (1931), were characterized by a stark simplicity, structural tautness, and mythic overtones. In 1926 she opened a studio on 5th Avenue between 12th and 13th streets, where she worked closely with the accompanist and composer Louis Horst, her intellectual advi-

Barbara Morgan, Martha Graham, Letter to the World (Kick) *(1940). Gelatin-silver print. Collection of the Museum of Modern Art. John Spencer Fund*

sor and the publisher of the journal *Dance Observer.* During the summers of 1936–41 she taught dance with Doris Humphrey, Hanya Holm, and Charles Weidman at the Bennington College School of Dance; there she met the classically trained dancer Erick Hawkins, who became the first male member of her company. At the same time she provided choreography for several distinctly American works, including *Frontier* (1935; sets by Isamu Noguchi), *American Document* (1938; featuring Hawkins), *Letter to the World* (1940), and *Appalachian Spring* (1944; featuring Hawkins and Merce Cunningham, music by Aaron Copland), in which she explored the roots of the American cultural experience and drew on her deep interest in religion and psychology. After 1944 Graham continued to work in the three dance styles that she explored early in her career: the abstract, the mythic, and the American. She continued in particular to explore themes derived from Greek mythology and Freudian psychology. More than forty of her dancers became choreographers and company directors, notably Hawkins, Cunningham, Sophie Maslow, and Anna Sokolow.

Elizabeth Kendall: *Where She Danced* (New York: Alfred A. Knopf, 1979)

Ernestine Stodelle: *Deep Song: The Dance Story of Martha Graham* (New York: Schirmer–Macmillan, 1984)

Peter M. Rutkoff, William B. Scott

Graham–Windham Services to Families and Children. Child welfare organization formed in 1977 by the merger of the Graham Home and Windham Children's Services. It helps six thousand children and families each year through adoption programs, foster boarding homes, group homes, family day care, pre-school and day-care centers, a family service center, a mental health clinic, and a residential campus and school.

Phyllis Barr

Gramercy Park. Neighborhood on the East Side of Manhattan, bounded to the north by 23rd Street, to the east by 3rd Avenue, to the south by 18th Street, and to the west by Park Avenue South. Dutch settlers once called the area Krom Moerasje (little crooked swamp), and the name was changed to Gramercy by the English. The land was bought from a descendant of Peter Stuyvesant by Samuel Ruggles, who drained the swamp, laid out streets in an English style around a private park (1831; Lexington Avenue between 20th and 21st streets), and offered sixty-six lots for sale. The park was opened to Union soldiers during the draft riots of 1863, the only occasion when nonresidents were allowed inside. Some of the first residents included Valentine Mott, the chief medical officer of the Union Army and the founder of Bellevue Hospital and New York University Medical School, George Templeton Strong, and James Harper, whose ornate "mayor's lights" still adorn his former residence at 4 Gramercy Park West. Some of the oldest luxury apartments in the city were built in 1884 at the southeast corner of the park (they were advertised as French flats to distinguish them from tenements). Residents and Republican legislators defeated several proposals by the city after 1890 to cut a road through the park, and into the 1920s many of the original townhouses were replaced by high-rise apartment buildings. Lexington Avenue between 14th and 20th streets was renamed Irving Place for Washington Irving, who never lived in the area but often visited a nephew who lived at Lexington Avenue and 17th Street.

The neighborhood became less fashionable after the extension of the 3rd Avenue elevated line (26 August 1878) and the onset of the Depression. From the 1940s most of the remaining nineteenth-century townhouses were remodeled and converted into apartments but several became private clubs, including 16 Gramercy Park (the Players, formed by Edwin Booth), 15 Gramercy Park (the National Arts Club, once owned by Samuel J. Tilden), and 3 Gramercy Park (the Nederlander Club). A Quaker meeting house on Gramercy Park South became the Brotherhood Synagogue. Many artists, writers, and performers lived in the neighborhood, including George Bellows, Robert Henri, Eugene O'Neill, O. Henry, David Graham Phillips, Ida Tarbell, Nathanael West, and Ludwig Bemelmans; other well-known residents have included Theodore Roosevelt, Eleanor Roosevelt, who was baptized at Calvary Episcopal Church at the northwestern edge of the park, Stanford White, who lived where the Gramercy Park Hotel now stands, and Elsie de Wolfe, who with White developed the field of interior design and lived in the Washington Irving house (southwest corner of 17th Street and Irving Place). The neighborhood became newly fashionable in the 1970s and 1980s; the park remains private and looks much as it did in the early nineteenth century.

4 Gramercy Park West, home of Mayor James Harper from 1847 to 1869

Stephen Garmey: *Gramercy Park: An Illustrated History of a New York Neighborhood* (New York: Routledge, 1984)

Carole Klein: *Gramercy Park: An American Bloomsbury* (Boston: Houghton Mifflin, 1987)

Harriet Davis-Kram

Grand Army Plaza (i). An oval plaza constructed in 1870 by Frederick Law Olmsted and Calvert Vaux as an approach to Prospect Park in Brooklyn, which they designed. Originally called Prospect Park Plaza, it was renamed in 1926 in honor of the Union Army. The plaza is the site of a triumphal arch eighty feet (twenty-four meters) high designed by John H. Duncan (1892). The arch is adorned with a four-horse bronze chariot group (1898) and sculptures on its southern façade (1901), both by Frederick MacMonnies. A fountain was designed by Egerton Swartwout north of the arch in 1932 and a bust of President John F. Kennedy by Neil Estern was installed in 1965. In between stands the Bailey Fountain, completed in 1932 and adorned with bronzed figures of Neptune and Tritons. The perimeter of the plaza is lined with apartment buildings.

Elliott B. Nixon, Stephen Weinstein

Grand Army Plaza (ii). A plaza at the southeast corner of Central Park, between 58th and 60th Streets. Its southern half includes the Plaza Hotel (1907); the most distinctive feature of the northern half is a statue

Grand Army Plaza, ca *1905*

of General William T. Sherman by Augustus Saint-Gaudens (1907).

Grand Central Terminal. From the earliest days of railroads in New York City locomotives hauled their cars as far into the city as was allowed, and with them came noise and dirt. In 1854 the Common Council forbade their operation south of 42nd Street, a boundary well north of the settled part of the city, and horses were used to haul the cars to their destinations farther downtown. By 1869 Cornelius Vanderbilt controlled all the railroads into the city, and he engaged the architect John B. Snook to design a "head house" at 4th Avenue and 42nd Street, which opened in 1871 as Grand Central Depot. The facility was never successful: it was in a constant state of rearrangement and enlargement, trains could exit only in reverse, and in spite of its name the depot was really in the hinterlands, an area that the city's horsecar lines had reached only recently. Shortly after the depot was built Vanderbilt began to lower the many tracks below street level, first in a deep cut roofed over and then in a tunnel that began at 96th Street and fanned out at 57th Street to a width of forty-one tracks on the upper level and twenty-six on the lower.

In 1889 the city demanded that the railroads either electrify their operations or move out of New York City altogether. A proposal to build a new depot was advanced by William Wilgus, the chief engineer responsible for submerging the tracks and electrifying the lines as far north as Mott Haven in the Bronx. He also proposed to raise revenues by selling and leasing the air rights over the tracks, between Madison and Lexington avenues from 42nd to 50th streets, to allow for the construction of office and apartment buildings. A limited competition for the design was won by the firm of Reed and Stem, which devised a system for separating automobile, pedestrian, train, and subway traffic by using ramps to route Park Avenue around the terminal on viaducts. Whitney Warren of the architectural firm of Warren and Wetmore designed the Beaux-Arts façade at 42nd Street as a triumphal triple archway facing south, allowing for a dramatic approach from Park Avenue. Sculpture is integral to the design rather than ornamental: above the entrance monumental statues of Minerva, Mercury, and Hercules in a pediment nearly fifty feet (fifteen meters) tall surround a clock with a diameter of thirteen feet (four meters). The interior of this terminal is equally dramatic: behind the main waiting room at the south entrance is the Main Concourse, a vast, vaulting space 120 feet (thirty-six meters) wide, 375 feet (114 meters) long, and 125 feet (thirty-eight meters) high, surmounted by a blue ceiling painted to resemble a starlit sky. At the west end a grand staircase allows the visitor to descend to the lower level; among the concessions there is the Oyster Bar, a popular restaurant that serves more than a thousand dozen oysters a day.

Because Grand Central Terminal is situated on a prime parcel of midtown real estate, its architectural integrity has occasionally been threatened by commercial development schemes. One advanced in 1960 would have divided the waiting room into four horizontal stories, with bowling alleys on the upper three. Soon after this proposal was put forward, Grand Central Terminal was designated a landmark. This status came to be resented by the owner, the Penn Central Railroad, because it empowered the Landmarks Commission to reject such proposals as one to build a fifty-four-story tower over the waiting room. A suit to have the landmark status revoked failed on the grounds that the city had the right to protect its architectural heritage. The interior of the building was cleaned in 1992, restoring some of its grandeur. In 1994 plans were announced to build additional entrances to the terminal several blocks north of 42nd Street, to afford quicker access to passengers riding toward the rear of arriving trains and the front of departing trains. More than 140,000 commuters a day pass through Grand Central Terminal, which remains one of the nation's most magnificent architectural monuments and one of the world's busiest train stations.

Grand Central Terminal, 1930s

Deborah Nevins, ed.: *Grand Central Terminal: City within the City* (New York: Municipal Art Society, 1982)

James E. Mooney

Perspective view of the proposed entrance to the Grand Boulevard and Concourse, East 161st Street and Mott Avenue, 1895

Grand (Boulevard and) Concourse. Thoroughfare in the western Bronx, and by extension the streets on either side of it. The street extends for four and a half miles (seven and a half kilometers) between 138th Street and Mosholu Parkway and has eleven lanes with a total width of 182 feet (fifty-five meters), two tree-lined dividers, and broad sidewalks. It was conceived by the engineer Louis Aloys Risse in 1870 and built between 1902 and 1909. An important innovation was the use of grade separations at the major cross streets, which allowed the traffic on the street to flow unimpeded by directing the traffic beneath it through underpasses. The concourse extended only as far south as 161st Street until 1927, when it came to include a newly widened portion of Mott Avenue. It soon became the main parade route for the borough, the site of its government, and the axis of an important shopping and entertainment district. Elegant apartment buildings were erected that offered cross-ventilation, large rooms, and uniformed doormen and attracted the wealthiest inhabitants of the Bronx, most of whom were Jewish. Among those who lived in the area were Mayor Joseph V. McKee, the opera singer Roberta Peters, the popular singer Eydie Gorme, the comedian Milton Berle, the baseball players Babe Ruth and Charlie Keller, and the novelist E. L. Doctorow. After the Second World War the population aged; children of local residents moved to the suburbs and in time were replaced by middle-class blacks and Latin Americans. Many synagogues were converted to churches; one became the Bronx Museum of the Arts. By 1990 a perceptible number of Koreans and Cambodians had moved to the area near Fordham Road.

Notable buildings along the Grand Concourse include Public School 31 (1899) at 144th Street, the Bronx General Post Office (1937) at 149th Street, the Mario Merola Bronx County Building (1934) at 161st Street, and the Edgar Allan Poe Cottage (*ca* 1812) at Kingsbridge Road.

Lloyd Ultan: *The Beautiful Bronx, 1920–1950* (New Rochelle, N.Y.: Arlington House, 1979)
Marion Risse Morris: "Always in My Heart: The Builder of the Grand Concourse," *Bronx County Historical Society Journal* 17 (spring 1980), 11–14
Gary Hermalyn and Robert Kornfeld: *Landmarks of the Bronx* (New York: Bronx County Historical Society, 1989)

Lloyd Ultan

Grand Hyatt. Hotel on 42nd Street in Manhattan, immediately to the east of Grand Central Terminal. Opened as the Hotel Commodore (1919; Warren and Wetmore, architects), it continued in operation under its original name until 1976, when the co-developers Donald Trump and the Hyatt Corporation used the structural shell of the building to create the Grand Hyatt. The new hotel opened in 1980 as a luxury convention hotel with fourteen hundred rooms. It has a façade of reflective glass sheathing and a space-frame cocktail lounge that forms a canopy over the main entrance.

May N. Stone

Grand Union Hotel. Hotel on the southeast corner of Park Avenue and 42nd Street, built in 1874. Its exterior had a mansard roof and reflected the Second Empire style of the Grand Central Depot across the street. The hotel was run on the European plan (in which meals are not included in the price of a room), and the restaurant became popular with politicians. The hotel closed on 2 May 1914 and was demolished during subway construction.

James Trager: *Park Avenue: Street of Dreams* (New York: Atheneum, 1990)

Val Ginter

Graniteville. Neighborhood in northwestern Staten Island, lying between Port Richmond and Bulls Head and bounded to the north by Forest and East Richmond avenues, to the east by the Martin Luther King Expressway, to the south by the Staten Island Expressway, and to the west by South Avenue. Once known as Bennett's Corners and then as Fayetteville, it was renamed for quarries operated from the 1840s to about 1896 to extract trap rock from the geological formation that includes the Palisades. From about the turn of the century until the 1940s there were many Italian and Greek dairy and truck farms in the area. The largest local employer until the end of the Second World War was the Unexcelled

Fireworks Company, which made munitions in a plant consisting of 167 buildings; the plant of the Weissglass Dairy stood at the northwestern edge of the neighborhood along Forest Avenue. The land is covered by townhouses and one- and two-family houses along new streets. Moore Catholic High School stands at the southern edge of the neighborhood. Baron Hirsch Cemetery, one of two large Jewish cemeteries in the borough, contains fifty thousand graves and covers eighty acres (thirty-two hectares) of land along Richmond Avenue, the major north–south thoroughfare. Little of the original grass and marshlands remains for development or conservation.

Harlow McMillen

Grant, Hugh J(ohn) (*b* New York City, 1852; *d* New York City, 3 Nov 1910). Mayor. He attended Catholic schools in the United States and Berlin and Columbia Law School, and inherited modest wealth and political connections from his father, a Democrat who owned several taverns on the West Side of Manhattan. After building a solid base in Irish-American fraternal organizations, he came to prominence by avoiding a scandal in 1882 in which many politicians were caught accepting bribes in exchange for contracts to operate streetcars, and he became the sheriff of New York County in 1885. With the backing of Tammany Hall he was elected mayor of New York City in 1888, defeating Abram S. Hewitt, who had earned a reputation for bigoted opposition to the Irish and other immigrants. He was reelected in 1890. Like earlier Irish mayors backed by Tammany Hall, Grant worked for limited government, low taxes, and investment in streets, sewers, water lines, and fire stations in areas undergoing real-estate development. In the 1890s he also played an important role in efforts by Tammany Hall to have the city build a harness racetrack. He did not seek reelection in 1892. Defeated in an attempt to regain his office in 1894 by William L. Strong and having lost control of Tammany Hall to Richard Croker, he retired from politics in 1897 to tend his real-estate investments.

David C. Hammack: "Hugh J. Grant," *Biographical Dictionary of American Mayors, 1820–1980*, ed. Melvin G. Holli and Peter d'A. Jones (Westport, Conn.: Greenwood, 1981), 138–39

David C. Hammack

Grant, Madison (*b* New York City, 19 Nov 1865; *d* New York City, 30 May 1937). Lawyer and political activist. The son of parents from two prominent families, he attended private schools in New York City and received a BA from Yale College (1887) and an LLB from Columbia Law School (1890). He lived on Park Avenue and spent most of his life in the city, where he helped to form the New York Zoological Society (1895), of which he was secretary (1895–1924) and president (1925–37). One of the most influential nativists of his time, he sought to restrict immigration on the basis of ethnicity. Through his writings he promoted the idea that immigrants from southern Europe were inferior to those from northern and western Europe and would destroy the country by eroding cultural values and reducing national achievement; he was especially hostile toward Jews. As vice-president of the Immigration Restriction League from 1922 he played an important role in the passage of the Immigration Act of 1924, which reduced the number of immigrants allowed to enter the country while increasing the proportion from northwestern Europe. Grant's published writings include *The Passing of the Great Race* (1916), *The Founders of the Republic on Immigration, Naturalization and Aliens* (with C. S. Davison, 1928), *The Alien in Our Midst* (with Davison, 1930), and *The Conquest of a Continent* (1933).

Walter Friedman

Grant, Ulysses S(impson) [Hiram Ulysses] (*b* Point Pleasant, Ohio, 27 April 1822; *d* New York City, 23 July 1885). Eighteenth president of the United States. He graduated from the U.S. Military Academy at West Point in 1843. A brilliant strategist, he won repeated victories in the West before President Lincoln made him commander of all Union forces in the Civil War. He became the country's first full general in 1866 and secretary of war in 1867. As the Republican presidential nominee he defeated Horatio Seymour in 1868 and was reelected against Horace Greeley in 1872. He retired to New York City in 1884, lived at 3 East 66th Street, and established Grant and Ward, an unsuccessful banking house. Grant's Tomb, a national memorial at Riverside Drive and 122nd Street that is the largest mausoleum in the United States, occupies a site donated by Mayor William R. Grace and houses the remains of Grant and his wife, Julia Dent Grant.

Arthur L. Conger: *The Rise of U. S. Grant* (New York: Century, 1931)
Jeannette Covert Nolan: *The Story of U. S. Grant* (New York: Grosset and Dunlap, 1952)

Neal C. Garelik

Grant City. Neighborhood in southeastern Staten Island (1990 pop. 4000), lying at the foot of Todt Hill and bounded to the west and north by Richmond Road and Jefferson Avenue, to the east by Hylan Boulevard, and to the south by Hylan Boulevard. Until after the Civil War the area was known as Frenchtown for its French population; it was renamed for President Ulysses S. Grant by a builder, John C. Thompson. About the turn of the century hotels and picnic grounds were clustered around a train station of Staten Island Rapid Transit at the center of the neighborhood. Semler's Hotel (1910) was a local landmark until it was demolished in 1965 and replaced by the Grant City Apartments, a complex of 305 units on Lincoln Avenue. Ballfields were added before the First World War. Many houses in the ranch and Cape Cod styles were built after the Second World War; they account for much of the housing, along with houses built after the Civil War and bungalows from the turn of the century. Grant City remains a closely knit residential community where small family stores and businesses line the streets near the railroad station.

Harlow McMillen

Grant's Tomb. Monument near the intersection of Riverside Drive and West 122nd

Grant's Tomb (designed by John H. Duncan), ca 1900

Street in Manhattan, the final resting place of President Ulysses S. Grant and his wife, Julia Dent Grant (1826–1902). As the result of an offer to the family from Mayor William R. Grace, the remains of President Grant were at first placed in a temporary vault in Riverside Park. The Grant Monument Association, formed shortly after Grant's death in 1885, raised about $600,000 from more than ninety thousand persons for the construction of a permanent tomb on the site of the vault. The association adopted a design proposed by the architect John Duncan, which was influenced by such famous mausoleums as those of Mausolus at Halicarnassus, Hadrian, and Napoleon, as well as the Garfield Memorial. On 27 April 1897, the seventy-fifth anniversary of Grant's birth, the tomb was dedicated in a ceremony attended by his widow and President William McKinley. The State of New York declared the day a full holiday, and the dedication proceedings were witnessed by about one million persons. Julia Grant was interred beside her husband in 1902. For many years Grant's Tomb was one of the most celebrated buildings in the nation, and it remained unsurpassed in popularity among the city's attractions until the end of the First World War. The Grant Monument Association continued to administer the site until 1959, when it was taken over by the National Park Service.

The monument is a neoclassical granite structure 150 feet (forty-five meters) tall. Among its elaborate features are Doric columns, a domed rotunda, and allegorical relief sculptures symbolizing aspects of Grant's life. On the exterior of the structure two figures representing victory and peace support Grant's epitaph, "Let Us Have Peace." The interior of the tomb is made of Lee and Carrara marble from Italy; within its center crypt are twin sarcophagi containing the remains of Grant and his wife. Grant is the only president buried in New York City, and his tomb is the second-largest mausoleum in the western hemisphere.

Frank Scaturro

graphic design. New York City became the capital of graphic design in the United States just before 1900. Graphic design was for many years a virtually anonymous activity, practiced by printers as an extra service to their customers and by art service studios. In 1914 the American Institute of Graphic Arts (AIGA) was formed in the city. The New York Art Directors Club, formed in 1921, became the largest organization of editorial and advertising art directors in the United States. The term "commercial art" was introduced about this time to refer to a wide range of graphic arts and crafts, including typography, advertising design, and package design. In the 1950s and 1960s the field of graphic design grew with extraordinary speed, owing partly to the need of large corporations to forge distinctive identities.

In part because of its many magazines, book publishers, and advertising agencies, New York City is also the site of a large number of graphic design firms, the largest of which have more than one hundred employees. Some of these offer a wide range of design services, while others specialize in such areas as corporate annual reports and retail packaging. Among the firms of longest standing are those of Milton Glaser, the Pushpin Group, Chermayeff and Geismar, Pentagram, Vignelli Associates, and Gipps, Balkind and Frankfurt; important younger firms include Smollan Carbone, Drentell Doyle, Doublespace, and Alex Isley Associates. The AIGA issues the quarterly critical journal the *AIGA Journal of Graphic Design*, and several trade publications are based in the city, notably *Print* (bimonthly), *U&lc* (Upper and lower case; published by the International Typeface Company), *Art Direction*, *Graphic Design U.S.A.*, and *Graphis*. Many schools and workshops in New York City offer training in the graphic arts. The largest are the Art Students League on 57th Street, the National Academy of Design on 5th Avenue, the Robert Blackburn Printmaking Workshop at 55 West 17th Street, the Pratt Institute in Brooklyn (offering undergraduate and graduate degrees in advertising and graphic design), the School of Visual Arts, the Parsons School of Design, Cooper Union (which houses the Herb Lubalin Study Center for training in typography), and the Fashion Institute of Technology, a branch of the State University of New York that offers courses in communication arts and advertising. Graphic design exhibitions are mounted at the Herb Lubalin Study Center and the galleries of the AIGA, the International Typeface Company, the School of Visual Arts, the Art Directors Club, the Shirley Goodman Resource Center at the Fashion Institute of Technology, the Museum of American Illustration (maintained by the Society of Illustrators), and the Parsons School of Design.

Steven Heller

Grasmere. Neighborhood in southeastern Staten Island (1990 pop. 4000), bounded to the north by the Staten Island Expressway, to the east and south by Hylan Boulevard, and to the west by the tracks of Staten Island Rapid Transit; it lies at the southern end of Clove Valley and is bisected from north to south by Clove Road and from west to east by Fingerboard Road. During the nineteenth century the area was the site of Sir Roderick Cameron's estate, and it was named for the village in the Lake District in England. The Durkee Manufacturing Company made marine hardware from the 1920s to 1951 in a plant on Clove Road (now the borough headquarters of the Salvation Army). An estate of the Goggi family on Hylan Boulevard became the Academy of St. Dorothy in 1932. Two privately owned ponds are surrounded by houses on rolling land: Brady's Pond, the only freshwater pond within the city limits fit for swimming, and Cameron's Pond. Nearby the Stonegate Condominiums were built on Fingerboard Road, as were the Elb Gardens apartments on Clove Road. The *Staten Island Advance*, the only daily newspaper in the borough, opened a publishing plant on Fingerboard Road in 1960. The Carmelite Sisters in 1973 opened the Carmel Nursing Home, the only Roman Catholic nursing home in the borough. Staten Island Rapid Transit has a station in Grasmere.

Harlow McMillen

Gravesend. Neighborhood in southwestern Brooklyn (1990 pop. 63,629), lying between Bensonhurst and Sheepshead Bay and bounded to the north by Avenue P, to the east by Ocean Parkway, to the south by Avenue Z, and to the west by Bay Parkway. One of the six original towns of Kings County, it was settled in 1643 by a group of English religious dissenters led by Lady Moody, who put forward a four-square plan centered at what is now the intersection of McDonald Avenue and Gravesend Neck Road. The town was named for a city at the mouth of the River Thames and was covered by farmland until 1875, when three racetracks and the resort of Coney Island were developed nearby. During the next two decades, when the local population was only six thousand, the area was known nationally for attracting on weekends crowds of 100,000 who were encouraged to visit by John Y. McKane, a local political figure. The neighborhood changed after its annexation to Brooklyn in 1894. Ocean Parkway, a tree-lined thoroughfare designed by Frederick Law Olmsted, was built in 1874–80. Residential development was spurred by the electrification of the Sea Beach (1898) and Culver (1899) rail lines, which reduced travel time to Manhattan to forty-five minutes, and eventually a large Italian community took shape.

Most of Gravesend remains a comfortable lower-middle-class and middle-class neighborhood. The Italian population remains large and lives in well-kept houses built after 1920; often children who grow up in the neighborhood marry and settle a few blocks from their parents. Ocean Parkway runs north to south and is the main thoroughfare; Avenue U is lined with bakeries, restaurants, and Italian delicatessens (*salumerias*). Moody's house stands at 27 Neck Road.

Jerry Della Femina: *An Italian Grows in Brooklyn* (Boston: Little, Brown, 1978)

Stephen Weinstein

Graziano, Rocky [Barbella, Thomas Rocco] (*b* New York City, 1 Jan 1921; *d* New York City, 22 May 1990). Boxer. He grew up on the Lower East Side and began boxing professionally in 1942 while absent without official leave from the army. He is best known for his three middleweight championship fights with Tony Zale, of which he lost the first, won the rematch on 16 July 1947, and lost the third in 1948, all by knockouts. After retiring in 1952 with a record of sixty-seven wins, ten losses, and six draws he became an entertainer and autobiographer. Graziano's boxing style was that of a street brawler, and his courage captivated the public.

Steven A. Riess

Great Atlantic and Pacific Tea Company [A&P]. Firm of food retailers. Formed as a partnership in 1859, it initially had one tea shop on Vesey Street. It later became the first major chain of grocery stores in the country and the largest enterprise of its kind in the world, operating more than fifteen thousand stores by 1929. For many years it was controlled by the Hartford family, and although it declined somewhat after the Second World War it remained the largest retailing firm in the country until 1965. After suffering a number of setbacks in the late 1960s and 1970s it was bought in 1979 by a German firm, the Tengelmann Group. In 1986 it bought the Shopwell–Food Emporium and Waldbaum grocery chains. In the mid 1990s A&P was the largest grocery chain in New York City and the fourth-largest in the country.

Richard S. Tedlow: *New and Improved: The Story of Mass Marketing in America* (New York: Basic Books, 1990), 182–258

Peter A. Coclanis

Great Britain. Transatlantic steamship, designed by the engineer and naval architect Isambard Kingdom Brunel and built in 1843 in Bristol, England; she was the first steamship made of iron and the first to have a propeller. After a profitable career she was converted into a sailing ship. The *Great Britain* was eventually wrecked in the Falkland Islands but was then salvaged, returned to Bristol, and restored in the same dry dock where she was built.

Frank O. Braynard

greater New York. A term that had a specific meaning in the late nineteenth century and gradually acquired a more general one. In the years preceding and immediately following the consolidation of New York City in 1898, it referred to the five boroughs of the city as newly defined: the Bronx, Brooklyn, Manhattan, Queens, and Staten Island. Over the years the term came to acquire a broader sense, connoting also the nearby suburbs of Westchester County, Long Island, New Jersey, and Connecticut. The term "greater New York" now has much the same imprecise sense as locutions like "greater Boston."

Greater New York Hospital Association. Nonprofit organization formed in 1904 as an advocacy group for hospital superintendents in New York City. After it absorbed the Hospital Conference of the City of New York and the Hospital Council of Brooklyn in 1937 it was formally organized to be the sole voice of nonprofit hospitals in the city. Among its first projects in this new role was an effort to obtain more funds from the city to provide care for indigent patients. It now represents more than a hundred hospitals in the metropolitan area and supports research and education, particularly in the areas of finance, health economics, and organization and management.

Brian Greenberg

Greater New York Savings Bank. Savings bank incorporated in Brooklyn in May 1897 by a group of businessmen led by Charles J. Obermayer. Its name referred to the forthcoming consolidation of New York City. The bank first occupied quarters in Park Slope at 7th Avenue and 1st Street, which it soon outgrew. It merged with the Guardian Savings Bank in 1908, City Savings in 1964, and the Flatbush Savings Bank in 1970. It became publicly owned in 1987 and later opened four branches on Long Island.

Stephen Weinstein

Great Fire. The fire of 16–17 December 1835 caused more damage to property than any other event in the history of New York City. It destroyed more than twenty square blocks of mostly wooden buildings bounded by Wall and Broad streets, Coenties Slip, and the East River. Every fire company in Manhattan and many from Brooklyn, Long Island, New Jersey, and other areas responded to the alarm, but their efforts were hampered by inadequate water supplies, primitive equipment, and bitterly cold temperatures that froze water pipes and leather fire hoses. Most of the fire was subdued on 18 December by nineteen hundred firemen, including four hundred from Philadelphia. Losses in the pier, warehouse, and commercial districts were estimated at $20 million to $40 million; the volume of claims forced twenty-three of the twenty-six fire insurance companies in the city to declare bankruptcy. The Great Fire led to demands for the reorganization of the volunteer force or its replacement with a paid one, and for the introduction of horse-drawn engines equipped with steam pumps. The cause of the fire was never determined.

Donald J. Cannon

Great Kill. Name used until the 1880s for a neighborhood in Manhattan, bounded to the north by 57th Street, to the east by 6th Avenue, to the south by 35th Street, and to the west by the Hudson River. It was named for a river of the same name that flowed from the Hudson into Manhattan along what is now West 41st Street. From the early eighteenth century to the late nineteenth the area was the site of the Great Kill Farm, a large estate owned by various members of the Hopper family. William F. Havemeyer lived near what is now Columbus Circle during the 1850s and 1860s. By the 1880s the Great Kill had been filled in and apartment buildings had replaced many houses.

Hopper Striker Mott: *The New York of Yesterday* (New York: Knickerbocker, 1908)

James Bradley

Great Kills. Neighborhood in southeastern Staten Island (1990 pop. 18,809), occupying a parcel of 2.5 square miles (6.5 square kilometers) bounded to the north by Arthur Kill

View of the Great Fire of 1835 from the top of the Bank of America, Wall and William streets

Road, to the east by Corbin Avenue, to the south by Great Kills Harbor, and to the west by Robinson Avenue. Great Kills Park and Crookes Point form a hook of land that shields most of the harbor from the Atlantic Ocean. The shoreline area was known as Clarendon and the inland area as Newtown until the two were combined under the name Gifford's, after the local commissioner and surveyor of roads Daniel Gifford; the current name was adopted in 1865. The neighborhood was relatively unaffected by the opening in 1964 of the Verrazano Narrows Bridge and remains spacious. Sycamore Street and its environs are covered by zoning laws that limit the construction of townhouses.

Stanford M. Forrester

Great North Side. See North side.

Greatorex [née Pratt], **Eliza** (*b* Manor Hamilton, Ireland, 25 Dec 1820; *d* Paris, 9 Feb 1897). Painter and etcher. She moved to New York City about 1840 and soon after married the musician Henry W. Greatorex (1816–58). On his death she began to produce oil paintings, drawings, and etchings, and became known for landscapes and especially scenes of New York City. One of her most successful series of etchings was "Old New York from the Battery to Bloomingdale" (1875). In 1869 she became the first woman elected an associate of the National Academy of Design. Greatorex resided on 5th Avenue during the 1860s and on East 32nd Street during the 1870s.

Elizabeth Pratt Greatorex: *Catalogue Sale of Private Collection of Paintings, Old Engravings, Old China, Studio Properties, and Furniture* (New York: n.pub., 1878)

Wendy Shadwell

Great Road. See Boston post road.

Greeks. New York City is the home of the largest Greek community in North America and perhaps the largest outside Greece itself. The exact number is in dispute: the federal census of 1990 counted 159,876 persons of Greek ancestry in New York State, whereas the Hellenic American Neighborhood Action Committee gave an estimate in 1984 of 439,640 for New York City alone, and various estimates for Astoria have ranged from sixty thousand to seventy thousand.

The first Greek immigrant to New York City on record was Basil Constantin, who settled in the city in July 1844. By 1855 several Greek merchants in the city imported currants and exported cotton and wheat as part of international trading firms. They also acted as representatives of the Greek government: Demetrius N. Botassi, who moved to New York City in 1856, was the Greek consul general for more than fifty-eight years. Perhaps the first Greek student in New York City was Christodoulos M. L. Evangelides, who graduated from Columbia College in 1836; welcomed into the homes of prominent New Yorkers, he was the subject of a poem by William Cullen Bryant. In 1857 the Peleponnesos opened as the first Greek restaurant in the city and the forerunner of a business in which thousands of Greek immigrants eventually distinguished themselves. After the Civil War the city became the preferred point of disembarkation for immigrants. In 1880 the Greek population of the city was nevertheless only sixty-nine. The first of many Greek flower shops opened in 1885.

Like other immigrants the Greeks traveled to North America because they lacked opportunity in their homeland and sought to escape political repression. Most were from rural areas and had only the skills of craftsmen or farmers, and few had ever lived in a large city. Until about 1910 almost all were men: those who were married sent for their wives and children from Greece when they felt financially secure; those who were unmarried often visited their village of origin in Greece and returned to the United States with a bride (during the first decades of immigration intermarriage with Americans of other ethnic backgrounds was uncommon). Few immigrants fulfilled their intentions of eventually resettling in Greece. Some young Greek boys seeking to emigrate to the United States fell victim to an exploitative practice similar to that maintained by the Italian padrones: systematically recruited by middlemen in Greece who arranged for their passage in return for a period of work as bootblacks or peddlers, once in the United States they were often crowded into unsanitary living conditions, and to be able to discharge their obligation they were forced to work long hours at low wages.

Strong family ties, fervent Greek nationalism, hard work, and upward mobility became characteristic of the Greek immigrants of New York City. The immigrants worked at the docks, sold flowers and fruit, and shined shoes. Their community was concentrated in lower Manhattan around Madison and Fulton streets, where men shared single rooms. Greeks entered the American middle class rapidly; for the most part they did not choose careers as wage earners but instead quickly sought to open shops or buy pushcarts. In 1873 a former sailor named Hatzikiris saved enough money to form the Greek–American Confectionery Company, which eventually supplied candy to retailers throughout the east coast. Worsening economic conditions in Greece caused the number of immigrants to increase sharply after 1891: there were 15,979 immigrants to the United States from Greece between 1890 and 1900, of whom at least 1309 settled in New York City, and by some estimates nearly one in four Greek males between fifteen and forty-five emigrated to the United States between 1900 and 1915. In 1891 about 450 members of the Brotherhood of Athena (the first Greek fraternal society in the city) raised funds to establish the Church of the Holy Trinity, the first Greek Orthodox church in the city and only the third in the United States. Through the efforts of Solon Vlasto, president of the Brotherhood of Athena, on 6 April 1893 the Greek flag was flown in honor of Greek Independence Day over City Hall and over Reiner Hall (475 Pearl Street), from which a crowd of three hundred Greeks marched to Broadway by way of Chambers Street. Vlasto also launched the Greek-language newspaper *Atlantis* in 1894 (it began daily publication in 1904 and remained in operation until 1972), which maintained a politically conservative stance to which the *National Herald* offered a liberal alternative from 1915. From 1904 a number of shipping lines scheduled service from the southern Greek port of Patras to New York City.

A survey of businesses in Manhattan owned by Greeks in 1909 recorded 151 bootblack parlors, 113 florists, 107 lunchrooms and restaurants, seventy confectioneries, sixty-two retail fruit stores, and eleven wholesale produce dealers. In 1911 there were at least twenty-four Greek fraternal organizations in the city, and the first Greek-language parochial school opened in the Bronx. By one estimate the Greek population of New York City was twenty thousand in 1913, and in 1920 the figure for the United States was more than 400,000. Unlike other immigrants the Greeks did not live in concentrated ethnic quarters or ghettos but were scattered throughout the boroughs, with some areas of concentration near the original settlement at Madison Street on the Lower East Side, along 6th Avenue in the West 30s, along 2nd and 3rd avenues in the 20s and 30s, and in Brooklyn. After the First World War most Greek immigrants settled along 8th Avenue between 14th and 45th streets. The English language spoken in the city combined with the Greek language of the immigrants to produce something of a dialect during the period of mass immigration, a subject that has yet to be fully explored. Early Greek-language films and sound recordings were made in New York City, and radio programs were first broadcast in the 1930s.

Like other immigrants from southern Europe Greek–Americans suffered from the nativist movements of the interwar period. Their long Greek names and heavily accented English made them identifiable targets for employment discrimination and other forms of prejudice. Greek businessmen were hurt when their competitors spread rumors accusing them of dishonesty and of operating establishments with unsanitary conditions. The Greeks of New York City fought back through their fraternal and business organizations, stressing to their members the importance of assimilation, American values, and American citizenship. Greek immigrants enrolled in English-language and civics courses

Revival style, along with several wooden shelters (including one in a Gothic Revival style, one resembling an Italian villa, and another resembling a Swiss chalet). Green-Wood Cemetery became fashionable after the body of De Witt Clinton was moved there in 1844 from Albany, New York. The natural beauty of the cemetery, its design and Victorian monuments, and the eminence of some of those buried there soon made the cemetery a popular tourist attraction. The success of Green-Wood inspired a competition to design a public park for New York City, to which Calvert Vaux and Frederick Law Olmsted submitted an entry for a park named "Greensward" (their plan was chosen and formed the basis for Central Park).

In the mid 1990s Green-Wood Cemetery covered 478 acres (194 hectares) and contained 550,000 interments; its facilities included community mausoleums, a crematorium, and columbariums. The cemetery continues to be an oasis of tranquility. Among those buried there are the political leaders Seth Low, Henry George, and William M. "Boss" Tweed, the inventors Peter Cooper, Elias Howe, and Samuel F. B. Morse, the artist George Bellows, the cabinetmaker Duncan Phyfe, the dancer Lola Montez (as Mrs. Eliza Gilbert), the birth control advocate Margaret Sanger, the composers Louis Moreau Gottschalk and Leonard Bernstein, the newspaper publisher Horace Greeley, and the organized-crime figures Albert Anastasia and Joey Gallo. For further illustration see CEMETERIES.

Edward F. Bergman

Grey Advertising. Advertising agency formed in 1917 by Larry Valenstein as Grey Studios. In its early years it focused on direct mail and designed monthly sales plans for department stores in New York City. One of the first agencies in the city to provide Jews with opportunities in advertising, the agency was incorporated as Grey Advertising in 1925, the year it became a full-service agency by acquiring the accounts of the magazine *Good Housekeeping* and the consumer products firm Mennen. As the agency grew it attracted such noted copywriters as William Bernbach, who became the copy chief in 1945 (and was later a principal in Doyle Dane Bernbach). By 1950 Grey was the twenty-eighth-largest agency in the United States, and in 1959 it opened its first office abroad, in Montreal. Grey was one of several agencies to become publicly owned in the mid 1960s. It formed Grey Public Relations (now Grey Com) in 1963 and in the 1970s and 1980s added subsidiaries in entertainment advertising, marketing, syndicated television programming, direct marketing, sales promotion, and medical advertising. In the mid 1990s Grey and its subsidiaries had 223 offices in eighty-four cities and thirty-four countries. Its income made it the tenth-largest advertising agency in the United States and the eleventh-largest in the world.

Stephen R. Fox: *The Mirror Makers: A History of American Advertising and Its Creators* (New York: William Morrow, 1984)

Chauncey G. Olinger, Jr.

grid plan. A far-reaching plan approved by the state legislature of New York in 1811, also known as the Commissioners' Plan. Devised by a commission made up of Gouverneur Morris, the surveyor Simeon De Witt, and the lawyer John Rutherford, it established a basis for the orderly sale and development of land in Manhattan between 14th Street and Washington Heights by establishing a rectangular grid of streets and property lines without regard for topography. Twelve numbered avenues, each a hundred feet (thirty meters) wide, ran north and south. In the interior 3rd, 4th, 5th, and 6th avenues were 920 feet (280 meters) apart; along the riverfronts the avenues were closer together in expectation of greater development. The signature of the plan was its 155 cross streets placed only two hundred feet (sixty meters) apart, producing a grid of about two thousand long, narrow blocks. Convinced that simple rectangular houses and lots were best, the commissioners avoided the addition of circles, ovals, and other features like those used by Pierre L'Enfant in his plan for Washington. The commission was instructed by the legislature to lay out streets and public squares of sufficient dimension to provide "free and abundant circulation of air" for public health. They provided small parks in the interior of the island at 53rd, 66th, 77th, and 120th streets and several large public spaces: one of twenty-six acres (eleven hectares) uptown for a reservoir, another of fifty-four acres (twenty-two hectares) on the Lower East Side for a wholesale market complex, and a third of 275 acres (111 hectares) extending from 23rd to 34th streets and from 3rd to 7th avenues for a military training ground, or "parade" (which it was hoped would eventually become a central park).

The grid plan of 1811 was repeatedly altered because it lacked the support of a formal planning commission. Union, Tompkins, Stuyvesant, and Madison squares were added, as were Lexington and Madison avenues to bisect the long blocks between 3rd and 5th avenues. More disruptive changes occurred with the elimination of the two large spaces provided for the market and militia. When plans for a park downtown were forestalled, the street plan was altered to allow for the extension of 4th, 5th, and 6th avenues south to 14th Street, and for the extension northward of Broadway. The angled course of Broadway later made possible the development of such areas as Times Square. Despite these changes the basic plan for most streets and blocks survived and continued to dominate the city's development. The one great exception was the building of Central Park in the late 1850s. Later modifications were made along the riverfronts, notably at Riverside Park.

Edward K. Spann: "The Greatest Grid: The New York Plan of 1811," *Two Centuries of American Planning*, ed. Daniel Schaffer (Baltimore: Johns Hopkins University Press, 1988), 11–39

See also STREETS.

Edward K. Spann

Grinnell, Minturn. Shipping firm formed in New York City in 1815 as Fish and Grinnell by Preserved Fish and Joseph Grinnell (1788–1885), formerly merchants in New Bedford, Massachusetts. It became Fish, Grinnell and Company when Grinnell's brothers Henry Grinnell (1799–1874) and Moses H(icks) Grinnell (1803–77) became partners. After Fish and Joseph Grinnell retired and Henry Grinnell's brother-in-law Robert Bowne

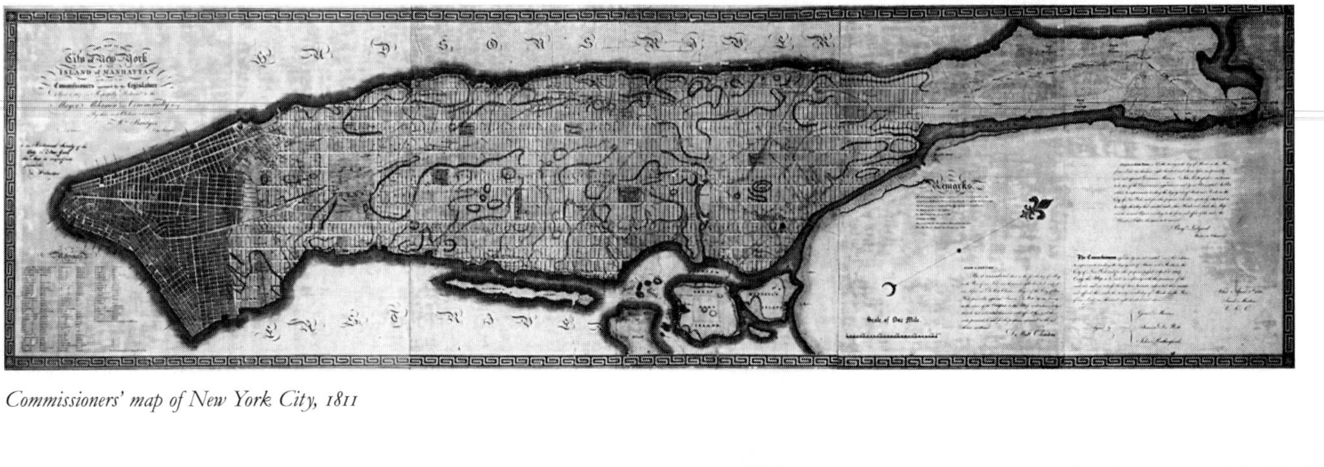

Commissioners' map of New York City, 1811

Minturn (1805–66) joined the firm, it was reorganized as Grinnell, Minturn and Company (1833) and became one of the city's great shipping firms. Its swallowtail flag flew over more than fifty vessels, including regular packet lines to Liverpool and London and the famous clipper the *Flying Cloud.* All three partners were officers of banks and insurance companies who were prominent in civic and philanthropic affairs. Henry Grinnell supported polar expeditions and was a founder of the American Geographical and Statistical Society, of which he became president. Minturn helped to establish organizations that aided immigrants and the poor in New York City and contributed to St. Luke's Hospital; he was both a president of the Union League Club and a member of the original Central Park Commission, as was Moses H. Grinnell, who was also president of the local Chamber of Commerce (1847, 1849–52) and the New England Society (1843–54). A close friend of Daniel Webster, Moses H. Grinnell became active in politics and in 1838 won election to Congress as a Whig. He later became a Republican, served on the Union Defense Committee at the outbreak of the Civil War, and in 1869 was appointed collector of the Port of New York by President Ulysses S. Grant. Among the junior partners in the firm was Franklin H. Delano, who married Laura Astor, daughter of William Backhouse Astor.

Allan Nevins, ed.: *The Diary of Philip Hone, 1828–1851* (New York: Dodd, Mead, 1927)

Robert Greenhalgh Albion: *The Rise of New York Port, 1815–1860* (New York: Charles Scribner's Sons, 1939)

Elaine Weber Pascu

Griscom, John Hoskins (*b* ?New York City, 14 Aug 1809; *d* 28 April 1874). Physician and public health official. He began a private practice in New York City in 1836. Appointed city inspector in 1842, he wrote the influential report *The Sanitary Condition of the Laboring Population of New York* (1845). During the following years he became a leader in the movement for public health and sanitation reform. Among the measures that he advocated was the establishment of a powerful, professionally staffed board of health that would systematically collect vital statistics and other data. Griscom was a founding member of both the New York Academy of Medicine and the New York Medical and Surgical Society. He was also a physician at New York Hospital from 1843 until about 1870.

Charles E. Rosenberg and Carroll Smith-Rosenberg: "Pietism and the Origins of the American Public Health Movement: A Note on John H. Griscom and Robert M. Hartley," *Journal of the History of Medicine and Allied Sciences* 23 (1968), Jan, 16–35

Allen J. Share

grocers. Most food in colonial New York City was sold by vendors in public markets. One of the first such markets was one opened on Pearl Street in lower Manhattan in 1656; more elaborate ones also opened but eventually were superseded by small shops that sold food and other items. As the population grew during the first half of the nineteenth century these shops were replaced by small specialty shops that sold produce, baked goods, meat, fish, dairy products, spirits, coffee, or tea. In 1882 James Butler opened a grocery store on 2nd Avenue; he had two hundred stores that grossed $15 million annually and eleven hundred stores by 1934. Chain grocery stores were introduced in the first decades of the twentieth century, and the most important ones had their own warehouses, distribution networks, and manufacturing plants by the 1920s, when economy stores were also increasingly common. In August 1930 the King Kullen Grocery Store was opened by Michael J. Cullen at 171st Street and Jamaica Avenue in Queens. Considered by many the first supermarket in the country, it had ample parking and was large and well stocked with a wide assortment of foods. It kept costs low by furnishing its stores sparsely and having customers serve themselves. Other stores adopted Cullen's methods and transformed the retail food industry, which operated with lower margins and much higher turnover than formerly and became more efficient and profitable. Supermarkets also took advantage of improvements in food processing, packaging, preservation, and distribution. By the 1940s most large chains such as A&P had adopted Cullen's methods. After the Second World War there was fierce competition in the city among such large chains as A&P, Daitch, D'Agostino, Pathmark, Pioneer, and Waldbaum. There were also several large cooperative and independent supermarket groups, as well as small convenience stores, "mom and pops," and bodegas. As their marketing techniques became increasingly sophisticated, supermarkets came to rely less on display advertising in newspapers and more on circulars and broadcast advertising. In the mid 1990s supermarkets accounted for about 63 percent of retail food sales in New York City, and A&P was the largest chain.

J. Tevere MacFadyen: "The Rise of the Supermarket," *American Heritage* 36 (Oct–Nov 1985), 22–32

Richard S. Tedlow: *New and Improved: The Story of Mass Marketing in America* (New York: Basic Books, 1990), 182–258

Peter A. Coclanis

Grolier Club. A club formed in 1884 by nine business and cultural figures who were collectors of books and prints. Named for the sixteenth-century French bibliophile Jean Grolier, its purpose was to encourage "literary study and the arts of the book." During its first century the club had more than three thousand members, mounted more than six hundred imaginative exhibitions on diverse topics, published about a hundred and fifty books, and held a large number of lectures and symposia in its impressive clubhouses. The first of these was in rented quarters; the second was built for the club at 29 East 32nd Street and is a designated landmark; the present building, designed by Bertram Grosvenor Goodhue, a member of the club, was completed in 1917 at 47 East 60th Street and enlarged in 1984.

James E. Mooney

Grosset and Dunlap. Firm of book publishers formed in 1898 as Dunlap and Grosset, a bookshop at 11 East 16th Street, by Alexander Grosset and George T. Dunlap. The name was changed to Alexander Grosset and Company when Dunlap left in 1899, and then to Grosset and Dunlap on his return in the following year. The first books published were pirated editions of Rudyard Kipling, most of which were already in the public domain because they had been republished earlier by other firms. In the first decade of the twentieth century the firm began the practice of reissuing the paperbound books of other publishers in hardcover form, and managed to sell the new hardcover editions at prices not much higher than those of the original paperbound editions. This innovation made it one of the leading reprint publishers in the United States. In 1903 it moved its offices to 52 Duane Street, and in 1907 it expanded into children's books by purchasing the firm of Chatterton and Peck, thus acquiring the rights to the Rover Boys series by Edward Stratemeyer, which sold more than five million copies; it later published popular children's series based on the characters Tom Swift, the Bobbsey Twins, the Hardy Boys, and Nancy Drew.

In 1910 the firm moved its offices and manufacturing operations to 518 West 26th Street and opened a retail shop on 26th Street and Broadway (moved in 1916 to 1140 Broadway). It introduced such techniques as selling books at newsstands, drugstores, and department stores, made extensive use of retail displays and posters, and was among the first publishers to coordinate the publication of popular novels with the release of their film versions. When Alexander Grosset died in 1934 Dunlap became president of the firm, which in 1939 moved to 1107 Broadway. In 1945 the firm joined with the Curtis Company, a nationwide book distributor, to form the paperback publisher Bantam Books, of which it became the sole owner in 1964. Grosset and Dunlap and Bantam were acquired in 1968 by the National General Corporation, which in 1974 sold Grosset to Filmways and Bantam to IFI International. In 1978 Grosset and Dunlap ranked third in hardcover sales and remained an important publisher of children's books, but in the next few years sales declined markedly. The firm was sold to the Putnam

Publishing Group in 1982. The offices are at 200 Madison Avenue.

Timothy Murray: "Grosset and Dunlap," *American Literary Publishing Houses, 1638–1899*, ed. Peter Dzwonkoski (Detroit: Gale Research, 1986)

Marjorie Harrison

Group Theatre. Experimental theater group formed in 1931 by Harold Clurman, Cheryl Crawford, and Lee Strasberg, members of the Theatre Guild. Modeled on the Moscow Art Theatre and influenced by the teaching methods of Konstantin Stanislavsky, it was intended to be a permanent acting company with a repertory that would involve more than aesthetics — it would create a tradition of common values. The group began as a summer workshop in Brookfield Center, Connecticut, with twenty-eight actors, including Stella Adler, Clifford Odets, J. Edward Bromberg, Sanford Meisner (later a director and acting teacher), and Morris Carnovsky and Franchot Tone of the Theatre Guild; the first directors were Clurman, Crawford, and Strasberg. The initial production was Paul Green's play *The House of Connelly*. Under Strasberg's direction and the auspices of the Theatre Guild the play was well received at its première at the Martin Beck Theatre on 23 September. It was followed by Claire and Paul Sifton's *1931–*, which opened at the Mansfield Theatre on 10 December 1931 and closed on 19 December. Others who soon became members were Adler's brother Luther Adler and Elia Kazan, Margaret Barker, Phoebe Brand, Lee J. Cobb, Frances Farmer, Jules Garfield (later known as John Garfield), Ruth Nelson, and Art Smith; Sylvia Sidney and Jane Wyatt performed occasionally, and Boris Aronson often designed sets. Summer retreats in Connecticut and upstate New York were crucial to the development of a style of acting called the Method. Members were paid whether or not they performed and regardless of the size of their parts. During its leanest year, 1932–33, the group even rented a ten-room walk-up apartment on West 57th Street. There was also talk of opening a restaurant.

The innovative approach of the directors and the renown of the actors earned the attention of critics, even for the company's least successful productions. Contrary to the wishes of many members, classic repertory was never attempted outside the summer camps, a policy that drew some criticism. The Group Theatre did introduce more than twenty new American plays by the most influential writers of the day, including Maxwell Anderson (*Night over Taos*, 1932, 48th Street Theatre), John Howard Lawson (*Success Story*, 1932, Maxine Elliot Theatre; *Gentlewoman*, 1934, Cort Theatre), Green and Kurt Weill (*Johnny Johnson*, 1936, 44th Street Theatre), Irwin Shaw (*Quiet City*, 1938, Belasco Theatre; score by Aaron Copland; *The Gentle People*, 1939, Belasco Theatre), and William Saroyan (*My Heart's in the Highlands*, 1939, Guild Theatre). The most important playwright was Odets, whose first play, *Awake and Sing!*, was performed in 1935 at the Belasco Theatre. He achieved critical success with *Waiting for Lefty*, a one-act play inspired by a strike of the city's taxi drivers in 1934. On its opening night at the Civic Repertory Theatre, 6 January 1935, the audience rose to its feet chanting "Strike! Strike!" as the main character, a strike leader, called to his workers. Within months the play was performed by leftist groups nationwide and by the Group Theatre in London, where it was an overwhelming success. The production was also an important example of the kind of cooperation between actors and the audience that the company sought to inspire.

Tension within the group increased as sacrifices became more difficult and disaffection spread. After studying in Paris with Stanislavsky, Stella Adler attended the company's summer workshop in 1933 in Ellenville, New York, where she initiated a quarrel with Strasberg over his interpretation of the Method that eventually helped to divide not only the company but American theater in general. The Group Theatre nonetheless earned critical and commercial success with Odets's *Golden Boy* (1937, Belasco Theatre). In 1937 Strasberg and Crawford resigned, disheartened by the defection to Hollywood of such members as Clurman, Tone, Garfield, and Odets. The actor Bobby Lewis briefly ran the Group Theatre School (or Studio) in 1937–38 and Clurman soon returned. Despite its many successes the Group Theatre never made enough money to establish a permanent company. Among its last productions were Shaw's *Retreat to Pleasure* (1940, Belasco Theatre, directed by Clurman) and Odets's *Rocket to the Moon* (1938, Belasco Theatre) and *Night Music* (1940, Broadhurst Theatre). Odets's *Clash by Night* (1941, Belasco Theatre, directed by Strasberg) is sometimes identified as the last production by the Group Theatre, but it was produced by Billy Rose with only two of the company's actors, and the name of the Group Theatre was deleted from the playbill. In 1941 the Group Theatre ceased operations. It is widely considered one of the most important American theater groups of the 1930s, having most clearly articulated the social, political, and theatrical spirit of its day in New York City.

Harold Clurman: *The Fervent Years: The Story of the Group Theatre and the Thirties* (New York: Alfred A. Knopf, 1945)

Brooks Atkinson: *Broadway* (New York: Macmillan, 1970)

Cindy Adams: *Lee Strasberg: The Imperfect Genius of the Actors Studio* (Garden City, N.Y.: Doubleday, 1980)

Elia Kazan: *A Life* (New York: Alfred A. Knopf, 1988)

Wendy Smith: *Real Life Drama: The Group Theatre and America, 1931–1940* (New York: Alfred A. Knopf, 1990)

For illustration see Odets, Clifford.

Grove Press. Firm of book publishers formed in 1948 on Grove Street in New York City by John Balcomb and Robert Phelps and purchased in 1951 by Barnet Rosset. It initially published reprints of the classics but early on began to acquire the rights to foreign works, including those of the writers Samuel Beckett, Marguerite Duras, Jean Genet, André Gide, Eugène Ionesco, and Alain Robbe-Grillet. In the 1950s and early 1960s it published banned works of D. H. Lawrence and Henry Miller over which it fought and won important obscenity cases. It also published the *Evergreen Review* from 1957 to 1973. Grove Press was acquired in 1985 by Ann Getty, who was later joined by George Weidenfeld. In the early 1990s the firm merged with the Atlantic Monthly Press.

Montana Katz

Grymes Hill. Neighborhood in northeastern Staten Island, overlooking Upper New York Bay and bounded to the northwest by Victory Boulevard, to the east by Richmond Road and Van Duzer Street, to the south by the Staten Island Expressway, and to the west by Clove Road; it is one of three hills in the northern half of the borough and is bisected by Howard Avenue. The area was choice land for estates from the early nineteenth century. Major George Howard bought the hill in 1830 and in 1836 it became the home of Mme Suzette Grymes, the widow of the first governor of Louisiana; Jacob Vanderbilt also lived in the area during the nineteenth century. The largest of the estates, Horrmann Castle, was built about this time and was a local landmark until the 1970s. A mansion was built by William Greene Ward, a general in the Civil War; with the estate of the Cunard family this became the campus of Wagner College in 1918. Notre Dame Academy opened in 1903 on the estate of the Wendt family at the northern end of Howard Avenue. In 1938 Notre Dame College bought the estate of John H. Gans, a shipping tycoon, and had a campus on the premises until 1971, when the land was taken over by the Staten Island branch of St. John's University. In the 1980s there was a modest settlement of immigrants from India, Korea, the Philippines, Honduras, and Yugoslavia. Housing developments in Grymes Hill include apartment buildings overlooking Silver Lake and the twelve-story Sunrise Towers Condominiums facing the Staten Island Expressway. Spacious one-family houses predominate, and the population is largely white.

Harlow McMillen

Guardian Angels. Volunteer crime-fighting organization of young men and women,

Alice Austen, View from Grymes Hill *(1897)*

formed by Curtis Sliwa (*b* New York City, 1954) in February 1979 as the Magnificent Thirteen Subway Safety Patrol. Members adopted a uniform of T-shirts and red berets and rode the subways to deter crime, making citizen's arrests when necessary. The group took its current name by September and membership increased, eventually exceeding a thousand. The organization caused debate between those who cited improvements in community empowerment and safety and others critical of vigilantism. In the mid 1990s the Guardian Angels operated forty chapters in the United States and seven abroad, and had headquarters at 628 West 28th Street and safety patrol offices at 302 West 46th Street.

James Hawkins: *The Guardian Angels* (Hillside, N.J.: Enslow, 1983)

Dennis J. Kenney: *Crime, Fear and New York City Subways: The Role of Citizen Action* (New York: Praeger, 1987)

Grai St. Clair Rice

Guardian Life Insurance Company of America. Firm of insurers formed on 10 July 1860 as the Germania Life Insurance Company to sell life insurance to German-speaking customers. The principal figure behind its formation was Hugo Wesendonck (1817–1900), a former member of the Frankfurt Parliament and a participant in its rump session who had fled Germany to escape a death sentence and settled in New York City as a political refugee in December 1849. He recruited for the board of directors a distinguished group of German-born New Yorkers that included the financier and diplomat August Belmont, the publisher Oswald Ottendorfer, the brewer Maximilian Schaefer, and the financier Joseph Seligman; he was also the first president of the firm (1860–97). The largest single holder of the firm's initial stock was his brother Otto Wesendonck, better known as a friend and benefactor of the composer Richard Wagner. With the onset of the First World War any identification with Germany became a distinct disadvantage: the firm ceased writing policies in Europe in December 1917 and on 1 March 1918 abandoned its original name in favor of its current one. Stock owned by German citizens, who were enemy aliens in 1918, was seized by the federal government and auctioned off in 1919. In the mid 1990s the firm had its headquarters in a building at 201 Park Avenue South designed by Albert F. D'Oench and opened in 1911.

Anita Rapone: *The Guardian Life Insurance Company, 1860–1920: A History of a German–American Enterprise* (New York: New York University Press, 1987)

Theresa Collins

Guerrilla Girls. Feminist group formed in 1985 to protest the exclusion of works by women from art exhibitions; the members keep their true identities secret by adopting the names of dead women artists and wearing gorilla masks when appearing in public. The group seeks to expose sexism, racism, and censorship in the art world. It drew widespread attention during the late 1980s when it plastered SoHo, Tribeca, and the East Village with posters that decried and poked fun at the travails of working in a male-dominated system. During the early 1990s the group expanded its focus to subjects not directly related to art, among them the riots in Los Angeles in 1992. Members also traveled worldwide exhibiting their work and giving lectures.

Roberta Smith: "Waging Guerrilla Warfare against the Art World," *New York Times*, 17 June 1990, §B, p. 1

"The Guerrilla Girls," *Ms.*, Sept–Oct 1990, pp. 60–63

Amanda Aaron

Guggenheim, Meyer (*b* Langnau, Switzerland, 1 Feb 1828; *d* Palm Beach, Fla., 15 March 1905). Businessman and philanthropist. He moved to the United States in 1847 and settled in Philadelphia, where with his father Simon Guggenheim he worked initially as a peddler of stove polish; soon he became wealthy as a lace and embroidery retailer, a coffee importer, and an investor in railroads, mining, and smelting. He demanded equal partnership for his sons, Isaac, Daniel (*b* Philadelphia, 1856; *d* near Port Washington, N.Y., 1930), Murry, Solomon, Benjamin, Simon, and William. In 1888 he moved to New York City, where he lived at 36 West 77th Street and opened a smelting firm. By investing through his firm, Guggenex, and dominating the smelting trust (1901) he amassed a large fortune in copper, tin, gold, diamonds, nitrates, and rubber. Among the many charities he supported were Mount Sinai Hospital and the Botanical Gardens. His daughter Peggy became an important patron of modern art; Solomon conceived the Guggenheim Museum and Simon was elected to the U.S. Senate from Colorado.

George J. Lankevich

Guggenheim Museum. See SOLOMON R. GUGGENHEIM MUSEUM.

guidebooks. Guides to New York City have always reflected changing attitudes toward the city and stages in its growth. The city's rise to commercial preeminence after the War of 1812 was confirmed by the appearance of competing guidebooks for visiting merchants published by A. T. Goodrich (1818) and Edmund M. Blunt (1828). Some guides for commercial visitors began to specialize according to trade, and in several fields the early guidebooks were replaced by commercial and professional directories. By 1860 New York City had grown so complex and its population was so large (more than 800,000) that general guidebooks found a market with local residents as well as business visitors. *Appleton's New York City and Vicinity Guide* provided thorough, brief accounts of places and institutions through a series of editions from 1849 to the 1890s that were widely imitated. *King's Handbook of New York City: An Outline, History and Description of the American Metropolis* (1891), edited by Moses King (*b* 1853; *d* 12 June 1909), was a profusely illustrated, comprehensive guide to New York City that went through many editions over three decades, and the companion volume *Views of New York* (1896; in later editions *Views of New York and Brooklyn*) was perhaps the most complete early portfolio of photographic views of the city. The growth of the city also inspired a new

H

Habad. See LUBAVITCHERS.

Hadassah. A women's volunteer organization formed in 1912 at Temple Emanu-El in New York City by Henrietta Szold and others to provide public health nursing in Palestine. It is the oldest and largest women's Zionist organization in the world. In 1913 it sent two nurses to Palestine to open a maternity center in Jerusalem, and in 1934 it founded Youth Aliyah to rescue German youths (of whom 4300 made their way to Palestine by the end of the war). Hadassah is committed to health care, Jewish education, and women's issues. It operates a teaching hospital and medical school affiliated with the Hebrew University in Jerusalem, as well as ninety clinics throughout Israel. At its headquarters in Manhattan the organization maintains an extensive film library documenting its projects and publishes *Hadassah Magazine*. In 1994 Hadassah had 385,000 members, including ten thousand in New York City, and an annual budget of $82 million.

Donald Miller: "A History of Hadassah New York" (diss., New York University, 1968)

Marlin Levy: *Balm in Gilead: The Story of Hadassah* (New York: Schocken, 1973)

Carol B. Kutscher: "The Early Years of Hadassah: 1912–1921" (diss., Brandeis University, 1976)

Jean Ulitz Mensch

Haddad, Rizq (George) [Risq; Rizk] (*b* Judeida, Marjayoun, Syria [now in Lebanon], 21 May 1873 / 15 Aug 1875; *d* New York City, 8 May 1943). Physician. Educated at the American University of Beirut, he moved to New York City in the 1890s and from 1907 lived at 56 Garden Place in Brooklyn. In addition to working as a physician he was an essayist, poet, and lecturer highly regarded in the Syrian–Lebanese community. Soon after his death the R. G. Haddad Foundation was established to fund college scholarships for young people of Syrian and Lebanese descent and later for medical students at Columbia University and Rutgers.

Paula Hajar

Haight, Charles C(oolidge) (*b* New York City, 17 March 1841; *d* Garrison, N.Y., 8 Feb 1917). Architect. The son of a rector at Trinity Church, he undertook many architectural commissions for clients associated with the church during the last quarter of the nineteenth century. His most notable designs include the midtown campus of Columbia University (1874–84, demolished), the quadrangle of General Theological Seminary in Chelsea (1883–1902), the New York Cancer Hospital (1884–86, 1889–90, 455 Central Park West), Trinity School (1894, 139 West 91st Street), and a series of warehouses for the Trinity Church Corporation near Canal Street. In his later years Haight designed the neo-Gothic 2nd Battalion, 105th Field Artillery Armory, in the Bronx (1910).

Marjorie Pearson

Haitians. As many as four thousand whites, free blacks, and slaves fled St.-Domingue (now Haiti) during the revolution there from 1791 to 1803 and settled in New York City. Among them were merchants, soldiers, civil servants, lawyers, doctors, plantation owners, priests, and skilled and unskilled laborers. Some settled at once in the city, while others went first to other countries (especially France) or to other colonies, including Jamaica, Trinidad, and Cuba. One of the immigrants, Médéric Louis Élie Moreau de Saint-Méry (1750–1819), a well-known legal scholar and historian of St.-Domingue, went to Le Havre, France, before settling briefly in New York City (25 May to 13 October 1794). Although many Haitians took little money to the city, hoping to return soon to Haiti to reclaim their property, after several years a few set up their own shipping businesses or opened boarding houses, and some worked in shops owned by French businessmen who had fled to the city during the French Revolution; but most Haitians did not speak English and could obtain only menial employment. The city gave shelter and financial aid to whites, about three hundred of whom lived without charge in a government house on Vesey Street until they were able to move to their own quarters. This aid was not extended to blacks.

During the first half of the nineteenth century the Haitian population became well established in Manhattan. Many Haitians met after Sunday Mass at St. Peter's Church, 16 Barclay Street, to renew their friendships and discuss recent events in Haiti. On 10 August 1801 about twenty Haitian refugees led by Marcel Sam attempted to stage a riot to liberate Haitian slaves in the custody of Jeanne Mathusine Droibillan Volunbrun. Their efforts aborted, they were arrested and sentenced to sixty days in jail, despite legal aid provided by the Manumission Society. The best-known and most widely respected immigrant of the period was Pierre Toussaint, a former slave who became a professional hairdresser to upper-class women and children. With money from his business he supported the widow of his former master, bought freedom for other slaves, gave to charities of the Catholic church, and helped orphaned, homeless, disabled, and sick people from many ethnic backgrounds. By 1850 the second generation of Haitians was integrated into the social and economic life of the city. Some owned businesses and others taught the Romance languages in high schools and colleges. As marriages to blacks from other backgrounds became more common, Haitians lost some of their ethnic distinctness. By the turn of the century political unrest and the *kako* (guerrilla) movement in Haiti resulted in the flight to New York City of much of the Haitian élite in business and politics, including Haitians of Syrian and Lebanese origin. Immigration increased during the American occupation of Haiti (1915–34).

Between 1916 and 1945 the Haitian community in New York City was notable for its diversity. Much of it was in Harlem and included students on scholarship at Teachers College who were expected to return to Haiti after completing their studies, businessmen who had lost their holdings to the kakos, and writers and artists attracted by the literary explosion of the Harlem Renaissance. Liberals and Marxist politicians found in Harlem a place where they could safely express their nationalist ideas and their discontent with the American occupation. Some Haitians supported the Universal Negro Improvement Association (UNIA), the "back to Africa" movement begun by Marcus Garvey; among its leaders were several Haitians, including Elie Garcia, who led a delegation of members of UNIA to Liberia in 1920 and later became the secretary of the Black Star Line, and the activist Jean-Joseph Adam, the secretary and interpreter for a delegation from UNIA to the League of Nations in Geneva in October 1922. One of the most influential Haitian activists in the city was Jacques Roumain, who while living there from 1939 to 1941 befriended black writers and activists in the Communist Party in Harlem and took part in several important literary and political events; he was himself a communist and often discussed his ideas and projects with his friends Paul Robeson and Ralph Ellison at the home of Louise Thompson. On 15 November 1939 he was honored at a banquet at the YMCA in Harlem by such well-known black writers and artists as Jessie Redmon Fauset, Langston Hughes, Alain Locke, and Richard Wright.

The Haitian immigrants in Harlem between the two world wars were middle and upper class. Some formed Utilités d'Haïti, a firm that imported Haitian goods into the American market and became extremely successful. They also organized several clubs, including Solidarité, the Club Aristocrate, the Club l'Arc-en-ciel, and the Club Clair de Lune, where they could reflect on their country, collect funds for various causes, and form a social bond that lessened the pain of racism. Even after the occupation of Haiti by the U.S. Marines ended, Haitian political organizations continued to flourish in Harlem. One of these, the Association Démocratique Haïtienne, organized a memorial service for Roumain in May 1945.

From 1957 to 1986 most Haitian immigrants in New York City were political refugees who had fled the brutal dictatorships of François and Jean-Claude Duvalier. More than 34,000 Haitians moved to the city between 1983 and 1989, and the influx continued into the 1990s as political life in Haiti became chaotic and violence erupted in the streets. Most who left during this time settled in Brooklyn, Manhattan, and Queens, with concentrations in Crown Heights, East Flatbush, the Upper West Side, and Cambria Heights. In these neighborhoods families opened many restaurants, barber shops, garages, grocery stores, record shops, bakeries, and various retail stores to cater to the Haitian population, often extending credit and speaking French or Creole during transactions. From the 1950s many Haitian women worked as domestics or in child care. A number of radio stations, television programs, and newspapers began to supply the Haitian community with information about events in New York City, in other Hâitian communities overseas, and in Haiti itself. *Haïti-Observateur*, established in 1971 in the city, was the first weekly newspaper for Haitian émigrés. It developed a large network of distribution in the United States, Canada, and France and was introduced in 1986 in Haiti itself, where it entered into competition with established local newspapers. *Haïti-Progrès* was first published in New York City in 1981.

Until the mid 1980s the Haitian population in New York City had a discreet presence, conducting only a few protests in front of the Haitian consulate and the United Nations against the Duvaliers, but in 1986 the collapse of the government of Jean-Claude Duvalier was celebrated in the streets by many of the 600,000 Haitians living in the city. The community was also highly visible on 20 April 1990, when 100,000 Haitians blocked traffic in Brooklyn and lower Manhattan to protest a recommendation by the U.S. Food and Drug Administration that blood banks reject donations from Haitian immigrants, who were presumed to be at a disproportionately high risk of carrying AIDS. At the same time Haitians with American citizenship became active in government and politics: some were appointed to municipal agencies and others sought elective office at the city and state levels.

Haitian–American social clubs in the city tend to attract people from one region in Haiti or one ideology. There are several groups in the city that give financial help to a specific Haitian region or town, among them Les amis des enfants de Lascahobas. Some political organizations are affiliated with political parties in Haiti and lend financial and logistical support to candidates there. A large network of social service organizations caters to Haitian immigrants: the poorest immigrants are helped to adjust to the city by Haitian Neighborhood Services Centers. The Catholic church, a potent force in the Haitian community, operates many charitable organizations. The social service center Charlemagne Péralte at 1156 Nostrand Avenue in Brooklyn was once run by the Haitian Fathers, who published *Sel*, a quarterly magazine written mostly in Creole. The community center Haitian–Americans United for Progress (HAUP), formed in October 1975 in Queens by the associate pastor Father Guy Sansaricq, took over the responsibility of running the National Office of the Haitian Apostolate in 1978. With the help of volunteers from the Sacred Heart Parish it publishes the quarterly newsletter *Laïcs engagés* (first issued in 1989). HAUP offers social services, counseling and referrals, family support services, immigration services, programs for senior citizens, training classes, cultural activities, and an information center. Perhaps the foremost parish in the city is the Holy Cross Church at 2530 Church Avenue in Brooklyn, presided over by Monsignor Rollin Darbouze. In the mid 1990s practitioners of Voodoo still lacked a temple where they could publicly worship their ancestral spirits. There are various Protestant churches and Masonic lodges, some of which offer social programs to help poor Haitians in the city.

Ira de A. Reid: *The Negro Immigrant: His Background, Characteristics and Social Adjustment, 1899–1937* (New York: Columbia University Press, 1939)

Moreau de Saint-Méry's American Journey (1793–1798) (New York: Doubleday, 1947)

Michel S. Laguerre: *American Odyssey: Haitians in New York City* (Ithaca, N.Y.: Cornell University Press, 1984)

Michel S. Laguerre

Hale, Nathan (*b* Coventry, Conn., 6 June 1756; *d* New York City, 22 Sept 1776). Soldier and spy. After graduating from Yale University he was commissioned a captain in 1776. His brigade, commanded by Major General William Heath, sought to gain information about British troops in New York City and its environs. After the city fell to the British he traveled through Long Island into Manhattan, and in Harlem he recorded details of British fortifications in Latin. Captured on 21 September 1776 while out of uniform, he was held at Provost Jail near the eastern boundary of City Hall Park and found guilty of spying. The statement he is purported to have made before being hanged near Chambers Street, "I only regret that I have but one life to lose for my country," made him a hero of the American Revolution. A statue of Hale by Frederick MacMonnies was placed in City Hall Park in 1890.

Charlotte Molyneux Holloway: *Nathan Hale: The Martyr–Hero of the Revolution* (New York: A. L. Burt, 1899)

William Ordway Partridge: *Nathan Hale: The Ideal Patriot: A Study of Character* (New York: Funk and Wagnalls, 1902)

Martin Ebon

Hale House Center. Facility for drug-addicted children at 152 West 122nd Street in Manhattan. It was opened in 1969 by Mother (Clara M.) Hale (1905–92) to care for the infant of a drug addict and was later expanded and managed by Hale and her daughter Lorraine E. Hale, a physician. A building at Manhattan Avenue and 113th Street was converted into temporary housing for reunited families in 1985, and during the same year Mother Hale was honored by President Ronald Reagan. Preferring foster homes to group homes, municipal agencies in October 1989 stopped sending children to Hale House, which by 1991 had helped more than eight hundred infants survive withdrawal and provided temporary housing for thirty-one families. Hale House receives federal, state, and private funds.

Alana J. Erickson

Hall, A(braham) Oakey (*b* Albany, N.Y., 26 July 1826; *d* New York City, 7 Oct 1898). Mayor. He was district attorney of New York City as a Whig and then as a Republican during the 1850s. In 1862 he joined the Democratic Party and became an ally of William M. "Boss" Tweed. As mayor from 1868 to 1872 he became entangled in the scandals of the Tweed Ring and was twice indicted for corruption. Although he was eventually exonerated his career was ruined, and he chose exile in London. Hall later returned to the United States.

Croswell Bowen: *The Elegant Oakey* (New York: Oxford University Press, 1956)

Alexander B. Callow Jr.: *The Tweed Ring* (New York: Oxford University Press, 1966)

Jerome Mushkat

Hall, Cornelius A(loysius) (*b* Staten Island, 1889; *d* Staten Island, 5 March 1953). Borough president. Unlike most of his predecessors, he was an independent Democrat. During the 1930s he served as the commissioner of public works in Staten Island. As borough president of Staten Island from 1945 to 1953 Hall saw the Staten Island Ferry Terminal to completion in 1951.

Andrew Wiese

Hall, George (*b* New York City, 21 Sept 1795; *d* Brooklyn, 18 April 1868). First mayor of Brooklyn. A painter and glazier by trade, he belonged to the Temperance and Whig parties. He served as mayor for one year at the adoption of the municipal charter in 1834. After the city was enlarged by the annexation of Williamsburgh and Bushwick he was elected in 1855 to a two-year term to the same office.

Ellen Fletcher

Halleck, Fitz-Greene (*b* Guilford, Conn., 8 July 1790; *d* Guilford, 19 Nov 1867). Poet. He moved to New York City in 1811. With Joseph Rodman Drake he published in the *New York Post* from March to July 1819 the

"Croaker Papers," which lampooned prominent local figures. On Drake's death in 1820 he wrote the famous monody "Green be the turf above thee." From 1832 to 1848 he was John Jacob Astor's confidential secretary. In 1849 he retired to Guilford. His best-known poems include "Fanny," "Marco Bozzaris," "Red Jacket," and "Young America." A statue of Halleck in Central Park was the first public sculpture in the city to commemorate a poet.

Nelson F. Adkins: *Fitz-Greene Halleck: An Early Knickerbocker Wit and Poet* (New Haven: Yale University Press, 1930)

Ormonde de Kay

Hallett, George (Hervey, Jr.) (*b* Philadelphia, 24 May 1895; *d* New York City, 2 July 1985). Reformer. A Quaker pacifist, he earned a doctorate in mathematics from the University of Pennsylvania in 1918. He worked for Citizens Union as its executive secretary (1934–67, 1970–71) and as a legislative liaison in Albany, New York (1934–61, 1963–72). A tireless advocate of electoral reform, he drafted provisions that ensured proportional representation on the City Council (1936) and on local school boards (1969) and worked for the development of community boards. In 1986 the Hallett Nature Sanctuary was designated on four acres (1.6 hectares) in the southeast corner of Central Park.

Dwight MacDonald: "Profile of George Hallett," *New Yorker*, 22 Aug 1953

Bernard Hirschhorn

Hallett's Cove. A small settlement in northwestern Queens near the ferry landing at the foot of Astoria Boulevard, established in the seventeenth century and incorporated into Astoria in 1839.

Vincent Seyfried

Hall of Fame for Great Americans. Monument in the Bronx, established to honor well-known Americans and dedicated on 30 May 1901 by Henry Mitchell MacCracken, president of New York University. It occupies a semicircular vaulted colonnade 630 feet (190 meters) long behind the Hall of Languages (1894), Gould Memorial Library (1899), and the Cornelius Baker Hall of Philosophy (1912) on the former campus of New York University. The first monument of its kind in the country, it relied on the public and an expert panel to choose its members. The first twenty-nine members were honored with tablets designed by Tiffany Studios, and in 1907 the first of ninety-seven busts was installed. In February 1966 the site was entered in the National Register of Historic Places. It fell under the jurisdiction of the City University of New York after the campus was taken over by Bronx Community College in 1973. Renovations costing $3 million were completed in 1985, but by the mid 1990s the Hall of Fame remained largely neglected by the public.

George J. Lankevich

Hall of Records. Name until 1962 of the building at the corner of Chambers and Centre streets now known as the SURROGATE'S COURT.

Halpern, Moyshe-Leyb (*b* Zolochev, Galicia [now in Ukraine], 2 Jan 1886; *d* New York City, 31 Aug 1932). Poet. He emigrated to the United States in 1908 and soon had his first poems published in the Yiddish press in New York City. He led an itinerant and impoverished life and remained a largely independent figure among the Yiddish literati, though he was associated with the circle of writers known as the Yunge. In his two collections of verse, *In Nyu-york* (1919) and *Di goldene pave* (The golden peacock, 1924), he displays a distinctively direct and unsentimental voice capable of both lyric and imaginatively probing modern verse.

Ruth R. Wisse: *A Little Love in Big Manhattan* (Cambridge: Harvard University Press, 1988)

Jeffrey Shandler

The Hall of Fame for Great Americans, ca 1910. Background, with domed roof *Gould Memorial Library (designed by McKim, Mead and White)*

Halston [Frowick, Roy Halston] (*b* Des Moines, Iowa, 26 April 1932; *d* San Francisco, 26 March 1990). Fashion designer. He began his career designing hats for Bergdorf Goodman in 1958 and in 1968 opened his own clothing company. Quickly recognized for his simple, modern designs, he popularized liquid silhouettes, natural colors, and relaxed separates, such styles as elongated sweater sets, halter dresses, tunics, and wrap-front coats in matte jersey, and materials such as charmeuse, cashmere, and Ultrasuede. After Halston relinquished rights to his name in a disastrous business arrangement in the early 1980s, his career faded and his designs were restricted to private commissions.

Caroline Rennolds Milbank

Hamburg–American Line. Firm of transatlantic shippers formed as the Hamburg-Amerikanische Paketfahrt Aktien-Gesellschaft (HAPAG) in Hamburg in 1847. It initially operated three copper-bottomed sailing ships including the *Deutschland*, which had a capacity of 220 passengers and first sailed for New York City on 15 October 1847. Monthly service between Hamburg and the city was offered from 1848; the average westbound sailing time was forty-one days. The firm commissioned its first steamship, the *Borussia*, in 1856 and soon bought others because they were larger, safer, faster, and more comfortable than sailing ships: the finest ones, including the *Fürst Bismarck*, the *Augusta Victoria*, the *Normannia*, and the *Columbia*, each registered at least ten thousand tons, had at least thirteen thousand horsepower, and could cross the Atlantic in as little as seven days. Several of its small lines offered service to Montreal, Boston, Philadelphia, and Baltimore. By 1897 HAPAG had opened lines to the Caribbean and South America and was the largest steamship company in the world. The largest and fastest ships were reserved for the American line, which had its offices at 37 Broadway and its main docking facilities in Hoboken, New Jersey. It provided service from Hamburg to Cherbourg and Southampton before docking in New York City and was crucial in encouraging immigration because it offered transatlantic fares for as little as $25: the line carried an average of 34,466 passengers a year from Hamburg to the city during the 1860s, 90,889 during the 1880s, and 60,041 during the 1890s. As the number of Germans emigrating to the United States declined before the turn of the century, southern and eastern Europeans accounted for an increasing number of the firm's passengers. With its rival, North German Lloyd of Bremen, HAPAG provided passage for a quarter of the European immigrants moving to the United States in 1906–7, and on its ships alone 150,633 emigrants sailed to New York City in 1907. Its largest steamships were admired throughout the world, among them the

Imperator (1912), which registered 52,000 tons, had six decks, and carried 3849 passengers. When much of the German merchant marine was seized by British and American forces during the First World War the pride of the line, the *Vaterland* (1914), became an American troop carrier and was renamed the *Leviathan.* The Hamburg–American Line resumed service in the 1920s and in 1934 combined its resources with North German Lloyd at the insistence of the Nazi government, operating under the name HAPAG–Lloyd Union; service was suspended during the 1940s. After resuming operations separately in the 1950s the firms merged in 1969. HAPAG–Lloyd (America), based at 1 Edgewater Place on Staten Island, runs a small airline, offers round-the-world cruises, and has a fleet of eighteen cargo liners.

Cecil Lamar: *Albert Ballin: Business and Politics in Imperial Germany, 1888–1918* (Princeton, N.J.: Princeton University Press, 1967)

Kevin Kenny

Hamilton, Alexander (*b* Nevis, British West Indies, 11 Jan 1755; *d* New York City, 12 July 1804). Secretary of the treasury and revolutionary leader. He settled in New York City in 1772 and studied at King's College (now Columbia University). When the American Revolution began he organized a city artillery company of which he became captain, and he later served as a lieutenant colonel on George Washington's staff. His marriage to Elizabeth Schuyler in 1780 connected him with one of the state's most powerful families; he was a delegate to the Continental Congress in 1782–83. From 1783 to 1790 he lived on Wall Street (the number of the house is given variously as 58 and 57). After the war he became a prominent lawyer, and in 1784 he successfully defended the British merchant Joshua Waddington in a case that helped to establish the principle of judicial review. In the same year he helped to form the Bank of New York (1784). A forceful advocate of a strong central government, he was a delegate to the Constitutional Convention in 1787 and a leader in the successful campaign to secure ratification of the Constitution in New York. To this end he wrote at least fifty-one papers in the *Federalist* (nos. 1, 6–9, 11–13, 15–17, 21–36, 59–61, and 65–85). When the new federal government assembled in New York City in 1789 Hamilton became its first secretary of the treasury (1789–95). During his tenure he supported policies favorable to business; these aided the growth of New York City as a financial center. He then returned to the city, where he practiced law. In 1800 he began construction in Harlem of his country home the Grange (the building is now called the Hamilton Grange National Memorial and is situated at 287 Convent Avenue, five hundred feet, or 150 meters, south of its original site). Active in Federalist politics as the leader of a wing opposed to John Adams, he helped to launch the *New York Evening Post* in 1801 to further his views. He was also a strong opponent of Aaron Burr, and helped to thwart his candidacy for the presidency of the United States in 1800 and for the governorship of New York in 1804. He lost his life in a duel with Burr in Weehauken, New Jersey, on 11 July 1804 and is buried in the graveyard of Trinity Church.

Broadus Mitchell: *Alexander Hamilton* (New York: Macmillan, 1957–62)

Harold C. Syrett, ed.: *The Papers of Alexander Hamilton* (New York: Columbia University Press, 1961–87)

Julius Goebel Jr. and Joseph H. Smith, eds.: *The Law Practice of Alexander Hamilton* (New York: Columbia University Press, 1964–81)

See also ABOLITIONISM.

Barbara A. Chernow

Hamilton Beach. Neighborhood in southwestern Queens (1985 pop. 1000), lying on a narrow peninsula separated from the eastern edge of Howard Beach by Hawtree Creek basin and bounded to the east by the Rockaway transit line and Kennedy Airport. Developed about 1926, it had a station on the Rockaway line of the Long Island Rail Road that closed in October 1955; municipal subway service began in 1956. In the mid 1990s Hamilton Beach lacked sewers and municipal sanitation service and had the only volunteer fire department in Queens. There are fewer than a dozen streets, which lie barely above the level of Jamaica Bay and flood easily. Nearly half the inhabitants are Irish and Catholic. Access to the area is provided by a wooden bridge from 102nd Street and a pedestrian bridge from 163rd Avenue.

Vincent Seyfried

Hamilton Grange. Historic house on Convent Avenue and 141st Street in Harlem Heights. A country residence commissioned by Alexander Hamilton, who named it after his family's ancestral home in Scotland, it was designed in the Federal style by John McComb Jr., an architect of City Hall, and stood nine miles (fourteen kilometers) from town at the time it was built. The estate was completed shortly after Hamilton's death in 1804 and remained in the family until 1834. After a succession of owners the house was given to St. Luke's Episcopal Church in 1889 and moved two blocks south to its present location. It was acquired in 1924 by the American Scenic and Historic Preservation Society and in 1933 opened as a public museum; its operation was taken over in 1962 by the National Park Service. In the mid 1990s there were plans to move the house again, possibly to St. Nicholas Park.

Hamilton Grange National Memorial: Report (Washington: U.S. Government Printing Office, 1988)

Jonathan Kuhn

Hamilton Heights. Neighborhood on the West Side of Manhattan, lying between Washington Heights and Morningside Heights; it includes the neighborhood of Sugar Hill and is itself often considered part of Harlem. The neighborhood is named for Alexander Hamilton, who spent the last two years of his life in what is now the Hamilton Grange National Monument. Most of the housing dates from the extension of elevated and subway lines to the neighborhood in the late nineteenth century and the early twentieth. This fairly elegant housing became less desirable to whites in the 1930s and 1940s as the black population rose. The brownstone revival of the 1960s and 1970s led to a new movement of middle-class

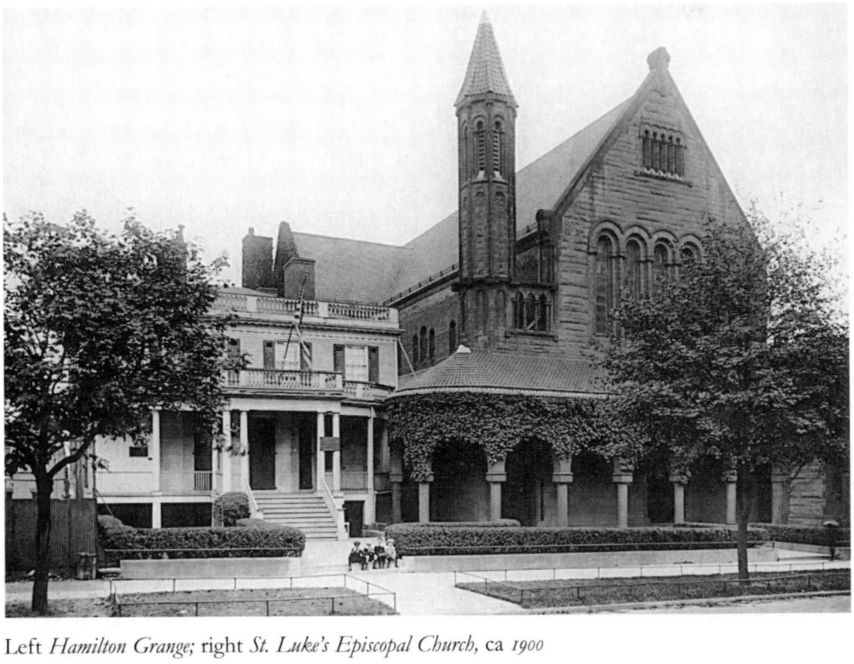

Left *Hamilton Grange;* right *St. Luke's Episcopal Church,* ca *1900*

blacks to the area. In the 1980s a large number of Latin Americans settled in the neighborhood; almost three quarters of all the immigrants who moved there were Dominican. Far smaller numbers arrived from Jamaica, Ecuador, Haiti, and China. One of the highest hills in Hamilton Heights slopes up from the Hudson River at 155th Street and contains the cemetery of Trinity Church. The campus of City College of New York lies along Convent Avenue between 132nd and 140th streets.

Hamilton Grange National Memorial: Report (Washington: U.S. Government Printing Office, 1988)

Lisa Gitelman

Hammels. Former name of a section of Rockaway Beach in southeastern Queens, lying on the Rockaway Peninsula around Beach 85th Street. It began as four or five boardwalks that ran from the bay to the ocean. A hotel, the Eldert House, was kept by Garret Eldert and faced the bay on the east side of what is now Beach 85th Street; in August 1869 it was leased to Louis Hammel of Elm Park on Staten Island. The railroad ran within a few paces of the hotel after a trestle was extended across the bay in 1880; a railroad station was then built, and trains carried thousands of visitors annually. A dock in front of the hotel, Fifth Landing, was a regular stop for boats of the Iron Steamboat Company carrying day visitors from Manhattan. In later years hotels on the bay declined as resorts along the shore attracted most beachgoers. Hammels was incorporated with Hollands into the Village of Rockaway Beach in 1897. A large housing project, Hammels Houses, was built in 1955.

Vincent Seyfried

Hammerstein, Oscar (*b* Stettin, Prussia [now Szezcin, Poland], 8 May 1846; *d* New York City, 1 Aug 1919). Opera impresario, grandfather of Oscar Hammerstein II. After emigrating as a penniless teenager to the United States and settling in New York City, he made a fortune in the tobacco business by inventing machines for the manufacture of cigars and launching a trade journal. He later designed and built theaters, first in Harlem and then in midtown. With profits from the Victoria, a vaudeville house managed by his son Willie, he financed the Manhattan Opera Company, which opened in 1906 in a theater that he built on West 34th Street west of 8th Avenue. His company posed a challenge to the Metropolitan Opera. It had a well-trained orchestra and chorus, leading soloists, and an adventuresome repertory: it not only mounted fine productions of the standard works but gave the American premières of Strauss's *Elektra* and Debussy's *Pelléas et Mélisande*. After three seasons of extravagant spending and the rejection of subsidies from wealthy members of fashionable society he was obliged to sell his interests to the Metropolitan. Hammerstein designed all his theater buildings, which were praised for their impressive interiors and excellent acoustics; none survive.

George A. Thompson, Jr.

Hammerstein, Oscar, II (*b* New York City, 12 July 1895; *d* Doylestown, Penn., 23 Aug 1960). Librettist and lyricist, grandson of Oscar Hammerstein. Born on East 116th Street, he attended Columbia University and collaborated on operettas and musical comedies with Rudolf Friml, Sigmund Romberg, and Jerome Kern. His most important contribution to the creation of the modern musical was *Show Boat* (1927, music by Kern), in which for the first time plot was a central element and the songs developed the characters. During the 1930s he worked primarily in Hollywood. He returned to Broadway with *Oklahoma!* (1943), the first in a series of collaborations with Richard Rodgers that included such works as *Carousel* (1945), *State Fair* (1945, film), *South Pacific* (1949), *The King and I* (1951), *Flower Drum Song* (1958), and *The Sound of Music* (1959), as well as several failures. His residences in New York City included buildings at Central Park West and 87th Street (1911), 509 West 121st Street (1917), 1067 5th Avenue (1930–31), and 157 East 61st Street (during the 1940s).

George A. Thompson, Jr.

Hammond, John (*b* New York City, 15 Dec 1910; *d* New York City, 10 July 1987). Record producer. A great-grandson of William H. Vanderbilt, he lived on Sullivan Street as a young man and promoted concerts at the Public Theatre. He worked from 1932 as a disc jockey for WEVD and from 1933 as the American recording director for the British division of Columbia Records; he used money from his own trust funds to produce records of performers he admired, including Fletcher Henderson, Bessie Smith, Billie Holiday, Charlie Christian, Teddy Wilson, and Count Basie. He encouraged racial integration in popular entertainment by supporting Benny Goodman's decision to engage Wilson and Lionel Hampton as members of his jazz ensemble in 1936, and organized the series of concerts known as "Spirituals to Swing" in 1938 and 1939 at Carnegie Hall. After his second marriage (1949) he lived at 444 East 57th Street. His determination to combat discrimination and his brief involvement in leftist politics led his name to be removed from the social register. In the 1960s and 1970s he launched the recording careers of Aretha Franklin, Bob Dylan, and Bruce Springsteen. Hammond is best known for his tireless advocacy of American popular music. He wrote a memoir, *John Hammond on Record* (1974).

Loren Schoenberg

Hampton, Lionel (Leo) (*b* Louisville, Ky., 20 April 1908). Bandleader and vibraphonist. He began his career as a drummer in Chicago and later Los Angeles. In November 1936 he moved to New York City to play the vibraphone in Benny Goodman's quartet, one of the first racially integrated groups in jazz; he settled in Harlem at the Doris E. Brooks Houses on 137th Street and lived there for more than thirty years. After leaving Goodman in the summer of 1940 he formed his own band, toured frequently, and made goodwill performances worldwide. With donated funds and his own funds he built a complex of 350 apartments called the Lionel Hampton Houses at 8th Avenue and 131st Street in 1971; he also sponsored a complex of 205 apartments known as the Gladys Hampton Houses on St. Nicholas Avenue and 130th Street in 1978. In addition to working as a musician and real-estate developer Hampton is well known in New York City for his longstanding involvement in Republican politics. He wrote *Hamp: An Autobiography* (with James Haskins, 1989).

Ira Berger

Hand, (Billings) Learned (*b* Albany, N.Y., 27 Jan 1872; *d* New York City, 18 Aug 1961). Jurist. He graduated from Harvard University (1893) and Harvard Law School (1896) and practiced law in Albany before moving in 1902 to New York City, where he joined the firm of Gould and Wilkie (1904). In 1909 he was named to the U.S. District Court for the Southern District of New York (1909). A supporter of Theodore Roosevelt in 1912, he unsuccessfully sought election as chief judge of the New York State Court of Appeals as a Progressive in 1913. He was appointed to the Federal Court of Appeals for the Second Circuit (1924) and became its senior judge in 1939 when disclosures of ethical violations forced the resignation of Martin T. Manton. During his tenure the court in 1950 upheld the constitutionality of the Smith Act. Only his age prevented his appointment to the U.S. Supreme Court by President Franklin D. Roosevelt. He retired from regular service on 15 May 1951 but continued to take on special assignments. He wrote almost three thousand opinions, including one in an antitrust case involving the Aluminum Company of America (in which he wrote that "Congress did not condone 'good trusts' and condemn 'bad' ones; it forbade all"), and another in *Masses Publishing Co. v. Patten* that sustained the right under the First Amendment to send antiwar leaflets through the mails. Hand gained national attention by delivering a speech entitled "The Spirit of Liberty" at "I Am an American Day" in Central Park (21 May 1944). He lived at 142 East 65th Street in Manhattan.

Gerald Gunther: *Learned Hand: The Man and the Judge* (New York: Alfred A. Knopf, 1994)

Jeffrey A. Kroessler

Handy, W(illiam) C(hristopher) (*b* Florence, Ala., 16 Nov 1873; *d* New York City, 28 March 1958). Composer, cornetist, and music publisher. A self-taught cornetist, he was widely known as a performer and composer by the late 1890s. He moved in 1918 to New York City, where he established the Pace and Handy Music Company as the leading publisher of music by black artists. During the Harlem Renaissance he lived on Strivers' Row. Handy's practice of incorporating syncopated rhythms into popular music earned him the nickname "father of the blues." He wrote more than 150 songs, including "Memphis Blues," "St. Louis Blues," and "Yellow Dog Blues," as well as the book *Father of the Blues: An Autobiography* (1941).

Harry A. Ploski and James Williams, eds. and comps.: *Reference Library of Black America*, vol. 3 (Detroit: Gale Research, 1990)

Cynthia Copeland

Hansberry, Lorraine (*b* Chicago, 19 May 1930; *d* New York City, 12 Jan 1965). Playwright. She moved to New York City in 1950 and achieved great success on Broadway in 1959 with her play *A Raisin in the Sun*, which depicts a black family struggling to leave a slum of Chicago for a better neighborhood. The first play produced on Broadway by a black woman, it won for her the distinction of being the first black and the youngest American to receive the New York Drama Critics' Circle Award. Her later plays, produced with the help of her former husband, Robert Nemiroff, include *The Sign in Sidney Brustein's Window* (1964), about white intellectuals in Greenwich Village. Among her posthumous works are *To Be Young, Gifted and Black* (1969), adapted from her letters, essays, and other writings, and *Les Blancs* (1970), about an African leader caught between the conflicting demands of his tribal traditions and modernity. A musical called *Raisin*, based on *A Raisin in the Sun*, was staged in 1973.

Lorraine Hansberry, 1959

Harold Cruse: *The Crisis of the Negro Intellectual* (New York: William Morrow, 1967), 267–84
Julius Lester: Introd. to *"Les Blancs": The Collected Last Plays of Lorraine Hansberry*, ed. Robert Nemiroff (New York: Random House, 1972)
Freedomways 19, no. 4 (1979), 183–304 [special issue on Hansberry]

E. G. Hill

Hapag–Lloyd. Shipping firm formed by the merger of Hamburg–America Lines and the NORTH GERMAN LLOYD STEAMSHIP LINES.

Hapgood, Hutchins (*b* Chicago, 21 May 1869; *d* Provincetown, Mass., 18 Nov 1944). Journalist. As a reporter from 1897 at the *New York Commercial Advertiser* (later the *New York Globe*) he practiced the "personal journalism" championed by his city editor Lincoln Steffens and was introduced to the Lower East Side by his fellow reporter Abraham Cahan. A collection of his vividly written articles about the lives of Jewish immigrants was published in 1902 as *The Spirit of the Ghetto: Studies of the Jewish Quarter in New York*. He also described the Bowery and its residents and worked for other newspapers in New York City, including the *Morning Telegraph* and the *Evening Post*, before turning his attention to radical causes, an interest encouraged by his having taken part in discussions of anarchism, the labor movement, and Freudian psychology at the salon of Mabel Dodge. After the First World War his career stagnated and he worked infrequently. In 1935 he exposed Theodore Dreiser's anti-Semitism in the *Nation*. Rischin described *The Spirit of the Ghetto* as "devoid of stereotype or sentimentality, sympathetic yet sober and realistic, intimate yet judicious and restrained." Hapgood's other published writings include *Types from City Streets* (1910) and an autobiography, *Victorian in the Modern World* (1939).

Moses Rischin: Introd. to *The Spirit of the Ghetto*, by Hutchins Hapgood (Cambridge: Harvard University Press, 1967), vii–xxxvi

Allen J. Share, Stephen Weinstein

happenings. Artistic events of the late 1950s and 1960s that combined drama, music, the visual arts, and written texts and were at least partially improvised. Both the term and the earliest such event are attributed to Allan Kaprow, who presented "18 Happenings in Six Parts" in a loft at the Reuben Gallery on lower 4th Avenue in the autumn of 1959. Frequently these impromptu spectacles included the audience, breaking down the distinction between viewer and art object. Their structure was inspired by the aleatory methods of the composer John Cage, whose seminars at the New School for Social Research drew many of the artists who made happenings in the city. Happenings were staged at diverse venues: by Kaprow in an abandoned brewery in the Bronx and in the courtyard of a derelict hotel in Chelsea, and by others in various lofts, art galleries, and public spaces. Claes Oldenburg staged his "Washes" in a swimming pool at Al Roon's Health Club and other happenings in his storefront on East 2nd Street.

Michael Kirby: *Happenings: An Illustrated Anthology* (New York: E. P. Dutton, 1965)

Kathleen Hulser

Happy Land fire. An arson fire on 25 March 1990 at the Happy Land Social Club on Southern Boulevard in the Bronx in which eighty-seven persons died. It was started by Julio Gonzalez, who after a quarrel with his companion, Lydia Feliciano, splashed gasoline through the front door of the club (its only exit) and set the gasoline afire. Feliciano, who worked at the club, and four others survived the fire, but others inside were trapped and died within minutes from smoke inhalation. The club had been shut in 1988 for a variety of fire code violations, including a lack of fire exits, sprinklers, and emergency lights, but reopened soon after. Gonzalez was convicted of all charges connected with the crime in September 1991 and sentenced to twenty-five years to life in prison. More people died in the fire than in any other in the city since the Triangle Shirtwaist fire.

Rachel Sawyer

Harcourt Brace. Firm of book publishers formed as Harcourt, Brace and Howe at 1 West 47th Street on 29 July 1919 by Alfred Harcourt and Donald Brace, both graduates of Columbia University and former employees of the publishers Henry Holt and Company, and Will D. Howe. Ellen Knowles Eayres, Harcourt's secretary and later his wife, also played an important role. The firm published *Main Street* (1920) by Sinclair Lewis, who had encouraged Harcourt to open his own firm: the book became its first best-seller. Howe concentrated on textbook publishing; in 1921 he left the firm (which was consequently renamed Harcourt Brace and Company), and his efforts were continued by S. Spencer Scott. In the following years the firm acquired the list of Brewer, Warren and Putnam (1932) and the entire firm of Reynal and Hitchcock (1948). After Harcourt resigned as president in 1942 the firm was led successively by Brace (to 1948), Scott (to 1954), and William Jovanovich, who had joined the firm as a textbook salesman and editor in 1947. In 1960 Harcourt Brace, now with publicly traded stock, merged with the World Book Company and was renamed Harcourt, Brace and World. In the following year Jovanovich began the first imprint arrangement in American publishing by issuing books with Kurt and Helen Wolff, formerly of Pantheon. The firm moved to its own twenty-seven-story building at 757 3rd Avenue in 1963, and in the following year had sales of more than $451 million (compared to $8 million in 1954). It acquired majority interests in the Canadian branch of Longmans, Green, in the English firm Rupert Hart-Davis (which ultimately was sold off), and in Grune and Stratton (1968) and Academic Press (1969). In 1970 the firm took the name Harcourt Brace Jovanovich, and in 1973 it purchased Pyramid Publications, which was renamed Jove Books and sold in 1978; it also acquired the History Book Club and the Instructor Book Club. In an effort to diversify, the firm acquired agriculture and business magazines, insurance companies, and television stations, as well as the profitable Sea World marine parks (1976), a purchase that met with some skepticism. The firm moved its trade department in 1982 from New York City to San Diego and in 1984 opened a newly constructed corporate headquarters in Orlando, Florida. It bought Holt Rinehart Winston–W. B. Saunders from the Columbia Broadcasting System in 1986, thus strengthening its position as one of the largest publishers of elementary, secondary, and college textbooks in the United States, and a world leader in medical and scientific books and journals. To prevent a hostile takeover by the British press magnate Robert Maxwell in 1987 Jovanovich took on $2600 million in debt, a controversial tactic.In 1989 his son Peter became president and chief executive officer of the firm. To reduce its huge debt the firm sold its four Sea World parks and two other parks for $1100 million in 1989. John S. Herrington, a former secretary of energy, replaced the elder Jovanovich as chairman of the board in 1990. In 1991 Peter Jovanovich recommended a sale to the General Cinema Corporation. Harcourt Brace Jovanovich had more than eleven thousand employees in 1990 and recorded $1800 million in sales. The firm took its current name in 1992.

Elizabeth Dzwonkoski: "Harcourt Brace Jovanovich," *American Literary Publishing Houses, 1900–1980: Trade and Paperback*, ed. Peter Dzwonkoski (Detroit: Gale Research, 1986)

Marjorie Harrison

hard-boiledness. The stereotype of the "hard-boiled" New Yorker expresses the fundamental differences between New York City and smaller places. It identifies the New Yorker as brash, rude, tough, and cynically indifferent or sometimes hostile to the fate of others, but at the same time sophisticated, streetwise, and able to survive amid the pressures and dangers of city life.

The stereotype exists primarily in oral culture and may be traced back at least as far as the 1840s through popular literature, journalism, and entertainment. In Benjamin Baker's play *A Glance at New York in 1848* the actor Francis Chanfrau portrayed Mose the Bowery B'hoy, a combative workingman from the East Side. Mose and other city characters — ruthless stock speculators and confidence men, shrewdly independent newsboys, remorseless prostitutes — were depicted in novels and urban sketches written in the 1840s and 1850s by Ned Buntline, George G. Foster, and others. Once established, all these types continued to embody popular conceptions of the skills and attributes necessary to navigate the perils of big-city life. Some popular authors, including the novelist Horatio Alger after the Civil War and later the short-story writers O. Henry, Damon Runyon, and Ring Lardner, softened the outlines of the hard-boiled stereotype with elements of sentimentality and humor. Others, who wrote fiction and nonfiction about the city in the realist tradition, made no such compromises. In works like Stephen Crane's *Maggie: A Girl of the Streets* and Jacob Riis's *How the Other Half Lives*, survival in the city's worst neighborhoods depends on the toughness and cynical indifference that form the grim core of the hard-boiled stereotype. Toughness and cynicism are central as well to a new popular genre of the twentieth century, the hard-boiled American detective story. This genre, which found its voice in the early 1920s in *Black Mask*, a magazine published in New York City, features a private detective who is both at war with the corruptions and other stern realities of the metropolis and embedded within them, and who like the earlier characters of Foster and Buntline is able to prevail, largely because he is an insider who knows how the evil city works.

Vaudeville, which flourished in New York City as nowhere else, built on the brashness and toughness of Mose and other traditional types to fill out the character of the "wiseguy" or "wiseacre," and to establish the wisecrack as the characteristic form of humor of the hard-boiled New Yorker. Tough, worldly Jewish women such as Sophie Tucker and Fanny Brice and such Irish–American performers as James Cagney helped to give this kind of humor specific ethnic dimensions, and more importantly to build ethnicity into the hard-boiled stereotype in ways that reinforced the city's distance from rural and small-town America. Like Mose before them, Cagney, Brice, and other vaudeville performers spoke in a distinctive accent that contributed to the image of the New Yorker as brash, cynical, and severe — a person apart from the rest of the country.

The hard-boiled stereotype has always been fluid and may now be changing in essential ways. The increasing violence and hostility of urban life seem to be transforming the image of the New Yorker into that of a person under siege, a "prisoner of 3rd Avenue" rather than a brash victor over the pressures and confusions of the city. It is also important that those who shape and perpetuate the stereotype are changing. The outsider is now much more likely to be the resident of a suburb or another city, and to stand in a relation to New York City very different from that of the innocent and awestruck countryman of earlier times. For this reason alone it can be expected that the stereotype of the hard-boiled New Yorker will not only change but lose much of its power to shape perceptions of the city and its people.

Stuart M. Blumin

Hardenbergh, Henry J(aneway) (*b* New Brunswick, N.J., 6 Feb 1847; *d* New York City, 13 March 1918). Architect. He designed such luxury hotels as the first Waldorf–Astoria at 5th Avenue and 34th Street (1891 and 1896, demolished), the Manhattan Hotel at Madison and 42nd Street (1896, demolished), and the Plaza Hotel at 5th Avenue and 59th Street (1905–7); each was dominated by a prominent mansard roof with gabled dormers. Under the patronage of Edward S. Clark he was an early developer of the Upper West Side: he planned such structures as the Dakota Apartments at Central Park West and 72nd Street (1880–84) and two blockfronts of houses on West 73rd Street (1879–80, 1882–85).

For illustration see Art Students League.

Marjorie Pearson

Harding, J. Horace (*b* Philadelphia, 31 July 1863; *d* New York City, 4 Jan 1929). Banker. In 1883 he joined his father-in-law's firm, C. D. Barney and Company, and soon became a senior partner. Respected for his financial acumen, he directed the New York, New Haven and Hartford Railroad Company, the New York Municipal Railways System, the American Beet Sugar Company, and the Bronx Gas and Electric Company; he was also the final trustee in closing the firm of Jay Cooke and took part in many corporate mergers and reorganizations. Harding supported a plan of the Long Island State Park Commission in the 1920s to build a scenic parkway from Queens to Lake Ronkonkoma in Nassau County (now the Northern State Parkway), and he also urged the construction of a highway from Shelter Rock Road in Nassau County to Queens Boulevard in Elmhurst to improve access to his country club; the road was named Horace Harding Boulevard after his death.

Alana J. Erickson

Hare Krishnas. The name for members of the International Society for Krishna Consciousness, a religious society based on Hindu ideals formed in New York City by Swami Prabhupada in 1966. The society draws on traditions of *bhakti* (devotion) and the worship of Krishna, a popular god considered an incarnation of Vishnu, a member of the Hindu Trinity. Members of the society often wear saffron robes and dance and chant in the street, and men shave their heads; they seek to spread their ideas to others, often by distributing written materials on the street and offering free vegetarian food. The society has headquarters in West Virginia and chapters worldwide, including one on Schermerhorn Street in Brooklyn.

Raymond Brady Williams: *Religions of Immigrants from India and Pakistan: New Threads in the American Tapestry* (Cambridge: Cambridge University Press, 1988)

Madhulika S. Khandelwal

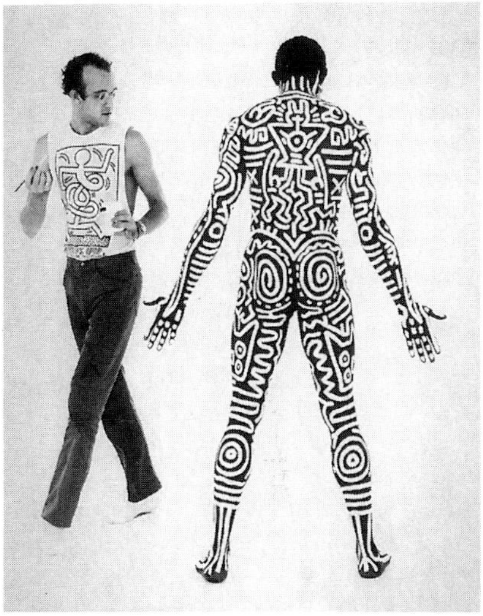

Keith Haring painting Bill T. Jones, 1984

Haring, Keith (*b* Kutztown, Penn., 4 May 1958; *d* New York City, 16 Feb 1990). Painter. He moved to New York City to study at the School of Visual Arts and became known for his graffiti; during the 1980s he drew chalk outlines of interlocking bodies in a blocky, simplified style in subway stations and was often arrested for spray-painting murals on the walls of buildings. He also provided choreography for music videos and designed body-paintings for the singer Grace Jones, a jacket for the entertainer Madonna, and coloring books and T-shirts for children. His work was shown in solo exhibitions worldwide, and three of his sculptures were installed at the United Nations. Haring's devotion to social causes gave his work a strongly political cast.

John Gruen: *Keith Haring: The Authorized Biography* (Englewood Cliffs, N.J.: Prentice Hall, 1991)

James E. Mooney

Harkness Ballet. Dance company formed in 1965, with headquarters in a townhouse at 4 East 75th Street. Its founder was Rebekah Harkness, whose family had become wealthy in the oil business; she prompted many directors and dancers to resign by meddling in the artistic affairs of the company, and critics complained of good dancing in bad ballets. Eventually the company was dissolved for lack of funds; its last performances were in 1974 in the lavishly renovated Harkness Theatre, formerly the Colonial Theatre, at Broadway and 63rd Street.

Clarissa L. Bushman

Harlem. Neighborhood in Manhattan, bounded to the north by the Harlem River, to the east by 5th Avenue, to the south by 110th Street (Central Park North), and to the west by Morningside and St. Nicholas avenues; it comprehends Bradhurst, Strivers' Row, Manhattanville, Hamilton Heights, and Sugar Hill. The area was settled by Dutch farmers who named it Nieuw Haarlem, and because of its remoteness from settled areas of New York City it remained a largely autonomous village for many years. During the eighteenth and nineteenth centuries it was known as Northern Manhattan, and 86th Street was sometimes considered its southern boundary. Many prominent families had estates there in colonial times, including the de Lanceys, the Bleekers, the Rikers, and the Hamiltons. At Harlem Heights in 1776 the Continental Army defeated British troops advancing to the city. The population was 203 in 1790. During the 1840s and 1850s the farmland became unproductive; many farms were deserted and taken over by Irish squatters. Transport to the city was provided by horsecar lines and a steamboat that ran during the summer from 125th Street to Peck Slip.

During the 1880s elevated railroads were extended along 2nd, 3rd, 8th, and 9th avenues, encouraging development during the next twenty-five years. Initially the most dramatic changes took place in adjoining neighborhoods: tenements were built in East Harlem, apartment buildings on the Upper West Side. As the population rose the neighborhood became predominately German; much of the housing consisted of brownstones. The boundaries of the neighborhood were generally placed at 155th Street, the East River, 110th Street, and Morningside Avenue and St. Nicholas Avenue. Attractive "new law" tenements and spacious apartment buildings with elevators were erected between 1898 and 1904, when subway lines were extended along Lenox Avenue. Oscar Hammerstein opened the Harlem Opera House in 1889 in the hope that middle-class families would move to Harlem in large numbers. Although this failed to occur the neighborhood did attract a large number of eastern European Jews seeking to avoid or escape from the tenements of the Lower East Side, who settled between 110th and 125th streets. About this time blacks first moved to the neighborhood, where they found better housing, a more attractive environment, and less racism and violence than in other parts of the city; most settled near 135th Street. Such organizations as the West Side Improvement Association tried to exclude blacks but had little impact, as tenants willing to pay full rent for vacant apartments were highly sought after by real-estate agents. Between 1904 and 1908 the Afro-American Realty Company of Philip Payton was especially active in encouraging black tenants to move into the neighborhood. In 1914 the St. James Presbyterian Church moved to Harlem from West 51st Street. Several black churches were formed in Harlem or moved there: the Abyssinian Baptist Church (1923), Canaan Baptist Church, St. Phillips Episcopal Church (formed 1818, moved to Harlem 1911), and St. Martin's Episcopal Church (formed 1928). There were also powerful black fraternal lodges and social clubs.

At its height in 1917 the Jewish population was eighty thousand; when combined with that of East Harlem (ninety thousand) it made up the second-largest Jewish neighborhood in the United States, after the Lower East Side. The most important institution was probably the Institutional Synagogue, formed in 1917 by Rabbi Herbert S. Goldstein. There were

Harlem, 1798, drawing by Archibald Robertson

several other highly influential congregations such as Temple Israel, Ohab Zedek, Shaare Zedek, and Anshe Chesed, along with scores of storefront synagogues. The neighborhood declined during the First World War owing to severe overcrowding, and after 1920 most Jews moved to newer neighborhoods on the West Side and in the Bronx, Brooklyn, and Queens. By 1930 the Jewish population had declined to about five thousand. All the large synagogue buildings were sold to churches during the 1920s and 1930s.

Between 1920 and 1930 the number of blacks in Harlem increased by 120,000 (to more than 200,000), while the number of whites decreased by an equivalent amount. Most of the new black residents were from the American South; others were from other parts of New York City (such as San Juan Hill) and the Caribbean. Blacks from throughout the nation were soon attracted to the area by economic opportunities and a flourishing cultural life. Langston Hughes, Countee Cullen, Zora Neale Hurston, and other writers launched a literary movement known as the Harlem Renaissance; distinctive styles of painting were forged by Romare Bearden, William H. Johnson, and Richmond Barthé; black theater and dance flourished; and comedians such as Jackie "Moms" Mabley and Pigmeat Markham performed their routines at the Apollo Theatre. Late in the second decade of the century James P. Johnson, Fats Waller, and Willie "the Lion" Smith helped to popularize Harlem stride, a vibrant form of early jazz piano, and jazz continued to flourish in the neighborhood for the next quarter-century. Fletcher Henderson, Duke Ellington, Chick Webb, and many other leaders performed big-band jazz at nightclubs in Harlem, and many famous jazz musicians lived in the neighborhood, among them Louis Armstrong, Coleman Hawkins, Bessie Smith, Ethel Waters, and the tap dancer Bill "Bojangles" Robinson. Critics such as Carl Van Vechten popularized the spirited musical and cultural life of Harlem and helped to attract a large white clientele, who patronized both segregated clubs such as Connie's Inn and the Cotton Club and integrated ones such as the Apollo Theatre, Small's Paradise, and the Savoy Ballroom. The local branch of the YMCA became a meeting place for black intellectuals, writers, and artists. In the early 1940s the innovative style of jazz called bebop was developed at local clubs by Charlie Parker, Dizzy Gillespie, and Thelonious Monk. During its heyday Harlem was not only a neighborhood but a symbol of black cultural success and independence.

Harlem was also a center of black economic and political life. For the middle third of the twentieth century the neighborhood was the site of some of the most successful businesses owned by blacks, among them the Carver Savings and Loan Association, the United Mutual Life Insurance Company, several funeral homes, law firms, and medical practices, and two well-known newspapers, the *Amsterdam News* and the *New York Age*. From 1930 politicians from the neighborhood dominated black politics in the city. They and their protégés led the most powerful black clubs and earned a disproportionate share of the important appointments for blacks in federal, state, and city government. Other political activists worked outside the system. A. Philip Randolph and W. E. B. Du Bois advocated civil rights for blacks. In the 1920s Marcus Garvey, a Jamaican immigrant, became the first leader of a mass black nationalist movement in the United States; although by 1930 the movement was largely ended Harlem remained a fertile ground for black nationalism. The Communist Party, forthright in its opposition to segregation, also attracted a large following in Harlem in the 1930s.

The Depression devastated the local economy. Blacks continued to settle in Harlem although work was scarce, and because the rents remained high apartments were subdivided into ever smaller units: at one point the population density in the neighborhood was more than twice that of the city as a whole. The economic distress perhaps contributed to a new political assertiveness, directed in particular at local stores that depended on black customers but had no black employees. Using the slogan "don't buy where you can't work" the National Urban League initiated a boycott against chain stores operated by whites. In the summer of 1934 more than nineteen thousand families were on relief; the unemployed gathered at the Tree of Hope (near the Lafayette Theatre) to touch its trunk. Churches were well attended and gained new members. Several religious leaders became powerful figures, among them Father Divine, Adam Clayton Powell Sr. of the Abyssinian Baptist Church, and George W. Becton. A riot broke out in March 1935 when a black youth who had been caught stealing a penknife in a department store on 125th Street was incorrectly rumored to have been beaten to death; a restless crowd smashed windows and looted major stores along the street, and businesses lost millions of dollars. A source of great pride to Harlem in the 1930s was the many successful title defenses of the heavyweight champion Joe Louis, which often sparked spontaneous celebrations. The nightlife for which the neighborhood was known continued to thrive at the Rockland Palace Ballroom and the Savoy Ballroom. In May 1932 the Renaissance Theatre gave the first showing of the film *Harlem Is Heaven* (with Robinson); and Waters, Bessie Smith, Mamie Smith, the Mills Brothers, Leadbelly, and others performed at the Lafayette.

The Second World War compelled blacks to fight abroad for rights they were denied at home. The armed forces were segregated, and the playwright Loften Mitchell articulated the views of many blacks when he spoke out against military service. Blacks were excluded from working in the munitions industry until late 1941, when Randolph effected a change in policy by threatening to march on Washington. After a white police officer shot a black soldier during a dispute a riot broke out on 1 August 1943: an angry crowd overturned automobiles and burned many businesses. At the same time blacks were increasingly able to exert political power. Adam Clayton Powell Jr. in 1944 won a seat in the House of Representatives, where he enjoyed a long, successful, and controversial career; J. Raymond Jones, known as the "Harlem fox," was for many years an influential figure in Democratic politics; and Hulan E. Jack was elected the first black borough president of Manhattan. A more militant brand of politics was espoused by the charismatic leader Malcolm X. By this time the population of Harlem was in a steady decline caused by crime, heroin addiction, and other social problems. The role of the neighborhood as the center of black cultural life in the city was eclipsed by Greenwich Village (where several black jazz musicians lived) and other areas such as Bedford–Stuyvesant. Civil rights demonstrations, protests, and boycotts to end de facto segregation were held from 1963. A riot occurred after the shooting of a black teenager by a white police officer in 1964, and there was another in 1968. Charles B. Rangel, a local black politician, defeated Powell for his seat in the House of Representatives in 1970. Social problems worsened and a riot occurred in 1977. As the public schools failed to prepare students adequately, the number of high school graduates declined. The unemployment rate among young working-class blacks consistently exceeded 30 percent, and many families were led by poor single mothers, a good number of them teenagers. There was an astoundingly high incidence of tuberculosis, AIDS, and cancer: in 1990 the *New England Journal of Medicine* reported that men in Harlem had a lower life expectancy than their counterparts in Bangladesh. In the 1990s the population of Harlem remained almost entirely black. Unlike most areas of heavy black population in New York City it attracted relatively few immigrants from the Caribbean. In 1989 the neighborhood gained in political stature with the election to the mayoralty of David N. Dinkins, a product of Democratic clubs in Harlem and the first black mayor of New York City.

The architectural record of Harlem is rich and varied. The Morris–Jumel Mansion (1765) is one of the few remaining buildings in Manhattan predating the American Revolution, and the High Bridge (1839–48), originally part of the Croton Aqueduct, is the oldest remaining bridge connecting Manhattan to the Bronx. Coogan's Bluff, at West 155th Street, was the site of the Polo Grounds, home of the baseball team the New York Giants. The residences of the élite of black Harlem may be seen at the Dunbar Apartments (1928), on Strivers' Row on West 139th Street, and in Sugar Hill at 155th Street and Edgecombe Avenue. Despite its difficulties Harlem has several thriving cultural institutions, including the Studio Museum of Harlem, the National Black Theatre, the Schomburg Center for Research in Black Culture, one of the most important research institutions of its kind, and the Dance Theatre of Harlem, one of the premier ballet companies in the nation.

Gilbert Osofsky: *Harlem: The Making of a Ghetto* (New York: Harper and Row, 1963)

Jeffrey S. Gurock: *When Harlem Was Jewish, 1870–1930* (New York: Columbia University Press, 1979)

Jeffrey S. Gurock, Calvin B. Holder

Harlem Commonwealth Council. An urban development corporation formed in 1967 with an initial grant of $400,000 from the Office of Equal Opportunity. Its organizers included Kenneth Marshall of the Metropolitan Applied Research Center, Billy Rolle of the United Block Association, Marshall England of Haryou–Act, Preston Wilcox, a professor at Columbia University, and Roy Innis, director of the Congress of Racial Equality. The council financed a study by Columbia of the feasibility of supporting business and industry in Harlem, and despite negative conclusions began operations, securing federal grants of nearly $1 million by 1968 under the direction of Donald Simmons. Under James H. Dowdy the council in the following year formed alliances with businesses in New York City that led to the establishment and refurbishment of several businesses in Harlem, including the Acme Foundry, the Schultz Company, Nigel Contracting and Construction, and Ben's Lumber Yard. In the mid 1990s the council was led by Barbara Norris. The diversified holdings of the Harlem Commonwealth Council, particularly in real estate, have enabled it to attract a number of popular franchises to the area.

Emilyn L. Brown

Harlem Hellfighters. The popular name of the 369th Regiment of the New York National Guard and the 15th Regiment, New York Guard. It was formed in 1913 as the 15th Regiment and during the First World War served with the 16th and 161st divisions of the French army, being redesignated the 369th U.S. Infantry. All the enlisted men were black and most of the officers white. By the end of the war the 369th had served 191 days in combat, longer than any unit in the armed forces. The first Croix de Guerre awarded to any Americans went to Corporal Henry Lincoln Johnson and Private Needham Roberts of the 369th, and the unit also earned the Croix de Guerre as a unit citation. It used French weapons, helmets, and equipment, and adapted so well that the American headquarters asked the French to apply American segregation policies, a request that was refused. The band of the unit, led by the composer James Reese Europe, helped to introduce jazz during its tours of France. The unit returned to the United States in 1919 and by the following year built its first armory (at 142nd Street and 5th Avenue), which remained in use into the 1990s. From 1936 the unit was commanded by Colonel Benjamin O. Davis Sr., who left in 1940 to become the first black American general. In that year the unit was mobilized for war, redesignated the 369th Coast Artillery (Anti-Aircraft), and sent to Hawaii, where it was known as "Hooper's Troopers" (after its commanding officer, Colonel Chauncey Hooper). Renamed the 369th and 870th Anti-Aircraft Artillery Battalions in 1943, the unit saw combat at Okinawa in 1945. The 15th Regiment of the New York Guard, under Colonel Woodruff Chisum, served stateside. In 1950 the 369th was mobilized for stateside active duty in the Korean War. It later became a field artillery group and (in 1974) the 369th Transportation Battalion. In 1990–91 both companies of the 369th and its headquarters detachment served in the Persian Gulf, earning a Meritorious Unit Citation, with the 15th New York Guard replacing it at home.

The Harlem Hellfighters marching over a bridge in Harlem, 1919

Emmett J. Scott: *Scott's Official History of the American Negro in the World War* (Chicago: Homewood, 1919)

Arthur W. Little: *From Harlem to the Rhine: The Story of New York's Colored Volunteers* (New York: Covici Friede, 1936)

Ulysses Lee: *The Employment of Negro Troops: U.S. Army in World War II: Special Studies* (Washington: U.S. Army, Office of the Chief of Military History, 1966)

Arthur E. Barbeau and Florette Henri: *The Unknown Soldiers: Black American Troops in World War I* (Philadelphia: Temple University Press, 1974)

Bernard C. Nalty: *Strength for the Fight: A History of Black Americans in the Military* (New York: Free Press, 1986)

Eleanor Hannah, Yarema Hutsaliuk

Harlem Hospital Center. Municipal hospital opened in 1877 in a house on East 120th Street to accommodate patients awaiting transfer to facilities on Wards and Randalls islands. It also soon served as an emergency branch for Bellevue Hospital. In 1907 the hospital moved to 506 Lenox Avenue, where it gradually developed a full range of medical services. Large numbers of southern blacks began moving into the neighborhood during the 1920s, but blacks were under-represented on the staff until well after the Second World War. Louis T. Wright joined the outpatient department in 1920 as the first black physician to serve in a hospital in New York City and was named director of surgery after twenty-three years of service. The hospital's national reputation for trauma care was dramatically tested in 1958, when it successfully treated Martin Luther King Jr. after he was stabbed during a visit nearby. It formed an affiliation with the College of Physicians and Surgeons of Columbia University in 1962. The hospital shared in many of the financial difficulties of the municipal health care system during the 1960s and mid 1970s; its fifty-year-old nursing school closed in 1977 for budgetary reasons, and the widespread poverty in Harlem placed special burdens on its community health clinics. In 1989 Harlem Hospital Center had more than seven hundred beds and was administered by the New York Health and Hospitals Corporation. It had a sickle cell anemia center, a burn unit, and more than eleven clinics in Harlem, and was noted for its research into tuberculosis, thoracic surgery, and rehabilitation medicine.

Aubre de L. Maynard: *Surgeons to the Poor: The Harlem Hospital Story* (New York: Appleton–Century–Crofts, 1978)

Sandra Opdycke

Harlem Renaissance. A literary and artistic movement that reached its high point between 1925 and the onset of the Depression in 1929. Writers and artists traveled to Harlem from throughout the United States to take part in the movement (Countee Cullen was its only important exponent who grew up in Harlem), not because it represented a single style or aesthetic but rather because it offered them the chance to become part of a vibrant community. Although the point at which the Harlem Renaissance began is open to debate, it is agreed that an important early influence was W. E. B. Du Bois's book *The Souls of Black Folk* (1903), which advanced the thesis that black American consciousness is composed of warring African and American influences. In 1917 the white playwright Ridgely Torrence staged his *Three Plays for the Negro Theatre*, which for the first time on stage depicted black characters with sympathy and depth. The Jamaican immigrant Claude McKay responded to widespread rioting against blacks in 1919 with his defiant sonnet "If We Must Die," and in 1921 the popular all-black musical *Shuffle Along* by Noble Sissle and Eubie Blake brought authentic black comedy, music, and dance back to the Broadway stage after more than a decade of exclusion. Jean Toomer's *Cane* (1923), a hybrid of prose, poetry, and drama, set new standards of accomplishment for modernist black writers.

These developments took place at a time when many northern industrial centers were expanding dramatically. Unstable real-estate conditions in Harlem before the First World War enabled blacks fleeing harsh conditions in the South to settle in the neighborhood, which at the time was populated by whites, mainly German Jews. A diverse community developed that included both blacks who had lived in other parts of New York City for generations and a large number of blacks from the Caribbean. Religious institutions played a prominent role in the community, notably the Abyssinian Baptist Church on 138th Street and St. Philip's Protestant Episcopal Church on 133rd Street; the weekly newspapers the *New York Age* and the *Amsterdam News* were also important, as was the local branch of the New York Public Library, which sponsored lectures and was the intellectual center of the neighborhood. Despite the relative freedom enjoyed by blacks in New York City, many were frustrated by high rents, crowded living conditions, and unemployment. The proposed remedies ranged from black nationalism, advocated by groups such as Marcus Garvey's Universal Negro Improvement Association, to eventual integration into American society, the goal of the National Association for the Advancement of Colored People (NAACP) and the National Urban League. As this debate continued, blacks regarded themselves as no longer needing to be subservient but aggressively urbane. Several publications played an important role in defining the militant, self-assertive image of what came to be called the "New Negro," among them the *Crisis* (1910), published by the NAACP and edited by Du Bois (later assisted by the novelist and literary editor Jessie Redmon Fauset) and *Opportunity* (1923), published by the National Urban League and edited by the sociologist Charles S. Johnson. Fauset, Johnson, the poet and diplomat James Weldon Johnson, and the aesthete Alain Locke advocated a genteel black art that would combat racism by proving that blacks were "civilized." With the backing of Charles Johnson, Locke in 1925 compiled and edited a special issue of the monthly periodical the *Survey Graphic* entitled "Harlem: Mecca of the New Negro." In the same year Locke expanded and published this material as *The New Negro: An Interpretation*, in which he called on black American artists to enhance their racial consciousness by studying African art and emulating its styles and themes.

Locke helped many visual artists to acquire patrons, such as Mrs. R. Osgood Mason (known as "Godmother") and the William E. Harmon Foundation (formed in 1922 by William Elmer Harmon, a millionaire from Ohio). The Julius Rosenwald Fund and the General Education Board also supported black artists and writers. Carl Van Vechten, author of the best-selling novel *Nigger Heaven* (1926), introduced many black writers to potential patrons, and a literary contest organized by *Opportunity* culminated in an awards dinner on 1 May 1925 where black writers and intellectuals met white authors and editors from leading magazines and publishing houses; a result was the publication of the books of poetry *Color*, by Cullen (1925, Harper and Brothers), and *The Weary Blues*, by Langston Hughes (1926, Alfred A. Knopf). Fiction soon replaced poetry as the dominant literary form of the Harlem Renaissance. From 1924 novels were published by writers such as Walter White (*Fire in the Flint*, 1924), Fauset (*There Is Confusion*, 1924), McKay (*Home to Harlem*, 1928), Nella Larsen (*Quicksand*, 1928), Wallace Thurman (*The Blacker the Berry*, 1929), Hughes (*Not without Laughter*, 1930), Cullen (*One Way to Heaven*, 1931), and Arna Bontemps (*God Sends Sunday*, 1931).

The Harlem Renaissance was marked by vigorous debate over literary tradition, folk culture, political responsibility, and sexual freedom. Cullen and McKay modeled their work on traditional literary forms; Zora Neale Hurston and Hughes championed black folk expression, including jazz, blues, and common speech. Du Bois insisted that black writers had an obligation to be propagandists for their race; Thurman and others pursued bohemian ideals that were largely divorced from issues of race. Locke believed that black artists must draw on African models to create a uniquely black art; others believed that the work of black artists was not essentially different from that of white artists, only that its development had been blocked by racial discrimination.

Among the painters associated with the Harlem Renaissance were Aaron Douglas, William H. Johnson, Palmer Hayden, and Malvin Gray Johnson. Douglas became known for his illustrations in Locke's *The New Negro* and James Weldon Johnson's *God's Trombones: Seven Negro Sermons in Verse* (1927), and for the covers of *Opportunity* and the *Crisis*. For the Countee Cullen branch of the New York Public Library (now the Schomburg Center for Research in Black Culture) he executed a stylized, multi-panel mural entitled *Aspects of Negro Life* (1934) intended to symbolize the strength of the "New Negro." William H. Johnson began his career in Paris and settled in Harlem in 1929, where he persuaded Locke to become his American agent. At first influenced by expressionism and later by primitivism, he was known for his treatment of southern religious and folkloric themes. Hayden moved to New York City in 1919 to study art at Cooper Union and at the urging of Locke treated African subjects in such paintings as *Fétiche and Fleurs* (1926) and *Nous Quatre à Paris* (1930). He lived in Paris for five years (1927–32) but continued to exhibit his works in New York City. In his later career he painted images of rural black life. Malvin Gray Johnson (1896–1934) studied at the National Academy of Design and became known for his interpretations of black genre themes and Negro spirituals. Although he was not black, the German artist Winold Reiss also was strongly associated with the Harlem Renaissance and greatly influenced the work of Douglas. He was commissioned to illustrate "Harlem: Mecca of the New Negro" and to produce (with Douglas) a series of portraits entitled "Harlem Residents and the 'New Negro': The Young Leaders of the Harlem Renaissance" (1925). The painter Archibald John Motley Jr. did not live in New York City, but an exhibition of his work at the New Gallery in 1928 was well received by both critics and artists. The most important sculptor of the Harlem Renaissance was Augusta Savage. After studying with George Brewster at Cooper Union she won a scholarship to study in France in 1923, but the invitation was later revoked because of her race. In 1930 she went to Europe on a grant from the Julius Rosenwald Fund and produced such works as *Gamin*, a bust of her young nephew that captured the exuberance of young artists in Harlem. She opened the Savage Studio of Arts and Crafts in Harlem in 1932 and worked to create opportunities for younger artists. Her heroic sculpture *The Harp* adorned the entrance to the Contemporary Arts building at the World's Fair of 1939–40. Three other sculptors were associated with the Harlem Renaissance although New York City was not their home. Meta Warrick Fuller (1877–1968) was born in Philadelphia, studied in Paris, and eventually settled in Framingham, Massachusetts. Her sculpture *Ethiopia Awakening* symbolized the restoration of the African heritage to a high place in black American consciousness. Sargent Johnson (1887–1967) lived in San Francisco, but his works were shown annually in New York City at the exhibitions of the Harmon Foundation. In pieces such as *Chester* (1931) and *Copper Mask* (1935), which were heavily influenced by African art, he aimed to portray the natural beauty and dignity of blacks to a black audience. Richmond Barthé, who was born in Mississippi in 1901, studied at the Art Students League and the Art Institute of Chicago. His elegant sculptures of dancers, such as *Feral Benga* (1935), and his busts of West Indian and black American men and women embodied the sensuous, racial themes favored by many artists of the Harlem Renaissance. The photographer James VanDerZee, who was born in Lenox, Massachusetts, in 1886, maintained a studio in Harlem and documented the lives of its residents. His black-and-white portraits of subjects ranging from Marcus Garvey and the heiress A'lelia Walker to black fraternities and funerals constitute the most complete visual record of Harlem in the period. The role of music in the Harlem Renaissance was important and at the same time peripheral: artists and writers heard jazz singers, instrumentalists, and bandleaders such as Bessie Smith, Louis Armstrong, Fletcher Henderson, and Duke Ellington at the Cotton Club, Smalls' Paradise, and the Renaissance Casino, but musicians were not normally associated with the goals of the movement.

Perhaps the most dramatic change wrought by the Harlem Renaissance was the sense that black artists gained by being part of a group linked by ethnic pride, political activism, and a shared cultural lineage. This sensibility was fostered by collective exhibitions such as those sponsored by the Harmon Foundation, which showed the work of leading black artists from Harlem and across the nation. At the same time there was great debate about how much freedom artists and writers really enjoyed given their heavy reliance on white patronage, a reliance made necessary by the failure of black artists and writers to sustain independent cultural institutions. Among those that were unsuccessful were *Fire!!: A Quarterly Devoted to the Younger Negro Artists* (1926), a magazine launched by Thurman and other writers that proclaimed radical intentions but appeared only once; the magazine *Harlem* (1928), also edited by Thurman; the Harlem African Art Museum; and the Salon of Contemporary Negro Artists. By 1930 the Harlem Renaissance was in sharp decline, but important work continued to be produced, notably novels by Hughes, Bontemps, Thurman, Hurston, and George Schuyler. The racially based riot that rocked Harlem in 1935 marked the definitive end of the movement.

A rich collection of materials related to the Harlem Renaissance was amassed by the bibliophile Arthur Schomburg and is now part of the Schomburg Center for Research in Black Culture.

"Harlem, Mecca of the New Negro," *Survey Graphic* 6, no. 6 (1925) [repr. Baltimore: Black Classic, 1980, as *Survey Graphic: Harlem, Mecca of the New Negro*]

Alain Locke, ed.: *The New Negro: An Interpretation* (New York: Albert and Charles Boni, 1925)

The World of James VanDerZee: A Visual Record of Black Americans (New York: Grove, 1969)

James A. Porter: *Modern Negro Art* (New York: Arno / New York Times, 1969)

Nathan I. Huggins: *Harlem Renaissance* (New York: Oxford University Press, 1971)

David Levering Lewis: *When Harlem Was in Vogue* (New York: Alfred A. Knopf, 1981)

An Independent Woman: The Life and Art of Meta Warrick Fuller (Framingham, Mass.: Danforth Museum of Art, 1984)

Arnold Rampersad: *The Life of Langston Hughes*, vol. 1, *1902–1941: I Too Sing America* (New York: Oxford University Press, 1986)

Bruce Kellner, ed.: *The Harlem Renaissance: A Historical Dictionary for the Era* (Westport, Conn.: Greenwood, 1987)

Harlem Renaissance: Art of Black America (New York: Studio Museum in Harlem / Harry N. Abrams, 1987)

Three Masters: Eldzier Cortor, Hughie Lee-Smith, Archibald John Motley Jr. (New York: Kenkeleba Gallery, 1988)

Augusta Savage and the Art Schools of Harlem (New York: Schomburg Center for Research in Black Culture, 1989)

Black Art: Ancestral Legacy: The African Impulse in African-American Art (Dallas: Dallas Museum of Art, 1989)

Leonard Harris, ed.: *The Philosophy of Alain Locke: Harlem Renaissance and Beyond* (Philadelphia: Temple University Press, 1989)

Jeffrey Stewart: *To Color America: Portraits by Winold Reiss* (Washington: Smithsonian Institution Press, 1989)

Novae: William H. Johnson and Bob Thompson (Los Angeles: California Afro-American Museum Foundation, 1990)

A Stronger Soul within a Finer Frame: Portraying African-Americans in the Black Renaissance (Minneapolis: University of Minnesota, University Art Museum, 1990)

Edmund Gaither, Arnold Rampersad

Harlem River. A navigable tidal strait about eight miles (thirteen kilometers) long between Manhattan and the Bronx, connecting the East River with Spuyten Duyvil Creek and the Hudson River. Its course was changed in 1923 when the Harlem River Ship Canal was cut through huge rock outcroppings between Inwood and Marble Hill in northern Manhattan, leaving Marble Hill attached to the Bronx. The river is spanned by six swing bridges, one lift bridge, and three arch bridges including High Bridge at East 173rd Street, built with massive stone arches in 1837–48 to carry the Croton Aqueduct system.

Harlem River: Its Use previous to and since the Revolutionary War (New York: J. D. Torrey, 1857)

Gerard R. Wolfe

Harlem River and Manhattan Bridge. Original name of the WASHINGTON BRIDGE.

Harlem River–Bronx State Park. Original name of ROBERTO CLEMENTE STATE PARK.

Harlem River Ship Canal [U.S. Ship Canal]. Waterway connecting the Hudson and Harlem rivers. Work began in 1826, with the purpose of promoting more efficient commercial shipping to Long Island Sound from the Hudson River and the system of barge canals criss-crossing upper New York State. In 1895 the first section was completed,

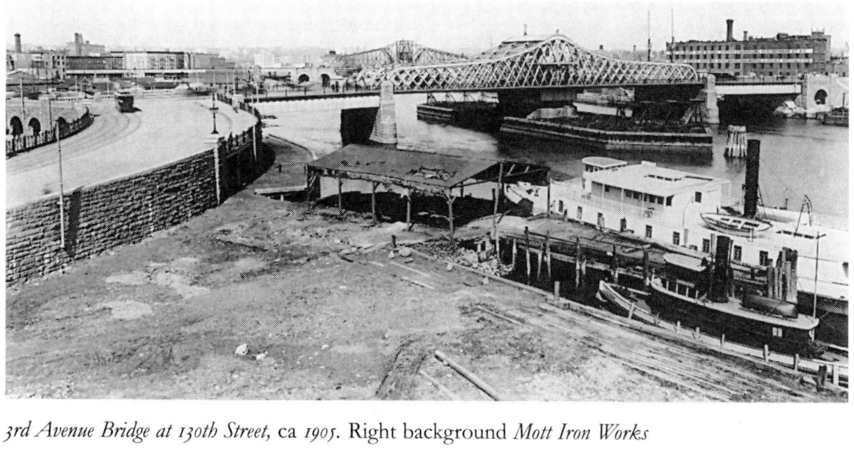

3rd Avenue Bridge at 130th Street, ca *1905.* Right background *Mott Iron Works*

making it possible for ships to circumnavigate Manhattan for the first time, and also separating Marble Hill from the rest of Manhattan. The entire project was completed in 1938.

Gary Hermalyn: "The Harlem River Ship Canal," *Bronx County Historical Society Journal* 20 (1983)

Gary D. Hermalyn

Harlem Savings Bank. Original name of the APPLE BANK FOR SAVINGS.

Harlem YWCA. A branch of the Young Women's Christian Association, formed in 1905. It met in rented rooms on West 63rd Street before following the city's black community north to Harlem, moving in 1913 to two rented buildings on West 132nd Street and in 1919 to a newly constructed building at 137th Street and Lenox Avenue. Housing a large cafeteria, reception and meeting rooms, classrooms, offices, a gymnasium, a swimming pool, showers, a laundry, and locker rooms, the new building was the best-equipped YWCA with a black membership in the United States. Later additions included an adjacent residence hall (1926) with a capacity of more than two hundred and an annex to the administration building (1932). The construction of the annex was funded by John D. Rockefeller Jr., a long-time supporter of the YWCA and of the Harlem branch in particular. In its earliest years the Harlem YWCA emphasized religious concerns: it sponsored vesper services and bible study and admitted as members only women who were also members in good standing of evangelical Protestant churches. Participation was extended in 1912 to non-evangelicals and non-Christians. In addition the organization held monthly public meetings at prominent churches in the city, where a musical program was followed by an educational address, often dealing with such issues as woman suffrage, anti-lynching legislation, American involvement in the First World War, education, and civil rights legislation. Speakers over the years included Ida B. Wells, Mary McLeod Bethune, Lucy Laney, T. Thomas Fortune, Bishop Alexander Walters, Mary Church Terrell, Madame C. J. Walker, and Booker T. Washington. Perhaps the greatest contribution of the Harlem YWCA to the life of black New Yorkers was its trade school, which trained women to become domestic servants, seamstresses, secretaries, beauticians, and nurses. For young girls there were team sports, after-school programs, a club called the Girl Reserve, and a camp in the Catskills, Fern Rock. The Harlem YWCA closed after the fiscal crisis that beset New York City in the 1970s.

Judith Weisenfeld

Harmonie Club. A social club formed in 1852 as the Harmonie Gesellschaft, a select German Jewish counterpart to the other social clubs in New York City; it took its current name in 1893. The club distinguished itself by having German as its official language and by hanging the kaiser's portrait in its hall for many years. In 1906 a clubhouse designed by Stanford White was constructed at 4 East 60th Street: although the building is not architecturally successful because it is crammed between large buildings in the middle of a block, the inside quarters have a comfortable, pleasant character. The Harmonie Club was the first men's club in the city to admit women at dinner, and it maintains a reputation for fine food.

James E. Mooney

Harper, James (*b* Newtown [now in Queens], 13 April 1795; *d* New York City, 27 March 1869). Mayor and businessman. With his brother John Harper he formed the publishing firm of J. and J. Harper and Brothers in 1817. In 1844 he was elected mayor as the nominee of the American Republican Party with Whig and Democratic support; during his term he lived at 50 Rose Street. A reformer, he advocated frugal government, limits on city services, low taxes, and social controls. His most noteworthy achievement while in office was the formation of the Municipal Police, or Night and Day Watch, one of the nation's earliest organized police forces. He returned to his publishing house in 1845 and worked there to the end of his life. Harper died after a carriage accident in Central Park.

James F. Richardson: *The New York Police: Colonial Times to 1901* (New York: Oxford University Press, 1970)

Edward K. Spann: *The New Metropolis: New York City, 1840–1857* (New York: Columbia University Press, 1981)

For illustration see GRAMERCY PARK.

Jerome Mushkat

Harper Collins. Firm of book publishers formed in 1817 as a printing firm called J. and J. Harper at the corner of Front and Dover streets by the brothers James and John Harper of Brooklyn. It soon began publishing books as well as printing them, and after the founders' younger brothers Fletcher Harper and Joseph Wesley Harper joined the firm in the 1820s it became the largest book publisher in the United States. In 1833 it changed its name to Harper and Brothers and moved into two buildings on Cliff Street, which eventually expanded as far as Pearl Street. By the early 1850s the firm occupied a number of five-story buildings, employed several hundred people, and handled all aspects of book publishing from editing to sales. The firm had become the world's largest publisher when a fire on 10 December 1853 destroyed its facility at 333 Pearl Street; it then moved to a fireproof building on Franklin Square, where a distinctive circular iron stairway became known as the "stairway to literary fame" because of the many major English and American writers published by the firm, including Dickens, Trollope, Melville, Poe, Mark Twain, William Dean Howells, and the Brontë sisters. The firm also launched the literary and intellectual journal *Harper's New Monthly Magazine* (1850); the politically oriented *Harper's Weekly* (1857), which published Dickens's *A Tale of Two Cities*, Wilkie Collins's *The Woman in White*, George Eliot's *Middlemarch*, and Thomas Hardy's *The Return of the Native*, as well as illustrations by Winslow Homer and Thomas Nast; *Harper's Bazar* (1867), a magazine for women eventually sold to William Randolph Hearst (who amended the spelling to *Harper's Bazaar*); and *Harper's Young People* (1879, later renamed *Harper's Round Table*). At its high point in the 1880s the firm had nearly eight hundred employees, more than four thousand titles in print, and annual sales of $4 million, but in the difficult economic climate of the 1890s it went into receivership, procured a loan of $850,000 from the financier J. P. Morgan, and was reorganized. It continued to publish well-known writers in the early twentieth century, including Presidents William Howard Taft and Woodrow Wilson, James Thurber, E. B. White, Aldous Huxley, and John Dos Passos. In 1913 it sold a million copies of Lew Wallace's *Ben-Hur* (1880) to Sears Roebuck, the largest single sale of a book in history.

The firm ceased printing its own books in 1923, reorganized the ownership of its stock, and moved its offices to 49 East 33rd Street, and in the following decades it branched out into religious books, bibles, textbooks, and books for young people. Twenty-one members of the Harper family spanning three generations worked for the firm until 1944, including James W. Harper, the first in the family to attend college (at Columbia). Cass Canfield, who joined the firm in 1924, was its president from 1931 to 1945, chairman of the board from 1945 to 1962, and then director emeritus. In 1962 Harper and Brothers merged with Row, Peterson, and Company to become Harper and Row. During the 1960s Canfield recruited managers with financial experience such as Winthrop Knowlton and Brooks Thomas in an effort to keep the house independent, as many publishers were bought up by corporate conglomerates. To this end he sold a large share of stock in the firm in 1965 to the Minneapolis Star and Tribune Company, owned by John Cowles Jr., which had earlier bought *Harper's Magazine*; Cowles became chairman of the board at Harper and Row in 1968 and later was chairman of its executive committee. The firm moved its offices to 10 East 53rd Street in 1972. In 1974 it sustained a seventeen-day strike by 320 of its employees in New York City, the first strike in the modern history of book publishing; there was also a weeklong strike in 1977 by 240 employees. Under the presidency of Winthrop Knowlton, Harper and Row acquired a number of other publishers, including Basic Books (1969), Thomas Y. Crowell (1977), and

J. B. Lippincott (1978). It was itself acquired in 1987 by the News Corporation, led by Rupert Murdoch. In 1989 the firm acquired the textbook publisher Scott, Foresman. It took its current name in June 1990 after forming an affiliation with William Collins, a British publisher also owned by the News Corporation. In 1990 Harper Collins ranked among the five largest publishers in the world: its imprints and divisions in the United States published about sixteen hundred titles a year; a large children's division publishes books by Maurice Sendak, Shel Silverstein, Margaret Wise Brown, and Laura Ingalls Wilder. There are about six hundred employees at the offices in New York City at 10 East 53rd Street.

Joseph Henry Harper: *I Remember* (New York: Harper and Brothers, 1934)
"The Houses of Harper," *Publishers Weekly*, 6 Nov 1967
Eugene Exman: *The House of Harper: One Hundred and Fifty Years of Publishing* (New York: Harper and Row, 1967)

Marjorie Harrison

Harper's Magazine. Literary magazine. Launched as *Harper's New Monthly Magazine* in 1850 by the firm of Harper and Brothers, it was intended to educate the general public while whetting its appetite for books published by Harper. The magazine contained articles on topics ranging from science to travel as well as reprints of fiction by such well-known English writers as Dickens, Thackeray, Trollope, Bulwer-Lytton, and George Eliot. It also included work by American writers as early as 1851 and increasingly stressed American contributions after the Civil War. Among its features were a humor section entitled "The Editor's Drawer" and such columns as George William Curtis's "The Editor's Easy Chair" and William Dean Howells's "The Editor's Study," which was introduced in 1886 and ran for six years. The magazine attracted such artists as Winslow Homer, Frederic Remington, Edwin A. Abbey, and John Singer Sargent. It chose its content carefully to appeal to educated middle-class families and became one of the most successful and influential magazines in the country's history. In 1900 it reached the peak of its success, was renamed *Harper's Monthly Magazine*, and published a fiftieth-anniversary issue that included pieces by Howells, Stephen Crane, Owen Wister, Mark Twain, and Theodore Dreiser. Adapting to changing tastes, during the next few years it stressed science, history, biography, and criticism over fiction and focused on current affairs after the First World War. In 1925 it took its current name, changed its format, and became a magazine of ideas and editorial comment. It focused on politics, sociology, science, and economics during the 1950s and published William Styron's *The Confessions of Nat Turner* and Norman Mailer's *Armies of the Night* in the late 1960s. The magazine experienced financial troubles in the following decades and periodically sought a new identity under a succession of editors.

Frank Luther Mott: *A History of American Magazines*, vol. 2, *1850–1865* (Cambridge: Harvard University Press, 1938), 383–405
Edward E. Chielens, ed.: *American Literary Magazines: The Eighteenth and Nineteenth Centuries* (New York: Greenwood, 1986), 166–71

For illustration see Nast, Thomas.

Alice Fahs

Harrigan and Hart. Team of comedians. Its members were the Irish musical comedy performers Ned (Edward) Harrigan (1845–1911) and Tony Hart (1855–91), who formed a highly successful partnership between 1871 and 1885. Harrigan wrote most of their material, including thirty-three plays that depicted life in New York City and particularly on the Lower East Side, where he was brought up. Although many of his plays such as the famous series on the "Mulligan Guards" centered on Irish immigrants, other ethnic groups such as Germans, Jews, Italians, and blacks were also treated sympathetically. Harrigan continued writing plays after the dissolution of his partnership with Hart and also owned several theaters in New York City.

Ely Jacques Kahn: *The Merry Partners: The Age and Stage of Harrigan and Hart* (New York: Random House, 1955)
Richard Moody: *Ned Harrigan: From Corlears Hook to Herald Square* (Chicago: Nelson–Hall, 1980)

John T. Ridge

Harriman, Edward H(enry) (*b* Hempstead, N.Y., 25 Feb 1848; *d* Arden, N.Y., 9 Sept 1909). Businessman, father of W. Averell Harriman and E. Roland Harriman. The son of an Episcopal minister, he left school to work as an office boy on Wall Street; he bought a seat on the New York Stock Exchange about 1870 and became an expert in rebuilding bankrupt railroads after 1879. By 1897 he was a director of the Union Pacific Railroad, and in the following year he became the head of its executive committee. Under his leadership the railroad regained financial stability and took control of the Southern Pacific Railroad and many connecting lines. A struggle with James J. Hill for control of the Northern Pacific Railroad in 1901 and an investigation of his railroad lines by the Interstate Commerce Commission in 1906–7 led to widespread disapproval of his business practices, and the federal government made efforts to halt abuses of the railroads. Known as a conservationist, he funded an important scientific expedition to Alaska in 1899. At his death Harriman had a fortune of more than $70 million and owned a forest preserve of twenty thousand acres (eight thousand hectares) in Orange County, New York.

Lloyd J. Mercer: *E. H. Harriman, Master Railroader* (Boston: Twayne, 1985)
Walter Isaacson and Evan Thomas: *The Wise Men: Six Friends and the World They Made* (New York: Simon and Schuster, 1986)

Mary E. Curry

Harriman, E. Roland (*b* New York City, 24 Dec 1895; *d* Arden, N.Y., 16 Feb 1978). Businessman and philanthropist, son of Edward H. Harriman and brother of W. Averell Harriman. He graduated from Yale University in 1917 and in the same year married Gladys Fries, daughter of a manufacturing chemist with interests in the South. He was a founding partner in 1927 of the banking firm of Harriman Brothers and Company. Its successor, Brown Brothers Harriman and Company (1931), was for many years the only large commercial bank in the United States owned and operated by a partnership instead of a corporation. In 1950 he was named by President Harry S. Truman to succeed General George C. Marshall as chairman of the American Red Cross, a position to which he was reappointed to seven more three-year terms by Presidents Dwight D. Eisenhower, John F. Kennedy, Lyndon B. Johnson, and Richard M. Nixon. He also served for twenty-three years as chairman of the Union Pacific Railroad and even longer as president and chairman of the Boys' Club of New York, founded by his father in 1876. In his philanthropic activity Harriman advanced the principle that "a trustee should either work, give, get or get out." He maintained a home in Manhattan but regarded his primary residence as his estate in Arden, where he was a leading patron of harness racing and the founder of the U.S. Trotting Association.

Kenneth T. Jackson

Harriman, W(illiam) Averell (*b* New York City, 15 Nov 1891; *d* Yorktown Heights, N.Y., 26 July 1986). Governor and investment banker, son of Edward H. Harriman and brother of E. Roland Harriman. He attended Yale University and was named to the board of the Boys' Club, an organization that his father had founded. As an undergraduate he donated to New York State ten thousand acres (four thousand hectares) of the family estate, "Arden," near West Point, as well as $1 million to transform the land into a state park; by his senior year (1913) he was a director of the Union Pacific. After his graduation he formed W. H. Harriman and Company (later Brown Brothers Harriman) and became a successful investment banker. A Republican in his early career, he supported the Democratic presidential candidacy of Alfred E. Smith in 1928 partly at the urging of his elder sister Mary, and in 1933 he was named chairman of the Emergency Reemployment Campaign in New York City by President Franklin D. Roosevelt. As the American ambassador to the Soviet Union from 1943 to 1946 he assiduously cultivated a relationship with Nikita Khrushchev. He sought the Democratic presidential nomination in 1952, losing to Adlai E. Stevenson, and in 1954 was elected governor of New York. After again being defeated for the Democratic presidential nomination by Stevenson in 1956, he sought reelection as governor in 1958 and was defeated by Nelson A. Rockefeller by 450,000 votes. On President John F. Kennedy's behalf he negotiated a limited but important nuclear test ban treaty with the Soviet Union in 1963. The W. Averell Harriman Institute for Soviet Studies at Columbia University is named for him.

Walter Isaacson and Evan Thomas: *The Wise Men: Six Friends and the Worlds They Made* (New York: Simon and Schuster, 1986)

Randy Abramson: *Spanning the Century: The Life of W. Averell Harriman, 1891–1986* (New York: William Morrow, 1992)

Marjory Potts

Harrington, (Edward) Michael (*b* St. Louis, 24 Feb 1928; *d* Larchmont, N.Y., 31 July 1989). Writer and political activist. He moved to New York City, where he edited the *Catholic Worker* and soon became a leading participant in the political culture of the city's leftist intelligentsia. Within a few years he shifted from Catholic radicalism to anticommunist democratic socialism, and after joining the Socialist Party in 1953 he cultivated ties with labor unions and liberal politicians and opposed groups that he felt did not understand the dangers of totalitarianism, including Stalinists and the founders of Students for a Democratic Society. He succeeded Norman Thomas as chairman of the Socialist Party in 1968. Despite his ardent anticommunism he increasingly battled elements within the party who supported the American intervention in Vietnam and rejected any collaboration with the New Left. In 1972 he resigned from the party, joining with other former members in the following year to form the Democratic Socialist Organizing Committee (DSOC). In 1982 he engineered its merger with the New American Movement, a group oriented toward the New Left, to form the Democratic Socialists of America, with headquarters in New York City. For many years Harrington taught at Queens College. The most influential of his many books is *The Other America* (1962), which describes the plight of those untouched by the economic boom in the United States after the Second World War.

Loren J. Okroi: *Galbraith, Harrington, Heilbroner: Economics and Dissent in an Age of Optimism* (Princeton, N.J.: Princeton University Press, 1988)

Richard Yeselson

Harris, Elisha (*b* Westminster, Vt., 5 March 1824; *d* Albany, N.Y., 31 Jan 1884). Public health official. With Stephen Smith he worked to improve sanitary conditions in New York City; their efforts led to the passage of the Metropolitan Health Act of 1866, which established the first effective health board for the city. He was the first registrar of records for the Metropolitan Board of Health (1866–69) and organized the first free public vaccination program for smallpox in 1869. Toward the end of his career he held several important posts: sanitary superintendent of the city (1869–70), registrar of vital statistics (1873–76), and original member of the New York State Board of Health (1880).

Joseph S. Lieber

Harrison, Hubert Henry (*b* St. Croix, Danish West Indies, 1883; *d* New York City, 1927). Activist. He moved to New York City in 1900, where he worked as a laborer during the day and studied at night. In 1909 he joined the Socialist Party, for which he wrote theoretical articles such as "Socialism and the Negro" (1912). In these he argued for the primacy of the black struggle in the socialist cause, and he became well known as a lecturer and soapbox orator. In 1914 he left the socialists, whom he saw as racist. He organized the Liberty League of Afro-Americans in June 1917, which was the first militant group of the "New Negro" movement, and in its newspaper the *Voice* he called for organizing labor, armed defense against lynch violence, federal action to protect civil rights, and socialism. When the league disbanded soon after, he briefly rejoined the Socialist Party, edited the radical black periodical *New Negro*, and led the Colored National Liberty Congress, which advocated laws against lynching. In 1920 he joined the United Negro Improvement Association, led by his former disciple Marcus Garvey, and he briefly edited its newspaper *Negro World*. Dissatisfied with Garvey's plans to establish colonies of American blacks in Africa, he attempted to organize a Liberty Party to work for civil rights. He took American citizenship in 1922 and became a lecturer for the New York Public Library, for which he helped to organize the Schomburg Collection for Research in Black Culture. He formed a group in 1924 called the International Colored Unity League that proved short-lived, and supported the creation of a black separatist state in the South. Harrison wrote two books of essays, *The Negro and the Nation* (1917) and *When Africa Awakes* (1920).

Theodore G. Vincent: *Black Power and the Garvey Movement* (Berkeley, Calif.: Ramparts, 1971)

Greg Robinson

Harrison, Wallace K(irkman) (*b* Worcester, Mass., 28 Sept 1895; *d* New York City, 2 Dec 1981). Architect. He moved in 1916 to New York City, where he was a draftsman for McKim, Mead and White and also worked in the atelier of Harvey Wiley Corbett and the firm of Bertram Grosvenor Goodhue. He developed a style that incorporated classical and space-age motifs in such structures as the Trylon and Perisphere at the World's Fair of 1939–40 and the main terminal at La Guardia Airport (1964). He helped to form the firm of Harrison, Fouilhoux and Abramovitz, which was responsible for many of the city's distinctive skyscrapers; with Raymond M. Hood he designed Rockefeller Center. Among Harrison's best-known buildings are the United Nations (1953; for illustration see UNITED NATIONS) and Lincoln Center for the Performing Arts (1966).

Victoria Newhouse: *Wallace K. Harrison, Architect* (New York: Rizzoli, 1989)

Edward A. Eigen

Harrisville. Obsolete name of SANDY GROUND.

Harry N. Abrams. Firm of book publishers formed in 1950 by Harry N. Abrams as the first American publisher devoted solely to books about art. It began its operations at a time when the American market for art books was limited, restricted in particular by the inferior quality and prohibitive cost of American color reproduction. By opening an office in Amsterdam in 1953 the firm was able to take advantage of European expertise and technology, and it became the first publisher to issue art books of high quality in large quantities and at moderate prices for the American market. The firm was acquired in 1966 by the Times Mirror Company, and Abrams left to set up a new firm, Abbeville. In the mid 1990s the offices were at 100 5th Avenue in Manhattan.

Eileen K. Cheng

Harsenville. Former neighborhood on the Upper West Side of Manhattan, bounded to the north by 81st Street, to the east by Central Park West, to the south by 68th Street, and to the west by the Hudson River. It was named after Jacob Harsen and his family, who moved to the area in 1763 and built a large farm there; such prominent families as the de Lanceys, the Dyckmans, and the Somerindycks owned farms nearby. In 1803 Harsenville Road was built through what later became Central Park. A Dutch Reformed church was formed by the Harsens in 1805. The rural character of the area changed when schools, churches, a post office, shops, and saloons were built during the 1830s and 1840s. In the 1860s Mayor Fernando Wood lived at 77th Street and 11th Avenue (now West End Avenue). The Dutch Reformed church was eventually demolished and Harsenville Road was torn up to make way for Central Park. By the 1880s the Upper West Side was developed and the name of the neighborhood disused.

James Bradley

Hart, Kitty Carlisle [Conn, Katherine] (*b* New Orleans, 3 Sept 1914). Arts administrator and actress. She studied at the Royal Academy of the Dramatic Arts and made her acting début in 1932 under the stage name Kitty Carlisle. In 1933 she signed a contract with Paramount Pictures, and she appeared in two films with Bing Crosby and in *A Night at* *the Opera* (1935) with the Marx Brothers. After marrying the playwright Moss Hart she continued to act for several years and was a regular panelist on the television quiz show "To Tell the Truth" from 1956 to 1977. She was named the head of the state conference on women by Governor Nelson A. Rockefeller in 1966, a vice-chairwoman of the New York State Council on the Arts in 1971, and the head of the council in 1976 (reappointed in 1982). She became best known as a prominent member of fashionable society and as an enthusiastic advocate for the arts in the state and city.

Rohit T. Aggarwala

Hart, Lorenz (Milton) (*b* New York City, 2 May 1895; *d* New York City, 22 Nov 1943). Lyricist. He grew up in Harlem and graduated from the Columbia University School of Journalism in 1917. His first important musical was *Dearest Enemy*, written with Richard Rodgers and performed at the Knickerbocker Theatre in 1925; the show included "Where the Hudson River Flows," one of his many songs inspired by New York City. He enjoyed a long partnership with Rodgers, whose romantic music he underpinned with wry and often cynical lyrics. Hart lived from 1943 at the Delmonico at 502 Park Avenue and 59th Street and during the last decade of his life at 320 Central Park West.

Samuel Marx and Jan Clayton: *Rodgers and Hart: Bewitched, Bothered, and Bedeviled* (New York: G. P. Putnam's Sons, 1976)

Marc Ferris

Hart Island. The site of the largest potter's field in the United States. Originally known variously as Spectacle Island and Little Minnefords and now sometimes called Hart's Island, it is situated in Long Island Sound, just northeast of City Island, and is part of the Bronx. Acquired by Oliver de Lancey of West Farms in 1774 and later owned by the Haight and Rodman families and by John Hunter, it was bought by the City of New York in 1869. The first interment was Louisa Van Slyke, an orphan who died in that year at Charity Hospital. More than 750,000 persons, all of them unclaimed and many of them unidentified, are now buried three deep in unmarked, mass graves. A granite cross erected in 1902 bears the inscription "He Calleth His children by name." At one time inmates from the Reformatory Prison on the island buried the dead; the task is now handled by prisoners from Rikers Island who volunteer. The only access to Hart Island is by a ferry run by the Department of Corrections from Fordham Street on City Island.

Kenneth T. Jackson

Hartley, Robert M(ilham) (*b* Cockermouth, England, 17 Feb 1796; *d* New York City, 3 March 1881). Philanthropist. After moving to New York City from England he opened a mercantile firm. Inspired by evangelical Protestantism, he retired to direct the New York City Temperance Society; he later became one of the city's most influential philanthropists as the general agent of the Association for Improving the Condition of the Poor from 1843 to 1876. Although he denounced indiscriminate charity and distinguished between the "worthy" and "unworthy" poor, he also recognized the evils of slum environments and focused the efforts of the association on public health and housing reform. Hartley helped to form the Society for the Relief of the Ruptured and Crippled.

See also Dairying.

Marilyn Thornton Williams

Hartmann, (Carl) Sadakichi (*b* Island of Deshima, Nagasaki Harbor, Japan, 8 Nov 1867; *d* St. Petersburg, Fla., 21 Nov 1944). Art critic and writer. Born to a Japanese mother and a German father, he was brought up by relatives in Germany and sent to Philadelphia when he was about fifteen. He reputedly worked as Walt Whitman's assistant before traveling in France, where he befriended the symbolist poet Stéphane Mallarmé. He spent most of his career in Greenwich Village, where he became known as a flamboyant personality and wrote esoteric plays that were considered sacrilegious. Widely respected nevertheless for his writings on painting and photography, he contributed frequently to Alfred Stieglitz's *Camera Work*, often using the pseudonym Sidney Allan, and wrote *A History of American Art* (1902), in which he evaluated American art with a prescient understanding of the evolving modernist movement. He spent his later years in southern California. Sadakichi's collected writings, edited by Jane Calhoun Weaver, were published in 1991.

Patricia Hills

Harugari. Fraternal order formed in New York City in 1847 by Philipp Merkle to promote German language and culture and the ideals of "friendship, affection, and humanity." Most of its members were artisans or skilled workers, and the group maintained close ties to the labor movement. By 1873 the order had sixty-two lodges with about seven thousand members in the metropolitan area. Although Harugari suffered a decline in membership during the next decade, it recovered and continued operating into the twentieth century.

Stanley Nadel

Harvard Club. A club formed in 1865 for persons associated with the university who lived or worked in New York City. Its clubhouse at 27 West 44th Street was designed by the firm of McKim, Mead and White and constructed in phases from 1893 to 1915. Of neo-Georgian design with dark red "Harvard" brick, it is a very handsome building inside and out, and its great Harvard Hall is one of the most impressive interior spaces in the city. The club has dining rooms of various types and sizes, a fine library and reading room, and accommodations for squash and other indoor activities.

James E. Mooney

Harvey, George (Brinton McClellan) (*b* Peacham, Vt., 16 Feb 1864; *d* Dublin, N.H., 20 Aug 1928). Newspaperman and businessman. He worked for a newspaper in Vermont before moving to New York City, where he joined the staff of the *New York World*; he became its editor in 1891. After a few years he left to work on Wall Street, where he made a fortune. In 1899 he bought the *North American Review*, naming himself its editor; he took over *Harper's Weekly* in 1901. A strong supporter of Woodrow Wilson's presidential candidacy in 1912, he later opposed the Fourteen Points and endorsed Warren G. Harding in the election of 1920. Appointed ambassador to London during the 1920s, Harvey also edited the *Washington Post* and wrote a biography of Henry Clay Frick that was published in 1928.

Willis Fletcher Johnson: *George Harvey: "A Passionate Patriot"* (Boston: Houghton Mifflin, 1929)

James E. Mooney

Haryou–Act. A comprehensive anti-poverty program launched in 1964. It combined the efforts of two organizations: Harlem Youth Unlimited (Haryou), inspired by a proposal of the psychologist Kenneth Clark and funded in 1964 with grants of $100,000 from the city (made by Mayor Robert F. Wagner) and $230,000 from the House Committee on Education and Labor (the results of effort by Representative Adam Clayton Powell Jr.); and Associated Community Teams (Act), established by the President's Committee on Juvenile Delinquency. The two groups differed in their methods, with Haryou focusing on education, job training, and lobbying and Act inclined toward rent strikes and the organizing of neighborhood boards. Haryou–Act achieved some success before ceasing operations in 1968, and its emphasis on community initiatives and youth programs proved influential.

Herbert Krasny: *Beyond Welfare: Poverty in the Supercity* (New York: Holt, Rinehart and Winston, 1966)

Emilyn L. Brown

Hasidim. Adherents of a mystical, revivalist form of Judaism that is inspired in part by the kabbala and that celebrates various aspects of everyday life, frequently with song and dance. Hasidism was founded in eighteenth-century Poland by Israel ben Eliezer, a rabbi known as the Baal Shem Tov. There are more than 100,000 Hasidic Jews in New York City, most of whom live in Brooklyn. Tensions among Hasidim stem from differences over doctrine and leadership; there is also conflict with other residents of Brooklyn, especially racial minorities, over such issues as the construction of schools and police protection. The largest Hasidic sects are the LUBAVITCHERS and the SATMARS; others include the Ger, the Bobov, the Belz, the Tzelem, the Stolin, and the Papa.

Haskins and Sells. Accounting firm established in New York City in 1886 by Charles Waldo Haskins, a resident of New York City and a relative of Ralph Waldo Emerson. It was one of the most prominent accounting firms in the United States with American rather than British sponsorship. In its early years the firm was commissioned to reorganize the accounting system of the federal government. It eventually became one of the "Big Eight" national accounting firms. In 1978 it merged with a British firm, Deloitte and Company, to form Deloitte, Haskins and Sells, serving international clients, while remaining known as Haskins and Sells in the United States. In 1989 the firm merged with Touche Ross to become Deloitte and Touche.

David Grayson Allen and Kathleen McDermott: *Accounting for Success: A History of Price Waterhouse in America, 1890–1990* (Boston: Harvard Business School Press, 1990)

Paul J. Miranti Jr.: *Accountancy Comes of Age: The Development of an American Profession, 1886–1940* (Chapel Hill: University of North Carolina Press, 1990)

Kathleen McDermott

Hassam, (Frederick) Childe (*b* Dorchester [now in Boston], 17 Oct 1859; *d* East Hampton, N.Y., 27 Aug 1935). Painter. After settling in New York City in 1889 he opened a studio on 5th Avenue and 17th Street, joined the Society of American Artists, and frequented the Players, where he met Julian Alden Weir and other artists with whom he formed the group known as Ten American Painters in 1898. He worked in an impressionist style and painted many street scenes of New York City, including *Fifth Avenue in Winter* (1899). In 1913 he displayed his work at the Armory Show. Hassam divided his time during the last forty years of his life between his home in East Hampton, Long Island, and his studio on West 57th Street in Manhattan.

Stephen Weinstein

Hastings. Name used from 1664 to 1683 by NEWTOWN.

hatting and millinery. The hatting and millinery industries became concentrated in New York City in the early nineteenth century. The styles of men's and women's hats were set in the city, which was the center for fashion in the United States. One of the first prominent men's hatters was Charles Knox, who began his career as an apprentice for Leary and Company, a firm on Broad Street in which he eventually became a foreman. At the age of nineteen he opened a small shop in 1838 that became known as "the hole in the wall" at 110 Fulton Street; he later moved successively to 128 Fulton Street and 212 Broadway. Competition arose about this time among the many small firms in the city making men's silk and beaver hats and led in 1850 to the "battle of the hatters," waged by Knox, John Genin, and Nicholas Espenscheid. In 1857 Robert Dunlap, an apprentice to Knox who had been denied a raise, opened his own business at 577 Broadway and became the most formidable competitor of Knox, with whom he dominated the hatting trade in the city by the 1870s; he eventually opened a large factory at 60 Nostrand Avenue in Brooklyn. In the 1870s Knox's firm was reorganized by his son Edward M. Knox, who opened a "business palace" beneath the Fifth Avenue Hotel at Madison Square. The Knox Hat Company opened two large factories in the 1890s in Brooklyn, at 340 Fulton Street and at the corner of Grand and St. Mark's avenues; its hats were sold throughout the United States, France, Germany, and South America. In 1919 it merged with Dunlap's firm. In addition to hat manufacturing New York City became the national center for importing and jobbing.

Like hatting, millinery (the making of women's hats) was a business conducted by small firms that competed intensely with each other; many retail shops were run by women and employed five persons or fewer. Prominent wholesale millinery manufacturers in the city in the late nineteenth century and the early twentieth included Hill Brothers, Ridley and Sons, and John Miles. Retail millinery offered unusual opportunities in business for women, and a few including Lilly Daché ran successful enterprises into the 1950s and 1960s.

Robert R. Updegraff: *The Story of Two Famous Hatters* (New York: Knox Hat Company, 1926)

Rebuilding an Industry: The History of the Eastern Women's Headwear Association (New York: Eastern Women's Headwear Association, n.d. [1951])

David Bensman: *The Practice of Solidarity: American Hat Finishers in the Nineteenth Century* (Urbana: University of Illinois Press, 1985)

Wendy Gamber

Havemeyer, Henry O(sborne) (*b* New York City, 18 Oct 1847; *d* Commack, N.Y., 4 Dec 1907). Businessman. He was the son of Frederick C. Havemeyer Jr. and made most of the deals that permitted his family to control the sugar industry. Ruthless and astute, he was the chief architect of the Sugar Trust (1887), which declined after his death. A street in the heart of Williamsburg is named for the family.

J. C. Havemeyer: *Life, Letters and Addresses of John Craig Havemeyer* (New York: Fleming H. Revell, 1914)

James Bradley

Havemeyer, William F(rederick) (*b* New York City, 12 Feb 1804; *d* New York City, 30 Nov 1874). Businessman and mayor. The son of the sugar refiner William Havemeyer (1770–1851), he was born at 31 Pine Street. In 1828 he formed a partnership in the sugar business with a cousin, which he left in 1842 to enter local politics. A Democrat and a member of Tammany Hall, he was elected mayor nonconsecutively in 1845 and 1848 largely on his reputation as a sound financial manager with integrity. After leaving office he resumed his career in business and then made a triumphant return to politics in 1872 when the scandals of the Tweed Ring prompted him to seek the mayoralty as a Republican. His independent style was not suited to the political patronage system of the time, and he lost the election.

J. C. Havemeyer: *Life, Letters and Addresses of John Craig Havemeyer* (New York: Fleming H. Revell, 1914)

See also UNEMPLOYMENT MOVEMENTS.

James Bradley

Sugar refinery of Havemeyer and Elder in Williamsburg, ca *1860*

Hawkins, Edler Garnet (*b* New York City, 13 June 1908; *d* Princeton, N.J., 13 Dec 1977). Minister and civil rights leader. He attended Bloomfield College in New Jersey (AB 1935) and Union Theological Seminary (BD 1938). As the pastor of St. Augustine Presbyterian Church in the Bronx in 1938–70 he was noted for establishing a church youth ministry and for confronting racism within the church. He helped to form the national Commission on Church and Race of the Presbyterian Church and in 1964 became the first black elected moderator of the General Assembly of the United Presbyterian Church in the United States of America. He spent the later years of his career, from 1970 to 1977, as a professor of theology at Princeton Theological Seminary.

David Meerse

Hawkins, Erick [Frederick] (*b* Trinidad, Colo., 23 April 1909; *d* New York City, 23 Nov 1994). Dancer, choreographer, and artistic director. In New York City he studied at the School of American Ballet and danced with the American Ballet (1935–37) and Ballet Caravan (1936–39). In 1938 he became the first male member of the modern dance company of Martha Graham, eventually becoming her dance partner and husband. By 1951 his associations with Graham ended and he formed his own company. He evolved an innovative choreographic style based on smooth, unhurried, meditative movement, reflecting his interest in Buddhist philosophy and American Indian culture.

Jean Morrison Brown, ed.: *The Vision of Modern Dance* (Princeton, N.J.: Princeton Book, 1979), 92–96

Brenda Dixon Gottschild

Hayden, Palmer (Cole) (*b* Wide Water, Stafford County, Va., 1890; *d* New York City, 18 Feb 1973). Painter. After serving in the First World War he moved to New York City in 1919 and studied art at Cooper Union and at the Boothbay Art Colony in Maine. At the urging of Alain Locke he painted marine subjects and then African subjects (*Fétiche and Fleurs*, 1926). In 1927 he went to Europe, but he continued to exhibit his works in New York City with the encouragement of the Harmon Foundation and to explore black subjects (*Nous Quatre à Paris*, 1930). He returned to New York City in 1932 and for the next decade concentrated on characterizations of rural black life. As his works became better known many blacks criticized his caricatured figures as being too close to prevalent white stereotypes of blacks.

Edmund Gaither

Hayden Planetarium. Planetarium built in 1935 on the grounds of the American Museum of Natural History, at 79th Street and Central Park West. Its centerpiece, a Zeiss projector, was used in programs to show the movements of stars, the rising and setting of the sun and moon, and the precession of the equinoxes. During the Second World War the U.S. Army and Navy used the planetarium as an instruction center for courses on celestial navigation. Exhibits of rockets, satellites, and astronautics were added in the 1950s. With the advent of laser technology the planetarium offered dramatic programs on black holes and supernovas in the 1980s, using special photography, synthesized sound and music, and a Zeiss VI Star Projector. The Hayden Planetarium is formally a part of the American Museum of Natural History.

Ronald Rainger

Hayes, Helen [Brown, Helen Hayes] (*b* Washington, 10 Oct 1900; *d* Nyack, N.Y., 17 March 1993). Actress. At the age of eight she moved to New York City and won her first role on Broadway as a mime in Victor Herbert's *Old Dutch*, which opened at the Herald Square Theatre on 22 November 1909. After her success in Norma Besant's *Coquette* (1927) she appeared in hundreds of productions, becoming best known for playing the leading roles in *Caesar and Cleopatra* (1925), *Mary of Scotland* (1935), and *Queen Regina* (1935). During a career of more than sixty years on the stage she won three Tony awards; she also won Academy awards for her performances in *The Sin of Madelon Claudet* (1931) and *Airport* (1970). Often called the "first lady of American theater," Hayes was president of the American Theater Wing and the American National Theater Academy and directed women's activities for the March of Dimes. In 1983 the Little Theater on West 44th Street was renamed in her honor.

Janet Frankston

Helen Hayes, 1977

Hayes, Patrick (Joseph) (*b* New York City, 20 Nov 1867; *d* Monticello, N.Y., 4 Sept 1938). Cardinal. Ordained on 8 September 1892, he graduated from Catholic University (STL 1894) and was the assistant of the Church of St. Gabriel in the East 30s (now defunct) from 1894 to 1902. He was John Farley's secretary before becoming the chancellor and president of Cathedral College (1903–14). On 24 November 1917 he was appointed bishop ordinary to the chaplains of the U.S. Army and Navy; on 10 March 1919 he was appointed an archbishop. One of his greatest concerns was social welfare: he signed the Bishops' Program of Social Reconstruction (1919), endorsed Irish independence but not violent revolution (1919–20), and promoted temperance but not Prohibition. He opposed a federal amendment prohibiting child labor on the grounds that it unduly restricted parental authority. On 1 May 1920 he launched the first fund-raising campaign for the Catholic Charities, an organization with which he remained closely associated. After his election as a cardinal on 24 March 1924 he remained active in workers' issues, encouraged the activities of the Catholic Worker movement begun by Dorothy Day and Peter Maurin and the Catholic Trade Union in his archdiocese, sponsored the Catholic Industrial Conference in 1933, and gave seminars to his clergymen in labor ethics (1937–38). He also denounced a proposal by the American Birth Control League to distribute contraceptives to welfare recipients on the grounds that the government should instead eliminate poverty (December 1935). A supporter of the Legion of Decency, he wrote a letter on moral standards in the theater that resulted in a measure of self-censorship (April 1937). Hayes is buried beneath St. Patrick's Cathedral.

John Bernard Kelly: *Cardinal Hayes: One of Ourselves* (New York: Farrar and Rinehart, 1940)

Mary Elizabeth Brown

Haynes, George Edmund (*b* Pine Bluff, Ark., 11 May 1880; *d* New York City, 8 Jan 1960). Reformer. He took part in the Association for the Protection of Colored Women (1905), the Committee for Improving the Industrial Conditions of Negroes in New York (1906), and the Committee on Urban Conditions among Negroes (1910), was a founder of the National Urban League (1911), and became the first black graduate of the New York School of Philanthropy (later the School of Social Work of Columbia University; 1910) and the first to receive a PhD from Columbia (in economics; 1912). Later he taught black history and social work at City College of New York (1951–59). Haynes stressed interracial cooperation. He wrote *The Negro at Work in New York City: A Study in Economic*

Progress (1912). His wife, Elizabeth Ross Haynes, was also a reformer.

Samuel Kelton Roberts: "Crucible for a Vision: The Work of George Edmund Haynes and the Commission on Race Relations" (thesis, Columbia University, 1975)

Thea Arnold

Hays, Jacob (*b* Bedford, N.Y., 5 May 1772; *d* New York City, 24 June 1850). Constable. Appointed marshal of New York City in 1798, he was named high constable in 1801 and held the position to the end of his life, even though the constabulary was abolished when the police force was formed in 1844. He became famous in the United States and England for his ability to control unruly mobs through sheer force of character, and for his abilities as a detective; he was particularly effective against counterfeiters, arsonists, and burglars. In a sensational court case in 1828 he proved the innocence of Timothy Redmond, a well-known hotel keeper who was widely believed to be guilty of fraud in a case of mistaken identity. From 1814 until his death Hays lived at several locations on Lispenard Street.

George A. Thompson, Jr.

HBO. See HOME BOX OFFICE.

headquarters. Corporate headquarters became concentrated in New York City at the end of the nineteenth century, when proximity to centers of transportation and communication was increasingly important to businesses with operations extending across the country. Because of its role in finance the city attracted a disproportionate number of the country's largest corporate headquarters, which initially were clustered in lower Manhattan around Wall Street. Its position was solidified when Standard Oil moved its headquarters to the city from Cleveland in 1882. After the rapid transit system opened and tracks north of Grand Central Terminal were covered (1910), publishers, chemical and drug companies, and eventually airlines formed a second business district between 42nd and 60th streets, and for the next fifty years construction east of 6th Avenue slowed only during the Depression and the Second World War. Corporate headquarters were widely seen as a symbol of lasting economic strength even though a study in 1959 showed that they employed only 12 percent of the city's office workers. By the mid 1960s New York City was home to the headquarters of 136 of the nation's five hundred largest firms, more than any other American city.

When an economic decline during the late 1960s and early 1970s severely hurt the city, a number of firms moved to suburban New York State, New Jersey, and Connecticut, where they found larger and cheaper facilities, a stabler work force, lower taxes, and less crime. Between 1969 and 1976 only four corporations opened headquarters in the city, and fifty-five corporations among the largest five hundred moved out. By the mid 1970s some companies moved to such cities as Dallas, Houston, Los Angeles, and Tulsa, Oklahoma, posing a serious threat to the economy of the metropolitan area. Despite economic growth during the 1980s the city suffered a net loss of corporate headquarters, but it also achieved some gains, as service industries such as banking, insurance, and transportation became stronger nationwide. Between 1981 and 1986 fifteen corporations among the largest five hundred moved out of the city, but eight cor-

Industrial Firms in the Fortune 500 Based in New York City

(Number in parentheses following the year indicates the total number of firms in the Fortune 500 based in New York City. Number in parentheses following the name of the firm indicates the rank of the firm in the Fortune 500.)

1955 (131)
1. Standard Oil of New Jersey (2)
2. U.S. Steel (4)
3. General Electric (6)
4. Western Electric (12)
5. Socony Mobil Oil (13)
6. Texaco (15)
7. Shell Oil (16)
8. National Dairy Products (20)
9. Union Carbide (22)
10. Sinclair Oil (25)

1960 (127)
1. Standard Oil (2)
2. General Electric (4)
3. U.S. Steel (5)
4. Socony Mobil Oil (6)
5. Texaco (8)
6. Western Electric (10)
7. General Dynamics (15)
8. Shell Oil (17)
9. National Dairy Products (20)
10. Union Carbide (24)

1965 (128)
1. Standard Oil (2)
2. General Electric (4)
3. Socony Mobil Oil (6)
4. U. S. Steel (7)
5. Texaco (8)
6. Western Electric (10)
7. Shell Oil (15)
8. Union Carbide (21)
9. RCA (24)
10. General Telephone and Electronics (25)

1970 (117)
1. Standard Oil (2)
2. General Electric (4)
3. Mobil Oil (6)
4. International Telephone and Telegraph (8)
5. Texaco (9)
6. Western Electric (10)
7. U.S. Steel (12)
8. Shell Oil (19)
9. General Telephone and Electronics (20)
10. RCA (21)

1975 (90)
1. Exxon (formerly Standard Oil of New Jersey) (1)
2. Texaco (3)
3. Mobil Oil (5)
4. International Telephone and Telegraph (11)

(continued)

Industrial Firms in the Fortune 500 Based in New York City *(Continued)*

5. Western Electric (18)
6. Union Carbide (21)
7. RCA (34)
8. W. R. Grace (47)
9. Borden (51)
10. Amerada Hess (54)

1980 (81)
1. Exxon (1)
2. Texaco (3)
3. International Telephone and Telegraph (13)
4. Western Electric (22)
5. Union Carbide (27)
6. RCA (41)
7. Amerada Hess (43)
8. Philip Morris (45)
9. W. R. Grace (51)
10. Gulf and Western Industries (57)

1985 (62)
1. Exxon (1)
2. Texaco (3)
3. American Telephone and Telegraph (8)
4. International Telephone and Telegraph (25)
5. Philip Morris (27)
6. Amerada Hess (48)
7. W. R. Grace (49)
8. Sperry Corp. (63)
9. Colgate–Palmolive (73)
10. Borden (77)

1990 (41)
1. Philip Morris (7)
2. RJR Nabisco Holdings (24)
3. Bristol–Myers Squibb (50)
4. Unilever U.S. (55)
5. Borden (64)
6. Amerada Hess (68)
7. American Home Products (70)
8. W. R. Grace (71)
9. Pfizer (73)
10. Hanson Industries (75)

Note: Firms included in the Fortune 500 derive more than 50 percent of their sales from manufacturing, mining, or both.
Source: Fortune Magazine

Compiled by James Bradley

porations in the service sector moved into it. Zoning changes eventually prompted the construction of offices west of 6th Avenue. A survey by the Regional Plan Association in 1987 of the one thousand leading firms in the country (including both the manufacturing and service sectors) showed that the city had 121 corporate headquarters, far more than any other city; another eighty were outside the city but within the metropolitan area. As many firms became part of conglomerates and multinational corporations or were decentralized, the role of the city as a hub of corporate headquarters remained unclear, especially as developments in communications diminished the importance of headquarters by permitting central operations to be carried out in offices across the country.

Wolfgang Quante: "The Relocation of Corporate Headquarters from New York" (diss., Columbia University, 1974)

Headquarters in the Region (New York: Regional Plan Association, 1987)

New York in the Global Economy (New York: Regional Plan Association, 1987)

Stanley Buder

health insurance. The earliest forms of health insurance in New York City date to the nineteenth century, when disability and income-replacement insurance became available and health care was directly provided by unions, employers, and mutual assistance societies. During the Depression the need for more reliable forms of insurance led to the development of a local branch of Blue Cross called the Associated Hospital Service (AHS), a nonprofit corporation formed in 1935 under the auspices of the United Hospital Fund (the philanthropic wing of the city's voluntary hospitals). From the outset the service covered twenty-one days a year of in-patient care at most acute-care hospitals in the city. By the early 1940s it had several million subscribers and was the largest branch of Blue Cross in the nation. From 1945 reimbursement for physicians' services was offered by a local branch of Blue Shield called the United Medical Service, set up with the sponsorship of the AHS and the city's medical professionals. The first health maintenance organization in New York City, the Health Insurance Plan (HIP), was formed in 1944 through the efforts of Mayor Fiorello H. La Guardia and the city's labor unions.

The early predominance of nonprofit health insurers in New York City was due in part to the subsidies they received from the state and federal governments, including Medicaid for the poor and Medicare for the elderly (both implemented in 1966). The state also controlled the rate of increase in hospital costs, thus allowing Empire Blue Cross and Blue Shield to continue offering open enrollment and remain competitive with commercial insurers such as the Guardian Life Insurance Company of America, Aetna Life and Casualty, the Prudential Insurance Company of America, and the New York Life Insurance Company, which entered the health insurance market in the 1940s. Unlike Blue Shield, which operated according to the principle of 100 percent reimbursement, commercial insurers covered only 80 percent of the cost of physicians' services, after the payment of a deductible. Eventually the commercial firms dominated the sale of major-medical policies, but the field remained highly competitive: no single commercial insurer in the city garnered more than a small share of the total market.

The primary market for health insurance shifted from individuals in the 1930s to employer-sponsored groups in the 1940s and 1950s, as labor unions increasingly demanded health insurance for their members and the federal government encouraged the purchase of group policies by making the cost of premiums tax-deductible for employers, and the value of benefits tax-exempt for employees. Employers in New York City responded early to these new developments, while at the same time changes were made in the means of setting premiums: the original system of "community rating," which spread risks across large pools and charged the same premium to all persons with the same policy, was replaced by one based on experience ratings and on the medical profile of each policyholder. The effects of the change were to increase premiums for policyholders in high-risk groups, increase the incentive for insurers to seek out customers who were healthy, and in general make the business more competitive. To avoid being driven from the market entirely, nonprofit health insurers were forced to use experience ratings for their larger employer groups; they derived sufficient profits from these customers to be able to retain community ratings for smaller groups and individuals, as well as an open enrollment policy.

The combination of community ratings, open enrollment, and a relatively generous state Medicaid program made for a higher rate of insurance coverage in New York City than in most other American cities. Achievements in the availability of medical insurance in the city were nonetheless called into question by steep increases in health care costs from the 1970s into the 1990s. Nonprofit insurers struggled to sustain their open enrollment policies, and many small groups and individuals were unable to afford health insurance at all. Most employers shifted part of the cost of premiums to their employees and implemented a variety of cost-cutting measures.

Health Insurance Plan of Greater New York: Health and Medical Care in New York City (Cambridge: Harvard University Press, 1957)

Robert A. Padgug

Health Insurance Plan [HIP]. Nonprofit health maintenance organization formed in 1944 under Mayor Fiorello H. La Guardia for the benefit of municipal workers and other middle-income wage earners. Organized and regulated under the state health code, it offers medical and hospital services through a network of more than fifty physician groups in the metropolitan region. In the mid 1990s the Health Insurance Plan had nearly one million members.

Amy Jo Schein: "Implications of Public Law 93-222 for a Prototype Health Maintenance Organization" (thesis, Yale University, 1978)

Robert A. Padgug

Health Policy Advisory Center [Health/PAC]. Research and advocacy organization formed in 1968. The impetus behind its formation was a report written by Robb Burlage for the Institute for Policy Studies that criticized the affiliation agreements between medical schools in New York City and the public hospitals that the agreements were intended to benefit. The center published the books *The American Health Empire* (1970) and *Prognosis: Negative* (1976) as well as the *Health/PAC Bulletin* (1968–). The premise underlying the proposals advanced by Health/PAC is that health care is a human right. Its offices are at 853 Broadway.

Lily M. Hoffman: *The Politics of Knowledge: Activist Movements in Medicine and Planning* (Albany: State University of New York Press, 1989)

Susan M. Reverby

Hearn's. Firm of retailers formed in 1842 at 425 Broadway near Canal Street by George Arnold Hearn Jr., an Englishman from the Isle of Wight who had earlier gone into business with his uncle Aaron Arnold. Under the stewardship of his son the establishment was renamed James A. Hearn and Son, moved to West 14th Street between 5th and 6th avenues, and became the prosperous rival of Macy's nearby. The stores fought a legendary price war: on one day in 1902 each tried to outdo the other by cutting the price of its silk, a yard of which sold at the beginning of the day for forty-one cents and by the end of the day for a penny. Hearn's closed in 1955.

Robert Hendrickson: *The Grand Emporiums* (New York: Stein and Day, 1979)

Leslie Gourse

Hearst, William Randolph (*b* San Francisco, 29 April 1863; *d* Beverly Hills, Calif., 4 Aug 1951). Newspaper publisher and political leader. After graduating from Harvard University he became highly successful as the proprietor in San Francisco of the *Enquirer*. He later moved to New York City, where he took up quarters at 1865 Broadway (now 1123 Broadway). Seeking to draw away readers from Joseph Pulitzer's *Evening World*, he bought the *Morning Journal* in 1895, retaining Arthur Brisbane as the editor. In the following years his heated competition gave rise to "yellow journalism," which was characterized by sensationalized and sometimes falsified news stories, trivialized reporting, and exaggerated editorials. By focusing on Spanish atrocities in Cuba, Hearst helped to mold public opinion against Spain, contributing to the country's drift toward the Spanish–American War in 1898. He considered his "new journalism" an answer to the needs of a democratic society, and in daily newspapers selling for one cent he offered expanded sports coverage and illustrations, introduced comic strips such as "The Katzenjammer Kids" (1897) that became extremely popular, and covered events ignored by the "élite" press, especially workers' issues. The circulation of his newspapers exceeded a million by 1900, and in 1901 he renamed the morning edition the *American* and the evening edition the *Journal*. During these years he lived at Worth House on the corner of 25th Street across from Worth Square (1897–1900) and at 123 Lexington Avenue (about 1900 to 1907, now the Arthur House National Historic Landmark).

After the turn of the century Hearst used his newspapers to advance his political career. Considering himself an urban Jeffersonian, he remained an independent Democrat with radical leanings during the Progressive era and was elected to two terms in the U.S. Congress (1903–7) from the eleventh district in Manhattan. In 1905 he sought the mayoralty as a member of the Municipal Ownership League but lost to George B. McClellan Jr., the candidate backed by Tammany Hall, in a disputed election; in 1906 he unsuccessfully sought the governorship as a Democrat. About 1907 he moved to the Clarendon Apartments at 137 Riverside Drive. He sought public office into the 1920s but never again won a nomination. He alternately supported Charles F. Murphy, the boss of Tammany Hall, and quarreled with him, but his bitterest political feud, which began in 1917 and lasted until 1925, was with Alfred E. Smith. Although the two differed little on policy issues, they clashed over patronage, judicial nominations, Smith's handling of the milk producers' strike while he was governor, the city's transit problems in 1919–20, support for Hearst's ally Mayor John F. Hylan, and the leadership of Tammany Hall after Murphy's death in 1924. George Olvany's ascendancy as the new boss later the same year and James J. Walker's defeat of Hylan in a primary in 1925 sealed Smith's victory over Hearst in controlling the Democratic Party in the city.

By 1922 Hearst's publishing empire included twenty daily newspapers, two wire services, the colossal King Features Syndicate, and half a dozen magazines, many of which were published in New York City. He remained active in politics, mainly on the national level, and toward the end of his life became a conservative critic and moved to California. Between 1928 and 1938 he occasionally lived at the Ritz Tower Hotel at 465 Park Avenue. At his death his organization (managed from 1937 by Clarence Shearn) still included two newspapers in New York City, the *Journal–American* and a tabloid, the *Mirror*.

W. A. Swanberg: *Citizen Hearst: A Biography of William Randolph Hearst* (New York: Charles Scribner's Sons, 1961)

Roy Everett Littlefield III: *William Randolph Hearst: His Role in American Progressivism* (Lanham, Md.: University Press of America, 1980)

For illustration see YELLOW JOURNALISM.

Robert F. Wesser

Hearst Magazines. A division of the Hearst Corporation with headquarters at 959 8th Avenue in Manhattan. It traces its origins to 1903, when William Randolph Hearst began publishing *Motor*. In the following years he acquired *Cosmopolitan* (1905), *Good Housekeeping* (1911), and other periodicals. Hearst Magazine became known for its diverse output, which it achieved in part by testing new magazines through sales of the first issue at newsstands rather than in costly direct-mail packages sent to potential consumers. Over the years its publications came to include the magazines *Colonial Homes*, *Country Living*, *Esquire*, *Harper's Bazaar*, *House Beautiful*, *Motorboating and Sailing*, *Popular Mechanics*, *Redbook*, *Smart Money*, *Town and Country*, and *Victoria*.

Melissa M. Merritt

Heartland Village. Neighborhood in west central Staten Island, bounded to the north by Rockland Avenue, to the east by Forest Hill Road, to the south by Richmond Hill Road, and to the west by Richmond Avenue. It is part of Community District 2. A middle-class residential neighborhood with a suburban character, it had its origins as a single development designed and built in the southeastern section of New Springville in 1968–71. The original development consisted of detached and semidetached one-family houses of two and three stories, with built-in garages and underground utility connections. The area adjoins the Staten Island Mall (1973) and centers on Public School 69 and Intermediate School 72 (1975).

Charles L. Sachs

Hebrew Free Loan Society. A nonprofit organization that grants interest-free loans, primarily to the Jewish community. It was formed in 1892 at the Wilner Synagogue on Henry Street by eleven Russian immigrants who began with working capital of $95. By the early 1990s the bank had lent almost $100 million to more than one million borrowers. Its offices are at 205 East 42nd Street.

The Poor Man's Bank (New York: Hebrew Free Loan Society, 1943)

Joyce Mendelsohn

Hebrew Immigrant Aid Society [HIAS]. International service for Jewish immigrants and refugees, formed in New York City on 16 March 1909 by the merger of the Hebrew Sheltering Society (1889), dedicated to helping eastern European Jews, and the Hebrew Immigrant Aid Society (1902), formed to provide traditional burial for Jewish immigrants who died on Ellis Island. Initially a modest welfare society with a budget of less than $10,000, during its first decade it helped immigrants to gain legal entry into the United States, obtain work and schooling, and find relatives. Its facilities included an information office at 229 Broadway that in 1912 had more than 150,000 visitors. During the same year the service helped survivors of the *Titanic*, received nearly fifteen thousand immigrants (of which it provided shelter for more than a fifth), and oversaw an English translation of its Yiddish-language bulletin, published under the auspices of the Connecticut Daughters of the American Revolution. By 1914 the service had a national membership and international affiliations. During and after the Second World War it opened offices to help refugees and displaced persons. It took its current name in 1954 after merging with the United Service for New Americans and the migration department of the American Jewish Joint Distribution Committee, consolidating all American Jewish refugee services. In 1965 the world headquarters were moved from Lafayette Street to 200 Park Avenue South. HIAS helped thousands of immigrants from Eastern Europe, the Soviet Union, and North Africa and was especially active during the Hungarian revolution in 1956, the Middle Eastern crises of 1956, 1967, and 1973, and the Iranian Revolution in the early 1980s. The headquarters are at 333 7th Avenue in Manhattan. The board of directors has had such influential members as Louis Marshall, Jacob Schiff, Oscar Straus, Cyrus Sulzberger, and Stephen S. Wise.

Mark Wischnitzer: *Visas to Freedom: The History of HIAS* (Cleveland: World, 1956)

Irving Howe: *World of Our Fathers* (New York: Harcourt Brace Jovanovich, 1976)

Michael N. Dobkowski, Allen J. Share

Hebrew Mutual Benefit Society. A burial and mutual aid association formed in 1820 by several members of Shearith Israel who broke away in 1825 to found B'Nai Jeshurun. The society established temporary quarters in Washington Hall at 533 Pearl Street, where it adopted a constitution in 1826. Organized to aid the needy, visit the sick, help new immigrants, and assist in burials, the society opened its membership to all Jews in 1845. In the mid 1990s it reimbursed medical expenses and provided funerals and graves at Hastings, New York, and Washington Cemetery in Brooklyn.

Israel Goldstein: *A Century of Judaism in New York* (New York: Congregation B'nai Jeshurun, 1930)

Hyman Grinstein: *The Rise of the Jewish Community of*

New York, 1654–1860 (Philadelphia: Jewish Publication Society of America, 1945)

Joyce Mendelsohn

Hebrew Union College–Jewish Institute of Religion. Rabbinical school formed in 1950 by the merger of the Jewish Institute of Religion (1922) of New York City and Hebrew Union College (1875) of Cincinnati. In 1979 it moved to 1 West 4th Street and became affiliated with New York University. The campus in New York City is one of four in the United States and Israel. A cantorial school, the School of Sacred Music, is also under its auspices. In 1991 the school had ninety-eight students.

Samuel E. Karff, ed.: *Hebrew Union College–Jewish Institute of Religion at One Hundred Years* (Cincinnati: Hebrew Union College Press, 1976)

Marc Ferris

Heck [née Ruckle], **Barbara** (*b* Ballingrane, County Limerick, Ireland, 1734; *d* Augusta, near Prescott, Ont., 17 Aug 1804). Religious leader. She moved to New York City on 11 August 1760 with her family. Dismayed at what she considered signs of spiritual poverty, including her brother's indulgence in card-playing, in 1766 she formed the city's first Methodist congregation with her cousin Philip Embury. This initially consisted of five members and met in Embury's home on Augustus Street; it later built Wesley Chapel (now John Street United Methodist Church). Considered by many the "mother of American Methodism," Heck later moved to Canada and helped to establish Methodism there.

Garwood Lincoln Caddell: *Barbara Heck: Pioneer Methodist* (Cleveland, Tenn.: Pathway, 1961)

Charles Yrigoyen, Jr.

Hecker, Isaac (Thomas) (*b* New York City, 18 Dec 1830; *d* New York City, 22 Dec 1888). Writer, editor, and religious leader. As a youth he worked in his father's bakery and took part in a number of religious movements including Methodism, Unitarianism, Mormonism, and transcendentalism; he was also briefly a member of the political movement known as the Locofocos. Religious stirrings and the writings of the German Romantics led him to seek fulfillment and social purpose in communitarian ventures at Brook Farm and the Fruitlands in Massachusetts. Dissatisfied with his experiences there, he looked to Orestes A. Brownson as a mentor and in 1844 converted to Catholicism and joined a congregation known as the Redemptorists; he was ordained in 1847 and spent several years on a mission circuit devoted to immigrants. He later sought to open a center in New York City devoted to the conversion of American-born non-Catholics. After his plan was rejected by his superiors he and three other Redemptorists formed a congregation known as the Missionary Priests of St. Paul the Apostle (Paulists). To advance their work he launched two monthly periodicals, the *Catholic World* (1865) and the *Young Catholic* (1870), and formed the Catholic Publication Society (1866, now Paulist Press). Illness in the 1870s prevented him from starting a Catholic daily newspaper. Hecker wrote *Questions of the Soul* (1855), *Aspirations of Nature* (1857), and *The Church and the Age* (1887).

Vincent F. Holden: *The Yankee Paul: Isaac Thomas Hecker* (Milwaukee: Bruce, 1958)

Robert Emmett Curran

Heeney, Cornelius (*b* County Offaly, Ireland, 1754; *d* Brooklyn, 3 May 1848). Merchant, philanthropist, and state legislator. After emigrating to the United States in 1784, penniless, he made a fortune selling furs in New York City. He gave sizable sums of money to churches and religious institutions, including his parish church, St. Paul's on Barclay Street, as well as St. Patrick's Old Cathedral, its school, and its orphanage. He also donated the land for the second Catholic church in Brooklyn, St. Paul's, and for the orphanage and industrial school that adjoin it. With a fellow parishioner, the soapmaker Andrew Morris, he donated the property that became the site of the present St. Patrick's Cathedral on 5th Avenue. The second Roman Catholic in the state legislature, he served from 1818 to 1822. He was instrumental in establishing a branch of the Sisters of Charity in New York City, and in 1820 he became the patron and guardian of a fatherless ten-year-old boy from Brooklyn, John McCloskey, who later became the second archbishop in New York City and the first cardinal in the United States. After the Great Fire of 1835 destroyed his mercantile establishment, he chose not to rebuild and instead retired to his house and farm in Brooklyn, where he continued his philanthropic work. In 1845 he formed the Brooklyn Benevolent Society, to which he left a bequest enabling it to distribute more than $2 million to the poor and homeless of Brooklyn.

Thomas F. Meehan: "A Self-effaced Philanthropist: Cornelius Heeney (1754–1848)," *Catholic Historical Review* 4, no. 1 (1918), 3–17

William Harper Bennett: "Cornelius Heeney," *Journal of the Irish American Historical Society* 17 (1918)

John J. Concannon

Heins and LaFarge. Firm of architects founded by George Lewis Heins and Christopher Grant Lafarge. It designed a number of religious and public buildings in New York City that were distinguished by their Guastavino tile vaulting. In 1891 the firm won a competition for executing the Byzantine–Romanesque design of the Cathedral of St. John the Divine (for illustration see CATHEDRAL OF ST. JOHN THE DIVINE); the choir, crossing, and two side chapels were added by the firm between 1892 and 1911, when the firm was replaced by Ralph Adams Cram. Heins and LaFarge also drew the plans for the administration building (1899) and six animal houses (1910) at the New York Zoological Gardens in the Bronx, and the underground stations and control houses of the city's first subway system (1901–4).

Marjorie Pearson

Heinzen, Karl Peter (*b* Grevenbroich, Germany, 22 Feb 1809; *d* Boston, 12 Nov 1880). Writer and newspaper editor. He was banished from Germany for his activities as a revolutionary and settled in New York City, where he edited *Die deutsche Schnellpost* before returning to Europe to take part in the revolution of 1848. He later returned to the city to launch *Der Volkerbund*, a radical publication that ceased operations after the first issue; he then returned to the *Schnellpost*, later editing the *New Yorker deutsche Zeitung* and then the *Janus*.

Carl Frederick Wittke: *Against the Current: The Life of Karl Heinzen* (Chicago: University of Chicago Press, 1945)

James E. Mooney

Held, John, Jr. (*b* Salt Lake City, 10 Jan 1889; *d* Belmar, N.J., 2 March 1958). Illustrator. He began his career in New York City in 1912 designing streetcar posters and advertisements for Wanamaker's department store. During the 1920s he became known for his absurd but forgiving caricatures of "flappers"; his comic strips "Rah Rah Rosalie" and "Margy" and other work appeared in such magazines as *Judge*, *Life*, the *Smart Set*, *Liberty*, *Vanity Fair*, *Harper's Bazaar*, and the *New Yorker*. He later turned away from illustrating to write novels and short stories, work with watercolors, and make wash drawings of animals. Held also raised horses on his farm near Weston, Connecticut, and in 1939 he exhibited several bronze sculptures of horses at the Bland Gallery in New York City.

Shelley Armitage: *John Held, Jr., Illustrator of the Jazz Age* (Syracuse, N.Y.: Syracuse University Press, 1987)

Michael Joseph

heliports. The same geographic features that make helicopters advantageous to use in New York City also make them difficult to use, even though in designing and locating heliports the city has been unusually resourceful. During the 1950s the helicopter was seen by some as the eventual successor to the private automobile; its more modest role as a means of transport between airports was foreseen in 1953 by New York Airways, which promised to inaugurate service by "skybus" as soon as adequate facilities were available. Small heliports were maintained by the police department at the Battery and on 34th Street at the East River, and from 1953 by the Port of New York Authority at its bus terminal on 8th Avenue; the first sizable facility opened at the foot of Wall Street in 1953. Service from commercial airports to a heliport atop the new headquarters of Pan American Airways began on 22 December 1965 after much controversy. The service proved unprofitable and was suspended in 1968. New York Airways used larger helicopters when it resumed service to the same site on 1 February 1977, but on 17 May the landing gear of a helicopter collapsed, killing four passengers and a passer-by. After service was moved to a rooftop heliport near the World Trade Center another helicopter crashed at Newark Airport on 18 April 1979, and service then ceased altogether. In 1981 a new company, New York Helicopter Airways, began airport service from the eastern end of 34th Street, in what represented perhaps the final concession that heliports were not compatible with the area that needed them most: central Manhattan.

Alex L. Hart: *Transportation by Helicopter, 1955–1975: A Study of Its Potential in the New Jersey–New York Metropolitan Area* (New York: Aviation Department, 1952)

Local Service Air Transportation and Metropolitan Helicopter Services: A Study of Two of the Newer Elements (New York: Investment Bankers' Association of America, 1954)

Paul Barrett

Heller, Joseph (*b* Brooklyn, 1 May 1923). Novelist. The son of Russian Jewish immigrants, he grew up in Coney Island, attended New York University (AB 1948) and Columbia University (MA in American literature 1949), and taught writing at City College. He drew on his experiences as a bomber pilot during the Second World War in his novel *Catch-22* (1961), an absurdist, antiwar black comedy that became a best-seller and was made into a popular film. His later writings include the novels *Something Happened* (1974), *Good as Gold* (1979), and *God Knows* (1984), as well as an account of his battle with Guillain–Barré syndrome, *No Laughing Matter* (1986).

B. Kimberly Taylor

Hell Gate. A narrow strait between Astoria and Ward's Island, connecting the East River with Long Island Sound. Its name is a corruption of the Dutch name Hellegat (hell channel). For many years the waterway was extremely hazardous to navigation because of its powerful tides and its many rocky outcroppings. Its treacherous waters were described by Adriaen Block, who made the first reported passage in 1612. In 1780 the British frigate *Hussar* ran aground and sank in the channel while carrying gold and silver for military paymasters in New York City (its treasure is still sought after by divers), and hundreds of other ships sank by the time the U.S. Army Corps of Engineers in 1876 blasted out most of the dangerous underwater rocks by setting off what was then the world's largest explosion ever detonated. The channel was later widened and deepened but remains difficult to navigate. One of two bridges spanning the waterway is the New York Connecting Railroad Bridge, commonly known as the Hell Gate Arch, which joins the Bronx and Queens and provides a direct rail link between New England and New York City. Completed in 1917 from plans by the engineer Gustav Lindenthal and the architect Henry Hornbostel, it is one of the finest steel arch bridges in the world. The Triborough Bridge nearby, designed by the engineer Othmar H. Ammann, opened in 1936 for vehicular traffic and connects Manhattan, the Bronx, and Queens. Both bridges pass over Wards Island and Randalls Island, which were once separated by a shallow tidal creek called Little Hell Gate.

Description of the Government Works at Hell Gate (New York: n.pub., 1873)

Gerard R. Wolfe

Hell Gate Bridge. The popular name for the New York Connecting Railroad Bridge, a steel arch bridge over Hell Gate Channel between Ward's Island and Queens. Opened in 1917, it was the longest steel arch bridge in the world at the time of its completion. The bridge has a massive arch of 1017 feet (311 meters) and a tower at either end, and carries four railroad tracks. The bridge is a segment of a system 2.5 miles (four kilometers) long that includes viaducts, overpasses, and two smaller bridges, all designed by Gustav Lindenthal and built by the Pennsylvania Railroad, to provide trains with access to Manhattan from Queens and the Bronx and direct passenger service to points in New England. Hell Gate Bridge serves trains on the heavily traveled northeastern corridor of the Amtrak train system.

Rebecca Read Shanor

Hellman, Lillian (*b* New Orleans, 20 June 1907; *d* Vineyard Haven, Mass., 30 June 1984). Playwright. She grew up in Manhattan, where she spent most of her life aside from brief stays in Hollywood and Westchester County; she lived from 1911 to 1925 at 330 East 95th Street and during the late 1930s at the Hotel Élysée (56–60 East 54th Street). A communist sympathizer and staunch apologist for Stalinism, she became well known for her contemptuous testimony in 1952 before the House Committee on Un-American Activities, leading her to be blacklisted in Hollywood. Her reputation revived during the 1970s when she published three volumes of memoirs, but she was harshly criticized by many liberal anticommunists, who accused her of distorting history. From 1970 to 1984 her principal residence was 630 Park Avenue. Hellman's published writings include the plays *The Children's Hour* (1934), *The Little Foxes* (1939), and *Watch on the Rhine* (1941), and the memoirs *An Unfinished Woman* (1969), *Pentimento* (1973), and *Scoundrel Time* (1976), which vividly depict her liaison with the writer Dashiell Hammett and the turbulence of the 1950s.

Doris V. Falk: *Lillian Hellman* (New York: Ungar, 1978)

Lawson Bowling

Hell's Kitchen. A largely disused name for a part of the West Side of Manhattan, bounded to the north by 59th Street, to the east by 8th Avenue, to the south by 30th Street, and to the west by the Hudson River. In colonial times most of the area was covered by forest and farmland. At the end of the eighteenth century the Hopper family owned the land north of the Great Kill (which met the Hudson at what is now 42nd Street); land south of the Great Kill to what is now 32nd Street was covered by the Glass House Farm, which contained a glass-bottle factory. During the first half of the nineteenth century these properties were divided into lots; a railroad station opened at 11th Avenue and 30th Street in 1851, and soon there were slaughterhouses, warehouses, lumberyards, factories, and tenements throughout. The Irish were the largest ethnic group, and there were also Scots, Germans, and blacks. By the end of the Civil War the area was one of the worst slums in the city, known for such notorious gangs as the Gophers. The name Hell's Kitchen was perhaps taken from that of a gang formed in the area in 1868, or adopted by local police in the 1870s. A black enclave in the northern part of the neighborhood became facetiously known as San Juan Hill. The 9th Avenue elevated line was extended about this time.

Greeks and eastern Europeans moved to the area after 1900, followed by blacks from the South and Puerto Ricans in the 1940s. Several public works projects were undertaken in the 1930s including the West Side Highway, the Lincoln Tunnel, the New York Central Railroad West Side Improvement Project, and the Port Authority Bus Terminal; many families were displaced and tenements destroyed, and the Paddy's Market, a well-known pushcart market, was forced to move in 1938 from the area under the 9th Avenue elevated line between 38th and 42nd streets; the elevated line closed in 1940. The rough-and-tumble reputation of the neighborhood was celebrated in popular culture, notably in the ballet "Slaughter on Tenth Avenue" (from the musical *On Your Toes*, 1936) and the musical *West Side Story* (1957). After two children were killed in gang wars in 1959 local organizations sought to improve the image of the neighborhood by giving it its current name (after De Witt Clinton Park, between 52nd and 54th streets west of 11th Avenue). With the decline of the ocean liner much of the waterfront and the piers were abandoned during the 1960s, and most of the housing in the northern section was demolished to make way for Lincoln Center and related development. Some efforts were made to renovate the neighborhood as a fashionable area in the 1980s, and it attracted a number of immi-

Shacks and tenements in Hell's Kitchen and Sebastopol (the Rock), ca *1890*

grants from the Dominican Republic, the United Kingdom, China, Israel, and France. At the same time a gang called the Westies carried on the area's more violent traditions. The neighborhood is still dotted with warehouses, Irish bars, and ramshackle tenements, and there is a large black and Latin American population. The Intrepid Sea, Air, Space Museum, aboard an aircraft carrier from the Second World War docked at Pier 86 on West 46th Street, is a popular tourist attraction.

George Winslow

Helmsley, Harry B(rakmann) (*b* New York City, 4 March 1909). Real-estate developer. He grew up in the Bronx. With Leon Spear, a manager of properties in the Garment District, he formed Helmsley–Spear in 1955. The firm became the city's largest in the business, and in 1961 it bought the Empire State Building in a complicated leaseback arrangement with the Crown family of Chicago (the owners of the building) and the Prudential Insurance Company (the owners of the land). As a partner of Lawrence Wien he bought several valuable office buildings and hotels, including the Fisk and Lincoln buildings and the Plaza Hotel. Later in the 1960s he bought Wien's financial interest in the Empire State Building as well as several of the city's leading real-estate brokerage and property management firms; he then erected the Pfizer Building and 1 Penn Plaza. In 1969 he bought the Furman–Wolfson real-estate trust for $165 million, thus gaining ownership of thirty large buildings in a number of cities including New York City, Chicago, and Los Angeles. In 1972 he divorced his first wife of thirty-two years and married one of his employees, Leona Roberts; she became the president of the Harley and Helmsley Hotels, a subsidiary of Helmsley–Spear that bought and refurbished twenty-one hotels in the city, including the Villard Houses (renamed the Helmsley Palace) and the Harley (renamed the Helmsley). By the 1980s the Helmsleys' real-estate assets were valued at more than $1000 million. The couple was indicted for tax evasion and mail fraud in 1988: he was declared incompetent to stand trial, but she was convicted of evading $1.2 million in federal taxes.

Richard Hammer: *The Helmsleys: The Rise and Fall of Harry and Leona* (New York: New American Library, 1990)

Lisa Gitelman, Marc A. Weiss

Helmsley [Roberts; née Rosenthal], **Leona (Mindy)** (*b* Marbletown, near Kingston, N.Y., 4 July 1920). Hotel and real-estate executive. She worked in real estate for several years before marrying Harry B. Helmsley in 1972. As the president of Harley and Helmsley Hotels, a subsidiary of his firm that manages twenty-one hotels in New York City, she became widely known for a series of advertisements that portrayed her as an exacting taskmaster intolerant of the slightest imperfections in hotel furnishings. Indicted for tax evasion in 1988, she was convicted of evading $1.2 million in federal taxes and sentenced to four years in prison after a celebrated trial at which many disgruntled employees and former employees testified about the Helmsleys' financial dealings and about construction work done on their mansion in Greenwich, Connecticut. One witness quoted her as having said that "only the little people pay taxes."

Richard Hammer: *The Helmsleys: The Rise and Fall of Harry and Leona* (New York: New American Library, 1990)

Henderson, Fletcher (Hamilton, Jr.) [Smack] (*b* Cuthbert, Ga., 1 Dec 1897; *d* New York City, 29 Dec. 1952). Bandleader, arranger, and pianist. After settling in New York City he toured with the singer Ethel Waters (1921–22) and recorded accompaniments for blues singers. At the Roseland Ballroom (on Broadway at West 51st Street) he led an innovative big band from 1924 that included the cornetist Louis Armstrong (1924–25), the tenor saxophonist Coleman Hawkins, and the arranger Don Redman. Until the late 1920s this was acclaimed as the best jazz band in New York City, but Henderson was indifferent to success. The membership changed often and in 1934 the group disbanded. His own arrangements, including *King Porter Stomp*, were crucial to the great popularity of Benny Goodman's big band in 1935. From 1936 he resumed working as a leader, except for a period as a staff arranger for Goodman.

Walter C. Allen: *Hendersonia: The Music of Fletcher Henderson and His Musicians: A Bio-Discography* (Highland Park, N.J.: Walter C. Allen, 1973)

Barry Kernfeld

Henri, Robert [Cozad, Robert Henry] (*b* Cincinnati, 25 June 1865; *d* New York City, 12 July 1929). Painter and teacher. Brought up in the western United States, he studied at the Pennsylvania Academy of the Fine Arts in Philadelphia and later in Paris. After returning to Philadelphia he became the teacher of the young painters John Sloan, George B. Luks, William James Glackens, and Everett Shinn, all of whom followed him to New York City after he moved there in 1900. He taught at the New York School of Art from 1902 to 1908 and then opened his own school. Rejecting impressionism and the genteel styles of painting favored by traditionalists, he urged the National Academy of Design to include the work of young realist painters in its annual shows. With Sloan in 1908 he organized an exhibition at the Macbeth Galleries of The Eight, which stirred controversy for its celebration of unconventional styles and its depictions of urban, working-class life. Henri's best-known works include *Laughing Child* (1907). His lecture notes and talks were published as *The Art Spirit* in 1930.

William Innes Homer: *Robert Henri and His Circle* (Ithaca, N.Y.: Cornell University Press, 1969)

Patricia Hills

Henri Bendel. Firm of specialty retailers. It was formed in 1896 when Henri Bendel (*b*

Lafayette, La., 1858; *d* 1939) opened a small millinery shop at 10 Bond Street, which he moved to 67 East 9th Street in the following year, to 5th Avenue in 1906, and to 10 West 57th Street during the First World War. The firm operated a number of boutiques that sold hats, women's clothing, perfumes, cosmetics, and home furnishings. Its elegant, imaginative window designs set the standard for other designers. After Bendel was bought in 1985 by the retailing firm the Limited, its main store moved in March 1991 to a building at 712 5th Avenue with three-story windows designed by the French glass designer René Lalique.

Leslie Gourse, Kenneth T. Jackson

Henry Holt. Firm of book publishers, formed in 1866 in New York City by Henry Holt and Frederick Leypoldt as the firm of Leypoldt and Holt; in 1873 it became Henry Holt and Company when Holt became the sole owner. The firm published literary works and a highly regarded list of books by prominent nineteenth-century American scientists and social scientists. It was also a leading publisher of poetry (notably that of Robert Frost) and of textbooks. In 1960 the firm strengthened its educational division by merging with Rinehart and Company and John C. Winston Company to form Holt, Rinehart and Winston. The new firm was acquired in 1967 by the Columbia Broadcasting System (CBS), which in 1985 sold its trade division of the company to the German firm Verlagsgruppe Georg von Holtzbrinck. The new trade house formed by this transaction reassumed the name Henry Holt and Company. CBS sold the school and college departments, still known as Holt, Rinehart and Winston, to Harcourt Brace Jovanovich in 1986. In the mid 1990s Henry Holt had offices at 115 West 18th Street in Manhattan.

See also Book publishing.

Eileen K. Cheng

Henry Street Settlement. Settlement house. It had its beginnings in the work of Lillian Wald and Mary Brewster, who from 1893 provided medical care at home for the indigent on the Lower East Side. Their work was financed by Betty Loeb and her son-in-law, the financier Jacob Schiff. As other nurses joined them, their need for larger quarters led them to move in 1895 to a building at 265 Henry Street that became known as the Henry Street Nurses' Settlement. Within a decade of its founding more than twenty nurses worked for the settlement, which was the first institution of its kind to have a visiting nurse service. The nurses lived in the neighborhoods where they worked and by the turn of the century attended to 4500 patients, made 35,035 home visits and 3542 convalescent visits, and gave 28,809 first-aid treatments. Their nursing services were available throughout the city from 9 a.m. to 6 p.m., seven days a week. Patients were usually visited daily or as often as needed; night nurses, cleaning, and laundry were provided for the gravely ill. The nurses ran first-aid stations where they treated burns, infections, and injuries, as well as convalescent homes. In some sections of the city they provided assistance twenty-four hours a day to women in childbirth and held health conferences for the mothers of infants. The settlement had forty-six residents by 1911, of whom forty-one were women.

In the following years the settlement developed into a neighborhood center for civic, social, and philanthropic work. By 1913 it occupied seven houses serving the Lower East Side and had branches in uptown Manhattan and the Bronx. Its citywide visiting nurse service made 200,000 home visits, and settlement clubs for boys, girls, and mothers had three thousand members and 25,000 participants in various programs. The settlement operated a dance school where national and folk dances were revived, a playground (one of the first in the nation), a gymnasium, debating clubs, literary societies, a kindergarten, a savings and loan fund, and a cooperative food store. The year 1915 marked the opening of the Neighborhood Playhouse (now at 340 East 54th Street). This became the first theater in the United States to present a play by a black author with a black cast before a racially integrated audience (*Rachel*, by Angelina Weld Grimké), and by the 1920s the playhouse was a leading experimental theater. By the time of Wald's retirement in 1933 the staff of 265 visiting nurses reportedly climbed 24,750,000 stairs, drove 140,000 miles (225,000 kilometers), and took 120,000 subway rides to make 550,000 home visits to 100,000 patients. Wald chose as her successors Helen Hull for the settlement and Marguerite Wales for the nursing service, which in 1944 achieved independent status, moved to 107 East 70th Street, and became known as the Visiting Nurse Service of New York.

In its first century of operation the settlement saw the ethnic composition of the Lower East Side change from roughly half eastern and central European to mostly Asian and Latin American (about 30 percent each). In the early 1990s it occupied eight buildings, operated two dozen programs for young people, families, and the elderly, had a budget of almost $13 million, and served 200,000 persons a year.

Lillian D. Wald: *Windows on Henry Street* (Boston: Little, Brown, 1934)

Robert H. Bremner: "Lillian D. Wald," *Notable American Women*, ed. Edward T. James et al. (Cambridge: Harvard University Press, 1971), vol. 3, pp. 526–29

Karen Buhler-Wilkerson

Hepburn, Katharine (Houghton) (*b* Hartford, Conn., 12 May 1907). Actress. She made her début on Broadway under the name Katherine Burns in *Night Hostess* in September 1928 before appearing in November under her own name in *These Days* at the Cort. After working as an understudy and acting in many plays that closed quickly, she had her first long run in *The Warrior's Husband* at the Morosco Theater in 1932, in which she played an Amazon warrior and made her entrance bounding down stairs with a stag over her shoulders. The exuberance and success of this performance won her a contract with Radio–Keith–Orpheum for George Cukor's film *A Bill of Divorcement* (1932). While filming *Woman of the Year* in 1941 she began an important relationship with Spencer Tracy (1900–67), with whom she made nine motion pictures. One of her most explicitly feminist works, *Adam's Rib* (1949, with Tracy), was shot in New York City. In 1962 she appeared in the film adaptation of Eugene O'Neill's *Long Day's Journey into Night* (1962), directed by Sidney Lumet, which was rehearsed on 2nd Avenue and shot in a house on City Island. Hepburn received Academy Awards for her films *Morning Glory* (1933), *Guess Who's Coming to Dinner* (1967, with Tracy), *The Lion in Winter* (1968), and *On Golden Pond* (1981). She wrote *Me: Stories of My Life* (1991).

Katharine Hepburn

Garson Kanin: *Tracy and Hepburn: An Intimate Memoir* (New York: Viking, 1971)

Christopher Andersen: *Young Kate: The Remarkable Hepburns and the Childhood That Shaped an American Legend* (New York: Henry Holt, 1988)

Grai St. Clair Rice

Herald Square. A section of midtown Manhattan, centered at the intersection of 6th Avenue, 34th Street, and Broadway, and encompassing Greeley Square. The area is named for the *New York Herald*, which from 1893 to the 1920s had its headquarters in a two-story, arcaded Italianate building on 35th Street designed by the firm of McKim, Mead and White. It became the heart of the Tenderloin

View of Herald Square, north from 34th Street along Broadway, 1904. Right *6th Avenue elevated railway;* background New York Times *building under construction*

during the 1870s and 1880s after the 6th Avenue elevated line was built, and it was known for theaters, dance halls, seafood restaurants, hotels like the Herald Square Hotel and the McAlpin Hotel, and the Manhattan Opera House. Reformers shut down the most risqué entertainments during the 1890s. The dry-goods firm of R. H. Macy bought and razed the opera house in 1901, and in the following year it opened the world's largest department store. Soon Gimbel's, Saks Fifth Avenue, and Ohrbach's moved in nearby, and the neighborhood became one of the best-known shopping districts in the nation. Many department stores closed in the 1980s. Herald Center Mall was built on the site of Saks in 1985, and the Gimbel's building was remodeled to accommodate the A&S Plaza in 1990. Herald Square remains an important shopping district. It is adorned by the elaborate Bennett Clock, named for James Gordon Bennett Jr., publisher of the *Herald.*

WPAG

Michele Herman

Herbert, Victor (August) (*b* Dublin, 1 Feb 1859; *d* New York City, 26 May 1924). Composer. He studied the cello and composition in Germany and moved to New York City in 1886 with his wife, Therese, a noted Viennese opera singer. He was a founder of the New York String Quartet and formed an orchestra for light music that came to be highly regarded. From 1898 to 1904 he conducted the Pittsburgh Symphony; he was also a guest conductor of the New York Philharmonic Society. Among his symphonic compositions are two cello concertos (1885, 1894) and the tone poem *Hero and Leander* (1901). In his mid thirties he began writing operettas, a genre at which he excelled: *Babes in Toyland* (1903), *Mlle Modiste* (1905), *The Red Mill* (1906), and *Naughty Marietta* (1910) were all successfully produced in New York City. He also wrote one grand opera, *Natoma* (1911), and a one-act opera, *Madeleine* (1913), and in 1916 composed music for the film *The Fall of a Nation.* Among his finest songs are "Kiss Me Again" (1905), "In Old New York" (known also as "The Streets of New York," 1906), "Ah, Sweet Mystery of Life" (1910), "I'm Falling in Love with Someone" (1910), and "Italian Love Song" (1910). He wrote almost forty operettas, known for their memorable tunes, adept orchestrations, full-sounding textures, resourcefully manipulated harmony and rhythm, and waltz and march meters reflecting his European background. Although the tonal polish of Herbert's songs made him the most popular composer of his day in New York City, his melodies have extended ranges, demanding leaps, and chromatic alterations that make them more difficult to sing than most music from Tin Pan Alley.

Edward N. Waters: *Victor Herbert: A Life in Music* (New York: Macmillan, 1955)

Nicholas E. Tawa

Hermannsöhne. Fraternal order formed by several Germans who belonged to the Independent Order of Odd Fellows in New York City in 1840. Named for a legendary founder of the German nation, it was prominent among German–American fraternal orders in the city and was a leader in organizing support for the revolution of 1848.

Stanley Nadel

Herter Brothers. Firm of furniture manufacturers and interior decorators, formed in 1864 by Gustave Herter (1830–98) of Stuttgart, Germany, and his half-brother Christian (1839–83). Its predecessor was a shop at 48 Mercer Street opened by 1851 by Gustave Herter, who moved to the city in 1848, reportedly worked for the firm of Tiffany, Young and Ellis, and had brief partnerships with Auguste Pottier and Erastus Bulkley. The shop expanded to 547 Broadway and produced furniture, architectural woodwork, and decorations for banks and private residences in the city between 1858 and 1864. Christian Herter joined the firm after studying in Stuttgart and possibly in Paris before moving to the city in 1859. In the years after the Civil War, Herter Brothers became known nationwide for the craftsmanship and innovative designs of its furniture. Christian Herter acquired his brother's interest in the firm in 1870, and under his direction from 1870 to 1883 it became known for suites of furniture in an Anglo-Japanesque style commissioned by such customers as the financiers Jay Gould and Mark Hopkins. The last and most important commission he accepted was the design and interior decoration of William H. Vanderbilt's house at 5th Avenue and 51st Street (1879–82); among the pieces he created for it was a mother-of-pearl inlaid rosewood library table (now in the Metropolitan Museum of Art). After he withdrew, the firm continued under William Baumgarten (1845–1908) until 1891 and William Gilman Nichols (*d* 1909) until it ceased operations in 1906.

Katherine S. Howe, Alice Cooney Frelinghuysen, Catherine Hoover Voorsanger, et al.: *Herter Brothers: Furniture and Interiors for a Gilded Age* (New York: Harry N. Abrams, in association with the Museum of Fine Arts, Houston, 1994)

Deborah Dependahl Waters

Herts and Tallant. Firm of architects, formed by Henry Beaumont Herts (1871–1933) and Hugh Tallant (1869–1952), both trained at the École des Beaux-Arts in Paris. Some of the finest theaters in New York City were designed by the firm, which sought to combine the elegance of French design with such technical innovations as the first cantilevered balconies. Among its principal works in the city were the New Amsterdam Theatre (1903), the most important example in the city of *art nouveau,* the Lyceum (1903), in a beaux-arts style, the Folies Bergère (1911, later the Helen Hayes; demolished), and the Brooklyn Academy of Music (1908). Among those who trained at the firm was Herbert J. Krapp, the most prolific architect of Broadway theaters.

See also THEATER ARCHITECTURE.

Anthony W. Robins

Heschel, Abraham J(oshua) (*b* Warsaw, 11 Jan 1907; *d* New York City, 23 Dec 1972). Rabbi, theologian, and author. He was born to a distinguished Hasidic family and received his doctorate in philosophy from the University of Berlin in 1933. In 1940 he fled the Nazis and moved to the United States, where he taught at Hebrew Union College in Cincinnati. He moved in 1945 to New York City and joined the faculty of the Jewish Theological Seminary of America, where he remained for twenty-seven years (residing at 425 Riverside Drive). Later he became one of the best-known and most widely respected Hasidic scholars, and also worked to bring about greater ecumenism between different branches of Judaism and between Jews and Christians. In 1964 he risked the anger of Jews by meeting with Pope Paul VI, as a result of which the second Vatican Council issued the statement *Nostra Aetate* condemning anti-Semitism and affirming the enduring validity of Judaism. In the following year he became the first rabbi to receive a visiting professorship at Union Theological Seminary. He was also active politically and spoke repeatedly against racism and the Vietnam War. In 1965 he marched with Martin Luther King Jr. in Selma, Alabama, and he took part in antiwar demonstrations in Washington in 1967 and 1968; he was also a chairman of Clergy Concerned about Vietnam. After the Arab–Israeli War he became an outspoken defender of Israel. Heschel wrote more than twenty books, among them *God in Search of Man: Philosophy of Judaism* (1955).

Fritz A. Rothschild, ed.: *Between God and Man: An Interpretation of Judaism, from the Writings of Abraham J. Heschel* (New York: Free Press, 1965)

John C. Merkle: *The Genesis of Faith: The Depth Psychology of Abraham Joshua Heschel* (New York: Macmillan, 1985)

Donald J. Moore: *The Human and the Holy: The Spirituality of Abraham Joshua Heschel* (New York: Fordham University Press, 1989)

Edward T. O'Donnell

Heterodoxy. A luncheon and lecture club formed in Greenwich Village in 1912 by the former Unitarian minister Marie Jenney Howe. Over the years it enlisted 110 known members, including the social reformer Crystal Eastman, the suffragist Inez Millholland Boissevain, the schoolteacher and activist Henrietta Rodman, the anarchist Rose Strunsky, the socialist, peace activist, and suffragist Katherine Anthony, the lawyer and theatrical producer Helen Arthur, the novelist and playwright Ida Wylie, the novelist and teacher Helen Hull, the suffragist and prison reformer Paula Jakobi, and the writer and radio commentator Mary Margaret McBride, as well as Elisabeth Irwin, director of the Little Red School House in Greenwich Village, S. Josephine Baker, director of the New York City Bureau of Child Hygiene, and the writer Mabel Dodge, who described the members as "unorthodox women . . . who did things and did them openly." The group met every other Saturday in local restaurants to discuss controversial topics. It was addressed in 1915 by Edith Lees, wife of Havelock Ellis, and in 1934 by Gertrude Stein and Alice B. Toklas. Although most members were feminists the club welcomed women regardless of their politics, background, or sexual orientation. It remained active until 1940.

Judith Schwarz: *Radical Feminists of Heterodoxy: Greenwich Village, 1912–1940* (Lebanon, N.H.: New Victoria, 1982)

Jan Seidler Ramirez

Hewitt, Abram S(tevens) (*b* Haverstraw, N.Y., 31 July 1822; *d* New York City, 18 Jan 1903). Mayor and industrialist. He graduated from Columbia College in 1842 and in 1845 opened an iron mill in Trenton, New Jersey, with Edward Cooper, a classmate whose father, the industrialist Peter Cooper, financed the operation. He produced a variety of new iron and steel products and invested in many firms, often serving on their boards. In 1855 he married Peter Cooper's daughter Sarah and began supervising the construction of the Union for the Advancement of Science and Art (later known as Cooper Union); he was chairman of its board of trustees until 1903. Influenced by Samuel J. Tilden, he began his political career as a Democrat and was active in the campaign against William M. "Boss" Tweed. He was elected to five congressional terms beginning in 1874 and was chairman of the Democratic National Committee in 1876 during Tilden's presidential campaign (when Peter Cooper mounted a rival campaign as the candidate of the Greenback Party). Backed by Tammany Hall in 1886, he was elected mayor in a dramatic campaign against the radical economic reformer Henry George and Theodore Roosevelt, the future president. Once in office he struggled to achieve his long-sought goals to unify business, labor, and taxpayers and to end corruption, improve municipal services (particularly rapid transit), and help the poor. In 1886 Hewitt ended his association with Tammany Hall after a dispute over patronage, and he was defeated for reelection. He remained active in philanthropic affairs and business to the end of his life.

Allan Nevins: *Abram S. Hewitt, with Some Account of Peter Cooper* (New York: Harper and Brothers, 1935)

Jerome Mushkat

Higgins, Vannie [Charles] (*b* Brooklyn, *ca* 1896; *d* Brooklyn, 19 June 1932). Bootlegger. During Prohibition he established himself as the major figure in the liquor trade in Brooklyn and Nassau County. One of his rum-running boats was believed to be the fastest in New York Harbor, and he was also an avid flyer and the owner of an immense seaplane. After attempting to extend his territory along the coast of New Jersey he was fatally shot while leaving a dance recital given by his seven-year-old daughter. Controversy surrounded the revelation that he had spent the previous night as a houseguest of the warden of the state penitentiary at Great Meadows.

George A. Thompson, Jr.

Highbridge. Neighborhood in the southwestern Bronx, bounded to the north by the Cross Bronx Expressway, to the east by Jerome Avenue and the Edward L. Grant Highway, to the south by East 161st Street, and to the west by the Harlem River; it is about six blocks wide and ten blocks long and lies northwest of Yankee Stadium. The area is named for a bridge of the same name (the oldest extant one in New York City) built across the Harlem River between 1840 and 1848 to carry water from the Croton Aqueduct to Manhattan. It was rural and in the mid nineteenth century became a resort, accessible by river steamer and favored by many residents of Manhattan. Bridges to Manhattan for railroads and other vehicles were built during the late nineteenth century, but development hastened only after the introduction of rapid transit service. The Jerome Avenue elevated line (1918) included a spur connection to the 9th Avenue elevated line that passed directly through the area; the Grand Concourse subway (1933) had a stop nearby at 161st Street. During these years many five-story walk-up apartment buildings and six-story buildings with elevators were erected. The rapidly growing population by 1940 consisted mostly of middle- and working-class descendants of Irish and Jewish immigrants. During the 1950s and 1960s the New York City Housing Authority built several high-rise apartment buildings overlooking the Harlem River. Many residents moved to the suburbs and the population became predominantly black and Latin American. Scores of apartment buildings were abandoned by landlords during the 1970s as fires ravaged the area and the population declined; in the 1980s the decline stabilized and some of the older housing was refurbished.

Peter Derrick

High Bridge. The oldest of the great bridges in New York City, spanning the Harlem River at 173rd Street. It was built between 1837 and 1848 to bring water to the city from the reservoirs of the Croton Aqueduct System to the north. The original High Bridge was Roman in conception, and its massive stone arches were favorite subjects for artists. In the early 1920s a single span of steel replaced the stone piers in the riverbed because they interfered with navigation. A pedestrian walkway, now closed, offers a fine view of the entire area. The High Bridge Watch Tower on the Manhattan side of the bridge is a landmark.

Kenneth T. Jackson

View of High Bridge from the Bronx to Manhattan at 174th Street, ca *1900*

Highland Park. Neighborhood in east central Brooklyn, bounded to the north by the border with Queens County, to the east by Force Tube Avenue, to the south by Liberty Avenue, and to the west by Pennsylvania Avenue; it is nearly coextensive with Cypress Hills, which is bounded to the east by Eldert Lane and to the south by Atlantic Avenue. Named for a park of 141 acres (fifty-seven hectares) at its northern edge, the neighborhood was developed in the second half of the nineteenth century and by the 1890s was a large suburb. It was neglected by the 1970s, and Jamaica Avenue was lined with abandoned houses and empty lots. During the 1980s the neighborhood and its environs attracted many immigrants from Guyana, the Dominican Republic, and Jamaica. In the mid 1990s the population was largely black, with a smaller number of Latin Americans, Italians, and other whites. Most of the housing in the area consisted of one- and two-family detached houses, along with some apartment buildings. The Lithuanian Cultural Center (455 Highland Boulevard) is frequented by the many Lithuanians living in the metropolitan area. Fulton Street and Jamaica Avenue are the main thoroughfares.

Ellen Marie Snyder-Grenier

High School of Music and Art. Original name of FIORELLO LA GUARDIA HIGH SCHOOL OF MUSIC AND ART AND PERFORMING ARTS.

Hill, John William (*b* London, 13 Jan 1812; *d* near West Nyack, N.Y., 24 Sept 1879). Painter and engraver. The son of the engraver John Hill (1770–1850), he moved with his family to New York City in 1822. After serving as an apprentice to his father he resettled in West Nyack in 1840. He worked as a topographical artist for the New York State Geological Survey in 1836–41, was influenced by John Ruskin's *Modern Painters*, and began to paint landscapes and still lifes in watercolor and oil directly from nature, becoming a leader in the American pre-Raphaelite movement. In 1863 he was elected president of the Association for the Advancement of Truth in Art. Hill was the father of the landscape painter and printmaker John Henry Hill (1839–1922).

John Henry Hill: *John William Hill: An Artist's Memorial* (New York: n.pub., 1888)

Susan M. Sivard

Hill and Knowlton. Public relations firm established in Cleveland in 1927 by John W. Hill, who in 1933 formed a partnership with Donald Knowlton. The firm opened a branch in New York City in 1938. During the mid 1940s Hill reorganized the firm and moved its headquarters to New York City. It later became a subsidiary of the firm J. Walter Thompson. Hill and Knowlton was the largest public relations agency in the United States until 1984. After acquiring the third-largest agency, Carl Byoir and Associates, in 1986 it was again the largest firm in its field, with combined revenues of more than $125 million. The headquarters are at 420 Lexington Avenue in Manhattan.

John W. Hill: *The Making of a Public Relations Man* (New York: David McKay, 1963)

Alan R. Raucher

Hillcrest. Neighborhood in central Queens, lying mostly in Jamaica and partly in Flushing and bounded to the north by Union Turnpike, to the east by Jamaica Estates, to the south by Hillside Avenue, and to the west by 164th Street. It was developed on two hundred acres (eighty hectares) of land in the spring of 1909 by William F. Wyckoff, who formed the Hillcrest of Jamaica Company. After the first two sections were prepared along Union Turnpike development was hastened by the incorporation on 9 March 1910 of the Jamaica–Hillcrest Company under the direction of Bryan L. Kennelly: in succeeding months the company paved streets north of Hillside Avenue, installed gas, water, and electricity, and built houses ranging in price from $6500 to $12,000. Lots were sold at auction from 1910 to 1915, and by 1913 there were sixty houses. Further development was aided by the growth of Jamaica Estates, and the opening of the elevated line along Jamaica Avenue in 1918 brought Hillcrest within the five-cent fare zone. The sale of houses in the northern section increased after Grand Central Parkway opened in 1933. By the Second World War Hillcrest had become densely built up with comfortable one-family houses. It became more ethnically diverse in the 1970s. About one fifth of the immigrants who settled in the area in the 1980s were from Guyana; others were from Haiti, China, India, and Colombia.

Vincent Seyfried

Hillman, Sidney (*b* Zagare, Russia, 1887; *d* New York City, 10 July 1946). Labor leader. A descendent of rabbis, he became a refugee of the revolution of 1905 in Russia; his experiences there led him to devote himself to the labor movement, and in 1914 he moved to New York City, where he became the first president of the Amalgamated Clothing Workers of America, a militant union that challenged the timidity, nativism, and craft élitism of the men's clothing trade union affiliated with the American Federation of Labor (AFL). For this he earned the enmity of Samuel Gompers, president of the AFL, but gained the support of such progressive reformers as Louis D. Brandeis, Lillian Wald, Florence Kelley, and Fiorello H. La Guardia, who were impressed with his commitment to "industrial democracy" and the "new unionism." Hillman became known as the country's foremost "labor statesman" for introducing a new method of collective bargaining and such innovations as unemployment insurance, the union bank, and affordable cooperative housing on the Lower East Side and in the Bronx. He worked closely with Governor Franklin D. Roosevelt and his aides, including Felix Frankfurter, Frances Perkins, and Rexford Tugwell. A ready supporter of the New Deal, he was appointed to the National Industrial Recovery Board by President Roosevelt, who relied on his political advice about labor and social welfare legislation. Hillman recognized the unique opportunity of the situation and with John L. Lewis formed the Committee for Industrial Organization (CIO; later renamed the Congress of Industrial Organizations) to introduce unionism to American heavy industry. He carefully built a relationship between the CIO and the Democratic Party and in New York City helped to form the American Labor Party, which proved more effective than the local Democratic machine in mobilizing the electorate. After a strike at Woolworth's department store in 1937 he helped to form the Department Store Workers Organizing Committee. During the Second World War he established the Political Action Committee of the CIO, which strengthened the alliance between the Democratic Party and the labor movement that endured for a quarter-century. At his death Hillman was recognized as a leader of both the national labor movement and the anti-fascist coalition abroad.

Steve Fraser: *Labor Will Rule: Sidney Hillman and the Rise of American Labor* (New York: Free Press, 1991)

Steve Fraser

Hillquit, Morris (*b* Riga, Latvia, 1 Aug 1869; *d* New York City, 7 Oct 1933). Lawyer and political leader. He moved to New York City in 1886 and built a law practice by working closely with garment workers' unions. A leader of the Socialist Party of America (SPA), he sought election to the U.S. House of Representatives five times from largely Jewish districts. He won 22 percent of the vote in the mayoral election of 1917 and sought the mayoralty again in 1933. Hillquit sought to preserve the SPA and the spirit of socialism in the city in the face of challenges from communism and the New Deal.

Norma Fain Pratt: *Morris Hillquit: A Political History of an American Jewish Socialist* (Westport, Conn.: Greenwood, 1979)

Melvyn Dubofsky

Hillside. Neighborhood in east central Queens east of Jamaica, bounded to the north by Hillside Avenue, to the east by 184th Street, to the south by Jamaica Avenue, and to the west by 175th Street. In the 1870s and 1880s it was variously called East Jamaica and Rockaway Junction (after the branch-off of the Rockaway line of the Long Island Rail Road at 178th Street). The developers of the Jamaica Estates extended 178th Street to the railroad; at their urging the railroad opened a station on 15 May 1911, named Hillside for its location at the foot of the terminal moraine below Hillcrest and the Jamaica Estates. The name was also given to a group of houses built on surrounding streets between 1922 and 1924 but eventually became disused.

Vincent Seyfried

Lewis Hine, Men at Work *(1930–31)*

Hine, Lewis (Wickes) (*b* Oshkosh, Wis., 26 Sept 1874; *d* Hastings-on-Hudson, N.Y., 4 Nov 1940). Photographer. He moved to New York City in 1900 to teach nature study at the Ethical Culture School, where he was given a camera as a teaching aid and later offered classes in photography; eventually he left the school to pursue photography himself. One of his first projects, a sympathetic depiction of immigrants at Ellis Island, inspired him to seek commissions from social agencies. In 1907 he was made the photographer for a sociological study that was published as *The Pittsburgh Survey* (1910–13). Later he became a staff photographer for the National Child Labor Committee, which had its headquarters in the city. Between 1907 and 1916 his work appeared in exhibitions, periodicals, and brochures sponsored by the supporters of child labor laws. After working for a year in the Balkans for the Red Cross (1918–19) he returned to the city to find that social photography was no longer in great demand and produced what he called "work portraits" of workers in various industries. In 1930 he was engaged to document the construction of the Empire State Building but in the following decade was employed only occasionally, mainly by the Tennessee Valley Authority, the Rural Electrification Agency, and the Works Progress Administration. Shortly before his death a retrospective exhibition of his photographs at the Riverside Museum briefly revived interest in his work, which treated unusual subjects with warmth of feeling and visual force. Hines wrote *Men at Work: Photographic Studies of Modern Men and Machines* (1932; 2nd edn, enlarged, 1977).

Judith Mara Gutman: *Lewis W. Hine and the American Social Conscience* (New York: Walker, 1967)
Walter Rosenblum, Naomi Rosenblum, and Alan Trachtenberg: *America and Lewis Hine: Photographs, 1904–1948* (Millerton, N.Y.: Aperture, 1977)
Daile Kaplan: *Lewis Hine in Europe: The Lost Photographs* (New York: Abbeville, 1988)

Naomi Rosenblum

Hines, James J. (*b* New York City, *ca* 1876; *d* Long Beach, N.Y., 26 March 1957). Political leader. A former blacksmith who boasted that he had shod forty thousand horses, he became the Democratic leader in 1912 of the eleventh assembly district (consisting of Morningside Heights and southwestern Harlem). Although a member of Tammany Hall he often opposed the reigning boss, Charles F. Murphy. By the mid 1930s he was the most powerful politician in Manhattan, known for his generosity, his success as a "fixer," and his public friendships with judges and organized-crime figures alike. Hines was eventually prosecuted by Thomas E. Dewey, district attorney of Manhattan, for protecting a numbers racket controlled by Dutch Schultz. He was convicted in 1939 and imprisoned; the case helped to make Dewey a national figure.

Jack Alexander: "District Leader," *New Yorker,* 25 July 1936; 1 Aug 1936; 8 Aug 1936

Frank Vos

Hinsdale. Name applied to FLORAL PARK from about 1870 to 1890.

HIP. See HEALTH INSURANCE PLAN.

Hippodrome. A theater on the east side of 6th Avenue between 43rd and 44th streets, built by Frederick Thompson and Elmer S. Dundy, who had also created Luna Park on Coney Island, and opened in 1905. Called the largest theatrical structure in the world, it had an auditorium with 5300 seats and a vast projecting stage with two circus rings and a large elliptical water tank. The exterior of the building was distinguished by two corner towers, each supporting a sparkling globe outlined in electric lights. The Hippodrome was well known as the site of theatrical extravaganzas, performances by dancing elephants, boxing matches, operas, and appearances by Annette Kellerman, the "million dollar mermaid." It closed in 1939.

Rebecca Read Shanor

Hirschfeld, Al(bert) (*b* St. Louis, 21 June 1903). Cartoonist. In 1925 he began an association with the *New York Times,* where his pen-and-ink caricatures of personalities in the performing arts appeared as frequently as four times a week into the 1990s. He also displayed his work at the Whitney Museum of American Art, the Museum of Modern Art, the Metropolitan Museum of Art, and various galleries, published several anthologies, designed postage stamps, and wrote Broadway shows with S. J. Perelman and others. Hirschfeld's work is characterized by a distinctive, spare style that combines long, sweeping lines, intricate curves, and extensive cross-hatching. Early in his career he began concealing the name of his daughter Nina in his drawings; the number of times that her name appears is given near his signature.

Sara J. Steen

Hispanics. See LATIN AMERICANS.

Hippodrome, ca 1910

Hispanic Society of America. Nonprofit organization dedicated to preserving and displaying the art and culture of Spain and Portugal, formed in 1904 by the philanthropist Archer Milton Huntington (1870–1955), son of the railroad magnate Collis P. Huntington. It maintains a free museum and reference library at its headquarters on Audubon Terrace in Manhattan, which it first occupied in 1908. The collection was largely assembled by Huntington and ranges from prehistory through the periods of Roman and Moorish domination to the twentieth century; it includes paintings by such artists as Goya, El Greco, Velázquez, Luís de Morales, Joaquín Sorolla y Bastida, and Francisco de Zurbarán, as well as sculptures, works of decorative art, and a collection of Spanish ceramics that is considered the foremost in the United States. The library holds several thousand manuscripts and more than 200,000 early and modern books, as well as prints, photographs, and maps. The exterior of the building was designed by Huntington's cousin Charles Pratt

Al Hirschfeld, Algonquin Round Table *(1962). Reproduced by special arrangement with Hirschfeld's exclusive representative, the Margo Feiden Galleries, New York.* From left: *Lynn Fontanne, Dorothy Parker, Alfred Lunt, Robert Benchley, Robert E. Sherwood, Frank Crowninshield, Alexander Woollcott, Heywood Broun, George S. Kaufman, Marc Connelly, Edna Ferber, Frank Case, Franklin P. Adams*

Hispanic Society

Huntington and conforms to the neoclassical style of Audubon Terrace as a whole. The skylit interior of the main gallery, finished in elaborately worked, dark red terra cotta, suggests a courtyard of the Spanish Renaissance.

A History of the Hispanic Society of America, Museum and Library, 1904–1954, with a Survey of the Collections (New York: Hispanic Society of America, 1954)

Carol V. Wright

historical societies. The following historical societies in New York City are the subjects of entries in the encyclopedia: BRONX COUNTY HISTORICAL SOCIETY, BROOKLYN HISTORICAL SOCIETY, NEW-YORK HISTORICAL SOCIETY, QUEENS HISTORICAL SOCIETY, and STATEN ISLAND HISTORICAL SOCIETY.

historic preservation. Early efforts to preserve monuments of the colonial and Federal eras in New York City began in the last quarter of the nineteenth century, in opposition to what Walt Whitman described as "the pull-down-and-build-over-again spirit." Hamilton Grange was moved to a new site (1889) and Fraunces Tavern was reconstructed on its original site (1907) by the architect William Mersereau for the Sons of the Revolution. During the expansion of the municipal government City Hall was protected, as were a few historic houses such as the Morris–Jumel Mansion and Dyckman House in upper Manhattan and the Bartow–Pell and Van Cortlandt mansions in the Bronx. The advent of the Works Progress Administration (WPA) in 1935 provided opportunities for artists, architects, and historians to record the city's historic monuments. Berenice Abbott produced *Changing New York* (1939), the Historic American Buildings Survey commissioned a collection of drawings that documented Federal and Greek Revival architecture in New York City, and the WPA published its well-known *New York City Guide* (1939).

The enormous scope of the projects undertaken by Robert Moses aroused public sentiment in favor of historic preservation in New York City. The Municipal Art Society encouraged this interest in the 1950s when it sponsored architectural walking tours and compiled information on the city's notable structures that was eventually published in Alan Burnham's *New York Landmarks* (1963). State legislation allowing municipalities to set up landmark commissions was initiated by Albert Bard in 1956; by 1961 New York City revised its zoning, and Platt and Harmon Goldstone (on behalf of the Municipal Art Society) urged James Felt, chairman of the City Planning Commission, to implement aesthetic zoning as a means of preserving noteworthy structures. Instead Felt helped persuade Mayor Robert F. Wagner to form the Mayor's Committee for the Preservation of Structures of Historic and Esthetic Importance in 1962, and separate legislation was drafted to establish a permanent Landmarks Preservation Commission.

Many notable buildings were lost and historic neighborhoods eroded in New York City before legal means were devised to halt their destruction. Pennsylvania Station was demolished in 1963–64, as were the château-like Brokaw mansions on 5th Avenue at 79th Street in 1965, both events that helped galvanize public opinion in favor of historic preservation. The Brooklyn Heights Association attempted to protect buildings from demolition by petitioning for designation of the neighborhood as a national historic landmark and as a Historic District; landmark status was achieved after Wagner signed a bill that formed the Landmarks Preservation Commission in 1965. In the following year the National Historic Preservation Act established the National Register of Historic Places.

Historic preservation was further encouraged in the 1970s by changes in federal law that allowed large income tax credits for federally certified preservation and restoration work. By 1968 James Marston Fitch established at Columbia University the nation's first professional program in the restoration of historic architecture. The next two decades saw challenges to the landmarks law in New York City and in particular to the commission's regulatory jurisdiction over Grand Central Terminal (1978) and St. Bartholomew's Church on Park Avenue (1991). Each case went to the U.S. Supreme Court, which upheld the landmarks legislation and affirmed the regulation of historic places as a valid

Historic Districts of New York City

Brooklyn Heights, Brooklyn, 1965
Sniffen Court, Murray Hill, Manhattan, 1966
Turtle Bay Gardens, Turtle Bay, Manhattan, 1966
Charlton–King–Vandam, Greenwich Village, Manhattan, 1966
Gramercy Park, Manhattan, 1966, extended 1988
St. Nicholas, Harlem, Manhattan, 1967
Macdougal–Sullivan Gardens, Greenwich Village, Manhattan, 1967
Treadwell Farm, Upper East Side, Manhattan, 1967
Hunters Point, Long Island City, Queens, 1968
St. Mark's, East Village, Manhattan, 1969
Greenwich Village, Manhattan, 1969
Henderson Place, Yorkville, Manhattan, 1969
Mott Haven, Bronx, 1969
Cobble Hill Brooklyn, 1969, extended 1988
Jumel Terrace, Hamilton Heights, Manhattan, 1970
Chelsea, Manhattan, 1970, extended 1981
Stuyvesant Heights, Bedford–Stuyvesant, Brooklyn, 1970
Mount Morris Park, Harlem, Manhattan, 1971
Central Park West–West 76th Street, Upper West Side, Manhattan, 1973
Riverside Drive–West 105th Street, Upper West Side, Manhattan, 1973
Park Slope, Brooklyn, 1973
SoHo–Cast Iron District, SoHo, Manhattan, 1973
Carroll Gardens, Brooklyn, 1973
Boerum Hill, Brooklyn, 1973
Carnegie Hill, Upper East Side, Manhattan, 1974, expanded 1993
Hamilton Heights, Manhattan, 1974
Stuyvesant Square, Manhattan, 1975
South Street Seaport (i), Manhattan, 1977
Fulton Ferry, Brooklyn, 1977
Central Park West–West 73rd and 74th streets, Upper West Side, Manhattan, 1977
Metropolitan Museum, Upper East Side, Manhattan, 1977
Albemarle–Kenmore Terraces, Flatbush, Brooklyn, 1978
Brooklyn Academy of Music, Fort Greene, Brooklyn, 1978
Fort Greene, Brooklyn, 1978
Fraunces Tavern Block Financial District, Manhattan, 1978
Audubon Terrace, Washington Heights, Manhattan, 1979
Prospect Park South, Flatbush, Brooklyn, 1979
Prospect–Lefferts Gardens, Brooklyn, 1979
Longwood, Pueblo de Mayaguez, Bronx, 1980, extended 1983
Upper East East Side, Manhattan, 1981
Ditmas Park, Brooklyn, 1981
Clinton Hill, Brooklyn, 1981
Greenpoint, Brooklyn, 1982
Morris High School, Morrisania, Bronx, 1982
West End–Collegiate, Upper West Side, Manhattan, 1984
New York City Farm Colony–Searview Heights, Willowbrook, Staten Island, 1985
Riverside Drive–West 80th and 81st streets, Upper West Side, Manhattan, 1985
Morris Avenue, Tremont, Bronx, 1986
Tudor City, Turtle Bay, Manhattan, 1988
West 71st Street, Upper West Side, Manhattan, 1989
Riverside–West End Avenue, Upper West Side, Manhattan, 1989
Ladies' Mile, Flatiron District, Manhattan, 1989
South Street Seaport (ii), Manhattan, 1989
Central Park West, Upper West Side, Manhattan, 1990
Riverdale, Bronx, 1990
Tribeca West, Manhattan, 1991
Tribeca East, Manhattan, 1992
Tribeca North, Manhattan, 1992
Tribeca South, Manhattan, 1992
African Burial Ground and City Hall, Manhattan, 1993
Jackson Heights, Queens, 1993
St. George, Staten Island, 1993
Clay Avenue, Morrisania, Bronx, 1994
Mott Haven East, Mott Haven, Bronx, 1994
Bertine Block, Mott Haven, Bronx, 1994

part of the city's land-use policy. Despite the rulings the commission remained controversial: some critics believed that historic status should be granted only to individual buildings and that by designating entire neighborhoods the commission was defeating the intent of zoning; others contended that historic preservation inhibited development and was too costly; and in the 1980s several religious organizations sought exemption from the landmarks law on the grounds that it interfered with their mission, as a result of which the Landmarks Conservancy set up a sacred properties fund to help religious organizations maintain, restore, and repair their properties.

By 1994 the Landmarks Commission had designated 920 individual landmarks, eighty-nine interiors, nine scenic landmarks, and sixty-five Historic Districts containing a total of 19,143 properties throughout the five boroughs. These included distinctive residential neighborhoods such as Greenwich Village and the Upper West Side in Manhattan, Cobble Hill and Park Slope in Brooklyn, and a section of Riverdale in the Bronx. Any proposed demolition or new construction within a Historic District was subject to review and approval by the commission. The Municipal Art Society, a public-interest advocacy and educational group dedicated to preservation, formed two related organizations in the 1970s: the Historic Districts Council, which joins representatives from designated Historic Districts to discuss preservation and advocate new Historic Districts; and the New York Landmarks Conservancy, a nonprofit entity that administers a revolving fund for restoration projects and offers technical advice on preservation matters. Several groups with interests in specific types and periods of architecture help to educate their members and the public about historic preservation through lectures, walking tours, and publications; among these are the Victorian Society, the Friends of Cast Iron Architecture, and the Friends of Terra Cotta.

Harmon H. Goldstone and Martha Dalrymple: *History Preserved: A Guide to New York City Landmarks and Historic Districts* (New York: Simon and Schuster, 1974)
Barbaralee Diamonstein: *The Landmarks of New York* (New York: Harry N. Abrams, 1988)
Guide to New York City Landmarks (Washington: Preservation Press, 1992)

Marjorie Pearson

Historic Richmond Town. Historic site and outdoor museum in Richmond Creek Valley on Staten Island, near the geographic center of the borough and bordered by Latourette Park to the north and Richmondtown to the east. It was formerly known as Richmondtown Restoration. The site covers twenty-five acres (ten hectares) of land that were once the county seat and seventy-five acres (thirty hectares) of Richmond Creek, an estuary of the Fresh Kills. Of its twenty-seven historic buildings eleven are on their original sites, including Voorlezer's House (1696), believed to be the oldest extant schoolhouse in the United States; the Third County Courthouse (1837), now a visitor's center; and the office of the county clerk and surrogate (1848, 1886, 1912), now the Historical Museum. On the shores of the Fresh Kills are the sites of Richmond Mill and various farm buildings. In the 1960s eleven other historic buildings were moved to the site to prevent their destruction, including the Britton Cottage (1677, 1765, 1800) and the Guyon–Lake–Tysen House (1740, 1820), both from New Dorp. The Jacob Crocheron House (1820) was moved from Woodrow in 1988. Fifteen buildings are restored and open to the public; the others were undergoing restoration in the mid 1990s. Guided tours and interpretive programs illustrate the development of the village and the daily life of its residents. The permanent exhibition "Made on Staten Island" covers the economy of the borough and its relation to the surrounding region. Historic Richmond Town is administered by the Staten Island Historical Society, and its land and buildings are owned by the city, which provides operational assistance through its department of cultural affairs.

Barnett Shepherd

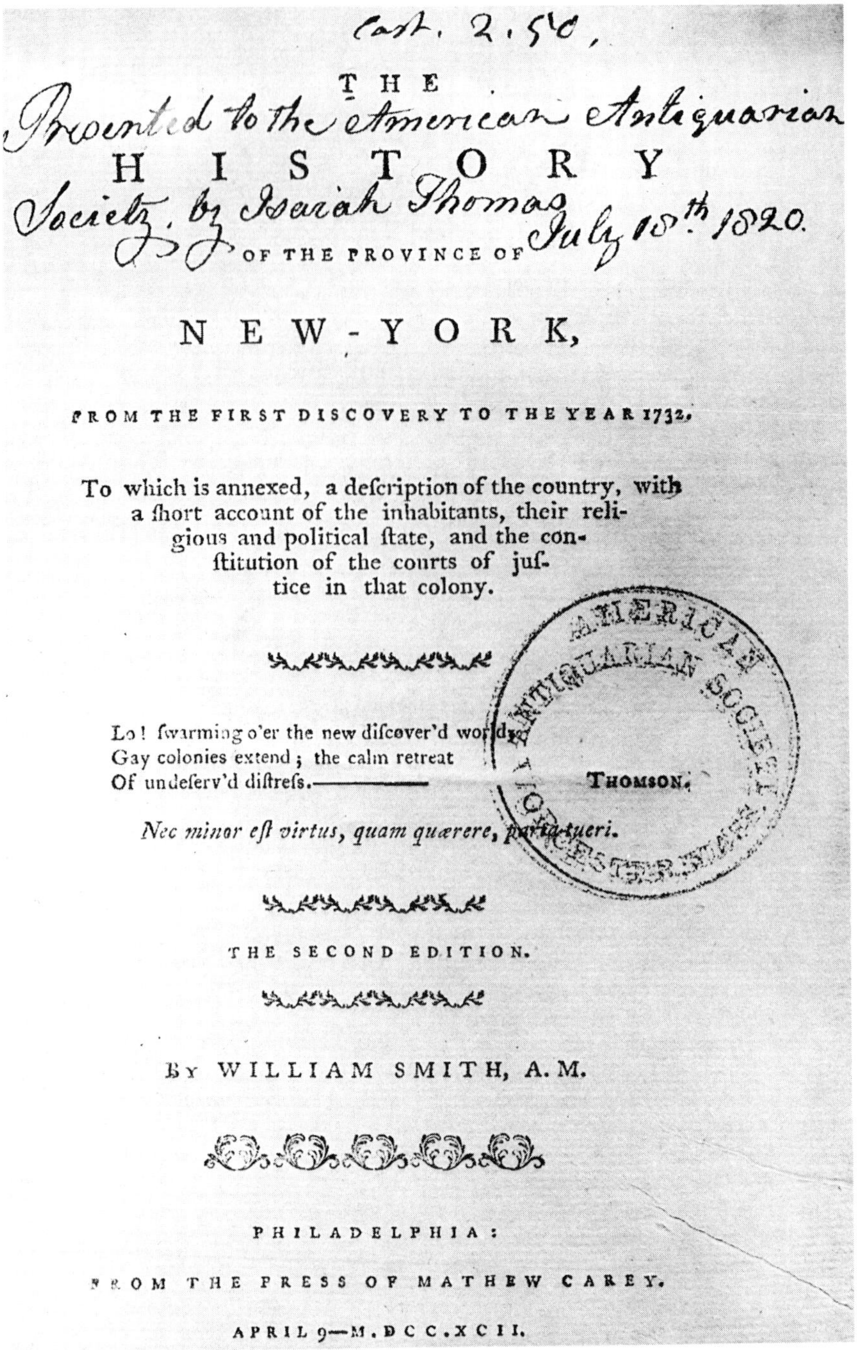

Cat. 2.50,

THE

Presented to the American Antiquarian Society, by Isaiah Thomas July 18th 1820.

HISTORY

OF THE PROVINCE OF

NEW-YORK,

FROM THE FIRST DISCOVERY TO THE YEAR 1732.

To which is annexed, a deſcription of the country, with a ſhort account of the inhabitants, their religious and political ſtate, and the conſtitution of the courts of juſtice in that colony.

Lo! ſwarming o'er the new diſcover'd world,
Gay colonies extend; the calm retreat
Of undeſerv'd diſtreſs.—— THOMSON.

Nec minor eſt virtus, quam quærere, parta tueri.

THE SECOND EDITION.

BY WILLIAM SMITH, A.M.

PHILADELPHIA:

FROM THE PRESS OF MATHEW CAREY.

APRIL 9—M.DCC.XCII.

Title page of the second edition of William Smith's The History of the Province of New-York *(1792)*

histories. The first serious attempt to trace the history of New York City was William Smith's *History of the Province of New-York* (London: Thomas Wilcox, 1757; rev. Philadelphia: Mathew Carey, 1792). Drawn from primary sources, this narrative gave particular attention to the early years of English control and extended down to the year 1732. Writers of the period such as Cadwallader Colden vigorously criticized the book because of the author's strong sympathies with the Whigs. Apart from reprints of Smith's book and collections of documents, historical writing on New York City after the American Revolution typically consisted of chapters in descriptive books such as Samuel L. Mitchell's *The Picture of New-York* (New York: I. Riley, 1807), the work that inspired Washington Irving's satiric *History of New York* (Philadelphia: Inskeep, Bradford, 1809). In the mid nineteenth century the first extended treatments of the city's history were written by Daniel Curry (1853), David T. Valentine (1853), Mary L. Booth (1859 and later editions), and William L. Stone (1872). With the exception of Joel T. Headley's *The Great Riots of New York, 1712 to 1873* (New York: E. B. Treat, 1873), the histories of this period stressed material progress, with little attention to social unrest and political corruption. Other laudatory interpretations of the city's history were written in the last quarter of the century by Benson J. Lossing (2 vols., 1884), Charles B. Todd (1888), and Martha Lamb (1877–96). R. S. Guernsey's *New York City and Vicinity during the War of 1812–15* (New York: C. L. Woodward, 1889–95) was recognized as one of the earliest works devoted to a specific historical period.

As New York City evolved into a world metropolis, historians increasingly combined hope for continued progress with a nostalgic celebration of simpler times. Works containing this more complex vision of the city were popular during the 1920s, among them Charles Hemstreet's *The Story of Manhattan* (New York: Charles Scribner's Sons, 1901) and the histories of William T. Bonner (1924) and Sarah M. Lockwood (1926). Henry C. Brown, founder of the Museum of the City of New York, wrote several historical volumes during the Depression, including *The Story of Old New York* (New York: E. P. Dutton, 1934). After the Second World War the manners and mores of New York City were recorded by such writers as Frank Weitenkampf in *Manhattan Kaleidoscope* (New York: Charles Scribner's Sons, 1947) and Lloyd R. Morris in *Incredible New York: High Life and Low Life of the Last Hundred Years* (New York: Random House,

1951). John A. Kouwenhoven wrote a careful pictorial history entitled *The Columbia Historical Portrait of New York* (Garden City, N.Y.: Doubleday, 1953); Benjamin A. Botkin, editor of *New York City Folklore* (New York: Random House, 1956), and Bayrd Still, editor of *Mirror for Gotham: New York as Seen by Contemporaries from Dutch Days to the Present* (New York: New York University Press, 1956), collected many useful sources.

Academic examinations of the political and social history of New York City proliferated from mid century. Among the most widely read were Charles Garrett's *The La Guardia Years: Machine and Reform Politics in New York City* (New Brunswick: N.J.: Rutgers University Press, 1961), Moses Rischin's *The Promised City: New York's Jews, 1870–1914* (Cambridge: Harvard University Press, 1962), Robert A. Caro's *The Power Broker: Robert Moses and the Fall of New York* (New York: Alfred A. Knopf, 1974), Charles Lockwood's *Manhattan Moves Uptown: An Illustrated History* (Boston: Houghton Mifflin, 1976), Thomas J. Archdeacon's *New York City, 1664–1710: Conquest and Change* (Ithaca, N.Y.: Cornell University Press, 1976), Thomas Kessner's *The Golden Door: Italian and Jewish Immigrant Mobility in New York City, 1800–1915* (New York: Oxford University Press, 1977), Gary B. Nash's *The Urban Crucible: The Northern Seaports and the Origins of the American Revolution* (Cambridge: Harvard University Press, 1979), Edward K. Spann's *The New Metropolis: New York City, 1840–1857* (New York: Columbia University Press, 1981), Amy Bridges's *A City in the Republic: Antebellum New York and the Origins of Machine Politics* (New York: Cambridge University Press, 1984), Thomas J. Davis's *A Rumor of Revolt: The "Great Negro Plot" in Colonial New York* (New York: Free Press, 1985), Thomas Bender's *New York Intellect: A History of Intellectual Life in New York City, from 1750 to the Beginnings of Our Own Time* (New York: Alfred A. Knopf, 1987), Joshua Freeman's *In Transit: The Transport Workers Union in New York City, 1933–1966* (New York: Oxford University Press, 1989), Kessner's *Fiorello H. La Guardia and the Making of Modern New York* (New York: McGraw–Hill, 1989), Richard Plunz's *A History of Housing in New York City: Dwelling Type and Social Change in the American Metropolis* (New York: Columbia University Press, 1990), and Roy Rosenzweig's and Elizabeth Blackmar's *The Park and the People: A History of Central Park* (Ithaca, N.Y.: Cornell Univerity Press, 1992). General histories of New York City for a mass market were written during this period by Susan E. Lyman, Stephen Longstreet, and Oliver E. Allen. Books with a more academic orientation included David Maldwyn Ellis's *New York, State and City* (Ithaca: N.Y.: Cornell University Press, 1979) and *A Brief History of New York City* (Port Washington, N.Y.: Associated Faculty Press, 1984), by George J. Lankevich and Howard B. Furer.

Neighborhoods, boroughs, and special topics about the history of New York City are discussed in books by Pamela Jones on the water system (1978), John G. Bunker on the port (1979), Jill Stone on Times Square (1982), Robert A. M. Stern, Gregory Gilmartin, and John Massengale on architecture in the late nineteenth century and the early twentieth (1983), David W. McCullough on Brooklyn (1983), Stephen Garmey on Gramercy Park (1984), Jill Jonnes on the South Bronx (1986), Stern, Gilmartin, and Thomas Mellins on architecture between the world wars (1987), and James Trager on the West Side (1987). Oral histories of the city include Jeff Kisseloff's *You Must Remember This: An Oral History of Manhattan from the 1890s to World War II* (San Diego: Harcourt Brace Jovanovich, 1989).

Harold Eugene Mahan

Hobart, John Henry (*b* Philadelphia, 14 Sept 1775; *d* Auburn, N.Y., 12 Sept 1830). Bishop. A leading Anglican advocate of High Church doctrine before the Oxford Movement, he helped to form the Protestant Episcopal Society for the Promotion of Religion and Learning in the State of New York (1802), the New-York Protestant Episcopal Bible and Common Prayer Book Society (1809), General Theological Seminary (1817), and many parishes and missions. Between 1816 and 1830 he was the bishop of the Episcopal Diocese of New York and the rector of Trinity Church. Known for his quick temper and iron hand, he wrote many books and took as his motto the phrase "Evangelical Truth and Apostolic Order." His proposal for a cathedral on Washington Square (1828) was later realized as the Cathedral of St. John the Divine.

Robert Bruce Mullin: *Episcopal Vision / American Reality: High Church Theology and Social Thought in Evangelical America* (New Haven: Yale University Press, 1986)

J. Robert Wright

Hoffman, Dustin (Lee) (*b* Los Angeles, 8 Aug 1937). Actor. He moved to New York City in 1958, lived on the Lower East Side, and made his début on Broadway in 1961. In the following years he worked off Broadway in productions of the American Place Theatre (1964–66) and the Circle in the Square (1967). After becoming widely known for his role in Mike Nichols's film *The Graduate* (1967) he continued to live and work at intervals in New York City, where he appeared in productions of Murray Schisgal's *Jimmy Shine* (1968–69), Arthur Miller's *Death of a Salesman* (1984), and *The Merchant of Venice* (1989).

Hoffman Island. A man-made island off the eastern shore of Staten Island. Built in 1872 on Orchard Shoals, it has an area of eleven acres (four and a half hectares) and is named for John T. Hoffman (mayor of New York City 1866–68, governor of New York State 1869–71). The island once housed a quarantine station used to isolate arriving immigrants suspected of having infectious diseases; for a time during the Second World War it was the site of a training facility of the U.S. Merchant Marine, as well as the anchorage of an antisubmarine net that extended across the entrance to the harbor. Now disused, it is part of the Gateway National Recreation Area and is inhabited by colonies of sea birds.

Gerard R. Wolfe

Hofstadter, Richard (*b* Buffalo, 6 Aug 1916; *d* New York City, 24 Oct 1970). Historian. After receiving his BA from the University of Buffalo in 1936 he moved to New York City to enroll in the graduate history program at Columbia University. With his wife he became active in the city's radical movement and joined a unit of the Communist Party at Columbia in 1938, but he had little interest in activist politics and left the party after a year. He taught part time at Brooklyn College and then full time at City College in the spring of 1941. His book *Social Darwinism in American Thought* (1944) became a classic work in American social history; in 1946 he joined the history department at Columbia, where in 1959 he became the De Witt Clinton Professor of American History. By the time of his death from leukemia he was widely recognized as the most important and influential historian of his generation. Hofstadter's published writings include *The American Political Tradition and the Men Who Made It* (1948), as well as *The Age of Reform* (1956) and *Anti-Intellectualism in American Life* (1963), both of which won Pulitzer prizes.

James Bradley

Hogan, Frank (Smithwick) (*b* Waterbury, Conn., 17 Jan 1902; *d* New York City, 2 April 1974). District attorney. After receiving his law degree from Columbia University in 1928 he worked for a private firm; he was later part of a two-man firm that became one of few of its size to survive the Depression. In 1935 he joined Thomas E. Dewey in a special investigation of organized crime, and after Dewey was elected district attorney of New York County in 1937 he became his administrative assistant. With Dewey's endorsement his own nomination for the office of district attorney was arranged in 1941 by the major political parties, perhaps largely because he had no strong political sympathies: he easily won the election and retained the office for thirty-two years, a tenure unmatched by any elected official in the city as late as the 1990s. He preserved the nonpartisan character of the office established by Dewey (whose reforms he expanded), emphasized the judicial nature of prosecution, and used extreme discretion in seeking indictments, thus helping to establish a model for prosecution throughout the country. Throughout the United States he was known as "Mr. District Attorney."

Mayer Mauer: "Hogan's Office Is a Kind of Ministry of Justice," *New York Times Magazine*, 2 Aug 1941, p. 16
Barry Cunningham: *Mr. District Attorney* (New York: Mason/Charter, 1977)

Emery E. Adoradio

Holiday, Billie [Fagan, Eleanora] (*b* Philadelphia, 7 April 1915; *d* New York City, 17 July 1959). Singer. The daughter of the guitarist Clarence Holiday, she began singing in nightclubs and bars in Harlem by the early 1930s. After gaining the attention of John Hammond she made her first recording in 1933 with Benny Goodman; during the 1930s she made recordings with small groups that included the pianist Teddy Wilson and several members of Count Basie's band, among them Lester Young, who gave her the nickname Lady Day. In 1937–38 she toured with the bands of Basie and Artie Shaw and also sang at nightclubs in Harlem. She later obtained long-term engagements at Café Society in Greenwich Village and as the principal performer at such nightclubs on 52nd Street as Kelly's Stables and the Onyx Club. Her impeccable timing, burnished tone, and profoundly expressive delivery made her the most important jazz singer after Louis Armstrong. Throughout her career she fought racism: she made critical remarks and was occasionally arrested for taking part in disputes after white nightclub patrons insulted her and attacked her companions. Her song "Strange Fruit" (1939) became well known at Café Society and was one of the first popular songs denouncing the treatment of blacks. At the height of her career she lived at 286 West 142nd Street. Heroin addiction and trouble with the police led her cabaret license to be revoked in 1949, and in the following years she performed less frequently, though she made several memorable appearances at Carnegie Hall. From 1957 Holiday lived at 26 West 87th Street. Her autobiography, *Lady Sings the Blues* (1956), indicts racism, ill-conceived drug policies, and hypocrisy.

Billie Holiday

Robert G. O'Meally: *Lady Day: The Many Faces of Billie Holiday* (New York: Little, Brown, 1991)

Douglas Henry Daniels

Holland House. Hotel at 276 5th Avenue, on the southwest corner of 30th Street. Designed in 1891 by the architects George Edward Harding and William Tyson Gooch as a reproduction of the Lords Holland Mansion in London, it was run on the European plan, in which meals are not included in the price of a room. The hotel had Gorham silver, Royal Worcester china, and Wilton carpeting and was said to be the grandest hotel in New York City until the Astoria was added to the Waldorf. A unique feature of the hotel was the Herzog Teleseme, an electromechanical indicator with which guests could dial any one of 140 services from their rooms. The Holland House closed with the onset of Prohibition and was converted into an office building.

Robert A. M. Stern, Gregory Gilmartin, and John Montague Massengale: *New York 1900: Metropolitan Architecture and Urbanism, 1890–1915* (New York: Rizzoli, 1983)

Val Ginter

Hollands. Neighborhood in south central Queens, lying on the Rockaway Peninsula around Beach 92nd Street. It was originally a parcel of sixty-five acres (twenty-six hectares) along Beach 92nd Street bought for $350 in 1855 by Michael P. Holland Sr., who had operated a hotel in Jamaica in the 1840s and 1850s and who opened a hotel on his newly acquired property in 1857. After his death his wife and his son Michael P. Holland Jr. speculated in real estate and operated the hotel, which was destroyed by fire on 9 April 1883 and then rebuilt. For twenty years the younger Holland was highly influential in Rockaway and initiated many improvements; he also operated Third Landing on the bay, the local point of embarkation for passengers of the Iron Steamboat Company. Hollands was incorporated with Hammels into the Village of Rockaway Beach in 1897. The extension of railroad service to Rockaway stimulated intensive development, and hundreds of hotels, boarding houses, and bathing pavilions were built along the beaches. In 1924 Cross Bay Boulevard opened for traffic, with a terminus at Beach 94th and Beach 95th streets. The Hollands subway station stands at Beach 90th Street.

Vincent Seyfried

Holland Tunnel. Double-tubed, underwater vehicular tunnel spanning the Hudson River between Canal Street in lower Manhattan and Jersey City, New Jersey. It was built over seven years by the Port of New York Authority and named after its engineer Clifford M. Holland, who died before its completion. When it opened in 1927 it was the longest underwater tunnel in the world, measuring 8557 feet (2610 meters) and having a maximum depth of ninety-three feet (28.4 meters). The greatest challenge in building the tunnel was the design of a ventilating system that would remove exhaust-filled air from the underground tubes and bring in fresh air. About two thousand tests were conducted to determine the amount of exhaust gases that would be produced and their effect on drivers. In the final stages of investigation an experimental tunnel was built to study the best method of ventilation: this study resulted in an innovative system in which fresh air is drawn from outside through four ventilating buildings and blown by fans into a duct under the tunnel roadway. The air is released through narrow slots above the curb and dilutes the exhaust gases, which are drawn out through an exhaust duct in the ceiling of the tunnel. The ventilating system of the Holland Tunnel became the model for other underwater tunnels in New York City and around the world.

Bernard J. Walker: "The Hudson River Vehicular Tunnel," *Scientific American*, Sept 1927, pp. 200–3

Rebecca Read Shanor

Holliday [Tuvim], **Judy** (*b* New York City, 21 June 1921; *d* New York City, 7 June 1965). Actress. She graduated from Julia Richman High School in Manhattan in 1938 and began working as a backstage switchboard operator for Orson Welles's Mercury Theatre. She then joined with Betty Comden, Adolph Green, John Frank, and Alvin Hammer to form a cabaret troupe called the Revuers, which performed in nightclubs such as the Village Vanguard and on radio from the autumn of 1938 until 1944. In 1945 she made her début on the stage in *Kiss Them for Me.* She replaced Jean Arthur in the role of Billie Dawn in the play *Born Yesterday* in 1946, which ran for almost four years and made her widely known; she also appeared in the film version of the play in 1950, winning an Academy Award for best actress. Her performance as the dim-witted Doris Attinger in the motion picture *Adam's Rib* (1949) was also highly regarded. Her liberal leanings caught the attention of the Senate Internal Security Subcommittee, which called her to testify in 1952, and her career suffered as a result; Garson Kanin later said of her appearance before the committee that no one was "more steadfast or less craven." She began rebuilding her career with the motion picture *It Should Happen to You* (1954) and appeared in the play *Bells Are Ringing* (1956) in a role written for her by Comden and Green, winning a Tony Award for her performance. Her last major film, a version of the play, was shot in 1960. Holliday was noted for her ability to convey shades of meaning with vocal inflections.

Gary Carey: *Judy Holliday: An Intimate Life Story* (New York: Seaview, 1982)

Will Holtzman: *Judy Holliday* (New York: G. P. Putnam's Sons, 1982)

Allen J. Share

Hollis. Neighborhood in central Queens, bounded to the north by Grand Central Parkway, to the east by Francis Lewis Boulevard, to the south by Hollis Avenue, and to the west by 184th Street. It was established in 1885 by Frederick W. Denton, a nephew of Austin Corbin who was a supervisor of Jamaica Town and a promoter of the Bicycle Railroad in East Patchogue, Long Island. He planned to name it Woodhull after a general who was captured by a British detachment in 1776 at what is now 197th Street and Jamaica Avenue, but to avoid confusion with another Woodhull in Steuben County he named it instead after his own birthplace in New Hampshire. A railroad station was built during the summer of 1885. A tollgate on the Hempstead and Jamaica Turnpike at Jamaica Avenue and 186th Street was used until 4 October 1895. Carpenter's Tavern (1710), the site of General Woodhull's capture, was replaced by housing in 1921. The neighborhood grew slowly as fine Victorian houses were erected along Woodhull Avenue between 188th and 198th streets. The extension of trolley service in May 1897 attracted developers of upper-middle-class houses: in 1906 Hollis Park Gardens was built between 192nd and 195th streets between Jamaica and Hillside avenues, and many similar developments were added during the next twenty years. The growing demand for housing stimulated the construction in 1921 of blocks of row houses, concentrated between Jamaica and Hillside avenues. By the Second World War no open land remained and Hollis was a commuter suburb. After 1955 the ethnic composition changed south of the railroad, and by 1980 the population was 80 percent black and Latin American. During the following decade the neighborhood attracted some immigrants from Guyana, Haiti, China, India, and Colombia. In the mid 1990s Hollis was a middle-class community of well-kept, one-family houses, with fewer than half a dozen high-rise apartment buildings.

Vincent Seyfried

Holliswood. Neighborhood in east central Queens, bounded to the north by Grand Central Parkway, to the east by Francis Lewis Boulevard, to the south by Hillside Avenue, and to the west by 188th Street. It was a hilly and heavily wooded area north of Hollis when it was promoted as a site for upper-middle-class housing in 1905 by the Grenoble Realty Company. Because the area was isolated and far from all means of transport, the sale of lots was slow and in 1918 the plan failed. As the need for housing grew during the 1920s, interest in development renewed and many houses were built. Growth slowed during the Depression but revived during the 1930s and continued after the Second World War. A number of Haitian, Chinese, and Indian immigrants settled in the neighborhood and its environs in the 1980s. In the mid 1990s Holliswood was an area of winding streets and irregular parcels; its many trees and elegant houses with large yards made it one of the most attractive neighborhoods in Queens.

Vincent Seyfried

Holm, Hanya (*b* Worms, Germany, 3 March 1893; *d* New York City, 3 Nov 1992). Choreographer. She settled in New York City in 1931 and opened a branch of the Wigman School, named for the German modern dancer Mary Wigman. In 1936 she opened her own school in New York City and developed a form of dance that combined Wigman's tradition of expressionism with her own gift for abstract design. She presented her first American work, *Trend* (1937), at the Bennington College School of Dance, where she taught with Martha Graham, Charles Weidman, and Doris Humphrey. Holm also provided choreography for the musical comedies *Kiss Me Kate* (1948) and *My Fair Lady* (1956). She retired from teaching in 1967 but continued to work with the Nikolais Dance Theater.

Walter Sorell: *Hanya Holm: The Biography of an Artist* (Middletown, Conn.: Wesleyan University Press, 1969)

Peter M. Rutkoff, William B. Scott

Holmes, John Haynes (*b* Philadelphia, 1879; *d* New York City, 3 April 1964). Minister and social activist. A descendant of Pilgrims, he graduated from Harvard College and the Harvard Divinity School. In February 1907 he was asked to take over the Church of the Messiah of New York City, which much of the conservative congregation had abandoned after Minot Savage's retirement. A pacifist during the First World War, Holmes was little understood even by his fellow ministers. After the war the church was destroyed by fire; when rebuilt it was renamed the Community Church of New York City. Holmes was a socialist with views similar to those of Norman Thomas. He was active in the American Civil Liberties Union and supported many other liberal causes, especially those concerning the plight of black Americans. He wrote an autobiography, *I Speak for Myself* (1959).

Walter Donald Kring

Holt, Rinehart and Winston. The history of the publishing house Holt, Rinehart and Winston is discussed in the entry HENRY HOLT.

Holy Name societies. For a discussion of Holy Name societies see ARCHDIOCESAN UNION OF THE HOLY NAME SOCIETY.

Holy Trinity Cathedral of the Ukrainian Autocephalic Orthodox Church. Cathedral at 117–85 South 5th Street in Williamsburg, built in 1906 as the main branch of the Williamsburg Trust Company by the architectural firm of Helmle and Huberty, which also designed the boathouse in Prospect Park. The building is an opulent terra cotta temple in the Roman Revival style inspired by the World's Columbian Exhibition of 1893. It was the main branch of Williamsburg Trust until 1911. After the bank was dissolved by the U.S. Supreme Court on 7 March 1922 the building stood vacant for some time. After remodeling it housed the Magistrate Court of the 5th District from 1928 and became a cathedral in the mid 1960s.

Brooke J. Barr

Home Box Office [HBO]. National cable television service launched in New York City in November 1972. It initially had headquarters in the Time Warner Building (50th Street and 6th Avenue) before moving them in 1983 to Times Square. The first successful venture of its kind, by the mid 1990s it operated a satellite system that provided service to more than seventeen million customers; its offerings included motion pictures, comedy programs, and sports broadcasts. In the summer comedians engaged by HBO provide entertainment at lunchtime in Bryant Park.

Janet Frankston

Homecrest. Neighborhood in southwestern Brooklyn, bounded to the north by Avenue U, to the east by East 21st Street, to the south by Avenue W, and to the west by Ocean Parkway. The area was originally farmland in the town of Gravesend and was developed from 1900, when it was advertised as "Homecrest by the Sea." Residents could walk to the shore in ten minutes and reach Manhattan by train in thirty. Large one-family Victorian houses on landscaped double lots had the latest modern conveniences. Of the many new immigrants who settled in the neighborhood and its environs during the 1980s more than a quarter were Chinese; others were from the Soviet Union, Israel, Korea, Italy, Syria, Egypt, and Lebanon. The quiet streets of Homecrest are lined with trees and modest one- and two-family brick houses, one-story bungalows, townhouses, and low-rise apartment buildings. The main commercial district lies along Avenue U and there is additional shopping along Coney Island Avenue.

Elizabeth Reich Rawson

Home Insurance Company. Firm of insurers incorporated in 1853. It grew steadily and became licensed throughout the United States as a provider of property and casualty insurance. In 1992 Home Insurance had total assets of $4200 million and $1300 million in net written premium, and was among the thirty-five largest property and casualty insurers in the United States. Its headquarters are at 59 Maiden Lane and its subsidiaries include the securities broker Gruntal Financial Corporation (also based in New York City) and Sterling Forest Corporation, a major landowner and developer in Orange County, New York.

Claude M. Scales III

homelessness. Provisions for the homeless in New York City date to the late seventeenth century, when the city and a number of its churches rented a building for emergency housing. In 1734 the city erected a "house of correction, workhouse and poorhouse" where residents were referred to as "family" in posted rules. The police routinely put up the shelterless before 1857, when each precinct was required to designate a station house to lodge "vagrant and disorderly persons." These were informal arrangements offering part-time shelter and required no submission to authority other than an agreement to behave oneself for the night. Although repeatedly denounced, these provisions did offer an alternative to the almshouse and the workhouse. This practice of offering the "soft side of a plank" to the vagrant poor gave rise to an enduring policy of improvisation. The demand for these refuges increased rapidly with economic downturns and declined chiefly when vagrancy statutes were enforced. Responding to the "great evil of homelessness among the honest poor," the Department of Charities and Corrections opened a lodging house for three months in early 1866. A similar facility was opened in 1877 by a citizens' group known as the Night Refuge Association. Organized charity did little to ease the lot of the "disreputable" poor, devoting itself instead to developing new methods of discipline. Aside from emergency measures to quell the rumblings of unemployed seamen, the first privately organized efforts were directed at "wild children" of the streets and at women suspected of prostitution.

In the years after the Civil War a host of evangelical "rescue missions" opened their doors, and in times of dire need citizens' groups organized drives to distribute food, fuel, and clothing to the desperately poor. Such efforts drew severe criticism from advocates of "scientific charity," who railed against "indiscriminate" almsgiving as well as the "tramp evil." In 1886 the state legislature passed the Municipal Lodging House Act, which empowered the city to open shelters for the homeless, excluding women, children, the elderly, and the infirm. To demonstrate the advantages of a well-ordered municipal shelter, the Charity Organization Society in 1893 opened the Wayfarer's Lodge, where guests paid for their stay by chopping wood. Other public shelters later adopted similar "work tests" but enforced them erratically. In February 1896 Police Commissioner Theodore Roosevelt abruptly closed the station houses, largely at the urging of the reformer Jacob A. Riis. No alternative facility had been prepared, and thousands of the homeless poor were left without shelter until a barge moored in the East River at 26th Street was hastily refurbished for their use. Other buildings were pressed into service until 1909, when the first Municipal Lodging House opened at 438 East 25th Street. It had the latest amenities, nearly a thousand beds, and a separate dormitory for women and children. Virtually from the start the Municipal Lodging House proved unequal to demand, and many of the homeless resorted to the old practice of "sleeping rough," usually in parks but also under bridges and in saloons, waiting rooms, churches, public toilets, and the subways. In times of severe economic depression the city lodged men on steamboats and piers along the East River, on Ellis Island, in jails, and even in the morgue. The Municipal Lodging House suffered from corrupt practices imposed by Tammany Hall but enjoyed a brief renaissance during reforms between 1914 and 1918. Stuart Rice, the superintendent and himself formerly homeless, described it as a "hybrid institution" saddled with the impossible task of providing emergency respite for men temporarily unemployed and rehabilitating those with crippling disabilities.

Homeless women at a temporary shelter attached to the 30th Street police station, ca *1885–90*

Measures of extraordinary scale were taken during the Depression. Two enormous "annexes" with nearly four thousand beds between them opened in 1930–32. A few facilities limited admission to the "better" classes, among them the "Gold Dust Lodge" of the Salvation Army. In 1935 separate provision was made for homeless women, and two work camps opened north of the city. In June nearly 21,000 persons, including transient families, were sheltered nightly by the city, more than ever before. Some needs went unmet: censuses at the time found thousands living in the streets, subways, and parks; shantytowns, some with hundreds of residents, were built in Riverside Park and Central Park, in Central Park, and along the East River. As workers were recruited to support the Second World War, the ranks of the homeless came to exclude nearly all but the elderly and disabled. Public shelters housed fewer than eight hundred men a night in 1944.

The nightly census in public shelters for men rose to about eight thousand in 1959. During the 1960s poor, elderly white men congregated along the Bowery, a grubby, mile-long "skid row" of flophouses, missions, and rough taverns. About eight thousand men lived in cheap lodgings. Most paid their way with pensions or by working in casual labor pools, panhandling, unloading trucks, or washing automobile windshields. Small groups of men pooled change for bottles of wine, repairing to streetcorners and vacant lots to drink it. The police made occasional sweeps for drunkards, but a more serious threat was the "jackrollers" who preyed on the unwary and the unconscious. Missionaries offered soup and sermons. The city's "Muni" on East 3rd Street housed six hundred men until 1964; in the following years scores of others slept in the lobby. The rest stayed in free missions, jails, and municipal hospitals, with only a few dozen sleeping outdoors. For the most part shelter was not a problem for

Hooverville in Queens, 1932

these homeless men. Sociologists took to defining homelessness in social terms, as "disaffiliation." In other words, although many of the men had stable sources of income, they had sundered the usual ties to work, family, and community and had no interest in forging new ones.

Despite confident predictions of its demise, visible homelessness extended well beyond the Lower East Side by the early 1970s. As neighborhoods were revitalized, flophouses gradually disappeared and affordable housing for the poor became scarce, especially after the loss of about 100,000 low-cost units in single-room occupancy hotels (SROs). These developments had severe repercussions for the city's shelters. From the early 1960s thousands of the mentally ill were discharged from institutions, some without provision for housing; unused to living on their own, they were easily exploited by unscrupulous landlords. By the mid 1970s severe psychiatric disorder rivaled alcoholism as the dominant affliction of homeless persons treated by clinicians in the city's shelters. Men were accommodated in the few remaining flophouses on the Bowery and on the floor of the lobby, or "Big Room," of the Muni on East 3rd Street; women were provided with only forty-seven beds in a shelter on Lafayette Street. Both facilities regularly turned applicants away. In October 1979 the case of *Callahan v. Carey* was brought against the city and the state by Robert Hayes, a young Wall Street lawyer, on behalf of three homeless plaintiffs, for violations of constitutional and statutory obligations to care for the indigent needy. New facilities were added after a preliminary ruling by the New York State Supreme Court late in 1979 that recognized a right to shelter and ordered the city to provide it to all eligible applicants (the ruling defined shelter as including "clean bedding, wholesome food and adequate security and supervision"). In August 1981 the case was settled by a consent decree reaffirming a right to shelter, setting minimal standards for its provision, and ensuring regular monitoring of conditions. This in turn became the basis of continuing legal disputes between city government and advocates for the homeless about the definition of adequate shelter. Similar protection was extended to women and families in later suits.

During the 1980s thousands of the homeless poor remained encamped on the streets. Many suffered from severe psychiatric disorders and were terrified of the city's warehouse-like shelters. For these persons a few innovative "supportive residences" were opened. The number of homeless families grew steadily and reached 5200 (17,800 persons) in January 1988, a virtually unparalleled number; most were led by one parent, and half were sheltered in costly "welfare hotels," half in congregate facilities and efficiency units. Pressured by the courts, a vocal advocacy movement, and the threatened loss of federal funds, Mayor Edward I. Koch expedited the renovation of tax-foreclosed properties for use by homeless families in the late 1980s; about twenty thousand units were reclaimed in this way between 1987 and 1991. The program was later diluted under Mayor David N. Dinkins, long a critic of shelter-based policy for the homeless. By this time the city had opened fifteen shelters for men and twelve for women. In 1990 combined occupancy reached more than eleven thousand. Need nonetheless far outstripped the housing supply.

Nels Anderson: *The Homeless in New York City* (New York: Welfare Council, 1934)

Howard Bahr: *Skid Row: An Introduction to Disaffiliation* (New York: Oxford University Press, 1973)

Rick Beard, ed.: *On Being Homeless: Historical Perspectives* (New York: Museum of the City of New York, 1987)

Kim Hopper

Home Life Insurance Company. Firm of insurers formed by several prominent residents of Brooklyn, including A. A. Low and John T. Stranahan (1808–98), a former congressman. It opened headquarters at the corner of Court and Joralemon streets on 1 May 1860, as well as a branch on Wall Street. The headquarters moved in 1870 to Manhattan and in 1892 to a new building at 256 Broadway designed by the firm of Napoleon Le Brun and Sons (this was among the tallest buildings in the world when it opened). The firm introduced guaranteed insurability for prospective policyholders and offered business insurance, pension planning, and life insurance plans that helped families to pay college tuition. Its headquarters moved in 1987 to 75 Wall Street. In 1990 Home Life had assets of $14,000 million and $45,000 million of policies in force.

James Bradley

Homeport–Stapleton. A base of the U.S. Navy in Staten Island. The name refers to a strategy called "homeporting," according to which vessels are dispersed among many ports as a safeguard against catastrophic losses that can result if a fleet is concentrated in only a few ports. The base opened in 1990 to provide a berth for battleships, destroyers, cruisers, and reserve frigates. It included a technologically advanced pier measuring 1410 feet (430 meters) by ninety feet (27.5 meters), with large maintenance buildings nearby. More than four thousand uniformed personnel working at the base were housed at Fort Wadsworth and elsewhere on Staten Island and in Brooklyn. As part of a nationwide policy to reduce and reallocate military spending, the federal government closed Homeport–Stapleton in 1994.

Barnett Shepherd

Homer, Winslow (*b* Boston, 24 Feb 1836; *d* Scarborough, Maine, 29 Sept 1910). Painter. After fulfilling an apprenticeship at the age of twenty-one in the lithography firm of Bufford, he moved to New York City and attended night school at the National Academy of Design. In 1859 he moved to 128 East 16th Street. During the first years of the Civil War he was sent to sketch scenes of the front, which were published in *Harper's Weekly.* On returning to the city he concentrated on war paintings and was elected to the National Academy of Design; his work was shown at a number of exhibitions there. Homer lived in a studio at 51 West 10th Street (erected 1857) during the 1870s and in another at Washington Square North and University Place from 1882 until 1884, when he moved to Prout's Neck, Maine.

Gordon Hendricks: *The Life and Work of Winslow Homer* (New York: Harry N. Abrams, 1979)

Nicolai Cikovsky: *Winslow Homer* (New York: Harry N. Abrams, 1990)

James E. Mooney

home rule. The legal term for local autonomy. The concept of home rule emerged in the nineteenth century in opposition to legal doctrines that treated cities as inferior creatures of their states, possessing only those powers expressly delegated to them, and subject to the plenary power of the states to alter, reduce, or abolish local authority. Home rule affirms the power of local governments to legislate regarding local matters, and limits the power of states to displace local decisions.

The constitution of New York State first provided a measure of home rule for New

Winslow Homer, The New Year *(1869)*

York City in 1894. The current home rule provision, article IX, was adopted in 1963. Among other provisions it prohibits the state from adopting special laws concerning the property, affairs, or government of New York City, except at the city's request. (There is no comparable restriction on general laws, by which the state may exert its authority over municipal matters.) Article IX also grants the city and other local governments the authority to adopt and amend local laws relating to local "property, affairs, or government," as well as other specifically enumerated local matters, including the "government, protection, order, conduct, safety, health, and well-being of persons or property" within the locality, as long as the local laws are not inconsistent with the state constitution or general laws.

Home rule has generally been effective in enabling local governments to take the initiative and legislate with respect to local matters without having to obtain express permission from the state government. It does not, however, provide the city with much legal protection from interference by the state legislature. The New York State Court of Appeals has held that the legislature may act by special law with respect to local "property, affairs, or government" without a request from the city "if the subject be in a substantial degree a matter of state concern . . . though intermingled with it are concerns of the locality" (*Adler v. Deegan*, 1929, concurring opinion of Chief Judge Cardozo). The court has also found that the property, affairs, and government of New York City are often matters of state concern. It has sustained special state laws regulating the city's multiple dwellings, mandating that a specific percentage of the city's budget be devoted to education, and displacing city residency requirements for municipal employees. Home rule also does not apply to local finances. Local governments in New York State are dependent on the legislature for the power to tax. Local spending, borrowing, taxing, and lending are subject to tight constitutional restraints, and may be further restricted by the legislature.

Richard Briffault

homoeopathy. A system of medical treatment in which small doses of medicines are administered that produce symptoms similar to those of the disease being treated, thus inducing the body to heal itself. It originated in the work of the German physician Samuel Hahnemann and was introduced in the United States by Hans Burch Gram (1786–1840), who began practicing medicine in New York City in 1825. Gram's efforts led to the formation in 1835 of the New York Homoeopathic Society and in 1841 of the New York Homoeopathic Physicians' Society. In 1844 homoeopaths in the city were instrumental in forming the national American Institute of Homoeopathy; the Homoeopathic Medical College of New York opened in 1860 (known from 1869 as the New York Homoeopathic Medical College). The number of homoeopaths in the city grew from 115 in 1860 to nearly a thousand by the turn of the century. Among the most prominent were Timothy F. Allen (1873–1902), William Tod Helmuth (1833–1902), Samuel Lilienthal (1815–91), and George S. Norton (1851–91). Several publishers in the city issued works about homoeopathy, including Boericke and Runyon, William Radde and Son, Hahnemann Publishing House, and Chatterton.

Having failed in their attempt in 1857 to have half the beds at Bellevue Hospital set aside for homoeopathic practice, homoeopaths in 1863 organized the New York Medical College for Women, one of only two institutions of its kind in the world. The first class of six was admitted in 1866 and a hospital for women and children was added a few years later, the whole institution now called the New York Medical College and Hospital for Women. This remained in operation until 1918, when the trustees decided to close the hospital and admit the remaining women to the Homoeopathic Medical College of New York, which until then had admitted only men. The opening of Hahnemann Hospital in 1869 at Lexington Avenue and 67th Street was followed by that of the New York Homoeopathic Surgical Hospital in 1874. In 1875 the two institutions merged and one hospital building on Wards Island was set aside for homoeopathy. By 1900 there were more than one hundred homoeopathic clinics, dispensaries, and hospitals in the city; these included Hahnemann Hospital and the Laura Franklin Free Hospital for Children at 17 East 111th Street, formed in 1886 by Franklin Delano and his wife (these two combined in 1922 to form the Fifth Avenue Hospital at 105th Street, advertised as the first hospital in the world to contain only rooms for individual patients rather than wards), as well as Flower Hospital, Metropolitan Hospital, Harlem Homoeopathic Hospital, and Ward's Island Homoeopathic Hospital.

The decline of homoeopathy in the city and the nation resulted in part from its convergence with traditional medicine and its consequently growing acceptance. By the early twentieth century the homoeopath was a well-trained physician primarily and a practitioner of homoeopathy only secondarily, and homoeopathy soon gained the approval of the medical establishment. The decision of the New York Homoeopathic Medical College to rename itself the New York Medical College in 1936 marked the end of a long period of influence for homoeopathy in the city.

Interest in homoeopathy revived in the early 1970s amid growing dissatisfaction with the American health system. By offering an alternative to the aggressive, highly technical methods of conventional medicine, homoeopathy won new followers attracted by its emphasis on health, natural medicines, and treating the whole person rather than the diseased organ. A National Center for Homoeopathy, offering information and referral, opened in 1974 in Alexandria, Virginia; in 1991 its listing of homoeopathic practitioners included thirteen in New York City.

William Harvey King, ed.: *History of Homoeopathy and Its Institutions in America* (New York: Lewis, 1905)
James J. Walsh: *History of Medicine in New York: Three Centuries of Medical Progress* (New York: National Americana Society, 1919)
Leonard P. Wershub: *One Hundred Years of Medical Progress: A History of New York Medical College, Flower and Fifth Avenue Hospitals* (Springfield, Ill.: Charles C. Thomas, 1967)

Martin Kaufman: *Homoeopathy in America: The Rise and Fall of a Medical Heresy* (Baltimore: Johns Hopkins University Press, 1971)

Phillip A. Nicholls: *Homoeopathy and the Medical Profession* (London: Croom Helm, 1988)

Francesco Cordasco: *Homoeopathy in the United States: A Bibliography of Homoeopathic Medical Imprints, 1825–1925* (Fairview, N.J.: Junius Vaughn, 1991)

Francesco Cordasco

Hondurans. The first Honduran immigrants in New York City were Garifuna, natives of an area along the Caribbean coast of mixed African, American Indian, and European ancestry who speak a creole language unrelated to Spanish. Garifuna from Honduras played an important role in the early 1960s in organizing hospital workers in Local 1199. Many Hondurans settled near Southern Boulevard and Van Cortlandt Park in the Bronx, and in Flatbush and near Pennsylvania Avenue in Brooklyn, where there were also Garifuna from other Central American countries. In 1980 the federal census counted 9500 Hondurans in the city, and during the next decade eleven thousand Hondurans moved there and became legal residents. By other estimates there were about forty thousand immigrants, and that of the Honduran consulate for the metropolitan area was seventy thousand. During war and upheaval in Central America from the late 1970s to the early 1990s Honduran mestizos of Spanish and Indian descent settled in the city, especially along Pennsylvania Avenue. A few were professionals; most were single, lacked permanent resident status, and worked in manufacturing and service industries. Racial discrimination and lack of documentation severely limited opportunities for Garifuna, who sought education and formed civic groups in Brooklyn. Hondurans accounted for most of the eighty-seven victims of a fire at the Happy Land social club on Southern Boulevard in the Bronx in 1990.

Graciela M. Castex

Hone, Philip (*b* New York City, 25 Oct 1780; *d* New York City, 5 May 1851). Businessman, mayor, and diarist. The son of a joiner, he became wealthy in an auction business that he formed with his brothers in 1797, and in 1821 he retired to pursue his artistic, cultural, and political interests. He served two terms as an assistant alderman and in 1825 was chosen by the Common Council for a one-year term as mayor, during which he presided over the opening of the Erie Canal and entertained the Marquis de Lafayette. After losing much of his fortune in the panic of 1837 he returned to work; he eventually received an appointment from President Zachary Taylor. Hone is best known for his diary, in which he wrote about political events and the social life of the city's élite from 1826 until his death.

Louis Auchincloss, ed.: *The Hone and Strong Diaries of Old Manhattan* (New York: Abbeville, 1989)

See also U.S. CUSTOMS SERVICE.

Evan Cornog

Honest Ballot Association. Organization formed in 1909 by Theodore Roosevelt and other civic leaders as a response to election fraud in New York City. It worked to ensure honest public elections by such measures as replacing paper ballots with voting machines. The association now occupies offices at 272-30 Grand Central Parkway in Floral Park and supervises balloting for unions, corporations, and organizations.

Alan Levin: "They Guard the Polls," *Sunday News*, 31 Jan 1965, pp. 76–77

Lawrence Van Gelder: "To Help Keep Elections Honest, a Former Politician Steps In," *New York Times*, 20 Jan 1985, §11 [Long Island Weekly]

Bernard Hirschhorn

Hood, Raymond M(athewson) (*b* Pawtucket, R.I., 21 March 1881; *d* Stamford, Conn., 15 Aug 1934). Architect. After studying at the École des Beaux-Arts and working for Henry Hornbostel in Pittsburgh he moved to New York City in 1914. With John Mead Howells he entered a competition to design the Chicago Tribune Building in 1922; their submission, a plan for a neo-Gothic tower, won the first prize of $50,000. Hood then designed a number of innovative skyscrapers in New York City, among them the American Radiator Building at 40 East 40th Street (1924, now American Standard), which he modeled after a medieval spire, clad in black brick and gold terra cotta ornament, and illuminated at night. Further experiments with color and pattern culminated in the Daily News Building at 220 East 42nd Street (1930, with J. M. Howells), with a façade of bold vertical stripes of white brick and dark window bands, and the McGraw–Hill Building at 330 East 42nd Street (1931), sheathed with blue-green terra cotta tiles. A member of the team that designed Rockefeller Center, he was largely responsible for the RCA Building and the concept of roof gardens. Hood was highly successful at persuading clients that his unusual ideas would return profits and gain wide publicity.

Walter H. Kilham Jr.: *Raymond Hood, Architect: Form through Function* (New York: Architectural Book Publishing, 1973)

For illustrations see ARCHITECTURE and MCGRAW–HILL BUILDING.

Carol Willis

Hook, Sidney (*b* New York City, 20 Dec 1902; *d* Stanford, Calif., 12 July 1989). Philosopher. He grew up in Williamsburg and studied with Morris Raphael Cohen at City College of New York and with John Dewey at Columbia University. He joined the faculty at New York University in 1927, remaining until 1972. Although initially an advocate of communism and a supporter of the Communist presidential candidate in 1932, by 1934 he was a tenacious anti-communist who believed that Stalin had betrayed the principles of socialism. After publishing *Towards the Understanding of Karl Marx* (1933) and *From Hegel to Marx* (1936) he was widely accepted as the preeminent American scholar of Marxism. During the 1930s he sought to counter the appeal of the Popular Front and in 1939 he organized the Committee for Cultural Freedom to emphasize the similarities between Stalinism and fascism; in 1949 he became the primary organizer and first leader of the American Committee for Cultural Freedom. Often near the center of intellectual controversies in the city and the nation, Hook was a proponent of philosophical pragmatism. He considered scientific thought the primary avenue to truth, argued vigorously for a definition of academic freedom that excluded communists, and supported nuclear deterrence, vigilance during the cold war, and an active welfare state. In 1987 he published the memoir *Out of Step: An Unquiet Life in the Twentieth Century*.

Paul Kurtz, ed.: *Sidney Hook and the Contemporary World: Essays on the Pragmatic Intelligence* (New York: John Day, 1968)

Terry A. Cooney

Hook Creek. A tributary of Jamaica Bay and by extension a neighborhood in the southeast corner of Queens, on a narrow neck of land fronting the bay on three sides. It is surrounded by marshes and consists of fishing shacks and boat supply outlets on three short streets. The neck is bisected by Rockaway Boulevard, a heavily traveled artery that gives access to the Rockaway Peninsula. Before 1920 the boulevard was a narrow turnpike road impassable during exceptional tides, and a trolley company that owned the road provided the sole access to the outside world.

Vincent Seyfried

Hoover, Herbert (Clark) (*b* West Branch, Iowa, 10 Aug 1874; *d* New York City, 20 Oct 1964). Thirty-first president of the United States. After a successful career in business he led the American relief effort in Europe during and after the First World War and after the civil war in the Soviet Union. He was later the secretary of commerce under presidents Warren G. Harding and Calvin Coolidge. As the Republican presidential candidate in 1928 he made one of his most successful campaign speeches at Madison Square Garden, declaring his unwavering support for an economy based on the "American system" rather than on European "collectivism," which he considered a threat to individual liberty and the spirit of free enterprise; he defeated the Democratic nominee, Alfred E. Smith, by a large margin. Unable to end the Depression, he failed to win reelection in 1932 against Franklin D. Roosevelt. He moved to New York City in 1934, took up residence in suite 31A of

Herbert Hoover taking part in the first public demonstration of intercity television broadcasting, 7 April 1927. His image was broadcast from Washington to Bell Telephone Laboratories in New York City

the Waldorf–Astoria Towers, and remained active in public life. After the Second World War he organized a relief effort and in 1947 was chosen by President Harry S. Truman to lead the Commission on the Organization of the Executive Branch, a bipartisan effort to streamline a federal government that had grown immense during the New Deal and the war. Known as the Hoover Commission, it had headquarters in Washington but was effectively run from Hoover's office at the Waldorf: he wrote most of the recommendations and most were adopted. After being reappointed in 1953 by President Dwight D. Eisenhower he remained in charge of the commission until 1955. For the last thirty years of his life Hoover lived at the Waldorf–Astoria, wrote books, met dignitaries, and advised leaders of the Republican Party.

George H. Nash: *Herbert Hoover* (New York: W. W. Norton, 1983–)

Edward T. O'Donnell

Hoovervilles. See SHANTYTOWNS.

Hopedale. Name formerly applied to a hamlet south of Queens Boulevard and north of Union Turnpike, where an inn called Hopedale Hall once stood. The Long Island Rail Road opened a station there in July 1875 and a depot in October; the Maple Grove Cemetery opened in the same year only a quarter of a mile (four hundred meters) away. After a railroad station opened there in May 1879 the Hopedale station closed and the hamlet dwindled. The name last appears on a map from 1886.

Vincent Seyfried

Hopkins, Harry (Lloyd) (*b* Sioux City, Iowa, 17 Aug 1890; *d* New York City, 29 Jan 1946). Social worker and public official. After moving to New York City in 1912 he worked at a settlement, Christodora House, and at the Association for Improving the Condition of the Poor; these experiences led him to believe that unemployment was the chief cause of poverty. In October 1931 he was appointed by Governor Franklin D. Roosevelt as the executive director of the Temporary Emergency Relief Association for New York State, and under his leadership the association provided work for thousands of residents of New York City. After Roosevelt was elected president Hopkins moved in May 1933 to Washington, where he led successively the Federal Emergency Relief Administration, the Civil Works Administration, and (from 1935) the Works Progress Administration.

George T. McJimsey: *Harry Hopkins: Ally of the Poor and Defender of Democracy* (Cambridge: Harvard University Press, 1987)

Sarah Henry Lederman

Hopper, Edward (*b* Nyack, N.Y., 22 July 1882; *d* New York City, 15 May 1967). Painter and printmaker. He studied painting with William Merritt Chase, Robert Henri, and Kenneth Hayes Miller at the New York School of Art, and worked initially as an illustrator and commercial artist; in the early years of the century he lived in a studio at 53 East 59th Street. After travels abroad in 1906–7 and 1909 he took part in the Exhibition of Independent Artists in 1910. From 1913 until his death he lived and worked at 3 Washington Square North; he exhibited frequently at the MacDowell Club (1912–18) and the Whitney Studio Club (1920–25). Hopper's cityscapes and interior scenes evoke the anonymity and isolation of modern life. The Whitney Museum of American Art owns the largest collection of his works. He was married to the painter Josephine Nivison.

Gail Levin: *Edward Hopper: The Complete Prints* (New York: W. W. Norton / Whitney Museum of American Art, 1979)
Gail Levin: *Edward Hopper: The Art and the Artist* (New York: W. W. Norton / Whitney Museum of American Art, 1980)
Gail Levin: *Hopper's Places* (New York: Alfred A. Knopf, 1985)

Judith Zilczer

Horace Mann School. Private elementary and secondary school opened in Manhattan in 1887 by Nicholas Murray Butler, who with the encouragement of Frederick A. P. Barnard (then president of Columbia University) had studied the educational theories of Horace Mann and others in Berlin. The school emphasized the training of public school teachers. Horace Mann–Barnard Elementary School and the Horace Mann School (high school) are now situated on eighteen acres (seven hectares) in the Bronx and enroll more than fourteen hundred students.

Richard Schwartz

Horne, Lena (*b* New York City, 30 June 1917). Dancer, singer, and actress. She became a dancer at the Cotton Club at sixteen and later had brief engagements with the orchestras of Noble Sissle and Charlie Barnet. In 1941 she had a seven-month engagement at the Café Society in Greenwich Village during which she became well known as a singer. In her many films she acted in roles that were not stereotypical, becoming one of the first black actresses to do so. In 1957 she had an engagement of unprecedented length at the

Edward Hopper, Night Shadows *(1921). Collection of the Whitney Museum of American Art. Gift of Gertrude Vanderbilt Whitney*

Waldorf–Astoria and made her début on Broadway in the musical *Jamaica,* which ran for a year and a half. She performed in 1981 in *Lena Horne: The Lady and Her Music,* a one-woman show that remained on Broadway for a year and won a Tony Award.

Donald Bogle: *Brown Sugar: Eighty Years of America's Black Female Superstars* (New York: Harmony, 1980)
James Haskins and Kathleen Benson: *Lena: A Personal and Professional Biography of Lena Horne* (New York: Stein and Day, 1984)

Ira Berger

Lena Horne and Cab Calloway

Horney [née Danielsen], **Karen** (*b* Hamburg, 16 Sept 1885; *d* New York City, 4 Dec 1952). Psychiatrist. After studying in Germany and living for two years in Chicago she moved to New York City in 1934, entered private practice, and until 1941 taught at the New School for Social Research. A critic of classical Freudianism, she argued in *The Neurotic Personality of Our Time* (1937) that social forces rather than psychosexual dynamics are responsible for personality disorders. She helped to form the Association for the Advancement of Psychoanalysis, taught at the American Institute for Psychoanalysis, edited the *American Journal of Psychoanalysis,* and wrote both scholarly and popular works. From the 1970s Horney's work received greater attention for its feminist implications. She lived at 240 Central Park South.

Jack L. Rubins: *Karen Horney: Gentle Rebel of Psychoanalysis* (New York: Dial, 1978)
Bernard J. Paris: *Karen Horney: A Psychoanalyst's Search for Self-Understanding* (New Haven: Yale University Press, 1994)

Mary Elizabeth Brown

Horowitz, Vladimir [Gorovitz, Vladimir (Samoliovich)] (*b* Kiev, Ukraine, 1 Oct 1903; *d* New York City, 5 Nov 1989). Pianist. After leaving the Soviet Union in 1925 he performed for several years in the major cities of Europe and made a sensational American début on 12 January 1928 at Carnegie Hall, playing Tchaikovsky's Piano Concerto no. 1 with the New York Philharmonic under Sir Thomas Beecham. He soon took up residence in New York City and in 1933 married Wanda Toscanini, daughter of the conductor. From 1944 he lived on East 94th Street near 5th Avenue. An idiosyncratic and often reluctant performer, he retired from the concert stage from 1953 to 1965 and again from 1969 to 17 November 1974, when he gave the first piano recital ever held at the Metropolitan Opera House. Horowitz's technique was supremely virtuosic; his performances often provoked controversy because of a tendency toward overly romantic gestures and a less-than-literal view of the written score. His repertory emphasized the late nineteenth century and the early twentieth, especially the music of the Russians Modest Mussorgsky, Alexander Scriabin, Sergei Rachmaninoff, and Serge Prokofiev. He played few large works of Mozart and Beethoven and seemed better suited to those on a small scale by Domenico Scarlatti and Muzio Clementi.

Glenn Plaskin: *Horowitz: A Biography* (New York: William Morrow, 1983)
Harold C. Schonberg: *Horowitz: His Life and Music* (New York: Simon and Schuster, 1992)

Barbara L. Tischler

horse-drawn vehicles. New York City quickly became the leading manufacturer of horse-drawn vehicles in the United States when the industry developed in the nineteenth century. John Stephenson in 1831 introduced the omnibus, a horse-drawn vehicle used for public transport, and in the following year developed horse-drawn streetcars that ran on tracks. He was also one of many manufacturers of private carriages in the city of which the foremost, Brewster and Company, became internationally known for providing elegant carriages to wealthy patrons. In addition to carriages many firms manufactured components: wheels, axles, boxing machines, carriage couplings, whipsockets, name plates, hubs, trimming and finishing hardware, gears, coach laces, and lamps were all produced in standard sizes and could be installed in any vehicle. New York City had the heaviest concentration of horse-drawn vehicle and component manufacturers in the country in 1850, at about the time when mechanical construction of vehicles for both public and private use began to replace construction by hand. By about 1875 the manufacture of horse-drawn vehicles had moved west, where land and raw materials were cheap and abundant: the proportion of vehicles produced on the east coast declined from 99 percent in 1820 to 33 percent in 1880.

Joanne Abel Goldman

horse racing. The beginning of thoroughbred horse racing in the metropolitan area dates to 1665, when Governor Richard Nicholls established the Newmarket Track at Salisbury Plain in what is now Hempstead, Long Island;

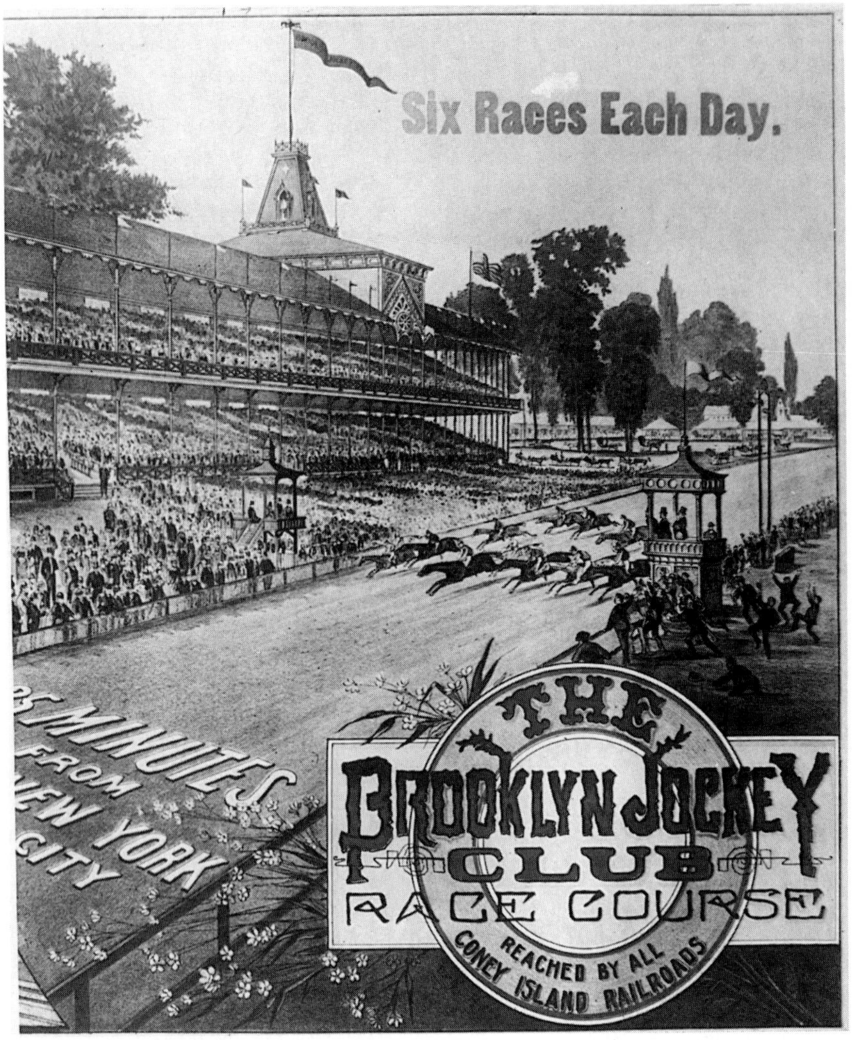

Poster for Brooklyn Jockey Club, 1886 (detail)

there races were contested for a silver cup over a course two miles (3.2 kilometers) long. The first track in what is now New York City was the Church Farm Course (probably in lower Manhattan), where from 1725 to 1753 the New York Subscription Plate was awarded. The sport continued during the American Revolution, which made it anathema to virtuous patriots who later banned it as aristocratic and immoral. The ban was repealed in 1820, and the Union Course opened on Long Island in the following year and became the scene of great match races, beginning with one between Eclipse and Sir Henry in 1823 before a crowd estimated at sixty thousand, and ending with another between Fashion and Peytona in 1845 before a crowd that was even larger. By this time thoroughbred racing was being surpassed in popularity by harness racing, which gained favor in the 1820s because the standardbred horses used in this sport were useful and cheaper than thoroughbreds: Lady Suffolk, the winner of more than $35,000 in purses, began her racing career after pulling a butcher's cart. Races were originally spontaneous events along 3rd Avenue and Harlem Lane, and were made more structured by the New York Trotting Club (1825), which built a course in Centerville, Long Island. As thoroughbred racing continued to suffer, virtually destroyed by the depression of 1837 and the westward migration of the breeding business, harness racing prospered: by 1860 there were seven trotting tracks in the metropolitan area, including the Fashion Course in Newtown (1854). The breeding of standardbreds by then could be quite expensive if middle-class owners wanted to compete with rich rivals like Cornelius Vanderbilt.

Thoroughbred racing enjoyed a renaissance under the auspices of the American Jockey Club, formed in 1865 by Leonard Jerome, August Belmont, and William R. Travers. Jerome built Jerome Park in Fordham, which became a lavish, upper-class resort. The track staged dashes and handicap races, offered large purses, and in 1871 introduced parimutuel betting, which failed to supplant auction-pool gambling and was abandoned. The feature event at the track was the Belmont Stakes (1867), a race 1⅝ miles (2.2 kilometers) long that eventually became the final event of the Triple Crown (the distance was changed to 1½ miles, or 2.4 kilometers, in 1926). The locus of racing shifted in 1879 to Coney Island, where William Engeman built the proprietary Brighton Beach racecourse, which was followed in 1880 by the élite Sheepshead Bay Track of the Coney Island Jockey Club and in 1885 by Mike and Philip Dwyer's Gravesend Track. Engeman and the Dwyers were entrepreneurs seeking large, plebeian audiences and large profits. In 1889, when Jerome was closed to make way for a reservoir, the Westchester Racing Association replaced it with a new, opulent resort, Morris Park Racetrack in the eastern Bronx. Its track 1⅜ miles (2.2 kilometers) long and grandstand (seating fifteen thousand) were the largest in the country. The growing popularity of racing led to the construction of four more tracks in or adjacent to New York City: Aqueduct Racetrack (1894), Jamaica Racetrack (1903), Empire City Racetrack in Yonkers, New York (1900), and Belmont Park in Elmont, Long Island (1905), built at a cost of $2.4 million, which replaced Morris Park.

From the 1880s the principal form of gambling at the tracks was bookmaking, which in 1887 was banned outside the tracks. The betting element tied the sport intimately to urban machine politicians and organized crime, and made racing a prime target of moral reformers. Élite horsemen in the city led by August Belmont responded by establishing the Jockey Club in 1894 to develop national standards for the sport. This became an adjunct of the new State Racing Commission (1895) and was recognized as the arbiter of the American turf. Nonetheless opposition continued, and in 1910 progressive reformers halted racing. It resumed in 1913, employing oral betting to circumvent the law, but without the tracks in Brooklyn, and the prestigious events formerly staged there shifted to Belmont.

American racing thrived after the First World War, and New Yorkers enjoyed the exploits of horses like Man o' War, yet local racing was held back because only oral bet-

Racetracks within the Present Boundaries of New York City

Union Course, Queens, 1821–51
Centerville (Eclipse) Course, Queens, 1830–59
National (Fashion), Queens, 1854–56
Jerome Park, Bronx, 1866–89
Morris Park, Bronx, 1889–1904
Brighton Beach, Brooklyn, 1879–1908
Sheepshead Bay, Brooklyn, 1880–1910
Gravesend, Brooklyn, 1886–1910
Aqueduct, Queens, 1894–1956, 1959–
Empire City, Bronx, 1900–42
Jamaica, Queens, 1903–59

ting with bookmakers affiliated with John Cavanagh was permitted at the tracks. Off-track gambling flourished under men like Arnold Rothstein, and bootleggers like Big Bill Dwyer emerged as the owners of out-of-town tracks. In 1940 parimutuel betting was legalized, leading to greater profits at the thoroughbred tracks and the establishment of harness racing at Roosevelt Raceway on Long Island (1940) and Yonkers Raceway (1950). Racing became the leading American spectator sport in the 1950s, but locally it was troubled by aging facilities and the state's relatively large "take" from the parimutuel pool (eventually raised to 17 percent). A nonprofit New York Racing Association established in 1956 to reinvigorate the sport took over all the tracks, closing Jamaica, rebuilding Aqueduct, and spending $30.7 million in 1968 to refurbish Belmont. Off-Track Betting began in 1971 and by 1989 was yielding $33 million for the city, but illegal gambling did not decline: attendance statewide fell from 6.5 million in 1970 to 4.7 million by 1985.

William H. P. Robertson: *The History of Thoroughbred Racing in America* (New York: Prentice Hall, 1964)

Melvin L. Adelman: *A Sporting Time: New York City and the Rise of Modern Athletics, 1820–1870* (Urbana: University of Illinois Press, 1986)

Steven A. Riess: *City Games: The Evolution of American Urban Society and the Rise of Sports* (Urbana: University of Illinois Press, 1989)

See also Sports.

Steven A. Riess

horses. Powerful, bulky horses were introduced into the colony of New Amsterdam by Dutch settlers and used for carrying heavy loads and operating gristmills and sawmills. In the 1660s finer-boned horses were imported by English colonists, who in 1665 opened a racetrack on Long Island to encourage the development of faster breeds. Trotting became immensely popular along the broad, straight roads of Manhattan. Elegant stagecoaches drawn by four horses each were introduced in 1830 between Bowling Green and Bleecker Street, helping to connect Greenwich Village and Yorkville more closely with the rest of the city. In 1833 the *New York Journal* established an express service to obtain news quickly from Washington and the South; its twenty-four horses covered the 227 miles (363 kilometers) between Washington and the city in twenty hours. In 1836 a horse-drawn street railroad, the first of its kind in the world, was inaugurated by the New York and Harlem Railroad, and tracks soon ran throughout the city. The New York and Harlem line offered regular service on a route running five miles (eight kilometers) along 4th Avenue to Yorkville and then to Harlem, and the Long Island Rail Road opened a line to Jamaica, a distance of ten miles (sixteen kilometers) that could be covered by a team of horses in less than an hour. By 1858 the city's five principal street railways carried nearly 35 million passengers a year, and in 1871 the Harlem Railroad opened Grand Central Depot on 42nd Street. Horses remained important in the city until the end of the First World War. They were widely used in firefighting after 1840, as well as in the growing industrial sections, where breweries were known for their wagons pulled by enormous draft horses. From 1900 automobiles were banned for a few years because they frightened horses. Private broughams and barouches filled the streets; horse-drawn, double-decker stagecoaches ran on 5th Avenue, and hacks and two-wheeled hansom cabs were available for hire throughout the city. The last horsecar ran on West Street in Manhattan until 1918.

Few horses remained in Manhattan by the mid 1990s. Riding continued to be popular at the Claremont Riding Academy on the Upper West Side and in Central Park. The mounted police kept horses at their stables on West 42nd Street. The use of horses to draw hansom cabs in the southern part of Central Park provoked criticism from animal-rights activists, who prevailed on the city to impose limits on the number of hours that horses could work, as well as a requirement that horses be taken off the streets during the hottest weather.

James Wilson: *The Memorial History of the City of New York* (New York: New York Historical Company, 1893)

James O. Drummond

Horsmanden, Daniel (*b* Purleigh, England, 4 June 1694; *d* Flatbush [now in Brooklyn], 23 Sept 1778). Judge. He studied law in England and by 1731 had a practice in New York City. In 1744 he published an account of the "Negro plot" of 1741. A supporter of the Livingston political faction, he was appointed recorder, supreme court judge, and admiralty judge. In 1747 he lost these offices during a time of political change and was nearly sent to debtors' prison. After regaining favor he was again made a judge during the 1750s and a chief justice during the 1760s.

James E. Mooney

horticulture. The Dutch who settled in America in the seventeenth century had a sophisticated understanding of horticulture and planted many gardens and orchards throughout New Amsterdam. One of the many orchards that they planted in Staten Island was raided by Indians in 1655 during a conflict known as the Peach War. In 1737 the first commercial nursery in America opened in what is now Flushing and soon offered fruit trees, shrubs, and ornamental plants. John Singleton Copley bought several varieties of shrubs, including mountain laurel, for his property on Beacon Hill in Boston. In the 1750s in what later became Queens the Newtown Pippin was developed into a prime apple for the London market. Several other new varieties of plants were grown in the country's first greenhouse, built in 1764 by James Beekman near what is now 51st Street and 1st Avenue in Manhattan.

The Elgin Botanical Garden, established in 1801 by David Hosack, a professor of botany and materia medica at Columbia College, was the first public botanical garden in the United States, covering twenty acres (eight hectares) of land on a site now occupied by Rockefeller Center. Its gardener, the taxonomist Frederick Pursh, helped to identify plants brought back from the expedition of Lewis and Clark. In the 1830s a nursery was opened in Brooklyn by a gardener of Belgian descent named Andrew Parmentier, and through the efforts of the Prince Nursery of Flushing the Isabella grape, found growing in Brooklyn Heights, became the most popular edible grape in the United States (until it was supplanted in the 1850s by the Concord grape). Many new plants were introduced to New York City with the opening of Central Park in 1858, including the Japanese maple, transported from Japan by Commodore Matthew C. Perry and grown by Samuel Bowne Parsons in his nurseries, one of which, Kissena Nurseries, became the site of Kissena Park.

Horticulture thrived in New York City between 1880 and 1940. Wealthy New Yorkers who owned large estates on Long Island and in Westchester County planted elaborate gardens, usually cared for by English-trained gardeners. One of these was Thomas H. Everett, who became chief of horticulture at the New York Botanical Garden and the author of *New York Botanical Garden Illustrated Encyclopedia of Horticulture* (1980–82). This same period saw the planting of the first flowerbeds in the city's parks. In 1891 Nathaniel Lord Britton, a professor of botany at Columbia, and his wife, Elizabeth Knight Britton, an expert on lichens, campaigned for the establishment of the New York Botanical Garden, designed by Calvert Vaux, John Charles Olmsted, and John R. Brinley at the northern end of Bronx Park along East Fordham Road. Among the many conservatories built in the city at this time was the one in Central Park (1899). The Horticultural Society of New York (1902) sponsored the first New York Flower Show, and in 1910 the Brooklyn Botanic Garden was built next to the Brooklyn Museum along Washington and Flatbush avenues, designed by Olmsted Brothers and Harold apRhys Caparn.

During the Depression resources for the city's parks, conservatories, and greenhouses could not be spared. Flowerbeds disappeared from the parks, and policies set by the park department after 1934 called for the destruction of all but three greenhouses. The great gardens on the outskirts of the city were also lost as suburban neighborhoods developed. A modest rebirth occurred after the Second World War, and in 1965 Wave Hill, an estate in

Riverdale with gardens and a greenhouse, became a city park; about the same time the Queens Botanical Garden moved to a site adjoining Flushing Meadow Park. The city acquired Sailors' Snug Harbor on Staten Island and its gardens and greenhouses in 1972 and 1974, and after a lapse the New York Flower Show was revived in 1985. The most visible addition to plant life in the city was made by the arrival of impatiens, an Indonesian species used in flower borders throughout the city.

Henry Hope Reed: *The Parks of New York City: A History and a Guide* (New York: Clarkson N. Potter, 1969)

See also BOTANICAL GARDENS.

Henry Hope Reed

Hosack, David (*b* New York City, 31 Aug 1769; *d* New York City, 22 Dec 1835). Physician. After attending Columbia University he graduated from Princeton University in 1789, studied medicine in the colonies and abroad, and in 1795 became a professor of botany and medicine at Columbia. In 1804 he was the attending physician at the duel between Aaron Burr and Alexander Hamilton. He resigned from Columbia in 1811 to take a position at the College of Physicians and Surgeons; he later held annual lectures and was influential in forming Bellevue Hospital. Hosack launched the *American Medical and Philosophical Register*, published a number of books, and helped to organize the New-York Historical Society.

Christine Chapman Robbins: *David Hosack, Citizen of New York* (Philadelphia: American Philosophical Society, 1964)

See also PUBLIC HEALTH.

James E. Mooney

hospitals. In the eighteenth century and the early nineteenth New York City had only a few hospitals. The almshouse infirmary opened in 1736, followed by New York Hospital in 1791. New York Hospital was generously supported by the Dutch gentry, and many of its trustees were descendants of the earliest Dutch settlers. Other medical facilities in the city included the Lying-In Hospital, which was organized after the yellow fever epidemic of 1798. Bellevue Hospital grew out of the almshouse infirmary: a separate institution from 1819, it was among the first public institutions to respond effectively to the medical needs of the rapidly increasing dependent and poor. King's County Hospital, which like Bellevue had begun as an almshouse infirmary, opened in Flatbush in 1831, and Brooklyn City Hospital was incorporated in 1845 under the auspices of the Brooklyn Association for Improving the Condition of the Poor. By the beginning of the Civil War there were twelve more hospitals, including St. Vincent's Hospital (1850), opened by the Sisters of Charity, the Jews' Hospital (1855, later renamed Mount Sinai Hospital), and St. John's Hospital (1861), the first hospital in Queens.

Brooklyn City Hospital, ca *1850*

Other charity hospitals with ethnic and religious affiliations included the French Hospital, Methodist Episcopal Hospital, Norwegian Lutheran Deaconess Home and Hospital, Beth Israel Hospital, Swedish Hospital, and the German Hospital (later renamed Lenox Hill Hospital). Although they drew patients from all economic levels these institutions served mostly the poor: members of the upper and middle classes were generally cared for in their homes.

Hospitals of the period offered warmth, shelter, regular meals, and minimal nursing, often provided by ill-trained staff in spartan surroundings. Because antisepsis was not widely practiced until late in the century, hospital care and particularly surgery carried a much higher risk of infection than home care did. Several children's hospitals were formed during these years, as was the Colored Home, which later became Lincoln Hospital. Homoeopathic institutions expanded and maternity hospitals were established to provide shelter and medical services for unwed mothers. In less settled areas like Blackwell's Island and Staten Island a number of special hospitals sponsored by local businessmen and members of the clergy were built for those suffering from tuberculosis and other contagious diseases, and from mental disorders.

Many hospitals of the late nineteenth century were small institutions that operated on minimal budgets, often in private homes, and treated "respectable" working-class patients who were wary of the stigma attached to the large charity hospitals. Some of these neighborhood hospitals prospered and expanded, but many faced difficulty as increasingly rigorous medical standards raised the cost of providing care, and as patients began using the expanding public transit system to move to outlying communities. Facilities with fewer than fifty beds lasted for an average of only five years, and by 1910 most of the smallest neighborhood hospitals closed. The larger ones expanded and new ones opened, steadily increasing the number of hospital beds in the city. By 1908 the State Charities Aid Association reported that there were sixty-three general hospitals in New York City, of which twenty-six were in Manhattan and twenty-three in Brooklyn.

The municipal hospital system in New York City underwent many changes in organization during the late nineteenth century. In 1875 hospitals for contagious diseases were transferred to the new Department of Health, and by the turn of the century mental hospitals and prisons also were placed under separate jurisdiction. Bellevue and its dependent facilities Gouverneur Hospital, Harlem Hospital, and Fordham Hospital were removed from the Department of Charities in 1902 and became governed by a separate board of trustees. The old charities department (renamed the Department of Public Welfare) retained control of the municipal facilities in Brooklyn, and the Department of Health directed those in Queens and the institutions for contagious diseases.

Private, nonprofit hospitals that survived into the twentieth century adopted antiseptic procedures that sharply reduced mortality rates after surgery. Large hospitals like Bellevue, Mount Sinai, New York, Lenox Hill, St. Luke's, and Presbyterian expanded their X-ray departments and clinical laboratories. Physicians increasingly encouraged their well-to-do patients to use the modern facilities, which became the focus of the new "scientific medicine"; between 1890 and 1905 the use of all hospital services increased by 85 percent. Although most new medical knowledge pertained to the classification of illness rather than its treatment, and although maternal death rates in the city's hospitals remained very high well into the 1930s, physicians and patients alike placed a great deal of trust in medical science, of which the modern hospital became a powerful symbol.

Private hospitals in New York City received much of their funding from the state until 1894, when state assistance to hospitals was banned. The city then began making fixed annual grants to the hospitals in recognition of their services to the poor. In 1908 Comptroller Bird S. Coler instituted a new system under which each patient had to be certified as destitute before the hospital was reimbursed by the city. Although total city outlays increased they lagged far behind rising costs, and by 1921 reimbursement by the city represented only 10 percent of the revenue of private nonprofit hospitals, with donations accounting for about 20 percent and patients' fees 69 percent (compared with 38 percent in 1911). One third of patients who paid a fee were in private rooms; the rest were in "pay wards," where they were excused from the housekeeping chores that were performed by convalescent patients who did not pay. To increase their revenue hospitals also developed graduated rate structures, sought increased municipal support for the charity care they provided, and advertised their private accommodations.

Free-standing dispensaries that had provided care during the nineteenth century fell victim to the same increasing specialization and technology that had brought an end to small neighborhood hospitals, and were gradually replaced by outpatient departments. By 1926 the outpatient department at Bellevue, the city's largest, had an average of nine hundred patients a day. Physicians in New York City found it increasingly difficult to sustain their practices independently of a hospital; as the hospital became more important to doctors, they in turn became more important to the hospital. At St. Luke's, Roosevelt Hospital, New York Hospital, and many others, trustees for the first time permitted doctors to charge private patients for hospital visits and accepted more physicians as visiting staff: the proportion of practitioners with admitting privileges at hospitals rose from one third in 1908 to one half in 1926.

The Department of Hospitals was formed in 1929 to administer all twenty municipal hospitals and health institutions and to inspect and license private health care facilities. By 1930 there were about 125 hospitals in New York City, with a total of about thirty thousand beds. Only a few hospitals had a daily census of more than 250 patients — Bellevue, Lincoln, St. Luke's, Mount Sinai, New York Hospital, New York Long Island College Hospital, and New York Post-Graduate Hospital (now University Hospital). Presbyterian Hospital and New York Hospital joined with leading medical schools to establish the city's first modern medical centers.

The nature of hospital care in New York City as elsewhere changed dramatically when nursing became professionalized. Before the late nineteenth century patients were tended by poorly paid and untrained workers, or by fellow convalescent patients who were required to assist with ward tasks in exchange for care. An exposé in the early 1870s of the

Hospitals in New York City with More Than 500 Beds in 1992

Bellevue Hospital Center (opened in 1736 as Almshouse Infirmary), 1st Avenue and 27th Street, Manhattan, 1242 beds (municipal)

Beth Israel Medical Center (formd in 1891), 1st Avenue and 16th Street, Manhattan, 949 beds (voluntary); merged in 1933 with Jewish Maternity Hospital (1906), in 1964 with Manhattan General Hospital, and in 1987 with Doctors Hospital (1953)

Bronx–Lebanon Hospital Center (formed in 1961 by merger of Lebanon Hospital, 1893, and Bronx Hospital, 1911), 1650 Grand Concourse, Bronx (Concourse Division), and 1276 Fulton Avenue, Bronx (Fulton Division), 725 beds (voluntary)

Bronx Municipal Hospital Center (opened in 1954), Pelham Parkway South and Eastchester Road, Bronx, 776 beds (municipal)

Brookdale Hospital Medical Center (opened in 1921 as Brownsville and East New York Hospital), Linden Boulevard, Brookdale Plaza, Brooklyn, 783 beds (voluntary)

Brooklyn Hospital Center (opened in 1847 as Brooklyn Hospital), 121 DeKalb Avenue, Brooklyn, 644 beds (voluntary); merged in 1923 with St. Christopher's Hospital for Babies (1881), in 1957 with Brooklyn Thoracic Hospital (1881), in 1963 with Cumberland Hospital (1903), in 1968 with Evangelical Deaconess Hospital (1923), and in 1982 with Caledonian Hospital (1910)

Catholic Medical Center of Brooklyn and Queens (opened in 1882 as St. Mary's Hospital), 88-25 153rd Street, Jamaica, 1063 beds (voluntary); merged in 1967 with Mary Immaculate Hospital (1902), in 1967 with St. John's Hospital (1891), and in 1985 with Hillcrest General Hospital (1882)

Columbia–Presbyterian Medical Center (opened in 1872 as Presbyterian Hospital), 622 West 168th Street, Manhattan, 1548 beds (voluntary); merged in 1925 with Sloane Hospital for Women (1887) and Babies Hospital (1887), in 1940 with Delafield Cancer Hospital (1940), and in 1945 with New York Orthopedic Hospital (1869)

Elmhurst Hospital Center (opened in 1832 as Penitentiary Hospital), 75-01 Broadway, Elmhurst, Queens, 628 beds (municipal)

Flushing Hospital and Medical Center (opened in 1884 as Flushing Hospital and Dispensary), 45th Avenue at Parsons Boulevard, Flushing, 524 beds (voluntary); merged in 1988 with Parsons Hospital

Harlem Hospital Center (opened in 1877 as Reception Hospital), 506 Lenox Avenue, Manhattan, 678 beds (municipal)

Interfaith Medical Center (formed in 1983 by merger of St. John's Hospital, 1873, and Brooklyn Jewish Hospital, 1906), 555 Prospect Place, Brooklyn, 620 beds (voluntary)

Kings County Hospital Center (opened in 1831), 451 Clarkson Avenue, Brooklyn, 1204 beds (municipal)

Lenox Hill Hospital (opened in 1868 as German Hospital), 100 East 77th Street, Manhattan, 640 beds (voluntary)

Lincoln Medical and Mental Health Center (opened in 1841 as Colored Home), 234 East 149th Street, Bronx, 597 beds (municipal)

Long Island College Hospital (opened in 1871), Atlantic Avenue at Hicks Street, Brooklyn, 567 beds (voluntary); merged in 1963 with Prospect Heights Hospital (1871)

Long Island Jewish Medical Center (opened in 1954), 270-05 76th Avenue, New Hyde Park, Queens, 825 beds (voluntary)

Lutheran Medical Center (opened in 1883 as Norwegian Lutheran Deaconess Hospital), 150 55th Street, Brooklyn, 532 beds (voluntary)

Maimonides Medical Center (opened in 1916 as New Utrecht Dispensary and Hospital), 4802 10th Avenue, Brooklyn, 705 beds (voluntary); merged in 1920 with Zion Hospital (1917) and in 1947 with Beth Moses Hospital (1921)

Methodist Hospital (opened in 1887 as Methodist Episcopal Hospital), 506 6th Street, Brooklyn 532 beds (voluntary); merged in 1970 with Carson Peck Memorial Hospital (1917)

Metropolitan Hospital Center (opened in 1875), 1901 1st Avenue, Manhattan, 569 beds (municipal)

Montefiore Medical Center (opened in 1884), 111 East 210th Street, Bronx, 1276 beds (voluntary)

Mount Sinai Medical Center (opened in 1855 as Jews' Hospital), 100th Street and 5th Avenue, Manhattan, 1122 beds (voluntary)

New York Hospital–Cornell Medical Center (opened in 1776), 525 East 68th Street, Manhattan, 1414 beds (voluntary); merged in 1932 with Lying-In Hospital (1799) and Manhattan Maternity and Dispensary (1905), and in 1934 with New York Nursery and Child's Hospital (1830)

(*continued*)

Hospitals in New York City with More Than 500 Beds *(Continued)*

New York University Medical Center (opened in 1886 as New York Post-Graduate Medical College and Hospital), 550 1st Avenue, Manhattan, 878 beds (voluntary)

Our Lady of Mercy Medical Center (opened in 1888), 600 East 233rd Street, Bronx, 605 beds (voluntary); merged in 1989 with Pelham Bay General Hospital (1955)

St. Luke's–Roosevelt Hospital Center (formed in 1979 by merger of St. Luke's Hospital, 1858, and Roosevelt Hospital, 1871), Amsterdam Avenue at 114th Street (St. Luke's Division) and 428 West 59th Street (Roosevelt Division), 1354 beds (voluntary)

St. Vincent's Hospital and Medical Center (opened in 1849), 163 West 11th Street, Manhattan, 813 beds (voluntary)

Sisters of Charity Health Care System (opened in 1849 as St. Vincent's Hospital of Richmond), 75 Vanderbilt Avenue, Staten Island, 644 beds (voluntary); merged in 1982 with Bayley Seton Hospital

Staten Island University Hospital (opened in 1861 as Staten Island Hospital), 475 Seaview Avenue, Staten Island, 658 beds; merged in 1987 with Richmond Memorial Hospital (1919)

Veterans Administration Medical Center (opened in 1947), 800 Poly Place, Brooklyn, 750 beds (federal)

Veterans Administration Medical Center (opened in 1922), 130 West Kingsbridge Road, Bronx, 775 beds (federal)

inadequately trained work force at Bellevue Hospital led the social reformer Louisa Schuyler to mobilize support for the Bellevue Training School for Female Nurses. Opened in 1873, the school was the first of hundreds in the United States designed according to the teachings of Florence Nightingale. Nearly every sizable hospital in New York City soon opened a "Nightingale school," and for more than half a century hospital wards were staffed primarily by nursing students, who worked long hours for little pay while most graduate nurses took private-duty assignments. Graduate nurses became numerous in hospitals only during the Depression, when the number of private-duty assignments dwindled.

During the Depression entire wings of private rooms stood empty and the demand for charity care soared. Of the city's more than thirty thousand hospital beds, half were in private institutions that relied extensively on fees from patients. A few hospitals closed, but most simply reduced their number of beds and increasingly looked to the city for assistance. The city reimbursed private hospitals more than $5 million for care to the indigent in 1933 and $6.4 million by 1940. Municipal hospitals also were hurt by the financial crisis of the 1930s, but their physical plants were improved with the help of funds from the Works Progress Administration and the Public Works Administration. Millions of dollars were spent on expanding and renovating the municipal hospital system, and by the end of the Second World War three thousand beds had been added. Professionalism in the Department of Hospitals increased during the tenure of S. S. Goldwater, formerly the nationally respected administrator of Mount Sinai, and the department's budget rose steadily from $17 million in 1934 to $36 million in 1945. Many more positions in the department came under civil service protection, new laboratory facilities were constructed, physicians in municipal outpatient departments earned salaries for the first time, maternity services and equipment were modernized, and a blood bank was established.

Public and private hospitals experienced soaring admissions during the decade following the Second World War: in 1948 the city reported an average occupancy rate of 102 percent in municipal facilities. The power and prestige of modern medicine were strongly reinforced by the new "miracle" sulfa drugs, penicillin and the tetracyclines, which eliminated many of the most feared diseases, permitted more difficult surgery, and sharply cut maternal mortality rates. As health benefits became a recognized issue for collective bargaining, Blue Cross and other hospital insurance systems that had begun in the 1930s expanded rapidly. In 1945 Mayor Fiorello H. La Guardia introduced the Health Insurance Plan of Greater New York (HIP), which was made available to city residents and workers earning less than $5000 a year; employers paid half the cost of coverage. By 1947 more than 110,000 members were enrolled in the plan, and New York City was considered a leader in the national effort to make hospital care more widely available to those who had long been excluded because of the high cost of private care and the stigma of wards.

During the postwar years private hospitals reopened wings closed during the Depression; they renovated old buildings and built new ones. The federal government expanded its veterans' hospitals in the city, and the municipal hospital system launched an ambitious renovation campaign. By 1968 the city had about 65,000 beds in 145 hospitals, of which eighty were nonprofit, eighteen were municipal, and forty-seven were federal or proprietary. About one quarter of the city's hospitals had more than five hundred beds (compared with 7 percent of the hospitals in 1924). Subsidized care was made available for the poor and elderly in 1965 with the passage of Medicare and Medicaid. Within a year these programs accounted for more than half the income received by hospitals in New York City and 86 percent of the income received by municipal hospitals. Medicare in particular enabled many people to afford private hospitals, but a large number of Medicaid patients as well as the uninsured remained in the public system. As a result the municipal hospitals continued to face shortages and understaffing even though they experienced a decline in their number of patients. Calls for a reorganization of the Department of Hospitals led to its replacement in 1970 by a new agency, the New York Health and Hospitals Corporation.

In the late 1950s and early 1960s powerful unions were organized by nonprofessional hospital workers, who for the most part were poorly paid women and members of racial minority groups. Local 1199 gained its first formal recognition at Montefiore Hospital in 1958, and in the following year led a bitter and ultimately successful strike against seven private hospitals. Meanwhile the Association of Federal, State, County and Municipal Employees gained ground in municipal hospitals. By 1970 collective bargaining was well established in the municipal hospital system and in most private hospitals. Several studies during these years demonstrated wide racial disparities in local hospitals: in 1964 the Department of Health found that whites accounted for 78 percent of the patients discharged from private, nonprofit hospitals but only 26 percent of those discharged from municipal hospitals, and that the proportion of patients with health insurance ranged from 80 percent among whites to 40 percent among blacks and 25 percent among Puerto Ricans. These inequities were accompanied by a growing animosity toward hospitals in New York City: in low-income neighborhoods such as Bedford–Stuyvesant and the southern Bronx local hospitals were condemned and even occupied by residents.

In the decades after 1965 a growing number of lawyers, insurers, social workers, bioethicists, and particularly patients claimed a role in health care decisions that until then had been left to physicians. At the same time the escalating cost of medical care led to governmental efforts to control costs, many focused on reimbursement rates for hospitals. State legislation in the late 1970s and the formation in 1983 of the federal Diagnosis-Related Group (DRG) system constrained hospitals by making external funding conditional on an increasing number of requirements; as the economy worsened, many hospitals reduced the number of beds for the first time since the Depression and consolidated to reduce administrative costs. By 1983 the number of general hospitals had fallen to seventy and the number of beds to 35,000. The financial crises of the early 1990s exacted a particularly heavy toll on the municipal hospital system of New York City. Repeated rounds of layoffs, cutbacks, and hospital closings led to demonstrations as well as strikes by hospital staff. An unusually high number of deaths in municipal emergency rooms in 1991 drew intense public scrutiny and caused the director of the Health and Hospitals Corporation to resign and the mayor to request a special investigation of the municipal system by the New York Academy of Medicine.

E. H. Lewinski-Corwin: *The Hospital Situation in Greater New York: Report of a Survey of Hospitals in New York City by the Public Health Committee of the New York Academy of Medicine* (New York: G. P. Putnam's Sons, 1924)

Haven Emerson: *The Hospital Survey for New York* (New York: United Hospital Fund, 1937)

Charles Garrett: *The LaGuardia Years: Machine and Reform Politics in New York City* (New Brunswick, N.J.: Rutgers University Press, 1961)

David Rosner: *A Once Charitable Enterprise: Hospitals and Health Care in Brooklyn and New York, 1885–1915* (Cambridge: Cambridge University Press, 1982)

Leon Fink and Brian Greenberg: *Upheaval in the Quiet Zone: A History of Hospital Workers' Union, Local 1199* (Urbana: University of Illinois Press, 1989)

Sandra Opdycke, David Rosner

Hospital Saturday and Sunday Association. Original name of the UNITED HOSPITAL FUND.

Hostos Community College. See EUGENIO MARIA DE HOSTOS COMMUNITY COLLEGE.

Hotel des Artistes. An elegant apartment building at 1 West 67th Street in Manhattan, between Central Park West and Columbus Avenue. Designed by George Mort Pollard, it opened in 1918. The apartments were intentionally designed without kitchens: instead residents ordered meals by telephone from the Café des Artistes on the ground floor, and these were sent up by dumbwaiter. The idea was to be able to dine in style without the bother of having a cook in residence. The system did not last, but by opening to the public the café flourished and became known as one of the most romantic and fashionable restaurants in Manhattan. Among the many famous residents of the hotel have been Rudolph Valentino, Isadora Duncan, Noël Coward, Zasu Pitts, Fannie Hurst, William Powell, and Norman Rockwell.

Kenneth T. Jackson

Hotel Employees and Restaurant Employees International Union. Labor union formed in 1891 and originally affiliated with the American Federation of Labor (AFL). Its numerous locals in New York City lost strength during Prohibition, when thousands of skilled restaurant positions were eliminated and craft-oriented locals of chefs and waiters proved ineffective in organizing unskilled workers at cafeterias and lunch counters. In 1934 independent industrial unions conducted a two-month strike against the city's hotels; this was unsuccessful but inspired a movement to merge the independent locals with those of the AFL. After an investigation led by Thomas E. Dewey in 1936 three local officers of the AFL were convicted of complicity in a labor racket organized by Dutch Schultz, allowing the former leaders of the independents to be elected to lead the restructured locals.

In the mid 1990s the union had two principal locals in New York City, Local 6 and Local 100. Local 6 was chartered in 1938 to represent hotel housekeeping, laundry, and food and beverage workers. To accommodate such employees as electricians who belonged to different unions, the New York Hotel Trades Council was formed to coordinate collective bargaining. Most of the city's hotels were unionized by 1946. Between 1947 and 1950 the international union expelled officials from three locals for their leftist politics. A decline in restaurant employment from 1972 led to the consolidation of ten specialized restaurant locals into Local 100. In the mid 1990s Local 6 represented nineteen thousand employees in 149 hotels and motels and fifty private clubs.

Matthew Josephson: *Union House, Union Bar: The History of the Hotel and Restaurant Employees and Bartenders International Union, AFL–CIO* (New York: Random House, 1956)

Morris A. Horowitz: *The New York Hotel Industry* (Cambridge: Harvard University Press, 1960)

Gilbert Tauber

Hotel Knickerbocker. Hotel opened in 1906. See 1466 BROADWAY.

Hotel Martinique. Hotel at 32nd Street and Broadway in Manhattan, designed in a French Renaissance style with a mansard roof by Henry J. Hardenbergh and built in 1897. It was enlarged in 1910–11 and for many years was known as a glamorous meeting place with ornate dining rooms and nightly entertainment. The hotel gradually fell into disrepair and by 1980 was being used as temporary housing for the homeless. In the early 1990s there were about fifteen hundred residents, most of them single mothers and their children; the city spent $2000 to $3000 a month for each unit, which usually contained two rooms and housed three to five persons.

Chad Ludington

Hotel Pennsylvania. Original name of the RAMADA HOTEL PENNSYLVANIA.

hotels. In the colonial period inns (also called taverns) were typically remodeled private houses. The first building in the United States to be erected specifically for use as a hotel was probably the City Hotel (begun in 1794) on the west side of lower Broadway between Thames and Cedar streets. Its large assembly room held prestigious social functions and until the early 1840s was also the city's principal site for concerts, including those of the third Philharmonic Society (1824–27); the hotel was demolished in 1849 to make room for shops. Luxury hotels began to appear in New York City by the mid nineteenth century: John Jacob Astor erected the Astor House on Broadway between Barclay and Vesey streets in 1834–36, and in the early 1850s even more palatial hotels were built on Broadway between Canal and 14th streets. Farther uptown at Madison Square, the Fifth Avenue Hotel (1859, six stories) had a marble façade and provided a setting for important social events into the next century. The success of this establishment led by the 1870s to a concentration of leading hotels nearby, and indirectly to the development of a fashionable shopping corridor on Broadway between 8th and 23rd streets later known as the Ladies' Mile. In the guidebook *Lights and Shadows of New York Life* (1872) James McCabe noted that the hotels of the city were exemplary in both quality and number; of the six to seven hundred hotels in the city about fifty were well known and about twenty-five were fashionable. Many of the finer establishments featured the European plan (without meals included in the cost of the room) rather than the more common American plan.

Most of the hotels built in the 1870s and 1880s were relatively undistinguished architecturally, but during the prosperous 1890s larger and more luxurious hotels were built. These reached heights of as much as seventeen stories, employed steel construction, and had telephones, electric lighting, and improved elevators. Residences at each end of the fashionable shopping district on 5th Avenue between Central Park and 34th Street were replaced with stylish hotels: at the southeast corner of Central Park were the original Plaza Hotel (1890), the Hotel Savoy (1892), and the New Netherland Hotel (1893); and between 33rd and 34th streets stood the Waldorf–Astoria (1893–97), which consisted of two conjoined hotels with about thirteen hundred guest rooms and forty public rooms. Two innovative hotels of a very different character were designed by Ernest Flagg to provide inexpensive accommodations to single working men: Mills House no. 1 (1896–97) at 160 Bleecker Street and Mills House no. 2 (1896–98) at Rivington and Chrystie streets.

After the turn of the century the wealthy found it fashionable to reside in fine hotels for either the winter or the entire year. The new Plaza Hotel (1907; Hardenbergh) was built on the site of an identically named former hotel at Grand Army Plaza in Manhattan and became particularly favored as a residence and meeting place. Apartment hotels, which had first appeared in the late nineteenth century, were extremely popular during this period. Most of them catered not to the wealthy but

Grand View Hotel, 1890. The hotel was built by the Brooklyn City Railroad Company near the base of what is now 5th Avenue and was eventually destroyed by fire

to the middle class, and were situated in the western part of midtown or on the Upper West Side, now more easily accessible because of the subway. Several popularly priced tourist hotels opened in Times Square. In the second decade of the twentieth century huge facilities were erected near the city's new railroad complexes to accommodate increasing numbers of middle-class travelers. These hotels were grandly decorated, affordable, convenient, and functional, and provided business services and such modern amenities as a bathroom with every bedroom. The first was the Hotel McAlpin (1912, fifteen hundred rooms) near Pennsylvania Station. The architectural firm of Warren and Wetmore became expert in hotels, and designed the Ritz–Carlton Hotel (1910), the Vanderbilt Hotel (1912), the Biltmore Hotel (1914), and the Hotel Commodore (1919, two thousand rooms), next to Grand Central Terminal; over the years the firm shifted its emphasis from Edwardian elegance to modern convenience. In 1919 the Hotel Pennsylvania (McKim, Mead and White) opened near Pennsylvania Station as the largest hotel in the world, with 2200 rooms.

After the First World War some commercial hotels were added near the railroad stations, but most were constructed around Times Square. Among several moderately priced hotels built on Lexington Avenue the first was the Shelton Hotel (1924, Arthur Loomis Harmon), intended as a clubhouse for bachelors; the building represented a skillful application to skyscraper design of the city's zoning laws of 1916. The St. George Hotel in Brooklyn, expanded in 1930, had 2632 rooms and was the largest hotel in the five boroughs, while the second Waldorf–Astoria on Park Avenue (1931, Schultze and Weaver) became one of the most luxurious hotels in the world. The postwar building boom had produced an excess of hotel accommodations, and thirty years passed before construction resumed in anticipation of the World's Fair of 1964–65. Then the first motor inns were opened on the West Side of Manhattan, and some new hotels were erected in midtown, including the first giant convention hotels: the Americana Hotel (1962) on 7th Avenue between 52nd and 53rd streets and the New York Hilton (1963) on 6th Avenue between 53rd and 54th streets. Older establishments found themselves threatened by declining occupancy rates, and as high-speed travel shortened the length of business trips and lessened the need for hotel accommodations, many hotels closed or were taken over by large chains.

During the 1980s and into the 1990s thousands of predominantly expensive hotel rooms were added in the city. Most of the new facilities were in midtown (such as the Marriott Marquis Hotel in Times Square, 1985), some farther downtown (such as the New York Vista Hotel, 1981, and the Hotel Millenium, 1991, near the World Trade Center). To meet requirements for the preservation of historic structures, the Helmsley Palace (1980, later renamed the New York Palace) on Madison Avenue incorporated sections of the Villard Houses at its base, and the Embassy Suites Hotel (1990) and the Hotel Macklowe (1990) near Times Square incorporated landmark theaters. Sometimes older structures were redesigned to lower construction costs: examples include the Grand Hyatt (1980), which used the steel structure of the Hotel Commodore, and the much smaller Morgans Hotel (1984) and Plaza Athenee (1984) on the East Side.

After the late 1980s room rates at hotels in New York City underwent a decline. An increasing number of budget hotels offered rooms for less than $100 a night to avoid a state luxury tax of 5 percent that took effect at that level. In 1993 the city had about sixty thousand hotel rooms. The average room rate was about $115, not including the combined city and state taxes of as much as 21.25 percent, which made hotel rooms in the city the highest-taxed in the nation until the rates were lowered in September 1994.

Robert A. M. Stern, Gregory Gilmartin, and John Montague Massengale: *New York 1900: Metropolitan Architecture and Urbanism, 1890–1915* (New York: Rizzoli, 1983)

Robert A. M. Stern, Gregory Gilmartin, and Thomas Mellins: *New York 1930: Architecture and Urbanism between the Two World Wars* (New York: Rizzoli, 1987)

May N. Stone

Hotel Theresa. Hotel thirteen stories tall at 7th Avenue and 125th Street in Harlem, designed with white brick and terra cotta facing by George Blum and Edward Blum. Initially the tallest building in Harlem, it opened in 1913 on the busiest thoroughfare in the neighborhood during a period of rapid growth, and at first it did not admit blacks. The hotel was popular for its double-height penthouse dining room, with views of the Palisades and Long Island Sound. It was bought in 1937 by Love B. Woods, a black businessman who ended its policy of racial discrimination; in the same year Joe Louis held a celebration there after winning the world heavyweight boxing title. In the following years the hotel became known as the "Waldorf of Harlem"; it thrived as the fashionable gathering place of prominent figures and also housed such important cultural institutions as the Organization of Afro-American Unity (led by Malcolm X) and the March Community Bookstore (run by A. Phillip Randolph). The hotel attracted international attention in 1960 when President Fidel Castro of Cuba moved his entourage there from downtown Manhattan during a visit to the United Nations; while at the hotel he met with Nikita S. Khrushchev, premier of the Soviet Union, and Gamal Abdel Nasser, president of Egypt. In 1966, after years of deterioration, the Hotel Theresa was bought by an investment group and converted into a modern office building, the Theresa Towers, which continued to house many community organizations.

Amanda Aaron

Houdini, Harry [Weiss, Ehrich] (*b* Budapest, 6 April 1874; *d* Detroit, 31 Oct 1926).

Harry Houdini in a packing box, 1914. From Houdini: His Life Story *(1928)*

Magician. Born to Hungarian immigrants, he performed as a trapeze artist before learning the art of illusion. He moved to New York City with his father in 1886 and briefly worked as a necktie cutter, and at sixteen he changed his name in honor of the French magician Jean-Eugène Robert-Houdin. In 1894 he married Wilhelmina Rahner, who became his assistant. He achieved moderate success during the 1890s by entertaining audiences in beer halls, theaters, and dime museums. In 1900 he embarked on a four-year tour of Europe during which he amazed audiences by extricating himself from a variety of shackles, ropes, handcuffs, prison cells, and locked containers. He was an international star by the time he returned to New York City, where he began performing elaborate stunts. On one occasion he freed himself after being shackled in chains, locked in a box, and submerged in the East River; on another he escaped from a straitjacket while suspended, head down, high above Broadway. From 1916 to 1923 he exhibited his skills in several motion pictures, including *The Master of Mystery* and *The Grim Game*. He lived for several years at 305 East 69th Street, and from 1904 until the end of his career in a brownstone at 278 West 113th Street, which he fitted with an oversized bathtub so that he could practice his underwater tricks. Although Houdini loved illusion he despised mediums and mind readers. In 1908 he wrote *The Unmasking of Robert-Houdin*, which exposed his former idol as a faker. His other published writings are *Handcuff Secrets* (1907) and *A Magician among the Spirits* (1924). He is buried in Machpelah Cemetery in Queens.

Harold Kellock: *Houdini: His Life Story* (New York: Harcourt, Brace, 1928)

Ruth Brandon: *The Life and Many Deaths of Harry Houdini* (London: Secker and Warburg, 1993)

Robert Sanger Steel

House, Edward (Mandell) (*b* Houston, 26 July 1858; *d* New York City, 28 March 1938). Businessman and presidential advisor. After meeting Woodrow Wilson, then governor of New Jersey, at the Hotel Gotham in New York City in 1910 he became his close friend and most trusted advisor. For the next few years House lived in the city, where he solicited the support of businessmen during Wilson's presidential campaign in 1912 and his first term as president. Known as Wilson's "silent partner," he played a vital role in securing the support of Wall Street for Wilson's financial legislation, particularly the Federal Reserve Act. He was also an advisor to Mayor William J. Gaynor. After Wilson's presidency he lived in Texas and New York City; he died in his apartment on East 68th Street. He was often known as Colonel House (the title was honorary). House wrote a memoir, *Intimate Papers* (1926–28).

James Bradley

Houseman, John [Haussmann, Jacques] (*b* Bucharest, 22 Sept 1902; *d* Malibu, Calif., 31 Oct 1988). Actor and director. He directed *Four Saints in Three Acts* by Virgil Thomson in 1934 and then collaborated with Orson Welles on a number of daring productions for the Federal Theater of the Works Progress Administration. In 1937 the two founded the Mercury Theatre, which on 31 October of the following year broadcast a radio dramatization of H. G. Wells's "The War of the Worlds" that many listeners mistook for a report of a Martian invasion. He returned to Broadway several times during his career and at the age of sixty-six helped to establish the school of drama at Juilliard. In 1972 he formed the Acting Company, of which he served as artistic director. The John Houseman Theater opened on West 42nd Street in 1986. Houseman wrote *Run Through: A Memoir* (1972), *Front and Center* (1979), and *Final Dress* (1982).

JillEllyn Riley

House Sparrow. A bird about six inches (fifteen centimeters) long: the male is white and chestnut and has a large black throat patch and a gray head; the female is dull brown and has a pale stripe over the eye. The bird was introduced to the metropolitan area in the early 1850s from Europe and soon became well established. By the 1890s its population had reached a peak: during the summer of 1892 Frank Chapman reported seeing about four thousand bathing in one small pool in Central Park. One of the most widely distributed land birds in the world, it lives in the city year round and has as many as three broods a year, laying from four to six eggs in each clutch between late March and mid August in birdhouses, in holes in trees and buildings, and less often in bulky, domed stick nests in trees.

John Bull: *Birds of the New York Area* (New York: Harper and Row, 1964)

John Bull: *Birds of New York State* (New York: Doubleday / Natural History Press, 1974)

John Bull: *Birds of New York State, including the 1976 Supplement* (Ithaca, N.Y.: Cornell University Press, 1985)

John Bull

housing. The diversity and density of New York City have made it unusually difficult to provide affordable, convenient housing for residents and profits for property owners and developers. In New Amsterdam the two most common types of dwelling were the farmhouse and the row house, squeezed on lots twenty-five feet (eight meters) wide as early as the late seventeenth century. The Dutch farmhouse was a single-story open barn of heavy timber, with clapboard siding and a

Dutch house on Williams Street dating from 1648, ca 1832

steep-pitched or sometimes gambrel-pitched loft, and a second-story door at the gabled end. The row house, patterned after the Dutch model, could accommodate a family with as many as eight members in a small space with low heating costs. It had a raised basement in which the family spent most of its time (the basement was warm because the kitchen was there), a parlor, and an upper story, sometimes with dormer windows, for sleeping. The roofs had the characteristic Dutch steep pitch, and the more costly were festooned with orange tiles and crow-stepped gambrels. At the front of the building was a stoop, from a Dutch word meaning step or platform, which included a staircase and landing outside the door to the parlor. The building was usually entered through a passage under the stoop: the stoop itself was used only on special occasions (Washington Irving wrote in *A History of New York* that the parlor was to be entered only for its weekly cleaning and that the brass lion's-head knocker on the front door was more often worn out from polishing than from use). The building was solidly built and had an adaptable design: either of its two lower stories could be converted into a shop or restaurant, rooms rented out to tenants when extra income was needed, the entire building converted into APARTMENTS for the middle class, and the building then restored to its former, one-family use.

Captain John Schenck House, built ca *1656 at what became Avenue U and East 63rd Street in Flatlands,* ca *1900*

The British built symmetrical red-brick residences of two and three stories, timber-framed and clad in masonry; the sashes and linteled doorways of these rowhouses gave them the look of prosperous provincial town residences. By the second decade of the nineteenth century the city was crowded with the Georgian and Federal row houses of middle- and upper-class residents: these buildings were of brick or wood or both and stood eighteen to twenty feet (five and a half to six meters) wide and two stories tall, with pitched roofs and dormer attics where the servants usually lived. Poor and working-class residents of the city lived off narrow streets and back alleys, in jerry-built one- and two-story wooden structures that had artisanal workshops on the ground floor and sleeping rooms for family and apprentices on the second floor or in the attic. The Commissioners' Plan of 1811 attempted to regulate the development of the congested and rapidly growing city by designating wide avenues and narrow cross streets, forming a grid that accommodated developers' preferences for lots of standard dimensions: a width of twenty-five feet (eight meters) and a depth of one hundred feet (thirty meters). Between 1820 and 1860 lower Manhattan changed considerably. The population of European immigrants quadrupled, leading many of the city's wealthy residents to move to developing neighborhoods in northern Manhattan; owners of residential housing and developers of business LOFTS and factories contended for space that was increasingly desirable to businessmen; and laissez-faire attitudes led to the development of housing that packed large numbers of people into small areas. South of Canal Street in the 1830s MANSIONS, churches, and breweries were converted to low-rent, multiple residences called rookeries, where families lived in cramped, dark, airless apartments. Rookeries provided the model for TENEMENTS, cheaply constructed, uniformly spartan buildings that contained small, uncomfortable apartments rented out to workers. Tenements spanned the width of the standard lot, extending back fifty to sixty feet (fifteen to eighteen meters); rear buildings, or "double houses," were often constructed on the remaining back area.

During the 1830s and 1840s large tenement neighborhoods took shape between Fulton Street and Corlear's Hook on the Lower East Side and to the west in the particularly squalid neighborhood of the Five Points. Residential density was so great in these neighborhoods that heavily used yard privies overflowed intermittently, contributing to the spread of cholera in 1832, 1849, and 1866. By mid century thousands of persons bunked in boarding houses, or "crib joints," along the Bowery, and upwards of eighteen thousand lived in quarters below street level.

Wealthy residents distanced themselves from lower Manhattan by moving uptown to exclusive neighborhoods of Federal and Greek Revival row houses: these stately buildings were made of red brick or wood, stood two or three stories tall, and had shallow basements, slope-roofed attics, and dormer windows. They sometimes stood on lots twenty feet (six meters) wide when builders put up five structures on land intended for four. The first BROWNSTONES were constructed in Washington Square and Gramercy Park during the 1840s and quickly became fashionable. During the Civil War housing reformers inspected the hygienic and fire-safety conditions of some fifteen thousand tenements and succeeded in having rudimentary fire and sanitary codes enacted. The Tenement House Law of 1867 defined a tenement as a multiple dwelling and required the owner to provide a fire ladder, a privy for every twenty tenants, and connections between inside rooms and those directly receiving outside air. Owners seeking to maximize their rental space complied with the law by combining front and back buildings and using shafts and transoms to ventilate the interior rooms. From 1879 reformers supported the "dumbbell" design of the architect James E. Ware, which was intended to raise hygienic standards by providing ventilation and light for interior rooms. The design was so named because the building resembled a dumbbell when seen from above: between the front and back rooms the exterior walls were indented, creating large air shafts of nearly ten by thirteen feet (three by four meters) between adjacent buildings that extended from the ground to the roof. The Tenement House Law of 1879 enforced these and other adjustments and led to the development of a thousand dumbbells a year on the Lower and Upper East Side and in Chelsea, Hell's Kitchen, and the southern Bronx. In Brooklyn and Williamsburg the fire codes were less restrictive and the population was sparser; a tradition of narrow house fronts in downtown Brooklyn spread across South Brooklyn as well, spurring the development on narrower lots of row houses only two rooms deep. In Brooklyn the philanthropist

Alfred T. White built low-rent housing for the "worthy poor," based on the "model tenement" experiments of such philanthropists as Silas Wood: he developed the Home Buildings (1877) and the Tower Buildings (1879) in Brooklyn Heights, incorporating interior courtyards that offered tenants more sunlight than tenements in Manhattan did. To the east and southeast of these developments lay the Navy Yard, or "Jungle," where three-story, wooden houses with rear buildings and outdoor privies were crowded together. These houses were of balloon-frame construction (characterized by widely spaced studs nailed together), a type characteristic of the housing stock in Brooklyn until the turn of the century.

By the 1830s some wealthy residents of Manhattan, particularly young married couples, began to reside in the more fashionable boarding houses and hotels, like the Astor House (completed in 1836) and the even more lavish St. Nicholas Hotel (opened in 1854). Eventually the upper classes overcame their prejudices against shared habitation, and during the 1870s and 1880s they developed a taste for luxury apartments with concierge services, known as French flats. The Stuyvesant (1870) and the Dakota (1884) resembled châteaux, with suites of several rooms and servants' quarters. Gilsey House (1871) and other hotels on Broadway between Madison and Herald squares offered comparable suites and concierge services; buildings such as the Apthorp Apartments (1908) were also luxurious but had rooms facing air shafts or gloomy Renaissance palazzos. In the late 1890s Elgin R. L. Gould led the City and Suburban Homes Company; others associated with it included the activists Jacob A. Riis, Felix Adler, and Robert W. De Forest. The firm built tenements at West 68th Street and Amsterdam Avenue on the hollow block plan (in which an apartment block in the European or French style surrounds an interior court), charged the tenants moderate rents, and promised dividends of 6 percent to "philanthropic" investors. In 1901 there were upwards of 83,000 rookeries, frame houses, and dumbbell tenements in New York City, of which sixty thousand had been built since the Tenement House Law of 1879. Half the city's population lived in buildings with six or more families, and less than one fifth lived in one-family houses. Under the guidance of De Forest and Lawrence Veiller, the Charity Organization Society successfully backed the Tenement House Law of 1901: this required fire escapes and separate privies for each family in already existing, or "old law," tenements; prohibited inside rooms without windows and required twelve-foot (four-meter) side courts and backyards for all buildings constructed according to the "new law"; made it uneconomical to install air shafts and build on lots twenty-five feet (eight meters) wide, leading to the development of lots forty to fifty feet (thirteen to fifteen meters) wide; and created the Tenement House Department, administered by De Forest and Veiller, which pressured the landlords of old law buildings to comply with the code by installing fire escapes, cutting open inside rooms, and replacing unsanitary privies.

The new law encouraged the construction uptown of solid, well-lit, six-story buildings containing apartments (known as flats) that had dumbwaiters, cooking ranges, and hot running water. The extension of the subway to Washington Heights, Brownsville, and Morrisania led to the introduction of improved tenements in developing neighborhoods. Henry Morgenthau's firm the American Real Estate Company developed flats near subway stations in Washington Heights and the southern Bronx; one complex called the South Bronx at 149th Street and Southern Boulevard had large, airy apartments surrounding a courtyard. In 1905–8 seventy thousand two- and three-story apartment buildings were built in northern Manhattan, thirty thousand in the Bronx. Many of these contained stylish flats with large rooms, parquet floors, and bathrooms with tubs, renting for $5 to $6 a room a month. The Queensboro Corporation (formed in 1913) built walkup apartments on a mass scale in Jackson Heights and Corona. The city zoning law of 1916 protected owners of apartment buildings from commercial and industrial developers, but it did not protect racial and ethnic minorities: housing covenants barred Jews from apartment buildings on Park Avenue and blacks from the streets surrounding Harlem. Rigid racial segregation guaranteed that the migration of blacks into Harlem would overload the neighborhood's stock of walkups and new law apartments of high quality. LIMITED-DIVIDEND HOUSING companies sheltered about eighteen thousand persons in Manhattan, or about 1 percent of the population of the borough. In 1918 the proportion of old law to new law housing varied widely in Manhattan (388,000 old law units, 153,000 new law units), the Bronx (33,000 old law, 106,000 new law), and Brooklyn (158,000 old law, 113,000 new law). In Queens and Staten Island about a million persons lived in steam-heated new law flats.

Shortages of credit and building materials during the First World War caused a decline in the construction of flats. The state legislature responded to unreasonable rent increases with emergency controls in 1920 (see RENT REGULATION) and revived the real-estate market by enacting a ten-year tax abatement for developers of apartments. During the prosperous administration of President Calvin Coolidge (1923–29) the government assisted the housing market; transit routes were extended through the outer boroughs and rows of art deco apartment buildings were erected along the Grand Concourse, as were luxury apartment buildings along Riverside Drive and on Central Park West (notably the Beresford, an impressive building designed by Emery Roth with three Baroque projections at the top lending it a twin-tower silhouette from the east and south). Tax incentives encouraged the construction of Spanish–Moorish flats on and around Northern Boulevard in Jackson Heights (the Metropolitan Life Insurance Company built Spanish Gardens, a complex of 2125 units designed by Andrew Thomas), and garden apartments were built along Queens Boulevard and Pelham Parkway. Throughout the period progressive builders worked closely with reformers to incorporate design improvements into the Multiple Dwellings Law of 1929. The law mandated larger courtyards, basic plumbing, and fire-resistant construction, and imposed bulk and setback requirements for high-rise residences.

In 1921–29 a total of 420,734 apartments were built, accounting for 30 percent of the city's multiple dwellings at the end of the period. New construction also accounted for 106,384 one-family and 111,662 two-family dwellings; many were built in Queens, where there was ample space. Under the guidance of municipal socialists like Paul Blanshard, who favored the public provision of housing as a vital service, some reformers attacked the subsidized housing market, which they contended was a benefit to the lower middle class but not to the one million occupants of old law buildings. The architect Clarence S. Stein, the economist Edith Elmer Wood, and the social critic Lewis Mumford advocated the development of satellite communities on the outskirts of New York City and petitioned Governor Alfred E. Smith to form a state commission that would consider this and other options. The legislature rejected a number of radical proposals and instead formed the State Board of Housing in 1926, to which it gave the power of eminent domain and the right to grant tax abatements to limited-dividend companies that built apartments renting for $12.50 a room or less. The board sponsored only a few projects, including the Amalgamated Dwelling (1930) in Manhattan and Academy Housing (1931) in the Bronx. The *Regional Plan of New York and Its Environs* (1931), an effort supported by mortgage bankers and transportation developers, envisioned a transit system that would connect Manhattan to the residential neighborhoods of the outer boroughs. The Depression devastated private construction, causing builders and mortgage firms to seek relief from state and federal authorities. The Reconstruction Finance Corporation invested in Knickerbocker Village (1934), a limited-dividend project that cleared slums on the Lower East Side, and supported federal insurance for home mortgages provided by the Federal

The transformation of an apartment building at Vyse Avenue and 178th Street in the Bronx, 1980 to mid 1990s

Housing Administration. Municipal socialists and the civic reformers Mary K. Simkhovitch and Louis H. Pink pressured Mayor Fiorello H. La Guardia to build low-rent housing. In 1936 the fledgling New York City Housing Authority completed the First Houses (a 210-unit development on the Lower East Side), and the Public Works Authority was ready to fund larger projects (see PUBLIC HOUSING). The housing authority accepted existing racial and income divisions, building the Harlem River Houses (1937) for blacks and locating other projects within acknowledged social boundaries. In 1938 the Citizens Housing Council led municipal reformers and advocates of publicly supported housing in gaining the voters' approval of article 18 of the State Constitution: this authorized comprehensive city planning, slum clearance, and urban redevelopment. The Williamsburg and Queensbridge Houses were completed in 1940. The housing authority sheltered forty thousand persons by 1941. Limited government subsidies caused planners to construct spartan, high-rise buildings like the East Harlem Houses (1941, ten stories), but these developments functioned more as warehouses than as communities.

In 1938 Robert Moses and Pink (now the state insurance superintendent) sought to convince lenders that government aid granted under article 18 made it possible to build modern, fireproof, low-rent developments that could have their construction costs amortized over forty years. The result was the Parkchester complex for 42,000 residents, developed by the Metropolitan Life Insurance Company and completed in 1940. In central Queens the City Planning Commission developed Forest Hills, the parkways around the World's Fair of 1939–40, and the Independent subway, reviving the speculative construction of semidetached houses and row houses. William Gutterman developed Kew Gardens Hills with houses that were eighteen feet (five and a half meters) wide, had six or more rooms and built-in garages, and sold for $5990; when working-class buyers hesitated to buy he added finished basements with "Kentile" floors and faucets that mixed hot and cold water. During the Second World War the Lanham Act (1940) increased government subsidies for projects like the Wallabout (1941) and Fort Greene (1944) houses (for shipyard workers and navy dependents in the area surrounding the Brooklyn Navy Yard), and for quonset villages housing thirty thousand residents at several sites (including Flushing Meadow Park and Manhattan Beach). Rent controls were imposed by the U.S. Office of Price Administration, which on 1 November 1943 froze rents outright, with some exceptions. Moses used the eminent domain and tax-subsidy provisions of the Redevelopment Companies Law of 1943 to enable Metropolitan Life to build Stuyvesant Town (1947; 8756 units). The project was highly regarded as an example of inner-city renewal by the private sector, but a decision by Metropolitan Life to limit it to white tenants caused a controversy that eventually led to municipal laws barring discrimination in publicly assisted housing. When the Office of Price Administration withdrew rent controls in 1947, militant tenants successfully petitioned the state to impose its own system of controls.

Moses and his allies had a far-reaching influence: they prevailed on the housing authority to support a housing bond issue of $215 million, transformed the Lower East Side by constructing ten-, twelve-, and fourteen-story projects named for Smith, La Guardia, Lillian Wald, and Bernard Baruch, cleared one third of East Harlem for the Taft, Jefferson, and Wagner complexes, and developed more low-rent units across Brownsville and the southern Bronx. The housing authority built 75,000 units during the 1950s and became the landlord to 500,000 low-income tenants. During the 1950s Moses funded slum clearance with federal subsidies from Title I of the Housing Act of 1949. He made secret arrangements with real-estate agents to develop projects for the upper middle class without concern for comprehensive planning or the tenants who were displaced. Although intended for residential reconstruction, funds granted under Title I were used to build housing for the staffs of Columbia University and New York University, as well as 28,000 units renting from $25 to $75 a room, and enabled the garment unions' consortium and the United Housing Foundation to build cooperative projects like the Hillman Houses on the Lower East Side and Penn South in midtown. Funds were also used to demolish 26,000 units that had rented for less than $10 a room, to offset the costs of the New York Coliseum, and to subsidize the performing arts at Lincoln Center. These developments anchored the middle class to the central business districts of Manhattan and Brooklyn, but some 200,000 persons, mostly black and Puerto Rican, were driven into public housing or new slums. After the war Moses continued to dominate the development plans of the municipal government. He encouraged the investment of savings banks in Parkway Village in Kew Gardens and of New York Life Insurance in the award-winning development Fresh Meadows. He also encouraged the construction of middle-income apartment buildings at Trump Village (1964; 3800 units) in Brighton Beach, and at Lefrak City (1967; five thousand units) near the Long

Island Expressway. Strengthened by the GI Bill, mortgage insurance from the Federal Housing Administration made possible the construction of six-room, semidetached houses in Flushing that sold for $7200 and of garden apartments in Glen Oaks Village that rented for $45 a month.

The excesses wrought by Moses bred resistance to government-assisted projects during the 1960s, but federal funds nevertheless allowed the housing authority to continue building nearly as aggressively as during the postwar years, to which the government responded with emergency measures. In 1965 the city recognized rent withholding as a valid means of forcing tenement repairs, and article 7A of the property laws was passed, permitting escrowed rents to fund tenant-run housing. The War on Poverty of the federal government, the Municipal Loan Program, and philanthropic efforts like those of the Bedford Stuyvesant Restoration Corporation extended urban renewal to the city's ghettos. The Mitchell–Lama Act subsidized middle-income projects like Co-op City (1968–70) in the Bronx, where 15,500 units rented for $20 a room, and added 138,849 units by the 1970s. During these years some activists organized against "bulldozer clearance"; owners of brownstones in Greenwich Village and on the Upper West Side and leaders of rent strikes in Harlem supported efforts to translate the housing needs of the poor into specific housing plans, and to promote control by the poor of neighborhood housing. In 1968 the legislature authorized the construction of Battery Park City, a complex of five thousand luxury apartments with set-asides for middle-income units. In the same year it chartered the Urban Development Corporation (UDC) to override zoning rules and expedite the construction of middle-income housing. The UDC built thirty-two projects, including Twin Parks in the Bronx and the cooperative apartments on Roosevelt Island, with mortgage subsidies that eventually endangered the state's credit. The legislature also adopted a system of maximum base rents, which exempted newly constructed apartments from rent regulation and allowed landlords greater profits despite fierce opposition from tenants.

The economic environment of the late 1960s and 1970s caused neighborhood development initiatives to fail. Although 33,000 units were erected in the early 1970s by church groups with mortgage subsidies from the Model Cities program, ownership under the provisions of article 7A redeemed only a handful of buildings. Even "sweat equity" could not make headway against rehabilitation costs that reached $30,000 a unit by the mid 1970s. Soaring mortgage and labor rates slowed the construction of private, medium-rent housing from twenty thousand units a year in the early 1960s to fewer than five thousand late in the decade. Buildings were abandoned at a staggering rate (an estimated 200,000 apartments were lost in 1960–75), and arsonists often destroyed the remains. Neighborhoods in the southern Bronx, central Harlem, and Bushwick became uninhabitable. The administration of President Richard M. Nixon ordered a moratorium on new public housing development in 1973, and the fiscal crisis of 1975 caused traditional sources of development money to disappear, weakening the UDC. President Jimmy Carter visited the devastated southern Bronx in 1977 and pledged to rebuild Charlotte Street; within six years several million dollars in federal money had funded a small number of ranch-style houses but failed to revitalize the neighborhood. Other efforts to reclaim apartments in the southern Bronx were led by the community activist Louis Gigante. Local Law 45 (1977) authorized the city to transfer foreclosed properties to tenant owners; by 1981 some 112,000 units had reverted to the city after being transferred to tenant owners when tenant managers failed to collect adequate rents from their neighbors. The Nehemiah Plan, initiated by East Brooklyn Congregations in 1984, built more than fifteen hundred houses on vacant land and became a national model for low-income homeownership.

Under President Ronald Reagan low-rent subsidies were nearly eliminated, and at the same time the state's mortgage authority reached its limit. The supply of housing in New York City was again determined by market forces and driven by inflation. Helmsley–Spear offered cooperative ownership plans to tenants in Tudor City and Parkchester in 1978, and during the 1980s landlords converted nearly 320,000 rental apartments to cooperative ownership in a process that became known as gentrification. The pressure to build high-priced housing eliminated two thirds of the city's 150,000 single-room occupancy units (SROs) by the late 1980s, and there was considerable new construction in Hell's Kitchen (which became known as Clinton) and along upper Broadway. Rising costs forced out thousands. By 1987 the market was glutted with 21,500 luxury apartments. A hard-pressed city kept five thousand homeless families in centers (ten families in each) and in sixty squalid hotels that charged exorbitant rates: the Hotel Martinique at Broadway and 32nd Street (390 units) became a notorious welfare hotel (see HOMELESSNESS). In the early 1990s the city ran out of subsidies for affordable housing. The median value of cooperatives in Manhattan reached $487,380 by 1989, a quadrupling in price since the late 1970s, and that of row houses in Kew Gardens $180,000. The number of homeless people was estimated to be between seventy thousand and 100,000; many of the homeless shunned municipal shelters and lived in shanties, under bridges, in parks and subways, and in the streets. The index of overcrowded domiciles had risen 50 percent since 1980, and 150,000 families awaited housing on the housing authority's waiting lists. An unknown number of families lived doubled up in public housing. Without the promise of new government subsidies and cheap land in the outer boroughs, the city was less able to provide decent housing than at any time since the days of Jacob A. Riis. In one more hopeful development, thousands of new dwellings were built after 1985 in formerly abandoned sections of Brooklyn and the Bronx, as the municipal government directed more money to affordable housing than the next fifty American cities combined.

Anthony Jackson: *A Place Called Home: A History of Low-cost Housing in Manhattan* (Cambridge: MIT Press, 1976)

Richard Plunz: *A History of Housing in New York City: Dwelling Type and Social Change in the American Metropolis* (New York: Columbia University Press, 1990)

Joel Schwartz

Howard Beach. Neighborhood in southwestern Queens (1985 pop. 18,000), bounded to the north by the Belt Parkway, to the east by 102nd Street, to the south by Jamaica Bay, and to the west by 78th Street. It was established in the 1890s by William J. Howard, a glove manufacturer in Brooklyn who operated a goat farm on 150 acres (sixty-one hectares) of meadow land near Aqueduct as a source of skins for kid gloves. In 1897 he bought more land and filled it in, and during the following year he built eighteen cottages and opened a hotel near the water, which he operated until it was destroyed by fire in October 1907. He gradually bought more land and in 1909 formed the Howard Estates Development Company; he dredged out Stillwell Basin (later Shellbank Canal) and used the dredgings for fill on the meadows. By 1914 Howard had reclaimed five hundred acres (two hundred hectares) of land, built several streets, laid out mains for water and gas, and built thirty-five houses priced between $2500 and $5000. A railroad station (opened in April 1913) and a post office were given the name Ramblersville; a casino, a beach, and a fishing pier were added in 1915. The railroad station and the post office took the name Howard Beach on 6 April 1916, and during 1916–17 more bungalows and cottages were built and several streets were paved. In 1922 a group of investors took over the development and sold lots for about $690 each.

The demand for more housing during the 1920s stimulated development and the construction of 150 houses each year, and there were 510 private houses at the end of 1935. In 1933 all street names were replaced by numbers to conform to the system used in the rest of Queens. After a fire destroyed the trestle across the bay the Long Island Rail Road terminated service to Howard Beach in October

Waterfront in Howard Beach, 1978

1955; subway service was inaugurated on 28 June 1956 from a station at 159th Avenue. During the 1950s a development called Rockwood was built in a large area west of Cross Bay Boulevard; cooperative housing and condominiums were built in the 1980s. Howard Beach received much unwanted attention after three black men passing through the area on 20 December 1986 were viciously assaulted by a group of white teenagers. One of the victims was killed while fleeing; the leaders of the attack were later convicted of manslaughter. Amid the ensuing controversy many residents grew resentful of what they believed to be a widely held assumption that they were all racists. It was the misfortune of Howard Beach to be an arena for issues that affect most of the city.

Many of the inhabitants of Howard Beach are Italian-American. The neighborhood has four elementary schools, two public and two parochial. The geographical isolation imposed by the bay, the airport, and the parkway gives the neighborhood a strong sense of community and local pride.

Vincent Seyfried

Howard J. Rubenstein Associates. Public relations firm established in Brooklyn in 1954 by Howard Rubenstein. After Rubenstein managed the successful mayoral campaign of Abraham D. Beame in 1973 the firm gained several major clients in municipal government and business. In 1984 it moved to Manhattan, where it served about two hundred clients, including many of the city's most powerful builders, trade associations, and labor unions. For thirty-four of these clients it worked as a registered lobbyist. By this time Howard J. Rubenstein Associates was one of the largest and most influential public relations firms in the city. It had seventy-two employees and headquarters at 1345 6th Avenue.

Alan R. Raucher

Howe [Horenstein], **Irving** (*b* Bronx, 11 June 1920; *d* New York City, 5 May 1993). Editor and critic. He grew up in a poor Jewish neighborhood in the eastern Bronx and joined the Young People's Socialist League at fourteen. During the late 1930s he attended City College of New York, where he became a leading Trotskyist activist and took part in rallies for many social causes; he later abandoned communism and embraced democratic socialism. After fulfilling military service he returned to the city and from 1948 to 1952 wrote reviews for *Time*. During the 1950s he taught at universities outside the city, and in 1954 he launched the magazine *Dissent*. He returned to the city in 1963 to join the English department at Hunter College, where he remained until 1986. He remained politically active as a lecturer, writer, and member of the Democratic Socialists of America, and continued to edit *Dissent*. Howe's published writings include *World of Our Fathers* (1975), a poignant account of Jewish life in New York City that was a best-seller and won many awards, and *A Margin of Hope: An Intellectual Autobiography* (1982).

James Bradley

Howell, James (*b* Bradford, Wiltshire, England, 16 Oct 1829; *d* Brooklyn, 27 Jan 1897). Mayor of Brooklyn. An iron founder by trade, he was elected the nineteenth mayor and served two consecutive terms (1878–81). His tenure was marked by retrenchment because of the effects of the financial crisis of 1873, but he did oversee the late stages of construction of the Brooklyn Bridge and was a trustee for the project.

Ellen Fletcher

Howells, William Dean (*b* Martins Ferry, Ohio, 1 March 1837; *d* New York City, 11 May 1920). Novelist and literary critic. He moved to New York City in 1865 and wrote briefly for the *New York Tribune* and the *Nation* before settling in Boston, where he became the assistant editor (1866–71) and then the editor (1871–81) of the *Atlantic Monthly* and wrote several novels, the best-known of which is *The Rise of Silas Lapham* (1885). In 1887 he endangered his career by publishing a letter to the editor of the *Tribune* in defense of the anarchists who had been condemned for the riots at the Haymarket in Chicago. He returned to New York City in 1888, took an apartment in an old house overlooking Livingston Place, and wrote several novels reflecting his disillusionment with a society that he saw as crippled by social and economic ills: *Annie Kilburn* (1888) was strongly pro-labor, and *A Hazard of New Fortunes* (1890) chronicled the "frantic panorama" of competitive life in the city. In the early 1890s he rented an apartment at 241 East 17th Street and in 1895 he moved to one overlooking Central Park, where he wrote articles in support of such authors as Tolstoy, Ibsen, Zola, and Stephen Crane. Howells became the first president of the American Academy of Arts and Letters in 1908 and remained active in controversial social and political causes. He lived the last ten years of his life at the Hotel St. Hubert, 120 West 57th Street.

Kenneth S. Lynn: *William Dean Howells: An American Life* (New York: Harcourt Brace Jovanovich, 1970)

See also LITERATURE.

Anthony Gronowicz

Howland Hook. Neighborhood in northwestern Staten Island, lying at the confluence of the Arthur Kill and the Kill van Kull; the Goethals Bridge (1928) stands at its southern edge. The neighborhood is also called Holland Hook, after Henry Holland, one of the representatives for Staten Island in the colonial assembly of New York. Ferries ran from the area to Elizabeth, New Jersey, between 1736 and 1961. In the mid 1990s Howland Hook was mostly industrial, the site of both the United States Lines container port, the largest facility of its kind in New York City, and Port Ivory, a disused plant and port of Procter and Gamble that was once the largest employer in the borough. Wetlands protected by the state account for some of the land.

Harlow McMillen

Hudson, Henry (*b* England; *d* after 23 June 1611). Explorer. He dedicated his life to finding a passage to China through North America. After unsuccessful voyages in 1607 and 1608 he made his third attempt in the early spring of 1609. With backing from the Dutch East India Company he set sail with a crew of eighteen from Amsterdam on the *Halve Maen*; icebergs north of Norway and the threat of

Henry Hudson

mutiny led him to seek shelter along the North American coast, and on 2 September he dropped anchor in the lower bay of what became New York Harbor, which he explored in small boats for ten days. He then sailed up the Hudson River (which he named) to the site of what became Albany, taking small boats as far as what became Troy, New York. Hudson made his last voyage in 1611; after discovering Hudson's Bay and claiming it for England his crew mutinied and cast him adrift. A statue of Hudson stands atop a tall shaft in Henry Hudson Park in Spuyten Duyvil.

Noel Bertram Gerson: *The Magnificent Adventures of Henry Hudson* (New York: Dodd, Mead, 1965)

James E. Mooney

Hudson River. A river bordering the western edge of New York City that is one of the most important waterways in the world. As an extension of the Atlantic Ocean it is technically an estuary, but because it results from glacial scouring it is also referred to as a fjord. From its source in upstate New York at Lake Tear of the Clouds in the Adirondacks the river flows for 315 miles (507 kilometers) in a generally southerly direction to Upper New York Bay. It is navigable for ocean vessels as far north as Albany, tidal for 154 miles (248 kilometers) as far north as Troy, and saline for about sixty miles (ninety-seven kilometers) as far north as Newburgh, depending on seasonal rain runoff. The river is the boundary between New York State and New Jersey for seventeen miles (twenty-seven kilometers). At its southern end it is known as the North River, and at its mouth it is 4400 feet (1340 meters) wide. The river traverses one of the oldest geological regions in the United States. For millions of years before the retreat of the last glacier, the Wisconsin Ice Sheet, it extended another 120 miles (193 kilometers) into the Atlantic to the edge of the Continental Shelf, but the rising seawater flooded the old river course, thus contributing to the navigability of the river. Despite years of pollution the river is rich in marine life. In the 1970s and 1980s strict controls on the dumping of toxic waste and strong efforts by environmentalists improved the quality of the water and enabled many varieties of fish to reestablish themselves, including striped bass, herring, sturgeon, and shad.

The Hudson was an important trade route for the Algonquin tribes, especially in its lower valley. The first European to see the river was the Florentine navigator Giovanni da Verrazano, who in 1524 sailed up the river in his ship the *Dauphine* for François I of France, for whom he claimed the land. In the following year the harbor was visited by Estéban Gómez, a Portuguese mariner sailing under the Spanish flag who named the river Río de San Antonio. In 1609 the Englishman Henry Hudson, sailing his ship the *Halve Maen* for the Dutch West India Company, explored much of the river as far north as Albany in search of a passage to the Orient. He provided an extensive report on the "Great River to the North," many details of which were chronicled in the log of his first mate, Robert Juet. The river was a major trade route for the early Dutch and English colonists, and later figured importantly in the American Revolution. Control of the river was vital for the survival of the rebellion, and one third of all the battles were fought along its shores. The capture near Tarrytown, New York, of the British major John André, who had the plans of West Point hidden in his boot, probably saved the American cause. In 1807 Robert Fulton inaugurated the era of steam navigation when he piloted his *North River Steamboat* (later known as the *Clermont*) up the Hudson. Traffic on the Hudson reached its peak in the mid nineteenth century when the Delaware and Hudson Canal and the Erie Canal were opened, but it declined when railroads were built on both sides of the river, and eventually the piers along the western shore of Manhattan all but disappeared. The striking beauty of the river, particularly along the Palisades and in the Hudson Highlands, inspired literary works by Washington Irving and the paintings of the Hudson River School.

William Bertrand Fink: *Getting to Know the Hudson River* (New York: Coward–McCann, 1970)

Gerard R. Wolfe

Hudson River lines. The business of transporting passengers by water from New York City to Albany and other points up the Hudson River developed quickly after the first voyage of Robert Fulton's steamship the *North River Steamboat* in 1807, and was profoundly altered by two developments in the early nineteenth century. Intense competition was spurred by the ruling of the U.S. Supreme Court in *Gibbons v. Ogden* (1824) that the official monopoly on steam travel in the waters of New York held by Fulton and Robert R. Livingston was unconstitutional, and improvements in the design of ships reduced the time needed to travel to Albany from upwards of thirty-two hours, which in turn brought about separate day and night lines. In 1832 the major operators of day lines formed a quasi-monopoly called the Hudson River Steamboat Association, which later evolved into the Hudson River Day Line under unified management. Night services began in 1832 with the sailings of the *James Kent*; service to Albany was offered by the People's Line Association from 1835. Among the ships sailing the Hudson in this period were the *Isaac Newton* (from 1846), the *Alida* (1847), and the *New World* (1848). From 1856 the Citizen's Line offered service to Troy.

After the Hudson River Railroad reached Albany in 1851, travel by sail and steam was undertaken less often for business and more often for recreation. Traffic was greatest between 1860 and 1920; among the best-known ships of this period was the *Mary Powell*, a beautiful sidewheel steamer known as the "speed queen of the Hudson." Built in 1861 by Michael S. Allison of Jersey City, New Jersey, for Captain Absalom L. Anderson of Kingston, New York, the ship had a length after modification of 288 feet (eighty-eight meters) and was powered by a vertical beam engine; she ran a daily round trip of 180 miles (290 kilometers) between Kingston and Manhattan, docking at noon. Remodeled in 1903 for excursion service, the *Mary Powell* ran on the Hudson River Day Line until 1917, when she was retired and dismantled. Other ships serving this route included the *St. John* (1864), the *Dean Richmond* (1865), the *Drew* (1866), and the *Adirondack* (1896).

In 1902 the night services were combined when the Hudson Navigation Company was formed by Charles Wyman Morse, known as the "ice king" for having made his fortune by supplying New York City with ice from Maine. The company operated under various names until 1939, although it was generally known as the Hudson River Night Line. In the early twentieth century the Hudson was served by such ships as the *C. W. Morse* (1903), the *Hendrick Hudson* (1906), the *Robert Fulton* (1909), and the *Washington Irving* (1913). The largest steamship was the *Berkshire* (in service from 1913 to 1937), which was noted for her classic interiors. Built by the New York Shipbuilding Company (Camden, New Jersey), the ship registered 4500 tons, measured 422 feet (129 meters) by fifty feet (fifteen meters), and was powered by a vertical beam engine with a cylinder of eighty-five inches (2.15 meters) and a stroke of twelve feet (3.66 meters). The

Berkshire provided night service between New York City and Albany. The *Alexander Hamilton* (1924) was the last operating sidewheel steamer on the Hudson River Day Line. Designed by J. W. Millard and built by the Bethlehem Shipbuilding Corporation of Maryland, she measured 349 feet (106 meters) by seventy-seven feet (twenty-three meters) and had a triple-expansion inclined engine and feathering sidewheels. The retirement of the *Alexander Hamilton* in September 1971 ended a long tradition of steam-powered travel on the Hudson.

Although the Hudson River Day Line was disbanded in 1949, the *Dayliner* was put into service in 1972 and successor companies continued regular sailings up the Hudson until 4 September 1989.

Donald C. Ringwald: *Hudson River Day Line: The Story of a Great American Steamboat Company* (Berkeley, Calif.: Howell–North, 1965)

Arthur G. Adams: *The Hudson through the Years* (Westwood, N.J.: Lind, 1985)

Arthur G. Adams

Jasper F. Cropsey, Castle Garden *(1851)*

Hudson River Railroad. Freight railroad chartered in 1846, merged in 1869 with the New York and Harlem Railroad to form the NEW YORK CENTRAL AND HUDSON RIVER RAILROAD.

Hudson River School. School of landscape painting that flourished between 1825 and 1870; the name, which appeared in print in 1879, was probably first used during the 1870s pejoratively by artists and critics who promoted European styles of painting and supported the Society of American Artists (1877–1906) as an alternative to the more conservative National Academy of Design. A sketching tour up the Hudson River to the Catskill Mountains by Thomas Cole and the purchase of several of his landscapes by John Trumbull, William Dunlap, and Asher B. Durand in the same year are considered to mark its beginning. Members subscribed to concepts of the sublime, the beautiful, the picturesque, and associationism articulated in the writings of such influential European critics as Edmund Burke (1729–97), William Gilpin (1724–1804), Sir Uvedale Price (1747–1829), and Archibald Alison (1757–1839). Cole was the first artist to treat the American landscape as a metaphor for the new nation. New York City was the center of the school, which was often called the "native," "American," or "New York" school. Many members had studios in the Tenth Street Studio Building (1857–1956) and belonged to such societies as the Sketch Club (1827–69) and the Century Association (formed in 1847). Their works were bought by art galleries in the city such as Williams, Stevens, Williams and Company and Goupil and Company (formed in 1846, reorganized as M. Knoedler and Company) and by patrons such as Jonathan Sturges and Robert Leighton Stuart. Several influential periodicals including the *Crayon* (1855–61) were published in the city, where a number of institutions promoted the works of the school, among them the American Academy of the Fine Arts (1802–42), the National Academy of Design (formed in 1826), and the American Art Union (1838–52).

Although most members of the school traveled and worked in Europe, they often chose the Hudson River as a subject for their works and also used it as a route to sketching sites in the Catskills, the Adirondacks, and the mountains of New England. Durand became the acknowledged leader of the school after Cole's death. He articulated its theories in "Letters on Landscape Painting," nine essays published in the *Crayon* in 1855 and based in part on the argument that the faithful depiction of nature reveals the presence of God. Cole's pupil Frederic E. Church sought to evoke cosmic truths by blending art and science in landscape paintings of grand scale; he became known internationally as the foremost American landscape painter for paintings that he completed after travels in North America, South America, Europe, and the Near East. Such artists as John Frederick Kensett, Martin Johnson Heade (1819–1904), and Sanford Robinson Gifford (1823–80) painted smaller landscapes in a "luminist" style characterized by careful study of light and atmosphere. They explored concepts of man's relation to nature and God and sought to represent the direct experience of a spiritual presence in nature by rendering their subjects with perceptual intensity.

The decline of the Hudson River School was brought about by the Civil War, which permanently altered Americans' perceptions of their country and its landscape, the influence of European academic training, the popularity of French Barbizon art and impressionism among American collectors, and a new emphasis on decorative design inspired by a movement in Britain. Although a few leading members remained popular into the early twentieth century, the school by the 1880s was widely viewed not as a contemporary force in American art but rather as a historic movement that had established an American tradition of landscape painting.

John K. Howat: *American Paradise: The World of the Hudson River School* (New York: Metropolitan Museum of Art, 1987)

Timothy Anglin Burgard

Hughes, Charles Evans (*b* Glens Falls, N.Y., 11 April 1862; *d* Barnstable, Mass., 28 Aug 1948). Justice of the Supreme Court. By the 1890s he earned a reputation as a lawyer unusually adept at reducing legal complexities to their essentials. He attracted public notice as the chief counsel on the Stevens Gas Commission (1905), which investigated utility practices in New York City, and as the counsel for the Armstrong Commission (1905–6), which mounted an inquiry by the state into insurance fraud. His findings led to unprecedented legislation to prevent corruption. In 1906 he was elected governor of New York; during his term he helped to formulate one of the most effective workers' compensation laws in the nation. He was appointed to the U.S. Supreme Court in 1910 and held his seat until 1916, when he resigned to become the Republican candidate for president. After his defeat by Woodrow Wilson he resumed private practice and did not reenter public life until 1921, when he became secretary of state. Reappointed to the Supreme Court, he met some of his greatest challenges as its chief justice from 1930 to 1941; he guided the court as it voided crucial aspects of the New Deal and incurred the anger of many liberals.

Largely because of his efforts the court salvaged its credibility and blunted President Franklin D. Roosevelt's plans to fashion a court sympathetic to the legislation of the New Deal. Hughes lived from 1886 to 1888 at 110 East 81st Street, for one year beginning in December 1888 at 129 East 62nd Street, from 1893 to 1905 on West End Avenue and 75th Street, and from 1917 to 1921 at 32 East 64th Street.

Merlo J. Pusey: *Charles Evans Hughes* (New York: Columbia University Press, 1963)

See also BUCKET SHOPS.

Frederick S. Voss

Hughes, Ellen [Mother Mary Angela] (*b* Annaloghan, County Tyrone, Ireland, *ca* 1806; *d* New York City, 5 Sept 1866). Nun. The sister of Archbishop John Hughes, she emigrated to the United States in 1818 and became a member of the Sisters of Charity in Maryland in 1825. She moved to New York City in 1846 and helped to establish the Sisters of Charity of Mount St. Vincent. Instrumental in the charity's early work, she opened St. Vincent's Hospital in 1849 and served as its superior until 1855, the year she became mother general of the Sisters of Charity of Mount St. Vincent.

Bernadette McCauley

Hughes, John (Joseph) (*b* Annaloghan, County Tyrone, Ireland, 24 June 1797; *d* New York City, 3 Jan 1864). Archbishop, brother of Ellen Hughes. Financial distress led his parents to apprentice him to a gardener, and by 1818 the family moved to Chambersburg, Pennsylvania. In 1820 he entered Mount St. Mary's Seminary near Emmitsburg, Maryland, where he supported himself as a gardener. He was ordained for the Diocese of Philadelphia on 15 October 1826 and appointed a coadjutor for the Diocese of New York on 7 January 1838. After John DuBois suffered a stroke in 1838 Hughes was put in charge of the diocese and in 1839 was given the title of apostolic administrator. His efforts to foster Catholic unity were complicated by the strength of ethnic loyalties. During his tenure he authorized a German parish staffed by diocesan clergy (St. Nicholas, 1833), a German parish staffed by clergy from a religious order (Most Holy Redeemer, 1844), a French parish (St. Vincent de Paul, 1840), and an Italian parish (Church of St. Anthony of Padua). In 1839 he toured Europe to seek funds and staff; he interested several religious orders in the city's mission, including the Ladies of the Sacred Heart (1841), the Sisters of Mercy (1846), and the Christian Brothers (1853). He also devoted himself to fighting anti-Catholicism. Arguing that Protestantism was being furthered by the Public School Society (a private organization that provided free education for poor children), he asked the state to give Catholics a share of the tax revenues that supported the society. When the legislature rejected his proposal he urged Catholics to vote for a slate of candidates who endorsed it (29 October 1841). They received few votes, but the fear of Catholic voting power led the legislature to introduce a public school system, to which Hughes responded by building parochial schools.

Appointed bishop on 20 December 1842, Hughes strengthened his authority by transferring ownership of parish property from lay corporations to a corporation in which the bishop was the principal trustee. He organized parishioners in 1844 to guard their churches against nativist rioters. In 1846 he laid the basis for Fordham University by placing St. John's College under the auspices of the Jesuits; during the same year he organized a diocesan community of sisters after the Sisters of Charity of St. Vincent de Paul informed him that the rules of their order prevented them from fulfilling his wishes to care for boys. When the archdiocese was formed on 19 July 1850 he was appointed archbishop, and he soon began the construction of St. Patrick's Cathedral. Although he favored religious liberty for Ireland he did not endorse the anti-British nationalist movement Young Ireland or the violent movement for independence. In 1861–62 he toured Europe as Abraham Lincoln's unofficial representative to promote the cause of the Union. Hughes last appeared in public on 17 July 1863, at Governor Horatio Seymour's request, to address participants in the city's draft riots. His remains were moved to St. Patrick's Cathedral in 1883.

John R. G. Hassard: *Life of the Most Reverend John Hughes, D.D., First Archbishop of New York, with Extracts from His Private Correspondence* (New York: D. Appleton, 1866)

Richard Shaw: *Dagger John: The Unquiet Life and Times of Archbishop John Hughes of New York* (New York: Paulist, 1977)

Mary Elizabeth Brown

Hughes, (James Mercer) Langston (*b* Joplin, Mo., 1 Feb 1902; *d* New York City, 22 May 1967). Poet and playwright. After graduating from high school in Cleveland he spent a year in Mexico with his father, briefly attended Columbia University, and worked in the United States and abroad. He won a poetry award sponsored by *Opportunity: A Journal of Negro Life* in 1925, and in the following year all his poems were published by Alfred A. Knopf as *The Weary Blues.* He earned his BA from Lincoln University in Pennsylvania in 1929 and then devoted himself entirely to writing. In his work he depicted the lives of black characters, often in the voice of the fictional character Simple. His play *Mulatto* ran on Broadway for two years; he also wrote songs and was a member of the American Society of Composers, Authors and Publishers. He won a Guggenheim Fellowship in 1935 and during the Second World War wrote radio scripts and toured with the United Service Organizations, often reading selections from his work. From 1942 to 1947 he lived at 634 St. Nicholas Avenue. He taught creative writing at Atlanta University in 1947 and was poet-in-residence at the University of Chicago Laboratory School in 1949. His last home was at 20 East 127th Street (from 1948). During the last decade of his life he devoted himself to such searching poetry as that collected in *The Panther and the Lash* (1967), which he dedicated to Rosa Parks. Among Hughes's works are the autobiographies *Big Sea* (1940) and *I Wonder as I Wander* (1956), and the book *The Sweet Flypaper of Life* (1955), which was well received for its humor and optimism.

Langston Hughes

Arnold Rampersad: *The Life of Langston Hughes* (New York: Oxford University Press, 1986–88)

James E. Mooney

Huguenot. Neighborhood in southwestern Staten Island, bounded to the north by Poillon Avenue, to the east by Hylan Boulevard, to the south by Foster Avenue, and to the west by Woodrow Road; it is bisected by Huguenot Avenue. The area was settled during the seventeenth and eighteenth centuries by Huguenots who built a church of native serpentine rock (still standing in the mid 1990s). It was called Bloomingview during the nineteenth century and before being renamed for a station of Staten Island Rapid Transit near the intersection of Amboy Road and Huguenot Avenue. The clean, sandy beaches in the area attracted vacationers, and in the early twentieth century several resorts opened, including the Terra Marine Hotel (one hundred rooms); John Kaltenmeier's Hotel stood near the railroad station. A miniature steam railway ran along Richmond Beach, where a boardwalk twenty feet (six meters) wide was built; eventually the beach became the site of St. Joseph by-the-Sea High School. Streets were laid out in the 1930s; development increased after Richmond Parkway opened in the 1970s, connecting Outerbridge Crossing with the center of the island. Residences in Huguenot range from undistinguished row houses to opulent estates. The neighborhood is the site of Intermediate School 7 (Bernstein), Intermediate School 75 (Paulo), and Tottenville High School. Small ponds of glacial origin are still found in the wooded sections remaining in eastern Huguenot.

Harlow McMillen

Huguenots. The first permanent European settlement in the metropolitan area was formed in Manhattan by a group of Walloons sponsored by the Dutch West India Company in 1624. Huguenot refugees from the Netherlands and the Germanys accounted for many of the colonists who moved to New Amsterdam in the following years; among them were Peter Minuit and the Bayard, Delanoy, and Delavall families. Harlem was settled in 1637 by the Walloon brothers Hendricus and Isaac DeForest and also became a Huguenot center. In 1650 Huguenots accounted for about a fifth of the population of New Amsterdam. Before the 1680s most French Calvinists moved to New York City after staying for a time in Protestant European countries. A number of refugees fled directly to the city after Louis XIV made a policy of eradicating Calvinism that culminated in the revocation of the Edict of Nantes in 1685; many of these refugees were merchants and craftsmen from the seaport of La Rochelle, the province of Aunis, and the Isle of Ré. Jacob Leisler, a German-born merchant with Huguenot roots, was the city's agent for settling the refugees, and from 1687 he bought land for them in Westchester County in what is now New Rochelle, New York. From 1658 to 1663 Harlem was the site of a French congregation under the ministry of Michel Cipierre. Pierre Daille moved to the city in 1682 and organized the first French congregation, which conducted services in Fort James and became defunct in the mid 1690s. Another congregation formed under Pierre Pieret in 1687 erected a French church on Petticoat Lane, the first in the city; it was replaced in 1704 by a stone building known as l'Église du St. Esprit at Church and Pine streets.

The toleration of ethnic and cultural diversity in the city led to the rapid assimilation of the Huguenots, and by the early eighteenth century such Huguenot merchants as Stephen de Lancey, Peter Jay, and Gabriel Laboyteaux were among the city's leaders. Huguenot craftsmen were also distinguished, especially such silversmiths as Bartholomew Le Roux, Simeon Soumaine, and Peter Quintard. Huguenots accounted for about 11 percent of the city's population by 1703 but after 1720 lost their independent religious identity: most became affiliated with other denominations, especially the Anglican church. In 1804 l'Église du St. Esprit became an Episcopal church; in the mid 1990s it continued to serve French-speakers. The Huguenot Society of America, formed in New York City in 1883, is dedicated to preserving Huguenot history.

Thomas J. Archdeacon: *New York City, 1664–1710: Conquest and Change* (Ithaca, N.Y.: Cornell University Press, 1976)

Jon Butler: *The Huguenots in America: A Refugee People in New World Society* (Cambridge: Harvard University Press, 1983)

David William Voorhees

Humphrey, Doris (*b* Oak Park, Ill., 17 Oct 1895; *d* New York City, 29 Dec 1958). Dancer and choreographer. She studied at Ruth St. Denis's dance school Denishawn until 1928, when she rejected exotic art dancing and opened up her own studio in New York City with Charles Weidman. While lecturing on modern dance at the New School for Social Research in 1931–40 she formed a circle of modernists in Greenwich Village that included the dance critic John Martin and the composers Aaron Copland and Henry Cowell. She articulated the idea that dance is the art of movement rather than pageantry, costume, or theatrical effects in the experimental dances *Water Study* (1928), *Life of the Bee* (1929), *Drama of Motion*, and *The Shakers* (1931). Because of severe arthritis she retired from dancing in 1946, but she continued to teach in her studio in New York City. In 1951 Humphrey joined the faculty of the Juilliard School of Music, where in 1955 she founded the Juilliard Dance Theater. She wrote *An Artist First: An Autobiography* (1972).

Peter M. Rutkoff, William B. Scott

Huneker, James Gibbons (*b* Philadelphia, 31 Jan 1857; *d* New York City, 9 Feb 1921). Critic. He taught piano at the National Conservatory in New York City and wrote for the *New York Recorder* (1891–95) and the *Morning Advertiser* (1895–97) before beginning a long association with the *Sun* (1900–17), for which he wrote criticism on music, art, literature, and the theater. He also worked for the *New York Times* as a foreign correspondent (for two years from 1912) and music critic (1918–19). Huneker wrote more than twenty books on music and other topics, including a study of New York City called *New Cosmopolis* (1915) and a novel about artists in the city, *Painted Veils* (1920).

Arnold T. Schwab: *James Gibbons Huneker, Critic of the Seven Arts* (Stanford, Calif.: Stanford University Press, 1963)

See also INTELLECTUALS and LITTLE MAGAZINES.

Hungarians. The first Hungarians arrived in New York City after the unsuccessful Hungarian Revolution of 1848–49. The great Hungarian revolutionary Louis Kossuth visited the city to muster support for his cause in December 1851, and he was greeted with several rousing receptions. The city's most notable Hungarian émigré after mid century was Imre Kiralfy, a producer and choreographer who with his brother Bolossy staged some of the city's most popular music and dance num-

Doris Humphrey center, *with Edith Orcutt, Katherine Litz, Letitia Ide, Miriam Raphael, Ada Korvin, Beatrice Seckler, and Joan Levy in* New Dance *(1935)*

bers of the period. Joseph Pulitzer, the reporter and newspaper owner who founded the Columbia School of Journalism, was also from Hungary.

Hungarians were a prominent part of the great European immigration movement in the late nineteenth century. Some ten thousand Hungarians settled in Manhattan in the 1870s, mostly on 2nd Avenue between 1st and 10th streets and between 55th and 72nd streets. The largest period of Hungarian settlement in New York City was the twenty-year-period beginning in 1890: by 1910 the federal census enumerated 76,625 persons of Hungarian origin in Manhattan and Brooklyn, and other estimates ranged as high as 110,000. Hungarian culture flourished, as churches, synagogues, restaurants, nightclubs, newspapers, and businesses were formed, mostly in lower Yorkville but also in parts of the Lower East Side.

Those who identified themselves as Hungarians before the First World War included many ethnic Slovaks, Romanians, Ruthenians, and Croatians from the Austro-Hungarian Empire. After the war many of the city's Hungarian-speaking residents were from Czechoslovakia, Austria, and Yugoslavia. Most of the city's Hungarians were Roman Catholic and Eastern Orthodox, though a large number were Protestant and Jewish. Hungarian Jews tended to identify more with their national origin than other eastern European Jews. Gypsies also contributed significantly to Hungarian culture, especially in the fields of music, dance, and literature.

Immigration declined after the First World War, and the center of the city's Hungarian life became Yorkville, in the upper 70s and lower 80s from 2nd Avenue to the East River, between the area's Czech and German communities. Hungarian communities also formed in the Bronx, Brooklyn, and Queens. In the area surrounding 2nd Avenue and 79th Street stood Hungarian churches, stores, butcher shops, and restaurants. By 1940 the city's Hungarian population surpassed 123,000, giving New York City the largest Hungarian community in the nation. During this period there were eight Hungarian daily, weekly, and monthly newspapers in the city.

In the 1980s only a few hundred immigrants from Hungary settled in New York City, but many of the 5440 immigrants from Romania were believed to be of Hungarian ancestry. After the collapse of the Eastern bloc governments in 1989 thousands of Hungarians settled in the city, for the most part in Queens (especially Ridgewood, Glendale, Long Island City, and Astoria); again, many of these immigrants were from Romania. Some gravitated to the old Hungarian neighborhood in Yorkville, though gentrification had long made this area too expensive for newcomers. In the mid 1990s several Hungarian institutions could still be found in Yorkville, which remained heavily frequented by Hungarians from throughout the region. The American Federation for Hungarian Education and Literature (also called Hungarian House) occupied two row houses on East 82nd Street, offering a library and other resources, and Puski-Corvin Magyar Konyveshaz remained the city's lone Hungarian bookstore. Weekly Hungarian newspapers included such established publications as Amerikai Magyar Nepszava (American Hungarian People's Voice; 1899) and the Hungarian Word (1902), as well as Szabdsag (Liberty; 1991). According to the federal census 75,721 New Yorkers in 1990 described themselves as being at least partly of Hungarian origin.

Prominent New Yorkers of Hungarian descent have included the magician Harry Houdini; the pediatrician Béla Schick; the composer Sigmund Romberg; the fencer Giorgio Santelli; the religious leader Stephen S. Wise; the composer Béla Bartók, who fled Hungary after the Nazi invasion and lived in the city from 1940 to 1945; two of Bartók's disciples, the composer Tibor Serly and the pianist Gyorgy Sandor; the sculptor Karl Illava, who created the War Memorial on 5th Avenue and 67th Street; the architect Emery Roth; the quarterback Joe Namath, who lived in the city while playing for the New York Jets; the actor Tony Curtis; and Ted Weiss, the liberal congressman who represented the Upper West Side from 1977 to 1992.

James Bradley

Hunt, Richard Morris (*b* Brattleboro, Vt., 31 Oct 1827; *d* Newport, R.I., 31 July 1895). Architect. He was the first American trained at the École des Beaux-Arts in Paris. After studying and traveling in Europe he moved to New York City in 1855 and in 1858 designed the Tenth Street Studios, where he introduced the French atelier system. Among those who worked with him there were such painters of the Hudson River School as Frederic E. Church. Hunt developed a lively, eclectic style and with such apprentices as William R. Ware, Frank Furness, and George B. Post designed several public buildings, including the Presbyterian Hospital on Madison Avenue (1872, commissioned by James Lenox), mansions (among them one commissioned by William K. Vanderbilt at 5th Avenue and 52nd Street, 1882), such commercial structures as the Tribune Building (1883), and the pedestal for the Statue of Liberty (1886). A member of the Century Club, he formed the American Institute of Architects, led the Municipal Art Society, and was a trustee and architect of the Metropolitan Museum of Art (1902). In 1898 a monument was erected in his honor by the Municipal Art Society at 5th Avenue and 70th Street facing the Lenox Library (1870), one of many commissions that he received from the Astors, Vanderbilts, and Lenoxes. None of the mansions Hunt designed along 5th Avenue and few of his public buildings survive.

Paul R. Baker: *Richard Morris Hunt* (Cambridge: MIT Press, 1980)

Edward A. Eigen

Hunter, Alberta (*b* Memphis, Tenn., 1 April 1895; *d* New York City, 17 Oct 1984). Singer and songwriter. At the behest of Paramount Records she moved to New York City in 1922, where she recorded her composition "Down Hearted Blues," later made famous by Bessie Smith. She worked in show business until 1956, when she studied nursing at the YWCA in Harlem and then worked as a licensed practical nurse for twenty years. She resumed her career as a performer in 1977 after being introduced to Barney Josephson, the owner of the Cookery (a restaurant and jazz club in Greenwich Village), and received the mayor's Award of Honor for Arts and Culture in 1983.

Frank C. Taylor with Gerald Cook: *Alberta Hunter: A Celebration in Blues* (New York: McGraw–Hill, 1987)

Val Ginter

Hunter College. College of the City University of New York. It began in 1869 as the Normal and High School for the Female Grammar Schools of the City of New York, renamed in the following year the Normal College of the City of New York and in 1914 Hunter College (after its first president, Thomas Hunter). From its inception the college operated a model school where prospective teachers could gain practical experience. The college held its first classes in rented space at Broadway and 4th Street; a neo-Gothic building opened at 68th Street and Lexington Avenue in 1873. Overcrowding during the 1920s led to the opening of extension centers in Queens and Brooklyn (the Brooklyn Collegiate Center of Hunter College in the building of the

Alberta Hunter

Chamber of Commerce at Court and Livingston streets, 1926), and of a satellite campus in 1931 in the northern Bronx (now Lehman College). By 1925 the college also offered evening classes at the freshman level open to all female high school graduates. After a fire at 68th Street the college operated temporarily out of rented space at 2 Park Avenue before opening a larger, modern building at 68th Street and Park Avenue in 1940: the repaired original structure became the home of Hunter High School. Two new towers were built during the presidency of Donna Shalala (1980–87). The college admitted only women until 1964, and as late as 1986 women received 74 percent of its undergraduate degrees and an even larger proportion of its master's degrees. In the mid 1990s Hunter College enrolled more than twenty thousand full- and part-time graduate and undergraduate students and operated two campus schools at 94th Street and Park Avenue for gifted children from pre-kindergarten to high school.

Samuel W. Patterson: *Hunter College: Eighty Five Years of Service* (New York: Lantern, 1955)

Selma Berrol

Hunter College High School. Secondary school opened in 1869 as part of the Female Normal and High School of the City of New York; it was the first school in the city to offer girls a free education beyond the eight grades of grammar school. In 1903 it changed its name to Normal College High School and was chartered by the New York State Board of Regents as an autonomous unit within Normal College (1870). Both the high school and the college were renamed in 1914 in honor of Thomas Hunter, a former president of the college. From 1943 the school enrolled students from the seventh to twelfth grades, and in 1955 it became a part of the college's teacher education program for intellectually gifted students, to which girls from all five boroughs were admitted by competitive examination. It began to admit male students in September 1974, and in 1977 it moved with the Hunter College Elementary School to 94th Street between Park and Madison avenues. In the mid 1990s the high school had about 1250 students.

Erica Judge

Hunter's Point. Neighborhood in northwestern Queens, lying within Long Island City; it is bounded to the north by 45th Avenue and abuts the East River and Newtown Creek. The land was owned in colonial times by Jacob Bennett, and after his death in 1817 it belonged to a parcel including all of Long Island City given over to his son-in-law George Hunter. The estate was sold after Hunter's death in 1825 to Jeremiah Johnson, a real-estate agent from Brooklyn acting for Eliphalet Nott, the president of Union College in Schenectady, New York. In 1853 Nott engaged the developers Jonathan Crane and Charles Ely to lay out Hunter's Point, and during the summer of the same year sand hills were leveled and swamps filled in. A map from 1858 shows only a few streets: 47th to 54th avenues, Vernon Boulevard, and 5th Street. Development hastened after railroad service was extended by the Flushing Railroad (1854) and the Long Island Rail Road (1861); visitors and commuters traveled there, and hotels, saloons, and stores were soon built around the ferry terminal at Borden Avenue. Oil refineries and factories for varnish, ceramic pipe, and cooperage were active along the waterfront, where ships from Europe docked regularly. The Steinway Tunnels under the East River at Hunter's Point were begun by William Steinway in 1892 as a trolley line. After several setbacks they opened in 1907 as the first connection between Manhattan and Queens, but they were not used regularly until being converted for subways in 1915 (they are now used by the no. 7 line). The area became less popular as a residential neighborhood after the Queensboro Bridge opened in 1909 and industrialization increased. Local industry declined after the Second World War. A former elementary school, Public School 1, was converted to artists' studios in 1976, and in 1984 an ambitious plan was adopted for the development of the waterfront. The Citicorp Building (1989) has forty-eight stories and is the tallest building in New York City outside Manhattan. Hunter's Point is an area of mixed industrial and residential use. One block of row houses dating from the 1870s is now a Historic District.

Vincent Seyfried

Huntington [née Hyatt], **Anna** (*b* Cambridge, Mass., 10 March 1876; *d* Redding, Conn., 4 Oct 1973). Sculptor. She studied sculpture in Boston with Henry Hudson Kitson (1863–1947) and in 1902 moved to New York City to study at the Art Students League with Hermon MacNeil (1866–1947) and privately with Gutzon Borglum (1867–1941), whose expertise in equestrian sculpture was a formative influence. In 1906 she went to Paris for further training; there her sculpture of Joan of Arc on horseback won an honorable mention at the Paris Salon of 1910 (a full-sized bronze replica was installed at Riverside Drive and 93rd Street in 1918). In 1923 she married the railroad heir Archer Milton Huntington, founder and director of the Hispanic Society of America, for which she executed the bronze sculptures *El Cid Campeador* (1927, Hispanic Society Courtyard) and *José Martí* (1958–59, Central Park South and 6th Avenue). She became the first woman artist elected to the American Academy of Arts and Letters (1932), which mounted a major retrospective of her work (1936). In addition to producing her own work Huntington was a collector and advocate of contemporary American sculpture. Much of her private collection was installed at Brookgreen Gardens, the coastal estate in South Carolina that she purchased with her husband in 1930. She remained active as a figurative sculptor well into her nineties.

Doris E. Cook: *Woman Sculptor: Anna Hyatt Huntington, 1876–1973* (Hartford, Conn.: D. E. Cook, 1976)

Jan Seidler Ramirez

Huntington, Daniel (*b* New York City, 14 Oct 1816; *d* New York City, 18 April 1906). Painter. A pupil of John Trumbull, Henry Inman, and Samuel F. B. Morse, he began his career in New York City, concentrating on landscapes, portraits, and genre pictures. His trip to Europe with Henry Peters Gray in 1839 inspired him to paint allegorical and didactic subjects such as *Mercy's Dream* (1841). In 1849 a group of leading artists and writers in New York City organized a show of his work at the Art Union Buildings. He attracted many prominent patrons in England during the 1850s, and after the Civil War he became the leading portraitist of the upper class in New York City. Huntington was president of both the National Academy of Design (1862–70, 1877–80) and the Century Association (1879–95). He also helped to found the Metropolitan Museum of Art, of which he was a vice-president in 1871–74 and 1876–1903.

Jay E. Cantor: *Drawn from Nature, Drawn from Life: Studies and Sketches by Frederic Church, Winslow Homer, and Daniel Huntington* (New York: American Federation of Arts, 1972)

Carrie Rebora

Huntington, William Reed (*b* Lowell, Mass., 20 Sept 1838; *d* Nahant, Mass., 26 July 1909). Priest. The rector of Grace Episcopal Church (802 Broadway) from 1883 to 1909, he was the principal architect of the Chicago–Lambeth Quadrilateral, a series of negotiations that proposed unity between Episcopal and other churches. He also helped to found the Cathedral of St. John the Divine, contributing its iconographic plans and serving as a trustee for twenty-two years, and was highly influential in revising the Book of Common Prayer in 1892. Huntington's ideas on the role of women in the church were far ahead of their time.

John Wallace Suter: *Life and Letters of William Reed Huntington: A Champion of Unity* (New York: Century, 1925)
J. Robert Wright: *Quadrilateral at One Hundred* (Cincinnati: Forward Movement, 1988)

J. Robert Wright

Hunts Point. Neighborhood in the southwestern Bronx (1990 pop. 34,551), bounded to the north by Westchester Avenue and the Bronx River, to the east by the Bronx River, to the south by the East River, and to the west by Prospect Avenue; it is bisected by the Bruckner Expressway and comprehends the residential neighborhood of Longwood. Once part of West Farms in lower Westchester County, the area was covered by large estates. It was annexed to New York City in 1874 and development began after a subway line to Manhattan was extended in 1904. An abundance of modern housing built about this time helped the Bronx to become known for its fine apartments. During the following decades the population was predominantly Jewish along with a few German, Irish, and Italian immigrants; later it became largely black and Puerto Rican. By the 1960s the housing was deteriorating, and many white residents left for the suburbs. The neighborhood was beset by poverty, drugs, and crime in the 1970s, and many apartment buildings were abandoned or destroyed by fire. Conditions later improved, although poverty and urban blight persisted. Some old buildings were later refurbished by organizations in the community, and funds from public programs were used to build many units of low-rise housing for middle- and low-income tenants. The neighborhood has an industrial section, a prison for juveniles, and a monastery. The Hunts Point Terminal Market is the largest produce market in the United States, built by the city in the mid 1960s along the shoreline of the East and Bronx rivers to rehouse the crowded and antiquated markets of lower Manhattan. The market was run by the city for twenty years before coming under the control of a merchants' cooperative in 1986.

Evelyn Gonzalez

Hunts Point Market. Market covering 329 acres (133 hectares) of land jutting into the East River, opened in the southern Bronx in 1967 to replace the Washington Wholesale Market in Manhattan. It was owned by the city until 1986, when it became cooperatively owned and run by its wholesale merchants. Its facilities include a terminal market where fruits, vegetables, and some meats are sold to retailers, a meat market cooperative, and several warehouses owned by private supermarket chains. In the mid 1990s it was the largest market of its kind in the world, selling more than $1000 million worth of produce a year that accounted for 50 to 60 percent of the nearly two million tons (1.814 million metric tons) consumed in the metropolitan area.

Suzanne R. Wasserman

Hurok [Gurkov], **Sol(omon Israelovich)** (*b* Pogar, Russia, 9 April 1888; *d* New York City, 5 March 1974). Impresario. He moved to New York City from Russia in 1906 nearly penniless, and for a while sold hardware and notions and took odd jobs, saving what money he could. In 1911 he arranged concerts for labor organizations and workers' clubs; in 1915 he became the manager of a series of Sunday evening concerts at the New York Hippodrome that featured such artists as Mischa Elman, Anna Pavlova, and Alma Gluck. For more than five decades he presented some of the world's most distinguished orchestras, concert artists, ballet and theater companies, and folk ensembles. He sponsored the first American performances of several groups from the Soviet Union, including the Bolshoi Ballet and the Moiseyev Dance Company. On 26 January 1972 his offices at 56th Street and 6th Avenue were firebombed, killing one employee and injuring thirteen. His life was the subject of the motion picture *Tonight We Sing* (1953). Hurok wrote *Impresario: A Memoir* (1946) and *S. Hurok Presents: A Memoir of the Dance World* (1953).

Harlow Robinson: *The Last Impresario: The Life, Times, and Legacy of Sol Hurok* (New York: Viking, 1994)

See also American ballet theater.

Allen J. Share

Hurston, Zora Neale (*b* Eatonville, near Orlando, Fla., 7 Jan 1901; *d* Fort Pierce, Fla., 6 Feb 1960). Novelist. She attended Howard University and from 1925 Barnard College, where she studied cultural anthropology with Franz Boas. A prominent figure of the Harlem renaissance who called herself the "queen of the Niggerati," she worked and socialized with such figures as Langston Hughes, Carl Van Vechten, and Alain Locke. Her first published work of fiction was the short story "Drenched in Light" (later retitled "Isis"), which appeared in 1925 in *Opportunity*; her novel *Their Eyes Were Watching God* (1937) is generally considered her most accomplished work. She lived in New York City until 1949, first on 131st Street and then West 66th Street. For most of her life she had financial difficulties and she died impoverished and unrecognized. Her work became the subject of renewed interest in the 1980s.

Zora Neale Hurston

Mary Lyons: *Sorrow's Kitchen: The Life and Folklore of Zora Neale Hurston* (New York: Charles Scribner's Sons, 1990)

Thea Arnold

Hussar. British frigate. The ship struck Pot Rock and sank near Hell Gate in November 1780. Reports that the *Hussar* carried gold to pay the British army led to a number of salvage attempts into the twentieth century. The exact location of the wreck is unknown.

Hutchinson [née Marbury], **Anne** (*b* Alford, England, 1591; *d* near Pelham Bay [now in the Bronx], 1643). Religious leader. She settled in the Massachusetts Bay Colony to seek religious freedom, and under the instruction of the Puritan divine John Cotton began teaching groups of women in her home. Her concept of the indwelling of the Holy Spirit was treated as antinomian heresy that threatened the moral structure of the colony. After her claim to direct revelations of the Spirit was repudiated by Cotton, she was excommunicated, tried, and banished in 1637. With her husband William Hutchinson she formed a community in Rhode Island; his death in 1642 and growing religious controversy led her to move with her children to a riverbank in Dutch territory adjoining Pelham Bay (near what is now the Boston Road Bridge). Soon after, she and all but one of her children were killed in an Indian raid. The river was named in Hutchinson's honor, as was the parkway that later ran along it.

Elizabeth Ilgenfritz: *Anne Hutchinson* (New York: Chelsea House, 1991)

Eileen W. Lindner

Hyde, Edward, Viscount Cornbury (*b* England, 28 Nov 1661; *d* London, 31 March 1723). Colonial governor. A first cousin to Queen Anne, he was appointed governor of New York and New Jersey and moved to New York City in 1702. He sided with the opponents of Jacob Leisler, a stand for which he received a gift of £2000 from the provincial assembly. Within six years the same body unanimously condemned his administration. In December 1708 he was recalled but his creditors had him arrested for debt; there was also scandal regarding his appearance in public dressed as Anne. The Loyalist historian William Smith wrote that the colony had never had a governor so universally detested.

See also Presbyterians.

James E. Mooney

Hylan, John F(rancis) (*b* Hunter, N.Y., 20 April 1869; *d* New York City, 12 Jan 1936). Mayor. While working as a motorman on the elevated line and attending law school he became friendly with John McCooey, who later became the Democratic boss of Kings County. After serving in several judicial positions in Brooklyn (1906–17) he was proposed as a mayoral candidate by McCooey and William Randolph Hearst. Supported by Tammany Hall, he defeated the incumbent, John Purroy Mitchel, in 1917 and was reelected in 1921. He inveighed against the "transit interests" but was widely considered Hearst's puppet and a man of minimal ability; he nonetheless won the admiration of Fiorello H. La Guardia. Hylan lost the Democratic mayoral primary in 1925 to James J. Walker, who later named him a justice of the Children's Court. Hylan Boulevard in Staten Island is named in his honor.

See also SUBWAYS.

Frank Vos

I

IATSE. See International Alliance of Theatrical Stage Employees and Moving Picture Operators of the United States.

IBEW. See International Brotherhood of Electrical Workers.

IBM. See International Business Machines.

ice harvesting. The harvesting of ice from rivers became an important part of the economy of New York City after Frederic Tudor in 1805 arranged a profitable shipment to Martinique of ice weighing 130 tons (118 metric tons). Shipments from the Port of New York to the American South, the Caribbean, and Asia increased in number from five in 1816 with a total weight of twelve hundred tons (1088 metric tons) to 363 in 1856 with a total weight of 146,000 tons (132,400 metric tons). A number of firms supplied ice to local residents, including the Knickerbocker Ice Company (1855), the Washington Ice Company, and the New York City Ice Company. Most households maintained deep wells to preserve their supply, which they stored in large blocks insulated by sawdust and hay to keep melting to a minimum. By 1882 the Knickerbocker Ice Company was the city's largest ice firm, with storage facilities at West 43rd Street, West 20th Street, Bank Street, 432 Canal Street, Delancey Street, East 33rd Street, 92nd Street, and East 128th Street. The city's annual consumption of ice was estimated at 1,885,000 tons (1,710,000 metric tons), some of which was sold by icemen from fifteen hundred horse-drawn carts. Icemen were often Italian immigrants who became known for the colorful manner in which they peddled their goods and were prominent additions to the city's street life. The winter harvesting season offered a supplemental income for fifteen to twenty thousand farmers who cut, dragged, and delivered ice from the Hudson River and lakes upstate to icehouses on riverbanks. In 1896 Charles W. Morse (1856–1933), an ice magnate from Maine, acquired control over most of the city's large-scale ice operations, which he incorporated as the American Ice Company. His trust became the target in 1899 of antitrust proceedings by New York State that also implicated Mayor Robert A. Van Wyck and Richard Croker, who owned large amounts of stock in American. Instead of contesting the charges Morse moved his operations to Chicago, which as the center of the nation's meatpacking business was its largest ice market.

The growing availability of refrigeration crippled the ice trade by the 1920s, but at least ninety firms continued to harvest and deliver ice until the Second World War.

Richard O. Cummings: *The American Ice Harvests: A Historical Study in Technology, 1800–1918* (Berkeley: University of California Press, 1949)

Marc Ferris

ice hockey. Ice hockey was first played in New York City in the late nineteenth century, when the best-known team was the St. Nicholas Athletic Club, an amateur team that regularly defeated teams from Canada. The first professional team was the New York Americans, which entered the National Hockey League (NHL) in 1925; it changed its name to the Brooklyn Americans to attract fans but suspended operations on 28 September 1942. The New York Rangers, formed in 1926, won the Stanley Cup in 1928, 1933, 1940, and 1994. During the 1970s the Greenleafs won four consecutive Metro Junior championships. Other teams in the city have included the Rovers, the Slapshots, and two members of the World Hockey Association — the Raiders (1972) and the Golden Blades (1973–74).

James Duplacey

Ice harvesters using horse-drawn blades on Silver Lake, Staten Island, ca *1905*

ice skating. City planners opened the first organized ice-skating rink in the United States in New York City in 1858, at the southeast corner of Central Park. Skating soon became a vogue among the upper and middle classes, and in 1859 the *New York Times* estimated that sixty thousand pairs of skates were sold in the city, ranging from cheaply made models to expensive imports from England and Germany. Conover and Walker, a hardware store at 474 Broadway, was one of the first businesses to sell imported skates, and Alexander Macmillan at 702 Broadway was the city's foremost skate manufacturer. Macmillan's iron and steel skates cost between $13 and $30; many New Yorkers fashioned homemade wooden skates for much less. City officials at first segregated the pond in Central Park by sex, but one intrepid female skater infiltrated the men's rink in 1860, and in 1870 separate areas for men and women were eliminated; the participation of women in ice skating helped to remove barriers that excluded them from other sports. As the popularity of skating increased, members of the upper class formed clubs and opened private rinks. The New York Skating Club, formed in January 1863 with 150 members, stressed the gracefulness of the sport and organized events at some of the many ponds on the East Side of Manhattan, including the Fifth Avenue Pond (between 5th and Madison avenues and 57th and 59th streets) and Beekman's Ponds (between 5th and 3rd avenues and 57th to 65th streets). Brooklyn also had many sites for skating, including Union Pond in Williamsburg and Washington Pond at 5th Avenue and 3rd Street. The stockbroker Leonard Jerome flooded a pond for skating at his famous racetrack in the Bronx in 1870, but by then interest in skating had waned. After it revived toward the end of the century the St. Nicholas Rink opened in December 1895 at 66th Street and 9th Avenue, and the New York Skating Club was re-formed as the New York Skate Club in December 1916. Indoor rinks opened during the 1920s, the most popular of which was the opulent Iceland Rink at 304 West 50th Street, which featured an orchestra, a restaurant, lockers, and annual ice carnivals and pageants.

After the Second World War skaters patronized such private facilities as Skyrink, on the sixteenth story of a building at 450 West 33rd Street. Private rinks remained outnumbered by city-built ones, which included the Wollman Memorial Rink (1950) at the southeast corner of Central Park, the Kate Wollman Memorial Rink (1962) in Prospect Park, and the Lasker Rink and Pool in northeastern Central Park (1966). In the early 1980s the city

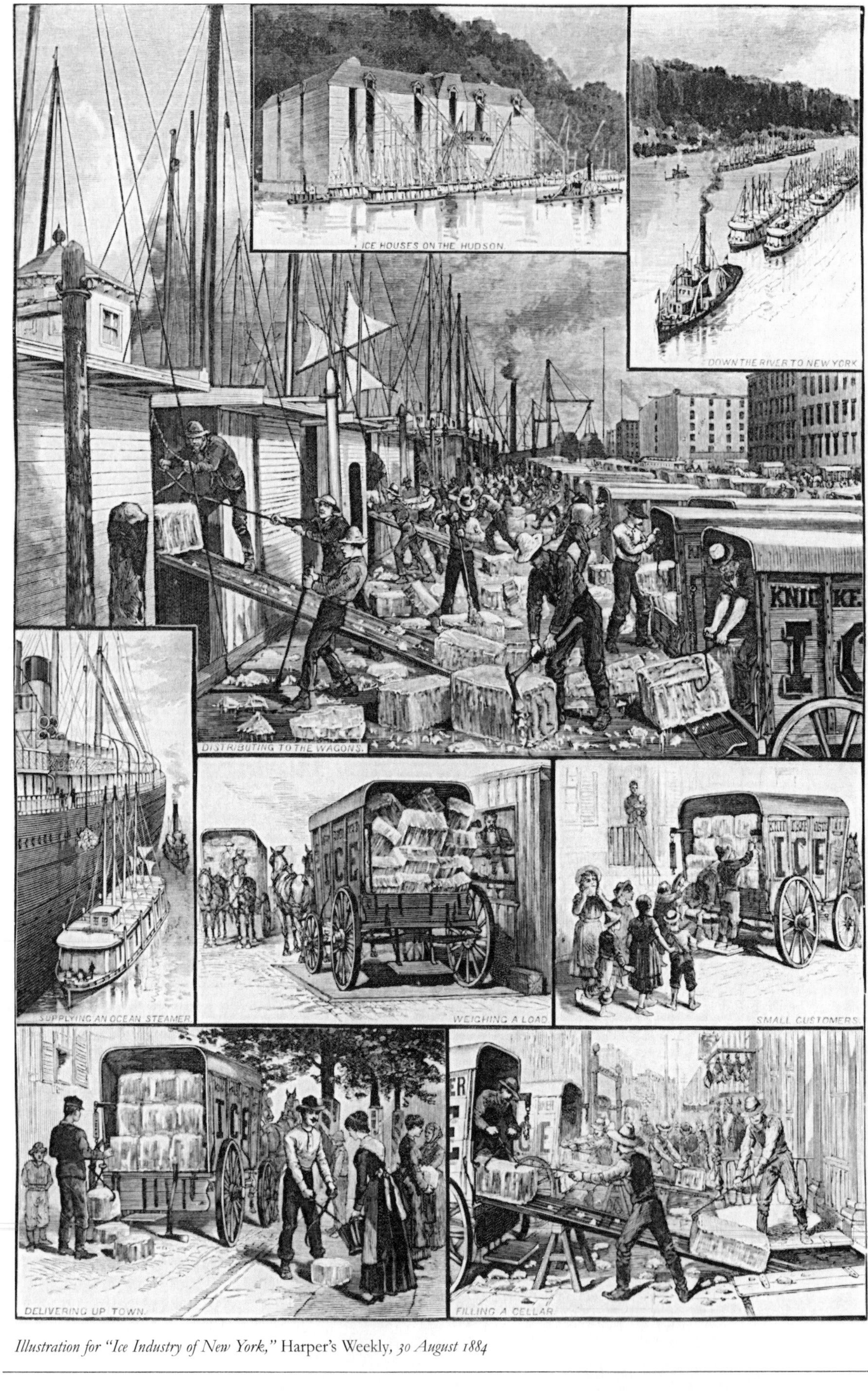

Illustration for "Ice Industry of New York," Harper's Weekly, *30 August 1884*

spent five years and $12 million in a blundering attempt to renovate Wollman Memorial Rink; the developer Donald J. Trump took over the rebuilding effort and reopened the rink after a few months. New York City is also the home of the outdoor rink at Rockefeller Center, which opened on Christmas Day 1936 and is probably the most famous skating rink in the world.

For illustration see DAKOTA.

Marc Ferris

Idlewild International Airport. Name used from 1948 to 1963 by JOHN F. KENNEDY INTERNATIONAL AIRPORT.

IEEE. See INSTITUTE OF ELECTRICAL AND ELECTRONICS ENGINEERS.

ILGWU. See INTERNATIONAL LADIES' GARMENT WORKERS' UNION.

Illustrated Daily News. Original name of the DAILY NEWS.

Il Progresso Italo-Americano. Daily Italian-language newspaper, launched in 1880 in Little Italy by Carolo Barsotti to publish news of interest to Italian immigrants. Its circulation reached 400,000 during the 1930s and 1940s, owing to the prominent role of Italy in world affairs. After several changes of ownership in the early 1980s the newspaper became embroiled in a labor dispute with its employees, forty of whom left to launch a competing daily newspaper called *Oggi*. *Il Progresso* ceased publication in 1988.

Leslie Gourse

Imbert, Anthony (*b* France, ?1794; *d* New York City, 21 Aug 1834). Lithographer. He probably arrived in the city in 1824, established one of the first lithography firms in the United States at 79 Murray Street, and produced a large amount of lithography of high quality. Early in his career he made lithographs of various fine-art images. Two of his most notable works were Cadwallader D. Colden's *Memoir* (1826), which depicted the opening ceremonies at the Erie Canal and contained illustrations by several artists, and Alexander Jackson Davis's *Public Buildings* (1827), the poor sales of which prompted him to produce cheaper, popular works for a middle-class audience, including sheet music, portraits, caricatures, and notably a series of prints entitled "Life in New York."

John Carbonell: "Anthony Imbert: New York's Pioneering Lithographer," *Prints and Printmakers of New York State, 1825–1940*, ed. David Tatham (Syracuse, N.Y.: Syracuse University Press, 1986), 11–41

For illustration see MARKETS.

Wendy Shadwell

immigration. New York City has long been the premier immigrant city in North America — settled as an Anglo-Dutch colony, transformed by millions of Irish, Germans, Italians, Jews, and others in the nineteenth century and the early twentieth, and transformed again after the Second World War by immigrants from the Caribbean, Latin America, and Asia.

Immigrants at South Ferry, ca 1900

1. 1624 to Early Twentieth Century

The first European settlers in New Amsterdam were Walloons who went there in 1624 with the sponsorship of the Dutch West India Company. During the next few decades they were joined by Huguenots, Dutch, English, and Germans, and New Amsterdam soon became the most culturally diverse European colony in North America. In 1643, when the population was about five hundred, a French Jesuit identified eighteen languages spoken in the city. By the 1680s the governor noted that there were "religions of all sorts, one church of England, several Presbiterians and Independents, Quakers and Anabaptists of Severall sects, [and] some Jews." There were ethnic and class conflicts such as Leisler's Rebellion (1689–91), in which Dutch artisans and small shopkeepers fought against English and Dutch merchants. As the city became the leading port in the nation during the eighteenth century it grew rapidly and remained culturally and ethnically diverse. The proportion of Africans rose steadily (reaching a peak of 20.9 percent by 1746) and slave rebellions broke out in 1712 and 1741. At the first census (1790) the city was the second-largest in the colonies (after Philadelphia): of its 33,131 inhabitants most were of English or Dutch descent, slightly less than a third were Scottish, Irish, or both, and many of the rest were German, French, or Welsh.

By the early nineteenth century economic conditions in much of northern and western Europe led many to leave their homelands: population increased; depressions recurred; families subdivided their farms for younger generations into plots too small for subsistence; small farms were replaced by larger ones run as businesses, and factories replaced handcraft workshops; crop failures and other agricultural crises became a constant affliction; and in Ireland British land policies and a devastating potato famine from 1845 to 1847 led to severe hardship. Some countries also experienced revolutions and religious persecution that led to emigration.

A tremendous need for labor accompanied the growth of New York City as a seaport and center for manufacturing. Between 1815 and 1915 about 33 million persons moved to the United States from all over the world, three quarters of them through the port of New York. A large number were Irish Catholics and German Catholics, and their presence in a city that was still strongly Protestant and Anglo-Saxon led to conflicts over temperance, city government, and the religious orientation of public education. Nativism, strongly influenced by anti-Catholicism, became an organized political movement through which James Harper was elected mayor in 1844. Led by such figures as Butcher Bill Poole, gangs of nativist brawlers fought often with the Irish. In response Catholic immigrants organized under the leadership of John Hughes, a bishop and archbishop who

Foreign-Born Population within the Present Boundaries of New York City by County, in Absolute Numbers and as a Percentage of Total Population, 1860–1890

	New York		Kings		Queens		Westchester		Richmond	
1860	386,345	47	109,077	39	14,090	25	27,823	27	8,575	33
1870	419,094	44	153,811	36	19,075	25	37,344	28	10,113	30
1880	478,670	39	188,312	31	22,001	24	23,710	21	10,961	28
1890	639,943	42	272,895	32	35,146	27	38,392	26	14,779	28

Total Foreign-Born Population of New York City by Borough, in Absolute Numbers and as a Percentage of Total Population, 1900–1980

	Manhattan		Brooklyn		Queens		Bronx		Staten Island		Total	
1900	850,884[1]	41	355,697	37	44,812	29	N/A	N/A	18,687	28	1,270,080	37
1910	1,104,019	47	571,356	35	79,115	28	148,935	34	24,278	28	1,927,703	40
1920	922,080	40	659,287	32	111,676	24	266,971	36	31,533	27	1,991,547	35
1930	641,618	34	868,770	34	266,150	25	477,342	38	39,520	25	2,293,400	33
1940	540,197	28	767,638	28	276,588	21	460,476	33	35,121	20	2,080,020	28
1950	461,102	23	630,526	23	288,197	18	373,894	26	30,487	16	1,784,206	23
1960	374,698	22	516,349	20	335,623	20	306,592	21	25,428	11	1,558,690	20
1970	307,630	20	456,636	17	416,887	21	229,210	20	26,695	9	1,437,058	18
1980	342,788	24	535,446	24	548,484	29	210,414	18	37,897	10	1,670,199	24

1. Includes the Bronx.
N/A = Not Available
Source: U.S. Bureau of the Census

Compiled by James Bradley

opposed nativists with stinging oratory and shrewd political tactics. Ethnic and racial animosity reached a peak during the draft riots of 1863. Protest by Irish immigrants against the inequities of the new conscription law soon unleashed long-standing hostilities toward blacks in the city. About 125 persons were killed, including eleven blacks; most of the remaining victims were rioters.

Almost half of all employed immigrants worked in the clothing industry or as manual laborers, servants, cooks, waiters, and household help. Irish immigrants arrived with less money than most other groups and larger numbers of them took unskilled work, and thousands of young, mostly Irish women sought work as domestic servants. About two fifths of all employed immigrants worked as craftsmen or in factories. Germans and other immigrants had been cabinetmakers, jewelers, tailors, shoemakers, bakers, and carpenters in their native countries, and some used capital that they had taken with them or accumulated to open their own shops, which often catered to other immigrants. Intense economic rivalry existed among immigrant groups, as well as between immigrant groups and the native-born. Often Irish workers came into competition with blacks for employment on the waterfront. In the late 1830s and 1840s Irish and German workers were accused of undercutting the wages of American-born laborers, and the recruitment of immigrants as strikebreakers led to violent clashes. Some immigrants helped to shape the labor movement by joining American trade unions or forming their own. During the 1850s German labor leaders instilled in the labor movement a militant class-consciousness and supported radical and socialist unions.

In the 1850s about two million immigrants moved through the Port of New York. Although most soon traveled to other parts of the country, others settled in the city because they found work or could not afford to travel any farther. Those who stayed often moved to the lower wards close to the docks, factories, foundries, and older immigrant neighborhoods, where they sought work, shelter, and kinship. In the area south of 14th Street they crowded into cellars, houses divided into tiny apartments, and newly built tenements that soon became overcrowded. New immigrant neighborhoods took shape: the central and lower wards near the southeastern tip of Manhattan were largely Irish, Kleindeutschland lay along the East River between 14th and Grand streets, and there were enclaves of English, Scots, Welsh, Dutch, Jews, French, Italians, Scandinavians, and Latin Americans. But all immigrant neighborhoods were heterogeneous: different nationalities often lived on the same street. In the 1850s a few people left the lower wards for Williamsburg and other parts of Brooklyn, upper Manhattan, and Hoboken, New Jersey. Immigrant neighborhoods often became slums owing to overcrowding, poverty, and the lack of basic services such as sewers and running water; the Five Points was the most notorious slum in the nation. Tuberculosis, pneumonia, and scrofula were perpetual afflictions, and epidemics of cholera, typhoid, and typhus occurred frequently, especially in the poorest neighborhoods. An inefficient city government and an inadequate public health system were unprepared to respond to these problems, and the rates of disease and death for immigrants were much higher than those for the American-born.

Immigrant neighborhoods had strong social networks, often formed in fraternal organizations, saloons, firehouses, political clubs, music halls, military companies, benevolent societies, beer gardens, theaters, sporting clubs, and churches. German and Irish immigrants supported the Democratic Party largely because it was opposed to nativism, temperance, and Sunday blue laws, and in return for their support Tammany Hall offered them work, food, shelter, minor political offices, and camaraderie. Through membership in saloons, fire companies, and strong-arm gangs the Irish became powerful and by the 1860s controlled Tammany Hall. By the last quarter of the nineteenth century the Irish and the Germans were well established in the economic and political life of the city.

After 1855 an official immigration center for the city was established at Castle Garden, a disused fortification off the southern tip of Manhattan. A new entity, the New York State Board of Commissioners of Emigration, initiated procedures at Castle Garden eliminating most of the exorbitant charges and fraudulent practices that had troubled earlier immigrants. By mid century New York City was the largest city in the western hemisphere. Its population stood at 622,924 in 1855 and included immigrants from most nations of the world, who accounted for more than half the total: 175,735 residents were from Ireland, 95,986 from Germany, 32,135 from Great Britain, and 21,790 from other countries including France, Prussia, Poland, Italy, and Canada.

A second phase of immigration began in the late 1880s, as Russian and Polish Jews, as well as southern Italians, Greeks, Poles, Hungarians, Romanians, Bohemians, and others from southern and eastern Europe, fled changes similar to those that had beset northern and western Europe in the first half of the century. In addition to dramatic increases in the population and the economic displacement wrought by industrialization there were periodic agricultural crises such as outbreaks of phylloxera, a blight that ravaged vineyards in southern Italy and led thousands of farm laborers and tenants to leave the land for the cities. The removal of restrictions on emigration encouraged millions to leave; others were forced out by political upheaval and religious persecution. Jews fled pogroms in eastern Europe and the Russian Pale of Settlement, where they were barred from farming and from most professions.

Between 1880 and 1919 more than 23 million persons emigrated to the United States, and of these, seventeen million entered through New York City. The two largest groups were Russian Jews and Italians. Unlike most immigrants of previous years who had moved to farmlands or smaller towns, most who immigrated during this period settled in cities, including five of six Russian Jews and three of four Italians, and a large number remained in New York City, where opportunities for employment were plentiful. As the largest port in the nation the city provided much employment along the waterfront. It was also a center for light manufacturing and supported a huge garment industry in which immigrants often found work, especially Jews and Italians. Families sewed garments at home, and young Italian and Jewish women worked in sweatshops and small factories, where they were supervised by Italian and Jewish foremen and tailors. Two thirds of Jewish immigrants were skilled (compared with 20 percent of other groups) and practiced trades such as butchery, carpentry, shoemaking, and tailoring. The expansion of the city's infrastructure also led to a demand for construction workers and manual laborers. Although immigrant workers were frequently exploited, most were compelled by work and wages to remain in the city.

The struggle of immigrant workers in the garment industry helped to shape the American labor movement in the early twentieth century. The International Ladies' Garment Workers' Union had only two thousand members in 1909 when more than fifteen thousand shirtwaist makers, most of whom were young Jewish and Italian women, went on strike in more than five hundred factories. The strike lasted for four months and galvanized the union movement, and in 1910 between fifty thousand and seventy thousand Jewish and Italian tailors in the cloakmaking industry went on strike, eventually securing the union shop. The abuse of workers in sweatshops became a matter of public concern after a fire at the Triangle Shirtwaist factory in 1911 killed 146 women, mostly young immigrants, trapped behind locked doors; the fire and labor strikes helped to stimulate interest in the union movement.

Immigrants of the late nineteenth century usually settled in ethnic neighborhoods. A "little Italy" took form in the area of Mulberry Street and another near East 110th Street; a sprawling Jewish neighborhood covered previously German sections of the Lower East Side, which became a district of theaters, foreign-language newspaper publishers, dance halls, churches and synagogues, nickelodeons, saloons, coffee houses, and ethnic and religious festivals. Tens of thousands of immigrants soon moved to the expanding working-class neighborhoods of upper Manhattan, the Bronx, and Brooklyn (accessible by the Brooklyn Bridge after 1883). About this time a Chinatown evolved in lower Manhattan; it remained small owing to the Chinese Exclusion Act of 1882, which denied entry into the United States to Chinese laborers, and was predominantly male because many men who had previously settled there were not allowed to bring their wives to join them. An immigration center opened on Ellis Island in 1892.

Many Americans were alarmed by immigration during the late nineteenth century. Because some believed that immigrants were now more difficult to assimilate than earlier immigrants had been, they introduced formal programs of Americanization. Punctuality, the value of hard work, and the superiority of the "American way" were taught in the city's public schools in addition to academic subjects. Fearing that their traditions would be undermined, some immigrants sent their children to parochial schools or to classes taught in their native language. In addition to attempting to eradicate some of the worst conditions in immigrant neighborhoods, settlement houses such as the Henry Street Settlement and Greenwich House also initiated assimilation programs. In response to such programs a few immigrants abandoned their own culture and others held firmly to it, but most integrated it with American culture. Vaudeville performers, songwriters of Tin Pan Alley, and operators of nickelodeons were often immigrants or the children of immigrants, and by introducing popular entertainment of an ethnic character they gained national audiences.

2. Early Twentieth Century to Mid 1990s

At the turn of the century the ethnic makeup of the population became increasingly diverse. In 1907 the number of immigrants was almost twice what it had been in 1882, and since then the proportion of all immigrants from northern and western Europe had declined from 87 percent to 19 percent. Immigrants in New York City made up 41 percent of the total population in 1910, a peak for recent years. Growing numbers of young men (sometimes called "birds of passage") moved to the United States to work for a few years before returning to their native countries, which about 20 to 30 percent of Italian, Hungarian, Greek, and Slavic immigrants did each year. The number of Chinese living in Chinatown in lower Manhattan stood at 6321 in 1900. Local politics began to take recent immigrants into account. Irish Democrats retained control of the patronage system and with other political operators recognized the advantages of gaining the support of the new immigrants, whose votes were soon sought by the Republican, Socialist, and Socialist Labor parties, and by various reform coalitions. Although Irish Democrats continued to dominate Tammany Hall, in the first decade of the century the Lower East Side was presided over by Jewish district leaders, assemblymen, aldermen, and local judges.

Like others before them immigrants of the early twentieth century were blamed for poverty, filth, disease, and crime in the slums. They were also subjected to social theories of race fashionable at the turn of the century: it was argued that nationalities possessed different traits, and that Anglo-Saxon traits risked being overwhelmed by southern and eastern European ones, which were considered inferior. In 1907 a "gentleman's agreement" was negotiated by the U.S. Department of State to end direct immigration between the United States and Japan. During the First World War the government played to fears of "mongrelization" as a means of strengthening national solidarity. German-Americans were hurt by pressure to end what was called hyphenated Americanism, and their culture weakened from attacks by the government and such campaigns as one to rename sauerkraut "liberty cabbage" during the war. But some intellectuals and writers in the city tended to esteem immigrants. Horace Kallen endorsed cultural pluralism and argued that compulsory assimilation was inconsistent with American democracy. Randolph Bourne wrote that immigrants could forge a dynamic federation of cultures in the United States. Israel Zangwill argued that immigrants should abandon their native characteristics and join forces to create a superior American nationality; his play *The Melting Pot* enjoyed a long run in the city in 1909, although the metaphor of its title was later criticized as assimilationist.

Nearly 40 percent of the city's population was foreign born in 1920. Russian Jews, the largest foreign-born group, numbered 480,000; there were 391,000 Italians, almost as many as the Irish-born and German-born combined. Half to two thirds of the southern

Selected Countries of Birth of the Foreign-Born Population of New York City and Brooklyn, 1855–1890, and of New York City, 1900–1990

	1855	1860	1870	1880	1890	1900	1910	1920
Africa	50	24		111	213	357		
Asia[1]	75	89		48	208	925		
Australia		64		253	474	484		
Austria[2]	376	533	3,078	5,371	28,686	71,427	190,237	126,739
Belgium	223	252		723	819	1,221		3,467
Canada	4,586	5,694	7,307	11,367	14,295	21,926	26,072	25,271
Central America				29	183	920		
China				870	2,648	6,080		
Cuba				2,073	3,439[3]	2,011	5,990[3]	2,815
Czechoslovakia[4]				8,223	8,233	15,005		26,437
Denmark	439	532		1,910	3,334	5,621	7,989	9,092
England	35,324	34,697	45,275[5]	49,988	62,400	68,836	78,135	71,404
Europe[6]				211	4,325	223		
Finland						3,733	7,409	10,240
France	7,326	6,940	10,306	11,846	12,937	14,755	18,265	23,020
Germany	116,691	135,883	191,328	218,821	305,521	322,343	278,114	194,154
Greece			49	78	301	1,309	8,038	21,455
Hungary			591	4,182	12,885	31,516	76,625	64,393
India			47	145	185	250		
Ireland	232,488	218,477	280,219	277,409	275,156	275,102	252,662	203,450
Northern Ireland								
Italy	1,039	1,067	3,019	13,411	49,514	145,433	340,765	390,832
Japan			5	21	164	311		
Lithuania								
Mexico	81	111	86	168	218	282		
Netherlands	971	1,059	2,011	2,848	2,011	2,608	4,191	4,750
Norway	351	355	673	1,767	6,448	11,387	22,280	24,500
Poland	1,276	1,357	2,602	9,521	8,646	32,873		145,679
Portugal	224	153	146	191	169	277		
Romania						10,499	33,584	38,139
Russia / Soviet Union[7]	163	369	1,224	4,760	52,187	155,201	484,189	479,797
Scotland	11,085	9,318		13,365	18,659	19,836	23,115	21,545
South America	221	238	307	570	721	995		5,742
Spain	501	527	682	1,048	1,413	1,491		10,980
Sweden	745	788	2,663	6,042	16,394	28,320	34,950	33,703
Switzerland	1,153	1,085	2,845	5,514	6,355	8,371	10,450	9,233
Syria								4,485
Turkey	41[10]	34	54	98	303	1,401	9,855	
Wales	1,273	907		1,354	1,475	1,686	1,778	1,510
West Indies	1,465	719	943	1,407		3,856		5,907
Yugoslavia[11]								5,271

1. Excluding China and Japan
2. Within present boundaries
3. Including West Indies
4. Within boundaries as of 1990
5. Including Wales
6. Excluding nations individually enumerated
7. Figures for 1855–1910 are for Russia; those for 1920–1990 are for Soviet Union
8. Including Central America
9. Including Palestine
10. Including Greece
11. Within boundaries as of 1990

Compiled by James Bradley

Italians and two thirds of the Slavs living in the city in 1920 were women, suggesting that families from southern and eastern Europe were moving to the United States to settle permanently. A depression after the First World War, the "red scare," and the fear of an influx of immigrants led to the passage in 1924 of laws restricting immigration. Quotas were set in proportion to the size of each country's contribution to the total population of the United States in 1920 (1890 became the base year in 1927), and a limit of 150,000 was imposed for all countries outside the western hemisphere. The law discriminated against Jews, Italians, and other southern and eastern European immigrants and ensured the continued exclusion of Asians. During the 1920s those immigrants already in the city became

1930	1940	1950	1960	1970	1980	1990
			13,029	23,578		
	5,107	31,977		42,459	122,410	
987			1,374			
127,169	145,106	124,256	84,389	48,024	26,263	11,877
	3,888			3,681		
39,622	40,345	35,860	29,034	20,545	15,874	13,919
				150,093		
			19,789	37,348	60,824	162,682
	13,344[3]		28,567	63,043	46,880	42,286
35,318	26,884	30,130	27,767	21,523	26,884	30,130
11,096	8,905	6,707		2,760		
78,003	63,115	53,614[5]	40,769	29,748	22,346	17,996
	5,757	41,099		14,173		
13,224	11,245	8,891		3,452		
23,285	19,696	20,461	19,016	15,514		
237,588	224,749	185,467	152,502	98,336	60,749	38,886
27,182	28,593	29,815	28,882	35,000	42,080	31,241
59,883	62,588	51,968	45,602	31,717	21,457	13,849
				5,032	21,880	42,367
192,810	150,325	141,723	114,163	68,778	41,354	29,853
27,821	21,501	3,085		6,604	1,409	
440,250	409,489	344,115	281,033	212,160	156,413	96,339
				7,843	9,549	12,433
	7,475	15,005	15,089	13,599	11,367	6,584
	2,973	3,234		3,541		
5,335	5,608	5,571		3,693		
38,130	30,750	25,552	18,532	10,229		
238,339	194,163	179,878	168,960	119,604	78,135	61,184
	2,676			3,040	4,678	3,581
46,750	40,655	29,409	24,784	21,165		17,566
442,431	395,696	314,603	204,821	117,363	88,415	79,701
38,535	33,292	26,405	19,615	11,683	6,408	
14,268[8]	12,429[8]	38,295[8]		71,429	153,714	
13,992	13,583		10,528	10,694		8,834
37,267	28,881	20,424	11,705	6,140	2,962	
9,895	8,551	7,151		3,930		
8,696[9]	8,598[9]			2,185		
15,115	17,663		11,803	10,069		6,561
1,903	1,296			763	444	
13,032			36,152	36,834		
6,450	6,475	6,736	12,399	16,491	21,419	20,364

more fully assimilated into American culture. Some formed new neighborhoods and ethnic enclaves that remained until the late 1940s, including the Grand Concourse in the Bronx, which was settled largely by Jews. The islands of Jamaica and Barbados and other parts of the West Indies were unaffected by the restrictive legislation: as colonial possessions of Great Britain they fell within its generous quota rather than under quotas of their own. Between 1900 and 1930 more than 300,000 West Indians emigrated to the United States, and almost half settled in New York City; in the 1920s they accounted for a quarter of the black population of Harlem. West Indians contributed much to the Harlem Renaissance and new political movements such as that led by Marcus Garvey. During these years many blacks from the South also moved to the city.

By the 1930s Italians were a political force in the city and helped to elect Fiorello H. La Guardia to the mayoralty. Women became the majority of immigrants about this time. The Depression led to a decline in immigration: during the entire decade only half a million persons moved to the United States, fewer than during the 1830s, and of these a good number later returned to their homelands. New York City was the destination of almost a third of those who moved to the United States during the Depression. A quarter of the immigrants of the 1930s were Jews fleeing Nazism. Immigration all but ceased during the Second World War but resumed afterward. Frequent airplane flights were offered between the city and Puerto Rico, the natives of which were citizens of the United States since 1917; in the 1950s the number of island-born Puerto Ricans in the city rose from 190,000 to 430,000. During the war many blacks moved to the city, later followed by displaced Germans, Italians, Poles, Greeks, and Jewish survivors of the Holocaust. Under the auspices of some programs refugees were to be dispersed throughout the country, but many and especially Jews wished to stay in the city. About one quarter of the immigrants who were admitted under the displaced persons acts of 1948 and 1950 remained there. Special laws for displaced persons and refugees also permitted the immigration of Italians and Greeks. Puerto Ricans were the largest Latin American group in the city after 1945, but later other Latin Americans also became numerous: Colombian professionals and members of the middle class in the 1950s in the face of escalating violence in the Colombian countryside (soon becoming the largest immigrant group from South America), Cubans after Fidel Castro's rise to power in 1959, and Dominicans, Salvadorans, and Guatemalans, especially after 1960. Pressured by political turmoil and economic difficulties in the Middle East, Arabs and Israelis also moved to New York City after 1960.

Immigration in the city changed dramatically after the passage of the Hart–Celler Act of 1965, which ended discrimination based on national origin: equal quotas of twenty thousand were set for each country in the eastern hemisphere, and for the first time restrictions were placed on immigration from the western hemisphere. Greeks and Italians benefited from the law, and about one third of Greek and Italian immigrants to the United States between 1965 and 1975 settled in New York City; there were also Eastern European refugees of communist regimes, including Czechs who fled the failed revolution against Soviet domination in 1968. Most Irish immigrants were unable to prove that their reason for seeking to immigrate was political, occupational, or family-related (as required by the new law), and they were further disinclined to leave Ireland because of its improved economic conditions. After 1965 immigration increased to the United States from Jamaica, Trinidad and Tobago, St. Vincent, Grenada, Barbados, Panama, Guyana, and other parts of the Caribbean. Nearly half of all West Indian immigrants settled in New York City. Some were descendants of immigrants from the Indian subcontinent who had settled in the Caribbean as contract workers, but most were English-speakers of African descent; there was also a large group of Haitians, who spoke French and Creole. The Hart–Celler Act also permitted more immigration from African nations, but most Africans lacked family networks in the United States and few qualified for entry. Nonetheless a small but growing number of Egyptians, Ethiopians, South Africans, Nigerians, and Senegalese settled in the city after 1965, and by the late 1980s they accounted for a few thousand inhabitants. Immigrants from nearly all parts of South Asia, East Asia, and the Middle East moved to the United States after 1965. The largest group were the Chinese; others included an increasing number of well-educated Indians and Filipinos, as well as Koreans, many of whom were doctors and greengrocers. Indochinese refugees also made their way to the city, although only twenty thousand settled there, as did some Pakistanis.

Immigrants accounted for only 18 percent of the city's population in 1970 (the lowest figure in years), after which about eighty thousand settled there annually. Although the total population of the city declined by 800,000 between 1970 and 1980, the number of immigrants rose by about 250,000, or 16 percent. Civil war, violence, and poverty in Central America after 1970 led thousands to move to the city. Some Peruvians, Uruguayans, Ecuadorans, Argentinians, and Portuguese-speaking Brazilians left their homelands to seek better economic opportunities. From the mid 1970s more than ninety thousand refugees of political turmoil and repression moved to the city from Cuba, Haiti, Vietnam, Cambodia, Poland, Romania, Afghanistan, Central America, and elsewhere; the number would have been greater had it not been for restrictive emigration policies. For most of the 1970s Soviet Jews had difficulty receiving permission to emigrate and those who succeeded usually settled in Israel. By 1981, when the Soviet government virtually ceased to grant exit visas, about 100,000 Soviet Jews had settled in the United States, most in New York City. The fundamentalist revolution in Iran in 1979 also led to large-scale emigration.

Of the many immigrants living in New York City in 1980, about 80 percent were from Asia, the Caribbean, and Latin America. Dominicans constituted the largest group, followed by Jamaicans, Chinese, Haitians, Italians, Trinidadians, Colombians, Ecuadorians, Soviet Jews, and Guyanese. More than half the Asians in the city in 1980 were Chinese. In the following decade the Chinese population, estimated at 300,000, was concentrated in three Chinatowns: the oldest around Canal Street on the East Side of Manhattan, another in Flushing, and the third near Bay Ridge. The temporary collapse of the labor movement Solidarity in 1981 led Poles to emigrate to the United States. After 1975 immigration from Greece and Italy declined, but the 1980s saw the settlement in the city of a few thousand Greeks and Italians, who were on the whole better educated and more highly skilled than their forerunners at the turn of the century had been. About the same time economic hardship prompted the emigration of thousands of Irish who settled in New York City. Those who could not obtain visas often became undocumented immigrants and found work and housing with the help of Irish-Americans and of immigrants who were already settled. The number of unauthorized immigrants rose as economic and political pressures encouraged emigration from countries that had long waiting lists for legal admission to the United States. Between 1980 and 1990 the population of the city grew by a quarter of a million: much of the increase was accounted for by immigrants, including some who were unauthorized but nonetheless were willing to be counted.

In 1980 immigrants made up 24 percent of the population of the city (most having settled there after 1965). Factories that formerly provided employment for native-born workers now employed immigrants even though manufacturing declined in the 1970s. Dominicans and Chinese opened small factories or became subcontractors in the garment industry, and as more labor was needed, shops and homework became common. Other immigrants found work providing services as nurses' aides, household workers, and beauticians. Grocery stores, restaurants, and other small businesses owned by immigrants served ethnic communities and provided work for family members whose inability to speak English hampered their search for employment elsewhere. Several immigrant groups came to be associated with one type of business or service: often Indians operated newsstands, Jamaicans worked as nurses' aides, and Dominicans owned bodegas. Work in households and in personal service was often taken by women recently settled in the United States and particularly by those who had emigrated alone. About 20 percent of immigrants who settled in the city after 1965 worked in the professions.

Immigration by Soviet Jews rose dramatically after the Soviet government in 1988 lifted its ban on exit visas, and in the following years thousands of Soviet Jews moved to New York City. More than three quarters of Dominican immigrants who moved to the United States settled in the city, most of them in upper Manhattan, and they were the city's largest group in the mid 1990s, when it was estimated that immigrants accounted for about a third of the population; the number of illegal immigrants was estimated at 400,000. Except for the Chinese, who remained concentrated on the Lower East Side and in other Chinese neighborhoods, most of those who moved to the city after 1965 were spread throughout Manhattan, Brooklyn, the Bronx, and Queens. West Indians, Soviets, Italians, Poles, and some Chinese (mainly from Hong Kong) settled in Brooklyn, Latin Americans and Irish in the Bronx. Queens had the largest immigrant population, with neighborhoods of nearly every nationality, the principal ones being Chinese, Korean, Indian, Greek, and Colombian.

Immigrants from more than a hundred nations lived in the city by the mid 1990s, and immigration continued to rise at a rate somewhat higher than that of the preceding decade. Ethnic rivalry and hostility played a persistent role, particularly as the city became more racially diverse. Immigrants continued to face difficult and dangerous conditions, such as those that led to a fire at the Happy Land Social Club in the Bronx in 1990 in which eighty-seven persons were killed, mostly Hondurans. At the same time the heterogeneity of the city permitted immigrants to mingle more easily than they could in other parts of the country. In a city where 121 languages were spoken, there were ethnic churches, political associations, social organizations, cultural events, festivals and parades, events, shops, and restaurants for every ethnic group, and dozens of foreign-language newspapers, magazines, and television and radio stations.

Sidney I. Pomerantz: *New York: An American City, 1783–1803: A study of Urban Life* (New York: Columbia University Press, 1938; 2nd edn Port Washington, N.Y.: I. J. Friedman, 1965)

Robert Ernst: *Immigrant Life in New York City, 1825–1863* (New York: Columbia University Press, 1949)

Thomas Kessner and Betty Boyd Caroli: *The Golden Door: Italian and Jewish Immigrant Mobility in New York City, 1880–1915* (New York: Oxford University Press, 1977)

Elizabeth Bogen: *Immigrants in New York* (New York: Praeger, 1987)

Nancy Foner, ed.: *New Immigrants in New York City* (New York: Columbia University Press, 1987)

Constance R. Sutton and Elsa M. Chaney, eds.: *Caribbean Life in New York City: Sociocultural Dimensions* (New York: Center for Migration Studies of New York, 1987)

David M. Reimers: *Still the Golden Door: The Third*

World Comes to America (New York: Columbia University Press, 1992)

Carol Groneman, David M. Reimers

Impellitteri, Vincent R(ichard) (*b* Isnello, Sicily, 4 Feb 1900; *d* Bridgeport, Conn., 29 Jan 1987). Mayor. Elected president of the City Council as the candidate of the Democratic and American Labor parties in 1945 and of the Democratic Party alone in 1949, he became the acting mayor of New York City on the resignation of Mayor William O'Dwyer in 1950. Although he lost the Democratic nomination for mayor in a special primary election later that year, he won the general election as the candidate of the Experience Party, becoming the first person elected mayor of New York City without the support of a major party. His administration was accused of incompetence, corruption, and links to organized crime, and he lost the Democratic mayoral primary in 1953 to Robert F. Wagner (ii). He was named a criminal court judge in 1954.

Warren Moscow: *The Last of the Big-time Bosses: The Life and Times of Carmine DeSapio* (New York: Stein and Day, 1971)

Chris McNickle

IND. See Independent subway system.

Independence League. Name taken in 1905 by the Municipal ownership league of greater new york.

Independent. Weekly newspaper launched on 7 December 1848 by the Congregationalist leaders Leonard Bacon, Joseph P. Thompson, and Richard S. Storrs and published until 13 October 1928. Among the leading contributors was Henry Ward Beecher. In the 1860s the newspaper was transformed by its owner Henry Chandler Bowen, Beecher, Joshua Leavitt, and especially the women's rights advocate Theodore Tilton from a denominational voice against slavery into a radical advocate of equality, abolition, and reform. It suffered during the scandalous breach between Tilton and Beecher that shook Congregationalism in the 1870s; Bowen then became the sole editor of the newspaper and renewed its emphasis on religion, but by continuing to publish the leading American poets he also maintained its literary appeal.

Mariam Touba

Independent Network News [INN]. A television news service that provides national and international news to television stations unaffiliated with the major networks, formed in 1980 by the television station WPIX. The service produces a half-hour national newscast called "USA Tonight," as well as thirty-five to forty news stories each day that local stations can incorporate into their local news broadcasts. In the mid 1990s more than 90 percent of American viewers were within the broadcasting range of at least one station that subscribed to INN.

George Winslow

Independent Order of Odd Fellows [IOOF]. A secret, ritualistic fraternal organization formed in 1819. Columbia Lodge no. 1 in Brooklyn was chartered in 1822, and in 1863 the order owned a large hall at the corner of Baxter and Grand streets. By 1924 there were 25,248 members in New York City in 157 lodges. Membership was increased by veterans of the Second World War to 29,978 in 1950 but declined in the following years. The IOOF offers insurance for members and their families, and supports heart research, a summer camp for children with cancer, and the United Odd Fellow and Rebekah Home at 1072 Havemeyer Avenue in the Bronx. In the early 1990s there were 11,534 members in New York State, with twenty-seven lodges in Manhattan and fourteen in Brooklyn.

Theodore A. Ross: *Odd Fellowship: Its History and Manual* (New York: M. W. Hazen, 1887)

Marc Ferris

independent schools. In addition to its public school system and its parochial schools, New York City has a large number of independent or "private" schools that provide a secular education. The independent schools are nonprofit, governed by a board of trustees, and primarily supported by tuition, charitable contributions, and endowment income. The Dutch opened the Collegiate School (1628), now the oldest independent school in the United States. Other early independent schools include Trinity School (1709) and Columbia Grammar and Preparatory School (1764), opened during British rule, and Friends Seminary (1784). In 1991 there were thirty-three independent schools providing comprehensive or secondary education, with a total enrollment of eighteen thousand; about one in six students received some form of financial assistance. (Another twenty-seven independent schools provided elementary education to seven thousand students.) About two thirds of the independent schools in the city date from between 1880 and 1930, a time of considerable advancement in both private and public education, and two thirds are coeducational; most of the rest are for girls. Some retain religious affiliations to promote moral development and ethical values. Several private schools have been established to serve the needs of the city's foreign and professional children, such as the Professional Children's School (1914) and the Lycée Français de New York (1935). Most of the schools are on the Upper East Side and Upper West Side of Manhattan. The independent schools in the city are generally noted for having high academic standards, small classes, many faculty members with advanced degrees, and large libraries, and for maintaining a focus on individual academic achievement and civic responsibility. Some require their students to take part in community service programs, and nearly all offer advanced college placement courses, study abroad, athletics, student publications, and instruction in the performing and fine arts. All but a few graduates of the independent schools attend four-year colleges, often in the Ivy League. Nearly all the independent schools in New York City belong to the Independent Schools Admissions Association of Greater New York (ISAAGNY) and the National Association of Independent Schools (NAIS).

Well-known independent schools in New York City include the Dwight School (1880), the Anglo-American International School (1980), the Riverdale Country School (1907), the Ethical Culture Fieldston Schools (1878), the Birch Wathen Lenox School (1916), Horace Mann School (1887), the Brearley School (1884), Elisabeth Irwin High School (1921), the Alexander Robertson School (1789), Polytechnic Preparatory Country Day School (1854), the Nightingale–Bamford School (1906), the Dalton School (1919), the Spence School (1892), Brooklyn Friends School (1867), the Packer Collegiate Institute (1845), and Staten Island Academy (1884).

Gerard Thomas Koeppel

Independent Subway System [IND]. The third underground railway system in New York City. It was conceived by Mayor John F. Hylan, who dominated transit politics during his two terms in office (1918–25) and who denounced the existing companies Interborough Rapid Transit (IRT) and Brooklyn Rapid Transit (later Brooklyn–Manhattan Transit, or BMT) as corrupt monopolies that ignored the needs of the people. The New York City Board of Transportation adopted a basic plan for the new system on 9 December 1924 and the first subway began service on 10 July 1932 as part of the 8th Avenue line, which was supplemented during the next eight years by four other lines: the Fulton Street, the Brooklyn–Queens crosstown, the Queensboro, and the 6th Avenue. Because the IND had to compete with both the IRT and the BMT its routes were confined primarily to built-up areas where heavy traffic could be generated: except for the Queensboro line and a segment of the 8th Avenue line that extended to Washington Heights it did not reach far into the outskirts of the city. Unlike the first two subway systems in the city the IND had relatively little impact on residential expansion. In June 1940 it merged with the IRT and the BMT to form a unified system; the IND was itself completed when the 6th Avenue line opened on 15 December.

Clifton Hood

India House. A luncheon club in the financial district, founded in 1918 by Willard Straight and other businessmen in interna-

India House, ca *1900*

tional trade. From 1921 it occupied a three-story Italianate brownstone at 1 Hanover Square, which contained a notable collection of maritime objects and Oriental art. Formerly the building was successively the headquarters of the Hanover Bank, the New York Cotton Exchange, and W. R. Grace and Company. The current name was taken after a merger in 1988.

Elliott B. Nixon

Indians. Immigrants from India and the Indian Subcontinent are discussed in the entry SOUTH ASIANS.

Industrial Workers of the World [IWW]. Federation formed in 1905 to organize destitute workers throughout the United States, including textile workers in the Northeast. It supported anarcho-syndicalism (the principle that labor organizations could regulate society and the economy, without formal state and political institutions) and often used militant tactics. The members were popularly known as Wobblies. In New York City the IWW drew many of its members from among Jewish and Italian immigrants working in the garment trade. In 1911–12 Elizabeth Gurley Flynn, Joseph Ettor, and Arturo Giovannitti, leaders of the organization in the city, led a strike of hotel and restaurant workers that was ultimately unsuccessful but disrupted service at some of the city's finest establishments and became known as one of the most tumultuous efforts of its kind before the First World War. An even better-known strike was one by silk workers in Paterson, New Jersey, organized in 1913 by such leaders of the IWW as Flynn and Big Bill Haywood with the support of such intellectuals as Mabel Dodge, John Reed, and Max Eastman. The Paterson Pageant, a dramatization of the strike, was proposed by Reed during a soirée held in Greenwich Village by Dodge and attended by Haywood; the pageant was later staged at Madison Square Garden. The Paterson strike itself failed and the alliance between leaders of the IWW and intellectuals in Greenwich Village disintegrated. After 1913 the IWW focused its efforts on workers in the West, but it retained a residual influence among both clothing workers and cultural rebels in the metropolitan area.

Patrick Renshaw: *The Wobblies: The Story of Syndicalism in the United States* (Garden City, N.Y.: Doubleday, 1967)

Melvyn Dubofsky: *We Shall Be All: A History of the IWW* (New York: Quadrangle, 1969)

Steve Golin: *The Fragile Bridge: Paterson Silk Strike, 1913* (Philadelphia: Temple University Press, 1988)

Melvyn Dubofsky

influenza. Influenza, commonly known as the flu, was named for a sixteenth-century Italian explanation of its presumed cause: the influence of the stars or occult astral bodies. It is a viral infection that visits New York City and almost everywhere else in the United States annually, generally during the late autumn and winter. In most cases the result is an all too familiar cold, cough, fever, and achiness, but those with serious underlying medical problems can become seriously ill and even die after infection with the influenza virus. About every eight to eighteen years the influenza virus mutates so significantly that pandemic outbreaks erupt. One historian of medicine estimates that about eighty-six influenza pandemics occurred between the years 1173 and 1874. Relatively few influenza epidemics have taken place in New York City, although influenza was recognized there as early as 1789. Perhaps the most serious outbreak of the flu was the worldwide pandemic of 1918, which took the lives of about fifteen to twenty-one million persons, including more than twelve thousand New Yorkers.

John Duffy: *A History of Public Health in New York City* (New York: Russell Sage Foundation, 1968, 1974)

A. C. Crosby: *The Forgotten Pandemic: The Influenza of 1918* (Cambridge: Cambridge University Press, 1989)

Howard Markel

Ingleside. Former name of a section to the east of downtown Flushing in north central Queens, bounded to the north by Northern Boulevard, to the east by Utopia Parkway, to the south by Kissena Park, and to the west by Murray Street, Sanford Avenue, and Kissena Boulevard. It was assembled and laid out by the Realty Trust Company of New York between 1893 and 1899; building lots had frontage of forty feet (twelve meters), fifty feet (fifteen meters), and sixty feet (eighteen meters). From 1896 to 1898 many elegant houses priced from $4000 to $6000 were built. After the line for the Flushing–Jamaica trolley was extended through Ingleside in 1899, travel to Manhattan and Brooklyn was facilitated and the value of property rose sharply. In 1908 Ingleside became one of the first developments to have sewers installed on all streets. As demand for housing increased during the 1920s and one-family houses were built it became indistinguishable from Flushing.

Vincent Seyfried

Inman, Henry (*b* Utica, N.Y., 20 Oct 1801; *d* New York City, 17 Jan 1846). Painter. He began an apprenticeship in 1814 with John Wesley Jarvis in New York City and in 1821 opened his own studio on Vesey Street. With a former student, Thomas Seir Cummings, he formed a partnership in 1824 and was granted many commissions for miniatures and portraits; both artists were on the first board of officers at the National Academy of Design. Inman lived in Philadelphia from 1831 until 1834, the year he painted four mayoral portraits for City Hall in New York City. The most talented portraitist of his generation, he attracted a large number of prestigious commissions during the last years of his life. Inman was honored by colleagues and patrons with a memorial exhibition at the American Art-Union, the first retrospective of one artist's works in the United States.

Theodore Bolton: "Henry Inman: An Account of His Life and Work," *Art Quarterly* 3 (1940), 353–74

William H. Gerdts: *The Art of Henry Inman* (Washington: National Portrait Gallery, Smithsonian Institution, 1987)

Carrie Rebora

INN. See INDEPENDENT NETWORK NEWS.

Inner City Broadcasting. Communications corporation formed in 1972 in New York City by Percy E. Sutton, a former borough president of Manhattan, through the purchase of the radio stations WLIB-AM and WLIB-FM (now WBLS-FM). During the 1970s WBLS developed a style of programming aimed at listeners between the ages of eighteen and thirty-four known as "urban contemporary," which made it one of the most popular radio stations in the city and was widely imitated. Inner City expanded when it purchased radio stations in California (in Berkeley, Glendale, and Los Angeles) and Detroit. In the mid 1990s Inner City was the largest minority-owned business in New York City. Its subsidiaries included Inner City America Music (ICAM), Apollo Entertainment Television (AET), and Inner City Cable Corporation, formed for joint cable ventures in Detroit, Philadelphia, and Washington; it also retained partial ownership of Queens Inner Unity Cable Television Systems.

Laura Gwinn

insignia. The Seal of the City of New York is affixed to official documents, publications, and stationery and depicted on buildings and other structures, vehicles, and the city flag.

Seal of New York City (revised in 1977)

The first seal was granted by the Duke of York to the Corporation of New York in 1664, to be used for the sealing of warrants, writs, executions, patents, grants, and other public acts. The symbol of the Imperial Crown was removed from the seal in 1783 and replaced by a federal eagle soaring over the northern hemisphere. By the early twentieth century the seal had suffered many variations and historical inaccuracies. To mark the 250th anniversary in 1915 of the English capture of New Amsterdam from the Dutch, the Associates of the Art Commission designed an official flag and conducted research for a historically correct seal to be executed by the sculptor Paul Manship. The new seal was blazoned on a flag of blue, white, and orange (the historic colors of the Netherlands) that was first raised at City Hall on 14 June 1915. In 1977 the City Council changed the date on the seal from 1664 to 1625, the year the Dutch founded New Amsterdam. The seal depicts a shield crossed with the vanes of a windmill (representing the first source of energy in Manhattan); on the shield are a beaver (the chief commodity of the fur trade) and barrels of flour (recalling the milling industry). On one side of the shield stands a sailor (representing the port and shipping), dressed in knee breeches and holding a lead plummet for sounding channels; opposite the shield to his left an Algonquin Indian holds a single curved bow, the weapon of the coastal tribes. Both figures stand on a laurel branch. Above the sailor is a cross-staff (a navigating instrument used to measure latitude) to recall the explorer Henry Hudson. The border of the seal consists of a laurel wreath, the heraldic symbol of triumph, and the legend "Sigillum Civitatis Novi Eboraci" (sometimes omitted). The seal is maintained by the office of the city clerk; the Municipal Archives hold previously used designs along with the seals of the five boroughs and other variations used by municipal departments. Unofficial use of the seal on any vehicle is subject to a fine of $25 or imprisonment not exceeding ten days.

John Buckley Pine: *Seal and Flag of the City of New York* (New York: G. P. Putnam's Sons, 1914)

Gordon Hyatt

Institute of Electrical and Electronics Engineers [IEEE]. Organization formed in 1962 by the merger of the American Institute of Electrical Engineers (AIEE) and the Institute of Radio Engineers (IRE). In 1990 it had 300,000 members worldwide.

Trudy E. Bell

Institute of Musical Arts. Original name of the JUILLIARD SCHOOL.

Institute of Public Administration. Private organization formed in 1906 as the Bureau of City Betterment of the Citizens Union to monitor the government of New York City at the departmental level. In 1907 it became the Bureau of Municipal Research, led by the reformers William H. Allen, Henry Bruère, and Frederick A. Cleveland. Its first administrative survey, *How Manhattan Is Governed* (1907), led to an improved budget system, and its social surveys resulted in more effective social service programs. In 1911 it opened the Training School for Public Service in New York City and began sending staff members to other cities to help improve the work of their governments. Luther Gulick succeeded Charles A. Beard as the director of the bureau in 1921, and in the same year the bureau and its training school were merged to form the National Institute of Public Administration. The organization took its current name in 1931, in part to reflect the international scope of its work, and Gulick became its president and chairman. The Institute of Public Administration occupies offices at 55 West 44th Street and engages in research and education; field surveys are still conducted under the name Bureau of Municipal Research.

Luther Gulick: *The National Institute of Public Administration: A Progress Report* (New York: National Institute of Public Administration, 1928)

Jane S. Dahlberg: *The New York Bureau of Municipal Research: Pioneer in Government Administration* (New York: New York University Press, 1966)

Bernard Hirschhorn

Institute of Radio Engineers [IRE]. Organization formed in 1912 to advance radio electronics, and eventually television, radar, control systems, and computers. It merged in 1963 with the American Institute of Electrical Engineers to form the INSTITUTE OF ELECTRICAL AND ELECTRONICS ENGINEERS.

Trudy E. Bell

Institute of Social Research. Experimental school founded as the Institut für Sozialforschung in 1923 at the University of Frankfurt and moved to Columbia University in 1934. Its members included the philosophers Walter Benjamin, Max Horkheimer, Herbert Marcuse, Theodor Adorno, Franz Neumann, and Otto Kirchheimer, who studied the relationship between contemporary society, culture, and politics through the lens of critical theory, an interpretation of Marxism influenced by the philosophy of Hegel. Members of the institute later fused the tradition of radical social critique with the psychological perspectives of Freud in works like Adorno's *The Authoritarian Personality* (1950) and Marcuse's *Eros and Civilization* (1955).

Martin Jay: *The Dialectical Imagination: A History of the Frankfurt School and the Institute for Social Research* (Boston: Little, Brown, 1973)

Peter M. Rutkoff, William B. Scott

Institute Park. Former name of a park in northwestern Brooklyn, lying on a triangular parcel bounded to the north by Eastern Parkway, to the east by Washington Avenue, and to the south and west by Flatbush Avenue. It was planned as the site of the Brooklyn Institute of Arts and Sciences by Frederick Law Olmsted and Calvert Vaux, the designers of Prospect Park nearby; they eventually used it instead for other institutions. It is the site of the Brooklyn Museum, the main branch of the Brooklyn Public Library, and the Brooklyn Botanic Garden.

Elizabeth Reich Rawson

insurance. The insurance business is discussed in HEALTH INSURANCE; LIFE INSURANCE; PROPERTY AND LIABILITY INSURANCE; and REINSURANCE.

intellectuals. Before the American Revolution intellectual endeavor in New York City was undertaken mostly by doctors, lawyers, and merchants who belonged to clubs and literary and scholarly societies, visited museums, and subscribed to periodicals; they excluded women from their circles. The work of these men was often ambitious. Cadwallader Colden, a graduate of the medical faculty at the University of Edinburgh and the lieutenant governor of the colony (1761–76), was an amateur physicist who wrote *The History of the Five Indian Nations* (1727), one of the first ethnographic studies. William Livingston launched the Whig magazine the *Independent Reflector* (1752–53) and was instrumental in forming the New York Society Library and King's College in 1754, the city's first intellectual institutions. As the city became a commercial center many discerned its potential as an intellectual center, although for years it remained overshadowed in most respects by Philadelphia. Some of its best-known thinkers were Alexander Hamilton and John Jay, who with Madison wrote the *Federalist* (1787–88). The leading intellectual circle of the late eighteenth century was the Friendly Club (1793–98), formed by the painter and art historian William Dunlap and the physician Elihu Hubbard Smith; other members included Samuel

Latham Mitchill, Samuel Miller, Charles Brockden Brown, and James Kent.

Intellectual societies flourished during the first half of the nineteenth century. The American Academy of Fine Arts was formed in 1801, the New-York Historical Society in 1804, and the Literary and Philosophical Society in 1814. The leading societies had quarters in the New York Institution of Learned and Scientific Establishments (1816). Most were dedicated to both practical and recondite matters and members were usually amateurs with many talents, among them Mitchill, Washington Irving, Samuel F. B. Morse, and Albert Gallatin. De Witt Clinton was the president of both the Literary and Philosophical Society and the American Academy of Fine Arts, and the vice-president of the New-York Historical Society. The best-known literary clubs were the Bread and Cheese, formed by James Fenimore Cooper in 1821, and the Sketch Club (1827), which became the Century Club in 1846 during the presidency of Gulian C. Verplanck.

Thinkers from the working class criticized various urban problems and particularly disparities of wealth. Inspired by Thomas Paine, they denounced property and privilege and argued that the value of goods and services should be determined by the labor necessary to produce and perform them. Cornelius Blatchly maintained in *An Essay on Common Wealths* (1822) that landlords, merchants, and bankers unfairly enriched themselves through the efforts of laborers. Thomas Skidmore, an English immigrant who wrote *The Rights of Man to Property* (1829), demanded that the egalitarian promise of the American Revolution be extended to the economic realm and called for an end to property rights and other inherited privileges. George Henry Evans, editor of the *Workingmen's Advocate*, urged that land be given to those who settled in the West. In his *Political Writings* William Leggett called for an end to privilege and monopoly and presented a scheme of equal rights and open competition that was adopted by the Locofocos of the Democratic Party. In an abandoned church on Broome Street the Scottish radicals Frances Wright and Robert Dale Owen opened the Hall of Sciences in 1829, an institute for workers that was extant until 1831; they later introduced the idea of communitarian socialism, which was revived in the 1840s by Albert Brisbane. The ideas he presented in the manifesto *The Social Destiny of Man* (1840) gained the support of Horace Greeley, the powerful editor of the *New York Tribune* and a supporter of most radical causes, including trade unionism, women's rights, and abolitionism. The University of the City of New York (later New York University), the first tuition-free institution in the city, opened in 1831. The German activist Wilhelm Weitling became well known in the late 1840s for arguing that the workers' movement was compatible with Christianity.

By mid century newspaper editors were prominent intellectual figures, journalism was considered a profession, and newspapers and magazines gradually became the center of intellectual life. Edgar Allan Poe and Margaret Fuller were among the first professional journalists, and Greeley and William Cullen Bryant, the editor of the *Evening Post*, helped to shift the focus of intellectual life toward magazines and newspapers. Rather than belong to the Century Club, Walt Whitman and Herman Melville took part in a nationalist literary movement led by Evert A. Duyckinck and known as "young America"; they also contributed to the *Democratic Review*, a journal edited by John O'Sullivan, who believed that literature should play a vital role in shaping the nation's democratic culture. Publishing was the fastest-growing business in the city between 1840 and 1860, and by the 1860s the city was a national center of journalism. *Harper's Weekly* began publication in 1857 and the *Nation*, another weekly newspaper, followed in 1865. By the 1870s many doubted the city's ability to accommodate its many European immigrants (especially poor Irish Catholics), to whom some intellectuals attributed the rise of political machines and municipal corruption. The corruption of William M. "Boss" Tweed's government was denounced by George William Curtis, editor of *Harper's Weekly*, and E. L. Godkin, editor of the *Nation* as the inevitable result of giving power to immigrants and workers; a fear that empowering former slaves would have similar results led them to abandon their commitment to Reconstruction and instead oppose any federal intervention in the South.

As Godkin predicted, the foremost question of the late nineteenth century became the relation between labor and capital; many intellectuals in the city sided with labor. During the 1870s the Marxists Friedrich Bolte, Friedrich Sorge, and Karl Speyer offered cogent critiques of social relations under capitalism, and German radicals played a central role in the International Workingmen's Association. The writer William Dean Howells took issue with the widespread condemnation of the anarchists arrested for rioting at the Haymarket in Chicago in 1886, who he believed were denied the right of public expression. Henry George, the author of *Progress and Poverty* (1879), urged that all profits from land ownership be taxed and redistributed. His mayoral candidacy in 1886 was strongly supported by the Irish radicals Edward McGlynn, a Catholic priest, and Patrick Ford, editor of the *Irish World and American Industrial Liberator* (1870); both were instrumental in forming the American Land League, an organization dedicated to land reform and Irish independence that was also supported by John Devoy, a leading Irish nationalist.

By the late nineteenth century there remained a few élite clubs and such magazines as the *Century*, launched in 1880 and edited by Richard Watson Gilder. Institutions of higher education, until 1890 unimportant for most professions and marginal to the intellectual life of the city, expanded at the urging of those who believed that the city needed at least one great university if it was to gain an international reputation. Between 1895 and 1905 New York University moved to University Heights in the Bronx, Columbia to Morningside Heights in upper Manhattan, and City College to a site twenty blocks north of Columbia. Columbia and New York University reorganized their professional schools along more stable lines and introduced graduate programs. During their terms as its president Seth Low (1890–1901) and Nicholas Murray Butler (1902–45) transformed Columbia into a nationally renowned university, where the newest methods of research and graduate training were introduced by such figures as John Burgess and William Dunning.

The most important intellectual circles were those that developed in Greenwich Village. James Gibbons Huneker led a bohemian circle based in cafés and saloons between Union Square and Tompkins Square and during the 1890s irreverently attacked the élite. The Progressive theorists Walter Lippmann and Herbert Croly began publishing the magazine the *New Republic* in 1914, and intellectuals like Randolph Bourne, Horace Kallen, and John Dewey articulated a philosophy rooted in the democracy and heterogeneity of city life. Novelists wrote works of social realism that drew on Progressive reforms. Prominent women included the feminists Charlotte Perkins Gilman, Harriet Stanton Blatch, and Rebecca Harding Davis, the reformer Lillian Wald, and the social activists Crystal Eastman, Margaret Sanger, and Emma Goldman. The *Jewish Daily Forward*, a Yiddish-language socialist newspaper, was edited by Abraham Cahan, who also wrote *The Rise of David Levinsky* (1917), a novel about immigrants' assimilation. In Greenwich Village during the years before the First World War, Mabel Dodge Luhan sponsored a literary salon, Alfred Stieglitz opened a gallery, Eugene O'Neill formed the Provincetown Players, and Goldman and Big Bill Haywood presented radical ideas in lectures. The *Masses*, a socialist journal in decline, was revitalized by a group that included Bourne, John Reed, Max Eastman, Floyd Dell, and Louise Bryant: under their direction it became an eclectic journal of socialism, feminism, and radical art that captured the buoyance of Greenwich Village. Because it opposed the entry of the United States into the war the magazine was denied postal privileges by the federal government and was eventually forced out of business.

After 1917 radical intellectuals focused on assessing the impact of the Bolshevik Revolution and gauging theories of progressivism, liberalism, and social engineering on the basis of evidence offered by the Soviet Union. In 1918 Max Eastman began publishing the journal the *Liberator*, which was more doctrinaire than the *Masses* and less dedicated to art. A few radical writers sought to preserve the link between art and politics established before the First World War, among them Michael Gold and Joseph Freeman, who worked together for the *Liberator* until it ceased publication in 1924 and in 1926 formed the *New Masses*, a magazine of proletarian literature. To encourage young proletarian writers they formed John Reed clubs across the country: the chapter in New York City, dominated by the radical young critics William Phillips and Philip Rahv, became the most influential. Radicalism was abandoned during the 1920s by most intellectuals, who devoted themselves instead to modernism. Some of the first studies of American modernism were *Axel's Castle* (1939) and *The Triple Thinkers* (1938; rev. and enlarged 1948) by Edmund Wilson, editor of the *New Republic*. Although intellectuals from throughout the country continued to move to Greenwich Village they generally eschewed politics; others sought to escape American materialism altogether by moving to Paris.

At the onset of the Depression the attitudes of the 1920s seemed self-indulgent, and interest in politics revived among intellectuals. Wilson wrote about the impact of the Depression in *The American Jitters: A Year of the Slump* (1932) and about the evolution of socialist theory in *To the Finland Station* (1940). The *New Masses* became a forum for renewed interest in the union of art and politics, and the *Nation* and the *New Republic* resumed a position to the left. Many Americans returned to New York City from Paris. Malcolm Cowley, who lived in Paris and Greenwich Village in the 1920s, replaced Wilson as the literary editor of the *New Republic*, joined the Communist Party, and drafted "Culture and Crisis" (1932), a statement supporting the Communist presidential candidate William Z. Foster and enlisting writers in the cause of revolution; the statement was signed by fifty-two leading intellectuals. Artists, writers, and critics joined radical parties and gave a political slant to their work.

In 1933 Phillips and Rahv persuaded Freeman to help sponsor a new literary magazine. *Partisan Review*, launched in the spring of 1934, was devoted to proletarian literature and had a communist orientation. Although the editors continued to write about the potential success of proletarian art, they eventually doubted the quality of much of it and had misgivings about the role of intellectuals and critics in the radical art movement, and they suspended publication of the magazine in 1936. Revived in 1937, the magazine now had an independent editorial position and four additional editors: F. W. Dupee, Dwight Macdonald, George L. K. Morris, and Mary McCarthy. From this time until the entry of the United States into the Second World War the magazine filled a void created by divisions within the left and enjoyed its greatest success. It attracted leftist writers representing a wide range of views, among them Wilson, Wallace Stevens, Lionel Trilling, Sidney Hook, and James T. Farrell; several others published their first work there, among them Delmore Schwartz, Saul Bellow, John Berryman, and Elizabeth Bishop. The magazine also sought to revive the literary reputations of modernist writers by embracing a new conception of radical art known as revolutionary modernism: according to its proponents a radical "sensibility" was as important as a political consciousness, and the avant-garde could steer the world toward socialism. This position permitted harmonious relations between the proletarian writer and the critic, who became essential for identifying the radical insights of writers of both left and right. It was applied to writers as diverse as Dostoyevsky, Kafka, Eliot, Dreiser, Hemingway, and André Malraux. A similar relationship between artist and critic was adopted in the visual arts.

The call for the formation of the Popular Front against fascism after 1935 led to a political shift among radicals. The League of American Writers of the Popular Front aimed to broaden the base of the radical art movement by uniting the left and the liberal center. The term "people" replaced "workers" and the works of American democrats such as Whitman and Emerson were studied in addition to those of European radicals. The Popular Front was destroyed by the Nazi–Soviet Pact of 1939, and the entry of the United States into the Second World War forced the literary left to think in national rather than ideological terms. Anti-Stalinist radicals supported the Allies; the patriotism of younger critics and writers is exemplified by Alfred Kazin's *On Native Grounds* (1942), a study that interprets American literature of the nineteenth century and the early twentieth as progressive and distinctly American.

About this time a number of European intellectuals moved to the city to escape fascism, among them Isaac Bashevis Singer, Hans Morgenthau, Hannah Arendt, Marc Chagall, W. H. Auden, and Bertolt Brecht. By the end of the war their ideas and those of other intellectuals in the city dominated American thought; writers associated with *Partisan Review* were especially influential. Scholars abandoned radicalism for liberal anticommunism and articulated new ideas about criticism. Trilling, the preeminent American literary critic of the time, wrote *The Middle of the Journey* (1947), a novel about the intellectual and political odyssey of his generation, and *The Liberal Imagination* (1949), in which the theories of Marx are supplanted by those of Freud as tools of literary analysis. Among those who influenced his work was Reinhold Niebuhr, a teacher at Union Theological Seminary who identified human "darkness" in Nazism and Stalinism and questioned the perfectibility of man. Arendt further linked bolshevism and fascism by equating totalitarianism of the left with that of the right. According to the sociologist Daniel Bell and others, ideology ended with the war and was replaced by a rough consensus among intellectuals who accepted the welfare state, decentralized power, a mixed economy, and political pluralism. Sociological studies by Bell and his colleague Seymour Martin Lipset suggested that class antagonism was becoming secondary to pluralism on the one hand and concerns for personal status on the other. Richard Hofstadter wrote that American history should be analyzed not according to conflict-based theories but rather by understanding a kind of "mute organic consistency." The American Jewish Committee sponsored *Commentary*, which was planned as a general-interest magazine but became more like *Partisan Review*: under the editorship of Elliot Cohen it offered political and literary analysis and discussion of modern Jewish identity. Those holding to democratic socialism, like the critic Irving Howe and the art historian Meyer Schapiro, helped to publish the magazine *Dissent*.

Intellectuals became nationally prominent and worked mostly in universities. No institution was more prominent than Columbia, which attracted Trilling, Dupee, Bell, Lipset, Hofstadter, Schapiro, and Niebuhr, as well as the critics Mark Van Doren and Richard Chase and the historian Jacques Barzun. Despite the emphasis on consensus and intellectual harmony, underground arts movements grew during the 1950s. During the late 1940s the beat movement developed from friendships among a number of writers, including Allen Ginsberg, Jack Kerouac, and William Burroughs. Many of its proponents moved to Greenwich Village, and the movement gained wider recognition after the publication of Ginsberg's *Howl* (1956) and Kerouac's *On the Road* (1957). Beat literature was considered subversive for its rejection of the social conformity and materialistic visions of the postwar years. These values were also rejected by a number of black writers who formed a literary movement inspired by black history: in the novel *Invisible Man* (1952) Ralph Ellison examined black history of the early twentieth century, ending with the radical and racial movements in Harlem during the 1930s. The Living Theater, formed in 1947 by Julian Beck and Judith Malina, rebelled against the conventions of Broadway. Young figurative painters were challenged by the abstract expressionism of Jasper Johns and Robert Rauschenberg and by the literal realism of the pop artists Andy Warhol, Roy Lichtenstein, and James Rosenquist. The sociologist C. Wright Mills, whose work was not generally accepted in the academy, argued in *White Collar* (1951) and *The Power Elite* (1956) for a continuation of radical analysis based on American themes.

During the 1960s notions of intellectual harmony were shattered. As the civil rights movement unfolded in the South, frustration and rage were evident in the work of the novelist James Baldwin and by the playwrights Lorraine Hansberry (*Raisin in the Sun*, 1959) and LeRoi Jones (*The Dutchman*, *The Slave*, and *The Toilet*, 1964). The work of such artists as Ginsberg, Warhol, and the Living Theater gained popularity, and young radicals found Mills's arguments compelling (some were incorporated by the activist Tom Hayden into the Port Huron Statement, the manifesto of Students for a Democratic Society). After becoming the editor of *Commentary* in 1960 Norman Podhoretz sought to infuse it with a new intellectual and political spirit: he published provocative articles on foreign policy along with excerpts of *Growing Up Absurd* (1960), a stinging criticism of education by Paul Goodman (Podhoretz later steered the magazine back toward the center and eventually to the right). During a newspaper strike in 1963 the *New York Review of Books* was begun by Jason Epstein, Barbara Epstein, and Robert Silvers. Once jokingly called the "New York Review of each other's books" by Hofstadter, it drew contributions from the city's most renowned intellectuals and took up the cause of the New Left. The Vietnam War, racial and ethnic conflicts (especially those fomented by the teachers' strike of 1968), and perceived excesses of the counterculture caused deep rifts in political and cultural life. William F. Buckley Jr. launched the *National Review*, a conservative journal, in 1965. In universities intellectuals who had become prominent after the war confronted the student movement. A strike at Columbia in 1968 engulfed Trilling, Dupee, Bell, and Hofstadter and split old friendships and alliances. Accusations flew among journals and editors: Rahv and Howe battled over politics of the left, *Partisan Review* offended many former contributors by supporting the literary counterculture, and *Commentary* criticized the *New York Review* for publishing leftist material, particularly a detailed cover illustration of a "Molotov cocktail."

By the 1970s intellectuals in the city were divided into several groups. Neoconservatism drew political essayists such as Podhoretz, Buckley, and Irving Kristol, and others like Hilton Kramer, an art critic for the *New York Times* who later edited the *New Criterion*. Former members of the New Left took academic posts and revitalized journals of the left, among them the *Nation*, which returned to its leftist perspective under the editorship of Victor Navasky. Women in the metropolitan area were highly active in the feminist movement, which gained a national following partly because of the popularity of *Ms.*, a magazine edited by Gloria Steinem. The materialistic outlook of the 1980s gave a primacy to business matters and conservative ideas, which were discussed in the *Wall Street Journal*, the *Public Interest*, and *National Review*, while specialized audiences turned to new magazines such as the literary journal *Grand Street*. In the mid 1990s *Commentary*, *Dissent*, the *New York Review*, and other major magazines of opinion continued to be published in the city but lacked the urgency and influence that they had enjoyed in earlier times.

Henry F. May: *The Enlightenment in America* (New York: Oxford University Press, 1976)
Sean Wilentz: *Chants Democratic: New York City and the Rise of the American Working Class, 1788–1850* (New York: Oxford University Press, 1984)
Alexander Bloom: *Prodigal Sons: New York Intellectuals and Their World* (New York: Oxford University Press, 1986)
Thomas Bender: *New York Intellect: A History of Intellectual Life in New York City from 1750 to the Beginnings of Our Own Time* (New York: Alfred A. Knopf, 1987)

Alexander Bloom, Kevin Kenny

Interborough Rapid Transit Company [IRT]. Operator of the first subways in New York City. The company was formed on 10 July 1902 by August Belmont, a wealthy society figure and financier who in 1900 had formed the Rapid Transit Subway Construction Company to build and equip his publicly owned subway. Opened on 27 October 1904, the new subway ran from City Hall up the East Side of Manhattan to Grand Central Terminal, then west along 42nd Street to Times Square, and up Broadway through the Upper West Side. At 96th Street it divided into two branches that continued to the Bronx, one terminating at Van Cortlandt Park and the other at Bronx Park. The IRT was the first subway in the world to have four-track service (separate express and local tracks in each direction), the success of which stimulated the residential growth of the Upper West Side, Harlem, northern Manhattan, and the Bronx. The express trains reached speeds as great as forty miles (sixty-four kilometers) an hour, making them the world's fastest form of urban mass transit.

From the outset the company's trains were badly overcrowded, and although the city government demanded that the IRT build more lines to alleviate the problem, Belmont refused so as not to dilute his company's earnings. In December 1905 he acquired his major competitor, the Manhattan Railway Company, which operated the island's elevated lines. Meanwhile the IRT continued to expand, building an extension from Manhattan to Brooklyn that opened in 1908. The company's monopoly ended in 1913, when it joined with a competitor, the Brooklyn Rapid Transit Company, to form a massive new network that doubled the size of the city's rapid transit system, increasing its length from 296 to 619 single-track miles (476 to 996 kilometers).

The Interborough Rapid Transit Company was profitable until the First World War but crippled by inflation after the war. It survived the 1920s only by deferring maintenance and cutting wages and entered bankruptcy in August 1932. After taking office in 1934 Mayor Fiorello H. La Guardia sought to bring the private subway companies under public ownership, but his efforts were delayed by opposition from Democrats in the state legislature loyal to Tammany Hall. The City of New York finally acquired the assets of Interborough Rapid Transit in June 1940, and the routes became part of the city's transit system.

Clifton Hood

Interchurch Center. A nineteen-story office building for religious organizations at 475 Riverside Drive in Manhattan (near 120th Street), opened in 1960 with funds largely provided by John D. Rockefeller Jr. The building is popularly known as the "God box." The governing board intended the center to be a visible symbol of ecumenical Christian unity that would house administrative offices of the National Council of Churches, several mainline Protestant and Orthodox denominations, and various interfaith agencies. The center did not attract support from the more conservative and evangelical churches. As Protestant denominations moved their offices out of New York City in the 1980s the center rented more of its space to educational, nonprofit, and social service agencies.

Peter J. Wosh

Interfaith Center on Corporate Responsibility. A national coalition of religious organizations that seeks to influence the business practices of corporations through shareholder investment. It was formed in 1971 under the auspices of the National Council of Churches after the Episcopal church called on General Motors to withdraw from South Africa in the first church-sponsored shareholder resolution on a social issue. The center encourages responsible corporate practices with respect to world debt, nuclear weapons, the environment, and the marketing of formula for infants. In the mid 1990s it had a membership of about 250 Protestant and Roman Catholic denominations, religious communities, health care agencies, and pension funds; its net worth was estimated at nearly $30,000 million.

Amie Klempnauer

interior design. In the United States interior design was centered in New York City when it was a fledgling field dominated by a few society decorators, and it remained so as it evolved into a profession with thousands of trained practitioners. Elsie de Wolfe, generally regarded as the first professional interior decorator, was neither an architect nor a craftsman but instead provided supervisory design services. She began working about 1905 and by 1913 had a successful practice catering to millionaires. In 1909 she decorated a "showcase" house with the architect Ogden Codman, author with Edith Wharton of *The Decoration of Houses* (1897); among their influential innovations was the replacement of the front stoop with an entrance at ground level and a small flagstone courtyard. Nancy McClelland (*d* 1959) inaugurated a decorating department at a branch of Wanamaker's in 1913, the first ever opened in a department store. Ruby Ross Wood (1880–1950), a disciple of de Wolfe, launched an influential practice. In 1924 Eleanor McMillen (later Eleanor McMillen Brown) formed a full-service firm under her own name that employed draftsmen, designers, and craftsmen who worked in diverse styles from many periods. Dorothy Draper (1889–1969) became the first woman who was not an architect to focus on nonresidential design: she played an important role to the end of the 1950s in developing partnerships with architects that eventually led to the evolution of such specialties as contract design and space planning. The New York School for Fine and Applied Arts (later the Parsons School of Design) placed a greater emphasis on interior design under the leadership of Frank Alvah Parsons from 1905 to 1930, and the New York School of Interior Design was formed in 1916. As decoration began to encompass some elements of architecture and the applied arts, magazines on interior design spread nationwide the innovative designs of New York City.

The field underwent another expansion in the 1950s and 1960s. There emerged specialties in office landscaping, color theory, lighting design, and acoustical design, and by the 1970s in store design, display design, and environmental psychology. The term "interior designer" came into widespread use in contrast to the more limited "interior decorator." Among the professional bodies formed were the Interior Design Educators Council (1962), to establish education standards, and the National Council for Interior Design Qualifications (1972), to administer examinations and accredit degree programs. In 1975 the National Society of Interior Designers (1957) merged with the American Institute of Interior Designers (formerly the American Institute of Decorators) to form the American Society of Interior Designers.

C. Ray Smith: *Interior Design in Twentieth-century America: A History* (New York: Harper and Row, 1987)

See also Decorative arts and Furniture.

Owen D. Gutfreund

International Alliance of Theatrical Stage Employees and Moving Picture Machine Operators of the United States and Canada [IATSE]. Labor union. Formed in New York City by stagehands in 1893, it later included such theatrical workers as carpenters, electricians, property crewmen, and ushers, as well as motion picture projectionists and other film, radio, and television employees. As the entertainment business evolved, the great variety of craftsmen working in it led to many jurisdictional disputes with other unions. In 1990 IATSE had 65,000 members in 750 locals nationwide. Its headquarters are at 1515 Broadway.

Martha S. LoMonaco

International Brotherhood of Electrical Workers. Labor union. Its branch in New York City, Local 3, was chartered by the American Federation of Labor in 1900 and soon became powerful. Under the leadership of Harry Van Arsdale Jr. it won the first pension funded by an employer, a five-hour day, and cooperative housing, and in 1962 it reserved a thousand apprenticeships for members of ethnic minorities. In 1965 it organized the city's taxi drivers. Local 3 remained the principal representative of electrical workers in the city in the mid 1990s. Apprentices are required to earn an associate degree from Empire State College.

Francis X. Gannon: *Joseph D. Kennan, Labor's Ambassador in War and Peace* (Lanham, Md.: University Press of America, 1984)

Colin J. Davis

International Brotherhood of Teamsters. The Teamsters set up the Joint Council of New York City soon after their union was formed in 1901. This council united all the branches of the Teamsters in New York City and was composed mostly of cartmen and later of truckers: it strongly supported regulation of the business and the exclusion from it of blacks, and wielded considerable political leverage. Eventually the union launched a drive to enroll members engaged in other trades, including taxi drivers, private carters, and warehousemen. By 1955 the Joint Council of New York City was the largest Teamster organization in the country, with 123,000 members belonging to sixty locals in greater New York. The Teamsters gained an unsavory reputation in the early 1960s because of racketeering scandals, mishandling of pension funds, and links to organized crime, with corruption in the national union mirrored locally in New York City. A turning point was marked in 1992 with the election as president of the union of Ron Carey, whose platform included promises to sell the union's limousines, luxury jets, and condominiums, cut his own salary from $225,000 to $125,000, and banish the mob from the union's national health insurance plan.

Graham Hodges

International Business Machines [IBM]. Firm of electronic data processing equipment manufacturers, incorporated on 16 June 1911 in New York City as the Computing–Tabulating–Recording Company (C–T–R). It set up offices in 1914 in a few small rooms on Broad Street; as sales grew, these offices were moved to another location on Broad Street and then to Broadway. In 1924 the firm took its present name and made New York City its headquarters. The earliest products were tabulating devices that allowed increasingly complex calculations; these were most useful for accounting functions, notably those connected with establishing the Social Security program in the 1930s. The firm also introduced the first electronic typewriter to enjoy wide commercial success. In 1938 the headquarters were moved to larger quarters at 590 Madison Avenue. During the Second World War the firm's accounting machines kept track of personnel and war equipment, and its plants produced war material such as control instruments, Browning automatic rifles, bombsights, and paper for war bonds. It introduced its first large-scale calculator, the Automatic Sequence Controlled Calculator (ASCC), in 1944. In the following year the Watson Scientific Research Laboratory (named for the president of the firm, James J. Watson Sr.) was dedicated at Columbia University. Another important technical innovation was the IBM 701, the first large vacuum tube computer (1952). In later years IBM worked in such diverse fields as navigational systems for spacecraft, personal computers, and superconductivity. Although the firm moved its corporate headquarters to Armonk, New York, in 1964, it remained one of the largest corporate tenants in New York City, with nearly five thousand employees. In 1983 a new and substantially larger building replaced the existing one at 590 Madison Avenue.

Shan Jayakumar

International Center of Photography. Museum and school opened in 1974 by the photojournalist Cornell Capa. It is the only institution in an important American city devoted to exhibiting, teaching, and collecting photography. The center has two facilities in New York City, one at 1130 5th Avenue at 94th Street (a neo-Georgian building designed in 1913 by Delano and Aldrich) and the other at 1133 6th Avenue. It sponsors about twenty exhibitions each year that reflect a commitment to "concerned photography," typified by the liberal, humanistic work of Robert Capa, Werner Bischof, and David Seymour ("Chim"); it also exhibits avant-garde photography, retrospectives of modern masters, and fashion and advertising photography, and circulates its materials to some sixty-five sites around the world. The center sponsors lectures, workshops, and documentary and experimental video programs, and offers a master's degree in conjunction with New York University. Its archives and collections contain about thirteen thousand prints.

Anne H. Hoy

International Design Center. Complex of several buildings in the former Dutch Kills Industrial Bank in Long Island City, occupied predominantly by showrooms for interior furnishings. Developed between 1981 and 1986 by Lazard Realty, it was planned by the firm of I. M. Pei and designed by Gwathmey Segal Associates and Stephen Lepp Associates. The oldest buildings were erected in 1914 by Michael J. Degnon, who also built the Sunnyside railroad yards and the subway tunnel between Manhattan and Steinway. Former tenants of the buildings include the American Chicle Company, American Eveready, and Bucilla. In the mid 1990s showroom tenants included Herman Miller and Knoll North America. Standing adjacent to the center is the Executone building, which was partly converted for offices but still contains factories and warehouses.

Ann L. Buttenwieser

International Exhibition of Modern Art. See ARMORY SHOW.

International Fur and Leather Workers Union. Labor union formed in 1913, one year after fur and leather workers in New York City led a strike and won a shorter work week and paid holidays. Conflict grew within the union between 1917 and 1927, as members became dissatisfied with unresponsive leaders and criminal elements sought to stifle dissent. Ben Gold, who managed the New York Joint Council and the Needle Trade Workers Industrial Union, became a central figure during this period when he coordinated a successful drive to weaken the influence of Louis "Lepke" Buchalter and other racketeers. The union entered the Congress of Industrial Organizations in 1937, merged with the National Leather Workers Association in 1939, and began building new locals and securing sizable wage increases during the Second World War. In 1947 the union's leadership strongly opposed American policy toward the Soviet Union, and it left the Congress of Industrial Organizations in 1950 in anticipation of being expelled. After Gold's conviction on perjury charges the union merged in 1955 with the Amalgamated Meat Cutters and Butcher Workmen.

Philip Foner: *The Fur and Leather Workers Union: A Story of Dramatic Struggles* (Newark, N.J.: Nordam, 1950)

Bert Cochran: *Labor and Communism: The Conflict That Shaped the American Unions* (Princeton, N.J.: Princeton University Press, 1977)

Harvey Levenstein: *Communism, Anticommunism and the CIO* (Westport, Conn.: Greenwood, 1981)

Ronald Mendel

International House. Residence and meeting place for foreign students at 500 Riverside Drive, opened in 1924 by Harry Edmonds, a leader in the Christian student movement, with the aid of John D. Rockefeller. It inspired the establishment of more than sixty similar facilities worldwide. International House can accommodate seven hundred residents. By the early 1990s more than 55,000 persons had lived there.

Elliot S. Meadows

International Ladies' Garment Workers' Union [ILGWU]. Labor union organized in New York City in 1900. It consisted at first of Jewish immigrants and drew many Italian immigrants during its first two decades. In its early years the union led successful strikes of shirtwaist workers (1909) and cloakmakers (1910). The cloakmakers' strike led the Joint Board of Sanitary Control to establish guidelines for hygiene and safety in the workplace and helped to create the "Protocol of Peace," which provided for the resolution of disputes between labor and management and the protection of workers' health; the union opened a health center in 1914. During the 1920s an attempted communist takeover led to intense conflict among members, and a disastrous strike by cloakmakers nearly destroyed the union. By this time Jewish men, who had initially made up a majority of the union's members, were outnumbered by young Jewish women and members of other ethnic groups. In 1932 David Dubinsky became president of the union, which from the following year benefited from the labor policies of President Franklin D. Roosevelt. The union organized its 150,000 members, repaid its loans, and in 1935 helped to form the Committee for Industrial Organization (CIO) within the American Federation of Labor (AFL); the CIO was later suspended by the AFL and became an independent group called the Congress of Industrial Organizations, which the ILGWU refused to join. In 1936 members of the union were instrumental in forming the American Labor Party in New York City; many eventually abandoned the party because of its increasingly leftist positions and formed the Liberal Party, with which the union was closely allied for twenty-five years. By the time Dubinsky retired in 1966 the ILGWU had grown to more than 450,000 members and had $571 million in assets. Having forsaken its socialist goals, it focused on securing benefits for its members, including health coverage, recreational facilities, a thirty-five-hour work week, retirement pensions, death benefits, and low-cost housing. From 1945 the union's ethnic composition continued to change as blacks, Puerto Ricans, Asians, and others entered the industry and Jews and Italians found other forms of work. In the late 1960s membership declined and the garment industry was increasingly driven overseas. Under Sol C. Chaikin (1977–86) and Jay Mazur (1986–) the ILGWU fought problems arising from the growing employment of illegal aliens, the return of industrial homework in New York City and elsewhere, worsened working conditions, and declining membership (less than 150,000 in 1993).

Louis Levine: *The Women's Garment Workers* (New York: B. W. Huebsch, 1924)

Benjamin Stolberg: *Tailor's Progress: The Story of a Famous Union and the Men Who Made It* (Garden City, N.Y.: Doubleday, Doran, 1944)

Leon Stein, ed.: *Out of the Sweatshop: The Struggle for Industrial Democracy* (New York: Quadrangle, 1977)

Robert D. Parmet

International Rescue Committee. Relief organization formed by Albert Einstein to rescue refugees of Hitler's regime and help "victims of racial, religious, and ethnic persecution and oppression, as well as people uprooted by war, violence, and famine to survive and rebuild their lives." It opened its first office at 11 West 42nd Street on 24 July 1933. Volunteers operating out of a hotel room in Marseilles rescued more than two thousand refugees, among them the philosopher Hannah Arendt and the artists Marcel Duchamp and Max Ernst. In the following years the committee provided assistance during crises in Hungary (1956), Cuba (1959), Czechoslovakia (1968), Bangladesh (1971), and Kurdistan (1991). In the mid 1990s it had offices on Park Avenue South and operated relief programs in Africa, Asia, Europe, and Central America, as well as domestic refugee resettlement programs in cities nationwide.

Jesse Drucker

International Telephone and Telegraph [ITT]. International conglomerate formed in New York City in 1920 as a holding company for several Caribbean telephone companies. Its founder, Sosthenes Behn, intended for it to be an international counterpart to American Telephone and Telegraph. From 1930 the headquarters were in a new building at 67 Broad Street. The firm acquired several Latin American and European telephone systems and after the Second World War shifted the focus of its acquisitions to electronics firms. Behn died in 1957, and from 1959 the firm was led by Harold Geneen, who stabilized its finances and began a large-scale effort at diversification that transformed the firm into a true conglomerate: among the businesses that he acquired were Sheraton Hotels, the Hartford Insurance Company, and the lumber firm Rayonier. The headquarters were moved in 1961 to a new building at 320 Park Avenue and in 1990 to 1330 6th Avenue. The building at 67 Broad Street is now the headquarters of ITT World Communications, which among other things operates the "hot line" between Washington and Moscow. In the mid 1990s the firm had about 2300 employees in New York City.

Robert Sobel: *ITT: The Management of Opportunity* (New York: Truman Talley, 1981)

Rohit T. Aggarwala

International Workingmen's Association. International labor organization, formed in London on 28 September 1864 by French and British labor leaders under the guidance of Karl Marx; its purpose was to help the working class "to conquer political power," beginning with such measures as trade unions and legislative campaigns for an eight-hour workday. After the Civil War it gained influence in New York City, a national center of unionism, and in 1868 section 1 of the International Workingmen's Association was formed from the General German Workingmen's Association, a group of German craftsmen and reformers in the city who adhered to the ideas of Marx and Ferdinand Lassalle. The section played a fundamental role in the trade union movement of the late 1860s by collecting strike funds, compiling labor statistics, helping to organize black workers, and providing leaders such as Friedrich Sorge, Adolph Douai, Friedrich Bolte, and Conrad Kuhn. Section 12, formed in 1871, was dominated by middle-class land reformers and anti-monopolists such as John Commerford, Lewis Masquerier, and William West. Another member was Victoria Woodhull, a flamboyant champion of equal rights for women who became influential in the organization by leading a memorial procession through the city for French Communards executed in 1871 and by reporting on labor affairs in *Woodhull and Claflin's Weekly* (financed by Cornelius Vanderbilt, a friend of her sister Tennessee Claflin). Her feminism was dismissed as a diversion from the issues of labor and wages by Sorge, Bolte, and other members of section 1, who viewed the members of section 12 as middle-class interlopers lacking in sympathy for the interests of the working classes. Sorge sought to deny admission to sections unless at least two thirds of their members were wage earners; West argued that only the middle class had the "experience and the intelligence" required for the success of the labor movement. This conflict led the association to divide in late 1871. The Hague Congress of 1872 gave its blessing to Sorge's faction, and the general council was moved to New York City and placed under his authority. Members of section 12 held their own assembly in Philadelphia and formed a competing International Workingmen's Association, which incorporated the land reformers' yearnings for a simple rural society and was sought out by the New York Workingmen's Assembly in 1872–73. By the mid 1870s the International Workingmen's Association was nearly extinct in Europe owing to government repression, and had been weakened in the United States because it raised the specter that open class warfare in the manner of the Paris Commune might spread across the Atlantic. It ceased functioning in 1876 after the movement for an eight-hour workday was defeated and hard times set in.

David Montgomery: *Beyond Equity: Labor and the Radical Republicans, 1862–1872* (New York: Alfred A. Knopf, 1967)

Iver Bernstein

Interstate Park. Name applied to BELLAIRE when it was first developed in 1899.

Intrepid Sea, Air, Space Museum. A decommissioned aircraft carrier nine hundred feet (275 meters) long, converted into a museum docked at Pier 86 on the West Side of Manhattan. Launched in 1942 at a cost of $44 million, the *Intrepid* carried more than a hundred aircraft and three thousand men. The carrier was modernized in 1954 and after serving in the Korean and Vietnam wars was scheduled in 1976 to be scrapped. To save and renovate the *Intrepid* a foundation was formed in 1978 by Zachary Fisher, a builder and philanthropist. Opened in August 1982, the museum recounts the history of the ship, which is a federal landmark and has propeller-driven aircraft and jet fighters displayed on deck.

Ann L. Buttenwieser

investment banking. A form of banking that meets the needs of business and government for long-term capital. An important function of investment bankers is to originate, underwrite, and distribute new issues of securities, which may then be traded on organized securities exchanges or over the counter. Although investment banking, commercial banking, and securities trading are distinct functions, some notable financial firms in New York City have engaged in more than one, and the city has long been a leader in all three.

Securities trading in the city began with the refinancing in 1790 of debts incurred during the American Revolution. In the early years of the nineteenth century there was some trading in the stock of private firms (principally banks and insurers) and new issues of stock were still sold by subscription. The beginnings of investment banking date to the second decade of the century, when some new issues were bought in large blocks by financiers who then resold them at a profit. Among the first to engage in this practice was John Jacob Astor, who with two other wealthy merchants contracted in 1813 with the federal government to take over and distribute for a commission the unsubscribed portion of a war loan of $16 million. From 1815 the states made several large offerings of securities to finance transportation enterprises such as the Erie Canal. The source of much of the demand for these government securities was Europe, where investment capital had accumulated. Several private banking houses in New York City organized the transfer to Europe of American securities before the Civil War: the firm known from 1826 to 1848 as Prime, Ward and King, formed in 1790 as a brokerage, dealt in foreign exchange by the 1820s and enjoyed close ties to Baring Brothers, a leading merchant banking house in Britain that distributed new issues of federal and state bonds to European investors; Winslow, Lanier and Company, formed in 1849, specialized in negotiating American railway securities and helped to make New York City the center of this important field of investment banking; and the firm of August Belmont was the agent in the United States for the Rothschilds.

Intrepid Sea, Air, Space Museum, 1990

The Civil War brought an unprecedented volume of government debt issues to financial markets in the United States, with lasting effects on investment banking. The firm of Jay Cooke in Philadelphia introduced the practice of offering federal war bonds to small retail customers throughout the nation, and several firms in New York City built retail investment banking businesses as Cooke's agents, among them Fisk and Hatch (1862), Vermilye and Company (1830), and Livermore and Clews (*ca* 1860). A second effect of war finance was the establishment of banking houses by German-born Jews who earlier had settled in the United States and prospered as merchants. The firm of J. and W. Seligman, formed in New York City in 1862, soon opened branches through family contacts in several American and European cities. The Seligmans dealt extensively in government debt, of which they sold $200 million in Germany during the war. Other prominent banking houses established in the war years by German Jews were Kuhn, Loeb and Company (1867), M. Goldman (1869, predecessor of Goldman Sachs), and Lehman Brothers (1865). A third group of new private banking houses that appeared in the city during the war were firms with origins in New England, called Yankee firms, of which the most prominent were the houses of J. P. Morgan and Levi P. Morton. Like the firm of Prime, Ward and King, that of Winslow, Lanier, and those formed by German Jews, the Yankee firms depended largely for their success on affiliations or other close ties with banking houses in Europe.

Legislation passed during the Civil War made possible the rise of national banks. These were commercial banks, but a few of the larger ones in New York City developed a business in investment banking as well. Foremost among these was the First National Bank, formed in 1863, which dealt as an investment banker in government war bonds and under the leadership of George F. Baker was a leading investment bank by the end of the century. In the 1890s National City Bank under James Stillman also became a major investment bank. The keys to the success of the national banks in investment banking were not European contacts but rather large corporate accounts and bankers' balances held as reserves.

After the middle of the century the focus of investment banking shifted from government finance to railroad finance. The large financial requirements of the railroads and the greater risks of dealing in securities of corporations rather than governments led to innovations in investment banking. The long-standing practice among financiers of forming cooperative syndicates to bid for and buy securities was extended after the Civil War to the sale of securities. Even more important was the formation in 1870 of the first underwriting syndicate: originally the bankers belonging to such a syndicate made a commitment to purchase at an agreed price and resell any portion of a corporate issue that could not be sold by the corporation itself. Because the bankers were assuming a greater risk they became more active in managing the affairs of the issuing corporations. Investment bankers in New York City had a decided edge in organizing and managing syndicates because of the development of money and capital markets there, and leaders such as Morgan, Baker, Stillman, and Jacob Schiff of Kuhn, Loeb wielded great power. From the 1890s to the First World War the emphasis in investment banking shifted gradually from railroad finance to industrial and public utility finance, and from bonds to common stocks: the number of industrial stocks listed on the New York Stock Exchange rose from twenty in 1898 to 173 in 1915. Leading bankers in the city became active in managing the industrial and utility corporations, much as they had done with the railroads. Allegations that investment bankers had formed a so-called money trust to control finance and industry were investigated by a committee led by Representative Arsène Pujo. The findings issued by the committee in 1913 had little immediate impact on federal legislation, but states began to enact "blue sky" laws regulating securities dealing.

The First World War forced the belligerent powers of Europe to turn to the United States to borrow money, buy war supplies, and sell accumulated financial assets. Huge loans to Britain, France, and other nations were made by syndicates led by the firm of J. P. Morgan, which also became the purchasing agent for the British and French governments. The massive transfer of money and financial assets from Europe made the United States a creditor nation, and New York City eclipsed London as the leading financial center in the world. After the United States entered the war in 1917 the federal government raised money through four "liberty" loans and a "victory" loan, amounting in all to $21,500 million in two years. Both investment bankers and commercial bankers were engaged in purchasing and distributing the bonds. As they had done in the Civil War, the bankers sold to small savers as well as to the wealthy individuals and institutional investors that were their traditional customers. The breadth and depth of the investment market in the United States that developed during the war was demonstrated in the 1920s, when syndicates led by firms in New York City originated and distributed numerous corporate stock and bond issues as well as foreign securities.

The stock market crash of 1929 and the worldwide depression that followed focused public attention on weaknesses in financial arrangements in the United States and on dubious practices in banking. From 1933 a series of federal laws were enacted to regulate investment banking. The Glass–Steagall Act (1933) mandated a separation of commercial banking (lending and the taking of deposits) from investment banking (securities underwriting and trading). As a consequence J. P. Morgan chose to remain in commercial banking, while some of its partners left to form the investment bank of Morgan Stanley and Company. Other federal laws of 1933 and 1934 required prior registration of public offerings of securities, full disclosure of all material facts, and the regulation of stock market trading by a new federal agency, the Securities and Exchange Commission. Investment banking did not recover from the Depression until the economic expansion of the 1950s. The Second World War had little impact on it because the legislation of the 1930s allowed commercial banks to continue originating and dealing in government debt: corporate finance was the area left to investment banking under Glass–Steagall. The leading investment banks in New York City, such long-established houses as Morgan Stanley, Goldman Sachs, Dillon Read, and Kuhn, Loeb, were protected by law from the competition of commercial banks. They organized, led, and managed major corporate underwriting syndicates and counseled leading corporations. In addition there were a number of smaller investment banks in the city, almost all in lower Manhattan.

By the 1960s growth and structural change brought newer firms to prominence. An increase in the number of individual shareholders gave a competitive advantage to retail firms such as Merrill Lynch, Pierce, Fenner and Smith that could distribute shares widely. At the same time institutional pension funds and mutual funds accounted for a growing share of securities holdings, and firms such as Salomon Brothers and Donaldson, Lufkin and Jenrette made a specialty of serving institutional customers. As conglomerate mergers became more common in the late 1960s investment bankers acted increasingly not only as underwriters but as advisors. There was also a change in the geography of investment banking, as many of the largest firms moved from lower Manhattan to midtown. The 1970s and 1980s were a period of inflation, disruptions in the supply of oil, fluctuations in interest rates and exchange rates, increased volatility in securities markets, and the return of the United States to the status of an international debtor. The regulatory system put in place during the 1930s began to unravel. Soaring interest rates in the 1970s stimulated financial innovation: money market mutual funds, introduced by retail investment firms such as Merrill Lynch, Pierce, Fenner and Smith, offered interest rates well above the regulated ones paid by commercial banks and thrift institutions, and gained a large amount of invested funds at their expense. In 1975 the federal government ended the long-standing tradition of fixed brokerage commissions, which led to competitive fees and to the liquidation or merger of several investment firms. By the 1980s there was considerable deregulation of financial services.

Competition, consolidation, and a shift from partnership to corporate organization were trends that affected the issuing and underwriting sector of investment banking in the 1980s. By the end of the decade there was a handful of large firms, instead of many of varying sizes led and managed by a few leaders. A number of changes accounted for this. The Securities and Exchange Commission had streamlined the process of security offerings with the practice of shelf registration, which promoted greater competition and lower commissions for investment bankers. Large, well-capitalized investment banking firms could sometimes underwrite large issues by themselves: syndicates made up of many smaller firms were needed neither to share risks and profits, because the larger firms could hedge their risks in newly developed financial futures and options markets, nor for distribution, because issues could be placed with the large institutional investors that had come to account for a large share of all securities held. At the end of the 1980s federal authorities restored the environment that had prevailed before Glass–Steagall by allowing commercial banks to establish affiliates that could underwrite and trade in securities; this made investment banking more competitive. Another development of the 1980s was a wave of corporate mergers, hostile takeovers, and leveraged buyouts (in which publicly held companies were taken private: their common stock was exchanged for bonds that were not publicly traded). These maneuvers were largely financed by what became known as junk bonds, which were of low grade and offered high yields. The firm of Drexel Burnham Lambert developed methods of selling this sort of high-risk debt before a collapse of the junk bond market led to the bankruptcy of the firm in 1990. Investment bankers on Wall Street sometimes became principals of a corporation rather than merely financiers of it, much as investment bankers had taken part in corporate affairs a century earlier. The decade also brought unprecedented attention to investment banking as a profession, as salaries rose dramatically. Investment bankers were cast as villains in such works of popular fiction as Tom Wolfe's *Bonfire of the Vanities* (1987) and in such films as Oliver Stone's *Wall Street* (1987).

New York City remains the international capital of finance and investment banking, despite the development of "Euromarkets" in London and the rise of the Japanese market in Tokyo.

Vincent P. Carosso: *Investment Banking in America: A History* (Cambridge: Harvard University Press, 1970)

Samuel L. Hayes III and Philip M. Hubbard: *Investment Banking: A Tale of Three Cities* (Boston: Harvard Business School Press, 1990)

Richard Sylla

Inwood. Neighborhood at the northern tip of Manhattan, bounded to the north and east by the Harlem River, to the south by Fairview Avenue, and to the west by Dyckman Street; it is bisected by Broadway. The area is thought by some to have been the site of Peter Minuit's purchase of Manhattan from the Indians. In the nineteenth century estates were built in the hilly western section, which was never leveled partly because of the efforts of Frederick Law Olmsted. During the early twentieth century tenements for Jewish and Irish immigrants were built in the flat eastern section after Interborough Rapid Transit extended its subway in 1906; the estates were replaced by apartment buildings for middle-class tenants after the "A" train began service in the 1930s. The population in 1990 of Inwood and of Washington Heights to its south was 198,192, of which 67 percent was Latin American and 11 percent black, with large numbers of Jews, Irish, and Greeks. Many of the residents were professionals. Almost 80 percent of recent immigrants who settled in Inwood in the 1980s were Dominican, with far smaller numbers of Cubans, Ecuadorians, Koreans, and Colombians. A branch of Columbia–Presbyterian Hospital opened in 1988 near Baker Field, and in the early 1990s the city planned to build a marina on the Hudson River at the foot of Dyckman Street. In 1992 Guillermo Linares became the first Dominican elected to public office in the United States when he won a seat representing Inwood on the City Council. Large sections of parkland in the neighborhood include Inwood Hill Park, which covers 196 acres (seventy-nine hectares) and contains the last remnant of primeval forest in Manhattan. Inwood is also the site of the Dyckman House (*ca* 1785), the last Dutch farmhouse in the borough.

Michele Herman

IOOF. See Independent Order of Odd Fellows.

Iranians. The first Iranians in New York City, a small group of diplomats, merchants, and students, arrived in the 1920s and 1930s. By the 1970s the community had grown substantially. It was then profoundly affected when the Iranian Revolution in February 1979 overthrew the monarchy of Shah Mohammad Reza Pahlavi (1910–80), who had been backed by the United States. Affluent families, many connected to the shah's regime, as well as members of Iranian religious minorities fled to the city in great numbers. By 1980 New York City had about seven thousand Iranian residents, more than any American city except Los Angeles. (The federal census of that year recorded 5400 persons of Iranian birth or ancestry in the city, of whom 3742 lived in Queens, but because the census was conducted during the hostage crisis it is almost certain that these figures were too low.) After the revolution Iranian businesses in New York City extended far beyond the traditional carpet, garment, and jewelry enterprises. A growing number of Iranians established new retail, real-estate, and engineering firms, and medical practices. The *Iranian Yellow Pages Directory* for greater New York was first published in 1984. The large number of Iranians forming new businesses and entering the professions and academia gave the community a tremendous concentration of wealth, education, and talent. Despite several decades of student activism in the city, political demonstrations and meetings diminished and cultural activities became more prominent. In New York City a growing number of musi-

Inwood Heights, 1913

and Stouffer's. After the administrations of Mayor William O'Dwyer (born in Ireland) and Robert F. Wagner (ii) (partly of Irish descent), there followed a long period, extending into the 1990s, during which the number of Irish municipal officeholders declined. Nevertheless the city still sent Irish–Americans like Daniel P. Moynihan, Robert F. Kennedy, John Rooney, Hugh L. Carey, and William F. Ryan to serve in Congress.

There were 450,000 first- and second-generation Irish in New York City in 1950, mainly in neighborhoods at the city limits. An active social center was the building of the Irish Institute on West 48th Street (1952). During the following decade the city's Irish residents began to organize along occupational lines through Emerald societies, in which employers ranging from the fire department and the courts to the Board of Education and New York Telephone Company were represented. By 1983 there were more than forty such societies (with about forty thousand members), overseen by the Grand Council of United Emerald Societies (1975).

The immigration law of 1965 placed Ireland at a disadvantage, and as a result only 7500 new Irish immigrants settled in the city between 1965 and 1980. The American Irish Immigration Committee (formed in 1967) worked to redress the inequity caused by the new law. From the 1970s a heightened focus on Irish ethnicity led to the formation of new cultural organizations in the city, like the Irish Arts Center, the Irish Repertory Theatre, and the New York Irish History Roundtable. Summer festivals in Snug Harbor, Rockaway, and Coney Island attracted thousands of spectators by featuring leading Irish traditional musicians, many of whom were born and brought up in the city. Social service programs also increased in number. The United Irish Counties Association in 1977 formed a Community Action Bureau with offices in three boroughs to assist elderly Irish New Yorkers in obtaining services from the city. In response to renewed immigration from Ireland during the 1980s, Catholic Charities opened an Irish Outreach Office, the Irish Immigration Reform Movement opened the Emerald Isle Immigration Center, and the city published a *Guide for Irish Immigrants.*

Although equal employment opportunities were more diverse for Irish-born men, especially those who had served in the armed forces or become citizens, both men and women continued to gravitate to traditional service employment, working as housekeepers, nannies, bartenders, doormen, and waitresses. The illegal status of new immigrants after 1985 reinforced this tendency, as did the presence of Irish employers in residual Irish enclaves like Woodside in Queens and Woodlawn in the Bronx. In the late 1980s the Irish Immigration Reform Movement began a campaign to increase the number of visas allotted to Ireland as a means of lessening the volume of illegal immigration, a legacy of the restrictive immigration law. Twenty to forty thousand or more undocumented Irish are estimated to have settled in New York City after 1985; many of these benefited from the work of the Irish Immigration Reform Movement when 48,000 visas were allotted to the Irish under the Immigration Act of 1990. The newspaper *Irish Voice* was launched in 1987 to cater to the city's new Irish immigrants.

The nationalist organization with the highest profile in New York City after 1969 was the Irish Northern Aid Committee (Noraid). It was formed to assist victims of violence in the north of Ireland, including political prisoners and their families, but repeatedly battled charges of illegal gun running. The legal efforts of Joseph Doherty, a member of the Irish Republican Army, to prevent extradition from the United States were mounted in New York City from 1983 until 1992. Doherty's controversial petition for political asylum was ultimately denied, but during nine years of incarceration his cause rallied an unusual coalition of supporters in the city and eventually across the country, including Irish nationalists, human rights activists, and politicians.

The city's St. Patrick's Day Parade, greatly expanded by the support of the Archdiocese of New York and the work of many new immigrants from Ireland during the 1950s, is a demonstration of Irish ethnic and religious pride that draws a large number of marchers and spectators from several generations. It is also something of a lightning rod for contemporary issues, particularly the troubles in Northern Ireland and gay and lesbian politics.

A trend toward outward migration hastened in the 1970s and 1980s, owing to changes in old Irish neighborhoods and the city's fiscal crisis. The Irish community scattered beyond the five boroughs and into neighboring Nassau, Westchester, Rockland, and Bergen counties. The federal census of 1980 found that 647,733 New Yorkers claimed Irish birth or descent. In 1990 the number was 535,846, of whom 8 percent were of Irish birth, 47 percent of pure Irish ancestry, and 45 percent partly of Irish ancestry.

Robert Ernst: *Immigrant Life in New York City, 1825–1863* (New York: King's Crown, 1949; rev. Port Washington, N.Y.: Ira J. Friedman, 1965)

Jay P. Dolan: *The Immigrant Church: New York's Irish and German Catholics, 1815–1865* (Baltimore: Johns Hopkins University Press, 1975)

Ronald H. Bayor: *Neighbors in Conflict: The Irish, Germans, Jews, and Italians of New York City* (Baltimore: Johns Hopkins University Press, 1978)

Joshua B. Freeman: "Catholics, Communists and Republicans: Irish Workers and the Organization of the Transport Workers Union," *Working-class America: Essays on Labor, Community, and American Society*, ed. Michael H. Frisch and Daniel J. Walkowitz (Urbana: University of Illinois Press, 1983)

Michael F. Funchion: *Irish American Voluntary Organizations* (Westport, Conn.: Greenwood, 1983)

Dennis J. Clark: *Hibernia America: The Irish and Regional Cultures* (Westport, Conn.: Greenwood, 1986)

Steven P. Erie: *Rainbow's End: Irish–Americans and the Dilemmas of Urban Machine Politics, 1840–1985* (Berkeley: University of California Press, 1988)

Ronald H. Bayor and Timothy J. Meagher, eds.: *The New York Irish: Essays toward a History* (Baltimore: Johns Hopkins University Press, 1995)

Marion R. Casey

Irish Advocate. Weekly newspaper launched in 1893 by John C. O'Connor, an Irish immigrant. The third and smallest newspaper of its kind, it was popular for its homey tone and format and its articles about Irish–American leaders and organizations. It relied heavily on columns, reprinted material, and voluntary contributions, and most of its readers were regular subscribers. Unlike its competitors the newspaper did not take strong editorial positions on Irish causes. When O'Connor died in October 1946 the newspaper was taken over by his daughters, Pearl and Elise, and his son, James. The *Advocate* ceased publication in April 1989.

John J. Concannon

Irish–American. Weekly newspaper launched in New York City in 1849 by Patrick Lynch, Edward Cole, and Patrick Meehan, and edited by Lynch and from 1857 by Meehan. It became the most popular publication of its kind in the city during the 1850s and 1860s, reaching a circulation of twenty thousand in 1854 and forty thousand by 1861. The newspaper was successful partly because it endorsed a moderate brand of Irish nationalism and thus maintained an uneasy truce with the Catholic church (its short-lived competitors the *Nation* (1848) and the *Citizen* (1854) were strongly opposed by Bishop John Hughes for urging armed struggle against British rule in Ireland). Increasing competition from the *Irish World* eventually forced it to narrow its scope. Like many other Irish publications the *Irish–American* was opposed to reform movements, especially abolitionism. It ceased publication in 1915.

William Leonard Joyce: *Editors and Ethnicity: A History of the Irish American Press, 1848–1883* (New York: Arno, 1976)

Kevin Kenny

Irish Echo. Weekly newspaper launched in New York City in 1928 by Charles Connolly, a printer of Irish background. It covered events in Ireland but gave greater attention to local news of the Irish in the city. In the 1980s the newspaper broadened its coverage of Irish–American activities outside New York City. After its purchase by Patrick Grimes the *Irish Echo* fell under the control of his family. In the early 1990s the publisher was Claire Grimes.

John T. Ridge

Irish Institute. Philanthropic society formed in 1948 by Paul O'Dwyer to promote cultural endeavors in the United States and Ireland; it was incorporated on 11 December 1950. The institute bought a four-story building at 326 West 48th Street in 1952 that was used as a headquarters by many Irish organizations until it was sold in 1982. From the proceeds of this sale the institute gave financial support to the first scholarly history of the Irish in New York City, published by Johns Hopkins University Press (1995).

Marion R. Casey

Irish Nation. Weekly publication launched in 1882 by John Devoy to promote militant Irish Republicanism. It soon became the foremost publication of its kind. For a time it promoted the "new departure" policy formulated in the late 1870s by Devoy, Michael Davitt, and Charles Stewart Parnell, which sought to unite three movements: those devoted to armed-force Republicanism, peaceful constitutional change, and reform of the system of landowning and tenanting in Ireland. After returning to a more militant stance in the 1880s and declaring that insurrection was the only means to achieve independence, the *Irish Nation* failed in 1886. Its causes were taken up by the *Gaelic American* (1903), which remained under Devoy's direction until his death.

Kevin Kenny

Irish Republicanism. Ideas about Irish Republicanism were introduced to New York City by such political exiles as Thomas Addis Emmet and William Sampson, veterans of the unsuccessful Irish uprising of 1798 who advocated ending British rule through armed struggle and forming an Irish republic. During the nineteenth century the city became the national center of Irish nationalism in the United States. In 1858 the Fenian Brotherhood (named for a mythical band of warriors) was formed there by John O'Mahony, an exile after the rebellion of 1848, as an affiliate of the Irish Revolutionary Brotherhood (IRB), formed in Dublin by James Stephens. There were Fenian circles in the Union Army and Navy, and by 1865 the Fenians had 250,000 followers, many of them veterans of the Civil War. On 1 March 1866 about 100,000 Fenians assembled at Jones's Wood. An Irish Republican government in exile modeled on the American government was set up in Philadelphia and supported by Fenians in New York City, who provided American money and manpower to the government in exile and also to Fenian insurrectionaries in Ireland. In the years after the Civil War a dissident Fenian faction sought to provoke a war with England by invading Canada, in the belief that with England at war an insurrection in Ireland might succeed and would in any event be certain to receive American support. On 12 April 1866 they tried to seize the island of Campobello, New Brunswick, off the coast of Maine; American troops dispersed them and the British and American navies intercepted a shipment of arms. After landing in New York City on 10 May, Stephens denounced the policy of attacking Canada, ousted O'Mahony, and called for restricting armed conflict to Irish soil. An attack on Canada was nonetheless mounted on 1 June by Colonel John O'Neill, who crossed the border with eight hundred men and defeated a Canadian militia company before retreating to Buffalo, leaving twelve Canadians dead and forty wounded, and eight Fenians dead and twenty wounded. Another attack was mounted on June 7 from St. Albans, Vermont, by a thousand Fenians.

The Fenian organizations in both the United States and Ireland nearly collapsed after their plans for an insurrection were discovered by police informants; there were only scattered rural uprisings on 5–6 March 1867. Many Irish Republicans went into exile in New York City, and in 1867 the Republican organization Clan na Gael was formed there by Jerome C. Collins. On 25 May 1870 O'Neill led a foray into Canada that according to the *New York Times* attracted thirty thousand Fenians from the city; only a few hundred appeared at the border and were easily repulsed by the thirteen thousand Canadian troops who met them. After Jeremiah O'Donovan Rossa and John Devoy were released from prison on condition of permanent exile in 1871 they moved to New York City, where they were met by Democrats and Republicans seeking to win the Irish vote: Tammany Hall reserved a suite for them at the Astor House (which they refused) and William M. "Boss" Tweed was the grand marshal of a parade in their honor. Under Devoy's leadership the Clan na Gael quickly became the most powerful Republican organization on either side of the Atlantic; by the late 1870s it had about ten thousand members and overshadowed the Fenians. In 1877 a seven-member council known as the Joint Revolutionary Directory was formed to bind it to the IRB. The city's Fenians, led by O'Donovan Rossa after 1877, adopted increasingly extreme policies, among them establishing a "skirmishing fund" to wage guerrilla warfare against the British empire. They also paid the Irish-born inventor John Phillip Holland \$23,000 to build a submarine that could cross the Atlantic and destroy the British fleet (his plans for another submarine were rejected by the U.S. Navy, which considered them unrealistic). The *Fenian Ram* was thirty-one feet (9.5 meters) long and designed for a three-man crew. After being launched in the Hudson River in May 1881 it made frequent runs beneath New York Harbor, diving to depths as great as sixty feet (eighteen meters) and remaining below the surface for as long as an hour, but was never put to its intended use.

Assuming that England would eventually be drawn into a war, the Clan na Gael continued sending money to Ireland for arms, and in 1916 a successful uprising was staged. The Anglo-Irish Treaty of 1922 was widely considered unsatisfactory, because although it established an independent Irish republic it left six mainly Protestant counties in the north of Ireland under British control, leading the IRB to launch a campaign to achieve their incorporation. During the late 1960s the issue was taken up by the Irish Republican Army, which used violent tactics supported by American groups such as the Irish Northern Aid Committee (Noraid).

During the 1980s and early 1990s much attention focused on the case of James Doherty, who in 1981 escaped from a jail in Belfast before standing trial for killing a British soldier. After making his way to New York City he was arrested at Clancy's Bar on 3rd Avenue near 56th Street in June 1983 by agents of the Federal Bureau of Investigation working undercover. A federal judge ruled in 1984 that Doherty should not be extradited because his crime was political, and the federal government sought to deport him as an illegal alien; he remained in prison while seeking an appeal. In 1988 the attorney general of the United States ruled that Doherty could be deported to Britain. The board of immigration appeals later held that the ruling should be reviewed. Doherty's case became an issue in the mayoral election of 1989: the Republican candidate, Rudolph W. Giuliani, was the U.S. attorney in charge of prosecuting him; the Democratic candidate, David N. Dinkins, called for granting him political asylum. Doherty's petition for asylum was denied in 1992, by which time he had spent nine years in detention without having been convicted of any crime.

Kevin Kenny

Irish World and Industrial Liberator. Weekly newspaper launched as the *Irish World* in 1870 by Patrick Ford; it was renamed in 1878. Like its predecessors the newspaper was devoted to Irish nationalism, but it also supported workers' movements and such causes as feminism, the eight-hour day, the right to strike, abolishing monopolies, the income tax, insuring greenbacks, and nationalizing land in the United States and in Ireland, where Ford hoped that such a policy would lead to independence. The *Irish World and Industrial Liberator* became the most important newspaper of its kind in the city and during the 1880s had a national circulation of 35,000. It ceased publication in 1951.

Kevin Kenny

IRT. See Interborough Rapid Transit Company.

Irving, Washington (*b* New York City, 3 April 1783; *d* Tarrytown, N.Y., 28 Nov 1859). Essayist and short-story writer. He spent his childhood in New York City and lived at 128 William Street until 1802, when

Washington Irving, ca *1819*

his family moved to a building at Ann and William streets. As a young man he studied law and traveled to the western frontier and to Europe. He later returned to the city, where he wrote for the *Morning Chronicle* and with James Kirke Paulding produced the humorous journal *Salmagundi* in 1807–8. His first well-known work was his *A History of New York* (1809), a collection of satirical essays written under the pen name Diedrich Knickerbocker. In the following years he again moved to Europe, remaining there for seventeen years and sending manuscripts to the city for publication, among them two collections of stories: *The Sketch Book of Geoffrey Crayon, Gent.* (1819–20), which included "Rip van Winkle" and "The Legend of Sleepy Hollow," and *Bracebridge Hall.* While working for the American embassy in Madrid he wrote *History of the Life and Voyages of Christopher Columbus.* His *A Chronicle of the Conquest of Granada* was published in 1829. He was later assigned to the embassy in London. On his return to the United States he published *A Tour on the Prairies* and other works about the frontier. In 1836 he moved from Colonnade Row in the city to Irvington, New York, where he lived until his appointment as minister to Spain in 1842. At the end of his assignment he returned to his home on the Hudson to complete his *Life of George Washington* (1855–59). On his many visits to the city Irving often stayed at his nephew's house at 46 East 21st Street.

Lewis G. Leary: *Washington Irving* (Minneapolis: University of Minnesota Press, 1963)

See also Classical music, §1.

James E. Mooney

Irving House. Hotel opened in 1848 at 281 Broadway in Manhattan, occupying the entire west side of the block-front between Chambers and Reade streets on the former site of A. T. Stewart's dry-goods emporium. Managed by Daniel D. Howard, it had several well-known guests, among them the Swedish soprano Jenny Lind (during her first American tour, September 1850) and the Hungarian revolutionary Louis Kossuth (December 1851). Commercial tenants included a druggist, a hatter, a tailor, and a bookshop. In September 1852 Howard was succeeded by William H. Burroughs as the manager of the hotel, which by the spring of 1856 was no longer in business. Wilson identifies Irving House as the "granite building" at 273 Broadway in which the printer Samuel Adams was slain by John Caldwell Colt in 1841.

T. Morehead: *New-York Mercantile Register for 1848–49* (New York: John P. Prall, 1848), 13
James Grant Wilson, ed.: *The Memorial History of the City of New-York,* vol. 4 (New York: New-York History Company, 1893), 394 n. 1

Joel Honig

Isaacs, Stanley M(yer) (*b* New York City, 27 Sept 1882; *d* New York City, 12 July 1962). City councilman, borough president, and civic leader. He graduated from Columbia College and New York Law School and led the campaign for enactment of the State Multiple Dwelling Law of 1929, which mandated improvements in tenement housing. A leader of the liberal wing of the Republican Party, he was borough president of Manhattan from 1938 to 1941 and oversaw the completion of the East River Drive (now the FDR Drive). He was elected to the City Council from the Upper East Side in 1941 and remained a member to the end of his life, serving as minority leader of the council and often as its only Republican. He was also the president of United Neighborhood Houses, an organization of settlement houses.

Edith S. Isaacs: *Love Affair with a City: The Story of Stanley M. Isaacs* (New York: Random House, 1967)

Mary B. Bowling

Island Hospital. Hospital on Blackwell's Island, a forerunner of Elmhurst hospital center.

Island of Meadows. Uninhabited island in the Arthur Kill off the western shore of Staten Island. In the mid 1990s it was on the verge of being absorbed by the Fresh Kills Landfill.

Spencer Smith: "The Harbor Islands," *South Street Reporter* 10, no. 2 (summer 1976)
Francis J. Duffy and William H. Miller: *The New York Harbor Book* (Falmouth, Maine: TBW, 1986)
Louise Tanner: "Islands of New York Harbor," *Seaport* 19, no. 4 (winter 1986)

Ellen Fletcher

Israelis. Few Israelis moved to New York City during the 1950s and early 1960s; most who did were Europeans for whom Israel was a temporary destination on the way to the United States. The number grew after the Six Day War of 1967 and consisted mostly of "sabras" seeking professional opportunities. These immigrants were attracted by the American emphasis on personal success and discouraged from staying in Israel by high taxes, a lower standard of living, a widespread sense of insecurity resulting from the protracted state of war, a cumbersome bureaucracy, political stagnation, and the erosion of the Zionist vision; there were also Israelis originating from Muslim countries who moved to the city to escape economic and social discrimination. Israeli immigrants usually settled in predominantly Jewish neighborhoods in Brooklyn and Queens; Borough Park became a popular destination for the Orthodox, Queens for secular Ashkenazim. Immigration increased again after the Yom Kippur War of 1973. In 1980 estimates of the population varied from 45,000 to 220,000, the wide range due in part to an unwillingness by both Jewish and Israeli institutions to make a systematic census: immigrants became stigmatized as *yordim* (those who abandon Israel) by Israeli and American Jewish organizations.

Immigrants in the 1980s were predominantly of Sephardic–Oriental extraction, had technical and blue-collar skills, and were drawn to the United States by the prospect of owning their own businesses. Many opened garment retailing firms, diamond and jewelry factories, electronics retail and wholesale firms, and taxicab, automobile, and moving services. Few community efforts were directed at Israelis owing to estrangement between them and other American Jews; efforts to bridge the gap led to the formation of two afternoon schools for Israeli children in Queens and in Brooklyn (Etgar and Nitsan) and of a communal Israeli club in the Central Queens YM-YWHA in Forest Hills. Israeli immigrants usually identify with national secularism, often travel between the city and Israel, and do not form communal organizations or join American Jewish ones. Israeli newspapers and a local Hebrew-language newspaper, *Israel Shelanu,* enjoy a wide audience. In the mid 1990s the United States remained the preferred destination of Israelis, and in New York City the population was estimated at 300,000.

Moshe Shokeid: *Children of Circumstances: Israeli Emigrants in New York* (Ithaca, N.Y.: Cornell University Press, 1988)

Hadassa Kosak

Italians. New York Harbor was explored in 1524 by Giovanni da Verrazano, an Italian employed by François I of France. As the area was settled during the next few centuries its small Italian population included such well-known figures as Lorenzo da Ponte, who wrote librettos for several of Mozart's operas before moving in 1805 to the city, where he later became the first professor of Italian language and literature at Columbia College. From the 1820s to the 1850s a few Italian political refugees lived in Staten Island, among them Giuseppe Garibaldi. The Archdiocese of New York formed a national parish for Italians in Greenwich Village in 1866.

Fewer than twenty thousand Italians lived in New York City in 1880, but immigration increased between 1899 and 1910, when about 1.9 million persons from southern Italy moved to the United States. About 77 percent were *contadini*, landless farmers fleeing bitter rural poverty. There were 220,000 Italians in New York City by 1900 and 545,000 by 1910; many later returned to Italy. Before the First World War women and girls often worked in the garment trade, men in construction. About four thousand Italian laborers worked on the Lexington Avenue subway, and many others dug tunnels, paved streets, and laid down subway track elsewhere in the city. Bosses known as padrones often found work for the laborers but also exploited them. As factories were built in the city more Italians were employed in manufacturing. Some craftsmen, especially tailors and barbers, opened shops, and entrepreneurs became street vendors and bootblacks; professionals were fewer in number. By the time of the First World War immigrants had sent about $750 million back to Italy.

Most Italians lived within walking distance of where they worked. The largest enclaves were formed before the turn of the century on the Lower East Side and in Greenwich Village and were known for their squalor, congestion, and disease. Other large Italian neighborhoods were in East Harlem, Williamsburg, and Greenpoint. Immigrants from the same Italian town often settled together, preserving their dialects and customs and forming mutual aid societies that helped members in the event of illness or death. The Sons of Italy was formed as a union of mutual aid societies in 1905. Because Italians competed with better-established immigrant groups for work, they were considered a threat to labor solidarity and encountered hostility in unions. Italians were however active in the labor movement, and Italian women and girls accounted for a large segment of the International Ladies' Garment Workers' Union. Some Italians gravitated toward anarchism and such radical movements as the Industrial Workers of the World. In 1913 the anarchist Carlo Tresca first published the newspaper *L'Avvenire* in the city; it was suppressed and its successor *Il Martello* was repeatedly confiscated.

Within the Catholic church Italians came into conflict with the Irish. Parish churches often refused to sponsor Italian religious festivals, which continued to be held by Italian societies. In ethnically mixed parishes Italians were often relegated to the church basement to worship. American Catholics rejected Italian brands of faith, which often incorporated animistic elements of folk religion. Among the second generation, family and community events were held in the parish church and many children attended the parish school. Italians were slow to move into municipal politics: of more than half a million Italians in the city in 1911 only fifteen thousand voted. Neglected by Irish politicians who governed the city through the Democratic Party, Italian immigrants remained loyal to patrons in their own neighborhoods. By contrast the American-born children of earlier immigrants learned the ways of machine politics. Their knowledge of Tammany Hall helped them to cultivate a political base among Italians who sought their patronage.

Italian racketeers formed crime syndicates that together made up La Cosa Nostra, which was modeled on secret societies in Italy but took shape as an American Mafia with bootlegging operations during Prohibition; it later became an arm for illegal gambling, loan sharking, pornography, drug smuggling, and labor racketeering. The influence of wealthy Mafiosi helped some Italian politicians to gain power. In 1931 Al Marinelli became the first Italian district leader in Tammany Hall, reportedly installed by the racketeer Lucky Luciano, who mistrusted the Irish Democrats in charge of city government.

After the First World War the number of Italian immigrants settling in the city declined sharply. Nevertheless by 1930 the 1,070,353 persons of Italian descent in New York City accounted for 17 percent of the city's population, the highest concentration of Italians in the United States. Their number increased slightly during the 1930s, when as many as 110,000 Italians lived east of Lexington Avenue between 96th and 116th streets and east of Madison Avenue between 116th and 125th streets. Working-class families improved their standard of living and spoke English as provincial loyalties dissipated and immigrant societies declined. According to the Wickersham Report on Crime and Criminal Justice (1931) the most common crimes in Italian neighborhoods were committed by youths and included violent crimes as well as delinquency and truancy; there were low rates of drunkenness, domestic violence, and property crimes. Although educational levels remained low, by the 1930s more Italians had skilled work than previously and a class of proprietors developed. Among the large ventures were clothing factories and construction firms, including a building supply firm owned by Generoso Pope that was the largest of its kind in the country. A survey conducted by the Works Progress Administration in 1938 identified ten thousand Italian grocery stores and about as many ice and coal dealers, some of which later sold heating oil.

The Republican Party and radicalism provided a route to city government for many Italians excluded from Tammany Hall, where Irish–Americans dominated. Fiorello H. La Guardia was elected mayor in 1933 for the first of three terms with the support of the Republican and American Labor parties. In addition to guiding reforms during the Depression he helped Italians gain political prominence; his protégé Vito Marcantonio, a fiery radical from East Harlem, held a seat in Congress from 1935 to 1937 and from 1939 to 1951. Other radicals included Tresca and Peter Cacchione, a Communist who held a seat on the City Council from 1941 to 1947. Pope became influential and widely known as the publisher of *Il Progresso Italo-Americano*, the city's major Italian-language newspaper, and in the 1930s sought to form a coalition of Italian Democrats. Both the Italian government and President Franklin D. Roosevelt sought his counsel regarding the attitudes of Italians in the United States toward Mussolini and fascism; he himself supported Mussolini at the outset and became less vocal only under pressure from Washington.

By the 1940s Luciano's successor Frank Costello had become a major power in Tammany Hall. Another was Carmine DeSapio, who broke with the Irish Democrats and became a district leader in Greenwich Village in 1939 and the county leader of Manhattan in 1949; a cover story in *Time* in 1956 called him "America's most celebrated boss." The political ascendance of the city's Italians was also reflected in the special mayoral election of 1950, contested by Vincent R. Impellitteri, Ferdinand Pecora, and Edward Corsi. The dispersion of the Italian population to the suburbs eventually undermined clubhouse politicians like DeSapio, who was defeated in an election for a district leadership in 1961 by a reform club that included among its members Edward I. Koch; in the 1950s DeSapio assisted in defeating a slum clearance project for Greenwich Village that was supported by Robert Moses and New York University.

The city's Italian–Americans demonstrated a capacity for political activism during the 1960s and 1970s, inspired in part by the black pride movement. The Italian American Civil Rights League gave expression to ethnic resentment among Italians during the late 1960s and early 1970s; its rally on "Unity Day" at Columbus Circle in June 1971 drew thousands of protesters angered by stereotypical images of Italians. Volunteers formed groups that became part of a new social and political network. The Congress of Italian–American Organizations was organized to procure social services and community development funds after a report in 1975 revealed that only 15 percent of Italian households below the poverty line were receiving public assistance. The Calandra Institute at the City University of New York was formed to promote the interests of Italian students whose levels of education lagged behind those of other ethnic groups in the city. The American Italian Historical Association was established in Manhattan, as was the Italian Academy for Advanced Studies in America at Columbia

University. The National Organization of Italian–American Women, formed in Manhattan in 1980, sought to provide a network for women in business and the professions. One of the first members was Geraldine A. Ferraro, a congresswoman from Queens who in 1984 became the first woman nominated by a major party for national office. Meade Esposito led a powerful Democratic coalition in Brooklyn until his retirement during Koch's third term as mayor. Peter Vallone of Queens became speaker of the City Council and John J. Marchi served in the state senate from the 1950s into the 1990s. Mario M. Cuomo lost an election for the mayoralty to Koch in 1977 but later became governor. Rudolph W. Giuliani, a federal attorney who prosecuted organized-crime figures, received overwhelming support from Italian voters in the mayoral election of 1989, which he narrowly lost to David N. Dinkins; Giuliani won a narrow victory over Dinkins in the next election, becoming mayor in 1994.

In 1980 the 1,005,304 persons of Italian descent in New York City were the largest national group, accounting for one seventh of the total population of the city and one twelfth the Italian population of the United States. Perhaps two million persons of Italian descent lived in the suburbs of New York City. About 67 percent of the Italians of New York City lived in Brooklyn and Queens; owing partly to the opening of the Verrazano Narrows Bridge in 1964, about 40 percent of the population of Staten Island was Italian. A large number were middle-class homeowners. Of those employed in the city 40 percent had administrative, retail, and technical occupations and 40 percent were blue-collar workers and laborers (26 percent of construction workers in the city were Italian), and 10 percent were professionals, mostly elementary- and secondary-school teachers. The poverty rate for Italians in 1980 was 9.7 percent, well below the rate of 12.9 percent for all whites in the city.

Although fewer than five thousand Italians moved to the United States annually during the 1980s, about 700,000 Italians remained in the city at the end of the decade, accounting for 10 percent of the population. Their social life continued to be defined by an ethnic family culture. The pull of traditional family values may account for low divorce rates, for the small numbers of elderly Italians in group homes and of working mothers with young children, and for the persistent presence of Italians in the metropolitan area. Italians have retained a high profile in a city where the ethnic mix has many built-in tensions; racial violence in predominantly Italian areas of Howard Beach (1986) and Bensonhurst (1990) drew national attention. Notwithstanding the long and distinguished tenure of Francis J. Mugavero as the archbishop of the Brooklyn and Queens archdiocese, there are still relatively few Italians in the clergy and the local church hierarchy. Despite successful federal prosecutions five organized-crime syndicates, or "families," maintain operations in the city; the largest is the Gambino family, which is believed to have four to five hundred members and perhaps three thousand affiliates and reportedly makes profits of more than $100 million annually, often through the infiltration of legitimate businesses, especially trucking, waste disposal, construction, and the garment trade.

Several institutions are dedicated to Italian culture in the city, including the Casa Italiana at Columbia University and the Italian Cultural Institute. Many Italians maintain cultural ties to Italy through Italian-language publications and television programs. The city is known for its Italian food, especially baked goods and pizza; some maintain that the first pizzeria in the city was Gennaro Lombardi's, opened on Spring Street in Manhattan in 1905. This food culture is the centerpiece of the Historic District in Little Italy. Important traditions include the annual parade on Columbus Day and the San Gennaro Festival on Mulberry Street in September.

Leonard Covello: *The Social Background of the Italo-American Schoolchild* (Leiden, Netherlands: E. J. Brill, 1967)

Donald Tricarico: *The Italians of Greenwich Village: The Social Structure and Transformation of an Ethnic Community* (New York: Center for Migration Studies, 1984)

Robert A. Orsi: *The Madonna of 115th Street: Faith and Community in Italian Harlem, 1880–1950* (New Haven: Yale University Press, 1985)

Donald Tricarico

ITT. See INTERNATIONAL TELEPHONE AND TELEGRAPH.

Ives, Charles (Edward) (*b* Danbury, Conn., 20 Oct 1874; *d* New York City, 19 May 1954). Composer. As a student at Yale University his experiments with unresolved dissonance left his teacher Horatio Parker nonplussed. He moved to New York City after his graduation in 1898 and with several colleagues from Yale lived in a series of apartments, each nicknamed "Poverty Flat," at 317 West 58th Street (to 1901), 65 Central Park West (1901–7), and 34 Gramercy Park (to 1908). As the organist at Central Presbyterian Church (1900–2) he took part in 1902 in the première of his cantata *The Celestial Country*, one of his few compositions to receive a public performance while he lived in the city. After his marriage to Harmony Twichell in 1908 the couple lived at 70 West 11th Street (to 1911), 118 Waverly Place (1911–12), and 29 West 11th Street (1914–15). During these years his music became increasingly dense and dissonant, and was for the most part ignored. He sustained his musical career by working in life insurance, first at the Mutual Insurance Company and then as a partner with Julian Myrick in the firm of Ives and Myrick, which at his instigation introduced a new form of annuity. He bought a house in West Redding, Connecticut, in 1912 but continued to spend winters in New York City; from 1917 to 1926 he lived at 120 East 22nd Street. After a heart attack in 1918 Ives retired from the insurance business, and his productive years as a composer ended about the same time. From 1926 he lived at 164 East 74th Street. Ives's music reflected his determination to overturn what he saw as the primly genteel conventions of the concert music of his day, as well as his deep affection for the secular and religious music of nineteenth-century America. He used polyrhythms and polytonality before many other composers did, and his works contain many allusions to hymn tunes, military marches, patriotic songs, and ragtime. New York City figured in such compositions as the orchestral works the *General Slocum* (1904) and *Central Park in the Dark* (1906), and the songs *Romanzo di Central Park* (1900) and *Ann Street* (1921). He achieved public recognition toward the last years of his life and was awarded the Pulitzer Prize in 1947 for his Symphony no. 3, an honor that he derided as being one of the "badges of mediocrity."

Frank Rossiter: *Charles Ives and His America* (New York: Liveright, 1975)

Barbara L. Tischler

IWW. See INDUSTRIAL WORKERS OF THE WORLD.

J

Jack, Hulan E(dwin, Sr.) (*b* St. Lucia, British West Indies, 23 Dec 1906; *d* New York City, 19 Dec 1986). Public official. After entering Democratic politics in the 1930s he was elected in 1940 to represent Harlem in the state assembly, from which he resigned when he was elected borough president of Manhattan in 1953; he was the first black borough president in New York City and the highest-ranking black elected official in the country in the 1950s. In 1957 he was elected to a second term, toward the end of which he was indicted and convicted for accepting an illegal gift valued at $4500, and in 1960 he resigned his office in disgrace. His conviction was bitterly criticized by many blacks, who accused the city government of racial discrimination. In 1968 he reentered politics, again winning election to the state assembly; he served one term. Jack was indicted for conspiracy and conflict of interest in 1970 by the federal government, which accused him of using improper means to promote certain products at groceries in Harlem; he was later convicted and sentenced to three months in prison. Toward the end of his life he was a political consultant to the conspiracy theorist Lyndon H. LaRouche Jr.

Calvin B. Holder: "The Rise of the West Indian Politician in New York City, 1900–1952," *Afro-Americans in New York Life and History* 4 (1980), 5–60

Calvin B. Holder: "The Rise and Fall of the West Indian Politician in New York City, 1900–1988" (New York: Medgar Evers College, Caribbean Research Center, 1991)

Calvin B. Holder

Jackson Heights. Neighborhood in northwestern Queens, bounded to the north by Astoria Boulevard, to the east by 94th Street and Junction Boulevard, to the south by Roosevelt Avenue, and to the west by the Brooklyn–Queens Expressway. It consisted originally of farmland rising sixty-five feet (nineteen meters) above the surrounding lowlands in the sparsely populated area of Trains Meadows. The land was bought in 1908 by a syndicate of bankers and real-estate agents called the Queensboro Realty Company, led by Edward A. MacDougal; Justice P. Henry Dugro was an agent. After the Queensboro Bridge opened in 1909 the area became more attractive to developers, and by the end of 1910 the syndicate had acquired 350 acres (140 hectares) of land. It prevailed on the city to close Trains Meadow Road and lay out streets in a regular grid pattern numbered consecutively (1st Street became the present 54th Street), and on Interborough Rapid Transit to extend a line into Queens, for which Roosevelt Avenue was specially built. The neighborhood was named for a street that ran through it, Jackson Avenue (now Northern Boulevard). An elevated line opened in May 1917 with four stations in Jackson Heights: 74th Street, 82nd Street, Elmhurst Avenue, and Junction Boulevard. The first apartment building was erected at 82nd Street and Northern Boulevard in 1911, and by 1912 there were eight miles (thirteen kilometers) of paved streets with sidewalks, curbs, and gutters, and five miles (eight kilometers) of sewers. During the next twenty years Queensborough Realty engaged prominent architects to design two-family houses and especially the apartment buildings for which the neighborhood became known, many bordering the street on two sides and separated from each other by a communal garden; there were also a golf course and a community center. An innovator in urban and suburban housing, the corporation offered cooperative apartments as early as 1920 and semidetached houses known as garden apartments from 1923; it also practiced exclusionary policies aimed at Jews, Catholics, and blacks. The neighborhood had 3600 residents in 1920, and in 1922 double-decker buses began offering service from 82nd Street to 5th Avenue in Manhattan. Suites of two to seven rooms in apartment buildings were rented for $90 to $200 a month in 1928. By the beginning of the Depression the entire tract had been built up except the northern section near Astoria Boulevard and the eastern section near Junction Boulevard, but these areas as well were gradually developed during the 1930s. The population increased during the 1930s from 44,000 to 54,290, in part because of the opening of the Independent subway to Roosevelt Avenue on 19 August 1933. A large number of immigrants settled in Jackson Heights in the 1980s, especially from Colombia, China, and the Dominican Republic and to a lesser extent from India, Ecuador, Korea, Guyana, Peru, Cuba, and Pakistan. The neighborhood is also the home of the largest Argentinian community in New York City. In the mid 1990s Jackson Heights was a well-maintained neighborhood with apartment buildings and expensive one-family houses.

Vincent Seyfried

Jacobi, Abraham (*b* Hartum, Germany, 6 May 1830; *d* Bolton Landing, N.Y., 10 July 1919). Physician. After completing his medical training he was imprisoned for taking part in the revolution of 1848; on his release he moved to New York City, where he taught at the College of Physicians and Surgeons and practiced medicine for sixty-six years, focusing his efforts on caring for the poor. Among his many concerns was teaching hygiene in schools, which he believed would slow the spread of tuberculosis among children. He was married to Mary Putnam Jacobi.

Rhoda Truax: *The Doctors Jacobi* (Boston: Little, Brown, 1952)

James E. Mooney

Jacobi, Mary Putnam (*b* New York City, 31 Aug 1842; *d* New York City, 10 June 1906). Physician. The daughter of a leading publisher, she grew up in the semirural suburbs of New York City, received the MD from the Female Medical College of Pennsylvania in 1864, and became a leading physician. She devoted herself to the welfare of children and to improving the status of women in medicine. With her husband, the German political refugee Abraham Jacobi, she was active and influential in the suffrage movement. In 1871–89 she taught at the Women's Medical College of the New York Infirmary for Women and Children, and in 1872 she founded the Women's Medical Association of New York City, serving as its president in 1874–1903.

Ruth Putnam, ed.: *Life and Letters of Mary Putnam Jacobi* (New York: G. P. Putnam's Sons, 1925)

Rhoda Truax: *The Doctors Jacobi* (Boston: Little, Brown, 1952)

Kathryn Kish Sklar

Jacob K. Javits Convention Center. Public convention complex in Manhattan, bounded by 38th Street, 11th Avenue, 34th Street, and 12th Avenue; it has 1.8 million square feet (167,220 square meters) of floor space contained under a vast frame and tinted-glass canopy. Commissioned by the New York State Urban Development Corporation from the firm of I. M. Pei in 1979 to replace the outmoded Coliseum on Columbus Circle and designed by a team under James Ingo Freed, it accommodates six events simultaneously and 85,000 visitors in various halls and more than a hundred meeting rooms. The center opened in 1986 at a cost of $500 million, $125 million over budget; the overrun was soon recovered in earnings from conventions. The number of visitors increased each year and by 1990 reached three million. In the mid 1990s it was estimated that the center accounted for nearly 2 percent of the city's economy.

Carol Willis

Jacob Ruppert Brewery. Firm of brewers opened in 1867 by Jacob Ruppert, the son of a German brewer. On the eve of Prohibition it sold beer locally and in New England and was the largest brewery in New York City. It was eventually taken over by Ruppert's son, who owned the New York Yankees and led efforts after 1933 to dissociate beer from saloons and promote its consumption in the home. In 1965 the firm closed its brewery at 92nd Street

Jacob K. Javits Convention Center. Photo by Nathaniel Lieberman. Courtesy of Pei Cobb Freed and Partners

and 3rd Avenue and sold its name to Rheingold.

Stanley Wade Baron: *Brewed in America: A History of Beer and Ale in the United States* (Boston: Little, Brown, 1962)

K. Austin Kerr

Jacques Marchais Center of Tibetan Art. Museum at 338 Lighthouse Avenue in Staten Island, opened in 1947. It contains the Asian art collection of Jacques Marchais (née Edna Koblentz, 1890–1948), who lived nearby and ran an art gallery on Madison Avenue, and is built to resemble a Tibetan monastery. The art is largely religious, with pieces ranging from elaborate, jewel-encrusted figures of deities to humble devotional objects made of human and animal bone.

Carol V. Wright

Jahn's. A chain of ice cream parlors, the first of which was opened in 1897 by John Jahn at Alexander Avenue and 138th Street in the Bronx. Outlets were later added in Brooklyn and in Jamaica, Flushing, and Richmond Hill in Queens. The parlors became well known for such extravagant ice cream dishes as the "Kitchen Sink," a gargantuan portion of ice cream, fruit, and syrups that serves eight. In the mid 1990s the oldest outlet was that in Richmond Hill, built in 1929 and decorated with Frank Jahn's paintings of New York City, a nickelodeon, gas lamps, and a soda fountain.

Stephen Weinstein

jails. The correctional facilities in New York City are technically jails rather than prisons because only a few of the inmates are serving time after having been convicted of crimes. The first jail in the city was opened in 1625 when the Dutch set aside dungeons in Fort Amsterdam to confine Indians and those who had been convicted of crimes. The Stadt Huys, the first city hall, erected in 1642 on the corner of Pearl Street and Coenties Slip, contained a jail in addition to courts, a tavern, and a school. In 1704 a jail for felons and debtors was installed in the basement of City Hall, then at the northern end of Broad Street. Because of overcrowding and poor conditions a new jail was built in 1758 in an adjacent field. This building served as the city prison until 1775, when the Bridewell was constructed. During the American Revolution the British used both the old and the new jails as military prisons. One of their first provost marshalls was Captain William Cunningham, who became infamous for the suffering that he imposed on prisoners. After the war the Bridewells again functioned as city jails. A state prison opened in 1797 in Greenwich Village for convicts sentenced to terms of three years or more. The Bridewell was converted into a debtor's jail in 1816, when a city penitentiary was installed in an almshouse at the Bellevue Establishment (26th Street and 1st Avenue). The penitentiary was the first prison to use the "stepping wheel," a mill wheel driven by prisoners that was both a form of punishment and a source of cheap labor. In 1832 the city established the Department of Charities and Corrections, and in 1836 a penitentiary opened on Blackwell's Island, allowing the jail at Bellevue to become reserved for female inmates. The Hall of Justice, later known as the Tombs, was constructed in 1838, at which time the Bridewell was converted into the Hall of Records.

In 1824 a philanthropic organization called the Managers of the Society for the Reformation of Juvenile Delinquents in the City of New York opened the House of Refuge as a reform institution that would "prevent pau-

Prisoners on Blackwell's Island, ca *1885–90*

City jail, 1940

New York State Correctional Facilities in New York City

Arthurkill Correctional Facility
2911 Arthurkill Road
Staten Island, New York 10309
Capacity 930; male inmates; medium security

Edgecombe Correctional Facility
611 Edgecombe Avenue
New York, New York 10032
Capacity 270; male inmates; minimum security

Fulton Correctional Facility
1511 Fulton Avenue
Bronx, New York 10457
Capacity 239; male inmates; minimum security

Lincoln Correctional Facility
133 West 110th Street
New York, New York 10026
Capacity 188; male inmates; minimum security

Parkside Correctional Facility
10 Mount Morris Park West
New York, New York 10027
Capacity 60; female inmates; minimum security

Queensboro Correctional Facility
4704 Van Dam Street
Long Island City, New York 11101
Capacity 480; male inmates; minimum security

Facilities of the New York City Department of Correction

Anna M. Kross Center
18-18 Hazen Street
East Elmhurst, New York 11370
Opened 1978; capacity 2862; sentenced inmates, male

Bellevue Hospital Prison Ward
1st Avenue and 30th Street
New York, New York 10016
Male inmates

Bronx House of Detention for Men
653 River Street
Bronx, New York 10451
Opened 1938; capacity 469; detainees, male

Brooklyn Correctional Facility
136 Flushing Avenue
Brooklyn, New York 11205
Opened during Second World War as navy brig; capacity 1254; detainees and sentenced inmates

Brooklyn House of Detention for Men
175 Atlantic Avenue
Brooklyn, New York 11201
Opened 1957; capacity 815; detainees, male

Cape Vincent
Cape Vincent, New York
Opened 1988; capacity 742; sentenced inmates, male

Elmhurst Hospital Prison Ward
79-01 Broadway
Queens, New York 11201
Female inmates

Forbell Street (Rose M. Singer annex)
East Elmhurst, New York 11370
Opened 1989; capacity 192; detainees, female

George Motchan Detention Center for Men
15-15 Hazen Street
East Elmhurst, New York 11370
Opened 1971; capacity 2829; detainees, male

George R. Vierno Center
Rikers Island
Opened 1991; capacity 850; detainees, male

Goldwater Memorial Hospital, chronic care facility
Roosevelt Island

Hart Island
10-10 Hazen Street
East Elmhurst, New York 11370
Capacity 63; sentenced inmates, male

James A. Thomas Center for Men
14-14 Hazen Street
East Elmhurst, New York 11370
Opened 1933; capacity 1200; sentenced inmates, male

Kings County Hospital Prison Ward
A451 Clarkson Avenue
Brooklyn, New York 11203
Male inmates

(*continued*)

Facilities of the New York City Department of Correction (*Continued*)

Manhattan Detention Center
125 White Street
New York, New York 10013
Opened 1983; capacity 881; detainees, male

North Infirmary Command
14-14 Hazen Street
East Elmhurst, New York 11370
Opened 1932; capacity 498

Otis Bantum Correctional Facility
16-00 Hazen Street
East Elmhurst, New York 11370
Opened 1985; capacity 1529; male inmates

Queens House of Detention for Men
126-02 82nd Avenue
Kew Gardens, New York 11452
Opened 1961; capacity 502; detainees, male

Rikers Island Adolescent Reception Detention Center
11-11 Hazen Street
East Elmhurst, New York 11370
Opened 1972; capacity 2788; detainees, male

Rikers Island Correctional Institution for Men
10-10 Hazen Street
East Elmhurst, New York 11370
Opened 1964; capacity 2312; detainees and sentenced inmates, male

Riverview
Ogdensburg, New York
Opened 1988; capacity 742; sentenced inmates, male

Rose M. Singer Center
19-19 Hazen Street
East Elmhurst, New York 11370
Opened 1988; capacity 1628; detainees and sentenced inmates, female

Wards Island (Rose M. Singer annex)
Opened 1989; capacity 207; sentenced inmates, female

Local Lockup Facilities in New York City

Rikers Island Transportation Division
10-10 Hazen Street
East Elmhurst, New York 11370

Queens House of Detention for Men
126-02 82nd Avenue
Kew Gardens, New York 11452

Hart Island
10-10 Hazen Street
East Elmhurst, New York 11370

Rose M. Singer Correctional Facility
19-19 Hazen Street
East Elmhurst, New York 11370

New York Police Department, Central Booking
1 Police Plaza
New York, New York 10038

New York Police Department, Mid-Town North Precinct
306 West 54th Street
New York, New York 10019

New York Police Department, Mid-Town South Precinct
357 West 54th Street
New York, New York 10019

New York Police Department, Brooklyn Central Booking
301 Gold Street
Brooklyn, New York 11201

Elmhurst Hospital Prison Ward
79-01 Broadway
Queens, New York 11201

Kings County Hospital Prison Ward
451 Clarkson Avenue
Brooklyn, New York 11203

New York Police Department, Queens Central Booking
68-40 Austin Street
Queens, New York 11374

Bellevue Hospital Prison Ward
1st Avenue and 30th Street
New York, New York 10016

New York City Transit Police, District 11
161st Street and River Avenue
Bronx, New York 10451

New York City Transit Police, District 12
180th Street and Morris Park Avenue
Bronx, New York 10461

New York City Transit Police, District 20
Roosevelt Avenue
Jackson Heights, New York 11377

New York City Transit Police, District 23
116th Street
Far Rockaway, New York 11356

New York City Transit Police, District 30
Hoyt and Schermerhorn streets
Brooklyn, New York 11201

New York City Transit Police, District 32
Franklin Avenue and Eastern Parkway
Brooklyn, New York 11225

New York City Transit Police, District 33
Broadway Junction
Brooklyn, New York 11238

(*continued*)

Local Lockup Facilities in New York City (*Continued*)

New York City Transit Police, District 34
Stillwell Avenue and Mermaid Avenue
Brooklyn, New York 11223

perism and [the] committing of crime" by young men and women. Situated at Madison Square Park on the grounds of a former arsenal, this facility of four acres (1.6 hectares) consisted of remodeled army barracks and originally housed six girls and three boys who had been gathered by the police. The refuge was moved successively to the site of the Bellevue Fever Hospital (1839) and to a parcel of ten acres (four hectares) on Wards Island (1850) before being exchanged in 1851 for thirty acres (twelve hectares) of land on Randalls Island, where separate buildings were built for girls and boys. In 1884 the city acquired an island of eighty-seven acres (thirty-five hectares) in the East River from the Ryker family to use as a prison farm. A separate department of correction was formed in 1895 with jurisdiction over five prisons, nine jails, and three prison farms.

The city's largest jail facility is Rikers Island, which has eleven units and a combined capacity of more than sixteen thousand inmates. The city also operates detention facilities in each borough except Staten Island (combined capacity 3137), prison wards at Elmhurst, Kings County, and Bellevue hospitals, and a work camp on Hart Island. In 1987 the city acquired two ferry boats formerly used by the Staten Island Ferry and two British prison barges to accommodate its inmates, who largely because of drug offenses increased in number to about 21,000 in 1991, about twice as many as in 1980.

Charles Sutton: *The New York Tombs*, ed. James B. Mix and Samuel A. Mackeever (New York: United States Publishing, 1874; repr. with an introd. by Thomas M. McDade, Montclair, N.J.: Patterson Smith, 1973)

Ekram U. Hague: "New York City Department of Correction," *American Jails*, winter 1989

Joseph P. Viteritti

Jamaica. The largest and most densely populated neighborhood in central Queens. It was first inhabited by Jameco, or Yamecah, Indians, whose name means beaver in Algonquian; they lived on the northern shore of Jamaica Bay and along Beaver Stream and Beaver Pond (filled in 1906). English colonists from Massachusetts and eastern Long Island moved to the area in 1656 and secured a patent for the land from the Dutch government, which named the area Rustdorp (rest-town). It soon became the seat of Queens County; the court and the county clerk's office were established there, and executions were carried out around Beaver Pond. After the English took control in 1683 the area became the seat of the Town of Jamaica, which included all the land south of what are now the Interborough and Grand Central parkways. In the mid eighteenth century horse races were held around the pond. The area was heavily Tory during the American Revolution and was occupied from 1776 to 1783 by British troops, whose huts lay in the foothills north of Hillside Avenue. It was incorporated as a village in 1814. Rail service to New York City provided by the Long Island Rail Road began in 1836. A farmhouse owned by the Smith family was acquired by Rufus King, who built a mansion nearby (now known as King Manor) that became part of Kings Park; his son John Alsop King, elected governor of New York State in 1856, also lived there.

After the Civil War Jamaica grew rapidly: the population grew to 780 in 1875, 3922 in 1880,

6500 in 1898, and 58,200 in 1910. Horse car service began in 1866 and a line for the electric trolley opened in 1888. Development increased further after an elevated line was extended in 1918 along Jamaica Avenue; the low fare (five cents) enabled people to live there and work in the city. Jamaica Avenue became known throughout central Queens for its department stores, and between 1920 and 1940 parcels along the avenue between 160th and 168th streets had the highest relative assessed valuations in Queens County (in relation to their frontage). Among the notable structures on the avenue was Loew's Valencia (1929), a magnificent art deco movie palace now used as a church. The avenue was also the site of the first modern supermarket, King Kullen, opened by Michael J. Cullen in 1930. Connections to the rapid transit lines of Manhattan, Brooklyn, and the Bronx were provided by the Independent subway, which opened in Jamaica on 24 April 1937. By 1940 there were five theaters and one nightclub.

After the Second World War Jamaica gradually declined as young people moved to Nassau County. Stores lacking adequate parking lost customers to shopping malls in Elmhurst and other suburbs, and the two largest department stores, Macy's and Gertz, left the neighborhood. After 1960 the ethnic composition of the area changed rapidly, and by 1980 its population was predominantly black and Latin American. The Greater Jamaica Development Corporation was formed to plan several developments, including York College, an eleven-story office of the U.S. Social Security Administration, a pedestrian mall on 165th Street, a subway extension along Archer Avenue, and a farmers' market; it also planned the restoration of King Manor and its surrounding park. During the 1980s Jamaica attracted many immigrants, of whom one fifth were from Guyana and many of the rest from Haiti, China, India, Colombia, Jamaica, the Philippines, the Dominican Republic, and Pakistan.

Vincent Seyfried

Jamaica Bay. A shallow tidal wetland of about twenty square miles (fifty square kilometers) between Brooklyn and Queens, consisting of grassy marshes sheltered from the Atlantic Ocean by Rockaway Peninsula. It forms a large part of the Gateway National Recreation Area. Within it are dozens of islands, of which only the largest, Broad Channel, is inhabited. On the northern half of this island is the Jamaica Bay Wildlife Refuge, which has two freshwater ponds and a remarkable number of shorebirds and is the largest urban refuge in the United States built on landfill wholly within the boundaries of a city. Before the arrival of the Dutch the bay was a favorite fishing and hunting ground for the Canarsee and Rockaway Indians. It was sparsely settled until 1880, when the New York, Woodhaven and Rockaway Railroad built a wooden trestle five miles (eight kilometers) long across the bay to connect the Rockaways to the rest of Queens. The bay became increasingly polluted by expanding industry along the shores and by two sewers, one in Canarsie (1886) that drained New Lots and one in Jamaica (1914). In 1916 fishing and swimming were banned by the board of health, and all the summer resort hotels closed. The opening in the mid 1920s of the Cross Bay Boulevard made Broad Channel accessible to automobiles and further development. After a fire in 1950 destroyed the railroad trestle the Metropolitan Transportation Authority acquired the property and rebuilt the line, connecting it to the subway system in 1953. In the 1980s efforts to clean up the waters achieved considerable success.

The Future of Jamaica Bay (New York: Department of Parks, 1938)

Gerard R. Wolfe

Jamaica Estates. Neighborhood in east central Queens, bounded to the north by Union Turnpike, to the east by 188th Street, to the south by Hillside Avenue, and to the west by Home Lawn Street. It was a tract of 503 acres (two hundred hectares) bought by the Jamaica Estates Company in 1907 and developed beginning in April 1908; backers included Timothy L. Woodruff, the lieutenant governor of New York State and the chairman of the Republican State Committee; Michael J. Degnon, builder of the Belmont Tunnel and a contractor for the municipal subways; Edward Grant, the comptroller of the City of New York; and many bankers. The development was designed as a "residential park" in which the streets were laid out to fit the contours of the land and only detached, one-family houses with an attic and two stories were built; it also included an elegant entrance with a stone gatehouse on Hillside Avenue. During the next twenty years many houses occupying at least three lots were built, the least expensive costing $6000. Grand Central Parkway was laid out through Jamaica Estates in the 1920s but was landscaped to blend with the neighborhood. In December 1929 the deed restrictions expired and the Jamaica Estates Association was formed to preserve the character of the neighborhood; the only apartment buildings allowed were along Hillside Avenue. There are now about seventeen hundred houses of various styles, shaded by trees on eighty-eight square blocks. Many of the inhabitants are doctors, lawyers, and political figures.

Vincent Seyfried

Jamaica Hills. Neighborhood in east central Queens (1990 pop. 10,700), bounded to the north by the Grand Central Parkway, to the east by Jamaica Estates, to the south by Hillside Avenue, and to the west by Briarwood; it lies along a terminal moraine extending the length of Long Island. Named for its hilly terrain, the area was developed in the 1920s and 1930s after subway lines were extended to Jamaica. After 1965 the population became ethnically more diverse. Almost a quarter of the new immigrants who settled in the neighborhood and its environs in the 1980s were from Guyana; many others were from Jamaica, the Dominican Republic, Colombia, El Salvador, China, and Haiti. The housing in the neighborhood consists mostly of old one-family frame houses and newer two- and three-family attached brick houses. A few apartment buildings stand near Hillside Avenue. There are three public high schools: Hillcrest, Thomas Edison, and Jamaica. To the north of Jamaica Hills are Queens Hospital Center and St. John's University, to the south the main commercial section of Jamaica.

Andrew Sparberg

Jamaica Hospital. Nonprofit hospital in Jamaica at 89th Avenue near the Van Wyck Expressway, opened in a small house by a group of women in 1891 to provide emergency care for local residents. It added an operating room and several more wards in 1899, and an orthopedic clinic in 1916 in response to the polio epidemic. The hospital had no male board members until 1920. The growth in population that followed the opening of the subway along Jamaica Avenue led to the building of a new facility with 123 beds in 1924. From 1950 until the late 1970s the hospital underwent further expansion, adding dental services and a nursing home. A major program of renovation and new construction was initiated in 1987. Jamaica Hospital had 270 beds in 1989.

Sandra Opdycke

Jamaicans. The first period of Jamaican immigration to the United States on a large scale began shortly after 1900, reached its peak about 1920, and was curtailed by restrictive legislation in 1924. About fifty thousand Jamaicans settled in the United States during these years, most in New York City. Jamaicans maintained an important presence in Harlem in the 1920s; they included Marcus Garvey, the black nationalist leader of the Universal Negro Improvement Association, and the poet and novelist Claude McKay, a leading figure in the Harlem Renaissance. Amendments to the Immigration and Nationality Act in 1965 brought about a second and much larger influx: according to census figures the number of Jamaican immigrants in New York City increased from eleven thousand in 1960 to 113,000 in 1990. These figures are conservative, for they exclude undocumented immigrants (who are undercounted by the Bureau of the Census and variously estimated to make up 20 to 50 percent of all immigrants), and people of Jamaican origin who were born in the United States. In the 1980s Jamaicans constituted the second-largest group of new immigrants in New York City, and between 1982 and 1989 more than seventy thousand settled there.

Jamaicans who moved to New York City early in the century generally lived in Harlem and Bedford–Stuyvesant; later immigrants settled along with other English-speaking West Indians principally in central Brooklyn, especially in Crown Heights, Flatbush, and East Flatbush. Large numbers also settled in the northeastern Bronx (Williamsbridge and Wakefield) and southeastern Queens, especially Laurelton, Springfield Gardens, and St. Albans. In the late twentieth century Jamaicans continued to face racial discrimination in housing, education, and employment. They found work mainly in low-wage service and clerical positions: an overwhelming number of Jamaican women worked in the lower ranks of nursing and health care and in private households as child-care workers and attendants to the elderly, as well as in clerical, keypunch, and data entry positions; men often worked as taxi drivers, clerks, security guards, and janitors, and in factories and hospitals.

Jamaicans in New York City have tended to set themselves apart socially and culturally from American-born blacks. The national identity that they have striven to maintain has to some extent been subsumed by a larger West Indian identity, one perhaps made inevitable by a common linguistic and cultural background: with other English-speaking West Indians, Jamaicans often attend churches rather than form congregations of their own, belong to groups in the workplace and to neighborhood associations, take part in the West Indian carnival every Labor Day in Brooklyn, and read the *New York Carib News*, a weekly newspaper with a diverse readership that numbered 62,000 in 1986. There is no locally published Jamaican newspaper in New York City, although a regional edition of the *Jamaican Weekly Gleaner* intended for North America enjoys wide circulation.

Reggae and other forms of Jamaican popular music have earned a large following in the city and have strongly influenced rap music. Prominent New Yorkers of Jamaican origin include Colin L. Powell, appointed chairman of the U.S. Joint Chiefs of Staff in 1989, who was born to Jamaican parents and grew up in the Bronx; Una Clarke, born in Jamaica and elected to the City Council in 1991; and Nick Perry, elected to the state assembly in 1992.

Ira de A. Reid: *The Negro Immigrant: His Background, Characteristics and Social Adjustment, 1899–1937* (New York: Columbia University Press, 1939; repr. Arno, 1969)

Nancy Foner: "The Jamaicans: Race and Ethnicity among Migrants in New York City," *New Immigrants in New York* (New York: Columbia University Press, 1987)

Philip Kasinitz: *Caribbean New York: Black Immigrants and the Politics of Race* (Ithaca, N.Y.: Cornell University Press, 1992)

Nancy Foner

Jamaica Pass. Obsolete name of Broadway Junction.

Jamaica Racetrack. Thoroughbred racetrack in Queens, opened on 27 April 1903 by the Metropolitan Jockey Club with fifteen thousand persons in attendance. It had nine thousand grandstand seats, costing $2 each, as well as field space costing 75 cents. Access was mainly by the Long Island Rail Road and local trolley lines. The oval track, one mile (1.6 kilometers) in circumference, was well drained and very fast. Jamaica was the least prestigious track of its time: the ambience was rather modest, and the large crowds were raucous, loud, and loyal. The gate of 64,670 on Memorial Day 1945 was a state record. Facilities deteriorated over time and the track closed on 1 August 1959.

Steven A. Riess

James, Charles [Boucheron, Charles; James, C. Haweis; James, C(harles) B. H.; Boucheron] (*b* Sandhurst, England 1905/6; *d* New York City, 23 Sept 1978). Fashion designer. The son of a British army officer and an American mother, he began his career at the age of eighteen as a milliner in Chicago under the name Boucheron before moving to New York City in 1938 to design hats and dresses for his select clientele. Between 1929 and 1940 he moved freely between the United States and Europe, gaining inspiration from legendary designers such as Paul Poiret and Christian Dior. In 1940 he settled in New York City, where he opened a custom-order shop. His reputation as a daring and innovative designer attracted such influential and fashionable customers as Mrs. William Randolph Hearst Jr., and he also designed the salon of Elizabeth Arden. As his career progressed James's contentious and eccentric character destroyed many relationships, including that with Arden, and he spent years engaged in contractual disputes while his customers waited for their orders. He retired in 1958 to lecture at the Rhode Island School of Design and the Pratt Institute, and spent the last years of his life in the Chelsea Hotel. James is regarded as one of the greatest couturiers of the twentieth century for having successfully combined European classical tradition and American individualism. Many of his most renowned designs, including his "Taxi" dresses of the 1920s and 1930s and his grand ball dresses of the 1940s and 1950s, are now held at the Smithsonian Institution and the Fashion Institute of Technology.

Anne E. Kornblut

James, Henry(, Jr.) (*b* New York City, 15 April 1843; *d* London, 28 Feb 1916). Novelist. Born at 21 Washington Place (now the site of the main building of New York University), he lived briefly in Europe and in Albany, New York, before moving with his family to West 14th Street; he also spent much of his childhood at his grandmother's house (now 18 Washington Square North). James saw New York City as a bastion of gentility but also scorned its limitations and parochialism, and in 1855 he left for Europe. He visited only rarely in the following years, staying for about six months at 111 East 25th Street in 1875 and with Edith Wharton's sister-in-law at 21 East 11th Street in 1904. His autobiographical novel *Washington Square* (1881) is set at his grandmother's house before the Civil War and reflects his lasting affection for Washington Square, which he described as possessing "an established repose . . . the look of having had something of a social history." His collection of essays *The American Scene* (1907) criticizes the city after the Gilded Age as a "steel-souled machine room" symbolized by skyscrapers and the ostentation of the Waldorf–Astoria.

R. W. B. Lewis: *The Jameses: A Family Narrative* (New York: Farrar Straus Giroux, 1991)

Fred Kaplan: *Henry James: The Imagination of Genius: A Biography* (New York: William Morrow, 1992)

See also Literature, §1.

Jeff Finlay

James McCreery. Dry-goods shop opened in 1837. It catered to wealthy women and built its reputation on service and on its stock of imported fabrics and dress materials, particularly silk. Like other stores it moved uptown in stages: from Canal Street, to Broadway and 11th Street, to what became its most prestigious address, the southeast corner of West 23rd Street and 6th Avenue. For more than two decades its gleaming marble building marked the northern edge of the shopping district. By the end of the nineteenth century it was considered the most elegant establishment of its kind. When the shopping district moved farther uptown during the first decade of the twentieth century McCreery's moved to 34th Street; it ceased to be popular after the Second World War and closed in 1954.

A Bird's Eye View of Greater New York, and Its Most Magnificent Store (New York: Siegel–Cooper, 1898)

Elaine Abelson

J. and W. Seligman. Firm of investment advisors. It began operations on 1 May 1864 as a merchant banking firm with headquarters at 59 Exchange Place and branches in San Francisco, New Orleans, London, Frankfurt am Main, and Paris. The founders were eight brothers from a Bavarian Jewish family who emigrated to the United States between 1837 and 1842, worked as peddlers, shopkeepers, merchants, and importers, and during the Civil War supplied the Union Army with clothing and sold federal securities in Europe. The firm, which raised capital for the city, its transit system, the nation's railroads, and the Panama Canal, was for many years under the control of the family, the members of which were prominent civic leaders. After Joseph Seligman's death the firm was run successively by his brother Jesse Seligman and his son Isaac Newton Seligman. From 1907 to 1919 it was based at its own building at 1 William Street (later occupied by Lehman Brothers and then by Banca Commerciale Italiana). In 1937 the last partner belonging to the family retired and the firm developed a specialty in investment fund advisement. After a leveraged buyout in January 1989 control passed to a group led by William C. Morris, and in March 1991 the management announced the formation of Chou Trust and Seligman Company in New York City, a joint venture with the Chou Trust and Banking Company of Tokyo. In the mid 1990s Seligman had its headquarters at 1 Bankers Trust Plaza.

Ross L. Muir and Carle J. White: *Over the Long Term: The Story of J. & W. Seligman and Co.* (New York: J. and W. Seligman, 1964)

Stephen Birmingham: *Our Crowd: The Great Jewish Families of New York* (New York: Harper and Row, 1967)

Theresa Collins

Japanese. Japanese immigrants began to enter the United States in the last quarter of the nineteenth century. In New York City they constituted a small, fast-growing, urban, predominantly male, middle-class population; unlike the Japanese that emigrated to Hawaii and the western United States they were seldom laborers from the four agricultural prefectures of southwestern Japan. Available statistics on Japanese immigrants vary greatly according to their source: in this entry figures for the years 1890 to 1920 are those of the Japanese Association, and for later years those of the U.S. Bureau of the Census.

In 1876 six Japanese businessmen arrived in the city to establish trade between Japan and the United States in wholesale and retail goods (primarily silk). During the following twenty years small numbers of Japanese businessmen continued to enter the city and some became permanent residents, though large-scale Japanese immigration continued to be limited by American and Japanese efforts to restrict the entry of Japanese labor. In 1890–91 there were six hundred Japanese in the city, more than half of whom lived in Brooklyn and worked at the Brooklyn Navy Yard. In the mid 1890s the number of Japanese began to increase, rising to more than one thousand in 1900, and 90 percent were employed in domestic work. In 1897 the first Japanese newspaper, a short-lived weekly, was published by a Japanese college student in Brooklyn. As the number of Japanese grew, church and social groups arose to meet their needs. The Japanese Christian Institute (1899) was the first of several organizations that offered room and board to Japanese immigrants and businessmen, and in 1907 Toyohiko Campbell Takami formed the Japanese Mutual Aid Society, a community welfare group; from this evolved the Japanese Association of New York (1914), sponsored by the Japanese government, which in addition to offering support for Japanese immigrants kept track of their numbers (its totals often differing considerably from those of the federal census). A number of newspapers were launched during these years, including the *Japanese American Commercial Weekly*, *Nyuyoku jiho* (1904–10), and the semi-weekly *Nyuyoku shimpo* (from 1911 until the outbreak of the Second World War).

The naval directives of 1907 increased the regulations on alien employment and led the Brooklyn Navy Yard to discharge large numbers of Japanese workers. This caused much of the Japanese community to move to Manhattan in search of new employment: by 1909 most of the three thousand Japanese in the city resided there. In 1908 Japan and the United States reached a "gentlemen's agreement" concerning immigration: as a result Japan issued two types of passport (one for skilled or unskilled laborers, the other for nonlaborers such as students, merchants, businessmen, and professionals, who were required to have a middle school education or its equivalent), and all Japanese citizens in the United States were required to register at Japanese consular offices. During the first fifteen years of the twentieth century 75 percent of those registered at the city's Japanese consulate held passports for nonlaborers: of these nonlaborers a fifth were from urban areas. Passport records suggest that many Japanese who visited New York City on temporary visas as students or businessmen chose to remain in the city permanently, even though many failed to finish school or succeed at business. Although racism was not as violent as it was on the Pacific coast, many Japanese were consigned to work as laborers because of anti-Japanese sentiment. The Japanese population in the city was 4652 in 1920, and about 75 percent of the Japanese were domestic workers in 1921. Most of the rest worked at semiskilled or unskilled jobs in small businesses such as amusement concessions at Coney Island, and not in the productive sectors of the city's economy. The Japanese were isolated from white European immigrants and scattered in areas such as southern Manhattan, 123rd Street, and downtown Brooklyn; some lived on large estates on Long Island. During the period from 1924 to 1952 when the National Origins Act was enforced and Japanese emigrants were excluded from the United States, the Japanese population in the city hovered between 2500 and 2900.

After the outbreak of the Second World War in 1941 all Japanese organizations were forced to cease operations, and during the war a number of their leaders and Japanese businessmen were detained at Ellis Island. The population at large was not interned as it was on the west coast, but many immigrant businesses failed amid a general hostility toward the Japanese. In the years following the war the Japanese Association of New York, the Christian churches, and Buddhist temples were revived, and several new organizations were formed, such as the Japanese American Citizens League, Japanese American Help for the Aging, and the Japanese American United Church. The *Nyuyoku nichibei* was launched as a weekly newspaper with sections in Japanese and English. In 1950 the number of Japanese in the city increased to more than 3800 as Japanese–Americans who had been interned in concentration camps in the western United States resettled in the East, but many began to return to the west coast as soon as they were able. A new but small influx from Japan began after 1952 and strengthened in 1965 when the Immigration Act abolished quotas on Japanese immigration. The number of Japanese in the city stood at about fourteen thousand in 1970 and about 21,000 in 1980, of whom seventeen thousand were Japanese born. In 1990 the total population was 16,828, of which 12,837 were Japanese born. Although the number of Japanese immigrants in the city steadily increased during this period, it declined as a percentage of total Asian immigration.

Prominent Japanese in New York City have included the art critic Sadakichi Hartmann, the bacteriologist Hideyo Noguchi, the sculptor Isamu Noguchi, the chemist Jokichi Takamine, the ministers Ernest Atushi Ohori, Sojiro Shimizu, and Alfred Saburo Akamatsu, and the lawyers George Yamaoka and G. Gentoku Shimamoto.

T. Scott Miyakawa: "Early New York Issei: Founders of Japanese–American Trade," *East across the Pacific: Historical and Sociological Studies of Japanese Immigration*, ed. Hilary Conroy and T. Scott Miyakawa (Santa Barbara, Calif.: ABC–CLIO, 1972), 156–86

Haru M. Reischauer: *Samurai and Silk: A Japanese and American Heritage* (Cambridge: Harvard University Press, 1986)

Mitziko Sawada: *Dreams of Change: Urban Japanese Visions of "Amerika," 1890–1924* (Berkeley: University of California Press, forthcoming)

Mitziko Sawada

Japanese American Association. Community organization formed in 1914 as the Japanese Association of New York to support the welfare of Japanese in greater New York. Inspired by similar organizations formed in the western United States from 1909, it sought to fight racism, help Japanese immigrants in their dealings with government, and obtain financial support from Japan. The association had offices on West 44th Street and originally drew most of its members from the Japanese Mutual Aid Society. Until 1940 it conducted periodic censuses at the request of the Japanese consulate. The racial makeup and activities of the association caused it to be perpetually under surveillance by the Federal Bureau of Investigation from 1920 to 1942, and with the onset of the Second World War the government closed its offices and confiscated its files. The association was revived after the war under its current name and now has offices at 15 West 44th Street.

Mitziko Sawada

inaugurated the Belmont Stakes, which continued to be run there until 1890. Wishing to provide a new elegance to the sport of horse racing, he provided the track with facilities for trap shooting, sleighing, and ice skating. The track closed in 1889 to make room for the Jerome Park Reservoir, and the eastern half of the property was ultimately used as the site for De Witt Clinton High School, the Bronx High School of Science, Harris Park, Hunter College in the Bronx (now Lehman College), Walton High School, and a local elementary school. In 1917 the Kingsbridge Armory, one of the largest armories in the world, was built at Kingsbridge Road and Jerome Avenue. The residential area south of the reservoir and west of the armory consists mostly of five- and six-story apartment buildings constructed in the 1920s for Irish and Jewish families attracted by the Lexington Avenue line of Interborough Rapid Transit. In later years the neighborhood became increasingly Latin American. The buildings along Kingsbridge Road have shops and restaurants at street level.

Lloyd Ultan

Jerome Park Racetrack. Thoroughbred racetrack opened on 25 September 1866 by Leonard Jerome and the American Jockey Club on the Bathgate estate in Fordham. It was a fashionable, élite course, and its opening marked the revival of thoroughbred racing in the metropolitan area. The track occupied 230 acres (ninety-three hectares) and had outstanding facilities, including a clubhouse comparable to luxury hotels. Innovations included handicapping, claiming races, races for two-year-olds, and parimutuel betting. The track also popularized sprint races and staged annual stakes events, beginning with the Belmont Stakes in 1867. The track closed in 1889 to make way for a reservoir, temporarily reopening in 1891 for the races of the Monmouth Park (New Jersey) Racing Association.

Steven A. Riess

Jervis, John B(loomfield) (*b* Huntington, N.Y., 14 Dec 1795; *d* Rome, N.Y., 12 Jan 1885). Civil and mechanical engineer. He worked on the Erie Canal and the Delaware and Hudson Canal under Benjamin Wright and proposed the first segment of the Delaware and Hudson Railroad, from Honesdale to Carbondale, Pennsylvania. Later he was the chief engineer of the Mohawk and Hudson Railroad (1831–35); the Croton Aqueduct (1836–42), an important part of the water system of New York City; the Hudson River Railroad from Manhattan to Poughkeepsie, New York (1847–50); and the Michigan Southern Railroad and the Chicago and Rock Island Railroad (1851–61). Port Jervis, New York, is named for him.

Neal Fitzsimmons, ed.: *The Reminiscences of John B. Jervis: Engineer of the Old Croton* (Syracuse, N.Y.: Syracuse University Press, 1971)

F. Daniel Larkin: *John B. Jervis: An American Engineering Pioneer* (Ames: Iowa State University Press, 1990)

Arthur G. Adams

Jesup, Morris K(etchum) (*b* Westport, Conn., 21 June 1830; *d* New York City, 22 Jan 1908). Philanthropist. He moved to New York City about 1838 and became a banker as a young man; after retiring in 1884 he devoted himself to dozens of religious and cultural institutions in the city. Jesup was the president of many organizations including the YMCA (1872–75), the Five Points House of Industry (1873–1908), the New York City Mission and Tract Society (1881–1903), the AMERICAN MUSEUM OF NATURAL HISTORY (1881–1908), which greatly expanded its programs and physical plant during his tenure, and the New York State Chamber of Commerce (1899–1907). He lived at 197 Madison Avenue with his wife, Maria De Witt Jesup, who was also active in charity and reform work.

William Adams Brown: *Morris Ketchum Jesup: A Character Sketch* (New York: Charles Scribner's Sons, 1910)

Alana J. Erickson

jewelry. During the eighteenth century a few jewelers in New York City worked in small workshops and foundries, and by 1795 a small jewelry district took shape at Maiden Lane. A number of retail jewelers worked on lower Broadway in the first half of the nineteenth century, including Marquand and Paulding (now Black, Starr and Frost), Tiffany and Company, and later Starr and Marcus. Larger pieces of jewelry set with gemstones became popular after the Civil War, as the nation prospered and manufacturing techniques improved, and with the discovery of gold and silver in the West and diamonds in South Africa. Between 1860 and 1890 the value of jewelry production increased from \$2.5 million to \$5.6 million. The new fashions largely reflected European tastes. By the turn of the century platinum was widely used and jewelry in the Edwardian style was in great demand. The firms of E. M. Gattle, Theodore A. Kohn, Charlton, Dreicer, and Udall and Ballou flourished, and the French firm of Cartier opened a branch in New York City in 1909. Dreicer introduced new ways of cutting diamonds, and Raymond C. Yard, who had worked at Marcus and Company, the foremost American art nouveau jeweler, founded his own firm, which specialized in finely crafted jewelry with precious stones.

Electricity and new machinery enabled emerging manufacturing jewelers to keep up with the demand for fashionable platinum and diamond jewelry. Prominent manufacturing jewelers included Jacob Mehrlust, Walter P. McTeigue, the firm of Oscar Heyman Brothers, which produced jewelry for leading retailers, Julius Wodiska, an innovator in platinum jewelry, and William Scheer, a supplier of more than half the fine jewelry in the United States. The geometric configurations of Parisian art deco were highly influential in the 1920s, and in the 1930s gold jewelry set with large, colored gemstones was popularized by Paul Flato and his designer Fulco di Verdura, who formed his own company in 1939. The same year marked the opening of a branch of Van Cleef and Arpels in New York City and of the World's Fair, where Tiffany, Black, Starr and Frost–Gorham, Udall and Ballou, Marcus, and Cartier contributed displays at the House of Jewels. Exuberant, figural jewelry with colored gemstones was made in the 1940s by the independent jewelers David Webb, Seaman Schepps, and John Rubel, who made jewelry for Van Cleef and Arpels before opening his own business. Harry Winston specialized in large gemstones and exhibited such well-known items as the Jonker and Hope diamonds. In the 1950s marketing became the key for the survival of the retail jeweler. Branches opened throughout the country and abroad, appealing to a wide clientele, and houses such as Black, Starr and Frost were acquired by large conglomerates.

Penny Proddow and Debra Healy: *American Jewelry: Glamour and Tradition* (New York: Rizzoli, 1987)

Dorothy T. Rainwater: *American Jewelry Manufacturers* (West Chester, Penn.: Schiffer, 1988)

Janet Zapata

Jewett murder. A notorious crime committed in New York City on 10 April 1836. The victim was Helen Jewett (*b* Augusta, Maine, June 1813), a strikingly beautiful, charming, witty, and literate woman who read poetry and literary magazines, and who had worked for about a year as a prostitute on the city's streets. The crime was committed late at night with an axe in a brothel at 41 Thomas Street. Circumstantial evidence showed that Jewett's companion Richard P. Robinson, a nineteen-year-old shop clerk, was the murderer. Great public interest surrounded the sensational trial: some observers were outraged by the openness and extent of prostitution in the city, others found Robinson an appealing character. The state presented a weak case, and Robinson was acquitted.

John D. Lawson, ed.: *American State Trials* (St. Louis: F. H. Thomas, 1919), vol. 11, pp. 426–87

Marilynn Wood Hill: *Their Sisters' Keepers: Prostitution in New York City, 1830–1870* (Berkeley: University of California Press, 1993)

George A. Thompson, Jr.

Jewish Board of Guardians [Jewish Board of Family and Children's Services]. Volunteer agency formed on 23 April 1921 by the merger of the Jewish Prisoners Aid Society (1893), the Jewish Protectory and Aid (1902), Jewish Big Brothers (1907), and Jewish Big Sisters (1913) to combat juvenile delinquency. Some of its first facilities were the Lakeview Home for unwed mothers, donated by Mrs. Joseph Proskauer, and the Hawthorne–Cedar Knolls reform school, built by Jacob Schiff. During the 1920s the agency shifted its focus to educational improvement, and under Mortimer Schiff it built a summer camp. Camp therapy was introduced during the 1930s, and the Madeline Borg centers opened based on the "quick response" approach to crisis intervention. Under the direction of Doris Rosenberg in the mid 1990s the organization had six hundred volunteers working in eighty programs that accommodated more than 45,000 persons a year. Its offices are at 120 West 57th Street.

S. R. Slavson: *An Introduction to Group Therapy* (New York: Commonwealth, 1943)

George J. Lankevich

Jewish Child Care Association. The successor to the Hebrew Benevolent Association (1822), formed in 1942 by the merger of nineteen organizations dedicated to children's welfare, including an orphanage (1860) and the Hebrew Sheltering Guardian Society (1879). Under the direction of Mary Boretz from 1918 to 1945 it introduced foster home care and help for neglected children. In 1990 the association served 10,632 persons, offering day care, a kinship foster home program, adoption placement, and services to help Soviet Jews in adjusting to life in the city. The Jewish Child Care Association runs outpatient mental health clinics and the Pleasantville Cottage School, a residential treatment center for children. It has headquarters at 575 Lexington Avenue.

Norman M. Block: *Recidivism in Foster Care* (New York: Child Welfare League, 1983)

George J. Lankevich

Jewish Defense League. Organization formed in 1968 by a small group of Orthodox Jews led by Meir Kahane of Brooklyn. During its first two years it taught self-defense and organized street patrols and neighborhood watches. The league became an advocate for Soviet Jews and by 1972 called for large-scale emigration to Israel of Soviet Jews. It also took a militant stance on Israeli defense and toward Palestinian refugees. A harsh critic of moderate Jews, it remained a marginal group.

Janet L. Dolgin: *Jewish Identity and the Jewish Defense League* (Princeton, N.J.: Princeton University Press, 1977)

Michael N. Dobkowski

Jewish education. Members of the small Jewish community in New Amsterdam were allowed to practice their religion and educate their children only at home. The first Jewish school was opened in 1731 by Shearith Israel, the city's first synagogue, which in 1755 opened a "publik school" to teach Hebrew and secular subjects; the school survived until the American Revolution and was reorganized in 1808 as the Polonies Talmud Torah Day School and in 1821 as a supplementary school that held classes in the afternoon. When many Ashkenazim moved to the city from central Europe in the mid nineteenth century, day schools were founded by several congregations including B'nai Jeshurun (1842), Ansche Chesed, Rodeph Sholem, and Sha'arei Hashamayim. Many Jewish parents placed their children in the public schools after changes in state laws severely limited Protestant influence in public education. A few congregational schools survived into the 1850s, but by 1860 all had closed. Parents remained committed to public schooling for more than a century, and Jewish education was offered largely in afternoon or Sunday schools. The 1880s saw an influx of eastern European Jews who were mostly Orthodox. They organized schools for basic religious instruction called *chedarim*, which thrived on the Lower East Side: there were hundreds by 1890, holding classes in the late afternoon after the public school session. The first religious secondary school in the city was Machazikai Talmud Torah (1883), the first yeshiva Etz Chaim (1886).

Such organizations as the Hebrew Free School Society (1865) and the Educational Alliance (1889), formed by Jews who had long lived in the city, sponsored training for the children of eastern European immigrants that was designed to provide religious instruction, counter the efforts of Christian missionaries, and hasten assimilation. By 1917 there were 277,000 Jewish children enrolled in public schools and fewer than a thousand in Jewish day schools, and less than a quarter of school-aged Jewish children received religious instruction. The Bureau of Jewish Education (1910) was formed by the Kehillah of New York (1909) and led by Samson Benderly, who with Mordecai Kaplan devised a modern Jewish curriculum to complement the offerings of the public school. Talmud Torah schools were based on modern pedagogical principles and introduced a new kind of religious and cultural education. From 1910 into the 1920s secular Jewish groups such as the Workmen's Circle established Yiddish-language schools; a few continued into the 1990s. From the 1920s increasingly the responsibility for Jewish education shifted from Talmud Torahs to congregations, which provided their own schools (most supplemental) and educational programs in Reform, Conservative, and Orthodox Judaism. Between the world wars a number of Orthodox day schools opened that became well known, including the Ramaz Academy, the Manhattan Day School, the Yeshiva of Flatbush, and several schools affiliated with Yeshiva University.

Many day schools were founded after the Second World War, especially by Hasidim and other strictly Orthodox sects. In the early 1990s about 131,000 children were enrolled in Jewish schools in the city: nearly 57 percent attended day schools, 39 percent supplementary schools, and 4 percent nursery schools.

Alexander M. Dushkin: *Jewish Education in New York City* (New York: Bureau of Jewish Education, 1918)

Judah Pilch, ed.: *A History of Jewish Education in America* (New York: National Curriculum Research Institute of the American Association for Jewish Education, 1969)

Stephan F. Brumberg: *Going to America, Going to School: The Jewish Immigrant Public School Encounter in Turn-of-the-Century New York City* (New York: Praeger, 1986)

Stephan F. Brumberg

Jewish Guild for the Blind. Charitable organization serving the blind and the visually impaired, as well as those with other disabilities. It was formed in 1914 as the New York Guild for the Jewish Blind to provide care and support for the Jewish blind, who were read to and received instruction in Braille in their homes. The organization opened a home for poor Jewish children in 1919 in Yonkers, New York, and later added residential services there for adults. In 1923 it moved to its own building in New York City at 172 East 96th Street; by this time it offered programs in sports, music, and handicrafts. The guild moved in 1944 to larger quarters at 1880 Broadway. After the Second World War it expanded its rehabilitative, social, educational, recreational, and medical services for the blind and also added programs for the multiply disabled. The Guild School for children and teenagers with visual, developmental, psychiatric, and orthopedic disabilities opened in 1951. After the guild began offering services to people of all faiths it adopted its current name in 1960 and in the following year opened the first psychiatric clinic in the country specializing in problems of blindness. It moved to a building at 15 West 65th Street in 1971.

Sandra Opdycke

Jewish Institute of Religion. Rabbinical and cantorial school founded in 1922 next to the Free Synagogue at 30 West 68th Street by Stephen S. Wise to train Reform rabbis and promote research and community service. It emphasized free inquiry, social reform, and Zionism and under Wise's direction launched the *Jewish Institute Quarterly* (1924–30) to report on social issues. Financial difficulties led Wise to negotiate a merger in 1950 with Hebrew Union College in Cincinnati, forming Hebrew union college–jewish institute of religion.

George J. Lankevich

Jewish Labor Committee. Organization formed on 25 February 1934 in New York City to represent Jewish workers. Initially it focused on rescue efforts and resistance to the Nazis in Europe. In the 1940s it joined with B'nai B'rith, the American Jewish Committee, and the American Jewish Congress to become an important Jewish defense organization. After the 1950s it became active in a wide range of concerns including civil and human rights, social justice, efforts to end the oppression of Soviet Jews, labor politics in Israel, and cultural activities. The Jewish Labor Committee is known for its liberal, secular views.

Samuel Halperin: *The Political World of American Zionism* (Detroit: Wayne State University Press, 1961)

Michael N. Dobkowski

Jewish Museum. Museum at 1109 5th Avenue in Manhattan, formed in 1904 by a gift of books and ceremonial objects to the Jewish Theological Seminary by Judge Meyer Sulzberger. On 8 May 1947 it moved into its current site, formerly the mansion of Felix M. Warburg. The museum expanded to an adjacent building in 1963 and renovated its entire facilities in 1993. The Jewish Museum is the largest and most comprehensive institution of its kind in the world. Its permanent collection includes more than 27,000 paintings, sculptures, drawings, photographs, artifacts, ceremonial objects, and other items documenting four thousand years of Jewish life and culture.

Jewish Theological Seminary. Seminary opened by Sabbato Morais (1823–97) in 1887 on West 19th Street to train Conservative rabbis and preserve traditional Judaism in the United States. It foundered when only eight students enrolled (one of whom became the chief rabbi of the British Empire), and after a reorganization it moved in 1902 to quarters at 531 West 123rd Street donated by Jacob Schiff. Its new president was Solomon Schechter, a leading scholar and rabbi from Europe who engaged Mordecai Kaplan to set up a teacher's institute (1909), promoted Zionism, and established the United Synagogue of America (1913). The seminary attracted some of the best faculty in the world, established a rigorous curriculum, and inspired its students to see Judaism as an "evolving religious civilization" with important ties to the United States. During Cyrus Adler's tenure as president (1915–40) the library was expanded and a museum of ceremonial objects opened in 1929 (later moved to the Jewish Museum). In 1930 the seminary moved to a building at 3080 Broadway designed by the firm of Gehron, Ross, Ashley. Under Louis Finkelstein (1940–72) it became known internationally, introduced interfaith study, and opened an institute for training cantors (1952) and a graduate division (1969). The library, which contained seventy thousand volumes, was destroyed in a fire in 1966; a new one was dedicated in 1983. As chancellor (1972–86) Gerson Cohen admitted women as candidates for ordination and strengthened ties to Israel. A national center of Conservative Judaism, Jewish Theological Seminary has a hundred faculty members and six hundred students.

Elliot N. Dorff: *A Living Tree: The Roots and Growth of Jewish Law* (Albany: State University of New York Press, 1988)

George J. Lankevich

Jews. The first Jews in New York City were twenty-three Sephardic refugees from Brazil who moved to the city in September 1654 and were granted asylum despite the protests of Governor Peter Stuyvesant. During the same year the first Jewish congregation in the country, Shearith Israel, was formed. The congregation prayed in private quarters; it built its first synagogue building in 1730 on Mill Street just south of Wall Street and was modeled in the Sephardic traditions in Amsterdam. In 1818 the synagogue on Mill Street was expanded. The congregation then erected buildings on Crosby Street (1834) and 19th Street (1860) before moving in 1897 to a new building at 70th Street and Central Park West. The city had the largest Jewish community in the colonies. Most Jews in New York City were patriots and many served in the Continental Army during the American Revolution. Because of the British occupation many fled to Philadelphia, which briefly had the largest Jewish community in the colonies. Jews accounted for 1 percent of the national population in 1789, when Gershom Mendes Seixas of Shearith Israel took part in President Washington's inauguration with fifteen Christian religious leaders. During the eighteenth and nineteenth centuries most Jews moving to the United States were Ashkenazim, and most settled in New York City. Congregation B'nai Jeshurun was formed by Ashkenazi immigrants in 1825. About this time Mordecai Manuel Noah was appointed high sheriff of New York City; he became well known as a proponent of a plan called Ararat to resettle oppressed Jews from overseas in northern New York State. The fraternal organization the Independent Order of B'nai B'rith was formed in 1843 on Essex Street on the Lower East Side.

In 1850 nearly one third of the fifty thousand Jews in the United States lived in New York City. Most had fled deprivation and persecution in Germany and other countries of central Europe; many were peddlers, storekeepers, craftsmen, and laborers, and some eventually became wealthy manufacturers and financiers. In 1850 there were fifteen synagogues of different groups. By 1859 there were twenty-seven, as well as forty fraternal organizations for education and mutual aid. The Jews' Hospital opened in 1852 (renamed Mount Sinai Hospital in 1866). Several Jewish newspapers were printed in the city, including the *Asmonean* (1849–58), the *Jewish Messenger* (1857–1902), and the *Hebrew Leader* (1859–74). Distributed throughout the country, these publications informed readers of the activities and opinions of religious and political

Congregation Orach Chaim, 1459 Lexington Avenue, near 95th Street

figures in the city and also provided a forum for protesting the mistreatment overseas of Jews such as Edgar Mortara, an Italian child abducted in 1859 by papal authorities. Several Jewish figures in the city gained national reputations through the newspapers; among the most notable were Jacques Judah Lyons, Isaac Bondy, Samuel Isaacs, Morris Raphall, Samuel Adler, Sampson Simson, and Henry Hendricks.

As frequent proponents of acculturation, German Jewish immigrants and their children adapted their religious practices to blend with American life, and until 1880 they controlled most congregations in the city. Reform Judaism predominated, although there were also some traditional synagogues. Temple Emanuel, Temple Rodef Sholom, Temple Anshe Chesed, Congregation Orach Chaim, Shearith Israel, and B'nai Jeshurun were among the most important synagogues uptown. During the late nineteenth century a wealthy Jewish élite took shape. Among its members were Jacob Schiff, Isidor Straus, Nathan Straus, Oscar Straus, Adolph Lewisohn, Louis Marshall, Felix Warburg, and the financier Joseph Seligman, a confidant of President Ulysses S. Grant. The views, exploits, and foibles of the group were reported in the *Jewish Times* (1869–78), the *American Hebrew* (1879–1950), and the *Jewish Herald* (1881–84).

Between 1880 and 1910 about 1.4 million Jews fleeing pogroms and economic discrimination in eastern Europe moved to the city. About 1.1 million stayed, and by 1910 Jews accounted for almost a quarter of the city's population. Between 1880 and 1890 three of four Jewish immigrants, or about sixty thousand altogether, settled on the Lower East

Side, where most lived in overcrowded, dumbbell, walk-up tenements of five stories each. Initially many immigrants were peddlers or found work in the garment and tobacco industries or in construction. By 1890 Jews from eastern Europe were the largest group and eastern European Orthodoxy predominated. Many eastern European Jews worshipped in *landsmanshaft* synagogues, transitory congregations established by immigrants from the same town seeking to preserve their traditions. As late as 1917 most Jews in the city worshipped in about eight hundred small synagogues formed by immigrants. Eventually a number of these congregations prospered and adapted to American life. A few of the best-known synagogues on the Lower East Side were Beth Hamidrash Hagadol (Norfolk Street), Kehal Adath Jeshurun (Eldridge Street), Ohab Zedek Congregation (Norfolk Street), and the First Roumanian–American Congregation (Rivington Street). During the first quarter of the twentieth century about 37,000 Sephardim moved to the city. Most were from Turkey and the Balkan countries and spoke Judeo-Spanish; there were some from Greece and others who spoke Judeo-Arabic and were mostly from Syria. They settled on the Lower East Side, where they formed support groups along with religious institutions patterned on those in their native cities; they also sponsored Judeo-Spanish theater and newspapers, among them *La America* and *La Vara*.

Rabbis from eastern Europe were dismayed at their lack of control over many aspects of religious life and at the difficulty of preserving Orthodoxy. Disaffection was particularly marked among the children of immigrants, who were educated in the United States and overwhelmingly repudiated the religious life of their elders. Many Jews wished to maintain a kosher diet, but there was no authority for inspecting kosher foods. To address these problems the Association of the American Orthodox Congregations was formed in 1887 and undertook a search for a highly respected rabbi to lead the older generation back to the Torah, inspire the younger generation to maintain the faith, and introduce order into the kosher food industry, which was often corrupt. In the same year Jacob Joseph of Vilna (Lithuania) accepted the post, which he retained until his death in July 1902. His efforts ultimately failed because many immigrants found American life appealing, and also because he lacked ecclesiastical authority to enforce his edicts. Within a week of his death the Union of Orthodox Rabbis of the United States and Canada was formed to continue his efforts. During Joseph's career a group of more acculturated Orthodox Jews addressed the problems of religious disaffection by integrating Jewish traditions into modern life. At the Talmud Torah, or communal afternoon school, they used the pedagogic methods of John Dewey to present the teachings of Moses and Israel; they also organized synagogues for a generation that spoke both Yiddish and English and had modern and traditional concerns. Many such congregations were organized by the Jewish Endeavor Society in the first decade of the century and by Young Israel after 1910. Mordecai Kaplan, a young rabbi, worked in both groups and later led the Reconstructionist movement. These experiments in integrating Judaism into American life soon became models for Conservative, modern Orthodox, and Reform synagogues throughout the country. The various groups cooperated closely with the Jewish Theological Seminary and the Union of Orthodox Jewish Congregations, a traditional organization in upper Manhattan, and Schiff and Marshall offered financial support to traditional groups if they agreed to promote Judaism in the most American manner. These alliances eventually led to the formation in 1909 of the Kehillah by German Jews in response to allegations by Thomas Bingham, the police commissioner, of widespread crime among Jewish immigrants. The group included immigrants and the German Jewish élite and eventually addressed not only criminality but anti-Semitism, philanthropy, Jewish education, and employment; it also attempted to supervise more closely the production of kosher foods.

The influx of poor Jews and Italians caused social tension in the city. Many reports studied health, housing, education, employment, crime, and mortality in Jewish neighborhoods, with the conclusion that overcrowding had to be eliminated. To this end recommendations were made to build the Brooklyn, Manhattan, and Williamsburg bridges, to set aside land for public parks, and to provide better housing. The work of such social reformers as Hutchins Hapgood, Norman Hapgood, Lincoln Steffens, and Jacob A. Riis helped to ensure that the recommendations were carried out, even though Riis and other reformers doubted whether Jews were committed to assimilation. Many people considered Jewish immigrants a threat to American culture, and there was an increasing number of outspoken critics of unrestricted immigration, among them Madison Grant. Partly because they feared for their own position in the city, leaders among German Jews were troubled by these events and in 1901 formed the Industrial Removal Office, which resettled sixty thousand Jews in other parts of the United States during the next decade. For those remaining in the city they developed a network of social welfare organizations to encourage assimilation: the United Hebrew Charities was their advocate on Ellis Island; the Hebrew Technical Institute, the Young Women's Hebrew Association, and settlement houses like the Educational Alliance urged them to abandon their culture, learn English, and be productive workers. Radicals also sought to attract immigrants. Many Jewish neighborhoods had a strong socialist culture rooted partly in traditions of European radicalism and partly in immigrants' anger at their exploitation in the United States. The best-known socialist newspaper, the Yiddish-language *Vorwert*, was instrumental in spreading socialism even as its editor, Abraham Cahan, worked to assimilate immigrants. The Arbeiter Ring, a socialist fraternal organization formed in 1892, was vital to the development and survival of radicalism.

By the turn of the century German Jews such as men of the Straus family were well established in politics. As a Russian–Polish enclave took shape on the Lower East Side and the Jewish population grew, Jews became a recognized force in politics, known for being independent voters. In presidential elections between 1888 and 1912 no party won the eighth assembly district in downtown Manhattan twice in a row. By the turn of the century Jewish votes were sought by Republicans supporting Theodore Roosevelt and by Democrats in Tammany Hall, who had often opposed Jews' efforts to gain access to political power and the city's payroll. In 1900 Henry Goldfogle, a resident of the Lower East Side chosen by Tammany Hall, became the first Jewish congressman to represent the area. Socialism flourished as Jewish labor unions became powerful, especially after 1900, when the International Ladies' Garment Workers' Union, the Amalgamated Clothing Workers, and the United Hebrew Trades developed a large membership among Jewish workers. After 1900 there was an influx of young immigrants more ideologically committed to socialism. Efforts at organizing unions about this time were marked by violence and divisive strikes, but in 1910 Jewish unionists and their bosses set a precedent for collective bargaining in the United States when with the aid of Schiff, Marshall, and Louis D. Brandeis they fashioned the "protocol of peace" that ended a massive strike by cloakmakers. In 1904 Moritz Graubard was elected to the state assembly on the Republican ticket; in 1906 Samuel Koenig, a Hungarian Jew, was elected secretary of state of New York as a Republican. Despite popular support for radical causes few radicals were elected to government, largely because of divisions between the American Socialist and Socialist Labor parties. The American Socialist Party lost the votes of Jewish immigrants because of its stance against unrestricted immigration, and it was not until 1914 that Meyer London, who repudiated his party's platform on immigration, capitalized on temporary disaffection with Tammany Hall to become the first Socialist congressman from the Lower East

Side. Many immigrants lost sympathy for radicalism during the seven years that they were required to maintain residency before qualifying to vote. Jewish socialists nonetheless continued to have a profound impact on city politics and the Jewish community through unions, newspapers, and scores of cultural and recreational organizations.

Even before the First World War Jews began leaving the crumbling Lower East Side for Yorkville, central Harlem, Williamsburg, and Brownsville. When the Lower East Side could no longer accommodate more people, poorer Jews moved to cramped quarters in East Harlem. By the time of the First World War there were more than 100,000 Jews in each of the new neighborhoods and 325,000 on the Lower East Side, where some blocks had a density of one thousand persons an acre (2500 persons a hectare). After the Bolshevik Revolution and the formation of the American Communist Party rifts developed between communists, socialists, liberals, and social democrats in the city, which became a national center of radical politics. Jews accounted for nearly 30 percent of the city's total population in 1920, the highest percentage until that time and for decades after. By the 1920s the focus of Jewish life in the city had shifted from the Lower East Side to neighborhoods in upper Manhattan, Brooklyn, the Bronx, and Queens; these neighborhoods ranged from upper middle class to working class and until the 1950s included the Grand Concourse, Fordham, Tremont, Morrisania, Jamaica, Astoria, Jackson Heights, and the Rockaways. Although the Kehillah was dismantled in 1922 its founding principal of blending Judaism into American life continued to influence Jewish educators and community workers, and the Bureau of Jewish Education and the New York Federation of Jewish Philanthropies (both formed under its auspices) remained in operation. Prosperous Sephardim often moved to Harlem, the Grand Concourse, and New Lots, and eventually there were Sephardic neighborhoods in Bensonhurst, Flatbush, and Forest Hills. Washington Heights, largely Jewish from the 1930s, attracted German Jewish refugees during the Second World War.

Although the children of Jewish immigrants suffered during the Depression many became prominent in the city in the garment industry. Vaudeville performers like Sophie Tucker, Groucho Marx, and George Burns became well known in radio, motion pictures, and television. A community of intellectuals included such scholars as Irving Howe and Alfred Kazin. Students were often radicals who joined the Socialist Party, Communist Party, and smaller splinter groups, or solid supporters of the Democratic Party, Mayor Fiorello H. La Guardia, and the New Deal. After the war a large number from this generation moved to the suburbs, but in doing so they only slightly decreased the Jewish population of the city. Many who stayed were committed to the city's middle class through their work as teachers, social workers, small businessmen, and professionals. At the same time the Union of Orthodox Rabbis became powerful as Hasidic refugees and survivors of the Holocaust supported their efforts to keep old-world traditions intact.

Beginning in the 1960s Sephardim moved to the city from North Africa and the Middle East, especially Morocco and Egypt. The 1960s and 1970s saw the transformation of Jewish neighborhoods and of ideas that had defined Jewish life in the city. The population of established Jewish neighborhoods in the Bronx and Brooklyn decreased as the inhabitants died or moved. Liberal politics became more divided as blacks and Latin Americans came into conflict with Jews over the distribution of political power. One of the bitterest conflicts was a public school strike in 1968 that pitted the United Federation of Teachers, which was heavily Jewish, against black advocates of community control of schools: the strike ended in a limited victory for the advocates of community control, and along with debates over affirmative action and support for Israel it influenced many formerly liberal Jews to embrace conservatism. They supported Edward I. Koch, a formerly liberal congressman from Greenwich Village who won the mayoralty in 1977 partly by pledging his support for the death penalty. Such political shifts and the rise of the violent and ultraconservative Jewish Defense League led many to conclude that Jews were abandoning radicalism and liberalism, an issue widely debated in the city. In the late 1980s New York City continued to have more Jews than any other city in the world: about 1.13 million, or 16 percent of the total population.

Many Jews moved to the city in the 1980s from the Soviet Union, Israel, Iran, and Arab countries. By the end of the decade Manhattan was the headquarters of more than a hundred Jewish organizations with various purposes — cultural, religious, community, and Zionist. Although Republicans aggressively sought their allegiance, Jews in the city remained loyal to the Democratic Party in the 1980s. About 70 percent voted for the Democratic candidate Michael S. Dukakis in the presidential election of 1988, despite their uneasiness about the role in Democratic politics of Jesse Jackson, who was widely criticized for having made remarks considered disparaging toward Jews in 1984 when he believed he was speaking off the record. In the mayoral election of 1989 only about 40 percent voted for the Democratic candidate David N. Dinkins, perhaps in part because of his political closeness to Jackson; this was nonetheless a higher figure than for any ethnic group in the city other than blacks and Latin Americans.

The Jewish population of the city remained roughly 1.13 million in 1990. About 420,000 Jews lived in Brooklyn, most in the neighborhoods of Borough Park, Bensonhurst, Flatbush, Sheepshead Bay, Canarsie, and Midwood (which included a large concentration of Syrian Jews). An influx of Jews from the Soviet Union increased the Jewish populations of Brighton Beach and Manhattan Beach, and Jewish enclaves were also formed in Park Slope and Brooklyn Heights by those working nearby in the business and financial districts of Manhattan. A large Hasidic population remained in Williamsburg. Most of the 321,000 Jews in Queens lived in Forest Hills and Kew Gardens; Flushing, Kew Garden Hills, and Hillcrest grew substantially, but older neighborhoods like Jamaica, Astoria, Jackson Heights, and the Rockaways declined. About 275,000 Jews lived in Manhattan, nearly half on the Upper West Side and Upper East Side; there were between 25,000 and thirty thousand on the Lower East Side and a large number in Washington Heights. Of the 85,000 Jews in the Bronx most lived in the growing neighborhoods of Riverdale, Van Cortlandt, and Kingsbridge; there were also many Jews in Co-op City and the neighborhoods along Pelham Parkway, but few remained in the Grand Concourse, Fordham, Tremont, and Morrisania. About 31,000 Jews lived in Staten Island, many in large enclaves near Richmond Avenue and Victory Boulevard.

Most Jews in New York City are third- and fourth-generation Americans who are solidly middle class and better educated than members of other groups: a survey taken in 1984 showed that a third of Jewish households had an annual income of more than $40,000, and that the heads of half the households had four or more years of higher education. Fewer Jews in the city marry outside their faith than in other parts of the United States: in 1984 the figure was about 5 to 9 percent among the children and grandchildren of Jewish immigrants, 16 percent among later generations. Many are somewhat uncertain about the tradition among Jews of support for liberal causes and the Democratic Party. A good number do not maintain a strong connection to the Jewish community, and in 1984 more than 40 percent of heads of households in Manhattan reportedly never attended synagogue. For those who are practicing, especially Orthodox Jews, the city has more facilities for Jewish communal living than any other place outside Israel, and many Jews are attracted to neighborhoods in Brooklyn, the Bronx, Queens, and Staten Island by their many synagogues, schools, ritual baths, and food stores. Most international and national Jewish organizations have their headquarters in the city, including the American Jewish Committee, the American Jewish Congress, the World Jewish Congress, and the Anti-Defamation League of B'nai B'rith, which lie within walking distance of one another on the Upper East Side; nearby are several Zionist organizations with various aims, including the United Jewish Appeal, Israel Bonds, Hadassah, and the Jewish National Fund. The city also has several facilities for training American rabbis: a branch of the Hebrew Union College–Jewish Institute of Religion (Reform) in Greenwich Village, the Jewish Theological Seminary (Conservative) in Morningside Heights, and the Rabbi Isaac Elchanan Theological Seminary of Yeshiva University (Orthodox) in Washington Heights. Hasidic yeshivas and others espousing more traditional forms of Orthodoxy are found mostly in Jewish sections of Brooklyn and Queens.

Hyman B. Grinstein: *The Rise of the Jewish Community of New York, 1654–1860* (Philadelphia: Jewish Publication Society of America, 1945)
Moses Rischin: *The Promised City: New York's Jews, 1870–1914* (Cambridge: Harvard University Press, 1962)
Irving Howe: *World of Our Fathers* (New York: Harcourt Brace Jovanovich, 1975)
Deborah Dash Moore: *At Home in America: Second Generation New York Jews* (New York: Columbia University Press, 1981)
Marc D. Angel: *La America: The Sephardic Experience in the United States* (Philadelphia: Jewish Publication Society, 1982)

Marc D. Angel, Jeffrey S. Gurock

JFK International Airport. See John F. Kennedy International Airport.

J. Levine Company. Bookstore at 5 West 30th Street in Manhattan, between 5th Avenue and Broadway. A family business for four generations, it moved to the Lower East Side from Lithuania in 1905. The business was once the largest manufacturer of Torah covers and Ark curtains in the United States and remains the country's largest retailer of Jewish books and Judaica.

Kenneth T. Jackson

J. M. Kaplan Fund. Charitable organization formed in 1945 by Jacob M. Kaplan (*b* 23 Dec 1891; *d* 18 July 1987), founder of the Welch Grape Juice Company and its owner from 1940 to 1958. Kaplan led the fund until 1977, when he was succeeded by his daughter, Joan K. Davidson. The fund donates exclusively to projects in New York State. In New York City it has been active in the arts, landmark preservation, social welfare, parks beautification, and civil liberties. It took part in the successful effort to save Carnegie Hall in 1960 and in the development of South Street Seaport, and has supported such organizations as the J. M. Kaplan Center for New York City Affairs at the New School for Social Research, Westbeth Artists' Housing, Mobilization for Youth (on the Lower East Side), the Association for Union Democracy, the Green Guerillas, and the Coalition for the Homeless. It has also supported greenmarkets in the city, the revitalization of 42nd Street, various clothing drives, and museum exhibitions. In 1990 the foundation had assets of $86.1 million and made grants totaling $6.3 million.

Kenneth W. Rose

Joffrey, Robert [Kahn, Anver Bey Abdullah Jaffa; Joffrey, Anver] (*b* Seattle, 24 Dec 1928; *d* New York City, 25 March 1988). Dancer and choreographer. He trained with Mary Ann Wells before moving in 1949 to New York City, where he studied ballet and modern dance and taught at the High School of the Performing Arts (1950–55). In 1952 he began providing choreography for ballets, galas, industrial shows, musicals, and operas (for the National Broadcasting Company and the New York City Opera) and in the following year he formed the American Ballet Center (now the Joffrey Ballet School). His first company, the Robert Joffrey Theatre Ballet, which began touring on 2 October 1956 with six dancers, grew slowly until it obtained support in 1962 from Rebekah Harkness for expansion, workshops, and international tours, but in 1964 she took over the company contracts to organize the Harkness Ballet. With Gerald Arpino (*b* Staten Island, 14 Jan 1923) Joffrey formed the Robert Joffrey Ballet in 1965; in the following years he increasingly devoted himself to administration while Arpino took over much of the choreography, which became characterized by athleticism and eroticism. The company stressed ballets intended to appeal to youth, including Joffrey's *Astarte* (1967), which was backed by a rock score and used innovative film technology; Arpino's sleek, ritualistic work *Trinity* (1971); and Twyla Tharp's first ballet, *Deuce Coupe* (1973). It also offered revivals of modern classics by Kurt Jooss (*The Green Table*), George Balanchine, Léonide Massine (*Parade*), Frederick Ashton, Bronislava Nijinska, and Vaslav Nijinsky, notably *Le Sacre du printemps* (1987). Although financial problems limited new productions and the size of the company, Joffrey encouraged experimental choreographers like Tharp, Oscar Araiz, and Laura Dean. In 1966 the company took up residence at the City Center; a small training company called Joffrey II was formed in 1970 and an affiliate was set up in Los Angeles in 1983.

Richard Philip and Mary Whitney: *Danseur: The Male in Ballet* (New York: McGraw–Hill, 1977)
Mary Whitney: *The Joffrey Ballet XXV, Celebrating 25 Years of the Joffrey Ballet from A to Z* (Greenwich, Conn.: Steelograph, 1981) [souvenir program]
George Dorris: "The Choreography of Robert Joffrey," *Dance Chronicle* 12 (1989), no. 1, pp. 105–39; no. 3, pp. 383–85
Anna Kisselgoff: "The Spirit of the Times," *Performing Arts Magazine*, March 1989

George Dorris

John Finley Walk. A promenade along the western bank of the East River between 63rd Street and 125th Street in Manhattan, including an elevated section at Carl Schurz Park. At the suggestion of Stanley M. Isaacs, borough president of Manhattan, it was named in 1940 for John H. Finley, an editor of the *New York Times*, president of City College, and education commissioner of New York State who reportedly had often walked the perimeter of Manhattan.

Owen D. Gutfreund

John F. Kennedy International Airport. Airport in southeastern Queens on the shores of Jamaica Bay. It was planned during the administration of Mayor Fiorello H. La Guardia and opened on 1 July 1948 as Idlewild International Airport. The airport was unprecedented in its distance from the center of the metropolitan area that it served (fifteen miles, or twenty-five kilometers, from the center of Manhattan) and in its size (eleven hundred acres, or 450 hectares, eventually expanded to 4930 acres, or two thousand hectares). It was also unique in its configuration: because American Airlines and other carriers had forcefully demanded that runways be laid out in every possible direction to allow for shifts in the wind, it was decided that the center of the airport should be given over to terminals and parking lots; these alone covered more area than the entire expanse of La Guardia Airport, until then the principal airport in the city. Idlewild was the point of origin for the first jet service provided by an American carrier when a Boeing 707 of Pan American Airways flew to London on 26 October 1958 in seven hours and twenty-seven minutes, a time then considered remarkably short. It was also the first airport at which airlines were encouraged to build their own terminals; some that resulted were of real architectural distinction, including those of Pan American Airways, Northwest Airlines, United Airlines, and notably Trans World Airlines, for which Eero Saarinen completed a terminal capturing the spirit of flight as experienced in 1960. The design of the new airport proved influential nationwide, particularly as passengers after 1950 became accustomed to making trips of several stages with a single carrier, rather than transferring from one to another as they had done in the days of widespread travel by rail. The airport took its current name in 1963. Later it saw the first service by "jumbo" jet (again by Pan American) and in the face of some reluctance accommodated the supersonic airplane the Concorde. In the 1970s and 1980s JFK became the busiest cargo airport in the world: by 1977 it had a cargo center of 344 acres (180 hectares) serving fifty-seven all-cargo airlines.

George Scullin: *International Airport: The Story of Kennedy Airport and U.S. Commercial Aviation* (Boston: Little, Brown, 1968)

For illustration see Trans World Airlines.

Paul Barrett

John Jay College of Criminal Justice. College of the City University of New York. Its forerunner was a police science program leading to an associate degree, begun in 1955 under the auspices of the Police Academy and the City College School of Business. The program was broadened soon after to offer courses of study leading to bachelor's and master's degrees and in 1965 was taken over by the College of Police Science, then newly formed. John Jay College opened in 1967 in rented space at 315 Park Avenue South and moved in 1973 to 59th Street between 9th and 10th avenues. The college offers undergraduate programs leading to bachelor of arts and bachelor of science degrees in fields related to criminal justice and fire science, as well as five similar programs leading to an associate degree. Graduate programs on the master's and doctoral level are also available. In the spring of 1991 the school enrolled 8416 students (of whom more than half were female), taught by a faculty of about 350 men and women. Although the college at its inception attracted many members of the police and fire departments seeking advancement, in later years most of its students were recent graduates of high schools in New York City.

Selma Berrol

John Reed Club. Social club formed in 1929 by artists and writers close to the Communist Party. Its members included the cartoonist William Gropper (1897–1977). The club was inspired by the Prolecult movement in the Soviet Union and soon launched chapters in ten other cities. The artists in the club organized exhibitions and opened an art school in New York City where the instructors included Louis Lozowick (1892–1973) and Raphael Soyer. By 1936 the club had disbanded in accordance with efforts by the Communist Party to encourage more nonsectarian and broad-based groups such as the American Artists' Congress.

Patricia Hills: *Social Concern and Urban Realism: American Painting of the 1930s* (Boston: Boston University Art Gallery, 1983)

Patricia Hills

Johns, Jasper (*b* Augusta, Ga., 15 May 1930). Painter. The only son of a failed farmer, he grew up with his relatives in rural South Carolina. After serving for two years in the Korean War he settled in New York City in 1952 and befriended Robert Rauschenberg, already an accomplished artist, with whom he worked part time designing window displays for Tiffany and Bonwit Teller. During the following years he turned his back on abstract expressionism and began depicting commonplace objects in paintings such as *Flag* (1955), *Target with Four Faces* (1955), and *Gray Numbers* (1959). He came to prominence in 1958 when the gallery impresario Leo Castelli gave him a one-man show that laid the basis for both pop art and minimalism. During the 1960s and 1970s he continued to explore new ways to blur the distinctions between art and everyday life; one of his sculptures, *Painted Bronze* (1960), depicts two beer cans. In 1977 he exhibited more than two hundred of his works in a retrospective at the Whitney Museum. "The Seasons," an autobiographical series of paintings that was acclaimed as a turning point in his career, was shown by Castelli in 1987. In 1988 his *Diver* (1962) was sold at public auction for $4.2 million, at the time the highest price ever paid for a work by a living artist.

Robert Sanger Steel

Johnson, Alvin (Saunders) (*b* Homer, Neb., 18 Dec 1874; *d* Upper Nyack, N.Y., 7 June 1971). Educator. He studied economics at Columbia University and in 1919 helped to found the New School for Social Research as an experimental institute that combined social research with adult education. As its director in 1922–63 he built the school into a thriving institution by replacing the permanent faculty with visiting lecturers and broadening the curriculum to include courses in literature, music, philosophy, psychology, and art. Johnson was also an editor of the *Encyclopedia of the Social Sciences* and the *Yale Review*. In 1933 he organized the University in Exile, a forerunner of the graduate faculty at the New School, which provided an academic sanctuary for refugee scholars from Nazi Germany. Johnson wrote *Pioneer's Progress* (1952).

Peter M. Rutkoff, William B. Scott

Johnson, Charles Spurgeon (*b* Bristol, Va., 24 July 1893; *d* Louisville, Ky., 27 Oct 1956). Sociologist and educator. He received a doctorate in sociology from the University of Chicago and moved to New York City in 1921 to work at the National Urban League. As the executive director of its Department of Research and Investigations he investigated the social and economic conditions of urban and rural blacks. From 1922 he edited the league's monthly journal *Opportunity*, giving special attention to issues relating to black migration. His published writings include *Shadow of the Plantation* (1934) and *Collapse of Cotton Tenancy* (1935). In 1928 Johnson left the league for Fisk University, of which he became president in 1946.

Nancy J. Weiss: *The National Urban League, 1910–1940* (New York: Oxford University Press, 1974)

See also HARLEM RENAISSANCE.

Seth M. Scheiner

Johnson, James P(rice) (*b* New Brunswick, N.J., 1 Feb 1894; *d* New York City, 17 Nov 1955). Pianist and composer. He played his first professional engagement in Far Rockaway in 1912 and later performed at rent parties and clubs in New York City; he began recording in 1921. He was the principal creator of Harlem stride, an early style of jazz piano that was looser and more improvisatory than classic ragtime, its immediate forebear. His best-known compositions include "Carolina Shout" (1918), the anthem of Harlem stride, the phenomenally popular song "Charleston" (1923), "Runnin' Wild" (1923), "If I Can Be with You" (1926), and "Keep Shufflin'" (1928). He also wrote a blues opera, "De Organizer" (1940), in collaboration with Langston Hughes, and several concertos and other classical compositions, among them *Yamekraw* for piano and orchestra (1928).

Scott E. Brown: *James P. Johnson: A Case of Mistaken Identity* / Robert Hilbert: *A James P. Johnson Discography, 1917–1950* (Metuchen, N.J.: Scarecrow / Institute of Jazz Studies, 1982–86)

Kathy J. Ogren

Johnson, James Weldon (*b* Jacksonville, Fla., 17 June 1871; *d* Darkharbor, Maine, 17 June 1930). Teacher and writer. Educated at Atlanta University, he was the first black member of the Florida bar. In 1901 he moved to New York City. After supporting Theodore Roosevelt in the presidential election of 1904 he received a consular position and left the city in 1906; he returned in 1913. For a number of years he lived at the Marshall Club (260 West 53rd Street). After writing *The Autobiography of an Ex-colored Man* (1912) he edited the newspaper the *New York Age* and published *Fifty Years and Other Poems* in 1917. During his fifteen-year tenure as secretary of the National Association for the Advancement of Colored People he published the *Book of American Negro Poetry* (1922), *Black Manhattan* (1930), and his autobiography, *Along This Way* (1933). During the early 1920s Johnson lived at 2311 7th Avenue, moving in 1925 to 187 West 135th Street, where he remained until the end of his life. He is buried in Green-Wood Cemetery in Brooklyn.

Jane Tolbert-Rouchaleau: *James Weldon Johnson* (New York: Chelsea House, 1988)

See also HARLEM RENAISSANCE and LITERATURE, §2.

James E. Mooney

Johnson, Philip (Cortelyou) (*b* Cleveland, 8 July 1906). Architect. The son of a wealthy family, he graduated from Harvard University in 1930 and then became associated with the Museum of Modern Art, where he directed the architecture department from 1932 to 1934. With Henry-Russell Hitchcock he organized the polemical exhibition on the International style in 1932 that introduced avant-garde European architecture to Americans. In 1943 he returned to Harvard for a degree in architecture. Among his first works was his own "Glass House" in New Canaan, Connecticut (1949). He resumed his directorship at the Museum of Modern Art from 1946 to 1954 and in 1964 designed its sculpture garden and East Wing addition. During the

1960s he accepted large commissions nationwide, especially from colleges and other cultural institutions; those in the city included the New York State Theater at Lincoln Center (1964, with Richard Foster), several buildings for the Washington Square campus of New York University, and the interior of the restaurant the Four Seasons (1959, in the Seagram Building), later designated a landmark. After entering a partnership with John Burgee (*b* 1933) in 1967 he focused on large commercial projects. He shocked many with his conversion to post-modernism in his design for the American Telephone and Telegraph Building at 550 Madison Avenue (1984, headquarters of Sony from 1991): its masonry cladding and "Chippendale" top marked a nostalgic revival of historical forms and ornament in skyscrapers of the 1980s. His other commissions include a castle-like office tower at 33 Maiden Lane (1986) and another at 885 3rd Avenue (1986), known informally as "the lipstick."

Carol Willis

Johnson, (William) Samuel (*b* Guilford, Conn., 14 Oct 1696; *d* Stratford, Conn., 6 Jan 1772). Minister and first president of King's College. At fourteen he was admitted to the Collegiate School (now Yale University), and after graduating he taught in Connecticut at Guilford and New Haven. In 1720 he was ordained a pastor of the Congregation Church in West Haven. Influenced by Timothy Cutler, he decided to join the Church of England, traveling to England for his ordination. He became a missionary for the Society for the Propagation of the Gospel in Foreign Parts, and settled in Stratford, where he led the only Anglican congregation in the colony. There he lived until 1763, when he became president of King's College and the assistant minister of Trinity Church on Wall Street. Early in his tenure at the college he became embroiled in a controversy with William Livingston, a Presbyterian who with others advocated a nonsectarian college; Johnson contributed essays against the plan to the *New-York Mercury* and the *New-York Gazette*. During the years leading to the American Revolution he supported the controversial plan to have bishops in the colonies. A prolific author of works of theology and Berkelian philosophy, Johnson wrote *Ethics, Elementa, or the First Principles of Moral Philosophy* (1746).

Morgan Dix: *A History of the Parish of Trinity Church in the City of New York* (New York: G. P. Putnam's Sons, 1898)

David C. Humphrey: *From King's College to Columbia, 1746–1800* (New York: Columbia University Press, 1976)

Peter N. Carroll: *The Other Samuel Johnson* (Rutherford, N.J.: Fairleigh Dickinson University Press, 1978)

Phyllis Barr

Johnson, William H(enry) (*b* Florence, S.C., 18 March 1901; *d* Long Island, N.Y., 13 April 1970). Painter. He moved to New York City in 1921 to study at the National Academy of Design and spent the summers of 1923–26 in Provincetown, Massachusetts, where he studied with Charles Hawthorne at the Cape Cod School of Art. His early works included still lifes and portraits in an academic realist style. In 1926 he went to Paris and became acquainted with the work of expressionists and European modernists such as Chaim Soutine: their influence is evident in such works as *Young Pastry Cook* (1927–28). On returning to New York City in 1929 he moved to Harlem, gained the backing of the Harmon Foundation, became associated with the Harlem Renaissance, and persuaded Alain Locke to become his American agent. In the following year he returned to Europe, and apart from painting excursions to North Africa (1931) and France he remained in Denmark, Norway, and Sweden until 1939, when financial distress forced him to return to the United States and accept commissions from the Works Progress Administration. Johnson painted religious scenes and war themes in a primitivist style until 1947, when he was hospitalized after a mental collapse. His work was the subject of a retrospective at the Studio Museum in Harlem in 1992.

Novae: William H. Johnson and Bob Thompson (Los Angeles: California Afro-American Museum Foundation, 1990)

Edmund Gaither

Johnson and Higgins. Firm of insurance brokers formed in 1845 as Jones and Johnson by Walter Restored Jones Jr. and Henry W. Johnson. It took its current name in 1854 when Jones left the firm and A. Foster Higgins joined it. During the early years the firm specialized in the adjustment of claims and the brokerage of marine insurance. In the late nineteenth century it gradually became engaged in the brokerage of fire insurance, a field that grew because of increasing urbanization and fires in Chicago (1871) and Boston (1872). The firm opened branch offices in several American cities and in 1899 changed its form of organization from partnership to privately held corporation, with all shares held by employees. In the early twentieth century it adjusted claims from the Baltimore fire of 1903, the San Francisco earthquake of 1906, and the sinking of the *Titanic* in 1912. It also provided marine and non-marine insurance to the federal government during both world wars. After the Second World War it grew domestically and abroad as it offered new services to an expanding market. Johnson and Higgins is the largest privately held insurance brokerage firm in the world. It has fifty-two offices in the United States and seventeen in Canada, and affiliates in a number of other countries. The headquarters are at 125 Broad Street in lower Manhattan.

Claude M. Scales III

John Street United Methodist Church. Methodist church at 44 John Street in lower Manhattan, erected in 1768 on the former site of Wesley Chapel (dedicated 30 October 1768), the first Methodist church in the United States. It was the site of sermons by many well-known Methodist leaders, including Francis Asbury. The church was rebuilt in 1818 and 1841 and renovated in 1975. It has an active congregation and a museum of portraits and artifacts.

Francis Bourne Upham: *The Story of Old John Street Methodist Episcopal Church* (New York: Cathedral, 1932)

Charles Yrigoyen, Jr.

John Wiley and Sons. Firm of book publishers formed in 1807 as a bookshop on Reade Street by Charles Wiley. By 1814 it published reprints of works by European authors. After the shop moved to 3 Wall Street its back room became a gathering place for intellectuals known as the "Den." The firm was beset by financial troubles and on Wiley's death in 1826 was taken over by his son John, who in 1824 formed a partnership with George Long; renamed Wiley and Long, it moved to 22 Nassau Street. George Palmer Putnam joined the firm in 1836, and Long left it in 1840; the firm then became known as Wiley and Putnam, with a branch in London established by Putnam. During this period the firm published the Library of American Books, a series dedicated to American writers both popular and unknown, including Hawthorne, Melville, and Poe. When Putnam returned from London in 1847 he dissolved his partnership with Wiley, who from that time concentrated on scientific and technological publications, an area in which the firm became preeminent by the end of the Civil War. Wiley's son Charles Wiley became a partner in 1865, as did his son William H. Wiley in 1875; the firm took its current name in 1876. In 1902 Major Wiley, then head of the firm, was elected to the first of three terms as a congressman from New Jersey. The first women joined the firm as a result of the labor shortage occasioned by the First World War. In the 1920s the firm began to expand into fields other than engineering and science. In the 1960s it opened offices overseas, with operations eventually extending into England, Canada, Mexico, South America, Australia, and Japan.

In the mid 1990s John Wiley and Sons maintained its role as a global publisher of print and electronic products, specializing in scientific and technical books and journals, professional and consumer books and subscription services, and textbooks and educational materials for colleges and universities. W. Bradford Wiley II, great-great-great-grandson of the founder, was the chairman of the firm, which had its corporate headquarters and main editorial offices at 605 3rd Avenue and subsidiaries in the United States, Canada, Europe, Asia, and Australia.

Edward J. Hall and David Dzwonkoski: "John Wiley and Sons," *American Literary Publishing Houses, 1638–1899*, ed. Peter Dzwonkoski (Detroit: Gale Research, 1986)

"Ellis Is President, CEO of Wiley," *Publishers Weekly*, 8 June 1990, p. 17

Marjorie Harrison

Jolson, Al [Yoelson, Asa] (*b* St. Petersburg, 26 May 1886; *d* San Francisco, 23 Oct 1950). Singer. After emigrating from Russia and working in circuses, minstrel shows, and vaudeville he appeared on Broadway in the musical *La Belle Paree* (1911). He became well known during the next fourteen years for his robust, emotional singing style and energetic clowning. After the 1920s he performed mostly in motion pictures and on radio. Jolson moved to an apartment at 36 West 59th Street in 1922 and during the 1920s kept a suite at the Ritz–Carlton (374 Madison Avenue).

Jones, J(ohn) Raymond (*b* St. Thomas, U.S. Virgin Islands, 1899; *d* New York City, 9 June 1991). Political leader. In the early 1920s he formed the Carver Democratic Club, which later became the most important black political organization in New York City, and he was in the vanguard of black Democrats who took control of elective politics in Harlem in the late 1930s. He was a district leader for much of the period from 1945 to 1967, served on the City Council from 1962 to 1967, and became the leader of the Democratic organization in Manhattan in the mid 1960s. Under his leadership the Carver Democratic Club promoted the careers of such influential black politicians as Representatives Charles B. Rangel and Adam Clayton Powell Jr. (his political rival in Harlem after the Second World War); Percy E. Sutton, borough president of Manhattan; the federal judges Constance Baker Motley and James Watson; Robert C. Weaver, secretary of housing and urban development; Basil Paterson, secretary of state of New York; and Mayor David N. Dinkins. Jones was a brilliant strategist sometimes known as the "Harlem Fox."

Calvin B. Holder: "The Rise of the West Indian Politician in New York City, 1900–1952," *Afro-Americans in New York Life and History* 4 (1980), 5–60

John C. Walter: *The Harlem Fox* (Albany: State University of New York Press, 1989)

Calvin B. Holder: "The Rise and Fall of the West Indian Politician, 1900–1988" (New York: Medgar Evers College, Caribbean Research Center, 1991)

Obituary, *New York Times*, 11 June 1991

Calvin B. Holder

Jones's Wood. The name given in the nineteenth century to an undulating, wooded, and sparsely populated tract in Manhattan, occupying about 160 acres (sixty-five hectares) and situated roughly between 3rd Avenue and the East River from 66th Street to 75th Street. Named after the country seat of the Jones family, it was proposed as the site of a public park in 1844 by William Cullen Bryant in an editorial in the *New York Evening Post*. In 1851 the state legislature authorized the city to acquire a portion of the land for this purpose, but opposition arose at once, and in 1854 the authorization was repealed. Nevertheless Jones's Wood remained popular as a pleasure ground frequented by private clubs, church groups, benevolent societies, and labor unions for organized excursions, sporting events, picnics, socials, and festivals; it was especially favored by the city's German population. On the grounds were amateur shooting galleries, bowling alleys, beer halls, and outdoor dancing stands, as well as the Jones's Wood Hotel (occupying the old Provoost Mansion) and the Coliseum, a large structure seating fourteen thousand designed in 1874 by the architectural firm of Kastner and Beach. The northward development of Manhattan brought about the eventual demise of the area. In 1894 fire destroyed some eleven acres (four hectares) of the neighborhood, including the Coliseum.

Clarence C. Cook: *A Description of the New York Central Park* (New York: F. J. Huntington, 1869; repr. Benjamin Blom, 1972)

Hopper Striker Mott: "Jones's Wood," *Valentine's Manual of the City of New York, 1917–1918*, new series no. 2, pp. 140–59

Ian R. Stewart: "Politics and the Park: The Fight for Central Park," *New-York Historical Society Quarterly* 61 (1977), 124–55

Joy M. Kestenbaum

Joplin, Scott (*b* northeastern Texas, first three months of 1868; *d* New York City, 1 April 1917). Composer. His early career was spent mostly in Missouri. His *Maple Leaf Rag* (1899) brought him to national prominence, and he became known as the "king of ragtime writers." He went to New York City in the summer of 1907 in an unsuccessful effort to find a producer for his still unfinished opera *Treemonisha* (1911). There he remained for the rest of his life, having more than twenty works published during these years, including the opera. He became closely associated with the city's leading black vaudevillians and had business contacts with such major figures in music publishing as Irving Berlin. During the half-century following his death Joplin was largely forgotten, although *Maple Leaf Rag* was retained in the jazz repertory. He was rediscovered in the 1970s, receiving both critical and popular acclaim. His opera was finally produced, selections of his music used in the film *The Sting* won an Academy Award in 1974, a piano recording of his rag *The Entertainer* (1902) won a Grammy Award for "best pop instrumental," and recordings of his music became best-sellers in both popular and classical categories. In 1976 he was awarded a special bicentennial Pulitzer prize for his contributions to American music.

James Haskins with Kathleen Benson: *Scott Joplin* (Garden City, N.Y.: Doubleday, 1978)

Edward A. Berlin: *King of Ragtime: Scott Joplin and His Era* (New York: Oxford University Press, 1994)

Edward A. Berlin

Jordanians. Immigrants from Jordan began settling in New York City in the late 1960s. They tended not to be highly visible, in part because they were overshadowed by a vibrant Jordanian community in Yonkers, New York (the most politically powerful in the United States), and in part because they associated themselves with the city's Palestinian community, which was better organized. Many Jordanians in the city own automobile repair shops and real-estate agencies, as well as small tobacco, stationery, and grocery stores; younger Jordanians work in the professions. In the mid 1990s the number of Jordanians in the city was estimated at ten thousand.

Paula Hajar

Joseph Papp Public Theater. A building at 425 Lafayette Street in lower Manhattan, near Astor Place. Constructed in stages between 1853 and 1881, it originally housed the Astor Library and then the Hebrew Immigrant Aid Society Service (HIAS). In the mid 1970s the building became the home of the New York Shakespeare Festival under the direction of Joseph Papp. It took its current name one year after Papp's death in 1991. The building houses five live performance spaces and one movie theater.

Josephson, Barney (*b* Trenton, N.J., *ca* 1902; *d* New York City, 29 Sept 1988). Nightclub owner. In December 1938 he opened Café Society at 2 Sheridan Square in Greenwich Village, one of the first racially integrated nightclubs under white ownership. During its first four years the club presented such boogie-woogie pianists as Pete Johnson, Meade "Lux" Lewis, and Albert Ammons, helping to inspire a vogue for the genre that spread nationwide. In 1940 he opened Café Society Uptown at East 58th Street, which like its counterpart downtown presented such performers as Billie Holiday, Lena Horne, Sarah Vaughan, and Zero Mostel. Josephson enjoyed great success until 1947, when his brother Leon, an acknowledged communist, was cited for contempt by the House Un-American Activities Committee. Vilified by such newspaper columnists as Walter Winchell and Lee Mortimer, he was compelled to sell his clubs. He then opened a restaurant called the Cookery at University Avenue and 8th Street, where from 1969 he again presented music. The best-known performer at the Cookery was the blues singer Alberta Hunter, who sang there from 1977 until her death in 1984.

Marc Ferris

Josiah Macy, Jr. Foundation. Charitable organization formed in April 1930 by Kate Macy Ladd (*b* 6 April 1863; *d* 27 Aug 1945) to honor her father, a well-known merchant. It sponsors medical research and education, as well as a series of interdisciplinary conferences begun in the 1930s. In 1993 the foundation reported assets of $123.1 million and made thirty-six grants totaling $4.4 million to such recipients as the City University of New York and Planned Parenthood of New York City. Health care institutions in the city have benefited from many of its grants. The offices are at 44 East 64th Street.

The Josiah Macy, Jr. Foundation, 1930–1955: A Review (New York: Josiah Macy, Jr. Foundation, 1955)

Kenneth W. Rose

Journal of Commerce. Daily newspaper, launched in 1827 by Samuel F. B. Morse, who intended it to promote moral virtues in licentious New York City. Based at the Merchant's Exchange Building on Wall Street, it sold for six cents a copy. The newspaper soon discarded its pietistic agenda and focused more on finance, particularly international trade and transportation. Under the editorship of Gerard Hallock (*d* 1865) it expanded, merging with the *New York Gazette and General Advertiser* in 1840. During the Civil War the newspaper gained much notoriety when it was harshly critical of Lincoln's war on the South, and on one occasion it printed details of Union military strategy. In 1861 a federal grand jury found the newspaper "disloyal," and the government subsequently refused to provide it with postal services. A settlement was reached when Hallock stepped down. In 1927 the *Journal of Commerce* was bought by the Ridders, who owned several newspapers in New York City, and it remained part of the Knight–Ridder chain into the 1990s. After many years on Wall Street the newspaper moved to the World Trade Center in 1991.

James Bradley

Jozef Pilsudski Institute of America for Research in the Modern History of Poland. Research institution formed in 1943 at 180 2nd Avenue in Manhattan. It maintains a research library and archives on Polish history since 1863, publishes books, sponsors lectures, and promotes research.

James S. Pula

J. P. Morgan. Merchant bank formed in 1843 as George Peabody and Company by George Peabody that helped to develop the railroads in the United States. J(unius) S(pencer) Morgan (1813–90) became a partner in 1854 and on Peabody's retirement in 1864 took control of the firm in London, which he renamed J. S. Morgan and Company. Dabney, Morgan and Company, the firm's affiliate in New York City at 53 Exchange Place, was managed by

Headquarters of J. P. Morgan at Wall and Broad streets, ca *1900*

his son J. P. Morgan, who in 1871 became a partner in Drexel, Morgan. This firm, allied with the bank Drexel and Company and strongly connected to European banks, soon became one of the most prosperous investment banks in New York City, important in both government and railroad finance; in 1873 it helped to refinance the Civil War debt by underwriting federal bonds worth $1400 million. Its headquarters were set up at 23 Wall Street during the same year. From 1875 the firm became to an increasing extent the engine of the Morgans' enterprises. It was the main underwriter of stock and bond issues for the railroads and controlled several important reorganizations, including that of the Northern Pacific Railroad Company. After 1890 the firm undertook more corporate financing, and in 1895 it rescued the federal government during a gold shortage; in the same year it was renamed J. P. Morgan and Company. The firm was also the primary underwriter in the mergers that formed General Electric in 1892, U.S. Steel in 1901, and International Harvester in 1902.

Assisted by his partners Henry P. Davison, George Perkins, and Charles Coster, J. P. Morgan became the central figure in national finance. He helped to limit bank failures during a panic in 1907 by permitting his firm to act as a sort of national bank. This action raised concern over the power of the country's largest banks, and Morgan became the primary target of an investigation conducted in 1912 by Representative Arsène Pujo into reported perfidies of the "money trust." Although exonerated, Morgan was distressed by the proceedings and died soon after. In 1913 the architectural firm of Trowbridge and Livingston erected a new building at 23 Wall Street that dominated the financial district (it was designated a landmark in 1965). Under the direction of Morgan's son J. P. Morgan Jr. (1867–1943) the firm ceased to function as a central bank after the formation of the Federal Reserve System and focused increasingly on investment banking in Asia, Latin America, and western Europe; it remained the preeminent investment bank in the country. Morgan himself was overshadowed by several partners, among them Dwight Morrow, Russell Leffingwell, and Thomas W. Lamont, the chairman after 1943.

During the Depression the firm ceased to dominate national finance. The Glass–Steagall Act (1933), passed in part to separate Morgan's interests, forced banks to choose between underwriting and lending. The firm then became a commercial bank and its investment services were taken over by its former partners, who established the firm of Morgan, Stanley in 1935. The firm of J. P. Morgan was incorporated as a commercial bank in 1940; its partnership was dissolved in 1941 and it became a publicly held company. Prosperous after the Second World War, it merged in 1959 with the Guaranty Trust. Its bank subsidiary, Morgan Guaranty, became a leader in international trade and in financing industries that developed in the United States after the war, among them defense contracting and the manufacture of plastics and airplanes. J. P. Morgan and Company was incorporated in 1969 as a one-bank holding company for Morgan Guaranty, which remained among the largest and strongest firms of its kind in the United States, catering exclusively to commercial clients. In 1990 its new headquarters at 60 Wall Street were completed and it became the first commercial bank allowed by the Securities and Exchange Commission to engage in limited investment banking. J. P. Morgan and Company remains a leading commercial bank and underwrites and trades securities to the extent allowed by law; it is also an important underwriter of securities in Europe.

Ron Chernow: *The House of Morgan: An American Banking Dynasty and the Rise of Modern Finance* (New York: Atlantic Monthly Press, 1990)

Susan Aaronson

Judd, Donald (Clarence) (*b* Excelsior Springs, Mo., 3 June 1928; *d* New York City, 12 Feb 1994). Sculptor. Born on his grandparents' farm, he served in the army in the Korean War, earned a BA in philosophy at Columbia University, and studied painting at the Art Students League. He returned to Columbia in the late 1950s for graduate study in art history with Meyer Schapiro and Rudolf Wittkower. By the 1960s he was one of the foremost American artists and a leading figure in the minimalist movement. His writings helped to identify a new generation of artists and lift the art world in New York City out of the doldrums of second-generation abstract expressionism and away from what he saw as tired European aesthetic conventions. For most of his active career Judd had a studio in a cast-iron building in SoHo.

Kenneth T. Jackson

Judge. Humor magazine launched by several cartoonists from *Puck*, including James Albert Wales. First issued on 29 October 1881, it sold for ten cents and soon became known for its political themes and full-page, brightly colored chromolithographic cartoons of leading political figures. Among its features was a series depicting the "Judge," a character drawn on the inside cover who attacked corruption and disparaged immigrants, especially Jews. Under Isaac M. Gregory the magazine became a publication of the Republican Party. It strongly supported William McKinley in the presidential election of 1896, in part through Grant Hamilton's "full dinner pail" cartoons. Circulation rose to 85,000 before the turn of the century. After the magazine's publisher was reorganized as the Leslie–Judge Company in 1909, James Lee became the editor and trod a politically independent course, choosing such topics of general humor as women's organizations and popular poets, and producing holiday issues. In 1922 the magazine merged with *Leslie's Weekly* and under new direction added crossword puzzles, contests, a man-about-town column called "Judge, Jr.," and a subtitle, "The Nation's Perpetual Smileage Book." By 1923 it sold for fifteen cents and circulation peaked at 250,000. It attracted such popular writers as Stephen Leacock, S. J. Perelman, Walter Trumbell, and Steven Vincent Benét, and such cartoonists as Oliver Herford and Theodor Seuss Geisel (who later wrote children's books as Dr. Seuss). During the Depression circulation declined, leading the publisher to reduce the price to ten cents and publish only monthly from July 1932. In 1937 the magazine was reorganized under Harry Newman, who changed the subtitle to "The National Magazine of Humor, Politics and Satire," raised the price to twenty-five cents, and sought to make the content more sophisticated; *Judge* nonetheless declined in popularity and ceased publication in 1949.

Walter Friedman

Judson Memorial Church. Baptist church at 55 Washington Square Park in Manhattan, formed in 1890 by Edward Judson, pastor of the Berean Baptist Congregation. In 1892 it moved into a building designed by the firm of McKim, Mead and White in the Romanesque Revival style and constructed of yellow Roman brick and limestone. This structure, a city, state, and federal landmark, is regarded as an architectural masterpiece, well known for its marble relief by Augustus Saint-Gaudens and stained-glass windows by John La Farge. Judson and his parishioners established a durable tradition of social activism, sponsoring cooking and sewing classes, a health center, and employment services. The church continued to advocate liberal reforms into the next century. In the 1960s its minister Al Carmines led a radical arts ministry, sponsoring modern dance and experimental music performances in the church's auditorium. Politically the church supported abortion rights, the peace movement, and gay and lesbian rights, and later donated space for trials of an experimental AIDS drug.

Aileen Laura Love

Judson Poets' Theatre. Theater formed in 1961 by members of the arts program at Judson Memorial Church in Greenwich Village. Led by the church's assistant pastor Al Carmines and its director Lawrence Kornfeld, the theater has presented an eclectic repertory ranging from plays by Strindberg, Gertrude Stein, and Sam Shepard to avant-garde musicals and performance events.

D. S. Moynihan

Juilliard School. Conservatory of music chartered in 1904 as the Institute of Musical Art by Frank Damrosch, head of music education for the public school system in New York City, with an endowment of $500,000 from James Loeb. Based on the European model and intended for American music students of the highest caliber, the school was planned for 150 students but within a year of its opening in October 1905 had nearly five hundred, who attended classes at the Lenox Mansion, a six-story brownstone at 53 5th Avenue, at 12th Street. The early faculty included such prominent figures as the violinists Franz Kneisel and Leopold Auer, the flutist Georges Barrère, the singer Georg Henschel, the composer Rubin Goldmark, the theorist Percy Goetschius, and the pianists Carl Friedberg, Josef Lhévinne, Rhosina Lhévinne, Olga Samaroff-Stokowski, Alexander Siloti, and Ernest Hutcheson (president of the school from 1933). The school moved in 1910 to 120 Claremont Avenue in Morningside Heights. The Juilliard Musical Foundation, formed in 1919 by a bequest of $20 million from the textile magnate August D. Juilliard and enlarged by a bequest of $10 million from Frederick A. Juilliard, oversaw the establishment in 1924 of the Juilliard Graduate School, which largely duplicated the offerings of the Institute of Musical Art; the two schools merged in 1926 to form the Juilliard School of Music (name abbreviated to its current form in 1968), which soon began to accept students from abroad, in part to compete with the Curtis Institute in Philadelphia.

From 1945 the school was led by the composer William Schuman, who oversaw the formation of the Juilliard String Quartet, the adoption of a basic-musicianship curriculum called "Literature and Materials of Music" that became widely imitated, and the establishment in 1951 of a dance division that numbered among its faculty Martha Graham, Agnes de Mille, and Antony Tudor. Schuman resigned in 1962 to become president of Lincoln Center. Under his successor Peter Mennin the school in 1968 opened a drama division led by John Houseman, in 1969 became a part of Lincoln Center, where it moved into a five-story complex encompassing several theaters and concert halls (including Alice Tully Hall), an extensive music library, and set and costume shops for staged productions, and in 1970 opened the Juilliard Opera Center. Joseph Polisi became the president of the school in 1984; an annex for student housing was added in 1991. Students from Israel, Russia, Korea, and other countries rose steadily in number, by 1993 accounting for 35 percent of total enrollment and 75 percent of the piano department.

Juilliard is generally regarded as the leading conservatory of music in North America. It enrolls some eight hundred students and offers the degrees of bachelor of music, bachelor of fine arts (in drama and dance), master of music, and doctor of musical arts; it also has an active pre-college division. Prominent members of the faculty have included Bessie Schönberg (dance), Michael Kahn (drama), and Wynton Marsalis, Milton Babbitt, the members of the Juilliard String Quartet, and Emanuel Ax (music). Among the better-known students have been Itzhak Perlman, Leontyne Price, Paul Taylor, Richard Rodgers, and Sarah Chang.

Frank Damrosch: *Institute of Musical Art, 1905–1926* (New York: Privately printed, 1936)

James M. Keller

Jujamcyn Theaters. Entertainment enterprise formed in 1956 by Virginia and James Binger; the name is derived from the names of the Bingers' children, Judy, James, and Cynthia. The firm owns and operates five Broadway theaters, and produces and invests in Broadway shows. It works closely with regional and resident theaters in developing new works for Broadway and is a member of the Broadway Alliance, a cooperative effort by theatrical unions, producers, and theater owners to produce dramas and comedies on Broadway at reasonable prices. The firm has produced such shows as *M. Butterfly*, *Grand Hotel*, *Into the Woods*, *The Secret Garden*, and *Angels in America*. In 1984 it inaugurated the Jujamcyn Award to recognize outstanding contributions by a resident theater.

Robert Seder

Julia (y Arcelay), Raul (Rafael Carlos) (*b* San Juan, 9 March 1940; *d* Manhasset, N.Y., 24 Oct 1994). Actor. He moved to New York City in 1964 and in 1971 won renown as Proteus in a modern, musical version of *Two Gentlemen of Verona* presented by the New York Shakespeare Festival. He then played the title role in *Othello* and appeared in plays by George Bernard Shaw, Noël Coward, Jean-Paul Sartre, and Harold Pinter, as well as Broadway musicals. He frequently took time away from the stage to act in films, notably *Kiss of the Spider Woman* (1985) and *The Addams Family* (1991), but he lived in Manhattan and regarded New York City as his home. Julia was active in political and social causes, including the Hunger Project.

Kenneth T. Jackson

Jumel [née Brown; Bowen], **Elizabeth** (*b* Providence, R.I., 1775; *d* New York City, 22 July 1865). Adventuress. Known for her beauty, she was reportedly the madam of a French bordello in her youth and was certainly a prostitute in Providence. She lived with the wine merchant Stephen Jumel in his mansion at Whitehall and Pearl streets for a number of years before marrying him. In 1810 she received as a gift from him the house of Roger Morris, which had been Washington's headquarters during the battle for Manhattan in 1776. Rejected in the city's social circles, she moved with her husband to France in 1815, where they were well received. She returned to New York City without her husband but then rejoined him in France. She moved back to New York City in 1826 with his power of attorney, sold his property, and kept the proceeds. She later married Aaron Burr, from whom she sought a divorce in 1834; this was granted on the day of his death in 1836. Jumel was reportedly the wealthiest woman in North America at mid century.

Leonard Faulkner: *Painted Lady: Eliza Jumel* (New York: E. P. Dutton, 1962)

James E. Mooney

Jumel, Stephen (*b* ?Bordeaux, *ca* 1754; *d* New York City, 22 May 1832). Wine merchant. The son of a merchant family from Bordeaux, he moved to New York City in 1795 and formed a partnership with Jacques Desobry. During the trade embargo of 1807–9 he found ways to conduct business that earned large profits. He was also known for marrying the stunning Eliza Brown, for whom in 1810 he purchased Roger Morris's house (Washington's former headquarters). With

The mansion of Stephen Jumel

her he moved to France in 1815. She returned to the city to gain his wealth and he returned to destitution.

Meade Minnegerode: *Lives and Times: Four Informal American Portraits* (New York: G. P. Putnam's Sons, 1925)

James E. Mooney

Junior League for the Promotion of Settlement Movements [Junior League for the Promotion of Neighborhood Work]. Organization that eventually became the ASSOCIATION OF JUNIOR LEAGUES INTERNATIONAL.

Junior Police. Original name of the POLICE ATHLETIC LEAGUE.

Junior's. Restaurant opened by Harry Rosen in 1950 at the corner of DeKalb and Flatbush avenues in Brooklyn. Situated across the street from the Brooklyn campus of Long Island University, it was a temporary classroom when a fire damaged a campus building in 1968, as well as a meeting place for the faculty during their strike in 1979. Junior's was renovated in 1981. It is known for its sandwiches, cheesecake, large portions, extensive menu, reasonable prices, and the many condiments placed on its tables.

Marjorie Harrison

J. Walter Thompson. Advertising and public relations firm. It was formed in 1878 by James Walter Thompson after he bought a firm for which he had worked for ten years. In 1896 the firm designed a symbol for the Prudential Life Insurance Company depicting the Rock of Gibraltar that remained in use into the 1990s. Thompson sold the agency in 1916 to Stanley Resor, who managed it with Helen Landsowne, a talented copywriter in the agency's office in Cincinnati whom he married in 1917. Resor took a scientific approach to advertising: he sought the advice of eminent behavioral psychologists, and was an innovator in using scientific and medical findings as a basis for copy. Among those associated with the firm during these years was the noted behavioral psychologist John B. Watson, who became a vice-president in 1924. Landsowne developed the advertising that introduced Crisco, Yuban Coffee, Lux Flakes, and Cutex to the American consumer; she attributed much of the firm's success to its having concentrated on products sold to women. In the 1920s the firm opened offices around the world. When radio and television became popular the firm produced many memorable advertisements. After the Second World War it gave greater attention to its international operations, which in 1973 surpassed those in the United States. During the 1970s and 1980s the firm made several acquisitions, notably that of the public relations firm Hill and Knowlton. J. Walter Thompson was itself acquired in 1987 by WPP.

James Playsted Wood: *The Story of Advertising* (New York: Ronald, 1958)
Stephen R. Fox: *The Mirror Makers: A History of American Advertising and Its Creators* (New York: William Morrow, 1984)

Chauncey G. Olinger, Jr.

K

Kahal Adas Jeshurun Anshe Lubz. Original name of the ELDRIDGE STREET SYNAGOGUE.

Kahane, Meir (*b* New York City, 1 Aug 1932; *d* New York City, 5 Nov 1990). Rabbi and political activist. He grew up in Brooklyn and as a youth became an ardent Zionist. After earning degrees from Brooklyn College, New York Law School, and New York University he became a rabbi at the Howard Beach Center, remaining there for two years before moving to Israel. He returned to the city in 1967, became a rabbi in Rochdale Village, and wrote a regular column for the *Jewish Press*. The eruption of anti-Semitism during a teachers' strike in 1968 inspired him to form the Jewish Defense League, a militant organization devoted to Jewish rights; he encouraged his followers to use violence, was often accused of vigilantism, and was jailed repeatedly for taking part in anti-Soviet demonstrations and for encouraging the use of explosives. He moved back to Israel and was elected to the Knesset after waging a campaign in which he advocated expelling Palestinians from the occupied territories. On one of his many visits to New York City he was fatally shot at a rally; the man accused of being his assailant was acquitted of homicide but convicted of illegal possession of a weapon.

Robert I. Friedman: *The False Prophet: Rabbi Meir Kahane* (New York: Lawrence Hill, 1990)

James E. Mooney

Kahn, Otto H(ermann) (*b* Mannheim, Germany, 23 Feb 1867; *d* New York City, 29 March 1934). Financier and arts patron. Born of Jewish ancestry to a family of merchant bankers, he settled in New York City in August 1893 and in January 1896 married Addie Wolff; her father, Abraham Wolff, was an elder partner at Kuhn, Loeb and Company who arranged for him to join the firm in January 1897. He soon emerged as an expert in railroad finance and a spokesman for both his firm and the conservative sensibilities of Wall Street. His accomplishments in finance were however overshadowed by his extraordinary patronage of the arts: more than anyone of his generation he promoted the arts as a worthy object of philanthropy (he once told Mayor John F. Hylan that a piano in every house would deter more crime than a policeman on every doorstep). His energetic chairmanship of the Metropolitan Opera from 1908 to 1931 secured its status as a nonprofit entity, and he helped to make the city an indispensable destination on the American tours of many influential theater and dance companies, including Serge Diaghilev's Ballets Russes, Jacques Copeau's Théâtre du Vieux Colombier, Konstantin Stanislavsky's Moscow Art Theatre, and Max Reinhardt's Repertory Company. He also supported such theater groups as the Washington Square Players (later the Theatre Guild), the Provincetown Players, and the New Playwrights Theatre, as well as many individual artists and writers, among them Hart Crane during his writing of *The Bridge*. Kahn's mansion at 1 East 91st Street is a landmark.

Mary Jane Matz: *The Many Lives of Otto Kahn* (New York: Macmillan, 1963)

John Kobler: *Otto the Magnificent: The Life of Otto Kahn* (New York: Charles Scribner's Sons, 1988)

Theresa Collins

Kalbfleisch, Martin (*b* Vlissingen, Netherlands, 8 Feb 1804; *d* Brooklyn, 12 Feb 1873). Mayor of Brooklyn. Born into a family of twenty-four children, he studied chemistry and settled in New York City in 1826. In 1835 he opened a color works in Harlem that he moved to Greenpoint in 1842: as the Brooklyn Chemical Works this became one of the most important chemical firms in the United States. He was the last supervisor of Bushwick (1851–55) and then mayor of Brooklyn for nearly seven years (1861–63, 1868–71). A Democrat, he remained active in civic affairs to the end of his life. Kalbfleisch was a controversial figure because of his contentious, emphatic personality.

Ellen Fletcher

Kaltenborn, H. V. [Hans von] (*b* Milwaukee, 9 July 1878; *d* New York City, 14 June 1965). News reporter. He began his career in 1922 by broadcasting news reports from the Statue of Liberty. He later covered many presidential campaigns and was a foreign correspondent for the Columbia Broadcasting System (CBS) and the National Broadcasting Company (NBC). During the Munich Conference in 1938 he moved a cot into the CBS studio at 485 Madison Avenue and remained on the air for eighteen consecutive days, broadcasting instantaneous translations of Hitler and Édouard Daladier along with his own analyses. He was controversial and opinionated, and advertisers avoided his programs. In 1940 he left CBS for NBC, from which he was forced to retire in 1958 after a dispute. He was known as the "dean of radio commentators."

Judith Adler Hennessee

Kane Street Synagogue. Conservative synagogue formed in Brooklyn in the 1850s by a largely Dutch and Bavarian congregation. It was originally known as the "Boerum Schule" and had quarters near Brooklyn Borough Hall before moving to Cobble Hill in 1905. The synagogue was a charter member of the United Synagogue of America. At one time the members included the family of Aaron Copland. The synagogue is reputed to be the oldest in Brooklyn.

Jenna Weissman Joselit

Kaplan, Mordecai M(enahem) (*b* Svencionys, Lithuania, 11 June 1881; *d* Bronx, 8 Nov 1983). Rabbi and theologian. After moving to the United States with his family in 1890 he was ordained in 1902 at the Jewish Theological Seminary, where in 1909 he was appointed dean of the Teachers Institute. He formed the Society for the Advancement of Judaism in 1922 and was the leading exponent of Reconstructionism, a branch of Judaism that views the faith as an "evolving religious civilization" in which cultural elements are as important as theological and legal ones. A teacher at the Jewish Teachers Seminary for fifty years, Kaplan influenced generations of rabbis, whom he urged to apply scriptural and rabbinical texts imaginatively to contemporary issues.

Ira Eisenstein: "Mordecai M. Kaplan," *Great Jewish Thinkers of the Twentieth Century*, ed. Simon Noveck (New York: B'nai B'rith, 1963)

Emanuel Goldsmith, Mel Scult, and Robert M. Seltzer: *The American Judaism of Mordecai M. Kaplan* (New York: New York University Press, 1990)

Thomas E. Bird

Karan [Faske], **Donna (Ivy)** (*b* New York City, 2 Oct 1948). Fashion designer. She gained much of her early experience in clothing design while working for Anne Klein. Her appreciation for sportswear enabled her to adapt sporty designs to the needs of executive women, and in 1985 she built one of the most prominent fashion businesses in New York City. Using stretch fabrics and building ensembles around a base of bodysuits, body blouses, and leggings, she designs separates that are comfortable, flattering, and easy to organize.

Caroline Rennolds Milbank

Käsebier [née Stanton], **Gertrude** (*b* Fort Des Moines [now Des Moines], Iowa, 18 May 1852; *d* New York City, 13 Oct 1934). Photographer. She developed a strong interest in photography while studying portrait painting at the Pratt Institute. From 1897 she photographed subjects in natural poses against a plain background, a rebellion against the painted backdrops and elaborate furniture used by photographers such as Napoleon Sarony. Working in successive studios on and near 5th Avenue, she soon became one of the best-known photographers in New York City, admired for her portraits of figures such as the architect Stanford White and the painter Arthur B. Davies, and for her timeless images of motherhood. Her work was highly regarded by Alfred Stieglitz, who featured it in the first issue of *Camera Work* (1903) as well as in various exhibitions at the Photo-Secession galleries. After breaking with Stieglitz in 1912 she aligned herself with Clarence H. White and

Gertrude Käsebier, Portrait (Miss N.) *(portrait of Evelyn Nesbit, 1902). Platinum print*

the Pictorial Photographers of America. Her activity dwindled after the First World War. In 1929 she was the subject of a retrospective exhibition at the Brooklyn Institute of Arts and Sciences (now the Brooklyn Museum).

W. I. Homer, ed.: *A Pictorial Heritage: The Photographs of Gertrude Käsebier* (Wilmington: Delaware Art Museum, 1979)

Barbara L. Michaels: *Gertrude Käsebier: The Photographer and Her Photographs* (New York: Harry N. Abrams, 1992)

See also PHOTOGRAPHY.

Barbara L. Michaels

Kaufman, George S(imon) (*b* Pittsburgh, 16 Nov 1889; *d* New York City, 2 June 1961). Playwright, essayist, director, and screenwriter. After his dismissal from the *Washington Times* he moved to New York City in 1913, where he lived at 241 West 101st Street and worked as a drama critic and columnist for several newspapers, including the *New York Tribune* and the *Evening Mail.* In 1917 he became the drama editor of the *New York Times,* a position he held until 1930. His reviews were well known for their wit; he once wrote that Raymond Massey, an impersonator of Lincoln considered overbearing by many, would not be satisfied until he had been assassinated. From 1921 he lived in an apartment at 200 West 58th Street. Quoted as having said that it was good to have company when locked in a room with a blank piece of paper, he almost always wrote in collaboration with others. With Marc Connelly he wrote the play *Dulcy* in 1921; the two continued to collaborate until 1924. He also worked with fellow members of the Algonquin Round Table, among them Edna Ferber, with whom he wrote *Royal Family* (1927), *Dinner at Eight* (1932), and four other plays. With Morrie Ryskind he wrote several comedies for the Marx Brothers (including *The Coconuts,* 1925; and *Animal Crackers,* 1928), as well as *Of Thee I Sing,* which opened at the Music Box Theatre on 26 December 1931 and was the first musical to win a Pulitzer Prize. On his own he wrote the play *Butter and Egg Man* (1925). He lived at 158 East 63rd Street from 1929 until 1932, when he moved to 14 East 94th Street. About this time he began working with Moss Hart (1904–61), with whom he wrote *Once in a Lifetime* (1930), *You Can't Take It with You* (1936), and *The Man Who Came to Dinner* (1939), which opened at the Music Box on 16 October 1939 and ran for 739 performances. Screen rights to most of his plays were bought by studios in Hollywood, where he eventually worked on such films as the Marx Brothers' *A Night at the Opera* (1935); he later directed *Guys and Dolls* (1950) and wrote *The Solid Gold Cadillac* (1953) with Howard Teichmann. Kaufman married the actress Leueen MacGrath, with whom he wrote *Silk Stockings* (1955). He moved to 410 Park Avenue during the mid 1940s and to 1035 Park Avenue about 1950, where he remained until the end of his life.

Scott Meredith: *George S. Kaufman and His Friends* (New York: Doubleday, 1974)

Walter Friedman

Kaufman, Irving R(obert) (*b* New York City, 24 June 1910; *d* New York City, 1 Feb 1992). Judge. He attended Fordham University (LLB 1931) and in 1949 became the youngest federal judge in the United States when President Harry S. Truman appointed him the chief judge of the U.S. Court of Appeals for the Second Circuit. He became widely known when in April 1951 he sentenced Julius and Ethel Rosenberg to death for espionage. In 1961 he issued the first order to desegregate an elementary school in the North (in Westchester County), and in the following decades he wrote several opinions in which he took a broad view of the First Amendment. He retired in 1987 but was designated a senior judge and remained active on the bench nearly to the end of his life.

B. Kimberly Taylor

Kaufmann, Sigismund (*b* Schotten [now in Germany], 8 Sept 1824; *d* Berlin, 17 Aug 1889). Lawyer. Of German Jewish background, he settled in New York City after the revolution of 1848 and in 1850 helped to form the New York Socialistischer Turnverein, a German organization that promoted physical fitness, radical politics, and religious skepticism. In 1852 he became an attorney and an officer of the German Society (president in 1873 and 1876–79). A prominent Republican, he was an elector for President Lincoln in 1860, a candidate for the state senate in 1869, and the Republican candidate for lieutenant governor in 1870. In the late 1870s he was the German representative on the State Board of Commissioners for Emigration and a trustee of Temple Beth Elohim.

Stanley Nadel

Kavookjian, Haik (*b* near Constantinople [now Istanbul], 20 Aug 1875; *d* New York City, 26 April 1977). Businessman and activist. In 1896 he fled Turkey and after arriving in New York City founded the Bingham Photo Engraving Company (1915), amassing a fortune as it became the largest firm of its kind in the city. He became the head of the Photo Engravers Board of Trade, founded or led half a dozen Armenian cultural and educational organizations, and financed the construction of St. Vartan Armenian Cathedral (1968, 34th Street and 2nd Avenue), headquarters of the Eastern Diocese of the Armenian Apostolic Church of North America.

Harold Takooshian

Kaye Scholer Fierman Hays and Handler. Law firm that began as a partnership formed in 1917 by Benjamin Kaye and Jacob Scholer. It became successful in part because Kaye was known for writing three comedies that were performed on Broadway. Harold L. Fierman and James S. Hays joined the firm in 1934, as did Milton Handler, a professor at Columbia University with expertise in antitrust law, in 1951. Soon associated with the Equitable Life Assurance Society of the United States, the firm also handled the refinancing of Allis–Chalmers, the takeover of Oscar Meyer and Entenmann's by General Foods, and a successful defense of the Xerox Corporation in a monopoly suit. It represented the State of New York in extended litigation over Westway, and for the real-estate firm of Olympia and York won the right to build the World Financial Center and Battery Park City. Because of its actions in advising Charles Keating and the Lincoln Savings and Loan, in March 1992 the firm was sued by the government for $275 million and its assets were frozen. Within a week it paid $41 million in settlement of all claims. In 1994 the firm had 111 partners and more than four hundred associates. The offices are at 425 Park Avenue.

George J. Lankevich

Kazan, Abraham E(li) (*b* Russia, 1889; *d* New York City, 21 Dec 1971). Real-estate developer. He moved to New York City from Russia and initially operated the credit union for the Amalgamated Clothing Workers of America. His first development, the Amalgamated Houses near Van Cortlandt Park in the Bronx, was financed with a long-term mortgage from the Metropolitan Life Insurance Company, municipal property tax abatements under a new state limited-dividend housing law, and additional funds from the *Jewish Daily Forward* and the Amalgamated Bank (owned by the Amalgamated Clothing Workers of America); the houses opened in 1927 and Kazan became president of the

Amalgamated Housing Corporation. In 1951 he formed the nonprofit United Housing Foundation, which during the 1960s used vacant land to build Rochdale Village in Queens and Co-op City, a housing development of 15,372 units on a site of three hundred acres (120 hectares) in the northeastern Bronx. Kazan led efforts to build limited-equity cooperative housing and became one of the city's foremost developers of low- and middle-income housing, producing more than 33,000 apartment units in six decades.

Kenneth G. Wray: "Abraham E. Kazan: The Story of the Amalgamated Houses and the United Housing Foundation" (thesis, Columbia University, 1991)

Marc A. Weiss

Kazan [Kazanjioglou], **Elia** (*b* Constantinople [now Istanbul], 7 Sept 1909). Director, actor, and teacher. With his family he moved to New York City in 1913 and lived briefly on West 136th Street. After earning an AB from Williams College (1930) and attending the Yale School of Drama (1930–32) he returned to the city and joined the Group Theatre (1931–41), with which he acted in Clifford Odets's *Waiting for Lefty* and directed Robert Ardry's *Casey Jones* and *Thunder Rock*. He also worked with several groups associated with the political left, including the Theatre of Action, the Federal Theatre, the League of Workers Theatre, and the Theatre Union. During the 1940s he first achieved critical acclaim on Broadway with Thornton Wilder's *The Skin of Our Teeth* (1942, Plymouth Theatre) and Arthur Miller's *All My Sons* (1947, Coronet Theatre) and *Death of a Salesman* (1949, Morosco Theatre). His most successful collaborations were with Tennessee Williams: *A Streetcar Named Desire* (1947, Barrymore Theatre), *Camino Real* (1953, Martin Beck Theatre), *Cat on a Hot Tin Roof* (1955, Morosco Theatre), and *Sweet Bird of Youth* (1959, Martin Beck Theatre). In 1945 he directed his first motion picture, *A Tree Grows in Brooklyn*. With Cheryl Crawford and Robert Lewis he formed the Actors Studio in 1947 and engaged several of its graduates in his productions, including Marlon Brando, James Dean, Julie Harris, and Eli Wallach. He directed several films in the following years that were well received: *A Streetcar Named Desire* (1951), *On the Waterfront* (1954), *East of Eden* (1955), and *Splendor in the Grass* (1961). In 1952 he testified about his association with the Communist Party before the House Un-American Activities Committee and in his own defense took out a full-page advertisement in the *New York Times* on 12 April. With Robert Whitehead he led the Repertory Theater of Lincoln Center from 1962 to 1965, and he directed its production of Miller's *After the Fall* (1962). Kazan gradually became disenchanted with both plays and films and increasingly devoted himself to writing novels, which include *The Arrangement* (1967) and *Beyond the Aegean* (1994).

For illustration see FILMMAKING.

Kazin, Alfred (*b* Brooklyn, 5 June 1915). Literary critic. The son of Jewish immigrants, he grew up in Brownsville and as an undergraduate at City College (graduated 1935) wrote book reviews for the *New York Times* and the *New York Herald Tribune*; he also worked closely with Malcolm Cowley at the *New Republic* and earned an MA from Columbia University (1938). In 1935 he began work on his book *On Native Grounds: An Interpretation of Modern American Prose Literature* (1942), for which he conducted research at the New York Public Library and which brought him recognition as an authority on American literature and culture. He also wrote for the *Partisan Review*, held editorial positions at *Fortune* and the *American Scholar*, and taught at New York University, Hunter College, and the City University of New York. At a time when most critics looked to Europe for artistic standards, Kazin proclaimed himself an independent, socially and politically aware "literary radical" who dealt with American culture on its own terms and wrote from his own experiences. The city has often been the subject of his writings. *A Walker in the City* (1951), written in a studio on Pineapple Street in Brooklyn Heights, describes his childhood in Brooklyn. *Starting Out in the Thirties* (1965) is an account of his work as a young man, including his years under Cowley. *New York Jew* (1978) addresses the fascination and fear that the city holds for him.

Naomi Wax

Keens Chophouse. Restaurant at 72 West 36th Street in Manhattan. Originally part of the select actors' club the Lambs, it became an independent establishment in 1885, catering to the actors, playwrights, and producers who worked at the theaters around Herald Square. Regular patrons joined the Keens Chophouse Pipe Club, which for a lifetime fee of $5 provided diners with their own long-stemmed clay pipes. Catalogued and stored in racks above the tables, the pipes were always at the ready for anyone who called for his "clay" after dinner. Over the years the club grew to include more than fifty thousand members, including Babe Ruth, Will Rogers, Enrico Caruso, and Douglas MacArthur. Keens remained an all-male preserve until 1901, when the actress Lillie Langtry sued the restaurant. She won, and the Langtry Room was named in her honor. Keens remained into the 1990s what it had always been: a restaurant, pub, and bar where a low-key, clubby ambience provided a respite from the bustle of midtown.

Kenneth T. Jackson

Keller, Helen (Adams) (*b* Tuscumbia, Ala., 27 June 1880; *d* Westport, Conn., 1 June 1968). Writer, lecturer, and philanthropist. At the age of nineteen months she lost her hearing and sight because of an unexplained illness. With her lifelong teacher Anne Sullivan she traveled to New York City in 1894 to improve her speech and lip reading at the Wright–Humason School on 76th Street, and became acquainted with many members of fashionable society, including the Rockefellers, the Parsons, Henry H. Rogers, John Burroughs, and Mark Twain. While attending Radcliffe College and living in New England she was a frequent visitor to the city; in 1915 she spoke at Washington Irving High School on behalf of the Labor Forum. She moved in 1917 to a house at 7111 112th Street in Forest Hills. During the following years she made several appearances with her teacher in vaudeville acts, including one at the Palace Theatre in 1920. She also worked with the American Federation for the Blind to solicit gifts for an endowment established in her name. In 1938 she left the city to live in Westport. Keller's published writings include two autobiographical works (*The Story of My Life*, 1901; *Midstream*, 1928) and *My Religion* (1926), about the teachings of Emanuel Swedenborg.

Elizabeth J. Kramer

Kelley, Florence (*b* Philadelphia, 12 Sept 1859; *d* New York City, 17 Feb 1932). Reformer. A member of an élite family from Philadelphia and the daughter of a powerful Republican congressman, she graduated from Cornell University in 1882 and became a prominent Progressive reformer in New York City. As the head of the National Consumers' League from 1898 until her death she fought at the state and federal levels for woman suffrage, a minimum wage for women, and other social legislation. Kelley lived at the Henry Street Settlement on the Lower East Side. Her autobiography was edited by Kathryn Kish Sklar and published in 1985 as *Notes of Sixty Years: The Autobiography of Florence Kelley*.

Josephine Goldmark: *Impatient Crusader: Florence Kelley's Life Story* (Urbana: University of Illinois Press, 1953; repr. New York: Greenwood, 1976)

See also OCCUPATIONAL HEALTH.

Kathryn Kish Sklar

Kelley Drye and Warren. Law firm begun in 1836 as the partnership of William Mulligan and Hiram Barney, President Abraham Lincoln's law agent; it is one of the oldest law firms in the city. Under Adrian Joline it helped to reorganize the Metropolitan Street Railroad system (1907–12), and it was also the primary outside counsel for the Chrysler Corporation from 1924 until the 1980s. Given its current name in 1975, the firm settled the chemical disaster in Bhopal, India, for the firm of Union Carbide, won a summary judgment in a case dealing with Agent Orange, handled the move of the football team the New York Giants to New Jersey, and represented the Rouse Company in the development of South Street Seaport. In the early 1990s Kelley Drye and Warren was known for its expertise in law pertaining to health care and represented New York Hospital, Memorial Sloan Kettering Cancer Center, New York Medical College, and the Terence Cardinal Cooke Health Center; it had seventy-one partners, 374 associates, and offices at 101 Park Avenue.

George J. Lankevich

Kellor, Frances (Alice) (*b* Columbus, Ohio, 20 Oct 1873; *d* New York City, 4 Jan 1952). Social scientist and reformer. She earned a law degree from Cornell University in 1897, studied sociology at the University of Chicago, and moved to New York City in 1905. In 1908 she was appointed to the New York State Commission of Immigration. She was a founder of the National Urban League and in 1910 became the first woman to lead the New York Bureau of Industries and Immigration. A close advisor to Theodore Roosevelt, she attracted attention during the presidential election of 1912 as the head of the National Service Committee of the Progressive Party. In 1916 she directed the National Americanization Committee, and after the First World War she became an authority on domestic and international arbitration. During the 1930s she was active in the American Arbitration Association. In her published writings Kellor analyzed women workers, black Americans, crime, unemployment, and immigration. Among her best-known works are *Experimental Sociology* (1901), *Out of Work* (1904), *Straight America: A Call to National Service* (1916), *Immigration and the Future* (1920), and *Arbitration in the New Industrial Society* (1934).

John Recchiuti

Kellum, John (*b* Hempstead, N.Y., 27 Aug 1809; *d* Hempstead, 24 July 1871). Architect. He began his career as a carpenter and became an architect several years after settling in Brooklyn in 1841. Initially he worked with Gamaliel King (1800–76), who was active in local business and political circles and designed the Brooklyn City Hall (1846–51, 209 Joralemon Street; now Borough Hall), the Kings County courthouse (1865, demolished), commercial buildings in Brooklyn and Manhattan including Kings County Savings Bank (1868, 135 Broadway), and such churches as St. Paul's (1838, Court and Congress streets, Brooklyn), the Twelfth Street Reformed Church (1869, Brooklyn), and the Sullivan Street Methodist Church (1860, West 4th Street, Manhattan). From 1850 the firm of King and Kellum had a varied practice. It received a commission for the Friends Meeting House (1859, 28 Gramercy Park South; later Brotherhood Synagogue) but was best known for its commercial cast-iron architecture, beginning with the Cary Building (1857, Chambers and Church streets). Kellum's independent career began in 1859 with a commission from A. T. Stewart for a new cast-iron department store (1859–62, 1867–68, demolished), which became nationally renowned. Other designs for Stewart, his most important client, included a mansion (1864–69, demolished), the innovative cast-iron Working Women's Hotel (1869–78, later the Park Avenue Hotel; demolished), and the suburb of Garden City, Long Island (1869–71). Among his commercial buildings were the Mutual Life Insurance Company (1863–65, demolished), Steinway Pianos (1863–64, demolished), the New York Stock Exchange (1864–65, demolished), the New York Herald (1865–67, demolished), Tiffany's (1869, 15th Street and Union Square East; later the Amalgamated Bank), McCreery's Store (1869, Broadway and 11th Street, converted into apartments), lofts with cast-iron façades in SoHo, and cast-iron ferry terminals on the East River. His only large public commission was the New York County, or "Tweed," Courthouse (1861–71, 52 Chambers Street; for illustration see TWEED COURTHOUSE).

Deborah S. Gardner: "The Architecture of Commercial Capitalism: John Kellum and the Development of New York, 1840–1875" (diss., Columbia University, 1979)
Deborah S. Gardner: "'A Paradise of Fashion': A. T. Stewart's Department Store, 1862–1875," *A Needle, a Bobbin, a Strike: Women Needleworkers in America*, ed. Joan M. Jensen and Sue Davidson (Philadelphia: Temple University Press, 1984), 60–80

Deborah S. Gardner

Kelly, John (*b* New York City, *ca* 1822; *d* New York City, 1886). Political leader. Self-taught and ambitious, he became an alderman in 1852. He was elected to the U.S. House of Representatives in 1854, where as the only Roman Catholic member he vigorously attacked the Know-Nothings. In 1858 he became sheriff of New York County. He left Tammany Hall in 1868 to protest the Tweed Ring but returned in 1871 as a reformer, and he became the organization's first Irish Catholic boss. He quashed other Democratic factions in the city and established party discipline by tightly controlling patronage. In 1876 he was elected comptroller of New York City. He supported and then opposed Samuel J. Tilden and tried to block Grover Cleveland's presidential nomination. During his tenure Kelly transformed Tammany Hall from a ring into a political machine. He was often known as Honest John Kelly.

Harold Zink: *City Bosses in the United States* (Durham, N.C.: Duke University Press, 1930)

See also TAMMANY HALL.

Frank Vos

Kennedy, Joseph P(atrick), Sr. (*b* Boston, 6 Sept 1888; *d* Hyannis, Mass., 18 Nov 1969). Financier, father of John F. Kennedy and Robert F. Kennedy. After a successful career as a financier and as a film producer in Hollywood he moved with his family to 252nd Street and Independence Avenue in Riverdale in 1927; in the following year he bought a mansion at 294 Pondfield Road in Bronxville, New York, and he also lived briefly in the 1920s at the Gramercy Park Hotel, 2 Lexington Avenue. He campaigned actively for Franklin D. Roosevelt in the presidential campaign of 1932 and from 1934 to 1935 was the head of the Securities and Exchange Commission, which had been recently formed to regulate the securities markets. In 1941 he sold his house in Bronxville and for the rest of his life lived in Washington and Hyannisport, Massachusetts. The firm of Joseph P. Kennedy Enterprises manages the family fortune of the Kennedys at 100 East 42nd Street in Manhattan.

Doris Kearns Goodwin: *The Fitzgeralds and the Kennedys* (New York: Simon and Schuster, 1987)

Edward T. O'Donnell

Kennedy, Robert F(rancis) (*b* Brookline, Mass., 20 Nov 1925; *d* Los Angeles, 6 June 1968). Attorney general, senator, and presidential candidate. The third son of Joseph Kennedy Sr., he grew up from 1927 to 1929 at 5040 Independence Avenue in Riverdale. In 1961 he was named attorney general of the United States by his brother, President John F. Kennedy. After his brother's assassination he resigned from office in 1964, moved to an apartment at United Nations Plaza in New York City, and in November was elected to the U.S. Senate from New York. As a senator he supported liberal social programs and institutions, among them the Bedford Stuyvesant Restoration Corporation, which sought to revitalize a poor neighborhood by achieving cooperation between business and community leaders. He also spoke out against President Lyndon B. Johnson's escalation of the war in Vietnam. In March 1968 he entered the race for the Democratic presidential nomination but was assassinated after winning the primary election in California. A Requiem was held in his honor at St. Patrick's Cathedral in Manhattan.

Arthur Schlesinger Jr.: *Robert F. Kennedy and His Times* (Boston: Houghton Mifflin, 1978)

For illustration see BEDFORD STUYVESANT RESTORATION CORPORATION.

Edward T. O'Donnell

Kennedy Airport. See JOHN F. KENNEDY INTERNATIONAL AIRPORT.

Kensett, John Frederick (*b* Cheshire, Conn., 22 March 1816; *d* New York City, 14 Dec 1872). Painter. In the 1820s and 1830s he trained and worked as an engraver in New

Haven, Connecticut; New York City; and Albany, New York. After studying art in Europe from 1840 he returned in 1847 to New York City, where he was elected to the National Academy of Design (1849), the Century Association (1849), the Sketch Club (1854), and the Union League Club (1863). His landscapes and paintings of coastal scenes from these years employ a "luminist" style characterized by a sensitive rendering of light and atmosphere and associate him with the second generation of the Hudson River School. A dramatic series of paintings from 1872 are often referred to as the "Last Summer's Work." In addition to working as an artist Kensett was a president of the Artists' Fund Society, a member of the National Art Commission (1859), a chairman of the Metropolitan Fair Art Committee (1864), and a founding member and trustee of the Metropolitan Museum of Art (1870).

John K. Howat, John Paul Driscoll, et al.: *John Frederick Kensett: An American Master* (New York: Worcester Art Museum / W. W. Norton, 1985)

Donna Ann Grossman

Kensington. Neighborhood in west central Brooklyn (1990 pop. 30,782), bounded to the north by Caton Avenue, to the east by Coney Island Avenue, to the south by Avenue H, and to the west by McDonald Avenue; it is bisected by Ocean Parkway. Once part of the town of Flatbush, it was developed after the northern reaches of Ocean Parkway were completed in 1875. The neighborhood is middle class and racially integrated. The housing is varied, but much of it was built in the 1920s and consists of row houses and six-story apartment buildings. In the 1980s Kensington and its environs attracted a diverse population, including immigrants from China, the Soviet Union, Haiti, and Guyana, as well as the Dominican Republic and Jamaica. A commercial district lies along Church Avenue, with additional retail outlets on Ditmas and 18th avenues.

John J. Gallagher

Kent, James (*b* Putnam County, N.Y., 31 July 1763; *d* New York City, 12 Dec 1847). Jurist. After being educated at Yale University he went to work as a lawyer. A Federalist, he was appointed recorder of New York City in 1797 and presided over the court of general sessions; he became a justice on the state supreme court in 1798, its chief justice in 1804, and chancellor of the Court of Chancery in 1814. In these positions Kent wrote opinions that helped to shape common law and equity law nationwide. After retiring in 1823 he lived in New York City and wrote *Commentaries on American Law* (1826–30), which earned him the nickname the "American Blackstone."

John T. Horton: *James Kent: A Study in Conservatism* (New York: D. Appleton–Century, 1939)

See also Lawyers.

James D. Folts

Rockwell Kent, Power of Electricity *(1939). Mural for the General Electric Building at the World's Fair of 1939–40*

Kent, Rockwell (*b* Tarrytown, N.Y., 21 June 1882; *d* Plattsburgh, N.Y., 13 March 1971). Painter, printmaker, and political activist. He studied architecture at Columbia University and realist painting under Robert Henri and Kenneth Hayes Miller. An opponent of the National Academy of Design, he championed progressive artists and in 1911 organized an independent exhibition at the Society of Beaux-Arts Architects in New York City. He drew inspiration from the wilderness of Newfoundland, Greenland, and Alaska to develop an austere, symbolic style of landscape painting; he also illustrated an edition of Shakespeare and completed a mural, *The Power of Electricity*, for the World's Fair of 1939–40. His ties to the Communist Party led to the revocation of his passport by the U.S. Department of State, which he contested; the decision was ultimately overturned by the U.S. Supreme Court. In 1967 he received the Lenin Peace Prize. Kent donated his collection of drawings to Columbia University.

David Traxel: *An American Saga: The Life and Times of Rockwell Kent* (New York: Harper and Row, 1980)
Fridolf Johnson, ed.: *Rockwell Kent: An Anthology of His Works* (New York: Alfred A. Knopf, 1982)
Richard V. West: *"An Enkindled Eye": The Paintings of Rockwell Kent: A Retrospective Exhibition* (Santa Barbara, Calif.: Santa Barbara Museum of Art, 1985)

Judith Zilczer

Kerensky, Alexander (Feodorovich) (*b* Simbirsk [now Ulyanovsk], Russia, 4 May 1881; *d* New York City, 11 June 1970). Revolutionary leader. He was prime minister of the Russian Provisional Government in 1917 before the Bolshevik takeover. Forced into exile, he lived in western Europe until 1940, when he emigrated to the United States and settled in New York City. For the last three decades of his life he lectured extensively at universities in New York City and elsewhere, and in 1949 he formed the League to Fight for National Freedom, which called for the restoration of democratic rule in Russia. From his apartment on Riverside Drive Kerensky wrote profusely on his revolutionary experiences: his published writings include *Russia and History's Turning Point* (1965) and *The Kerensky Memoirs* (1966).

Richard Abraham: *Alexander Kerensky: The First Love of the Revolution* (New York: Columbia University Press, 1987)

Paul Robert Magocsi

Kern, Jerome (David) (*b* New York City, 27 Jan 1885; *d* New York City, 11 Nov 1945). Composer. He lived at 411 East 56th Street until his family moved to Newark, New Jersey, in 1897. He received a thorough education in music at the New York College of Music and in Germany. After working on Broadway as a song plugger and rehearsal pianist he moved to London to adapt English musicals for performance on Broadway. His first hit song was "How'd You Like to Spoon with Me?" (1905). He returned to New York City and lived in an apartment at 107 West 68th Street in 1907, then achieved his first success on the stage with *The Red Petticoat* (1911). After a brief move farther uptown in 1912 he occupied 226 West 70th Street, his last residence in New York City; he lived there until 1915, when he moved to Bronxville, New York. His most outstanding and influential score was that for *Show Boat* (1927), a musical with book and lyrics by Oscar Hammerstein II based on a novel written by Edna Ferber in 1926. Its songs, including "Ol' Man River," "Can't Help Loving Dat Man of Mine," "Why Do I Love You?," and "Bill," joined lyrical European operetta with American vernacular genres, including folk ballad, syncopated dance, and the music of Tin Pan Alley. *Show Boat* greatly influenced younger composers on Broadway, including George Gershwin, Richard Rodgers, and Cole Porter, who admired its distinctively American plot and integration of narrative and characterization. Its vivid and sensitive portrayal of blacks was unusual for its time. In 1954 the New York City Opera added *Show Boat* to its repertory, making it arguably the first musical to be presented by an opera company. Kern wrote more than seventy scores for screen and stage, some in collaboration with Hammerstein, Guy Bolton, and P. G. Wodehouse, and more than nine hundred songs, including "Smoke Gets in Your Eyes" (from his musical *Roberta*, 1933, made into a film in 1935), "They Didn't Believe Me" (1914), "Look for the Silver Lining" (1920), "The Song Is You" (1932), and "All the Things You Are" (1940). At least two of his songs were inspired by places in New York City: "Nestin' Time in Flatbush" (1917) and "Bojangles of Harlem" (1936). The spontaneity of Kern's music belies its careful crafting and sophistication.

Gerald Martin Bordman: *Jerome Kern: His Life and Music* (New York: Oxford University Press, 1980)

Nicholas E. Tawa

Kerouac, Jack [Jean-Louis] (*b* Lowell, Mass., 12 March 1922; *d* St. Petersburg, Fla., 21 Oct 1969). Novelist. He moved to New York City at seventeen and spent a year at the Horace Mann School before attending Columbia University on a football scholarship. In 1944 he met William Burroughs and Allen Ginsberg, then a student at Columbia; the three formed the nucleus of the group of writers that became known as the beats. Kerouac described his life in New York City in *The Town and the City* (1950), *Lonesome Traveler* (1960), and *Vanity of Duluoz* (1969). In three weeks during April 1951 he wrote his best-known novel, *On the Road* (published 1957), in an apartment at 454 West 20th Street in Manhattan. Kerouac lived at intervals from 1952 to 1963 at 94-21 134th Street in Queens and in 1953 at 501 East 11th Street in Manhattan.

Ann Charters: *Kerouac: A Biography* (San Francisco: Straight Arrow, 1973)

Tom Clark: *Jack Kerouac: A Biography* (New York: Harcourt Brace Jovanovich, 1984)

Ann Charters

Keteltas affair. A political scandal of 1796 that facilitated the rise to power of the Jeffersonian Democratic Republicans. The controversy arose when the Federalist alderman Gabriel Furman ordered that two allegedly insolent ferrymen should be whipped and jailed without the right to counsel or the right to testify in their own defense, and the Republican attorney William Keteltas demanded that the state assembly remove Furman from office. When the assembly later absolved Furman, Keteltas condemned it for "flagrant abuse of rights" and was jailed for contempt. Along with many poor craftsmen and laborers, Jeffersonians berated the Federalists for the incident, which they saw as evidence of Federalist disregard for the middling and poorer classes.

Alfred F. Young: *The Democratic–Republicans of New York: The Origins, 1763–1797* (Chapel Hill: University of North Carolina Press, 1967)

Howard Rock

Passengers boarding a morning train at the Kew Gardens Station of the Long Island Rail Road, ca *1920s*

Kew Gardens. Neighborhood in central Queens, bounded to the north by the Interborough Parkway and Queens Boulevard, to the east by Kew Gardens Road, to the south by Myrtle Avenue, and to the west by Forest Park. Much of the area was acquired in 1868 by Albon P. Man, who developed the neighborhood of Richmond Hill to the south, chiefly along Jamaica Avenue, while leaving undeveloped the hilly land to the north. Maple Grove Cemetery on Kew Gardens Road opened in 1875. A station was built for mourners in October and trains stopped there from mid November. The station was named Hopedale, after Hopedale Hall, a hotel at what is now Queens Boulevard and Union Turnpike. In the 1890s the executors of Man's estate laid out the Richmond Hill Golf Course on the hilly terrain south of the railroad. This remained in use until it was bisected in 1908 by the main line of the Long Island Rail Road, which had been moved six hundred feet (180 meters) to the south to eliminate a curve. The golf course was then abandoned and a new station was built in 1909 on Lefferts Boulevard. Man's heirs Alrick Man and Albon Man Jr. decided to lay out a new community and called it at first Kew and then Kew Gardens after the well-known botanical gardens in England. The architects of the development favored English and neo-Tudor styles, which still predominate in many sections. In 1910 the property was sold piecemeal by the estate and during the next few years streets were extended, land graded, and water and sewer pipes installed. The first apartment building was the Kew Bolmer at 80-45 Kew Gardens Road, erected in 1915; a clubhouse followed in 1916 and a private school in 1918. In 1920 the Kew Gardens Inn at the railroad station opened for resident guests, who paid $40 a week for a room and bath with meals, and $85 a week for two rooms and bath with meals. Elegant one-family houses were built in the 1920s, as were apartment buildings such as Colonial Hall (1921) and Kew Hall (1922) that numbered more than twenty by 1936.

In July 1933 Grand Central Parkway opened from Kew Gardens to the edge of Nassau County; this road was extended in 1935 as the Interborough Parkway to Pennsylvania Avenue in East New York. Because the parkways used part of the roadbed of Union Turnpike no houses were sacrificed. The greatest change was wrought by the opening of the Independent subway along Queens Boulevard to Union Turnpike on 31 December 1936; four months later the subway was extended to Jamaica. Residents could now reach Manhattan and Brooklyn twenty-four hours a day for five cents. The immediate effect was to stimulate the construction of larger apartment buildings like Kent Manor and high-rise buildings along Queens Boulevard, and the last vacant land disappeared. A large community of Jewish refugees from Germany took shape during the Second World War. In 1964 the neighborhood received a measure of unwanted notoriety when a bar manager named Kitty Genovese was fatally assaulted there before thirty-eight witnesses, none of whom came to her aid. The incident focused attention on the growing crime problem in New York City and the increasing insularity and apathy of its residents. The neighborhood attracted many Chinese immigrants after 1965, about 2500 Iranian Jews after the Iranian revolution of 1979, and immigrants from China, Iran, Afghanistan, Israel, the Soviet Union, India, Colombia, and Korea during the 1980s. Kew Gardens remains a densely populated, upper-middle-class residential community. Private, one-family houses line the sidestreets near Queens Borough Hall, a courthouse on Queens Boulevard.

Vincent Seyfried

Key Food. A cooperative chain of supermarkets formed in 1937 by a group of independent grocers in Brooklyn who hoped by joining forces to lower their expenses and compete with the growing national chains like the Great Atlantic and Pacific Tea Company (A&P). The original outlet was at 2nd Avenue and 45th Street in Sunset Park. In the mid 1990s the members of Key Food operated nearly 160 stores in the metropolitan area, most in the five boroughs. The warehouse is in the Brooklyn Terminal Market at Avenue D and East 89th Street in East Flatbush.

Stephen Weinstein

Kidd, William (*b* Greenock, Scotland, *ca* 1645; *d* London, 23 May 1701). Pirate and privateer. He went to sea early in life. When war broke out between France and England in 1688 he received from the governor of the English colony of Nevis a commission as a privateer, empowered to harass and plunder enemy shipping in times of war. He then attacked and plundered French ships and colonies until the members of his crew abandoned him, taking with them his ship and treasure (most were pirates who preferred piracy to war). He acquired another ship and during an unsuccessful pursuit of his former crew landed in New York City in time to aid the forces sent to end Leisler's Rebellion. His alliance with the new government worked to his advantage, and he profited from the friendship of such rich and powerful residents of the city as Robert Livingston. In 1691 he married the wealthy widow Sarah Bradley Cox Oort, with whom he moved to what is now 119–21 Pearl Street and bought a pew in Trinity Church. A summer home, "Saw Kill," stood near the East River at what is now 74th Street.

In 1695 Kidd embarked on a trading voyage to London in the hope of obtaining a royal privateering commission. When he left London in the following year he had a commission to hunt pirates, along with financial backing from the leaders of the Whig government, an alliance that he owed to the intervention of Livingston and the newly appointed governor for New York and Massachusetts, the Earl of Bellomont. He sailed to New York City, enlisted more men for a crew, and set out for the Indian Ocean, but instead of hunting pirates he turned pirate himself, capturing five ships off the coast of India before heading for Madagascar. By the time he sailed for home the East India Company had set the English government against him, and when he met with Bellomont in Boston he was arrested and sent to England. His well-publicized and highly political trial ended in his conviction and hanging. Only a small part of Kidd's reputedly large treasure was ever recovered by authorities, and a popular belief that the rest remains buried has inspired searches ranging from the Indian Ocean to New York City.

Graham Brooks, ed.: *The Trial of Captain Kidd* (London: William Hodges, 1930)
Harold T. Wilkins: *Captain Kidd and His Skeleton Island: The Discovery of a Strange Secret* (London: Cassell, 1935)
Dunbar M. Hinrichs: *The Fateful Voyage of Captain Kidd* (New York: Bookman, 1955)
Robert C. Ritchie: *Captain Kidd and the War against the Pirates* (Cambridge: Harvard University Press, 1986)

Robert Ritchie

Kildare, Owen (Frawley) (*b* New York City, 1864; *d* New York City, 4 Feb 1911). Journalist. Born on Catharine Street and orphaned at birth, he was abandoned on the streets of the city by his foster family when he was seven. After supporting himself as a newsboy he became a brawler, a "bouncer" in bars on the Bowery, a prizefighter, and a "slugger" in election campaigns. He learned to read and write at the age of thirty and by the age of thirty-seven was able to work as a newspaperman. During his short career Kildare published six books, including a play, the autobiography *My Mamie Rose* (1903), and *My Old Bailiwick* (1906), a collection of articles on life along the Bowery.

George A. Thompson, Jr.

Kill van Kull. A tidal strait about three miles (five kilometers) long and one thousand feet (three hundred meters) wide between Staten Island and Bayonne, New Jersey, connecting Upper New York Bay with Newark Bay. It is traversed by the Bayonne Bridge, and at its western end is Shooters Island. The Kill van Kull is one of the busiest waterways in New York Harbor, used by oil tankers and by container ships bound for Port Newark and Port Elizabeth in New Jersey.

Gerard R. Wolfe

Kimball, Francis (*b* Kennebunk, Maine, 24 Sept 1845; *d* 20 Dec 1919). Architect. Known as a theater designer, he moved to New York City in 1879 to refurbish the Madison Square Theatre and later built the Casino Theatre at Broadway and 39th Street (1882). He designed the Montauk Club in Brooklyn in a Venetian neo-Gothic style (1890; for illustration see MONTAUK CLUB) and after working with the English architect William Burges was inspired to use a French neo-Gothic style for the Rhinelander Mansion on Madison Avenue (1899). With George Thompson he built a tower for the Manhattan Life Insurance Company (1892) that was the first skyscraper in the city with a frame made entirely of steel. Kimball also designed the tower of the United States Trust Company (1907).

Edward A. Eigen

King, Rufus (*b* Scarborough, Maine, 24 March 1755; *d* New York City, 29 April 1827). Lawyer, senator, and diplomat. He represented Massachusetts at the Constitutional Convention and earned a reputation as a strong nationalist and gifted orator. After moving to New York City he was appointed to the first U.S. Senate; as minister to Great Britain (1796–1803) he intervened to prevent Irish political exiles from receiving asylum in the United States. In 1805 he purchased on Jamaica Avenue in Queens land and a house (still standing in the mid 1990s). He later served again in the Senate (1813–25) and again as minister to Britain (1825–26); he was also the Federalist candidate for the vice presidency in 1804 and 1808 and an unofficial candidate for the presidency in 1816, and he sought the governorship of New York in 1816. King's role in the politics of New York City was circumscribed by hostility from Irish voters who resented his role in suppressing Irish immigration. Although he opposed the declaration of war in 1812 his patriotic response in raising money for the city's defense won him respect as a Federalist elder statesman long after his party ceased to be a political force. King was an early member of the New-York Historical Society, a warden of Trinity Church, a trustee of Columbia College, the first president of the Queens County Society for the Promotion of Agriculture and Domestic Manufactures, and an instrumental supporter of Grace Church in Jamaica, where he is buried in the churchyard. King Street in Manhattan was named for him in 1807. His eldest son, John A. King, was governor of New York (1857–59), and a second son, Charles, was the editor of the *New-York American* (1823–45) and president of Columbia College (1849–64).

Robert Ernst: *Rufus King: American Federalist* (Chapel Hill: University of North Carolina Press, 1968)

Mariam Touba

King Manor. Historic house at 153rd Street and Jamaica Avenue in King Park in Jamaica, built as a farmhouse in a Dutch style between 1733 and 1755. It was bought in 1805 by Rufus King, a signer of the Constitution who oversaw the remodeling and expansion of the house. Among the additions were a three-story structure with a gambrel roof and a Greek Revival portico. The house remained with King's heirs until 1896, was deeded to the city in 1898, and later became a museum with many furnished period rooms. After an extensive exterior and interior renovation that restored the manor to its early-nineteenth-century appearance, the museum reopened to the public in 1994.

Historic Houses in New York City Parks (New York: Department of Parks and Recreation / Historic House Trust of New York City, 1989)

Jonathan Kuhn

King Model Houses. See STRIVERS' ROW.

Kingsborough Community College. Junior college of the City University of New

York, opened in 1963 at 2001 Oriental Boulevard, on a campus of sixty-seven acres (twenty-seven hectares) at the eastern tip of Coney Island. It offers a highly regarded program in marine and fisheries technology, as well as programs in environmental health and science and in print journalism and broadcast technology (the only one at a two-year college in the city). In 1990 Kingsborough enrolled 6560 full-time and 7760 part-time students.

Marc Ferris

Kingsbridge. Neighborhood in the northwestern Bronx, bounded to the north by Mosholu, to the east by Broadway, to the south by Marble Hill, and to the west by the hills of Spuyten Duyvil. It is named for the King's Bridge, the first bridge connecting Manhattan with the mainland, built by Frederick Philipse in 1693 over Spuyten Duyvil Creek at what is now Kingsbridge Avenue and 230th Street. A strategic area and the site of frequent battles during the American Revolution, it was largely farmland until the 1860s, when the Johnson Iron Foundry along the banks of Spuyten Duyvil Creek made munitions for the Union Army. Increasing migration into the area was stimulated by the construction of the 7th Avenue subway line by Interborough Rapid Transit in 1908. In 1913 the Church of the Mediator (Episcopal) was consecrated on Kingsbridge Avenue at 231st Street; St. John's Church (Catholic) was built next door to the south. In the mid 1990s the population was mostly Irish; 231st Street and Broadway was the center of the commercial district, which included restaurants and a movie theater. The housing stock consists of one-family houses and interspersed five- and six-story apartment buildings dating from the 1920s, as well as a few high-rise apartment buildings from the 1950s and 1960s.

Lloyd Ultan

Kingsbridge, ca *1900*

King's College. Original name of COLUMBIA UNIVERSITY.

Kings County. One of the five counties of New York City, coextensive with the borough of Brooklyn.

Kings County Hospital Center. Municipal hospital in Brooklyn, one of the oldest in the metropolitan area. It began in 1831 as a one-room infirmary in the town of Flatbush that expanded in 1837. In 1929 Mayor James J. Walker approved funds to construct a new complex: built in 1931, this covered an entire block along Clarkson Avenue between New York and Albany avenues. The institution continued to expand, establishing affiliates in Bedford–Stuyvesant and East New York. In 1956 the hospital formed an affiliation with the Downstate Medical Center (renamed the Health Science Center in 1986), a medical school of the State University of New York. The hospital encountered financial and other problems in the 1980s and 1990s, notably a controversy surrounding its treatment in 1991 of Yankel Rosenbaum, a victim of the riots in Crown Heights whose death was attributed to a stab wound that had gone unattended at the hospital. This incident and others led to a series of investigations and calls for the hospital to be privatized. In the mid 1990s Kings County served nearly a million persons a year and was the third-largest hospital in the United States.

James Bradley

King's Highway. See BOSTON POST ROAD.

Kings Highway. Neighborhood in southwestern Brooklyn, bounded to the north by Avenue M, to the east by Nostrand Avenue, to the south by Avenue T, and to the west by Ocean Parkway; it lies mostly within the original boundaries of Gravesend. The neighborhood is named for a road bisecting it that was once an Indian trail running east from the Narrows; this linked the small villages of New Utrecht, Flatbush, Flatlands, and Bushwick and was used by British troops as an approach during the Battle of Long Island. A farm of a hundred acres (forty hectares) owned by the Wyckoff family was bought in 1835 by Cornelius W. Bennett, who moved there from Gowanus. Potato farms predominated until 1903, when a large portion of Bennett's land was sold by his descendant Edward Bennett to the development firm of Wood, Harmon. During the 1920s the studios of Vitagraph, Warner Brothers, and Ace Films stood near Avenue M, and silent-film stars such as Lillian Walker, Maurice Costello, and Clara Williams built grand houses in the neighborhood. Most new immigrants settling in the neighborhood and its environs in the 1980s were from the Soviet Union, Israel, and China. The population of Kings Highway is mostly Jewish, and there are many elderly residents. Much of the housing consists of small apartment buildings and one- and two-story houses standing along tree-lined streets. A commercial district lies between Ocean Avenue and Ocean Parkway. The Wyckoff–Bennett homestead remains at 1669 East 22nd Street at Kings Highway.

"Kings Highway for Satisfied Living," *New York Herald Tribune*, 21 Feb 1965

"Kings Highway," *New Brooklyn* 2, no. 1 (summer 1979), 55

"City Plans to Better Shopping Ambiance," *Daily News*, 21 May 1982

Elizabeth Reich Rawson

Kingsland, Ambrose C(ornelius) (*b* New York City, 24 May 1804; *d* New York City, 13 Oct 1878). Mayor. In 1820 he opened a dry-goods store with his brother that soon expanded into international trade. The business flourished as an importer of sperm oil, and it also acquired and operated whaling vessels. Nominated for the mayoralty by the Whig Party in 1851, he defeated his Democratic opponent, Fernando Wood, because of divisions within Tammany Hall. The election was the first held under a new municipal charter forced on the city by a state legislature dominated by Whigs, which diminished the powers of the mayor and increased those of a bicameral city council. The limitations imposed by the charter helped to make Kingsland an ineffective mayor: during his tenure police officers were appointed by aldermen, nearly autonomous city departments were riddled with corruption, and the members of the city council, known as the "Forty Thieves," ran the city for their own profit. His main achievement was his endorsement of the plan to build Central Park. He failed to be renominated after one two-year term, and he returned to his business, now called A. C. Kingsland and Sons, which expanded into trade with Great Britain, China, and the East Indies. Kingsland never again held elective office, but he remained active in the Whig Party during its final years, was a commissioner of the Croton Aqueduct, and served on the Chamber of Commerce.

Melvin G. Holli and Peter d'A. Jones, eds.: *Biographical Dictionary of American Mayors, 1820–1980: Big City Mayors* (Westport, Conn.: Greenwood, 1981)

Rohit T. Aggarwala

Kingsland House. Historic house at 143-35 37th Avenue in Flushing. It was built by Charles Doughty about 1785 and named for his son-in-law Joseph King, a British sea captain who bought it in 1801. The house has two and a half stories, a gambrel roof, a split front door in the Dutch style, and a columned front porch. It was twice moved because of development: in 1923 to a site formerly occupied by a stable after being displaced by a proposed subway extension, and in 1968 to property once owned by the nurseryman Samuel Parsons, near a weeping beech that he planted in 1847. In 1968 the house became the headquarters of the Queens Historical Society, which sponsors exhibitions there.

Historic Houses in New York City Parks (New York: Department of Parks and Recreation / Historic House Trust of New York City, 1989)

Jonathan Kuhn

Kips Bay. Neighborhood on the East Side of Manhattan (1990 pop. 9000), bounded to the north by 34th Street, to the east by the East River, to the south by 27th Street, and to the west by 3rd Avenue. It is named for Jacobus Kip, who in the mid seventeenth century owned a large farm extending to a bay of the East River. Among the affluent and influential residents during the nineteenth century were Horace Greeley and Francis Bayard Winthrop. About the turn of the century many estates were replaced by tenements, and elevated railways were built along 2nd and 3rd avenues. After the 1960s large apartment complexes were erected, including Kips Bay Plaza (1965), which contains the first exposed concrete structures in the city. Kips Bay is dominated by hospitals, among them Bellevue Hospital and New York University Medical Center.

James Bradley

Kiralfy, Imre (*b* Pest [now in Budapest], 1845; *d* Brighton, England, 27 April 1919). Choreographer and producer. With his brother Bolossy Kiralfy (*b* Pest, 1848; *d* London, 27 March 1932) he made his début in New York City in 1869 at the head of a family troupe that performed Hungarian and Slavic dances. In the 1870s and 1880s the brothers became the most important producers of musical spectacles in the city: their productions used large contingents of dancers, elaborate scenery, and special effects to illustrate biblical and historical themes, and eventually grew too large for ordinary stages and were moved to outdoor amphitheaters on Staten Island and in the Palisades. From 1886 the brothers worked separately: Imre moved to London, where he built the Earl's Court and White City, and Bolossy produced shows for international exhibitions, circuses, and world's fairs in New York City and London and on the Continent.

For further illustration see MUSICAL THEATER.

Barbara Barker

Kirstein, Lincoln (*b* Rochester, N.Y., 4 May 1907). Arts patron. While a student at Harvard University (BS 1930) he launched the literary magazine *Hound and Horn* and formed the Harvard Society for Contemporary Art, a forerunner of the Museum of Modern Art in New York City. In 1933 he invited the Russian dancer and choreographer George Balanchine to New York City, and the two formed the School of American Ballet and several ballet companies, including the American Ballet, the American Ballet Caravan, Ballet Society, and the New York City Ballet (1948). Kirstein was also the president of the School of American Ballet and the general manager of the New York City Ballet. His published writings include *Dance* (1935) and *Thirty Years: Lincoln Kirstein's the New York City Ballet* (1978), an account of his partnership with Balanchine.

Montana Katz

Imre Kiralfy's "Columbus and the Discovery of America" at the Barnum & Bailey Greatest Show on Earth, 1891

Kissinger, Henry (Alfred) (*b* Fürth, near Nürnberg, Germany, 27 May 1923). Diplomat. With his parents, Louis and Paula Kissinger, he fled Nazi Germany in August 1938 and settled in an apartment on Fort Washington Avenue in Washington Heights. While attending George Washington High School he worked in a factory downtown that made bristles for shaving brushes. After graduating in 1941 with highest honors he enrolled in the business school of City College of New York on 23rd Street. He was drafted by the army in 1943 and after his military service transferred to Harvard University, where he began his career as an expert in foreign policy. He was the national security advisor to President Richard M. Nixon (1969–73) and secretary of state under Nixon and President Gerald R. Ford (1974–77). Kissinger Associates, an international consulting firm, was formed in the early 1980s with headquarters at Park Avenue and 51st Street. Kissinger was a winner of the Nobel Peace Prize in 1973.

Bernard Kalb and Marvin Kalb: *Kissinger* (Boston: Little, Brown, 1974)

Walter Isaacson: *Kissinger: A Biography* (New York: Simon and Schuster, 1992)

James Bradley

Kitchen (Center for Video, Music, Dance, Performance, Film and Literature). Performing arts center. It opened in 1971 at the Broadway Central Hotel on Mercer Street as a center for video art but soon offered live performances as well. The facility later moved to Broome Street and in 1986 to 512 West 19th Street near the Hudson River. Among those whose work it has featured are the composers Laurie Anderson and Philip Glass, the director Robert Wilson, the choreographers Trisha Brown and Meredith Monk, and the performance artist Eric Bogosian. In 1994 it opened an annex in SoHo, the Kitchenette, which presents daily video exhibitions. Known as one of the most sophisticated centers of its kind, the Kitchen presents more than a hundred live performances a year, administers a video archive and a touring program, and takes part in occasional television projects.

Joan Acocella

Klein, Anne [Golofski, Hannah] (*b* New York City, 1923; *d* New York City, 19 March 1974). Fashion designer. She worked from 1948 at Junior Sophisticates, where she first designed sporty separates for petites, for which she became noted. In 1963 she opened her own company on 7th Avenue and began designing several lines of modern, practical clothes aimed primarily at young women; the basis of her outfits was often a bodysuit.

Caroline Rennolds Milbank

Klein, Calvin (Richard) (*b* Bronx, 19 Nov 1942). Fashion designer. He attended the High School of Art and Design and the Fashion Institute of Technology, then served an apprenticeship in a coat and suit house in Manhattan. In 1968 he opened a coat business with Barry Schwartz, in the following year becoming president of a firm bearing his name. The success of his coats prompted him to expand his designs to include sportswear and eventually fragrances, eyewear, swimwear, lingerie, and a fashionable line of men's and women's clothing sold under the marque "cK." Despite the popularity of his designs he incurred huge debts when sales of designer jeans declined in 1992. He was able to recover, in part by means of an advertising campaign that featured young, scantily clad models. Klein has won three Coty awards (1973, 1974, 1975) and several other awards for men's and women's fashions.

Anne E. Kornblut

Kleindeutschland. Former neighborhood on the Lower East Side of Manhattan, bounded to the north by 16th Street, to the east by the East River, to the south by Division and Grand streets, and to the west by the Bowery; it was also known as Little Germany, Deutschlandle, and Dutchtown. A German enclave took form there in the 1830s and 1840s near what was the northeastern edge of the city. Immigrants from various German regions often settled together, and the population grew to hundreds of thousands. Kleindeutschland was a vital cultural center for two generations of German immigrants and became the foundation of the Jewish neighborhood that took form on the Lower East Side at the end of the nineteenth century.

Stanley Nadel

Kline, Ardolph L(oges) (*b* Sussex County, N.J., 21 Feb 1858; *d* New York City, 13 Oct 1930). Mayor. He was a colonel in the Spanish–American War, an unsuccessful candidate for sheriff, and an alderman from 1904 until his appointment as acting mayor in late 1913. After working as a tax commissioner between 1914 and 1918 he won a seat in the U.S. Congress in 1920 as a Republican; he returned to New York City after being appointed a local agent for the U.S. Shipping Board.

James E. Mooney

Kline, Franz (Joseph) (*b* Wilkes-Barre, Penn., 23 May 1910; *d* New York City, 13 May 1962). Painter. He studied painting in Boston, Paris, and London before moving to New York City in 1938, where he became known for woodcuts, watercolors, and oil paintings executed in a realistic mode. His work was shown at outdoor exhibitions in Washington Square and won awards from the National Academy of Design. With Willem de Kooning he led the Painters' Club. By 1950 he worked primarily on large canvases using black paint applied with wide house-painting brushes. A leader of the abstract expressionist movement, he taught at the Pratt Institute

Kleindeutschland, 1914. George Ehret's restaurant and café at 130–32 3rd Avenue, just north of 14th Street

Franz Kline, Mahoning *(1956). Whitney Museum of American Art*

from 1953. A number of his works were shown in an exhibition at the Museum of Modern Art in 1955 and in a traveling exhibition in 1958–59. Kline had a studio on West 14th Street.

Fielding Dawson: *An Emotional Memoir of Franz Kline* (New York: Pantheon, 1967)

James E. Mooney

Knapp Commission. An investigative body with five members formed in May 1970 by Mayor John V. Lindsay to examine allegations of corruption in the New York Police Department. Its formation followed an exposé in April in the *New York Times* alleging that the police received millions of dollars a year in illegal payments from drug dealers, bookmakers, businessmen, and organized crime. The central figure in the investigation was Frank Serpico, a police detective who with a few colleagues between 1967 and 1970 gathered extensive evidence of corruption in the department, in particular the collection of payoffs from owners of small businesses; he divulged the evidence to the *Times* only after repeatedly failing to elicit a response from the police and City Hall. The chairman of the commission, Whitman Knapp, and his chief investigating counsel, Michael Armstrong, conducted an investigation that lasted two years, and held hearings that produced three stinging reports. The last of these attacked city officials for failing to investigate charges of misconduct by the police and alleged that more than half of all police officers were corrupt. Serpico's battle against corruption is recounted in Peter Maas's riveting book *Serpico* (1973).

George Winslow

Knickerbocker Base Ball Club. A group formed on the East Side of Manhattan in 1842 that played a game believed to be the precursor of modern baseball; the rules of the game were standardized by Alexander J. Cartwright and several other members in 1845. In the autumn of 1845 members of the club competed against each other in Manhattan before moving to the Elysian Fields in Hoboken, New Jersey. They lost the first game that they played against another team, the New York Club, in June 1846. During the late 1850s the members helped to form the National Association of Base Ball Players. In the face of a growing tendency toward professionalism and commercialism in baseball, the Knickerbockers remained an amateur social and athletic club until they disbanded in the mid 1870s.

George B. Kirsch

Knickerbocker Club. Club formed in quarters on 5th Avenue in 1871 by eighteen members of the Union Club who had reservations about some of the changes being made there. Among its founders were Alexander Hamilton (grandson of the secretary of the treasury), John Jacob Astor, Moses Lazarus, and August Belmont. In 1875 members interested in driving four-horse teams formed a subgroup known as the Coaching Club. In 1915 the club moved to a building at 5th Avenue and 62nd Street designed by William Adams Delano of the firm of Delano and Aldrich. In the mid 1990s there were about eight hundred members.

James E. Mooney

Knickerbocker Fire Insurance Company. Name used from 1846 by the UNITED INSURANCE COMPANY OF THE CITY OF NEW YORK.

Knickerbocker Magazine. Literary journal launched in 1833 by Samuel Langtree. It advanced the ideas of the Knickerbocker Group, which consisted mainly of Whigs from New England who sought to create a national literature and make New York City an important literary center. The magazine became the first well-respected literary periodical in the United States after it was taken over by Lewis Gaylord Clark in 1834. To make it competitive with English publications (which were cheaper in the city than in London) Clark sought to infuse it with a distinctively American flavor; he used no reprints but did not object when its contents were reprinted by others, with the result that the literary pieces he published were soon circulated nationally. Among those who wrote for the magazine were Henry Wadsworth Longfellow (who published his first poems in it), Francis Parkman (whose *Oregon Trail* was published serially in 1847), William Cullen Bryant, James Fenimore Cooper, Fitz-Greene Halleck, Nathaniel Hawthorne, Washington Irving, and John Greenleaf Whittier. The magazine declined with the Knickerbocker Group after 1850; never profitable, it ceased publication in 1861. The *Knickerbocker Magazine* is best known for having set standards of intellectual taste for the emerging middle class in New York City.

The Letters of Willis Gaylord Clark and Lewis Gaylord Clark, ed. Leslie W. Dunlap (New York: New York Public Library, 1940)

Kendall Taft: *Minor Knickerbockers: Representative Selections, with Introduction, Bibliography and Notes* (New York: American Book Campany, 1947)

Perry Miller: *The Raven and the Whale* (New York: Harcourt, Brace, 1956)

Jeff Finlay

Knights of Columbus. Roman Catholic fraternal order. The first local unit within what is now New York City was Brooklyn Council no. 60 (formed 23 Sept 1891), followed by the Long Island Chapter (Brooklyn, 19 Jan 1897), New York Council no. 124 (Manhattan, 12 May 1895), the New York Chapter (12 Dec 1899), and the Staten Island Chapter (13 Oct 1913). In its early years the organization overcame a fear by local bishops that their ecclesiastical authority would be undercut. During the Spanish–American War it began a tradition of attending to members of the armed services. Later it organized blood-donation campaigns and sports programs for youths, promoted spiritual activities, and articulated Catholic opinion on social issues. The Long Island and Staten Island chapters raise funds for programs for handicapped children offered by the Catholic Charities; the New York Chapter does the same for the Foundling Hospital. In 1944 the New York Chapter became the holder of the permit for the Columbus Day Parade. The Knights of Columbus had more than seventeen thousand members in New York City in 1990.

Knights of Columbus in the State of New York, 1891–1945 (New York: New York State Council, Knights of Columbus, 1945)

Eugene Finucane and James A. Foy: *History of the Knights of Columbus in New York State, 1891–1987* (New York: New York State Council, Knights of Columbus, 1987), 6–9, 61–80

Mary Elizabeth Brown

Knights of Labor, District Assembly 49. Labor union, formed in 1869 in Philadelphia as a union of skilled garment workers; the full name was Noble and Holy Order of the Knights of Labor. Seeking to transcend divisions of occupation, race, and sex, the union later extended membership to all "producers," which included most workers (although not lawyers, bankers, or liquor dealers). District Assembly 49 was formed in 1882 and had about sixty thousand members, accounting for most of the Knights in New York City and Brooklyn; it was perhaps the most influential assembly in the national organization, which in 1886 had 700,000 members. Unlike the national leadership, the local one, known as the "home club," rejected trade unionism because it considered craft unions a regressive form of organization destined to be replaced by mixed assemblies based on producerism. It nonetheless sought and gained the affiliations of the city's trade unions, which also belonged to their own international unions. Cooperation between the assembly and the unions eventually disintegrated, owing largely to jurisdictional disputes that arose when District 49 encouraged local unions to leave their international organizations for exclusive membership in the Knights. In 1886 a conflict erupted between the district assembly and the Cigar Makers' International Union (CMIU) that fractured the labor movement in the city. After locking out fifteen thousand workers in January, the United Cigar Manufacturers Association canceled its contract with the CMIU in February and signed another one for lower wages with the Cigarmakers' Progressive Union, a rival organization supported by District 49, which negotiated to have its own label used on cigars rather than that of the CMIU. During the spring and summer the CMIU exerted its influence in the trade to force employers to renegotiate its contracts, and in August the Cigarmakers' Progressive Union itself voted to join the international union rather than meet the ultimatum of District 49 to merge with the Knights.

Despite these divisions the district worked with the craft unions to promote the mayoral candidacy in 1886 of Henry George, a social reformer nominated by the newly formed Independent Labor Party. District 49 however weakened, largely through the efforts of Samuel Gompers, who opposed dual unionism and undertook a national speaking tour to excoriate the Knights. It remained in operation into the 1890s, forming an alliance with the Socialist Daniel DeLeon in 1894 that was short-lived, but never again challenged the tenets of American trade unionism.

Norman Ware: *The Labor Movement in the United States, 1860–1895: A Study in Democracy* (New York: Appleton, 1929)
Philip S. Foner: *The History of the Labor Movement in the United States* (New York: International, 1947)
Stuart B. Kaufman: *Samuel Gompers and the Origins of the American Federation of Labor, 1848–1896* (Westport, Conn.: Greenwood, 1973)

Richard Yeselson

Koch, Edward I(rving) (*b* New York City, 12 Dec 1924). Mayor. He graduated from City College of New York and New York University Law School, was a leading Democratic reformer in the 1950s, and in 1963 and 1965 defeated Carmine DeSapio in primary elections for district leaderships. In 1968 he became the first Democrat in thirty-four years to represent the Silk Stocking District in the U.S. Congress. He opposed Mayor Abraham D. Beame and several other candidates for the Democratic mayoral nomination in 1977; after narrowly finishing first in the primary election he defeated Mario M. Cuomo in a runoff and won the general election by advocating fiscal discipline and emphasizing his support of the death penalty and opposition to public unions. Koch developed a conservative Democratic political base by gaining the support of white Catholics and Jews and some Latin Americans and blacks. He accused his predecessor John V. Lindsay of fiscal irresponsibility and blamed him for having been excessively beholden to interest groups. During his first term he helped to restore financial stability to the city, and he was reelected in 1981 with the support of both the Democratic and Republican parties. A few weeks into his second term he decided to seek the governorship when Governor Hugh L. Carey declined to seek reelection. He lost a bitterly fought primary election to Cuomo after an interview was published in which he had spoken disparagingly of upstate New York. In 1985 he became only the third mayor since consolidation to win a third term. After his reelection his political reputation suffered because of an economic crisis, racial turmoil, and a scandal in the Parking Violations Bureau in which his ally Donald Manes was embroiled. His attempt to win a fourth term failed when he was defeated in the Democratic primary in 1989 by David N. Dinkins.

Edward I. Koch

Koch was a colorful mayor who provoked strong emotions. He frequently attacked political pieties and sometimes endorsed Republican candidates. His supporters found his outspokenness and independence refreshing, and his frequently shouted signature question "How'm I doing?" gave him an air of unpretentiousness. But liberal Democrats and racial minorities believed that he was hostile toward them, excessively close to real-estate interests, and given to intemperate statements on foreign policy and other issues beyond his purview. For most of his mayoralty he enjoyed favorable coverage by the press and an unusually high degree of support on the editorial pages. His book *Mayor* (1984) was a best-seller.

John Mollenkopf: *A Phoenix in the Ashes: The Rise and Fall of the Koch Coalition in New York City Politics* (Princeton, N.J.: Princeton University Press, 1992)

Martin Shefter

Kohn Pedersen Fox. Firm of architects formed in 1976 by Eugene Kohn, William Pedersen, and Sheldon Fox. It specialized in office buildings and became known for using rich materials and innovative designs; one building at 125 East 57th Street incorporated a concave corner façade and a circular colonnaded pavilion with neoclassical details. The firm designed studios for WABC at 7 Lincoln Square (1977) and Shearson Lehman Brothers Plaza at 388 Greenwich Street (1985). Pedersen oversees the designers, Kohn and Fox the marketing and management.

Sonia R. Chao and Trevor D. Abramson, eds.: *Kohn Pedersen Fox, Building and Projects, 1976–1986* (New York: Rizzoli, 1987)

Edward A. Eigen

Kommunisten Klub. A radical German political organization formed by Albert Komp in New York City in 1857. Its members included the playwright Max Cohnheim and the music teacher Friedrich A. Sorge. The group helped to organize a demonstration attended by fifteen thousand unemployed workers on 5 November. Despite its strong start the club became inactive until 1867, when it joined a group of Lassallean socialists in forming the Social Party of New York City.

Stanley Nadel

Koreans. About ten thousand Koreans entered the United States, mostly through Hawaii and California, before the National Origins Act of 1924 barred the entry of Asians. Of the few who settled in New York City many were Protestants, students, and political refugees; they banded together to protest the Japanese takeover of the Korean peninsula. In 1920 they established the New York Korean Church, the first Korean church in the city, near Columbia University. The church became a center for anti-Japanese political activities and counted among its members students at Columbia who later became prominent political leaders after Korean independence. The community declined somewhat as its members aged, until after the Korean War, when there was an influx of students from South Korea. Most of these stayed after finishing their studies and many became influential businessmen, Protestant ministers, publishers of Korean-language newspapers, and leaders of such important organizations as the Korean Association of New York, an umbrella organization representing all Koreans in the metropolitan area. The number of immigrants increased after the Immigration Act of 1965 allowed the reunion of families. The new immigrants settled throughout the city but were concentrated in Flushing, Jackson Heights, and Elmhurst, and after achieving success most moved to the suburbs; these patterns prevented Koreans from achieving a sizable electoral influence anywhere in the city. Koreans achieved solidarity by organizing religious, professional, recreational, business, family, and alumni associations, as well as informal clubs. Among the most important were revolving credit associations known as *kye*, which provided business capital and money for consumer goods. These were derived from traditional cooperatives designed to promote mutual assistance, friendship, and good will.

Owing largely to community self-help networks supportive of business, Koreans acquired more small businesses than most other groups of immigrants did. Many bought greengroceries, retail fish stores, and dry-cleaning stores. Often these were in predominantly black neighborhoods, drawing protest from some blacks who sought to retain control of their communities. In 1979 a few organizations distributed anti-Korean leaflets and picketed Korean shops. According to the Korean American Small Business Service, 70 percent of employed Koreans in the area worked in Korean businesses in 1986, and such important associations as the Korean Produce Retailers Association, the Korean Seafood Association, and the Korean Dry Cleaners Association used their large annual budgets to provide group insurance, tax guides, legal services, and seminars to members. The most comprehensive services were offered by the Korean Produce Retailers Association, which sponsored the first *Chusok* festival of thanksgiving in 1982. In later years the festival was held annually at Flushing Meadow Park on a Sunday in October (and on the 15th of the eighth lunar month in Korea). In 1967 *Hangkook Ilbo*, a Korean-language daily newspaper in South Korea, began to publish an edition based in New York City.

From the 1970s immigrants were drawn mainly from the élite of such South Korean cities as Seoul and Pusan. According to a survey by the *Hangkook Ilbo* in 1987 most Korean immigrants moved to the city with their families; 89 percent of Korean householders were married and lived with their spouses, 74 percent had completed college in Korea, and 96 percent were employed (as were 80 percent of the spouses). The presence of two and often three generations in the household was important to the economic success of many Koreans, nearly half of whom eventually moved to the suburbs. Racial tensions continued to rise, and in 1988 a Korean greengrocery in Brooklyn was driven out of business by a black boycott. Another boycott of two Korean groceries on Church Avenue in Brooklyn began in January 1990 and attracted national attention. The federal census of 1990 recorded 134,180 Koreans in the metropolitan area, including 69,718 living in the city; the figure was placed at 210,000 by the Korean Foreign Ministry. In 1991 about 41 percent of the Korean population ran about ten thousand small businesses. According to the survey by *Hangkook Ilbo* 63 percent of the population attended Protestant churches, mostly Presbyterian, which became important social centers. In the metropolitan area in 1991 there were 390 Korean Protestant churches, fifteen Korean Catholic churches, and eleven Buddhist temples.

By the early 1990s the Korean news media were a vital source of cohesion in the Korean community. In addition to *Hangkook Ilbo* these included local editions of three Korean-language newspapers based in Seoul (*Joong Ang Ilbo*, *Chosun Ilbo*, and *Sae Gae Ilbo*), three weekly newspapers, three radio stations (one of which was operated by *Hangkook Ilbo*), and three television stations that broadcast news and South Korean entertainment programs on channels 25, 31, and 53.

Illsoo Kim: *New Urban Immigrants: The Korean Community in New York* (Princeton, N.J.: Princeton University Press, 1981), 181–225

Illsoo Kim

Kosciuszko Bridge. Truss bridge of steel and reinforced concrete spanning Newton Creek between Brooklyn and Queens, near but unconnected to Kosciuszko Street. Opened on 23 August 1939 as the Meeker Avenue Bridge on the former site of Penny Bridge (an old drawbridge), it was renamed on 10 July 1940 in honor of the Polish patriot Tadeusz Kościuszko. At first part of the Brooklyn–Queens Connecting Highway, it later became part of the Brooklyn–Queens Expressway, providing rapid access between the Midtown Tunnel and the Williamsburg Bridge. The bridge has a maximum span of three hundred feet (91.5 meters) and a maximum height of 125 feet (38.1 meters), and the approaches are quite steep; this and the huge traffic capacity make it a hazardous stretch of expressway. The Kosciuszko Bridge is operated by the New York State Department of Transportation.

Andrew Sparberg

Kosciuszko Foundation. Polish–American cultural and educational institution formed in New York City in 1925. It was named in honor of Tadeusz Kościuszko, who designed the fortress at West Point and was instrumental in the American victory in Saratoga, New York, during the American Revolution. The foundation provides scholarships to Americans of Polish heritage, supports exchanges of students and scholars between the United States and Poland, publishes books, and operates summer sessions for Americans to study at Polish universities. The Kosciuszko Foundation has its offices at 15 East 65th Street in Manhattan.

James S. Pula

kosher foods. The production of matzo in New York City expanded rapidly during an influx of Jewish immigrants between 1880 and 1920. Most matzo bakeries were on the Lower East Side, including that of Horowitz Brothers and Margareten, which had factories on East 4th Street, Meyer London's Matzos Bakery on Bayard Street, and the Finsilver Matzoth Baking Company on Pitt Street. Soon the slaughtering and meatpacking industry in the city also expanded to accommodate a rising demand for kosher meat. The wholesale value of kosher food increased 70 percent between 1900 and 1909, and by 1916 kosher meat retailers in the city had $50 million in sales. The number of butcher shops selling kosher meat increased from fifteen hundred in 1902 to 7500 in 1930; some of the largest kosher butchers and meat wholesalers were the firms of Isaac Gellis on Essex Street and S. Ershowsky and Brothers on East Houston Street. By 1934 there were about twelve thousand kosher food processors and dealers, with annual sales of more than $200 million. Because demand for kosher food was sudden and large, kosher certification remained problematic for decades. The first efforts at regulation were made at the turn of the century by Rabbi Jacob Joseph of the Association of the United Hebrew Congregation. Later efforts continued to provoke controversy, including those of the New York Kehillah between 1910 and 1920, the Union of Orthodox Jewish Congregations in the 1920s, and the Kashruth Association in the 1930s.

Disputes over the cost of kosher meat resulted in several "kosher meat riots." The most severe occurred in May 1902, when butchers in the city closed their shops after

Matzo factory in Brooklyn, ca *1990*

Berenice Abbott, Chicken Market *(1937), 55 Hester Street*

packers raised the price of kosher meat. A settlement was reached, but many customers still considered prices too high and organized a citywide boycott. Although this led to lower prices similar incidents took place in 1910, 1929, and 1937. Resentment arose when the power to regulate the kosher food business was given to the federal government by the National Industrial Recovery Act (NIRA) of 1933, and in 1934 a suit was brought by the Schechter Brothers, kosher poultry wholesalers in Brooklyn convicted of violating the Live Poultry Code: the NIRA was ruled unconstitutional by the U.S. Supreme Court in the case of *Schechter Poultry Corporation v. United States* (1935). In the 1940s the Union of Orthodox Jewish Congregations and the Kosher Law Enforcement Bureau (1944) became the primary monitors of the kosher food business. Dealers and manufacturers in the city declined in the following decade, as kosher products were introduced by large food producers, including such national kosher producers outside the city as the B. Manischewitz Company. The demand for kosher food remained high in the city, and eventually most kosher food was bought by gentiles, who recognized that koshering was associated with high standards. In the 1980s the largest firm of matzo bakers was that of Aron Streit (1924) on Rivington Street in Manhattan; matzo was also made by Horowitz Brothers and Margareten, which maintained a factory in Queens, and by many small firms in Borough Park. Glatt kosher food, prepared according to more stringent standards than other kosher food, was at first sold mostly in Williamsburg, Borough Park, and other neighborhoods in Brooklyn, but later spread to the other boroughs. Many kosher restaurants opened in the city in the 1980s and early 1990s, offering not only traditional kosher foods but kosher versions of Chinese, Italian, and other types of cuisine. The city also has a number of kosher wine distributors, including Shapiro Wine on Rivington Street and the Royal Corporation in Brooklyn, the makers of Kedem, Monfort, and Bartenura wine.

Harold P. Gastwirt: *Fraud, Corruption and Holiness: The Controversy over the Supervision of Jewish Dietary Practice in New York City* (Port Washington, N.Y.: Kennikat, 1974)

Paula E. Hyman: "Immigrant Women and Consumer Protest: The New York City Kosher Meat Boycott of 1902," *American Jewish History* 70 (1980), 91–105

James Bradley, Hadassa Kosak

Kosinski, Jerzy (Nikodem) (*b* Łódź, Poland, 14 June 1933; *d* New York City, 3 May 1991). Novelist and photographer. After earning an MA in history and another in political science at the University of Łódź he became a doctoral candidate in sociology at the Polish Academy of Sciences (1955–57). He arrived in New York City on 20 December 1957 and in the following months worked as a parking lot attendant, taxi driver, paint scraper on excursion boats, chauffeur, and cinema projectionist. He wrote a number of nonfiction works (the first two published under the pseudonym Joseph Novak), including *The Future is Ours, Comrade: Conversations with the Russians* (1960), and in 1965 he became an American citizen. His works of fiction include *The Painted Bird* (abridged edn 1965, complete edn 1970), *Steps* (1968, National Book Award), *The Devil Tree* (1973), and *The Hermit of* 69th Street (1988). He also adapted two of his novels for the screen (*Being There*, 1971; *Passion Play*, 1979) and won prizes for his photographs, which were exhibited in many countries. Kosinski gathered material for his books by prowling the streets of New York City and other cities, sometimes in disguise. He died by his own hand.

Norman Lavers: *Jerzy Kosinski* (Boston: Twayne, 1982)

Paul R. Lilly Jr.: *Words in Search of Victims: The Achievement of Jerzy Kosinski* (Kent, Ohio: Kent State University Press, 1988)

Tom Teicholz, ed.: *Conversations with Jerzy Kosinski* (Jackson: University Press of Mississippi, 1993)

Allen J. Share

Kossuth, Louis [Lajos] (*b* Monok, Hungary, 16 Sept 1802; *d* Turin, Italy, 20 March 1894). Revolutionary. After leading the failed Hungarian revolution of 1848 he fled Hungary as it was occupied by Russian troops, and in 1851 he embarked on a seven-month tour of the United States to seek support for Hungarian independence. He landed at Staten Island on 5 December and was greeted with an elaborate procession and public reception. The following day a crowd of thousands attended Mayor Ambrose C. Kingsland's reception for him at Castle Garden and the Battery, where he was saluted with a fusillade of cannon fire and reviewed the assembled militia companies before proceeding up Broadway by carriage, cheered by tens of thousands of spectators. A municipal banquet was held in his honor on 11 December at the Irving House (Broadway and Chambers Street), and he was also given receptions at Columbia College and Plymouth Church in Brooklyn before leaving the city for Philadelphia on 23 December. Although his visit to New York City was brief it had a wide impact: news of it dominated the city's newspapers for the entire month, and his ideas influenced "young America," a Romantic nationalist literary movement led by Evert A. Duyckinck and John O'Sullivan. The wide-brimmed, soft felt hats that he often wore became fashionable among young men, and long cloaks known as Kossuths were worn into the 1860s. On 15 March 1928 an audience of 25,000 attended the dedication of a bronze statue erected in his honor at 113th Street and Riverside Drive, including a delegation of 520 Hungarians who had traveled to the city for the occasion.

Donald S. Spencer: *Louis Kossuth and Young America* (Columbia: University of Missouri Press, 1977)

Kevin Kenny

KPMG Peat Marwick. The largest accounting firm in the world, formed in 1987 by the merger of Peat, Marwick, Mitchell and Copartners of New York City with KMG of Amsterdam. The firm has its headquarters in Amsterdam but retains important ties to New York City, where its main offices are at 767 5th Avenue.

Chad Ludington

Kramer, Larry [Laurence D.] (*b* 1935). Playwright and activist. He attended Yale University, graduating in 1957. He gained notoriety when he helped to form the Gay Men's Health Crisis (1982) and the AIDS Coalition to Unleash Power (1987), becoming widely known for his attacks on the government and the health care system, which he held responsible for failing to halt the spread of AIDS. Kramer's published writings include the novel *Faggots* (1978), the play *The Normal Heart* (1985), and the essays *Reports from the Holocaust: The Making of an AIDS Activist* (1989).

Robert A. Padgug

Krapp, Herbert J. (*b* New York City, 21 Feb 1886; *d* Stuart, Fla., 16 Feb 1973). Architect. After working for the firm of Herts and Tallant he formed his own practice and became the principal architect for the Shubert and Chanin organizations, which dominated Broadway theater between the two world wars. He specialized in designing functional theaters on limited sites, with excellent acoustics and sightlines and restrained ornamental designs. Krapp was the most prolific architect of legitimate theaters on Broadway. Of his twenty-one theaters in New York City sixteen remained extant into the 1990s, including the Ambassador Theatre, the Barrymore Theatre, the Broadhurst Theatre, the Plymouth Theatre, the Imperial Theatre, the Eugene O'Neill Theatre, and the Ritz Theater (all for Shubert), and the Biltmore Theatre, the Brooks Atkinson Theatre, the 46th Street Theatre, the Golden Theatre, the Majestic Theatre, and the Royale Theatre (all for Chanin).

See also THEATER ARCHITECTURE.

Anthony W. Robins

Krasner, Lee [Krassner, Lenore] (*b* Brooklyn, 27 Oct 1908; *d* New York City, 19 June 1984). Painter. The daughter of Russian immigrants, she entered the Women's Art School of Cooper Union in 1926 (graduating in 1929) and became active in the art world of New York City in the 1930s. She worked on the Federal Art Project of the Works Progress Administration from 1934 (the poet Harold Rosenberg was a fellow assistant in 1935), studied with Hans Hofmann in 1937, and exhibited her work with the American Abstract Artists in 1940. Her cubist abstractions made her a well-known figure in the avant-garde. She married Jackson Pollock in 1945, and with him she moved in the same year to Springs, Long Island. She continued to spend winters in New York City at various addresses until she purchased an apartment at 180 East 79th Street. Between 1945 and 1949 she completed her "little image" paintings, abstract expressionist works in which she perfected her own version of Pollock's "all-over" composition. In the 1950s she incorporated collage into her work, creating bold, innovative paintings that represent a high point in her career. She had her first solo exhibition in 1951 at the Betty Parsons Gallery; with her nephew Ronald Stein she executed in mosaic a mural commissioned for the Uris Building (completed in 1959).

Ellen G. Landau: "Lee Krasner's Early Career," *Arts Magazine* 56 (1981), no. 2, pp. 110–22; no. 3, pp. 80–89

Barbara Rose: *Lee Krasner: A Retrospective* (Houston: Museum of Fine Arts / New York: Museum of Modern Art, 1983)

Mona Hadler

Kreischerville. Name applied until 1927 to CHARLESTON.

Kriege, Hermann (*b* Westphalia, 25 June 1820; *d* Hoboken, N.J., 31 Dec 1850). Revolutionist. A member of the communist Bund der Gerechten in Berlin, he emigrated to the United States in 1845 and settled in New York City, where he organized the Sozialreformassoziation, an offshoot of the Bund and the city's first radical German–American association. Members of the group backed his short-lived newspaper the *Volkstribun* and affiliated with the National Reform Association, but they were expelled from the Bund for giving too much attention to land reform and not enough to communism. In 1846 Kriege declared the Sozialreformassoziation the "left wing of Tammany Hall" and abandoned communism. After the Sozialreformassoziation sent him to Germany to take part in the revolution of 1848 he returned to the United States, where he suffered a mental breakdown.

Stanley Nadel

Kuhn, Abraham (*b* Herscheim, Bavarian Rhein-Pfalz, 20 June 1819; *d* Frankfurt am Main, 30 May 1892). Banker. A German Jewish immigrant, he worked in the dry-goods trade in Cincinnati about 1850. After sending his second cousin Solomon Loeb to New York City to look into business opportunities he operated a clothing store at 158 Chambers Street in 1859–66. Kuhn and Loeb each married the other's sister; in 1867 the two formed the banking firm Kuhn, Loeb at 31 Nassau Street. The Kuhns lived at 50 West 21st Street from 1860 to 1870. Kuhn then returned to Germany with his family but remained a partner in the firm until 1887.

A Century of Investment Banking (New York: Kuhn, Loeb, 1967)

Stephen Birmingham: *Our Crowd* (New York: Harper and Row, 1967)

Joyce Mendelsohn

Kuhn, Conrad (*fl* 1866–72). Labor leader. He was president of the cigarmakers' union (1866–72) and helped to organize the Association of United Workers (1868), a German labor council that sponsored the *Arbeiter Union*, the first daily German labor newspaper in New York City. Under his leadership the German unions became the most active participants in the city's labor movement, taking the lead in strikes for an eight-hour work day in 1872. Kuhn delivered the major address of the campaign, which helped to attract more than 100,000 city workers to the strike. His career as a labor leader ended when the movement was crushed and he was blacklisted.

Stanley Nadel

Kuhn, Loeb. Firm of investment bankers. It was formed as a private bank in 1867 by Abraham Kuhn and Solomon Loeb, German immigrants who owned dry-goods stores in Indiana and Ohio; the first offices were at 31 Nassau Street. Jacob Schiff became a partner in 1875 and was a senior partner by 1885. Under his leadership the firm raised capital in Europe for American industry and refinanced almost every important railroad in the country, including the Pennsylvania Railroad, the Louisville and Nashville, and the Baltimore and Ohio. It also worked with Edward H. Harriman on the reorganization of the Union Pacific Railroad. A number of partners were added in the late nineteenth century, including Abraham Wolff, Felix Warburg, Paul Warburg, and Otto H. Kahn. During a struggle for control of the Northern Pacific Railroad in 1901 Schiff advised Harriman, and J. P. Morgan advised his rival James J. Hill, leading to the formation of a holding company called Northern Securities that was declared an illegal combination by the U.S. Supreme Court in 1904. Paul Warburg retired in 1914 to become the first president of the Federal Reserve Bank of New York. Unlike many other investment banks, Kuhn, Loeb remained small during the 1920s. It specialized in railroad and industrial issues until the 1940s, when public sealed bidding became required for railroad securities. By the mid 1970s the firm's capital was becoming depleted, and in 1977 the partners agreed to merge with Lehman Brothers to form Lehman Brothers Kuhn Loeb.

Investment Banking through Four Generations (New York: Kuhn, Loeb, 1955)

Ken Auletta: *Greed and Glory on Wall Street: The Fall of the House of Lehman* (New York: Random House, 1986)

Mary E. Curry

Ku Klux Klan [KKK]. The name of three secret societies, formed in 1866, in 1915, and in the years following the Second World War. The second of these was the largest, gaining nationwide influence and millions of members between 1921 and 1925, when it was especially strong in Indianapolis, Denver, Portland (Oregon), Chicago, Detroit, Atlanta, Memphis, and Dallas, and also achieved some success in New York City. Lloyd P. Hooper, "grand goblin" of the Klan, set up headquarters at the Hotel Embassy in March 1921 and oversaw an initiation as early as 10 June. In July a klavern was formed in Brooklyn, and in September one began meeting in the Bronx as the American Civic Association. According to C. Anderson Wright, a defector from the Klan, there were twenty-one operative klaverns in the city in December 1922. Many members were inspired by the anti-Catholic and anti-Semitic ideology of the local newspaper the *American Standard.* A typical diatribe declared: "To receive into your home Roman Catholics, to give them employment in your office, is to put your home and your office at the mercy of the Roman Catholic system." Even so William Joseph Simmons, "imperial wizard" of the Klan, described New York City as "the most un-American city of the American continent" and Columbia University as the "least American of all schools."

The Ku Klux Klan made stronger inroads into the suburbs, especially Yonkers in Westchester County and Stamford, Greenwich, and Bridgeport in Connecticut. On Long Island it won elections in 1923 in Islip, Babylon, Oyster Bay, and Brookhaven, and in 1924 it took temporary control of the Suffolk County Republican Committee. In New Jersey the state headquarters were in West Hoboken, and the order won many adherents in Newark, Paterson, and Elizabeth.

Kenneth T. Jackson: *The Ku Klux Klan in the City* (New York: Oxford University Press, 1967), 175–79

Kenneth T. Jackson

Kunstler, William (Moses) (*b* New York City, 7 July 1919). Lawyer. He grew up on the West Side, attended De Witt Clinton High School, and earned his law degree from Columbia University in 1948. His commitment to the civil rights movement in the 1960s led him to defend a number of celebrated radicals, including the Catonsville Nine, the Chicago Eight, the black activists Stokely Carmichael and H. Rap Brown, and the militant American Indians of Wounded Knee, South Dakota. He became a highly controversial figure in New York City for being present at the revolt at Attica State Prison in 1971, filing suit on behalf of the protesters at Tompkins Square, and defending controversial figures such as Larry Davis (accused of the attempted murder of six police officers), the youths who accosted the subway vigilante Bernhard Goetz, and the gang members accused of attacking the "Central Park jogger." In 1989–90 he won a case before the U.S. Supreme Court after arguing that burning the American flag is protected by the First Amendment.

George J. Lankevich

Kurds. After the failure of the Kurdish revolution in Iran in 1975 the U.S. Department of State was responsible for resettling about seven hundred Kurds to the United States, some of whom took up residence in New York City. In time some sent for relatives, and by the early 1990s the community numbered about two thousand. The city's Kurds are nationals of Iraq, Iran, Syria, and Turkey who are overwhelmingly male and maintain a low profile. Many work in engineering, some in medicine and business. Most live around the far reaches of Ocean Parkway and Coney Island Avenue in Brooklyn; others live in various parts of Queens. The Kurdish Library, established in a brownstone in Brooklyn in 1986 by Vera Beaudin Saeedpour, is a center for the study of Kurdish history, culture, and contemporary affairs that has worked to increase American awareness of the Kurds' existence and was an important source of information for the American news media during the Kurdish refugee crisis that followed the Gulf War in 1991.

Marc Ferris

L

labor. New York City became a national center of labor activity in colonial times. Some of the first labor conflicts were slave insurrections in 1712 and 1741. Three craft strikes were recorded before 1788, and in 1794 a group of journeymen printers formed the Franklin Typographical Society, the city's first permanent association of wage earners. A citywide labor movement did not begin until the presidency of Andrew Jackson. Journeymen, small masters, and radicals banded together to form the Working Men's Party (1829–31), which sought egalitarian political and social reforms and briefly had many supporters among the electorate. After its demise the city's craft unions organized the General Trades' Union, a confederation that between 1833 and 1836 joined with various unaffiliated unions (including several led by women) in carrying out nearly forty strikes to combat declining wages and working conditions. In 1834 it led efforts to form the National Trades' Union, the country's first organization uniting workers in different cities. The panic of 1837 crushed this national movement and abetted a nativism during the 1840s that divided unions and forced many to cease operations; a few survived the decade and undertook new efforts, ranging from George Henry Evans's land reform movement to the Subterranean Democracy of the Bowery radical Mike Walsh, an insurgent faction within the Democratic Party. After the late 1840s the city's work force grew enormously and soon came to consist largely of immigrants from Ireland and Germany and their children. Labor advocates disagreed over whether and how to organize immigrants, especially the unskilled, and over forming relationships with the city's political parties, especially the Democrats, who aggressively fought for the immigrants' loyalty. Compounded by ethnic and cultural tensions, these questions defined debates over the relative merits of craft unionism, industrial unionism, and broader political action. Immigrants, especially Germans, offered ideas about organizing that confirmed the city's importance as a center of activism. In 1850 the labor movement regained its strength through several bitter strikes and the formation of the Industrial Congress, a coalition of unionists, reform groups, and intellectuals that lasted until 1852.

Efforts to organize intensified as industrialization accelerated. As early as 1850 the city was the most productive manufacturing center in the United States and an attractive location for the needle trades, printing, and other industries. During the Civil War alone its trade unions undertook more than ninety strikes, mainly for higher wages to offset rising prices. Despite these shows of solidarity deep divisions remained. As the number of whites increased with immigration, blacks accounted for a dwindling share of the work force and were subjected to worsening discrimination: this reached a crisis during the draft riots of 1863, when crowds of white workers who had gathered to protest the draft swept through the city terrorizing black residents. Although denounced by labor leaders the incident long remained a source of bitterness.

Labor won several important victories during the last decades of the nineteenth century. In 1872 a hundred thousand workers in the BUILDING TRADES waged a successful three-month strike for the eight-hour day. Nearly every major labor organization was well represented in the city, notably the socialist International Workingmen's Association, which had its headquarters there, the Knights of Labor, and several individual craft unions. Such prominent editors as John Swinton and Patrick Ford launched newspapers devoted to labor issues. The city's union and labor reformers adopted a political approach that soon proved highly successful in gaining widespread support, despite economic downturns, disagreements over strategy and tactics, and periodic repression by the police (such as that in the Tompkins Square riot of 1874). In 1882 a group of Irish–American workers joined with union delegates and German–American socialists to form the Central Labor Union (CLU), which quickly became the leading organization of its kind in the country. Through boycotts and such measures as the observance of Labor Day in 1882, it eventually included more than two hundred groups and maintained friendly relations with its chief rivals, most importantly the Knights of Labor. After a court ruling against a boycott in 1885 the CLU and other groups focused on fielding candidates for political office: they chose the reformer Henry George to run in the mayoral election of 1886. His campaign, based in part on instituting a single tax on land, nearly prevailed and seemed to presage even broader political activity, but the movement collapsed owing to dissent among labor leaders and the timely introduction of state reforms.

After George's defeat the labor movement took a more conservative course. Skilled craft unions dominated; the most important leader in the city was Samuel Gompers, who had become well known as an organizer for the Federation of Organized Trades and Labor Unions in 1881. Initially a supporter of the CLU, he grew wary of focusing on political elections and organizing poor, unskilled workers, especially immigrants. In 1886 conflicts led to the rapid decline of the Knights of Labor and the formation of the American Federation of Labor (AFL), which represented only a fraction of the country's workers but under Gompers's leadership became the leading labor confederation, largely through its emphasis on organizing craft workers. About this time a large influx of immigrants settled in the city from southern and central Europe and Russia, leading to sharp ethnic antagonism among these groups and with longer-established ones. By the early twentieth century the new immigrants launched their own activist movement centered in the needle trades. The International Ladies' Garment Workers' Union (ILGWU) was formed as an affiliate of the AFL, and locals proliferated. Helped in their efforts by such reform groups as the Women's Trade Union League, the unions staged strikes that gradually changed the industry: one of the most successful, the "uprising of the thirty thousand," was led by young Jewish and Italian women and resulted in important gains. Radicalism in the labor movement was revived by a Yiddish-speaking milieu of socialists, anarchists, and reformers on the Lower East Side, the base of such important publications as Abraham Cahan's newspaper *Vorwerts*. Italians and other immigrants also formed radical circles, and the cause of labor was championed by a number of other groups, including settlement house workers, writers in Greenwich Village for such publications as the *Masses*, and the Socialist Party.

The First World War marked a change in the fortunes of the labor movement nationwide. The political left was put on the defensive by a general reaction against radicalism. Disagreements over whether to support the Bolshevik Revolution broke out among labor leaders, ending in thuggery and gunfights during the mid 1920s. Hostile government investigations into several unions, especially in the building trades, produced a sordid picture of widespread graft and racketeering. After the war many employers sought to reverse the gains of labor by taking part in an aggressive "open shop" campaign. Several unions survived, notably those in the garment trades, and the conservatism of the AFL was challenged by Sidney Hillman, president of the Amalgamated Clothing Workers of America (ACWA). Hillman called for grouping workers along industry rather than craft lines and also introduced a form of collective bargaining, sometimes called "industrial democracy," that invited workers to settle disputes on the shop floor; his ideas were well received and became known as "new unionism." Under Hillman the ACWA also offered unemployment insurance, low-cost housing for members in Manhattan and the Bronx, and group health care, and opened the Amalgamated Bank, which provided workers with low-interest credit. By the late 1920s the city's labor movement was nonetheless severely weakened. The Depression brought more serious problems, as even

Important Strikes in History of New York City

Date	*Participants*	*Number of Workers*	*Outcome*
1677	Cartmen	12	Strikers held in contempt of court. First criminal prosecution for a strike in the colonies.
1684	Cartmen		Fined for violation of the law.
7 April 1741	Bakers		Prosecuted as criminal conspiracy.
May 1833 to June 1833	Journeymen carpenters		Wage increase. General Trades Union of the City of New York (GTU) founded 14 Aug 1833.
Feb 1836	Tailors		National Guard called in. Twenty journeymen tailors indicted for illegal combination, denied right to unionize. Largest protest meeting in United States to date (thirty thousand participants). Call for new political party.
15 July 1850	Tailors	2000	First time in history of United States that worker is killed in a trade dispute. Few concrete gains. Cooperative Union of Tailoring Estates founded.
1886	Various		Many workers win eight-hour day or ten-hour day.
Jan 1887	Longshoremen		Wages and benefits cut. One year after strike not one longshoremen's organization left in Port of New York.
11 Feb 1887	Knights of Labor District Assembly 49		
20 July 1899	Newsboys, bootblacks		Wage increase.
7 March 1904 to 11 March 1904	Amalgamated Association of Street and Electric Railway Employees (AASERE), Brotherhood of Locomotive Firemen (BLF), Brotherhood of Locomotive Engineers (BLE)		Defeated. Open shop.
24 Nov 1909 to 15 Feb 1910	International Ladies' Garment Workers' Union (ILGWU)	30,000	Higher wages, better conditions, fifty-two-hour work week.
7 July 1910 to 2 Sept 1910	International Ladies' Garment Workers' Union (ILGWU)	60,000	"Protocol of Peace." Fifty hour work-week, overtime pay, ten legal holidays, compulsory arbitration, joint labor–management board. Foundations laid for long, stable unionism.
Nov 1910	Brooklyn Boot and Shoe Workers	3000	Defeated. No concessions.
18 March 1911	Industrial Workers of the World, Local 168		
7 May 1912	Hotel Workers Industrial Union	18,000	A few contracts signed.
28 June 1912	Industrial Workers of the World		
21 June 1912	United Hebrew Trades	9000	Union recognition, forty-nine-hour week, overtime pay, ten paid holidays, ban on home work, permanent board of arbitration, joint board of sanitary control. Almost complete unionization of fur industry.
16 April 1916	International Ladies' Garment Workers' Union (ILGWU)	60,000	Full representation of ILGWU, binding two-year contracts, standard collective bargaining agreements
4 Aug 1916 to 27 Sept 1916	Amalgamated Association of Street and Electric Railway Employees (AASERE)		No concrete gains.
7 Aug 1919 to 6 Sept 1919	Actors' Equity Association (AEA)	3000	Secured unpaid rehearsal time, closed shop, strict eight-performance week. Membership in Actors' Equity reaches fourteen thousand, creating a stable union in theater.
July 1932	Amalgamated Clothing and Textile Workers (ACTW)	30,000	Decline of ILGWU in New York City is arrested.
Aug 1932	Amalgamated Clothing and Textile Workers (ACTW)	15,000	Strengthens ILGWU on east coast.

(continued)

Important Strikes in History of New York City (*Continued*)

Date	*Participants*	*Number of Workers*	*Outcome*
6 Feb 1934 to 12 March 1934	Taxi drivers		Violence, destruction of property, eventual wage increase.
10 March 1941 to 21 March 1941	Transportation Workers Union (TWU)		Wage increase.
3 Oct 1945 to 19 Oct 1945	International Longshoremen's Association (ILA)	35,000	Wage gains, improved working conditions, challenge to Joseph P. Ryan's control of union.
1959	Local 1199		
7 Nov 1960 to 8 Nov 1960	United Federation of Teachers (UFT)	5000	Collective bargaining agreement promised. Challenge to Condon–Waldin Act against public employee strikes.
12 April 1962	United Federation of Teachers (UFT)	20,000	Wage increase. Violation of Condon–Waldin Act begins era of public employee strikes.
6 Dec 1962 to 31 March 1963	International Typographical Union (ITU)	20,000	Small wage increase, new technology allowed. *Mirror* ceases publication after strike displaces fourteen hundred employees.
2 Jan 1965 to 1 Feb 1965	Social Service Employees Union (SSEU)	8000	Salary increase, welfare fund for educational purposes, caseload reductions, end to "midnight" raids on welfare recipients.
1 Jan 1966 to 13 Jan 1966	Transportation Workers Union (TWU)	35,000	Wage increase, fare increase.
Jan 1968	Uniformed Sanitationmen's Association (USA)		Binding arbitration, large pay increase.
9 Sept 1968	United Federation of Teachers (UFT)	54,000	Strike leaders jailed. Teachers allowed back into classrooms in Ocean Hill–Brownsville.
18 March 1970 to 25 March 1970	United Federation of Postal Clerks (UFPC), National Postal Union (NPU)	57,000	Wage increase, full health benefits, locally based wages, amnesty for striking workers. Postal Reorganization Act requires collective bargaining on all issues and binding arbitration.
June 1971	American Federation of State, County and Municipal Employees (AFSCME)	8000	Public disapproval, union fined.
Dec 1971 to 1972	Communication Workers of America (CWA)		
14 Jan 1971 to 19 Jan 1971	Patrolmen's Benevolent Association (PBA)	25,000	Salary increase, prosecutions under Taylor Law, police unions strengthened.
1991	Employees of *Daily News*		The British publisher Robert Maxwell buys the newspaper on 15 March and settles with union leaders on 31 March. Thirty-five management workers are laid off.

unions that had remained relatively strong suffered enormous losses. The ACWA lost fifty thousand members between 1929 and 1933, and wages fell to between 40 and 50 percent of what they had been before the Depression. Earlier abuses returned, and labor leaders struggled to preserve their gains and combat sweatshops, destructive competition, and the movement of businesses to rural areas.

Change came with the election of President Franklin D. Roosevelt and Mayor Fiorello H. La Guardia. Organized labor was greatly strengthened by the Wagner Act (1935), introduced by Senator Robert F. Wagner. The act was among the most progressive pieces of labor legislation ever enacted at the national level: it guaranteed the right to collective bargaining, allowed free speech in advocating unionism, and gave unions and their members the right to protest unfair labor practices and seek redress of grievances through the National Labor Relations Board. In 1936 the Congress of Industrial Organizations (CIO) was formed to compete with the AFL; it borrowed and extended innovative practices of the new unionism. During the same year its branch in the city gave institutional support to Roosevelt by organizing the American Labor Party, which delivered votes to him as well as to La Guardia and Governor Herbert H. Lehman. Encouraged by a sympathetic government and the increasing militancy of workers (often led by members of the Communist Party), several local affiliates of the CIO, including the United Textile Workers and the United Electrical Workers, organized workers in manufacturing. La Guardia, a Republican supporter of Roosevelt, publicly backed labor and in the first few years of the New Deal alone provided more than 200,000 jobs for the city's unemployed. He also supported the right to collective bargaining and the right to strike (although not for municipal workers). Such figures as Hillman and David Dubinsky, president of the ILGWU, served on several government boards and were influential in elections throughout the New Deal. Although overshadowed in politics somewhat by the CIO, the AFL retained as members most of the city's organized workers, counting largely on its unions in the building trades for its strength. In response to successes of the CIO a few unions in the AFL, including the ILGWU and the International Brotherhood of Electrical Workers (IBEW), organized factory workers according to the industrial model of the CIO; otherwise there was little overlap between the two organizations. Several leaders of the AFL in the city who were not entirely opposed to industrial organizing eventually held the highest positions in organized labor. One was George Meany, president of the State Federation of Labor and later the AFL.

Unions prospered with the return of economic stability during the Second World War. A precedent for civil service unions was set by the Transport Workers Union of America, which despite its small size enforced contract provisions made when the city took over public transit in 1940. By 1945 labor groups in the city were firmly allied with the Democratic Party. New problems arose after the war, when an influx of black workers from the South and immigrants from the Caribbean coincided with the flight of manufacturers from the city. Because of personal differences and its committed anti-communism, the AFL remained divided from the CIO until 1955, when Meany orchestrated a merger of the two groups to form the AFL–CIO. From the mid 1950s municipal unions made important gains. Under Mayor Robert F. Wagner they won the right to organize, and in 1958 Executive Order 49 gave many of them the right to collective bargaining. The transport workers brought the city to a halt with a twelve-day strike in 1966; strikes during the next three years by social workers and sanitation workers led to the passage of the Taylor Law (1967), which outlawed strikes by municipal employees. The most divisive conflict of the time was the teachers' strike of 1968 in Ocean Hill and Brownsville, which marked a turning point in race relations in the city (see Teachers' unions). After nineteen teachers were dismissed by the Ocean Hill–Brownsville school board, a strike by the United Federation of Teachers (UFT) was called by their controversial leader Albert Shanker. The UFT and the Afro-American Teachers Association squared off over the issue of community control of schools, trading charges of racism and anti-Semitism. Shanker was sentenced to fifteen days in prison for defying a court injunction; the strike ended after the nineteen teachers were reinstated, but the experiment with local control was reduced, straining relations between the UFT and some black community groups well into the 1990s.

In the following years labor gained strength on only a few fronts. Under the direction of Victor Gotbaum the American Federation of State, County and Municipal Employees (AFSCME), the largest representative of municipal employees, launched an ambitious unionization drive, aided by the expansion of municipal government and service industries. By the early 1970s the power base of District Council 37 of AFSCME shifted from motor vehicle operators, most of whom were white men, to hospital, clerical, and administrative workers, most of whom were black women. Workers became more militant, and divisions formed over such ideologically charged issues as the Vietnam War and support for undemocratic regimes in Latin America, which were favored by the conservative building trades unions but not by those in the public sector (AFSCME was the only union on the executive council of the AFL–CIO that regularly opposed Meany in his support for the war). The municipal unions became important power brokers in city politics by contributing money and organizers to electoral campaigns, but they were vulnerable to budget cuts during times of austerity: in negotiations prompted by the fiscal crisis in 1975 they accepted reductions in wages and benefits, and agreed to invest pension funds in municipal bonds to keep the city from bankruptcy.

The strength of unions diminished again during the 1980s, when the city and state cut their budgets, hostility toward labor took root under Presidents Ronald Reagan and George Bush, and the economy slowed late in the decade. Building trades unions focused on retaining control of large projects and became more vulnerable than ever to cancellations of plans for new office buildings. They did manage to remain strong beyond their numbers: although representing less than a fifth of the city's organized work force, the building trades unions held most of the major political positions open to labor leaders, controlling the Central Labor Council and the State Federation of Labor, two influential partners in the coalition that helped elect Governor Mario M. Cuomo in 1982. In 1989 the municipal unions achieved an important victory in electing David N. Dinkins as mayor with help from District Council 37 and Local 1199.

In the mid 1990s New York City remained a stronghold for labor. According to a survey in 1988 more than 30 percent of its regular work force was unionized, while in the same year the corresponding figure for the United States as a whole was 16.8 percent. Some unions sought to expand their jurisdiction, among them the IGLWU, which competed with others to represent the city's office workers. Militant unionism returned with a strike of workers at the *Daily News* in 1991. Among the greatest challenges facing the labor movement were its relations with recent immigrants and the need to recapture the interest of intellectuals, which had declined with the idealism of the CIO.

Vernon H. Jensen: *Strife on the Waterfront: The Port of New York since 1945* (Ithaca, N.Y.: Cornell University Press, 1974)

Jewell Bellush and Bernard Bellush: *Union Power and New York: Victor Gotbaum and District Council 37* (New York: Praeger, 1984)

Joshua Freeman: *In Transit: The Transit Workers Union in New York City, 1933–1966* (New York: Oxford University Press, 1989)

Richard J. Attenbaugh: *Education for Struggle* (Philadelphia: Temple University Press, 1990)

See also Child labor, Maritime unions, and Occupational health.

Kerry Candaele, Sean Wilentz

Laboratory Institute of Merchandising. Private, independent college opened in 1939 in an ornate townhouse at 12 East 53rd Street by Maxwell F. Marcuse (1889–1978), an immigrant from England who worked as an executive at R. H. Macy and was a member of the state Board of Higher Education. The college trains students for careers in the fashion business and offers associate degrees and a bachelor of professional studies. Students at the institute visit showrooms, fashion magazines, buying offices, and cosmetics firms as part of their education.

Marc Ferris

Labor Temple. Community center. Established by the Presbyterian church in 1910 at 14th Street and 2nd Avenue, it sponsored adult education classes, lecture series, and community service programs. Its popular forums stimulated a dialogue between church activists, disaffected Marxists, and communist labor organizers, and the temple was an important community center during strikes. The attendance and budget of the temple declined by the late 1930s. The Institute of Industrial Relations was established there in 1944 by the Presbyterian church before being moved to Chicago in 1952. The Labor Temple ceased to function after a vote of the Presbytery of New York City in 1957.

Peter J. Wosh

Laconia. Name formerly applied to a section of Williamsbridge lying between the Boston Road and Wakefield in the northwestern Bronx. Originally named Laconia Park, it was a real-estate development built in the late

1880s on the estates of William Blodgett and Marmaduke Tilden.

John McNamara: *History in Asphalt: The Origin of Bronx Street and Place Names* (New York: Bronx County Historical Society, 1984)

Gary D. Hermalyn

Ladies' Mile. The name retrospectively applied to a shopping district along Broadway and 6th Avenue that took form in the mid nineteenth century, as wealthy residents of lower Manhattan moved north. The anchor of the district was the store of R. H. Macy, which opened in 1858 at 6th Avenue and 14th Street, near wealthy customers who lived on 5th Avenue. During the next twenty years other stores followed, marking off a district between the stores of A. T. Stewart at 9th Street and Stern Brothers at 23rd Street. The retailers of the Ladies' Mile occupied cast-iron palaces of different styles, and their display windows were designed to imitate those of Europe. Some of the most elegant stores were those of Lord and Taylor, B. Altman, and Arnold Constable. The opening of the 6th Avenue elevated line in 1878 provided convenient access for customers throughout the city. Spurred by the construction of the Flatiron Building (1902–3), commercial establishments such as publishers and booksellers gradually replaced the residences on 5th Avenue, and by the time of the First World War the Ladies' Mile had been abandoned by department stores for sites farther north.

Jennifer Dunning: "Browsing in Phantom Emporiums along the Ladies' Mile," *New York Times*, 5 Nov 1976, §C, p. 19

Amanda Aaron

La Farge, John (*b* New York City, 31 March 1835; *d* Providence, R.I., 14 Nov 1910). Painter. Born near Washington Square, he was educated at home before attending St. John's College (now Fordham University) and Mount St. Mary's in Maryland; he completed his artistic training in France. On his return to the city he settled near Washington Square and produced drawings for *Riverside Magazine*. He became known for his murals at the Church of the Incarnation, St. Thomas's Church (now destroyed), and the Church of the Ascension and also for his thousands of stained-glass windows. La Farge had a studio at 51 West 10th Street.

H. Barbara Weinberg: *The Decorative Work of John La Farge* (New York: Garland, 1977)

See also TIFFANY, LOUIS COMFORT.

James E. Mooney

Lafayette, Marquis **de** [Du Motier, Marie Joseph Paul Yves Roch Gilbert] (*b* château of Chavaniac, Auvergne, 6 Sept 1757; *d* Paris, 20 May 1834). Statesman. He first visited New York City from 4 August to 8 August 1784. On his return on 11 September he was given a banquet by officers of the Continental Army at Capes Tavern, and during receptions by municipal officials and Mayor James Duane on the following day he was presented with the "freedom of the city" in a golden box. He left the city on 15 September, returned three months later, and before his departure on 21 December was escorted to his frigate by a select committee, honored with a parade and artillery salute, and presented with a farewell ode. Lafayette returned to the city on 14 August 1824 for a six-day visit that included a "triumphal procession" to City Hall, a reception by the mayor, and a state banquet on 16 August. During another visit from 5 September to 14 September a performance of *Lafayette; or, The Hero of Olmutz* was given at the Park Theatre on 9 September, the Lafayette Museum at 11 Park Street was illuminated on 13 September, and the next evening a "grand fete" and reception at Castle Garden drew six thousand guests. Lafayette stayed in the city again for three days beginning on 20 September. He made his last visit from 3 July to 14 July 1825. On 4 July a reception for him at City Hall was followed by performances at the Park Theatre and Castle Garden. He remarked to one audience during the course of the day that he was greatly impressed by the "prodigious progress" of the city. Samuel F. B. Morse was commissioned to paint a full-length portrait of Lafayette to hang in City Hall; Walt Whitman, then six years old, later recounted that Lafayette had picked him up and kissed him while visiting Brooklyn.

J. Bennett Nolan: *Lafayette in America Day by Day* (Baltimore: Johns Hopkins University Press, 1934)
Fred Somkin: *Unquiet Eagle: Memory and Desire in the Idea of American Freedom, 1815–1860* (Ithaca, N.Y.: Cornell University Press, 1967)

Allen J. Share

Lafayette Theatre. Theater in Harlem, opened in 1912. From 1915 to 1932, when there were few serious roles for blacks on Broadway, it was the venue for various black stock companies, most known by the name the Lafayette Players. Under the leadership of a white director, A. C. Winn, they presented a range of one-act plays and adaptations of lightweight successes from Broadway. The Lafayette became the most celebrated theater in Harlem. Many members of the Lafayette Players gained recognition as serious dramatic actors. From 1935 to 1939 the theater was the headquarters in Harlem of the Federal Theatre Project of the Works Project Administration and housed productions including *Voodoo Macbeth*, directed by Orson Welles (for further illustration see WELLES, ORSON). After being abandoned in the late 1930s the theater was used temporarily as a church, and while being restored as the New Lafayette it was destroyed by fire in 1968.

Loften Mitchell: *Black Drama: The Story of the American Negro in the Theatre* (New York: Hawthorn, 1967), 66–72
Sister M. Francesca Thompson: "The Lafayette Players," Ronald Ross: "The Role of Blacks in the Federal Theatre, 1935–1939," *The Theatre of Black Americans: A Collection of Critical Essays*, ed. Errol Hill (New York: Applause Theatre Books, 1987), 211–46

E. G. Hill

Lafever, Minard (*b* near Morristown, N.J., 1797; *d* 1854). Carpenter, draftsman, architect, and writer. He moved to New York City in 1828 and in the following year published a builder's guide, the first in a popular series that helped to inspire the Greek Revival in the United States. The Old Merchant's House (1832) and St. James Roman Catholic Church (1837) include details from his handbooks.

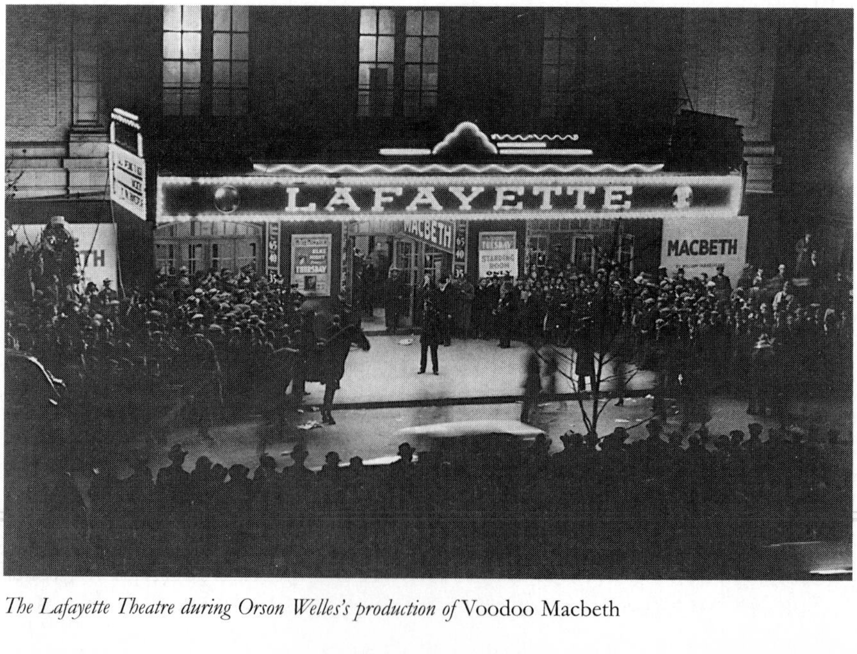

The Lafayette Theatre during Orson Welles's production of Voodoo Macbeth

During his later career he designed Gothic buildings in Brooklyn, including the Church of the Saviour (1844), Holy Trinity Protestant Episcopal Church (1847), and Packer Collegiate Institute (1854), his final commission.

Talbot Hamlin: *Greek Revival Architecture in America* (New York: Dover, 1964)

David Gebhard and Deborah Nevins: *200 Years of American Architectural Drawing* (New York: Whitney Library of Design, 1977)

Val Ginter

La Guardia, Fiorello (Raffaele) H(enry) [Enrico]

(*b* New York City, 11 Dec 1882; *d* New York City, 20 Sept 1947). Mayor and congressman. The son of an Austrian Jewish mother and an Italian agnostic father, he was born at 177 Sullivan Street in lower Manhattan and brought up in the American West, where his father, Achille, was a bandmaster in the U.S. Army. He studied law at New York University and was admitted to the bar in 1910. In 1916 he became the first Italian–American elected to Congress, as a Republican opposed to Tammany Hall and representing a working-class district in lower Manhattan. While holding office he commanded American air forces on the Italian–Austrian front during the First World War. By the end of the 1920s he led a progressive minority in the House that fought against Prohibition, racism, and the prevailing economic doctrine of laissez faire. His ideas won increasing acceptance during the Depression and eventually helped shape the recovery and relief programs of the New Deal. After a brief tenure as president of the city's Board of Aldermen (1920–21) he was reelected to Congress in 1922; there he sponsored the Norris–La Guardia Act, which prohibited injunctions in labor disputes. In 1932 he lost his seat to James Lanzetta in the Democratic landslide that elected Franklin D. Roosevelt to the presidency.

La Guardia turned to municipal politics and was elected mayor in 1933 as a fusion candidate, helped by the investigations that forced Mayor James J. Walker from office, the city's financial troubles, and the Depression. He disclaimed loyalty to the Fusion Party, became known for his aggressive political leadership, and was suspicious of those who threatened his power. Recognizing on taking office that the city was divided into haphazardly administered political fiefdoms and had inadequate social and health services, he completely modernized and centralized its government, consolidated departments, and eliminated unnecessary borough and county offices. He was frustrated by what he considered a hostile press and saw radio broadcasting as a means of reaching the people directly: in what became the best-remembered act of his mayoralty he gave a dramatic reading of the comic strip "Dick Tracy" during a newspaper strike on 8 July 1945. He assumed a far larger role than preceding mayors had done by taking up local needs not with the board of aldermen or the state but with the White House: he persuaded President Roosevelt to grant billions of dollars in funds to the city for the construction of bridges, tunnels, reservoirs, sewer systems, parks, highways, schools, hospitals, health centers, and airports. For the first time in the city's history it had a unified transit system and could provide public housing for its poor and training and subsidies for its artists. As president of the U.S. Conference of Mayors for nearly a decade La Guardia led a national coalition that fought for a generous federal urban policy. In the spring of 1941 Roosevelt appointed him director of the Office of Civilian Defense, a position he assumed while seeking a third term as mayor. After war broke out he could no longer balance both tasks, and in February 1942 he resigned from his position in Washington. After leaving office at the end of 1945 he served briefly as the director general of the United Nations Relief and Rehabilitation Administration.

Mayor Fiorello H. La Guardia, 1942. The mayor was well known for reading comic strips over the radio. One newspaper wrote that his popularity was attributable to his "lusty mugging and robust histrionics."

La Guardia was a colorful, forceful figure who provided honest, inspired, impassioned leadership. He embodied some contradictions: although he enjoyed a reputation as a civil libertarian, he cracked down on gamblers (for illustration see GAMBLING), closed burlesque houses, and used his powers of "garbage collection" to rid newsstands of sexually explicit magazines. He also failed to consider sufficiently the long-term effect of his progressive policies, and by the time he left office New York City was plagued with debt, facilities too expensive to maintain, and a rapidly growing bureaucracy. La Guardia's residences in New York City included 39 Charles Street (from 1914 or 1915 to 1921), 1852 University Avenue in Riverdale (1921 to the early 1930s), 23 East 109th Street (1929–32), 1274 5th Avenue (1933–42), Gracie Mansion (which became the official mayoral residence during his third term as mayor, 1942–45), and 5020 Goodridge Avenue in Riverdale (from 1945). He is buried in Woodlawn Cemetery in the Bronx.

Thomas Kessner: *Fiorello H. La Guardia and the Making of Modern New York* (New York: McGraw–Hill, 1989)

See also BUSES, CIVIL SERVICE UNIONS, MARKETS, and NO DEAL PARTY.

Thomas Kessner

La Guardia Airport.

Airport in north central Queens, opened on 2 December 1939 as North Beach Airport and given its current name soon after. It was the first airport in the United States to have been financed, designed, and built with the full participation of the federal government and the first viable commercial airport in New York City. Plans for the airport were promoted by Mayor Fiorello H. La Guardia, an enthusiastic advocate of aviation who overcame the objections of Robert Moses and won the support of the city's Board of Estimate to acquire a site formerly occupied by the Gala Amusement Park and owned by the Curtis Flying School and Airport. Despite poor soil and obstructing buildings near two of its sides, the site offered easy access to the Triborough Bridge and to proposed highways. The airport was built with $45 million from the Works Progress Administration and initially covered 558 acres (226 hectares), part of which consisted of seventeen million cubic yards (thirteen million cubic meters) of landfill from Rikers Island and from subway excavations. The airport originally included a seaplane station, a circular structure 144 feet (forty-four meters) high of three stories, the third of which was built of steel and glass; although soon abandoned the station remained intact into the 1990s. In an effort to make the airport self-sustaining La Guardia insisted that spectators pay to be admitted to the observation deck of the airport (a decision that proved highly successful) and that the airlines pay high landing fees. He also persuaded banks, hairdressers, gift shops, and other businesses to set up concessions at the airport, which because of the layout of the terminal would be seen by passengers meeting their flights. Although the collapse of three runways by 1942 led many to believe that the airport would never be suitable for large postwar aircraft, the adaptability of aircraft technology and of the airport itself allowed for the eventual lengthening and reinforcement of the runways so that all but the largest commercial aircraft could be accommodated. Nevertheless it became evident that the airport could not sustain itself economically, and in 1947 it was taken over by the Port of New York Authority. Air cargo service was at first a

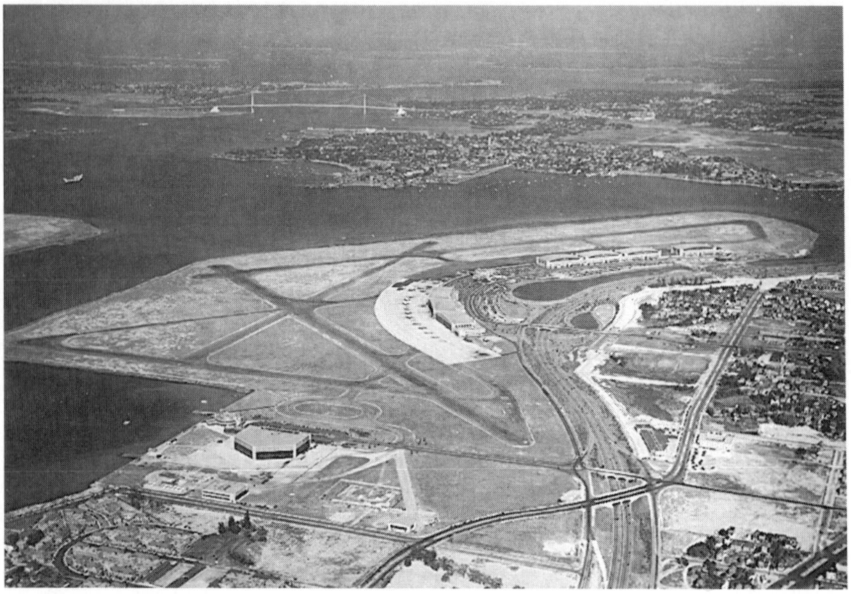

La Guardia Airport, 1941

mainstay of the airport but later declined in importance. In passenger traffic between 1960 and 1990 La Guardia Airport was by turns the leading airport in the metropolitan region and the second after Kennedy Airport. In 1990 it served nearly 23 million travelers, more than twice the number served in 1968.

Paul Barrett

La Guardia Community College. Junior college of the City University of New York, opened in 1971 in Long Island City. It is the only community college in the city to require internships for graduation. The college oversees two high schools on its campus, Middle College and International High School. Its division of continuing education offers programs in Astoria, Harlem, and Chinatown, and on the Upper East Side. In 1990 La Guardia enrolled 7461 full-time and 1781 part-time students.

Marc Ferris

La Mama Experimental Theatre Club. Theater company on East 4th Street, formed in a basement apartment in 1961 by Ellen Stewart, a clothing designer interested in the collaborative nature of theater. When building inspectors threatened to close the theater Stewart circumvented municipal regulations by nominally converting her theater into a café. Despite recurring problems with municipal authorities La Mama eventually became one of the foremost producers of experimental theater. The company presented a wide range of international companies and nurtured the early careers of such figures as Sam Shepard, Lanford Wilson, Tom O'Horgan, Wilford Leach, Peter Brook, Andrei Serban, Robert Wilson, Elizabeth Swados, and Philip Glass.

D. S. Moynihan

La Marqueta. Indoor market in El Barrio, under the Park Avenue viaduct of Metro-North Commuter Railroad between 111th and 116th streets. Built as part of Mayor Fiorello H. La Guardia's program to eliminate pushcarts, it opened in 1936 and became known as the "life of East Harlem." The number of vendors declined in the 1960s, and from the mid 1970s the complex fell into disrepair, leading Mayor Edward I. Koch to talk of refurbishment. In 1990 the city dissolved its contract with the firm responsible for the market, La Marqueta Development Associates, for failing to begin renovations. By the mid 1990s another contract was signed with the Puerto Rican Association for Community Affairs, which planned to renovate the complex (still lacking hot water) and spend $12 to $15 million to add a day-care center, a health clinic, and a movie theater. The area outside the market became a Greenmarket in 1994. Vendors at La Marqueta sell clothing, fish, and tropical produce.

Melissa M. Merritt

Lamb, Thomas W(hite) (*b* Dundee, Scotland, 1871; *d* New York City, 26 Feb 1942). Architect. He designed more than three hundred movie theaters in New York City and around the world, including the Regent Theater (1913, seating 1800), now on Adam Clayton Powell Jr. Boulevard at 116th Street, which has a façade modeled after that of the Doges' Palace in Venice and is generally considered the first true movie palace, and many theaters for Marcus Loew, the leading movie theater operator in the city, with whom he was associated from 1908. His work for Loew included Loew's State Theatre (1921, seating 3300; demolished) at the headquarters of the company in Times Square and such exotic venues as the Pitkin Theatre (1929) in Brooklyn and the 175th Street Theatre (1930, seating 3560) in upper Manhattan. He also designed several legitimate stage theaters, including the Cort Theatre (1912) and the Hollywood Theater (1929; now the Mark Hellinger Theatre) on Broadway, the theater used by Warner Brothers to show its first "talkies," and the Albee Theatre in downtown Brooklyn (1925, seating 3200; demolished).

Anthony W. Robins

Lambs. A club formed in 1874 by five theatrical figures at Delmonico's restaurant. The members met at various restaurants around Union Square before moving to rented quarters at 34 West 26th Street. The club was situated for generations at 134 West 44th Street in the theater district. The architect and club member Stanford White, who had been responsible for the alterations to a clubhouse at 70 West 36th Street, was asked to design a new

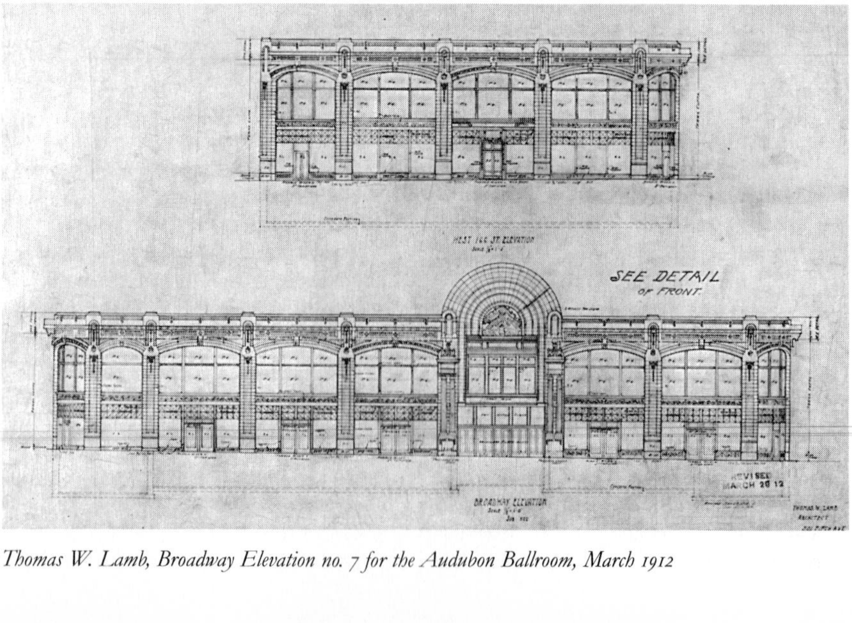

Thomas W. Lamb, Broadway Elevation no. 7 for the Audubon Ballroom, March 1912

clubhouse, which was completed just in time for the Christmas Gambol of 1904. White's portrait was placed in the position of honor in the Grille, the spiritual center of the club. The present address is 3 West 51st Street. Members of the Lambs take part in monthly "Lambastes," four annual stage productions in their theater, and the Lambs Foundation, which supports classes for actors. The club steward is called the Shepherd, the membership the Flock, and the clubhouse the Fold.

James E. Mooney

Lamont, Thomas (William) (*b* Claverack, N.Y., 30 Sept 1870; *d* Boca Grande, Fla., 2 Feb 1948). Journalist, financier, and diplomat. He moved to New York City in 1893 to work as a reporter for the *New York Tribune.* After two years he left to form the consulting firm of Lamont, Corliss, which soon became prominent on Wall Street and helped him to become treasurer of the Bankers Trust Company (1903–9), vice-president of First National Bank (1909–11), and a partner in the firm of J. P. Morgan and Company (1910–48). He and his wife, Florence, rented Franklin D. Roosevelt's house on East 65th Street until 1921, when they bought a townhouse at 107 East 70th Street. He remained interested in journalism and for a time owned the *New York Evening Post* (1918–22) and the *Saturday Review of Literature* (1922–38). By the 1920s he was one of the city's most powerful financiers, overshadowing even J. P. Morgan Jr. A well-known diplomat, Lamont represented the United States at the peace talks in Paris in 1919 and helped to formulate the Dawes Plan for German reparations in 1924.

James Bradley

La Motta, Jake [Jacob] (*b* New York City, 10 July 1921). Boxer. He grew up on the Lower East Side and in Philadelphia and moved to the Bronx in the late 1930s, beginning his professional boxing career in 1941. His aggressive, brawling style made him one of most popular fighters in the city, and he was soon considered one of the best and most exciting middleweight fighters in the country. He became known as the "Bronx bull" and fought frequently at Madison Square Garden, where he had two of his six bouts with Sugar Ray Robinson. In 1947 he deliberately lost a bout there with Billy Fox, resulting in his temporary suspension from boxing. He became the middleweight champion of the world in 1949 but lost the title to Sugar Ray Robinson in 1951. La Motta is considered by many to have been one of the greatest middleweights in the history of boxing. He wrote *Raging Bull: My Story* (1970), and his career was the subject of Martin Scorsese's motion picture *Raging Bull* (1980).

James Bradley

landfill. During the seventeenth century Manhattan was bounded to the north by the North River, which ran along sections of Greenwich and Washington streets and what are now 10th, 11th, and 12th avenues; the southern boundary was the high-water mark, which on the East River was at Pearl and Cherry streets and 1st Avenue. Large coves and inlets pierced Corlear's Hook and East 12th, 25th, and 90th streets. Landfill was first added by the Dutch, who excavated canals, filled in swamps for building sites, and built piers into the East River that became foundations for new land when commerce expanded under English rule. The charter of Governor Thomas Dongan (1686) gave to the city all state-owned land under water between low and high tide. Streets were elongated and new blocks built according to the British grid pattern. Just before the American Revolution development began along the shoreline of the East River in Brooklyn, and industries moved to landfill between Fulton Street and Atlantic Avenue. Atlantic Basin, which was modeled after British and European ports, pushed new blocks into Buttermilk Channel. During the first half of the nineteenth century more land was added in the East River to accommodate facilities for the Port of New York, the busiest port in the nation; beyond this area longer docks were built for large new sailing and steam-powered ships. With dredgings from the Erie Basin in Brooklyn, Red Hook was transformed from an island into a peninsula. Market spoil and debris from fires and demolished buildings were used to build several blocks between Greenwich and West streets and between Vesey and Liberty streets. Land was added to eastern Staten Island, southern Brooklyn, and lower Manhattan to build fortifications along New York Bay, and the northern shore of Staten Island was also expanded.

Most maritime-related landfill was complete by the Civil War; the next phase of landfill created municipal facilities, highways, and parks. Industrial materials were deposited in swamps to provide land for building. During the late nineteenth century the Brooklyn Ash Removal Company extended northern Queens by depositing coal ash from Manhattan in Flushing Bay. Abundant and cheap, ash was also dumped along Randalls Island to form a bridge to Wards Island. At the turn of the century subway excavations provided cheap fill for extending Governors Island southward into New York Bay, and Riverside Park westward into the Hudson. An ambitious landfill program was begun in the 1930s and carried out mainly by Robert Moses during the following twenty years. Garbage, ash, earth from excavations for highways and buildings, and sand from the Rockaways were used in filling in parts of New York and Jamaica bays, wetlands, and rivers to build parks (Ferry Point, Soundview, Dreier Offerman, Marine, Owls Head, Spring Creek, East River, Flushing Meadows, and Fresh Kills), highways (the Brooklyn–Queens Expressway, Henry Hudson Parkway, and East River and Franklin D. Roosevelt drives), and beaches (South, Orchard, and Oakland). The Port of New York Authority filled in parts of Flushing and Jamaica bays to enlarge La Guardia and Idlewild (now John F. Kennedy) airports.

After 1960 development on new land was increasingly opposed by those concerned for the environment. The expansion of Idlewild Airport was halted largely because of efforts by supporters of the Jamaica Bay Wildlife Refuge. Gaps were filled between several piers in South Brooklyn to build a staging area for containerized cargo shipments. In 1974 the construction of Waterside, a housing complex on pilings, added a block to the edge of the East River between 25th and 30th streets. Dredgings from the harbor and earth excavated from the site of the World Trade Center provided the fill between Battery Park and Harrison Street for what in the 1980s became Battery Park City. Plans for an extension of several blocks into the Hudson between Harrison and West 34th streets were part of the proposal for Westway, a large-scale development incorporating a highway and a park that was canceled in 1990. In the mid 1990s landfill accounted for 33 percent of the land in lower Manhattan and a large portion of the city's shoreline.

Report upon the Sanitary Condition of the City (New York: D. Appleton, 1865)

Ann L. Buttenwieser: *Manhattan Water-bound: Planning and Developing Manhattan's Waterfront from the Seventeenth Century to the Present* (New York: New York University Press, 1987)

Ann L. Buttenwieser

Landmarks Preservation Commission. Public body formed in 1965 to identify and protect landmarks and Historic Districts; the law establishing it amended section 534 of the Charter and title 25, chapter 3, of the Administrative Code. The formation of the commission was inspired by the rapid growth in building after the Second World War and the loss of such valued structures as Pennsylvania Station. Designations of structures at least thirty years old are made on the basis of aesthetic, architectural, cultural, and historic significance to the city, state, or nation. In 1973 jurisdiction was extended to interiors customarily open to the public and to scenic landmarks on property owned by the city. Designations are preceded by public hearings and reviewed by the City Council. Once a designation has been made, alterations to a protected feature are prohibited without the prior approval of the commission. The mayor appoints the full-time, paid head of the commission and ten part-time, unpaid commissioners, all of whom serve three-year terms. The commission must include at least three architects, one historian, one city planner or landscape architect, and one real-estate agent or developer, and at least one resident from each of the five boroughs. It is supported by a paid professional staff. In 1978 the U.S. Supreme Court upheld the constitutionality of the landmark preservation law in a notable case concerning Grand Central Terminal. As of 15 April 1994 the commission had designated 920 individual landmarks, eighty-nine interiors, nine scenic landmarks, and sixty-five Historic Districts containing a total of 19,143 properties. (For a list of Historic Districts see HISTORIC PRESERVATION.)

David Listokin: *Landmarks Preservation and the Property Tax* (New York: New York Landmarks Conservancy, 1982)

Joseph B. Rose: "Landmarks Preservation in New York," *Public Interest*, winter 1984, 132–45

Brooke J. Barr

landsmanshaftn. Associations formed by Jewish immigrants from eastern Europe. The members of each one had the same town of origin, and often one town was represented by several landsmanshaftn, reflecting political, religious, and generational divisions among its former residents. From the 1880s the landsmanshaftn provided members with health and death benefits, loans, and help in securing employment and housing. Before the turn of the century most landsmanshaftn were religious congregations or lodges of larger fraternal orders; later independent mutual aid associations and branches of radical orders became more numerous, but the older groups survived as well. Although most groups were exclusively for men, some women's and mixed groups were also formed. After the First World War landsmanshaftn provided large sums of money as well as technical assistance to the beleaguered Jewish communities of eastern Europe. In 1938 the groups numbered nearly three thousand, with a total membership of about half a million. After the Second World War they absorbed many survivors of the Nazi persecution and published memorial books (or *yizker-bikher*) to record for posterity the local history and folklore of former Jewish towns. There were never many American-born members of the landsmanshaftn, and as the immigrant generation vanished so did most of the associations, but several hundred of them survived into the 1990s.

Isaac Elchanan Rontch, ed.: *Di idishe landsmanshaften fun Niu York* (New York: I. L. Peretz Yiddish Writers Union, 1938)

Michael R. Weisser: *A Brotherhood of Memory: Jewish Landsmanshaftn in the New World* (New York: Basic Books, 1985)

American Jewish History 76, no. 1 (1986) [special issue]

Hannah Kliger, ed.: *Jewish Hometown Associations and Family Circles in New York: The WPA Yiddish Writers' Group Study* (Bloomington: Indiana University Press, 1992)

Daniel Soyer: "Jewish Landsmanshaftn (Hometown Associations) in New York, 1880s to 1924" (diss., New York University, 1994)

See also FRATERNAL ORGANIZATIONS.

Daniel Soyer

Landsteiner, Karl (*b* Vienna, 14 June 1868; *d* New York City, 26 June 1943). Immunologist and physician. In Vienna he worked with a group of scientists who discovered the polio virus in 1908. In 1900 he identified and classified the human blood groups A, B, AB, and O, a discovery that allowed for the successful administration of blood transfusions. Affiliated with the Rockefeller Institute for Medical Research from 1922 to 1943, he was awarded the Nobel Prize in medicine in 1930.

Renee D. Mastrocco

Lane, Gertrude Battles (*b* Saco, Maine, 21 Dec 1874; *d* 25 Sept 1941). Magazine editor. She moved to New York City in 1903 to work at *Woman's Home Companion* and in 1911 became the editor, a position she held until her death. Through the magazine she called for improved health care for mothers and infants and fought against child labor. During the First World War she led the Magazine and Feature Section of the Education Division of the U.S. Food Administration. In 1929 Lane was appointed vice-president of the magazine's publisher, the Crowell Publishing Company.

Mary Ellen Zuckerman

Lane Bryant. Firm of women's clothing retailers. It began as a private dressmaker's shop in the apartment on Gouverneur Street of Lena Bryant (1879–1951), a Lithuanian immigrant widowed in 1900 and the mother of a young son. She designed what was probably the first maternity dress in the United States by attaching an accordion-pleated skirt to the bodice of a dress with an elastic band, and was overwhelmed with customers. In 1905 she moved to 38th Street near 5th Avenue, specializing initially in maternity clothes and later in clothes for larger women. About this time she reportedly signed her name Lane Bryant inadvertently when opening a bank account for her growing business and decided not to correct the euphonious error. Her firm evolved into a large and successful operation and in 1947 modernized its store at 455 5th Avenue. After surviving many changes in retailing it was bought by the firm the Limited in 1982.

Leslie Gourse, Kenneth T. Jackson

Lansky, Meyer [Suchowljansky, Maier] (*b* Grodno, Belarus, 1902; *d* Miami, 15 Jan 1983). Organized-crime figure. He moved with his family to New York City in 1911; the ascription to him of 4 July as a date of birth was made arbitrarily by an immigration officer. He worked on the Lower East Side at disguising stolen automobiles, and after the onset of Prohibition formed a gang with Bugsy Siegel known as the "Bugs and Meyer mob" that hijacked and transported bootleg whiskey. After the repeal of Prohibition he worked with Frank Costello in illegal gambling and with Lucky Luciano in racketeering, which he helped to transform into a nationwide enterprise. He also channeled profits from organized crime into real estate, resorts, and gambling in Las Vegas, Cuba, and the Bahamas and was closely associated with the contract killers of Murder Incorporated. In 1950–51 he became widely known when he testified before the investigatory committee of Senator Estes Kefauver. After a brief prison term in 1953 he moved to Florida and spent little time in New York City. Of short stature and unpretentious, Lansky was an anomaly at a time when most leaders of organized crime were ostentatious, and he concealed his important role in the underworld by living modestly. Although he was considered ruthless his rise was based more on his reputation for reliability and intelligence. He lived from the late 1930s to 1943 at 411 West End Avenue, from 1943 to 1948 at 211 Central Park West, and for six years beginning in 1948 at 40 Central Park South.

Hank Messick: *Lansky* (New York: G. P. Putnam's Sons, 1971)

Robert Lacey: *Little Man: Meyer Lansky and the Gangster Life* (Boston: Little, Brown, 1991)

Warren Sloat

Lapchick, Joe [Joseph Bohomiel] (*b* Yonkers, N.Y., 12 April 1900; *d* Monticello, N.Y., 10 Aug 1970). Basketball coach. He was a player with the Original Celtics in New York City before serving from 1936 to 1947 as the head coach of St. John's College (later St. John's University); during his tenure the team appeared seven times in the National Invitation Tournament (NIT), which it won in 1943 and 1944. From 1947 to 1956 he coached the New York Knickerbockers, compiling a record of 326 wins and 247 losses. He was again the head coach at St. John's from 1956 to 1965, during which his teams twice more won the NIT. For his entire career at St. John's his record was 334 wins and 130 losses. In 1973 St. John's and the Basketball Hall of Fame began awarding the annual Joe Lapchick Award to the outstanding collegiate basketball player in the country.

Sandy Padwe: *Basketball's Hall of Fame* (Englewood Cliffs, N.J.: Prentice Hall, 1970)

Larry Fox: *Illustrated History of Basketball* (New York: Grosset and Dunlap, 1974)

Neil D. Isaacs: *All the Moves: A History of College Basketball* (Philadelphia: J. B. Lippincott, 1975)

Albert Figone

Lasker, Mary Woodward (*b* Watertown, Wis., 1902; *d* Greenwich, Conn., 23 Feb 1994). Philanthropist. She moved to New York City in 1923. In 1940 she married Albert Davis Lasker, who owned the advertising agency Lord and Thomas, and in 1942 the two established the Lasker Foundation, donor of the annual Albert Lasker Awards for outstanding contributions to medical research. Lasker was also a leader in urban beautification efforts in the city and once donated three hundred Japanese cherry trees to the United Nations.

Kenneth T. Jackson

Lathrop, Rose Hawthorne [Mother Mary Alphonsa] (*b* Lenox, Mass., 2 May 1851; *d* Hawthorne, N.Y., 8 July 1926). Nun and humanitarian. A daughter of Nathaniel Hawthorne, she moved with her husband, George Lathrop, to New York City in 1876 and converted to Catholicism in 1891. After separating from him in 1894 she began working with cancer victims on the Lower East Side and became a Dominican nun in 1895. She helped to open St. Rose's Free Home for Incurable Cancer on Cherry Street in 1899 (moved to Jackson Street in 1912) and the Rosary Hill Home in Hawthorne, New York, also for cancer patients. With other members of her order she formed Servants for the Relief of Incurable Cancer in 1901.

Paricia Dunlavy Valenti: *To Myself a Stranger: A Biography of Rose Hawthorne Lathrop* (Baton Rouge: Louisiana State University Press, 1991)

Bernadette McCauley

Latimer, Lewis (Howard) (*b* Chelsea, Mass., 8 Sept 1848; *d* Queens, 11 Dec 1928). Inventor. The son of fugitive slaves, he served in the Union Navy and learned drafting while working for a firm of patent solicitors in Boston. In 1876 he helped Alexander Graham Bell to prepare his application for a patent for the telephone. As an employee of the U.S. Electric Lighting Company in Bridgeport, Connecticut, from 1879 to 1883 he took out patents for a long-lasting, inexpensive carbon filament and an improved electric lamp, and supervised the installation of street lighting in New York City, Philadelphia, Montreal, and London. From 1884 he was the chief draftsman and an expert witness on patents for the Edison Electric Light Company (65 5th Avenue). He wrote and illustrated one of the earliest scientific books on electric lighting (*Incandescent Electric Lighting*, 1890) and later was a founding member of the Edison Pioneers. Latimer lived at 64 Holly Avenue in Flushing.

Louis Haber: *Black Pioneers of Science and Invention* (New York: Harcourt, Brace and World, 1970)
Glennette Tilley Turner: *Lewis Howard Latimer* (Englewood Cliffs, N.J.: Silver Burdett, 1991)

Joyce Mendelsohn

Latin Americans. Although people from Spain and its possessions settled in New York City in the earliest times, the community grew especially rapidly in the mid nineteenth century, when the United States expanded trade in Latin America and the Caribbean. Between 1845 and 1870 the number of Latin Americans in the city increased from 508 to 2062, with the majority consisting of Spaniards, Cubans, and other immigrants from the Spanish-speaking West Indies. Their numbers continued to rise after the Spanish–American War, when the United States acquired Puerto Rico and increased its influence in the Caribbean.

The first immigrants included many exiled political leaders, among them José Martí of Cuba and Ramón Betances and Eugenio Maria de Hostos of Puerto Rico, who from the late 1860s to the late 1890s were based in the city and fought for Cuban and Puerto Rican independence. Their activism also gave rise to civic and political organizations concerned primarily with issues affecting Latin Americans in the United States. Among the most successful of the early organizations was an association of cigar makers who organized a "populist committee" (1893) that became active in the city's electoral politics.

In 1900 half of the more than 7500 Latin Americans in New York City were immigrants from the Caribbean. Many arrived with entrepreneurial skills, and opened boarding houses and small businesses that catered to newcomers. On the Lower East Side and in Chelsea nearly five hundred Latin Americans owned tobacco factories by 1900; other businesses included restaurants, grocery stores called bodegas, and botánicas (stores that sold items such as herbs, religious statues, and candles). Among the many publications issued in Spanish were several newspapers; the oldest and largest was *La Prensa* (1913), which covered both New York City and Latin America. In 1923 the Guía Hispana, a guide to commercial and professional services offered by Latin Americans, listed 275 businesses and 150 professionals, including physicians, dentists, and lawyers.

Latin Americans first became active in Democratic and Republican politics in New York City in the 1890s. Among the political organizations then emerging were the Caribe Democratic Club, the Hispanic–American Democratic Club, the Puerto Rican and Hispanic League, and the Federation of Puerto Rican Democratic Clubs. In the late 1920s the Republican Party supported the candidacies of two Puerto Rican politicians, Rafael Bosch (for the state assembly) and Victor Fiol Ramos (for the City Council). Latin Americans made their first strong impact on the city's elections during the reform period of the late 1930s and early 1940s. Mayor Fiorello H. La Guardia and Representative Vito Marcantonio, whose congressional district in East Harlem included El Barrio, the city's largest Latin American community, encouraged Latin Americans to take part in politics and supported the successful candidacy of Oscar García Rivera, a Puerto Rican state assemblyman from East Harlem (1937, 1939).

Puerto Ricans became the largest Latin American group in New York City by the early 1940s. Already accounting for 18 percent of the total Spanish-speaking population in 1920, they increased their share to 46 percent in 1940 and 81 percent by 1960; between 1940 and 1970 they grew in number from 61,463 to 811,843. Thus for several decades the city's Latin American community was synonymous with its Puerto Rican community. Puerto Rican migration accelerated with the island's worsening economic and social crises during the Depression, postwar expansion in the United States, and industrialization efforts in Puerto Rico during the 1950s. Some of those who left the island were political exiles, but most were escaping its troubled economy. The number of Latin Americans from countries other than Puerto Rico increased during the 1960s after the Cuban Revolution (1959) and the Dominican civil war (1965), and was reflected in the growth of several Latin American neighborhoods in New York City.

During the late 1940s and 1950s Puerto Rican politicians were appointed to district leaderships and supported for political office by the Democratic Party. Mayor Robert F. Wagner opened up city government to Latinos, appointing Herman Badillo and others to high posts in his administration. His successor, John V. Lindsay, also reached out to Latinos. The 1960s saw the birth of a more activist brand of politics. Groups such as the Young Lords, the Puerto Rican Student Union, and the Puerto Rican Socialist Party addressed issues such as housing, education, health, and civil rights. They also heightened the political awareness of the younger generation and provided models for greater political assertiveness. By the late 1960s Puerto Rican and other Latino politicians entered the political establishment. With the support of reform Democrats, Badillo was elected the first Puerto Rican congressman in 1970. His success and the changes within the Democratic and Republican parties during the 1970s and 1980s led to more support for other Puerto Rican and Latino candidates. Many entered politics at the most local level, successfully running for positions on community school boards.

During these years Puerto Ricans in the city opened businesses of many kinds: factories that made garments, food products, and soft drinks, large retail furniture and department stores, jewelry shops, real-estate offices, garages and used car businesses, travel agencies, resort communities in the Catskills, and theaters. There were also more than two hundred Puerto Rican ministers and greater numbers working in the professions. Business owners aided emerging institutions such as regional societies and neighborhood clubs, and helped to form new ones.

Although Spanish had long been taught as a foreign language in the city's schools and universities, the large influx of Puerto Ricans in the 1940s and 1950s brought Spanish and Hispanic language and culture out of the universities and into the city's streets. In much the same way that large-scale Cuban immigration made Miami a bilingual city, the large Puerto Rican migration to New York City made some observers refer to the city as the "Big Mango."

Many of the Latin American neighborhoods in New York City and particularly the southern Bronx were hurt by postwar federal policies that sponsored badly planned housing projects for poor and working-class communities and emphasized the construction of highways, such as the Cross Bronx Expressway, which destroyed neighborhoods and initiated a period of middle-class flight to remotely situated developments such as Co-op City. Further damage was inflicted in the 1970s by the city's fiscal crisis and in the 1980s by bank redlining, arson, drugs, and crime. Many once prosperous Puerto Rican businesses were closed or sold.

At the same time the city's Latin American population continued to rise, from 1,406,024 in 1980 to 1,783,511 in 1990. Most of the new immigrants originated from countries other than Puerto Rico, especially Ecuador, Colombia, El Salvador, and the Dominican Republic, and settled in Brooklyn and Queens. These newer immigrants showed the same entrepreneurial tendencies of earlier Latin American immigrants in the city, and many opened small businesses and formed organizations. The Puerto Rican population, which accounted for 72 percent of the total Latin American population in 1980, declined in 1990 to 50 percent, as greater numbers began leaving the city for the suburbs and other parts of the country.

The predominance of Caribbean Latinos in the last 1980s gave the city's Latino community a decidedly Antillean cast. Despite this trend Latin Americans of various backgrounds in New York City continued to share many cultural institutions, often attending the same concerts and films and listening to the same radio stations. Latin music, in particular Latin jazz and salsa, incorporates diverse musical styles and appeals to a wide audience, as do such popular Latin dance styles and rhythms as danza, plenas, mambos, cha cha cha, and boogaloo. The Museo del Barrio and the Bronx Museum of the Arts, which were created in neighborhoods that were once predominantly Puerto Rican, sponsor exhibitions by artists from Latin America, Mexico, and Spain. The Puerto Rican Traveling Theater stages productions by Latin American playwrights and features Latin American actors. Spanish-language radio and television programs are popular among Latin Americans in New York City, and the television stations WNJU (channel 47) and WXTV (channel 41) broadcast almost entirely in Spanish. Leading Spanish-language periodicals include the newspapers *El Diario–La Prensa* and *Noticias del Mundo* (see SPANISH-LANGUAGE PRESS).

Roberto E. Villareal and Norma G. Hernández, eds.: *Latinos and Political Coalitions* (New York: Greenwood, 1991)

Latin American Music (Redlands, Calif.: Libros Latinos, 1992)

Rodney E. Hero: *Latinos and the U.S. Political System* (Philadelphia: Temple University Press, 1992)

Clara Rodríguez, Gabriel Haslip-Viera (with David L. González)

Latvians. A Latvian community took form in New York City during the second half of the nineteenth century. Most immigrants were peasants, sailors, and craftsmen; many of their children became professionals. In 1902 Latvian Lutherans formed their first parish on the Upper East Side. After the failed revolution of 1905 in Russia there was an influx of political exiles including many socialists, who soon launched the publications *Briva Tribuna* (Free Tribune, 1907–8) and *Proletarietis* (1917–19). A number of Latvian anarchists in France moved to the city and launched *Briviba* (Liberty, 1908–13) and *Melnais Karogs* (The Black Flag, 1912–14). There was also the scholarly journal *Gaisma* (The Light, 1912) and the religious publication *Lauzu Kancelis* (People's Pulpit, 1912). Latvians in the city vigorously campaigned for Latvian independence after the First World War. Seeking to combat the influence of the political left, Baptists introduced the publication *Drauga Bals* (Voice of a Friend, 1917–19) and later *Draugas Vests* (Message from a Friend, 1942–47); both became popular and stressed ethnicity and education, as did *Amerikas Atbalss* (American Echo, 1920–22). The city became a center of international efforts to preserve Latvian language and culture: the First Congress of the American Latvian League was held there (1919), and the city was also the site of a youth club (1922) and a library society that circulated Latvian books (1923). The newspaper *Amerikas Latviesu Zinals* (American Latvian News, 1926) ceased operations for lack of funds. A Latvian chamber of commerce opened in 1938. Independence efforts intensified after Latvia was annexed by the Soviet Union in 1940.

Political refugees of the communist regime in Latvia, including many professionals, settled in the city after the Second World War and issued a number of publications. *Laiks* (Time, 1949–) was begun in Brooklyn by Helmers Rudzitis, who also formed Gramatu Draugs, soon the most important Latvian publishing house in the United States. Other periodicals included *Latviju Zurnals* (1951–56), the political journal *Latvijas Brivibat* (Freedom for Latvia, 1955–68; later moved to Switzerland), and *Brivibas Talcinieris* (Helper for Youth Freedom, 1957–60). A professional Latvian theater (1950) and a summer camp for children (1956) were also established in the city. Nine hundred singers in thirty-eight choruses took part in the Second Latvian Song Festival in USA (1958), and a program of song and dance was presented on Latvian Day at the World's Fair of 1964–65.

In the mid 1990s there were between three and four thousand Latvians in New York City. About 85 percent were Lutheran (concentrated from the 1960s in the Latvian Evangelical Lutheran Church in Brooklyn); the rest were Baptist, Catholic, and Eastern Orthodox. Well-known Latvians in the city have included the sculptor Augustus Annus, the painter Janis Gailis, the landscape architect Vilhelms Purvitis, the violinist Uldis Baumanis, the composer Gundars Poné, and the actress Laila Roberts.

Maruta Karklis, Liga Streips, and Laimonis Streips: *The Latvians in America, 1640–1973: A Chronology and Fact Book* (Dobbs Ferry, N.Y.: Oceana, 1974)

Vladimir Wertsman

Lauder, Estée [née Mentzer, Josephine Esther] (*b* Queens, 1 July 1908). Businesswoman. After growing up on Hillside Avenue and attending Public School 14 and Newtown High School she entered the cosmetics business in 1924 with her uncle John Schatz, who had developed a facial cream and formed a company called New Way Labs in Brooklyn. Early in her career she developed a modest line of fragrances, skin cream, cleansing oil, lipstick, face powder, and turquoise eye shadow that she aimed specifically at well-to-do Jewish women, and she prevailed on the department store Bonwit Teller to sell six of her products. She married Joseph Lauder in 1930 and incorporated her business in 1947. In 1953 she achieved great success with a bath oil called Youth Dew, manufactured at two small plants in upper Manhattan. She introduced the practice of offering promotional gifts with purchases and was the first cosmetics maker to feature a single fashion model throughout a series of advertisements. In 1965 she introduced a line of twenty-one products for men under the marque Aramis; by this time her firm had gross sales of $14 million and was encroaching on a market formerly controlled by Revlon, with which she engaged in a heated rivalry. She moved her corporate headquarters to the General Motors building at 767 5th Avenue in 1968. During these years she also became a member of fashionable society. By 1982 her business was the largest privately held cosmetics firm in the world, with annual sales of $1000 million. One of Lauder's sons, Leonard, became chief executive officer of the firm in 1971; another son, Ronald, who also worked for the firm, was an unsuccessful Republican mayoral candidate in 1989.

Lee Israel: *Estée Lauder: Beyond the Magic* (New York: Macmillan, 1985)

Marc Ferris

Laurel Hill. Small industrial neighborhood in northwestern Queens, lying between Long Island City and Maspeth and bounded to the north by the Long Island Expressway, to the east by 58th Street, to the west by Laurel Hill Boulevard, and to the south by Maspeth

Creek. It was originally the farm of Edward Waters and was bought in 1853 by Jacob Rapalye, who renamed it and built an imposing mansion on high ground between 44th and 46th streets on 55th Drive; his son August Rapalye lived there until 1890. After the Civil War the South Side Railroad cut a track through the property, and later F. Haberman's National Enameling and Stamping Company built chemical and enameling plants on the banks of Newtown Creek that poisoned the air with corrosive fumes. The farmland behind the mansion was sold in the 1880s for development as the village of Laurel Hill to cater to travelers and visitors to the cemetery. In the mid 1990s the area remained commercial and industrial and had few private houses. The Long Island Expressway and the Calvary Cemetery isolate Laurel Hill, to which access is provided only on the side near Maspeth.

Vincent Seyfried

Laurelton. Neighborhood in southeastern Queens (1990 pop. 28,000), bounded to the north by Francis Lewis Boulevard, to the east by Laurelton Parkway, to the south by 147th Avenue, and to the west by Springfield Boulevard. In 1906 three hundred acres (120 hectares) just east of Springfield Gardens at the junction of the Atlantic and Montauk divisions of the Long Island Rail Road were acquired by William H. Reynolds, a former state senator, who incorporated the Laurelton Land Company to develop the tract. In January 1907 the company paid $8000 for an elegant railroad station just east of 222nd Street, which opened in April 1907. Lots were priced from $500 to $750 and sold in parcels of three; only one-family houses costing at least $4000 could be built. A few expensive houses costing between $5500 and $17,500 were constructed during the next ten years, and Reynolds abandoned Laurelton to develop Long Beach. As the demand for housing rose during the 1920s Laurelton revived and became the site of many more middle-class houses. In 1928 the grounds of the golf club were developed as blocks of houses in a Spanish style with tile roofs. Predominantly Jewish from the 1940s and 1950s, Laurelton attracted middle-class blacks from Springfield Gardens in the following decades. During the 1980s Laurelton drew many immigrants from Jamaica (almost half of all immigrants settling in the neighborhood), Haiti, Guyana, and Trinidad and Tobago, and by the early 1990s the population was 70 to 80 percent black. The houses are mostly well-maintained English Tudors and Spanish stuccos; a garden club planted the malls.

Vincent Seyfried

Lauren [Lifshitz], **Ralph** (*b* Bronx, 14 Oct 1939). Fashion designer. He grew up in New York City and began his career on the business side of fashion, working during the day as both a salesperson at Brooks Brothers and a buyer for Allied Stores while taking business classes at night at City College. By 1967 his lifelong interest in design and his creativity prompted Beau Brummel Neckwear to have him create his own line of men's ties, which he named Polo. In 1968 he founded Polo Fashions and Polo Men's Wear, expanding his designs to include men's clothing, shoes, and luggage. He later established a marque of women's clothing, Ralph Lauren (1971), and designed costumes for the film *The Great Gatsby* (1973). By the mid 1980s Polo Fashions had reached $600 million in sales and his salary reportedly exceeded $15 million. In 1986 he restored the Rhinelander Mansion on Madison Avenue, which he made the site of a boutique featuring his fashions. A leading exponent of a traditional, "Ivy League" style characterized by aristocratic simplicity, Lauren has likened his approach to that of Coco Chanel. Although he has earned many fashion awards, including several Coty awards, his success as a designer has been more popular than critical. Apart from his designing career he has supported several philanthropic projects, including the breast cancer research center of Georgetown University.

Anne E. Kornblut

lawn bowling. A Dutch pastime popular from the time of European settlement in what is now New York City. Perhaps the first matches were held in 1626 in the area at the southern end of Broadway later known as Bowling Green. Lawn bowling was very popular in the early eighteenth century but virtually disappeared during the nineteenth. It was revived by the New York Lawn Bowling Club, which established the first bowling green in Central Park at 69th Street in 1926 and opened a second green at the same location in 1930. The club's membership declined in the 1980s; in the mid 1990s it stood at about 150.

James Weir Greig: *The Game of Bowling on the Green, or Lawn Bowls* (New York: American Sports Publishing, 1904)

Laura Lewison

Lawrence, Cornelius Van Wyck (*b* Flushing [now in Queens], 18 Feb 1791; *d* Flushing, 20 Feb 1861). Mayor. He moved to New York City in 1812 and worked in business before his election to the House of Representatives as a Jacksonian Democrat in 1832. In 1834 he became the first directly elected mayor of New York City when he defeated the Whig candidate Gulian C. Verplanck by 174 votes; he remained in office until 1837. Lawrence also directed several corporations and was collector of New York from 1845 to 1849.

James E. Mooney

law schools. Legal training during the eighteenth century was usually accomplished by apprenticeship that lasted as long as seven years. Students paid a fee and served a lawyer in return for instruction in the principles and practice of law; they copied, drafted, and filed documents and read legal treatises and textbooks. Such an apprenticeship was required well into the nineteenth century. Efforts to establish more formal training were undertaken by James Kent, who gave a series of lectures on law at Columbia College in 1794 and 1795. After retiring as chancellor of New York he gave another series of lectures between 1824 and 1826 that became the basis of his *Commentaries on American Law*. Benjamin Butler opened the city's first law school in 1838 at the University of the City of New York (now New York University); it closed after a year. During the Jacksonian era efforts were made to abolish the stringent controls on admission to the bar that fostered élitism. The New York State constitution of 1846 abolished the training requirement and allowed any male citizen twenty-one years old or more to practice law after passing a public examination. Although self-directed reading became an acceptable means of preparation, apprenticeships continued to predominate and were eventually replaced by "clerkships," in which students were sometimes paid for their services. Admission to the bar solely on the basis of office study was allowed until the 1970s. In 1858 law schools were established by New York University and Columbia. Largely independent, they were supported almost entirely by tuition. To compete with clerkships they adopted lax admissions standards (applicants did not need a high school education), set a curriculum oriented toward the practice of law, and scheduled classes at times convenient for working students. Lessons were based on textbooks, treatises, lectures, and recitations.

The late nineteenth century saw the establishment of new standards and the expansion of the city's law schools. In 1871 the state court of appeals was empowered to set requirements for admission to the bar. Under Theodore W. Dwight during the 1870s and 1880s Columbia College School of Law became one of the country's two largest law schools and an important influence on the city's bar. Before 1890 the law school at New York University seldom had more than seventy-five students. After the first woman was admitted to the bar in 1886 the university cooperated with the Women's Legal Education Society to introduce a special one-year course in 1890. Women were also admitted to the regular law school for the first time in the same year, and the first women graduated in 1892. The growth of law schools, the development of the typewriter and stenography, and the introduction of women to clerical work led to the decline of clerkships. More students were pushed into law school after 1894 with the introduction of a uniform written bar examination that emphasized academic skills, and between 1889 and 1899 enrollments rose from six hundred to about eighteen hundred. Under Seth Low, who became president of Columbia College in 1890, the law school adopted policies similar to those introduced at Harvard Law School by Christopher Columbus Langdell: it raised its admissions requirements, broadened the curriculum, adjusted the schedule to discourage students from working, and added a third year of study. Columbia also adopted the "case method" of legal instruction developed at Harvard, which focused on the written opinions of judges. Columbia became more exclusive and academically rigorous, and enrollment declined.

In response to Low's reforms most of the faculty and many students left Columbia in 1891 to form New York Law School. It was known for its focus on practice, its lax admissions, and its flexible class schedule, as was the first night school, Metropolis Law School, which was chartered in the same year and merged with New York University in 1895. Enrollments continued to rise and new schools opened that focused on practice, among them Brooklyn Law School (1901), Fordham University School of Law (1905), and St. John's University School of Law (1925). Like New York University and New York Law School these attracted immigrants and a small but increasing number of women, and enrollments increased rapidly between 1910 and the late 1920s: by 1928 there were almost eleven thousand law students in the city. These developments, especially the enrollment of immigrants, provoked a reaction by the bar. In the mid 1920s the New York State Bar Association sought to prevent students without the equivalent of two years of college education from studying law in school or an office; the state court of appeals adopted such a rule in 1927, which went into effect in 1929. At the same time most schools adopted admissions and curricular policies similar to those of Columbia and Harvard. In 1928 only Columbia among schools in New York City was approved by the Section of Legal Education of the American Bar Association; by 1938 New York Law School was the only school in the city without approval. The new policies and the Depression reduced enrollments by half between 1928 and 1938, and the Second World War exacerbated conditions. New York Law School was closed until the end of the war, and similar action was considered by both Brooklyn Law School and New York University.

Enrollments quickly returned to their previous level after the war. During the late 1940s and 1950s legal education became standardized according to the model set by the exclusive schools. Institutions in the city improved their facilities, expanded their faculty, raised entrance requirements, and reformed their curricula. Enrollments fell slightly in the 1950s and rose again in the 1960s. These enrollments continued to rise in the 1970s, largely because more women and ethnic minorities were attracted to the profession. The Cardozo School of Law of Yeshiva University opened in 1976, followed by the City University of New York Law School at Queens College in 1983.

Paul M. Hamlin: *Legal Education in Colonial New York* (New York: New York University, Law Quarterly Review, 1939)

Robert B. Stevens: *Law School: Legal Education in America from the 1850s to the 1980s* (Chapel Hill: University of North Carolina Press, 1983)

James A. Wooten

lawyers. The legal profession grew slowly in colonial New York City, where initially conveyancing and debt collection accounted for most legal work. Between 1695 and 1769 there were forty-nine practicing lawyers, many of them poorly trained; preparation for a career in law consisted of an apprenticeship of as long as seven years with a lawyer. Judges were appointed by the executive rather than elected. The profession was not well regarded until the 1730s, when commerce expanded rapidly and the demand for skilled lawyers increased. Commercial and maritime law grew in importance, and on the eve of the American Revolution lawyers were few but well established. Among the most important were the editors of the *Independent Reflector* (1752–53): William Smith Jr., William Livingston, and John Morin Scott, who was also a leader of the Sons of Liberty. Many other leaders opposed the revolution.

After the war such men as Alexander Hamilton, John Jay, and Aaron Burr became active in national politics, and a career in law became a path to social, economic, and political success. By the early nineteenth century lawyers were prominent figures in the city; these included Thomas Addis Emmet and William Sampson, who sought to codify the law and simplify the process for admission to the bar, and the legal scholar James Kent. Under the new state constitution of 1846 the systems of apprenticeship and judicial appointment were abolished: male citizens twenty-one and older were allowed to practice law after passing a public examination, and judges were elected by popular vote. A code of civil law was drafted by David Dudley Field, a lawyer in the city who believed that undue complexity made the law inaccessible to everyone outside the profession. Usually known as the Field Code, it simplified civil law by combining the practice of common law and equity and was adopted by the state assembly in 1848. During the next twenty-five years it became the basis of civil codes in twenty-four states.

Largest Law Firms in New York City, 1990, with Number of Lawyers in Metropolitan Region

1. Skadden, Arps, Slate, Meagher and Flom 560
2. Shearman and Sterling 472
3. Simpson Thatcher and Bartlett 426
4. Weil, Gotshal and Manges 408
5. Paul, Weiss, Rifkind, Wharton and Garrison 395
6. Davis Polk and Wardwell 371
7. Millbank, Tweed, Hadley and McCloy 354
8. Proskauer Rose Goetz and Mendelsohn 341
9. Sullivan and Cromwell 320
10. Debevoise and Plimpton 307
11. White and Case 304
12. Cravath, Swaine and Moore 298
13. Kaye Scholer Fierman Hays and Handler 288
14. Willkie Farr and Gallagher 279
15. Cleary Gottlieb Steen and Hamilton 270
16. Stroock and Stroock and Lavan 259
17. Fried Frank Harris Shriver and Jacobson 258
18. Mudge Rose Guthrie Alexander and Ferdon 256
19. Dewey Ballantine 253
20. Cahill Gordon and Reindel 248
20. Wilson, Elser, Moskowitz, Edelman and Dicker 248
22. Rogers and Wells 235
23. Shea and Gould 232
24. Rosenman and Colin 221
25. Kelley Drye and Warren 217

Source: *Crain's New York Business* 6, no. 53, pp. 52–53. Metropolitan region includes New York City; Westchester, Nassau, and Suffolk counties in New York; and Bergen, Essex, Husdon, and Union counties in New Jersey.

Compiled by Kevin Kenny

The influence of trial lawyers in the city increased during the nineteenth century and reached a pinnacle about the 1880s. The partners William F. Howe and Abe Hummel became well known for their spectacular success in defending clients charged with arson, murder, and involvement in organized crime. William M. Evarts defended President Andrew Johnson in his impeachment trial in 1868 and was appointed attorney general of the United States (1868–69). Perhaps the best-known trial lawyer in the city was Charles O'Conor, who led the prosecution against William M. "Boss" Tweed in the early 1870s. Joseph Choate continued to try cases into his eightieth year in 1912. In 1870 the Association of the Bar of the City of New York was formed by fewer than five hundred of the four thousand lawyers practicing in the city; Evarts was president from 1870 to 1880. A private club, it sought to protect the profession for the élite. Its members blamed the reforms of 1846 for a decline in professional standards, called for more rigorous ethics and training, and were prominent in fighting corruption in municipal government during the 1870s. Among them were Samuel J. Tilden, a vice-president of the association who as chairman of the Democratic Party in New York State (1866–74) investigated the Tweed Ring, and James C. Carter, who helped to prosecute Tweed. Carter also led the opposition to proposals for codification in the 1870s and 1880s, which many lawyers in the city (especially those of the bar association) considered an encroachment on the legal profession by government. Field defended Tweed after members of the bar association rejected his offer to work for the prosecution.

During the 1870s the importance of business law increased with the number of large public corporations. The firms of Cravath (now Cravath, Swaine and Moore), which moved to the city in 1854, and Shearman and Sterling (1873) opened offices on Wall Street and made innovations that were soon widely imitated. Cravath was among the first to focus on offering advice to corporate clients in such areas as financial management and the prevention of lawsuits. It also introduced the "Cravath system," adopted by many firms by 1900, in which not only partners, associates, and clerks but also law students working in the firm were paid a salary beginning at $30 a month. By the 1890s business law and especially corporate law dominated the practices of many lawyers, who spent less time in court than formerly and often worked as associates and partners in large corporate firms such as those on Wall Street, the most powerful in the city.

A degree in law rather than a clerkship soon became the prerequisite for a career as a lawyer. Columbia Law School became increasingly rigorous and exclusive; many of its graduates found work in the city's most prominent firms, which employed mostly white Republican Protestant men from the upper middle class. A number of them eventually had careers in government, including Elihu Root, secretary of war under presidents William McKinley and Theodore Roosevelt, and John W. Davis, the Democratic presidential nominee in 1924. Members of ethnic minorities were employed by some corporate firms including Cravath, where William D. Guthrie, a Roman Catholic, and Charles M. Da Costa, a descendant of West Indian Jews, were important figures. A few firms employed mainly Catholics or Jews, among them Proskauer Rose Goetz and Mendelsohn (1875). Women were allowed to practice law in New York State in 1886 and were admitted by New York University Law School from 1890; Melle Titus, who enrolled there in 1891, was the first woman in the city to graduate from law school and become a lawyer. The university also sponsored the Women's Legal Education Society, which offered an introductory course in law for women. A number of law schools opened in the city during the first decades of the twentieth century: Brooklyn Law School in 1903, Fordham University School of Law in 1905, St. John's University School of Law in 1925. Legal education became more accessible to women, immigrants, and workers, especially through classes at night, and women were first admitted to Columbia in 1927. But corporate law remained largely the preserve of the élite.

Lawyers became well known for their roles in reforms undertaken during the first two decades of the twentieth century. Charles Evans Hughes was a member of the Stevens Gas Commission (1906), which investigated the practices of utilities in the city, and became known nationally as the counsel for the Armstrong Commission in its investigation of insurance fraud (1906–7); he served as governor of New York (1907–10), sought the presidency as a Republican in 1916, and was chief justice of the United States from 1930 to 1941. Samuel Untermyer led a congressional investigation of the Wall Street banking system in 1912. Some of the best-known public interest lawyers were women, most of them graduates of the New York University Law School. Among them were Crystal Eastman (graduated 1907), a feminist and labor activist who formed the American Civil Liberties Union with Roger Baldwin in the city in 1920, and Dorothy Kenyon, an advocate of civil liberties and one of several women lawyers who worked for Mayor Fiorello H. La Guardia. Helen L. Buttenwieser (graduated 1936) was employed by Cravath, Swaine and Moore and joined the bar association in 1937, the first year it accepted women as members. One of the first women to work as an associate in a corporate firm, she was also well known for her work in civil liberties. Prominent trial lawyers during these years included Samuel Leibowitz, who defended the Scottsboro Boys during the 1930s, and William J. Fallon.

The legal profession in the city strengthened in the years before and after the Second World War. Lawyers were needed during the Depression to work for the government and handle an unprecedented number of bankruptcies. As a federal prosecutor appointed to investigate organized crime in the city, Thomas E. Dewey in the mid 1930s gained seventy-two convictions on racketeering charges in seventy-three cases brought against restaurateurs, poultry producers, bakers, and truckers; he was later elected to three terms as governor of New York and nominated for the presidency by the Republicans in 1944 and 1948. Two important organizations formed in the city were the National Lawyers Guild (1937), which played an important role in drafting and implementing New Deal policies, and the NAACP Legal Defense and Educational Fund (1939). The number of immigrants and children of immigrants becoming lawyers grew rapidly. Among them was La Guardia, who worked while attending law school at New York University before being elected mayor in 1933. Ferdinand Pecora, a graduate of the same law school, was counsel to the U.S. Senate in its investigation of banking (1934–35) that led to the formation of the Securities and Exchange Commission; he later became a justice of the Supreme Court of New York. Corporate firms continued to grow after the Second World War and reached the height of their strength in the 1950s and 1960s, when most opened offices in plush modern buildings on and near Park Avenue. They drew their clients from among the largest domestic and international corporations and formed a network unmatched in wealth and power that exerted considerable influence on national legislation. Several members of the city's corporate firms became national public figures, including John Foster Dulles, Henry L. Stimson, John McCloy, and Cyrus Vance. The 1960s saw a rapid increase in the number of blacks and women employed as lawyers in the city. During the late 1960s students at New York University formed the Women's Rights Committee, which helped to make several important scholarships available to women. They also formed the National Conference of Law Women, which successfully fought sex discrimination in admissions to law school and in employment. A prominent legal activist in the city during the 1970s was Florynce Kennedy, who was known for her confrontational style. Radical causes were also taken up by such lawyers as William M. Kunstler and Arthur Kinoy. Most of the country's radical law organizations established their base in the city, such as the Center for Constitutional Rights.

Changes in the practice of law during the 1970s and 1980s led the city's legal profession to expand rapidly. Aggressive strategies for mergers and acquisitions were developed by Joseph Flom of Skadden, Arps, Slate, Meagher and Flom and his colleague Marty Lipton; their approach was soon adopted by such leading firms as Cravath, Swaine and Moore, Shearman and Sterling, and Sullivan and Cromwell. Arranging and preventing hostile takeovers became tremendously lucrative for these firms, and to reduce rising legal costs some large corporations expanded their own legal departments. Tort litigation increased after the U.S. Supreme Court ruled in 1977 that lawyers could advertise their services. Plaintiff lawyers often won enormous damages for their clients and earned contingency fees averaging 33 to 40 percent. Between the early 1970s and 1990 the number of lawyers in the city increased from thirty thousand to more than sixty thousand, and by 1980 women accounted for 40 percent of the student body at New York University, more than ever before. In 1990 Conrad K. Harper became the first black president of the bar association. By the same year the five largest firms in the city each employed at least four hundred lawyers in the metropolitan area and offered starting salaries of at least $83,000.

Anton-Hermann Chroust: *The Rise of the Legal Profession in America* (Norman: University of Oklahoma Press, 1965)
George Whitney Martin: *Causes and Conflicts: The Centennial History of the Association of the Bar of the City of New York, 1870–1970* (Boston: Houghton Mifflin, 1970)
Lawrence M. Friedman: *A History of American Law* (New York: Simon and Schuster, 1973)
Paul Hoffman: *Lions in the Street: The Inside Story of the Great Wall Street Law Firms* (New York: E. P. Dutton, 1973)
Karen Berger Morello: *The Invisible Bar: The Woman Lawyer in America, 1638 to the Present* (New York: Random House, 1986)
Michael J. Powell: *From Patrician to Professional Elite: The Transformation of the New York City Bar* (New York: Russell Sage Foundation, 1988)

Kevin Kenny

Lazard Frères. Firm of investment bankers. Formed as a dry-goods company in New Orleans in 1848 by Alexandre Lazard, Simon Lazard, and Élie Lazard, it became a firm of bankers in the 1850s and opened offices in San Francisco (1851), Paris (1852), and London (1870); an office was opened in New York City in 1880 by Simon Lazard and his cousin Alexandre Weill. Under the direction of André Meyer from the 1950s to the 1970s the firm became known for arranging mergers and acquisitions. Its general partner Felix Rohatyn oversaw the restructuring of the city's debt and finances during the fiscal crisis of the mid 1970s and served for nearly twenty years as the chairman of the Municipal Assistance Corporation (MAC). Under the direction of its senior partner Michel David-Weill, the firm took part in the buyout of RJR Nabisco in 1989, the merger in the same year of Time Inc. and Warner Communications, and the acquisitions in the 1990s of McCaw Cellular by American Telephone and Telegraph, Snapple by Quaker Oats, and Paramount by Viacom. In the mid 1990s Lazard Frères remained small and exclusive; it was devoted primarily to financial advising and was active in corporate banking and capital and asset management. The headquarters are at Rockefeller Plaza, and the firm maintains offices in Paris, London, Frankfurt am Main, Milan, and Tokyo.

"The Last Emperor of Wall Street: Michel David-Weill," *Business Week*, 30 May 1988, pp. 64–75

Mary E. Curry

Lazarsfeld, Paul F(elix) (*b* Vienna, 13 Feb 1901; *d* New York City, 30 Aug 1976). Sociologist. He moved to the United States in 1933 and from 1940 was the chairman of sociology at Columbia University, where in 1945 he became the director of the Bureau of Applied Social Research. He was profoundly influential in shaping the methodology of social research and in developing institutes for training and research in the social sciences. His use of surveys as an analytical tool helped to make opinion polling a scientific endeavor.

Thomas E. Bird

Lazarus, Emma (*b* New York City, 22 July 1849; *d* New York City, 19 Nov 1887). Poet. She was educated by private tutors and published her first poems during her early teens; these attracted the attention of Ralph Waldo Emerson, to whom she dedicated her second book of poems. A number of her poems were published in *Scribner's Monthly* and *Lippincott's Magazine*. During the Russian pogroms of the 1880s she began to write about Jewish issues and became known for defending the oppressed and organizing relief efforts for refugees at Wards Island. By far her best-known work is the sonnet "New Colossus," which was chosen as an inscription for the pedestal of the Statue of Liberty in 1886.

Dan Vogel: *Emma Lazarus* (New York: Twayne, 1980)
Diane Lefer: *Emma Lazarus* (New York: Chelsea House, 1988)

James E. Mooney

LDCs. See LOCAL DEVELOPMENT CORPORATIONS.

leather. The tanning of leather and the manufacture of leather products are discussed in the entry SHOES, BOOTS, AND LEATHER.

Lebanese. The Lebanese community in New York City is treated in the entry SYRIANS AND LEBANESE.

Lebanon Hospital. Private hospital in the Bronx, incorporated in 1890 and opened in 1893 with fifty beds in a disused Ursuline convent on the corner of Westchester Avenue and 151st Street. It originally served Jewish immigrants. In 1894 a school of nursing was added. A new building opened in 1932 on the Grand Concourse; another completed in 1943 at the intersection of 173rd Street, Mount Eden Parkway, and Selwyn Avenue was used by the army until 1946. The hospital merged in 1962 with Bronx Hospital to form BRONX–LEBANON HOSPITAL CENTER.

Tina Levitan: *Islands of Compassion* (New York: Twayne, 1964)

Andrea Balis

LeBoeuf, Lamb, Greene and Macrae. Law firm, founded in the late 1920s by Randall LeBoeuf, a former assistant attorney general of New York State. Initially his practice was oriented toward water, energy, and public utilities. Horace Lamb joined the firm in 1934, later followed by Adrian Leiby (1952) and Cameron MacRae (1958). In the mid 1990s LeBoeuf, Lamb, Greene and Macrae had 240 lawyers and offices at 125 West 55th Street in Manhattan.

Le Brun, Napoleon (Eugene Henry Charles) (*b* Philadelphia, 2 Jan 1821; *d* New York City, 9 July 1901). Architect. He studied architecture with Thomas U. Walter and worked in Philadelphia for about twenty years before moving to New York City in 1864, where he designed the Church of the Epiphany in a Romanesque style, the Episcopal Church of St. Mary the Virgin (West 46th Street) in a French Gothic style, and an imitation of Dutch Renaissance for the engine house in Old Slip near the foot of Wall Street, the Home Life Insurance building on Broadway, and firehouses at East 67th Street. Le Brun's office building for the Metropolitan Life Insurance Company at Madison Square received an award from the American Institute of Architects (for illustration see MADISON SQUARE).

James E. Mooney

L'Eco D'Italia. An Italian-language daily newspaper launched in New York City in 1849 by Giovanni Francesco Secchi de Casali (*b* Piacenza, Italy, 1818), a revolutionary in exile who arrived in New York City in 1843. The newspaper favored Italian unification and for many years was an important chronicle of Italian–American news. Although largely supplanted after 1880 by *Il Progresso Italo-Americano* it continued to appear at irregular intervals until 1896.

Giovanni Fumagalli: *La Stampa periodica Italiana All'Estero* (Milan: Carriolo e Massimino, 1909)
Francesco Cordasco and Eugene Bucchioni: *The Italians: Social Backgrounds of an American Group* (Clifton, N.J.: Augustus M. Kelley, 1974)

Francesco Cordasco

Lederberg, Joshua (*b* Montclair, N.J., 23 May 1925). Geneticist and educator. The son of a rabbi, he grew up in Washington Heights and attended Stuyvesant High School. While an undergraduate and medical student at Columbia University he discovered how to conduct genetic crosses in bacteria, a finding that became one of the foundations of modern biotechnology and molecular biology. He received his PhD from Yale University in 1947 and became a professor of genetics at the University of Wisconsin in the same year. In 1958 he was awarded the Nobel Prize in medicine for his research at Columbia and Yale. He taught at Stanford University from 1959 to 1978, when he returned to New York City to assume the presidency of Rockefeller University, a post he held until 1990. After his retirement he resumed his research in molecular genetics.

Lee, Ivy L(edbetter) (*b* Cedartown, Ga., 16 July 1877; *d* New York City, 9 Nov 1934). Public relations executive. Educated at Princeton University, he worked in New York City as a newspaper reporter. During the mayoral campaign of 1903 he was a press representative for Seth Low. Later he opened a publicity firm through which he provided services for several corporate clients and the Rockefeller family. His firm worked on behalf of the Interborough Rapid Transit in the 1920s to win an increase in fares from government regulators.

Ray Eldon Hiebert: *Courtier to the Crowd: The Story of Ivy Lee and the Development of Public Relations* (Ames: Iowa State University Press, 1966)

Alan R. Raucher

Lee, Spike [Shelton Jackson] (*b* Atlanta, 20 March 1957). Director, writer, producer, and actor. He lived from the age of two in Fort Greene in Brooklyn. As a student at the New York University film school he received a Student Academy Award from the Academy of Motion Picture Arts and Sciences for his thesis film, "Joe's Bed–Stuy Barbershop: We Cut Heads" (1982). After forming his own production company at 124 DeKalb Avenue, Forty Acres and a Mule Filmworks, he made a number of motion pictures focusing on the contemporary black experience and interracial conflict, many of them set in Brooklyn. His first commercial success was *She's Gotta Have It* (1986), followed by *School Daze* (1988), *Do the Right Thing* (1989), *Mo' Better Blues* (1990), *Jungle Fever* (1991), *Malcolm X* (1992), and *Crooklyn* (1994); these works helped to open Hollywood studios to black directors. In 1990 he opened a store, Spike's Joint, at 1 South Elliot Place in Brooklyn to sell T-shirts, jackets, hats, and postcards celebrating his films and black identity. During the same year he produced a concert at the Brooklyn Academy of Music and the related record album *Do It Acappella.*

Grai St. Clair Rice

Lefcourt, Abraham E. (*b* Birmingham, England, 1877; *d* New York City, 13 Nov 1932). Real-estate developer. He began developing lofts and warehouses in 1910 and by 1924 owned property worth more than $10 million, including more properties than any other landowner in the area bounded by 39th Street, Broadway, 35th Street, and 8th Avenue; his Lefcourt Clothing Center, a building of twenty-seven stories at 275 Broadway, became the anchor of the new garment district, where he was soon a leading developer. During the 1920s he also erected several tall office buildings in Manhattan and some of the first large apartment buildings and hotels in Newark, New Jersey. Lefcourt expanded into finance, forming the Lefcourt Normandie National Bank in 1928; many of his enterprises declared bankruptcy during the Depression.

Marc A. Weiss

Lefferts Homestead. Historic house on Flatbush Avenue near Empire Boulevard in Prospect Park. It was built as a farmhouse in a Dutch style between 1777 and 1783 by Peter Lefferts, a lieutenant in the Continental Army and later a judge on the county court and a delegate to the Constitutional Convention. The house has a gambrel roof and front and back porches, and its rooms are arranged symmetrically. It once stood on Flatbush Avenue near Maple Street, then was moved to Prospect Park after Lefferts's descendants deeded the house to the city in 1918. Lefferts Homestead is one of the few houses of its style remaining in Brooklyn.

Teunis G. Bergin: *Genealogy of the Lefferts Family* (Albany, N.Y.: Jo Munsell, 1878)
Historic Houses in New York City Parks (New York: Department of Parks and Recreation / Historic House Trust of New York City, 1989)

Jonathan Kuhn

Lefrak City. Housing development in Rego Park (1990 pop. 14,000), covering forty acres (sixteen hectares) and bounded to the north by 57th Avenue, to the east by 99th Street, to the south by the Long Island Expressway, and to the west by Junction Boulevard. It was built between 1960 and 1968 as a complex offering "total facilities for total living" for working- and middle-class tenants by the Lefrak Organization, led by the prominent developer Samuel Lefrak. Twenty towers of eighteen stories each contain five thousand apartments with one to three bedrooms; there are also playgrounds between buildings, three tennis courts, a swimming pool, 2800 outdoor parking spaces, a public garage with 750 spaces, a security service, a branch of the Queens Borough Public Library, a post office (Elmhurst branch), two office buildings with 500,000 square feet (46,500 square meters) of space in which the main tenant is the New York City Department of Environmental Protection, and 325,000 square feet (thirty thousand square meters) of retail space. The development also offers several organizations for tenants and senior citizens, as well as little league baseball.

James O. Drummond

Legal Aid Society. Nonprofit legal service organization, established in March 1876 as the Deutscher Rechtesschutz Verein to provide legal advice to German immigrants. It was formed at the suggestion of Edward Salomon, a former governor of Wisconsin, in a meeting on Wall Street of German merchants eager to help German immigrants to assimilate. Charles K. Lexow, a graduate of Columbia Law School (1875), was engaged by the society on 31 March and earned $1000 for a year's work. Initially the society focused on cases dealing with citizenship, seamen's rights, and child labor. During Arthur von Brieson's twenty-six-year tenure as president after 1890 it extended its services to all poor people in the city, shifted its emphasis to defense work provided by a paid legal staff, and developed a system for case assignment that won wide support. German sponsorship ended in 1896. In 1916 the society handled 41,646 cases, or 40 percent of all legal-aid cases in the nation, by which time it was a model for organizations in thirty-seven cities. Successes achieved under Harrison Tweed between 1936 and 1945 helped to attract young lawyers to its staff. In 1962 a juvenile division was formed to take on cases in family court. The society focused on criminal defense after the federal government took over other legal services for the poor, and after the U.S. Supreme Court required states to appoint lawyers for defendants unable to pay legal fees (*Gideon v. Wainwright*, 1963). Under a contract negotiated with Mayor John V. Lindsay in September 1966 the society remained a private institution but received public funds, and in 1974 it became the model for a federal body known as the Legal Services Corporation.

In its efforts to improve services for clients the Legal Aid Society has fought to improve the quality of detention facilities, establish rooms for conferences between lawyers and clients, and increase the rate of reimbursement for court-appointed attorneys. Through a bitter strike in 1982 it forced New York City to consider setting up a public defender system, a plan ultimately rejected as impractical; it also forced the city to act on the problem of homelessness, won higher shelter allowances for welfare recipients, and was itself forced to defend wealthy clients charged with drug dealing (because they claimed to have no assets). By the mid 1990s it had argued thirty-five cases before the U.S. Supreme Court. The oldest organization of its kind in the country, the Legal Aid Society in 1991 had 1180 lawyers, a budget of $100 million, and 300,000 clients. In 1994 Mayor Rudolph W. Giuliani reduced its budget and staff.

George Whitney Martin: *Causes and Conflicts: The Centennial History of the Bar Association of the*

City of New York (Boston: Houghton Mifflin, 1970)
Michael J. Powell: *From Patrician to Professional Elite: The Transformation of the New York City Bar Association* (New York: Russell Sage Foundation, 1988)
David T. Wasserman: *A Sword for the Convicted: Representing Indigent Defendants on Appeal* (Westport, Conn.: Greenwood, 1990)

George J. Lankevich

Le Gallienne, Eva (*b* London, 11 Jan 1899; *d* Weston, Conn., 3 June 1991). Actress, director, writer, and producer. She moved to New York City in 1915 and in 1926 formed the Civic Repertory Theater (on 14th Street west of 6th Avenue), which for six seasons until 1933 presented classic plays at low prices and supported an acting school. There she took the role of Peter Pan, in which she was the first actress to appear to fly, and presented *Alice in Wonderland*, which she adapted for the stage with Florida Friebus.

Martha S. LoMonaco

Leggett, William (*b* New York City, 30 April 1802; *d* New Rochelle, N.Y., 29 May 1839). Political writer. He first gained public attention in 1829 for his editorials in the *Evening Post*, edited by William Cullen Bryant, a supporter of President Andrew Jackson. In 1834 he was temporarily put in charge of the newspaper and quickly adopted a radical stance. Believing that the division between monopolists and workers was growing, he called for political reforms to remove all economic privilege and legal favoritism. His views, delivered in an unsparing, vitriolic style, pushed well beyond the conventional boundaries of egalitarian principle (he was called an agrarian by his opponents) and inspired dissenting Democrats who in 1835 seceded to form the Equal Rights Party in New York City (nicknamed the Locofocos by their enemies). Leggett's health failed as the movement began; he regained sufficient strength late in 1836 to launch another newspaper, the *Plaindealer*, and to endorse the abolition of slavery. After his death he was considered a martyred hero among the city's radical Democrats until the Civil War, when he faded into obscurity.

Sean Wilentz

Lehman, Herbert H(enry) (*b* New York City, 28 March 1878; *d* New York City, 5 Dec 1963). Governor, brother of Irving Lehman. He was the son of Mayer Lehman, a German Jewish immigrant who after settling in the United States in 1849 made a fortune in textiles and finance and helped to found the investment banking firm of Lehman Brothers. In his early career he was lieutenant governor of New York State under Governor Franklin D. Roosevelt and chairman of the finance committee of Alfred E. Smith's presidential campaign in 1928. Elected governor as a Democrat in 1932, 1934, and 1936 and again in 1938 with the endorsement of the American Labor Party (after the term of office had been extended to four years), he initiated and signed legislation pertaining to labor relations, the minimum wage, and unemployment insurance. Between 1942 and 1946 he was the director of the United Nations Relief and Rehabilitation Agency. Although he lost a race for a seat in the U.S. Senate in 1946, he won a special election in 1949 and was reelected to a full term in 1950. During his tenure he fought for liberal social policies and courageously challenged the accusations of Senator Joseph R. McCarthy. With Eleanor Roosevelt and Thomas Finletter he began a reform movement in 1959 that led in 1961 to the ouster of Carmine DeSapio from Tammany Hall. He then retired from politics and dedicated himself to more than twenty-five philanthropic causes with which he had been associated throughout his life, many of them Jewish charities. He received the Presidential Medal of Freedom, the nation's highest peacetime medal.

Chris McNickle

Lehman, Irving (*b* New York City, 28 Jan 1876; *d* New York City, 22 Sept 1945). Judge, brother of Herbert H. Lehman. He won election to the New York State Court of Appeals in 1923 and was reelected in 1937. During his tenure he earned a reputation as a brilliant legal scholar. In 1939 he was elected chief justice of the Court of Appeals. An active philanthropist, Lehman served on the Jewish Welfare Board (1921–40) and was president of the 92nd Street Y for eight years.

Chris McNickle

Lehman Brothers. Firm of investment bankers. Initially it was a mercantile goods company, formed in 1850 in Montgomery, Alabama, by three German Jewish immigrants, Henry, Emmanuel, and Mayer Lehman. In 1868 Mayer and Emmanuel Lehman left the war-ravaged South to form a cotton brokerage firm in New York City at 133–35 Pearl Street. In 1870 the firm helped to form the New York Cotton Exchange, becoming the first to trade commodities futures. It had an underwriting partnership from 1908 to 1926 with the firm of Goldman Sachs and Company. In 1928 Lehman Brothers moved its headquarters to 1 William Street, a building designed in 1907 by Francis H. Kimball and Julian C. Levi for the Seligman brothers. For many years the firm was run by members of the Lehman family; the most influential were Philip Lehman (1861–1947), who supervised the firm's entrance into investment banking, and Robert Lehman (1891–1969), the senior partner from 1926 to 1969. It made several innovations in investment banking during the 1930s, introducing among other services "private placements," a system for matching prospective corporate borrowers with corporate investors such as insurance companies. The firm became a leader in commercial paper after Lehman Commercial Paper was formed in 1964 by Lewis L. Glucksman (later the president of Lehman Brothers). After merging with its powerful rival Kuhn, Loeb in 1977 Lehman Brothers was bought in 1984 by Shearson–American Express and renamed Shearson Lehman Brothers. During the 1980s it acquired and merged with many firms, among them E. F. Hutton and Company in 1987, and its headquarters were moved in 1985 to the World Financial Center at Vesey Street in Manhattan. In May 1994 American Express divested itself of the firm, which became an independent, publicly owned corporation again named Lehman Brothers.

James Bradley

Lehman College. College of the City University of New York. It began in 1931 as an extension in the Bronx of Hunter College at Bedford Park Boulevard West. When separated from Hunter in 1968 it was named after Herbert H. Lehman, former governor of New York. In the 1970s the campus underwent a rapid expansion during which a successful Center for the Performing Arts was added. By the autumn of 1990 the college enrolled 10,238 graduate and undergraduate students, full and part time. In the same year a branch campus opened in Hiroshima, Japan, funded by Japanese sponsors who were impressed with the college's program in English as a second language. Lehman grants bachelor of arts, bachelor of science, bachelor of fine arts, and master's degrees.

Selma Berrol

Leisler's Rebellion. The term used to refer to political unrest from 1689 to 1691 in the province of New York after the Glorious Revolution. Colonial politics were thrown into disarray after the overthrow of James II in 1688 and the subsequent downfall of the Dominion of New England, which included New York. After the New York City militia rebelled and seized Fort James on 31 May 1689 a committee of safety was formed, and from June 27 a convention of representatives from East Jersey and all counties in New York except Albany governed the province. On 28 June the convention chose Jacob Leisler (1640–91), a captain of the militia and a successful German-born merchant, to become "captain of the fort," and on 16 August it made him the chief military commander. Leisler led a militantly anti-Catholic faction that strongly supported the claims of William of Orange to the English throne. The city government, however, remained in the hands of appointees of James II until September, when the provincial convention called for elections in which Peter Delanoy became the first elected mayor. After the arrival of several ambiguously addressed royal letters Leisler assumed the title of lieutenant governor and dissolved the convention on 16 December. The city became bitterly divided over this and other actions by him. He further antagonized his opponents by making summary arrests of alleged "papists," and alienated a number of his supporters through his tax policies. In May 1690 the city was the site of an intercolonial conference organized by Leisler, the first of its kind, to plan a military and naval expedition against Canada. This was undertaken in the summer of 1690 but ended without success. Leisler then faced increasingly vocal resistance. In January 1691 the former city officials returned from exile with the arrival of a contingent of English regulars commanded by Richard Ingoldsby. Leisler's refusal to surrender the fort to Ingoldsby and a violent battle between pro- and anti-Leislerians for control of the city led the new royal governor, Henry Sloughter, to arrest Leisler and many of his sympathizers after he took control on 17 March. At the urging of such opponents as Nicholas Bayard, Leisler was tried for treason and executed on 16 May with an associate, Jacob Milborne; their sentences were later reversed by Parliament. Leisler's Rebellion was the most divisive conflict in New York and helped to develop the bitter factionalism that shaped city politics for several decades.

Jerome R. Reich: *Leisler's Rebellion: A Study of Democracy in New York, 1664–1720* (Chicago: University of Chicago Press, 1953)

Thomas J. Archdeacon: *New York City, 1664–1710: Conquest and Change* (Ithaca, N.Y.: Cornell University Press, 1976)

Robert C. Ritchie: *The Duke's Province: A Study of New York Politics and Society, 1664–1691* (Chapel Hill: University of North Carolina Press, 1977)

Charles Howard McCormick: *Leisler's Rebellion* (New York: Garland, 1989)

David William Voorhees

Lennon, John (Winston Ono) (*b* Liverpool, 9 Oct 1940; *d* New York City, 8 Dec 1980). Singer and songwriter. He sang with a number of groups before joining the Beatles, for which he and Paul McCartney wrote songs including "Help," "Revolution," "Strawberry Fields," and "Lucy in the Sky with Diamonds." He married the performance artist Yoko Ono in 1969 and moved with her to New York City in 1971 after the Beatles disbanded; the two lived at the St. Regis Hotel (2 East 55th Street) in 1971–72 and recorded a number of songs, among them "The Dream Is Over," "Come Together," and "Imagine." From 1975 they lived at the Dakota at 1 West 72nd Street, where they also had an office and a studio on the ground floor. Among Lennon's last songs was "Starting Over," which he recorded a month before he was fatally shot in front of the Dakota by a deranged fan. A garden in Central Park named Strawberry Fields is dedicated to his memory.

John Robertson: *The Art and Music of John Lennon* (New York: Carol Publishing, 1991)

James E. Mooney

Lenox, Robert (*b* Kirkcudbright, Scotland, December 1759; *d* New York City, 13 Dec 1839). Merchant. He emigrated to America as a youth and was educated in New Jersey. In 1784 he set up a business as a general merchant in New York City, where he became successful through trade and investments in real estate. He became the vice-president of the Chamber of Commerce in 1817 and its president in 1827, a position he retained until the end of his life; he was also a trustee of the Presbyterian College in Princeton, New Jersey. At his death Lenox was one of the city's five wealthiest men. His son James Lenox established the Lenox Library.

James E. Mooney

Lenox Hill. Neighborhood on the East Side of Manhattan, bounded to the north by East 77th Street, to the east by Lexington Avenue, to the south by East 60th Street, and to the west by 5th Avenue. The farm of Robert Lenox once covered thirty acres (twelve hectares) bounded by what are now East 74th Street, 4th Avenue, East 68th Street, and 5th Avenue; the hill for which the neighborhood is named stood at what became 70th Street and Park Avenue. A parcel bounded by what are now East 68th Street, 3rd Avenue, East 60th Street, and 5th Avenue was named Hamilton Square and set aside as public space in 1807. At his death in 1840 Lenox left his estate to his son James, who donated land on 4th Avenue between East 71st Street and East 69th Street for Union Theological Seminary and Presbyterian Hospital. The area attracted several charitable and religious institutions during the 1860s, when fashionable New Yorkers lived below 59th Street: the German Hospital (1869; later renamed Lenox Hill Hospital) on East 77th Street off 4th Avenue; the Normal School (later Hunter College), Hahnemann Hospital, and Mount Sinai Hospital in Hamilton Square; the Lenox Library (1877) at 5th Avenue and East 70th Street; and the Seventh Regiment Armory (1879) on 4th Avenue at East 66th Street. In the 1880s elegant townhouses lined the sidestreets, and lavish mansions along 5th Avenue faced the newly completed Central Park; 4th Avenue, renamed Park Avenue in 1888, became a grand boulevard known for its handsome residences after the New York Central Railroad was electrified (1907) and placed entirely underground (1913). The avenue still has luxury apartment buildings erected between 1910 and 1920. Lenox Hill is served by Lexington Avenue, a thoroughfare of shops and restaurants, and Madison Avenue, known for its boutiques, art galleries, and luxury hotels. The Whitney Museum of American Art, the Asia Society, and the Frick Collection are major cultural attractions.

James Trager: *Park Avenue* (New York: Atheneum, 1990)

Joyce Mendelsohn

Lenox Hill Hospital. Hospital on the Upper East Side of Manhattan. It opened in 1868 as an offshoot of the German Dispensary, a facility opened at 132 Canal Street in 1857 by German doctors to serve Germans on the Lower East Side. Known as the German Hospital and Dispensary of New York, the hospital was a private facility that occupied a site owned by the city at 77th Street and Park Avenue (formerly the Robert Lenox farm). It moved to larger quarters at 8 East 3rd Street, but these became overcrowded and plans were made to build new ones. A corporation led by Carl Gottfried Gunther (later the mayor) was formed; its members included the pediatrician Abraham Jacobi, the gynecologist Emil Noeggerath, the surgeon Ernst Krackowizer, the ophthalmologist Herman Althof, the publishers Anna Ottendorfer and Oswald Ottendorfer, and the newspaper editor Carl Schurz. Initially the hospital served mostly indigent patients. During the 1860s it stood next to a swamp and across from the stables of the New York Cab Company. Most of the patients were from Yorkville, a growing German neighborhood east of Park Avenue. After the First World War the neighborhood became fashionable as open railroad tracks along the avenue were covered and elegant houses were built. The first private pavilion opened in 1901; the hospital took its current name and after 1949 a number of beds became semi-private. After the Second World War the in-patient and outpatient facilities expanded to fill the block bounded by 77th Street, Lexington Avenue, 76th Street, and Park Avenue.

Ann L. Buttenwieser

Lenya, Lotte [Blamauer, Karoline (Wilhelmine)] (*b* Vienna, 19 Oct 1898; *d* New York City, 27 Nov 1981). Actress and singer. After becoming well known in Berlin for her performances in the theatrical works of her husband, Kurt Weill, she fled with him from Nazi Germany and arrived in New York City on 10 September 1935; they lived at the St. Moritz Hotel (50 Central Park South) before moving to an apartment at 231 East 62nd Street. After her husband's death in 1950 she continued to appear on stage and in films, and won a Tony Award for her portrayal of Jenny the prostitute in a production by the Theatre de Lys of *The Threepenny Opera*, which ran for 2611 performances between 1954 and 1961. During these years she divided her time between her home in Rockland County and several apartments on the East Side, the last at 404 East 55th Street. Lenya later appeared as Fräulein Schneider in the Broadway production of *Cabaret* (John Kander, Fred Ebb, and Joe Masteroff), which in 1966–69 ran for 1165 performances at the Broadhurst Theatre.

Donald Spoto: *Lenya: A Life* (Boston: Little, Brown, 1989)

Marc Ferris

Leo Baeck Institute. Independent nonprofit center formed in 1955 and devoted to the political, economic, social, and cultural history of German-speaking Jews to the time of the Nazis. It provides annual research fellowships, presents exhibits, sponsors lectures, international symposia, and monthly faculty seminars, and publishes books, lectures, and exhibition catalogues as well as *Library and Archives News* (two to three times a year), the *LBI News* (occasionally), a yearbook, and a quarterly bulletin. Its building at 129 East 73rd Street houses a library containing about sixty thousand volumes, periodicals, and serials, more than thirty thousand photographs, and a collection of prints, drawings, paintings, and sculptures. The institute also has an extensive archive of unpublished manuscripts and memoirs.

Allen J. Share

Leonard, Benny [Leiner, Benjamin] (*b* New York City, 7 April 1896; *d* New York City, 18 April 1947). Boxer and referee. Of Russian Jewish background, he grew up on the Lower East Side. He turned professional in 1911 under a pseudonym because of the opposition of his parents. Under the management of Billy Gibson he won the world lightweight championship by knocking out Freddy Welsh on 28 May 1917 in New York City. He retired as champion in 1925 after several memorable defenses, although financial troubles inspired a brief return to the ring in 1931. Leonard compiled a record of eighty-eight wins, five losses, and one draw (with 115 fights declared no decision). He was elected to the Boxing Hall of Fame, and is generally regarded as the second-best lightweight in the history of boxing.

Steven A. Riess

Lerner, Max (*b* Minsk, Russia, 20 Dec 1902; *d* New York City, 5 June 1992). Political scientist, writer, and journalist. He emigrated to the United States in 1907, attended Yale University and Washington University in St. Louis, and received the PhD from the Robert Brookings School of Economics and Government. An adherent of the political left who for a time advocated economic planning through "democratic collectivism," he edited the *Nation* in the 1930s and the newspapers *PM* and the *Star* in the 1940s, was a contributing editor for the *New Republic* and the managing editor of the *Encyclopedia of the Social Sciences*, and from 1948 until his death wrote a syndicated column for the *New York Post.* He also taught briefly at several colleges and universities, among them Sarah Lawrence College in Westchester. Lerner's published writings include *It Is Later Than You Think: The Need for a Militant Democracy* (1938), *Ideas Are Weapons: The History and Uses of Ideas* (1939), *The Mind and Faith of Justice Holmes* (1943), *Actions and Passions: Notes on the Multiple Revolution of Our Time* (1949), *America as a Civilization* (1957), and *The Age of Overkill* (1962), as well as modern editions of works by Aristotle, Machiavelli, Adam Smith, Alexis de Tocqueville, and Thorstein Veblen.

John Recchiuti

Lesbian Herstory Archives. The world's largest collection of materials relating to lesbians, formed in New York City in 1973 by the Lesbian Herstory Educational Foundation and opened to the public in the following year. It receives more than a thousand visitors a year, publishes a newsletter, and in addition to a reading room houses a museum and art gallery. The archives are at Park Slope in Brooklyn.

Lee Hudson, Joan Nestle

lesbians. In 1665 the Duke of York included in the laws governing what later became New York City the capital offense of sodomy, defined as "unnatural lusts of men with men and women with women." This "buggery" law remained in effect until 1797, when the death penalty for the offense was abolished. By 1890 lesbians (scornfully referred to as tribadists or sexual perverts) were documented as part of the city's criminal culture: mannish women were often found among the "social undesirables" who gathered nightly in the Bowery at the Artistic Club, the Slide, and Walhalla Hall, and at Paresis Hall on 4th Avenue. Theories about women who had lost their true womanly nature abounded; throughout the 1890s speakers at conferences in the city such as the international medico-legal congress of 1893 recommended hysterectomies as a cure. Frequent references to practitioners of tribadism suggest that the city had a large lesbian population. When a farcical play called *A Florida Enchantment* by A. C. Gunter opened on Broadway in April 1896, critics reviled it for its presentation of a masculine woman who cursed, smoked a cigarette, and tried to seduce all the other women on stage. Although the play did not depict lesbianism directly (the female character swallowed magical seeds to change her sex), it clearly implied that lesbianism and the liberation of women were linked. In 1899 a special investigative committee questioned Mayor Robert A. Van Wyck about his knowledge of lesbian meeting places. Some lesbians survived by "passing," or living their public and sometimes private lives disguised as men. The most famous passing woman of the nineteenth century was Murray Hall, who masqueraded as a man for more than a quarter-century and was a respected politician in the thirteenth senatorial district and an important member of Tammany Hall. She married two women who did not reveal her secret, and because of her disguise was able to register and vote many years before women were enfranchised. She died of breast cancer after refusing to see a doctor, even when the pain in her chest was unbearable. The *New York Times* wrote in her obituary (19 January 1901) that "she even had a reputation as a man about town, a bon vivant, and all around good fellow."

In 1912 a group of women writers, activists, journalists, health reformers, socialists, and advocates of "free love" formed Heterodoxy, a club for "unorthodox" women that met for biweekly lunches in Greenwich Village until 1940. At least twenty-four of the club's 110 members were lesbians. Among those who often visited the club were Edith Lees, the wife of Havelock Ellis (1915), and Gertrude Stein and Alice B. Toklas (1934). Some lesbians became part of the city's social élite, such as Elsie de Wolfe and her companion Elisabeth Marbury. In 1922 a lesbian character was featured in Sholem Asch's Yiddish drama *The God of Vengeance*; after the play moved uptown from Greenwich Village it was quickly closed and the entire cast was arrested. *The Captive*, a play by the French writer Édouard Bourdet about the breakup of a marriage by the wife's lesbian suitor, opened on Broadway on 29 September 1926. According to local newspapers hundreds of female couples attended each performance, and local florists sold large quantities of violets, symbolic in the play of the lesbian character. As part of Mayor James J. Walker's campaign against vice, the police joined with religious groups and John S. Sumner, secretary of the New York Society for the Suppression of Vice, to close the play on obscenity charges and arrest its star, Helen Mencken. On 6 April 1927 the New York State Legislature passed the Padlock Law forbidding the presentation of any work depicting the subject of "sex perversion" on stage; this law remained in effect until 1967. A complaint by Sumner in December 1929 prompted the police to remove Radclyffe Hall's novel *The Well of Loneliness* from all bookstores, and in February of the following year a local judge ruled the book obscene in a trial that kept the theme of lesbianism on the front page of the *Times.* A higher court later reversed the opinion.

From the 1920s lesbians gathered at bars and dinner clubs such as Tony Pastor's and Howdys, an exotic bar where lesbians, bohemians, and tourists watched the lesbian performers Blackie and Bubbles Kent impersonate men. This tradition of male impersonation continued during the next two decades at Club 82 on East 4th Street and later at the 81 Club nearby. As a result of the northward migration of blacks during the First World War Harlem became a cultural mecca for young black lesbians. In the 1920s and well into the 1930s lesbians there congregated at rent parties where performers sang "sissy man" and "bull dagger" blues; a well-known hostess was A'lelia Walker, the daughter of the entrepreneur and social activist Madame Walker. Other clubs featured lesbian entertainers such as Gladys Bentley and Ma Rainey; literary gatherings attracted such poets as Gladys May, Casely Hayford, Mae v. Cowdery, Georgia Douglas Johnson, and Angelina Weld Grimké. Lesbians in Harlem were not safe from police raids and intimidation by the vice squad: in 1922 the lesbian activist Mabel Hampton was arrested at an all-women's party and sent to the reformatory in Bedford Hills for two years on a charge of prostitution.

The public lesbian social life of Harlem continued into the 1930s and 1940s, with "drag" balls, yearly trips up the Hudson, and dances. Mona's, a bar in midtown, became a gathering place for lesbians in the 1940s. By the following decade bars catering openly and exclusively to lesbians proliferated in Greenwich Village, among them the Pony Stable, Laurel's, Swing Rendevous, Bagatelle, Seven Steps, Bohemia, Kookie's, Gianni's, the Three, and the Sea Colony on Abingdon Square. Dancing with a partner of the same sex was illegal, and women who did not wear three pieces of women's clothing were periodically arrested for transvestism. There was an uneasy collaboration between the vice squad, the police, and the organized-crime figures who often owned and managed the bars. The Sea Colony had a backroom for dancing equipped with a red light, which flashed on when the police arrived each week to collect their bribes; often the police did not leave after the money was exchanged, and many lesbians reported being beaten and sexually assaulted.

Lesbians in Greenwich Village referred to the Women's House of Detention, a red-brick building on the corner of 6th Avenue and 8th Street, as the "country club." During the 1950s it became the scene of public displays of affection as women on the street called up to their incarcerated girlfriends. The prison was considered an embarrassment by city officials and closed in the early 1970s. From the 1950s working-class lesbians met in Riis Park on the weekends to play softball and enjoy the beach. A more established community catered to artistic, affluent lesbians in the beach town of Cherry Grove on Fire Island, where Janet Flanner and others rented summer homes; police raids in both communities were common. Barbara Gittings in 1958 formed a local chapter of the Daughters of Bilitis, the first incorporated membership organization for lesbians in the city. Intimidation and harassment by the Federal Bureau of Investigation and other authorities occurred frequently, and for fear of being exposed most members used only their first names or pseudonyms. Shortly after Ruth Simpson moved the Daughters of Bilitis to its own loft on Prince Street, internal disagreements led the group to disband.

The city subjected lesbians to raids, entrapment, verbal abuse, and physical threats into the early 1960s. The last raid on a lesbian bar reported in the newspapers was in March 1964: on a Friday night the police entered MaryAngela's on 7th Avenue South and took away forty-three women in steel-windowed police vans. Charged with disorderly conduct and disturbing the peace, they were held overnight and forced to walk a gantlet of jeering officers the next morning. The judge dismissed the case when a detective was unable to identify the women who he alleged had been dancing together at the bar. In 1964 Rene Cafiero, Nancy Garden, and other lesbian members of the New York League for Sexual Freedom demonstrated in front of the U.S. Army Building against the exclusion of homosexuals from the military. Lesbians took part in the first protest sponsored by a gay-rights organization when the Mattachine Society picketed the United Nations on 16 April 1965 to protest the Cuban government's imprisonment of homosexuals in labor camps. One first-person account in the *Village Voice* credited a lesbian with having instigated the Stonewall Rebellion (27 June 1969), in which gay men and lesbians resisted a police raid on the Stonewall Inn in Greenwich Village, an event considered by some as having begun the lesbian and gay liberation movement. New lesbian bars opened in the 1970s, such as Bonnie and Clyde's, Ariel, and the Dutchess in Greenwich Village, and Peaches and the Sahara uptown. In addition several restaurants catered only to women, among them Mother Courage on the Hudson River, the Women's Coffeehouse, and Bonnie's, and women's bookstores opened in Greenwich Village (Djuna Books) and on 92nd Street and Amsterdam Avenue (Womanbooks). Dances for women only were held monthly at the Woman's Center and the bars were no longer the most popular place for lesbians to meet.

Lesbians belonged to the Gay Liberation Front (1969–70) and the Gay Activists Alliance (1970–74), which met in a disused firehouse on Wooster Street, but because these organizations were dominated by men the women soon grew restless and formed their own group, the Lesbian Liberation Committee. In 1971 a group of lesbians including Ginny Vida and Nath Rockhill formed the Lesbian Feminist Liberation, an organization that provided social alternatives to the bars. A group of lesbians and gay academicians met in 1972 to form the Gay Academic Union, the first national organization that aimed to integrate lesbian and gay studies into the college curriculum and to represent the concerns of lesbian and gay teachers and students; the union encouraged the work of such lesbian theorists as Karla Jay, Esther Newton, Julia Penelope, and Catherine Stimpson, and helped to form the Center for Lesbian and Gay Studies (CLAGS) at the Graduate School of City University of New York. Other groups included Women against Rape, Gay Women's Alternative, and Radicalesbians, which published the most influential lesbian document of the 1970s, a four-page pamphlet entitled "The Woman-Identified Woman." Several books with lesbian themes reached a wide readership: *Sappho Was a Right-On Woman* (1972) by Barbara Love and Sidney Abbott, *Lesbian Nation* (1973) by Jill Johnston, and *Rubyfruit Jungle* (1973) by Rita Mae Brown, which is set in New York City. The Lesbian Herstory Archives, formed in 1973 and opened to the public in the following year in the apartment of Joan Nestle and Deborah Edel in Manhattan, became the largest archive of its kind in the world.

Political gains were achieved in the early 1970s by the Gay Activists Alliance, the Lesbian Feminist Liberation, the New York Political Action Committee, and the Study Group, and by such activists as Meryl Friedman, Martha Shelley, Kitty Cotter, and Blue Lunden. Councilmen Carter Burden and Eldon Clingan introduced the first gay-rights bill in the country before the City Council on 6 January 1971 (not passed until 20 March 1986). Cafiero and Dallice Covello in 1972 were the first openly lesbian delegates to the national convention of a major political party (as supporters of the Democratic candidate George McGovern). The Coalition for Lesbian and Gay Rights, formed in 1977, was led by Hunter, Eleanor Cooper, and Betty Santoro. Salsa Soul Sisters, the first social and political organization in the United States exclusively for lesbians from racial minority groups, was formed in September 1974 by Dolores Jackson; now known as African-American Wimmin United for Social Change, it meets weekly at the lesbian and gay community center on 13th Street in Manhattan. Black lesbians who became prominent in the city during these years included the poets Audre Lorde, Jewelle Gomez, Cheryl Clarke, Pat Parker, and Sapphire, the performers Storme DeLarverie, Edwina Lee Taylor, and Pamela Sneed, and the community leaders Betty Powell, Joyce Hunter, Candace Boyce, Sandra Lowe, Joan Gibbs, and Marjorie Hill. Lesbian activists served on the city's Commission on the Status of Women, among them Jean O'Leary (1975), Charlotte Bunch, and Vida (1980–91). The first openly lesbian candidate for public office was Ginny Apuzzo, who unsuccessfully sought a seat in the state assembly in 1978. From 1986 the openly lesbian judges Mary Bednar, Joan Lobis, Marci Kahn, Karen Burstein, and Roz Richter were appointed to the city's civil, criminal, and family courts, and the Office for the Lesbian and Gay Community, the first of its kind in the United States, was formed in 1989 by Mayor Edward I. Koch, who appointed a lesbian director, Lee Hudson. A community liaison position created by the police department was filled by Detective Vanessa Ferro, and Jacquelyn Shaffer and later Katy Doran served as community liaison in the office of the district attorney of Manhattan. In 1990 Deborah Glick became the first openly lesbian candidate to win election to the state assembly, and in 1993 gay and lesbian couples were granted the right to register with the city as domestic partners. In the same year city employees also received medical benefits for domestic partners, ending a long lawsuit against the Board of Education.

In the mid 1990s there were more than four hundred political, social, and religious organizations for lesbians in New York City, ranging from Queer Nation, the Pink Panthers, and Dyke Action Machine (DAM) to Las Buenas Amigas, Asian Lesbians of the East Coast, and We Wah and Bar Chee Ampe, a group for lesbian and gay American Indians. Jewish lesbians attended Congregation Beth Simchat Torah, a predominantly gay and lesbian synagogue on Bethune Street with a lesbian rabbi, Sharon Kleinbaum. The city also supported several lesbian publications, of which the best-known were *Womenews*, *Sappho's Isle*, *Visibilities*, and the lesbian separatist publication *Tribade*.

Jonathan Ned Katz: *Gay American History* (New York: Thomas Y. Crowell, 1976)
Judith Schwarz: *Radical Feminists of Heterodoxy: Greenwich Village, 1912–1940* (Lebanon, N.H.: New Victoria, 1982)
Gay/Lesbian Almanac (New York: Harper and Row, 1983)
Kaier Cartin: *We Can Always Call Them Bulgarians* (Boston: Alyson, 1987)
Joan Nestle: *A Restricted Country* (Ithaca, N.Y.: Firebrand, 1988)
Will Roscoe, ed.: *Living the Spirit: A Gay American Indian Anthology* (New York: St. Martin's, 1988)
Eric Garber: "A Spectacle in Color: The Lesbian and Gay Subculture of Jazz Age Harlem," *Hidden Histories*, ed. Martin Bauml Duberman, Martha Vicinius, and George Chauncey Jr. (New York: New American Library, 1989)
Maureen Honey, ed.: *Shadowed Dreams: Women's Poetry of the Harlem Renaissance* (New Brunswick, N.J.: Rutgers University Press, 1989)
Lillian Faderman: *Old Girls and Twilight Lovers* (New York: Penguin, 1991)

Lee Hudson, Joan Nestle

Lescaze, William (*b* Geneva, 27 March 1896; *d* New York City, 9 Feb 1969). Architect. After training in Switzerland he moved to New York City in 1923 and opened a firm with George Howe in 1929. One of the first proponents of the International style in the city, he submitted a plan for a "tower in the park" housing development between Chrystie and Forsyth streets (1931) that was shown at the International Exhibition at the Museum of Modern Art in 1932; he designed the Williamsburg Houses in Brooklyn (Public Works Administration, 1938) in a similar style. Sleek modern lines characterize Lescaze's designs for the Aviation Building at the World's Fair of 1939–40 and a number of retail outlets and private houses, including his townhouse at East 48th Street (1933), as well as renovations he made to the lobby and Egyptology library of the Brooklyn Museum.

Lorraine Welling Lanmon: *William Lescaze, Architect* (Philadelphia: Art Alliance Press / Cranbury, N.J.: Associated University Presses, 1987)
Robert A. M. Stern, Gregory F. Gilmartin, and Thomas Mellins: *New York 1930: Architecture and Urbanism between the Two World Wars* (New York: Rizzoli, 1987)

Edward A. Eigen

Leslie, Frank [Carter, Henry] (*b* Ipswich, England, 21 March 1821; *d* New York City, 10 Jan 1880). Magazine publisher. He became a skilled news illustrator in London, using the pseudonym Frank Leslie to conceal his trade from his disapproving father. In 1848 he settled in New York City, where he worked as a wood engraver and illustrator for several publications and in 1854 published the *Illustrated News* with P. T. Barnum. A more successful venture was *Frank Leslie's Lady's Gazette of Fashion and Fancy Needlework*, launched in the following year as the first in a series of magazines bearing his name; later in the year he began publishing *Frank Leslie's Illustrated Newspaper*, the first weekly news magazine in the United States and an enormous success. Leslie attacked the "swill milk" interests of the city in 1858 — he inveighed against the use of distillery refuse as feed and published graphic pictures of diseased cows — but in general his publications refrained from taking political stands and were neutral during the Civil War. During his career Leslie published about forty periodicals in English and German, most of which emphasized humor, crime, gossip, and fiction of interest to women and children. The depression of the 1870s hurt his business, which after his death was restored to profitability by his second wife, Miriam Follin Squier.

Frank Luther Mott: *A History of American Magazines*, vol. 1, *1741–1850* (New York: D. Appleton, 1930)
Budd Leslie Gambee Jr.: *Frank Leslie and His Illustrated Newspaper, 1855–1860* (Ann Arbor: Department of Library Science, University of Michigan, 1964)

Robert Stinson

Leslie [Squier; née Follin], **Miriam** [Leslie, Frank] (*b* New Orleans, 5 June 1836; *d* New York City, 18 Sept 1914). Magazine publisher. Born into a wealthy family and expected to enter fashionable society, she moved to New York City at the age of fourteen. Highly literate, artistic, and personally captivating, she was frequently the subject of scandal, as when she openly carried on a relationship with Frank Leslie while still married to one of his associates. She skillfully edited *Frank Leslie's Chimney Corner* (1865) and *Frank Leslie's Lady's Journal* (1871) and married Leslie in 1874; on his death in 1880 she assumed control of his business, which was still suffering from the depression of the 1870s, and restored it to profitability. She herself took the name Frank Leslie in 1881. After a brief marriage in 1891 to Oscar Wilde's brother Willie Wilde she resumed her career in journalism, then leased some of her publications, sold others, and worked as a writer and lecturer. Leslie left an estate valued at $2 million to the woman suffrage movement.

Frank Luther Mott: *A History of American Magazines*, vol. 1, *1741–1850* (New York: D. Appleton, 1930)
Madeline B. Stern: *Purple Passage: The Life of Mrs. Frank Leslie* (Norman: University of Oklahoma Press, 1953)

Robert Stinson

Letterman, David (*b* Indianapolis, 12 April 1947). Comedian and entertainer. He attended Ball State University (graduating in 1969), worked as a weatherman in Indianapolis and as a comedian in Los Angeles, and then moved to New York City. He also appeared frequently as a guest host of Johnny Carson's "Tonight Show." In 1980 he became the host of his own daytime program for the National Broadcasting Company (NBC); he moved to a nighttime program, "Late Night with David Letterman," in 1982. During the following years he became known for a wry, irreverent, and self-deprecating humor, replete with topical references to New York City, that proved especially popular with young adults. It was widely assumed that he would become the host of the "Tonight Show" on Carson's retirement, and the decision by NBC to choose another host instead prompted Letterman to move to the Columbia Broadcasting System (CBS) in 1993. For his new program, "Late Show," CBS renovated the Ed Sullivan Theater on Broadway and 53rd Street.

Lever House. Skyscraper at 390 Park Avenue in Manhattan, between 53rd and 54th streets. Designed by Gordon Bunshaft, a partner in the firm of Skidmore, Owings and Merrill, and completed in 1952 as the headquarters for the soap manufacturer Lever Brothers, it was the first glass skyscraper on Park Avenue. The building's stunning geometry of metal and glass prompted architects to reconsider traditional skyscraper design, and within a decade of its construction it had inspired numerous imitations in New York City and around the world. The building has twenty-one stories atop a horizontal slab supported by columns. It is encased in a blue-green skin of glass banded in stainless steel. At night the skyscraper takes on a crystalline beauty and seems to float above Park Avenue. Lever House was designated a city landmark in 1982.

Rebecca Read Shanor

Leviathan. Steamship built in 1914 in Hamburg and owned by the Hamburg American Line. Initially called the *Vaterland* by her owner, she was the largest ship in the world and one of the fastest. When the United States entered the First World War the ship was seized, renamed, and refitted to carry fourteen thousand troops at a time. Considered by many the greatest ship in the world, she was returned to service as an express liner for the firm of United States Lines after the war, carrying as many as 2700 passengers on a single crossing. The *Leviathan* ceased to earn profits during the Depression and was scrapped in 1938.

Frank O. Braynard

Lewisohn, Leonard (*b* Hamburg, 1847; *d* London, 5 March 1902). Industrialist. Of German Jewish background, he arrived in Manhattan in 1865 and opened an importing business at 251 Pearl Street. In 1867 he formed a partnership with his brothers Julius Lewisohn and Adolph Lewisohn (*b* Hamburg, *ca* 1849; *d* New York City, 17 Aug 1938). The three purchased a copper mine in 1879 that was the first of several profitable mining ventures; they also acquired smelting firms and virtually controlled the industry until successfully challenged by the Guggenheims in 1900. Lewisohn was a prominent contributor to the Jewish Theological Seminary. His daughters Irene and Alice in 1915 organized the Neighborhood Playhouse of the Henry Street Settlement at 466 Grand Street, an early promoter of experimental theater.

Alice Lewisohn Crowley: *The Neighborhood Playhouse* (New York: Theatre Arts Books, 1959)
Stephen Birmingham: *Our Crowd* (New York: Harper and Row, 1967)

Joyce Mendelsohn

Lewisohn Stadium. The stadium of City College of New York, between West 136th and West 138th streets and Convent and Amsterdam avenues. Built at the instigation of John H. Finley, president of the college from 1903 to 1913, it was named after the philanthropist Adolph Lewisohn (*b* Hamburg, *ca* 1849; *d* New York City, 17 Aug 1938), who donated $50,000 for construction and presented the stadium to the college on 29 May 1915. The stadium was designed by Arnold W. Brunner as a half-oval of reinforced concrete with twenty-four tiers of seats below a row of sixty-four doric columns. It seated six thousand and had standing room for fifteen hundred. The stadium was best known as the site of reasonably priced orchestral concerts presented each summer from 1918 to 1966. It was demolished in 1973.

Laura Lewison

Lexow, Rudolf (*b* Schleswig–Holstein, 10 Jan 1821; *d* Brooklyn, 16 July 1909). Editor and novelist. He emigrated from Germany to the United States and settled in New York City after the revolution of 1848. In 1852 he founded the *Criminal Zeitung und Belletristisches Journal*, which became a leading German–American newspaper and literary journal under his editorship (circulation reached twenty thousand in 1855 and more than seventy thousand in the 1880s). His published writings include the novels *Amerikanische Criminal-Mysterien oder das Leben der Verbrecher in New-York* (1854) and *Annies Prüfungen* (1860), and histories of the revolution of 1848 and the U.S. Civil War. One of his sons was Clarence Lexow, a state senator who investigated municipal corruption in the 1890s.

Stanley Nadel

Lexow Committee. An investigative body that between January 1894 and January 1895 investigated allegations of corruption by the police department in New York City. Composed of five Republican and two Democratic members of the state senate, it was led by State Senator Clarence Lexow of Rockland County. Its counsel was John William Goff. The committee was designed to embarrass Democrats aligned with Tammany Hall. It disclosed evidence that the police were engaged in vice operations and were responsible for rigging elections and for physical brutality. One result of its findings was the defeat of Tammany Hall in the municipal elections of 1894.

Joseph P. Viteritti

liability insurance. For information on liability insurance see PROPERTY AND LIABILITY INSURANCE.

Liberal Club. Organization formed in September 1913 by Henrietta Rodman and others as a radical offshoot of a club of the same name that earlier had met in Gramercy Park. Its headquarters were on the ground floor of 137 MacDougal Street. The members of the club called it a "meeting place for those interested in new ideas." Until 1918 it sponsored programs of a radical nature ranging from discussions of Freud to lectures on birth control, and also functioned as an art gallery, a poker parlor, a dance hall, and an experimental theater. Prominent members included Floyd Dell, Mary Heaton Vorse, Max Eastman, Louise Bryant, and George Cram Cook.

Jan Seidler Ramirez

Liberal Party. Statewide political party formed in New York City in 1944. Former members of the American Labor Party who had become disaffected by its increasingly left-wing stance made up most of the initial membership; the principal organizers were Alex Rose and David Dubinsky. The party evolved into a reformist group largely controlled by Rose that sometimes nominated its own candidates for public office and at other times provided a second line on the ballot to a liberal Democrat or Republican. In the 1940s and 1950s it promoted rent control and consumer protection laws, and in the 1960s it took part in a suit for congressional reapportionment favorable to racial minorities, a suit eventually upheld by the U.S. Supreme Court. Later it opposed the Vietnam War and called for the impeachment of President Richard M. Nixon during the Watergate scandal. A high point for the party was marked in 1969 when it was the vehicle for the reelection of Mayor John V. Lindsay, who had been denied renomination by the Republican Party. With the end of the Vietnam War the party lost much of its focus, and it declined in membership and influence during the following years, especially after Rose's death in 1976. The party's fortunes revived in 1993, when it endorsed the Republican mayoral candidate Rudolph W. Giuliani: he received 62,469 votes on the Liberal line, more than the 53,581 votes by which he defeated the Democratic incumbent, Mayor David N. Dinkins. Mayor Giuliani appointed Fran Reiter, the party's state chairman, to the position of deputy mayor for planning and community relations. The Liberal Party is believed to be the longest-standing third party in the United States. In early 1994 there were 26,704 registered Liberals in New York City, representing 0.8 percent of all registered voters. The headquarters are at 381 Park Avenue South in Manhattan.

Chad Ludington

libraries. New York City has more than a thousand libraries and multi-branch library systems, including several of the finest in the world.

The first libraries in New York City were private collections, some of substantial size by the eighteenth century. The earliest known non-private library, a small deposit of books in Trinity Church, was mentioned in 1698; there were a few other feeble library enterprises early in the eighteenth century. The first institutional library of consequence was the New York Society Library, founded in 1754 during a period of cultural awakening and modeled on the Library Company of Philadelphia established by Benjamin Franklin in 1731. For many years the New York Society Library, a subscription, or social, library (charging a membership fee), was an enclave for the city's élite. Many of its first directors were also founders in 1754 of King's College (later Columbia University), which had a library by 1757. The bookseller Garret Noel in 1763 opened the first for-profit lending library and reading room in the city, the third in the colonies, and from 1797 to 1804 Hocquet Caritat operated the best commercial lending library in eighteenth-century North America. Several specialized libraries also began in the late eighteenth century and the early nineteenth, notably at the New-York Historical Society, Union Theological Seminary, New York Hospital, and the New York Academy of Medicine (1847).

Additional social libraries appeared in the early nineteenth century, several of them for the education and moral improvement of urban workers. Among the best-known was the Mercantile Library Association of New York, organized by merchants' clerks in 1820; it later was transformed into a general subscription library. The General Society of Mechanics and Tradesmen in 1820 opened the Apprentices' Library, a free institution that eventually de-

Columbia College Library, ca *1895*

veloped a large collection of general literature; in 1972 it became a subscription library. An apprentices' library organized in Brooklyn in the 1820s was the predecessor of the Brooklyn Mercantile Library, which began in 1857 and was later converted into the Brooklyn Library, a general subscription library that merged with the Brooklyn Public Library in 1902. Other social libraries in outlying areas were the Harlem Library (1825), the Washington Heights Library (1868), and several libraries in Queens.

The first privately endowed, independent, free public reference library in the United States, the Astor Library, was formed in New York in 1848 by the will of John Jacob Astor and incorporated in 1849. Opened in 1854, the Astor ranked among the foremost American libraries in the scope and quality of its collections. During the years preceding the Civil War the Cooper Union for the Advancement of Science and Art and the YMCA offered free reading rooms to the public, Charles Loring Brace opened a reading room for the uplift of the poor, and the Maimonides Library of the Jewish fraternal organization B'nai B'rith operated a public circulating collection that survived until 1906. New York City was also the site of the earliest known librarians' convention: in 1853 eighty-two American librarians and other interested men met to discuss common concerns, library development, and plans for a librarians' association.

By 1876 there were some ninety small collections in clubs, academies, asylums, schools, and other organizations in the city. Among these was another endowed free reference library, the Lenox Library, a collection of Americana, bibles, and rarities incorporated by James Lenox in 1870. The major academic library in the city was at Columbia, which by 1876 reached ninth in holdings among American libraries. The librarian at Columbia from 1883 to 1889 was the famous Melvil Dewey, a founder of the modern library profession. At Columbia he began the first institution to educate librarians, the School of Library Economy (1887), which in defiance of college policy enrolled women. Owing in part to this conflict Dewey left Columbia for Albany, New York, to become the secretary of the University of the State of New York and the director of the State Library. He took with him the library school, which was reconstituted as the New York State Library School. In 1926 it combined with the New York Public Library Library School (1911) to form the School of Library Service of Columbia University. These schools operated distinguished programs, and the library science library at Columbia was the world's finest until the university dismantled the school in 1992.

Between the 1870s and 1890s several free lending libraries were established under private auspices, some independent and some operated by agencies such as settlement houses. Many of these libraries eventually received municipal appropriations allowed under state law and from 1892 received state aid; to get these funds several subscription libraries were converted into free public libraries. The most prominent free libraries were three multi-branch systems (all later consolidated with the New York Public Library): the New York Free Circulating Library (1878, incorporated 1880); the Aguilar Free Library (1886), formed by German–American Jews to aid assimilation by eastern European Jewish immigrants; and the Cathedral Library (1887), sponsored by the Roman Catholic Archdiocese and from 1893 open to the public. In Brooklyn the Pratt Institute ran a free public library from 1888 to 1940, and a few communities in the Bronx, Queens, and Staten Island also had small libraries. But New York City did not have the central, tax-supported, municipal library common by the late nineteenth century in many other American cities and commensurate with its status as the nation's largest city and cultural metropolis. Efforts to establish such a library had foundered.

Events beginning in the early 1890s culminated in not one but three public library systems shortly after New York City was consolidated in 1898: the Brooklyn Public Library, the Queens Borough Public Library, and the New York Public Library. The key impetus was the founding of the New York Public Library in 1895 as a privately endowed free public reference library, the result of a merger of the Astor Library, the Lenox Library, and the Tilden Trust, a legacy of Governor Samuel J. Tilden. The city agreed to build and maintain a central building in Manhattan for the new institution, and in 1901, under pressure from municipal officials seeking to systematize tax-supported library service, the New York Public Library began to assume responsibility for local circulating library service in Manhattan, the Bronx, and Staten Island; Brooklyn and Queens kept their own recently founded library systems. A catalyst for the absorption by the New York Public Library of most of the city's free lending libraries and for the advancement of public libraries in the outer boroughs was Andrew Carnegie's gift of funds in 1901 to construct branch library buildings throughout the city. In turn the municipality contracted to provide annual maintenance for public library service in addition to sites for the Carnegie branches. Public libraries were thus firmly established as essential public services. Although substantial state aid was forthcoming after 1950, the Brooklyn and Queens Borough public libraries and the New York Public Library branch system depended mainly on municipal funds. The wide-ranging research collections of the New York Public Library, preeminent in the city and among the world's largest, remained for the most part privately supported.

The branch system of the New York Public Library initially overshadowed the other two public libraries. By the mid twentieth century the Brooklyn Public Library had become an important institution; later, as Queens became widely settled, the Queens Borough Public Library grew into a major system with the highest circulation of any municipal library in the United States. The years after the Second World War saw substantial growth in municipal library service: by 1990 there were more than two hundred library branches citywide.

The three systems serve persons of all ages with collections and programs of many kinds aimed at diverse groups. Among these are projects to promote literacy and to teach English as a second language, and special programs and services for schoolchildren, residents of nursing homes, the blind and physically handicapped, the homebound, and the homeless. The public libraries supply state-subsidized library service and educational programs to prison inmates in all five boroughs. At times city officials have considered consolidating all the public libraries, but studies indicated that few advantages would result. Although they have cooperated in some ways, the three systems remain distinct.

The public libraries support the city's educational systems, public and private, by serving legions of students from the elementary level to the graduate and professional, especially when the schools have weak libraries or none at all (as was true of public elementary schools until the 1960s). With the opening of the Mid-Manhattan Library of the New York Public Library in 1970, New York City finally had the very large, central, college-level lending collection commonly available in other cities. Columbia University remains the city's predominant academic library. Strong in most subjects, it has extensive holdings in law, health sciences, East Asian studies, business, architecture, social welfare, rare books, and manuscripts. One of the great collections in education (founded in 1887) is at Teachers College. The main library of New York University (1835) was considerably strengthened for research purposes by the opening in 1973 of the Elmer Holmes Bobst Library and Study Center, which includes the Avery Fisher Center for Music and Media (1986) and resources for the study of American radicalism and the labor movement in New York City; New York University also has important collections in medicine, law, art history, and mathematics. In 1961 the Graduate School and University Center of the new City University of New York (CUNY) was organized; at its headquarters, opposite the central building of the New York Public Library, the school developed a collection in aid of graduate study but not a comprehensive research library.

The advent of hundreds of specialized libraries in New York City was a twentieth-century phenomenon that followed the city's progress as a center of the visual and performing arts, communications, finance, advertising, medicine and science, international affairs, law, design, commerce, and corporate management. World-renowned collections in the performing arts are at the New York Public Library for the Performing Arts at Lincoln Center. In the visual arts the Metropolitan Museum of Art houses important collections, dating from 1880, of books, slides, and photographs; the Frick Art Reference Library (1920) encompasses the fine arts of western Europe and the United States; the Museum of Modern Art Library covers art after 1880; and the New York Public Library has art, picture, fine print, and photograph collections. A premier collection of prints, drawings, rare books, and manuscripts is at the Pierpont Morgan Library, incorporated in 1924 as an endowed public reference library.

The libraries and information centers in banking and investment houses in the financial district constitute an informal library network for the financial community, which is also served by the Business Library of the Brooklyn Public Library. In the health sciences major resources include the collections of universities and medical centers, and the great public reference library of the New York Academy of Medicine, a node in the national system of access to biomedical information. Other notable science collections are at the Chemists' Club, the New York Botanical Garden, and the American Museum of Natural History. The Science, Industry and Business Library (SIBL) of the New York Public Library, a facility consolidating the public library's collections and services in scientific and economic fields and employing the latest electronic technology, is scheduled to open in the former B. Altman building in 1995.

New York City has nearly a hundred libraries in law firms and associations, courts, and law schools. The Dag Hammarskjöld Library at the United Nations has important holdings in international affairs. Major local history collections are at the New-York Historical Society and the Brooklyn Historical Society (founded in 1863 and until 1985 known as the Long Island Historical Society). The Municipal Reference and Research Center, a source of information on municipal affairs, was initiated by urban reformers in 1913 as the Municipal Reference Library and operated by the New York Public Library from 1914 to 1967, when it reverted to the city. The American Geographical Society transferred its library to the University of Wisconsin at Milwaukee in 1978; the Map Division of the New York Public Library remains a rich geographical resource. Research collections reflecting the city's ethnic and religious diversity began to develop in the 1890s, when the library of the Jewish Theological Seminary and the Jewish and Slavonic Divisions of the New York Public Library were established. The Schomburg Center for Research in Black Culture, a division of the New York Public Library, dates to the mid 1920s. Collections relating to eastern European Jewish culture are at the YIVO Institute for Jewish Research (1925), to German-speaking Jewry at the Leo Baeck Institute (1955). The library of the Center for Migration Studies on Staten Island (1964) is strong in Italian–American materials; that of the Hispanic Society of America (1904) documents the culture of Spanish- and Portuguese-speaking peoples. The Museum of the American Indian (1916) transferred its library in 1930 to the Huntington Free Library and Reading Room in the Bronx; the American Museum of Natural History has American Indian materials.

Although informal understandings have long existed among the city's libraries, formal cooperative arrangements date from after the Second World War. Biomedical libraries established the Medical Library Center of New York in 1959 for cooperative storage and service. The New York Public Library, Columbia University, Yale University, and Harvard University in 1974 formed the Research Libraries Group, a consortium eventually of national scope that other libraries in New York City later joined. New York State has been a strong proponent of interlibrary cooperation in the public interest, and in its interlibrary loan system (NYSILL) a number of the city's libraries serve as referral resources. Several hundred libraries of all types belong to the New York Metropolitan Reference and Research Library Agency (METRO), formed in 1964 under a state program of support for reference and research library resource systems. These and other local, regional, and national library networks in which libraries in New York City take part have been active in the application of new technology — computers, telecommunication, and photoduplication — to enhance library resources and services.

George Watson Cole: "Early Library Development in New York State (1800–1900)," *Bulletin of the New York Public Library*, Nov–Dec 1926 [repr. n.p. [New York]: New York Public Library, 1927]
Frank L. Tolman: "Libraries and Lyceums," *History of the State of New York*, ed. Alexander C. Flick, vol. 9, *Mind and Spirit* (New York: Columbia University Press, 1937), 47–91
Robert B. Downs: *Resources of New York City Libraries: A Survey of Facilities for Advanced Study and Research* (Chicago: American Library Association, 1942)
Cornelia Marwell, ed.: *Library Resources in New York City: A Selection for Students* (New York: School of Library Service, Columbia University, 1979)

See also ARCHIVES.

Phyllis Dain

Library and Museum of the Performing Arts. Former name of the NEW YORK PUBLIC LIBRARY FOR THE PERFORMING ARTS.

licensing. In the seventeenth and eighteenth centuries licensing in New York City was concerned mostly with examining and sealing weights and measures, inspecting food, and regulating markets. The Bureau of Licenses was established in 1904, after a state investigation uncovered a notorious operation on the Lower East Side in which businesses posing as employment agencies were steering young women, mostly immigrants, to prostitution and other illegal enterprises. But the bureau was given regulatory jurisdiction only over employment agencies, and reformers called for one centralized municipal department to oversee all the city's licensing duties. The Department of Licenses was formed as a result in 1914, although some licensing responsibilities remained with other municipal entities. The new department had as its purpose to regulate businesses and other operations so as to protect consumers, public health, and public safety. It was given licensing jurisdiction over places of entertainment (theaters, movie theaters, cabarets), hacks and truck drivers, and businesses that were potential outlets for stolen property (junk dealers, pawnbrokers). But the office's first commissioner, George H. Bell (1878–1965), was actually less a consumer advocate than a self-professed guardian of the city's morals. During his tenure (1914–17) he worked with the National Board of Censorship to ensure that no films shown in New York City depicted crime, lewdness, or even slapstick. In 1916 the department closed down twenty film productions, and threatened to revoke the license of any theater that showed Margaret Sanger's film *Birth Control.* Bell even demanded that hurdy-gurdy players have their instruments in tune before they could receive a license. After Bell left office the department issued a growing number of licenses (117,884 in 1924, compared with 29,157 in 1914), and it continued to censor the entertainment business well into the 1930s. In 1922 it shut down a play entitled *The Demi-Virgin*, an action eventually overturned by the New York State Court of Appeals. Later Mayor Fiorello H. La Guardia worked with the department to close down burlesque houses. When shows did resume it was only under the commissioner's strict supervision.

During the 1950s the Department of Licenses focused more on business regulation, and licensing responsibilities became more diffused: by 1960 it issued less than 13 percent of the 833 types of licenses distributed by twenty-four municipal agencies. In 1968 the department was abolished outright, its duties transferred to the Department of Consumer Affairs. The new department expanded licensing responsibilities, implemented education programs, and focused more on consumer protection.

By the time of the city's fiscal crisis in the mid 1970s politicians increasingly resorted to licensing fees to raise revenue, to the great resentment of the city's businesses. An underground economy took shape to circumvent the city's licensing requirements, a phenomenon that sometimes had baleful consequences. In 1990 eighty-seven persons were killed in a fire at the Happy Land Social Club in the Bronx, an unlicensed operation that did not meet the city's fire protection codes. During the 1990s there were many calls for a reform of the city's licensing apparatus, which was increasingly seen as unfair and burdensome to small businesses. In 1994 Mayor Rudolph W. Giuliani created a task force to eliminate some of the unnecessary and antiquated licensing requirements still in place. At the time there were more than five hundred types of license issued by municipal agencies.

Milton M. Carrow: *The Licensing Power in New York City* (South Hackensack, N.J.: Fred R. Rothman, 1968)

James Bradley

Lichtenstein, Roy (*b* New York City, 27 Oct 1923). Painter. He attended Benjamin Franklin High School, studied with Reginald Marsh at the Art Students League, and in 1940 left the city to attend the School of Fine Arts at Ohio State University (MFA 1950). He then moved to Cleveland to work as an engineering draftsman, and in 1951 he had his first one-man show in New York City, at the Carlebach Gallery. By the early 1960s he was associated with the pop art movement, and his works were exhibited at the Leo Castelli Gallery and other venues. He moved his studio in 1965 to 26th Street in Manhattan and in the following year to the Bowery. Lichtenstein's best-known works are large paintings in the style of comic strips, in which the subject's thoughts are often revealed in an accompanying "thought bubble."

Chad Ludington

Liebling, A(bbott) J(oseph) (*b* New York City, 18 Oct 1904; *d* New York City, 28 Dec 1963). Essayist. Brought up in Far Rockaway, he worked for the *New York World* (1930–31) and the *New York World–Telegram* (1931–35) and then became an essayist and humorist for the *New Yorker* (1935–63). He wrote his best work about the low life of New York City: the customers at I. and Y.'s, an all-night tobacco store on the Lower East Side, unscrupulous promoters of Broadway shows, prizefighters, gamblers, and habitués of the racetrack. A close friend of Alger Hiss, Liebling derided the anti-communist fervor of the late 1940s. Published collections of his essays include *The Wayward Pressman* (1947), *The Sweet Science* (1956, on boxing), and *Liebling at Home* (1982).

Stephen Weinstein

Liebmann Breweries. Original name of RHEINGOLD BREWERIES.

Lienau, Detlef (*b* Schleswig–Holstein, 17 Feb 1818; *d* New York City, 29 Aug 1887). Architect. He received his training in Germany and France and in 1848 emigrated to the United States. Highly regarded by his contemporaries for the quality of his work, he introduced the French Second Empire style and the mansard roof to New York City when he designed the Hart Schiff house at 32 5th Avenue (1850–52, demolished). Other influential works by Lienau include the houses of William and Edmund H. Schermerhorn, 49 and 45–47 West 23rd Street (1859 and 1868–70, demolished), and a row of marble-fronted houses designed as an ensemble for Rebecca Colford Jones, 5th Avenue at 55th Street (1868–70, demolished).

Marjorie Pearson

Lievre, Eugen (*fl* 1848–60). Political activist and hotel owner. A German immigrant, he bought the Shakespeare Hotel at the corner of Duane and William streets in Manhattan in 1848 and made it a center of social activities for Germans. He was a member of the Befreiungsbund, a group formed by the utopian communist leader Wilhelm Weitling in 1847–48, and allowed many German radicals to use his hotel as a meeting place throughout the 1850s; their activities were depicted in a play by Max Cohnheim. He later sold the hotel and opened the Hôtel Hansa in Hoboken, New Jersey.

Stanley Nadel

Life. Weekly magazine published in New York City from November 1936 by Time. Its publisher was Henry R. Luce, a vigorous advocate of photojournalism who for several years had recognized the market for a generously illustrated periodical available at a low price (*Life* at first sold for five cents a copy). The magazine overcame many production problems to become the first popular "picture weekly" in the United States and one of the most widely read periodicals of any kind. It offered weekly photographic summaries of the news and such features on the popular arts as "*Life* Goes to the Movies." Luce insisted that his readers be "educated" with lavish essays on history and culture, but he also published photographs of young actresses and the humorous efforts of amateur photographers. Circulation and advertising reached their peak in the 1950s despite the advent of television, but the magazine was hurt by the rising costs of production and postage. In the 1960s *Life* attracted new subscribers only through deeply discounted subscriptions, which displeased advertisers. Late in the decade it gave less emphasis to photographs and more to longer essays, but by sacrificing the visual and the irreverent it became dull. At the same time the growing use of satellite transmission improved the ability of television to cover breaking stories, which had once been a specialty of the magazine. *Life* ceased publication in December 1972. Although it was revived as a monthly magazine in October 1978, its circulation of 1.7 million in 1988 was only a fifth of that claimed by its weekly predecessor in 1970.

Loudon Wainwright: *The Great American Magazine: An Inside History of Life* (New York: Alfred A. Knopf, 1986)

James L. Baughman

life insurance. Short-term life insurance policies for travelers embarking on hazardous journeys were sold in New York City and elsewhere in the colonies by colonial and English underwriters. A corporation set up in 1759 by the Presbyterian Synod of New York City offered policies for Presbyterian ministers and their families, financed largely by church members (contributions were also expected from ministers). At the Tontine Coffee House, built in 1792 at Wall and Water streets, the New York Insurance Company was organized in 1796 as a contributory fund called a tontine: the fund grew as members of the pool died, and eventually reverted to the last survivor. The twenty-one members of the board of directors fixed values on the members' slaves, sailing vessels, houses, and other property. In the early nineteenth century whole-life policies (as opposed to policies for finite terms), financed with level premiums, were sold in urban centers including New York City by British insurers, who left the United States during the War of 1812 and did not return until the 1840s. After the Erie Canal was completed (1825) the city prospered and the insurance industry expanded. A charter for the New York Life Insurance and Trust Company was granted in March 1830 to William Bard, who hoped to channel Dutch capital into real estate in the city. He assembled $1 million in capital and set up a network of sales agents throughout New York State, and until 1843 the firm had the highest sales in the country (it ceased selling life insurance before merging with the Bank of New York). In 1840 benefits paid to widows from policies sold in New York State were exempted from creditors' claims by the state legislature.

Recovery from a depression in 1837–42 spurred the formation of mutual companies, which required little capital and offered policyholders a share in profits. In April 1842 a charter for the Mutual Life Insurance Company of New York was granted to Morris Robinson, formerly a cashier in the city's branch of the Second Bank of the United States, and Alfred Pell, an agent for an English marine insurer. The firm's sales increased steadily even though its policies were invalidated by travel south of Virginia. The bylaws of the Nautilus Insurance Company, a marine and fire insurer chartered in 1841, were amended in 1848 to permit sales of life insurance, and in 1849 the firm was renamed the New York Life Insurance Company. Soon after its formation the firm accepted risks on slaves, and in 1860 it became the first company to provide a contractual nonforfeiture benefit, guaranteeing the policyholder a cash value if the policy lapsed. A need for regulation developed during the 1840s as competition among mutual companies increased, and in 1849 the first law in New York State regulating insurance was passed, stating that no insurance firm could be formed in the city or Kings County with less than $100,000 in capital. Life insurance was made separate from fire and marine insurance in 1853. The first American mortality table was compiled by Charles Gill, an actuary for Mutual Life, whose work was continued by Sheppard Homans and incorporated into a table based on the mortality rates of policyholders of Mutual Life from 1843 to 1858.

Most firms were organized under the general agency system, under which an agent controlled a territory, recruited and trained a sales force at his or her own expense, and received a percentage of sales from a home office. Agents appointed by New York Life during the 1850s included Hugh McCulloch, Thomas Hendricks, and Lew Wallace. During the late 1850s fraudulent practices were attacked in the *Insurance Monitor*, a publication begun by Thomas Jones Jr., whose criticisms led to the formation of a state insurance department in 1859, the first in the nation. Critical of both the "cold-hearted speculator" and the "leech-like stockholder," William Barnes, the commissioner, established links between the department, the insurance industry, and the state legislature. On leaving office he was berated by George Miller, his successor and an associate of William M. "Boss" Tweed, for having acquired enough wealth to build a mansion. The Equitable Life Assurance Society was formed in July 1859 by Henry Hyde, a former agent and cashier for Mutual Life, who appointed wealthy fellow members of the Fifth Avenue Presbyterian Church to the board of directors and raised capital by promising the positions of medical director and company lawyer to men able to sell stock in the company; as president of the firm he selected William Alexander, brother of the minister of his church.

The population of the city exceeded a million by 1860, when the first report by the insurance department showed that the ten firms based in New York State employed 1257 agents, including 439 within the state. During the same year the Germania Life Insurance Company was formed by a group under the direction of Hugo Wesendonck. The first company to appoint agents in the Caribbean and Central America, it opened offices in Germany in 1868 and acquired an impressive building in Berlin for the headquarters of its European branch, which by 1873 accounted for a quarter of total sales. In 1867 Hyde secured legislation authorizing the sale of deferred dividend, or tontine, contracts, which quickly became popular for their offer of both death claim protection and high investment earnings to those survivors who did not lapse their policies and continued to pay premiums. The Metropolitan Life Insurance Company received a charter in 1868 and sold policies, which required weekly premiums, to members of a German-speaking association. During the same year the state insurance department adopted the mortality table devised by Homans and Gill. Mutual Life introduced tontine contracts and competed for business with Equitable and New York Life. The prosperity of the 1860s was followed by a decade of decreasing sales and intense competition, and between 1867 and 1873 twenty-two life insurers operating in New York State declared bankruptcy.

From 1860 to 1870 sales to New Yorkers increased tenfold, to 650,000 policies worth $1800 million. Led by United States Life of New York, firms based in New York City expanded overseas. Contracts were issued by Equitable in England in 1869, in France in 1870, and in Germany in 1871. In 1875 industrial, or home service, life insurance was introduced by John Dryden: his policies had low face value and required small weekly premiums collected at customers' homes. From 1879 industrial policies were sold on an increasing scale in the city by Metropolitan Life, which modeled its operations on those of the British firm London Prudential. Large companies became major sources of investment funds, and in 1883 the state legislature permitted insurers based in New York State to buy railroad securities, which by 1897 accounted for 16 percent of investments by the "Big Three": Mutual Life, Equitable, and New York Life. Unlimited bank deposits by insurers based in New York State were allowed in 1892. In the late nineteenth century a strong pro-industry bias developed within the system of regulation. John McCall held the post of insurance commissioner when named comptroller of Equitable in 1886, Darwin Kingsley was the superintendent of insurance in Colorado when engaged by New York Life in 1888, and before 1906 four incumbent commissioners faced charges of misconduct (none were dismissed).

Mutual Life set up a foreign department in 1886 under the direction of the firm's president, Richard McCurdy, after expansion overseas by Equitable and several smaller insurers. Many insurers met with obstacles abroad, including costs and mortality rates higher than expected and problems with currency and exchange rates. Life insurance was sponsored by the German state under Bismarck, and in 1893 the Prussian government revoked the licenses of Mutual Life and New York Life (only Germania Life continued operating without severe restrictions). During these years a number of firms built impressive headquarters in Manhattan. Additions were made to the offices of Equitable at 120 Broadway in 1887 and to those of Mutual Life at 34 Nassau Street in 1892. An annex designed by McKim, Mead and White was installed next to the headquarters of New York Life at 346 Broadway. And in 1893 Metropolitan Life completed the first section of a massive building on Madison Square, which by 1897 accommodated 1081 workers. A tower added in 1909 was at the time the tallest in the world.

By the turn of the century Mutual Life expanded into Asia and George Perkins led the overseas expansion of New York Life, which in 1899 was supervised by eighty-two governments. By 1905 New York Life had 24 percent of its life insurance in force abroad and $35.6 million in foreign securities; Equitable had 21 percent of its life insurance in force abroad and Mutual Life 18 percent; and the Big Three together had $64 million in foreign securities. In the city insurance firms, investment firms, and large banks formed close ties. Among the investment bankers appointed to the boards of life insurance firms were Jacob Schiff of Kuhn, Loeb at Equitable, and George F. Baker of First National Bank at Mutual Life; Perkins and McCall of New York Life were appointed to the board of National City Bank, and in 1901 Perkins became a full partner in the investment banking house of J. P. Morgan, which during the next five years sold almost $39 million in securities to a subsidiary of New York Life. Sales of industrial contracts surged, leading to the publication in 1906 of the first industrial mortality table, based on statistics gathered by Metropolitan Life from 1896 to 1905 (the table was prescribed by most states until 1948). In 1905 New York Life had $2100 million of life insurance in force and was the nation's leading firm. The next-largest firms were Metropolitan Life (directed by John Hegeman and Haley Fiske) with life insurance in force of $1600 million and 8.1 million industrial policies; Mutual Life; and Equitable. At New York Life McCall replaced the general agency system with a system of branch offices, the transition directed by Perkins, a strong advocate of centralized management. Although many insurers retained the general agency system, by the mid 1930s five of the six leading insurers in the nation employed salaried managers exclusively. A larger staff was needed for the home office, which as the center of operations for the branches recruited, trained, and supervised the sales force, processed contracts, handled premiums, decided the legitimacy of claims, and invested reserve funds. In 1906 Mutual Life had 645 employees at its headquarters.

Concern about abuses culminated during the career of Hyde's son James. Appointed chairman of the finance committee of Equitable at the age of twenty-seven, James Hyde became the director of forty-five corporations. His lavish expenditures, especially for a widely publicized French ball, were denounced by Thomas Lawson and other members of the press. Under attack, Hyde in 1905 sold his holdings in Equitable to the financier Thomas Ryan, prompting State Senator William Armstrong to form the Legislative Insurance Investigating Committee. The committee examined the conduct of leading insurance executives and through the questioning of Charles Evans Hughes, the chief counsel, established that the cost of insurance was excessive in New York State, that commissions and executive salaries were similarly excessive, and that there was graft, extensive lobbying, and stock manipulation. As a result of the committee's findings the state legislature forced insurers to sever their ties with financial intermediaries and outlawed political contributions and tontines; it later restricted the powers of company officials, required that general expenditures be reduced, and also required that each policy declare its loan value (how much could be borrowed against it), its surrender value (its value when the policyholder canceled coverage), and the grounds and time limits for contesting the contract by the insurer. A welfare division was organized at Metropolitan Life in 1909 by Lee Frankel, a sociologist specializing in workers' insurance. Through his efforts pamphlets on preventable diseases were made available to holders of industrial policies, and in June 1909 he established a free visiting nurse service for policyholders in Manhattan that was later extended to the other boroughs.

Most insurers prospered during the years between 1910 and 1920. Germania Life in 1911 completed a twenty-story building at 4th Avenue and 17th Street. The first group contract was issued in June 1911 to the Pantasote Leather Company (a firm of 121 employees) by Equitable, which during the next year sold more than twenty such contracts including one to the New York and Queens Electric Light and Power Company. After the United States entered the First World War, Germania Life was separated from its large operation in Germany, and some questioned the loyalty of its executives. The firm responded by abandoning its overseas market and changing its name to Guardian Life in 1918. Metropolitan Life became a mutual company in 1915 and in 1917 introduced group policies (of which it soon sold more than Equitable). The newly formed War Risk Bureau spurred sales of life insurance by valuing the life of each serviceman at $10,000, thus serving as an example to the civilian population. In 1918 the Teachers Insurance and Annuity Association (TIAA) was formed in New York City as a nonprofit corporation by the Carnegie Foundation for the Advancement of Teaching to provide inexpensive insurance and pension benefits for college teachers. An epidemic of influenza after the war stimulated sales, and prosperity continued during the 1920s. Eight of the nation's ten leading insurers were mutual firms, including Equitable, which mutualized in 1925. Among the forty leading insurers were the mutual firms Guardian Life (converted in 1924) and Home Life. By 1929 Metropolitan Life had $2250 million in group policies that insured more than 1.3 million customers. The 1920s saw an increasing number of charitable projects undertaken by insurers. The most ambitious firm in this regard was Metropolitan Life, the first to provide inexpensive housing: under the provisions of special legislation it used $7 million to build housing for 2125 families in Queens.

The Depression endangered insurance reserves, as policyholders borrowed heavily against the cash value of their policies and sometimes terminated them outright. After banks were closed in the city on 5 and 6 March 1933, George Van Schaick, the insurance superintendent, drew up emergency state legislation that virtually prohibited loan and surrender payments: this action, combined with conservative investments by insurers, allowed the industry to survive. After the National Labor Relations Act was passed in 1935, agents of Metropolitan Life formed a union that went unrecognized by management, which contended that agents were not included in the legislation: this position was rejected by the New York State Court of Appeals and the union was recertified in 1942. To increase investment income and provide housing at moderate cost, Metropolitan Life built an apartment complex called Parkchester (1939–42) on a parcel of 129 acres (fifty-two hectares) in the Bronx. The largest development of its kind in the nation, it eventually housed twelve thousand families. Savings Bank Life Insurance (begun 1939) commanded an increasing share of the market in the city and by 1953 had 146,196 policies valued at $215.3 million. Sales of group and individual annuity plans increased rapidly during the Second World War, in part because of the increased employment of women. National Service Life Insurance was made available to members of the armed forces.

To help insurers to increase their investment income, the state legislature allowed them to make direct investments in some kinds of real estate (1945) and to invest as much as 3 percent of their assets in common stock (1951). In 1957 this amount was raised to 5 percent of assets or half of accumulated earnings, whichever was smaller. These measures allowed insurers to enter the diversified markets of financial service and encouraged ventures that were more innovative but riskier than earlier ones. Concern about reduced buying power led TIAA in 1952 to charter the College Retirement Equities Fund (CREF), which was permitted to invest in common stock, public housing, redevelopment projects, and other equities. In 1953 Mutual of New York (MONY) offered a group plan for small businesses that provided pensions, disability income, and major medical coverage. During the same year the Institute of Life Insurance reported that the eighteen firms based in the city had more than $90,000 million in life insurance in force and more than $25,000 million in assets, and paid more than $2000 million annually to American families. Customers in the city owned policies worth $25,000 million and received $350 million annually in benefits. After reaching a peak in the early 1950s sales of industrial life insurance declined as customers increasingly chose larger policies and ceased to use home service collections of premiums. The cost of debit operations rose, and in the early 1970s industrial life insurance was largely discontinued. MONY in 1965 became the first firm in the city to sell group variable annuity insurance, providing for annuity payments that varied according to investment earnings. Individual variable annuity insurance was sold by Equitable in 1968 and by Metropolitan Life soon after.

During the 1970s and 1980s large firms expanded the scope of their operations. They competed with firms that offered high investment yields by developing universal life insurance (which included both a protection element — term insurance — and a savings element — cash value), selling casualty and property insurance and variable life contracts with fixed and flexible premiums, managing health care facilities and pension funds through subsidiaries, entering merchant banking, and supplying venture capital. Home and automobile insurance was offered in 1972 by Metropolitan Life and in 1974 by Equitable, which during the same year introduced property and casualty insurance that was discontinued in 1981 after occasioning losses estimated at $100 million. New York Life discontinued its flexible-premium deferred annuities in 1982. Metropolitan Life formed a brokerage subsidiary to sell other firms' products in 1983 and in 1985 bought Century 21, the largest real-estate franchise sales organization in the world. In 1985 Equitable bought the investment firm of Donaldson, Lufkin and Jenrette. To sell innovative forms of insurance, Mutual Life bought a stock company in Arizona and later organized the Legacy Life Insurance Company in the city. By 1990 TIAA–CREF was the largest retirement plan in the world: it had 1.4 million policies and assets of $87,900 million, and paid annuity income to 236,000 customers. An economic recession in the early 1990s hurt firms that had invested in commercial mortgages, real estate, and high-yield "junk" bonds. Equitable was burdened with many guaranteed investment contracts sold during the early 1980s requiring high yields regardless of interest rates at the time of payment. In December 1990 the chairman, Richard Jenrette, announced plans to convert from a mutual company to a stock company, with the hope of raising $500 million in capital. This was accomplished in 1992.

Terence O'Donnell: *History of Life Insurance in Its Formative Years* (Chicago: American Conservation, 1936)

J. Owen Stalson: *Marketing Life Insurance: Its History in America* (Cambridge: Harvard University Press, 1942)

Morton Keller: *The Life Insurance Enterprise, 1885–1910: A Study in the Limits of Corporate Power* (Cambridge: Harvard University Press, 1963)

Jack Blicksilver

light and power. In the early nineteenth century in New York City gas manufactured from coal replaced oil burned in street lights and domestic lamps. The first gas company in the city, the New York Gas Light Company, was incorporated by the state legislature on 26 March 1823 at the behest of the banker Samuel Leggett and others. It obtained a thirty-year exclusive franchise from the city that gave it the right to lay underground gas pipes in the area south of Grand Street (which at the time encompassed most of the city); it also constructed a gas works at the corner of Hester Street and Rhynders (now Centre) Street, on what is now the Lower East Side. This monopoly proved politically controversial and was criticized by the Workingmen's Party in 1829. The Manhattan Gaslight Company was formed in the following year, and the competition between the two companies led to a reduction in the price of gas. The rivalry ended in 1833 when the city awarded the Manhattan Gaslight Company an exclusive franchise for all territory north of Grand Street, allowing each company to prosper.

A number of other gas companies sought and received franchise rights between 1858 and 1878. In August 1878 the Knickerbocker Gas Light Company sharply reduced the price of gas, triggering a price war that proved so unsettling to the industry that all the companies in the city agreed in 1880 to pool a portion of their revenues. In the same year the threat of competition from electricity became clear: on the evening of 20 December the Brush Electric Light Company demonstrated electric arc street lights in New York City for the first time, and it was soon granted permission by the Gas Commission to erect street lamps along Broadway from 14th to 34th streets; it also built the city's first central electric station at 133 West 25th Street. After providing street lighting free of charge for six months the Brush Electric Illuminating Company received a contract from the city, and in the following years it erected electric stations at West and Bank streets, 48–50 Washington Street, and 204 Elizabeth Street.

Arc lighting was quickly superseded in importance by Thomas Edison's incandescent lighting. The Edison Electric Illuminating Company of New York was incorporated on 17 December 1880 and was awarded the city's first electricity franchise by the Board of Aldermen on 19 April 1881; the board overrode the veto of Mayor William R. Grace, who believed that the compensation being offered by Edison's company for this right was inadequate. On 3 May 1881 the board again overrode Grace's veto in awarding franchises to both the Brush Electric Illuminating Company and the United States Illuminating Company. All three companies were given the right to serve Manhattan south of 136th Street, a huge area given their limited technical and financial capabilities. On 4 September 1882 the Edison Electric Illuminating Company opened its first station at 257 Pearl Street, initiating the modern era of electricity.

Concerted efforts were made over the next two decades to encourage competition and stimulate the spread of electrification: twenty-eight political subdivisions in what is now New York City granted at least ninety-two franchises for the provision of electricity. Of the twenty-five franchises awarded in Manhattan all but one included the right to serve the entire island.

The city's gas companies faced potentially devastating competition from the advent of electrical power as well as from a new rival, the Equitable Gas Light Company, formed by William Rockefeller and others in 1882. In response the gas companies that had pooled their revenues sought to make their alliance more formal: on 10 November 1884 the New York, Manhattan, Harlem, Knickerbocker, Metropolitan, and Municipal gaslight companies merged to form the Consolidated Gas Company of New York and made Charles Roome the company's first president. The Mutual Gas Light Company declined to be part of the merger but was later absorbed by Consolidated. Public outrage at the consolidation led the State Senate to appoint an in-

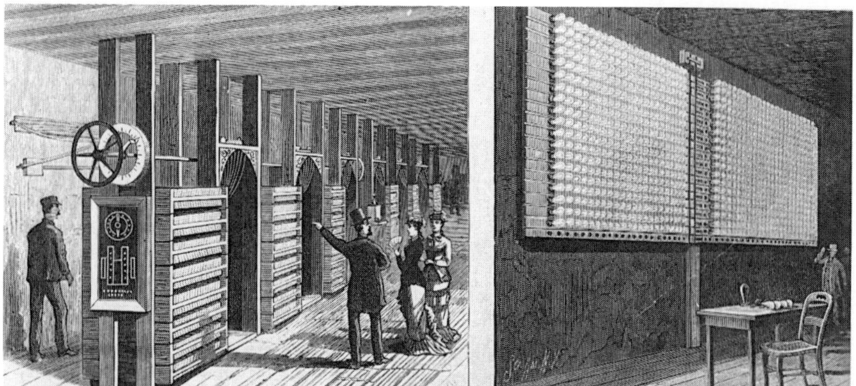

Consolidated Edison plant at Pearl Street

vestigating committee, which ruled that the gas companies had made excessive profits. In 1886 the state legislature passed a bill reducing the price of gas from $1.75 to $1.25 per thousand cubic feet (twenty-eight cubic meters) but did nothing to alter the structure of the Consolidated Gas Company.

In the late 1880s the electricity business was divided by a battle between the system invented by Edison, which used direct current, and that of the Westinghouse and Thomson–Houston companies, which used alternating current. Edison contended publicly that alternating current was more dangerous than direct current. Westinghouse generators were installed in 1887 by the Safety Electric Light and Power Company, the name of which was chosen to spite Edison and prompted him to sue — under court order it was changed to the United Electric Light and Power Company in 1889. Alternating current eventually prevailed over direct current because it could be transmitted economically over much longer distances. At the same time Consolidated Gas sought to control the electric lighting business: in 1890 it absorbed United Electric Light and Power, which had recently taken over the Brush Electric Illuminating Company.

Consolidated was faced with new competition in the gas business between 1886 and 1898. The Standard Gas Light Company under the direction of Russell Sage received valuable rights from the state legislature, and in 1897 the New Amsterdam Gas Company was formed with the support of J. P. Morgan from the merger of the Equitable Gas Light Company, the New York and East River Gas Company of Long Island, and several other firms. A rate war that broke out in 1899 between Consolidated, Standard, and New Amsterdam ended in the following year when Consolidated absorbed the other two, thus gaining complete control of the gas business in Manhattan and major portions of the rest of the city (except Brooklyn). It later acquired the New York and Queens Gas Company (1913) and New York Mutual Gas (1922).

The electric utility industry in New York City was fundamentally restructured at the beginning of the twentieth century. Anthony N. Brady purchased the Block Lighting and Power Company, the Borough of Manhattan Electric Company (formerly the Excelsior Steam Power Company), the North River Electric Light and Power Company, and the Mount Morris Electric Light Company to form the New York Gas and Electric Light, Heat and Power Company, which along with the Edison Electric Illuminating Company and United Electric Light and Power supplied virtually all the electricity used in Manhattan and the Bronx. A controlling interest in all three firms was acquired between 1899 and 1901 by Consolidated Gas, led by Harrison E. Gawtry, and in 1901 New York Gas and Electric and the Edison Electric Illuminating Company merged to form the New York Edison Company.

Consolidated Gas and the electric companies under its control met with frequent challenges. In 1902 Mayor Seth Low charged them with price gouging, and an investigation in 1905 led by Charles Evans Hughes caused adverse publicity for Consolidated Gas. In the same year a state law created a Commission of Gas and Electricity with the authority to set rates, but the state supreme court ruled the law unconstitutional. In 1907 Hughes, now governor, signed legislation establishing one of the first state public service commissions in the United States: one of two district commissions was given jurisdiction over the city, including the authority to set rates.

Between 1900 and 1935 demand for electricity increased markedly, and gas came to be used exclusively for cooking and heating. Consolidated Gas continued to expand under the direction of George B. Cortelyou, acquiring the New York and Queens Electric Light and Power Company (1913), Bronx Gas and Electric (1921), and Brooklyn Edison (1928), and in 1936 it changed its name to Consolidated Edison (usually known as Con Edison). After the Second World War it successfully converted from manufactured gas to natural gas (1951–56). It also purchased Staten Island Edison (1952), three power plants owned by the transit authority (1959), and the Consolidated Telegraph and Electric Subway Company (1960). The only company to stave off acquisition by Consolidated Edison was the Long Island Lighting Company. By the 1960s Con Edison provided electricity to all of New York City except the Rockaways; gas to Manhattan, the Bronx, and part of Queens; and steam to part of Manhattan. It also served most of Westchester County.

Concerns about plant safety and the environment made it difficult for Con Edison to maintain sufficient generating capacity in the 1960s and 1970s, and as a result the city was beset by a series of major power Blackouts. A number of construction projects became so controversial that they were abandoned, including a one-thousand megawatt nuclear plant at Ravenswood in Queens (1962) and a two-thousand megawatt pumped-storage hydroelectric plant at Storm King Mountain in

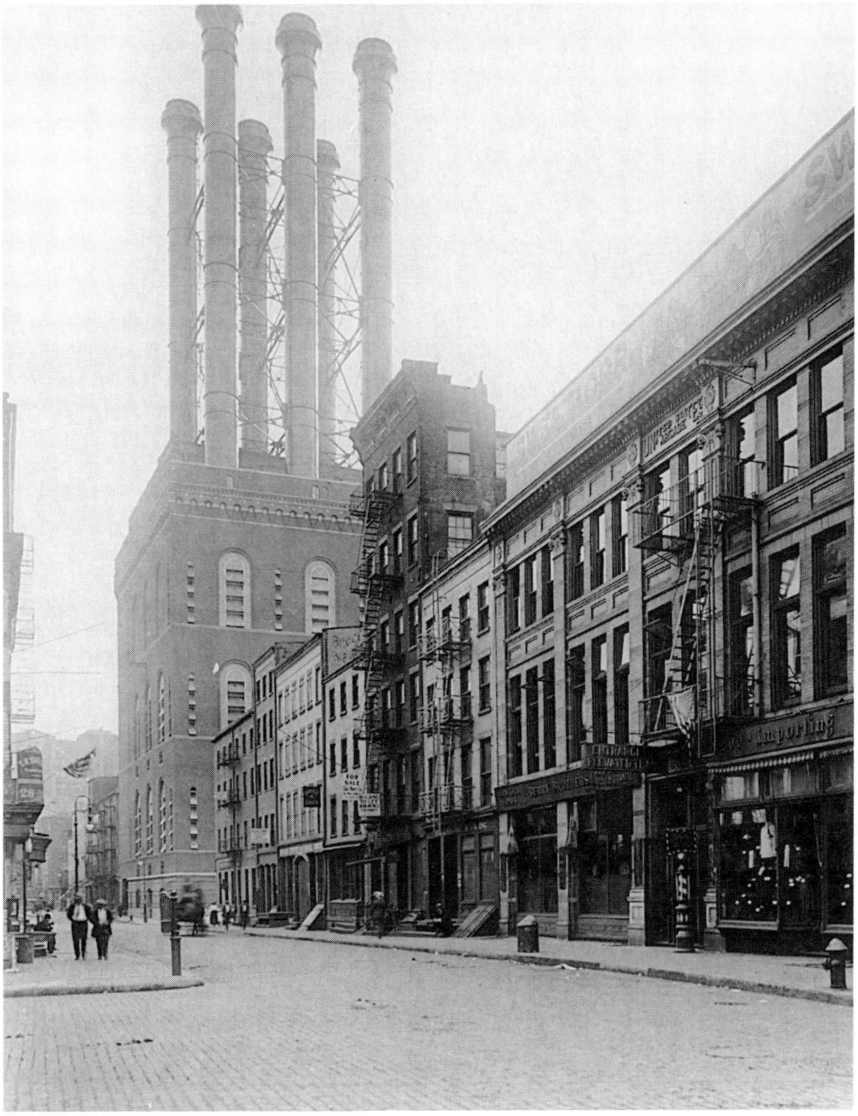

Consolidated Edison plant, 1917

Cornwall on Hudson (1963). Con Edison was hard hit by the oil embargo of 1973–74. Of its three nuclear plants (all at Indian Point, up the Hudson from New York City in Buchanan) one was sold in 1974 and another was shut down. In the mid 1990s the Consolidated Edison Company of New York had more than $10,000 million in assets and nineteen thousand employees, and sold nearly 40,000 million kilowatt-hours of electricity to about three million customers.

Frederick L. Collins: *Consolidated Gas Company of New York* (New York: Consolidated Gas, 1934)
Alexander Lurkis: *The Power Brink: Con Edison: A Centennial of Electricity* (New York: Icare, 1982)
Joseph A. Pratt: *A Managerial History of Consolidated Edison, 1936–1981* (New York: Consolidated Edison, 1988)

William J. Hausman

lighterage. The movement of freight by lighterage became a major enterprise early in the history of New York City: there was no land crossing of the East River until 1883 or of the Hudson until 1908–9, and even then the crossings did not accommodate freight railroad cars. Lighter fleets consisting of barges and tugboats were formed to carry cargo within the port. A barge was usually a wooden scow of ninety by thirty feet (twenty-seven by nine meters) that had a shed overhanging most of the deck to protect the cargo; a cabin at one end housed the captain and often his family as well. The largest fleets were operated by the railroads between large freight facilities along the shore of the Hudson River in New Jersey and smaller terminals in the city; lighter fleets were also operated by independent terminal and lighterage firms. Some had hundreds of barges and tugboats. During the 1930s lighter barges were gradually replaced by trucks that used the Holland and Lincoln tunnels and the George Washington Bridge. The last barge operating in the harbor, which carried bagged coffee from Brooklyn to Hoboken, New Jersey, ceased operation in the 1980s.

See also Port of new york.

Norman J. Brouwer

Lighthouse. Nonprofit vision rehabilitation agency, the largest in the United States. It was formed in 1904 by the sisters Winifred and Edith Holt, who from the preceding year had operated the Ticket Bureau for the Blind from their home at 44 East 78th Street to help the visually impaired attend musical performances. The agency was incorporated in 1906 as the New York Association for the Blind. The Holts adopted the instructional methods they had seen used in Europe to help the blind become self-supporting. They established a program to teach skills to the blind in their homes, organized the first formal census of blind people in New York City, opened the Bourne Workshop (later Lighthouse Industries), persuaded the Board of Education to accept blind students in the public schools, published the first Braille magazine for children, and opened the summer camp River Lighthouse for blind adults at Cornwall-on-Hudson, New York. Winifred Holt successfully argued for a state law requiring vision screening for newborns, a procedure that significantly reduced the incidence of blindness among children. The work of the Lighthouse led in 1908 to the formation of the National Society to Prevent Blindness. In 1913 President William Howard Taft dedicated a new building for the Lighthouse at 111 East 59th Street.

During the 1920s the Lighthouse introduced special classes for blind children and opened a new camp for blind girls in Waretown, New Jersey; other facilities for children were added to River Lighthouse during the 1940s. In 1951 a branch of the Lighthouse was established in Queens, and Lighthouse Industries moved to a large factory at 36-20 Northern Boulevard in Long Island City. Other branches were added in Westchester County (1961), Staten Island (1977), and Dutchess County (1985). The Child Development Center of the Lighthouse (later renamed the National Center for Vision and Child Development) opened in 1964. Later the Lighthouse expanded several programs to help the growing elderly population: it offered programs for the partially sighted, many of whom were elderly, and helped to form the National Center for Vision and Aging in 1984 to make vision problems among the elderly more widely known. More than 2500 persons attended low-vision clinics in 1990, by which time 54 percent of those helped by the Lighthouse were sixty-five or older. In the same year the organization adopted its popular name, the Lighthouse, as its official name.

Sandra Opdycke

Lighthouse on North Brother Island, ca *1880–90*

Lighthouse Hill. Neighborhood in central Staten Island, bounded to the north by Forest Hill Road, to the east by Rockland Avenue, to the south by the base of a hill in Richmondtown, and to the west by Latourette Golf Course; it lies in the hills that run northeast toward Upper New York Bay. Named for the Staten Island Lighthouse (1907), it is also called Richmond Hill. At the southern end stands Latourette Mansion, built in the 1830s and now the clubhouse of the Latourette Golf Course. Fine houses line the streets along the crest of Lighthouse Hill to the golf course. The northern section, called Meisner Hill, is the site of the Eger Health Care Center of Staten Island. At the northwestern edge is the Greenbelt, a large area of forest criss-crossed by remains of farmers' stone walls.

Harlow McMillen

lighthouses. Reefs and shifting sandbars often caused shipwrecks in the winding channels leading to the Port of New York during the eighteenth century. Frequent loss of life and property led merchants in the city to organize a lottery in 1764 to pay for the construction of a stone lighthouse at the entrance to Lower Near York Bay near the outer end of Sandy Hook, New Jersey (in the mid 1990s this was the oldest lighthouse in use in the country). Early lighthouses were powered by oil lamps and candles. In Britain in 1772 William Hutchinson developed the use of reflectors to magnify oil and candle light; this advance spread rapidly. The federal government assumed responsibility for lighthouses in 1789. Increased traffic during the 1820s led to the construction of lighthouses on Fire Island and the heights of Navesink, New Jersey, and to the installation of a lightship anchored off Sandy Hook, the first device of its kind in the United States. From the 1880s lighthouses were built in Lower New York Bay; among these was the Robbins Reef Lighthouse in Upper New York Bay off Bayonne, New Jersey, operated for almost thirty years by Kate Walker, a widow who brought up two children there. The first electric arc lamp in the United States was introduced in 1898. After Ambrose Channel was opened in 1908 to provide a deeper and more direct route to the port, the lightship at Sandy Hook was replaced. Lighthouses were automated in the 1950s. The last lightship in Ambrose Channel was replaced in 1967 with a light on a platform supported by four legs screwed into the ocean floor; this was one of the last manned lights when it was automated in 1988.

Lila Wallace–Reader's Digest Fund. Charitable organization formed in 1987 by the reorganization of the L. A. W. Fund (1956) and the High Winds Fund (1966), both established by Lila Acheson Wallace (*d* 8 May 1984), a founder of *Reader's Digest.* It supports programs in the performing arts and the visual arts, and museums. In 1992 it reported assets of $867.5 million and grants totaling $40.1 million.

Kenneth W. Rose

Lilienthal, Max (*b* Munich, 16 Oct 1815; *d* Cincinnati, 5 April 1882). Rabbi. He earned a doctorate in philosophy at the University of Munich at sixteen and became well known in Europe before moving to New York City in 1845. Soon elected the principal rabbi of three congregations, he stressed separation of church and state and supported ecumenism, becoming the first rabbi to deliver sermons to Christian congregations. In 1855 he moved to Cincinnati, where he formed the Union of American Hebrew Congregations and Hebrew Union College.

David Philipson: *Max Lilienthal, American Rabbi: Life and Writings* (New York: Bloch, 1915)

James E. Mooney

Lily Pleasure Club. Original name of UNIVERSITY SETTLEMENT.

limited-dividend housing. Private housing for limited profit developed in New York City in the mid nineteenth century to increase the availability of housing for low- and middle-income tenants. The first such project, the Workingmen's Home (1855, John W. Ritch), was built for black families as a philanthropic enterprise by the Association for Improving the Condition of the Poor; of many similar projects that followed, the largest was sponsored by Alfred T. White in Brooklyn between 1877 and 1890. Eventually White's Improved Dwellings Company housed almost five hundred families at rents well below the market level. In return tenants were expected to follow a moral canon that prescribed religion and forbade alcohol. Like others who followed, White focused his efforts on the "deserving poor," families on the threshold of the middle class, and used a highly selective screening process.

Limited-dividend firms such as William Field and Son added innovative features to subsidized housing during the late nineteenth century. In designing the Home, Tower, and Riverside buildings (1877–90) for White the firm employed designs developed in England and sought to provide shared garden space. Other projects were built by the Improved Dwellings Association in Manhattan and Charles Pratt in Brooklyn. The City and Suburban Homes Company (1896) maintained tenements of high quality on the Upper East Side through its subsidiaries New York Avenue Estate and First Avenue Estate; by 1915 it owned almost three thousand apartments in Manhattan and another 250 in Brooklyn, and it remained one of the largest philanthropic organizations in the United States until the New Deal. Smaller limited-profit companies included the New York Fireproof Tenement Company (1899), the Open Stair Dwellings Company (1910), which built the Mesa Verde in Jackson Heights (1926, Henry Atterbury Smith), and the City Housing Corporation (1924), which planned the low-density development Sunnyside (1924, Clarence S. Stein, Henry Wright, Frederick Ackerman).

The construction of limited-dividend housing was greatly stimulated when the state legislature in 1922 passed a law permitting life insurance companies to invest in it. The Metropolitan Life Insurance Company soon built a large development in Brooklyn with more than two thousand units (1924, Andrew Thomas). In 1926 the law was amended to encourage the participation of labor unions and workers' cooperatives. The result was affordable housing that was remarkably well built, including the Amalgamated Estate in the Bronx (1927) and Grand Street Housing on the Lower East Side (1930), both sponsored by the Amalgamated Clothing Workers and designed by the firm of Springsteen and Goldhammer. Other notable limited-dividend efforts included the Workers Cooperative Colony in the Bronx (1927, Herman J. Jessor), Thomas Garden Apartments in the Bronx (1928, Andrew Thomas), and the Phipps Garden Apartments in Queens (1928, Stein). After the limited-dividend law was further amended Metropolitan Life built Parkchester in the Bronx (1940, Richmond H. Shreve), and Peter Cooper Village (1947, Gilmore D. Clarke) and Stuyvesant Town (1949, Clarke) in Manhattan. The years following the Second World War saw the development of more projects by insurers, notably at Fresh Meadows by New York Life Insurance (1949, Vorhees, Walker, Foley and Smith) and at Fordham Hill in the Bronx by Equitable Life Assurance (1949, Leonard Schultz).

The Limited-profit Housing Companies Law of 1955 (known as MITCHELL–LAMA) greatly expanded limited-dividend development. Many of the housing projects built during the two following decades were financed by Mitchell–Lama mortgages and tax exemptions, in return for which landlords agreed to accept limited rents. The best-known middle-income projects of these years were Penn Station South in Manhattan (1962, Jessor), Co-op City in the Bronx (1968–70, Jessor), Starrett City in Queens (1976, Jessor), Riverbend in Manhattan (1967, Davis, Brody), and 1199 Plaza in Manhattan (1974, Hodna/Stageburg). Mitchell–Lama was eventually terminated because of inflation during the mid 1970s, rent increases, and tenant strikes. In later years the principles of limited-dividend housing were adopted by such nonprofit entities as the Urban Development Corporation (1968), the Battery Park City Authority (1966), and local development corporations.

James Ford: *Slums and Housing* (Cambridge: Harvard University Press, 1936)

Richard Plunz: *A History of Housing in New York City: Dwelling Type and Social Change in the American Metropolis* (New York: Columbia University Press, 1990)

Richard Plunz

Limited-profit Housing Companies Law. See MITCHELL–LAMA.

Limón, José (Arcadia) (*b* Culiacán, Mexico, 12 Jan 1908; *d* Flemington, N.J., 2 Dec 1972). Dancer and choreographer. He emigrated to the United States at the age of seven, in 1928 moved to New York City to study painting, and learned modern dance at the studio of Doris Humphrey and Charles Weidman. In 1947 he formed his own company, which became the first to tour internationally under the auspices of the U.S. Department of State. He also taught at the Juilliard School and the American Dance Festival at Connecticut College. Limón's majestic bearing contributed to his lyrical yet powerful style. He emphasized human dignity and worth in such works as *The Moor's Pavane*, *Emperor Jones*, *Missa Brevis*, and *The Traitor*. His company continued to thrive after his death.

Margaret Latimer

José Limón in Day on Earth *by Doris Humphrey*

Lincoln, Abraham (*b* Hardin County, Ky., 12 Feb 1809; *d* Washington, 15 April 1865). Sixteenth president of the United States. He made his first visit to New York City on 26 February 1860, while campaigning for the Republican presidential nomination. He stayed at the Astor House on Barclay and Vesey streets, attended services at Plymouth Church in Brooklyn, where he heard a sermon by Henry Ward Beecher, and visited the Five Points. The next day he had his photograph taken at Mathew Brady's studio on 643 Broadway, and then delivered one of the most important speeches of his career before an audience of about fifteen hundred in the Great Hall of Cooper Union. In his speech he defended the federal government's constitutional authority to control slavery in the territories, and denounced what he said were false accusations against the Republican Party. He concluded by declaring: "Let us have faith that right makes might, and in that faith, let us, to the end, dare to do our duty as we understand it." He left the city on 28 February. After being elected president with about one third of the city's votes, he returned on 19 February 1861, en route from his home in Springfield, Illinois, to his inauguration in Washington. He stayed again at the Astor House, where he delivered a brief address on the day of his arrival. On 20 February, after having breakfast at the mansion of Moses Hicks Grinnell on 5th Avenue and 14th Street, he attended a reception at City Hall given by Mayor Fernando Wood. That night he heard Giuseppe Verdi's opera *Un Ballo in Maschera* at the Academy of Music on 14th Street before leaving the city early the next morning.

After Lincoln's assassination his funeral train arrived in New York City early on 24 April. The cortège followed a route from Desbrosses Street to City Hall Park, and Lincoln's body lay in state at City Hall from 1 p.m. until noon the next day, when the cortège traveled up Broadway to the depot of the Hudson River Railroad.

Frank Scaturro

Lincoln Center for the Performing Arts. The largest performing arts complex in the United States, situated on the West Side of Manhattan and bounded by 66th Street, Columbus Avenue, 62nd Street, and Amsterdam Avenue. Plans for the center took shape in 1954, at a time when the Metropolitan Opera, the New York Philharmonic, and the Juilliard School were all in need of new facilities. The site was chosen by Robert Moses with the aim of revitalizing a decaying area consisting largely of retail stores and tenements; financial backing was provided by John D. Rockefeller Jr., John D. Rockefeller III, and several others. A charter was granted in 1955, construction began on 21 May 1959, and over the following decade the buildings were completed and occupied: Philharmonic Hall (first performance on 23 September 1962, name changed to Avery Fisher Hall in 1973), the New York State Theatre (performance venue of the New York City Ballet from 1964 and of the New York City Opera from 1966), the Library and Museum of the Performing Arts (completed 1965, later renamed New York Public Library for the Performing Arts), the Metropolitan Opera House (first performance on 16 September 1966), the Juilliard School (completed 1969 and including Alice Tully Hall), and the Lincoln Center Theater (housing what eventually became the Vivian Beaumont and Mitzi E. Newhouse theaters). Lincoln Center Plaza, an amphitheater, and an underground parking garage were also built. Two affiliated companies were formed in 1969: the Film Society of Lincoln Center and the Chamber Music Society of Lincoln Center, a resident ensemble that undertook a schedule of regular performances at Alice Tully Hall.

During the following decades Lincoln Center became nationally and internationally known through features such as the "Mostly Mozart Festival" and broadcasts of concerts through public radio and television programs such as "Live at Lincoln Center." The School of American Ballet became an affiliate in 1987. All the organizations at Lincoln Center collaborated on a project for the first time in 1991–92, when they devised an ambitious program to honor the bicentenary of Mozart's death by performing all his works in more than five hundred concerts. A series of jazz concerts was inaugurated in 1991, and in the same year the Samuel B. and David Rose Building (twenty-eight stories) was completed, the first new building on the site in more than twenty years. The building houses

name, is now the borough headquarters of the department of parks and recreation.

John J. Gallagher

Litchfield Villa. Historic house in Brooklyn, at Prospect Park West between 4th and 5th streets. It was built between 1853 and 1857 as a country residence for Edwin C. Litchfield, an attorney, railroad financier, and real-estate speculator who invested in land in Brooklyn from the 1850s. Designed in an Italianate style by the distinguished architect Alexander Jackson Davis, it was called Grace Hill by the Litchfield family. The house was incorporated into Prospect Park and in 1892 was made the headquarters of the parks department of Brooklyn; it received a two-story addition in 1911. In the 1940s the stucco exterior and imitation stone façade were removed. The villa is notable for its size, square tower, and rich detailing. Carriage houses and a stable are nearby.

Historic Houses in New York City Parks (New York: Department of Parks and Recreation / Historic House Trust of New York City, 1989)

Jonathan Kuhn

literary agents. The rise of the literary agent in England and the United States coincided with the growth of the literary marketplace in the early nineteenth century. The Scottish émigré James Lawson arrived in New York City in 1815 and worked with authors like William Cullen Bryant, James Kirke Paulding, Edgar Allan Poe, and John Greenleaf Whittier; he made contacts with publishers and editors by doing them small favors and did not charge authors a fee for his services. Park Benjamin, best known as the editor of *Brother Jonathan*, established an informal agency in the city in the 1840s. By the 1860s his advertisements announced that for $10 he would give advice on a manuscript, which if it appealed to him he would recommend to a publisher. Writers were also assisted in their dealings with publishers by the Atheneum Bureau of Literature (1878), the New York Bureau of Literary Revision (1882), the Writer's Literary Bureau (1887), and the Author's League of America (1912), which later came to include the Authors Guild and the Dramatists Guild. With the passage of the International Copyright Act in 1891 the need for agents grew. Between 1892 and 1898 Paul Revere Reynolds (1864–1944) represented a number of leading British publishers in New York City, as well as such English authors as H. G. Wells and Joseph Conrad and (from 1895) the American authors Stephen Crane, Ellen Glasgow, and Frank Norris. Reynolds's authors paid him 10 percent of the money they earned on sales of their books but had no contracts with him. Before the turn of the century many of the leading agents were women: Flora May Holly (1868–1960), who began as an editorial assistant at the *Bookman* in the mid 1890s and by the end of the decade established a literary agency at 156 5th Avenue, worked with authors like Gertrude Atherton, Noël Coward, and Theodore Dreiser, edited romances and detective stories to make them more salable, and at her home held regular gatherings for literary figures; Elisabeth Marbury (1856–1933) represented many French dramatists and the dramatic works of English authors like George Bernard Shaw and Oscar Wilde; and Alice Kauser began as an employee of Marbury and later opened her own agency. Notwithstanding the objections of publishers like Henry Holt who maintained that agents were ruining publishing, in the 1930s literary agents became increasingly important in placing manuscripts with book and magazine publishers, and women continued to be strongly represented in the field: Ann Watkins, a leading agent in the 1940s, built her business on knowing the preferences of editors, Elizabeth Nowell of the Maxim Lieber Agency shaped Thomas Wolfe's drafts into magazine-length segments, and Helen M. Strauss in 1944 became the first literary agent to work at the William Morris Agency, where later Berta Kaslow also worked. Other important literary agents included Harold Ober, who edited some of F. Scott Fitzgerald's magazine pieces, Elizabeth McKee of the Harold Matson Company, Bernice Baumgarten of Brandt and Brandt, Alan C. Collins and Edith Haggard of the Curtis Brown Agency, Bertha Lausner, and Andrew Wylie.

James Hepburn: *The Author's Empty Purse and the Rise of the Literary Agent* (London: Oxford University Press, 1968)

James L. W. West III: *American Authors and the Literary Marketplace since 1900* (Philadelphia: University of Pennsylvania Press, 1988)

Marc H. Aronson

Literary Digest. Weekly periodical of news, art, and politics, launched in 1890 by Isaac Kauffman Funk (1839–1912), a southern clergymen and a founder of Funk and Wagnalls Publishing Company. It was one of the first publications to take extensive public opinion polls, and it accurately forecast the results of the presidential elections of 1924 and 1928. By 1927 it had a circulation of more than 1.5 million, a figure surpassed only by the *Saturday Evening Post.* The publication received unwelcome notoriety in 1936 when it predicted that the Republican presidential candidate Alfred M. Landon would defeat President Franklin D. Roosevelt, a prediction that proved embarrassingly inaccurate when Roosevelt was reelected in a landslide. This along with the ascendancy of *Time* and *Newsweek* irrevocably damaged the fortunes of *Literary Digest*, which merged with *Time* in 1938.

James Bradley

literature. New York City became a literary center in colonial times. Its natural features were celebrated in the national literature of the Knickerbocker group during the early nineteenth century; its growth and colossal scale in later years became symbols of both hope and despair, darkness and light.

1. To 1900

The first literary description of Manhattan was written by Giovanni da Verrazano about his exploration of the surrounding waterways in 1524:

> In termine di leghe cento trovammo un sito molto ameno posto in fra dui piccoli colli eminenti . . . La gente . . . vestiti di penne di uccelli di varii colori, venivano verso di noi allegramente, mettendo grandissimi gridi di admiratione.
>
> After a hundred leagues we found a very agreeable place between two small but prominent hills . . . The people . . . dressed in birds' feathers of various colors, and they came toward us joyfully, uttering loud cries of wonderment.

One of the first poets in New Amsterdam was Jacob Steendam, a clerk for the Dutch West India Company who sent "The Complaint of New Amsterdam to Her Mother" to the Netherlands for publication in 1659, followed by "The Praise of New Amsterdam" in 1661. Freedom of the press in the colonies was first established in New York in 1735 by the trial of John Peter Zenger, editor of the *New-York Weekly Journal*, who had been charged with libel for attacking Governor William Cosby but acquitted by a colonial court. Philosophers and polemicists of the American Revolution were some of the first writers in English in the city, which had a strong faction of militant revolutionaries as well as the largest Tory population in the colonies. One well-known political satirist was Philip Freneau, who wrote poetry and fiction as a student at Princeton University and in 1775 returned to the city to write such poems as "American Liberty" and "Libera Nos Domine." During a varied career that included a stint as the captain of a privateer during the war, he focused on lyrical poetry that became his best-known work, some of it suffused with a sense of the sea. Under the name Publius the statesmen Alexander Hamilton, John Jay, and James Madison (one of Freneau's eleven classmates at Princeton) wrote eighty-five essays in 1787 and 1788 urging the ratification of the Constitution; these were published in the city's newspapers and collected as *The Federalist*, the country's first literary classic.

After the revolution New York City grew popular as the setting for works of fiction. Susanna Rowson, a writer from New England, based her novel *Charlotte Temple, a Tale of Truth* (1791) on a story from the city; it went through two hundred editions and was unequaled as a best-seller until the publication in 1852 of Harriet Beecher Stowe's *Uncle Tom's Cabin.* The yellow fever epidemic of 1798 provided material for such Gothic novels as

Arthur Mervyn (1799) by Charles Brockden Brown, who moved to the city from Philadelphia and boarded with the critic and playwright William Dunlap. From 1809 installments of Washington Irving's satiric *A History of New York* were published as a hoax under the pseudonym Diedrich Knickerbocker by the *New York Evening Post*; the entire collection was later published as a book about New Amsterdam "from the Beginning of the World to the End of the Dutch Dynasty" and became the first work of American fiction known abroad. The name "Knickerbocker" became a nickname for New Yorker and was adopted by a group of writers seeking to develop a national literature from the 1820s. One of its principal exponents was James Fenimore Cooper, who in 1821 published *The Spy*, a novel based on a story told to him by Jay. By 1825 the Cooper Club, or the Lunch, was formed by such literary men as Cooper, Dunlap, Fitz-Greene Halleck, the poet William Cullen Bryant, the inventor Samuel F. B. Morse, the publisher Charles Wiley, and James Kent, author of the *Commentaries on American Law* (1826–30). The Knickerbockers looked to the landscape as a source of national pride and set much of their writing in woods, fields, rivers, prairies, and mountains. The first American sea novel, *The Pilot* (1823), was written by Cooper, who had served in the navy and sought to improve on Sir Walter Scott's *The Pirate*.

The growth of newspaper publishing from the 1830s helped to make the city the nation's publishing capital by the 1840s, attracting some of the most important writers of the day. The most influential newspaper was the *New York Tribune*, launched in 1841 by Horace Greeley to educate readers morally, politically, and culturally. It was the first newspaper distributed nationally and had many readers in the frontier states, where its influence was said to be second only to that of the Bible. As a young man Walt Whitman worked for the *Aurora* in Manhattan and for several newspapers in Brooklyn including the *Brooklyn Eagle*, which he edited in 1846–47. After booksellers refused to handle *Leaves of Grass* he published it himself in 1855. He called himself "manhattanese" and wrote of the city in the poem "Mannahatta":

My city's fit and noble name resumed,
Choice aboriginal name, with marvelous beauty, meaning,
A rocky founded island — shores where ever gayly dash the coming,
going, hurrying sea waves.

After visiting the city in 1831 to publish his third book of poetry, Edgar Allan Poe settled there in 1844 to become the editor of the *Broadway Journal*. During the same year he wrote a series of letters about the city for the *Columbia Spy* in Pennsylvania. He extolled the natural beauty of the area, especially the eastern edge of Manhattan, which he said contained some of the most picturesque sites for villas; he nonetheless pronounced such places "doomed" by the "spirit of Improvement," which he felt had "withered them with its acrid breath," and predicted that "in some thirty years every noble cliff [would] be a pier, and the whole island [would] be densely desecrated by buildings of brick, with portentous *facades* of brown-stone." Poe later based his book *The Mystery of Marie Rogêt* on a murder that occurred in Manhattan. He also became one of the city's best-known literary critics and by the end of his life had edited five magazines and made contributions to thirty more.

Other writers became influential in the following years. At Greeley's invitation Margaret Fuller moved from Cambridge, Massachusetts, to the city in 1844 to write for the *Tribune*. With Poe she was one of the most important literary critics of the day, and reviewed his work along with that of Carlyle, Shelley, Robert Browning, Lord Tennyson, Henry Wadsworth Longfellow, Nathaniel Hawthorne, Ralph Waldo Emerson, and James Russell Lowell; she also wrote exposés on local hospitals and prisons as well as *Woman in the Nineteenth Century* (1845), a treatise that was one of the principal intellectual inspirations for the American feminist movement. On leaving for Europe in 1846 she wrote: "New York is the focus, the point where American and European interests converge . . . Twenty months have presented me with a richer and more varied exercise for thought and life, than twenty years could in any other part of these United States." Herman Melville, a descendent of British, Dutch, and French settlers, grew up in the city and left to work as a sailor. After returning in 1845 he wrote the novels *Typee* (1846) and *Omoo* (1847), inspired by his adventures in the Marquesas and in Moorea, Tahiti. During these years he sought out such writers as Irving and Bryant and enjoyed spirited evenings with Evert A. Duyckinck, who wrote the *Cyclopaedia of American Literature* (1855) and worked as an editor for the publishers John Wiley and G. P. Putnam. Between 1847 and 1850 Melville wrote *Mardi*, *Redburn*, and *White-Jacket* and began *Moby-Dick*, which he completed after moving to the Berkshires.

Writers were attracted to the city by the growing Book publishing industry, which during the nineteenth century consisted of such firms as D. Appleton; Dodd, Mead; Doubleday, Page; E. P. Dutton; Harper and Brothers; Henry Holt; G. P. Putnam's Sons; and Charles Scribner's Sons. After mid century a number of writers rose to prominence from the newly fashionable area around Gramercy Park and Madison Square. As a boy in the late 1840s Henry James spent much time at his grandmother's house on Washington Square and heard Poe's stories from his elder brother William; he spent most of his life in Europe and returned only periodically to New York City, where he feared that provincialism would make him into a literary hack. He wrote about life in the city's upper classes during the 1830s and 1840s in the novel *Washington Square* (1881). One of his associates was Edith Wharton, who was born at 14 West 23rd Street and related to the city's most prominent families. As a child she read the collected works of Irving, an old family friend, and while living on Madison Avenue as a young woman she published some of her first poems in *Scribner's*, *Harper's*, and the *Century*. Emma Lazarus, whose father formed the Knickerbocker Club, in 1886 saw her sonnet "New Colossus" inscribed on the pedestal of the Statue of Liberty. In 1888 William Dean Howells took an apartment in Stuyvesant Square, signaling that the country's literary center had shifted from New England to New York City. He called for a new realism and strove for it in *A Hazard of New Fortunes* (1890), which he wrote while working as a columnist for *Harper's New Monthly Magazine*. Considering the city the only one that belonged to the whole country, he often depicted it as a place of limitless opportunity where capitalists and revolutionaries and the rich and the poor coexisted and came into conflict. By the turn of the century Washington Square drew writers from all over the country; Mark Twain, at the height of his popularity, lived on 10th Street.

During the last decade of the nineteenth century themes of disillusionment dominated literary works produced in the city. In a series of articles for the *Sun* and in his book *How the Other Half Lives* (1890), Jacob A. Riis described the dire conditions in neighborhoods inhabited by immigrants, especially the Five Points, a slum so loathsome that it had shocked even Charles Dickens during a visit in 1842. Riis's work influenced Lincoln Steffens, who moved to the city from San Francisco in 1892 after attending universities in Europe, and Stephen Crane, who wrote the first draft of *Maggie: A Girl of the Streets* (1893) before he ever saw the Bowery. Crane lived with friends in a studio at the Art Students League on East 23rd Street, where he wrote *The Red Badge of Courage* (1895) before going to war. The building was also the setting of Howells's novel *The Coast of Bohemia* (1893). After moving to the city from Chicago, Theodore Dreiser settled in Greenwich Village in 1895. Living on West 102nd Street from 1899, he wrote about the sparsely populated West Side in *Sister Carrie* (1900), the first "city novel," which treated themes of alienation, materialism, mechanization, the breakdown of tradition, and the conflict between the artist and society; these ideas preoccupied novelists in the following decades. About this time *McClure's Magazine* was launched by S. S. McClure, a publisher from Illinois shaped by the abolitionist, feminist, and temperance movements. He assembled a staff of writers that included Steffens, Ida Tarbell, William Allen White, Ray Stannard Baker, and Frank Norris, who on moving to the city from San Francisco in 1898 commented: "Of all the ambitions of the Great Unpublished, the one that is strongest, the most abiding, is the ambition to get to New York." McClure infused muckraking with art and authority and named Willa Cather, a teacher in Pittsburgh, the managing editor of the magazine. The issue dated January 1903 included articles that set a standard in journalism, including those on the Standard Oil Company by Tarbell, on corruption in Minneapolis by Steffens, and on the violent union struggles in the Pennsylvania coal fields by Baker. The Tenderloin, an area of bars, dance halls, brothels, and gambling houses along 6th Avenue between 14th and 47th streets, was romanticized in the short stories of O. Henry (pseudonym of William Sydney Porter), who moved to the city in 1902 and wrote: "Silent, grim, colossal, the big city has ever stood against its revilers. They call it hard as iron, they say that no pulse of pity beats in its bosom; they compare its streets with lonely forests and deserts of lava." By 1903 Porter produced a story a week for $100 for the *Sunday World.*

2. After 1900

Literature in the city took new directions after the turn of the century. Howells complained of commercialism in 1902: "New York society has not taken to our literature. New York publishes it, criticizes it, and circulates it, but I doubt if New York society much reads it or cares for it, and New York is therefore by no means the literary centre that Boston once was, though a large number of our literary men live in or about New York . . . New York is a vast mart, and literature is one of the things marketed here." Ambitious literary ventures were undertaken in other quarters. In 1910 W. E. B. Du Bois moved to the city to edit the *Crisis*, published by the National Association for the Advancement of Colored People as the first magazine devoted to the work of black writers. For a number of years James Weldon Johnson lived in the neighborhood of black artists and writers between 33rd and 23rd streets and 6th and 7th avenues. Of the city he wrote: "New York City is the most fatally fascinating thing in America. She sits like a great witch at the gate of the country, showing her alluring white face and hiding her crooked hands and feet under the folds of her wide garments — constantly enticing thousands." He published the novel *The Autobiography of an Ex-colored Man* in 1912 and moved to Harlem in 1914. During these years the row houses and elegant apartment buildings of the West Side attracted Ellen Glasgow, Sara Teasdale, Edna Ferber, and Marc Connelly and later Sinclair Lewis and Fanny Hurst; this was also the neighborhood where Anaïs Nin, Nathanael West, J. D. Salinger, and Dorothy Parker grew up. Literary circles also formed in Greenwich Village, a center for artists and intellectuals described as an "American bohemia" by Max Eastman, a professor of philosophy at Columbia University. Journals and "little magazines" began publication and thrived there between 1910 and 1920. One of the first was the *Masses*, a leftist magazine of politics, art, literature, and humor edited by Eastman from 1912. Among its contributors were the painter John Sloan, the poet Louis Untermeyer, and the war correspondent John Reed. The government eventually charged the staff of the *Masses* with resisting the First World War and interfering with enlistment.

Many writers came to prominence as contributors to publications in Greenwich Village. The *Smart Set* was taken over in 1914 by George Jean Nathan and H. L. Mencken, for fifteen years one of the most authoritative voices in American letters. Mencken wrote a column for the magazine and as one of its editors published work by Eugene O'Neill, F. Scott Fitzgerald, and Joyce. From about 1915 a number of writers in the city were associated with the Provincetown Players, including Steffens, Reed, O'Neill, Dreiser, Edna St. Vincent Millay, Walter Lippmann, and John Dos Passos. About 1916–17 writers whom Gertrude Stein called the "lost generation" first moved to Greenwich Village, which according to Malcolm Cowley was attractive for its literary culture, cheap living, and welcoming environment for young writers. Among them were Hart Crane, Edmund Wilson, Matthew Josephson, and E. E. Cummings. *Others* published some of the first work by William Carlos Williams, Wallace Stevens, and Marianne Moore. *Seven Arts*, a magazine that lasted for only a year in 1917, engaged Waldo Frank and Van Wyck Brooks as editors and published O'Neill's first short story, Sherwood Anderson's Winesburg stories, and Claude McKay's "Harlem Dancer" (printed under the pseudonym Eli Edwards), signaling the beginning of the Harlem Renaissance; the magazine also published work by Dos Passos, D. H. Lawrence, S. N. Behrman, Robert Frost, Carl Sandburg, Amy Lowell, and Stephen Vincent Benét. Reed wrote *Ten Days That Shook the World* (1919), his account of the Russian Revolution, while awaiting trial on charges of sedition in connection with articles that he had written for the *Masses*. A number of Jewish newspapers published on the Lower East Side were also important venues for fiction writers. As the editor of the *Jewish Daily Forward* Abraham Cahan published work by Sholom Aleichem, Sholem Asch, I. J. Singer, and Isaac Bashevis Singer; he also produced a novel, *The Rise of David Levinsky* (1917). Emma Goldman published the work of Strindberg and Ibsen in *Mother Earth*. Several publishing firms opened to handle the work of European writers as well as experimental literature and works about radical politics, a subject that often plunged them into conflict with censors. Among these firms was Boni and Liveright, the first to publish the work of Eastman, Reed, and O'Neill.

Stylish literary entertainments were the hallmark of such magazines as the *Smart Set*, the *American Mercury*, and *Vanity Fair*, which began publication before 1920 and included on its staff Parker, Robert Benchley, and Robert E. Sherwood; the three ate lunch together every day at the Algonquin Hotel and were soon joined by Alexander Woollcott, drama critic for the *New York Times*, the columnist Heywood Broun, and Franklin P. Adams, who reported the group's witticisms in his column for the *New York World*, "The Conning Tower." Later called the Algonquin Round Table, the group also included such playwrights as Ferber, Connelly, and George S. Kaufman. The *Little Review*, a magazine begun in Chicago by Margaret Anderson, moved to the city in 1917 and accepted experimental fiction and poetry by such writers as Hart Crane and Djuna Barnes. Its editors gave Joyce's *Ulysses* its first printing, in installments from 1918 to 1920, and were fined $100 in an obscenity suit brought by John S. Sumner, head of the New York Society for the Suppression of Vice. The foremost little magazine was the *Dial*, a publication initially associated with transcendentalists in Boston and edited by Fuller and Emerson. It moved to New York in 1917 and by 1920, under Scofield Thayer and J. Sibley Watson Jr., was a nonpolitical monthly magazine devoted to the "best of European and American art, experimental and conventional" in the words of Moore, its editor from 1925 until it ceased publication in 1929.

The 1920s saw the flourishing of a literary aesthetic rooted in the vast array of experiences available in the growing city. Inspired in part by James, Wharton wrote of the élite of Washington Square during the Gilded Age in *The Age of Innocence* (1920, Pulitzer Prize). Fitzgerald's *This Side of Paradise* (1920) set a tone for what Wilson called "jazz-age romanticism." In *The Bridge* (1930) Hart Crane celebrated the Brooklyn Bridge as a symbol of the beauty made possible by a fusion of art and technology. Dos Passos depicted city life in *Manhattan Transfer* (1925) as a panorama of disparate lives and voices, interwoven and simultaneous, that was described by Jean-Paul Sartre as a "social voice." The same year saw the publication of Fitzgerald's *The Great Gatsby*, Dreiser's *An American Tragedy*, and Lewis's *Arrowsmith*. Several writers became known for their works based on experiences outside the city: Cather, who wrote about Nebraska, Sherwood Anderson, who wrote about Ohio, and Thomas Wolfe, who moved to the city in 1923 and wrote about North Carolina. The city attracted such writers in part because it was by this time acknowledged as the country's publishing center. By 1924 Boni and Liveright was one of the most influential publishers. It produced works by Freud, Dreiser, O'Neill, Sherwood Anderson, George Moore, Gertrude Atherton, Robinson Jeffers, Henrik Van Loon, and Rose Macaulay, and also founded the Modern Library, a series that sold more than 300,000 copies a year of works by such renowned writers as Freud, Faulkner, Anderson, Hemingway, O'Neill, Cummings, and Hart Crane. The editors were appreciated for their attentiveness and for their "vivid, impetuous, high-living" style, according to Lillian Hellman, who worked there as a reader. Another important house was Alfred A. Knopf, which published Mencken, Nathan, and Cather.

The literary world of the city became increasingly fashionable from the mid 1920s. One of its most important outlets was the *New Yorker*, a magazine aimed at sophisticated readers that began publication in 1925. Edited by Harold Ross, the magazine published E. B. White, James Thurber, and Dwight Macdonald. Other well-known critics and editors of these years included Cowley and Josephson, the editors of *Broom*, an international magazine of the arts, and Mark Van Doren, literary editor of the *Nation*. Wilson took over as literary editor of the *New Republic* in 1928 and was succeeded in 1929 by Cowley, who made the magazine a literary force; he often wrote the lead reviews himself and was admired by such writers as Alfred Kazin, who began his career as a reviewer for the magazine. Commercial publishing and the theater were centered in midtown Manhattan, where writers, journalists, playwrights, critics, and actors stayed in the great hotels and gathered in restaurants, speakeasies, and salons. A well-known figure of the literary high life was John O'Hara, who moved to the city in 1927 and frequented speakeasies, Sardi's, and the Algonquin; during the 1930s he wrote *Butterfield 8*, named for the telephone exchange for the fashionable East Side, and *Appointment in Samarra*.

The Harlem Renaissance reached its height during the 1920s and 1930s. Some of the most important figures in the movement were Charles Johnson, editor of *Opportunity* (the magazine of the National Urban League), Jessie Redmon Fauset, editor of the *Crisis*, and Alain Locke; they encouraged black writers and helped them to get their work published. Zora Neale Hurston, the daughter of a tenant farmer, moved to Harlem and won a prize for a story in *Opportunity*; she later became an anthropologist and wrote the novels *Jonah's Gourd Vine* (1934) and *Their Eyes Were Watching God* (1937). Rudolph Fisher, who moved to the city to study bacteriology and pathology at the Columbia College of Physicians and Surgeons, became a radiologist, ran a hospital, and also wrote *The Walls of Jericho* and *The Conjure Man Dies*, the first mystery dealing entirely with black characters. In 1925 Fauset, Locke, and Charles Johnson produced the anthology *The New Negro*, which included work by Fisher, Hurston, Countee Cullen, Arna Bontemps, Wallace Thurman, Nella Larsen, and Jean Toomer. The writer and photographer Carl Van Vechten published *Nigger Heaven* in 1926, and in 1928 McKay's *Home to Harlem* became a best-seller. After Richard Wright published *Uncle Tom's Children* in 1938 many black writers turned to social realism in the 1940s. On his first day in Harlem in the summer of 1936 Ralph Ellison met Langston Hughes, who arranged for him to meet Wright; Ellison was later one of the first to read Wright's manuscript for *Native Son* (1940). Ellison considered Harlem of the late 1930s and early 1940s both a haunting "ruin" and a place of liberation and light. The neighborhood became the setting for his novel *Invisible Man* (1952), in his words the story of a man traveling "through blackness to light . . . from ignorance to enlightenment; invisibility to visibility." Harlem of the same era was also used by James Baldwin as the setting for his novel *Go Tell It on the Mountain* (1953).

The vibrancy and contrasts of life in the city continued to preoccupy writers in the 1930s. Dashiell Hammett finished writing *The Maltese Falcon* there in 1930, and Hellman achieved success with the plays *The Children's Hour* (1934) and *The Little Foxes* (1939). *Esquire* was launched in 1933 by Arnold Gingrich and in its first issue included pieces by Hemingway, Dos Passos, Hammett, and Erskine Caldwell. The magazine became immediately successful and in 1936 published Fitzgerald's *The Crack-up* in three installments. In describing the city during these years John Steinbeck wrote: "All of everything is concentrated here, population, theater, art, writing, publishing, importing, business, murder, mugging, luxury, poverty. It is all of everything. It goes all night. It is tireless and its air is charged with energy." White marvelled at the city's variety and complexity: "I am twenty-two blocks from where Rudolph Valentino lay in state, eight blocks from where Nathan Hale was executed, five blocks from the publisher's office where Ernest Hemingway hit Max Eastman on the nose, four miles from where Walt Whitman sat sweating out editorials for the *Brooklyn Eagle*, thirty-four blocks from the street Willa Cather lived in when she came to New York to write books about Nebraska." For Wolfe the city aroused fascination but also feelings of "naked homelessness, rootlessness, and loneliness." His books *Of Time and the River* (1935), *The Web and the Rock* (1939), and *You Can't Go Home Again* (1940) were edited meticulously by Maxwell Perkins of Scribner's. For John P. Marquand the city was an "indefinable combination of triumph, discouragement and memories" and provided the setting for the novels *So Little Time* (1943) and *Point of No Return* (1949). His work was also edited by Perkins, as was that of Fitzgerald, Hemingway, and Caldwell. A group of Jewish writers, many of them from families of immigrants in Brooklyn, became well-known critics. Among these were Kazin, Irving Howe, editor of *Dissent*, Norman Podhoretz, editor of *Commentary*, and Delmore Schwartz, who described some of these writers' conflicts in the story "In Dreams Begin Responsibilities," published in 1937 to great acclaim in the first issue of *Partisan Review* (launched by Philip Rahv and William Phillips). Henry Roth wrote of a childhood spent on "snug, homogeneous, orthodox 9th Street" and in Harlem in *Call It Sleep* (1934).

The 1940s saw another generation of writers emerge in the city. Barnes settled at Patchin Place after a number of years in Paris, where in 1936 she published *Nightwood*. After winning a Rockefeller Fellowship and moving to the city in 1939, Tennessee Williams found work waiting on tables and reciting poetry; he produced a series of plays during the 1940s and 1950s that were well received, including *The Glass Menagerie* (1944) and *A Streetcar Named Desire* (1947). James Agee lived in Greenwich Village and worked for *Fortune* while writing a book published posthumously as *A Death in the Family* (1957). Nin left Paris for New York City, where she published *Winter of Artifice* (1939) and *Under a Glass Bell* (1944). William Styron arrived from North Carolina in 1947, took a writing class at the New School taught by Hiram Haydn, and finished *Lie Down in Darkness* (1951) at twenty-six. Columbia University became a literary center where Van Doren, winner of the Pulitzer Prize for poetry in 1940, taught such students as John Berryman, Thomas Merton, Herb Gold, Allen Ginsberg, and Jack Kerouac. His brother Carl Van Doren, also a literary editor of the *Nation* and a teacher at Columbia, urged Kazin to write his critical work *On Native Grounds: An Interpretation of Modern American Prose Literature* (1942). Lionel Trilling succeeded Van Doren as the preeminent literary figure at Columbia.

After the Second World War the *New Yorker* became more serious under the direction of William Shawn. In 1946 it published John Hersey's *Hiroshima*, the first in a series of influential nonfiction pieces that began as articles in the magazine and later appeared in book form; others included Rachel Carson's *Silent Spring* (1963) and Jonathan Schell's *The Fate of the Earth*. The magazine was also known for its profiles by A. J. Liebling, Lillian Ross, Joseph Mitchell, and Truman Capote, whose piece on Marlon Brando was especially revealing.

By the 1940s many of the city's writers moved to Brooklyn. For five years a house in Brooklyn Heights was shared by Carson McCullers, W. H. Auden, the theatrical designer Oliver Smith, and Jane and Paul Bowles; Wright also lived there briefly while writing

Native Son. In another house in Brooklyn, Norman Mailer wrote *The Naked and the Dead* (1948) and Arthur Miller wrote *All My Sons* (1947), which was followed by *Death of a Salesman* (1949, Pulitzer Prize) and *A View from the Bridge* (1955, Pulitzer Prize), a work set in Red Hook. *Partisan Review* attracted articles by such critics as Macdonald, F. W. Dupee, Mary McCarthy, Harold Rosenberg, Meyer Schapiro, and Lionel Abel. In 1953 it published a translation of Isaac Bashevis Singer's "Gimpel the Fool" by Saul Bellow, a Canadian who moved to the city and made it the setting of his novels *The Victim* (1947), *Seize the Day* (1956), *Herzog* (1964), *Mr. Sammler's Planet* (1969), and *Humboldt's Gift* (1975), an account of Schwartz's career as a *poète maudit.* The low rents of the East Village drew Mailer and members of a literary movement known as the beats during the 1950s. One of the first to live there was Ginsberg, in an apartment on East 7th Street; he was joined there in 1953 by William Burroughs, who wrote *Junkie* under the pseudonym William Lee. The year 1957 saw the publication of Kerouac's *On the Road* and Ginsberg's poem "Howl" in the *Evergreen Review.* During the same year Capote moved into the basement apartment of the house owned by Smith and wrote *Breakfast at Tiffany's* (1958), as well as the "nonfiction novel" *In Cold Blood* (1966). Kerouac wrote about the Lower East Side in *The Subterraneans* (1958), in a style that he called "spontaneous bop prosody."

During the 1950s the West Side came to be associated with a group of thinkers and writers that included Podhoretz, Howe, Kazin, Susan Sontag, Jason Epstein, Barbara Epstein, Murray Kempton, and Elizabeth Hardwick. Bellow and Joseph Heller also lived there, and a younger generation of poets settled on the East Side, among them Tuli Kupferberg, LeRoi Jones, Hubert Selby, Gilbert Sorrentino, Robert Creeley, and Diane Di Prima, who with Alan Marlowe opened the American Theatre for Poets. This theater produced Di Prima's one-act plays and those of Jones, Robert Duncan, Frank O'Hara, and Michael McClure, as well as dance programs and "happenings." Poetry readings were often given at Cafe le Metro and St. Mark's Church in the Bowery. The magazine *Umbra* attracted many black writers, including Jones, Larry Neal, Ishmael Reed, Toni Cade, and Nikki Giovanni. The *Paris Review* moved to the city toward the end of the decade and during the 1970s published a series of illuminating interviews with writers. During the 1960s George Plimpton's apartment on East 72nd Street became the one of the city's liveliest literary salons, and the only one, according to the journalist Gay Talese, that regularly drew together Hellman, Mailer, Macdonald, Styron, James Jones, Irwin Shaw, Philip Roth, Jack Gelber, Peter Matthiessen, Terry Southern, John Marquand Jr., and Blair Fuller.

In 1963 *Esquire* devoted an entire issue to literature that included pieces by and about Southern, Baldwin, Mailer, Bellow, Styron, Heller, Burroughs, Salinger, James Jones, John Cheever, Vladimir Nabokov, Robert Penn Warren, Edward Albee, Flannery O'Connor, and John Updike; the issue helped to establish the city as the country's preeminent literary center. The offerings of *Esquire* and the *New Yorker* led to a new brand of novelistic journalism in such works as Mailer's *The Armies of the Night* (1968, Pulitzer Prize) and *The Executioner's Song* (1979, Pulitzer Prize) and Tom Wolfe's *The Kandy-Kolored Tangerine-Flake Streamline Baby* (1965) and *The Right Stuff* (1979). Elements of fiction and journalism were also combined by E. L. Doctorow in *Ragtime* (1975). Works in more conventional forms included McCarthy's *The Group* (1963) and Shirley Hazzard's *The Transit of Venus* (1980).

Many of the writers who had become well known in the 1960s left the city during the 1970s and 1980s. In the mid 1990s New York City nonetheless remained the world's largest literary marketplace and a popular destination of those seeking to hone their skills and test their talents.

Susan Edmiston and Linda D. Cirino: *Literary New York: A History and Guide* (Boston: Houghton Mifflin, 1976; rev. Layton, Utah: Gibbs Smith, 1991)

See also Popular fiction.

Susan Edmiston

Lithuanians. Lithuanians first moved to New York City in large number during the second half of the nineteenth century; many were socialists and other revolutionaries fleeing a failed uprising against Russian domination in Lithuania and Poland. From the 1880s to 1914 a new majority consisted of farmers and unskilled workers who found employment in shipyards, manufacturing, and the garment industry. The newspapers *Lietuwiszka Gazieta* (Lithuanian Gazette, 1879–80) and *Unija* (Unity, 1884–85) were short-lived because of financial difficulties and internal editorial conflicts. The pro-socialist newspaper *Lietuwiszkasis Balsas* (The Lithuanian Voice, 1885–89; Jonas Sliupas, publisher) stressed the importance of Lithuanian heritage and called for the formation of a national Lithuanian organization. Soon after, the Lithuanian Alliance of America (1886–) was begun in Pennsylvania; it survived internal conflicts between clerics and communists and moved to New York City, where it became a fraternal and mutual benefit society and published the periodical *Tevyne* (Motherland, 1889–). Catholics accounted for much of the population and formed several churches: St. Mary of Angels (1894), St. George (1905), and the Annunciation of the Blessed Virgin (1914) in Brooklyn; Our Lady of Vilnius (1905) in Manhattan; and the Church of Transfiguration (1908) in Queens. The Roman Catholic Alliance issued the publication *Garsas* (The Sound, 1917–30). Liberals and moderates rallied around the privately run newspaper *Vienybe* (Unity, 1911–) and formed the Lithuanian National League in Brooklyn, which was associated with the Lithuanian Alliance of America. Under Antanas Bimba, editor of *Laisve* (Liberty, 1911–87), communists who supported the government in Moscow joined the Communist Party of America and launched a number of publications: *Darbas* (Labor, 1919–20) of Local 54 of the Amalgamated Workers Union, *Kommunistas* (1920–21), *Kova* (The Struggle, 1920–22), *Tiesa* (The Truth, 1922), *Sviesa* (Light, 1933–40), and *Siuvejas* (The Tailor, 1934). Communists who opposed Moscow published *Darbininku Tiesa* (Worker's Truth, 1922) and *Nauja Gadyne* (New Era, 1931–43). After the First World War the city became an international center of efforts for Lithuanian independence.

Many Lithuanians lived in Williamsburg before the Second World War and later moved elsewhere, especially to Long Island and New Jersey. In the World Fairs of 1939–40 and 1964–65 thousands of folk singers, hundreds of folk dancers, and dozens of choirs took part in the Lithuanian Days organized by local groups. The independence movement in the city intensified with the annexation of Lithuania by the Soviet Union in 1940. The years after the war saw an influx of refugees strongly opposed to communism, including many businessmen, bankers, government officials, teachers, architects, engineers, lawyers, scholars, musicians, writers, and artists; they formed a number of professional organizations, youth groups, and the Committee for a Free Lithuania (1951–). The Franciscan Fathers, based in Brooklyn, offered comprehensive social and cultural programs and also issued the publications *Aidai* (Echoes, 1950–), devoted to Lithuanian art, science, and politics, and *Darbininkas* (The Worker, 1955–), covering religious topics and local and international news. Local groups sponsored courses in Lithuanian language and culture at Fordham University (1957–69) and opened the Lithuanian Citizens Club in Queens and the Lithuanian Cultural Center (1974–) in Brooklyn, which amassed materials for extensive archives. Manyland Books, a publisher of works in Lithuanian and English, also opened in the city.

In the mid 1990s Lithuanians in New York City numbered between ten and twelve thousand, forming the largest Baltic community in New York City and the second-largest Lithuanian one in the United States (after that of Chicago). Most lived in central Brooklyn and in Woodhaven, Richmond Hills, and Jamaica in Queens. More than 90 percent were Catholic, the rest including a few evangelical Lutherans. Well-known Lithuanians in the city have included the writer and publisher Jonas Valaitis, the tennis player Vitas Gerulaitis, the composer Elizabeth Swados, and the film critic and producer Jonas Mekas.

Algirdas M. Budreckis: *The Lithuanians in America, 1651–1975: A Chronology and Fact Book* (Dobbs Ferry, N.Y.: Oceana, 1975)

Antanas Kucas: *Lithuanians in America* (Boston: Encyclopedia Lituanica, 1975)

Vladimir Wertsman

Little, Jacob (*b* 1796/7; *d* 1865). Speculator. During the 1830s he became the most prominent figure on Wall Street by developing innovative techniques for manipulating the price of stocks, especially those of railroad and canal companies. Because he specialized in making prices fall he was known as "the great bear of Wall Street," but he was equally adept at making prices rise: in 1834 he drove the price of the Morris Canal and Banking Company from $10 to $185 in less than two months. Little's schemes were not always successful, and after declaring bankruptcy three times he was effectively ruined by the crash of 1857 and died in poverty.

George Winslow

Little Africa. Name given to several black communities in New York City. It was first applied to what became the Five Points, an area composed of land grants made to Africans in 1659 by the Dutch West India Company. This area, adjacent to the Collect, was also known as Stagg Town, and remained a black area until the mid nineteenth century. It was the original site of the Abyssinian Baptist Church, opened on Worth Street in 1808 by free Anglo-Africans and Ethiopian sailors. The African Burial Ground was part of this community.

Toward the end of the eighteenth century many blacks left to settle in the area now bounded to the north by Bleecker Street, to the east by Mercer Street, and to the west by Thompson, Sullivan, MacDougal, and Carmine streets. It had been given to eleven Africans including Big Manuel in 1644 by the Dutch West India Company and was a buffer for the Dutch colony against local Indians, who repeatedly destroyed Europeans' farms. Abyssinian Baptist Church moved to this new Little Africa by the 1850s, first to Thompson Street and then to Waverly Place. The enclave eventually included the African Grove Theatre, an independent branch of the YMCA, and many businesses.

During the 1890s the name Little Africa was also applied to the area near Broadway and Harrison streets in Williamsburg.

Gilbert Osofsky: *Harlem: The Making of a Ghetto* (New York: Harper and Row, 1963)

M. A. Harris: *A Negro History Tour of Manhattan* (New York: Greenwood, 1968)

Jervis Anderson: *This Was Harlem: A Cultural Portrait, 1900–1950* (New York: Farrar, Straus and Giroux, 1982)

Sule Greg C. Wilson

Little Church around the Corner. See CHURCH OF THE TRANSFIGURATION (ii).

Little Germany. Alternative name of KLEINDEUTSCHLAND.

Little Italy. Neighborhood in lower Manhattan, bounded to the north by Houston Street, to the east by Mulberry Street, to the south by Canal Street, and to the west by Broadway. Italians first settled in the Five Points during the 1850s and efforts to set up a Roman Catholic parish for Italians began in 1858; the Church of St. Anthony of Padua was formed in 1866 by Franciscans of the Province of the Immaculate Conception, and its current Romanesque church at 153–57 Sullivan Street was dedicated on 10 June 1888. *Il Progresso*, an Italian-language daily newspaper, was launched in the neighborhood in 1880 by Carolo Barsotti. The parish of the Church of the Transfiguration (formerly Zion Episcopal Church) at 25 Mott Street was largely Italian by the 1880s, and a chapel that later became the Church of Our Lady of Pompeii opened at 25 Carmine Street on 8 May 1892. By the 1920s the neighborhood occupied an area roughly bounded to the north by West 4th Street and Houston Street, to the east by the Bowery, to the south by the Five Points and Canal Street, and to the west by Greenwich Village (which also was a large Italian settlement). Genoans, Calabrians, Neapolitans, and Sicilians settled in an area bounded by Houston Street, the Bowery, the Five Points, and Broadway; Piedmontese, Tuscans, and Neapolitans settled in an area bounded by West 4th Street, West Broadway, Canal Street, and the Hudson River. Immigrants from southern Italy first celebrated the Feast of San Gennaro along Mulberry Street about 1926.

In later years Little Italy diminished in size. The parish of the Church of the Transfiguration was largely Chinese by the 1950s, and much of Little Italy became part of Chinatown after 1968. In the mid 1990s the western boundary of Little Italy continued to recede as Chinatown expanded. The neighborhood remains well known for such restaurants as Umberto's Clamhouse (129 Mulberry Street), where in 1972 the organized-crime figure Joey Gallo was shot to death during a family dinner, and for its bakeries (including the Parisi Bakery on Mott Street).

John Horace Mariano: *The Italian Contribution to American Democracy* (Boston: Christopher, 1921), 18–22

Mary Elizabeth Brown

little magazines. Literary and political magazines devoted to work deemed unacceptable by publications of general circulation; their name, which became popular about the time of the First World War, came into use because the magazines rarely paid their contributors. The first little magazine in New York City was *M'lle New York* (1895–99), edited by Vance Thompson but dominated by its iconoclastic associate editor James Gibbons Huneker, the leader of a bohemian circle near Union Square. Printed on buff paper and illustrated in black and pink, it had an air of *fin de siècle* decadence tempered by the philosophy of Wilde and Nietzsche, and it poured scorn in equal measure on the city's literary élite and the notion of democratic culture. There were few little magazines from the time *M'lle New York* ceased publication until the "little renaissance" after 1910, when many magazines were published in Greenwich Village by intellectuals in revolt against conventional aesthetic, moral, and political standards. The editors delighted in outraging public taste and were will-

Mulberry Street, 1994

ing to lose money to do so. Although a few of the magazines became popular, most had a thousand subscribers or fewer and survived for less than a year. In addition to unknown writers they often published the most distinguished writers in the United States and Europe.

New York City soon became the national center of little magazines. Among the best-known were the *Masses* (1911–17), which focused on art and radical politics and was edited by Max Eastman from 1912; the *Pagan* (1916–22), which published such poets as Malcolm Cowley and Hart Crane; *Seven Arts* (1916–17), which published criticism by Waldo Frank, Van Wyck Brooks, and Randolph Bourne; and the *Quill* (1917–29). Among the less successful were *Rongwrong* (1917), the *Lyric* (1917–19), and several magazines published by Angelo Bruno. The *Little Review* began publication in Chicago in 1914 and in 1917 moved to New York City, where it published work by Ezra Pound, William Butler Yeats, T. S. Eliot, and Wyndham Lewis; after issuing James Joyce's *Ulysses* in serial form the editors, Margaret Anderson and Jane Heap, were prosecuted and fined, and the magazine moved to Paris in 1922.

Little magazines reached the height of their influence during the 1920s and 1930s. *Contact* (1920–23; 1932) published critical essays and poetry by William Carlos Williams, Robert McAlmon, E. E. Cummings, and S. J. Perelman. The *Dial* (1920–29) issued the work of Eliot, Pound, Cummings, Yeats, Marianne Moore, and D. H. Lawrence. Under the direction of Samuel Roth *Two Worlds* (1925–27) also published poetry as well as some of the first sections of Joyce's *Finnegans Wake* and engaged Pound as a contributing editor. *Fire!!: A Quarterly Devoted to the Younger Negro Artists* (1926), the most important little magazine of the Harlem Renaissance, was overseen by Wallace Thurman with Langston Hughes and Zora Neale Hurston. Like the *Masses* and the *Liberator*, the *New Masses* dealt with politics, satire, and aesthetics under the direction of Joseph Freeman (1926–28) and Michael Gold (1926–33); after 1933 it abandoned the little magazine format by turning away from art and the avant-garde and focusing exclusively on politics. A number of magazines were launched in the 1930s: the *Miscellany* (1930–31), *Fifth Floor Window* (1931–32), the *American Spectator* (1932–37), *Blast* (1933–34), the *Greenwich Villager* (1933–34), the *Latin Quarterly* (1933–34), *Manhattan Poetry Parade* (1936), and *Acorn* (1938). *Twice a Year* (1938) published articles on the arts and work by new writers, and staunchly defended civil liberties. *Partisan Review*, launched in 1934, was sympathetic to the left and soon became one of the most important literary journals in the country, publishing work by leading American and European writers. The little magazines of the early 1940s included *Vice Versa* (1940–42), which published new poetry and inveighed against established journals; *Decisions* (1941–42), a magazine dedicated to defending democracy, especially against Nazism, that published essays and poetry by Thomas Mann, W. H. Auden, and Somerset Maugham; *VV* (1942), which was devoted entirely to the plastic arts and promoted surrealism and psychology; and *Politics* (1944–49), edited by Dwight Macdonald. After the Second World War the influence of little magazines declined. Many left the city to become affiliated with universities.

Frederick J. Hoffman et al., eds.: *The Little Magazine: A History and Bibliography* (Princeton, N.J.: Princeton University Press, 1946)

Arthur F. Wertheim: *The New York Little Renaissance* (New York: New York University Press, 1976)

Elliot Anderson and Mary Kinzie, eds.: *The Little Magazine in America: A Modern Documentary History* (Yonkers, N.Y.: Pushcart, 1978)

Abby Arthur Johnson and Ronald Maberry Johnson: *Propaganda and Aesthetics: The Literary Politics of Afro-American Magazines in the Twentieth Century* (Amherst: University of Massachusetts Press, 1979)

Kevin Kenny

Little Neck. Neighborhood in the northeast corner of Queens, bounded to the north by Little Neck Bay, to the east by Nassau County, to the south by Grand Central Parkway, and to the west by 247th Street. It was originally inhabited by Matinecock Indians, a tribe of the Algonquin nation. With what is now Douglaston it was assigned in 1663 by the Dutch to Thomas Hicks, Thomas Ellison, and John Ellison; Richard Cornell soon settled there as well. During the American Revolution the area remained Loyalist but was despoiled by the thievery of Hessian and British soldiers. The best-known resident in the nineteenth century was Bloodgood H. Cutter, a wealthy and eccentric poet. In the 1850s and 1860s oystermen operated more than a dozen sloops and schooners at the foot of Old House Landing Road (now Little Neck Parkway) to supply clams and oysters to the surrounding population. The Old House was destroyed by fire on 31 May 1865; the railroad was extended to the area in the following year. Beers's map of 1873 shows Little Neck as a hamlet of twenty-three houses, a hotel, and a church at the intersection of Northern Boulevard and Little Neck Parkway. In 1906 the Rickert–Finlay Company laid out Westmoreland south of the railroad station, and in the following year Marathon Park was laid out just to the west. Waverly Hills was developed in 1908 south of Northern Boulevard between Little Neck Parkway and the Nassau line, followed by Little Neck Hills in 1914 between Browvale Lane and Little Neck Parkway. A large tract to the west between Browvale Lane and Douglaston Parkway was promoted as Douglaston Hills in 1924.

Vincent Seyfried

Little Red School House. Private elementary and secondary school opened by Elisabeth Irwin on East 16th Street in 1921 as an experiment in progressive education. The school stressed learning through experience, play, and self-expression and eschewed tests and grades. It was sponsored by the Public Education Association and was at first part of the city's public school system. Mayor John F. Hylan's hostility toward the school led to the condemnation of its first site, and the school was forced to move to Public School 61 and then to Public School 41 on Greenwich Avenue. In 1932 the Depression and a withdrawal of private funds led to attempts to close the school by the city's Board of Superintendents, but parents raised enough money to keep it open as a private school on 196 Bleecker Street. Students in the secondary grades of the Little Red School House attend the Elisabeth Irwin School, which occupies a building at 40 Charlton Street purchased in 1941.

Agnes De Lima: *The Little Red School House* (New York: Macmillan, 1942)

Alfonso J. Orsini

Little Review. Literary journal launched in Chicago in 1914 and moved in 1917 to New York City, where it was published from a basement office on West 14th Street. Under the astute leadership of its editor Margaret Anderson and her assistant Jane Heap, it sponsored experimental fiction and poetry. From March 1918 to 1920 it published James Joyce's *Ulysses* in installments, which led to the editors' conviction on charges of pandering obscenity and the destruction of four offending issues by the U.S. Post Office. The journal moved to Paris in the 1920s and ceased publication in 1929.

Margaret C. Anderson: *My Thirty Years' War: An Autobiography* (New York: Covici, Friede, 1930)

Jan Seidler Ramirez

Livermore, Jesse L(auriston) (*b* Shrewsbury, Mass., 26 July 1877; *d* New York City, 28 Nov 1940). Speculator. Brought up on a farm in Massachusetts, he began speculating in stocks as soon as he left school and became a millionaire before his thirtieth birthday. An expert in selling stocks short, he declared bankruptcy in 1915 but soon recovered and became one of the most famous speculators on Wall Street before the Depression by working with other large speculators to manipulate stock prices. In one of his largest deals he made more than $10 million by speculating on a fall in the price of wheat; at another time he increased the price of shares in the grocery firm Piggly-Wiggly by fifty points in one day. He did not recover from his fourth bankruptcy, in 1934, because the reforms of the New Deal outlawed stock market manipulation. In 1940 he published a book about his investment techniques called *How to Trade in Stocks*.

Paul Sarnoff: *Jesse Livermore, Speculator–King* (New York: Investors' Press, 1967)

George Winslow

Livingston. Neighborhood in north central Staten Island, bounded to the north by the Kill van Kull, to the east by the Snug Harbor Cultural Center, to the south by Castleton Avenue, and to the west by West New Brighton. It was developed as Elliotville in the 1840s by Samuel MacKenzie Elliot, a prominent eye surgeon who treated such prominent literary figures as George William Curtis, Sidney Howard Gary, and Francis George Shaw. The name was changed when the railroad established a station on the northern shore in the Livingston homestead. The city operates Walker Park, a recreation area with tennis courts and playing fields that draws many visitors. The population is largely white.

Marjorie Johnson

Livingston, (Henry) Brockholst (*b* New York City, 26 Nov 1757; *d* Washington, 19 March 1823). Justice of the Supreme Court, son of William Livingston. A member of one of the most influential families in New York City, he was an officer in the Continental Army during the American Revolution and a secretary to his brother-in-law, John Jay, during a mission to Spain. His intrigues against Jay there caused bitterness between the two men that inspired Livingston's anti-Federalist politics in the 1790s and his opposition to Jay's campaigns for the governorship of New York. Livingston was a capable lawyer who in 1802 became a judge on the Supreme Court of New York State. As a justice of the U.S. Supreme Court from 1807 he abandoned anti-Federalism for a brand of conservative nationalism compatible with the views of Chief Justice John Marshall.

Gerald T. Dunne: "Brockholst Livingston," *The Justices of the United States Supreme Court, 1789–1969*, ed. Leon Friedman and Fred L. Israel (New York: R. R. Bowker, 1969)

Frederick S. Voss

Livingston, Edward (*b* Clermont, Columbia County, N.Y., 28 May 1764; *d* Rhinebeck, N.Y., 23 May 1836). Statesman, brother of Robert R. Livingston. After attending schools along the Hudson and graduating from Princeton College in 1781 he studied law, was admitted to the bar, and won election to Congress as a Democrat in 1794, serving until 1801. In that year he received simultaneous appointments as mayor and as U.S. attorney for the New York District. While in office he contracted yellow fever; on recovering he learned that municipal funds had been stolen by an aide and assumed responsibility by repaying the city with all his property. He then moved to New Orleans to rebuild his career but was troubled by debts for the next twenty-four years. After resolving his financial problems he returned to New York City. He later served in the U.S. Senate from Louisiana and was secretary of state under President Andrew Jackson.

William B. Hatcher: *Edward Livingston: Jeffersonian Republican and Jacksonian Democrat* (Baton Rouge: Louisiana State University Press, 1940)

James E. Mooney

Livingston, Philip (*b* Albany, N.Y., 15 Jan 1716; *d* New York City, 12 June 1778). Merchant and statesman. After graduating from Yale College in 1737 he became an importer in New York City, where he lived in a townhouse on Duke Street; he also had a country house in Brooklyn Heights. A member of the state assembly, he attended the First and Second Continental Congresses and signed the Declaration of Independence. In New York City he helped to organize King's College, New York Hospital, the New York Society Library, the Chamber of Commerce, and the first Methodist church in the colonies. He was also the president of St. Andrew's Society, the city's oldest benevolent institution.

James E. Mooney

Livingston, Robert R(obert) (*b* New York City, 27 Nov 1746; *d* Clermont, Columbia County, N.Y., 26 Feb 1813). Jurist and diplomat, brother of Edward Livingston. After studying at King's College (now Columbia University) he became a law partner of John Jay, served as the recorder of the City of New York, and later was a delegate to the Continental Congress. As chief judge of the Court of Chancery of New York State (1777–1801) he administered the presidential oath of office to George Washington on the steps of Federal Hall. During the peace negotiations with Britain he was secretary for foreign affairs (1781–83). He became active in Republican politics because of his opposition to Alexander Hamilton's economic policies and because his family had received little patronage from the Federalists. As Jefferson's minister to France (1801–4) he conducted negotiations that led to the Louisiana Purchase. Livingston was also interested in agriculture and steamboat navigation. He supported the experiments of Robert Fulton that led to the launching of the *North River Steamboat* in 1807, and he used his influence to secure a monopoly for himself and Fulton on steamboat operations in New York State.

Clare Brandt: *American Aristocracy: The Livingstons* (Garden City, N.Y.: Doubleday, 1986)

Barbara A. Chernow

Livingston, William (*b* Albany, N.Y., 30 Nov 1723; *d* Elizabethtown, N.J., 25 July 1790). Writer and political leader, father of Brockholst Livingston. He graduated from Yale University in 1741 and moved to New York City, where he established himself as a leading lawyer. With William Smith Jr. and John Morin Scott he wrote and published one of the first American magazines, the *Independent Reflector* (1752–53), a lively periodical that opposed efforts by the Anglican church to establish a colonial episcopacy and to gain control over a proposed institution eventually established as King's College (later Columbia University). He also worked with Smith to publish in 1752 and 1762 the first digest of the laws of provincial New York, covering the period from 1691 to 1756. Until a political reversal in 1768 he was active in politics in New York City; he then moved to New Jersey, where he was later governor for fourteen years.

Dorothy Rita Dillon: *The New York Triumvirate: A Study of the Legal and Political Careers of William Livingston, John Morin Scott, William Smith, Jr.* (New York: Columbia University Press, 1949; repr. New York: AMS, 1968)

Barbara A. Chernow

Living Theatre. Theater company formed in 1946 by Judith Malina, a former pupil of the director Erwin Piscator, and her husband, Julian Beck. It began by producing poetic dramas but eventually developed an improvisational style in works such as *The Connection* (1959), about drug addiction, and *The Brig* (1963), about life in the U.S. Marines. In 1963 the theater was closed for nonpayment of taxes and the company went abroad, where it created works of an increasingly political and confrontational nature. When the company returned to the United States in 1968 it was both praised and criticized for its work. The Becks moved to Brazil in 1970 but were later expelled for their controversial theatrical activities and returned to the United States. The theater eventually reopened under the direction of Malina.

Edwin Milson and Alvin Goldfarb: *Living Theatre: An Introduction to Theatre History* (New York: McGraw–Hill, 1983)

D. S. Moynihan

local development corporations [LDCs]. Nonprofit corporations that provide affordable housing, deliver social services, offer planning assistance in low- and middle-income neighborhoods, and work to improve commercial districts by encouraging public and private investment; they are also known as community development corporations (CDCs). The first corporation in the city, the Bedford Stuyvesant Restoration Corporation, was formed in Brooklyn in 1966 with political support from Senator Robert F. Kennedy and technical assistance from the Pratt Center for Community Improvement. Like many of its counterparts elsewhere the corporation was an outgrowth of programs devised to combat juvenile delinquency, such as Mobilization for Youth, Harlem Youth Opportunities Unlimited, and the Gray Areas program of the Ford Foundation. During its first two decades the corporation built and renovated sixteen hundred dwellings, assisted seventeen hundred homeowners and 130 businesses, and created sixteen thousand jobs. In 1966 Senators Kennedy and Jacob K. Javits sponsored an amendment to the Economic Opportunity Act that created the Special Impact Program, which provided federal funding for community development corporations.

Local development corporations devoted to urban renewal were set up during the 1970s and 1980s in response to housing abandonment and arson in the southern Bronx, Harlem, and other neighborhoods. Groups such as the Banana Kelly Community Improvement Association and the South East Bronx Community Organization, led by Father Louis Gigante, renovated and managed apartment buildings and constructed owner-occupied housing for low-income families in the Bronx. These corporations received technical assistance from the Urban Homesteading Assistance Board (1975) and additional support from the Association for Neighborhood and Housing Development (1974). Private financial intermediaries were established to complement and support the activities of development corporations. The Community Preservation Corporation, formed in 1974 at the behest of David Rockefeller, pooled resources from more than fifty commercial banks, savings banks, and life insurance companies in New York City to finance 26,000 new and renovated apartments. The Local Initiatives Support Corporation (1979), a project of the Ford Foundation, and the Enterprise Foundation, formed by the developer James Rouse in 1982, created the New York Equity Fund in 1989 to attract corporate investment for rental housing through a federal program providing tax credits for the development of low-income housing.

Although reductions in federal urban spending weakened the corporations during the 1980s, many groups maintained and expanded their activities with increased municipal, state, and private funds. In Williamsburg the St. Nicholas Neighborhood Preservation Corporation invested $30 million to develop more than six hundred housing units. The New York City Housing Partnership, formed in 1982 as an affiliate of Rockefeller's New York City Partnership, worked with local development corporations to finance and sell new housing to middle-income families. To strengthen the local economy, development corporations assisted merchants in neighborhood commercial areas and built urban industrial parks. In 1982 they began to manage business improvement districts (BIDs), authorized by the state legislature to raise funds for revitalizing commercial and industrial areas. By 1992 twenty BIDs were operating in Manhattan and the outer boroughs. The expertise of local development corporations and their intermediaries became increasingly important to the management of such city and state initiatives as the municipal housing plan (1986), a ten-year program providing $5000 million for housing.

Local development corporations in New York City are nationally recognized in neighborhood revitalization and urban redevelopment. The Nehemiah Plan, initiated by East Brooklyn Congregations in 1982, has built more than fifteen hundred houses on vacant land and is a national model for low-income homeownership. Charlotte Street in the southern Bronx, once a stark symbol of inner-city decay visited by Jimmy Carter and Ronald Reagan, is the site of Charlotte Gardens, a cluster of eighty-nine one-family houses.

Neal R. Peirce and Carol F. Steinbach: *Corrective Capitalism: The Rise of America's Community Development Corporations* (New York: Ford Foundation, 1987)

Roberta Brandes Gratz: *The Living City* (New York: Simon and Schuster, 1989)

John T. Metzger

Local 1199. Local chapter of the Drug, Hospital and Health Care Employees Union, formed in New York City in 1932 by pharmacists and drugstore employees. It first successfully organized nonprofessional hospital workers in 1958 under the leadership of Leon J. Davis at Montefiore Hospital in the Bronx. On 8 May 1959 about 3500 hospital workers began a strike against seven large private hospitals in New York City that lasted forty-six days. This unprecedented action ended when both sides agreed that labor relations in the hospitals would be supervised by a quasi-public agency, the Permanent Administrative Committee. The committee was successfully challenged in 1962; the local began organizing professional and technical workers in the autumn of 1963, and in the same year won the right to collective bargaining under provisions of the state's labor relations act. It was granted the power in 1965 to represent workers throughout New York State, won a contract in 1968 that for the first time secured a minimum salary for workers of $100 a week, and in 1973 began to organize registered nurses. An attempt by the national union to merge with the Service Employees International Union in the early 1980s prompted the local to declare itself independent. Internal struggles within the local persisted until 1988, when Dennis Rivera became its president. Local 1199 was an important supporter of David N. Dinkins's successful mayoral campaign in 1989.

Leon Fink and Brian Greenberg: *Upheaval in the Quiet Zone: A History of Hospital Workers' Union, Local 1199* (Urbana: University of Illinois Press, 1989)

Brian Greenberg

Locke, Alain (Leroy) (*b* Philadelphia, 13 Sept 1885; *d* New York City, 9 June 1954). Critic. Born to an educated, well-traveled family, he became the first black recipient of a Rhodes scholarship in 1907, taught at Howard University from 1912, and received his PhD from Harvard University in 1918. He considered New York City his second home and helped to shape the HARLEM RENAISSANCE through his influential book *The New Negro* (1925). His education and contacts enabled him to support young black writers and artists. Locke was a visiting professor at the New School for Social Research in 1947 and at City College of New York in 1948.

Russell J. Linnemann, ed.: *Alain Locke: Reflections on a Modern Renaissance Man* (Baton Rouge: Louisiana State University Press, 1982)

Johnny Washington: *Alain Locke and Philosophy: A Quest for Cultural Pluralism* (Westport, Conn.: Greenwood, 1986)

Thea Arnold

Locofocos [Equal Rights Party]. Egalitarian faction of the Democratic Party formed in the autumn of 1835. It began as a group opposing the nomination of a slate of candidates at a meeting of Tammany Hall; party regulars managed the meeting so as to nominate their slate before the opposition could gain control. The regulars then fled, extinguishing the gaslights as they left. The opposing group proceeded with the meeting by candlelight, using matches called locofocos. The name was later applied derisively by Democrats allied with Tammany Hall and eventually adopted by the dissidents themselves. The Locofocos drew some members from the former Workingmen's Party and were sympathetic to workers and labor unions, but they focused primarily on restoring Jefferson's standards to the Democratic Party. They opposed monopolies (particularly chartered banks and transportation companies) and supported Martin Van Buren's plan for an independent treasury. In the mid 1830s it appeared that the group might hold the balance of power between the Democrats and their newly formed competitors the Whig Party and the Native American Democratic Association. After Van Buren brought about a reconciliation with Tammany Hall the Locofocos disbanded; the result was a stronger and less conservative Democratic organization in the city.

Leo Hershkowitz: "The Locofoco Party of New York: Its Origins and Career, 1835–1837," *New-York Historical Society Quarterly* 46 (1962), 305–29

Jerome Mushkat: *Tammany: The Evolution of a Political Machine, 1789–1865* (Syracuse, N.Y.: Syracuse University Press, 1971)

Amy Bridges: *A City in the Republic: Antebellum New York and the Origins of Machine Politics* (Cambridge: Cambridge University Press, 1984)

Evan Cornog

locomotives. In the nineteenth century many manufacturers of marine engines in New York City also made steam engines for locomotives. Most locomotive construction was concentrated in New Jersey and Pennsylvania, but in 1901 the formation of the

American Locomotive Company through the merger of eight formerly independent companies brought the city to the forefront of the industry. Although the firm had its executive offices in Manhattan, its factories continued to operate outside the city. American Locomotive dominated much of domestic production between 1901 and 1950, remaining second only to Bishop Manufacturing of Pennsylvania.

Joanne Abel Goldman

Locust Point. Neighborhood in the northeastern Bronx (1994 pop. 400), on a peninsula in Throgs Neck facing Long Island Sound. It is named for the indigenous locustwood trees, which because of their resistance to rot were esteemed by early settlers. The area was called Horse Neck in 1667 and later Locust Island, for it was cut off from the mainland during high tide. In 1848 the local landowner John Wright built a causeway to the mainland. The present name prevailed when the land was subdivided in 1910, after which summer bungalows were replaced by permanent houses. In 1961 the building of an approach to the Throgs Neck Bridge considerably changed the area.

John McNamara: *History in Asphalt: The Origin of Bronx Street and Place Names* (New York: Bronx County Historical Society, 1984)

John McNamara: *McNamara's Old Bronx* (New York: Bronx County Historical Society, 1989)

John McNamara

Loeb, Jacques (*b* Prussia, 7 April 1859; *d* New York City, 11 Feb 1924). Physiologist. He moved to the United States in 1891 and joined the Rockefeller Institute for Medical Research in 1910. During his years at the institute he was known as a champion of the mechanistic conception of life. He conducted research in artificial parthogenesis and protein chemistry, and was the editor of the *Journal of General Physiology*.

Philip J. Pauly: *Controlling Life: Jacques Loeb and the Engineering Ideal in Biology* (New York: Oxford University Press, 1987)

Lee R. Hiltzik

Loehmann's. Firm of clothing retailers. It began in 1921 when Charles Cord Loehmann became a co-owner of his mother's store in Brooklyn; he was in charge of retail sales until 1931, when he opened his own store, Charles C. Loehmann, to sell annual surplus stock of women's apparel manufacturers. The firm took its current name in 1964, opened a chain of stores, and became known throughout the metropolitan area for the fine quality and low prices of its merchandise. It opened headquarters in the Bronx in 1968 and became a division of the Associated Dry Goods Corporation of New York in 1983. In 1990 Loehmann's had 3400 employees and sales of about $70 million.

James E. Mooney

Loesser, Frank (Henry) (*b* New York City, 29 June 1910; *d* New York City, 26 July 1969). Composer. The son of German immigrants, he grew up on West 107th Street, taught himself to play the piano, and compiled an undistinguished academic record at Townsend Harris High School and City College. For a time he wrote songs in Tin Pan Alley, including "Heart and Soul," a perennial favorite of neophyte pianists. In 1936 he moved to the west coast, where he wrote songs for Universal and Paramount; between 1937 and 1938 eight of his compositions reached the Lucky Strike Hit Parade, and while in the service during the Second World War he wrote the hit song "Praise the Lord and Pass the Ammunition." He soon returned to New York City, where he wrote the score for *Where's Charley?*, an adaptation of a British stage comedy. His best-known musical, *Guys and Dolls*, based on Damon Runyon's stories of amiable ne'er-do-wells in New York City, opened at the 46th Street Theater in November 1950 and achieved great success for its flawless integration of book and song. His later works include *The Most Happy Fella*, given its première in 1956, and *How to Succeed in Business without Really Trying* (1961), a spoof of the corporate life that won a Pulitzer Prize. After Loesser's death a number of his musicals were given popular revivals.

Susan Loesser: *A Most Remarkable Fella* (New York: Donald I. Fine, 1993)

Thomas M. Hilbink

Loews Corporation. Diversified holding company, formed in 1911 by Marcus Loew (1870–1927) as Loew's Theatrical Enterprises, an entertainment firm with holdings in New York City ranging from vaudeville theaters to nickelodeons. The firm responded to the increasing popularity of motion pictures by opening several movie theaters in the city between 1915 and 1920. It became nationally known in 1924 when it bought Metro Pictures and merged it with Goldwyn Pictures and Louis B. Mayer Pictures to form Metro–Goldwyn–Mayer (MGM), a Hollywood studio that became enormously successful. In the 1920s and 1930s Loew's built dozens of lavish movie theaters throughout the city, most having elegant interiors and distinctive terra cotta ornaments. After antitrust suits forced it to relinquish MGM the firm was bought in 1946 by Laurence Tisch and Preston Tisch, who then bought a number of hotels including the McAlpin and the Belmont–Plaza. During the 1960s Loew's diversified, acquiring the tobacco manufacturer Lorillard (1968), the insurance firm CNA Financial Corporation (1974), and the watchmaker Bulova (1977); it sold its movie theaters in 1985 (although they continued to use the name Loews until 1994) and in the following year bought nearly 25 percent of the stock in the Columbia Broadcasting System. The firm had sales in 1990 of more than $12,000 million. By the mid 1990s it had abandoned the motion picture industry but continued to operate six hotels in the city, including the Regency (Park Avenue and 61st Street) and the Loew's Summit (51st Street and Lexington Avenue). One of the most visible firms in the city, Loew's remains under the management of the Tisch family. Several of its former theaters in the city survive.

James Bradley

Loew's Paradise. Movie theater built in 1929 in the Bronx, on the Grand Concourse and 188th Street. Designed by John Eberson and built at a cost of $4 million, the theater had a lavish auditorium (seating 4200) and a lobby resembling a Spanish patio. In later years Loew's Paradise was divided into four theaters. It closed in the early 1990s.

David Nasaw

lofts. The popular meaning of the term "loft" changed completely during the 1970s. Formerly it was applied to multi-story buildings used for light manufacturing, storage, and showrooms; from that time it came to refer to spacious, stylish apartments without traditional rooms, usually in renovated commercial buildings.

Most lofts were constructed between the 1870s and 1930, first in lower Manhattan and near port facilities, and later in midtown. Typically lofts are built as adaptable space and rented by the story; the structure is sturdy to support heavy loads and interiors are plain and unpartitioned, with high ceilings. Windows are large, but the deep interior space lacks natural light and is thus undesirable for offices. Façades are often ornamented, especially in the central business district, but lobbies are spare and there are more elevators for freight than for passengers.

The most famous loft district in New York City is SoHo, where many six- to eight-story buildings were erected during the 1870s and 1880s for light manufacturing and storage. Cast iron was used for façades, with rich architectural effects and iron columns supporting beams, but the main load-bearing structure remained masonry until metal skeletal construction was approved by the building code in 1888. From the 1890s lofts of twelve stories and more proliferated, especially south of 14th Street, where the garment industry concentrated after laws were passed to regulate sweatshops and restrict work at home. Between 1910 and 1914 more than two hundred lofts were constructed, most of them on cross streets in the area between 23rd and 34th streets and 5th and 6th avenues. These buildings rose sheer above the sidewalk, often twenty or more stories, and cast shadows over sidewalks and buildings below. The thousands of workers spilled onto the fashionable avenues during lunch hour, leading local merchants to join reformers in calling for regulation. This movement led to the passage of a zoning law in 1916 that restricted the height and bulk of buildings and banned various uses in some areas. The volume of construction increased again during the 1920s, especially in the second half of the decade in the new garment district west of 6th Avenue between 34th and 42nd streets. Zoning requirements shaped these buildings into forms that stepped back at upper levels, and the vogue for art deco inspired a rich variety of ornament; showrooms were an important feature in these buildings. After reaching a peak in 1931 the amount of loft space in Manhattan decreased, mirroring the decline of the manufacturing sector.

The conversion of lofts into residences began in the 1950s, when artists seeking low rents and large spaces set up studios in old commercial structures. In violation of codes, many inhabited their comfortless quarters and petitioned to legalize occupancy, a change approved for certain areas in 1968. This proved the first step in the gentrification of former manufacturing districts such as SoHo and Tribeca; lofts became fashionable for the well-to-do and the demands for space drove out older businesses. In 1980 the City Planning Commission adopted a policy designed to maintain some zones for manufacturing while allowing for more conversions into residences. A few lofts were built for manufacturing in Manhattan after 1960; some survive in the outer boroughs.

Sharon Zukin: *Loft Living: Culture and Capital in Urban Change* (Baltimore: Johns Hopkins University Press, 1982)

Carol Willis

Logue, Edward J(oseph) (*b* Philadelphia, 7 Feb 1921). Urban planner. After serving as the head of the New Haven Redevelopment Agency and the Boston Redevelopment Authority he was persuaded by Governor Nelson A. Rockefeller to become the head of the Urban Development Corporation on its formation in 1968. Under his leadership (to 1975) the corporation planned and constructed major projects throughout New York State, including several "new towns." In New York City its most important project was Roosevelt Island. Logue was later president of the South Bronx Development Organization (1978–85) and the president of his own development company, Logue Boston.

I. Steen

Lohman, Ann Trow (*b* Painswick, England, 1812; *d* New York City, 1 April 1878). Abortionist. She moved from England to New York City in 1831, and by the end of the decade advertised in local newspapers and directories as Madame Restell, "female physician and professor of midwifery." She lived first on Chambers Street and from 1864 in a four-story brownstone at 52nd Street and 5th Avenue, where she provided desperate and needy women with contraceptives, abortions, and help with deliveries and in arranging clandestine adoptions. Because of her activities she was vilified in several sensationalistic tracts as the "wickedest woman" in New York City, and imprisoned on Blackwell's Island. She took her own life on the eve of another trial; Anthony Comstock, secretary of the New York Society for the Suppression of Vice, called her suicide a "bloody ending to a bloody life." The size of her estate was estimated at between $600,000 and $1 million.

Clifford Browder: *The Wickedest Woman in New York: Madame Restell, the Abortionist* (Hamden, Conn.: Archon, 1988)

Allen J. Share

Lombardi, Vince(nt Thomas) (*b* Brooklyn, 11 June 1913; *d* Washington, 3 Sept 1970). Football coach. He played football at Fordham University as part of the defensive line known as the "seven blocks of granite" (1934–36). In 1947 he coached the freshman squad at Fordham, for which he installed the "T" formation, and in the following year he coached the varsity offense. He worked for five seasons as an assistant coach at the U.S. Military Academy in West Point before joining the coaching staff of Jim Lee Howell with the New York Giants in 1954. Given complete control of the Giants' offense, he helped them in 1956 to win their first championship in eighteen years. He later became the head coach of the Green Bay Packers (1959–67), who under his leadership won the first two Super Bowls ever played.

Michael O'Brien: *Vince: A Personal Biography* (New York: William Morrow, 1987)

Joseph A. Horrigan

Lombardo, Guy [Gaetano Albert] (*b* London, Ont., 19 June 1892; *d* Houston, 5 Nov 1977). Bandleader. He made his début in New York City with his band the Royal Canadiens in 1929 at the Roosevelt Hotel Grill Room, where he performed each winter for the next thirty-three years. His well-known New Year's Eve celebrations were broadcast first on radio and then on television by the Columbia Broadcasting System until 1976. Lombardo performed at Carnegie Hall in 1969 and owned Lombardo Music Company, a publishing firm at 1619 Broadway.

Herndon Booton: *The Sweetest Music This Side of Heaven: The Guy Lombardo Story* (New York: McGraw–Hill, 1964)

Marc Ferris

London, Meyer (*b* Russia, 29 Dec 1871; *d* New York City, 6 June 1926). Lawyer and political leader. He moved in 1888 to New York City, where he built a career as an attorney for garment workers' unions and became an active member of the Socialist Party of America. In 1914 he became the first Socialist candidate elected to the U.S. House of Representatives from New York State, winning reelection in 1916 and 1920. London was killed in an automobile accident.

Harry Rogoff: *An East Side Epic: The Life and Work of Meyer London* (New York: Vanguard, 1930)

Melvyn Dubofsky

London Bridge. Former name of BULL'S HEAD.

London Plane Tree. The London Plane Tree (*Platanus × acerifolia*) is a hybrid of two closely related plane trees prized for their beauty, the American Sycamore (*Platanus occidentalis*) and the Oriental Plane Tree (*Platanus orientalis*); it is hardier and better adapted to harsh urban environments than the parent species. A depiction of its maple-like leaf in a circle is the logotype of the Department of Parks and Recreation.

Steven D. Garber: *The Urban Naturalist* (New York: John Wiley and Sons, 1987)

Steven D. Garber

London Terrace. Apartment complex in Manhattan, erected in 1930 between 23rd and 24th streets and 9th and 10th avenues. It contains 1670 apartments in fourteen buildings of sixteen stories each, and at the time of its construction was one of the largest developments of its kind in the world. The complex includes a private garden a block long, a swimming pool, a solarium, shops, and banks. The name is derived from that of a fashionable row of four-story townhouses built in 1845 on the same site by Alexander Jackson Davis, and at first the management sought to evoke associations with Britain by having the doormen wear the uniforms of bobbies in London.

Sandra Opdycke

Long Island City. Neighborhood in northwestern Queens, bounded to the west and the north by the East River, to the east by Hazen Street, 49th Street, and New Calvary Cemetery, and to the south by Newtown Creek. In area it is the largest neighborhood in the borough and comprehends several smaller ones: Hunter's Point, Ravenswood, Astoria, Steinway, and Sunnyside. Before 1853 most of the low-lying area flooded easily, and in colonial

Mayors of Long Island City, 1870–1898

Abram D. Ditmars 1870–72
Henry S. DeBevoise 1872–75
Abram D. Ditmars 1875
John Quinn 1876
Henry S. DeBevoise 1876–83
George Petry 1883–86
Patrick J. Gleason 1887–92
Horatio S. Sanford 1893–95
Patrick J. Gleason 1896–97

Compiled by James Bradley

times there were few roads or settlers. During the American Revolution the British army dug itself in along what is now 39th Avenue and its continuation through the railroad yards in Sunnyside. In 1837 the farm of the Hunter family was sold to two developers, Neziah Bliss and Eliphalet Nott, who in 1853 leveled sand hills and laid out streets. Terminals were built for the Flushing Railroad (1854) and the Long Island Rail Road (1861), and a ferry to Manhattan offered service from 1859. During the Civil War Hunter's Point was industrialized and in 1869 a street railway connected it with Astoria. In May 1870 Long Island City became an incorporated municipality, the fourth within the current boundaries of New York City (after New York City itself, Brooklyn, and Williamsburgh); for much of the late 1880s and 1890s Patrick J. Gleason was its feisty and influential mayor. The Steinway family in 1870 erected a plant on the East River at what is now Steinway Street and laid out Steinway Village, which became heavily German. In the 1870s and 1880s large oil refineries, lumber yards, and factories for asphalt, ceramic pipe, barrels, tinware, and light manufacturing were built in Hunter's Point, where schooners and sailing ships delivered raw materials and carried finished products from docks along the shore; in later years chemical and glass factories and gas plants lined the shore to Astoria. Between 1874 and 1880 swamps were drained and the land filled in to a depth of ten to thirty feet (three to nine meters) to end flooding. The notorious Hell Gate Reef, a deadly trap for ships, was dynamited in 1876 and again in 1885. Construction began on the Steinway Tunnel but was delayed by an explosion on 28 December 1892.

After 1900 heavy industry moved out because of crowding, but the highways, ferries, and proximity to commercial waterways attracted other manufacturers. The Long Island Rail Road in 1905 erected a large plant on 2nd Street to electrify its suburban routes and from 1908 to 1910 laid out the yards in Sunnyside. The Steinway Tunnel was finally completed in 1907, but wrangling with the City of New York over valuation delayed its opening until 1915. After the Queensboro Bridge opened in 1909 new streets were laid out, blocks of houses were built, and land values rose; inland development was especially intense. In 1914 the first apartment building was constructed in Astoria, and aircraft parts were produced in the neighborhood during the First World War. Interborough Rapid Transit extended elevated lines to Astoria and to Corona along Queens Boulevard in 1917, and the five-cent subway fare stimulated further growth; during the 1920s the last open land in Astoria was developed. During a time when the local economy was severely affected by the Depression, the Independent subway extended service to the neighborhood in 1933 and the Triborough Bridge opened in 1936 after some delay. The manufacture of aircraft parts revived during the Second World War.

Long Island City after the war underwent marked changes. Many of the large factories closed, and some were converted to other uses: the Silvercup Bakery became the Silvercup Studios, used for video production; such large factories on Thomson Avenue as those of Adams Chewing Gum and Sunshine Biscuits became part of the International Design Center, a complex of showrooms for furniture and interior design firms; and La Guardia Community College took over the disused factories of the White Motor Company and the Equitable Bag Company. There was some growth in the residential population as older apartments and factories were refurbished as living spaces. The neighborhood attracted a few immigrants from Asia and Latin America in the 1980s. Long Island City remains the most heavily industrialized area in Queens County, with railroad yards, the Queens–Midtown Tunnel, one end of the Queensboro Bridge, and blocks of factories in its lower reaches. North of the bridge and Northern Boulevard are private homes, apartments, and commercial buildings; the housing in Astoria consists almost entirely of apartments interspersed with older private houses, many of which are attached. A high-rise residential complex on the waterfront from Newtown Creek to 45th Avenue was proposed in 1984 as part of the Hunter's Point Redevelopment Project and approved in 1990. The Citicorp Building (1989) on Jackson Avenue, erected in 1989, has forty-eight stories and is the tallest building in New York City outside Manhattan.

Vincent Seyfried

Long Island City High School. Original name of WILLIAM CULLEN BRYANT HIGH SCHOOL.

Long Island Historical Society. Original name of the BROOKLYN HISTORICAL SOCIETY.

Long Island Rail Road [LIRR]. Passenger railroad, running from New York City to points east. It is the third-oldest railroad in the country and the only one to carry its original name. Early on it merged with two of its competitors, the South Side Railroad and the Flushing, North Shore and Central Railroad. The first train ran on 18 April 1836. The route was planned to shorten the time needed to travel from New York City to Boston (passengers rode to Greenport, then took a ferry to Connecticut) and was built through the sparsely populated center of the island rather than through the villages along the shore. Track was extended to Hicksville in 1837, to Hempstead in 1838, and to Greenport in 1844. An insufficient number of passengers led the railroad to declare bankruptcy in 1850, and it did not recover until several branches were built, including those to Northport (1868), Sag Harbor (1870), and Port Jefferson (1873). After reaching the height of its prosperity between 1880 and 1914, when it had a monopoly on passenger and freight traffic, the railroad declined slowly before again declaring bankruptcy in 1965. In the same year the state took over the railroad and initiated improvements that were carried out during the next few decades, including electrification of a line from Mineola to Huntington and the introduction of reverse signaling between Pennsylvania Station and Jamaica. Construction projects included a new yard at Ronkonkoma, a lay-up yard on the West Side, a large modern repair facility to replace shops in Morris Park, and a new tower at the Harold control tower in Long Island City.

In the mid 1990s the Long Island Rail Road operated about 350 miles (560 kilometers) of

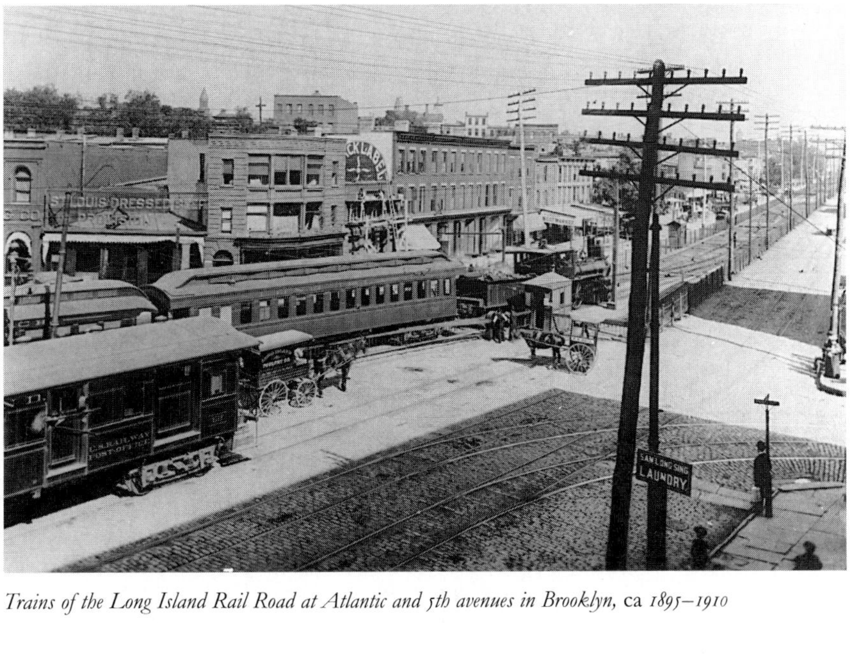

Trains of the Long Island Rail Road at Atlantic and 5th avenues in Brooklyn, ca *1895–1910*

Long Island Rail Road

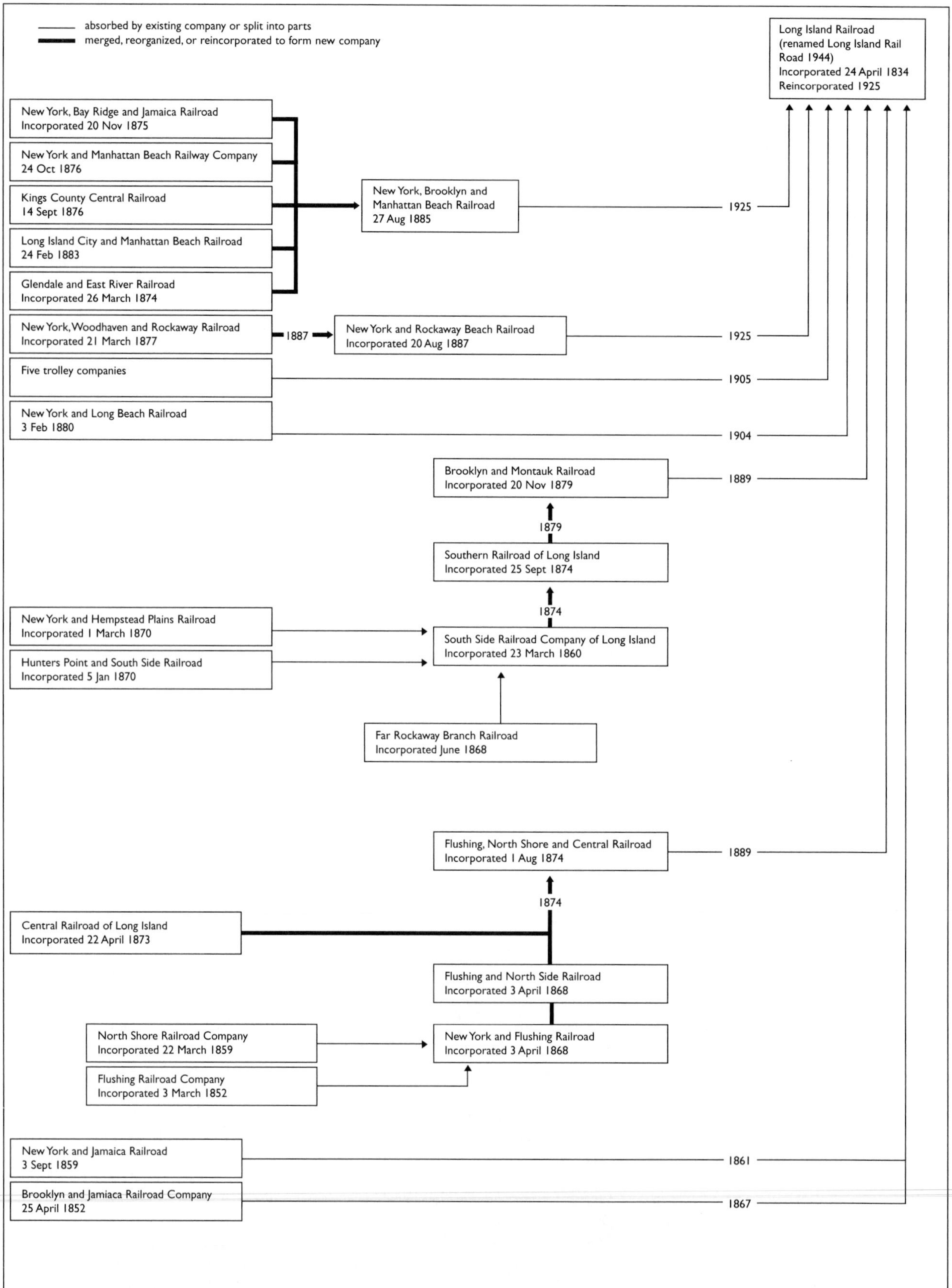

Compiled by Vincent Seyfried with the assistance of Laura Lewison

track and was the largest commuter railroad in the United States, carrying about sixty thousand commuters a day and thousands more during the summer. About three hundred of its 640 daily trains enter Pennsylvania Station through two tunnels. Unlike most lines the railroad has three terminals in New York City: Pennsylvania Station and stations at Flatbush Avenue and Hunter's Point Avenue. Except for the North Side line all passenger routes pass through Jamaica Station, which has eight passenger tracks serving its five platforms, a pair of express tracks bypassing the station, six lay-up tracks for storing trains, and a network of crossings, switches, and bridges. The main line extends ninety-five miles (150 kilometers) from Pennsylvania Station to Greenport. Branches include the Montauk division from Long Island City, the Port Jefferson branch from Hicksville, the Oyster Bay branch from Mineola, the North Side branch from Woodside to Port Washington, the Hempstead branch from Floral Park, the West Hempstead branch from Valley Stream, the Long Beach branch from Lynbrook, the Atlantic branch from Flatbush Avenue to Laurelton, the Far Rockaway branch from Valley Stream, and the Bay Ridge branch for freight from Glendale. By the 1990s the fleet had been almost entirely replaced with modern M-1 and M-3 cars and diesel engines, and renovations were under way at Pennsylvania Station.

See also RAILROADS.

Vincent Seyfried

Long Island University. Private university established in Brooklyn in 1926; the name was adopted at the outset because Brooklyn belongs geographically to Long Island. The impetus for opening the school was a recommendation by a committee formed in 1925 by the incoming mayor of New York City, James J. Walker, at the request of Representative Emanuel Celler of Brooklyn. Ralph Jonas, chairman of the committee and president of the Brooklyn Chamber of Commerce, pledged half a million dollars for the new university, which also had the support of Theodore Roosevelt. The university opened in downtown Brooklyn on a site of twenty-two acres (nine hectares). In 1928 it launched one of the first academic honors programs in the United States, and in the following year it formed an affiliation with the Brooklyn College of Pharmacy (absorbed in 1979 as the Arnold and Marie Schwartz School of Health Sciences). William Zeckendorf, the real-estate developer for whom the downtown campus is named, was elected to the university's board of trustees in 1942 and eventually became its chairman. The university dedicated large campuses on Long Island in Brookville (1954, the campus of C. W. Post College) and Southampton (1963) and smaller ones in Suffolk County (1959, now at Brentwood), Dobbs Ferry in Westchester County (1975), and Rockland County (1980), as well as administrative offices in Greenvale, Long Island. The student body is ethnically diverse, and many students are the first in their family to attend college. Degrees are offered in the liberal arts, the sciences, business, public administration and information sciences, communications, the visual and performing arts, education, and health sciences. In 1990 Long Island University was the nation's ninth-largest private university, with a combined undergraduate and graduate enrollment of 22,000 and 606 faculty members; of these, 5500 students and 198 faculty members were associated with the campus in Brooklyn.

Elliot S. M. Gatner: "Long Island: The History of a Relevant and Responsive University, 1926–1968" (diss., Teachers College, Columbia University, 1974)

Marjorie Harrison

Long Neck. Name applied to TRAVIS during the Civil War.

longshoremen. A strike in 1836 was the first documented effort by longshoremen in New York City to organize themselves. They soon formed benevolent societies and unions such as the Alongshoremen's United Benefit Society (1853) and the Longshoremen's Union Protective Association (1866). Half a dozen unions formed before the turn of the century were short-lived and unable to secure stable wages for their members. By 1874 hourly rates rose as high as forty cents for day work and eighty cents for night work, but hours were so irregular that longshoremen earned only $12 to $13 a week. After receiving a cut in pay in 1874, between eight and ten thousand members of the Longshoremen Union Protective Association went on strike, but their efforts failed, crippling the union. In 1887 the ocean and maritime associations of the Knights of Labor were crushed after fifty thousand members organized a strike in sympathy with 150 longshoremen in the city and coal handlers in Newark, New Jersey. Longshore work remained dangerous and brutally strenuous well into the twentieth century. A congressional investigation for the U.S. Industrial Commission in 1912 showed that longshoremen on the West Side hauled cargo for as many as twenty hours a day, at times carrying on their backs sacks of sugar, coffee, and other commodities weighing as much as 350 pounds (160 kilograms).

Hiring was done in "shape-ups" at each pier head, where bosses chose a few men for a single day's work to round out the regular work gangs from hundreds of applicants, leading to discrimination, kickbacks, loansharking, and racketeering. Conditions on the waterfront became notorious under Joseph Patrick Ryan, who became president of the Atlantic District of the International Longshoremen's Association (ILA) in 1918. Ryan made "sweetheart" contracts with employers and had convicts paroled into his custody, whom he used as strong-arms to ensure that there were no major strikes on the waterfront between 1919 and 1945; he was elected president-for-life of the ILA in 1943. Wildcat strikes occurred in 1945, 1946, 1948, and 1951, supported by the articles of Malcolm Johnson in the *Sun* and the efforts of the Jesuit priest John M. Corridan (depicted in the film *On the Waterfront*, 1954); as a result Governor Thomas E. Dewey formed the New York Crime Commission in 1951. In 1953 Ryan was expelled from office and the New York–New Jersey Waterfront Commission was formed to replace shape-ups with government-run hiring halls; in the same year the American Federation of Labor revoked the charter of the ILA and formed the International Brotherhood of Longshoremen, which failed in three elections to decertify the ILA as a collective bargaining agent and ceased operations in 1959.

After containerization was introduced in the 1960s hours became more regular, but the number of positions on the waterfront in the city and New Jersey declined from 48,000 in the 1950s to twelve thousand in the mid 1980s, at the same time as the volume of cargo rose from 22 million to 27 million tons (20 million to 24 million metric tons). Important benefits were won by Teddy (Thomas) Gleason, president of the ILA from 1963 to 1987, including a guaranteed annual income that by 1968 assured pay for 2080 hours of work annually (more than $31,000 a year by the mid 1980s). In the 1990s about four thousand members of the ILA in greater New York received the guaranteed annual income.

Charles Larrowe: *Shape-up and Hiring Hall: A Comparison of Hiring Methods and Labor Relations on New York and Seattle Waterfronts* (Berkeley: University of California Press, 1955)

Allen Raymond: *Waterfront Priest* (New York: Henry Holt, 1955)

William DiFazio: *Longshoremen, Community, and Resistance on the Brooklyn Waterfront* (South Hadley, Mass.: Bergin and Garvey, 1985)

Joe Doyle

Longwood. Neighborhood in the southwestern Bronx (1990 pop. 23,969), bounded to the north by Westchester Avenue, to the east and south by Southern Boulevard, and to the west by Prospect Avenue; it is part of the neighborhood of Hunts Point. During the nineteenth century the area was part of the town of West Farms. It received its name from one of many large estates: part of this estate, which occupied what is now the western part of the neighborhood, was acquired in the 1870s by S. B. White and renamed Longwood Park. Just before 1900 a few townhouses were built on a section of the former estate that later became a landmark district. After the subway reached the area in 1904 the rest of the estates were subdivided and apartment buildings were erected. The population remained predominantly Jewish until blacks and Puerto Ricans moved in during the 1950s. In the 1960s and 1970s drugs, crime, and the abandonment of housing devastated the neighborhood, but through public programs and community efforts much housing was built and refurbished by the 1990s.

Evelyn Gonzalez

Loral Corporation. Firm of electronics and aerospace equipment manufacturers, formed in 1948 in the Bronx by William Lorenz and Leon Alpert. In the mid 1960s its offices moved to Manhattan. The firm won several lucrative contracts with the U.S. Air Force in the late 1960s and early 1970s, and excelled in providing advanced electronics equipment and aerospace technology. It became a member of the New York Stock Exchange in 1963. In the mid 1990s Loral was one of the nation's leading defense contractors, with sales of $4000 million in 1993.

James Bradley

Lord and Taylor. Firm of retailers that began in 1826 as a small dry-goods shop on Catherine Street. Its owners were Samuel Lord and his junior partner George Washington Taylor, who retired from the business in 1852. The shop moved successively to the corner of Grand and Chrystie streets (1853), where it became known as the city's "fashion emporium," and to a five-story marble building on Broadway that became the focus of the Ladies' Mile (1860). Lord's clerk and his eldest son John T. Lord became partners in the firm; when the Lords retired after the Civil War younger members of the family succeeded them. Lord and Taylor moved in 1872 to a building at Broadway and 20th Street that was the first in New York City to have an iron frame. After the panic of 1873 the firm was taken over by Edward P. Hatch, who annexed a building nearby that made Lord and Taylor the first retailer on 5th Avenue. A store opened in 1914 on 5th Avenue between 38th and 39th streets and became the principal retail facility. Dorothy Shaver, who joined the firm in 1924, became the first woman ever to lead a major American retailer when she was elected president in 1945. She greatly enhanced the reputation of the store and made it the leading supporter of American fashion designs throughout the world. In the mid 1990s Lord and Taylor had more than fifty stores in fifteen states.

Leon A. Harris: *Merchant Princes: An Intimate History of Jewish Families Who Built Great Department Stores* (New York: Harper and Row, 1979)

Robert Hendrickson: *The Grand Emporiums: The Illustrated History of America's Great Department Stores* (New York: Stein and Day, 1979)

Joseph Devorkin: *Great Merchants of Early New York: "The Ladies' Mile"* (New York: Society for the Architecture of the City, 1987)

Laura Gwinn

Lord and Thomas. Advertising agency formed in 1873 in Chicago by Daniel M. Lord and Ambrose L. Thomas. It eventually set up headquarters in both Chicago and New York City (at 5th Avenue and 28th Street). In 1910 the agency was purchased by Albert Lasker (1880–1952), who bought the firm of Thomas Francis Logan in New York City in 1926. Under Lasker's guidance the agency became an important force in expanding the advertising: it produced advertisements detailing to the consumer the advantages of products and services, and emphasized research to measure the effect of advertising on sales. After Lasker sold his stake in the business in 1943 for $10 million three of his executives formed the firm of Foote, Cone and Belding.

George Winslow

Lord Day and Lord Barrett Smith. Law firm, founded in 1848 as Lord, Day and Lord by Daniel Lord (1795–1868), a graduate of Yale College (1814) and Litchfield Law School (1815), in partnership with his son Daniel DeForest Lord and his son-in-law Henry Day. The firm built its reputation on maritime law: it successfully handled the prize-ship cases during the Civil War and numbered among its clients the Cunard Lines, John Jacob Astor, Samuel F. B. Morse, and Cyrus W. Field. It also acquired expertise in estates and trusts, and real estate. Just before the Depression the firm added departments specializing in tax law, corporate law, antitrust law, and litigation. The families of the founders dominated the firm until after the Second World War. A vigorous international practice was developed by such partners as Herbert Brownell, attorney general under President Dwight D. Eisenhower. The firm took the name Lord Day and Lord Barrett Smith after a merger in 1988. In September 1994 it announced its dissolution.

Paul H. Mattingly

Lorillard. See P. LORILLARD AND COMPANY.

Lotos Club. Literary club formed in 1870. Initially based at 2 Irving Place, it moved successively to 21st Street in 1876, 46th Street in 1893, West 57th Street in 1910, and 5 East 66th Street in 1947, where it occupied a building designed by Richard Howland Hunt about the turn of the century as a private home. Women were first admitted in 1976. The club offers lodging and meals, monthly exhibitions, special dinners for mayors, literary evenings, art exhibitions, musical recitals, and lectures on public affairs; it is one of the oldest literary clubs in the country.

James E. Mooney

lotteries. Lotteries became popular in the early days of colonial America. In 1611 the financially pressed Virginia Company held a lottery to fund the Jamestown colony. The New York State Assembly passed its first legislation regulating lotteries in 1721. In New York City receipts from lotteries were put to diverse purposes: protection of the city against attacks by the French and Indians (1746), education (Columbia University was founded with lottery money), repairs for City Hall (1761), a church in Brooklyn (1774), the American Revolution, relief for Loyalist refugees (1781), and a poor house (1795). Between 1797 and 1817 sixteen lotteries in New York State raised $217,400 for canals, schools, roads, churches, and public works. Lotteries also played an important role in the development of investment banking and the city's financial system. Many pioneers in banking and finance, such as John Thompson, founder of the First National Bank of New York and Chase National Bank, began their careers by selling lottery tickets, and in the early nineteenth century stockbrokers on Wall Street sold more lottery tickets than securities. The profitability of lotteries for their sponsors and several scandals led to widespread criticism and in 1833 and 1834 to legislation outlawing lotteries. In the 1840s and 1850s John Frink and Reuben Parsons popularized poor people's "casinos," and the NUMBERS, or policy, racket became an important source of profits for organized crime. In 1876 it was reported that more than thirty-three agencies sold more than a million illegal lottery tickets each year in New York City. A syndicate of gamblers based in New York City also sold

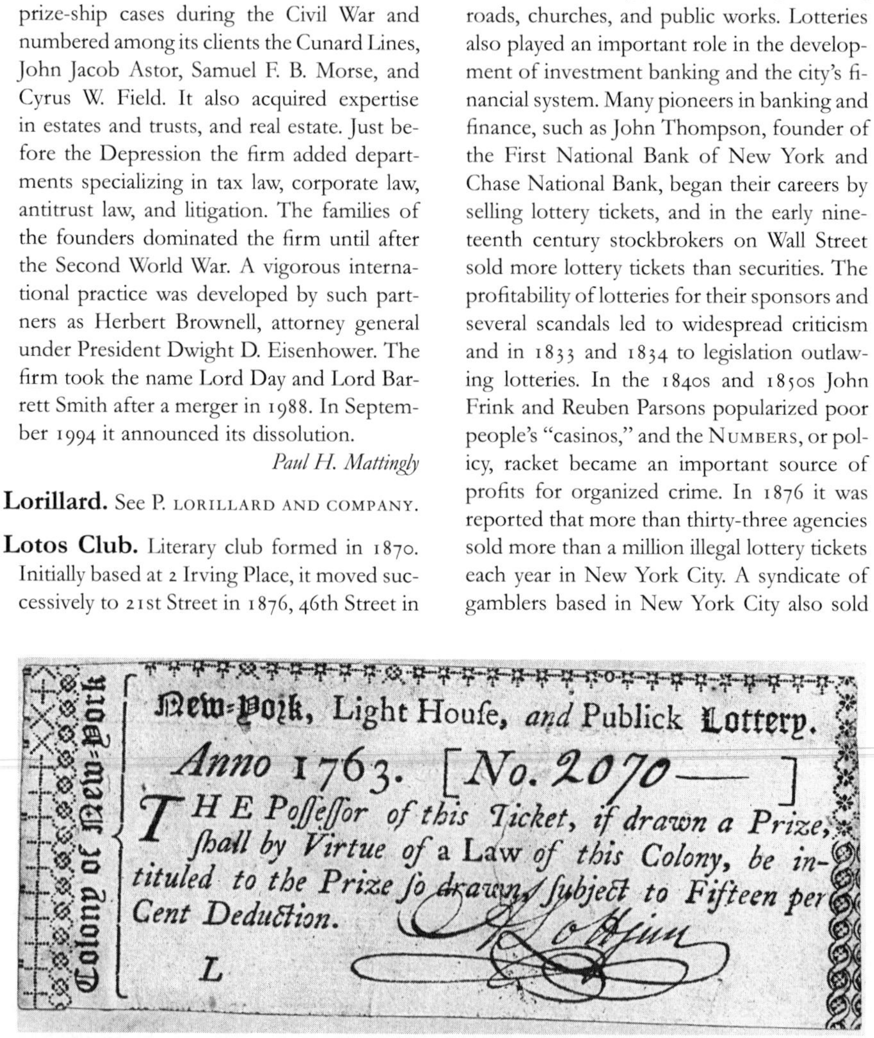

Lottery ticket, 1763

tickets of the Louisiana Lottery Company nationwide between 1868 and 1892.

In part to compete with the numbers racket and in part to raise funds for education, New York State established a lottery in 1967 that eventually expanded to include games of many types. Between 1977 and 1990 the city received more than $1900 million in educational aid from state-run lotteries.

George Winslow

Lovelace, Francis (*b* Hurley, England, *ca* 1621; *d* Oxford, England, 1675). Colonial governor. A staunch royalist, he was appointed governor of New York in 1667, moved to New York City in March 1668, and took office in August. He improved ferries and roads, regulated trade, extended commerce, opened the first mercantile exchange, promoted shipbuilding, and bought Staten Island from Indians. While overseeing the building of a post road to Boston Lovelace left the city, which was recaptured by a Dutch squadron; he was then recalled and imprisoned in the Tower of London.

James E. Mooney

Lovestone, Jay [Liebstein, Jacob] (*b* Lithuania, 24 Dec 1897; *d* 7 March 1990). Political and labor leader. At nine he moved to New York City with his family. Drawn to socialist activism as a teenager, he entered City College and became president of its socialist club. In 1919 he attended the first convention of the Communist Party of America and was elected to the central committee. A master of political manipulation, he became general secretary in 1927 and soon after expelled a rival Trotskyist faction; in 1929 he himself was stripped of his office and membership in the party after a confrontation with Stalin in Moscow. During the 1930s he challenged Stalinism and formed links with many unions, eventually rejecting communism entirely and seeking the expulsion of communists from unions. Working closely with George Meany, he coordinated the foreign policy of the American Federation of Labor and managed the international affairs department of the AFL–CIO from 1955 until his retirement in 1974.

Robert Jackson Alexander: *The Right Opposition: The Lovestoneites and the International Communist Opposition of the 1930s* (Westport, Conn.: Greenwood, 1981)

Richard Yeselson

Low, A(biel) A(bbot) (*b* Salem, Mass., 7 Feb 1811; *d* Brooklyn, 7 Jan 1893). Merchant, father of Seth Low. Born at a time when ambitious merchants were abandoning New England for growing opportunities to the south, he moved to Brooklyn in 1829 with his father. In 1840 he completed a visit to Canton and sought to dominate trade with China by building fast clipper ships, beginning with the *Houqua* in 1844. The swiftness of his ships the *Samuel Russell*, the *Oriental*, and the *Surprise* allowed him to buy fresh tea in Canton later than his competitors, at low prices, and sell it in the United States earlier, at high prices. At the peak of his career in 1849 he moved his firm into new quarters on Burling Slip in lower Manhattan. In the following year one of his ships was the first to ply the newly opened route from China to London, soon making slower ships obsolete. When trade with China declined in the 1860s he dedicated himself to other pursuits, becoming president of the New York Chamber of Commerce and of a private school in Brooklyn; he retired from business in 1887. Low's house stands at 3 Pierrepont Place in Brooklyn Heights, and the building occupied by his business is at 167–71 John Street in Manhattan, at South Street Seaport.

Tribute of the Chamber of Commerce of the State of New-York to the Memory of Abiel Abbot Low, President, 1883–1887 (New York: Chamber of Commerce, 1893)
Helen Augur: *Tall Ships to Cathay* (New York: Doubleday, 1951)
Ellen Fletcher Rosebrock: "Abiel Abbot Low: A New York Merchant in the China Trade," *Seaport* 14, no. 2 (summer 1980), 15

Ellen Fletcher

Low, Seth (*b* Brooklyn, 18 Jan 1850; *d* Bedford Hills, N.Y., 17 Sept 1916). Mayor and educator, son of A. A. Low. Educated at Brooklyn Polytechnic Institute and Columbia College (AB 1870), he undertook legal studies that he later abandoned to enter his father's business. In 1881 he was elected mayor of Brooklyn as a reformist Republican, after two Republican candidates withdrew in his favor. During his two two-year terms he achieved de facto home rule and implemented civil service and public school reforms. His sympathy for the mugwumps in 1884 and his hostility to patronage did not sit well with regular Republicans, and he decided not to seek reelection in 1885. A trustee of Columbia College since 1881, he became its president in 1890. During his tenure the college promoted graduate education, absorbed several professional schools, and formed an affiliation with Barnard College. He was chiefly responsible for having Columbia move in 1897 from 49th Street to Morningside Heights, and he financed the centerpiece of the new campus, Low Memorial Library (named for his father). At the same time he helped to draft the charter for a consolidated New York City, and in 1897 he campaigned in the first election in which its mayoralty was at stake, losing to Robert A. Van Wyck, a Democrat backed by Tammany Hall. He prevailed in a second attempt for the mayoralty, defeating the Democratic candidate E. M. Shephard in 1901 after a campaign in which he advocated reform and spending for capital improvements. He failed to win reelection in 1903, losing to George B. McClellan Jr., a Democrat supported by Tammany Hall who attacked Low's enforcement of blue laws and his purported Republican partisanship. In 1914 he resigned his trusteeship at Columbia in a dispute over the right of Jewish groups to have access to the university's facilities. Low retired to Bedford Hills, where he organized a farmer's cooperative, mediated labor disputes, and was chairman of the board of trustees of the Tuskegee Institute, the New York Chamber of Commerce (which his father had also led), and the committee on cities of the New York State Constitutional Convention of 1915.

Benjamin R. C. Low: *Seth Low* (New York: G. P. Putnam's Sons, 1925)
Steven C. Swett: "The Test of a Reformer: A Study of Seth Low, New York City Mayor, 1902–1903," *New-York Historical Society Quarterly* 44 (1960), 5–41
Gerald Kurland: *Seth Low: The Reformer in an Urban and Industrial Age* (New York: Twayne, 1971)
Harold S. Wechsler: *The Qualified Student: A History of Selective College Admission in America, 1870-1970* (New York: Wiley Interscience, 1977), chaps. 3, 4

Harold Wechsler

Lowell, Josephine Shaw (*b* West Roxbury [now in Boston], 16 Dec 1843; *d* New York City, 12 Oct 1905). The wife and sister of Union officers, she was widowed at twenty. She later became interested in conditions in poorhouses and jails of New York State and joined a county visiting committee of the State Charities Aid Association, for which she helped to write a report on a poorhouse near her home in Staten Island: she was appalled at the conditions there, where men, women, children, vagrants, alcoholics, the insane, and the retarded were crowded together with minimal care, and believed strongly that intermingling of this sort would lead to hereditary pauperism, perpetual dependence among vagrants, and a negative attitude toward work. In 1876 she became the first woman appointed commissioner of the State Board of Charities, and for thirteen years she worked tirelessly through reports, letters, lectures, and personal contacts to carry out such reforms as opening separate reformatories for women, moving the retarded and the insane to separate institutions, excluding children from jails, and ensuring that overseers of poorhouses were paid a salary rather than according to the number of persons lodged each night. Under her leadership the board in 1882 formed the Charity Organization Society of the City of New York to reduce waste and duplication; she remained associated with the society until her death. In 1886 she led an effort to form the Working Women's Society (later the Consumers' League), which advocated a code of working conditions for young women employed in retail stores and urged customers to boycott stores that refused to honor it. During a bitter depression in the winter of 1893–94 she formed the East Side Relief Work

Committee, which initiated such employment projects as street cleaning and the whitewashing of tenement buildings. She was also active in the mayoral campaign of 1894 in which the candidate endorsed by Tammany Hall was defeated. About 1884 Lowell wrote *Public Relief and Private Charity.*

W. R. Stewart, ed.: *The Philanthropic Work of Josephine Shaw Lowell* (New York: Macmillan, 1911)
Margaret Elden Rich: *Josephine Shaw Lowell, 1843–1905* (New York: Arno, 1954)
Lloyd C. Taylor Jr.: "Josephine Shaw Lowell and American Philanthropy," *New York History* 44 (1964), 336–64

Jane Allen

Lowenstein, Allard K(enneth)

[Allard Augustus] (*b* Newark, N.J., 16 Jan 1929; *d* New York City, 14 March 1980). Lawyer and congressman. He taught at City College and was active in the civil rights and antiwar movements. In 1968 he was a leading supporter of the presidential candidacy of Senator Eugene J. McCarthy and helped to bring about President Lyndon B. Johnson's decision not to seek reelection. Although he mounted seven campaigns for Congress in and around New York City he was elected only once (on Long Island in 1968). After working at the United Nations he joined the law firm of Layton and Sherman. He was fatally shot in his office at Rockefeller Center by a former colleague.

Richard Cummings: *The Pied Piper: Allard K. Lowenstein and the Liberal Dream* (New York: Grove, 1985)
William H. Chafe: *Never Stop Running: Allard Lowenstein and the Struggle to Save American Liberalism* (New York: Basic Books, 1993)

Lisa Gitelman

Lower East Side. Neighborhood in Manhattan, bounded to the north by 14th Street, to the east by the East River, to the south by Fulton and Franklin streets, and to the west by Pearl Street and Broadway; it comprehends the East Village, Chinatown, Little Italy, Tompkins Square, Astor Place, and the housing development Knickerbocker Village. Some of the first settlers in the area were free black farmers who moved to the Bouwerie. After smaller plots were consolidated into larger ones during the seventeenth century, much of the area was covered by James de Lancey's farm, which was confiscated and sold after the American Revolution. An enclave of craftsmen developed around the Collect at the intersection of Baxter, Worth, and Park streets and later became known as the Five Points. The first tenements in the city were erected near Corlear's Hook in 1833, and Irish immigrants settled in the northern section along the Bowery. Kleindeutschland developed north of Houston Street in the 1840s. The 1880s saw an influx of Italians, Jews from eastern Europe, Russians, Romanians, Hungarians, Ukrainians, Slovaks, Greeks, and Poles. One of the largest ethnic enclaves was a Jewish one that in 1920 had a population of 400,000. The Yiddish theater flourished along 2nd Avenue between Houston Street and 14th Street. Pushcart vendors sold inexpensive clothing and ethnic food on Orchard Street, and household items on Grand Street.

Alice Austen, Hester Street Egg Stand Group *(18 April 1895)*

The burgeoning population found housing in the many tenements built in the area after 1850. The neighborhood remained a prototypical big-city slum, despite such attempts at mandating improvements as the introduction of "dumbbell" tenements in 1878 and reforms in 1901 that led to the construction of "new law" tenements with improved sanitary conditions and more comfortable living space. Conditions in the area were decried by reformers such as Jacob A. Riis, author of *How the Other Half Lives* (1890); attempts to ameliorate them led to the formation of service and welfare organizations such as the Educational Alliance, and a number of settlement houses, the best-known of which were the University Settlement and the Henry Street Settlement. In 1936 the First Houses at 3rd Street and 1st Avenue were the first housing project built by the city's housing author-

Orchard Street between Stanton and Rivington streets, 1991

ity. This and subsequent efforts to replace tenements with city housing had at best a mixed record in attacking the underlying causes of poverty on the Lower East Side.

At the same time the neighborhood became known for its artists and its radical politics. Anarchism, capitalism, socialism, and communism were widely discussed on the streets and in newspapers such as the *Jewish Daily Forward* and *Morgen Freiheit*, which also reported news and gossip. Performances from many cultures were given at the Henry Street Playhouse (opened in 1915), and several important entertainers lived in the area, among them Eddie Cantor, George Gershwin, Ira Gershwin, Irving Berlin, Jimmy Durante, Al Jolson, and the Marx Brothers. Alfred E. Smith and Big Tim Sullivan were among the best-known political figures. Tens of thousands of immigrant families settled in the neighborhood despite unprecedented overcrowding and rampant tuberculosis, cholera, and poverty.

The neighborhood became the first racially integrated section of the city after the Second World War, when thousands of blacks and Puerto Ricans moved there. As the Spanish-speaking population increased, the area sometimes came to be referred to as Loisida, derived from the phonetic spelling of the original name as pronounced by Spanish-speakers. Poets, writers, and musicians found social tolerance and cheap food and housing in the northern section, which became the center of the beat movement (see BEATS); 4th Avenue was soon the site of many secondhand bookstores. By the 1960s most Jewish and eastern European residents had moved out of the neighborhood, which in the following decade was beset by persistent poverty, crime, drugs, and the abandonment of housing. The area stabilized to some degree in the 1980s, and its inexpensive housing attracted venturesome students and members of the middle class, as well as immigrants from China, the Dominican Republic, the Philippines, the United Kingdom, Poland, Japan, Korea, India, and Bangladesh. In its southern reaches the Lower East Side is heavily Chinese.

Moses Rischin: *The Promised City: New York's Jews, 1870–1914* (Cambridge: Harvard University Press, 1962)

Irving Howe: *World of Our Fathers* (New York: Harcourt Brace Jovanovich, 1975)

Thomas Kessner: *The Golden Door: Italian and Jewish Immigrant Mobility in New York City, 1880–1915* (New York: Oxford University Press, 1977)

Stanley Nadel: *Little Germany: Ethnicity, Religion, and Class in New York City, 1845–1880* (Urbana: University of Illinois Press, 1990)

Graham Hodges

Lower East Side Tenement Museum. Museum at 97 Orchard Street in Manhattan, founded in 1988 by Ruth J. Abram and Anita Jacobson. Situated in the heart of what was the most crowded neighborhood in the world about 1910, it represents the nation's first effort to preserve a tenement. The building itself dates to 1863, making it a rare example of a structure that predated virtually every housing law in the United States. The two lower stories were used for commercial purposes; each of the four upper stories was divided into four apartments of three rooms each. Even though the building itself occupied sixty-eight feet (20.7 meters) of a lot that was eighty-eight feet (26.8 meters) deep, the largest rooms in the apartments were only twelve by eleven feet (3.7 by 3.4 meters), and the bedrooms were eight feet (2.4 meters) square. Thus each apartment totaled only about 325 square feet (thirty square meters), within which as many as fifteen persons might have lived, some of them lodgers taken in to supplement family income. For more than four decades the building provided no running water, flush toilets, or electric lights, and most of its rooms lacked windows. Although the so-called dumbbell tenement law of 1879 required that every room have an opening to the outside, the law did not apply to existing buildings, and thus residents of 97 Orchard Street continued to live in primitive circumstances. About 1905 running water and flush toilets were finally installed as a result of the tenement law of 1901. The building was condemned as a residence in 1932, and the upper floors were sealed until 1988. In 1994 the tenement rooms were opened to the public, by which time the museum was scattered over three locations, featuring a gallery, a theater, an archive, and a full program of walking tours, plays, multimedia shows, and exhibitions.

Kenneth T. Jackson

Lower New York Bay. The principal waterway leading into New York Harbor, bounded by the curving arm of Sandy Hook, New Jersey, by Rockaway Point in Queens, by Coney Island and southwestern Brooklyn, by the eastern shore of Staten Island, and by Raritan Bay. The bay follows the preglacial route of the Hudson River. Several dredged channels lead into the harbor: the largest of these is Ambrose Channel, which has a depth of about forty feet (twelve meters), a width of two thousand feet (six hundred meters), and a length of seven miles (11.5 kilometers) and extends as far north as the Narrows. At the entrance to Lower New York Bay is Ambrose Light Station, which is anchored to the sea floor.

Gerard R. Wolfe

Lowry, Edith E(lizabeth) (*b* Plainfield, N.J., 23 March 1897; *d* Claremont, N.H., 11 March 1970). Reformer. After attending Wellesley College she worked for a number of Protestant home mission organizations and in 1926 found her life's work as an advocate for exploited migrant farm laborers. Consolidation of Protestant home mission efforts brought her to the National Council of Churches, where she worked from 1950 to 1962. In 1939 she became the first woman to speak from the National Radio Pulpit. Lowry retired in 1965 to a farm in Vermont. Among her published writings is *Migrants of the Crops: They Starve That We May Eat* (1938).

Mary Elizabeth Brown

Loyalists. Before and during the American Revolution New York had more Loyalists, or Tories, than any other province, in both relative and absolute terms. The views of Loyalists were shaped by pride in the Empire, a belief that resistance was morally wrong, adherence to Anglicanism, an eagerness to sustain valuable commercial ties overseas, and for some a desire to retain a high office. The revolution shattered their hopes: soon after the battles of Lexington and Concord, several leading Loyalists left for England; many others urged conciliation, and some became equivocal on the issue of independence or fell discreetly silent. The Loyalists' situation deteriorated further after 6 October 1775, when the Continental Congress recommended the arrest of persons deemed dangerous to colonial liberty. In the spring of 1776 the Loyalists were disarmed. Resentment of their opinions and a fear that they were British spies led to riots, and Loyalists in all classes of society were attacked, forced out of town, and jailed; many fled the country. Loyalist families were disrupted after the Declaration of Independence made it impossible to remain loyal to the Crown and yet support the American cause.

After Sir William Howe's troops occupied New York City in September 1776 fugitive Loyalists returned, and during seven years of British occupation the city and the surrounding countryside became the focus of Loyalism in America. More than a thousand civilians signed an address of loyalty in October 1776, and 3020 swore allegiance to the Crown in February 1777. Loyalists then moved to the city from the interior of New York and other provinces. At least three thousand accompanied the British army that evacuated Philadelphia in June 1778, and some 25,000 were in the city by 1781. After abandoning Savannah, Georgia, in July 1782 the British moved most of their officers and civilians to New York City; in January 1783 more Loyalists moved there from Charleston, South Carolina. Martial law prevailed during the entire British occupation. Although appointed chief justice in 1779 Judge William Smith did not serve, and the director of police Andrew Elliot depended on the commandant for the execution of his orders. Loyalists lacked an effective organization — a Loyalist council formed in 1781 to advise the military governor was riven by factionalism — but they nonetheless supported British war operations by contributing money and supplies, outfitting privateers, and spying. Samuel Seabury, the author of pamphlets urging peaceful change, held several chaplaincies and acted as a guide to British forces on Long Island and in Westchester. The British recruited perhaps half of their 25,000 provincials in the colony of New York, where Loyalists were conscripted into militia companies and impressed into the royal navy. A few obtained military commissions; others served in the ranks, the majority in the provincial corps. Among the more than 3100 provincial troops in New York City were the Queen's Rangers, the Loyal American Regiment, and three brigades raised by Oliver de Lancey. These forces served chiefly as guards but also scouted, skirmished, and foraged in outlying areas. The Associated Loyalists were notorious for their depredations: organized in 1781, they conducted punitive expeditions under their own board of directors and engaged in ruthless plunder.

After George III acceded to independence the Loyalists felt betrayed and abandoned, and feared reprisals. As many as eleven thousand departed before 1783, including probably six thousand for the British Isles. A mass exodus began on 27 April 1783, when seven thousand civilians and soldiers sailed for Nova Scotia. Of the more than 29,000 who left New York State in 1783 at least 28,000 went to Canada, mostly to Nova Scotia and New Brunswick. Perhaps as many as forty thousand Loyalists left New York State during and after the American Revolution, most from New York City and four fifths of them civilians. A few who had suffered property losses, including several attainted in 1779 by the state legislature, were eventually reimbursed by the British government for a fraction of their claims. The de Lancey estate in Manhattan was broken up and sold to more than two hundred purchasers. Loyalists remaining in New York City faced forfeitures and anti-Tory laws that denied them the right to vote and hold office, restricted their ability to collect debts, and facilitated suits against them for wartime damages.

Prosperity and the emergence of new issues after the war led to the reintegration of the Loyalists, who accounted for perhaps a third of the city's inhabitants. The Chamber of Commerce readmitted Loyalist members, and disbarred Loyalists were allowed to resume the practice of law on taking an oath of allegiance. As conservative New Yorkers welcomed their assistance former Loyalists gradually gained influence, shared in the Federalist dominance of New York City, and advocated ratification of the federal constitution. By the time the state's anti-Tory laws were fully repealed in 1788 the hatred of Loyalists had abated, and an élite of former Loyalists took part in the city's cultural and social life.

Alexander C. Flick: *Loyalism in New York during the American Revolution* (New York: Columbia University Press, 1901; repr. Arno, 1969)

Oscar T. Barck: *New York City during the War for Independence with Special Reference to the Period of British Occupation* (New York: Columbia University Press, 1931; repr. Port Washington, N.Y.: Ira J. Friedman, 1966)

Thomas J. Wertenbaker: *Father Knickerbocker Rebels: New York City during the Revolution* (New York: Charles Scribner's Sons, 1948)

Robert Ernst

Loyola High School. Secondary school at 980 Park Avenue in Manhattan, between 83rd and 84th streets. Founded in 1900 as a boys' school by the Society of Jesus, it became coeducational in 1973. In 1994 the enrollment was about two hundred. Prominent figures who have attended the school include Mayor Robert F. Wagner and Wellington Mara, owner of the New York Giants. Loyola is the only coeducational Jesuit high school in the metropolitan region.

Gladys Chen

Lubavitchers. Members of the largest Hasidic sect in the world, founded in eastern Europe in the nineteenth century by Shneur Zalman; they are also known as the Habad. After the Holocaust many of the surviving members emigrated from eastern Europe and settled in Brooklyn and especially in Crown Heights, where the movement maintains its world headquarters at 770 Eastern Parkway. The leader of the sect for many years was Menachem Schneerson. Most members speak Yiddish and are strongly oriented toward their community. They emphasize reason and study as a path toward union with the divinity. As in other Hasidic sects men dress in black suits and wear beards and often *peyes* (long sidelocks), married women cover their heads, and children are segregated by sex from an early age. The Lubavitchers are active in persuading nonobservant Jews to embrace Orthodoxy, and are the only Jews who engage in such efforts; older Lubavitcher students often work as street missionaries.

Lisa Gitelman

Luce, (Ann) Clare Boothe (*b* New York City, 10 April 1903; *d* Washington, 9 Oct 1987). Playwright and public official. She attended schools in Garden City and Tarrytown, New York, and edited the magazines *Vogue* and *Vanity Fair* from 1930 to 1935; she also wrote newspaper columns and such plays as *The Women* (1936), *Kiss the Boys Goodbye* (1938), and *Margin for Error* (1939), which were well received on Broadway. She lived at River House (435 East 52nd Street) from 1935 until 1938, when she moved to the Waldorf–Astoria Towers at 100 East 50th Street. In 1942 she was elected as a Republican to the U.S. House of Representatives, representing Connecticut until 1947. After serving as ambassador to Italy from 1953 to 1957 she was a consultant on foreign affairs to the White House during the 1970s and 1980s. Luce was married to the magazine publisher Henry R. Luce.

Wilfrid Sheed: *Clare Boothe Luce* (New York: E. P. Dutton, 1982)

Joseph Lyons: *Clare Boothe Luce* (New York: Chelsea House, 1989)

James E. Mooney

Luce, Henry R(obinson) (*b* Tengchow [now P'eng-lai], China, 3 April 1898; *d* Phoenix, 28 Feb 1967). Magazine publisher. He was the son of missionaries and attended Yale University. With the help of Briton Hadden and $86,000 from the families of his classmates he launched the weekly magazine *Time* in New York City in March 1923 while living with his parents at 514 West 122nd Street. This became the first successful news magazine, and apart from a period in the mid 1920s when its editorial offices were moved to Cleveland it continued to be published in New York City into the 1990s. In the year following Hadden's death in 1929 Luce launched *Fortune*, a generously illustrated monthly magazine that refined business journalism by offering long essays on individual firms along with features unrelated to business. He also oversaw the introduction in 1931 of the weekly radio news program "The March of Time," first intended to promote the magazine, and of a newsreel version of the program for movie theaters in 1935. His most successful publishing venture was *Life*, a weekly picture magazine published from November 1936 that in the 1940s and 1950s was one of the most widely read magazines in the country. In 1954 he introduced the weekly magazine *Sports Illustrated*, also based in New York City, which became profitable after ten years. With his wife, the playwright Clare Boothe Luce, he was active in Republican causes and in the so-called China lobby. He lived successively at 234 East 49th Street (from 1927 to about 1933), 4 East 72nd Street (to about 1935), 435 East 52nd Street (to 1960), and 5th Avenue near 77th Street (to the end of his life).

W. A. Swanberg: *Luce and His Empire* (New York: Charles Scribner's Sons, 1972)

James L. Baughman: *Henry R. Luce and the Rise of the American News Media* (Boston: Twayne, 1987)

James L. Baughman

Lüchow's. The best-known German restaurant in New York City, opened in 1882 at 110 East 14th Street at Irving Place. The building was constructed in 1840, when the neighborhood was still residential, but by the late nineteenth century it was at the southern edge of the thriving Gashouse District. The restaurant was almost adjacent to the Academy of Music and became especially popular among figures in the entertainment world. Paderewski and Caruso were frequent patrons, and in 1914 Victor Herbert founded the American Society of Composers, Authors and Publishers (ASCAP) in the restaurant. The songwriter Gus Kahn wrote "Yes, Sir, That's My Baby" in one of its rooms. The décor was reminiscent of a German beer hall, "oompah" bands played constantly, and the waiters wore *lederhosen* year round. In June 1982 Lüchow's moved uptown, to a site near Times Square. The change was not successful and the restaurant closed in 1984.

Kenneth T. Jackson

Luciano, Lucky [Charles; Ross, Charles; Lucania, Salvatore] (*b* Lercara Friddi, Sicily, 11 Nov 1896; *d* Naples, 26 Jan 1962). Organized-crime figure. He moved to New York City at the age of nine and settled with his family on 1st Avenue near 14th Street in Manhattan, where in his teens he became a member of the Five Points Gang. During Prohibition he helped to distribute illicit alcohol nationwide. He worked closely with Louis "Lepke" Buchalter and Arnold Rothstein and assumed control over many of Al Capone's interests after Capone was imprisoned for tax evasion. He himself was ordered arrested by Mayor Fiorello H. La Guardia but eluded the authorities until 1936, when he was successfully prosecuted on charges of running a prostitution ring by the district attorney of Manhattan, Thomas E. Dewey, and sentenced to thirty to fifty years in Sing Sing Prison; Luciano consistently maintained that he was falsely convicted. After the unexplained burning and sinking in 1942 off a pier in Manhattan of the *Normandie*, a French liner converted to a troop ship, he allegedly ordered tighter security on the waterfront, then controlled by organized crime, and there were no further incidents of sabotage in New York Harbor during the Second World War. Although the navy denied that Luciano's assistance had been sought, his sentence was commuted after less than ten years by Dewey, now governor of New York. He was deported in 1946 to Italy, where he resumed his criminal career. He did not return to New York City during his lifetime but was buried in St. John's Cemetery in Queens. Luciano conformed to the popular image of an organized-crime leader: he favored custom-made shirts and sleek cars and bore facial scars from a beating he had received in the gang wars. He disdained the rivalry and parochialism of criminals from the older generation, whom he derisively termed "mustache Petes," and consistently allied himself with younger, more energetic ones, including Jews such as Meyer Lansky and Bugsy Siegel. In the late 1920s he lived at the Barbizon–Plaza Hotel, 101 West 57th Street; under the alias Charles Ross he lived from 1933 to 1936 in suite 39D of the Waldorf–Astoria Towers, 100 East 50th Street.

Sid Feder and Joachim Joesten: *The Luciano Story* (New York: D. McKay, 1954)

See also ITALIANS and ORGANIZED CRIME.

Warren Sloat

Ludwig, Daniel K(eith) (*b* South Haven, Mich., 24 June 1897; *d* New York City, 27 Aug 1992). Industrialist. The nephew of four captains on the Great Lakes, he bought a small boat for $75 at the age of nine, which he repaired and then leased out for more than $150. After finishing the eighth grade he left school to sell shipping supplies and at nineteen borrowed $5000 to finance his first business, converting steamers into freight barges to transport molasses and wood. He became wealthy after starting a tanker business, which he expanded even during the Depression; his primary corporate enterprise, National Bank Carriers, was based in New York City, and he eventually extended his investments into wood products, oil, gas, coal, minerals, real estate, and agriculture. Named one of the country's two wealthiest men in 1976, he lost much of his fortune in a development venture in the Brazilian jungle during the 1970s. Ludwig spent the last years of his life in Manhattan and was known for his strolls through midtown and his solitary lunches.

Amanda Aaron

Luhan [née Ganson], **Mabel Dodge** (*b* Buffalo, 26 Feb 1879; *d* Taos, N.M., 13 Aug 1962). Writer. As the wife of Edwin Dodge she became known as a hostess in Paris and Florence before moving to New York City in 1912, where she set up a salon at 23 5th Avenue that became well known for attracting such members as Emma Goldman, Alfred Stieglitz, Margaret Sanger, and John Reed. After her divorce she moved to Taos. She wrote a four-volume autobiography, *Intimate Memories* (1933–37).

Lois Palken Rudnick: *Mabel Dodge Luhan: New Woman, New Worlds* (Albuquerque: University of New Mexico Press, 1984)

James E. Mooney

Luks, George (Benjamin) (*b* Williamsport, Penn., 13 Aug 1867; *d* New York City, 29 Oct 1933). Painter. He studied art in Pennsylvania and in Europe before moving to New York City, where he worked in 1896 as a cartoonist for the *New York World*. In 1913 he exhibited work with The Eight at the Armory Show. For many years he taught at the Art Students League; he later offered classes at 7 East 22nd Street.

James E. Mooney

Lumet, Sidney (*b* Philadelphia, 15 June 1924). Theater, film, and television director. He made his acting début at the age of four at the Yiddish Art Theatre, where his father also acted. As a child he worked in radio, on Broadway, and eventually in films, and after the Second World War he directed Off Broadway plays. He worked on several television series for the Columbia Broadcasting System, including "Danger" and "You Are There," and wrote and directed television plays for such programs as "Playhouse 90" during the 1950s. The first motion picture that he directed was *12 Angry Men* (1957), with Henry Fonda. His film adaptations of Broadway plays include *The Fugitive Kind* (1960, from Tennessee Williams's *Orpheus Descending*) and *Long Day's Journey into Night* (1962, with Katharine Hepburn). In the following decades he shot nearly all his films in the city: the gritty urban locales of *The Pawnbroker* (1965) and *The Group* (1966) helped to establish his

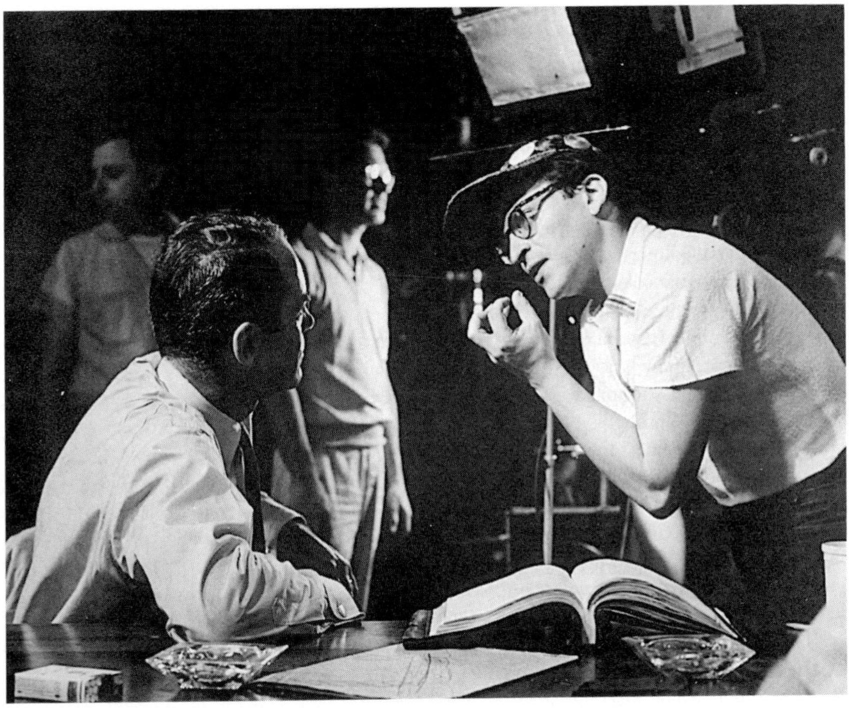

*Sidney Lumet (*right*) and Henry Fonda on the set of* 12 Angry Men *(United Artists, 1957). Collection of the American Museum of the Moving Image. Gift of Ronald A. and Randy P. Munkacsi*

tions into political corruption. After his election he became known as a witty promoter of the Bronx who often used clever phrases and stunts: he once planted a flag of the Bronx in Marble Hill to claim the neighborhood from Manhattan. Reelected six times before retiring in 1961, he served on the Board of Estimate for twenty-eight years, longer than any member before him.

Jill Jonnes: *We're Still Here: The Rise, Fall, and Resurrection of the South Bronx* (New York: Atlantic Monthly Press, 1986)

Chris McNickle

Lyons Law. Municipal law enacted in 1937, sponsored by James J. Lyons, borough president of the Bronx. It required municipal employees to have been residents of the city for three years at the time of their appointment and to maintain a residence within the city limits. Because of personnel shortages in the areas of public health and education, by the late 1950s various city and state exemptions were passed that freed more than half the city's employees from its provisions. The law had also come under increasing attack as an example of provincialism. The Lyons Law was repealed in 1962 during the administration of Mayor Robert F. Wagner.

Matthew Kachur

M

MAC. See MUNICIPAL ASSISTANCE CORPORATION.

McAdoo, William Gibbs (*b* near Marietta, Ga., 31 Oct 1863; *d* Santa Barbara, Calif., 1 Feb 1941). Lawyer, public official, and senator. He moved to New York City in 1892 to practice law; to save money he frequently walked from his home on West 87th Street to his office on Wall Street. He organized and oversaw the construction of the first tunnel under the Hudson River in 1904 and in the same year founded the Hudson and Manhattan Railroad, making sure that women who sold tickets earned the same pay as their male counterparts. An early supporter of Woodrow Wilson, as secretary of the treasury from 1913 to 1918 he played a critical role in establishing the Federal Reserve, set up the program known as Liberty Loans, and introduced life insurance for members of the armed forces. After the First World War he moved to California and in 1924 sought the Democratic presidential nomination; he led through much of the voting at the Democratic convention in Madison Square Garden but lost to John W. Davis. McAdoo later became a senator from California.

John J. Broesamle: *William Gibbs McAdoo: A Passion for Change* (Port Washington, N.Y.: Kennikat, 1973)

Ashbel Green

McAllister, (Samuel) Ward (*b* Savannah, Ga., December 1827; *d* New York City, 31 Jan 1895). Lawyer and society figure. He moved to New York City at twenty to be introduced in élite circles, later returning to Savannah, where he practiced law and became wealthy. After living in Europe and Newport, Rhode Island, for a few years he settled again in New York City, where by the late 1860s he helped to choose members for an élite group known as the "four hundred," named for the number of guests who could be accommodated in Mrs. William Astor's ballroom. He reflected on his successes in this circle in the book *Society As I Have Found It* (1890).

James E. Mooney

MacAndrews and Forbes Holdings. Holding company of the financier Ronald O. Perelman (*b* 1943), with headquarters at 35 East 62nd Street in Manhattan. It takes its name from a licorice processing firm in New Jersey that Perelman bought in 1979. After buying Technicolor in 1982 (sold 1988) it was taken private in 1983 by Perelman through financing with "junk" bonds and transformed into a holding company. In 1985 it made a hostile takeover of Revlon for $1800 million. The firm received help from the federal government in 1988 in taking over five troubled savings and loan companies that it merged to form First Gibraltar. It also bought Marvel Comics and Coleman, a manufacturer of camping equipment. In 1989 MacAndrews and Forbes had holdings valued at more than $7000 million.

Gilbert Tauber

McAneny, George (*b* Jersey City, N.J., 24 Dec 1869; *d* Princeton, N.J., 29 July 1953). Newspaperman and public official. He was a correspondent for the *New York World* who supported initiatives to make government more efficient through reform of the civil service, formation of the Bureau of Municipal Research, and zoning and regional planning. As an assistant secretary of the New York Civil Service Reform Association in 1892–94 and its secretary in 1894–1902 he drafted new civil service rules. In 1908 he was a member of the committee that revised the city charter. Elected borough president of Manhattan on a fusion ticket (1910–13), he earned a law degree from Hobart College, was president of the Board of Aldermen under the reform mayor John Purroy Mitchel (1914–16), and was the city's acting mayor for several months. In 1916–21 he was the executive manager of the *New York Times*, and from the 1920s he was active in city planning and finance. In later years McAneny led the Regional Plan Association (from 1930), was the city's sanitation commissioner and briefly its comptroller (in the early 1930s), and was chairman of the board of the Title Guarantee and Trust Company. He also helped to plan the World's Fair of 1939–40 and was active in the landmark preservation movement.

Richard Skolnick

MacArthur, Douglas (*b* Little Rock, Ark., 26 Jan 1880; *d* Washington, 5 April 1964). General. After leading the Allied forces in the Southwest Pacific during the Second World War and being relieved of command on 11 April 1951 for insubordination, he was welcomed in New York City with a ticker-tape parade on 21 April. An unsuccessful presidential candidate in 1952, he accepted a position on the board of Remington Rand and moved to a suite in the Waldorf Towers, where he spent the last years of his life, and where his widow, Jean MacArthur, remained into the 1990s. After his death MacArthur lay in state at the Seventh Regiment Armory.

D. Clayton James: *The Years of MacArthur* (Boston: Houghton Mifflin, 1970–85)

Andrew Wiese

McBride, Henry (*b* West Chester, Penn., 25 July 1867; *d* New York City, 31 March 1962). Art critic. After moving to New York City in 1889 to study art, he formed an art department for the Educational Alliance in 1900 and in the following year became the director of the School of Industrial Arts in Trenton, New Jersey. He made frequent trips abroad, often to Paris, where he became acquainted with Gertrude Stein and her circle. In 1913 he joined the *Sun* as an art writer and he soon became its chief critic, a position he held until 1950. He also contributed to the *Dial* and to *Creative Art* (which he edited from 1930 to 1932), and wrote a monthly column for *Art News* from 1950 to 1955. McBride wrote favorably about modern artists from Constantin Brancuşi to Jackson Pollock. A collection of his essays, *The Flow of Art: Essays and Criticisms of Henry McBride*, was published in 1975.

Patricia Hills

McCall's Magazine. Women's magazine launched in 1873 in New York City by the tailor James McCall as *The Queen: Illustrating McCall's Bazar Glove-fitting Patterns.* Originally it supplied its readers with new dressmaking patterns produced by James McCall and Company ten times a year. In 1890 the firm became the McCall Publishing Company and George H. Bladworth became its president. When James Henry Ottley took over in 1893 he increased the size of the magazine by adding a section of fiction and changed the title to *McCall's Magazine: The Queen of Fashion* (1897): circulation surpassed one million in 1908. Ottley sold the magazine in 1913, it underwent several changes in format, and circulation declined. Sections on home decoration, food, child care, and fashions were later added to expand the readership. From the 1970s *McCall's Magazine* broadened its scope to appeal to working women. In the mid 1990s it was published in New York City by the New York Times Magazine Group.

Frank Luther Mott: *A History of American Magazines* (New York: D. Appleton, 1930 [vol. 1] / Cambridge: Harvard University Press, 1938–68 [vols. 2–5])

Sandra Roff

McCann–Erickson. Advertising agency. Its precursor was the H. K. McCann Company, formed in 1911 to serve the divisions of the Standard Oil Company, newly separated by a decision of the U.S. Supreme Court. The plan for the agency was advanced by Harrison McCann, a young employee of the oil company. In 1930 the agency merged with the Alfred W. Erickson Company and took its current name; it was made one of four divisions of the Interpublic Group in 1960 by its chairman Marion Harper. In the mid 1990s McCann–Erickson was the largest division of the Interpublic Group, with more than one hundred offices in more than sixty countries.

Stephen R. Fox: *The Mirror Makers: A History of American Advertising and Its Creators* (New York: William Morrow, 1984)

Chauncey G. Olinger, Jr.

McCardell, Claire (*b* Frederick, Md., 24 May 1905; *d* New York City, 22 March 1958). Fashion designer. From 1930 she worked for the designer Robert Turk. With him she later joined the firm Townley Frocks, where she became head designer. She was well known for her designs of both ready-to-wear and custom-made clothing, and Townley produced clothes under her name from 1940. McCardell's designs were comfortable and affordable.

Caroline Rennolds Milbank

McCarren, Patrick (Henry) (*b* East Cambridge, Mass., 18 June 1847; *d* Brooklyn, 23 Oct 1909). Political leader. A state senator, he ousted Hugh McLaughlin as the Democratic boss of Brooklyn with support from Tammany Hall after its candidates were successful in the municipal elections of 1903. Later he declared that he would "rather be a serf in Russia than a satrap of Tammany" and opposed Tammany Hall until the end of his life.

Frank Vos

McCarthy, Mary (Therese) (*b* Seattle, 21 June 1912; *d* New York City, 25 Oct 1989). Novelist. After graduating from Vassar College in 1933 she became a literary figure in New York City and a freelance writer for the *Nation* and the *New Republic.* She lived at 52 Gramercy Park North during the early 1940s and at 14 Henderson Place in 1944. After unintentionally becoming involved with a committee that defended Leon Trotsky, she became a steadfast anti-Stalinist, leading her to help reshape the *Partisan Review.* Her views were at the center of a literary feud during the 1970s with Lillian Hellman over Hellman's discussion in her memoirs of having been a communist sympathizer during the 1950s. McCarthy's published writings include the novels *The Group* (1963) and *Birds of America* (1971). She was married to Edmund Wilson.

Carol W. Gelderman: *Mary McCarthy: A Life* (New York: St. Martin's, 1988)

Lawson Bowling

McCarthyism. As the largest city in the nation, the center of its communications industry, and the home of the Communist Party of the United States and at least 40 percent of its members, New York City was profoundly affected by the repressive anticommunist ideology known as McCarthyism. Although the term was inspired by the anticommunist charges of Senator Joseph R. McCarthy of Wisconsin between 1950 and 1954, in New York City as elsewhere the climate in which McCarthyism flourished was in evidence at least a decade before the hearings began. In 1940–41 the Rapp–Coudert investigations by the state legislature into schools and colleges in the city led to the dismissal of about sixty faculty members. Anticommunist fervor diminished during the Second World War but resumed soon after. In 1949 the state legislature passed the Feinberg Law, which mandated the elimination of members of the Communist Party from public school and college faculties. The Board of Education administered the measure by engaging a separate staff to oversee the political investigation of its employees. Suspected communists were questioned in internal hearings before the counsel to the board and often forced to disclose the names of other alleged communists. More than 435 public school and college teachers in the city were discharged as a result of these hearings, as were most of about fifty others who were questioned in public by the Internal Security Subcommittee of the U.S. Senate and invoked the Fifth Amendment. Social workers, other municipal employees, and many American citizens who worked for the United Nations were similarly persecuted, as political tests as a condition of employment became widespread.

The entertainment industry was an inviting target for McCarthyism. Blacklists were enforced by radio and television networks, their commercial sponsors, and advertising agencies, who feared retaliation from the political right if they did not comply. The book *Red Channels* (1950) included the names of 151 entertainers alleged to be subversive, only some of whom had ever belonged to the Communist Party. In 1951 and 1952 the House Un-American Activities Committee held several highly publicized hearings on the entertainment industry.

The federal courthouse in Foley Square in Manhattan was the site of the most important political trials of the McCarthy period. In 1949 the federal government prosecuted the eleven highest-ranking members of the Communist Party under the Smith Act (1940), which prohibited advocating the overthrow of the government; the conviction of the defendants was upheld by the U.S. Supreme Court in a decision now widely regarded as a grave infringement of free speech. In the following year Alger Hiss, a former official in the U.S. Department of State, was convicted of perjury in Manhattan in connection with allegations that he had transmitted government documents to the Soviet Union. There was widespread skepticism regarding the motives of the prosecutors, the soundness of the evidence, and the fairness of the proceedings in Hiss's case, as there was in that of Julius and Ethel Rosenberg, charged with atomic espionage in 1950, convicted in 1951, and executed in June 1953.

Although New York City had a reputation for liberalism, opposition to communism was so intense and pervasive that the violation of the civil rights of communists and former communists was generally tolerated.

Lawrence H. Chamberlain: *Loyalty and Legislative Action: A Survey of Activity by the New York State Legislature, 1919–1949* (Ithaca, N.Y.: Cornell University Press, 1951)

David Caute: *The Great Fear: The Anti-communist Purge under Truman and Eisenhower* (New York: Simon and Schuster, 1978)

Ellen W. Schrecker

McCay, (Zenas) Winsor (*b* Canada, 1867 / Spring Lake, Mich., 26 Sept 1871; *d* Peekskill, N.Y., 26 July 1934). Illustrator and animator. He was best known for his full-page Sunday comic strip "Little Nemo in Slumberland," first published in James Gordon Bennett's *New York Herald* on 15 October 1905; it remained there until 23 July 1911, when it was transferred to William Randolph Hearst's *New York American* under the title "In the Land of Wonderful Dreams." McCay discontinued the comic strip in 1913 but published it again from 1924 to 1926. Inspired by flipbooks, he produced the animated film *Little Nemo* (1911), which required four years to complete and is widely considered the first animated cartoon. He followed this with another, *Gertie the Dinosaur* (1914). McCay's phantasmagoric imagery endeared him to his readers and influenced such illustrators as Maurice Sendak and the filmmakers Paul Terry, Walter Lantz, and Walt Disney.

John Canemaker: *Winsor McCay* (New York: Abbeville, 1987)

Michael Joseph

McClellan, George B(rinton), Jr. (*b* Dresden, 23 Nov 1865; *d* Washington, 30 Nov 1940). Mayor. He was named for his father, the well-known Civil War general, and spent his childhood in several places, including New York City. After attending Princeton University and New York Law School he entered local politics in 1889 and later won election as president of the Board of Aldermen. For several terms beginning in 1894 he served with distinction in Congress. In 1903 he was persuaded to accept the Democratic mayoral nomination by the new boss of Tammany Hall, Charles F. Murphy, who sought to oust the fusion incumbent, Seth Low. McClellan was elected by a large majority and reelected in 1905 to a four-year term after a bitter contest with the newspaper publisher William Randolph Hearst. He ran an efficient, honest government that was highly praised even by his critics: he introduced an ambitious program of public works, fought to expand the subway system, and inaugurated a construction project in the Catskills to increase the city's water supply. After quarreling with Murphy over patronage and Murphy's support of Hearst for the governorship in 1906, McClellan retired from politics. He later became a professor of economic history at Princeton and a well-known writer. Although he brought a touch of cynicism into public life, McClellan is remembered for having served the city well.

Robert F. Wesser

McCloskey, John (*b* Brooklyn, 10 March 1810; *d* Mount St. Vincent-on-Hudson [now in the Bronx], 10 Oct 1885). Cardinal. With his parents he moved to Manhattan in 1817, and after his father's death in 1820 he entered Mount St. Mary's Seminary near Emmitsburg, Maryland, in 1821. On 12 January 1834 he became the first man born in the metropolitan area to be ordained for the secular (diocesan) priesthood. He toured Europe from 1834 to 1837, was the pastor of St. Joseph's (now on 6th Avenue) from 1837 to 1841, and from 1841 to 1847 was the first president of St. John's College (now Fordham University). He received into the Catholic faith James Roosevelt Bayley (1842) and Isaac Hecker (1844) before his appointment as the first bishop of Albany, New York, on 21 May 1847, a position he resigned to become the archbishop of New York on 6 May 1864. Although many Irish Catholics in the city supported the movement for Irish independence, he condemned Fenian violence (1866). He endorsed Levi Silliman Ives's Catholic Protectory and John Drumgoole's Mission of the Immaculate Virgin, and authorized the city's first permanent parishes for Italians (St. Anthony of Padua), Poles (St. Stanislaus, 1872), and blacks (St. Benedict the Moor); he also attended the First Vatican Council (1869–70), was elected the first American cardinal on 15 March 1875, and dedicated St. Patrick's Cathedral on 25 May 1879. By his intervention in 1884 the Italian government was prevented from confiscating the North American College in Rome, which the hierarchy in the United States supported financially and to which it sent seminarians for training. He retired during the same year to Mount St. Vincent-on-Hudson. McCloskey is buried beneath St. Patrick's Cathedral.

John Cardinal Farley: *The Life of John Cardinal McCloskey, First Prince of the Church in America, 1810–1885* (New York: Longmans, Green, 1918)

Mary Elizabeth Brown

McCloy, John J(ay) (*b* Philadelphia, 31 March 1895; *d* Stamford, Conn., 11 March 1989). Lawyer, government official, and businessman. After earning an undergraduate degree from Amherst College in 1916 he graduated from Harvard Law School in 1921 and in the same year joined the law firm Cadwalader, Wickersham and Taft. There he remained until joining the firm of Cravath, De Gersdorff, Swaine and Wood in November 1924, often traveling to Europe on business. From the 1920s he specialized in corporate law, and he played an important role during the 1930s on behalf of the Bethlehem Steel Company in litigation resulting from the Black Tom explosion. He left his practice in October 1940 to become a consultant to the secretary of war, Henry L. Stimson, and in April 1941 he was appointed assistant secretary of war. Toward the end of the Second World War he helped to plan the occupation of Germany and the trials for war crimes at Nuremberg. He resigned from the war department in November 1945 and joined the firm of Milbank, Tweed, Hope, Hadley and McCloy in New York City, leaving in February 1947 to become president of the International Bank for Reconstruction and Development. He returned to the United States in August 1952, was named chairman of Chase National Bank in January 1953, and oversaw its merger with the Bank of Manhattan Company in March 1955 to form the Chase Manhattan Bank, the second-largest commercial bank in the country. After his retirement from the bank in December 1960 he returned to private practice with Milbank, Tweed. During his long career McCloy advised every American president from Franklin D. Roosevelt to Ronald Reagan. Brinkley wrote that he was "involved in more areas of national policy, in more critical decisions, than perhaps any figure of his generation."

Alan Brinkley: "Minister without Portfolio," *Harper's*, Feb 1983, pp. 30–46
Walter Isaacson and Evan Thomas: *The Wise Men: Six Friends and the World They Made: Acheson, Bohlen, Harriman, Kennan, Lovett, McCloy* (New York: Simon and Schuster, 1986)
Thomas Alan Schwartz: *America's Germany: John J. McCloy and the Federal Republic of Germany* (Cambridge: Harvard University Press, 1991)
Kai Bird: *The Chairman: John J. McCloy, the Making of the American Establishment* (New York: Simon and Schuster, 1992)

Allen J. Share

McClure, S(amuel) S(idney) (*b* County Antrim, Ireland, 17 Feb 1857; *d* Bronx, 21 March 1949). Magazine publisher. Educated in Illinois, he moved in 1885 to New York City, where he formed a syndicate for newspaper features and in 1893 launched *McClure's*, one of the first magazines of mass circulation. In addition to sentimental fiction the magazine published early work by Stephen Crane, Frank Norris, O. Henry, and Willa Cather; essays about scientific wonders, historical figures, art, and business; and the work of such prominent "muckrakers" as Ida M. Tarbell, Ray Stannard Baker (1901–6), and Lincoln Steffens, whose well-known series "The Shame of the Cities" appeared in 1902–3. McClure's penchant for articles on municipal corruption, trusts, labor unions, and the "white slave" trade stemmed from their marketability rather than any ethical commitment. Much of his time was spent visiting foreign capitals in search of editorial material. His attempt to form a corporate conglomerate that would have included an insurance firm, a bank, a textbook publisher, and a model housing project prompted his staff to leave in protest in 1906, and his plans failed. After losing control of *McClure's* in 1912 he bought into the *Evening Mail* in 1915 as its editor-in-chief; embarrassed by the pro-German sympathies of the newspaper's principal owner during the First World War, he sold his interest in 1917. He briefly regained control of *McClure's* in 1922 but failed to halt its decline: it ceased publication in 1929. McClure retired on a trust fund established by his former colleagues. He wrote *My Autobiography* (1914).

Peter Lyon: *Success Story: The Life and Times of S. S. McClure* (New York: Charles Scribner's Sons, 1963)
Harold S. Wilson: *McClure's Magazine and the Muckrakers* (Princeton, N.J.: Princeton University Press, 1970)

Robert Stinson

McComb, John(, Jr.) (*b* New York City, 17 Oct 1763; *d* New York City, 25 May 1853). Architect. He built a lighthouse at Montauk Point, New York (1795), and also designed the home of Alexander Hamilton known as the Grange (1801–2, now on 143rd Street). On 4 October 1802 an entry he designed with Joseph François Mangin won a competition to design City Hall (for illustration see CITY HALLS); he was appointed the sole architect in charge of construction on 22 March 1803, generating a controversy about whether he or Mangin was the principal designer. Other commissions included St. John's Chapel, formerly on Varick Street (1803–7), and Castle Clinton (1811–15), as well as engineering and surveying projects. As a city surveyor (1813–21) and as the street commissioner he planned streets, sewers, canals, and piers. McComb is often considered the city's most important architect of the Federal period.

Mary Beth Betts

McCooey, John (Henry) (*b* New York City, 18 June 1864; *d* Brooklyn, 21 Jan 1934). Political leader. In 1909 he succeeded Patrick McCarren as the Democratic leader of Brooklyn, a position he held for twenty-five years. Under his direction the organization cooperated with Tammany Hall, long its enemy, to distribute patronage. In the mayoral primary election of 1925 he backed the incumbent mayor, John F. Hylan, but in the general election he shifted his support to the winner, James J. Walker. In 1932 he defused attempts by Tammany Hall to block Herbert H. Lehman's nomination for the governorship. A consummate politician known as "Uncle John," McCooey avoided controversy whenever possible. Although never elected to office, he remained on the public payroll from 1887 until 1930, when he retired as chief clerk of the Kings County Surrogate's Court.

Frank Vos

McDougall, Alexander (*b* Islay, Scotland, July/Aug 1732; *d* New York City, 9 June 1786). Soldier. After moving to New York City he commanded privateers during the Seven Years' War and in 1763 became a merchant. An avid opponent of the Crown, he was jailed for libel, became a popular hero, and served on a committee of correspondence. During the American Revolution he

Alexander McDougall by John Ramage, ca 1785. Miniature on ivory

rose to the rank of major general in the Continental Army and commanded the highlands along the Hudson. After a court-martial for insubordination he became more conservative, served in the national and state legislatures, organized the Bank of New York, and until the end of his life directed the New York State Society of the Cincinnati.

James E. Mooney

MacDowell, Edward (Alexander) (*b* New York City, 18 Dec 1860; *d* New York City, 23 Jan 1908). Composer. Born at 220 Clinton Street, where he lived until about 1876, he studied in France and Germany and then returned to New York City in 1896 to become the first professor of music at Columbia University; during these years he lived near 96th Street and Central Park West. He was president of the Society of American Musicians and Composers from 1899 to 1900, and a conductor and composer for the Mendelssohn Glee Club at Barnard College. After leaving the faculty in 1904 because of differences with the president of Columbia, Nicholas Murray Butler, he remained in New York City to teach privately. An accident with a hansom cab at Broadway and 20th Street in 1904 brought about his mental and physical decline. In 1905 a number of friends and admirers formed the MacDowell Club, which attracted four hundred members. MacDowell was the first American composer to achieve renown in Europe. In his symphonic poems, piano sonatas, and two piano concertos he forged a distinctive American style influenced by his European contemporaries Brahms and Lizst but by no means derivative of them.

Margery M. Lowens: "The New York Years of Edward MacDowell" (diss., University of Michigan, 1971)

Barbara L. Tischler

McEnroe, John (Patrick, Jr.) (*b* Wiesbaden, Germany, 16 Feb 1959). Tennis player. He grew up in Queens and lived successively in Flushing on Northern Boulevard and in Douglaston on Beverly Road, Rushmore Avenue, and Manor Road; he attended the Trinity School in Manhattan. As an amateur with a powerful left-handed serve and volley he entered the international tennis circuit in 1977 by advancing to the semifinals at Wimbledon, and until 1982 he was one of the two best players in the world; Björn Borg of Sweden was often his closest rival. He won the U.S. Open in Flushing in 1979, 1980, and 1981 and was the champion at Wimbledon in 1981. His aggressiveness and short temper led to frequent disputes with game officials and the tennis hierarchy. When he was in his mid twenties back injuries caused his game to decline. Although he had not won a major tournament since 1982 he remained a competitive player into the 1990s.

Joseph S. Lieber

Macfadden, Bernarr [McFadden, Bernard Adolphus] (*b* near Mill Spring, Mo., 16 Aug 1868; *d* Jersey City, N.J., 12 Oct 1955). Writer and publisher. Without benefit of formal schooling he moved to New York City in 1894 to work as a health crusader and publisher and in 1899 launched a popular monthly magazine called *Physical Culture*. In later years his publications included the first confession magazine in the United States, *True Story* (1919), which made him a millionaire, *True Detective Mysteries* (1924), *Liberty* (which he acquired in 1931), and a tabloid newspaper, the *New York Evening Graphic* (1924). He also wrote and published more than 150 books on diet, fitness, and sex and sponsored an encyclopedia of physical culture. Macfadden reveled in publicity: he gave lectures, promoted "health homes," denounced alcohol and tobacco, accused the American Medical Association of being a self-interested monopoly, and advocated fasting, natural healing, and exercise. His frankness about nudity and his exhibitions of healthy bodies affronted moral censors.

Robert Ernst: *Weakness Is a Crime: The Life of Bernarr Macfadden* (Syracuse, N.Y.: Syracuse University Press, 1991)

Robert Ernst

McGlynn, Edward (*b* New York City, 27 Sept 1837; *d* Newburgh, N.Y., 7 Jan 1900). Priest. After attending public schools in New York City and the Urban College of Propaganda in Rome, he was ordained on 24 March 1860 and became associated with a group of liberal clergymen. During his tenure as the pastor of St. Stephen's, 149–55 East 28th Street (1866–87), the longest pastorate of his career, he served a parish of twenty thousand known for patronizing the arts and commissioned Constantine Brumidi to paint frescoes for the church. Economic hardship caused by deflation in the late nineteenth century led him to study contemporary proposals for abolishing poverty. A supporter of the economic theories of Henry George and the Irish Land League, he came into conflict with Archbishop Michael A. Corrigan that led to his excommunication on 4 July 1887; public protest inspired an investigation by the Vatican and his reinstatement in 1892. Although he refused to build a parochial school that he considered unnecessary, one did open at St. Stephen's in 1887. McGlynn was appointed by Corrigan to St. Mary's in Newburgh, New York, in 1894.

Sylvester Malone: *Dr. Edward McGlynn* (New York: Dr. McGlynn Monument Association, 1918; repr. New York: Arno, 1978)
Stephen Bell: *Rebel Priest and Prophet: A Biography of Dr. Edward McGlynn* (New York: Devin–Adair, 1937)
St. Stephen Church, One Hundred Twenty-five Years: 1848–1973 (New York: Park, 1973)

Mary Elizabeth Brown

McGraw, John J(oseph) (*b* Truxton, N.Y., 7 April 1873; *d* New Rochelle, N.Y., 25 Feb 1934). Baseball manager. He played third base for the Baltimore Orioles from 1891 to 1900, helping the team to win three National League pennants and compiling a lifetime batting average of .334. From 1902 to 1932 he managed the New York Giants during their most successful years, winning ten pennants and finishing second in the league eleven times. A diminutive player nicknamed "Little Napoleon" and "Black John," McGraw was tyrannical and abusive: he taunted players, berated umpires, and incited crowds. As both a player and a manager he was feared and widely hated but also respected for a cunning and pugnacious brand of baseball that stressed the bunt, the steal, the hit-and-run play, and sheer intimidation. Off the field he consorted with showmen and gamblers and attended college. He wrote a memoir, *My Thirty Years in Baseball* (1923; repr. 1974). Connie Mack, for many years the manager of the Philadelphia Athletics, said in 1927: "There has been only one manager — and his name is McGraw."

Charles Blair Cleveland: *The Great Baseball Managers* (New York: Thomas Y. Crowell, 1950)
Harold Seymour: *Baseball: The Early Years* (New York: Oxford University Press, 1960)
Harold Seymour: *Baseball: The Golden Age* (New York: Oxford University Press, 1971)
Charles C. Alexander: *John McGraw* (New York: Viking, 1988)
John Thorn and Pete Palmer: *Total Baseball* (New York: Warner, 1989)
Joseph Durso: *Casey and Mr. McGraw* (New York: Sporting News, 1989)

Jeffrey Scheuer

McGraw–Hill. Firm of book, magazine, and multimedia publishers formed in New

McGraw–Hill Building on West 42nd Street, 1957

York City in 1917 by James H. McGraw and John Hill as the McGraw–Hill Book Company. When Hill died in 1917 McGraw changed the name to the McGraw–Hill Publishing Company and expanded its services. It later became one of the world's largest college and professional book publishers, also issuing magazines such as *Business Week*, *Aviation Week and Space Technology*, *BYTE*, and *Architectural Record*, and informational services in the fields of finance (Standard and Poor's), construction (F. W. Dodge), law (Shepard's), and computers (Datapro Research). In 1930 the company commissioned Raymond M. Hood to design a new headquarters at 330 West 42nd Street. Designed in an art deco style and decorated with horizontal bands of blue and green terra cotta, the building was among the first to use curtain-wall construction (the structure is partly supported by interior walls). McGraw–Hill opened its present headquarters in Rockefeller Center in 1972. It was designated a city landmark in 1990. In the mid 1990s McGraw–Hill had about four thousand employees in New York City and had published books written or edited by eighteen winners of the Nobel Prize.

Roger Burlingame: *Endless Frontiers: The Story of McGraw–Hill* (New York: McGraw–Hill, 1959)

Donald S. Rubin

McGuire, Peter J(ames) (*b* New York City, 6 July 1852; *d* Camden, N.J., 18 Feb 1906). Labor leader. The son of Irish immigrants, he became the family's primary wage earner at the age of eleven when his father enlisted in the Union Army; he found work selling newspapers, shining shoes, cleaning stables, and running errands for the department store Lord and Taylor. After attending courses and lectures at Cooper Union he was apprenticed to a carpenter and later became a journeyman. He joined the labor movement out of concern about rising unemployment, horrendous working conditions, and attacks by the police on workers' rallies. A tireless organizer and talented speaker and writer, he traveled along the East Coast urging unions to cooperate and fighting for workers' rights, labor laws, and an eight-hour work day. In August 1881 he formed the United Brotherhood of Carpenters and Joiners; he also helped to establish Labor Day as a national holiday (1882) and to form the American Federation of Labor, of which he was the first secretary (1886). McGuire died in poverty and obscurity. He is remembered for his motto, "Organize, Agitate, Educate."

Mark Ehrlich: "Peter J. McGuire: The Story of a Remarkable Trade Unionist," *Carpenter*, March 1982

L. A. O'Donnell: "Peter J. McGuire, Architect of the House of Labor," *Irish Echo*, 2 Sept 1989

John J. Concannon

Machito [Grillo, Raúl Frank] (*b* Tampa, Fla., 16 Feb 1909; *d* London, 15 April 1984). Bandleader. Soon after his birth he went with his parents to Cuba, where as a young man he played the piano and percussion and sang. In 1937 he settled in Manhattan; there he worked as a singer with Xavier Cugat's band and in 1940 formed his own band, the Afro-Cubans, with his brother-in-law Mario Bauzá as its music director. The band performed at the Park Palace Ballroom in Harlem and made many recordings. After serving in the U.S. Army in 1943–45 he returned to New York City, where his band gave weekly performances at La Conga Club that were broadcast nationwide. His work during the 1940s with the saxophonists Charlie Parker and Flip Phillips and the trumpeter Dizzy Gillespie proved highly influential in the evolution of Latin jazz. In later years Machito lived in the Bronx, toured the United States, Latin America, and Europe, and played at the Casa Blanca in Manhattan.

Chad Ludington

McKane, John Y(oung) (*b* County Antrim, Ireland, 10 Aug 1841; *d* Brooklyn, 5 Sept 1899). Political leader. He grew up in Sheepshead Bay and first held political office as a commissioner of common lands in Gravesend, where he was a powerful town supervisor from 1878 to 1893. He also served as the chief of police of Coney Island, which during his lenient tenure became known as a center of unrestricted and sometimes licentious behavior. His political career declined when politicians and businessmen in Brooklyn sought to annex Gravesend, regulate commercial amusements, and undertake suburban development for the middle class. After a celebrated trial for election fraud in 1893 McKane served five years in prison.

See also SHEEPSHEAD BAY.

Stephen Weinstein

Mackay, Clarence Hungerford (*b* San Francisco, 17 April 1874; *d* New York City, 12 Nov 1938). Philanthropist. Educated abroad by Jesuits, he moved to New York City to work in his father's mining business, which he eventually inherited. Under his auspices a trans-Pacific cable was completed in 1904. During the Depression he suffered many losses. An avid cellist, he became chairman of the Philharmonic Society and was influential in attracting Arturo Toscanini as its conductor. Mackay lived in the city except during grouse, quail, and partridge seasons. At his mansion in Roslyn, Long Island, he entertained such personages as Charles A. Lindbergh and the Prince of Wales. He is buried in Green-Wood Cemetery.

James E. Mooney

McKee, Joseph V(incent) (*b* 8 Aug 1889; *d* New York City, 28 Jan 1956). Acting mayor. A Wall Street lawyer, he became president of the Board of Aldermen in 1926 through the Democratic organization of Edward J. Flynn in the Bronx. He became acting mayor on the resignation of Mayor James J. Walker in September 1932 and remained in office until December, striking a popular chord among citizens with demands for municipal economy and political reform (among other measures he reduced his mayoral salary from $40,000 to $25,000). Although not a candidate in the special election held on 8 November 1932 that was won by John P. O'Brien, he received 232,501 write-in votes. As the mayoral nominee of the Recovery Party in the regular election of the following year he drew Democratic votes from O'Brien, thus facilitating the election of Fiorello H. La Guardia. A noted Roman Catholic layman after leaving office, McKee was sometimes known as "Holy Joe."

Andrew Wiese

Mackerelville. Nineteenth-century neighborhood on the Lower East Side of Manhattan, lying near Avenue A south of 14th Street. It was named for its many fish businesses and fish peddlers. The population was mostly Irish and poor, and the neighborhood had some gangs and its share of crime. In the 1880s European Jews moved in after new tenements were built; Irish residents moved out and Mackerelville soon disappeared.

James Bradley

McKim, Charles Follen (*b* Isabelle Furnace, Penn., 27 Aug 1847; *d* St. James, N.Y., 14 Sept 1909). Architect. Born to idealistic leaders of the abolitionist movement, he was instilled with high principles in childhood. As a young man he did not feel inclined toward any profession and left the Lawrence Scientific School at Harvard University after a year to go to Paris in 1867, having abandoned his studies in mining to become an architect. Encouraged by his father, who planned to build a few suburban houses, he studied diligently at the Atelier Daumet and at the École des Beaux-Arts. After settling in New York City he focused during the 1880s on introducing historical European styles to the United States and sought to build noble homes for the wealthy and grand public buildings, including museums, universities, hospitals, and libraries: he eventually became the principal designer of the University Club, the Harvard Club, and the campus of Columbia University in Morningside Heights. He built many houses in the city in styles ranging from Italian Renaissance to neo-Federal. Known for his precision, he looked to history to validate the details of his buildings, largely ignoring popular French styles and instead seeking inspiration in the styles of Italy and eighteenth-century America. He lived in the city for most of his life, and most of his commissions were there and in Newport (Rhode Island), Boston, and later Washington. After the dissolution of his first marriage and the death of his second wife in childbirth, he led an austere personal life when not in the company of clients, renting rooms in row houses east and west of 5th Avenue on 35th Street but never owning a home. He devoted his energy to making America beautiful in the sense of major European capitals.

By the 1890s McKim was regarded as the dean of American architecture and the embodiment of all that was noble in the nation's artistic direction, admired in part because he devoted himself to architecture rather than family. In the late 1890s he became frail but nevertheless traveled to Europe, where he formed the American Academy in Rome and won the gold medal of the Royal Institute of British Architects in 1903. His reputation saved the firm from collapse after Stanford White's murder and the lurid publicity that followed, but McKim suffered a nervous breakdown from which he never recovered and died at the home of Mrs. Stanford White.

Charles Moore: *The Life and Times of Charles Follen McKim* (Boston: Houghton Mifflin, 1929)

Leland M. Roth: *McKim, Mead and White* (New York: Harper and Row, 1983)

Mosette G. Broderick

McKim, Mead and White, elevation of the waiting room at Pennsylvania Station

McKim, Mead and White. Firm of architects. It was initially a loose partnership between Charles Follen McKim and William Rutherford Mead (1846–1928); they were soon joined by William B. Bigelow, who was replaced on his retirement in 1879 by Stanford White. The firm operated from a small office at 57 Broadway and during the next few years designed mostly resort and suburban houses in the metropolitan area, but after their Villard houses at 451–57 Madison Avenue were widely acclaimed they received many more commissions in the city, especially from wealthy businessmen for fine houses along and just off 5th Avenue. Eventually assistants handled much of the drawing and site work, and during prosperous times there were almost a hundred employees. The firm became known for the pronounced order of its designs, many based on Italian palazzi and Bostonian brick houses, and for its workmanship: McKim himself meticulously arranged for the dry-jointed walls of J. P. Morgan's library. Refittings of existing houses were undertaken for favored clients such as W. C. Whitney (1889–90 and 1898–1902). Other commissions included several apartment buildings erected as investments by insurance companies, row houses at 7th Avenue and 139th Street (1891–92) for middle-class tenants designed for the contractor David H. King, and a few tenement buildings, including two remaining ones on West 83rd Street (1885–86) and at 359 West 47th Street (1886–87).

The firm designed a few commercial buildings during the 1880s but did not receive commissions for skyscrapers in the following decades, perhaps because its buildings were expensive to build. It built the Imperial Hotel at Broadway and 32nd Street (1889–94, demolished) and in the late 1880s converted the unoccupied Plaza apartment building into a luxury hotel. The firm entered several architectural competitions but initially lost most of them. White designed and invested in Madison Square Garden (demolished 1925). During the 1890s the firm received commissions for the campuses of Columbia University in Morningside Heights (McKim) and New York University on a hill in the Bronx (now used by Bronx Community College); in the 1890s and the early twentieth century it also designed buildings for the Century Association, the University Club, the Harvard Club, the Metropolitan Club, and the Harmonie Club. Many designs were executed in the "free classical" style, including the Judson Memorial Baptist Church (1888–96) at Washington Square, one of few churches designed by the firm. Other commissions for public buildings included the Brooklyn Museum (1893–1915) and the wings of the Metropolitan Museum of Art (1904–20) along 5th Avenue (members of the firm supported the formation of art collections and often served on the boards of museums). In 1903 the firm built two tall showroom buildings on 5th Avenue for the jewelers Gorham and Tiffany. Perhaps the best-known architectural firm of the late nineteenth century, McKim, Mead and White helped to transform New York City from a city of brownstone into one of white marble and tawny brick. The firm underwent changes of name after the death of its principals; it remained in operation into the 1990s.

Leland M. Roth: *McKim, Mead and White* (New York: Harper and Row, 1983)

For further illustrations see BROOKLYN MUSEUM; HALL OF FAME FOR GREAT AMERICANS; METROPOLITAN MUSEUM OF ART; MUNICIPAL BUILDING; PENNSYLVANIA STATION; POST OFFICES; ST. BARTHOLOMEW'S CHURCH; and TIFFANY, LOUIS COMFORT.

Mosette G. Broderick

McKinney-Steward [née Smith], **Susan (Maria)** (*b* Brooklyn, 1847; *d* Xenia, Ohio, 7 March 1918). Physician. She was the daughter of Sylvanus Smith, a trustee of the African Free Schools of Brooklyn whose landholdings in the ninth ward helped to open central Brooklyn to African–Americans, and a sister-in-law of Henry Highland Garnet. After teaching school in Washington she attended the New York Medical College, where she graduated as valedictorian in 1870; she completed graduate work at the Long Island Medical College, becoming the first African–American physician in the state and the third in the country. A practitioner of homoeopathic medicine, she was a member of the King's County and New York State homoeopathic societies and had an office at 205 DeKalb Avenue, which she later moved to her home at 178 Ryerson Street in Brooklyn. In 1881 she helped to form the Women's Homoeopathic Hospital and Dispensary at Myrtle and Grand avenues. She was also a physician for the Brooklyn Home for Aged Colored People (now the Brooklyn Home for the Aged) at Kingston Avenue and St. John's Place. For twenty-eight years she was the organist and choir director for the Bridge Street African Methodist Episcopal church. McKinney-Steward later moved to Wilberforce, Ohio, where her husband was a professor, and worked as a resident physician at Wilberforce University until the end of her life.

Susan Smith McKinney-Steward, 1870

Sule Greg C. Wilson

McKinsey and Company. Firm of management consultants formed in Chicago in 1925 by the noted consultant James O. McKinsey. It quickly gained a reputation in both Chicago and New York City as a leader in its field and continued to flourish after McKinsey's death in 1937. In the early 1990s the firm had forty-four offices in twenty-two countries and 2300 consultants. Its headquarters are at 55 East 52nd Street in Manhattan.

William B. Wolf: *Management and Consulting: An Introduction to James O. McKinsey* (Ithaca, N.Y.: New York State School of Industrial and Labor Relations, 1978)

McLaughlin, Hugh (*b* Brooklyn, 25 April 1823; *d* Brooklyn, 7 Dec 1904). Political leader. Originally a fishmonger, he worked as a master foreman at the Brooklyn Navy Yard and later became a millionaire through real-estate speculation. He won election three times as register of Kings County (1861–67, 1871–73) and dominated politics in Brooklyn for almost half a century. Known as the "sage of Willoughby Street," he opposed Tammany Hall (led by William M. "Boss" Tweed, John Kelly, Richard Croker, and Charles F. Murphy during his career) and the incorporation of Brooklyn into New York City. McLaughlin is considered the founder of the Democratic organization in Brooklyn.

Frank Vos

McLoughlin Brothers. Firm of children's book publishers formed in 1858 by Edmund McLoughlin and John McLoughlin. Unlike the city's older publishers it emphasized graphic vibrancy over literary taste and originality, issuing flashy inexpensive books in quantities without rival. Its success was confirmed after John McLoughlin adapted progressive color printing technology to produce some of the first chromoxylographs, chromotints, and chromolithographs. In 1870 the firm opened a factory for color printing in Brooklyn, the largest of its kind to that time. By 1894 a plant devoted to color lithography was added, employing a staff of seventy-five artists. After John McLoughlin's death in 1905 the firm was taken over by his sons James G. McLoughlin and Charles McLoughlin; it soon sank into mediocrity, and on Charles McLoughlin's death in 1920 it was sold to the firm of Milton Bradley in Springfield, Massachusetts.

Michael Joseph

Macmillan. Communications conglomerate. It traces its origins to a bookshop opened at 53 Bleecker Street in 1869 by the English bookseller George Edward Brett as an American division of Macmillan, the publisher in London. The firm began its own publishing operations in 1886 and was incorporated as P. F. Collier and Son in 1898. Under Brett's son George Platt Brett revenues rose from $50,000 in 1890 to more than $10 million in 1935, and by 1920 sales of elementary, high school, and college textbooks accounted for about half the firm's income. In 1923 the firm moved into offices at 60 5th Avenue, near 12th Street. It remained the largest publisher in the country from the 1930s until the Second World War, when it was surpassed by Doubleday. In 1934 Collier merged with Crowell Publishers to form Crowell–Collier. It became a publicly held company in 1950 and gained independence from the British division in 1952, absorbing the Free Press of Glencoe, Illinois, in 1961. During the 1960s the firm bought such operations as the Berlitz Language Schools, Uniforms by Ostwald (a manufacturer of uniforms for marching bands), the Katharine Gibbs secretarial schools, and the Brentano chain of bookstores. Headquarters were moved to 866 3rd Avenue in 1966. After the parent company shortened its name to Macmillan in 1973 the publishing subsidiary became the Macmillan Publishing Company. In April 1984 it took over Scribner Book Companies. Macmillan was bought by Robert Maxwell of Maxwell Communication Corporation of Great Britain for $2600 million in November 1988. It later became part of the conglomerate Viacom.

Charles Morgan: *The House of Macmillan (1843–1943)* (New York: Macmillan, 1944)

John Tebbel: *A History of Book Publishing in the United States* (New York: R. R. Bowker, 1972–81), vol. 2, pp. 354–55; vol. 3, pp. 101–3, 535–37; vol. 4, pp. 118–30, 513–15

See also Book publishing.

Allen J. Share

MacMonnies, Frederick (William) (*b* Brooklyn, 28 Sept 1863; *d* New York City, 22 March 1937). Sculptor. Although he spent most of his professional life in Paris, he executed several important works of sculpture in New York City. Among the works that best represent his style are the quadriga (1898) and army and navy groups (1901) on the Soldiers' and Sailors' Memorial Arch at Grand Army Plaza, and his *Horse Tamers* (for the Pan-American Exposition of 1901, later moved to Prospect Park). In 1922 MacMonnies completed his most controversial work, *Civic Virtue* (1922), a monumental fountain with a sculpted image of a male nude trampling two females personifying Vice. The protest of several women's groups led to its removal from City Hall Park to the grounds of the Queens Municipal Building in 1941.

Edith Pettit: "Frederick MacMonnies: Portrait Painter," *International Studio* 29 (1906), 319–24

Edward J. Foote: "An Interview with Frederick W. MacMonnies, American Sculptor of the Beaux-Arts Era," *New-York Historical Society Quarterly* 61 (1977), 102–23

E. Adina Gordon and Sophie Fourny-Dargère: *Frederick William MacMonnies (1863–1937) / Mary Fairchild MacMonnies (1858–1946): deux artistes américains à Giverny* (Vernon, Eure, France: Musée Municipal A.-G. Poulain, 1988)

Susan Rather

MacNeven [McNevin], **William James** (*b* Aughrim, County Galway, Ireland, 21 March 1763; *d* New York City, 12 July 1841). Physician. He received his education in Vienna and Prague before opening a medical practice in Dublin in 1784. In Ireland he worked for Catholic emancipation and joined the United Irishmen in 1797; while traveling to France to solicit help for the organization his plans were uncovered by England, and he was jailed in Ireland and Scotland. Freed in 1802, he emigrated to the United States and settled in New York City in 1805. He was appointed professor of midwifery at the College of Physicians and Surgeons and worked to assist Irish immigrants. He died at the home of Thomas Addis Emmet Jr.

Pieces of Irish History, Illustrative of the Condition of the Catholics of Ireland (New York: B. Dornin, 1807)

William McGimpsey

Macombs Dam. Dam built in 1813 by Robert Macomb to power a mill on the Harlem River near a site now occupied by Yankee Stadium. It blocked boats sailing the river, and in 1838 residents of the riverbank led by Lewis G. Morris chartered a coal barge and paid the crew to break through the dam with axes: when the owners of the dam sued for damages the New York State Court of Appeals ruled that the federal government had jurisdiction over navigable waterways and that the state should not have permitted the dam to be built. A park at the Bronx landing bears the name of the dam, as does the drawbridge built near the site.

Lloyd Ultan

Macombs Dam Bridge, ca *1900*

Macombs Dam Bridge. Swing drawbridge spanning the Harlem River between 155th Street at 7th Avenue in Manhattan and Jerome Avenue at 161st Street in the Bronx. Completed in 1896 at a cost of $1.36 million as the third bridge on the site, it is named for Robert Macomb (who built a dam there in 1813). The bridge has a maximum span of 408 feet (125 meters) and rises 29.2 feet (8.9 meters). In Manhattan a long approach descends from Edgecombe Avenue to 7th Avenue. The bridge is well known to baseball fans as a link from Manhattan to Yankee Stadium. It is operated by the New York State Department of Transportation.

WPAG

Andrew Sparberg

McSorley's Old Ale House. Saloon opened in 1854 at 15 East 7th Street by John McSorley, a Quaker immigrant from Ireland. During the nineteenth century it attracted a diverse group of patrons: German and Irish immigrants, skilled craftsmen, Wall Street brokers, and politicians, including Abraham Lincoln. The back room was used for weekly bible meetings that McSorley encouraged. Originally the saloon operated under the motto "Good Ale, Raw Onions, and No Ladies," which it changed to "Good Ale and Raw Onions" after admitting women in 1970. The oldest establishment of its kind in Manhattan, McSorley's draws many visitors, not only for its beer and food but also for its collection of memorabilia, which include theater programs, political cartoons, menus, newspaper cuttings, furniture, and photographs.

Joseph Mitchell: *McSorley's Wonderful Saloon* (New York: Grosset and Dunlap, 1943)

Kevin Kenny

Macy, Josiah (*b* Nantucket, Mass., 28 Feb 1785; *d* Rye, N.Y., 15 May 1872). Merchant and banker. The son of a prominent whaling and shipping family in Nantucket, he worked in virtually every aspect of the maritime trade. He began his career as a common sailor before becoming a ship's master and later the owner of a shipping and commissions business. After the end of the War of 1812 he moved to New York City in 1815 to take part in the "triangular trade." One of the leading commercial shippers of his time, Macy operated a packet service that served Liverpool and Charleston, South Carolina, owned a fleet of whaling vessels, directed the Tradesman's Bank, and managed a trading house in Manhattan. In the 1860s his firm entered the petroleum business; its refinery was purchased by the Standard Oil Company in 1872.

David A. Balcom, Andrew Wiese

Macy Foundation. See Josiah Macy, Jr. Foundation.

Macy's. See R. H. Macy.

Mad. Humor magazine launched in April 1955 by Harvey Kurtzman and William M. Gaines, who in 1952 had published a satirical comic book called *Tales Calculated to Drive You Mad: Humor in a Jugular Vein.* Published by E.C. Publications at 485 Madison Avenue, it lampooned advertisements and popular culture and adopted as its mascot the fictitious character Alfred E. Newman, a freckle-faced boy with a moronic grin whose only pronouncement was "What, me worry?" The magazine thrived by perfecting an anarchic brand of humor closely associated with New York City and aimed largely at preadolescent males. It became known for its irreverent comic strips, parodies of films and television programs, and especially its "fold-ins," seemingly innocuous illustrations on the inside back cover that depicted something different and usually derisive when folded. In addition to its regular, monthly issues *Mad* publishes six special issues a year, as well as a large number of paperback anthologies.

Maria Reidelbach: *Completely Mad: A History of the Comic Book and Magazine* (Boston: Little, Brown, 1991)

Patricia A. Perito

Mad Bomber. The popular name of George P. Metesky, who between 1940 and 1956 planted thirty-three homemade bombs throughout New York City, of which twenty-three detonated before being found; six of these caused injuries to a total of fifteen persons. Some targets were attacked more than once: Grand Central Terminal (five times), Pennsylvania Station (three times), Radio City Music Hall (twice), and the Port Authority Bus Terminal (twice). Metesky was fifty-four years old when arrested at his home in Waterbury, Connecticut, on 18 January 1957. A former employee of Consolidated Edison, he was disgruntled about the rejection of a claim for workers' compensation that he had filed in 1934. He was traced through a series of letters about the claim that he wrote to the *New York Journal–American* from 1956. Metesky served seventeen years in an asylum for the criminally insane and was released in December 1974.

Rohit T. Aggarwala

Madison Avenue. Major avenue in Manhattan between 23rd Street and 138th Street. Its width is seventy feet (21.4 meters) south of 42nd Street and eighty feet (24.4 meters) north of 42nd Street. Construction during the 1840s was called for because few lots were still available on large avenues, and because of the wide distance between Park Avenue to the west and 5th Avenue to the east. In the last half of the nineteenth century the avenue became a residential street for the upper middle class, and it had some commercial establishments by the turn of the century; these extended as far north as 59th Street in 1910–30 and included such exclusive hotels as the Biltmore, the Roosevelt, and the Ritz–Carlton, as well as fashionable men's shops. After the Second World War the avenue became identified with the advertising business, although only two major agencies ever had their offices there (Young and Rubicam; and Batten, Barton, Durstine and Osborn). In the mid 1990s Madison Avenue was lined with fashionable shops and residences between 59th and 96th streets.

Martin Mayer: *Madison Avenue, USA* (New York: Harper and Brothers, 1958)

John Tauranac

Madison Square with Metropolitan Life Insurance Building (designed by Napoleon Le Brun), 1910

Madison Square. Neighborhood on the East Side of Manhattan, centered at a park occupying 6.8 acres (2.75 hectares) that is bounded to the north by 26th Street, to the east by Madison Avenue, to the south by 23rd Street, and to the west by Broadway and 5th Avenue. It was once part of the Parade, a tract of about 240 acres (ninety-seven hectares) set aside in 1807 for an arsenal, a barracks, and a potter's field; the tract was pared to ninety acres (thirty-six hectares) and renamed for President James Madison in 1814. The playing field of the Knickerbocker Base Ball Club once stood at 27th Street and Madison Avenue. Soon all that remained of the original tract was the square, which opened on 10 May 1847 and was from the 1850s to the 1870s the center of an aristocratic neighborhood of brownstones where Theodore Roosevelt and Edith Wharton were born. Across from the western edge of the park an obelisk was erected in 1857 over the grave of General William J. Worth, who fought in the Mexican War. The luxurious Fifth Avenue Hotel opened nearby in 1859. The intersection of Madison Avenue and 26th Street was occupied successively by a depot of the New York and Harlem Rail Road, Barnum's Hippodrome (1873), the first Madison Square Garden (1879), and the second Madison Square Garden (1890, Stanford White). About the turn of the century the area became a commercial district. Madison Square is known for its toy, china, and insurance companies and for several architecturally distinguished buildings, among them an art deco skyscraper and campanile of the Metropolitan Life Insurance Company, a building of the New York Life Insurance Company topped with a gilded pyramid, and the Flatiron Building (1902), erected on a triangular lot at Broadway and 23rd Street. A building housing the Appellate Division of the New York State Supreme Court on Madison Avenue is adorned with several fine sculptures.

Marcus Benjamin: *A Historical Sketch of Madison Square* (New York: Meridian Britannia, 1894)
Charles Lockwood: *Manhattan Moves Uptown* (Boston: Houghton Mifflin, 1976)

See also SPORTS, §§3, 4. For further illustration see DEWEY ARCH.

Joyce Mendelsohn

Original site of Madison Square Garden

Madison Square Garden. The name of four major indoor sporting and entertainment facilities in New York City. The first was a grimy, drafty structure opened by William Vanderbilt on 31 May 1879 at 26th Street and Madison Avenue, on a site used since 1874 by the impresarios P. T. Barnum and Patrick S. Gilmore. Vanderbilt emphasized sport, and his most popular athletic attraction was the boxing champion John L. Sullivan. After he razed the building in 1889 because it was losing money, officials of the Horse Show Association replaced it with one designed in a Moorish style by Stanford White and erected at a cost of $3 million. The second-tallest building in New York City, it had the largest auditorium in the United States (seating eight thousand), a theater, a concert hall, apartments, a roof cabaret, and the city's largest restaurant, topped by Augustus Saint-Gaudens's *Diana.* The facility was the site of the Horse Show, the shows of the Westminster Kennel Club, bicycle races, long-distance footraces, boxing matches, physical culture exhibitions, and political rallies, but it was still losing money, having a mortgage of $2 million and requiring $20,000 a month to operate while rentals seldom brought in more than $1500 a day. The F&D Real Estate Company purchased the structure in 1911 for $3.5 million and went bankrupt in 1916, when the New York Life Insurance Company foreclosed on the property.

Business turned around in 1920, when the promoter Tex Rickard leased the building for $200,000 a year for ten years. The newly legalized sport of boxing was the key to his success, bringing in $5 million in five years, but other attractions were also important, including the circus, track meets, six-day bicycle races, and the rodeo. The facility was the site in 1924 of the Democratic National Convention, which lasted seventeen days; in the following year it was razed to make way for the new headquarters of New York Life Insurance. Rickard raised $6 million for a new arena at 50th Street and 8th Avenue, which opened on 28 November 1925 and was profitable immediately. Earnings surpassed $1 million in 1927, and the building remained profitable to the end of 1931 despite the Depression. New attractions included professional hockey (the New York Rangers) and the Ice Show. From 1931 to 1933 the journalist Ned Irish staged an annual college basketball tripleheader for charity: the event was so successful that in 1934 he scheduled six doubleheaders between local and national teams. Irish made Madison Square Garden a renowned venue for basketball, especially after it became the site of the National Invitational Tournament in 1938. Yet the main attraction was still boxing, and thirty-two championship fights were staged between 1925 and 1945. The single largest crowd (23,306) was for the welterweight championship fight between Henry Armstrong and Fritzie Zivic on 17 January 1941.

After the Second World War Madison Square Garden was filled almost daily with crowds attending familiar attractions like the circus (which alone had seventy-seven shows

Madison Square Garden (designed by Stanford White), ca *1900*

a year) and new ones like professional basketball (the New York Knicks). But the college basketball scandals of 1951 were a major setback, ending the popular intercollegiate doubleheaders, and the boxing business declined in the late 1950s because of antitrust violations, the influence of organized crime, and overexposure on television. The building had poor sightlines and lacked modern amenities, and in 1968 it was replaced by a new, circular complex atop Pennsylvania Station, costing $116 million, that had an arena seating 20,344 and a smaller facility called the Felt Forum.

In 1977 Madison Square Garden was purchased for $60 million by the conglomerate Gulf and Western (later renamed Paramount). Top ticket prices rose sharply, from $8.50 in 1970 to $45 in 1990. In 1992 the facility underwent a renovation costing $200 million, during which ninety-eight box suites were constructed, each renting for as much as $190,000. Madison Square Garden has its own cable television network that broadcasts games of the Rangers, Knicks, and New York Yankees. Television rights to the Yankees alone cost $486 million for the period 1989–2000.

Joseph Durso: *Madison Square Garden: 100 Years of History* (New York, 1979)

For further illustration see AMERICAN LABOR PARTY.

Steven A. Riess

Mafia. The activities of the Mafia are discussed in the entry ORGANIZED CRIME.

magazines. The first magazines in New York City were published by James Parker during the 1750s. These were followed in 1787 by Noah Webster's *American Magazine*, which ceased after a year, and *New-York Magazine* (1790–97), which published theater reviews, poetry, and a monthly listing of local events. By the 1790s the city was a national center of commerce, culture, and publishing, and the number of magazines increased. Nearly all publications at the time were plagued by financial problems and a chronic scarcity of contributors and readers; many new ones appeared after postal regulations were changed in 1794 to allow magazines to be sent through the mail. A number of these sought a national audience, often imitating British journals and even copying their material. The first American medical journal, the *Medical Repository* (1797–1824), was published quarterly in the city. Other specialized magazines appeared during the first decades of the nineteenth century, many of them devoted to such varied topics as science, literature, art criticism, politics, satire, and fiction. Charles Brockden Brown's *Monthly Magazine and American Review* (1799–1800) printed fiction, poetry, and articles about literature, science, and politics. One of the city's first WOMEN'S MAGAZINES, the *Lady's Weekly Miscellany*, was published from 1805 to 1808. A journal of satire,

Magazine vendor, ca *1935–40*

Salmagundi (1807–8), was offered by Washington Irving, his brother William Irving, and James Kirk Paulding; *Analectic* (1813–21) was edited for its first two years by Washington Irving and solicited pieces from Paulding. One of the city's first religious magazines, the *Methodist Review*, was introduced in 1818 and was soon followed by the *New York Observer* (1823) and the *Methodist Christian Advocate* (1826). The weekly *Ladies' Literary Cabinet* (1819–22) was edited by Samuel Woodworth. Short-lived but important journals included the *American Monthly and Critical Review* (1817–19), the *Literary and Scientific Repository* (1820–22), and the weekly magazine *New-York Mirror* (1823–57; from 1823 to 1840 edited by Samuel Woodworth and Nathaniel Parker Willis, and published by George Pope Morris), which supported the Knickerbocker literary group and reported news of the élite.

By 1825 more magazines were published in New York City than in Boston or Philadelphia. Innovations in printing between 1825 and 1850, especially the development of the cylinder press, helped the magazine business to grow rapidly, as did the expansion of literacy. Magazines for a general audience became common. The *New-York Review and Atheneum Magazine* (1825–26) was a magazine of culture edited by William Cullen Bryant and Robert C. Sands that drew contributions from Fitz-Greene Halleck and Nathaniel Willis. The first magazine aimed at the city's black residents, *Freedom's Journal*, began publication in 1827. The country's first general sports magazine, *Spirit of the Times* (1831–1902), was introduced in the city by William Porter. There were also a number of religious magazines, such as the *New York Evangelist* (1832) and later the *Church Review* (1848). Under Lewis Gaylord Clark the literary magazine the *Knickerbocker* (1833–65) published such writers as Paulding, Bryant, Sands, Willis, and James Fenimore Cooper, many of them writing about life in the city. The *Ladies' Companion* (1834–44) of William Snowden received contributions from Edgar Allan Poe and Henry Wadsworth Longfellow. Political journals also appeared: the *Democratic Review* (1837–59), which moved to the city in 1841, printed political and literary pieces, including stories by Poe and Nathaniel Hawthorne. The *Mirror of Liberty* (1838–41), a magazine for blacks, was edited by the abolitionist and civil rights leader David Ruggles. The literary and satirical journal *Arcturus* (1840–42) was published by the critics Cornelius Mathews and Evert A. Duyckinck. New specialized periodicals included the *American Agriculturalist* (from 1842), *Scientific American* (from 1845), and *American Whig Review* (1845–52). The weekly publication *Broadway Journal* (1845–46) offered literary criticism, political commentary, poetry, and art, theater, and music reviews; it attracted such writers as James Russell Lowell and Poe, who edited the last issues. The *Home Journal* (from 1846; edited by Morris and Willis) was the most sophisticated publication for the home; renamed *Town and Country* in 1901, it continued into the 1990s. The *Congregationalist Independent* was published from 1848 to 1928.

The mid nineteenth century saw a marked change in the city's magazines. Book publishers, growing in number and influence, issued magazines of their own, and the books and magazines often shared material. Harper and Brothers introduced *Harper's Monthly* in 1850, followed by *Harper's Bazar* (1867) and *Harper's Weekly* (1875). An important rival was *Putnam's Monthly*, a magazine of literature and political commentary begun in 1853 by the firm of G. P. Putnam; one of its most popular features was "The World of New York," introduced in 1856. During the 1850s Frank Leslie began publishing some of the first illustrated magazines and newspapers. These provided news about international, national, and local events, accompanied by vivid and timely illustrations. *Leslie's Weekly* was especially thorough in its coverage of the city. It undertook such ambitious projects as investigating Mayor Fernando Wood's activities and the events of Election Day in 1858, and leading a successful campaign against unsanitary conditions in dairies. One of the first trade publications was the *Hardware Man's Newspaper and American Manufacturer's Circular* (from 1855), later renamed *Iron Age*.

The panic of 1857 caused a number of magazines to fail, including the *Democratic Review* and the *New York Mirror*. The scholarly publication *Anglo-African Magazine* (1859–60) was edited and published by Thomas Hamilton. During the Civil War the issues of slavery, states' rights, and the tariff dominated many magazines; some such as *Leslie's Weekly* and *Harper's Monthly* lost their southern readership. Other hardships included the rising cost of paper and ink, and competition from newspapers, which provided more immediate coverage of the war. The *Nation*, a journal of political commentary, was begun in 1865. Among new trade publications were the *Telegrapher* (1864–77), issued weekly, and the *Publishers' and Stationers' Weekly Trade Circular* (from 1872), which later became *Publishers Weekly*, the leading publication of the book trade.

In the decades after the war, production technology improved and magazine publishers sought wider audiences and adopted aggressive marketing techniques. Subscription prices were reduced, the amount of advertising increased, and circulation numbers rose markedly. Some of the first figures to adopt new practices were in New York City, such as Frank Munsey, S. S. McClure, and the publishers of the women's magazines *McCall's* and the *Delineator*. Publications devoted to woman suffrage and other feminist issues appeared during these years, notably the *Revolution* (1868–72), edited by Susan B. Anthony, Elizabeth Cady Stanton, and George Trainor, and the more radical magazine *Woodhull and Claflin's Weekly* (1870–76). *Appleton's Journal* (1869–81) was issued by the book publisher D. Appleton, as was *Scribner's Monthly* (later renamed the *Century*) by Charles Scribner in 1870. Scientific, technical, and trade journals of the time included *American Garden*, which began publication in 1871 in Brooklyn, and *Popular Science Monthly* (1872). After the war the most influential religious magazines were published elsewhere, but a few appeared in the city. Some of the best-known were Henry Ward Beecher's *Christian Union* (1870–93, later renamed the *Outlook*) and the *Brooklyn Magazine* (1884–89) of Edward Bok and Frederic Colver, which printed Beecher's sermons.

As early as 1880 publishers in the city produced a quarter of the country's magazines and two thirds of those with a circulation of more than 100,000. Cheaper delivery by mail was made possible after postal rates for second-class mailings were reduced in 1885. Most magazines begun about this time, such as *Munsey's*, *McClure's*, *Cosmopolitan*, and *Everybody's*, appealed to the middle class and emphasized national politics, the economy, and social issues rather than articles on travel, history, literature, and the arts. Many of the city's magazines covered both local and national news. New publications that reported and analyzed contemporary events included the *Literary Digest* (1890–1938) and the *Review of Reviews* (1891–1937). The center of women's magazine publishing moved to New York City from Philadelphia, and the number of women's magazines grew as women, especially those in the middle class, sought advice about their role in society. The *Delineator*, *McCall's*, and the *Pictorial Review* began publication during the late nineteenth century, followed by the *Woman's Home Companion* and *Good Housekeeping* in the early twentieth. Fashion magazines like *Harper's Bazar* and *Vogue* grew with the emerging fashion industry. The *Smart Set* (1890) chronicled news of the city's élite; under the editorial direction of George Jean Nathan and H. L. Mencken it published literary reviews, essays, and satirical pieces. Bernarr Macfadden built an empire based on magazines about health and sex, starting with *Physical Culture* in 1899.

After the turn of the century a number of magazines, most of them published in the city, became known nationally for their investigative reporting, termed "muckraking" by President Theodore Roosevelt. Articles on the country's social and economic problems appeared in *Collier's*, *Everybody's*, *Leslie's Monthly*, *Cosmopolitan*, *Pearson's*, *Scribner's*, the *Delineator*, and *Broadway*, attracting public attention and more subscribers. Some of the most ambitious efforts were undertaken by *McClure's* in January 1903, when it published articles on Standard Oil by Ida Tarbell, on the United Mine Workers by Ray Stannard Baker, and on corruption in Minneapolis by Lincoln Steffens, prefaced with an editorial piece by McClure. The early decades of the century saw the introduction of the *Crisis* (1910), the publication of the National Association for the Advancement of Colored People, and of the radical journals the *Masses* (1911) and the *New Republic* (1914), which with the *Nation* offered sharper criticism of society than most other magazines did. Under Frank Crowninshield *Vanity Fair* (1913–36) reported on cultural affairs. Increasingly supported by advertising, magazines began to conduct market research and use advertising agents, leading to the establishment of the first advertising agencies in the city. In 1914 the Audit Bureau of Circulation was organized to meet advertisers' demands for verified circulation figures. Advertising became even more influential after the First World War, determining the size, distribution, and even the content of magazines. Macfadden introduced the first confession magazine, *True Story*, in 1919; it appealed to a wide audience and with a number of successful imitations flourished during the 1920s and 1930s. Other "pulps" devoted to adventure, mystery, Western themes, and romance also became popular, many of them produced by the firm of Street and Smith; science fiction pulps were introduced in the late 1920s.

Economic and cultural change in the decades between the world wars radically altered the magazine market. Two of the most successful publications were intended to give the reader information quickly and easily: *Reader's Digest* (1922), begun by Lila Wallace and DeWitt Wallace in a basement in Greenwich Village and soon moved to Westchester County, and the news magazine *Time* (1923) of Henry R. Luce and Briton Haddon. The *American Mercury* (1924) was edited by Nathan and Mencken and consistently debunked the middle class. The *New Yorker* (1925), edited by Harold Ross, began as a humor magazine and eventually took on a literary emphasis. A number of business publications were introduced during these years: *Tide* (1927) for advertisers and *Fortune* (1930) for businessmen, both published by Luce, and *Business Week* (1929), published by McGraw–Hill. These were among the first magazines to maintain editorial standards as high as those of consumer publications. The year 1933 marked the introduction of *Newsweek*, by Thomas Martyn and Samuel Williamson, and of *United States News* (later *U.S. News and World Report*). As one of the country's most important intellectual centers, the city supported the *Partisan Review* (formed 1934), a magazine devoted to works of the avant-garde as well as those by European writers. Many publications suffered during the first months of the Depression when advertisers reduced their spending, and some were forced out of business, among them *Scribner's*, the *Review of Reviews*, and the *Century*. Hearst's empire, which owned *Good Housekeeping* and *Cosmopolitan*, faltered and ceased publishing the *Pictorial Review–Delineator* in 1939 owing to insufficient advertising revenues. The industry suffered further during the Second World War because of shortages of paper and consumer goods.

After the war magazines were forced to compete with television for audiences and advertising. The competition proved fatal for *Look*, *Life*, the *Saturday Evening Post*, and all the magazines published by Crowell–Collier, including *Collier's*, the *Woman's Home Companion*, and the *American*. During the 1960s postal rates and paper prices rose and advertising revenues declined. Publishers raised subscription prices and emphasized to prospective advertisers that magazines had more of an impact than television because they were read at leisure, and that unlike television they had a secondary, "pass-along" audience. Competition from television also accelerated a trend toward specialization. Some general-interest magazines were transformed for a narrower audience. One of the most successful examples of this trend was *Cosmopolitan*, which under the direction of Helen Gurley Brown from 1965 aimed at aspiring single women. From the 1960s women's magazines sought to adjust to the changes wrought by the feminist movement, which inspired the politically oriented magazine *Ms.* and eventually more traditional magazines such as *Working Woman*, *Self*, *Lear's*, and *Victoria*. The introduction of ink-jet printing, selective binding, and computers allowed publishers to customize magazines for different readers. As television became the primary provider of entertainment, many magazines abandoned fiction and focused exclusively on news and information. The market for business publications outstripped that for consumer magazines: *Money*, *Fortune*, *Forbes*, *Crain's New York Business*, and *New York City Business* provided detailed coverage of financial and corporate activity, much of it centered in the city.

Many publications were absorbed during the 1970s and 1980s by media conglomerates like Time–Warner and Thomson and Maxwell, and became increasingly national in their focus. At the same time some publishers introduced publications for segments of the population that had been largely ignored, especially Latin Americans and gays. *Vanity Fair*, revived by Condé Nast in 1983, achieved great success under the direction of Tina Brown, who later moved to the *New Yorker*. The most successful magazines published in the city in the 1980s and 1990s were devoted to money, diet, fitness and health, child-rearing, travel, the home (*HG*, *Metropolitan Home*, *Architectural Digest*), fashion (*Vogue*, *Harper's Bazaar*, *Women's Wear Daily*, *Esquire*, *GQ*), sex (*Penthouse*), and the magazine business itself (*Magazine Age*).

Theodore Peterson: *Magazines in the Twentieth Century* (Urbana: University of Illinois Press, 1956)
John William Tebbel and Mary Ellen Zuckerman: *The Magazine in America, 1741–1990* (New York: Oxford University Press, 1991)

See also LITTLE MAGAZINES and SCIENTIFIC PUBLISHING.

Mary Ellen Zuckerman

magdalen societies. Charitable organizations formed to help prostitutes and lead them to respectability. The New-York Magdalen Society, the first organization of its kind in the United States, was formed on 1 January 1830 by John R. McDowall, a missionary of the American Tract Society working in the Five Points. With several wealthy women he opened a "house of refuge" for prostitutes in 1831. The society's first annual report accused genteel New Yorkers of frequenting prostitutes and caused an enormous uproar, leading the women members to close the house of refuge. Undeterred, McDowall called for a moral crusade in his tract *Magdalen Facts* (1832) and began publishing *McDowall's Journal*, which inspired middle- and upper-class women to launch a number of reform societies in local churches. These groups merged in May 1834 and became the New York Female Moral Reform Society under the direction of Lydia Andrews Finney, the wife of the evangelist Charles Grandison Finney. A new house of refuge opened on West 25th Street but did not become very active, perhaps because its sponsors were highly moralistic and unrealistic. In 1836 the society shifted its focus to preventing prostitution and doing charity work. Renamed the New-York Magdalen Asylum, the house of refuge moved in 1850 to East 88th Street and in 1893 to a building on West 139th Street with room for 125 persons.

Several magdalen homes were organized in the mid nineteenth century. The House of Mercy at Inwood-on-the-Hudson (1850) was an important one that moved successively to East 86th Street and in 1891 to larger quarters on 206th Street. The House of the Good Shepherd, established in 1857 by five nuns of the Order of Our Lady of the Good Shepherd of Angers, was the largest home in the city (with a capacity of five hundred) and admitted women regardless of creed. The Florence Crittenton Mission for Fallen Women, which occupied a building on Bleecker Street near the Bowery, was well known and sought to reclaim prostitutes with lodging and nightly Gospel meetings. In 1866 the Midnight Mission opened at 208 West 46th Street; in 1891 St. Joseph's Night Refuge was founded on West 14th Street by Friends of the Homeless, which was among the first agencies to assume that women were driven to prostitution by poverty rather than moral weakness. St. Joseph's provided beds and meals for 3500 homeless women a year. Magdalen homes reached the height of their influence during the late nineteenth century. In the following decades prostitution came to be seen as a criminal activity, and by the 1950s the remaining magdalen homes abandoned moral reform and concentrated instead on providing shelter for unwed mothers.

Alana J. Erickson

Magnes, Judah L(eon) (*b* San Francisco, 5 July 1877; *d* New York City, 27 Oct 1948). Rabbi. Educated in the United States and abroad, he attended Hebrew Union College and later worked there as an instructor and librarian. Between 1906 and 1912 he was the rabbi at Temple Israel in Brooklyn and at Temple Emanu-El and B'nai Jeshurun in Manhattan. Magnes led the Society for the Advancement of Judaism for the next eight years, after which he moved to Jerusalem to become chancellor of Hebrew University.

William M. Brinner and Moses Rischin: *Like All the Nations?: The Life and Legacy of Judah L. Magnes* (Albany: State University of New York Press, 1987)

James E. Mooney

Maidenform. Firm of intimate-apparel manufacturers, formed in 1922 by the dressmakers Ida Rosenthal and William Rosenthal with Enid Bissett. It was based at 36 West 57th Street in Manhattan and during its first year introduced the Maiden Form Brassiere, the first uplift brassiere. In 1927 the firm was renamed the Maiden Form Brassiere Company and moved to 245 5th Avenue. During the next decade it became one of the largest intimate-apparel manufacturers in the world. Known for its astute marketing, it ran ingenious advertising campaigns, among them one based on the slogan "I dreamed . . . in my Maidenform bra," which lasted from 1949 to 1969. The headquarters were moved to 90 Park Avenue in 1964.

James Bradley

Mailer, Norman (Kingsley) (*b* Long Branch, N.J., 31 Jan 1923). Novelist. He grew up in Brooklyn, attended Harvard College, and was an infantryman in the Second World War. In 1948 he published *The Naked and the Dead*, widely regarded as one of the most compelling novels about the war. He was a founder in 1956 of the *Village Voice*, for which he wrote a column, and became known for developing a style of journalism that described events through the subjective eye of the novelist. The hero of his essay "The White Negro" (1957), published in *Dissent*, is an existential "hipster" who finds American society totalitarian and rejects it. He provoked controversy with such works as *Advertisements for Myself* (1959), a collection of essays, unfinished stories, and other pieces; *An American Dream* (1965), a novel set in New York City; *Miami and the Siege of Chicago* (1968), about the Democratic and Republican conventions in 1968; and *Armies of the Night* (1968), a personal history of an antiwar protest in 1967 for which he won the National Book Award, the Polk Award, and the Pulitzer Prize. He also directed several experimental films, unsuccessfully sought the mayoralty of New York City in 1969, wrote a highly publicized book about Marilyn Monroe and a murder mystery (*Tough Guys Don't Dance*, 1984), cultivated a reputation as an amateur boxer, and championed a talented writer who was a convicted murderer. A resident of Greenwich Village in the 1950s, he later moved to Brooklyn Heights, where he remained into the 1990s. Mailer's egotism, quick temper, and costly divorces brought him much publicity. His later work includes the long, critically praised novel *Harlot's Ghost* (1991).

Leslie Gourse

Mainbocher [Bocher, Main (Rousseau)] (*b* Chicago, 9 Oct 1891; *d* Munich, 27 Dec 1976). Fashion designer. He began his career in Paris as a fashion artist in haute couture. When he returned to the United States he worked as an editor at *Harper's Bazaar* for several years before opening his own couture house in 1930. The best known of his many dresses was worn by Wallis Simpson during her marriage to the Duke of Windsor in 1937. His gold lamé lumberjack jacket and aproned evening dresses reflected his ability to juxtapose down-to-earth designs and ornate materials. From 1940 to 1971 Mainbocher was known for having one of the most elegant and expensive couture houses in New York City.

Caroline Rennolds Milbank

Malamud, Bernard (*b* Brooklyn, 26 April 1914; *d* New York City, 18 March 1986). Novelist and short-story writer. The son of Russian Jewish immigrants who operated a small grocery store, he grew up speaking both English and Yiddish. From 1928 to 1932 he attended Erasmus Hall High School. After graduating from City College of New York (BA in English 1936) he worked as a clerk, in a factory, and as a shop assistant while writing fiction in his spare time. His short stories were published in a number of magazines, including the *New Yorker*, *Harper's*, and the *Atlantic*, and he also contributed articles to the *New York Times*. During the 1950s and 1960s he became one of the leading figures in Jewish American letters through his novels *The Natural* (1952), *The Assistant* (1957), and *The Fixer* (1966, National Book Award and Pulitzer Prize) and the collection of short stories *The Magic Barrel* (1958, National Book Award), often drawing inspiration from his life in New York City. In addition to working as a writer Malamud taught at Erasmus Hall (1940–48), Harlem High School (1948–49), Oregon State College (1949–61), and Bennington College in Vermont (from 1961 until the end of his life).

Jeffrey Helterman: *Understanding Bernard Malamud* (Columbia: University of South Carolina Press, 1985)

Harold Bloom, ed.: *Bernard Malamud* (New York: Chelsea House, 1986)

Edward A. Abramson: *Bernard Malamud Revisited* (New York: Twayne, 1993)

Allen J. Share

Malba. Neighborhood in north central Queens, bounded to the north by the East River (Powell's Cove), to the east by the Whitestone Expressway, to the south by 15th Avenue, and to the west by 138th Street. Its name is derived from the first letters of the surnames of the five founders, all residents of New Haven, Connecticut: George A. Maycock, Samuel R. Avis, George W. Lewis, Nobel P. Bishop, and David R. Alling. The land was acquired in 1883 by William Ziegler, president of the Royal Baking Powder Company; a subsidiary, the Realty Trust Company, developed 163 acres (sixty-six hectares) in 1908 for wealthy boaters and fishermen, and in the same year railroad service was extended. There were thirteen houses by the time of the First World War and more than a hundred were built in the 1920s. The railroad station closed in 1932. In the mid 1990s Malba had about four hundred houses, ranging in value from $500,000 to $1 million; a group of homeowners, the Malba Association, attends to the interests of the neighborhood.

Vincent Seyfried

Malbone Street crash. A subway accident that occurred on 1 November 1918, the first day of a strike by workers of Brooklyn Rapid Transit that led to the temporary employment of untrained dispatchers. During the evening rush a train bound for Brooklyn on what is now the Franklin Avenue shuttle line jumped the track as it approached the Malbone Street Station (now the Prospect Park Station), after reaching a speed of more than thirty miles (forty-eight kilometers) an hour on a downgrade ending in several curves where the speed limit was six miles (ten kilometers) an hour. Ninety-seven persons died at the scene and five died later.

George A. Thompson, Jr.

Malcolm–King Harlem College Extension. College opened in 1968 at 2090 Adam Clayton Powell Jr. Boulevard in Harlem. It is supported by Marymount Manhattan College, the College of Mount St. Vincent, and Fordham University, and its faculty consists entirely of volunteers. The college offers several associate degree programs and has free day care and a study skills center that provides tutoring in remedial reading, writing, and mathematics. In the mid 1990s Malcolm–King Harlem College Extension had one thousand students, of whom 95 percent received financial aid.

Erica Judge

Malcolm X [Shabazz, el-Hajj Malik el-; Little, Malcolm] (*b* Omaha, Neb., 19 May 1925; *d* New York City, 21 Feb 1965). Political and religious leader. When he was six, local whites killed his father, a minister and disciple of Marcus Garvey in Lansing, Michigan. He was brought up by white foster families and in the early 1940s moved to Boston to live with his sister Ella. He often traveled to New York City while working as a "numbers runner," a thief, a drug dealer, and a procurer. Convicted and imprisoned for conducting a burglary of a house in Boston in 1946, he became acquainted with the precepts of the Nation of Islam, changed his name (the "X" representing the lost African name of his ancestors), and began to read voraciously. After his release in 1952 he founded several temples for the Nation of Islam, promoted its newspaper *Muhammad Speaks*, and became its most popular and effective minister. In 1954 he moved to 23-11 97th Street in East Elmhurst, where he remained for the rest of his life. During the next decade he denounced nonviolence and integration, characterized whites as devils, and advocated black self-defense against racist violence. His success aroused jealousy and tension within the Nation of Islam, and in December 1963 he was publicly reprimanded by its leader Elijah Muhammad for having described the assassination of President John F. Kennedy as an instance of "the chickens coming home to roost." At the same time he was shaken by revelations of Muhammad's extramarital affairs, and he left the Nation of Islam in March 1964.

Malcolm X during a press conference at the National Memorial African Book Store, 3 March 1964

In the spring of 1964 Malcolm X made a pilgrimage to Mecca, where he was surprised to find people of all races mixing amicably. Two subsequent trips to Africa convinced him that the problems of black Americans had a kinship with those of the third world. After returning to the United States he formed the Muslim Mosque, an Orthodox Islamic organization, and the Organization of African-American Unity, designed to promote black nationalism worldwide. He announced that he no longer believed all whites to be evil but continued to regard them with suspicion. His uncompromising stances on black pride and black control of community institutions hindered alliances with civil rights groups, and he was placed under surveillance by the federal government. On 14 February 1965 his house was firebombed while he and his family were inside. He was assassinated one week later while speaking at the Audubon Ballroom in Manhattan. The teachings of Malcolm X proved influential in the Black Power movement of the late 1960s, and he remained an important symbol of black pride in the decades that followed. *The Autobiography of Malcolm X* (1965), written with Alex Haley, is a classic of black literature.

Karl Evanzz: *The Judas Factor: The Plot to Kill Malcolm X* (Emeryville, Calif.: Thunder's Mouth, 1992)

Greg Robinson

Malcom [Melkonyan], **M(elkon) Vartan** (*b* Sivas, Turkey, 12 Sept 1883; *d* Sawyer's Island, Maine, 21 June 1967). Lawyer and activist. In 1895 he fled Sivas because of the massacre of the Armenians by the Turkish. He graduated from the University of Massachusetts in 1907, earned a law degree from Harvard University in 1910, and opened law offices at 32 Liberty Street in New York City in 1912, becoming a prominent business lawyer and a champion of the rights of immigrants, especially Armenian refugees. His work *The Armenians in America* (1919) helped to shape a consciousness of Armenian-American history. With the anthropologist Franz Boas of Columbia University he was an expert witness in the case *U.S. v. Cartozian* (1925), in which some Asian immigrants were recognized as "free white persons" entitled to naturalization in the United States.

Harold Takooshian

Maltese. Emigrants from the Maltese islands began to settle in New York City during the early twentieth century, with the largest concentrations in Astoria. In the mid 1990s the exact number of Maltese in the city was unknown; the number in New York State was estimated at 33,000.

Antonia S. Mattheou

Mamma Leone's. Restaurant in Manhattan, opened on 26 April 1906 as Leone's on Broadway at 39th Street (near the Metropolitan Opera) by Luisa Leone (*b* 2 Nov 1873; *d* 2 May 1944), the wife of a wine merchant named Gerolamo Leone. The tenor Enrico Caruso was the first of many prominent customers. The restaurant moved shortly after the First World War to 239 West 48th Street and in 1988 to 261 West 44th Street. After the death of Luisa Leone her sons Gene and Celestine gave the restaurant its current name. In 1959 Gene Leone sold it to Restaurant Associates. Mamma Leone's became the best-known Italian restaurant in New York City, although perhaps frequented more by tourists than by residents. In 1994 it closed while its owners considered moving to a new location.

Mary Elizabeth Brown

Mamoulian, Rouben (*b* Russia, 8 Oct 1897; *d* New York City, 4 Dec 1987). Stage and film director. Educated in England, he emigrated to the United States in 1923 when George Eastman invited him to direct the National Opera Company in Rochester, New York. He directed DuBose Hayward's play *Porgy* in 1927 and later the musical adaptation of it on Broadway by George Gershwin, *Porgy and Bess* (1936). After directing films in Hollywood he returned to Broadway to direct two musicals by Richard Rodgers and Oscar Hammerstein II, *Oklahoma!* (1943) and *Carousel* (1945). He was relatively inactive during the last decades of his life.

Tom Milne: *Rouben Mamoulian* (Bloomington: Indiana University Press, 1969)

Robert Seder

Mandel, Henry (*b* Russia, 1884; *d* New York City, 10 Oct 1942). Real-estate developer. During the 1920s he erected office buildings, apartment buildings, and hotels throughout New York City, including the Pershing Square Building near Grand Central Terminal (1923, twenty-seven stories), the Hearst Building at Columbus Circle, and the Brittany, Lombardy, and Tuscany hotels in Manhattan. In 1929 he razed tenements on a large site in Chelsea to build London Terrace, fourteen twenty-story buildings containing two thousand apartments for middle-class workers. Mandel also built the luxurious Parc Vendome complex of six hundred apartments on West 57th Street, completed in 1931 at a cost of $4.5 million.

Marc A. Weiss

Mandelbaum, Marm [Frederika] (*b* ?Hessen-Kassel, *ca* 1830; *d* Hamilton, Ont., 26 Feb 1894). Dealer in stolen goods. For about twenty years she ran a dry-goods store at the corner of Clinton and Rivington streets where she sold stolen shawls, scarves, fashion accessories, jewelry, bolts of silk, and (occasionally) negotiable bonds. On 22 July 1884 she was arrested with one of her sons on the basis of evidence gathered by Pinkerton detectives at the behest of Peter Olney, district attorney of Manhattan. That the police had not arrested her sooner led to public controversy and a clash between Olney and the police inspector Thomas Byrnes. Mandelbaum's trial was delayed for several months by her lawyers William F. Howe and Abe Hummel, during which she was able to flee to Canada.

George W. Walling: *Recollections of a New York Chief of Police* (New York: Caxton, 1888), 279–91

George A. Thompson, Jr.

Manes, Donald R. (*b* Brooklyn, 18 Jan 1934; *d* Queens, 13 March 1986). Borough president. He began his career in 1957 as an assistant district attorney of Queens, an aide in the state legislature, and a city councilman (1965). Elected borough president of Queens in 1971, he worked to encourage economic development, decentralize city offices, and expand educational, athletic, and cultural facilities. In 1974 he sought the Democratic gubernatorial nomination, and in the same year he became chairman of the Democratic Party in Queens, a position that prepared him to serve as President Jimmy Carter's campaign chairman in New York City (1980). Two days after being sworn in for his fourth term as borough president in 1986, his career collapsed when he attempted suicide. In the following weeks it was revealed that he stood to be indicted by federal and city prosecutors for having accepted bribes since 1979 from vendors seeking contracts with the Parking Violations Bureau. Manes resigned from office and took his own life a few weeks later. The scandal dominated the last years of the administration of Mayor Edward I. Koch and led to a law prohibiting government officials from holding party office.

Jack Newfield and Wayne Barrett: *City for Sale: Ed Koch and the Betrayal of New York* (New York: Harper and Row, 1988)

Nora L. Mandel

Mangin, Joseph François (*b* France; *d* after 1818). Engineer and architect. Admitted to New York City as a freeman in May 1795, he was a partner in the architectural firm of Mangin Brothers, which designed the Park Theatre (1795–98, often inaccurately credited to Marc Isambard Brunnel). Soon appointed a city surveyor and the chief engineer of fortifications, he designed the New York State prison on the Hudson River at Christopher Street in 1797. During the same year he began work on a city map with Casimir Goerk, which was published in 1803 and delineated the shoreline and street layout of Corlear's Hook. As a technical advisor to the war department in 1798 he planned the city's fortifications and probably made the first design for the fort later known as Castle Garden. With John McComb he submitted the plan that won the design competition for City Hall (for illustration see CITY HALLS); only McComb's name was inscribed on the foundation stone, and the denial of credit to Mangin became a matter of controversy, especially because of the building's resemblance to his earlier works. Mangin also helped to build St. Patrick's Cathedral (1809–15) on Mott Street. Nothing is known of his life after 1818.

Jonathan Aspell

Manhattan. The smallest in area of the five boroughs making up New York City. It consists principally of the island of Manhattan, which extends about thirteen miles (twenty-one kilometers) from north to south and about two miles (three kilometers) from east to west, surrounded by the Harlem River to the northeast and north, the East River to the east, Upper New York Bay to the south, and the Hudson River to the west. The borough of Manhattan is coextensive with New York County. In addition to the island of Manhattan it includes several smaller islands (among them Governors Island, Randalls Island, Wards Island, Roosevelt Island, and U Thant Island) and the neighborhood of Marble Hill, which is geographically part of the Bronx. Manhattan occupies about 22.6 square miles (58.5 square kilometers), or 7.1 percent of the municipality. It is the site of virtually all of the hundreds of skyscrapers that are the symbol of the metropolis, and it is also the oldest, densest, and most built-up part of the entire urbanized region. The population of Manhattan is ethnically, religiously, economically, and racially diverse. It grew from 33,000 in 1790 to 2.33 million in 1910, then began a slow decline. A low point of 1.43 million was reached in 1980, after which the population again began to increase.

Uncertainty surrounds the origin of the name, which has been variously traced to the Munsee words *manahactanienk* ("place of general inebriation"), *manahatouh* ("place where timber in procured for bows and arrows"), and *menatay* ("island"). It is in any event the earliest known Munsee place name, appearing in 1610 as Manahatta on a map prepared by a Spanish spy in the English court, where Henry Hudson was detained before his return to the Netherlands.

Manhattan was the first part of New York City to be settled by Europeans when the Dutch West India company established a permanent outpost on the southeastern tip of the island in 1624. There they built Fort Amsterdam to defend the community, and from there the population slowly moved north. New Amsterdam fell to the British in 1664, who renamed the settlement New York. Even though most of the island was well north of the area that the settlers occupied, from that time the city and the island of Manhattan were essentially the same, until New York City in 1874 began annexing parts of what is now the Bronx.

Most of the streets of lower Manhattan are narrow and twisting, reflecting their having been laid out before Boston, Philadelphia, and Williamsburg, Virginia, even existed. Everything north of Houston Street, however, is marked by a grid pattern. In 1807 the state legislature passed an act providing for the appointment of three commissioners "to lay out . . . the leading streets and great avenues" of the city. The result was the famous grid plan of 1811 (also known as the Commissioners' Plan), which imposed a kind of waffle-iron system on Manhattan from Houston Street to what later became 155th Street (and later to the northernmost tip of the island). This decision changed Manhattan irrevocably. The straight, right-angled street plan simplified surveying, minimized legal disputes over lot boundaries, maximized the number of lots fronting each thoroughfare, and stamped New York City with a standard plot of twenty-five by one hundred feet (eight by thirty meters).

The physical organization of Manhattan is relatively simple. Twelve major avenues, each a hundred feet (thirty meters) wide, run north and south: the longest is 10th Avenue, reaching as far north as Fort George at the tip of the island, and the most elusive 12th Avenue, which does not begin until 23rd Street. Four short avenues (A, B, C, and D) exist only on the Lower East Side. Because at the time of the Commissioners' Plan two diagonal thoroughfares, Broadway and the Bowery Road,

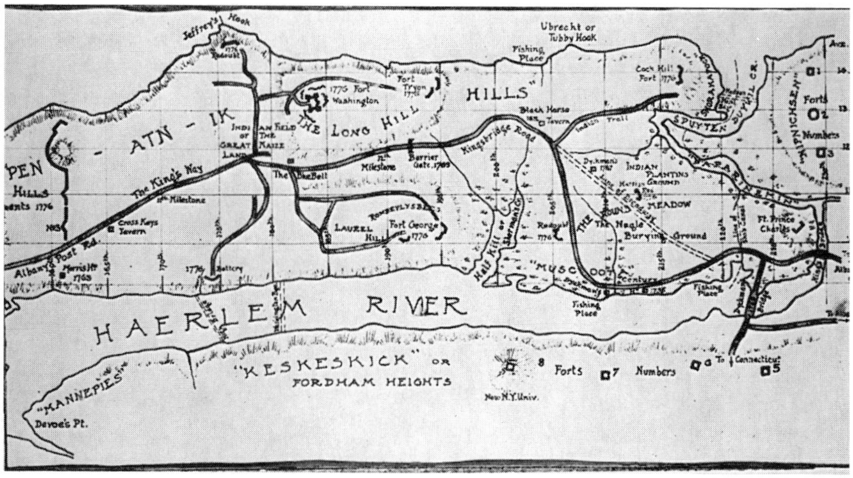

Map of colonial sites in northern Manhattan

Aerial view of Manhattan

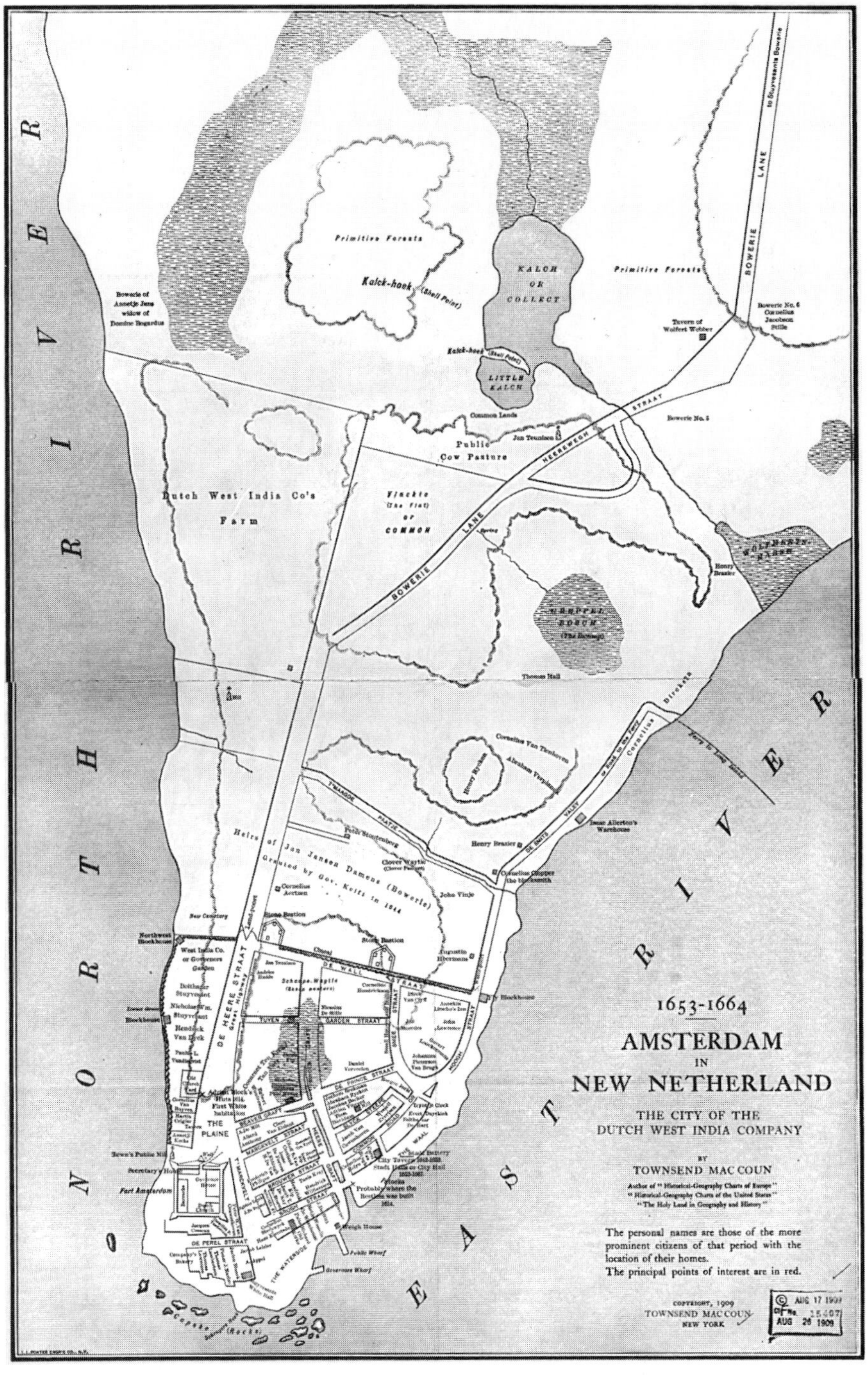

Map of New Netherland by Townsend MacCoun, 1909

were already in place and heavily used, they were left unchanged and their junction at 17th Street was set aside for Union Square. Intersecting the avenues at right angles and running east and west between the East River and the Hudson River are 220 consecutively numbered streets, most of them sixty feet (eighteen meters) wide. The exceptions are the streets that intersect Broadway as it crosses one of the avenues: 14th, 23rd, 34th, 42nd, 57th, 72nd, 86th, 96th, 106th, 125th, and 145th streets. These streets are one hundred feet (thirty meters) wide and are also the site of subway stations.

Manhattan is in many respects different from the rest of New York City, and the differences have sometimes been a source of friction. Despite its small size the borough is the business and financial heart of the United States, as well as the home of most of the institutions, buildings, and neighborhoods that have made New York City famous. It is politically more liberal than the city's other boroughs, and more affluent (in 1989 the median family income was $36,831, 7.2 percent higher than the comparable figure of $34,360 for the city as a whole; and the borough's per capita income, $27,862, was second only to Marin County, California, in the entire United States). The borough has also exerted a disproportionately large political influence in relation to the city as a whole, and has been the home of most of the city's mayors and political leaders. Tammany Hall, for example, which was practically synonymous with powerful big-city political machines for more than a century, operated only in Manhattan and not in the outer boroughs.

Because it has streets that are narrow by American standards, buildings that are closely spaced and tall, and an enormous level of pedestrian and vehicular traffic, Manhattan often overwhelms visitors. Certainly it is unlike any other place in the United States, and in all the world only Tokyo and Hong Kong rival it for intensely concentrated activity in a small area. Among the many famous neighborhoods in Manhattan are Chinatown, the Lower East Side, Greenwich Village, SoHo, Chelsea, Harlem, Morningside Heights, Little Italy, Yorkville, and the Upper West Side.

Kenneth T. Jackson

Manhattan Beach. Neighborhood in southwestern Brooklyn (1990 pop. 4464), lying on a peninsula at the eastern end of Coney Island and bounded to the north by Sheepshead Bay, to the east and south by the Atlantic Ocean, and to the west by Corbin Place. It was developed in 1877 as a self-contained summer resort on five hundred acres (two hundred hectares) of salt marsh by Austin Corbin's firm, the Manhattan Beach Improvement Company. During its heyday the Manhattan Beach Hotel and the Oriental Hotel offered entertainment by Patrick S. Gilmore and John Philip Sousa (who commemorated the resort in his *Manhattan Beach March*). Several factors contributed to the decline of the resort during the early years of the twentieth century: amusement parks opened in West Brighton, many parts of Brooklyn became suburban, and the three racetracks on Coney Island closed in 1910. Residential development began after 1907, when Manhattan Beach Improvement divided its land north of the hotels into building lots. During the Second World War the federal government operated an important training station for the U.S. Coast Guard at the eastern end on land later occupied by Kingsborough Community College. From the 1970s the large community in Brighton Beach of Jews from the Soviet Union extended into the neighborhood. Most of the population of Manhattan Beach lives in one-family houses on twenty tree-lined streets arranged in alphabetical order and named after places in England. The neighborhood is quiet and has few commercial establishments.

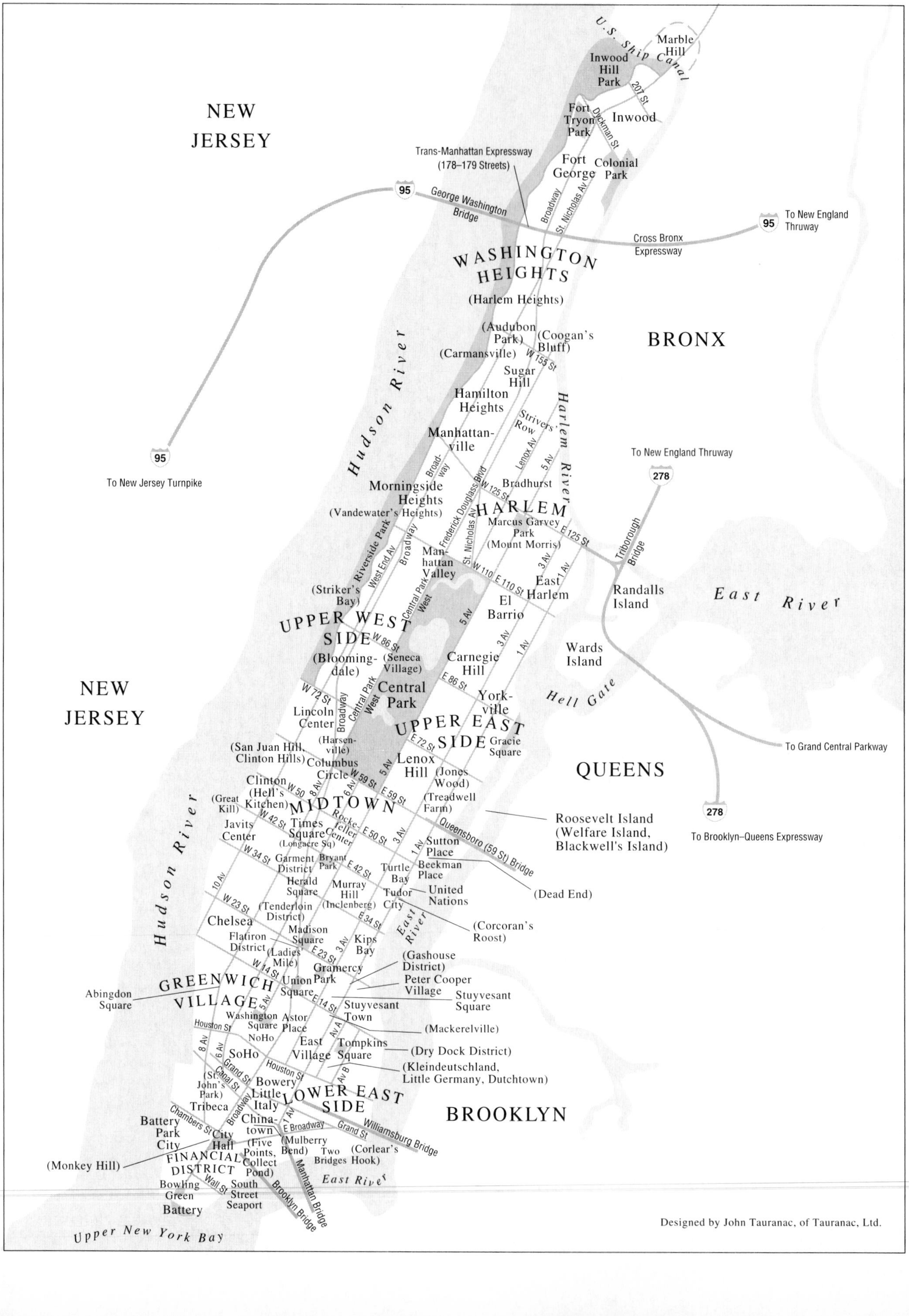
NEW JERSEY
NEW JERSEY
BRONX
QUEENS
BROOKLYN
U.S. Ship Canal
Marble Hill
Inwood Hill Park
207 St
Inwood
Fort Tryon Park
Dyckman St
Fort George
Colonial Park
Trans-Manhattan Expressway (178–179 Streets)
95
George Washington Bridge
Broadway
St. Nicholas Av
95
To New England Thruway
Cross Bronx Expressway
WASHINGTON HEIGHTS
(Harlem Heights)
(Audubon Park)
(Coogan's Bluff)
(Carmansville)
W 155 St
Sugar Hill
Hamilton Heights
Hudson River
Harlem River
Strivers' Row
Manhattan-ville
Lenox Av
5 Av
95
To New Jersey Turnpike
To New England Thruway
278
Broad-way
Frederick Douglass Blvd
W 125 St
Bradhurst
Morningside Heights
(Vandewater's Heights)
HARLEM
Marcus Garvey Park
(Mount Morris)
E 125 St
Triborough Bridge
Riverside Park
West End Av
Broadway
St. Nicholas Av
Man-hattan Valley
W 110
E 110 St
3 Av
1 Av
East Harlem
Randalls Island
East River
(Striker's Bay)
Central Park West
5 Av
El Barrio
UPPER WEST SIDE
W 86 St
3 Av
1 Av
(Blooming-dale)
(Seneca Village)
Carnegie Hill
Wards Island
E 86 St
Central Park
W 72 St
Broadway
Central Park West
York-ville
Hell Gate
Lincoln Center
UPPER EAST SIDE
Gracie Square
(Harsen-ville)
E 72 St
To Grand Central Parkway
(San Juan Hill, Clinton Hills)
Columbus Circle
Lenox Hill
(Jones Wood)
W 59 St
5 Av
E 59 St
Clinton (Hell's Kitchen)
W 50
8 Av
6 Av
(Treadwell Farm)
MIDTOWN
(Great Kill)
W 42 St
Rocke-feller Center
E 50 St
3 Av
Queensboro (59 St) Bridge
Roosevelt Island (Welfare Island, Blackwell's Island)
278
To Brooklyn–Queens Expressway
Javits Center
Times Square
(Longacre Sq)
1 Av
Sutton Place
W 34 St
Garment District
Bryant Park
E 42 St
Turtle Bay
Beekman Place
(Dead End)
10 Av
Herald Square
Murray Hill
(Inclenberg)
Tudor City
United Nations
W 23 St
(Tenderloin District)
E 34 St
East River
(Corcoran's Roost)
Chelsea
Madison Square
Flatiron District
(Ladies' Mile)
E 23 St
3 Av
Kips Bay
(Gashouse District)
W 14 St
Gramercy Park
Peter Cooper Village
GREENWICH VILLAGE
Abingdon Square
Union Square
5 Av
E 14 St
Stuyvesant Square
Stuyvesant Town
Washington Square
Astor Place
Houston St
NoHo
Av A
(Mackerelville)
8 Av
6 Av
SoHo
East Village
Tompkins Square
(Dry Dock District)
Houston St
Av B
(Kleindeutschland, Little Germany, Dutchtown)
Grand St
Canal St
(St. John's Park)
Bowery
Little Italy
LOWER EAST SIDE
Tribeca
Broadway
Chambers St
China-town
1 Av
E Broadway
Grand St
Williamsburg Bridge
Battery Park City
City Hall
(Five Points, Collect Pond)
(Mulberry Bend)
Two Bridges
(Corlear's Hook)
(Monkey Hill)
FINANCIAL DISTRICT
Manhattan Bridge
East River
Bowling Green
Wall St
South Street Seaport
Brooklyn Bridge
Battery
Upper New York Bay

Designed by John Tauranac, of Tauranac, Ltd.

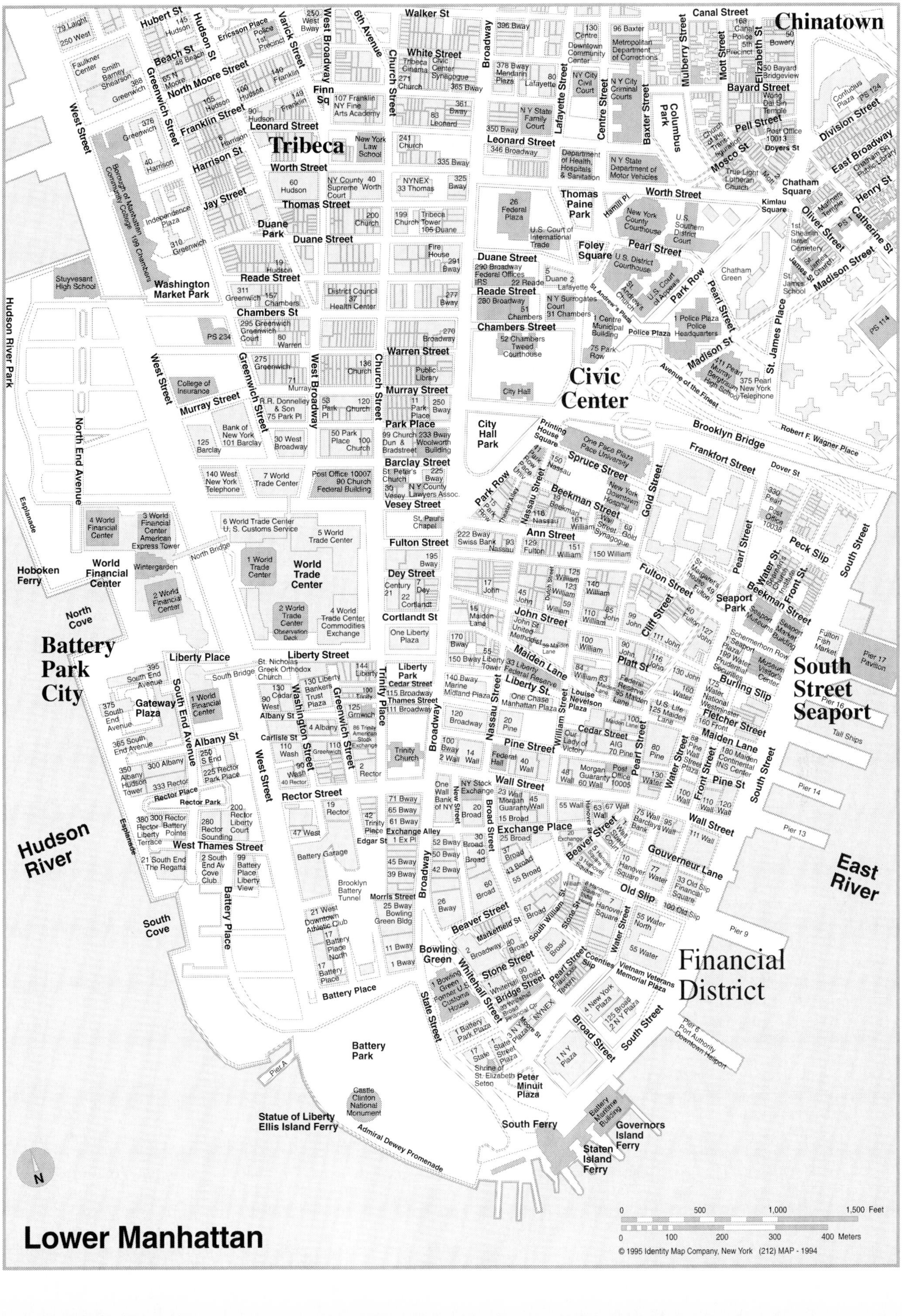

Lower Manhattan
Chinatown
Tribeca
Civic Center
Battery Park City
South Street Seaport
Financial District
Hudson River
East River
Hudson River Park
Walker St
Canal Street
White Street
Hubert St
Beach St
North Moore Street
Franklin Street
Harrison St
Jay Street
Leonard Street
Worth Street
Thomas Street
Duane Street
Reade Street
Chambers St
Chambers Street
Warren Street
Murray Street
Park Place
Barclay Street
Vesey Street
Fulton Street
Dey Street
Cortlandt St
Liberty Street
Liberty Place
Albany St
Carlisle St
Rector Street
Rector Place
West Thames Street
Battery Place
West Street
Greenwich Street
Hudson St
Varick Street
West Broadway
6th Avenue
Church Street
Broadway
Lafayette Street
Centre Street
Baxter Street
Mulberry Street
Mott Street
Elizabeth St
Bayard Street
Pell Street
Mosco St
Doyers St
Division Street
East Broadway
Henry St
Oliver Street
Catherine St
Madison Street
St. James Place
Pearl Street
Park Row
Madison St
Worth Street
Kimlau Square
Chatham Square
Columbus Park
Thomas Paine Park
Foley Square
Police Plaza
Avenue of the Finest
Duane Park
Washington Market Park
City Hall Park
Brooklyn Bridge
Frankfort Street
Dover St
Robert F. Wagner Place
Spruce Street
Beekman Street
Gold Street
Nassau Street
Ann Street
John Street
Maiden Lane
Liberty St.
Cedar Street
Pine Street
Wall Street
Exchange Place
Beaver Street
Stone Street
Bridge Street
Whitehall Street
State Street
Broad Street
William Street
Water Street
Front St.
South Street
Peck Slip
Fulton Street
Cliff Street
Platt St
Burling Slip
Fletcher Street
Pine St
Gouverneur Lane
Old Slip
Coenties Slip
Pearl Street
Peter Minuit Plaza
Bowling Green
Battery Park
South Ferry
Staten Island Ferry
Governors Island Ferry
Statue of Liberty Ellis Island Ferry
Admiral Dewey Promenade
Castle Clinton National Monument
Pier A
Pier 6
Pier 9
Pier 13
Pier 14
Pier 16
Pier 17 Pavilion
Tall Ships
Fulton Fish Market
Seaport Park
World Trade Center
World Financial Center
Wintergarden
North Bridge
South Bridge
North Cove
South Cove
Hoboken Ferry
Esplanade
North End Avenue
South End Avenue
Gateway Plaza
Rector Park
Stuyvesant High School
Borough of Manhattan Community College
Trinity Church
Trinity Place
Liberty Park
Federal Hall
Chase Manhattan Plaza
Louise Nevelson Plaza
Vietnam Veterans Memorial Plaza
Brooklyn Battery Tunnel
N
0 500 1,000 1,500 Feet
0 100 200 300 400 Meters
© 1995 Identity Map Company, New York (212) MAP - 1994

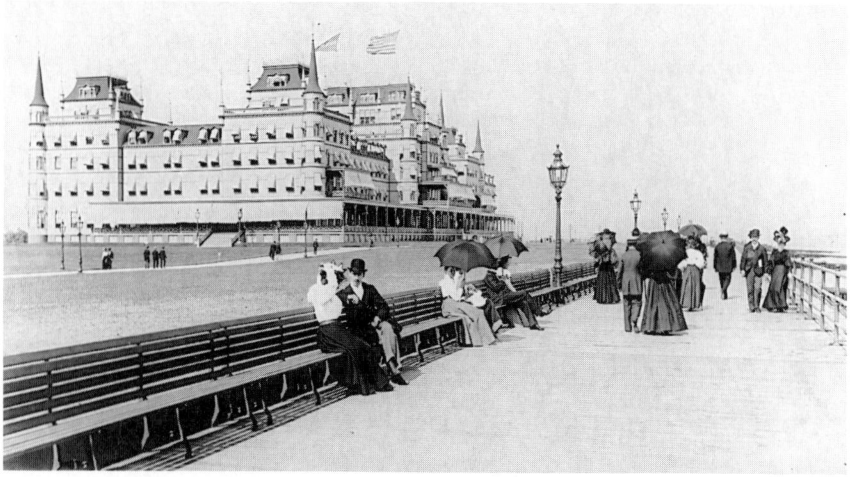

Oriental Hotel in Manhattan Beach, ca *1905*

Manhattan Beach Estates, ca *1900*

Stephen Weinstein: "The Nickel Empire: Coney Island and the Creation of Urban Seaside Resorts in the United States" (diss., Columbia University, 1984)

Stephen Weinstein

Manhattan Beach Hotel. A summer resort hotel constructed in 1877 on the eastern end of Coney Island by the Manhattan Beach Improvement Company, a firm led by Austin Corbin. Designed by J. Pickering Putnam in the Queen Anne style, the hotel had 150 rooms on four stories and attracted upper-class customers of the sort who frequented Newport (Rhode Island) and Long Branch (New Jersey), among them August Belmont and Leonard Walter Jerome. The hotel offered entertainment ranging from displays of scenic fireworks presented by the Pain family to performances by John Philip Sousa, whose *Manhattan Beach March* is named for the resort. The Manhattan Beach Hotel was adjacent to the fashionable Sheepshead Bay racetrack and near two others: their closing in 1910 led to the demise of the hotel, which was razed in 1911.

Stephen Weinstein

Manhattan Bridge. Steel, two-level suspension bridge spanning the East River between Canal Street in Manhattan and Flatbush Avenue in Brooklyn. Designed by Leon Moisseiff and opened in 1909, it is often mistakenly attributed to Gustav Lindenthal, who submitted a plan for the bridge in 1903 that was rejected by city administrators for its structural innovations. The entrance to the bridge on Canal Street is decorated by a grand arch and flanking colonnades designed by Carrère and Hastings. The bridge is 6855 feet (2091 meters) long, with a main span of 1470 feet (462.3 meters), and clears the East River at 135 feet (41.1 meters). The upper level has four lanes and a pedestrian walk; the lower level has three vehicular lanes and four subway tracks. The Manhattan Bridge stands north of the Brooklyn Bridge and south of the Williamsburg Bridge.

Rebecca Read Shanor

Manhattan Chess Club. The oldest chess club in the United States. Formed in 1877 by three dozen casual players who met regularly in the back room of a café in the Bowery, it came to number among its members almost every American master of the next hundred years, including the world champions José (Raúl) Capablanca and Bobby Fischer. The club also played a major role in organizing such historic events as the first official chess World Championship match (1886) and the famous New York Tournaments of 1924 and 1927. Now occupying quarters in Carnegie Hall, it remains one of the most active chess clubs in the United States.

The Manhattan Chess Club of the City of New York, Organized, 1877, Incorporated 1883 (New York: Manhattan Chess Club, 1894)

James Glass

Manhattan College. Private liberal arts college in Riverdale, opened by the Brothers of the Christian Schools in 1853 at 131st Street and Broadway in Manhattan as the Academy of Holy Infancy. After moving to the Bronx in 1923 the college expanded its liberal arts offerings and added schools of engineering, business, and education and human services. It developed a cooperative arrangement with the College of Mount St. Vincent in 1964 and became coeducational in 1973. The college's athletic teams are nicknamed the Jaspers, after the college's first baseball coach, Brother Jasper of Mary (who according to school tradition invented the "seventh-inning stretch"). In 1991 there were about three hundred faculty members, 3100 undergraduate students, and six hundred graduate students.

Marc Ferris

Manhattan Company. A company formed in 1799 at 23 Wall Street, originally to provide water for New York City. Permitted to pursue other interests as a result of a clause in the charter that many attribute to Aaron Burr (one of the founders of the company), it opened a bank on 1 September 1799 that became an unexpected competitor of Alexander Hamilton's Bank of New York. By 1840 the company had ceased to function as a water utility and the bank was one of the most important commercial banks in the city. The headquarters were at 40 Wall Street at the turn of the century, by which time the bank had attained national prominence. It later merged with and incorporated several local banks, including the Bank of the Metropolis (1871) in 1918 and the Merchants National Bank (1803) in 1920. In 1930 it had seventy-eight branches throughout all five boroughs and carried deposits of $404 million. It merged with the Chase National Bank in 1955 to form the Chase Manhattan Corporation.

Ann C. Gibson

Manhattan Eye, Ear and Throat Hospital. Private hospital chartered in 1869 as a clinic for the poor. First housed in a rented brownstone on East 34th Street, it moved to Park Avenue and 41st Street in 1881, by which time it was already nationally

Manhattan Bridge, 1910

recognized, and to East 64th Street in 1906. A renovation in 1980 greatly expanded the facilities to provide space for research and development in diagnostics and treatment. The hospital is the regional center for specialty care in ophthalmology, otolaryngology, and plastic and reconstructive surgery. It offers educational services and free screening for city residents.

Andrea Balis

Manhattan Institute. Nonprofit research and education organization formed in 1978 by William Casey, later the director of central intelligence. It is generally associated with conservative ideas, but is nonpartisan and has attracted contributors and staff members from diverse political backgrounds. The institute studies issues such as choice in public education, the privatization of municipal services, and the limits of multiculturalism. It also publishes a quarterly magazine, *City Journal*, that is devoted entirely to urban issues. The institute met with some success in the mayoral election of 1993, when Rudolph W. Giuliani espoused its proposals to reduce local business taxes, decentralize the public school system, assume a tougher stance toward homeless drug addicts, and privatize some municipal services. In the mid 1990s the institute had a budget of $5 million and about thirty staff members. Its offices are at 52 Vanderbilt Avenue in Manhattan.

Chad Ludington

Manhattan Life Insurance Company. Firm of insurers formed on 28 February 1850 by thirty prominent citizens of New York City, including Caleb S. Woodhull, Ambrose C. Kingsland, and Edwin D. Morgan. The charter was approved on 29 May and operations began at 108 Broadway on 1 August. The firm experienced steady growth in its early years. In March 1865 it moved to 156–58 Broadway, and by 1870 assets reached $6.9 million. A new headquarters at 66 Broadway stood 347 feet (105.8 meters) high and was the tallest building in the United States at the time of its completion in 1894. The value of all policies exceeded $101 million in 1930. In 1936 the firm moved its offices to 120 West 57th Street. It was an issuing agent for War Savings Bonds during the Second World War. The value of all policies rose successively to $400 million (1953), $629.5 million (1955), $1000 million (1957), $2000 million (1963), and $3400 million (1974, after the purchase of Grosten–Schlesinger Agencies).

Elizabeth J. Kramer

Manhattan Opera House. An opera house at 315 West 34th Street, opened on 3 December 1906 with a performance of Bellini's *I Puritani*. Designed and financed by Oscar Hammerstein, it was often referred to as Manhattan Center. Hammerstein's attempt to compete with the Metropolitan Opera was artistically successful but financially disastrous, and in 1910 he sold his interest in the theater to the Metropolitan Opera and agreed never again to produce opera in New York City.

John Frederick Cone: *Oscar Hammerstein's Manhattan Opera Company* (Norman: University of Oklahoma Press, 1966)

Marc Ferris

Manhattan Plaza. Apartment complex between 42nd and 43rd streets and 9th and 10th avenues, containing 1689 units in two buildings, one of forty-six stories and the other of forty-five. Designed by the firm of David Todd and built by Richard Ravitch, it was intended to provide market-rate housing for the affluent but was later reconceived as a subsidized facility for artists, actors, and musicians. The complex opened on 1 June 1977 and soon helped to revitalize the area. Its prominent residents have included the jazz musician Charles Mingus and the playwright Tennessee Williams.

Jesse Drucker

Manhattan Psychiatric Center. State mental hospital. It began in 1899 as Manhattan State Hospital when the State of New York consolidated two hospitals on Wards Island that it had taken over in 1896 (one at the eastern end for men and the other at the western end for women). The new hospital had 4400 patients and was the largest psychiatric institution in the world; as admissions far outnumbered discharges the hospital became overcrowded and inadequately staffed, and its buildings deteriorated. A fire in 1923 that killed twenty-two patients and three attendants helped rouse public support for a bond issue to improve the safety of all state hospitals. In 1926 the hospital had seven thousand patients. To prepare for the reversion to the city in 1943 of the land on which the hospital stood, more than half the patients were moved in 1940 to other psychiatric hospitals. The city in turn donated the land to the state, and in 1955 the hospital moved into three new buildings on Wards Island.

During the 1960s the number of patients declined after the introduction of tranquilizers and antidepressants. With the decentralization of the state hospital system in December 1969 the hospital was divided into the Dunlap Manhattan Psychiatric Center, the Kirby Manhattan Psychiatric Center, and the Meyer Manhattan Psychiatric Center; the reversal of this policy in 1976 by the Department of Mental Hygiene of New York State led the centers to be consolidated in 1979 into the Manhattan Psychiatric Center, which in the same year became affiliated with New York University Medical Center. The center emptied one of its three buildings in 1981 and made it available to the Kirby Forensic Psychiatric Center, a specialized facility for mental patients who have had involvement with the criminal justice system. Although the center introduced several innovative programs during the 1970s and the 1980s, it was repeatedly criticized for inadequate staffing, minimal standards in its programs, and other problems. These complaints culminated in the case of *Doe v. Cuomo*, which was settled in 1988 with an agreement to increase the clinical staff at the hospital and expand its therapeutic programs. In the same year the center began the largest renovation project in the history of the state, according to which its buildings were to be gutted and completely refitted over eight years. The number of in-patients in 1991 was about 850.

Sandra Opdycke

Manhattan Savings Bank. A savings bank formed in 1942 by the merger of three banks chartered in the 1850s. The oldest of these, the Manhattan Savings Institution, was founded on 10 April 1850 at Constitution Hall (650 Broadway) by Mayor Ambrose C. Kingsland and Caleb S. Woodhull, a former mayor, to serve customers of modest means. Its offices were situated first at 648 Broadway before moving in 1855 to 644 Broadway. The two other banks, the Metropolitan Savings Bank and Citizens Savings Bank, also began in lower Manhattan with a similar purpose; all three institutions prospered during the late nineteenth century and the early twentieth. After the merger the new bank set up headquarters at 754 Broadway, which moved in 1951 to 385 Madison Avenue. The Manhattan Savings Bank had seventeen branches in New York City and Westchester and $2800 million in deposits by 1990, when it was acquired by the Republic New York Corporation. It continued to operate as a subsidiary, with headquarters at 452 5th Avenue.

Chad Ludington

Manhattan School of Music. Conservatory of music opened in 1917 on the Upper East Side as the Neighborhood Music School by the philanthropist Janet D. Schenck, who served as its director until 1956. It took its current name in 1939 and in 1969 moved to 120 Claremont Avenue in Morningside Heights, the building formerly occupied by the Juilliard School. Under the direction of the baritone John Brownlee (1956–69) and his successors, the conservatory developed programs in opera, accompanying, and jazz. The Manhattan School enrolls more than eight hundred students and grants bachelor's, master's, and doctoral degrees in performance and composition.

James M. Keller

Manhattan State Hospital. Hospital that later became the MANHATTAN PSYCHIATRIC CENTER.

Manhattan Transfer. A defunct interchange station in the Meadowlands in New Jersey, where passengers could change between trains of the Pennsylvania Railroad heading for the line's new tunnels under the Hudson River to Pennsylvania Station in New York City and those still bound for the old Exchange Place station in Jersey City. This near mythic station later gave its name to a novel written by John Dos Passos, as well as to a popular singing group.

Kenneth T. Jackson

Manhattan Valley. Neighborhood on the Upper West Side of Manhattan, bounded to the north by 110th Street, to the east by Central Park West, to the south by 100th Street, and to the west by Broadway. The name became popular in the 1960s and refers to the sloping of Manhattan Avenue, which runs north from 100th Street. The area was once inhabited by squatters who were evicted in the 1850s for the construction of Central Park. After 1878 it was the site of asylums for the elderly and the poor, and eventually of the New York Cancer Hospital was built (later moved and now known as the Memorial Sloan Kettering Cancer Center). In the mid 1990s most of the residents were black and Latin American, and many were from Puerto Rico, Cuba, and Haiti. The neighborhood is largely working class and poor, with some enclaves of gentrification. Much of the housing consists of "old law" tenements and public housing, including the Frederick Douglass Houses. Row houses on Manhattan Avenue and the building that once housed the hospital remain.

Elliott Sclar

Manhattanville. A nineteenth-century village that flourished during the industrial revolution on what is now the Upper West Side. Surrounded by open land and country residences, it was in the valley centered near the present intersection of 125th Street and Broadway. The community was the site of churches, a grade school, and Manhattan College (1853). A ferry terminus on the Hudson River, a mill, and a brewery contributed to a thriving enclave that had about five hundred residents at mid century.

Karen E. Markoe

Mannes College of Music. Conservatory opened in 1916 as the David Mannes Music School by the violinist David Mannes and his wife, Clara Damrosch. It moved in 1919 to East 74th Street and took its current name in 1953. In addition to bachelor's and master's degrees in music performance the school offers training in composition and theory (it is a noted bastion of Schenkerian musical analysis) and is one of few American conservatories to encourage studies in early-music performance. The school moved to West 85th Street in 1984 and in 1989 became an independent division of the New School for Social Research. In the mid 1990s it had an enrollment of about two hundred.

David Mannes: *Music Is My Faith* (New York: Privately printed, 1949)

James M. Keller

Manning, William Thomas (*b* Northampton, England, 12 May 1866; *d* New York City, 18 Nov 1949). Bishop. He moved to Nebraska with his family at sixteen and earned a bachelor of divinity degree in 1891 from the University of the South in Sewanee, Tennessee. After serving as a parish priest in California, Pennsylvania, and Tennessee he was assigned to Trinity Parish in New York City, the wealthiest Episcopal parish in the country, of which he became rector in 1908. He was elected bishop of New York in 1921 and held the office until 1946; his diocese included not only Manhattan, the Bronx, and Staten Island but also seven counties north of New York City, consisting of 336 clergymen, 252 parishes and chapels, and 103,000 communicants. His priority was the construction of the Cathedral of St. John the Divine, on which he was consulted for every detail. He raised $13 million for the project, and despite a decrease in funds during the Depression the nave and the choir were completed by 1939. Frail and ascetic in appearance, Manning was noted for his conservative theology and strict interpretation of church tenets. As an adherent of the High Church and a militant practitioner of his faith, he was often at the center of controversy, especially on such issues as remarriage after divorce and the rules of propriety in church services.

Obituary, *New York Times*, 19 Nov 1949

William Dudley Foulke Hughes: *Prudently with Power: William Thomas Manning, Tenth Bishop of New York* (New York: Holy Cross Publications, 1963)

Jane Allen

Man-o'-War Reef. An outcropping in the East River that later became U THANT ISLAND.

Man Ray [Radnitsky, Emmanuel] (*b* Philadelphia, 27 Aug 1890; *d* 18 Nov 1976). Painter and photographer. He moved to Brooklyn with his family in 1897 and as a young man was influenced by the realistic paintings of John Sloan and Robert Henri. In 1911 he began visiting "291," a gallery run by Alfred Stieglitz, who became his mentor. At the age of twenty-six he attended a salon organized by Walter Arensberg on West 67th Street where he met Marcel Duchamp, who became a close friend for the next fifty years. He spent most of the rest of his life in Paris, where he was at the forefront of the Dadaist and surrealist movements and enjoyed a flourishing career as a commercial photographer.

Stephen Weinstein

Manship, Paul (*b* St. Paul, Minn., 24 Dec 1885; *d* New York City, 28 Jan 1966). Sculptor. He trained in New York City in 1905 and spent the period 1909–12 as a fellow at the American Academy in Rome. After his return he produced the bronze sculpture *Dancer and Gazelles* (1916, Metropolitan Museum of Art) and other small-scale decorative sculptures for private homes and gardens. His major public commissions date to the 1930s, when he executed the Paul J. Rainey Memorial Gateway (1934) for New York Zoological Park, the Prometheus Fountain (1934) for Rockefeller Center, and several large sculptural groups for the World's Fair of 1939–40. His sculpture was typically in an archaistic style, combining a naturalistic treatment of anatomy with stylized, linear details that revealed his admiration for Greek sculpture. Manship served terms as president of the National Sculpture Society (1939–42), vice-president of the National Academy of Design (1942–48), and president of the American Academy of Arts and Letters (1948–54). Among his late works are the gates for the William Church Osborn Memorial Playground (1952) in Central Park and the Children's Zoo (1961). He lived at 319 East 72nd Street.

John Manship: *Paul Manship* (New York: Abbeville, 1989)

Harry Rand: *Paul Manship* (Washington: Smithsonian Institution Press, 1989)

Susan Rather

mansions. The first mansion in New York City was the home of Stephen de Lancey, built in 1719 at 115 Broadway and converted into the Queen's Head Tavern in 1762. Country residences were built north of the city by wealthy families before the American Revolution, among them Whitehall, owned by Governor Peter Stuyvesant (destroyed by fire in 1715); the home of Nicholas Bayard near Grand, Broome, Crosby, and Lafayette streets in what is now SoHo (built 1735; demolished 1821); the Rutgers–Crosby mansion on Cherry Street (built 1754; demolished 1875); the Apthorpe mansion on the West Side (built 1764; demolished 1892); James Beekman's Mount Pleasant on the East Side (built 1763; demolished 1874); the Roger Morris–Jumel mansion in northern Manhattan (1765); and Richmond Hill, built in 1769 on the west side of Broadway for Abraham Mortier and later occupied by Aaron Burr and John Jacob Astor (moved in 1820 during the development of Charleton Street). Many well-known personages stayed at the mansion of Captain Archibald Kennedy at 1 Broadway (1760), which became the Washington Hotel in 1830 and was demolished in 1882. Across Bowling Green from the Kennedy house stood Government House (1790), designed by John McComb as the Executive Mansion but never occupied by a president: it became a boarding house in 1798. A mansion built for Archibald Gracie in 1804 at Bridge and State streets was demolished in 1879.

Broadway remained the most fashionable street well into the Federal period. During the first half of the nineteenth century the only large house built in the city was that of John Cox Stevens at College Place, designed by Alexander Jackson Davis, built in 1846–47, and soon demolished. The first mansion on 5th Avenue was a marble palace built by John Kellum for the businessman A. T. Stewart in 1864–69; it remained the wonder of the city until the death of Cornelius Vanderbilt in 1877, when members of his family decided to end their exclusion from society by building ornate houses along the west side of 5th Avenue between 50th and 58th streets. There soon followed a frenzy of construction along 5th Avenue that lasted from the 1880s to the First World War and culminated in a mansion for Henry Clay Frick designed by the firm of Carrère and Hastings and built between 70th and 71st streets. Commissioned mostly by clients desirous of social status, the houses were designed in historical European styles and usually built of white stone; ornaments were often made by craftsmen who had moved to the city from Europe. The houses were rarely sold but rather left to the owner's heirs, who often had them demolished, especially during the mid 1920s when the construction of apartment buildings virtually guaranteed a fortune. Some of the mansions became consulates and museums, including those of Frick (now the Frick Collection) and Andrew Carnegie (now the Cooper–Hewitt Museum).

William A. Clarke Mansion (designed by Lord, Hewlett and Hull and Henri Deglane), 5th Avenue and 77th Street, ca 1910. With a cost of $5 million, it was reportedly the most expensive private residence ever built in New York City.

I. N. Phelps Stokes: *The Iconography of Manhattan Island, 1498–1909, Compiled from Original Sources and Illustrated by Photo Intaglio Reproductions of Important Maps, Plans, Views and Documents in Public and Private Collections* (New York: Robert H. Dodd, 1915–28; repr. Arno, 1967)

Robert A. M. Stern, Gregory Gilmartin, and John Massengale: *New York 1900: Metropolitan Architecture and Urbanism* (New York: Rizzoli, 1983)

Mosette G. Broderick

Manteo Sicilian Marionette Theater. Theater devoted to *opera dei pupi*, a style of puppetry developed in Sicily during the early nineteenth century. It was opened by the Manteo family of Catania, Sicily, in Argentina about 1894 and moved to New York City in 1919. Using the "rod control" technique known in Roman times, the family built life-size marionettes and opened a theater on the Lower East Side in 1923, later moving to Little Italy. They performed Tasso's *Gerusaleme Liberata* and Ariosto's *Orlando Furioso*, which was divided into 394 episodes that required thirteen months of nightly performances to complete. In 1936 the entire season consisted of fifty-six episodes of *Orlando Furioso* performed in a theater at 107 Waverly Place seating three hundred; admission was twenty-five cents. In the summer the theater toured the east coast. After Aggrippino Manteo's death the title of Papa Manteo passed to his son Miguel Manteo, who led the troupe

The Manteo Sicilian Marionette Theatre

until his death in 1990. Electricians by day, the family performed for the Festival of American Folklife at the Smithsonian Institution (1975), the World Puppetry Festival (1980), the American Museum of Natural History (1982), and the Staten Island Institute of Arts and Sciences. The Manteo Sicilian Marionette Theater is the last surviving company of its kind in North America.

Barbara Kirshenblatt-Gimblett

Manton, Martin T(homas) (*b* New York City, 2 Aug 1880; *d* Fayetteville, N.Y., 17 Nov 1946). Judge. He earned a law degree at Columbia University (1901), formed the law firm of Cochran and Manton, and was appointed by President Woodrow Wilson to a federal judgeship (1916) and then to the U.S. Circuit Court of Appeals for the Second Circuit (March 1918). In March 1928 he sat on the Federal Statutory Court, a special tribunal formed to rule on the attempt by Interborough Rapid Transit (IRT) to raise the subway fare to seven cents; his ruling in favor of the increase was reversed by the U.S. Supreme Court. He later oversaw the receivership of the IRT: this was overturned by Judge John M. Woolsey, who ruled that his intervention had usurped the authority of the U.S. District Court for the Southern District of New York, which had jurisdiction over bankruptcy cases. After years of rumors that he was engaged in unethical conduct he became the subject of an investigation in 1938 by the district attorney Thomas E. Dewey, who sent a list of charges to the House Judiciary Committee; he resigned when the charges became public (January 1939) and was indicted by a federal grand jury (April 1939) on charges of accepting loans and gifts of $186,146 from litigants in eight cases, most involving patent law. Manton was convicted and fined $10,000; he served one year and seven months in prison. After his release he lived with his son in Fayetteville.

Jeffrey A. Kroessler

Manufacturers Hanover. Commercial bank, formed in 1961 by a merger of Manufacturers Trust and the Hanover Bank, both of which had a long history in New York City. The origins of Manufacturers Trust may be traced to the founding in 1812 of the New York Manufacturing Company, a textile company with a charter authorizing banking activities. This bank gradually evolved into the Chatham and Phenix Bank, with which J. P. Morgan was associated. In 1932 Chatham and Phenix was absorbed by Manufacturers Trust, a bank in Brooklyn founded in 1853. In 1950 Manufacturers purchased the Brooklyn Trust Company, which had been largely responsible for financing the construction of the Brooklyn Bridge. The Hanover Bank was founded in 1851 and grew tremendously from loans and investments in the Reconstruction South and the expanding West. In 1912 it merged with Gallatin Bank, chartered in 1829 as the National Bank of the City of New York, funded largely by John Jacob Astor, and first led by Albert Gallatin, secretary of the treasury under Presidents Thomas Jefferson and James Madison. The merger of Manufacturers and Hanover proceeded despite a ruling by the U.S. Department of Justice that it violated antitrust laws. The new bank continued to expand during the 1960s and 1970s, but by 1979 it was excessively dependent on delinquent international loans. In 1992 a weakened Manufacturers Hanover Bank became a division of Chemical Bank under the parent company, the Chemical Banking Corporation.

Chad Ludington

Mapleton. Neighborhood in west central Brooklyn, bounded to the north by Washington Cemetery, to the east by 23rd Avenue, to the south by 63rd Street, and to the west by 17th Avenue. Once part of New Utrecht, the neighborhood stands on high ground and when first settled offered fine views of Lower New York Bay. It was a sparsely populated farming area until the Sea Beach, West End, and Culver divisions of Brooklyn–Manhattan Transit were modernized between 1913 and 1919. Small apartment buildings and one-family houses built by the firm of New Utrecht Improvement soon filled empty lots. The population is primarily Italian and Jewish, with a growing number of Chinese.

Stephen Weinstein

Mapplethorpe, Robert (*b* Queens, 4 Nov 1946; *d* Boston, 9 March 1989). Photographer. He attended Pratt Institute from 1963 to 1970. After solo exhibitions at the Light Gallery (1976), the Holly Solomon Gallery (1977), and the Robert Miller Gallery he achieved prominence and exhibited internationally. He lived at 24 Bond Street in Manhattan. Although Mapplethorpe's work covered a wide range of subjects, including portraits, still lifes, and female nudes, his name is inextricably associated with his often explicitly homoerotic male nudes, some of which caused a furor when they were included in an exhibition that received federal funds. Published collections of his photographs include *Robert Mapplethorpe: Photographs* (1978), *Lady: Lisa Lyon* (1983), *Robert Mapplethorpe: Certain People* (1985), and *Robert Mapplethorpe* (1988).

Mara, Tim(othy James) (*b* New York City, 29 July 1887; *d* New York City, 17 Feb 1959). Football executive. He was born on the Lower East Side, became a successful bookmaker (at the time a legal trade), and in 1925 bought the New York Giants of the National Football League (NFL) for $500. The team was financially unsuccessful in its first season until more than seventy thousand spectators attended its last game, against the Chicago Bears at the Polo Grounds; this convinced Mara that professional football could succeed in New York. On four occasions his efforts to build a following for the Giants were threatened by leagues that sought to compete with the NFL: the American Football League nearly destroyed his team in 1926, two other leagues of the same name had franchises in New York City in 1936–37 and 1940–41, and the All-America Football Conference caused serious financial problems for the Giants in 1946–49. Mara's son Wellington was later the president of the team.

Joseph A. Horrigan

Marble Collegiate Church. The first Dutch Reformed church in North America, formed in 1628 by Jonas Michaëlius, the first ordained clergyman in New Amsterdam. It was at the center of several controversies during colonial times, especially after the English conquest of 1664, and issues of class, political loyalty, and language divided the congregation and diminished its influence. The church lost all four of its pastors immediately after the American Revolution: John Ritzema went to Kinderhook, Archibald Laidlie to Red Hook, Lambertus De Ronde to Saugerties, and John Livingston to Albany, Livingston Manor, and Poughkeepsie. As a leader of the "chapel movement" during the nineteenth century the church built chapels in impoverished and immigrant neighborhoods, and eventually added social programs and English classes to aid assimilation. The struggling congregation of two hundred was taken over in 1932 by Norman Vincent Peale, whose optimistic theology drew audiences of four thousand and more by the 1950s. The interior of the church, which features stained-glass windows designed by Frederick Wilson for Louis Comfort Tiffany in 1900–1, was extensively restored in 1984.

A Monograph to Commemorate the Three Hundredth Anniversary of the Organization in 1628 (New York: Marble Collegiate Church, 1928)

Randall Balmer

Marble Hill. Neighborhood lying on a rocky mound overlooking the Harlem River and bounded to the north by West 230th Street, to the east by Exterior Street, and to the west by Johnson Avenue. Although situated on the land mass making up the Bronx it belongs to New York County and is part of the borough of Manhattan for most administrative purposes. Its unique status derives from its history. Once part of the island of Manhattan, it was bounded by the Harlem River and Spuyten Duyvil Creek and connected to the mainland at 230th Street and Kingsbridge Avenue by the Kings Bridge (1693); the Farmers' Free Bridge (1759) was built to the mainland near Exterior Street. The neighborhood was the site of a marble quarry in the early nineteenth century. After June 1895 it was severed from Manhattan when the Harlem River Ship Canal was dug, and it became an island surrounded by the canal and Spuyten Duyvil Creek. Before the First World War the canal was filled in, leaving Marble Hill part of the mainland, and for many years residents were listed in the telephone directories of both Manhattan and the Bronx. The neighborhood did not become populous until the subway was extended along Broadway to 225th Street. Apartment buildings erected in the 1920s and 1930s soon replaced most of the existing one-family frame houses. About this time a velodrome was built east of Broadway; in 1950 it became part of the site of the Marble Hill Houses, a low-income housing project that initially attracted many municipal employees. In the mid 1990s the population was mostly black and Latin American.

Gary D. Hermalyn

Marble Palace. Term applied to the first department store in the world, a four-story structure situated on the southeast corner of Broadway and Reade Street and opened in 1846 as the dry-goods emporium of A. T. Stewart. The building was of Anglo-Italianate design and featured white Tuckahoe marble. Stewart introduced several merchandising practices at the store, including those of organizing a store by departments, offering money-back guarantees, and advertising on a large scale. Eventually the Marble Palace occupied the entire block, as far south as Chambers Street. It was the largest store in the world by the 1850s. In 1862 Stewart moved his store to Broadway and 9th Street; the Marble Palace became the home of the *Sun* from about 1911 to 1950. The building was later bought by the city, which converted it into municipal offices.

Kenneth T. Jackson

Marcantonio, Vito (*b* New York City, 12 Dec 1902; *d* New York City, 8 Aug 1954). Congressman. He was born near East 112th Street in a predominantly Italian immigrant neighborhood and began his career in the early 1920s as an aide and protégé of Representative Fiorello H. La Guardia, who like him was a Republican sympathetic toward the left. After La Guardia was defeated by a Democrat in 1932 Marcantonio ran successfully for the seat in 1934, having gained the endorsement of La Guardia's organization, the City Fusion Party. Defeated in the Democratic landslide of 1936, he was reelected in 1938 as the candidate of the Republicans and the American Labor Party. A fiery speaker, he successfully broadened his support to include not only Italians but also blacks and Puerto Ricans, who represented an increasing share of the voters in his district. He was a staunch supporter of civil rights, Puerto Rican independence, and the New Deal and embraced many policies of the American Communist Party, including its unpopular stand against war after the Soviet Union made its pact with Germany in 1939. As the cold war began he faced stiff opposition and was only narrowly reelected in 1948. As the mayoral candidate of the American Labor Party in the following year he won 13.8 percent of the vote across the city and a majority in East Harlem. He lost his seat in Congress in 1950, when the Democrats, Republicans, and Liberals sponsored a single candidate against him.

Gerald Meyer: *Vito Marcantonio: Radical Politician, 1902–1954* (Albany: State University of New York Press, 1989)

Maurice Isserman

Marchi, John J(oseph) (*b* Staten Island, 20 May 1921). Lawyer and legislator. The son of Italian immigrants, he graduated from Manhattan College (1942), St. John's Law School (1949), and Brooklyn Law School (1953). In 1956 he was elected to the State Senate, where he became chairman of the Senate Finance Committee (1973–88) and president pro tempore (from 1989). He defeated Mayor John V. Lindsay in the Republican mayoral primary in 1969, but he lost the general election to Lindsay, who had the endorsement of the Liberal Party. In 1973 he was again the Republican mayoral nominee. An authority on government finance, he was instrumental in writing the laws that saved New York City from financial collapse in the 1970s. Marchi is regarded as the founder of a movement to have Staten Island secede from New York City. In 1989 the State of New York Charter Commission for Staten Island was established and he was elected its chairman, and in 1993 the residents of the borough voted to accept the charter proposed by the commission, by a margin of two to one.

Barnett Shepherd

March of Dimes Birth Defects Foundation. Charitable organization formed in 1938 in New York City as the National Foundation for Infant Paralysis by President Franklin D. Roosevelt and Basil O'Connor with the goal of fighting polio. It occupied offices in the Equitable Life Assurance Building at 120 Broadway and acquired the name March of Dimes after a national radio broadcast by the comedian Eddie Cantor, who urged listeners to send dimes for the organization to the White House. After polio vaccines were developed by Jonas Salk and Albert Sabin the organization shifted its emphasis in 1958 toward fighting birth defects through research and education. The current name dates from 1979.

Montana Katz

marinas. Private boats were kept in undeveloped shoal coves and bays in the metropolitan area during the nineteenth century. After the New York Yacht Club was formed in 1884 other private boating facilities were soon provided. As parks commissioner, Robert Moses opened the first public marinas in 1937 at the 79th Street Boat Basin (now primarily used by houseboats) as part of a project known as the West Side Improvement; he added the World's Fair Marina in Flushing Bay in the early 1960s. Recreational boats may be stored and serviced for a fee at more than seventy facilities with more than 7750 slips in the East Bronx, North Queens, Staten Island, and Jamaica Bay.

Ann L. Buttenwieser

Marine Air Terminal. Facility at La Guardia Airport completed in 1939 to accommodate seaplanes, on the western end of the airport abutting Bowery Bay. Designed by the architectural firm of Delano and Aldrich in the art deco style, it has a prominent circular waiting area decorated with a mural by James Brooks entitled *Flight.* The terminal now serves the passengers of intercity shuttle flights. Both the building and its interior have

79th Street Boat Basin, 1991

been designated historic sites by the New York City Landmarks Preservation Commission.

Lisa Gitelman

Marine Midland Bank. Commercial bank formed in 1850 by eight businessmen to finance the growing shipping trade along the Great Lakes. It has headquarters in New York City and Buffalo. In the mid 1990s Marine Midland was the thirtieth-largest commercial bank in the United States, with $16,100 million in assets and 315 branches in New York State, of which eighty-three were in New York City and Long Island.

Gladys Chen

Marine Park. Neighborhood in southeastern Brooklyn (1990 pop. 19,992), bounded to the north by Flatlands Avenue, to the east by Flatbush Avenue, to the south by Avenue U, and to the west by Gerritsen and Nostrand avenues; it lies adjacent to an expanse of the same name occupying 1024 acres (415 hectares) in the Gateway National Recreation Area. A parcel of 140 acres (fifty-seven hectares) was bought and donated in 1916 to the city for use as a public park by the philanthropists Alfred T. White and Frederic B. Pratt in response to a wave of speculation along Jamaica Bay, which some hoped to transform into a major port. Although Mayor John F. Hylan initially resisted the gift, development of the park began and in 1939 the recreation area opened. Residential development increased in the 1930s after the completion of the Belt Parkway, the extension of Flatbush Avenue south of Avenue U, and the opening of the Marine Parkway Bridge to the Rockaways. Streets were laid out at an oblique angle to the grid of surrounding neighborhoods. Public transit was inadequate, and houses were built with driveways and garages so that owners could easily keep automobiles. In 1970 the neighborhood was transformed by the opening of Kings Plaza, the first suburban mall in Brooklyn. The section of the park south of Avenue U remained undeveloped except for a golf course and a nature trail. Among the churches in the area are St. Thomas Aquinas Roman Catholic Church and St. Columba Roman Catholic Church. Most of the population is Italian, Irish, and Jewish.

The Gerritsen Creek Nature Trail (New York: City of New York Parks and Recreation Natural Resources Group, 1989)

Stephen Weinstein

Mariners Harbor. Neighborhood in northwestern Staten Island, bounded to the north by the Kill van Kull, to the east by the approach to the Bayonne Bridge, to the south by Forest Avenue, and to the west by the Goethals Bridge. The area was long associated with maritime businesses: commercial fishing and the harvesting of oysters (curtailed about 1900 by pollution of the harbor), shipbuilding (at its height during the Second World War, notably at the Bethlehem Steel Shipyard, but later of declining importance), and boat repair. There are small businesses along Richmond Terrace, the main thoroughfare. The housing stock consists of older one-family houses, some attached housing, and two subsidized housing projects. In 1980 the population was 67 percent white, 23 percent black, and 10 percent Latin American.

Marjorie Johnson

Maritime College. Public college in the Bronx that trains officers for the U.S. Merchant Marine. Formed in 1874 as the New York Nautical Training School, its first home was aboard the *St. Mary's*, moored in the East River. In 1938 classes were moved ashore to Fort Schuyler in the Bronx, and in 1948 the college became a fully accredited branch of the State University of New York. The college had about nine hundred students in the mid 1990s.

Arnold Markoe

maritime unions. Seamen in New York City first went on strike in 1802 seeking to increase their monthly wage from $10 to $14. They took part in a labor convention in 1850, and in 1895 offices were opened in the city by the International Seamen's Union (ISU), a national federation that included craft unions for deckhands, stewards, and engine room personnel, and such organizations as the Harbor Boatmen's Union of New York (chartered in 1907). The National Industrial Union of Marine Transport Workers, which was affiliated with the Industrial Workers of the World, opened a branch in the city in 1913 that by 1916 had five thousand members. In 1928 communists began organizing seamen into the Marine Workers Progressive League, reorganized in 1930 as the Marine Workers Industrial Union (MWIU); it competed with the Marine Transport Workers for recruits among unemployed seamen, who congregated around South Street and took lodging at the Seamen's Church Institute. The MWIU disbanded in 1935 to infiltrate the ISU, leading to two bitter strikes in 1936 and the formation of the National Maritime Union (NMU) in 1937. After gaining nearly all the members of the ISU, the NMU had nearly 100,000 members in 1945. Between 1947 and 1950 it was weakened by infighting between communists and their opponents that led to the expulsion of communist leaders (Joseph Curran, the founding president, remained in control); it was also challenged by the Seafarer's International Union (SIU), formed in the city in 1938 by members of the Sailor's Union of the Pacific, who were opposed to the communists. The NMU and the SIU had contradictory racial policies: the NMU sought to end racial segregation in shipping on the east coast, and the SIU barred blacks from working in the deck and engine room departments until the early 1950s. Both unions suffered terrible casualties in the Atlantic during the Second World War. Containerization, ships sailing under foreign registry, and the decline of passenger service diminished the NMU to 22,000 members by 1988, at which time it closed its headquarters in New York City and merged with District 1 of the Marine Engineers Benevolent Association. In the mid 1990s membership stood at about 85,000.

William L. Standard: *Merchant Seamen: A Short History of Their Struggles* (New York: International Publishers, 1947)

William Gottlieb: *This Is the NMU* (New York: William P. Gottlieb, 1956)

Bruce Nelson: *Workers on the Waterfront: Seamen, Longshoremen, and Unionism in the 1930s* (Urbana: University of Illinois Press, 1989)

Joe Doyle

markets. The first regularly appointed marketplace in New Amsterdam occupied an area of vacant land between the warehouse of the West India Company and Fort Amsterdam. Known as Market Street or Market-Field, it was used by Indians and country people

Hiring hall of the National Maritime Union

Pushcart peddlers on the Lower East Side, ca *1935*

(called "strangers" by the colonists) to sell pelts, corn, and fish daily to local residents until 1641, when officials seeking to regulate the trade established a weekly market day. They also introduced two annual autumn fairs for the sale of cattle and hogs and set aside ten days at the end of August for the sale of homemade goods. Because local farmers grew only tobacco, food shortages were common, and by 1650 on market day residents waited along the shore between Whitehall and Broad Street, known as the Strand, for farmers and Indians to arrive. The authorities responded by opening the first public market there in 1656; it was replaced by the Custom-House Bridge Market-House in 1675, which remained the primary market until it was razed in 1708. Officials established the first public meat market in 1658 after charges of corruption were leveled against the store of the Dutch West India Company. Known as the Broadway Shambles, it stood in front of Fort Amsterdam and was staffed by twelve "sworn butchers" authorized to slaughter all cattle within the city limits. By 1683 produce and meat could be sold every day, but unauthorized peddlers, or "hucksters," and residents were prohibited from transacting any sales outside the official markets, a rule that remained in place until 1841. Butchers paid a tax for the exclusive right to make sales in the markets.

Initially the Common Council recommended sites for new markets, and at its request the court designated several in 1691: the Broad Street Market, the Coenties Slip Fish Market, and the Old Slip Market, which sold only meat. Customs changed when the Fly Market was formed in 1699 in response to a petition by residents of Pearl Street. Similar arrangements were made elsewhere, and once neighborhoods were granted permission to build a market they often raised money for it by selling lottery tickets. Those built during the first half of the eighteenth century included the Wall Street Market, the Flatten Barrack Market, the Broadway Market, where trading between Indians and slaves was outlawed in 1740 for promoting "disease," the White Hall Slip Market, built in 1746 on the former site of the Custom-House Bridge Market, the Exchange Market, and the Peck Slip Market, erected by residents of the wealthy neighborhood facing Water Street as the first brick market in the city. By mid century a large volume of business was done at the Fly Market, which stood next to the ferry, attracting farmers from Long Island, and which also functioned as a slave market. Overcrowded, filthy, and dilapidated by 1795, it closed in 1816 and was replaced by the Fulton Market. Markets built during the second half of the eighteenth century included the Bear (or Hudson), Crown, Oswego, Catherine, and Spring Street markets; those built during the first half of the nineteenth included the Grand-Market Place and the Corlear's Hook (Grand Street), Collect, Greenwich, Goveneur, Washington, Fish, Centre, Essex, Franklin, Manhattan, Clinton, Tompkins, Jefferson, Monroe, and Harlem markets. Butchers were among the most influential figures in markets during these years; they usually wore high hats and long-tailed coats.

Corruption and graft abounded. Speculators known as "forestallers" took advantage of desperate farmers who could not find or afford stalls in the markets. During yellow fever epidemics in the late eighteenth century and the early nineteenth, butchers and farmers deserted the markets in the infected districts, leaving them vulnerable to unlicensed "shark" butchers. From the beginning of the nineteenth century itinerant peddlers and hucksters, especially poor widows and children, sold fruit, vegetables, candies, and cakes in the streets. There were about forty markets by 1861, and the need for food increased rapidly as the local population and economy expanded after the Civil War. Perishables were delivered without regard for demand, quality, or price, and gluts became common. After four peddlers installed pushcarts on Hester Street in 1866, stationary open-air pushcart markets were set up in many parts of the city, used by peddlers and hucksters selling food surpluses; the best-known was one on the Lower East Side. An area near Gansevoort Street became a farmers' market in 1882, and in 1889 the West Washington Market was built for wholesaling, especially of poultry. Peddling attracted 25,000 immigrants by 1900, mostly because it required little capital or knowledge of English. Although an alternative to the sweatshop, it entailed long, hard hours of work and often became a means to exploit oneself and one's family members. Peddlers bought surpluses from wholesalers at dawn and often worked by lantern light past midnight; they sold many different kinds of goods, including pickles, sweet potatoes, soda water, halvah, arbis (hot chick peas), and used clothes.

Few municipal regulations or local statutes governed the markets before 1900. By this time crops from nearby farms no longer met the city's needs. Produce was delivered by rail and steamship from all over the country and abroad, sometimes as much as three hundred carloads a day. It was collected, graded, shipped, and distributed by shippers, commission merchants, wholesalers, and jobbers and often had to pass through several dealers before reaching the retailers. Secondary wholesale distributing points, or jobbers' markets, were at the Harlem Market and in Brooklyn at the Wallabout Market. Corruption remained unchecked, and markets were also known for their filth and stench and for the congestion that they caused on local streets. The city established a pushcart commission in 1905 and another one in 1912, which recommended

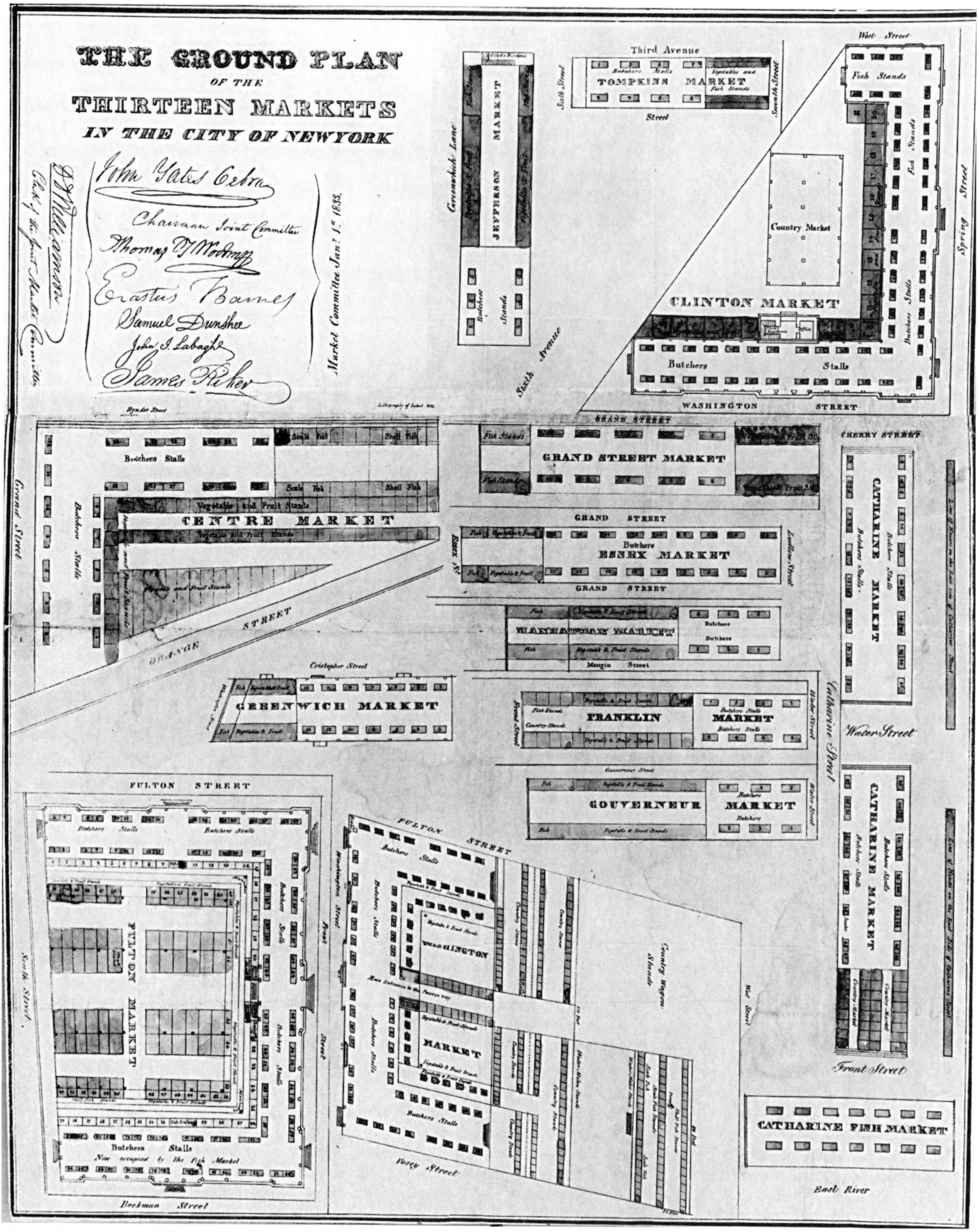

Anthony Imbert, Ground Plan of the Thirteen Markets in the City of New York

Nicolino Calyo, The Butcher

that there be a wholesale terminal market in each borough; only one resulted, the Bronx Terminal Market, and not until 1929. One of few other changes was the formation of the Department of Markets in 1917, which eventually operated and supervised the city's wholesale markets, including the Bronx Terminal, Wallabout, West Washington, Gansevoort, and Fulton Fish markets.

The city had more than fifty open-air markets by 1923 and fifteen thousand peddlers in 1933, leading Mayor Fiorello H. La Guardia to make a number of controversial changes. Although many of the city's poor depended on peddling for a living, especially during the Depression, La Guardia abolished open-air pushcart markets in the late 1930s. With federal funds the city erected several indoor municipal retail markets and banned all pushcarts on 1 December 1938, and by 1945 there were only twelve hundred peddlers left. The indoor markets soon languished: the rents for stalls were too high. Later customers preferred the convenience of bodegas and supermarkets, and refrigeration obviated daily shopping. The Hunts Point Market replaced the Washington Market as the city's wholesale food center in 1967. A farmers' market sponsored by Greenmarket, a program of the nonprofit Council on the Environment, opened in Union Square in 1976 and eventually drew twenty thousand regular customers. The Bronx Terminal Market became mainly a supplier of Latin American grocers who carted produce in pick-up trucks. In the mid 1990s the city's indoor markets catered mostly to the poor, and a growing number of immigrants worked, like their predecessors, as peddlers.

Thomas F. De Voe: *The Market Book* (New York: Burt Franklin, 1862; repr. 1969)
Suzanne R. Wasserman: "'The Good Old Days of Poverty': The Battle over the Fate of New York City's Lower East Side during the Depression" (diss., New York University, 1990)

Suzanne R. Wasserman

Markham, Edwin [Charles Edward Anson] (*b* Oregon City, 23 April 1852; *d* Staten Island, 7 March 1940). Poet and lecturer. Born in a log cabin, he was brought up by his mother in California and worked as a teacher and school administrator. After seeing Jean-François Millet's painting *The Man with the Hoe* on exhibit in San Francisco he was moved to write a poem of the same title; its publication in the *San Francisco Examiner* (1899) made him famous across the nation and allowed him to write and give lectures full time. His poem "Lincoln, Man of the People" (1901) was equally successful, but his later efforts were less well received. Near the end of his life he settled in Staten Island, where in 1930 his birthday was proclaimed a holiday.

Leslie Gourse

Marot, Helen (*b* Philadelphia, 9 June 1865; *d* New York City, 3 June 1940). Writer and reformer. She moved to New York City in 1902 to investigate child labor conditions for the Neighborhood Workers of New York City. In 1905 she led the school visiting committee of the Public Education Association of New York. As executive secretary of the Women's Trade Union League of New York (1906–13) she organized the shirtwaist strike of 1909–10. She wrote two books, *American Labor Unions* (1914) and *Creative Impulse in Industry* (1918), and was an editor of the radical newspaper the *Masses* (1916–17) and the journal the *Dial* (1918–19).

Nancy Schrom Dye: *As Equals and as Sisters: Feminism, the Labor Movement, and the Women's Trade Union League of New York* (Columbia: University of Missouri Press, 1980)

Sarah Henry Lederman

Marquand and Company [Marquand and Paulding]. Firm of jewelers that later became Black, Starr and Frost.

Marquis, Don(ald Robert Perry) (*b* Walnut, Ill., 29 July 1878; *d* Queens, 29 Dec 1937). Humorist, poet, and playwright. From 1913 to 1922 he wrote a popular newspaper column for the *Sun*, "The Sun Dial," in which he created fictional characters to represent typical city dwellers. Among these were Hermione, a dilettante from Greenwich Village; Clem Hawley, a heavy drinker critical of Prohibition; Archy, a cockroach who wrote verse by jumping from one typewriter key to the next (his writings always uncapitalized because of his inability to hold down two keys at once); and Mehitabel, an adventurous alley cat. In addition to his newspaper columns (reissued in several compilations including *the lives and times of archy and mehitabel*, 1940) Marquis wrote poems, novels, short stories, and plays (the first and most successful of which was *The Old Soak*, 1922, in which Hawley is the main character).

Lynn Lee: *Don Marquis* (Boston: Twayne, 1981)

Patricia A. Perito

Marsh, Reginald (*b* Paris, 15 March 1898; *d* Dorset, Vt., 3 July 1954). Painter and illustrator. The son of two American artists, he grew up in Nutley, New Jersey, and graduated from Yale University in 1920. He moved to New York City in the same year and became a cartoonist for the *Daily News* and later for the *New Yorker*. In 1921 he studied with John Sloan at the Art Students League, but he was most influenced by Kenneth Hayes Miller. He also taught at the league from 1935 to 1954. His sketches and careful paintings depict working-class life of the 1930s and 1940s in the Bowery and on 14th Street, in burlesque halls and subways, and at local beaches. In 1937 he was commissioned by the U.S. Department of the Treasury to paint panels for the rotunda of the U.S. Customs House in lower Manhattan. His illustrations in 1946 for an edition of John Dos Passos's *U.S.A.* successfully captured the picaresque quality of the trilogy. Marsh was elected to the National Institute of Arts and Letters in 1946.

Marilyn Cohen: *Reginald Marsh's New York: Paintings, Drawings, Prints and Photographs* (New York: Whitney Museum of American Art / Dover, 1983)

For illustrations see Bowery, Burlesque, and Movie theaters.

Patricia Hills

Marshall, Louis (*b* Syracuse, N.Y., 1856; *d* Zurich, 1929). Lawyer and civic leader. The son of immigrants, he graduated from Columbia University Law School in 1877 and in 1894 became a partner in the firm of Guggenheimer, Untermyer and Marshall in New York City. He was a prominent member of the German Jewish élite and president of the American Jewish Committee from 1912 to 1929. Under his leadership the committee submitted legal briefs in cases concerned with religious freedom, fought against anti-Semitism and denounced Henry Ford, took part in Leo Frank's legal defense, and opposed restrictions on immigration. Marshall attended the peace conference in Paris and was instrumental in ensuring that guarantees of minority rights were written into the constitutions of all the newly created eastern European states. He was president of Temple Emanu-El and chairman of the board of the Jewish Theological Seminary.

Mortin Rosenstock: *Louis Marshall, Defender of Jewish Rights* (Detroit: Wayne State University Press, 1965)

Michael N. Dobkowski

Marshall, Thurgood (*b* Baltimore, 2 July 1908; *d* Washington, 25 Jan 1991). Justice of the Supreme Court and civil rights lawyer. He began working in New York City in 1935 as a lawyer for the National Association for the

Advancement of Colored People (NAACP) at 69 5th Avenue. After becoming the chief counsel of the association he settled in the city in 1938, taking a one-room flat at 409 Edgecombe Avenue in Harlem. While living in the city he worked with other leaders of the NAACP to plan the lawsuit that led to the overturning of racial segregation in public schools (*Brown v. Board of Education*, 1954). After the death of his first wife in 1955 he remarried and moved to Morningside Gardens on 123rd Street. He was nominated to the U.S. Court of Appeals for the Second Circuit by President John F. Kennedy in 1961 and left the city for Washington in 1965 when named solicitor general by President Lyndon B. Johnson in 1965.

Michael D. Davis and Hunter R. Clark: *Thurgood Marshall* (New York: Birch Lane, 1992)

Thomas M. Hilbink

Marshall Chess Club. One of the oldest and most active chess clubs in the United States. Formed in 1915 by Frank J. Marshall, national chess champion from 1909 to 1936, it moved in 1931 to its own brownstone building at 23 West 10th Street, which it continued to occupy into the 1990s. The club has sponsored several memorable events, including rounds of national championships and a tournament in 1956 in which Bobby Fischer defeated Donald Byrne in what became known as the "game of the century." Leading American players who have developed at the club include Reuben Fine, Arthur Dake, Larry Evans, Edmar Mednis, and Andrew Soltis.

Chess: The Game of the Ages (New York: Marshall Chess Club, 1932)

James Glass

marshals. The marshal system was established by ordinance in 1665. Marshals are responsible for executing mandates of the Civil Court in cases involving $10,000 or less. They are appointed by the mayor to six-year terms and are unsalaried: their income consists of fees set by statute and poundage paid by the debtor. In the early 1990s there were eighty-three marshalships.

Neal C. Garelik

Marsh and McLennan. Firm of insurance brokers. It was formed in 1904 in a merger of insurance agencies controlled by Henry W. Marsh and Donald R. McLennan. From an office in New York City that he opened in 1901, Marsh managed insurance for U.S. Steel. McLennan, whose office was in Chicago, was an expert in railroad insurance. When the two joined forces they captured the insurance accounts for all major railroads in the Midwest. The firm's main offices were in New York City and Chicago, and others opened to serve a growing number of corporate clients such as American Telephone and Telegraph, Armour, Canadian Pacific, the Ford Motor Company, and American Can. A public stock offering in 1962 enabled the firm to acquire many regional insurance agencies and major subsidiaries in related businesses, such as Guy Carpenter, a reinsurance broker, Putnam, a firm of investment managers, William T. Mercer, consultants on employee benefits, and C. T. Bowring, an insurance broker in London. By the mid 1990s Marsh and McLennan was one of the largest insurance organizations in the world.

Robert J. Gibbons

Martí [y Pérez], **José** [Julián] (*b* Havana, 28 Jan 1853; *d* Dos Ríos, Cuba, 19 May 1895). Poet and revolutionary. He was educated in Havana, published his first poems by the age of fifteen, and launched the newspaper *La patria libre* at sixteen. For supporting Cuban nationalism during an uprising in 1868 he was imprisoned by Spanish authorities and deported to Spain, where he continued to write and earned a degree in law. He moved to New York City on 3 January 1880 and remained there for most of the next fifteen years, working from his headquarters at 120 Front Street to end slavery and Spanish rule in Cuba. While in the city he was the editor of *Patria*, a Cuban nationalist weekly newspaper launched in 1892, and wrote poetic works such as *Versos sencillos* (1890–91); he also led the Partido Revolucionario Cubano in Brooklyn and helped to form La Liga (1890) to promote the rights of Cuban and Puerto Rican blacks. After leaving the city for the Caribbean on 31 January 1895 he outlined plans for a Cuban insurrection in the *Manifesto of Montecristo*, issued from Santo Domingo on 25 March. He led an expeditionary force to Cuba on 11 April and was killed while fighting the Spanish. An equestrian statue of Martí stands in Central Park.

Peter Turton: *José Martí, Architect of Cuba's Freedom* (London: Zed Books, 1986)

Kevin Kenny

Martin, Mary (*b* Weatherford, Texas, 1 Dec 1914; *d* Rancho Mirage, Calif., 3 Nov 1990). Actress. She attended school in Nashville and moved to New York City, where in 1938 she became known for singing "My Heart Belongs to Daddy" in Cole Porter's *Leave It to Me* on Broadway. After making several motion pictures in Hollywood she returned to the Broadway stage, where she performed in *South Pacific* (winning a Tony Award in 1949), *Annie Get Your Gun* (1947), *Peter Pan* (1954), and *The Sound of Music* (1959); she also toured with such productions as *A Celebration of Richard Rodgers* and had many roles on television. Martin was known for the vivacity and precision of her performances. She wrote an autobiography, *My Heart Belongs* (1976).

Shirlee P. Newman: *Mary Martin on Stage* (Louisville, Ky.: Westminster, n.d. [?1969])

James E. Mooney

Marvel Comics. Firm of comic book publishers, formed in 1939 in New York City as Timely Publications. It introduced the characters the Human Torch and the Sub-Mariner in the same year, its "superhero" Captain America in 1941, and the Fantastic Four in 1961. The firm sought to distinguish itself from its competitor DC Comics by imbuing its superheroes with human frailties. Some of its most memorable characters were introduced in 1962, including the Incredible Hulk, Thor the Thunder God, and Spider-Man. It also developed the first black superhero, the Black Panther, who began as a member of the Fantastic Four in 1966 and was given his own series in 1973. In 1971 the firm published an issue that focused on drug abuse (*The Amazing Spider Man Comics* no. 96) without the seal of approval of the Comics Code (adopted in 1954), as a result of which the code was relaxed. Later publications by Marvel Comics include *X-men* (1975), *Marvel Graphic Novel* (1982), a comic "album" based on the European model, and *Epic Comics*.

Reinhold Reitberger and Wolfgang Fuchs: *Comics: Anatomie eines Massenmediums* (Munich: H. Moss, 1971; Eng. trans. Boston: Little, Brown, n.d. [1972])

Will Jacobs and Gerard Jones: *The Comic Book Heroes* (New York: Crown, 1985)

Mike Benton: *The Comic Book in America: An Illustrated History* (Dallas: Taylor, 1989)

Patricia A. Perito

Marx Brothers. Team of comedians. Its members, all born in New York City, were Chico (Leonard) Marx (*b* 26 March 1886; *d* Beverly Hills, Calif., 11 Oct 1961), Harpo (Adolph) Marx (*b* 23 Nov 1888; *d* Hollywood, 28 Sept 1964), Groucho (Julius) Marx (*b* 2 Oct 1890; *d* Los Angeles, 19 Aug 1977), Gummo (Milton) Marx (*b* 23 Oct 1893; *d* Palm Springs, Calif., 21 April 1977), and Zeppo (Herbert) Marx (*b* 25 Feb 1901; *d* Palm Springs, 30 Nov 1979). Groucho was born at 239 East 114th Street; from 1895 to 1910 the family lived at 179 East 93rd Street. Some of the brothers attended Public School 86 on 96th Street; none graduated. Groucho began his career in show business at fifteen as a singer in a vaudeville trio and was soon followed by Gummo. The two formed the Nightingales in 1907 with a female singer (soon replaced by a male singer) and in the following year were joined by Harpo. In 1910 the brothers moved to Chicago with their mother, Minnie Marx, who was also their manager; Chico had his own act in Pittsburgh before joining the others in 1912. Gummo, the "straight man" of the group, was drafted during the First World War and replaced by Zeppo. The brothers toured the vaudeville circuit and won a performance at the Palace Theatre in 1915. After returning to New York City they appeared on Broadway in the phenomenally successful musical revue *I'll Say She Is!* (1924), in George S. Kaufman's *The Cocoanuts* (1925; film version, Astoria Studios,

The Marx Brothers in The Cocoanuts. From left*: Zeppo, Groucho, Chico, Harpo*

1929), which satirized financial speculation in Florida, and in *Animal Crackers* (1928; film version, Astoria Studios, 1930), a satire by Kaufman and Morrie Ryskind of efforts by Jews to assimilate into genteel society. From 1924 to 1926 Groucho lived in an apartment building at Riverside Drive and 161st Street. The brothers signed a lucrative contract with Paramount Pictures in 1931 and moved to California. After Zeppo's retirement they returned to New York City in 1935 to film *A Night at the Opera* by Kaufman and Ryskind. The Marx Brothers perfected an anarchic brand of comedy that relied on physicality, rapid timing, and verbal repartee and came to be strongly associated with ethnic New York City. Each brother had a distinctive persona that varied little from one film to the next: Groucho portrayed a wiseacre and ne'er-do-well, Chico an Italian immigrant with an unorthodox style of playing the piano, and Harpo a frenetic harpist who never spoke. Off screen Harpo was an occasional member of the Algonquin Round Table.

Harpo Marx with Rowland Barber: *Harpo Speaks* (New York: Random House, 1961; rev. Freeway, 1974)

Hector Arce: *Groucho* (New York: G. P. Putnam's Sons, 1979)

Wes D. Gehring: *The Marx Brothers: A Bio-bibliography* (New York: Greenwood, 1987)

Groucho Marx and Richard J. Anobile: *The Marx Brothers Scrapbook* (New York: Harper and Row, 1989)

Charles Musser, David Nasaw

Mary Louis Academy. Catholic high school for girls at 176-21 Wexford Terrace in Jamaica Estates, opened in September 1936 and run by the Sisters of St. Joseph; it was named for the superior of the order who chose the site, formerly the Adikes estate. Classes were held in the faculty convent (formerly the main house on the estate) until a new building was completed. An addition completed in 1956 doubled the size of the school. About a thousand students were enrolled in 1991.

Gilbert Tauber

Marymount Manhattan College. Roman Catholic college opened in 1936 on 5th Avenue and 84th Street. One of six women's colleges in the United States founded by the Religious of the Sacred Heart of Mary (a Catholic order formed in France in the mid nineteenth century), it began as a junior college affiliated with Marymount College in Tarrytown, New York. In 1947 the school was granted a charter from New York State as Marymount College New York City and began offering a four-year program leading to a bachelor's degree. The college moved to its present site at 221 East 71st Street in 1948 and became independent of Marymount in Tarrytown in 1961. The main building was designated a city landmark; the Joseph C. Nugent Building was erected adjacent to it in 1975. The school offers a liberal arts curriculum, a teacher certification program, and graduate degrees through an affiliation with Iona College. It first admitted men in 1989 and by the mid 1990s had about fourteen hundred students.

Katherine Kurz Burton: *Mother Butler of Marymount* (New York: Longmans, Green, 1944)

Bernadette McCauley

Mary Powell. Sidewheel steamboat, built in 1861 by Michael S. Allison of Jersey City, New Jersey. Known as the "speed queen of the Hudson," she was three hundred feet (ninety-one meters) long and had a vertical-beam engine made by the firm of Fletcher, Harrison. Each day from Monday to Saturday between 1861 and 1912 she made a round trip of 180 miles (290 kilometers): from Rondout, New York, to Manhattan, where she docked at noon, and back to Rondout by 9 p.m. She earned a reputation for punctuality and safety under the exacting command of Absalom L. Anderson. The ship was later remodeled and used for various excursions by the Hudson River Day Line. She was retired in 1917 and dismantled, her whistle acquired by the steamboat *Robert Fulton*.

Donald C. Ringwald: *The Mary Powell* (Berkeley, Calif.: Howell–North, 1992)

Arthur G. Adams

Masliansky, Zvi Hirsch (*b* Slutsk [now in Belarus], 16 May 1856; *d* Brooklyn, 11 Jan 1943). Preacher. A religious Zionist and a brilliant speaker whose rhetoric bridged the gap between traditional Jewish preaching and modern oratory, he was forced because of his political activities to flee Russia in 1895. He settled in New York City, where he became active in Zionist circles and gained enormous popularity as a speaker among eastern European Jewish immigrants. From 1898 he delivered a Yiddish sermon on Friday nights at the Educational Alliance, and in 1902 he helped to launch *Di yidishe velt*, a daily newspaper in Yiddish and English. Masliansky published several volumes of sermons and memoirs.

Daniel Soyer

Masons. See Freemasons.

Maspeth. Large neighborhood in west central Queens (1991 pop. 40,000), bounded to the north by the Brooklyn–Queens Expressway, to the east by 69th Street, to the south by Metropolitan Avenue, and to the west by Newtown Creek and Brooklyn. It is named for the Mespat Indians, who inhabited the headwaters of Newtown Creek. The first European settlement in Queens County (1642), it was attacked by Indians in 1643 and abandoned in 1644. Several roads were laid out during the eighteenth century. De Witt Clinton, a governor of New York State (1817–28), had a summer home at 56th Terrace and 56th Avenue, where he planned the Erie Canal. In 1852 Mount Olivet Cemetery was opened and development escalated: the population grew from 1449 in 1875 to 4300 in 1898. Fertilizer works and lumber yards were built along the creek; inland were a linoleum plant and rope walks (long, narrow buildings where hemp was spun into rope). The eastern edge of Maspeth abutting Newtown Creek remained industrial and commercial, especially along Grand and Maspeth avenues. In the mid 1990s the population was mostly Catholic,

Polish, Lithuanian, German, Irish, and Italian, with increasing numbers of Koreans, Puerto Ricans, Dominicans, and Greeks. Many residents were sanitation workers, firefighters, truck drivers, factory workers, laborers, and small shopkeepers. The Long Island Expressway and the belt of cemeteries nearby isolated the northern section of Maspeth from northern and central Queens and kept it suburban; the sidestreets were lined with one-family detached houses. There is a large amount of industry in the area. Grand Avenue, the main shopping street, provides a route to Brooklyn and Elmhurst.

Vincent Seyfried

Masses. A monthly magazine launched in 1911 as the reinvigorated descendant of an earlier muckraking socialist publication of the same name. It was published from offices situated first on Nassau Street and from June 1913 at 91 Greenwich Avenue. Edited by Max Eastman and his associate editor Floyd Dell, the magazine was organized under a system of collective ownership and editorship. It became known for its bold, powerful graphics, advocacy of class warfare, and relentless satire of bourgeois values. The magazine's opposition to the First World War resulted in its suppression by federal censors, and it ceased publication in December 1917.

Rebecca Zurier: *Art for the Masses: A Radical Magazine and Its Graphics, 1911–1917* (Philadelphia: Temple University Press, 1988)

Jan Seidler Ramirez

Massine, Léonide [Miassin, Leonid (Fedorovich)] (*b* Moscow, 8 Aug 1895; *d* Cologne, 16 March 1979). Choreographer. He first visited New York City with the Ballets Russes in 1916, when ballet was virtually unknown in the United States. By the time of his third visit in 1933 ballet was immensely popular and he was widely known. In the city he joined Ballet Theatre in 1942 and provided choreography for a production in 1948 of *The Red Shoes*, in which he also danced. Believing that a ballet should incorporate art and music of high quality, he was as comfortable in the classical idiom as he was at creating choreography for the short features shown in movie theaters. Although his later works were too didactic for his audiences, such earlier ones as *Gaîeté Parisienne* and *Parade* are still performed regularly. Massine was a pivotal figure in the popularization of classical dance in the city. He wrote *My Life in Ballet* (1968).

Clarissa L. Bushman

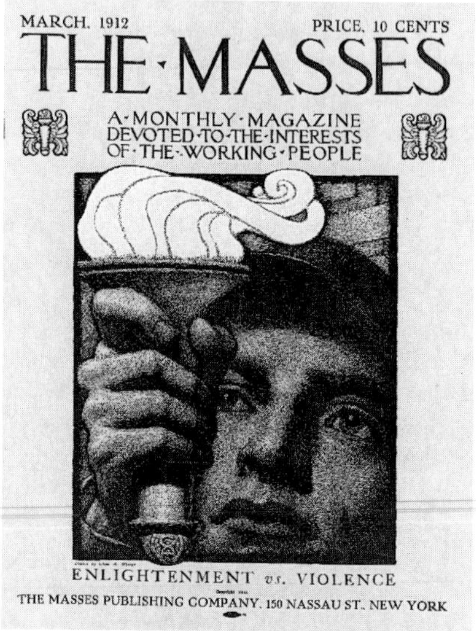

MARCH, 1912
PRICE, 10 CENTS
THE·MASSES
A·MONTHLY·MAGAZINE
DEVOTED·TO·THE·INTERESTS
OF·THE·WORKING·PEOPLE
ENLIGHTENMENT vs. VIOLENCE
THE MASSES PUBLISHING COMPANY, 150 NASSAU ST. NEW YORK

Cover designed by Charles Allen Winter for the Masses, *March 1912*

Masterson, Bat [William Barclay] (*b* Iroquois County, Ill., 24 Nov 1853; *d* New York City, 25 Oct 1921). Peace officer, gambler, and newspaper reporter. After a career as a gunfighter and gambler in the West he moved to New York City in 1902, where he became a sportswriter and editor at the *Morning Telegraph*. At the time of his death he was the sports editor of the newspaper and secretary of the company. Masterson is buried in Woodlawn Cemetery in the Bronx.

Kenneth T. Jackson

Mathewson, Christy [Christopher] (*b* Factoryville, Penn., 12 Aug 1880; *d* Saranac Lake, N.Y., 7 Oct 1925). Baseball player. After attending Bucknell University he was a pitcher for the New York Giants, managed by John J. McGraw, from 1900 to 1916. Nicknamed "Big Six" after a well-known fire engine in New York City, he was noted for his superb control and particularly for his "fadeaway" (screwball) pitch. During his career he won 373 games and lost only 188, compiling a lifetime earned run average of 2.13. He threw eighty shutout games, including three against Philadelphia in the World Series in 1905, won twenty or more games in twelve consecutive seasons, and won thirty or more games in four seasons. Religious and college-bred, he enjoyed a wholesome image and may have been a model for William Gilbert Patten's series of dime novels "Frank Merriwell at Yale." He was treated like a son by the ruthless and controversial McGraw. Mathewson wrote *Pitching in a Pinch: Baseball from the Inside* (1912) and a play that opened on Broadway, *The Girl and the Pennant: A Base-ball Comedy on Four Acts* (1913). Exposure to poison gas during a training accident in the First World War contributed to his death from tuberculosis. In 1936 he was one of five original members inducted into the Baseball Hall of Fame.

Harold Seymour: *Baseball: The Early Years* (New York: Oxford University Press, 1960)

Harold Seymour: *Baseball: The Golden Age* (New York: Oxford University Press, 1971)

"Baseball in the Dead Ball Era," *The National Pastime: A Review of Baseball History* (Cooperstown, N.Y.: Society for American Baseball Research, 1986)

Victoria Earle Matthews

Charles C. Alexander: *John McGraw* (New York: Viking, 1988)

Ray Robinson: *Matty, an American Hero: Christy Mathewson of the New York Giants* (New York: Oxford University Press, 1993)

Jeffrey Scheuer

Matthews, Victoria Earle (*b* Fort Valley, Ga., 27 May 1861; *d* New York City, 10 March 1907). Journalist and reformer. Born into slavery, she moved to New York City in 1873 and worked sporadically for large daily newspapers such as the *New York Times*, the *New York Herald*, the *New York Age*, and the *New York Globe*. She is best known for having established the White Rose Industrial Association in 1897, a mission that offered employment advice to black female migrants, a kindergarten, a library, and classes in cooking, sewing, and black history. The association was at 86th Street in 1900 and later moved to 262 West 137th Street in Harlem. Matthews wrote *The Awakening of the Afro-American Woman* (?1897).

Thea Arnold

Maurer, Louis (*b* Biebrich [now in Germany], 21 Feb 1832; *d* New York City, 19 July 1932). Lithographer and painter. He arrived New York City in 1851, worked briefly for the publisher Thomas Strong, spent eight years with Currier and Ives, joined Major and Knapp in 1860, and in 1872–84 produced commercial lithography for his own firm, Maurer and Heppenheimer. A draftsman, illustrator, and printer, he specialized in figures and animals (especially horses): his series "Life of a Fireman" is one of his finest. Maurer was a central figure within printing circles for eighty years and lived his last fifty-seven years at 404 West 43rd Street. His son Alfred H. Maurer (1868–1932) was a well-known painter in New York City.

Wendy Shadwell

Maxwell, William Henry (*b* Stewartstown, Ireland, 5 March 1852; *d* New York City, 3 May 1920). Educator. After moving to the metropolitan region in 1874 he became the superintendent of schools for the City of Brooklyn and then the first superintendent of the public schools of New York City after consolidation (1898–1917). Faced with shortages of space and funds brought on by the massive immigration of the early twentieth century, he initiated programs for immigrants and the poor, including kindergartens, recreation centers, courses in English, and vocational training. He was president of the National Education Association from 1904 to 1905 and a member of two of its important committees on curriculum; he also edited the *Educational Review* and fought to prohibit child labor. Maxwell lived at Park Avenue and 59th Street.

Samuel Abelow: *Dr. William Henry Maxwell* (New York: Scheba, 1934)

Selma Berrol

Maxwell's Plum. Restaurant and bar in Manhattan, opened in April 1966 on 1st Avenue and 64th Street by Warner LeRoy. For many years the best-known "singles bar" in New York City, it was known for attracting large crowds and for its deliberately garish décor, which included Tiffany lamps, ornate mirrors, and large expanses of stained glass. At the peak of its popularity in the 1970s the restaurant served 350,000 meals a year. Business fell off sharply in the following decade, and the restaurant closed in July 1988.

Mayflower Madame. The nickname given by tabloid newspapers in New York City to Sidney Biddle Barrows, who was arrested in 1984 for running a prostitution ring that was ostensibly an escort service called Cachet at 307 West 74th Street. She was so called for being a descendant of two original settlers of the Plymouth Colony, John Howland and William Brewster, as well as of Nicholas Biddle, president of the Second Bank of the United States (1823–36).

Timothy J. Gilfoyle

mayoralty. The first mayor of New York City was Thomas Willett, appointed by the English governor Richard Nicolls in 1665. For a century and a half the mayor was appointed annually, first by the colonial governor and then by the governor of New York State. The early mayors had limited powers: they sat on the Common Council, where they were at best first among equals. In the nineteenth century the powers and responsibilities of the office fluctuated wildly through many charter revisions, but in general they increased. The mayor in 1820 became elected by the Common Council and in 1830 was given the power to veto the decisions of the council, of which he was no longer a member. When the first direct mayoral elections were held in 1834 the

Returns of Mayoral Elections in New York City, 1834–1894

1834	
Cornelius W. Lawrence (Democrat)	17,576
Gulian C. Verplanck (Whig)	17,395
Others	18
Total	34,989
1835	
Cornelius W. Lawrence (Democrat)	17,696
Others	2,500
Total	20,196
1836	
Cornelius W. Lawrence (Democrat)	15,754
Seth Geer (Whig)	6,136
Alexander Ming Jr. (Locofoco)	2,712
Samuel F. B. Morse (Native American)	1,497
Others	75
Total	26,174
1837	
Aaron Clark (Whig)	16,140
John I. Morgan (Democrat)	12,974
Moses Jacques (Locofoco)	3,911
Others	28
Total	33,053
1838	
Aaron Clark (Whig)	19,723
Isaac L. Varian (Democrat)	19,204
Richard Riker (Conservative)	395
Others	19
Total	39,341
1839	
Isaac L. Varian (Democrat)	21,072
Aaron Clark (Whig)	20,005
Others	36
Total	41,113
1840	
Isaac L. Varian (Democrat)	21,243
J. P. Phoenix (Whig)	19,622
Others	36
Total	40,901
1841	
Robert H. Morris (Democrat)	18,605
J. P. Phoenix (Whig)	18,206
Samuel F. B. Morse (Native American)	77
Others	45
Total	36,933
1842	
Robert H. Morris (Democrat)	20,633
J. P. Phoenix (Whig)	18,755
Thomas F. Field (Abolition)	136
Others	63
Total	39,587
1843	
Robert H. Morris (Democrat)	24,395
Robert Smith (Whig)	19,516
Others	73
Total	43,984

(*continued*)

Returns of Mayoral Elections in New York City, 1834–1894 (*Continued*)

1844	
James Harper (Native)	24,606
Jonathan I. Coddington (Locofoco)	20,726
Morris Franklin (Whig)	5,207
Others	22
Total	50,561
1845	
William F. Havemeyer (Democrat)	24,183
James Harper (Native)	17,472
Dudley Selden (Whig)	7,082
Others	226
Total	48,963
1846	
Andrew H. Mickle (Democrat)	21,675
Robert Taylor (Whig)	15,111
William B. Cozzens (Native)	8,301
Others	757
Total	45,844
1847	
William V. Brady (Whig)	21,310
J. Sherman Brownell (Democrat)	19,877
E. G. Drake (Native)	2,078
Others	433
Total	43,698
1848	
William F. Havemeyer (Democrat)	23,155
William V. Brady (Whig)	22,227
Others	848
Total	46,230
1849	
Caleb S. Woodhull (Whig)	21,656
Myndert Van Schaick (Democrat)	17,535
Others	103
Total	39,294
1850	
Ambrose C. Kingsland (Whig)	22,546
Fernando Wood (Democrat)	17,973
Others	335
Total	40,854
1852	
Jacob A. Westervelt (Democrat)	33,251
Morgan Morgans (Whig)	23,719
Others	1,088
Total	58,058
1854	
Fernando Wood (Soft Shells–Hard Shells)	19,993
James W. Barker (Know Nothing)	18,553
Wilson G. Hunt (Reform)	15,386
Others	5,828
Total	59,760
1856	
Fernando Wood (Democrat)	34,860
Isaac O. Backer (American)	25,209
Anthony J. Bleecker (Republican)	9,654
James S. Libby (Bog Democrat)	4,764

(*continued*)

Returns of Mayoral Elections in New York City, 1834–1894 *(Continued)*

James R. Whiting (Municipal Reform)	3,646
Others	84
Total	78,217
1857	
Daniel F. Tiemann (Independent)	43,216
Fernando Wood (Democrat)	40,889
Others	103
Total	84,208
1859	
Fernando Wood (Mozart Democrat)	29,940
William F. Havemeyer (Tammany Democrat)	26,913
George Opdyke (Republican)	21,417
Others	106
Total	78,376
1861	
George Opdyke (Republican)	25,380
C. Godfrey Gunther (Tammany Democrat)	24,767
Fernando Wood (Mozart Democrat)	24,167
Others	81
Total	74,395
1863	
C. Godfrey Gunther (Independent Democrat)	29,121
Francis I. A. Boole (Tammany Democrat)	22,597
Orison Blunt (Republican)	19,383
Others	65
Total	71,166
1865	
John T. Hoffman (Tammany Democrat)	32,820
Marshall O. Roberts (Republican)	31,657
John Hecker (Mozart Democrat)	10,390
C. Godfrey Gunther (Independent Democrat)	6,758
Others	77
Total	81,702
1867	
John T. Hoffman (Tammany Democrat)	63,061
Fernando Wood (Mozart Democrat)	22,837
William A. Darling (Republican)	18,483
Others	100
Total	104,481
1868	
A. Oakey Hall (Democrat)	75,109
Frederick A. Conkling (Republican)	20,835
Others	321
Total	96,265
1869	
A. Oakey Hall (Democrat)	65,568
Others	1,051
Total	66,619

(continued)

Returns of Mayoral Elections in New York City, 1834–1894 *(Continued)*

1870	
A. Oakey Hall (Tammany Democrat)	71,037
Thomas A. Ledwith (Anti-Tammany Democrat)	46,392
Others	1,989
Total	119,418
1872	
William F. Havemeyer (Republican)	53,806
A. R. Lawrence (Liberal–Republican)	45,398
James O'Brien (Apollo Hall Democrat)	31,121
Total	130,325
1874	
William H. Wickham (Democrat)	70,071
Salem H. Wales (Republican)	36,953
Oswald Ottendorfer (Independent)	24,226
Others	443
Total	131,693
1876	
Smith Ely Jr. (Democrat)	111,880
John Dix (Republican)	57,811
Others	552
Total	170,243
1878	
Edward Cooper (Republican)	79,986
August Schell (Democrat)	60,485
Others	2,793
Total	143,264
1880	
William R. Grace (Democrat)	101,760
William Dowd (Republican)	98,715
Others	1,827
Total	202,302
1882	
Franklin Edson (Democrat)	97,802
Allan Campbell (Republican)	76,385
Others	4,124
Total	178,311
1884	
William R. Grace (Independent)	96,288
Hugh J. Grant (Tammany Hall Democrat)	85,361
Frederick S. Gibbs (Republican)	44,386
Others	1,300
Total	227,335
1886	
Abram S. Hewitt (Democrat)	90,552
Henry George (Labor Union)	68,110
Theodore Roosevelt (Republican)	60,435
Others	895
Total	219,992
1888	
Hugh J. Grant (Democrat)	114,111
Joel B. Erhardt (Republican)	73,037

(continued)

Returns of Mayoral Elections in New York City, 1834–1894 *(Continued)*

Abram S. Hewitt (Citizens Democrat)	71,979
Others	13,643
Total	272,770
1890	
Hugh J. Grant (Democrat)	116,581
Francis M. Scott (Republican)	93,382
Others	7,846
Total	217,809
1892	
Thomas F. Gilroy (Democrat)	173,510
Edwin Einstein (Republican)	97,923
Henry Hicks (People's)	2,466
Others	12,250
Total	286,149
1894	
William L. Strong (Republican)	154,094
Hugh J. Grant (Democrat)	108,907
Others	11,315
Total	274,316

Sources: *Manual of the Corporation of the City of New York*, 1870 [for years 1834–70]
The City Record [for years 1872–94]

Compiled by James Bradley

Democrat Cornelius Van Wyck Lawrence defeated Gulian C. Verplanck by 181 votes; in 1849 the mayoral term was extended to two years. Most mayors in the nineteenth century were businessmen, and the best-known ones, such as Philip Hone, William F. Havemeyer, and William R. Grace, are remembered more for their accomplishments out of office than in it. One of few dominant mayors during these years was Fernando Wood (1854–57, 1859–60). No head of Tammany Hall attained the office during the organization's long period of influence, which lasted until after the Second World War.

The mayor became the symbolic head of government at consolidation in 1898 but continued to operate under severe constraints for decades, especially regarding appointments and budgets: the newly created borough presidents' offices circumscribed the ability of the mayor to control the city's payroll, and other powers were now shared with a strengthened Board of Estimate. The mayoral term was extended to four years in 1905. The person chiefly responsible for defining the modern mayoralty was Fiorello H. La Guardia, who by declaring his independence from political bosses and determinedly seeking publicity made himself the focus of power and attention throughout his long tenure (1934–45). Mayoral power was further strengthened by reforms to the city charter in 1961 that gave mayors the authority to prepare the capital budget (formerly prepared by the City Planning Commission), to alter the operating budget (an authority formerly shared with the

Returns of Mayoral Elections in New York City by Borough, 1897–1993

1897

	Robert A. Van Wyck (Democrat)	Seth Low (Citizens Union)	Benjamin Tracy (Republican)
Manhattan and Bronx	143,666	77,210	55,834
Brooklyn	76,185	65,656	37,611
Queens	9,275	5,876	5,639
Staten Island	4,871	2,798	2,779
Total	233,997	151,540	101,863

Others, 44,230
Total Vote: 531,630

1901

	Seth Low (Fusion)	Edward M. Shephard (Democrat)
Manhattan and Bronx	114,625	88,858
Brooklyn	162,298	156,631
Queens	12,757	13,321
Staten Island	7,133	6,367
Total	296,813	265,177

Total vote: 561,990

1903

	George B. McClellan (Democrat)	Seth Low (Fusion)
Manhattan and Bronx	188,681	132,178
Brooklyn	102,569	101,251
Queens	17,074	11,960
Staten Island	6,458	6,697
Total	314,782	252,086

Others, 28,417
Total vote: 595,285

1905

	George B. McClellan (Democrat)	William R. Hearst (Independent)	William M. Ivins (Republican)
Manhattan and Bronx	140,264	123,292	64,289
Brooklyn	68,778	84,835	61,192
Queens	13,228	13,706	7,213
Staten Island	6,127	3,096	4,499
Total	228,397	224,929	137,193

Others, 15,676
Total Vote: 606,195

1909

	William J. Gaynor (Democrat)	Otto T. Bannard (Fusion)	William R. Hearst (Independent)
Manhattan and Bronx	134,075	86,497	87,155
Brooklyn	91,666	73,860	49,040
Queens	17,570	11,907	15,186
Staten Island	7,067	5,040	2,806
Total	250,378	177,304	154,187

Others, 22,198
Total vote: 604,067

1913

	John Purroy Mitchel (Fusion)	Edward E. McCall (Democrat)
Manhattan	131,280	103,429
Bronx	46,944	25,684
Brooklyn	137,074	77,826
Queens	34,279	20,097
Staten Island	8,640	6,883
Total	358,217	233,919

Others, 34,991
Total vote: 627,127

(*continued*)

Returns of Mayoral Elections in New York City by Borough, 1897–1993 (*Continued*)

1917

	John F. Hylan (Democrat)	John Purroy Mitchel (Fusion)	Morris Hillquit (Socialist)
Manhattan	113,728	66,748	51,176
Bronx	41,492	19,247	30,374
Brooklyn	114,487	52,921	48,880
Queens	35,399	13,641	13,477
Staten Island	8,850	2,940	1,425
Total	313,956	155,497	145,332

Joseph Bennett (Republican), 56,438; Others, 20,586
Total vote: 691,809

1921

	John F. Hylan (Democrat)	Henry H. Curran (Republican)	Jacob Panken (Socialist)
Manhattan	261,452	124,253	28,756
Bronx	118,235	34,919	21,255
Brooklyn	260,143	128,259	29,580
Queens	87,676	36,415	2,741
Staten Island	22,741	9,000	275
Total	750,247	332,846	82,607

Others, 31,242
Total vote: 1,196,942

1925
Democratic Primary

	James J. Walker	John F. Hylan
Manhattan	102,835	27,802
Bronx	45,308	21,228
Brooklyn	65,671	60,814
Queens	28,203	32,163
Staten Island	6,321	12,197
Total	248,338	154,204

General Election

	James J. Walker (Democrat)	Frank D. Waterman (Republican)	Norman Thomas (Socialist)
Manhattan	247,079	98,617	9,482
Bronx	131,226	39,615	11,133
Brooklyn	244,029	139,060	16,809
Queens	103,629	58,478	1,943
Staten Island	22,724	10,794	207
Total	748,687	346,564	39,574

Others, 26,272
Total Vote: 1,161,097

1929

	James J. Walker (Democrat)	Fiorello H. La Guardia (Republican)	Norman Thomas (Socialist)
Manhattan	232,370	91,944	37,316
Bronx	159,948	52,646	39,181
Brooklyn	283,432	132,095	71,145
Queens	166,188	75,911	24,807
Staten Island	25,584	15,079	3,248
Total	867,522	367,675	175,697

Others, 53,795
Total Vote: 1,464,689

1932

	John O'Brien (Democrat)	Lewis H. Pounds (Republican)	Morris Hillquit (Socialist)	Joseph McKee (write-in)
Manhattan	308,944	116,729	40,011	42,299
Bronx	181,639	48,366	68,980	50,212
Brooklyn	358,945	157,152	113,622	73,431
Queens	176,070	105,068	24,981	61,648

(*continued*)

Returns of Mayoral Elections in New York City by Borough, 1897–1993 *(Continued)*

Staten Island	30,517	16,586	2,293	6,782
Total	1,056,115	443,901	249,887	234,372

Others, 269,585
Total Vote: 2,253,860

1933

	Fiorello H. La Guardia (Republican–City Fusion)	Joseph McKee (Recovery)	John O'Brien (Democrat)
Manhattan	203,479	123,707	192,649
Bronx	151,669	131,280	93,403
Brooklyn	331,920	194,558	194,335
Queens	154,369	141,296	90,501
Staten Island	27,085	18,212	15,784
Total	868,522	609,053	586,672

Charles Solomon (Socialist), 59,846; Others, 81,309
Total Vote: 2,205,402

1937

	Fiorello H. La Guardia (City Fusion–Progressive–American Labor–Republican)	Jeremiah T. Mahoney (Democrat–Trades Union–Anti-Communist)
Manhattan	328,995	237,006
Bronx	272,322	166,805
Brooklyn	494,516	286,647
Queens	213,939	172,973
Staten Island	34,858	27,325
Total	1,344,630	890,756

Others, 64,834
Total Vote: 2,300,220

1941

	Fiorello H. La Guardia (City Fusion–United City–American Labor–Republican)	William O'Dwyer (Democrat)
Manhattan	298,225	227,717
Bronx	259,607	185,295
Brooklyn	439,856	348,048
Queens	166,364	259,239
Staten Island	22,249	33,876
Total	1,186,301	1,054,175

Others, 53,250
Total Vote: 2,293,726

1945

	William O'Dwyer (Democrat–American Labor)	Jonah J. Goldstein (Republican–Liberal–Fusion)	Newbold Morris (No Deal)
Manhattan	253,371	100,591	100,064
Bronx	227,818	95,582	88,404
Brooklyn	386,335	161,119	136,262
Queens	228,275	65,240	77,687
Staten Island	29,558	9,069	5,931
Total	1,125,357	431,601	408,348

Others, 71,385
Total Vote: 2,036,691

1949

	William O'Dwyer (Democrat)	Newbold Morris (Republican–Liberal–Fusion)	Vito Marcantonio (American Labor)
Manhattan	278,343	219,430	123,128
Bronx	254,014	185,248	82,386

(continued)

Returns of Mayoral Elections in New York City by Borough, 1897–1993 (*Continued*)

Brooklyn	425,225	332,433	113,478
Queens	270,062	200,552	34,677
Staten Island	38,868	18,406	2,957
Total	1,266,512	956,069	356,626

Others, 83,710
Total Vote: 2,662,917

1950

	Vincent Impellitteri (Experience)	Ferdinand Pecora (Democrat–Liberal)	Edward Corsi (Republican)
Manhattan	246,608	214,610	102,575
Bronx	215,913	217,254	54,796
Brooklyn	357,322	362,246	113,392
Queens	303,448	129,223	99,225
Staten Island	37,884	12,018	12,384
Total	1,161,175	935,351	382,372

Paul L. Ross (American Labor), 147,578; Others, 70,429
Total Vote: 2,696,905

1953

	Robert F. Wagner (Democrat)	Harold Riegelman (Republican)	Rudolph Halley (Liberal–Independent)
Manhattan	236,960	147,876	84,532
Bronx	206,771	97,224	122,678
Brooklyn	339,970	183,968	175,537
Queens	207,918	208,829	80,548
Staten Island	31,007	23,694	3,809
Total	1,022,626	661,591	467,104

Clifford T. McAvor (American Labor), 53,045; Others, 39,780
Total Vote: 2,224,146

1957

	Robert F. Wagner (Democrat–Liberal–Fusion)	Robert K. Christenberry (Republican)
Manhattan	316,203	112,173
Bronx	316,299	96,726
Brooklyn	494,078	163,427
Queens	341,212	191,061
Staten Island	40,983	22,381
Total	1,508,775	585,768

Others, 129,511
Total Vote: 2,224,054

1961
Democratic Primary

	Robert F. Wagner	Arthur Levitt
Manhattan	122,607	66,917
Bronx	78,626	47,885
Brooklyn	136,440	103,296
Queens	102,845	64,157
Staten Island	15,498	10,471
Total	456,016	292,726

General Election

	Robert F. Wagner (Democrat–Liberal–Brotherhood)	Louis J. Lefkowitz (Republican–Civic Action–Non-Partisan)	Lawrence E. Gerosa (Independent–Citizens Party)
Manhattan	265,015	174,471	36,893
Bronx	255,528	134,964	67,213
Brooklyn	396,539	251,258	105,232

(*continued*)

Returns of Mayoral Elections in New York City by Borough, 1897–1993 *(Continued)*

Queens	290,194	243,836	99,987
Staten Island	30,145	31,162	12,279
Total	1,237,421	835,691	321,604

Others, 72,830
Total Vote: 2,467,546

1965
Democratic Primary

	Abraham D. Beame	Paul R. Screvane	William F. Ryan	Paul O'Dwyer
Manhattan	53,386	66,444	48,744	6,775
Bronx	66,064	54,260	16,632	5,976
Brooklyn	128,146	79,485	24,588	8,332
Queens	82,601	63,680	22,570	6,895
Staten Island	6,148	7,512	1,204	697
Total	336,345	271,381	113,738	28,675

General Election

	John V. Lindsay (Republican–Liberal–Independent Citizen)	Abraham D. Beame (Democrat–Civil Service–Fusion)	William F. Buckley (Conservative)
Manhattan	291,326	193,230	37,694
Bronx	181,072	213,980	63,858
Brooklyn	308,398	365,360	97,679
Queens	331,162	250,662	121,544
Staten Island	37,148	23,467	20,451
Total	1,149,106	1,046,699	341,226

Others, 115,420
Total Vote: 2,652,451

1969
Democratic Primary

	Mario Procaccino	Robert F. Wagner	Herman Badillo	Norman Mailer	James H. Scheuer
Manhattan	26,804	40,978	74,809	17,372	7,117
Bronx	50,465	33,442	48,841	4,214	10,788
Brooklyn	87,630	81,833	52,866	10,299	11,942
Queens	79,002	61,244	37,880	8,700	8,994
Staten Island	11,628	6,967	2,769	703	509
Total	255,529	224,464	217,165	41,288	39,350

Republican Primary

	John J. Marchi	John V. Lindsay
Manhattan	12,457	44,236
Bronx	16,132	12,222
Brooklyn	33,694	20,575
Queens	40,469	26,658
Staten Island	10,946	3,675
Total	113,698	107,366

General Election

	John V. Lindsay (Liberal–Independent)	Mario Procaccino (Democrat–Non-Partisan–Civil Service Independent)	John J. Marchi (Republican–Conservative)
Manhattan	328,564	99,460	61,539
Bronx	161,953	165,647	76,711
Brooklyn	256,046	301,324	152,933
Queens	249,330	245,783	192,008
Staten Island	16,740	19,558	59,220
Total	1,012,633	831,772	542,411

Others, 71,387
Total Vote: 2,458,203

(continued)

Returns of Mayoral Elections in New York City by Borough, 1897–1993 (*Continued*)

1973

Democratic Primary

	Abraham D. Beame	Herman Badillo	Mario Biaggi	Albert H. Blumenthal
Manhattan	45,901	73,676	17,830	41,906
Bronx	41,508	55,432	39,462	18,400
Brooklyn	96,621	57,836	48,352	31,913
Queens	73,520	33,990	45,992	28,960
Staten Island	8,912	2,902	7,524	2,062
Total	266,462	223,836	159,160	123,241

Democratic Primary Runoff

	Abraham D. Beame	Herman Badillo
Manhattan	77,928	112,482
Bronx	97,415	86,482
Brooklyn	201,866	93,140
Queens	153,415	57,658
Staten Island	17,999	4,819
Total	548,623	354,581

General Election

	Abraham D. Beame (Democrat)	John J. Marchi (Republican)	Albert H. Blumenthal (Liberal)	Mario Biaggi (Conservative)
Manhattan	158,050	45,803	101,117	17,882
Bronx	160,774	37,609	32,661	50,805
Brooklyn	321,477	73,776	60,340	51,713
Queens	283,474	90,942	66,059	60,490
Staten Island	37,355	28,445	5,120	9,096
Total	961,130	276,575	265,297	189,986

Others, 7,883

Total Vote: 1,700,871

1977

Democratic Primary

	Edward I. Koch	Mario M. Cuomo	Abraham D. Beame	Bella Abzug	Percy Sutton	Herman Badillo
Manhattan	49,855	25,056	23,507	54,591	34,742	26,895
Bronx	23,237	22,939	25,534	20,429	24,588	34,246
Brooklyn	49,894	55,439	62,921	37,790	42,215	28,838
Queens	51,515	56,719	44,342	33,623	28,286	8,961
Staten Island	5,747	10,335	7,306	4,286	1,366	868
Total	180,248	170,488	163,610	150,719	131,197	99,808

Democratic Primary Runoff

	Edward I. Koch	Mario M. Cuomo
Manhattan	114,084	61,555
Bronx	69,230	55,017
Brooklyn	131,583	112,862
Queens	107,182	105,149
Staten Island	9,770	19,639
Total	431,849	354,222

General Election

	Edward I. Koch (Democrat)	Mario M. Cuomo (Liberal)	Roy M. Goodman (Republican)
Manhattan	184,842	70,717	19,324
Bronx	116,436	75,754	6,102
Brooklyn	204,934	153,134	11,491
Queens	191,894	186,590	18,460
Staten Island	19,270	36,747	3,229
Total	717,376	522,942	58,606

Barry Farber (Conservative), 57,437; Others, 13,781

Total Vote: 1,370,142

(*continued*)

Returns of Mayoral Elections in New York City by Borough, 1897–1993 *(Continued)*

1981

	Edward I. Koch (Democrat–Republican)	Frank J. Barbaro (Unity)
Manhattan	189,631	56,702
Bronx	132,421	22,074
Brooklyn	261,292	48,812
Queens	275,812	31,225
Staten Island	53,466	3,906
Total	912,622	162,719

Others, 147,303
Total Vote: 1,222,644

1985

	Edward I. Koch (Democrat–Independent)	Carol Bellamy (Liberal)	Diane McGrath (Republican–Conservative)
Manhattan	170,198	41,190	17,491
Bronx	136,263	14,092	12,358
Brooklyn	246,748	29,256	25,738
Queens	246,854	25,098	36,032
Staten Island	62,163	3,835	10,049
Total	862,226	113,471	101,668

Others, 29,397
Total Vote: 1,106,762

1989
Democratic Primary

	David N. Dinkins	Edward I. Koch	Harrison J. Goldin	Richard Ravitch
Manhattan	151,113	96,923	6,889	17,499
Bronx	101,274	66,600	4,951	5,946
Brooklyn	170,440	139,268	9,619	13,214
Queens	113,952	129,262	5,857	9,443
Staten Island	11,122	24,260	1,493	1,432
Total	547,901	456,313	28,809	47,534

General Election

	David N. Dinkins (Democrat)	Rudolph W. Giuliani (Republican–Liberal–Independent Fusion)
Manhattan	255,286	157,686
Bronx	172,271	99,800
Brooklyn	276,903	237,832
Queens	190,096	284,766
Staten Island	22,988	90,380
Total	917,544	870,464

Henry Hewes (Right-to-Life), 17,460; Ronald S. Lauder (Conservative), 9,271; Others, 85,106
Total Vote: 1,899,845

1993
General Election

	Rudolph W. Giuliani (Republican–Liberal)	David N. Dinkins (Democrat)
Manhattan	166,357	242,524
Bronx	98,780	162,995
Brooklyn	258,058	269,343
Queens	291,625	180,527
Staten Island	115,416	21,507
Total	930,236	876,896

George J. Marlin (Conservative–Right-to-Life), 15,926; Others, 65,945
Total vote: 1,889,003

Mayors of New York City

Thomas Willett 1665
Thomas Delavall 1666
Thomas Willett 1667
Cornelius Van Steenwyck 1668–70
Thomas Delavall 1671
Matthias Nicolls 1672
John Lawrence 1673–74
William Dervall 1675
Nicholas De Meyer 1676
Stephanus Van Cortlandt 1677
Thomas Delavall 1678
Francis Rombouts 1679
William Dyre 1680–81
Cornelius Van Steenwyck 1682–83
Gabriel Minvielle 1684
Nicolas Bayard 1685
Stephanus Van Cortlandt 1686–88
Peter Delanoy 1689–90
John Lawrence 1691
Abraham De Peyster 1692–94
Charles Lodwik 1694–95
William Merrett 1695–98
Johannes De Peyster 1698–99
David Provost 1699–1700
Issac De Reimer 1700–1
Thomas Noell 1701–2
Philip French 1702–3
William Peartree 1703–7
Ebenezer Wilson 1707–10
Jacobus Van Cortlandt 1710–11
Caleb Heathcote 1711–14
John Johnson 1714–19
Jacobus Van Cortlandt 1719–20
Robert Walters 1720–25
Johannes Jansen 1725–26
Robert Lurting 1726–35
Paul Richard 1735–39
John Cruger 1739–44
Stephen Bayard 1744–47
Edward Holland 1747–57
John Cruger Jr. 1757–66
Whitehead Hicks 1766–76
David Matthews 1776–84
James Duane 1784–89
Richard Varick 1789–1801
Edward Livingston 1801–3
De Witt Clinton 1803–7
Marinus Willett 1807–8
De Witt Clinton 1808–10
Jacob Radcliff 1810–11
De Witt Clinton 1811–15
John Ferguson 1815
Jacob Radcliff 1815–18
Cadwaller D. Colden 1818–21
Stephen Allen 1821–24
William Paulding 1825–26
Philip Hone 1826–27
William Paulding 1827–29
Walter Bowne 1829–33
Gideon Lee 1833–34
Cornelius W. Lawrence 1834–37
Aaron Clark 1837–39
Isaac L. Varian 1839–41

(continued)

Mayors of New York City
(Continued)

Robert H. Morris 1841–44
James Harper 1844–45
William F. Havemeyer 1845–46
Andrew F. Mickle 1846–47
William V. Brady 1847–48
William F. Havemeyer 1848–49
Caleb S. Woodhull 1849–51
Ambrose C. Kingsland 1851–53
Jacob A. Westervelt 1853–55
Fernando Wood 1855–58
Daniel F. Tiemann 1858–60
Fernando Wood 1860–62
George Opdyke 1862–64
C. Godfrey Gunther 1864–66
John T. Hoffman 1866–68
T. Coman 1868 (acting)
A. Oakey Hall 1869–72
William F. Havemeyer 1873–74
S. B. H. Vance 1874 (acting)
William H. Wickham 1875–76
Smith Ely 1877–78
Edward Cooper 1879–80
William R. Grace 1881–82
Franklin Edson 1883–84
William R. Grace 1885–86
Abram S. Hewitt 1887–88
Hugh J. Grant 1889–92
Thomas F. Gilroy 1893–94
William L. Strong 1895–97
Robert A. Van Wyck 1898–1901
Seth Low 1902–3
George B. McClellan 1904–9
William J. Gaynor 1910–13
Ardolph L. Kline 1913 (acting)
John Purroy Mitchel 1914–17
John F. Hylan 1918–25
James J. Walker 1926–32
Joseph V. McKee 1932 (acting)
John P. O'Brien 1933
Fiorello H. La Guardia 1934–45
William O'Dwyer 1946–50
Vincent R. Impellitteri 1950–53
Robert F. Wagner 1954–65
John V. Lindsay 1966–73
Abraham D. Beame 1974–77
Edward I. Koch 1978–89
David N. Dinkins 1990–93
Rudolph W. Giuliani 1994–

Source: The Green Book

Board of Estimate), and to reorganize municipal offices (also formerly shared with the Board of Estimate). Reforms in 1975 encouraged decentralization within the executive branch by allowing commissioners greater discretion than previously in decisions about staffing and the budget, which had formerly been made by the central budget and personnel offices; mayors rarely implemented these reforms, because they undermined mayoral control over the commissioners. The mayor's powers of appointment were slightly weakened in 1975, when approval by the City Council became necessary for some positions that had fallen entirely under mayoral jurisdiction, including several on the Municipal Arts Commission, the Board of Health, the Board of Standards and Appeals, the City Planning Commission, the Civil Service Commission, the Landmarks Preservation Commission, the Tax Commission, the Taxi and Limousine Commission, and the Environmental Control Board. Reforms to the charter in 1989 abolished the Board of Estimate and divided its powers between the mayor and the City Council: the budgeting powers of the council were increased, and the power to award contracts was assigned to the mayor.

The mayor of New York City is elected to a four-year term in years following national presidential elections. A limit of two terms was approved by referendum in 1993. In addition to preparing and administering the operating and capital budgets the mayor is responsible for collective bargaining with municipal unions and for appointing staff members, deputy mayors, and most commissioners of municipal agencies, as well as for appointing and funding special commissions. The mayor is assisted by a budget unit led by the director of the Office of Management and Budget, a management unit led by the director of the Office of Operations (which supervises the operations of municipal agencies), the Office of Labor Relations (which conducts collective bargaining on the mayor's behalf), and legislative liaison offices in Washington and Albany, New York. In 1990 the mayor's office had a budget of $129.5 million and 1736 employees; the mayor was paid $130,000 a year and had many perquisites including a chauffeured limousine, a chef, and quarters in Gracie Mansion, a residence owned by the city. Rudolph W. Giuliani was elected in 1993 as the 107th mayor in the city's history.

Wallace Sayre and Herbert Kaufman: *Governing New York City: Politics in the Metropolis* (New York: Russell Sage Foundation, 1960)
Wallace Sayre: "The Mayor," *Agenda for a City: Issues Confronting New York*, ed. Lyle C. Fitch and Annmarie Hauck Walsh (Beverly Hills, Calif.: Sage, 1970)
David Eichenthal: "Changing Styles and Strategies of the Mayor," *Urban Politics New York Style*, ed. Jewel Bellush and Dick Netzer (Armonk, N.Y.: M. E. Sharpe, 1990)

Charles Brecher

MCA [Music Corporation of America]. A corporate conglomerate that began as a talent agency formed in 1924 in Chicago by Jules Stein. It booked popular big bands in New York City and in the 1930s was the largest musical talent agency in the United States; from 1945 it also booked performers for the theater, films, and television. After the firm left the booking business in 1962 it grew under the leadership of Lew Wasserman into a diversified entertainment company with subsidiaries in television (WWOR-TV, channel 9, acquired in 1987), motion pictures (Universal Pictures), music (MCA Records), and book publishing (G. P. Putnam's Sons); it was also active in cable television and movie theaters through its ownership of 50 percent of the USA Network and Cineplex Odeon. In 1991 MCA was acquired for $6100 by the Japanese electronics firm Matsushita Electric Industrial Company million, which sold WWOR-TV. The offices are at 1755 Broadway.

George Winslow

Mead, Margaret (*b* Philadelphia, 16 Dec 1901; *d* New York City, 15 Nov 1978). Anthropologist. After moving to New York City she graduated from Barnard College in 1923 and earned an MA in psychology (1924) and a PhD in anthropology (1929) from Columbia University. She studied with Franz Boas and Ruth Benedict and did cultural research in the South Pacific, conducting her most intensive fieldwork between 1925 and 1939. In 1926 she began a lifelong association with the American Museum of Natural History as an assistant curator in the department of anthropology; she rose to the rank of curator by 1964. The publication in 1928 of her first book, *Coming of Age in Samoa*, brought her widespread acclaim. In 1940 she became a professor at Columbia, and in 1944 she formed the Institute for Intercultural Studies, a nonprofit organization that supported cultural research. She directed the Institute for Contemporary Culture at Columbia from 1948 to 1952 and was an adjunct professor there from 1954 until her death. She also taught at Fordham University (1968–70), lectured widely, and wrote an autobiography, *Blackberry Winter: My Earlier Years* (1972). Her residences in New York City included 72 Perry Street (during the 1940s and early 1950s), 193 Waverly Place (in the 1960s), and the Beresford at 211 Central Park West (from 1966). The Hall of Pacific Peoples at the American Museum of Natural History includes an exhibit on her fieldwork, and the park surrounding the building bears her name. Mead is regarded as the most influential anthropologist of her generation.

Mary Catherine Bateson: *With a Daughter's Eye: A Memoir of Margaret Mead and Gregory Bateson* (New York: William Morrow, 1984)

Jane Howard: *Margaret Mead: A Life* (New York: Simon and Schuster, 1984)

Ira Jacknis

Meagher, Thomas Francis (*b* Waterford, Ireland, 23 Aug 1823; *d* Fort Benton, Mont., 1 July 1867). Lawyer and public official. After escaping from Tasmania, where he was serving a sentence of life imprisonment for his role in the rebellion of 1848, he settled in New York City in 1852. He prospered as a lawyer and journalist and established himself as a leader among Irish immigrants. During the Civil War he commanded the Irish Brigade, which was built around a core of volunteers from the city. At the time of his death he was the acting governor of the Montana Territory.

John Paul Jones: *The Irish Brigade* (New York: R. B. Luce, n.d. [1969])

William D. Griffin

Meany, (William) George (*b* New York City, 16 Aug 1894; *d* Bethesda, Md., 10 Jan 1980). Labor leader. He lived in Harlem until the age of five, when his family moved to 695 East 135th Street in Port Morris. As a child he became interested in the union activities of his father, the president of the Plumbers' Bronx Local no. 463. He left school at fourteen and later attended trade school while working as a plumber's helper. After becoming a journeyman plumber he joined the union in 1916, winning election as a member of the local executive board in 1920 and as its business agent in 1922. Believing that membership in craft unions should be restricted, he zealously safeguarded his members' employment and also mastered the arcane contractual minutiae of the building trades. As the secretary from 1923 of the New York City Building Trades Council, he impressed labor leaders and politicians with his intelligence and deference. He was a vice-president of the New York State Federation of Labor by 1932 and became its president in 1934. Through alliances with such powerful figures as Governor Herbert H. Lehman and Mayor Fiorello H. La Guardia he successfully pressed for legislation guaranteeing unemployment insurance and workers' compensation. He became the secretary–treasurer of the American Federation of Labor (AFL) in 1940, was elected its president in 1952, and in 1955 oversaw the merger of the AFL with the Congress of Industrial Organizations to form the AFL–CIO, becoming the country's most important trade unionist even though he had never organized a shop union, taken part in a strike, or even walked a picket line. Meany was the first president of the AFL–CIO, a position he held until his retirement in 1979.

Joseph C. Goulden: *Meany: The Unchallenged Strong Man of American Labor* (New York: Atheneum, 1972)

"George Meany: Labor's Organization Man," *Labor Leaders in America*, ed. Melvyn Dubofsky and Warren Van Tine (Urbana: University of Illinois Press, 1987)

Richard Yeselson

meatpacking. Meat was produced for local consumption in New York City from colonial times. Independent butchers bought animals from drovers or outlying stockyards and brought them to slaughter in the city, where they had access to "baulks," spaces in slaughterhouses containing a hoist, a table, and gutters. Slaughterhouses were poorly lit and ventilated and impossible to clean thoroughly because they were built of wood; they often stood near residential neighborhoods and filled the surrounding streets with wastes and with the sounds of animals dying, usually at night. Blood eventually flowed into ponds, streams, and rivers, and large waste pieces were carried away to dumping grounds or sold to tanners, soap and tallow makers, and sugar refiners. By 1656 the first measures regulating slaughterhouses were passed. Private slaughterhouses were banned in 1676 and replaced by a single public facility on Pearl Street north of Wall Street, where licensed butchers operated under controlled conditions. Additional public slaughterhouses were built at the outskirts and moved northward as the city grew, to Peck Slip in 1696, Roosevelt and Water streets in 1720, the Bowery near the Bull's Head Tavern in 1850 (where a livestock market was set up near several small illegal

Stockyards on the East River below 46th Street, 1942

slaughterhouses), Mulberry Street in 1776 (which became known as "slaughterhouse row" when private slaughterhouses opened there), and Moore and Water streets during the British occupation. Cattle were driven along a route from Westchester and Putnam counties over the King's Bridge to the Bull's Head Market, and drovers often stayed at the Dyckman House (*ca* 1784) at the northern end of Broadway. The public slaughterhouse, moved to Corlear's Hook near Jackson and Water streets in 1784, was abolished in 1790 in the face of opposition from butchers.

A meat industry developed in the city from 1791. The Bull's Head Market was moved in 1825 to a larger site near East 24th Street and 3rd Avenue, and when the local supply of livestock became inadequate, cattle were driven to the city from stockyards as far west as Ohio; the best-known driver was Daniel Drew. The drives increased in size until 1845, when they became unable to compete with railroad transport and were discontinued. In 1848 the cattle market was moved to 44th Street. After large stockyards were built at railheads in New Jersey, the number of slaughterhouses increased along both sides of the Hudson River, especially on West Street in Manhattan. By the 1850s New York City was the largest center of beef production in the country. Slaughterhouses were a major public health issue, and when the Board of Health adopted the first sanitary code in 1870 they became regulated, and banned outright between 2nd and 10th avenues. Large new companies developed factories for slaughtering and processing meat: known as abattoirs after model public slaughterhouses built near Paris in 1807–10 and 1868, these were large buildings with improved but still deficient sanitation. Animals were herded along ramps to the upper stories to be slaughtered and cleaned by teams of butchers working in long rows of baulks; finished pieces were stored in ice rooms in the lower stories, and waste parts were processed by other workers. The firm of Schwarzchild and Sulzberger was formed in 1870; it later moved to the Midwest. From the 1870s large quantities of fresh meat were shipped from the city to Europe in containers cooled with harvested ice.

By 1877 the city designated an offal pier on West 38th Street, and there were four major abattoirs in the area: the one at the Central Stockyard and Transit Company in Jersey City, New Jersey (established in 1874 by the Pennsylvania Railroad), the Manhattan Abattoirs on West 34th Street, the Butcher's Hide and Melting Association on East 44th Street, and the Union Stock Yard Abattoir on West 60th Street. There also remained fifty-two small, private slaughterhouses, which became the focus of intense efforts at reform. In 1884–85 the Ladies' Health Protective Association led a campaign to replace slaughterhouses and rendering-plants in the East 40s with abattoirs. The slaughter of poultry was forbidden in markets and restricted to licensed slaughterhouses in 1894, and in 1898 slaughtering in Manhattan was restricted to an area known as Abbatoir Center in the East 40s near the East River and to another area between 39th and 41st streets including Abattoir Place (39th Street) near the Hudson; slaughterhouses were also concentrated along Newtown Creek and in English Kills in Brooklyn. After refrigeration was improved in 1882 national companies based in the Midwest found that dressed meat was cheaper to send east than live animals. They built huge, efficient plants in the Midwest and forced eastern producers out of business, but a growing demand for kosher meat, which could be kept no more than three days after being butchered, allowed meatpacking in New York City to survive.

About the turn of the century the "beef trust" of Chicago became widely resented. In 1902 the Ladies Anti-Beef Trust Association led consumer riots against kosher markets that passed on higher prices from wholesalers. A group of retail butchers organized the New York Butchers Dressed Meat Company to compete with four of the largest Midwestern meatpackers that dominated the local market (including Schwarzchild and Sulzberger). An abattoir was built at West 39th Street and 11th Avenue by the company according to scientific standards of sanitation and efficiency. Opened in 1905, it was called the "model abattoir of the world" during a national debate following the publication of *The Jungle*, Upton Sinclair's novel about meatpacking. The company was bought out within a few years; its plant met new standards that were also adopted in the construction of such abattoirs as those of Wilson and Company on the East Side (1906) and Joseph Stern and Sons on the West Side (1912). These plants were fireproof and had their own stockyards, power stations, rendering houses, transportation links, and cold-storage facilities for keeping meat until prices were favorable. Inside they were finished with impermeable, washable materials and equipped with elaborate plumbing, cooling, and ventilating systems and tracks for moving animal parts. The tasks of butchering were divided among as many as twenty-four employees.

In 1906 New York City had 240 sites for slaughtering cattle and hogs. Packers in the city produced the third-largest volume of dressed meat in the country during the 1920s and 1930s, but after the Second World War their share in the market declined as the cost of labor rose and the industry became increasingly dependent on trucking and new technology. At the same time more cold-storage plants were built in the metropolitan area. The slaughtering district on the East Side was cleared for the United Nations in the late 1940s and the one on the West Side was closed by strikes about 1960; slaughtering was later banned in the city. Meat dealers declined in number and in the mid 1990s were concentrated around West 14th and West 125th streets in Manhattan and at Hunt's Point in the Bronx.

Thomas F. DeVoe: *Abattoirs: A Paper Read before the Polytechnic Branch of the American Institute, June 8, 1865* (Albany, N.Y.: Van Benthuysen and Sons, 1866)

Fred William Wilder: *The Modern Packing House: A Complete Treatise* (Chicago: Nickson and Collins, 1905)

John Duffy: *A History of Public Health in New York City* (New York: Russell Sage Foundation, 1968, 1974)

Michael R. Corbett

Medgar Evers College. College of the City University of New York, founded in 1969. The main campus is at 1650 Bedford Avenue in Brooklyn, with another at 1150 Carroll Street. The college was intended principally for the residents of central Brooklyn and was to offer only associate degrees, but at the urging of local residents it was eventually designated a four-year institution by the state Board of Higher Education. This status was revoked when the state legislature refused to assume financial responsibility for the college during the city's fiscal crisis in 1978, but the college had its status as a four-year institution restored in 1994. Medgar Evers offers programs in business, education, the health sciences, the humanities, the natural sciences and mathematics, and the social sciences. It is the only college in the city's university system to work with a community council composed of citizens, faculty members, students, and public officials. In 1990 the school enrolled 1710 full-time and 1830 part-time students, nearly half of whom traced their ancestry to the West Indies.

Marc Ferris

medical examiner. Until the early twentieth century there were eleven county coroners in what became the five boroughs of New York City, all of whom were elected. Reports in the press of their corruption and incompetence along with the efforts of the reformers Richard S. Childs and Robert S. Binkerd led to an investigation in 1914 by Leonard M. Wallstein, the commissioner of accounts under Mayor John Purroy Mitchel. In the following year the state legislature replaced the system of elected coroners with a centralized medical examiner's office, the first of its kind in the nation. The chief medical examiner was required to be a skilled physician, pathologist, and microscopist, and was to be appointed by the mayor. The first to hold the office was Charles Norris (1918–35), who was followed by Thomas A. Gonzales (1935–54), Milton Helpern (1954–73), Dominick DiMaio (1973–78), Michael Baden (1978–79), Elliot M. Gross (1979–87), Beverly Leffers (1987–88), and Charles S. Hirsch (1989–). A long-standing connection between the medical examiner's office and New York University was established in 1947, when the university acquired a parcel of land of eleven acres (five hectares) between 1st Avenue and East River and between 30th and 34th streets. The university agreed to donate a portion of the land for the construction of the Institute of Forensic Medicine, which came to house the medical examiner's office and the city MORGUE, and the city agreed in return to close the streets in the area and to transfer their title to the university; the medical examiner's office moved to 520 1st Avenue in 1960. In addition the Department of Forensic Medicine at the New York University School of Medicine made it a policy to recruit faculty members from the Office of Chief Medical Examiner. The office was beset by controversy in 1985, when Gross was alleged to have produced misleading or inaccurate autopsy reports, some for people who had died while in police custody. The allegations led to federal, state, and city investigations that cleared Gross of willful wrongdoing.

About 250 persons work for the medical examiner's office in its offices covering the five boroughs.

William G. Eckert: "Medicolegal Investigation in New York City: History and Activities, 1918–78," *American Journal of Forensic Medicine and Pathology* 4 (1983), 33–54

Bernard Hirschhorn: "Richard Spencer Childs: His Role in Modernization of Medicolegal Investigation in America," *American Journal of Forensic Medicine and Pathology* 4 (1983), 245–54

Bernard Hirschhorn

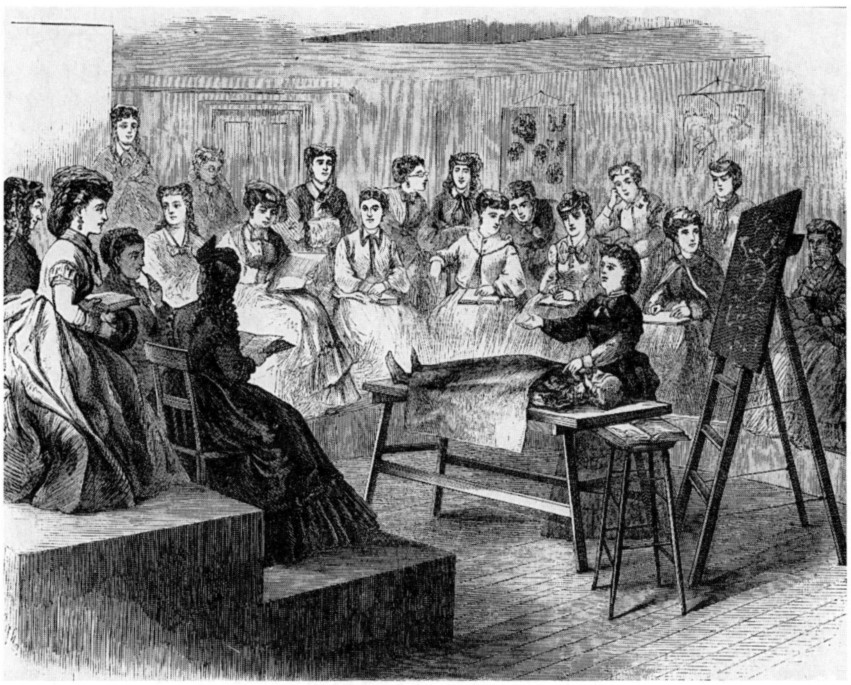

Anatomy lesson at the New York Medical College for Women, 1870

medical schools. Formal medical instruction was first offered in New York City in the mid eighteenth century by physicians who taught private courses in anatomy to supplement a three-year apprenticeship. The first formal medical school in North America was organized in 1767 with six faculty members by King's College (later Columbia College). Like all medical schools for the next century it was affiliated with a college only so that it could award degrees, and it remained financially and administratively independent. Most physicians in colonial America continued to receive their training at hospitals rather than medical schools. Until the late nineteenth century medical students were required to complete two courses lasting four or five months, in addition to an apprenticeship with a physician. The medical school at Kings College closed during the American Revolution and reopened in 1792, attracting few students. A second medical school, the College of Physicians and Surgeons, was opened in 1807 by the New York County Medical Society and in 1813 absorbed the medical school at Columbia. The college was independent until 1860, when it merged nominally with Columbia College. Among the many other medical schools established before the mid nineteenth century only one survived for more than a few years: the Medical Department of the University of the City of New York (later New York University), formed in 1841.

As the apprenticeship system declined in New York City during the second quarter of the nineteenth century, new methods of clinical instruction were devised to supplement medical lectures. The most important programs were developed at Bellevue Hospital, where a medical board composed of faculty members was formed in 1847. In 1855–60 the hospital added a teaching building and an amphitheater for lectures and surgical operations, and took control of a city hospital on Wards Island that it used as a teaching facility. The Homoeopathic Medical College of New York opened in 1860, as did the Long Island College Hospital Medical School in Brooklyn. Bellevue Hospital Medical College (1861) was the first medical school in the United States tied closely to a large hospital.

Women were denied admission into medical schools until the opening in 1863 of the New York Medical College and Hospital for Women, which was homoeopathic. A second medical school for women, the Women's Medical College of New York Infirmary, opened in 1865. A number of other short-lived medical schools were organized in New York City after the Civil War. After a fire destroyed the medical school at New York University in 1869 it was rebuilt opposite Bellevue Hospital to allow greater access to the hospital's clinical facilities. In 1882 Bellevue was divided into units for clinical instruction staffed by each of the three leading non-homoeopathic medical schools in the city. This period marked the beginning of the arrangement whereby faculty members at medical schools provided medical care at hospitals in return for being allowed to use hospital facilities for teaching and research.

Two postgraduate schools were organized in 1882 to train physicians in medical specialties: the New York Post-Graduate Medical School and Hospital, and the New York Polyclinic Medical School and Hospital. The College of Physicians and Surgeons merged with Columbia University in 1891. The merger in 1898 of the medical school at New York University with Bellevue Hospital Medical College to form the University and Bellevue Hospital Medical College (later renamed the New York University School of Medicine) was unacceptable to several faculty members of New York University, who responded later that year by organizing the Cornell University Medical College with the financial support of Oliver H. Payne. During this period medical schools improved their curriculum and their clinical training and expanded their facilities. With gifts from William Vanderbilt the College of Physicians and Surgeons built the Vanderbilt Clinic and the Sloane Maternity Hospital in the 1880s. Fordham University added a medical school in 1905 (forced by financial troubles to close in 1921). Columbia in 1928 opened a medical center based at Presbyterian Hospital on the Upper West Side (with contributions from Edward Harkness and his mother), as did Cornell University Medical College and New York Hospital in 1932 in midtown (with contributions from Payne Whitney and others).

The admission of women to medical

schools in the early twentieth century led to the closing of the two women's medical schools in New York City. The Homoeopathic Medical College of New York, which loosened its ties to homoeopathy, became the New York Medical College and created a medical center on the Upper East Side with the Flower Free Surgical Hospital and later the Fifth Avenue Hospital. Medical education in New York City rose to national prominence largely because of the internship and residency programs offered in its municipal hospitals, and state licensing of physicians brought about the demise of less reputable schools; by the early 1920s almost all physicians took hospital internships immediately after graduating from medical school.

After the Second World War New York State assumed a greater role in medical education. Evidence of discrimination against Jews and Italians seeking admission to medical schools prompted the state to enact laws prohibiting discrimination in 1948, and also led to the establishment of the Albert Einstein College of Medicine as part of Yeshiva University in the Bronx in 1955. In response to the growing shortage of physicians the state in 1950 transformed Long Island College Hospital in Brooklyn into the State University of New York (SUNY) Downstate Medical Center (later renamed the SUNY Health Science Center at Brooklyn). It also granted annual subsidies to private medical schools in the city to help increase enrollment, and developed programs to provide financial aid and to increase the number of black and Spanish-speaking students. Among the most successful programs for racial minorities was one at the Sophie Davis School of Biomedical Education (1973, later part of the City University of New York), where two years of undergraduate education at the university were combined with education at an affiliated medical school.

Federal support of health research in the 1950s increased biomedical research in schools and research institutes in New York City. Soon New York State was receiving more federal funds for health research than any state except California. Degrees were granted from 1954 by the Rockefeller Institute, an internationally renowned medical research laboratory (in 1965 renamed Rockefeller University). Both Rockefeller and the Memorial Sloan Kettering Cancer Center established joint teaching and research programs with Cornell University Medical College. In an effort to improve the quality of care in municipal hospitals, medical schools and their affiliated teaching hospitals in the early 1960s agreed to provide them with designated services. The early results were discouraging, and public officials, community leaders, and the press accused the participating medical schools and teaching hospitals of mismanagement, misuse of funds, and lack of commitment to improving the quality of care, but in time the affiliation agreements brought better results. The Mount Sinai School of Medicine was established in 1968 largely because the management at Mount Sinai Hospital believed that a medical school was needed to maintain the hospital's stature. The New York Medical College, which moved in part to Valhalla, New York, in 1968, was purchased by the Archdiocese of New York in 1978 to improve the staffing of its hospitals.

In the mid 1990s the six medical schools in New York City were important providers of health care; the SUNY Health Science Center at Brooklyn enrolled more students than any other medical school in the state. Two medical schools on Long Island, the SUNY Health Sciences Center at Stony Brook (1971) and the New York College of Osteopathic Medicine of the New York Institute of Technology in Old Westbury (1977), both use hospitals in New York City for clinical training.

James J. Walsh: *History of Medicine in New York: Three Centuries of Medical Progress* (New York: National Americana Society, 1919)

Kenneth M. Ludmerer: *Learning to Heal: The Development of American Medical Education* (New York: Basic Books, 1985)

William G. Rothstein: *American Medical Schools and the Practice of Medicine: A History* (New York: Oxford University Press, 1987)

Medina, Harold (Raymond) (*b* Brooklyn, 16 Feb 1888 *d* Westwood, N.J., 15 March 1991). Judge. He graduated from Princeton University (1909) and Columbia Law School (1912) and taught law at Columbia from 1915 to 1940. He built a private practice that earned him $100,000 a year by 1947, when he accepted an appointment to the U.S. District Court for the Southern District of New York. In 1949 he presided over the trial of eleven communists indicted under the Smith Act. He served on the Circuit Court of Appeals for the Second Circuit from 1951 until he became a senior circuit judge in 1958; he retired in 1980. Medina wrote *Judge Medina Speaks* (1954) and *The Anatomy of Freedom* (1959). For many years he lived at 14 East 75th Street in Manhattan.

Jeffrey A. Kroessler

Meeker Avenue Bridge. Original name of the KOSCIUSZKO BRIDGE.

Megalopolis. A term coined by the French geographer Jean Gottman, whose book *Megalopolis: The Urbanized Northeastern Seaboard of the United States* (1961) defined the corridor six hundred miles (one thousand kilometers) long between Boston and Washington, centered at New York City, and its thirty-eight million residents as a new social, economic, and political entity. He credited the word to the ancient Greeks, who used it for a newly founded city intended to be their largest. According to Gottman the Megalopolis was the "richest, best-educated, best-housed, and best-serviced" urbanized region in the world.

Kenneth T. Jackson

Meiers Corners. Neighborhood in north central Staten Island, near the intersection of Victory Boulevard, Jewett Avenue, and Watchogue Road. It took shape about the turn of the century as a transfer point when trolley lines were built along Victory Boulevard and Jewett Avenue. The neighborhood is named for Joachim Meier, who lived in the Martling–Cozine House, a stone house built before the American Revolution that survived into the 1980s. Small shops line Victory Boulevard, to the south of which is a residential area of small one-family houses. The population is largely white.

Marjorie Johnson

Mellon Foundation. See ANDREW W. MELLON FOUNDATION.

Melrose. Neighborhood in the southwestern Bronx (1990 pop. 18,245), bounded to the north by the intersection of Brook and Park avenues, to the east by Brook Avenue, to the south by 149th Street, and to the west by Park Avenue; its center is a commercial area on 149th Street at a former transfer point between the subway and the 3rd Avenue elevated line. When the area was developed in the 1850s as a suburb for those who worked in Manhattan the population was mostly German. The village was transformed into an urban neighborhood in the 1890s, when cheap rapid transit was provided by the 3rd Avenue elevated line. Development increased again after the subway was extended to the area in 1904. The site of beer gardens, German churches, and *Turnvereine*, Melrose retained its German character until the 1940s. The commercial district around 149th Street, known as the Hub, was for the first half of the twentieth century the commercial and entertainment center of the Bronx: it was the site of theaters and of several department stores, including the first Alexander's (1928). By then Morris Avenue was known as a Little Italy and the population also included some Russian Jews and Irish. Blacks and Puerto Ricans first moved in after 1950. The area saw a period of urban renewal in which low-income public housing projects were built. During the 1960s and 1970s tenements crumbled and were abandoned, slum clearance and arson left behind rubble-filled lots, crime and drugs rose, and the population was largely poor. A small Italian section remained. In the mid 1990s plans had been made for a civic center, a new police academy, and thousands of units of new and renovated housing.

Joel Schwartz: "Community Building on the Bronx Frontier: Morrisania, 1848–1875" (diss., University of Chicago, 1972)

Evelyn Gonzalez

Melville, Herman (*b* New York City, 1 Aug 1819; *d* New York City, 28 Sept 1891). Novelist. He was born at 6 Pearl Street and as a child lived at 33 Bleecker Street (1824–28) and 675 Broadway (1828). From 1834 he worked as a bank clerk, farmhand, and schoolteacher, and spent several years at sea before settling in Boston. After returning to New York City in 1845 he wrote the acclaimed novel *Typee* (1846) and settled at 103 4th Avenue; he also spent much of his time at 20 Clinton Place, the home of Evert A. Duyckink. During these years he wrote *Omoo* (1847), *Mardi* (1849), *Redburn* (1849), and *White-Jacket* (1850). He had little tolerance for the factionalism of the city's patrons, editors, and publishers and was especially torn between Duyckink's interests and the literary nationalism of the Knickerbocker Group, and after the cholera epidemic of 1849 he left for the Berkshires. On his return in 1863 he moved to 104 East 26th Street, where he lived in obscurity. Between 1866 and 1885 he was a customs inspector on the piers at Gansevoort Street, during which time he wrote *Battle Pieces* (1866), *Aspects of the War* (1866), and *Clarel* (1876). After retiring he produced a number of books including *Billy Budd, Sailor*, which was not published until 1924.

Perry Miller: *The Raven and the Whale* (New York: Harcourt, Brace, 1956)
Edwin Haviland Miller: *Melville* (George Braziller, 1975)

Jeff Finlay

Melvina. Former neighborhood in west central Queens. It was originally the farm of the Van Cott family and became one of the first real-estate developments in Maspeth. On a map published in October 1852 by a real-estate agent from New York City, John H. Smith, the area was shown as being bounded to the north by Maspeth Avenue and to the south by Flushing Avenue, and extending 257.5 feet (78.5 meters) on either side of 59th Street. There are twenty-five houses on Beers's map of 1873. Melvina was later absorbed by Maspeth.

Vincent Seyfried

Memorial Fund Association. Original name of the Milbank Memorial Fund.

Memorial Sloan Kettering Cancer Center. Hospital established in 1884 as the New York Cancer Hospital, the first institution in the United States devoted exclusively to the care of cancer patients. Its original location was Central Park West and 106th Street. The hospital became the first in the country to use radiation therapy in 1904, only six years after the discovery of radium. Renamed the Memorial Hospital for the Treatment of Cancer and Allied Diseases in 1917, it moved in 1937 to its present site on land donated by John D. Rockefeller and bounded by 67th Street, 68th Street, 1st Avenue, and York Avenue. A laboratory devoted to cancer research and financed by two executives from General Motors, Alfred P. Sloan Jr. (chairman of the company) and Charles F. Kettering, opened in 1945 as the Sloan–Kettering Institute; in 1960 the hospital took its current name. Experiments at the hospital during the Second World War into the effects of chemical warfare led to chemotherapy treatments for various types of cancer. In 1971 the Congress designated the hospital the prototype of a comprehensive cancer center. Memorial Sloan Kettering offers screening and diagnostic services to the community and maintains a mobile mammography unit. A survey in 1994 rated it the finest cancer hospital in the United States.

Martha Fay: *A Mortal Condition* (New York: Coward–McCann, 1983)

Andrea Balis

Mendes, Henry Pereira (*b* Birmingham, England, 13 April 1852; *d* New York City, 20 Oct 1937). Rabbi. He led the Sephardic congregation of Manchester, England, before moving to New York City, where he led Congregation Shearith Israel from 1877 until his death. A man of broad culture, he was a rabbinic teacher and writer as well as a physician and helped to form the Jewish Theological Seminary, the Lexington School for the Deaf, and Montefiore Hospital. He was a leading voice of Orthodox Judaism and a founder and president of the Union of Orthodox Jewish Congregations, as well as an outspoken and active Zionist. Mendes urged his followers to commit themselves to both religion and culture. He lived at 90 Central Park West.

David de Sola Pool: *An Old Faith in the New World: Portrait of Shearith Israel* (New York: Columbia University Press, 1955)

Marc D. Angel

mental health. In New York City the treatment of mental illness was first made a public responsibility in 1665, when a provincial law authorized towns within the colony of New York to share the cost of maintaining "distracted persons." For more than a century those who required public maintenance were confined in cellars, attics, strongrooms in poorhouses, and jails. Hospital care for the insane first became available in the state when New York Hospital began admitting mental patients in 1792, and by 1808 the hospital opened a separate lunatic asylum on its grounds, funded by the state legislature. Demand from communities throughout the state eventually exceeded the supply of beds, and most insane indigent persons were forced to remain in local almshouses and jails. From the early 1820s reformers such as Thomas Eddy, treasurer of New York Hospital, advocated the new methods of "moral treatment" introduced in Europe, which stressed humane care of the mentally ill, and cure rather than confinement. This approach required adequate space, comfortable surroundings, and trained staff, all of which were available from 1821 at Bloomingdale Asylum of New York Hospital, on Broadway and 116th Street (where Columbia University now stands).

In the mid 1820s most of the insane paupers at Bloomingdale and the almshouse were transferred to Bellevue Hospital, the city's largest municipal hospital. Repeated public complaints about overcrowding at Bellevue eventually led to the opening of a separate lunatic asylum with 164 beds on Blackwell's Island (1839), the first public mental hospital in New York State and the first municipal mental institution in the country. In Flatbush the insane were placed in the county poorhouse, an arrangement that was criticized by the reformer Dorothea Dix during her state tour of asylums in 1844. The poorhouse was replaced by separate buildings for the insane on the same site in 1845 and 1855, each of which suffered from overcrowding and minimal staffing. When Charles Dickens visited the asylum on Blackwell's Island in 1842 he found it little better than the asylum in Brooklyn and noted its "lounging, listless, madhouse air." Each enlargement of the facilities was quickly followed by a flood of new admissions: in 1848 the asylum on Blackwell's Island held more than four hundred patients. A separate building for women was added to the asylum in the same year and by 1860 the facility held 750 patients and conditions were appalling. More than 80 percent of the asylum patients were foreign born at this time, compared with 45 percent of the city's total population. When the number of patients reached thirteen hundred, additional facilities were built on Wards Island (1871, later the Manhattan Psychiatric Center) and Hart Island (1878), but these rapidly became as grim and overcrowded as the facility on Blackwell's Island.

Periodic reforms did little to improve the conditions of the city asylums, which became infamous for their bad food, frequent epidemics, graft-ridden administration, and an incompetent staff that included convicts from the city prison. The reporter Nellie Bly attempted to provoke change in the system by committing herself to the city asylum in 1887 and then writing the widely read series "Ten Days in a Mad-house." The only governmental action taken during the 1880s to improve asylums was a law empowering the State Board of Charities to deport alien and nonresident paupers who were insane. This power was later extended to the State Commission on Lunacy and resulted in thousands of deportations, with seventeen hundred in 1912 alone. Growing complaints during the 1880s helped bring about the passage of the State Care Aid Act (1890), under which the insane were placed in state hospitals as space became available. Asylums in Manhattan and Brooklyn were taken over by the state and became state hospitals. In 1894 Bloomingdale Asylum, which had about four hundred patients, moved from the city to larger quarters in White Plains, New York.

Organized psychiatric research was first conducted in the United States at the Pathological Institute of New York State Hospitals (1895). Initially the institute examined only morbid materials (cadavers, organs, and tissue samples), but in 1902 its new director Adolf Meyer moved the institute to Wards Island, where it became affiliated with the state hospital; in 1929 the institute moved to the Columbia–Presbyterian Medical Center. From 1909 the mental hygiene movement gave a new emphasis to finding a cure for mental illness. It was led by Clifford Beers, who described his own experiences as a mental patient in the widely read book *A Mind That Found Itself* (1908) and launched the National Committee for Mental Hygiene at the Manhattan Hotel. The movement stressed research, public education, and better institutional care, and the use of the term "mental hygiene" reflected a conviction that mental problems could be cured. Within twenty years similar societies were formed in thirty countries around the world. Child guidance clinics were set up for the mentally ill in 1919, community services for the mentally ill expanded in the 1920s, the city's Vocational Adjustment Bureau established its first workshop for the emotionally disturbed in 1925, and the New York Academy of Medicine persuaded the Board of Education to augment its services for emotionally disturbed children. The Payne Whitney Psychiatric Clinic opened at New York Hospital in 1932, and in 1944 a large after-care clinic was set up at the New York State Psychiatric Institute (the descendant of the Pathological Institute) to serve patients released from the many state hospitals in and around New York City. The term "mental health" was adopted in the late 1930s.

The growing acceptance of psychoanalysis had a strong impact on mental health care. In spite of opposition from most psychiatrists in the United States, A. A. Brill (who first translated Freud's work into English), Smith Ely Jelliffe, and others in New York City formed the New York Psychoanalytical Society in 1911, the second such organization in the United States. The city's psychoanalytic community, which grew rapidly during the 1920s, was riven by several controversial issues, such as whether psychoanalysts should be required to be physicians and whether culture plays an important role in individual development; Karen Horney, Clara Thompson, William Silverberg, and others who stressed the importance of culture formed the Association for the Advancement of Psychoanalysis (1941), which later established the American Institute of Psychoanalysis as its teaching branch. Psychoanalytic treatment became much sought after by the city's affluent residents. It exerted a profound influence on literature and the arts, and the psychoanalyst became a stock figure in accounts of neurosis and anxiety among the privileged.

Institutional services for the mentally ill expanded in New York City at the turn of the century, and by 1912 the Manhattan Psychiatric Center was the world's largest mental hospital, with more than 4500 patients. Another twelve thousand New Yorkers were cared for in other state hospitals. Admission rates rose abruptly in the 1920s, and the patient population included a growing number of children suffering from encephalitis. By the early 1930s more than 25,000 city residents lived in state institutions, occupying two thirds of the beds in the system. During these years the state initiated various reforms and expanded facilities within the city (opening Creedmoor State Hospital in Queens), but it failed to accommodate the growing number of people needing care. Overcrowding continued, buildings deteriorated, and care remained primarily custodial. Local governments often referred the large population of dependent elderly persons to the state-funded facilities, even if their primary problems were not psychiatric; by 1945 three fifths of the patients at Manhattan Psychiatric Center were older than sixty. In 1947 Albert Deutsch published his influential exposé of American mental institutions, *The Shame of the States*, devoting one chapter each to Manhattan State Hospital and to the psychiatric unit at Bellevue.

The growing interest in community-based care for the mentally ill led the state legislature to pass the Community Mental Health Services Act in 1954, the first act of its kind in the United States. It called for local boards to develop community mental health programs, with state aid covering as much as 50 percent of the costs. The city's Department of Mental Health, Mental Retardation and Alcoholism Services was formed in 1955 as part of this effort. The trend toward community care was aided greatly by the availability from 1955 of psychotropic medications (tranquilizers and antidepressants). In the mid 1950s state mental institutions, including those in New York City, experienced the first annual declines in their number of patients. A phase of construction of large state hospitals ended with the opening of Bronx State Hospital in 1955. When South Beach Psychiatric Center opened on Staten Island in 1974, community services were as much a part of its program as the care of in-patients. The pace of "deinstitutionalization" was quickened by a growing body of court decisions stressing patients' rights. Epidemiological studies in New York City in the early 1960s by Leo Srole and Bruce Dohrenwend supported the idea that mental illness and health were part of a continuum rather than discrete conditions, and that illness responded to varying kinds of treatment and was not necessarily disabling.

The 1970s and 1980s brought new challenges. Community mental health services strained to support the large number of patients newly released from state hospitals. Divisions among psychoanalysts continued, and by 1979 there were at least eleven training groups for psychoanalysis within greater New York. By the early 1990s fiscal problems, jurisdictional disputes between state and city agencies, a shrinking job market, and drastic reductions in the city's stock of affordable housing made it increasingly difficult for the city to meet the needs of its mentally ill, many of whom were homeless and suffered from alcoholism and drug abuse. In 1991 the city's Department of Mental Health, Mental Retardation and Alcoholism Services supported 870 community programs (most provided under contract by voluntary agencies) at a combined cost of $680 million drawn from city, state, and federal funds. Numerous other services were funded through charitable contributions, private insurance, and patients' fees. Within the city were more than three thousand licensed psychologists, about the same number of psychiatrists, and more than twelve thousand social workers.

Albert Deutsch: *The Mentally Ill in America* (Garden City, N.Y.: Doubleday, Doran, 1937)

David M. Schneider and Albert Deutsch: *The History of Public Welfare in New York State, 1867–1940* (Chicago: University of Chicago Press, 1941)

Albert Deutsch: *The Shame of the States* (New York: Harcourt, Brace, 1948)

Nina Ridenour: *Mental Health in the United States: A Fifty-year History* (Cambridge: Harvard University Press, 1961)

Norman Dain: *Concepts of Insanity in the United States, 1789–1865* (New Brunswick, N.J.: Rutgers University Press, 1964)

Franz G. Alexander and Sheldon T. Selesnick: *The History of Psychiatry* (New York: Harper and Row, 1966)

John Duffy: *A History of Public Health in New York City* (New York: Russell Sage Foundation, 1968, 1974)

Gerald N. Grob: *Mental Institutions in America: Social Policy to 1875* (New York: Free Press, 1973)

Reuben Fine: *A History of Psychoanalysis* (New York: Columbia University Press, 1979)

Gerald N. Grob: *Mental Illness and American Society* (Princeton, N.J.: Princeton University Press, 1983)

Sandra Opdycke

Mercantile Library Association. An organization formed by merchant clerks in 1820 that opened a circulating library in rented rooms at 49 Fulton Street in the following year. It accepted members from diverse backgrounds but allowed only merchant clerks to vote and hold office. In 1828 a number of its prominent members formed the Clinton Hall Association to raise funds and manage real estate acquired for a permanent library building, and in 1830 a new building called Clinton Hall opened to the public at the corner of Nassau and Beekman streets. The

Clinton Hall at Astor Place and Lafayette Street, site of the Mercantile Library Association, ca *1890 (demolished 1890)*

library moved in 1854 to the Italian Opera House at Astor Place, a more convenient location for most of its patrons. It became a cultural center that offered lectures and evening classes. Membership reached a peak of more than twelve thousand in 1870, and the library's collection of 120,000 volumes made it the leading circulating library in the United States. The reading room had more than four hundred newspapers and periodicals and three thousand reference works and was reportedly used by a thousand persons a day in 1871. After the Opera House was demolished a new Clinton Hall opened on the same site in 1891. In addition to the main library the association had a downtown office and seven branch libraries. Although the establishment of free public libraries led to a decline in membership, a new Clinton Hall opened in 1933 at 17 East 47th Street that included 230,000 volumes available to three thousand members. In the mid 1990s the Mercantile Library Association continued to operate a circulating library with a reading room open to all subscribers; the collection held 150,000 volumes, including fifty thousand novels and 55,000 works of nonfiction relating to literature. It also maintained a writers' studio and offered a series of literary programs open to the public.

John Rose Greene Hassard: "The New York Mercantile Library," *Scribner's Monthly*, Feb 1871, pp. 353–67

Fiftieth Anniversary Celebration of the Mercantile Library Association (New York: G. F. Nesbitt, 1871)

Elaine Weber Pascu

Mercer, Mabel (*b* Burton-on-Trent, England, 3 Feb 1900; *d* Pittsfield, Mass., 20 April 1984). Singer. In the 1920s she entertained expatriates such as F. Scott Fitzgerald and Cole Porter at Bricktop's renowned nightclub in Paris. After emigrating to the United States in the late 1930s she settled in New York City in 1941. She developed a large following for her performances in cabarets and nightclubs, becoming known as the "queen of the intimate supper clubs" for her flawless diction, elegance, and emotional sensitivity to lyrics, as well as for her attention to forgotten repertory. Her influence extended to many popular songwriters and singers, including Frank Sinatra. Mercer's papers are held at the Schomburg Center for Research in Black Culture.

William Livingstone: "Mabel Mercer: William Livingstone Visits with the Singer's Singer," *Stereo Review*, Feb 1975, pp. 60–65

Whitney Balliett: "Profile: A Queenly Aura," *New Yorker*, 6 Sept 1982, pp 40–49

Eileen Southern, ed.: *Biographical Dictionary of Afro-American and African Musicians* (Westport, Conn.: Greenwood, 1982)

Obituary, *New York Times*, 21 April 1984, p. 24

Darlene Clarke-Hine, ed.: *Black Women in America: An Historical Encyclopedia* (New York: Carlson, 1993)

Cynthia Copeland

Merchants Association of New York. Trade association. It was formed by wholesale traders in an effort to attract dry-goods firms to New York City and assist those already there. After 1900 it developed into a powerful group with influence over governmental affairs.

Arnold J. Bornfriend: "The Business Group in Metropolis: The Commerce and Industry Association of New York" (diss., Columbia University, 1967)

Donald R. Stabile

Mercury Theater. A repertory company for classical drama formed in the autumn of 1937 by Orson Welles, then twenty-two years old, and John Houseman. Its first production was *Julius Caesar*, mounted in a theater at Broadway and 41st Street in an abbreviated, ninety-minute version that was staged as an allegory of Europe under fascism. This as well as an all-black version of *Macbeth* and other productions were critically and popularly successful, but the company's commitment to repertory work and cheap tickets soon undermined its finances, and with the failure of Georg Büchner's *Danton's Death* in 1938–39 it was forced to close. The company made Welles nationally renowned, and he was offered a weekly radio program presenting adaptations of famous novels. Houseman and actors from the company took part in the program, which was often referred to as the Mercury Theater on the Air. Its rendition of H. G. Wells's *The War of the Worlds* (31 October 1938) caused panic across the nation when many mistook it for a news bulletin relating an invasion by Martians.

George A. Thompson, Jr.

Merkle, Philipp (*b* Rheinpfalz, 20 March 1811; *d* New York City, 3 May 1899). Political activist and minister. He studied theology at the University of Heidelberg before emigrating to the United States and settling in New York City in 1833. He was a Lutheran minister until 1835, when he organized and became the "speaker" of a congregation of freethinkers known as the German Universal Christian Church and operated a pharmacy. In 1847 he helped to form the Harugari, the largest German fraternal order in America, which he led. A prominent figure among Germans in the Democratic Party, he held a series of patronage positions: appraiser of drugs for the federal government (appointed 1853), city excise commissioner (appointed 1878), and coroner (elected 1881).

Stanley Nadel

Merman [Zimmermann], **Ethel (Agnes)** (*b* Queens, 16 Jan 1909; *d* New

Ethel Merman in Annie Get Your Gun, *1946*

York City, 15 Feb 1984). Singer and actress. She made her début in the musical comedy *Girl Crazy* (1930) and during the next forty years delighted audiences with her powerful singing and good-humored acting in such shows as *Anything Goes* (1934), *Annie Get Your Gun* (1946), and *Gypsy* (1959). She moved to the Century Apartments at 25 Central Park West in 1933 and during the 1960s lived at the Park Lane Hotel at 36 West 59th Street; she spent the last year of her life at the Surrey (20 East 76th Street).

Merrick [Margulois], **David (Lee)** (*b* St. Louis, 27 Nov 1911). Producer. In St. Louis he graduated from Washington University and worked as a lawyer. After settling in New York City in 1946 he began his career as a producer of plays and musicals; his most successful included *Fanny* (Harold Rome, 1954), *Gypsy* (Jule Styne and Stephen Sondheim, 1959), *Hello, Dolly!* (Jerry Herman, 1964), *Marat/Sade* (Peter Weiss, 1965), *Play It Again, Sam* (Woody Allen, 1969), and *42nd Street* (Gower Champion, 1980), at 3486 performances one of the longest-running shows on Broadway. He produced a revival of George Gershwin's *Oh, Kay!* in 1991. Merrick's astute management and shrewd use of publicity have made him one of the most successful producers on Broadway, with more than eighty-five productions to his credit.

Howard Kissel: *David Merrick: The Abominable Showman: The Unauthorized Biography* (New York: Applause Books, 1993)

Martha S. LoMonaco

Merrill Lynch, Pierce, Fenner and Smith. Firm of stockbrokers formed in the early 1940s through the merger of the firms Merrill Lynch (1915), Fenner and Beane (1916), and E. A. Pierce and Company (1927). Winthrop Smith, who worked for Merrill Lynch in the 1920s and for E. A. Pierce in the 1930s, was instrumental in arranging the merger; his name replaced that of Alpheus Beane in the name of the firm in 1958. Charles E. Merrill was the key figure in mapping the strategy of the firm, which emphasized service to middle-class investors and long-term investment in blue-chip securities. The firm maintained its headquarters in New York City and had more than a hundred branch offices nationwide; it became the nation's most successful brokerage firm in the 1940s. At a time when brokerage suffered from a disreputable image, it introduced a number of innovations that later became widely imitated, including publication of an annual report, aggressive advertising, the preparation of research reports, and training for new brokers. Donald T. Regan, who enrolled in the training program at the end of the Second World War, became chief executive officer of the firm in 1971 before leaving to serve as President Ronald Reagan's secretary of the treasury and chief of staff. In the mid 1990s Merrill Lynch, Pierce, Fenner and Smith was the largest brokerage firm in the United States, with more than five hundred branches worldwide.

Henry Hecht, ed.: *A Legacy of Leadership: Merrill Lynch, 1885–1985* (New York: Merrill Lynch, 1985)

Edwin J. Perkins

Merton, Robert K(ing) (*b* Philadelphia, 5 July 1910). Sociologist. A son of Jewish immigrants from eastern Europe, he received his graduate education at Harvard University and began teaching at Columbia University in 1941, where he remained for the rest of his career and rose to the rank of university professor. In dozens of books and articles he defended sociology as a science capable of being tested by empirical evidence. His many awards include a Guggenheim Fellowship (1962) and the Career Distinguished Service Award (1980) of the American Sociological Association. Merton is regarded as the greatest sociologist of his time, and his best-known works, *Social Theory and Social Structure* (1949) and *The Sociology of Science* (1973), are considered standards in the field.

Piotr Sztomka: *Robert K. Merton: An Intellectual Profile* (New York: St. Martin's, 1986)

Andrew Wiese

Merton, Thomas (*b* Prades, France, 31 Jan 1915; *d* Bangkok, 10 Dec 1968). He enrolled at Columbia College in January 1935 (BA 1938, MA 1939), where he studied literature with Mark Van Doren and philosophy with Daniel Walsh; he also took part in communist activities and helped to produce a student humor magazine. On 16 November 1938 he converted to Catholicism in a ceremony in the parish of Corpus Christi, 531–35 West 121st Street. In 1939–40 he lived at 35 Perry Street. He entered the Trappist monastery of Our Lady of Gethsemani in Kentucky on 10 December 1941 and wrote poetry (including *Figures for an Apocalypse*, 1949), an autobiography (*The Seven Story Mountain*, 1948), meditations on Eastern mysticism (*Seeds of Contemplation*, 1949), and essays on war and peace. While attending a conference of Buddhist contemplatives he was accidentally electrocuted.

Michael Mott: *The Seven Mountains of Thomas Merton* (Boston: Houghton Mifflin, 1984)

Mary Elizabeth Brown

Merzbacher, Leo (*b* Fürth [now in Germany], 1810; *d* New York City, 1856). Rabbi. He emigrated from Bavaria to the United States and became the first professionally trained rabbi in New York City in 1841. He was a teacher for the German Orthodox congregation Rodeph Shalom and for Anshe Chesed, the earliest German congregation in the city. In 1845 a disagreement with Rodeph Shalom led to his departure and to his founding of the Reform synagogue Temple Emanu-El. He was an organizer of the Independent Order of B'nai B'rith and is credited with having originated its name. Merzbacher published a revised prayerbook in 1855 and is regarded as the first Reform rabbi in the United States.

Stanley Nadel

metal founding and metalworking. During the colonial period New York City became an important center for tinsmiths and coppersmiths, and later for iron founders. The early iron foundries were small operations (ten workers or fewer) that also wrought copper, brass, and tin. Wrought iron and cast iron were both produced at the New York Air Furnace (in the 1780s) and the Phoenix Foundry (by 1800), and in the early nineteenth century the growth of shipbuilding made iron founding a major industry. The Allaire Ironworks (opened by James P. Allaire in 1816) was the first of several huge foundries where boilers weighing several tons were constructed for the steamships of the 1820s and 1830s. The first ironworks to specialize in steam engines was that of Robert McQueen (a protégé of Robert Fulton), whose Columbian Foundry was one of the leading manufacturers in New York City (eighty-two employees in 1820). By 1830 employment at Allaire reached two hundred. Other notable ironworks included the Novelty Ironworks (opened by Thomas Stillman in 1830), the Delameter Works (the only major ironworks on the Hudson, opened in 1835), the Morgan Ironworks (1838), and the Cornell Ironworks (1847). But even operations like McQueen's were too small to build engines for the oceangoing vessels of the 1840s, and to obtain more space most of the large foundries and other firms that were connected to shipbuilding moved to sites along the East River. The industry was hurt by the depression of 1837 (by 1847 Allaire had only 250 employees), but the unprecedented prosperity of the late 1840s created a boom in shipbuilding and manufacturing and a vast expansion of the city's iron foundries. By 1850 the Novelty Works had 938 employees, the Allaire Works five hundred.

By the middle of the nineteenth century foundries that in some cases covered several city blocks became the subject of newspaper and magazine articles and even tourist attractions. The organization of these huge enterprises greatly impressed observers. *Harper's Magazine* described the Novelty Works in 1851 as "having like any state or kingdom, its gradations of rank, its established usages, its written laws, its police . . . its rewards and its penalties." At the top of these "kingdoms" were the proprietors, men like Allaire and Stillman whose knowledge and industriousness helped to make the East River one of the most advanced and technologically innovative centers for founding and machining in the 1850s. Laborers at ironworks worked in highly specialized departments, yet it was necessary for them to remain versatile because most large engines were custom-built, and parts cast or turned on lathes required extensive chipping and filing to achieve acceptable tolerances. The élite workers were molders and machinists who accounted for about 50 percent of the work force; in the 1850s these men received $10 to $12 weekly, about twice as much as their many semiskilled helpers. Foundries also employed blacksmiths, pattern makers, instrument makers, carpenters, and unskilled laborers. Many of the workers were immigrants from England (especially among molders and machinists), Ireland, and Germany, who often lived in the wards near the East River. Allaire, Novelty, and Morgan alone accounted for one third of the 7770 metalworkers in the city in 1860. In 1863 seven thousand machinists closed the Novelty, Allaire, and Delameter ironworks in a strike for higher wages, and in the following year the Iron Molders' Union campaigned to prevent the manufacture of castings at the state prison in Sing Sing, but generally the mixture at ironworks of skilled and semiskilled employees thwarted unity, and a traditional coolness between molders and machinists limited the influence of each group on management and on fellow workers in the labor movement.

The Civil War marked the high point for the ironworks. Guns and warships were ordered, and the Delameter Ironworks built the Union ironclad the *Monitor* (1861). The war obscured such problems as the spiraling price of land and the high cost of doing business in Manhattan, and when it ended most of the industry began to move to the Delaware River, where proximity to coal and other advantages made production cheaper. The Novelty Works closed in 1870, its machinery outmoded and its real estate on the East River too valuable for heavy industry. The Allaire Works failed during the depression of 1873: its site on the river became a stable. Surviving businesses included tinsmiths, coppersmiths, and iron and brass foundries such as the Delameter works that had fifty to a hundred employees and flourished by doing repair work and custom architectural and ornamental ironwork, and producing hardware for "modern conveniences" like indoor plumbing, central heating, and gas lighting. Firms like Daniel Badger's Architectural Ironworks (1846) that had begun specializing in moldings for cast-iron buildings before the war found themselves in the primary area of growth when the war ended. The Cornell works (1847), known as the "iron university," had plants on Centre and 26th streets, which in 1870 produced sixteen thousand castings for the inner and outer walls of the new Tiffany Building on Union Square at 15th Street. But over time the costs of operating in the city doomed the foundries in Manhattan; some moved elsewhere, especially to New Jersey, but in most cases the huge fixed capital investment in buildings, cupolas, and air furnaces made moving economically unfeasible. By 1928 only five foundries remained in Manhattan, though several others continued to operate in Queens. Smaller metalworking firms exhibited a surprising vitality because of their ability to produce small batches of cast iron, wrought iron, and brass. The manufacturing census of 1920 counted 657 metalworking shops in the city with 26,562 employees.

The military buildup brought on by the two world wars greatly increased the demand for metal production and benefited what remained of the industry. One of the five women who are the subject of the well-known documentary film *Rosie the Riveter* (1944) made shell casings in a machine shop in Manhattan. In 1954 there were 53,000 workers in the city producing fabricated metal products, including ornamental ironwork, heating and plumbing fixtures, and stamps and wire; at the same time only seven thousand workers produced primary metals. During the following decades employment in metalworking declined, primarily because of rising rents. In 1982 nineteen thousand workers in the city made fabricated metal products at 882 firms, and three thousand made primary metals at seventy-eight firms (none of them in Manhattan).

John Leander Bishop: *A History of American Manufacturers from 1608 to 1860* (Philadelphia: Edward Young, 1868)

Edward Ewing Pratt: *Industrial Causes of Congestion of Population in New York City* (New York: Columbia University, 1911; repr. AMS, 1968)

Vincent W. Lanfear: "The Metals Industry," *Regional Survey of New York and Its Environs*, ed. Robert Murray Haig and Roswell McCrea (New York: Regional Plan of New York and Its Environs, 1928)

Richard Stott

Methfessel Institute. Original name of STATEN ISLAND ACADEMY.

Methodists. The first Methodist congregation in New York City was established in 1766 by Barbara Ruckle Heck and her cousin Philip Embury, Irish immigrants who settled in the city in August 1760. Distressed by what she considered signs of indifference to religion (including her brother's fondness for cards), Heck urged Embury to give sermons lest all "go to Hell together." She gathered a congregation of five that initially met at Embury's home on Augustus Street. A larger room was rented nearby, and a Methodist organization was formed and led by Embury and Thomas Webb, a British army captain. The congregation met in a sail-rigging loft on William Street from 1767 until Wesley Chapel was completed and dedicated at 44 John Street on 30 October 1768.

In the following years the city became one of the country's most important centers of Methodist activity. It was a base for such missionaries as Richard Boardman, Joseph Pilmoor, and Francis Asbury, who were sent to the colonies by John Wesley. Membership rose to about two hundred by the eve of the American Revolution. Sermons were offered in Queens and Brooklyn as early as 1768 by Thomas Webb and on Staten Island in 1771 by Francis Asbury. By 1784, the year the Methodist Episcopal Church in America was organized in Baltimore, there were only sixty Methodists in New York City, but the number grew steadily in the following years. Churches opened in Queens in 1785, Staten Island in 1787 (Woodrow Church), and Brooklyn in 1794. In the early nineteenth century Wesley Chapel became known as the John Street Methodist Episcopal Church. Disaffected by discrimination there, black members under Peter Williams, James Varick, and Christopher Rush left to hold their own services in 1796, and in 1800 they erected their own building, Zion Church. A denomination was organized formally in 1821 and in 1848 was named the African Methodist Episcopal Zion church.

The nineteenth century saw an expansion of Methodism. A congregation of the African Methodist Episcopal church was organized in 1817 under William Lambert and eventually became the Bethel African Methodist Episcopal Church. By 1830 the Methodist Episcopal Church set up the Harlem Mission, which included all of Manhattan north of 23rd Street and became the site of some of the most influential congregations, including those of St. Paul, St. Andrew, Madison Avenue, and Park Avenue. Among the first churches in the Bronx were several opened between 1850 and 1865 on Willis Avenue and in Morrisania, Fordham, and Tremont. One of the first Methodist urban missions in the country was the Five Points Mission, opened in 1844 by the Ladies' Home Missionary Society of the Methodist Episcopal Church to provide housing, food, clothing, and Christian guidance for adults and children. From 1845 to 1879 the society also sponsored Bethel Ship, a mission for Scandinavian immigrants and seamen aboard a vessel docked in New York Harbor. In 1888 the Woman's Home Missionary Society of the Methodist Episcopal Church opened a shelter for "worthy female immigrants" near Battery Park; it moved to Greenwich Village in 1927 and became known as Alma Mathews House, after its most prominent deaconess. The Madison Avenue congregation was renamed Christ United Methodist Church and moved to Park Avenue and 60th Street, where it became the city's best-known Methodist church under the nationally known minister Ralph W. Sockman from 1917 to 1961. In 1963 Methodists opened the Church Center for the United Nations on United Nations Plaza, a facility devoted to such ecumenical activities as seminars on world affairs.

In 1968 the Methodist Church united with

the Evangelical United Brethren Church to form the United Methodist Church. There were a number of United Methodist congregations in the city in the mid 1990s, with about forty thousand members in 1994. Some of the most important Methodist agencies are the General Board of Global Ministries and the General Commission on Christian Unity and Interreligious Concerns; both have offices in the Interchurch Center at 475 Riverside Drive.

Samuel A. Seaman: *Annals of New York Methodism* (New York: Hunt and Eaton, 1892)

Charles Yrigoyen, Jr.

Metromedia. Corporate conglomerate with interests in technology, entertainment, telecommunications, and restaurants. Originally called Metropolitan Broadcasting Company, it was formed in 1959 when John W(erner) Kluge bought from Paramount Pictures its interest in the broadcasting stations that had belonged to the defunct DuMont Broadcasting Corporation, among them WNEW-AM, WNEW-FM, and WNEW-TV. The firm took its current name in 1960 when it entered such fields as outdoor advertising and publishing. After Metromedia shifted its emphasis, the broadcast group was purchased in 1986 for $2000 million by the Australian magnate Rupert Murdoch, also the owner of Twentieth Century Fox, who created the Fox Broadcasting Company. Some offices of the firm are in the original Central Turn-Verein at 205 East 67th Street in Manhattan, as are the studios of WNYW-TV (formerly WNEW-TV), which is owned by Fox. The corporate headquarters are in Jackson, Mississippi.

Metromedia and the DuMont Legacy: W2XWV, WABD, WNEW-TV (New York: Museum of Broadcasting, n.d.)

Walter Spencer: "Why Diversification Is the Name of the Game: A Study of the Conglomerates Emerging in Television," *Television Magazine*, Oct 1967, p. 41

Judith Adler Hennessee: "Tabloid TV," *Manhattan, Inc.*, Oct 1986, 151–56

Christine Craft: *Too Old, Too Ugly, and Not Deferential to Men* (Rocklin, Calif.: L. Prima, 1988)

Mary Billard and Patricia O'Toole: "Best Friends at War," *Manhattan, Inc.*, April 1989, pp. 65–72

Val Ginter

Metro-North Commuter Railroad. Subsidiary of the Metropolitan Transportation Authority, formed on 1 January 1983. Under a capital program of the Metropolitan Transportation Authority it received $1662 million between 1982 (when the lines were still being operated by Conrail) and 1991, and the number of riders increased as service improved. In 1992 the railroad carried 57.6 million passengers and was the second-largest commuter system in the United States (after the Long Island Rail Road). Using the former lines of the New York Central Railroad and the New York, New Haven and Hartford

Riverdale station of Metro-North, 1992

Railroad, it provides service between Grand Central Terminal and the Bronx, Connecticut, and Westchester, Putnam, and Dutchess counties. Under contract to the New Jersey Transit it also provides service between Hoboken, New Jersey, and Orange and Rockland counties. Metro-North has 118 passenger stations, 788 locomotives and rail cars, and 737 miles (1179 kilometers) of track covering 338 miles (540 kilometers) of routes.

Peter Derrick

Metropolitan. Former neighborhood in west central Queens, surrounding the intersection of Metropolitan and Flushing avenues in what is now Ridgewood and an area near Maspeth Creek. It was an unprosperous hamlet that was the site of a tollhouse for Flushing Avenue. The two main avenues were turnpikes from 1816 until about 1870. The name fell into disuse after the First World War.

Vincent Seyfried

Metropolitan Baptist Church. Church at 151 West 128th Street in Manhattan. It occupies an arch-and-vault Romanesque Revival building originally owned by the Presbyterian church, designed by John R. Thomas and built in 1884. The church is a white stone edifice with orange granite columns at the entrance and a coned-roof side chapel. Its auditorium was built in 1890 under the design of Richard

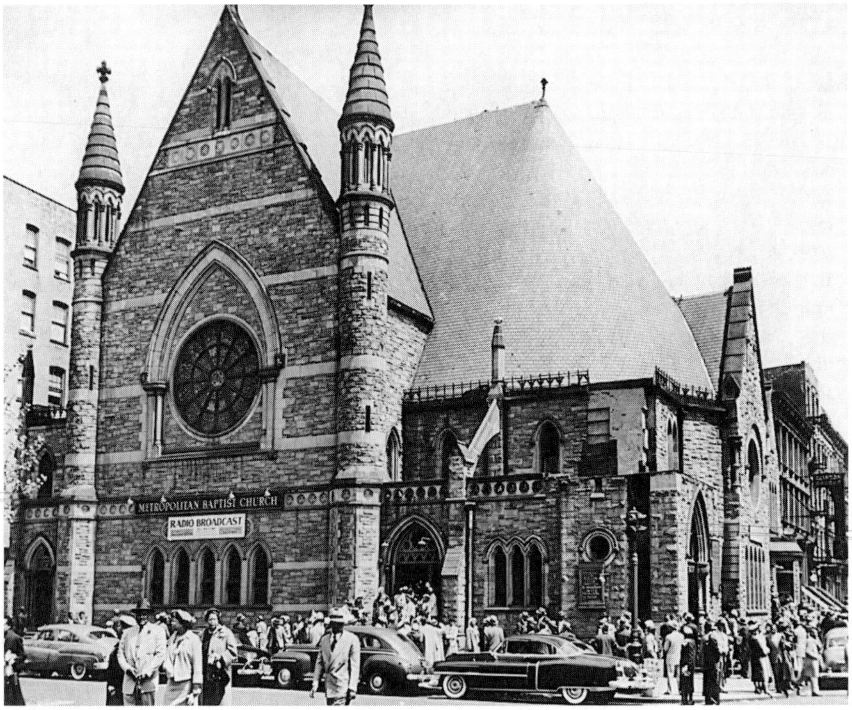

Metropolitan Baptist Church

R. Davis. In 1912 the congregation of the Metropolitan Baptist Church was formed through the merger of the Zion Baptist Church and the Mercy Seat Baptist Church of Harlem. The members of the newly formed church originally worshipped at 45–47 West 134th Street. Under the leadership of W. W. Brown (1914–30) the church secured its present location and the congregation grew to more than a thousand members. Brown was a founder of the Baptist Negro Education Center, a cooperative between white and black Baptists. The church's social and political activism continued, especially in the 1960s when black Baptist ministries helped support the civil rights movement. Metropolitan Baptist Church is a city, state, and federal landmark. Under the pastorship of John A. Smith in the mid 1990s it served the local community, while its choir and gospel soloists attracted an international audience.

Aileen Laura Love

Metropolitan Club. Private club in Manhattan, founded in 1891. It occupies a building built in 1894 at the corner of 5th Avenue and 60th Street overlooking Grand Army Plaza and Central Park. Commissioned by J. P. Morgan and designed by Stanford White, the building cost almost $2 million, a sum covered by the pledges of the seven hundred members originally enrolled, who included Morgans, Vanderbilts, Hamiltons, Cromwells, Browns, Whitneys, and Roosevelts. The lavish club has many dining rooms, a library, thirty-four bedrooms on the top floor, and a bowling alley in the basement. Membership is extended to both men and women. In the mid 1990s there were about fifteen hundred members.

Paul Porzelt: *The Metropolitan Club of New York* (New York: Rizzoli, 1982)

Thea Arnold

Metropolitan Council on Housing. A nonprofit tenants' advocacy group formed in 1959 by Jane Benedict, a supporter of rent control. Its forerunner was a coalition of neighborhood tenant advocacy groups formed in response to Title I of the Federal Housing Act of 1949, which required the U.S. Housing and Home Finance Administration to absorb more than half the costs incurred by private concerns in redeveloping residential properties in poor neighborhoods. Redevelopment accelerated under Robert Moses, who directed the Committee on Slum Clearance, and caused 100,000 New Yorkers to be driven from their homes by 1960. Owing largely to the efforts of the council the Rent Stabilization Law was passed in 1969, limiting annual rent increases for housing built after 1947. Initially an important voice for public housing, the council eventually shifted its support to what it called "housing in the public domain," or housing owned publicly and controlled by tenants rather than private landlords.

Ronald Lawson, ed.: *The Tenant Movement in New York City, 1904–1984* (New Brunswick, N.J.: Rutgers University Press, 1986)

Melissa M. Merritt

Metropolitan Hotel. A six-story hotel on the northeast corner of Broadway and Prince Street. Designed in the Italian palazzo style by the firm of Trench and Snook, it opened in 1852 as the second great luxury hotel in New York City (after the Astor House, 1836). The hotel had lavishly furnished public parlors and about five hundred guest rooms, with hot and cold running water and steam heat provided throughout. The building also housed Niblo's Garden, an entertainment center consisting of a theater, ballroom, and refreshment room. The hotel and its garden complex were demolished in 1895.

May N. Stone

Metropolitan Life Insurance Company. Financial institution formed in New York City in 1863, with headquarters on lower Broadway. In 1879 it began selling "industrial," or workingman's, insurance, which brought it much of its early success. Millions of industrial policies were sold, usually for a fee of five or ten cents a week collected at the policyholder's home. The firm moved its offices in 1893 to 1 Madison Avenue; the Metropolitan Life Tower, a well-known building, was completed in 1908, and in the same year the firm set up a welfare division to provide home nursing services to policyholders. A campaign begun by the firm in 1922 to provide affordable housing to city dwellers led to the construction of a large-scale housing project in Long Island City and of a complex of eleven thousand apartments in Stuyvesant Town and Peter Cooper Village (1947). During the Depression the firm rehabilitated more than seven thousand foreclosed farms and made loans to finance the construction of the Empire State Building and Rockefeller Center. It became the first life insurer to install a large-scale electronic data processing system in 1954. The firm in the 1980s acquired the Goldman Sachs Building near Wall Street and the Pan Am Building (200 Park Avenue, now known as the Met Life Building), the headquarters for the management of its wide-ranging real-estate holdings. In the early 1990s Metropolitan Life had sales offices throughout the five boroughs and more than $130,000 million in assets under management, and provided life insurance coverage for more than 45 million policyholders in the United States, Canada, Europe, and the Far East.

Daniel May

Metropolitan Life Building (formerly Pan Am Building), 1994

Metropolitan Museum of Art. Art museum on 5th Avenue between 80th and 84th streets, formed in 1870 by members of the Union League Club, including John Jay, the poet William Cullen Bryant, William T. Blodgett, the lawyer Joseph H. Choate, the railroad executive John Taylor Johnston, Henry W. Bellows, and the painters John Frederick Kensett and Worthington Whittredge. The museum was proposed by Jay in Paris in 1865 as an educational institution and cultural monument for the city and the nation. The board of trustees, formed in 1870, included the founders as well as the painters Frederic E. Church and Eastman Johnson, the sculptor John Quincy Adams Ward, and the architects Russell Sturgis and Richard Morris Hunt. Johnston was elected the first president in 1870, and in the following year a site along 5th Avenue was chosen, largely because of its proximity to Central Park. The first important collection, 174 European paintings (mostly Dutch and Flemish), was acquired in 1871 and helped the museum to become widely known. By levying a tax the city raised $500,000 for construction costs. Calvert Vaux was engaged as the architect and with Jacob Wrey Mould designed a small, red-brick building in a neo-Gothic style with a steel and glass roof reminiscent of that on the Crystal Palace in London (1851).

The museum was organized largely by George Fiske Comfort, founder of the College of Fine Arts at Syracuse University, who sought to provide enrichment, especially for workers, and drew up a detailed plan for establishing curatorial departments, a series of loan exhibitions, and lectures and school programs (his plan was later adopted by other American museums). A department of casts and reproductions was set up to provide copies of works unavailable for display. As early as 1883 a bequest was made to buy architectural casts, engravings, and photographs. The first director of the museum was the art collector Luigi Palma di Cesnola, elected in 1879. After a curator was appointed in 1882, followed by two others in 1889, the collection was divided into three departments: paintings, drawings, and prints; sculpture, antiquities, and objets d'art; and casts and reproductions (which lasted until the 1930s). The museum opened schools throughout the city that offered instruction in woodwork, metal work, drawing and design, modeling and carving, carriage drafting, and plumbing; these closed in 1892, when the museum shifted its focus to the study and enjoyment of authentic works of art. In 1888 and 1894 Theodore Weston and Arthur Tuckerman made additions to the building.

The museum expanded rapidly, adding to its holdings the Crosby Collection of musical instruments, the Marquand and Altman collections of paintings (mostly by old masters), and the Garland Collection of Asian porcelains. An estate of about $7 million was bequeathed to the museum by the manufacturer Jacob Rogers in 1901 and produced income that was used to buy books and works of art. One of the museum's most important benefactors was J. P. Morgan, who as president (1904–13) continued to expand the collections and the plant. Under his direction the museum acquired a magnificent collection of European art, and excavations begun in 1906 furnished its first Egyptian artifacts. He also commissioned the firm of McKim, Mead and White to build a wing (completed 1910) that would house the collection of decorative arts and his own collection of medieval and Renaissance works, and to complete the flanking wings of the façade on 5th Avenue (1926). In 1909 the museum mounted the Hudson–Fulton exhibition, the first comprehensive examination of American art by a major museum. Attended by more than 300,000 visitors, the show commemorated the Dutch and American heritage of the city with Dutch and early American paintings and American industrial arts.

As the collections grew, the curatorial departments were subdivided into categories that reflected the evolution of art history. In 1924 the American wing opened, and American art became a separate department. The Cloisters, a museum of medieval art and architecture assembled by George Grey Barnard, became a branch of the Metropolitan Museum after it and Fort Tryon Park, a tract of fifty-six acres (twenty-two hectares) surrounding it, were bought for the city by John D. Rockefeller in 1926. A larger building was erected to accommodate both the original collection and one donated by Rockefeller; designed by Charles Collens with Rockefeller and James Rorimer, an associate curator of decorative arts, it incorporated the many architectural fragments assembled by Barnard in France and opened in 1938. In 1929 the museum acquired an outstanding collec-

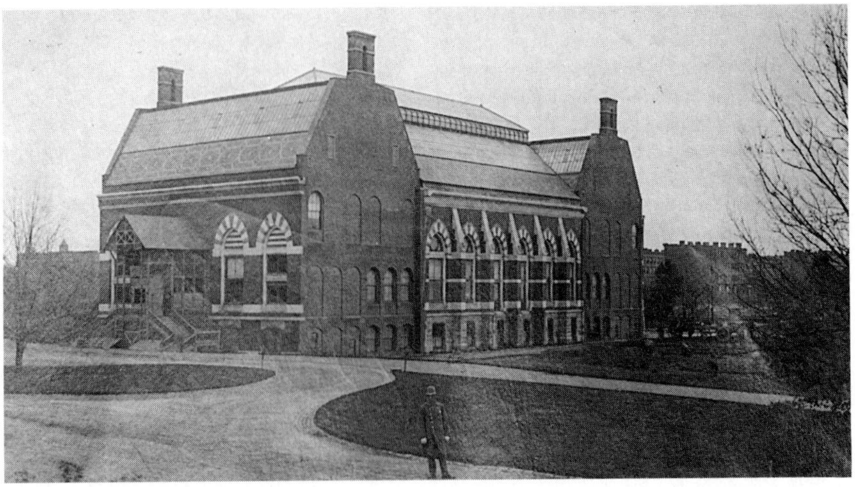

Metropolitan Museum of Art, ca *1880*

Façade on 5th Avenue (designed by McKim, Mead and White), Metropolitan Museum of Art, 1909

Metropolitan Museum of Art, 1994

tion of French impressionist paintings from Louisine Havemeyer.

For many years the Metropolitan rejected modern American and European art; in 1930 it refused Gertrude Vanderbilt Whitney's offer of her collection of American paintings and money to build a wing for it. After the Second World War the museum merged with the Whitney Museum of American Art and the Museum of Modern Art under the "three museum agreement," which collapsed largely because the administration of the Metropolitan rejected the tenets of modern art, especially abstraction. At the same time the museum in the 1940s even explored the possibility of moving entirely, an idea vetoed by the parks commissioner Robert Moses.

The focus of the museum changed after the war. Organizational changes were proposed by Francis Henry Taylor, the director during the 1940s, who first envisioned the Metropolitan as a series of many smaller museums within a single structure. He was followed in 1955 by Rorimer and in 1967 by Thomas P. F. Hoving, who sought to reshape the museum to serve a more diverse population. Hoving's style of administration often provoked controversy, and his somewhat cavalier attitude toward acquisitions led to an investigation by New York State into the practice of selling collections to raise purchasing funds. He enlarged the education department and opened a department of community programs and a department of contemporary and twentieth-century art (1967). Exhibitions during his tenure such as "Harlem on My Mind" treated broader themes than formerly, and with the exhibitions "In the Presence of Kings" and "Tutankhamun" (1978) Hoving developed an approach that drew enormous audiences and was soon imitated by other museums. He also secured Robert Lehman's collection of European art, considered by many the finest private collection of its kind in the United States, and undertook the construction of six new wings (Kevin Roche and John Dinkeloo, 1967–90). In 1982 Ruth Uris and Harold Uris gave money for an educational center, which opened in the basement of the museum. Under Philippe de Montebello efforts to attract broad audiences continued but the number of community programs decreased. From financial necessity the museum sought to sell reproductions of works displayed in such popular exhibitions as "The Vatican Collections" and "Van Gogh in St. Remy and Auvers."

The Metropolitan Museum of Art is the largest and most comprehensive art museum in the western hemisphere. It had 4.5 million visitors in 1989 and in the mid 1990s owned more than two million objects. Its collection of Egyptian art is second only to the one in Cairo.

Winifred E. Howe: *A History of the Metropolitan Museum of Art* (New York: n.pub., 1913 [vol. 1] / Columbia University Press, 1946 [vol. 2])

Calvin Tomkins: *Merchants and Masterpieces: The Story of the Metropolitan Museum of Art* (New York: E. P. Dutton, 1970)

Peter L. Donhauser

Metropolitan Opera. Opera company formed in 1883. Its first season coincided with the opening at Broadway and 39th Street of the Metropolitan Opera House, a structure seating 3700 that was built when a number of wealthy residents of New York City were unable to obtain boxes at the Academy of Music on 14th Street. Designed by J. C. Cady in a conservative Italian Renaissance style, the new building was criticized as a "yellow brick brewery" by James H. Mapleson, impresario at the Academy of Music, which eventually ceased operations owing to the pressure of competition. The first season at the Metropolitan Opera was managed by Henry E. Abbey and consisted of standard Italian and French operas along with Wagner's *Lohengrin*, all sung in Italian. In the interest of economy the holders of boxes at the opera house consigned the next seven seasons to a company based in Germany and led successively by Leopold Damrosch and Edmond C. Stanton. The repertory again included Italian and French works and Wagner, now all sung in German (except in some tour performances) by such singers as Marcella Sembrich and Lilli Lehmann. In 1891–92 Abbey returned to the company with the European impresario Maurice Grau to mount Italian and French operas in their original languages and to introduce the singers Emma Eames, the brothers Jean and Édouard de Reszke, Nellie Melba, and Emma Calvé. He continued as the manager until his death in 1896, which led to a reorganization under the leadership of Grau alone and to the cancellation of an entire season in 1897–98.

As the manager of the opera until 1903, Grau presented the singers Joanna Gadski and Antonio Scotti and signed a contract with Enrico Caruso, a mainstay of the company under Grau's successor Heinrich Conried (1903–8), whose other singers included Olive Fremstad, Geraldine Farrar, Feodor Chaliapin, and Louise Homer. Conried was responsible for a number of achievements, notably the unauthorized American stage première of Wagner's *Parsifal* (1903), which the composer's heirs failed to prevent by lawsuit; he retired in the face of ill health and some criticism. The financier Otto H. Kahn, one of the most loyal backers of Conried and the company, chose as the new manager of the opera house Giulio Gatti-Casazza, who introduced Emmy Destinn and Frances Alda, and later Lucrezia Bori, Claudia Muzio, Rosa Ponselle, Elisabeth Rethberg, Ezio Pinza, Lily Pons, Tito Schipa, Maria Jeritza, Giovanni Martinelli, Beniamino Gigli, Lauritz Melchior, Freidrich Schorr, Giuseppe De Luca, Lawrence Tibbett, Rose Bampton, and Grace Moore. The role of chief conductor of the company was filled by Arturo Toscanini (1908–15) and then Artur Bodanzky (1915–39), who later shared his responsibilities with Tullio Serafin and Ettore Panizza. Gatti-Casazza believed in novelties, a few of them durable, including the world premières of Puccini's *La fanciulla del West* (1910) and *Il Trittico* (1918).

In the following decades the company acquired a broad appeal that belied its reputation as a bastion of wealth and snobbery (a reputation to some extent surely deserved):

Metropolitan Opera House at Broadway and 39th Street, ca *1937*

immigrants were eager to hear singers from their homelands, some of whom were immigrants themselves; the first regular radio broadcasts of performances were made in 1931, and a long-running sponsorship by Texaco of broadcasts on Saturday afternoons began in December 1940; and the Metropolitan Opera Ballet solidified its reputation as one of the most important ballet companies in the city. At the same time the company was buffeted by the Depression, and its very existence was threatened by 1935, when Gatti-Casazza retired. Plans to move the company to new quarters at Radio City (originally designed by Joseph Urban as an opera house), Rockefeller Center, or another location were deferred owing to a lack of funds. In time the company was placed on surer financial footing, owing in part to the formation in 1935 by Mrs. August Belmont (1878–1979) of the Metropolitan Opera Guild, which began issuing the magazine *Opera News* in December 1936. The company was also helped during these lean years by the introduction of two of the greatest Wagner singers of the century, Kirsten Flagstad and Lauritz Melchior. Gatti-Casazza's successor as the manager of the company, Edward Johnson, was a former tenor who brought to the stage such well-known singers as Bidù Sayão, Jussi Björling, Zinka Milanov, Giuseppe Di Stefano, and Ljuba Welitsch, as well as an abundance of American talent: Jan Peerce, Helen Traubel, Risë Stevens, Leonard Warren, Eleanor Steber, Astrid Varnay, Richard Tucker, Dorothy Kirsten, and Robert Merrill. With the Second World War, the loss of some European artists was compensated for by such new residents as the singers Licia Albanese and Jarmila Novotná and the conductors Bruno Walter and Fritz Busch. The company was stable during the 1940s and enjoyed a remarkable esprit de corps. Johnson undertook few experiments in repertory, but he did introduce Benjamin Britten's *Peter Grimes* (1947–48) and Modest Mussorgsky's *Khovanshchina* (1949–50) and oversaw a raising of production standards in the performance of operas by Mozart, whose music was then enjoying a resurgence of popular interest.

Rudolf Bing became the manager of the company in 1950 and initiated a shift in emphasis toward prominent conductors (Leonard Bernstein, Zubin Mehta) and stage directors (including some not usually identified with opera, such as Margaret Webster and Alfred Lunt). Although Bing disclaimed the "star system," he did avail himself of well-known singers dating from Johnson's tenure and introduced others of the same caliber: Cesare Siepi, Mario Del Monaco, Renata Tebaldi, Victoria de Los Angeles, Carlo Bergonzi, Nicolai Gedda, Leonie Rysanek, Birgit Nilsson, Mirella Freni, Joan Sutherland, Renata Scotto, and Montserrat Caballé. In 1955 he engaged the first black soloist with the company, the contralto Marian Anderson, who was followed by Leontyne Price and others. He also presented the world premières of two operas by Samuel Barber, *Vanessa* (1958) and *Antony and Cleopatra* (1966), and of Marvin David Levy's *Mourning Becomes Electra* (1967). The première of *Antony and Cleopatra* marked the opening at Lincoln Center on 16 September 1966 of a new Opera House, designed by Wallace K. Harrison and built at a cost of $50 million. Important débuts were made on its stage, including those of Plácido Domingo (1966) and Marilyn Horne (1970). After Bing the company was managed successively by Schuyler Chapin (1972–75), who introduced the singers Kiri Te Kanawa and José Carreras, by Anthony Bliss (1975–85), who introduced José Van Dam, Tatiana Troyanos, Jessye Norman, and Samuel Ramey, and briefly by Bruce Crawford and then Hugh Southern. The conductor James Levine was then named artistic director and exerted a decisive influence. In the 1980s the Metropolitan discontinued its extensive national tours, a practice as old as the company itself. The assistant manager Joseph Volpe was named to the highest administrative position in the company in 1990–91.

In the mid 1990s the continuing visibility of the Metropolitan Opera was assured by regular radio broadcasts and a growing role in television. It remained the dominant opera company in the United States and one of the most important in the world.

Gerald Fitzgerald, ed.: *Annals of the Metropolitan Opera* (Boston: Metropolitan Opera Guild / G. K. Hall, 1989)

John W. Freeman

Metropolitan Transportation Authority [MTA]. Public authority created by the State of New York in 1968 to set policies and budgets for transportation agencies in New York City and seven suburban counties. Its board of directors has jurisdiction over the New York City Transit Authority, the Staten Island Rapid Transit Operating Authority, the Long Island Rail Road, Metro-North Commuter Railroad, the Metropolitan Suburban Bus Authority, and the Triborough Bridge and Tunnel Authority. During its first decade the authority improved commuter rail service and made plans to build subway lines to Queens and under 2nd Avenue; these projects were suspended in the mid 1970s owing to lack of funds. Richard Ravitch, who became chairman in 1979, focused instead on refurbishing existing facilities. In response to a decline in the number of transit passengers the authority launched a large capital program, which allotted $16,300 million between 1982 and 1991 to restore safe and reliable transit service. By the end of the 1980s the number of passengers stabilized and even increased on many lines. On an average weekday in 1992 the facilities of the MTA were used by more than five million passengers and 781,000 motor vehicles.

Peter Derrick: "Catalyst for Development: Rapid Transit in New York," *New York Affairs* 9, no. 4 (1986), 27–59

Peter Derrick

Metrotech Center. Office complex in downtown Brooklyn, bounded to the north by Tillary Street, to the east by the Flatbush Avenue Extension, to the south by Willoughby Street, and to the west by Jay Street. It comprises twelve buildings on ten blocks, on a total area of sixteen acres (6.5 hectares). The aim of the project was to provide back-office space for businesses at prices lower than those prevailing in lower Manhattan. Construction took place in 1986–87; the total cost of roughly $1000 million was borne by the city and by Polytechnic University, which renovated two buildings and built a third to house its Center for Advanced Technology in Telecommunications and its Dibner Library of Technology and Science. Among the firms that moved their headquarters to Metrotech were Brooklyn Union Gas and the Securities Industry Automation Corporation; other tenants include operations centers for Chase Manhattan Bank and Bear, Stearns and Company, and a training center for the New York Telephone Company. Metrotech was designed by the development firm of Forest City Ratner. Among the architects who took part in the project were Swanke Hayden Connell; Skidmore, Owings and Merrill; Davis, Brody and Associates; and Haines Lundberg Waehler. The firm of Ehrenkrantz, Eckstut, and Whitelaw designed and landscaped the open space, which includes a central commons of 3.3 acres (1.3 hectares). In the early 1990s the project was intended eventually to comprise 8.1 million square feet (750,000 square meters) of office space.

John Voelcker

Meucci, Antonio (*b* Italy, 13 April 1808; *d* Staten Island, 18 Oct 1889). Inventor. He lived for a time in Havana, where in 1841 he saw electrified wires transmitting sound. He moved to Staten Island in 1850 and provided housing there for Giuseppe Garibaldi. While he was recovering from a boiler explosion in 1864 his wife sold his experimental telephone equipment to a junk dealer for $6. On reading an announcement in 1876 that Alexander Graham Bell had invented the telephone, Meucci sought legal redress but was hampered by poverty and his poor knowledge of English. Meucci's accomplishments are detailed at the Garibaldi–Meucci Museum at 420 Tompkins Avenue in Rosebank, where he is buried.

Giovanni Ermenegildo Schiavo: *Antonio Meucci: Inventor of the Telephone* (New York: Vigo, 1958)

Patrick J. Gallo: *Old Bread, New Wine: A Portrait of the Italian–Americans* (Chicago: Nelson–Hall, 1981), 70–74

Mary Elizabeth Brown

Mexicans. Few Mexicans settled in New York City until after the Second World War. About ten thousand lived in the metropolitan area by 1960, most of them unskilled laborers. Slightly more than three thousand Mexicans settled in New York during the 1980s, accounting for only 0.5 percent of the city's immigrants and 0.6 percent of Mexican immigrants in the United States; only seven hundred were naturalized. Many worked in Mexican restaurants, which gained popularity during the 1980s.

Chad Ludington

Meyer [née Nathan], **Annie (Florance)** (*b* New York City, 19 Feb 1867; *d* New York City, 23 Sept 1951). Philanthropist. Born into a prominent Sephardic Jewish family, she traced her American ancestry to revolutionary patriots. In 1887 she married and took up residence on Park Avenue. With her husband she supported charitable, artistic, political, and civic causes; she played a prominent role in founding Barnard College (1889), of which she was a lifelong trustee and which she helped Zora Neale Hurston to attend. She also worked against woman suffrage and for the civil rights of all minorities, and opposed both Nazism and Zionism. Meyer was a prolific writer of essays, novels, short stories, letters to the editor, and plays, several of which had short runs on and off Broadway.

Dora Askowith: *Three Outstanding Women* (New York: Bloch, 1941)

Lynn D. Gordon

Meyer, Cord (i) (*b* Germany, 4 Dec 1823; *d* Maspeth [now in Queens], 10 June 1891). Businessman, father of Cord Meyer (ii). He emigrated to the United States as a boy and moved to Maspeth, Long Island, in 1852. In 1873 he opened the Acme Fertilizer Company, a factory on Newtown Creek where animal bones were burned to produce an ingredient necessary in sugar refining and fertilizer manufacture. Later he became a part owner of a profitable sugar refinery.

Vincent Seyfried

Meyer, Cord (ii) (*b* Maspeth [now in Queens], 9 Oct 1854; *d* Great Neck, N.Y., 14 Oct 1920). Businessman, son of Cord Meyer (i). He became the superintendent of his father's company, the Acme Fertilizer Company, when he was twenty years old and later entered into private banking with C. L. Rathbone and Company. In 1890 he formed the Cord Meyer Company and began to speculate in real estate. He developed Elmhurst on a large tract of land north of the village of Newtown and in 1893 formed the Citizens Water Company, a borough-wide utility of which he was president. Meyer became active in politics and was chairman of the Democratic State Committee in 1904–6. He created the neighborhood of Forest Hills from farmland in 1906–10 and was active in its development. Meyer lived in Great Neck, Long Island.

Vincent Seyfried

Michaëlius, Jonas (*b* Grootebroek, Netherlands, 1584; *d* after 1637). Minister. He was educated at the University of Leiden and set sail from Texel on 24 January 1628, landing on 7 April in New Amsterdam, where he became the first minister of the Dutch Reformed church in North America; his first communion drew fifty Walloon and Dutch communicants. He is best known for a letter that he wrote about the colony on 11 August 1628 to colleagues in Amsterdam (published in 1904 as *Manhattan in 1628, as Described in the Recently Discovered Autograph Letter*); he found the climate "good and pleasant" but lamented the state of civil government, the barbarity of the natives, and the lack of provisions. Michaëlius left New Netherland in 1632. A message from the Assembly of Nineteen in 1637 to the Classis of Amsterdam, which had recommended his reappointment, contains the last known record of his name.

Randall Balmer

Mickle, Andrew H. (*b* New York City, 1805; *d*?New York City, ?25 Jan 1863). Mayor. He spent his childhood in poverty in the sixth ward and married the daughter of a tobacco dealer whose business he later inherited, increasing his fortune to more than $1 million. Although he had little political experience when elected mayor in 1846 he supported many reforms. He sought to build an insane asylum and a new workhouse and provide the city with new fire engines.

James E. Mooney

Middleburgh. Name used from 1652 to 1664 by Newtown.

Middletown (i). Neighborhood in the eastern Bronx, bounded to the north by Pelham Bay Park, to the east by Country Club, to the south by Tremont Avenue, and to the west by the Hutchinson River Parkway. Middletown Road was the route of General William Howe's march to Eastchester Bay in October 1776 that led to the Battle of Pell's Point. Large private estates covered most of the area into the early twentieth century, when the completion of the Lexington Avenue subway to Pelham Bay along Westchester Avenue spurred the development of one- and two-family houses and small apartment buildings. In the mid 1990s the population was largely Italian, Irish, and Greek. Most who live in the neighborhood consider themselves residents of Pelham Bay.

Gary D. Hermalyn

Middletown (ii). Neighborhood in Queens during the American Revolution and the early nineteenth century, lying within Long Island City and centered at the junction of Ridge Road (now 46th Street) and Newtown Avenue. It consisted of three or four houses and a one-room school.

Vincent Seyfried

Middle Village. Neighborhood in west central Queens, bounded to the north by Eliot Avenue, to the east by Woodhaven Boulevard, to the south by Cooper Avenue and the Long Island Rail Road, and to the west by the Lutheran Cemetery. It began as a hamlet of families of English descent and was named for its location at the midpoint of the Williamsburgh and Jamaica Turnpike (now Metropolitan Avenue), which opened in 1816 and ran from Bushwick Avenue to Jamaica; the hamlet was established in the same year. In 1852 a Lutheran church in Manhattan bought several farms north and south of Metropolitan Avenue that were made into a large cemetery. After the Civil War the population of the hamlet became mostly German. In 1879 the Roman

Yard shrine on Furmanville Road in Middle Village, 1992

Midland Beach, 1903

Catholic diocese laid out St. John's Cemetery east of 80th Street. The growth of Middle Village was limited by the cemeteries and by Juniper Swamp (filled in 1915 to make Juniper Park), and it came to cater almost exclusively to visitors to the cemeteries. For years Metropolitan Avenue was lined with monument works, flower shops, small hotels, and saloons. Working farms in the outskirts along Dry Harbor Road and Caldwell Avenue lasted until the First World War. The need for housing in the 1920s spurred development, and blocks of one-family detached houses were built south of Metropolitan Avenue and on all four sides of Juniper Valley Park. After the Second World War the population became heavily Jewish and Italian, and Christ the King Catholic High School was built just east of the elevated station. Rentar Plaza, a shopping mall, was built on open space west of the Lutheran Cemetery. By the early 1990s a number of immigrants from Yugoslavia and the Balkans had moved to the area. Housing from the 1920s survives and is well maintained. The neighborhood still caters to visitors to the cemeteries.

Vincent Seyfried

Midland Beach. Neighborhood in east central Staten Island, lying southeast of Hylan Boulevard. By 1900 it was one of the finest summer resorts in the metropolitan area. Along with summer bungalows a pier was built to accommodate excursion boats carrying visitors from the other boroughs and New Jersey. Disastrous fires and ocean pollution contributed to the demise of the resort after the Second World War. The beach is now administered by the parks department, which maintains ballfields, picnic grounds, and parking areas nearby. The original bungalows have been insulated for year-round use and many one-family houses have been built as far inland as Hylan Boulevard. The population is largely white.

Marjorie Johnson

midtown. The center of Manhattan, roughly bounded to the north by 59th Street, to the east by 3rd Avenue, to the south by 34th Street, and to the west by 8th Avenue. The eastern section is dominated by office buildings, among them the Empire State, Chrysler, Seagram, International Business Machines, American Telephone and Telegraph, and Helmsley buildings, and the Met Life Building (200 Park Avenue, formerly the Pan Am Building). At the center of the neighborhood is Rockefeller Center and to the west the theater and garment districts. Other well-known buildings include St. Patrick's Cathedral, the New York Public Library, the Museum of Modern Art, Grand Central Terminal, and Carnegie Hall. Many hotels are situated in midtown, including the Plaza and the Waldorf–Astoria. Important intersections include Herald Square, Times Square, Grand Army Plaza, and Columbus Circle.

Elliott Sclar

midwifery. In colonial New York City most infants were delivered by midwives, who lacked formal medical training but were required by law to take an oath promising good behavior, conscientious care, and equitable fees. Physicians took a strong interest in midwifery from the 1790s. Valentine Seaman, a surgeon from New York City, opened a school for midwives at the new maternity ward of the Almshouse (1798) and two other physicians from the city published manuals for midwives. From the mid nineteenth century physicians sought to supplant midwives altogether: the New York County Medical Society voted against licensing midwives in 1860, and the New York Midwifery Dispensary (1890) limited its staff to medical students. The share of all deliveries made by midwives dwindled during the 1880s, but immigration in the 1890s brought to the city hundreds of European women who were formally trained in midwifery, which many immigrants saw as a traditional and respected profession. Despite the growing professionalization of medical care, midwives presided at 42 percent of the births in New York City in 1905.

A study conducted by F. Elisabeth Crowell estimated that one thousand midwives were in New York City in 1907, of whom only 4 percent were born in the United States. Like many physicians Crowell viewed midwives as ill-trained and of low character, and she associated midwifery with illegal and unsafe abortion practices. Even defenders of midwives such as S. Josephine Baker of the city's health department agreed that midwives should be screened, trained, and licensed. The New

Rush hour at 3rd Avenue and 42nd Street, 1957

York Committee for the Prevention of Blindness argued that midwives should be required to put silver nitrate in the eyes of newborns to prevent conjunctivitis; with its support Bellevue Hospital opened a free School for Midwives in 1911, the only such school in the United States operated by a municipality. In 1914 the health department established strict licensing requirements, allowing only midwives trained in certified schools to practice in the city. Bellevue was the only certified school in the United States.

By 1910 the number of licensed midwives working in New York City reached 1344, of whom 9 percent were American born. The New York Academy of Medicine passed a resolution supporting the education and registration of midwives in 1911, and in the following year one of the nation's foremost professors of pediatrics, Abraham Jacobi of New York City, spoke in favor of midwifery in his opening address as the president of the American Medical Association. Stricter regulation of midwives did little to silence the controversy over their qualifications raging in medical and popular journals throughout the period 1910–30, and the midwives' lack of influence and funds put them at a disadvantage in the struggle against those seeking to eradicate their profession. A widely publicized study by the New York Academy of Medicine (1933) inflamed the controversy by finding that of all the maternal deaths in the city in 1930–32 two thirds had been preventable, of which physicians had been responsible for 61 percent and midwives for only 2 percent. The academy criticized physicians for excessive intervention during childbirth, and maintained that the growing trend of hospital deliveries was accompanied by greater risk of infection. The report was passionately debated, and criticized especially strongly by the New York Obstetrical Society. At the same time the trend away from home deliveries by midwives and toward hospital deliveries by physicians continued; it accelerated as new hospital maternity wards opened, limits on immigration were imposed in 1924, and transportation from home to hospital improved. The proportion of childbirths in the United States taking place in hospitals increased from nearly 40 percent in 1935 to 50 percent in 1940, 90 percent in 1950, and 99 percent by the early 1970s.

Nurse midwifery was established as a profession about the time when traditional midwifery began to die out. First practiced by members of the Frontier Nursing Service in Kentucky in 1925, it was introduced in New York City by the Maternity Center Association (MCA), which opened a school of midwifery for registered nurses in Harlem in 1931. In the 1950s nurse midwives based at the MCA continued to deliver infants at home; in 1958 the training program moved to Downstate Medical Center–Kings County Hospital in Brooklyn, and increasingly the nurse midwife came to be seen as a member of the obstetrical team. During the 1970s interest in midwifery and home births revived as many expressed disillusionment with organized medicine, but in 1988 there were still only fifteen hundred nurse midwives certified and practicing nationwide, of whom about 250 were in greater New York.

The Midwife in the United States (New York: Josiah Macy, Jr. Foundation, 1968)

Sandra Opdycke

Midwood. Neighborhood in south central Brooklyn (1990 pop. 165,863), bounded to the north by Avenue H and the campus of Brooklyn College, to the east by Flatbush Avenue, to the south by Kings Highway, and to the west by Coney Island Avenue. Originally covered by thick forest, the area was named Midwout (middle woods) by Dutch settlers and lay between the towns of Gravesend and Flatlands. The residence of Johannes Van Nuyse (1128 East 34th Street; also known as the Coe House) was begun in 1744 with additions made in 1793 and 1806. The Van Nuyse–Magaw residence was built in 1800 (moved in 1916 to a site at 1041 East 2nd Street). The area remained largely undeveloped until apartment buildings and large tracts of detached houses were built in the 1920s. At the same time the film industry established itself in the neighborhood. The Vitagraph company occupied a studio at Avenue M and East 14th Street until 1925, when the company moved to Hollywood and the studio was taken over by Warner Brothers.

During these years the population of Midwood was largely Italian and Jewish. The following decades saw a marked increase in the number of Jews of various backgrounds, notably Hasidim and other Orthodox Jews and a large Sephardic population that included the largest settlement of Syrian Jews anywhere in the world (by some estimates said to number about thirty thousand in 1992). Some houses and apartment buildings were erected after the Second World War. In 1953 the National Broadcasting Company set up studios in the area, from which it broadcast the programs of Perry Como and Steve Allen; later the soap opera "Another World" and the situation comedy "The Cosby Show" were also made there. Another entertainment figure associated with Midwood is the filmmaker Woody Allen, who grew up in Midwood and graduated from Midwood High School. The neighborhood underwent a period of decline in the 1970s, when many of its residents moved to the suburbs and the commercial districts declined. There was a resurgence in the 1980s, as new residents were drawn to the area by its quiet, middle-class ambience. The largest single group of new immigrants who settled in Midwood during the decade were from the Soviet Union; there were also large numbers from China and Haiti, and to a lesser extent Israel, Pakistan, Guyana, Jamaica, Iran, and India. The main shopping areas lie along Avenue M, Kings Highway, and Flatbush, Nostrand, and Coney Island avenues.

Elizabeth Reich Rawson

Milbank, Tweed, Hadley and McCloy. Law firm. It traces its origins to the firm of Anderson, Adams and Young (formed in 1866) and has long been associated with its two most important clients, the Rockefeller family and Chase Manhattan Bank. George Welwood Murray (1856–1925), who became a partner in 1888, brought in John D. Rockefeller as a client and remained his legal advisor and confidant for decades. Winthrop W. Aldrich (1885–1974), son of Senator Nelson Aldrich of Rhode Island and brother of Abby Aldrich Rockefeller, played a similar role for John D. Rockefeller Jr. In 1929 Albert G. Milbank (1873–1949) joined the firm: a college friend of John D. Rockefeller Jr., he had served as senior counsel to Chase and its predecessors. John J. McCloy, assistant secretary of war during the Second World War and later high commissioner of Germany, chairman of Chase, and president of the World Bank, moved to the firm from Cravath, Swaine and Moore in 1946. Milbank, Tweed is regarded as the prototypical "white shoe" law firm. It is a longtime supporter of the New York Legal Aid Society and of cultural institutions in New York City, to many of which it also gives legal advice. In the mid 1990s Milbank, Tweed, Hadley and McCloy had about 270 lawyers in New York City and offices at 1 Chase Manhattan Plaza.

Ellen Joan Pollock: *Turks and Brahmins: Upheaval at Milbank, Tweed* (New York: Simon and Schuster, 1990)

Jonathan G. Cedarbaum

Milbank Memorial Fund. Charitable organization formed as the Memorial Fund Association on 3 April 1905 by Elizabeth Milbank Anderson (*b* 20 Dec 1850; *d* 22 Feb 1921), who inherited nearly $10 million from her father, Jeremiah Milbank. The death of her young son from diphtheria led her to focus her philanthropic efforts on public health and child welfare: a gift of $150,000 to the Association for Improving the Condition of the Poor enabled the construction of the Milbank Memorial Baths, opened in 1904 on East 38th Street, which became a model for other public baths in the city. The *Milbank Quarterly*, begun in 1923, evolved into an international journal of health policy. In the 1930s and 1940s the fund developed programs in nutrition and mental health, and in the 1960s it shifted its focus toward professional education and training. New efforts over the following two decades included a fellowship program in epidemiology and clinical medicine, a program in occupational health, and the publication of the *Milbank Health Policy Reviews* (1988–89). In 1991 the fund had assets of $46.7 million, made grants totaling $370,085, and expended $803,000 on four foundation-administered programs.

Howard S. Miller: "Anderson, Elizabeth Milbank," *Notable American Women, 1607–1950: A Biographical Dictionary*, vol. 1 (Cambridge: Harvard University Press, 1971), 42–43

Clyde V. Kiser: *The Milbank Memorial Fund: Its Leaders and Its Work, 1905–1974* (New York: Milbank Memorial Fund, 1975)

Kenneth W. Rose

military companies. See TARGET COMPANIES.

Mill Basin. Neighborhood in southeastern Brooklyn (1990 pop. 6404), lying along Jamaica Bay and bounded to the north by Avenue U, and to the east, south, and west by the Mill Basin Inlet. The area was called Equandito (broken lands) by the local Canarsee Indians who sold it in 1664 to John Tilton Jr. and Samuel Spicer. During the seventeenth century it became part of Flatlands and tidal mills were built on it; the land was owned from 1675 by Jan Martense Schenck and between 1818 and 1870 by the wife of General Phillip S. Crooke. The Crooke–Schenck House, which stood at East 63rd Street, was dismantled in the early 1960s and reassembled at the Brooklyn Museum. The area retained its rural character until Robert L. Crooke built a lead-smelting plant in 1890. The Crooke Smelting Company was bought out by the National Lead Company, and Crooke sold the remainder of the land to the firm of McNulty and Fitzgerald, which erected bulkheads and filled in the marshes.

Until the early twentieth century the chief resources were the abundant crabs, oysters, and clams in Jamaica Bay. In 1906 the Flatbush Improvement Company bought marshland and engaged the firm of Atlantic, Gulf and Pacific to dredge creeks and fill in meadows. Eventually the parcel had an area of 332 acres (135 hectares) and was fit for industrial development, and within a decade National Lead, Gulf Refining, and other leading firms engaged in heavy industry opened plants there. Atlantic, Gulf and Pacific bought the land in 1909 and built three large drydocks employing a thousand workers; it also began promoting Jamaica Bay as a major harbor but failed to attract a large volume of shipping. A project begun in 1913 and completed in 1923 to extend Flatbush Avenue to Rockaway Inlet provided an additional 2700 feet (823 meters) of dock facilities and a strip of land for a road across the marshes. In 1915 a channel was dredged to the main channel of Jamaica Bay, and a bulkhead and wharfage platform were built on the mainland side of Mill Creek. By 1919 Mill Island was the site of at least six manufacturing and commercial concerns. During the late 1920s and 1930s the docks were rented to a number of small industrial firms. The neighborhood remained a grimy industrial area for thirty years, but its further development was hindered when plans for rail service to the rest of Brooklyn went unrealized. Residential development began after the Second World War when Atlantic, Gulf and Pacific sold to the firm of Flatbush Park Homes the land bounded to the north by Avenue U, to the east by East 68th Street and East Mill Basin, to the south by Basset Avenue, and to the west by Strickland Avenue and Mill Avenue. Brick bungalows were built in the late 1940s and early 1950s, many of which were later replaced by large, custom-built, detached one-family houses on lots measuring fifty by a hundred feet (fifteen by thirty meters). Mill Basin is now one of the most exclusive residential areas in Brooklyn. It is primarily Irish and Italian, with shopping along Avenue U and Flatbush and Ralph avenues. The streets are circular and many homeowners dock their boats behind their property.

Elizabeth Reich Rawson, Stephen Weinstein

Miller, Arthur (*b* New York City, 17 Oct 1915). Playwright. He grew up in Harlem and Brooklyn and became a member of the Federal Theatre Project in 1938. His first successful Broadway play, *All My Sons* (1947), received the Drama Critics Circle Award. He is best known for his play *Death of a Salesman* (1949), an exploration of the American myth of money and success that earned a number of prizes (among them the Pulitzer Prize and the Tony Award). *The Crucible* (1953), a powerful account of the witch trials in Salem, Massachusetts, in 1692, is an allegory of the McCarthy period; *A View from the Bridge* (1955) recounts the story of a Sicilian–American family in Red Hook. From 1956 to 1961 he lived at 444 East 57th Street and from 1962 to 1968 at the Chelsea Hotel at 222 West 23rd Street. He married the actress Marilyn Monroe in 1956 and the photographer Inge Morath in 1962. Miller's is a rare and consistent voice of conscience in American theater. He wrote an autobiography, *Timebends* (1988).

Robert Seder

Miller, Kenneth Hayes (*b* Oneida, N.Y., 11 March 1876; *d* New York City, 1 Jan 1952). Painter and teacher. He grew up in the utopian community of Oneida, New York, and studied at the Art Students League and the New York School of Art under William Merritt Chase. Influenced by Albert Pinkham Ryder, he painted symbolic subjects before adopting a classic style of figure painting. He endowed scenes of life in Union Square with an underlying orderly structure, and his figures with a simplicity that verges on the monumental. He taught at the New York School of Art (1900–11) and the Art Students League (at intervals, 1911–51). A leader of the "Fourteenth Street School," he introduced the subject of the city shopper — young working woman or mature matron — to American painting. Some of his work is owned by the Whitney Museum of American Art.

Lloyd Goodrich: *Kenneth Hayes Miller* (New York: Arts Publishing, 1930)

Lincoln Rothschild: *To Keep Art Alive: The Effort of Kenneth Hayes Miller, American Painter (1876–1952)* (Philadelphia: Art Alliance, 1974)

Judith Zilczer

Miller, Samuel (*b* near Dover, Del., 31 Oct 1769; *d* Princeton, N.J., 7 Jan 1850). Minister. He served at First Presbyterian Church in 1793–1813, during which time he helped to publish the *New York Magazine* (1790–97) as a member of the Friendly Society and to organize the Free School Society (1805), which advocated parochial schools. A spokesman for the gradual abolition of slavery, he was a member of the New York Manumission Society and led a national denominational committee that studied the compatibility of slavery and Christianity (1835); the findings of the committee led to the division within the Presbyterian church between Old School and New School (1837–38). Miller became a professor of ecclesiastical history and church government at Princeton Theological Seminary and wrote a history of the eighteenth century and a biography of John Rodgers, his predecessor at First Presbyterian Church.

David Meerse

millinery. For a discussion of millinery see HATTING AND MILLINERY.

Mill Rock. An island in the East River opposite East 96th Street in Manhattan, and the site of the only city park accessible only by boat. It is about two acres (eighty ares) in size and remains undeveloped. A neighboring island called Little Mill Rock was joined with it at the outbreak of the War of 1812, when a blockhouse was erected as part of the harbor defenses. In the late nineteenth century the Army Corps of Engineers manufactured explosives on the site to be used for blasting rocks from Hell Gate Channel. Mill Rock was deeded to the city in 1958.

Gerard R. Wolfe

Millrose Games. An annual winter track meet first held in 1908, and moved to Madison Square Garden in 1914. It initially was organized by the Millrose Athletic Association, which was itself formed by employees of Wanamaker's department stores; the name Millrose was that of Rodman Wanamaker's summer home. Over the years the meet became a prestigious event sometimes called the "indoor olympics." Controversy attended the meet in 1950, when the judges reversed their ruling on the outcome of the mile race (the issue was not settled for nine months), and in 1955, when the running of the Wanamaker Mile resulted in both a world indoor record (by Gunnar Nielsen, 4:03.6) and a fierce shoving match. Among those who have taken part in the Millrose Games are Paavo Nurmi, Frank Shorter, Marty Liquori, Steve Scott, Eammon Coghlan, Carl Lewis, Mary Decker, Said Aouita, Jackie Joyner-Kersee, and Noureddine Morceli.

Robert Hillenbrand

Mills, C(harles) Wright (*b* Waco, Texas, 28 Aug 1916; *d* West Nyack, N.Y., 20 March 1962). Sociologist and social critic. After receiving an MA in philosophy from the University of Texas at Austin (1939) and a PhD in sociology from the University of Wisconsin (1942) he was an associate professor of sociology at the University of Maryland (1941–45). He spent the summer of 1943 in New York City, where he lived in Greenwich Village and made the acquaintance of such well-known intellectuals as Daniel Bell, Dwight Macdonald, Philip Rahv, and Irving Howe. In 1945 he began a lifelong association with Columbia University as the director of the Labor Research Division of the Bureau of Applied Research, a position he held until 1948. Between 1945 and 1962 he was a professor of sociology at Columbia, where he taught mostly undergraduates, and held visiting appointments at the University of Chicago (1949), Brandeis University (1953), and the University of Copenhagen (1956–57). In his early work he argued that the powerful forces controlling the United States had become devoid of knowledge and moral wisdom: he examined labor leaders in *The New Men of Power* (1948), the new middle class in *White Collar* (1951), and military, political, and corporate leaders in *The Power Elite* (1956). An energetic scholar long associated with left-wing intellectuals in Greenwich Village, he disliked what he perceived as snobbery at Columbia and saw himself as a solitary combatant against the smug, intellectually apathetic America of the 1950s. In his well-known "Letter to the New Left" he appealed to young radicals to join his cause. Mills lived for a time on 114th Street. His other published writings include *The Causes of World War III* (1958) and *Listen, Yankee: The Revolution in Cuba* (1960).

Irving Louis Horowitz: *C. Wright Mills: An American Utopian* (New York: Macmillan / Free Press, 1983)

Marjorie Harrison

Mingus, Charles (*b* Nogales, Ariz., 22 April 1922; *d* Cuernavaca, Mexico, 5 Jan 1979). Double bass player, pianist, and composer. He grew up in Los Angeles and became a virtuoso double bass player in the 1940s; from 1951 he lived at a series of addresses in New York City, including 5 Great Jones Street (in the mid 1960s) and Manhattan Plaza (for the last several years of his life). He composed ambitious works that melded such diverse influences as the lush orchestral textures of Duke Ellington's writing and the raw, emotionally charged music heard in many black churches. He appeared frequently at the Five Spot, the Half Note, the Showplace, and the Village Vanguard. His most important recordings include *The Black Saint and the Sinner Lady* (1963) and *Meditations on Integration* (1964). Mingus redefined the role of the double bass soloist in the jazz ensemble and was probably the most ambitious composer of his generation to work in jazz. Much of his writing represented a radical departure from the jazz tradition, embracing atonality, extended forms, and an unusual degree of rhythmic freedom; yet he also created a body of compositions that in their hard-swinging directness hark back to the very roots of black American music.

Brian Priestley: *Mingus: A Critical Biography* (New York: Da Capo, 1984)

Peter Keepnews

mining. Deposits of iron ore in the serpentine hills of Staten Island were discovered by Dutch settlers, who gave the name Yserberg (iron hill) to what later became Todt Hill. Staten Island became an important center of mining and quarrying in the nineteenth century. The ore was exported and used primarily in blast furnaces; if screened, ground, and washed it could be used to produce red ochre paint. By the 1920s about 300,000 tons (272,000 metric tons) had been extracted, primarily from the mines at Todt Hill, Ocean Terrace, the Serpentine Road (Emerson Hill), and Jewett Avenue. Deposits of precious stones were reported in the hills but attempts to recover them were futile; the area eventually produced eighty tons (seventy-three metric tons) of fibrous serpentine that was used as asbestos. From 1841 to 1896 granite-like rock was quarried from the secondary stratum of sandstone under the island and used to pave Whitehall Street, sections of Broadway, and Bowling Green in Manhattan, as well as the streets of Charleston, South Carolina. Hand-broken stone from Staten Island was used for paving the streets of Brooklyn, and tens of thousands of tons were sold for building foundations, docks, and sea walls. Gypsum was quarried on Staten Island as late as the 1960s.

Kevin Kenny

Minsky, Billy [Michael William] (*b* New York City, 1891; *d* Brooklyn, 12 June 1932). Impresario. He was a society reporter for the *World* before beginning his career in the theater, for a good part of which he worked with his brothers Abe (*b* New York City, 1881; *d* New York City, 1949), Herbert (*b* New York City, ?1892; *d* New York City, 1959), and Morton (*b* New York City, 1902; *d* New York City, 1987). He produced shows with Abe at the National Winter Garden on East Houston Street (1913), which was owned by their father, at the Park Theatre on Columbus Circle (for one year beginning in 1922), again at the National Winter Garden (1923–24), where he installed a runway to give his patrons a closer look at the chorus girls, and at the Apollo Theatre (from 1924). In 1931 he staged one of the first burlesque shows on Broadway, at the Republic Theatre on 42nd Street. Minsky was a leading producer of burlesque in New York City, and the greatest showman of all the impresarios in his family. His shows were noted for their freshness, the high caliber of their performances, and their risqué quality. The slim, attractive chorus girl was a mainstay of his productions.

Rowland Barber: *The Night They Raided Minsky's* (New York: Simon and Schuster, 1960)
Morton Minsky and Milt Machlin: *Minsky's Burlesque* (New York: Arbor House, 1986)

William Green

minstrelsy. The American minstrel show has its roots in eighteenth-century theater. Beginning in the 1760s some British plays, regularly performed in New York City, included black

Miners on Staten Island, 1890

well's Island and was due to be deported under the Espionage Act when he died during a speaking tour.

Frederic Trautmann: *The Voice of Terror: A Biography of Johann Most* (Westport, Conn.: Greenwood, 1980)

Kevin Kenny

Mostel, Zero [Samuel Joel] (*b* New York City, 28 Feb 1915; *d* Philadelphia, 8 Sept 1977). Actor and comedian. From 1942 he worked as a stand-up comedian in Greenwich Village and became noted for a zany, exaggerated, improvisational style influenced by the Yiddish theater of the 1930s. During the McCarthy period he was blacklisted as a communist (1952–58); forced to take up painting to support his family, he rented a studio on 28th Street (his experiences during these years are depicted in Martin Ritt's film *The Front* (1976), in which he appeared). His acting career revived in the early 1960s and he won Tony awards for his performances in the Broadway musicals *A Funny Thing Happened on the Way to the Forum* (1962) and *Fiddler on the Roof* (1964), often considered his best work.

Gerald Bordman: *The Concise Oxford Companion to American Theatre* (New York: Oxford University Press, 1987)
Jared Brown: *Zero Mostel: A Biography* (New York: Atheneum, 1989)

Tina Margolis

Mother African Methodist Episcopal Zion Church. Church formed by blacks who withdrew from the John Street Methodist Episcopal Church in 1796. Legally established in 1801, it moved from lower Manhattan to Harlem, where buildings were bought and built on 136th and 137th streets in 1915 and 1925. The church occupied seven buildings, of which three were built and four were purchased. Membership increased from three hundred to more than a thousand owing to the efforts of the pastor James W. Brown, who became a bishop in 1936.

William J. Walls: *The African Methodist Episcopal Zion Church: Reality of the Black Church* (Charlotte, N.C.: A.M.E. Zion Publishing House, 1974)

Dennis C. Dickerson

Mother Horn [Horn, Rosa Artimus] (*b* Sumter, S.C., 1886; *d* Baltimore, 11 May 1976). Religious leader. After becoming known as a faith-healer in Georgia she moved to Illinois and then to Indiana, where she was ordained a Pentecostal minister. After forming a church in Evanston, Illinois, she moved to Brooklyn in 1926 and to Harlem in 1930, where she formed Mount Calvary Assembly Hall of the Pentecostal Faith Church at 400 Lenox Avenue. During the 1930s she became well known for her impassioned evangelical meetings at the church, which regularly attracted audiences of three thousand and were broadcast for half an hour every Wednesday and Sunday by the radio station WHN; the program was soon carried by several other stations along the eastern seaboard, and Horn eventually opened branches of her church in five cities.

Kevin Kenny

Motherwell, Robert (*b* Aberdeen, Wash., 24 Jan 1915; *d* Provincetown, Mass., 16 July 1991). Painter. He grew up in San Francisco and became noted for using black, white, and ochre in his paintings because of his love for the scenery of California. Influenced by Cézanne and Matisse, he traveled to France and formed connections with the European surrealists Marcel Duchamp, Max Ernst, and André Breton before settling in Greenwich Village in 1932. A leader with Jackson Pollock, Willem de Kooning, and Mark Rothko of the American abstract expressionist movement in the 1930s and 1940s, he exhibited paintings and collages in galleries and museums in Japan, Europe, and the United States; an exhibition devoted to his work was mounted at the Musée National d'Art Moderne in Paris in 1977. Motherwell was married to the painter Helen Frankenthaler. He taught at Hunter College.

Leslie Gourse

Motley, Constance Baker (*b* New Haven, Conn., 14 Sept 1921). Judge. The daughter of a family from the British West Indies, she was educated at New York University and earned a law degree from Columbia University in 1946. During her tenure from 1948 to 1965 as a representative of the NAACP Legal Defense Fund she won seven lawsuits before the U.S. Supreme Court. With her family she moved in December 1961 into an apartment building in New York City where they were the first black residents; she also supported a one-day boycott of the public schools to protest de facto segregation in 1964. After winning a special election to the state senate in February 1964 she became borough president of Manhattan (1965–66) and then a judge of the U.S. District Court (1966). As a senior judge (from 1986) she ruled in 1991 that quick-printing businesses cannot copy articles for profit without first obtaining permission from the holders of copyright.

George J. Lankevich

Mott, Valentine (*b* Glen Cove, N.Y., 20 Aug 1785; *d* New York City, 26 April 1865). Physician and surgeon. He began his medical studies in 1804 at Columbia College (MD 1806). Because physicians in New York City at the time could acquire clinical experience mainly in prisons and almshouses under the supervision of largely corrupt politicians, he promptly left for London and Edinburgh. On his return to the city in 1809 he was offered the chair of surgery at Columbia College. He remained until 1826, when he resigned over disagreements with the administration. With a few associates he then founded Rutgers Medical College, which disbanded a few years later. He returned in 1830 to Columbia and then taught at the University Medical College. Mott was a champion of the poor and a proponent of the use of cadavers in surgical instruction, a notion then considered sacrilegious. He was a president of the New York Academy of Medicine, a fellow of the Imperial Academy of Paris and the Medical Society of London, and a Knight of Constantinople.

Shan Jayakumar

Mott Haven. Neighborhood in the southwestern Bronx (1990 pop. 48,951), bounded to the north by East 149th Street and St. Mary's Park, to the east by the southeasterly continuation of East 149th Street and the East River, and to the south and west by the Harlem River. Developed in 1850 as an industrial village and as a suburb for people working in Manhattan by Jordan L. Mott, the owner of a nearby ironworks, it soon included the residential and industrial sections of North New York and Port Morris. After the 3rd Avenue elevated line was extended in 1886 it became a fashionable area with elegant new row houses, and the industrial section became a center of piano manufacturing. Germans and Jews settled throughout; Alexander Avenue was largely Irish and the northwestern section Italian. Despite a thriving commercial section and the convenience of new subways, by 1940 the piano industry had disappeared, the neighborhood was less affluent than formerly, and much of the old housing was scheduled for demolition under slum clearance programs. After 1950 the population became increasingly black and Puerto Rican, and many areas were rebuilt with low-income public housing. The neighborhood suffered less housing devastation than other parts of the Bronx in the 1960s because of its mix of row houses (often owner-occupied) and new public housing for the poor. In the mid 1990s Mott Haven was the site of vacant lots and abandoned buildings, low- and high-rise public housing, a landmark district, old tenements and row houses, an industrial waterfront, and two historic churches, St. Ann's Episcopal Church (1841; built under the auspices of Gouverneur Morris Jr.) and St. Jerome's Roman Catholic Church. The population was mostly poor, but a growing number of middle-class blacks were moving into renovated row houses.

Joel Schwartz: "Community Building on the Bronx Frontier: Morrisania, 1848–1875" (diss., University of Chicago, 1972)

Evelyn Gonzalez

Mould, Jacob Wrey (*b* Chislehurst [now in London], 1825; *d* New York City, 14 June 1886). Architect. After emigrating to the United States he achieved immediate success in New York City for his polychromatic design of the All Souls Church, popularly called the "Church of the Holy Zebra," at 4th Avenue and 20th Street (1853–55). Among the many structures he designed were several in Central Park with Frederick Law Olmsted and Calvert Vaux: Bethesda Terrace (1858–71), the Music Stand (1863–65, demolished), the Boathouse (1870–71, demolished), the Sheepfold (1870–71), the Stable (1870–71), and the Casino (1870–71, demolished). He also designed the initial buildings for the Metropolitan Museum of Art (1874–80) and the American Museum of Natural History (1874–77; for illustration see AMERICAN MUSEUM OF NATURAL HISTORY) and translated from Italian to English some librettos of Mozart's operas.

Marjorie Pearson

Mount, William Sidney (*b* Setauket, N.Y., 26 Nov 1807; *d* Setauket, 19 Nov 1868). Painter. He was trained as a portrait painter in New York City in the late 1820s and elected to the National Academy of Design in 1832 after his first major exhibition of genre paintings in the city in 1830. Although not the first artist to treat rural America as a repository of virtue, he developed rural themes and character types that influenced other American artists, leading many to consider him the most important American genre painter. For most of his career Mount worked in Stony Brook, New York, where his papers and more than seven hundred of his works are held in a museum.

Alfred Frankenstein: *William Sidney Mount* (New York: Harry N. Abrams, 1975)

Timothy Anglin Burgard

Mount Eden. Neighborhood in the west central Bronx, lying within Tremont. Named for Rachel Eden, who bought a hilly farm there in 1820, the area was farmland into the early decades of the twentieth century. During the 1920s and 1930s apartment buildings were built that were occupied mostly by wealthy Jews, and Bronx–Lebanon Hospital opened in 1942. After 1975 the population became mostly black and Latin American. Mount Eden Avenue and Mount Eden Parkway form the main thoroughfare. The novelist E. L. Doctorow grew up in the neighborhood.

Lloyd Ultan

Mount Hope. Neighborhood in the central Bronx, lying within Tremont along Tremont Avenue and bounded to the west by the Grand Concourse. The land once belonged to the Morris family and for many years was used for farming. In 1868 it became known as the Western Reserve. In the 1920s and 1930s a large number of Jews moved to five- and six-story apartment buildings in the area. By the early 1990s most of the inhabitants were black and Latin American. The neighborhood is the site of a public school, the Mount Hope School.

Lloyd Ultan

Mount Loretto–Mission of the Immaculate Virgin. Orphanage opened in 1870 by John Drumgoole as St. Vincent's Home for Homeless Newsboys, in response to the prevailing policy of children's aid groups of sending thousands of Irish Catholic homeless children to western states in the late 1860s. In 1882–83 the orphanage moved from 80 Lafayette Street in Manhattan to Pleasant Plains on the southern shore of Staten Island. In the mid 1990s it was coeducational and primarily served blacks, Latin Americans, and non-Catholics. The institution caters to children with social, emotional, and mental handicaps in its residential treatment center and in group homes and offers long-term foster care and adoptive services; it remains affiliated with the New York City Archdiocesan Catholic Charities.

Nancy Flood

Mount Pleasant. An obsolete name for a neighborhood in northwestern Queens east of Maurice Avenue, just northeast of Maspeth. It appears only in the Beers's atlas of 1873 and on Beers's wall map of 1886. The land rises steeply from Maspeth Creek to a height of 132 feet (forty meters) above sea level; the hill is now traversed by 69th Street. As late as 1922 the area formed Maurice's Woods, a tract of seventy-two acres (twenty-nine hectares) donated to the Episcopal church for a seminary by James Maurice, a former congressman; the tract is now covered by houses.

Vincent Seyfried

Mount Prospect. A hill on the terminal moraine in Brooklyn, just east of the intersection of Eastern Parkway and Flatbush Avenue. Before the Battle of Long Island (August 1776) it was used as an observation post by the American forces. In 1856 a reservoir was built on the site to supply the western part of the borough. The city took part of the land for a park in 1937 and designated the rest for the Brooklyn Central Library. The name inspired those of Prospect Park and Prospect Heights.

John J. Gallagher

Mount Sinai Hospital. Hospital incorporated in 1852 as the Jews' Hospital in the City of New York and opened on West 28th Street between 7th and 8th avenues in 1855. Initially it admitted only patients who were Jewish, but after treating a large number of Union soldiers during the Civil War it admitted patients regardless of their background and in 1866 took its current name. In 1872 the hospital moved from a building that held only forty-five beds to much larger quarters on Lexington Avenue between 66th and 67th streets, where it opened a modern laboratory, a training school for nurses (1881–1971), an outpatient department, a house staff system, and specialty departments that included the first pediatrics department (1878) established in a general hospital and the first neurological service (1900) in a hospital in New York City. The site at Lexington Avenue was ideal at first and the number of beds eventually expanded from 120 to 225, but the hospital was nevertheless unable to meet the demands of a rapidly growing city. In 1898 land was purchased at 5th Avenue and 100th Street and a new hospital consisting of ten buildings with 456 beds was completed in 1904. During the world wars Mount Sinai sponsored the Base Hospital no. 3 of the American Expeditionary Forces and the 3rd General Hospital of the U.S. Army, both composed of a core group of physicians and nurses from the hospital. Research assumed a larger role at 100th Street and many medical contributions were made: twenty-one diseases, tests, instruments, and phenomena were named after doctors at the hospital who described them, including Crohn's Disease, Tay–Sachs Disease, the Shwartzman Phenomenon, and the Rubin Test. Medical education also grew in importance as medical students from schools in New York City served clerkships at the hospital. In 1910 postgraduate training of physicians began in conjunction with Columbia University, and in 1953 Mount Sinai was named a major affiliate of the university. The Mount Sinai Medical School received its first charter in 1963, became affiliated with the City University of New York in 1967, and opened in 1968. Authorized to grant the MD and the PhD, it was the first medical school in New York City since the Flexner Report (1910) to be developed by a hospital rather than a university. With the founding of the school the hospital complex became known as the Mount Sinai Medical Center.

Joseph Hirsh and Beka Doherty: *The First Hundred Years of the Mount Sinai Hospital of New York, 1852–1952* (New York: Random House, 1952)

Janie Brown Nowak: *The Forty-seven Hundred: The Story of the Mount Sinai Hospital School of Nursing* (Canaan, N.H.: Phoenix, 1981)

Barbara J. Niss

movie theaters. The first movie theaters in New York City were opened in storefronts about the end of the nineteenth century. Nickelodeons became popular in the following decade and the city soon had hundreds. These began with little more than a projector, a screen, a piano, and camp chairs but soon became small yet fancifully decorated auditoriums. The nickelodeon took on some of the characteristics of the vaudeville hall and the stage theater and evolved into what became known as the movie palace. The first movie palace is generally considered to have been the Regent Theater (1913, seating 1800), now on Adam Clayton Powell Jr. Boulevard at 116th Street. Designed by Thomas W. Lamb with a façade modeled after that of the Doges' Palace in Venice, it was managed by Samuel "Roxy" Rothafel.

The American movie theater reached its peak in the 1920s as a luxurious and often exotic place. Theaters seating several thousand offered weekly programs including not only motion pictures but vaudeville, organ re-

Reginald Marsh, Twenty Cent Movie *(1936). Whitney Museum of American Art*

citals, orchestras, comedians, and magicians; they also served as civic centers for such events as high school graduation ceremonies. In New York City there were more than a thousand theaters, most concentrated in Times Square and others on the "subway circuit" in various neighborhoods. The theaters were built by a small group of entrepreneurs, all of whom had enjoyed unimportant careers as entertainers and had come to control hundreds of theaters in regional and national circuits. They included the vaudeville promoters B. F. Keith and E. F. Albee; William Fox, founder of 20th Century Fox; and Marcus Loew, builder of the largest chain of theaters in the city. Rothafel managed only a few theaters, among them the Roxy Theater at 50th Street and 7th Avenue, known as the "cathedral of the motion picture" (Walter Ahlschlager, 1927, seating six thousand; demolished) and Radio City Music Hall at Rockefeller Center (Associated Architects, 1932). Showcase theaters were later built by such corporations as Paramount and Warner Brothers. The leading theater architects in the city were Lamb, John Eberson, C. Howard Crane, G. Albert Lansburgh, and the firm of Rapp and Rapp. Crane, Lamb, and Eberson began as architects of legitimate stage theaters; these and their early movie palaces relied on plaster ornamental designs in the Adam style. Three of Lamb's early movie theaters on Broadway—the Strand (1914, seating three thousand; demolished), the Rivoli (1917, seating two thousand; demolished), and the Capitol (1919, seating five thousand; demolished) — helped to make Times Square the focus not only of the stage theaters of the city but also of its movie theaters. His later work, in a similar style, included the Loew's State (1921, seating 3300; demolished) at the headquarters of Loew's firm in Times Square and the Albee Theatre in downtown Brooklyn (1925, seating 3200; demolished).

Other architects stressed the exotic: theaters called the Rialto, the Tivoli, the Oriental, the Paradise, and the Valencia were designed in styles reminiscent of Baroque Spain, ancient Egypt, India, and the Far East. Rapp and Rapp designed theaters for Paramount and Loew's in a regal French manner, among them the Paramount Theater (1926, seating 3700; gutted) in the Paramount building on Times Square and the Brooklyn Paramount (1928, seating 4100; converted) in the theater district of downtown Brooklyn. Crane's series of immense theaters for Fox included the Brooklyn Fox Theatre (1928, seating four thousand; demolished), combining Baroque, South Asian, and art deco ornament, and the Roxy Theater, designed by Ahlschlager, which combined elements from a variety of ancient Egyptian, Greek, and Roman sources. Eberson developed the so-called atmospheric theater: in place of a domed classical ceiling was a blue plaster surface on which cloudlike images were projected by a hidden machine; electric lightbulbs simulated stars and the walls resembled the backdrops of a stage. The effect was described by Eberson as that of being in "an Italian garden, a Persian Court, a Spanish patio, or a mystic Egyptian templeyard, all canopied by a soft moonlit sky." His work included Loew's 72nd Street Theatre on the East Side of Manhattan (1932, seating 3200; demolished), designed in an extravagant southeast Asian style.

Among the largest and most elaborate movie palaces in New York City were five "wonder theaters" built for Loew's in 1929–30 in the major population centers outside midtown Manhattan: Brooklyn was served by the Kings Theatre in Flatbush (Rapp and Rapp, seating 3670), Queens by the Valencia Theatre on Jamaica Avenue (Eberson, seating 3550), the Bronx by the Paradise Theatre on the Grand Concourse at Fordham Road (Eberson, seating 3885), upper Manhattan by the 175th Street Theatre on Broadway (1930, Lamb, seating 3560), and New Jersey by the Jersey Theatre in Jersey City (Rapp and Rapp, seating 3300). The style of the Kings Theatre and the Jersey Theatre was French, of the 175th Street Theatre Oriental, of the Valencia Theatre Spanish, and of the Paradise Theatre Italian (its sources included Michelangelo's tombs for the Medici). There were various reasons for the explosion of exotic designs. The architectural settings of the theaters unquestionably added to the fantasy of moviegoing. The theater owner A. J. Balaban, who formed the firm of Balaban and Katz in Chicago and later operated the Roxy Theater, spoke of bringing the fabulous sights of the world to the masses. Marcus Loew once remarked: "We sell tickets to theaters, not movies." Moreover movie palaces flourished at a time when historically derived styles were generally accepted, before eclecticism gave way to modernism.

During the Depression the building of large movie palaces ceased, and architects of smaller theaters turned from the extravagance of the 1920s to the abstract, streamlined styles of the 1930s. Eberson produced a series of small, modernistic theaters, including the Lane Theatre in Staten Island (1938, seating six hundred). With the advent of television after the Second World War movie theaters no longer dominated urban entertainment. Enormous movie palaces seating thousands could no longer function economically, and gradually fell victim to conversion and demolition.

Carrie Balaban: *Continuous Performance* (New York: G. P. Putnam's Sons, 1942)

Ben M. Hall: *The Best Remaining Seats: The Story of the Golden Age of the Movie Palace* (New York: Clarkson N. Potter, 1961)

David Naylor: *American Picture Palaces: The Architecture of Fantasy* (New York: Van Nostrand Reinhold, 1981)

David Naylor: *Great American Movie Theaters* (Washington: Preservation Press, 1987)

See also THEATER ARCHITECTURE.

Moving Day. The English custom of celebrating May Day led to the practice of signing leases on 1 May in New York City. From the nineteenth century a chronic housing shortage and high rents led tenants in the city to move frequently in the hope of improving their situation; all trade ceased that day because the streets were so heavily filled with traffic. After the economic depression of 1873 ended, more housing was built and tenants gradually moved less often. Commercial leases are still effective on 1 May or (in keeping with the English tradition of paying land rents at Michaelmas) 1 October.

Alana J. Erickson

Moynihan, Daniel P(atrick) (*b* Tulsa, Okla., 16 March 1927). Senator, educator, and diplomat. He grew up in Hell's Kitchen, attended Tufts University (BA 1948, MA 1949, PhD 1961), and in 1965 was an unsuccessful candidate for the presidency of the City Council of New York City. He held various positions under Presidents John F. Kennedy, Lyndon B. Johnson, Richard M. Nixon, and Gerald R. Ford, including those of ambassador to India (1973–75) and ambassador to the United Nations (1975–76); he also taught at Harvard University (1966–73). As the Democratic nominee for the U.S. Senate in New York in 1976 he defeated Senator James L. Buckley. Reelected in 1982 and 1988, he became chairman of the Senate Committee on Finance in 1993. His many books on politics, ethnicity, race relations, and poverty include *Beyond the Melting Pot: The Negroes, Puerto Ricans, Jews, Italians and Irish of New York City* (with Nathan Glazer, 1963) and *The Politics of a Guaranteed Income* (1973).

Douglas E. Schoen: *Pat: A Biography of Daniel Patrick Moynihan* (New York: Harper and Row, 1979)

Lee R. Hiltzik

Mozart Hall. Political organization formed in 1858 by Fernando Wood after his expulsion from Tammany Hall, named for a building at the corner of Bleecker Street and Broadway in Greenwich Village. A force in city politics throughout the 1860s, the organization provided Wood with the popular support he needed to do battle with Tammany Hall. It was intended by him to be the true representative of the Democratic Party and of Irish and German immigrants. The most notable achievement of the organization was to secure school wards for Germans. More closely allied with Tammany Hall after the Civil War, Mozart Hall lost much of its power and disbanded in 1867.

James Bradley

Ms. Semimonthly magazine. Launched by the publisher Patricia Carbine and the founding editor Gloria Steinem at the height of the feminist movement in 1972, it began as a monthly publication that covered previously undiscussed topics such as the domestic battering of women and alternatives to mastectomy, encouraged untraditional advertisements aimed at female readers, and broke with a long-standing policy among women's magazines by making relatively few references to its advertisers in its editorial pages. *Ms.* was sold to an Australian publisher in November 1987, which sold it in turn to Lang Communications in October 1989. In the early 1990s the magazine had a circulation of 100,000 and carried no advertising.

Laura Gwinn

MTA. See METROPOLITAN TRANSPORTATION AUTHORITY.

MTV [Music Television]. A cable television service based in New York City that broadcasts music videos twenty-four hours a day. It was conceived by John Lack, an executive at Warner Amex Satellite Entertainment Company, and began showing programs on 1 August 1981. The service quickly won the support of record companies, who saw it as a vehicle for promoting their artists, and of corporate sponsors eager to reach its audience of fifteen- to twenty-five-year-olds. It claimed fifteen million subscribers by the end of its first year in operation. In 1985 the service was taken over by Viacom International, a media conglomerate that expanded it to Europe, Australia, Latin America, the Middle East, Asia, and Japan. By the summer of 1993 it was beaming videos into 210 million households in seventy-one countries. Throughout its history MTV has sidestepped accusations that its programming promotes explicit sex and violence and inhibits musical and ethnic diversity. The offices are at 1515 Broadway in Manhattan.

R. Serge Denisoff: *Inside MTV* (New Brunswick, N.J.: Transaction, 1988)

Mark Landler and Geoffrey Smith: "The MTV Tycoon," *Business Week*, 21 Sept 1992

Robert Sanger Steel

muckraking. A term coined by Theodore Roosevelt in 1906 to describe journalism that exposes corruption, exploitation, and health hazards; he likened its practitioners to the nameless character in John Bunyan's *The Pilgrim's Progress* who stared only at the muck and missed the sky above. The style of journalism to which he referred began about the turn of the century, when idealistic young writers from small cities and towns moved to New York City to build their careers. They made the large, complex city the subject of many exposés in such mass-circulation magazines as *McClure's*, *Everybody's*, *Ladies Home Journal*, *Hampton's*, *Collier's*, and *Cosmopolitan*. In January 1903 an editorial in *McClure's* signaled the beginning of a journalistic movement that aspired toward social criticism, and the same issue contained installments of stories by Lincoln Steffens, Ida M. Tarbell ("History of the Standard Oil Company"), and Ray Stannard Baker ("Right to Work"). Corruption was exposed in Tammany Hall in Steffens's series "The Shame of the Cities" (1902–3) and at the New York Life Insurance Company and the Equitable Life Assurance Society in Thomas Lawson's "Frenzied Finance" (1904). George Kibbe Turner's "Daughters of the Poor" (1909) focused on the "white slave" trade, the practice of forcing immigrant girls into prostitution. During the Progressive era the muckrakers were distinguished by their number and the quality and extent of their research.

Louis Filler: *The Muckrakers* (University Park: Pennsylvania State University Press, 1976)

Robert Stinson

Mudge Rose Guthrie Alexander and Ferdon. Law firm. Its forerunner was opened on Wall Street by Simon Hunt Sterne in 1869. During its first fifty years in operation the firm represented the Bank of Manhattan Company, Chase National Bank, and the New York Counting House. Among its partners was Charles Rushmore, a trial lawyer for whom the mountain in South Dakota was named after he won an investor's suit. The firm survived the Depression largely through the efforts of Alfred Mudge; it was not considered élite again until it merged with the firm of Baldwin Todd in 1955. During the 1960s Richard M. Nixon became a partner and the firm introduced municipal bond offerings under the direction of John N. Mitchell, later President Nixon's attorney general. After settling the claims of the Erie Lackawanna Railroad against Conrail in 1982 the firm doubled in size in the 1980s. About the same time it became instrumental in promoting bonds for city transit and the Jacob K. Javits Convention Center and financing for hospitals and nursing homes. In the mid 1990s Mudge Rose Guthrie Alexander and Ferdon had eight-six partners and 266 associates; it was known as the country's leading defense firm in cases brought under the Racketeer Influenced and Corrupt Organizations (RICO) laws and also represented the city pro bono in negligence suits. The offices are at 180 Maiden Lane.

George J. Lankevich

mugwumps. A term applied to Republicans who in 1884 deserted their party's presidential nominee, James G. Blaine, and supported the Democratic candidate, Grover Cleveland. The term is a corruption of the Algonquin word *maqquomp* (chief). Mugwumps were upper-class men who denounced corrupt political machines and the excesses of corporate monopolies and supported civil service reform and tariff reductions. Prominent mugwumps in New York City included E. L. Godkin, George William Curtis, R. R. Bowker, Richard Watson Gilder, and Albert Shaw. Many mugwumps joined municipal reform movements at the beginning of the twentieth century.

Gerald W. McFarland: *Mugwumps, Morals, and Politics, 1884–1920* (Amherst: University of Massachusetts Press, 1975)

Richard Skolnick

Muhlenberg, William Augustus (*b* Philadelphia, 16 Sept 1796; *d* St. Johnland [now in Kings Park], N.Y., 8 April 1877). Clergyman. He moved to New York City in 1828 and formed the Flushing Institute, an Episcopal boys' preparatory school. In 1846 he became the rector of the Church of the Holy Communion (6th Avenue and 20th Street), where he developed the practice of "Evangelical Catholicism," an attempt to combine, in the Episcopal church, Protestant evangelicalism with traditional Catholic ritual and order. He wrote the Muhlenberg Memorial (1853), which called the Episcopal church to greater evangelical and ecumenical commitment, planned and opened St. Luke's Hospital on 5th Avenue between 54th and 55th streets (1858), and in 1870 organized St. Johnland, a utopian industrial community on Long Island.

Alvin Wilson Skardon: *Church Leader in the Cities: William Augustus Muhlenberg* (Philadelphia: University of Pennsylvania Press, 1971)

Allen C. Guelzo

Mulberry Bend. Former neighborhood in Manhattan, lying near the Five Points along Mulberry Street between Park and Bayard streets. A predominantly Italian area with many wretched tenements and liquor stores, it was known for some of the worst overcrowding in nineteenth-century New York City. In *How the Other Half Lives* (1890) Jacob A. Riis described Mulberry Bend as the most dangerous place in the city. In 1894 Mulberry Bend Park replaced buildings condemned on a parcel bounded by Bayard Street, Mulberry Street, Park Street, and Bexter Street; this was renamed Columbus Park in 1911.

Carol Groneman

Mulberry Street Boys. Name sometimes given to the DEAD RABBITS.

Mullaly, John (*b* Belfast, 1835; *d* New York City, 2 Jan 1915). Reformer. He moved to New York City as a young man and began his career as a correspondent for the *New York Herald.* From 1857 to 1858 he was a secretary to Samuel F. B. Morse. He later became the editor of the Catholic newspaper *Metropolitan Record* (remaining for fourteen years), worked for other newspapers, was the commissioner of health of New York City, and served on the board of tax assessors. In 1881 he formed the New York Park Association, which argued successfully for the creation of parks in what is now the Bronx. The city in 1888 acquired Van Cortlandt, Pelham Bay, Bronx, Crotona, and Claremont parks, as well as four parkways. Mullaly Park, dedicated in 1932, is bounded by Jerome Avenue, McClellan Street, River Avenue, and East 162nd Street in the Bronx. Mullaly wrote *The Milk Trade of New York and Vicinity* (1853) and *The New Parks beyond the Harlem* (1887).

Jonathan Kuhn

Mumford, Lewis (*b* Flushing [now in Queens], 19 Oct 1895; *d* Amenia, N.Y., 26 Jan 1990). Writer and critic. He studied at City College, Columbia University, and the New School and published the book *The Study of Utopias* in 1922. He edited the yearbook *American Caravan* from 1927 to 1936 and was a member of the Board of Higher Education from 1935 to 1937. For more than a decade until the mid 1930s he lived in the model community of Sunnyside Gardens in Queens. Disgusted with the city, he then moved permanently to Amenia. In the article "Call to Arms" in the *New Republic* (May 1938) and the books *Men Must Act* (1939) and *Faith for Living* (1940), he urged the United States to pledge its help to other democracies in repelling attacks by totalitarian powers. From the late 1930s he concentrated on writing a philosophy of civilization culminating in *The Conduct of Life* in 1951. After the Second World War, in which his son was killed, he spoke out against the atomic bomb as a visiting professor at Stanford University, North Carolina State University, and the University of Pennsylvania and gave the Bampton Lectures at Columbia in 1951. For many years he was an architectural critic for the *New Yorker*; his *The City in History* (1961) won the National Book Award. During the 1960s and 1970s Mumford explored the theme of moral renewal in his writings. His autobiographical works include *Findings and Keepings* (1975), *Works and Days* (1978), and *Sketches from Life* (1982).

Donald L. Miller: *Lewis Mumford: A Life* (New York: Weidenfeld and Nicholson, 1989)

James E. Mooney

Jacob A. Riis, Mulberry Bend *(ca 1888–89)*

Municipal Archives. The Municipal Archives of New York City hold valuable records created or received in the course of transacting official city business, with particular emphasis on the city's built environment and criminal justice system. Among the materials held by the archives are plans for the construction and alteration of the Brooklyn Bridge; the original design drawings of Central Park; the papers of Robert Moses, commissioner of the parks department, 1934–60; records of the Manhattan Department of Buildings; assessed valuation ledgers, 1789–1975; district attorneys' files and criminal court records from as early as 1683; mayoral records from 1849 to the present; petitions, minutes, and accounts of the legislative branch from as early as 1625; ledgers of nineteenth-century almshouse and charity hospitals; films and sound recordings from the municipal broadcasting system WNYC; vital records; and manuscript materials and photographs from the local branch of the Federal Writers' Project of the Works Progress Administration. There is also photographic documentation covering the period from about 1900 to about 1950 in collections from the Department of Bridges and Public Works, the Department of Docks and Ferries, the Department of Taxes, the Department of Sanitation, the Law Department, and the offices of the borough presidents of Manhattan, Brooklyn, and Queens. The holdings of the Municipal Archives total ninety thousand cubic feet (2500 cubic meters). A public reference room is at 31 Chambers Street.

Kenneth R. Cobb

Municipal Assistance Corporation [MAC]. A public finance corporation formed by the state legislature in 1975 to resolve the fiscal crisis in New York City. The first chairman of the corporation was Felix G. Rohatyn, who was succeeded in 1993 by Eugene J. Keilin. The corporation monitors the city's finances and borrows money on its behalf; because its bonds are guaranteed by a first lien on tax revenues, its debt is more secure than bonds issued by the city itself and it is able to borrow even when the city is excluded from the municipal capital market. The corporation continued refinancing its securities into the 1990s, but after the city regained access to the capital market its influence diminished.

Martin Shefter: *Political Crisis, Fiscal Crisis: The Collapse and Revival of New York City* (New York: Basic Books, 1985)

Martin Shefter

Municipal Building. Skyscraper at the intersection of Chambers and Centre streets. Its construction followed an architectural competition that the city sponsored in 1907–8 for a large office building to consolidate various agencies. Urged by Mayor George B. McClellan to enter, the firm of McKim, Mead and White won with a proposal for a classically detailed skyscraper, an irony given that Charles Follen McKim disdained high-rise buildings as destroyers of civic beauty. The U-shaped structure was designed by a younger partner, William Mitchell Kendall (1856–1941), and adroitly placed on an irregular site bisected by Chambers Street and criss-crossed by underground transit connections. Completed in 1913, the twenty-five-story block was surmounted by a central "wedding-cake" tower and adorned with Adolf A. Weiman's sculpture *Civic Fame*. In the second-story wedding chapel 13,786 couples were married in 1990.

Municipal Building at Chambers and Centre streets, ca *1914*

Carol Willis

municipal courts. See COURTS, §1.

Municipal Ownership League of Greater New York. Organization formed on 22 December 1904 at a conference of reform groups in Albany, New York, to advocate public, nonprofit operation of gas, electricity, and mass transit. It was part of a nationwide public power movement, spurred by a decade of dissatisfaction with privately owned companies because of the rates they charged and the quality of service they provided. Among those who helped to organize the league were Judge Samuel Seabury, author of a two-hundred-page study of monopoly abuses by the Consolidated Gas Company and the New York Edison Company, and the newspaper publisher William Randolph Hearst, an advocate of municipal ownership since the late 1890s who became chairman of the league in 1905. Other prominent members included reformers like J. G. Phelps Stokes and State Senator John Ford. The league had more than 100,000 members in 1905, when it waged an aggressive campaign to deny reelection to Mayor George B. McClellan, a Democrat backed by Tammany Hall. After an unsuccessful attempt to join forces with the Republican Party the league decided to support its own independent candidate: its nomination was declined by Seabury and then accepted by Hearst at a convention on 12 October 1905, twenty-six days before the election, which Hearst narrowly lost after a vigorous campaign (prompting him to accuse the Democrats of fraud). The league also sponsored public education activities, including a forum in October 1905 at Cooper Union, and supported a well-publicized investigation into the mismanagement of gas utilities serving the city by a committee of the state legislature to which Charles Evans Hughes was counsel. The league changed its name to the Independence League in December 1905, perhaps to attract the support of voters upstate for Hearst's gubernatorial campaign in the following year, when he defeated McClellan for the Democratic nomination and lost the general election to Hughes. After that time it ceased to have a public presence.

Herbert Mitgang: *The Man Who Rode the Tiger: The Life and Times of Judge Samuel Seabury* (Philadelphia: J. B. Lippincott, 1963)

Marjorie Harrison

Munsey, Frank A(ndrew) (*b* Mercer, Maine, 21 Aug 1854; *d* New York City, 22 Dec 1925). Publisher. After arriving in New York City in 1882 he launched the weekly children's magazine *Golden Argosy*, for which he wrote many stories relating the progress of a protagonist from poverty to wealth. Among his later magazines was *Munsey's* (1889), a profitable monthly publication that sold for ten cents a copy and provided funds for other enterprises, including a chain of grocery stores, banks in Baltimore and Washington, and various newspapers. The magazine was one of the first to have a mass circulation and to be driven by advertising; it printed lavishly illustrated articles on art, business, and European royalty as well as sentimental fiction, and avoided the "muckraking" that characterized its competitors. From 1901 to 1925 Munsey bought, merged, sold, and ruined a dozen newspapers, several of which were based in New York City. His more successful acquisitions included the *New York Press* (1912), which he made into an organ of support for Theodore Roosevelt's presidential candidacy, the *Sun* (1916, which absorbed the *New York Press* to obtain a franchise from the Associated Press), the *New York Herald* (1918, later merged with the *Sun*), the Paris edition of the *Herald* (1918), the *Telegram* (1918), the *Globe* (1923, merged with the *Sun*), and the *Evening Mail* (merged with the *Telegram*). In 1924 he attempted to buy the *New York Tribune* in the hope of merging it with the *Herald* but in the end sold the *Herald* to the owner of the *Tribune*, Mrs. Ogden Reid, who effected the same merger herself. During his career Munsey owned eighteen newspapers, including daily publications in Boston, Philadelphia, Baltimore, and Washington. *Munsey's* ceased publication in 1929.

George Britt: *Forty Years, Forty Millions: The Career of Frank A. Munsey* (New York: Farrar and Rinehart, 1935)

Frank Luther Mott: *A History of American Magazines*, vol. 4, *1885–1905* (Cambridge: Harvard University Press, 1957)

Robert Stinson

murals. There were few murals in New York City before the late nineteenth century. A number with themes inspired by the Italian Renaissance were painted by John La Farge, who during the 1880s received mural commissions for the Union League Club House, the Vanderbilt Houses, and the Whitelaw Reid Music Room. His best-known mural was *Ascension of Our Lord* (1889) in the Church of the Ascension. With Edwin Blashfield and Kenyon Cox he formed the National Society of Mural Painters in 1893, which between 1895 and 1902 encouraged a number of muralists; most treated academic themes and were not innovative. Murals were commissioned from Frederick Crowninshield, Will H. Low, George W. Maynard, Frank Fowler, D. Maitland Armstrong, and C. Y. Turner by the Waldorf–Astoria and from Edwin Abbey and Thomas W. Dewing by the Hotel Imperial and the Hotel Manhattan. Ten artists painted murals in the appellate courtroom of the Criminal Courts Building (1899). The Vanderbilts, the Huntingtons, and the Lewisohns were among the few families at the time who com-

Mural designed by the Farm Security Administration to promote the sale of defense bonds, Grand Central Terminal, 1941

missioned murals for their homes. The first two decades of the twentieth century saw more commissions, especially by banks, insurance companies, department stores, and courthouses.

Most private commissions were suspended during the Depression; exceptions included those for Rockefeller Center, where Radio City Music Hall was decorated with modernist murals painted by Stuart Davis and Yasuo Kuniyoshi and with photographic murals by Edward Steichen. In the adjoining RCA Building were photographic murals by Margaret Bourke-White and a fresco in the lobby by Diego Rivera (1931) that incorporated portraits of Lenin, Marx, and other communist leaders (destroyed in 1932 and replaced in 1937 with a mural by José María Sert less distasteful to Rockefeller). Most murals of the time were narrative. The New School for Social Research commissioned works from José Clemente Orozco and Thomas Hart Benton, whose mural *America Today* (1931) was later moved to the Equitable Life Assurance Center (for illustration see BENTON, THOMAS HART).

The success of Rivera, Orozco, and David Siqueiros inspired the federal government to sponsor a mural program in 1933. The Section of Fine Arts of the U.S. Department of the Treasury was responsible for many murals painted in the city, as was the Federal Art Project of the Works Progress Administration, which sponsored more than two hundred murals in the metropolitan area between 1935 and 1943. These agencies provided unprecedented opportunities for artists and drew broad public attention to murals, which for the first time were painted in schools, hospitals, libraries, and prisons. Some works were abstract, but most dealt with general subjects such as the progress of civilization or were tailored to the institutions that made the commissions. Simple styles were favored over the allegorical ones used previously. Among the best-known muralists supported by the Federal Art Project in the city were Davis, Ilya Bolotowsky, James Brooks, Byron Browne, Philip Evergood, Arshile Gorky, Balcomb Greene, Philip Guston, Lee Krasner, Anton Refregier, and Moses Soyer. The Second World War saw the end of the New Deal projects, and eventually some murals painted under its auspices were destroyed. Everett Shinn completed several realist murals for the Oak Room of the Plaza Hotel in 1944, but for the most part private commissions declined.

Interest in large-scale outdoor murals revived during the late 1960s. A mural association called City Walls was formed by professional artists wishing to improve the city's appearance and support artists financially; the first mural painted under its auspices was *East 9th Street Wall* (1967) by Allan d'Arcangelo. Others who received commissions included Jason Crum, Richard Anuszkiewicz, Nassos Daphnis, Tania, Robert Wiegart, and Mel Pekarsky. Another association, City Arts Workshop (1968), organized projects carried out by amateurs and overseen by professional artists. The first mural that it sponsored was *Anti-drug* (1969) by Susan Kiok, followed by *Chinatown Today* (1973) and *Chi Lai Arriba* (1974) by Alan Okada, *Wall of Respect for Women* (1974) by Tomie Arai, and projects in Queens and Manhattan by J. Braun-Reinitz in 1990. *Trompe l'oeil* was made popular by Richard Haas, whose first mural in the city was painted outside a loft on Prince Street in SoHo in 1974; his later work included a series of storefronts along Mulberry Street and murals for Prospect Place in Brooklyn, a substation of Consolidated Edison at Peck Slip, Barney's clothing store, and a number of private residences. Large indoor works also became popular. One of the most striking, Roy Lichtenstein's *Mural with Blue Brushstroke* (1985), was painted five stories high in the lobby of the Equitable Life Assurance Center and is visible from the street.

By the early 1990s City Arts Workshop had sponsored more than 120 public art works. At the same time a number of murals from the 1930s had been restored, including Brooks's *Flight* at the Marine Terminal of La Guardia Airport, a group of paintings at Harlem Hospital, Abraham Champanier's mural for Gouverneur Hospital (one panel is now at the New York Public Library at Lincoln Center), and abstract murals for the radio station WNYC and the Williamsburg Housing Project in Brooklyn.

Pauline King: *American Mural Painting* (Boston: Noyes, Platt, 1902)

Eva Cockcroft, Jim Cockcroft, and John Weber: *Toward a People's Art: The Contemporary Mural Movement* (New York: E. P. Dutton, 1977)

Greta Berman: *The Lost Years: Mural Painting in New York City under the Works Progress Administration's Federal Art Project, 1935–1943* (New York: Garland, 1978)

Grace Glueck: "A Guide to the City's Depression Murals," *New York Times*, 7 Jan 1994, §C, p. 1

Greta Berman

Murder Incorporated. A nickname applied to an organization of criminals based in Brownsville in the 1930s that carried out contract killings for a nationwide organized-crime syndicate. It was directed for the most part by Sicilians and Jews and had ten leaders, including Lucky Luciano (the most powerful), Meyer Lansky, Joe Adonis, and Frank Costello; Louis "Lepke" Buchalter and Albert Anastasia, popularly known as the "lord high executioner," were in charge of operations. Estimates of the number of murders committed by the organization range from four hundred to one thousand. It disbanded in 1940 when a number of lower-level criminals were arrested: Abe "Kid Twist" Reles, a lieutenant in the organization, provided information to the district attorney that led to the prosecution and execution of Buchalter and several other members, but before he was able to testify against Anastasia he fell to his death under mysterious circumstances from the window of the Half Moon Hotel in Coney Island on 12 November 1941.

Burton B. Turkus and Sid Feder: *Murder, Inc.: The*

Story of "The Syndicate" (New York: Farrar, Straus and Young, 1951)

See also Organized crime.

Warren Sloat

Murphy, Arthur H. (*b* New York City, 1868; *d* New York City, 6 Feb 1922). Political leader. Of Irish descent, he attended Ottawa University and in 1893 moved to the Bronx, where he opened a liquor, cigar, and real-estate business. He served on the city's Board of Aldermen from 1903 to 1909, became a member of the general committee of Tammany Hall, and unsuccessfully sought the borough presidency of the Bronx in 1909. When the Bronx became a separate county in 1914 Murphy was elected its first Democratic leader, a position he held until his death. He cooperated closely with the leadership of Tammany Hall in Manhattan and had his own political club in his saloon near Bronx Borough Hall.

Gary Hermalyn and Laura Tosi: *Elected Public Officials of the Bronx since 1898* (New York: Bronx County Historical Society, 1989)

Stephen A. Stertz

Murphy, Charles F(rancis) (*b* New York City, 20 June 1858; *d* New York City, 25 April 1924). Political leader. Born in a tenement on the East Side, he became a horsecar driver and a successful saloon owner and political worker. He was named leader of the Gashouse District in 1892, and in 1897 Mayor Robert A. Van Wyck appointed him dock commissioner (the only salaried municipal position he ever held). Intelligent, taciturn, and somewhat straightlaced, he became the leader of Tammany Hall at a time (1902) when scandals and political defeat had severely damaged its authority. In 1903 he named Representative George B. McClellan Jr. (son of the general) as a mayoral candidate and also recruited to the ticket two prominent reformers, the incumbent comptroller and aldermanic president; the opposition was soundly defeated. In 1905 his organization used fraudulent ballots to block William Randolph Hearst's mayoral candidacy. He placed Mayors William J. Gaynor and John F. Hylan in office, as well as Governors John A. Dix, William Sulzer, and Alfred E. Smith. When Sulzer turned against Tammany Hall, Murphy had him impeached, a mistake that contributed to John Purroy Mitchel's victory in the mayoral election of 1913. Widely regarded as the most effective machine politician in the city's history, Murphy also launched and guided the careers of Senator Robert F. Wagner, Edward J. Flynn, Democratic leader of the Bronx, and the nationally respected probate judge James A. Foley. During his tenure Democratic legislators opposed Prohibition and passed progressive labor laws. Toward the end of his life he exerted considerable influence in national Democratic politics: he hoped to send Smith to the White House but died weeks before the Democratic National Convention met (and deadlocked) at Madison Square Garden. Murphy left an estate valued at more than $2 million, the sources of which remain unclear. For many years he lived at 305 East 17th Street.

Nancy J. Weiss: *Charles Francis Murphy, 1858–1924: Respectability and Responsibility in Tammany Politics* (Northampton, Mass.: Smith College Press, 1968)

Frank Vos

Murray, Arthur [Teichman, Arthur Murray] (*b* New York City, 4 April 1895; *d* Honolulu, 3 March 1991). Dancer and entrepreneur. Brought up in East Harlem, he developed a talent for ballroom dancing while a student at Morris High School. By the early 1920s he offered dance instruction kits by mail order: these contained detailed charts indicating where each dancer's feet should be placed and in which sequence. From the beginning he aimed at a clientele that was socially insecure. His first advertisement was headed "How I Became Popular Overnight" and ran in the magazine *True Story*. He based his business in Atlanta but used a mailing address in New York City to create a cosmopolitan image, and eventually broadened its scope from mail-order instruction to dance studios, which opened in 1928 in New York City and eventually numbered in the hundreds throughout the United States. In 1950–60 he was the host of a "dance party" on television. Sales representatives working for his company were accused in 1960 of using high-pressure tactics to manipulate the lonely and the aged. Murray sold the company in the early 1960s.

Milton Mackaye: "The Wallflower's Friend," *New Yorker*, 6 Jan 1934, pp. 27–30

George A. Thompson, Jr.

Murray, John (*b* Swatara Creek, Penn., 1737; *d* New York City, 11 Oct 1808). Merchant. He moved to New York City in his teens to set up an importing business with his brother, which by the time of the American Revolution owned more ships than any other firm in the colonies. During the British occupation he and other members of the Chamber of Commerce handled the internal affairs of the city, and he was president of the Chamber of Commerce from 1798 to 1806. Murray also directed the Bank of New York and was active in such humanitarian causes as the Free School for Poor Children, the Humane Society, and prison reform. By the end of his life he had a fortune of $500,000 and valuable land in Murray Hill, named for him.

James E. Mooney

Murray, Thomas Edward (*b* Albany, N.Y., 21 Oct 1860; *d* New York City, 21 July 1929). Engineer. After working for power companies in upstate New York he moved to New York City and helped to organize a firm that became the Brooklyn Edison Company, where he was a vice-president until a merger with the New York Edison Company. He later designed power stations throughout the country and set up corporations to manufacture some of the eleven hundred inventions for which he received patents. Murray was inducted into the American Institute of Electrical Engineers and won the gold medal of the American Museum of Safety.

James E. Mooney

Murray Hill (i). Neighborhood on the East Side of Manhattan, bounded to the north by 40th Street, to the east by 3rd Avenue, to the south by 34th Street, and to the west by Madison Avenue. During colonial times the area was known as Inclenberg, after an estate of twenty-five acres (ten hectares) owned by the Quakers Robert and Mary Murray. From the 1830s to the 1890s the tracks of the New York and Harlem Railroad ran along 4th Avenue; a tunnel was dug in the early 1850s to hide the trains from view and to obviate pulling cars uphill. The Common Council ordered the addition of a grassy mall forty feet (twelve meters) wide at the center of 4th Avenue between 34th and 38th streets. The avenue was renamed Park Avenue, and its gracious width and planted mall stimulated development. By the end of the century such prominent families as the Belmonts, the Rhinelanders, the Tiffanys, the Havemeyers, the Phelpses, the Delanos, and the Morgans had brownstone mansions along 5th, Madison, and Park avenues. Many professional, political, and social clubs followed, including the Union League Club at 38 East 37th Street. The picturesque 71st Regiment Armory (1905; Clinton and Russell) on Park Avenue between 33rd and 34th streets was replaced in 1976 by Norman Thomas High School and an office tower at 3 Park Avenue. Murray Hill is the site of many clubs, churches, high-rise apartment buildings, and restaurants. Landmarks include the Pierpont Morgan Library (1906; McKim, Mead and White) and townhouses built in the early twentieth century, among them the De Lamar mansion (Madison and 37th Street), now the Polish consulate.

Tales of Murray Hill (New York: Irving Trust, 1952)

Joyce Gold

Murray Hill (ii). Neighborhood in north central Queens, lying within Flushing near 150th and Murray streets south of Northern Boulevard. It was once owned by M. B. Parsons and M. A. Murray, and much of it was the site of King and Murray's Nursery. After the nursery closed, the area was developed in 1889 as Murray Hill and a railroad station opened in April of the same year. Additional streets were laid out and more than two hundred lots were sold. During the next twenty-five years the sale of lots continued, and the developer built houses according to buyers' specifications.

Vincent Seyfried

Murray Hill Hotel. Hotel on Park Avenue between 40th and 41st streets, completed in 1884 after plans by Stephen Hatch. It stood eight stories tall, including two ornamental towers, and had six hundred guest rooms. In 1893 *King's Handbook of New York City* called the hotel "an establishment of the highest class." Its façade was of brownstone, granite, and red brick, the interior furnished with red and white marble floors, burgundy and gold carmine plush, gilt-framed mirrors, and rococo walls. In its heyday the Murray Hill Hotel was patronized by Mark Twain, Senator George Hearst, Jay Gould, Diamond Jim Brady, and Presidents Grover Cleveland and William McKinley. It did not survive the redesigning of lower Park Avenue into a business district and was demolished in 1945–46 to make way for an office building.

Chad Ludington

Murray's Roman Gardens. Cabaret and hotel at 228–32 West 42nd Street in Manhattan, opened after the remodeling in 1908 of a disused school building. The architect, Henri Erkins, altered the exterior to resemble the Hôtel de Strasbourg in Paris and designed an exotic, mirrored interior. With the onset of Prohibition the building was occupied by Hubert's Flea Circus. In the early 1990s it was a candidate for incorporation into the urban renewal plan for 42nd Street.

Charles R. Bevington: *New York Plaisance: An Illustrated Series of New York Places of Amusement* (New York: New York Plaisance Company, 1908)
Michael Batterberry and Ariane Batterberry: *On the Town in New York, from 1776 to the Present* (New York: Charles Scribner's Sons, 1973)
Rem Koolhaas: *Delirious New York: A Retroactive Manifesto for Manhattan* (New York: Oxford University Press, 1978)
Jill Stone: *Times Square: A Pictorial History* (New York: Collier, 1982)

Val Ginter

Murrow, Edward [Egbert] **R(oscoe)** (*b* Greensboro, N.C., 25 April 1908; *d* Pawling, N.Y., 27 April 1965). Broadcaster. He arrived in New York City in 1930 and worked from 1932 at the Institute of International Education on West 45th Street, where he helped scholars persecuted by the Nazis. In 1935 he joined the Columbia Broadcasting System (CBS) at 485 Madison Avenue, and in 1937 he went to London to take charge of its European bureau. He organized the network's first news team in Europe and during the Second World War became well known for his radio reports, which were broadcast live from London rooftops during German bombing raids. After the war he returned to New York City, where he became a vice-president at CBS in charge of news. Uncomfortable with his role as an executive, he returned to broadcasting in 1947 with the nightly radio series "Edward R. Murrow with the News." At studios above Grand Central Terminal he joined with Fred Friendly as his co-producer in 1951 to begin the television series "See It Now," which set the standards for television documentaries and contributed to the fall of Senator Joseph R. McCarthy. He also appeared on the television series "Person to Person" (1953) and "Small World" (1957, also produced with Friendly), and worked with Friendly on the series "CBS Reports" (1960), with Morrow as the reporter on the classic documentary "Harvest of Shame." Increasingly distressed by the growing commercialism of television, Murrow left CBS in 1961 to become the director of the United States Information Agency, remaining until January 1964. His programs may be viewed at the Museum of Television and Radio.

Edward R. Murrow reporting results of the presidential election of 1948

Erik Barnouw: *A History of Broadcasting in the United States* (New York: Oxford University Press, 1967, 1970)
Fred W. Friendly: *Due to Circumstances beyond Our Control* (New York: Random House, 1967)
A. M. Sperber: *Murrow: His Life and Times* (New York: Bantam, 1987)

A. M. Sperber

Muscular Dystrophy Association. Nonprofit organization formed in 1950 in New York City by a group of parents to advocate research into hereditary muscle-destroying disorders. In the same year its first branch was chartered in Flatbush. On Labor Day of 1966 the association broadcast the first of many annual fund-raising programs on television, from the Americana Hotel on 6th Avenue. In 1986 it was announced that researchers sponsored by the association had identified the gene that when defective causes the most common form of muscular dystrophy, Duchenne dystrophy. In the early 1990s the association sponsored weekly clinics at eight leading hospitals in New York City, at which patients received treatment from hospital staff; a coordinator from the association oversaw these services and in most cases also arranged for payment. The association continued to be funded almost entirely by private contributions and worked to cure forty neuromuscular diseases, including nine kinds of muscular dystrophy. The headquarters were moved in January 1991 from 810 7th Avenue in Manhattan to Tucson, Arizona; at the time there were 160 chapters nationwide.

Sandra Opdycke

Museo del Barrio. Museum at 1230 5th Avenue in Manhattan, between 104th and 105th streets. Founded in 1969 in a classroom in East Harlem, it is dedicated to preserving and documenting the art of Puerto Rico and Latin America. The museum maintains a permanent collection of paintings, sculptures, photographs, and other objects ranging from pre-Columbian times to the present, and has a large number of folk materials, including an important group of *santos de palo* (carved and painted wooden figures of saints). The exhibition program emphasizes the work of contemporary Puerto Rican and Latin American artists, especially those working locally, as well as the folk heritage, history, and community life of the people of El Barrio.

Carol V. Wright

Museum of Modern Art. Museum at 11 West 53rd Street in Manhattan, founded in 1929 by Abby Aldrich Rockefeller, Mary Quinn Sullivan, and Lillie P. Bliss. The first

Sculpture garden at the Museum of Modern Art, 1994

exhibition, "Cézanne, Gauguin, Seurat and van Gogh," opened in the Heckscher Building at 730 5th Avenue on 7 November. Under its first director, Alfred H. Barr Jr., the museum devoted itself to presenting all the visual arts, a notion considered radical at the time. In 1932 the exhibition "Modern Architecture: International Exhibition," directed by Philip Johnson, introduced the International style of architecture to the American public. In the same year the museum began circulating exhibitions to other American institutions and moved to a townhouse at its current address leased from John D. Rockefeller Jr. A bequest from Bliss in 1934 formed the core of the permanent collection. The museum outgrew its new quarters by 1937 and in 1939 dedicated a new building on the same site designed by Philip L. Goodwin and Edward Durell Stone. Under its second director, René d'Harnoncourt, it expanded its exhibition program in the 1950s, and the curator William Rubin placed a major emphasis on abstract expressionism. Later additions to the building included the Abby Aldrich Rockefeller Sculpture Garden in 1953 (designed by Johnson), a lobby, two wings, and an enlarged sculpture garden in 1964 (also by Johnson), and a garden hall and galleries that effectively doubled the size of the museum in 1984 (designed by Cesar Pelli). Richard E. Oldenburg became the director in 1972 and organized important exhibitions on primitivism (1984), Cézanne (1988), Picasso and Braque (1992), and Matisse (1992).

The permanent collection of the museum contains more than 100,000 paintings, sculptures, drawings, prints, and photographs from the post-impressionist period and later, and is the most comprehensive collection of modern art in the world. The film division holds all the surviving original negatives of the Biograph Company and the Edison Company, as well as works by a wide range of directors including Louis Lumière, Edwin S. Porter, D. W. Griffith, Hans Richter, and Sergei Eisenstein, and sponsors regular screenings at the Roy Titus Theatre. There is also an active publications program.

The Museum of Modern Art, New York: The History and the Collection (New York: Harry N. Abrams / Museum of Modern Art, 1984)

Sharon Zane

Museum of Natural History. See AMERICAN MUSEUM OF NATURAL HISTORY.

Museum of Television and Radio. Museum opened in 1975 as the Museum of Broadcasting by William S. Paley, founder and chairman of the Columbia Broadcasting System, to collect and preserve radio and television programs and make them available to the public. Its collection covers more than seventy years of broadcast history and has more than forty thousand programs, including news, public affairs, documentary, performing arts, children's, sports, comedy, and dramatic programming, as well as advertising. Exhibitions and seminars highlighting the museum's extensive collection are presented annually. In 1991 the museum took its current name and moved into a new building at 23 West 52nd Street.

Laura Gwinn

Museum of the American Indian. Museum at Audubon Terrace in Manhattan, founded in 1916 by George Gustav Heye (1874–1957), the son of an oil baron who became interested in American Indian culture while working as an engineer in Arizona. The museum opened in 1922 and grew quickly. It eventually came to include nearly a million items, including horn, wood, and stone carvings of Northwest Coast Indians, Kachina dance masks and dolls, rare Caribbean archaeological objects, textiles from Peru and Mexico, Southwestern basketry, gold work from Colombia, Mexico, and Peru, and such memorabilia as Sitting Bull's drum and Geronimo's hat. Severe overcrowding and declining attendance prompted the museum in the 1980s to consider moving, and an agreement was reached in 1990 with the Smithsonian Institution, which stipulated that the building at Audubon Terrace would close and that some of the museum's holdings would remain in New York City (as required by Heye's will). In October 1994 the George Gustav Heye Center of the National Museum of the American Indian opened in the building formerly known as the U.S. Custom House. At the time most of the holdings of the museum were to move to Washington, to become part of the National Museum of the American Indian (scheduled to open about the year 2001). The museum also maintains two facilities in the Bronx: a research center in Pelham Bay and a library attached to the Huntington Free Library in Westchester Square.

Kevin Wallace: "Slim-Shin's Monument," *New Yorker*, 19 Nov 1960, p. 104

Carol V. Wright

Museum of the City of New York. Museum incorporated on 21 July 1923 to preserve the history of New York City, inspired by the Carnavalet in Paris and by city museums in London, Berlin, and Hamburg. At first confined to cramped quarters in Gracie Mansion, it mounted an exhibition at the Fine Arts Building on West 57th Street called "Old New York" (1926), characterized in the annual report of 1927 as an effort to describe the city's development in an arresting manner and "awaken in the schoolboy and immigrant an understanding and pride in his citizenship." The exhibition was so successful that supporters of the museum began an effort to find new, more spacious quarters. A site along 5th Avenue was donated by the city and funds for a new building were raised by public subscription. The trustees' original plans were drastically reduced after the stock market crash of 1929. A building designed in the Georgian colonial style by Joseph H. Freedlander was dedicated on 11 January 1932. In the decades after the dedication of the new building several large collections were added, including the J. Clarence Davies Collection of more than fifteen thousand paintings, prints, and maps, the photographic collections of Percy Byron, Jacob A. Riis, and Berenice Abbott, the Harry T. Peters Collection of more than three thousand prints by Currier and Ives, and furnishings for period rooms donated by the Rockefeller family. Many costumes, theater pieces, and decorative objects were also acquired, and the museum became the first in the nation to set up a curatorial department for toys. The museum has one of the world's finest collections of objects relating to theater in the city; its holdings are strongest in objects from the nineteenth century and the early twentieth. A plan to merge the museum with the New-York Historical Society was abandoned in 1992.

Once upon a City: New York from 1890 to 1910 (New York: Macmillan, 1958)

Rick Beard

museums. The number, quality, and variety of its museums has helped to identify New York City as the cultural capital of the United States. The first nonprofit educational museum in the city was the short-lived Tammany Museum, formed in 1790 to collect Americana including Indian artifacts for the Society of St. Tammany, the city's first cultural organization. Gardiner Baker (*d* 1798), a collector of zoological specimens, mechanical devices, and books, became the keeper of the museum with the support of John Pintard, a merchant, philanthropist, and scholar. Exhibitions were held initially in the building on Wall Street formerly occupied by the federal government. The museum was later renamed the American Museum and expanded its collections to include a live mountain lion, a preserved orangutan fetus, copper engravings, and a model of a Scottish threshing and winnowing machine. After abandoning its scholarly emphasis it was turned over by the society to Baker to run as a private profit-making venture.

Art academies often housed collections (mostly plaster copies of classical sculptures) and mounted exhibitions of members' work. One of the first was the American Academy of the Fine Arts (1802); this was overshadowed from 1826 by the National Academy of Design, which continued to sponsor exhibitions into the 1990s. Under the direction of Pintard the New-York Historical Society was chartered in 1804 as a library of national and local history and a meeting place for prominent men. Interest mounted to assemble a permanent collection devoted to science, leading to the formation of the Lyceum of Natural History in 1817 (destroyed by fire some years later). Small collections were assembled by individuals, cultural clubs, and literary and scientific societies.

In addition to public galleries before the Civil War the city had several "dime" museums, which were dedicated to entertainment and showed curiosities for a fee. The best-known in the city was Barnum's American Museum, opened by P. T. Barnum with the collections of failed ventures that he bought in 1841. It offered curiosities of both art and nature, such as fleas, jugglers, dioramas, the spurious "Feejee mermaid," and Charles Stratton, who stood twenty-five inches (sixty-three centimeters) tall and was

American Museum at City Hall Park, 1825

Museums of New York City

Abigail Adams Smith Museum (1939), 421 East 61st Street, Manhattan (historical)
African–American Institute (1953), 833 United Nations Plaza, Manhattan
Alice Austen House (1966), 2 Hylan Boulevard, Staten Island (historical)
Alternative Museum (1975), 17 White Street, Manhattan
American Academy and Institute of Arts and Letters (1904), Audubon Terrace, Broadway at 155th Street, Manhattan (historical)
American Craft Museum (1956), 40 West 53rd Street, Manhattan
American Irish Historical Society (1897), 991 5th Avenue, Manhattan (historical)
American Museum of Immigration (1972), Statue of Liberty National Monument, Liberty Island, Manhattan (historical)
American Museum of Natural History (1869), Central Park West at 79th Street, Manhattan (historical, scientific)
American Museum of the Moving Image (1988), Astoria Studios, 36-01 35th Avenue, Astoria, Queens (historical)
American Numismatic Society (1858), Audubon Terrace, Broadway at 155th Street, Manhattan (historical)
American Society (1965), 680 Park Avenue, Manhattan (historical)
Anthology Film Archives (1970), 32 2nd Avenue, Manhattan
Arnold and Marie Schwartz College of Pharmacy and Health Services (1967), 75 DeKalb Avenue, Brooklyn (historical, scientific)
Asia Society Galleries (1956), 725 Park Avenue, Manhattan (art)
Asian American Arts Centre (1974), 26 Bowery, Manhattan
AT&T InfoQuest Center (1986), 550 Madison Avenue, Manhattan (scientific)
Aunt Len's Doll and Toy Museum (*ca* 1930), 6 Hamilton Terrace, Manhattan (art)
Bartow–Pell Mansion Museum and Gardens (1947), Shore Road, Pelham Bay Park, Bronx (historical)
Baruch College Gallery (1981), 135 East 22nd Street, Manhattan
Bowne House Historical Society (1945), 37-01 Bowne Street, Flushing (historical)
Bronx County Historical Society (1955), 3309 Bainbridge Avenue, Bronx 10467 (historical)
Bronx Museum of the Arts (1971), 1040 Grand Concourse, Bronx
Brooklyn Children's Museum (1988), 145 Brooklyn Avenue, Brooklyn (historical, scientific)
Brooklyn Historical Society (1863), 128 Pierrepont Street, Brooklyn (historical)
Brooklyn Museum (1823), 200 Eastern Parkway, Brooklyn (art, historical)
Center for African Art (1982), 54 East 68th Street, Manhattan
Children's Museum of Manhattan (1973), 212 West 83rd Street, Manhattan (historical)
China House Gallery of China Institute in America (1966), 125 East 65th Street, Manhattan

(continued)

Museums of New York City *(Continued)*

City Island Museum (1964), 190 Fordham Street, City Island, Bronx (historical)
Cloisters (1938), Fort Tryon Park, Fort Washington Avenue, Manhattan (art)
Con Edison Energy Museum (1979), 145 East 14th Street, Manhattan (scientific)
Conference House Association (1927), 7455 Hylan Boulevard, Staten Island (historical)
Cooper–Hewitt Museum (1897), Smithsonian Institution National Museum of Design, 2 East 91st Street, Manhattan (art, historical)
Dyckman House Museum (1915), 4881 Broadway, Manhattan (historical)
Edward C. Blum Design Laboratory of the Brooklyn Museum (1975), 7th Avenue at 27th Street, Manhattan (historical)
Ellis Island Immigration Museum (1990), Ellis Island, Manhattan (historical)
Federal Hall National Memorial (1955), 26 Wall Street, Manhattan (historical)
Franklin Furnace (1976), 112 Franklin Street, Manhattan (historical)
Fraunces Tavern Museum (1907), 54 Pearl Street, Manhattan (historical)
Frick Collection (1920), 1 East 70th Street, Manhattan (art)
Galleries at FIT (1975), 7th Avenue at 27th Street, Manhattan (historical)
Garibaldi–Meucci Museum (1956), 420 Tompkins Avenue, Staten Island (historical)
General Grant National Memorial [Grant's Tomb] (1897), Riverside Drive and West 122nd Street, Manhattan (historical)
Godwin–Ternbach Museum at Queens College (1981), 65-30 Kissena Boulevard, Flushing, Queens (art)
Gracie Mansion (1927), East End Avenue and 88th Street, Manhattan (historical)
Grand Army Plaza Memorial Arch (1892), Grand Army Plaza, Brooklyn
Grey Art Gallery and Study Center (1958), New York University Art Collection, 33 Washington Place, Manhattan (art)
Guinness Book of World Records Exhibit Hall (1978), 350 5th Avenue, Empire State Building, Manhattan (historical)
Hall of Fame for Great Americans (1900), University Avenue and West 181st Street, Bronx (historical)
Hamilton Grange National Memorial (1924), 287 Convent Avenue, Manhattan (historical)
Harbor Defense Museum of New York City (1980), Fort Hamilton, Brooklyn (historical)
Hayden Planetarium (1935), Central Park West at 81st Street, Manhattan (scientific)
Hispanic Society of America (1904), Broadway between 155th and 156th streets, Manhattan (art, historical)
IBM Gallery of Science and Art (1983), 590 Madison Avenue, Manhattan (art, scientific)
Institute for Contemporary Art: Clocktower Gallery (1973), 108 Leonard Street, Manhattan; P.S. 1 Museum (1976), 46-01 21st Street, Long Island City (art)
International Center of Photography (1974), 1150 5th Avenue, Manhattan (art)
International Theatre Institute of the United States, (1948), 220 West 42nd Street, Suite 1710, Manhattan (historical)
Intrepid Sea, Air, Space Museum (1982), Pier 86, West 46th Street at 12th Avenue, Manhattan (historical)
Isamu Noguchi Garden Museum (1985), 32-37 Vernon Boulevard, Long Island City, Queens (art)
Jacques Marchais Center of Tibetan Art (1945), 338 Lighthouse Avenue, Staten Island (art, historical)
Jamaica Arts Center (1972), 161-04 Jamaica Avenue, Queens
Japan Society Gallery (1907), 333 East 47th Street, Manhattan
Jewish Museum (1904), 1109 5th Avenue, Manhattan (art, historical)
King Manor (1900), 150-03 Jamaica Avenue, Queens (historical)
Kingsborough Historical Society (1972), Kingsborough Community College, 2001 Oriental Boulevard, Brooklyn (historical)
Lladró Museum and Galleries (1988), 43 West 57th Street, Manhattan (art)
Lefferts Homestead (1918), Prospect Park, near Flatbush Avenue and Empire Boulevard, Brooklyn (historical)
Living Memorial to the Holocaust (1994), Museum of Jewish Heritage, Battery Park City, Manhattan (historical)
Lower East Side Tenement Museum (1988), 97 Orchard Street, Manhattan (historical)
Metropolitan Museum of Art (1874), 5th Avenue and 82nd Street, Manhattan (art)
Morris–Jumel Mansion (1904), 1765 Jumel Terrace between 160th and 162nd streets, Manhattan (historical)
Mossman Collection of Locks (1903), 20 West 44th Street, Manhattan (historical)
Museo Del Barrio (1969), 1230 5th Avenue, Manhattan (art, historical)

(continued)

renamed Tom Thumb by Barnum. Such presentations led the public to associate showmanship and theatricality with museums, and the distinction between dime museums and public galleries was sometimes blurred according to directors' tastes. Rigorous standards were upheld by the New York Gallery of Fine Arts, formed in 1844 as a permanent public art gallery around the private collection of Luman Reed. Acquired in 1858 by the New-York Historical Society, the collection was later augmented by such diverse objects as marble bas-relief sculptures from the palace of Sardanapalus at Nineveh (donated by James Lenox), a collection of Egyptian antiquities (donated by Henry Abbott), and John James Audubon's watercolor originals for the engravings used in *Birds of America* (1827–38). The society rivaled some European galleries after Thomas J. Bryan and Louis Durr donated paintings by European masters. In 1846 a permanent art gallery was opened by the Brooklyn Institute (formerly known as the Apprentices' Library). From its inception the Cooper Union for the Advancement of Science and Art, chartered in 1859 to provide free education for workers, included among its facilities a public art gallery free of charge; it opened the Museum for the Arts of Decoration at Astor Place in 1897.

Most of the city's museums were established by industrialists who amassed fortunes in the decades of prosperity after the Civil War. Advances in the natural sciences during the 1860s by such theorists as Charles Darwin, Thomas Huxley, and Charles Lyell inspired Albert Smith Bickmore, a naturalist trained at Harvard, to form the American Museum of Natural History. The museum was conceived as a partnership between the city, which erected the building and supplied funds for maintenance, and the trustees, who supported the collections, staff, and programs. Bickmore and a few associates used their own money to buy the first exhibits, a collection of stuffed birds and mammals owned by the German naturalist Maximillian zu Wed-Neuwiebl and originally housed at the Arsenal in Central Park. The museum opened in 1869 as an institution dedicated to research and public instruction in the natural sciences and ethnology. Collections there and at other natural history museums eventually included big-game trophies and entire families of monkeys, birds, insects, and plants.

In 1870 members of the Union League Club including John Jay (grandson of the chief justice) and William Cullen Bryant proposed a public art museum to promote education and social and moral betterment. To these ends a museum was incorporated by the state legislature, and the city raised $500,000 toward construction costs. The first collection consisted of American and European paintings formerly owned by William T. Blodgett, and in 1880 the museum opened its first building

Museums of New York City *(Continued)*

Museum of African American History and Arts, 352 West 71st Street, Manhattan (art, historical)
Museum of American Folk Art (1963), 2 Lincoln Square, Manhattan (art)
Museum of the American Indian (1916), George Gustav Heye Center, U.S. Custom House, Manhattan (historical)
Museum of the American Piano (1984), 211 West 58th Street, Manhattan (historical)
Museum of the City of New York (1923), 5th Avenue at 103rd Street, Manhattan (art, historical)
Museum of Colored Glass and Light (1975), 72 Wooster Street, Manhattan (art)
Museum of Holography (1976), 11 Mercer Street, Manhattan (art, scientific)
Museum of Migrating People (1974), 750 Baychester Avenue, Co-op City, Bronx (historical)
Museum of Modern Art (1929), 11 West 53rd Street, Manhattan (art)
Museum of Television and Radio (1975), 25 West 52nd Street, Manhattan (historical)
National Academy of Design (1982), 1083 5th Avenue, Manhattan
New Museum of Contemporary Art (1977), 583 Broadway, Manhattan
New York Aquarium (1896), Surf Avenue and West 8th Street, Brooklyn (scientific)
New York City Fire Museum (1987), 278 Spring Street, Manhattan (historical)
New York City Police Museum (1929), 235 East 20th Street, Manhattan (historical)
New York Genealogical and Biographical Society (1869), 122 East 58th Street, Manhattan (historical)
New York Hall of Science (1964), 47-01 111th Street, Corona, Queens (scientific)
New-York Historical Society (1804), 170 Central Park West, Manhattan (art, historical)
New York Public Library (1911), 5th Avenue at 42nd Street, Manhattan
New York Public Library for the Performing Arts (1965), Lincoln Center Plaza North, Manhattan (historical)
New York Transit Museum (1976), beneath Boerum Place and Schermerhorn Street, Brooklyn Heights (historical)
Nicholas Roerich Museum (1958), 319 West 107th Street, Manhattan (art)
North Wind Undersea Institute (1978), 610 City Island Avenue, Bronx (scientific)
Old Merchant's House (1936), 29 East 4th Street, Manhattan (historical)
Pierpont Morgan Library (1924), 29 East 36th Street, Manhattan
Prospect Park Boathouse (1905), Prospect Park, near Lincoln Road Entrance, Brooklyn
Queens County Farm Museum (1975), 73-50 Little Neck Parkway, Floral Park, Queens (historical)
Queens Historical Society (1968), 143-35 37th Avenue, Flushing, Queens (historical)
Queens Museum of Art (1972), Flushing Meadows–Corona Park, Queens
Rotunda Gallery (1981), 1 Pierre Plaza at Clinton Street, Brooklyn
Romanian Library (1971), 200 East 38th Street, Manhattan
Schomburg Center for Research in Black Culture (1925), 515 Lenox Avenue, Manhattan (art, historical)
Snug Harbor Cultural Center (1976), 1000 Richmond Terrace, Staten Island (art)
Solomon R. Guggenheim Museum (1937), 1071 5th Avenue, Manhattan (art)
Society of Illustrators Museum of American Illustration (1981), 128 East 63rd Street, Manhattan (art, historical)
South Street Seaport Museum (1967), 207 Front Street, Manhattan (historical)
Staten Island Children's Museum (1974), 1000 Richmond Terrace, Staten Island
Staten Island Institute of Arts and Sciences (1881), 75 Stuyvesant Place, Staten Island
Studio Museum in Harlem (1967), 144 West 125th Street, Manhattan (art)
Theodore Roosevelt Birthplace National Historic Site (1923), 28 East 20th Street, Manhattan (historical)
Trinity Museum (1982), Trinity Church, Broadway at Wall Street, Manhattan (historical)
Ukrainian Museum (1976), 203 2nd Avenue, Manhattan (historical)
Van Cortlandt House (1896), Van Cortlandt Park, Broadway at 246th Street, Bronx (historical)
Visual Arts Museum (1965), School of Visual Arts, 209 East 23rd Street, Manhattan
Wave Hill (1965), 675 West 252nd Street, Bronx
Whitney Museum of American Art (1931), 945 Madison Avenue, Manhattan (art)

Source: Fred W. McDarrah: *Museums in New York: A Descriptive Reference Guide to Seventy-nine Fine Arts Museums, Local History Museums, Specialized Museums, Natural History and Science Museums, Libraries, Botanical and Zoological Parks, Commercial Collections, and Historical Houses and Mansions Open to the Public within the Five Boroughs of New York City* (New York: E. P. Dutton, 1967; 5th edn St. Martin's, 1990)

along 5th Avenue in Central Park. With the Museum of Fine Arts in Boston and the Corcoran Gallery in Washington the museum helped to make social aims a central concern of museum planning.

During the late nineteenth century the Brooklyn Institute became the Brooklyn Institute of Arts and Sciences, which encouraged research and public education and had a museum of art, natural history, and ethnology dedicated to assimilating immigrants. Its building, designed by in a Roman Revival style by McKim, Mead and White, was erected between 1892 and 1925. Gradually the art collections took precedence over the scientific ones, and the museum, eventually named the Brooklyn Museum, was known for its collections of Egyptian, African, pre-Columbian, American, and decorative art. One of its branches was the Brooklyn Children's Museum, the first of its kind in the world. Opened in 1899 in several Victorian mansions, it mounted displays with materials to touch, arranged to emphasize relationships and accompanied by brief labels in large, readable type.

A number of wealthy patrons left large bequests during the first decades of the twentieth century to form and maintain museums. In 1901 the railroad magnate Jacob S. Rogers left $5 million to the Metropolitan Museum of Art, making it the wealthiest museum in the world. The collections of Benjamin Altman and J. P. Morgan, donated in 1913 and 1917, established it as a museum of international importance, with holdings eventually including musical instruments, arms and armor, primitive art, and art from Asia, the Middle East, Europe, and the United States. In 1926 part of the medieval collection was installed at the Cloisters, a section of a Romanesque Benedictine monastery from southern France bought by John D. Rockefeller and reconstructed in Fort Tryon Park. The Hispanic Society of America, founded in 1904 by Archer Milton Huntington (1870–1955), established a free public museum and library for the study of Hispanic culture, one of the first institutions devoted to ethnic studies. This was soon followed by the Museum of the American Indian, which opened in 1916 (its holdings eventually taken over by the Smithsonian Institution). A number of collections held in private residences became public museums, among them the Frick Collection of European paintings and sculptures, maintained in the former residence of the industrialist Henry Clay Frick on 5th Avenue (designed by Thomas Hastings), and the Pierpont Morgan Library, holding books and art formerly owned by J. Pierpont Morgan and housed in his Renaissance mansion on East 36th Street (1906, McKim, Mead and White). The Museum of the City of New York, opened in Gracie Mansion in 1923 to preserve local history, amassed fine examples of clipper ships, colonial portraits, furniture, toys, costumes, and fire engines; in 1932 it moved to 5th Avenue at 103rd Street. The Museum of Natural History added astronomy to its areas of study in 1937 with the gift of the Hayden Planetarium from the philanthropist Charles Hayden.

During the 1920s several collectors took measures to preserve and promote the work of modern artists. The Whitney Studio was founded to display the work of young artists by the sculptor Gertrude Vanderbilt Whitney, daughter of the railroad magnate Cornelius Whitney. She later made her collection the basis of the Whitney Museum of American Art (1930). The Museum of Modern Art was set up in 1929 to collect not only paintings and sculptures but also drawings, prints, photographs, films, stage designs, furniture, and work in architecture and commercial design. Its initial holdings were donated by Lillie P. Bliss. Abby Aldrich Rockefeller later donated her collection and with Mrs. Simon R. Guggenheim provided generous funds to buy avant-garde works by twentieth-century artists. The holdings of Solomon R. Guggenheim evolved into the Solomon R. Guggenheim Museum of Non-objective Painting (1939), which occupied rented quarters before moving to a building on 5th Avenue between 88th and 89th streets designed by Frank Lloyd Wright. The collections of the Museum for the Arts of Decoration were taken over by the Smithsonian Institution during the 1960s and installed in a mansion on 5th Avenue (formerly owned by Andrew Carnegie) that became known as the Cooper–Hewitt Museum of Decorative Art and Design. Several museums opened during the mid twentieth century, among them the International Center of Photography, the Museum of Contemporary Crafts, the Museum of American Folk Art, and the Museum of Broadcasting (now the Museum of Television and Radio). Smaller institutions devoted to modern art often lacked permanent collections but offered educational programs to the public and opportunities for lesser-known artists to exhibit their work. The Bronx Museum of the Arts was formed in 1972 by the Bronx Council on the Arts to display traveling exhibitions from other museums and the work of local artists. Other popular exhibition spaces included Public School 1 in Long Island City and the New Museum of Contemporary Art, Artists Space, and Franklin Furnace in lower Manhattan.

Other museums were dedicated during the same years to house collections of works by national, ethnic, and cultural groups, notably the Asia Society, the Japan Society Gallery, the Jewish Museum, the Ukrainian Museum, the Museo Del Barrio, the Studio Museum in Harlem, and the Jacques Marchais Center of Tibetan Art. Historic houses throughout the city were also preserved, often through local efforts. Among those restored in Manhattan were the Abigail Adams Smith Museum, the Morris–Jumel Mansion, and the William Dyckman, Frederick Van Cortlandt, and Seabury Tredwell (or Old Merchant's) houses; more survived in the outer boroughs, including the Lefferts Homestead (now in Prospect Park), the Valentine–Varian farmhouse, which became the headquarters of the Museum of Bronx History, and Poe Cottage in the Bronx, and the Queens Quaker Meeting House, a rare example of seventeenth-century architecture and one of the country's oldest places of worship. Work also began on the restoration of forty buildings from Richmondtown, a project sponsored locally and directed by the Staten Island Historical Society to trace the development of a village from the seventeenth century to the nineteenth.

By the mid 1990s some institutions sought new sources of funds and explored new systems of management. The Brooklyn Children's Museum became independent of the Brooklyn Museum in 1979 and provided a model for institutions in Manhattan and Staten Island. Corporations and the government accounted for an increasing portion of museums' funding. The Museum of Modern Art expanded its holdings through donations by collectors as well as artists, architects, and gallery owners. To accommodate the additions it renovated its existing galleries in the first six stories of a residential tower built by a private developer and in 1984 opened its west wing (designed by Cesar Pelli). As natural habitats were destroyed and many species faced extinction, natural history museums reevaluated their practices and ceased to harvest specimens for display. The American Museum of Natural History adopted many new exhibition formats, among them habitat groups, dioramas, and grand-scale Naturemax screens. It also opened a research laboratory and school for advanced study and expanded its programs in publications and field exploration.

Nathaniel Burt: *Palaces for the People: A Social History of the American Art Museum* (Boston: Little, Brown, 1977)

Joel J. Orosz: *Curators and Culture: The Museum Movement in America, 1740–1870* (Tuscaloosa: University of Alabama Press, 1990)

Ella M. Foshay

music. For information on music in New York City see the entries Bands, Choruses, Classical music, Folk music, Gospel music, Jazz, Opera, Ragtime, Rap, and Rock, as well as entries on individual figures and institutions.

musical instruments. The manufacture of lutes and violins in New York City was reported as early as the 1690s. During the eighteenth century the workshops were concentrated around South Street, and most instrument makers were immigrants who com-

Advertisement for Firth, Hall and Pond, Pianoforte and Music Warehouse

bined the manufacture of new instruments with the repair of older ones and the sale of imported instruments and music. After 1750 artisans such as Christian Claus (1789–99), Thomas Dodds (1785–99), and Archibald Whaites (1793–1816) frequently placed newspaper advertisements proclaiming their ability to make as many as a dozen kinds of instrument. On its introduction into the city in the 1770s the piano replaced the harpsichord as the standard keyboard instrument: although only two of the twenty-one instrument makers active in the city in the 1790s made pianos (most made wind and stringed instruments), within a decade an enormous demand for pianos led to a rapid expansion of the business. John Gelb, an organ builder from 1798, formed a business with his brothers Adam and William that made pianos until 1872. About 1800 many instrument makers and dealers moved to the fashionable area around the new City Hall, and by the 1820s instrument making was the city's fifth-largest industry, after shipbuilding, sugar refining, metalworking, and furniture making. At the same time the origin of instrument makers in the city changed from predominantly British in the 1820s to German and central European in the 1830s and 1840s. Most German-speaking workers entered the trade as journeymen but many later became shop supervisors, and some opened shops of their own. A census in 1855 found that 553 of the 836 instrument makers living in New York City were immigrants, and of these 58 percent were German. Some of the leading piano-making firms of the period included Dubois and Stodart (founded 1819), Bacon (1841), Hardman (1842), Haines

(1851), Weber (1852), Mathusek (1857), Steck (1857), Behning (1861), Sohmer (1872), and Behr (1881). Other firms made violins (August and George Gemunder), flutes (E. Riley, A. G. Badger), woodwinds (Firth and Pond, 1848–65), and brass instruments (Schreiber Cornet Company, Stratton).

As pianists began to demand greater volume and tone from their instruments, piano makers experimented with various methods of reinforcing their pianos. The firm of Steinway and Sons, formed in 1853 by Heinrich E. Steinweg, patented a cast-iron piano frame in the 1850s that won a gold medal at the World's Fair in London in 1862. Steinway's success directed attention to the innovations of other artisans in New York City and led to the expansion of instrument shops, which required larger spaces and more craftsmen to manufacture pianos with cast-iron frames. The district where retail musical instrument shops were centered moved progressively northward, extending to Cooper Square in the 1850s and to 14th Street in the 1870s and 1880s, and the expansion of the trade in the city continued unabated until the 1890s. According to the federal census of 1890 New York City had 131 instrument firms employing 5958 craftsmen, who produced $12,824,451 worth of instruments.

In the late 1890s the city's instrument business suffered from a succession of technological and economic changes, despite which it expanded as far north as West 57th Street by about 1900. It initially benefited from the introduction of automated player pianos, but the benefit was soon offset by the increased popularity of phonographs and radios. Instrument making declined throughout the Depression, and during the Second World War many of the larger piano factories were requisitioned for the production of war materials (very few reopened). When Sohmer left the city in the early 1980s Steinway became the only remaining piano maker. In the mid 1990s a few small ateliers in the city made wind, string, and percussion instruments of high quality. Among the best-known were the Français Gael Violin Workshop, Matt Umanov Guitars, and the stringed instruments makers Rutig and Oster.

Nancy Groce: *Urban Craftsmen: Musical Instrument Makers in New York City* (New York: Pendragon, 1991)

Nancy Groce

Members of the chorus in The Black Crook *(1866) preparing to "fly" on wires across the stage*

musical theater. The first known musical theater performances in New York City were ballad operas such as *The Beggar's Opera* (London, 1728) by John Gay and Johann Pepush, presented by the Hallam Company at the New Theatre in Nassau Street in 1753. Touring companies avoided the city during the American Revolution but returned afterward, and in 1796 the Old American Company performed the first important American musical comedy, *The Archers*, with libretto by William Dunlap and music by Benjamin Carr. The musical stage was dominated by English and European works well into the nineteenth century, but the number of American works grew by the 1840s. *A Glance at New York* (1848) depicted neighborhoods in New York City and character types associated with them, including the well-known "Mose the Bowery B'hoy." Burlesques on American themes became popular after John Brougham presented *Pocahontas; or, the Gentle Savage* (1855). Minstrel companies made regular visits by the 1850s, and several minstrel houses opened in the city. The number of musical productions declined during the Civil War but increased rapidly in the years after. *The Black Crook* (1866) featured melodrama, spectacle, music, and ballet dancers clad in flesh-colored tights; it was an enormous success and inspired a number of imitations. Other spectacles known as extravaganzas combined elaborate settings with a burlesque of a literary work and were popular among the upper class. One of the best-known was *Evangeline*, which opened in 1874 and toured until the end of the century. By the 1870s New York City was the country's most important center for musical theater. Productions attracted a large number of spectators locally and a growing number from elsewhere, and also toured the country.

After the triumphant première of *HMS Pinafore* by Gilbert and Sullivan in 1879 English comic opera dominated musical theater in the city until the turn of the century. Popular among upper-class audiences, it inspired such works as *Robin Hood* (1891), by the American composer Reginald De Koven. Minstrel shows

West Side Story *at the Winter Garden Theater, 1959*

were favored by immigrants and workers, as was vaudeville, which evolved after Tony Pastor transformed variety shows into family entertainment. At the Theatre Comique, Edward Harrigan and Tony Hart produced musical plays depicting life among Irish, Germans, and blacks in the city. As immigration reached a peak at the turn of the century the number of ethnic theaters increased, especially those for German- and Yiddish-speakers. Ethnic characters also became a mainstay of the English-language musical stage in the Irish musicals of W. J. Scanlan and Chauncey Olcott, the "Fritz" musicals of J. K. Emmet, and the "Dutch" comedy burlesques of Weber and Fields. By the end of the nineteenth century there were a few works by blacks, among them *The Origin of the Cakewalk; or, Clorindy* (1898) by Paul Lawrence Dunbar and Will Marion Cook. *The Passing Show* (1894) was produced by George W. Lederer, who declared it a "review" of the political, social, and theatrical events of the year. Based on the olio section of the minstrel show and on the vaudeville variety show, it was soon widely imitated in shows known as revues, which with comic operas, operettas, and musical comedies dominated musical theater at the turn of the century. The English comic opera *Florodora* (1900), a production in the style of Gilbert and Sullivan, ran for many years. The operettas of Victor Herbert, such as *Babes in Toyland* (1903) and *Naughty Marietta* (1910), were also highly successful. The urban settings and characters of Harrigan and Hart were brought up to date by George M. Cohan in such comedies as *Little Johnny Jones* (1904). In 1907 Florenz Ziegfeld produced the first of his annual *Follies*, a revue known for its comedians, dancers, singers, chorus girls, and elaborate scenery.

About the time of the First World War composers of musical comedies rejected European styles in favor of American ones. Ragtime was incorporated into a few songs on the musical stage and was widely adopted in musical comedy after Irving Berlin composed an entire score of modified ragtime for the revue *Watch Your Step* in 1914. The composer Jerome Kern and the librettist Guy Bolton (later joined by P. G. Wodehouse) experimented with small casts, simple settings, and contemporary characters and situations in musicals at the intimate Princess Theatre. One of their best-known productions was *Very Good Eddie* (1915). More traditional operettas remained among the most popular forms, and a number were written for the American stage by composers trained in Europe, including Rudolf Friml (*Rose-Marie*, 1924) and Sigmund Romberg (*The Student Prince*, 1924). After the success of *Shuffle Along* (1921) by Noble Sissle and Eubie Blake other musicals written and performed by blacks were presented during the early 1920s; they introduced many new dance steps as well as early jazz, which supplanted ragtime. Later in the decade George and Ira Gershwin incorporated jazz-inspired music and satirical lyrics like those of W. S. Gilbert in a series of successful musicals culminating in *Of Thee I Sing* (1931), which won a Pulitzer Prize. Several productions of the songwriters Richard Rodgers and Lorenz Hart were highly successful, including *A Connecticut Yankee* (1927). One of the longest-running productions of the 1920s was *Good News* (1927), a musical by B. G. DeSylva, Lew Brown, and Ray Henderson about college life. Traditional and contemporary styles were blended in *Show Boat* (1927), a musical by Kern and Oscar Hammerstein II about a family of showboat performers from the 1880s to the 1920s.

The number of musicals produced in the city fell drastically after the stock market crashed, and many of the most important figures in musical theater moved to Hollywood to make motion pictures. Broadway nonetheless saw some of its finest productions between 1929 and 1960. Cole Porter wrote insinuating melodies and clever lyrics for such musical comedies as *Fifty Million Frenchmen* (1929) and *Anything Goes* (1934), and a sophisticated style of topical revue was introduced by Arthur Schwartz and Howard Dietz in *The Little Show* (1929) and *The Band Wagon* (1931). Some writers and composers sought to explore the country's growing unrest in their work. *Johnny Johnson*, a musical with a strong antiwar message by Kurt Weill, was produced by the Group Theatre in 1936; *The Cradle Will Rock*, a musical by Marc Blitzstein dealing with conflicts between workers and capitalists, caused controversy in a production by Orson Welles's Mercury Theatre Company in 1938. Social and political themes yielded to escapist ones with the advent of the Second World War. In 1943 Rodgers and Hammerstein produced *Oklahoma!*, a nostalgic operetta

A Chorus Line, *1987*

Herschel Bernardi in Fiddler on the Roof

about the simple life of cowboys and farmers in 1907 in the Oklahoma Territory. It enjoyed unprecedented popularity and was the first work of its kind to include a violent death on stage and a "dream ballet" (choreography by Agnes de Mille) to explain and enhance the dramatic action. Other "musical plays" by Rodgers and Hammerstein included *Carousel* (1945), *South Pacific* (1949), *The King and I* (1951), and *The Sound of Music* (1959).

Although some composers and lyricists sought to imitate Rodgers and Hammerstein, a more traditional style of musical comedy also flourished during the 1940s and early 1950s. Berlin wrote the score for *Annie Get Your Gun* (1946), in which Ethel Merman played the character of Annie Oakley; other popular comedies included Frank Loesser's *Guys and Dolls* (1950), about Broadway gamblers and their girlfriends; *Wonderful Town* (1953), a depiction of life in Greenwich Village during the 1930s by Leonard Bernstein, Betty Comden, and Adolph Green; and *The Pajama Game* (1954) by Richard Adler and Jerry Ross, a story about personal and professional relationships between managers and employees in a pajama factory. In 1956 Alan Jay Lerner and Frederick Loewe adapted George Bernard Shaw's comedy *Pygmalion* into a musical, *My Fair Lady*, that had a record-breaking run. Their show helped to revive interest in operettas set in bygone eras, encouraged adaptations of other successful plays, novels, and motion pictures, and inaugurated the practice of using actors rather than singers for important roles. Musical comedies continued to draw audiences into the mid 1960s, as did operettas, which tended to be more experimental and ambitious. The story of Romeo and Juliet provided the inspiration for the musical *West Side Story* (1957) by the composer Leonard Bernstein, the librettist Arthur Laurents, the lyricist Stephen Sondheim, and the director Jerome Robbins. Jerry Bock and Sheldon Harnick wrote an ironic version of the European operetta in *She Loves Me* (1963) and in 1964 joined with Robbins to create *Fiddler on the Roof*, which soon became one of the country's most popular musicals. New subjects and settings were also used in a number of musical comedies, notably *Gypsy* (1959), a story based on the life of the stripper Gypsy Rose Lee; *How to Succeed in Business without Really Trying* (1961), a satire of the corporate world; *Cabaret* (1966), set in Berlin during the 1930s; and *Hair* (1968), which introduced rock music and nudity to Broadway.

During the early 1970s concern arose about the failure of Broadway to attract new artists and audiences. Revues based on songs by well-known composers and revivals of old productions predominated. Some of the few new works were created by Sondheim, whose innovative shows were often considered controversial: *Company* (1970), *Follies* (1971), *A Little Night Music* (1973), *Pacific Overtures* (1976), *Sweeney Todd* (1979), *Sunday in the Park with George* (1984), *Into the Woods* (1987), and *Passion* (1994). His early collaborations with the director Harold Prince, known as "concept musicals," shaped the work around an idea or visual image rather than a libretto and score. In some musicals that followed this model the directors and choreographers were the primary creative figures: examples include *Pippin* (1972) and *Dancin'* (1978) by Bob Fosse and *A Chorus Line* (1975) and *Dreamgirls* by Michael Bennett. As production costs and ticket prices rose during the 1980s, some writers, performers, and producers preferred to work in the more relaxed environment of Off Broadway, Off Off Broadway, and regional theaters outside the city. The most successful productions were often European or British: *Cats* (1981) and *The Phantom of the Opera* (1989) by Andrew Lloyd Webber played in London before being shown in New York City, and *Les Misérables* (1987) and *Miss Saigon* (1991) were presented by a team of French songwriters. In 1990 Tommy Tune used elements of the concept musical in *Grand Hotel*, his adaptation of a popular motion picture.

By the early 1990s some observers were predicting the demise of musical theater in the city, but as a series of revivals in the following years joined the imports and a few new productions, the Broadway musical stage again prospered.

Cecil Smith and Glenn Litton: *Musical Comedy in America* (New York: Theatre Arts Books, 1950; rev. 1981)

Gerald Bordman: *American Musical Theatre: A Chronicle* (New York: Oxford University Press, 1978; 2nd edn 1992)

Allen Woll: *Black Musical Theatre: From Coontown to Dreamgirls* (Baton Rouge: Louisiana State University Press, 1989)

Margaret M. Knapp

Music Corporation of America. See Mca.

music criticism. Reviews of the first concerts in New York City appeared in such early newspapers as John Peter Zenger's *New-York Weekly Journal* (founded in 1733) and Hugh Gaine's *New-York Mercury* (founded in 1752). Initially most articles about music were unsigned; during the early nineteenth century these ceded to signed, subjective reviews printed by such newspapers as the *Evening Post*, the *Gazette and General Advertiser*, and the *Herald* and a number of other publications including the *Albion*, the *New-York Musical Journal*, and the *New-York Mirror*. On its introduction to the city by Manuel García in 1825, grand opera was greeted by anonymous reviews in the *Evening Post*.

By the time the New York Philharmonic Orchestra began operations in 1842 the foundation for a circle of music critics had been laid by Henry C. Watson, an eloquent English writer who contributed reviews to such newspapers and journals as the *Albion*, the city's leading literary periodical at the time. The first prominent figure in this circle was William Henry Fry, a columnist for the *New York Tribune* between 1852 and 1863 who fervently campaigned for American music, often in effusive, self-serving prose that was nonetheless informed by his compositional talent. His successor at the *Tribune* was Watson, followed in 1867 by John Hassard, who provided insightful reviews of Wagner's *Der Ring des Nibelungen* from Bayreuth in 1876. The late nineteenth century saw the rise of powerful critics in New York City, owing largely to the city's growth as a cultural center, the proliferation of its musical institutions, and the growth of its newspapers. Music criticism was offered by the *Tribune*, the *New York Herald*, the *New York Times*, the *Sun* and the *New York World*, which were among the most widely read newspapers of the day, and by literary journals such as *Harper's* (1850–), *Scribner's Magazine* (1887–1900), and the *Dial* (1880–1929). Several publications dominated the musical press, including *Watson's Art Journal* (1864–1905), the *New York Figaro* (1881–1900), *Musical America* (1898–), the *Musical Observer* (1907–31), and the *Musical Quarterly* (1915–).

For more than forty years after 1880 the work of such critics as Henry T. Finck, Henry Krehbiel, William James Henderson, Richard Aldrich, and James Gibbons Huneker made New York City the country's leader in music criticism. These critics had similar training, and their extensive knowledge and lucid reasoning won wide respect for their initially progressive ideas. Reports from the Bayreuth Festival in 1876 were cabled to the *New York Times*, the first music criticism to be transmitted in this way between Europe and North America. Finck's enthusiastic reports from the festival for the *Tribune* helped to make

Wagner popular in North America. Although often in disagreement with Finck, Krehbiel also gave favorable reviews of Wagner's work, as well as that of Brahms. As Hassard's successor at the *Tribune* from the mid 1880s until his death in 1923, he was known for his vivid prose style, but a growing conservatism hindered his understanding of such "modernists" as Stravinsky and Schoenberg. The *New York Times* gained authority in music criticism after engaging Henderson in 1887. A brilliant stylist with solid musical training, he shared Krehbiel's affinity for Wagner and Brahms and his distaste for the work of modernists like Debussy and Strauss. In reviews of such works as *Salome* he stressed moral value as an important criterion for music criticism. He worked for the *Sun* from 1902 until his death in 1937 and often gave lectures about music at the New York Musical College and the Institute of Musical Art. His successor at the *Times* was Aldrich, who was milder and more open-minded but nevertheless opposed radical manifestations of modernism. Unlike his peers he wrote in a witty, entertaining style. Huneker, the youngest critic in the circle, wrote music, art, and drama reviews in turgid prose for the *Sun* from 1900 to 1912; he was the only critic active in the city before the First World War who outspokenly supported contemporary composers, including Strauss and Schoenberg.

A new group of critics came to prominence during the troubled 1920s as their predecessors retired, at the same time as the circulation of the city's daily newspapers began its decline. Music in the city became divided between advocates of modern music and the conservatives, who saw the concert hall as a sort of museum. The conflict was carried into the city's press and its venerable musical institutions. During these years the League of Composers emerged as the leading defender of modern music and launched the important publication *Modern Music* (1924–46), which attracted prominent composers as contributors, among them Aaron Copland and Henry Cowell.

In the years between the world wars a more moderate approach was taken by Deems Taylor at the *World* (1921–25), Lawrence Gilman at the *Tribune* (1923–37), and Olin Downes at the *Times* (1924–55). They cultivated an elevated literary style like that of their predecessors, but except for Gilman they were usually more straightforward; they were also less dogmatic and more likely to accept the modernism of Stravinsky, Bartók, and Prokofiev. Downes was the first major music critic in the city to adopt a simple and direct style aimed less at the cultural élite than at the average reader. The most radical critic of the time was Paul Rosenfeld, a supporter of the avant-garde composers Charles Ives, Edgar Varèse, and Wallingford Riegger. Primarily a contributor to literary journals and *Modern Music*, he used complex constructions, striking metaphors, and invented vocabulary.

Music criticism in the city changed after the appointment of Virgil Thomson as Gilman's successor at the *Herald Tribune* in 1940. A francophile and himself a composer, Thomson was known for the wit, clarity, and depth of his reviews and became one of the country's leading voices in music criticism. On his retirement in 1954 he was succeeded by the musicologist Paul Henry Lang, who offered a scholarly perspective during his tenure of six years. After Downes's death in 1955 Howard Taubman served as the chief music critic for the *Times* until 1960. His replacement was Harold C. Schonberg, who dominated music criticism in the city for two decades and won a Pulitzer Prize in 1971 for reviews distinguished not only by wide-ranging expertise but also by fine literary craft.

Music critics were forced to adapt to the changing interests of their readers in the decades after 1960. One of the city's few surviving daily newspapers, the *Times*, sought to expand its readership by offering reviews of jazz and rock; among its most versatile critics was John Rockwell, who worked in both classical and popular genres. On his retirement in 1980 Schonberg was succeeded by Donal Henahan, who was himself followed by Edward Rothstein in 1991. The number of full-time critics at the *Times* gradually declined by 1994 to six (four for classical music, two for popular music), and the newspaper increasingly used freelance writers to cover important musical events. The *Village Voice* attracted such well-known jazz and rock reviewers as Robert Christgau and Gary Giddins, as well as younger writers such as Ann Powers. The *New Yorker* became a dominant force in music criticism in 1972 when Andrew Porter joined the magazine. He often discussed several related events in a longer essay drawing on his extensive musical background and musicological inclinations. His reviews, known for their engaging style and incisiveness, tended to favor opera, contemporary music, and obscure or unknown works of the past. In 1992 he was succeeded by Paul Griffiths, also an expert on contemporary music. *Rolling Stone* eventually became a primary source for rock criticism. Despite the city's prominence as a musical center, music critics there in the mid 1990s faced a continuing threat in the steady erosion of the daily press.

Hermann Klein: *Unmusical New York: A Brief Criticism of Triumphs, Failures and Abuses* (London: J. Lane, 1910)

Henry T. Finck: *My Adventures in the Golden Age of Music* (New York: Funk and Wagnalls, 1926)

Michael Sherwin: "The Classical Age of New York Musical Criticism, 1880–1920: A Study of Henry T. Finck, James G. Huneker, W. J. Henderson, Henry E. Krehbiel, and Richard Aldrich" (thesis, City College of New York, 1972)

Barbara Mueser: "The Criticism of New Music in New York, 1919–1929" (diss., City University of New York, 1975)

Edward O. D. Downes and John Rockwell: "Criticism," *The New Grove Dictionary of American Music*, ed. H. Wiley Hitchcock and Stanley Sadie (London: Macmillan, 1986)

James Deaville

Muslims. Islam is one of the fastest-growing religions in New York City, owing both to conversions and to immigration from regions of the world where the religion is dominant, including Africa, parts of eastern Europe, Turkey, central Asia, the Middle East, the Indian subcontinent, most of Indonesia and Malaysia, and parts of China, the Philippines, and Latin America (especially Guyana).

It is probable that there were Muslims among the Africans transported to New York City during the colonial period, and that Muslim seamen passed through the Port of New York. The first Islamic institution in the city was established by Alexander Russell Webb, a white journalist who converted to Islam while serving as the American consul to the Philippines (from 1887). After moving to New York City in 1893 he set up a missionary headquarters at 30 East 23rd Street and formed the Moslem World Publishing Company, which issued the periodicals *Moslem World: Dedicated to the American Islamic Propaganda* and *Voice of Islam.* Immigrants from Muslim countries arrived in New York City soon after the turn of the century. In 1907 Polish, Russian, and Lithuanian immigrants formed the American Mohammedan Society, which at its peak had about four hundred members; the society worshipped at 108 Powers Street in Williamsburg from 1931. A tiny community of Druze (an offshoot of Islam) settled in the city before 1924. In 1939 Sheik Daoud Ahmed Faisal, born in Morocco and later a resident of the island of Grenada, opened the Islamic Mission of America on State Street in Brooklyn Heights (the mosque survived into the 1990s). The group rented a former mansion at 143 State Street in Brooklyn that it purchased in 1947. A large number of Arab Muslims settled in the city after 1948.

By this time Islam had gained converts among the city's blacks. Followers of Marcus Garvey were influenced by the Moorish Science Temple, formed in 1913 in Newark, New Jersey, and led by Noble Drew Ali. After the founder's death in 1929 the movement split, and some Moors in 1933 opened Temple no. 21 at Livonia Avenue in Brooklyn (later moved to 349 Bainbridge Avenue), which was probably the first black mosque in New York City. Members of the movement later opened temples no. 54 in Brooklyn, no. 72 in Manhattan, and no. 69 in the Bronx. Black conversions to Islam increased in number after the Nation of Islam, based in Chicago and led by Elijah Muhammad, opened Temple no. 7 at the YMCA in Harlem in 1946, and especially after it sent Malcolm X to the city in June 1954 as the imam of Mosque no. 7, which was now

The Islamic Center at East 96th Street in Manhattan, 1992

situated at 102 West 116th Street. The Nation of Islam appealed to many blacks because of its emphasis on black identity and empowerment, but some of its practices and tenets proved highly controversial, especially its exclusion of whites and its espousal of black separatism and racial superiority.

More conventional Islamic traditions were maintained during the 1950s by representatives from Muslim countries to the United Nations. Under the auspices of the Pakistani League of America (formed in 1954) the Pakistani delegation sponsored ceremonies at Pakistan House (12 East 65th Street) and several local hotels during the feast marking the end of the holy month of Ramadan. In 1955 the Pakistanis joined with representatives from Indonesia, Egypt, and other Islamic countries to organize the Islamic Center of New York, based temporarily at Pakistan House and moved to 1 Riverside Drive in 1957. At Columbia University the first Muslim student organization in New York City was formed in 1956.

After a pilgrimage to Mecca in 1964 Malcolm X embraced Sunni Islam, severed his ties with Elijah Muhammad, and established a mosque at the Theresa Hotel on 125th Street and 7th Avenue (now Adam Clayton Powell Jr. Boulevard). For a brief period his successor as the imam of Mosque no. 7 and as the spokesman in the city for the Nation of Islam was Louis Farrakhan. The assassination of Malcolm X in 1965 left the followers of the Nation of Islam irrevocably fragmented. A blast of dynamite ignited a fire that destroyed Mosque no. 7, which was rebuilt into a complex of stores, classrooms, and a prayer space in 1970. After it reopened, Mosque no. 7 was also called Mosque no. 7A before being renamed Masjid Malcolm Shabazz in 1976. Other mosques of the Nation of Islam in the city included Mosques no. 7B at 103-05 Northern Boulevard in Queens, no. 7C at 120 Madison Street in Brooklyn, and no. 7D at 2000 Morris Avenue in the Bronx (later moved to 960 Woodycrest Avenue). Muhammad was succeeded after his death in 1975 by his son Wallace D. Muhammad, who guided his followers away from racial confrontation and toward Sunni orthodoxy. The Nation of Islam then became divided into factions, with Farrakhan leading one adhering closely to the teachings of Elijah Muhammad.

Many mosques opened during these years, principally in black neighborhoods. Several in Brooklyn were allied with Dar-ul-Islam (House of Islam), a Sunni group formed in 1963 by former members of the Islamic Mission of America; its principal place of worship was the Ya Sin Mosque, opened in 1967 at 52 Herkimer Street and later moved to 342 Van Siclen Avenue. After the federal government relaxed immigration restrictions in 1965 a large number of Muslim immigrants from around the world settled in the city. The Elmhurst Muslim Society, formed in 1969 by Pakistanis in the basement of an abandoned school building at 85-37 Britton Avenue, was also frequented by Muslims from Syria, Afghanistan, Egypt, Africa, and Bangladesh. In 1972 the Albanian–American Islamic Center of New York and New Jersey converted a former mansion at 1325 Albemarle Road in Flatbush into a mosque where Pakistani, Turkish, and Arab Muslims also worshipped. Pakistanis and Bangladeshis in 1976 opened the Islamic Center of Corona (Masjid al-Falah), situated first at 101-03 43rd Avenue and moved in 1983 to 42-12 National Street.

Although Muslims in New York City were generally able to practice their religion freely they were also subject to occasional hostility. During the 1960s and 1970s the Nation of Islam was invariably cast in a negative light by the press, and its social and neighborhood programs were routinely ignored. Local newspapers gave inordinate attention to violent acts committed by Muslims: a shootout in 1972 between Muslims and the police at Mosque no. 7 that left one officer dead, and the attempted robbery by five black Muslims in 1973 of a sporting goods store in Brooklyn that led to the taking of hostages. Sometimes violence was directed toward mosques: in 1974 the imam of the Ya Sin Mosque was killed in a shootout, during the Iranian hostage crisis of 1979 assailants set fire to the Islamic Center of Corona, causing slight damage, and in 1988 there was violence between Latin Americans and Pakistanis near the Islamic Center at 50-11 Queens Boulevard.

In spite of these incidents Islam continued to thrive in New York City. The *Minaret*, a fortnightly newspaper first published in 1974, and the Islamic Circle of North America, formed in Queens in 1971 to spread Islamic teaching throughout the continent, expanded their activities in the late 1980s. A group aligned with Dar-ul-Islam in 1983 opened the Masjid al-Muminun and a school at 1221 Atlantic Avenue in Bedford–Stuyvesant, which eventually ministered to about forty families. In 1985 the United Muslims' Day parade was held in midtown Manhattan, beginning a practice repeated each year in September, and an Islamic radio program was launched on the radio station WNWK-FM. An organization of Latin American Muslims was formed by a Puerto Rican woman in 1987, and the Islamic Cultural Society in Manhattan sponsored frequent talks about Islam for American audiences at the United Nations and at Riverside Church.

In the mid 1990s the number of Muslims in New York City was estimated at 400,000 to 600,000, the great majority of whom adhered to the Sunni tradition. Muslim organizations in the city varied considerably in size and composition, from the overwhelmingly elderly American Mohammedan Society to the Islamic Mission of America, which had one of the most diverse congregations in the city. There were about sixty mosques in New York City, most of which occupied basements, storefronts, or disused factories. The largest was the Mosque of New York of the Islamic Center of New York, planned over a period of almost forty years with most of its financing from Kuwaitis, designed by the firm of Skidmore, Owings and Merrill in a style incorporating both traditional elements (such as a minaret and dome) and modernist ones, and opened in September 1991 at 96th Street and 3rd Avenue. Other well-known mosques and masjids (places of prayer) in the city included the Masjid al-Farouq on Atlantic Avenue and the Islamic Community Center in Flatbush; a mosque at 137-64 Geranium Avenue in Flushing was being built by the Muslim Center of New York (a predominately Pakistani organization). The city's Druze community, which consisted of about five hundred families of refugees from the civil war in Lebanon, were served by the head of the Druze Council of North America (based in New Jersey). Islam remained an important force among the city's blacks, who accounted for 25 to 40 percent of all the Muslims in New York City.

Earle H. Waugh et al., eds: *The Muslim Community in North America* (Edmonton: University of Alberta Press, 1983)

Marc Ferris

Muste, A(braham) J(ohannes) (*b* Zierikzee, Netherlands, 8 Jan 1885; *d* New York City, 11 Feb 1967). Minister, labor leader, and peace activist. He grew up in Michigan and studied to become a Dutch Reformed minister. Eventually he moved to New York City, where his first pastorate was the Fort Washington Collegiate Church in Washington Heights. He opposed the First World War and became a Quaker and pacifist. During the 1920s and 1930s he took part in efforts to form unions and establish training programs for textile workers. From 1921 to 1933 he directed Brookwood Labor College in Westchester County; for a brief time he also led a radical organization called the American Workers Party. He renounced Marxism in 1936 for radical pacifism and returned to the city, where he settled with his family in the Bronx in an apartment complex of the Amalgamated Clothing Workers. For several years he worked at the Presbyterian "Labor Temple" at 14th Street and 2nd Avenue. As chairman of the Fellowship of Reconciliation (1940–53) he was instrumental in forming the Congress of Racial Equality in 1942 and influenced the Ghandian education of such civil rights leaders as Bayard Rustin, James Farmer, Martin Luther King Jr., and Coretta Scott King. After the Second World War he led many protests against the proliferation of nuclear arms, including acts of civil disobedience during air-raid drills. In 1956 he helped to launch *Liberation*, a monthly magazine of the New Left. Muste worked during the mid 1960s to organize some of the first large-scale protests against the Vietnam War and traveled to North and South Vietnam on peace missions in 1966 and 1967.

Nat Hentoff, ed.: *The Essays of A. J. Muste* (New York: Simon and Schuster, 1967)

Jo Ann Robinson: *Abraham Went Out: A Biography of A. J. Muste* (Philadelphia: Temple University Press, 1981)

Jonathan D. Bloom

mutual aid societies. Organizations formed by various ethnic, religious, and racial groups to give social and economic support to their members. They were especially active during the peak years of immigration to the United States in the late nineteenth century and the early twentieth, when they offered advice to immigrants seeking to adjust to life in the United States. Most of the societies provided members with some form of health and accident insurance for a small fee; almost all also ensured a decent burial by defraying expenses and providing mourners.

The Present Status of Mutual Benefit Associations (New York: National Industrial Conference Board, 1931)

See also FRATERNAL ORGANIZATIONS and LANDSMANSHAFTN.

Robert A. Slayton

Mutual Broadcasting System. Radio network launched in 1934 by the station WOR in New York City. It began with three stations and within two years extended from coast to coast, attracting listeners and affiliates with popular programs such as "Lum and Abner," "The Lone Ranger," "Dick Tracy," and "The Shadow." The network was praised for its coverage of the Second World War and its extensive sports broadcasting. Unlike WOR it did not expand into television after the war. In the 1950s and 1960s the Mutual Broadcasting System changed ownership and declared bankruptcy. It moved its headquarters to Washington in 1972 and closed its news bureau in New York City in 1974.

JillEllyn Riley

Mutual Life Insurance Company of New York [MONY]. Firm of life insurers, formed in 1843 by Morris Robinson (1784–1849) and Alfred S. Pell (1805–69) at 44 Wall Street. The first president was Robinson, who introduced new methods of marketing and advertising, including door-to-door soliciting. By 1870 the firm had $242 million of policies in force and was the leading insurer in the country. It lost much of its market during the last quarter of the nineteenth century, when several companies introduced tontine plans and competition increased. In 1884 the firm bought headquarters at 34 Nassau Street. Under the direction of Richard McCurdy (1835–1916; president 1885–1905) it introduced a deferred dividend plan in 1885 that allowed dividends to be paid at the end of a specified period rather than only on the policyholder's death. An aggressive manager, McCurdy expanded the firm's agency force, strengthened its investment portfolio, and liberalized contracts. MONY was one of many life insurance firms in the city examined by the Legislative Insurance Investigating Committee led by State Senator William Armstrong in 1905; as a result of the committee's findings most of the firm's executives including McCurdy resigned under pressure and were replaced by a group led by Charles A. Peabody (1849–1931; president 1905–27). Under Peabody's direction the firm expanded its investments in real estate in New York City: by 1943 property in the city accounted for 70 percent of its mortgage loans and 89 percent of its land holdings. The headquarters were moved in 1950 to Broadway between 55th and 56th streets. In 1990 MONY had about $63,000 million of policies in force and assets of $23,000 million and was the fourteenth-largest life insurance firm in the country.

Shephard B. Clough: *A Century of American Life Insurance: A History of the Mutual Life Insurance Company of New York, 1843–1943* (New York: Columbia University Press, 1946)

James Bradley

Muzak. A firm that offers background music to subscribers. It traces its roots in New York City to 1922, when George O. Squier, a retired army major-general, conceived of transmitting news, music, lectures, and advertising directly into private homes by means of electric wires. The result of his plan was Wired Radio Inc., out of which the Muzak Corporation was formed in 1934. By this time wireless radio was already widespread in American homes, and consequently Muzak concentrated on selling its pre-recorded "functional music" to hotels and restaurants. In 1938 the firm introduced music for offices and factories that was intended to offset boredom and monotony in the workplace, and franchises were licensed throughout the United States. After the Second World War the firm moved from 151 West 46th Street to 229 Park Avenue South. Industrial psychologists in the 1950s promoted the virtues of music in the workplace, and President Dwight D. Eisenhower had Muzak installed in the White House. During these years Muzak began using FM radio side channels instead of direct wiring for transmitting its pre-recorded programs. In 1966 Muzak moved into new headquarters at 100 Park Avenue South; there the firm remained until the mid 1980s, when it was purchased by Westinghouse. The last location in New York City was at 888 7th Avenue. In 1986 Muzak was purchased by the Field Corporation of Chicago and moved to Seattle.

Chad Ludington

Myers, Myer (*b* New York City, 1723; *d* New York City, 12 Dec 1795). Silversmith and goldsmith. The son of Dutch Sephardic immigrants, he executed tableware as well as religious objects for both Jewish and Protestant congregations; his work was often characterized by Rococo flourishes. He was also a merchant and land speculator, and a leader of the synagogue Shearith Israel. During British occupation he was in patriotic exile in Philadelphia. In 1786 he was elected chairman of the Gold and Silver Smith's Society in New York City. Myers lived successively at 14 Pearl Street and 17 Pearl Street. Examples of his craft may be seen at the Metropolitan Museum of Art, the Museum of the City of New York, and the New-York Historical Society.

Jeanette W. Rosenbaum: *Myer Myers, Goldsmith, 1723–1795* (Philadelphia: Jewish Publication Society of America, 1954)

Robert I. Goler

Myerson [Grant], **Bess** [Elizabeth] (*b* New York City, 16 July 1924). Miss America and public official. Born into poverty in the Bronx, she became the first Jew to win the Miss America pageant in 1945. In the following years she often appeared on television game shows and worked as a consumer advisor for several corporations. In 1980 she sought election to the U.S. Senate, and although at first heavily favored to win the Democratic primary she eventually lost to Elizabeth Holtzman. Appointed consumer affairs commissioner by Mayor Edward I. Koch in 1983, she was forced to resign in 1987 amid allegations that she had given a municipal job to the daughter of Hortense Gabel, the judge handling the divorce of her companion, the sewer contractor Carl "Andy" Capasso; she was indicted later the same year for conspiring to bribe Gabel but was acquitted.

Jesse Drucker

N

NAACP. See NATIONAL ASSOCIATION FOR THE ADVANCEMENT OF COLORED PEOPLE.

Nabisco. Forerunner of the firm RJR NABISCO.

Namath, Joe [Joseph William] (*b* Beaver Falls, Penn., 31 May 1943). Football player. The son of Hungarian immigrants, he played football for the University of Alabama. In 1965 he signed an unprecedented three-year contract with the New York Jets worth $427,000 a year. He remained with the team as a quarterback for twelve years, during which he set many records for passing.

In 1969 he fulfilled his own audacious prediction that the Jets would win the Super Bowl by leading his team to victory against the Baltimore Colts in Miami, who had been heavily favored. His flamboyant way of life and charismatic personality earned him the nickname "Broadway Joe" and made him one of the most popular and controversial athletes of his time. While playing for the Jets he lived at 370 East 76th Street in Manhattan. After finishing his career as a player with the Los Angeles Rams he worked from 1977 as an actor and sports announcer.

Joseph S. Lieber

Nash, (Frederic) Ogden (*b* Rye, N.Y., 19 Aug 1902; *d* Baltimore, 19 May 1971). Poet. He attended Harvard College for one year, moved to New York City, and worked as a bond salesman and an advertising copywriter. In 1930 he published in the *New Yorker* "Spring Comes to Murray Hill," which began with the lines "I sit in an office at 244 Madison Avenue / And say to myself You have a responsible job, havenue?"; most of his later work was similarly characterized by fractured meter and outlandish rhyme. After marrying and moving to Baltimore in 1933 his poems became less metropolitan as he increasingly took on the role of suburban paterfamilias. In 1943 he revisited New York City during performances of Kurt Weill's musical *One Touch of Venus*, for which he wrote the lyrics, and from 1956 to 1965 he maintained a residence at 333 East 57th Street. Among the collections of Nash's verse dating from his years in New York City are *Free Wheeling* (1931), *Hard Lines* (1931), and *Happy Days* (1933).

Archibald MacLeish: Introd. to *I Wouldn't Have Missed It: Selected Poems of Ogden Nash* (Boston: Little, Brown, 1975)

Ormonde de Kay

Nassau Heights. An obsolete name for a part of northwestern Queens lying within Elmhurst south of Queens Boulevard and east of Grand Avenue. The name first appears on a map of the Bretonniere farm published in December 1853 by its developer W. E. Caldwell; the farm occupied a parcel now bounded by the tracks of the Long Island Rail Road (northeast), 58th Avenue (southeast), 83rd Street (southwest), and 55th Avenue (northwest). On some maps the neighborhood extended as far south as Caldwell Avenue. The tract was slow to develop: streets were not laid out until 1896 and houses were not built until the 1920s.

Vincent Seyfried

Nast, Thomas (*b* Landau, Germany, 27 Sept 1840; *d* Guayaquil, Ecuador, 7 Dec 1902). Cartoonist. He moved to New York City as a boy and attended the National Academy of Design. At fifteen he showed some sketches to Frank Leslie, who engaged him to work for his *Illustrated Newspaper*; Nast submitted work to other publications and eventually left Leslie for the *New York Illustrated News*, for which he provided illustrations of John Brown's funeral, a prizefight in England, and Garibaldi's campaigns in Italy. In 1861 he joined *Harper's Weekly* and traveled to the front to make sketches that were praised by President

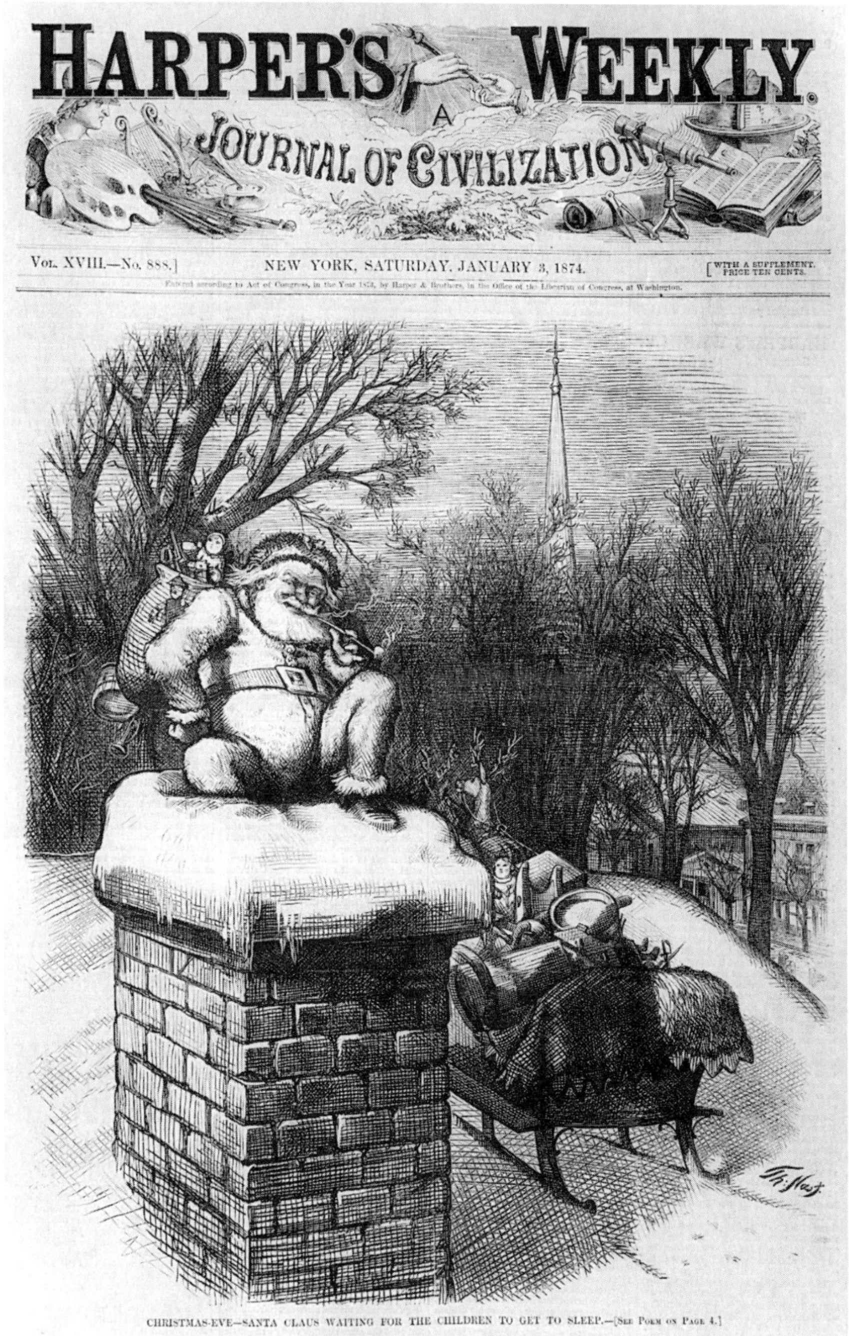
HARPER'S WEEKLY.
A JOURNAL OF CIVILIZATION.

Vol. XVIII.—No. 888.] NEW YORK, SATURDAY, JANUARY 3, 1874. [WITH A SUPPLEMENT. PRICE TEN CENTS.

Entered according to Act of Congress, in the Year 1873, by Harper & Brothers, in the Office of the Librarian of Congress, at Washington.

CHRISTMAS-EVE—SANTA CLAUS WAITING FOR THE CHILDREN TO GET TO SLEEP.—[See Poem on Page 4.]

Thomas Nast's cover drawing for Harper's Weekly, *3 January 1874*

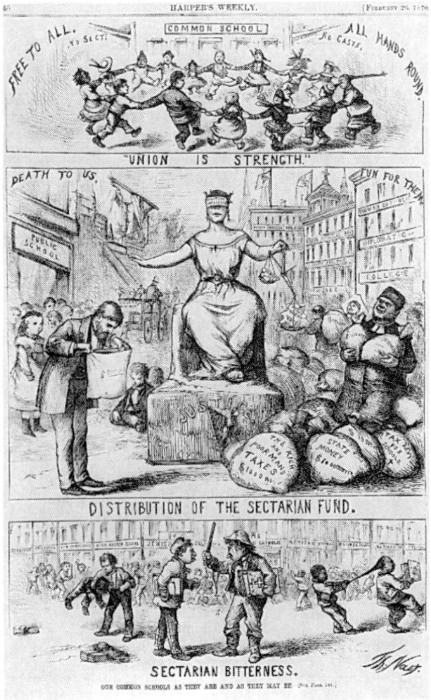

Thomas Nast, "Our Common Schools as They Are and as They May Be," Harper's Weekly, *26 February 1870*

Nathan's, Coney Island, ca *1958*

Abraham Lincoln. He lived in Harlem from 1864 to 1873 and later bought a house on 125th Street near 5th Avenue, where he also built a studio. Between 1869 and 1872 he became well known for caricatures of politicians and businessmen (some depicted as vultures) that helped to expose the Tweed Ring. A staunch Republican, he attacked Horace Greeley, supported Presidents Rutherford B. Hayes and Grover Cleveland, advocated sound money policy, municipal reform, and restrictions on immigration, and sought to end what he saw as the pope's malign influence on the country's affairs. After a disagreement with his editors he left *Harper's* in 1886; he later gave lectures and for a short time issued a journal called *Nast's Weekly.* His savings depleted, he accepted an appointment from President Theodore Roosevelt as American consul to Ecuador. Nast was the first illustrator to depict the Democratic Party as a donkey, the Republican Party as an elephant, and Santa Claus as plump, jolly, and white-haired.

Morton Keller: *The Art and Politics of Thomas Nast* (New York: Oxford University Press, 1968)

For further illustrations see NATIVISM, PUBLIC SCHOOLS, and 7TH REGIMENT.

James E. Mooney

Nathan, Maud (*d* New York City, 20 Oct 1862; *d* New York City, 15 Dec 1936). Reformer. A member of an established Sephardic Jewish family, she began a long career in charitable activity and social reform at the age of seventeen. Soon after her marriage to her first cousin she became a director at the nursing school of Mount Sinai Hospital, which her father-in-law had helped to found. Between 1890 and 1925 much of her attention was devoted to the Consumers' League of New York City, an organization of élite and working-class women that fought to improve women's working conditions. She was also a major force in the woman suffrage movement and worked for Theodore Roosevelt's Progressive presidential candidacy in 1912. She wrote a memoir, *Once upon a Time and Today* (1933).

Kathryn Kish Sklar

Nathan's. A hot dog stand on Surf Avenue in Coney Island, opened in 1916 by Nathan Handwerker, a former employee of the entrepreneur Charles Feltman. It became popular because of its low prices, garish architecture, and hectic ambience. The owners later licensed a franchising operation, which by the early 1990s had sixty-two outlets nationwide. In 1991 the original stand on Surf Avenue sold 1.05 million frankfurters.

Stephen Weinstein

Nation. Weekly magazine launched in 1865 to support the cause of former slaves after the Civil War. In its early years the editor was E. L. Godkin and the literary editor Wendell Phillips Garrison (son of William Lloyd Garri-

Nathan's, Coney Island, ca *1922*

son). The magazine established itself as a consistent supporter of civil rights, civil liberties, and free expression. Until the First World War it published only unsigned articles in the interest of nonpartisanship. In spite of its national focus the magazine often covered issues relevant to New York City, such as the corruption of the Tweed Ring, the policies of Robert Moses, and the revision of the municipal charter. Prominent contributors have included Harold Laski, Frederick Law Olmsted, and Freda Kirchwey, who edited, owned, and published the magazine from 1937 to 1955. The *Nation* is the oldest continuously published weekly magazine in the United States.

Alan Pendleton Grimes: *The Political Liberalism of the Nation, 1865–1932* (Chapel Hill: University of North Carolina Press, 1953)

Sara Alpern: *Freda Kirchwey: A Woman of "The Nation"* (Cambridge: Harvard University Press, 1987)

Amanda Aaron

National Academy of Design, 23rd Street and 4th Avenue, ca *1885*

National Academy of Design. Organization formed on 14 January 1826 by Samuel F. B. Morse and others after unsuccessful attempts to merge the American Academy of the Fine Arts and the New York Association of Artists (also known as the Drawing Association). Dedicated to promoting artistic design in America, it limited its membership to artists and exhibited the work of living artists exclusively. In 1863 the academy erected a building designed by P. B. Wight at the corner of 23rd Street and 4th Avenue. Despite its sympathy for modern art several artists criticized the academy for becoming increasingly conservative, and in rebellion they formed the Society of American Artists in 1877. The academy then suffered a severe decline in activity and respect, but toward the end of the century it reclaimed its reputation and absorbed the Society of American Artists. The National Academy of Design now operates an important art school and gallery at 5 East 89th Street, with a permanent collection that features the work of its members. Among the prominent artists who have taught at the academy in addition to Morse are Jasper F. Cropsey, Asher B. Durand, J. Alden Weir, and Abbott Thayer.

Thomas Cummings: *Historical Annals of the National Academy of Design* (New York: Kennedy Galleries, 1969)

Peter Hastings Falk, ed.: *The Annual Exhibition Record, 1901–1950* (Madison, Conn.: Sound View, 1990)

Carrie Rebora

National Allied Publications. Original name of Dc comics.

National Archives–Northeast Region. Regional archives of the National Archives and Records Administration, housing records of courts in New York State, New Jersey, Puerto Rico, and the Virgin Islands. It traces its origin to 1950, when the National Archives and Records Service (NARS) established federal records centers in Linden, New Jersey, and Brooklyn. Within a few months the facility in Linden was closed and records were transferred to the Brooklyn Naval Supply Activities Depot, where they remained until being moved in 1952 to 641 Washington Street in Manhattan. In 1969 NARS created an archives branch of the Federal Records Center–New York for permanent records. A destructive fire at the National Personnel Records Center in St. Louis prompted the moving of the records in New York City to safer quarters in Bayonne, New Jersey (1974–75). When NARS became the National Archives and Records Administration in 1985, the archives branch was made separate from the Federal Records Center and became the National Archives–New York Branch (later the National Archives–Northeast Region). In 1992–93 the Northeast Regional Archives moved to the federal building at 201 Varick Street in lower Manhattan. One of thirteen such federal depositories in the United States, the archives for the Northeast Region maintain more than 63,000 cubic feet (eighteen hundred cubic meters) of records generated by forty-seven federal agencies and courts. Among the holdings are extensive manuscript materials (including provincial admiralty records dating from 1685) and forty thousand rolls of microfilm containing publications of the National Archives.

Donald R. McCoy: *The National Archives: America's Ministry of Documents* (Chapel Hill: University of North Carolina Press, 1978)

Robert C. Morris

National Association for the Advancement of Colored People [NAACP]. Civil rights organization formed in 1909 by the merger of the Niagara Movement, led by W. E. B. Du Bois, and a group of prominent white liberals angered by a race riot in Springfield, Illinois. Discussions for the merger began at the National Negro Conference in New York City, which was called for on the centenary of the birth of President Lincoln (12 February 1909) by Henry Moskowitz, Mary White Ovington, and William English Walling. Black and white participants at the conference demanded equal educational opportunity, enforcement of the Fourteenth Amendment, and protection of voting rights under the Fifteenth Amendment; they appointed the Committee of Forty, which incorporated the association in the following year. An important victory was achieved in 1915 in the case of *Guinn v. U.S.*, in which the Supreme Court outlawed a "grandfather clause" limiting the right to vote in several southern states to men whose grandfathers had voted before the Civil War. In the same year Joel E. Spingarn, chairman of the board of the association, endowed the Spingarn Medal, to be awarded annually to a black person of distinction. The association in 1917 prevailed on New York City to abolish ordinances that segregated municipal housing, and in 1918 it appointed as its first full-time secretary John R. Shillady, who was succeeded by James Weldon Johnson, the first black secretary of the association (1920–30). Oswald Garrison Villard, grandson of the abolitionist William Lloyd Garrison and publisher of the *New York Evening Post*, helped to pay the salaries of these early officers. The *Crisis*, a monthly publication edited by Du Bois, had a circulation of more than 100,000 by 1920.

The NAACP fought racial injustice by legislative, judicial, and educational means. It mounted a campaign against lynching in the 1930s that led to a decline in incidents but

Members of the National Association for the Advancement of Colored People. Left *Walter White;* second from left *Mary White Ovington;* third from right *William Pickens;* right *Joel E. Spingarn*

failed to have anti-lynching legislation enacted. The association then turned its attention to securing equal funding for black and white school systems and fighting segregation in public accommodations and transportation. In 1939 the NAACP Legal Defense and Educational Fund was formed as an independent body; its greatest accomplishment was winning the case of *Brown v. Board of Education* (1954), in which the Supreme Court overturned the doctrine of "separate but equal" and declared school segregation unconstitutional. Southern reaction to this decision almost crippled the association: several southern states tried to retaliate by seeking out its membership rolls, leveling accusations that it was infiltrated by communists, and seeking to have the association banned outright. In the 1960s and 1970s it continued to work through the courts and the Congress for equal opportunity in education, employment, housing, and politics, at a time when other civil rights organizations such as the Congress of Racial Equality, the Southern Christian Leadership Conference, and the Student Nonviolent Coordinating Committee were more outspoken and visible. The NAACP during the 1980s shifted its attention to economic development and the fight against poverty. Because of escalating costs it moved its national headquarters from Manhattan to Brooklyn Heights in 1982 and to its own building in Baltimore in 1986. The NAACP has been led by Walter White (1931–55), Roy Wilkins (1955–77), Benjamin L. Hooks (1977–93), and Benjamin F. Chavis Jr. (1993–94). In the mid 1990s it had half a million members throughout the United States.

Charles F. Kellogg: *NAACP: A History of the National Association for the Advancement of Colored People*, vol. 1, *1909–1920* (Baltimore: Johns Hopkins University Press, 1967)

R. L. Harris, Jr.

National Association of Social Workers. The leading professional organization of social workers, founded in New York City in 1955. Its formation resulted from the merger of the American Association of Social Workers (originally the National Social Workers Exchange, an offshoot of the Intercollegiate Bureau of Occupations renamed in 1922), which offered a national placement service, published a journal, and held annual conferences; the American Association of Group Workers; and five other organizations. In late 1972 the National Association of Social Workers moved its headquarters to Washington.

Judith Ann Trolander: *Professionalism and Social Change: From the Settlement House Movement to Neighborhood Centers, 1886 to the Present* (New York: Columbia University Press, 1987)

Judith Ann Trolander

National Audubon Society. Wildlife conservation society. Its forerunner was formed in 1886 by George Bird Grinnell, editor of the magazine *Field and Stream*, to halt the destruction of the North American bird population by hunters and hat manufacturers. The group attracted more than 38,000 members during its first three months of operation, overwhelming Grinnell and leading him to disband it in 1888. Other Audubon societies were organized in seventeen states by 1899; these were loosely connected through the magazine *Bird Lore*, launched in 1899 by Frank Chapman of the American Museum of Natural History, and the first national Christmas bird count, sponsored by Chapman in 1900. The state societies became part of the National Association of Audubon Societies for the Protection of Wild Birds and Animals in 1901; this organization played an important role in helping to pass the New York State Audubon Plumage Law (1910) and the federal Migratory Bird Treaty Act (1918) and in forming the Paul J. Rainy Sanctuary, a preserve of 26,000 acres (10,530 hectares) in Louisiana (1926). During the 1930s the association began supporting research on endangered birds. It took its current name in 1940 and during the 1960s focused on promoting such environmental protection laws as the Clean Air, Clean Water, Wild and Scenic Rivers, and Endangered Species acts. In the mid 1990s the National Audubon Society had fifteen regional offices and five hundred local chapters, offered educational programs for more than half a million children, and was active in preserving woodlands, supporting the Endangered Species Act, and protecting the forests of the Pacific Northwest and the Arctic National Wildlife Refuge. One of the oldest and largest organizations of its kind in the United States, the society has its headquarters at 700 Broadway in Manhattan.

Eric Wm. Allison

National Broadcasting Company [NBC]. The oldest permanent radio and television network in the United States, formed in 1926 by a group of highly influential businessmen representing the Radio Corporation of America (RCA), General Electric, and Westinghouse. It began radio broadcasts with a gala at the Waldorf–Astoria on 15 November. The network grew so quickly that by 1927 it began building permanent studios at 711 5th Avenue, and in time the amount of programming could not be accommodated on one network alone. The result was the creation of two separate entities: the Blue Network, which offered mostly cultural programs (music, drama, and commentary), and the Red Network, which specialized in comedy and light entertainment. The number of affiliates also increased, from twenty-five when operations began to sixty-one across the United States in 1931, by which time the network reported a net profit of $2,346,766. In the following year RCA, under the leadership of David Sarnoff, bought out General Electric and Westinghouse to become the sole owner. From the outset NBC featured popular vaudeville entertainers of the day on its broadcasts: Rudy Vallee, Fred Allen, Jack Benny, Ed Wynn, Eddie Cantor, Al Jolson, Groucho Marx, Bob Hope, Bing Crosby, Red Skelton, Edgar Bergen and Charlie McCarthy, and George Burns and Gracie Allen all had regular programs. The series "Amos 'n' Andy," recorded on Chicago, secured the network's position as the most popular radio network in the United States. Sporting events and political speeches were also mainstays of its broadcast offerings. In spite of the Depression NBC enjoyed unabated success, and in 1931 it made plans to move into Rockefeller Center, then under construction in midtown Manhat-

Master control board at the National Broadcasting Company, ca *1937*

tan. By 1933 the division NBC News had been created by Lowell Thomas.

With the encouragement of Sarnoff NBC began experimental television broadcasts from the Empire State Building in 1932, and in 1939 it began its first regular television service with a broadcast of President Franklin D. Roosevelt opening the World's Fair. In 1941 the network obtained a commercial television license from the Federal Communications Commission (FCC) for WNBT-TV in New York City, which became the world's first commercial television station. Although the development of television was interrupted by the Second World War, radio continued to grow. In 1943 the FCC ruled that no organization could own more than one radio network. As a result NBC sold the weaker Blue Network, which eventually became the American Broadcasting Company (ABC). After the war the growth of television resumed, and many radio programs were adapted to the new medium. "Meet the Press," begun as a radio program in 1945, moved to television in 1947 and eventually became the longest-running program in television history. The number of American homes equipped with television increased from fourteen thousand in 1947 to 175,000 in 1948. During the 1950s the radio division at NBC focused on news, sports, and public affairs programs, while the television division was expanding its broadcast day beyond the afternoon and evening hours to include mornings as well. "Today," begun in 1952, was the first morning program to offer news, human interest stories, and entertainment in a format that became widely imitated. NBC Television transmitted the first coast-to-coast color broadcast in 1953 and aired the first videotape in 1956, and in 1962 the Telstar communications satellite made it possible to relay live broadcasts from one continent to another almost instantaneously.

By the 1960s television was as much a part of American life as radio had been since the 1930s, and NBC was the leader in the burgeoning industry with programs such as "Rowan and Martin's Laugh-In" and "Star Trek." But the popularity of radio was declining by the 1970s. Although the network succeeded in its efforts to revive NBC Radio, which became profitable by 1985, it decided in 1988 to sell eight of its nine radio stations, retaining only WNBC in New York City. In 1986 General Electric, one of the original part-owners of the network, purchased RCA for $6300 million and thereby became the sole parent company of NBC. The headquarters of NBC are at 30 Rockefeller Plaza.

Erik Barnouw: *A History of Broadcasting in the United States* (New York: Oxford University Press, 1966–70)

Robert Campbell: *The Golden Years of Broadcasting: A Celebration of the First 50 Years of Radio and Television on NBC* (New York: Charles Scribner's Sons, 1976)

Chad Ludington

National City Bank of New York. Name used from 1865 by a bank later known as CITIBANK.

National Conference of Christians and Jews. Organization formed in 1927 by Charles Evans Hughes, S. Parkes Cadman, and Roger W. Straus to combat bias, bigotry, and racism in the United States and promote tolerance and understanding between different races, religions, and cultures. Initially aimed at bringing together Catholics, Protestants, and Jews, the organization broadened its focus over the years as the nation became more religiously and ethnically diverse. In the 1980s it placed a particular emphasis on including Muslims in its interfaith programs. In addition to its national headquarters at 71 5th Avenue in Manhattan, the National Conference also operates sixty-seven regional offices in thirty-two states and the District of Columbia.

National Consumers' League. Organization formed in New York City in 1898 by women active in the Consumers' League of New York City (1890). It had its headquarters in the Charities Building at 44 East 23rd Street. Under the innovative leadership of its first secretary general, Florence Kelley, the league quickly became a highly effective proponent of social and labor legislation to improve the working conditions of women and the health of mothers and infants, and to eliminate child labor. It rapidly gained members from the social élite, the middle class, and trade unions. By 1906 the league had more than sixty national affiliates. It published influential studies of exploitative working conditions, and its advisory board prepared an annual agenda that guided the efforts of local affiliates in state legislatures and state and federal courts. The league's influence diminished in the 1920s, and on Kelley's death in 1932 its offices were moved to Cleveland.

Josephine Goldmark: *Impatient Crusader: Florence Kelley's Life Story* (Urbana: University of Illinois Press, 1953; repr. Westport, Conn.: Greenwood, 1976)

Kathryn Kish Sklar

National Council of Churches of Christ in the USA [NCC]. Association formed in 1950 by the merger of the Federal Council of Churches and seven other interdenominational agencies. It made its headquarters at Riverside Drive and 120th Street in Manhattan and was influential in persuading members of the Rockefeller family to establish the Interchurch Center opposite Riverside Church and Union Theological Seminary. In 1952 it authorized the publication of the Revised Standard Version of the Bible. The council in the mid 1990s was the country's largest ecumenical agency, with thirty-two Protestant, Anglican, and Orthodox member organizations and a combined membership of more than forty million persons. A vehicle for action, education, and service in the United States and abroad, it has sparked controversy for its public statements on such issues as civil rights and American foreign policy.

Peggy L. Shriver: *Having Gifts That Differ: Profiles for Ecumenical Churches* (New York: Friendship Press, 1989)

Eileen W. Lindner

National Council of Negro Women. Federation formed on 5 December 1935 by representatives of twenty-nine black organizations at the YWCA on 137th Street in Harlem at the initiation of the educator Mary McLeod Bethune, an advisor to President Franklin D. Roosevelt. Its purpose was to coordinate the work of its members and to encourage black women to take part in government and politics, education, and business. As the leader of the council from 1957 into the 1990s Dorothy I. Height oversaw an expansion of its activities into such diverse fields as on-the-job training, preventing drug abuse and teenage pregnancy, and African relief.

Tracey A. Fitzgerald: *The National Council of Negro Women and the Feminist Movement, 1935–1975* (Washington: Georgetown University Press, 1985)

Larry A. Greene

National Foundation for Infant Paralysis. Original name of the MARCH OF DIMES.

National Industrial Conference Board. Original name of the CONFERENCE BOARD.

National Institute of Public Administration. Former name of the INSTITUTE OF PUBLIC ADMINISTRATION.

National Lampoon. Monthly humor magazine launched in April 1970 by Henry Beard, Doug Kenney, and Rob Hoffman, graduates of Harvard University who had worked on the *Harvard Lampoon*, and published by Matty Simmons and Leonard Mogul, owners of Twenty-first Century Communications. Known as the "Humor Magazine for Adults," it attracted such cartoonists and writers as Gahan Wilson, John Hughes, and Michael O'Donohue and aimed to attack everything and offend everyone, especially adolescents, popular culture, celebrities, and other magazines. The magazine became known for its preoccupation with sex and its tasteless treatment of sensitive topics: notable features included "Famine Circle" (about starvation in Africa, July 1974) and "Better Homes and Closets, the Idea Magazine for Women of All Sexes" (May 1977). Its best-known cover showed a dog with a gun to its head accompanied by the caption "If you don't buy this magazine, we'll shoot this dog" (April 1973). The magazine chose as its mascot a cartoon by Sam Gross of a frog that lost its legs working in a French restaurant. Circulation peaked at 842,000 in 1974 but then declined rapidly. In 1978 P. J. O'Rourke became the editor-in-chief and made the magazine more professional, introducing such standard features as "News on the March," "True Facts," "Straight Talk," "Canadian Corner," and "Foto Funnies." After reaching half a million the circulation again declined, and in March 1990 the *National Lampoon* was bought by James P. Jimirro of J2 Communications.

Al Sarrantonio, ed.: *The National Lampoon Treasury of Humor* (New York: Simon and Schuster, 1991)

Walter Friedman

National Lead Industries. Former name of NL INDUSTRIES.

National Memorial African Book Store. Bookstore at 2107 7th Avenue opposite the Hotel Theresa in Harlem. Run by Lewis H. Michaux, it was in business from 1930 to 1974. The store was well known for its selection of books by African, black American, and nationalist writers and served as an art gallery and meeting place for black intellectuals. It faced what is now called "African Square," a site where community news was given and soapbox orators made speeches.

Sule Greg C. Wilson

National Puerto Rican Forum. Nonprofit organization formed in 1957 as the Puerto Rican Forum by a group of educators including Herman Badillo to assist the large number of Puerto Ricans settling in New York City. Over the years it established several vocational and academic training programs: its Puerto Rican Community Development Project, launched in the early 1960s, led to the establishment of Boricua College in Manhattan and of other advocacy and nonprofit organizations in the city. The organization took its current name when offices opened in other cities in 1971. In the mid 1990s the National Puerto Rican Forum was the nation's largest nonprofit organization serving the Latin American community. In addition to its national headquarters at 31 East 32nd Street the organization maintains a chapter in the Bronx.

James Bradley

National Railroad Passenger Corporation. See AMTRAK.

National Review. Fortnightly magazine launched in November 1955 in New York City by William F. Buckley Jr. as a forum for conservative thought, both traditional and libertarian. It attracted contributions from such noted conservatives as Clare Boothe Luce and George F. Will, as well as disenchanted leftists such as John Dos Passos and Max Eastman, and was a respected journal by the early 1970s. The *National Review* continues to be identified with Buckley and remains central to the development of American conservatism.

John Chamberlain: *The National Review Reader* (New York: Bookmailer, 1957)

Lawson Bowling

National Rifle Association. Organization formed in New York City in 1871. There were several causes underlying its formation: the prominent role of the rifle in the Civil War; advocacy by William Connant Church, the influential editor of the *Army and Navy Journal*, of marksmanship training as practiced by Captain George Wood Wingate of the New York National Guard; and the Orange Riot of 1871, which revealed how inadequately members of the National Guard were trained. The association benefited from an increased interest in shooting skills among militia and professional soldiers after the Battle of Little Bighorn in 1876 and helped to make riflery an important sport in the 1870s and 1880s, but after failing to obtain federal funding or form a partnership with the army it became moribund in 1892. It revived in 1901 and established headquarters in Washington.

Russell S. Gilmore

National Social Workers Exchange. Original name of the NATIONAL ASSOCIATION OF SOCIAL WORKERS.

National Tuberculosis Association. Original name of the National Lung Association, of which the NEW YORK LUNG ASSOCIATION is an affiliate.

National Urban League. Social service and civil rights organization with headquarters in New York City. Formed on 16 October 1911 as the National League on Urban Conditions among Negroes, it resulted from the merger of the National League for the Protection of Colored Women (1906), the Committee for Improving the Industrial Condition of Negroes in New York (1906), and the Committee on Urban Conditions among Negroes (1910). The founders included both blacks and whites, notably Ruth Standish Baldwin, William Bulkley, Frances Kellor, and George Edmund Haynes. Reflecting the approaches of both the Progressive movement and Booker T. Washington, the league sought to further its goals through careful investigation, advocacy, negotiation, and education. It formally adopted its current name on 4 February 1920. The league set up local affiliates, including one in New York City, where it sponsored youth programs, health clinics, and adult education programs and sought to integrate unions and improve housing (often unsuccessfully). Through its national office it provided social welfare and employment services for black migrants to northern cities and worked to broaden employment opportunities for blacks; later it led vocational opportunity and voter education campaigns and supported marches on Washington (one was planned in 1941 but canceled; another took place in 1963). Activities increased under the direction of Whitney Young in the 1960s, when the league sought to mediate between civil rights groups and white legislative and business leaders. It also organized community-based programs under the rubric "New Thrust" to promote economic and political opportunity in the inner cities.

Over the years the National Urban League developed and supported such programs as the National Skills Bank, the Leadership Development Program, the Labor Education Advancement Program, and the Street Academies, and in New York City the Visiting Nurses, the Utopia Neighborhood Club, Big Brothers and Big Sisters, and the Juvenile Park Protective League. It continues to work for community improvement and civil rights.

Guichard Parris and Lester Brooks: *Blacks in the City: A History of the National Urban League* (Boston: Little, Brown, 1971)

Thomas Nast, "The American River Ganges: The Priests and the Children," Harper's Weekly, *30 September 1871*

Nancy Weiss: *The National Urban League, 1910–1940* (New York: Oxford University Press, 1974)

Jesse Moore Jr.: *A Search for Equality: The National Urban League, 1910–1961* (University Park: Pennsylvania State University Press, 1981)

Nancy Weiss: *Whitney M. Young, Jr. and the Struggle for Civil Rights* (Princeton, N.J.: Princeton University Press, 1989)

Cheryl Greenberg

nativism. Most nativist violence in New York City during the nineteenth century was directed at Irish Catholic immigrants. In one of the first incidents, which took place on Christmas night in 1806, a mob of native-born Protestants gathered outside St. Peter's Church and threatened the Irish congregation into fleeing. In the mid 1830s violence against Irish immigrants increased, and the Native American Democratic Association was formed. The Whig Party, which had sought to attract immigrants in 1834, turned against them after attacks on Whigs by immigrants were publicized. Whig newspapers printed excerpts from *Six Months in a Convent* and *Awful Disclosures*, false accounts of sexual escapades among nuns that inflamed anti-Catholic sentiment. In the mayoral election of 1836 the Native American Democratic Association chose Samuel F. B. Morse as its candidate after Philip Hone declined; it lost many supporters after Morse received only a tenth as many votes as the winning Democrat. A number of issues promoted by nativists remained important in political debate, especially temperance and the question of control over the public schools. The American Republican Party, formed in 1843, attracted nativists and promised reform at a time when dissatisfaction with government was widespread. In the elections of 1844 it nominated as its mayoral candidate the publisher James Harper, who gained the support of such influential Whig journalists as James Watson Webb and Thurlow Weed; Harper won the election, and the party also gained a majority on the Common Council. Nativism declined in the city after riots against immigrants in Philadelphia in May 1844 became bloody. Harper and other Native American Democrats failed to fulfill their campaign promises and were replaced by Democrats in the elections of 1845.

During the next six years nativists retreated from politics and formed secret societies opposed to immigration, of which there were at least sixty in Manhattan and Brooklyn by 1852. Members of the Order of the Star-Spangled Banner were supposedly instructed to answer "I know nothing" to all questions about their organization; the term Know Nothing was apparently first applied as a political label to the nativists by the *New York Tribune* in November 1853. The Know Nothings failed to elect a mayor in the city but became strong nationwide as dissatisfaction with the existing party system spread. In the city nativism gained support in all classes but especially among craftsmen and mechanics, who felt threatened economically and politically by the rising number of immigrants. Many nativists feared that Catholics would undermine the republic by answering to the pope rather than the United States; others hoped that by reducing the rate of immigration, progress toward industrialization would be slowed or even halted. Most groups called for the exclusion of immigrants from appointive and elective office and advocated a waiting period of twenty-one years for citizenship.

The most lasting effect of nativism was to strengthen the Democratic Party, which generally accepted immigrants. By 1855 the majority of the city's population was foreign born, and nativism ceased to be an important force in politics. A few candidates including Mayor Abram S. Hewitt (1887–88) adopted a nativist stance later in the century but generally enjoyed little success.

Louis Dow Scisco: *Political Nativism in New York State* (New York: Columbia University Press, 1901)

Amy Bridges: *A City in the Republic: Antebellum New York and the Origins of Machine Politics* (Cambridge: Cambridge University Press, 1984)

Tyler Anbinder: *Nativism and Slavery: The Northern Know Nothings and the Politics of the* 1850s (New York: Oxford University Press, 1992)

Evan Cornog

NBC. See NATIONAL BROADCASTING COMPANY.

Nederlander Organization. The second-largest theater management firm in the United States, founded by David Nederlander, a jeweler from Detroit, and developed by his son James. At one time the firm and its rival the Shubert Organization together owned about 70 percent of the theaters on Broadway. In the 1970s and 1980s rising costs and declining attendance forced the organization to produce fewer shows and rent out its theaters to concert producers and religious organizations; some of its theaters closed altogether. In the 1980s and early 1990s the Nederlander Organization fought attempts by preservationists to have theaters near Times Square designated as landmarks. The Nederlanders no longer own the firm but remain prominent in its management.

Sara J. Steen

Nedick's. A chain of restaurants in New York City, which began in the early 1920s as a business at 27th Street and Broadway that made and sold orange drink. Known for its orange and white décor and its slogan "Good food is never expensive at Nedick's," the firm quickly expanded to more than one hundred outlets in the five boroughs. During the 1950s it also opened outlets in Newark (New Jersey), Albany (New York), Philadelphia, Baltimore, and Washington. The popularity of Nedick's was due to its quick and inexpensive menu: orange drink, coffee, and doughnuts, and later frankfurters in an effort to compete with successful chains such as Nathan's. During the 1970s growing national chains such as McDonald's and Dunkin Donuts provided stiff competition, and after a concession that Nedick's operated at the Central Park Zoo was criticized in 1981 for the quality of its food and service, the firm ceased operations.

Robert Sanger Steel

Neel, Alice (*b* Colwyn, near Philadelphia, 28 Jan 1900; *d* New York City, 13 Oct 1984). Painter. After studying from 1921 to 1925 at the Philadelphia School of Design for Women (now Moore College of Art) she was briefly married to the Cuban artist Carlos Enriquez.

In 1932 she settled in Greenwich Village, where she painted portraits of left-wing activists and intellectuals such as Kenneth Fearing and Joe Gould, and expressionist renderings of street scenes that conveyed a message of social protest. She moved to Spanish Harlem in 1938 and to West 106th Street in the late 1950s, just as interest in her work was reviving. Neel became notorious for her satirical portraits of artists, critics, and collectors. The Whitney Museum of American Art held an exhibition of her work in 1974, and in 1976 she was elected to the National Institute of Arts and Letters.

Patricia Hills: *Alice Neel* (New York: Harry N. Abrams, 1983)

Patricia Hills

Negro Ensemble Company. Theater company. Formed in 1967 with a grant from the Ford Foundation, it began as a repertory company of fourteen and held workshops for actors and playwrights in St. Mark's Playhouse in the East Village; the actor and playwright Douglas Turner Ward was its artistic director. Although its repertory activities were discontinued in 1972 owing to a lack of funds, the directorate of the company continued to operate in a new location uptown. In its first twenty years the company staged more than two hundred productions, including workshops. During this period plays presented by the company won four Obie awards, two Tony awards, and a Pulitzer Prize (*A Soldier's Play* by Charles Fuller, 1982).

Ellen Foreman: "The Negro Ensemble Company: A Transcendent Vision," *The Theatre of Black Americans: A Collection of Critical Essays*, ed. Errol Hill (New York: Applause Theatre Books, 1987), 270–82

Ron Howell: "The Negro Ensemble Company: 20 Years of Theatrical Excellence," *Ebony*, March 1987, pp. 90–98

See also THEATER, §6.

E. G. Hill

"Negro plot." An alleged conspiracy by black slaves to burn New York City and murder its white inhabitants. The accusations were leveled in March 1741, after authorities discovered an interracial theft ring and illegal interracial meetings and implicated slaves in several fires and robberies. That some of the slaves were Spanish-speaking caused particular concern at a time when public attention was focused on the Anglo-Spanish War. Officials convened the provincial supreme court, which indicted more than 170 persons on charges of conspiracy based largely on hearsay and circumstantial evidence. Thirty-one blacks and four whites were executed, and more than seventy blacks and seven whites were banished from the city.

Thomas J. Davis: *A Rumor of Revolt: The "Great Negro Plot" in Colonial New York* (New York: Free Press, 1985)

Cynthia A. Kierner

Nehemiah Plan Homes. An organization that builds two-story, one-family row houses for working-class and low-income families on land formerly owned by the city. It was conceived by the retired commercial builder and civic activist I. D. Robbins and launched by East Brooklyn Congregations, a nonprofit, community-based coalition of mostly black churches formed in 1982–83. By 1992 more than 2300 houses had been built in Brownsville and East New York and another 540 were planned by the group South Bronx Churches.

Sydney H. Schanberg: "Bricks and Local Power," *New York Times*, 21 Feb 1984

Margot Hornblower: "Homes, Hope Rising from N.Y. Rubble," *Washington Post*, 12 July 1985

I. D. Robbins: "Affordable Single-family Housing Grows in Brooklyn," *Real Estate Finance Journal*, winter 1987, pp. 49–55

Bernard Hirschhorn

Neighborhood Guild. Former name of UNIVERSITY SETTLEMENT.

Neighborhood Music School. Original name of the MANHATTAN SCHOOL OF MUSIC.

Neighborhood Playhouse. Theater company formed in 1915 by Alice and Irene Lewisohn to serve the large immigrant population of the Henry Street Settlement. The repertory of the amateur company reflected the diverse nature of the audience and included Japanese and Hindu dramas as well as works by George Bernard Shaw, Eugene O'Neill, and Leonid Andreyev. The troupe gradually became more professional, but the theater faced financial problems that finally forced it to close in 1927. The Neighborhood School of Theatre opened in 1928; under the direction of Sanford Meisner, a member of the Group Theatre, it became an important training ground for young actors.

Alice Lewisohn Crowley: *The Neighborhood Playhouse: Leaves from a Theatre Scrapbook* (New York: Theatre Arts Books, 1959)

D. S. Moynihan

neighborhoods. In New York City neighborhoods range widely in size and composition. Some cover a few square blocks and have only several hundred residents (such as Hook Creek in Queens and Emerson Hill in Staten Island); others take in large sections of boroughs (such as Flushing and Jamaica in Queens and Harlem in Manhattan). Most neighborhoods in the city have a generally recognized central district, but the boundaries of neighborhoods are often difficult to define, especially if the population is transient and heterogeneous, the neighborhood is centrally situated, or the question of boundaries is politically sensitive. Some large neighborhoods encompass smaller neighborhoods: examples include Bedford–Stuyvesant and Williamsburg in Brooklyn and Morrisania in the Bronx. The number of neighborhoods in New York City is impossible to measure precisely but is almost certainly greater than three hundred.

The origin of neighborhoods in the city may be traced to the charter granted under Governor Thomas Dongan (1686), which divided lower Manhattan into six wards (North, South, Dock, East, West, and Out). Although the city was small, intimate, unified, and essentially classless, residentially there was some differentiation: in the very poorest areas, like the waterfront district of the Lower East Side, residents formed urban villages that were largely self contained; throughout the eighteenth century many residents lived and worked in the same house. The wards became more distinct as the markets, churches, and taverns of different ethnic groups gradually clustered in separate areas. Early in the eighteenth century ethnic communities took shape around local churches (Dutch in the North and West wards, English and Huguenots in the East and Dock wards). But for the most part the wards remained ethnically and economically diverse, and by the end of the century most ethnic groups had been assimilated (except for Jews and blacks, whose communities were isolated). The ethnic neighborhoods gave way to ones based on trade and class: by 1800 carters, coachmakers, and building artisans had become situated on inexpensive land north of Chambers Street, shipbuilding and maritime crafts in Corlear's Hook, printers in Franklin Square, and "nuisance" industries like brewing and tallow making in the sixth ward. Residents of Manhattan also maintained social ties and transacted business in an area extending west to Newark and the Meadowlands in New Jersey, north to what is now Yonkers, and east to the borders of what is now Nassau County. During the early nineteenth century industrial districts were systematically developed along the advancing northern periphery of the city, and residential areas like Gramercy Park were designed after the Georgian private parks of London, with restrictive residential covenants and blocks of one-family housing for the wealthy.

The years before the Civil War saw an enormous geographic mobility, which allowed the affluent to isolate themselves in residential enclaves and made the neighborhoods of Manhattan economically segregated, and often racially segregated as well, with black residents concentrated in the fifth ward and especially the Five Points. Landowners dispersed to neighborhoods that were removed from those of their tenants; wealthy merchants who had previously resided in lower Manhattan sold their homes to expanding businesses and moved to newly fashionable districts like Madison Square and 5th Avenue; and the new middle- and upper-class inhabitants of the city moved to newly constructed housing in uptown Manhattan, as old artisan neighborhoods like the West Side, the fifth ward, and the eighth ward were rebuilt as warehouse districts. "Moving Day," on 1 May of each year, became a mass ritual. During the late nineteenth century tenement neighborhoods were developed, including the Lower East Side, Hell's Kitchen (Irish), and Yorktown (German), each replete with ethnic saloons, churches, benevolent societies, and clubs.

Despite increased class division and the emergence of separate residential districts (much of the East Side north of 14th Street was primarily residential), neighborhood identities remained vague until late in the century, except at the extremes of the economic spectrum: New Yorkers did have a sense of what were the boundaries of affluent residential parks and of notorious slums like the Five Points. Members of the working class continued to define neighborhoods by such local landmarks as alleyways and saloons. The awareness of neighborhoods became sharper in the 1850s and 1860s, when journalists and reformers focused their attention on the conditions of the slums, and sharper still after the Civil War.

In the outer boroughs many neighborhoods began as cities and towns that were eventually absorbed as the boroughs expanded. These included industrial communities (such as Williamsburg and Astoria), villages (Bushwick, Flatbush, and Morrisania), suburban resorts (Bensonhurst and Bayside), suburbs built between 1910 and 1940 for Italians, Jews, Poles, and other immigrants from the crowded tenements of Manhattan, many of whom continued to travel to Manhattan by subway to work (the Grand Concourse, Jackson Heights, and Greenpoint), and speculative building ventures for the middle class (Forest Hills and Rego Park before the Second World War, Kew Gardens and Canarsie after the war). The most distinct neighborhoods tended to be those populated by racial and ethnic minorities and the working class, such as Canarsie and Bensonhurst.

Perceptions play a large role in shaping the evolution of neighborhoods: areas that are perceived as desirable for the middle class tend to grow and prosper, which in turn makes them more desirable. At the same time the boundaries of a prosperous neighborhood inevitably expand, which serves the interests of residents of adjoining areas, of real-estate brokers and speculators, and sometimes of government. A similar process works in reverse to the detriment of declining neighborhoods. Sometimes neighborhoods are renamed in an effort to improve their image: Yellow Hook became Bay Ridge in 1853 to avoid associations with the yellow fever epidemic of 1848–49, and Hell's Kitchen became Clinton after gang violence in the late 1950s. The historic preservation movement, which took hold in the 1950s, focused attention on the architectural integrity of neighborhoods and led to the designation of Historic Districts. The methods developed by preservationists later helped community activists to prevent the "gentrification" of poor neighborhoods.

From the 1960s into the 1990s neighborhoods were prominent in political and social controversies. The bitter public school strike of 1968 in Ocean Hill and Brownsville revolved around the issue of community control, an issue that continues to affect the debate over community school and community planning districts. The mayoral candidacy in 1969 of the writer Norman Mailer employed the slogan "Power to the Neighborhoods." Although the idea of the neighborhood has considerable popular appeal in New York City, it betrays a longing for a sense of local community that may never have existed.

New York City Planning Commission, Plan for New York City, vol. 6 (Cambridge: MIT Press, 1969)
Elizabeth Blackmar: *Manhattan for Rent, 1785–1850* (Ithaca, N.Y.: Cornell University Press, 1989)
Nan A. Rothschild: *New York City Neighborhoods: The 18th Century* (San Diego: Academic, 1990)
Kenneth A. Scherzer: *The Unbounded Community: Neighborhood Life and Social Structure in New York City, 1830–1875* (Durham, N.C.: Duke University Press, 1992)

Kenneth A. Scherzer

Neponsit. Neighborhood in southwestern Queens on the Rockaway Peninsula, bounded to the east by Adirondack Boulevard (Beach 142nd Street) and to the west by Beach 149th Street; Belle Harbor lies to the east and Jacob Riis Park to the west. The neighborhood began as a tract laid out in January 1910 by the Neponsit Realty Company, which first sold lots and houses in July 1911; houses costing less than $3000 were prohibited, as were hotels and stores. Unlike other areas in Rockaway the development was designed for year-round suburban living, the houses built of vitrified block and cement stucco for protection against fire and salt air. During the 1920s and 1930s the area became fully built up; in the mid 1990s it remained a wealthy neighborhood.

Vincent Seyfried

Nesbitt, George F(ash) (*b* 13 Jan 1809; *d* New York City, 7 April 1869). Printer. In 1832 he opened a firm of stationers, printers, lithographers, and envelope and card manufacturers that bore his name. For eighty years this was the leading printer for the maritime market of the city: it printed broadsides, calendars, tickets, bills of lading, and colorful, imaginative clipper ship cards (which advertised vessels sailing out of New York City). In 1855 the firm moved from the Tontine Building at Wall and Water streets to the Haggerty Building at Pearl and Pine streets, where it remained until it closed in 1912. Nesbitt died in his home at 89 Lexington Avenue.

Wendy Shadwell: "George F. Nesbitt: Maritime Specialist," *Billheads and Broadsides* (New York: South Street Seaport Museum, 1985), 21–28

Wendy Shadwell

Nevelson, Louise [née Berliawsky, Leah] (*b* Kiev, Ukraine, 23 Sept 1900; *d* New York City, 17 April 1988). Sculptor. After arriving in New York City in 1920 she began to construct large-scale wooden sculptures usually composed of crates, moldings, and other objects found in the streets, and painted uniformly in matte black. She opened a studio on Prince Street, where for many years she worked largely in obscurity. From about 1960 her work gained wide recognition and she executed several large public sculptures, including *Night Presence IV* (1972, Cor-ten steel) at Park Avenue and 92nd Street; a group of seven sculptures called *Shadows and Flags* (1977, Cor-ten steel painted black) at Louise Nevelson Plaza, a triangular park at the intersection of Maiden Lane, William Street, and Liberty Street (the first space in New York City to be named for an artist); her largest relief, *Sky Gate — New York* (1977–78, wood painted black), in the lobby of 1 World Trade Center, which evokes the city at night; and the interior of the Erol Beker Chapel of the Good Shepherd in St. Peter's Lutheran Church (1977, Citicorp Center, Lexington Avenue and 54th Street), for which she used white reliefs and free-standing sculptures. Her work was the subject of major exhibitions at the Whitney Museum of American Art in 1967, 1970, and 1980 and at the Guggenheim Museum in 1986. Nevelson was a dramatic figure known for her thick black eyelashes and exotic dress.

Laurie Lisle: *Louise Nevelson: A Passionate Life* (New York: Summit, 1990)

Harriet F. Senie

Nevins, Allan (*b* Camp Point, Ill., 20 May 1890; *d* Menlo Park, Calif., 5 March 1971). Historian. He wrote editorials for the *Evening Post* in 1913–23 and published a history of the newspaper in 1922; he became literary editor of the *Sun* in 1924 and a staff writer of the *New York World* in 1925. After teaching for a year at Cornell University he joined the faculty at Columbia University as an assistant professor of history in 1928 and became the De Witt Clinton Professor of American History in 1931. At Columbia he formed the Society of American Historians (1939) and launched the country's first oral history program (1948). A leading authority on the Civil War, he led the Civil War Centennial Commission in 1961 and wrote more than seventy books, including biographies of John D. Rockefeller and Henry Ford; his *Grover Cleveland: A Study in Courage* (1932) and *Hamilton Fish: The Inner History of the Grant Administration* (1936) won Pulitzer prizes. Nevins retired in 1958 and was honored by the Century Association and the New-York Historical Society for his contributions to the city.

Janet Frankston

New Alliance Party. Political party formed in 1979 by the social therapist Fred Newman to support such causes as feminism and gay rights. It challenged restrictive ballot access laws but used the same laws to challenge the ballot petitions of rival parties. With its antecedent the International Workers Party, it formed alliances with the conspiracy theorist Lyndon LaRouche, the activist Al Sharpton, and the Brooklyn Democratic boss Vander Beatty (before his conviction for election fraud). Its first presidential candidate, Dennis Serrette, was on the ballot in thirty-three states in 1984 and received 35,000 votes; Lenora Fulani received 250,000 votes in 1988 and 100,000 in 1992. The New Alliance Party has been accused of attempting to take over other progressive groups and grass-roots political organizations; it has also attracted criticism for its social therapy practices, considered by some to be cult-like.

Jesse Drucker

New American Library. Firm of book publishers formed in 1947 by Kurt Enoch and Victor Weybright, who had been in charge of the American office of Penguin Books. It was set up with two imprints: Signet for fiction of high quality and reference books, and Mentor for classics and serious nonfiction. Under the slogan "Good Reading for the Millions" the firm published paperbacks by such authors as William Faulkner, Thomas Mann, Eugene O'Neill, George Bernard Shaw, and Truman Capote. With "double volumes" selling for fifty cents a copy the firm broke the traditional twenty-five-cent barrier for paperbacks. Sales reached 33 million copies in 1959, but in 1966 the original partnership disbanded in a dispute over a takeover by Times–Mirror. In the late 1960s New American Library published "broadsides" against the Vietnam War, as well as Ian Fleming's highly successful series of James Bond novels. In 1979 it published three hundred titles.

Victor Weybright: *The Making of a Publisher: A Life in the 20th Century Book Revolution* (New York: Reynal, 1967)

James E. Mooney

New Amsterdam. The former name of New York City, first used in the mid 1620s. On 2 February 1653 the settlement was granted legal autonomy as a city distinct from the surrounding province. The name fell into disuse when the British defeated the Dutch in 1664.

New Blazing Star. An early name for the ferry landing on the Arthur Kill near Long Neck in Staten Island (later called Linoleumville; now called Travis). The New Blazing Star Ferry to New Jersey was established in 1757 by Jacob Fitz Randolph and was operated for several decades by John Mersereau. From the ferry landing a road led to the Port Richmond Ferry, which in turn led to Bergen Point and then to New York City, making for a short route to Philadelphia.

Barnett Shepherd

New Brighton. Neighborhood in northeastern Staten Island. The Village of New Brighton, incorporated in 1866, consisted of the six northeastern wards of the Town of Castleton and was four miles (six kilometers) long and two miles (three kilometers) wide. Variously known as Goosepatch, Vinegar Hill, and Tuxedo, it included West New Brighton, Elliotville, parts of Tompkinsville and St. George Landing, and Sailors' Snug Harbor. A village hall erected in 1871 at Lafayette Avenue and 2nd Street (now Fillmore Street) was later designated a landmark. Pauw Street is named for the Dutch patroon of Staten Island; Hamilton Park, an enclave of Victorian houses built before the Civil War, is nearby. The Goodhue Center of the Children's Aid Society stands on about forty-five acres (eighteen hectares) of land. The neighborhood is also the site of several fine old churches: Christ Episcopal Church, the Brighton Heights Reformed Church, which is a landmark atop a hill overlooking the harbor, and St. Peter's Church, the oldest Roman Catholic church on Staten Island.

Martha S. Bendix

New Dorp. Neighborhood in southeastern Staten Island, lying southeast of a portion of the hill that rises above Richmond Road. It was settled by the Dutch about 1671 as Niewe Dorp (new town), ten years after the settlement of Oude Dorp (old town). The early settlers were Dutch, French, and English farmers and fishermen. In the early eighteenth century the area near the junction of Richmond Road and Amboy Road became an important stop for horse-drawn carriages and the site of several inns and taverns, of which the Rose and Crown and the Black Horse were owned by the forebears of Cornelius Vanderbilt; during the American Revolution both taverns were occupied by British officers. In the 1850s horse racing became popular in large part because of the enthusiasm of William H. Vanderbilt, who lived and worked on a large farm near the beach from about 1842 to about 1863, and a trotting track was laid out on the southern portion of his property near the beach. The Seaview Association had a track near Richmond Road, races were held on lower New Dorp Lane (now the main street), and several hotels were built to accommodate sportsmen and spectators from New York City.

The development of New Dorp and the rest of the southern shore was slow, but aided greatly by the construction in 1860 of a railroad line that ran through the area with a station at New Dorp Lane. Vanderbilt was instrumental in establishing the line and assumed control of it when it was declared bankrupt. With the advent of railroad service real-estate development began, a grid of streets and lots was laid out, and shops opened around the station and then on New Dorp Lane. The railroad also facilitated access to the beach, and hotels with large picnic groves were built nearby. Most shops, restaurants, and theaters in the area were north of Hylan Boulevard until the Second World War, after which pollution and erosion took their toll on the beach and shopping malls were built on the empty land south of the boulevard.

Among the structures that have been designated landmarks by the city are the Gustav Mayer House (an Italianate residence from the 1840s), the New Dorp lighthouse on the hill above Richmond Road (a replacement for the Elm Tree Beacon, which stood on the beach), and the Lane Theater, in art deco style. Nearby is the Jacques Marchais Center of Tibetan Art (1947), built in the style of a Tibetan Buddhist monastery. Other notable sites include the New Dorp Moravian Church (of which the Vanderbilts were among the founders), its cemetery, and the Vanderbilt Mausoleum adjoining it. The mausoleum was designed by Richard M. Hunt and the grounds were landscaped by Frederick Law Olmsted. The Britton Cottage and the Guyon–Lake–Tysen House, which predate the American Revolution, were moved in the 1960s to Richmondtown Restoration (now Historic Richmond Town). A branch of the Gateway National Recreation Area is on land that was once the site of the Vanderbilts' farm and was later part of Miller Field, an airfield maintained by the federal government; New Dorp High School occupies the rest of the property. The residential area north of Hylan Boulevard includes mainly one-family houses on tree-lined streets. South of the boulevard are several large apartment buildings and bungalows inhabited year round. The population is mostly white, and the main ethnic group is Italian.

Marjorie Johnson

New Dublin. Obsolete name of EGBERTVILLE.

Newhouse [Neuhaus], **S(amuel) I(rving)** (*b* New York City, 24 May 1895; *d* New York City, 29 Aug 1979). Newspaper publisher. The son of Russian and Austrian Jewish immigrants, he grew up on the Lower East Side and went to work at thirteen. By twenty he was the general manager of the *Bayonne Times* in New Jersey, and he soon had a share in its profits. He bought a controlling interest in the *Staten Island Advance* in 1922 and owned it outright from 1927; in 1932 he bought the *Long Island Press*, becoming unpopular with unions for reportedly having the police attack striking workers in 1937. With the help of his brothers Theodore, Louis, and Norman he began operations in Syracuse, New York, in 1939 and Oregon in 1950, expanded into broadcasting, and bought Condé Nast's magazines in 1959. By cutting costs and keeping profits in his family Newhouse built one of the country's largest chains of newspapers, magazines, and broadcasters. He also donated more than $25 million to philanthropic causes and built the Mitzi E. Newhouse Theatre (named for his wife) at Lincoln Center. In the mid 1990s his conglomerate was run by his sons S. I. Newhouse Jr. and Donald E. Newhouse.

Alana J. Erickson

New Left. A term applied to the participants in a number of protest movements of the 1960s, especially the movements for civil rights in the South and against the Vietnam War. Although accounts of the activities of the New Left focus mainly on college campuses in place like Madison (Wisconsin), Berkeley (California), and Ann Arbor (Michigan), New York City was also an important center and many members of the New Left in other parts of the nation were originally from there. Some of the first demonstrations in the North for civil rights took place in the city in 1960, when college students and other protestors picketed Woolworth's department stores to protest segregation at lunch counters in the South. In the early 1960s groups like Student SANE and the Student Peace Union (SPU) protested the atmospheric testing of nuclear weapons, and pacifist groups gathered annually in City Hall Park to protest civil defense drills. Students for a Democratic Society (SDS), the main organizational body of the New Left, had its national office in the city from its formation in 1962 until 1965, when it moved to Chicago. During the spring of that year SDS sponsored a demonstration in front of the headquarters of Chase Manhattan Bank against its policies of investment in South Africa; forty-three demonstrators were arrested in the protest, the first of any magnitude in the United States against apartheid.

When the war in Vietnam escalated in 1965 the New Left began to grow dramatically. In October 25,000 persons marched down 5th Avenue in the first major protest in the city against the war. A few days later David Miller burned his draft card in front of the Army Induction Center on Whitehall Street in lower Manhattan, an act for which he was later tried and imprisoned. In April 1967 about 250,000 persons took part in the "spring mobilization" against the war by marching from Central Park to the United Nations. Students at Columbia University took over five buildings on campus in April 1968 to protest the cooperation of the university in research related to the war and the plans of the administration to build a gymnasium in Morningside Park; the occupation lasted for a week, until the police cleared the buildings of protestors, arresting 711 persons and injuring more than one hundred.

The protest at Columbia became a model for others at dozens of campuses during the next few years and also led to the rise of the "Weathermen," a militant faction that took control of SDS in 1969 and dissolved it within a few months. On 6 March 1970 an explosion destroyed a makeshift bomb factory in the basement of a townhouse on West 11th Street in Greenwich Village. Three members of the "Weather Underground" were killed, including Ted Gold, who had been an activist at Columbia. New York City was also the headquarters of groups like the Yippies, which were formed by Jerry Rubin and Abbie Hoffman; the Young Lords, a Puerto Rican radical group; and the local chapter of the Black Panther Party, of which twenty-one members were indicted for a bombing conspiracy and later acquitted. Radicalism in the 1960s culminated in the national student strike of May 1970, which followed the invasion of Cambodia by American troops and the killing of four students at Kent State University in Ohio by members of the National Guard. In New York City protests were largely peaceful until 8 May 1970, when students demonstrating in lower Manhattan against the war were attacked by a group of about two hundred construction workers who injured seventy protesters and passers-by. During the following autumn radicalism on college campuses began to subside, and by the mid 1970s there were few organizational traces of the New Left, but its impact on American politics and culture was considerable.

Kirkpatrick Sale: *SDS* (New York: Random House, 1973)

Nancy Zaroulis and Gerald Sullivan: *Who Spoke Up?: American Protest against the War in Vietnam, 1963–1975* (Garden City, N.Y.: Doubleday, 1984)

Maurice Isserman

New Lots. Neighborhood in northeastern Brooklyn, bounded to the north by New Lots (Sutter) Avenue, to the east by Fountain Avenue, to the south by Linden Boulevard, and to the west by Pennsylvania Avenue; it is sometimes said to overlap East New York. A special patent for the area was granted by Governor Edmund Andros in 1677 to Dutch settlers from the town of Flatbush, who changed the name from Oostwoud to distinguish the land from that which they had left behind. A village was built that remained part of Flatbush until it was made a separate town in 1852; it eventually came to include parts of what are now Brownsville, East New York, and Cypress Hills. In 1886 the village was annexed to the City of Brooklyn. Much of the housing consists of two- and four-family attached houses. The main commercial thoroughfare, New Lots Avenue (especially between Pennsylvania and Van Siclen avenues), was once lined with family businesses. In the 1980s about half the immigrants settling in New Lots and its environs were from the Dominican Republic and Jamaica; many others were from Guyana, Haiti, and Honduras. The Reformed Protestant Dutch Church (also called the New Lots Community Church) stands at 620 New Lots Avenue.

Ellen Marie Snyder-Grenier

Newman, Pauline M. (*b* Papilé, Lithuania, ?1889; *d* New York City, 8 April 1986). Labor leader. She emigrated to the United States in 1901 and settled in New York City, where she took up work in the factory that was later the site of the Triangle Shirtwaist fire in 1911. After eight years at the factory she was employed as an organizer by the International Ladies' Garment Workers' Union (ILGWU) and became active in the Women's Trade Union League and the Socialist Party. A lecturer on workers' rights and woman suffrage, she sought a seat in Congress in 1918 and became the education director of the new Union Health Center opened by the ILGWU. Newman provided workers with health education services for sixty-five years.

Robert D. Parmet

New Orange. Former Dutch name of New York City. It was given by the Dutch governor general Anthony Clove, who on 8 August 1673 had commanded a fleet that took the city from the English. Under the Treaty of Westminster (19 February 1674) the province returned to English rule and the name New York was restored.

Robert Seder

New Republic. Weekly magazine launched in New York City in 1914 by Herbert Croly, Walter Weyl, and Walter Lippmann as a forum for progressive thought. It sought to influence young intellectuals and espoused the upper-middle-class liberal cosmopolitanism of the Northeast. The magazine supported the entry of the United States into the First World War (although some of its writers such as Randolph Bourne opposed it) and embraced the status quo, which it hoped to improve through enlightened reform devised and implemented by an educated élite. Among its first writers were Felix Frankfurter and Raymond Moley. The magazine moved to Washington in 1950–51.

David Seideman: *The New Republic: A Voice of Modern Liberalism* (New York: Praeger, 1986)

Lawson Bowling

newsboys. The emergence of the penny press in the 1830s made newsboys essential to the distribution of newspapers in New York City. Often the orphaned and abandoned children of immigrants, newsboys (also called newsies) plied the streets of the city for the next century. The newsboys were loud, tough, self-reliant entrepreneurs who spoke a distinct dialect, used colorful nicknames, and frequented the city's theaters; their subculture was often celebrated in novels, plays, and paintings. Homeless newsboys were subject to the malevolent influences of the saloon and the gambling den and soon drew the attention

Alice Austen, Children Selling "Extra" Edition at City Hall *(1896)*

of reformers: in 1854 the Children's Aid Society opened the first of several Newsboys' Lodging Houses, which offered bed, board, and a minimum of night-schooling, and newsboys were sometimes sent west on orphan trains. The mass-circulation evening newspapers that catered to the commuters and theatergoers of the 1890s were especially dependent on newsboys. By then the typical newsboy was an Italian or Jewish immigrant boy eleven to fifteen years old who lived at home and could hawk the evening papers after school. Girls also sold newspapers, but the practice was discouraged as unsafe. Boisterous newsboys were common in the heavily traveled areas near City Hall, Times Square, and the bridges across the East River. Attempts by reformers to license newsboys and reduce their late hours were only moderately successful: newsboys always preferred to police themselves and in 1899 organized a successful strike against the *Evening World* and the *New York Journal.* The newsboy eventually succumbed to adult competition, suburban home delivery, and the enclosed newsstand.

Charles Loring Brace: *Short Sermons to News Boys: With a History of the Formation of the News Boys' Lodging-house* (New York: Charles Scribner, 1866)

Jacob A. Riis: "The New York Newsboy," *Century Magazine* 85 (1912), 247–55

David Nasaw: *Children of the City: At Work and at Play* (Garden City, N.Y.: Doubleday, 1985)

Mariam Touba

New School for Social Research. Private college at 66 West 12th Street in Greenwich Village, formed in 1919 as an experimental institute to provide an alternative to the "academic authoritarianism" of Columbia University. From its earliest years the school prided itself on its unconventional character. Early faculty members included the economist Wesley Mitchell, the social theorist Thorstein Veblen, the philosopher Horace Kallen, and the historians Charles A. Beard and James Harvey Robinson. In 1922 it became clear that courses in the social sciences were not attracting enough students to meet expenses; Alvin Johnson, an economist trained at Columbia, took over the directorship and quickly transformed the school into a thriving institution by replacing the permanent faculty with visiting lecturers and allowing all to enroll in noncredit evening courses for a modest fee.

In the 1920s Johnson broadened the curriculum to include courses in literature, music, philosophy, psychology, and art. The interdisciplinary environment of the New School proved especially valuable to artists interested in collaborative efforts. In the interwar years the school attracted several important figures in the arts, including the composers Aaron Copland and Henry Cowell, the dancers Doris Humphrey and Charles Weidman, the art historian Leo Stein, the architectural historian Lewis Mumford, the painters Stuart Davis and Thomas Hart Benton, and the sculptor William Zorach. The school helped to popularize psychoanalysis, Marxism, expressionist drama, Keynesian economics, structuralism, Weberian sociology, and feminist theory.

After 1933 the New School became a sanctuary for Jewish and socialist scholars persecuted by Hitler. To provide an academic sponsor for displaced European scholars who would otherwise be denied entry into the United States, Johnson formed the University in Exile with the support of the Rockefeller Foundation; authorized by the State of New York in 1935 to grant graduate degrees, this later became the school's graduate faculty. The Dramatic Workshop was formed in 1940 to give the radical dramatist Erwin Piscator, a refugee from Berlin, a place to practice his craft. During its eleven-year history the workshop provided a training ground for such actors and playwrights as Marlon Brando, Tennessee Williams, Rod Steiger, and Shelley Winters. In 1942 the École Libre des Hautes Études was formed as an autonomous division of the school by several leading intellectuals opposed to the Vichy government, among them the theologian Jacques Maritain, the philosopher Alexandre Koyré, the linguist Roman Jakobson, and the anthropologist Claude Lévi-Strauss, who developed his structuralist theory while teaching in New York City.

After the Second World War many of the academic innovations of the New School were adopted by conventional colleges and universities. Its adult education division attracted distinguished lecturers and permanent faculty such as the literary critic Alfred Kazin, the political theorist Hannah Arendt, the economist Robert Heilbroner, and the composer John Cage. In the mid 1990s the New School for Social Research had 25,000 students and one thousand faculty members.

Peter M. Rutkoff and William B. Scott: *New School: A History of the New School for Social Research* (New York: Free Press, 1986)

Peter M. Rutkoff, William B. Scott

Newspaper Row. A name applied from the 1840s to the early twentieth century to an expanse of Park Row in lower Manhattan where the offices of many daily newspapers were situated, including the *Globe and Commercial Advertiser*, the *New York Times*, the *Recorder*, and more than a dozen others. The area was also occupied by paper manufacturers, advertising agencies, photographers, printers, and printmakers, including the renowned firm of Currier and Ives at 152 Nassau Street. Immediately south of the entrance to the Brooklyn Bridge stood the great golden dome of Joseph Pulitzer's World Building (1890, demolished). Nearby, extending above the skyline at Spruce and Nassau streets, was the red-brick clock tower of the Tribune Building (1870s, demolished). The demise of Newspaper Row began when the city's major daily newspapers moved uptown. The *New York Herald* was one of the first, moving in 1894 to 34th Street and Herald Square, and the *Times* followed in 1904, leaving Park Row for new quarters at Times Square. Some vestiges of Newspaper Row remain: the Associated Press was founded beneath the twin cupolas of the Park Row Building (1899), at 15 Park Row; 38 Park Row is the Potter Building (1883), where the *New York Press* and the *New-York Observer* were published; 41 Park Row, the former New York Times Building (1889; later remodeled), is now part of the campus of Pace University.

Rebecca Read Shanor

newspapers. The first newspaper in New York City was the *New-York Gazette* (8 November 1725) of William Bradford, a member of a prominent family of newspaper publishers in Philadelphia who had moved to the city to become the government printer. New York was the third colony to have a newspaper, after Massachusetts and Pennsylvania. Displeased by the royalist leanings of the *Gazette*, a number of wealthy merchants and landowners supported the *New-York Weekly Journal*, which was printed from 5 November 1733 by John Peter Zenger, Bradford's former apprentice and partner. He challenged the actions of the colonial government and was arrested on charges of seditious libel on 17 November 1734; his wife, Anna Catherine Zenger, continued the newspaper while he was in jail. His trial was the first of its kind in the colonies. Begun on 4 August 1735 and ending in his acquittal, it helped to win support for the American Revolution. From 1766 the *New-York Journal* was published by John Holt, one of the most influential printers outside Boston. In 1768–69 it was one of several colonial newspapers to print the "Journal of Occurrences," a series of anti-British articles written by Samuel Adams and the Sons of Liberty. In the years before the revolution, Holt led efforts to distribute such tracts to printers from Boston to Charleston, South Carolina, and fled New York City as British troops moved in. The newspaper *Rivington's New-York Gazetteer; or, the Connecticut, New-Jersey, Hudson's River, and Quebec Weekly Advertiser* was first published in 1773 by James Rivington, a Tory who had opened the first chain of bookshops in the colonies; he renamed it the *Royal Gazette* after patriots refused his invitation to resolve the colonial conflict through negotiation. The *New York Gazette and Mercury* was published by the Tory printer Hugh Gaine.

After the revolution the number of newspapers in the city increased. Holt returned in 1783 and resumed publishing the *Journal*, which on his death in 1784 was run until the following year by his widow, Elizabeth Holt. The articles by Alexander Hamilton, John Jay, and James Madison that were later compiled

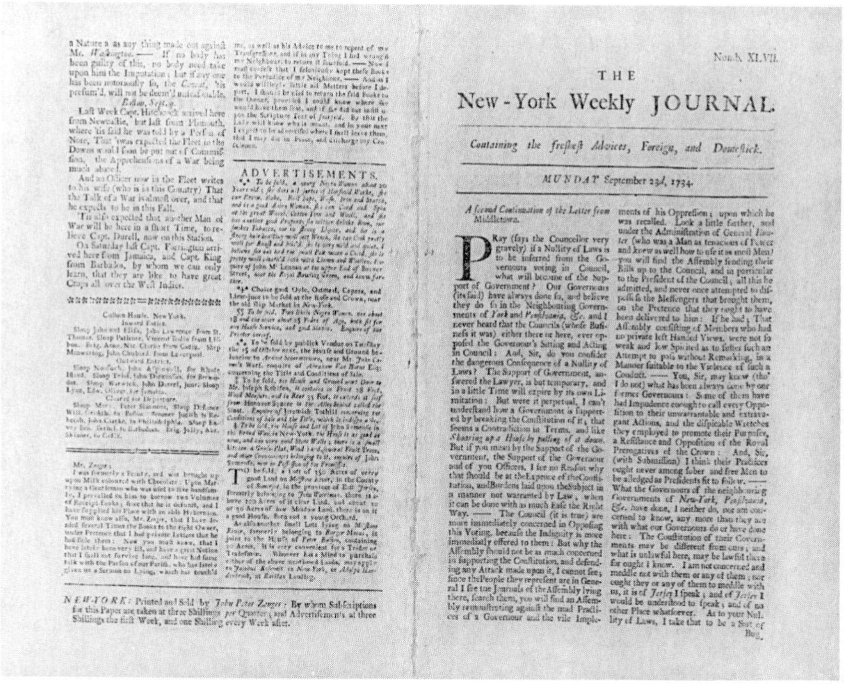

a Nature a as any thing made out against Mr. *Washington*. —— If no body has been guilty of this, no body need take upon him the Imputation; but if any one has been notoriously so, the *Censure*, 'tis presum'd, will not be deem'd unseasonable.

Boston, Sept. 9.

Last Week Capt. Hitchcock arrived here from Newcastle, but last from Plimouth, where 'tis said he was told by a Person of Note, That 'twas expected the Fleet in the Downs would soon be put out of Commission, the Apprehensions of a War being much abated.

And an Officer now in the Fleet writes to his wife (who is in this Country) That the Talk of a War is almost over, and that he expects to be in this Fall.

'Tis also expected that another Man of War will be here in a short Time, to relieve Capt. Durell, now on this Station.

On Saturday last Capt. Farrington arrived here from Jamaica, and Capt. King from Barbados, by whom we can only learn, that they are like to have great Crops all over the West Indies.

Custom House, New York.

Inward Entries.

Sloop John and Eliza, John Lawrence from St. Thomas. Sloop Patience, Vincent Bodin from Lisbon. Brig. Anne, Nic. Clarke from Cadiz. Sloop Mainwaring, John Chubard from Leverpool.

Outward Entries.

Sloop Neufuch, John Aspinwall, for Rhode Island. Sloop Trial, John Dickinson, for Bermudas. Sloop Warwick, John Darrel, jun. Sloop Lyon, Edw. Oliver, for Jamaica.

Cleared for Departure.

Sloop Mary, Peter Simmons, Sloop Defiance Will. Griffith, to Boston. Scooner Judith & Rebecah, John Clarke, to Philadelphia. Sloop Every [illegible] to Barbadoes. Brig. Jolly, Ant. Skinner, to Cadiz.

Mr. Zenger;

I was formerly a Beauty, and was brought up upon Milk coloured with Chocolate; Upon Marrying a Gentleman who was used to live handsomely, I prevailed on him to borrow two Volumes of Receipt Books; since that he is defunct, and I have supplied his Place with an able Hybernian. You must know also, Mr. Zenger, that I have denied several Times the Books to the right Owner, under Pretence that I had private Letters that he had stole them: Now you must know, that I have lately been very ill, and have a great Notion that I shall not survive long, and have had some talk with the Parson of our Parish, who has lately given us a Sermon on Lying, which has touch'd me, as well as his Advice to me to repent of my Transgression, and if in any Thing I had wrong'd my Neighbour, to return it fourfold. —— Now I must confess that I feloniously kept these Books to the Prejudice of my Neighbour. —— And as I would willingly settle all Matters before I depart, I should be glad to return the said Books to the Owner, provided I could know where she would have them sent, and if she did not insist upon the Scripture Text of fourfold. By this the Lady will know who is meant, and in your next I expect to be advertised where I shall leave them, that I may die in Peace, and discharge my Conscience.

ADVERTISEMENTS.

*** *To be sold, a young Negro Woman about 20 Years old; she does all sorts of Houshold Work, she can Brew, Bake, Boil Soft, Wash, Iron and Starch, and is a good Dairy Woman, she can Card and Spin at the great Wheel, Cotton Linen and Woollen, and she has another good Property she neither drinks Rum, nor smokes Tobacco, nor is Strong Liquor, and she is a strong healthy well set Wench, she can Cook pretty well for Roast and boil'd, she is very mild and quiet, I believe she has had the small Pox when a Child, she is pretty well match'd with Linen and Woollen. Enquire of John Mc Lennan at the upper End of Beaver Street, near the Royal Bowling Green, and know further.*

\$ Choice good Oyle, Oatmeal, Capers, and Lime-juice to be sold at the Rose and Crown, near the old Slip Market in *New-York*.

§§ *To be sold, Two likely Negro Women, one about 18 and the other about 25 Years of Age, both fit for any House Service, and good Slaves. Enquire of the Printer hereof.*

*** To be sold by publick Vendue on Tuesday the 15 of *October* next, the House and Ground belonging to *Arnout Schermerhorn*, near Mr. *John Cruger's* Warf, enquire of *Abraham Van Horne* Esq; concerning the Title and Conditions of Sale.

‡ To be sold, *the House and Ground next Door to* Mr. Joseph Robinson, *it contains in Front 28 Foot, Wood Measure, and in Rear 33 Foot, it extends it self from* Hanover Square *to the Alley behind called the* Sloat. *Enquire of* Jeremiah Tuthill *concerning the Conditions of Sale and the Title, which is indisputable.*

§ *To be sold, the House and Lot of* John Symonds *in the Broad Way, in* New-York, *the House is as good as new, and has very good Stone Walls; there is a small Kitchen a Grass-Plat, Wood Yard, several Fruit Trees, and other Conveniencies belonging to it, enquire of* John Symonds, *now in Possession of the Premises.*

TO be sold, a Lott of 350 Acres of very good Land on *Millstone River*, in the County of *Somerset*, in the province of *East Jersey*, formerly belonging to *John Wortman*, there is above 100 Acres of it clear Land, and about 20 or 30 Acres of low Meadow Land, there is on it a good House, Barn and a young Orchard.

As also another small Lott lying on *Millstone River*, formerly belonging to *Burger Meuse*, it joins to the House of *Peter Bodine*, containing 10 Acres, It is very convenient for a Trader or Tradesman. Whoever has a Mind to purchase either of the above mentioned Lands, may apply to *Jacobus Kiersted* in *New York*, or *Adolph Hardenbrook*, at *Raritan* Landing.

NEW-YORK: Printed and Sold by *John Peter Zenger*; By whom Subscriptions for this Paper are taken at three Shillings *per* Quarter; and Advertisements at three Shillings the first Week, and one Shilling every Week after.

Numb. XLVII.

THE

New-York Weekly JOURNAL.

Containing the freshest Advices, Foreign, and Domestick.

MUNDAY September 23d, 1734.

A second Continuation of the Letter from Middletown.

PRay (says the Councellor very gravely) if a Nullity of Laws is to be inferred from the Governours voting in Council, what will become of the Support of Government? Our Governours (its said) have always done so, and believe they do so in the Neighbouring Governments of *York* and *Pensilvania*, &c. and I never heard that the Councils (*whose* Business it was) either there or here, ever opposed the Governour's Sitting and Acting in Council: And, Sir, do you consider the dangerous Consequence of a Nullity of Laws? The Support of Government, answered the Lawyer, is but temporary, and in a little Time will expire by its own Limitation: But were it perpetual, I can't understand how a Government is supported by breaking the Constitution of it; that seems a Contradiction in Terms, and like *Shoaring up a House by pulling of it down.* But if you mean by the Support of the Government, the Support of the Governour and of you Officers, I see no Reason why that should be at the Expence of the Constitution, and Burdens laid upon the Subject in a manner not warranted by Law, when it can be done with as much Ease the Right Way. —— The Council (it is true) are more immediately concerned in Opposing this Voting, because the Indignity is more immediatly offered to them: But why the Assembly should not be as much concerned in supporting the Constitution, and defending any Attack made upon it, I cannot see; since the People they represent are in General I see the Journals of the Assembly lying there, search them, you will find an Assembly remonstrating against the mad Practices of a Governour and the vile Implements of his Oppression; upon which he was recalled. Look a little farther, and under the Administration of General *Hunter* (who was a Man as tenacious of Power and knew as well how to use it as most Men) you will find the Assembly sending their Bills up to the Council, and in particular to the President of the Council; all this he admitted, and never once attempted to dispossess the Messengers that brought them, on the Pretence that they ought to have been delivered to him: If he had, That Assembly consisting of Members who had no private left Handed Views, were not so weak and low Spirited as to suffer such an Attempt to pass without Remarking, in a Manner suitable to the Violence of such a Conduct. —— You, Sir, may know (tho' I do not) what has been always done by our former Governours: Some of them have had Impudence enough to call every Opposition to their unwarrantable and extravagant Actions, and the dispicable Wretches they employed to promote their Purposes, a Resistance and Opposition of the Royal Prerogatives of the Crown: And, Sir, (with Submission) I think their Practices ought never among sober and free Men to be alledged as Presidents fit to follow. —— What the Governours of the neighbouring Governments of *New-York*, *Pensilvania*, &c. have done, I neither do, nor am concerned to know, any more than they are with what our Governours do or have done here: The Constitution of their Governments may be different from ours; and what is unlawful here, may be lawful there for ought I know. I am not concerned and meddle not with them or any of them; nor ought they or any of them to meddle with us, it is of *Jersey* I speak; and of *Jersey* I would be understood to speak; and of no other Place whatsoever. As to your Nullity of Laws, I take that to be a Sort of

Bug,

The New-York Weekly Journal, *23 September 1734*

as the *Federalist* were printed in the *New York Independent Journal* before being circulated throughout the states in 1787–88. The best-known Federalist newspaper was the *Gazette of the United States*, published in the city by John Fenno. The prominent Federalist Noah Webster was the editor of several newspapers, including the *Minerva* (daily, 1793). During the 1790s newspapers provided accounts of feuds between Federalists and the anti-Federalist supporters of Thomas Jefferson. After the Alien and Sedition acts were passed in 1798 some anti-Federalist newspapers ceased publication, among them the *Time Piece* of John Burk; most of the city supported the Federalists. Hamilton began publishing the *New York Evening Post* in 1801 and in 1805 defended Harry Croswell (editor of the *Wasp*, a Federalist newspaper in Hudson, New York), who was accused of reprinting material from the *Evening Post* and committing libel against President Jefferson. Hamilton prevailed by maintaining that in libel cases the truthfulness of what a defendant had written or published was relevant and therefore admissible; this led to changes in New York State law in 1805 and later in federal law.

By 1800 there were five daily newspapers in New York City, which rapidly became the nation's leading commercial center. One of the

Stacks of the Sunday New York Times *near a newsstand in Greenwich Village on a Saturday night, 1991*

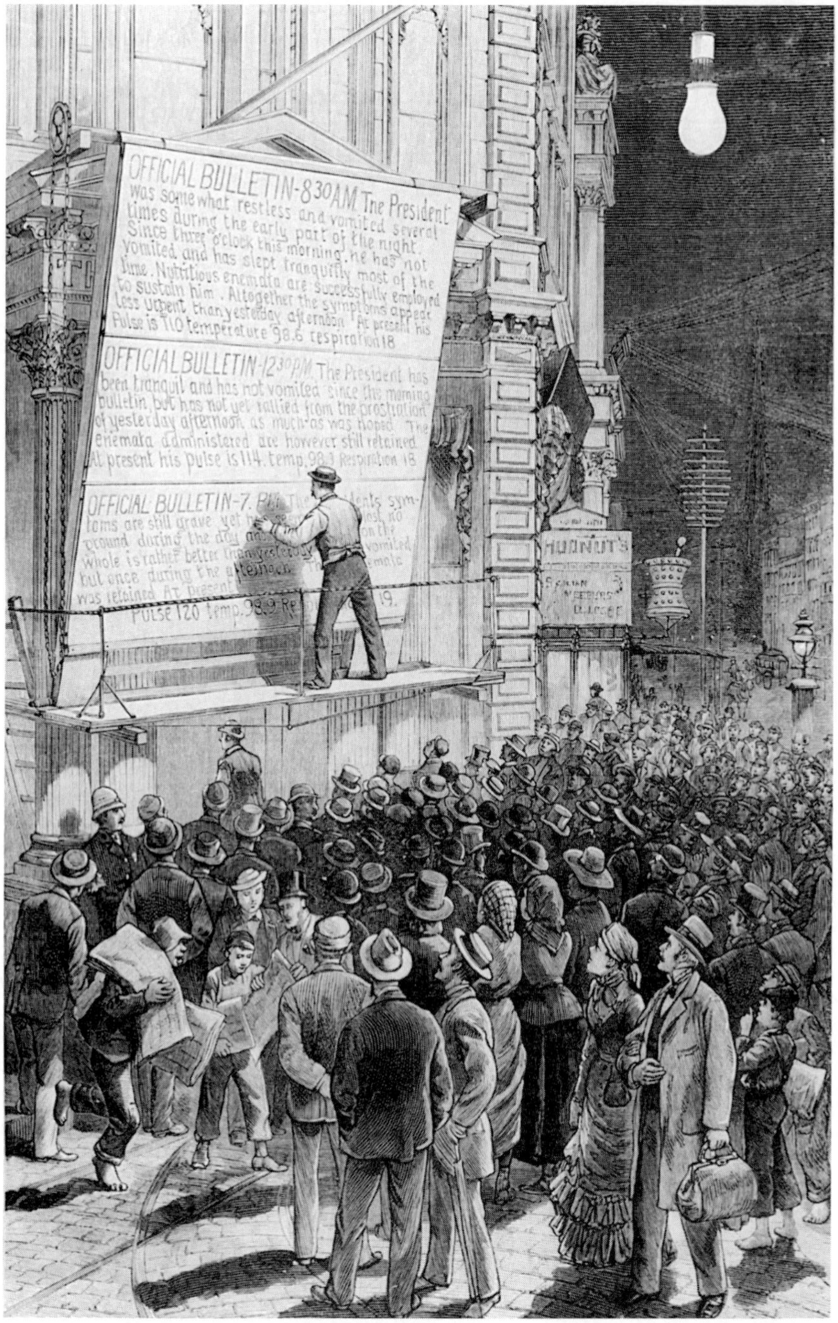

News bulletin outside the New York Herald *at Park Row and Ann Street, 3 September 1881. A reporter brings information from the telegraph in the office about President James A. Garfield's condition several weeks after he was shot by a disgruntled office seeker.*

few that took up the cause of workers was the *Evening Post*, edited by the poet William Cullen Bryant from 1825; others included the *Working Man's Advocate* (1829) of George H. Evans and the *Free Enquirer* (1829) of Fanny Wright, which was supported by Walt Whitman. The country's first newspaper owned by blacks was *Freedom's Journal*, launched in the city on 16 March 1827 by John B. Russwurm, who was the first black American to graduate from college (Bowdoin College, 1826), and the Presbyterian minister Samuel Cornish; it ceased publication in October 1829, and from 1837 Cornish was an editor of the *Weekly Advocate*, published by Phillip A. Bell and renamed the *Colored American* before ceasing operations in 1842.

Gradually presses were improved and printing became more efficient. Samuel Rust invented the Washington hand press (1827) in New York City, and steam-driven presses were introduced a few years later. By the late 1830s the presses manufactured by the firm of Robert Hoe produced more than four thousand double impressions an hour. On 3 September 1833 Benjamin H. Day brought out the first issue of the *Sun*, which carried mostly human-interest stories and was aimed at a wide audience. Similar newspapers became popular in cities nationwide and were known as the PENNY PRESS. Of the thirty-five penny newspapers in New York City during the 1830s the largest and most widely respected was the *New York Herald* (1835). Under the direction of James Gordon Bennett Sr. it aggressively gathered news and offered thorough coverage of sports, financial news, and foreign news. In 1841 it introduced regular Sunday editions. Soon there were ten daily newspapers in the city. The main rival of the *Herald* was the *New York Tribune*, which began in 1841 under Horace Greeley and became known for its thorough reporting and its global perspective on farming, labor, and business. During the 1830s and 1840s aggressive coverage was also provided by the *Courier and Enquirer* of James Watson Webb and the *Journal of Commerce*, published by Arthur Tappan and later by David Hale and Gerard Hallock. The *New York Times* was launched in 1851 by Henry J. Raymond. Fierce competition led editors to use the Pony Express, pigeons, railroads, and steamboats in gathering news.

Of the penny newspapers introduced in the 1830s only the *Herald* and the *Sun* survived, but the development of the popular press changed journalism profoundly. Regular reports from Washington were begun in 1822 by the *New-York Statesman* under the direction of Nathaniel Carter. Eliab Kingman became the first permanent Washington correspondent (1830–61) and wrote for such publications as the *Journal of Commerce*. The Harbor News Association, the first cooperative organization for gathering news, was formed in 1849. A number of women journalists gained influence, including Margaret Fuller of the *Tribune*. Advertising became more sophisticated. By 1860 the *Herald* had a circulation of 77,000 and was the world's largest daily newspaper. The *Tribune* was one of the most popular newspapers outside New York City.

Journalism played an important role in the Civil War. The weekly edition of the *Tribune* had a national circulation of more than 200,000 as early as 1852 and provided extensive coverage of the intense debates in the West before the war. By 1861 the *Herald* was able to print 135,000 copies a day. Greeley inveighed against slavery, the abolition of which he saw as a moral issue that transcended the preservation of the Union. Bennett supported President Abraham Lincoln's policies halfheartedly. Censorship was pervasive, and when the *New York World* and the *Journal of Commerce* in 1864 published a forged document concocted by a stock market speculator they were forced to suspend publication for two days. Coverage of the draft riots of 1863 was sensational, and the presidential election year of 1864 saw angry debates over the poli-

Eighteenth-Century Newspapers in New York City, by Date of First Publication
(Frequencies of publication are given in chronological order.)

New-York Gazette (1725–44), weekly; pubd by William Bradford, later with H. DeForeest; continued by New-York Evening-Post

New-York Weekly Journal (1733–51), weekly; pubd by John Peter Zenger

New-York Weekly Post-Boy (1743–47), weekly; pubd by James Parker; continued by New-York Gazette, revived in the Weekly Post-Boy

New-York Evening-Post (1744–52), weekly; pubd by Henry DeForeest

New-York Gazette, revived in the Weekly Post-Boy (1747–52), weekly; pubd by James Parker; continued by New-York Gazette; or, the Weekly Post-Boy

Independent Reflector (1752–53), weekly; pubd by James Parker

New-York Mercury (1752–68), weekly;[1] pubd by Hugh Gaine; continued by New-York Gazette and the Weekly Mercury

Occasional Reverberator (1753), weekly; pubd by J(ames) Parker

New-York Gazette; or, the Weekly Post-Boy (1753–59), weekly; pubd by James Parker and William Weyman; continued by Parker's New-York Gazette; or, the Weekly Post-Boy

Instructor (1755), weekly; pubd by J(ames) Parker and W(illiam) Weyman

John Englishman. In Defence of the English Constitution (1755), weekly; pubd by J(ames) Parker and W(illiam) Weyman

Weyman's New York Gazette (1759), weekly; pubd by William Weyman; continued by New-York Gazette

Parker's New-York Gazette; or, the Weekly Post-Boy (1759–62), weekly; pubd by Samuel Parker; continued by New-York Gazette; or, the Weekly Post-Boy

New-York Gazette (1759–67), weekly; pubd by William Weyman

American Chronicle (1762), weekly; pubd by Samuel Farley

New-York Gazette; or, the Weekly Post-Boy (1762–66), weekly; pubd by John Holt; continued by New-York Journal; or, General Advertiser

New-York Pacquet (1763), weekly; pubd by John Mecom, printer

New-York Gazette; or, the Weekly Post-Boy (1766–73), weekly; pubd by James Parker

New-York Journal; or, General Advertiser (1766–82), weekly; pubd by John Holt; continued by Independent New-York Gazette

New-York Gazette and the Weekly Mercury (1768–83), weekly; pubd by Hugh Gaine

New-York Chronicle (1769–70), weekly; pubd by Alexander and James Robertson

Rivington's New-York Gazetteer; or, the Connecticut, New-Jersey, Hudson's River, and Quebec Weekly Advertiser (1773–75), weekly; pubd by James Rivington; continued by Rivington's New-York Gazette; or, the Connecticut, New-Jersey, Hudson's River, and Quebec Weekly Advertiser

Constitutional Gazette (1775–76), semiweekly, pubd by John Anderson

New-York Packet, and the American Advertiser (1776–84), weekly, semiweekly; pubd by Samuel Loudon; continued by Loudon's New-York Packet

Rivington's New-York Loyal Gazette (1777), weekly; pubd by James Rivington; continued by Royal Gazette

Rivington's New-York Gazette; or, the Connecticut, New-Jersey, Hudson's River, and Quebec Weekly Advertiser (1777), weekly; pubd by James Rivington; continued by Rivington's New-York Loyal Gazette

Royal Gazette (1777–83), semiweekly, weekly; pubd by James Rivington; continued by Rivington's New-York Gazette, and Universal Advertiser

Royal American Gazette (1777–83), weekly, semiweekly; pubd by James Robertson

New-York Mercury; or, General Advertiser (1779–83), weekly; pubd by William Lewis

Brooklyne Hall Super-Extra Gazette (1782), irregular; pubd by Charles Loosely

New-York Evening Post (1782–83), thrice weekly; pubd by (Christopher) Sower (Jr.), (William) Morton, and (Samuel) Horner; continued by New-York Morning Post

Independent New-York Gazette (1783), weekly; pubd by John Holt; continued by Independent Gazette; or, the New-York Journal Revived

Rivington's New-York Gazette, and Universal Advertiser (1783), semiweekly; pubd by James Rivington

Town and Country Journal; or, the American Advertiser (1783), weekly; pubd by W(illiam) Ross

Independent Gazette; or, the New-York Journal Revived (1783–84), weekly, semiweekly; pubd by John Holt; continued by New-York Journal, and State Gazette

New-York Morning Post (1783–85), semiweekly; pubd by (William) Morton and (Samuel) Horner; continued by New-York Morning Post, and Daily Advertiser

New-York Gazetteer(, and Country Journal) (1783–86), weekly, semiweekly, thrice weekly;[2] pubd by Shepard Kollock; continued by New-York Gazetteer, or Daily Evening-Post

Independent Journal; or, the General Advertiser (1783–88), semiweekly, weekly; pubd by (Charles) Webster and (John) M'Lean; continued by New-York Daily Gazette

New-York Journal, and State Gazette (1784–85), weekly; pubd by Elizabeth Holt; continued by New-York Journal, and the General Advertiser

Loudon's New-York Packet (1784–85), semiweekly; pubd by Samuel Loudon; continued by New-York Packet

Daily Advertiser, Political, Commercial and Historical (1785), daily; pubd by F(rancis) Childs; continued by Daily Advertiser; Political, Historical and Commercial

New-York Journal, and the General Advertiser (1785), weekly; pubd by Elizabeth Holt; continued by New-York Journal; or, the Weekly Register

New-York Journal; or, the Weekly Register (1785–87), weekly; pubd by Eleazar Oswald; continued by New-York Journal, and Weekly Register

Daily Advertiser; Political, Historical and Commercial (1785–87), daily; pubd by F(rancis) Childs; continued by Daily Advertiser

New-York Morning Post, and Daily Advertiser (1785–88), daily; pubd by (William) Morton and (Samuel) Horner; continued by Morning Post, and Daily Advertiser

New-York Packet (1785–92), weekly, semiweekly, thrice weekly; pubd by Samuel Loudon; continued by Diary, or Loudon's Register

American Price-Current (1786), weekly; pubd by Francis Childs for Aeneas Lamont; continued by New-York Price-Current

New-York Gazetteer; or, Daily Evening-Post (1786), daily; pubd by (Shepard) Kollock, (George) Carroll, and (John) Patterson; continued by New-York Gazetteer; and, Public Advertiser

New-York Price-Current (1786), weekly; pubd by Francis Childs

New-York Gazetteer; and, Public Advertiser (1786–87), semiweekly; pubd by (George) Carroll and (John) Patterson

New-York Journal, and Weekly Register (1787), weekly; pubd by Thomas Greenleaf; continued by New-York Journal, and Daily Patriotic Register

New-York Journal, and Daily Patriotic Register (1787–88), daily; pubd by Thomas Greenleaf; continued by New-York Journal, and Weekly Register

Daily Advertiser (1787–1806), daily;[3] pubd by F(rancis) Childs; continued by People's Friend and Daily Advertiser

Impartial Gazetteer, and Saturday Evening Post (1788), weekly; pubd by (John)

(continued)

Eighteenth-Century Newspapers in New York City, by Date of First Publication *(Continued)*

Harrisson and (Stephen) Purdy; continued by New-York Weekly Museum

New-York Museum (1788), semiweekly; pubd by John Russell

New-York Journal, and Weekly Register (1788–90), weekly; pubd by Thomas Greenleaf; continued by New-York Journal, and Patriotic Register

Morning Post, and Daily Advertiser (1788–92), daily; pubd by William Morton; continued by New-York Morning Post

New-York Daily Gazette (1788–95), daily; pubd by J(ohn) and A(rchibald) M'Lean; continued by New-York Gazette and General Advertiser

(New-York) Weekly Museum (1788–1817), weekly; pubd by John Harrisson and Stephen Purdy Jr.;[4] continued by Ladies' Weekly Museum

Gazette of the United States (1789–93), semiweekly; pubd by John Fenno; continued by Gazette of the United States and Evening Advertiser[5]

New-York Journal, and Patriotic Register (1790–93), weekly; pubd by Thomas Greenleaf; continued by Greenleaf's New York Journal, and Patriotic Register

New-York Morning Post (1792), daily; pubd by William Morton

Diary, or Loudon's Register (1792–95), daily; pubd by Samuel Loudon Jr.; continued by Diary, and Universal (Daily) Advertiser

Evening Mercury (1793), daily; pubd by John Buel

Journal des Révolutions de la Partie Française de Sainte-Domingue (1793), semiweekly; ed. Tanguy de la Boissiere; pubd by Thomas Greenleaf, printer

Columbian Gazetteer (1793–94), semiweekly; pubd by John Buel and Company; continued by New-York Evening Post

American Minerva (1793–96), daily;[6] pubd by George Bunce, and Company; continued by Minerva, and Mercantile Evening Advertiser

New-York Evening Post (1794–95), thrice weekly; pubd by L(evi) Wayland

Herald, a Gazette for the Country (1794–97), semiweekly;[7] pubd by George Bunce, and Company; continued by Spectator

Greenleaf's New York Journal, and Patriotic Register (1794–1800), weekly; pubd by Thomas Greenleaf; continued by Republican Watch-Tower

Argus and Greenleaf's New Daily Advertiser (1795), daily; pubd by Thomas Greenleaf; continued by Argus; or, Greenleaf's New Daily Advertiser

New-York Weekly Chronicle (1795), weekly; pubd by William Hurtin Jr. and Andrew Commardinger

Mott and Hurtin's New-York Weekly Chronicle (1795), weekly; pubd by Jacob S. Mott and William Hurtin Jr.; continued by New-York Weekly Chronicle

Gazette Française et Américaine (1795–96), thrice weekly; pubd by J(ohn) Delafond and by Labruère, Parisot and Company; continued by Gazette Française

Diary, and Universal (Daily) Advertiser (1795–96), daily; pubd by Samuel Loudon Jr.; continued by Diary

Argus; or, Greenleaf's New Daily Advertiser (1795–96), daily; pubd by Thomas Greenleaf; continued by Greenleaf's New Daily Advertiser

New-York Gazette and General Advertiser (1795–1820), daily; pubd by A(rchibald) M'Lean; continued by New York Gazette and General Advertiser[8]

New-York Prices Current (1796–97), weekly; pubd by James Oram; continued by Oram's New-York Price-Current, and Marine Register

Diary (1796–97), daily; pubd by Cornelius C. Van Alen and Company; continued by Diary and Mercantile Advertiser

Minerva, and Mercantile Evening Advertiser (1796–97), daily; pubd by George Bunce and Company; continued by Commercial Advertiser

Register of the Times (1796–98), weekly;[9] pubd by Cornelius C. Van Alen and Company

Gazette Française (1796–99), thrice weekly; pubd by (Claude) Parisot and Company

Greenleaf's New Daily Advertiser (1796–1800), daily; pubd by Thomas Greenleaf; continued by American Citizen and General Advertiser

Youth's News Paper (1797), weekly; pubd by J(acob) S. Mott and C(harles) Smith

Diary and Mercantile Advertiser (1797–98), daily; pubd by (John) Crookes and (Robert) Saunders; continued by Mercantile Advertiser

Tablet; and Weekly Advertiser (1797–98), weekly; pubd by (John) Tiebout and (Thomas) Burling

Time Piece (1797–98), thrice weekly; pubd by Philip Freneau and Alexander Menut[10]

Oram's New-York Price-Current, and Marine Register (1797–99), weekly; pubd by James Oram; continued by New-York Price-Current

Spectator (1797–1804), semiweekly;[11] pubd by George F. Hopkins; continued by New-York Spectator

Commercial Advertiser (1797–1804), daily;[12] pubd by George F. Hopkins; continued by New-York Commercial Advertiser

Mercantile Advertiser (1798–1829), daily; pubd by John Crookes; continued by New-York Mercantile Advertiser[13]

Columbian Gazette (1799), weekly; pubd by (Robert M.) Hurtin and (Monteith) M'Farlane for J(ohn) M(ason) Williams

Courier, and Long Island Advertiser (1799), weekly; pubd by Thomas Kirk; continued by Courier, and New-York and Long Island Advertiser

Courier, and New-York and Long Island Advertiser (1799–1800), weekly; pubd by Thomas Kirk; continued by Long Island Courier

New-York Price-Current (1799–1802), weekly; pubd by James Oram; continued by Oram's New-York Price-Current[14]

Porcupine's Gazette (1800);[15] pubd by William Cobbett

Forlorn Hope (1800), weekly;[16] pubd by William Keteltas

Prisoner of Hope (1800), weekly, semiweekly; pubd by William Sing

American Citizen and General Advertiser (1800–2), daily; pubd by D(avid) Denniston; continued by American Citizen (daily, 1802–10)

Temple of Reason (1800–3), weekly; pubd by D(ennis) Driscol

Long Island Courier [Brooklyn] (1800–3), weekly; pubd by Thomas Kirk

Republican Watch-Tower (1800–10), semiweekly;[17] pubd by D(avid) Denniston; continued by Morning Star (semiweekly, 1810–13)

1. Other title was "No Stamped Paper to be Had."
2. Title varies.
3. Continued to 1809 under various titles.
4. Subsequently published by John Harrisson alone, by his wife Margaret Harrisson after his death, by his son C. Harrisson, and finally by James Oram (1814–17).
5. Published in Philadelphia.
6. Title varies. Companion to semiweekly Herald.
7. Companion to daily Minerva.
8. See table of daily newspapers.
9. Companion to the daily Diary.
10. Subsequent publishers were Philip Freneau and M. L. Davis and Company; M. L. Davis and Company; and R. Saunders for John D. Burk and James Smith.
11. Companion to daily Commercial Advertiser.
12. Companion to semiweekly Spectator.
13. See list of daily newspapers.
14. Continued under varying titles until 1817.
15. Published in Philadelphia; last issue published in New York City 13 Jan 1800.
16. Published in "the Prison, New York."
17. Companion to the daily American Citizen and General Advertiser. Published with James Cheetham from 1801 and by Cheetham alone from 1803.

Sources: Clarence S. Brigham: *History and Bibliography of American Newspapers, 1690–1820*, vol.

(continued)

Eighteenth-Century Newspapers in New York City, by Date of First Publication *(Continued)*

1 (Worcester, Mass.: American Antiquarian Society, 1947)
Edward Connery Lathem, comp.: *Chronological Tables of American Newspapers,* 1690–1820 (Barre, Mass.: American Antiquarian Society / Barre Publishers, 1972)
Newspapers in Microform, United States, 1948–1983 (Washington: Library of Congress, 1984)
United States Newspaper Program, National Union List, 3rd edn, June 1989 (Dublin, Ohio: Online Computer Library Center)
United States Newspaper Program, New-York Historical Society Holdings, April 1990 (Dublin, Ohio: Online Computer Library Center)

Compiled by Alana J. Erickson

cies of Lincoln, who was strongly endorsed by only five of the seventeen daily newspapers in the city: the *Times,* the *Tribune,* the *Sun,* the *Evening Post,* and the *Commercial Advertiser.* New formats were introduced by *Frank Leslie's Illustrated Newspaper* (weekly, 1855) and *Harper's Weekly* (1857), which incorporated large illustrations printed from wood engravings. Greeley and Bennett both died in 1872; James Gordon Bennett Jr. took over the *Herald* and remained in charge until his death in 1918. Newspaper staffs became larger and the telephone was used more widely for gathering news. The city was known as a national center for writers, who were drawn by the quality of the morning daily newspapers (the *Post* under the direction of E. L. Godkin was the only evening newspaper of high quality at the time). The city's dailies provided extensive reports on local party politics. In 1871 the Tweed Ring was exposed by the *Times* and ridiculed by Thomas Nast in cartoons for *Harper's Weekly.*

Circulations continued to grow toward the end of the nineteenth century. The most important issue in the city was the large influx of immigrants: by 1890 about 80 percent of the population had foreign-born parents, and the number of foreign-language newspapers increased accordingly. In 1880 the first halftone photograph of good quality appeared in the *New York Daily Graphic* (for illustration see Shantytowns). Joseph Pulitzer bought the *World* in 1883 and by 1887 had morning, evening, and Sunday newspapers that allowed him to dominate the newspaper business (the Sunday edition alone had a circulation of 250,000, the largest of any newspaper in the nation). In 1888 the *Sun* published photographs of life in the slums by Jacob A. Riis (see Photojournalism). The *Wall Street Journal* was begun in 1889 by the Dow Jones financial service. The *New York Age,* published by T. Thomas Fortune from 1890, became a leading newspaper of the black press.

By 1890 stereotyped plates invented during the Civil War were used in new kinds of presses, allowing 48,000 twelve-page newspapers to be produced in an hour. Color printing was first used by the *World* in 1893 and color comics became a feature of the Sunday edition. The best-known comic strip was "Hogan's Alley" by R. F. Outcault, which depicted life in a tenement. The central character, a toothless child wearing a nightshirt dotted with blobs of yellow ink, became known to readers as the "Yellow Kid." In 1895 William Randolph Hearst moved to the city from San Francisco and purchased the *New York Journal,* which attracted leading contributors from Pulitzer and published the "Yellow Kid" as well. The *Journal* and the *World* became sensational, cramming pages with enormous headlines and photographs. Named Yellow journalism by critics, their style was adopted by daily newspapers nationwide during the Spanish–American War. Along with the *Sun* under Charles A. Dana and the *Herald* under Bennett, the *Journal* and the *World* nonetheless attracted some of the best writers of the day, who gathered in the newspaper offices on Park Row and at neighboring steakhouses. Well-known reporters included Nelly Bly, Lincoln Steffens, and Stephen Crane.

Competition among newspapers increased during the following decades. The *New York Times,* which had been strong under Raymond, lost considerable prestige in the 1880s and 1890s until it was taken over in 1896 by Adolph S. Ochs, who appointed Carr Van Anda as his managing editor and moved operations to a new building on Broadway known as the Times Tower (1904). Of the $100 million that the *Times* earned between 1896 and 1921 Ochs reinvested $96 million in the newspaper, which was widely regarded as the city's finest and most dependable by the end of the First World War. Hearst began newspapers in other cities, and Pulitzer devoted the last years of his life to relentless crusades in the Muckraking spirit. The *Jewish Daily Forward* was launched in 1897, the *Amsterdam News* in 1909. The *Herald* continued to offer comprehensive coverage, but the quality of the *Tribune,* the *Sun,* and the *Post* deteriorated. A number of press associations were formed about this time. The Associated Press, the successor to the Harbor News Association, was reorganized in 1900. It had cooperative agreements with foreign news agencies and controlled much of the flow of news until E. W. Scripps formed the United Press (1907) and Hearst the International News Service (1909). The socialist daily newspaper the *New York Call* began publication in 1908 and became popular, but it suffered after 1918, when the *Times* led the major daily newspapers in promoting a wave of anti-Bolshevik hysteria nationwide. The *Call* lost its mailing privileges under provisions of the Espionage Act of 1917; its offices were later ransacked by government agents and it was forced out of business in 1923. Foreign-language newspapers were also attacked, especially German ones. Hearst's newspapers and the *World* were among the few publications that condemned these events. The communist newspaper the *Daily Worker* was formed in 1924 and later renamed the *Daily World.*

The 1920s saw the introduction of tabloid newspapers that incorporated large photographs and wild headlines (see Tabloids). One of the first was the *Illustrated Daily News* (26 June 1919), soon renamed the *Daily News*; its circulation reached 750,000 by 1924 and two million before the Second World War. In 1924 tabloid newspapers were introduced by Hearst (the *Mirror*) and Bernarr Macfadden (the *New York Evening Graphic*). Popular for their columnists and bold format, tabloids put tremendous pressure on other newspapers: the *Herald* and *Tribune* merged in 1924, the *World* declared bankruptcy in 1931, and the *Sun* was absorbed by the *World–Telegram* in 1950. After Ochs's death in 1935 the *Times* was taken over by the Sulzberger family. It soon offered the most comprehensive coverage of major stories and had more foreign correspondents and won more Pulitzer prizes than any competitor. The largest foreign-language newspaper was the *New York Staats-Zeitung* (1945), which at one point had a circulation of 250,000. The *Village Voice* began in 1955 as a weekly alternative to the daily press (see Alternative press). Radio and television increased the importance of the press associations, and in 1958 the United Press and the International News Service merged to form United Press International, which soon fell heavily into debt.

A series of strikes during the early 1960s severely hurt newspapers in the city. The newspaper business retained an unusually complicated structure, with pressmen, drivers, reporters, and typographers each represented by a different union. The number of daily newspapers decreased from eight to three; among those that declared bankruptcy were the *Mirror* in 1963, the *Herald Tribune* in 1966, and the *Journal–American* (owned by Hearst) and *World–Telegram and Sun* (owned by Scripps–Howard) in 1967, which together were known

Daily Newspapers Published within the Present Boundaries of New York City, by Date of First Publication

New-York Gazetteer[1] 1783–87
New-York Morning Post (, and Daily Advertiser)[2] 1783–92
New York Journal (i)[3] 1784–93
(New York) Daily Advertiser[4] 1785–1809
New-York Gazette (and General Advertiser) (i)[5] 1788–1840; continued by New York Journal of Commerce and Commercial
Diary[6] 1792–98; continued by (New-York) Mercantile Advertiser
American Minerva 1793–96; continued by Commercial Advertiser
Evening Mercury 1793
Argus. Greenleaf's New Daily Advertiser[7] 1795–1800; continued by American Citizen
(New-York) Commercial Advertiser 1797–1804
(New-York) Mercantile Advertiser 1798–1833; continued by Mercantile Advertiser and New-York Advocate
American Citizen (and General Advertiser) 1800–10; continued by New-York Morning Post
New York (Evening) Post (i) 1801–
Morning Chronicle (i) 1802–7
Public Advertiser[8] 1807–13
(New-York) Columbian[9] 1809–21; continued by New-York Statesman
New York (Morning) (Daily) Post (ii) 1810–12; continued by Statesman
Daily Telegraph (i) 1812–13
National Advocate 1812–29; continued by New York Morning Herald
Statesman 1812–13; continued by Daily Express
Daily Express 1813
Mid-day Courier 1814
Daily Items, for Merchants 1815–16
New York Commercial[10] 1815–1926; continued by New York Journal of Commerce and Commercial
New-York Courier 1815–17; continued by New-York Daily Advertiser
New-York Daily Advertiser 1817–36; continued by New York (Daily) Express
Republican Chronicle (and City Advertiser) 1817–19
New-York American, for the Country[11] 1819–45
New-York Statesman[12] 1822–29; continued by New-York Morning Herald
New York Patriot (and Morning Advertiser) 1823–24
New York National Advocate 1824–26
New-York Enquirer 1826–29; continued by Morning Courier and New-York Enquirer
Times 1826–27
Brooklyn Evening Star 1827–63
(New York) Journal of Commerce (and Commercial) 1827–
Morning Chronicle (ii) 1827
Morning Courier 1827–29; continued by Morning Courier and New York Enquirer
(New-York) Standard 1827–34; continued by New York Times (i)
Merchants' Telegraph 1828
Morning Courier and New-York Enquirer 1829–61; continued by World
New-York Evening Journal 1829–32; continued by New-York Advocate and Journal
New-York Morning Herald 1829–30; continued by New York Standard (i)
New York Daily Sentinel[13] 1830–33
New-York American Advocate 1831–32; continued by New-York Advocate and Journal
New York Whig 1831–32
Democrat (i) [Brooklyn] 1832
Franklin Daily Advertiser 1832
New-York Advocate and Journal 1832–33; continued by Mercantile Advertiser and New-York Advocate
New York Citizen 1832
New York Globe 1832
Evening Star (i) 1833–40; continued by New York Times and Evening Star
Mercantile Advertiser and New-York Advocate 1833–38
Morning Post and Family Gazette 1833
Sun[14] 1833–1950; continued by New York World–Telegram and the Sun
Adopted Citizen 1834
American Whig 1834
Brooklyn (Daily) (Morning) (Evening) Advertiser 1834–35; continued by American Citizen and Brooklyn Evening Advertiser
Constitution 1834
Democratic Chronicle 1834
Eagle 1834
Humorist; or, Real Life in New York 1834
Jeffersonian 1834–36
Major Downing's Advocate (and Mechanics' Journal) 1834
Man[15] 1834 to ?1835
New York Daily Bee 1834 to ?1836
New York Mechanic 1834
New York Times (i) 1834–39
New York Transcript[16] 1834–39
Penny Daily Gazette (i) 1834; continued by Constitution
Transcript and Wasp 1834–39
Truth (i) 1834
American Citizen and Brooklyn Evening Advertiser 1835; continued by Native American Citizen (and Brooklyn Evening Advertiser)
Business Reporter and Merchants' and Mechanics' Advertiser 1835
Mechanic 1835
Native American and Democratic Citizen 1835
Native American Citizen (and Brooklyn Evening Advertiser) 1835–[1837]
Native American Democrat 1835
New York General Advertiser and Daily Commercial Register 1835
New York (Morning) Herald[17] 1835–1924; continued by New York Herald Tribune
Williamsburgh Gazette 1835–53
Age (i) 1836
American Banker[18] 1836–
Democrat (ii) 1836
(Ladies) Morning Star (i) 1836–37
New York (Daily) (Morning) Express 1836–64
Union (i) 1836
Daily News (i) 1837
Daily News (ii) 1837–38
Examiner 1837
New York Daily Whig 1837–40; continued by New York Gazette and General Advertiser
Omnium Advertiser 1837
Age (ii) 1838
Censor 1838
(New York) Times and Commercial Advertiser 1838–40; continued by New York Times and Evening Star
Evening Tattler (i) 1839–40; continued by Dispatch and Tattler
Morning Dispatch 1839–40; continued by Dispatch and Tattler
New York Evening Express ?1839 to 1881; continued by Mail and Express
Penny Daily Gazette (ii) 1839
Ballot Box [campaign paper] 1840
Brooklyn Daily News (and Long Island Times) (i) 1840–43
Corsair 1840
Democratic Press 1840
Dispatch and Tattler 1840; continued by Evening Tattler (ii)
Evening Tattler (ii) 1840 to ?1842
Long Island Daily Times [Brooklyn] 1840–41
Morning Chronicle (and Tippecanoe Advertiser) (iii) 1840 to ?1841
New-York Planet 1840–41
New York Standard (i) 1840–44
New York Times and Evening Star [semiweekly] 1840–41; continued by Commercial Advertiser
Brooklyn (Daily) Eagle[19] 1841–1955
Evening Mail (i) 1841
New York Advertiser ?1841 to ?1842
New York Democrat (i) 1841
New-York (Daily) Tribune 1841–1924; continued by New York Herald Tribune
New York Trumpet 1841
Penny Press 1841
Truth (ii) 1841
Daily Plebian 1842–45; continued by New York Morning News

(*continued*)

Daily Newspapers Published within the Present Boundaries of New York City, by Date of First Publication *(Continued)*

Flushing (Evening) Journal 1842–1931; continued by North Shore Daily Journal
Morning Chronicle (and New York Penny-a-Line Advertiser) (iv) 1842–43
Morning Star (ii) 1842
New York Arena 1842–45; continued by Daily Plebian
New York Aurora 1842–44; continued by Daily Plebian
New York Commercial Transcript 1842
New-York Daily News (i) 1842
Union (ii) 1842–43; continued by New York Aurora
Washingtonian Daily News 1842–43
American Patriot 1843–45; continued by Evening Gazette
(New-York) American Republican[20] 1843–45
Brooklyn Daily News (ii) 1843
Evening Tribune 1843–65
New-York Cynosure and Morning Chronicle 1843
True Sun[21] 1843–48
American Advocate for Equal Rights to Man 1844 to ?1845; continued by Daily Plebian
American Ensign 1844
Brooklyn Daily Advertiser (i) 1844–54; continued by United States Daily Freeman
Evening Mirror (i) 1844–59
(New York Daily) Evening Mirror (ii) 1844–45
New York Morning News 1844–46
Republic (i) 1844–45
(New-York) Daily Globe 1845–51
Daily Long Islander 1845
Evening Gazette 1845–46; continued by Gazette and Times
Evening Star (ii) 1845
Morning Telegraph (i) 1845–46; continued by Daily Telegraph (ii)
Daily Telegraph (ii) 1846
Daily Times 1846; continued by Gazette and Times
Gazette and Times 1846–47
New York Evening Ledger 1846
Daily American Artisan 1847
(New-York) (Evening) Day-Book 1848–61
Morning Star (iii) 1848–52
Williamsburgh Times[22] 1848–55; continued by Brooklyn Daily Times
Brooklyn Daily Freeman[23] 1849–50
Daily Dispatch 1849
Merchants' Day Book 1849
New-Yorker 1849–51
True National Democrat and Morning Star 1849–54
Daily Independent Press [Williamsburgh] 1850–55
New York Standard (ii) 1850
Brooklyn Morning Journal 1851–55
Journal of Commerce Jr. 1851–65
(Daily) National Democrat 1851–[1854]
New York Evening Times[24] 1851–57
New York Times (ii)[25] 1851–
Brooklyn Daily Journal 1852
Daily Half-Cent 1853
Woodhaven Advertiser and Literary Gazette 1853
United States Daily Freeman 1854
Brooklyn Daily Signal 1855–[1867]
Brooklyn Daily Times 1855–1932; continued by Brooklyn Times–Union
Dawn 1855
New York Daily News (ii) 1855 to ?1906
New York Daily Era (and Hotel Register) 1856–66
Daily Museum 1858–59
Gerrit Smith Banner [campaign banner] 1858
Brooklyn City News 1859–63; continued by Brooklyn Daily Union
New York Daily Transcript 1859–[1872]
World[26] 1860–1931; continued by New York World–Telegram
Brooklyn Daily Standard 1861
Brooklyn Daily Programme 1863–75
Brooklyn (Daily) Union (i) 1863–77; continued by Brooklyn Daily Union–Argus
Brooklyn Daily Advertiser (ii) 1864–72
Brooklyn Daily Whig 1864–65
Drum Beat 1864
(New York) Daily Commercial Bulletin and Auction Record[27] 1865–93; continued by New York Journal of Commerce and Commercial
Flushing Daily Times 1865 to ?1925
New York Evening Star and American Advertiser 1865
New York (Evening) Gazette (ii) 1866–67
Brooklyn Press 1867
Evening Telegram[28] 1867–1931; continued by New York World–Telegram
(New York) (Evening) Mail 1867–81; continued by Mail and Express
Evening Press 1868–70; continued by Globe and Evening Press
Every Afternoon 1868
New York Democrat (ii)[29] 1868–71
(New York) (Daily) Star 1868–91; continued by Daily Continent
Evening Republic 1869
Globe 1870 to ?1871
Globe and Evening Press 1870; continued by Globe
Journal of the Day 1870–71
New York Evening Free Press 1870–71
New-York Standard (iii) 1870–72
Evening Leader 1871
New York Daily Register 1871–89
New York Daily Witness 1871–79
Brooklyn Daily Argus 1873–77; continued by Brooklyn Daily Union–Argus
City Record 1873–
Daily Graphic 1873–89
Brooklyn Daily Post 1874
Republic (ii) 1874
(Long Island City) Daily Star 1876–1938; continued by Long Island Star–Journal
Brooklyn Daily Union–Argus 1877–83; continued by Brooklyn Union (ii)
Hotel Reporter 1877–[1925]
Truth (iii) 1879–84
Wall Street Daily News 1879–1907
Greenpoint Daily Star [1881] to ?1900; continued by Daily Star
Mail and Express 1882–1904; continued by Evening Mail (ii)
New York (Morning) Journal (ii) 1882–97; continued by New York Journal and Advertiser
American Metal Market[30] 1883–
Brooklyn Union (ii) 1883–87; continued by Standard–Union
Dial 1884 to ?1885
Brooklyn Standard 1885–87; continued by Standard–Union
Daily Telegraph (iii) 1885
Up-Town News ?1885 to ?1889
Brooklyn Citizen[32] 1886–1947
Brooklyn Daily News (iii) 1886–1947
Daily Voice 1886
Staten Island Advance[31] 1886–
Argus 1887
Evening Sun 1887–1920
Evening World 1887–1931; continued by New York World–Telegram
Investigator 1887 to ?1913
(New York) Press 1887–1916; continued by Sun
Standard–Union [Brooklyn] 1887–1932
New York Law Journal 1888–
Wall Street Journal 1889–
Journal of Finance (i) 1890 to ?1904
Bond Buyer 1891–
Daily Continent 1891; continued by Morning Advertiser
Journal of Finance (ii) 1891–1914
Morning Advertiser 1891–97; continued by New York Journal and Advertiser
New York Advocate 1891–93
New York Recorder 1891–96
Daily Trade Record 1892–1916; continued by Daily News Record
Daily America 1893–94
Daily Mercury 1893–97
Wall Street Summary 1893–1910; continued by Financial America
Daily Tattler 1896
New York (Evening) Journal (iii) 1896–1937; continued by New York Journal American
Morning Telegraph (ii) 1897–1972
New York Journal and Advertiser 1897–1901; continued by New York Journal and American
Wall Street Daily Investigator ?1898 to 1904
Daily People 1900–14
Daily Metal Reporter ?1901 to 1961

(continued)

Daily Newspapers Published within the Present Boundaries of New York City, by Date of First Publication *(Continued)*

Daily North Side News [Bronx] 1901 to ?1958
New York Journal and American 1901–2; continued by New York American and Journal
New York American and Journal 1902–3; continued by New York American
New York American 1903–37; continued by New York Journal–American
Evening Mail (ii) 1904–24; continued by Evening Telegram
Globe and Commercial Advertiser 1904–23
Wall Street Daily Investor 1905 to ?1914
(Bronx) Home News 1906–48; continued by New York Post Home News
Wall Street Daily Ticker 1906 to ?1907
Bromley Morning News 1908
New York (Evening) Call 1908–23; continued by New York Leader
Financial America 1910–24; continued by Wall Street News
Women's Wear Daily 1910–
Daily Long Island Democrat [Jamaica] 1911–12
Long Island Daily Advocate (i)[33] 1911–66
Film (and Television) Daily[34] 1915–72
Queens (County) (Evening) News 1915–39
Daily News Record 1916–
Daily Tank 1917
Evening Call[35] 1917–18
Daily News (iii)[36] 1919–
Market News ?1919 to ?1920
Long Island Daily Press and Daily Long Island Farmer 1921–26; continued by Long Island (Daily) Press
Combined New York Morning Newspapers[37] 1923
New York Leader 1923
Daily Mirror 1924–57
New York Evening Bulletin 1924–[1925]
New York Evening Graphic 1924–32
New York Herald Tribune[38] 1924–66; continued by World Journal Tribune
Sunday Worker 1924 to ?1956
Wall Street News 1924–30; continued by Wall Street Journal
Long Island (Daily) Press [Jamaica] 1926–77
Daily Worker[39] 1927–58
New York Repository[40] 1931–33
New York World–Telegram[41] 1931–50; continued by New York World–Telegram and the Sun
North Shore Daily Journal 1931–38; continued by Long Island Star–Journal
Brooklyn Times–Union 1932–37
Brooklyn Daily 1933–63
Harlem Heights Daily Citizen ?1933 to ?1934
Westchester Globe (i) [campaign paper] 1933
Westchester Globe (ii) [campaign paper] 1935
New York Journal–American[42] 1937–66; continued by World–Journal Tribune
Long Island Star–Journal [Flushing][43] 1938–[1948]
PM 1940–48; continued by New York Star
Long Island Daily Advocate (ii) [Ridgewood] 1948–66
New York Post Home News[44] 1948–49
New York Star[45] 1948–49; continued by Daily Compass
Retailing Daily 1948–57; continued by Home Furnishings Daily
Daily Compass 1949–52
New York World–Telegram and the Sun 1950–66; continued by World Journal Tribune
Daily Bulletin 1955–
Home Furnishings Daily 1957–
New York Mirror 1957–63
New York and Brooklyn Daily ?1963–[1971]
New York Standard (iv) 1963
World–Journal Tribune 1966–67
Daily World 1968–86; continued by People's Daily World
New York (Daily) Column (and the New York Knickerbocker) 1968–73
Daily Mirror 1971–73
Black American[46] 1972–
City News [1978]
New York Daily Press 1978
New York Graphic 1978
Trib 1978
New York City Tribune[47] 1983–92
Investor's Daily 1984–
New York Newsday 1985–
People's Daily World 1986–
National 1989–91

Note: Parts of names in parentheses used during some part of a newspaper's run. Bracketed dates indicate first or last extant copy of a newspaper. List may not be comprehensive for business newspapers.

1. Daily in 1786; title varies.
2. Daily in 1785–92.
3. Daily in 1787–88; title varies.
4. Known as People's Friend 1806–7, L'Oracle and Daily Advertiser 1808.
5. Known as the New-York Daily Gazette 1788–95; title and publishers vary.
6. Title varies.
7. Title varies; see table of eighteenth-century newspapers.
8. Known as American Patriot and Public Advertiser 1811–12; frequency varies.
9. Known as the New York Evening Journal and Patron of Industry 1821.
10. Known as the Shipping and Commercial List and New York Price Current 1826–98.
11. Daily in 1820–45.
12. Known as the New York Statesman and Evening Advertiser 1822–23.
13. Daily edition of the weekly Working Man's Advocate (1830–36).
14. Merged in 1920 with Herald to form Sun and New York Herald (1920), which then divided again.
15. Daily edition of the weekly Working Man's Advocate (1830–36).
16. Known as the New York Transcript and Wasp 1839.
17. Founded as the weekly Thompson's Bank Note and Commercial Reporter (1836–87).
18. Merged in 1920 with the Sun to form Sun and New York Herald (1920), which then divided again.
19. Known as Brooklyn Eagle and King's County Democrat 1841–46.
20. Known as New York Citizen and American Republican 1844.
21. Published by striking compositors of the Sun.
22. Also known as East Brooklyn Daily Times.
23. Began as a weekly, became daily in 1849 or 1850.
24. Companion to the morning edition of the New York Daily Times.
25. Known as the New York Daily Times 1851–57, companion of the New York Evening Times.
26. Known as the World, Morning Courier and New York Enquirer 1861–63.
27. Title varies.
28. Known as the New York Telegram (1925–31).
29. Title varies.
30. Weekly 1883–1901. Also known as American Metal Market and (Daily) Iron and Steel Report 1902–26.
31. Sometimes known as the Richmond County Advance.
32. Daily to 1931.
33. Also known as Knickerbocker News, Greater Ridgewood News.
34. Weekly to 1918.
35. The "night edition" of the New York Call.
36. Also known as the News, Illustrated Daily News.
37. Joint issue of morning newspapers during printers' strike (19–26 Sept).
38. Known as the New York Herald, New York Tribune 1924–26.
39. Published in Chicago 1924–27.
40. Published to retain franchise of Associated Press but never circulated.
41. Known as the Evening World, the World, the New York Telegram 1931.
42. Known as the New York Journal and American 1937–41.
43. Known as North Shore Daily Journal and Long Island Star 1938.

(continued)

Daily Newspapers Published within the Present Boundaries of New York City, by Date of First Publication *(Continued)*

44. Name during this period of the New York (Evening) Post.
45. Known as New York Star, formerly PM 1948.
46. May not be daily throughout the run.
47. Also known as New York Tribune 1983.

INDEX

Adopted Citizen 1834
Age 1836 (i)
Age 1838 (ii)
American Advocate for Equal Rights to Man 1844 to ?1845
American Banker 1836–
American Citizen (and General Advertiser) 1800–10
American Citizen and Brooklyn Evening Advertiser 1835
American Ensign 1844
American Metal Market 1883–
American Minerva 1793–96
American Patriot 1843–45
(New-York) American Republican 1843–45
American Whig 1834
Argus 1887
Argus. Greenleaf's New Daily Advertiser 1795–1800
Ballot Box [campaign paper] 1840
Black American 1972–
Bond Buyer 1891–
Bromley Morning News 1908
Brooklyn (Daily) (Morning) (Evening) Advertiser 1834–35
Brooklyn City News 1859–63
Brooklyn Daily 1933–63
Brooklyn Daily Advertiser (i) 1844–54
Brooklyn Daily Advertiser (ii) 1864–72
Brooklyn Daily Argus 1873–77
Brooklyn Daily Freeman 1849–50
Brooklyn Daily Journal 1852
Brooklyn Daily News (and Long Island Times) (i) 1840–43
Brooklyn Daily News (ii) 1843
Brooklyn Daily News (iii) 1886–1947
Brooklyn Daily Post 1874
Brooklyn Daily Programme 1863–75
Brooklyn Daily Signal 1855–[1867]
Brooklyn Daily Standard 1861
Brooklyn Daily Times 1855–1932
Brooklyn Daily Union–Argus 1877–83
Brooklyn Daily Whig 1864–65
Brooklyn Citizen 1886–1947
Brooklyn (Daily) Eagle 1841–1955
Brooklyn Evening Star 1827–63
Brooklyn Morning Journal 1851–55
Brooklyn Press 1867
Brooklyn Standard 1885–87
Brooklyn Times–Union 1932–37
Brooklyn (Daily) Union (i) 1863–77
Brooklyn Union (ii) 1883–87
Business Reporter and Merchants' and Mechanics' Advertiser 1835
Censor 1838
City News [1978]
City Record 1873–
(New-York) Columbian 1809–21
Combined New York Morning Newspapers 1923
(New-York) Commercial Advertiser 1797–1904
Constitution 1834
Corsair 1840
(New York) Daily Advertiser 1785–1809
Daily America 1893–94
Daily American Artisan 1847
Daily Bulletin 1955–
Daily Compass 1949–52
Daily Continent 1891
Daily Dispatch 1849
(New York) Daily Commercial Bulletin and Auction Record 1865–93
Daily Express 1813
(New-York) Daily Globe 1845–51
Daily Graphic 1873–89
Daily Half-Cent 1853
Daily Independent Press [Williamsburgh] 1850–55
Daily Items, for Merchants 1815–16
Daily Long Island Democrat [Jamaica] 1911–12
Daily Long Islander 1845
Daily Mercury 1893–97
Daily Metal Reporter ?1901 to 1961
Daily Mirror 1924–57
Daily Mirror 1971–73
Daily Museum 1858–59
Daily News (i) 1837
Daily News (ii) 1837–38
Daily News (iii) 1919–
Daily News Record 1916–
Daily North Side News [Bronx] 1901 to ?1958
Daily People 1900–14
Daily Plebian 1842–45
(Long Island City) Daily Star 1876–1938
Daily Tank 1917
Daily Tattler 1896
Daily Telegraph (i) 1812–13
Daily Telegraph (ii) 1846
Daily Telegraph (iii) 1885
Daily Times 1846
Daily Trade Record 1892–1916
Daily Voice 1886
Daily Worker 1927–58
Daily World 1968–86
Dawn 1855
(New-York) (Evening) Day-Book 1848–61
Democrat (i) [Brooklyn] 1832
Democrat (ii) 1836
Democratic Press 1840
Democratic Chronicle 1834
Dial 1884 to ?1885
Diary 1792–98
Dispatch and Tattler 1840
Drum Beat 1864
Eagle 1834
Evening Call 1917–18
Evening Gazette 1845–46
Evening Leader 1871
Evening Mail (i) 1841
Evening Mail (ii) 1904–24
Evening Mercury 1793
Evening Mirror (i) 1844–59
(New York Daily) Evening Mirror (ii) 1844–45
Evening Press 1868–70
Evening Republic 1869
Evening Star (i) 1833–40
Evening Star (ii) 1845
Evening Sun 1887–1920
Evening Tattler (i) 1839–1840
Evening Tattler (ii) 1840 to ?1842
Evening Telegram 1867–1931
Evening Tribune 1843–65
Evening World 1887–1931
Every Afternoon 1868
Examiner 1837
Film (and Television) Daily 1915–72
Financial America 1910–24
Flushing Daily Times 1865 to ?1925
Flushing (Evening) Journal 1842–1931
Franklin Daily Advertiser 1832
Gazette and Times 1846–47
Gerrit Smith Banner [campaign banner] 1858
Globe 1870 to ?1871
Globe and Commercial Advertiser 1904–23
Globe and Evening Press 1870
Greenpoint Daily Star [1881] to ?1900
Harlem Heights Daily Citizen ?1933 to ?1934
Home Furnishings Daily 1957–
(Bronx) Home News 1906–48
Hotel Reporter 1877–[1925]
Humorist; or, Real Life in New York 1834
Investigator 1887 to ?1913
Investor's Daily 1984–
Jeffersonian 1834–36
(New York) Journal of Commerce (and Commercial) 1827–
Journal of Commerce Jr. 1851–65
Journal of Finance (i) 1890 to ?1904
Journal of Finance (ii) 1891–1914
Journal of the Day 1870–71
Long Island Daily Advocate (i) 1911–66
Long Island Daily Advocate (ii) [Ridgewood] 1948–66
Long Island Daily Press and Daily Long Island Farmer 1921–26
Long Island Daily Times [Brooklyn] 1840–41
Long Island (Daily) Press [Jamaica] 1926–77
Long Island Star–Journal [Flushing] 1938–[1948]
(New York) (Evening) Mail 1867–81
Mail and Express 1882–1904
Major Downing's Advocate (and Mechanics' Journal) 1834
Man 1834 to ?1835
Market News ?1919 to ?1920
Mechanic 1835

(continued)

Daily Newspapers Published within the Present Boundaries of New York City, by Date of First Publication *(Continued)*

(New-York) Mercantile Advertiser 1798–1833
Mercantile Advertiser and New-York Advocate 1833–38
Merchants' Day Book 1849
Merchants' Telegraph 1828
Mid-day Courier 1814
Morning Advertiser 1891–97
Morning Chronicle (i) 1802–7
Morning Chronicle (ii) 1827
Morning Chronicle (and Tippecanoe Advertiser) (iii) 1840 to ?1841
Morning Chronicle (and New York Penny-a-Line Advertiser) (iv) 1842–43
Morning Courier 1827–29
Morning Courier and New-York Enquirer 1829–61
Morning Dispatch 1839–40
Morning Post and Family Gazette 1833
(Ladies) Morning Star (i) 1836–37
Morning Star (ii) 1842
Morning Star (iii) 1848–52
Morning Telegraph (i) 1845–46
Morning Telegraph (ii) 1897–1972
National 1989–91
National Advocate 1812–29
(Daily) National Democrat 1851–[1854]
Native American and Democratic Citizen 1835
Native American Citizen (and Brooklyn Evening Advertiser) 1835–[1837]
Native American Democrat 1835
New York Advertiser ?1841 to ?1842
New York Advocate 1891–93
New-York Advocate and Journal 1832–33
New-York American, for the Country 1819–45
New York American 1903–37
New-York American Advocate 1831–32
New York American and Journal 1902–3
New York and Brooklyn Daily ?1963–[1971]
New York Arena 1842–45
New York Aurora 1842–44
New York (Evening) Call 1908–23
New York Citizen 1832
New York City Tribune 1983–92
New York (Daily) Column (and the New York Knickerbocker) 1968–73
New York Commercial 1815–1926
New York Commercial Transcript 1842
New-York Courier 1815–17
New-York Cynosure and Morning Chronicle 1843
New-York Daily Advertiser 1817–36
New York Daily Bee 1834 to ?1836
New York Daily Era (and Hotel Register) 1856–66
New-York Daily News (i) 1842
New York Daily News (ii) 1855 to ?1906
New York Daily Press 1978
New York Daily Register 1871–89
New York Daily Sentinel 1830–33
New York Daily Transcript 1859–[1872]
New York Daily Whig 1837–40
New York Daily Witness 1871–79
New York Democrat (i) 1841
New York Democrat (ii) 1868–71
New-York Enquirer 1826–29
New-Yorker 1849–51
New York Evening Bulletin 1924–[1925]
New York Evening Express ?1839 to 1881
New York Evening Free Press 1870–71
New York Evening Graphic 1924–32
New-York Evening Journal 1829–32
New York Evening Ledger 1846
New York Evening Star and American Advertiser 1865
New York Evening Times 1851–57
New York (Daily) (Morning) Express 1836–64
New-York Gazette (and General Advertiser) (i) 1788–1840
New York (Evening) Gazette (ii) 1866–67
New-York Gazetteer 1783–87
New York General Advertiser and Daily Commercial Register 1835
New York Globe 1832
New York Graphic 1978
New York (Morning) Herald 1835–1924
New York Herald Tribune 1924–66
New York Journal (i) 1784–93
New York (Morning) Journal (ii) 1882–97
New York (Evening) Journal (iii) 1896–1937
New York Journal–American 1937–66
New York Journal and Advertiser 1897–1901
New York Journal and American 1901–2
New York Law Journal 1888–
New York Leader 1923
New York Mechanic 1834
New York Mirror 1957–63
New-York Morning Herald 1829–30
New York Morning News 1844–46
New-York Morning Post (and Daily Advertiser) 1783–92
New York National Advocate 1824–26
New York Newsday 1985–
New York Patriot (and Morning Advertiser) 1823–24
New-York Planet 1840–41
New York (Evening) Post (i) 1801–
New York (Morning) (Daily) Post (ii) 1810–12
New York Post Home News 1948–49
New York Recorder 1891–96
New York Repository 1931–33
New York Standard (i) 1840–44
New York Standard (ii) 1850
New-York Standard (iii) 1870–72
New York Standard (iv) 1963
New York Star 1948–49
New-York Statesman 1822–29
New York Times (i) 1834–39
New York Times (ii) 1851–
New York Times and Evening Star [semiweekly] 1840–41
New York Transcript 1834–39
New-York (Daily) Tribune 1841–1924
New York Trumpet 1841
New York Whig 1831–32
New York World–Telegram 1931–50
New York World–Telegram and the Sun 1950–66
North Shore Daily Journal 1931–38
Omnium Advertiser 1837
Penny Daily Gazette (i) 1834
Penny Daily Gazette (ii) 1839
Penny Press 1841
People's Daily World 1986–
PM 1940–48
(New York) Press 1887–1916
Public Advertiser 1807–13
Queens (County) (Evening) News 1915–39
Republic (i) 1844–45
Republic (ii) 1874
Republican Chronicle (and City Advertiser) 1817–19
Retailing Daily 1948–57
(New-York) Standard 1827–34
Standard–Union [Brooklyn] 1887–1932
(New York) (Daily) Star 1868–91
Staten Island Advance 1886–
Statesman 1812–13
Sun 1833–1950
Sunday Worker 1924 to ?1956
Times 1826–27
(New York) Times and Commercial Advertiser 1838–40
Transcript and Wasp 1834–39
Trib 1978
True National Democrat and Morning Star 1849–54
True Sun 1843–48
Truth (i) 1834
Truth (ii) 1841
Truth (iii) 1879–84
Union (i) 1836
Union (ii) 1842–1843
United States Daily Freeman 1854
Up-Town News ?1885 to ?1889
Wall Street Daily Investigator ?1898 to 1904
Wall Street Daily Investor 1905 to ?1914
Wall Street Daily News 1879–1907
Wall Street Daily Ticker 1906 to ?1907
Wall Street Journal 1889–
Wall Street News 1924–30
Wall Street Summary 1893–1910
Washingtonian Daily News 1842–43
Westchester Globe (i) [campaign paper] 1933
Westchester Globe (ii) [campaign paper] 1935
Williamsburgh Gazette 1835–53
Williamsburgh Times 1848–55
Women's Wear Daily 1910–
Woodhaven Advertiser and Literary Gazette 1853
World 1860–1931
World–Journal Tribune 1966–67

Sources: Winifred Gregory, ed.: *American Newspapers, 1821–1936: A Union List of Files Available*

(continued)

Daily Newspapers Published within the Present Boundaries of New York City, by Date of First Publication *(Continued)*

in the United States and Canada (New York: H. W. Wilson, 1937; repr. Kraus, 1967)
Clarence S. Brigham: *History and Bibliography of American Newspapers, 1690–1820*, vol. 1 (Worcester, Mass.: American Antiquarian Society, 1947)
Newspapers in Microform, United States, 1948–1983 (Washington: Library of Congress, 1984)
United States Newpaper Project, National Union List, 3rd edn, June 1989 (Dublin, Ohio: Online Computer Library Center)
United States Newspaper Project: New-York Historical Society Holdings, April 1990 (Dublin, Ohio: Online Computer Library Center)

Compiled by Alana J. Erickson

Foreign-Language Daily Newspapers in New York City

ARABIC
Kawkab Amirka [Star of America], 1892–1909, daily 1897–1909
Al-Hoda [American Journal], 1898–, daily 1915
Mir'at al gharb [Mirror of the West; Daily Mirror], 1899–[1961], daily ?1913 to 1932
Jurab-Ul Kurdy, 1907 to ?1913, daily 1912 to ?1913
As-Sayeh [The Traveler], 1912–58, daily 1928–30
Syrian Eagle [New York City Eagle], 1914–[1920]
As-Sameer [The Entertainer] [1945]

CARPATHO-RUSYN
Den [The Day], 1922–26

CHINESE[1]
Mei hua shin pao [Mei hua ri bao; Chinese American], 1883
Chinese Daily News [Chinese Republic Daily], 1912
Chinese Nationalist, 1915–58
Mei-chou jih pao [Mei-zhou ri bao; Chinese Journal], 1926–[1976]
Min ch'i jih pao [Min qi ri bao; Chinese Nationalist Daily], 1927–58
Kung ho (jih) pao [Gong he (ri) bao, Kong wo (yat) bo; Justice (Daily) News], 1928–37, daily 1928–29
Mei-chou Hua ch'iao jih pao [Mei-zhou Hua qiao ri bao, Hua ch'iao jih pao; China Daily News], 1940–[1989]
Lian he ri bao [United Journal], 1940–
Hua mei ri bao [China Tribune], 1943–
Min chih jih pao [Min zhi ri bao; Min chih Journal], 1960–66
Sing Tao jih pao [Sing Tao Newspaper], pubd in New York City 1968–
Shi jie ri bao [World Journal], 1976–
Pei Mei jih pao [Bei Mei ri bao; Peimei news], 1978–[1989]
Zhong guo ri bao [China Daily], 1981–

CROATIAN
Narodni List [National Gazette], 1898–1922
Jugoslovenski Svijet [Southern Slav World], 1908–23;[2] continued by Svijet
Svijet [The World], 1924–38

CZECH
Delnik Americky [American Worker], 1882–85
Hlas Lidu [Voice of the People], 1886 to ?1921, daily 1905 to ?1921
New Yorske Listy, 1886–1966, daily 1886–1923; continued by Americke Listy (weekly, 1962–)

FRENCH
Le Courrier des États-Unis, 1828 to ?1937, daily 1851–1932
Le Républicain, 1853–[1854]
Le Progrès, 1855–[1855]
Le Messager Franco-Américain, 1860–83, daily 1860–83
Le Progrès [Le Journal Français aux États-Unis], 1909–[1910]

GERMAN
New Yorker Staats-Zeitung, 1834–1934; continued by New Yorker Staats-Zeitung und Herold
New-Yorker Staats-Demokrat, 1845–56, daily 1846–56; continued by New-Yorker Demokrat
Deutsche Schnellpost, 1848–51, daily 1850–51; continued by New-Yorker Deutsche Zeitung
New-Yorker Deutsche Zeitung, 1851 to ?1851
New-Yorker Demokrat, 1856–1876; continued by New Yorker Allgemeine Zeitung
New Yorker Handels-Zeitung, 1857–58
New Yorker Journal, 1866 to ?1878
New-Yorker Tages-Nachrichten, ?1870 to ?1896
New-Yorker Presse, 1873 to ?1876
Brooklyner Freie Presse (und Long Island Anzeiger), 1873 to ?1918
Brooklyner Presse, ?1875 to ?1876
New Yorker Allgemeine Zeitung, 1876 to ?1878; continued by New-Yorker Zeitung
New Yorker Volkszeitung, 1878–1932; continued by Neue Volks-Zeitung (weekly, 1932–49)
New-Yorker Zeitung, ?1879 to 1896; continued by Gross-New-Yorker Zeitung
New Yorker Herold Abend Zeitung, 1880–1934; continued by New Yorker Staats-Zeitung und Herold
Morgen Journal, 1890–1912; continued by Deutsches Morgen-Journal
Abendblatt der New Yorker Staats-Zeitung, 1892–1914; continued by New-Yorker Staats-Zeitung Abendblatt
Gross-New-Yorker Zeitung, 1896–1908; continued by New-Yorker Zeitung
New-Yorker Zeitung, 1908 to ?1913; continued by New Yorker Herold Morgenblatt
Deutsches Morgen Journal, 1912; continued by Deutsches Journal
Deutsches Journal, 1912–17; continued by New Yorker Deutsches Journal
New Yorker Herold Morgenblatt, ?1913 to 1919; continued by New Yorker Staats-Zeitung und Herold Morgenblatt
New Yorker Deutsches Journal, 1917–18
New Yorker Staats-Zeitung und Herold Morgenblatt, 1919 to ?1921; continued by New Yorker Staats-Zeitung
New Yorker Staats-Zeitung, 1921–34; continued by New Yorker Staats-Zeitung und Herold
New Yorker Staats-Zeitung und Herold, 1934–, daily 1934–75

GREEK
Atlantis, 1894–1972, daily 1905–72
Thermopylae ?1900 to ?1907, daily ?1907
Ethnikos Kerux [National Herald], 1915–
Proini [Morning Paper], 1976–

HEBREW
Hadoar [The Post], 1921–, daily 1921–22

HUNGARIAN
Amerikai Magyar Nepszava [Hungarian American People's Voice], 1899–1969, daily 1904–69
Amerikai Magyar Vilag [Hungarian Daily World], 1901–[1938]
Elore [The Forward], 1904–21; continued by Uj elore
Egyetertes [The Concord], [1911]–1931; continued by A Kereszt-Egyetertes (weekly, 1932)
Uj elore [The New Forward], 1921 to ?1938
Magyar Ujsag [Hungarian News], 1932–[1933]
Magyar Jovo [Hungarian Daily Journal], [1945]–[1950]

ITALIAN
L'Eco d'Italia, 1849 to ?1896, daily 1881 to ?1896; continued by L'Eco D'Italia: Rivista Italo-Americana (weekly, ?1896–[1896])

(continued)

Foreign-Language Daily Newspapers in New York City *(Continued)*

Il Progresso Italo-Americano, 1880–1988
Cristoforo Colombo, 1887–97; continued by Il Progresso Italo-Americano
L'Araldo Italiano, 1889–1921
Bolletino Della Sera, 1898–1932
Il Movimento, ?1901–[1909]
Il Telegrafo, 1902–19
Corriere Della Sera, 1909 to ?1933
Il Giornale Italiano, 1909–22
Corriere d'America, 1922–[1937]
Il Nuovo Mondo, 1925–31; continued by La Stampa Libera
La Stampa Libera, 1931–38
Il Mondo, 1940–[1941]
America Oggi, 1988–[3]

KOREAN

Hangkook Ilbo New York Pan [Korea Times, New York Edition], 1967–
Korea Herald, U.S. Edition, 1975–
Sae gae Ilbo, 1982–, daily 1987–

POLISH

Telegram Codzienny [Daily Telegram], 1913–1925; continued by Nowy Swiat
Nowy Swiat [Polish Morning World], ?1919 to 1971; continued by Nowy Dziennik
Nowy Dziennik [Polish Daily News], 1971–

RUSSIAN

Russkoe Slovo, 1910–20; continued by Novoye Russkoe Slovo
Novyi Mir, 1911–38, daily 1914 to ?1918; continued by Russkii Golos
Russkii Emigrant, 1911–15
Rodnaia Riech [Native Language], 1913–18
Russkaia Zemlia, 1915–[1916], daily 1916
Russkii Golos [Russian Voice], 1917–, daily 1917 to ?1963
Rassvet [The Dawn], 1918–26; continued by Russkii Vestnik I Rassvet
Novoye Russkoe Slovo, 1920–
Iskra [The Spark], 1921–[1921]
Utro [Morning], 1922
Russkaia Mysl [Russian Thought], 1923–[1924]
Rossiia, 1933–73, daily 1935–64
Novosti [1984]

SERBIAN

Srpski Dnevnik [Serbian Daily], 1911–[1932]

SLOVAK

(Dennik) Slovak v Amerike, 1899–[1989], daily 1913–1936, 1951
Slovenski Narod [Slovenic People], 1906–17, daily 1906–15
New Yorksky Dennik, 1913–62

SLOVENIAN

Glas Naroda [People's Voice], ?1893 to ?1963

SPANISH

Diario Cubano, 1870–[1870]
El Democrata (de Nueva York), 1870
Iberia, 1894–[1894]
(Diario de) las Novedades, 1876–1918, daily 1909 to ?1910
La Prensa, 1913–63, daily 1917–63; continued by El Diario de Nueva York, La Prensa
La Voz, 1937–39; continued by La Nueva Voz
La Nueva Voz, 1939–41
El Diario de Nueva York, 1948–63; continued by El Diario de Nueva York, La Prensa
El Diario de Nueva York, La Prensa, 1963; continued by El Diario–La Prensa
El Diario–La Prensa, 1963–
Noticias del Mundo, 1979–

UKRAINIAN

Ukrain'ski Shchodenni Visti [Ukrainian Daily News], 1919–56; continued by Ukrain'ski Visti (weekly, 1957–)
Svoboda Ukrainian Daily, 1919–[4]

YIDDISH[5]

Yudishe gazeten, 1876–1927
Yiddisches Tageblatt [Yidishes tageblat], 1885–1928; continued by Der Morgen Zhurnal, Yidishes Tageblat
Der daily telegraf [Der Deyli telegraf], 1894–[1894]
Der Taglicher Herold [Der Teglikher herold], 1894–1905; continued by Der Tog, di Varhayt
Abend Blatt fur die Arbeiter Zeitung [Abend-blatt fun di Arbayter tsaytung], 1894–1902[6]
Forverts [Jewish Daily Forward], 1897–, daily 1897–1986
Tagliche Presse [Teglikhe prese], [1898]
Idische Welt [Idishe velt], 1899–1905; continued by New Yorker Morgenblatt un Idische Welt
New Yorker Abend Post, 1899 to ?1901
Morgen Zhurnal, 1901–1928; continued by Der Morgen Zhurnal, Yidishes Tageblat
Di yidishe velt, 1902–5
Morgen-zeitung [Morgen-tsaytung], 1906
Die Abend Zeitung [Di Abend tsaytung], 1906
New Yorker Morgenblatt un Idische Welt [Nyu-yorker morgenblat un Idishe velt], 1905
Di Varhayt [Jewish Daily Warheit], 1905–19; continued by Der Tog, di Varhayt
Der Tog, 1914–19; continued by Der Tog, di Varhayt
Der Fihrer, 1915
Der Tog, di Varhayt, 1919–22; continued by Der Tog
Heint [Haynt], 1920
Die zeit [Di tsayt], 1920–22
Der Tog, 1922–53; continued by Der Tog, Morgen Zhurnal
Freiheit [Frayhayt], 1922–29; continued by Morgen Freiheit
Neue Warheit [Di Naye varhayt], 1925[7]
Der Morgen Zhurnal, Yidishes Tageblat, 1928–38; continued by Morgen Zhurnal
Morgen Freiheit [Morgn frayhayt], 1929–[1931]
Der Morgen Zhurnal, 1938–53; continued by Der Tog, Morgen Zhurnal
Der Tog, Morgen Zhurnal, 1953–72; continued by Der Morgen Zhurnal, Yidisches Tageblat

1. Names are transliterations used by the newspaper; Pinyin transliteration, where different, follows in brackets.
2. Also contains articles in Slovenian.
3. Published in New Jersey.
4. Published in New Jersey.
5. Names are transliterations used by the newspaper; YIVO transliteration, where different, follows in brackets.
6. Also in German and English.
7. Also in Hebrew.

Note: Bracketed dates indicate first or last extant copy of a newspaper. Dates when a newspaper was daily are given only if the newspaper was not daily during its entire run.

Sources: Winifred Gregory, ed.: *American Newspapers, 1821–1936: A Union List of Files Available in the United States and Canada* (New York: H. W. Wilson, 1937; repr. Kraus, 1967)
Newspapers in Microform, United States, 1948–1983 (Washington: Library of Congress, 1984)
United States Newpaper Project, National Union List, 3rd edn, June 1989 (Dublin, Ohio: Online Computer Library Center)

Compiled by Erica Judge

briefly in 1966 as the *World Journal Tribune.* The *New York Times* won two important cases in the U.S. Supreme Court: one concerning libel (*New York Times v. Sullivan,* 1964), the other an attempt by the federal government to prevent the release of the Pentagon Papers (1971). In 1982 United Press International moved its offices to Washington.

In the mid 1990s New York City had four major daily newspapers, more than any other American city. There was intense competition for readers and advertisers, especially among the three tabloids: *New York Newsday,* the *New York Post,* and the *Daily News.* After a long strike the *News* was bought first by Robert Maxwell and then by Mortimer B. Zuckerman, and the *Post* underwent several changes of management before being acquired in 1993 by Rupert Murdoch, who had owned the newspaper from 1976 to 1988. Both newspapers faced uncertain futures because of pressures to wrest concessions from labor unions and to introduce color printing, a step already being taken by their better-capitalized competitors the *Times* and *Newsday*. In addition to its major daily newspapers the city was also served by foreign-language newspapers ranging from the *Jewish Daily Forward* to *Sing Tao* (with a circulation of sixty thousand), and by a large number of weekly neighborhood newspapers, most of which consisted largely of advertisements and were distributed free of charge.

See also SPANISH-LANGUAGE PRESS.

Michael Emery

New Springville. Neighborhood in central Staten Island, adjoining the Greenbelt and bounded by Bull's Head, Travis, Willowbrook, Lighthouse Hill, and the Fresh Kills at Greenridge. It is part of Community District 2. The area was first settled in the 1680, when it was called Carle's Neck, for the extension of land between Main Creek and Richmond Creek. By about 1840 it included a small hamlet, a dock, a Methodist church, and several freshwater springs, surrounded by a patchwork of modest farmsteads, and was known variously as Springville and New Springville. Extant structures from the nineteenth century include the former Asbury Methodist Church (1849, replacing an earlier building) and the Sylvanus Decker Farmhouse (*ca* 1810), both designated landmarks by the city, and the Basketmaker's House (*ca* 1810, now at Historic Richmond Town). New Springville remained an agricultural district and the center of truck farming in Staten Island until the end of the 1950s, when subdivision for tract housing accelerated. From 1926 to 1964 two small airports were situated on Richmond Avenue, the main thoroughfare of the neigborhood and the focus of commercial development into the late twentieth century. The population grew rapidly after the opening of the Verrazano Narrows Bridge in 1964 and became increasingly diverse after 1970, as many residents of Brooklyn moved to the area to occupy new townhouses, garden apartments, and condominiums built near the Staten Island Mall, which opened on Richmond Avenue in 1973. In the 1980s a large number of Korean and Chinese immigrants settled in New Springville. Among the residents in the mid 1990s Jewish and Korean families predominated.

Charles W. Leng and William T. Davis: *Staten Island and Its People: A History, 1609–1929* (New York: Lewis Historical Publishing, 1930)

Staten Island: A Resource Manual for School and Community (New York: Board of Education of the City of New York, 1964)

John E. Hurley: "New Springville," *Staten Island Advance*, 19 June 1989, §B, pp. 1–2

Robert V. Wolf: "Island's Ethnic Mix Increasing, Census Shows," *Staten Island Advance*, 24 Feb 1991

Charles L. Sachs

Newsweek. Weekly international news magazine launched in Manhattan in 1933 by Thomas J. C. Martyn, formerly a foreign editor of *Time*. After the death in 1961 of its owner Vincent Astor it was sold to the Washington Post Company. The magazine made its reputation by incorporating objective reporting, signed commentaries, and (from 1967) advocacy issues. It publishes several editions overseas, including one in Japanese. The circulation worldwide is more than four million and the readership more than twenty million. The offices are at 444 Madison Avenue.

Elliot S. Meadows

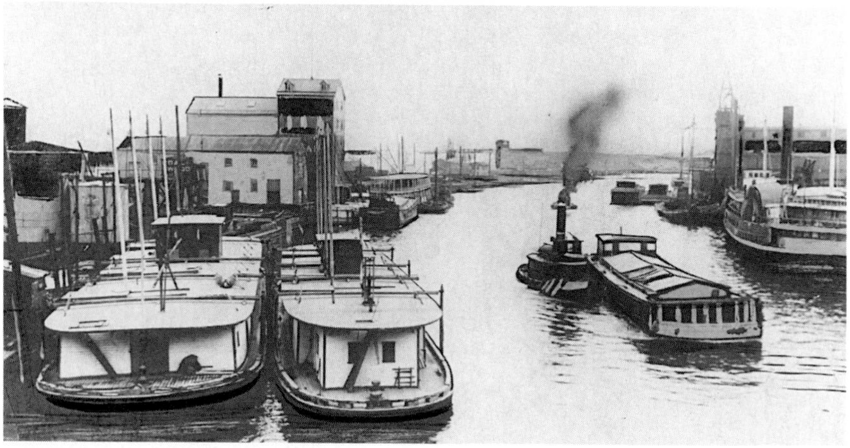

Newtown Creek through Greenpoint, 1908

News World. Original name of the NEW YORK CITY TRIBUNE.

Newtown. Name used in colonial times for Elmhurst and for one of the three towns that made up what is now Queens County. The first European settlement in Queens was made at Maspeth in 1642, attacked by Indians in 1643, and abandoned in 1644. Another settlement was made in 1652 at what is now Queens Boulevard and Broadway, a site well inland and less vulnerable to raiding; it was at first named Middleburgh and in 1664 renamed Hastings. Settlers often referred to it as the "new town" to distinguish it from the first settlement, and when the English system of towns and counties was established in 1683 the name Newtown was given to the village and the township. In 1895–96 an area north of Newtown was developed by Cord Meyer (ii), a real-estate promoter who did not want his development to be associated with the pollution of Newtown Creek; in 1896 he prevailed on federal authorities to rename the area Elmhurst, although the name Newtown is retained by a high school and a subway station.

Vincent Seyfried

Newtown Creek. Tributary of the East River. It extends inland for a distance of three miles (five kilometers) including a number of canals into Brooklyn, and is the boundary between Brooklyn and Queens. The creek was the route by which European colonists first reached Maspeth in 1642. During the American Revolution the British spent the winter near the creek, and the British military road that crossed Queens to what is now the Marine Air Terminal began at the town dock in Maspeth. Commercial vessels and small boats sailed the creek in the early nineteenth century. About 1860 the first oil and coal oil refineries opened along the banks and began dumping sludge and acids into the water; sewers were also built to accommodate the growing neighborhoods of Williamsburg and Greenpoint and discharged their wastes directly into the creek, which by 1900 was well known for its pollution and foul odors. The water corroded the paint on the undersides of ships and noxious deposits were left on the banks by the tides. High-level bridges over the creek were built from 1903 (some remain). State and city commissions sought unsuccessfully to improve the creek as it became one of the busiest commercial waterways in the country, second only to the Mississippi River in tonnage: 5,435,016 tons (4,929,560 metric tons) were transported in 1915 by 102,270 ships, which passed so frequently that traffic over the drawbridges was seriously disrupted. The channel was dredged constantly and widened by the federal government to accommodate marine traffic. After the Second World War the creek ceased to be important for shipping, as trucks and airplanes replaced waterborne transport, but it continued to be the site of many industrial plants. The water quality improved dramatically after all sewage was diverted to waste treatment plants. A high-rise residential city at the confluence of Newtown Creek and the East River was proposed as part of the Hunter's Point Redevelopment Project.

Vincent Seyfried

New Utrecht. Neighborhood in southwestern Brooklyn, lying within Bensonhurst. The land was inhabited by Nyack Indians in 1647 when the governor of New Netherland granted a deed for it to Anthony Jansen van Salee. It became one of the first six towns in

Old farm in New Utrecht

Kings County and included what became Bensonhurst, Bath Beach, Dyker Heights, Mapleton, and Bay Ridge. The first European settlement was a house and a mill built in 1652 by Cornelius van Werckhoven (a schepen, or alderman, in Utrecht in the Netherlands), his two children, and their tutor, Jacques Cortelyou. After van Werckhoven's death in 1655 Cortelyou assumed leadership of the settlement, secured patents for land later occupied by Fort Hamilton, and divided the parcel into twenty plots of fifty acres (twenty hectares) each, the last of which he reserved for the town's poor. In 1677 residents formed the Reformed Protestant Dutch Church: its building, erected in 1828, stands at 18th Avenue and 83rd Street.

By 1738 there were 282 inhabitants of whom 119 were slaves. Farmers raised cattle and grew grains and tobacco. The population grew to 907 in 1810, 1009 in 1820, 2129 in 1850, and 4742 in 1880 as residents gradually sold land to developers who built suburban houses. The remaining truck farmers grew vegetables to sell to the growing population of Brooklyn. The opening of the Sea Beach, Coney Island, and West End steam railroads in the 1870s accelerated the development of the area as a suburb. It lost its identity when it was annexed by the City of Brooklyn in 1894 and is now considered a small neighborhood of Bensonhurst.

Mrs. Bleecker Bangs: *Reminiscences of Old New Utrecht and Gowanus* (New York: Brooklyn Daily Eagle Press, 1912)

Ellis Lawrence Raesly: *Portrait of New Netherland* (Port Washington, N.Y.: Ira J. Friedman, 1965)

Stephen Weinstein

New Utrecht Reformed Church. Dutch Reformed church in southwestern Brooklyn, at 18th Avenue between 83rd and 84th streets. It opened in 1677 in the village of New Utrecht (1661) and was the fourth Dutch Reformed church in Kings County. The original building, erected in 1700, was repaired in 1774 and used as a hospital by the British during the American Revolution; it was demolished owing to structural weakness in 1827 and replaced in 1829 by a Georgian Gothic church built of granite with Victorian milk glass windows in brick frames. A parsonage in the Dutch shingle style was added on 83rd Street in 1885 and a parish house in a Romanesque Revival style on 84th Street in 1892.

Mrs. Bleecker Bangs: *Reminiscences of Old New Utrecht and Gowanus* (New York: Brooklyn Daily Eagle Press, 1912)

Kevin Kenny

New Venice. Original name of EDGEMERE.

New Year's Eve. The first celebration of New Year's Eve in Times Square took place in 1906, sponsored by the *New York Times* to mark the completion of its new headquarters. The event was staged by the newspaper's publisher Adolph Ochs, who conceived of an elaborate "time ball" that would descend from atop a building precisely at midnight, intentionally recalling the globes used in most American cities during the 1870s and 1880s to keep time and synchronize watches. The brightly lit ball of Times Square became an annual feature of the celebration, except for two years during the Second World War. Each New Year's Eve the spectacle draws hundreds of thousands of persons to Times Square and millions of television viewers from across the nation.

Michael O'Malley: *Keeping Watch: A History of American Time* (New York: Viking, 1990)

Michael O'Malley

New York. Weekly magazine. It originated in 1963 as a supplement to the Sunday edition of the *New York Herald Tribune*; in 1964 Clay S. Felker became the editor, and in 1967 he bought the rights to the name. With his partner, the graphic designer Milton Glaser, he launched *New York* as an independent magazine in the following year: they mixed humor and seriousness in a format that emphasized graphics and typography and made the magazine one of the most widely imitated publications of its time. In the first issues it printed stories on subjects as diverse as celebrity watching in the Hamptons (by Jimmy Breslin) and the conditions of skid row (by Tom Wolfe). Felker supported efforts by Wolfe and others to propound a style of writing known as "new journalism," which employed the tone and descriptive techniques of fiction writing. Nicholas Pileggi, who became a contributing editor in 1968, wrote investigative pieces on corruption in city government and organized crime. The magazine became known for its opinionated and at times sardonic tone. Among its more popular writers were Breslin, Gloria Steinem, Pete Hamill, Gael Greene, who used sensual images in her restaurant reviews, and the theater critic John Simon. In January 1977 the magazine was bought by the Australian newspaper magnate Rupert Murdoch, who merged it in 1980 with *Cue*, a weekly guide to cultural events and entertainment.

Thomas Kiernan: *Citizen Murdoch* (New York: Dodd, Mead, 1986)

Richard Kluger: *The Life and Death of the New York Herald Tribune* (New York: Alfred A. Knopf, 1986)

Rachel Sawyer

New York, New Haven and Hartford Railroad. Railroad formed in 1872, the first to connect New York City with Boston. It superseded the New York and New Haven Railroad, which was chartered in 1844 to operate between Canal Street and New Haven, Connecticut, and in New York City used track owned by the New York and Harlem Railroad. Service to Boston and New England was taken over by Amtrak in 1971; the line between New York City and New Haven continued to serve commuters and became administered by the Connecticut Department of Transportation and the Metropolitan Transportation Authority of New York State.

John L. Weller: *The New Haven Railroad: Its Rise and Fall* (Mamaroneck, N.Y.: Hastings House, 1967)

See also RAILROADS.

John Fink

New York, Westchester and Boston Railroad. Railroad operating from 24 May 1912 as a modern, four-track subsidiary of the New York, New Haven and Hartford Railroad. It inherited the rights of the New York, Housatonic and Northern Railroad and the New York and Portchester Railroad, both defunct, and was built at a high price. The operators of the railroad believed that the commercial center of the city would continue to move north, but the zoning law of 1916 contained the central business district below 59th Street and the line ran no farther south than 133rd Street at the Harlem River in the Bronx. Hindered by their inability to transport passengers into Manhattan, the directors abandoned the line on 31 December 1937. The portion of the line in the Bronx reopened on 15 May 1941 as the Dyre Avenue shuttle of Interborough Rapid Transit. The New York, Westchester and Boston was the last important railroad built in New York City.

Roger Arcara: *Westchester's Forgotten Railway, 1912–1937* (New York: Quadrant, 1962)

John Fink

New York Academy of Arts. Original name of the AMERICAN ACADEMY OF THE FINE ARTS.

New York Academy of Medicine. Nonprofit corporation formed in 1847 to raise the standards of medical education and promote the health of the public. It originated at a time when physicians were struggling to establish themselves as members of an ethical and scientific profession. The academy's status rose with that of the profession, and by the time it moved into a large building at 119 West 43rd Street in 1890 it was renowned for its expertise on issues of municipal health in New York City. The academy advocated improved public hygiene and sanitation as a means of staving off epidemics. It moved in 1926 into a handsome building designed by the architects York and Sawyer at 2 East 103rd Street. Recommendations by special committees of the academy helped give rise to the Department of Hospitals (1928), to a review of maternal deaths in the 1930s, and to the New York City Health and Hospitals Corporation (1970). During the mid 1990s the academy was particularly well known in the field of medical education. Its health library, the second-largest in the United States, contains more than fourteen miles (twenty-three kilometers) of shelves and nearly 700,000 catalogued works, including one of the world's finest collections of rare medical Americana and early European medical materials, and one of the world's largest collections of cookbooks (donated by a physician concerned with nutrition). Besides offering a wide range of information services to its fellows and to the general public, the institution serves as a regional library of medicine and coordinates cooperative services among health sciences libraries in ten northeastern states and Puerto Rico. In 1991 the New York Academy of Medicine installed its first full-time president, Jeremiah A. Barondess, who at the request of Mayor David N. Dinkins launched a new study of the city's municipal hospital system.

Sandra Opdycke

New York Academy of Sciences. Organization formed as the Lyceum of Natural History by Samuel Latham Mitchill, who convened the first meeting on 29 January 1817; most of the early members were students at the College of Physicians and Surgeons. Progress came haltingly, and it was not until 1823 that the lyceum began regular publication of its journal the *Annals*. In 1836 it moved from rented rooms at the New York Dispensary to its own building on Broadway, which financial pressures forced the members to sell in 1844. Despite this setback the lyceum by 1860 maintained a library and a natural-history museum; it also counted among its members such prominent scientists as John William Draper, Wolcott Gibbs, and William Cox Redfield. Eventually some functions of the lyceum ceased: it no longer had any role as a natural history museum after its museum was destroyed by fire in 1866, and no scientific research was carried on within it after a professorate oriented toward research emerged at Columbia. Its role was also changed by the formation of the American Museum of Natural History (1868), the increasing specialization of science and the growth of societies devoted to individual disciplines, and the emergence of science as a profession. In 1876 the lyceum reorganized as the New York Academy of Sciences. The new organization was controlled not by weekly membership meetings but by an elected council, and was divided into four sections: biology; chemistry and technology; geology and mineralogy; and physics, astronomy, and mathematics. As a general scientific society the academy was responsible in 1887 for the organization of the first meeting of the American Association for the Advancement of Science to be held in New York City. Under the leadership of Nathaniel Lord Britton the academy in 1891 organized the Scientific Alliance, a federation of scientific societies that published a monthly bulletin and from 1906 occupied quarters at the American Museum of Natural History. The early decades of the twentieth century were a time of unparalleled prosperity for the academy; such scientists as Edmund Beecher Wilson, Thomas Hunt Morgan, Franz Boas, James McKeen Cattell, and Michael Pupin were active members. In 1912 the academy organized a survey of the geology, anthropology, and natural history of Puerto Rico and the Virgin Islands that continued for three decades. Under the auspices of the academy, scientists from many institutions in New York City conducted expeditions, the results of which the academy published.

From 1938 into the 1990s the New York Academy of Sciences sponsored scientific conferences, notably on biomedical topics, as a means of communicating research results to the scientific community; in 1965 this educational role expanded. The academy publishes the magazine the *Sciences* (1961) and has twenty-four sections, which hold monthly meetings. It also sponsors the Scientists in Schools and Science Research Training programs, and the Junior Academy of Sciences engages high school students in a variety of scientific activities.

Herman Le Roy Fairchild: *A History of the New York Academy of Sciences* (New York: Herman Le Roy Fairchild, 1887)

Simon Baatz: *Knowledge, Culture, and Science in the Metropolis: The New York Academy of Sciences, 1817–1970* (New York: New York Academy of Sciences, 1990)

Simon Baatz

New York African Society for Mutual Relief. Mutual benefit organization formed in New York City in 1808. It was incorporated in 1810 when Mayor De Witt Clinton carried a special petition to the state legislature at Albany, making the organization the first to be incorporated by black Americans. Early members included the influential Methodist minister Peter Williams Jr.; the businessman William Hamilton Sr.; John Teasman, an instructor at the New York African School; James McCune Smith, the nation's first black physician; Christopher Rush, one of the first African Methodist Episcopal bishops; Phillip A. Bell, the antislavery journalist and editor of the *Colored American*; and Thomas Downing, proprietor of one of the most exclusive restaurants in Manhattan. All the members staunchly opposed slavery and promoted the black national convention movement and the independent black church movement. African Society Hall, a building constructed in the rear of the society's first property in lower Manhattan, was the meeting place of most of the African associations of antebellum New York City and contained a trap door so that it could fulfill its dual role as a stop on the Underground Railroad.

After the Civil War the society was struck by a number of internal scandals that shook its members' faith in mutual relief as a principle and collective action as a strategy. It came close to disbanding on more than one occasion but was saved by the inspired work of its oldest members: the printer John J. Zuille, one of the leading antislavery spokesmen in the city; E. V. C. Eato, grand master of the state's black Masons; William P. Powell, owner of a seaman's home and a nationally known abolitionist; and Peter Vogelsang, a veteran of the Union Army. Together they brought a new unity to the society and a new commitment to their struggle for equality. By 1900 Booker T. Washington could refer to the New York African Society for Mutual Relief as the most influential and successful financial association among black Americans. In the decades that followed, the society became active in the politics of black New York City and made public declarations on such national issues as the Scottsboro case in Alabama. Its membership included the city's leading ministers, businessmen, politicians, and intellectuals. Among these were the real-estate dealer John Nail and the dentist Walter N. Beekman.

From the 1880s to 1945 the already sizable holdings of the New York African Society increased by $1000 annually, and the value of membership increased commensurately. By 1910 each membership was worth several thousand dollars, although the initiation fee was far smaller. The members of the society therefore faced a dilemma: either the initiation fees and dues would need to rise to a prohibitive level, or each new membership would reduce the worth of all existing ones. The society struggled with declining membership for four decades, until many of the society's benefits were duplicated by the New Deal. In 1945 the remaining members began the sad work of dismantling the society and liquidating its impressive holdings.

Craig Steven Wilder

Engraving of four-track viaduct over Harlem flats between 98th and 112th streets, New York and Harlem Railroad

New York Age. Weekly newspaper launched in 1887 as an organ of blacks who advocated equal rights. It was edited from 1889 to 1907 by the distinguished black journalist T. Thomas Fortune, who urged blacks to take part in the political process. In 1907 he sold his interests to Fred R. Moore, secretary and national organizer of the National Negro Business League, who continued to edit and publish the newspaper with his son-in-law Lester A. Walton as its managing editor. In 1949 black ownership ended when the newspaper was purchased by V. P. Bourne-Vanneck and his wife.

Sandra Roff

New York and Harlem Railroad. The first railroad in New York City, originating in 1832 with horses for motive power and connecting Union Square with 23rd Street and 4th Avenue. Steam-powered operations began in 1835 when the railroad extended its line to 125th Street and 4th Avenue in Harlem. It built the city's first major train station, at 27th Street and 4th Avenue, and eventually built as far north as Chatham, New York, and as far east as Albany. The railroad was at best only marginally profitable, and in 1857 it merged with the New York and Hudson River Railroad to form the New York Central and Hudson River Railroad. The tracks of the railroad between New York City and Dover Plains through the Bronx River Valley formed the backbone of the Metro-North commuter railroad into the late twentieth century.

See also Railroads, §1.

John Fink

New York and Mississippi Valley Printing Telegraph Company. Forerunner of Western union.

New York and Sea Beach Railway. A railway that began operations on 18 July 1877 as a small steam line for transporting passengers from New Utrecht Avenue in Brooklyn to Coney Island over 4.5 miles (seven kilometers) of private track. It was the last line built expressly to profit from the enormous summer traffic. The railroad's depot at Coney Island was the Sea Beach Palace, a building constructed for the Centennial Exposition of 1876. The line was extended from New Utrecht Avenue to the ferry terminal at 65th Street in 1879 and was reasonably profitable to the end of the 1880s, but during the 1890s it was undermined by the development of trolley lines. The line was leased to the Brooklyn Rapid Transit system (BRT) in 1897, electrified, and linked to the elevated lines in Brooklyn. Its track was used by trolleys until 1907 and in 1915 was integrated into the 4th Avenue subway line. Now known as the Sea Beach or "N" line, the line has four tracks, of which two furnish the normal service; there are nine stations and a terminus at Stillwell Avenue, Coney Island.

Vincent Seyfried

New York Aquarium. Aquarium opened by the City of New York at Castle Clinton in Battery Park in 1896. The New York Zoological Society took over the administration of the facility at the city's request in 1902; under the first director elected by the society, Charles H. Townsend, steps were taken to alleviate crowded conditions and problems of maintenance. Charles M. Breder Jr. succeeded Townsend in 1937 and helped to establish the aquarium's international reputation for scientific research. Aided by its location, the aquarium flourished for many years and drew seven thousand visitors a day until the parks commissioner Robert Moses temporarily closed it in 1941 to allow construction of the Brooklyn–Battery Tunnel; ensuing plans to demolish Castle Clinton and close the aquarium permanently aroused such strong protest that the castle was spared and the aquarium moved to the Bronx Zoo. Because of pressures to distribute funds for cultural attractions evenly among the boroughs, the Bronx was rejected as the site for a new aquarium in favor of Coney Island, where a new facility opened in 1957 near the boardwalk. An affiliated marine laboratory opened nearby in 1964 and was dedicated in 1967 as the Osborn Laboratory for Marine Sciences, named for Henry Fairfield Osborn: there research was conducted in fish genetics, fish pathology, aquaculture, and pharmacological applications of marine science. In its new site the aquarium could accommodate more than three hundred species in more than one hundred indoor and outdoor habitats; it was the first aquarium to breed and exhibit Beluga whales. The aquarium draws more than 750,000 visitors a year and is active in education, scientific research, and conservation.

Terry Collins and Steven P. Johnson: *Guide to the Archives of the New York Zoological Society* (New York: New York Zoological Society, 1982)

Elliot S. Meadows

New York Association for New Americans [NYANA]. Resettlement agency. Formed in 1949, it became the largest agency of its kind in the United States by assisting more than a quarter of a million persons referred by the Hebrew Immigrant Aid Society, including Jewish refugees from Europe (1949–53), Greece (1955–56), Hungary (1956–58), Egypt and Romania (1956–63), Cuba (1961–67), Czechoslovakia (1968–69), Poland (1968–69), the Soviet Union and Russia (from 1969), which eventually accounted for the largest number of refugees, Syria (1977), and Iran (from 1983). In 1975 the association began receiving federal funds to aid in the resettlement of non-Jewish refugees from Southeast Asia; it also received funds from the United Jewish Appeal, the United

Way, private foundations, and government grants.

Joseph S. Lieber

New York Association for the Blind. Name used from 1906 to 1990 by the LIGHTHOUSE.

New York Athletic Club. Private club at Central Park South and 6th Avenue, formed in 1868 by William B. Curtis, Henry E. Buermeyer, and John C. Babcock in the backroom of the Knickerbocker Cottage on 6th Avenue between 27th and 28th streets. On 11 November 1868 the club sponsored the New York Athletic Games, the first indoor amateur athletic meet in the United States, in the unfinished Empire Skating Rink on 3rd Avenue. On a cold, rainy night the meet drew more than a thousand spectators, who saw six track and eight field events; among the innovations introduced at the meet were cleated athletic shoes and an early bicycle with a large front wheel called the velocipede. The club built a boathouse on the Harlem River in 1870, opened a clubhouse in Mott Haven in June 1874, and in 1880 purchased an island of thirty acres (twelve hectares) in Long Island Sound as a training retreat for its élite competitors. Called Sheffields Island (later renamed Travers Island for the club's president William R. Travers), the island had two buildings in which as many as seventy athletes could live and train while carrying on business in New York City. By 1898 the club had many prominent businessmen in the city as members. The club's building on Central Park South, opened with great fanfare on 22 January 1929, houses extensive athletic facilities, restaurants, and guest rooms.

Robert Hillenbrand

New York Bible Society. Organization formed on 4 December 1809 at the home of Theodorus Van Wyck to distribute English-language bibles without note or comment in New York City. An auxiliary of the American Bible Society from 1829 to 1912, it had offices in the society's Bible House on Astor Place until 1919. After briefly occupying quarters on Madison Avenue it moved in 1921 into a building at 5 East 48th Street donated by James Talcott and later named for him.

David J. Fant: *The Bible in New York: The Romance of Scripture Distribution in a World Metropolis from 1807 to 1948* (New York: New York Bible Society, 1948)

Alana J. Erickson

New York Botanical Garden. Public botanical garden in the Bronx. See BOTANICAL GARDENS.

New York Central and Hudson River Railroad. The principal route for passengers and freight traveling west from New York City during the late nineteenth century. In New York City its origins may be traced to the New York and Harlem Railroad (1832) and the Hudson River Railroad (1846), and it was itself known as the New York Central Railroad until Cornelius Vanderbilt merged it in 1869 with the Hudson River Railroad. The railroad followed the course of the Hudson River and the Erie Canal and because of its easy grades gained a competitive advantage over other railroads and canals. In 1871 passenger train operations were consolidated at the new Grand Central Depot. Like its competitor the Pennsylvania Railroad, the New York Central and Hudson River cut to sixteen hours the travel time between New York City and Chicago in the 1930s with its fastest train, the Twentieth Century Limited. In 1893 its Empire State Express set a speed record of 112 miles (180 kilometers) an hour. When the new Grand Central Terminal opened in 1913 the railroad's suburban electric trains, which carried commuters, used the lower level and its intercity trains the main level. In 1968 the railroad merged with the Pennsylvania Railroad to form the Penn Central, which declared bankruptcy in 1970. Its intercity routes were taken over in 1971 by the National Railroad Passenger Corporation (Amtrak), its commuter routes in 1972 by the Metropolitan Transportation Authority (MTA), and its freight operations in 1976 by the Consolidated Rail Corporation (Conrail).

Joseph R. Daughen and Peter Binzen: *The Wreck of the Penn Central* (Boston: Little, Brown, 1971)
Carl W. Condit: *The Port of New York: A History of the Rail Terminal System* (Chicago: University of Chicago Press, 1980, 1981)
Freeman H. Hubbard: *Encyclopedia of North American Railroading* (New York: McGraw–Hill, 1981)
Aaron E. Klein: *The History of the New York Central System* (New York: Bonanza, 1985)

See also RAILROADS.

Robert A. Olmsted

New York Central Railroad freight terminal between 59th and 72nd streets, ca *1910–20*

New York Chamber of Commerce and Industry. Association for the development of business in New York City, formed on 5 April 1768 as the New York Chamber of Commerce by twenty merchants at Fraunces Tavern and granted a royal charter on 13 March 1770 by George III. It was the first business association in the city to be unaffiliated with any government body. From its earliest days the chamber mediated business disputes, and supported public works and legislation that promoted business. Meetings were held at various sites, such as the Royal Exchange, the Merchants' Coffee House, the Tontine Coffee House, and the Merchants' Exchange. The first president was the Loyalist and former mayor of New York City John Cruger. During the American Revolution a rift arose between the Loyalists and the revolutionary members, who fled when the British captured the city. The chamber was an administrative base for the Loyalists until their defeat, and because of this function it lost its power at the end of the war. It was reorganized on 13 April 1784 and renamed the Chamber of Commerce of the State of New York (the latter part of the name reflecting the source of its charter rather than any statewide orientation). On 3 January 1786 it issued the first proposal for the Erie Canal, which it continued to support until construction was carried out by Governor De Witt Clinton in the 1820s. Membership increased from one hundred in 1840 to 550 in 1858, and in 1861 the state legislature declared that the judgments of the chamber's Committee of Arbitration could be made the basis of a judgment in a court of record.

During the sixty years after the Civil War the chamber was deeply engaged in the affairs of the city. It funded the Committee of Seventy (many members of which also belonged to the chamber), and from 1872 it investigated the political corruption of the Tweed Ring. In 1874–75 the state legislature passed laws creating a Court of Arbitration, under which the secretary of the chamber was appointed to the position of arbitration clerk, but this system lapsed; it was revived in 1911 when the chamber's Committee of Arbitration was reinstituted. The chamber proposed the consolidation of New York City in 1888 and various civic improvements. Seven of the eight members on the Rapid Transit Commission that developed plans for the subway system in 1894–1907 belonged to the chamber, including Mayor Abram S. Hewitt. In November 1902 the chamber constructed its first building, a four-story structure of Vermont marble at 65 Liberty Street that had a great hall and several impressive meeting rooms. The chamber encouraged the development of the Catskill Aqueduct in 1912, and in 1916 its president Eugenius Outerbridge proposed the formation of the Port of New York Authority, of which he became the first chairman in 1921.

During the Depression and the New Deal the popular image of the businessman worsened, and the power of the chamber decreased accordingly. Permanent staff members were first employed during the 1920s and completely displaced volunteer workers after the Second World War, and a research staff gathered authoritative information on the economy of the city. The exterior of the chamber's building was declared a landmark in 1969, but the organization moved to rented quarters at 200 Madison Avenue in 1979 and sold the building in 1989. It took its current name in 1973 and merged in 1979 with the New York Partnership, an organization concerned with housing, education, and alleviating social problems. The New York Chamber of Commerce and Industry had nearly fifteen hundred member firms in 1988.

Joseph Bucklin Bishop: *A Chronicle of One Hundred and Fifty Years: The Chamber of Commerce of the State of New York, 1768–1918* (New York: Charles Scribner's Sons, 1918)

Donald R. Stabile

New York City Ballet. Dance company formed by George Balanchine and Lincoln Kirstein in 1948 as a resident company of the City Center of Music and Drama. It performed several masterpieces by Balanchine, including *Serenade*, *Concerto Barocco*, *Symphony in C*, *Apollo*, *The Four Temperaments*, and *Agon*, as well as such favorites as *The Nutcracker*. In 1964 it moved to the New York State Theatre at Lincoln Center. Balanchine trained his dancers to move forcefully and developed an athletic style that contrasted sharply with the old "grand manner." Music was the most important element of his choreography, and among composers Stravinsky provided the greatest inspiration. For his brilliant Stravinsky festival (1972) Balanchine produced four major new ballets. He also provided choreography to the music of Bach, Mozart, Tchaikovsky, Ravel, Ives, Gershwin, Sousa, Alexander Glazounov, and Mikhail Glinka. Connoisseurs of music often attended performances of the New York City Ballet to hear scores that were not played in concert halls. Balanchine's aesthetic predominated even when the company worked with other choreographers, such as Frederick Ashton, Antony Tudor, John Taras, Todd Bolender, Peter Martins, and Jerome Robbins, an associate director of the company from 1949 to 1956 and again from 1969 to 1990. Robbins's work with the company was characterized by humor, introspection, and an impressive command of dance values. Among his most successful early ballets were *Cage*, *Concert*, and *Afternoon of a Faun*, an adaptation of the controversial work by Nijinsky. His later important ballets included *Dances at a Gathering*, *Goldberg Variations*, *Glass Pieces*, and *I'm Old Fashioned*, a tribute to Fred Astaire.

On Balanchine's death in 1983 Robbins and Martins became ballet masters of the company. After several early pieces reflecting Balanchine's influence, Martins developed a number of highly original ballets, including *Ecstatic Orange* (1987) and *Fearful Symmetries* (1990), both to minimalist scores. Kirstein retired as the general director in 1989 (at the age of eighty-two) and Robbins resigned in 1990. The New York City Ballet has more than one hundred dancers and offers more than twenty weeks of performances annually in the city alone.

Lincoln Kirstein: *The New York City Ballet* (New York: Alfred A. Knopf, 1973; rev. 1978 as *Thirty Years: Lincoln Kirstein's The New York City Ballet*)
Nancy Reynolds: *Repertory in Review* (New York: Dial, 1977)

Nancy Reynolds

New York City Community College of Applied Arts and Sciences. Former name of NEW YORK CITY TECHNICAL COLLEGE.

New York City Farm Colony–Seaview Hospital Historic District. The first Historic District designated by the New York City Landmarks Preservation Commission on Staten Island. It occupies an elevated site abutting and partly within the Greenbelt and bounded to the north by Walcott and Brielle avenues, to the east by Manor Road, to the south by Rockland Avenue, and to the west by Colonial Avenue and Forest Hill Road; it is bisected by Brielle Avenue. Built on the former site of the Richmond County Poor Farm for the "able-bodied indigent," the Farm Colony was built west of Brielle Avenue by the Department of Public Charities between 1903 and 1914. Its large, gambrel-roofed fieldstone dormitories and service buildings were designed by a number of firms including Renwick, Aspinwall and Owen to evoke colonial domestic architecture, contrasting with the severe institutional almshouses formerly used on Blackwell's Island. Four large neo-Georgian dormitories were added in 1934. The complex was used as a geriatric facility until being closed in 1975. Seaview Hospital, built on the opposite side of Brielle Avenue, was the country's largest and most expensive municipal facility for treating tuberculosis. The original portion consisted of patients' pavilions, dining halls, nurses' and doctors' residences, and a surgical pavilion and was carefully designed by Raymond F. Almiral for maximum efficiency and exposure to air, light, and pleasant vistas. The patient pavilions had capacious sleeping porches and solaria and were enlivened by distinctive tile roofs and mosaic friezes. The hospital was dedicated in 1913; later additions, including a number of open-air pavilions (1917), increased the capacity of the hospital to two thousand patients. In 1951 the first successful clinical trials of a non-toxic cure for tuberculosis were undertaken at Seaview, which was converted to other uses after 1961. In the mid 1990s portions of the complex and several modern buildings continued to be used for health services, including geriatric care.

Shirley Zavin

New York City Federation of Women's Clubs. Organization of women's clubs convened in February 1903 by the suffragist and clubwoman Belle (Mrs. John) De Rivera. It was affiliated with the New York State Federation of Women's Clubs and the General Federation of Women's Clubs; delegates represented a wide range of clubs from throughout the city, among them groups devoted to politics, careers, civic improvement, and reform. The federation hoped to assist member clubs by providing material for meetings and inviting them to contribute time and money to projects of common interest. In 1909 it began subsidizing a hotel at 462 West 22nd Street for working women. The federation sponsored annual conferences and distributed a newsletter until its dissolution in 1990.

Karen J. Blair

New York City Health and Hospitals Corporation. Nonprofit corporation created by state law on 27 May 1969 to administer all municipal health facilities in New York City. It began operations on 1 July 1970 with a board of fifteen, of whom five members were municipal officials, five were appointed by the mayor alone, and five were appointed by the mayor with the approval of the City Council. Like its predecessor the Department of Hospitals the corporation was required to focus on serving the city's poor.

Its formation followed a decade of increasingly strident criticism of the municipal hospital system, and it was believed that a quasi-independent corporation would encounter fewer of the bureaucratic constraints that many investigative commissions had identified as a major difficulty in providing health care. The corporation did have somewhat more autonomy than its predecessor, but not to the extent hoped for by its supporters. In addition to political obstacles it was impeded by the city's severe fiscal crisis. Caught between municipal deficits and rising medical costs, it was forced during the late 1970s and 1980s to close some hospitals and consolidate others. A series of untoward deaths in municipal emergency rooms in 1991 drew intense public scrutiny, as a result of which the director of the corporation resigned and Mayor David N. Dinkins requested an investigation of the municipal system by the New York Academy of Medicine. At that time the system contained about nine thousand beds, barely half the number managed by the Department of Hospitals in 1929, and ambulatory facilities that served more than twenty thousand persons a day. The corporation managed eleven acute-care hospitals (accounting for 20 percent of the city's acute-care beds), five long-term care facilities, five neighborhood family care centers, forty outreach clinics, and the city's emergency medical service. Together its facilities cared for 30 percent of the city's newborn and pediatric patients, 40 percent of its substance abuse patients, and 50 percent of its psychiatric patients, as well as 10 percent of the patients hospitalized for AIDS in the entire United States.

Health Care Needs and the New York City Health and Hospitals Corporation (New York: New York City Health and Hospitals Corporation, 1973)

Sandra Opdycke

New York City Marathon. An annual footrace first staged in 1970. See Running.

New York City Mission Society. Missionary organization formed on 19 February 1827 to encourage religious conversions by distributing religious tracts. Originally known as the New York City Tract Society, it was most active south of 14th Street and began operating mission stations in 1852. It was renamed the New York City Mission and Tract Society in 1866 and in 1870 shifted its efforts to opening churches in poor neighborhoods; the first, Mount Olivet, was at 63 East 2nd Street. With the Association for Improving the Condition of the Poor, the Charity Organization Society, and the Children's Aid Society, the New York City Mission and Tract Society received the United Charities Building at 105 East 22nd Street as a gift from John M. Kennedy in 1891. Given its current name in 1913, it advised churches and social service agencies into the 1990s.

Kenneth D. Miller and Ethel Prince Miller: *The People Are the City: 150 Years of Social and Religious Concern in New York City* (New York: Macmillan, 1962)

Alana J. Erickson

New York City Opera. Opera company formed in 1943 as the City Center Opera Company by Mayor Fiorello H. La Guardia and other prominent citizens. Its purpose was to bring opera of a high quality to lower- and middle-class New Yorkers who could not afford the Metropolitan Opera, and to provide a forum for emerging American singers, conductors, and composers. In its early years and under the direction of Julius Rudel (1957–79) the company gave the premières of works by Dominick Argento, Jack Beeson, Lee Hoiby, Leon Kirchner, Robert Kurka, Gian Carlo Menotti, Douglas Moore, Thomas Pasatieri, Ned Rorem, Robert Ward, and Hugo Weisgall, and introduced many American singers (including the soprano Beverly Sills and the basses Norman Treigle and Samuel Ramey), as well as Plácido Domingo and José Carreras. The company performed at City Center on West 55th Street until 1966, when it moved to the New York State Theater at Lincoln Center. After retiring from the stage Sills managed the company from 1979 to 1989: she built a large audience by programming works from the operatic mainstream and musical comedies, and by introducing "supertitles" (displaying below the proscenium arch an English translation of the text being sung), as a result of which a large deficit was eliminated and the company's operating budget was nearly tripled (to $28 million). Sills was succeeded in 1990 by the conductor Christopher Keene, who emphasized adventurous repertory of the sort that had characterized the company's early years; his first seasons included noteworthy productions of operas by Ferruccio Busoni, Arnold Schoenberg, Leoš Janáček, and Bernd Alois Zimmermann. The New York City Opera has proved resilient in the face of financial challenge, protracted union strikes, and the loss of its costumes in a warehouse fire in 1985.

Martin L. Sokol: *The New York City Opera: An American Adventure, with the Complete Annals* (New York: Macmillan, 1981)

James M. Keller

New York City Partnership. A coalition of leaders in business, nonprofit organizations, and education formed in 1979 by David Rockefeller to work with government agencies on economic development, education, and housing. It introduced a summer employment program for low-income youth and developed housing for middle-income families through the New York City Housing Partnership, formed in 1982. The organization has studied obstacles to development in New York City, especially those posed by the environmental review process and those that discourage technologically advanced industries. Rockefeller was succeeded as chairman by James D. Robinson III (1987) and Preston Tisch (1990).

Perry Davis, ed.: *Public–Private Partnership: Improving Urban Life* (New York: Academy of Political Science / New York City Partnership, 1986)

Rosalie Genevro

New York City Technical College. College of the City University of New York at 300 Jay Street in Brooklyn, formed in 1946 by the state legislature as the New York State Institute of Applied Arts and Science, one of five experimental technical schools intended for returning veterans of the Second World War. In 1948 it became part of the State University of New York. The New York City Board of Estimate assumed responsibility for its administration in 1953 and changed the name to the New York City Community College of Applied Arts and Sciences, and the college joined the city university system in 1964. In 1971 it absorbed the Voorhees Technical Institute (originally the New York Trade School) and opened a branch campus at 450 West 41st Street in Manhattan (closed in 1987). Bachelor's degrees were first awarded in 1980, when the school took its current name. New York City Technical College is the only technical college in the city university system. It offers bachelor's degrees in hotel and restaurant management, legal assistant studies, telecommunications, and graphic arts. There were 6442 full-time and 4485 part-time students enrolled in 1990, when the school completed an extensive renovation and construction program.

Marc Ferris

New York City Transit Authority. Public authority created by the State of New York to operate and maintain the public transit system in New York City; it took responsibility for running the city's subways on 15 June 1953. In 1968 the authority became part of the Metropolitan Transportation Authority (MTA). In addition to the city's subways it operates local buses, express bus routes, and the Staten Island rapid transit line. From 1982 the authority oversaw a massive capital renewal program, accompanied by management changes, that revitalized the city's bus and subway systems.

Peter Derrick: "Catalyst for Development: Rapid Transit in New York," *New York Affairs* 9, no. 4 (1986), 29–59

Peter Derrick

New York City Tribune. Daily newspaper, founded in 1976 as the *News World* by the Korean spiritual leader and businessman Sun Myung Moon. It had its headquarters at 401 5th Avenue in Manhattan and was printed in Long Island City. The newspaper was promoted as an alternative to the other daily newspapers in New York City and became

New York Naval Shipyard. Official name of the BROOKLYN NAVY YARD.

New York Newsday. Daily newspaper launched in 1985. Its parent newspaper, *Newsday*, was founded in 1940 in Hempstead, Long Island, by Alicia Petterson, who as the editor and publisher shaped it into a tabloid best known for its local investigative reporting. The newspaper began expanding its circulation into New York City after being purchased by the Times–Mirror Company in 1970. New York Newsday maintains its own headquarters in Manhattan and a separate editorial staff. In the mid 1990s it had a circulation of about 250,000 in New York City and several widely read columnists, including Sydney Schanberg, Murray Kempton, Jimmy Breslin, and Liz Smith.

Robert F. Keller: *Newsday: A Candid History of the Respectable Tabloid* (New York: William Morrow, 1990)

Madeline Rogers

New York Newspaper Guild. Labor organization formed in New York City in November 1933; its members elected Allen Raymond of the *New York Herald Tribune* their first president and Heywood Broun of the *New York World–Telegram* their vice-president. The organization was instrumental in forming the American Newspaper Guild.

Michael Green

New York Observer (i). Weekly newspaper launched on 17 May 1823 by Sidney E. Morse and Richard C. Morse and published until 30 May 1912. It reflected Presbyterian orthodoxy and was the first religious newspaper published in New York City. Soon after it began publication the newspaper drew attention for its fervent campaign against the city's theaters. For many years it was edited by Samuel Irenaeus Prime, who published a popular series of letters under the pseudonym "Irenaeus" and exploited anti-Catholic sentiment among evangelical Protestants. By mid century he broadened the scope of the newspaper beyond a denominational readership. The founders of the newspaper, sons of the geographer Jedidiah Morse, introduced in 1839 a wax-engraving technique suitable for printing maps. Their brother, the artist and inventor Samuel F. B. Morse, was a contributor to the *Observer*: his letter from Paris published on 20 April 1839 was the first American report of the daguerreotype.

Mariam Touba

New York Observer (ii). Weekly newspaper launched in 1987 by Arthur L. Carter. Printed on peach-colored paper in a broadsheet format, it aimed to offer bold, irreverent coverage of cultural, social, political, and business life in New York City. The newspaper catered unabashedly to the wealthy and powerful élite of Manhattan. It became well-known for its regular columns on politics by Joe Conason and Terry Golway, on the arts by Hilton Kramer, on nightlife by Rex Reed, and on film by Andrew Sarris. In 1994 the *Observer* had a circulation of fifty thousand.

James Bradley

New York Palace. Luxury hotel on Madison Avenue between 50th and 51st streets, designed by the firm of Emery Roth and Sons and completed in 1986; it is built over the Villard Houses, a palazzo designed by the firm of McKim, Mead and White in 1882. Known as the Helmsley Palace from 1981 to 1992, the hotel has fifty-five stories, 962 rooms, a courtyard facing Madison Avenue, and a façade of dark bronzed glass and anodized aluminum; its two-story marble lobby was designed by Tom Lee. Four antique Florentine lanterns adorn the main entrance, and two tiers of nineteenth-century bronze and glass marquees overhang the other two. The great hall of the palazzo is known for its spectacular features, including a red Verona marble fireplace in the grand foyer of the upper lobby (designed by Augustus Saint-Gaudens) and a clock decorated with the signs of the zodiac (Saint-Gaudens and Stanford White). Some of the most elegant rooms are the Drawing Room and the Madison Room, designed by White for the newspaper publisher Whitelaw Reid.

Janet Frankston

New York Peace Society. Forerunner of the AMERICAN PEACE SOCIETY.

New York Philharmonic. Orchestra in New York City, the oldest in continuous existence in the United States and one of the oldest in the world. It was formed in 1842 as the Philharmonic Society, a cooperative organization of musicians led by the American-born conductor Ureli Corelli Hill. The first concert took place on 7 December in the Apollo Rooms on lower Broadway, with sixty-three musicians performing before an audience of six hundred. The concert began with Hill conducting Beethoven's Symphony no. 5. German music and musicians dominated the orchestra in its early years, during which the conductor's post was shared by several men, chiefly Theodore Eisfeld and Carl Bergmann. In 1877–78 and 1879–91 performances were brought to a virtuoso level by Theodore Thomas, born in Germany and trained in the United States, who also conducted his own orchestra from 1867 to 1891. His successor Anton Seidl (1891–98) was a renowned conductor of Wagner whose romantic interpretations inspired both adulation and controversy, and during his tenure the orchestra enjoyed unprecedented success and prosperity.

After a group of wealthy patrons formed the Guarantors' Committee in 1909 the orchestra enjoyed far more financial stability than it had as a cooperative. The guarantors were responsible for engaging Gustav Mahler as the principal conductor of the orchestra and for expanding the season from eighteen concerts a year to fifty-four, some of which were given on tour in New England. Under the leadership of Josef Stransky (1911–23) the orchestra broadened its repertory to include works by American composers, as well as new Europeans such as Debussy, Schoenberg, and Stravinsky, and made its first commercial recording in January 1917. Willem Mengelberg first conducted the orchestra in 1921 and was an important figure for nine years, although half the concerts each season were conducted by others, among them Stravinsky, Wilhelm Furtwängler, and Arturo Toscanini. The orchestra absorbed several others: in 1921 the National Symphony Orchestra (formed as the New Symphony in 1919), in 1923 the City Symphony Orchestra (formed in 1922), and in 1928 the Symphony Society of New York (formed in 1878 by Leopold Damrosch). This period marked the beginning of a greatly expanded educational program, radio broadcasts (1922), summer concerts at Lewisohn Stadium (1922), and children's concerts under the direction of Ernest Schelling that became a model for similar efforts by other orchestras (1924).

Toscanini became the conductor of the newly combined orchestra in 1929 and was the sole conductor for its European tour in 1930. Nationwide radio broadcasts began in the same year and continued without interruption until 1967. On Toscanini's resignation in 1936 the orchestra was led principally by John Barbirolli and by Artur Rodzinski (to 1947), whose assistant conductor Leonard

Music Directors, Music Advisors, and Principal Conductors of the New York Philharmonic

Ureli Corelli Hill 1842–47
Theodore Eisfeld 1848–65
Carl Bergmann 1855–76
Leopold Damrosch 1876–77
Theodore Thomas 1877–91
Anton Seidl 1891–98
Emil Paur 1898–1902
Walter Damrosch 1902–3
Wassily Safanoff 1906–9
Gustav Mahler 1909–11
Josef Stransky 1911–23
Willem Mengelberg 1922–30
Arturo Toscanini 1928–36
John Barbirolli 1936–41
Artur Rodzinski 1943–47
Bruno Walter 1946–49
Leopold Stokowski 1949–50
Dimitri Mitropoulos 1949–58
Leonard Bernstein 1958–69
George Szell 1969–70
Pierre Boulez 1971–77
Zubin Mehta 1977–91
Kurt Masur 1991–

Bernstein made a spectacular début leading the orchestra as a substitute for Bruno Walter, who had been taken ill. The years following Rodzinski's resignation were dominated by Walter, Leopold Stokowski, Dimitri Mitropoulos, and Bernstein (from 1957), whose tenure was a period of great change and growth. Two television series were begun in 1958, and in September 1962 the orchestra left Carnegie Hall after sixty-nine years and moved to Philharmonic Hall (later known as Avery Fisher Hall) at Lincoln Center. In 1964 it became the first American orchestra to offer a year-round contract to its members. This led to expanded programming: André Kostelanetz led a series of popular-music concerts called "Promenades" from 1964 to 1978, and free concerts were given in the parks in all five boroughs from 1965. In the autumn of 1969 Bernstein was given the lifetime position of laureate conductor, the first in the history of the orchestra. Pierre Boulez, the music director from 1971, became known for his emphasis on music of the twentieth century and for innovative programming: from 1972 to 1978 the orchestra performed "Rug Concerts" and took part in a series of "Prospective Encounters" both in the concert hall and at other venues throughout the city. Zubin Mehta, who held the post of music director longer than anyone else in the twentieth century (1978–91), specialized in late Romantic composers. He led the orchestra in its ten-thousandth concert on 7 March 1982 (an achievement unmatched by any other orchestra) and in 1983 inaugurated a new series of chamber music concerts by the Philharmonic Ensembles. Kurt Masur, music director of the Gewandhaus Orchestra Leipzig, became the music director in September 1991. The New York Philharmonic has 106 permanent musicians and performs about 190 concerts a season.

Walter Damrosch: *My Musical Life* (New York: Charles Scribner's Sons, 1923)

Howard Shanet: *Philharmonic: A History of New York's Orchestra* (Garden City, N.Y.: Doubleday, 1975)

Vera Brodsky Lawrence: *Strong on Music: The New York Music Scene in the Days of George Templeton Strong, 1836–1875*, vol. 1, *Resonances, 1836–1850* (New York: Oxford University Press, 1988)

Vera Brodsky Lawrence: *Strong on Music: The New York Music Scene in the Days of George Templeton Strong, 1836–1875*, vol. 2, *Reverberations, 1850–1856* (Chicago: University of Chicago Press, forthcoming)

Barbara Haws

New York Port of Embarkation. Military command. During the Second World War it organized the shipping overseas of three million troops and their equipment, and more than sixty-three million tons (fifty-seven million metric tons) of additional war supplies. Its facilities included a complex network of railroad lines, highways, waterways, wharves, and warehouses. At its peak in 1944 the port comprised ten terminals and three areas for staging troops, and employed more than 55,000 men and women. The three principal terminals of the port were the Brooklyn Army Terminal, where the commander of the port, Major General Homer M. Groninger, had his headquarters; Bush Terminal, which extended from 28th to 50th streets along 1st and 2nd avenues in Brooklyn and comprised twenty-six eight-story warehouses built between 1895 and 1926; and Staten Island Terminal. Together these terminals handled about half the wartime shipments from the port. Other facilities on Staten Island included Fox Hills Terminal and Howland Hook Terminal, the principal point from which petroleum, oil, and lubricants were shipped. In Manhattan the North River Terminal, at 12th Avenue and 46th Street, was an important point of embarkation for troops. Seven piers on the Hudson permitted the loading of troop ships and liners. The Army Postal Terminal, at 464 Lexington Avenue in Manhattan, handled more than 3000 million pieces of mail during the war. Across the harbor in New Jersey were the terminals of Port Johnson and Claremont, and the Special Service Supply Terminal had offices in Manhattan and Brooklyn. Troops bound overseas were routed into the port from three staging areas: Camp Kilmer (New Brunswick, New Jersey), Camp Shanks (Orangeburg, New York), and Fort Hamilton (Brooklyn).

"Staging Area — Brooklyn: Record of a Borough at War," *Brooklyn Eagle*, 9 Dec 1945

Joseph F. Meany Jr.

New York Post. Daily newspaper. Launched in 1801 by Alexander Hamilton as the *Evening Post* with William Coleman as its first editor, it was produced in offices on Pine Street and published shipping notices and anti-Jeffersonian invective. Coleman was succeeded on his death in 1829 by William Cullen Bryant, under whose guidance the newspaper abandoned its conservative politics and broadened its appeal. During the party realignments of the 1820s and 1830s it supported Andrew Jackson and the Democratic Party, and opposed high tariffs, the Bank of the United States, and the nullification acts of South Carolina. Bryant tempered the blustery, radical brand of Jacksonianism embraced by his associate William Leggett (to 1836), and avoided the sensationalism of the penny press, notably the *Herald* of James Gordon Bennett Sr. With his later associate John Bigelow (from 1848) he opposed slavery and expressed increasing frustration with the Democrats for equivocating on the issue. In 1850 the offices of the newspaper were moved to the corner of Liberty and Nassau streets. Bigelow introduced a broad range of new issues through a weekly column of fictional interviews with a "Jersey ferryman" that related political gossip, and in 1851 he published an exposé of Jared Sparks's sanitized edition of George Washington's correspondence.

In 1855 the *Post* became a supporter of the Republican Party. Bigelow left the newspaper in 1860 and was replaced by Charles Nordhoff, who supported Abraham Lincoln and advocated the vigorous prosecution of the Civil War. During the draft riots (1863) he wrote an account of eight thousand words suggesting that the riots had been instigated by Copperhead Democrats, and after attaching a hose to the steam boiler of the newspaper's offices he threatened to repel attackers with blasts of scalding water. After the war Bryant and Nordhoff backed President Andrew Johnson's mild Reconstruction program and the Fourteenth Amendment, and opposed Johnson's impeachment and a silver-based monetary system. The offices of the *Post* were moved to Broadway and Fulton Street in 1875, at a time when the newspaper was faring well commercially. Bryant died in 1878 and was succeeded as the chief editor of the newspaper by his son-in-law Parke Godwin. In 1881 the newspaper was purchased by Henry Villard, who installed the editorial triumvirate of Horace White, E. L. Godkin, and Carl Schurz. Under their leadership the newspaper continued to oppose free silver and supported lower tariffs and civil service reform. As the sole editor from 1883 Godkin waged a relentless and popular attack against Tammany Hall: in 1890 he published a series of scathing biographical sketches of its leaders, whom he described as "liquor-dealers," "pugilists," "dive-keepers," and "convicted murderers."

The Villard family relinquished control of the *Post* in 1917, which under the ownership of Thomas Lamont (1917–22) and Cyrus Curtis (from 1924) became a forum for more conservative views. The political perspective changed again in 1936 when the newspaper was bought by J. David Stern, a supporter of the New Deal. By this time the newspaper was declining in profitability, and when Dorothy Schiff assumed control in 1939 it ranked third in circulation among afternoon newspapers in the city. In an effort to attract readers Schiff and her third husband, Theodore O. Thackrey, emphasized scandal and human-interest stories, and in 1942 the format was changed from broadsheet to tabloid. James A. Wechsler, the chief editor from 1949, crusaded for civil liberties, attacked Senator Joseph R. McCarthy, and was himself attacked for his early association with the Young Communist League; in 1954 vandals splashed red paint on the newspaper's building on West Street. Paul Sann assumed the editorship in 1961 and increased coverage of crime and sports.

By 1967 the *New York Post* was the only afternoon newspaper left in the city. It benefited little from the demise of its competitors, because the same demographic and cultural changes that had driven them out of business were hurting the *Post* as well. Financial losses led Schiff to sell the newspaper in 1976 to the Australian press magnate Rupert Murdoch, who sought to replace the newspaper's traditional readership, which was largely white, middle class, and aging, with a newer one that was racially diverse, working class, and young. Murdoch introduced marked changes: a stridently conservative editorial stance, frequent blurring of the distinction between reporting and opinion, sensationalistic and at times smirking coverage of crime, sex, accidents, scandal, and celebrities, and deliberately outrageous headlines, of which perhaps the most memorable was "Headless Body in Topless Bar." The newspaper also ran sweepstakes that it promoted aggressively, and within a few years circulation increased sharply. The *Post* nevertheless remained unprofitable, largely because of its inability to sell display advertising to large retailers (who recognized that most readers of the *Post* also read other newspapers, and therefore believed that advertising in the *Post* was redundant). Murdoch lost about $150 million by 1988, when he was forced to sell the newspaper because of a federal regulation barring common ownership of television stations and newspapers in the same market. The *Post* was purchased by the real-estate investor Peter Kalikow, who won $22 million in concessions from the newspaper's labor unions. Kalikow in turn was compelled to sell the newspaper in 1993 when he became bankrupt. Granted a waiver of the regulation that had forced him to sell the newspaper years before, Murdoch again became the owner in 1993.

Allan Nevins: *The Evening Post: A Century of Journalism* (New York: Boni and Liveright, 1922)

James A. Wechsler: *The Age of Suspicion* (New York: Random House, 1953)

Charles H. Brown: *William Cullen Bryant* (New York: Charles Scribner's Sons, 1971)

Jeffrey Potter: *Men, Money, and Magic: The Story of Dorothy Schiff* (New York: Coward, McCann and Geoghegan, 1976)

Robert Stinson

New York Press Club. Fraternal organization of newspaper reporters. Formed in 1872 as the New York Journalistic Fraternity, it was incorporated in 1874 under its current name. Its activities included charity work as well as banquets and shows at which such speakers as Governor Alfred E. Smith and Mayor James J. Walker appeared. The club disbanded in 1933 after going into receivership but was revived in 1948. Later it undertook charity work for underprivileged children and the Muscular Dystrophy Association, sponsored debates and speeches, and aided reporters charged with libel or contempt.

New York Times, 10 Jan 1933, 16 April 1933, 31 Dec 1933

Michael Green

New York Printers' Union. Original name of NEW YORK TYPOGRAPHICAL UNION NO. 6.

New York Produce Exchange. A commodities market formed in 1861 as the New York Commercial Association by merchants and ship brokers who gathered outside the Merchants' Exchange, and renamed in 1868. It was at first a cash spot market: merchants based their transactions on samples from individual lots of grain rather than on inspection, grades, and negotiable warehouse receipts (the system used in Chicago). Members included agents of European firms buying for shipment abroad, often through other ports. The leaders of the exchange overcame the resistance of exporters and in 1874 established trading "pits" for transactions in inspected and graded grains. From 1885 the exchange was housed in a building erected at 2 Broadway. As the nation's leading export market for wheat, flour, lard, and cottonseed oil, the exchange attracted many respected merchants. In the 1870s Franklin Edson, later mayor of New York City, was its president for three terms. Shrinking foreign trade after 1920 forced the exchange to broaden its scope and offer both spot and futures trading in such commodities as hay, hops, butter, and cheese. Later retrenchment confined its operations by the 1950s to trading in cottonseed oil, tallow, fishmeal, and pepper. After several years of heavy losses the New York Produce Exchange was reorganized in 1973 into a real-estate investment trust, and its commodities business was taken over by other exchanges.

Richard Wheatly: "The New York Produce Exchange," *Harper's New Monthly Magazine*, July 1886, pp. 189–218

Morton Rothstein

New York Public Interest Research Group [NYPIRG]. Statewide nonprofit organization. It began in 1973 as one of several consumer and environmental advocacy groups formed by the consumer advocate Ralph Nader on college campuses throughout the country. In 1977 the group launched the Straphangers Campaign to monitor the mass transit system and make recommendations for improvements in service. It opposed the building of a trash incinerator for the Brooklyn Navy Yard proposed by Mayor Edward I. Koch, the dredging of Wallabout Channel, and the expansion of the Fresh Kills landfill on Staten Island. In the 1980s it issued environmental reports assessing sewage treatment plants, toxic dumps, municipal landfills, and the effects of burning garbage, and in the early 1990s it supported local legislation that imposed regulations on the placement of cigarette vending machines. The group began issuing semiannual reports called the "State of the Subways" in 1990, and in the same year it petitioned the Metropolitan Transit Authority to cancel proposed reductions in service and a plan to close the Transit Museum. It also undertook voter registration efforts.

In the mid 1990s NYPIRG had its main office on Murray Street in Manhattan and eight chapters in New York City, at the College of Staten Island, Hunter College, City College, the Pratt Institute of Art and Technology, New York City Technical College, Brooklyn College, Queens College, and Queensboro Community College. The group is run by a board of students and carries on its work through the efforts of paid organizers, attorneys, volunteers, and various experts. It publishes a bimonthly newsletter, "Councilwatch," about the City Council.

Marjorie Harrison

New York Public Library [NYPL]. Library formed in 1895 by the consolidation of the Astor and Lenox libraries and the Tilden Trust. New York City had no major library when John Jacob Astor provided a bequest of $400,000 for one in the 1830s. A building was erected in 1854 on Astor Place for a noncirculating library open to the public free of charge. Although members of the Astor family continued to make contributions, the library often suffered financial difficulties. James Lenox (1800–80) transferred land and his collection of books and art to the Lenox Library, incorporated in 1870. Opened in 1877 in a building designed by Richard Morris Hunt, the library was used primarily for art exhibitions, because its books were so poorly catalogued that they could not easily be consulted. Under public pressure the library gradually extended its hours and eased its admission policies even as it faced recurrent financial problems. A trust to set up a free library was left to the city in 1886 by Samuel J. Tilden, the former Democratic governor and presidential candidate. Family members contested the will and were awarded the entire estate by a court decision in 1891, but one heir donated Tilden's personal library and more than $2 million to the trust. Negotiations were undertaken to merge the trust and the Astor Library and were eventually extended to include the Lenox Library; they ended on 23 May 1895 with the formation of the New York Public Library, Astor, Lenox and Tilden Foundations, a private institution open to the public.

Confronted with the task of building a strong institution from two weak ones, the board of trustees appointed as their first director John S. Billings, a former army surgeon who had built the country's foremost medical library. He combined the inadequate and often inaccessible Astor and Lenox collections into the reference department, a major noncirculating research library intended as a library of record. Maintained by the Astor, Lenox, and Tilden endowments, it was especially strong in Americana, English and Amer-

Branch of the New York Public Library at 7th Avenue, ca *1910*

South Reading Room, New York Public Library

New York Public Library, 40th Street and 5th Avenue, 1911

ican literature, music, dance, theater, foreign languages, and genealogy, and had comprehensive collections of illustrated books, periodicals, government publications, maps, and newspapers. Billings reorganized the staffs of the former libraries, built new collections, devised a unique classification scheme, and drew a sketch that became the basis for the main building at 5th Avenue and 42nd Street, which was designed by John M. Carrère and Thomas Hastings and opened to the public on 23 May 1911. The trustees left open the possibility of adding neighborhood branches. The free libraries were small, independent institutions sponsored primarily by charitable and religious organizations to promote the moral, civic, and intellectual growth of immigrants and workers; they were popular but lacked coordination and financial support. The branches of the New York Free Circulating Library (formed 1878), the largest of the city's free libraries with eleven branches by 1899, were absorbed by the New York Public Library in 1901 and converted into a circulation department.

A month after the circulation department was formed Andrew Carnegie offered $5.2 million to erect sixty-five buildings for branches if the city would provide the sites and maintenance. The city agreed, and between 1902 and 1914 thirty-seven branches operated by the New York Public Library under contract with the city were built in Manhattan, the Bronx, and Staten Island. In 1906 the superintendent of work with children (now the office of children's services) was established, one of the first libraries to welcome children regardless of age. During the same year the superintendent of work with schools (now the office of young adult services) was also established, the first office of its kind in the United States. By 1921 there were forty-three branches. Shifts in population placed new demands on the library: in such areas as the Lower East Side, where there were several branches, the population was decreasing, while in others such as the Bronx there were few libraries for a population that was rapidly expanding. Seven branches opened between the world wars, but inflation and a lack of municipal funds left some needs unmet. The library responded by opening fourteen subbranches with abbreviated hours and deposit stations in community institutions, and by providing "bookmobiles" to remote areas of the Bronx and Staten Island. Severe strains developed during the Depression. The branches were used less and staff was furloughed, hours were shortened, and book purchases declined. At the same time the reference department experienced such an increase in use that it became known as the "people's university." Some library operations were maintained in part by workers in federal relief programs.

After the Second World War renovations

New York Public Library (designed by Carrère and Hastings), 42nd Street and 5th Avenue, ca *1945*

and additions were needed in the branch system, forcing the library to seek new sources of income. During the 1940s it shifted its goals from large gifts to a greater number of small gifts in annual campaigns. It also revamped its administration, adding an office of adult services (1946) and departments of public relations and personnel. After 1950 state and city funding for the circulating department rose sharply. Between 1945 and 1956 the number of branches grew from fifty to eighty. They increasingly gave attention to such materials as films, discs, and tapes; developed radio and television programs for audiences of all ages; and expanded their range of free programs to include film screenings, concerts, dramatic readings, art exhibitions, and lectures. The branch libraries during the 1960s intensified their efforts in neighborhoods dominated by ethnic minorities. The New York Public Library in 1965 established a Library for the Performing Arts at Lincoln Center (now the New York Public Library for the Performing Arts). The reference department developed programs in book preservation, microfilming, exhibits, and bibliographic publications, and was renamed the research libraries in 1966. In 1974 the library helped to form the Research Libraries Group, a cooperative for sharing resources.

As the city's fiscal situation deteriorated during the late 1960s the library experienced serious financial problems. Nevertheless a full-blown crisis was averted, and in 1970 the first large circulation building opened in midtown Manhattan. The branch staffs were reduced by 20 percent in the early 1970s because of budget cuts, and the situation was exacerbated by high inflation and the city's fiscal crisis of the mid 1970s. From 1975 branch programs and hours were sharply curtailed, the research libraries' deficits grew, and hours for the central building, until then open eighty-four hours a week, were reduced by nearly half. Finances improved in the late 1970s with an influx of funds from New York State, the federal government, and private contributors. Circulation and hours did not increase again until the early 1980s, and the system did not fully regain its earlier service levels. The appointment of Vartan Gregorian as president in 1981 was an important step toward revitalization. During his tenure the library renovated the central building and many branches, introduced new programs, reduced cataloguing backlogs, increased its hours, and successfully completed a campaign to raise $300 million. The research libraries continued to be supported primarily by private endowment, the branch libraries by the city.

The New York Public Library is considered one of the five greatest libraries in the world, holding 49.5 million items, including 17.9 million books (in both the research centers and the branch libraries). The main facility at 42nd Street and 5th Avenue houses research divisions and sections devoted to economics and public affairs; the history of the United States, local history, and genealogy; the humanities and social sciences; Judaica; the Far East; the Slavic and Baltic regions; periodicals; maps; and science and technology. Nearly one million rare items are held in the library's special collections, including the Miriam and Ira D. Wallach Division of Art, Prints, and Photographs; the Rare Books and Manuscripts Division; the Carl H. Pforzheimer Collection of Shelley and His Circle; the George Arents Collection on the History of Tobacco and Tobacco-Related Literature; the Spencer Collection of Illustrated Books, Illuminated Manuscripts, and Fine Bindings; and the Berg Collection of English and American Literature. In addition to the main research library and the Library for the Performing Arts, the NYPL operates the Schomburg Center for Research in Black Culture, the Science, Industry, and Business Library (in formation; scheduled to open in late 1995), and eighty-two branch libraries.

The library issues borrowers' cards to anyone who lives, works, or attends school in New York State. In fiscal year 1994 there were 1,916,009 library card holders and a total circulation of 10,712,582 items.

Harry Miller Lydenberg: *History of the New York Public Library* (New York: New York Public Library, 1923)

Phyllis Dain: *The New York Public Library: History of Its Founding and Early Years* (New York: New York Public Library, 1972)

Henry Hope Reed: *The New York Public Library: Its Architecture and Decoration* (New York: W. W. Norton, 1986)

Robert Sink

New York Public Library for the Performing Arts. Research center of the New York Public Library, opened in 1965 at Lincoln Center for the Performing Arts as the Library and Museum of the Performing Arts. Its research divisions comprise the Rodgers and Hammerstein Archives of Recorded Sound, the Billy Rose Theater Collection, the world's largest dance archive, and a large music division. A lending library circulates more than 200,000 books, records, tapes, compact discs, video cassettes, children's materials, and music scores. There are also seven exhibition spaces where materials related to music and dance are displayed, and a small auditorium.

Rosine Raoul: *The Library and Museum of the Performing Arts at Lincoln Center* (New York: Library and Museum of the Performing Arts, n.d. [?1965])

New York Rangers. Ice hockey team formed on 15 May 1926, sometimes called the "Broadway Blues." The team played its first game on 16 November 1926 in Madison Square Garden under the direction of Lester Patrick, the coach and manager. In 1928 it won the Stanley Cup after defeating the Montreal Maroons in five games; it also reached the Stanley Cup finals in 1929 and 1932 owing largely to the plays of Frank Boucher, scoring by Bill Cook and his brother Bun Cook, and defense by Ivan "Ching" Johnson. The team won the Stanley Cup in 1933 and again in 1940 when it defeated the Toronto Maple Leafs in six games: members of the team included

Babe Pratt, Lynn Patrick, Art Coulter, Neil Colville, and Bryan Hextall. The Rangers finished first in the National Hockey League (NHL) in 1941–42 and reached the finals in 1949–50, but despite excellent performances by Andy Bathgate, Harry Howell, and Gump Worsley they failed to reach the finals again until 1965–66, when Emile Francis became the coach. In the 1960s and 1970s the team had such well-known players as Rod Gilbert, Jean Ratelle, Brad Park, Ed Giacomin, and Phil Esposito. It entered the finals for the Stanley Cup in 1972 and 1979 and in 1989–90 finished first in the Patrick Division. In the early 1990s such leading players as Brian Leetch, Mike Gartner, Brian Messier, and John Vanbiesbrouck played for the team. It finished the season with the best record in the NHL in 1991–92 and was favored to win the Stanley Cup, but it lost to the Pittsburgh Penguins. In the following season the team failed to qualify for the playoffs altogether.

In 1993–94 the Rangers compiled the best record in the National Hockey League during the regular season, and in the playoffs successively defeated the New York Islanders, the Washington Capitals, the New Jersey Devils, and the Vancouver Canucks to win the Stanley Cup for the first time in fifty-four years.

Stan Fischler: *New York Rangers: The Iceman Cometh* (Englewood Cliffs, N.J.: Prentice Hall, 1974)

James Duplacey

New York Review of Books. Fortnightly literary magazine, launched as a book review by Robert Benjamin Silvers and Barbara Epstein during a newspaper strike in February 1963. Once jokingly called the "New York review of each other's books" by the historian Richard Hofstadter, it took up the cause of the New Left and was soon one of the most influential publications of its kind among members of academe. Its rise coincided with the decline of the intellectuals of New York City as a cohesive group. The *Review* became known for publishing long, wide-ranging essays in which several books were discussed. In the 1960s it was criticized by the magazine *Commentary* for publishing leftist material, particularly a detailed cover illustration of a "Molotov cocktail." Among those who contributed frequently were Noam Chomsky, Joan Didion, Theodore Draper, Stephen Jay Gould, Andrew Kopkind, Felix G. Rohatyn, and I. F. Stone, and the cartoonist David Levine. Over the years the *Review* evolved into a sober journal of ideas open to different political points of view and not strongly oriented toward writers from New York City. In the mid 1990s the circulation was about 130,000 and Silvers and Epstein remained the editors.

Philip Nobile: *Intellectual Skywriting: Literary Politics and the New York Review of Books* (New York: Charterhouse, 1974)

Thomas E. Bird

New York School. Name given to a group of abstract expressionist artists in New York City who became well known after the Second World War and were active throughout the 1950s; they included William Baziotes, Elaine de Kooning, Willem de Kooning, Arshile Gorky, Adolph Gottlieb, Philip Guston, Grace Hartigan, Franz Kline, Lee Krasner, Norman Lewis, Robert Motherwell, Barnett Newman, Jackson Pollock, Ad Reinhardt, Mark Rothko, and Clyfford Still. The group drew inspiration from diverse sources: the work of abstract and surrealist artists living in New York City during the late 1930s, including such Europeans as John Graham, Max Ernst, Marcel Duchamp, and Yves Tanguy, and the Chilean artist Matta (Roberto Matta Echaurren); shows on cubism and surrealism at the Museum of Modern Art during the same period; the psychoanalytic theories of Carl Jung; Greek myth; existentialism; and American Indian art. Its members repudiated the social relevance and communitarian ideals that pervaded social realism, regionalism, and "American scene" painting of the 1930s, and instead saw painting as a means of expressing their own inner emotions. In the 1950s the work of the New York School was shown at the art galleries of Peggy Guggenheim, Betty Parsons, Charles Egan, Sam Kootz, and Julien Levy, and championed by the art critics Clement Greenberg, Harold Rosenberg, and Meyer Schapiro. Several critics celebrated the seemingly apolitical art of the New York School as an art of freedom that contrasted sharply with the socialist realism of the Soviet bloc.

Dore Ashton: *The New York School: A Cultural Reckoning* (New York: Penguin, 1979)
David Shapiro and Cecile Shapiro, eds.: *Abstract Expressionism: A Critical Record* (New York: Cambridge University Press, 1990)

Patricia Hills

New York School for Fine and Applied Art. Former name of the Parsons School of Design.

New York School of Chiropody. Original name of the New York College of Podiatric Medicine.

New York School of Interior Design. A private college at 155 East 56th Street, founded in 1916 as the School of Interior Decoration by the architect Augustus Sherrill Whiton (1887–1961) and several other designers, artists, and decorators. It offers certificates, associate degrees, and bachelor's degrees, and has the largest faculty of any college in the United States specializing in interior design. In 1991 the school had 602 students.

Marc Ferris

New York School of Social Work. Institution that later became the School of Social Work at Columbia University.

New York Shakespeare Festival. Theater company formed in 1954 by the producer and director Joseph Papp. It began by giving free performances of Shakespeare's plays, which were staged successively in a church basement, on a flatbed truck, and at the Delacorte Theatre in Central Park, built in 1962 as a permanent summer facility. In 1967 Papp opened the Public Theater in a building formerly occupied by the Astor Library in Greenwich Village. Dedicated to new American plays, the theater opened on 29 October 1967 with the controversial musical *Hair* (book and lyrics by Gerome Ragni and James Rado, music by Galt MacDermott): this later was produced on Broadway as the first of several commercial vehicles that subsidized both the Shakespeare Festival and the more adventurous programming of the Public Theater. The theater's successful production of *A Chorus Line* (James Kirkwood and Nicholas Dante, 1975) ran on Broadway for 6137 performances, becoming the longest-running show in Broadway history and enabling Papp to present the work of the emerging playwrights David Rabe, John Guare, James Lapine, and David Henry Hwang. Other notable productions included Rabe's *The Basic Training of Pavlo Hummel* (1971) and *Sticks and Bones* (1971), Jason Miller's *That Championship Season* (1972), and musical productions of *Two Gentlemen of Verona* (1971), *The Pirates of Penzance* (1980), and *The Mystery of Edwin Drood* (1985). Important programs at the theater have included an exchange with the Royal Court Theatre of London featuring the work of such authors as David Hare and Caryl Churchill; the Festival Latino, an annual celebration of music, dance, and film; and the Shakespeare Marathon, a project begun in 1987 to produce all of Shakespeare's plays over six years. Shortly before his death Papp resigned from the theater and named as his successor JoAnne Akalaitis, former member of the theater company Mabou Mines. She was in turn replaced by George C. Wolfe in March 1993.

D. S. Moynihan

New York Society Library. Public library opened by subscription in 1754 in City Hall to members who paid an annual fee. Most of its holdings were destroyed or lost during the American Revolution, after which it experienced financial problems and faced competition from the increasingly popular free public libraries. The library moved to Nassau Street in 1795 and in 1839 absorbed its rival, the New York Athenaeum. The city's upper classes accounted for most of its members, and as they moved uptown the library followed, to Broadway and Leonard Street in 1840 and then to University Place in 1856. From 1850 the library received several generous bequests that ensured its long-term prosperity, and from 1882 it offered delivery service to its patrons. The trustees considered leaving University Place as early as 1900 but delayed moving until 1937, when they renovated and expanded a five-story townhouse at 53 East 79th Street. By the time of its bicentenary the New York Society Library owned roughly 200,000 items, including many rare books and manuscripts. It is the oldest library in New York City and the fourth-oldest in the United States.

Austin Baxter Keep: *History of the New York Society Library* (New York: De Vinne, 1908)
Marion King: *Books and People: Five Decades of New York's Oldest Library* (New York: Macmillan, 1954)

Cynthia A. Kierner

New York Society of Umbra. An artistic and literary organization formed in the summer of 1962, having evolved from a series of weekly workshops, readings, and informal meetings on the Lower East Side. The society was influenced both by currents in African–American culture and by the social activism of the 1960s. Its original members included Mildred Hernton, Albert Hayes, Joseph Johnson, Tom Feelings, Brenda Walcott, and the editors Thomas C. Dent, Calvin C. Hernton, and David Henderson. From 1963 to 1968 the organization issued *Umbra*, a cooperatively published quarterly journal of contemporary art, photography, poetry, drama, and opinion that aimed to publish works "as radical as society demands the truth to be." Among the early contributors were Julian Bond, Lerone Bennett, Ann Shockley, Amiri Baraka, Ishmael Reed, Clarence Major, Conrad Kent Rivers, and Alice Walker.

Emilyn L. Brown

New York State Institute of Applied Arts and Science. Original name of NEW YORK CITY TECHNICAL COLLEGE.

New York Stock Exchange [NYSE]. The principal securities market in the United States, accounting for about 85 percent of all transactions in the securities listed on it.

New York City had an active securities market by 1790, stimulated by the issuance in that year of bonds by Alexander Hamilton, the first secretary of the treasury, to consolidate and refund debts incurred during the American Revolution. There is however little evidence to support the claim that the "Buttonwood Agreement" of 1792 (signed by twenty-two stockbrokers and merchants on 17 May and by two more later in the year) marks the beginning of the NYSE itself. Within a few months of the bankruptcy of William Duer in the spring of 1792 the city's securities market was largely inactive, not to be revived until after the War of 1812.

The New York Stock Exchange was organized on 8 March 1817, when a group of twenty-eight brokers adopted a constitution and set up formal membership rules. The initial name was the New York Stock and Exchange Board; the present name dates to 1863, and the exchange is popularly referred to as the Big Board. In its early years the exchange functioned as a call market, in which the name of each stock was called out in turn as brokers bid on only one security at a time. Its business at first consisted almost entirely of bank and insurance stock. Railroad securities began to dominate by the 1830s and 1840s and continued to do so until the end of the century. The early exchange was a small operation: only a few dozen brokers regularly attended the twice-daily calls, and daily volume was only a few thousand shares. Between 1817 and 1865, when the exchange opened its first permanent headquarters on its current site at Broad and Wall streets, it moved its base of operations ten times.

The 1860s were a decade of major change at the NYSE. Fueled by wartime speculation, trading flourished at the exchange and at other sites in lower Manhattan. A number of rival exchanges opened, among them the Open Board of Stock Brokers, which from 1863 to 1869 often matched the NYSE in trading volume. When the NYSE absorbed its rival in 1869 it became a body of 1060 members, more than ten times the number of a decade earlier. Membership on the exchange became a salable property right in 1868, with seats selling for $4000 in the 1870s. (The price remained relatively stable over the years, al-

Trading floor at the New York Stock Exchange, from Harper's Weekly, *10 September 1881*

Trading floor of the New York Stock Exchange

though it did surpass $1.1 million in 1987.) The number of seats increased to eleven hundred in 1880, and in another sign of growth the call-market was replaced in 1871 by a continuous-auction market, which remains the principal means of trading.

Growth continued in the late nineteenth century, with occasional reverses. In 1873 the exchange closed for ten days after the failure of Jay Cooke and Company. On 15 December 1886 the volume of shares traded first exceeded one million, and by the turn of the century industrial securities were traded for the first time. The coming of age of industrial listings was confirmed in 1901, when the newly formed U.S. Steel Corporation became the first company capitalized at more than $1000 million. In the same year the exchange witnessed perhaps the most remarkable of several attempted "corners," when Edward H. Harriman and Jacob Schiff battled James Hill and J. P. Morgan for control of the North Pacific Railroad: in the course of a single trading session the price of a share quintupled, to more than $1000. The struggle took place in borrowed quarters, the exchange having moved out of its former building while a new one was being erected on the same site. The new building, the current home of the NYSE, was designed by George B. Post and completed in 1903 at a cost of $2 million, and features a magnificent Renaissance façade on Broad Street and a trading floor one hundred feet (thirty meters) wide, 183 feet (fixty-six meters) long, and seventy-nine feet (twenty-four meters) tall.

The NYSE was closed for six months in 1914 because of war, but the exchange emerged from the war much stronger, as did the economy of the United States, which for the first time became a creditor nation. The exchange was in the forefront of the great securities boom of the 1920s, and 275 new seats were created in 1929. The boom ended abruptly with the stock market crash of the same year. On "Black Tuesday," 29 October, more than sixteen million shares were traded (a record that stood for nearly forty years), and by the end of the trading session the Dow Jones Industrial Average (DJIA) had declined more than 23 percent from its closing level of the preceding week. This marked only the beginning of the Depression: by the time the DJIA reached its lowest level in the summer of 1932, it had only about one tenth its value of three years earlier. Public confidence in the exchange was shaken, and after extensive congressional hearings the Securities and Exchange Commission (SEC) was formed in 1934. The commission tightened reporting and listing requirements and implemented other reforms, arousing considerable opposition from an exchange that for decades had operated with little or no governmental oversight. The leader of the opposition was Richard Whitney, president of the exchange from 1930 to 1935, who in the view of his many enemies received his just reward in 1938 when he was convicted of swindling his customers. After his downfall the exchange accepted the reforms of the SEC, and in 1938 it initiated random supervisory audits of member firms to protect customers' assets in brokerage accounts.

After the Second World War the exchange mounted extensive advertising and promotional campaigns in an effort to attract small investors. But by the 1960s the dominant force was the institutional market, comprising private pension funds, trust funds, insurance companies, and open-end investment companies, or mutual funds. The reputation of the exchange as dependable and secure was reinforced by the successful resolution of the so-called salad-oil scandal in 1963. The crisis was brought on when the failure of a member firm, Ira Haupt and Company, endangered $450 million worth of its customers' cash and stock, which were pledged to banks as security for loans. Although under no legal obligation to do so, the NYSE set up a special trust fund to protect the firm's customers. When four member firms were liquidated in 1969 and ten more followed in 1970, customers were protected against losses by the trust fund and by the Securities Investors Protection Corporation. In 1971 the NYSE was incorporated for the first time, as a nonprofit corporation. A long-standing rule mandating fixed commissions for stock transactions was repealed in 1975, leading to the rapid growth of discount brokers and to negotiable commissions from full-service brokers.

Further changes were brought about by the stock market crash of 1987, which followed an extended "bull market" during which prices and trading volume rose sharply. On 20 October 608 million shares were traded, with a value of about $21,000 million, and the DJIA declined by more than five hundred points. Because much of the sudden decline in the market had been caused by "program trading," under which transactions are executed by computer when prices reach a certain level, the exchange implemented "trading collars" to make the market less volatile. Among these were special controls that take effect when the DJIA declines by fifty points from the closing level of the preceding day. By the early 1990s program trading still accounted for 12 percent of all trading volume on the exchange, but its tendency to exaggerate swings in the market had apparently been neutralized.

In a twelve-year period beginning in the early 1980s the NYSE spent more than $1000 million on technology, to increase the volume of trading that could be handled to more than 1000 million shares each day, about four times the average daily volume in 1993. In the mid 1990s about 90 percent of all customer's orders were processed electronically, with the trade confirmed in seconds and a record of the transaction instantaneously made available to investors worldwide.

In 1993 the NYSE listed 191 new issues that raised more than $40,000 million, and by the following year the total number of listed firms reached 2361. The combined value of all firms listed on the exchange stood at $4,500,000,000,000, representing 83 percent of the capitalization of all publicly held equities in the United States. Foreign stocks listed on the exchange numbered 153 and accounted for 8.3 percent of trading volume in 1993. In 1994 the exchange had 1366 members, a number fixed in 1953.

The NYSE neither buys nor sells securities. A firm seeking to have its shares traded on the exchange must satisfy very strict requirements with respect to financial condition, reporting, and registration with the SEC. Membership on the NYSE is generally considered an endorsement of a firm's status and is eagerly sought after. The exchange is governed by a board consisting of ten directors from the securities industry and ten directors representing the public, who elect a president and a full-time paid chairman. Educational programs offered by the exchange include a weeklong series called "Teach the Teacher" and summer seminars attended by thousands of graduate and undergraduate students.

Robert Sobel: *N.Y.S.E.: A History of the New York Stock Exchange, 1935–1975* (New York: Weybright and Talley, 1975)

Walter Werner and Steven T. Smith: *Wall Street* (New York: Columbia University Press, 1991)

Peter Eisenstadt: "Forgetting the Origins of the New York Stock Exchange: How the Buttonwood Tree Grows," *Prospects* 19 (1994)

For illustration see WALL STREET.

New York Theological Seminary (i). Original name of UNION THEOLOGICAL SEMINARY.

New York Theological Seminary (ii). Nondenominational Protestant seminary formed in 1900 as the Bible Teachers College in Montclair, New Jersey, by Wilbert Webster White (1863–1944), a minister of the United Presbyterian Church. It moved in 1902 to New York City, where its classes were held first at the Broadway Tabernacle on 6th Avenue and 34th Street (built 1859), then at an optician's office nearby, at a building on 49th Street between Lexington and 3rd avenues (from 1918), and at the Marble Collegiate Church on 5th Avenue and West 29th Street (from 1976). The seminary was renamed successively the Bible Teachers Training School (to bring it into compliance with regulations of the New York Board of Regents) and the Biblical Seminary in New York (1921) before adopting its current name in 1965. The course of instruction reflected White's belief that scriptural study belonged at the center of the theological curriculum. As president of the seminary until 1940 White oversaw the training of scores of pastors, directors of Christian education, teachers, and missionaries. Although enrollment declined in the 1950s and 1960s the fortunes of the seminary revived after it radically restructured its programs in 1970 to provide an affordable theological education for the growing black, Spanish-speaking, and Asian population in the metropolitan area. Although bible study remained central to the curriculum, various experimental offerings sought to equip members of the clergy and lay leaders for diverse urban ministries; one innovative program known as the seminary behind bars was established to train prison ministers.

Charles Richard Eberhardt: *The Bible in the Making of Ministers* (New York: Association Press, 1949)

George W. Webber: *Led by the Spirit* (New York: Pilgrim, 1990)

Peter J. Wosh

New York Times. Daily newspaper launched on 18 September 1851 by a group of bankers from Albany, New York, led by Henry J. Raymond, who had worked for Horace Greeley's newspaper the *New York Tribune* and James Watson Webb's *Courier and Enquirer.* Although less influential and widely read than the *New York Tribune* and the *New York Herald* of James Gordon Bennett Sr., it quickly became successful by offering comprehensive reporting, while at the same time reflecting Raymond's sympathy toward the Whig and Republican leaders William H. Seward and Thurlow Weed. Its coverage during the Civil War lent the newspaper increased importance and respect and helped Raymond not only to win a seat in the U.S. Congress but also to become the Republican national chairman. After the war Raymond's hesitancy to break with the conservative Reconstruction policies of President Andrew Johnson alienated him from the mainstream of the party and diminished the newspaper's circulation and power, though he reconciled with the Republican Party when he supported Ulysses S. Grant for the presidency in 1868. After Raymond's death in 1869 control of the newspaper passed to George Jones, who with Louis Jennings as his editor aggressively pursued and exposed William M. "Boss" Tweed in the early 1870s (this despite Tweed's demands that they desist and notwithstanding the risk of financial ruin). In 1884 the newspaper sided with liberal Republicans who endorsed the Democratic presidential candidate Grover Cleveland over his Republican opponent James G. Blaine, as a result of which the newspaper lost its old Republican support. Jones died in 1891; by 1896, in the unbusinesslike hands of its editor Charles R. Miller and several other staff members, daily circulation was down to nine thousand and the newspaper was nearly bankrupt.

New York Times Building (designed by Eidlitz and MacKenzie), 1905

Fortunes changed when Adolph S. Ochs became the principal owner of the *New York Times* in the hopes of earning revenue for his struggling newspaper the *Chattanooga Times.* This was done with the proviso that he could become the sole owner if he were able to retire all the newspaper's debt. Having satisfied this condition he assumed control on 19 August 1896, promising to "give the news impartially, without fear or favor, regardless of any party, sect or interest involved." Ochs improved the layout, increased the amount of financial news, and used the editorial page to print letters to the editor and articulate his own conservative Democratic positions. He also sponsored a contest for a slogan but eventually chose his own, "All the News That's Fit to Print," which first appeared on the front page on 10 February 1897. By late 1898 the sensational coverage of the Spanish–American War in the newspapers of William Randolph Hearst and Joseph Pulitzer cut into the circulation of the *Times.* In response Ochs reduced its price from three cents to one cent, without resorting to "yellow journalism," and readership tripled within a year. Shortly after the turn of the century the newspaper moved from 41 Park Row in lower Manhattan to Long Acre Square, which soon became known as Times Square. In the 1920s it moved again, to its present site on 43rd Street between 7th and 8th avenues.

Carr Van Anda became the managing editor in 1904 and in the next twenty years strove to make the *Times* the "paper of record," in part by emphasizing such scientific events as Robert Peary's exploration of the North Pole and Albert Einstein's discoveries. The newspaper was recognized for its able coverage after the sinking of the *Titanic* and again during the First World War when Van Anda's planning often enabled his reporters to reach battle sites before the armies did. After Miller's death in 1922 his position as editorial page editor was filled successively by Rollo Ogden, John Finley, and Charles Merz. In 1923 Lester Markel began a forty-year tenure as editor of the Sunday newspaper: he introduced the "News of the Week in Review" among other sections. After Van Anda retired in 1925 his assistant Frederick Birchall discharged the duties of managing editor, while formally remaining acting managing editor owing to his British citizenship. At the end of 1932 the position of managing editor was assumed by Edwin L. James, a foreign correspondent distinguished for his coverage of the war and the "lead" of his story about the first solo flight across the Atlantic: "Lindbergh did it." In the same year Arthur Krock became the chief of the Washington bureau: later a columnist, he enjoyed a career at the newspaper that lasted until 1966, during which he won four Pulitzer prizes.

The new publisher of the *Times* after Ochs's death in 1935 was Arthur Hays Sulzberger, who had married Ochs's only child, Iphigene, and served a long apprenticeship as his assistant. With the assistance of the general manager, Julius Ochs Adler (Ochs's nephew), he made important, subtle changes: he modernized the printing plants, named Anne O'Hare McCormick foreign affairs columnist, and added a crossword puzzle and sections on fashion and food. He made a large commitment of money and staff to covering the Second World War at a time when other newspapers were cutting back on the space devoted to news, thus helping the newspaper to maintain its leadership. Turner Catledge, a leading reporter in Washington, became the managing editor after James's death in 1951 and later served as editor in chief until 1968. Aware that its tradition of including exhaustive facts had given the *Times* a reputation for accuracy yet dullness, and envious of the praise that its rival the *New York Herald Tribune* had earned for its writing, he sought to enliven the newspaper. In the following years he added a feature called "Man in the News," demanded sharper writing, and gave charge of design and copy-editing to Theodore Bernstein, a crusader for grammatical rectitude. He also chose the next generation of editors, mostly foreign correspondents: Clifton Daniel, his successor as managing editor; Harrison Salisbury, the first editor of the "op-ed" page when it began in 1970; and A. M. Rosenthal, who became city editor in 1963 and dominated news coverage at the newspaper until the mid 1980s. James Reston succeeded Krock as head of the Washington bureau in 1953, became one of the nation's most influential and popular columnists, and engaged the reporters and columnists Russell Baker, Tom Wicker, and Anthony Lewis. In 1954 C. L. Sulzberger, a nephew of the publisher, became the foreign affairs columnist. After Merz retired in 1961 Ochs's nephew John B. Oakes took charge of the editorial page: he gave it a noticeably more liberal cast and was an early opponent of the Vietnam War and a supporter of environmentalism.

In the early 1960s the newspaper changed publishers twice in two years: first in 1961 when Sulzberger was succeeded by his son-in-law Orvil Dryfoos, then in 1963 when Dryfoos died, just after the settlement of a printers' strike that lasted 114 days. About the same time an advertisement placed in the *Times* concerning civil rights in Montgomery, Alabama, led to a lawsuit against the newspaper for libel. The case resulted in a ruling in favor of the newspaper by the U.S. Supreme Court, which in *New York Times Company v. Sullivan* (1964) narrowed the definition of libel in cases concerning public figures and reaffirmed the principle of freedom of the press. Sulzberger's son Arthur Ochs Sulzberger, who became the publisher in 1963, introduced changes in the newspaper's format and helped the owners to expand into other fields such as magazine publishing and broadcasting. In 1966 the *Herald Tribune* ceased publication, a victim of management problems and an inability to secure advertising, especially from department stores. An indirect result of this was the recruitment to the *Times* of new staff, including the renowned sports columnist Red Smith. The *Times* was left as the only choice for New Yorkers who preferred restrained news coverage to the sensationalism of the tabloids.

Rosenthal became managing editor of the *Times* in 1969 and was executive editor from 1976 until he retired in 1986. With his longtime aide Arthur Gelb he oversaw the restructuring of the newspaper's format: after several years of being printed in only two sections, local editions were now being printed in four, which allowed more space for full-page advertising and increased revenues that underwrote the paper's commitment to worldwide reporting. Rosenthal directed major investigative stories about the Central Intelligence Agency and about the "Pentagon papers" in 1971, a government record of the Vietnam War that the federal government tried to prevent the *Times* and the *Washington Post* from publishing. By a decision of the U.S. Supreme Court publication was allowed to proceed on the grounds that efforts to suppress the papers constituted "prior restraint" of free speech.

Restructuring continued under the executive editor Max Frankel, who during a decade in charge of the editorial page had made it more politically moderate and more literary, and the managing editor Joseph Lelyveld. The *Times* maintained the traditional appearance that earned it the nickname the "great grey lady" while at the same time increasing the use of photography and of lively headlines and writing. It also expanded coverage of local news and sports in response to continuing competition from the tabloids – the *Daily News*, the *New York Post*, and especially *New York Newsday*. The *Times* also continued to dominate the Pulitzer prizes: in 1991 it won its sixty-third, bringing to about 10 percent its share of all the prizes awarded since they began in 1917.

In 1991 the *New York Times* had a daily circulation of nearly 1.2 million and a Sunday circulation of 1.7 million. By the terms of a trust set up by Iphigene Ochs Sulzberger, on her death in 1991 at the age of ninety-seven control of the newspaper passed to her four children, Arthur Sulzberger, Judith Sulzberger, Marian Heiskell, and Ruth Holmberg; on their death control would pass to their thirteen children, including Arthur Ochs Sulzberger Jr., who succeeded his father as publisher in 1992.

The *Times* publishes a national edition in half a dozen satellite plants around the country and shares ownership with the *Washington Post* of the *International Herald Tribune*. It also owns television and radio stations, magazines, and more than thirty newspapers: apart from the *Boston Globe* most of these are small and profitable and serve the South and Southwest. By the mid 1990s the *Times* used color printing in most of its Sunday sections.

Gay Talese: *The Kingdom and the Power* (New York: World, 1969)

Harrison E. Salisbury: *Without Fear or Favor: The New York Times and Its Times* (New York: Times Books, 1980)

Joseph C. Goulden: *Fit to Print: A. M. Rosenthal and His Times* (Secaucus, N.J.: L. Stuart, 1988)

W. Wat Hopkins: *Actual Malice: Twenty-five Years after*

Times v. Sullivan (New York: Praeger, 1989)
James Reston: *Deadline: A Memoir* (New York: Random House, 1991)
Nan Robertson: *The Girls in the Balcony: Women, Men, and the New York Times* (New York: Random House, 1992)

Harrison Salisbury

New York Titans. Name by which the NEW YORK JETS were known from 1960 to 1963.

New York Trade School. Original name of VOORHEES TECHNICAL INSTITUTE.

New York Transit Museum. A museum in Brooklyn, operated under the auspices of the New York City Transit Authority and displaying the history of mass transit in New York City. It is situated in the disused Court Street station of the Independent subway, at the corner of Schermerhorn Street and Boerum Place. Exhibits at the museum include antique signals, fareboxes, and turnstiles, and rapid transit maps dating from as early as 1892 (before the opening of the subway system). The museum holds an extensive collection of mosaics, friezes, and terra cotta plaques inspired by the "city beautiful" movement of the early twentieth century, and architectural drawings of ticket booths and stations that reveal a uniformly high quality of design. One section of the museum houses models of trolley cars and modern buses, as well as subways and elevated railway cars dating to 1903.

Barbara Grcevic

New York Tribune. Daily newspaper launched by Horace Greeley in 1841. It supported Whig politics and reformist causes favored by its publisher, including temperance, the labor movement, utopian socialism, and opposition to the expansion of slavery. The staff during the 1840s included Solon Robinson and George "Gaslight" Foster, who together wrote about the plight of the city's slum dwellers and sweatshop workers, and the feminist Margaret Fuller. It also published a weekly edition that was the most influential Republican newspaper in the nation and by the 1850s had a circulation of more than 200,000. The newspaper was instrumental in persuading Lincoln to enact the Emancipation Proclamation in 1863. It was purchased by the editor Whitelaw Reid in 1872, under whose direction it took a more conservative turn and engaged in an eight-year battle (1884–1892) with striking printers. In 1886 the *Tribune* was the first newspaper to install Ottmar Mergenthaler's slug-casting linotype machine, which revolutionized typesetting. Reid's son Ogden Reid Sr. became the president and managing editor in 1912; with his wife Helen (Miles) Rogers Reid he revamped the newspaper's news coverage and layout. In 1924 the Reid family bought the *New York Herald* and merged it with the *Tribune* to form the *New York Herald Tribune.*

Steven H. Jaffe

New York Typographical Union no. 6. Trade union representing typographers, organized as the New York Printers' Union in New York City in 1850 by Horace Greeley, its first president. In 1852 it formed an affiliation with the National Typographical Union (renamed the International Typographical Union in 1869). Known as the "Big Six," the union at first included all craftworkers in the trade; eventually it included only compositors and book and job printers when pressmen, bookbinders, stereotypers and electrotypers, and photoengravers formed their own unions. Separate unions formed by women typesetters in 1868 and by German–American printers in the following year were later reincorporated into Big Six. Although the union was dominated by newspaper compositors it also maintained a presence in about half of all book and job offices in the city. It was known for its aggressiveness and engaged in prolonged strikes against city newspaper offices in 1934 and 1962–63. The union had a membership of about 8900 active journeymen and nineteen hundred pensioners in 1965. It agreed in 1974 to an eleven-year contract that virtually guaranteed workers a lifetime income and allowed newspaper companies to reduce their work force by introducing computerized typesetting. In 1990 the union had about 750 active members and 185 retirees.

George A. Stevens: *History of New York Typographical Union No. 6* (Albany, N.Y.: J. B. Lyons, 1914)
Harry Kelber and Carl Schlesinger: *Union Printers and Controlled Automation* (New York: Free Press, 1967)

William S. Pretzer

New York University. Private university formed in 1831 in Washington Square as the University of the City of New York by a committee led by Albert Gallatin, secretary of the treasury under Presidents Thomas Jefferson and James Madison. From the beginning it was the subject of a debate over the purpose of education. The banker John Delafield and Dutch merchants such as Myndert Van Schaick argued that the university should provide practical instruction for those who could not afford to attend an expensive college; an influential group of Presbyterian and Dutch Reformed ministers advocated a religious approach to education and resisted any separation of science and morality. The first chancellor was James M. Mathews (1785–1870), a minister whose adoption of a traditional religious orientation for the university prompted Gallatin to resign as a trustee. He was followed by a succession of Dutch Reformed and Presbyterian ministers who tried to sustain the evangelical character of the institution and who were opposed by such prominent faculty members as Samuel F. B Morse, professor of fine arts and inventor of the telegraph, and John Draper, chemist, historian, and an early developer of photography. In spite of the religious commitments of its leaders, the university's curriculum was nondenominational: religion was a central feature of it, but so were classics, natural history, and mathematics.

The first students reflected the evangelical inclinations of the first chancellors. During the 1830s and 1840s Presbyterian students were twice as numerous as those of any other denomination, and nearly all were from outside the city until the 1850s, when the proportion decreased to one half. By the 1890s the university drew 65 percent of its students from New York City and began to reflect the heterogeneity of the city. Virtually every Protestant denomination including Quakers was represented, as were Catholics and Jews. Henry Mitchell MacCracken (*b* 28 Sept 1840; *d* 24 Dec 1918), a professor of philosophy from 1884, became a vice-chancellor in 1885 and chancellor in 1891: in nineteen years he transformed the university into a modern institution by moving the undergraduate college to a campus designed by Stanford White in University Heights, and developing a graduate school of arts and sciences, a law school, and a medical school (which forged an affiliation with Bellevue Hospital). In addition he founded the university's graduate school of education (the first in the United States) and a school of commerce, accounts, and finance. These changes were effected without benefit of endowment, in part because enrollment increased from less than one hundred to nearly four thousand, and in part because a change in the by-laws authorized the university to acquire investment property. This rapid growth made for overcrowded classrooms, transient faculty, and fluctuating standards, and yet opened the university to students who had neither the means nor the preparation to study at more selective institutions. In 1896 the university took its current name.

Elmer Ellsworth Brown resigned from his position as commissioner of education under President William Howard Taft to succeed MacCracken in 1911. During his long tenure (to 1933) the university became one of the largest in the United States: between 1912 and 1917 alone enrollment increased from 4300 to 9300. Brown continued the emphasis on professional training by moving the school of business to Wall Street (1920), opening a school of dentistry (1925) and a school of fine arts (1928), and imposing more stringent requirements for admission to the schools of law (two years of college) and medicine (a college degree as of 1930). He also established New York University Press (1916) and strengthened the libraries. By the university's centenary in 1931 enrollment reached a peak of forty thousand.

After the Depression the chancellors Harry W. Chase (1883–1955) and Henry T. Heald

(1904–75) reduced building and curtailed enrollment in an effort to raise academic standards. The School of Continuing Education (1934) and the School of Public Administration (1938, now the Robert F. Wagner Graduate School of Public Service) were the only new structures erected during their tenures. The GI Bill brought an influx of older students after the Second World War who tended to raise the academic quality of the university. During the McCarthy period two popular professors were dismissed for their political views, bringing about a censure by the American Association of University Professors that was not lifted until the 1960s. Carroll V. Newsom (1905–90), an outspoken critic of McCarthyism, was inaugurated the university's tenth chancellor in 1956.

Efforts to improve academic standards and make the university a leading research institution were undertaken in the following decades by the chancellors James Hester, John Sawhill, and John Brademas. Visible symbols of these efforts were the construction of Warren Weaver Hall for the Courant Institute of Mathematical Sciences and of the Elmer Holmes Bobst Library on Washington Square (1967–72), a twelve-story structure of red sandstone designed by Philip Johnson and Richard Foster. Sawhill and Brademas also mounted a successful campaign to increase the university's endowment. The campus at University Heights was sold to the city in 1973 and eventually housed Bronx Community College. Several additional developments further concentrated the university's presence near Washington Square, notably the reorganization of the Tisch School of the Arts nearby and of the Robert F. Wagner Graduate School of Public Service, and the removal of the Leonard N. Stern School of Business to a modern facility designed by Robert Geddes. The construction of dormitories and the acquisition of apartments to enable students and faculty to reside on campus aroused protests from community groups, as well as from alumni who feared that the university's commitment to the commuting student would be undermined. Another sign of academic self-confidence was the appointment in 1991 of the historian L. Jay Oliva, the first president ever chosen from the ranks of the academic faculty.

James M. Mathews: *Recollections of Persons and Events, Chiefly in the City of New York, Being Selections from His Journal* (New York: Sheldon, 1865)

Theodore Francis Jones: *New York University, 1832–1932* (New York: New York University Press, 1933)

Thomas Bender: *New York Intellect: A History of Intellectual Life in New York City from 1750 to the Beginning of Our Own Time* (New York: Alfred A. Knopf, 1987)

Paul H. Mattingly

New York University Medical Center. Teaching hospital of the New York University School of Medicine, opened in 1947 in Manhattan, between 30th and 34th streets and 1st Avenue and Franklin D. Roosevelt Drive. In 1948 the New York Post-Graduate Medical School and Hospital (renamed University Hospital) joined the center and the Howard A. Rusk Institute of Rehabilitation Medicine opened. Tisch Hospital (1963) is an acute-care general hospital. The center is nationally recognized for its cooperative care unit (1979).

Jane E. Mottus

New York Women's Trade Union League. Labor organization formed in 1903 by Jane Addams and other social reformers to help working women organize unions. During its early years the league was mistrusted by union leaders and working-class women because its executive board was dominated by reformers from the middle class. Leonora O'Reilly, an Irish shirtmaker and union organizer and the league's most influential working-class member, set out to remedy this by attracting talented trade union women to the league. In 1905 she recruited as a member Rose Schneiderman, a Jewish immigrant capmaker who brought solid credentials as an organizer and as the first woman elected to the executive board of a national union (the United Cap and Hat Makers). Elected vice-president of the league in the following year, Schneiderman brought a new perspective to the league's organizing work. She suggested that the league extend aid only to those working women who asked for it, and asserted that previously they had acted more like social reformers than union organizers, studying which industries had the worst conditions and then attempting to organize their workers. Despite a severe depression in 1907–8 Schneiderman made great progress among Jewish immigrant garment workers, laying the groundwork for a strike led by shirtwaist makers in 1909–10 called the "uprising of the thirty thousand." This was the largest strike by American women to that time.

The uprising brought a dynamic group of women workers into the league, among them the Lithuanian-born shirtwaist maker Pauline Newman, and Clara Lemlich, a Ukrainian immigrant whose fiery speech moved the workers to strike over the objections of both male union leaders and the middle class leadership of the league. But the emergence of a strong working-class core led to conflict. Some middle-class members, particularly the league's secretary Helen Marot, argued that too much energy was being devoted to Russian Jewish immigrant women at the expense of American-born workers. This conflict highlighted the tensions of class and ethnicity that plagued the league in its early years. Schneiderman and Newman, supported by O'Reilly, complained that middle-class "allies" were too domineering and that the league should be run by working women. They contemplated resigning when Marot supported her arguments by accusing Russian Jews of being too emotional and unused to constructive work. Before the First World War working-class members were unable to successfully challenge the middle-class officers, because the league drew its financial support not from unions but from wealthy women.

After 1917 the working-class leaders attracted a new group of wealthy supporters to the league who shared their belief that the organization should be run by working women themselves. In 1917 Schneiderman was elected president, Newman vice-president. The two gathered around them an executive board made up almost entirely of working women, which shaped the policies of the league for the rest of its life. From the 1920s until the 1940s the league adopted a strategy for improving the lives of working women that was based on education, organization, and legislation. It ran a school for working women from 1923 to 1955 that offered courses in history, literature, current events, and economics, as well as labor relations, labor history, and lobbying, and the school became a model for adult education in the United States. The league sought both to train women academically and to encourage the growth of a professional network that would extend beyond the classroom. In its organizing drives it took a special interest in unskilled workers overlooked by the American Federation of Labor and the Congress of Industrial Organizations. League organizers helped build the garment unions and supported them during the 1920s and 1930s; they embarked on a decades-long campaign to unionize the city's largely black and Puerto Rican laundry workers and hotel maids, and during the 1940s they were advocates for women in the defense industries.

Finally the league was instrumental in making New York State a testing ground for labor legislation. During the second decade of the twentieth century it successfully lobbied for maximum hours and occupational safety legislation for women workers. Over the next thirty years it fought long but ultimately successful campaigns for minimum wage, fire safety, and equal pay laws, maternity insurance, and the extension of social security to domestic workers. It also fought for publicly funded child care and comparable worth (the principle that jobs of equal worth to an employer should be equally paid). The league benefited from the support of Franklin D. Roosevelt and Eleanor Roosevelt, who gave it influence on a national level. It also enjoyed close relations with municipal and state officials, and during the late 1930s and early 1940s the state department of labor was dominated by league members. Dwindling financial support and the postwar "red scare" combined to cripple the league by the 1950s, and it disbanded in 1955.

Nancy Schrom Dye: *As Equals and as Sisters: Feminism, Unionism and the Women's Trade Union League of New York* (Columbia: University of Missouri Press, 1980)
Annelise Orleck: *Common Sense and a Little Fire: Working Class Women's Activism in the 20th Century United States* (Chapel Hill: University of North Carolina Press, 1995)

Annelise Orleck

New York World–Telegram. Daily newspaper launched in 1931 by Roy W. Howard, director of the Scripps–Howard chain, through a merger of the *New York Telegram*, which he acquired in 1925, with the *New York World*, formerly owned by Joseph Pulitzer. In the tradition of its politically liberal founder, Edward W. Scripps, the chain gave the newspaper autonomy in local news coverage but maintained strict control over national coverage and the editorial page. The staff of the *World–Telegram* also adhered to the crusading tradition of Scripps even though Howard made the newspaper somewhat more conservative and was critical of the New Deal. The Pulitzer Prize was awarded to the newspaper in 1933 for its campaign against local misgovernment, in 1940 and 1941 to a group of its writers including Westbrook Pegler for helping to convict dishonest public officials, and in 1947 to Frederick Woltmann for exposing communist activity in the United States. In 1950 the newspaper absorbed Charles A. Dana's *Sun*, becoming the *World–Telegram and Sun*. Although a team of reporters won another Pulitzer Prize in 1963 for their coverage of an airplane disaster, the newspaper lost much of its circulation and advertising revenue by 1966 because of shifts in population. In 1966 the *World–Telegram* combined with the *New York Herald Tribune* and the *New York Journal–American* to form the *World–Journal Tribune*, which lasted less than a year. For many years the newspaper was published at 125 Barclay Street in lower Manhattan.

Frank Luther Mott: *American Journalism: A History of Newspapers in the United States through 260 Years, 1690–1950* (New York: Macmillan, 1941; 3rd edn 1962)
Joseph Sage: *Three to Zero: The Story of the Birth and Death of the World Journal Tribune* (New York: American Publishers Association, 1967)
John Hohenberg: *The Pulitzer Prizes* (New York: Columbia University Press, 1974)

Julian S. Rammelkamp

New York Yacht Club. Organization formed in 1844 by the sportsman John Cox Stevens and eight fellow yachtsmen aboard the schooner *Gimcrack* anchored off the Battery; their meeting probably marked the beginning of organized yachting in the United States. The first clubhouse was on Stevens's property in the Elysian Fields in Hoboken, New Jersey, and was moved several times until its removal in 1901 to land given to the club by J. P. Morgan at 37 West 44th Street. The building was designed with a nautical motif by Whitney Warren of Warren and Wetmore. In the nineteenth century the club was one of the most exclusive associations in the city: its commodores included first Stevens and later men of the Morgan, Vanderbilt, and Astor families. From 1857 to 1983 the America's Cup was on display in the clubhouse. The New York Yacht Club remains the preeminent yacht club in the country. In the mid 1990s it had about 2650 members.

John Parkinson Jr.: *The History of The New York Yacht Club* (New York: New York Yacht Club, 1975)

Joseph S. Lieber

New York Yankees. Baseball team. It began in 1903 as the New York Highlanders when Frank Farrell and Bill Devery acquired the Baltimore Orioles for $18,000 and moved them to New York City. The team played its home games at Hilltop Park, on the west side of Broadway between 165th and 168th streets. Its first outstanding player was the pitcher Jack Chesbro, who won forty-one games in 1904, a major league record. The Highlanders played well for a few years but gradually weakened and ended last in their league in 1912. In the following year they were renamed the Yankees and abandoned Hilltop Park for the Polo Grounds. Farrell and Devery sold the club in 1915 for $460,000 to Colonel Tillinghast L'Hommedieu Huston, a wealthy engineer, and Colonel Jacob Ruppert, a millionaire who owned a brewery and had served four consecutive terms as a Democratic congressman from New York City (1899–1907). In 1920 Ruppert and Huston bought from the Boston Red Sox the contract of Babe Ruth, with whom the Yankees, managed by Miller Huggins, won their first American League pennant in 1921 and their first World Series in 1923. With his teammates on what became known as "murderer's row" he helped the team win six American League pennants and three World Series titles in the 1920s. Ruth electrified the world of baseball with his unprecedented skill at hitting home runs. His popularity led the Yankees to build their own ballpark, Yankee Stadium, at River Avenue between 157th and 161st streets in the Bronx, across the Harlem River from the Polo Grounds. More than 74,000 fans attended its dedication on 23 April 1923; nearly 25,000 others were turned away. The sportswriter Fred Lieb of the *New York Evening Telegram* referred to the magnificent new stadium as "the house that Ruth built," a name that continued to be used into the late twentieth century. Ruppert bought Huston's share in the team in 1923 and remained the sole owner until his death in 1939.

In 1927 the Yankees won 110 games and lost only 44, one of the best records in the history of baseball, but in 1929 Huggins died and the early 1930s saw the retirement of many players, including Ruth. By the mid 1930s another strong team had been assembled: led by Joe DiMaggio, Tommy Henrich, Charlie Keller, and Bill Dickey and managed by Joe McCarthy, it was acquired in 1939 for $2.8 million by Dan Topping and Del Webb. This team won seven pennants and six World Series between 1936 and 1943. The team that emerged in the late 1940s was also highly successful; it was managed first by Casey Stengel and later by Ralph Houk, and included Phil Rizzuto, Mickey Mantle, Roger Maris, Whitey Ford, and Yogi Berra. The team won the World Series every year from 1949 to 1953, and between 1954 and 1964 won four World Series and nine pennants. Elston Howard became the first black member of the Yankees in 1955. Topping and Webb sold the team to the Columbia Broadcasting System (CBS) for $14 million in 1964.

The Yankees were mediocre in the late 1960s and early 1970s but improved when a syndicate controlled by George Steinbrenner, a shipbuilder from Cleveland, bought them from CBS in 1973, reportedly for $10 million. In 1974 and 1975 the team played at Shea Stadium while Yankee Stadium was being renovated. When the cost of the project reached $100 million, well over its budget, the City of New York agreed to assume ownership of Yankee Stadium and pay for its renovation; the Yankees signed a lease to remain there for thirty years beginning in 1976. Under Steinbrenner's ownership the Yankees aggressively sought free agents, and with Catfish Hunter, Reggie Jackson, Thurman Munson, Sparky Lyle, and Ron Guidry the team won the World Series in 1977 and 1978 and pennants in 1976 and 1981. The Yankees played poorly in the 1980s, a period marked by Steinbrenner's summary dismissal of several managers: Billy Martin (1928–89) alone was dismissed five times. In 1990 Steinbrenner was ordered by the commissioner of baseball to relinquish control of the Yankees for having associated with a gambler, but he was allowed to retain a financial interest in the team. He resumed active control of the club in 1993. The New York Yankees, often known as the "Bronx Bombers," dominated baseball from the early 1920s to the mid 1960s and are perhaps the most famous team in the history of sport. By 1990 they had won twenty-two World Series and thirty-three American League pennants, a record in American baseball.

Frank Graham: *The New York Yankees: An Informal History* (New York: G. P. Putnam's Sons, 1948)
Donald Honig: *The New York Yankees* (New York: Crown, 1981)
Mark Gallagher: *Day by Day in New York Yankees History* (Champaign, Ill.: Leisure Press, 1983)

See also SPORTS, §3; and YANKEE STADIUM.

Lawrence S. Ritter

Niblo's Garden. Entertainment center at Broadway and Prince Street. When purchased in 1823 by the Irish impresario William Niblo the site was known as the Columbian Gardens and frequented for open-air events. Niblo added the Sans Souci Theatre to the landscaped grounds in 1827; with the further addition of a saloon and hotel the complex was renamed Niblo's Garden and opened on 18 May 1829. The facility could seat three thousand and soon became famous for fashionable entertainment. It was the site of first performances by Joseph Jefferson, Charles Kean, Edwin Forrest, James and Lester Wallack, Charlotte Cushman, Dion Boucicault, and Adelina Patti and of early performances by the Philharmonic Society, and the polka was reportedly introduced there in 1844. Destroyed by fire in 1846, the facility reopened in 1849. On 27 September 1855 George F(rederick) Bristow's *Rip van Winkle*, the first American opera on an American subject, was given its première there. Niblo retired in 1858, Niblo's Garden was soon acquired by A. T. Stewart, and the last performance in the theater was given on 23 March 1895.

Abram Child Dayton: *Last Days of Knickerbocker Life in New York* (New York: G. W. Harlan, 1882), 303–8

Rufus Osgood Mason: *Sketches and Impressions: Musical, Theatrical, and Social, 1799–1885* (New York: G. P. Putnam's Sons, 1886), 275–91

Marion R. Casey

Nicholas Brothers. Team of tap dancers, consisting of the brothers Fayard (Antonio) Nicholas (*b* Mobile, Ala., 20 Oct 1914) and Harold Nicholas (*b* Winston–Salem, N.C., 17 March 1921). Their parents were musicians in a vaudeville pit band, and they learned to dance by watching other performers. The family moved from Philadelphia to Harlem in 1932, and the brothers were soon the regular final act at the Cotton Club. They combined classical tap dancing with ballet and rigorous acrobatics, using their entire bodies with the grace and agility of the most skilled adult tap dancers. In 1930 they made their début on Broadway in the first production of *Babes in Arms* (choreography by George Balanchine). They performed at the Cotton Club throughout the 1930s even while they made their first motion pictures; they also appeared in many musicals in Hollywood, among them *Stormy Weather* (1943) and *The Pirate* (1948).

Rusty E. Frank: *Tap!: The Greatest Tap Dance Stars and Their Stories, 1900–1955* (New York: William Morrow, 1990)

Amanda Aaron

nickel fare. By the late nineteenth century most urban railways in the United States charged passengers a standard fare of five cents for a single ride of unlimited distance. This uniform nickel fare was adopted in 1900 in the original contract between the City of New York and the Interborough Rapid Transit Company (IRT) and retained in 1913 when the IRT and its competitor, the Brooklyn Rapid Transit Company, signed contracts for additional lines. Inflation during and after the First World War lowered the real value of the nickel of 1904 to 2.25 cents by 1920, so that in the 1920s and 1930s even the city's poor residents could ride the subway frequently. But the low fare also deprived the transit companies of income that was badly needed to maintain service: between 1916 and 1919 the cost of steel increased from $30 to $90 a ton ($33 to $99 a metric ton) and that of coal from $3.23 to $6.07 a ton ($3.56 to $6.70 a metric ton), and the cost of brake shoes increased by 150 percent. Lacking direct municipal subsidies, the companies were forced to keep wages low, introduce labor-saving machinery such as turnstiles and automatic door openers, and defer maintenance. The result was that the subways physically declined. The subway companies' demands for an increase in the fare were extremely unpopular. In his reelection campaign in 1921 Mayor John F. Hylan called the nickel fare a "property right" for middle- and working-class citizens; his landslide victory was widely attributed to his strong position on the issue. As a result the five-cent fare became an article of faith honored by every mayor until 1948, when Mayor William O'Dwyer reluctantly doubled it.

Clifton Hood

Niebuhr, Reinhold (*b* Wright City, Mo., 21 July 1892; *d* Stockbridge, Mass., 1 June 1971). Theologian and social theorist. The son of a Midwestern German pastor, he graduated from Elmhurst College (1910) and Eden Theological Seminary (1913) and earned a bachelor's degree in divinity (1914) and a master of arts (1915) at Yale University. From 1915 to 1928 he was the pastor of a progressive, middle-class congregation at Bethel Evangelical Church in Detroit, where he was known an energetic writer and speaker. He moved to New York City in 1928 to teach "applied Christianity" at Union Theological Seminary, remaining there until 1960. While in the city he wrote more than a dozen books and hundreds of articles, and was a speaker and consultant for many groups. From its formation in 1941 he edited *Christianity and Crisis*, a religious journal of social and political commentary. He sought election to Congress as a Socialist in 1930 but by 1936 gravitated to the Democratic Party; he later became a consultant to the state department and after the Second World War helped to form the group Americans for Democratic Action. Considered "neo-orthodox" by many, he renounced the ideals of human goodness, inevitable progress, and adaptive personality that were central to liberal Protestantism and urged his followers to embrace a brand of realism that recognized and repented the evils it necessarily committed. He considered life fraught with paradox and tension and explicable only by dialectical analysis, believing that God demands mankind's intense engagement in history, which nonetheless acquires meaning only through his transcendent purposes. Liberal in his theological method, to which he gave broad secular applications, Niebuhr was instrumental in reshaping Protestantism to protest an age of totalitarianism, economic depression, and impersonality. A part of West 120th Street between Broadway and Riverside Drive is named in his honor.

Charles W. Kegley, ed.: *Reinhold Niebuhr: His Religious, Social, and Political Thought* (New York: Macmillan, 1956)

Richard W. Fox: *Reinhold Niebuhr: A Biography* (New York: Pantheon, 1985)

James D. Bratt

Nightingale Bamford School. Private girls' elementary and secondary school opened in 1920 in Manhattan by Frances N. Nightingale, a teacher since 1906, and Maya Stevens Bamford. It moved in 1929 to 20 East 92nd Street, where in 1989 the original school house was renovated and an adjacent brownstone was added. The school offers a classical, thirteen-year college preparatory program for 475 students; it had only five headmistresses in its first seventy years.

Richard Schwartz

92nd Street Y(M-YWHA). Jewish community center at 1395 Lexington Avenue in Manhattan, formed in 1874 as the Young Men's Hebrew Association (YMHA) by German Jews as a social and literary society for Jewish young adults. In 1882 a branch for Russian Jewish immigrants opened on the Lower East Side, which evolved into the Educational Alliance (1889). A broad range of social, religious, educational, and recreational activities were developed in the late 1890s to appeal to young people who were not reached by synagogues and to encourage support from the Jewish community. Jacob H. Schiff purchased property at the present site and paid for construction of a building, occupied from 1900 to 1928. This facility was replaced in 1930 by the present structure, to which an addition was made in 1968. In 1942 the 92nd Street Y absorbed the Young Women's Hebrew Association (YWHA, founded in 1902), which moved its programs to 92nd Street from Harlem and at the same time opened Jewish neighborhood centers in other areas of the city. Reincorporated in 1945 as the YM-YWHA, the 92nd Street Y merged in 1962 with the Clara de Hirsch Home for Working Girls (1897), which had begun as a trade school and residence for immigrants and become solely a residence in the 1920s.

The 92nd Street Y is a nonsectarian agency offering diverse cultural, educational, and recreational activities, including concerts, lectures, and films, and classes in Jewish education, the humanities, dance, fine arts, and music. It also operates a nursery school and kindergarten, after-school programs, summer day camps, adult travel programs, a health and fitness center, a senior adult center, a residence for young adults, and a library and archives.

Alfred Stern, ed.: *Building Character for Seventy-five Years* (New York: YM-YWHA, 1949)

Steven W. Siegel

Nixon, Richard M(ilhous) (*b* Yorba Linda, Calif., 9 Jan 1913; *d* New York City, 22 April 1994). Thirty-seventh president of the United States. After graduating from law school at Duke University in 1937 he failed to secure a position with a law firm on Wall Street, and he returned to California to work for a law firm in Whittier and enter politics. He served in the U.S. Congress from 1947 to 1953 and as vice president of the United States under Dwight D. Eisenhower from 1953 to 1961. After running unsuccessfully for the presidency in 1960 and for the governorship of California in 1962 he moved with his family to New York City, where he lived at 810 5th Avenue and worked for the law firm of Mudge, Rose, Guthrie and Alexander. He soon became a partner in the firm and began to rebuild his political career with the help of his colleague John N. Mitchell. After being elected president of the United States in 1968 he left the city for Washington (Mitchell served as his attorney general). Reelected in 1972, he resigned in 1974 during the Watergate scandal and moved to San Clemente, California. In 1980 he returned with his wife to New York City, where he took up residence in a cooperative apartment at 142 East 65th Street and rented an office suite at 26 Federal Plaza. He sold the apartment in 1981 to the Syrian government and moved to New Jersey. In 1984 he attempted to buy a cooperative apartment at 760 Park Avenue but withdrew his offer in the face of objections from other residents. He moved his office in 1988 to Short Hills, New Jersey.

Stephen E. Ambrose: *Nixon* (New York: Simon and Schuster, 1987–89)

Edward T. O'Donnell

Nizer, Louis (*b* London, 6 Feb 1902; *d* New York City, 10 Nov 1994). Lawyer. After moving to New York City he lived in Brooklyn, where his father had a cleaning and dyeing shop. After graduating from Columbia College and Columbia Law School (1924) he studied copyright and worked for such entertainers as Charlie Chaplin and Mae West. In 1954 he won a libel suit on behalf of Quentin Reynolds against the columnist Westbrook Pegler and the Hearst Corporation, inspiring a play on Broadway, *A Case of Libel* (1963). The Motion Picture Association of America became his client in 1966. Nizer's published writings include *My Life in Court* (1961).

George J. Lankevich

NL Industries [National Lead Industries]. Firm of lead and titanium producers. Incorporated in New Jersey on 7 December 1891 as the National Lead Company, by 1920 it operated plants in Brooklyn, Long Island City, Staten Island, and four cities around the United States. It became one of four firms that produced 90 percent of all American-made white lead used in the manufacture of paint. After heavy investment in titanium pigments the firm acquired the Titanium Pigments Company (1932), which soon became a major division. In 1935 the largest titanium pigment plant in the United States opened at Sayreville, New Jersey. Additional foreign and domestic acquisitions further diversified the firm, and on 16 April 1971 it took its present name. In the mid 1990s the firm maintained its headquarters at 445 Park Avenue in Manhattan.

David B. Sicilia

Noah, Mordecai M(anuel) (*b* Philadelphia, 19 July 1785; *d* New York City, 22 March 1851). Journalist, public official, and playwright. He edited six newspapers in New York City, including the lively and influential *National Advocate* (1817–24), the *New-York Enquirer* (1826–29), and the *Evening Star* (1833–40). His variable political loyalties ranged across the spectrum from Tammany Democrat to Jacksonian to Whig, and he served the city in various short-lived patronage positions: sheriff, judge, and surveyor of the Port of New York. His promotion of Jewish causes and his successful presidency of the Hebrew Benevolent Society (1842–51) made him the most visible spokesman of American Jewry. Among his plays are *She Would Be a Soldier* (1819) and *Marion; or, the Hero of Lake George* (1821). Noah was a spirited nationalist with an interest in many social and municipal reforms.

Mariam Touba

No Deal Party. Political party formed in 1945 by Mayor Fiorello H. La Guardia to provide a position on the ballot for Newbold Morris, president of the City Council and a candidate to succeed La Guardia as mayor. Morris's candidacy was a deliberate effort to draw votes away from the Republican Party, with which La Guardia was engaged in a dispute. The party drew 21 percent of the vote and disbanded soon after the election.

Chris McNickle

Noguchi, Hideyo [Seisaku] (*b* Inawashiro, Japan, 24 Nov 1876; *d* Accra [now in Ghana], 21 May 1928). Bacteriologist, parasitologist, and immunologist. He moved to the United States in 1899 after meeting the American microbiologist Simon Flexner, with whom he joined the Rockefeller Institute at its inception in 1904; he remained there for the rest of his career and conducted innovative studies of syphilis, rabies, polio, and yellow fever. On a trip to Africa to study the relationship between the South American and African strains of the virus that causes yellow fever he contracted the disease and died.

Joseph S. Lieber

Noguchi, Isamu (*b* Los Angeles, 17 Nov 1904; *d* New York City, 30 Dec 1988). Sculptor. His father was a Japanese poet and his mother an American writer. In 1923 he moved to New York City to study medicine at Columbia University and turned to sculpture after taking classes at Leonardo da Vinci Art School. From 1935 to 1966 he built set designs for the choreographer Martha Graham and made delicate lighting fixtures out of paper, for which he coined the term *akari*. In 1940 he built the stainless-steel relief *News* for the entrance of the Associated Press Building at 50 Rockefeller Plaza, as well as his first fountain (for the Ford Foundation). In *Ceiling and Waterfall* (1955–57, aluminum and steel) he incorporated sound and light into the design of a lobby installation at 666 5th Avenue. His first sculpture garden in the city, at Chase Manhattan Bank Plaza (1961–64), used granite and basalt rocks imported from Kyoto and placed in a glass enclosure. In 1968 a major retrospective of his work was held at the Whitney Museum of American Art. In the same year his sculpture *Red Cube* was permanently installed at 140 Broadway. He also made unrealized plans for playgrounds at the United Nations, Riverside Park, and the plaza of Lever House. From the early 1950s until the end of his life he divided his time between studios in New York City and Japan; in 1985 a studio that he designed and built at 32-37 Vernon Boulevard, Long Island City, became the Isamu Noguchi Garden Museum, where many of his works are displayed. Noguchi's autobiography *A Sculptor's World* was published in 1968.

Nancy Grove and Diane Botnick: *The Sculpture of Isamu Noguchi, 1924–1979* (New York: Garland, 1980)

Harriet F. Senie

NoHo. Neighborhood in lower Manhattan (1990 pop. 5000), bounded to the north by 8th Street, to the east by 3rd Avenue and the Bowery, to the south by Houston Street, and to the west by Mercer Street; its name stands for the phrase "north of Houston." The land was once the site of Jacob Sperry's Botanic Gardens, which were purchased in 1803 by John Jacob Astor for development. In the 1830s the area attracted such well-known residents as Warren Delano, Philip Hone, and Julia Ward Howe and became known as Astor Place. Commercial ventures such as publishing moved in after the Civil War. Later the area was variously considered part of the Lower East Side and part of the East Village. In the 1970s it became a fashionable residential area after artists such as Robert Rauschenberg and Frank Stella moved into century-old loft

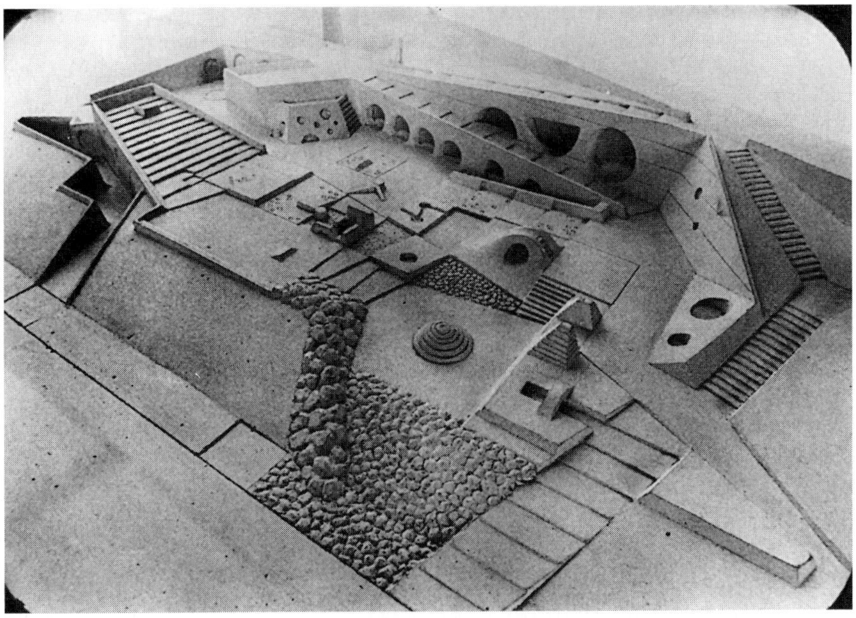

Isamu Noguchi with Louis I. Kahn, model for a playground on Riverside Drive (1961–66, unbuilt)

buildings. The population is economically diverse and there are many artists. Well-known residents have included the entertainers Cher and Keith Richards.

I. N. Phelps Stokes: *The Iconography of Manhattan Island, 1498–1909, Compiled from Original Sources and Illustrated by Photo Intaglio Reproductions of Important Maps, Plans, Views and Documents in Public and Private Collections* (New York: Robert H. Dodd, 1915–28; repr. Arno, 1967)

Paul Goldberger: "Astor Place: A Mingling of Theaters, Ghosts, and Phoenixes" *New York Times*, 7 May 1976, §C, p. 21

David W. Dunlap: "Stepping into the 1800s on Broadway in NoHo," *New York Times*, 16 Nov 1990, §C, p. 28

Val Ginter

Nooten Eylandt. Former name of GOVERNORS ISLAND.

Norddeutscher Lloyd. See NORTH GERMAN LLOYD STEAMSHIP LINES.

Norell [Levinson], **Norman** (*b* Noblesville, Ind., 20 April 1900; *d* New York City, 25 Oct 1972). Fashion designer. He worked as a designer for the firm of Traina–Norell in 1941–60 and became well known for his fine ready-to-wear clothes. Designing under his own name from 1960 to 1972, he distinguished himself through the use of simple lines and spectacular fabrics. His work was often based on an amusing conceit, such as using gray flannel for evening wear, and had a large influence on couturiers in France.

Caroline Rennolds Milbank

Normal College High School. Former name of HUNTER COLLEGE HIGH SCHOOL .

Normal College of the City of New York. Name used from 1870 to 1914 by HUNTER COLLEGE.

Normandie. Ocean liner built in France in 1931–32. At more than one thousand feet (three hundred meters) and 83,000 tons, she was the largest and heaviest vessel to that time. The ship crossed the Atlantic regularly until 1939, when the outbreak of the Second World War prevented a return to Europe. Moored at Pier 88, the ship was boarded by the coast guard toward the end of 1941 and claimed by the federal government. While being converted into a troopship the *Normandie* in 1942 caught fire and rolled onto one side, remaining thus until the superstructure was stripped and the hull raised and taken to Columbia Pier in Brooklyn. Two portals salvaged from the ship are now part Our Lady of Lebanon Maronite Cathedral.

Harvey Ardman: *Normandie: Her Life and Times* (New York: Watts, 1985)

James E. Mooney

Norris, Charles R. (*b* Hoboken, N.J., 4 Dec 1867; *d* New York City, 11 Sept 1935). Pathologist. He received his MD in 1892 from the College of Physicians and Surgeons and was appointed the first chief medical examiner of New York City in 1918 after the system of local coroners was discontinued. With Thomas A. Gonzales and Alexander O. Gettler he achieved notable advances in forensic techniques. Although his popular reputation was that of a sleuth who exposed murder, in several of his most celebrated cases he determined that murder had not occurred. Norris was deeply concerned with issues of public health and taught many medical examiners.

William C. Eckert: "Medicolegal Investigation in New York City: History and Activities, 1918–1978," *American Journal of Forensic Medicine and Pathology* 4, no. 1 (1983), 33–54

George A. Thompson, Jr.

North American Reinsurance Corporation. Firm of insurers. It began in 1910 as a branch office in New York City of the Swiss Reinsurance Company and in the following year became the first reinsurer of casualty insurance in the United States. The firm was reorganized in 1940 under its present name and took over the parent firm's American business. In 1993 it had assets in excess of $1000 million, making it the largest reinsurance firm based in New York City. The headquarters are at 237 Park Avenue.

Claude M. Scales III

North Beach. A former resort in northwestern Queens, lying along the shoreline of Bowery Bay and the East River from 80th Street to the shore of Flushing Bay. It was opened on 19 June 1886 as Bowery Bay Beach by the piano maker William Steinway, who wished to provide a local beach resort for workers, with financial support from the brewer George Ehret. The resort was renamed North Beach in February 1891. Between 1895 and 1915 it reached its peak: there were hotels, carousels, scenic railways, restaurants, shooting galleries, dance halls, beer gardens, Ferris wheels, swimming pools, theaters, bowling alleys, picnic grounds, weekly fireworks displays, and boat rides known as chutes. Steamboats carried large crowds from Manhattan and the Bronx, and trolleys ran from Long Island City and Brooklyn. Attendance decreased in 1917 after the United States entered the First World War and ceased altogether during Prohibition. In the 1920s some of the land was used for Glenn L. Curtiss Airport, which opened in 1939 and was later renamed La Guardia Airport. The runways entirely cover the old pleasure grounds and beach.

Vincent Seyfried

North Brother Island. An island in the eastern arm of the East River, at the entrance to Long Island Sound. It has an area of 20.5 acres (8.3 hectares) and is part of the Bronx. The Dutch called the island and its neighbor South Brother Island (about a third of a mile, or half a kilometer, to the west) the Gezellen (companions). For many years North Brother Island was in private hands, until it was purchased in 1871 by the Town of Morrisania. A tuberculosis hospital built there by the Sisters of Charity closed in 1885 when the city took possession of the island and built Riverside Hospital for the treatment of infectious diseases; the best-known patient was Typhoid Mary (Mary Mallon). The *General Slocum* ran aground on the island on 15 June 1904. After the Second World War the city rented out the disused hospital and some quonset huts to returning veterans studying under the GI Bill. The hospital was later used as a drug rehabilitation center before closing in 1964. In 1970 the city put the island up for sale.

For illustration see LIGHTHOUSES.

Gerard R. Wolfe

Northern Dispensary. A privately funded clinic opened in 1827 to provide health care for the residents of Greenwich Village at little or no cost. The clinic moved in 1831 to a triangular building at the intersection of Waverly Place, Grove Street, and Christopher Street. It became a dental clinic after the Second World War and remained so until 1989, when a shortage of funds compelled it to cease operations and transfer its land and building to the Roman Catholic Archdiocese of New York.

Northern Dispensary: By-laws for the Government of the Board of Trustees (New York: William Van Norden, 1829)

Elliott B. Nixon

Northfield. Former administrative district in northwestern Staten Island, bounded to the north by the Kill van Kull, to the east by Rockland Avenue and Brielle Avenue, to the south by Richmond Road, Richmond Creek, and Fresh Kills Creek, and to the west by the Arthur Kill. The area was known variously as the North Side, the North Division, and the North Quarter until after the American Revolution, when it became one of four administrative districts on the island. Towns within its boundaries included Port Richmond, Mariners Harbor, Old Place, Graniteville, Bulls Head, Travis, Chelsea, and New Springville. The district became obsolete when the city was consolidated in 1898; the last seat was Port Richmond.

Marjorie Johnson

North German Lloyd Steamship Lines [Norddeutscher Lloyd]. A German shipping firm formed in 1858 to connect its home port of Bremen with New York City. Service began in June with crossings by the *Bremen*, the first of three steamships, and in 1863 the firm acquired extensive dock facilities in Hoboken, New Jersey. From the 1860s emigrants from Germany and eastern Europe accounted for much of the westbound traffic. When the United States was still neutral during the early years of the First World War, several of the firm's ships sought refuge in New York City, only to be seized by the U.S. Navy when the United States entered the war in 1917. Service to New York City resumed in 1920 but was later interrupted by the Second World War, when several ships again sought refuge in the city; one that did not was the *Bremen*, which raced across the North Atlantic to Murmansk in the Russian SFSR before safely reaching Bremen several months later. After service resumed in 1951 Lloyd ran the *Bremen* (reconditioned), the *Europa*, and the *Berlin* from New York City to Bremerhaven until 1971. In 1970 it merged with its longtime competitor Hamburg–America Lines. The new firm, Hapag–Lloyd, continued into the 1990s to offer container service to New York City and to operate the *Europa* as a cruise ship. The fleet of North German Lloyd included some ships that held speed records: in 1881 the steamer *Elbe* sailed from Southampton to New York City in eight days, a record that held until 1900, and in 1929 the new *Bremen* set a record for the fastest transatlantic crossing.

Otto J. Seiler: *Bridge across the Atlantic: The Story of Hapag–Lloyd's North American Liner Services* (Herford, Germany: Mittler and Sohn, n.d.)

Rohit T. Aggarwala

North New York. A disused name for a part of the southwestern Bronx lying within the present Mott Haven and bounded to the north by 147th Street, to the east by the neighborhood of Port Morris, to the south by 134th Street, and to the west by 3rd Avenue. Irish factory workers settled the area in the 1840s, the name North New York first being used as a postal address in 1862. After the Second World War the neighborhood became the site of two low-income, high-rise housing projects, John Purroy Mitchel Houses and Mott Haven Houses. Some brick apartment buildings from the turn of the century survive; the northern section is more commercial. The population in the early 1990s was mostly black and Latin American.

Lloyd Ultan

North River. Name by which the HUDSON RIVER is known at its southern end.

North River Steamboat. See CLERMONT.

North Side [Great North Side]. Name applied between 1874 and 1898 to the land north of the East River in what is now the Bronx. Its use was promoted by the North Side Board of Trade (organized on 6 March 1894) as an alternative to the name Annexed District, which many residents disliked. Among the organizations and businesses that used the name were the North Side Savings Bank, the North Side Brewing Company, the North Side Hotel, and the *North Side News*, a Democratic newspaper launched in April 1897. The name fell into disuse after the Bronx became a borough in 1898.

The Great North Side (Bronx: North Side Board of Trade, 1897)

Gary D. Hermalyn

Northside Center for Child Development. Social service organization formed in 1946 to provide psychological counseling for black youths in Harlem. It is now in the Schomburg Houses on 5th Avenue and 110th Street.

David Rosner

North Side News. Democratic newspaper launched on 4 April 1897 and published weekly; it was the first important newspaper in the North Side, the familiar name for the Annexed District, which later became part of the Bronx. The newspaper appeared daily from October 1901 until it ceased publication in the mid 1950s.

Stephen Jenkins: *The Story of The Bronx* (New York: G. P. Putnam's Sons, 1912)

Gary Hermalyn: "The Bronx at the Turn of the Century," *Bronx County Historical Society Journal* 26 (1989), 92–103

Gary D. Hermalyn

North Side Savings Bank. Savings bank founded in 1905 in the Bronx, where there were few similar institutions at the time. The first president was John J. Barry, a wealthy builder born in Ireland, and the first office was at 3196 3rd Avenue (near 161st Street), moved in 1910 to 3230 3rd Avenue (near 163rd Street). The bank grew along with the population of the Bronx and in 1951 the main office was moved to 185 West 231st Street, adjacent to the Major Deegan Expressway. In 1986 the bank was converted from mutual to stock ownership. Now based in Floral Park, the North Side Savings Bank has many branch offices in Manhattan and Westchester County as well as in the Bronx. In 1993 its assets were $1420.5 million.

Chad Ludington

Norton, C(harles) McKim (*b* Lake Forest, Ill., 6 Jan 1907; *d* Lexington, Mass., 10 May 1991). Planner. The son of the influential urban planner Charles Dyer Norton, he graduated from Harvard College in 1929 and Harvard Law School in 1932. He set out to practice law in New York City but gravitated toward a career as a planner after being elected in 1937 to the board of directors of the Regional Plan Association (RPA), of which his father had been the founding chairman. In 1940 he was appointed to the chief staff position at the association, where he worked for almost thirty years before retiring as president in 1969. During the late 1950s he was responsible for developing a second regional plan for greater New York that used the first plan as a point of departure but took into account the changes that had affected the region since the Second World War. The plan was notable for the extent to which the public was involved in formulating it — an involvement that transformed the process of urban planning — and for its acknowledgment of the dangers of urban sprawl. Norton advocated clustered urban development, strong downtowns, and public parks (he was instrumental in creating the Gateway National Recreation Area, the nation's first urban national park). A supporter of public transit, he also helped to form the Metropolitan Transportation Authority (MTA).

Shan Jayakumar

Norwegian Lutheran Deaconesses' Home and Hospital. Forerunner of the LUTHERAN MEDICAL CENTER.

Norwegians. Norwegian settlers emigrated to the New Netherland in the seventeenth century. In New Amsterdam they became shopkeepers, innkeepers, carpenters, traders, and shipbuilders, and introduced a style of clapboard house that became common in the colony. One immigrant was Anneken Henriksen from Bergen, who in 1650 married Jan Arentzen van der Bilt, forebear of the Vanderbilt family. The Port of New York attracted sailors, carpenters, and those skilled in other aspects of maritime industry.

A large number of Norwegians settled in the city and its environs after 1825. About six thousand lived there in 1869, and by the end of the century many were concentrated in Brooklyn. The largest neighborhood was around the docks, piers, and shipyards along Hamilton Avenue near what is now Red Hook. Several humanitarian organizations were formed, including the Independent Order of Good Templars (1879), a secret temperance society in Brooklyn. The Voluntary Relief Society for the Sick and Poor among Norwegians in New York and Brooklyn, organized in 1883 by the Lutheran deaconess Sister Elizabeth Fedde (1850–1921) and eight clergymen, was incorporated in 1892 as the Norwegian Lutheran Deaconesses' Home and Hospital and situated at 4th Avenue and 46th Street in Brooklyn. Important churches in Brooklyn included the Trinity Lutheran Church (411 46th Street), established in 1890, and Our Saviour's Lutheran Church (414 80th Street). For many years the Norwegian Seamen's Church owned an impressive edifice at 33 1st Place in Carroll Gardens before moving to smaller quarters in Manhattan. The weekly newspaper *Norway Times / Nordisk Tidende*, one of the major Norwegian newspapers in the country, began publication in 1891; among its influential editors was Andreas Nilsson Rygg (1912–29). Many Norwegians settled about the turn of the century in Bay Ridge, a community that supported a wide range of Norwegian cultural institutions and businesses. The year 1895 saw the formation of the national fraternal order the Sons of Norway and of the American–Scandinavian Foundation, with headquarters in Manhattan; the foundation in 1913 began publishing the quarterly journal *Scandinavian–American Review* (now known as *Scandinavian Review*) and also distributed books, translations, and scholarly works about the five Scandinavian countries. Social clubs and athletic clubs became an essential part of Norwegian culture in the city. The Norwegian National Federation, formed in 1905, had forty societies affiliated with it by 1914.

As many as 55,000 first- and second-generation Norwegians lived in New York City in 1940, most of them in Bay Ridge. From 1940 to 1963 Carl Soyland was the editor of the *Norway Times* and was instrumental in promoting Norwegian cultural affairs, especially plays produced with the help of the actress Borgny Hammer. During the Second World War tons of food and clothing were sent to Norway by American Relief for Norway, which became a large organization. The Norwegian Lutheran Deaconesses' Home and Hospital merged in 1956 with the Lutheran Hospital of Manhattan, was renamed the Lutheran Medical Center, and later became a city hospital at 2nd Avenue in the 50s in Brooklyn. Other health facilities included the Norwegian Children's Home on 84th Street in Dyker Heights, the Norwegian Christian Home and Health Center for the elderly on 67th Street in Brooklyn, and the Eger Home on Staten Island. Bay Ridge lost some of its Scandinavian character during the later decades of the twentieth century as second- and third-generation Norwegians moved to the suburbs. In the mid 1980s the *Norway Times* began to print most of its contents in English, and by 1990 the Norwegian population in the city had fallen to about ten thousand. The Sons of Norway continued to operate six lodges in the metropolitan area.

Prominent Norwegian immigrants to the city and its environs have included Ole Singstad, who built the Holland Tunnel, and Thor Solberg, a pioneer aviator who in 1935 was the first person to fly solo from the United States to Norway.

John O. Evjen: *Scandinavian Immigrants in New York, 1630–1674* (New York: K. C. Holter, 1916; repr. Genealogical Publishing, 1972)

A. N. Rygg: *Norwegians in New York, 1825–1925* (New York: Norwegian News, 1942)

Erik J. Friis, ed.: *They Came from Norway* (New York: Norwegian Immigration Sesquicentennial Commission, 1975)

Erik J. Friis

Norwood. Neighborhood in the northwestern Bronx, bounded by to the north by Van Cortlandt Park and Woodlawn Cemetery, to the east by Bronx Park, and to the southwest by Mosholu Parkway. The name is probably a contraction of "north wood." During the American Revolution the area was the site of several skirmishes around the Valentine–Varian House. Although the Williamsbridge Reservoir was built in the area by the city in 1888, most of the land until 1905 was part of a dairy farm belonging to the Varian family. Development began in the early twentieth century after the extension of the 3rd Avenue elevated line and the subway system created shopping streets along 204th Street and Jerome Avenue. Montefiore Hospital was built in the neighborhood in 1912. In the 1980s Norwood attracted a diverse population of new residents, including many from Puerto Rico, the Dominican Republic, India, Cambodia, Vietnam, Korea, the Philippines, and Ireland. There is also a sizable Jewish and Irish population. The housing stock consists of apartment buildings and one- and two-family houses.

Lloyd Ultan

Noticias del Mundo. Daily Spanish-language newspaper, launched in 1980 by the Korean spiritual leader and businessman Sun Myung Moon. The newspaper covers local, national, and international news from a politically conservative point of view. In 1994 it was the second-largest Spanish-language newspaper in New York City, with a circulation of 42,000. The offices are at 401 5th Avenue in Manhattan.

James Bradley

Novelty Ironworks. Firm of iron founders between 12th and 14th streets on the East River in Manhattan, just north of where the Jacob Riis Houses now stand. It was formed in the mid 1830s by the president of Union College, Eliphalet Nott, to build an engine for his anthracite-burning steamboat the *Novelty* (1836), and under the leadership of Thomas B. Stillman and Horatio Allen from 1842 it became the city's largest foundry. The firm made castings for a variety of machinery, and because it specialized in steam engines for oceangoing ships it benefited greatly from the shipbuilding boom of the early 1850s. Eighteen departments occupied two city blocks and two slips along the river and employed more than a thousand men, most of whom were highly skilled machinists earning some of the highest wages in the city. Operations were carried out on a vast scale: the bedplate alone for the engine of the steamboat *Arctic* weighed sixty tons (fifty-four metric tons). The immensity of operations at the works and the consequent need for thorough organization and supervision made it the best-known industrial workplace in New York City and a symbol of industrial progress. From the late 1850s engine-building businesses moved their most technologically advanced operations to the Delaware River, and although the iron industry prospered during the Civil War most of the large works in the city were in financial straits by the late 1860s. The Novelty Ironworks closed in 1870, its machinery obsolete and its property now too valuable for a factory site.

Jacob Abbott: "The Novelty Works," *Harper's New Monthly Magazine*, May 1851, pp. 721–34

Richard Stott

Novoye Russkoye Slovo. Independent, illustrated Russian-language daily newspaper, launched in 1910 as *Russkoye Slovo*; it is the oldest continuously published newspaper of its kind in the world. Renamed in 1920, it was edited for fifty years by Mark Weinbaum and from 1973 by Andrei Sedych. Until the last years of the Soviet Union the newspaper published material that could not be published there. In the early 1990s the circulation was about 45,500. Local news is emphasized, but there are also reports on international and national events as well as pieces on literary and historical topics. *Novoye Russkoye Slovo* remains the most influential Russian-language newspaper in North America.

Sally M. Miller, ed.: *The Ethnic Press in the United States: A Historical Analysis and Handbook* (Westport, Conn.: Greenwood, 1987)

Robert A. Karlowich: *We Fall and Rise, 1889–1914: Russian-Language Newspapers in New York City* (Metuchen, N.J.: Scarecrow, 1991)

Thomas E. Bird

Novy Zhurnal. Russian-language quarterly journal launched in June 1942 in New York City by Mark Aldanov and Mark Zetlin. Initially known for publishing a wide range of items, it later espoused values of traditional Russian culture and advocated the defense of individual freedoms. It was edited for about twenty-five years by Roman Gul and in the early 1990s by Yuri Kashkarov. The journal is especially important to Russians living in the city, who contribute memoirs, correspondence, and bibliographies.

Thomas E. Bird

NOW Legal Defense and Education Fund. Organization formed in 1970 in New York City by the National Organization for Women (NOW), from which it remains distinct. It administers legal, educational, and public information programs aimed at achieving equality for women in schools, the courts, the workplace, and the family. Among the areas in which the fund is active are sexual harassment, reproductive rights, violence against women, and pension reform. Its offices are at 99 Hudson Street in Manhattan.

Nowy Dziennik [Daily News]. Polish-language newspaper, launched in 1971 and published six days a week in New York City. It focuses on Polish and Polish–American affairs. During the early 1990s it was one of three major Polish-language daily newspapers in the United States.

James S. Pula

Nowy Swiat [New World]. Polish-language newspaper published in New York City from 1919 to about 1971. It provided detailed coverage of Polish politics and during the interwar period was a leading supporter of Joseph Pilsudski's regime.

James S. Pula

NRA. See National rifle association.

numbers. A term used for illegal gambling operations that usually involve wagers on three-digit numbers from 001 to 999. The winning number, or "hit," is a well-publicized number agreed on by custom: sometimes it is taken from the financial or sports pages (for example the last three digits of the daily handle, or total amount wagered, at a racetrack). The bettor chooses a number and places a "policy" (a nickname derived from the penny insurance once popular in poor neighborhoods); a "runner" or "writer" usually records bets on slips of paper and takes them to a "spot" (where bets are also accepted) or "store." Betting slips are then collected by "pick-up men" and taken to a "controller" who takes them to the "policy bank," a central facility where the day's hits are tallied and the split of the profits among the spots and runners is figured. Timing is crucial to a successful numbers operation. Because the payoff on a winning number is usually six hundred to one, about 40 percent of the total amount wagered accrues to the operators, a higher return than in other forms of gambling.

One of the first well-known numbers operators in New York City was Al Adams, who dealt in favors for Tammany Hall and William M. "Boss" Tweed. He had about a thousand policy shops in the 1880s and was known as the meanest gambler in the city, because by rigging the numbers he drove other operators out of business. During the 1920s penny ante numbers, a game intended for residents of the poorest neighborhoods, was invented, probably by Meyer Lansky (according to Lucky Luciano); it became popular and was soon the most lucrative kind of numbers game for its operators. Another influential figure was Madame St. Clair, an operator based in Harlem. Her racket was eventually taken over by Dutch Schultz, who terrorized her "bankers" into buying his protection and then took control of their businesses. His underling, Otto "Abbadabba" Berman, later developed a rigging system that prevented numbers heavily bet on from winning. After Schultz's murder in 1935 the racket in Harlem was taken over by Luciano and Lansky, and supervised by Luciano's lieutenant, Vito Genovese.

The numbers game is a durable institution that has resisted efforts by the government to outlaw it or displace it with state lotteries. It has also given rise to an industry that provides advice to bettors: among the most popular guides are booklets that recommend lucky numbers based on common dream images. In the mid 1990s it was estimated that far more gamblers played the numbers than the state lottery.

Jesse Drucker

numismatics. Numismatics first became popular in the United States about 1857, when the replacement of the large cent by the flying-eagle cent led many enthusiasts to collect a coin from each year beginning with 1793. The American Numismatic Society, formed in the city in April 1858 as the second such society in North America (after one in Philadelphia), was for many years a collectors' club. Under the direction of Archer Milton Huntington, John Sanford Saltus Jr., Daniel Parish Jr., and Edward Theodore Newell about 1906–8 it moved to its own building on 155th Street and focused on scholarship; under Newell, the greatest American numismatist, it produced a number of excellent works, especially concerning Greek, Roman, and Islamic coins. This shift in emphasis led to the formation of the New York Numismatic Club in 1908, which included among its members Victor D. Brenner, the designer of the Lincoln cent. The Brooklyn Coin Club was organized in 1932, followed by the Bronx Coin Club in 1933. After Newell's death in February 1941 the American Numismatic Society established a summer graduate seminar in his memory and under George Carpenter Miles and Margaret Thompson trained many historians and classicists.

Howard L. Adelson: *The American Numismatic Society, 1858–1958* (New York: n.pub., 1958)

See also Stamp and coin dealers.

John M. Kleeberg

Nurses' Settlement. Name by which the Henry street settlement was known from 1898 to 1913.

nursing. Until the early twentieth century medical and nursing care was usually administered at home. At the first hospitals in New York City, opened during colonial times primarily to quarantine infected sailors and immigrants, nursing care was provided by untrained attendants and recovering patients. The first recorded effort to train nurses in the United States was made at New York Hospital in 1798 by Valentine Seaman, a doctor who taught a course in maternity and child care. Nursing of a more professional sort was provided in 1817 by the Sisters of Charity, who were sent to the city from their motherhouse in Maryland by Mother Elizabeth Bayley Seton. After serving in schools, hospitals, and orphanages they founded St. Vincent's Hospital (1849), the Half Orphan Asylum (1856), and New York Foundling Hospital (1869); they also worked at the contagion hospitals on Wards Island, Blackwell's Island, and Randalls Island during outbreaks of smallpox, cholera, and yellow fever.

Racial segregation led to the founding in 1839 of Lincoln Hospital by the Society for the Relief of Worthy, Aged, Indigent Colored Persons. Only black women were admitted to the training program for nurses offered there from 1898. A training program for nurses was established at the New York Infirmary for Women and Children (1857) by three doctors: Elizabeth Blackwell, the first woman in the United States to earn a medical degree, her sister Emily Blackwell, and their colleague Marie E. Zakrzewska. Elizabeth Blackwell also trained nurses at Bellevue Hospital in 1861 for service in army hospitals during the Civil War. The brutality of war demonstrated the need for better nursing care. The State Charities Aid Association, formed after the war by the philanthropist Louisa Lee Schuyler, sponsored visiting committees to investigate conditions in schools, asylums, and hospitals in the city. After finding filth and depravity at Bellevue Hospital the association in 1873 opened there the first Nightingale school for nurses' training in the United States. Student nurses cared for patients under the supervision of only a superintendent and one or two head nurses, who taught them procedures. Their formal education consisted of lectures delivered sporadically by hospital physicians at night. Admitting women students of good character and holding them to a strict regime of discipline was considered critical to the success of the school's reform mission.

Nightingale schools opened at many other hospitals in the city, where by the 1920s most nursing was provided by students. Graduates of the nursing programs found work mainly in private households but also joined the public health sector and filled the few positions available on hospital staffs. The women's branch of the New York City Mission and Tract Society established Visiting Nursing in 1877, the first organization in the United States to send trained nurses into the homes of indigent patients. The American School for Male Nurses opened in 1886 in connection with the City Training School on Blackwell's Island, followed by the Mills Training School for Male Nurses in 1888 at Bellevue. In 1893 the National League for Nursing was formed and Lillian Wald, a graduate of the nursing school at New York Hospital, organized a settlement later known as the Henry Street Settlement, which became the model for visiting nursing programs in the United States. The American Nurses Association was formed in the city in 1896. The *American Journal of Nursing* was first published there in 1899, and during the same year a course on hospital economics was given at Teachers College, from which a program in higher education for nurses evolved: the Division of Nursing Education at Teachers College later granted advanced degrees and led the effort to professionalize nursing during the first half of the twentieth century. Legislation was passed to set standards (in 1903 for New York State), control practice, and register nurses. M. Adelaide Nutting became the first professor of nursing in the world at Teachers College in 1906. The first meeting of the National Association of Colored Graduate Nurses (NACGN) was held in New York City in 1908. Fifty-eight organizations employed 372 visiting nurses by 1909 to serve the city's neighborhoods. From 1912 to 1950 the National Organization of Public Health Nurses had its headquarters in the city.

Pregnant women were cared for principally by midwives and nurse–midwives, some of whom were immigrants trained at Bellevue Hospital, which had a program in midwifery from 1911 to 1935. Despite opposition, community-based maternity centers were organized, such as the Maternity Center Association in 1915. The first birth control clinic in the nation was opened in Brooklyn on 16 October 1916 by Margaret Sanger, a nurse who led the struggle to provide birth control to women. Nurses in the city's health department initiated preventive care in school health and child hygiene programs and home visits to postpartum women and their infants.

By the 1920s Lincoln Hospital had the largest nursing school for blacks in the United States. Before closing in 1961 it granted diplomas to 1864 nurses. Another nursing school for black women opened in 1923 at Harlem Hospital, which was run by the city. Through the efforts of the NACGN under the leadership of the nurses Adah Belle Thoms, Geneva Estelle Massey Riddle, and Mabel Keaton Staupers discrimination against black nurses was contested and racial quotas in the armed services were eliminated during the Second World War.

After the war nursing care became increasingly complex. Several levels of certification developed, including those of licensed practical nurse and research nurse (which requires a doctorate). The GI Bill and federal grants financed college education for nurses, and university and college programs gradually replaced the hospital schools: only two of the twenty-six programs that trained registered nurses in the city in 1989 were offered by hospitals; of the rest nine were senior (baccalaureate) programs and fifteen were associate degree programs in community colleges. Nursing remained attractive to immigrants. By 1989 a survey of registered nurses in New York State showed that of those in New York City 49 percent were white, 29 percent black, 18 percent Asian, 5 percent Puerto Rican and Latin American, and fewer than 1 percent American Indian. More than two million nurses were registered in the United States in 1991, of whom 233,369 were in New York State. About one third of those registered in the state were employed in New York City.

In the mid 1990s nurses in New York City earned doctorates, conducted research, and managed large hospital budgets, in addition to providing bedside care in hospitals, visiting the sick in their homes, and ministering to the needy in the community.

Philip A. Kalisch and Beatrice J. Kalisch: *The Advance of American Nursing* (Boston: Little, Brown, 1978)

Jane Mottus: *New York Nightingales: The Emergence of the Nursing Profession at Bellevue and New York Hospital, 1850–1920* (Ann Arbor, Mich.: UMI Research Press, 1981)

Susan M. Reverby: *Ordered to Care: The Dilemma of American Nursing, 1850–1945* (New York: Cambridge University Press, 1987)

Darlene Clark Hine: *Black Women in White* (Bloomington: Indiana University Press, 1989)

Ellen D. Baer: "Nurses," *Women, Health and Medicine in America: A Historical Handbook*, ed. Rima D. Apple (New York: Garland, 1990)

Ellen D. Baer, Susan M. Reverby

nursing-home scandals. Nursing homes in New York City have been the subject of several major scandals. In the late 1950s night raids by the city's department of investigations revealed poor living conditions and lax management at several nursing homes, and other investigations by the welfare department uncovered millions of dollars in overcharging by the owners of the homes. Several nursing homes were closed as a result, including ten owned by Bernard Bergman (1911–84). In 1960 a report by the city's investigations commissioner, Louis I. Kaplan, depicted widespread abuse and neglect at the city's nursing homes. None of these investigations attracted much publicity or led to major reforms. The government's initial failure to crack down on rogue nursing home operations had serious repercussions, because illegal activities continued in New York City throughout the 1960s and early 1970s, particularly after the advent of Medicaid and its system of reimbursements in 1967.

In October 1974 a four-part series in the *New York Times* by John L. Hess broke open the nursing-home scandals. The stories detailed how the owners of nursing homes were making millions of dollars by cheating on Medicaid billings and engaging in other illegal activities, while the patients lived in abject conditions. Other journalists also exposed nursing-home fraud, including Jack Newfield of the *Village Voice* and Steve Bauman of the television station WNEW. Governor Hugh L. Carey then appointed a special prosecutor, Charles J. Hynes, to investigate nursing homes throughout New York State, and Assemblyman Andrew Stein of Manhattan held dramatic hearings that brought widespread corruption to light. The most notorious figure to emerge from the scandals was Bergman, who controlled thirty-seven nursing homes in the city, notably the Park Crescent and the Towers on the Upper West Side. Convicted of Medicaid fraud and bribery, he served a year in prison and paid nearly $2 million in fines. Another owner to be implicated was Eugene Hollander, who owned four nursing homes in the city and achieved particular notoriety for having purchased valuable paintings with Medicaid payments. Although indicted he avoided prison by agreeing to divest himself of all his nursing-home interests.

In the end several reforms were implemented: the city's worst nursing homes, including Bergman's, were closed, and a permanent office of special prosecutor was established to oversee the business. The nursing-home scandals also played a role in bringing down two leaders of the state assembly: Stanley Steingut of Queens was criticized for his affiliation with Bergman and voted out of office in 1978; Albert H. Blumenthal of Manhattan was indicted on charges of making illegal payments for a nursing-home license, and although the charges were dismissed he resigned in 1976. The scandals also launched the political careers of Stein, who became borough president of Manhattan and president of the City Council, and Hynes, who became district attorney of Brooklyn.

James Bradley

Nutten Island. Former name of GOVERNORS ISLAND.

Nutting, M(ary) Adelaide (*b* Waterloo [now in Quebec], 1 Nov 1858; *d* New York City, 3 Oct 1948). Nursing educator. She moved to New York City in 1899 after becoming known at Johns Hopkins University as a champion of improved nursing education and better working conditions for nurses. She taught in various departments at Teachers College, Columbia University (1899–1925), and in 1906 became the first professor of nursing in the world. One of the most prominent figures in modern nursing, she was instrumental in establishing the Department of Nursing and Health at Teachers College and was the first person to lead it (1910–25).

Joseph S. Lieber

Nuyorican Poets Cafe. A meeting and performance space opened in October 1975 at 505 East 6th Street in Manhattan. It was an outgrowth of a salon held from 1972 by Miguel Algarin and Richard August at their apartment in the East Village, which attracted such writers as Lucky Cienfuegos, Miguel Piñero, Pedro Pietri, Tato Laviera, Bimbo Rivas, and Sandra Esteves, and where works such as Piñero's *Short Eyes* (1974) and Pietri's *Puerto Rican Obituary* (1974) were written and revised. Although many of the writers associated with the café were Spanish-speaking, it also drew such figures as Allen Ginsberg, Gregory Corso, Amiri Baraka, and Ntoszake Shange. The café moved in 1980 to an abandoned tenement building at 236 East 3rd Street. Closed in 1983, it reopened in 1989. In addition to sponsoring readings of poems and screenplays the Nuyorican Poets Cafe has produced more than two dozen plays and published poetry anthologies such as *Aloud: Voices from the Nuyorican Poets Cafe* (1994).

Roland Legiardi-Laura

N. W. Ayer and Partners. Advertising agency formed in 1869 in Philadelphia as N. W. Ayer and Son. It is the oldest agency in continuous operation in the United States. The firm opened an office in the Flatiron Building in New York City in 1903, and the city gradually became its unofficial headquarters; the headquarters were formally moved to New York City in 1973. Over the years the firm became known for several innovations in advertising, including the first color print advertisement (1893) and the first radio advertisement (1922), for long-running campaigns on behalf of such clients as the National Biscuit Company, Steinway and Sons, and American Telephone and Telegraph (an association that began in 1908 and continued into the 1990s), and for several memorable advertising slogans, including "A Diamond Is Forever" (for DeBeers Consolidated Mines), "Reach Out and Touch Someone" (for American Telephone and Telegraph), and "Be All That You Can Be" (for the U.S. Army). In 1994 N. W. Ayer was one of few privately held advertising agencies in the United States, with six hundred employees nationwide and annual billings of $945.2 million.

NYANA. See NEW YORK ASSOCIATION FOR NEW AMERICANS.

NYPIRG. See NEW YORK PUBLIC INTEREST RESEARCH GROUP.

NYPL. See NEW YORK PUBLIC LIBRARY.

O

Oakland Gardens. Neighborhood in northeastern Queens (1989 pop. 33,000), bounded to the north by 48th Avenue, to the east by Alley Pond Park, to the south by Union Turnpike, and to the west by Cunningham Park. A housing development of the same name lies within the neighborhood and is bounded by the Long Island Expressway, Cloverdale Boulevard, 69th Avenue, and Springfield Boulevard. The area was settled in 1645 by John Hicks, one of the original patentees of Flushing. In the early nineteenth century his property passed into the Lawrence family, and about 1847 Frederick Newbold Lawrence built a mansion named the Oaks. A restaurateur from Manhattan, John Taylor, bought the estate in 1859 and with John Henderson transformed it into a horticultural establishment of more than thirty greenhouses specializing in roses and orchids. The property was inherited in 1886 by Taylor's son John H. Taylor, who organized the Oakland Golf Club in 1896 and became its first president. Among the members were Alfred E. Smith, Robert F. Wagner (i), and Bernard Baruch. After 1911 the club bought the golf course; the Draper Realty Company of Manhattan bought the rest of the land and divided it into building lots. In 1952 the club was bought by Morton Pickman of Forest Hills. His plan to erect high-rise apartment buildings was blocked, and he sold the property to Marvin Krattner in 1958. The City of New York bought the golf club in the early 1960s and on its land built Queensborough Community College, Benjamin Cardozo High School, and Public School 203; several houses were moved to the area from the path of the Clearview Expressway by the Triborough Bridge and Tunnel Authority. In 1963 the firm of Alexander Muss and Sons bought the remaining sixty-five acres (twenty-six hectares) of the golf course and built about seven hundred one-family houses (initially selling for $33,745) and two-family houses (selling for $36,240 to $45,240). Overdevelopment threatened during the 1980s, but zoning changes limited new construction and residents were able to preserve the environment around Oakland Lake.

Jeffrey A. Kroessler

Oakwood. Neighborhood in east central Staten Island (1990 pop. 9300), lying near the southern shore and bounded to the north by Ebbitts Street, to the east by the Atlantic Ocean, to the south by Great Kills Park, and to the west by the tracks of Staten Island Rapid Transit (SIRT); it stretches along a flat corridor between the Atlantic Ocean and the hilly interior of the island. During the nineteenth century the area was an ocean resort. Development increased for a time after a subway tunnel under the Narrows was proposed in the 1920s that would have linked the SIRT and the 4th Avenue subway. In the mid 1990s Oakwood was a middle-class neighborhood of one- and two-family houses and garden apartments, with an important commercial section along Hylan Boulevard.

Andrew Sparberg

Obelisk. See Cleopatra's needle.

Obie Award. An award instituted in 1955 by the *Village Voice* to acknowledge the achievements of theater off Broadway (and later off off Broadway). Citations are given for acting, directing, playwriting, and design, with special awards for distinguished or sustained achievement.

Ross Wetzsteon, ed.: *The Obie Winners: The Best of Off-Broadway* (New York: Doubleday, 1980)

D. S. Moynihan

O'Brien, John P(atrick) (*b* Worcester, Mass., 1 Feb 1873; *d* New York City, 22 Sept 1951). Mayor. After a successful career as the corporation counsel of New York City and surrogate he won a special election in 1932 to finish James J. Walker's unexpired term as mayor. The problems of the Depression and his ineptitude in public relations turned voters against him, and he finished third in the election of 1933, which was won by Fiorello H. La Guardia.

Frank Vos

occupational health. In the late nineteenth century and the early twentieth, reformers working with the urban poor focused on improving health and safety in the workplace. Such crusaders as Alice Hamilton and Florence Kelley, who were associated with the settlement movement, paid particular attention to the link between illness and working conditions. In 1890 workers for charities and settlement houses in New York City found that nearly one person in every four families died of tuberculosis (then called consumption); in poorer neighborhoods the toll was much higher and entire communities were left devastated by the disease. In 1911 a tragic fire at the Triangle Shirtwaist Company that took 146 lives shocked the public and persuaded the state legislature to organize a factory inspection commission to visit dangerous work sites. The commission held hearings on the dangers of several occupations and issued a report that marked a turning point in efforts to prevent occupational disease and accidents. The publicity surrounding these hearings spurred the passage of workers' compensation laws in New York City, and several members of the commission later played an important role in the administration of Franklin D. Roosevelt, including Kelley, Frances Perkins, and Robert F. Wagner (i).

During the second decade of the twentieth century the Consumer's League joined forces with the International Ladies' Garment Workers' Union to seek better working conditions and control the spread of communicable diseases in the workplace: the "union label" attached to garments came to symbolize clean working conditions. Activist organizations like the Workers' Health Bureau of America continued to aid labor groups such as the Bakers' and Confectioners' Union and the Amalgamated Clothing Workers in investigating hazards in the workplace. At the same time the widespread introduction of lead into paint and gasoline and the increased smelting of ores heightened awareness of the danger to workers and the public. John B. Andrews and the American Association for Labor Legislation, which had its headquarters in the city, led the campaigns against "phossy jaw" and lead poisoning, and industrial hygienists and occupational physicians tested the exposure to lead of painters and battery workers.

As the political power of progressive reformers waned in the 1920s, professional industrial hygienists replaced labor advocates as custodians of health and safety in the workplace. Such organizations as the National Safety Council and the Industrial Hygiene Association encouraged workers and management to assume greater responsibility in reducing injuries and disease. The Workers' Health Bureau, based in New York City and led by progressive women, was one of the few organizations that maintained the traditional alliance with labor; it helped in particular to focus public attention on the plight of watchmakers who were suffering from chronic diseases because of their ingestion of radium. During the Depression labor unions regained much of their earlier power, and the number of liability suits increased. Among occupational diseases silicosis was of particular concern because it affected large numbers of workers who inhaled silica dust in foundries, steel plants, and sandblasting operations. The Congress of Industrial Organizations used the deplorable health and safety conditions of these heavy industries as a vehicle for organizing unions.

The decline of heavy industry after the Second World War and the rise of white-collar and service industries led to a general belief that occupational diseases would be virtually eliminated. Instead occupational health problems took on new forms. Dangers associated with the telecommunications and electrical industries received much attention, as did the proliferation of video display terminals: in the 1980s some studies suggested a link between exposure to low-level radiation from the terminals and miscarriages, and many office workers became afflicted with carpal-tunnel syndrome, a condition caused by repetitive motions of the hand.

See also Physical disabilities.

David Rosner

Ocean Breeze. Neighborhood in east central Staten Island, lying southeast of Hylan Boulevard. It was originally a summer beach colony of bungalows and tents; the beach is now part of the city parks system. The adjacent inland area, long a marshy meadow, is now occupied by the New York State Mental Hygiene Center. Farther inland is the Staten Island University Hospital and other health care facilities. Seaview Avenue is the main thoroughfare. Near Hylan Boulevard is a residential area of small one-family houses. The population is largely white.

Marjorie Johnson

Ocean Hill. Neighborhood in east central Brooklyn, bounded to the north by Broadway, to the east by Van Sinderen Avenue, to the south by East New York Avenue, and to the west by Ralph, Atlantic, and Saratoga avenues. It was developed as an exclusive neighborhood in the 1890s. By the early twentieth century there were department stores, theaters, and some industrial facilities, and Broadway and Rockaway Avenue were the main thoroughfares. With neighboring Brownsville the neighborhood formed one of three districts designated in the 1960s to test community control over local schools, with support from the Ford Foundation. Conflict ensued between school leaders, members of the community, and the United Federation of Teachers, sparking one of the bitterest teachers' strikes in the history of New York City. After 1970 the number of vacant lots rose as houses were abandoned, and many stores along Broadway were destroyed by fire during a blackout in 1977. In the mid 1990s two- to four-family houses predominated; the city planned to rebuild one- and two-family houses on vacant lots and to renovate vacant apartment buildings along Eastern Parkway and multifamily houses. The East Broadway Merchants' Association and the Ocean Hill Bushwick Bedford–Stuyvesant Development Corporation undertook the improvement of Broadway, which remained an important thoroughfare. The population is largely black; a few Latin Americans live in the northern section near Broadway.

Ellen Marie Snyder-Grenier

Ocean Parkway. Neighborhood in west central Brooklyn, lying along a thoroughfare of the same name running about six miles (ten kilometers) north to south from Prospect Park to the southeastern edge of Coney Island. The parkway was suggested in the 1860s in reports to the park commissioners of Brooklyn by Frederick Law Olmsted and Calvert Vaux, who together drew up a plan influenced by boulevards in Paris and Berlin. Begun in 1874 and completed by 1880, the parkway resembled Eastern Parkway: it had a width of 210 feet (sixty-four meters), a central roadway, two malls, two side roads, and two sidewalks, and was lined with trees, benches, playing tables, and a bicycle path. It ran through several neighborhoods including Parkville and Windsor Terrace; later other neighborhoods such as Kensington were built along the parkway. About the turn of the century houses were constructed along the edges, attracting buyers from Bushwick, Bedford–Stuyvesant, and Brooklyn Heights. Many grand houses were built about the time of the First World War, which marked the end of a period of suburban affluence in the neighborhood. In the 1920s rows of one- and two-family houses and small apartment buildings were erected, and the upper reaches of the parkway became the site of luxury apartment buildings with elevators; after the Second World War apartment buildings replaced older houses on streets near the parkway. Parallel to Ocean Parkway and several blocks to the east is Coney Island Avenue, an important commercial street.

Ellen Marie Snyder-Grenier

Ochs, Adolph S(imon) (*b* Cincinnati, 12 March 1858; *d* Chattanooga, Tenn., 8 April 1935). Newspaper publisher. He began his career in journalism in 1872 as a printer's devil at the *Knoxville Chronicle* in Tennessee and worked as a printer in Knoxville and Chattanooga until 1878, when he borrowed money and bought the struggling daily newspaper the *Chattanooga Times*. The newspaper thrived under his stewardship, but after the financial panic of 1893 he became nearly bankrupt and was forced to seek new sources of capital. In 1896 he rescued the *New York Times* from receivership, quickly making the newspaper profitable and respectable by emphasizing objective news rather than opinion and sensationalism. He coined the slogan "All the News That's Fit to Print" and resolved to keep the newspaper in his family, which retained control into the 1990s. For many years he resided at 308 West 75th Street (later the site of the Manhattan Day School); he was active as the publisher of the *Times* to the end of his life.

Gerald W. Johnson: *An Honorable Titan: A Biographical Study of Adolph S. Ochs* (New York: Harper and Brothers, 1946)

See also New year's eve.

Harrison Salisbury

O'Connor, John (Joseph) (*b* Philadelphia, 15 Jan 1920). Cardinal. Ordained in 1945, he was a chaplain in the navy from 1952 to 1979, when he was consecrated a bishop. New York City was then the military vicariate, and he became the auxiliary for military chaplains. Appointed successively bishop of Scranton, Pennsylvania (1983), archbishop of New York City (1984), and a cardinal (1985), he engaged politicians on issues of sexual and reproductive morality, opposing those who said that their personal opinions on abortion should not interfere with their public obligation to uphold existing laws. In 1990 he warned Catholic politicians who favored abortion rights that they risked excommunication. His archdiocese in 1984 took part in a coalition that successfully challenged in the courts a directive prohibiting employment discrimination based on sexual orientation. He attacked the problem of Catholic fragmentation in 1986 by forbidding parishes to sponsor Catholic speakers whose presentations conflicted with church doctrine. In 1986 he opened an archdiocesan hospice for people with AIDS, but the homosexual activity often associated with AIDS proved difficult for the church: in 1990 the activist group ACT-UP made O'Connor the target of a protest against what it perceived as the lack of support by the church for efforts to prevent AIDS. O'Connor collaborated with Mayor Edward I. Koch on the book *His Eminence and Hizzonor* (1989).

Nat Hentoff: *John Cardinal O'Connor: At the Storm Center of a Changing American Catholic Church* (New York: Charles Scribner's Sons, 1988)

Mary Elizabeth Brown

O'Conor, Charles (*b* New York City, 22 Jan 1804; *d* Nantucket, Mass., 12 May 1884). Lawyer. The son of an Irish immigrant who had been active in the rebellion of 1798 against British rule, he grew up in poverty. His quick mind and tenaciousness allowed him to overcome a meager education. By the 1840s he began earning a reputation as an unusually capable lawyer known especially for his humorless combativeness. One of his best-known cases was a divorce suit in 1851–52 in which he successfully defended Catherine Forrest against charges of infidelity made by her husband, the actor Edwin Forrest. A leading member of the Bar Association of the City of New York, he was appointed to lead the prosecution of the Tweed Ring in 1871. O'Conor was a defender of slavery and the Confederacy, and he was promoted as a presidential candidate by a faction of the Democratic Party in 1872.

Henry Ellsworth Gregory: "Charles O'Conor," *Great American Lawyers: The Lives and Influence of Judges and Lawyers*, ed. William Draper Lewis (Philadelphia: John C. Winston, 1908)

Frederick S. Voss

Octagon Tower. A ruin on Roosevelt Island, built in 1839 as the New York City Lunatic Asylum. It consists of a rotunda sixty-two feet (nineteen meters) tall surrounded by a spectacular flying staircase. The structure once served as the hub between the southern and western wings of a much larger building. The wings were demolished in 1970, and the dome was destroyed by fire in 1982. In 1994 the Roosevelt Island Operating Corporation asked for permission to stabilize the building and open part of it to the public.

Kenneth T. Jackson

O'Day, Caroline (Love Goodwin) (*b* Georgia, 22 June 1869; *d* Rye, N.Y., 4 Jan 1943). Congresswoman. She moved to New York City in 1886 to study art and also studied in Europe before marrying Daniel O'Day in 1901. With her husband she lived in Rye until his death in 1916; she then became an active participant in the New York Consumer League, the New York Women's Trade Union League, and the women's division of the state Democratic Party. She led the state delegation at the Democratic National Convention in New York City in 1924, and in 1934 was elected to the U.S. Congress. During four terms in office she was a committed proponent of the New Deal and of pacifism.

Marion Dickerman: "Caroline O'Day," *Notable American Women: A Biographical Dictionary*, ed. Edward T. James, Janet Wilson James, and Paul S. Boyer (Cambridge: Harvard University Press, 1971)

Lois Scharf

Odets, Clifford (*b* Philadelphia, 18 July 1906; *d* Los Angeles, 14 Aug 1963). Theater director, playwright, and actor. He began his career as an apprentice actor in New York City with the Group Theatre, an experimental troupe led by Harold Clurman, Lee Strasberg, and Cheryl Crawford. In 1933 he rented an apartment at 82 Horatio Street, where he lived until moving to 1 University Place. He gained national prominence in 1935 for his militant one-act play *Waiting For Lefty*; several weeks later the Group Theatre mounted his second play, *Awake and Sing!*, with the actors Stella Adler, Morris Carnovsky, and John Garfield. During an association with the company that lasted seven years he wrote *Golden Boy* (1937) and several other plays. He then moved to Hollywood, where he struggled as a screenwriter. His success as a playwright nevertheless continued, and his play *The Country Girl* (1950) was staged on Broadway. In 1952 Odets testified before the House Un-American Activities Committee about his political activities in the 1930s.

Margaret Brenman-Gibson: *Clifford Odets, American Playwright: The Years from 1906 to 1940* (New York: Atheneum, 1981)

Peter M. Rutkoff, William B. Scott

John Garfield, Morris Carnovsky, J. E. Bromberg, Stella Adler, Luther Adler, Sanford Meisner, and Art Smith in Clifford Odets's Awake and Sing *at the Belasco Theatre, 1935*

O'Donovan Rossa, Jeremiah (*b* Rosscarbery, Ireland, 14 Sept 1831; *d* New York City, 29 June 1915). Political activist. A member of the Irish Republican Brotherhood, he was imprisoned by the British in 1859 and again in 1865. After his release in 1870 on condition of lifetime exile he moved to New York City, where he was greeted with a rousing ceremony at Cooper Union. He spent the rest of his life in the city, where he led the Fenian movement, edited the *United Irishman* (launched in 1881), and promoted dynamite and assassination as the only means to obtain Irish independence. He lived at 194 Richmond Terrace in New Brighton. After his death his body was taken to Ireland, where he was eulogized by Patrick Pearse as personifying the Fenian dead who would inspire Ireland to freedom.

Kevin Kenny

O'Dwyer, (Peter) Paul (*b* Bohola, County Mayo, Ireland, 29 June 1907). Lawyer and reformer, brother of William O'Dwyer. He grew up in Brooklyn, attended law school at St. John's University, and worked as a lawyer in behalf of miners in Kentucky and blacks in Mississippi and Alabama; he also smuggled arms to Israel in 1948. In 1958 he joined with Eleanor Roosevelt, Herbert H. Lehman, and others in establishing the Committee for Democratic Voters, which marked the beginning of the Democratic reform movement in New York State. As the Democratic nominee for the U.S. Senate in 1968 he was defeated by Senator Jacob K. Javits. He was president of the City Council of New York from 1974 to 1977. He wrote *Counsel for the Defense: An Autobiography* (1979).

B. Kimberly Taylor

O'Dwyer, William (*b* Bohola, County Mayo, Ireland, 7 July 1890; *d* New York City, 24 Nov 1964). Mayor, brother of Paul O'Dwyer. As the district attorney of Brooklyn in 1940–41 he successfully prosecuted members of Murder Incorporated. He won the Democratic mayoral nomination in 1941 but was defeated in the general election by Fiorello H. La Guardia. In 1945 he was elected mayor as the candidate of the Democratic and American Labor parties. As a mayor he had a reputation as a capable administrator with an unpredictable personality. His career was marked by allegations of complicity with organized crime, and after his reelection in 1949 he was forced to resign in 1950 to become ambassador to Mexico.

George Walsh: *Public Enemies: The Mayor, the Mob and the Crime That Was* (New York: W. W. Norton, 1980)

See also Nickel fare.

Chris McNickle

Off-Track Betting (Corporation, New York City) [OTB]. Public-benefit corporation formed in April 1971 by the state legislature of New York to allow wagering at locations away from the racetrack on thoroughbred and harness races. Although objections were raised by opponents of gambling and by the New York Racing Authority, which represented racetracks throughout the state, the supporters of off-track betting promoted it as a means of producing revenue for the city and state, weakening the illegal gambling operations of organized crime, and reviving horse racing. The corporation was overseen by a board of directors appointed by the mayor. The first head of OTB was Howard Samuels, a successful businessman active in Democratic politics. Patrons could bet on local races and on events outside the state including the Kentucky Derby and the Preakness; they placed their bets at small outlets, modeled after betting parlors in Britain, that were the first of their kind in the United States, as well as by telephone. Although the betting outlets were not initially intended as gathering places they eventually included restrooms, snack bars, and television monitors on which races were broadcast. By 1978 there were 157 branches scattered throughout the city. From that time the volume of wagers declined because of competition from the state lottery and other forms of gambling, the general decline in popularity of horse racing, and the imposition by OTB of an unpopular surtax on winnings. In 1990 OTB had a hundred branches in the city, employed seventeen hundred workers full time and six hundred part time, and raised $40 million for the city, $17 million for the state, and $8 million for other local governments.

In the early 1990s OTB became unprofitable. During the mayoral campaign in 1993 Rudolph W. Giuliani frequently attacked the corporation as a bloated, inefficient bureaucracy, and after the election his administration explored the possibility of selling OTB to a private buyer.

Edward T. O'Donnell

Ogilvy, David (Mackenzie) (*b* West Horsley, near Guildford, England, 23 June 1911). Advertising executive. After attending Oxford University he worked in Paris as a chef and in Scotland as a door-to-door stove salesman until his brother Francis helped him secure a position with the advertising firm Mather and Crowther in London in 1935. He went to the United States in 1938 to learn about American advertising and decided to stay; from the following year he conducted 439 nationwide surveys for George Gallup. He served during the Second World War in the intelligence arm of the British embassy in Washington. In 1948 he formed the advertising agency Hewitt Ogilvy Benson and Mather with Anderson Hewitt in New York City: he became well known for distinctive campaigns such as one for Hathaway shirts featuring a man with an eye-patch, and for placing advertisements in respected publications such as the *New Yorker.* In 1975 he retired as the chairman of Ogilvy and Mather International and became its worldwide creative head, a position from which he retired in 1983; he moved in the 1970s to France, where he took up residence in a twelfth-century château south of Paris. Ogilvy is the author of *Confessions of an Advertising Man* (1963), *Ogilvy on Advertising* (1983), and an autobiography, *Blood, Brains, and Beer* (1978).

"A Disease Called Entertainment," *Forbes*, 7 March 1988, pp. 150–51

Marjorie Harrison

Ogilvy and Mather. Advertising agency formed as Ogilvy Benson and Mather in 1948 by David Ogilvy and Anderson Hewitt. It occupied offices at 345 Madison Avenue and received the financial support of two advertising firms based in London: Mather and Crowther, for which Ogilvy had worked from 1935 to 1938, and S. H. Benson. During its first year the name was changed successively to B&M Incorporated, Benson and Mather, and Hewitt, Ogilvy, Benson and Mather. Early accounts included Sun Oil and Chase Bank. In 1953 the agency became Ogilvy, Benson and Mather after Hewitt resigned as its president and chief executive officer. Throughout the 1950s and 1960s the agency won important accounts such as Bristol–Myers, Maxwell House, Rolls Royce, Shell Oil, and American Express, for which it devised a long-running and successful campaign. After a merger in November 1964 with Mather and Crowther (the fifth-largest agency in the United Kingdom), each agency operated as a subsidiary of the new parent firm Ogilvy and Mather, now the tenth-largest advertising firm in the world. Both firms changed their names to Ogilvy and Mather in 1965, with the parent company called Ogilvy and Mather International. In the following year the company's stock was sold publicly for the first time.

In 1972 Ogilvy and Mather opened a Yellow Pages division in Pleasantville, New York, which placed advertisements for more than one hundred of its leading national and regional customers in local telephone directories. During the 1970s its accounts came to include Sears Roebuck, International Business Machines, and Merrill Lynch, Pierce, Fenner and Smith. Ogilvy retired as the chairman of Ogilvy and Mather International in 1975, and over the next ten years the firm acquired a number of other advertising agencies. It changed its name to the Ogilvy Group in 1985, which included Ogilvy and Mather Worldwide (also a new name). In 1989 the firm was acquired by the WWP Group of London, led by Martin Sorrell, of which it became an independently run subsidiary. In the same year Ogilvy and Mather opened one of the first offices of a Western advertising agency in the Soviet Union (Tisza, Ogilvy and Mather). In 1990 the firm's billing reached $4700 million dollars. About eight hundred persons work for Ogilvy and Mather New York, which occupies offices at Worldwide Plaza on West 49th Street and represents NYNEX, Cotton Incorporated, Smith Barney, Seagram's, and Time Warner. Ogilvy and Mather Worldwide, with 284 offices in fifty-six countries and more than ten thousand employees, is the third-largest agency network in the world.

Marjorie Harrison

O'Hara, Frank [Francis Russell] (*b* Baltimore, 27 March 1926; *d* Mastic Beach, N.Y., 25 July 1966). Poet. He studied at Harvard University (AB 1950) and served in the navy during the Second World War. Deeply influenced by the paintings of the abstract expressionists, he cultivated friendships with Jackson Pollack and Franz Kline and became associated with the New York School of poetry. He developed an unconstrained poetic style characterized by spontaneous observations of everyday life; the collection *Lunch Poems* (1964) provides a quasi-photographic view of New York City at midday. Many of his other works, such as *Love Poems* (1965), celebrate his homosexuality. After O'Hara's death in an automobile accident his friend Allen Ginsberg paid tribute to him in the poem "City Midnight Junk Strains" (1966).

Brad Gooch: *City Poet: The Life and Times of Frank O'Hara* (New York: Alfred A. Knopf, 1993)

Shan Jayakumar

O'Hara, John (Henry) (*b* Pottsville, Penn., 31 Jan 1905; *d* Princeton, N.J., 11 April 1970). Novelist and short-story writer. He moved to New York City in 1928 and wrote for newspapers and magazines such as the *New Yorker.* His novel *Appointment in Samarra* (1934), composed in his hotel room at 230 East 51st Street, brought him literary recognition; his popular stories of a roguish nightclub singer in New York City eventually made him wealthy. With Richard Rodgers and Lorenz Hart he adapted his novel *Pal Joey* (1940) for Broadway. O'Hara was a prolific writer of short stories, of which the *New Yorker* published 225.

Matthew J. Bruccoli: *The O'Hara Concern* (New York: Random House, 1975)

Robert Morrow

O. Henry [Porter, William Sydney] (*b* Greensboro, N.C., 11 Sept 1862; *d* New York City, 5 June 1910). Short-story writer. After leaving school at fifteen he lived in Texas and Honduras and spent three years in prison in Ohio, where he wrote many stories. On his release he lived briefly in Pittsburgh before settling in New York City in 1902. He lived at 55 Irving Place from 1903 and in 1906 moved to the Caledonia Hotel at 28 West 26th Street; he kept a room there for writing after moving to the Chelsea Hotel at 222 West 23rd Street. O. Henry wrote dozens of stories a year, many of them inspired by life in the city, and published them in such collections as *The Four Million* (1906) and *The Voice of the City* (1908).

Richard O'Connor: *O. Henry: The Legendary Life of William S. Porter* (New York: Doubleday, 1970)

James E. Mooney

Ohrbach's. Firm of clothing retailers. It began as a store opened in 1923 in Union Square by Nathan M. Ohrbach (*b* Vienna, 31 Aug 1885; *d* New York City, 19 Nov 1972), who sold ready-to-wear clothing at low prices. He made large profits by selling in bulk for cash, offering minimal sales service, and forgoing delivery, decorative wrappings, and alterations. His slogan was "more for less, or your money back"; customers who could prove that another store had undersold him were refunded their money and also received 10 percent of the competitor's selling price. After the store moved to 5 West 34th Street its annual sales exceeded $30 million. Ohrbach later specialized in inexpensive copies of European designer clothes and fulfilled his aspiration of becoming to discount retailing what Bergdorf Goodman was to high-priced retailing. The firm was later sold to the Brenninkmeyer family of the Netherlands, then ceased operations in February 1987.

Nathan Ohrbach: *Getting Ahead in Retailing* (New York: McGraw–Hill, 1935)

Leslie Gourse

O'Keeffe, Georgia (*b* Sun Prairie, Wis., 15 Nov 1887; *d* Santa Fe, N.M., 6 March 1986). Painter. She moved to New York City in 1907 to study at the Art Students League with William Merritt Chase and first encountered modern art in the following year at Alfred Stieglitz's gallery "291." After working as an illustrator in Chicago (1909–10) and studying at the University of Virginia (1912) she returned to the city in 1914 to study with Arthur Wesley Dow (1857–1922) at Teachers College, Columbia University. In South Carolina she completed abstract drawings that in 1916 gained the attention of Stieglitz, who included her work in two group exhibitions, presented the first solo exhibition of her drawings and watercolors in 1917, and invited her to leave a teaching post in Texas and return in 1918 to New York City, where from July to the end of 1920 she lived and worked at 114 East 59th Street. After the two were married in 1924 she moved into the Hotel Shelton at 525 Lexington Avenue, which became her residence in the city for the next ten years. During this period she also spent time in Lake George (New York) and New Mexico. Her work from these years ranges from organic abstractions to floral still lifes, stark landscapes, and "precisionist" paintings and drawings inspired by the dramatic architecture of the city (1924–29). She lived from the autumn of 1936 at 405 East 54th Street and from October 1942 at 59 East 54th Street. On Stieglitz's death in 1946 she organized and dispersed his art collection, and operated the American Place gallery, which lasted until 1950. The Metropolitan Museum of Art and the Whitney Museum of American Art own important examples of O'Keeffe's work.

Lloyd Goodrich and Doris Bry: *Georgia O'Keeffe Retrospective Exhibition* (New York: Whitney Museum of American Art, 1970)

Laurie Lisle: *Portrait of an Artist: A Biography of Georgia O'Keeffe* (New York: Seaview, 1980)

Patterson Sims: *Georgia O'Keeffe: A Concentration of Works from the Permanent Collection* (New York: Whitney Museum of American Art, 1981)

Jack Cowart, Juan Hamilton, and Sarah Greenough: *Georgia O'Keeffe: Art and Letters* (Washington: National Gallery of Art / New York: Graphic Society Books / Boston: Little, Brown, 1987)

Charles C. Eldredge: *Georgia O'Keeffe* (New York: Harry N. Abrams, 1991)

Judith Zilczer

Olatunji, Babatunde Michael (*b* Adjido-Badagry, Nigeria, 7 April 1927). Drummer. After attending Baptiste Academy in Lagos he earned his BA from Morehouse College in 1954 and in 1958 opened the Center for African Culture at 43 East 125th Street, which became a national center for African drumming and culture; for more than twenty-five years he taught students from all over the world and introduced to new audiences such performers as John Coltrane, Ladji Camara, and Yusef Lateef. His first album, *Drums of Passion* (1959), brought traditional African music into the commercial mainstream, and his song "Jingo-lo-ba" became well known through a version done by Carlos Santana in 1968. Olatunji's students and associates have included the percussionists Chief James Hawthorne Bey, Taiwo Duvall, Moses Miann, Ladji Camara, Kehinde Stewart O'Uhuru, Montego Joe, Sonny Morgan, Sule Greg C. Wilson, and Mickey Hart of the Grateful Dead.

Sule Greg C. Wilson

Olcott, Chauncey [Chancellor John] (*b* Buffalo, 21 July 1860; *d* Monte Carlo, Monaco, 18 March 1932). Actor and singer. He was the star of the Irish musical stage in the United States from the late 1890s to the mid 1920s. His splendid singing voice and magnetic stage personality assured the success of several highly patriotic and sentimental plays, including *Sweet Inniscarra* and *O'Neill of Derry*. Olcott introduced such popular songs as "My Wild Irish Rose," which became his signature, and "Mother Machree" during his frequent appearances at the 14th Street Theatre in Manhattan and the Bijou in Brooklyn.

Rita O'Donovan Olcott: *Song in His Heart* (New York: House of Field, 1939)

John T. Ridge

Old Blazing Star. An early name for the area on the shore of the Arthur Kill near Rossville in Staten Island. The name refers to a comet, but its origin is unknown. The Blazing Star Ferry to New Jersey docked there from 1722 and later there was also a Blazing Star Tavern. When a new ferry service was begun at Long Neck north of Blazing Star the "old" was added and after 1837 the name was changed to Rossville.

Barnett Shepherd

Oldenburg, Claes (Thure) (*b* Stockholm, 28 Jan 1929). Sculptor. He studied at Yale University (BA 1951) and the Art Institute of Chicago (1952–54). His early works include *The Street* (1960), constructed of debris from the streets of New York City. In the 1960s he became widely known for his oversized soft sculptures of everyday objects, often made of vinyl or canvas and stuffed with kapok or a similar material. Typical examples include *Soft Typewriter* (1963) and *Bacon, Lettuce and Tomato* (1963). He maintained a studio in New York City and had several important exhibitions there, at the Martha Jackson Gallery (1960, 1961), the Reuben Gallery (1960), the Green Gallery (1962), the Museum of Modern Art (1963), the Metropolitan Museum of Art (1969), the Leo Castelli Gallery (1974, 1976, 1980), and Wave Hill (1984).

Shan Jayakumar

Old Merchant's House. Historic house at 29 East 4th Street erected in 1832 by Joseph Brewster in a synthesis of the Federal and Greek Revival styles. Built in what was then a fashionable neighborhood, it was purchased in 1835 by Seabury Treadwell, retired from a successful career as a marine-hardware merchant, and was occupied by various members of the family for the next ninety-eight years; his youngest daughter Gertrude is credited with having kept the contents of the household intact. Opened as a museum in 1936, the house contains an extensive collection of furnishings and personal items from the Federal and Victorian periods. For more than twenty years before his death in 1988 the architect Joseph Roberto worked to restore the house and bring it to public attention. A city landmark listed on the National Register of Historic Places, the Old Merchant's House is the only nineteenth-century dwelling in Manhattan that contains the furniture and possessions of its original owners.

The Old Merchant's House and the Tredwell Family (New York: Historic Landmark Society, n.d. [?1936])

Joyce Gold

Old Place. Neighborhood in northwestern Staten Island, near the approach to the Goethals Bridge. The original settlement grew up around a tide mill built by the 1750s on Old Place Creek, which empties into the Kill van Kull. The eastern portion of the settlement, along Forest Avenue, was given the attractive name of Summerville. Old Place was never populous because of its marshes, swamps, and creeks, and the mosquitos with which they were infested. Much of the marsh was filled in and the land zoned for industrial use. The remaining marshland has been designated as wetlands. A permanent trailer park, the only one in New York City, is near the approach to the bridge.

Marjorie Johnson

Old Town. Neighborhood in northeastern Staten Island, lying east of Richmond Road. The first permanent European settlement on the island was made near the beach adjoining Fort Wadsworth in 1661 by Dutch, French, and English farmers and fishermen. The town was called Dover by the English but became known as Old Town when a new town was formed at New Dorp. In the late nineteenth century the beach area was developed as a summer resort and amusement park known as South Beach and a spur line of the railroad was built to accommodate tourists. After the turn of the century many western, war, and adventure films were shot at the farm of Fred Scott just inland from the beach. Hylan Boulevard, which runs the length of Staten Island, bisects the neighborhood and is its principal commercial thoroughfare. Below Hylan Boulevard is a large marshy area that has been designated a protected wetlands. Staten Island Rapid Transit crosses the northern section of the neighborhood, with a station at Old Town Road. Near the station are the Carmel–Richmond Nursing Home and the Carmel–Richmond Apartments for senior citizens. The housing stock of Old Town consists mainly of one-family houses and the population is largely white.

Marjorie Johnson

Olinville. Neighborhood in the north central Bronx, bounded to the north by 215th Street, to the east by White Plains Road, to the south by Burke Avenue, and to the west by the Bronx River. It began as Olinville no. 1 and Olinville no. 2, two villages named for Stephen Olin, a bishop in the Methodist church, that were formed in the 1840s after a railroad station of the New York and Harlem River Railroad opened nearby in Williamsbridge. The villages were separated by Olin Avenue (formerly Gun Hill Road between the Bronx River and White Plains Road) and incorporated between 1852 and 1854. The population grew after the 3rd Avenue elevated line was extended to meet the recently completed branch of the subway to White Plains Road. In the mid 1990s most of the population was black. Many who live in the neighborhood consider themselves residents of Williamsbridge.

John McNamara: *History in Asphalt: The Origin of Bronx Street and Place Names* (New York: Bronx County Historical Society, 1984)

Gary D. Hermalyn

Eastern Parkway (designed by Frederick Law Olmsted), ca *1895*

Olmsted, Frederick Law (*b* Hartford, Conn., 26 April 1822; *d* Belmont, Mass., 28 Aug 1903). Landscape architect. After moving to New York City in 1840 he worked as a clerk in a mercantile house and lived from 1848 to 1854 in Staten Island at what is now Woods of Arden Road (his farmhouse stands at 4515 Hylan Boulevard). Several accounts of his travels in the southern United States were published in the 1850s and 1860s. He became best known for his work as a landscape architect from 1858 with Calvert Vaux: together they designed Central Park (the construction and use of which Olmsted oversaw as its architect-in-chief and superintendent; for illustration see CENTRAL PARK), Riverside Park, and smaller recreational areas in Manhattan, proposed a street plan for Washington Heights, and were the landscape architects of Prospect Park, Fort Greene Park, Ocean Parkway, Eastern Parkway, and several smaller parks in Brooklyn. Olmsted also prepared comprehensive plans for the Bronx (with the engineer J. J. R. Croes) and Staten Island and for a resort at Rockaway Point. In addition to working as an architect he was an experimental farmer on Staten Island and a founder of the Union League Club and the Metropolitan Museum of Art.

Olmsted's career in the city was hindered and eventually cut short by politics. He fought bitterly against Tammany Hall, reform Democrats (notably Andrew Haswell Green), and Republicans, whom he accused of interfering with his designs and according more importance to patronage than to the proper administration of the parks. After his dismissal by the Department of Public Parks in 1878 he moved in 1882 to Brookline, Massachusetts, but continued to concern himself with the fate of the public parks in New York City: in his last years he opposed the addition to the parks of neoclassical structures designed by McKim, Mead and White and other architects, and oversaw the construction of parks that he had designed in southern Brooklyn. Insanity forced his retirement in 1895.

In his designs Olmsted sought to provide relief from the density, congestion, and incessant pace of New York City. He considered his landscapes both works of art and social experiments that would have a civilizing influence. He denounced the gridiron system of streets as a relic of an earlier stage of urbanization and envisioned instead a compact business district surrounded by more open residential neighborhoods and spacious, naturalistic parks; this vision is most clearly set forth in his proposals for the Bronx and for the parkways in Brooklyn. Although often frustrated by political maneuvering and competing ideas of what a park should be, Olmsted and his collaborators had a profound influence on New York City.

Laura Wood Roper: *FLO: A Biography of Frederick Law Olmsted* (Baltimore: Johns Hopkins University Press, 1973)

Charles C. McLaughlin et al., eds.: *The Papers of Frederick Law Olmsted* (Baltimore: Johns Hopkins University Press, 1979–)

See also U.S. SANITARY COMMISSION.

David Schuyler

Olvany, George W(ashington) (*b* New York City, 20 June 1873; *d* New York City, 15 Oct 1952). Lawyer and political leader. He rose through the ranks of the Democratic Party to become alderman (1906), district leader, counsel to the sheriff of New York County (1916–23), and judge of special sessions. After Charles F. Murphy's death in 1924 he was named head of Tammany Hall with the backing of Governor Alfred E. Smith. In 1925 he contributed to the defeat in a primary election of Mayor John F. Hylan, a critic of Smith. Citing poor health, he resigned in March 1929 after Smith had failed to win sufficient support in the city in the presidential election of 1928. An investigation of municipal government by Samuel Seabury in 1931 revealed that during Olvany's tenure as the boss of Tammany Hall his law firm had secretly collected large fees from real-estate interests seeking variances from the Board of Standards and Appeals.

Alfred Conable and Edward Silverfarb: *Tigers of Tammany* (New York: Holt, Rinehart and Winston, 1967)

Frank Vos

Olympia and York. Real-estate development firm based in Toronto and owned by Albert, Paul, and Ralph Reichmann. It attracted widespread attention for buying eight distressed skyscrapers on prime sites in Manhattan during a real-estate slump in 1977. This risky purchase helped to launch a wave of foreign investment in the city's real estate during the 1980s after a boom in financial services led the eight buildings to triple in value. Olympia and York became an important force in the local real-estate market; it later built the World Financial Center in Battery Park City, a complex of four towers completed between 1985 and 1988 containing seven million square feet (650,000 square meters) of office space. The firm is one of the largest of its kind in the world.

Susan Goldenberg: *Men of Property: The Canadian Developers Who Are Buying America* (Toronto: Personal Library, 1981)

Peter Foster: *The Master Builders: How the Reichmanns Reached for an Empire* (Toronto: Key Porter, 1986)

Marc A. Weiss

omnibuses. See BUSES.

Omnicom Group. Advertising holding group formed in 1986 by the merger of Batten, Barton, Durstine and Osborn; Doyle Dane Bernbach; and Needham Harper. It operates three independent agency networks: BBDO Worldwide Network, DDB Needham Worldwide Network, and TBWA International (acquired in 1993). It also manages specialty advertising companies through Diversified Agency Services (DAS) and Omnicom UK. In the mid 1990s Omnicom had total billings of about $5000 million and offices at 437 Madison Avenue in Manhattan.

Janet Frankston

Onassis [Kennedy; née Bouvier], **Jacqueline (Lee)** (*b* East Hampton, N.Y., 28 July 1929; *d* New York City, 19 May 1994). Editor. As a young woman she lived in her family's apartment on Park Avenue. She married John F. Kennedy in 1953 and moved to Washington in 1961 after his election to the presidency. After choosing to reside permanently in New York City she purchased a co-operative apartment on 5th Avenue in 1964, but she often lived abroad while married to Aristotle Onassis (1968–75). She was a consulting editor at Viking Press until she moved to Doubleday in 1978, where she became a senior editor. A leader in the city's landmarks preservation movement, she was instrumental in protecting Grand Central Terminal from destruction. She also helped to form the 42nd Street Development Corporation and became a member of the Municipal Art Society, the International Center of Photography, and the Century Association. After her death the reservoir in Central Park was renamed in her honor.

Patricia U. Bonomi

Onderdonck House. Historic house at 1820 Flushing Avenue in Queens, built in 1731 in the Dutch Colonial style, a blend of English Georgian and Dutch styles found only in the metropolitan area and along the Hudson River. It was bought in the 1820s by Adrian Onderdonck, a farmer who had married a member of the Wyckoff family, and was occupied by his descendants until 1905. After a devastating fire in the late 1970s the house was restored by the Greater Ridgewood Historical Society between 1979 and 1982. Onderdonck House is the last surviving farmhouse of its time in the area.

Eric Wm. Allison

O'Neill, Eugene (Gladstone) (*b* New York City, 16 Oct 1888; *d* Boston, 27 Nov 1953). Playwright. Born in room 236 of Barrett House, on 43rd Street off Broadway, he spent much of his life in New York City. As a child he toured with his father, the romantic actor James O'Neill (1847–1920), and after a year at Princeton University he worked in a variety of jobs and as a seaman. He contracted tuberculosis and while recovering in a sanitarium decided to become a playwright. In 1916 he became the leading writer for a theater group on Cape Cod that moved to Greenwich Village as the Provincetown Players. He joined the troupe in New York City, living at 38 and 42 Washington Square South and spending time at Jimmy the Priest's, a boarding house at 252 Fulton Street that is the setting for his play *Anna Christie*, and at the Hell Hole (on 4th Street and 6th Avenue), an Irish saloon where he often slept. The Provincetown Players gave the premières in off Broadway theaters at 133 and 139 MacDougal Street (1916–19) of ten of his one-act plays, and on Broadway of his first full-length play, *Beyond the Horizon* (1920), for which he won a Pulitzer Prize; he also won the prize for *Anna Christie* (1921), *Strange Interlude* (1928), produced by the Theatre Guild, and *Long Day's Journey into Night*, his best-known work, completed in 1941 and produced posthumously in 1956. Other major works include *The Emperor Jones* (1920), *Desire under the Elms* (1924), *Mourning Becomes Electra* (1931), and *The Iceman Cometh*, first produced in 1946 but not recognized as a work of genius until its revival in 1956 at the Circle in the Square, staged by José Quintero and featuring Jason Robards.

Although he experimented in a wide range of theatrical genres and production styles, O'Neill is best known for his stark, realistic drama. His plays offer intense psychological treatments of alcoholism, insanity, suicide, and sexual passion. Most of his works are autobiographical and draw on his experiences in waterfront hovels and in Greenwich Village. He received the Nobel Prize for literature in 1936.

Arthur Gelb and Barbara Gelb: *O'Neill* (New York: Harper and Brothers, 1960)

Martha S. LoMonaco

Opdyke, George (*b* Kingwood Township, near Frenchtown, N.J., 7 Dec 1805; *d* New York City, 12 June 1880). Merchant and mayor. He became a prosperous clothing manufacturer and moved to New York City in 1832 to open the first large clothing factory there. In 1846 he turned the business over to his brother-in-law and became an importer of wholesale dry goods. A millionaire by 1853, he later organized a bank and was elected to the state assembly, where he advocated various reforms. As mayor during the draft riots of 1863 he refused to compromise with rioters and abandoned City Hall for the St. Nicholas Hotel. Opdyke was also known for his work on colonial economics.

James E. Mooney

opera. Although rooted in a repertory and a tradition dating largely from the nineteenth century, opera in New York City is as cosmopolitan and varied as its audience. The earliest opera performances in the city took place in 1750, when the Nassau Street Theatre presented ballad operas such as John Gay's *The Beggar's Opera*, musical plays, and pastiches (which consisted of selections or movements by different composers). Carl Maria von Weber's *Der Freischütz* was performed in English at the Park Theatre in 1825 by a troupe led by the celebrated tenor Manuel García and including four members of his family, of whom the youngest, Maria Felicia (then seventeen), achieved early success in the city before building an important career in Europe as Maria Malibran. In November of the same year the troupe began the first foreign-language operas staged in the city, a series of eighty performances sponsored by the wine importer Dominick Lynch with encouragement from Lorenzo da Ponte, now living and teaching in New York City after having written librettos for Mozart; this series consisted largely of operas by Rossini and also included Mozart's *Don Giovanni*, all sung in Italian. Operas were performed at the Park Theatre soon after by a French company and at several other theaters as well, including the Chatham Garden, near City Hall, where Signora Bartolini sang "operatic airs between the plays," and the Richmond Hill, Aaron Burr's former mansion at Varick and Charlton streets, where in 1832 the French tenor Jacques Montresor presented an Italian series, again emphasizing Rossini.

Because important singers were expensive, Italian operas fared better when staged in English. The Austin–Wood and Inverarity companies, run by English and Scottish singers, performed at the Park Theatre in the 1830s, while the Shireff–Seguin–Wilson troupe (also English) followed at the National and at Niblo's Garden (at Broadway and Prince Street), where admission cost only fifty cents. Da Ponte helped to form the Rivafinoli troupe and in 1833 raised money to build the Italian Opera House, the first in the city. The venture was short-lived, with a single season of sixty performances, and the theater burned in 1839. Palmo's Opera House on Chambers Street came to a similarly abrupt end in 1844. In late 1847 the Astor Place, characterized by Richard Grant White as an "elegant little house" at Broadway and 8th Street, also opened for a single, brief season. Although its boxes were likened to "pens for wild beasts," the Park Theatre remained the principal venue for opera in New York City until 1848, when it also burned. The same year was marked by more encouraging developments: the return of Montresor between visits to Mexico and Havana and the staging by his company of performances at Castle Garden (where Jenny Lind made her American début in 1850), a venue that appealed to the masses much as the Park Theatre had appealed to the élite, and the first of many important visits by the conductors Luigi Arditi and Max Maretzek. During these years the influence of immigrants from Italy, Germany, and to a lesser extent France gave imported culture a cachet and indigenous culture something of a stigma; among the few American operas to receive performances were George Frederick Bristow's *Rip van Winkle* (1855) and William Henry Fry's *Leonora* (1858).

As the city grew northward its first major opera house was built on Irving Place at 14th Street: the Academy of Music (seating 4600), where operas and concerts by leading performers were staged, despite managerial problems. The inaugural season began in October

1854 with Vincenzo Bellini's *Norma* sung by a cast including Giulia Grisi and her husband, the tenor Mario Grisi. In the same year Adelina Patti made her opera début at the age of sixteen in Gaetano Donizetti's *Lucia di Lammermoor*; she was a mainstay of the Academy of Music through its years under the management of Maretzek and later of the English impresario James H. Mapleson. Destroyed by fire in 1866, the house was rebuilt but eventually succumbed when wealthy residents of the city, resentful of the small number of boxes there, built the Metropolitan Opera House in 1883. As the nineteenth century progressed, the dominance of European singers was challenged by performers born and trained in the United States, among them Clara Louise Kellogg, Minnie Hauk, and Annie Louise Cary. At the same time the Metropolitan Opera consolidated its position as the leading company in the city. Its only serious competitor was the Manhattan Opera House, opened on 34th Street by Oscar Hammerstein in 1906, where the performers included Mary Garden, Emma Calvé, Luisa Tetrazzini, and John McCormack and much of the repertory was French; backers of the Metropolitan Opera bought out Hammerstein in 1910. The City Center Opera, formed in 1943 at the former Mecca Temple on 54th Street, established itself as the second-most important company in the city when it moved to Lincoln Center in 1966 and became the New York City Opera.

Dozens of local opera companies have come and gone in New York City, many small and some having an ethnic orientation. The most prominent include the Amato Opera Theater, the Bronx Opera, the Brooklyn Lyric Opera, the Queens Opera, and the New York Grand Opera. The Opera Orchestra of New York, formed in 1968 by Eve Queler, specializes in concert readings of rarely heard works. Operas are also performed by students at the Juilliard American Opera Center, the Manhattan School of Music, and the Mannes College of Music, and the Brooklyn Academy of Music became an active presenter of operas in the late 1980s.

Richard Grant White: "Opera in New York," *Century Magazine*, March–April 1882

Julius Mattfeld: "100 Years of Opera in New York," *New York Public Library Bulletin* 29, no. 10 (1925)

Lillian Moore: "New York Academy of Music: A Centenary," *Opera News*, 6 Dec 1954, 13 Dec 1954, 20 Dec 1954

Ann M. Lingg: "Great Opera Houses: Old New York," *Opera News*, 3 Feb 1962

John Dizikes: *Opera in America: A Cultural History* (New Haven: Yale University Press, 1993)

John W. Freeman

Opportunity. The journal of the National Urban League, launched in 1923 and issued monthly for most of its duration. Its full name was *Opportunity: A Journal of Negro Life*. The journal published news of the National Urban League and its local affiliates, results of research, and the work of black artists and writers, and discussed issues of interest to blacks. Its first editor, Charles Johnson, was succeeded in 1928 by Elmer Carter. In 1943 the journal became a quarterly. Editorial direction was assumed in 1945 by Madeline Aldridge and in 1947 by Dutton Ferguson. In 1949 *Opportunity* ceased publication.

Cheryl Greenberg

Orange Order. Fraternal organization formed in Ireland in 1795 "to maintain and uphold the Protestant faith." Named for William III, prince of Orange, who defeated James II at the Battle of the Boyne in Ireland (1690), it advocates the continued membership of Northern Ireland in the United Kingdom. During its early years in New York City the order organized an annual parade on 12 July: in 1824 Thomas Addis Emmet, an exiled member of the United Irishmen, recorded that the marchers received a "humiliating thrashing" from the "green" Irish. More violent disruptions in 1870 and 1871 became known as the Orange riots. A sharp decline in Irish Protestant immigration during the late nineteenth century weakened the order in the city, and the parades were eventually discontinued.

Tony Gray: *The Orange Order* (London: Bodley Head, 1972)

Michael A. Gordon: *The Orange Riots: Irish Political Violence in New York City, 1870 and 1871* (Ithaca, N.Y.: Cornell University Press, 1993)

William McGimpsey

Orange riots. Violence that occurred during parades in 1870 and 1871 to commemorate the anniversary of a major victory of the Protestants over the Catholics in Ireland, that of William III, king of England and prince of Orange, over James II at the Battle of the Boyne. On 12 July 1870 a group of Irish Protestants (Orangemen) held a parade up 8th Avenue to Elm Park at 19th Street; they were followed and harassed by two hundred Catholic Irish, who with three hundred Irish laborers working near the park attacked the Orangemen. The police intervened but eight persons were killed in several skirmishes nearby. In the following year the police commissioner, James J. Kelso, banned the parade, fearing another outbreak of violence. He was quickly overruled by Governor John T. Hoffman, who ordered that the marchers be protected by the police and the militia: Tammany Hall was then under attack from reformers and felt obliged to prove that it could maintain order among the people who were the source of its power. The parade went forward with an escort of several hundred police officers and five regiments of the National Guard. With provocation but without orders many of the guardsmen fired into the crowd. Sixty-seven persons (including militiamen and police officers) were killed and more than 150 were injured. The incident further compromised Tammany Hall and led to efforts to improve the National Guard.

Stephen J. Sullivan: "The Orange and Green Riots (New York City: July 12, 1870 and 1871)," *New York Irish History* 6 (1991–92), 3–12, 46–59

Russell S. Gilmore

Oratorio Society of New York. The oldest amateur chorus in New York City, founded in 1873 by Leopold Damrosch. In its early years it inaugurated a series of performances each Christmas of Handel's *Messiah*, and also gave the American premières of Berlioz's *Romeo and Juliet* (1882) and Wagner's *Parsifal* (1886). Early performances were given at the Metropolitan Opera House and Steinway Hall. In 1888 Andrew Carnegie became president of the society, a position he retained for thirty years, and in 1891 he built it a new home, Carnegie Hall. Many famous conductors have led the Oratorio Society, including Tchaikovsky, Leonard Bernstein, and Aaron Copland.

James Bradley

O'Reilly, Leonora (*b* New York City, 16 Feb 1870; *d* New York City, 3 April 1927). Labor activist. Her father died shortly after her birth and she was brought up by her mother, a garment worker who introduced her to radical politics. Active at an early age, in 1886 she organized the Working Women's Society, both a trade union and a mutual aid society. The organization greatly impressed the philanthropist Josephine Shaw Lowell, who drew O'Reilly into social reform circles, where she won the admiration of influential reformers like Lillian Wald of the Henry Street Settlement and Felix Adler of the Ethical Culture Society. In 1897 O'Reilly organized the first women's local of the United Garment Workers of America and an experimental garment workers' cooperative. She helped to form the New York Women's Trade Union League in 1903 and remained an active member until 1915, attracting thousands to unionism with her moving speeches. She was also an impassioned antiwar activist and a founder of the National Association for the Advancement of Colored People (NAACP), formed the industrial division of the state's Woman Suffrage Party, and worked to the end of her life for the independence of Ireland.

Annelise Orleck

organized crime. The business of crime in New York City is defined by three eras. From the mid nineteenth century to the early twentieth its rackets were locally oriented and conducted with the approval of political organizations. With the onset of Prohibition in the 1920s organized-crime figures in the city became pivotal in national organizations, so powerful that they influenced city government. After the 1960s a combination of law enforcement initiatives, the aging and weakening of old criminal families, and the emergence of new criminal combinations forced a restructuring of organized crime in the city.

During the first of these three stages the distinction between ward leader and gang leader sometimes blurred. Street gangs controlled the ballot box in behalf of politicians, who in return gave protection to saloons, brothels, and gambling houses. Gambling was the major source of revenue for these combines, which provided a base for more than a generation of politicians. Among the best-known was John Morrissey, a prizefighter and Democratic politician who opposed efforts by the Anti-Gambling Society to raid gambling houses in 1867. Leaders of Tammany Hall, police officers, and gamblers cooperated, and the chain of influence reached from the neighborhoods, where gamblers made deals with leaders of assembly districts, to the county party organizations, to the highest levels of municipal government. Morrissey amassed wealth and power through his scheming, as later did others such as Big Tim Sullivan, a district leader from the Bowery. But their machinations were highly local, rooted in backroom politics and the give and take of the city streets, and had little impact beyond New York City and its environs.

The first generation of Jewish and Italian criminals about the turn of the century did little to alter the localism of organized crime. Like their predecessors they formed gangs: the Five Points Gang of Paul Kelly, mostly Italian, included such criminals as Al Capone, Lucky Luciano, Frankie Yale, and Johnny Torrio; a rival group, the Eastmans, was controlled by the Jewish gang leader Monk Eastman. Both gangs enjoyed connections to Democratic organizations. Shadowy "black hand" gangs run by Italians were in charge of extortion rackets, but they confined their activities to Italian neighborhoods and in retrospect it seems likely that their power and cohesion were exaggerated. In the early twentieth century a number of widely publicized murders linked to organized crime helped to give the city a reputation as a source of evil, corruption, and intrigue. The murder in 1909 of the police lieutenant Joseph Petrosino while he was pursuing an investigation in Palermo, Sicily, was suspected by some of being part of an international conspiracy, and the suspicions were probably correct. In a case of official corruption a few years later the police lieutenant Charles Becker and four accomplices were executed for the killing in 1912 of the gambler Herman Rosenthal. Becker's guilt was later called into question, but not before his case had advanced the career of Charles Whitman, the Republican district attorney who prosecuted Becker and was later elected governor.

Italian gangs in the early 1920s were parochial and somewhat inflexible. Old gang leaders such as Giuseppe "Joe the Boss" Masseria recruited members according to what their place of origin was in Sicily and the rest of Italy. They disdained cooperation with those who were not Italian but were not unwilling to wage gang wars against those who were: in the late 1920s, for example, Masseria fought for control of the rackets against Salvatore Maranzano in what was known as the Castellammarese war.

With the onset of Prohibition organized crime became more sophisticated in the 1920s. Those who controlled the rackets in the city were now national figures in charge of a national operation, and neighborhood hoodlums became businessmen who put aside their ethnic and regional differences and agreed to divide responsibilities and territories rather than do battle with each other. Within the Mafia there developed a peculiarly American institution known as the "family." In most American cities one Mafia family was in control; in New York City there were five families, known by the surnames of their leaders — Genovese, Bonanno, Gambino, Profaci, and Lucchese. The new generation of organized-crime leaders included Lucky Luciano, Meyer Lansky, Frank Costello, and Joe Adonis, and followed the businesslike example set by the gambler Arnold Rothstein. Luciano took charge of efforts to eliminate the influence of the older generation by ingratiating himself with Masseria and then engineering in 1931 the killing of both Masseria (at a restaurant in Coney Island) and Maranzano. He also cultivated his power in city government, as in 1931 when his gunmen threatened Harry Perry, a district leader from the Lower East Side who subsequently chose not to seek reelection and was replaced by Luciano's preferred candidate, Albert Marinelli.

The actions of Luciano and his organization of enforcers, known in the tabloid newspapers as Murder Incorporated, became a source of fascination and speculation among the press, in works of fiction and films, on radio, and later on television. Perhaps for this reason they have sometimes been exaggerated: the killing of older organized-crime leaders was not indiscriminate, and the new national crime syndicate did not run as smoothly as a legitimate business. Nevertheless Luciano and his accomplices did give to organized crime in New York City a stability and structure that it had lacked, and helped to make it a formidable force in American life.

Mayor Fiorello H. La Guardia inveighed against organized crime during the 1930s and campaigned successfully to ban Costello's slot machines. At the same time Thomas E. Dewey launched his own political career by winning convictions of Luciano on charges of prostitution in 1936 and of the Democratic district leader James J. Hines on charges of protecting the numbers racket of Dutch Schultz. Although Luciano managed to retain some of his power when he went to prison in 1936, his enforced absence made possible a grander role for Costello, who like others was compelled by the repeal of Prohibition in 1933 and the consequent end of the vast bootlegging business to seek different sources of profit. Gambling, loan-sharking, labor racketeering, and prostitution were reinvigorated, most organized-crime leaders were involved in the sale of illegal drugs (contrary to widespread belief), and Lansky used his financial and organizational abilities to channel illegitimate gains into legitimate businesses such as casinos and resorts. Criminals infiltrated the garment industry, vegetable markets, and other businesses that were disorganized and decentralized. Often they entered a business by force; at other times they were invited by labor or management.

In the 1940s organized-crime leaders used their newly gained wealth to colonize Tammany Hall. Whereas earlier the racketeers had flourished with the sufferance of political leaders, they were now political leaders themselves. Adonis wielded political influence in Brooklyn while controlling the drug trade and the docks. Costello established even more extensive connections in government, and used the money he made in gambling and from a slot machine network in Louisiana to function as a kind of political patron. He gained a large measure of control over a Tammany Hall weakened by La Guardia's reform mayoralty and appears to have rigged some judicial appointments. During the 1950s Costello lost power in the rackets to Vito Genovese, who had fled the United States for Italy to avoid a murder charge but returned after the Second World War. Genovese failed in an attempt on Costello's life but succeeded in one against Costello's ally Albert Anastasia in the Park Sheraton Hotel, and Costello was eventually persuaded to retire. Genovese was soon undone by internal struggles with rivals: Costello, Lansky, and Luciano are widely believed to have arranged the arrest on a federal drug charge that led to his imprisonment in 1959.

The 1950s and early 1960s saw repeated challenges to organized crime in New York City, from within the city and without. Mayor William O'Dwyer, who became well known for prosecuting the members of Murder Incorporated, was forced to resign from office in 1950 because of allegations that he himself had links to organized crime and gamblers. In that year an investigatory committee in Washington led by Senator Estes Kefauver began hearings on organized crime. Costello's testimony before the committee revealed his connections to Tammany Hall and also gave credence to the allegations surrounding O'Dwyer. In the city political reforms weakened the bonds between organized crime and politics. From 1952 district leaders were chosen by direct election, which lessened the chances that the process could be manipulated and freed the office of district leader from its disreputable past. Mayor Robert F. Wagner, a product of the political machine, eventually repudiated his sponsors. By the middle of the decade the long-standing ties between organized crime and the city's political machine had been broken.

Organized crime in New York City was further weakened in the 1960s by the vigorous enforcement efforts of Robert F. Kennedy during his tenure as attorney general of the United States, the extent of information about criminal activities revealed by Joseph Valachi to the U.S. Department of Justice and in testimony before an investigatory committee of the U.S. Senate, and the aging of the organized-crime families, which often fought brutally for control of the rackets. Early in the decade the Profacis prevailed against the Gallos in a violent dispute over the rackets in Brooklyn; later in the decade the Bonannos unsuccessfully waged the so-called banana war in an effort to expand their power.

By the late 1960s Carlo Gambino emerged as the dominant organized-crime leader in the city (he died of natural causes in 1976). Joey Gallo, imprisoned during the struggle with the Profacis, was freed in 1971 and soon became something of a celebrity. He advocated bringing blacks into organized crime to broaden the base and effectiveness of criminal combinations, much as Luciano had once advocated an alliance between Italians and Jews. About the same time Joe Colombo, who had emerged as the head of the Profaci family, organized the Italian–American Civil Rights League to bring pressure to bear against stereotypes of Italians as organized-crime figures. Carmine Galante, who had taken charge of the Bonanno family in the mid 1970s, moved to expand his power at the end of the decade. Colombo was shot and paralyzed at a rally in 1971; Gallo was fatally shot in Little Italy in 1972; and Galante was fatally shot at a restaurant in Brooklyn in 1979.

The means of prosecuting organized crime changed radically after the U.S. Congress passed the Racketeer Influenced and Corrupt Organizations laws, better known as RICO, as part of the Organized Crime Control Act of 1970. The laws severely limited the freedom of action of organized crime: they made it easier for the government to prove criminal conspiracies and to prosecute criminal organizations instead of only individuals; they also imposed heavy penalties on those convicted and enabled prosecutors to seize the assets of criminal enterprises. After the death in 1972 of J. Edgar Hoover, director of the Federal Bureau of Investigation, the bureau no longer focused its energies on the fight against communism and began to work more closely with the Drug Enforcement Agency. Local police also devoted more of their resources to fighting organized crime.

In New York City the federal prosecutor Rudolph W. Giuliani gained renown and political power from a series of highly publicized cases. Organized crime incurred major losses nationwide and especially in New York City, and it also became less glamorous in the city owing to its heavy involvement in the heroin trade, which by the early 1970s had caused a drug-abuse problem of dangerous proportions. Some of the glamour attached to organized crime was restored by Mario Puzo's novel *The Godfather* and the motion pictures that it inspired: organized-crime leaders were no longer depicted only as parasites who preyed on the city but also as exemplars of ethnic pride, old-fashioned men of honor, and businessmen who supplied needed if morally questionable services.

As organized-crime families continued to weaken they came to be governed increasingly by younger and inexperienced criminals. At the same time new rackets and new gangs appeared. Asian gangs based in Chinatown thrived on extortion, racketeering, gambling, and drug dealing. Black and Latin American gangs gained enough power to control drug operations once dominated by the Mafia, which was weakened by the breaking in 1987 of a heroin-smuggling ring known as the "pizza connection" that operated under the cover of pizza parlors. Criminal immigrants from Russia and Cuba transferred their illicit operations to the United States. The five original organized-crime families continued to pursue illegal activities ranging from waterfront rackets to the theft of stock certificates, and to infiltrate legitimate businesses in the meat-packing, garbage disposal, construction, and garment industries. John Gotti, who acquired a growing reputation as a racketeer after the assassination in 1985 of Paul Castellano, leader of the Gambino family, became a symbol of the enduring presence of organized crime in New York City and evaded repeated prosecutions until 1992, when he was convicted on several felony charges and sent to prison. In the mid 1990s organized crime in New York City was in the process of being restructured, but it was not disappearing.

Warren Moscow: *What Have You Done for Me Lately?: The Ins and Outs of New York City Politics* (Englewood Cliffs, N.J.: Prentice Hall, 1967)

Humbert S. Nelli: *The Business of Crime: Italians and Syndicate Crime in the United States* (New York: Oxford University Press, 1976)

Alan A. Block: *East Side, West Side: Organizing Crime in New York, 1930–1950* (New Brunswick, N.J.: Transaction, 1983)

Robert W. Snyder

orphanages. For information on orphanages see CHILD WELFARE.

Orphan Asylum Society. Charitable organization formed in 1806 by a group that included Isabella Graham, her daughter Johanna Bethune, Sarah Hoffman, and Elizabeth Hamilton (widow of Alexander Hamilton). It occupied a small rented house on Raisin Street where six recently orphaned children were given care and instruction. Rapid growth prompted the society to purchase land for a new building on Bank Street in 1807; in the following year the state legislature raised $5000 for its orphanage by lottery. The orphanage moved in 1836 to spacious quarters at Riverside Drive and 73rd Street, where there was room for about two hundred children. In 1899 the society named its first professional superintendent as part of a plan to emphasize higher education. Scholarship support was soon provided by a legacy from Mrs. R. G. Dun, wife of the founder of Dun and Bradstreet. In 1902 the society decided to sell its property in Manhattan to Charles Schwab and buy a site in rural Hastings-on-Hudson in Westchester County.

The Orphan Asylum Society was an innovative institution that was among the first to employ the "cottage system," under which about twenty children of various ages, divided by sex, lived in a cottage under the supervision of house parents. At the age of eleven or twelve each child was indentured to a family, which paid $25 at the outset and an additional $25 to the child when he or she turned eighteen. The program required that each family taking part in it belong to the Protestant church and that the father be employed. In 1929 the society was renamed the Graham School in honor of its founder.

Joanna H. Mathews: *A Short History of the Orphan Asylum Society in the City of New York, Founded 1806* (New York: A. D. F. Randolph, 1893)

Phyllis Barr, Page Putnam Miller, Stephen Weinstein

Osborn, Henry Fairfield (*b* Fairfield, Conn., 8 Aug 1857; *d* Garrison, N.Y., 6 Nov 1935). Biologist. He was appointed in 1891 to a dual position at Columbia University and the AMERICAN MUSEUM OF NATURAL HISTORY, where he established programs in biology and vertebrate paleontology. As president of the museum in 1908–33 he promoted worldwide expeditions and oversaw the construction of massive exhibition halls. Osborn was also president of the New York Zoological Society and took part in opening and administering the Bronx Zoo.

Ronald Rainger

Oscar of the Waldorf. The nickname of the headwaiter Oscar (Michel) Tschirky (*b* Switzerland, 28 Sept 1866; *d* New York City, 6 Nov 1950). He arrived in New York City with his mother on 14 May 1883, and the next day began working as a busboy at the Hoffman House. Over the next four years he advanced to the rank of waiter in its private dining room, and he then worked as a waiter at Delmonico's. In 1893 he became the headwaiter at the Waldorf Hotel (which had recently opened) and eventually he was the most famous one in New York City. He originated the

Waldorf salad and many other recipes, which he published in a collection of nearly a thousand pages called *The Cook Book, by "Oscar" of the Waldorf* (1896). In 1943 he took an advisory position with the hotel.

Karl Schriftgiesser: *Oscar of the Waldorf* (New York: E. P. Dutton, 1943)

Allen J. Share

O'Sullivan, John Louis (*b* Harbor of Gibraltar, November 1813; *d* New York City, 24 Feb 1895). Writer and diplomat. He earned degrees from Columbia University in 1831 and 1834, practiced law, and in 1837 launched the *Democratic Review*, a literary journal in which he coined the term "manifest destiny." He was elected to the state legislature and with Samuel J. Tilden launched the *New York Morning News*, which he edited from 1844 to 1846, and was a regent of New York State University until 1854. O'Sullivan was a diplomat in Portugal until 1879, when he returned to the city.

Sheldon Howard Harris: "The Public Career of John Louis O'Sullivan" (diss., Columbia University, 1958)

James E. Mooney

Oswald, Lee Harvey (*b* New Orleans, 18 Oct 1939; *d* Dallas, 24 Nov 1963). Assassin. He lived in New York City for seventeen months about a decade before his presumed role in the assassination of President John F. Kennedy. In August 1952 he moved to the city with his mother, the two living successively with his half-brother at 325 East 92nd Street in Manhattan, in a basement apartment at 1455 Sheridan Avenue in the Bronx, and at 825 East 179th Street in the Bronx (from January 1953). During this period he attended Trinity Evangelical Lutheran School (to 26 September 1952), Public School 117 (from 30 September 1952 to 16 January 1953), and Public School 44 (from 23 March 1953), but because of his perpetual truancy he was remanded to Youth House for psychiatric evaluation on 16 April 1953. His problems at school continued after he enrolled at Public School 44 on 24 September. Oswald and his mother left New York City for New Orleans in early January 1954.

OTB. See Off-track betting.

Ott, Mel(vin Thomas) (*b* Gretna, La., 2 March 1909; *d* New Orleans, 21 Nov 1958). Baseball player. A popular outfielder for the New York Giants from 1926 to 1947, he was one of the leading power hitters in the National League, leading the league in home runs six times and compiling a lifetime batting average of .304. He became known for a distinctive batting style that involved raising the front leg before swinging. Ott retired with 511 career home runs, a league record at the time. From 1942 to 1948 he managed the Giants. He was inducted into the Baseball Hall of Fame in 1951.

Milton J. Shapiro: *The Mel Ott Story* (New York: Messner, 1959)
John Thorn and Pete Palmer: *Total Baseball* (New York: Warner, 1989)

Jeffrey Scheuer

Ottley, Roi (*b* New York City, 2 Aug 1906; *d* 1 Oct 1960). Writer and broadcaster. Born to immigrants from the British West Indies, he became a reporter for the *Amsterdam News* during the Depression. After being discharged in 1935 by one of the new owners of the newspaper, C. B. Powell, he worked for the Federal Writers Project while conducting research for his book *New World a-Coming* (1943), which called for full racial equality. He was the host of a radio program and during the Second World War was one of the first black writers to work for the established press. Ottley's published writings include *Black Odyssey* (1948), *No Green Pastures* (1951), *The Lonely Warrior* (1955), and (with William J. Weatherby) *The Negro in New York: An Informal Social History* (1967).

Mario A. Charles

Our Lady of Lebanon Maronite Cathedral. Cathedral at the intersection of Remsen and Henry streets in Brooklyn. Designed in a Romanesque Revival style by Richard Upjohn, it was built between 1844 and 1846 and opened as the Church of the Pilgrims (Congregational). When the congregation merged with that of the Plymouth Church the Tiffany windows of the original building were removed in 1934 to Hillis Hall behind the Plymouth Church of the Pilgrims. The doors at the western and southern portals, which depict Norman churches, were salvaged from the oceanliner *Normandie*, which caught fire in 1942. The church took its current name in June 1977. The building is one of the oldest of its style in the country.

Thomas E. Bird

Our Lady of Mercy Medical Center. General-care hospital opened by the Misericordia Sisters of Montreal in 1887. It was originally a home for unwed mothers known as the New York Mothers' Home of the Sisters of Misericordia. The facility spent its first year on Staten Island before moving in 1888 to 106 West 123rd Street in Manhattan and in 1889 to East 86th Street. It expanded to a general-care hospital known as Misericordia Hospital by the turn of the century. In 1958 the hospital moved to its present location on East 233rd Street in the Bronx; in 1976 the Archdiocese of New York assumed control of the hospital, which took its current name in 1984. The center is a major secondary health-care facility with thirteen departments, forty-five outpatient clinics, an ambulatory surgery center, an acute-care psychiatric unit, and an emergency room. The Misericordia Sisters continue to sponsor Rosalie Hall, a residential program for unwed mothers.

Bernadette McCauley

Richard Fenton Outcault, The Yellow Kid

Outcault, R(ichard) F(elton) (*b* Flushing [now in Queens], 14 Jan 1863; *d* Lancaster, Ohio, 5 Sept 1928). Cartoonist. He is regarded as having created the first comic strip: a series of cartoons about immigrants in New York City that appeared in the *New York World* as "Hogan's Alley" from the mid 1880s to 1896. Retitled "The Yellow Kid" after its central character, the strip was published from 1896 to 1898 in a color supplement to the *New York Journal* called *American Humorist.* He also drew the comic strip "Buster Brown" (*New York Herald* 1902–5, *New York Journal* 1906–20); Buster Brown, his friend Mary Jane, and his bulldog Tige were among the first comic strip characters used to merchandise products. Outcault lived in Flushing.
See also Cartooning.

Patricia A. Perito

outdoor advertising. Billboards promoted circuses and theaters as early as the 1840s, when P. T. Barnum used huge banners and woodcuts to advertise his American Museum at Broadway and Ann Street. In the antebellum period the first sandwichmen, or "walking billboards," paraded on busy thoroughfares such as Broadway, often advertising entertainments or patent medicines. Gaslight signs, favored especially by entertainment halls, taverns, and tobacco shops, became widely used by the end of the Civil War. The development of roads, streetcars, and elevated lines spurred larger and more numerous billboards, often in color. Posters covered the pillars of the elevated trains, and fences lining streetcar routes were covered with bills promoting such products as Hood's sasparilla, Quaker oats, Dutch cleanser, Sapolio soap, St. Jacob's oil, Bull Durham tobacco, and five-cent cigars. The largest early outdoor advertising firms in New York City were those of Kissam and Allen (1872–78), Bradbury and

Houghtaling (1870–83), and O. J. Gude of Brooklyn. Until the business began to regulate itself in the late nineteenth century, bill stickers would post their advertisements atop those of competitors.

When chromolithography was developed in the 1880s advertisements grew larger and more colorful. The first lithograph for a billboard was an illustration for a theatrical production of *Uncle Tom's Cabin*, depicting Eliza fleeing the bloodhounds across the ice floes. O. J. Gude put up the first electric sign in 1891 on a rooftop in Madison Square, composed of 1457 lamps that read "Manhattan Beach Swept by Breezes." By 1910 posters covering more than two hundred square feet (nineteen square meters) were common, and often posted in multiple copies. Riverside Drive and Central Park, where carriages paraded on Sundays, were bordered with huge signs, and posters were affixed to fences surrounding construction sites. Reformers criticized these large displays as an eyesore and complained that they provided a hiding place for "immoral acts." In response outdoor advertisers erected neater, permanent signboard stands of metal and often landscaped the area around them.

During the Progressive era the Municipal Art Society and adherents of the "city beautiful" movement raised a great outcry against outdoor advertising. Raymond Fosdick, the commissioner of accounts for New York City, led a commission that investigated the "billboard nuisance" in 1912. By 1918 the city had passed an ordinance regulating billboards, allowing them only outside residential and scenic areas and prohibiting the posting of small bills by individuals; far from ruining the billboard business, this helped it by eliminating a source of informal competition. Neon signs were popular by the 1920s, and Times Square became well known as a center of outdoor advertising, where an advertisement for Wrigley's Spearmint chewing gum that depicted a "spearman" launching his weapon took up more than two blocks along Broadway. In the 1930s movie theaters in midtown erected enormous lighted signs to promote their attractions. The spot beneath the Budweiser sign, which showed a team of Clydesdale horses hauling a great wagon of barrels, was a favorite meeting place in Times Square, as was that beneath the Pepsi-Cola waterfall atop the Bond Building. During both world wars giant outdoor displays urged the public to buy war bonds.

Theaters and movie houses in the 1950s continued to commission both lighted displays and giant billboards, which often depicted shapely, reclining actresses and provoked some public indignation. Outdoor advertising became the subject of several films: *It Should Happen to You* (1953), directed by George Cukor, tells the story of an actress who rents a billboard on Columbus Circle to promote herself, and the signs of Times Square are featured in William Klein's *Broadway by Light* (1958). Audacious cut-out figures and moving designs appeared on billboards during the 1960s, and in 1966 the Sunkist "smellacular" sign emitted a citrus aroma over the West Side Highway. In the following decades Times Square increasingly became the site of advertisements for the products of Japanese electronics firms.

The large, bright outdoor advertising of Times Square was to be protected under a redevelopment plan under way in the early 1990s, and a billboard museum was planned for one of the skyscrapers to be built.

Frank Presbrey: *The History and Development of Advertising* (Garden City, N.Y.: Doubleday, Doran, 1929)

W. G. Rogers and Mildred Weston: *Carnival Crossroads: The Story of Times Square* (Garden City, N.Y.: Doubleday, 1960)

Kathleen Hulser

Outerbridge Crossing. Steel cantilevered bridge spanning the Arthur Kill between southwestern Staten Island and Perth Amboy, New Jersey. It was designed by Alexander Waddell and opened to traffic on 29 June 1928 at the same time as the smaller Goethals Bridge (built upstream and also designed by Waddell). The two bridges were the first crossings for motor vehicles between Staten Island and the mainland. The bridge has a span of 750 feet (229 meters), clears Arthur Kill by 135 feet (41.1 meters), and has a long-graded viaduct, making the total length of the bridge 10,140 feet (3093 meters). Outerbridge Crossing is named for Eugenius Outerbridge, the first chairman of the Port of New York Authority and a resident of Staten Island.

Rebecca Read Shanor

Overseas Press Club of America. Club based in New York City for both foreign correspondents and American reporters. Its formation was first suggested by Charles Ferlin, a longtime reporter for the Associated Press and the United Press, at a meeting on 2 April 1939 at the Algonquin Hotel, where the club first set up offices. The club holds banquets and meetings, gives annual awards for outstanding reporting; it has also published several volumes of reporting and recollections by its members, including *The Inside Story* (1940). In 1990 it had more than a thousand members. The offices are at 3 West 51st Street.

H. L. Stevenson: "OPC at 50: Years of Crisis — and Good Fun," *Dateline*, 11 May 1989, pp. 8–11

Michael Green

Ovington, Mary White (*b* Brooklyn, 11 April 1865; *d* Newton Highlands, Mass., 15 July 1951). Writer, social worker, and civil rights activist. After becoming the registrar at the Pratt Institute in 1893 and the head social worker at the Greenpoint Settlement in 1895, she helped to form the National Association for the Advancement of Colored People (NAACP) in 1909, of which she was later an interim executive secretary, vice-president, treasurer, and for thirteen years chairman of the board. Her book *Half a Man: The Status of the Negro in New York* (1911) examined racial discrimination encountered by blacks seeking employment or housing. She also wrote a novel, children's books, and *The Walls Came Tumbling Down* (1947), both a memoir and a history of the NAACP.

Daniel W. Cryer: "Mary White Ovington and the Rise of the NAACP" (diss., University of Minnesota, 1977)

R. L. Harris, Jr.

Oxford University Press. University press in England, the American branch of which was formed in 1896 at 91 5th Avenue to facilitate the marketing and sale of Oxford Bibles in the United States. In the following year the branch took over from Macmillan the American marketing of all books published by its parent. The American office underwent rapid growth between 1928 and 1936, eventually becoming one of the leading university presses in the United States. Its primary emphasis is on scholarly and reference books, bibles, and college and medical textbooks. In the early 1990s it announced plans to move its offices from 200 Madison Avenue to the former B. Altman building.

Eileen K. Cheng

oyster bars. From the 1830s to the 1870s oyster bars enjoyed great popularity in New York City, which was surrounded by waters containing enormously rich oyster beds. The English visitor Charles McKay noted the marked appreciation of New Yorkers for this "gift of oysters." At the entrance to oyster bars in vaults and cellars throughout the city was a distinctive "balloon" of red and white muslin, stretched over a wire frame and illuminated by a candle when the bar was open. In the 1840s a large number of bars in Canal Street offered the "Canal Street Plan," which allowed patrons to consume as many oysters as they wished for six cents; other oyster bars such as Thomas Downing's on Broad Street and Florence's on Broadway were considerably more expensive. Most New Yorkers enjoyed their oysters raw and their tables furnished with pepper, lemons, mustard, and oil and vinegar, though oysters were also popular fried, stewed, roasted, and scalloped; lager beer was favored by most customers, champagne by the wealthy. By the 1850s about $6 million worth of oysters were consumed annually by New Yorkers. The merits of different varieties of oyster were heatedly debated: many preferred Saddle Rock oysters (some almost as large as a hand), others the oysters of Cold Spring, Cow Bay, and Oyster Bay. Most of the established beds off Long Island and New Jersey were completely dredged by the 1870s, and newly discovered beds were quickly depleted. Most

Oyster vendor, ca *1890*

oysters consumed in the 1880s were from the Chesapeake Bay, but these were more expensive than the local variety and devotees found them to be of inferior quality. Although the oyster eventually lost its prominent place in the cuisine of the city, the Grand Central Oyster Bar at Grand Central Terminal remained world-renowned into the 1990s.

Charles Mackay: *Life and Liberty in America* (New York: Harper and Brothers, 1859)

Joan Reardon: *Oysters: A Culinary Celebration* (Orleans, Mass.: Parnassus Imprints, 1984)

Richard Stott

Ozone Park. Neighborhood in southwestern Queens, bounded to the north by Atlantic Avenue, to the east by 104th Street, to the south by Liberty Avenue, and to the west by 96th Street. It was developed by the music publisher Benjamin W. Hitchcock and Charles C. Dunton after railroad service was extended to the area in 1880 by the New York, Woodhaven and Rockaway Railroad, which provided a direct route to Brooklyn and Rockaway Beach. Hitchcock and Dunton filed a survey map in July 1882, and their land was divided into 316 lots, each measuring twenty-five by one hundred feet (eight by thirty meters). In 1883–84 they bought more land, enlarging Ozone Park to 630 lots that were sold at auction; streets and sidewalks were laid out and shade trees planted. A post office opened in 1889 when the number of residents reached the required level of six hundred. The population reached eleven hundred by 1900 and three thousand by 1910, and consisted mostly of young families from Brooklyn. Development was spurred by the need to house workers at the tinware plant of Lalance and Grosjean in Woodhaven.

The success of Ozone Park led to the development in 1896 of Ozone Park Heights, which extended as far south as Rockaway Boulevard, and the formation of the Ozone Park Home Company. The popularity of the area for housing increased after the Brooklyn Rapid Transit extended the Fulton Street elevated line along Liberty Avenue to Lefferts Boulevard (119th Street) in September 1915, enabling residents to commute to work in Manhattan for only five cents. The area became entirely built up as the demand for housing continued to rise during the 1920s; the last open spaces were used for blocks of row houses and attached houses. In April 1956 the Independent subway was connected at Grant Avenue to the Fulton Street elevated line, which became obsolete. There were 132,353 residents in Ozone Park, South Ozone Park, and Richmond Hill South in 1957. Aqueduct Racetrack at Rockaway Boulevard and Southern Parkway, the last remaining venue for horse racing in New York City, opened in 1894 and was extensively renovated in 1959. In the mid 1990s Ozone Park was a modest, middle-class community of one- and two-family frame houses. Most inhabitants were of German, Irish, Italian, and eastern European ancestry, and there was also a growing number of blacks and immigrants from the Caribbean and Latin America.

Vincent Seyfried

P

Pace University. University incorporated as Pace College in 1947. Its forerunner was a course developed by Homer St. Clair Pace to tutor candidates for state certifying examinations for public accountants. With his brother Charles Ashford Pace he opened a school of accountancy in 1906 at the New York Tribune Building in lower Manhattan. The two also offered the Pace Standardized Course in Accounting at YMCAs in Brooklyn, Manhattan, and New Jersey. Enrollment in the metropolitan area exceeded three hundred by 1909 and four thousand by 1919, and in 1927 the school moved from the Hudson Terminal Building on Church Street to the new Transportation Building on Broadway. Pace Institute was incorporated in 1935 as a nonprofit institution of higher education. In 1942 it received its permanent charter and the administration was taken over by Homer Pace's sons Robert Scott Pace, who became president, and C. Richard Pace, who became secretary. When the institute became Pace College Edward J. Mortola was appointed an assistant dean. The college bought the New York Times Building on Park Row in 1951; in 1953 it moved into its new quarters and was authorized to grant BA degrees. It offered the MBA from 1958 and in 1961 inaugurated Mortola as its third president. During his administration the school opened a campus in Pleasantville, New York (1962), and schools of arts and sciences, education, and nursing (1966), introduced graduate programs in education (1969), completed the Pace Plaza building in lower Manhattan (1970), attained university status (1973), effected a merger with the Colleges of White Plains (1975), opened a law school and a midtown campus (1976), acquired the former campus of Briarcliff College (1977), and began a doctoral program in school and community psychology (1979) and a school of computer science and information systems (1983). On being named chancellor in 1984 Mortola was succeeded by William B. Sharwell, who oversaw the introduction of a master's program in publishing (1985) and new programs in information systems (1986), as well as the opening of the Lubin Graduate Center in White Plains, New York (1987). In 1990 Patricia O'Donnell Ewers was named president of the university.

Marilyn E. Weigold

Packer Collegiate Institute. Private, coeducational elementary and secondary school opened in 1854 as the Brooklyn Female Academy. It is the oldest independent school in Brooklyn and the fifth-oldest in New York City. The college division of the school in 1919 became the first junior college to be approved by the Regents of the State of New York. In 1972 the school became coeducational and the junior college was discontinued. Packer is known for its magnificent neo-Gothic chapel and for its alumni garden, awarded the National Nurserymen's Prize for best urban school garden in 1980.

Richard Schwartz

Paderewski, Jan Ignace (*b* Kuryłowka, Podolia, 12 Nov 1860; *d* New York City, 29 June 1941). Pianist, composer, and statesman. The most popular pianist in the world during his lifetime, he made many concert tours to New York City and lived there on several occasions. He died in the city shortly after returning to the United States to plead the case for Poland when the nation was overrun by the German army in the early days of the Second World War.

Kenneth T. Jackson

Paerdegat Basin. A channel in Brooklyn one and a quarter miles (two kilometers) long that empties into Jamaica Bay, and by extension the surrounding neighborhood, which is bordered by Canarsie, Flatlands, and Bergen Beach. After the city failed to transform Jamaica Bay into a major port in the 1920s the area remained undeveloped until the 1960s. In 1972 local residents defeated a proposal to construct a city-sponsored complex of garden apartments for nearly four thousand residents. Paerdegat Basin now consists of one- and two-family suburban houses.

Stephen Weinstein

Page, Geraldine (*b* Kirksville, Mo., 22 Nov 1924; *d* New York City, 13 June 1987). Actress. The daughter of middle-class parents, she attended the Goodman Theater Dramatic School in Chicago. In 1945 she moved to New York City and made her début in a production of *Seven Mirrors* by the Blackfriars Guild. She studied voice with Alice Hermes and acting with Uta Hagen at the Berghof Studios and the Theater Wing School. In 1952 she became well known for her performance in Tennessee Williams's *Summer and Smoke* at the Sheridan Square Theater in Greenwich Village. In the following year she played the role of Lily Barton in Vina Delmar's *Midsummer* at the Vanderbilt Theater, for which she won the Theater World Award, the Donaldson Award, and the Drama Critics Award; after this she seldom left the city or the public eye. She made her first motion picture, *Hondo* (with John Wayne), in 1954. During the 1960s she worked with the Actors Studio in the city and played many roles on Broadway in productions directed by Lee Strasberg. With her second husband, the actor Rip Torn, she formed the Sanctuary Theater Company. Known for the enthusiasm she brought to her roles, she performed in dozens of plays, films, and television productions and won two Emmys, as well as an Academy Award for her performance in *A Trip to Bountiful* in 1985. At the end of her life she lived at 435 West 22nd Street and appeared on Broadway as Madame Arcate in Noël Coward's *Blithe Spirit.*

Chad Ludington

Paine, Thomas (*b* Thetford, England, 29 Jan 1737; *d* New York City, 8 June 1809). Political theorist and writer. After a series of false starts as a corset maker, excise official, and pamphleteer, he left England in 1774 and settled in Philadelphia. He was drawn into political controversy and became a brilliant proponent for American independence. His enormously popular pamphlet *Common Sense* (1776) laid out the patriot case and galvanized public opinion. Regarded as a leading spokesman for democracy well into the 1790s, he ran afoul of respectable opinion for his activities in connection with the French Revolution and especially after publishing *The Age of Reason* (1795), a deist critique of Christianity. This and other writings were condemned in the United States as irrelevant to American political concerns by some, and as blasphemy by others. After returning to the United States in 1803 he settled at his farm in New Rochelle, New York, a gift from the state assembly after the American Revolution. He was drawn back to New York City repeatedly to spend time with sympathetic freethinkers and Republicans, and also to escape his pious, unfriendly neighbors. In 1804 he lived at 16 Gold Street before moving to 36 Cedar Street. He settled permanently in the city in 1806, moving successively from 85 Church Street to 63 Partition Street (now West Fulton Street) in 1807 and to 309 Bleecker Street in 1808. During the following year he lost many friends in quarrels and suffered bouts of apoplexy that left him an invalid; he also wrote prolifically, replying to personal attacks, lambasting the Federalists, and encouraging his friends and supporters. (His fiery example inspired several young admirers who became leading radical spokesmen during the 1820s and 1830s.) Lonely and ill, in May 1809 he begged a long-time friend from his days in France, Marguerite Bonneville, to take him into her household. She grudgingly agreed and rented a house for him at 59 Grove Street adjoining her own.

Sean Wilentz

Paine Webber. Firm of securities brokers, formed in 1942 as Paine, Webber, Jackson and Curtis by the merger of Jackson and Curtis (1879) and Paine, Webber and Company (1880). Originally based in Boston, the firm moved its headquarters to New York City in 1963. It became a publicly owned corporation in 1972 and took its current name in 1974. Although best known for its nationwide network of retail brokerage offices, the firm also provides institutional investment banking services. Shares in Paine Webber are traded on the New York Stock Exchange. The headquarters are at 1285 6th Avenue in Manhattan.

Paine, Webber and Company, 1880–1930: A National Institution (Boston: Paine, Webber, 1930)

Owen D. Gutfreund

painting. During the eighteenth century in New York City several artists made their living painting portraits of wealthy residents. The most successful of these were the members of the Duyckinck family, especially Gerardus Duyckinck II (1723–97), who was skilled at varnishing, Japanning, gilding, silvering, and glazing. Several painters trained in Europe visited the city, including John Smibert, who had settled in Boston, and John Watson, from Perth Amboy, New Jersey. The most cosmopolitan artist of the period was John Wollaston, who was born in London and worked in New York City from 1749 to about 1752, when he moved to Maryland. The English portraitist Lawrence Kilburn (active until about 1775) was also prominent. Thomas McIlworth, born in the colonies, probably learned the trade from Wollaston; some fifteen of his portraits executed between 1757 and 1762 are recorded. Others born in New York City were John Mare (*b* ?1739; *d* 1795/1802), who learned painting from his brother-in-law William Williams of Philadelphia, and Abraham Delanoy, who studied portraiture with Benjamin West in London; among Delanoy's well-known sitters were members of the Livingston, Beekman, and Stuyvesant families. Artists who worked briefly in the city included John Durand (*fl* 1766–82), Matthew Pratt, and Gilbert Stuart and John Singleton Copley of Boston. The portraiture of the time was not as sophisticated as the work of West, Joshua Reynolds, and Thomas Gainsborough, but it was nevertheless as strong as that of any major provincial city in England.

In the early years of the republic portraiture continued to provide the main source of income for painters such as Samuel Lovett Waldo and his student William Jewett, who formed a portraiture business together. By the second decade of the nineteenth century many painters also pursued other interests. Robert Fulton (1765–1815) and Samuel F. B. Morse both abandoned active careers as portraitists to become engineers, and William Dunlap had been a playwright, worked as the librarian of the American Academy of the Fine Arts, and later helped to found its rival, the National Academy of Design. His *History of the Rise and Progress of the Arts of Design in the United States* (1834) set the standard for critical writing about art in the United States. John Trumbull, who aspired to develop the genre of American history painting, had a studio in New York City (1804–8, 1816–35) and was the president of the American Academy of Fine Arts. After years of living in France John Vanderlyn settled in New York City in 1815 and also became a portraitist. He attempted unsuccessfully to tour the country with his masterwork *Ariadne* (1812, Pennsylvania Academy of the Fine Arts), the first major painting of a nude in America, and to promote his panorama of Versailles (Metropolitan Museum of Art), which he installed in a specially built rotunda in City Hall Park in 1818. Because of the invention of the daguerreotype in 1839 the more expensive oil portraits were less in demand, although Charles Loring Elliott and Daniel Huntington continued to fill major commissions.

Views of the city achieved popularity in the early years of the republic with both residents and visitors and were frequently commissioned by publishers. William Guy Wall (*b* Ireland, 1792; *d* ?1864) painted scenes for *Hudson River Portfolio* (1820–28), and Nicolino Calyo, who trained in Naples and moved to New York City in 1835, became known for *Street Cries* (Museum of the City of New York) and his depictions of the Great Fire of 1835 (New-York Historical Society). Francis Guy (*b* Burton-in-Kendal, England, 1760; *d* Brooklyn, 1820), although he spent much of his career in Baltimore painting country estates, also painted *Winter Scene in Brooklyn* (*ca* 1817–20, Brooklyn Museum) and a view of Wall Street.

A rising élite of merchants, bankers, and railroad directors such as Luman Reed, Jonathan Sturges, Philip Hone, and Marshall O. Roberts gradually became interested in landscape, genre, and idealized figurative painting in the European tradition. These new cultural patrons encouraged and bought the work of the artists of the Hudson River School, including Thomas Cole, Asher B. Durand, John Frederick Kensett, and later Jasper F. Cropsey (1823–1900), Sanford Robinson Gifford (1823–80), Albert Bierstadt (1830–1902), Thomas Worthington Whittredge (1820–1910), and Frederic E. Church. They also favored such historical painters and idealized figurative painters as Henry Peters Gray (1819–77), Daniel Huntington, Thomas P. Rossiter (1818–71), and Emanuel Leutze (1816–68), whose *Washington Crossing the Delaware* (1850–52, Metropolitan Museum of Art) became a rallying point for unionist sentiment. Patrons became acquainted with artists through several clubs in the city, notably the Century Association, and with literary figures such as the poet and journalist William Cullen Bryant they promoted American art through organizations such as the American Art-Union.

Although landscape painting dominated in terms of numbers at the annual exhibitions of the National Academy of Design, genre paintings appealed to art writers and journalists at mid century and during the two decades following the Civil War. The outstanding members of the first generation of genre painters were the banker and artist Francis Edmonds (1806–63), William Sidney Mount, Henry Inman, James H. Cafferty (1819–96), Arthur Fitzwilliam Tait (1819–1905), who often drew for Currier and Ives, and the eccentric John Quidor (1801–81), who painted scenes from the Knickerbocker stories of Washington Irving. Two artists from Ohio also became successful in New York City: William Holbrook Beard (1824–1900) specialized in humorous depictions of anthropomorphized animals such as *Bulls and Bears of Wall Street* (New-York Historical Society), and Lilly Martin Spencer (1822–1902) painted sentimental pictures of domestic subjects that were distributed as lithographs through the print publisher William Schaus. Many of the genre artists in New York City who achieved prominence during the 1840s studied in such European centers of art as London, Düsseldorf, and Paris, where the French painter Thomas Couture found particular favor with the Americans. John George Brown (1831–1913), Thomas Hicks (1823–90), John Whetten Ehninger (1827–89), and Eastman Johnson, the most celebrated genre painter of the 1860s, combined European techniques with American subjects to produce genre scenes praised for their faithfulness to contemporary life.

At the onset of the Civil War the artists Sanford Gifford and Jervis McEntee enlisted in the Union Army. Johnson and Edwin Forbes followed the troops—Johnson to find subjects for his genre scenes and Forbes as a staff artist for *Frank Leslie's Illustrated Newspaper*. Artists and patrons together organized the art exhibition of the Metropolitan Fair (1864) to raise funds for the U.S. Sanitary Commission. The artist most closely associated with war scenes was Winslow Homer, whose sketches were reproduced in *Harper's Weekly*; his *Prisoners from the Front* (1866, Metropolitan Museum of Art) established him as an important painter and was exhibited in 1867 in the American section of the Exposition Universelle in Paris.

The moralizing genre painting and the detailed nativist landscape painting of the Hudson River School drew few new adherents after the Civil War. Although Homer continued to paint subject pictures in the 1870s and 1880s, he deemphasized their narrative elements. At the same time younger American painters flocked to Paris and Munich to learn cosmopolitan European styles and new attitudes about art that critics began to call "art for art's sake." The transition to the new art was not smooth. Artists returning from Europe to New York City such as William Merritt Chase and Julian Alden Weir (1852–1919) found that their art was not welcomed by the older generation that controlled the National Academy. In 1877 Augustus Saint-Gaudens, Walter Shirlaw (1838–1909), Wyatt Eaton (1849–96), and Helena de Kay Gilder (1848–1916) formed the Society of American Artists to promote new trends in art. From 1878 the society held annual exhibitions that displayed the work of Chase, Weir, Will Hicok Low (1853–1932), Maria Richards Oakey (1845–1927), George Inness (1825–94), Albert Pinkham Ryder (1847–1917), John La Farge, Homer Dodge Martin (1836–97), Thomas Dewing (1851–1938), and John Singer Sargent (1856–1924). The critics Charles de Kay, Clarence Cook, and Mariana Griswold van Rensselaer praised the young artists, many of whom were eventually elected to the National Academy, which absorbed the Society of American Artists in 1906.

The major tendencies in painting in New York City were exemplified at the end of the nineteenth century by the poetical landscapes of Ryder and Ralph Blakelock and the impressionism of artists such as Chase and Childe Hassam, a founding member of the group Ten American Painters (1898). An academic, neoclassical style of painting still flourished: its exponents included artists such as Edwin Howland Blashfield (1848–1936) and Kenyon Cox (1856–1919), who painted murals for the numerous private mansions and public buildings then being constructed.

Early in the twentieth century a group of artists in New York City led by Robert Henri rejected impressionism, which they saw as too genteel, and insisted on a realism that represented the "spirit" of the people and the new age of urbanization. Influenced by Walt Whitman, the European tradition of graphic realism, and the realist novelists, the painters George Luks, William James Glackens, John Sloan, and Everett Shinn depicted the leisure life of the working classes. To counter the conservatism of the National Academy, Sloan and Henri organized an exhibition at the Macbeth Gallery (1908) that included their own work as well as that of Luks, Glackens, Shinn, Arthur B. Davies (1862–1928), Ernest Lawson (1873–1939), and Maurice Prendergast (1859–1924); the participants in this show became known as The Eight. In 1910 a large exhibition was organized by a group of artists who called themselves Independents and identified with the progressive movement. Sloan joined the Socialist Party and from 1912 to about 1916 worked without pay as the art director of the radical bohemian publication the *Masses*, which was edited by Max Eastman and also featured the work of George Bellows, Stuart Davis, and the other Independents.

The early twentieth century also saw the development of a semi-abstract style that expressed the responses of artists to the increasing mechanization of the modern era. The photographer Alfred Stieglitz was instrumental in bringing European cubism to the attention of many artists in New York City through exhibitions at the Little Galleries of the Photo Secession at 291 5th Avenue (commonly known as "291"), which he directed. He also showed the work of avant-garde photographers and the paintings of John Marin (1870–1953), Abraham Walkowitz (1878–1965), Max Weber, and Georgia O'Keeffe, which conveyed the vitality of the city through expressive depictions of its skyscrapers and people. Other early modern artists included Alfred H. Maurer (1868–1932) and Joseph Stella, who borrowed from Italian futurism in his paintings of Coney Island and the Brooklyn Bridge.

The realists and semi-abstractionists together organized the International Exhibition of Modern Art, known as the Armory Show, which opened at the 69th Regiment Armory in New York in 1913 with more than sixteen hundred European and American works. The critical reception of the show was largely negative: most controversial of all was the work of the French artist Marcel Duchamp, whose *Nude Descending a Staircase* (1912, Philadelphia Museum) was humorously called "Explosion in a Shingle Factory." Duchamp and the American artist Man Ray were part of the Dadaist movement, which grew out of a wartime cultural malaise, emphasized the mental conception of the artwork over its craftsmanship, and was often highly irreverent. Many of the avant-garde artists frequented the weekly salons of Louise and Walter Arensberg, Mabel Dodge, and the Stettheimer sisters — Ettie, Carrie, and Florine, who became a well-known eccentric painter of small-scale group portraits known as conversation pieces.

During the 1920s and 1930s Charles Sheeler, Charles Demuth (1883–1935), and Niles Spencer (1893–1953) depicted industrial America in a modernist style often called precisionism or cubist realism, and characterized by precise lines and reductive forms. O'Keeffe, Marsden Hartley, and Arthur B. Dove (1880–1946), who lived in Connecticut but frequented New York City, developed a style based on natural forms; Stieglitz acted as a dealer for all three. In the years between the two world wars Maurer and Milton Avery (1893–1965) created their own brand of abstracted figuration. About the same time the society figure and sculptor Gertrude Vanderbilt Whitney created many important exhibition spaces, including the Whitney Studio (1914–17), the Whitney Studio Club (1918–28), and the Whitney Studio Galleries (1928–30), which regularly showed the paintings of Sloan, Alexander Brook (1898–1980), and Guy Pène du Bois (1884–1958). In 1930 she founded the Whitney Museum of American Art. Both Sloan and du Bois as well as Kenneth Hayes Miller taught at the Art Students League, the most influential art school of the 1920s and 1930s.

When the Depression began many artists in New York City became part of the political left. A number joined the John Reed Club, which served as a social club and forum for revolutionary artists and advocated an art by and for the working classes. Among those active as organizers or as cartoonists and writers for political journals were the artists Rockwell Kent, Hugo Gellert (1892–1985), William Gropper (1897–1977), Louis Lozowick (1892–1973), Ben Shahn, Bernarda Bryson Shahn (*b* 1903), and Philip Evergood; the most prominent journal was *Art Front*, the monthly magazine of the Artists' Union, edited successively by Davis, Joe Solman (*b* 1909), and Clarence Weinstock (1910–64). Lozowick, Raphael Soyer, and Philip Reisman (1904–92) were among the teachers at the John Reed Club School of Art. Politically oriented artists organized protests when the mural *Man at the Crossroads* by the Mexican painter Diego Rivera was covered over and then destroyed in 1933–34.

After urging artists in the city toward revolutionary struggle in the early 1930s, the Communist Party by 1935 adopted a more conciliatory tone and formed alliances with liberal groups. This change in political direction ended the John Reed clubs and brought about the formation of the American Artists' Congress, which organized a conference in February 1936 that was attended by artists, musicians, and such writers as Lewis Mumford and Meyer Schapiro. Davis became the executive secretary of the congress, a position he held until 1940. Not all figurative artists at the time were overtly political in their painting: Isabel Bishop (1902–88) was more inclined to paint the shop girls of Union Square; Reginald Marsh depicted bathers at Coney Island and derelicts of the Bowery; Thomas Hart Benton, who lived in the city for the first half of the 1930s and influenced artists through his teaching at the Art Students League and his murals at the New School for Social Research, vigorously opposed Marxism and social realism; and Edward Hopper, who was not inclined to join groups, avoided politics altogether.

Harlem during the late 1920s and 1930s was a lively artistic center. Aaron Douglas and Charles Alston (1907–77) painted murals that incorporated African and black American imagery with modernist techniques. Romare Bearden and Jacob Lawrence (*b* 1917) were heirs to the ideals and institutions of the Harlem Renaissance and learned from such dynamic figures as the sculptor Augusta Savage. Both young painters developed their styles by drawing on cubist models, with Lawrence specializing in series paintings of the heroes and heroines of black American history. Other painters associated with Harlem were William H. Johnson, Palmer Hayden, Malvin Gray Johnson, and Norman Lewis (1909–79).

The major patron for artists in New York City in the late 1930s was the federal government. In December 1933 the Public Works of Art Project was formed to provide relief for unemployed artists; in New York City the project was directed by Juliana Force (then head of the Whitney Museum) and lasted until June 1934. A more ambitious program, the

Federal Art Project of the Works Progress Administration (WPA), began in August 1935. In exchange for regular wages painters worked in the easel division, painting works to be hung in government offices, or the mural division, executing projects for public schools, housing projects, and radio stations. The "Section," a program operated by the Department of the Treasury, commissioned murals for post offices, other federal buildings, and airports. These government programs for the most part subsidized figurative painting, but they also employed such abstract artists as Burgoyne Diller (1906–65) and Ilya Bolotowsky (1907–81). The WPA ended in 1943, but some murals commissioned by the Section were not completed until after the end of the Second World War.

In the late 1930s and the 1940s the Museum of Modern Art presented exhibitions of modern European abstract, cubist, and surrealist paintings, yet its curators tended to ignore American abstraction. As a result an organization called American Abstract Artists was formed in 1936; its members, including George L. K. Morris, worked in a hard-edged abstract style like that of Bolotowsky and Diller. A more expressive form of abstraction developed owing in part to the influence of émigré abstract and surrealist artists who lived in New York City in the late 1930s, including Duchamp, John Graham (1881–1961), Max Ernst, Yves Tanguy, Hans Hoffman (1880–1966), and the Chilean artist Matta (Roberto Matta Echaurren). Its adherents, who became known as the New York School, drew on mythology, American Indian art, and their experiences with psychoanalysis to create paintings that focused on self-examination and the work of art itself. Jackson Pollock and Willem de Kooning emerged as the leading exponents of this new style, variously called abstract expressionism and "action painting" (a term coined by the critic Harold Rosenberg). Other members of the New York School included Lewis, William Baziotes, Elaine de Kooning (*b* 1920), Arshile Gorky, Adolph Gottlieb, Philip Guston (1913–80), Grace Hartigan, Franz Kline (1910–62), Lee Krasner, Norman Lewis, Robert Motherwell, Barnett Newman, Ad Reinhardt, Mark Rothko, and Clyfford Still.

Painting after the Second World War was marked by a diversity of styles, and art galleries were more numerous and active in New York City than anywhere else in the world. Artists such as Yasuo Kuniyoshi, Stephen Greene (*b* 1918), and Rico LeBrun (1900–64) focused on the human figure, often brutalized and disfigured or placed in barren landscapes; Alice Neel and Fairfield Porter (1907–75) practiced a more straightforward figurative art; the German-born painter Richard Lindner (1901–78) developed a figurative art that was intensely sardonic; and Larry Rivers (*b* 1923) emphasized draftsmanship. Robert Rauschenberg and Jasper Johns drew on images from popular culture, foreshadowing the movement later known as pop art.

A number of new painting styles influential in the 1960s took hold in New York City. Pop art by Andy Warhol, Roy Lichtenstein, and James Rosenquist (*b* 1933) celebrated the banality of everyday objects; the hard-edge painting of Ellsworth Kelly (*b* 1923), Jack Youngerman (*b* 1926), and Jules Olitski (*b* 1922) was based on simple shapes; minimal works by Frank Stella, Agnes Martin (*b* 1912), and Robert Ryman (*b* 1930) used stripes, grids, and patterns in the shape of protractors; and the lyrical abstraction of Helen Frankenthaler was characterized by broad areas of thin paint that penetrated the surface of the canvas. New realists included Philip Pearlstein (*b* 1924), Alex Katz (*b* 1927), and Janet Fish (*b* 1938); photorealists included Richard Estes (*b* 1936) and Audrey Flack (*b* 1931). Political art by Rudolf Baranik (*b* 1920), Leon Golub (*b* 1922), Nancy Spero (*b* 1926), and May Stevens (*b* 1924) criticized imperialism, sexism, and racism. A number of women, blacks, Asian-Americans, American Indians, and Latin Americans also came to the forefront of painting, notably Emma Amos (*b* 1938), Ida Applebroog (*b* 1929), Luis Cruz Azaceta (*b* 1942), Jean-Michel Basquiat (1960–88), Margo Machida, Howardena Pindell (*b* 1943), Katherine Porter (*b* 1941), Faith Ringgold (*b* 1930), Juan Sanchez (*b* 1954), Miriam Schapiro (*b* 1923), Joan Semmel, Sylvia Sleigh, Joan Snyder (*b* 1940), and Kay Walkingstick (*b* 1947).

Henry T. Tuckerman: *Book of the Artists: American Artist Life, Comprising Biographical and Critical Sketches of American Artists: Preceded by an Historical Account of the Rise and Progress of Art in America* (New York: G. P. Putnam and Son, 1867; repr. New York: James F. Carr, 1967)

Milton W. Brown: *American Painting from the Armory Show to the Depression* (Princeton, N.J.: Princeton University Press, 1955)

George C. Groce and David H. Wallace: *The New-York Historical Society's Dictionary of Artists in America, 1564–1860* (New Haven: Yale University Press, 1957)

Barbara Rose: *American Art since 1900* (New York: Praeger, 1967; rev. 1975)

Wayne Craven: "Painting in New York City, 1750–1775," *American Painting to 1776: A Reappraisal*, ed. Ian M. G. Quimby (Charlottesville: University Press of Virginia, 1971)

Dore Ashton: *The New York School: A Cultural Reckoning* (New York: Viking, 1972)

Patricia Hills: *Turn-of-the-century America: Paintings, Graphics, Photographs, 1890–1910* (New York: Whitney Museum of American Art, 1977)

Matthew Baigell: *Dictionary of American Art* (London: John Murray, 1980)

Doreen Bolger Burke: *American Paintings in the Metropolitan Museum of Art*, vol. 3, *A Catalogue of Works by Artists Born between 1846 and 1864* (New York: Metropolitan Museum of Art, 1980)

Patricia Hills and Roberta K. Tarbell: *The Figurative Tradition and the Whitney Museum of American Art: Paintings and Sculpture from the Permanent Collection* (New York: Whitney Museum of American Art, 1980)

Charlotte Streifer Rubinstein: *American Women Artists from Early Indian Times to the Present* (Boston: G. K. Hall, 1982)

Patricia Hills: *Social Concern and Urban Realism: American Painting of the 1930s* (Boston: Boston University Art Gallery, 1983)

Matthew Baigell: *A Concise History of American Painting and Sculpture* (New York: Harper and Row, 1984)

Natalie Spassky: *American Paintings in the Metropolitan Museum of Art*, vol. 2, *A Catalogue of Works by Artists Born between 1816 and 1845* (New York: Metropolitan Museum of Art, 1985)

The Decade Show: Frameworks of Identity in the 1980s (New York: Museum of Contemporary Hispanic Art / New Museum of Contemporary Art / Studio Museum in Harlem, 1990)

Patricia Hills

paints, dyes, and varnishes. There was little demand for paints, dyes, and varnishes in New York City during the colonial period: for cultural reasons early settlers refrained from painting buildings, and as of 1712 lampblack was the only pigment legally produced in the colony of New York. In 1754 William Post began mixing, grinding, and importing pigments at a shop on Fletcher Street that was the forerunner of the Devoe and Raynolds Company. New Yorkers in the 1770s made dyes from dogwood, redwood, and indigo and had halted much of the importation of dyed goods, linseed oil, and related products. William Partridge began grinding dyestuffs at a horse-propelled capstan mill in Greenwich Village in 1798 and introduced into the United States argols, lac dye from India, Nicaragua wood, and potassium dichromate for use as a mordant; his enterprise was the precursor of the American Dyewood Company (1904), the first giant in the field. Several patents were issued for dyes and leads during the early nineteenth century. In 1819 Mordecai Lewis began making lead pigments, and Joel West opened a turpentine distillery. The New York Chemical Manufacturing Company (1823) made paints and dyes, and by 1825 several small plants ground imported white lead and colored paints. Pascal B. Smith developed a spar varnish at his shop on East 6th Street in 1827 and built a large business. In the same year the merchant David Leavitt, the distillers Augustus and John Bell Graham, and others formed the Brooklyn White Lead Works, and in 1827 the brothers Whitehead Cornell, Peter Cornell, and George Cornell formed the Union White Lead Company of Brooklyn (incorporated in 1841).

Several large lead factories opened between 1840 and 1850: Robert Colgate formed the Atlantic White Lead Company of New York (which became the nucleus of the National Lead Company), and John Jewett and Sons

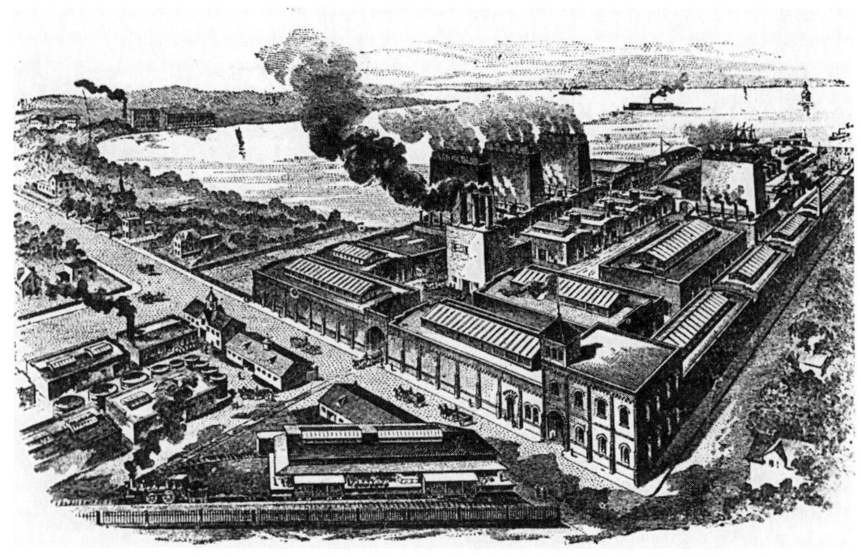

The Standard varnish works in Elm Park, Staten Island, ca *1911*

opened a plant on Staten Island. After the Civil War Hall, Bradley and Company built a large plant in Brooklyn, the Bradley White Lead Company. In 1865 the production of aniline dyes began in Brooklyn at the plant of Thomas and Charles Holliday, and by 1880 factories in New York State accounted for all of the eighty thousand pounds (36,000 kilograms) of aniline dyes produced in the United States. But manufacturers of dyes could not compete with the flood of German imports, which eliminated most domestic producers by 1900; one of few that remained was the American Dyewood Company, which in 1904 had sales of $3 million. From about the turn of the century factories moved from Manhattan to Brooklyn and other surrounding communities where tall stacks carried off the noxious fumes. Paint and varnish manufacturers in New York City continued to prosper: between 1890 and 1919 they increased in number from twenty-seven to 113, in employment from 783 to 5243, and in the total value of their products from $3.8 million to $31.2 million (an increase only partly explained by the consolidation of the city in 1898), and in 1919 the metropolitan area accounted for half of all the varnish made in the United States. In 1929 the value added for the 206 paint and varnish makers in the region was $58.6 million. Production levels in New York City were uneven in the 1970s and 1980s, but there was a clear trend toward the consolidation of firms. In the late 1970s only 115 producers of paint and allied products remained in the metropolitan area, with a total value added of $78.4 million.

Notes for a History of Lead (New York: D. Van Nostrand, 1888)

Williams Haynes: *American Chemical Industry,* vol. 1, *Background and Beginnings, 1609–1911* (New York: D. Van Nostrand, 1954)

David B. Sicilia

Pakistanis. Immigrants from Pakistan are discussed in the entry South Asians.

PAL. See Police Athletic League.

Palace Theatre. Theater at 7th Avenue and 47th Street, built by the impresario Martin Beck. It opened in 1913 and through several questionable transactions was taken over by E. F. Albee, head of the Keith vaudeville circuit, under whose management it became the pinnacle of vaudeville. Performers who were well received at the theater could win a national audience, and the sidewalks outside were often crowded with those seeking bookings. The top floor was used for offices by agents preparing cross-country tours for performers. During the Depression vaudeville declined and was largely replaced by sound motion pictures, and in 1932 the Palace became a movie house. The management then introduced a combination of films and live acts before offering films alone from 1935 to 1949. After a performance in the 1950s by Judy Garland the theater became a national stage for Danny Kaye, Jerry Lewis, Harry Belafonte, and others. From 1960 to 1965 it reverted to showing motion pictures. It was bought by the Nederlander family and reopened as a theater for live performance in 1966. During a complicated review of its historic status the interior was named a landmark, but the building surrounding the auditorium was destroyed and replaced by a hotel. The auditorium reopened in 1991 for a performance of the musical *The Will Rogers Follies.*

Marian Spitzer: *The Palace* (New York: Atheneum, 1969)

Louis Botto: *At This Theatre: An Informal History of New York's Legitimate Theatres* (New York: Dodd, Mead, 1984)

Robert W. Snyder: *The Voice of the City: Vaudeville and Popular Culture in New York* (New York: Oxford University Press, 1989)

Robert W. Snyder

Palestinians. A few Palestinians lived in New York City by the early twentieth century. Among them was Abdelhameed Shoman, who moved to the city with little money in 1911 and later opened the Arab Bank. Palestinians initially lived near Syrian and Lebanese enclaves in lower Manhattan but later settled primarily in Brooklyn. After the formation of Israel in 1948 a large number of Palestinians including many professionals moved to the United States, especially in the 1970s and 1980s. They became the fastest-growing group of Arab immigrants after being forced from their homes by Israel's military presence in the occupied territories, bloodshed in refugee camps during the Lebanese civil war, the invasion of Lebanon by Israel in 1982, and the Gulf War. Organizations such as the Union of Palestinian Women's Associations (1986), the Palestinian American Youth Club, the Palestinian–American Community Center, and various student groups encouraged their members to be politically active, especially in working toward an independent Palestinian state. In the mid 1990s the largest Palestinian community in the city was in Sunset Park. Many Palestinians belong to village clubs like the Al-Bireh and Beit Hanina clubs and the Ramallah Federation. Palestinians are among the better educated Arab immigrants in the city. Religious institutions that they frequent include the Al-Faruq Mosque and St. Nicholas Cathedral. Because a Palestinian may carry a passport from one of several nations, estimates of the Palestinian population in the city are rough, ranging from ten to forty thousand. One of the most distinguished Palestinians in the city is Edward Said: born in Jerusalem, he teaches English and comparative literature at Columbia University and is a member of the Palestinian National Council and a forceful spokesman for Palestinian rights.

Inea Bushnaq

Paley, William S. (*b* Chicago, 28 Sept 1901; *d* New York City, 26 Oct 1990). Entrepreneur. He moved to New York City in 1928 and consolidated a loosely connected group of radio stations to form the Columbia Broadcasting System (CBS). Under his direction the firm invested in Broadway musicals and made acquisitions ranging from the New York Yankees to the piano makers Steinway and Sons. Paley was also an art collector and the longtime president and trustee of the Museum of Modern Art. From the mid 1960s until his death he lived at 820 5th Avenue in Manhattan. Paley Park is on 53rd Street.

David Halberstam: *The Powers That Be* (New York: Alfred A. Knopf, 1979)

Sally Bedell Smith: *In All His Glory: The Life of William S. Paley* (New York: Simon and Schuster, 1990)

JillEllyn Riley

Palmer [née Worrall], **Phoebe** (*b* New York City, 18 Dec 1807; *d* New York City, 2 Nov 1874). Theologian. Born to a devout Methodist family, she married Warren C. Palmer, a Methodist physician, and with him underwent a religious renewal from 1832 to 1837 that led her to believe in "entire sanctification," an ideal of total personal consecration achieved in a distinct experience. Her idea adapted Wesleyan perfectionism to Victorian standards of urban domesticity and moderate social reform, and was crucial in shaping the American holiness tradition. She spread her ideas in books, in her magazine *Guide to Holiness* (1864–74), and in weekly meetings at her home. She held revival meetings across the eastern United States and Canada during the 1850s and in the British Isles during the Civil War but otherwise lived in the city for her entire life.

Charles Edward White: *The Beauty of Holiness: Phoebe Palmer as Theologian, Revivalist, Feminist, and Humanitarian* (Wilmore, Ky.: Francis Asbury, 1986)

James D. Bratt

Palmo's New York Opera House. Opera house opened in February 1844 at 67 Chambers Street by Ferdinand Palmo (1785–1869), an Italian immigrant. It initially attracted a genteel clientele and was the focus of a brief vogue for Italian opera during the mid nineteenth century. The house was the site in 1845 of the local début of the German Opera Company (in productions that were a critical success and a popular failure), and in 1847 of the first performance in New York City of an opera by Verdi (*I Lombardi*). In the end Palmo's was hurt by its location too far downtown, and in 1848 it was sold to William Burton, who abandoned opera in favor of dramatic performances.

Marc Ferris

Panamanians. There were a few Panamanians of West Indian origin before 1950 in New York City, inasmuch as the city was a principal terminus of shipping and air routes from Panama. Further, as an independent nation of the western hemisphere, Panama was exempt from the immigration quotas imposed in 1924 and 1952. During the 1950s a sizable number of Panamanians emigrated to the United States because of changes in employment in the Canal Zone, a large-scale retirement of older workers, and the voluntary entry of young men looking to serve in the armed forces of the United States during the Korean War. Much of what is known about Panamanian immigration dates from after 1960, when the U.S. Bureau of the Census first recorded the country of origin of immigrants from Central and South America. The largest number of Panamanian immigrants to the United States settled in New York City.

Most Panamanians who arrived before 1970 were educated people, presumably West Indian, black, or of mixed race, who originated from the Canal Zone and the cities of Panamá and Colón. They settled in the Haitian and Caribbean enclaves and black neighborhoods of Brooklyn, and in Spanish-speaking enclaves in Queens, Manhattan, and the Bronx. A military coup in 1968 spurred an influx of Panamanians of European ancestry who settled mostly in Miami and in wealthy neighborhoods in Manhattan and Queens. During the 1970s and 1980s the number of poor Panamanian immigrants increased, accounting for part of the purportedly large undocumented population in the city before the passage of the Immigration Reform and Control Act of 1986. Legal status was granted to canal workers (many of West Indian origin) who were displaced by the terms of a treaty signed by General Omar Torrijos and President Jimmy Carter in 1979. One of few organizations in New York City intended strictly for Panamanians was Las Servidoras, formed by Sarah Anesta Samuel in Brooklyn in 1953; later renamed the Dedicators, by the mid 1990s it had provided hundreds of thousands of dollars in college scholarships for Panamanian immigrants and other minority students. Panamanians in the city also joined alumni associations affiliated with secondary schools in the Canal Zone, and organized large groups that traveled to Panama for an annual festival. The *Panama Chronicle*, a bilingual quarterly newspaper published from 1977 to 1992, was distributed free of charge and provided news about the Panamanian community in the city and events in Panama.

Panamanians often adjusted more easily to life in New York City than members of other groups because of their urban and cosmopolitan background, work habits, multilingualism, and exposure to American culture (due in large part to the American presence in the Canal Zone for most of the twentieth century). Most were Roman Catholic, Anglican, or Episcopalian; a smaller number were Methodist, Baptist, and Adventist, and some were quite visibly involved with Afro-Caribbean religions. From the 1980s a number converted to Pentecostalism. Over the years many Panamanians bought houses and commercial real estate, opened retail stores, and worked in the highest levels of insurance, travel, and real-estate sales and public service. Prominent Panamanians in the city have included the state assemblyman Ed Griffith, the former state senator Waldaba Stewart, the composer Roque Cordero, the singer and actor Rubén Blades, the playwright Carlos Quintero, the classical pianist Jaime Ingram, the baseball players Hector Lopez and Rod Carew, the bantamweight boxing champion Panama Al Brown, and the basketball player Rolando Blackman. According to the federal census there were 22,707 Panamanians in New York City in 1990, most of whom lived in Brooklyn and Queens.

Marcia Bayne-Smith, Roy S. Bryce-Laporte

Pan American Airways. International airline, formed in 1927 by Henry "Hap" Arnold and taken over in the same year by Juan Trippe, a naval pilot in the First World War who had strong political and financial backing. From the outset the headquarters were at East 42nd Street. The airline was so successful in cultivating the favor of regulators in the United States and Latin America that by 1931 its routes covered 20,308 miles (32,676 kilometers) in twenty countries. As the only international carrier in the United States from 1931 to 1942 it helped to establish New York City as a center of international aviation and was responsible for a number of innovations in air travel. Scheduled transatlantic service from New York City began on 20 May 1939 from the Marine Air Terminal at La Guardia Airfield (at the time unfinished) and was provided by Boeing 314 seaplanes that traveled at 193 miles (311 kilometers) an hour and could carry seventy-four passengers or provide berths for forty. Between 1942 and 1945 the airline was active in the planning of what later became John F. Kennedy International Airport. Service around the world was inaugurated in 1947; the airline also introduced jet service from New York City to London with the Boeing 707 (26 October 1958) and the first "jumbo" jet, the Boeing 747 (from Kennedy Airport in 1969). In 1964 it opened a new headquarters in Manhattan, at the time the largest office building in the world. Pan American was the dominant international airline in the United States until the early 1980s but toward the end of the decade encountered financial difficulties. Its headquarters building was acquired by the Metropolitan Life Insurance Company. In 1991 it sold its European routes to Delta Airlines in an effort to reposition itself as a regional carrier to South America but was forced to cease operations in 1992.

Marylin Bender and Selig Altschul: *The Chosen Instrument: Pan Am, Juan Trippe, the Rise and Fall of an American Entrepreneur* (New York: Simon and Schuster, 1982)

R. E. G. Davies: *Pan Am: An Airline and Its Aircraft* (New York: Orion, 1987)

See also W. R. GRACE.

Paul Barrett

Panorama of New York City. A huge, three-dimensional reproduction of New York City at the Queens Museum in Flushing Meadows–Corona Park. Constructed as the New York City exhibit for the World's Fair of 1964–65, it is the world's largest scale model, occupying 9335 square feet (867 square meters). At a scale of 1200:1 it reproduces the city's 830,000 buildings, thousands of streets and parks, and dozens of major bridges. The project was conceived by Robert Moses, the long-time municipal builder and president of the World's Fair Corporation, and fabricated by the model-making firm of Lester Associates. The task took more than three years and required the full-time labor of hundreds of workers. Visitors to the museum may observe the model from overhead. Regularly brought up to date and completely renovated between 1992 and 1994, the Panorama of New York remains a popular attraction.

Kenneth T. Jackson

Pantoja, Antonia (*b* San Juan, 1921). Activist. Born into a working-class family, she moved to New York City in 1944. The example of the militant tobacco workers of Puerto Rico inspired her to form a network of Puerto Rican social and cultural organizations, which she viewed as a tool for progressive struggle: these included the Puerto Rican Association for Community Affairs (1953), the Puerto Rican Forum (1958), Aspira (1961), and Boricua College (1970). In the 1980s Pantoja moved to San Diego, where she organized the Graduate School for Community Development. Later she returned to Puerto Rico, where with Wilhelmina Perry she formed an economic development corporation called Producir. With Barbara Blourock she wrote *Events in the History of Puerto Rico* (1967).

Virginia Sánchez Korrol

Papanicolaou, George N(icholas) (*b* Kimi, Greece, 13 May 1883; *d* Miami, 18 Feb 1962). Physician and medical researcher. After earning his MD from the University of Athens (1904) and PhD from the University of Munich (1910) he moved to New York City and became a professor in the department of anatomy at Cornell University Medical College. During an association with the college lasting forty-seven years he invented a gynecological procedure called the "pap test" that allows for the early detection of uterine cancer. He also perfected the diagnostic techniques of exfoliative cytology, which are used to find malignant cells in many other areas of the body, and wrote the *Atlas of Exfoliative Cytology* (1954). His work is considered a prodigious contribution to modern cancer research.

Daniel Erskine Carmichael: *The Pap Smear: Life of George N. Papanicolaou* (Springfield, Ill.: Thomas, 1973)

Adele A. Lerner

paper. Although it lacks sufficient wood, water, and land for papermaking, New York City early in its history became a center for the manufacture and sale of specialized paper products such as cardboard and wrapping paper. The supply of paper during the colonial period was subject to a highly irregular supply of rags. After the American Revolution supplies were more dependable, and Jonathan Seymour became the city's first important paper merchant after he began selling paper from his print shop at 49 John Street in 1820. In the same year a stationery shop at 110–12 Nassau Street was opened by Samuel Campbell, who maintained paper mills in Millburn, New Jersey, and floated his goods across the Hudson River to his warehouses in Manhattan. The business was continued after his death by his son Jonathan. The center of the city's paper trade was the area east of Printing House Square (now Park Row), where many newspapers were based. Some of the larger wholesalers included Hudson River Pulp and Paper (154 Nassau Street), the Diamond Mills Paper Company (44 Murray Street), and the Berlin and Jones Envelope Company (134 and 136 William Street).

Germans perfected the wood-pulp method of papermaking about 1869, and an abundant supply of paper became available in New York City and the United States by the 1880s. Some Americans saw paper as a miracle fabric and experimented with paper clothes, coffins, and even boat hulls. In 1882 Augustine Smith, who reorganized Samuel Campbell and Company after Jonathan Campbell's death, became the city's most renowned stationer and supplied a steady flow of paper to the presses of leading book and magazine publishers. Smith acquired an interest in the Chelsea Paper Manufacturing Company of Greenville (now Norwich), Connecticut, which transported its wares to New York City by rail. Bulkley, Dunton and Company moved from 111 Beekman Street, then known as "paper street," to 75 and 77 Duane Street in 1891 and grew into the city's largest paper supply firm. The firm next door, Louis DeJonge and Company, manufactured fancy paper at its factory in Tompkinsville and employed about four hundred workers in 1903. After the turn of the century New York City became the base of trade groups such as the Paper Merchants' Association of New York (incorporated in 1902 by fifteen of the city's largest paper merchandisers and periodicals) and of trade periodicals such as the *Paper Trade Journal* (1872–1986). The International Paper Company, formed in 1898, made New York City the site of its corporate headquarters until the firm moved to Memphis in 1987.

In 1991 there were 245 firms in the city producing paper products ranging from envelopes and greeting cards to large paperboard boxes. The industry employed more than ten thousand persons and produced goods worth $888.1 million.

Irmengarde Eberle: *The New World of Paper* (New York: Dodd, Mead, 1969)

Marc Ferris

Papp, Joseph [Papirofsky, Yosl] (*b* Brooklyn, 22 June 1921; *d* New York City, 31 Oct 1991). Theater producer. Brought up in poverty in Williamsburg, he began staging free performances of Shakespeare at Emmanuel Presbyterian Church on the Lower East Side in 1954. His troupe became known as the New York Shakespeare Festival and from 1957 mounted shows every summer in Central Park. The right of the festival to perform there became the subject of an acrimonious lawsuit against the parks commissioner Robert Moses; after a compromise was reached the Delacorte Theater was built for use by the festival in 1962. Papp oversaw the conversion of the Astor Library on Lafayette Street into a theater complex designed by Giorgio Cavaglieri and opened in 1966 as the Public Theater. From the late 1960s to the end of his life he staged both works by young playwrights such as Miguel Piñero, David Mamet, and Sam Shepard and innovative interpretations of standard works by Bertolt Brecht and Chekhov. He skillfully used receipts from the financially successful musical *A Chorus Line*, which ran for a record 6137 performances on Broadway from 1975 to 1990, to subsidize more adventurous productions with less commercial appeal. Papp was strongly concerned with social issues, which he brought to the fore through his choice of productions and his support of actors and playwrights from minority groups. After his death the Public Theater was renamed the Papp Public Theater, and Lincoln Center received a large collection of his documents, audio and videotapes, and memorabilia.

Helen Epstein: *Joe Papp: An American Life* (Boston: Little, Brown, 1994)

George A. Thompson, Jr.

parades. Among the first parades in New York City were military reviews and musters, which were common during the seventeenth century. The first St. Patrick's Day Parade was held in 1766 by Irish soldiers in the British army. Large annual parades during the late eighteenth century commemorated events of national importance: American independence, Evacuation Day (marking the evacuation of the British from the city in 1783 and celebrated with parades and a ceremonial flag raising at the Battery), and the ratification of the Constitution of the United States in 1788. Parades and pageants soon became massive civic and ethnic celebrations sponsored by political parties, immigrant groups, and city government. In the first half of the nineteenth century the city became a customary stop for personages who toured the United States, and parades and festivities in their honor became an enduring aspect of city life. A large parade was given in 1824 to welcome the Marquis de Lafayette to the city, another in 1851 for the Hungarian revolutionary Louis Kossuth. Important public works projects were also celebrated with parades, including the opening of the Erie Canal in 1825 and of the Croton Water Works in 1842. Steuben Day and other holidays were celebrated with parades by immigrants. The sponsorship of the St. Patrick's Day Parade was taken over in the 1850s by the Ancient Order of Hibernians.

Fireworks became an important part of the celebration of Independence Day and other holidays during the second half of the nineteenth century. Many displays were presented by Italian–American exhibitors such as the Grucci family of Long Island, who had first opened their fireworks company in southern Italy in the 1850s. From about this time colorful parades served to advertise circuses; these were discontinued in the first quarter of the twentieth century owing to congestion in the streets and the use of other forms of advertising. A spectacular parade in 1860 welcomed to the city the Prince of Wales (later Edward VII), and the end of the Civil War was celebrated with a large parade in 1865. The Easter Parade, first held in the 1870s, became an annual event in which marchers (or more accurately strollers) gathered along 5th Avenue on Easter Sunday to display new outfits and hats for spring.

TICKER-TAPE PARADES were first organized by the city in the 1880s around Wall Street. Union Square was the site of many rallies and parades on May Day sponsored by radical groups and labor organizations; the first Labor Day parade was held there in 1882. The frequency of these gatherings diminished after the Second World War as the American left declined, but an annual Labor Day Parade lasted until 1986, when it was canceled because of its lessened popularity among union members. The one hundredth anniversary of Evacuation Day was celebrated with several elaborate parades and ceremonies, including a marine parade of naval and commercial vessels off Manhattan. By this time parades, particularly torchlight processions, were an important aspect of politics in the city. More than 110,000 marchers took part in the Business Men's Republican and Sound Money Parade of 1896 in support of William McKinley's presidential candidacy. In 1899 an elaborate triumphal arch was erected on 5th Avenue at 23rd Street for a celebration of Admiral George Dewey's victorious return from the Philippines. Henry Hudson's explorations and Robert Fulton's invention of the steamboat were celebrated in 1909 with parades and performances in city parks. A ticker-tape parade was given for Theodore Roosevelt in 1910. The last celebrations of Evacuation Day date from the early years of the First World War, when civic leaders concluded that the alliance of the United States with Great Britain was not well served by an anti-British holiday. Parades sponsored by commercial firms began in the twentieth century, including the Macy's parade on Thanksgiving Day (annual from 1924). Ticker-tape parades honored Charles Lindbergh (1927), the New York Mets (1969, 1986), Pope John Paul II (1979), Nelson Mandela (1990), and veterans of the Gulf War (1991).

The Halloween Parade in Greenwich Village was organized by the performance artist Ralph Lee in 1974 and became an annual event. Its success depended on wide participation (anyone in costume could march) and

Major Parades in New York City

African–American Day Parade (1969), Adam Clayton Powell Boulevard, 111st to 142nd streets, Manhattan, September
American Ethnic Parade, Columbus Circle, along Central Park South to 6th Avenue to 43rd Street, Manhattan
Armenian Martyr's Day (1965), Times Square, Manhattan, April
Brazilian Summer Carnival Parade (1986), Lower East Side, Manhattan
Bronx Week Parade (1971), Grand Concourse, 198th to 153rd streets, Bronx, May–June
Captive Nations Week Parade (1959), 5th Avenue, Manhattan, July
Children's Parade for Peace, Manhattan, October
Chinese New Year Parade, Chinatown, Manhattan, February
Columbus Day Parade (1909), 5th Avenue, 44th to 86th streets, Manhattan, 12 October
Cuban Day Parade (1904), Madison Avenue, 56th to 37th streets, Manhattan, May
Dominican Day Parade (1981), Madison Ave, 57th to 37th streets, Manhattan, August
Easter Parade (*ca* 1870), 5th Avenue near St. Patrick's Cathedral and 50th Street, Manhattan, April
Ecuador Day Parade (1984), 35th Avenue, 70th to 89th streets, Queens, August
Flag Day Parade, Fulton and Water streets to Fraunces Tavern Museum, Manhattan, June
Greek Independence Day Parade (1893), 5th Avenue, 62nd to 79th streets, Manhattan, March–April
Greenwich Village Halloween Parade (1974), Houston Street from West Street to 6th Avenue, north to 14th Street, east to Union Square, Manhattan, 31 October
Hispanic American Day Parade (1984), 4th Avenue, 50th to 40th streets, Brooklyn, June
Hispanic Parade (1977), 35th Avenue, 70th to 89th streets, Queens, Sept
India Day Parade, Madison Avenue, 54th to 26th streets, Manhattan, August
International Cultures Parade, June
International Immigrants Parade (1986), Madison Avenue, 37th to 56th streets, Manhattan, October
Korean Day Parade (1980), Broadway and Times Square, Manhattan, September
Krishna Procession, 5th Avenue and 59th Street to Washington Square Park, Manhattan
Labor Day Parade (1882), 5th Avenue, Manhattan, September
Lesbian and Gay Pride Day Parade (1970), 5th Avenue, Columbus Circle, and Christopher Street, Manhattan, June
Loisaida Fair (1986), Avenue C, 3rd to 10th streets, Manhattan, May
Macy's Thanksgiving Day Parade (1924), Central Park West, 77th to 59th streets, down Broadway to 34th Street, Manhattan, November
Martin Luther King Jr. Parade (1968), 5th Avenue, 44th to 86th streets, Manhattan, May
Memorial Day Parade (1896), 72nd Street and Broadway, west on 86th Street to Soldiers' and Sailors' Monument, Manhattan, May
Mermaid Parade (1983), Steeplechase Park to West 5th Street, Brooklyn, June
Norwegian Constitution Day Parade (1951), 5th Avenue, 95th to 67th streets, Brooklyn, May
Pakistan Independence Parade, Lexington Avenue, 33rd to 21st streets, Manhattan, August
Parade of Liberty, 4 July
Puerto Rican Day Parade (i) (1956), 5th Avenue, 44th to 86th streets, Manhattan, June
Puerto Rican Day Parade (ii) (1988), Grand Concourse, 161st to 185th streets, Bronx, July
Pulaski Day Parade (1937), 5th Avenue, 26th to 52nd streets, Manhattan, October
Queens Purim Parade (1980), Main Street, 68th Drive to 73rd Avenue, Kew Gardens, Queens, March
Ragamuffin Day Parade, Brooklyn, October
St. Patrick's Day Parade (1853), 5th Avenue, 44th to 86th streets, Manhattan, 17 March
Salute to Israel Parade (1964), 5th Avenue, 57th to 86th streets, Manhattan, May–June
Solidarity Day Parade, 5th Avenue, Manhattan, May
Steuben Day Parade (1958), 5th Avenue, 63rd to 86th streets, Manhattan, September
Three Kings Parade (1977), 5th Avenue, 104th to 116th streets, Manhattan, January
Turkish–American Day Parade (1982), 5th Avenue, Manhattan, April
United Hispanic American Day Parade (1965), 5th Avenue, 44th to 72nd streets, Manhattan, October
Veteran's Day Parade (1918), 5th Avenue, 39th to 24th streets, Manhattan, November
Washington's Birthday Parade, Manhattan, February
West Indian–American Day Parade and Carnival (1967), Eastern Parkway, Utica Avenue to Washington Avenue, Brooklyn, September

parks. New York City has by far the largest urban parks system in the United States, occupying some 26,000 acres (10,530 hectares) exclusive of state and federal lands, and comprising more than fifteen hundred parks and playgrounds, as well as recreation centers, golf courses, ballfields, zoological and botanical gardens, monuments, historic houses, beaches, forests, meadows, and wetlands. The charter of Governor Thomas Dongan provided for municipal stewardship of all "waste, vacant, unpatented and unappropriated lands" in 1686, when urban settlement was still largely confined to the southern tip of Manhattan. As a result the city acquired a marketplace and military parade ground (at Bowling Green) and a public commons (later City Hall Park). On 12 March 1733 the Common Council established at Bowling Green the oldest public park in New York City: this oval plot was leased for one peppercorn a year to three citizens with the stipulation that the landscape be upgraded "for the beauty and ornament of the said street as well as for the recreation & delight of the inhabitants of this City." In the following year building was restricted along the southern shoreline, the area that eventually became Battery Park. Shortly after New York City became the first national capital in 1785 the new park was finally landscaped and a public promenade was added. The city laid out a potter's field in Greenwich Village in 1797 on land now occupied by Washington Square Park, and acquired a small triangular parcel at Duane and Hudson streets specifically to promote "health and recreation." The grid plan of 1811 did not provide for a central park but did roughly define several public squares that are the current sites of Tompkins Square Park, Union Square Park, Madison Square Park (which is only one tenth as large as was originally intended), and Marcus Garvey Park (originally Mount Morris Park).

Similar efforts were under way in Brooklyn. Green-Wood Cemetery opened in 1838 and became a popular site for strolling and picnics, and in the following year eleven park sites were proposed by a three-member commission. The first major park in Brooklyn was Fort Greene Park (1848); the effort to acquire this hilly site well-known for its role during the American Revolution had been championed by Walt Whitman, then the editor of the *Brooklyn Daily Eagle*. The success of Green-Wood Cemetery inspired William Cullen Bryant, Andrew Jackson Downing, and others to recommend the construction of a large public park in Manhattan. At first attention focused on Jones's Wood, an area extending from 3rd Avenue to the East River and from 66th to 75th streets, but efforts to build a park there were thwarted by real-estate interests. In 1853 the state finally authorized the first appropriation of the land that eventually became Central Park. Hardly central at the time, the property occupied 840 acres (340 hectares) of swampy land with rocky outcroppings. The Albany Post Road ran along the eastern edge of the site, and within the park were small communities of lower-class property owners, a state arsenal, and in the northern section a tavern, a convent, a mill, farms, and abandoned military fortifications. A board of commissioners formed to oversee the construction of the park sponsored a design competition in 1857 and in the following year chose as the winning entry the Greensward plan of Frederick Law Olmsted and Calvert Vaux. Their landscape design was based on the English pastoral style and by the early 1870s was fully implemented. Olmsted and Vaux also designed Riverside Park in Manhattan (Olmsted having been responsible for the laying out and Vaux for many of the details) and Prospect Park in Brooklyn (often considered their masterpiece), and planned a system of parkways, or landscaped routes, intended to link parks within a system: Eastern Parkway (1868–74) and Ocean Parkway (1869–76) in Brooklyn were early examples.

New York City formed a department of public parks in 1870. Brooklyn had its own department, which also administered Forest Park in Queens and other lands. Lower Westchester (later the Bronx) was largely undeveloped and became the focus of parks advocates in the 1880s. Union Square Park and Tompkins Square Park in Manhattan were popular venues for political rallies. A group of citizens who formed the New York Park Association in 1881 pointed to the example of Central Park in arguing that parks not only improved the quality of life in the city but also raised the value of adjacent property. Their efforts led in 1888 to the signing of a law authorizing six new parks and four parkways, thus quintupling the area of parkland in the city. In 1895 the first municipal golf course in the United States opened at Van Cortlandt Park, as did the first bicycle path (along Ocean Parkway). PLAYGROUNDS were sponsored privately from 1898 and publicly from 1903, when one opened at Seward Park on the Lower East Side.

During the second and third decades of the twentieth century interborough athletic championships drew as many as ten thousand spectators to the parks of New York City. The parks became the sites of outdoor concerts, historical pageants, and even showings of films. Farm gardens introduced children from the city to country living and neighborhood parks soon replaced the streets as gathering places. The Park Association of New York City, a privately sponsored parks advocacy group, was formed in 1926; it later evolved into the Parks Council (incorporated in 1970). Robert Moses became the parks commissioner in 1934 and consolidated the separate borough departments. He formed a large professional staff and with federal relief work funds employed tens of thousands of laborers. Over the ensuing decade hundreds of new playgrounds were built. Eleven large outdoor pools opened, miles of beachfront were improved for swimming, and Flushing Meadows rose on what had once been industrial ash heaps and became the third-largest park in the city. Outlying areas such as Jamaica Bay and Marine Park were rescued from development and kept in a largely natural state. Construction slowed during the Second World War, but in the 1950s new indoor recreation centers in Brownsville, Bedford–Stuyvesant, and Mott Haven addressed the need for year-round places of play, especially in poor, underserved neighborhoods. By the time Moses retired from office in 1960 the parks system had nearly tripled in size.

Many experiments were introduced in the late 1960s: as land grew scarcer the city looked to vacant lots for places to build what became known as VEST POCKET PARKS, new types of equipment were tried in "adventure" playgrounds, and the planning of parks took into account as never before the concerns of local residents. Central Park and the other large parks became used for concerts and other events that drew large, diverse audiences. Growing concern for the environment and a desire to preserve forests and wetlands led to the securing of the Greenbelt in Staten Island and Udalls Cove in Queens. The decline in port traffic inspired proposals to build waterfront parks, while a greater concern for existing historic parks gave rise to private groups such as the Central Park Conservancy. The parks came to be regarded not only as an amenity without which the city would be a poorer place, but as a civic right.

In the early 1990s three urban parks opened with the sponsorship of the state and public authorities: Riverbank State Park (May 1993), occupying twenty-eight acres (eleven hectares) atop a waste treatment plant in Harlem; Octagon Park (October 1992), a sports complex and community garden of fifteen acres (six hectares) at the northern end of Roosevelt Island; and Hudson River Park (June 1992), an eight-acre (three-hectare) park in lower Manhattan with a fine view of New York Harbor.

Elizabeth Barlow Rogers: *Frederick Law Olmsted's New York* (New York: Praeger, 1972)

A Timeline of New York City Park History (New York: Department of Parks and Recreation, 1988)

Jonathan Kuhn

Parks, Sam(uel J.) (*b* County Down, Ireland, 1864; *d* Ossining, N.Y., 4 May 1904). Labor leader. He moved to Chicago in 1892 and to New York City in 1896, where he learned the housesmith's trade. Known for his enormous size and strength, he helped to win for the Housesmiths and Bridgemen's Union an increase in the daily wage advance from $2.50 to $4.50 as he worked his way through the building trades. Later he was the president of the union and of the New York City Board of Building Trades and became a well-known racketeer, often sending workers out on strike to help a contractor destroy its competitors. He remained popular among union members because of his success at enforcing union rules, maintaining job security, and helping ironworkers to win wage advances and increases: through his efforts daily wages rose from $1.50 to $5. Parks was indicted for blackmail in 1903 and sentenced to two and a half years in prison, where he died.

Ray Stannard Baker: "Trusts and Labour in America: The Amazing Story of Sam Parks," *World's Work* 3 (1903), 40–52

Kerry Candaele

Parks Council. Nonprofit organization for preserving open spaces and improving recreational facilities, formed in New York City in 1970 by a merger of the Park Association of New York City and the Council for Parks and Playgrounds, a neighborhood organization dedicated to improving play facilities.

Ann L. Buttenwieser

Park Slope. Neighborhood in northeastern Brooklyn (1990 pop. 48,427), bounded to the north by 4th and Flatbush avenues, to the east by Flatbush Avenue and Prospect Park West, to the south by Prospect Park West and 15th Street, and to the west by 4th Avenue. It was developed after Prospect Park was completed and street railways were extended to the area in the 1870s. Mansions and four-story row houses were built north of 9th Street near Grand Army Plaza for professionals and entrepreneurs, many of whom used new streetcar lines that extended over the Brooklyn Bridge (1883) to travel to work in downtown Brooklyn and Manhattan. From about this time Prospect Park West from the plaza to 1st Street was known as the "gold coast." Modest row houses and apartment buildings were built west of 7th Avenue and south of 9th Street to house workers in local factories like that of Ansonia Clock at 12th Street and 7th Avenue, which for a while was the largest clock factory in the world. Development slowed about the time of the First World War, when real-estate firms took interest in open land south of Prospect Park that had become accessible by subway and automobile. The lower, less elegant working-class sections of Park Slope were largely Irish. The neighborhood became less fashionable after the Second World War with the increase of suburban settlement on Long Island. Working-class families moved into the residences in the northern sections, many of which were used as rooming houses.

In the 1960s 8th Avenue between the Plaza and 1st Street became known as "doctor's row," and in the following years row houses were bought cheaply and restored. On 16 December 1960 a commercial airliner that had collided with another airplane over Staten Island crashed near 7th Avenue and Sterling Place, killing eighty-four passengers and six persons on the ground. A landmark district (the largest in Brooklyn) was formed in 1974 in an area containing about sixteen hundred historic buildings and bounded by Flatbush Avenue, Prospect Park West, 14th Street, and 8th Avenue. The Ansonia Clock factory was converted into a housing cooperative in 1982.

Park Slope is primarily residential, with many renovated row houses and apartment buildings. The population consists of young professionals near Prospect Park, attracted by the proximity of the neighborhood to Manhattan and the low cost of housing; Latin Americans west of 7th Avenue; and many Irish–Americans in an enclave south of 9th Street. The neighborhood is the site of the largest Irish–American Day parade in Brooklyn. The commercial districts lie along 7th Avenue and on 5th Avenue, especially south of 9th Street. Many noteworthy buildings are in the landmark district near Grand Army Plaza, including the Montauk Club (designed after the Ca d'Oro in Venice) and Romanesque Revival and neo-Classic row houses (many built before 1916) along sidestreets. The area attracted a small number of new immigrants in the 1980s, principally from the Dominican Republic and Jamaica.

Henry Reed Stiles, ed.: *The Civil, Political, Professional and Ecclesiastical History, and Commercial and Industrial Record of the County of Kings and the City of Brooklyn, N.Y. from 1683 to 1884* (New York: W. W. Munsell, n.d. [1884])

Henry W. B. Howard: *The Eagle and Brooklyn: The Record of the Progress of the Brooklyn Daily Eagle, Issued in Commemoration of its Semi-centennial and Occupancy of Its New Building, together with a History of the City of Brooklyn from Its Settlement to the Present Time* (Brooklyn: Brooklyn Daily Eagle, 1893)

John J. Gallagher

Brownstones on Carroll Street in Park Slope, 1991

Park Theatre. A theater on Park Row facing City Hall Park, designed by Joseph François Mangin and built in 1798. It became one of the city's most important entertainment venues, where English stock companies produced farces, musical plays, and melodramas and helped introduce the "star system" in the city's entertainment business. From 1825 the theater's custodian Edward Simpson staged operas and classical music performances, including the local première in 1839 of Beethoven's *Fidelio* and the début in 1843 of the Norwegian violinist Ole Bull. The theater was destroyed by fire on 16 December 1848 and rebuilt as a row of retail shops.

Charles Nevers Holmes: "The Park Theatre, New York," *Magazine of History* 22 (1916), 72–75

See also Theater, §2.

Marc Ferris

Park Versailles. A disused name for a part of the eastern Bronx bounded to the north by East Tremont Avenue, to the east by White Plains Road, to the south by Westchester Avenue, and to the west by Croes Avenue. The area was once occupied by the Archer–Mapes farm, which was auctioned off in the 1860s, and was named by developers who believed that its wide, tree-lined avenues recalled the grounds of Versailles.

John McNamara: *History in Asphalt: The Origin of Bronx Street and Place Names* (New York: Bronx County Historical Society, 1984)

Gary D. Hermalyn

Parkville. Neighborhood in central Brooklyn, bounded to the north by Ditmas Avenue, to the east by Coney Island Avenue, to the south by Avenue H and Walsh Court, and to the west by McDonald Avenue; it is considered part of Flatbush. Known as Greenfield until 1870, the neighborhood was laid out on land purchased in 1851 and 1852 from the Tredwell and Ditmas families by the United Freeman's Association. With Windsor Terrace it lay on both sides of what is now Ocean Parkway from Brooklyn to Coney Island. After streets were laid out in 1853 the area became a comfortable, middle-class suburb of Brooklyn, largely Jewish and Italian. In the 1980s many immigrants from China moved to the neighborhood and its environs, as did smaller numbers of immigrants from the Soviet Union, Italy, Israel, and Poland.

Edmund D. Fisher: *Flatbush Past and Present* (New York: Flatbush Trust, 1901)

Ellen Marie Snyder-Grenier

parkways. Limited-access highways bordered and often divided by strips landscaped with trees, grass, and other plantings, common in New York City and its environs and unknown in most of the United States. They are generally closed to trucks and commercial traffic and free of advertising billboards. The term was originally applied to the roads built for pedestrians and carriages in public parks at the end of the nineteenth century. The first modern parkway was the Bronx River Parkway (1916–24), which formed the basis for an innovative network of landscaped parkways in the metropolitan area, many built by Robert Moses. The network came to encompass Westchester and Long Island and was a forerunner of the interstate highway system. Among the best-known parkways in New York City are the Grand Central Parkway, the Henry Hudson Parkway, and the Hutchinson River Parkway.

See also STREETS.

Owen D. Gutfreund

Parrish, (Frederick) Maxfield (*b* Philadelphia, 25 July 1870; *d* Plainfield, N.H., 30 March 1966). Painter and illustrator. Educated abroad and at Haverford College and the Pennsylvania Academy, he achieved his first commercial success with a cover for *Harper's Weekly* and was soon engaged by the magazines *Collier's*, *Scribner's*, and *Ladies' Home Journal*; he later illustrated such books as Edith Wharton's *Italian Villas* and Francis Turner Palgrave's *Golden Treasury* (1911). During the winter of 1918–19 he painted at 49 East 63rd Street. He became known for advertisements for tires, light bulbs, and Jell-O desserts and for a mural twenty-eight feet (8.5 meters) long at the Hotel Knickerbocker, *Old King Cole*, depicting the legendary king of the nursery tale surrounded by his court; this was moved to the St. Regis Hotel in 1933 and became a favorite of New Yorkers for decades. An exhibition of his work was held at the Gallery of Modern Art in 1964. Parrish received the gold medal of the Architectural League.

Coy L. Ludwig: *Maxfield Parrish* (New York: Watson–Guptill, 1973)

James E. Mooney

Parsons [née Clews], **Elsie (Worthington)** (*b* New York City, 27 Nov 1874; *d* New York City, 19 Dec 1941). Sociologist, anthropologist, and folklorist. Born to a wealthy and socially prominent family, she graduated from Barnard College in 1896 and earned a PhD in sociology from Columbia University in 1899. Under the influence of Franz Boas she began to concentrate on anthropology about 1915, becoming known for her studies of the Indians of the southwestern United States. She helped to found the New School for Social Research and the magazine the *New Republic* and was active in the salon of Mabel Dodge and other artistic and intellectual circles. Parsons was also a noted feminist, pacifist, and social critic. Her published writings include *The Family: An Ethnographical and Historical Outline with Descriptive Notes* (1906), *Mitla, Town of the Souls, and Other Zapoteco-Speaking Pueblos at Oaxaca, Mexico* (1936), and *Pueblo Indian Religion* (1939).

Rosemary Lévy Zumwalt: *Wealth and Rebellion: Elsie Clews Parsons, Anthropologist and Folklorist* (Urbana: University of Illinois Press, 1992)

Ira Jacknis

Parsons, William Barclay (*b* New York City, 15 April 1859; *d* New York City, 9 May 1932). Civil engineer. He graduated from Columbia University (AB 1879, civil engineering degree 1882). As the chief engineer for the Rapid Transit Commission of New York (1894–1905) he supervised the planning and construction of the city's first subway line, the Interborough Rapid Transit (IRT). A trustee of Columbia (from 1897) and later the chairman of the board of the Columbia Medical Hospital, he took an active role in establishing the university's campus on Morningside Heights at the turn of the century and in the building of Presbyterian Hospital. He was also a surveyor for the Chinese railway system (1898–99), the chief engineer for the Cape Cod Canal (1905–14), a consulting engineer for the Panama Canal (1905), and chairman of the Chicago Transit Commission. Parsons's practice was a forerunner of the firm of consulting engineers Parsons–Brinkerhoff. His published writings include *Track* (1885), *Turnouts* (1885), *American Engineering in China* (1900), *Rapid Transit in Foreign Cities* (1895), *American Engineers in France* (1920), and *Robert Fulton and the Submarine* (1923). A vestryman at Trinity Church, he lived for many years at 35 East 50th Street.

Shan Jayakumar

Parsons School of Design. Private art school at 5th Avenue and 13th Street in Manhattan, opened in 1896 as the Chase School of Art by the painter and art teacher William Merritt Chase. The school was known as the New York School for Fine and Applied Art when it was led from 1905 to 1930 by Frank Alvah Parsons (1866–1930), who shifted the emphasis away from painting and sculpture and toward design and the applied arts, and introduced a unique curriculum that included courses in interior decoration, costume design, teacher training, and advertising design. By 1922 the school had established a full-time program in Paris that was the first program for study abroad supported by an American art institution. The current name dates to 1940. About two thousand students are enrolled at the school, which offers undergraduate and graduate degrees in design, the visual arts, and the fine arts. The work of students and of artists and designers from the United States and abroad is shown at the Parsons Exhibition Center, one of the largest public galleries in lower Manhattan. Parsons became an affiliate of the New School for Social Research in 1970.

Frank Alvah Parsons: "The New York School of Fine and Applied Arts, Its Twenty-five Years of Growth," *Portfolio*, Dec 1921

David C. Levy: *An Historical Study of Parsons School of Design and Its Merger / Affiliation with the New School for Social Research* (New York: New York University Press, 1979)

Linda Elsroad

partisan press. An openly partisan form of journalism developed during the nineteenth century as political parties began to subsidize and control newspapers across the country and particularly in New York City. The *Evening Post*, a Federalist newspaper, was launched in the city in 1801 by Alexander Hamilton to counteract Republican opposition. John D. Burk, anti-Federalist editor of the *Time Piece*, feared prosecution for his political outspokenness under the Alien and Sedition Acts and went underground for two years. Both newspapers blurred the distinction between news and opinion, and commonly printed party slogans on their mastheads. During the 1830s the *Evening Post* shifted its allegiance from the Federalists to the Democrats and lent critical eastern support to Andrew Jackson. Partisan journalism took its extreme form in short-lived campaign newspapers that existed solely to promote candidates, among them the Whig newspaper the *Log Cabin*. To counteract the domination of Democratic newspapers in New York City the Whigs founded the *New York Tribune* (1841), which by the 1870s turned Republican and engaged its opponent, the Democratic *World*, in heated partisan headline warfare. Journalists who displayed loyalty toward a party were often rewarded with lucrative state printing contracts and appointments to political office.

The economic ties between the press and political parties weakened as newspapers increasingly relied on advertising for revenues, a trend that began in New York City during the mid nineteenth century. While partisan journalism continued, editors such as Horace Greeley of the *New York Tribune* seized control over the political content of their newspapers from the parties. The labor press in New York City began promoting objective journalism in the 1830s, which it maintained would enable citizens to make independent political judgments. In the 1840s the use of wire services in New York City made news more homogeneous than before and partisan distortions all the more obvious. The *New York Times* led efforts to professionalize journalism in the 1870s by making objective, independent reporting its highest goal. It led a crusade against the Tweed Ring in 1870–71 and later against political parties themselves. Partisanship in journalism was further disclaimed by editors such as E. L. Godkin who led a movement for liberal reform in the late nineteenth century. By the 1880s New York City emerged as a center of independent journalism, as large daily newspapers embraced objectivity and symbolically replaced partisan mastheads with ones extolling factuality.

Edwin Emery and Michael Emery: *The Press and America: An Interpretive History of the Mass Media* (Englewood Cliffs, N.J.: Prentice Hall, 1978)
Michael Schudson: *Discovering the News: A Social History of American Newspapers* (New York: Basic Books, 1978)
Michael McGerr: *The Decline of Popular Politics: The American North, 1865–1928* (New York: Oxford University Press, 1986)

Becky M. Nicolaides

Partisan Review. Quarterly magazine launched by the John Reed Club in 1935. It was reshaped in 1937 as an independent radical publication by Philip Rahv and William Phillips, who objected to the treatment of culture as a political issue by many communists. The magazine challenged the communists' domination of leftist thought, quickly becoming the most important forum for anti-Stalinism and the most influential publication of its kind in the nation. In May–June 1954 it sponsored an influential symposium, "Our Country and Our Culture," that included such participants as Norman Mailer, Reinhold Niebuhr, David Riesman, and Lionel Trilling. Its influence declined after 1960; Phillips remained the editor into the 1990s.

James Burkhart Gilbert: *Writers and Partisans: A History of Literary Radicalism in America* (New York: John Wiley and Sons, 1968)
Partisan Review: The Fiftieth Anniversary Edition (New York: Stein and Day, 1984)

Lawson Bowling

Pastor, Tony [Antonio] (*b* New York City, ?1834; *d* Queens, 26 Aug 1908). Theater manager and variety performer. He began his career in 1846 at P. T. Barnum's Museum; later he operated several concert saloons in New York City, the first of which opened in 1865 at 201 Bowery. In the last concert saloon that he operated, situated on 14th Street and opened in 1881, he promoted vaudeville suitable for families. Often called the "father of vaudeville," Pastor was chiefly responsible for adapting the boisterous, largely male performances of the concert saloons to the more genteel world of vaudeville.

See also VAUDEVILLE.

Don B. Wilmeth

PATH [Port Authority Trans-Hudson Corporation]. Rapid transit system formed in 1962 that connects stations in New Jersey at Newark and Hoboken to midtown and lower Manhattan. It uses fourteen miles (twenty-two kilometers) of route built between 1874 and 1909 and formerly used by the Hudson and Manhattan Railroad. The system is a subsidiary of the Port Authority of New York and New Jersey, which covers capital expenses. In the early 1990s about 200,000 passengers each weekday paid a fare of $1 to ride the PATH.

Gilbert H. Gilbert, Lucius I. Wightman, and W. L. Saunders: *The Subways and Tunnels of New York* (New York: John Wiley and Sons, 1912)
Brian J. Cudahy: *Rails under the Mighty Hudson: The Story of the Hudson Tubes, the Pennsy Tunnels and Manhattan Transfer* (Brattleboro, Vt.: Stephen Greene, 1975)
Daniel L. Schodek: *Landmarks in American Civil Engineering* (Cambridge: MIT Press, 1987)

Robert A. Olmsted

Pathmark. A chain of supermarkets operated by Supermarkets General Corporation, and one of the ten largest grocery chains in the United States. It was formed in 1968 under the direction of Milton Perlmutter by several members of the Wakefern Cooperative, which operated supermarkets in New York City and its environs under the name Shop Rite. The firm encouraged the operators of its stores to heed local preferences, and also followed a policy of community involvement. In 1977 it entered into an agreement with the Bedford Stuyvesant Restoration Corporation to build a supermarket in one of the most severely depressed parts of Brooklyn. Pathmark opened a supermarket at Pike Slip in Manhattan in the mid 1980s after persuading local merchants that the store would help the local economy rather than drive competitors out of business.

Chad Ludington

Patrolmen's Benevolent Association [PBA]. Labor organization formed as a protective society in 1894 to assure proper burials for police officers who died during the influenza epidemic. In 1911 it won its first important legislative victory when it secured passage of a "three platoon" law, which replaced the system of two twelve-hour work shifts with three eight-hour shifts. From 1914 to 1935 the president of the PBA was Joseph Moran; his retirement was followed by a period of instability that lasted until John Carton was elected president in 1947 by defeating Raymond Donovan, who advocated that the PBA break with tradition by declaring itself a union. In 1951 Donovan led a small faction of officers who joined the United Patrolmen's Association, an affiliate of the Transit Workers Union; their insurgency ended when the police commissioner, George P. Monaghan, threatened to take disciplinary action. Carton remained president until 1958 and won large pay increases for his men. His successor, John Cassese, soon revived the controversy over the formal status of the organization: he threatened to form an affiliation with the International Brotherhood of Teamsters, owing to the city's refusal in 1958 to have the PBA collect membership dues through payroll deductions, a source of operating income that most other municipal unions had been granted. In 1964 Mayor Robert F. Wagner extended this right to the PBA and recognized it as the exclusive collective bargaining unit for police officers. The years 1966 to 1973 were a tumultuous period for the PBA, during which the most volatile issue was the demand of firefighters and sanitation workers that their salaries match those of police officers. After Cassese retired in 1969 the PBA experienced another period of instability until Philip Caruso's election as president in 1980.

Emma Schweppe: *The Firemen's and Patrolmen's Unions in the City of New York* (New York: King's Crown, 1948)
Margaret Levi: *Bureaucratic Insurgency: The Case of Police Unions* (Beverly Hills, Calif.: Sage, 1973)

Joseph P. Viteritti

patronage. For a discussion of patronage see CIVIL SERVICE.

pattern making. The first unsized clothing patterns appeared in fashion magazines in the early 1850s; sized patterns were introduced in 1864 and made it possible for amateur seamstresses and women working at home to produce fashionable clothes tailored to the wearer. During the second half of the nineteenth century the focus of the pattern business shifted to New York City when the three largest companies moved there (E. Butterick and Company, Madame Demorest, and McCall), as did several smaller ones. Patterns were a practical and economical alternative to drafting systems and dressmakers and became popular throughout the United States and Europe, especially among women who lived far from cities; Butterick's patterns sold for ten to seventy-five cents each in 1867, Demorest's skirt and bodice patterns for as little as thirty cents each in 1877. At its height in the 1870s Demorest purchased five thousand reams of tissue paper and two million envelopes at a time and reportedly sold fifty thousand copies of its most popular styles. Demorest's rival, E. Butterick and Company, sold between four and six million patterns annually. The pattern business helped to make New York City the fashion capital of the United States and to set national standards of style and taste by reinterpreting Parisian vogues for American consumers. Fashion magazines were sometimes issued by pattern manufacturers: *Mme. Demorest's What to Wear*, *Demorest's Monthly Magazine*, and *The Quarterly Mirror of Fashion* by Demorest; *The Ladies' Quarterly Report of Fashions*, *The Metropolitan*, and *The Delineator* by Butterick; and *The Queen* and *The Bazar Dressmaker* by McCall. These reached a combined readership of nearly 400,000 by the 1880s. In the early twentieth century women's ready-made apparel replaced pattern making as the primary fashion enterprise in New York City. A few of the large pattern manufacturers continued into the late twentieth century, including Butterick and McCall.

Claudia B. Kidwell: *Cutting a Fashionable Fit: Dressmakers' Drafting Systems in the United States* (Washington: Smithsonian Institution Press, 1979)

Margaret Walsh: "The Democratization of Fashion: The Emergence of the Women's Dress Pattern Industry," *Journal of American History* 66 (1979), 299–313

Nancy Page Fernandez: "'If a Woman Had Taste . . .': Home Sewing and the Making of Fashion, 1850–1910" (diss., University of California, Irvine, 1987)

For illustration see BUTTERICK, EBENEZER.

Wendy Gamber

Patterson, Alicia (*b* Chicago, 15 Oct 1906; *d* New York City, 2 July 1963). Newspaper editor and publisher. She learned the newspaper business from her father, Joseph Medill Patterson, founder of the *Daily News*. In a financial partnership with her husband, Harry Guggenheim, in 1940 she launched *Newsday*, a tabloid newspaper that she made into a powerful force on Long Island by means of local reporting, aggressive efforts to increase regular readership through home delivery, and coverage that treated the island as a unified political and economic region. In her later years she opposed the isolationist views of her father, who responded by reneging on plans to give her control of the *Daily News*.

Robert F. Keeler: *Newsday: A Candid History of the Respectable Tabloid* (New York: William Morrow, 1990)

Madeline Rogers

Patterson, Joseph Medill (*b* Chicago, 6 Jan 1879; *d* New York City, 26 May 1946). Newspaper publisher, father of Alicia Patterson. A grandson of Joseph Medill, founder of the *Chicago Tribune*, and son of Robert Wilson Patterson, its editor-in-chief, he attended Groton and Yale University (class of 1901) and went to work as a reporter for the *Tribune*. Fascinated by socialist politics and literature, he was elected to the state legislature of Illinois in 1903, managed Eugene V. Debs's presidential campaign in 1908, wrote two proletarian novels, and had three of his plays produced on Broadway before returning to the *Tribune* as a co-editor in 1912. From 1914 he worked as a war correspondent in Mexico, Belgium, Germany, and China. After returning to the United States he set out to publish a daily newspaper with mass appeal along the lines of Lord Northcliffe's *Daily Mirror*, and in 1919 he launched the *Illustrated Daily News*, published in New York City while he remained in Chicago. Renamed the *Daily News*, the newspaper became the first successful American tabloid and by 1924 was the most popular newspaper in the United States, reaching 750,000 readers daily. In 1925 he moved to New York City to manage it full time. Circulation exceeded one million by 1926 and almost two million by 1940. As an editor Patterson was often known as dictatorial and suspicious, yet he paid his trusted employees uncommonly high salaries and took pride in staying in touch with the common people, frequenting nightclubs in Coney Island, Times Square, and the Bowery. During the Depression he was a close advisor to President Franklin D. Roosevelt and an outspoken supporter of the New Deal, and his series of editorials defending Roosevelt's candidacy for a third term in 1940 helped him win a Pulitzer Prize. The relationship between the two worsened when Patterson espoused an editorial policy of ardent isolationism during the Second World War. He ran the *Daily News* until his death.

Jack Alexander: "Vox Populi," *New Yorker*, 6 Aug 1938, 13 Aug 1938, 20 Aug 1938

Frank Luther Mott: *American Journalism* (New York: Macmillan, 1941)

John Tebbel: *An American Dynasty* (New York: Greenwood, 1968)

Leo E. McGivena et al.: *The News: The First Fifty Years of New York's Picture Newspaper* (New York: News Syndicate, 1969)

Steve Rivo

Paul, Weiss, Rifkind, Wharton and Garrison. Law firm established in 1927 when the partnership of John Wharton and Louis Weiss merged with the firm of Cohen, Cole and Weiss to become Cohen, Cole, Weiss and Wharton. At a time when most law firms in New York City were either overwhelmingly Jewish or gentile, the firm chose its staff without regard to religious background. Early on it developed a thriving entertainment practice led by Wharton, who devised the standard form of agreement used to finance theatrical productions. Randolph Paul, a tax specialist and former undersecretary of the treasury, became a partner in 1946; the former federal judge Simon H. Rifkind followed in 1950, the year the firm took its current name, and set up the firm's litigation department. Several lawyers in the firm were active in national and international politics, including Adlai Stevenson, Lloyd K. Garrison, former head of the War Labor Board, Arthur Goldberg, justice of the Supreme Court and ambassador to the United Nations, and Ramsey Clark, former attorney general. During the city's fiscal crisis in 1975 lawyers at the firm drafted legislation that created the Municipal Assistance Corporation, the agency responsible for stabilizing the city's finances. Public figures who were members of the firm during the early 1990s included Rifkind, the Democratic leader Edward N. Costikyan, Theodore C. Sorensen, special counsel to Presidents John F. Kennedy and Lyndon B. Johnson, and Matthew Nimetz, former undersecretary of state. In 1991 Paul, Weiss, Rifkind, Wharton and Garrison employed 372 lawyers, including eighty-seven partners, and maintained six offices in the United States and abroad.

Fay Rosenfeld

Paulding, James Kirke (*b* Great Nine Partners, Putnam County, N.Y., 22 Aug 1778; *d* New York City, 6 April 1860). Writer and naval officer, brother of William Paulding Jr. He grew up in Tarrytown, New York, where he became a friend of Washington Irving; together they published the whimsical journal *Salmagundi* in 1807–8. Paulding soon wrote *The Diverting History of John Bull and Brother Jonathan* and poetry that he defended in *The United States and England* (1815). He was later appointed secretary of the navy commissioners (1815–23), naval agent for New York State (1824–38), and secretary of the navy (1838–41). His works include a life of Washington, studies of the South, dozens of tales, and such novels about New York City as *The Dutchman's Fireside* and *The Old Continental*. He is buried in Green-Wood Cemetery.

Larry J. Reynolds: *James Kirke Paulding* (Boston: Twayne, 1984)

James E. Mooney

Paulding, William, Jr. (*b* Tarrytown, N.Y., 7 March 1770; *d* Tarrytown, 11 Feb 1854). Congressman and mayor, brother of James Kirke Paulding. He studied law and practiced in New York City for several years before his election to the U.S. House of Representatives as a Democrat from the twelfth district (1811–13). During the War of 1812 he was a brigadier general in the state militia. A delegate to the state constitutional convention of 1821, he was the state's adjutant general before his election as mayor in 1824; he remained in office until 1825, when he was replaced by Philip Hone, but won reelection and held office again from 1826 to 1829.

James E. Mooney

paving. The first recorded paving of a street in New Amsterdam took place in 1658, when at the request of nearby residents cobblestones were laid along what later became Stone Street between Whitehall and Broad streets. In May 1684 the Common Council ordered that principal streets be paved, the expense to be borne by the owners of adjacent property. Legislation passed on 20 May 1708 mandated stricter enforcement of paving regulations and noted that earlier measures had

Paving blocks on 28th Street between Broadway and 6th Avenue, 2 October 1930

gone unheeded. In 1748 the streets of New York City were said by visitors to be spacious and well paved, but they were reported to be filthy and often impassable on 6 April 1787 when the state legislature granted the power to pave the streets to the Common Council. Legislation passed by the council in April 1789 imposed severe penalties for the breach of paving regulations. From the 1830s experiments were undertaken with different paving materials, including macadam, woodblocks, and cut stone block. Square, granite paving stones called Belgian blocks and rectangular blocks made of trap stone became widespread in 1852, replacing the common round cobblestones. In 1876 there were 299 miles (481 kilometers) of paved streets in New York City, of which Belgian and trap blocks accounted for 146 miles (235 kilometers), cobblestones for eighty-six miles (138 kilometers), and other materials including concrete, wood, macadam, and gravel for sixty-seven miles (108 kilometers). Asphalt pavement was introduced in the city in 1884 and represented a marked improvement over stone block, which was bumpy and noisy; it was officially adopted on 6 January 1890 for streets not extensively used for business purposes and remained in use more than a century later to pave the more than 6300 miles (10,100 kilometers) of streets and highways in the five boroughs.

I. N. Phelps Stokes: *The Iconography of Manhattan Island, 1498–1909, Compiled from Original Sources and Illustrated by Photo Intaglio Reproductions of Important Maps, Plans, Views and Documents in Public and Private Collections* (New York: Robert H. Dodd, 1915–28; repr. Arno, 1967)

James Ford: *Slums and Housing, with Special Reference to New York City: History, Conditions, Policy* (Westport, Conn.: Negro Universities Press, 1971)

Craig D. Bida

Pavlova, Anna (Pavlovna) (*b* St. Petersburg, 12 Feb 1881; *d* The Hague, 23 Jan 1931). Dancer. She was trained at the Imperial School of Ballet in St. Petersburg. In 1909 her performance with Serge Diaghilev's Ballets Russes was seen by Otto H. Kahn, director of the Metropolitan Opera, who signed her and her partner Mikhail Mordkin to a one-month contract; the two opened on 28 February 1910 in *Coppélia* to great success. Although Pavlova occasionally returned to Russia before the First World War she spent much of her career in New York City. She is considered the greatest ballerina of the early twentieth century.

Keith Money: *Anna Pavlova: Her Life and Art* (New York: Alfred A. Knopf, 1982)

Barbara Barker

pawnshops. The first pawnshop in New York City was opened in 1822 at 25 Chatham Street by an Englishman named William Simpson. The many secondhand shops operated by usurers at the time also lent money on personal property, but unlike pawnshops they required customers to sign conditional bills of sale. Typically customers exchanged items such as jewelry or clothing for money and agreed to repay the amount borrowed plus interest to redeem their property, which those who could not pay would forfeit. Pawnbrokers appraised merchandise and gave their customers pawn tickets, which were either used to redeem pledges or sold to hock-ticket peddlers (pawnshops were also known as hockshops). In 1838 Simpson paid $5 for coats, $1 for watches, and fifty cents for pants. A typical business day in 1841 brought in 153 items valued at $655.71, and in 1842 his vault held jewelry on which $34,504.31 was lent. Other pawnshops soon opened and in time enjoyed a virtual monopoly of the lending field, in part by remaining open twenty-four hours a day. They ran the risk that the property they accepted would later be found to have been stolen, and they were sometimes embroiled in disputes over the ownership of valuables in businesses that were jointly owned. From 1891 to 1916 Simpson made $100,000 to $200,000 a year.

In the late 1980s pawnshops experienced a resurgence, as members of the middle class and the affluent turned to them in a period of layoffs, bankruptcies, foreclosures, tight credit, high medical bills, and costly divorce settlements. Nationwide the number of pawnshops increased by more than half from 1986 to 1991. At the same time there was a trend toward publicly owned operators of pawnshops, such as Cash American Investments and Ezcorp. Edward Lewis Wallant's novel *The Pawnbroker* (1961), which was made into a popular film, is set in New York City.

William R. Simpson, Florence K. Simpson, and Charles Samuels: *Hockshop* (New York: Random House, 1954)

Mary Ann Romano

Payton, Philip A. (, Jr.) (*b* Westfield, Mass., 1876; *d* Allenhurst, N.J., 29 Aug 1917). Businessman. A graduate of Livingston College (1898), he moved in 1899 to New York City, where as the president of the Afro-American Realty Company (incorporated 1904) he was the first real-estate agent to rent apartments in Harlem to blacks. His success inspired other blacks to become real-estate agents, including John E. Nail and Henry C. Parker. Afro-American Realty declared bankruptcy in 1908, after which Payton bought and managed buildings from an office at 67 West 134th Street.

Alana J. Erickson

peace movements. Organized opposition to war began in New York City during the colonial period, when Dutch Mennonites, Quakers, and Moravians from central Europe refused to take up arms or pay taxes specifically intended for war. On 14 August 1815 the Christian pacifist and wealthy merchant David Low Dodge formed the New York Peace Society, one of the first organizations in the world to hold the abolition of war as its single goal. The society condemned all warfare as opposed to the example of Jesus, and insisted that all its members be affiliated with an evangelical church. A kindred organization, the American Peace Society (1828), had its headquarters for a time in New York City. The peace movement declined at the onset of the Civil War, as most of its adherents had an equally strong commitment to the crusade against slavery.

When the peace movement was revived in the late nineteenth century its earlier religious basis was replaced by a secular internationalism. The emergence of New York City as a center of international finance and trade made many local businessmen become more concerned with foreign affairs, and the New York Peace Society was revived and under Andrew Carnegie's leadership soon became the largest branch of the American Peace Society. The society campaigned for the international arbitration treaties negotiated during the presidency of William Howard Taft and organized the highly successful National Arbitration and Peace Congress held in New York City on the eve of the conference at The Hague in 1907. Carnegie donated $10 million in 1910 to form the Carnegie Endowment for International Peace, but the conservative leadership of the organization favored scholarly research and had little enthusiasm for pacifist activity. The peace movement before the First World War was mostly sustained by an élite who sought to avoid a war among the great powers: they equated peace with the preservation of a stable international order and were generally accepting of the existing imperial system.

The outbreak of war produced an extraordinary transformation of the pacifist movement, as women emerged in leadership roles. On 29 August 1914 fifteen hundred women in mourning dress marched in silence down 5th Avenue behind a large white banner depicting a dove holding an olive branch. A coalition of women's groups in 1915 formed the Women's Peace Party under the leadership of Jane Addams and Carrie Chapman Catt; the group was founded in Washington but had a very active branch in New York City. Many members were suffragists, and most believed that the nurturing role of women led them naturally to oppose violence and war. Ignoring the wrath of critics, they organized a conference at The Hague that brought together women from the warring nations. Leaders of the conference met with heads of state in an unsuccessful effort to mediate the conflict. In later years participants in the conference formed the Women's International League for Peace and Freedom, which had an active, sometimes faction-ridden chapter in New York City and remained active into the 1990s. At the same time a branch of the Women's Peace Party in the city led by Crystal Eastman campaigned against a buildup of American armed forces, fearing that it would lead to involvement in the war. Another activist organization, the American Union against Militarism (1916), grew out of a meeting of reformers at the Henry Street Settlement. Led by Lillian Wald and Paul Kellogg, editor of the magazine the *Survey*, the group argued that war would prevent the implementation of domestic reforms, and sought to mobilize public pressure on President Woodrow Wilson to mediate among warring nations to end the conflict. A group of well-known internationalists led by Taft and A. Lawrence Lowell, the president of Harvard University, formed the League to Enforce Peace in 1915 during a series of meetings at the Century Club in New York City. The league urged that after the war nations should settle their disputes through an international tribunal, failing which it favored collective retaliation against offenders. The carnage in Europe lent weight to this message, and the league became the catalyst for the formation of a postwar league of nations.

American entry into the war dealt a series of blows to organizations that had opposed it: many suffragists in the pacifist movement aided the war effort as a means of winning public support and gaining the vote, and the city's trade unions were faced with the choice between making gains by cooperating with the war effort and being persecuted for opposing it. After the war internationalists in 1919 organized the League of Free Nations Association (which became the Foreign Policy Association in 1921): its program favored planned reconstruction, liberalized trade, and social democracy. Although some pacifists continued to press for American membership in the League of Nations after the U.S. Senate blocked it, many others were discouraged by the punitive Treaty of Versailles and by postwar xenophobia.

During the 1920s and 1930s the Women's Peace Union, based primarily in New York City and led by Elinor Byrns, campaigned for a constitutional amendment that would limit American participation in future wars. The Fellowship of Reconciliation, formed in 1915 in Garden City, New York, advocated an absolute pacifism; its leaders, including A. J. Muste and John Haynes Holmes, successfully appealed to many Protestant clergymen who had come to regret their enthusiasm for the war. Pacifist groups had substantial appeal during the 1930s until Hitler's stunning conquest of France and the Battle of Britain in 1940, and above all the Japanese attack on Pearl Harbor. Pacifists were now a tiny, embattled minority, their efforts reduced to protecting the rights of conscientious objectors.

With the end of the Second World War and the beginning of the atomic age many internationalists believed that American membership in the United Nations was insufficient to achieve world peace. The United World Federalists, formed in 1947 at a convention in Asheville, North Carolina, by the end of the following year claimed 659 chapters and forty thousand members, many of whom were in New York City. The group advocated a world government with the authority to create an international police force, and it grew rapidly when it enlisted a number of scientists fearful of an atomic arms race. In 1957 Norman Cousins, editor of the *Saturday Review*, brought together at the Overseas Press Club in New York City a coalition of pacifists, liberals, and scientists disturbed by the dangers of radiation from atmospheric nuclear testing; the psychologist Erich Fromm named the group the Committee for a Sane Nuclear Policy (SANE). Peace activism was unpopular during the cold war. Critics demanded that SANE purge its ranks of communists, and when Cousins acquiesced some leaders like Linus Pauling resigned and several chapters in New York City refused to investigate their own members. SANE survived the purge but was weakened in the process.

President Lyndon B. Johnson's escalation of the Vietnam War led to protests from peace organizations, and opposition broadened when the demands imposed by the war led to the sacrifice of domestic programs. Residents of New York City organized candlelight vigils, public readings, "teach-ins" on college campuses, petition campaigns, and marches on Washington. Columbia University was the scene of a violent confrontation between students and police in 1968. Leading antiwar organizations active in the city included Women Strike for Peace, the Fifth Avenue Peace Parade Committee, Vietnam Veterans against the War, and Clergy and Laymen Concerned about Viet Nam. President Richard M. Nixon's continuation of the war led to mass protests known as moratoriums in October and November 1969. The protests diminished only when Nixon began to withdraw forces from Vietnam and discontinued the military draft.

A widespread reluctance among Americans to become embroiled in military conflicts after the Vietnam War took some of the urgency from the peace movement, which in the 1980s focused its efforts on slowing the buildup in nuclear arms by the United States and the Soviet Union. One of the stronger organizations in New York City was Physicians for Social Responsibility, formed in 1982 in Boston. On 12 June 1982 peace advocates from every region of the country gathered in New York City for the United Nations Special Session on Disarmament, and nearly one million persons marched from the United Nations to Central Park to call for a nuclear freeze.

During the crisis in the Persian Gulf in 1990, New York City was the focus of considerable dissent against President George Bush's decision to deploy troops. The calls for sanctions rather than war mirrored the spirited debate taking place in the U.S. Congress.

Peter Brock: *Pacifism in the United States, from the Colonial Era to the First World War* (Princeton, N.J.: Princeton University Press, 1968)

Charles DeBenedetti: *The Peace Reform in American History* (Bloomington: Indiana University Press, 1980)

Charles DeBenedetti and Charles Chatfield: *An American Ordeal: The Antiwar Movement of the Viet-*

nam Era (Syracuse, N.Y.: Syracuse University Press, 1990)

Michael A. Lutzker

Peale, Norman Vincent (*b* Bowersville, Ohio, 31 May 1898; *d* Pawling, N.Y., 24 Dec 1993). Preacher, writer, and religious counselor. The son of a Methodist physician who became a minister, he lived in several small towns in Ohio during his childhood and attended Ohio Wesleyan University (BA 1920) and Boston University (MA, STM 1924); he was ordained a Methodist minister in 1922. After leading parishes in Rhode Island, Brooklyn, and Syracuse, New York, he became the pastor of Marble Collegiate Church in 1932, where he developed "positive thinking," a program that blended popular psychology and Christian idiom into a practical philosophy that found many adherents, especially among professionals in Manhattan. Peale proposed that a willful and practiced change in attitude can bring about prosperity, inner peace, health, and popularity, views that he articulated in his book *The Power of Positive Thinking* (1952). As a member of various local organizations he opposed the New Deal in the 1930s, communism in the 1950s, and the presidential candidacy of John F. Kennedy in 1960. Despite such controversies he concentrated on spreading his message: he launched a radio program (which became nationally syndicated) and the monthly magazine *Guideposts*, and also had a newspaper column, wrote more than twenty books, and gave many speeches. He was president of the Protestant Council of the City of New York from 1965 to 1969. Toward the end of his life Peale had the largest outpatient psychiatric clinic in the country and remained one of the country's best-known religious figures. In 1984 he received the Presidential Medal of Freedom.

Donald B. Meyer: *The Positive Thinkers: A Study of the American Quest for Health, Wealth and Personal Power from Mary Baker Eddy to Norman Vincent Peale* (Garden City, N.Y.: Doubleday, 1965; rev. Middletown, Conn.: Wesleyan University Press, 1988)

James D. Bratt

Peat, Marwick, Mitchell and Copartners. Accounting firm. Its formation in New York City in 1911 was the result of a chance meeting on a transatlantic crossing between William Peat, who ran a successful accounting firm in London, and James Marwick. The two and their fellow Scotsman Robert Mitchell had established a similar firm in New York City in 1897 and agreed to work together again. The firm grew slowly during the Depression but boomed after the Second World War, becoming the second-largest accounting firm in the world. In 1987 it merged with KMG of Amsterdam to form KPMG PEAT MARWICK.

Chad Ludington

Peckham, Wheeler H(azard) (*b* Albany, N.Y., 1 Jan 1833; *d* New York City, 27 Sept 1905). Lawyer. He studied at Albany Law School, was admitted to the bar in 1854, and in 1864 entered into a partnership with George M. Miller and John A. Stoutenburgh in New York City. In 1873 he was a key figure in the successful prosecution of William M. "Boss" Tweed. He was a founder of the Association of the Bar of the City of New York (1869), of which he also served as president (1892–94). In 1894 Peckham was nominated to the U.S. Supreme Court by President Grover Cleveland, but his confirmation was blocked by both senators from New York, who resented his opposition to Tammany Hall.

Pecora, Ferdinand (*b* Nicosia, Italy, 6 Jan 1882; *d* New York City, 7 Dec 1971). Judge. He moved to New York City with his family in 1887 and later earned a degree from New York Law School. After working in the district attorney's office for twelve years he was appointed counsel to the committee on banking of the U.S. Senate in 1933–34; his investigations uncovered questionable practices on Wall Street and led to the passage of the securities acts of 1933 and 1934. He was the first director of the Securities and Exchange Commission, resigning to become a justice of the Supreme Court of New York. In 1950 he sought election as mayor. He was also counsel to the law firm of Schwartz and Frolich and a director of Freedom House. Pecora's writings include *Wall Street under Oath* (1939).

See also CIVIL SERVICE UNIONS.

James E. Mooney

Peerce, Jan (*b* New York City, 3 June 1904; *d* New York City, 15 Dec 1984). Singer. He began his career singing and playing the violin at resorts in the Catskills and with dance bands, often using the pseudonym Pinkey Pearl. After singing briefly at Radio City Music Hall he made his operatic début in 1939 and first sang at the Metropolitan Opera in 1941 as Alfredo in *La Traviata*. His career encompassed 324 performances in eleven operas, including *La Bohème*, *Carmen*, and *Rigoletto*. A favorite of the conductor Arturo Toscanini, Peerce was known for his refinement and rich tone, and gave concerts into the 1970s. He was related by marriage to Richard Tucker.

David J. Weiner

Pei, I(eoh) M(ing) (*b* Canton, China, 26 April 1917). Architect. After graduating from the Massachusetts Institute of Technology he began practicing architecture in New York City in 1939. In 1955 he formed I. M. Pei and Associates (now Pei Cobb Freed and Partners), one of the best-known architectural firms in New York City. His projects in the city include the Jacob K. Javits Convention Center, a spectacular glass monument (for illustration see JACOB K. JAVITS CONVENTION CENTER), the National Airlines Terminal at John F. Kennedy International Airport, New York University Plaza, and Kips Bay Plaza. His offices are at 600 Madison Avenue.

Carter Wiseman: *I. M. Pei: A Profile in American Architecture* (New York: Harry N. Abrams, 1990)

Elliot S. Meadows

Pelham Bay. Neighborhood in the northeastern Bronx, south of Pelham Parkway and east of Pelham Bay Park. It took shape about 1920 around a recently completed terminal station of Interborough Rapid Transit. The housing stock consists of brick apartment buildings dating from the 1920s and the years following the Second World War, along with some one-family houses. The population is mostly Italian and Irish. Westchester Avenue is the principal commercial thoroughfare. One well-known resident of Pelham Bay was George Meany, first president of the AFL–CIO.

Lloyd Ultan

Pelham Bay Park. Public park in the northeastern Bronx, bounded to the north by Westchester County, to the east by City Island and Long Island Sound, to the south by Watt Avenue and Bruckner Boulevard, and to the west by the Hutchinson River Parkway. Including Orchard Beach it comprises 2764 acres (1120 hectares), making it three times the size of Central Park in Manhattan and among parks in New York City second in area only to the Federal Gateway National Recreation Area. The land was the site in 1776 of the Battle of Bell's Point, in which Colonel John Glover and his militia held off the Hessian army of Sir William Howe, allowing General Washington and his army to escape to White Plains. It was acquired by the state legislature at the urging of the New York Park Association in 1888, when the surrounding area was largely undeveloped. Within the park are the Bartow–Pell Mansion (1836–42), the only surviving estate from among more than two dozen that once overlooked Pelham Bay, the Pelham Bay Golf Course (1914), and the Split Rock golf course (1936), which is named for a nearby boulder and Indian trail and has a clubhouse reminiscent of a mansion on a southern plantation. Orchard Beach, a large public bathing facility on Long Island Sound opened in the mid 1930s by dredging of the nearby waters, links the mainland to Hunter's Island, now a wooded nature sanctuary. The inlet formerly connected to the sound became a lagoon where the trials for the U.S. Olympic rowing team were held in 1964. Pelham Bay Park has more than nine miles (fourteen kilometers) of shoreline, two public golf courses, ballfields, bridle paths, tennis courts, nature preserves, and a firing range of the New York Police Department at Rodman's Neck; two important highways and the Boston line of Amtrak run through it.

Aerial view of Pelham Bay Park and Orchard Beach

John Mullaly: *The New Parks beyond the Harlem* (New York: Records and Guide, 1887)
Gary Hermalyn: "The Bronx at the Turn of the Century," *Bronx County Historical Society Journal* 26 (1989), 92–107

Gary D. Hermalyn, Jonathan Kuhn

PEN. See POETS, PLAYWRIGHTS, EDITORS AND NOVELISTS.

Penfield, Edward (*b* Brooklyn, 2 June 1866; *d* Beacon, N.Y., 8 Feb 1925). Painter and illustrator. He studied at the Art Students League before becoming the art editor in 1890 of Harper's magazines, a position he resigned in 1901 to devote himself to his own work. In his murals and posters he used designs based on Japanese principles of simplicity. His illustrations for John Kendrick Bangs's book *Dreamers* (1899), and for *Holland Sketches* (1907) and *Spanish Sketches* (1911), are well known. Penfield lived at 163 West 23rd Street and then in Pelham Manor, where a small collection of his work is preserved at a high school.

James E. Mooney

Penn Central Transportation Co. v. City of New York. Case decided in 1978 (438 U.S. 104) by the U.S. Supreme Court, which upheld the application of the Landmarks Preservation Law of New York City to a proposed development involving Grand Central Terminal. The law prevented the owner of the building, the Penn Central, from constructing a fifty-five-story office tower over the terminal and stripping off part of its façade. The court held that the restriction on the development, which did not interfere with the use of the terminal and permitted the owner to transfer the air rights over the terminal to other parcels of land in the vicinity, was "substantially related to the promotion of the general welfare" and did not constitute a "taking" of property without just compensation.

Richard Briffault

Pennington, J(ames) W(illiam) C(harles) (*b* Maryland, 1807; *d* Jacksonville, Fla., 20/22 Oct 1870). Minister and writer. After escaping from slavery in Maryland about 1828 he was educated by Quakers, worked as a blacksmith, and was a pastor on Long Island, in Connecticut, and then at the First (Shiloh) Presbyterian Church on Prince Street in New York City (1847–55). A strong supporter of John Brown, he was among the most radical black ministers in antebellum New York City. He received the doctorate of divinity from the University of Heidelberg in 1851 and later wrote an important narrative of his years as a slave and a history of blacks in colonial America. In 1855 he helped to form the New York Legal Rights Association, which sued the city to secure the right for blacks to use public transit facilities.

Graham Hodges

Pennsylvania Railroad. A mainline railroad that joined New York City and Philadelphia by 1863. It purchased a majority of the shares in the Long Island Rail Road in 1900 and connected to Pennsylvania Station in Manhattan through tunnels built under the Hudson River in 1910. The completion of the tunnel was a feat of civil engineering; it put an end to the need for passengers and freight destined for New York City from points south and west to disembark in New Jersey and cross the Hudson by ferry or by the Hudson and Manhattan Railroad (1909). Like its competitor the New York Central Railroad, in the 1930s the Pennsylvania Railroad cut to sixteen hours the travel time between New York City and Chicago (setting the record with the Broadway Limited). In 1968 the railroad was forced by growing competition from air and highway travel to merge with the New York Central Railroad. The new railroad, the Penn Central, declared bankruptcy in 1970, after which its passenger routes were taken over in 1971 by the National Railroad Passenger Corporation (Amtrak), its commuter routes to New Jersey by New Jersey Transit, and its freight operations in 1976 by the Consolidated Rail Corporation (Conrail).

George H. Burgess and Miles C. Kennedy: *Centennial History of the Pennsylvania Railroad Company* (Philadelphia: Pennsylvania Railroad Company, 1949)
Carl W. Condit: *The Port of New York: A History of the Rail Terminal System from the Beginnings to Pennsylvania Station* (Chicago: University of Chicago Press, 1980)

See also RAILROADS.

Robert A. Olmsted

Pennsylvania Station. Name used by a station of the Pennsylvania Railroad and later by a station of the National Railroad Passenger Corporation (Amtrak). The first of the two was designed by the firm of McKim, Mead and White and covered two blocks bounded by 33rd Street, 7th Avenue, 31st Street, and 8th Avenue. The Pennsylvania Railroad long wished to build a station in New York City to compete with Grand Central Terminal of the New York Central Railroad, but could not build a bridge or tunnel across the Hudson River from its terminal in Hoboken, New Jersey. In the 1890s the use of electric tracks and advances in civil engineering permitted a tunnel to be dug to Manhattan. By 1895 Alexander Cassatt, president of the railroad, made plans for a station that would be the first in the United States to accommodate large-scale use of electric traction. McKim, Mead and White designed a monumental gateway to the city modeled after the Baths of Caracalla and consistent with principles of the "city beautiful" movement (for illustration see MCKIM, MEAD AND WHITE): they provided for a rational distribution of space and traffic, took into account the civic function of the building, and incorporated references to classical precedents. Construction began in 1902 and was hastened by legislation in 1908 banning steam locomotion on passenger trains.

At its completion in 1911 the station facilitated the orderly movement of both commuters using the Long Island Rail Road and passengers traveling to New England and southern cities along the east coast. Access streets running through the building enabled passengers and baggage to be let off and

Façade of Pennsylvania Station on 7th Avenue, 1915

picked up with minimal disruption of city traffic. The tracks were laid below grade about eighteen feet (six meters) under a concourse for the Long Island Rail Road. Above this was the austere, monumental waiting room of the Pennsylvania Railroad, adjacent to a concourse of glass and wrought iron. Flights of stairs connected the various levels. A row of colossal Tuscan columns extended across the eastern frontage, behind which a shopping arcade led to the waiting room. The railroad decided in 1962 to replace the station with a new one that would also house offices and Madison Square Garden, and despite heated objections from preservationists Pennsylvania Station was demolished in 1965. As a result the city formed the Landmarks Preservation Commission in 1965, and a national interest developed in preserving historic buildings. Photographs of Pennsylvania Station survive in the work of Berenice Abbott.

The second Pennsylvania Station was completed in 1968 between 31st and 33rd streets and 7th and 8th avenues as part of a complex that also houses Madison Square Garden and offices. The railroad functions are confined to the cramped basement levels. In 1993 the U.S. Postal Service announced that it would no longer use its building directly west of the station, designed by McKim, Mead and White in 1908–13. The administrators of Amtrak decided to remodel the post office building as an expanded and more elegant Pennsylvania Station, and commissioned designs from the architectural firm of Hellmith, Obata and Kassabaum. Pennsylvania Station is the busiest train station in North America. Its twenty-one tracks handle some 600,000 passengers a day, sometimes at the rate of one thousand every ninety seconds.

Leland M. Roth: *McKim, Mead and White, Architects* (New York: Harper and Row, 1983)

Mary Beth Betts

Interior of Pennsylvania Station, 1911

penny arcades. Enclosed areas in amusement parks and other bustling places filled with machines offering entertainment bought by dropping a coin (usually a penny) into a slot. They were well known at Coney Island as early as the 1880s. Some machines played a tune while model locomotives and steamboats ran in place; others depicted such sights as "Munich's Beer Drinking Festival," "The Island of Pango-Pango," "Mountain Climbing in Switzerland," and "Life among the Head Hunters in Borneo." Other machines allowed customers to measure the strength of their grip, the size of their chest, or the force of their punch; they could also view pictures of the golfer Bobby Jones demonstrating good form and scenes from fights between such well-known boxers as Jack Dempsey and Gene Tunney. For a dime the "photomat" produced framed portraits. The "love teller" rated a customer's capacity as a lover on a scale from hot to cold, and in other machines risqué scenes were shown under such titles as "Artists and Models," "Red Hot Momma," "Jazz Baby," "They Forgot to Lower the Curtain," "The Girls and the Burglar," "Cleo, Queen of the Harem," "The Chemise Girl," "The Queen of Sin," and "Bare in the Bear Skin." Machines also told fortunes and provided horoscopes. To the dismay of some, penny arcades and burlesque theaters moved to the formerly elegant area around Times Square during the Depression. The arcades survived in slightly altered form into the 1960s, until they finally disappeared with the advent of more sophisticated electronic machines.

Sodom by the Sea: An Affectionate History of Coney Island (Garden City, N.Y.: Doubleday, Doran, 1941)

Jill Stone: *Times Square: A Pictorial History* (New York: Macmillan, 1982)

James O. Drummond

penny papers. A term used to describe the mass circulation daily newspapers that revolutionized American journalism during the 1830s; New York City played a dominant role in their development. The penny papers were intended to have broader popular appeal than the conventional political and mercantile daily newspapers that sold expensive annual subscriptions and catered to an élite readership. Horace Greeley's experimental newspaper the *Morning Post*, launched in January 1833 and sold at two cents a copy, was unsuccessful. The *Sun*, begun in September by Benjamin Day and priced at one cent, achieved an unparalleled circulation of twenty thousand by 1835. Day's innovations included an avowedly nonpolitical editorial stance, a heavy emphasis on local crime and sports, and the use of newsboys to sell the *Sun* in the city's streets. The *Sun* inspired numerous imitators, the most successful of which were the *Transcript* (1834–39) and the *New York Herald* of James Gordon Bennett Sr. Rising circulation led these newspapers to experiment with new forms of printing technology, such as steam power and presses with several cylinders. The most politically radical of the penny papers was George Henry Evans's *Man* (1834–35). Although often sympathetic to the city's working class, the *Sun*, the *Transcript*, and the *New York Herald* were racist and sometimes nativist. Their sensationalistic exploitation of murder trials led to boycotts and denunciations of the "gutter press," and their editorial attacks prompted numerous libel suits. At the same time they competed to obtain the latest and most accurate national and international news by means of horse expresses, trains, and newsboats. The *New York Tribune* (1841) and the *New York Times* (1851) inaugurated an era of more restrained penny papers. Most of these newspapers eventually raised their daily price to two or three cents. The penny papers invigorated competitive news gathering in New York City, freed the press from the necessity of political partisanship, and created a new mass readership that included workers and artisans. Many of their innovations prefigured the methods of yellow journalism and the tabloids.

Frank Luther Mott: *American Journalism: A History of Newspapers in the United States through 250 Years, 1690 to 1940* (New York: Macmillan, 1941; 3rd edn 1962)

Dan Schiller: *Objectivity and the News: The Public and the Rise of Commercial Journalism* (Philadelphia: University of Pennsylvania Press, 1981)

Alexander Saxton: *The Rise and Fall of the White Republic: Class Politics and Mass Culture in Nineteenth-century America* (London: Verso, 1990)

Steven H. Jaffe

Pentecostal and Holiness churches.

The Holiness and Pentecostal movements began in New York City, where the Methodist sisters Sarah Worrall Langford Palmer and Phoebe Worrall Palmer developed a doctrine that united the perfectionism of the 1830s with Methodist ideas of Christian perfection (or entire sanctification) as a religious experience following conversion. From 1835 Sarah Langford held Tuesday meetings for women in the home at 54 Rivington Street that she shared with her sister and brother-in-law. Palmer took over these meetings by the late 1830s and after 1839 opened them to men. They became popular and were moved to 23 St. Mark's Place and then to 316 East 15th Street in 1871 but were still being held as late as 1914. During the 1830s Palmer helped to organize the Five Points Mission, which consisted of a home, a school, a work room, and a chapel. Offshoots of the Holiness Movement formed outside Methodism. One known as "Oberlin perfectionism" began in the city under Charles G. Finney, pastor of the Chatham Street Chapel (1832–35) and the Broadway Tabernacle (1836–37). His *Lectures to Professing Christians* were delivered at the Broadway Tabernacle in 1837 and serialized in the *New York Evangelist*. Another strand of perfectionism developed after prayer meeting revivals of 1857–59 that began in a Dutch Reformed church on Fulton Street and quickly spread to cities across the United States, Canada, and Great Britain. One of its most important exponents was William E. Boardman, a Presbyterian minister who often attended Palmer's Tuesday meetings and wrote *The Higher Christian Life* (1858), a widely circulated treatise that united Methodistic and Oberlin perfectionism.

The prayer meeting revival also led to the formation of the Antioch Baptist Church at 264 Bleecker Street by the minister John Quincy Adams. It operated a press and bookstore and circulated the *Christian*, a monthly publication dedicated to advancing the gospel of Holiness. The movement also found adherents among several small Methodist splinter groups. The Wesleyan Methodist Connection (now Wesleyan church) was organized in 1843 by Methodist Episcopal Church abolitionists and from 1844 to 1852 had its national headquarters, a publishing house, and a church on King Street. After attending Palmer's meetings during the 1860s and experiencing entire sanctification, Amanda Smith (1837–1915) gave sermons in a number of the city's black churches. Congregations of the Free Methodist Church were formed in Manhattan and Brooklyn during the 1860s and worked extensively among the city's poor. In 1860 Jane Dunning, a Free Methodist laywoman, became the superintendent of the Providence Mission at 329 West 37th Street, which served the black community. One of her converts, Jerry McAuley, organized the Water Street Mission in 1872; its principal financial sponsor was Joseph Mackey, editor of the *United States Dry Goods Reporter*, and its first supervisors were Mr. and Mrs. Frank Smith. The mission also issued a newsletter edited by the Free Methodist pastor J. S. Bradbrook. During these years the Salvation Army was formed and through its rescue work became the best-known exponent of Holiness. In 1881 the Christian and Missionary Alliance Church was founded in the city by A. B. Simpson, a pastor of the Thirteenth Street Presbyterian Church from 1879 to 1881 who also oversaw a missionary training school, a home for faith healing, a mission board, an interdenominational mission publication, and the evangelical Gospel Tabernacle.

By the 1880s resistance mounted against Holiness teaching in a number of churches, including the Methodist Episcopal Church. One of the first new denominations was the Church of God Reformation Movement (1881), founded by Daniel Sidney Warner. Later known as the Church of God (Anderson), it began a ministry in the city under Charles James Blewitt in 1897. The ministry of the Church of the Nazarene was begun in the city by William Howard Hoople, son of a prominent leather merchant. He and Charles BeViev opened a mission at 123 Schenectady Avenue in Brooklyn on 4 January 1894 that was soon organized into the Utica Avenue Tabernacle. A second congregation was formed on Bedford Avenue in 1895 and a third in the following year; the three congregations merged into the Association of Pentecostal Churches of America on 31 March 1896.

Pentecostalism developed after 1900 as an offshoot of the Holiness Movement emphasizing glossolalia as evidence of the "baptism of the Holy Spirit." After a manifestation of glossolalia in 1901 the Holiness evangelist Charles F. Parham sent Marie Burgess to work in a Holiness mission at 416 West 42nd Street in New York City in 1907 and to spread his teachings concerning spirit baptism. There she met and married Robert Brown, with whom she formed the Glad Tidings Tabernacle. The Church of God (Anderson) moved to rented quarters at 2450 Grand Avenue in 1906 and by 1908 added a missionary home and chapel. In 1907 the Association of Pentecostal Churches of America united with the Church of the Nazarene to form the Pentecostal Church of the Nazarene, which took the name Church of the Nazarene in 1919 to dissociate itself from Pentecostalism. As early as 1908 Pentecostal ministries were launched among Italians by the evangelist Peter Ottolini.

A number of black Pentecostal and Holiness churches opened after an influx of black workers from the South during the First World War. In 1919 R. C. Lawson formed a congregation of the Refuge Churches of Our Lord in Harlem (renamed the Church of Our Lord Jesus Christ of the Apostolic Faith in 1931). During the 1920s and 1930s congregations of the predominantly black Church of God (Spreading Gospel), Churches of God in Christ, and United Holy Church were established. Glad Tidings Tabernacle was the largest Pentecostal Church in New York City by the 1920s, giving rise to congregations in a number of the city's ethnic communities. Ivan

Voronaev, a Russian Baptist pastor, opened the first Russian Pentecost Church in the city after being introduced to Pentecostalism by the Browns in 1920. Another was Hans R. Waldvogel, who in 1925 took over a struggling German Pentecostal mission, the Ridgewood Pentecostal Church at 815 Seneca Avenue, and transformed it into a thriving congregation that eventually led to the formation of other congregations throughout the metropolitan area. A Finnish church was organized in the 1920s and the Salvation Army was highly successful in its mission work among Swedish immigrants in Brooklyn. Pentecostal evangelism was also taken up by Puerto Ricans who settled in the city during the 1920s. One of the first pastors, Juan Lugo, began his ministry in Greenpoint in 1929.

From the 1930s a number of Pentecostal leaders became prominent. One of the most important was Mother Horn, who opened the Mount Calvary Assembly Hall of Pentecostal Faith Church in Brooklyn in 1930. She later established a second church in the old Olympia Sports Club in Harlem, which became her headquarters, and broadcast a radio program. Under Charles Manuel ("Sweet Daddy") Grace (1881–1960) the United House of Prayer for All Nations on the Rock of the Apostolic Faith Church provided low-income housing and employment in church industries. During the 1930s a Spanish-speaking congregation was organized by Francisco Olazabel as the Bethel Christian Church; it became the Assembly of Christian Churches and made its headquarters in the city in 1939. After failing to succeed his father as the general overseer of the Church of God of Prophecy, Homer A. Tomlinson (1894–1968) formed the Church of God (Queens, New York) in 1943. In 1954 he traveled to more than a hundred countries to proclaim his reign as "King of the World." He also sought the presidency as the candidate of the Theocratic Party. After his death the church moved its headquarters to Huntsville, Alabama. The converted organized-crime figure and drug addict Billy Roberts opened the Soul Saving Station in Harlem in 1940. By 1973 it had eleven thousand members, took the name Soul Saving Station For Every Nation Crusaders of America, and had ties to the Pentecostal Holiness Church.

New churches took shape after the Second World War. By 1950 there were eight Church of God (Anderson) congregations in the city. A ministry known as Teen Challenge was organized in 1958 in Brooklyn by David Wilkerson, an Assemblies of God minister whose work with young drug addicts gained attention through his book *The Cross and the Switchblade* (1963, later the subject of a motion picture). The Bible Church of Christ was formed in 1961 by Roy Bryant, as was the House of Our Lord Church in Brooklyn by the activist pastor Herbert Daughtry. In 1975 the Church of the Nazarene bought the clubhouse of the Lambs in Times Square and under Paul Moore and Sharon Moore focused its efforts on performing artists as well as the homeless in Times Square and Hell's Kitchen. George Baker, known as Father Divine, established the Father Divine Peace Mission in Harlem during the 1930s, which became known for its service to the poor, claims of faith healing, teachings on racial equality, and strict moral code. In 1942 it moved its headquarters to Philadelphia. Reverend Ike used the media extensively to promote his doctrine of material prosperity as the leader of the United Christian Evangelistic Association, which made its headquarters in Washington Heights.

Charles Edwin Jones: *A Guide to the Study of the Pentecostal Movement* (Metuchen, N.J.: Scarecrow, 1983)

Charles Edwin Jones: *Black Holiness: A Guide to the Study of Black Participation in Wesleyan Perfectionist and Glossolalic Pentecostal Movements* (Metuchen, N.J.: Scarecrow, 1987)

William C. Kostlevy

Penthouse. Monthly men's magazine launched in 1965 by Bob Guccione, a native of Brooklyn. It was conceived in London and originally distributed in England. In 1969 Guccione opened an office at 909 3rd Avenue in New York City and began selling the magazine in the United States. The first American issue sold more than 230,000 copies, and the magazine's combination of nude photography and investigative journalism quickly attracted a devoted male readership, providing strong competition for Hugh Hefner's *Playboy*. In 1994 *Penthouse* had 1.2 million subscribers in the United States and claimed a readership of nearly ten million worldwide. It has won a National Magazine Award, four awards from the Overseas Press Club, and more than forty citations for excellence in graphic design. The offices are at 1965 Broadway.

Robert Sanger Steel

People's Institute. Institute formed in New York City in 1897 by Charles Sprague Smith, a professor at Columbia University. It was closely associated with progressive reform and played a role in efforts by the state legislature to improve the conditions of workers. Soon it focused on the provision of leisure activity as an important element of social progress and the elimination of crime. With the Women's Municipal League it investigated the spread of "cheap amusements" in the city, leading to the formation of the National Board of Review of Motion Pictures in 1908. To provide alternatives to these amusements it sponsored the Cooper Union Forum and the People's Symphony concerts, designated "play streets," offered discounted theater tickets, and set up community centers in public schools. The People's Institute closed in 1934.

John Collier and Edward M. Barrows: *The City Where Crime Is Play* (New York: People's Institute, 1914)

Benjamin Charles Gruenber, ed.: *Modern Science and People's Health* (New York: W. W. Norton, 1926)

Robert B. Fisher: "The People's Institute of New York City, 1897–1934: Culture, Progressive Democracy, and the People" (diss., New York University, 1974)

Peter G. Buckley

People's Institute Publishing Company. Original name of the firm W. W. NORTON.

People's Weekly World. Newspaper of the American Communist Party, and historically the most influential newspaper of the American left. Known during its heyday as the *Daily Worker*, it was launched in Chicago in 1924 and moved to New York City in 1927. The newspaper wielded its greatest influence in the 1930s, when it had a circulation of more than 100,000 and defended the "Scottsboro boys," and during the Second World War, when it agitated against fascism and racism. After the war many members of its staff were harassed and jailed by federal authorities. Absorbed in 1958 by the *Worker*, it resumed publication in 1968 as the *Daily World*, became the *People's Daily World* in 1986, and took its current name in 1990.

Anthony Gronowicz

Pepsico. Conglomerate of snack-food and soft-drink makers and restaurateurs formed by the merger of the Pepsi-Cola Company and Frito-Lay in 1965. A forerunner was the Pepsi-Cola Company, which formulated the soft drink Pepsi-Cola in 1893. Under the direction of Alfred Steele and his wife, Joan Crawford, corporate headquarters were moved in 1948 from Long Island City to Manhattan. In 1990 the firm had annual sales of nearly $13,000 million and more than 225,000 employees. Pepsico has its headquarters in Purchase, New York.

James O. Drummond

Perelman, S(idney) J(oseph) (*b* New York City, 1 Feb 1904; *d* New York City, 17 Oct 1979). Essayist and playwright. He grew up in Providence, Rhode Island, and after graduating from Brown University worked as a cartoonist for the weekly magazine *Judge* in New York City before devoting himself to writing. A master of language and wordplay, he contributed comic essays to the *New Yorker* and with his wife, Laura West, wrote the play *All Good Americans* (1933). He also wrote a number of comic plays, including the musical *One Touch of Venus* (1943) and the play *The Beauty Part* (1962), as well as screenplays for the Marx Brothers' *Monkey Business* (1931) and *Horse Feathers* (1932); he won an Academy Award for his screenplay of *Around the World in Eighty Days* (1956). One of his best-known books is *Acres and Pains*, a collection of humorous essays about life in Exurbia, Pennsylvania. His published writings also include *Westward Ha!* (1948) and *Baby It's Cold Inside* (1970), in which he introduced the Irish poet Shameless McGonigle. Perelman lived at 134 West 11th Street from 1955 until 1966 and at the Gramercy Park Hotel (52 Gramercy Park North) from 1972.

Walter Friedman

performance art. An art form developed in the 1970s that combined elements from diverse media such as music, dance, sculpture, film, and videotape. It challenged the conception of art as a commodity and often blurred the boundary between performer and audience. A performance art event could be as short as several minutes (often dozens of short pieces were presented in an evening) or as long as several days. The roots of performance art may be traced to such art movements of the early twentieth century as constructivism, Futurism, Dada, and surrealism, and more immediately to conceptual art, happenings, and the Fluxus movement, in which Dick Higgins, Alison Knowles, and Nam June Paik were leading figures in New York City from the 1950s to the 1970s. Performance art events took place in private, public, official, and unofficial spaces: the artist Jean Dupuy presided over many events at his loft at 405 East 13th Street and later at 537 Broadway; performers from many nations appeared in festivals and performance events at the Judson Memorial Baptist Church on Washington Square; the composer Charlie Morrow once led a band of players blowing conch shells through the Port Authority Bus Terminal; and one summer afternoon the "sanitation artist" Mierle Laderman Ukeles staged a "wedding" of two barges at a refuse transfer station on the Hudson River. Dancers such as Yvonne Rainer, Trisha Brown, Simone Forti, and Steve Paxton became known for a style of movement that drew on everyday gestures, and Vito Acconci staged "self-dramatizations": these included "Following Piece," in which he followed a person on the street chosen at random, and "Conversions," in which he burned off his chest hairs and hid his penis so that he could experience the sense of not being a man.

By the mid 1970s a second generation of performance artists appeared at small performance spaces and clubs in SoHo and Tribeca such as the Kitchen on Broome Street, Artist's Space, Franklin Furnace, the Mudd Club, TR 3, and Roulette. Feminist ideas influenced the performance art of Martha Wilson, Linda Montano, and Adrian Piper, who experimented with disguises and perceptions of women's appearance, and Vanalyne Green and Joan Jonas, who combined live and videotaped performances to examine the intersection of the personal and the political. A number of performance artists began their careers in obscurity in New York City and later became nationally known, among them Wilson, Piper, Laurie Anderson, and Michael Smith.

Gregory Battcock and Robert Nickas, eds.: *The Art of Performance: A Critical Anthology* (New York: E. P. Dutton, 1984)

Kathleen Hulser

Perkins, Frances (*b* Boston, 10 April 1880; *d* New York City, 14 May 1965). Reformer and public official. Brought up in Worcester, Massachusetts, and educated at Mount Holyoke College, she worked for the New York City Consumers League from 1910 and in 1912 prevailed on the state legislature to pass an important bill limiting the work week for women and children to fifty-four hours. Under the league's director Florence Kelley she investigated sanitary conditions in the city's bakeries and fire hazards in factories. After the Triangle Shirtwaist fire in 1911 she was an expert witness and later an inspector for the Factory Investigating Commission of the state legislature, which included Robert F. Wagner (i) and Alfred E. Smith. In 1918 her concern over inadequate care for poor pregnant women and infants led her to help form the Maternity Center Association in New York City, for which she worked as an unpaid executive secretary. She became the first woman to hold high state office in New York in 1919 when Smith, now governor, appointed her to the Industrial Board (forerunner of the Department of Labor), citing her command of facts and figures. As Governor Franklin D. Roosevelt's industrial commissioner from 1928, her priorities included occupational health and safety, enforcement of workers' compensation, and an end to child labor. After Roosevelt became president in 1933 he named her secretary of labor, then the highest public office ever held by a woman in the nation. Perkins served until 1945, and as the head of the Committee on Economic Security she was a leading force behind the drafting of the Social Security Act. In Washington the main building of the U.S. Department of Labor is named for her.

George Whitney Martin: *Madam Secretary: Frances Perkins* (Boston: Houghton Mifflin, 1976)

Marjory Potts

Perkins, (William) Maxwell (Everts) (*b* New York City, 20 Sept 1884; *d* Stamford, Conn., 17 June 1947). Editor. He attended Harvard University and in 1910 joined the advertising department at Charles Scribner's Sons, where he became an editor in 1914 and worked to the end of his life. After persuading the firm in 1919 to publish F. Scott Fitzgerald's *This Side of Paradise* he became the editor for such writers as Erskine Caldwell, Ernest Hemingway, James Jones, Ring Lardner, Marjorie Kinnan Rawlings, and Alan Paton. He is perhaps best known as the editor for Thomas Wolfe, whose manuscripts for *Look Homeward, Angel* and *Of Time and the River* he subjected to aggressive editing that reduced their length by several hundred thousand words, and to whom he remained loyal despite Wolfe's violent outbursts. Perkins's dedication to his authors and his insightful criticism set a standard for modern editors. Some scholars have questioned whether his editing might not have hampered Wolfe's artistic development, and have emphasized the conflicts in the friendship between the two. From 1932 to 1938 Perkins lived at 246 East 49th Street in Manhattan.

A. Scott Berg: *Max Perkins, Editor of Genius* (New York: E. P. Dutton, 1978)

David Herbert Donald: *Look Homeward: A Life of Thomas Wolfe* (New York: Fawcett Columbine, 1987)

James L. W. West III: *American Authors and the Literary Marketplace since 1900* (Philadelphia: University of Pennsylvania Press, 1988)

Marc H. Aronson

Perlea, Ionel (*b* Ograda, Romania, 13 Dec 1900; *d* New York City, 29 July 1970). Conductor. He completed his studies in music in Germany and before the Second World War directed the Bucharest Opera. He moved to the United States in 1949 and soon made his American début conducting *Tristan and Isolde* at the Metropolitan Opera in New York City. In 1952 he joined the faculty of the Manhattan School of Music, where he taught until the end of his life. After a heart attack and a stroke paralyzed his right hand he continued conducting using his left hand. Perlea made more than fifty recordings of orchestral works for Vox and RCA.

Vladimir Wertsman

Peruvians. The recorded settlement of Peruvian immigrants in New York City began in the early 1970s. Only about a quarter of all Peruvian immigrants settled in the city, a smaller proportion than other Latin American groups such as Ecuadorians. There were about forty thousand Peruvians in New York City before the late 1980s, when many arrived, fleeing terrorism and economic crisis in Peru. According to the Peruvian consulate there were about a hundred thousand Peruvians in the metropolitan area by the early 1990s. More than half of those in the city lived in Queens between Sunnyside and Elmhurst. There were many professionals, especially physicians, but most Peruvians lacked permanent resident status, knew little or no English, and worked in service industries, in manufacturing, and as domestic servants. Several weekly and monthly newspapers cater to Peruvians, among them *Nueva Imagen*, *Imagen del Sur*, and the *Prensa Peruana*. Community groups include religious fraternities and athletic and professional organizations. The feast of El Señor de los Milagros is celebrated with a street fair on West 53rd Street in Manhattan during the last week in October.

Graciela M. Castex

Peter Cooper Village. Housing project in Manhattan (1990 pop. 5000), adjacent to Stuyvesant Town and bounded to the north by 23rd Street, to the east by Franklin D. Roosevelt Drive, to the south by 20th Street, and to the west by 1st Avenue. Planned in 1943 as part of a project to redevelop the Gashouse District, it was built by the Metropolitan Life Insurance Company at the city's request. After more than five hundred existing buildings in the area were demolished in the autumn of 1945, construction began on twenty-one apartment buildings ranging in height from twelve to fifteen stories and containing 2495 apartments, many with a view of the East River. The development was landscaped with lawns, paths, and play areas adorned with trees and shrubs and offered fifteen recreational facilities. The first tenants moved in on 1 August 1947 and by 1 June 1949 all the apartments had been leased. In the mid 1990s Peter Cooper Village remained highly desirable because of its proximity to the business districts of Manhattan, and was considered a model for high-density development.

James O. Drummond

Peter Luger Steak House. Restaurant at 178 Broadway in Williamsburg, opened in 1887 as Charles Luger's Cafe, Billiards, and Bowling Alley. It is known for its wood-paneled walls, ornate pressed-tin ceilings, and what Alfred Hitchcock once called "the best steak in the world."

Kenneth T. Jackson

Pete's Tavern. The oldest continually operating drinking establishment in New York City, opened in 1864 on the corner of 18th Street and Irving Place, near Gramercy Park. The tavern once offered nightly lodging and stables for horses in addition to food and drink. It was a favorite meeting place of politicians connected with Tammany Hall, which was situated a few blocks south. At the turn of the century O. Henry lived in a nearby boarding house and spent many hours at the tavern, where he wrote *The Gift of the Magi* (1905). During Prohibition (1920–33) the front of the tavern was converted into a sham florist shop while in the back rooms, entered through a dummy refrigerator door, a speakeasy catered to local politicians. In later years Pete's Tavern was used in many television commercials and films, including parts of Milos Forman's *Ragtime.*

Chad Ludington

petroleum. The presence of the petroleum industry in New York City dates to 1859, when John D. Rockefeller, a partner in a small refinery, opened a sales office in the city after oil was discovered near Titusville, Pennsylvania. His brother William joined the firm and in 1867 moved to New York City to handle domestic sales, develop foreign markets, and aggressively buy up shares in oil concerns. The firm eventually became the banker for the Standard Oil Alliance, which disbanded in 1882 to form several companies, including the Standard Oil Company of New York (Socony); William Rockefeller was named president of Socony and soon brought about the merger of the firm with that of Charles Pratt. Conservative and shrewd, Pratt proved to be an outstanding director, and he and his partner, the entrepreneur Henry Huttleston Rogers, made major additions to the Standard Trust. By 1899 Socony was the most important company in the Standard network. In later years the growth of the oil industry in New York City was hindered by adverse state laws governing joint stock companies and partnerships. Despite these obstacles the city's oil businesses flourished. Many oil corporations availed themselves of more lenient corporate laws in New Jersey and Delaware while transacting most of their business in the city. Among these were two of the giants in the industry, Mobil Oil and the Exxon Corporation. Although both these firms moved away in 1990 (Exxon to Texas and Mobil to Virginia), the city remained a center for the petroleum industry.

Paul H. Giddens: *The Birth of the Oil Industry* (New York: Macmillan, 1938)

Ralph W. Hidy and Muriel E. Hidy: *History of Standard Oil Company (New Jersey)*, vol. 1, *Pioneering in Big Business, 1882–1911* (New York: McGraw–Hill, 1955)

Oil's First Century (Cambridge: Harvard Graduate School of Business Administration, 1960)

Bennett H. Wall

Petrosino, Joseph (*b* Padula [now in Italy], 30 April 1860; *d* Palermo, Sicily, 12 March 1909). Detective. He emigrated to the United States in 1873, settling in New York City, and became a police officer on 19 October 1883 and a detective on 20 July 1895. In December 1908 he was appointed to lead a secret service charged with eliminating the criminal organization known as the Black Hand. His work disproved the widespread notion that there was an international criminal syndicate based in Sicily that had a branch in the city. Petrosino was murdered while checking criminal records in Palermo during a deportation inquiry. The case remained unsolved; the most likely suspect, Don Vito Cascio Ferro, died in 1943. A small plaza just north of the old police headquarters at 240 Centre Street is dedicated to Petrosino's memory.

Arrigo Petacco: *Joe Petrosino*, trans. Charles Lam Markmann (New York: Macmillan, 1974)

Humbert Nelli: *The Business of Crime: Italians and Syndicate Crime in the United States* (New York: Oxford University Press, 1976), 95–98

Mary Elizabeth Brown

Pfaff's Cellar. Restaurant opened in 1856 by Charley Pfaff at 647 Broadway, then within the entertainment district. It became the meeting place of a famous roundtable led by Henry Clapp, editor of the literary magazine the *Saturday Press*; the members called themselves "bohemians" and included the actresses Ada Clare and Adah Isaacs Menkin, the future French premier Georges Clemenceau, the journalist Horace Greeley, the novelist William Dean Howells, and the poet Walt Whitman. Pfaff's closed because of the Civil War and the northward expansion of the city. The building is extant.

Stephen Jenkins: *The Greatest Street in the World: The Story of Broadway, Old and New* (New York: G. P. Putnam's Sons, 1911)

Michael Batterberry and Ariane Batterberry: *On the Town in New York, from 1776 to the Present* (New York: Charles Scribner's Sons, 1973)

Elizabeth Kray: *Four Literary–Historical Walks* (New York: Academy of American Poets, 1982)

David W. Dunlap: *On Broadway: A Journey Uptown over Time* (New York: Rizzoli, 1990)

Val Ginter

Pfizer. Firm of pharmaceutical manufacturers formed in Brooklyn in 1849 by Charles Pfizer and Charles Erhart, chemists trained in Germany. During the nineteenth century its main factory was at Bartlett Street and Harrison Avenue in Williamsburg, then a mostly German area; its administrative office was at 81 Maiden Lane in Manhattan. The firm was known for the fine quality of its chemicals, especially its santonin, tartaric acid, and citric acid, which it sold in bulk to pharmaceutical wholesalers. It was incorporated in 1900 but remained essentially a family business until 1942. During the First World War the firm developed a method of producing citric acid with sugar (later molasses) rather than imported limes, and in the 1930s and 1940s its research led to the production of vitamins. During the Second World War the firm was part of a consortium led by the government to produce penicillin, which was scarce. The president of the company, John L. Smith, risked government sanctions by supplying penicillin to the physician Leo Lowe at Brooklyn Jewish Hospital. After the war the major products of the firm were vitamins and antibiotics (including Terramycin) rather than iodides, mercurials, and citric acid. The marketing of pharmaceuticals abroad began in 1946. Under its president John McKeen the firm in the 1950s and 1960s acquired manufacturers of petroleum, paints, rubber, composite metals, plastics, cosmetics, toiletries, and baby care products. International headquarters opened in 1961 on 2nd Avenue and 42nd Street. In the 1970s and 1980s John Powers and Ed Pratt oversaw the sale of divisions unrelated to the production of pharmaceutical, agricultural, consumer, and chemical products. The firm made 46 percent of its sales abroad in 1989, by which time it was the only pharmaceutical firm that continued to manufacture its products in New York City. In the mid 1990s Pfizer had sales of more than $7000 million.

Pfizer Quality: 100th Anniversary, 1849–1949 (New York: Pfizer, 1949)
Samuel Mines: *Pfizer: An Informal History* (New York: Pfizer, 1978)

David J. S. King

pharmaceuticals. The first pharmaceutical firm in New York City was formed in 1781 by Effingham Lawrence and survived well into the twentieth century as Schieffelin and Company. Five druggists were listed in the city directory of 1786: Lawrence and the firm of Besley and Goodwin on Pearl (Queen) Street, and Francis Wainwright, Timothy Hurse, and Oliver Hull in Hanover Square. By the early nineteenth century druggists stocked not only chemicals used to prepare medicines but such goods as glassware, oils, and paints. The most important of these early firms included Lawrence and Keese, J. A. and W. B. Post, Thomas S. Clark, John and William Penfold, John M. Bradhurst, R. and S. Murray, Silas Carle, and John C. Morrison. Medicines were produced in small laboratories attached to druggists' shops, and some firms eventually specialized in making common preparations on a large scale. Most pharmacies derived their preparations from plants and found a market for herbal remedies such as jalap, ipecac, sarsaparilla, and balsam. Firms kept pace with their European counterparts, introducing European drugs in the city soon after they were developed. In 1825, only five years after Pierre Joseph Pelletier and Joseph B. Caventou published their methods for isolating quinine from cinchona bark to treat malaria, John Currie set up a factory to produce quinine sulfate in New York City. Quinine extracted from cinchona bark remained an important product until synthetic antimalarials were developed in the 1940s.

In the mid nineteenth century the city became the national center of the pharmaceutical industry. Patent medicines such as William Brandeth's Life-Extension pills were manufactured and advertised there. The New York College of Pharmacy opened in 1829, and the firm of Olcott and McKesson (later McKesson and Robbins) was formed in 1833 to produce gelatin-coated pills. From 1846 a naval hospital in Brooklyn operated a laboratory to assure the purity of its medicines; production there increased between 1852 and 1856 during the tenure of E. R. Squibb, who formed a company in Brooklyn to continue his work after the naval laboratory ceased to be funded. In 1849 the firm of Pfizer and Company was formed in Brooklyn by Charles Pfizer and Charles F. Erhart, chemists trained in Germany. A shop for laboratory supplies was opened in 1851 at 3rd Avenue and 18th Street by Bernard G. Amend, once an assistant to the influential German chemist Justus Liebig; it was expanded by Amend and Carl Eimer in 1856 into one of the first prescription laboratories in the area. In 1885 Charles Robbins formed the New York Quinine and Chemical Works, which became a leading manufacturer of quinine. Foreign companies were attracted to New York City by its port; among them was E. Merck, a German firm that established an agency in the city in 1890. The large local market prompted the William R. Warner Company and many other American firms to open sales offices, and the city became the largest center for distribution in the country.

During the First World War American firms were spurred to develop synthetic substitutes for raw materials that had become difficult to import, such as limes for the manufacture of citric acid. After German companies (which had dominated the industry) and their patents ceased to be protected by law, the American branch of the Bayer Company was acquired by Sterling Products, incorporated in the city in 1901. American firms grew rapidly after the war and established active research laboratories. Several firms in the city including Pfizer, Warner–Lambert, Squibb, and Bristol–Meyers remained national leaders, and many began producing cosmetics and other consumer goods. Manufacturing, research, and development gradually moved outside the city, which continued into the 1990s to be a center for administration, marketing, and finance.

Williams Haynes: *American Chemical Industry* (New York: D. Van Nostrand, 1945–54)
Tom Mahoney: *The Merchants of Life: An Account of the American Pharmaceutical Industry* (New York: Harper and Brothers, 1959)

David J. S. King

Phelps, Dodge. Firm of metallurgists formed in 1833 by William Earl Dodge and Anson G. Phelps. It remained under the control of family members and expanded its operations to England. In the first decade of the twentieth century it produced 77,500 tons (70,300 metric tons) of copper a year and owned a number of railroads. James Douglas, a mining engineer, became president in 1908. By 1949 the firm had thirty thousand stockholders and fifteen thousand employees; in 1990 it had sales of more than $2000 million and about eleven thousand employees.

Robert Glass Cleland: *A History of Phelps, Dodge, 1834–1950* (New York: Alfred A. Knopf, 1952)

James E. Mooney

Phelps Stokes Fund. Foundation organized in 1911 with a bequest from Caroline Phelps Stokes (1854–1909) to improve low-income housing in New York City and expand educational opportunities for American Indians, black Americans, Africans, and poor whites; it is one of the oldest foundations in New York City. Members of the Phelps Stokes family served on the board of directors and played a major role in shaping the agenda of the fund, especially I. N. Phelps Stokes (member of the board from 1911 to 1938) and his brother Anson Phelps Stokes Jr. (member from 1911 to 1946). Some of the first initiatives were studies of educational policy, aid to southern black colleges, and competitions for better housing design in New York City. The fund also subsidized James Ford's research for *Slums and Housing* (1936). After the Second World War it concentrated on social policy, seeking to better race relations and to encourage racially integrated housing in New York City. During the 1970s and 1980s it shifted its focus to broadening educational opportunities for American Indians and black South Africans. Members of the Phelps Stokes family remained active on the board into the 1990s.

Deborah S. Gardner: "Practical Philanthropy: The Phelps Stokes Fund and Housing," *Prospects* 15 (New York: Cambridge University Press, 1990), 359–411

Deborah S. Gardner

philanthropy. The history of philanthropy in New York City reflects the city's tradition of active government, its wealth, its religious diversity, and its central position in American society. Such philanthropy as occurred during the colonial period was usually directed toward religious institutions, for educational and humanitarian as well as religious purposes, and generally supplemented government support. The notable public and private gifts to Trinity Church and King's College under British rule were clearly intended to establish the Anglican church in the colony, and met with criticism from New Yorkers who adhered to other religious traditions. The American Revolution created conditions that encouraged an expansion of private philanthropy by popularizing the notions of limited government, low taxes, separation of church and state, and eventually the First Amendment freedoms of speech and assembly, but it did not end the philanthropic role of municipal government. Most early social welfare institutions received more funds from the city and state than from private donors. These included the Humane Society (1787), which helped to free debtors from jail and find them work and also provided food and medicine to the poor; New York Hospital (1791); the Free School Society (1805); the Society for the Prevention of Pauperism (1818); the African Free School; the Bloomingdale Asylum; and the New York Institution for the Instruction of the Deaf and Dumb, formerly the almshouse, where in 1815 the city allowed learned societies and museums free use of space. Jacksonians opposed to public spending condemned this as a wasteful subsidy of wealthy dilettantes and evicted the societies in 1831, just as they cut municipal subsidies to nonprofit charities and sought to shift responsibility for social welfare from the city to private organizations, including workers' mutual benefit organizations, which were often formed along craft lines.

Protestant revivals after 1816 encouraged evangelicals to give generously, and New York City became the national center of a "benevolent empire" of new organizations devoted to Protestant causes, including the American Bible Society, the American Tract Society, and the American Sunday School Union. Arthur and Lewis Tappan and other evangelical merchants also financed abolitionists, as well as many western colleges. Within the city evangelicals (very often women) created missions and strongly Protestant organizations, schools, and homes for orphans, widows, unwed mothers, the handicapped, and the unemployed. Among these were the Five Points House of Industry and the Association for Improving the Condition of the Poor (1843). To evangelicals these were philanthropies that offered disinterested aid, spiritual as well as material; to nonevangelicals they were aggressively sectarian. Catholics (especially orders of nuns) and Jews accordingly created their own institutions, which evangelicals in turn saw as commendable but clannish, and not contributing to general philanthropy. In 1875 the state legislature sought to resolve religious conflicts by stipulating that orphans be sent to institutions "of the same religious faith as the parents." Episcopalians generously supported many institutions within the mainstream; Quakers developed notable institutions for blacks and others excluded from the mainstream. The religious character of all these organizations largely explains why their staffs of teachers, missionaries, social workers, and nurses accepted such low wages, as a result of which they became perhaps the most indispensable philanthropists in the city.

The great commercial and industrial growth of New York City produced large fortunes that enabled individuals to act independently. One of the earliest large private gifts was a bequest in 1801 by Captain Robert Richard Randall of twenty acres (eight hectares) of land around Washington Square. The trustees of the bequest, who included the rector of Trinity Church and the minister of the First Presbyterian Church, used the income from the land to open Sailors' Snug Harbor, a large home for seamen on Staten Island. In 1849 John Jacob Astor's will provided $400,000 for a library, and Peter Cooper used much of the fortune amassed from his glue business to endow the Cooper Union for the Advancement of Science and Art (1859). Similar gifts created the Lenox Library, the Pratt Institute, Carnegie Hall, the "five percent philanthropy" houses funded by Alfred T. White of Brooklyn and others, and several settlement houses. Many New Yorkers owed their wealth to business elsewhere, and a number of entrepreneurs moved to the city after making fortunes in the West: both groups tended to give to institutions outside the city, including universities and such evangelical entities as the YMCA.

Meanwhile Democrats and Republicans alike restored the city's earlier pattern of government subsidies. In the 1860s the Central Park Commission provided city-owned land and city building funds to such private cultural institutions as the Metropolitan Museum of Art and the American Museum of Natural History, and similar subsidies were later provided to the New York Zoological Society, the Brooklyn Museum, and the Brooklyn Botanical Garden. Under what was known as William M. "Boss" Tweed's welfare program (which was also supported by his opponents) many private welfare organizations relied on the city government for much of their income in the late 1860s. By 1894 the city was supplying twenty-three private institutions for children with 69 percent of their budgets, and it was alleged that perhaps a dozen of these received more money from the city than they spent on charity. In 1899 the city provided a total of $3.25 million to more than 280 institutions.

Women played key roles in nineteenth-century philanthropy, and women led the two most important efforts to bring some order to it at century's end. The State Charities Aid Association, under Louisa Lee Schuyler, monitored both government agencies and private charities. It argued in 1899 that the city's appropriations to private charities deprived public hospitals and almshouses of needed funds and discouraged private support for private charities. The Charity Organization Society of New York, founded by Josephine Shaw Lowell, also promoted order among Protestant charities (and to some extent Jewish and Catholic ones) through the annual *Charities Directory* and a clearing house for individual aid applications at the central United Charities Building. Its New York School of Social Work and the research facilities of the Russell Sage Foundation, with which it was closely associated, served charities of all kinds. Parallel and separate Jewish organizations included the United Hebrew Charities, which had its own building not far from the United Charities Building. The Catholic Charities of the Archdiocese of New York (1920) and a similar organization in the Diocese of Brooklyn appeared at the same time. This pattern of distinct organization along religious lines remained a pronounced characteristic of philanthropy in New York City, as did the presence of strong mutual benefit organizations ranging from the Workmen's Circle, which served Yiddish-speaking residents, to the black churches.

Throughout much of the nineteenth century the law and the courts of New York State discouraged the creation of endowments, forcing nonprofit organizations to rely heavily on annual contributions. "Charity balls" grew so prominent by the 1880s that they were perhaps less important in raising funds for charities than in defining who belonged to fashionable society. New legislation passed by New York State after the disputed probate of the estate of Samuel J. Tilden made it easier to create endowments, and also made general-purpose foundations legal for the first time (see FOUNDATIONS). A few foundations followed the example of the Russell Sage Foundation and focused much of their philanthropy on New York City, but most took the entire United States or the world as their territory. By 1920 New York City was the great national center of foundation activity.

As New York City became ever more diverse in religion and ethnicity, some philanthropic efforts were aimed at specific communities; Beth Israel Hospital and Yeshiva University, for example, were identified with Jews from eastern Europe. Yet on the whole large-scale philanthropy did not become organized along ethnic lines, even as black, Latin American, and Asian New Yorkers became increasingly prominent. Some Catholics and Jews, like many Protestants, shifted their focus from religion to the more secular and less controversial fields of education, medicine, science, and art, giving in some cases to established universities, hospitals, and museums and in others to new entities like the John Simon Guggenheim Memorial Foundation. Much of the most highly publicized philanthropy in the early twentieth century benefited art museums, which unlike schools and hospitals remained relatively small and independent of government support. The palatial homes of J. P. Morgan and Henry Clay Frick were envisioned as art museums when they were first designed; the Museum of Modern Art, the Solomon R. Guggenheim Museum, and the Whitney Museum of American Art were intended to celebrate art that appealed to their donors; the Cloisters and the Asia Society, like several other institutions, were the products of philanthropy by the Rockefeller family. Robert Lehman and others put their personal stamp on the Metropolitan Museum by donating galleries complete with collections. Another group of major donors supported the renewal of old institutions, notably Elmer Holmes Bobst and Laurence Tisch (New York University), and Lila Acheson Wallace and Brooke Astor (the New York Public Library).

After the Second World War the city's position as the American center for the evaluation of grant proposals was strengthened when the library of the Russell Sage Foundation evolved into the Foundation Center in 1947, the Ford Foundation moved to the city in 1953, and big business developed corporate foundations and other forms of giving. At the same time national policy reinforced the city's strong traditions of government and private philanthropy. Anti-poverty programs begun in the 1960s and aimed at black and Latin

First known photographic image of New York City, attributed to Richard Lewis. It is a half-plate daguerreotype with the hand-printed title Chatham Sq.—New York *on the reverse*

Broadway between Fulton and Canal streets. There salons were opened by some of the best-known portraitists, among them Mathew B. Brady and in the 1860s Jeremiah Gurney and the Meade brothers. Eventually more than seventy firms offered a range of facilities and prices, and in 1856 the *Cosmopolitan Art Journal* reported that there was "scarcely the humblest cottage but ha[d] some beautiful image of friend and relative." During the 1840s businesses in the city made and distributed equipment, chemicals, and photographs. The city also became a center for publishing photographs and works on photography: the first portfolio of portraits of national figures (1847), based on photographs by John Plumbe Jr. (1809–57); *The History and Practice of the Art of Photography* (1849), by Henry Hunt Snelling (1817–97); the *Daguerreian Journal* (1850; later *Humphrey's Journal*); Brady's *Gallery of Illustrious Americans* (1851); and the *Photographic Art Journal* (1851), edited by Snelling.

About 1851 a process was introduced by which albumen paper prints were made from a negative of collodion and glass. This supplanted the earlier processes and remained the most commonly used one in the city until the late 1880s. Portraitists in New York City were the first in the nation to use the new technology for commercial purposes. They responded to sharp competition and periods of economic depression between 1860 and 1890 by offering a choice of processes and a range of sizes and formats: ambrotypes, tintypes, cartes de visite, and cabinet- and imperial-size portraits. Some photographers including Brady and Napoleon Sarony sold small and large prints of well-known personages (President Lincoln maintained that a carte-de-visite portrait made during his visit to the city on 27 February 1860 by Brady helped him to win the presidential election). Sarony and one of his competitors, Jose Mora (active in the 1880s), paid well-known figures in the theater for the right to make and sell their portraits. After the Civil War periodicals published in the city relied increasingly on photographs, first as models for drawn illustrations and later in direct reproduction. The first lithographic transcription of a photograph appeared in the *Daily Graphic* in 1873. The halftone process plate was introduced in the late 1880s, and publishers soon became interested in recording with pictures what the *Illustrated American* called "contemporaneous history." Images taken with cameras were eventually the most widely used kind of illustration, especially valued in the growing field of advertising. The development of new technology for printing also coincided with the advent of documentary photographs of slums in New York City. Among the first reproductions using the halftone process plate were those made in the late 1880s for Jacob A. Riis's *How the Other Half Lives.*

Scenes of the city were often photographed, especially views of midtown Manhattan, the Bowery and Broadway, and the waterfront along the East River. Photographs of the city were frequently used by real-estate developers and illustrators and were also sold for use in stereoscopes. Well-known landscape photographers included Edward T. Anthony (1818–88) and John S. Johnston (active in the 1870s). After simplified equipment and procedures were introduced in the late 1880s views of the city were photographed by amateurs, who organized such groups as the Society of Amateur Photographers (later the Camera Club of New York) to promote pictorialism, or the practice of photography as an art form. Among those who photographed buildings and street life in the late nineteenth century were Alice Austen, Robert Bracklow (1849–1920), and Alfred Stieglitz; they favored picturesque scenes reproduced in a "straight" style, with little manual or chemical manipulation. As pictorialism evolved under Stieglitz's auspices within the group known as the Photo-Secession, artistic photographers used soft focus and hand retouching in their city views. Alvin Langdon Coburn (1882–1956), Gertrude Käsebier, and Karl Struss (1886–1980) were members of the Photo-Secession who sought to symbolize rather than depict the unique vitality of the city. Commercial photographs of the city continued to be produced by firms such as that of the Byron family (Joseph, 1844–1923, and Percy, 1878–1959), which supplied private patrons and publishers with photographs of many aspects of urban life, including the homes of the wealthy. Just before the turn of the century commercial portraiture suffered from a depressed economy and from the popularity of snapshots. It was revitalized by Käsebier and Zaida Ben-Yusuf (active between 1896 and 1915), whose studios on 5th Avenue catered to the wealthy and set an elegant style imitated into the 1920s by Arnold Genthe (1868–1942) and others. Documentary photography was used in the early twentieth century by Lewis Hine and by Jessie Tarbox Beals to promote the social policies of the Progressive era.

After 1912 the pictorialist movement gave way to a modernist aesthetic that relied on abstraction and geometric form to portray the city as a vital center. Some of the best-known examples of the clean, precise modernist style occur in the early work of Charles Sheeler and Paul Strand (1890–1976), who photographed streets and buildings in the years surrounding 1920; they made the first short art film about the city, *New York the Magnificent* (1921; later known as *Manhatta*). During the 1920s notable works by amateur photographers included portraits by Doris Ulmann (1882–1934) of Sinclair Lewis and other literary figures and by Carl Van Vechten of prominent black New Yorkers. Celebrity portraiture was later taken over by photographers working for magazines like *Vogue* and *Vanity Fair* and became linked with fashion photography. The sleekness of photographs by Edward Steichen and the surreal mystique of those by George Platt Lynes (1907–55) inspired such later photographers as Richard Avedon, Arnold Newman (*b* 1918), and Irving Penn (*b* 1917) to develop unique styles in their work with celebrities. Hine was one of few in the 1920s who considered working people suitable subjects for art photography. Neighborhood life was documented by such portraitists as James VanDerZee, who photographed blacks in business and the professions in Harlem.

The establishment in Manhattan of major news bureaus, advertising agencies, and fashion and entertainment firms between 1925 and 1950 led to a greater role for photography in publishing. The color process Kodachrome was invented in 1935 by the musicians and amateur chemists Leopold Godowsky and Leopold Mannes. PHOTOGRAPHIC AGENCIES were formed: the firm of E. and H. T. Anthony (which later merged with the Scovill Manufacturing Company to form Ansco) provided pictures and equipment. Black Star, Underwood and Underwood, and Magnum expanded the business and supplied specialized products.

Interest in social documentation revived during the 1930s. Late in the decade photographers abandoned pictorialist conventions to record the street life of working-class neighborhoods in projects under the aegis of the Photo League and the Works Progress Administration. Hine, Berenice Abbott, and Margaret Bourke-White (1904–71) were commissioned in the 1930s to photograph new skyscrapers, notably the RCA, Chrysler, and Empire State buildings; Abbott used her photographs to examine architectural connections and transformations in *Changing New York*, for which text was provided by the art historian Elizabeth McCausland. In some of his last photographs of buildings in midtown Manhattan, Stieglitz expressed his deepest feelings about the city. At this time Walker Evans began photographing urban street scenes and street signs. Picturebooks about the city by such photographers as Alexander Alland (1902–89) and Andreas Feininger (*b* 1906) were also popular.

The launching of the magazines *Fortune*, *Life*, and *Look* in the late 1920s and 1930s helped to make New York City the center of photojournalism, which attracted among others Bourke-White, Feininger, and W. Eugene Smith (1918–78). The demand for photographs was great, and several photographers escaping upheaval in Europe found work in the city as photojournalists, including Alfred Eisenstaedt, Philippe Halsman (1906–79), André Kertész (1894–1985), Otto Hagel, and Hansel Mieth Hagel. City life also attracted unaffiliated photographers who supported their projects with exhibitions, publications, teaching, and grants. Helen Levitt (*b* 1918) and Lisette Model (1906–83) photographed street life; Diane Arbus and Bruce Davidson (*b* 1933) explored intimate subjects. A department of photography was set up in 1939 at the Museum of Modern Art, and photographs became widely considered worthy of collection and exhibition by other museums, galleries, dealers, and auction houses, some of which specialized in photographs. Encouraged by the respect accorded to photography, many photographers experimented with color, multiple exposure, and unusual scale; graphic artists began to combine different media. Photography and the history of photography were introduced into the curricula of major universities and art schools in the city, and publishers offered a greater number of books on photography. Centers for teaching, publication, and exhibition were established, among them the International Center for Photography, and the Aperture Foundation moved to the city in 1980. As new electronic imaging techniques were developed in the mid 1990s, New York City continued to be a center for producing, publishing, and distributing photographic art.

Berenice Abbott: *Changing New York*, with text by Elizabeth McCausland (New York: E. P. Dutton, 1939; repr. New York: Dover, 1973, as *New York in the Thirties, as Photographed by Berenice Abbott*)
Felix Riesenberg and Alexander Alland Sr.: *Portrait of New York* (New York: Macmillan, 1939)
Andreas Feininger and Susan E. Lyman: *The Face of New York* (New York: Crown, 1954)
Grace M. Mayer: *Once upon a City* (New York: Macmillan, 1958)
Roger Whitehouse: *New York: Sunshine and Shadow* (New York: Harper and Row, 1974)
Reese V. Jenkins: *Images and Enterprise: Technology and the American Photographic Industry, 1839 to 1925* (Baltimore: Johns Hopkins University Press, 1975)
William Welling: *Photography in America: The Formative Years, 1839–1900* (New York: Thomas Y. Crowell, 1978)
Roy Meredith: *Mathew Brady's Portrait of an Era* (New York: W. W. Norton, 1982)
Peter B. Hales: *Silver Cities: The Photography of American Urbanization, 1839–1915* (Philadelphia: Temple University Press, 1984)
Alan Trachtenberg: *Reading American Photographs: Images as History, Mathew Brady to Walker Evans* (New York: Hill and Wang, 1989)

Naomi Rosenblum

photojournalism. The use of photographs to convey news became important in New York City during the 1860s. *Frank Leslie's Illustrated News* and *Harper's Weekly* regularly illustrated articles with wood engravings adapted from daguerreotype portraits and other photographs. Photomechanical methods, in which photographic images are used directly in the preparation of ink printing plates, were employed as early as 1873 by experimental processes in the *Daily Graphic*, but photographs were not widely used in newspapers until a patent was granted in 1878 for the halftone process, which reduced continuous tones into patterns of dots and produced images of a quality similar to that of original photographs. By the turn of the century photojournalism was well established. Among early professionals were several women including Jessie Tarbox Beals, the first woman press photographer, who opened a studio in the city in 1905 and contributed often to the *New York Herald* and the *New York Tribune*, and Francis Benjamin Johnston (1864–1952), who was well known for her work before the First World War and worked on many freelance assignments including a documentation of the building of the New Theatre in 1909.

Photojournalism changed after small, hand-held cameras with fast lenses were introduced in the 1920s, permitting photographers to take candid photographs and to cover news events as they happened. The new style of photojournalism led to the success of picture magazines, most of which had headquarters in the city and began publication during the 1930s and 1940s. One of the first was *Fortune* (1929), which engaged as its first staff photographer Margaret Bourke-White (1904–71), a former pupil at the Clarence White School of Photography who was admired for her simple, bold compositions. She executed many photographic essays on industrial and social subjects and was one of the first four staff photographers for *Life*, which used her photograph of Fort Peck Dam as the cover illustration for its first issue (23 November 1936). At its peak *Life* had more than forty staff photographers, including Alfred Eisenstaedt, Andreas Feininger (*b* 1906), and W. Eugene Smith (1918–78). Other magazines influential in the development of photojournalism were *Look*, *Focus*, and *Holiday*. The format of picture magazines led to the development of fashion photography and photography for advertising. In 1932 Anton Bruehl (1900–83) made some of the first color photographs for editorial work and advertisements under contract with Condé Nast. The work of Richard Avedon, Louise Dahl-Wolfe, and Paul Outerbridge was reproduced in *Vogue* and *Harper's Bazaar*.

By the middle of the twentieth century some of the most distinctive photojournalism in the city was the work of Weegee, whose gritty images were featured in the *Daily News*. By using a police radio he often reached the scene of a crime before the police did and became renowned for his stark images of murders, fires, and the chaos of urban life. In 1945 he published *Naked City*, a collection of photographs of crime. Picture magazines declined during the 1960s, after television began to provide immediate coverage of news. *Look* ceased publication in 1971, as did *Life* in 1972. By the mid 1990s interest in photojournalism had revived owing to the demand for images more vivid than those of television, and often photojournalists concentrated on issues of social reform. Photographic agencies became important to photojournalism for directing photojournalists to parts of the world discussed in the news and matching photographers with buyers for their images. Magnum (formed in the city in 1947) and other leading agencies helped to shape the future of photojournalism.

Tim N. Gidal: *Modern Photojournalism: Origin and Evolution, 1910–1933* (New York: Collier, 1973)

Lee D. Witkin and Barbara London: *The Photograph Collector's Guide* (Boston: New York Graphic Society, 1979)

See also DOCUMENTARY PHOTOGRAPHY.

Dale L. Neighbors

Photo League. A group of photographers formed in 1936 to document working-class life in New York City and to photograph social and political events from a liberal perspective. Eventually it attracted a diverse group of photographers, including Berenice Abbott, Dorothea Lange, Beaumont Newhall, Nancy Newhall, W. Eugene Smith, Paul Strand, and Edward Weston, who considered the league a lively alternative to the conservatism of the Camera Club of New York and the Pictorial Society of America. The league sponsored several projects concerned with city life; it also had a gallery and publication. In a school directed by Sid Grossman amateurs learned about basic problems in documentation by executing structured projects such as "Men at Work," supervised by Lewis Hine, and the Harlem Document, supervised by Aaron Siskind; pupils included Morris Engel, Arthur Leipzig, Walter Rosenblum, and Dan Weiner. The avant-garde photographers John Heartfield and Barbara Morgan and the photojournalist Weegee were among those who had exhibitions at the gallery. The publication *Photo Notes* informed members of activities and published criticism by Elizabeth McCausland, the Newhalls, and Strand, among others. At its peak in 1948 the league was listed as a "subversive" organization and in 1952 it was forced to close.

Anne Tucker: "The Photo League," *OVO Magazine* (Montreal) 10, nos. 40–41 (1981), 3–59

Naomi Rosenblum

phrenology. A pseudo-science that purports to analyze character by studying the shape of the skull. It was introduced to New York City in 1835 by the brothers Lorenzo and Orson Squire Fowler, who opened an office, museum, lecture hall, and examination room at 135 Nassau Street, a brick building called Clinton Hall. In the same year Orson Fowler published the book *Phrenology Proved, Illustrated and Applied*, which sold tens of thousands of copies and went through sixty-two editions during the next two decades. The business of "practical phrenology" proved lucrative, and the two brothers called on their sister Charlotte to join them. She helped Lorenzo on the lecture circuit and with head-reading while Orson dashed off more books, among them *Matrimony; or, Phrenology and Physiology Applied to the Selection of Congenial Companions for Life, including Directions to the Married for Living Together Affectionately and Happily* (1843). The Fowlers' enterprise attracted widespread interest (one of their customers was Walt Whitman, whom they described as having "friendship and sympathy," as well as "indolence and a tendency to the pleasures of voluptuousness"), and they moved to larger quarters at 308 Broadway. Others were more skeptical: as early as 1838 David Meredith Reese denounced phrenology in his book *Humbugs of New-York; Being a Remonstrance against Popular Delusion, Whether in Science, Philosophy, or Religion*. Lorenzo's wife Lydia joined the business in 1844, and during the same year the Fowler brothers formed a partnership with Samuel Roberts Wells, who married Charlotte, and with him set up the publishing house of Fowler and Wells. All five gave lectures and wrote books that sold millions of copies. In 1855 Orson and Lorenzo Fowler sold their interests in the publishing house to the Wellses. Fowler and Wells Phrenological Museum moved to successively larger quarters at 389, 737, 753, and 775 Broadway; the Lorenzo Fowlers and the Wellses eventually shared an elegant residence at 233 East Broadway. In 1860 Lorenzo and Lydia Fowler moved to London. On Lydia's death in 1879 their daughter Jessie helped her father in phrenological undertakings. Fowler and Wells continued to publish phrenological tracts into the first decade of the twentieth century. Jessie Fowler, a resident of New York City from 1896, was for many years the vice-president of the American Institute of Phrenology, wrote a number of books on phrenology, and as late as 1928 was listed as a phrenologist in local

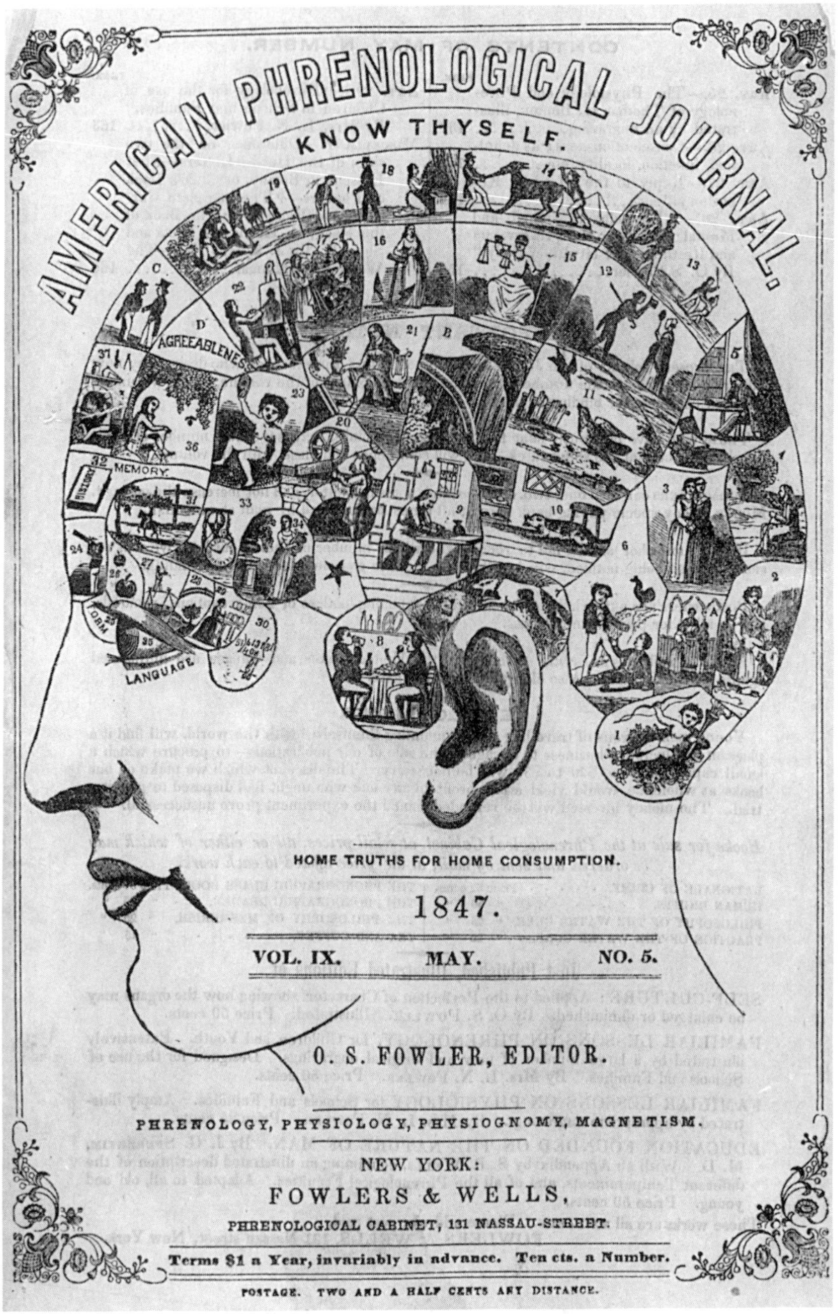

American Phrenological Journal, *May 1847*

directories. She died at her home at 843 West 179th Street on 16 October 1932, the last of the phrenological Fowlers.

Carl Carmer: "That Was New York: The Fowlers, Practical Phrenologists," *New Yorker*, 13 Feb 1937, pp. 22–27

Madeleine B. Stern: *Heads and Headlines: The Phrenological Fowlers* (Norman: University of Oklahoma Press, 1971)

Allen J. Share

Phyfe [Fife], **Duncan** (*b* Scotland, 1768; *d* New York City, 16 Aug 1854). Cabinetmaker. He moved from Albany, New York, to New York City by 1792, when he joined the General Society of Mechanics and Tradesmen. He was first listed in city directories in 1793 and by 1795 moved his shop to 35 Partition (now Fulton) Street. He employed many apprentices and journeymen, who struck when he reduced wages during the panic of 1819. He marketed his work in the city and in ports of the South and the West Indies. Between 1817 and 1822 he had customers in Savannah, Georgia, and briefly stationed an agent there to take orders and sell furniture. Phyfe was well known in his day for his elegant designs; his name now identifies American neoclassical furniture generally. In *Wealth and Biography of the Wealthy Citizens of New York City* (1845) his estate was valued at $300,000 and his firm was described as the largest and most fashionable in the country. He retired from the trade in 1847.

Nancy McClelland: *Duncan Phyfe and the English Regency, 1795–1830* (New York: W. R. Scott, 1939)

Deborah Dependahl Waters

physical disabilities. Before the mid nineteenth century there were few services in New York City to assist the physically disabled. The number of handicapped people in the city became particularly evident during the winter of 1842, and clinics for the disabled were set up at local medical colleges. In the 1850s James Knight, a physician who made home visits for the Association for the Improvement of the Condition of the Poor (AICP), reported that a large number of crippled persons could not leave their homes. In response the AICP formed the New York Society for the Relief of the Ruptured and Crippled (1862), which opened an asylum for twenty-five crippled children and supplied trusses and bandages for the disabled in a small building at 97 2nd Avenue. The society eventually moved to new quarters at Lexington Avenue and 42nd Street, where it established an asylum and hospital that housed two hundred children and a dispensary for the handicapped. The financial support provided by the city and by private sources such as the Hospital Sunday Fund allowed the society to offer most of its services free of charge. The society later evolved into the Hospital for Special Surgery.

In 1868 the New York Orthopedic Dispensary opened at 126 East 59th Street to provide free mechanical and surgical treatment of diseases and deformities of the spine and joints, infantile paralysis, bow-legs, club-feet, and other physical handicaps. In 1875 the dispensary opened a hospital with fifty beds that offered most of its services to children aged four to fourteen suffering from curable handicaps; Theodore Roosevelt was the organization's treasurer for several years in the 1870s. During this same period the city's Charity Hospital on Blackwell's Island set up a paralytic hospital to provide chronic care for those permanently disabled by paralysis or epilepsy. The Hospital for Deformities and Joint Diseases opened in 1905 at Madison Avenue and 123rd Street (it now operates as the Hospital for Joint Diseases–Orthopedic Institute at 301 East 17th Street). Among the many residential programs established for crippled children about the turn of the century were the House of St. Giles the Cripple at 417 Clinton Street in Brooklyn (by Episcopalians in 1891), the House of the Annunciation for Crippled and Incurable Children on the Upper West Side (by the Sisters of the Annunciation of the Blessed Virgin Mary in 1893), the Darrach Home for Crippled Children (1903), and the New York Home for Destitute Crippled Children (1904). The Association for the Aid of Crippled Children (1899) at Stuyvesant Square provided home nursing and transportation assistance, and helped handicapped children, especially the blind, to obtain care elsewhere.

By the late 1890s there was a growing emphasis on helping physically handicapped children become self-sufficient. The Children's Aid Society organized the Guild for Crippled Children of the Poor of New York City (1896) at 224 West 63rd Street; renamed Classes for Crippled Children, this organization had a kindergarten and offered vocational training for older children. Vocational training was also provided by the William H. Davis Free Industrial School for Crippled Children at 471 West 57th Street, the Crippled Children's East Side Free School at 157 Henry Street (1902, later known as the New York Service for the Orthopedically Handicapped), and the Brearley League Industrial School for Cripples at 350 East 88th Street (1908, later known as the Rhinelander School). In 1903 the city's health department began routine screening of schoolchildren for orthopedic and visual problems. The city's first public school classes for crippled children opened in 1905, and in the following year Henry Goldman, head of the East Side Free School, persuaded the Board of Education to establish a special public school for children with physical disabilities. Services for handicapped adults were much slower to develop than those available for children: a state commission revealed that only 12 percent of the 414,000 workers injured in industrial accidents from 1906 to 1908 received compensation. Reform legislation established local industrial commissions to adjudicate compensation cases impartially, but in the 1930s an exposé of these agencies in New York City and Chicago by the legal scholar Walter Dodd revealed exploitation of the immigrants who filed most of the claims, and a marked tendency to favor the interests of insurance companies rather than those of the injured workers. Righting these wrongs became a new priority of reformers.

Medical advances helped to reduce the number of seriously handicapped children,

Duncan Phyfe, sideboard and cellarette, ca *1825*

but even as late as 1912 nearly one third of schoolchildren in New York City had physical disabilities. Special classes for children with cardiac problems were begun in 1917 (discontinued in 1941 by recommendation of a mayoral commission). State support became available to assist the city's school programs in the same year, when New York became one of only two states in the country to pass laws aiding handicapped children not confined to institutions. In 1925 the New York Academy of Medicine reported that the efforts of private agencies such as the Association to Aid Crippled Children were reaching only about one sixth of the estimated eighteen thousand disabled children in the city, a gap in services that was confirmed in 1938 by the Commission for the Study of Crippled Children, appointed by Mayor Fiorello H. La Guardia. At the recommendation of the new commission the mayor formed the Division of Physically Handicapped Children in the health department, which was made responsible for maintaining a central registry of physically handicapped children in the city set up by the commission. As death rates from infectious diseases diminished, public health officials gave greater attention to broader issues of health and welfare in the city. This change of emphasis was highlighted in 1945 when the responsibility of administering state aid to the handicapped was moved from the city's Domestic Relations Court to its health department.

Although New York State provided more financial assistance than many other states for disabled adults, it did not significantly improve its vocational training programs for the disabled until after the First World War, when the needs of wounded veterans sparked public interest and generated federal grants for state training programs. This support led to the formation of the city's Rehabilitation Center for the Disabled in 1924 and of the Rehabilitation Bureau in the state education department, both of which received vocational rehabilitation funds granted under the Social Security Act of 1935. The training programs developed during these years focused on workers who could be restored to ordinary functioning. Several important steps were taken in the 1950s to improve health care for disabled children. The Division for Physically Handicapped Children in the health department was given the status of a bureau in 1951, and city and state funds were set aside to cover medical and rehabilitation costs for children with severe orthopedic problems, congenital heart disease, cleft palates, harelips, and conditions requiring plastic surgery; state funds supported the opening in 1953 of a cleft-palate rehabilitation center at Mount Sinai Hospital. Classes were offered in the public schools for brain-injured children, amputees, and children with cerebral palsy, and programs for the handicapped were extended into high school. The development of Medicare and Medicaid in 1965 expanded the health care available to disabled adults. Additional benefits were provided for the city's handicapped residents by amendments to the Vocational Rehabilitation Act (1965), which provided the federal support to cover 90 percent of the cost of programs that trained the physically handicapped.

A new emphasis was placed on social equality for the disabled during the civil rights movement. The claim by advocacy groups in New York City that the disabled had a right to full participation in the life of the city met with growing acceptance from the federal government and the public. The Housing Act of 1972 extended subsidies to make new housing accessible to the handicapped; the Vocational Rehabilitation Act of 1973 increased funding for vocational programs and in Section 504 mandated an end to all discriminatory exclusion of the disabled from community services. How and where to apply Section 504 became a matter of bitter controversy in New York City. The disclosure that fewer than a third of the city's 3600 buses had wheelchair lifts led to a lawsuit by advocacy groups in 1982, as a result of which lifts were installed on 80 percent of the city's buses by 1991. The Americans with Disabilities Act, passed by the U.S. Congress in 1990, required that all new mass transit vehicles be accessible to the disabled, and in the following year the city installed elevators or ramps in ten of its fifty-four major subway stations (it was required to do the same in the remaining stations by 1995). The Education for Handicapped Children Act of 1978 (Public Law 94-142) affirmed the equal right of all disabled children to publicly funded education. By 1991 special education classes were offered in nearly every public elementary school in New York City, and the city was moving toward expanding its preschool programs for the disabled.

Henry J. Cammann and Hugh N. Camp: *The Charities of New York, Brooklyn, and Staten Island* (New York: Hurd and Houghton, 1868)

David M. Schneider and Albert Deutsch: *The History of Public Welfare in New York State, 1867–1940* (Chicago: University of Chicago Press, 1941)

John Duffy: *A History of Public Health in New York City* (New York: Russell Sage Foundation, 1968, 1974)

Aliki Coudroglou and Dennis L. Poole: *Disability, Work and Social Policy: Models for Social Welfare* (New York: Springer, 1984)

Edward D. Berkowitz: *Disabled Policy: America's Programs for the Handicapped* (Cambridge: Cambridge University Press, 1987)

Sandra Opdycke

physics. Creative genius in the physical sciences in the eighteenth- and nineteenth-century United States was isolated rather than sustained, as exemplified by the work of Benjamin Franklin, Benjamin Thompson ("Count Rumford"), Joseph Henry, Josiah Willard Gibbs, and A. A. Michelson. There was nothing yet comparable with either the established tradition of Europe or its recent growth and scientific professionalization. The situation was such that at a meeting in New York City in 1880 of the American Association for the Advancement of Science, Henry Rowland, the first American professor of physics (at Johns Hopkins University), described American science as "a thing of the future and not of the present or the past." But soon the scene quickly began to change, and many of the changes radiated from New York City and its environs.

The rapid transformation of physics was fueled by a series of sensational discoveries in the burgeoning field of electrical science and applied electricity (x-rays in 1895, radioactivity in 1896, the electron in 1897, quantum phenomena from 1900), by the inexorable transformation of the United States from an agricultural to a manufacturing society, and by the steady growth of population in the metropolitan area, adding to its wealth and reinforcing its ambitions. Early work in industrial physics was conducted in the city by Thomas Edison, Alexander Graham Bell, Nikola Tesla, and others. Columbia University contributed ideas, students, and teachers to academia and industry: the American Physical Society was founded at the university in 1899 and held many of its meetings there for several decades; George Pegram of Columbia in 1927 became the treasurer of the society; the university for many years housed the editorial offices of the *Physical Review*, the leading professional journal; and in 1905 the university awarded its first PhD in physics to R. A. Millikan, later much celebrated. At Columbia Michael Pupin, although himself essentially an engineer, vigorously defended basic scientific research. In 1927 Columbia opened splendid new physics laboratories, named in honor of Pupin after his death in 1934. Many of the accomplishments of the 1930s and after in the new laboratories were overseen by Pegram and inspired by I. I. Rabi. One landmark was the discovery by Harold C. Urey in 1932 of heavy-hydrogen. This was closely followed by spectacular developments in the field of molecular-beam physics by Rabi and his disciples, who brought the field to a new level of precision and sophistication. Their work earned the Nobel Prize in 1944.

The Second World War diverted scientific energies. The Pupin laboratories became the site in 1940 of the Manhattan Project, in which Pegram, Urey, and Enrico Fermi played leading roles. After the war the new molecular-beam techniques were applied to the investigation of the refined properties of atoms, molecules, nuclei, and electrons (by Polykarp Kusch and Willis Lamb) and to new precision methods of measuring time (by Norman Ramsay). And the study of the subtleties of electromagnetic interactions launched the era of masers and lasers. In this same period new and increasingly powerful techniques were used to explore the new field of "elementary particle" physics, and especially to examine the basic symmetries of these particles and their interactions. In this important work physicists at Columbia figured prominently, notably T. D. Lee, Chien-shiung Wu, Melvin Schwartz, Leon Lederman, and Jack Steinberger. By this time physics had become part of a huge international enterprise. Columbia maintained some close links with the giants of industrial physics, especially Bell Telephone Laboratories (now greatly expanded in New Jersey) and International Business Machines (through its on-campus research institute, the Watson Laboratory).

By the late twentieth century several trends had combined to diminish the former significance of New York City as a center of physics: the enormous growth and globalization of physical research, the immensely more elaborate and extensive involvement of physical science in industry and government, and social, economic, and demographic changes in the metropolitan region. The gargantuan machines used for "elementary particle" research had outgrown the confines of a university campus or city, perhaps even of a single country. Much of the nuclear science and technology that emerged from the Manhattan Project had become environmentally inappropriate to an urban setting. And the headquarters of the American Physical Society and later of the Institute of Physics left New York City entirely for enlarged premises strategically closer to Washington.

Celebration of the Fiftieth Anniversary of the Pupin Laboratories (New York: Columbia University, 1978)
Melba Phillips: "The American Physical Society: A Survey of Its First 50 Years," *American Journal of Physics* 58, no. 3 (1990)

Samuel Devons

East Room of the Pierpont Morgan Library

Pierpont Morgan Library. Rare-book and manuscript library in Manhattan, on 36th Street between Madison and Park avenues. It is part of a complex of buildings housing the book and art collections of J. Pierpont Morgan, including his works of sculpture and porcelain and his old-master paintings and drawings. Designed in a neoclassical style by the firm of McKim, Mead and White and completed in 1906, the library embodies Morgan's identification with the princely collectors of the Renaissance. At a disused entrance are large bronze doors that once opened to the portico. Morgan's study, the West Room, has red damask walls, sculpture, and old-master paintings. In the East Room three galleried tiers of bookshelves contain books acquired by Morgan and added to by the museum's curators (notably Belle da Costa Greene, who from 1905 to 1948 had as much impact on the collections as Morgan did); the room has a coved ceiling, an enormous stone fireplace, walnut tables, and bronze exhibition cases. In a corner is the Stavelot Triptych, a reliquary crafted in the twelfth century in what is now Belgium. A display case contains one of Morgan's three copies of the Gutenberg Bible (*ca* 1455). The lectern cases display exemplars from the library's collection of more than one thousand illuminated medieval and Renaissance manuscripts; early printed books and literary manuscripts, music manuscripts, rare children's books, and old bindings also are frequently displayed in the room. The Pierpont Morgan Library holds more than nine thousand prints and drawings by Leonardo, Michelangelo, Dürer, Andrea Mantegna, and others, some of which are exhibited in the galleries.

Joseph Blumenthal: *The Art of the Printed Book* (New York: Pierpont Morgan Library, 1973)

Pierre Hotel. Hotel at 5th Avenue and 61st Street in Manhattan. Opened in October 1930, it joined a group of luxury hotels near the southeastern corner of Central Park, including the Sherry–Netherland, the Plaza, and the Savoy (now demolished). The architects, Schultze and Weaver, designed a conservative forty-four-story tower to replace the château-like mansion of Commodore Elbridge T. Gerry. Named for its owner, the celebrated restaurateur Charles Pierre, who was backed in the venture by a group of Wall Street financiers, the hotel contained more than seven hundred rooms, most of which were leased annually by its wealthy clientele. By 1960 most of the suites were sold as cooperatives; the hotel came under the control of Four Seasons Hotels in 1981.

Carol Willis

Pierrepont, Henry E(velyn) (*b* Brooklyn, 8 Aug 1808; *d* Brooklyn, 28 March 1888). City planner and businessman, second son of Hezekiah B. Pierrepont. In addition to managing his family's properties he worked to establish ferry connections across and up the East River and was a founder and later a trustee of Green-Wood Cemetery. He is regarded as one of the first city planners in the United States: active in planning the expansion of Brooklyn and known as its "first citizen," he also studied many European cities firsthand. His elder brother, William Constable Pierrepont, dedicated himself to managing the family properties in upstate New York.

In Memoriam: Henry Evelyn Pierrepont of Brooklyn (New York: G. P. Putnam's Sons, 1888)

John J. Gallagher

Pierrepont [Pierpont], **Hezekiah B(eers)** (*b* New Haven, Conn., 1768; *d* Brooklyn, 1838). Merchant, father of Henry E. Pierrepont. Born to a family long established in New England, he settled in Brooklyn in 1802 and restored the spelling of his surname to its original, French form. He amassed a small fortune as a merchant adventurer and was once captured by French privateers in the China Sea. Through his marriage to Anna Maria Constable, the daughter of a prominent merchant in Manhattan, he inherited considerable properties in upstate New York. In Brooklyn Ferry (now Brooklyn Heights) he bought sixty acres (twenty-four hectares) of the Benson farm and built a mansion on the heights above the East River. He was a prominent investor in Robert Fulton's steam ferry connecting Brooklyn to Manhattan, as well as in the local development that ensued. Pierrepont was the first important suburban real-estate developer in American history, and he was advertising and selling lots in Brooklyn Heights to prominent businessmen from Manhattan by 1823. Among the proposals that he made but did not see realized was one for a promenade along Brooklyn Heights.

Kenneth T. Jackson: *Crabgrass Frontier: The Suburbanization of the United States* (New York: Oxford University Press, 1985)

John J. Gallagher

pigeons. For information on the species of pigeon most common in New York City see Rock pigeon.

Pigtown. Name applied during the nineteenth century and the early twentieth to two neighborhoods in Flatbush, one near Bedford Avenue and Montgomery Place and the other about half a mile (one kilometer) to the east near Lincoln Terrace Park. The neighborhoods were far from urban development and had many wooden shacks, pigpens, and chicken coops. In 1908 Charles Ebbets, owner of the Brooklyn Dodgers, began buying lots in anticipation that Interborough Rapid Transit would extend its subway along Eastern Parkway and by 1913 completed Ebbets Field. After the subway was extended into East Flatbush in 1914 both Pigtowns disappeared.

Stephen Weinstein

Piñero, Miguel (Antonio Gomez, Jr.) (*b* Puerto Rico, 19 Dec 1946; *d* New York City, 17 June 1988). Playwright. He moved with his family from Puerto Rico to the Lower East Side in 1950. His arrest and imprisonment for burglary in 1964 began a ten-year series of convictions for petty crimes related to his drug addiction. He was eventually sent to the Otisville State Training School for Boys and earned his high school equivalency diploma while an inmate at Manhattan State Hospital. In 1971 he took part in Clay Stevenson's acting workshop at Ossining Correctional Facility and began writing plays. Prison life became the basis of his best-known work, *Short Eyes* (1974), which was presented off Broadway and made into a motion picture; brutally realistic portrayals of life in prison and on the city streets characterize twelve other plays, including *Eulogy for a Small-time Thief* (1977), two screenplays, and two books of poetry. Piñero helped to form the Nuyoricans, a group of Puerto Rican poets based in the city. In 1974 he won an Obie Award, the New York Drama Critics Circle Award, and the Drama Desk Award.

James Pelton

Ping Chong (*b* Toronto, 2 Oct 1946). Playwright, choreographer, and visual artist. In 1972 he formed the Fiji Company (also known as Ping Chong and Company), which in the same year staged its first production, *Lazarus.* In the following years he created more than thirty performance pieces and installations as the company's principal writer, director, and choreographer. His work was presented at the Brooklyn Academy of Music, La Mama Experimental Theatre Club, the Kennedy Center in Washington, the Walker Arts Center in Minneapolis, the Cabaret Voltaire in Turin, the Togamura Theatre Festival in Japan, the Holland Festival in Amsterdam, and the International Theatre Festival in Bogotá. Chong won an Obie Award in 1977 for *Humboldt's Current,* the Outstanding Achievement Award of the National Institute of Music Theatre in 1986 for *The Games,* a collaboration with Meredith Monk, and the USA Playwrights Award in 1987 for *Kind Ness*; he also won a Winton Fellowship, a fellowship from the Guggenheim Foundation, two from the McKnight Foundation, and five from the National Endowment for the Arts. His highly eclectic works draw on such disparate sources as *Alice in Wonderland* and Indonesian puppet plays and explore such themes as alienation and cultural conflict.

Luis H. Francia

Pintard, John (*b* New York City, 18 May 1759; *d* New York City, 21 June 1844). Businessman. After graduating from Princeton College in 1776 he entered business, focusing his efforts in the China and East India trade, and by 1792 he was one of the most successful merchants in New York City. He later declared bankruptcy and was imprisoned for debt before finding work as an auctioneer of books and as an editor of the *Daily Advertiser*; he was eventually engaged as the secretary of the city's first fire insurance company. As clerk of the corporation and inspector for the city he developed a system for keeping vital statistics. Under the auspices of the Tammany Society, in which he was a sagamore and grand sachem, he organized a historical museum; he also helped to organize the New-York Historical Society in 1804 and General Theological Seminary, served for many years as the secretary of the American Bible Society, and was influential in strengthening the Chamber of Commerce. An alderman and a member of the state legislature, Pintard promoted the Erie Canal and organized the city's first savings bank, of which he was president.

Miniature of John Pintard by John Ramage (1787)

James E. Mooney

Pinto, Isaac (*b* 12 June 1720; *d* New York City, 17 Jan 1791). Merchant and scholar. With his family he moved to Connecticut in 1724 and settled in New York City in 1736, where he became a member of Congregation Shearith Israel. Known for his scholarship, he taught Spanish and worked as a translator, producing the first Jewish prayer book printed in English in the colonies and publishing the texts of Rosh Hashana and Yom Kippur services in 1761 and 1766. Pinto is buried in the Spanish and Portuguese cemetery on 21st Street.

Janet Frankston

Planetarium. See Hayden planetarium.

Planned Parenthood of America. Nonprofit organization devoted to reproductive health care, the oldest and largest of its kind in the United States. Among its forerunners was the country's first birth-control clinic, opened in Brooklyn in 1916 by Margaret Sanger. After her prompt arrest and indictment for distributing contraceptive devices the organization continued in various forms until 1939, when the Birth Control Clinical Research Bureau of America merged with the American Birth Control League to form the Birth Control Federation of America. Headquarters were established in the city and the current name was adopted in 1942. Planned Parenthood has its offices at 810 7th Avenue and operates more than nine hundred centers nationwide that provide medically supervised reproductive health services, information, and educational programs.

See also FAMILY PLANNING.

Chad Ludington

Platt, Thomas C(ollier) (*b* Oswego, N.Y., 15 July 1833; *d* New York City, 6 March 1910). Political leader. He was well known in business and politics when he moved to New York City in 1880. Soon elected to the U.S. Senate, he led the New York State delegation to the Republican National Convention in 1888. Through political maneuvering he unsuccessfully sought an appointment as secretary of the treasury. As a leading figure in city politics he gained power in state government and became the leader of the Republican Party in New York State. After Platt's reelection to the Senate in 1904 his influence declined and he left politics. He lived at 2 Rector Street.

See also FIFTH AVENUE HOTEL.

James E. Mooney

Players. A club incorporated in 1888 for men active in the theater, music, literature, and the arts. One of its founders, the actor Edwin Booth, purchased a building for the club on Gramercy Park. Erected in 1845 in the Gothic Revival style as one of the first brownstones in New York City, the building was remodeled by Stanford White to resemble an Italian Renaissance palace, leaving the proper residents of the neighborhood aghast. Inside the building are comfortable quarters and a working library of theater history that is based on the collection of Booth, much augmented. Quotations from Shakespeare are on the walls of every room.

James E. Mooney

playgrounds. The movement to build playgrounds for children living in densely populated tenement districts was begun in the 1880s to offer an alternative to the street for outdoor play. The first playgrounds were sponsored by settlement houses and consisted of backyard spaces with sandboxes and other simple equipment. Charles Stover in 1891 helped to form the New York Society for Parks and Playgrounds, which demonstrated new play equipment and pressured the city to build playgrounds. In 1897 the city appointed the journalist, photographer, and social activist Jacob A. Riis to lead the Small Parks Advisory Committee, which urged the city to build playgrounds for their "healthful influence upon morals and conduct." Stover in 1898 joined with Lillian Wald, director of the Henry Street Settlement, to form the Outdoor Recreation League, which built nine privately sponsored playgrounds that the parks department agreed to improve and operate in 1902. In the following year the first permanent playground built by the city opened in Seward Park at Essex Street and East Broadway on the Lower East Side.

Playground at 10 West 28th Street, ca *1890*

As the parks commissioner from 1910 to 1913 Stover formed the Bureau of Recreation in 1911 to accommodate the growing role of athletics in the design and operation of parks. About the same time the city opened playgrounds atop active commercial waterfront piers. Between 1910 and 1920 thousands of children took part in interborough sports tournaments at playgrounds that drew large crowds of spectators. The first playgrounds in Central Park were built in the 1920s. During the tenure of Robert Moses as the parks commissioner (1934–60) the number of playgrounds in the city rose from 119 to 777. Many were built by federal relief workers during the 1930s; the standard designs of mass-produced sandboxes, wading pools, swings, and benches gave them a uniform look throughout the city. Employees of the city known as "parkies" led children's activities and conducted preschool classes. In 1938 the parks department worked with the Board of Education to develop additional playgrounds on sites adjacent to schools.

From the 1960s designers experimented with new equipment and materials. The first "adventure playground" in the city opened in 1967 on the west side of Central Park; like its European forerunners, it was built after a planning stage during which the opinions of children were solicited. Temporary playgrounds were set up on vacant lots. The Playground for All Children at Flushing Meadows–Corona Park (1984) was the first playground in the nation designed specifically for physically disabled children; another was added at Asser Levy Recreation Center in 1993. Efforts increased to involve communities in the design, construction, and maintenance of playgrounds. In addition to the many outdoor playgrounds throughout New York City, a number are indoors, including one at the Pelham Fritz Recreation Center in Marcus Garvey Park.

A Playground for All Children: City of New York (Washington: U.S. Department of Housing and Urban Development, 1976–78)

Jonathan Kuhn

Plaza Hotel. Hotel at 59th Street and 5th Avenue, overlooking Grand Army Plaza. The site was once occupied by a shallow pond that the wealthy used for ice skating. Because of its splendid view of Central Park, it was considered too valuable even for developing fine row houses of the sort commonly built along 5th Avenue. The land was bought in 1880 by a group of real-estate speculators including Jared Bradley Flagg who hoped to erect an apartment building; their insistence on a large profit deterred investors, and Flagg sold the property to John Charles Anderson, who took a mortgage from John C. Pfyfe and James Campbell. The two planned to build a fashionable apartment hotel designed by Carl Pfeiffer and were given a loan for it by the New York Life Insurance Company. When their funds were depleted they abandoned Pfeiffer's design and undertook the construction themselves but were unable to complete it. After New York Life foreclosed on the building it was fitted as a hotel by the firm of

McKim, Mead and White and opened on 1 October 1890, soon becoming well known for its four hundred guest rooms and grand public spaces. It was sold to the George A. Fuller Company in 1902, demolished in 1905, and replaced in 1907 with a building designed by Henry J. Hardenbergh, an architect well known for his apartment buildings and hotels. The structure had about eight hundred rooms with some grand entertaining areas and became the best-known Edwardian hotel in the city, especially after the first Waldorf–Astoria was demolished. Among the guests were the Duke and Duchess of Windsor, Frank Lloyd Wright, and the Beatles; the hotel was also the setting of several stories by F. Scott Fitzgerald. In the 1980s the Plaza Hotel was bought by Donald Trump, who maintained its reputation for exclusivity and style.

Eva Brown: *The Plaza: Its Life and Times* (New York: Meredith, 1967)

Mosette G. Broderick

Pleasant Plains. Neighborhood in southern Staten Island, northeast of Tottenville. The area was named after the Staten Island Railroad built a station in the 1860s at a bend in the Amboy Road; the business and entertainment district took shape nearby. Most of the housing consists of one-family houses, among them a number built in the nineteenth century. Late in the century John C. Drumgoole formed Mount Loretto, a home for destitute orphaned boys from Manhattan, which covered six hundred acres (240 hectares) near the neighborhood; part of the property became the Cemetery of the Resurrection in 1988. Pleasant Plains retains its rural character. Well-known residents have included the harpist Maud Morgan and the opera manager Max Maretzek.

Marjorie Johnson

P. Lorillard and Company. Firm of tobacco products manufacturers. It began as a snuff factory opened in 1760 by Pierre Lorillard (*b* 1742; *d ca* 1778) in a rented house on Chatham Street in Manhattan. After Lorillard was killed by British troops seeking refuge in the house, his sons Peter and George took over the firm in 1792; they maintained the building in Manhattan as their headquarters and moved the factory to a wooden grist mill in Westchester County along the Bronx River (now in the Bronx), where they experimented with using water power in production. The mill produced more tobacco than any other facility in the country by the end of the eighteenth century and was later replaced with a larger granite building, which was sold in 1870. The firm left the city in 1891 and became part of a trust formed by the American Tobacco Company; when the trust was declared illegal in 1911 by the U.S. Supreme Court Lorillard again became independent. The mill was acquired by the New York Botanical Garden in 1937 and converted into a restaurant. In 1959 the firm's headquarters were moved to Manhattan. Lorillard was bought by the Loews Corporation in 1969.

Lorillard and Tobacco: 200th Anniversary, P. Lorillard and Company, 1760–1960 (New York: P. Lorillard, 1960)

James Bradley

Plum(b) Beach. Former neighborhood in southeastern Brooklyn, connected to Sheepshead Bay by a neck of land extending east from the foot of Emmons Avenue. Named for the beach plums growing in the area, the site was known variously as Plum Island and Plumb Island until it was joined to the mainland with dredgings from the construction of the Belt Parkway. In the late 1890s it was bought by the federal government as a site for a mortar fortification, but after this project was abandoned the land was leased with the stipulation that it be used as a summer resort. It became a bungalow colony that by 1934 still had no electricity, gas, or telephone service. In the 1950s the U.S. Department of Agriculture opened a laboratory there to study animal diseases. No longer inhabited, the area lies within the Gateway National Recreation Area and is partly owned by the city.

Ellen Marie Snyder-Grenier

Plunders Neck. Former neighborhood in southeastern Brooklyn, lying within New Lots and bordered to the north by East New York and the Queens county line, to the east by Spring Creek, to the south by Jamaica Bay, and to the west by Betts Creek (Fountain Avenue). The area was the site of farming and fishing, and during the late nineteenth century about fifty families lived in wooden houses isolated from the rest of Kings County. A small hotel stood at Forbells's Landing adjacent to Mill Pond. The land is now the site of the Louis H. Pink housing project and the Pitkin Avenue subway yards.

Stephen Weinstein

Plunkitt, George Washington (*b* New York City, 16 Nov 1842; *d* New York City, 19 Nov 1924). Political leader. Known as "the sage of Tammany Hall," he held office as an alderman and state senator; for many years he was a Democratic district leader on the West Side and a sachem of the Tammany Society, of which he became Father of the Council. Plunkitt is remembered for his frank statements about "honest graft" and why reform movements are doomed in New York City. Many of his views are recorded in William Riordan's book *Plunkitt of Tammany Hall* (1905). Plunkitt lived at 323 West 51st Street.

Frank Vos

Plymouth Church of the Pilgrims. Congregational church organized on 13 June 1847 by a group of merchants, most of them abolitionists from New England. It opened in a building at the corner of Orange and Hicks streets in Brooklyn Heights, with Henry Ward Beecher as its minister. After being destroyed

Plymouth Church of the Pilgrims (designed by Joseph C. Wells), Brooklyn Heights, ca *1900*

by fire on 13 January 1849 the building was replaced in 1850 by a much larger one, which had ample standing room and a large semicircle of pews around a platform that served as a pulpit. The number of full members rose from twenty-one in 1847 to 1460 in 1859, when the congregation on Sundays reached nearly three thousand (many Congregational churches had fewer than a hundred communicants at the time). The congregation took keen interest in temperance and abolition and opened the church as a station on the Underground Railroad to offer asylum to runaway slaves. During the Kansas–Nebraska crisis of the mid 1850s it dispatched rifles to the antislavery settlers; the rifles quickly became known as "Beecher's bibles," the church as the "church of the holy rifles." Most members supported Beecher when accusations of adultery were brought against him in the 1870s, and when he died in 1887 fifty thousand mourners passed through the church. The church continued to thrive under his successor, Lyman Abbott. A parish house enclosing a garden court was added in 1914. After merging with the Congregational Church of the Pilgrims in 1934 the church was renamed Plymouth Church of the Pilgrims; it remained in its building on Orange Street, where in Hillis Hall the Tiffany windows from the former Congregational Church of the Pilgrims (113 Remsen Street) were installed. In the mid 1990s Plymouth Church sponsored a YMCA youth program, a day clinic for patients with Alzheimer's disease, several programs for recovering addicts, and services for disabled children offered in conjunction with the Lamm Institute of Long Island.

Stephen Morrell Griswold: *Sixty Years with Plymouth Church* (New York: Revell, 1907)

Kevin Kenny

PM. Daily newspaper launched in New York City in 1940 and shaped by the idealism of its editor and publisher, Ralph Ingersoll, who had worked for the publishers of *Time* as an editor of *Fortune* and a founder of *Life*. It had a magazine format, carried no advertising, and became known for its crusading journalism.

Among the newspaper's innovations were its coverage of the labor movement and its features of interest to consumers. Its prominent writers and photographers included Ben Hecht, Ernest Hemingway, Max Lerner, I. F. Stone, James A. Wechsler, Margaret Bourke-White, and Weegee. Despite these strengths the newspaper was not profitable, owing largely to Ingersoll's inability to manage the company. When it began accepting advertising in 1946 at the insistence of the investor Marshall Field III, Ingersoll resigned in protest. The newspaper became the *Star* in 1948 and ceased publication later that year.

Roy Hoopes: *Ralph Ingersoll: A Biography* (New York: Atheneum, 1985)

Madeline Rogers

Podhoretz, Norman (*b* Brooklyn, 16 Jan 1930). Editor and writer. A son of immigrants, he graduated from high school at sixteen and studied with Lionel Trilling at Columbia University, where he earned a BA in English. He later studied for two years at Cambridge University with the literary critic F. R. Leavis. He returned to New York City and became one of the youngest members on the staff of *Commentary*, a monthly magazine edited by Elliot Cohen. In 1956 he married Midge Decter, Cohen's secretary and later an editor and political analyst. Bitterness erupted among the staff during a search for another editor after Cohen took his own life in 1959. Podhoretz became the editor although he was only thirty, remaining for thirty-five years. For a short time he was allied with the New Left, publishing critical essays on the cold war, the Vietnam War, and American life. His memoir *Making It* (1968) was widely denounced by his colleagues, in large part because of his assertion that among intellectuals in the city sexual energy was displaced by ambition. He moved back toward the political center and to the right during the mid 1960s; by the early 1970s he abandoned literary interests for political ones and became a leading spokesman for neoconservatism. He accused critics of Israel of "faithlessness to the interests of the United States and . . . Western civilization as a whole."

Alexander Bloom

Poe, Edgar Allan (*b* Boston, 19 Jan 1809; *d* Baltimore, 7 Oct 1849). Short-story writer, poet, and critic. Orphaned in 1811, he grew up in Virginia and England. His early career was marked by frequent changes of residence and a conspicuous lack of success as a writer. He lived in New York City in 1837–38 and spent the summers of 1843 and 1844 in a farmhouse on West 84th Street, just west of Broadway. He again took up permanent residence in the city in 1844. While living at 85 Amity Street (now West 3rd Street) he wrote the poem "The Raven," which he published anonymously in February 1845 in the *American Review* to critical success. During the same year he became the editor of the *Broadway Journal*, a weekly publication through which he sought to challenge the city's best-known literary journals, especially the *Knickerbocker Magazine*, leading him into several damaging controversies. His charge that Henry Wadsworth Longfellow's poetry was plagiary contributed to the demise of the journal in December. In 1846 he moved to Fordham Cottage at 2640 Grand Concourse near East Kingsbridge Road; the building is now known as Poe Cottage. Critical intrigue continued to influence his work. For the popular magazine *Godey's Lady's Book* he wrote the series "The Literati of New York," which resulted in a libel suit against him by Thomas Dunn English, one of his subjects. *Godey's* dropped the series but published his short story "The Cask of Amontillado," a veiled parody of his literary troubles. After the death of his wife Poe left the city in 1849.

Kenneth Silverman: *Edgar A. Poe: A Mournful and Never Ending Remembrance* (New York: Harper Collins, 1991)

See also LITERATURE, §1.

Jeff Finlay

Poe Cottage. The last home of Edgar Allan Poe (from 1846 to 1849), built about 1812 on the Grand Concourse and East Kingsbridge Road in the Bronx. Poe moved to the site in the hope that its setting would prove salutary to his wife, who was gravely ill, and because of its access to Manhattan by the New York and Harlem River Railroad. While living in the cottage Poe wrote such well-known poems as "Annabel Lee," "Ulalume," "The Bells," and "Eureka." Poe's wife died of tuberculosis at the cottage in 1847. In 1913 the cottage was moved to Poe Park across the street to avoid demolition, and in 1917 it opened as a historic house museum. Now a national and city landmark, it is administered by the Bronx County Historical Society.

Gary D. Hermalyn

Poets, Playwrights, Editors and Novelists [PEN]. International literary organization formed in 1921 by the English writer Catherine Amy Dawson as a dining club in London, and later including eighty-five branches in fifty-five countries. Its activities in the United States are centered in New York City, where it operates two committees: Freedom to Write, which defends writers against government interference, and Writer's Watch, which monitors government censorship. The group often meets at the Salmagundi Club at 47 5th Avenue. In the mid 1990s the president was Louis Begley.

Anthony Gronowicz

Poles. The Polish presence in New York City dates to the early seventeenth century, when a number of merchants, soldiers, and teachers from Poland settled in New Amsterdam. Among them were Alexander Curtius, founder of the first school in Manhattan; Daniel Litscho, a leading supporter of Peter Stuyvesant on the council of burgomasters and schepens; Olbracht Zaborowski, a landowner who held title to much of New Jersey; and Marcin Krygier, who was elected burgomaster at least three times. In 1834 two Austrian warships arrived in New York Harbor carrying 234 Polish exiles from the failed uprising of November 1830. Some settled in the city, where they worked to free Poland from foreign domination; Gaspard Tochman founded the Polish–Slavonian Literary Association (1846) and several others published literary and historical works. More groups of Polish immigrants settled in New York City after the unsuccessful Polish revolts of 1846 and 1848 and the January Resurrection of 1863. Many of the immigrants were highly educated, eventually entered the professions, and often took part in reform movements such as that against slavery. During the Civil War Colonel Wladimir Krzyzanowski raised the 58th New York

Poe Cottage, ca *1915*

Infantry, known as the Polish Legion, and Major Alexander Raszewski led a Polish unit, Company C of the 31st New York Infantry.

Most of the Poles settling in New York City between 1870 and 1920 were rural laborers seeking economic opportunity who were originally from parts of Poland occupied by Austria and Russia. Called the *za chlebem* ("for bread") immigrants, they generally found employment in construction and manufacturing (especially textiles). Once established they proved to be enthusiastic supporters of the labor movement, many becoming leaders in union locals. The first neighborhood of the za chlebem took form on the Lower East Side, where St. Stanislaus Bishop and Martyr Church was erected in 1872. Gradually these immigrants expanded into the southern and northeastern Bronx, Fort Greene, South Brooklyn, Elmhurst, and in 1890 Greenpoint, where they established St. Stanislaus Kostka Church in 1896. The Catholic church proved important in the daily lives of Polish immigrants, providing a social focus as well as a religious one. Two parishes of the Polish National Catholic Church were eventually formed in the city: Holy Cross Parish in South Brooklyn and the Church of the Resurrection in Greenpoint. The Polish population of New York City was swelled by refugees from Nazi atrocities during the Second World War, displaced persons after the war, refugees from communist persecution during the cold war, and the rise of the labor movement Solidarity. These new immigrants tended to be educated and highly skilled, and many settled in traditional Polish neighborhoods. In 1970 about 292,000 residents of New York City were of Polish birth and about 500,000 others were of Polish heritage. Among those of Polish birth 38 percent lived in Brooklyn, 33 percent in Queens, 14 percent in Manhattan, 11 percent in the Bronx, and 4 percent in Staten Island. The largest Polish neighborhood was Greenpoint. One of the most influential Polish-language newspapers, *Nowy Dziennik*, was launched in the city in 1971.

In the mid 1990s Polish fraternal, cultural, and educational organizations in New York City included the Kosciuszko Foundation, the Polish Institute of Arts and Sciences of America, the Polish National Alliance of Brooklyn, the Roman Dmowski Institute, and the Joseph Pilsudski Institute of America for Research in the Modern History of Poland. There were also twenty-four Roman Catholic parishes recognized as Polish, eight major Polish veterans' organizations, ten Polish political organizations, nine professional associations, six artistic and theatrical societies, and twelve periodicals. The most important Polish social and cultural celebration of the year is the annual Pulaski Day Parade in October.

James S. Pula

Policeman of 1693, from Harper's New Monthly Magazine

police. For the first two hundred years of its existence New York City had a system for maintaining public order much like that of other colonial cities, designed to protect citizens from external as much as internal threats. In New Amsterdam a *schout fiscal* (sheriff attorney) administered the rules established by the Dutch West India Company, and a burgher guard looked out for Indians at times of expected raids. When fears of Indians became widespread Governor Peter Stuyvesant initiated a paid nighttime foot patrol consisting of a captain and eight men armed only with rattles. The patrol was intended to alert residents of impending raids, to control rowdy sailors, drunkards, and prostitutes, and to watch for fires. Under British control in the late seventeenth century New York City was subject to military rule; a notable exception to the pattern was a night watch, forty-five strong, that patrolled from 1684 to 1689 and briefly made the city perhaps the best-protected in the colonies, a distinction of which the city was soon deprived by political unrest and war. From the end of the seventeenth century until well into the nineteenth New Yorkers falteringly sought to navigate between competing approaches to policing. Under the charter promulgated by John Montgomerie in 1731 all citizens residing south of the Fresh Water Pond could be called on for night-watch duty. A constable in each ward took eight men with him every night to serve watch (although women were eligible there is no record of any having served). The reluctance of local residents to be pressed into service, even for a night, abruptly ended the citizens' watch in 1734, when it was replaced by a paid force of three to a dozen men standing guard over a city of ten thousand.

From the 1740s residents believed their city to be besieged by crime and disorder and were unsure of the remedy. The "Negro plot" in 1741 frightened the city into organizing a temporary militia, which was immediately succeeded by another paid force, this time of

Number of Police Officers in New York City, 1826–1990

1826	200
1840	948
1844	1,132
1850	901
1855	1,116
1860	1,473
1865	2,474
1870	2,325
1875	2,544
1880	2,159
1885	2,898
1890	3,525
1895	3,825
1900	7,426
1905	8,766
1910	10,173
1915	10,664
1920	10,905
1925	14,216
1930	18,595
1935	17,842
1940	19,747
1945	15,579
1950	19,789
1955	22,024
1960	26,993
1965	29,407
1970	38,927
1975	42,165
1980	28,691
1985	30,705
1990	26,911

Compiled by Edward T. O'Donnell

thirty-six men, a dozen of whom were on duty on any given night. Within a year the paid force was replaced by another citizens' watch; like its predecessors this proved both inadequate to the task at hand and overly burdensome on the citizenry, particularly the poor, who could ill afford the time needed to serve or the money to secure a substitute. As a result impoverished residents found themselves guarding their more affluent neighbors, an arrangement that continued when the state government in 1747 set up a force with characteristics of both a militia and a citizens' watch, prompting the city to organize yet another paid police force in 1762. In 1774 there was a force with the equivalent of twenty full-time positions: sixteen regular watchmen served nightly for £32 a year, and eight served on alternate nights for £16 a year. The force looked out for fires but was scarcely able to control the city's burgeoning, boisterous populace. When the British army occupied New York City in 1776 it assumed primary responsibility for policing, but many residents maintained a voluntary watch throughout the war. A formal constabulary system and night watch were reintroduced after the British evacuated in 1783. To provide incentives for enforcing the law the state legislature soon established a fee schedule by which constables were paid according to each task: fees were set for serving a warrant (1*s.* 6*d.*, plus 6*d.* for each mile traveled), issuing fines, making arrests, detaining prisoners, serving summonses, and performing similar duties.

In 1800 sixteen constables patrolled the city by day along with about forty marshals appointed by the mayor. Together they were responsible for suppressing riots, maintaining order in the streets, acting as court officers, and arresting offenders. Much of the work of law enforcement in the early nineteenth century was done by one man, Jacob Hays, who governed the small constabulary force for nearly fifty years after Mayor Edward Livingston appointed him high constable in 1801. Born in Bedford, New York, in 1772, Hays gained an international reputation for his autocratic rule; he made many single-handed arrests and dispersed rebellious crowds with a minimum of physical force.

At night a ragtag force of seventy-two men served in the watch in 1800 under two captains and two deputies, and was entrusted with lighting the street lamps, subduing wrongdoers, looking out for fires, and guarding Potter's Field from grave-robbing medical students. Paid too little to support themselves on watch work alone, the watchmen labored during the day as mechanics, teamsters, stevedores and the like, then often dozed their way through guard duty. Records show that 120 watchmen were fined for sleeping while on duty in 1803, and 140 were caught in the following year. Like the constables and marshals the watchmen wore no uniform apart from leather helmets, for which they became known as leatherheads.

During the first half-century after independence New Yorkers tolerated their meek and modest police system and accepted a remarkable degree of unchallenged lawlessness in the streets, largely because their fears of a standing army made them wary of delegating greater coercive power to local government. But by 1830 many came to see their fractured police force as woefully incompetent and ineffective. As poor immigrants, tenements, and factories became more numerous, tensions relating to class, race, and ethnicity heightened and crime increased accordingly. There were frequent riots, robberies around the wharves and businesses of the first ward, violence and vice in the slums of the Five Points, and rampant prostitution and gambling throughout the city, all signaling the breakdown of communal order. At the same time the constables and night watch were increasingly criticized for paying less attention to public safety than to the fees they could earn and the political favors they owed to the politicians who had appointed them. Inspired by the example set in London, officials in the early 1840s resolved to make New York City the first American city to adopt a full-time, professional police force that could effectively prevent crime as well as respond to it. A measure to reorganize the force introduced by Mayor Robert H. Morris and signed into law in 1845 by Mayor William F. Havemeyer established a "Day and Night Police" of as many as eight hundred men, identified by a star-shaped badge that gave the new force the nickname "star police."

Reformers were still fearful that the power vested in a strong, independent police department could be abused, and they sought to make the police strictly accountable to the public by subjecting them to the control of elected officials. In solving one problem they nevertheless created others. By commingling control of the police and partisan politics they made the mayor's authority to appoint policemen dependent on the recommendations of aldermen; patrol districts coincided with ward boundaries, local politicians used the police for their own venal purposes, party officials controlled the appointment of magistrates to the police courts that had original jurisdiction in criminal cases, and aldermen enjoyed the right to have criminal charges dismissed. Because the fee schedule was replaced by a system of fixed salaries, the most lucrative part of police work was now the taking of bribes from those engaged in gambling, prostitution, and other illicit businesses. There were other problems as well. The same reformers who were eager to organize a police force were reluctant to pay for it, and the force remained surprisingly small in relation to the city's population, numbering only twelve hundred in 1855 (when the city's population exceeded 600,000). Further, the absence of a modern system of social services forced the police to shoulder many duties having little relation to crime fighting: patrolmen directed traffic, found shelter for the homeless, searched for lost children, settled domestic disputes, and escorted drunkards home or to the precinct house. In 1850 the police were outfitted with uniforms.

The police in 1853 were placed under the control of a board of commissioners composed of the mayor, the recorder, and the city judge. In the same year some formal training began, and officers were armed with nightsticks. It was hoped that the new board would wrest control over law enforcement from the corrupt council, but soon Mayor Fernando Wood demonstrated his capacity to use the police for his own purposes. In 1857 a state legislature dominated by Republicans decided to take power away from the city's Democrats and into its own hands when it established the Metropolitan Police District. Composed of New York, Kings, Westchester, and Richmond counties, the new district was governed by a board of five gubernatorial appointees and the mayors of New York City and Brooklyn. Wood, a Democrat, resisted the establish-

Police Commissioners of New York City after Consolidation

Bernard J. York 1898–1901
John B. Sexton 1898–1901
Theodore L. Hamilton 1898
William E. Philips 1898
Jacob Hess 1898–1901
Henry E. Abell 1899–1901
Michael C. Murphy 1901–2
John N. Partridge 1902–3
Francis V. Greene 1903–4
William McAdoo 1904–5
Theodore A. Bingham 1906–9
William F. Baker 1909–10
James C. Cropsey 1910–11
Rhinelander Waldo 1911–13
Douglas I. McKay 1913–14
Arthur Woods 1914–17
Frederick Burgher 1918
Richard E. Enright 1918–25
George V. McLaughlin 1926–27
Joseph A. Warren 1927–28
Grover A. Whalen 1928–30
Edward P. Mulrooney 1930–33
James S. Bolan 1933
John F. O'Ryan 1934
Lewis J. Valentine 1934–45
Arthur W. Wallander 1945–49
William P. O'Brien 1949–50
Thomas F. Murphy 1950–51
George P. Monaghan 1951–53
Francis W. H. Adams 1954–55
Stephen P. Kennedy 1955–61
Michael J. Murphy 1961–65
Vincent L. Broderick 1965–66
Howard R. Leary 1966–70
Patrick V. Murphy 1970–73
Donald F. Cawley 1973–74
Michael J. Codd 1974–77
Robert J. McGuire 1978–83
William J. Devine 1983
Benjamin Ward 1984–89
Richard Condon 1989–90
Lee P. Brown 1990–92
Raymond Kelly 1992–94
William Bratton 1994–

ment of a state force within the city and vowed to maintain a municipal counterpart. The two forces coexisted for several months, until the Metropolitans in June sought to arrest the recalcitrant mayor for inciting a riot and a bloody battle ensued on Broadway. The confrontation ended when the state militia intervened, and the crisis was resolved a month later when the New York State Court of Appeals upheld the constitutionality of the state force. In the same year officers were authorized to carry a service revolver. The seats on the board reserved for the mayors of New York City and Brooklyn were eliminated in 1860 and the total number of members was reduced to three (all appointed by the governor), thus guaranteeing that Republicans would have unlimited access to the patronage afforded by the police department. The Metropolitan Police District was abolished in 1870 by the state legislature, now controlled by the Democrats, and the governance of the department was returned to a local board composed of Democrats loyal to Tammany Hall and a few Republican allies, giving impetus to a reform movement already under way. All precinct detectives in 1883 were placed under the jurisdiction of the Central Detective Bureau at the request of its commanding officer Thomas Byrnes, ostensibly to fight corruption, and in the following year the police came under the jurisdiction of civil service regulations already applicable to other municipal agencies. After a long campaign by the Women's Temperance Union, New York City in 1891 became one of the last large American cities to employ police matrons.

The city's police department was a symbol of corruption in the late nineteenth century and for much of the twentieth, owing largely to the close connections between policing and politics. An investigative commission led by State Senator Clarence Lexow in 1894–95 disclosed involvement by the police in vice operations and found officers responsible for rigging elections and for physical brutality. In 1930 an investigation led by Samuel Seabury uncovered widespread corruption, as well as the harassment of innocent women by police vice squads. Periodic scandals inspired attempts to reform the police force and make it more professional, but these proved slow and difficult to bring about.

One effort to instill professionalism was the formation of specialized, technically trained units with specific functions. Traffic control was adopted as an official activity in 1908. In response to a spate of anarchist terrorism, a bomb squad was created in 1914. Radio motor patrol cars (RMPs) were introduced in 1917, followed in 1927 by the Air Service Unit, equipped with helicopters and small airplanes, and in 1930 by the Emergency Services Division. Two-way communication between patrol cars and precincts began in 1937; a fully automated communications system known as the Special Police Inquiry Network (SPRINT) became operational in 1969. In 1959 the department organized the Tactical Patrol Force, a specially trained corps of physically imposing, college-educated police officers intended to deal with a serious outbreak of gang violence. By the mid 1960s this became an important instrument for the suppression of civil unrest. The force was admired by some for its proficiency and resented by others, especially among racial minorities, as an army of occupation. Skepticism toward the department among minority groups stemmed from its long history as an all-white organization: it did not appoint its first black officer, Samuel Battle, until 1911, and its first black precinct commander, Lloyd Sealy, until 1964.

Efforts at reform took on a new urgency in the 1960s with the onset of the civil rights movement, racial unrest, and charges of police brutality. Demands that the police be sensitive to the concerns of racial and ethnic minorities became widespread. In 1966 the Patrolman's Benevolent Association became embroiled in a heated political battle over a referendum to form a civilian review board. By the end of the decade two national commissions had stressed the need for urban police departments to recruit more officers from racial minority groups. A commission led by Whitman Knapp in 1972 confirmed allegations that the leadership of the police department had tolerated and condoned systemic corruption, and that many officers routinely collected payoffs from owners of small businesses; the findings of the commission made clear that breaking the ties between politics and the police left other opportunities for corruption that were rooted in the structure of the police department itself. The growing pressure for change had some effect. In 1972 the Civil Rights Act was amended to bring state and local governments under federal guidelines for employment, and between 1974 and 1983 the Guardians, an association of black officers, filed four successful lawsuits against the city because of racial bias in entry-level and promotional examinations. The city's first black police commissioners were named in the following years: Benjamin Ward in 1984 and Lee P. Brown in 1990. In 1985 Mayor Edward I. Koch appointed a committee led by John E. Zuccotti to investigate management and personnel practices in the department. The committee found that the major obstacle to achieving a racially balanced police force was an overreliance on written civil service examinations for selection and promotion. It also found that systematic corruption in the department had been essentially eliminated. Other problems facing the department included charges by female officers of sex discrimination and renewed concerns about police brutality. There was also a large number of officers shot in the line of duty, even as the number of deaths declined owing largely to the use of bulletproof vests (which were introduced in the early 1980s and made compulsory in 1991). In 1992 seventeen officers were shot in the line of duty, only one fatally. In response to an increase in suicides among uniformed personnel (thirteen in the period 1991–93) the department expanded its suicide prevention program in 1993 in conjunction with the Patrolmen's Benevolent Association.

A surge in violent crime that began in the 1970s and culminated in increased drug-related shootings in the 1990s earned New

York City a reputation as a dangerous place. Brown and Mayor David N. Dinkins responded by reintroducing foot patrols in many neighborhoods and developing a plan called "Safe Streets, Safe City," which called for the number of police to be raised to 32,000 between 1991 and 1996. The new emphasis on community policing was consistent with a national trend, but it also increased the risk of corruption. In a direct contradiction of the recommendations made by the Knapp Commission, it placed more officers on foot patrol and closer to the people at a time when the drug trade put an unprecedented volume of tainted money on the street. When drug-related corruption in several precincts was uncovered in 1992, Mayor Dinkins appointed an investigatory panel led by Judge Milton Mollen of the New York State Supreme Court. Although the panel did not find the widespread, systemic corruption of the sort unearthed by the Knapp Commission twenty years earlier, it warned that the department had failed to uproot corruption and tolerated a culture that fostered misconduct and concealed lawlessness. The release of these findings in 1993 and the election as mayor in the same year of Rudolph W. Giuliani, a former federal prosecutor who pledged to be tough on crime, signaled that major changes in the department were likely to be made.

Unlike most American cities, New York City has not one police department but three. In 1993 there were 26,926 members in the city's regular force, the New York Police Department (which reports directly to the mayor), in addition to 4214 in the Transit Authority Police Department (a part of the Transit Authority that patrols the subways) and 2027 in the Housing Authority Police Department (a part of the Housing Authority that patrols the city's housing projects). The three departments together made for a force of 4.53 officers per one thousand residents of New York City, a figure higher than that of any American city except Washington. Periodic attempts to merge the three departments in the interest of efficiency and economy all faltered, but a renewed attempt was pledged in the mid 1990s by Mayor Giuliani and his police commissioner, William J. Bratton. Despite efforts to make the force more representative of the city's population, it remains 74 percent white, 11.6 percent black, 13.5 percent Latin American, 0.6 percent Asian, and 0.1 percent American Indian; about 13.9 percent of the force is female. In addition to its professional force the city has the Auxiliary Police, an unarmed, volunteer force of about 4500 civilians, formed in 1951 as a civil defense measure during the Korean War and fully integrated into the command structure of the department in 1971. Members of the Auxiliary Police receive fifty-four hours of training from the department, carry a walkie-talkie and a baton when on duty, and wear uniforms that are indistinguishable from regular uniforms except for the presence of an arm patch and a differently shaped shield; they perform patrol duties and other support functions.

The basic unit of command from which officers are deployed for patrol duty is the precinct. There are seventy-five precincts in New York City, organized within seven borough commands. Both the borough and precinct command structures are under the Patrol Services Bureau, the most important subdivision in the department. Other major units include the Detective Bureau, the Organized Crime Control Bureau, and the Internal Affairs Bureau, which investigates charges of corruption. Other specialized units include the Harbor Patrol, the Bomb Squad, the Aviation Unit, the Mounted Police, a specially equipped Emergency Services Unit, and a Joint Terrorist Task Force, operated in conjunction with the Federal Bureau of Investigation. There are four civil service ranks in the department that are granted on the basis of a written examination: police officer, sergeant, lieutenant, and captain. A member of the force is awarded a gold shield of the detective rank for meritorious service at the discretion of the police commissioner. All promotions to executive ranks above captain are also at the discretion of the commissioner: these ranks include deputy inspector, inspector, deputy chief, assistant chief, and chief.

In 1993 the starting salary at the rank of police officer was $27,772, the average salary $39,495. These amounts were high by national standards, but perhaps no more so than the local cost of living, and they were lower than the salaries paid by suburban departments in the metropolitan area, particularly on Long Island. After being sworn in, police recruits receive twenty-seven weeks of training at the Police Academy in law, police science, and social science. The academy also offers in-service training, courses in human relations, and an executive development program. In the mid 1990s the department was planning to build a new police academy in Melrose, between 153rd and 156th streets east of the Grand Concourse.

James F. Richardson: *The New York Police: Colonial Times to 1901* (New York: Oxford University Press, 1970)
Joseph P. Viteritti: *Police, Politics, and Pluralism in New York City* (New York: Sage Publications, 1973)
Robert M. Fogelson: *Big City Police* (Cambridge: Harvard University Press, 1977)
Wilbur R. Miller: *Cops and Bobbies: Police Authority in New York and London, 1830–1870* (Chicago: University of Chicago Press, 1977)
Thomas A. Reppetto: *The Blue Parade* (New York: Free Press, 1978)
Joseph P. Viteritti: *Police Professionalism in New York City: The Zuccotti Committee in Historical Context* (New York: Center for Research in Crime and Justice, New York University School of Law, 1987)

Joseph P. Viteritti

Police Athletic League [PAL]. A non-profit organization run by volunteer police officers and dedicated to the educational, cultural, and recreational enrichment of disadvantaged children in New York City, formed in 1914 as the Junior Police by Captain John Sweeney of the New York Police Department. It became well known for its programs in athletics, notably boxing, and later added employment training, courses in remedial reading, drug-abuse counseling, creative writing contests, day-care centers, after-school clubs, and educational summer day camps. More than sixty thousand youths a year take part in activities sponsored by the league.

Stephen Weinstein

poliomyelitis. A viral infection that attacks the anterior horn cells of the spinal cord and can cause paralysis, brain damage, and death. Although cases of poliomyelitis were commonly observed and treated by physicians in New York City during the eighteenth and nineteenth centuries, the first recorded epidemic of polio in the city did not occur until 1907. In 1910 the New York City Board of Health classified polio as a communicable disease requiring immediate reporting and isolation of the patient. The city suffered its worst polio epidemic during the summer of 1916. Before its demise in late October the epidemic claimed 8991 victims, with 2449 deaths. About 95 percent of all the polio cases in the city that summer were children under the age of ten. By declaring that the city was in a "state of great and imminent peril" Mayor John Purroy Mitchel justified the closing of theaters and parks, a postponement in the opening of the city's public schools, the forcible removal of victims from their homes by the city's health department, and other harsh measures. Less severe epidemics of poliomyelitis occurred in New York City during the summers of 1931, 1935, and 1936, with sporadic outbreaks during the 1940s and 1950s. Although poliomyelitis was already waning before the advent of the Salk and later the Sabin polio vaccines, their implementation between 1955 and 1965 led to its demise as a major killer of children.

John Duffy: *A History of Public Health in New York City* (New York: Russell Sage Foundation, 1968, 1974)
John R. Paul: *A History of Poliomyelitis* (New Haven: Yale University Press, 1971)
Naomi Rogers: *Dirt and Disease: Polio before FDR* (New Brunswick, N.J.: Rutgers University Press, 1992)

Howard Markel

Polish Institute of Arts and Sciences of America. Research institution formed in 1942 by Polish scholars exiled by the Nazi invasion of their homeland. It had more than thirteen hundred members from throughout the world in the mid 1990s, including the former national security advisor Zbigniew Brzezinski, the poet Czeslaw Milosz, and the ambassador John Gronouski. The institute sponsors an annual scholarly meeting, maintains a library and archives for research on Polish history and culture, publishes books, supports lectures and art exhibitions, and publishes the internationally recognized journal *Polish Review*. Its offices are at 208 East 30th Street in Manhattan.

James S. Pula

Polish Legion. Popular name for the 58th New York Volunteer Infantry, recruited in 1861 from among Polish, German, and other immigrants in New York City and organized by Colonel Wladimir Krzyzanowski. It fought during the Civil War at Cross Keys, Groveton, Second Bull Run, Chancellorsville, Gettysburg, Lookout Mountain, and Wauhatchie.

James S. Pula

Polish National Alliance of Brooklyn. Fraternal organization formed in 1905 to provide immigration services and cultural activities for Poles. From the outset it offered insurance, provided scholarships for college students, and promoted Polish heritage. In the mid 1990s it was the largest Polish fraternal organization in New York City, with members throughout New England and the eastern states. Its headquarters are at 155 Noble Street in Brooklyn.

James S. Pula

political clubs. The first political clubs in New York City were caucuses formed during the American Revolution to support the Livingstons (patriots) and the de Lanceys (Loyalists). After the first formal party system took shape in the early 1790s clubs supported the Democratic Republicans (led by Thomas Jefferson) and the Federalists (led by Alexander Hamilton). The Democratic Republicans dominated the civic activities of New York City, and their influence increased after the War of 1812. Their success was due to the ward system, which enabled a quasi-democratic political system to develop. Political clubs ranged in size from those covering one ward (such as the Young Hickory Association in the eighth ward) to citywide organizations like the Democratic Empire Club; the more powerful ones conducted meetings in their own halls or saloons. By the 1840s even the Catholic Church had its own political club, Carroll Hall, run by Bishop John Hughes. The Empire Club, led by Captain Isaiah Rynders, actively supported the annexation of Texas: it strove to forge its worker membership into a fighting force for the Democratic Party that could be used against the party's political opponents or against Mexico, an opponent of slavery. Its members frequently hooted down speakers and physically attacked rival political processions on horseback. The other political organization that enjoyed both popular support and the approval of the Democratic leadership was Mike Walsh's Spartan Club, which drew its membership from newly arrived, exploited Irish immigrants.

The political club grew in importance in the nineteenth century, reaching a peak when the Democratic Party became institutionalized and the city in the early 1840s underwent unprecedented population growth. In 1849 the refusal of the Spartan Club to support the mayoral candidate of Tammany Hall led to the victory of Fernando Wood, a Whig sponsored by Mozart Hall. A resumption of growth after the Civil War resulted in a more centralized and less democratic politics, in part a reaction to the scandals of the Tweed Ring. Political clubs diminished in importance. Many citizens became involved instead in reform efforts mounted by a large number of good-government associations, voters' leagues, and city clubs. In the late nineteenth century political clubs nevertheless remained active in Brooklyn; in addition to those allied to the Democratic and Republican parties Brooklyn had clubs organized around specific issues such as Prohibition (the Anti-Saloon Republican League, 1888) and women's rights (the Equal Rights Club, 1890). In the first half of the twentieth century some socialist and communist clubs were formed.

After the Second World War the influence of political clubs declined precipitously. Their number fell from 2819 in 1933 to 268 in 1972, with the largest number in Queens. Much of the clubs' residual power, especially within the Democratic Party, accrued because organized crime had filled a patronage vacuum left by the federal government, which saw its role formally eliminated when the Hatch Act (1940) forbade federal employees to contribute money to political organizations. Frank Costello became the covert head of Tammany Hall, and organized-crime figures were dominant in Democratic clubs in Brooklyn and Manhattan.

Roy V. Peel: *The Political Clubs of New York City* (New York: G. P. Putnam's Sons, 1935)
Norman Adler: *Political Clubs in New York City* (New York: Praeger, 1975)
Anthony Gronowicz: "Labor's Decline within New York City's Democratic Party from 1844 to 1884," *Immigration to New York*, ed. William Pencak, Selma Berrol, and Randall M. Miller (London: Associated University Press, 1991)

Anthony Gronowicz

politics. For an outline of the political history of New York City see GOVERNMENT AND POLITICS.

Pollock, (Paul) Jackson (*b* Cody, Wyo., 28 Jan 1912; *d* East Hampton, N.Y., 11 Aug 1956). Painter. After following two of his brothers to New York City in 1930 he studied at the Art Students League with Thomas Hart Benton, whose figurative painting influenced his early style. In 1935 he worked on the Federal Art Project of the Works Progress Administration, and in the following year he joined an experimental workshop run by David Alfaro Siqueiros. Shortly after leaving the Federal Art Project he met his future patron, Peggy Guggenheim, who had recently opened her gallery Art of This Century at 30 West 56th Street. In 1943 the Museum of Modern Art purchased his painting *The She-Wolf*. He married the artist Lee Krasner in 1945, with whom he moved to Springs, Long Island; there he set up a studio in a barn, where he developed a technique of pouring paint directly on the canvas that became typical of his mature works and proved highly influential. He died in an automobile accident. Although controversial during his life, Pollock achieved great recognition after his death as a key figure in the American abstract expressionist movement. His residences in New York City included 46 Carmine Street (1932–33), his brother's apartment at 46 East 8th Street (1935–45), and a carriage house at 9 MacDougal Alley (1949 and 1950).

Francis Valentine O'Connor and Eugene Victor Thaw: *Jackson Pollock: A Catalogue Raisonné of Paintings, Drawings, and Other Works* (New Haven: Yale University Press, 1978)
Ellen G. Landau: *Jackson Pollock* (New York: Harry N. Abrams, 1989)

Mona Hadler

pollution. Environmentally hazardous contamination of the water and air is one of the more serious and complex issues facing New York City, where as in other urban centers its effects on public health, property values, and the quality of life are magnified by the density of population. The purity of drinking water was an early concern. Although clear ponds, streams, and freshwater wells provided an adequate supply for American Indians and Dutch and English colonists, by the mid eighteenth century surface waters and some public and private wells were becoming fouled by seepage from cesspools and street runoff. A shortage of potable water in 1832 contributed to a cholera epidemic that killed 3513 city residents. Most of the populace still depended on well water when voters in New York City approved plans in 1835 to dam the Croton River in Westchester County and construct an aqueduct to transport clean water to the city (completed 1842). During the twentieth century the city markedly expanded its upstate supply of pristine water, building six large reservoirs in the Catskill and Delaware watersheds from 1907 to 1964. Over the following decades these upstate supplies provided the city with water of high quality, which consistently met state and federal standards and was frequently preferred to expensive bottled waters in blind taste surveys. But by the late twentieth century development and sewage discharges, especially in the suburbanized Croton watershed, resulted in some declines in the quality of reservoir water, leading to a commitment by the city to filter Croton water by 1999. To protect the city's water supply at its source, government officials sought from the early 1990s to accelerate a pollution-prevention program in the upstate watershed, elements of which included the purchase of critical buffer lands and the control of sewage discharges.

The rivers and bays of New York City have been polluted for many years, mostly by sewage and to a lesser extent by toxins and garbage. The city's first, primitive sewer was constructed along Broad Street in lower Manhattan in the late seventeenth century, but a comprehensive network of underground sewers was not laid until the mid nineteenth. Although in the following decades rudimentary devices were installed at outflow pipes to filter solid biological wastes, virtually all raw sewage generated by the city was dumped directly into local waterways until the early twentieth century, by which time it had largely destroyed a prosperous shellfish industry and was endangering the health of bathers. In 1935 the city opened its first modern sewage treatment plant on the shores of Coney Island. By the time the North River plant in western Harlem began operating in 1986, fourteen sewage plants were treating nearly all the raw waste generated in New York City during dry weather, or upwards of 1700 million gallons (6435 million liters) a day. In most parts of the city rainwater and sewage are carried in the same underground mains; during wet weather, to prevent plants from being overloaded, several hundred million gallons of effluent are flushed directly into the city's waterways. Although unhealthy bacteria levels still contaminate shellfish beds and limit swimming along sections of the waterfront, pollution related to sewage began a steady decline in the 1970s. Sewage sludge, the end product of sewage treatment, was for many years dumped twelve nautical miles (22.2 kilometers) offshore and later 106 miles (170.6 kilometers) offshore; because of its likely damage to the marine ecosystem ocean dumping of sewage sludge is now prohibited by federal law.

The waters surrounding New York City are also subject to toxic pollution. From the late 1940s to the mid 1970s two manufacturing plants operated by General Electric north of Albany, New York, sent more than 500,000 pounds (227,000 kilograms) of polychlorinated biphenyls (PCBs) directly into the Hudson River. These toxic PCBs were detected in more than twenty species of fish taken from the river, of which more than half a dozen were declared off limits to commercial fishing in New York State. Hundreds of businesses drain chemical wastes into the city's sewers: as many as seven thousand pounds (3178 kilograms) of heavy metals such as zinc, copper, lead, chromium, and nickel were entering the city's sewage plants every day in 1990, and much of this load was discharged into nearby waters. Oil spills in the Arthur Kill along Staten Island and ubiquitous urban runoff such as automotive fluids add to the toxic flow dumped into New York Harbor.

Garbage has been another source of water pollution. In the 1850s the city began loading trash on barges to be jettisoned offshore, a practice that was halted in 1934 by order of the U.S. Supreme Court after garbage repeatedly washed onto the New Jersey coast. For decades the city relied on landfilling as the primary means of trash disposal, ultimately destroying tens of thousands of acres of saltwater wetlands; as a result ecologically sensitive marshes in all five boroughs vanished and pollution seepage ("leachate") from uncontrolled dumps contributed to the contamination of waterways. The number of landfills in the city peaked at eighty-nine in 1934, after which landfills began closing as they reached capacity and their damaging effects were recognized. In 1990 the city generated about 26,000 tons (23,582 metric tons) of municipal solid waste a day; and in 1994 the Fresh Kills landfill in Staten Island, the city's last active land disposal site, was receiving fourteen thousand tons (12,698 metric tons) a day, with most of the rest being shipped to landfills out of state. This unlined facility had been discharging nearly two million gallons (7.5 million liters) a day of leachate into surrounding waters; in 1990 SANITATION officials agreed to stem the flow. In the mid 1990s the landfill was projected to reach capacity early in the twenty-first century, and measures aimed at reducing pollution such as RECYCLING and waste reduction were still gathering momentum, with the official residential recycling rate having reached 15 percent.

The air in New York City after the American Revolution was often foul: pungent odors were emitted by overflowing outhouses, open sewers, manure and refuse in the streets, and fat, bones, and other wastes discarded by butchers, fishmongers, and tradesmen. The unpleasant smells caused by the rending of tallow and other aspects of soap making were one reason why the city in 1796 restricted the manufacture of soap and candles to the residential outskirts. Until the mid nineteenth century garbage was often left for pigs and other scavengers in streets and alleys, dumped in low-lying lands, or discarded at the water's edge. The nation's first refuse incinerator was built on Governors Island in 1885, and the use of incinerators increased after the U.S. Supreme Court banned ocean dumping of garbage. By the early twentieth century the burning of coal to power utility plants and heat residences often filled the city's skies with plumes of dark smoke. A boom in automobile travel after the Second World War compounded the problem. In November 1953 a temperature inversion trapped sulfur dioxides, particulates, and other contaminants over the city, resulting in perhaps two hundred deaths and the hospitalization of many more. During the 1960s more than seventeen thousand incinerators in apartment buildings and eleven municipal garbage-burning plants were adding soot and toxins to the atmosphere. A mayoral task force warned in 1966 that in proportion to its area New York City was pumping more poisons into its air than any other major city in the United States. Important steps to reduce pollution were taken during the next three decades. The City Council lowered the sulfur content allowed in coal and heating oil in 1966 and 1971, yielding significant reductions in sulfur dioxide and soot. Lead in gasoline was reduced by the U.S. Environmental Protection Agency, and as a result airborne lead concentrations in the metropolitan region fell by 95 percent. The City Council prohibited new incinerators in apartment buildings as of 1970; those that remained were phased out by 1993. In 1988 and 1995 the council restricted tobacco smoking, a leading source of indoor pollution, in nearly all enclosed public spaces in the city. By the mid 1990s federally required pollution controls on automobiles and annual automobile inspections had helped to lower official carbon monoxide readings from the harmful levels of the preceding decades. But although the air quality in the city had markedly improved, it continued to violate national health standatds for particulates and ozone smog. Among the major contributors to the problem were diesel-powered buses and trucks, and a steady growth in regional motor vehicle travel.

Noise pollution became a problem in New York City with the introduction of elevated railways in the 1870s and worsened with increased traffic, construction, and population density, especially after the Second World War. Some improvements resulted when the city adopted one of the nation's first noise control codes in 1972, and in the mid 1990s the city was issuing nearly a thousand summonses a year for noise code violations. But excessive noise from roaring subways, honking horns, piercing sirens, and takeoffs from Kennedy and La Guardia airports remains an annoyance in many neighborhoods and sometimes interferes with hearing and sleep.

After the environmental movement took hold in the 1960s tens of thousands of residents of New York City joined environmental groups; Mayor John V. Lindsay in 1968 formed what later became the Department of Environmental Protection. During the 1970s and 1980s the city's most prominent environmental controversies focused on potential new sources of pollution, including the Westway highway project along the Hudson (eventually abandoned) and a proposed garbage incinerator at the Brooklyn Navy Yard. At the same time there was a growing recognition that some of the more troubling environmental problems (such as lead in paint) were having a disproportionate impact on the poor and minorities. By the mid 1990s the city's immediate pollution dangers were less acute than those in most cities of comparable size, but long-term assaults on its water and air continued.

Freedom To Breathe: Report of the Mayor's Task Force on Air Pollution in the City of New York (New York: City of New York, 1966)

John Duffy: *A History of Public Health in New York City* (New York: Russell Sage Foundation, 1968, 1974)

Charles H. Weidner: *Water for a City: A History of New York City's Problem from the Beginning to the Delaware River System* (New Brunswick, N.J.: Rutgers University Press, 1974)

Eric A. Goldstein and Mark A. Izeman: *The New York Environment Book* (Washington: Island, 1990)

Eric A. Goldstein, Mark A. Izeman

Polo Grounds. The name of several sporting facilities in New York City. The first opened in 1876 between 110th and 112th streets between 5th and 6th avenues in Manhattan for polo and became the home of the baseball Giants and Metropolitans in 1883, but was abandoned when streets were cut through in 1889. The name was revived in 1891 when the Giants took over Brotherhood Park overlooking the Harlem River at 157th Street, then a year old. This structure was destroyed by fire on 13 April 1911 and replaced on 28 June by a structure of concrete and steel seating 38,000 (eventually 55,987) and notable for its unusual dimensions (279 feet, or eighty-five meters, to left field; 483 feet, or 147.2 meters, to center field; 258 feet, or 78.6 meters, to right field). This facility was the home of the baseball Giants (to 1957), the football Giants (1925–55), and the New York Mets (1962–63) before being demolished in 1964 to make way for apartment buildings.

For further illustration see BASEBALL.

Steven A. Riess

Polytechnic Preparatory Country Day School. Private, coeducational secondary school opened in 1854 on twenty-five acres (ten hectares) in Bay Ridge. It was one of the first private schools in the United States to adopt the model of the country day school: a full day's program of academics, arts, athletics, and college preparation, and shared responsibility with the family in providing guidance to students.

Richard Schwartz

Polytechnic University. Private educational institution opened in 1854 as the Brooklyn Collegiate and Polytechnic Institute, a college preparatory school for boys at the edge of Brooklyn Heights. The school was led in its first decade by John H. Raymond, later the first president of Vassar College; it gradually focused on scientific and technical education under its second president, David H. Cochran, and as the industrial economy of Brooklyn expanded in the 1880s it implemented a four-year scientific curriculum emphasizing engineering. In 1890 the name was changed by state charter to the Polytechnic Institute of Brooklyn. Graduates of the school readily found employment in the developing industry and governmental services of the growing metropolitan area, especially after Brooklyn became a part of New York City in 1898. At the same time inadequate physical resources kept the school crowded into downtown Brooklyn. In the early decades of the twentieth century the school had a distinguished scientific and technical faculty that included an extraordinary group of Viennese refugees from fascism, under whose leadership the PhD was first offered in several fields in the 1930s and important research was carried on in the 1940s. Advances were made in the field of polymers by the chemist Herman F. Mark. Developments in microwave research by the electrical engineer Ernst Weber were crucial to the development of American radar during the Second World War. The school's achievements in these years helped its reputation extend as far as India, Taiwan, and Iran.

Women were admitted as students in the 1940s. During the administration of its fifth president, Harry Rodgers, the school acquired nearby facilities that had been vacated in the late 1950s by the American Safety Razor Company. Baccalaureate degrees in the humanities and social sciences were added in the late 1960s. Severe financial problems in the following years limited the school's ability to attract students and retain faculty, even after a merger in 1973 with the engineering school of New York University strengthened the faculty and increased the amount of state aid. Under the presidency of George Bugliarello (1973–) a wrenching confrontation between the trustees and the administration on the one hand and the faculty on the other brought about the dissolution of the faculty's collective bargaining unit, an affiliate of the American Association of University Professors. During Bugliarello's tenure the school took its current name. In addition to engineers the faculty of Polytechnic University has included the poet Louis Zukofsky, the anthropologist Eleanor Burke Leacock, the economist Murray Rothbard, and the historian Eugene Genovese.

John J. O'Connor: *Polytechnic Institute of Brooklyn: An Account of the Educational Purposes and Development of the Institute during Its First Century* (New York: Polytechnic Institute, 1955)

Marvin E. Gettleman

The Harlem River Speedway (center) *and the Polo Grounds* (right), *1914*

Pomander Walk. Private row of sixteen two-story cottages in a Tudor style from 94th to 95th streets between Broadway and West End Avenue, built by the developer Thomas Healy. The land was acquired on a ninety-nine-year lease by Healy, who engaged the firm of King and Campbell to design a development based on the quaint English village depicted in Louis N. Parker's popular play *Pomander Walk* (opened in New York City in 1911). Along Broadway Healy built one of the first indoor skating rinks in Manhattan and the restaurant Sunken Gardens. Pomander Walk stands out from its surroundings for its style and ambience: it is ornamented with colorful trim (including shutters of aqua, blue, red, and green), old-fashioned lampposts, a small wooden sentry box, and hedges and flower boxes lining the walk. Its residents

Pomander Walk, early 1990s

have included such actors as Dorothy Gish, Lillian Gish, Mary Martin, Humphrey Bogart, and Rosalind Russell.

See also Taxpayers.

Amanda Aaron

Pomonok. Neighborhood in central Queens; it is part of Flushing and is served by Jewel Avenue, Parsons Boulevard, Kissena Boulevard, and Main Street. The name derives from an Indian word applied to an area of eastern Long Island and probably means "land of tribute" or "land where there is traveling by water." In early deeds it is spelled Pommanocc (1639), Paumanacke (1659), and Pommanock (1665). By 1919 there was a country club with a golf course named Pomonok by the members, who in 1949 voted to sell the land. The two major buyers were the Electrical Workers Union, which built on it a cooperative apartment development, and the City of New York, which built a low- and middle-income housing project. The neighborhood is the site of several educational facilities, including Queens College of the City University of New York.

Patricia A. Doyal

Pondiac Democratic Club. Political club formed in the Bronx in 1921 by Albert Cohn at the behest of Edward J. Flynn, the Democratic leader of Bronx County (1922–53). It was intended to erode the political base of the rival Democratic district leader Patrick Kane, who unsuccessfully challenged Flynn for the office of sheriff of the Bronx in 1921. The club met on the second floor of 809 Westchester Avenue and was originally called the Pontiac Club after an American Indian chief of the Ottawa tribe (the name was misspelled when the club was registered). At first the two hundred dues-paying members of the club were predominantly Jewish and Irish. The club gained influence because of its ability to guarantee an extraordinarily high turnout among voters and was the first Democratic club to draw members from the growing Latin American community in the Bronx. In 1953 its member Felipe Torres became the first Latin American elected to the state assembly, and in 1967 its leader Eugene Rodriquez, also an assemblyman, became the first one elected to the state senate. Rodriquez's conviction of attempted extortion in 1967 led to the collapse of the club, and it disbanded when his rival Louis Gigante was elected a Democratic district leader in 1972 with the backing of a neighboring club. Other members of the Pondiac Club included James J. Lyons, Stanley Friedman, Clara Gompers, Ed Gilhooley, Robert Garcia, Salvador Almeida, and David Ross.

Jill Jonnes: *We're Still Here: The Rise, Fall, and Resurrection of the South Bronx* (New York: Atlantic Monthly Press, 1986)

Neal C. Garelik

Poole, Butcher Bill [William] (*b* ?1829; *d* New York City, 8 March 1855). Nativist. A butcher, a notoriously ferocious street fighter, and a gang leader, he was involved in gambling and liquor sales but was best known for his association with various anti-immigrant groups, including the Bowery Boys. He was also a "shoulder hitter" (strong-arm man) for nativist political causes. His dispute with the Irish-born heavyweight boxer John Morrissey led to his fatal shooting by Lewis Baker, a Welshman; his last words were reportedly "Good-bye boys, I die a true American." Nativist newspapers exploited the incident by glorifying Poole and portraying him as the innocent victim of an Irish conspiracy. As many as 250,000 persons attended his funeral, and the trial that followed his death led to increased tension between Irish immigrants and native-born Americans.

Elliott J. Gorn: "'Good-bye Boys, I Die a True American': Homicide, Nativism, and Working-class Culture in Antebellum New York City," *Journal of American History* 74 (1987), 388–410

Elliott J. Gorn

poorhouses. See Almshouses.

Pope, Generoso (*b* near Naples, 1 April 1891; *d* New York City, 28 April 1950). Businessman and community leader. He moved to New York City in 1906 and first worked as a waterboy for the Colonial Sand and Gravel Company, a tunnel excavation company that he owned by 1920; he had enterprises in real estate, banking, and communications. He bought the leading Italian–American daily newspaper, *Il Progresso Italo-Americano*, in 1928 and weekly newspaper, *Il Corriere d'America*, in 1929. A supporter of Mussolini, he received medals from the Italian fascists in 1926, 1928, and 1930, and in 1931 leftists tried to assassinate him with a letter bomb. In 1936 he voiced his support for neutrality, thus aiding the fascists in the Italo-Ethiopian War. He was a powerful figure in Tammany Hall politics, and his friendship with Mayor James J. Walker prompted his investigation by the Seabury Commission (he was eventually cleared). Initially opposed to Fiorello H. La Guardia's mayoral candidacy, he later supported it; in later years he returned to endorsing Democratic candidates. He repudiated fascism in an editorial in *Il Progresso* in 1941. During the late 1940s he organized Italian relief efforts and established a college scholarship fund for graduates of the city's Catholic schools. In 1949 he bought the radio station WINS. Pope left the bulk of his estate to charity.

Philip V. Cannistraro: "Generoso Pope and the Rise of Italian–American Politics, 1925–1936," *Italian Americans: New Perspectives in Italian Immigration and Ethnicity*, ed. Lydio F. Tomasi (New York: Center for Migration Studies, 1985), 264–88

Mary Elizabeth Brown

Poppenhusen, Conrad (*b* Hamburg, 1 April 1818; *d* College Point [now in Queens], 12 Dec 1883). Businessman. The son of a prosperous textile trader, he moved to New York City in 1843 to run the offices of the whalebone merchant H. C. Meyer and in 1844 became a partner in the firm of Meyer and Poppenhusen. At its plant in Brooklyn the firm processed whalebone into buttons, corset stays, combs, spoons, medical products, and various other articles, and in 1852 it secured a license for the manufacture and sale of hard rubber (developed by Charles Goodyear). With the assistance of a new partner, Frederick Koenig, the plant was converted to the manufacture of hard-rubber household goods, but it soon proved too small for the rapidly expanding business and in 1854 the firm was reestablished in Queens as the India

Rubber Comb Company, later the Enterprise Works. The new location easily accommodated the factory workers, and in the following years Poppenhusen built streets, houses, businesses, and schools (including the Poppenhusen Institute, 1868, which remained open into the 1990s). In 1870 the community became the village of College Point, incorporating the neighborhoods of Flammersburg and Strattonport. Poppenhusen built the Flushing and North Side Railroad and entrusted it to his sons, but their inexperience in management and fierce competition led to ruin. Although he tried to remedy the damage, in 1877 he was forced to declare bankruptcy; in his final years he made a limited financial recovery.

U.S. Circuit Court, Trial of the Case of Conrad Poppenhusen vs. N.Y. Gutta Percha Comb Co. (New York: India Rubber Comb Company, 1858)

Vincent Seyfried

popular entertainment. Parades, festivals, and informal recreations in streets and taverns were some of the popular entertainments available in New York City during the colonial period. Most participants were men. The growth of the city in the first half of the nineteenth century encouraged some entrepreneurs to open theaters, and soon melodramatic plays and minstrel shows were introduced. Both genres relied on a range of ethnic, racial, and regional stereotypes (the worst of which were reserved for blacks), and by the early 1830s they were well established. To accommodate the wide audience that the performances attracted, theaters were divided into an upper tier, or gallery, for rowdies and prostitutes and a mezzanine for families. By the middle of the century there were many theaters and different kinds of entertainment for each social class: the Bowery became the entertainment district for immigrants and the working class, Broadway that for the middle and upper classes. In the 1880s entrepreneurs hoping to appeal to all segments of the population developed vaudeville theater, in which old-fashioned variety shows were presented in new settings; there was enough propriety and enough raciness to suit most tastes and offend few, and drunkenness was not tolerated. Manhattan soon became a national center for vaudeville, which along with amusement parks, cafés, dance halls, and nickelodeons helped to subvert Victorian ideas of propriety and sexuality by permitting working women to mingle unsupervised with men. After the introduction of sound motion pictures in the late 1920s vaudeville theater declined and could not survive the Depression, and by the 1930s motion pictures became the most popular form of entertainment. Virtually every commercial district had its own movie house, usually a renovated vaudeville theater or an enormous new motion picture "palace" with extravagant décor. Many New Yorkers went to the movies weekly. After the Second World War popular culture in the city changed immensely. Racial and ethnic minorities demanded an end to offensive stereotypes in theatrical productions and broadcasts. After television was introduced popular forms of entertainment were usually broadcast rather than performed in public for audiences. Fear of crime and racial conflict also decreased the public nature of popular entertainment.

Despite these changes, New York City in the mid 1990s remained a center for live entertainment. The popularity of nightclubs grew (one well-known club called the Rainbow Room was refurbished), and bars offered televised sports, billiards, and other diversions. Rap music was developed on the streets and spread worldwide. Movie theaters showed first-run films from Hollywood and classic and foreign films, and public celebrations for the Fourth of July and other occasions were well attended.

Paul Buhle, ed.: *Popular Culture in America* (Minneapolis: University of Minnesota Press, 1987)

Robert W. Snyder

popular fiction. In the mid nineteenth century New York City emerged as the center of American popular fiction. About half the popular books written on urban subjects in 1820–70 were set in New York City, which was presented with all its promises and threats as the archetypal American city. Fiction was commonly published by some magazines and newspapers, including *Brother Jonathan* (1839), the *New York Ledger* (1855), and the *New York Weekly* (1859). In a period of widespread moral evangelism the city was seen by some as harboring all the temptations of sin: greed on Wall Street, licentiousness on the Bowery, and artifice on Broadway. The city was the ultimate proving ground for personal character—a challenge to the innocent and a lure to the weak. Many early authors of popular fiction contrasted images of the smoke-shrouded city with sentimental notions of the idyllic countryside, and used this contrast to promote the supposed rural virtues of simplicity, chastity, honesty, industry, and frugality. Frequently a country-born protagonist approached the city with a mixture of awe and dread: in Cornelius Mathews's *Moneypenny* (1849) the title character regarded it "with fear and trembling, as though it were some beast of prey crouching on the river-bank in the dark." Another common device was to relate a tale of heroism from the perspective of an innocent, virtuous child, as in *The Newsboy* (1854) and other works by Elizabeth Oakes Smith, or of a sober, religious wife, as in the works of Ann Sophia Stephens and Maria Susanna Cummins, in which the heroine provides shelter from the immorality of the streets. A harsher genre of popular fiction known as "rogue fiction" featured the outlaw or cowboy as its protagonist.

In the mid nineteenth century the details of vice, poverty, and squalor were accentuated. Across the United States readers of popular fiction became familiar with such stock details of the city as the Five Points, the Tombs, gambling houses, concert saloons, dance halls, oyster cellars, prostitutes, newsboys, and firemen, and the prevalent style in popular fiction shifted from sentimentalism to realism. The standards of the period were set in such bestsellers as *Letters from New-York* (1843) by Lydia Maria Child and *The Mysteries and Miseries of New York* (1848) by Ned Buntline (a pseudonym of Edward Zane Carroll Judson), which combined elements of fiction, journalism, realism, and sensationalism. The author of journalistic exposés George G. Foster employed a symbolism of sunlight and shadows to denounce the filth and misery of the city in the novel *Celio; or, New York Above-ground and Under-ground* (1850), and the city was portrayed as "part Paradise, part Pandemonium" in works such as John D. Vose's *Seven Nights in Gotham* (1852), a luridly detailed chronicle of the nightlife and sexual adventures of the wealthy and sophisticated. The less decadent lives of the working class were explored in novels that romanticized the hardy workman and his virtuous wife. Although many writers deplored the exploitation of the working class and sympathized with the downtrodden, they did not champion radical social reform. Working-class readers were assured that they would eventually be rewarded and that the idle rich would be punished. In works like *Celio* and George Lippard's *New York: Its Upper Ten and Lower Million* (1853) the salvation of the working-class hero comes from above, perhaps in the form of an inherited fortune, rather than from such active remedies as politics, strikes, riots, or crime.

One of the most sensational portrayals of the suffering of the poor in the shadow of splendor was Solon Robinson's *Hot Corn: Life Scenes in New York Illustrated* (1854), which sold fifty thousand copies in six months. William Wirt Howe wrote in his popular novel *The Pasha Papers* (1859) that the city had "more trade, more wealth, more houses, more dirt, more misery, more political corruption than any other great city in the country," that it was "a place of very great importance — particularly self-importance." By 1865 the publishing house of Beadle and Adams had produced four million copies of "dime novels." Writers of popular fiction in the 1860s and 1870s began to share the concerns of civic reformers, and denounced incompetent civil servants, corrupt policemen, and self-serving politicians. Howe's *The Pasha Papers* and Henry L. Williams's *Gay Life in New York; or, Fast Men and War Widows* (1866) blasted Tammany Hall and wistfully recalled a supposed golden era of enlightened rule. In the last third of the century popular fiction contributed to the emerging image of the city as a place of civilization and progress. The urban mysteries that had entranced and bewildered earlier generations of readers were now explained in fictional works that doubled as success manuals. Foremost among these were the novels of Horatio Alger, which were so popular that after his death his name was attached to the works of other writers. In *Ragged Dick; or, Street Life in New York* (1867) and about 120 subsequent novels, Alger provided a mostly rural audience with detailed descriptions of the city and practical information on employment, transportation, and lodging. He reassured his readers that anyone could get along in the city with enough "street smarts," charm, aggressiveness, and good fortune.

After the Civil War improvements in law enforcement led to a more favorable view of policemen and detectives, who were no longer seen as unsavory types consorting with criminals and meddled in marital affairs and labor disputes. The detective story, a genre developed earlier in the century by Edgar Allan Poe, became an important form of popular fiction in the late 1880s. Individual wit and will triumphed in a dangerous and deceitful world in such stories as *Lady Kate, the Dashing Female Detective* (1886), in which a female protagonist in New York City alternates between explicitly male and female roles and flirts with the objects of her professional and romantic attention. The celebrated head of the detective bureau of the city police, Thomas Byrnes (1880–92), was instrumental to boosting the reputation of real and fictional detectives through his collaboration with Julian Hawthorne (son of Nathaniel Hawthorne) on five novels loosely based on his own casework and published in 1887–88. Over time the detective genre evolved to reflect changing attitudes toward law and order in the big city, and detectives were variously incarnated in such stock roles as those of spy, scientist, vigilante, and police officer, all adept at disguising themselves and infiltrating milieus ranging from fashionable society to the underworld. In *Black Tom, The Negro Detective; or, Solving a Thompson Street Mystery* (1893) the hero is "a mysterious individual who came and went into and out of the negro quarters of the city" and unravels the mystery of a white woman found dead in the black part of town, only to be revealed himself as a white detective in disguise.

Government regulation and a changed marketplace brought a rapid end to the dime novel in the 1890s and led to the development of the pulp magazine. One of few fictional detectives to enjoy popularity in both the old and new types of publication was Nick Carter, a hardy, all-American Protestant youth from New York City who appeared in more than a thousand stories from the 1890s to the 1920s. The character was created in "The Old Detective's Pupil; or, The Mysterious Crime of Madison Square," published in the *New York Weekly* in September 1886, and remained a constant for seventeen years under the byline of Frederick Marmaduke Van Rensselaer Dey. Carter was pictured in various disguises, including those of a farmer, an Irish political boss, a Chinese boy, and a woman. In a time of imperialism, nativism, and moralism, he embodied traditional middle-class values, eschewing all vice including alcohol, tobacco, and profanity: Dey boasted that he "never wrote a Nick Carter story that he wouldn't read to a Bible class." After the turn of the century the widely held opinion that science was a remedy for urban ills helped to transform the detective from a disguise artist into a scientist. Arthur B. Reeve began a successful series of novels with *The Silent Bullet* (1912), about a professor of "criminal science" at Columbia University who solves crimes with such advanced techniques as "soul analysis." The detective as a force for Progressivism was exemplified by Average Jones, created by the prominent muckraking journalist Samuel Hopkins Adams. After inheriting a fortune on condition that he live in New York City for ten years, Jones became an "Ad-Visor," using his powers of detection to ferret out fraud in newspaper advertising; much as earlier detectives had protected New Yorkers from the hidden menaces of the industrial metropolis, Jones protected them from quack doctors, greedy trusts, and corrupt politicians.

As the city grew more complex the craft of the fictional detective grew more esoteric: having at first consisted of knowledge of the street and disguises and then of scientific techniques, it now further evolved into an ability to solve crimes through pure analytical reasoning. The detective as a gentleman of leisure who lent his intellectual powers to solving bizarre and sophisticated crimes was exemplified in Willard Huntington Wright's *The Benson Murder Case* (1926), the first novel featuring his highly popular detective Philo Vance, the scion of an aristocratic family in New York City who recalled such characters from British detective fiction as Hercule Poirot and Lord Peter Wimsey. Vance solved crimes nonchalantly with the aid of psychology, criminal anthropology, and a sound knowledge of art; his popularity continued through several sequels until Wright's death in 1933. Frederic Dannay and Manfred B. Lee wrote a long series of novels beginning with *The Roman Hat Mystery* (1929) in which both the pseudonymous author and the detective were Ellery Queen, who lived with his father on West 87th Street and regarded the city with scientific detachment through rimless pince-nez. Rex Stout introduced Nero Wolfe in *Fer-de-lance* (1934), and by 1975 there were more than sixty sequels. Unsoiled by the street life of the city, Wolfe was an obese, cerebral detective who remained ensconced in his apartment on West 35th Street while his energetic assistant Archie Goodwin did the legwork. In an increasingly confounding and hazardous world of crime, Wolfe's renowned brownstone was a fortress from which reason continued to rule. The detective became an antihero in the work of Dashiell Hammett, who made New York City the setting for parts of *The Glass Key* (1931) and for his last novel, *The Thin Man* (1934), which inspired a series of motion pictures. Its central character is a retired detective named Nick Charles, who while on vacation amid the decadent leisure class of New York City is thrust into the investigation of a murder. Clearly more enthusiastic about drinking and cavorting than about pursuing the case, Charles nevertheless solves it while doing hardly any investigative work of his own. Several other fictional detectives became popular in the 1930s and 1940s: Hildegarde Withers, a spinster schoolteacher and police buff introduced in Stuart Palmer's *The Penguin Pool Murder* (1931) who later appeared in a series of books and films; Bill Crane, a private detective created by John Latimer in *Murder in the Madhouse* (1935); and Scott Jordan, a lawyer and classical music aficionado in New York City created by Harold Q. Masur in *Bury Me Deep* (1947).

At the same time as Vance and Wolfe relied on their deductive powers, the brawling, "hard-boiled" private investigator of pulp fiction pulled the genre of detective fiction in the opposite direction. The most extreme example of the detective as a vengeful urban vigilante is Mike Hammer in more than twenty novels by Mickey Spillane beginning with *I, the Jury* (1947); the character helped to make Spillane the best-selling mystery writer in the world. The ingredients of these stories are deserted, rainy streets, a few luxury penthouses, and an endless maze of tenements, bars, and alleyways, as well as a distrust of lawful authority and a rejection of liberal idealism. In *My Gun Is Quick* (1950) Spillane wrote: "There isn't a Coliseum any more, but the city is a bigger bowl, and it seats more people . . . The razor-sharp claws aren't those of wild animals but man's can be just as sharp and twice as vicious." The leading postwar writer of the "police story" was Ed McBain (pseudonym of Evan Hunter), who in *Cop Hater* (1956) and later novels drew a similarly bleak portrait of the city. The citizens of "Isola," McBain's version of New York City, are vulnerable "cave-dwellers" who cower in their apartments while the city crumbles around them. Unlike Spillane, whose despair over the individual's loss of power led him to create an armed and dangerous outlaw in Hammer, McBain abandoned individual heroics altogether in favor of the collective authority of the police. His fictional 87th Precinct replaced the lone detective, and teamwork and the power of law replaced individual will.

In the 1950s the detective story began to depict Harlem. Chester Himes created the police detectives Grave Digger Jones and Coffin Ed Johnson and broached the subject of racism. In *Blind Man with a Pistol* (1969) and *The Real Cool Killers* (1985) the possibilities for heroism are tightly circumscribed by the drugs, prostitution, filth, and despondence of Harlem, but Jones and Johnson are nevertheless able to fight crime by relying on the law and their partnership. Ernest Tidyman introduced the first fictional black private detective in *Shaft* (1971), the original cover of which announced: "Shaft has no prejudices . . . He'll kill anyone — black or white." Against a backdrop of racial unrest, Shaft and a team of black revolutionaries confront a band of kidnappers seeking to take over the heroin trade in Harlem. Like many other detective stories *Shaft* is infused with sardonic humor: at one point the main character ignites a riot by running through the streets crying "The niggers are coming!" Other detectives specialized in the sort of crime found only in the international capital of finance: under the pseudonym Emma Lathen, Mary J. Latis and Martha Hennisart wrote a series of books including *Banking in Death* (1961) in which the expertise of John Putnam Thatcher, an executive at a bank on Wall Street, allows him to uncover elaborate financial chicanery. Arthur Maling wrote several novels, including *Ripoff* (1976), in which the hero is Brock Potter, a partner in the fictional brokerage house of Price, Potter, and Petacque.

Adrienne Siegel: *The Image of the American City in Popular Literature, 1820–1870* (Port Washington, N.Y.: Kennikat, 1981)

T. J. Binyon: *"Murder Will Out": The Detective in Fiction* (Oxford: Oxford University Press, 1989)

Jeff Sklansky

Popular Library. Firm of book publishers, formed in 1942 by Ned Price and specializing in paperbound editions. In the mid 1950s it created a stir in the book trade by purporting to have the "fastest selling pocket-size book line in the nation." Although the firm did sell as many as 85 million books a year by publishing the work of such varied authors as Fulton Sheen and Polly Adler, it was never as successful as it claimed. It became a profitable imprint of Fawcett and the Columbia Broadcasting System (CBS) before being acquired by Warner Books.

James E. Mooney

population. According to the first known colonial census, the land making up what is now New York City probably had about ten thousand inhabitants in 1698, including 4937 in New York County (Manhattan, settled mostly at the southern tip), 2017 in Kings County (Brooklyn), 727 in Richmond County (Staten Island), and a few others in Queens County (which extended into what is now Nassau County) and the part of southern Westchester County that later became the Bronx. Within the present boundaries of the

Population of New York City by Race and Nativity, 1900–1960 (in Thousands)

	Puerto Rican		Non–Puerto Rican			
	Birth	Parentage	White	Black	Other	Total
1900	—	—	3,369	61	7	3,437
1910	1	—	4,668	92	6	4,767
1920	7	N/A	5,453	152	8	5,620
1930	49*	N/A	6,540	328	13	6,930
1940	61	N/A	6,925	450	19	7,455
1950	187	58	6,891	728	28	7,892
1960	430	183	6,052	1,060	57	7,782

Dash denotes zero; asterisk denotes estimate.
N/A = Not Available
Sources: Nathan Kantrowitz: "New York City Migration, 1900–1960," *Social Statistics for Metropolitan New York*, no. 3 (1969)
Ira Rosenwaike: *Population History of New York City* (Syracuse, N.Y.: Syracuse University Press, 1972)
U.S. Bureau of Labor Statistics, New York Region, *A Half Century of Change* (1992)

Compiled by Nathan Kantrowitz

Average Number of Persons per Household in New York City, 1940–1990

	Number of Households (in Thousands)	Population in Households (in Thousands)	Persons per Household (Calculated from Unrounded Numbers)
1940	2,050	7,217	3.52
1950	2,360	7,554	3.20
1960	2,654	7,632	2.88
1970	2,837	7,770	2.74
1980	2,789	6,948	2.49
1990	2,819	7,155	2.54

Note: Before 1940 consistent definitions are lacking for persons in households and families. The number of persons per household has been estimated at 4.5 in 1900 and 4.0 in 1930. Approximations for the non-slave populations in earlier years are 5.1 in 1790 and 4.5 in 1703. See U.S. Bureau of the Census, Census of Population 1900, 1930; U.S. Bureau of the Census, *A Century of Population Growth* (1909); and Robert Wells: *Population of the British Colonies in America before 1776* (Princeton, N.J.: Princeton University Press, 1975).
Sources: U.S. Bureau of the Census, Census of Population 1940, 1950, 1960, 1970, 1980, 1990

Compiled by Nathan Kantrowitz

Women as a Percentage of the Population of New York City by Age, Race, and Hispanic Origin, 1990

			Non-Hispanic		Other
	All Races	Hispanic	White	Black	
All Ages	53.1	52.3	52.8	55.2	49.3
0–4	49.0	49.2	48.5	49.5	47.9
5–9	49.0	49.1	48.5	49.5	48.1
10–14	49.4	49.2	48.7	50.4	48.7
15–19	49.6	48.8	49.3	50.9	49.2
20–24	51.4	49.9	51.0	53.8	50.2
25–29	51.3	51.0	49.8	54.8	49.2
30–34	51.4	52.5	49.0	55.9	48.0
35–39	51.9	53.5	49.2	56.6	47.5
40–44	53.1	54.4	50.7	57.5	49.6
45–49	53.9	54.6	51.9	58.0	48.8
50–54	54.1	55.1	52.1	58.2	48.6
55–59	54.7	56.3	52.8	58.8	50.5
60–64	56.2	58.1	54.4	60.4	53.3
65–69	58.3	60.9	57.0	61.9	52.6
70–74	61.0	63.6	59.8	65.0	54.4
75+	66.7	67.0	66.3	70.2	57.8

Source: U.S. Bureau of the Census, Census of Population 1990, Modified Age, Race, Sex (MARS) file

Population of New York City by Race and Hispanic Origin, 1970–1990 (in Thousands)

	Hispanic			Non-Hispanic			
	Puerto Rican	Other	Total	White	Black	Other	Total
1970*	847	432	1,279	4,973	1,526	118	7,895
1980	853	554	1,406	3,703	1,695	268	7,072
1990	897	887	1,784	3,163	1,847	529	7,323

Asterisk denotes estimate.
Figures may not add because of rounding.
Sources: U.S. Bureau of the Census, Census of Population 1970, 1980, 1990
Ira Rosenwaike: *Population History of New York City* (Syracuse, N.Y.: Syracuse University Press, 1972)

Compiled by Nathan Kantrowitz

Children under 18 in New York City, by Type of Family, 1970–1990

	Number of Children (in Thousands)	Percent Living with Married Couple	Percent Living with Single Parent	Percent Living with Other Relative	Other
1970	2,235	72.6	21.1	4.8	1.2
1980	1,765	58.0	33.4	7.1	1.3
1990	1,687	52.2	32.6	12.4	2.5

Note: Of 2,167,000 children under 18 in 1960, an estimated 83.4 percent were living with a married couple and 9.1 percent with a single parent.
Percentages may not add to 100 because of rounding and because of exclusion of children under 18 who were themselves already married.
Sources: U.S. Bureau of the Census, Census of Population 1960, 1970, 1980, 1990

Compiled by Nathan Kantrowitz

Median Family Income in New York City and the United States, 1949–1989

	In Current Dollars		In Constant 1989 Dollars		New York City Income as a Percentage of
	New York City	U.S.	New York City	U.S.	U.S. Income
1949	$3,526	$3,091	$18,371	$16,104	114.1
1959	6,091	5,660	25,955	24,118	107.6
1969	9,682	9,590	32,713	32,402	101.0
1979	16,818	19,917	28,725	34,018	84.4
1989	34,360	35,225	34,360	35,225	97.5

Sources: U.S. Bureau of Labor Statistics, Consumer Price Index, All Urban Consumers, U.S. City Average, All Items, 1982–84 = 100
U.S. Bureau of the Census, Census of Population 1950, 1960, 1970, 1980, 1990

Population of New York City by Borough, 1900–1990

	Manhattan	Bronx	Brooklyn	Queens	Staten Island	Total
1900	1,850,093	200,507	1,166,582	152,999	67,021	3,437,202
1910	2,331,542	430,980	1,634,351	284,041	85,969	4,766,883
1920	2,284,103	732,016	2,018,356	469,042	116,531	5,620,048
1930	1,867,312	1,265,258	2,560,401	1,079,129	158,346	6,930,446
1940	1,889,924	1,394,711	2,698,285	1,297,634	174,441	7,454,995
1950	1,960,101	1,451,277	2,738,175	1,550,849	191,555	7,891,957
1960	1,698,281	1,424,815	2,627,319	1,809,578	221,991	7,781,984
1970	1,539,233	1,471,701	2,602,012	1,986,473	295,443	7,894,862
1980	1,428,285	1,168,972	2,230,936	1,891,325	352,121	7,071,639
1990	1,487,536	1,203,789	2,300,664	1,951,598	378,977	7,322,564

Sources: U.S. Bureau of the Census, Census of Population 1960 (vol. 1, part A, table 28), 1970, 1980, 1990

Percentage of Foreign-Born in New York City, 1890–1990

1890*	36.0
1900*	37.0
1910	40.8
1920	36.1
1930	34.3
1940	28.7
1950	23.6
1960	20.0
1970	18.2
1980	23.6
1990	28.4

Asterisk denotes estimate.
Sources: U.S. Bureau of the Census, Census of Population 1910, 1920, 1930, 1940, 1950, 1960, 1970, 1980, 1990
Walter Laidlaw: *Population of the City of New York, 1890–1930* (New York: Cities Census Committee, 1932)
Ira Rosenwaike: *Population History of New York City* (Syracuse, N.Y.: Syracuse University Press, 1971)

city in 1698 black slaves were about 12 percent of the population overall, perhaps more in view of a probable undercount; there were seven hundred black residents in New York County, 296 in Kings County, 199 in Queens County, 146 in Westchester County, and seventy-three in Richmond County. In colonial times free blacks were rarely recorded, and Indians usually not at all (although 715 were enumerated in the census of 1731 in Suffolk County). By 1771 blacks made up nearly a fifth of the total population, which probably stood at more than thirty thousand. The census of 1786 indicated a stable population throughout the American Revolution and also enumerated four Indians "who pay taxes."

More detailed information was collected in 1790 for the first federal decennial census. This showed the city itself with a population of 32,328 (in addition to about nineteen thousand in the outlying settlements and farms in areas that later became part of the city), or 0.8 percent of the new nation's population; the next-largest cities were Philadelphia (28,522), Boston (18,320), Baltimore (13,503), and Providence, Rhode Island (6380). Blacks accounted for about 14 percent of the population, and for the first time a distinction was made between free blacks ("all other free persons," who were neither white nor slave) and slaves. Blacks, whether free or slave, made up 32.9 percent of the population of Kings County, about 25 percent of what is now the Bronx, 25 percent of present-day Queens, 23.1 percent of Richmond, and 10.5 percent of New York County. It is believed that the category "all other free persons" consisted mostly of free blacks, although some may have been Indians; they accounted for 1.7 percent of present-day Queens, 3.5 percent of what is now the Bronx, 3.3 percent of New

Percentage Distribution of the Population of New York City by Age, 1900–1990

	0–14	15–44	45–64	65+
1900	30.6	53.5	13.1	2.8
1910	28.7	54.6	13.7	2.8
1920	28.3	52.4	16.0	3.1
1930	24.4	54.5	17.3	3.8
1940	19.6	52.9	21.9	5.6
1950	20.8	46.6	24.9	7.7
1960	23.9	39.8	25.9	10.4
1970	23.7	41.1	23.2	12.0
1980	20.1	45.3	21.1	13.5
1990	19.4	48.3	19.4	13.0

Percentages may not add to 100 because of rounding and ages not reported.
Sources: U.S. Bureau of the Census, Census of Population 1900, 1910, 1920, 1930, 1940, 1950, 1960, 1970, 1980, 1990

Population of Selected Counties of the Colony of New York, 1698–1786

	New York	Kings	Queens	Richmond	Westchester
1698	4,937	2,017	3,565	727	1,063
1703	4,375	1,912	4,392	504	1,946
1712	5,841	1,925	N/A	1,279	2,818
1723	7,248	2,218	7,191	1,506	4,409
1731	8,622	2,150	7,995	1,817	6,033
1737	10,664	2,348	9,059	1,889	6,745
1746	11,717	2,331	9,640	2,073	9,235
1749	13,294	2,283	7,940	2,154	10,703
1756	13,046	2,707	10,786	2,132	13,257
1771	21,863	3,623	10,980	2,847	21,755
1786	23,614	3,986	13,084	3,152	20,554

N/A = Not Available

Source: U.S. Bureau of the Census, *A Century of Population Growth* (1909)

York and Richmond counties, and 1 percent of Kings County.

The population increased by well over 50 percent each decade except for 1810–20 until the Civil War, largely because of the city's importance as a commercial center. By 1850 New York City had a population of 515,000, in addition to 181,000 persons living in what later became the other boroughs. Despite the movement of settlers westward it remained the largest city in the United States, followed by Baltimore (169,000), New Orleans (169,000), Boston (137,000), and Philadelphia (121,000).

Just after consolidation (1898) the population of New York City stood at 3.437 million, compared with 1.699 million for Chicago, 1.294 million for Philadelphia, 575,000 for St. Louis, and 561,000 for Boston. There were 61,000 blacks and about seven thousand Asians, mostly Chinese. Some indicators declined after 1900: the average number of persons in a household reached 4.5 in that year before becoming steadily smaller; the proportion of children under the age of fifteen also began its decline, after reaching 30.6 percent in the same year.

Between 1900 and 1910 the population increased by 1.330 million, to 4.767 million. In 1910 the population of Manhattan reached a peak of 2.332 million; at the same time it ceased to account for a majority of the population of the city, as completed subways encouraged settlement in the outer boroughs.

The city reached a population of 6.93 million by 1930 and fluctuated between seven and eight million in later years. The Second World War marked a turning point in growth: in every decade from the 1940s to the 1980s the city experienced a net migration loss. The suburbs grew while the city stabilized. For some time, probably after the Second World War, net gains in population were among im-

Labor Force Participation in New York City by Sex, 1930–1990 (in Thousands)

	Females			Males		
	Total	Number in Labor Force	Percent in Labor Force (Calculated from Unrounded Numbers)	Total	Number in Labor Force	Percent in Labor Force (Calculated from Unrounded Numbers)
1930	2,680	863	32.2	2,675	2,324	86.9
1940	3,113	1,050	33.7	2,990	2,425	81.1
1950	3,305	1,138	34.4	3,028	2,383	78.7
1960	3,200	1,276	39.9	2,826	2,212	78.3
1970	3,209	1,355	42.2	2,685	1,976	73.6
1980	3,049	1,435	47.1	2,494	1,726	69.2
1990	3,154	1,694	53.7	2,663	1,886	70.8

Note: Figures are based on civilian labor force (from 1950 exclusive of armed forces), both employed and unemployed, aged 14 and older in 1930–60 and aged 16 and older in 1970–90. Figures for 1930 are estimates based on the category Gainful Workers, defined as persons who usually have an occupation.
Source: U.S. Bureau of the Census, Census of Population 1930, 1940, 1950, 1960, 1970, 1980, 1990

Blacks as a Percentage of Total Population in Selected Counties of New York State, 1790–1890

	New York	Kings	Queens	Richmond	Westchester
1790	10.47	32.88	19.46	23.10	7.42
1800	10.53	31.55	17.52	16.61	6.35
1810	10.19	22.32	16.36	13.30	6.38
1820	8.80	15.74	14.90	9.94	5.65
1830	6.90	9.77	13.77	7.79	5.80
1840	5.23	5.98	11.57	4.40	4.73
1850	2.68	2.93	9.37	3.92	3.56
1860	1.55	1.79	5.90	2.59	2.28
1870	1.39	1.35	5.14	2.38	1.91
1880	1.63	1.53	4.20	2.39	2.37
1890	1.56	1.35	2.76	1.86	2.33

Note: During the period 1790–1890 New York, Kings, and Richmond counties are assumed to be substantially equivalent to the present Manhattan, Brooklyn, and Staten Island. Queens included what is now Nassau County, and Westchester included what is now the Bronx.
Sources: U.S. Bureau of the Census, Reports for 1790, 1800, 1810, 1820, 1830, 1840, 1850, 1860, 1870, 1880, 1890
Ira Rosenwaike: *Population History of New York City* (Syracuse, N.Y.: Syracuse University Press, 1972)

Youth Population of New York by Race and Hispanic Origin, 1970–1990 (in Thousands)

	Hispanic	Non-Hispanic White	Non-Hispanic Black	Other	Total
Ages 0–4					
1970*	166	266	165	18	616
1980	143	158	141	23	465
1990	166	153	152	38	510
Ages 5–17					
1970*	404	738	437	40	1,619
1980	360	475	411	52	1,299
1990	378	338	374	87	1,177

Asterisk denotes estimate.

Figures may not add because of rounding.

Sources: U.S. Bureau of the Census, Census of Population 1970, 1980, 1990

Compiled by Nathan Kantrowitz

Population of Boroughs of New York City
(as Defined by Consolidation of 1898), 1790–1890

	Manhattan	Bronx	Brooklyn	Queens	Staten Island	Total
1790	33,131	1,781	4,495	6,159	3,835	49,401
1800	60,515	1,755	5,740	6,642	4,564	79,216
1810	96,373	2,267	8,303	7,444	5,347	119,734
1820	123,706	2,782	11,187	8,246	6,135	152,056
1830	202,589	3,023	20,535	9,049	7,082	242,278
1840	312,710	5,346	47,613	14,480	10,965	391,114
1850	515,547	8,032	138,882	18,593	15,061	696,115
1860	813,669	23,593	279,122	32,903	25,492	1,174,779
1870	942,292	37,393	419,921	45,468	33,029	1,478,103
1880	1,164,673	51,980	599,495	56,559	38,991	1,911,698
1890	1,441,216	88,908	838,547	87,050	51,693	2,507,414

Note: From 1874 to 1895 New York City consisted of Manhattan and part of the Bronx. The total population of the city was 1,206,299 in 1880 and 1,515,301 in 1890.

Sources: U.S. Department of Commerce, Bureau of the Census, Census of Population 1960 (vol. 1, part A, table 28), 1970, 1980, 1990

Black Population as a Percentage of Total Population in Selected Counties of the Colony of New York, 1698–1786

	New York	Kings	Queens	Richmond	Westchester
1698	14.2	14.7	5.6	10.0	13.7
1703	14.4	17.9	9.7	19.2	10.2
1712	16.7	N/A	N/A	N/A	11.8
1723	18.8	20.0	15.6	16.9	10.2
1731	18.3	22.9	15.8	16.7	11.5
1737	16.1	24.0	14.5	18.5	12.6
1746	20.9	27.7	16.4	18.4	7.3
1749	17.8	34.3	16.7	19.0	10.8
1756	17.5	31.2	20.1	21.8	10.1
1771	14.3	32.1	20.4	20.9	15.8
1786	8.9	33.0	16.7	22.0	6.1

N/A = Not Available

Note: Counties are not necessarily coextensive with present counties.

Source: U.S. Bureau of the Census, *A Century of Population Growth* (1909)

migrants, net losses among the native-born. The outward movement of population from the urban center affected all the boroughs except Staten Island, and after the Second World War the population reached a peak in Brooklyn (1950), the Bronx (1970), and Queens (1970).

During these postwar years the city's racial and Hispanic composition also changed, owing in part to a large influx from Puerto Rico, the Caribbean, Latin America, and Asia. Only limited information on Puerto Ricans was collected before 1970. The Puerto Rican population reached a quarter-million by 1950, when there were perhaps another 100,000 persons in the city who were Hispanic but not Puerto Rican. By 1960 there were well over 600,000 Puerto Ricans and probably 200,000 other Hispanics, and the number of Hispanics exceeded 1.25 million by 1970, at which time the number of Asians exceeded 100,000 for the first time. From then on the Hispanic population continued to grow at a slower rate, comparable to that of the non-Hispanic black population. In contrast to the continued decline of non-Hispanic whites and the more moderate growth of Hispanics and non-Hispanic blacks, the category called "other races" (mostly Chinese) grew sharply, roughly doubling between 1970 and 1980, and again between 1980 and 1990. By 1990 non-Hispanic whites were a minority of the population (43.2 percent), followed by non-Hispanic blacks (25.2 percent), Hispanics (24.4 percent), and Asians (6.7 percent).

The decennial census provides some of the most valuable information about the people of New York City, even with such limitations as its undercounting. This remains an important obstacle, especially among ethnic minorities and the poor: it omitted as many as half a million persons in 1980 and possibly as many or more in 1990. In 1990 New York City was the center of a metropolitan area extending across three states and containing a population of about nineteen million; it remained the largest city in the United States, followed by Los Angeles, Chicago, Houston, and Philadelphia.

Nathan Kantrowitz

Population Council. Nonprofit organization formed in 1951 by John D. Rockefeller III to study and control population. Initially its goal was to expedite population policies in the third world, but it eventually sought also to control fertility in the United States in the interest of preserving advances in education, culture, and development. The first benefactors were Rockefeller (who gave $1,893,000), chairman for the first twenty-five years, the Ford Foundation ($600,000), the Rockefeller Brothers Fund ($120,000 a year for three years), and several large corporations. By 1985 the council had received $63 million from the

the world; in August it began operating between the city and Albany, and Fulton was granted a monopoly on the operation of steam-powered vessels in New York State and to points in adjoining states. He designed ferries for use on routes from the city to Jersey City, New Jersey, and to Brooklyn, and in 1813 he launched the *Fulton*, a steamboat intended to run on Long Island Sound between the city and southern New England; it ran on the Hudson during the War of 1812 and with the steamship *Connecticut* was later used on the route between the city and New Haven, Connecticut.

The growth of the port accelerated after the war. The world's first steam-powered warship, designed by Fulton, was under construction in the city by 1815. A steam towing service for becalmed sailing ships was introduced in 1818 by the *Nautilus*, a ferry to Staten Island that towed ships into Upper New York Bay. During the same year the first packet service began between the city and Europe: a fleet of four ships was assembled by the Black Ball Line, allowing it to schedule regular sailings in each direction between New York City and Liverpool (previous sailings were unpredictable, because they were undertaken whenever the loading of cargo was completed). Although it was more expensive than others the service was soon in demand, and a number of new firms provided service to Liverpool, London, and ports in continental Europe, where grain and cotton were delivered, emigrants embarked, and manufactured goods bound for the city were loaded. Regular steam service was initiated in 1819 between the city and Charleston, South Carolina, by the *Robert Fulton*, a sidewheel steamer fitted with sails; the service was abandoned after five years. The first transatlantic crossing by a ship with steam capability was made in 1819 by the *Savannah*, a packet ship built in the city; the ship's engine was used little and regular service was not established, largely because the amount of fuel required for steam power left insufficient space for cargo. The ferry route from the city to New England was extended to Providence, Rhode Island, in 1822. The development of steamboat travel was hindered by Fulton's monopoly, which was declared unconstitutional by the U.S. Supreme Court in *Gibbons v. Ogden* (1824).

Berenice Abbott, Watuppa *(1936)*

The port expanded at an unprecedented rate after the Erie Canal was completed from Albany to Buffalo in 1825. Goods could be shipped from Buffalo to the city in eight days rather than twenty, and the cost was reduced from $100 to $15 a ton ($90 to $13.50 a metric ton); the most important commodity was grain from the Western Reserve of Ohio. A second canal was built from the Hudson River to Lake Champlain, and several other states built canals that also served the Port of New York: the Delaware and Hudson Canal was built with money from investors in New York City to carry coal to the port from northeastern Pennsylvania, as was the Morris Canal, which ran across northern New Jersey; and the Delaware and Raritan Canal connected the Delaware and Raritan rivers in New Jersey, permitting cargo to be shipped into Lower New York Bay. Most boats used on the canals were pulled by horses or mules and required steamships to tow them to the port. The first vessel designed as a towboat was the *Rufus King*, a sidewheel steamboat built in the city in 1825. Larger ships were later developed to tow canal boats to the port in rafts of forty or more moored together. Steam travel was introduced on most waterways and there was keen competition among shippers on the Hudson. A variety of services were offered at the port, which became a railroad terminus after the successful run of a steam train between Albany and Schenectady, New York, on 9 August 1831.

By the mid nineteenth century the port handled more goods and passengers than all the other ports in the country combined and was one of the most important ports in the world. Transatlantic steamship service began in 1838, when vessels of two rival British companies arrived at the port within hours of each other. American companies were unable to offer such service before the Civil War. Railroads connected Albany and Buffalo by 1842, and in 1846 the Fall River Line was introduced to provide overnight ferry service from lower Manhattan to Fall River, Massachusetts, where passengers boarded an express train to Boston; this became the most successful ferry company operating in the Sound. Sailing ships continued to dominate long trade routes, and in 1845 one of the world's first clipper ships, the *Rainbow*, was launched from the city to engage in trade in China. Many clippers were built after gold was discovered in California, but construction ceased during a depression in shipping in 1857. A railroad line that later became the New York Central Railroad was completed in 1851 from Albany to New York City. The fastest service across the North Atlantic during the 1850s was provided by the Collins Line, which operated a fleet of wooden sidewheel steamboats between the city and Liverpool. Shipbuilding facilities opened on East 14th Street and in Williamsburg and Greenpoint, and before the Civil War the city was the leading center of wooden shipbuilding in the nation. Atlantic Basin and Erie Basin, the first large-scale cargo terminals, were built in Red Hook during the 1850s and 1860s.

Industrial activity increased during and after the war. Wooden shipbuilding declined, and the centers of iron and steel shipbuilding gradually moved elsewhere, although a few shipbuilders remained in the city as late as the 1970s. The harbor was altered to accommodate ever larger steamships; dangerous reefs were blasted out of Hell Gate in 1876 and 1885 and work on the Harlem River Ship Canal was conducted between 1826 and 1938. By the early 1870s the shoreline of Brooklyn from the navy yard to Red Hook was lined with multi-story brick warehouses. Three companies garnered most of the shipping on the Hudson: overnight ferries were operated between the city and Albany by the Peoples' Line and between the city and Troy, New York, by the Citizens' Line, and day ferries were operated by the Hudson River Day Line between New York and Albany. By the 1880s eleven major railroads built terminals in the city. Those of the New York Central and the New Haven railroads were in Manhattan, that of the Long Island Railroad in Brooklyn at the foot of Atlantic Avenue and later in Long Island City; the Baltimore and Ohio railroad had a freight terminal on Staten Island; and the other lines had terminals on the shore of the harbor in New Jersey. Until tunnels were built under the Hudson after the turn of the century, railroads in New Jersey operated thousands of ferries and lighterage vessels that ran from freight and passenger terminals in New Jersey (many built on landfill) to terminals in Manhattan and Brooklyn. Entire trains were moved on the East River from Jersey City to the Bronx, and strings of freight cars were carried on barges called car floats and moved by tugboats. Cargo also traveled in open scows, covered barges, hold barges, derrick lighters, and steam lighters, and was transferred to ships by crane barges and floating elevators.

The Port of New York became the busiest port in the world shortly after 1900 and remained so for more than fifty years. Ferry companies on the Hudson and the Sound operated some of the largest and most elegant sidewheel steamboats ever built. Many had a length of about three hundred feet (ninety meters; that of the *Commonwealth*, built in 1908 and operated by the Fall River Line, was 456 feet, or 140 meters), and they were furnished and decorated so splendidly that they became known as "floating palaces." To accommodate such large vessels piers were built on the Hudson in Manhattan, along the shore of Brooklyn beneath Brooklyn Heights, and in Jersey City and Hoboken, New Jersey, many of them covered with sheds to protect cargo from the weather and theft. The Ambrose Channel, completed in 1912 to provide a deeper and more direct entrance to the port, was later used by enormous passenger liners. Sailing ships continued to use berths off the East River in Manhattan into the early twentieth century. The year 1921 marked the formation of the Port of New York Authority (later renamed the Port Authority of New York and New Jersey), which was intended to improve terminals in the port and related transportation facilities. The handling of goods and passengers remained largely unchanged into the 1950s, and the port gradually lost business to truck transport after the George Washington Bridge, the Lincoln and Holland tunnels, and various roads were built in the 1930s. The Fall River Line ceased operations in 1937 and overnight services on the Hudson were discontinued in 1939; the Hudson River Day Line retired its last sidewheel steamer, the *Alexander Hamilton*, in 1971. The port operated to full capacity during the Second World War, handling half the troops and a third of the supplies sent overseas.

About 1960 steel containers of standard size were introduced to speed the handling of freight. Designed for use on specially adapted ships, trains, and trucks, they were forty feet (twelve meters) long, required much open space for storage and maneuvering, and protected cargo from weather and theft. As modern terminals were built in southern Brooklyn and Howland Hook, and in Bayonne and Elizabeth, New Jersey, the covered piers and warehouses along the shores of Manhattan and Brooklyn became obsolete; some were demolished and replaced by such developments as Battery Park City and South Street Seaport. Cargo facilities were abandoned, among them the vast railroad freight yards along the western bank of the Hudson; new uses were found for large ferry terminals in Manhattan and warehouse complexes in Brooklyn and Staten Island. Sailors' Snug Harbor, formerly a home for retired seamen on Staten Island, became a cultural center in 1976, and the immigrant processing station on Ellis Island reopened in 1990 as a museum administered by the National Park Service. As it ceased to be used by commercial traffic the central harbor increasingly attracted sailboats and excursion vessels. High-speed launches carried passengers between lower Manhattan and points as far away as Sandy Hook (New Jersey), Jamaica Bay, and the northern shore of Long Island. A few double-ended ferry boats continued to run from Manhattan to Staten Island and to the U.S. Coast Guard base on Governors Island. In the mid 1990s the future of a number of abandoned facilities remained undecided, including that of shipyards, a lighthouse depot, and a quarantine station on Staten Island, grain and coal handling facilities in Brooklyn, and the Brooklyn Navy Yard. Commercial traffic continued to flow through the Narrows, most of it approaching or leaving the container terminals, oil depots, and refineries of New Jersey.

A Maritime History of New York (Garden City, N.Y.: Doubleday, Doran, 1941)

Norman J. Brouwer

Port Richmond. Neighborhood in northwestern Staten Island, lying south of the Kill van Kull. The area was known in 1700 as the Burial Place, after a cemetery of the Dutch Reformed church near the shore on Richmond Avenue. It was a transfer point for freight and passengers traveling by boat between New York City and New Brunswick, New Jersey, and a ferry landing known variously as Ryer's Landing, Mersereau's Landing, and Decker's Landing was built as a terminus for a route to Bergen Point (now in Bayonne), New Jersey; ferries ran continually until shortly after the Bayonne Bridge was built in 1931. The area also became the site of an important stop on a coach route between the city and Philadelphia. A public park was built in 1836. Irish and Germans settled in the neighborhood in the mid nineteenth century. Some small industries were established, including the only whaling company on the island in 1838. Its whale-oil processing plant was destroyed by fire in 1842 and replaced by a factory of the Jewett White Lead and Linseed Oil Company, which operated into the twentieth century. Lumber and coal yards moved near the waterfront during the nineteenth century. A large cloth-dyeing plant was built inland in 1851 by the Barrett Nephews Company, an offshoot of the New York Printing and Dyeing Company in West New Brighton that flourished until the early twentieth century (a shopping mall now stands on the site).

The neighborhood was incorporated as Port Richmond in 1866 and in 1883 was described as a model village. In the 1880s the Staten Island Railroad built a northern line with a station at Richmond Avenue, the main shopping area. By the 1890s there was a black church. Port Richmond Square eventually became a transfer point for streetcars and later for bus lines, encouraging the growth of a prosperous commercial center and a large population. Italians, Poles, Norwegians, and Swedes moved into the neighborhood at the turn of the century. Several buildings soon lined three sides of the park: Public School 20 (now a city landmark), a public library built by Andrew Carnegie in 1902, and three churches. A synagogue was built in 1907. Faber Park and Pool were built by the city in 1932; sporting events were held during the 1940s and 1950s at Weinglass Stadium (privately owned).

In 1990 the population was 75 percent white, 12 percent black, 10 percent Latin American, and 3 percent Asian. The housing consists of modest one-family houses on small lots, especially in the downtown. Larger Victorian houses line Herberton Avenue, and attractive one-family houses built in the 1920s are just north of Forest Avenue (Port Richmond Center). Two lumberyards remain. There are ten churches in the area.

Marjorie Johnson

Post [née Price], **Emily** (*b* Baltimore, 27 Oct 1872; *d* New York City, 25 Sept 1960). Writer. She grew up in New York City, where she attended Miss Graham's Finishing School for Young Ladies and from the age of twelve lived at 12 West 10th Street. After her marriage ended in divorce she devoted herself to writing. By 1921 she was commissioned to write a book on etiquette; more than 666,000 copies were sold, and she later wrote columns for *McCall's* and 150 newspapers and had a weekly radio program on which she answered questions about etiquette. By 1946 she opened the Emily Post Institute. She lived at 39 East 79th Street from about 1925 until the end of her life.

James E. Mooney

The World Building, designed by George B. Post at Park Row and Frankfort Street, ca *1900 (demolished)*

U.S. Post Office at 34th Street (designed by McKim, Mead and White), 1994

Post, George B(rowne) (*b* New York City, 15 Dec 1837; *d* Bernardsville, N.J., 28 Nov 1913). Architect. He graduated from New York University in 1858 and was engaged as the consulting architect in charge of elevators and ironwork for the Equitable Building (1868–70, demolished), considered the first skyscraper in New York City. He later designed the Western Union building (1872–75, demolished) and used metal-framed interior walls in his New York Produce Exchange (1881–84, demolished) that prefigured the skeleton framing later adopted for skyscraper construction. Post is also known for such works as the Williamsburgh Savings Bank in Brooklyn (1869–75), the Pulitzer Building (1889–90, demolished), the New York Stock Exchange (1901–4), and the campus of City College (1897–1907; for illustration see CITY COLLEGE OF NEW YORK).

Winston Weisman: "The Commercial Architecture of George B. Post," *Journal of the Society of Architectural Historians* 31 (1972), 176–203

Sarah Bradford Landau

post offices. Postal service was first offered in New Amsterdam in 1660. The rotunda on Chambers Street housed the city's only post office until 1835, when a branch opened near Wall Street. In 1845 the main post office was moved to the former Middle Dutch Church on Nassau Street and the branch office to Chatham Square. Post offices were first erected by the federal government during the mid nineteenth century, and after the Civil War the Office of the Supervising Architect of the Treasury designed and built a number of large post offices, many of them also containing courthouses. In 1875 the main post office on Nassau Street was replaced by an enormous facility in City Hall Park designed in the Second Empire style by Alfred Mullet (demolished). During Mifflin Bell's tenure as supervising architect of the Treasury, work began in 1885 on the Brooklyn Post Office, built in the Romanesque Revival style (in the mid 1990s this remained the city's oldest post office in use). The Tarnsey Act of 1893 authorized the federal government to award commissions to private architects, and before its repeal in 1912 two of the city's largest post offices were erected: Grand Central Station (1909), designed by Warren and Wetmore, architects of the adjoining railroad terminal; and the General Post Office (1913), designed in a Classical Revival style and built of granite by the firm of McKim, Mead and White (William Kendall, partner in charge) to complement Pennsylvania Station. In the late 1920s Congress authorized the construction of a large number of branch offices, including those in Long Island City (1929) and Staten Island (1932).

Postal service expanded rapidly during the Depression, when money was allotted for building post offices under the New Deal. Between 1932 and 1941 twenty-nine post offices were erected in the city, four designed by Louis Simon, the supervising architect of the Treasury, and the rest by local architects employed by work relief programs. The number of commissions for federal buildings increased so rapidly that Simon's office became unable to handle them, and in 1930 Congress again permitted commissions to be awarded to private architects. Dwight James Baum designed the Flushing post office (1934); the firm of Cross and Cross designed the Jamaica post office (1934) and collaborated with the firm of Pennington, Lewis and Mills on Church Street Station, both a post office and an office building (1938). By 1934 funds for so many new post offices had been allocated that the government was forced to undertake a novel plan to acquire designs: some of the most important commissions were given to a group of unemployed architects who were moved temporarily to Washington; architects from New York City, including Thomas Harlan

Old Post Office (designed by Alfred Mullett; demolished), ca *1910*

Branch U.S. Post Office Station "S" in the Bronx, ca *1880*

Ellett, William Dewey Foster, Eric Kebbon, Alan Balch Mills, Carroll Pratt, and Lorimer Rich, were responsible for at least twenty buildings.

Most of the new post offices were designed in the Colonial Revival style popular in federal architecture. Rich designed branches in Flatbush (1936) and West Farms (1936) to resemble farmhouses from the eighteenth century and the early nineteenth; Kebbon designed Lenox Hill (1935) and Planetarium (1936) stations to resemble townhouses and was also responsible for the branch in Far Rockaway (1936), an adaptation of Monticello. A few post offices in the city were designed in the austere "Modern Classical" style that became popular for public buildings during the 1930s, including Madison Square Station (1937, Rich) and the main post office in the Bronx (1937, Ellett), and a few were examples of modernism, notably Forest Hills Station (1938, Rich). The Treasury also commissioned works of art for ten of the new buildings, including the painting *First Amendment* (Woodhaven Station) and the fresco cycle *American at Work* (Bronx post office), both by Ben Shahn; two murals with scenes of the city by Louis Lozowick (General Post Office); and eight murals with urban street scenes by Kindred McLeary (Madison Square Station). Fewer post offices were built after the relief projects were discontinued in 1941, and in later years the U.S. Postal Service erected few notable buildings, preferring instead to lease space in existing buildings.

Andrew S. Dolkart

Potter, Edward T(uckerman) (*b* Schenectady, N.Y., 25 Sept 1831; *d* New York City, 21 Dec 1904). Architect, brother of Henry Codman Potter and half-brother of William A. Potter. He was known for designing churches and college buildings, many in the High Victorian Gothic style. In New York City his buildings include the Church of the Heavenly Rest (1868–71, demolished), St. Paul's Memorial Church and rectory on Staten Island (1866–70), and the original Brown Brothers building (1864–65, demolished), a marble palazzo on Wall Street.

Sarah Bradford Landau: *Edward T. and William A. Potter* (New York: Garland, 1979)

Sarah Bradford Landau

Potter, Henry Codman (*b* Schenectady, N.Y., 25 May 1834; *d* Cooperstown, N.Y., 21 July 1908). Bishop, brother of Edward T. Potter and half-brother of William A. Potter. He graduated from Virginia Theological Seminary in 1857. He was the rector of small parishes in Pennsylvania and New York State before becoming successively the assistant rector of Trinity Church in Boston (1866); the rector of Grace Church in New York City (1868), one of the most distinguished positions in the largest and wealthiest Episcopal parish in the nation; an assistant bishop of the Diocese of New York (1883); and the bishop of the diocese (1888), a position he held to the end of his life. During his career in the city he became known for his conviction that urban churches must concern themselves not only with wealthy, educated parishioners but also with workingmen, prisoners, the poor, and the uneducated. Although his church was supported by the wealthy he became identified with the cause of labor and joined forces with religious and civic leaders who were trying to improve the conditions of the poor. Among the organizations for social betterment that he supported or helped to form were the Church Association for the Advancement of the Interests of Labor (CAAIL), the Seamen's Church Institute, and the Actors' Church Alliance; he was also an important figure in the settlement and institutional church movements and came to be known by some as the "people's bishop" and "citizen bishop." Potter tended toward the Low Church and was theologically liberal, but through his tolerance, skill, diplomacy, and strong personality he was able to secure the cooperation of diverse elements in the diocese. He eagerly pursued the construction of the Cathedral of St. John the Divine, hoping that a great metropolitan cathedral would join with other educational, religious, cultural, and philanthropic institutions to make the city a leader in moral ideas, letters, science, and art; he secured a site, raised the initial funds, and in 1892 laid the cornerstone. His episcopate is considered by some the height of the Episcopal church in the city. He published *Brilliants: Selected from the Writings of Henry Codman Potter* in 1893.

George Hodges: *Henry Codman Potter, Seventh Bishop of New York* (New York: Macmillan, 1915)
James Sheerin: *Henry Codman Potter, an American Metropolitan* (New York: Fleming H. Revell, 1933)

Jane Allen

Potter, William A(ppleton) (*b* Schenectady, N.Y., 10 Dec 1842; *d* Rome, 19 Feb 1909). Architect, half-brother of Henry Codman Potter and Edward T. Potter. He was known for designing church and college buildings, including the Holy Trinity Church complex (1887–89; now St. Martin's Church) on Lenox Avenue and 122nd Street, the campus of Teachers College (1892–97), and the Universalist Church of the Divine Paternity and parish house (1897–98; now Universalist Church of New York City) at Central Park West and 76th Street.

Sarah Bradford Landau: *Edward T. and William A. Potter* (New York: Garland, 1979)

Sarah Bradford Landau

potter's fields. New York City had its first known potter's field in Washington Square, which was replaced successively by one at Madison Square and another in Bryant Park; some nearby towns had their own sites. A small field was shared during the nineteenth century by Jamaica, Flushing, Newtown, Hempstead, North Hempstead, and Oyster Bay (it is now a schoolyard in Queens Village). In 1869 the city adopted as its potter's field Hart Island, an island of forty-five acres (eighteen hectares) in Long Island Sound that had a million interments by the mid 1990s. Convicts from Rikers Island perform the burials of the indigent, which number about fifteen hundred a year; they volunteer for the duty and are transported to the site by ferry from City Island. There are no stones but the dead are numbered; about a hundred bodies a year are identified by friends or relatives. Hart Island is not accessible to the public.

Edward F. Bergman

Jacob A. Riis, The Potter's Field; The Common Trench *(ca 1890). Convicts lower wooden coffins into a common grave on Hart Island.*

Pottier and Stymus. Firm of furniture manufacturers and decorators, formed in 1859 as the partnership of the upholsterer William Pierre Stymus and Auguste Pottier (1823–96), a wood sculptor trained in France who settled in New York City in 1850. By 1871 it operated an integrated factory on Lexington Avenue between 41st and 42nd streets to handle large contracts for complete interiors in diverse styles. In 1876 it showed neo-Grec and Henry II wares at the Centennial Exhibition in Philadelphia, including two black walnut chairs (*ca* 1875, now at the Metropolitan Museum of Art). Its customers included President Ulysses S. Grant and the financier Henry Morrison Flagler. After a fire in 1888 Pottier left the firm, which reorganized, rebuilt its factory, and remained in operation until 1918–19.

Deborah Dependahl Waters

poverty. Efforts were made to alleviate poverty in New Amsterdam in the early seventeenth century, when the Dutch Reformed church established a poor-relief system. Under the system orphans were apprenticed, medical services were provided, and an almshouse was built for the aged poor (see ALMSHOUSES). Laws enacted by the colony in 1661 required that each community collect donations to maintain a poor fund, a system that was replaced in 1683 by poor-law legislation that shifted the responsibility for caring for the poor to counties. The wardens of the Anglican church who administered the new system listed only thirty-five permanent paupers in 1700, a number that increased to about one hundred during the 1730s. City relief cost an average of £500 a year and commonly took the form of food, firewood, shoes, clothing, medical care, funeral expenses, and small cash payments for those who met the residency requirements.

Poverty became a more serious problem in New York City during the eighteenth century, as immigration brought to the city indentured servants and other dependent people such as orphans, the elderly, and the blind. In 1734 the Common Council responded by authorizing the construction of an almshouse that by 1772 sheltered 425 paupers. Large numbers of "outdoor" poor were also supported, making the poor-relief effort one of the city's largest annual expenditures. The Humane Society was one of many charitable organizations in the city that supplemented public assistance after the American Revolution: formed in 1787 to aid imprisoned debtors, the society broadened its activities after 1800 to include medical care for the poor, child labor reform, and the support of a soup house.

During the first half of the nineteenth century economic difficulties, rising immigration, and periodic epidemics increased the welfare burden dramatically in New York City. Severe winters caused annual emergencies in the city as construction workers and other outdoor laborers became unemployed and appealed to relief officials for food and fuel. A three-story poorhouse completed in 1797 was replaced in 1816 by a much larger structure called the Bellevue Establishment, which by the 1820s housed about seventeen hundred paupers. Hundreds of other dependents were confined in a public hospital, an orphanage, an insane asylum, and a juvenile reformatory. Throughout this period public welfare accounted for about a fourth of the city's annual budget, more than any other item. By 1825 several dozen specialized charities were formed, including religious and medical philanthropies,

"Stepping mill" for grinding grain, operated by convicts, 1823

James Henry Cafferty, The Sidewalks of New York *(1859; also known as* The Encounter*)*

societies to provide for orphans and widows, and mutual benefit associations.

The growing belief that poverty was the result of individual moral failure was reflected in these groups' efforts to reform paupers. Adherents of a vigorous urban missionary movement of Bible and tract societies, Sunday schools, and temperance crusades dedicated themselves to providing moral education for the poor; groups such as the New York Society for the Prevention of Pauperism discouraged material assistance by emphasizing the social dangers of dependency. New attitudes toward social welfare led to the enactment of state laws in 1824 that abolished "outdoor" relief and required that the truly needy be placed in institutions. Work was viewed as a means of combating public dependency and cutting welfare costs by the Common Council, which from 1830 required that even the most feeble paupers in the almshouse perform some kind of work. Changing public attitudes toward benevolence also underlay the formation of the Association for Improving the Condition of the Poor, founded by religious leaders in 1843. Under the direction of Robert M. Hartley, it introduced the district visitor system to provide moral and spiritual advice to the poor.

Poverty intensified during the 1870s and 1880s. Immigration contributed to overcrowded slums, and economic depressions brought unemployment, in response to which New York City sponsored work relief efforts. During the winter of 1893–94 police stations in the city provided temporary shelter for more than twenty thousand persons. A Catholic periodical estimated that forty thousand children lived as vagrants in New York City during the late nineteenth century, a deplorable condition captured by Jacob A. Riis's photographs of street children in the city during the 1890s. Robert Hunter argued in *Poverty* (1904), his classic study of the urban poor, that outside forces such as low wages kept most working-class families on the edge of subsistence. By 1907 New York City had four almshouses that sheltered almost five thousand persons, as well as a number of specialized institutions that provided care for the blind and the physically handicapped, and housed juvenile delinquents. Moralistic views about poverty nevertheless continued to shape welfare programs in New York City. Those temporarily unemployed were often unable to find public assistance, the city suspended outdoor relief during a depression in 1874 (as did Brooklyn in 1878), and the new charter that took effect on consolidation in 1898 prohibited home relief.

Private philanthropy was transformed when the Charity Organization Society introduced "scientific charity" to New York City during the late nineteenth century. Initiated in Buffalo in 1877, the charity organization movement sought to make private relief systematic by investigating the merits of each recipient's case and weeding out the unworthy; its "friendly visitors" provided counseling for poor families. The director of the charity organization in New York City, Josephine Shaw Lowell, became a national spokeswoman for reform. Officials of the organization formed the nucleus of the National Conference on Charities and Correction in 1874 (renamed the National Conference of Social Work in 1917). Toward the end of the century the settlement house movement, begun in London in 1884, increasingly saw poverty as the product of structural problems in the urban economy. The movement found support in New York City among such members of the Social Gospel churches as Stanton Coit, who in 1886 opened the first settlement house in the United States, known as the Neighborhood Guild. Others settlement houses soon followed, including the College Settlement (1889), East Side House (1891), the Henry Street Settlement (1893), the Lenox Hill Settlement (1894), the Union Settlement (1895), and Greenwich House (1902). In addition to promoting child labor reform, tenement house legislation, and the building of parks and playgrounds, the settlement houses worked to improve education and public health. Tensions between the Charity Organization Society and the settlement houses grew during the second decade of the twentieth century when progressive reformers in the state legislature enacted a law that created "mothers' pensions," cash assistance for dependent mothers. The Charity Organization Society denounced the law, which they viewed as an incursion on private philanthropy.

Attitudes toward poverty that began to form during the Progressive era became more widespread during the Depression. Several studies on poverty in New York City reinforced the notion that relief was not a charity but a right, and that caring for the poor was not the responsibility of the municipality but rather that of the state. In his book *The American Poorfarm and Its Inmates* (1926) Harry C. Evans shocked New Yorkers with his descriptions of children living among the insane in poorhouses. The state legislature ordered an inquiry in response to this and to a study that showed 50 to 75 percent of the almshouse population to be chronically ill. By 1929 the legislature passed the New York State Public Welfare Act, which restored home relief for the poor. In the following year it passed the Old Age Security Act, making New York the first state to provide benefits for the elderly. Factory wages fell 50 percent in the state between 1929 and 1933, and between 1930 and 1933 the number of unemployed workers grew from 656,000 to 2,061,000. With a population of almost seven million in 1930, New York City faced especially severe problems with welfare, unemployment, and housing. A shantytown called Hoover Valley was built on the Great Lawn of Central Park. Groucho Marx said that he knew things were bad when he saw pigeons in the park feeding people.

Mayor James J. Walker responded to the city's economic problems in 1930 by forming a committee to raise cash grants for the needy. In 1931 the Board of Aldermen appropriated $80 million for work relief programs on roads and parks, but by summer the money was exhausted and to avoid bankruptcy the city appealed for unemployment relief to the state, which was sympathetic because a number of its officials were reformers who had spent much of their life in the city. Shortly after Governor Franklin D. Roosevelt asked the state legislature for emergency action in 1931, the Temporary Emergency Relief Administration was formed and New York became the first state to provide unemployment relief. After state funds too were exhausted in 1932, leaving 88,000 approved applicants waiting for work relief, Representative Fiorello H. La Guardia and Senator Robert F. Wagner secured a relief appropriation of $2000 million from the U.S. Congress. New York City obtained additional sums of federal money for public works after the election of La Guardia as mayor and Roosevelt as president, and eventually it became known as the unofficial capital of the New Deal. Programs developed by Roosevelt such as the Works Progress Administration in 1935, Aid to Families with Dependent Children, and the Social Security Act temporarily revived the social welfare system in New York City.

In the economic boom of the 1940s and 1950s poverty steadily decreased in New York City, but gradually changes in demographics and manufacturing weakened the economy and profoundly affected welfare policy. Large numbers of southern blacks were drawn to New York City by the promise of better economic conditions, but many were disappointed by the scarcity of unskilled work. While total employment in the city increased, the manufacturing sector began to decline. Tensions mounted over the high level of unemployment in cities throughout the United States and finally led to the race riots of the 1960s. To alleviate poverty, welfare benefits were expanded during the administration of President Lyndon B. Johnson. In New York City Mayor John V. Lindsay raised welfare benefits to the highest level in the nation and relaxed requirements for eligibility, in part to ease racial tension. The number of persons receiving public assistance in New York City increased from 328,000 in 1960 to 1.1 million in 1972. Public resentment grew as reports showed that the welfare system created a disincentive to work; some argued that it encouraged births out of wedlock.

By the time of the fiscal crisis of the mid 1970s many New Yorkers refused to tolerate the high cost of welfare. Mayor Edward I. Koch and his administration began cutting the welfare rolls and limiting payments to recipients in 1978. These measures contributed to widespread HOMELESSNESS, as did the continued erosion of manufacturing employment and the destruction of low-income housing throughout the city: tax concessions granted to developers by Koch, an incentive to encourage new commercial and residential development and improve the city's tax base after the fiscal crisis, led to the destruction of as many as 100,000 single-room-occupancy units (SROs) that had served as cheap housing for the mentally ill and the elderly. During the 1980s the federal government also sharply reduced its housing programs, and families were increasingly forced to double up in cramped apartments. The Coalition for the Homeless and the Legal Aid Society successfully sued the city to establish a legal right to housing for the poor; they forced the city to open and maintain shelters for the homeless. Soup kitchens opened in hundreds of churches for the first time since the Depression, abandoned psychiatric institutions were reclaimed to house the mentally ill, and orphanages, called "congregate care facilities," were built to house homeless and abandoned children.

After Ronald Reagan was elected president in 1980 the federal government restricted welfare, disability payments, school hot-lunch programs, and food stamps. Many families in New York City and throughout the nation that had come to rely on these sources of aid slipped further into poverty, and at the same time the manufacturing sector in the city continued to decline. David N. Dinkins was elected mayor in 1989 after pledging to improve the lot of the poor, but his promise to finish a massive public housing program begun by Koch was forestalled by another fiscal crisis. Public sentiments toward the poor, initially sympathetic when the homeless first became visible in the early 1980s, turned as beggars seemed more threatening and demanding; there was little opposition when Dinkins closed several public shelters and removed encampments of homeless persons from Tompkins Square Park and Columbus Circle. The election of two Republicans, Mayor Rudolph W. Giuliani in 1993 and Governor George E. Pataki in 1994, brought new attacks on welfare programs. Both sought major cuts in relief and medical care for the poor. In January 1995 there were 1.15 million New Yorkers on welfare rolls.

David Moses Schneider: *History of Public Welfare in New York State* (Chicago: University of Chicago Press, 1938–41)

Raymond A. Mohl: *Poverty in New York, 1783–1825* (New York: Oxford University Press, 1971)

Miriam Ostow and Anna B. Dutka: *Work and Welfare in New York City* (Baltimore: Johns Hopkins University Press, 1975)

Emanuel Tobier: *Changing Face of Poverty: Trends in New York City's Population in Poverty, 1960–1990* (New York: Community Service Society, 1984)

Michael B. Katz: *In the Shadow of the Poorhouse: A Social History of Welfare in America* (New York: Basic Books, 1986)

Rick Beard et al.: *On Being Homeless: Historical Perspectives* (Museum of the City of New York, 1987)

Robert E. Cray Jr.: *Paupers and Poor Relief in New York City and Its Rural Environs, 1700–1830* (Philadelphia: Temple University Press, 1988)

Clara J. Hemphill, Raymond A. Mohl

Powell, Adam Clayton, Jr. (*b* New Haven, Conn., 29 Nov 1908; *d* Bimini, 4 April 1972). Congressman, minister, and civil rights leader, son of Adam Clayton Powell Sr. He grew up in New York City and attended Colgate University. His complexion was light, and at college he allegedly tried for a time to be taken as white. He graduated in 1930, became an assistant pastor at the ABYSSINIAN BAPTIST CHURCH in New York City (where his father was the pastor), and received a master's degree in religious education from Teachers College in 1932 and a doctor of divinity degree from Shaw University in 1938. After leading a night school, an employment bureau, and a soup kitchen at his church he took over the pastorate in 1938. He helped to organize the Equal Employment Coordinating Committee and led boycotts of companies in Harlem and elsewhere that refused to employ black workers. An adroit politician, he secured backing for his movement from opposing groups of communists and black nationalists. In 1941 he became the first black member of the City Council, and after a congressional district with a black majority was drawn in Harlem he was elected to represent it in 1944. During more than two decades in Congress he unsuccessfully introduced many amendments intended to ensure nondiscrimination in federally funded programs. In 1960 he became the first black chairman of a major com-

Adam Clayton Powell Jr. with Haile Selassie

mittee, that on education and labor; he used this position to further the Great Society by helping to design and pass legislation in support of education, housing, and civil rights.

Powell alienated many of his white colleagues. They considered his brash, assertive style arrogant and disapproved of his reputation as a libertine, which was furthered by his marriage to the entertainer Hazel Scott. He retained his post as the pastor of the Abyssinian Baptist Church, and his weekly trips to New York City and frequent vacations on the Caribbean island of Bimini left him little time for legislative and committee work. His amendments sometimes killed progressive legislation by costing it the votes of southerners and conservatives. In 1960 he was sued for slander by a woman in Harlem whom he had accused of collecting racketeering payoffs for the police; he ignored the suit and claimed congressional immunity. Convicted in 1966 of contempt of court for refusing to answer a subpoena, he responded by remaining outside of New York City except on Sundays, when legal papers could not be served. In the following year Congress voted to deny him his seat on the grounds that he had misused campaign funds. Asserting that he was the victim of a "Northern-style lynching," he sought reelection to his seat in the special election that followed, won by a huge margin, but declined to take his seat. In 1968 he won the seat again in a regular election, but Congress denied him seniority and committee assignments. The U.S. Supreme Court ruled in 1969 that Powell's exclusion in 1967 had been unconstitutional. In the following year Powell was defeated in the Democratic primary by Charles B. Rangel, and he retired to Bimini.

Charles V. Hamilton: *Adam Clayton Powell: The Political Biography of an American Dilemma* (New York: Atheneum, 1992)

Wil Haywood: *King of Cats: The Life and Times of Adam Clayton Powell, Jr.* (Boston: Houghton Mifflin, 1993)

Greg Robinson

Powell, Adam Clayton, Sr. (*b* Franklin County, Va., 5 May 1865; *d* New York City, 12 June 1953). Minister, father of Adam Clayton Powell Jr. He graduated from Wayland Seminary in 1892, and briefly assumed the pastorate at Ebenezer Baptist Church in Philadelphia in 1893. In the same year he was named a minister by the Immanuel Baptist Church in New Haven, Connecticut, and in 1895–96 he attended Yale Divinity School as a special student. He moved in 1908 to the Abyssinian Baptist Church in New York City, then on West 40th Street. A dynamic, powerful figure, he attempted repeatedly to persuade the congregation to move to the developing black neighborhood of Harlem. For this purpose he raised a large sum of money, and in 1920 the congregation bought land on West 138th Street where a new church was completed in June 1923 at a cost of some $350,000. He also built an old-age home on St. Nicholas Avenue, which was named in his honor. During the 1930s Abyssinian Baptist Church became the largest Baptist church in the United States, and he became widely known and much sought after as a speaker. A political moderate, he was influential in the Republican Party. After retiring as a pastor in favor of his son in 1938 he wrote several books, including *Riots and Ruins* (1945), a discussion of race riots; *Upon this Rock* (1949), a history of the Abyssinian Church; and an autobiography, *Against the Tide* (1938).

Greg Robinson

Powell, Bud [Earl] (*b* New York City, 27 Sept 1924; *d* New York City, 1 Aug 1966). Pianist. After leaving high school to work as a pianist in Coney Island, Greenwich Village, and Harlem he lived on St. Nicholas Avenue between 140th and 141st streets and soon was taking part in jam sessions at Minton's Playhouse (West 118th Street). He toured and recorded in the big band of the trumpeter Cootie Williams (1942–44) and then worked with swing and bop musicians on 52nd Street. Continuing psychological troubles were worsened by a head injury in 1945, and he spent extended periods in mental institutions. Nonetheless he played regularly into the 1950s, and he became the foremost piano soloist in bop owing to an unparalleled ability to transfer to the keyboard the improvisational style of the alto saxophonist Charlie Parker. Powell lived in Paris from 1959 to 1964 and then spent the rest of his life in New York City.

Marc Ferris, Barry Kernfeld

Powell, Colin L(uther) (*b* New York City, April 1937). Military leader. The son of Jamaican immigrants, he grew up on Kelly Street in Longwood and in 1954 graduated from Morris High School. In 1958 he earned a BS from City College of New York and enlisted in the army; he later fought in Vietnam, where he won many citations. A White House Fellow in the early 1970s, he worked in the Pentagon by the late 1970s and quickly became the highest-ranking black member of the military. He was named national security advisor in 1987 by President Ronald Reagan; in 1989 he became a four-star general and the first black chairman of the Joint Chiefs of Staff. Powell was instrumental in conducting the Gulf War in 1991.

James Bradley

Powell, Samuel S. (*b* New York City, 16 Feb 1815; *d* 6 Feb 1879). Mayor of Brooklyn. Born to a family from Long Island, he moved to Brooklyn at thirteen and enjoyed a successful career in business: he was a director of insurance companies, of a utility, and of a bank. He was elected mayor as a Democrat and served from 1857 to 1861 and from 1872 to 1873; the total length of his tenure, six years and four months, was one of the longest of any mayor of Brooklyn.

Ellen Fletcher

Power Memorial Academy. Catholic high school for boys, opened in 1931 and run by the Congregation of Christian Brothers. It was named for James Power, the pastor of All Saints Church in Harlem who introduced the order to the United States in 1906. Originally at 15–19 West 124th Street, the school moved in 1938 to a former hospital building ten stories tall at Amsterdam Avenue and West 61st Street. The school was known for its consistently strong athletic teams until it ceased operations in 1984. One of its best-known alumni was the basketball player Lew Alcindor (class of 1965), who later took the name Kareem Abdul-Jabbar.

Gilbert Tauber

Prall's Island. Uninhabited island in the Arthur Kill off the western shore of Staten Island. It is named for a family that grew hay there in the nineteenth century. The parks department maintains the island as a bird sanctuary.

Spencer Smith: "The Harbor Islands," *South Street Reporter* 10, no. 2 (summer 1976)
Francis J. Duffy and William H. Miller: *The New York Harbor Book* (Falmouth, Maine: TBW, 1986)
Louise Tanner: "Islands of New York Harbor," *Seaport* 19, no. 4 (winter 1986)

Ellen Fletcher

Pratt, Charles (*b* Watertown, Mass., 2 Oct 1830; *d* New York City, 4 May 1891). Businessman and philanthropist. As a young man he worked as a salesman in a number of mercantile establishments in Watertown and New York City, to which he moved in 1851. He formed a partnership with Henry Huttleston Rogers, and the two entered the oil business in 1867 as the firm of Charles Pratt and Company. Their refinery at Green Point, Long Island, producing fifteen hundred barrels a day, quickly established its product, Pratt's Astral Oil, as among the best on the market. In 1874 John D. Rockefeller bought the company, not only because of the good reputation of its product but to obtain the talents of the two owners, who proved to be outstanding executives with Standard Oil. Pratt's concern with the education of young people, especially their engineering training, often took him to western European nations to study their secondary technical training systems. After several years of such study he founded the Pratt Institute, which opened on 12 October 1887, and of which he served as president until his death. He also founded the Pratt Institute Free Public Library at a time when no such institution existed in Brooklyn or Manhattan, and in 1888 he organized the Thrift, one of the first savings and loan institutions. As a leader of Standard Oil Pratt promoted increased efficiency and product marketing throughout the corporation, and he was known for his attention to detail.

Paul H. Giddens: *The Birth of the Oil Industry* (New York: Macmillan, 1938)
Allan Nevins: *John D. Rockefeller: The Heroic Age of American Enterprise* (New York: Charles Scribner's Sons, 1940)
Ralph W. Hidy and Muriel E. Hidy: *History of Standard Oil Company (New Jersey)*, vol. 1, *Pioneering in Big Business, 1882–1911* (New York: McGraw–Hill, 1955)

Bennett H. Wall

Pratt [née Baker], **Ruth (Sears)** (*b* Ware, Mass., 24 Aug 1877; *d* Glen Cove, N.Y., 23 Aug 1965). Congresswoman. The daughter of a cotton manufacturer in Massachusetts, she married John Pratt (1903), son of Charles Pratt of the Standard Oil Company. She became an active Republican and refused several entreaties from the party to become a candidate for office before agreeing to seek a seat on the Board of Aldermen, to which she became the first woman elected in 1925. As an avowed reformer and a vigorous opponent of Tammany Hall she received much attention from the press, particularly when her analysis of the municipal budget revealed that the city could save $50 million a year by cutting back on inflated salaries, "no-show" jobs, and nonessential automobiles. A cartoon in the *New Yorker* depicted her in an arena, whip in hand, taming a tiger representing Tammany Hall. In 1928 she became the first woman elected to the U.S. Congress from New York State, representing the city's seventeenth district (then known as the Silk Stocking District). She was reelected in 1930 over stiff opposition, but then lost her seat in the Democratic landslide of 1932.

Susan J. Tolchin: *Women in Congress, 1917–1976* (Washington: U.S. House of Representatives, 1976)

Marjory Potts

Pratt Institute. Private college in Brooklyn, opened in 1887 by the oil baron Charles Pratt to provide training in practical vocations. From the outset it was coeducational and admitted students of all races. The institute began with twelve students and one drawing class and soon had several thousand students; it offered courses in mechanical and applied arts, domestic arts and sciences, library training, and kindergarten training. The institute had the first public library in Brooklyn and the first manual training high school in New York City. Many of its programs were among the first of their kind in the United States, and they inspired similar programs at such schools as the Drexel Institute and the Carnegie Institute of Technology. In the early 1990s Pratt had about 3700 students and four hundred faculty members and granted degrees at its schools of art and design, architecture, information and library science, liberal arts and sciences, and professional studies.

Margaret Latimer: "Field of Influence: A Centennial History of Pratt Institute" (1988) [unpubd, Pratt Institute]

Margaret Latimer

"preppy murder." A notorious crime that occurred on the morning of 26 August 1986, when Jennifer Dawn Levin, the eighteen-year-old daughter of a wealthy family, was strangled to death during a sexual encounter in Central Park near the Metropolitan Museum of Art. The assailant was Robert E. Chambers, a nineteen-year-old man she had met several hours earlier at Dorian's Red Hand, a bar on East 84th Street. The case attracted widespread notice because of the youth and privileged background of both Chambers and Levin. Chambers pleaded guilty to manslaughter but was sentenced to five to fifteen years in prison for two counts of second-degree murder.

Melissa M. Merritt

Presbyterian Hospital. Charitable hospital opened in 1872 by James Lenox (1800–80) and other philanthropists to serve "the poor of New York without regard to race, creed, or color." Situated between 70th and 71st streets and Madison and 4th (Park) avenues on land donated by Lenox, it opened with thirty-two available ward beds and several private rooms. Expansion began with an outpatient dispensary (1888), two ward buildings that increased capacity to two hundred beds (1892), a school of nursing (1892), and a surgical pavilion (1893). By 1908 the medical board recommended construction of a new hospital on a larger plot of land, and in 1910 a member of the board of managers, Edward S. Harkness (1874–1940), proposed an affiliation with the

College of Physicians and Surgeons of Columbia University. In 1922 Harkness and his mother, Mrs. Stephen Harkness, donated a site occupying twenty-two acres (nine hectares) in Washington Heights between 165th and 168th streets and between Broadway and Fort Washington Avenue, along with funds for construction. During construction it was decided that a new state psychiatric institute and hospital would be associated with the medical center and built in Washington Heights (1924), and affiliation agreements were signed with the Sloane Hospital for Women, the Vanderbilt Clinic, Babies Hospital, and the Neurological Institute (1925). When the COLUMBIA–PRESBYTERIAN MEDICAL CENTER was completed in 1928 Presbyterian moved to a 694-bed facility that included Harkness Pavilion (150 private rooms) and the Squier Urological Clinic.

Albert R. Lamb: *The Presbyterian Hospital and the Columbia–Presbyterian Medical Center, 1868–1943: A History of a Great Medical Adventure* (New York: Columbia University Press, 1955)

Jane E. Mottus

Madison Avenue Presbyterian Church (designed by James E. Ware), ca *1904*

Presbyterians. Organized Presbyterianism in New York City began with the founding in Queens of First Presbyterian Church, Newtown (1652), and of First Presbyterian Church, Jamaica (1662). During the early eighteenth century the Anglican colonial governors Benjamin Fletcher and Lord Cornbury sought to suppress Presbyterians, who were classed as "dissenters," by forcing Newtown and other Presbyterian congregations to accept Anglican pastors. When services were led in a private home on 20 January 1707 by Francis Makemie, the father of American Presbyterianism and moderator of the first American presbytery (at Philadelphia in 1706), Cornbury arrested him for preaching without a license. Jailed for three months before trial, Makemie defended himself under the English Toleration Act (1689) and was acquitted, although forced to pay all costs of the trial, the unpopularity of which contributed to Cornbury's removal (1708). The First Presbyterian Church, Manhattan, formed in 1716, began holding services at its site on Wall Street in 1719; a Presbyterian church in Staten Island was formed in 1717 (destroyed during the American Revolution and rebuilt in 1856).

Presbyterian laymen were active in the political, economic, and intellectual life of New York City during the revolutionary period. Leaders in the war such as William and Philip Livingston, William Smith Jr., John Morin Scott, and Alexander McDougall were members of First Presbyterian in Manhattan, which became known as the "church of the patriots." The revolutionary activities of John Rodgers, pastor of First Presbyterian in 1765–1811, caused him to flee the city during the British occupation. Rodgers was later a vice-chancellor of the New York Board of Regents (1784), president of the Society for the Relief of Distressed Debtors (1787), and moderator of the first Presbyterian General Assembly (1789). He and others in the General Assembly took steps to educate the clergy and laity during the late eighteenth century. To make a "priesthood of all believers" the church leadership opened the James Robertson School (1788), the first school for blacks (1787), the first Sunday schools in Manhattan (1793, run by a black woman at Scotch Presbyterian Church), and in Brooklyn (1824), the Free School Society (1805), the New York Sunday School Union (1816), and the first free school for infants (1827, at the Canal Street Presbyterian Church).

In 1836 Samuel Miller's report to the General Assembly on slavery and the church contributed to a denominational schism. On one side was the New School, which dominated Union Theological Seminary; it opposed slavery, was receptive to revivalism, advocated a union with Congregationalism under a plan put forth in 1801, and supported such ecumenical organizations as the American Board of Commissioners for Foreign Missions, the American Tract Society, and the American Sabbath School Union. The Old School disapproved of revivalism, supported missionary work and the expansion of frontier churches, and was not openly opposed to slavery; it was centered at Princeton Theological Seminary and a number of congregations in New York City were aligned with it, among them Brick Presbyterian Church, Fifth Avenue Presbyterian Church, and First Presbyterian Church, Manhattan. New School churches such as Spring Street Presbyterian Church (Manhattan), Laight Street Presbyterian Church (Manhattan), and First Presbyterian Church, Brooklyn, were threatened by mob violence because of their opposition to slavery. Unity within the Old School was maintained until 1861, when a resolution in support of the Union by Gardner Spring, the pastor of Brick Presbyterian, split the Old School General Assembly and created the Southern Presbyterian Church. In 1869 the faction that supported the Union sought reconciliation with the New School during a joint communion service of the General Assemblies led by Spring at the Brick and Covenant churches.

The period after the Civil War saw renewed Presbyterian leadership in social, missionary, and political causes. Among the institutions formed were Presbyterian Hospital (1868, now Columbia–Presbyterian Medical Center), by James Lenox, elder of First Presbyterian Church, Manhattan; the Presbyterian Home for Aged Women (1866), forerunner of the James Lenox House (49 East 73rd Street), by the Lenox family; and the Riverdale Neighborhood House (1872), by the Dodge family. In 1884 Horace Underwood was commissioned as the first Presbyterian missionary to Korea by the Lafayette Avenue Presbyterian Church, and in the 1890s Charles H. Parkhurst of the Madison Square Presbyterian Church became a champion of municipal reform. The Presbyterian national headquarters opened at 156 5th Avenue in Manhattan on 1 May 1895. The Social Gospel movement, enunciated by Henry Sloane Coffin and others, took root in the Labor Temple, led by Charles Stelzle and formally organized as the American International Church in 1915. Presbyterians were also embroiled in two major controversies over theology when Charles A. Briggs of Union Theological Seminary (1893) and Harry Emerson Fosdick, pastor at First Presbyterian Church, Manhattan (1923), were brought to trial before the General Assembly. The church saw remarkable growth during these years despite increasing divisions: the Church Extension Committee of the Presbytery and the Presbyterian Progress Foundation provided buildings for Featherbed Lane Presbyterian Church (1919), Eastchester Presbyterian Church (1930) in the Bronx, Fort George Presbyterian Church (1918), and Rendall Memorial Presbyterian Church (1927), and transferred declining congregations to congregations in other neighborhoods. The activity of William Adams of the national Board of Home Missions drew many other Presbyterian agencies to the city in the mid 1950s.

More than thirty moderators of the General Assembly have been residents of New York City, including Rodgers (1789), Miller (1806), Coffin (1943), Edler Hawkins (1964, the first black moderator), Thelma Adair (1976, the first black female moderator), and Robert Davidson (1981). Among those who have contributed to the rich musical heritage of the church are Clarence Dickinson of Brick Church, founder of the American Guild of Organists and editor of the *Presbyterian Hymnal* published in 1933, and John Weaver, organist at Madison Avenue Presbyterian Church and a major contributor to the *Hymnal* published in 1990. In 1983 the Presbyterian Church (United States) reunited with the United Presbyterian Church (United States of America) to end the division that began during the Civil War, and the reunited Presbyterian Church (United States of America) moved the denominational headquarters to Louisville, Kentucky. During this period the church reaffirmed its commitment to including members of minority groups in its congregations. Of the 113 Presbyterian churches in New York City during the early 1990s two were Chinese, thirteen Korean, fifteen Latin American, and twenty-seven black. Although Presbyterian congregations nationwide were still overwhelmingly white in 1990, about 52 percent of the 21,974 Presbyterians in New York City were nonwhite.

Theodore Fiske Savage: *The Presbyterian Church in New York City* (New York: Presbytery of New York, 1949)

Robert Hastings Nichols: *Presbyterianism in New York State: A History of the Synod and Its Predecessors* (Philadelphia: Westminster, 1963)

Dorothy Ganfield Fowler: *A City Church: The First Presbyterian Church in the City of New York, 1716–1976* (New York: First Presbyterian Church in the City of New York, 1981)

David E. Meerse

presidents. A number of presidents of the United States have had associations with New York City. The first Executive Mansion, at 3 Cherry Street in Manhattan, was the home of President Washington from April 1789 to February 1790. While serving as his vice president John Adams lived in the Mortier House (also known as Richmond Hill) at what is now Charlton Street in Greenwich Village, and when he became president himself he moved to the Vincent–Halsey House in Eastchester (now in the Bronx) for two months in 1797 to avoid a yellow fever epidemic in Philadelphia. As Washington's secretary of state, Thomas Jefferson lived briefly at 57 Maiden Lane in 1790. James Monroe retired to his son-in-law Samuel Gouverneur's home, a small, Dutch-roofed house at Lafayette and Prince streets where he remained for the rest of his life. While campaigning for the presidency in 1860 Abraham Lincoln delivered one of the most important speeches of his career at the Great Hall of Cooper Union; after his assassination his funeral cortège passed through the city, and his body lay in state at City Hall. From 1881 to 1885 Ulysses S. Grant lived in a brownstone at East 66th Street where he wrote his memoirs and made several disastrous investments; he is the only president buried in the city. Chester A. Arthur built his career in the city, where he first worked as a civil rights lawyer and eventually oversaw the New York Customs House; after his term as president he lived out his life in the city. Between his two presidential terms Grover Cleveland lived on Madison Avenue and 68th Street and worked for a prominent law firm on Wall Street. Born on East 20th Street near Gramercy Park, Theodore Roosevelt spent his childhood in the city and was active in city politics as a state assemblyman, police commissioner, and mayoral candidate. Calvin Coolidge was never a resident of the city, but after his presidency he became a director of the New York Life Insurance Company and often stayed in a reserved suite in the Vanderbilt Hotel. After his presidency Herbert Hoover lived in a suite in the Waldorf Towers on East 50th Street from 1934. Franklin D. Roosevelt began his career in the city, where he lived from 1905 until he was inaugurated in 1933, entering politics as a lawyer and later becoming a state legislator and governor of New York State. As the president of Columbia University, Dwight D. Eisenhower lived at 60 Morningside Drive from 1948 until he became a presidential candidate in 1952. John F. Kennedy lived in Riverdale as a boy, from 1926 to 1929. During his brief retirement from politics Richard M. Nixon moved to the city in 1963 to join the law firm of Mudge, Rose, Guthrie and Alexander, and he lived in the city again from 1980 to 1981. George Bush lived in the Waldorf Towers from 1970 to 1972 while he was the American ambassador to the United Nations.

James Bradley

Press Club. See New York Press Club.

Prial, Frank J. (*b* 11 Aug 1875; *d* Brooklyn, 24 Feb 1948). Labor leader. A deputy city comptroller from 1918 to 1933, he formed and led the Civil Service Forum and also published and edited the *Chief*, a civil service newspaper. He was the most influential spokesman of city workers in the years before municipal unionism. He opposed collective bargaining, preferring instead to achieve his goals through politics and personal connections. A well-known figure in the Democratic Party, he ran unsuccessfully in several elections. Prial's influence diminished after the election of Fiorello H. La Guardia as mayor, especially during the late 1930s as civil service unions grew.

Joshua B. Freeman

Price, Bruce (*b* Cumberland, Md., 12 Dec 1845; *d* Paris, 29 May 1903). Architect. He studied architecture with the firm of Niernsee and Neilson in Baltimore, where he began his career before moving to New York City in 1877. His major contribution in the city was his exploration of the design of "tower" skyscrapers, set forth in a series of projects that treated the building as a tripartite column. These included the Sun Building (1890, unexecuted), the American Surety Building at 100 Broadway (1894–96), the St. James Building at 1133 Broadway (1896), the International Bank Building at Broadway and Cedar (1899, demolished), and the Bank of the Metropolis at Union Square West (1902–3). Price's skill in designing urban residences is displayed in the King Model Houses, built in two rows on West 138th and 139th streets (1891, with Clarence S. Luce) and now known as Strivers' Row.

Lamia Doumato: *Bruce Price, 1845–1903* (Monticello, Ill.: Vance, 1984) [bibliography]

Marjorie Pearson

Price, (Mary) Leontyne (*b* Laurel, Miss., 10 Feb 1927). Singer. The daughter of a sawmill worker and a midwife, she graduated from Central State College in Wilberforce, Ohio, and embarked on a career as a classical soprano. She studied for four years at the Juilliard School of Music in New York City, where she was coached by Florence Page Kimball, and sang the part of Alice in Verdi's *Falstaff*. Her début in the city in Virgil Thomson's *Four Saints in Three Acts* (April 1952) attracted the attention of Ira Gershwin; he chose her to sing the role of Bess in his revival of his brother's opera *Porgy and Bess*, which played in the city from 1952 to 1954 before touring the rest of the country and western Europe. Known for her soaring phrasing and subtle inflections, she was chosen for the title role in a production of Puccini's *Tosca* broadcast on television in 1955. Although some American opera houses were hesitant to engage her because she was black, in Europe she was welcomed and cast in the lead role of Verdi's *Aïda*, to which her vocal sheen, stamina, and phrasing were well suited. She later earned tremendous acclaim singing the role in Vienna (1959), at Covent Garden (1959), and at La Scala (1960). In January 1961 she was given a forty-five-minute ovation after her début at the Metropolitan Opera as Leonora in Verdi's *Il Trovatore*, opposite the tenor Franco Corelli. During the following decades she spent most of her career at the Metropolitan Opera and lived in New York

Leontyne Price in Verdi's La forza del destino

City. She sang leading roles in operas by Mozart, Puccini, Massenet, and Tchaikovsky but was most admired for her performances of Verdi's music. She made successful recordings as Aïda, Tosca, Carmen, and Verdi's Leonoras.

S. D. R. Cashman

Price Waterhouse. Accounting firm, begun as a British entity that opened a branch office in New York City in 1890 to investigate and audit American companies for British investors. The firm became an independent American partnership by the turn of the century and began working for several of the nation's largest corporations, including U.S. Steel in 1902. During the 1920s the firm evolved into a distinctly American entity. By the following decade it had become the most highly respected accounting firm in the United States because of its many successful clients and the reputation of its senior partner, George O. May, the foremost accounting theorist of his time. In the mid 1990s Price Waterhouse was one of the six largest accounting firms in the United States. It maintained its chief administrative offices in New York City and had more than a hundred offices and nine hundred partners worldwide.

David Grayson Allen and Kathleen McDermott: *Accounting for Success: A History of Price Waterhouse in America, 1890–1990* (Boston: Harvard Business School Press, 1990)

Kathleen McDermott

Primerica Corporation. The name used from 1987 by the financial services firm that had originated as the packing company American Can. The firm used the name until 1993, when it became the TRAVELERS.

Janet Frankston

Prince, Hal [Harold Smith] (*b* New York City, 30 Jan 1928). Producer. After attending the University of Pennsylvania (AB 1948) he collaborated with Frederick Brisson and Robert E. Griffith on productions of *The Pajama Game* (1954), *Damn Yankees* (1955), and *New Girl in Town* (1957). He also produced works by Jerry Bock and Sheldon Harnick (*Fiorello!*, 1959, with Griffith; and *Fiddler on the Roof*, 1964) and became an especially frequent collaborator of Stephen Sondheim (*A Funny Thing Happened on the Way to the Forum*, 1962; *Company*, 1970; *Sweeney Todd*, 1979). By the mid 1990s Prince had won sixteen Tony awards. He wrote an autobiography, *Contradictions* (1974).

Prince's Bay. Neighborhood in southwestern Staten Island, bounded to the north by Amboy Road and to the south by Raritan Bay. The area is probably named for an English prince who anchored his ship there during the American Revolution. From the earliest times fishing was an important activity, particularly the harvest of clams and oysters that were considered the best in the metropolitan area. A plant for processing palm oil and making candles was built at Seguine Point in 1846. The Johnson Brothers Supply Company was formed after the Civil War and in 1888 was taken over by S. S. White Dental Works, which became the world's largest manufacturer of dental equipment. In the 1860s the Staten Island Railroad built a line through the area with a station on Seguine Avenue near Amboy Road. A small business district took form around the station. After 1900 state officials banned all fishing in the bay because of pollution. The buildings of the dental works were demolished in the 1970s after the firm moved to New Jersey, and a luxury townhouse complex was planned for the site. Elegant houses were built inland and on the waterfront in the 1980s. Richmond Memorial Hospital (1919) became part of Staten Island Hospital in 1988 (later Staten Island University Hospital).

Many older one-family houses remain near the railroad station. The neighborhood has several recreational facilities: Wolfe's Pond Park, extending from the shore to Hylan Boulevard, Lemon Creek, which has berths for four hundred pleasure boats (being redeveloped in the early 1990s), and the Seguine Mansion at Lemon Creek, built in the Greek Revival style and designated a landmark by the city. Nearby stands Manee–Purdy House, built in the eighteenth century and also a landmark.

Marjorie Johnson

Princeton Club. A club incorporated in 1899 as an outgrowth of a local alumni association. It occupied the former home of Stanford White in Gramercy Park for ten years before moving to the corner of Park Avenue and 39th Street, where it remained for forty years. During the First World War, when many members were serving overseas, the club shared facilities and membership with the Yale Club. By 1955 there were about four thousand members and the old facilities were crowded. A new building at 15 West 43rd Street opened in 1963; its facilities include dining rooms, library and reading rooms, squash courts and other sporting facilities, and sleeping accommodations. The club has associate members who belonged to defunct sister clubs, such as that of Columbia University.

James E. Mooney

printing. The first printing press on Manhattan Island was set up in 1693 by William Bradford (1663–1752), who had earlier trained in London and introduced printing in Pennsylvania. He began his operation in a shop near what is now 81 Pearl Street, and soon printed pamphlets concerning a trial that he faced in Philadelphia (for printing material critical of the Quaker faith). Bradford held the position of royal printer until 1742, and in the course of nearly fifty years was responsible for printing the first legislative proceedings in America (1694), the first paper money in New York City (1709), the first American edition of the *Book of Common Prayer* (1710), the first edition of an American play (Governor Robert Hunter's *Androboros*, 1714), the first newspaper in New York City (the *Gazette*, 1725–44), and the first map of the city (by James Lyne, 1731). Bradford's former apprentice John Peter Zenger, who served for a short period as the public printer in Maryland, returned to New York City in 1725 and opened a printing shop. Opponents of Governor William Cosby, who despised Bradford's newspaper for representing the government, asked Zenger to launch another paper in 1733. Zenger's *Weekly Journal* appeared on 5 November 1733, edited by James Alexander, a leader of the opposition. Its insistent attacks on Cosby's administration led after a year to Zenger's imprisonment for seditious libel, and to a trial (4 August 1735) at which the renowned Andrew Hamilton of Philadelphia secured Zenger's acquittal. News of the trial spread quickly; Alexander's *A Brief Narrative* (1736), in which it was described, was widely reprinted in America and abroad and required some twenty editions before 1800. Although Zenger's trial had no force as legal precedent, it became a highly popular symbol of the struggle for free speech in America.

Another former apprentice of Bradford, James Parker (1714–70), established the third printing office in New York City in 1742 and the third newspaper, the *Weekly Post-Boy*, in 1743. After Bradford's retirement in 1744 and Zenger's death in 1746 a new generation took over the printing trade in New York City. Under Bradford's successor Henry DeForeest (*b* 1712; *d ca* 1766), the first American-born printer in the city, the *Gazette* became the *Eve-*

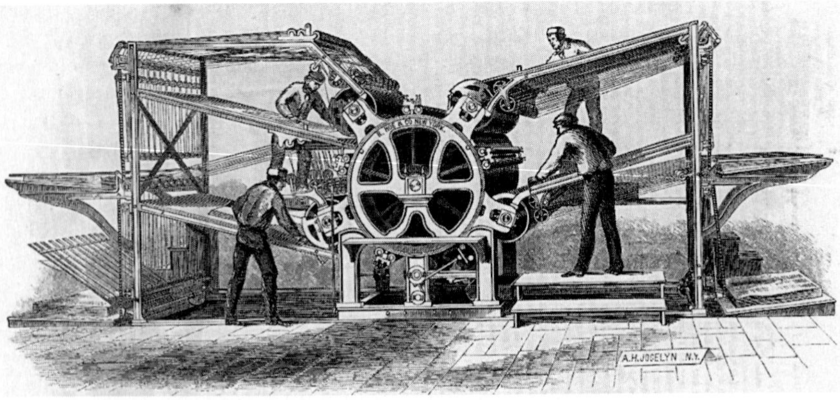

Hoe Rotary Press, from Harper's New Monthly Magazine, *1865*

ning Post (1744–53). Parker printed a number of substantial books in the 1740s, including Richardson's *Pamela* (the earliest "best seller" in New York City), entered into a partnership with William Weyman (1753), and opened printing offices in New Jersey and Connecticut. His firm produced the earliest magazine in New York City, the *Independent Reflector* (1752–53), noted for publishing the essays of William Livingston. In 1760 Weyman left Parker's firm, and John Holt (1721–84), who worked for the firm in New Haven, Connecticut, moved to New York City to edit Parker's newspaper (now called *New-York Gazette and Weekly Post-Boy*). Holt became one of the most active supporters among printers of the revolutionary cause, serving as a printer to the province and continuing his own newspaper (the *New-York Journal*, launched 1766) outside the city during British occupation.

In 1776 the prolific printer Hugh Gaine left the city (as did many other printers); he supported the revolution from Newark, New Jersey, where he published his own newspaper, begun as the *Mercury* in 1752. To the shock of many patriots he returned to New York City seven weeks later and transformed his newspaper into an outlet for Loyalist sentiment. His equivocation prevented him from being named the royal printer during the war; in 1777 the position went instead to James Rivington (1724–1802), a bookseller specializing in books from England who also published the *Gazetteer* (from 1773), a widely circulated newspaper that he later renamed the *Loyal Gazette* and then the *Royal Gazette*. The most prominent Loyalist printers in New York City during the war were the brothers James Robertson (*b* 1740; *d ca* 1810) and Alexander Robertson (1742–84), who opened a shop and published two newspapers, the *Chronicle* (1769) and the *Royal American Gazette*; leading patriots included John Anderson (*d* 1798), who printed an edition of Paine's *Common Sense* (1776), and Samuel Loudon (*b ca* 1727; *d ca* 1813), who created a furor by printing a reply to Paine—both of whom were forced to leave the city in 1776.

The typical printing shop of the colonial and revolutionary periods had one or two presses and four or five fonts of type, and employed two journeymen besides family members and apprentices. It printed forms, almanacs, primers, literary and political writings, and (if it was an official printer) government documents. From 1693 to 1783 there were about 2500 known items printed in New York City (excluding forms and newspapers); about two dozen printers' names appear on these items, but nearly half the total was produced by the two largest printers and 90 percent by the seven largest (in decreasing order of output: Bradford, Gaine, Parker, Holt, Weyman, Rivington, Zenger). Most materials produced during the period are typographically undistinguished, but the number of significant books produced is impressive.

The printing trade was profoundly transformed by technological innovations made in New York City after the revolution. In 1790 Adam Mappa introduced typefounding and in 1795 Alexander Anderson popularized boxwood engraving, a process used to produce woodcut illustrations. By 1800 there were about fifteen printing offices in the city, together employing seventy or eighty journeymen printers. Knowledge of the art of stereotyping was imported in 1813 from England by the printer David Bruce, who made molds of composed type and engravings for cast printing plates. David and George Bruce shifted from the printing business to typefounding about 1814, and by 1820 there were nine foundries operating in the city. Although New York City had two hundred printers in 1820, its trade was subordinate in output and reputation to that of Boston and Philadelphia. R. Hoe and Company introduced an iron toggle-jointed hand press in 1822 and by the mid 1830s produced the Washington press, which became the standard iron hand press for the rest of the century; the company also made flatbed cylinder presses for newspaper work.

In 1820–40 the printing trade diversified into a number of branches, including newspaper, book, and commercial printing; at the same time bookbinding, typefounding, equipment manufacturing, and other auxiliary trades expanded. The city's reputation as a center of book and periodical printing was enhanced by the formation of several influential firms with national distribution: the Methodist Book Concern, the Tract Society, and Harper and Brothers. Faster production methods gave rise in the 1830s to the penny press, a term used to describe inexpensive daily newspapers that focused on commercial information and gossip. James Gordon Bennett Sr. and Horace Greeley were two of the city's most successful newspaper editors at the time. George Bruce Jr. in 1838 introduced his pivotal typecasting machine, a device that mechanized typefoundries and increased productivity by 600 percent. By 1847 Richard M. Hoe developed a large rotary, type-revolving press for metropolitan newspapers. A successful treadle-driven press invented by George P. Gordon in 1851 encouraged the production of job work and the proliferation of small shops. The presence of these aggressive entrepreneurs, industrial growth, and the commercial and financial influence of New York City made it the printing center of the United States by the 1850s, when there were more than one thousand printers in the city.

By the mid nineteenth century different sectors of the printing trade became concentrated in different parts of New York City. Newspaper companies clustered around Printing House Square at the intersection of Park Row and Nassau Street, and job shops spread from Park Row to the East River along John, Fulton, Ann, Beekman, and Spruce streets; their proximity reinforced competition and promoted the growth of unions. In 1852 journeymen printers formed New York Typographical Union no. 6, which became the longest-lasting printers' organization in the city. Master printers organized a short-lived employers' association, the Typothetae of the City of New York, in 1865. Dominated by entrepreneurial book and job printers such as Theodore Low De Vinne, the Typothetae opposed the growth of trade unionism. By the 1860s the city had fifty-one newspaper offices (employing about 2400), seventeen book publishers (employing more than 2100 production workers), and eighty-one job offices (employing 870). New York City also became the center of periodical publishing and printing, owing both to the large number of advertisers there and the presence of writers and skilled printers; the number of magazines quintupled to 3300 between 1865 and 1885.

A number of book publishers moved to the city in the late nineteenth century, including E. P. Dutton and Thomas Y. Crowell. Four independent foundries were consolidated in 1893: American Type Founders Company, J. Conners, D. and G. Bruce, and A. D. Farmer and Son. By the mid 1890s pressmen, electrotypers and stereotypers, and bookbinders who were members of New York Typographical Union no. 6 organized their own unions and then formed the Allied Printing Trades Council. After an acrimonious strike in 1906 a group of master printers led by Charles Francis formed the Printers' League. It joined forces with the Typothetae in 1916 to form the New York Employing Printers' Association, forerunner of the New York Employing Printers Association and the Association of the Graphics Arts (formerly the Printing Industries of Metropolitan New York). During the first half of the twentieth century nearly 20 percent of all workers in printing and publishing in the United States were employed in New York City. Increasingly publishers of magazines and books moved into offices in Manhattan but commissioned their printing to businesses in the surrounding counties, whereas newspaper and commercial printing remained centrally situated. In 1940 the federal census of manufactures found that New York City had more than 18,400 compositors and typesetters, 7700 other printing craftsmen, seven hundred electrotypers and stereotypers, 3600 photoengravers and lithographers, and 3400 pressmen and plate printers.

The printing industry in New York City underwent a major shift as periodical and newspaper publishers became less numerous and commercial printers more numerous. The number of daily newspapers decreased from forty-three in 1892 (when there were also 294 weekly newspapers) to seven in the 1950s and four in 1990. Book and periodical printing continued to move to surrounding counties, although publishing and administrative staff remained concentrated in Manhattan. More than four thousand firms engaged in printing and publishing in New York City in 1972 had together more than 110,000 employees, about half of them production workers, with a total annual payroll of nearly $1300 million; the industry contributed nearly $3200 million to the city's economy. Computerized printing and xerographic technology increased the amount of in-house printing done in large firms in the city in the 1970s. Commercial printers served legal and financial firms near City Hall, retail stores near 8th Avenue and 34th Street, and advertising firms east of Madison Avenue above 42nd Street (see FINANCIAL PRINTING). By 1988 New York City had fewer than three thousand printing and publishing firms, including seventeen hundred commercial printers and companies specializing in business forms, greeting cards, and bookbinding. Of these, twelve hundred establishments were in Manhattan.

Charles R. Hildeburn: *Sketches of Printers and Printing in Colonial New York* (New York: Dodd, Mead, 1895)

Lawrence C. Wroth: *The Colonial Printer* (New York: Grolier Club, 1931; rev. Portland, Maine: Southworth–Anthoensen, 1937)

Douglas C. McMurtrie: *A History of Printing in the United States* (New York: R. R. Bowker, 1936)

Eric W. Gustafson: "Printing and Publishing," *Made in New York: Case Studies in Metropolitan Manufacturing*, ed. Max Hall (Cambridge: Harvard University Press, 1959)

G. Thomas Tanselle: *Guide to the Study of United States Imprints* (Cambridge: Harvard University Press, 1971)

Bernard Bailyn and John B. Hench, eds.: *The Press and the American Revolution* (Worcester, Mass.: American Antiquarian Society, 1980)

William S. Pretzer, G. Thomas Tanselle

printmaking. There were no printmakers of note in New York City before the American Revolution, when most art sold there consisted of reproductions issued by European presses. In the seventeenth century a number of Dutch artists made prints of Manhattan. A copper engraving by the Englishman William Burgis, "A South Prospect of the Flourishing City of New York" (1717), depicts the history of the port in four combined images printed from four plates. A few caricatures of political figures were also produced in the eighteenth century. During the first decades of the nineteenth century a group of artists made topographic albums of the city that were published as the collections of aquatints *Picturesque Views of American Scenery* (1819–21) and *The Hudson River Portfolio* (1821–25) and the collection of lithographs *Itinéraire pittoresque du fleuve Hudson* (1828–29).

The quality of topographic views made in the city improved through the work of several artists trained in England, including William James Bennett, Francis Guy, John Hill, William Guy Wall, and William Winstanley; their prints later inspired the artists of the Hudson River School. Alexander Anderson and Cornelius Tiebout were among the first engravers who resided in the city. Formal training in printmaking was first offered by the National Academy of Design (1826), which was modeled on the Royal Academy of Art in London and had a gallery devoted to exhibitions of prints. Members included such printmakers as Bennett, F. O. C. Darley, Alfred Jones, J. F. E. Prud'homme, and James Smillie. Etchings and lithographs lampooning President Andrew Jackson increased the popularity of political caricatures. The Apollo Association, formed in 1839 and later renamed the American Art-Union, awarded many commissions to engravers for reproductions of American paintings, which were distributed to the organization's subscribers, and print exhibitions held in its galleries became fashionable.

As the market for prints expanded during the nineteenth century, the number of printmakers increased and thousands of prints were issued by the firms of John Bachman, Lewis P. Clover, Charles Magnus, Ferdinand Mayer and Sons, H. R. Robinson, and Endicott. The most successful firm was that of Currier and Ives, which had its plant at Spruce and Nassau streets and remained in operation from 1857 to 1907. The firm was best known for more than seven thousand lithographs depicting scenes of daily life, many of them executed by such well-known artists as George Catlin, George Inness, Eastman Johnson, Louis Maurer, Fanny Palmer, Charles Parsons, and Arthur F. Tait. It was also the best-known publisher of political caricatures, many issued about the time of the Civil War, by popular artists such as Thomas Worth. The introduction of wood engraving, a process using the grain side of boxwood blocks, allowed illustrations to be printed on the steam-powered presses used to print periodicals and books. Scenes of city life appeared in such periodicals as the *Mirror*, *Family Magazine*, the *Picture Gallery*, *Godey's Lady's Book*, *International Monthly*, *National Magazine*, *United States Magazine*, *Frank Leslie's Illustrated Newspaper*, *Harper's Weekly*, and the *Illustrated News*. The largest illustrations required several blocks prepared by different engravers and screwed together for printing; among the illustrators who became widely known was Winslow Homer. In addition to wood engraving, intaglio and planographic techniques were used to make illustrations for books. During the 1850s Darley became extremely popular for his illustrations of works by Shakespeare, Dickens, Poe, Longfellow, Washington Irving, James Fenimore Cooper, and Joseph C. Neal. A growing number of illustrators were women, who were able to learn printmaking techniques in workshops and classes offered by large cultural institutions such as the National Academy of Design.

Etching became a popular technique in the city after mid century, when artists in France and England demonstrated its expressive possibilities in rendering landscapes. It was embraced by Thomas Moran, Mary Nimmo Moran, Robert Swain Gifford, Samuel Colman, and Stephen Parrish. Their prints were made on fine paper in small runs in print dealers' shops and soon became much sought after, leading in 1877 to the formation of the New York Etching Club, an exclusive organization that sponsored exhibitions until 1893. Many painters were influenced by the work of James McNeill Whistler, whose first exhibition of prints in the United States was held at the Wunderlich Gallery in the city in 1883. About this time political cartoons became popular nationwide in a number of periodicals issued in the city, among them *Yankee Doodle*, *Phunny Phellow*, *Vanity Fair*, the *Daily Graphic*, *Frank Leslie's Illustrated Newspaper*, the *New York Herald*, *Scribner's*, and especially *Puck*, which developed a format that later became the basis for the editorial page of the *New York Times*. The best-known cartoonist was Thomas Nast, who produced a biting series of cartoons about the Tweed Ring and the first cartoon of a fat, jovial, bearded Santa Claus.

During the 1890s posters became the most popular form of graphic art. Posters by French artists were exhibited in 1890 and 1893 at the Grolier Club. A poster by Edward Penfield advertising the April issue of *Harper's Monthly Magazine* in 1893 set a standard for a bold, simple style that was soon adopted by other American artists. Will H. Bradley, Elisha Brown Bird, Howard Chandler Christy, Arthur Wesley Dow, John Christian Leyendecker, Florence Lundorg, Maxfield Parrish, and John Louis Reed became well known for their posters, many of which were commissioned by publishers in the city. Posters reached the height of their popularity about 1895: nearly fifteen hundred were shown in an exhibition at the Fidelis Club in Manhattan in 1899. Several members of the exclusive Society of Illustrators including Christy, Leyendecker, Charles Dana Gibson, James Montgomery Flagg, and Jessie Willcox Smith used the grand style popular at the turn of the century for posters designed to encourage support for the entry of the United States into the First World War. By this time prints had been supplanted by photographs as a medium for illustrating newspapers and periodicals. Some artists such as Joseph Pennell expanded the scope of printmaking as an art form; other printmakers and art studios accepted commissions for advertising.

Many innovations in printmaking date from the Depression. Under the auspices of the Works Progress Administration workshops were organized between 1935 and 1941 to encourage experimentation with different techniques. More than 300,000 prints were made nationwide during those years, many of them by a workshop in the city that was the country's largest. American prints became noted for their original compositions, lush colors, and technical innovation, and New York City, known as a center for printmaking, attracted such prominent artists as John Sloan, Edward Hopper, John Marin, George Bellows, Martin Lewis, Louis Lozowick, and Reginald Marsh, and later Andy Warhol, Helen Frankenthaler, Robert Indiana, and Ellsworth Kelly. More workshops were formed; one of the most important was Atelier 17, opened in 1940 by the English printmaker Stanley William Hayter, which promoted new approaches to printmaking until it closed in 1955. A workshop called Universal Limited Art Editions, opened in 1957 by Tatyana Grosman, attracted major painters to printmaking, among them Larry Rivers, Robert Rauschenberg, and Jasper Johns, and became a model for later workshops.

Eighteenth-century views of the city are held by the Museum of the City of New York, the New-York Historical Society, the New York Public Library (in the Stokes and Eno collections), and the Metropolitan Museum of Art (in the Clarence J. Davies Collection). Several galleries specialize in prints, among them the Hirschl and Adler Galleries near Madison Avenue and the Susan Sheehan Gallery on 57th Street.

Frank Weitenkampf: *American Graphic Art* (New York: Henry Holt, 1912)

I. N. Phelps Stokes: *The Iconography of Manhattan Island, 1498–1909, Compiled from Original Sources and Illustrated by Photo Intaglio Reproductions of Important Maps, Plans, Views and Documents in Public and Private Collections* (New York: Robert H. Dodd, 1915–28; repr. Arno, 1967)

Maureen C. O'Brien and Patricia C. F. Mandel: *The American Painter–Etcher Movement* (Southampton, N.Y.: Parish Art Museum, 1984)

James Watrous: *American Printmaking: A Century of American Printmaking, 1880–1980* (Madison: University of Wisconsin Press, 1984)

Gloria Gilda Deák: *Picturing America, 1497–1899: Prints, Maps and Drawings Bearing on the New World Discoveries and on the Development of the Territory That Is Now the United States* (Princeton, N.J.: Princeton University Press, 1988)

Walton H. Rawls: *Wake Up, America!: World War I and the American Poster* (New York: Abbeville, 1988)

Gloria Deák

Priscilla. Steamboat designed by George Peirce and built in 1893 for $1.5 million. She measured 440 feet (134 meters) by fifty-two feet (sixteen meters), her sidewheels thirty-five feet (eleven meters) by fourteen feet (four meters). The ship had five boilers, a four-cylinder double-inclined compound engine, and 8500 horsepower. There were fifteen hundred berths and the ship could carry eight hundred tons of freight; the interior was designed in a Renaissance style by Frank Hill Smith. The *Priscilla* was operated by the Fall River Line from 1894 until 1937 and ran between Manhattan and Fall River, Massachusetts.

Arthur G. Adams

prison ships. Between 1776 and 1783 British ships that lay at anchor in New York Harbor caused more deaths than all the land and sea battles and campaigns in all the years of the American Revolution combined. The British chose to keep their prisoners in New York City because it was the one city under their control for virtually the entire war, it was easily accessible to the Royal Navy, and most American prisoners were already being held nearby. The largest number of captives were taken during the Battle of Long Island (26–31 August 1776), which was disastrous for the patriot cause. Other Americans fell into the hands of the British after the debacle of 16 November at Fort Washington. And the captive ranks continually swelled as British cruisers swept the seas of American vessels and brought the captured seamen back to the city. Because the city was short of habitable structures the British commandeered barns, sugar houses, churches, and even private residences as temporary stockades. These proved inadequate, especially after two great fires destroyed one third of the city in the autumn of 1776, and the British then set out to convert broken-down transports and warships into floating prisons. The first conversion was of the *Whitby*, which became a prison ship on 20 October 1776 and burned in the following year. She was followed by the *John*, *Glasgow*, *Preston*, *Good Intent*, *Good Hope*, *Prince of Wales*, *Grovnor*, *Falmouth*, *Stromboli*, *Lord Dunlace*, *Scorpion*, *Judith*, *Myrtle*, *Felicity*, *Chatham*, *Kitty*, *Frederick*, *Woodlands*, *Scheldt*, *Clyde*, *Hunter*, *Perseverance*, and *Bristol Packet*.

Usually anchored in and around Wallabout Bay, these vessels presented grim silhouettes with their rigging, spars, masts, and rudders removed, and with iron bars placed across their lower portholes. The most notorious ship was the *Jersey*, a seventy-four-gun veteran of wars with the French that was little more than a rotting hulk with a broken bowsprit and flagstaff when she became a prison ship late in 1776. She sat in the mud flats of the East River for seven years, and portions of her timbers could still be seen well into the nineteenth century.

The routine on the *Jersey* and other prison ships varied according to the whims of the captors. Sometimes the prisoners were kept below from sunrise to sunset. After dark, one or two captives at a time were occasionally allowed to stretch their legs on deck. Otherwise the only light they saw came from the openings along the hull, twenty inches (fifty centimeters) square. Fresh air was in short supply because of overcrowding, and contagious diseases were rampant, especially yellow fever, typhus, dysentery, and smallpox. The food was often simply the refuse from the English ships of war that also nested in the harbor.

Although the conditions aboard prison ships were not much worse than those in prisons on land or those endured by redcoats captured by the Continental forces, the prison ships inflicted suffering on an unprecedented scale. It is believed that eleven thousand American prisoners died aboard the rotting ships in New York Harbor, far more than the 6824 American troops killed in combat. The *Jersey* alone gave up six or eight corpses every day. Every morning a gang of prisoners known as the "working party" went from one ship to the next collecting bodies, which they then buried along the shore.

Forgotten even during their own time, the prisoners of the American Revolution have been all but obliterated from the historical record. Although in 1907 a Martyr's Monument was put up in Fort Greene to house their remains after a public subscription, the monument had deteriorated even before the Second World War, and by the mid 1990s it remained forgotten and forlorn at the center of Fort Greene Park.

Kenneth T. Jackson: "The Forgotten Saga of the Prison Ships," *Seaport Magazine* 24 (summer 1990), 25–28

For illustration see FORT GREENE.

Kenneth T. Jackson

private schools. For a discussion of private schools see INDEPENDENT SCHOOLS.

Procter and Gamble. Firm of household products manufacturers. Formed in Cincinnati in 1837, it opened an industrial plant at Port Ivory in 1907, which manufactured soaps, detergents, toilet goods, vegetable oil, and food and paper products. At its height in the 1920s the plant occupied 129 acres (fifty-two hectares) and employed fifteen hundred workers to manufacture soap bars, flakes, and granules (most under the brand name Ivory), vegetable shortening (Crisco), and related products for the northeastern United States. As the firm diversified during the following decades the factory also made synthetic detergents and cleansers (such as Tide), cooking oils, baking goods under the name Duncan Hines, and orange juice (Citrus Hill). Because of mounting costs the firm began phasing out selected operations in the mid 1980s, and it closed all of Port Ivory in 1991. Procter and Gamble was an innovator in developing close relations with advertising and communications firms in Manhattan; it was the first firm to use direct radio promotion (1923) and produce daytime serial "soap operas" on radio (1933) and television (1950). In the mid 1990s the firm owned and produced three major television soap operas in New York City.

Robert Davidson: *"Alive at 75": A Short History of the Port Ivory Plant of Procter & Gamble* (New York: Procter and Gamble, 1973)
Oscar Schisgall: *Eyes on Tomorrow: The Evolution of Procter and Gamble* (Chicago: J. G. Ferguson, 1981)
Charles L. Sachs: *Made on Staten Island: Agriculture, Industry, and Suburban Living in the City* (New York: Staten Island Historical Society, 1988)
Stephania Cleaton: "P&G to Close by February '92," *Staten Island Advance*, 13 July 1990

Charles L. Sachs

Produce Exchange. See NEW YORK PRODUCE EXCHANGE.

progressive education. The progressive education movement began in the decades following the Civil War as a reaction to the corrupt political control and rote instruction that characterized most public schools in the United States. Many of the goals and tenets of progressive education were conceived and implemented in experimental schools in New York City. The early focus of the movement on hands-on experience was inspired by a display of the Moscow Imperial Technical School at the Philadelphia Centennial Exposition of 1876, where Victor Della Vos exhibited tools, models, and drawings to stress the importance of manual training in instruction shops. Interest in manual training led to the opening of the New York Trades Schools by Richard T. Auchmuty in 1881, and of the Pratt Institute in Brooklyn and the Baron de Hirsch School in the 1890s. The drive to open new schools gained further momentum in 1892 when Joseph Mayer Rice of New York City wrote a series of muckracking articles about the conditions of public schools in the monthly publication the *Forum.*

In the 1880s progressive educators focused on improving the lives of the many rural Americans and immigrants pouring into New York City and other American cities. They formed settlements modeled on those of England, where university students in the 1880s assisted and lived with the poor. In 1886 the Lily Pleasure Club (later renamed the University Settlement) was opened at 146 Forsyth Street in Manhattan by Stanton Coit (*b* 11 Aug 1857; *d* 15 Feb 1944), followed by the New York College Settlement (1889), Everett Wheeler's East Side House (1891), Lillian Wald's Nurses' Settlement (1895, later renamed the Henry Street Settlement), the Hudson Guild (1895), and Greenwich House (1902). The settlements' kindergarten programs, health and nutrition classes, cultural activities, manual training, and clubs and courses for entire families led to reforms in schools throughout the city.

The growth of progressive education, the development of psychology as a discipline, and the influence of John Dewey gave rise to professional schools of education, notably Teachers College of Columbia University (1887) and the Bank Street College of Education, formed by Lucy Sprague Mitchell in 1916 as the Bureau of Educational Experiments. The graduates of these colleges founded and taught at such experimental schools in New York City as the Play School (1914), the Walden School (1915), the Lincoln School of Teachers College (1917), the Dalton School (1919), and the Little Red School House (1921). At these schools traditional, formalist methods were rejected in favor of programs stressing self-expression and learning by doing. The progressive movement waned in the 1950s, but many progressive schools continued to operate according to the principles on which they were founded.

Lawrence A. Cremin: *The Transformation of the School* (New York: Alfred A. Knopf, 1961)
Merle Curti: *The Social Ideas of American Educators* (Lanham, Md.: Littlefield, 1978)

Alfonso J. Orsini

Progressive Party. A political party formed in 1912 and best known for its role in the presidential election of the same year; it is often referred to as the Bull Moose Party. The party advocated far-reaching regulatory and social reforms, including the abolition of sweatshops; laws regulating employer liability, child labor, and wages and hours; public ownership of natural resources; a graduated income tax; the direct election of U.S. senators; woman suffrage; and old-age, health, and unemployment insurance. New York City played an important role in the history of the party. The national headquarters were on 42nd Street, and the party's presidential nominee, Theodore Roosevelt, often consulted with party leaders in Manhattan from his residence at Oyster Bay on Long Island. Leading social scientists and social reformers from the city were instrumental in writing the party's politi-

Star Naphtha soap assembly line at the Procter and Gamble factory in Port Ivory, Staten Island, 1919

cal platform. Frances Kellor, executive director of the party's Progressive Service (based in Manhattan), directed research, education, and legislative efforts. Samuel McCune Lindsay, professor of social legislation at Columbia University, and John B. Andrews, secretary of the American Association for Labor Legislation (also based in Manhattan), addressed delegates at the national convention and were notable contributors to the party's agenda. Other New Yorkers prominent in the party included Edward T. Devine, George W. Kirchwey, and E. R. A. Seligman, all professors at Columbia, and the social reformers Florence Kelley, Pauline Goldmark, Henry Moskowitz, and Homer Folks. The philosopher John Dewey was briefly a co-director of the party's Committee on Education. In addition Herbert Croly had a formative influence on Roosevelt through his book *The Promise of American Life* (1909).

The Progressive Party engaged in internecine battles with the Republican Party, from which it had broken, and had slight support from organized labor (Samuel Gompers and the American Federation of Labor endorsed Woodrow Wilson's candidacy). As a result the Progressives fared poorly in New York State and elsewhere, electing only one governor, two senators, sixteen representatives, and a few hundred local officials nationwide. Nevertheless the Progressive Party retains a central role in the rise of the modern welfare state and the history of party politics in the twentieth century.

John Recchiuti

Prohibition. The Eighteenth Amendment to the Constitution of the United States went into effect in 1920, making illegal the manufacture, sale, and transport of all alcoholic beverages. The sympathy toward the temperance movement of the national majority thus overrode an antipathy toward it in New York City that was personified by Fiorello H. La Guardia, who as a congressman excoriated the "noble experiment" of Prohibition as unenforceable, discriminatory toward immigrants and workers, and likely to breed contempt for the law. Prohibition did create new opportunities in the city for leaders of organized crime, who recognized the advantages of the harbor for the illegal importation of alcohol, known as rumrunning: their fleets ran liquor past the coast guard, their trucks transported it nationwide, and bootlegging replaced gambling as their main source of revenue. The city provided the country not only with much of its liquor but also with many of its organized-crime leaders, among them Johnny Torrio and Al Capone, who had criminal careers in Brooklyn before moving to Chicago, Charles "King" Solomon, who used his connections in the city to dominate the rackets in New England from his base in Boston, and the members of the Purple Gang of Detroit.

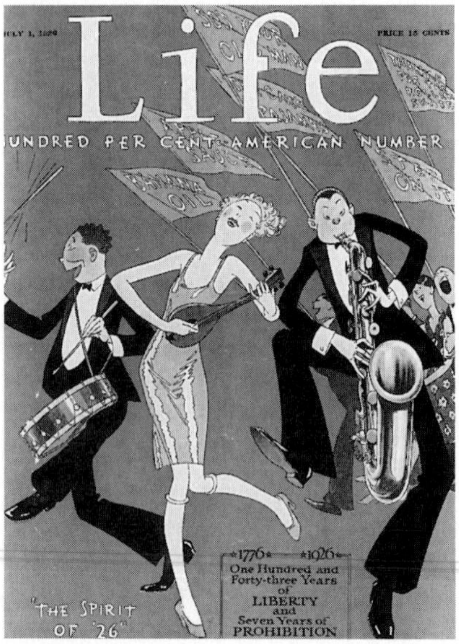

"One Hundred and Forty-three Years of Liberty and Seven Years of Prohibition," cover for Life, *1 July 1926*

In addition New York City was a leading source of demand for illegal alcohol, and with the onset of Prohibition speakeasies opened throughout the city, ranging from squalid to elegant. Police Commissioner Grover Whalen estimated that the city had 32,000 speakeasies, twice the number of the legal saloons in the city before Prohibition. Some speakeasies restricted their clientele to males, others encouraged the mingling of the sexes, and still others aimed at college students. The part of 52nd Street between 5th and 6th avenues was reputed to have the city's greatest concentration of speakeasies, which to the chagrin of the proper old families in the neighborhood took over many of the fine brownstone townhouses. The best-known speakeasy on the block and indeed in the city was Jack and Charlie's 21, favored by such literary figures as Robert Benchley, Dorothy Parker, and Alexander Woollcott: it was equipped with a chute so that if it were raided the evidence could be disposed of quickly. The owners of speakeasies had to pay off not only the precinct police captains but the leaders of organized crime, some of whom like Jack "Legs" Diamond made extortion a specialty. They also had to look out for operatives of the Prohibition Bureau, a federal strike force with fifteen hundred agents, of whom the best-known were two partners from the Lower East Side, Izzy Einstein and Moe Smith. Short, fat, and balding, they slipped into speakeasies by disguising themselves as milk-wagon drivers, streetcar conductors, visiting musicians, icemen, and once as gravediggers to raid a speakeasy across from Woodlawn Cemetery. Newspapers given to sensational coverage of crime found them colorful, and in time they staged their raids to accommodate newspaper deadlines. In 1925 the Prohibition Bureau was sufficiently embarrassed by their celebrity to discharge them "for the good of the service." By this time the local police had largely relinquished its role in enforcing Prohibition and left it to an increasingly ineffectual federal force.

It is unsurprising that the first presidential candidate to call for the repeal of Prohibition should have been Alfred E. Smith, a product of the immigrant Lower East Side and Tammany Hall. Although he lost the election of 1928 Prohibition had by then nearly run its course and was repealed in 1933. It left no discernible impact on the drinking habits of New Yorkers but unquestionably invigorated organized crime in the city, and gangs that profited on bootlegging during Prohibition were later able to diversify their operations.

Herbert Asbury: "The Noble Experiment of Izzy and Moe," *The Aspirin Age, 1919–1941*, ed. Isabel Leighton (New York: Simon and Schuster, 1949)
John Kobler: *Ardent Spirits: The Rise and Fall of Prohibition* (New York: G. P. Putnam's Sons, 1973)

Warren Sloat

property and liability insurance. The insurance business was established in New York City in the early eighteenth century as maritime insurance became a routine element of commerce. Colonial merchants usually bought their insurance from underwriters in Amsterdam and London, which perfected marine insurance practices; often the distance imposed a long delay, and gradually agents in the ports of Boston, New York, Philadelphia, Baltimore, and Charleston, South Carolina, accepted applications for marine insurance and offered them to local underwriters in a manner similar to that of Lloyd's of London, where individual insurers wrote their names under descriptions of the voyages they were willing to guarantee. In 1719 Parliament prohibited the formation of stock insurance companies in the colonies, and underwriters in the colonial ports had insufficient capital of their own to meet the demand for insurance.

After the American Revolution joint stock companies that were organized with limited liability raised more capital for insurance operations. The formation of the Insurance Company of North America in Philadelphia in 1792 freed American shipowners from relying on insurers in London, and the success of the firm inspired entrepreneurs to provide marine insurance in other port cities. Within two years the United States Insurance Company and the Pacific Insurance Company began marine insurance operations in New York City. The city's expansion also led to the formation of several fire insurers: the United Insurance Company (1787), the New York Insurance Company (1798), the Columbian Insurance Company (1801), and the Eagle Fire Insurance Company (1806). By the end of the eighteenth century marine insurance, fire insurance, and life insurance were established lines of business in the United States.

Fire insurers were crippled by the Great Fire of 1835 in the city. Nearly six hundred buildings were destroyed, generating losses of about $15 million. Of the twenty-six fire insurers in business at the time, twenty-three exhausted their reserves by paying claims and declared bankruptcy. Another severe fire in 1845 destroyed 450 buildings and caused the failure of more insurers, most of which were joint stock companies. The mutual form of organization later came to dominate but proved no more stable. A general insurance law passed by New York State in 1849 placed the licensing and supervision of companies under the authority of the state controller and abolished chartering by the legislature. In the following years a number of companies were organized imprudently: forty-seven of fifty-four formed after 1849 failed by 1860 and together left unpaid losses of more than $2 million. To protect policyholders the state moved to regulate companies. In 1859 the office of the superintendent of insurance was established, and companies were required to submit financial reports and meet minimum standards.

The New York Board of Fire Underwriters was chartered on 9 May 1867 by the state legislature to "inculcate just and equitable principles in the business of insurance, operate the Fire Patrol and assess all companies writing fire insurance in the City for maintenance of the Patrol." For a short time the board attempted to control rates but ceased to do so in 1877 because members frequently deviated from established rates. The board did succeed in reducing fire hazards by inspecting buildings, investigating arson, and researching technology for fire fighting. A standard fire policy was drafted by a committee of the board and in 1888 made mandatory by the state legislature for all fire insurers.

Marine insurers benefited from the great success of American clipper ships but suffered during the era of free trade after the Civil War, when British steam-propelled metal ships carried an increasing share of American exports and British insurers captured most of the market for American marine insurance. Of the thirteen domestic marine insurers listed in the first report of the state insurance department in 1864, only Atlantic Mutual survived to the end of the century. British insurers held almost all policies for hull insurance, since most ships were British; American insurers continued to provide large amounts of insurance for cargo.

The city's property and liability insurers did not achieve the same degree of national prominence during the second half of the nineteenth century as its life insurers did. Resentment in the Midwest of eastern financiers led to the establishment there of local and regional insurance companies that competed vigorously with companies in New York City; many states taxed insurers from out of state. Regional distrust was exacerbated by the findings of the Armstrong Committee (1905) of abuses by major life insurers, and those of the Merritt Committee (1910), which examined the sharp increases in fire insurance rates in the city during the 1890s and the early twentieth century.

The revival of the American merchant marine early in the twentieth century improved conditions for American marine insurers. The American Institute of Marine Underwriters, formed in 1920, helped American companies to regain some hull insurance business through syndication. New kinds of insurance were developed about this time, against automobile accidents and theft, burglary, public liability, and inland marine losses; insurers in the city also provided fidelity and surety bonds. Workers' compensation resulted from the efforts of reformers and from the mistrust of business spurred by the investigations by the Armstrong Committee; the first law in the United States establishing workers' compensation was enacted in New York State in 1910. Several new private insurers and a state fund were formed to provide coverage, in part because many traditional insurers supported employers' resistance to the principle that compensation for work-related injuries should be provided regardless of fault. Eventually many of the traditional insurers did provide workers' compensation insurance.

Insurers became limited to underwriting either fire and marine insurance or casualty and surety by the Appleton rule, first promulgated in 1901 by the deputy superintendent of insurance for New York State, H. D. Appleton, and incorporated into the insurance law of 1939. This rule led to the adoption nationwide of the insurance practices of New York State, although other states were less stringent. The first law in the nation for insurance guaranty was passed in 1947 and assessed all insurers a percentage of their premiums for a guaranty fund to pay the unsatisfied claims against insolvent insurers; it became an important consumer protection measure and was later adopted by all the other states. In 1949 a new law granted full underwriting powers to both fire and marine insurers and casualty and surety insurers, enabling firms to combine different types of coverage in a single policy.

Those Who Underwrite Metropolitan New York (New York: Roberts, 1943)

Robert J. Gibbons

Proskauer Rose Goetz and Mendelsohn. Law firm, founded in 1875 by William Rose. Walter Mendelsohn became a partner in 1921, followed in 1925 by Norman Goetz and in 1930 by Joseph Proskauer, a justice of the New York State Appellate Division and a close advisor to Governor Alfred E. Smith who led the firm's litigation department until 1971. The firm took its current name in 1942. In 1991 the firm defended the publishing house of Simon and Schuster in a case that led to the invalidation by the U.S. Supreme Court of the "Son of Sam law," which prohibited persons in New York State from profiting from the publication of works about crimes of which they were accused or convicted. In the mid 1990s Proskauer Rose Goetz and Mendelsohn had 425 lawyers and offices at 1585 Broadway.

Prospect Heights. Neighborhood in northwestern Brooklyn, lying along the northern edge of Prospect Park and bounded to the north by Atlantic Avenue, to the east by Washington Avenue, to the south by Eastern Parkway (which begins in the neighborhood at Grand Army Plaza), and to the west by Flatbush Avenue. It was developed after Prospect Park was completed in the 1870s. The population consisted mostly of middle-class Italians, Irish, and Jews until after the Second World War, when it became predominantly black. Eventually many buildings were abandoned and the neighborhood declined, and during the 1960s Washington Avenue was the site of severe race riots and arson that destroyed many buildings. In the mid 1980s the city sold off clusters of abandoned buildings to encourage the development of middle-income housing. A wave of speculation resulted, and during the next eight years almost a third of the neighborhood's housing was renovated, becoming unaffordable for most residents, many of whom were forced from their homes by rising prices. The middle class grew, attracted by relatively inexpensive condominiums and cooperatives, and by the proximity of the neighborhood to Park Slope, Prospect Park, and Manhattan. Most of the immigrants who settled in Prospect Heights during the 1980s were from the Caribbean, especially from Jamaica, Haiti, and Guyana and to a lesser extent from Trinidad and Tobago, the Dominican Republic, Barbados, and Panama. The population in the mid 1990s included working-class and middle-class homeowners and low-income renters and was largely black, with some whites, West Indians, and Latin Americans. Along Eastern Parkway stand the Brooklyn Museum, the Brooklyn Botanic Garden, and the Brooklyn Public Library; the sidestreets are lined with brownstones and townhouses built at the turn of the century, along with small apartment buildings.

Judith Berck

Prospect–Lefferts Gardens. Neighborhood in northwestern Brooklyn, lying within northern Flatbush and bounded to the north by Empire Boulevard, to the east by New York Avenue, to the south by Clarkson Avenue, and to the west by Ocean Avenue. The area was farmland until the 1890s, when row-house development began. F. B. Norris and

Realty Associates were the principal developers, responsible for nearly one third of the two- and three-story one-family houses of brick and stone. The most active period for construction was between 1905 and 1911, when more than five hundred limestone houses were built. The area was called Lefferts Manor during this time but was later renamed for Prospect Park, the Lefferts Homestead (on which the neighborhood was built), and the nearby Brooklyn Botanic Garden.

Prospect–Lefferts Gardens is racially integrated and middle class and is a Historic District. The housing consists of row houses and some semidetached and detached houses, as well as apartment buildings with storefronts along Rogers Avenue; most of the housing was built between the 1890s and the 1920s. Flatbush Avenue is the main thoroughfare and there is additional shopping along Nostrand Avenue.

Andrew S. Dolkart: *This Is Brooklyn: A Guide to the Borough's Historic Districts and Landmarks* (New York: Fund for the Borough of Brooklyn, 1990)

Elizabeth Reich Rawson

Prospect Park. Public park in west central Brooklyn, bounded to the north by Eastern Parkway, to the east by Washington Avenue and Ocean Avenue, to the south by Parkside Avenue, and to the west by Prospect Park Southwest and Prospect Park West. It occupies 526 acres (213 hectares). Part of the site was acquired by the City of Brooklyn in 1860; the present configuration of the park was first sketched by Calvert Vaux in February 1865 at the behest of James S. T. Stranahan, president of the Prospect Park Commission. A comprehensive plan for development was submitted in the following year by Vaux and Frederick Law Olmsted. The principal features of their design were the Green, or Long Meadow, a rolling expanse of lawn and trees; a rocky, heavily wooded area called the Ravine; and Prospect Lake. The Meadowport Arch, Endale Arch, East Wood Arch, and other arches throughout the park separated traffic. The Parade, across Franklin Avenue from the park, provided additional facilities for recreation, and the Plaza (now Grand Army Plaza) routed traffic into and around the park and served as a grand ceremonial space. From 1866 Olmsted supervised construction, a massive undertaking that employed as many as eighteen hundred men to move earth, lay an underground drainage system, pave miles of roads and paths, plant grass, trees, and shrubs, and erect bridges. Vaux and a number of associates designed the Thatched Shelter, the Dairy, the Concert Grove and its pavilions, and numerous rustic arbors. Shortly after its opening Prospect Park became a favorite place of resort. In 1868 about two million persons visited to enjoy the scenery or a family picnic, sail or skate on the lake, listen to weekly concerts, and take part in athletic contests on the Parade. By the end of the nineteenth century there were perhaps as many as fifteen million visitors each year.

Olmsted and Vaux considered Prospect Park integral to the future of Brooklyn and the metropolitan area. As early as 1866 they urged that it be connected to Central Park in Manhattan by a series of wide boulevards, and although this plan was never realized they were able to forge a comprehensive park and avenue system by rearranging the streets approaching Prospect Park, constructing Ocean Parkway and Eastern Parkway, and designing other public spaces. In later years Olmsted was distressed by changes made to the park, particularly the addition of gateways and structures designed by McKim, Mead and White and other architects and the more formal treatment of parts of the landscape. In the twentieth century the advent of the automobile made it necessary to widen and straighten the drives, and playgrounds and other recreational facilities were added. During the Depression the city's parks commissioner, Robert Moses, rehabilitated the landscape and restored many buildings; he also added such new structures as the Wollman Skating Rink (on part of the Concert Grove) and the zoo. Despite these major changes to the original landscape Prospect Park remains the centerpiece of the park system in Brooklyn and perhaps the greatest of the urban parks designed by Olmsted and Vaux.

Clay Lancaster: *Prospect Park Handbook* (New York: W. H. Rawls, 1967)

David Schuyler et al., eds.: *The Papers of Frederick Law Olmsted*, vol. 6, *The Years of Olmsted, Vaux and Company, 1865–1874* (Baltimore: Johns Hopkins University Press, 1992)

David Schuyler

Prospect Park and Coney Island Rail Road [Culver Line]. Railroad formed by Andrew Culver in 1874 after consolidating the Park Avenue Horsecar Line in Brooklyn and the steam-operated Greenwood and Coney Island Rail Road, which joined at 20th Street and 9th Avenue in Brooklyn. Horsecar routes served ferry slips at Catherine Street and Hamilton Avenue. In 1879 the railroad leased the New York and Coney Island Rail Road, which ran between Coney Island and Norton's Point near Sea Gate. It was bought by Brooklyn Rapid Transit in 1893 and electrified in 1899. Faster service to Manhattan was initiated in 1919 after an elevated line on McDonald Avenue was completed. During the early 1930s the railroad tested along its routes a new trolley car known as the PCC car (for Presidents Conference Committee, an organization of electric railway presidents that redesigned trolleys so that they could compete with automobiles and buses). Trolley service was offered on McDonald Avenue until 1956.

James C. Greller and Edward B. Watson: *The Brooklyn Elevated* (Hicksville, N.Y.: N.J. International, 1986)

James C. Greller and Edward B. Watson: *Brooklyn Trolleys* (Hicksville, N.Y.: N.J. International, 1986)

John Fink

Prospect Park South. Neighborhood in northwestern Brooklyn (1990 pop. 28,991), covering sixty acres (twenty-four hectares) and bounded to the north by Church Avenue, to the east by the tracks of the "D" and "Q" subway lines, to the south by Beverly Road, and to the west by Coney Island Avenue. Once owned by the Dutch Reformed church of Flatbush, the area was developed in 1899 by Dean Alvord after the extension of rail service from Manhattan and downtown Brooklyn. He planned the neighborhood to resemble a spacious suburb, engaged John Aitkin to provide landscaping, and established stringent architectural standards. The houses are set back thirty feet (nine meters) from the sidewalk; many were built at the turn of the century in a variety of styles, including Georgian, Prairie, Queen Anne, Elizabethan, neo-Tudor, Pediment, Japanese, Colonial Revival, French Revival, and Mission. A strip of land eight feet (2.4 meters) wide lies between the street and the sidewalk for planting. The streets are lined with trees, and Buckingham and Albermarle roads have central planting malls. The neighborhood is upper middle class and the main commercial thoroughfares are Church and Coney Island avenues.

Herbert F. Gunnison, ed.: *Flatbush of To-day* (New York: Privately printed, 1908), 37

John J. Gallagher

prostitution. The earliest evidence of prostitution in New York City is reports by late-seventeenth-century visitors who noticed Dutch and English "lasses" soliciting along the Battery. Throughout the colonial period "disorderly houses" along the waterfront catered to sailors who frequented taverns and saloons nearby. By the time of the American Revolution prostitutes did most of their business with British soldiers. Commercial sex in the eighteenth century and the early nineteenth was concentrated in three areas: the "holy ground" adjacent to St. Paul's Chapel and a block east of the Hudson River on land owned by Trinity Church; George Street (later Spruce Street) on the northern edge of the city near the Park Theater and the "Common" (later City Hall Park); and East George Street (later Market Street) along the East River. Prostitution flourished after 1810. Property owners willingly rented space to prostitutes because they had more money and proved more stable than working-class tenants. Under common law, landlords who owned houses of prostitution were not considered accessories. Prostitution was treated as vagrancy or disorderly conduct, both misdemeanors for which most participants went

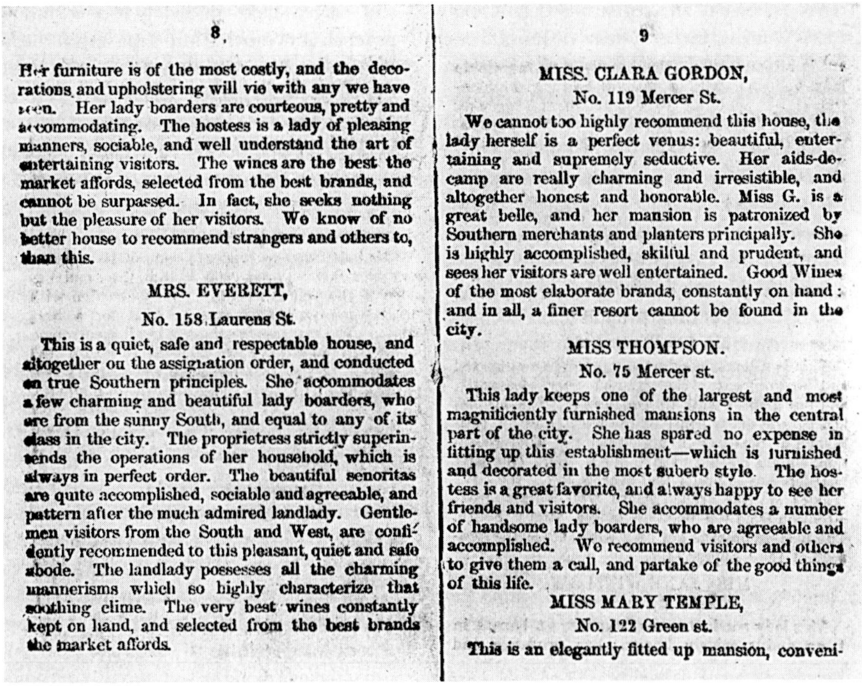

8

Her furniture is of the most costly, and the decorations and upholstering will vie with any we have seen. Her lady boarders are courteous, pretty and accommodating. The hostess is a lady of pleasing manners, sociable, and well understand the art of entertaining visitors. The wines are the best the market affords, selected from the best brands, and cannot be surpassed. In fact, she seeks nothing but the pleasure of her visitors. We know of no better house to recommend strangers and others to, than this.

MRS. EVERETT,

No. 158 Laurens St.

This is a quiet, safe and respectable house, and altogether on the assignation order, and conducted on true Southern principles. She accommodates a few charming and beautiful lady boarders, who are from the sunny South, and equal to any of its class in the city. The proprietress strictly superintends the operations of her household, which is always in perfect order. The beautiful senoritas are quite accomplished, sociable and agreeable, and pattern after the much admired landlady. Gentlemen visitors from the South and West, are confidently recommended to this pleasant, quiet and safe abode. The landlady possesses all the charming mannerisms which so highly characterize that soothing clime. The very best wines constantly kept on hand, and selected from the best brands the market affords.

9

MISS. CLARA GORDON,

No. 119 Mercer St.

We cannot too highly recommend this house, the lady herself is a perfect venus: beautiful, entertaining and supremely seductive. Her aids-de-camp are really charming and irresistible, and altogether honest and honorable. Miss G. is a great belle, and her mansion is patronized by Southern merchants and planters principally. She is highly accomplished, skilful and prudent, and sees her visitors are well entertained. Good Wines of the most elaborate brands, constantly on hand: and in all, a finer resort cannot be found in the city.

MISS THOMPSON.

No. 75 Mercer st.

This lady keeps one of the largest and most magnificiently furnished mansions in the central part of the city. She has spared no expense in fitting up this establishment—which is furnished and decorated in the most suberb style. The hostess is a great favorite, and always happy to see her friends and visitors. She accommodates a number of handsome lady boarders, who are agreeable and accomplished. We recommend visitors and others to give them a call, and partake of the good things of this life.

MISS MARY TEMPLE,

No. 122 Green st.

This is an elegantly fitted up mansion, conveni-

Excerpt from the Directory to the Seraglios

unpunished. A Victorian double standard sanctioned male sexual activity outside marriage and divided women into two groups: the respectable, who were considered "passionless," and the unrespectable, who were irredeemable and available for purchase.

Nineteenth-century urban prostitution thrived for several reasons. The number of single, underemployed young women who moved to New York City from rural areas and abroad grew dramatically after 1820. They earned such low wages for what was considered legitimate work that many were forced to seek additional income. Probably 5 to 10 percent became prostitutes because they earned more in an evening than other employment might bring in a week, sometimes a month. Most were prostitutes for only a short time, eventually securing more socially acceptable employment or marriage. Some women attained a social or economic status that transcended their identity as prostitutes. Eliza Bowen abandoned prostitution to marry the wealthy French wine merchant Stephen Jumel in 1804 and became the wealthiest woman in the United States on his death in 1832 (she married Aaron Burr in 1833). Before the Civil War the madames Julia Brown, Adeline Miller, and Rosina Townsend were celebrated figures. The murder of the courtesan Helen Jewett in 1836 and the ensuing trial of her lover and alleged killer Richard Robinson attracted national interest, exposing the popularity of prostitution among men from all ranks of life. By the end of the century Rosie Hertz, the reputed "godmother" for prostitutes in the city, ran several brothels on the Lower East Side while living in an affluent neighborhood of Brooklyn. Few women involved in prostitution attained this glamour and success.

As factory work undercut the craft system and unregulated boarding houses replaced the patriarchal artisan household, young men enjoyed new freedoms. Increasingly commercialized leisure activities appealed to a young, transient male population with indiscriminate sexual mores. After the Civil War leading concert saloons like Harry Hill's used "waiter girl" prostitutes to attract these "Bowery B'hoys" as well as prominent businessmen and politicians. From the 1830s procurers, or "pimps," managed prostitutes and lived off their earnings. Nicknamed "Broadway statues," "bullies," and the "fancy men" of prostitutes, they were fixtures in the sexual underworld by mid century. Prostitution was preeminent in the city's underground economy. Brothels, unlicensed saloons, and illegal gambling dens corrupted neighborhood politicians and police, and antebellum theater proprietors routinely allowed prostitutes to conduct business in the "third tier" of their establishments. The leading "parlor houses" employed fifteen to twenty women on weekends, the smaller establishments four or six. Many even advertised their services in local newspapers and guidebooks. From 1820 to 1850 the largest concentrations of prostitutes were found in the Five Points and at Corlear's Hook, Water Street, Church Street, and Chapel Street. By 1860 New York City reportedly had five hundred brothels.

After 1850 the city's first exclusive sex and entertainment district took shape in the streets north of Canal Street and parallel to Broadway (the area now known as SoHo). It was eclipsed in importance shortly after the Civil War by the Tenderloin, an area in the heart of Manhattan between 5th and 8th avenues, extending as far south as 23rd Street and as far north as 34th Street by 1870, 42nd Street by 1880, and 50th Street by 1900. Allen Street on the Lower East Side and Union Square were similar centers of prostitution. Despite controversy prostitution was never segregated: concert halls, saloons, cigar stores, restaurants, masquerade balls, and later cabarets resorted to commercial sex to attract patrons, and elegant bordellos could be found in élite areas like Gramercy Park. In 1896 the assemblyman and district leader Martin Engel of Tammany Hall and his ally Max Hochstim formed the Independent Benevolent Association. The first "syndicate," it had a membership of several hundred madames, landlords, doctors, and municipal officials, and collected dues to pay for "protection" and legal expenses, settled disputes, and organized prostitution on the Lower East Side.

Anti-prostitution movements took different forms. In 1831 the young Presbyterian minister John McDowall formed a Magdalen society to reform prostitutes, followed within a decade by the New York Female Benevolent Society, the New-York Society of Public Morals, and the New-York Female Moral Reform Society (see MAGDALEN SOCIETIES). In 1843 the Roman Catholic Sisters of Mercy and the Sisters of the Good Shepherd began efforts to reform and assist prostitutes, and in 1854 evangelical Methodists converted the notorious "Old Brewery" into the Five Points House of Industry. Other anti-prostitution movements were linked to temperance and emphasized conversion to a morally pure way of life. These purity crusades were however sporadic and ineffective in diminishing prostitution. To Judge Charles Daley in 1849 and the newspaper editor Walt Whitman in the 1850s legalizing the trade was the only way to control it. Doctors like William Sanger supported regulation to protect public health and prevent venereal disease. Measures to legalize prostitution were debated by the state legislature in 1871 and 1875 but defeated by a coalition led by the women's rights advocate Susan B. Anthony.

At century's end vice crusades grew in number and significance. The Presbyterian pastor Charles H. Parkhurst instigated an anti-prostitution campaign that contributed to an electoral defeat for Tammany Hall in 1892, and within a decade committees led by State Senator Clarence Lexow and Assemblyman Robert Mazet further exposed links between the city's sex entrepreneurs and law enforcement officials. Wealthy businessmen, university professors, and other progressive reformers organized the Committee of Fifteen (1900–2) and the Committee of Fourteen (1905–32), which helped pass the Tenement House Law (1901), establish a women's night

tals and uninhabited islands in Lower New York Bay.

Chad Ludington

Queen Mary. Transatlantic passenger liner. She was owned by the Cunard Line, which wanted to name her the *Victoria.* The current name was reportedly given after Sir Percy Bates and Sir Ashley Sparks, leading officials of the firm, told George V that they planned to name the ship after the greatest queen of England, to which the king replied, "My wife would be delighted"; the ship became the company's first to have a name ending in letters other than "ia." After her maiden voyage to New York City in 1936 she became known as one of the greatest liners, for many years holding the transatlantic speed record. She was used to ferry troops to Britain during the Second World War and in the mid 1990s was a museum and hotel docked at Long Beach, California.

Frank O. Braynard

Queens. The largest borough in land area, comprising 37 percent of the territory of New York City; it covers about 120 square miles (311 square kilometers) and is almost as large as Manhattan, the Bronx, and Staten Island combined. From east to west it measures 13.75 miles (twenty-two kilometers) and from north to south fifteen miles (twenty-four kilometers). It is bounded to the north by the East River and Long Island Sound, to the east by Nassau County, to the south by the Atlantic Ocean, to the southwest by Brooklyn, and to the west by the East River.

Population of Selected Towns in Queens, 1790–1890

	Flushing	Jamaica	Long Island City	Newtown
1790	1,607	1,675	N/A	2,111
1800	1,818	1,661	N/A	2,282
1830	2,822	2,376	N/A	2,610
1840	4,124	3,781	N/A	5,054
1850	5,376	4,247	N/A	7,208
1860	10,188	6,515	N/A	13,725
1870	14,650	7,745	3,867	20,274
1880	15,960	10,088	17,129	N/A
1890	19,803	14,441	30,506	17,549

NA = Not Available

Note: Population figures for towns were not included in the censuses of population of 1810 and 1820.

Compiled by James Bradley

1. To the Civil War

The first inhabitants were American Indians, who lived near bays and inlets along the coast, including what is now Flushing Bay, Little Neck Bay and Oakland Lake, Douglaston, Jamaica Bay, Rockaway Peninsula, and Maspeth at the headwaters of Newtown Creek. Between 1609 and 1624 the Dutch explored the region and established the colony of New Netherland. They initially occupied the southern tip of Manhattan and a few farms in what is now Brooklyn; between 1633 and 1638 some farming began in Queens along the East River in what became Hallett's Point in Astoria. None of these pioneer settlements in Queens endured. But the loamy soils, oak forests, and salt marshes of Long Island soon lured others seeking to raise hay, grain, and livestock and extract timber and firewood. After receiving approval from the Dutch government English settlers entered Queens in the 1640s. Some from New England took up land in 1642 in the area of Maspeth, only to be driven out in the following year by Indian attacks that probably also expelled the farmers of Astoria. In the mid seventeenth century the Dutch and the English forced out the Indians, who left little behind but place names and trails that later became wagon roads and major streets; for a while Indian wampum served European settlers as a local currency.

The Dutch authorities gave each village a Dutch name and installed the Dutch form of government. English families settled Vlissingen (Flushing) in 1645, Middleburgh (later Newtown and Elmhurst) farther inland in 1652, and Rustdorp (Jamaica) in 1656. Queens became more culturally diverse as Dutch farmers from Brooklyn settled among the English. By the late seventeenth century many families that later became prominent were established, including the Halletts of Newtown, the Lawrences of Flushing, and the Van Siclens of Jamaica.

English settlers disliked Dutch rule. Residents of Flushing in particular resented Dutch meddling in matters of religion and local administration. Their grievances gave rise to the most famous event in the early history of Queens: the Flushing Remonstrance. On 27 December 1657 they formally protested the denial to Quakers of freedom of worship guaranteed by the town charter. The Dutch immediately arrested and fined several petitioners. In 1662 they imprisoned John Bowne for allowing Quaker meetings in his home, then banished him from the colony. Bowne traveled to the Netherlands and appealed his banishment to the Dutch West India Company, which upheld him and guaranteed religious freedom for all Protestant sects in the colony. Vindicated, Bowne returned to Flushing.

The English took over the colony in 1664 and in 1683 divided it into ten counties, among them Queens County, named after the queen of King Charles II, Catherine of Braganza, and consisting of what later became Queens and Nassau counties. The western portion, corresponding to the present-day borough (excluding Rockaway Peninsula), was divided into three large governing units, or towns: Newtown, Flushing, and Jamaica. The boundaries separating the three towns reflected natural features of the terrain, which continued into the twentieth century to influence the social divisions in Queens and the movement of goods and people. Newtown lay to the northwest and Flushing to the northeast of the terminal moraine extending across the borough and running the length of Long Island (now the route of the Interborough Parkway and, east of Kew Gardens, the Grand Central Expressway). The two towns were divided from each other by Flushing Creek, which meandered southward from Flushing Bay through three miles (five kilometers) of salt marsh (now under landfill beneath Flushing Meadows–Corona Park) until it reached the moraine. In colonial times Flushing Meadows prevented continuous travel by land along the northern shore of Queens; the first bridge crossing was built in 1800 at what became Northern Boulevard. On the sandy outwash plain to the south of the moraine lay Jamaica, divided from the Atlantic Ocean by Jamaica Bay, a vast saltwater lagoon shielded from the ocean by Rockaway Peninsula and noted for its fish, shellfish, salt-marsh meadows, and low islands.

The chief village of the town, also called Jamaica, was the county seat and a popular stopping point along the road that began twelve miles (nineteen kilometers) from Jamaica in Brooklyn at the ferry across the East River to Manhattan and ran east along an Indian trail to Jamaica. In 1703 the colonial legislature designated this road the King's Highway and authorized its continuation to East Hampton at the far end of Long Island; in Queens it became Jamaica Avenue.

Some inhabitants of the towns lived in villages but most lived on outlying farms. In the late seventeenth century and the early eighteenth land prices rose steadily and the size of farms decreased as more land was taken up, much of it tightly held by established families. Many farmers' sons who could not afford to buy a tract large enough to farm learned trades or moved where farmland was cheaper. A growing number of rural families owned slaves, although few owned more than two. The first census (1790) recorded 5393 inhabitants in the three towns, including 1095 slaves.

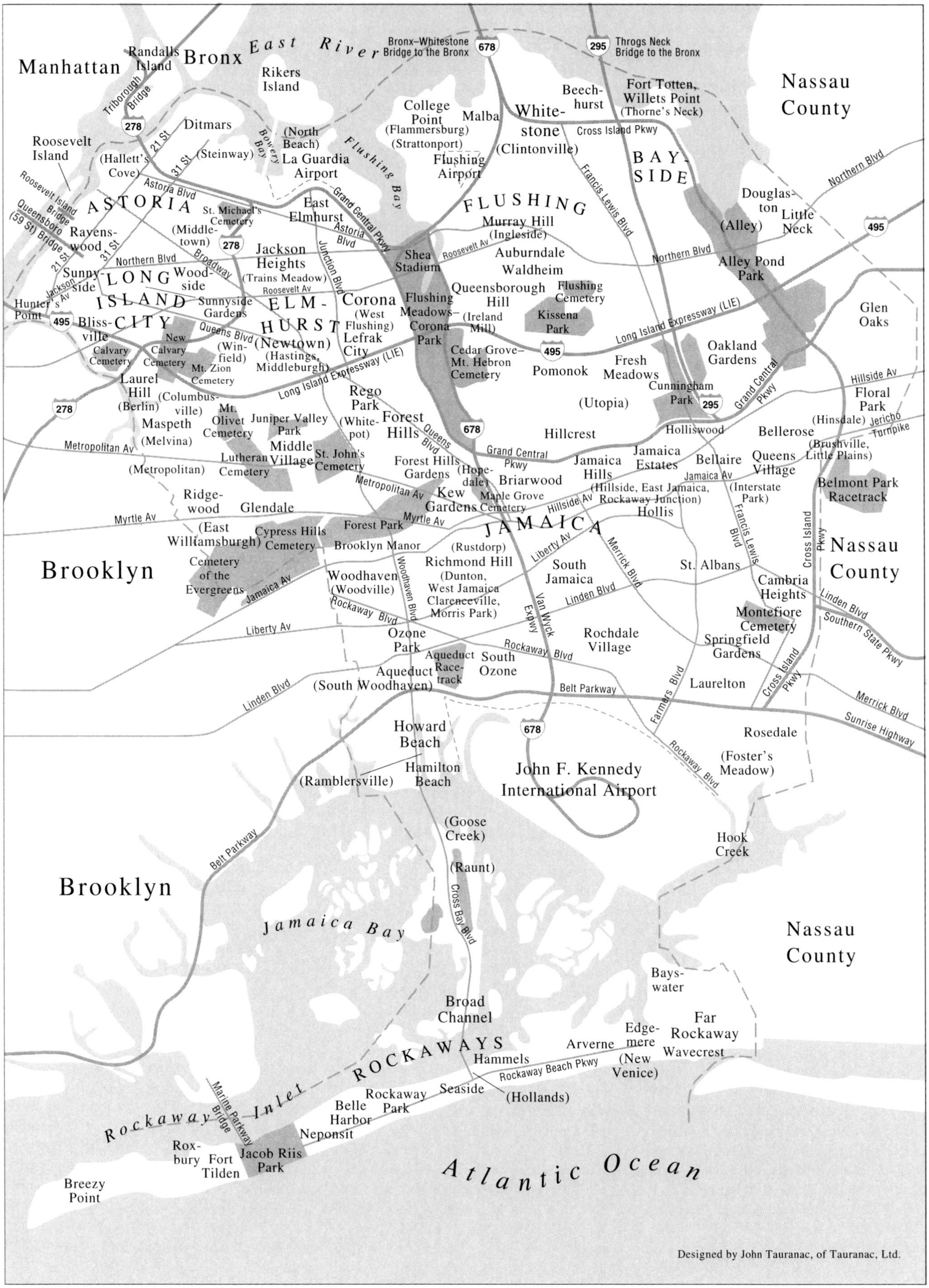
Manhattan
Randalls Island
Bronx
East River
Bronx–Whitestone Bridge to the Bronx
678
295
Throgs Neck Bridge to the Bronx
Nassau County
Rikers Island
Triborough Bridge
278
Ditmars
Roosevelt Island
21 St
31 St
(Steinway)
Bowery Bay
(North Beach)
La Guardia Airport
(Hallett's Cove)
Flushing Bay
College Point
(Flammersburg)
(Strattonport)
Malba
Flushing Airport
White-stone
(Clintonville)
Beech-hurst
Fort Totten, Willets Point
(Thorne's Neck)
Cross Island Pkwy
BAYSIDE
Francis Lewis Blvd
Northern Blvd
Roosevelt Island Bridge
Queensboro (59 St) Bridge
Astoria Blvd
ASTORIA
St. Michael's Cemetery
East Elmhurst
Grand Central Pkwy
FLUSHING
Murray Hill
(Ingleside)
Douglas-ton
Little Neck
(Alley)
495
Ravens-wood
(Middle-town)
Broadway
Jackson Heights
(Trains Meadow)
Junction Blvd
Shea Stadium
Roosevelt Av
Auburndale
Waldheim
Alley Pond Park
Sunny-side
Jackson Av
LONG ISLAND CITY
Wood-side
Sunnyside Gardens
ELMHURST
(Newtown)
Corona
(West Flushing)
Flushing Meadows–Corona Park
Queensborough Hill
(Ireland Mill)
Flushing Cemetery
Kissena Park
Glen Oaks
Long Island Expressway (LIE)
Hunter's Point
Bliss-ville
Queens Blvd
(Win-field)
New Calvary Cemetery
Calvary Cemetery
Mt. Zion Cemetery
(Hastings, Middleburgh)
Lefrak City
Cedar Grove–Mt. Hebron Cemetery
Pomonok
Fresh Meadows
Oakland Gardens
Laurel Hill
(Berlin)
(Columbus-ville)
Rego Park
Cunningham Park
Hillside Av
Floral Park
Maspeth
(Melvina)
Mt. Olivet Cemetery
Juniper Valley Park
(White-pot)
Forest Hills
Queens Blvd
(Utopia)
Hillcrest
Holliswood
Bellerose
(Hinsdale)
Jericho Turnpike
(Brushville, Little Plains)
Metropolitan Av
Middle Village
Lutheran Cemetery
St. John's Cemetery
Forest Hills Gardens
(Hope-dale)
Briarwood
Jamaica Hills
(Hillside, East Jamaica, Rockaway Junction)
Jamaica Estates
Bellaire
Queens Village
(Interstate Park)
Jamaica Av
Belmont Park Racetrack
(Metropolitan)
Ridge-wood
(East Williamsburgh)
Glendale
Kew Gardens
Maple Grove Cemetery
Hollis
Myrtle Av
Cypress Hills Cemetery
Forest Park
JAMAICA
Cross Island Pkwy
Nassau County
Brooklyn
Cemetery of the Evergreens
Brooklyn Manor
(Rustdorp)
Richmond Hill
(Dunton, West Jamaica Clarenceville, Morris Park)
Liberty Av
Merrick Blvd
South Jamaica
St. Albans
Cambria Heights
Woodhaven
(Woodville)
Woodhaven Blvd
Van Wyck Expwy
Linden Blvd
Montefiore Cemetery
Southern State Pkwy
Rockaway Blvd
Ozone Park
Rochdale Village
Springfield Gardens
Aqueduct Race-track
South Ozone
Aqueduct
(South Woodhaven)
Belt Parkway
Laurelton
Farmers Blvd
Sunrise Highway
Howard Beach
Hamilton Beach
(Ramblersville)
John F. Kennedy International Airport
Rosedale
(Foster's Meadow)
(Goose Creek)
(Raunt)
Hook Creek
Brooklyn
Cross Bay Blvd
Jamaica Bay
Nassau County
Bays-water
Broad Channel
Far Rockaway
Edge-mere
(New Venice)
Arverne
Wavecrest
ROCKAWAYS
Hammels
Rockaway Beach Pkwy
Seaside
(Hollands)
Rockaway Park
Belle Harbor
Neponsit
Rockaway Inlet
Marine Parkway Bridge
Rox-bury
Fort Tilden
Jacob Riis Park
Breezy Point
Atlantic Ocean
Designed by John Tauranac, of Tauranac, Ltd.

In the early eighteenth century some farmers began growing specialty crops. A new variety of apple, the Newtown Pippin, became available after 1730 and soon grew in many orchards on Long Island. It was the first American-grown apple exported to England, where it was considered a luxury and commanded a high price. As early as 1737 William Prince opened in Flushing the first commercial nursery for trees and plants in America. In the nineteenth century the firms of Prince, Parsons, and other families in Flushing introduced ornamental trees and shrubs from Europe, Asia, and other parts of the world.

The American Revolution divided Queens. Except in Newtown most residents strongly favored the British, whose army defeated the American troops under George Washington on 27 August 1776 in the Battle of Long Island (fought in Brooklyn). This defeat enabled the British to use western Long Island, especially the territory of what is now Queens, for quartering their troops and staging their American operations. They enjoyed nearly absolute military security, disturbed only by the inconsequential raids of rebels from Connecticut in whaleboats. The British occupied the territory for seven years, leaving behind a ravaged countryside and lasting memories of hardship. Officers billeted themselves at farmhouses and in villages. The troops, of whom there were thousands, encamped at many sites, where they survived the winters in huts and the summers in tents. The army requisitioned crops and livestock, and soldiers acting on their own stole produce. In the course of the war they stripped Queens of timber and even took fenceposts. After the British had abandoned most other areas Queens became a staging ground for the evacuation of thousands of Loyalists from all over America and their resettlement in Nova Scotia and Newfoundland. Fearful of retribution by the revolutionaries, many Loyalists from Queens joined the flight.

From the final withdrawal of the British in November 1783 until the 1830s Queens remained a district of farms and villages and grew slowly as it rebuilt. In 1788 the county seat was transferred from Jamaica to Mineola (now in Nassau County). Access to urban markets was improved for farmers by six turnpikes built between 1801 and 1816, including two running end to end between Flushing and Brooklyn through Newtown and two separately linking Jamaica and Brooklyn. Between 1800 and 1830 the population rose only from 5791 to 7806, suggesting that many young adults continued to seek their fortunes elsewhere. New York City was then growing at an extraordinary pace: soon it became the economic and cultural capital of the nation and sent increasing numbers of settlers to Queens, as did Brooklyn.

The 1830s began the decline of rural Queens as Brooklyn and New York City exploited its resources. The population increased markedly, by 5153 between 1830 and 1840. The Long Island Rail Road began running between Brooklyn and Jamaica in 1836. In 1839 Astoria became the first village to be incorporated in Queens since the seventeenth century. Ravenswood began as a fashionable suburb along the East River in 1848 and became the first town of the "gold coast," which eventually expanded to the east along the northern shore of Long Island through parts of Flushing, Malba, Bayside, and Douglaston and into Nassau County. Other kinds of growth also fueled rural decline. In the 1850s three racetracks in western Queens served urban sportsmen; the most popular was the Union Course in Woodhaven, just over the line from Brooklyn. Several large cemeteries for religious groups in Manhattan and Brooklyn were laid out in western Queens after burial grounds were banned from lower Manhattan in 1848 for sanitary reasons. Manufacturers scattered widely, building factories in Whitestone, Woodhaven, and College Point. By the 1850s Far Rockaway had become a well-established seaside resort for wealthy visitors during the summer.

Urbanization accelerated notably during the 1850s. Speculators bought up farms between 1852 and 1854 for resale as village lots in Hunter's Point, Maspeth, Winfield, and West Flushing (Corona) along the proposed route of the Flushing Railroad. The railroad, financed by wealthy residents of Flushing, began offering service in 1854 to Hunter's Point, and in the late nineteenth century Flushing became preeminent as a commuter suburb and genteel summer colony. Large numbers of Irish and German immigrants moved into Queens about this time. Those displaced by the potato famine in Ireland in the late 1840s settled mostly in Astoria but also in Jamaica and Flushing. Many Germans moved to Queens from Brooklyn, settling along Metropolitan and Myrtle avenues. Middle Village, which had been English in the 1840s, became almost entirely German by 1860. By then the population of Queens reached 30,429.

2. After the Civil War

Growth was only briefly interrupted by the Civil War, and from 1865 to 1890 pervaded much of western Queens but was spotty elsewhere. Kerosene fuel refineries developed along Newtown Creek and the waterfront in Long Island City from the 1860s. Glendale began in 1868–69, Richmond Hill in 1869, and to the east Queens Village in 1871. In the early 1870s the piano maker William Steinway opened a factory and manufacturing village in East Astoria, along what is now upper Steinway Avenue. Some large farms in Bayside in northeastern Queens were converted into building lots in 1872, and South Flushing between the old village and what is now Kissena Park was subdivided in the following year. New, privately owned excursion parks catered to working-class German families, and on weekends thousands of visitors went to College Point and Ridgewood, both heavily German, to enjoy the waterfront, the picnic and clambake groves, the dance pavilions, and the beer of the celebrated resorts. After the depression of the mid 1870s Ridgewood became a prosperous residential community, and this trend accelerated when the Brooklyn City Railroad built its car barns there in 1881. The growing number of residents in Richmond Hill and Woodhaven who had moved from Brooklyn led to the establishment of Ozone and Morris parks (1882, 1884). In eastern Queens, Hollis (1885) began as a suburb at a station stop of the Long Island Rail Road. In 1888 the Myrtle Avenue elevated railroad enhanced the attraction of Ridgewood as a residential community, and the population in Queens expanded accordingly, from 45,468 in 1870 to 56,559 in 1880 and 87,050 in 1890.

Still shifting from rural to urban, Queens by 1890 had emerged as a civic fringe area of dramatic contrasts. Newtown Creek had become a major industrial waterway notorious for its polluting refineries. Agriculture still flourished in eastern sections and in some western ones through an emphasis on large-scale truck gardening for urban markets. In Astoria Chinese-run vegetable farms grew bitter melon, bottle squash, bok choy, and other produce for homes and restaurants in Chinatown in Manhattan. Large greenhouses in Flushing and Bayside provided cut flowers to wholesalers in the city. Floral Park, in far eastern Queens, supplied tulips and carnations from vast fields to hotels and restaurants in Manhattan. An amusement park similar to Coney Island at North Beach (now occupied by La Guardia Airport) served Long Island City and other industrial neighborhoods nearby. At the close of the nineteenth century 152,999 persons lived in Queens, including Rockaway, the site of popular resorts and new beach towns.

In 1894 the residents of Queens voted in a nonbinding referendum on whether to consolidate with other districts into New York City: Jamaica, Newtown, and the city of Long Island City were in favor; Flushing, Hempstead, and other communities in eastern Queens were opposed. After consolidation on 1 January 1898 the municipal borough of Queens, and the new Queens County with which it was coextensive, lacked a distinct identity: the new jurisdiction was ethnically diverse, had many areas of farmland and open territory, and was separated from communities to the east that had formerly been part of Queens but were now in Nassau County.

During its first decade as a borough Queens increased its already high rate of growth, owing largely to the expansion of rapid transit. The Pennsylvania Railroad bought the Long Island Rail Road in 1900, electrified its route through Queens (1905–8), and opened tunnels under the East River in 1910, bringing most of Queens within commuting distance of Manhattan, whereas previously the sole links had been two ferries. The opening of the Queensboro Bridge in 1909 provided access to the borough by automobile and trolley. The value of land rose and more homes were built; 284,041 persons lived in Queens by 1910. To accommodate the increasing traffic a new road system was built, of which Queens Boulevard, a road two hundred feet (sixty-one meters) wide, was designed to be the main highway. The borough government promised to devise a uniform system for naming and numbering streets, which it hesitated at first to impose in the face of local opposition.

Much of western and southern Queens was incorporated into the city's subway system in the following decades. Service from Manhattan reached Hunter's Point in 1915, Bridge Plaza in 1916, and Astoria in 1917; another branch extending along Queens Boulevard and Roosevelt Avenue reached Corona in 1917 and Flushing in 1928. The fare from Queens to Manhattan was five cents. In southern Queens the Brooklyn Rapid Transit Corporation (from 1922 Brooklyn–Manhattan Transit) built an elevated line along Liberty Avenue through Ozone Park and Woodhaven to Richmond Hill in 1915, and along Jamaica Avenue from Brooklyn through Woodhaven and Richmond Hill to Jamaica in 1917–18.

During the 1920s the population of Queens grew 130 percent, from 469,042 to 1,079,129. More houses (many of which were brick and wood-frame) were built at this time than at any other in the history of the borough. Queens was by now mostly urban but remained rural in places. By 1930 it had eighteen golf courses (mostly in its eastern sections), more than any other borough. Its diverse and picturesque landscapes, both urban and rural, appealed to the silent-film industry, for which Queens became the national center of production. At least twenty studios, some rather small, operated there before Hollywood became the center of American filmmaking in the late 1920s. By the end of the decade there were four airports: Grand Central Air Terminal, Glenn H. Curtiss Airport, Jamaica Sea Airport, and Flushing Meadows Airport.

Development was slowed by the Depression, but the concentration of public facilities in Queens established the borough as a place of considerable importance. The Triborough Bridge and the Grand Central Parkway from the bridge to Kew Gardens opened in 1936. In the same year the city began preparing for the World's Fair of 1939–40 by leveling Flushing Meadows, for two decades used as a dump by the Brooklyn Ash Removal Company for ash, garbage, and dredgings from subway excavations in Brooklyn. The established networks of transportation were improved: Astoria Avenue was widened and made into a boulevard, the Bronx–Whitestone Bridge was built, and La Guardia Airport opened in 1939. With these additions and the existing rail and subway services north central Queens became readily accessible to residents from the rest of the city, and an ideal location for sports arenas and recreational facilities. The site of the World's Fair became Flushing Meadow Park, later renamed Flushing Meadows–Corona Park. In 1937 the borough became the site of Queens College.

The population continued to grow after the Second World War. Garden apartments the size of a city block were built in many areas, and tracts of land remaining in northeastern Queens, including former golf courses, filled up with one-family and attached housing. In Fresh Meadows, between Flushing and Jamaica, the New York Life Insurance Company purchased a golf course where the United States Open had been held in 1932 and in its place erected a garden apartment and shopping complex for fourteen thousand residents (1946–49) that received high praise. In the late 1950s and early 1960s many parts of central Flushing that had once been spacious and suburban were built up with blocks of four- and five-story apartment complexes. Postwar growth culminated in the opening of Shea Stadium in 1964 and the World's Fair of 1964–65, both in Flushing Meadows–Corona Park. The following years saw less development and more replacement and renovation of existing structures.

In the quarter-century after the Immigration Act of 1965 many immigrants settled in Queens, especially Asians and Latin Americans. The foreign-born population increased by nearly 30 percent during the 1970s, making Queens the city's most ethnically diverse borough. About 56 percent of the foreign-born residents of Queens in 1980 had arrived in the preceding fifteen years. Two fifths of all Asian immigrants in the city lived in Queens, including 29 percent of the total Chinese population, many Koreans, Filipinos, and Indians, and an increasing number of refugees from Cambodia and Vietnam. Many Asian immigrants settled in Jackson Heights, Elmhurst, and Corona. By 1990 there were nearly 100,000 Chinese and Koreans in Queens, who invested in Flushing, revived its shopping district, and made it one of the most important Asian neighborhoods in North America. The Spanish-speaking population expanded greatly in the borough as in the rest of the city: in 1980 half the city's Latin Americans lived in Queens, where there were communities of Peruvians, Bolivians, Argentinians, Colombians, Ecuadorans, Panamanians, Hondurans, Guatemalans, Nicaraguans, Salvadorans, Mexicans, Dominicans, Cubans, and Puerto Ricans. Many blacks settled in Hollis, Jamaica, Cambria Heights, St. Albans, and South Jamaica, one of the largest black neighborhoods in the city. Haitians from Manhattan and Brooklyn and recent immigrants from Haiti, the West Indies, and Africa also moved into these neighborhoods, as well as Springfield Gardens. Jamaicans settled in southeastern Queens, principally in Laurelton, Springfield Gardens, and St. Albans. Despite the influx of immigrants the population of the borough declined in the 1970s for the first time in recorded history before increasing again in the 1980s to 1,986,473, nearly equaling the figure for 1970. In 1988 the population was 49 percent white, 21 percent black, 16 percent Latin American, and 14 percent Asian.

With the growth of population in the twentieth century a political machine developed and the borough took an active role in city government. In the 1970s and 1980s Donald Manes became one of the most powerful politicians in the city as the borough president and the chairman of the local Democratic Party; in 1973 he appointed to public office Mario M. Cuomo, who in the early 1970s had forged compromises in Corona and Forest Hills between middle-class homeowners and advocates of low-income housing, and who later became governor of New York.

In 1990 about 36 percent of the population of Queens was foreign born, the highest proportion of any borough. Asians accounted for about a third of all immigrants and Latin Americans for about a quarter. The nation with the largest group of immigrants was China, followed by Guyana, the Dominican Republic, Colombia, Jamaica, Korea, India, Haiti, Ecuador, the Philippines, Romania, Peru, Pakistan, Iran, El Salvador, and Greece. The strongest and most varied patterns of immigration were in Astoria, Woodside, Jackson Heights, Elmhurst, and Flushing in the northwestern part of the borough. Jews and European immigrants were numerous in Astoria, Forest Hills, and Kew Gardens, as were Guyanese in the southwestern and south central neighborhoods of Richmond Hill, South Ozone Park, and Jamaica, Dominicans in Corona, Greeks in Astoria, and Irish in Woodside. In South Jamaica, Cambria Heights, Laurelton, and Springfield Gardens in the southern part of the borough the pattern of immigration was increasingly dominated by Jamaicans and other black immigrants from the Caribbean.

Queens remains a predominantly residential borough where the identity of the neighborhood is stronger than that of the borough. Industry continues in Long Island City, Maspeth, and College Point. The borough is the site of Aqueduct Race Track, the National Tennis Center (1978), and a large part of the Gateway National Recreation Area (Jamaica Bay). There are also several colleges and universities, including St. John's University, which is private, and four branches of the City University of New York: Queens College, York College, La Guardia Community College, and Queensborough Community College. The only working farm is Adriance Farmhouse, restored as a museum in Floral Park.

William Munsell, ed.: *A History of Queens County, New York* (New York: W. W. Munsell, 1882)

Vincent F. Seyfried: *Queens: A Pictorial History* (Norfolk, Va.: Donning, 1983)

Jon A. Peterson, ed., and Vincent F. Seyfried, consultant: *A Research Guide to the History of the Borough of Queens, New York City* (New York: Department of History, Queens College, City University of New York, 1987)

Jeffrey Kroessler: "Building Queens: The Urbanization of New York's Largest Borough" (diss., City University of New York, 1991)

Vincent F. Seyfried and William Asadorian: *Old Queens, N.Y. in Early Photographs* (New York: Dover, 1991)

Jon A. Peterson, Vincent Seyfried

Queensboro Bridge. Steel, two-leveled bridge with two cantilevered lengths spanning the East River between 59th Street in Manhattan and Long Island City in Queens, by way of an intermediate link on Roosevelt Island. Completed in 1909, it was designed by Gustav Lindenthal and decorated with ornate ironwork and finials by the architect Henry Hornbostel. The bridge was the first major one in New York City to depart from the suspension form and the third of eight bridges built across the East River. It has a total length, including approaches, of 7450 feet (2272 meters) and a height above water of 135 feet (41.1 meters). The Queensboro Bridge, often referred to as the 59th Street Bridge, is a city landmark.

Rebecca Read Shanor

Queensborough Community College. Junior college of the City University of New York, opened in 1958 on the grounds of the Oakland Golf Course. Students attended classes at several locations nearby until a new campus of thirty-four acres (fourteen hectares) was completed in 1978 at 56th Avenue and Springfield Boulevard. The college offers the only program in the state in laser and fiber optics and is highly regarded for its program External Education for the Homebound. In 1991 the college enrolled 4823 full-time and 7423 part-time students.

Marc Ferris

Queensborough Hill. Neighborhood in north central Queens, lying within Flushing and bounded to the north by Booth Memorial Drive, to the east by Main Street, to the south by Mount Hebron Cemetery and Cedar Grove Cemetery, and to the west by College Point Boulevard. The land rises steeply from Flushing Creek to a height of eighty-one feet (twenty-five meters) above sea level. In the nineteenth century the area was called Ireland Mill after a grist mill on the creek at what is now College Point Boulevard.

Vincent Seyfried

View of the Queensboro Bridge from Manhattan, ca *1910*

Queens Borough Public Library. The origins of the public library system in Queens date to the mid nineteenth century. Three libraries joined to form the Long Island City Public Library, chartered in 1896. About the turn of the century four other libraries joined the system, now called the Queens Borough Library. Andrew Carnegie donated $240,000 in 1901 to build eight additional branches, and New York City was authorized to provide operating funds. The Flushing Library, organized in 1858, joined the system in 1902. In 1907 the enlarged system was incorporated under its present name. The library had administrative offices in Long Island City until 1908, when they were moved to Jamaica. The Central Library, built in 1966 at 89-11 Merrick Boulevard in Jamaica, acquired collections in art, music, history, language, literature, the social sciences, science, and technology. In 1978 the Queens Borough Public Library became the first automated library system in the city, and from 1986 into the 1990s it had the highest circulation of any municipal library in the United States (13.2 million items circulated in 1993). By 1994 it was also the fifth-largest public library system in the country, with sixty-two branches, about a million registered patrons, and a collection of nearly 9.5 million items. Its adult literacy program was the first to use computers and offer driver's education and classes for the deaf. Through its New Americans Project the library also offered cultural programs and classes in English for immigrants, who in the mid 1990s accounted for a third of the population of the borough. The Chinese-language "Ni Hao" collections were available in twenty-four branches, the Spanish-language "Say Sí" collections in sixteen.

In addition to books the Central Library circulates films, videocassettes, compact discs, and magazines and has divisions for teenagers and children; in the Toddler Learning Center

Bus to the Queens Borough Public Library, ca *1937*

children aged one to three years can play with educational toys while their parents meet with child-care professionals. A special collection called the Long Island Division focuses on the history of the four counties of Long Island (Brooklyn, Queens, Nassau, and Suffolk) and contains photographs, slides, manuscripts, maps, postcards, reference books, newspapers, and genealogies. The Langston Hughes Community Library and Cultural Center houses the Black Heritage Reference Collection. The library mails books to the homebound and maintains Kurzweil readers, which convert printed text into synthesized speech, and telecommunications devices for the deaf. In 1993 an on-line public access catalogue was introduced at the Central Library, providing access to databases, listings of library programs, community information, and library catalogues worldwide. Each branch has Quick Cat, a CD-ROM catalogue that provides access to all catalogued materials in the collections of the Central Library and the branches; on-line databases may be used free of charge.

How Far That Little Candle . . . : The Queens Borough Public Library: Fifty-five Years, 1896–1951 (New York: Queens Borough Public Library, 1951)

GraceAnne A. DeCandido

Queens College. College of the City University of New York. It began as a group of extension centers formed by Hunter College and City College in the 1920s and became autonomous in 1937, when it first occupied a campus off Kissena Boulevard in Flushing on grounds used initially as a school for juvenile delinquents. The original complex of cottages in the Spanish style was supplemented during the next half-century by a modern campus that now includes the well-known music auditorium the Colden Center, Townsend Harris High School (part of City College until 1942), and the City University Law School. The college emphasizes the liberal arts and has a larger proportion of white students than any other four-year college in the city university system. Its faculty of thirteen hundred has included such distinguished figures as the writer Michael Harrington (from 1972 until his death), the geologist Barry Commoner, the composer Thea Musgrave, and the mathematician Dennis Sullivan, who holds the Albert Einstein Chair in Science.

Florence Neumann: "Access to Free Public Education in New York City, 1847–1961" (diss., City University of New York, 1984)

Selma Berrol

Queens Historical Society. Organization formed in 1968. In the year of its founding it moved to the Kingsland House, a historic house in Flushing. The society sponsors exhibitions, lectures, and walking tours, publishes a quarterly newsletter, and maintains a library and archive.

Queens–Midtown Tunnel. A double tunnel under the East River between 36th Street in Manhattan and Long Island City in Queens. Designed by Ole Singstad and opened to traffic in 1940, it is the third of four tunnels built to provide access to Manhattan for motor vehicles. The tunnel has a length of 6300 feet (1921 meters); ventilation towers with large, computer-controlled fans at either end of the tunnel provide a complete change of air every minute and a half. Advanced construction techniques made it possible to complete the Queens–Midtown Tunnel in four years.

Rebecca Read Shanor

Queens Museum of Art. Center for the visual arts in Flushing Meadows–Corona Park. Dedicated in 1972, it occupies the New York City Building constructed for the World's Fair of 1939–40. Although best known for its extraordinary PANORAMA OF NEW YORK CITY, the largest three-dimensional model of an urban area in the United States, the museum offers a wide array of exhibitions, from classical sculpture to the avant-garde. It also maintains a permanent collection, operates an extensive school tour and workshop program, and offers gallery talks, performances, and films.

Kenneth T. Jackson

Queens Village. Neighborhood in east central Queens, bounded to the north by Union Turnpike, to the east by the Cross Island Parkway (also known as the Belt Parkway), to the south by Murdock Avenue, and to the west by Francis Lewis Boulevard. The area was known during colonial times as the Little Plains because it marked the western edge of the treeless plain that extended to Wantagh. Thomas Brush opened a wheelwright and blacksmith shop in 1824 and later built a tavern, a country store, and a shed for curing tobacco. These enterprises became the center of a hamlet on Springfield Boulevard that came to be called Brushville. In April 1854 residents voted to change the name to Queens; Callister's Wagon Works opened in the same year. Extensive development began in 1870 when Scott R. Sherwood subdivided a parcel south of the tracks of the Long Island Rail Road into seven hundred building lots and Colonel Alfred Wood persuaded the railroad to build a station. A map of 1873 shows fifty houses; the population increased from 675 in 1891 to nine hundred in 1898. Growth accelerated after the construction of Interstate Park (1902) and the opening of Belmont Park (1905), and many streets and houses were added during the 1920s. To obviate confusion with the name of the county the Long Island Rail Road added "village" to the name of its local station, a change that was soon made to the name of the neighborhood as well. After the Second World War blacks from Hollis and St. Albans moved in, along with Latin Americans. Queens Village remains suburban and residential. In the 1980s many new immigrants settled in Queens Village, especially from Guyana, Haiti, India, and Jamaica, and to a lesser extent the Philippines and Colombia.

Vincent Seyfried

Queens West. A proposed redevelopment project along the Queens side of the East River in Hunters Point, authorized by the state legislature in 1984. The site occupies seventy-four acres (thirty hectares), including more than one mile (1.6 kilometers) of shoreline between 47th Road and 54th Avenue. The proposal calls for apartment towers of as much as forty-two stories, as well as a four-block hotel and office complex intended to keep agencies of the United Nations in New York City. Ground was not broken until September 1994, and then only for a sliver of park two blocks from the river.

Kenneth T. Jackson

Quill, Michael J(oseph) (*b* Ireland, 18 Sept 1906; *d* New York City, 28 Jan 1966). Labor leader. As a young man he fought in the Irish Republican Army before moving in 1926 to New York City, where he worked in the subway system. He helped to form the Transport Workers Union (TWU) in 1934 and the next year was elected its president. He won a seat on the City Council as a candidate of the American Labor Party in 1937 and failed to win reelection in 1939, but he was returned to office in 1943, remaining until 1949. He worked closely with the Communist Party, an influential force in the TWU, until renouncing it in 1948. As a vice-president of the Congress of Industrial Organizations and the head of its council in the city, he was a leading labor spokesman and liaison between unions and city government during the 1950s. Quill's ties to communists, outspoken Irish nationalism, strong support for civil rights and other liberal causes, and repeated threats to call subway strikes made him a controversial figure throughout his career. Sharp-tongued and humorous, he was constantly an object of attention from the press and appeared often on radio and television. He died shortly after leading a twelve-day strike of bus and subway workers during which he was imprisoned for contempt of court.

Joshua B. Freeman: *In Transit: The Transport Workers Union in New York City, 1933–1966* (New York: Oxford University Press, 1989)

Joshua B. Freeman

Quinn, Anthony (Rudolph Oaxaca) (*b* Chihuahua, Mexico, 21 April 1915). Actor. He made his début on Broadway in 1947. Although best known for his work in films he appeared in Broadway and touring productions of several plays, including Tennessee Williams's *A Streetcar Named Desire* (1961) and *Zorba* (1983–84), and maintained his prin-

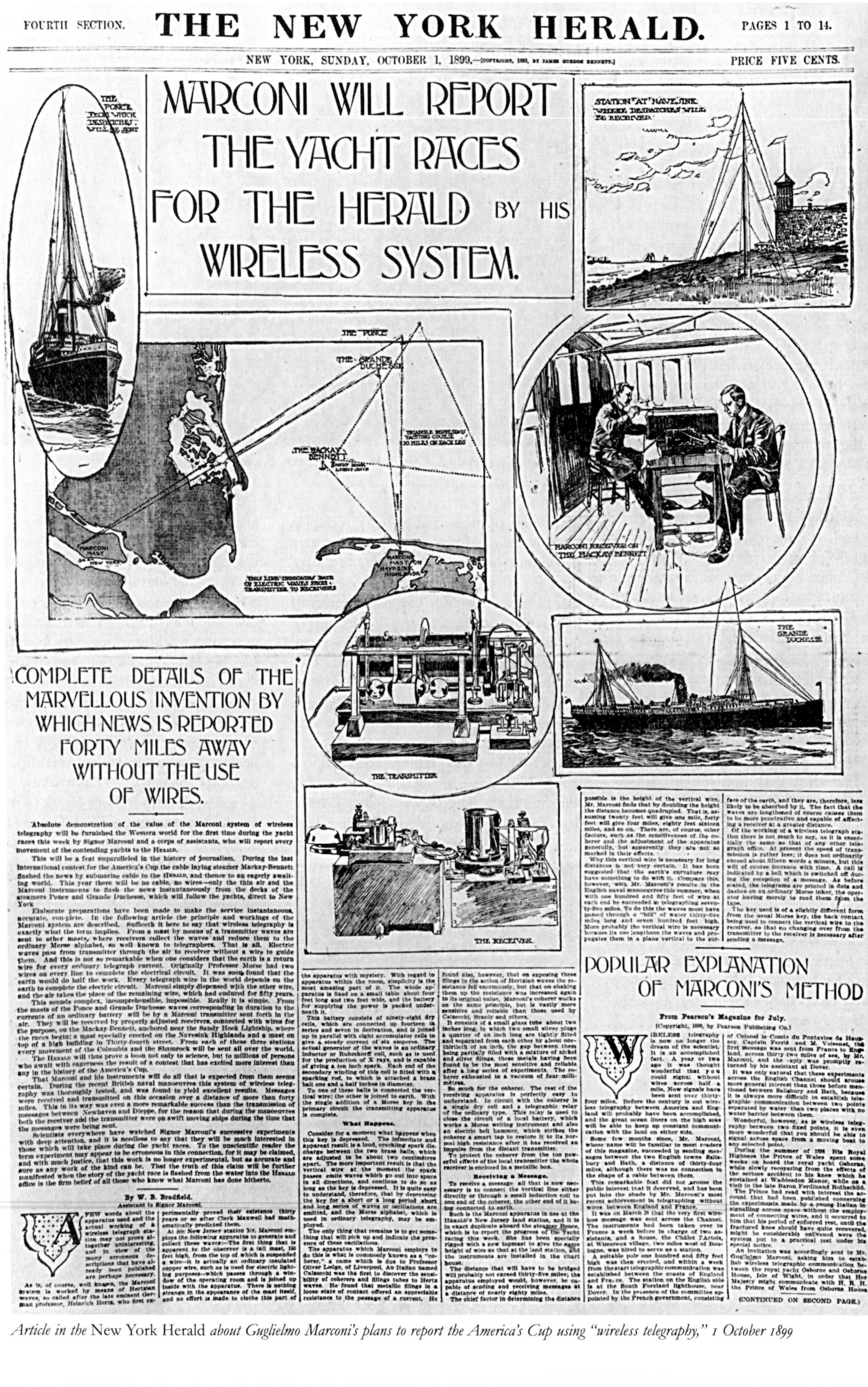

FOURTH SECTION. **THE NEW YORK HERALD.** PAGES 1 TO 14.

NEW YORK, SUNDAY, OCTOBER 1, 1899.—[COPYRIGHT, 1899, BY JAMES GORDON BENNETT.] PRICE FIVE CENTS.

MARCONI WILL REPORT THE YACHT RACES FOR THE HERALD BY HIS WIRELESS SYSTEM.

THE PONCE FROM WHICH DESPATCHES WILL BE SENT

STATION AT NAVESINK WHERE DESPATCHES WILL BE RECEIVED.

THE PONCE

THE GRANDE DUCHESSE

THE MACKAY BENNETT

MARCONI MAST ON NAVESINK HIGHLANDS

MARCONI RECEIVER ON THE MACKAY BENNETT

THE TRANSMITTER

THE GRANDE DUCHESSE

THE RECEIVER

COMPLETE DETAILS OF THE MARVELLOUS INVENTION BY WHICH NEWS IS REPORTED FORTY MILES AWAY WITHOUT THE USE OF WIRES.

Absolute demonstration of the value of the Marconi system of wireless telegraphy will be furnished the Western world for the first time during the yacht races this week by Signor Marconi and a corps of assistants, who will report every movement of the contending yachts to the Herald.

This will be a feat unparalleled in the history of journalism. During the last international contest for the America's Cup the cable laying steamer Mackay-Bennett flashed the news by submarine cable to the Herald, and thence to an eagerly awaiting world. This year there will be no cable, no wires—only the thin air and the Marconi instruments to flash the news instantaneously from the decks of the steamers Ponce and Grande Duchesse, which will follow the yachts, direct to New York

Elaborate preparations have been made to make the service instantaneous, accurate, complete. In the following article the principle and workings of the Marconi system are described. Sufficeth it here to say that wireless telegraphy is exactly what the term implies. From a mast by means of a transmitter waves are sent to other masts, where receivers collect the waves and reduce them to the ordinary Morse alphabet, so well known to telegraphers. That is all. Electric waves pass from transmitter through the air to receiver without a wire to guide them. And this is not so remarkable when one considers that the earth is a return wire for every ordinary telegraph current. Originally Professor Morse had two wires on every line to complete the electrical circuit. It was soon found that the earth would do half the work. Every telegraph wire in the world depends on the earth to complete the electric circuit. Marconi simply dispensed with the other wire, and the air takes the place of the remaining wire, which had endured for fifty years.

This sounds complex, incomprehensible, impossible. Really it is simple. From the masts of the Ponce and Grande Duchesse waves corresponding in duration to the currents of an ordinary battery will be by a Marconi transmitter sent forth in the air. They will be received by properly adjusted receivers, connected with wires for the purpose, on the Mackay-Bennett, anchored near the Sandy Hook Lightship, where the races begin; a mast specially erected on the Navesink Highlands and a mast on top of a high building in Thirty-fourth street. From each of these three stations every movement of the Columbia and the Shamrock will be sent all over the world.

The Herald will thus prove a boon not only to science, but to millions of persons who await with eagerness the result of a contest that has excited more interest than any in the history of the America's Cup.

That Marconi and his instruments will do all that is expected from them seems certain. During the recent British naval manoeuvres this system of wireless telegraphy was thoroughly tested, and was found to yield excellent results. Messages were received and transmitted on this occasion over a distance of more than forty miles. This in its way was even a more remarkable success than the transmission of messages between Newhaven and Dieppe, for the reason that during the manoeuvres both the receiver and the transmitter were on swift moving ships during the time that the messages were being sent.

Scientists everywhere have watched Signor Marconi's successive experiments with deep attention, and it is needless to say that they will be much interested in those which will take place during the yacht races. To the unscientific reader the term experiment may appear to be erroneous in this connection, for it may be claimed, and with much justice, that this work is no longer experimental, but as accurate and sure as any work of the kind can be. That the truth of this claim will be further manifested when the story of the yacht race is flashed from the water into the Herald office is the firm belief of all those who know what Marconi has done hitherto.

By W. B. Bradfield.

Assistant to Signor Marconi.

A FEW words about the apparatus used and the actual working of a wireless telegraph station may not prove altogether uninteresting, and in view of the many erroneous descriptions that have already been published are perhaps necessary.

As is, of course, well known, the Marconi system is worked by means of Hertzian waves, so called after the late eminent German professor, Heinrich Hertz, who first experimentally proved their existence thirty years or so after Clerk Maxwell had mathematically predicted them.

At his New Jersey station Mr. Marconi employs the following apparatus to generate and collect these waves:—The first thing that is apparent to the observer is a tall mast, 150 feet high, from the top of which is suspended a wire—it is actually an ordinary insulated copper wire, such as is used for electric lighting purposes—which passes through a window of the operating room and is joined up inside with the apparatus. There is nothing strange in the appearance of the mast itself, and no effort is made to clothe this part of the apparatus with mystery. With regard to apparatus within the room, simplicity is the most amazing part of it. The whole apparatus is fixed on a small table about four feet long and two feet wide, and the battery for supplying the power is packed underneath it.

This battery consists of ninety-eight dry cells, which are connected up fourteen in series and seven in derivation, and is joined up in parallel with eight accumulator cells to give a steady current of six amperes. The actual generator of the waves is an ordinary inductor or Ruhmkorff coil, such as is used for the production of X rays, and is capable of giving a ten inch spark. Each end of the secondary winding of this coil is fitted with a sparking rod, to which is attached a brass ball one and a half inches in diameter.

To one of these balls is connected the vertical wire; the other is joined to earth. With the single addition of a Morse key in the primary circuit the transmitting apparatus is complete.

What Happens.

Consider for a moment what happens when this key is depressed. The immediate and apparent result is a loud, crackling spark discharge between the two brass balls, which are adjusted to be about two centimètres apart. The more important result is that the vertical wire at the moment the spark passes emits waves which go out into space in all directions, and continue to do so as long as the key is depressed. It is quite easy to understand, therefore, that by depressing the key for a short or a long period short and long series of waves or oscillations are emitted, and the Morse alphabet, which is used in ordinary telegraphy, may be employed.

The only thing that remains is to get something that will pick up and indicate the presence of these oscillations.

The apparatus which Marconi employs to do this is what is commonly known as a "coherer," a name which is due to Professor Oliver Lodge, of Liverpool. An Italian named Calzecchi was the first to discover the sensibility of coherers and filings tubes to Hertz waves. He found that metallic filings in a loose state of contact offered an appreciable resistance to the passage of a current. He found also, however, that on exposing these filings to the action of Hertzian waves the resistance fell enormously, but that on shaking them up the resistance was increased again to its original value. Marconi's coherer works on the same principle, but is vastly more sensitive and reliable than those used by Calzecchi, Branly and others.

It consists of a small glass tube about two inches long, in which two small silver plugs a quarter of an inch long are tightly fitted and separated from each other by about one-thirtieth of an inch, the gap between them being partially filled with a mixture of nickel and silver filings, these metals having been found to be the most sensitive and reliable after a long series of experiments. The coherer exhausted to a vacuum of four millimètres.

So much for the coherer. The rest of the receiving apparatus is perfectly easy to understand. In circuit with the coherer is a single dry cell and a telegraphic relay of the ordinary type. This relay is used to close the circuit of a local battery, which works a Morse writing instrument and also an electric bell hammer, which strikes the coherer a smart tap to restore it to its normal high resistance after it has received an impulse from the distant transmitter.

To protect the coherer from the too powerful effects of the local transmitter the whole receiver is enclosed in a metallic box.

Receiving a Message.

To receive a message all that is now necessary is to connect the vertical line either directly or through a small induction coil to one end of the coherer, the other end of it being connected to earth.

Such is the Marconi apparatus in use at the Herald's New Jersey land station, and it is in exact duplicate aboard the steamer Ponce, which is to report the progress of the yacht racing this week. She has been specially rigged with a new topmast to give the same height of wire as that at the land station, and the instruments are installed in the chart house.

The distance that will have to be bridged will probably not exceed thirty-five miles; the apparatus employed would, however, be capable of sending and receiving messages at a distance of nearly eighty miles.

The chief factor in determining the distance possible is the height of the vertical wire. Mr. Marconi finds that by doubling the height the distance becomes quadrupled. That is, assuming twenty feet will give one mile, forty feet will give four miles, eighty feet sixteen miles, and so on. There are, of course, other factors, such as the sensitiveness of the coherer and the adjustment of the apparatus generally, but apparently they are not so marked in their effects.

Why this vertical wire is necessary for long distances is not very certain. It has been suggested that the earth's curvature may have something to do with it. Compare this, however, with Mr. Marconi's results in the English naval manoeuvres this summer, when with one hundred and fifty feet of wire at each end he succeeded in telegraphing seventy-five miles. To do this the waves must have passed through a "hill" of water thirty-five miles long and seven hundred feet high. More probably the vertical wire is necessary because its use lengthens the waves and propagates them in a plane vertical to the surface of the earth, and they are, therefore, less likely to be absorbed by it. The fact that the waves are lengthened of course causes them to be more penetrative and capable of affecting a receiver at a greater distance.

Of the working of a wireless telegraph station there is not much to say, as it is essentially the same as that of any other telegraph office. At present the speed of transmission is rather less; it does not ordinarily exceed about fifteen words a minute, but this will of course increase with time. A call is indicated by a bell which is switched off during the reception of a message. As before stated, the telegrams are printed in dots and dashes on an ordinary Morse inker, the operator having merely to read them from the tape.

The key used is of a slightly different form from the usual Morse key, the back contact being used to connect the vertical wire to the receiver, so that no changing over from the transmitter to the receiver is necessary after sending a message.

POPULAR EXPLANATION OF MARCONI'S METHOD

From Pearson's Magazine for July.

[Copyright, 1899, by Pearson Publishing Co.]

WIRELESS telegraphy is now no longer the dream of the scientist. It is an accomplished fact. A year or two ago it was thought wonderful that you could signal without wires across half a mile. Now signals have been sent over thirty-four miles. Before the century is out wireless telegraphy between America and England will probably have been accomplished, and the great ocean liners on the high seas will be able to keep up constant communication with the land on either side.

Some few months since, Mr. Marconi, whose name will be familiar to most readers of this magazine, succeeded in sending messages between the two English towns Salisbury and Bath, a distance of thirty-four miles, although there was no connection in the shape of a cable between them.

This remarkable feat did not arouse the public interest that it deserved, and has been put into the shade by Mr. Marconi's most recent achievement in telegraphing without wires between England and France.

It was on March 28 that the very first wireless message was sent across the Channel. The instruments had been taken over to France a week before in charge of two assistants, and a house, the Châlet l'Artois, at Wimereux village, two miles west of Boulogne, was hired to serve as a station.

A suitable pole one hundred and fifty feet high was then erected, and within a week from the start telegraphic communication was established between the coasts of England and France. The station on the English side is at the South Foreland lighthouse, near Dover. In the presence of the committee appointed by the French government, consisting of Colonel le Comte du Pontavice de Heussey, Captain Ferrié and M. Voisenet, the first message was sent from France to England, across thirty-two miles of sea, by Mr. Marconi, and the reply was promptly returned by his assistant at Dover.

It was only natural that these experiments across the English Channel should arouse more general interest than those before mentioned between Salisbury and Bath, because it is always more difficult to establish telegraphic communication between two points separated by water than two places with no water barrier between them.

Wonderful, however, as is wireless telegraphy between two fixed points, it is even more wonderful that you should be able to signal across space from a moving boat to any selected point.

During the summer of 1898 His Royal Highness the Prince of Wales spent some weeks on board the royal yacht Osborne, while slowly recovering from the effects of the serious accident to his knee which he sustained at Waddesdon Manor, while on a visit to the late Baron Ferdinand Rothschild.

The Prince had read with interest the account that had been published concerning the experiments made by a young Italian in signalling across space without the employment of connecting wires, and it occurred to him that his period of enforced rest, until the fractured knee should have quite recovered, might be considerably enlivened were the system put to a practical test under his special notice.

An invitation was accordingly sent to Mr. Guglielmo Marconi, asking him to establish wireless telegraphic communication between the royal yacht Osborne and Osborne House, Isle of Wight, in order that Her Majesty might communicate with H. R. H. the Prince of Wales from Osborne House

(CONTINUED ON SECOND PAGE.)

Article in the New York Herald *about Guglielmo Marconi's plans to report the America's Cup using "wireless telegraphy," 1 October 1899*

for ten minutes in the afternoon for $50 or in the evening for $100, and eventually there would be a chain of stations. The first station to be licensed under the plan was WEAF (based during its first year on lower Broadway and then at 711 5th Avenue), which on 28 August 1922 broadcast the first paid advertisement (sold for $50), for a cooperative housing complex in Jackson Heights, and which aggressively exploited the commercial potential of radio: Marion Davies gave a talk called "How I Make Up for the Movies" for the beauty product Mineralava and offered autographed pictures that drew hundreds of requests, and Will Rogers was reportedly paid $1000 to speak during the "Eveready Hour."

Initially advertising over the radio was controversial, but by the late 1920s it was the primary financial support for broadcasting. The city became the center of commercial radio after the first networks were formed there: the National Broadcasting Company (NBC; November 1926), led by David Sarnoff and comprising WEAF as its "flagship" and twenty-five affiliates nationwide, and the Columbia Broadcasting System (CBS; 1927), which had WOR as its flagship. In 1927 NBC was divided into the Red Network (with nineteen affiliates) and the Blue Network (which offered cultural and public service programs; it was sold by NBC in 1942 and later evolved into the American Broadcasting Company). From 1927 CBS and then NBC broadcast performances at the Cotton Club by Duke Ellington and later Cab Calloway. As governor of New York in the 1920s Franklin D. Roosevelt made broadcasting an important force in politics by discussing his decisions over the radio.

Programming for radio was influenced by cultural activities in the city. After 1929 many unemployed performers and musicians were engaged for radio programs. A brand of urban, ethnic humor made popular on the vaudeville stage in New York City by Al Jolson, George Burns and Gracie Allen, Ed Wynn, Jack Benny, Fred Allen, and Jack Pearl (as Baron Munchausen) was introduced on the radio to a national audience. Music programs were a staple for most stations: the performances of Bing Crosby, Rudy Vallee, and Arturo Toscanini with the New York Philharmonic were heard throughout the country, and from 1935 Martin Block, one of the first disc jockeys, broadcast his "Make Believe Ballroom" on WNEW, on which he played selections by several bands rather than only one (the program became one of the most popular of the following decade). Probably the most notorious program of the time was "War of the Worlds," Orson Welles's highly realistic radio play about an invasion of New Jersey by Martians, broadcast on the eve of Halloween in 1938. Public reaction to the play demonstrated how much New Yorkers relied on radio for news bulletins and live reports; residents created havoc as they fled their homes. After the outbreak of the Second World War radio became a vital source of information about world events. Radio was still being broadcast by amplitude modulation (AM): the commercial development of FM was thwarted by RCA until the 1950s and 1960s, when it became used mostly to broadcast classical music.

After the introduction of television the popularity of radio comedies, dramas, and variety programs broadcast by the networks declined while that of local programs featuring the music of Tin Pan Alley increased. Recorded music gained in importance and by the early 1960s accounted for some of the most popular programming in the city. Disc jockeys such as Alan Freed, Murray the K, Cousin Brucie, and Scott Muni played rock-and-roll and popular music on powerful stations like WINS, WABC, and WMCA, which adopted a format known as "top forty" (their playlists always consisted of the forty best-selling records). Many considered the new programs emblematic of the frenzied pace of life in the city and its growing youth culture. As AM radio was increasingly given over to top forty, FM stations like WNEW and WOR developed a new format known as "underground," or "progressive rock," in which advertisements, the banter of disc jockeys, and station identification were kept to a minimum. By the mid 1970s AM had declined in popularity. In the following decades FM stations directed their programming at narrow segments of the audience and specialized increasingly in one type of programming: top forty (which remained the dominant format), "oldies," easy listening, country, rhythm-and-blues, rap, jazz, classical music, foreign-language programming, news, and talk. Controversial disc jockeys like Howard Stern also became popular for developing a genre known as "shock," or "raunch," radio, characterized by savage humor and sexual innuendo. Broadcasters in the mid 1990s sought to cater to the diverse population of the city, which remained a national center for radio broadcasting.

Erik Barnouw: *A History of Broadcasting in the United States* (New York: Oxford University Press, 1966–70)

Christopher H. Sterling and John M. Kittross: *Stay Tuned: A Concise History of American Broadcasting* (Belmont, Calif.: Wadsworth, 1978)

Susan J. Douglas

Radio City Music Hall. The largest and most famous theater in the United States, situated at Rockefeller Center. Conceived by Samuel Rothafel as a palatial entertainment center affordable to the general public, it was designed by Donald Deskey in the art deco style with an opulent interior and 5874 seats, and opened on 27 December 1932 with a gala performance by Martha Graham, Ray Bolger, and Gertrude Niesen. The ceiling gives the illusion of a giant sunset; three large elevators on an enormous stage make possible fast and extensive scene changes and such dazzling effects as whole choruses rising up through the floor. The opulence of the foyer stunned theatergoers during the Depression: it has a ceiling sixty feet (eighteen meters) high and drapes extending from the ceiling to the floor, ornate mirrors, and long, slender chandeliers. Soon after its opening the theater offered programs combining feature films with stage shows, a format that remained popular for almost fifty years. In 1979 the interior was declared a landmark and restored. Under Robert Jani's direction the theater became principally a venue for live spectacles and tele-

Radio City Music Hall, ca *1937*

New York Railways System ("Green Lines")

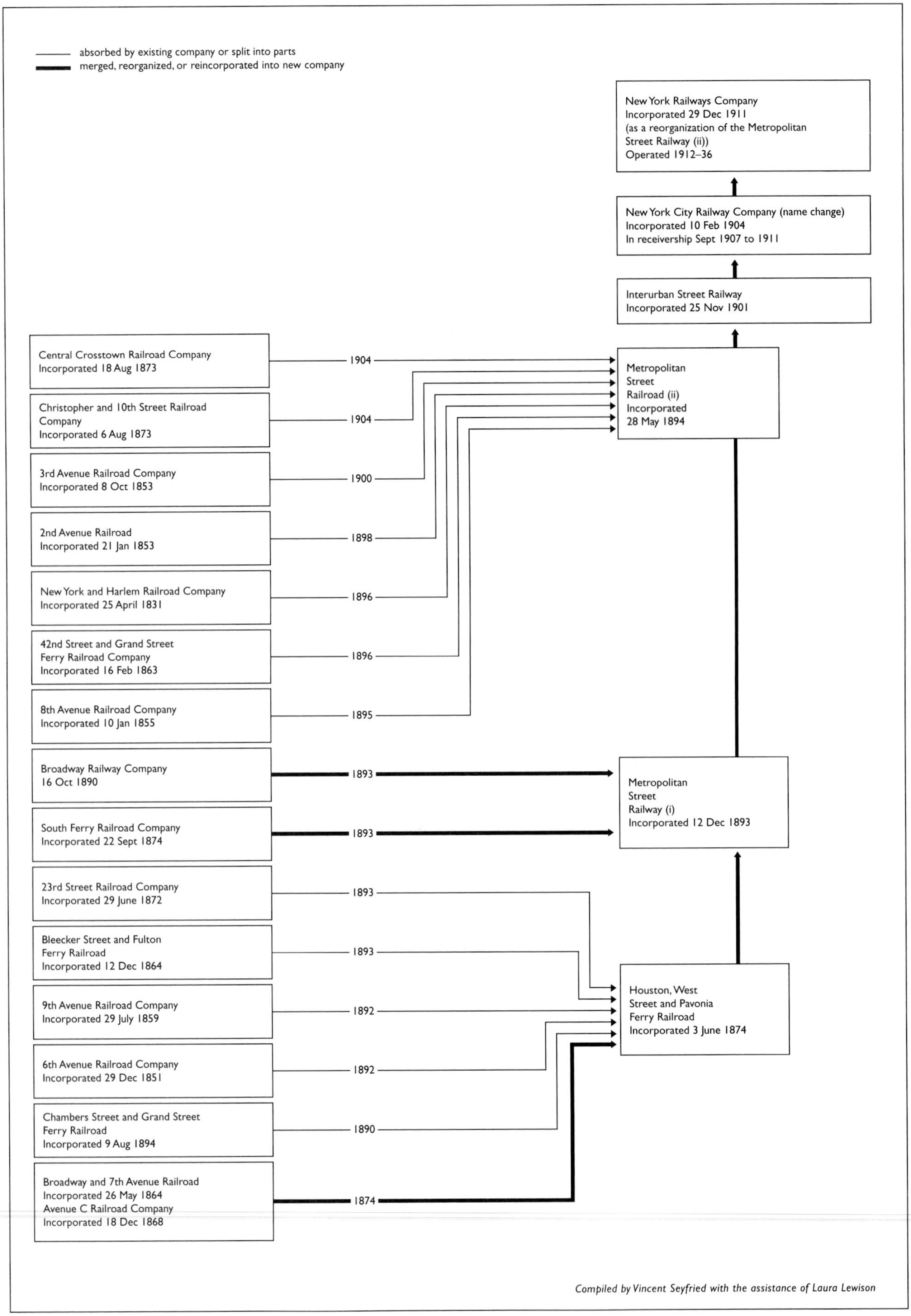
absorbed by existing company or split into parts
merged, reorganized, or reincorporated into new company
New York Railways Company Incorporated 29 Dec 1911 (as a reorganization of the Metropolitan Street Railway (ii)) Operated 1912–36
New York City Railway Company (name change) Incorporated 10 Feb 1904 In receivership Sept 1907 to 1911
Interurban Street Railway Incorporated 25 Nov 1901
Metropolitan Street Railroad (ii) Incorporated 28 May 1894
Central Crosstown Railroad Company Incorporated 18 Aug 1873
1904
Christopher and 10th Street Railroad Company Incorporated 6 Aug 1873
1904
3rd Avenue Railroad Company Incorporated 8 Oct 1853
1900
2nd Avenue Railroad Incorporated 21 Jan 1853
1898
New York and Harlem Railroad Company Incorporated 25 April 1831
1896
42nd Street and Grand Street Ferry Railroad Company Incorporated 16 Feb 1863
1896
8th Avenue Railroad Company Incorporated 10 Jan 1855
1895
Broadway Railway Company 16 Oct 1890
1893
South Ferry Railroad Company Incorporated 22 Sept 1874
1893
Metropolitan Street Railway (i) Incorporated 12 Dec 1893
23rd Street Railroad Company Incorporated 29 June 1872
1893
Bleecker Street and Fulton Ferry Railroad Incorporated 12 Dec 1864
1893
9th Avenue Railroad Company Incorporated 29 July 1859
1892
6th Avenue Railroad Company Incorporated 29 Dec 1851
1892
Chambers Street and Grand Street Ferry Railroad Incorporated 9 Aug 1894
1890
Broadway and 7th Avenue Railroad Incorporated 26 May 1864 Avenue C Railroad Company Incorporated 18 Dec 1868
1874
Houston, West Street and Pavonia Ferry Railroad Incorporated 3 June 1874
Compiled by Vincent Seyfried with the assistance of Laura Lewison

Third Avenue Railway System

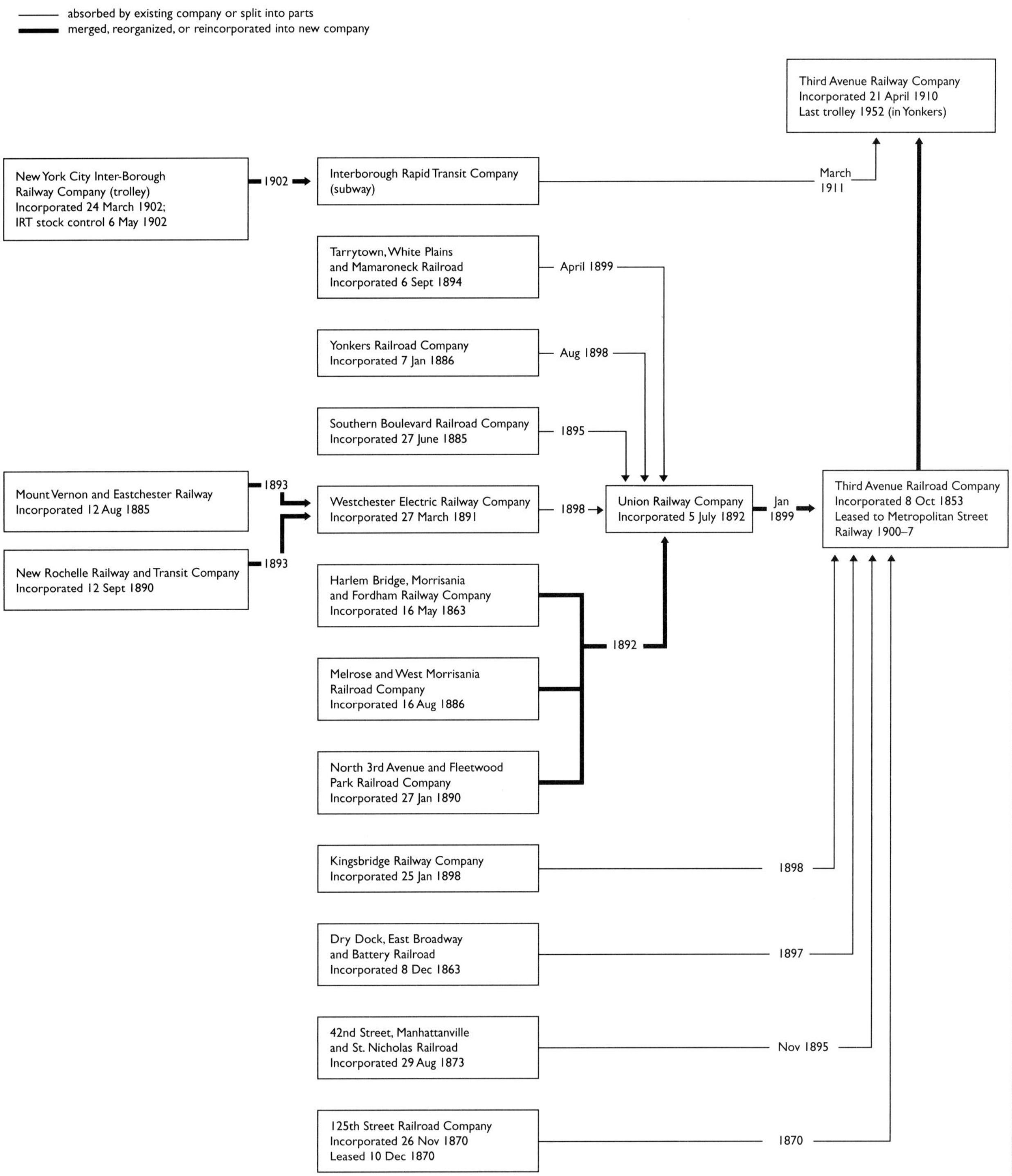

Compiled by Vincent Seyfried with the assistance of Laura Lewison

grounds were illuminated and used for concerts, fireworks, and other entertainments. Samuel Francis was the lessee in 1769, apparently its last year in operation. Rutgers's heirs sold the property in 1790; the house, which stood at what is now 232–36 Church Street, was demolished in 1796.

Gilbert Tauber

Rangel, Charles B(ernard) (*b* New York City, 11 June 1930). Congressman. He served in the U.S. Army from 1948 to 1952 and received the Bronze Star for Valor and the Purple Heart during the Korean War. After graduating from New York University (1957) and St. John's University School of Law (1960) he was an assistant U.S. attorney for the Southern District of New York (1961–62). He was elected as a Democrat to the New York State Assembly in 1966 from Harlem and to the U.S. Congress in 1970 from the nineteenth congressional district after defeating Adam Clayton Powell Jr. in the Democratic primary. He was a member in 1974 of the House Judiciary Committee that voted articles of impeachment against President Richard M. Nixon. In 1983 he was appointed deputy whip of the Democratic Party in the House of Representatives and in July 1984 he was named a chairman of the Democratic presidential campaign of Walter F. Mondale. He was elected to a thirteenth term in 1994. Rangel sits on the House Select Committee on Narcotics Abuse and the House Ways and Means Committee.

Larry A. Greene

rap. A popular and primarily urban form of music in which one or more performers chant rhyming verses in counterpoint to a highly rhythmic musical accompaniment, usually recorded. It evolved in the mid 1970s in the Bronx and other urban centers and became closely associated with black residents of New York City. The form had many antecedents: patter by Jamaican disc jockeys at open-air parties, between musical selections and eventually during them (a practice known as "toasting"); a long-standing black convention of verbal sparring called "the dozens," characterized by insults (often about parentage) and braggadocio (often sexual); and a tradition in black poetry of consciously evoking jazz, the blues, and popular music in language and orthography, a tradition that comprehends the poetry of Langston Hughes and Sterling Brown, of black writers such as Amiri Baraka who from the late 1950s read or improvised texts to musical backing, and of the improvised, militant, black-power declarations of the group the Last Poets in Harlem in the late 1960s.

Rap flourished in the 1970s at parties that resembled the rent parties held in Harlem before the Depression. Using several turntables and recordings by such musicians as James Brown and George Clinton, disc jockeys devised elaborate, layered musical patchworks that provided a backing for rapping and dancing. Among the techniques that they mastered was "scratching," a sound effect created by moving a record clockwise and counterclockwise while the stylus is held against it. At the same time and within the same circles there developed a highly rhythmic, acrobatic form known as break dancing. Rap soon evolved from a live genre to a recorded one, as recordings were made of rappers performing over other recordings. Some of the first widely popular rap recordings were made by musicians from New York City, including the Sugar Hill Gang ("Rapper's Delight") and Grandmaster Flash and the Furious Five ("The Message"). Although rap began as a true popular music that used inexpensive, widely available resources and could in theory be mastered by the diligent, as it became more complex and increasingly dependent on synthesizers and other sophisticated equipment, particularly in the brand of rap known as hip-hop, the number of musicians with access to the needed equipment became smaller. In the mid 1980s the popularity among white audiences of rap songs like "Rock Box" by Run–D.M.C. made large record companies recognize that rap had commercial potential. As commercial interests changed the nature of rap, less authentic entertainers came to dominate the form, which moved from the streets and small clubs and into large commercial venues; eventually adulterated forms of rap found their way into broadcast advertising. In the mid 1990s a number of prominent rap musicians continued to be associated with New York City, including LL Cool J, Big Daddy Kane, and the members of Public Enemy, and several radio stations in the city emphasized rap programming, notably WQHT and WRKS.

Gene Santoro

Rapelye, George Bernard (*b* New York City, 1784; *d* New York City, 27 March 1863). Antiquarian and real-estate magnate. He worked as a merchant's clerk from 1802 to 1806 before setting up a real-estate business in 1807. He owned nearly all the houses in the area bounded by 40th Street, 8th Avenue, 13th Street, and 11th Avenue but lived in miserly circumstances in a one-room apartment on Broadway; he also bought stocks and collected materials associated with the history of the city, including autographs, maps, and directories. Rapelye was a friend of John Pintard, an organizer of the New-York Historical Society, and a vestryman of St. Thomas's Church on Broadway.

James E. Mooney

Rapp–Coudert Committee. Committee of the state legislature active in 1940–41. It was led by George Rapp of upstate New York and his staff; Frederic R. Coudert, of the law firm Coudert Brothers, was the relatively inactive co-chairman. The committee originally was charged with investigating allegations of excessive spending in schools but soon shifted its focus toward purging communists from the municipal colleges and particularly from City College of New York and Brooklyn College. In addition to being centers of student radicalism, these colleges had large faculty and staff communist units that published lively shop papers, demanded improved working conditions, led local chapters of the College Teachers Union (affiliated with the American Federation of Labor), and supported the positions of the Soviet Union on major issues. The committee induced informers to testify about communists on the campuses and then called those who were implicated to testify themselves; uncooperative faculty members were dismissed by the New York City Board of Higher Education. The committee abruptly halted its investigations when the Nazis invaded the Soviet Union, but after the war its work was continued by such arms of the U.S. Congress as the Internal Security Subcommittee of the Senate Judiciary Committee, which also adopted many of its techniques and employed some of its staff members. With the cooperation of the Board of Higher Education several professors at Brooklyn College who had been overlooked earlier were dismissed in the 1950s, as were scores of teachers in the city's elementary and secondary schools.

Ellen W. Schrecker: *No Ivory Tower: McCarthyism and the Universities* (New York: Oxford University Press, 1986)

Marvin E. Gettleman

Raritan Bay. A body of water at the extreme southern limit of New York City. It is at the confluence of the Raritan River, the Arthur Kill, and the Atlantic Ocean, abutting Middlesex County, New Jersey, and the southeast corner of Staten Island at the neighborhoods of Tottenville and Pleasant Plains. The name of the bay and the river derives from an Algonquin word meaning "stream overflows." Raritan was also the name of an Indian tribe on Staten Island that existed before European settlement.

Clyde L. Mackenzie Jr.: *The Fisheries of Raritan Bay* (New Brunswick, N.J.: Rutgers University Press, 1992)

Andrew Sparberg

Raunt. Former neighborhood in south central Queens, lying on several marshy islands along a wide channel of the same name in Jamaica Bay; the name is of unknown origin. A fishing platform once stood on the southern shore of a marshy island facing the channel, and from July 1888 it was a station on the Cross Jamaica Bay line of the Long Island Rail Road. Small hotels on piles accommodated weekend fishing parties and the area was soon favored by rod and gun clubs, but it was abandoned after the Board of Health declared Ja-

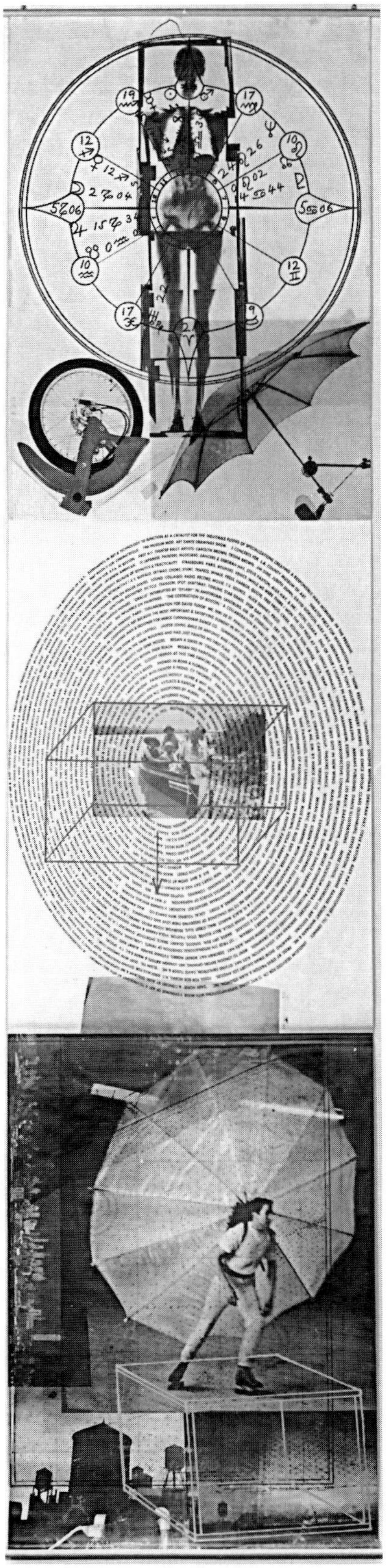

Robert Rauschenberg, Autobiography *(1967). Collection of Whitney Museum of American Art. Gift of Broadside Art, Inc.*

maica Bay too polluted for fishing in 1916. Railroad service was suspended after the railroad trestle was destroyed by fire on 7 May 1950. When the city rebuilt the line in 1956 as part of the rapid transit system the channel was filled in; it is now a plot of land opposite East 1st Road and the visitor center in Broad Channel.

Vincent Seyfried

Rauschenberg, Robert (*b* Port Arthur, Texas, 22 Oct 1925). Painter. He first saw European paintings in 1943. After moving to New York City in 1949 he became acquainted with the composer John Cage and the choreographer Merce Cunningham (with whom he later collaborated) and began to experiment with the economical medium of blueprint paper. His display windows for the clothing store Bonwit Teller brought him to the attention of *Life* in 1951; critics disdained his exhibition of white oil paintings in the same year and his all-black paintings soon after. He then executed a series of "combine-paintings," in which he sought to communicate a coherent message through disparate images. These wildly imaginative, bizarre collages juxtaposed diverse everyday objects (one consisted of a paint-splattered bed and pillow). He won prizes at the Venice Biennale (1954) and the Corcoran Gallery (1955) and in 1958 was given a one-man show by Leo Castelli. Rauschenberg is a leading figure in the avant-garde movement and one of the founders of pop art.

Leslie Gourse

Rauschenbusch, Walter (*b* Rochester, N.Y., 4 Oct 1861; *d* Rochester, 25 July 1918). Theologian. Educated as a minister in Rochester and abroad, he moved to New York City in 1886 as a pastor of the Second German Baptist Church. While ministering to his congregation during the blizzard of 1888 he contracted influenza that left him deaf. He had a strong social conscience, and after becoming acquainted with Henry George and studying economics and theology he helped to formulate the Social Gospel, a theology based on social reform. He became known nationally for his book *Christianity and the Social Order* (1907). After moving to the Rochester Theological Seminary he continued to write. Toward the end of his life Rauschenbusch was deeply disillusioned by the social breakdown that he believed had contributed to the First World War.

Janet Forsythe Fishburn: *The Fatherhood of God and the Victorian Family: The Social Gospel in America* (Philadelphia: Fortress, 1981)

Paul M. Minus: *Walter Rauschenbusch, American Reformer* (New York: Macmillan, 1988)

James E. Mooney

Ravenswood. Former name for the shore of LONG ISLAND CITY in Queens along the East River. The land was acquired in 1814 and developed by Colonel George Gibbs, a businessman from New York City. After his death in 1833 his land was divided by three developers into nine estates, and from 1848 there were several fine mansions lining the shore. In 1875 the first commercial buildings were erected, and the mansions eventually became offices and boarding houses. The area was heavily commercial by 1900. The name Ravenswood survives in that of the large housing project bounded by 34th Avenue, 24th Street, 36th Avenue, and 12th Street.

Vincent Seyfried

Raymond, Henry (Jarvis) (*b* Lima, N.Y., 24 Jan 1820; *d* New York City, 18 June 1869). Newspaper editor and congressman. He began his career in journalism as an assistant to Horace Greeley at the weekly journal the *New Yorker* and in 1841 helped Greeley to publish the first *New York Tribune*; in 1843 he joined the *Courier and Enquirer*, published by James Watson Webb. With George Jones and several other bankers from Albany, New York, he launched the *New York Times* on 18 September 1851. The newspaper thrived by providing detailed news and maintaining a high level of objectivity; it avoided both the sensationalism of the *New York Herald*, published by James Gordon Bennett Sr., and the crusading tone of the *New York Tribune*, while at the same time providing a forum for Raymond's Republican politics. The success of the newspaper helped his political career: he replaced Greeley as the principal advocate for such prominent Republicans as William H. Seward and Thurlow Weed, and he became a state assemblyman and lieutenant governor. In 1864 he led President Lincoln's reelection campaign and was elected to the U.S. Congress, but after Lincoln's death he espoused President Andrew

Proposed development along the East River in Ravenswood, Long Island, near Hallett's Point, ca *1836*

Johnson's Reconstruction policy at a time when most Republicans had abandoned its racist principles, and as a result his influence and that of the newspaper declined. Raymond eventually returned to the mainstream of the Republican Party and worked on rebuilding the *Times* until the end of his life.

Francis Brown: *Raymond of the Times* (New York: W. W. Norton, 1951)

Harrison Salisbury

"His Master's Voice," advertisement for Victor Phonograph

Razaf, Andy [Razafinkeriefo, Andreamenentania (Paul)] (*b* Washington, 16 Dec 1895; *d* New York City, 3 Feb 1973). Lyricist. The son of a Malagasy nobleman and a black American woman, he moved to Manhattan in 1905, where for more than fifty years he was a songwriter in Harlem and Tin Pan Alley and on Broadway. Over the years he collaborated with many musicians: his principal songwriting partners were Fats Waller and Eubie Blake. Some of Razaf's most popular lyrics are those to the songs "Ain't Misbehavin'," "Honeysuckle Rose," and "Memories of You."

Barry Singer: *Black and Blue: The Life and Lyrics of Andy Razaf* (New York: Schirmer, 1993)

Barry Singer

RCA Corporation. Firm of radio and television equipment manufacturers, formed in 1919 as the Radio Corporation of America at the urging of the U.S. Navy, which was convinced by wartime experience of the need for a communications system under American ownership. The new corporation was a monopoly that held all the patents in the new field of wireless communication. Its stock was controlled by such companies as General Electric and American Telephone and Telegraph under the leadership of Owen D. Young, later joined by Westinghouse. In broadcasting it also competed with Westinghouse, on the whole unsuccessfully until 1921, when David Sarnoff, then thirty years old, was brought in as the general manager and promptly broadcast the heavyweight boxing match between Jack Dempsey and Georges Carpentier to an audience of three million. Sarnoff then carried out his intention to manufacture radio receiver sets for less than $100 each and had sales in the hundreds of thousands each year. In 1926, with one station in Providence, Rhode Island, RCA went on the air as the newly incorporated National Broadcasting Company (NBC), which within a few months was operating on two networks. The federal government broke up the firm in the 1930s, and RCA became an independent corporation with NBC as its sole property. Among its many successes was the "Amos 'n' Andy Show," to which half the receivers in the United States were tuned for each program.

While having great success in broadcasting and the manufacture of radios, RCA allocated $1 million in 1935 for testing television, largely in an important research laboratory founded by Sarnoff. The firm launched commercial television in July 1941, but only a few hundred sets were able to receive the signals, and when war broke out the full production effort of RCA was given over to military purposes: its research staff had experience in developing radar and such other electronic systems as loran, sonar, and walkie-talkies, and many of the tubes designed for television sets were used in radar rooms. Sarnoff also went off to war, using as his entry a commission as a lieutenant colonel in the reserve of the Signal Corps that he had received in 1924 and his promotion to colonel in 1930. He served with General Dwight D. Eisenhower as a communications expert for the invasion of northern Europe and went with the troops to France, where he restored communications. Promoted to the rank of brigadier general, he returned to RCA by the end of 1944, where he resumed full control from his office at 30 Rockefeller Plaza.

Postwar life for RCA and Sarnoff meant television, and the first sets began to reach the public in late 1946. During the next year a

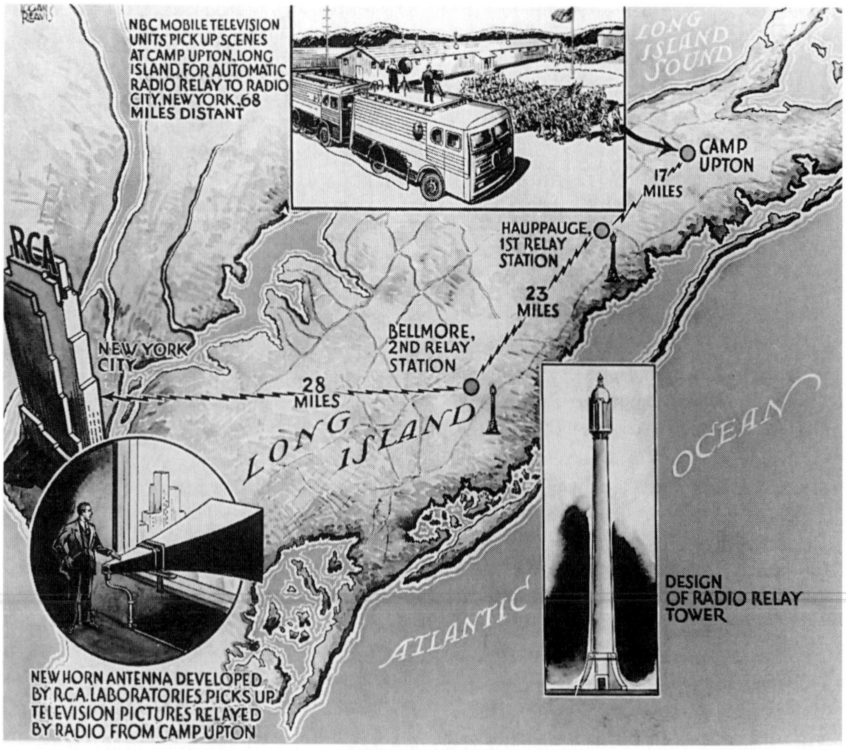

Illustration of RCA television relay

quarter-million sets were sold, four fifths of them made by RCA and all of them black-and-white. The Columbia Broadcasting System (CBS) was working on a color television but could not get its mechanical system approved by the Federal Communication Commission. Benefiting from this delay and from the resources of its electronics laboratory at Princeton, New Jersey, RCA prevailed in the race to develop color television by successfully arguing to regulators that the approach to color television taken by CBS would be incompatible with the millions of monochrome sets in American homes. As a result of this victory RCA had annual sales in the range of $100 million in the late 1950s, and twice that in 1965 (by which time color sets accounted for half of total sales). In that year Sarnoff resigned as chief executive of the firm and became chairman. His son took over as president and introduced a number of changes, two of which were scorned by his father: the adoption by the firm of its acronym as its official name, and its expansion into such disparate businesses as automobile rentals, frozen foods, greeting cards, and office buildings. In 1971 Sarnoff died after years of hospitalization. His son's contract was not renewed by the board in 1975, and change and turmoil marked the late 1970s; the firm had a debt of $1000 million by 1981. After a series of changes in management the firm reverted to its original businesses: electronics, communications, and entertainment. Sales and profits increased by the mid 1980s, but soon afterward a plan to acquire RCA was put forth by General Electric, and despite protests by some staff and stockholders the acquisition was realized in mid 1986.

Kenneth Bilby: *The General: David Sarnoff and the Rise of the Communications Industry* (New York: Harper and Row, 1986)

James E. Mooney

Reader's Digest. Monthly magazine, launched in 1922 from a basement office on Minetta Lane in Greenwich Village by DeWitt Wallace (1889–1981) and Lila Acheson Wallace (1889–1984). Only a few issues were published in New York City: by the end of 1922 the office moved to Pleasantville in Westchester County, where it remained into the 1990s.

James Bradley

real estate. From colonial times the development of New York City was heavily influenced by shortages of land and housing that led city and state government aggressively to encourage investment and private development through urban planning, the provision of infrastructure, tax abatement, and other incentives. One of the city's first efforts toward this end was the implementation of a street plan in 1811. As the population and number of buildings grew, land in the city gradually became scarce and valuable. During the first half of the nineteenth century John Jacob Astor became the wealthiest man in the United States largely by buying up land in the city; he built his empire in part by foreclosing on mortgages and buying land during the panic of 1837, when others could not afford to keep distressed property until it regained value. During the second half of the century real-estate developers gained readier access to debt and equity capital, as the city became the most important financial center in North America. The intense demand for increasingly limited space led developers to erect ever taller buildings, and during the 1860s multi-story office buildings, apartment buildings, and TENEMENTS were introduced. APARTMENTS were generally designed for middle- and upper-class tenants; many began as luxury units for rent and were later owned cooperatively. Tenements covered virtually the entire lot on which they were built and could accommodate many tenants, allowing landlords to collect a large rental income; the high value of such properties deterred architects from incorporating open spaces and recreational facilities into their design. Overcrowding became so severe that the city enacted tenement regulations in 1867, the first in the United States. Efforts to relieve the housing crisis were made by a number of private concerns, among them the City and Suburban Homes Company of Alfred T. White, which during the late nineteenth century built model housing projects for workers. At the same time the number of skyscrapers increased, as did the number of loft buildings, which had rooms with open floors and high ceilings for use as workshops and showrooms.

As the rate of development increased, real-estate interests became more highly organized, and public concern grew for controlling building standards more closely. One of the first trade publications, the weekly *Real Estate Record and Builders Guide*, was launched in 1868 by the Real Estate Record Association, which later published the influential books *A History of Real Estate, Building, and Architecture in New York City* (1898) and Richard M. Hurd's *Principles of City Land Values* (1903), the first systematic attempt to analyze patterns of urban development in the United States. Hurd, president of the Lawyers Mortgage Company and vice-president of the Mortgage Bond Company, was a leading lender for office and apartment buildings at the turn of the century. The Real Estate Board of New York (1896) was one of the first organizations of its kind in the country. From the 1890s private developers in the city vied with each other to build the world's tallest buildings, and successively taller skyscrapers were built: the Pulitzer and Flatiron buildings, the Times Tower, the Singer Building, the Metropolitan Life Tower, and the Woolworth Building (1913), which at nearly eight hundred feet (243 meters) held the record for almost two decades. Large-scale projects such as the Equitable Building, built by the du Pont family in 1915, received a great deal of publicity and aroused much public concern, leading to demands for public control. About this time reformers sought to regulate development more tightly. Efforts to improve building standards, eliminate unsanitary conditions, and relieve overcrowding in tenements culminated in the Tenement House Law of 1901, which prescribed minimum standards for light, air, indoor plumbing, and other housing improvements. In the first decade of the twentieth century owners and tenants of office buildings, hotels, department stores, and boutiques fought to prevent the garment industry from building lofts in commercial districts; they eventually won such protection through ZONING. In 1916 the city implemented the country's first comprehensive zoning regulations controlling the height, bulk, and use of all private structures. The new zoning law required skyscrapers to be built with setbacks above a certain height, thus allowing more light, air, and open space between buildings, and also leading to fundamental changes in the design of skyscrapers.

The 1920s saw a tremendous increase in the construction of residential housing and commercial buildings. Large-scale projects were undertaken by such developers as Fred F. French, Harry Black, Henry Mandel, Abraham E. Lefcourt, Irwin Chanin, Leo Bing, and Alexander Bing, financed by such lenders as Chase Manhattan Bank, Bowery Savings Bank, and Dime Savings Bank. Skyscrapers were concentrated near Wall Street and on lower Broadway until the 1920s, when the first ones were built around Grand Central Terminal. Midtown Manhattan soon flourished and became the site of the Garment District after a number of developers led by Lefcourt built lofts along 7th Avenue. By this time the city had more buildings of at least twenty stories than all other American cities combined. Competition to build the world's tallest building escalated, and the Woolworth Building was surpassed by the Bank of Manhattan (1929), followed by the Chrysler Building (1930).

An acute housing shortage led the city to introduce property tax benefits and bold policies for encouraging the construction of more housing. Various philanthropic organizations and limited-dividend ventures also sought to promote innovative residential planning and to reduce rents and the cost of housing. They built such developments as Forest Hills Gardens, a middle-income community in Queens financed by the Russell Sage Foundation and designed by Frederick Law Olmsted Jr. and Grosvenor Atterbury; the Paul Lawrence Dunbar apartment buildings in Harlem, built by the Rockefeller family; and Sunnyside Gardens in Queens, sponsored by the City Housing Corporation and planned by Alexander Bing and the architects Clarence S. Stein and

Henry Wright. Large-scale developments were also undertaken by such life insurance companies as Equitable Life, New York Life, and Metropolitan Life, which in 1924 under Frederick H. Ecker built Sunnyside, a 2125-unit apartment complex in Queens. The greatest number of units were built by limited-dividend cooperative housing organizations, often formed by labor unions; the largest was the United Housing Foundation of the Amalgamated Clothing Workers, directed for six decades by Abraham E. Kazan. Its first projects, completed in the 1920s, were the Amalgamated Houses in the Bronx and the Amalgamated Dwellings on the Lower East Side. Building codes for apartment buildings improved, especially under the Multiple Dwellings Law of 1929, which strengthened minimum housing quality and development standards.

Real-estate developments grew in scale and increasingly attracted the public's attention. Publicity focused on such projects as the Empire State Building, financed by the du Pont family, which at 1250 feet (381 meters) was the world's tallest building from its completion in 1931 until the World Trade Center surpassed it in the mid 1970s. Rockefeller Center, built by the Rockefeller family in the 1930s, was even more ambitious and costly and became a model for mixed-use projects with buildings containing offices and retail space. In addition to these spectacular successes, the high cost of property and the importance of the real-estate market in the local economy also caused devastating failures, such as that of French in the Depression. During these years the New York City Housing Authority began erecting PUBLIC HOUSING; the number of units reached 175,000 by the mid 1990s. City government also encouraged private development by expanding public infrastructure, a practice engaged in to an unprecedented degree by Robert Moses, who oversaw the construction and maintenance of bridges, highways, parks, and such public projects as the world's fairs of 1939–40 and 1964–65 in Flushing Meadow. Government agencies and special public authorities also built tunnels, airports, and convention centers. The Metropolitan Life Insurance Company sponsored Parkchester, a complex of more than twelve thousand apartments in the Bronx opened in 1941, as well as Stuyvesant Town and Peter Cooper Village on the East Side and Riverton in Harlem, which became prototypes for national redevelopment programs. In the 1950s the state and city introduced the MITCHELL–LAMA program of subsidized mortgages and property tax abatements for the construction of middle-income rental housing. Urban renewal projects were undertaken by the private developer William Zeckendorf, who assembled the land for the site of the United Nations in 1946 and built such residential developments as Kips Bay Plaza, Lincoln Towers, and Park West Village. During the 1940s and 1950s thirty major skyscrapers were completed in New York City (many of them in midtown Manhattan), compared with ten in the rest of the United States. By mid century multi-family housing occupied most of Manhattan and much of Brooklyn, the Bronx, and Queens.

The pace of development accelerated and the price of property in the city rose. By the 1960s office towers dominated midtown Manhattan, especially Park Avenue, and the redevelopment of lower Manhattan resulted in the construction of the Chase Manhattan Bank and the planning of the World Trade Center. The city cleared a number of sites for urban renewal projects, among them the site of Lincoln Center for the Performing Arts. Many developers prospered, including HRH–Starrett, Tishman Speyer, Rose Associates, the Trump Organization, Levitt and Sons, the Durst Organization, and Helmsley–Spear; a decline in the market forced Zeckendorf into bankruptcy in 1965. Under the leadership of Austin Tobin the Port of New York Authority built much of the region's infrastructure as well as the World Trade Center, an office complex dominated by twin towers 1350 feet (411 meters) tall. Programs to build and rehabilitate rental housing, condominiums, and cooperatives were begun by nonprofit community development corporations, sometimes using "sweat equity," under which prospective owners and tenants rehabilitated buildings with their own labor. During the 1960s and 1970s the city led the nation in generating capital for Real Estate Investment Trusts (REITs). Under Kazan the United Housing Foundation in the late 1960s and early 1970s built Co-op City in the Bronx, one of the largest residential complexes in the world (15,372 units). During a slump in the city's real-estate market in 1977 the Canadian firm of Olympia and York attracted international attention by buying eight office buildings at "distress" prices: when the market later improved, the value of the buildings quadrupled. In the 1980s public authorities built the new communities of Roosevelt Island and Battery Park City, both highly successful; Battery Park City in the mid 1980s became the site of the World Financial Center, a flourishing development by Olympia and York. Homeownership programs for low- and middle-income families in the outer boroughs were sponsored by the East Brooklyn Congregations and churches in the southern Bronx, and by the New Homes Program of the New York City Housing Partnership, inspiring similar efforts by other community builders. The developer Donald Trump amassed real-estate holdings worth thousands of millions of dollars; he experienced severe financial difficulties, as did Olympia and York, after a decline in the real-estate market brought on by the stock market crash of 1987 and the loss of jobs in financial services.

In 1990–91 the assessed valuation of real estate in New York City ranged from $47,226,648,735 in Manhattan to $2,668,664,967 in Staten Island.

Eugene Rachlis and John E. Marqusee: *The Land Lords* (New York: Random House, 1963)
Tom Shachtman: *Skyscraper Dreams: The Great Real Estate Dynasties of New York* (Boston: Little, Brown, 1991)

See also HOUSING.

Marc A. Weiss

Real Estate Board of New York

[REBNY]. Trade association of real-estate brokers formed in 1896 as the Real Estate Board of Brokers. Among its forerunners were the New York Real Estate Exchange (1847), the first real-estate trade organization in the United States (which lasted only a year), and the Real Estate Exchange of the City of New York, formed in 1885 by property owners and brokers to standardize practices and win the public's confidence in real-estate transactions; this exchange worked closely with the weekly trade magazine *Real Estate Record and Builders' Guide* (1868). In 1904 the board introduced an education program at the West Side YMCA that was one of the first of its kind in the country; it also supported the city's important zoning law of 1916 and took part in national efforts to introduce licensing for real-estate agents. In the mid 1990s it had more than 5600 members, including developers, brokers, property owners, managers, and lenders. The board works primarily as an advocate for tax policies and other public programs to encourage real-estate development in the city; it also supports education and research programs and operates the "Creators of New York" hall of fame.

Pearl Janet Davies: *Real Estate in American History* (Washington: Public Affairs Press, 1958)
Tom Schachtman: *Skyscraper Dreams: The Great Real Estate Dynasties of New York* (Boston: Little, Brown, 1991)

Marc A. Weiss

Real Estate Record and Builder's Guide.

Weekly trade publication for the real-estate and building industries of greater New York. It was launched in 1868 by Clinton W. Sweet, the publisher for four decades. The journal was at its peak during the late nineteenth century, when Manhattan developed into the hub of the integrated metropolitan area. It made itself indispensable to large development interests in the city by publishing regular, accurate, and geographically comprehensive reports of lot transactions, mortgage rates, and failures; copies of building plans and tabulations of building costs that helped to rationalize the metropolitan markets in real estate, credit, and building supplies; and "insider" columns and editorials. With the West Side Association, the powerful defender of property owners' interests, it advocated a visionary program of planned growth through comprehensive park, street, transit, and other public improvements, and it was an early supporter of using planning and landscape design to coordinate private development. Although its influence over development policies and planning debates declined early in the twentieth century, the *Record and Guide* continued to be published into the 1990s.

David Scobey

Recovery Party. Party label used on the three-way election of 1933 by Joseph V. McKee and his mentor Edward J. Flynn, Democratic boss of the Bronx. McKee, who had served briefly as acting mayor of New York City after James J. Walker resigned in September 1932, had counted on support from the White House. This never materialized, and although McKee outpolled the incumbent mayor, John P. O'Brien, who was connected with Tammany Hall, the winner was the Fusion candidate, Fiorello H. La Guardia.

Frank Vos

recreation piers. According to its charters New York City initially had use of its waterfront only for shipping and commerce, but in 1892 these restrictions were eased by the state legislature, which permitted the upper stories of certain piers to be set aside for public use. In 1897 the 3rd Street Recreation Pier at Corlear's Hook was built by the Dock Department; measuring 350 by sixty feet (107 by eighteen meters), it had space on the first story for landing produce and a pavilion in a French Renaissance style with seating for five hundred on the second story. Similar facilities were soon opened on the East River at 112th Street and on the Hudson River at Christopher and 50th streets. Attendants were present and offerings included music on weekday evenings, inexpensive food concessions, and free milk. By the time of the Second World War the oldest recreation piers were closed.

The city and state in the 1980s opened unused piers in Manhattan, Brooklyn, and Queens for fishing, sunning, and jogging. Food concessions, shopping, and cultural programs were introduced at the foot of Wall Street (at Piers 15–17 in South Street Seaport); a pavilion built by Robert Moses at 107th Street was refurbished for fishing and community events; and indoor sports were offered in the Cromwell Recreation Center, a renovated commercial pier shed built in 1936 in an art deco style at the foot of Victory Boulevard in Tompkinsville. Pier 84 on the Hudson became the site of rock concerts during the summer. In the early 1990s the city and state began implementing a plan to renovate piers on the Hudson between Battery Park City and the Intrepid Sea, Air, Space Museum at 42nd Street for recreational and commercial use.

Ann L. Buttenwieser

Ayude a reducir la basura
de Nueve York. Recicle por favor.
NEWS
Papel
Plástico
Vidrio
Metal
Aluminio
Mi Día de Reciclaje es:
SÁBADO
NYC Departamento de Sanidad

Refrigerator magnet to promote recycling, also issued in English and Chinese, 1992

recycling. New York City generates more refuse than any other city in the United States (24,000 tons, or 21,768 metric tons, each day), and its recycling plan is the nation's most ambitious. The need to recycle became especially pressing in the 1980s, as the environmental hazards of incinerating garbage became more apparent and landfills rapidly neared capacity (the city's only operating landfill, at Fresh Kills on Staten Island, was likely to close by the year 2000). A state law requiring a deposit on most glass bottles and aluminum cans in which beverages are sold was enacted in 1982 and took effect in the following year. Supermarkets and groceries designated as redemption centers were not equipped to accept the large volume of containers collected and brought in by the city's large homeless population, and at least one entrepreneur set up redemption centers where such large quantities were accepted. Because many consumers chose to discard containers on which they had paid a deposit, several million dollars in unredeemed deposits accrued to the beverage companies: these funds became the subject of political wrangling when Governor Mario M. Cuomo sought to have them used to defray the cost of recycling.

The city's recycling program began in earnest with the passage in 1989 of Local Law 19, a measure intended to combat the air pollution caused by large-scale incineration of garbage. In 1992 the city called for the phasing in of mandatory recycling by late in the following year. About 13 percent of the city's refuse was diverted from landfills and incinerators to recycling plants by 1993; at the time plans called for the city to have spent roughly $300 million on recycling by 1996, and to have diverted 41 percent of its refuse to recycling by 2000.

Local legislation requires residents of all five boroughs, who account for more than 2.6 million households, to bundle newspapers, magazines, and corrugated cardboard and to place rinsed glass, metal, and plastic containers and aluminum foil into special containers. The materials are collected by sanitation workers, then stored until they can be processed for resale to manufacturers. Superintendents in apartment buildings must provide space and bins for their residents, and the police are authorized to ensure that recyclable materials are not discarded along with garbage; fines for violations range from $25 to $100.

Edward A. Gargan: "State Bottle Deposit Law in Full Effect Tomorrow," *New York Times*, 11 Sept 1983, §1, p. 42

Joanna Molloy: "How Bad Is New York's Environment?," *New York*, 16 April 1990, p. 30

John Schall: "Recycling, Minus the Myths," *New York Times*, 22 Aug 1992, §1, p. 21

Jacqueline Lalley

Redemptorists. Members of the Congregation of the Most Holy Redeemer, a Roman Catholic men's order formed in Italy in 1732 by St. Alphonsus Liguori. In 1832 the first Redemptorists traveled to the United States to do missionary work with German immigrants. The first Redemptorist parish in New York City was the Church of the Most Holy Redeemer, on 3rd Street on the Lower East Side. During the nineteenth century the group operated missions at the church and established a permanent foundation in New York City. The Redemptorists were invited into the Archdiocese of New York by Archbishop John Hughes in 1841.

Joseph Wissel: *The Redemptorist on the American Missions* (New York: Arno, 1979)

Margaret M. McGuinness

Red Hook. Neighborhood in southwestern Brooklyn, occupying a peninsula of 680 acres (275 hectares) that is bounded to the northeast by the Gowanus Expressway and the entrance to the Brooklyn–Battery Tunnel, to the south by Gowanus Bay, to the west by Upper New York Bay, and to the northwest by Buttermilk Channel. Settled in 1636, the area was called Roode Hoek for the color of its soil and its shape, and for two hundred years it remained a marshy, rural enclave. The opening of Atlantic Basin brought about rapid maritime, industrial, and residential development in the 1850s, and the area became one of the busiest shipping centers in the nation; it was the second rowhouse district to be extensively developed in Brooklyn (after Brooklyn Heights). By the time of the Civil War ships from all over the world docked at Red Hook to receive and unload cargo and for repair and service, and hundreds of grain barges from the Erie Canal clustered at the mouth of the Gowanus Canal; there were also a few shipyards. The neighborhood at the turn of the century was a tough, lively, bustling place where Al Capone worked as a petty criminal before moving to Chicago. Although dominated by Italian dockworkers it also had a small but thriving colony of immigrants from the Middle East, centered along Atlantic Avenue. In 1936 the Red Hook Houses were built for the families of the dockworkers. This was one of the first housing projects in the city and also one of the largest, and continued into the 1990s to house most of the local residents. The ambience of the neighborhood in the 1930s and 1940s is conveyed in Arthur Miller's play *The View from the Bridge*, Elia Kazan's film *On the Waterfront*, and H. P. Lovecraft's short story "The Horror at Red Hook."

The deterioration of Red Hook was brought on by the construction of the Gowanus Expressway (1946), the Belt Parkway, and the Brooklyn–Battery Tunnel, which separated the waterfront from the rest of the neighborhood, and the neighborhood from the rest of the city. After reaching 25,000 in 1960 the population declined sharply. The chief means of employment, break-bulk shipping, was displaced in the 1960s by container shipping. In 1964 the city decided to replace much of the neighborhood with a container port that opened in 1981, but although this consumed much land it provided little employment, as most shipping activity had already shifted to New Jersey. The neighborhood became desolate and poor; eventually some 90 percent of the population was black and Latin American. The Fishport at Erie Basin, operating briefly in 1987–88, did little to help, but the late 1980s saw a slow, hopeful renaissance along Columbia Street. The principal commercial thoroughfares are Atlantic Avenue and Court and Smith streets.

WPAG

Toby Sanchez: *Red Hook Neighborhood Profile* (New York: Brooklyn in Touch Information Center, 1986)

Ellen Fletcher, John J. Gallagher

Redtke, Martin (*b* Lithuania, 13 Nov 1883; *d* New York City, 15 March 1973). Financier and philanthropist. He moved to the United States before the First World War and for a time worked as a gardener in New Jersey. Later he settled in New York City, where he spent his leisure time in the New York Public Library reading about economics, science, literature, history, and the arts. He made a fortune on Wall Street, lost it in 1929, and regained it after the Second World War. Redtke left his entire estate (valued at $368,000) to the New York Public Library; on 1 October 1974 a commemorative plaque in his honor was placed in the main entrance hall of the research library on 5th Avenue.

Vladimir Wertsman

Reed, John (*b* Portland, Ore., 22 Oct 1887; *d* Moscow, 19 Oct 1920). Revolutionist. Educated at Harvard University, he moved to New York City to work for the *American Magazine*, where he became acquainted with Lincoln Steffens and Ida M. Tarbell; he then went to work for the *Masses*, was imprisoned for supporting strikers, and worked as a war correspondent in Mexico and Europe for *Metropolitan Magazine*. He lived at 42 Washington Square South (1911–12) until moving to the mansion of Mabel Dodge at 23 5th Avenue (1913–14). In January 1916 he went to live with Louise Bryant at 43 Washington Square South. Declared ineligible for military service for reasons of health, he traveled to Russia, witnessed the October Revolution, and wrote articles for the *Masses* that led to charges of sedition. On his return to the city he lived briefly at 1 Patchin Place before settling in the autumn of 1918 at 147 West 4th Street, where he wrote his best-known work, *Ten Days That Shook the World* (1919). After a number of problems with the law he escaped to Russia using a forged passport. He is buried in the Kremlin.

David C. Duke: *John Reed* (Boston: Twayne, 1987)

James E. Mooney

Reed, Lou(is Alan) (*b* Brooklyn, 2 March 1942). Singer and songwriter. He grew up on Long Island, learned to play the guitar, and earned his BA at Syracuse University, where he studied with the poet Delmore Schwartz. With John Cale he led the Velvet Underground from 1965 to 1970, a rock group inspired by the work and ideas of the artist Andy Warhol. The poignant and often lurid imagery of its music violated taboos by evoking such themes as sadomasochism and heroin addiction, and stood in sharp contrast to the innocence and optimism of much popular music of the late 1960s. After the group disbanded his work was extremely erratic; his most accomplished record albums include *The Blue Mask* (with the guitarist Robert Quine) and *Songs for Drella* (with Cale), a tribute to Warhol. Although best known for his low monotone voice and abrasive guitar style, Reed is more highly regarded by critics for his lyrics and his poetry.

Gene Santoro

Reed, Luman (*b* Green River, N.Y., 4 Jan 1785; *d* New York City, 7 June 1836). Merchant and art patron. Brought up in Coxsackie, New York, on the Hudson River, in 1815 he moved to New York City, where in 1821 he opened the mercantile firm of Reed and Lee at 125–27 Front Street. He later built a mansion at 13 Greenwich Street and converted the third story into a private art gallery. Initially a collector of works by Flemish, Dutch, German, and Italian masters, he was inspired by patriotism to buy paintings by American artists. From Thomas Cole he commissioned "The Course of Empire," a series of five paintings, and he gathered portraits and historical and genre paintings by Asher B. Durand, William Sidney Mount, and George W. Flagg (1816–97) to fill his gallery, which opened to the public once a week (it was one of few institutions with public viewing hours). He was a member of the Sketch Club (*ca* 1834) and a patron and honorary member of the National Academy of Design (1834). In 1844 Reed's collection was bought by his son-in-law Theodore Allen (1800–50) and his business partner Jonathan Sturges to form the New-York Gallery of the Fine Arts (1844–58); it was given to the New-York Historical Society in 1858.

Wayne Craven: "Luman Reed, Patron: His Collection and Gallery," *American Art Journal* 12 (spring 1980), 40–59

Ella M. Foshay: *Mr. Luman Reed's Picture Gallery: A Pioneer Collection of American Art* (New York: Harry N. Abrams / New-York Historical Society, 1990)

Timothy Anglin Burgard, Ella M. Foshay

Reformed Church in America. Protestant denomination originally known as the Dutch Reformed church. Its first congregation in New Amsterdam was formed in 1628 and administered by Jonas Michaëlius, who reported fifty communicants at the first communion that he celebrated there. This was the official church of the colony, and through its influence Dutch Calvinism expanded steadily under the supervision of the Classis of Amsterdam. After the English assumed control in 1664 they aggressively replaced Dutch customs and institutions with English ones. Little resistance was offered by Dutch merchants and traders eager to protect their interests or by Dutch ministers, or dominies, who felt compelled to cooperate in the interest of preserving their freedom to worship: they generally won a measure of autonomy from English magistrates, despite Governor Edmund Andros's efforts to install a dominie with Anglican orders in the Dutch Reformed church in Albany, New York. Irked by the economic hardship incurred during the English conquest, many congregations disputed the salaries of dominies willing to assimilate. In 1689 Jacob Leisler led an uprising of lower-class Dutch settlers against Andros, English rule, and a perceived threat of papism, and soon the rebels also found themselves pitted against the dominies and the Dutch mercantile élite. When the rebellion was put down in 1691 Henricus Selyns, minister of the Dutch Reformed church in New York City, lambasted Leisler and praised the restoration of political order. He later persuaded Governor Henry Sloughter to sign the warrant for Leisler's execution.

During the following decade the Dutch Reformed church was torn by feuding between supporters and opponents of Leisler, whose rebellion came to be viewed as a protest against assimilation to English ways; control of church offices was sought by both factions. In 1698 supporters were permitted by the governor to exhume the bodies of Leisler and Jacob Milborne, his lieutenant, which were reinterred in the city's Dutch church after a cavalcade through the streets. Tensions within the Reformed church eased somewhat as many of Leisler's supporters moved to New

Jersey to escape political and ecclesiastical factionalism. A greater degree of harmony was restored after Selyns's death in 1701. For the first half of the eighteenth century Gualtherus Du Bois led the city's Dutch Reformed churches, which faced steady attrition owing in part to the success of the Society for the Propagation of the Gospel (1701), an organization of Anglican missionaries who distributed the Book of Common Prayer in Dutch and also opened schools that taught Anglican theology and English. The society's efforts were reinforced by several governors who sought to advance Anglicanism, which they considered the official religion of the colony according to the Ministry Act of 1693.

Education was left increasingly to Anglicans as the Dutch churches allowed their own schools to decline. Recognizing that the future of the colony lay with the English, many young people became Anglicans and Presbyterians, and to encourage their return to the Dutch church, congregants at mid century called on Du Bois to appoint an English-speaking minister. William Livingston, publisher of the *Independent Reflector*, lamented the "melancholy declension" of the Dutch churches because the young, "forgetting the religion of their ancestors, wandered in search of new persuasions"; he himself had left the Dutch Reformed church because he could not understand the Dutch language. In 1763 the Dutch church in the city engaged Archibald Laidlie, an English-speaking minister who had graduated from the University of Edinburgh. His sermons soon drew three times as many congregants as those of Dutch dominies. By the time of the American Revolution the Dutch Reformed church was one denomination among many in the city.

The denomination took its present name in 1867 and remained active into the 1990s. One of its better-known congregations is the Marble Collegiate Church in Manhattan.

John M. Murrin: "English Rights as Ethnic Aggression: The English Conquest, the Charter of Liberties of 1683, and Leisler's Rebellion in New York," *Authority and Resistance in Early New York*, ed. William Pencak and Conrad Edick Wright (New York: New-York Historical Society, 1988), 56–94

Richard W. Pointer: *Protestant Pluralism and the New York Experience: A Study of Eighteenth-century Religious Diversity* (Bloomington: Indiana University Press, 1988)

Randall Balmer: *A Perfect Babel of Confusion: Dutch Religion and English Culture in the Middle Colonies* (New York: Oxford University Press, 1989)

Randall Balmer

Reformed Church of South Bushwick. Church at 15 Himrod Street in Brooklyn, organized in 1851. Known as the White Church, it is a white-frame structure with Greek Revival elements, a central tower, and a steeple.

Kenneth T. Jackson

Reformed Dutch Church of Newtown. One-story church at 85-15 Broadway in Elmhurst, erected in 1831 in a Greek Revival style with a pitched roof and a flat-roofed porch supported by columns and decorated with cornices; it is one of the city's few remaining churches built entirely of wood. The building replaced a small octagonal church, built in 1735, that stood at the center of the colonial settlement of Newtown and was used in 1780 as a powder magazine by the British. Built by volunteers, the new church was designed to incorporate the bell tower and cornerstone of the original one. In 1858 a separate chapel, Fellowship Hall, was built to the south. During a renovation in 1906 the church was enlarged, Fellowship Hall was moved back from the street, and the columned porches of the two buildings were aligned and connected with a hallway. Another chapel was added during the 1940s to honor three members of the congregation who died in the Second World War. The 1970s saw an influx of Asian immigrants in the neighborhood, and a Taiwanese ministry was initiated in August 1980. Between 1988 and 1991 the church underwent another restoration and the congregation bought two houses for further expansion.

Amanda Aaron

Reformed Episcopal church. Religious movement launched at a meeting in the Young Men's Christian Association Hall (4th Avenue and 23rd Street) on 2 December 1873 by George David Cummins. Its formation was the result of a breach opened in the 1840s between the Evangelical wing of the Protestant Episcopal church (of which Cummins, the assistant bishop of Kentucky, was a member) and the Anglo-Catholic movement (which entered the church through the General Theological Seminary of New York City), and more immediately of Cummins's participation in the closing communion service of the Evangelical Alliance in New York City (2–12 October 1873), for which he received a severe censure from Bishop Horatio Potter that led him to resign from the church on 10 November. The new movement advocated a moderate episcopacy but failed to attract many Evangelicals and suffered a serious setback when Cummins died in 1876; its national membership never grew beyond twelve thousand (in the 1920s). The Reformed Episcopalians at one time had twelve parishes in New York City, but in the mid 1990s only the First Reformed Episcopal Church on East 50th Street remained.

Allen C. Guelzo: *For the Union of Evangelical Christendom: The Irony of the Reformed Episcopalians, 1873–1930* (University Park: Pennsylvania State University Press, 1994)

Allen C. Guelzo

Reformed Protestant Dutch Church. Church at 630 New Lots Avenue in Brooklyn, also known as the New Lots Community Church and the New Lots Reformed Dutch Church. The building was erected in 1823 by local Dutch farmers who had grown weary of the weekly trek to the Flatbush Reformed Church. A registered landmark, it is a simple wood clapboard church with a pitched roof, an impressive steeple, and Gothic Revival stained-glass windows. In 1994 its predominantly black congregation had 250 active members.

Kenneth T. Jackson

Regional Plan Association of New York [RPA]. A private organization formed in 1929 to implement the *Regional Plan of New York and Its Environs*, a study comprising ten preliminary and two final volumes proposed by the Committee on the Regional Plan. It superseded the Committee on the Regional Plan (formed in 1922), which continued to function until the two organizations completed their merger in 1931. Among the many experts in urban development who contributed to the plan were Edward Bassett, the attorney who wrote the zoning law of 1916; Clarence Arthur Perry, who developed the concept of the "neighborhood unit"; Raymond Unwin, founder of the urban planning program at Columbia University; and other well-known planners such as Harland Bartholomew, Edward Bennett, and George Ford. The authors of the plan proposed a detailed system of land use and transportation improvements for Manhattan, the outer boroughs, and surrounding areas in New York State, New Jersey, and Connecticut. They intended to maintain the metropolitan region as the economic center of the United States by strengthening the financial and commercial centers, improving the upper-income residential areas of Manhattan, and dispersing manufacturing throughout the region. Special attention was given to highway and bridge construction and to the preservation of open space. On the release of the plan funds for monitoring its success were granted to the RPA by the Russell Sage Foundation. With the support of the Ford Foundation and the Rockefeller Brothers Fund the association sponsored further planning studies during the 1950s and early 1960s, including the New York Metropolitan Region Study, directed by the economist Raymond Vernon, and *Spread City*, an influential forecast of suburban sprawl published in 1962.

C. McKim Norton, son of Charles Dyer Norton and president of the RPA, guided the preparation of *The Second Regional Plan* in 1968. The plan proposed to control suburbanization in the region and revitalize its core, by coordinating the construction of office buildings and the planning of public transit, building the Citicorp Center, the World Trade Center, and new plazas and arcades in Manhattan, reviving downtown Brooklyn, and redeveloping the region's waterfronts.

In 1990 the RPA began preparing for a third regional plan intended to emphasize the role of New York City in an increasingly global economy.

Forbes B. Hays: *Community Leadership: The Regional Plan Association of New York* (New York: Columbia University Press, 1965)

David Alan Johnson: "The Emergence of Metropolitan Regionalism: An Analysis of the 1929 Regional Plan of New York and Its Environs" (diss., Cornell University, 1974)

John T. Metzger, Marc A. Weiss

Regis High School. Jesuit day school for boys at 55 East 84th Street, opened in 1914. Its building, designed by the firm of Maginnis and Walsh, was completed in 1917 and later designated a city landmark. The school is known for its competitive admissions and rigorous academic program, and all its students receive scholarships covering all expenses except laboratory and activity fees. In the mid 1990s there were five hundred students drawn from the entire metropolitan area, including New Jersey and Connecticut.

Gilbert Tauber

Rego Park. Neighborhood in east central Queens, bounded to the north by Queens Boulevard, to the east by Yellowstone Boulevard, to the south by the intersection of Yellowstone and Woodhaven boulevards, and to the west by Woodhaven Boulevard. The name is derived from that of the Real Good Construction Company, which developed the neighborhood in the 1920s. Until 1920 the area was covered by farms and had one road, Remsen's Lane (now 63rd Drive, Fleet Court, and 64th Road), which abutted the Zeiler farm; for several years Chinese farmers who kept strictly to themselves grew vegetables there for sale in Chinatown. The Rego Construction Company bought out the farms during the 1920s and built one-family row houses, multi-family houses, and apartment buildings, and in 1923 the area was named by the developers Henry Schloh and Charles I. Hausmann. The core of the development was 525 eight-room houses costing $8000 each; the first stores were built in 1926 on Queens Boulevard and 63rd Drive. Apartment buildings were erected in 1927–28, among them Jupiter Court, Remo Hall, and Marion Court. A railroad station opened in 1928, the expressway was extended to Queens in 1935, and a subway line to Union Turnpike began service on 31 December 1936. In 1939–40 the World's Fair spurred development: apartments filled the last open land on 99th Street and on Queens Boulevard. Rego Park has a diverse mix of apartment buildings and private housing, including Lefrak City (1962–67), a huge housing complex astride the Long Island Expressway that at first was predominantly Irish, German, and Italian and from 1970 attracted many immigrants from the Soviet Union and Asia. About 15 percent of the immigrants settling in Rego Park in the 1980s were Chinese. There was also a large number of immigrants, many of them Jewish, from the Soviet Union, Iran, and Israel, as well as enclaves of Indians, Colombians, Koreans, and Romanians.

Vincent Seyfried

Reich, Steve [Stephen Michael] (*b* New York City, 3 Oct 1936). Composer. He studied philosophy at Cornell University (BA 1957) and composition at Mills College and the Juilliard School with Darius Milhaud and Luciano Berio. His interest in non-Western music inspired him to study drumming in Ghana, and from the 1960s he composed a number of experimental works influenced by John Cage. In the late 1960s his music became characterized by the repetition of short motivic cells, rhythmic regularity punctuated by syncopations, gradual harmonic change, and the use of percussive timbres; with Philip Glass he was one of the early exponents of minimalism. Reich's best-known works include *Drumming* (1971), *Music for 18 Musicians* (1976), and *Tehillim* (1981).

Wim Mertens: *American Minimal Music: La Monte Young, Terry Riley, Steve Reich, Philip Glass* (New York: Broude, 1983)

Frank Morrow

Reid, Helen (Miles) Rogers (*b* Appleton, Wis., 23 Nov 1882; *d* New York City, 27 July 1970). Newspaper publisher. After graduating from Barnard College (1903) she became the social secretary of Elisabeth Mills Reid, whose husband, Whitelaw Reid, was the publisher of the *New York Herald Tribune.* In 1911 she married their son Ogden Reid, who took over the newspaper after his father's death in 1912, and she began working for it in 1918. She recruited women as reporters and executives and helped to make the *Herald Tribune* into a profitable venture by developing a suburban readership, introducing features for female readers, and establishing the Herald Tribune Forum, an annual conference in which national and world leaders addressed women on the issues of the day. Known as "Queen Helen," she played an important role at the newspaper until its sale in 1957. Reid actively supported woman suffrage, Republican candidates for political office (notably Wendell Willkie in 1940 and Dwight D. Eisenhower in 1952), internationalist causes, and Barnard College.

Richard Kluger: *The Paper: The Life and Death of the New York Herald Tribune* (New York: Alfred A. Knopf, 1986)

Lynn D. Gordon

Reid, Whitelaw (*b* near Xenia, Ohio, 27 Oct 1837; *d* London, 15 Dec 1912). Journalist and diplomat. After covering the Civil War for the *Gazette* (Cincinnati) he joined the staff of the *New York Tribune* in 1868. On Horace Greeley's death in 1872 he became the principal owner and editor-in-chief of the newspaper and was considered by many to be the nation's most influential Republican editor. He relinquished active editorship of the *Tribune* in 1889 but retained financial control. In the same year he was appointed minister to France by President Benjamin Harrison, and in 1892 he returned to the United States and was the unsuccessful Republican candidate for vice president. He became President Theodore Roosevelt's ambassador to Great Britain in 1905, a position he held until his death.

Bingham Duncan: *Whitelaw Reid: Journalist, Politician, Diplomat* (Athens: University of Georgia Press, 1975)

Steven H. Jaffe

Reinhardt, Ad(olf D. Frederick) (*b* Buffalo, 24 Dec 1913; *d* New York City, 30 Aug 1967). Painter. He grew up in Brooklyn and Queens and studied at Columbia University from 1931 to 1935. While working in a studio next to Stuart Davis's in 1938 he began a series of brightly colored abstract paintings inspired partly by what he called Davis's "loud ragtime jazz records" and "loud colored shirts on the clothes-line." He had his first major exhibition in 1946 at the Betty Parsons Gallery and in 1952 was a visiting critic at the Yale School of Art. Unlike most other painters of the New York School, he opposed painterly expressionism and decried what he considered the corrupt relationship of artists, dealers, and critics (especially Clement Greenberg). He drew cartoons for the newspaper *PM* in the 1940s that satirized the art world and was himself the subject of "Pure Paints a Picture" (1957), a spoof written by Elaine de Kooning. He also took part in a protest in November 1940 against the Museum of Modern Art because of its reluctance to exhibit contemporary abstract painting. From 1947 to 1967 he taught at Brooklyn College. Reinhardt's paintings were eventually acknowledged as some of the most theoretically rich work produced by the New York School: while taking Greenberg's formalism to an extreme degree, his work also directly influenced the anti-formalist minimal and conceptual movements that took shape in the decade after his death. In 1991 he was given a posthumous retrospective exhibition at the Museum of Modern Art. Reinhardt is best known for a series of black monochrome paintings exhibited at a retrospective exhibition at the Jewish Museum in Manhattan in 1966 and for his writings on art, which address notions of autonomy and purity in painting and set forth a dogma of radical formalism.

Lucy R. Lippard: *Ad Reinhardt* (New York: Harry N. Abrams, 1981)

Melissa M. Merritt

reinsurance. Insurance by firms that spread their risks by transferring some of them to other insurers. The validity of reinsurance contracts was recognized by the supreme court of New York State in *New York Bowery Insurance Company v. New York Fire Insurance Company* (1837). One of the first companies to offer reinsurance was Atlantic Mutual, which had a reinsurance agreement with the Insurance Company of North America that enabled both companies to provide larger amounts of insurance for single ships. Reinsurance became vital for fire insurers after the fires of 1835 and 1846 in New York City and of 1871 in Chicago, when companies that wrote most of their policies in a single geographic area found that they had to pay losses on many of the policies simultaneously. Lower Manhattan was found to be a convenient location for firms offering primary insurance and reinsurance. The opportunities there about the turn of the century also attracted many foreign firms, such as Cologne Re and Munich Re in 1898, Skandia in 1900, and North American Re, a branch of Swiss Re that in 1910 opened offices in the city to transact business throughout the nation. New York City has emerged as one of the leading reinsurance centers in the world.

Bernard L. Webb et al.: *Principles of Reinsurance* (Malvern, Penn.: Insurance Institute of America, 1990)

Robert J. Gibbons

Reisman, Philip (*b* Warsaw, 1904; *d* New York City, 17 June 1992). Painter and printmaker. After arriving in New York City in 1908 he studied at the Art Students League in the 1920s and had his first solo show at the Painters and Sculptors Gallery in 1931. He worked in the tradition of the Ashcan School and was especially known for his views of the teeming streets, tenements, parks, and bars of the city. In 1979 an exhibition of Reisman's work was held at the Museum of the City of New York.

Kenneth T. Jackson

religion. A tradition of religious diversity was established in New York City by Dutch colonists and strengthened by the position of the city as a trading post. The colonists espoused toleration, and the Dutch West India Company did not want the enforcement of the Dutch Reformed faith to interfere with trade. The difficulty of attracting settlers led the company to accept a religiously diverse population that included Italians, Danes, Dutch from the lower classes, and refugees of religious persecution, including thirty Protestant Walloon families in 1624. The practice of Dutch pietism, as represented by the Reformed church, was not enforced by the first governor, Peter Minuit, a nominal Huguenot. For this he drew criticism from Jonas Michaëlius of the Dutch Reformed church, with whom he often disagreed. After becoming governor in 1647 Peter Stuyvesant tried unsuccessfully to establish the exclusive rights of the Dutch church, which was poorly staffed and attended. Most able *predikanten* (pastors) were unwilling to cross the Atlantic for a frontier ministry, and less able ones in the colony attracted few congregants. At this time the city was rapidly evolving from a trading post into a diverse, international community. In 1654 Stuyvesant protested the emigration to the city of Jews from Recife, Brazil, for fear of encouraging other immigrants who did not belong to the Dutch Reformed church, but the Dutch West India Company welcomed Brazilian Jews for their knowledge of international affairs; that the company had Jews among its prime stockholders in Amsterdam may also have played a part. One of Stuyvesant's supporters was Dominie Johannes Megapolensis, who in 1655 complained to officials in Amsterdam: "We have here Papists, Mennonites and Lutherans among the Dutch [and] also many Puritans or Independents and many atheists and various other servants of Baal."

When the English took control of the city in 1664 they made efforts to establish the Church of England, which had a growing number of adherents in the colony. In the 1680s the Dutch Reformed church in New York City was led by Dominie Hendrik Selijns, who had integrity and was popular among merchants. At times fierce disputes arose between members of the Anglican, Dutch Reformed, and Presbyterian faiths, but in general there was widespread tolerance of religious difference. The African Methodist Episcopal Church (also known as the Zion church), incorporated in 1800, was the first African-American church in the city. The

Easter Service at Holy Trinity Ethiopian Orthodox Church in the Bronx, 1991

Hindu Temple Society in Flushing, 1992

New York City Mission Society was formed as an interdenominational organization in 1812 by the clergy and laymen to help the poor. Members raised funds for charitable causes and worked in slums to promote good health and education; they also used religious motivations grounded in congregants' understanding of benevolence, and formed religious organizations to combat urban problems. Several other charitable organizations were formed during these years, among them the New York City Mission and Tract Society, the New York Female Moral Reform Society, and the New York Society for the Relief of Widows and Orphans of Medical Men. The American Bible Society was formed in 1816. After the founding of Union Theological Seminary by Presbyterians in 1836 Protestantism developed a new intellectual focus. Scholars at the seminary were pioneers in ecumenism who experimented with liberal theology. Among the faculty members was the religious historian Philip Schaff, who urged American Protestant churches to join in a federation.

Like most other parts of the United States, New York City remained heavily Protestant until emigrations of Catholics from Ireland and continental Europe began in the 1830s. The leaders of the city were highly reluctant to welcome immigrants whom they considered poor, apt to concentrate in areas of crime and delinquency, resistant to evangelistic appeals, and unwilling to adopt such Protestant customs as observing a quiet Sabbath and abstaining from alcohol. In 1833 there were five Catholic churches in New York City. Tension between Catholics and Protestants in the city peaked after controversies over religion in public schools and an attack on Catholics in Philadelphia in the early 1840s. Bishop John Hughes staved off attacks in New York City by threatening to arm his churches. By 1863 the city was the Catholic center of the country and had thirty-two Catholic churches, many of which drew large congregations. Some Protestant evangelists attempted to convert Catholics in the city, as they had done in small towns upstate and in other parts of the nation. The best-known evangelist of the day, Charles G. Finney, worked closely with wealthy merchants including Arthur and Lewis Tappan, who built for him on Broadway a tabernacle that resembled a theater and attracted large crowds. Nevertheless few Catholics attended his sermons: most of his adherents were Protestants displaced from small towns.

In the second half of the nineteenth century hundreds of thousands of Jews fleeing pogroms in eastern Europe emigrated to the United States and settled in New York City, where they lived on the Lower East Side and in Harlem. Most were from *shtetls* and ghettos and were desperately poor. German Jews, in general wealthier and longer established in the city, were at the time forming Conservative and Reform congregations and often came

Estimated Number of Houses of Worship for Principal Faiths in New York City

	1855	1901	1926	1960	1986	1990
PROTESTANT						
Adventist Christian					6	3
African Methodist Episcopal	11	15	22	36	37	5
African Methodist Episcopal Zion			13	16	25	4
Apostolic				9	35	72
Assembly of God			6	67	131	47
Baptist	46	118	88	250	606	471
Bible					10	10
Christian and Missionary Alliance			3	10	24	14
Christian Church (Disciples of Christ)	1	5	15	26	41	2
Christian Church of North America					11	63
Christian Scientist		7	33	35	27	47
Church of Christ					23	50
Church of Christ, Disciples of Christ					25	26
Church of God				28	115	37
Church of God (Anderson)				4	14	
Church of God in Christ				17	52	29
Church of Jesus Christ of Latter Day Saints		1	3	3	6	47
Church of the Nazarene			8	6	15	16
Congregationalist / United Church of Christ	22	54	52	42	64	26
Divine Science			2	2	2	
Episcopal	88	180	194	169	149	163
Evangelical	4	9	14	22	15	36
Friends	9	4	5	4	5	3
Jehovah's Witnesses				16	57	54
Lutheran	7	114	192	199	175	161
Mennonite				4	11	10
Methodist	93	149	145	127	136	123
Moravian	3	8	12	12	9	9
Pentecostal		4	3	36	324	391
Plymouth Brethren		1	19	15	19	12
Presbyterian	69	132	138	103	113	159
Reformed	52	87	85	70	69	37
Seventh-Day Adventist			17	38	70	116
Spiritualist			61		11	12
Unification					6	3
Unitarian	5	7	10	8		
Unitarian Universalist					9	12
United Holy Church of America					5	
Universalist	5	8	5	2		
Other Denominations	50	30	31	165	308	248
ORTHODOX						
African Orthodox			6	9		
Greek Orthodox			6	30	27	40
Russian Orthodox			11	18	11	69
Other Orthodox		4	16	19	37	1
CATHOLIC						
American Catholic Church			2			
Liberal Catholic			2	2	3	3
Roman Catholic	53	224	430	442	430	403
Other Catholic		4				23
Synagogues	11	104	1,044	1,240	410	437

(*continued*)

Estimated Number of Houses of Worship for Principal Faiths in New York City *(Continued)*

	1855	1901	1926	1960	1986	1990
Baha'i Temples			1		2	1
Hindu Temples				7	9	
Buddist Temples	15[1]			4	30	16
Mosques			1	5	50	60

1. Figure is for 1906.
Sources: Walter Laidlaw, ed.: *Population of the City of New York, 1890–1930* (New York: Cities Census Committee, 1932)
1960 Protestant Church Directory [Protestant Council of the City of New York]
Religious Distribution in the New York City Metropolitan Area (New York: Protestant Council of the City of New York, Department of Church Planning and Research, 1965)
1986–87 Church Directory [Council of Churches of the City of New York]

Compiled by Marc Ferris

into conflict with the Jewish immigrants from eastern Europe, who either remained Orthodox and organized small *shuls* or ceased to practice their religion altogether. Reform and Conservative Judaism later became influential: about the turn of the century the founding of the Jewish Theological Seminary established an intellectual focus for Conservatism; Reform temples were built on fashionable avenues and presided over by rabbis who became known throughout the nation.

In 1892 Episcopalians laid the foundation on Morningside Heights for the Cathedral of St. John the Divine. Designed to overshadow St. Patrick's Cathedral, it was the third-largest cathedral in the world. Churches well known for their fine music and splendid architecture drew many tourists. Protestant ministers who hoped to influence élite New Yorkers and become known through religious publications aspired to a fashionable pulpit in the city. There were also a number of well-known ministers in Brooklyn, the "city of churches," among them Henry Ward Beecher. Some ministers including William S. Rainsford (1850–1933) of St. George's Episcopal Church became known as reformers. They attacked Tammany Hall and other corrupt political organizations and fought against prostitution, liquor trafficking, and other social vices. Rainsford and others solicited funds from philanthropists like J. P. Morgan to found "institutional churches" that offered gymnasiums, health centers, game rooms, and educational facilities for the poor. Charles A. Briggs of Union Theological Seminary was tried in 1892–93 for heresy by his fellow Presbyterians for offering new, critical views of the Bible. After his acquittal the seminary became interdenominational and eventually led the mainstream of the Protestant ministry in the city; in 1910 the seminary moved to Morningside Heights next to Columbia University.

The city was a major center after the 1890s for the Social Gospel, a movement begun by liberal Protestants. Its best-known leader, Walter Rauschenbusch, was a Baptist who worked in Hell's Kitchen, where he could occasionally be seen leading his fellow Baptist John D. Rockefeller through the streets to gain his support for ministries to immigrants. For members of many ethnic groups that settled in the city, religion became a way of preserving ethnicity and finding community. They continued to practice the religions of their native countries and also used their houses of worship for social gatherings. Christians from Russia, Greece, eastern Europe, and the Middle East erected Orthodox and national Catholic churches (independent of papal authority) that were highly influential in their neighborhoods, although less so in the nation. Chinese houses of worship were first recorded in the census of 1890.

About the time of the First World War large numbers of poor blacks moved from the South to New York City. Most settled in Harlem, sometimes displacing Jews. Black Protestant congregations often met in disused churches and synagogues that became rallying points for the concerns of the community. Some ministers, including Adam Clayton Powell Sr. and Adam Clayton Powell Jr. of the Abyssinian Baptist Church, inspired their large followings to take up political causes: the younger Powell was elected to the U.S. Congress. In the 1920s Marcus Garvey formed a "back to Africa" movement that incorporated religious imagery, attracted the support of some ministers, and led to the rise of the African Orthodox church, which remained a small denomination. Many black radicals active in the Harlem Renaissance found religion confining and became averse to it, but African–American spiritual lore did find its way into the work of some poets, soul and gospel musicians, and playwrights. After 1920 many Puerto Ricans moved into an area of New York City that became known as Spanish Harlem. Most remained Catholic but did not practice Catholicism the way Europeans did: one estimate suggested that only 4 percent of Puerto Rican Catholics attended church regularly, less than one tenth the proportion for all Catholics in the nation.

Religious and social conscience took new forms in New York City in the mid twentieth century. George Baker assumed the name Father Divine and in the 1930s formed the Father Divine Mission, which attracted a largely black congregation and became known nationally. Dorothy Day, a convert to Catholicism, began publishing the *Catholic Worker* in 1933 and with her colleagues ministered to the poor and promoted social justice. The best-known liberal Protestant minister of the century, Harry Emerson Fosdick, was helped by John D. Rockefeller Jr. to build Riverside Church at 120th Street and Riverside Drive in Morningside Heights. This interdenominational church helped to shape American theology for decades. At mid century the faculty of Union Theological Seminary included the preeminent religious thinkers Reinhold Niebuhr and Paul Tillich; Francis Cardinal Spellman was the head of the Archdiocese of New York and often regarded as the leader of American Catholicism; and Rabbi Abraham J. Heschel dominated Jewish theology. With funds from John D. Rockefeller Jr. Protestants opened the Interchurch Center in 1958 in Morningside Heights at 475 Riverside Drive, nicknamed the "God box" for its architecture and function.

In 1957 the evangelist Billy Graham began the Billy Graham Crusade in Madison Square Garden, where he held nightly gatherings that were broadcast on national television. His large audiences were drawn from churches in the city and even from congregations hundreds of miles away. He made thousands of conversions and gained the approval of the Protestant Council of New York, which was often skeptical of conservative evangelists. He also won many friends, some of them celebrities, and fended off criticism from theologians like Niebuhr who found his evangelism lacking in social justice and relevance to the modern world. Eventually Graham left the city, and the impact of his ministry there was ultimately inconsequential.

By the 1960s other Protestant evangelists, many of them Pentecostalists, came into conflict with the Catholic church by attracting Puerto Ricans and other Latin Americans. In the same decade a ministry of the Nation of Islam (the members of which were known as the Black Muslims) was formed in the city and led by Malcolm X, a charismatic leader who was assassinated in 1965 during a struggle for power within the Nation of Islam.

Pluralism continued to flourish in the city in the late twentieth century, but many believers found it difficult to build and sustain a community as they left their neighborhoods and moved to other parts of the city, where the size of the population and the consequent crowding resulted in anonymity. In many aspects of modern city life religion counted little in matters of personal identity, but New York City remained an important religious center for the nation. Some denominations and many interdenominational agencies continued to make their headquarters there, including the National Council of Churches and Church Women United USA (both at the Interchurch Center on Riverside Drive). Other less ecumenical Christian organizations also were well established in the city. The Watchtower in Brooklyn Heights became the international headquarters of the Jehovah's Witnesses, and many evangelical denominations were strongly represented in the mid 1990s, including the American Bible Society (at 1865 Broadway). The Young Women's Christian Association (YWCA), not as explicitly religious as it had been in its early years, established its national headquarters on Broadway. The major interfaith organization in the United States, the National Conference of Christians and Jews, maintained offices on 5th Avenue, and Religion in American Life, also a national organization, had offices on 2nd Avenue. Many of the world's religions continued to be practiced in the city, including Islam, Buddhism, and Hinduism. The largest denomination was Catholicism, with 2.35 million adherents. The Archdiocese of New York was not the largest in the country, but its location made it one of the most important. The city continued to have the largest Jewish community in the nation. There were also large constituencies of black Protestants, and white Protestants retained a minor influence. Although the city retained its reputation for secularity and for being preoccupied with commerce and material pursuits, some observers like the sociologist Peter Berger saw a continuing spirituality in its vibrant universalism.

George L. Smith: *Religion and Trade in New Netherland: Dutch Origins and American Development* (Ithaca, N.Y.: Cornell University Press, 1973)

Martin E. Marty

Remsen Village. Neighborhood in northeastern Brooklyn, bounded to the north by Linden Boulevard, to the east by Rockaway Parkway, to the south by Ditmas Avenue, and to the west by Ralph Avenue; it is named for an avenue that bisects it. Modest attached and semidetached brick houses were built during a rush of development in the 1920s and 1930s. In the 1970s there was a large Jewish population that formed an active community council. Many Jews moved out in the 1980s, as the area attracted a large number of immigrants from the Caribbean, chiefly from Jamaica, Haiti, and Guyana. The main commercial district lies along Remsen Avenue; there are also small industries and shopping areas along Ditmas Avenue and Linden Boulevard.

Elizabeth Reich Rawson

rent regulation. Government regulation of the amount of rent charged for housing and the procedures for eviction began in New York City during the 1920s. A housing shortage and high rents after the First World War prompted the state legislature to pass emergency laws enabling tenants to challenge "unjust, unreasonable and oppressive" rent increases in magistrates' courts. These laws were annually renewed until 1928; residents of "old law" tenements that were in violation of these rent regulations gained further protection under the Minkoff Law (1939), which prohibited rent increases in old law housing that did not fully comply with the Multiple Dwellings Law of 1929 (an omnibus code for structural, maintenance, and hygienic standards in apartment housing).

During the Second World War the U.S. Office of Price Administration (OPA) declared the city a "defense rental area" to encourage landlords to maintain fair rents voluntarily. Tenant groups demanded a "freeze" on rent increases in 1942, and the Metropolitan Fair Rent Committee, an influential group of large apartment owners formed in the same year, promised that the landlords whom it represented would comply, but the administration of Fiorello H. La Guardia nevertheless received frequent reports of exorbitant rents. Soaring rents precipitated a riot in Harlem in August 1943. On 1 November the OPA froze the rents of 1.4 million dwellings at the level of 1 March, with some exceptions: landlords were permitted to increase rents by 15 percent in cases of hardship and to evict tenants to provide housing for their immediate families. As the war came to an end tenant groups began to organize, often to defend themselves against landlords who charged extortionate rates for installing fixtures and furnishings. Despite charges that rent controls were creating a black market, they were maintained by the OPA until 1947, whereupon tenant groups persuaded Governor Thomas E. Dewey and Mayor William O'Dwyer to impose a state-run system that placed controls on apartments built before 1947 (landlords were allowed a "catch-up" rent increase of 15 percent); it was at this point that the year when a building was constructed became a factor in determining how much rent could be charged. Under the new system the vacancy rate was measured at three-year intervals: a rate below 5 percent constituted a housing emergency that could justify a renewal of rent controls by the state legislature. Landlords were granted occasional rent increases of as much as 15 percent.

The city resumed the administration of rent regulation in 1962. In 1967 and 1969 it lifted controls on some high-rent apartments and imposed a new system called "rent stabilization" on apartment buildings with six or more dwelling units. Rent increases were subject to self-enforcement by landlords belonging to the Rent Stabilization Association. Fears that housing abandonment would become chronic moved the legislature to weaken rent controls — in 1971 it allowed a rent increase of 15 percent and an inflation adjustment of 7 percent, and linked stabilized rents to a "maximum base" calculated according to a reasonable return on investment; and in 1972 it adopted "vacancy decontrol," under which apartments were removed from rent control altogether when they became vacant — but owing to pressure from tenant groups it reimposed rent stabilization on decontrolled apartments in 1974. Landlords in the 1980s increasingly perceived rent control as permanent, and as a result many converted rental apartments to cooperatives and condominium units. In the early 1990s there were 840,000 rent-stabilized and 155,000 rent-controlled apartments in the New York City, housing two fifths of all its residents. Apartments covered by both forms of regulation rented on the average for 15 percent less than their market rate, the actual difference ranging from $40 a month in the outer boroughs to $400 a month in Manhattan below 110th Street.

Rent regulation continues to be fiercely debated. Opponents of the system contend that it contributes to abandonment and reduces revenues from property taxes. It is also argued that rent regulation benefits the middle class rather than the poor: regulated rents do not take into account a tenant's income (except in the highest-priced rent-stabilized apartments, because of a limited provision passed in 1993), and the higher turnover of apartments in poor neighborhoods allows for more frequent rent increases. Defenders of the system maintain that the inadequate supply of affordable housing stems not from regulation but from more fundamental problems, and that in any case rent regulation does not apply to new construction. They also doubt whether a repeal of regulation would achieve its purported benefits, arguing that rents in poor neighborhoods would still be higher than what local residents could afford to pay, and that a repeal would lead to widespread price gouging. Rent-regulated apartments in the city are highly sought after and are often the subject of legal disputes, especially concerning tenants' principal domicile, subletting, and rights of succession.

George Sternlieb and James W. Hughes: *Housing and Economic Reality: New York City, 1976* (New Brunswick, N.J.: Rutgers University Center for Urban Policy Research, 1976)

Ronald Lawson, ed.: *The Tenant Movement in New York City, 1904–1984* (New Brunswick, N.J.: Rutgers University Press, 1986)

Joel Schwartz

Renwick, James (*b* New York City, 1 Nov 1818; *d* New York City, 23 June 1895). Architect. After graduating from Columbia College he oversaw the construction of a reservoir on the site now occupied by the New York Public Library. He soon won a competition to design Grace Church, a success that led to commissions for St. Bartholomew's Church and St. Patrick's Cathedral (for illustration see St.

PATRICK'S CATHEDRAL); he also designed the fountain at Bowling Green, the Free Academy, hotels including the St. Denis, banks, such palatial residences as that of Charles Morgan, and buildings on Blackwell's, Wards, and Randalls islands for the Board of Charities and Correction. Toward the end of his life he was a senior warden of Grace Church. See also TERRA COTTA.

James E. Mooney

Republican Party. The Republican Party became a national organization in 1854, and in the same year it opened a New York State chapter in New York City that was controlled by such adherents of the free-soil movement as Hamilton Fish, Daniel D. Barnard, and Horace Greeley (publisher of the *New York Tribune*). For many years the party was overshadowed in New York City by the Democratic machine and especially by Tammany Hall, and Republicans were able to win elections only by forging coalitions with disgruntled Democrats and independent reformers. Irish, Jewish, and other immigrants in the city were mistrustful of the party because it indulged in anti-Catholic rhetoric and favored a twenty-five-year residency requirement for voting, and because it consisted mostly of Anglo-Saxon Protestants, including remnants of the nativist Know-Nothing Party. In 1857 the state legislature, dominated by Republicans, imposed a new charter on the city, which resulted in the following year in the election of Daniel F. Tiemann, who became the city's first Republican mayor by running on a fusion ticket with the Know-Nothings and Tammany Hall. During his administration relations between Republicans and the predominantly Irish working class further deteriorated over the issues of slavery and participation in the Civil War. Republican opposition to slavery provoked fears among the Irish that they might someday have to compete with a large number of unskilled freed slaves. These fears were heightened when the Republicans sponsored the Conscription Act of 1863, which led in July to the draft riots. After the Civil War the Republican Party had little success in city politics, winning only a single mayoral election between 1863 and 1892. Republicans nonetheless had an impact on local politics that was greater than their numbers. Able to exercise influence through newspapers and civic organizations, they attacked Tammany Hall as corrupt and were sometimes powerful enough to enact reforms and effect changes in municipal administration. Often they held the balance of power in the delicate relations between the city and state governments.

Republicans fared somewhat better when the reform movement gained strength toward the end of the century, and in 1894 the reformist Republican William L. Strong was elected mayor. Among the reforms undertaken during his administration was a reorganization of the city police by the newly appointed president of the police board, Theodore Roosevelt. In 1901 the Republican Seth Low, president of Columbia University, was elected mayor as a fusion candidate. In office he enforced the tenement laws, markedly increased expenditures for public education, improved public transit and the water supply, and made diligent attempts to attract professionals to city government. Nevertheless he was defeated for reelection in 1903 by a candidate supported by Tammany Hall. In the succeeding decades the Republican Party had little success in the city: in 1909 it backed fusion candidates for the Board of Aldermen and won a majority, but at the same time lost the mayoralty to the independent Democrat John Purroy Mitchel. In the 1920s the party was damaged by its support for Prohibition, while Democrats benefited from the popularity of Alfred E. Smith and Franklin D. Roosevelt. As a Republican presidential candidate in 1924 Calvin Coolidge was the last Republican to carry the city for many years (Democratic nominees carried the city in the next seventeen elections).

During these years Republicans in New York City forged a political ethic that was at once fiscally conservative and socially progressive. This brand of Republicanism was exemplified by such figures as Henry L. Stimson, Wendell Willkie, Thomas E. Dewey, and later Jacob K. Javits and Nelson A. Rockefeller. The most successful Republican politician in New York City in the 1930s and 1940s, Mayor Fiorello H. La Guardia, was only nominally a Republican. A proponent of the New Deal and of nonpartisan government, he enjoyed strong support among the working class during three terms in office (1934–45). The Republicans were then excluded from City Hall until the election in 1965 of John V. Lindsay, a liberal congressman from the Upper East Side who won reelection in 1969 only after being denied renomination by the Republicans, and who later became a Democrat.

In the 1970s and early 1980s the Republican Party in New York City gradually changed both its ideology and its ethnic composition. The liberal, affluent wing of the party aged and declined in importance, and some of its members became Democrats or independents. Increasingly the party became rooted in the middle class and the outer boroughs (it was especially strong in Staten Island); its new base included many Italians and some Latin Americans and Jews (particularly the Orthodox) who took conservative stands on taxes and on crime and other social issues. The leading spokesmen of the party included such diverse figures as Vito Battista, John J. Marchi, and later Guy Molinari. In Manhattan the tradition of liberal Republicanism persisted on the Upper East Side (traditionally known as the Silk Stocking District), which was represented in the U.S. Congress from the late 1970s to 1993 by the liberal Republican Bill Green. Citywide Republican candidates continued to fare poorly: in a four-candidate mayoral election in 1977 the Republican nominee Roy M. Goodman received only 4.7 percent of all votes cast, and in the election of 1981 the party endorsed the Democratic incumbent, Edward I. Koch.

In the late 1980s and early 1990s the Republican Party in New York City was revitalized. In 1989 the Republican mayoral nominee, Rudolph W. Giuliani, received 49 percent of the vote against David N. Dinkins, and when the two candidates faced each other again in 1993 Giuliani prevailed. During the first year of his term the Republicans had seven seats on the City Council, giving it more political influence than at any time since the 1960s.

In early 1994 there were 468,410 registered Republicans in New York City, representing 14.2 percent of all registered voters.

James C. Mohr: *The Radical Republicans and Reform in New York during Reconstruction* (Ithaca, N.Y.: Cornell University Press, 1973)

Hendrik Booraem: *The Formation of the Republican Party in New York: Politics and Conscience in the Antebellum North* (New York: New York University Press, 1983)

Peter Field

Republic New York Corporation. Commercial bank, formed in 1966 as the Republic National Bank of New York by Edmond J. Safra (*b* 1914) with headquarters at the Knox Hat Building on 5th Avenue and 42nd Street (declared a landmark in 1980 and incorporated in 1986 as the National Bank Tower). The bank undertook a series of mergers and acquisitions beginning in 1974, when it bought the Kings Lafayette Bank, based in Brooklyn. Later acquisitions included twelve branches from Bankers Trust Company (1980), the Williamsburgh Savings Bank (1987), and the Manhattan Savings Bank (1990). In 1990 the bank adopted its current name. By 1991 Republic was the eighth-largest commercial bank in the city, with nearly $31,000 million in assets.

James Bradley

Resor, Stanley B(urnet) (*b* Cincinnati, ?1879; *d* New York City, 29 Oct 1962). Advertising executive. He joined the firm of J. Walter Thompson in 1908, was transferred to its office in New York City in 1912, and became its president in 1916, a position he retained until 1955; he was also a director until 1961. Resor sought public acceptance of advertising and in 1917 helped to form the American Association of Advertising Agencies. Under his direction J. Walter Thompson became the largest agency in the world, owing to its successful use of market research. His wife, Helen Lansdowne Resor (*b* ?1886; *d* New York City, 2 Jan 1964), was a vice-president and director of the agency and a proponent of testimonial advertising: she promoted Pond's

testimony sessions were held at noon and drew audiences of thousands, including many businessmen. These meetings were linked by telegraph to meetings in other large cities across the country. Although the movement soon waned, it left a widespread interest in urban missions. The Water Street Mission, the first of its kind in the city, was formed in October 1872 by Jerry McAuley, a former alcoholic, and emphasized the spiritual power to overcome addiction. Branches soon opened throughout the city, and by 1892 there were hundreds nationwide. The Crittenden (1883) and the Door of Hope (1890), homes for "fallen women," were established in the city by members of the Water Street missions. These homes grew into national organizations linked by the *Christian Herald*, a magazine published in the city from 1878 that by 1900 had a circulation of 250,000 and was one of the most popular magazines in the world. Several missions gave rise to denominations, including the Christian and Missionary Alliance, which began as a mission in the 1880s led by the Presbyterian minister Albert B. Simpson and eventually became one of the largest evangelical denominations in the country. This and other missionary denominations were marked by the theology of personal consecration that developed in 1857–58.

In his campaign from 7 February to 19 April 1876 Dwight L. Moody adapted music hall entertainment to a brand of revivalism carefully fashioned for the middle class. The local clergy made detailed preparations for his campaign, which was financed by local business magnates. Moody spoke to audiences of ten thousand a day in P. T. Barnum's Hippodrome at Madison Avenue and 27th Street and claimed to inspire five thousand conversions. Because most members of the audience were respectable churchgoers rather than the poor and alienated whom Moody had hoped to attract, the campaign showed Protestants making revivalism a ritual of pious reaffirmation that withdrew from the world, in contrast to Finney's revivalism that sought to change the world. With the help of meticulous planning by a professional staff, Billy Sunday became the best-known revivalist in the city during his career from 1896 to 1935: his comic rhetoric, frenzied stagecraft, and adaptation of vaudeville entertainment attracted audiences of 1.4 million to his meetings, where there were 65,000 conversions (nonetheless few subsequently became churchgoers). He equated Christianity with good citizenship, especially during the First World War, and reached the height of his career during a rally that lasted ten weeks from April to June 1917. His zealotry and anti-intellectualism eventually cost evangelism respect with the public, and his popularity diminished.

During the 1950s Billy Graham built his career on themes of Christianity, good citizenship, and peace of mind. He demonstrated his calmer style during a rally at Madison Square Garden in 1957. From 15 May to Labor Day he addressed two million persons among whom he claimed 55,000 as converts (although most were already churchgoers). He made his national début on television in the city on 1 June 1957, launching the "electronic church," which grew quickly and by the early 1990s was the largest outlet for revivalism. Graham's return visits in 1960 and 1969 were not as successful. More notable was a mission to drug addicts begun in the city in 1958 by the Pentecostal pastor David Wilkerson, popularized in his book *The Cross and the Switchblade* (1963) and expanded into the nationwide ministry Teen Challenge.

William G. McLoughlin: *Modern Revivalism: From Charles Grandison Finney to Billy Graham* (New York: Ronald, 1959)

Carroll Smith Rosenberg: *Religion and the Rise of the American City: The New York City Mission Movement, 1812–1870* (Ithaca, N.Y.: Cornell University Press, 1971)

Norris A. Magnuson: *Salvation in the Slums: Evangelical Social Work, 1865–1920* (Metuchen, N.J.: Scarecrow, 1977)

James D. Bratt

Revlon. Firm of cosmetics manufacturers formed in 1932 by Charles Revson (1906–75), a salesman who had moved to New York City from Massachusetts in 1923 to work for the Pickwick Dress Company. Based in its early years at 125 West 45th Street, the firm achieved quick success with a unique opaque nail polish developed by Revson, his brother, and his friend Charles Lachman. Revson saw an untapped market in the large number of women unable to afford the products of Helena Rubinstein and Elizabeth Arden. He sold his nail polish in drug stores, in 1940 introduced the first color-coordinated nail polish and lipstick ("matching lips and fingertips") and the first pink nail polish, and by 1941 achieved a near-monopoly for his products in beauty salons. Borrowing some of the techniques used to sell automobiles, he introduced new color lines each spring and autumn, devised advertisements that associated his products with heightened sexuality (an advertising campaign in 1952 based on the slogan "fire and ice" caused a sensation and was highly influential), and was the first cosmetics manufacturer to sponsor a television program ("The $64,000 Question"). The firm also led a trend in the cosmetics industry toward diversification by expanding into vitamins, toilet bowl cleaners, and shoe polish in the 1950s and eye shadow in the 1960s. For many years the firm enjoyed a heated rivalry with Lauder; at one time both firms had their headquarters in the General Motors building at 767 5th Avenue. By 1970 Revlon was the second-largest cosmetics firm in the world, with sales reaching $605 million in 1974. In the mid 1990s it employed more than thirty thousand persons in ninety-seven countries. Revson was active as a philanthropist and donated large sums for Temple Emanu-El, the Albert Einstein College of Medicine, Revson Plaza at Columbia University, and the fountain at Lincoln Center for the Performing Arts. In 1985 Revlon was acquired by MacAndrews and Forbes Holding and its chairman, Ronald O. Perelman, in a hostile takeover valued at $2700 million.

Andrew P. Tobias: *Fire and Ice: The Story of Charles Revson, the Man Who Built the Revlon Empire* (New York: William Morrow, 1976)

Marc Ferris

Revolution. Weekly periodical launched in 1868 in New York City by Susan B. Anthony. It emphasized news of the reform movement and favored an informed electorate and the abolition of standing armies. The publication was edited by Elizabeth Cady Stanton and Parker Pillsbury until Laura J. Curtis Bullard took charge in 1870; under her direction the focus was more on the well-being of women than on their equality. In 1871 *Revolution* was bought by W. T. Clarke, who tried unsuccessfully to transform it into a literary journal. It merged in February 1872 with the *Liberal Christian*.

For illustration see ALTERNATIVE PRESS.

Sandra Roff

Rheingold Breweries. Firm of brewers formed in Brooklyn in 1855 by Samuel Liebmann, a German immigrant. After his death in 1872 the firm of Liebmann Breweries was taken over by his sons, who expanded it by buying smaller local breweries, and during the 1880s Rheingold became its principal marque. From 1940 to 1965 the firm achieved wide publicity by running a promotional beauty contest in which customers cast ballots to choose Miss Rheingold. Like other smaller brewers it could not survive the competition from large firms with modern facilities, national distribution, and enormous advertising budgets. In 1964 it took its current name after being sold by the family to Pepsi-Cola United Bottlers. Sales declined, the firm was put up for sale in 1974, and a purchase by Chock Full O'Nuts was arranged by the city. Under the new ownership sales continued to decline, and the factory in Brooklyn closed in 1976 when operations were moved to Orange, New Jersey. In 1977 Rheingold was bought by C. Schmidt and Sons, a brewer in Philadelphia that soon left the business.

Stanley Wade Baron: *Brewed in America: A History of Beer and Ale in the United States* (Boston: Little, Brown, 1962)

K. Austin Kerr

R. H. Macy. Department store founded in 1858 by Rowland H. Macy. It began as a small shop on 6th Avenue between 13th and 14th streets, far north of the existing dry-goods district bounded by Broome Street, the Bow-

Macy's food counter, 1902

ery, Grand Street, and Broadway. The early Macy's was an innovative operation. Specializing in "fancy" and imported dry goods for women, the store was known for odd pricing (setting prices only one cent or a few cents below a full-dollar amount), cash sales, a money-back guarantee, and good values. Throughout the nineteenth century there was a factory on the premises, and before ready-to-wear women's clothing was introduced more than two hundred employees, mostly women, sewed made-to-measure suits, coats, jackets, and undergarments for women and shirts for men. The store grew rapidly and by the 1870s had an unprecedented number of departments, among them a large and profitable one devoted to home furnishings, and a range of merchandise that included toys, china, glassware, men's furnishings, jewelry, candy, and books. It also helped to secularize the American Christmas. Illuminated window displays, introduced in 1874, became a tradition that signaled the beginning of the Christmas shopping season; a Santa Claus first appeared in the store during the 1870s and remained a fixture of the modern Macy's Thanksgiving Day Parade. The firm was taken over in 1888 by Isidor and Nathan Straus, who moved the store from the declining shopping district on 14th Street to a building that they erected in 1902 at 34th Street and Broadway. This was the first large store north of 23rd Street, and despite the proximity of the 6th Avenue elevated line it initially had to run a steam wagonette between 14th and 34th streets for customers reluctant to make the trip.

For many years Macy's was characterized by a remarkable continuity of ownership. The Straus brothers' partnership became a family partnership in 1919 and a public corporation in 1922. The firm became again became privately held in 1986, after a leveraged buyout led by senior management. The buyout put such a strain on the operations of the firm that on 27 January 1992 it filed for bankruptcy, and two years later it was still operating under the protection of the bankruptcy court.

Macy's at Herald Square remains the largest department store in the world. The main floor of the building was refurbished in 1983. There is also one local branch, on Queens Boulevard.

Ralph M. Hower: *History of Macy's of New York, 1858–1919: Chapters in the Evolution of the Department Store* (Cambridge: Harvard University Press, 1943)

Elaine Abelson

R. Hoe and Company. Firm of printing-equipment manufacturers formed in New York City in 1822. It developed several of the chief printing presses used in the nineteenth century, including the Washington press, a toggle-jointed iron hand press; a flatbed cylinder newspaper press; and a type-revolving, rotary press invented in 1847 by Richard M. Hoe (1812–86). The firm occupied buildings at 29 and 31 Gold Street on the Lower East Side to 1869, when it moved to the block bounded by Grand, Sheriff, Broome, and Columbia streets. In 1930 it moved its three thousand employees to the southeastern Bronx, where it remained until it was dissolved by bankruptcy in 1977.

Frank E. Comparato: *Chronicles of Genius and Folly: R. Hoe and Company and the Printing Press as a Service to Democracy* (Culver City, Calif.: Labyrinthos, 1979)

William S. Pretzer

Rice [née Stevens], **Gertrude** (*b* New York City, 1841; *d* New York City, 24 March 1926). Reformer. A founder of the Charity Organization Society, she worked to improve public charities and help dependent children. In 1875 she joined the board of directors of the Central Committee of State Charities Aid Association, of which she was later vice-president and president (1885–87). She also served on the boards of the National Committee for the Prevention of Blindness and the Russell Sage Foundation, and was a vice-president of both.

Obituary, *New York Times*, 25 March 1926, p. 23

Erica Judge

Rice, (Henry) Grantland (*b* Murfreesboro, Tenn., 1 Nov 1880; *d* New York City, 13 July 1954). Sportswriter. He studied classics at Vanderbilt University (BA 1901) and worked for newspapers in Nashville, Washington, Atlanta, and Cleveland before moving to New York City in 1911 to write for the *New York Evening Mail.* In 1914 he joined the *New York Tribune*, with which he remained associated until 1930. Rice's effusive, hyperbolic writing style, often painting the athlete in heroic terms, was immensely popular and influenced an entire generation of sportswriters. He wrote three volumes of verse and an autobiography, *The Tumult and the Shouting: My Life in Sport* (1954). In New York City he lived at 616 West 116th Street (for a brief period after his arrival in the city), 450 Riverside Drive (1911–30), and 1158 5th Avenue (from 1930).

Charles Fountain: *Sportswriter: The Life and Times of Grantland Rice* (New York: Oxford University Press, 1993)
Mark Inabinett: *Grantland Rice and His Heroes: The Sportswriter as Myth-maker in the 1920s* (Knoxville: University of Tennessee Press, 1994)

Rice, William Marsh (*b* Springfield, Mass., 14 March 1816; *d* New York City, 23 Sept 1900). Businessman and philanthropist. He moved to Houston in 1838 and became a partner in the mercantile firm of Nichols (renamed Rice and Nichols), and then moved to Mexico at the beginning of the Civil War and to New York City in 1865, where he oversaw finances and purchases for the Houston and Texas Central Railroad. For many years he lived in hotels but by 1883 he had an apartment in the Grenoble on 57th Street. After his wife's death in 1896 he moved to an apartment at 500 Madison Avenue. He was murdered by his valet, Charles F. Jones, at the instigation of a lawyer, Albert T. Patrick, who hoped to gain some of his wealth through a forged will. Most of Rice's estate went to form the William Marsh Rice Institute in Houston, which opened in 1912 and is now Rice University.

Sylvia Stallings Morris, ed.: *William Marsh Rice and His Institute: A Biographical Study* (Houston: William Marsh Rice University, 1972)

Eileen K. Cheng

Rice High School. Catholic high school for boys in Harlem, opened in 1938 and run by the Congregation of Christian Brothers. Named for the founder of the Christian Brothers, Edmund Ignatius Rice (1762–1844), it once occupied three buildings on West 124th Street that had previously been the campus of Power Memorial Academy. In 1940 it moved to its current facility (formerly occupied by the YWCA). In 1991 it had 360 students.

Gilbert Tauber

Richmond, Frederick W(illiam) (*b* Boston, 15 Nov 1923). Businessman and congressman. He moved to New York City during the early 1950s and from 1955 to 1959 was the president of the Urban League of Greater New York. In 1960 he helped to prevent the demolition of Carnegie Hall and for fifteen years he led the Carnegie Hall Corporation. After his election to the U.S. House of Representatives in 1974 as a Democrat from the fourteenth district he organized the Congressional Arts Caucus. In August 1982 he resigned from office after pleading guilty to charges of tax evasion and bribery. After serving nine months in prison Richmond returned to the city to resume business and charitable pursuits.

Alana J. Erickson

Richmond, Mary E(llen) (*b* Belleville, Ill., 5 Aug 1861; *d* New York City, 12 Sept 1928). Social worker. She moved to New York City in 1909 as the first director of the charity organization department of the Russell Sage Foundation. She believed that the complex problems of impoverished people could be solved only by trained case workers in privately funded social service agencies, and not by public welfare programs. A pioneer in the professionalization of social work, she developed case work techniques while opposing popular measures for public assistance, such as widows' pensions. Her books *Social Diagnosis* (1917) and *What Is Social Case Work?* (1922) greatly influenced the first generation of academically trained social workers. Richmond lived in an apartment on West 120th Street, near Columbia University.

Joanna C. Colcord and Ruth Z. S. Mann, eds.: *The Long View: Papers and Addresses by Mary E. Richmond* (New York: Russell Sage Foundation, 1930)

Sarah Henry Lederman

Richmond County. One of the five counties of New York City, coextensive with the borough of Staten Island.

Richmond Hill. Neighborhood in east central Queens, lying adjacent to Jamaica and bounded to the north by Myrtle and Hillside avenues, to the east by the Van Wyck Expressway, to the south by Linden Boulevard, and to the west by 100th Street. The area was mostly farmland until it was developed by Albon P. Man, a wealthy lawyer of the firm of Man and Parsons in New York City who in 1867 engaged the landscape architect Edward Richmond to buy land and lay out a community. Between 1868 and 1874 streets, a school, and a church were built, trees were planted, and a railroad station began service. The settlement was incorporated as an independent village in 1894. Most residents were businessmen from Manhattan who erected large houses costing from \$2500 to \$5000 each on generous plots. By 1900 the high school had opened and a hilly section toward Kew Gardens was covered by luxurious houses costing \$8000 each. More houses were built and Jamaica Avenue became commercialized after the Jamaica Avenue elevated line was extended to the area in 1918. By 1920 there was no open land and the only sort of development possible was infilling (building new houses in between older ones, often on substandard lots, or demolishing large houses and putting up smaller ones in their place). The population was mostly German and Irish until an influx of Latin Americans began after 1975. In the 1980s almost 40 percent of the immigrants who settled in Richmond Hill were from Guyana; others were from the Dominican Republic, Colombia, Ecuador, India, and Jamaica. Richmond Hill is a well-maintained residential neighborhood that retains many elegant structures from the turn of the century. The center of the neighborhood is the Triangle, formed by the intersection of Lefferts Boulevard with Myrtle and Jamaica avenues. Nearby is the Triangle Hofbrau (1864), reputed to be one of the oldest inns in continuous operation on Long Island.

Vincent Seyfried

Richmondtown. Neighborhood in Staten Island, near the geographic center of the borough. Its main streets are Richmond Road and Clarke Avenue. In the 1690s the area was the site of a crossroads settlement known as Cocclestown because of its abundance of oyster shells. It later became Richmond Town, the county seat and the site of the county jail (1710) and courthouse (1728). The first building of the Church of St. Andrew (Episcopal) was constructed from 1711 to 1713. In 1837 a local entrepreneur named Henry Seaman bought the Swaim farm, divided it into lots, and constructed five houses (four of which remained standing in the mid 1990s). In the same year a new Greek Revival courthouse was also built, followed by a new jail in 1860 (later demolished). The Church of St. Patrick (Roman Catholic) was erected in 1868. Consolidation in 1898 led to the gradual removal of county government operations to St. George, and the neighborhood continued to grow slowly after Staten Island Rapid Transit was built well to its south. Richmondtown is a middle-class residential neighborhood, with some new townhouses south of Clarke Avenue. The firehouse at 3664 Richmond Road is the home of one of the two remaining volunteer fire companies in New York City.

Barnett Shepherd

Richmondtown Restoration. Former name of HISTORIC RICHMOND TOWN.

Richmond Valley. Neighborhood in southwestern Staten Island, bounded to the north by Outerbridge Crossing Plaza and the exchanges of the Richmond Parkway and West Shore Expressway, to the south by Mill Creek and Amboy Road, and to the west by the Arthur Kill. A mill that stood on the creek for several hundred years was run by the Dissosway, Weir, and Cole families. The area was named by the Staten Island Railroad, which opened a station there in the 1860s. Luxury houses and warehouses were built in the 1980s, and a large hotel was planned for the waterfront in the early 1990s. Richmond Valley retains its rural character.

Marjorie Johnson

Richter, Erhard (*fl* 1848–57). Political activist. In 1848 he formed the Deutscher Arbeiter Verein, an organization influenced by French socialist ideas. By 1854 he became the leader of a faction of German radicals who split with the Democratic Party over the Kansas–Nebraska Act and joined the Republican Party. With the leaders of the Freethinkers' League he organized a mass meeting to demand government action in behalf of the unemployed in 1857. His saloon at 55–57 Forsyth Street was a popular meeting place for Germans in the 1850s and 1860s.

Stanley Nadel

Rickard, Tex [George Lewis] (*b* Leavenworth, Kansas, 2 Jan 1871; *d* Miami, 6 Jan 1929). Promoter. The first boxing match that he promoted in New York City was that for the heavyweight championship between Jess Willard and Frank Moran on 25 March 1916 at Madison Square Garden, the first heavyweight title fight in the city since 1900. In the following years he made Madison Square Garden into the best-known boxing venue in the nation, especially when he made it the site of Jack Dempsey's defense of the heavyweight title against Georges Carpentier on 2 July 1921, the first fight to draw \$1 million in gate receipts. This figure was exceeded by a fight that he promoted between Dempsey and Luis Firpo on 14 September 1923 at the Polo Grounds before 75,000 fans. In 1925 Rickard's syndicate built a new Madison Square Garden that featured boxing, ice hockey, and six-day bicycle races.

Steven A. Riess

Rickey, (Wesley) Branch (*b* Little California [now in Stockdale], Ohio, 20 Dec 1881; *d* Columbia, Mo., 9 Dec 1965). Baseball executive. After a career as a player and manager he spent twenty-six years as an executive with the St. Louis Cardinals. As president and general manager from 1942 of the Brooklyn Dodgers he was influential in having Jackie Robinson enter the major leagues in 1947. Forced from the Dodgers in 1950 by the team's owner Walter O'Malley, he attempted with the lawyer William A. Shea to form a new baseball league in the late 1950s; their efforts led indirectly to the admission of the New York Mets into the major leagues in 1962. From 1943 to 1950 Rickey lived at 215 Montague Street in Brooklyn Heights.

Murray Polner: *Branch Rickey: A Biography* (New York: Atheneum, 1982)

Joseph S. Lieber

Ridder, Hermann (*b* New York City, 5 March 1851; *d* New York City, 1 Nov 1915). Newspaper publisher. He left school, worked for fourteen years as an insurance agent, and launched the weekly publication *Katholisches Volksblatt*, which after eight years he renamed the *Catholic News*, soon the leading Catholic newspaper in the United States. He later became the manager and owner of the *New Yorker Staats-Zeitung*. An active Democrat, he opposed Tammany Hall and was active in national politics. Ridder helped to form the Associated Press and was a president of the American Newspaper Publishers Association.

James E. Mooney

Ridgewood. Neighborhood in Brooklyn and Queens (1990 pop. 109,231), bounded to the north by Metropolitan Avenue, to the east by the tracks of the Long Island Rail Road and Conrail, to the south by Central Avenue, and to the west by Flushing Avenue. The area was inhabited by Mespachtes Indians and during the seventeenth and eighteenth centuries was tilled by Dutch farmers. The only surviving Dutch farmhouse is the Adrien Onderdonck House (1731). Arbitration Rock was set at Onderdonk and Montrose avenues to end a dispute that lasted from 1660 to 1769 over the boundary between Brooklyn and Queens. English settlers in the early eighteenth century named the area for its high wooded terrain. It began to grow after transportation to Brooklyn improved: the horsecar line along Myrtle Avenue was extended to Broadway in 1855, as were elevated rapid transit lines in 1879; the Brooklyn City and Bushwick trolley lines built large depots at Myrtle and Wyckoff avenues in 1881; and the Myrtle Avenue elevated line was extended to Wyckoff Avenue in 1888. From the late 1880s until the end of the First World War the area was sometimes known as Evergreen, in deference to a community on Long Island that claimed priority in using the name Ridgewood. The population was largely middle class and German and supported many local businesses, including several breweries and knitting mills. At first small frame houses were erected, and from 1906 Gustav Mathews acquired the remaining farmlands and built the Mathews Flats, a complex of more than eight hundred six-family brick row houses of three stories each. The houses sold for more than $11,000 or rented for $15 a month. Paul Stier built a similar development from 1908 to 1914 between 67th and 70th avenues, using tan brick and lumber of the highest quality (much of the housing in the neighborhood consists of his row houses, about half of which are occupied by their owners).

After the Second World War a large number of Romanians, Italians, and Slovenes settled in the neighborhood. In an effort to disassociate themselves from Bushwick, a largely black area to the south with high rates of crime and arson, the local residents in 1979 voted to change from a postal zone in Brooklyn to one in Queens. In September 1983 an area comprising 2980 buildings was designated the largest Historic District in the nation. Some six-family apartment buildings were converted into cooperatives in the late 1980s to attract young working-class families. In addition to its large German community Ridgewood during the 1980s attracted many immigrants from eastern Europe, especially Romania (accounting for more than a quarter of all immigrants settling there), the former republics of Yugoslavia, and Poland. The neighborhood also drew large numbers of Chinese, Dominicans, Italians, Koreans, and Ecuadorians. In the mid 1990s it remained solidly working class and lower middle class.

Vincent Seyfried, Stephen Weinstein

Ridiculous Theatrical Company. Theater company formed in 1967 by Charles Ludlam as an offshoot of John Vaccaro's Play-House of the Ridiculous. As the company's producer, director, playwright, and leading actor, Ludlam took much of his material from popular culture and used exaggerated characterizations and sexual ambiguity in his performances. After Ludlam's death his duties were assumed by his companion Everett Quinton.

D. S. Moynihan

Right to Life Party. Political party formed in 1969 to oppose abortion for any reason. It became an official political party in New York State after the gubernatorial election of 1978, when its candidate, Mary Jane Tobin, received the fifty thousand votes required for official party status. The party had 22,000 registered members in New York State at a peak in the early 1980s; in 1994 there were 9208 members in New York City, representing 0.3 percent of all registered voters. Although eligible to nominate its own candidates, the Right to Life Party instead usually endorses candidates of the major parties.

Melissa M. Merritt

Rihani, Ameen [Amin] **(Fares)** (*b* Freika, near Bikfaya, Lebanon, 24 Nov 1876; *d* Freika, 14 Sept 1940). Writer. After moving to New York City in 1888 he worked in his father's dry-goods shop on Washington Street. He became a member of al-Rabitah al-Qalamiyya (the Pen League), an influential literary circle of Syrian émigré writers, and wrote *The Book of Khaled* (1911), believed to be the first novel about the earliest Syrian immigrants in America. As a writer he sought to bridge two cultures and therefore returned often to the Middle East. Rihani was one of the first Syrians in New York City to speak out against militant Zionism. His writings on the Arab world include the book *Maker of Modern Arabia* (1928) and articles in the *New York Times*, *Harper's Weekly*, and the *Nation*.

Paula Hajar

Riis, Jacob A(ugustus) (*b* Ribe, Denmark, 3 May 1849; *d* Barre, Mass., 26 May 1914). Social reformer, photographer, and writer. After emigrating to the United States from Denmark in 1870 he worked as a police reporter for the *New York Tribune* from 1877 to 1888 and became known for his vivid descriptions of crime in Mulberry Bend and the Five Points. The unspeakable poverty and overcrowding that he witnessed there led him to become an advocate for immigrants. In 1887 he built a house at 84-41 120th Street in Richmond Hill, his home until 1911. From this time Riis took photographs in tenements to illustrate his stories, stunning his subjects with the bright light of the flash and forcing his middle-class readers to confront the filth and degradation of the slums. His article "Flashes from the Slums" (1888) in the *Sun* was highly successful, and in 1890 he became nationally known for his book *How the Other Half Lives*, an account of the squalid conditions endured by immigrants on the Lower East Side. An engaging storyteller and entertainer, he also gave lantern slide lectures to religious and charitable organizations, seeking to close police lodging houses and promoting tenement regulation, care for homeless children, and the construction of playgrounds. He eventually left newspaper work to write and give lectures full time. Among his supporters was Theodore Roosevelt, who as the city's police commissioner closed the police lodging houses. Riis lived at 524 North Beech Street in Richmond Hill.

Alexander Alland: *Jacob A. Riis, Photographer and Citizen* (Millerton: Aperture, 1974)

For further illustrations see ALMSHOUSES, AMERICAN INDIANS, CHILD LABOR, CHILDREN'S AID SOCIETY, FOUNDLINGS, GANGS, HELL'S KITCHEN, JAILS, LIGHTHOUSES, MULBERRY BEND, PLAYGROUNDS, POTTER'S FIELDS, TENEMENTS, and WARING, GEORGE E.

Bonnie Yochelson

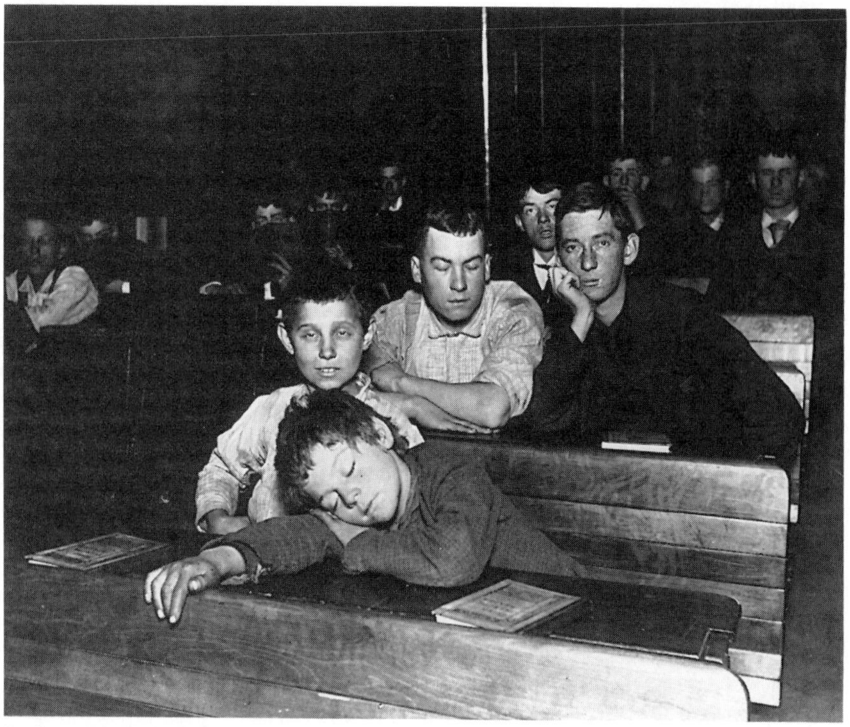

Jacob A. Riis, Night School in the Seventh Avenue Lodging House *(ca 1890). The school was run by the Children's Aid Society.*

Rikers Island. Island in the East River off the southeastern edge of the Bronx, to which it belongs. It originally covered eighty-seven acres (thirty-five hectares) of land and belonged to the Ryker family, descendants of Abraham Rycken, a settler who moved to Long Island in 1638. The city bought the island from the family in 1884 and used it as a prison farm; in 1932 it opened a prison for men there to replace its crumbling one on Blackwell's Island. After 1954 landfill was added to enlarge the area of the island to 415 acres (168 hectares), enabling the prison facilities to expand. The only transport was a ferry to the Bronx until 1966, when a three-lane bridge 4200 feet (1280 meters) long was extended to Queens. In 1994 about fifteen thousand inmates were held on Rikers Island in eleven jails (eight for men awaiting trial, one for convicted men whose terms do not exceed a year, one for women, and one for youths between sixteen and twenty) and a hospital. The facility also has a bakery, a laundry, a tailor shop, a print shop, maintenance and transportation units, a power plant, a methadone detoxification unit, a mental health center, an infirmary for patients with AIDS, and a nursery. By most measures Rikers Island is the largest jail facility in the United States.

"Inquiry into Disturbances on Rikers Island: October, 1986" (Albany: New York State Commission on Correction, 1987)

Joseph P. Viteritti

Rio de San Antonio. Former name of the HUDSON RIVER.

riots. Although New York City was considered a center of Loyalist sentiment during the American Revolution, British imperial policy frequently drove the local populace into the streets in the years preceding armed revolt. The English traditions that shaped colonial New York sanctioned rioting, and in the eighteenth century and the early nineteenth it was an established part of the city's political culture. On 1 November 1765 mobs demonstrated against the Stamp Act by parading with effigies of Cadwallader Colden, the lieutenant governor of New York; they controlled the streets until the act was repealed the next spring. Other effigy processions took place in opposition to the Townshend Duties on 14 November 1768, 10 May 1770, and 5 November 1770. On 15 June 1774 a crowd paraded with effigies of British officials to protest the Boston Port Bill. British soldiers and residents of New York City defending the Liberty Pole clashed several times from 10 August 1766 to 18 January 1770 (the Golden Hill Riot). Crowds harassed royal officials, whom they threatened with bodily harm and sometimes tarred and feathered.

The end of hostilities with Britain and the departure of the redcoats did not bring peace to the streets. On 26 July 1788 enraged supporters of the proposed Constitution gutted the printing office of the anti-Federalist Thomas Greenleaf. Political differences led to several disturbances in the 1790s, including a demonstration against the Jay Treaty at which Alexander Hamilton maintained that the crowd pelted him with stones. The Doctors' Riot of 1788 began on 13 April when five thousand persons marched on New York Hospital to protest the purported theft of cadavers for dissection. Searching for evidence of illegal behavior, the rioters destroyed laboratories, ransacked offices, and buried (or reburied) every cadaver they found. They took into custody a group of medical students (whom they later surrendered to the authorities for "safe keeping"), returned the next day to search the homes of physicians and other facilities, and then disarmed a small militia detachment and threatened to storm the jail where the students were being held. The au-

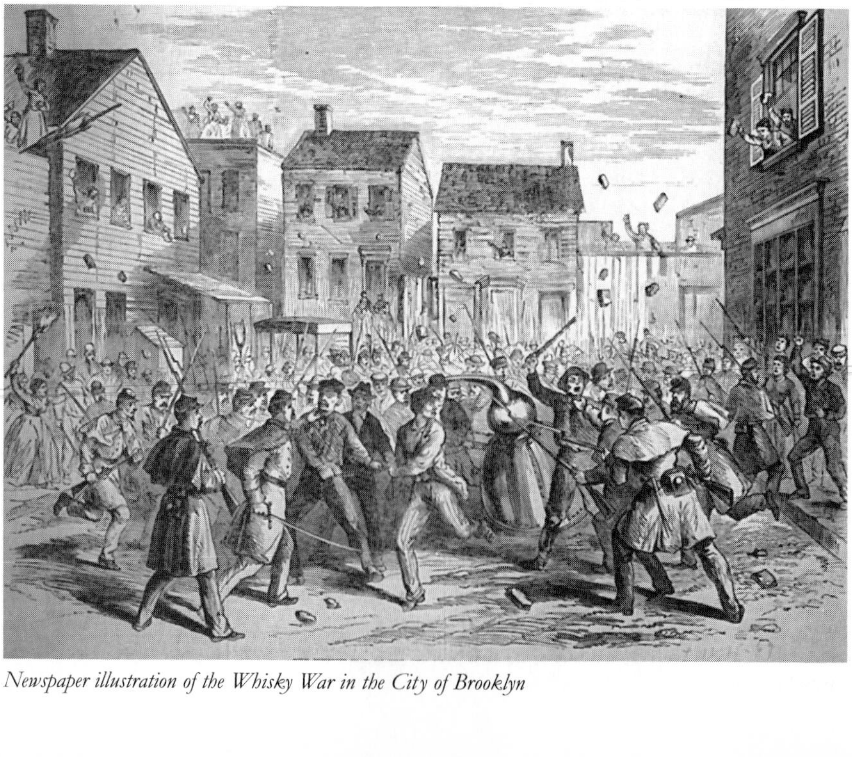

Newspaper illustration of the Whisky War in the City of Brooklyn

thorities reacted by firing on the crowd and killing three persons. Concerns about immoral behavior inspired two riots aimed at bawdyhouses (14–15 October 1793 and 17–20 July 1799).

During the nineteenth century ethnic and religious differences, politics, and racial prejudice led to the most violent rioting in the city's history, typified by a battle on Christmas Day 1806 in the sixth ward between Catholics (mostly Irish) and Protestants (mostly native born). There were also violent strikes by stevedores (1825 and 1828), weavers (1828), and stonecutters (1829). Many regard 1834 as the city's worst year for riots because of election rioting between Whigs and Democrats (9–10 April) and mob attacks on abolitionists and blacks (7–11 July). Both these disturbances and several others in the 1830s were marked by intense physical violence. The Flour Riot (12 February 1837) was different: after a political meeting decrying the plight of the poor a large crowd attacked Eli Hart's warehouse and gave away flour; two other warehouses also were attacked. The police were powerless to stop fights on 4–5 July 1857 between the Protestant street gang the Bowery Boys and the Catholic gang the Dead Rabbits, and twelve lives were lost as a result.

By this time widespread crowd violence had become commonplace, setting the stage for the second-most serious riot in the city's history. The Astor Place Riot (10–11 May 1849) began when supporters of the American actor Edwin Forrest interrupted a performance by his English rival, William C. Macready. Protests both in and outside the Astor Place Opera House brought forth the militia and the police, who killed twenty-two persons (nine more may have died later of their injuries) and wounded forty-eight when they fired into a crowd that refused to disperse, and fifty to seventy policemen were injured when the crowd retaliated. The riot reflected deep ethnic and class resentments within the city. In the Kleindeutschland Riot (12–13 July 1857) the police killed one man and wounded several others in a disturbance in a German neighborhood that began when police officers attempted to break up a street brawl.

The Draft riots of 13–17 July 1863, the bloodiest riots in American history, began in front of a conscription office on 3rd Avenue and 47th Street when the city's Irish poor arose against a new law exempting from conscription anyone who paid a fee of $300. A mob went on a rampage through the city, attacking such symbols of privilege and power as police stations, arsenals, and the homes and shops of the wealthy. Soon the riot assumed a racial dimension: some blacks were hanged or mutilated, many were assaulted, and black institutions and homes were destroyed. The riot was put down only after pitched battles in the streets in which the police, the militia, and the army used artillery to destroy barricades. Contemporary estimates reported from 105 to a thousand deaths, though the most widely accepted figure is 125. Eight persons were killed and fifteen were injured in the Orange Riot of 12 July 1870, in which Irish Catholics attacked Irish Protestants commemorating the victory of William of Orange over French and Irish forces in 1690 (see Orange riots). In the following year Catholics assaulted a truncated Protestant parade on the same anniversary despite the presence of a large police and militia guard; sixty-seven persons were killed, three of them militiamen.

Hard times following the Civil War prompted a resurgence of labor strife, which became the principal source of rioting in the late nineteenth century. The Tompkins Square Riot (13 January 1874) was the result of a demonstration planned by the Committee of Safety, a political group with many members in the communist organization the International Workingmen's Association, or First International. The police board and the parks commissioner at first seemed cooperative but at the last moment denied the necessary permits. Although the organizers revised their plans and canceled part of the proceedings, most of the participants were left uninformed of any changes, and in the ensuing confusion about seven thousand men and women gathered in Tompkins Square. The demonstrators were ordered to disperse by the police commissioner and soon after were charged by a force of sixteen hundred police officers, who indiscriminately beat and arrested demonstrators and bystanders. News of the riot spread and hundreds of demonstrators converged on police headquarters to demand the release of those arrested, but city officials were aware that the behavior of the police was largely sanctioned by middle-class New Yorkers and ignored the demands for an inquiry. On 22 April 1886 eastern European sugar refinery workers attacked delivery wagons and fought with police in Williamsburg.

The employees of the city's many privately owned streetcar and elevated railroad companies were particularly noted for aggressive behavior, especially during strikes over wages and working conditions. Although riots took place on several occasions (notably in Manhattan in 1886) the most serious were the Brooklyn Surface Railroad Riots (14 January to 2 February 1895), in which strikers tore down electrical wires, damaged tracks, beat nonunion workers, and confronted the police and militia. Shots fired by rioters on 21 January wounded two policemen, and in partial retaliation soldiers charged into the crowd with bayonets and injured many people. Almost seven thousand militiamen were deployed along the rail lines to guard the streetcar tracks against sabotage, and on 23 January the militia shot and killed one man. Race relations remained a persistent problem. Whites attacked blacks in 1889 and in response to an arrest did so again in 1900 in San Juan Hill.

In the early and mid twentieth century riots in New York City resulted less from conflict between whites and blacks than from attacks on property that pitted blacks against the city's police force. On the whole riots caused fewer deaths than they had previously. There were riots in Harlem in 1935 (killing three persons), 1943 (killing six), 1964, 1965, and 1977 (during a power blackout). At the same time protests of the antiwar movement and the student left in the 1960s and early 1970s sometimes resulted in politically motivated riots. The best-known incident of the period took place between 23 April and 1 May 1968 at Columbia University, where students protested the university's cooperation with the Institute for Defense Analysis and its decision to build a gymnasium in Morningside Park to serve students rather than the poor residents of Harlem. The students staged large rallies, destroyed fences at the construction site, occupied campus buildings, held three university officials hostage for more than twenty-four hours, and ransacked several offices, including that of President Grayson Kirk in Low Library. With classes mostly suspended and the university in turmoil, police began to remove the protestors forcibly on 30 April. Four faculty members, 132 students, and twelve police officers were injured in clashes on the first day, as were five more police officers and six students the next day. The confrontation did not subside until the end of the spring semester, and the bitterness on both sides remained for many years. Another violent incident connected with the Vietnam War occurred in 1970, when construction workers attacked antiwar demonstrators on Wall Street.

Disagreement about a park curfew and its impact on the homeless led to a confrontation between the community and the police in the Tompkins Square Riot of 6 August 1988, characterized as a "police riot" because of the manner in which the police dealt with the protestors. During the summer of 1991 an automobile driven by a Hasidic Jew in Crown Heights struck and killed a black child, black youths were charged with killing a Hasid in retaliation, and several days and nights of rioting embroiled blacks, Hasidim, and the police.

Joel Tyler Headley: *The Great Riots of New York, 1712–1873* (New York: E. B. Treat, 1873; repr. Indianapolis: Bobbs–Merrill, 1970)

Richard Moody: *The Astor Place Riot* (Bloomington: Indiana University Press, 1958)

Herbert Gutman: "The Tompkins Square 'Riot' in New York City on January 13, 1874," *Labor History* 6 (1965), 44–70

Richard Hofstadter and Michael Wallace, eds.: *American Violence: A Documentary History* (New York: Vintage, 1970)

Adrian Cook: *The Armies of the Streets: The New York City Draft Riots of 1863* (Lexington: University Press of Kentucky, 1974)

Paul O. Weinbaum: *Mobs and Demagogues: The New York Response to Collective Violence in the Early Nineteenth Century* (Ann Arbor, Mich.: UMI Research Press, 1979)

Peter G. Buckley: "To the Opera House: Culture and Society in New York City, 1820–1860" (diss., State University of New York, Stony Brook, 1984)

Paul A. Gilje: *The Road to Mobocracy: Popular Disorder in New York City, 1763–1834* (Chapel Hill: University of North Carolina Press, 1987)

Paul A. Gilje

Ritz Tower. Luxury hotel and apartment building at 57th Street and Park Avenue, opened in October 1926. Its forty-one stories and height of 540 feet (165 meters) made it the world's tallest residential building at the time and the embodiment of luxury. Although several stories accommodated transient guests, the hotel offered full domestic services to the wealthy who leased apartments annually. Suites of four to twelve rooms rented for about $3000 a room. The developer Arthur Brisbane, a popular columnist for William Randolph Hearst's publications, assembled the site in 1924 and engaged the architect Emery Roth (later joined by Thomas Hastings) to design the building, then leased the venture to the Ritz–Carlton hotel interests. Brisbane reserved for himself a spectacular eighteen-room duplex apartment; this was later occupied by Hearst, who purchased the hotel. The building became a cooperative in 1956 but reopened as a hotel in 1983.

Carol Willis

Riverdale. Neighborhood in the northwestern Bronx, lying on the ridge mostly to the north and west of the Henry Hudson Parkway and bounded to the north by Westchester County, to the south by 239th Street, and to the west by the Hudson River. It began as a railroad station of the Hudson division of New York Central called Riverdale-on-Hudson. In the 1860s the high ground overlooking the Hudson was an ideal site for the summer mansions of the city's industrial and mercantile élite, who could travel easily by rail to and from their offices in Manhattan. Before the Second World War a number of luxurious one-family houses were built on landscaped grounds near the mansions. The construction in the 1930s of the Henry Hudson Parkway spurred development, as did the addition of a bus line connecting the neighborhood to the 7th Avenue line of Interborough Rapid Transit at 231st Street and to the 8th Avenue line of the Independent subway in northern Manhattan. In the years after the war most of the estates were sold to institutions and developers. Fewer high-rise apartment buildings were erected than in Spuyten Duyvil.

Many structures dating from the nineteenth century are local landmarks: Fieldston Hill (*ca* 1865) at the western end of 246th Street, Greyston (1864) at 247th Street and Independence Avenue, Wave Hill (1844) at 249th Street and Independence Avenue, and Stonehurst (1861). From the same period are Christ Church (1866) and the Riverdale Presbyterian Church (1863), which stand on either side of the Henry Hudson Parkway. The College of Mount St. Vincent, operated by the Sisters of Charity, has a castle originally built in 1852 for the well-known Shakespearean actor Edwin Forrest, as well as his cottage and stable. The college's administration building was built in stages from 1857 to 1908. Along Sycamore Avenue between 252nd and 254th streets is the Riverdale Historic District, the residences of which were originally the barns and carriage houses of the nearby estates. Major institutions in Riverdale include the Riverdale Country School, the Wave Hill Center, the Henry Ittleson Center for Child Research, the Cardinal Spellman Retreat House, and the Hebrew Home for the Aged.

Riverdale is a neighborhood of fine houses on landscaped grounds that is distinguished by its affluence and by the geographical separation from the rest of the city that is effected by its ridge. Apart from such major commercial thoroughfares as Riverdale Avenue most of its roadways are pleasantly winding and have no sidewalks, which imparts to the neighborhood a distinctive suburban character.

William A. Tieck: *Riverdale, Kingsbridge, Spuyten Duyvil: New York City* (Old Tappan, N.J.: Fleming H. Revell, 1968)

Lloyd Ultan and Gary Hermalyn: *The Bronx in the Innocent Years, 1895–1925* (New York: Harper and Row, 1985)

Gary Hermalyn and Robert Kornfeld: *Landmarks of the Bronx* (New York: Bronx County Historical Society, 1989)

Lloyd Ultan

Bus serving the Riverdale Country School, ca *1913*

Riverdale Country School. Coeducational elementary and secondary school opened in 1907 by Frank Sutcliff Hackett and his wife, Frances Hackett. With $500 in savings the two rented a country estate high above Van Cortlandt Park and employed four teachers to instruct twelve boys. In 1935 the Riverdale Country School for Girls opened on a nearby estate west of the original campus. Riverdale Country School became fully coeducational in 1972: the original campus became the site of its secondary school, the former girls' school the site of its elementary school. The enrollment stood at 981 students in 1994.

Richard Schwartz

Riverdale Presbyterian Church. Church formed in 1863 at 4765 Henry Hudson Parkway West by J. Joseph Eagleton, Samuel W. Dodge, William Earl Dodge Jr., Robert Colgate, and John Mott. The building was designed by James Renwick on land donated by Joseph Delafield. With the active support of the philanthropist Grace Hoadley Dodge, church members established Riverdale Neighborhood House (1872) and the Riverdale Neighborhood and Library Association. Notable members of the congregation included Cleveland H. Dodge and George W. Perkins. In 1965 the city designated the church building and the attached Grace H. Dodge Church House as landmarks. In 1991 the church had 295 members.

William A. Tieck: *Riverdale, Kingsbridge, Spuyten Duyvil* (Old Tappan, N.Y.: F. H. Revell, 1968)

David Meerse

Rivers, Thomas M(ilton) (*b* Jonesboro, Ga., 3 Sept 1888; *d* New York City, 12 May 1962). Virologist and public health official. He moved to New York City in 1922 to direct the infectious disease ward at the Rockefeller Institute and rose to several prominent positions there and at the Rockefeller Foundation. One of the first to recognize the importance of viruses as a distinct group of infective agents, he urged the establishment of virology as a separate field within microbiology. In 1929 he fought the outbreak in New York City of psittacosis (parrot fever), which spread quickly among public health workers in laboratories. He helped form the Public Health Research Institute of the City of New York (1942) and was a member of the board of health (1944–62).

Joseph S. Lieber

Riverside Church. An interdenominational church on the east side of Riverside Drive between 120th and 122nd Streets. It occupies a huge, steel-framed Gothic building, financed by John D. Rockefeller Jr. and completed in 1930, that is the most impressive structure along the Hudson River between midtown and the George Washington Bridge. The congregation began as a Baptist church in 1841 in lower Manhattan and soon became known for its interracial and international character. The first minister at the new site uptown was the controversial and influential Harry Emerson Fosdick. The church seats 2500 persons and is notable for the excellence of its stone carving and stained glass. The Laura Spelman Rockefeller Memorial Carillon, the largest in the world, contains seventy-four bells and occupies a space extending from the twenty-third story to what would be the twenty-eighth; it was the first carillon in history to achieve a compass of five octaves, and its Bourdon, or hour-bell, is the largest and heaviest carillon bell ever cast. An observation platform 355 feet (108 meters) above the ground is served by the tallest elevators in any church in the world. Riverside Church is affiliated with both the American Baptist Churches in the United States and the United Church of Christ.

Kenneth T. Jackson

Riverside Park. Public park in Manhattan, situated on a narrow strip of land along the Hudson River from 72nd Street to 125th Street and from 135th Street to 158th Street, and occupying more than 323 acres (131 hectares). Prehistoric glaciers left rocky outcroppings and steep bluffs on the site, and before European settlement the rough terrain was only sparsely populated by American Indians. In 1846 the Hudson River Railroad was built along the shoreline. A proposal for a scenic drive and park was advanced in 1865 by William R. Martin, a commissioner on the Board of Central Park. During the next two years the city acquired land between the railroad and the bluffs, for which a park was commissioned in 1873 by the park board from the chief designer of Central Park, Frederick Law Olmsted. His proposal calling for a parkway that would adapt to the rolling contours of the

Riverside Church, 1936

Soldiers' and Sailors' Monument (designed by Stoughton and Stoughton with Paul E. M. Duboy) on Riverside Drive, ca *1900*

land was accepted in 1875; the final plans were drawn up by others, including Samuel Parsons, Julius Munkwitz, and Calvert Vaux, and implemented during the next twenty-five years. The park was built in English pastoral style, with a rustic retaining wall and informally arranged plantings and meandering paths.

Dockside industries and noisy railroads along the riverfront threatened the park. A plan made as early as 1891 to build a bridge over the tracks was neglected for more than forty years. Proponents of the "city beautiful" movement at the turn of the century introduced formal elements into the park, including the Soldiers' and Sailors' Monument and its plaza at 89th Street, Grant's Tomb at 121st Street, and the Firemen's Memorial at 100th Street. Between 1934 and 1937 a plan known as the West Side Improvement was executed along the riverfront under the guidance of Robert Moses, who expanded earlier proposals, including one by McKim, Mead and White from the 1920s, to build a rotunda and a marina at 79th Street and to double the size of the park by adding to it the West Side Highway and Henry Hudson Parkway. The architect and engineer Clinton Lloyd replaced rustic stone with granite, bluestone, and concrete to give the park a more orderly appearance; the landscape architect Gilmore Clarke contributed a complementary planting scheme. Most of the labor was provided by relief workers, who enclosed the railroad tracks and built a promenade over them, and added a lower level on landfill for athletic fields and tennis courts. When their work was completed the park incorporated elements of several styles of landscape design.

In the mid 1990s Riverside Park was one of the most heavily used open spaces in the city. Community groups were active in planting the park and restoring its historic features.

Jonathan Kuhn

RJR Nabisco. Firm of food processors formed in 1890 as the New York Biscuit Company by the lawyer William Henry Moore. In 1898 it acquired the brands Fig Newtons and Premium Saltines when it merged with the American Biscuit Company to form the National Biscuit Company, a group of 114 bakeries with total capitalization of $55 million. Under the direction of Adolphus Greene during the following decade it introduced small, sealed cardboard boxes of soda crackers known as Uneeda Biscuits, which were tremendously successful owing largely to an advertising campaign handled by the firm of N. W. Ayer and Son; it also developed uniform production standards, innovative packaging, and trademarks. The firm moved its headquarters from Chicago to New York City in 1906 and introduced several brands, among them Oreo cookies and Barnum's Animal Crackers, and was soon the leading manufacturer of cookies and crackers in the United

Advertisement for Barnum's Animal Crackers, 1923

States. It also operated a bakery at 10th Avenue and 14th Street in Manhattan that was the largest in the world; the name Nabisco became a trademark in 1941. After a period of losses during the 1930s, followed by the Second World War, the firm recovered by expanding its line of products and marketing them aggressively. By the 1970s it was again the country's leading cookie and cracker manufacturer; the headquarters were moved to East Hanover, New Jersey, in 1975. In 1980 the firm had annual sales of $2400 million. It merged in 1981 with Standard Brands, a food and beverage manufacturer, to form Nabisco Brands. After being acquired by R. J. Reynolds Industries in 1985 Nabisco Brands became part of RJR Nabisco, a firm with annual sales of more than $19,000 million that was the largest consumer products company in the United States. An attempt in 1988 by F. Ross Johnson, president of the firm, to take it private led to one of the costliest corporate bidding wars in history; Johnson's group eventually lost out to another led by the brokerage firm Kohlberg Kravis Roberts, which prevailed by bidding nearly $25,000 million in cash, notes, and securities. Despite the debt incurred by its new owners RJR Nabisco remained successful. The headquarters were moved to Manhattan, with those of the Nabisco division remaining in East Hanover.

Peter A. Coclanis

Robards, Jason (Nelson, Jr.) (*b* Chicago, 26 July 1922). Actor. After attending the American Academy of Dramatic Arts (1946) he performed at the Circle in the Square in 1953 under the direction of José Quintero. On Broadway he appeared in *The Iceman Cometh* (1956) and *Long Day's Journey into Night* (1956–58) by Eugene O'Neill, the playwright with whom he became most strongly associated. He also won a Tony Award for his performance in Budd Schulberg's *The Disenchanted* (1958–59). In later years Robards appeared in Arthur Miller's *After the Fall* (1964) and revivals of *Long Day's Journey* (1976, 1988), as well as many films.

Robbins [Rabinowitz], **Jerome** (*b* New York City, 11 Oct 1918). Dancer, choreographer, and director. He joined Ballet Theatre in 1940, became a soloist in 1941, and in 1949 joined George Balanchine's NEW YORK CITY BALLET, of which he became the associate artistic director. From the 1940s to the 1960s he was the choreographer and director of many productions on Broadway, including *On the Town* (1944; based on *Fancy Free*, his ballet about sailors on shore leave in the city), *Billion Dollar Baby* (1945), *High Button Shoes* (1947), *The King and I* (1951), *Peter Pan* (1954), *West Side Story* (1957, film version 1961), *Gypsy* (1959), and *Fiddler on the Roof* (1964). In 1958 he formed the Lena Robbins Foundation to bring new choreographers to the public's attention. For the Spoleto Festival of the same year he formed his own company, Ballets USA, which he reconvened for the Spoleto Festival of 1961. After returning to New York City Ballet in the 1960s he became its balletmaster in 1969. With Peter Martins he became ballet-master-in-chief on Balanchine's death in 1983, a position he retained until 1990. Robbins's work includes more than fifty ballets, among them *The Cage* (1951), *Interplay* (1952), *Afternoon of a Faun* (1953), *New York Export: Opus Jazz* (1958), *Moves* (1961), *Dances at a Gathering* (1969), *In the Night* (1970), *The Goldberg Variations* (1971), *Watermill* (1972), *In G Major* (1975), *The Four Seasons* (1979), *Glass Pieces* (1983), *I'm Old Fashioned* (1983), and *In Memory of. . .* (1985). *Jerome Robbins' Broadway* (1989) was a retrospective of his choreography from nearly a dozen musicals. By the mid 1990s Robbins had won the Tony Award five times, the Donaldson Award four times, and the Academy Award twice, as well as the Emmy Award, the Screen Directors' Guild Award, the New York Drama Critics' Circle Award, the Kennedy Center Honors (1981), and the National Medal of Art.

Christena Schlundt: *Dance in the Musical Theater: Jerome Robbins and His Peers, 1934–1965: A Guide* (New York: Garland, 1989)

For illustration see AMERICAN BALLET THEATER.

Norma Adler

Roberto Clemente State Park. Public park opened in August 1973 as Harlem River–Bronx State Park, the first state park in New York City, on twenty-five acres (ten hectares) of land along the Harlem River north of the Washington Bridge in the Bronx. The site was occupied by boating clubhouses and shipyards in the nineteenth century. It was given its current name in September 1974 in memory of the baseball player for the Pittsburgh Pirates killed in a plane crash while on a relief mission to earthquake victims in Nicaragua.

Edward Steichen, Paul Robeson in "The Emperor Jones" *(1933). Gelatin-silver print. Collection of the Museum of Modern Art. Gift of the photographer. Copyright 1933 (renewed 1961) by Condé Nast Publications*

The park has a large outdoor pool, a gymnasium, and ballfields, and abuts the River Park Towers.

John McNamara: *History in Asphalt: The Origin of Bronx Street and Place Names* (New York: Bronx County Historical Society, 1984)

Gary D. Hermalyn

Robertson, R(obert) H(enderson) (*b* Philadelphia, 29 April 1849; *d* New York City, 4 June 1919). Architect. An early association with the architect William A. Potter helped him to achieve a reputation as a skilled designer of religious and commercial buildings. His most important projects included St. Luke's Church, a Romanesque Revival structure at 285 Convent Avenue (1892–95), and the classically inspired St. Paul's Methodist Church (now the Church of St. Paul and St. Andrew) at West End Avenue and 86th Street (1896). Robertson explored diverse solutions to the problems encountered in designing tall office buildings while working on the Lincoln Building (1889–90, Union Square West), the McIntyre Building (1890–92, 874 Broadway), the Corn Exchange Bank (1892–94, Beaver and William streets, demolished), the American Tract Society Building (1894–95, Nassau Street), and the Park Row Building (1896–99, 15 Park Row), on its completion the world's tallest building.

Marjorie Pearson

Robeson, Paul (Leroy) (*b* Princeton, N.J., 9 April 1898; *d* Philadelphia, 23 Jan 1976). Actor, singer, athlete, and political activist. The son of a runaway slave and Methodist minister, he won a scholarship to attend Rutgers College, where he was the only black student, earned twelve varsity letters in four sports, was elected to the All-America football team in 1918, and graduated as the valedictorian of his class. While working as a professional football player and heavyweight boxer he entered Columbia University Law School in 1920. His talent for acting was noticed by Eugene O'Neill during an amateur play at the YMCA, and his acting career was launched when O'Neill cast him in *Taboo* and *The Emperor Jones*; he later became known as one of the first actors to portray realistic, nuanced black characters in motion pictures. One of the most popular singers of his time, he mastered more than twenty languages and performed classical repertory, spirituals, and folk songs from around the world in concert. From 1939 to 1941 he lived at 555 Edgecomb Avenue in Harlem (the house was later designated a National Historic Landmark). Inspired by his experience of discrimination in law and by the perspectives he gained while touring abroad, he joined several causes devoted to labor and anti-fascism; his passport was subsequently suspended from 1950 to 1958, cutting short his career. In protest Robeson spent many years in England and the Soviet Union. His last home in the city was at 16 Jumel Terrace in Manhattan, where he lived from 1963 to 1966.

Martin Bauml Duberman: *Paul Robeson* (New York: Alfred A. Knopf, 1988)

Amanda Aaron

Robinson, Bill (Luther) "Bojangles" (*b* Richmond, Va., 25 May 1878; *d* Los Angeles, 25 Nov 1949). Tap dancer. After spending years in vaudeville he played leading roles in such all-black Broadway revues as *Blackbirds of 1928* and *The Hot Mikado* (1939). He refined tap dancing and performed in a seemingly effortless manner in such routines as the staircase dance. Nicknamed the "Mayor of Harlem," he was also known for his dapper appearance. He is best remembered for his dances with Shirley Temple, considered controversial at a time when interracial performances were rare, in the motion pictures *The Littlest Rebel* (1935) and *Rebecca of Sunnybrook Farm* (1938), and for his role in *Stormy Weather* (1943).

Bill "Bojangles" Robinson, 1935, with a pearl-handled gold revolver given to him by the 32nd police precinct of New York City, a platinum key to the city of Richmond, Virginia, two gold deputy sheriff's badges from New York City and Brooklyn, and a gold badge for the honorary mayoralty of Harlem, all awarded to him for charitable work

James Haskins and N. R. Mitgang: *Mr. Bojangles: The Biography of Bill Robinson* (New York: William Morrow, 1988)

David J. Weiner

Robinson, Boardman (*b* Somerset, near Berwick, Nova Scotia, 6 Sept 1876; *d* Stamford, Conn., 5 Sept 1952). Painter and illustrator. He studied art in Boston and Paris and settled in New York City in 1904, where he worked as a cartoonist for the *Morning Telegraph* and the *Masses* and provided illustrations for books published by Random House, among them *The Idiot* and *The Brothers Karamazov*. In 1915 his book *Cartoons of the War* was published by E. P. Dutton. He traveled with John Reed and made illustrations for Reed's book *War in Eastern Europe* (1916). During the 1920s he painted such murals as *Man and His Toys* at the RKO Building and taught at the Art Students League. Robinson received the gold medal of the New York Architectural League in 1930 and was a leader in the federal art programs of the New Deal; he moved to Colorado in 1936.

Albert Christ-Janer: *Boardman Robinson* (Chicago: University of Chicago Press, 1946)

James E. Mooney

Robinson, Jackie [John Roosevelt] (*b* Cairo, Ga., 31 Jan 1919; *d* New York City, 24 Oct 1972). Baseball player. When he was sixteen months old his mother, Mallie, moved the family to California, where he became the first student at UCLA to earn four letters (one each in football, baseball, basketball, and track). During the Second World War he was nearly court-martialed when he refused to play on the football team at Fort Hood in Texas, an act of protest prompted by having been forced to move to the back of an army bus. After the war he played baseball in the Negro Leagues for the Kansas City Monarchs; soon many believed that he would become the first black player in the major leagues. At the East–West Game of the Negro Leagues in 1945 he was approached by a scout for Branch Rickey, president of the Brooklyn Dodgers. After secret negotiations Rickey announced on 23 October 1945 in Montreal that he had signed Robinson, who soon joined the Dodgers' farm team the Montreal Royals. He was promoted to the major leagues on 9 April 1947. In ten years as a second baseman for the Dodgers he batted .311, stole 197 bases, had 1518 hits in 1382 games, and played in six World Series. His performance on the field and his ability to handle the pressures of his role became an inspiration to all who fought bigotry. He was elected to the Baseball Hall of Fame in 1962, the first year he was eligible. From 1947 to 1949 he lived at 5224 Tilden Street in Flatbush; for most of his years as a player he lived in St. Albans. After his retirement from baseball he was a business executive, a founder of Freedom National Bank in Harlem (1964), a civil rights activist, and a prominent Republican. In 1990 *Life* named him one of the hundred most influential Americans of the twentieth century. Robinson wrote an autobiography, *I Never Had It Made* (1972).

Arthur Ashe: *A Hard Road to Glory* (New York: Amistad/Warner, 1988)

Arthur Ashe

Robinson, Sugar Ray [Smith, Walker, Jr.] (*b* Detroit, 3 May 1921; *d* Culver City, Iowa, 12 April 1989). Boxer. At the age of twelve he moved with his mother to New York City, where he attended De Witt Clinton High School for three years. After a successful career as an amateur boxer he turned professional in 1940 and won the world welterweight title in 1946 in a fifteen-round decision over Tommy Bell. In 1951 he defeated Jake La Motta in a contest for the world middleweight title, a championship he held five times during his long career. Although he retired several times, financial problems forced him back into the ring. At the time of his final retirement in 1965 after a loss to Joey Archer his record stood at 174 wins, nineteen losses, six draws, one no-decision, and one no-contest. He was elected to the Boxing Hall of Fame in 1967. With Dave Anderson he wrote *Sugar Ray* (1970).

Randy Roberts

Rochdale Village. Apartment village in southeastern Queens (1990 pop. 13,185), lying within South Jamaica and bounded to the north by Baisley Boulevard and Bedell Street, to the east by Bedell Street, to the south by 137th Avenue, and to the west by Guy R. Brewer Boulevard. The Jamaica Racetrack was demolished in 1960 to make way for the complex, which was built for $86 million as a middle-income cooperative. Twenty brick buildings of fourteen stories each were erected on thirty-three acres (thirteen hectares). In addition to several recreational facilities there were three public schools. When the village opened in 1963 it was the largest private housing complex in the world (later surpassed by Co-op City). The population was at first heavily Jewish but became mostly black in the early 1970s.

James Bradley

rock. New York City played an important role in the development of rock and of its precursors rock-and-roll and rhythm-and-blues. In the 1940s and 1950s rhythm-and-blues recorded in Kansas City, East St. Louis (Illinois), Chicago, Cincinnati, New Orleans, Texas, and California was transferred to disc at Bell Studios. Atlantic Records began in the city as a small independent record label led by Ahmet Ertegun, Nesuhi Ertegun, Herb Abramson, and (later) Jerry Wexler; it recorded such rhythm-and-blues musicians as Big Joe Turner. Record companies in the city helped to develop a style of rhythm-and-blues that was more polished and jazz-oriented than its counterpart elsewhere by engaging as studio musicians a number of sidemen from big bands, including those of Duke Ellington and Count Basie: among the best-known studio players were the guitarist Mickey Baker and the saxophonist King Curtis (both of whom recorded for Atlantic), the guitarist Cornell Dupree and the drummer Bernard Purdie (both members of Curtis's band), and the guitarist Jimmy Spruill (who recorded for the labels Fire, Joy, and Fury, all owned by Bobby Robinson). Early rhythm-and-blues recordings by Fats Domino and Little Richard were broadcast on the radio station WINS in New York City from 1954 by the disc jockey Alan Freed (who is believed to have originated the term "rock-and-roll"); he later organized concerts at the Paramount Theater in Brooklyn. Other disc jockeys in the city included Murray the K (Murray Kaufman), Cousin Brucie (Bruce Morrow), and B. Mitchell Reid.

The line between rhythm-and-blues and rock-and-roll became increasingly blurred by white performers like Elvis Presley, Chuck Berry, Buddy Holly, and Bill Haley, who found a wide audience by combining elements of rhythm-and-blues and country music. Berry and Holly were among the few rock-and-roll performers who wrote their own songs: most relied on material written by other songwriters that adhered closely to the popular-song formulas of Tin Pan Alley. Many of these songwriters worked in the Brill Building at 1619 Broadway, including Jerry Lieber and Mike Stoller, Gerry Goffin and Carole King, Neil Sedaka, Bert Berns, Ellie Greenwich, Barry Mann, Bobby Darin, and Neil Diamond (all employed by Don Kirshner's firm Aldon Music), Doc Pomus and Mort Shuman, and Burt Bacharach and Hal David. By the early 1960s songwriters were powerful figures in the music business, and many began performing themselves: among those who did was Paul Simon. Doo-wop emerged as a genre of rock-and-roll that combined the smooth, intricate harmonies of the barbershop quartet, the rhythmic drive of black gospel music, and often ludicrous lyrics. Early doo-wop groups included the Mills Brothers and the Ink Spots; the gospel element predominated in the work of later groups like the Ravens, the Orioles, the Dominos, the Clovers, the Drifters, the Platters, and the Coasters. Popularized by Freed and often performed on street corners, doo-wop had an enormous impact on white, black, and Latin American teenagers in New York City in the late 1950s and early 1960s. Italian groups were especially numerous, among them Johnny Maestro and the Crests (1958–60, best known for their recording "16 Candles"), the Brooklyn Bridge (also formed by Maestro), Dion DiMucci and the Belmonts (named for the predominantly Italian neighborhood in the Bronx), Frankie Valli and the Four Seasons, Joey Dee and the Starlighters (whose recording "Peppermint Twist" was named for the Peppermint Lounge, a discothèque in the city), and Danny and the Juniors (well known for their recording "At the Hop"). In the early 1960s doo-wop was largely eclipsed by the music of the Beatles and other groups from Britain.

At the same time small clubs like Gerde's Folk City, the Bitter End, the Cafe Wha?, and the Gaslight achieved success as venues for folk music and blues, both associated in the popular mind with the bohemianism then fashionable and the brand of leftist populism embodied by such folk musicians as Woody Guthrie and Pete Seeger. The clubs drew college-educated listeners familiar with the music of Doc Watson, Bill Monroe, Sonny Terry and Brownie McGhee, Elizabeth Cotten, Mississippi John Hurt, Skip James, Muddy Waters, and the Reverend Gary Davis. Among the more distinctive performers were Phil Ochs and Dave Van Ronk; others were dutiful imitators of genres ranging from Scottish ballads to Mississippi Delta blues. Bob Dylan, who began his career by performing folk music on the acoustic guitar, took up the electric guitar at the Newport Folk Festival in 1965 and soon gained a large following. His album *Highway 61 Revisited* and such songs as "Like a Rolling Stone" had a profound influence on the Beatles, the Rolling Stones, and other groups, who in their music and especially their lyrics now gave greater attention to irony and political topicality. Rock was first played on FM radio in New York City in 1966 on the classical-music station WOR by the disc jockey Scott Muni; he later moved to WNEW-FM, where he became known for innovative programming that demanded rather more from his listeners than the steady regimen of pop singles to which they were accustomed. Rock was also broadcast by WBAI, which combined highly eclectic music programming with counterculture politics.

The musical explorations of the Beatles in their albums *Revolver*, *Rubber Soul*, and *Sgt. Pepper's Lonely Hearts Club Band* contributed further to the growing selfconsciousness and diversity of rock. Musicians largely abandoned the conventions of Tin Pan Alley in favor of adventurous material of their own composition. Their lyrics became more sophisticated and ambitious, and they freely drew on inspirations as diverse as the music of Erik Satie and the cacophony of the city. On disc and at clubs like the Electric Circus, Lou Reed and his influential band the Velvet Underground sang about sadomasochism and drugs to the accompaniment of shrieking, microtonal viola lines, guitar feedback, and a thundering rhythm section. The Fugs and the Mothers of Invention engaged in anarchic musical satire; blues and soul were performed by the Blues Project, by Aretha Franklin and B. B. King (both of whom recorded with Curtis), and by a number of "garage" bands, including the Young Rascals, Vanilla Fudge, and Mountain. The recording studio took on a more prominent role as overdubbing and editing were used to create increasingly dense sounds. From the late 1960s the producer Bill Graham presented concerts featuring three or four widely disparate groups at the Fillmore East, a converted vaudeville house on lower 2nd Avenue, and a club called the Scene in a basement in the West 40s offered performances by Buddy Guy, Johnny Winter, Jerry Garcia, and Jimi Hendrix, who regularly played at the Cafe Wha? and had a recording studio at 55 West 8th Street called the Electric Lady Studio. Inspired by the innovative guitar playing of Hendrix, the jazz trumpeter Miles Davis added electric instruments to his band and helped to launch a genre known as jazz-rock, which was heard at venues like the Fillmore East and appealed to a broader audience than jazz had reached for some time.

The music of many rock groups had become vapid and pretentious by the mid 1970s, in response to which there emerged a new genre called punk rock, centered on the Lower East Side and in particular at a rundown bar on the Bowery called CBGB-OMFUG (the abbreviation standing for Country, Bluegrass and Blues, and Other Music for Uplifting Gourmandizers). Inspired by the garage bands of the 1960s, the Velvet Underground and the New York Dolls, and often the jazz musicians John Coltrane, Ornette Coleman, and Albert Ayler, punk musicians created a raw, stripped-down sound; among the better-known were Television (which included the guitarists Tom Verlaine and Richard Lloyd), Richard Hell and the Voidoids (including the guitarist Robert Quine), Patti Smith, the Ramones, Talking Heads, and Blondie. The music influenced English bands like the Clash and the Sex Pistols (overtly modeled after the Voidoids by Malcolm McLaren, a former manager of the New York Dolls), some of which performed in New York City in the late 1970s, achieving success that in turn helped some bands from New York City to sign record contracts with Sire (Talking Heads and the Dead Boys), Chrysalis (Blondie), Elektra (Television), Arista (Smith), and Capitol (Mink DeVille). A few bands were heard on commercial radio (Blondie and Talking Heads made hit recordings), but locally most were broadcast on college stations and briefly in 1978 on WPIX-FM. At the end of the decade punk rock thrived at such clubs as Max's Kansas City, Hurrah, the Mudd Club, Danceteria, and the Ritz (on East 11th Street), though by this time the musical differences among the bands had become accentuated and punk rock soon fragmented into such genres as new wave, noise rock, hardcore, and thrash. Although punk rock was a spent force by 1981 it achieved a lasting impact by bringing more women into rock and animating nightlife in lower Manhattan.

Other rock musicians were more difficult to categorize. Elements from such disparate sources as avant-garde jazz, the music of John Cage, and conceptual art were incorporated into the work of Eugene Chadbourne, Glenn Branca, Laurie Anderson, and the groups Curlew, DNA, the Lounge Lizards, and Naked City (consisting of the saxophonist John Zorn and the guitarists Fred Frith and Bill Frisell). An amalgam of punk rock and funk was forged by Material (the electric bass guitarist Bill Laswell and the electric guitarist Ronnie Drayton) and the Music Revelation Ensemble (the saxophonist David Murray and the electric guitarist James Blood Ulmer). James Chance, a white saxophonist, led a largely black band at the Squat Theater called James White and the Blacks that evolved into Defunkt, led by the trombonist Joseph Bowie. By the early 1990s New York City had become inhospitable to rock musicians, and few had contracts with major record companies. A prominent exception was Living Colour: led by the virtuoso electric guitarist Vernon Reid, it developed a distinctive style by drawing on jazz, calypso, and heavy metal. The band was active in the Black Rock Coalition, a group formed in the city to combat racism in the record business.

Gene Santoro, George Winslow

Rockaway. Peninsula consisting of a barrier beach four miles (six kilometers) long in southern Queens, bounded to the north by Rockaway Inlet, to the east by Nassau County, and to the south and west by the Atlantic Ocean; it includes Fort Tilden and Jacob Riis Park as well as the neighborhoods of Breezy Point, Neponsit, Belle Harbor, Rockaway Park, Hollands, Hammels, Arverne, Edgemere, and Far Rockaway. The area was uninhabited until a fishing shack was built in 1856. Transportation for the first summer visitors was provided by a ferry from Canarsie in 1864. After the railroad was extended hotels were built between 1872 and 1875, and the area was a resort by the late nineteenth century.

Vincent Seyfried

Rockaway Junction. Former name of HILLSIDE.

Rockaway Park. Neighborhood in southern Queens, lying on the Rockway Peninsula and bounded to the north by Rockaway Inlet, to the east by Beach 110th Street, to the south by the Atlantic Ocean, and to the west by Beach 126th Street. There was rapid development after the New York, Woodhaven and Rockaway Railroad was extended to the area in 1880. On 25 July 1889 Austin Corbin, president of the Long Island Rail Road, set aside three hundred acres (120 hectares) with half a mile (one kilometer) of beachfront for an exclusive residential neighborhood. The failure of the Hotel Imperial, built for $1 million, slowed development. In 1900 the owners of the beach resumed promotional efforts and invested $500,000 to fill in twenty-three acres (nine hectares) of the bay and build a boulevard along the ocean and a boardwalk twelve blocks long; fourteen streets were laid out, utilities were installed, and Rockaway Beach Amusement Park in Rockaway Beach nearby opened in 1901. Soon there were large crowds of summer visitors, and hundreds of houses by the time of the First World War. A smaller amusement park called Rockaway Playland, also in Rockaway Beach, lasted until 1987. Rockaway Park, an attractive residential neighborhood, now draws fewer vacationers and has a larger permanent population.

Vincent Seyfried

Rockefeller, David (*b* New York City, 12 June 1915). Banker and businessman. The youngest of five sons of John D. Rockefeller Jr. and Abby Aldrich Rockefeller, he graduated from Harvard College and studied for a year at the London School of Economics before taking his PhD in economics at the University of Chicago in 1940. He served as an intelligence officer in North Africa and southern France during the Second World War and then as an assistant military attaché at the American embassy in Paris until late 1945. In the following year he returned to New York City to work in the international department of Chase National Bank. He was the chairman in the late 1940s and 1950s of a coalition of educational and religious groups that sought to improve conditions in Morningside Heights by building low-cost cooperative apartments with federal funds. In the early 1950s he was instrumental in having Chase remain in lower Manhattan and build a new headquarters there rather than in midtown or outside the city, a decision that led most of the large banks and brokerage houses in the city to remain there as well. In 1956 he took part in the negotiations that led to the merger of Chase with the Bank of Manhattan. He became president and vice-chairman of Chase in 1959 and chairman of the board and chief executive officer in 1969. Under his direction the bank expanded its activities overseas, markedly increased its capitalization and asset base, and began lending to the third world after the first Arab oil embargo in 1973. During the city's fiscal crisis of the mid 1970s he joined with Walter Wriston of Citicorp, Felix G. Rohatyn of Lazard Frères, and many others to form the Municipal Assistance Corporation, which stabilized the city's finances. After retiring from Chase in 1981 he continued to serve as the chairman of its international advisory committee; he was also chairman of the Downtown–Lower Manhattan Association, which helped to plan the South Street Seaport, the World Trade Center, and Battery Park City, and of the New York City Partnership, an organization of major corporations that constructs low-cost housing and works with city agencies to improve the delivery of services. An important collector of modern art, Rockefeller became a patron of the Museum of Modern Art in the 1940s and continued his association with it into the 1990s.

Alvin Moscow: *The Rockefeller Inheritance* (New York: Doubleday, 1977)
John Willson: *The Chase* (Boston: Harvard Business School Press, 1986)

Peter J. Johnson

Rockefeller, John D(avison) (*b* near Richford, N.Y., 8 July 1837; *d* Ormond Beach, Fla., 23 May 1937). Businessman and philanthropist. In 1859 he opened a sales office in New York City that was the forerunner of the Standard Oil Company of New York, of which he became the principal shareholder. He organized the firm as a holding company, or trust, with national and international networks of production, refining, transportation, and distribution. Under his guidance Standard Oil reached a position of near-monopoly in an industry that had previously been characterized by ruinous competition. He moved with his family to New York City in 1884, taking up residence at 4 West 54th Street (now the site of the garden of the Museum of Modern Art). He also had an estate of five thousand acres (two thousand hectares) in Westchester County. In the late 1880s he made large charitable donations to the churches of the Northern Baptist Convention and the educational and welfare agencies affiliated with it. On the advice of his associate Frederick T. Gates he shifted his support in the late 1890s to such causes as the settlement house movement, public health, education, housing, and municipal reform. For many years he was the principal supporter of the Bureau of Municipal Research, which had a profound influence on the structure of the city's government and led to reform of the police force, schools, and public health system. He remained active in the daily management of Standard Oil until 1897 and retained the title of president until 1912, the year following the dissolution of the firm by the U.S. Supreme Court. Rockefeller later formed several major philanthropic foundations: the Rockefeller Institute for Medical Research (1901), the General Education Board (1903), and the Rockefeller Foundation (1913).

Allan Nevins: *John D. Rockefeller: A Study in Power* (New York: Charles Scribner's Sons, 1953)
John Ensor Harr and Peter J. Johnson: *The Rockefeller Century* (New York: Charles Scribner's Sons, 1988)
John Ensor Harr and Peter J. Johnson: *The Rockefeller Conscience: An American Family in Public and in Private* (New York: Macmillan, 1991)

Peter J. Johnson

Rockefeller, John D(avison), Jr. (*b* Cleveland, 28 Jan 1874; *d* Tucson, Ariz., 12 May 1960). Businessman and philanthropist, father of John D. Rockefeller III, Nelson A. Rockefeller, and David Rockefeller. He was the only son and principal heir to the fortune of John D. Rockefeller. In his early thirties he married Abby Green Aldrich, the daughter of Senator Nelson W. Aldrich of Rhode Island, and devoted himself to managing his father's business and philanthropic affairs. He was deeply influenced by his friend Harry Emerson Fosdick, who advocated Christian involvement in social problems, and by Frederick W. Taylor's writings on scientific management. His personal involvement with the events surrounding the "Ludlow Massacre" in Colorado in 1914–15 turned him toward a greater involvement with issues of reform. His personal fortune, which peaked at $1000 million in 1929, enabled him to help finance the Paul Lawrence Dunbar Houses in Harlem, the Thomas Garden Apartments in the Bronx, and Sunnyside Gardens in Queens. He was also active in creating public parks and open spaces: Fort Tryon Park, site of the Cloisters, was developed with his personal funds and then contributed to the city in the 1930s, and in 1946 he donated to the United Nations a parcel of land in Turtle Bay that he had purchased for $8.5 million, which became its permanent site. He also supported the early efforts of Margaret Sanger and her colleagues to promote contraception. Rockefeller Center, built almost entirely with his own money during the Depression, became a focus of the city's life and had an enduring effect on urban design. Rockefeller's residences in New York City included 13 West 54th Street (1901–8), 10 West 54th Street (1908–36), and 740 Park Avenue (from 1936).

Raymond B. Fosdick: *John D. Rockefeller, Jr.: A Portrait* (New York: Harper and Brothers, 1956)
John Ensor Harr and Peter J. Johnson: *The Rockefeller Conscience: An American Family in Public and in Private* (New York: Macmillan, 1991)

Peter J. Johnson

Rockefeller, John D(avison), III (*b* New York City, 21 March 1906; *d* Tarrytown, N.Y., 10 July 1978). Philanthropist. The eldest son of John D. Rockefeller Jr. and Abby Aldrich Rockefeller, he graduated from Princeton University in 1929 and embarked on a world tour. He returned to the United States just after the stock market crash and went to work for his father, serving on the boards of more than thirty foundations and nonprofit organizations. He also took part in the development of Radio City Music Hall and the other theaters in Rockefeller Center. After the Second World War he prevailed on the Rockefeller Foundation to conduct research on world population growth, agriculture, and agricultural economics. Frustrated by the resistance of the foundation's trustees and officers, he used his own funds to form the Population Council and the Agricultural Development Council in the early 1950s. Both organizations made enormous contributions to the development of safe and effective contraceptives and to a better understanding of economic development. During the 1950s and 1960s he formed the Asia Society, revived the Japan Society, and was a leader of the group that planned and built Lincoln Center for the Performing Arts (of which he later served as chairman for almost fifteen years). In the early 1970s he was the chairman of the Commission on Population Growth and the American Future. He lived at 1 Beekman Place from 1934 to 1978. Rockefeller believed that philanthropy should reclaim its tradition of voluntarism and distance itself from both government and business.

Alvin Moscow: *The Rockefeller Inheritance* (New York: Doubleday, 1977)
John E. Harr and Peter J. Johnson: *The Rockefeller Century* (New York: Charles Scribner's Sons, 1988)
John Ensor Harr and Peter J. Johnson: *The Rockefeller Conscience: An American Family in Public and in Private* (New York: Macmillan, 1991)

Peter J. Johnson

Rockefeller, Nelson A(ldrich) (*b* Bar Harbor, Maine, 8 July 1908; *d* New York City, 26 Jan 1979). Governor and vice president of the United States. A grandson of John D. Rockefeller, he was born to a background of immense wealth and privilege. His close association with New York City began at childhood. One of the family's three homes was at 10 West 54th Street, and from 1917 to 1926 he attended the Lincoln School, a private school in Manhattan. After graduating from Dartmouth College in 1930 he returned to the city in the following year, settling into an apartment on East 67th Street; he later moved to 5th Avenue and 63rd Street. In 1932 he became a trustee of the Museum of Modern Art, marking the beginning of an increasingly active career as an art collector and patron. Under his presidency in 1939 and 1959 the museum developed into a prominent and popular cultural institution. He also assembled an exceptional private collection of modern and primitive art, and used his own collection of primitive sculpture to found the Museum of Primitive Art in 1954. From 1931 he worked at various branches of the family's business. He focused in particular on Rockefeller Center, becoming its president in 1938. His political career grew out of his investment in 1935 in Creole Petroleum, the Venezuelan subsidiary of Standard Oil. Because of his involvement in Latin American affairs he was appointed coordinator of Inter-American Affairs in the U.S. Department of State in 1940, and assistant secretary of state for the American Republics in 1944.

After serving in appointed posts under Presidents Harry S. Truman and Dwight D. Eisenhower, Rockefeller turned his attention to elective office. Nominated by the Republicans for the governorship of New York in 1958, he defeated the incumbent, W. Averell Harriman. He became a leader of the moderate wing of the Republican Party, and mounted unsuccessful campaigns for the Republican presidential nomination in 1960, 1964, and 1968. Despite these setbacks he was reelected governor in 1962, 1966, and 1970. Rockefeller was the first governor to establish a permanent office in New York City, and he governed the state largely from headquarters at 22 West 55th Street, staying in Albany mainly for legislative sessions. He also became embroiled in local politics. For many years he feuded with Mayor John V. Lindsay (initially an ally) and with Robert Moses, who lost his commanding influence over the city's politics in 1968 when Rockefeller established the Metropolitan Transit Authority, which absorbed Moses's last base of power, the Triborough Bridge and Tunnel Authority. In 1973 he resigned as governor to lead the National Commission on Critical Choices for Americans. He returned to public office in the following year as vice president of the United States, succeeding Gerald R. Ford, who had himself succeeded Richard M. Nixon as president. Rockefeller withdrew from consideration as Ford's running mate in 1976, and when Ford's term ended in 1977 he retired from politics.

Eileen K. Cheng

Rockefeller Center. Complex of nineteen commercial buildings in midtown Manhattan, on a site bounded by 52nd Street, 5th Avenue, 49th Street, and 7th Avenue. Planned and built from 1929, it is a widely known site that has inspired developers of other areas, including Battery Park City. The land was initially occupied by tenements and theaters and was leased by Columbia University to John D. Rockefeller Jr., who in early 1929 planned to revitalize the area by erecting three tall office buildings and a new Metropolitan Opera House around a plaza. After the stock market crash in the following autumn the opera could not afford to move, and Rockefeller was forced to devise an alternative plan. Seeking to preserve his original goals, he reconceived the development as an entirely commercial complex and engaged the firm of Todd, Robertson and Todd as a consultant, as well as a team of architecture firms: Reinhard and Hofmeister (expert in dividing office spaces), Corbett, Harrison and MacMurray (known for civic concern and sober design), and Hood, Godley and Fouilhoux (known for innovative design). The first group of buildings was completed in 1939 and consisted of office towers and theaters, among them Radio City Music Hall, surrounding a sunken plaza and bounded by 51st Street, 5th Avenue, 49th Street, and 6th Avenue. Along the west side of the plaza the architects placed the office towers, including the tallest (the RCA Building, now known as the GE Building); these stood near two theaters (including the Center Theater, demolished in 1954) visible from the theater district and occupying less desirable lots along 6th Avenue. To improve this area elegant shops were added along 5th Avenue and the plaza. Four low buildings on the two northern blocks provided an entrance of inviting scale, and a downward slope in the center block between these buildings was built to lead pedestrians past shop windows toward the sunken plaza, where plants, flags, sculptures, benches, and fountains were installed; an outdoor restaurant was opened in summer and an ice skating rink in winter. A new street west of the plaza eased traffic and provided access to the adjacent buildings. To produce income, gardens and an observation deck were planned for the rooftops. A restaurant called the Rainbow Room opened in 1934 and became one of the most glamorous in the city. The owner commissioned many murals and works of sculpture, including a massive figure of Atlas by Lee Lawrie with René Chambellan (1937) at the entrance to 630 5th Avenue.

Seeking to take advantage of a subway line proposed for 6th Avenue, the firm of Todd, Robertson and Todd planned a series of underground corridors leading to the subway station at 47th–50th streets and flanked by shops and services. A second underground system cleared traffic from the area by providing for off-street truck loading and deliveries. The imaginative design and high standards for construction and maintenance attracted tenants and tourists, and Rockefeller Center became a bustling commercial area even in inclement weather. Its increasing profitability during the Second World War inspired the owners to buy the site and add buildings on the northern and western sides after 1947, including four office towers on 6th Avenue between 48th and 52nd streets, the first erected in 1960, the three south of it in 1973. The northern and southern towers bracket the two central ones (all are by Harrison and Abramovitz). They are tall, prismatic towers surrounded by open space, reflecting the new standards permitted by the zoning regulations of 1961 and drawing less admiration than the original buildings. In the mid 1990s Rockefeller Center was owned by Japanese and American interests.

Alan Balfour: *Rockefeller Center: Architecture as Theater* (New York: McGraw–Hill, 1978)

Carol Herselle Krinsky: *Rockefeller Center* (New York: Oxford University Press, 1978)

Carol Herselle Krinsky

Rockefeller Foundation. Charitable foundation, one of the oldest and largest in the United States. It was formed in 1913 "to promote the well-being of man-kind through out the world" by John D. Rockefeller and his advisors Frederick T. Gates (1853–1929) and John D. Rockefeller Jr., who had also formed the Rockefeller Institute for Medical Research (1901; later Rockefeller University), the General Education Board (1903), and the Rockefeller Sanitary Commission for the Eradication of Hookworm Disease (1909). The work of these institutions influenced the direction of the fund: its trustees set up the International Health Division (1913–51) to enable the sanitary commission to combat malaria, tuberculosis, and yellow fever in addition to hookworm, and the China Medical Board (1914–28) to promote modern Western medicine in China; the fund also financed the construction of the Peking Union Medical College. Under the leadership from 1917 to 1929 of George E. Vincent (1864–1941) the fund was active principally in public health and medical education. A reorganization of the Rockefellers' various philanthropies in 1928 left the fund with five divisions, devoted to international health, the medical sciences, the natural sciences, the social sciences, and the humanities. It merged with the Laura Spelman Rockefeller Memorial, a foundation formed in 1918 by John D. Rockefeller in honor of his late wife, and also continued the work of the International Education Board, formed by John D. Rockefeller Jr. in 1923. The China Medical Board became an independent foundation charged with operating the Peking Union Medical College, and by 1991 it had assets of $122.4 million and made grants totaling $2.6 million.

The efforts of the Rockefeller Foundation in the natural and medical sciences were strengthened during the presidencies of Max Mason (1877–1961) from 1929 to 1936 and of Raymond B. Fosdick (1883–1972) from 1936 to 1948. Under the direction of Dean Rusk from 1952 to 1961 and J. George Harrar (1906–82) from 1961 to 1972 attention shifted to agricultural development, equal opportunity, and population concerns. Led from 1972 to 1979 by John H. Knowles (1926–79), the foundation began to fund social history projects, established a fellowship program in the humanities, and expanded its work in agricultural and medical science in the third world. The next president, Richard Lyman (*b* 1923), served from 1980 to 1988, during which the foundation continued its work in developing countries with scientifically based development programs, and also undertook new initiatives in secondary education and the fight against persistent urban poverty. The selection of Peter C. Goldmark Jr. as president in 1988 brought about a clearer focus on housing, education, and the environment. In 1992 the Rockefeller Foundation held assets of $2140 million and made grants totaling $93.1 million. Many universities, health care facilities, and cultural institutions in New York City have received support from the foundation for experimental and model programs, and in recognition of their national leadership roles.

The Rockefeller Foundation is one of several independent foundations based in New York City that carry the Rockefellers' name. The Rockefeller Brothers Fund, formed in 1940 by John D. Rockefeller's grandchildren, had assets in 1991 of $317.9 million and made grants totaling $10.9 million; one component of its programs focuses on New York City. Rockefeller's great-grandchildren in 1967 formed the Rockefeller Family Fund, which in 1992 held assets of $39.1 million and made grants totaling $1.7 million.

Kenneth W. Rose

Rockefeller University. Research institute offering graduate training in the physical and medical sciences. Founded in 1901 by John D. Rockefeller as the Rockefeller Institute for Medical Research, it first occupied quarters on Lexington Avenue and 50th Street. In 1906 the institute moved to its present site at 1230 York Avenue, between 63rd and 68th streets, where it opened Central Laboratory (now Founder's Hall). A hospital built in 1910 combined the study and treatment of human disease. Rockefeller's two chief philanthropic advisors, his son John D. Rockefeller Jr. and Frederick T. Gates, were determined to create a research institute of international caliber on American soil. Initially pledging $20,000 a year over ten years, Rockefeller eventually gave $2.6 million in 1907 and $3.8 million in 1910.

At its inception the institute functioned as a grant-giving body that supported private and public scientific research. One of its first grants supported a study of the sanitary conditions of the city's milk supply, in cooperation with the city's health department. The institute's early research emphasis on the biology of infectious disease broadened by 1935 to keep pace with new developments in biological research. The first director, Simon Flexner (1901–35), worked closely with the Rockefeller family and other institutions that they sponsored, and also developed the institute's administrative organization. By the 1950s the institute was recognized as one of the leading research facilities in the nation; it became a degree-granting institution in 1954 and first awarded the PhD in 1959. The current name was adopted in 1965, reflecting a commitment to the academic exploration of science. Nineteen Nobel laureates have been associated with the institution, among them Alexis Carrel, Karl Landsteiner, Peyton Rous, Fritz Lipmann, Joshua Lederberg, and David Baltimore. Other prominent scientists who have worked there include Rebecca Lancefield, Hideyo Noguchi, Louise Pierce, Oswald Avery, and René Dubos. The university and its hospital have been the site of important developments in diverse areas: the identification of human blood groups, the production of antibiotics, the discovery of viral cancers and of the first effective treatment for African sleeping sickness, and research into vision, taste, and smell, methadone-based drug rehabilitation, aging, tuberculosis, poliomyelitis, yellow fever, heart disease, diabetes, leukemia, arthritis, AIDS, alcoholism, parasitic diseases, and genetic disorders.

At Rockefeller University the laboratory led by a senior professor is the basic unit of organization. There are no academic departments, and graduate courses, discussion groups, tutorials, and research apprenticeships all revolve around the laboratory. Students attend tuition-free and in addition receive a yearly stipend. University research encompasses the fields of cellular and molecular biology, genetics, biochemistry, neurobiology, immunology, mathematics, physics, and the behavioral sciences. The university also sponsors programs and events in conjunction with neighboring medical institutions. Unlike most universities it is dedicated exclusively to graduate study, conferring only the PhD, medical degrees, and honorary degrees. A program offering a joint MD and PhD is offered with the Cornell University Medical College in New York City.

George W. Corner: *A History of the Rockefeller Institute: 1901–1953, Origins and Growth* (New York: Rockefeller Institute Press, 1964)

See also SCIENCE.

Lee R. Hiltzik, Renee D. Mastrocco

Rockettes. Precision dance team. Modeled on the sixteen Missouri Rockettes, the group was formed by Russell Markert for the opening of Radio City Music Hall at Rockefeller Center on 27 December 1932. When motion pictures were shown in the theater they performed at least three times a day and learned new routines every week. After the hall suspended production in the 1970s the troupe found success performing at pop concerts, at Disney World, and on tour. Decades of controversy over the all-white membership of the troupe ended when Jennifer Jones became the first black member in December 1987. In the mid 1990s the group had thirty-six members and was directed by Violet Holmes; it performed in the Christmas and Easter shows at Radio City Music Hall, in the Macy's Thanksgiving Day Parade, and at many theatrical, municipal, and sporting events.

Charles Francisco: *The Radio City Music Hall: An Affectionate History of the World's Greatest Theater* (New York: E. P. Dutton, 1979)

Barbara Cohen-Stratyner

Rock Pigeon [Domestic Pigeon]. A plump bird about thirteen inches (thirty-three centimeters) long with a short, fan-shaped tail, a white rump, two black wing bars, and an iridescent green neck patch; it is usually blue-gray but the color varies from black to white. Originally a cliff-dweller, it was introduced to New York City from Europe at an unknown time and soon proliferated. The bird builds nests sometimes in trees but more often on windowsills and cornices and usually produces clutches of two eggs three times a year; eggs have been reported during every month. Pigeons are especially common in larger parks such as Central and Prospect parks.

John Bull: *Birds of the New York Area* (New York: Harper and Row, 1964)
Wendell Mitchell Levi: *Encyclopedia of Pigeon Breeds* (Jersey City, N.J.: TFH, 1965)
John Bull: *Birds of New York State* (New York: Doubleday / Natural History Press, 1974)
John Bull: *Birds of New York State, including the 1976 Supplement* (Ithaca, N.Y.: Cornell University Press, 1985)

John Bull

Rockwell, Norman (*b* New York City, 3 Feb 1894; *d* Stockbridge, Mass., 9 Nov 1978). Painter and illustrator. He was born at Amsterdam Avenue and 103rd Street and lived there until the age of two; his family later lived in apartments in Harlem, including one at St. Nicholas Avenue and 147th Street from 1896 to 1900. He spent much of his childhood in Westchester County and was educated at the Art Students League. Rockwell won the affection of the public for his nostalgic portrayals of life in small towns and sought above all to provoke an emotional response in his audience, leading some to criticize him for avoiding the stark realities of his time. He is best known for 317 cover illustrations executed for the *Saturday Evening Post* between 1916 and 1963. In 1964 he made a cover illustration for *Look* depicting the murder of three civil rights workers in Mississippi.

Donald Walton: *A Rockwell Portrait: An Intimate Biography* (Kansas City, Kansas: Sheed Andrews and McMeel, 1978)

Andrew Wiese

Rodgers, Richard (*b* Queens, 28 June 1902; *d* New York City, 30 Dec 1979). Composer. He attended Columbia College and the Institute of Musical Art in New York City but learned music largely through his own study of the operettas of Victor Herbert and the musicals of Jerome Kern. He wrote the music for several successful Broadway shows to which Lorenz Hart contributed the lyrics: *Garrick Gaieties* (1925); *On Your Toes* (1936), well known for the dance sequence "Slaughter on Tenth Avenue" and the song "There's a Small Hotel"; and *Babes in Arms* (1937), which included the songs "The Lady Is a Tramp," "My Funny Valentine," and "Where or When." Their show *Pal Joey* (1940, book by John O'Hara) was considered bold for its time: it tells the story of an unprincipled protagonist in a trashy environment and features a ballad of troubled love, "Bewitched, Bothered and Bewildered." Many of the works of Rodgers and Hart celebrate life in New York City, among them their first hit song, "I'll Take Manhattan" (1925), the show *Fifth Avenue Follies* (1926), and the songs "Coney Island" (1930), "Harlemania" (1930), "I Gotta Get Back to New York" (1933), "Manhattan Melodrama" (1934), "The Circus Is on Parade" (1935), "Memories of Madison Square Garden" (1935), "There's a Boy in Harlem" (1938), "At the Roxy Music Hall" (1938), and "Give It Back to the Indians" (1939). After Hart's death Rodgers wrote a number of successful musicals with Oscar Hammerstein II, including *Oklahoma!* (1943), *Carousel* (1945), *South Pacific* (1949), *The King and I* (1951), and *The Sound of Music* (1959). He wrote *Musical Stages: An Autobiography* (1975).

David Ewen: *Richard Rodgers* (New York: Holt, Rinehart and Winston, 1957)

Nicholas E. Tawa

Rodman, Henrietta (*b* Astoria [now in Queens], 1878; *d* New York City, 23 March 1923). Schoolteacher and activist. She was instrumental in forming both the Feminist Alliance, a group based in Greenwich Village dedicated to abolishing sex discrimination, and the Liberal Club (1913), in which she caused a split by insisting on the admission of blacks. A socialist, suffragist, member of the Women's Trade Union League, and advocate of dress reform, she prevailed on the Board of Education to allow female teachers to marry, bear children, and retain their positions, and also fought to secure cooperative housing and child care for professional women. Rodman's apartment on Bank Street was a popular gathering place for bohemians and social reformers before the First World War.

Jan Seidler Ramirez

Rodman's Neck. A section of Pelham Bay Park in the Bronx, jutting prominently into Eastchester Bay. After the late seventeenth century it was given several names, including Ann Hoeck and Ann's Neck (after Anne Hutchinson, who settled nearby in 1643). The land was acquired in 1888 with the intention of making it a park, but it was used for various purposes in the following century: as a naval training station between 1917 and 1919, as a park in the 1920s, as the site between 1930 and 1936 of Camp Mulrooney, the summer home of the New York City Police Academy, and as a firing range for the police department between 1959 and 1989. In the mid 1990s it was unclear whether Rodman's Neck would remain a police facility or again be used as a park.

Kenneth T. Jackson

Roebling, John Augustus (*b* Mühlhausen in Thüringen, Germany, 12 June 1806; *d* Brooklyn, 22 July 1869). Engineer, inventor, and bridge designer, father of Washington Roebling. The son of a poor tobacconist, he studied in Berlin and emigrated to the United States in 1831, where he settled with other Thuringians in a farming colony near Pittsburgh and took up farming. While working as an engineer in the canals of Pennsylvania he developed wire cable as a sturdier substitute for rope made of hemp, which often caused accidents when boats were pulled uphill. He tested his invention on a series of suspended aqueducts over the Allegheny River, then formed a wire-cable works in Trenton, New Jersey (the firm remained in business until the 1980s). Later he built iron suspension bridges over Niagara Gorge and across the Ohio River at Cincinnati. He put forward a plan in 1867 for a steel suspension bridge across the East River between Brooklyn and Manhattan and oversaw the early stages of its construction before suffering a fatal accident. The bridge eventually became known as the Brooklyn Bridge.

Hamilton Schuyler: *The Roeblings: A Century of Engineers, Bridge-builders and Industrialists* (Princeton, N.J.: Princeton University Press, 1931)
David B. Steinman: *The Builders of the Bridge: The Story of John Roebling and His Son* (New York: Harcourt, Brace, 1945)

Ellen Fletcher

Roebling, Washington (Augustus) (*b* Saxonburg, Penn., 26 May 1837; *d* Trenton, N.J., 21 July 1926). Engineer, son of John Augustus Roebling. He studied engineering at Rensselaer Polytechnic Institute, worked as a bridge builder for the Union Army during the Civil War, and on the death of his father took charge of the construction of the Brooklyn Bridge. After becoming gravely ill with the bends in the summer of 1872 he depended on his wife, Emily Warren Roebling, to relay his instructions to workers and managers.

Hamilton Schuyler: *The Roeblings: A Century of Engineers, Bridge-builders and Industrialists* (Princeton, N.J.: Princeton University Press, 1931)
David Steinman: *The Builders of the Bridge: The Story of John Roebling and His Son* (New York: Harcourt, Brace, 1945)

Ellen Fletcher

Rogers and Wells. Law firm. Its forerunner was the practice of Walter S. Carter (1833–1904), which opened in 1871 and after his death was led by his son-in-law Charles Evans Hughes. In 1937 it split into two firms, one known as Rogers and Wells and the other as Hughes, Hubbard and Reed. Kenneth C. Royall (1894–1971), who joined the firm in 1949, was the country's last secretary of war and first secretary of the army. William P. Rogers (*b* 1913) joined the firm in 1951 and was later attorney general under President Dwight D. Eisenhower and secretary of state under President Richard M. Nixon. William Casey, a partner from 1976, left the firm in 1981 to direct the Central Intelligence Agency. The firm is at 200 Park Avenue and has about 320 lawyers, of whom sixty-six are partners.

Gilbert Tauber

Rohatyn, Felix G(eorge) (*b* Vienna, 29 May 1928). Investment banker. After graduating from Middlebury College in 1948 he went to work for Lazard Frères, where he became a partner in 1960. During the 1970s he was a member of the board of governors of the New York Stock Exchange. In 1975 he was appointed chairman of the Municipal Assistance Corporation (MAC) by Governor Hugh L. Carey, and during the fiscal crisis of the following years he played a critical role in returning the city to solvency. He left the MAC in May 1993.

Janet Frankston

Rolling Stone. Monthly magazine launched in 1967 in San Francisco by Jann Wenner, a twenty-year-old former student at the University of California, Berkeley. Begun as a small alternative newsletter, it featured John Lennon on the cover of its first issue, which sold six thousand copies. The magazine soon became a voice for the counterculture in the Haight–Ashbury district of San Francisco. In the early 1970s it turned to more serious topics such as the Vietnam War and corruption in American politics. It also boosted the career of several journalists, including Greil Marcus, Tim Cahill, Joe Eszterhas, Hunter S. Thompson, and P. J. O'Rourke, as well as the photographer Annie Liebovitz. Articles on the murders committed by Charles Manson and his followers, the presidential campaign of 1972, and the abduction of Patricia Hearst attracted critical accolades and a broader audience. In 1977 Wenner moved the magazine to 745 5th Avenue in New York City, where he began developing a slicker, more commercial style and cultivating major advertisers. The magazines's circulation rose from half a million in 1977 to 1.5 million in 1988 before stabilizing at 1.2 million in 1993. By this time *Rolling Stone* had won five national magazine awards, including one for David Black's feature on AIDS in 1985 and another for Richard Avedon's essay on the family in 1976. Its offices are at 1290 6th Avenue.

Robert Draper: *Rolling Stone Magazine: The Uncensored History* (New York: Doubleday, 1990)

Robert Sanger Steel

Rollins, Sonny [Theodore Walter] (*b* New York City, 9 Sept 1930). Saxophonist. He attended public schools in New York City and performed with Miles Davis in 1949 and at intervals throughout the 1950s. His early recordings *Saxophone Colossus* (1956) and *Freedom Suite* (1958) made him known for his rich tone on the tenor saxophone and his ability to transcend the harmonic limitations of "hard bop." He took several leaves from his career as a performer, during one of which in the early 1960s he practiced in the early morning on the Williamsburg Bridge (a period commemorated by his album *The Bridge*, 1962).

Charles Blancq: *Sonny Rollins: The Journey of a Jazzman* (Boston: Twayne, 1983)

Marc Ferris

Roma. See Gypsies.

Romanians. A Romanian community took form in New York City between about 1900 and the First World War. The largest number of Romanians were immigrants from Transylvania and Banat, regions under Austro-Hungarian rule, and a few were Macedo-Romanians from Greece and Albania. Most were factory workers, craftsmen, and innkeepers. The community was served by several general-interest publications: *Curierul Romano-American* (Romanian–American Courier, 1900), *Vremea Noua* (New Time, 1900), and *Ecoul Americei* (America's Echo, 1904), which provided cultural and political news. Some of the first organizations were cultural and mutual aid societies, among them Dorul (1903–), Farsarotul (1903–; Macedo-Romanian), Unirea (1909–), Perivolea (1909; Macedo-Romanian), and Avram Iancu (1909–). Specialized publications covered diverse topics: religious news was given in *The Romanul American* (1910–12), edited by a Roman Catholic (Eastern Rite) priest; *Desteapta-te Romane* (Awake Thee Romanian, 1911–16) took a pro-Hungarian stand on the issue of Transylvania; *Steaua Noastra* (Our Star, 1911–24) promoted Romanian books sold in the bookstore of the editor, P. Axelrad, the compiler of a Romanian–English dictionary; and *Curierul Roman* (1923–24) provided news of the city's Macedo-Romanians. From the time of the First World War Romanians in the city strongly supported Romanian sovereignty over Transylvania. Improving relations with Romania was the goal of the Society of Friends of Romania (1928–32), which published the periodical *Romania*, and of the Sons of Romania (1932–34), which issued a bulletin. The publications *Porunca Vremii* (Imperative of the Time, 1937–), *Fii Daciei* (Sons of Dacia, 1938–), and later the *Romanian Boian News* (1968–) were launched by an editorial staff that opposed communism and sought to promote chauvinism; they enjoyed limited circulation.

Romanians in the city strenuously protested the fascist regime in Romania of Ion Antonescu (1940–44) and the communist regimes of Gheorghe Gheorghiu-Dej and Nicolae Ceausescu. The Free Romania Committee (1941–44) and the Democratic Union of Free Romania (1948–56) sought to revive the Romanian monarchy; the Romanian National Committee (1951–67) attacked the communist government; and the Romanian Welfare Organization (1948–74) helped refugees to settle in the United States. Formed to preserve Romanian heritage, the Iuliu Maniu Romanian American Foundation (1952–) amassed a library and a collection of Romanian costumes and set up a scholarship program. Refugees and political exiles moved to the city in the 1950s and late 1980s. In 1970 an association called Truth about Romania was formed to monitor violations of human rights and international treaties by the government of Romania. Devoted to local, national, and international news, the periodicals *Micro-Magazin* (1972–), *Lumea Libera* (Free World, 1987–), and *Epoca* (1987–) became popular; the political journals *Dreptatea* (Justice, 1973–) and *Spectatorul* (1975–) found smaller audiences. Through its newspaper *Actiunea Romaneasca* the Romanian National Council (1974–) sought to publicize Romanian achievements and help immigrants to adjust to life in the United States. The Romanian Cultural Center (1980–) was formed to organize celebrations of Romanian national holidays and other cultural events. In December 1989 Romanians in the city celebrated the fall of the Romanian communist government.

In the mid 1990s the Romanian population of New York City was estimated at upwards of twenty thousand, concentrated in northern Manhattan, Astoria, Sunnyside, and Ridgewood. Its members were professionals, engineers, musicians, writers, teachers, office workers, small businessmen, taxi drivers, and maintenance workers. About 80 percent of Romanian churchgoers were Eastern Orthodox and belonged to six churches: St. Dumitru, formed in Manhattan before the Second World War; and St. Maria, Holy Trinity, Descending of the Holy Ghost, St. Nicholae, and Three Hierarchs in Queens. Other churches in Queens were the St. Mary Roman Catholic Church, two Baptist churches, a Pentecostal church, and a Seventh-Day Adventist church. Well-known Romanians in the city have included the soprano Stella Roman, the broadcaster Liviu Floda, the stage director Andrei Serban, and the graphic artist Eugen Mihaesco.

Vasile Hategan: "The Romanians of New York City," *New Pioneer* 3, no. 2 (1945), 28–50

Vladimir Wertsman: *The Romanians in America, 1748–1974: A Chronology and Fact Book* (Dobbs Ferry, N.Y.: Oceana, 1975)

Vladimir Wertsman

Romberg, Sigmund (*b* Nagy Kanizsa, Hungary, 29 July 1887; *d* New York City, 9 Nov 1951). Composer. In 1909 he arrived in New York City, where he composed, arranged, and adapted more than seventy revues and operettas, most of which were performed on Broadway. His style of sentimental, Viennese operetta faded in popularity by the time of the Second World War, and he then formed an orchestra that performed on radio and toured the United States performing light classics, which he termed "middle-brow music." Romberg's works include *The Student Prince* (1924), *The Desert Song* (1926), *The New Moon* (1927), and more than two thousand songs, among them "Stouthearted Men," "Lover, Come Back to Me," and "One Alone." He was the president of the Song Writers Protective Association for fifteen years and had one of the largest libraries of musical scores in the world, containing more than five thousand works.

Sara J. Steen

Ronson Ship. A vessel used in the trade between New York City and the Caribbean, sunk in the 1740s for use as landfill. It was recovered in 1982 during the archaeological excavation of 175 Water Street.

Nan A. Rothschild and Diana diZerega Rockman: "Method in Urban Archaeology: The Stadt Huys Block," *Archaeology of Urban America*, ed. Roy S. Dickens Jr. (New York: Academic, 1982), 3–18

Nan A. Rothschild, Joan H. Geismar, and Diana diZ. Wall, eds.: "Urbanization and Social Change in Historical Archaeology," *American Archeology* 5 (1985), 162–221

Nan A. Rothschild

Roosevelt, (Anna) Eleanor (*b* New York City, 11 Oct 1884; *d* New York City, 7 Nov 1962). Humanitarian. She was orphaned at the age of ten and brought up at 11 West 37th Street by her maternal grandmother, who sent her to a fashionable boarding school outside London. A débutante in 1901, she married her cousin Franklin D. Roosevelt in 1905 and lived successively at 125 East 36th Street (1905–8) and in a townhouse at 47–49 East 65th Street. Her husband's political career took the family to Albany, New York, in 1910, to Washington in 1913, and again to New York City in 1920. During 1921 her husband was stricken with polio. In the same year she became involved with the League of Women Voters. Through her work with this group and with the New York Women's Trade Union League, the New York Women's City Club, and the women's division of the state Democratic Party she deepened her political skills and her commitment to social activism. In 1924 she was the head of the women's platform committee at the Democratic National Convention in Madison Square Garden, and in 1928 she worked at the national party headquarters on the presidential campaign of Alfred E. Smith. After her husband's successful campaign for governor took her back to Albany in 1928 she traveled to the city each week to teach at the Todhunter School; during his tenure as the thirty-second president of the United States (1933–45) she traveled frequently to New York City from Washington for speaking engagements and official appearances. After her husband's death in 1945 she divided her time between Hyde Park (New York) and several addresses in the city, including 29 Washington Square West (from 1945), the Park Sheraton at 870 7th Avenue (1949–53, 1958), and 211 East 62nd Street (1953–59). In 1946–52 she was a delegate to the United Nations and a regular presence at its headquarters. In addition to her official duties she was embroiled in notable disputes with figures such as Francis Cardinal Spellman and Carmine DeSapio, whose ouster from Tam-

Eleanor Roosevelt reviews the Waves at the Naval Training School for Women's Reserves in the Bronx, 2 August 1943

many Hall she engineered with Herbert H. Lehman and Mayor Robert F. Wagner. In 1959 she moved to a townhouse at 55 East 74th Street, where she spent the rest of her life.

Lois Scharf: *Eleanor Roosevelt: First Lady of American Liberalism* (Boston: Twayne, 1987)

Lois Scharf

Roosevelt, Franklin D(elano) (*b* Hyde Park, N.Y., 30 Jan 1882; *d* Warm Springs, Ga., 12 April 1945). Thirty-second president of the United States and governor, great-great-grandson of Isaac Roosevelt. Born on his family's estate in Duchess County, he was educated at Groton Preparatory School and Harvard University and moved to New York City to study law at Columbia University. He married his cousin Eleanor in 1905 and lived with her at 125 East 36th Street (1905–8) before moving to a townhouse at 47–49 East 65th Street. As a state senator in Albany from 1910 he enraged Tammany Hall by leading party insurgents in blocking the legislative election of its candidate William P. Sheehan. The insurgents refused to attend the binding party caucus, which Tammany Hall dominated, and voted for the opposition, reform candidate; a stalemated state senate chose a third candidate in a compromise. He served as an assistant secretary of the navy from 1913 and returned to New York City in 1920. Stricken with polio in 1921, he recovered with the help of his wife and resumed his political career. He supported Alfred E. Smith's candidacy for the governorship in 1924 and for the presidency in 1929 but pointedly ignored him after becoming governor himself (elected 1928, reelected 1930). Nominated by the Democrats for the presidency in 1932, he defeated President Herbert Hoover by a wide margin. During the Depression he greatly assisted the city through the Works Progress Administration (which sponsored important programs in the arts, music, theater, and literature) and the Public Works Administration (the Triborough Bridge was its largest project yet at the time of construction in 1936). He also set up the Securities and Exchange Commission, which lent stability to the financial markets on Wall Street. Roosevelt's personal connection to the city was minimal: he preferred the genteel life of the Hudson Valley, his political career took him away from the city for long periods, and he had mixed feelings about the city's culture and its leaders. Nevertheless his attention to the city helped to make it a stronghold of labor, ethnic, and black support for the Democratic Party.

Lois Scharf

Roosevelt, Isaac (*b* New York City, 8 Dec 1726; *d* New York City, 13 Oct 1794). Political and mercantile leader, great-great-grandfather of Franklin D. Roosevelt. He opened a wholesale sugar refinery on Wall Street in 1745, soon became one of the most successful businessmen in New York City, and helped to form the New York Chamber of Commerce and the Society of the New York Hospital (the first hospital in the city). A leading patriot during the American Revolution, he represented the city during the state constitutional convention of 1776. In his later years he was a close ally of Alexander Hamilton; he helped to form the Bank of New York in 1784 and was a strong supporter of Federalist causes.

Allen Churchill: *The Roosevelts: American Aristocrats* (New York: Harper and Row, 1965)

James Bradley

Roosevelt, Theodore(, Jr.) (*b* New York City, 27 Oct 1858; *d* Oyster Bay, N.Y., 6 Jan 1919). Twenty-sixth president of the United States. He was born at 28 East 20th Street in the home of his parents. His family was one of the oldest and most prominent in the city, influential for six generations in politics, business, and society. His grandfather Cornelius Van Schaanck Roosevelt (1794–1871) was a real-estate investor, a founder of Chemical Bank, and one of the city's wealthiest citizens. His father, Theodore Roosevelt Sr. (1831–78), was a leading philanthropist who supported many charitable and cultural institutions, notably the Metropolitan Museum of Art and the American Museum of Natural History. In his youth Roosevelt suffered from asthma, and in 1873 his family moved to a larger home at 6 West 57th Street so that he could practice his physical conditioning. His health gradually improved, and in 1876 he entered Harvard University. After graduating he married Alice Lee, and the couple moved to New York City to live with his widowed mother. At this point Roosevelt enrolled at Columbia Law School, became involved in local politics, and joined the district Republican club; this and his family's reputation helped him to win a seat in the state assembly in 1882, where he represented the relatively wealthy twenty-first district of midtown Manhattan. He became a member of the city affairs committee and received extensive publicity when he accused the financier Jay Gould of corrupting a state supreme court judge in an attempt to control the Manhattan Elevated Railroad; he persuaded the assembly's judiciary committee to hold investigative hearings, and although Gould was exonerated Roosevelt secured a reputation as a reformer and fighter of corruption. In February 1884 his political career was interrupted by the death of his mother and wife on the same day, and later that year he chose not to seek reelection.

Roosevelt returned to politics in 1886 as a candidate for the mayoralty against the Democrat Abram S. Hewitt and the Union Labor candidate Henry George, an economist who advocated a "single tax" on land, but Hewitt won the election and Roosevelt finished third. He was the city's civil service commissioner in 1889–95, and in 1895 he was appointed president of the police board in the reform administration of Mayor William L. Strong. Roosevelt's boundless energy and impromptu social visits to policemen made him popular with the press, but he faced clamorous opposition when he decided to enforce the Sunday closing law on saloons, and his imperious, determined nature made for troubled relationships with the mayor and other members of the police board. In 1897 he resigned his office to accept an appointment as the assistant secretary of the navy under President William McKinley. During the Spanish–American War he was one of the organizers of the

Rough Riders and earned fame for his efforts in the Battle of San Juan Hill. In 1898 he was elected governor of New York, and in 1900 he was selected as McKinley's vice-presidential candidate; he became president after McKinley was assassinated in 1901, serving for seven and a half controversial years. The most notable events of his presidency were his numerous antitrust battles with big business, the building of the Panama Canal, and his mediation of the Russo-Japanese War in 1905, which earned him the Nobel Peace Prize. In 1909 he left office and traveled extensively abroad. On his return to the United States in June 1910 his ship docked at New York City, and he was greeted with a thunderous reception and a ticker-tape parade of unprecedented size. Roosevelt became an editor at *Outlook*, with an office on 4th (now Park) Avenue, and a contributor to *Metropolitan Magazine*. His remaining years were marked by an unsuccessful campaign as the presidential candidate of the Progressive Party in 1912 and his open criticism of President Woodrow Wilson. Roosevelt's birthplace was demolished in 1916 but replicated by Theodate Pope Riddle in 1923, and in 1962 it was named a National Historic Site and opened to the public. A memorial statue of Roosevelt designed by John Russell Pope and erected in 1940 stands fifteen feet (four and a half meters) tall in front of the American Museum of Natural History. Roosevelt is the only native of New York City to have achieved the nation's highest office.

John Morton Blum: *The Republican Roosevelt* (Cambridge: Harvard University Press, 1954)

Henry F. Pringle: *Theodore Roosevelt* (Norwalk, Conn.: Easton, 1987)

Nathan Miller: *Theodore Roosevelt: A Life* (New York: William Morrow, 1992)

Richard Skolnick

Roosevelt Hospital. Private hospital incorporated in 1864 and funded by a bequest from James H. Roosevelt, an uncle of Theodore Roosevelt. It opened in 1871 at its present location between 58th and 59th streets and 9th and 10th avenues and became the site of many medical innovations: William Halstead in the 1880s was the first surgeon in the United States to use rubber gloves during surgery; the Syms Operating Pavilion, opened in 1891, was the first modern operating theater in New York City and is now a landmark; William McBurney developed the technique for performing an appendectomy in the 1890s (an operation performed at the hospital on the Duchess of Windsor in 1944); and Karl Connell developed the gas mask used by American troops during the First World War. The Smithers Alcoholism Treatment and Training Center opened in 1968; it is named for R. Brinkley Smithers, who donated more than $10 million to the center. The in-patient unit of Roosevelt Hospital is housed in a mansion in the East 90s formerly owned by the showman Billy Rose. The hospital merged with St. Luke's Hospital in 1979 to form ST. LUKE'S–ROOSEVELT HOSPITAL CENTER.

Andrea Balis

Institutions on Blackwell's Island

Roosevelt Island. An island in the East River (1990 pop. 8190), equidistant between the Upper East Side of Manhattan (51st Street to 86th Street) and Long Island City in Queens. It is about eight hundred feet (240 meters) wide and 1.75 miles (2.8 kilometers) long. The Queensboro Bridge crosses overhead, carrying an aerial tramway that connects the island to Manhattan. The island was called Minnehanonck by the Indians and Varcken Eylandt by the Dutch. Its first European owner was Wouter van Twiller, who bought it from the Indians, as he had done with what are now known as Wards, Randalls, and Governors islands. In 1668 the island was bought by Captain John Manning, who retired to it in disgrace after having surrendered the colony of New York to the Dutch in 1673. By the early eighteenth century title to the property was taken by Robert Blackwell, who had married Manning's daughter Mary. He lived and farmed on the island, which came to bear his name; a farmhouse believed to have belonged to his descendants still stands just south of the Queensboro Bridge. Blackwell's Island was acquired in 1828 by the city, which by 1860 built on it a prison, an almshouse, a workhouse, and three hospitals: Metropolitan Hospital (A. J. Davis, 1839), designed as a lunatic asylum with an octagonal tower that survived into the 1990s (without its original wings); City Hospital (James Renwick Jr., 1859), a charity hospital built of stone quarried on the island by convicts imprisoned there; and Smallpox Hospital (James Renwick Jr., 1856), a small Gothic Revival structure that is now a gray, crenelated ruin. Later structures include the Chapel of the Good Shepherd (Frederick Clarke Withers, 1889), which served patients and staff, and the Blackwell Lighthouse (James Renwick Jr., 1872) at the northern tip of the island. By 1921 the prison and the workhouse had achieved such a reputation for overcrowding, violence, and drug trafficking that the city renamed the island Welfare Is-

Main Street, Roosevelt Island, 1992

Roosevelt Island tram, 1992

land. A series of new hospitals was begun in the 1920s, of which the most important is Goldwater Memorial for the chronically ill (Isadore Rosenfield; Butler and Kohn; York and Sawyer, 1939). The prison was moved to Rikers Island in 1935, leaving Welfare Island to the aged and the sick.

The Urban Development Corporation (UDC) of New York State in 1971 undertook to transform Welfare Island into a densely developed residential community to be called Roosevelt Island. A master plan by Philip Johnson and John Burgee called for a neighborhood free of automobiles, with apartment buildings and stores connected by a central street, restored historic buildings, river views, and a park at each end of the island. Because of changes to the plan, inflation, and the fiscal collapse of the UDC, only part of the plan was realized in the mid 1970s. Southtown (Sert, Jackson and Associates; Johansen and Bhavnani, 1975–76), a complex of four large apartment buildings with both subsidized and market-rate apartments, is built around a quiet street paved with brick. Higher-priced apartments face the Upper East Side, lower-priced ones Long Island City. Roosevelt Island was slow to achieve popularity but by the 1980s had become sought after as a quiet neighborhood offering fine views of Manhattan. Automobiles can reach the island only from Queens and are allowed to go no farther than the Motorgate garage and entry complex; the tramway was the only means of access from Manhattan until a subway station opened on the island in 1989. Some new apartments were built in 1988 (designed by Gwathmey and Siegel).

Roosevelt Island Tramway System Assessment (Washington: U.S. Department of Transportation, 1979)

For further illustrations see ALMSHOUSES and JAILS.

Ellen Fletcher

Root, Elihu (*b* Clinton, N.Y., 15 Feb 1845; *d* New York City, 7 Feb 1937). Statesman. After graduating from Hamilton College he attended New York University Law School and became successful on Wall Street. From 1871 to 1878 he lived at 20 Irving Place. Theodore Roosevelt sought his legal advice while serving as the city's police commissioner and later as governor of New York. Under President William McKinley he was appointed secretary of war in 1899, a position he retained until Roosevelt, now president, made him secretary of state in 1905. He was elected to the U.S. Senate from New York State in 1909 and won the Nobel Peace Prize in 1912. Root worked for the Allied cause during the First World War and was active in the Carnegie benefactions; he returned to private life in 1915. His homes in New York City included a house that he built at 733 Park Avenue in 1903 and another at 998 5th Avenue, where he lived from about 1912 until the end of his life.

Richard W. Leopold: *Elihu Root and the Conservative Tradition* (Boston: Little, Brown, 1954)

James E. Mooney

rope and cordage. The manufacture of rope and cordage is closely linked to the port economy and requires large amounts of land. In colonial Manhattan ropeyards lined the northern fringes of Broadway and the banks of the Collect Pond. By 1824 eight ropewalks in Brooklyn that operated one mile (one and a half kilometers) inland employed two hundred workers and each year produced about 1130 tons (1025 metric tons) of cordage. John Good, a ropemaker in Brooklyn, received the first American patent for spreaders and breakers in 1869, and within ten years his inventions revolutionized the manufacture of cordage. Large ropemakers included Tucker, Carter and Company, Elizabethport Steam Cordage, and William Wall and Sons in Brooklyn (1830). Increased output and fierce competition prompted four firms in Manhattan to organize a cartel in 1887 called the National Cordage Company, which lasted until 1893; a similar effort led to the formation of the United States Cordage Company, which passed into receivership in 1895. The shift from sailpower to steam, spiraling land costs in the city, and the nationwide railroad network drove rope factories from New York City, and few mechanized plants remained by the turn of the century. The largest was the Waterbury Rope Company, which operated a fortress-like factory in Brooklyn where it made several grades of cordage from Philippine manila and Yucatan sisal. The industry benefited from the building boom of the 1920s, but many firms such as the American Manufacturing Company and the Chelsea Fibre Mills nevertheless diversified into related products like twine, shoelaces, and wire rope. The Depression essentially ended ropemaking the city.

"The Manufacture of Cordage," *Scientific American*, 19 Oct 1901
Solveig Paulson Russell: *Twist and Twine: The Story of Cordage* (New York: Parents' Magazine, 1969)

Marc Ferris

Rorem, Ned (*b* Richmond, Ind., 23 Oct 1923). Composer and writer. He grew up in Chicago and studied music in New York City at the Juilliard School and with Virgil Thomson, who exerted a strong influence on his style. After living in Paris and Morocco he returned to the city in 1958. During the following decades he became known as a composer of emphatically tonal works, particularly art songs, and as an essayist who wrote provocatively about music and other topics in such collections as *New York Diary* (1966) and *Paris Diary* (1967). In 1976 he won a Pulitzer Prize for his orchestral composition *Air Music.*

Janet Frankston

Rose, Alex [Royz, Olesh] (*b* Warsaw, 15 Oct 1898; *d* New York City, 28 Dec 1976). Labor leader. He arrived in New York City in 1913, became a millinery worker, and in 1914 joined the Millinery Workers Union. A leading organizer in 1936 of the American Labor Party, he became increasingly concerned that the party was being infiltrated by communists, and after a leftist faction gained control in 1944 he left with David Dubinsky to form the Liberal Party. Despite a lack of mass support and funds, Rose used his political skills to make the party a powerful force in politics at both the city and state levels. In addition to leading the party he was president of the

United Hatters, Cap and Millinery International Union from 1950 until his death.

Eileen K. Cheng

Rose, Billy [Rosenberg, Samuel Wolf] (*b* New York City, 6 Sept 1899; *d* New York City, 10 Feb 1966). Songwriter, theater and nightclub owner, and producer. The son of Russian Jewish immigrants, he acquired an expertise in shorthand as a youth that enabled him to secure a position in Washington as the head of the Reports Division of the War Industries Board, then led by Bernard Baruch. After the war he returned to New York City, where he lived at a church mission on 46th Street and studied popular songs at the New York Public Library. He published his first song in 1921 and over the years he took credit for nearly four hundred more, although in many cases he was probably no more than a co-author of the lyrics. In February 1929 he married the entertainer Fanny Brice, with whom he moved to an apartment at 15 East 69th Street (now the Westbury Hotel). During the same period he helped to form the Songwriter's Protective Agency (serving as its first president) and used his money from songwriting to purchase the Back Stage Club.

Rose's club was supported by organized crime and highly profitable. He had similar support at the Casino de Paree and the Billy Rose Music Hall, and when he eventually tried to break free from criminal influence he was forced to seek protection from the Federal Bureau of Investigation. In 1931 he had his first success as a producer with the show *Crazy Quilt*, a touring production that was able to make money during the Depression. He next joined with Jimmy Durante and an elephant in the Broadway spectacular *Jumbo* (1935) and produced shows in Cleveland and in Fort Worth, Texas, where he met Eleanor Holm, the star of an aquatic musical revue; she became his second wife in 1939 and was featured in New York City in his next "aquacade," at the World's Fair of 1939–40. From 1939 to 1952 he lived at 33 Beekman Place and managed the popular nightclub the Diamond Horseshoe. His Broadway productions during these years included *Carmen Jones* (1943), an all-black version of Bizet's opera set in a parachute factory during the Second World War, and *The Seven Lively Arts* (1944), produced in collaboration with Igor Stravinsky, Cole Porter, Benny Goodman, Bert Lahr, and Beatrice Lillie. Between 1947 and 1959 he wrote a newspaper column focusing on show business. The improbable Rose also had a brief career as a stockbroker: during one five-month period in 1963–64 he earned almost $9000 for every hour that the New York Stock Exchange was in session.

From 1956 until his death Rose lived at 56 East 93rd Street. He bequeathed almost his entire estate of $54 million to the Billy Rose Foundation, which gave major support to the Billy Rose Theatre Collection at the New York Public Library for the Performing Arts, and to other causes in the arts and medicine.

Earl Conrad: *Billy Rose, Manhattan Primitive* (Cleveland: World, 1968)

Polly Rose Gottlieb: *The Nine Lives of Billy Rose* (New York: Crown, 1968)

Chad Ludington

Rosebank. Neighborhood in northeastern Staten Island (1990 pop. 16,000), bounded to the east by Upper New York Bay, to the southwest by the Staten Island Expressway, and to the northwest by Clifton. Until 1880 the area was part of Peterstown, so named by the German settlers who lived in the southern part of the town; Irish immigrants lived in the northern part. In 1873 New York State purchased eight and a half acres (three and a half hectares) of waterfront for a maritime quarantine facility, which was the principal facility of its kind in the United States from the late 1930s until quarantine functions were transferred to Governors Island in 1971. The neighborhood is the site of the home of Alice Austen, portions of which date to the eighteenth century; the house was extensively renovated in 1846, perhaps by James Renwick, and it opened to the public in 1985 as a place of exhibit for some of Austen's finest photographs. The Italian revolutionary Giuseppe Garibaldi lived in the area for several years during his exile from Italy, and a later resident, Antonio Meucci, is credited by some as the rightful inventor of the telephone; both are commemorated in the Garibaldi–Meucci Museum. In the late 1880s families who had lived in the area for many years and Irish and German residents were displaced from parts of Rosebank by immigrants from southern Italy who intended to farm the land but found that the small plots made even truck farming difficult; many soon sought other work. Although some Irish–Americans remain, Rosebank retains a strong Italian–American identity and has well-maintained small houses, gardens, grape arbors, and fig trees. Catholic and Italian festivals are important events in the neighborhood, St. Mary's Catholic school is a stable institution, and the shrine of Our Lady of Mount Carmel stands near St. Joseph's Roman Catholic Church. The neighborhood is working class and has experienced some tensions because of pollution, noise, drugs, and racial incidents. Tompkins Avenue is the principal thoroughfare in the neighborhood, which abuts Von Briesen Park and Fort Wadsworth.

Diana E. Thompson: "The Italian–American Immigrants of Rosebank, Staten Island, 1890–1920" (thesis, Richmond College, 1972)

Geoffrey Mohan: "The Old Neighborhood Remembered," *Staten Island Advance*, 15 Oct 1984, §B, pp. 5, 8

Alexis Jetter: "Race, Fear and Death on Staten Island," *New York Newsday*, 18 Oct 1988, §2, pp. 4, 5

Howard Weiner

Rosedale. Neighborhood in southeastern Queens, bounded to the north by Merrick Boulevard, to the east and south by Hook Creek, and to the west by Brookfield Park. The area was settled in 1647 by Thomas and Christopher Foster and became known as Foster's Meadow. A hamlet was built after a railroad station opened in 1870; developers changed the name to Rosedale in 1892. Most of the housing was erected in the 1920s, and until the 1930s the population was Irish and German. After the Second World War the neighborhood attracted a more diverse population, including Italians, Jews, and blacks. In the 1980s a number of immigrants from the Caribbean moved to Rosedale and its environs, almost half from Jamaica and many others from Haiti and Guyana.

Vincent Seyfried

Roseland Ballroom. Dance hall. It opened on 1 January 1919 at 1658 Broadway, near 51st Street, and became a notable venue for jazz bands including McKinney's Cotton Pickers and the bands of Sam Lanin, Fletcher Henderson, A. J. Piron, Claude Hopkins, Earl Hines, and Ella Fitzgerald. The hall was considered safer and more elegant than the taxi dance halls where patrons paid ten cents for each dance; its location in the theater district, lavish décor, and national radio broadcasts made it especially prominent. The building that housed the ballroom was demolished in December 1956 and superseded by Roseland Dance City in 1957. This new dance hall remained popular into the 1990s and entertained a diverse clientele, presenting ballroom dancing on weeknights, occasional rock shows, and Latin dancing on weekends.

Samuel B. Charters and Leonard Kunstadt: *Jazz: A History of the New York Scene* (Garden City, N.Y.: Doubleday, 1962; repr. New York: Da Capo, 1981)

Kathy J. Ogren

Rosenberg case. The most celebrated court case of the cold war, in which a husband and wife were convicted of spying for the Soviet Union and executed at Sing Sing Prison (Ossining, New York) on 19 June 1953. In 1950 the Federal Bureau of Investigation arrested Julius Rosenberg (1918–53), his wife, Ethel (1915–53), and his brother-in-law David Greenglass after revelations about a spy ring in New York City that included the atomic scientist Klaus Fuchs. The Rosenbergs were accused of conveying atomic secrets to the Soviet Union while Julius Rosenberg, a devoted communist, was a civilian employee of the U.S. Signal Corps from 1940 to 1945; Greenglass had had access to classified information while working at atomic facilities in Los Alamos, New Mexico, in 1944. Greenglass became a federal witness, testified against the Rosenbergs, and received a prison sentence. The death sentence imposed on the Rosenbergs was widely regarded as severe.

Julius and Ethel Rosenberg leaving the U.S. Courthouse after being found guilty of spying for the Soviet Union, 30 March 1951

Ronald Radosh and Joyce Milton: *The Rosenberg File: A Search for the Truth* (New York: Holt, Rinehart, 1983)
Joseph H. Sharlitt: *Fatal Error: The Miscarriage of Justice That Sealed the Rosenbergs' Fate* (New York: Charles Scribner's Sons, 1989)

Martin Ebon

Rosenblatt, Yossele (*b* Ukraine, 9 May 1882; *d* Jerusalem, 18 June 1933). Cantor. Brought up in Galicia in Austro-Hungary, he became known for his wide tenor range and coloratura. After arriving in New York City in 1912 he began a lengthy service as the cantor of the First Hungarian Congregation Ohab Zedek in Harlem, also serving briefly at Congregation Anshe Sfard in Borough Park. He performed arias, Jewish folk songs, and liturgical pieces on the concert stage, recorded for the record label Victor, and supplied the voice of the father in Al Jolson's film *The Jazz Singer*. Rosenblatt died while making a film.

Samuel Rosenblatt: *Yossele Rosenblatt: The Story of His Life as Told by His Son* (New York: Farrar, Straus and Young, 1954)

Daniel Soyer

Rosenfeld, Morris (*b* Boksze, near Suwałki, Poland, 28 Dec 1862; *d* New York City, 22 June 1923). Poet. After living in Warsaw he emigrated to the United States in 1886 and worked for a time in the garment industry in New York City. He wrote verses about the travails of the sweatshop, immigrant longings, and socialist ideals that were often published in the Yiddish press and sung at workers' meetings and rallies: he was regarded as the bard of the Jewish labor movement. Several collections of his work were issued. In 1898 Rosenfeld became the first American Yiddish writer to achieve fame beyond the immigrant community when Leo Weiner translated his verses in *Songs from the Ghetto*.

Hutchins Hapgood: *Four Poets of the Ghetto* (Berkeley Heights, N.J.: Oriole, 1963)

Jeffrey Shandler

Ross, Charles. Alias of LUCKY LUCIANO when he lived at the Waldorf–Astoria Towers.

Ross, Harold (Wallace) (*b* Aspen, Colo., 6 Nov 1892; *d* Boston, 6 Dec 1951). Editor. During the First World War he worked in Paris with Alexander Woollcott as a member of the editorial board of the military newspaper the *Stars and Stripes*. After settling in New York City he launched the *New Yorker* with his wife, Jane Grant, who had written for the *New York Times*; in this endeavor he drew on the literary talents of the members of the Algonquin Round Table and the financial resources of Raoul Fleischmann, who had earned his fortune in the baking business. As the editor of the magazine for the next twenty-six years he acquired a reputation for intelligence, brusqueness, and fanatical dedication to good writing. Although he seldom was publicly outspoken, just before his death he successfully protested the broadcasting of advertisements over loudspeakers in Grand Central Terminal. Ross lived from 1919 to 1920 at 56 West 11th Street in Manhattan, from August 1920 to August 1922 at 231 West 58th Street (at the same time also living for about a year at 333 West 85th Street), from 1922 to 1928 at 412 West 47th Street, and in the early 1930s at the Ritz–Carlton Hotel, 374 Madison Avenue.

James Thurber: *The Years with Ross* (Boston: Little, Brown, 1957)
Jane Grant: *Ross, the New Yorker, and Me* (New York: Reynal, 1968)
Thomas Kunkel: *Genius in Disguise: Harold Ross of the New Yorker* (New York: Random House, 1995)

Brenda Wineapple

Rossville. Neighborhood in southwestern Staten Island (1990 pop. 5000), bounded to the north by the Fresh Kills Landfill, to the east by Woodrow, to the south by Charleston, and to the west by the Arthur Kill. The area was settled during the seventeenth century and was known before the American Revolution as Blazing Star for a local tavern of the same name. It was linked to the mainland by the Blazing Star ferry and later by coastal steamships, and during the nineteenth century it became a prosperous farming community; in 1836 it was renamed for the wealthy landowner William E. Ross. Passed over by rapid transit in the early twentieth century, it declined until the mid 1970s, when the opening of the West Shore Expressway stimulated development. The population is predominantly Italian, Jewish, Indian, Pakistani, Filipino, and Korean. There are two historic cemeteries, as well as a number of nineteenth-century houses on Arthur Kill Road; condominiums and large, one-family houses stand along Rossville Avenue and near Bloomingdale Road. Along the Arthur Kill are automobile repair shops, correctional facilities, a power transformer, and a marine junkyard.

Charles W. Leng and William T. Davis: *Staten Island and Its People: A History, 1609–1929* (New York: Lewis Historical Publishing, 1930)

Carol V. Wright

Roth, Henry (*b* Tysmenia, Galicia, 8 Feb 1906). Novelist. He grew up on the Lower East Side and in Harlem, and moved to Maine while in his twenties. In 1934 he published *Call It Sleep*, a novel in a documentary realist style set on the Lower East Side in the first decades of the twentieth century. The book was reissued in 1960 and 1964 and sold more than a million copies. Roth's second book, *Shifting Landscape: A Composite (1925–1987)* (1987), includes stories, interviews, and correspondence. In 1994 he published *A Star Shines over Mount Morris Park*, the first volume in a quasi-autobiographical fictional work called "Mercy of a Rude Stream."

Bonnie Lyons: *Henry Roth: The Man and His Work* (New York: Cooper Square, 1976)

B. Kimberly Taylor

Roth, Philip (*b* Newark, N.J., 19 May 1933). Novelist and short-story writer. He studied at Bucknell University (AB 1954) and the University of Chicago (MA 1955) and gained renown after the publication of *Goodbye, Columbus* (1959), a collection of short stories that won a National Book Award, and the comic novel *Portnoy's Complaint* (1969). These and other works, including *My Life as a Man* (1974),

The Professor of Desire (1975), *Zuckerman Unbound* (1981), and *The Counterlife* (1987), reflect his preoccupations with American Jewish identity and with the shifting boundaries between fiction and reality. He became a professor at Hunter College in 1989.

Shan Jayakumar

Rothko, Mark [Rothkowitz, Marcus] (*b* Dvinsk [now Daugavpils, Latvia], 25 Sept 1903; *d* New York City, 25 Feb 1970). Painter. After emigrating to the United States in 1913 he lived in Portland, Oregon, and in 1925 moved permanently to New York City, where he became a pupil of Max Weber at the Art Students League. He frequented Milton Avery's studio and in 1935 joined Adolph Gottlieb and other artists in a group called The Ten. With Gottlieb and Barnett Newman he wrote a letter on 7 June 1943 to Edward Alden Jewell, the art critic for the *New York Times*, that described their art as "the simple expression of the complex thought." His first solo exhibition was held in 1945 at Art of This Century, a gallery owned by Peggy Guggenheim. After the gallery closed he was represented by the Betty Parsons Gallery, which from 1947 mounted five solo exhibitions of his works. By 1950 he had eliminated all vestiges of representational imagery from his art and developed the style for which he became known, characterized by large rectangles of color hovering in the canvas field. Toward the end of the decade his work became progressively more somber, as evidenced by a series of large-scale canvases that he painted in 1958–59 for the restaurant the Four Seasons in the Seagram Building. Soon after completing his last series of paintings, limited in color to black, gray, and brown, he took his own life. Rothko's residences in New York City included 19 West 102nd Street (1924–29), 137 West 72nd Street (1932–36), 313 East 6th Street (1936–40), 29 East 28th Street (1940–43), 22 West 52nd Street (from 1945), 1288 6th Avenue (from late 1946 to 1954), 102 West 54th Street (from 1954), 118 East 95th Street (1960–64), and his studio at 157 East 69th Street (where he worked from 1964 and lived from January 1969 until his death).

Diane Waldman: *Mark Rothko, 1903–1970: A Retrospective* (New York: Harry N. Abrams / Solomon R. Guggenheim Foundation, 1978)

Anna G. Chave: *Mark Rothko: Subjects in Abstraction* (New Haven: Yale University Press, 1989)

James E. B. Breslin: *Mark Rothko: A Biography* (Chicago: University of Chicago Press, 1993)

Mona Hadler

Rothstein, Arnold (*b* New York City, 1882; *d* New York City, 6 Nov 1928). Gambler and organized-crime figure. Born into a wealthy family, he spent time as a youth in the poolrooms and gambling parlors of the Lower East Side, where he met the gang leader Monk Eastman and Big Tim Sullivan, a leader of Tammany Hall. He used his connections to Eastman, Sullivan, and others to become a leading gambler, bootlegger, drug dealer, and labor racketeer. Dapper and refined, he applied techniques of business to crime that were later perfected by Meyer Lansky, Lucky Luciano, and others. He was widely accused of having engineered the outcome of the World Series of 1919, although he denied having done so. He almost certainly supplied strong-arms and finances for communist unionists in the garment industry, in which he apparently mediated labor disputes. Rothstein was shot and mortally wounded in room 349 of the Park Central Hotel (7th Avenue and 56th Street), perhaps for refusing to pay a gambling debt. Although the police investigation was supervised by Mayor James J. Walker the assailant was never found, leading some to conclude that Tammany Hall had sabotaged the investigation to keep hidden Rothstein's links to city government. He lived in the 1920s at 355 West 84th Street and at the Ritz–Carlton Hotel, 374 Madison Avenue, and to end of his life at 912 5th Avenue.

Leo Katcher: *The Big Bankroll: The Life and Times of Arnold Rothstein* (New York: Harper and Brothers, 1959)

Robert W. Snyder

rotisserie baseball. A game played by baseball enthusiasts, invented in New York City in 1979 by a group including the writer Daniel Okrent, the editor Cork Smith, and Robert Sklar, a professor of film at New York University, at La Rotisserie Française, a restaurant on 52nd Street between 3rd Avenue and Lexington Avenue. Participants in the game form fictitious teams that include real baseball players: by means of statistical formulas the performance of the teams is determined according to that of the players in the major leagues. In 1991 the *New York Times* estimated that one million persons played the game nationwide.

Joseph S. Lieber

Rowell, George P(resbury) (*b* Concord, Vt., 4 July 1838; *d* Poland Springs, Maine, 28 Aug 1908). Publisher. After moving to New York City he set up an advertising firm and published a directory of accurate circulation figures for newspapers at a time when many publishers used false ones. He launched *Printers' Ink*, a trade journal for advertisers, and fought for truth in advertising. After selling the firm to his employees he bought into it again to stave off bankruptcy but again sold his shares in 1905. Rowell wrote an autobiography, *Forty Years an Advertising Agent* (1906).

See also ADVERTISING.

James E. Mooney

row houses. The type of row house characteristic of New York City was introduced in New Amsterdam by the Dutch in the mid seventeenth century. The earliest Dutch row houses in America were simpler than those in the Netherlands: they were twenty feet (six meters) wide, were built of brick in Flemish bond with their gable end on the street (often pictured showing their distinctive Dutch stepped roof lines), and had a kitchen in the basement (the top of which extended above ground level), a parlor on the first story, and sleeping quarters on the upper story. Flush with either the left or right side of the building was a grand exterior staircase called the stoop (from a Dutch word for step or platform) that led from the street to the first story, with benches on either side of the landing; the family entered and left the building through a passage under the stoop and spent most of its time in the basement. Two-part Dutch doors allowed for ventilation while keeping children in and animals out; initially chimneys were made of wood with a clay lining and required frequent cleaning. Stepped gables were a convenience for chimney sweeps and for the fire brigade, and were important for householders before fire-resistant brick and tile became readily available.

The Dutch row house offered a practical means of housing large families in a small space: it was sturdily built, cost little to maintain and heat, had separate family and reception areas, and was more comfortable than the English row house that was common in Boston and Philadelphia. In addition the design of the row house was highly adaptable: the building could be appointed lavishly for a wealthy family or sparely for a worker's family with as many as eight members; it could also be subdivided into several rental units and then converted back again into a one-family house, and the lower stories could be rented out to shops or restaurants. The parlor on the first story was used only for occasions of great importance such as St. Nicholas Day, weddings, and funerals; Washington Irving wrote in *A History of New York* that the parlor was so inviolable that it was to be entered only for its weekly cleaning and that the brass lion's-head knocker on the front door was worn out from polishing more often than from use.

After the British invasion of 1664 the row house evolved into a simplified Georgian style characterized by brickwork in English bond, dormer windows, eaves parallel to the street, a low stoop of three or four steps, and railings and gates in wrought iron. The Federal style that took hold after independence was similar to the Georgian, except that the brickwork was now done in American running bond, and applied decoration often included an eagle. The appearance of the row house changed again with the onset of the Greek Revival. Used first in churches, courthouses, and other public buildings, the new style became popular in private houses in the 1820s, when the rising up of the Greek people against the Ottoman Empire in 1821–28 rekindled an interest in ancient Greece (in the same period a number of American cities were given Greek names). During the Greek Revival the row house acquired such classical features as egg-and-dart moldings, eaves featuring the beamlike triglyph and metope of the Greek pediment, lights atop and beside the main entrance, and balanced colonettes with capitals on either side. Pineapples, symbols of hospitality, were commonly used as finials on the newel posts. The windows had flat lintels, sometimes with a Greek key or other geometric fretwork, and the basement was visually separated from the rest of the house by a distinctive string course. The brickwork was frequently in American running bond. As in the Federal style the stoop was low, the railings were of wrought iron, and there was a high proportion of window space to wall. The Gothic Revival enjoyed a brief popularity due partly to the writings of John Ruskin (1785–1864), who believed that people's actions were in great part determined by their surroundings and that human simplicity and goodness were at their peak during the high Middle Ages. Although the Gothic Revival in the United States is associated principally with rectories and manses, a small number of private row houses were built in this highly decorative style, which is characterized by broken arches, trefoils and quatrefoils in railings and ballisters, crockets on finials, and the triescalon motif in frets. In New York City the windows of Gothic Revival buildings were invariably surmounted by balanced, L-shaped drip moldings designed to keep rainwater away from the opening.

By the 1840s the first story was divided by sliding doors, which separated the parlor (often called the salon in wealthy families and the front room in working-class families) from the rooms to the rear. Behind the parlor and in front of the dining room was a music room, a space about six or eight feet (two to two and a half meters) deep marked off by columns, demi-walls, or a scrollwork lattice. The room usually contained a piano and was the center of family entertainment. During this period architects exploited the easy reversibility of the floor plan of the row house: the stoops in a row would be on the right side between the left-hand cap house (a more substantial building at the end of the row) and the middle of the row, those in the other half of the row would be on the left, and a combined stoop would be formed in the middle.

The row houses built of soft, brownish sandstone and known as BROWNSTONES became popular during the Anglo-Italianate period that began in the late 1860s. The style was derived from that of English rows and crescents, which was in turn influenced by the style of Italian palazzi visited by young Britons in the eighteenth century. In New York City the Italianate buildings were distinguished by deep cornices over the windows, an impressive cornice over the main door (often supported by S-shaped console brackets), a heavy, imposing stoop with cast-iron baluster and newel posts, floor-to-ceiling windows on the parlor story, and arched windows in an elevated basement. Two new styles called Romanesque Revival and Queen Anne vied for popularity from the mid 1870s, at a time when architecture became established as a profession. Romanesque Revival was also known as Richardson Romanesque, after H. H. Richardson, one of the first Americans to study at the École des Beaux-Arts in Paris (with Eugène Viollet-le-Duc). The style was a late Victorian interpretation of the buildings of the later Roman Empire, particularly the fortified buildings. Its features included bases of heavy, rusticated stone, masonry arches (usually for the entrance), tower-like elements, engaged colonettes, elaborate floral panels of curved stone (called Byzantine scrollwork), and sometimes gargoyles. Buildings were generally constructed of Roman bricks (which were longer and slimmer than common bricks). The Queen Anne was an eclectic, Anglophile style that strove to use all the motifs associated in the popular imagination with historical England. Its buildings were constructed of such diverse materials as cast iron, terra cotta, carved stone, force-molded concrete, and decorative burnt brick. Many were asymmetrical and combined antithetical elements; they could include Flemish gables and bulbous, Victorian towers. Both the Romanesque Revival and the Queen Anne emphasized texture and the voluptuous use of materials (especially brick), as well as large buildings or at least the appearance of large buildings: a row of houses would often be designed with a unified front to make the final product resemble a palace. During these years the interior design of the row house underwent one of its few changes, as the affordability of furnaces and central heating from the 1870s made it practical to dig cellars.

Innovative builders in the late 1880s added to the grandeur of the row house by introducing the box stoop, which at first had two levels and eventually as many as three or (very rarely) four. At the same time a new style of row house was imported from England, called variously the London Basement Plan and the American Basement Plan. Its main departure from earlier designs was the location of the grand ceremonial staircase inside the house, and of the entrance at ground level or at most two or three steps above it. Some of the row houses built according to the new plan were Georgian (a classic style filtered through English sensibilities of the eighteenth century); others were neo-Classic (based on Greek and Roman styles as viewed by the École des Beaux-Arts).

The row house housed many Irish and Italian immigrants in Brooklyn and the Bronx in the early twentieth century. It continued to be used much as it had been by the Dutch: the family spent most of its waking hours near the kitchen in the basement, reserved the front room for Sunday dinner and other important events, and used the stoop as a meeting place. In most families the parents slept in the quieter bedroom, at the rear of the second story; the front bedroom was used by children and other relatives. Over the years stories could be added and interior modifications made, but the floor plan and the use of the rooms remained essentially the same. Grander row houses often had two stories for receiving guests, the parlor story and the one above. On the parlor story the salon was in the front and the library in the rear. In imitation of the customs of grand English houses, the family ate its daytime meals in the library, served by a dumbwaiter from the basement kitchen. On the story above the front room might be a drawing room to which the women could withdraw after supper, or a billiard room for the men (in which case the women used the library). At the back of this story was the formal dining room, also served by dumbwaiter, with a butler's pantry next to it used for the final preparation and reheating of food. The latter Georgian and neo-Classic row houses were the grandest ever built in New York City: fine examples are on West 74th Street off Central Park West (1904).

The row house began its decline about 1916. Then the subways were reaching into the unsettled parts of Brooklyn and the Bronx, where there was sufficient space to build semidetached and free-standing houses with larger lawns and backyards. At the same time the automobile was becoming affordable to an upwardly mobile middle class, which was increasingly likely to buy a house with a driveway and a garage. To accommodate this new development the design of row houses sacrificed living space. The garden cottage, developed in the 1940s, had a garage built below ground level that was reached by an inclined driveway; the automobile occupied the basement, the family was forced upstairs, and the upper stories and separate reception area disappeared. By the 1950s the family automobile was so large and important that the garage was moved to street level and seemed to be the most important design element of the building.

John J. Gallagher

rowing. Competitive rowing in New York City dates from colonial times, when races were staged between harbor and river workers, many of whom rowed passengers and goods across the water for a living. In the early nineteenth century rowing became a popular sport in the city. Ferrymen from Whitehall Landing, at the Battery, enjoyed great success in racing against local crews on the Hudson River in the years after 1810. These races attracted huge crowds as rowing became one of the first spectator sports in the United States.

Businesses sometimes closed during races, and wagering was widespread. In 1825 New York City was the site of the first international rowing contest, in which the English captain of the *Hussar*, docked in the East River, challenged the crew from Whitehall Landing to a race from Bedloe's Island to Hoboken, New Jersey, to the Battery; as many as fifty thousand spectators saw the New Yorkers win. From the 1830s wealthy residents formed competitive rowing clubs throughout the city, and in 1834 a group of the clubs banded together to form the Castle Garden Amateur Boat Club Association. Its most successful crew was the Wave Club, which rowed boats built by Clarkson Crolius. The Independent Boat Club Association, a somewhat less élitist and less competitive group of clubs, was also formed about this time. In 1837 the New Yorkers Stephen Roberts and Sidney Dorlan squared off on a round-trip course from Castle Garden to Bedloe's Island in the first recorded individual championship race. More clubs were formed at mid century, notably the Atalanta Boat Club in 1848 and the Empire City Regatta Club in 1855. The first collegiate crew in the city was formed at Columbia College in 1859. Some rowing clubs were more social and recreational than competitive, including the Hudson Amateur Rowing Association (1866). The National Association of Amateur Oarsmen, organized at a meeting in the city in 1872, first codified rules and defined amateurism in the sport. With the rise of professional rowing in the United States such individual athletes as James Lee and Charles Thomas of New York City became popular public figures. Like other professional sports of the time rowing had a seamy underside, and gambling, drinking, and fighting were prevalent. By the early twentieth century professional rowing in the city had ceased to exist. Amateur rowing continued to thrive for some time: there were thirty-one boathouses in the city in 1905, and rowing clubs were active on the western bank of the Harlem River, known as the Speedway, and the eastern bank of the Hudson between 125th and 135th streets, known as Scullers' Row. Most of Scullers' Row was demolished when bulkheads were built in 1928; a few clubs moved uptown, to near Dyckman Street south of Sherman Creek.

The popularity of rowing among ethnic social clubs in all five boroughs continued into the 1950s but eventually diminished owing to the growth of spectator sports, the increasing use of powerboats, and the rising cost of organizing and staging events. The last wooden Victorian boathouse owned by the Fordham Rowing Association was lost to arson in 1978. Although New York City by the 1990s was no longer a center of rowing, a few groups were active. The New York Athletic Club, with a boathouse in Westchester, rowed in the popular waters of Orchard Beach Lagoon and remained competitive at the national level. A group called the Power Ten occasionally competed as the New York Rowing Association and used the boathouse of the fire department near Gracie Mansion on the East River. The Empire State Rowing Association, formed in the early 1980s and based at Roberto Clemente State Park in the Bronx, sponsored community rowing programs, some in conjunction with the Police Athletic League. Several local colleges had crews, including Columbia, Manhattan College, Fordham University, St. John's University, and Maritime College. Although St. Helena's High School in the Bronx had a competitive crew for many years, in the mid 1990s the only high school in the city with a crew was Beach Channel High School in Far Rockaway.

Arthur Ruhl and Samuel Crowther: *Rowing and Track Athletics* (New York: Macmillan, 1905)

Melvin L. Adelman: *A Sporting Time: New York City and the Rise of Modern Athletics, 1820–1870* (Urbana: University of Illinois Press, 1986)

Joseph S. Lieber

Roxbury. Neighborhood in southwestern Queens, lying near the western end of Rockaway Peninsula and bounded to the north by Rockaway Inlet, to the east by a station of the U.S. Coast Guard, to the south by State Road, and to the west by a section of the Gateway National Recreation Area. It was developed in the early 1960s as part of the Breezy Point Cooperative. Most of the housing consists of small bungalows; the population is largely Irish and middle class.

James Bradley

Roxy Theater. Movie theater opened in 1927 on 50th Street and Broadway at a cost of about $12 million. It was designed by the architect W. W. Ahlschlager and promoted and managed by Samuel Rothafel. Called the "cathedral of the motion picture," the theater seated more than six thousand and had the largest music library found in any theater, an advanced refrigeration and ventilation system, its own infirmary, and a power plant large

Interior of Roxy Theater

enough to light a city of 250,000. The Roxy Theater was razed in 1961.

Roxy: A History (New York: Film Daily, 1927)

David Nasaw

RPA. See Regional plan association of new york.

Rubin, I(sidor) C(linton) (*b* Vienna, 8 Jan 1883; *d* London, 10 July 1958). Gynecologist. He settled in New York City as a child. In 1919 he developed a test for sterility in women for which he became internationally known; he also conducted important research in cervical cancer. Rubin taught at the College of Physicians and Surgeons (1937–47), was chief of gynecology at Mount Sinai Hospital (1937–46), and was also associated with Beth Israel Hospital, Montefiore Hospital, and Harlem Hospital.

Joseph S. Lieber

Rubinstein, Helena (*b* Kraków, Poland, *ca* 1871; *d* New York City, 1 April 1965). Businesswoman. She moved to New York City in 1914 by way of London and in the following year opened the Maison de Beauté de Valaze at 14 East 49th Street, which featured her Crème Valaze. Her factory-made but narrowly marketed products soon became successful, and she expanded her salons and product line to several American and European cities. Advertisements that showed her wearing a white laboratory coat and inspecting her products extolled a scientifically designed beauty program, a marketing strategy that became widely imitated. She also offered the first line of cosmetics for oily, dry, and normal skin, and introduced a mascara applicator that remained in use into the 1990s. Rubinstein was well known for her idiosyncrasies and for most of her career had a highly publicized rivalry with Elizabeth Arden. From her headquarters at 655 5th Avenue she oversaw a cosmetics empire that by the time of her death included more than five hundred products and employed about 26,000 persons in salons, factories, and laboratories in fourteen countries. She also owned the building at 625 Park Avenue, which was one of her many residences throughout the world.

Marc Ferris

Ruder Finn. Public relations firm, formed in 1948 by Bill Ruder (*b* 1921) and David Finn (*b* 1921). Based in a small room at the Lombardy Hotel on East 56th Street, it began as an organization called Art in Industry that was intended to promote business sponsorship of the arts. The firm soon took its current name and became successful as a public relations firm for entertainers such as Perry Como, Dinah Shore, the Mills Brothers, and Jack Lemmon. It later acquired a more diverse list of clients, including large corporations, colleges and universities, and foreign governments. Ruder served as an assistant secretary of commerce under President John F. Kennedy. In 1994 Ruder Finn was one of the largest public relations firms in New York City, with headquarters at 301 East 57th Street in Manhattan and more than a hundred offices worldwide.

James Bradley

Rudin, Samuel (*b* 1896; *d* New York City, 22 Dec 1975). Real-estate developer. He erected apartment buildings in New York City before the Second World War and became known after the war for his modern apartment towers on the Upper East Side, furnished with such conveniences as insulated plumbing, air-conditioned hallways, and street-level stores; he promoted the apartments as "walk-to-work" residences for executives. He also erected such office buildings as 1 Battery Park Plaza, the New York Merchandise Mart, and 345 Park Avenue, chosen by the firm of Bristol–Myers as its headquarters over properties outside the city. An active philanthropist, Rudin helped to form the Association for a Better New York and sponsored the New York City Marathon. His sons Lewis Rudin and Jack Rudin also became prominent developers.

Marc A. Weiss

Ruffian. Thoroughbred racehorse. Born on 17 April 1972, she was a large, strong, fast, black horse who easily won all ten of her races against other fillies, including the "fillies' triple crown." In an effort to extend her popularity Belmont Park sponsored a match race of one and a quarter miles (two kilometers) on 6 July 1975 between her and Foolish Pleasure, a winner of the Kentucky Derby. The race was promoted as a battle between the sexes and drew extensive press coverage and an immense crowd. Ruffian broke her right ankle less than halfway through the race and was destroyed. She is buried in the infield at Belmont Park, near the finish line.

George A. Thompson, Jr.

Rugby. Neighborhood in central Brooklyn, encompassing the land north of Holy Cross Cemetery and that surrounding Kings County Hospital and bounded to the north by Church Avenue, to the east by 57th Street, to the south by Clarendon Road, and to the west by Albany Avenue; it is considered one of the four sections of East Flatbush. The area was once covered by potato farms and was renamed in the late 1890s by developers who thought Flatlands an unattractive name. In 1900 the real-estate firm of Wood, Harmon bought many acres of farmland for development as suburban lots and contracted with Brooklyn Rapid Transit to build fifty houses within a year in return for the extension to the area of a trolley line along Reid Avenue. Growth increased after Interborough Rapid Transit extended the subway to Nostrand Avenue in 1912. The housing stock consists of one- and two-family detached and semidetached houses built mostly in the 1920s and 1930s and a few apartment buildings from after the Second World War. The main retail shopping area developed along Utica Avenue and Church Avenue. From the 1920s to the 1960s many Italians and American-born Jews moved to the neighborhood, and the population became increasingly diverse after 1965, with a large number of blacks and immigrants from the Caribbean (especially Jamaica, Haiti, and Guyana).

Ellen Marie Snyder-Grenier

Ruggles, David (*b* Norwich, Conn., 15 March 1810; *d* Florence, Mass., 26 Dec 1849). Writer, publisher, and abolitionist. He grew up in Norwich and in 1827 moved to New York City, where he operated a grocery. In 1834 he opened a bookshop at 67 Lispenard Street that served blacks and abolitionists until it was destroyed by a mob in the following year. He launched the first black magazine in the United States, the *Mirror of Liberty*, in 1838, and wrote numerous pamphlets satirizing American colonialism. In 1835 he became the leader of the New York Vigilance Committee, which helped fugitives from slavery such as Frederick Douglass to evade capture.

Dorothy B. Porter: "David Ruggles, 1810–1849: Hydropathic Practitioner," *Journal of the National Medical Association* 49 (1957), 67–72, 130–34

Graham Hodges

Ruggles, Samuel B(ulkley) (*b* New Milford, Conn., 11 April 1800; *d* Fire Island, N.Y., 28 Aug 1881). Lawyer and public official. He moved to New York City in 1821 and by 1831 had bought Gramercy Farm, occupying twenty-two acres (nine hectares) between 3rd and 4th avenues and 20th and 22nd streets. He then subdivided the land into 108 lots, with forty-two set aside for a private park to be held in perpetuity by the residents of the surrounding sixty-six lots. The result was Gramercy Park, a patch of green that became one of the most pleasant small spaces in Manhattan. Ruggles was active in promoting the creation of Union Square, one of the city's first public parks, and he was also a commissioner of the Croton Aqueduct and a longtime trustee of Columbia College.

Kenneth T. Jackson

Rumsey, Mary Harriman (*b* 17 Nov 1881; *d* 18 Dec 1934). Philanthropist and political advisor. The eldest of six children of the railroad magnate Edward H. Harriman, she graduated from Barnard College, for which she was a trustee from 1911 until her death. She founded the Junior League in 1901 and was its chairman until 1904. In 1910 she married the sculptor Charles Cary "Pad" Rumsey. In 1920 she formed the Welfare Council to bring together overlapping social agencies in New York City; this later became the Community Council of Greater New York. She persuaded her brother W. Averell Harriman to go to Washington in 1933 to help restructure the National Recovery Administration. Later he largely attributed his having pursued a career in government to her influence. Although she usually lived with her three children in suburban Sands Point, Long Island, shortly before her death she worked and lived with Frances Perkins in Washington, where the two worked to pass the Social Security Act.

Kenneth T. Jackson

running. Organized footraces were held in New York City in the early nineteenth century. The first cash prize was won in 1835 by Louis Bennett, who emphasized his half-Senecan background by competing under the name Deerfoot while wearing a loincloth and a feather headdress: he covered the distance of ten miles (sixteen kilometers) in fifty-six minutes. By 1850 "pedestrianism" had become something of an obsession. Large prizes were offered to professional runners, who competed under such colorful names as the "American Deer," the "Welsh Bantam," and the "Yankee Clipper"; one runner who called himself the "Grand American Union" ran in an outfit bearing the stars and stripes. A popular event was the six-day race, which was run continuously and usually indoors. Prizes were as high as $30,000 and competitors covered upwards of four hundred miles (640 kilometers). At one six-day race in 1888 George Littlewood ran 623.75 miles (1003.6 kilometers), setting a record that lasted for nearly a century (it was broken in New York City in 1984, when Yannis Kouros covered 635 miles and 1023 yards, or 1022.8 kilometers, at a six-day race on Randalls Island). A race of about thirty-five miles (fifty-six kilometers) from Stamford, Connecticut, to New York City in 1896 was won by John McDermott, who later that year won the Boston Marathon, and between November 1908 and April 1909 four professional and five amateur marathons were run in and around the city. The last of these was the "Marathon Derby" run on a dirt track at the Polo Grounds, where in a steady rain the Frenchman Henri St. Yves handily defeated some of the greatest runners in the world in a time of 2:40:50. The Millrose Athletic Association, formed as the Wahna Athletic Association by employees of Wanamaker's department stores, held its first meet in Madison Square Garden in 1914.

The New York Road Runners Club was formed in 1958 by a small group of dedicated runners and grew into a large organization when running became widely popular in the 1970s. On 13 September 1970 it organized the first running of the New York City Marathon: 127 runners started the course, which was run entirely in Central Park. The president of the club, Fred Lebow, later persuaded the city to have the course of the marathon run through each of the five boroughs beginning in 1976, with the starting line in Staten Island at one end of the Verrazano Narrows Bridge and the finish line in Central Park near Tavern on the Green. By the 1990s the New York City Marathon was among the largest marathons in the world, with more than twenty thousand participants from throughout the United States and the world, and as many as two million spectators.

Beginning of the New York City Marathon on the Verrazano Narrows Bridge, late 1980s

Central Park and Prospect Park remain important centers of recreational running in New York City. In Central Park many runners train at the reservoir, surrounded by a dirt track with a perimeter of 1.58 miles (2.54 kilometers); races are frequently run on the main, paved road in the park, which has a perimeter of 6.03 miles (9.7 kilometers) and is closed to motor vehicles for much of the week during the summer. The New York Road Runners Club on East 89th Street sponsors group runs and meetings on athletic topics and is the nation's largest organization of its kind, with more than 29,000 members. Two runners from New York City who have achieved renown in international competition are Abel

Winners of New York City Marathon

	MEN		WOMEN	
1970	Gary Muhrcke	2:31:39	No Finisher	
1971	Norman Higgins	2:22:55	Beth Bonner	2:55:22
1972	Sheldon Karlin	2:27:53	Nina Kucsik	3:08:42
1973	Tom Fleming	2:21:55	Nina Kucsik	2:57:08
1974	Norbert Sander	2:26:31	Kathrine Switzer	3:07:29
1975	Tom Fleming	2:19:27	Kim Merritt	2:46:15
1976	Bill Rodgers	2:10:15	Miki Gorman	2:39:11
1977	Bill Rodgers	2:11:28	Miki Gorman	2:43:10
1978	Bill Rodgers	2:12:12	Grete Waitz	2:32:30
1979	Bill Rodgers	2:11:42	Grete Waitz	2:27:33
1980	Alberto Salazar	2:09:41	Grete Waitz	2:25:41
1981	Alberto Salazar	2:08:13	Allison Roe	2:25:29
1982	Alberto Salazar	2:09:29	Grete Waitz	2:27:14
1983	Rod Dixon	2:08:59	Grete Waitz	2:27:00
1984	Orlando Pizzolato	2:14:53	Grete Waitz	2:29:30
1985	Orlando Pizzolato	2:11:34	Grete Waitz	2:28:34
1986	Gianni Poli	2:11:06	Grete Waitz	2:28:06
1987	Ibrahim Hussein	2:11:01	Priscilla Welch	2:30:17
1988	Steve Jones	2:08:20	Grete Waitz	2:28:07
1989	Juma Ikangaa	2:08:01	Ingrid Kristiansen	2:25:30
1990	Douglas Waikihuri	2:12:39	Wanda Panfil	2:30:45
1991	Salvador Garcia	2:09:28	Liz McColgan	2:27:33
1992	Willie Mtolo	2:09:29	Lisa Ondieki	2:24:40
1993	Andres Espinosa	2:10:04	Uta Pippig	2:26:24
1994	German Silva	2:11:21	Tegla Loroupe	2:27:37

Kiviat, who won the silver medal in the 1500 meter run in the Olympic games in 1912, and Ted Corbitt, who competed for the United States in the Olympic marathon in 1952.

Robert Hillenbrand

Runyon [Runyan], **(Alfred) Damon** (*b* Manhattan, Kansas, 3 Oct 1880; *d* New York City, 10 Dec 1946). Journalist and short-story writer. He worked for newspapers in Colorado before moving to New York City in 1910. In the following year he joined the *New York American*, owned by William Randolph Hearst, as a sportswriter. He gained a loyal readership and then took on a wide range of assignments, working as a war correspondent, crime reporter, and syndicated feature writer for Hearst's other newspapers. He is best known for his short stories, which recount the misadventures of petty criminals, gamblers, chorus girls, and other colorful characters in New York City. His most popular collection, *Guys and Dolls* (1931), was made into a musical by Frank Loesser. Runyon's short stories are considered exemplars of the "hard-boiled" style. Among the addresses in New York City where he is reported to have lived are 111th Street and Broadway (1913); 251 West 95th Street, 320 West 102nd Street, and 113th street and Riverside Drive (all in the 1920s); 224 West 49th Street (1928–32); the Hotel Forrest, 224 West 49th Street (from 1928); 350 West 57th Street (1940); and the Hotel Buckingham, 101 West 57th Street (toward the end of his life).

Edwin P. Hoyt: *A Gentleman of Broadway* (New York: Little, Brown, 1964)
Tom Clark: *The World of Damon Runyon* (New York: Harper and Row, 1978)
Jimmy Breslin: *Damon Runyon* (New York: Ticknor and Fields, 1991)

Russell Sage Foundation. Charitable organization formed in 1907 by Olivia Sage and named after her late husband, a prominent financier. Encouraged by her friend and advisor Robert De Forest, president of the Charity Organization Society, she gave the foundation a broad mandate to improve social and living conditions in the United States that allowed it to become a leader in the reforms of the Progressive era. Her original endowment of $10 million was increased by $5 million on her death in 1918. Among those who served the foundation in its early years were De Forest (first chairman of the board), John Glenn of the Charity Organization Society of Baltimore (general director), Louisa Lee Schuyler, founder of the New York State Charities Aid Association, and Gertrude Rice, a founder of the Charity Organization Society of New York (all original board members), Mary Richmond, a dominant figure in the Charity Organization Society (director of the Charity Organization Department), and Luther Gulick, organizer of the Camp Fire Girls (director of the Department of Child Hygiene). In its early years the foundation sought to promote the new profession of social work and to develop practical applications of social welfare theories. The first extensive project that it funded was the Pittsburgh Survey, which inspired important social and industrial reforms in Pittsburgh and legitimated the survey as a research tool. In response to suggestions from C. McKim Norton, an authority on city planning appointed to the board in 1918, the foundation donated $1.2 million to the Committee on the Regional Plan between 1921 to 1932 to conduct a comprehensive survey of the metropolitan region and an additional $500,000 to promote adoption of the committee's recommendations. From 1913 the headquarters were at Lexington Avenue and 22nd Street. As part of a major reorganization the foundation in 1948 shifted its focus toward the funding of social science research and sold its main building to the Catholic archdiocese. The foundation continues to support research in fields ranging from means of escaping poverty to the success rates of second-generation immigrants, and has an active publications program. In 1992 it had assets of $122 million and made grants totaling $1.9 million. The offices of the foundation are at 112 West 64th Street, former headquarters of the Asia Society.

John M. Glenn, Lilian Brandt, and F. Emerson Andrews: *Russell Sage Foundation, 1907–1946* (New York: Russell Sage Foundation, 1947)

Melissa A. Smith

Russians. New York City was the principal point of entry at the time of the first large-scale emigration of Russians to the United States, which began in the 1880s and continued until the outbreak of the First World War. About 60 percent of these immigrants were Jews and spoke Yiddish. Townspeople without specific trades, called *luftmenschen*, arrived soon after the assassination of Tsar Alexander II in 1881, which the Russian government and populace used as a pretext for subjecting Jews to persecution and pogroms. Many of the first immigrants were also fleeing poverty and seeking better economic conditions in the United States; a large number settled on the Lower East Side and across the East River in Williamsburg. They found employment in clothing factories, in the fur business, and in the building trades as bricklayers, carpenters, house painters, and house wreckers. A sense of Russian identity among Jews and non-Jews was sustained by the publication of *Novoe russkoe slovo* (1910–), the oldest and most widely read Russian-language newspaper outside the homeland. The Russian Social-Democratic Society was formed in the city in 1891 and became the basis for a Russian division of the American Socialist Party. Its aggressively leftist newspaper *Novyi mir* (1911–20, 1927–38) included on its editorial staff Leon Trotsky, who resided in the Bronx in early 1917 before returning to Russia to join Lenin in leading the Bolshevik Revolution. During the "red scare" of 1919–20 Russian immigrants were generally assumed to be communist agitators, and many were arrested and deported.

In the early decades of the twentieth century the city was a center of religious activity for Russians of various faiths. It became the headquarters of the Russian Orthodox Church in North America in 1905, and the headquarters of all three groups into which the church split as a result of political changes in Russia (the Metropolia, later the Orthodox Church in America; the Moscow Patriarchal Exarchate; and the Russian Orthodox Synod Abroad). Among the earliest and largest organizations was the Russian Orthodox Christian Immigrant Society of North America (1908), which for many years occupied a five-story building on East 14th Street and provided shelter and social services to immigrants. Basic and advanced adult education was available through the Russian Collegiate Institute (1919), the Russian Technical Institute (1920), and the Russian–American Technicum (1924). The Russian Student Fund (1921) provided assistance to students in American colleges and universities.

A second group of Russians settled in the city during the early 1920s and was largely made up of political exiles forced out of their country during the Bolshevik Revolution. Many of these immigrants were professionals (lawyers, doctors, engineers, professors), businessmen, clergymen, performing artists, and wealthy aristocrats. While some of the professionals were able to retrain themselves and continue their work, others worked as taxi drivers, watchmen, and house painters, and in retail sales; the more enterprising became restaurant managers, shop owners, and hotel managers. The best-known existing landmark from this period of immigration is the Russian Tea Room on 57th Street in Manhattan. Russians who settled in New York City in the late 1940s and early 1950s included refugees from the Bolsheviks who had spent the interwar years in Europe, as well as "displaced persons" who had escaped from the Soviet Union during the Second World War. Although these immigrants were from social and economic backgrounds similar to those of earlier immigrants, they found it easier to secure skilled work. Their Russian-language skills were highly valued by American and international government agencies during the cold war, and they entered professions such as interpreting, translating, and teaching. This group of immigrants launched the first Russian literary and public affairs quarterly outside Russia, *Novyi zhurnal* (1942), and formed the Association of Russian–American Scholars (1947) to promote scholarly research and publications, as well as several organizations dedicated to political change in the Soviet Union and the United States.

The popular image of Russian–Americans as communist prevailed even though many of the immigrants were fiercely anti-communist. Among the best-known Russian immigrants from these years was Alexander Kerensky, who settled in New York City in 1940, where in 1949 he formed the League to Fight for National Freedom. In the 1970s and 1980s the Soviet Union allowed many Jews to emigrate, and of these a large number settled in New York City and specifically in Brighton Beach. As Russian became the dominant language in the neighborhood and signs in the Cyrillic alphabet were hung from the façades of its shops and restaurants, Brighton Beach replaced the Lower East Side as the principal Russian neighborhood in New York City. The Society of New Russian Immigrants, an educational and cultural organization, was formed in 1975.

Of the prominent Russians who have lived in New York City many have been artists and musicians, including the composer Igor Stravinsky, the pianist Vladimir Horowitz, the choreographer and founder of the New York City Ballet George Balanchine, the sculptor Louise Nevelson, and the artistic director of the American Ballet Theatre Mikhail Baryshnikov.

Jerome Davis: *The Russian Immigrant* (New York: Macmillan, 1922)

Paul Robert Magocsi: *The Russian Americans* (New York: Chelsea House, 1989)

Paul Robert Magocsi

Russian Tea Room. Restaurant at 150 West 57th Street next to Carnegie Hall in Manhattan, opened in 1927 as a meeting place for Russian émigrés and later expanded to a full-size restaurant by its proprietor Sammy Kaye. On Kaye's death in 1967 control of the restaurant passed to his widow, Faith Stewart-Gordon, who continued to operate it into the 1990s. The décor of the restaurant is meant to evoke a Russian Christmas before the Bolshevik Revolution and includes dark green walls, samovars, and Christmas decorations. A number of films have been made there, among them Woody Allen's *Manhattan*. The restaurant's clientele has included such well-known figures as George Balanchine, Leonard Bernstein, Anita Loos, and Harold Clurman.

Rachel Sawyer

Russwurm, John B(rown) (*b* Port Antonio, Jamaica, 1 Oct 1799; *d* Liberia, 17 June 1851). Newspaper editor, abolitionist, and government official. After moving with his father to Maine he attended the Hebron Academy and graduated from Bowdoin College in 1826. He moved to New York City in the following year and helped to found *Freedom's Journal*, the city's first black newspaper, which he published first with Samuel Cornish and from late 1827 by himself. His despair over what he saw as the grim future of blacks in the United States led him to accept a position in the Liberian department of education in February 1829, a decision that caused a scandal among blacks in the city.

Graham Hodges

Rustin, Bayard (*b* West Chester, Penn., 17 March 1912; *d* New York City, 24 Aug 1987). Civil rights activist. He was brought up as a Quaker and embraced communism during the 1930s before turning to socialism during the 1940s. After being imprisoned for refusing to serve in the Second World War he devoted himself to pacifism and was an aide to Martin Luther King Jr. from 1955 to 1960. He helped to organize successful demonstrations, including a march on Washington that drew 200,000 participants in 1963 and a school boycott in New York City on 3 February 1964 involving 464,000 students. Believing that the oppression of blacks was due primarily to economic injustice rather than racial prejudice, he sought to form a coalition led by blacks, white liberals, and workers. He favored cooperation with the federal government and supported the domestic and international policies of President Lyndon B. Johnson, including the Vietnam War. For his approach to these issues he was criticized by many black activists including black nationalists, whom he steadfastly opposed; he later maintained that their criticism was also due to his homosexuality. Rustin lived for many years in Chelsea. At the end of his life he was a director of the A. Philip Randolph Institute, an organization devoted to education, civil rights, and labor. In 1983 Bayard Rustin High School for the Humanities opened at 351 West 18th Street.

Kevin Kenny

Rutgers, Henry (*b* near New York City, 7 Oct 1745; *d* New York City, 17 Feb 1830). Landholder and philanthropist. A descendant of Dutch immigrants who settled in New York City in 1636 and prospered as brewers, he graduated from King's College in 1766 and became active in politics, serving in the state assembly as a Jeffersonian Republican and political ally of Aaron Burr. He was a colonel during the American Revolution and in 1811 helped raise funds for the construction of Tammany Hall. He also gave land and funds to his own Dutch Reformed church, to Presbyterian and Baptist churches, and to schools for children of the poor. He became president of the Public School Society in 1828. At the time of his death Rutgers's estate in Chatham Square was valued at more than $900,000. Queen's College in New Jersey was renamed in his honor.

Elaine Weber Pascu

Rutgers v. Waddington. A case decided in 1784 in which a state law called the Trespass Act of 1783 was overturned. The act allowed persons whose premises had been occupied by the British during the American Revolution to recover damages, and Mrs. Elizabeth Rutgers invoked its provisions in filing suit for £8000 against Joshua Waddington, a British merchant who during the war had resided in her brewery in Maiden Lane. Alexander Hamilton successfully argued for the defendant before the mayor's court that the act was a violation of the Articles of Confederation and of international law. The case helped to establish the principle of judicial review.

Julius Goebel, ed.: *The Law Practice of Alexander Hamilton*, vol. 1 (New York: Columbia University Press, 1964)

Peter Eisenstadt

Ruth, Babe [George Herman] (*b* Baltimore, 6 Feb 1895; *d* New York City, 16 Aug 1948). Baseball player. He came from a poor background and began his career in the major leagues in 1914 as a pitcher for the Boston Red Sox. To capitalize on his ability as a hitter he was shifted to the outfield so that he could play every day. He became widely known as a hitter during his career with the New York Yankees (1920–34). Nicknamed the "Sultan of Swat" and the "Bambino," he hit so many home runs that he changed the way baseball was played. For the Yankees he hit 659 of his 714 home runs; in three of his best seasons he hit fifty-four, fifty-nine, and sixty. He led his team to seven pennants and four world championships at the Polo Grounds and at Yankee Stadium (known as "the house that Ruth built" because it was made large enough to seat his many fans and designed partly to accommodate his style of hitting). His colorful personality often put him in the public eye. After joining the Yankees he always lived on the Upper West Side, for many years at the Ansonia Hotel on Broadway and 73rd Street and then successively at 345 West 88th Street, 173 Riverside Drive, and 110 Riverside Drive (at 83rd Street). Ruth is regarded by many as the greatest baseball player in history, and he remains the most celebrated figure in American sport. He is buried in Gate of Heaven Cemetery in Westchester County.

Robert W. Creamer: *Babe* (New York: Simon and Schuster, 1974)

Marshall Smelser: *The House That Ruth Built* (New York: Quadrangle, 1975)

Lawrence S. Ritter and Mark Rucker: *The Babe: A Life in Pictures* (New York: Ticknor and Fields, 1988)

Lawrence S. Ritter

RWDSU. See Retail, wholesale and department store union.

Ryan, Thomas Fortune (*b* Lovingston, Va., 17 Oct 1851; *d* New York City, 23 Nov 1928). Businessman. Orphaned and impoverished as a youth, he arrived in New York City in 1870 and formed an investment syndicate that dominated the transportation franchises in the city through the Metropolitan Traction Company (formed in 1886, reorganized in 1902 as the Metropolitan Securities Company). Essentially he consolidated the city's various street railway firms into a single entity. He also controlled the State Trust Company, investigated in 1900 by banking authorities, and the Equitable Life Assurance Company, investigated in 1905 by the state legislature of New York. After withdrawing from the Metropolitan Traction Company in 1906 he became embroiled in many legal actions when it was placed under receivership in the following year: among these was an investigation by the Public Service Commission into charges of bribery, overcapitalization, and fraudulent accounting. He was also a founder of the American Tobacco Company, dissolved as a monopoly in 1911 by the U.S. Supreme Court. Ryan was best known during his life for his colossal personal wealth and his questionable business practices but was perhaps more influential for having developed the holding company. He lived at 60 5th Avenue and had a country house in Sulfern, New York.

Robert T. Swaine: *The Cravath Firm and Its Predecessors, 1819–1947* (New York: Ad Press, 1946)

Theresa Collins

Ryan, William F(itts) (*b* Albion, N.Y., 28 July 1922; *d* New York City, 17 Sept 1972). Congressman. After working as a lawyer in New York City he was elected to the U.S. Congress in 1960 from the West Side, the first reform Democrat elected to public office from the city. Labeled a radical and a firebrand by opponents, he remained in office for six terms and consistently worked for civil rights, peace, social justice, and the environment. His first vote was to end funding for the House Un-American Activities Committee. Ryan was one of the first elected officials to speak out against the Vietnam War and in 1964 went to Mississippi at great hazard to investigate the disappearance of three civil rights workers. In 1965 he was an unsuccessful mayoral candidate. Having won renomination in 1972 against Bella S. Abzug, whose own congressional seat had been eliminated by redistricting, he died before the general election.

Andrew Wiese

S

Saatchi and Saatchi. Advertising agency formed in 1970 in London by the brothers Charles Saatchi and Maurice Saatchi. Soon known for its innovative advertising copy, it was perhaps even better known for its acquisition of several agencies in New York City, including Compton Communications (1982), Dancer Fitzgerald Sample (1986), Backer and Spielvogel (1986), and Ted Bates (1986). It was the largest advertising firm in the world by 1986. In the late 1980s huge debts and a worldwide decline in advertising revenues forced the Saatchis to sell off assets and entrust management of the firm to an outsider, Robert Louis-Dreyfus. In 1990 Saatchi and Saatchi was the world's second-largest advertising agency, with $11,900 million in billings. Its offices in New York City are at 375 Hudson Street.

Ivan Fallon: *The Brothers: The Saatchi and Saatchi Story* (Chicago: Contemporary, 1989)

George Winslow

Sadlier, Mary Anne Madden (*b* Cootehill, Ireland, 31 Dec 1820; *d* Montreal, 5 April 1903). Novelist. She wrote more than sixty popular novels depicting the lives of poor Irish immigrants in America and especially New York City. Her characters typically rise to success while remaining faithful to the religion and traditions of the old country. She also translated many religious works. Her husband, James, was a founder of the book publishers William H. Sadlier.

John T. Ridge

Sage [née Slocum], **(Margaret) Olivia** (*b* Syracuse, N.Y., 8 Sept 1828; *d* New York City, 4 Nov 1918). Philanthropist. She worked as a schoolteacher in Syracuse, New York, and moved to New York City when she married the financier Russell Sage in 1869. On the death of her husband in 1906 she inherited $65 million but continued to live modestly on 5th Avenue near what is now Rockefeller Center. At the age of seventy-seven she embarked on a career in large-scale philanthropy: in 1907 she formed the Russell Sage Foundation, to which she ultimately donated more than $15 million. Her giving totaled more than $80 million, much of it going to New York City and the Northeast.

Melissa A. Smith

Sage, Russell (*b* Oneida, N.Y., 4 Aug 1816; *d* Lawrence, near Cedarhurst, N.Y., 22 July 1906). Financier. Successful in business as a young man, he was elected to Congress as a Whig in 1852 and later joined with Jay Gould in building the railroads. After moving to New York City he helped to make "puts" and "calls" popular on the stock market. Shrewd and conservative, he lent money on an immense scale and amassed a fortune worth $70 million; most of it was given by his wife, Olivia Sage, to such charities as the YMCA, the YWCA, Women's Hospital, the American Museum of Natural History, and the Metropolitan Museum of Art, and to the Russell Sage Foundation, which she organized in 1907.

James E. Mooney

sailing. Boats were first sailed and raced for pleasure in New York City in the mid 1830s. About this time the first boats intended specifically for pleasure were made in the city, which soon became the national center for the sport. In 1844 the well-known sportsman John Cox Stevens and eight fellow enthusiasts formed the New York Yacht Club. From its inception the annual regatta held by the club attracted large crowds of spectators and considerable press coverage, largely because of the high social standing of the participants. Most sailing enthusiasts were men from old, wealthy families, including the founders of the club, George L. Schuyler, Hamilton Wilkes, and John C. Jay. In 1851 George Steers of William H. Brown's boatyard (at the foot of 12th Street, on the East River) built for a syndicate of club members the *America*, which had an innovative design that marked a new era in yacht construction. After the victory of this yacht in the Royal Yacht Squadron Cup in 1851 the sport enjoyed a heightened status: although remaining beyond the means of the average New Yorker it aroused the interest of the newly wealthy industrial class, including members of the Bennett, Gould, and Vanderbilt families. The Union Boat Club was formed in 1852 at the basin at Hamilton Avenue and the Gowanus Canal and in 1861 was renamed the Brooklyn Yacht Club.

The growth of yachting ceased during the Civil War but resumed soon after the war ended, when several clubs were established, including the Atlantic Yacht Club in Brooklyn (1865) and the Columbia Yacht Club at 86th Street on the Hudson River (1867). In 1866 the New York Yacht Club sponsored the first transatlantic race, in which three boats set sail from Sandy Hook, New Jersey, with much fanfare and press coverage. This race and the controversial challenge by yachtsmen from Britain for the America's Cup in 1870 brought sailing to a height of popularity in the city. Although the New York Yacht Club remained the most influential yachting organization there were also many others, among them the Harlem Yacht Club at 123rd Street on the Harlem River (1883), the Corinthian Yacht Club in Tompkinsville (1886), the Canarsie Yacht Club on Sands Bay Point (1887), and the City Island Yacht Club at the eastern end of Cross Street (1905). Public interest in sailing diminished in the late nineteenth century and the early twentieth with the rise of baseball and other spectator sports but revived in later years. The Mayor's Cup was established in 1967 and gained the sponsorship of the South Street Seaport Museum; only yachts built before 1960 were made eligible, with most entrants residing in greater New York. In 1984 the Harbor Festival Foundation sponsored the first Liberty Cup, which evolved into an annual race in New York Harbor attracting competitors from around the world. The Manhattan Yacht Club, formed in 1987 at 207 Front Street, became the sponsor of various races in New York Harbor. The America's Cup continued to be regarded as the most prestigious event in the sport and made New York City an international capital of sailing competition. The New York Yacht Club, long influential in the development of sailing in the United States, remained the preeminent yacht club in the country.

Douglas Phillips-Birt: *The History of Yachting* (New York: Stein and Day, 1974)
John Parkinson Jr.: *The History of the New York Yacht Club* (New York: New York Yacht Club, 1975)
Melvin L. Adelman: *A Sporting Time: New York City and the Rise of Modern Athletics, 1820–1870* (Urbana: University of Illinois Press, 1986)

Joseph S. Lieber

Sailors' Snug Harbor. Retirement home formerly in Livingston in Staten Island. It was created by a bequest of Robert Richard Randall (*d* 1801), a resident of Manhattan who made a fortune in the maritime industry, as a home where care would be provided for "aged, decrepit, and worn-out sailors." The trustees of the bequest, who included the rector of Trinity Church and the minister of the First Presbyterian Church, funded the project by leasing twenty acres (eight hectares) of farmland left by Randall at Washington Square North and 5th Avenue. In 1831 the home opened with twenty-seven residents, and by 1900 it housed one thousand. It was one of the best-funded eleemosynary institutions in the United States and an innovator in care for the aged. The years after the Second World War saw a gradual decline in enrollment, and legal battles with the New York City Landmarks Commission caused the property to be sold to New York City in 1975. The home was moved to Sea Level, North Carolina, where there were 150 residents in the mid 1990s. Its former site in Snug Harbor was taken over by the Snug Harbor Cultural Center in 1976.

Barnett Shepherd: *Sailors' Snug Harbor, 1801–1976* (New York: Snug Harbor Cultural Center / Staten Island Institute of Arts and Sciences, 1979; repr. 1994)

Barnett Shepherd

St. Albans. Neighborhood in southeastern Queens, bounded to the north by Hollis Avenue, to the east by Springfield Boulevard, to the south by Merrick Boulevard, and to the west by Farmers Boulevard. A syndicate of developers from Manhattan bought the Francis farm on Linden Boulevard in 1892 and laid out streets and building lots. A railroad station opened along Linden Boulevard on 1 July 1898, and a post office was built in April 1899, when the population stood at six hundred. The section of Linden Boulevard beyond the railroad station was paved in July 1912. The Lenox Development Company in 1916 promoted a tract now covering thirty-five blocks east of Farmer's Boulevard on 195th and 196th streets and 115th Road. The St. Albans Golf Club opened in 1919 for residents along Merrick, Linden, and Baisley boulevards. Between 1924 and 1926 a few hundred small one-family houses were built by several firms, including Blattmacher–Porth, Richmond Homes, St. Albans Gardens Homes, and Mezik Homes. Addisleigh Park was developed overlooking the golf course in 1926 by the Burfrey Realty Company: its half-timbered and stucco houses stood on lots forty by a hundred feet (twelve by thirty meters) and each sold for $13,000 or more. Development slowed during the 1930s as land was used up and the Depression worsened. The golf course closed during the Second World War and became the site of a large naval hospital that was eventually converted by the Veterans Administration into an extended care center. During the 1940s the population became more ethnically diverse as Lena Horne, Count Basie, Fats Waller, Roy Campanella, and other prominent blacks bought property in Addisleigh Park nearby, and the neighborhood was racially integrated in the 1950s and 1960s. Apartment buildings were built nearby, among them Merrick Park Gardens (1952) and the Addisleigh (1960). In the early 1970s St. Albans became almost exclusively black. A large number of black immigrants settled in the neighborhood and its environs during the 1980s, almost half from Jamaica and the rest from Haiti, Guyana, Trinidad and Tobago, and the United Kingdom. The economic status of the neighborhood is middle class and the character suburban.

Vincent Seyfried

St. Bartholomew's Church. Name given to several Episcopal churches occupied successively by a congregation established in 1835 on Lafayette Place and Great Jones Street. The congregation was one of the wealthiest and most fashionable in New York City when it moved in 1872 to Madison Avenue and 44th Street. In the late nineteenth century and the early twentieth the pastors reshaped "St. Bart's" into a model "institutional church" supporting a wide range of educational and social services. In 1918 the congregation moved to a church in the Romanesque style designed by Bertram Grosvenor Goodhue on Park Avenue at 50th Street, which incorporated the portals designed by McKim, Mead and White for the church on Madison Avenue. Members of the church vestry proposed during the 1980s to raise money by replacing the Community House on 50th Street (1927) with a high-rise office tower. Their application was twice refused by the municipal Landmarks Preservation Commission, which was upheld in its decision by the U.S Supreme Court (1991). The low, spacious church of St. Bart's remains an anomaly in a neighborhood of skyscrapers.

Peter J. Wosh

St. Bartholomew's Episcopal Church (designed by McKim, Mead and White), 1994

St. Clair, Arthur (*b* Thurso, Scotland, 3 April 1736; *d* Westmoreland County, Penn., 31 Aug 1818). General and statesman. He settled in the colonies in 1757 and developed close ties with George Washington as a major in the Continental Army during the American Revolution. From 1785 a delegate from Pennsylvania to the Continental Congress, on 2 February 1787 he was elected president of the congress, which then met at City Hall in Manhattan. After the draft of the Constitution was completed on 17 September it was sent to him with a letter from Washington reviewing the principles delineated by the framers. St. Clair was appointed the first governor of the Northwest Territory in October 1787, a position he held until 1802.

Richard B. Morris: *The Forging of the Union, 1781–1789* (New York: Harper and Row, 1987)

Grai St. Clair Rice

St. Denis, Ruth (*b* Englewood, N.J., 20 Jan 1879; *d* Hollywood, 21 July 1968). Dancer. She received her professional training in New York City and worked as a "skirt dancer." Featured in 1904 by David Belasco in the revue *Madame DuBarry*, she developed an exotic dance that became known as the Radha, which she performed on a tour of Europe in 1906–7. From 1909 to 1914 she worked in New York City, where with Ted Shawn she formed Denishawn, the premier American dance company until the 1930s. Among the many dancers that trained with the company were Doris Humphrey, Martha Graham, and Charles Weidman.

Suzanne Shelton: *Divine Dancer: A Biography of Ruth St. Denis* (Garden City, N.Y.: Doubleday, 1981)

Peter M. Rutkoff, William B. Scott

St. Francis College. Catholic school at 180 Remsen Street. Originally a boys' school, it was opened in 1859 at 300 Baltic Street in Brooklyn by the Franciscan Brothers and offered instruction on all levels from elementary school to college. By 1884, when it was authorized to grant degrees, it had expanded to Smith and Butler streets. In 1902 the lower divisions split off to form St. Francis Academy. The college became coeducational with the admission of nuns in 1953; lay women were admitted from 1969. It moved in 1963 to its present site, formerly the headquarters of Brooklyn Union Gas Company. In 1992 the school had 1911 students, including 1330 who attended full time. St. Francis College is the oldest Catholic school in Brooklyn.

Gilbert Tauber

Saint-Gaudens, Augustus (*b* Dublin, 1 March 1848; *d* Cornish, N.H., 3 Aug 1907). Sculptor. The son of a French shoemaker and a working-class Irishwoman, he lived from 1848 to 1860 in lower Manhattan. He moved to 22 Washington Place in 1880, remaining there until 1890. His first public commission, *Admiral David Glasgow Farragut* (1881, Madison Square Park), was a collaboration with Stanford White that set a standard for American

Memorial to William Tecumseh Sherman by Augustus Saint-Gaudens, ca *1905*

sculptors: the first major public work in the country influenced by a French beaux-arts aesthetic, it strove for an ideal esteemed after the Civil War of integrating sculpture, architecture, and landscape to promote urban harmony. He had a studio at 148 West 36th Street from 1884 and lived at 51 West 45th Street from 1890 to 1897. Among his municipal commissions were *Robert Randall* (1884, Sailors' Snug Harbor) and *Diana* for the tower of Madison Square Garden (1894, Philadelphia Museum of Art), both with White; *Peter Cooper* (unveiled 1897, Cooper Square); and *William Tecumseh Sherman* (1903, pedestal by Charles Follen McKim; Grand Army Plaza, Manhattan). Private commissions included angels for St. Thomas Church (1877, destroyed), decorations for the mansions of Cornelius Vanderbilt II (1883, Metropolitan Museum of Art) and the publisher Henry Villard (1883, 451 Madison Avenue), tomb reliefs for the importer David Stewart (1883, Green-Wood Cemetery, Brooklyn), and bronze bas-relief portraits of many prominent New Yorkers. Saint-Gaudens drew unprecedented international attention to American sculpture, especially through his public works.

Lois G. Marcus: "Studies in Nineteenth-century Sculpture: Augustus Saint-Gaudens (1848–1907)" (diss., City University of New York, 1979)

Kathryn Greenthal: *Saint-Gaudens: Master Sculptor* (New York: Metropolitan Museum of Art, 1985)

Burke Wilkinson: *Uncommon Clay: The Life and Works of Augustus Saint-Gaudens* (New York: Harcourt Brace Jovanovich, 1985)

Michele H. Bogart: *Public Sculpture and the Civic Ideal in New York City, 1890–1930* (Chicago: University of Chicago Press, 1989)

Michele H. Bogart

St. George. Neighborhood lying on hills on the northeastern shore of Staten Island (1990 pop. 7000), bounded to the north and east by Upper New York Bay, to the south by Tompkinsville, and to the west by New Brighton. One of the hills, Fort Hill, was fortified by the British during the American Revolution, and the federal government opened a quarantine station on Bay Street in 1799. The area remained rural until the 1830s, when the section facing the Kill van Kull became a fashionable resort. Several elegant hotels were built successively on St. Mark's Place across from what was later the site of Curtis High School; the last and most imposing was the Hotel Castleton (1889; destroyed by fire in 1907). In 1868 the land occupied by the quarantine station was taken over by the U.S. Lighthouse Service. The neighborhood was considered part of New Brighton until the 1880s, when Erastus Wiman (1834–1904) consolidated local ferry lines and rail routes; he reportedly renamed the area for George Law, an investor in railroads and ferries whose land he needed for the ferry terminal. Between 1886 and 1888 Wiman offered athletic events, an illuminated fountain, and spectacular pageants at the Staten Island Amusement Company on Richmond Terrace, near the ferry slips.

St. George grew rapidly in the early twentieth century. Curtis High School, named for George William Curtis, opened in 1904 at St. Mark's Place on the corner of Hamilton Avenue. Municipal ferry service to Manhattan began in 1905. The firm of Carrère and Hastings erected several public buildings: a branch of the New York Public Library (1906) at 10 Hyatt Street; Borough Hall (1906), at Borough Place facing Richmond Terrace; and the Richmond County Courthouse (1919), at Schuyler Place on Richmond Terrace. The Staten Island Institute of Arts and Sciences (1881) moved to 75 Stuyvesant Place in 1918 (where it now oversees the Staten Island Museum). In 1936 the lighthouse service was taken over by the U.S. Coast Guard, which operated the facility on Bay Street until moving to Governors Island in 1967. The opening of the Verrazano Narrows Bridge in 1964 and of the Staten Island Expressway led to development of the interior and the decline of the neighborhood. Commercial property remained vacant and important institutions moved out.

The most densely developed neighborhood on Staten Island, St. George faces many problems, including homelessness. Nonetheless it remains the center of government and transportation for the borough. It has terminals for buses and Staten Island Rapid Transit as well as one for the Staten Island Ferry. A few blocks uphill from the terminal is an area of small businesses and government buildings, among them the Richmond County Family Courthouse (Richmond Terrace between Wall Street and Hamilton Avenue), the 120th Precinct of the New York Police Department, a building of the New York City Department of Health, and a federal building at 95 Bay Street that houses offices of the Federal Bureau of Investigation and the Internal Revenue Service. In the mid 1990s the waterfront, which commands fine views of Manhattan, was to be redeveloped: there were plans for a large ferry repair facility as well as a public esplanade on the former property of the coast guard. Fort Hill is residential, with housing consisting of apartment buildings and older one- and two-family houses. The population is economically and racially diverse; many residents are young professionals who work in Manhattan.

William T. Davis and Charles W. Leng: *Staten Island and Its People: A History, 1609–1929* (New York: Lewis Historical Publishing, 1930)

Carol V. Wright

St. George Hotel. A hotel erected in Brooklyn Heights in 1884 by Captain William Tumbridge. By 1930 it comprised eight buildings bounded by Hicks, Henry, Clark and Pineapple streets, contained 2632 rooms (the most of any hotel in New York City), and had a grand ballroom, an indoor saltwater swimming pool, and a rooftop for dining and dancing. The hotel's busiest years were during and just after the Second World War because of the city's role as a port of embarkation. In the 1980s the St. George was in decline and the owners converted two wings into cooperative residential units.

Stephen Weinstein

St. George's Episcopal Church (i). Episcopal church at 16th Street and Stuyvesant Square, formed as a chapel of Trinity Church in 1752 and made independent in 1811. From early on it emphasized the Protestant nature of the Episcopal church. Under the leadership of William Rainsford (1850–1933) it was a leader at the end of the nineteenth century in the institutional-church movement, offering such services to the community as sewing classes, soup kitchens, and fitness and health programs. The financier J. P. Morgan was for decades its most influential parishioner. In the mid 1970s it formed a united parish with Calvary Church and the Church of the Holy Communion; the building continued to be used for worship services.

Robert Bruce Mullin

St. George's Episcopal Church (ii). Church built in 1746 in Flushing, an area where Quakers were heavily concentrated but where Episcopal services were held from 1704. During the nineteenth century the parish maintained vital Sunday schools and established important educational institutions, including the Academy (1803) and the Flushing Institute (1828). Later St. George's moved to a Gothic Revival church known for its grand interior (1854, on Main Street between

St. George's Episcopal Church (i) (designed by Otto Blesch and Leopold Eidlitz) and Stuyvesant Square, 1905

38th and 39th avenues). Parishioners undertook ambitious missionary work and helped to establish Episcopal churches in Bayside, College Point, Whitestone, Queens Village, and Fresh Meadows. In the late 1980s they organized a ministry program for the growing Chinese community in Flushing.

Peter J. Wosh

St. James Cathedral. Roman Catholic cathedral church of the Diocese of Brooklyn, at 250 Cathedral Place, built in a neo-Gothic style by Catholic laymen under the leadership of Peter Turner and dedicated by Bishop John Connolly in 1823. It is the oldest church in the Diocese of Brooklyn, the third-oldest Catholic church in New York City, and the sixth-oldest Catholic church in New York State. When the Diocese of Brooklyn separated from the Archdiocese of New York in 1853 St. James became its procathedral. The first bishop to administer the cathedral was John Loughlin, who served from 1853 to 1891.

Margaret M. McGuinness

St. James Hotel. Luxury hotel built during the 1860s at 26th Street and Broadway. It was one of several elegant hotels, including Astor's 5th Avenue Hotel, the Grand, and the Gilsey, that were clustered near Madison Square, then the city's most fashionable district. As late as the 1890s the St. James catered mostly to personages of the local theaters.

Andrew Wiese

St. John's Evangelical Lutheran Church. Church at 79–83 Christopher Street between 7th Avenue and Bleecker Street; it is built of painted brownstone and metal in a Romanesque style and has a cupola in a Federal style. Completed in 1821 for the congregation of the Eighth Presbyterian Church, it was sold in 1857 to St. John's Evangelical Lutheran Church, a German Lutheran congregation organized in 1855.

Alana J. Erickson

St. John's Park. Former neighborhood in Manhattan, bounded to the north by Laight Street, to the east by Varick Street, to the south by Beach Street, and to the west by Hudson Street. It was developed in the early nineteenth century in the area around St. John's Chapel (built 1804, demolished 1918–19), in a speculative venture directed by the vestrymen of Trinity Church and modeled after the fashionable neighborhoods found in the residential parks of London. About 1807 it became referred to as Hudson Square, and during the 1820s the neighborhood was one of the most fashionable areas of New York City. It declined during the late 1840s, and in 1866 Cornelius Vanderbilt covered much of the area with a railroad freight yard. The land was later paved over to provide access to the Holland Tunnel.

Kenneth A. Scherzer

St. John's University. Roman Catholic university opened in 1870 by the Vincentian Fathers at the request of the first bishop of Brooklyn, John Loughlin. Originally called St. John's College, under its first president, John T. Landry, it occupied a newly constructed building on Willoughby Street and Lewis Avenue in Brooklyn. The college awarded its first baccalaureate degree in 1881 and opened a separate seminary building on Lewis Avenue and Hart Street in 1891. After being chartered as a university in 1906 it added a law school (1925), a college of pharmacy (1929), and a downtown division on Schermerhorn Street (1929). In 1936 the school purchased the disused Hillcrest Golf Club in Jamaica and in 1954 it began construction of a new campus, completed in 1956. It assumed control of Notre Dame College of Staten Island in 1971 and closed the school on Schermerhorn Street. In the mid 1990s St. John's had more than 21,000 students, the largest enrollment of any Roman Catholic university in the United States, and the lowest tuition of any private university in the state. It had eleven colleges and institutes offering degrees in more than sixty undergraduate and thirty graduate subjects. The school is well known for its basketball team, the Redmen, a frequent contender in the athletic conference known as the Big East and in the annual tournament of the National Collegiate Athletic Association.

Frederick Ernst Hueppe: *"The Radiant Light": A History of Saint John's College* (New York: C. H. Helmken for St. John's University, 1956)

Bernadette McCauley

St. Joseph's College. Four-year Catholic college, opened in 1916 at 286 Washington Avenue in Brooklyn as a women's college by the Sisters of St. Joseph. It moved to 245 Clinton Avenue in 1918 and became coeducational in 1970; a branch campus opened in Patchogue, New York, in 1979. In 1992 there were 860 students enrolled at the main campus, nineteen hundred at the branch. The college has a predominantly lay faculty and offers preprofessional programs in business, education, law, and health administration.

Gilbert Tauber

St. Luke's Hospital. Private hospital formed by Episcopalians in 1858. It stood at 5th Avenue and 54th Street before moving in 1896 to 113th Street and Amsterdam Avenue, where it occupied five buildings. Additions to the hospital were built in 1906 and 1933. At the request of the U.S. Army in January 1942 it collaborated with Roosevelt Hospital in planning a field hospital with 750 beds called the Second Evacuation Hospital; this was deployed five miles (eight kilometers) from Omaha Beach in Normandy on 17 June 1944. The hospital became affiliated with the College of Physicians and Surgeons at Columbia University in the early 1950s, expanded in 1954 and 1957, and entered into an affiliation with Women's Hospital in 1965. Throughout the 1970s it responded to the changing needs of the community by expanding its clinic programs and its emergency room facilities. It also became well known for its research and for such medical innovations as the first open-heart surgery in New York City. The hospital merged with Roosevelt Hospital in 1979 to form St. Luke's–Roosevelt Hospital Center.

John Petit West: *Surgeons and Surgery: St. Luke's Hospital* (New York: Woodhaven, 1978)

Andrea Balis

St. Luke's–Roosevelt Hospital Center. Hospital formed in 1979 by the merger of two of the oldest and largest hospitals in New York City. It serves the West Side of Manhattan from 34th Street to 142nd Street. The merger of St. Luke's Hospital and Roosevelt Hospital made it possible to consolidate some services. At the time of the merger both institutions were teaching affiliates of the College of Physicians and Surgeons at Columbia University, and this function continued uninterrupted. Facilities added after the merger include the Kathryn and Gilbert Miller Health Care Institute for the Performing Arts at Roosevelt Hospital (the only full-service center for performing-arts medicine in New York City and the largest in the nation) and the largest center for AIDS at any private hospital in New York City. In the mid 1990s the hospital had 1313 beds.

Andrea Balis

St. Mark's Church in the Bowery. Episcopal parish church at East 10th Street and 2nd Avenue in the East Village. Its site, formerly occupied by Peter Stuyvesant's family chapel, is reportedly the oldest in continuous use by Christian congregations in the city. The building was completed in 1799; a steeple in a Greek Revival style was added in 1828, a Georgian interior in later years. During the mid 1960s the St. Mark's Poetry Project was established to explore aesthetic and social concerns. The interior was restored after a serious fire in 1978, and stained-glass windows in a striking abstract design by Harold Edelman were installed in the balcony in 1982. St. Mark's in the Bowery is the second-oldest church in the city, after St. Paul's Chapel. The churchyard contains Stuyvesant's grave.

Memorial of St. Mark's Church in the Bowery (New York: Thomas Whittaker, 1899)

J. Robert Wright

St. Mark's Church in the Bowery, ca *1910*

St. Michael's Church. Episcopal parish church at 99th Street and Amsterdam Avenue in Manhattan, founded in 1807. The present building, designed by Robert W. Gibson in a Byzantine Romanesque style and built of Indiana limestone with a square bell tower 160 feet (fifty meters) high, opened in 1891 and became known for its interior and its stained-glass windows by Louis Comfort Tiffany (installed mostly between 1893 and 1900, restored 1989–90). The seven lancet windows in the chancel (1895), which depict the victory of St. Michael in Heaven, are widely considered Tiffany's ecclesiastical masterpiece in glass. St. Michael's grew under the direction of its rector Frederick Hill during a period of recovery on the Upper West Side that began about 1980.

J. Robert Wright

St. Moritz Hotel. Hotel at 50 Central Park South, on the east side of 6th Avenue. Designed by Emery Roth and built by the Harper organization (representing Harris H. Uris and Percy Uris), it was completed in October 1930, stands thirty-eight stories tall, has one thousand rooms, and is named for the resort in the Swiss Alps. Chase described the hotel as "a picturesque cliff, amidst towering trees to the north and other soaring skyscrapers to the south." The Bowery Savings Bank took over the hotel in 1932 and then sold it to the Engadine Corporation, led by S. Gregory Taylor. In 1950 the hotel completely redecorated and redesigned its rooms, and from the following year it housed the Café de la Paix, said to be the first sidewalk restaurant in New York City. The hotel also houses Rumpelmayer's, a well-known tea and pastry shop decorated by the German–American interior designer and artist Winold Reiss. In 1990 the hotel became operated by Interstate Hotels Corporation, based in Pittsburgh.

W. Parker Chase: *New York: The Wonder City* (New York: Wonder City, 1931)
Steven Ruttenbaum: *Mansions in the Clouds: The Skyscraper Palazzi of Emery Roth* (New York: Balsam, 1986)

Allen J. Share

St. Nicholas Kirche. The first German Catholic church in New York City, founded in 1833 on East 2nd Street by Johann Stephen Raffeiner, a wealthy Austrian priest. In 1842 he abandoned the parish because of disputes with the congregation; in the same year the church was formally recognized by the diocese. Raffeiner's successor Gabriel Rumpler, appointed by Bishop John Hughes, left in 1844 after battling church members and trustees to form the Most Holy Redeemer Church on East 3rd Street. This became the leading German Catholic church in the city and St. Nicholas Kirche declined in importance.

Stanley Nadel

St. Nicholas Magazine. Monthly children's magazine launched by Roswell Smith of the publishing house of Charles Scribner in November 1873. It became highly successful under its first editor, Mary Mapes Dodge, who assembled a staff of illustrators that included Palmer Cox, Arthur Rackham, Reginald Birch, and Thomas Nast and attracted contributions from leading writers, including stories by Louisa May Alcott and Rudyard Kipling (later published as *The Jungle Book*), as well as Mark Twain's *Tom Sawyer Abroad*, which it serialized. In 1880 Smith formed the Century Company to publish the most popular selections from the magazine as books; in 1884 Theodore Low De Vinne, one of the city's finest printers, was engaged to work for both the magazine and Century. At Dodge's death in 1905 William Fayal Clarke, a member of the staff for many years, was chosen to replace her. He successfully continued her policies but the magazine fell into decline after he resigned in 1927. *St. Nicholas Magazine* left the city after being sold in 1930 and ceased publication in June 1943.

Alice M. Jordan: "Good Old St. Nicholas and Its Contemporaries," *From Rollo to Tom Sawyer* (Boston: Horn Book, 1948), 131–43

Michael Joseph

St. Nicolas Hotel. Hotel built in 1853 at Spring Street and Broadway. Constructed of white marble, containing six hundred rooms, and employing more than three hundred servants, it was one of the world's largest hotels and eclipsed the Astor House as the most luxurious hotel in New York City. Even as the wealthy gradually moved north of Houston Street the hotel continued to attract exclusive guests and residents, largely because of the Crystal Palace Exhibition of 1853, and the increasing cost of private homes and servants. During the draft riots of 1863 Mayor George Opdyke abandoned City Hall for more commodious headquarters in the hotel.

Andrew Wiese

St. Patrick's Cathedral, 1923

St. Patrick's Cathedral. Roman Catholic cathedral church of the Archdiocese of New York, on 50th Street and 5th Avenue in Manhattan. It was built by the architect James Renwick during the administration of Archbishop John Hughes. Although it was estimated that building the cathedral would take eight years when work began in 1859, the project took much longer because of its interruption by the Civil War. During construction St. Patrick's Old Cathedral on Prince and Mott streets was destroyed by fire (1866) and then rebuilt and rededicated by John Cardinal McCloskey (1868), who also dedicated the new cathedral on its completion on 25 May 1879; the final cost of construction was $1.9 million. McCloskey appointed William Quinn, vicar of the archdiocese, as the first pastor of the new cathedral. The archbishop's house and the rectory were added from 1882 to 1884 and the school opened in 1882. Major additions to St. Patrick's were completed under Archbishop Michael Corrigan. The building of the spires was begun in 1885 at a cost of $200,000. Funds for building the Chapel of St. John were donated to the cathedral by Corrigan, who also began construction of the Lady Chapel in 1901, completed during the tenure of John Cardinal Farley. In 1945 the exterior of the cathedral was renovated extensively at a cost of more than $3 million. Later improvements included the great rose window, bronze doors on the 5th Avenue side of the cathedral, and an elevator to the choir loft. The cathedral was visited by Popes Paul VI (1964) and John Paul II (1979). Wakes were held there for Senator Robert F. Kennedy, Governor Alfred E. Smith, and Prime Minister Jan Ignace Paderewski of Poland. St. Patrick's Gothic exterior is four hundred feet (120 meters) long and 174 (fifty-three meters) wide and seats about 2400. The parish is bounded by 59th Street, 3rd Avenue, 44th Street, and 7th Avenue and encompasses 302 city blocks.

Leland A. Cook: *St. Patrick's Cathedral* (New York: Quick Fox, 1979)

Margaret M. McGuinness

St. Patrick's Day Parade. The first St. Patrick's Day parade in New York City was held in 1766 by Irishmen in a military unit recruited to serve in the American colonies. Military units continued to organize the parade each year until after the War of 1812, when local Irish fraternal and beneficial societies began sponsoring the event. In the early nineteenth century the parade was a relatively simple affair in which the members of individual Irish societies joined together at their meeting rooms and moved in a procession toward St. Patrick's Old Cathedral, St. James Church, or one of the many other Roman Catholic churches in New York City. The size of the parade increased sharply from 1851, as individual societies merged under a single grand marshal. In keeping with the parade's military origins, each year a unit of soldiers marched at the head, followed by the Irish societies of the city. In the 1850s the Irish 69th Regiment (now the 165th Infantry) became the parade's primary escort unit and the Ancient Order of Hibernians its chief sponsor. Other major participants in the parade have included the thirty Irish county societies, and various Emerald, Irish-language, and Irish nationalist societies. Floats, automobiles, and exhibits are not permitted in the parade, in which more than 150,000 marchers take part each year. Attendance at the St. Patrick's Day Parade had become a tradition among politicians of various ethnic backgrounds and political leanings.

John T. Ridge: *The St. Patrick's Day Parade in New York* (New York: St. Patrick's Day Parade Committee, 1988)

John T. Ridge

St. Paul's Chapel. A "chapel of ease" completed in 1766 at Broadway and Fulton Street for Anglicans living beyond convenient walking distance of Trinity Church. It was designed by Thomas McBean in the Georgian style and often used for extraordinary ceremonies, including a thanksgiving service for George Washington on 30 April 1789 after his inauguration as president; his customary pew in the north aisle remains a popular tourist attraction. The chapel is the oldest public building in continuous use in Manhattan and sponsors daily services, ministries for travelers and business people, weekday concerts, occasional lectures, and programs for the homeless.

Peter J. Wosh

St. Peter's Church. Episcopal church in the Bronx. Its beginnings may be traced to 1693, when Episcopalians in what is now the Bronx began meeting for worship. They erected a church in 1700 and received a minister from the Society for the Propagation of the Gospel in 1702. From its establishment St. Peter's chose to follow the rites of the High Church, retaining the Anglo-Catholic sacraments and liturgical traditions. Several of its rectors became bishops, notably Samuel Seabury (1801–72). By the mid nineteenth century its wealthy congregation was concentrated in Throgs Neck. A new church in the Gothic Revival style at 2500 Westchester Avenue was designed by Leopold Eidlitz and opened in 1855. St. Peter's continued to occupy this structure into the 1990s.

Peter J. Wosh

St. Philip's Episcopal Church. Episcopal church at 134th Street off Adam Clayton Powell Boulevard, formed in 1818 by a group of blacks who separated from Trinity Church on Wall Street. Its first minister was Peter Williams Jr., whose association with the abolition movement led to an attack by an anti-abolitionist mob in 1834 that left the church partly destroyed. The oldest and among the largest black congregations of the Episcopal church in New York City, St. Philip's is noted for its commitment to providing housing for the poor.

Robert Bruce Mullin

St. Raymond's Cemetery. Roman Catholic cemetery laid out in 1856 beside the Church of St. Raymond at Castle Hill and East Tremont avenues in the Bronx. In 1877 a noncontiguous parcel of more than sixty acres (twenty-four hectares) with its main gate at Whittemore and East Tremont avenues was added; this became known as Old St. Raymond's when another noncontiguous parcel of roughly the same size with its main gate at Lafayette Avenue and East 177th Street was added in 1954. In the mid 1990s about five thousand burials a year were performed at the two newer sites. Among the well-known figures buried at St. Raymond's are Francis P. Duffy, Billie Holiday, and Typhoid Mary (Mary Mallon). The cemetery was where the ransom was delivered in connection with the kidnapping of the son of Charles A. Lindbergh.

Howard Kaplan

St. Regis. Hotel erected in 1904 at 5th Avenue and 55th Street. Designed in a beaux-arts style by Trowbridge and Livingston and containing 316 rooms in nineteen stories, it was built to replace the Waldorf–Astoria as the city's most elegant hotel. The hotel was one of the first in the city that was a skyscraper, a structure that until that time had been used primarily for offices; it was also one of the first hotels in its neighborhood, in which mansions were soon displaced by fashionable shops and businesses. Considered one of the most elegant and sophisticated buildings of its style, the hotel was designated a landmark in 1988. The St. Regis is among the most elegant and costly hotels in New York City, with prices ranging from $390 to $595 a night in 1994. Among the well-known residents have been Salvador Dali, John Lennon, and Yoko Ono.

Andrew Wiese

Sts. Cyril and Methodius. Croatian Roman Catholic church formed in 1913 by Irenej Petricak, a Franciscan priest, at 552 West 50th Street in Manhattan. It was bought, renovated, and sustained with funds donated by parishioners. Missionary sisters in 1922 joined the parish to prepare children for the sacraments and teach them folk songs, the Croatian language, and the *kolo* dance, and a church hall opened as a religious, educational, and national center. During the Second World War the church became a center of opposition to the communist government in Yugoslavia and a staunch supporter of the Croatian independence movement. From 1946 an organization known as United American Croats was based there to preserve the national culture and support the struggle for freedom. The church in 1971 set up a Croatian center at 40th Street and 10th Avenue. In 1974 it moved to larger quarters at St. Raphael's Church (502 West 41st Street) and began a biweekly radio program. The area in front of the building on 41st Street was named in honor of Aloysius Cardinal Stepinac on 10 February 1980.

After services the congregation has a meal together and discusses politics. The church has a library, a reading room, and a choir and holds many works by Croatian artists; it also runs the Cardinal Stepinac Croatian School, where children are taught the tamburica (a stringed musical instrument), dance, and folk songs. Each summer Sts. Cyril and Methodius sponsors a picnic at Hrvatska Zemija ("Croatian lands"), its park of forty-two acres (seventeen hectares) in New Jersey; barbecued lamb (*joryitina*) and a kind of spicy beef patty, *ćevapčići*, are served.

Frances Kraljic

St. Stanislaus Bishop and Martyr Parish. Roman Catholic church founded in 1872 at St. Mark's Place and 3rd Avenue on the Lower East Side. It was the mother church of later Polish congregations in New York City. In the early 1950s the parish began a steady decline as young Polish-Americans left the neighborhood. The current address is 101 East 7th Street.

James S. Pula

St. Thomas Church. Episcopal parish church at 5th Avenue and 53rd Street, formed in 1823. During the late nineteenth century parishioners first carried flowers used in the Easter service to St. Luke's Hospital (then at 5th Avenue and 54th Street), thus beginning the tradition of an Easter parade along 5th Avenue. The current building, designed in a French Gothic Revival style by the firm of Cram, Goodhue and Ferguson, was built of Kentucky limestone and consecrated in 1916. A boarding school to train choirboys was added in 1919 and in 1989 moved to a fourteen-story building for fifty students at 202 West 58th Street; in the mid 1990s this was the only school of its kind affiliated with a church in the United States. Under John Andrew, the rector from 1972, attendance on Sundays rose to about 1450. Services draw heavily on Anglican heritage. Notable features of the church include the reredos, which stands about eighty feet (twenty-four meters) tall and is pierced by three stained-glass windows, and features rows of statues centering on an empty cross, symbol of the Resurrection; the statues on the façade, completed in 1963; the chime of twenty-one bells in the great tower; and the statue of Our Lady of Fifth Avenue, dedicated by many of the city's church leaders in a joint service on 17 January 1991.

George E. Demille: *Saint Thomas Church in the City and County of New York, 1823–1954* (Austin, Texas: Church Historical Society, 1958)

J. Robert Wright

St. Vincent's Home for Homeless Newsboys. Forerunner of MOUNT LORETTO–MISSION OF THE IMMACULATE VIRGIN.

St. Vincent's Hospital and Medical Center of New York. Roman Catholic hospital in Manhattan, on the corner of West 11th Street and 7th Avenue. Opened by the Sisters of Charity of New York in 1849 on 13th Street between 3rd and 4th avenues, it housed thirty patients at the outset and seventy by 1852. The first administrator was Mary Angela Hughes, who left when she was elected superior general of the Sisters of Charity in 1855 and returned to the hospital as its head administrator in 1861. In 1856 the hospital moved into a building at its current site that had earlier housed St. Joseph's Half Orphan Asylum. Costs were defrayed through private contributions, fees from patients, and public appropriations. One of the most successful fund-raising efforts was organized by Catholic laywomen at the Crystal Palace in 1856. In 1880 a group of prominent Catholic laymen organized St. Vincent's Advisory Board; its first chairman was Eugene Kelly, nephew of Mary Angela Hughes and Archbishop John Hughes. A school of nursing, opened in 1892 with a class of eight students, was led by Katherine Sanborne, a graduate of the New York Hospital School of Nursing. St. Lawrence Hospital in the Bronx, an affiliated convalescent hospital opened in 1907, was sold to the Missionary Sisters of the Sacred Heart in 1920 and became an extension of Columbus Hospital. Additions were also made in Manhattan: the Cardinal Spellman Pavilion (1941), the Alfred E. Smith Memorial Building (1950), the John J. Rascob Building (1952), the John A. Coleman Pavilion (1983), and the George Link, Jr. Pavilion (1988).

In 1975 St. Vincent's fell under the joint sponsorship of the Archdiocese of New York and the Sisters of Charity, and in 1977 it became a teaching affiliate of the New York Medical College. Its specialties include cardiac surgery, oncology, and obstetrics. The hospital is designated a "level one" trauma center and an AIDS center by New York State, and its cystic fibrosis center is one of the largest on the east coast. The nursing school is one of few in New York State based in a hospital.

Bernadette McCauley

Saks Fifth Avenue. Firm of clothing retailers. It began in 1902 as a store on 34th Street near Herald Square opened by Andrew Saks (1847–1912), who had been born in Baltimore, worked as a newsboy and peddler in Washington, and operated men's stores in several cities. With Bernard Gimbel, a grandson of the founder of Gimbel's, his son Horace Saks agreed to a merger arrangement in 1923 under which Gimbel's bought out Saks's store; this enabled Horace Saks in 1924 to open a lavish store on 5th Avenue catering to the wealthy. On the death of Saks in 1925 Adam Gimbel became the president of the business, which he expanded according to Saks's plans. After changing hands several times the firm was bought in July 1990 by Investcorp, an investment group based in Bahrain. Saks Fifth Avenue has set a standard for elegance for generations of shoppers and remains one of the best-known retailers in the world.

Leslie Gourse

salad-oil swindle. A notorious incident that occurred in 1963, involving the securities firm Ira Haupt and Company. After accepting warehouse receipts as collateral, the firm approved loans to a salad-oil company in New Jersey for which it traded commodities futures. When futures prices for soybean and cottonseed oil declined, the firm discovered that the receipts had been forged; the salad-oil company declared bankruptcy. Ira Haupt could not repay millions of dollars in loans taken to cover the declining futures prices and was liquidated in late November by the New York Stock Exchange, which covered the losses of the firm's 20,700 customers and set up a trust fund to pay for similar liquidations in the future.

Norman C. Miller: *The Great Salad Oil Swindle* (New York: Coward–McCann, 1965)

Mary E. Curry

Saks Fifth Avenue

Salisbury, Harrison E(vans) (*b* Minneapolis, 14 Nov 1908; *d* near Providence, R.I., 5 July 1993). Newspaper editor, reporter, and essayist. He began his career in 1930 at the United Press in Minneapolis, became head of its bureau in London during the Second World War, and worked after the war as a foreign editor. He joined the *New York Times* in 1949 and reported from the Soviet Union for five years. In 1955 he won a Pulitzer Prize for a series of stories about the country, written after his return to New York City to work as a reporter for the *Times*. He was promoted to national news editor in 1962 and assistant managing editor in 1964, and in 1966 he became the first American newspaperman to report from North Vietnam, outraging Washington by reporting that contrary to official claims Vietnamese civilians had been bombed. In 1970 he became the first editor of the "op-ed" page, and after retiring from the newspaper he retraced Mao Zedong's "long march" of 1934, which became the subject of *The Long March* (1985), one of his more than two dozen books.

Michael Green

Salmagundi Club. Club formed in 1871 by a group of artists and their patrons, incorporated in 1880 as the Salmagundi Sketch Club. Its members rented a brownstone at 14 West 12th Street from 1895 until 1917, when they bought a brownstone at 47 5th Avenue (designated a national landmark in 1974). Women were first admitted in 1973. In the mid 1990s there were about six hundred members. The club holds a number of events open to the public, including exhibitions of members' work and competitions for nonmembers; it also sponsors lectures, demonstrations, and sketch classes and has a reference library. The building reputedly has the only remaining stoop on 5th Avenue.

James E. Mooney

Salomon. Firm of investment bankers. Its forerunner was a small brokerage opened on Exchange Place in the 1880s by Ferdinand Salomon, a German Jewish immigrant. The firm of Salomon Brothers and Hutzler, formed at 80 Broadway in 1910 by his sons Arthur Salomon (1990–1928), Percy Salomon, and Herbert Salomon and by Morton Hutzler, began after the First World War to trade securities of the U.S. government, which remained its chief source of income for the next fifty years. The headquarters were moved to 60 Wall Street in 1922 and by the mid 1920s Arthur Salomon was a leading financier on Wall Street, one of few who did not need an appointment to meet with J. P. Morgan. By underwriting bonds for Swift and Company in 1935 the firm was the first to break the "Wall Street strike" (the refusal of investment bankers to underwrite securities to protest regulations of the of New Deal). Among those who led the firm during the 1940s and 1950s were Benjamin Levy (1888–1966) and Rudolph Smutny (1897–1974), whose aggressive style of management led to his replacement in 1957 by William Salomon (*b* 1914).

The firm was reshaped by several men who joined it as partners in the 1950s, including Sidney Homer, Gedale B. Horowitz, Henry Kaufman (*b* 1927), John Gutfreund (*b* 1929), and William Simon (*b* 1927; later secretary of the treasury under President Gerald R. Ford). By the late 1960s the firm made "block trades" involving unprecedentedly large amounts of stock. In 1970 it moved its headquarters to 1 New York Plaza (near Battery Park City) and became known as Salomon Brothers. The firm helped to end a fiscal crisis in the city in 1975 by underwriting more than $1000 million in bonds of the Municipal Assistance Corporation. After William Salomon retired he was succeeded in 1978 by Gutfreund, who in 1981 oversaw a $550 million merger with the Phibro Corporation (a commodities firm formed in the city in 1892 by Julius and Oscar Philipp): this provided the capital that allowed Salomon Brothers to become the largest firm of securities underwriters by the mid 1980s. It took its current name in 1987. The largest brokerage house in the city, Salomon in 1991 had more than $109,000 million in assets. Its prosperity was imperiled in August of the same year by revelations that illegal bids had been made for treasury securities, leading to the resignation of some of the firm's most important officials, including Gutfreund.

James Bradley

Salomon, Haym (*b* Leszno, Poland, *ca* 1740; *d* Philadelphia, 6 Jan 1785). Patriot and financier. After moving to New York City he opened a brokerage and became a patriot. Imprisoned during the British occupation as a spy, he was released on parole to serve as an interpreter for Hessian troops, whom he encouraged to desert; after being freed he was arrested again, confined to the Provost prison, and condemned to death. He escaped to the American lines and traveled to Philadelphia, where he gave large sums to finance the patriot cause and died nearly penniless.

Laurence R. Schwartz: *Jews and the American Revolution: Haym Salomon and Others* (Jefferson, N.C.: McFarland, 1987)

James E. Mooney

saloons. On saloons generally see BARS, TAVERNS, AND SALOONS; the type of saloon offering entertainment in the nineteenth century is discussed in the entry CONCERT SALOONS.

Salvadorans. Few Salvadorans lived in New York City until a mass migration from El Salvador occasioned by a civil war that broke out in 1979. In the following years Salvadorans in the city increased in number from 7260 (federal census of 1980) to more than 100,000, many living in Far Rockaway, Jamaica, Flushing, and upper Manhattan. Unlike their forerunners in New York City, who were largely from the middle class, the newer immigrants were of the urban working class. Few were granted political asylum, though under a law passed in 1990 they were given "temporary protected status" from deportation. By the early 1990s fewer than fifteen thousand Salvadorans had acquired legal residency and most remained fearful of being deported. Like other immigrants before them many Salvadorans do unskilled work as dishwashers, factory workers, domestic workers, and carpenters. Some men travel to Long Island and Westchester County to work as landscape gardeners. Because of their long workdays Salvadorans enjoy few voluntary associations. Soccer clubs and Salvadoran restaurants called *pupuserias* offer a place for social gatherings.

Sarah Mahler

Salvation Army. Charitable organization formed in 1878 in England by William Booth (1829–1912). It began as an evangelical Christian movement for the urban working class and poor and had titles, ranks, brass bands, and uniforms modeled on those of the British military. A small corps was set up in Philadelphia in 1879, but the first authorized missionary to the United States was George Scott Railton, who disembarked at Battery Park in March 1880 with seven women "soldiers." From this time to 1905 New York City was the national headquarters of the organization. There the corps sought the spiritual salvation of the "fallen, degraded, and forsaken" at meetings held outdoors and in rented halls, where large crowds were drawn by popular tunes and hymns, parades, bands, and the testimony of the repentant. The organization focused almost exclusively on evangelism during its early years and met with some opposition. By the late 1880s it sponsored several charitable endeavors, including shelters for "fallen women" and homeless men and assistance by women members to families in slums. In 1890 large cities in thirty-five states had 410 corps. During the same year Booth published *In Darkest England and the Way Out*, which described how the organization's doctrines could be applied practically and marked the shift of the organization almost entirely toward social work.

During the next twenty-five years the Salvation Army became widely known and respected in the United States for its efficient administration of many services. At its workingmen's hotels (temporary shelters opened in the 1890s in New York City, Chicago, San Francisco, Buffalo, and Newark, New Jersey) a bed, a wash, and a meal were made available to men for eleven cents or two hours' work at the shelter or at a woodyard. These hotels inspired industrial homes, where homeless or unemployed men (often alcoholic) were employed to salvage and repair used clothing, which was resold at low prices to the poor. Rescue homes helped prostitutes and desperate women, and prison brigades helped prisoners and former prisoners. By 1895 the American branch of the organization was the largest and most successful overseas mission and had its own national headquarters at 120 West 14th Street. Booth named several of his children and their spouses national commanders in the United States. He and his son Bramwell were sometimes considered rigid and autocratic for dictating from London without understanding the needs of the army in the United States. A schism occurred in 1896, when Booth's son Ballington, national commander from 1887 to 1896, and his wife resigned to form the Volunteers of America. Booth's son-in-law Frederick Booth-Tucker became the national commander in 1896 and held the post until 1904, when Booth's daughter Evangeline took over; her tenure ended in 1934.

The First World War marked the heyday of the Salvation Army in the United States. Its "lassies" baked doughnuts, wrote letters, sewed, and provided other services for American troops in Europe. Public contributions to its welfare projects increased greatly, and eventually the organization became a beneficiary of fund drives by the Community Chest and the United Way. By the 1920s it operated twenty-six homes for unwed mothers that provided prenatal care, delivery and recovery services, infant care, and an adoption service. As the organization grew it became decentralized, and in 1920 the United States was divided into four independent territories. The tremendous extent of homelessness and unemployment during the Depression put a severe strain on resources, and the organization gradually declined in importance as its mix of services and evangelizing came to be perceived as outmoded and as the government assumed a greater role in social welfare. During the Second World War it joined with the Red Cross, the YMCA, the YWCA, and other groups to form the United Service Organizations, which provided a range of personal services to American troops. After the war the industrial homes were superseded by adult rehabilitation centers, which provided both men and women with shelter, food, clothing, medical care, psychiatric counseling, meaningful work, and vocational training, as well as practicing Christian evangelism. Rescue homes disappeared as the stigma attached to unwed mothers diminished, and the Salvation Army opened maternity and general hospitals, day-care centers, and residences for young working women. A rescue home opened in 1892 on the Lower East Side eventually became Booth Memorial Hospital and Medical Center.

In 1990 the Salvation Army had 1821 soldiers, 156 officers, and thirty-five halls in the metropolitan area, which is part of its Eastern Territory. Among the services of the Salvation Army are emergency disaster relief, aid to poor families and teenagers, housing for the elderly, and unemployment and missing persons bureaus. Because of its widely recognized social services the Salvation Army is often thought to be primarily an agency for social welfare, but it is also a Christian denomination with 1.5 million adherents in ninety nations.

William H. Tolman and William Hull: *Handbook of Sociological Information with Special Reference to New York City* (n.p.: n.pub., 1894)

Edward H. McKinley: *Marching to Glory: The History of the Salvation Army in the United States of America, 1880–1980* (New York: Harper and Row, 1980)

Clark C. Spence: *The Salvation Army Farm Colonies* (Tucson: University of Arizona Press, 1985)

Edward H. McKinley: *Somebody's Brother: A History of the Salvation Army Men's Social Service Department, 1891–1985* (Lewiston, N.Y.: Edwin Mellen, 1986)

Jane Allen

Sampson, William (*b* Londonderry [now in Northern Ireland], 17 Jan 1764; *d* New York City, 28 Dec 1836). Lawyer. Exiled from Ireland, he settled in New York City in 1806. In his law practice he often represented poor clients and was a champion of individual rights: among the cases that he argued successfully was one establishing the principle that Catholic priests should not have to divulge information revealed in confession. Sampson ridiculed excessive reliance on English common law and promoted reform and codification of the law to meet American needs. He unsuccessfully argued against English precedents in defending the Journeymen Cordwainers, a trade union indicted for conspiracy. He was also a skilled stenographer who published reports of the city's more engrossing trials. His flamboyant eloquence and whimsy in argument furthered public interest in the law.

See also Irish republicanism.

Mariam Touba

Sandy Ground. Neighborhood in southwestern Staten Island, centered at Bloomingdale Road between Rossville and Charleston. Settled in the 1830s as the first free black community in New York State and perhaps the nation, it was known as Harrisville and then as Little Africa before being given its current name because of the poor quality of its soil. Only a few descendants still live in the area. The early settlers included a few local families along with oystermen from New Jersey, Delaware, Virginia, and Snow Hill, Maryland, who were attracted by the rich oysterbeds in the area and by business opportunities not available in the South. The area was served by the Underground Railroad, and the Zion African Methodist Episcopal Church (1850) at Bloomingdale and Woodrow roads became a community center. Food crops and farm animals were kept near well-maintained homes on large plots, and relations with white neighbors were cordial. As the oysterbeds of Raritan Bay became overworked many oystermen moved their operations to the Arthur Kill; when these oysterbeds were condemned in 1916 some residents turned to well digging, ironworking, smithing, and midwifery. Homes fell into disrepair, and a fire in 1964 destroyed many dwellings. New condominiums now stand in the area. The neighborhood is listed on the National Register of Historic Places. Historic sites include a seventeenth-century private school, the home of William Pedro, who died in 1988 at the age of 106, and the Bishop Forge, the last private blacksmith shop in New York City. The Sandy Ground Historical Society was formed in 1979. Many blacks visit the area as an affirmation of their historical connection to Staten Island. Developers have proposed a number of schemes for both affordable and expensive houses in the area.

Howard Weiner

Sandy Hook. A narrow sandspit five miles (eight kilometers) long just off the New Jersey shore at the entrance to Lower New York Bay, regarded as the outer limit of the Port of New York. It resembles a fishhook curving inward from the sea and pointing toward lower Manhattan, which is seventeen miles (twenty-seven kilometers) to the north. Between Sandy Hook and Coney Island lies a broad sandbar, in some places perilously close to the surface, and large vessels must stay within the few hundred yards of the Main–Gedney Ship Channel. Only experienced harbor pilots who know the location of every sandbar may navigate large ships past Sandy Hook and into the Narrows and Upper New York Bay.

Kenneth T. Jackson

San Gennaro Festival. An annual festival held in mid September along Mulberry Street in Manhattan, organized from 1926 and perhaps earlier by a men's club and mutual benefit society of immigrants from southern Italy. The food offered at the festival has become more international as immigrants from many countries have settled in New York City and taken up the vending trade. The festival is not primarily a religious one, but a statue of San Gennaro (Januarius), the patron saint of Naples, is still enshrined on an outdoor altar to preside over the affair. There is a shrine to San Gennaro at the Church of the Most Precious Blood, 113 Baxter Street.

"Festa," *New Yorker,* 5 Oct 1957, pp. 34–36

Mary Elizabeth Brown

Sanger, [née Higgins], **Margaret (Louise)** (*b* Corning, N.Y., 14 Sept 1879; *d* Tucson, Ariz., 6 Sept 1966). Political activist. One of eleven children, she married an architect and had three children. She moved in 1910 with her family to Manhattan, where she embraced radical politics and bohemian culture and lived successively at 135th Street in Washington Street, Post Avenue near Dyckman Street (from 1914), and 14th Street between 7th and 8th avenues (from 1916). While working as a visiting nurse on the Lower East Side she saw the suffering inflicted on women by unwanted pregnancies and became convinced that it would be alleviated only by making contraceptives widely available. Defying state and federal "Comstock laws," she advocated contraception in her journal the *Woman Rebel* (1914) and published explicit information on contraceptive methods in her pamphlet *Family Limitation* (1914). She helped to coin the phrase "birth control" and with her sister Ethel Byrne, a registered nurse, opened a birth control clinic at 46 Amboy Street in Brownsville on 16 October 1916, the first in the country. It printed advertisements in English, Italian, and Yiddish and served more than four hundred women before being closed by the police on 25 October. The two were arrested and convicted of violating state laws prohibiting the distribution of contraceptives and information about them. Byrne was sentenced to thirty days in the workhouse in Blackwell's Island on 22 January 1917, Sanger to thirty days in the Queens County Penitentiary on 5 February 1917, where she gave lectures on birth control to her fellow inmates. During the same year her family moved to 236 West 14th Street. In 1918 the New York State Court of Appeals upheld Sanger's conviction but allowed physicians to prescribe contraceptives to women to cure or prevent disease.

Margaret Sanger before her hearing in the Court of Appeals in Brooklyn, 1917

After a trip to Europe Sanger formed the American Birth Control League at 104 5th Avenue in 1921 to provide education about contraception. On 13 November she attracted widespread publicity during a rally, when a riot nearly broke out after police removed her from the stage of Town Hall. She also sought the support of the city's physicians, in part by fighting for legislation giving them the exclusive right to dispense contraceptives. Sanger married J. Noah Slee, a millionaire who supported her work, in 1922 and on 2 January 1923 opened the Birth Control Clinical Research Bureau (later renamed the Margaret Sanger Bureau) at 17 West 16th Street, a facility staffed by such women physicians as Hannah Stone (1893–1941), who provided gynecological services as well as contraceptives. For some time Sanger lived in an apartment above the bureau, which gathered detailed statistics on the effects of contraceptives on women's health. At the urging of Catholic leaders the bureau was raided on 15 April 1929 by the police, who seized its confidential medical records. Outraged at this violation of the confidentiality of patients' records, the medical establishment rushed to Sanger's defense, and charges against her were dropped. She continued to promote social, economic, and medical justifications for birth control, which she argued would result in a population free of poverty, disease, crime, and insanity. Seeking the support of eugenics leaders, she advocated forced sterilization of the mentally incompetent, stressed the value of birth control for the poor, and opposed all efforts to promote increased fertility.

By 1938 Sanger was dismayed with the increasingly conservative male leadership of the birth control movement, which shifted its focus from female empowerment toward "child spacing" and infertility. She remained an active supporter of Planned Parenthood but retired to Tucson. In 1952 concerns about overpopulation and global stability led her to help form the International Planned Parenthood Federation. She also encouraged the research that led to the development of the first birth control pill.

David M. Kennedy: *Birth Control in America: The Career of Margaret Sanger* (New Haven: Yale University Press, 1970)

Linda Gordon: *Woman's Body, Woman's Right: A Social History of Birth Control in America* (New York: Grossman, 1976)

James Reed: *From Private Vice to Public Virtue: The Birth Control Movement and American Society since 1830* (Princeton, N.J.: Princeton University Press, 1978)

Ellen Chesler: *Woman of Valor: Margaret Sanger and the Birth Control Movement in America* (New York: Simon and Schuster, 1992)

Esther Katz

Sanitary Commission. See U.S. SANITARY COMMISSION.

sanitation. Colonists were responsible for disposing of their own wastes in New Amsterdam, where sanitation was not an important issue until the 1650s. In 1657 the Common Council forbade the disposal of offensive materials in the streets (including dirt and animal carcasses), established proper dumping sites, and required residents to clean the streets in front of their homes. Efforts to ban the emptying of privies in the streets were made as early as 1658 but for years remained unsuccessful. Most SEWERS were simply open or closed ditches for draining surface water; they often overflowed after becoming clogged with solid wastes and the contents of illegally

Thomas Nast's depiction of the departure of the 7th Regiment for the Civil War, 19 April 1861

finest surviving examples of American interior design of the time.

The armory remains privately owned and is a military facility for the 107th Support Group of the New York National Guard. It also houses other military organizations, a tennis club, a rifle club, and a public restaurant, presents exhibitions of art and antiques, and serves as a shelter for homeless women.

Clarence C. Buel: "The New York Seventh," *Scribner's Monthly* 20 (May–Oct 1880), 63–80

William C. Brownell: "Decoration in the Seventh Regiment Armory," *Scribner's Monthly* 22 (May–Oct 1881), 374

For further illustrations see Armories.

Lisa Weilbacker

sewers. The problems of maintaining a pure water supply and safely disposing of household and commercial wastes arose early in the history of New York City. For most of the eighteenth century kitchen slops were generally poured on the ground or emptied into cesspools, and sewage was collected in pails and dumped into the river. What is now Broad Street in Manhattan was originally a brook that was widened by the Dutch into a canal and then paved over for a road to create the city's first "common sewer," primarily designed to carry off storm water. As the city grew, a network of sewer pipes made first of wood and later of stone and brick expanded, but without a coherent plan. Criticism of the system increased during the early nineteenth century, when the city's population neared 300,000, real-estate development disrupted the island's natural drainage, backyard privies overflowed, and riverbanks became reeking cesspools. The completion of the Croton Aqueduct in the 1840s aggravated the problem by increasing the flow of water in the already overburdened sewers. Wealthy householders further contributed by installing the city's first water closets and flushing their effluent into the storm sewers.

Although some thought was given to converting sewage into fertilizer, the abundant water carried through the Croton Aqueduct made it easier to float away the city's wastes through underground pipes. Years of debate and a massive cholera epidemic that dramatized the need for improved sanitation led to the reorganization of the Croton Aqueduct Department (1849), which was given responsibility for building a comprehensive sewer system. Seventy miles (112 kilometers) of sewers were constructed in 1850–55, yet the Association for Improving the Condition of the Poor estimated that three quarters of the city's five hundred miles (eight hundred kilometers) of streets lacked sewers. The Metropolitan Health Board (1866) greatly expanded the system and by the early 1890s New York City had 464 miles (747 kilometers) of sewers, more than any American or European city except Chicago. In 1894 half the residents of the city's tenements lived in houses with flush toilets, and by 1902 the city had more than fourteen hundred miles (2240 kilometers) of sewers and most newly constructed tenements had private flush toilets.

After an elaborate system of sewer lines was constructed in New York City, the Metropolitan Sewerage Commission (1910–14) turned its attention to the problem of sewage disposal. Each day a flood of sewage from six million residents flowed directly into New York Harbor. Recommendations by the commission for a sophisticated system of collection and purification were often reiterated, but in 1930 the city was still pouring 1.3 million gallons (4.9 million liters) of raw sewage into the harbor every day. The growing urgency of the problem and the availability of public works funds during the New Deal finally led to the construction of seven sewage treatment plants, the first opening on Coney Island in 1937. When it was discovered that seven facilities could treat only about half the city's sewage in 1942, a master plan was drawn up that recommended a system of fourteen plants. The Interstate Sanitation Commission ordered the city in 1948 to hasten the pace at which the plants were being constructed. Three more plants opened in 1952, but by 1962 one quarter of the city's sewage still went untreated. The last two of the fourteen plants did not open until 1986 and 1987: North River (on the Hudson at 137th Street in Manhattan) and Red Hook (in Brooklyn). With all its plants operating the system was able to handle the nearly 1600 million gallons (6050 million liters) of sewage carried every day through 6200 miles (9975 kilometers) of pipe, but it did not end the pollution of the waters surrounding the city. Six of the largest plants operated at or above capacity in 1991, and odors emanating from the Newtown Creek plant in Brooklyn and the North River plant in Manhattan caused resentment among local residents, who argued that the facilities had been deliberately placed in poor neighborhoods. Plants with purification processes that met specific requirements continued to dump final-stage sewage precipitate at sea until 1992, when the practice was banned.

Joseph Duffy: *A History of Public Health in New York City, 1866–1966* (New York: Russell Sage Foundation, 1974)

Edward K. Spann: *The New Metropolis: New York City, 1840–1857* (New York: Columbia University Press, 1981)

Jon C. Teaford: *The Unheralded Triumph: City Government in America, 1870–1900* (Baltimore: Johns Hopkins University Press, 1984)

See also Sanitation.

Sandra Opdycke

sewing machines. New York City played a role in developing the sewing machine when Walter Hunt, a resident of the city, invented a mechanized device in 1834 that made a lock stitch with sewing thread. The region became a leading center for the manufacture of sewing machines soon after the sewing machine itself was invented in 1846 by Elias Howe of Boston. I. M. Singer formed I. M. Singer and Company in 1851 with Edward Clark, a lawyer who took charge of finances, and opened his main office in Manhattan, where production facilities were moved in the following year. Singer took out twenty patents between 1851 and 1863; with his competitors (among them several firms in the city such as Grove and Baker, and Wheeler and Wilson) he set up the Sewing Machine Combination in 1856, the first patent pool in the country, which lasted until 1877. Although his machines were the only ones that could stitch continuously they sold poorly at first, prompting Clark to launch a marketing system that was one of the most innovative in the country. The firm was one of the first to have its own distribution network and developed techniques for promoting, repairing, and financing durable goods. It both responded to the demand of the rapidly growing apparel industry in the city and persistently developed the household market: in the mid 1850s company headquarters featured lavish showrooms where sewing machines were demonstrated by young women. In 1863 the firm was renamed the Singer Manufacturing Company. The sewing machine and the availability of textiles allowed the average family to own more clothing than even the wealthy had been able to own several generations earlier. As a global market emerged Singer built factories abroad, first in Glasgow (1867) and then in Canada. The primary manufacturing operation was moved to a factory complex opened in 1873 in Elizabethport, New Jersey. By 1875 the firm was the largest manufacturer of sewing machines in the world. It moved into a building designed by Ernest Flagg and completed at 561 Broadway in lower Manhattan in 1904; the Singer Tower (also designed by Flagg) was completed at 149 Broadway in 1908.

From the 1880s many clothing factories with hundreds of sewing machines opened, as New York City solidified its position as the center of the garment industry in the United States. Specialized devices such as the buttonhole machine made manufacturing more efficient by allowing for increased division of labor and reducing the skills that each worker required. Because the sewing machine was compact and had low power requirements, it was often operated by women both in sweatshops and in the home (where work was paid for by the piece, often at exploitative rates). From the 1950s the use of the household machine declined in New York City, largely as a result of the increasing numbers of women who worked outside their homes, but the garment industry nevertheless remained dependent on the sewing machine into the 1990s.

David A. Hounshell: *From the American System to Mass Production: The Development of Manufacturing Technology in the United States* (Baltimore: Johns Hopkins University Press, 1984), 67–123

Darwin H. Stapleton

Shaarey Zedek. Conservative synagogue opened in 1839 by Polish Jews who seceded first from B'nai Jeshurun. The congregation prospered during the nineteenth century and the early twentieth and had two branches, one in a remodeled Quaker meeting house on Henry Street on the Lower East Side, the other in a building in an exuberant Moorish style on 118th Street in Harlem. Shaarey Zedek moved to the Upper West Side during the 1920s.

Jenna Weissman Joselit

Shahn, Ben(jamin) (*b* Kaunas, Lithuania, 12 Sept 1898; *d* New York City, 14 March 1969). Painter and illustrator. After settling in Brooklyn with his family in 1906 he worked for a lithographer and attended New York University and City College of New York. He left school to study at the National Academy of Design and the Art Students League, then traveled in Europe during the 1920s and returned to New York City in 1929. His series of twenty-five gouache paintings depicting the trial of Sacco and Vanzetti were exhibited at the Downtown Gallery in 1932, evoking favorable criticism, and from the same year he assisted Diego Rivera in painting a mural at Rockefeller Center (later destroyed). During the 1930s he worked as a photographer for the Resettlement Administration and as a muralist for projects sponsored by the federal government in New York and New Jersey, and during the Second World War he designed posters for the Office of War Information. Although his graphic depictions of socially relevant subjects angered many conservative politicians and critics, he was chosen to represent the United States (along with Willem de Kooning) at the Venice Biennale in 1954. In 1956–57 he delivered the Charles Eliot Norton lectures at Harvard University, which were later reprinted as *The Shape of Content.* Shahn was elected to the National Institute of Arts and Letters in 1956 and to the American Academy of Arts and Letters in 1959.

Bernarda Bryson Shahn: *Ben Shahn* (New York: Harry N. Abrams, 1972)

Patricia Hills

Shakespeare Festival. See NEW YORK SHAKESPEARE FESTIVAL.

Shalom Aleichem Houses. A cooperative housing project at Sedgwick Avenue and 238th Street in the Bronx, organized in 1927 by the Yiddishe Cooperative Heim Geselshaft (an offshoot of the Workmen's Circle). Named for the prominent Yiddish writer, the building contained artists' studios, an auditorium with a stage, meeting rooms, and housing for 240 families; many of the residents were artists, performers, and writers. The cooperative failed financially in 1929, but its members maintained the organization after the property was taken over, and they defeated the landlord's attempts to evict unemployed tenants in 1932. The residents continued to operate the meeting rooms, auditorium, cooperative kindergarten, and Yiddish schools until the 1960s.

Stanley Nadel

Shanker, Albert (*b* Queens, 14 Sept 1928). Labor leader. He grew up in New York City, attended Stuyvesant High School and the University of Illinois, and did graduate work at Columbia University. After becoming a substitute teacher in 1952 he soon took an interest in the Teachers' Guild and from 1959 worked as a union official full time. He helped to form the United Federation of Teachers (UFT) in 1960, played an important role in securing its collective bargaining election, and was elected its president in 1964. He consistently argued that as professionals teachers deserve adequate pay and the authority to make decisions, and during the 1960s and 1970s he led several strikes to secure higher wages and an effective grievance procedure. In 1968 he led the UFT in a bitter strike after nineteen school employees, including thirteen teachers, were transferred involuntarily by the Ocean Hill–Brownsville school board, which sought greater control over its staff. Charges of racism and anti-Semitism were traded, and Shanker was sentenced to fifteen days in prison for defying a court order; his position was strengthened after the teachers were reinstated, and during the 1970s he made the UFT a powerful force in politics and extended membership in it to a group of assistants to classroom teachers known as paraprofessionals. He became president of the American Federation of Teachers in 1974, continuing to lead the UFT until January 1986. In 1975 he led the UFT in a plan to save the city from bankruptcy by using pension funds to buy bonds of the Municipal Assistance Corporation. Shanker has continued his efforts to improve teachers' pay and status and the quality of education.

Philip Taft: *United They Teach: The Story of the United Federation of Teachers* (Los Angeles: Nash, 1974)

Irwin Yellowitz

shantytowns. During the 1850s a shantytown inhabited mostly by German, Irish, and black squatters covered almost the entire West Side between 65th and 85th streets. There were many shantytowns during the 1870s and 1890s throughout the city. More than twenty were built during the Depression, and these attracted a great deal of attention. Named "Hoovervilles" after President Herbert Hoover, they had about two thousand residents, most of them men, during the 1930s. The largest was the "Hard Luck Town" at 9th Street and the East River, which housed about 450 men in 1933. The best-known Hooverville, set up after the Lower Reservoir was drained to make way for the Great Lawn, was variously called "Hoover Valley," "Shanty Village," "Shack Town," "Squatters Village," and "Forgotten Man's Gulch." Twenty-two men were arrested for vagrancy in July 1931 after residents of 5th Avenue complained about the "hobos" sleeping in Central Park; a sympathetic judge suspended their sentences and sent the men back to the park after giving $2 of his own money to each one. By the autumn of 1932 there were seventeen shacks in the area, each furnished with chairs, beds, and a chimney. There was also a shack known as the "Rockside Inn," built of brick with an inlaid roof by unemployed bricklayers. One well-

"A Scene in Shantytown, New York," from the New York Daily Graphic, *4 March 1880, the first halftone photograph printed in a newspaper*

known resident was Ralph Redfield, an unemployed vaudeville performer who charged visitors a fee to watch him walk a tightrope stretched across the shantytown. His act inspired Robert Nathan's novel *One More Spring*, which was made into a motion picture in 1935 and became the basis for Al Jolson's successful musical *Hallelujah I'm a Bum*. After the Second World War public intolerance of shantytowns increased. Between the late 1980s and the mid 1990s those near Columbus Circle, Tompkins Square Park, the Port Authority Bus Terminal, the United Nations, and the base of the Manhattan Bridge were razed, forcing many of the city's 25,000 homeless to seek shelter elsewhere.

Roy Rosenzweig and Elizabeth Blackmar: *The Park and the People: A History of Central Park* (Ithaca, N.Y.: Cornell University Press, 1992)

Chad Ludington

Sharpton, Al(fred Charles, Jr.) (*b* Brooklyn, 3 Oct 1954). Minister and civil rights activist. He began preaching at the age of four, and soon began touring as the "wonder boy preacher." In 1964 he was ordained, preached at the World's Fair, and toured with the gospel singer Mahalia Jackson. In the late 1960s he became a follower of Adam Clayton Powell Jr., and in 1969 he was appointed youth director of Operation Breadbasket, a group led by Jesse Jackson for which he spent two years organizing boycotts and demonstrations to force businesses to employ blacks. In 1971 he formed an offshoot of the organization called the National Youth Movement. He met the soul singer James Brown in 1973, and for the next eight years he worked variously as the manager of Brown's singing tours and for the National Youth Movement, at the same time forging political connections in the black community of New York City. In 1978 he was an unsuccessful candidate for the state senate. He worked as a community activist in the early 1980s and first became widely known in 1987, when he led protests after the racially motivated murder of a black man in Howard Beach and served as an advisor to Tawana Brawley, a young woman whose allegations that she had been raped by white men in upstate New York became a cause célèbre; his reputation suffered when an investigation found that Brawley's charges were baseless and that he had engaged in financial impropriety. He regained notoriety when he led marches in Bensonhurst after the murder of a black man in 1989. In 1992 Sharpton mounted a campaign for the Democratic nomination for the U.S. Senate in which he cultivated a moderate image, avoided an acrimonious debate indulged in by his three opponents, and won about 15 percent of the vote. He was again a candidate for the Senate in 1994, losing the Democratic primary to Senator Daniel Patrick Moynihan.

Michael Klein: *The Man behind the Soundbite: The Real Story of Rev. Al Sharpton* (New York: Castillo, 1991)

Catherine Manegold: "The Reformation of a Street Preacher," *New York Times Magazine*, 24 Jan 1993, p. 18

Greg Robinson

Shea, William A(lfred) (*b* New York City, 21 June 1907; *d* New York City, 2 Oct 1991). Lawyer. He grew up in Washington Heights, graduated from New York University, and was admitted to the New York State bar in 1932. After several years of work for the Democratic Party in Brooklyn and for insurance companies he entered private law practice in 1941. He is best known for having restored National League baseball to New York City after the departure of the Dodgers and the Giants in 1957: his efforts led to the formation of the New York Mets in 1962, and the team's new ballpark in Flushing was named Shea Stadium in his honor in 1964. In the same year he joined with the trial lawyer Milton S. Gould to form the law firm of Shea, Gallop, Climenko and Gould (from 1979 Shea and Gould), with offices at Rockefeller Center; the firm became one of the largest and most powerful in the city before being dissolved in the mid 1990s. Although less active in his later years Shea retained an important role in his firm and took part in philanthropic activities.

James Bradley

Shearith Israel. The first Jewish congregation in North America, formed in 1654 in New Amsterdam by a small group of Sephardim from Recife, Brazil, seeking refuge from the Inquisition. The congregation was initially denied permission by both the Dutch and the British to build a house of worship; legal impediments were gradually removed and by 1729 it built its first synagogue on Mill Street, which remained in continuous use for almost a century. Shearith Israel was for many years the most important institution in the Jewish community: it supervised the preparation of kosher food, educated Jewish children, provided charity for the poor, adjudicated internal disputes, and supervised all Jewish marriages and burials. It ceased to be the city's only synagogue in 1825, when several Ashkenazim seceded to form B'nai Jeshurun after becoming disgruntled by what they considered an undemocratic system for distributing communal honors; this schism inspired the formation of twenty-seven other congregations before the Civil War. By 1833 the city's Jewish population grew and moved northward, and the synagogue moved to Crosby Street and then to 19th Street. In 1897 it moved to a building at Central Park West and 70th Street. Designed by Arnold Brunner, the new building was said to be inspired by Greco-Roman synagogues discovered in the Mediterranean basin during the late nineteenth century. In the mid 1990s Shearith Israel remained a vital center of Jewish religious life.

Jenna Weissman Joselit

Shearman and Sterling. Law firm, founded in 1873 by Thomas G. Shearman (1834–1900) and John William Sterling (1844–1918). In its early years the firm represented railroads, industrial corporations, and financial institutions, and it was involved in litigation arising from the Bolshevik Revolution. In 1994 the firm represented Viacom in its acquisition of Paramount Communications. Shearman and Sterling was the third-largest law firm in New York City in the mid 1990s, with 425 lawyers and large practices in banking, corporate, and securities law. The offices are at 599 Lexington Avenue in Manhattan.

Shea Stadium. A municipally owned stadium at Flushing Meadows–Corona Park in Queens, opened on 17 April 1964 as the new home of the New York Mets. Named for William A. Shea, a lawyer instrumental in helping New York City to regain a National League baseball team in 1962, it seats 55,101. In addition to the Mets the stadium has accommodated the New York Yankees (in 1974–75, during renovations of Yankee Stadium) and the football teams the New York Jets (1967–83) and the New York Giants (1975), and has been the site of special events including rock concerts by the Beatles in 1965 (which drew 53,275 persons) and the Who in 1982 (which drew 70,346).

Steven A. Riess

Sheeler, Charles (*b* Philadelphia, 16 July 1883; *d* Dobbs Ferry, N.Y., 7 May 1965). Painter and photographer. He began his career in Philadelphia and in 1908 exhibited his work at the Macbeth Galleries in New York City. He took part in the Armory Show (1913) and was associated with the photographer Alfred Stieglitz and the art collectors Louise and Walter Arensberg. In 1916 he began work as an assistant at Marius de Zayas's Modern Gallery, and he moved permanently to New York City in 1919. With the photographer Paul Strand he produced the film *Manhatta* (1921). Sheeler used cubist abstraction in his painting and photography and often depicted urban and industrial architecture. The crisp geometry of his work inspired other American artists known as the "immaculates," or "precisionists." The Whitney Museum of American Art owns several of Sheeler's works.

Martin Friedman, Bartlett Hayes, and Charles Millard: *Charles Sheeler* (Washington: Smithsonian Institution Press for the National Collection of Fine Arts, 1968)

Carol Troyen and Erica E. Hirshler: *Charles Sheeler: Paintings and Drawings* (Boston: Museum of Fine Arts, 1987)

Judith Zilczer

Sheen, Fulton (John) (*b* El Paso, Ill., 8 May 1895; *d* New York City, 9 Dec 1979). Bishop. Educated at St. Viator College in Illinois, the Catholic University of America, and universities in Louvain (Belgium) and Rome, he was ordained in 1919. In 1926 he moved to Washington, where he joined the faculty of the Catholic University of America. During the 1930s and 1940s his outstanding oratory made him one of the foremost Catholic priests in the United States. He often spoke from the pulpit of St. Patrick's Cathedral, and from 1951 he appeared on the popular weekly television program "Life Is Worth Living," which reached a national audience from studios in New York City. He received into the Catholic church such notable converts as the journalists Heywood Broun and Clare Boothe Luce. In 1950 he was appointed national director of the Society for the Propagation of the Faith (an agency for the funding of Catholic missionaries); he moved to New York City and in 1951 was appointed bishop. A strong-minded man of deep convictions, Sheen clashed with Francis Cardinal Spellman over the financial management of the Society for the Propagation of the Faith, leading to his virtual banishment from the pulpit of St. Patrick's Cathedral. In 1966 he was named the bishop of Rochester, New York, and began a new career as a diocesan administrator, but after three unhappy years he resigned the post, was appointed a titular archbishop, and spent his remaining years in New York City, occasionally emerging from retirement to impress audiences with his oratorical skill. He wrote *Treasure in Clay: The Autobiography of Fulton J. Sheen* (1980).

D. P. Noonan: *The Passion of Fulton Sheen* (New York: Dodd, Mead, 1972)

John Tracy Ellis: *Catholic Bishops: A Memoir* (Wilmington, Del.: Michael Glazier, 1983)

T. J. Shelley

Sheep Meadow. A clearing in Central Park between 66th and 69th streets, occupying twenty-two acres (nine hectares) of relatively flat tableland. It was set aside as a parade ground originally named the Green by the principal designer of the park, Frederick Law Olmsted, to meet a requirement imposed in 1857 that all designs for the park must include an area for military exercises. Although the National Guard used the grounds for this purpose in 1864, a state law passed later that year banned military drills in the park. The way was then clear for the introduction of a flock of 150 sheep, a crook-carrying herdsman, and a Victorian sheepfold. During the next six decades the area was also the site of such recreational activities as dancing, baseball, and lawn tennis. A cast-iron pavilion provided mineral springs to visitors from 1870. In 1934 the parks commissioner Robert Moses exiled the sheep to Prospect Park and converted the sheepfold into the restaurant Tavern on the Green. The elegant pavilion was replaced in 1961 by a conventional concession stand. During the 1960s and 1970s a succession of rallies and concerts destroyed much of the grass, reducing the area to a dustbowl. Part of the field was then fenced in, replenished with new topsoil and sod, and installed with drainage and irrigation systems. Loud noise and team sports were prohibited in 1986. The lush lawn and extraordinary skyline views of Sheep Meadow make it one of the park's most popular and picturesque attractions.

Elizabeth Barlow Rogers: *Rebuilding Central Park: A Management and Restoration Plan* (Cambridge: MIT Press, 1987)

Roy Rosenzweig and Elizabeth Blackmar: *The Park and the People: A History of Central Park* (Ithaca, N.Y.: Cornell University Press, 1992)

Robert Sanger Steel

Sheepshead Bay. Neighborhood in southeastern Brooklyn (1990 pop. 61,544), overlooking an ocean inlet of the same name to its south and bordered to the north by Marine

Sheepshead Bay, 1992

Park, to the east by Shell Bank Creek, to the south by Manhattan Beach, and to the west by Gravesend. The area was the site of a large Canarsee Indian village and remained undeveloped for more than a century and a half after the English settled Gravesend in 1645 only a short distance to the northwest. The Wycoff–Bennett residence (1766) is one of the most striking of the extant Dutch farmhouses in Brooklyn. In the early nineteenth century a cluster of wooden shacks took shape around the inlet, which provided a sheltered anchorage for small boats. Shortly after the Civil War the village began to attract visitors from the city during the summer, who were drawn by the cool sea breezes and the seafood that had become a local specialty. Although two hotels were built there was no permanent growth until 1877, when a farm of fifty acres (twenty hectares) by the bay was subdivided and developed. The same fate soon befell other farms, and by the end of the century the village had some four hundred houses served by stores, churches, and a post office. During the 1870s John Y. McKane, the notorious political "boss" of Gravesend, arranged for the extension of several railroads and boulevards to Coney Island, making the whole southern shore more accessible than it had been before. He also opened the Coney Island Jockey Club Race Track on a site of 2200 acres (one thousand hectares). This was replaced in 1915 by the Sheepshead Speedway, which was demolished in 1923; the site was then subdivided into small building lots and developed.

In 1931 the city took title to the area around the basin as the first step toward revitalizing it. Aging structures on stilts above the water were restored, and Emmons Avenue was wid-

Greenlawn Colony in Sheepshead Bay, 1992

ened. When work was completed in the summer of 1937 the *Brooklyn Eagle* characterized the renovated neighborhood as "clean, tidy and practically odorless." The character of the neighborhood changed again after 1954 as wooden houses were replaced by six- and seven-story red-brick apartment buildings for middle-income residents. By 1960 Sheepshead Bay was the fastest-growing community in Brooklyn. It became widely known as the center of recreational fishing in New York City, and a number of private boats moored at its ten piers and used it as a port from which to launch cruises for bluefish, snappers, and striped bass. In the 1980s the city announced new development plans for Sheepshead Bay that provided for the improvement of the piers, private residential and retail construction, an esplanade along Emmons Avenue, and a park and ferry landing at the foot of Knapp Street; these plans remained unrealized several years later. The population of the neighborhood in the 1980s and early 1990s was mostly Italian and Jewish, though there were increasing numbers of Asians and Caribbeans. In the neighborhood and its environs there was considerable settlement by immigrants from the Soviet Union, China, India, Pakistan, Vietnam, Israel, the Philippines, Poland, and Guyana.

Ellen Fletcher

shellfish. A great variety of shellfish inhabit the varied estuarine environments around New York City, especially the glacially created outwash plain of Jamaica Bay and the terminal moraine landscape of the northern shore of Queens and Staten Island. The many species of bivalves include the American Oyster (*Crassostrea virginica*), the Hard-shelled Clam (*Mya arenaria*), the Surf Clam (*Spisula solidissima*), the Razor Clam (*Ensis directus*), the Blue Mussel (*Mytilus edulis*), the Periwinkle (*Littorina littorea*), and the Channeled Whelk (*Busycon canaliculatum*). Other common invertebrates are the Blue Crab (*Callinectes sapidus*), the Common Spider Crab (*Libinia emarginata*), the American Lobster (*Homarus americanus*), young Sand Shrimp (*Crangon septemspinoa*), and the Fiddler Crab (*Uca pugnax*), which is usually found in salt marshes.

D. J. Zinn: *The Handbook for Beach Strollers* (Old Saybrook, Conn.: Pequot, 1975)

John T. Tanacredi

Sheridan, Martin (Joseph) (*b* Bohola, County Mayo, Ireland, 28 March 1881; *d* New York City, 28 March 1918). Track and field athlete. After emigrating to the United States in 1900 he joined the New York Police Department and became a detective. He trained at the New York Athletic Club and competed in the Olympic Games of 1904 (St. Louis) and 1908 (London), winning two gold medals, one silver medal, and one bronze; in unofficial games at Athens in 1906 he won three gold medals and two silver medals, a performance exceeding that of any national team. He competed in nine events and excelled in the shot put, discus, broad jump, long jump, pole vault, and stone and javelin throws. During a career lasting sixteen years he set sixteen world records and won twelve national championships in the United States and thirty in Canada. In 1918 the police department named for him its highest award for valor. Sheridan is buried in Calvary Cemetery.

John J. Concannon

sheriff. The sheriff of New York City executes mandates issued by city courts. Until 1943 positions as volunteer and paid county sheriffs were awarded to political supporters. Mayor Fiorello H. La Guardia consolidated the offices and created the first salaried sheriff's office in the United States subject to civil service. On 12 July 1990 the sheriff became a mayoral appointee.

Edward J. Flynn: *You're the Boss* (New York: Viking, 1947)
Richard S. Childs: "First Civil Service Sheriff," *National Municipal Review* 38 (1948)

Neal C. Garelik

Sherry Netherland Hotel. Hotel built in 1927 at 59th Street and 5th Avenue. Designed by the firm of Schultze and Weaver and containing 525 rooms in forty stories, it was erected at one of the country's most distinguished addresses as the first graceful skyscraper hotel in the area. It was largely a residential hotel, advertised as "more than a place to live — a new way of living." Like other hotels of the time the Sherry Netherland became known for its opulent interiors and elegant appointments and helped to make luxury high-rise apartments fashionable.

Andrew Wiese

Sherry's. Restaurant and apartment hotel opened in 1890 at 5th Avenue and 37th Street by Louis Sherry, the owner of a confectionery shop near the Metropolitan Opera House that expanded into a home catering service for the wealthy. A competitor of Delmonico's, the restaurant was the site of many elaborate parties, including a breakfast that followed the wedding of Consuelo Vanderbilt to the Duke of Marlborough in 1895, and a dinner given by Herbert Barnum Seeley for men only that was raided by the police because of the presence of a nude female dancer. Delmonico's soon moved uptown and Sherry followed on 10 October 1898, opening diagonally across the street from it a twelve-story restaurant and apartment hotel designed by Stanford White at the southwest corner of 5th Avenue and 45th Street. At its new site it continued to stage outlandish events, including a dinner for the New York Riding Club at which diners ate on horseback. Sherry's closed on 17 May 1919, one week before Delmonico's. The building survived for a time as the Guaranty Trust Company of New York.

Grace M. Mayer: *Once upon a City* (New York: Macmillan, 1958)
Allen Churchill: *The Upper Crust: An Informal History of New York's Highest Society* (Englewood Cliffs, N.J.: Prentice Hall, 1970)
Waverly Root and Richard de Rochemont: *Eating in America: A History* (New York: Ecco, 1976)

Rohit T. Aggarwala

Shinn, Everett (*b* Woodstown, N.J., 7 Nov 1876; *d* New York City, 1 May 1953). Painter. After beginning his career as an artist and reporter in Philadelphia he moved in 1897 to New York City, where he worked for the *New York World* and later for *Harper's Weekly*. He initially painted urban street scenes, but after a trip to Paris in 1900 he turned his attention to the theater and society in New York City. Eventually he came to prefer a realist style, which he used to depict the life of the working class. In 1908 he took part in an exhibition of The Eight at the Macbeth Gallery. He also executed murals for the Stuyvesant Theatre (1907) and the Plaza Hotel (1945) and was active as a playwright, a costume designer, and an art director for motion pictures. In 1912 he formed the Waverly Street Players, a theatrical group that performed out of his home at 112 Waverly Place in Greenwich Village. The life of Eugene Witla, the central character in Theodore Dreiser's novel *The Genius* (1915), was purportedly based on Shinn's early career.

Warren Kent: "The Versatile Art of Everett Shinn," *American Artist* 9 (Oct 1945), 8–13, 35–37

Joseph J. Kwait: "Dreiser's *The Genius* and Everett Shinn the 'Ash-Can' Painter," *PMLA* 67 (March 1952), 15–31

Edith DeShazo: *Everett Shinn, 1876–1953: A Figure in His Times* (New York: Clarkson N. Potter, 1974)

Carol Lowrey

shipbuilding. New York City was the busiest port in the world between 1830 and 1960 and long supported a vibrant shipbuilding and repair industry.

Naval vessels were first built in New York City in the 1790s. The normalization of commerce after the American Revolution led several shipbuilders including Forman Cheeseman, Samuel Ackerly, and Thomas Vail to operate yards along the East River in lower Manhattan, below Corlear's Hook; they prospered for a while but succumbed to the maritime depression that accompanied the blockade by the British before and during the War of 1812. The New York Navy Yard (later the New York Naval Shipyard, popularly the Brooklyn Navy Yard) opened in 1806, and the navy's first steam warship, named *Demologos*, was built there in 1814 by Adam and Noah Brown with machinery provided by Robert Fulton. Shipbuilding flourished after the War of 1812, and as trade expanded, new shipyards opened and many of the established yards moved north, some as far as 14th Street. Until the end of the Civil War more than thirty shipbuilders were active along the East River, among them the firms of Adam, Noah, and Charles Brown(e); Henry Eckford; Christian Bergh; Jacob A., Daniel, and Aaron Westervelt; Isaac and William H. Webb; Stephen Smith; Jeremiah Simonson; Rosevelt and Joyce; Smith and Dimon; and Brown and Bell. In the first half of the nineteenth century there were many well-known shipyards on the eastern bank of the East River at Greenpoint, Williamsburgh, and Brooklyn, including those of C. and R. Poillon; Perrine, Patterson and Stack; Eckford Webb (brother of William H. Webb); Jabez Williams; and Henry Steers. A number of small shipyards also operated on Staten Island in Tottenville and along the Kill van Kull, and in Hoboken and Jersey City, New Jersey.

Ships were continually launched into local waters to carry cargo from the city and to transport passengers from Europe. Many shipbuilders built ferries and steamboats for inland transport, among them George, Thomas, and William Collyer, John Englis and Son, Devine Burtis, Lawrence and Foulks, and Samuel Sneden. In 1851 William H. Brown built in his shipyard at the foot of 12th Street on the East River the schooner yacht *America*, designed by George Steers, for which the America's Cup was named. The best-known naval vessel built in New York City was John Ericsson's *Monitor*, outfitted at the Continental Iron Works in Greenpoint in 1862 and provided with machinery by Delamater. The most renowned shipbuilder in the city was William H. Webb (1816–99), who in 1840 took over the business of his father, Isaac. His yard, one of the largest in the city, extended from East 5th Street to East 7th Street and employed about four hundred men during its peak years in the early 1850s; three vessels could be built there simultaneously. Webb is best remembered for his clipper ships *Challenge*, *Young America*, and *Comet*; he also built the immense ironclad *Dunderberg*, launched in 1865 for the U.S. Navy and later sold to France. The packet *Charles H. Marshall*, completed by Webb in 1869, was the last square-rigged sailing ship built in New York City.

Early shipyards for building wooden vessels were little more than open waterside areas in which hulls could be erected and launched, and spars and rigging installed. A shipyard included a mold loft, a blacksmith's workshop, offices, warehouses, and sheds for storage. Although a few iron hulls were built in the city in the 1850s and 1860s it never became a center for iron shipbuilding, which was more common along the Delaware River; the small group of local builders who survived the maritime depression after the Civil War continued to build in wood because they were far from the sources of iron plates and shapes, there were few skilled ironworkers in New York City, and the prospects for shipbuilding were bleak. During this time many yards on the East River closed, and most of the ship carpenters and wood crafters in the city moved or were forced to leave the industry. A few shipyards that built harbor craft remained in Brooklyn and Staten Island. The yard of John Englis in Greenpoint built the last large wooden hulls in the area: the steamship *City of Vera Cruz* in 1874 was the last for oceangoing service and the Hudson River steamboat *Adirondack* in 1896 was the last for inland waters. By the end of the nineteenth century shipbuilders in New York City turned increasingly to steel as a construction material.

Propulsion machinery for the locally built hulls was provided by engineers in the city, including the Allaire, Etna, Fulton, Morgan, Neptune, Novelty, and Quintard ironworks. Fletcher, Harrison and Company (later W. and A. Fletcher Company), the city's most renowned engine builder, was first situated on West Street and later moved to Hoboken. Many of these firms also built steam engines, boilers, and other machinery for use ashore. Their shops were near the shipyards, and a large number had their own piers where engines and boilers were installed in recently launched vessels. A typical engine works consisted of a pattern shop, iron and brass foundries, boiler and machine shops, and storehouses. There were also sail, spar, and block makers, rope-making establishments, and paint factories. Mechanics, ironworkers, and riveters were employed in increasing numbers as iron and steel displaced wood in the construction of ships. Apprentices and journeymen worked in all sectors of the industry.

The building of naval and merchant vessels revived in New York City during the First World War. The Staten Island Shipbuilding Company built cargo ships, minesweepers, and naval tugs; other builders such as Standard Shipbuilding and Downey Shipbuilding in the city and others in New Jersey also contributed to the war effort. The Staten Island Shipbuilding yard, later owned by Bethlehem Steel, was the only important firm in the city to survive the 1920s and 1930s. In the Second World War Bethlehem Staten Island was a major builder of destroyers. Other shipyards on the Harlem River and in Brooklyn turned out patrol craft, tugs, and barges. On City Island yacht builders skilled in the construction of wooden ships produced minesweepers and similar vessels, and large fighting ships — battleships, aircraft carriers, and cruisers — were built in the Brooklyn Navy Yard. Toward the end of the twentieth century the city continued to be an important maritime center, but the only remnants of the shipbuilding industry were a few small ship repair firms; the major ones, Todd Shipyards and Bethlehem Steel, had closed their yards in the 1980s.

Robert Greenhalgh Albion: *The Rise of New York Port [1815–1860]* (New York: Charles Scribner's Sons, 1939; repr. 1970)

Edwin L. Dunbaugh and William duBarry Thomas: *William H. Webb, Shipbuilder* (Glen Cove, N.Y.: Webb Institute of Naval Architecture, 1989)

William duBarry Thomas

shoes, boots, and leather. The leather industry in New Amsterdam became centered as early as 1680 in the Swamp, a section of lower Manhattan near the East River and the Brooklyn Bridge. The tanning pits were considered a nuisance and were moved to Maiden Lane and William and Gold streets, names later used in the marketing of leather goods. Tanneries were small operations that relied mostly on local hides and skins; leather for shoe and boot soles was imported from Britain. By 1813 these stocks were no longer adequate for the demands of shoe, saddlery, and harness manufacturers, and as a result tanners, especially those in the Catskill Mountains, sought out importers of Latin American

Advertisement for Donaldson Brothers' cable screw wire boots and shoes, ca *1875*

hides as suppliers. According to the federal census of 1810 there were nine tanneries in Manhattan and six in Brooklyn; they used lighter skins for shoe and boot uppers and darker, hemlock-tanned ones for soles. By the 1840s and 1850s the brokers who bought and sold this sole leather were clustered in the Swamp under such names as Gideon Lee, Charles M. Leupp, and the "Long Firm" of Thorne, Watson, Corse. Shoe factories in the city before the Civil War were small and hand-operated and usually stood near the leather brokers, who also provided sole leather to firms in New Jersey, Philadelphia, and Massachusetts. In 1860 about 70 percent of the firms in the metropolitan area were in Manhattan, and the 5500 workers in the leather industry accounted for 5 percent of the city's labor force in manufacturing. Leather manufacture was transformed during the war by new technology and an increased demand for leather goods.

Between 1860 and the First World War the city's leather industry expanded. It employed twenty thousand workers, about 3 percent of those in manufacturing, and in 1913 footwear accounted for 53 percent of employment in the leather industry in New York City, ranking the city among the five largest shoe centers in the country; it was known especially for its fine women's shoes. Although the factories in Brooklyn were fewer in number than those in Manhattan, they were larger and employed about two thirds of the city's shoe workers. Several firms in the city came to dominate the national market. Shoes of higher quality were made possible by the Goodyear welt machine, which was invented by Charles Goodyear Jr. (1833–96) and improved the method of attaching uppers to soles. The shoe firm of John H. Hannan (*b* 1849) in Brooklyn, one of the largest in the country, was among the first to use trademarks, national advertising, and its own retail stores to increase sales. Hannan also helped to organize the United Shoe Machinery Company in 1899, of which he was vice-president until 1907, and became the first president of the National Boot and Shoe Manufacturers Association in 1904. Mark Hoyt (1834–96), the youngest child in a well-known family of tanners, helped in 1893 to form the United States Leather Company, a firm known as the "leather trust" and based in the city.

Bolstered by the presence of the city's fashion industry, leather manufacturers remained strong and employed more than 31,000 workers in the decade after the Second World War; a third of these produced footwear, another third produced such items as handbags, and more were employed in Manhattan than in Brooklyn. From the mid 1960s the leather industry declined as the number of imported shoes increased and consumers turned to less expensive canvas and rubber footwear. The number of leather workers fell from nineteen thousand in 1967 to 5800 in 1988, representing about 2.5 percent of the city's manufacturing sector. Handbags and other small goods accounted for almost 60 percent of the labor force; there were fewer than a thousand shoe workers, and only one firm employed more than a hundred. As a capital of fashion the city nonetheless remained an important center for products requiring skilled labor and fresh ideas.

Frank W. Norcross: *A History of the New York Swamp* (New York: Chiswick, 1901)

Charles H. McDermott: *A History of the Shoe and Leather Industries of the United States* (Boston: John W. Denehy, 1918)

Edgar Malone Hoover: *Location Theory and the Shoe and Leather Industries* (Cambridge: Harvard University Press, 1937)

James L. Wiles

Sholem Aleichem [Rabinowitz, Sholem] (*b* Pereyaslavl, Russia [now Pereyaslav–Khmelnitski, Ukraine], 3 March 1859; *d* New York City, 13 May 1916). Short-story writer. He emerged as a major prose writer and leading pioneer of modern Yiddish culture during the late nineteenth century. His stories of Jewish life in eastern Europe were widely popular in the United States as well, but although he twice resided in New York City (1906–7, 1914–16) his attempts to write for an American immigrant audience were largely unsuccessful. His funeral, which took place in the city, was attended by more than 150,000 mourners, and after his death he was venerated as an icon of European Yiddish culture. Sholem Aleichem's works have been extensively translated into English, and the Broadway musical *Fiddler on the Roof* is based on his work. A system of secular Yiddish schools and a cooperative apartment complex in the Bronx are named after him.

Joseph and Frances Butwin: *Sholom Aleichem* (Boston: Twayne, 1977)

Jeffrey Shandler

Shooters Island. An island off the northwestern shore of Staten Island in the Kill van Kull. It has a land area of fifty-one acres (twenty-one hectares), of which one third lies in New Jersey and the rest in New York State. The island was popular for duck hunting during colonial times and during the American Revolution was a haven for spies. In the late nineteenth century it became a shipbuilding center: the Townsend Downey Shipyard launched Kaiser Wilhelm's yacht the *Meteor* from the island in 1907. The industry declined after the First World War and the island was abandoned; it is now covered with derelict piers, dry docks, and rotting debris. Five species of heron and other sea birds are found on Shooters Island, which is protected as a wildlife sanctuary. In the mid 1990s the New York Audubon Society was responsible for wildlife research on the island.

Gerard R. Wolfe

shopping malls. Regional shopping malls were developed throughout greater New York between 1970 and 1980. The three largest malls in the city itself are the Queens Center at Queens Boulevard and Woodhaven Boulevard, the King Plaza Mall in Mill Basin, and the Staten Island Center in Heartland Village. There are also smaller malls in Manhattan, which lack the large parking lots of their counterparts in the outer boroughs: A&S Plaza at 6th Avenue and 33rd Street, the World Financial Center at Battery Park City, Herald Center at 34th Street and Broadway, Trump Tower at 5th Avenue and 56th Street, and the Market and Citicorp Center at 53rd Street and Lexington Avenue.

Richard Kobliner

Shop Rite. The name used from the 1950s by several supermarkets in New York City and its environs belonging to the Wakefern Cooperative, a group formed by several small grocers in New Jersey to counter the proliferation of large grocery chains. The supermarkets grew rapidly in the 1950s and 1960s by using such innovative techniques as maintaining butcher departments and stocking frozen foods and nonfood items. In 1968 a group within the Wakefern Cooperative broke away to form the chain known as Pathmark.

Chad Ludington

Shor, Toots [Bernard] (*b* Philadelphia, 6 May 1903; *d* 23 Jan 1977). Restaurateur. He attended the Drexel Institute and the Wharton School of Business, worked as a salesman, and in 1930 moved to New York City. In 1940 he opened the first of several restaurants named Toots Shor's at 51 West 51st Street. The establishment became popular with tourists and celebrities such as Joe DiMaggio, Frank Sinatra, and Jackie Gleason. Shor himself was loud and brash and often insulted customers, notably the football player Joe Namath and the film producer Louis B. Mayer. In 1959 he sold the lease on the original restaurant, and in the following year he opened a new one with virtually identical décor at 33 West 52nd Street; he later opened a restaurant at 5 East 54th Street that was less successful than the two earlier ones had been. At the time of his death Shor operated three restaurants, at 1 Penn Plaza, 64 West 52nd Street, and 44 East 43rd Street.

Eric Wm. Allison

Shore Acres. Neighborhood in northeastern Staten Island, lying on a bluff overlooking the Verrazano Narrows Bridge and bounded to the north by Harborview Place, to the east by Upper New York Bay, to the south by Von Briesen Park, and to the west by Bay Street; it is near Fort Wadsworth. The land belonged to the estate of Henry Alexandre during the nineteenth century and was developed in the 1930s by Cornelius G. Kolff, an entrepreneur who lived at 15 Harbor View Place South. Known for its views inland and toward the Narrows, Shore Acres is an exclusive residential neighborhood. The principal street is Sea Gate Road.

Barnett Shepherd

Shubert Organization. Theater syndicate formed in the late nineteenth century in Syracuse, New York, by Sam S. Shubert (*b* ?1877; *d* 12 May 1905), Lee Shubert (*b* ?1875; *d* 25 Dec 1953), and J(acob) J. Shubert (*b* ?1879; *d* 26 Dec 1963), the sons of Jewish immigrants from East Prussia. After operating theaters in upstate New York for several years they began in 1900 to work in New York City and to present light theatrical entertainment. Soon they controlled the Herald Square Theatre on Broadway and 35th Street, the Casino Theatre on Broadway and 39th Street, and the Lyric Theatre on 42nd Street. Sam Shubert was generally considered the head of the firm, which came into conflict with the Theatrical Syndicate, a powerful organization operated by Marc Klaw and Abraham Erlanger. After Sam Shubert was killed in a railroad accident most expected his brothers to sell their business to Klaw and Erlanger; instead they moved to expand it. By the late 1920s they owned more than a hundred theaters around the country. Among those in the city were the Shubert Theatre (1913) and the Broadhurst Theatre (1917), both on 44th Street, the Booth Theatre (1913) on 45th Street, and the Barrymore Theatre (1928) on 47th Street (all of which the organization retained into the 1990s). Some of their most successful presentations included the summer revue *The Passing Show* (1912–22), *Artists and Models* (1923), and *The Student Prince* (1924). Performers who were associated with the organization included Alla Nazimova, Al Jolson, Ethel Barrymore, the team of Olsen and Johnson, and Carmen Miranda. Jacob Shubert's son John Shubert (*b* 13 Dec 1908; *d* 17 Nov 1962) ran the company in the 1950s, followed by a great-nephew of the Shubert brothers, Lawrence Shubert Lawrence Jr. (*b* 18 Feb 1916). In the 1970s the company produced plays under the direction of its chairman Gerald Schoenfeld (*b* 2 Sept 1924) and its president Bernard Jacobs (*b* 13 June 1916). Productions during the 1970s and 1980s included *Ain't Misbehavin'* (1978), *Cats* (1982), and *Jerome Robbins' Broadway* (1989). In the mid 1990s the Shuberts owned and operated sixteen Broadway theaters and had produced more than five hundred comedies, melodramas, musicals, operettas, and revues. They had offices at 234 West 44th Street above the Sam H. Shubert Theatre in what had once been Lee Shubert's living quarters, the entrance to which was on Shubert Alley (which runs west of Broadway from 44th Street to 45th Street next to the Shubert and Booth theaters).

Jerry Stagg: *The Brothers Shubert* (New York: Random House, 1968)

Brooks McNamara: *The Shuberts of Broadway* (New York: Oxford University Press, 1990)

Brooks McNamara

"sick chicken case." See SCHECHTER V. UNITED STATES.

Sickles, Daniel E(dgar) (*b* New York City, 20 Oct 1823; *d* New York City, 3 May 1914). Legislator and major-general. As a state senator from New York City he sponsored legislation in 1855 authorizing the acquisition of the land that became Central Park. From 1856 to 1861 he represented the city in the U.S. House of Representatives as a Democrat. His most notable act during his tenure was killing Philip Barton Key (a son of Francis Scott Key) for having an affair with his wife; in a bizarre trial Sickles became the first defendant in the United States acquitted on grounds of temporary insanity. At the request of President Abraham Lincoln he raised a volunteer brigade during the Civil War. Promoted to major-general, he played an important role at Gettysburg, where his questionable strategies at the battle of Little Round Top resulted in many casualties, as well as the loss of his own leg. In later positions in the United States and abroad he was often accused of incompetence and impropriety. After returning to the city he was elected to another term in Congress (1893–95). Bankrupt and separated from his family, Sickles spent the rest of his life in the city, where he died in his home at 5th Avenue and 19th Street.

W. A. Swanberg: *Sickles the Incredible* (New York: Charles Scribner's Sons, 1956)

James Bradley

Siegel–Cooper. Firm of retailers, occupying a store on 6th Avenue between 18th and 19th streets. Known as the "big store," this had eighteen acres (seven hectares) of floor space and was the largest department store in the city at its opening in 1896; it stood in the heart of the Ladies' Mile. In addition to a vast selection of merchandise the store provided such amenities as a post office, a dental parlor, a theater, an art gallery, and a nursery. In 1903 the management published one of the first newspapers for employees, *Thought and Work*. The store relied on elaborate advertising gimmicks and high-volume sales but also promoted its elegance and fashionable address with the slogan "Meet Me at the Fountain." Siegel–Cooper declared bankruptcy in 1915.

Elaine S. Abelson

Sigel, Franz (*b* Sinsheim, Baden, 18 Nov 1824; *d* New York City, 22 Aug 1902). Soldier, editor, and public official. He moved to the United States after the German Revolution of 1848 and in May 1852 settled in New York City, where he worked as a tobacconist, surveyor, draftsman, and musician. With his father-in-law, Rudolph Dulon, he formed the German–American Institute in 1855; he also taught in the city's public schools and at the German Turner Society, belonged to the 5th New York Militia, and wrote for the *New Yorker Staats-Zeitung* and the *New York Times*. In August 1857 he moved to St. Louis to teach at the German–American Institute. When the Civil War broke out he joined the Union Army and became a major-general after fighting in several campaigns. He returned to New York City after the war and in 1869 worked for the Brooklyn Steamship and Emigration Company and the Metropolitan Railway Company. In June 1870 he was appointed internal revenue collector for the 9th New York District by President Ulysses S. Grant. Elected to one term as register of the city in 1871, he served during Grover Cleveland's presidency as chief clerk in the county clerk's office (May 1885 to June 1886) and pension agent for the New York District (March 1886 to May 1889). After retiring from politics Sigel published the *New Yorker Deutsches Volksblatt* and edited the *New York Monthly* from 1897 to 1904. An equestrian statue of him was dedicated at 106th Street and Riverside Drive in 1907 and a park bounded by 158th Street, the Grand Concourse, 153rd Street, and Walton Avenue in the Bronx was named for him.

Stephen D. Engle: *Yankee Dutchman: The Life of Franz Sigel* (Fayetteville: University of Arkansas Press, 1993)

Stephen D. Engle

Silk Stocking District. A loose term usually applied to the congressional district that includes the Upper East Side of Manhattan and sometimes to state and local legislative districts in the same area. First recorded in 1897, the name arose because of the great concentration of wealthy residents along 5th and Park avenues and dozens of nearby streets, making the district the wealthiest in the United States. Because of decennial redistricting the boundaries of the congressional district have changed repeatedly, as has the number by which the district is designated (successively eighteen, seventeen, fifteen, and fourteen). Representatives from the district have exerted a disproportionately large influence in Washington because of their many prominent and wealthy constituents. In general they have exemplified the liberal, patrician brand of Republicanism with which the district has long been associated. John V. Lindsay represented the district from 1959 to 1965 before his election as mayor; Edward I. Koch, who also later became mayor, in 1968 was the first Democrat elected to represent the district in thirty-four years. After Koch was elected mayor in 1977 the district was represented by Bill Green, a liberal Republican. Redistricting brought about by the federal census of 1990 enlarged the district and diluted its liberal Republican character, and in 1992 Green was defeated by a Democrat, Carolyn B. Maloney.

Andrew Sparberg

Sills, Beverly [Silverman, Belle] (*b* Brooklyn, 25 May 1929). Singer and administrator. As a child she performed on the first radio advertisement to include singing, and in 1947 she made her début as an operatic soprano with the Philadelphia Civic Opera. With the New York City Opera she sang the role of Rosalinde in Johann Strauss's *Die Fledermaus* in 1955 and that of Cleopatra in Handel's *Giulio Cesare* in 1966. She also performed at the Metropolitan Opera. In 1979 she became the general director of the New York City Opera, and she devoted herself to the position full time after retiring from the stage in the following year. She became a managing director of the Metropolitan Opera in 1991.

B. Kimberly Taylor

silver. The first goldsmith recorded in New Amsterdam was Jeuriaen Blanck Sr., who was noted by trade in 1643 but may not have practiced his craft in the colony. Only after the English conquest, when silver coin, bullion, and outmoded plate became widely available, was there enough wealth to support several smiths. The first silversmith who was not from the Netherlands was Bartholomew LeRoux (1663–1713), a Huguenot refugee who settled in the city in 1687. He trained his son John, another son, Charles (1689–1745), who was the silversmith for the Common Council from 1720 to 1743, and Peter Van Dyck (1684–1750). Charles LeRoux in turn trained succeeding generations of apprentices. Between 1723 and 1745 the city supported as many as twenty-three silversmiths at once. Before 1750 about sixty silversmiths worked in the city, of whom thirty-two were of Dutch heritage, ten French Huguenot, and seven English. They produced a wide range of objects, usually in the prevailing English fashion; they also developed distinctive forms like the brandywine bowl, as well as an ornamental vocabulary encompassing meander wire, cut-card work, and cast appliqués. Silversmiths in New York City used distinctive marks, such as the trefoil of Gerrit Onckelbag, the stylized initials of Peter Van Dyck, and the conjoined initials of Cornelius Vander Burch. During the mid eighteenth century silversmiths in the city kept abreast of international fashions by importing silver and plated wares and engraved designs, and by employing British and European craftsmen who settled in the city, among them Daniel Christian Fueter, a Swiss Moravian, who worked from 1754 to 1769, and his chaser John Anthony Beau of Geneva. British designs predominated in the products of such mid-century silversmiths as Myer Myers, who won commissions from churches, synagogues, and prominent families.

Brandywine Bowl by Gerrit Onckelbag, ca *1710*

The production of silver declined during the American Revolution. Patriots including Myers sought safety in Philadelphia, New Jersey, and Connecticut; such Loyalists as Charles Oliver Bruff remained until the British evacuated the city in 1783. After the revolution international neoclassicism was quickly adopted by the city's craftsmen, among them Daniel Van Voorhis (1751–1824) and Ephraim Brasher (1744–1810), who seamed sleek surfaces from rolled or "flatted" sheet silver and decorated them with bright-cut engraving and beading. During the early decades of the nineteenth century the silver trade reorganized, as smaller manufacturers ceased to sell their wares directly to customers, instead supplying them to retailers who often advanced capital to buy bullion and also shared in any profits. Large firms dominated by mid century. According to the state census of 1855 the firm of William Gale and Son employed sixty-five men and ten boys and produced goods valued at $175,000; its competitors, Charles Wood and Jasper W. Hughes, employed sixty men, twenty women, ten boys, and fifteen girls and produced goods valued at $225,000. Products were distributed throughout the Midwest and the South. In 1851 the firm of Tiffany and Company made an exclusive arrangement with a leading silversmith, John Chandler Moore, to make hollowware pieces. Moore's son Edward C. Moore directed the manufactory. After the Civil War Tiffany and Company secured much of the luxury trade, particularly for objects in the "testimonial ostentatious" style. During the late nineteenth century and the early twentieth the industry consolidated and many plants left Manhattan. Silver continued to be hand wrought in the studios of such craftsmen as the German-born Peter Müller-Munk (1904–67) and the jeweler Marie Zimmermann (1878–1972), and in classes at the Craft Students League.

Deborah Dependahl Waters

Silver Beach. Neighborhood in the eastern Bronx, lying on a bluff near the tip of Throgs Neck overlooking the East River. The land was used as a lookout during the American Revolution. A farm in the area owned by the Stephenson family was sold in 1795 to Abijah Hammond, who built a mansion (later the offices of the Silver Beach Garden Corporation). In the 1920s the Peters and Sorgenfrei families formed Silver Beach Garden (named for the color of the beach at low tide), a summer colony of bungalows that were later adapted for year-round use; most of the streets were named for flowers and trees found on the Hammond estate. Residents owned their houses but rented the land until 1972, when they joined together to buy it. In the mid 1990s there were 350 small houses lying along narrow lanes. The neighborhood is not easily accessible.

John McNamara: *History in Asphalt: The Origin of Bronx Street and Place Names* (New York: Bronx County Historical Society, 1984)

Gary Hermalyn and Robert Kornfeld: *Landmarks of the Bronx* (New York: Bronx County Historical Society, 1990)

Gary D. Hermalyn

Silver Lake. Neighborhood in northwestern Staten Island, comprising the area around Silver Lake Park. In the late nineteenth century the area now occupied by the park was a popular resort for boating, fishing, picnics, and ice skating, and the site of a hotel. The lake once supported a thriving ice-harvesting business. The main thoroughfares are Victory Boulevard, where there are several attractive one-family houses. All of the neighborhood is at high elevation, giving sweeping views to the north. The recreation area is maintained by the parks department and has a golf course, tennis courts, and walking trails; it is also the site of summer concerts. The population of the neighborhood is largely white.

For illustrations see Ice harvesting and Works progress administration.

Marjorie Johnson

Simkhovitch [née Kingsbury], **Mary (Melinda)** (*b* near Boston, 8 Sept 1867; *d* New York City, 15 Nov 1951). She was educated in Massachusetts and Berlin and in 1899 married Vladimir G. Simkhovitch. In 1902 she formed the Cooperative Social Settlement Society on Jones Street, later known as Greenwich House; she was its head resident until 1946. By the 1930s she concentrated on national housing reform: she led the Public Housing Conference from 1932 to 1943 and was vice-chairman of the New York City Housing Authority from 1934 to 1947.

Betty Boyd Caroli

Simon, Kate [Grobsmith, Kaila] (*b* Warsaw, 5 Dec 1912; *d* New York City, 4 Feb 1990). Writer. In 1917 she moved to New York City with her mother and younger brother to join her father, who had settled there in 1914. After growing up near 178th Street and Lafontaine Avenue in Tremont she earned a BA from Hunter College and became known as a writer, editor, and book reviewer. She wrote a number of books about the city, including *New York Places and Pleasures: An Uncommon Guidebook* (1959; 4th edn 1971), which became a best-seller, *New York* (1964, illustrated with photographs of the city by Andreas Feininger), and *Fifth Avenue: A Very Social History* (1978). Among her autobiographical works are *Bronx Primitive: Portraits in a Childhood* (1982), *A Wider World: Portraits in an Adolescence* (1986), and *Etchings in an Hourglass* (1990).

Allen J. Share

Simon, (Marvin) Neil (*b* New York City, 4 July 1927). Playwright. He began his career as a sketch writer for the "Phil Silvers Arrow Show" (1948), contributed sketches to the Broadway revue *Catch a Star* (1955), and collaborated with his brother Daniel on the revue *New Faces of 1956*. His first full-length play was *Come Blow Your Horn* (1961). During the following decades he wrote more than a dozen comedies set in New York City, including *Barefoot in the Park* (1963), *The Odd Couple* (1965), and *Prisoner of Second Avenue* (1971), all of which were adapted for film, television, or both. The play *Lost in Yonkers* (1990) was critically acclaimed and received a Tony Award for best play.

Sara J. Steen

Simon, Paul (*b* Newark, N.J., 13 Oct 1941). Singer and songwriter. He grew up in Forest Hills, graduated from Queens College, and briefly attended Brooklyn Law School. From 1964 to 1971 he belonged to a duo with Art Garfunkel that forged a distinctive genre known as folk–rock: among their well-known songs is *The 59th Street Bridge Song (Feelin' Groovy)* (1966). After embarking on a career as a soloist he continued to maintain a residence in New York City and gave several concerts there, including one at Radio City Music Hall in April 1987 and another at Central Park on 15 August 1990 before 750,000 spectators. He also performed with Garfunkel in Central Park in September 1981.

Simon and Schuster. Firm of book publishers, formed in 1924 by Richard L. Simon (1899–1960) and Max Lincoln Schuster (1897–1970) in a three-room office at 37 West 57th Street. Its first title was a crossword puzzle book that became a best-seller. A paperback division called Pocket Books began operations in 1939. Over the years the firm published such writers as William Shirer (*The Rise and Fall of the Third Reich*), Joseph Heller (*Catch-22*), Joan Didion, Margaret Atwood, John Gregory Dunne, Larry McMurtry, and Anthony Burgess. It also became noted for its aggressive advertising efforts. In 1975 the firm was acquired by Gulf and Western Industries, which later became Paramount Communications. After Paramount was in turn acquired by Viacom, Simon and Schuster in 1994 took over all the publishing operations of Viacom worldwide. In the mid 1990s the headquarters of Simon and Schuster were at 1230 6th Avenue in Rockefeller Center. Among the books published by the firm are Mary McCarthy's *The Company She Keeps* (1942), Nikos Kazantzakis's *Zorba the Greek* (1953) and *The Odyssey: A Modern Sequel* (1958), Joseph Heller's *Catch-22* (1961), Ray Bradbury's *Fahrenheit 451* (1967), Graham Greene's *The Honorary Consul* (1973) and *The Human Factor* (1978), and many works of S. J. Perelman.

Peter Schwed: *Turning the Pages: An Insider's Story of Simon and Schuster* (New York: Macmillan, 1984)

James Bradley

Simplicity Pattern Company. Firm of pattern makers formed in New York City in 1927 by James J. Shapiro. Specializing in simple designs sold at low prices, it opened a foreign subsidiary in 1928 and a large manufacturing plant in Michigan in 1931, and soon became the largest pattern company in the world. In the early 1990s the firm had its executive offices at 200 Madison Avenue in Manhattan, where it had about 180 employees.

Marc Ferris

Simpson Thacher and Bartlett. Law firm. It was formed in 1884 by John W. Simpson, Thomas Thacher, and William M. Barnum. Initially associated with railroads, it prospered during the era of railroad consolidation and later gained clients among electric utilities and in industry and finance. The firm took its current name in 1904. Whitney North Seymour (1901–83), well known for his work in civil liberties and antitrust law, joined the firm in 1923 and argued more than fifty cases before the U.S. Supreme Court. Cyrus R. Vance (*b* 1917), who joined the firm in 1947, was later secretary of state under President Jimmy Carter.

Gilbert Tauber

Sims, J(ames) Marion (*b* Lancaster County, S.C., 25 Jan 1813; *d* New York City, 13 Nov 1883). Gynecologist. He spent the first part of his career in Alabama, where he developed surgical techniques for which he became prominent. In 1853 he moved to New York City and founded the Woman's Hospital of the State of New York at 83 Madison Avenue (1855). Torn by dual loyalties, he moved to Europe during the Civil War. He was the president of the American Medical Association in 1876 and is considered one of the first modern gynecologists. A statue of Sims stands in Central Park, at 5th Avenue and 103rd Street.

Joseph S. Lieber

Singer, I(saac) M(erritt) (*b* Pittstown, N.Y., 27 Oct 1811; *d* Torquay, England, 23 July 1875). Inventor. After several years in upstate New York, where he trained as a machinist and cabinetmaker in Oswego and pursued an acting career in Rochester, he moved first to New York City and then to Boston. There he unsuccessfully promoted a device to carve wooden printer's type and became aware of Elias Howe's sewing machine. In 1851 he returned to New York City, where his firm I. M. Singer and Company opened an office and facilities where sewing machines were manufactured. By marketing its machines to women for use in the home and by continually improving its product, the firm quickly became the leader in its field in the United States. In the mid 1850s young women demonstrated the operation of sewing machines in lavish showrooms at the firm's headquarters. A custom-built factory opened on Mott Street in 1858, soon followed by a foundry on Delancey Street. More than 100,000 machines were produced in 1870, and in 1873 a new factory opened in Elizabethport, New Jersey. As its global market developed, the firm built factories abroad, first in Scotland and then in Canada. Although Singer was sued for infringement by Howe in 1851, his company was already well established and continued to prosper. Singer patented twenty innovations for his machines, including a yielding presser foot and a foot treadle, and remained active in the business until he moved to Great Britain in 1863.

Ruth Brandon: *A Capitalist Romance: Singer and the Sewing Machine* (Philadelphia: Lippincott, 1977)

Darwin H. Stapleton

Singer, Isaac Bashevis (*b* Leoncin, near Warsaw, 14 July 1904; *d* New York City, 24 July 1991). Novelist. He grew up in Warsaw and emigrated to the United States in 1935. Like his older brother, the author Israel Joshua Singer, he began publishing his prose fiction in the Polish Yiddish press during the years between the world wars. Many of his stories and novels were first printed in serial form in the *Forverts* and later issued in English translation. Singer is best known for his gothic tales of the sexual and supernatural set in a mythic, eastern European Jewish past. A long-time resident of the Upper West Side, he also wrote about his life as a refugee. He received the Nobel Prize for literature in 1978.

Paul Kresh: *Isaac Bashevis Singer: The Story of a Storyteller* (New York: E. P. Dutton, 1984)

Jeffrey Shandler

Singer Building. Ornate skyscraper 612 feet (186.5 meters) tall at 149 Broadway, designed by Ernest Flagg and completed in 1911. It was the first building designed after zoning laws were passed limiting the height of new buildings relative to the area that they covered and to their frontage along the street. With the Woolworth Building (Cass Gilbert, 1913) it helped to make setbacks and terraces standard elements in the design of skyscrapers in Manhattan during the following decades. The Singer Building remained the tallest building in the world for eighteen months.

Susan Lyman: *The Story of New York* (New York: Crown, 1964)
Barbaralee Diamonstein: *The Landmarks of New York* (New York: Harry N. Abrams, 1988)

James O. Drummond

single-room occupancy hotels. See SROS.

Singleton, Anne. Pseudonym under which RUTH BENEDICT published poetry.

Sing Tao. Chinese-language newspaper launched in 1965 and published six days a week. Aimed at immigrants, business people, and students, it covers news in Chinese communities worldwide and offers financial news and articles on leisure, tourism, medicine, and entertainment. In the mid 1990s it had a circulation of sixty thousand; about 80 percent of its readers speak Cantonese and 20 percent Mandarin. *Sing Tao* is owned by a parent company in Hong Kong and distributed in New York City and eleven other major cities in the United States.

Jacqueline Lalley

Sisters of Charity of Mount St. Vincent. Roman Catholic women's order formed in New York City in 1846. Its original members were adherents of the American Sisters of Charity (formed in 1809 by Elizabeth Ann Seton in Emmitsburg, Maryland) who first worked in New York City in 1817 at the Roman Catholic Orphan Asylum. The first superior was Elizabeth Boyle (1788–1861), and the first motherhouse was at McGowan's Pass in what is now Central Park. The members of the order were responsible for much of the charitable work of the Catholic church in child care, health care, and education in New York City. They earned a reputation as effective nurses during cholera epidemics in 1832 and again in 1849, when they opened their first hospital, St. Vincent's Hospital, in Manhattan. The motherhouse was moved to its present location at Mount St. Vincent in Riverdale in 1859. Some members left to form orders in Halifax, Nova Scotia (1849), and Convent Station, New Jersey (1859). During the Civil War the order volunteered its services to the war department and operated St. Joseph's Military Hospital at McGowan's Pass. In 1868 the members opened St. Mary's Female Hospital in Brooklyn (reorganized to provide general care as the Hospital of the Holy Name in 1909 and transferred to the Daughters of Wisdom in 1955). They also opened and taught at several schools in Manhattan and Brooklyn and formed other institutions such as the New York Foundling Home (1869) and the College of Mount St. Vincent (1901). On Staten Island the order established several other health services, later combined as the Sisters of Charity Services Corporation. The membership grew steadily during the 1950s to a peak of fourteen hundred, declined in the 1960s, and numbered about five hundred in the early 1990s, when most members worked in schools and hospitals.

Sister Marie De Lourdes Walsh: *The Sisters of Charity of New York, 1809–1959* (New York: Fordham University Press, 1960)

Bernadette McCauley

Sisters of Charity Service Corporation. Nonprofit health services organization in Staten Island, owned and operated by the Roman Catholic Sisters of Charity. It maintains two general hospitals: St. Vincent's Medical Center of Richmond (440 beds), established in 1903 by sisters from St. Vincent's Hospital in Manhattan, is a certified trauma center and provides the only psychiatric emergency service on Staten Island; Bayley Seton Hospital (204 beds), named for Richard Bayley, one of the first public health officers in New York City (1795–1804), and for his daughter, St. Elizabeth Seton, who founded the Sisters of Charity, was established in 1982 as a general-care facility in a disused hospital of the U.S. Public Health Service. The corporation also administers the Sister Elizabeth Boyle Child Learning Center, the Olivet–St. Vincent's Housing Development Fund Company, and the Pax Christi Hospice.

Sandra Opdycke

Sisters of Mercy. Roman Catholic women's order formed in 1831 in Dublin by Mary Catherine McAuley to serve the poor. Initially dedicated to setting up schools and hospitals in the poorest parts of Ireland, it established a branch in Pittsburgh in 1843 before opening another in New York City in 1845 under Mary Agnes O'Connor, who was persuaded to move to the city from England by Bishop John J. Hughes. In 1848 the order took over the former convent of the Sisters of the Sacred Heart on the corner of Houston and Mulberry streets and renamed it St. Catherine's Convent of Mercy. During the following years it focused on the care, training, and placement of young women, especially immigrants. In 1855 nuns of St. Catherine's under Mary Vincent Haire established the Sisters of Mercy in the Convent of St. Francis of Assisi in a brick house at Jay and Chapel streets in Brooklyn.

Kathleen Healy, ed.: *Sisters of Mercy: Spirituality in America, 1843–1900* (New York City: Paulist Press, 1992)

Melissa M. Merritt

69th Regiment. Military unit privately formed in 1848 in New York City. It joined the New York Militia in 1849. At the outset the regiment consisted largely of Irish-Americans, and it became the military escort of the St. Patrick's Day parade in 1851 (a status that it retained into the 1990s). During the Civil War the regiment fought in the battles of Bull Run, Antietam, and Appomattox. The regiment earned the nickname the "Fighting 69th" during the First World War, when as part of the 42nd Division of the American Expeditionary Forces (AEF) it fought with distinction in the Argonne. During the Second World War it served in the Pacific theater, fighting on Makin, Saipan, and Okinawa. From 1904 the 69th had its headquarters at 68 Lexington Avenue in Manhattan.

William Francis Stanton Root: *The 69th Regiment in Peace and War* (New York: Blanchard, 1905)

Eleanor Hannah

Skadden, Arps, Slate, Meagher and Flom. Law firm, formed in 1948 by Marshall Skadden (1907–58), Leslie H. Arps (1907–87), and John Slate (1914–67). All had previously worked at the firm of Root Ballantine, and much of their early business came from Pan American Airways, where the general counsel was Henry Friendly, also formerly of Root Ballantine. The first associate at the firm was Joseph H(arold) Flom (*b* 1923). During the 1950s and 1960s he developed an expertise in struggles over corporate control, an area many older Wall Street firms considered ungentlemanly, by working with William Timbers (*b* 1915), formerly general counsel of the Securities and Exchange Commission and later a federal judge. During the wave of mergers, acquisitions, and selloffs that began in the mid 1970s and continued in the 1980s, the firm was well positioned for the explosive growth that made it one of the largest and most profitable firms in the country. In the mid 1990s Skadden, Arps, Slate, Meagher and Flom was the largest law firm in New York City, with about five hundred lawyers and offices at 919 3rd Avenue.

Lincoln Caplan: *Skadden: Power, Money, and the Rise of a Legal Empire* (New York: Farrar, Straus and Giroux, 1993)

Jonathan G. Cedarbaum

Skene, Alexander J(ohnston) C(halmers) (*b* Fyvie, Aberdeenshire, Scotland, 17 June 1837; *d* Highmount, N.Y., 4 July 1900). Gynecologist. He emigrated to the United States in 1846 and lived for many years on Clinton Street in Brooklyn; he was a teacher, dean, and president at the Long Island College Hospital and taught at the New York Post-graduate Hospital. A founder and president of the American Gynecological Society (1886–87) and of Skene's Hospital for Self-supporting Women on President Street (1899), he was influential for having discovered the urethral glands that were later named for him and for having invented thirty-one surgical instruments. A bust of Skene by John Massey Rhind (1905) stands at the base of Grand Army Plaza in Prospect Park.

Joseph S. Lieber

Skidmore, Owings and Merrill. Firm of architects begun in 1935 as the partnership of Louis Skidmore (1897–1962) and Nathaniel Owings (1903–84), later joined by John Ogden Merrill (1896–1975). The firm received many commissions from corporations and prospered, engaging four more partners in 1949 including Gordon Bunshaft, who was in charge of designing Lever House (completed 1952), a relatively low, thin, slab-shaped office tower on slender supports at Park Avenue and 52nd Street. This was the first glass-faced commercial building in the city and introduced modern European design to American businessmen. Its prismatic shape, contrasting with that of the customary setback skyscrapers, and the open space at its base helped to promote new zoning regulations in 1961. Bunshaft was also responsible for Manhattan House (1950), the Veterans Administration Hospital at Fort Hamilton (1951), a building of Manufacturers Trust Company at 43rd Street and 5th Avenue (1954), the Pepsi-Cola building (1960), Chase Manhattan Bank (1961), the Library and Museum of the Performing Arts at Lincoln Center (1965), 140 Broadway (1967), and 9 West 57th Street (1984). In later years a number of other partners joined the firm, among them David Childs, Raul de Armas, and Michael McCarthy, who designed such conspicuous office towers as Liberty Plaza (1974), the Olympic Tower (1976), Park Avenue Plaza (1981), the Wang building (1984), the Citicorp Building in Queens (1990), and Worldwide Plaza (1990). Skidmore, Owings and Merrill is also well known for its hospitals and several structures at John F. Kennedy Airport.

Albert Bush-Brown: *Skidmore, Owings and Merrill: Architecture and Urbanism, 1973–1983* (New York: Van Nostrand, 1983)

Carol Herselle Krinsky: *Gordon Bunshaft of Skidmore, Owings and Merrill* (Cambridge: Architectural History Foundation / MIT Press, 1988)

Carol Herselle Krinsky

skyline. Masts and steeples defined the skyline of New York City from the 1830s until the 1870s, when steel-frame construction and improved elevator design allowed tall office towers to be built. An arresting skyline developed that included the thirteen-story Tower Building at 50 Broadway (1889), the Woolworth Building (1913), the Paramount Building (1927), and the Empire State Building (1931, 102 stories), often called the "cathedral of the skies." The massiveness of the Equitable Building at 120 Broadway (1915), which covered a full block in the heart of the financial district, led the city to pass a law in 1916 that limited the height of buildings according to their frontage on the street, required setbacks allowing for more light, and separated commercial and residential areas. These requirements led to the construction of skyscrapers resembling ziggurats in an art deco style adorned with iconic towers adapted from Gothic cathedrals, Roman temples, Strozzi palaces, and Mayan pyramids. The Chrysler Building (1930) was among the most striking, known for its tower of polished chrome steel. During these years the skyline was dominated by a cluster of skyscrapers at the tip of Manhattan and another between 32nd Street and Central Park. In the late 1920s and early 1930s, when competition to erect ever taller buildings was fierce, the skyscrapers in the financial district were dwarfed by new ones built for such firms as the Bank of Manhattan Company, Cities Service, City Bank Farmers Trust, and Irving Trust Company. On seeing the area at night the Swiss architect Le Corbusier described it in *Quand les Cathédrales Étaient Blanches* (1937) as a Milky Way brought down to earth. After the war glass-walled skyscrapers in the International style dominated the area, among them the United Nations Secretariat building (1950), Lever House (1952), the Seagram Building (1958), the World Trade Center (1976), and the Citicorp Center (1977), known for the forty-five-degree slope of its roof. The historian Jacques Barzun called the skyline the "most stupendous unbelievable manmade spectacle since the hanging gardens of Babylon."

Sheldon Cheney: *The New World Architecture* (New York: Longmans, Green, 1930)

Paul Goldberger: *The Skyscraper* (New York: Alfred A. Knopf, 1981)

Jan Morris: *Manhattan '45* (New York: Oxford University Press, 1986, 1987)

Robert A. M. Stern, Gregory Gilmartin, and Thomas Mellins: *New York 1930: Architecture and Urbanism between the Two World Wars* (New York: Rizzoli, 1987)

Allen J. Share

skyscrapers. New York City is inextricably associated with skyscrapers, and it has more of them than any other city in the world.

1. 1870–1916

The demand for tall office buildings arose during the 1860s as the commercial district along Broadway between the Battery and City Hall became more congested, and as large businesses, among them insurance and communications firms, sought more impressive and larger corporate headquarters.

Skyscrapers were made possible by technological advances, especially the passenger elevator, used successfully in the late 1850s. As the first office building to include elevators in its initial design, the Equitable Building (1868–70, Gilman and Kendall with George B. Post; demolished), seven and a half stories tall, opened the age of the skyscraper. By 1875 the city had several ten-story buildings, notably the Western Union building (1872–75, Post; demolished) at Broadway and Dey Street and the Tribune building (1873–75, Richard Morris Hunt; demolished) at Nassau and Spruce streets, both of which had a mansard roof and a tower. The 1880s saw the construction of such massive commercial blocks as Temple Court (1881–83, Silliman and Farnsworth; enlarged 1890) at Beekman and Nassau streets, which has twin towers. The Produce Exchange (1881–84, Post; demolished) overlooking Bowling Green, innovative in its "modified Renaissance" design, incorporated iron-framed inner court walls that were a forerunner of skeleton construction.

A cluster of skyscrapers had formed next to City Hall Park with the completion of the ebulliently ornamented Potter Building

Skyscrapers in midtown along 42nd Street, ca *1940*

(1883–86, N. G. Starkweather) on Park Row and the mansarded, neo-Romanesque New York Times Building (1888–89, Post; altered). Using as its structural base the iron-framed floors of the newspaper's old five-story building (1857–58, T. R. Jackson), the new Times building at the intersection of Park Row and Chatham and Nassau streets combined load-bearing walls with cage framing. The narrow, eleven-story Tower Building (1888–89, Bradford L. Gilbert; demolished) at 50 Broadway introduced full skeleton, or skyscraper, construction to the city: the metal frame carried both walls and floors, allowing the walls to be reduced in thickness and the site to be used more efficiently. The Pulitzer, or World, Building at Park Row and Frankfort Street (1889–90, Post; demolished), known for its gilded dome, was less innovative structurally, but with a reported height of 309 feet (ninety-four meters) it was briefly the city's tallest building.

The word "skyscraper" came into common usage during the 1890s when skeleton construction was widely adopted, building methods were refined, and competition intensified to build ever higher buildings. The steel-skeleton-framed Manhattan Life Building (1893–95, Kimball and Thompson; demolished) at 66 Broadway was the city's first skyscraper erected on pneumatic caisson foundations. Others soon followed, among them the American Surety Building (1894–96, Bruce Price; enlarged 1921) at 100 Broadway, an elegant, column-like tower of twenty-one stories. R. H. Robertson, who designed the twenty-three-story American Tract Society Building (1894–95) at Nassau and Spruce streets with a distinctive arcaded top, set a new height record with his formidable thirty-story Park Row Building (1896–99). Neoclassical designs with three-part façades also became fashionable, and were used in such distinctive buildings as the Bowling Green Offices (1895–98, W. and G. Audsley; altered), decorated with crisp Grecian motifs, and the slablike Empire Building (1897–98, Kimball and Thompson) south of Trinity Church at Broadway and Rector Street. Standing thirteen stories tall, the Bayard Building (1897–99) at 65–69 Bleecker Street was designed by Louis Sullivan with slender, structurally revealing piers and lush, fluid ornamentation (it was Sullivan's only work in New York City). The Broadway Chambers building (1899–1900), a colorful brick- and terra-cotta-clad tower across from City Hall Park, was the first of several stunning skyscrapers in New York City designed by Cass Gilbert.

During the first decade of the twentieth century skyscrapers were built in areas beyond lower Broadway. At twenty-one stories the Flatiron Building (1901–3, D. H. Burnham and Company), just south of Madison Square, was the tallest building north of the financial district. Designed to conform to its triangular site, it was likened to the bow of a "monster ocean-steamer" by the photographer Alfred Stieglitz. The neo-Gothic Trinity and U.S. Realty buildings (1904–7, 1906–7, Francis Kimball) were erected north of Trinity churchyard on Broadway. As the Broadway subway neared completion (opened 1904) the Times Tower (1903–4, Eidlitz and McKenzie; altered 1966) was built on a midtown site that soon became known as Times Square. Elegant skyscrapers were also erected in lower Manhattan: the neo-Gothic West Street Building (1906–7, Gilbert), which set a new standard of opulence, as well as the neoclassical Whitehall Building at Battery Place and West Street (1902–3, Henry Hardenbergh; 1909–11, Clinton and Russell) and the flamboyant City Investing Company Building (1906–9, Kimball; demolished) at Broadway and Cortlandt Street. As the narrow streets off Broadway became more densely built up, the loss of light and air emerged as an increasingly serious problem. A solution was offered by Ernest Flagg, who determined that adequate light and air would be let in if a skyscraper tower, no matter how high, occupied only 25 percent of its site. He demonstrated the effectiveness of this principle in his needle-like Singer Tower (1906–8), which at forty-seven stories was the tallest building in the city. But not for long: the Metropolitan Life Tower (1907–9, Napoleon Lebrun and Sons) on Madison Square, modeled after the Campanile of San Marco in Venice, was three stories higher.

The last unregulated office buildings were completed about the time of the First World War, among them the new Equitable Building (1913–15, E. R. Graham), which rose thirty-eight stories and was said to cast a noonday shadow four blocks long; the colossal Municipal Building (1909–14, W. M. Kendall of McKim, Mead and White), at Chambers and Centre streets; and the romantic neo-Gothic Woolworth Building (1910–13, Gilbert), which has a mounted tower and with a height equal to sixty stories remained the world's tallest commercial building until 1930. The design of skyscrapers was transformed in 1916 when the city passed a zoning law restricting the height and bulk of buildings.

2. After 1916

A formula called the "zoning envelope" required that upper stories be stepped back above a prescribed level. A tower of unlimited height was allowed over only 25 percent of the site. These regulations produced the "setback" or "wedding cake" profiles (some with a slender tower) that dominated design until the next major zoning change, in 1961. During the 1920s architects developed an aesthetic of simple, sculptural mass expressed in pyramidal forms clad in brick or stone; early examples of the "setback style" were the Shelton Hotel (1924, Arthur Loomis Harmon) and the New York Telephone Building at 140 West Street (1923–25, Ralph Walker). Fueled by national prosperity and easy financing, the volume of construction increased in the second half of the 1920s. This increase coincided with the peak of art deco design to produce a spate of modernistic skyscrapers. Most activity took place in the burgeoning business district of midtown Manhattan. Within a few blocks of Grand Central Terminal rose the Chanin, Chrysler, Lincoln, Graybar, Fred F. French, and Daily News buildings, while projects such as Rockefeller Center and the Empire State Building opened up new areas distant from transportation centers. Speculation drove up land prices and led to the construction of taller towers. Downtown in the financial district several structures of fifty to seventy stories were shoe-horned into narrow sites, among them the Bank of Manhattan Company and the Cities Service buildings. The race to build ever taller buildings resulted in the Chrysler Building (1046 feet, or 319 meters) and the Empire State Building (1250 feet, or 381 meters). Between 1920 and 1935 the amount of office space in the city nearly doubled, from 74 million square feet (seven million square meters) to 138 million square feet (thirteen million square meters); at least two thirds of this amount was in speculative construction. Skyscrapers also accommodated hotels, apartments, and even hospitals. Most high-rise buildings in the outer boroughs were residential, although a number of office towers were built in Brooklyn.

Construction virtually ceased during the Depression and the Second World War. When building resumed, the new aesthetic of the International Style was firmly established. Design changes both external and internal were made possible by advances in curtain-wall technology, air conditioning, and other mechanical and structural systems. The United Nations Secretariat (1947) and the corporate headquarters Lever House (1952, Gordon Bunshaft) and the Seagram Building (1958, Ludwig Mies van der Rohe) on Park Avenue established the prismatic glass box as the modern paradigm. Unlike older buildings that usually filled their lots, these were sited away from the street in plazas. Acclaimed by planners, the "tower-in-the-plaza" arrangement was encouraged by the zoning law of 1961, a sweeping revision that imposed a maximum volume for a building based on a multiple of the area of the lot, known as the Floor Area Ratio, or FAR; bonus floors could be added by including public spaces and amenities. Under the new code in the 1960s and 1970s sheer metal and glass shafts such as those on 6th Avenue at Rockefeller Center proliferated. Skyscrapers of the 1960s were often big and bland; the construction of the Pan Am Building exploited the air rights above Grand Central Terminal to create 2.4 million square feet (222,960 square meters) of floor space.

Redevelopment in lower Manhattan did not begin until Chase Manhattan Bank built new headquarters, designed by Bunshaft, in 1960. During the late 1960s large speculative buildings on Water Street boxed in the skyline along the East River. On Broadway the Singer Tower became the tallest building ever demolished, making way for 1 Liberty Plaza (1974). Plans for the World Trade Center, announced in 1964, called for twin towers 110 stories and 1350 feet (412 meters) tall. Designed by Minoru Yamasaki and completed in 1973, the complex added ten million square feet (929,000 square meters) of office space just before a collapse of the real-estate market that persisted until the late 1970s.

Changing tastes and technology dictated new forms and styles in skyscrapers of the 1980s. Reacting against the anonymity of modernist slabs and spurred by the theories of post-modernism, many architects revived historical references and lavish ornamentation. Masonry cladding was used in the headquarters of American Telephone and Telegraph (1978–84, Philip Johnson; now the Sony Building) and the Heron Tower (1987, Kohn Pedersen Fox); others such as the Carnegie Hall Tower (1990, Cesar Pelli) reflected the character of an adjacent landmark or neighborhood. With the demand for "smart buildings" wired for computers and for large floor areas of thirty to forty thousand square feet (three to four thousand square meters), buildings became bulkier. Sites at the edges of the dense business districts permitted such buildings, among them the four giants of the World Financial Center (1985–88, Pelli) at Battery Park City and the full-block development of Worldwide Plaza (1989, Skidmore, Owings and Merrill; David Childs) west of 8th Avenue between 49th and 50th streets. Other towers more centrally situated, such as the headquarters of the Morgan Bank on Wall Street (1988, Kevin Roche), were able to achieve the same expanded volume by using the air rights of adjacent low-rise buildings or landmarks. Special zoning incentives made the west side of midtown Manhattan especially attractive to developers. From 1978 to 1991 more than 59 million square feet (six million square meters) of commercial space was constructed in Manhattan.

In 1990 New York City had twenty-five of the one hundred tallest buildings in the world.

Winston Weisman: "A New View of Skyscraper History," *The Rise of an American Architecture*, ed. Edgar Kaufmann Jr. (New York: Praeger, 1970), 115–60

Paul Goldberger: *The Skyscraper* (New York: Alfred A. Knopf, 1981)

Sarah Bradford Landau: "The Tall Office Building Artistically Reconsidered: Arcaded Buildings of the New York School, c. 1870–1890," *In Search of Modern Architecture: A Tribute to Henry-Russell Hitchcock*, ed. Helen Searing (New York: Architectural History Foundation / Cambridge: MIT Press, 1982)

Robert A. M. Stern et al.: *New York 1900* (New York: Rizzoli, 1983)

Robert A. M. Stern et al.: *New York 1930* (New York: Rizzoli, 1987)

Sarah Bradford Landau and Carl W. Condit: *Rise of the New York Skyscraper, 1865–1913* (New Haven: Yale University Press, forthcoming)

Sarah Bradford Landau (§1), Carol Willis (§2)

slang. From the early nineteenth century various aspects of life in New York City inspired the formation of slang words and phrases. The wealthy were known in the 1840s as the *Upper Ten (Thousand)*; many lived on 5th Avenue and by 1850 were known as *Avenoodles*, which played on the local pronunciation of "avenue" as two syllables. In the 1880s *Astorbilt* (a form combining Astor and Vanderbilt) became a generic surname for the wealthy. The words *ritz* and *ritzy* and the phrase *puttin' on the ritz* were inspired by the high style of the Ritz hotels. During the 1890s the wealthy were often called the *Four Hundred* in newspapers, after the society figure Ward McAllister remarked that Mrs. William Astor limited her guest list to four hundred names. Chorus girls (often called *Dumb Doras* from 1890) accompanied *sugar daddys* (1905), who took them to late-night dinners of champagne and lobster at *lobster palaces* in Times Square. From the Cockney use of the verb *to hook*, meaning to solicit for prostitution, the noun *hooker* was formed in the 1840s; the term was later reinforced by the reputation of brothels in Corlear's Hook, where residents were known as "Hookers." About this time the terms *O.K.*, *shyster*, and *smart aleck* came into use in the city. From the 1860s being *sent up the river* meant going to Sing Sing Prison, which stood on the Hudson River at Sing Sing, now known as Ossining. Pesky, loud-mouthed newsboys prompted the phrase *go peddle your papers*, meaning "get lost."

In the 1880s *hokey pokey* came to mean "penny serving of ice cream" rather than simply "trickery"; the ice cream vendor became known as the *hokey-pokey man*. Some newspapers in the city gained a reputation for *yellow journalism*, after the policies of two sensational newspapers that also printed the comic strip "The Yellow Kid." *Skyscraper* was coined in the 1880s, and its adoption was influenced by the spectacle of tall buildings in New York City. The phrase *to do a Brodie* was inspired by the false claim of Steve Brodie, a saloonkeeper from the Bowery, that he had dived from the Brooklyn Bridge in 1886. *Hot dogs*, introduced at Coney Island about 1890, were perhaps so named because according to urban folklore they were made with dog meat. Gawking tourists became known as *rubberneckers* in the 1890s. At the turn of the century the elevated lines, or *els*, were so crowded that the hours when most people traveled to and from work became known as *rush hours*; many riders stood clinging to overhead straps, inspiring the word *straphanger*. About this time *breadline* came into use, after Fleischmann's bakery began giving bread and coffee to the poor each night at the side door of its shop on Broadway at 10th Street.

By 1915 country residents of upstate New York were called *appleknockers*, after a putative method of harvesting apples by knocking them down with long sticks; the name of the town of Herkimer, New York, inspired the term *Herkimer Jerkimer*, meaning both a hick and a jerk. Nightlife after the First World War focused on the activities of *Café Society*, a name first used in a gossip column and generally popular in the 1930s. Younger members of fashionable society who had apartments were called *cliff dwellers* and older ones who lived in mansions on Murray Hill were known as *cave dwellers*. A Broadway musical of the 1920s helped to make popular the expression *makin' whoopee* for risqué behavior, including that of the *butter-and-egg man*, a big spender in nightclubs, who was so named because he seemed to have become wealthy in the dairy business. The term *g-string* came into use in the 1930s in the burlesque theater and derives from the name of a loincloth used by an American Indian male. Young men and women of little means sunbathed at *tarpaper beach*, the tarred and graveled rooftops of apartment buildings. *Dumbbell* tenements were named for the shape of their floorplan. *Sidewalk superintendents* watched the progress of local construction sites. Homeless women in the 1960s became known as *shopping bag ladies* or simply *bag ladies*. *Yuppies*, a term coined in New York City in 1983, came to symbolize the 1980s.

Irving Lewis Allen: *The City in Slang: New York Life and Popular Speech* (New York: Oxford University Press, 1993)

Irving Lewis Allen

slaughterhouses. For a discussion of slaughterhouses from colonial times to the late twentieth century see Meatpacking.

slavery. Slavery was introduced in Manhattan by the Dutch, who settled eleven African men there in 1626 and three women in 1628, all of whom had been captured in war. The Dutch West India Company was among the foremost slave traders in the world but provided only a few Africans to New Netherland, where slaves commanded lower prices than in the Caribbean. Most slaves taken before the 1650s were captured by Dutch or French privateers from Spanish or Portuguese ships. Initially the company, the main employer in the colony, used slaves for projects such as building the fort of New Amsterdam, laying roads, carrying merchandise, and providing officers with domestic services like cooking and laundering. During these years slaves were married in church and their children were registered with the company. As the settlement became established and public works slackened, the need for slaves diminished and the eleven men of the first cargo petitioned for their freedom. On 25 February 1644 they and their wives received their conditional release in return for services on demand and lifelong payments due annually in cash or kind. The company surrendered none of its claims to service, shifted living costs to the petitioners, and bound to service their children, born and unborn; it later freed some of the nearly two dozen persons affected by this arrangement, and a comparable number were freed privately by 1664 when the English took control of the colony. At this time at least 9 percent of the eight thousand settlers were Africans, and there were communities of slaves and free blacks.

Free Black and Slave Population of New York, Kings, Queens, Richmond, and Westchester Counties, 1790–1820

	1790		1800		1810		1820	
	Slaves	Free Blacks	Slaves	Free Blacks	Slaves	Free Blacks	Slaves	Free Blacks
New York	2,369	1,101	2,868	3,499	1,686	8,137	518	10,368
Kings	1,432	46	1,479	332	1,118	735	879	882
Queens	2,309	808	1,528	1,431	809	2,354	559	2,648
Richmond	759	127	675	83	437	274	532	78
Westchester	1,419	357	1,259	482	982	948	205	1,638
Total	8,288	2,439	7,809	5,827	5,032	12,448	2,693	15,614
Total Black Population	10,727		13,636		17,480		18,307	
Slaves as Percentage of Black Population	77.3		57.3		28.8		14.7	

Source: U.S. Bureau of the Census, Census of Population 1790, 1800, 1810, 1820

Compiled by James Bradley

The Articles of Capitulation formalizing the surrender of the Dutch preserved all the property rights that they recognized, and the ownership of slaves was transferred to the English, who soon institutionalized slavery by endorsing it as a system of property rights in the Laws of 1665, the first legal code in the colony. Slaves were classified as chattel bound to serve involuntary, indefinite, and heritable tenure, and their marriages were no longer recognized as legal. American Indians and Africans were enslaved, but the laws made "slaves" synonymous with "Negroes," and the Iroquois Confederacy, the Hurons, and the Delawares made pacts with the English to return runaways. To help keep peace the colonial governor Edmund Andros prohibited the enslavement of Indians from local tribes in 1679; others continued to be enslaved until the 1740s.

White working men protested the increasing use of slaves in shops, along the docks, and in skilled and unskilled trades, and eventually municipal licensing ordinances banned blacks from driving wagons and selling goods in public markets. The restrictions mostly affected free blacks, since slaves continued to be employed in these ways by their masters. Restrictions on slavery were proposed as early as the 1680s. Many people resented the power of the Royal African Company (chartered in 1672), which had a monopoly in the slave trade: a tax was levied on the importing of slaves, though smuggling made this ineffective. By the beginning of the eighteenth century about 14.2 percent of the population was black. The number of slaves entering the port was 225 between 1701 and 1704, and 185 between 1710 and 1712; all were from Africa, and unlike those who had entered on earlier shipments from the West Indies they had no experience with slavery. Between 1700 and 1774 the city legally admitted about 6800 slaves, 2800 of whom were from Africa. Slave markets at the foot of Wall Street were named after prominent families involved in slave trading, including the Crommelins, Schuylers, Van Zandts, and Waltons. Other families that made high profits legally and illegally in the slave trade were the Beekmans, Crugers, Livingstons, Philips, Van Hornes, and Van Cortlandts.

Slaves did have a very few rights: those who willfully killed or maimed them were punished under a law passed in 1686. But the purpose of most laws was to control rather than to protect slaves. A set of laws passed in 1702 prohibited salves from escaping, taking part in conspiracies or insurrections, trafficking in stolen goods, assembling in groups larger than three, bearing arms, and traveling without permission. In 1705 the state assembly declared baptism ineffective for slaves and from the following year endorsed conversion. Local ordinances barred slaves from various activities.

Despite the laws slaves often stole, gambled, drank, evaded curfew, and disturbed the peace; less frequently they committed serious crimes such as assault, battery, murder (usually of whites), and arson. After a time in which the number of slaves increased dramatically, recently arrived Africans led an uprising on the night of 6 April 1712, in which eight whites were killed and more than twenty others seriously injured. In addition fires were set in the east ward, although only a few outbuildings burned and property damage was light. Twenty-five blacks paid for the incident with their lives: six were hunted down and nineteen were later executed. During the same year and again in 1730 more laws were passed to tighten the control of slaves.

The division of families was a principal cause of hardship for slaves. Like those in many other cities, slave families in New York City seldom shared one household. Mothers and young children lived together but men were housed separately. Visiting privileges were granted for Sundays, but husbands and wives frequently negotiated weeknight meetings, usually at the woman's quarters. Often men were denied visits and violence resulted; in 1741 Roosevelt Quack was kept from seeing his wife, the governor's cook, and burned the governor's house. The separation of mothers and children at sale, especially beyond visiting distance, was also a source of great distress.

Slaves recognized and respected their own family unions regardless of law, and networks of kin developed early. The proximity of houses to each other also encouraged networks for friendship and recreation. Some slaves organized theft rings such as the Geneva Club of the 1730s; members conspired with whites and caroused with them in notorious taverns where they held private celebrations. Some celebrations were public, but carnivals such as Pinkster and Election Day that were held by rural blacks were restrained in Manhattan, perhaps because officials feared that they could not assure public safety.

Between 1730 and 1740 at least 1429 slaves were brought to the city. By 1741 the ratio of men to women had become imbalanced: because of the growing use of slaves in business the number of men for every hundred women rose from ninety-nine in 1731 to 120 in 1741. On 18 March 1741 an uprising began that lasted more than six months and resulted in massive property damage. The seat of royal government was destroyed by fire, including the governor's residence and the rest of Fort George on the southwestern tip of Manhattan; other homes and businesses burned during the following three weeks. The only death was that of a soldier at the fort. An investigation led by Justice Daniel Horsmanden of the supreme court blamed a conspiracy of slaves aided by white accomplices for the fires, and trials on various charges resulted in the execution of thirty black men, two white men, and two white women, as well as the deportation of seventy-two blacks. Misgivings arose almost immediately that the punishments had exceeded the crimes, and the episode remained controversial. In the 1740s the proportion of slaves in the population peaked at 20.9 percent.

Just before the American Revolution New York City was second only to Charleston, South Carolina, among urban centers of slavery. There were 3137 blacks in Manhattan, about 14.3 percent of the population, and the number grew during the war as thousands of runaways and Loyalists' slaves flooded Manhattan, hopeful for freedom that had been promised by the British. Many bore arms against patriots who owned slaves. The local Black Brigade was housed at several sites, including 18 Broadway and 10 Church Street, and distinguished itself variously as the Royal African Regiment and the Ethiopian Regiment in battles in New York State and New Jersey. Many slaves won their freedom from one side or the other during the war. Nearly five thousand blacks sailed with the British in the evacuation of the city in November 1783.

In the decades after the revolution the effects of national liberty eventually eroded slavery in New York City. Large numbers of white workers who moved to the city forced gradual emancipation but like many others refused to extend civil rights to blacks, which were omitted from legislation passed by the state in 1785. There were 2369 slaves in the city in 1790.

The first step toward ending slavery in the city was an act of 1799, which declared free the children of slaves born on or after 4 July, granted freedom to slaves born before that date at the age of twenty-four for women and twenty-eight for men, and required the registration of children indentured to their masters until the age of manumission. A law passed in 1809 recognized the legality of marriages between slaves and prohibited for the first time the forced separation of slave families. In 1817 the state legislature and Governor Daniel D. Tompkins agreed to abolish slavery in New York on 4 July 1827, a date followed by two days of singing, parades, and fireworks. Complete abolition was not achieved until 1841, when the state rescinded provisions allowing nonresidents to hold slaves for as long as nine months. Slavery nonetheless remained a part of the economy in New York City until the Civil War. The slave states had strong economic ties to the city, which the *New York Times* described as "the spot most tainted by Southern poison." Blacks lived in fear of the notorious "blackbirders," who until the war seized victims from the streets for sale in the South. Other hardships also persisted for former slaves, who had to eke out a living amid racial hostility that flared into such violent incidents as the draft riots of 1863.

Edgar J. McManus: *Negro Slavery in New York* (Syracuse, N.Y.: Syracuse University Press, 1966)

Thomas J. Davis: "Slavery in Colonial New York City" (diss., Columbia University, 1974)

Vivienne L. Kruger: "Born to Run: The Slave Family in Early New York, 1626 to 1827" (diss., Columbia University, 1985)

See also Abolitionism.

Thomas J. Davis

sliver buildings. A term used in New York City during the late 1970s and early 1980s to describe tall, slender apartment buildings on small parcels in mid block, built by real-estate developers to maintain high profits at a time when the city's residential housing market was at its peak. The structures rose as high as thirty stories, usually contained only one apartment on each floor, and could be as narrow as twenty-two feet (seven meters). They were especially common on the Upper East Side. Sliver buildings were criticized for disrupting the visual harmony of low-rise residential streets, and after a campaign by activists the city's zoning laws were amended in 1983 to prohibit their construction in designated areas of the city, including the Upper East Side. Some examples of sliver buildings are 350 East 86th Street, 344 East 63rd Street, and 266 East 78th Street.

Rebecca Read Shanor

Sloan, John (French) (*b* Lock Haven, Penn., 2 Aug 1871; *d* Hanover, N.H., 7 Sept 1951). Painter. Brought up in Philadelphia, he left school to support his family by doing lettering and advertisements. In 1892 he became an illustrator and art editor for the *Inquirer* and in 1895 he moved to the *Press*. During the 1890s he studied with Robert Henri, who encouraged him to paint in a realist style. He joined Henri in New York City in 1904 and worked for several magazines as a freelance illustrator while completing a series of etchings depicting life in the city (including "New York City Life," 1905–6) and various paintings. With Henri in 1908 he organized an exhibition at the Macbeth Galleries of eight realist and independent painters; he also helped to organize the Exhibition of Independent Artists in 1910. He took part in the Armory Show of 1913 and in the first exhibition of the Society of Independent Artists in 1917, and was also a president of the society. Sloan was a Socialist candidate for the state assembly in 1910, and in 1912 he joined the staff of the radical publication the *Masses*, edited by Max Eastman. He did his best illustrations for the magazine but resigned in 1916 over a policy dispute and eventually left the Socialist Party. During the 1920s and into the 1930s he was an influential teacher at the Art Students League. He was elected in 1919 to the National Institute of Arts and Letters and in 1942 to the Academy of Arts and Letters. The Whitney Museum of American Art held a retrospective exhibition of Sloan's work in 1952.

David W. Scott and E. John Bullard: *John Sloan, 1871–1951* (Washington: National Gallery of Art, 1971)

Patricia Hills

Sloane. For information on the carpet and furniture retailers see W. J. Sloane.

Slovaks. The first Slovaks in New York City were immigrants from the Austro-Hungarian Empire who settled in Manhattan about 1848, especially around 14th Street and 2nd Avenue. In the 1880s Slovak communities took shape in the 70s and 80s between York and 3rd avenues, in Long Island City, Astoria, and Sunnyside (Queens), and in Greenpoint, particularly the section bounded by Newtown

John Sloan, Sixth Avenue Elevated at Third Street *(1928). Collection of the Whitney Museum of American Art*

Creek, the East River, Grand Street, and McGinnis Boulevard. The first Slovak organization in New York City, Živena (1883), was absorbed in 1887 by the St. John the Baptist Society. A large number of organizations soon followed, by the early 1890s including the Catholic Ženská Jednota (Women's union, 1892), St. Catherine's Society for Slovak Women, the Social Society of St. Francis, St. Peter's Society, and the St. Matthew's and St. Joseph's Society; these were joined in 1905 by the Central Slovak National Council and in 1915 by the Slovenská Telovičná Jednota Sokol (Slovak gymnastic union falcon). National Slovak organizations also opened branches in the city, among them the Prvý Bednársky Výpomocný Spolok (First cooper's benefit society, 1888), the Slovak Evangelical Union (a Lutheran organization, 1893), the Slovak Calvinist Union (1894), Národný Slovenský Spolok (National Slovak society), Jednota (Union), and the American Fund for Czechoslovak Relief (founded 1948). A Slovak American Cultural Center was formed in the city in 1968.

Religious institutions included the St. Elias Greek Catholic parish (1883) and three Roman Catholic churches: the Church of St. Elizabeth of Hungary (1891), the Church of St. John Nepomucene (1895), and the Church of the Holy Family (1895). The Holy Trinity Evangelical Lutheran parish was formed in lower Manhattan in 1902. Slovaks also launched a number of local newspapers, notably *Slovák v Amerike* (1889–), *Newyorský denník* (New York Daily, 1895–1974), and *Slobodný orol* (Free eagle, 1900–4), published by Jozef Kossalko.

The Slovak population in New York City reached 10,504 in 1910 and increased sharply after the formation of Czechoslovakia in 1918. The issue of Slovak independence sharply divided the Slovak community in New York City, with one group supporting Tomáš Masaryk and the ideal of one democratic Czechoslovak state, while others argued that only through independence could the Slovaks avoid being taken advantage of by the Czechs. By 1970 Slovaks in the city accounted for more than 1 percent of the total population, and in 1977 they numbered 85,000. Among the prominent members of the Slovak community in New York City are the writer Thomas Bel, the journalist John Sciranka, the social leader Daniel Sustek, the actress Pauline Novomeská, and the editor and political leader Andrew J. Valusek.

John S. Scíranka, ed.: *Slovenski pioneri v New Yorku, z poverenia Spolku sv. Matúša Ev., čís. 45. I. K. S. J. vydal výbor 35. ročného jubileumu; Sostavil J. C. Scíranka Dňa 6. novembra 1927 v halle osady sv. Jána Nepomuckého* (New York: Slovák v Amerike, 1927)

Vrastislav Busek and John Shintay: *The Czechs and Slovaks of New York* (Cicero, Ill.: Czechoslovak National Council of America, 1969)

"The History of Slovak Catholic Parishes of Greater New York," *Katolícky Sokol*, 22 Oct 1975, p. 13

John Andrew Bertha: "Slovaks of New York City" (thesis, Florida State University, Center for Yugoslav–American Studies, 1977)

Mark Stolarik: *Immigration and Urbanization: The Slovak Experience* (New York: AMS, 1989)

Edward Kasinec

Slovenes. The Slovenes, a southern Slavic people, first emigrated from the Austro-Hungarian Empire and settled in greater New York at the end of the nineteenth century. Because they were for the most part poorly educated and of peasant background, their earliest occupations were in the straw-hat industry in New York City. During the 1920s and 1930s some Slovenes were successful in establishing their own hat manufacturing firms in the city. Other entrepreneurs opened retail and service businesses such as groceries, bars, bakeries, craft shops, travel agencies, and shipping companies. Some of these firms evolved into banks. Community life focused on the Slovenian parish of St. Cyril (Franciscan Fathers), formed in July 1916. There were also mutual assistance organizations (such as the League of Slovenian Americans, founded in the early 1970s) and singing and dramatic societies. The Society for Slovene Studies was established in 1973 at Columbia University as a national association of American scholars, devotees, and supporters. In 1979 it began sponsoring the journal *Slovene Studies.* In the mid 1990s a group of Slovenian–American professionals in the city began planning a national organization to be known as the American Slovene Congress. Among the notable Slovenian intellectual and cultural leaders who have resided or worked in New York City are the prolific writer and political activist Louis Adamic (1899–1951), the musician Anton Schubel (1899–1965), and the editor and community leader Frank Sakser (1859–1937). Sakser was also the founder and publisher of *Glas naroda* (The People's Voice), published in New York City between 1893 and 1963, and of its *Slovenski-Amerikanski koledar.*

John Arnez: *Slovenci v New Yorku* (New York: Studia Slovenica, 1966)

"Society for Slovene Studies: Ten Years of Activity, 1973–1983," *Slovene Studies: Journal of the Society for Slovene Studies* 5 (1983), 3–103

Edward Kasinec

SLP. See Socialist labor party.

smallpox. Public health records for New York City reveal that epidemics of smallpox, a viral infectious disease that is easily transmitted from person to person, wreaked havoc among the public from the colonial period well into the nineteenth century. The disease had a high mortality rate and left its survivors with disfiguring scars along the exposed parts of the body. One of the most devastating smallpox epidemics of the colonial period was one lasting three months in the late summer and autumn of 1731, when 5 to 8 percent of the city's ten thousand inhabitants were killed. During this epidemic a smallpox inoculation was first used in New York City, beginning a debate between proponents and opponents of vaccination that lasted in some fashion into the late twentieth century.

By the mid eighteenth century smallpox visited the city almost annually. Lazarettos or "quarantine hospitals" were established by the city during the nineteenth century on remote islands off Manhattan such as Blackwell's Island (1828) and North Brother Island (1880), to care for smallpox patients and more importantly to remove them from the healthy population at large. By 1850 smallpox accounted for 25.4 of every one thousand deaths in New York City. The settlement in the city of immigrants from countries such as Ireland, Great Britain, and Germany in the early to mid nineteenth century, followed by a huge influx of eastern Europeans and Italians between 1880 and 1924, soon became the most frequent vector of smallpox. Many immigrants and anti-vaccinationists distrustful of American medicine avoided the inoculations sponsored by the public health department, creating a susceptible reservoir for the continued spread of the disease. Mandatory vaccination laws during the late nineteenth century, better screening methods, and educational programs that explained the importance of smallpox prevention helped bring about the decline of smallpox by the beginning of the twentieth century. It was eventually eradicated by vaccination programs from the 1920s to the 1940s aimed at children entering the public schools, and efforts by the World Health Organization from the 1950s to the 1980s.

John Duffy: *Epidemics in Colonial America* (Baton Rouge: Louisiana State University Press, 1953; repr. 1979)

John Duffy: *A History of Public Health in New York City* (New York: Russell Sage Foundation, 1968, 1974)

Howard Markel

Smalls' Paradise. Jazz club, opened on 22 October 1925 at 2294½ 7th Avenue by Ed Smalls. It seated about fifteen hundred and was racially integrated, although because of its relatively high prices the clientele was largely white. Advertised as "Harlem's House of Mirth and Music," the club featured performances by such musicians as Willie "the Lion" Smith, Fletcher Henderson, and James P. Johnson, as well as elaborate floor shows, Chinese food, and singing waiters. It attracted leading figures of the Harlem Renaissance, including Countee Cullen and Carl Van Vechten. Smalls' operated under the same name until 1986.

Marc Ferris

Alfred E. Smith's campaign poster for the Democratic National Convention, 1924

Smith, Alfred E(manuel) (*b* New York City, 30 Dec 1873; *d* New York City, 4 Oct 1944). Governor and presidential candidate. The son of immigrants, he attended St. James Parochial School but left before graduating to help support his family. After various employments he entered politics and soon became a favorite of Charles F. Murphy, the boss of Tammany Hall. During these years he lived at 83 Madison Street (1900–1, now the site of St. Joseph's Convent) and 28 Oliver Street (1904–9) before moving to 25 Oliver Street in 1909, where he remained until 1924. From 1904 to 1915 he served as a Democrat in the state assembly, where he gradually assumed important leadership positions. He introduced legislation beneficial to New York City, especially his district, and was named vice-chairman of the Factory Investigating Commission formed in 1911 after the Triangle Shirtwaist fire; he and the chairman, Senator Robert F. Wagner, helped to improve the conditions of the city's workers by ensuring that the state labor code was revised. In 1915 he attended the state constitutional convention, where he vigorously defended the city's interests in the matters of apportionment and home rule. The proposed constitutional revisions were defeated at the polls, but he was widely praised for his constructive approach to public affairs. During the same year he won election as sheriff of New York County, a position that offered him generous compensation but little challenging work. As president of the Board of Aldermen in 1918 he had few responsibilities but remained active as a speaker at benefits and rallies. He won his first gubernatorial election in 1918 but was defeated for reelection. In 1921 he was a member of the commission that guided through the state legislature a plan for a port authority run jointly by New York and New Jersey.

After regaining the governorship in 1922 Smith championed progressive policies for New York City. He sought to transfer ownership of the transit system to the city but settled for legislation allowing the city to build, operate, and regulate subway lines. He also sponsored laws on rent control, tenant protection, and the construction of low-cost housing, an initiative that met with modest success, and ensured the passage of laws that improved workers' compensation, set a maximum number of hours that women could work, and increased aid to mothers, infants, and dependent children. After he put Robert Moses in charge of parks statewide many recreational areas were built in the metropolitan area. His policies often cut deeply into city politics and led to feuds with the newspaper publisher William Randolph Hearst and Mayor John F. Hylan; these did not subside until 1925, when Hearst retreated and Hylan's attempt to win a third term ended in a loss in a primary election to James J. Walker. Smith was the unsuccessful Democratic presidential nominee in 1928. Soon after his defeat he returned to the city with his family, where they took up residence on 5th Avenue. In the following years he became president of the Empire State Building Corporation, undertook many charitable projects, gave lectures, and was active in the affairs of the Catholic church; he also sponsored a housing development, the Alfred E. Smith Houses, that was built at 174 South Street, the site of his birth. Smith remained immensely popular in the city, which named him its "First Citizen."

Matthew Josephson and Hannah Josephson: *Al Smith: Hero of the Cities: A Political Portrait* (Boston: Houghton Mifflin, 1969)

David R. Colburn: "Alfred E. Smith: The First Fifty Years, 1873–1924" (diss., University of North Carolina, 1971)

Robert F. Wesser: *A Response to Progressivism: The Democratic Party and New York Politics, 1902–1918* (New York: New York University Press, 1986)

For further illustration see Catt, Carrie Chapman.

Robert F. Wesser

Smith, Bessie [Elizabeth] (*b* Chattanooga, Tenn., 15 April 1895; *d* Clarksdale, Miss., 26 Sept 1937). Singer. She began her career in 1912 as a dancer with Moses Stokes's traveling show and toured with the Theatre Owners Booking Agency (TOBA) and the Liberty Belles. She sang with Charlie Taylor's Band in New York City in 1920 and with the revue "How Come?" in 1923. Her recording career began when Clarence Williams and Frank Walker of Columbia Records persuaded her to record "Down Hearted Blues" (1923); her subsequent collaborations with Louis Armstrong, Fletcher Henderson, and Tommy Ladnier sold millions of copies. She achieved a level of popularity unusual for a jazz and blues singer; Carl Van Vechten, a patron of the Harlem Renaissance who was white, promoted her work among white intellectuals and leaders in entertainment. She made her début on Broadway in *Pansy* (1929) and performed in the revue "League of Rhythm" in 1936 at the Apollo Theatre. Smith is remembered for her rich, expressive voice and her dramatic stage presence. Many of her songs describe the experiences of southern black migrants, especially the struggles of black women to adjust to urban life in the North. Langston Hughes considered her songs exemplars of the creativity inherent in black vernacular culture.

Chris Albertson: *Bessie Smith: Empress of the Blues* (New York: Schirmer, 1975)

Kathy J. Ogren

Smith [née Keogh], **Betty** [Elizabeth] **(Wehner)** (*b* Brooklyn, 15 Dec 1904; *d* Shelton, Conn., 17 Jan 1972). Novelist. After leaving school in her early teens she attended the University of Michigan (1927–30) as a special student and the Yale School of Drama (1930–34). She is best known for her novel *A Tree Grows in Brooklyn* (1943), a poignant account of childhood in the tenements of Williamsburg. Her later works include *Tomorrow Will Be Better* (1948), *Maggie — Now* (1958), *Joy in the Morning* (1963), and more than forty plays.

B. Kimberly Taylor

Smith, David (Roland) (*b* Decatur, Ind., 6 March 1906; *d* near Bennington, Vt., 23 May 1965). Sculptor. He arrived in New York City in 1926, studied painting at the Art Students League in 1927–32, and began welding metal sculptures in his studio at the Brooklyn Terminal Iron Works in 1933. His first sculptures were innovative works influenced by his experience as a welder in an automobile plant and by illustrations of the work of Julio Gonzalez. In 1938 he moved to Bolton Landing. His *Hudson River Landscape* (1951, welded steel), inspired by frequent train trips along the Hudson into New York City, is at the Whitney Museum of American Art. Smith worked in several styles inspired by cubism and constructivism. His last works, in stainless steel, are characterized by an unusual finish, first polished and then abraded, creating abstract marks that reflect the light around them. Many consider Smith the greatest modern American sculptor.

Karen Wilkin: *David Smith* (New York: Abbeville, 1984)

Harriet F. Senie

Smith, Red [Walter Wellesley] (*b* Green Bay, Wis., 25 Sept 1905; *d* Stamford, Conn., 15 Jan 1982). Sportswriter. He studied journalism at the University of Notre Dame (graduated 1927) and began his career at the *Milwaukee Sentinel*, the *St. Louis Star*, and the *Philadelphia Record*. In 1945 he moved to New York City to write a sports column for the *New York Herald Tribune* that was syndicated in ninety newspapers. After the dissolution of the successor to the *Herald Tribune*, the *World Journal–Tribune*, he joined the *New York Times* in 1971, for which he wrote a column until the end of his life. Smith strove for simplicity in his writing and disdained hyperbole, sentimentality, and cliché. He avoided both the tendency to lionize athletes and the "wiseguy" style affected by many urban sportswriters. Although he wrote about virtually all sports, he was especially fond of baseball, football, boxing, and horse racing, and disliked basketball. The most respected sportswriter of his generation, he won a Pulitzer Prize for commentary in 1976. Collections of his writings include *Out of the Red* (1950), *Views of Sport* (1954), *The Best of Red Smith* (1963), and *The Red Smith Reader* (1982).

Ira Berkow: *Red: A Biography of Red Smith* (New York: Times Books, 1986)

Smith, Stephen (*b* near Skaneateles, N.Y., 19 Feb 1823; *d* Montour Falls, N.Y., 26 Aug 1922). Surgeon and public health official. A graduate of the College of Physicians and Surgeons (1850), he was an attending surgeon at Bellevue Hospital from 1854 to 1896, and from 1861 to 1872 he taught surgery and anatomy at Bellevue Hospital Medical College. His leadership of the campaign to establish the Metropolitan Board of Health (1866) is regarded as one of the most notable achievements in the history of public health in New York City and the United States; he was a member of the board from 1868 to 1875. Smith designed the plan for Roosevelt Hospital (1866) and promoted improvements at Bellevue Hospital. He edited the *New York Journal of Medicine* and founded the American Public Health Association. In 1892 he was president of the New York Medical Association. His book *The City That Was* (1911) describes his many battles to improve public health in New York City. He lived for many years at 300 Central Park West.

Gert H. Brieger: "Sanitary Reform in New York City: Stephen Smith and the Passage of the Metropolitan Health Bill," *Bulletin of the History of Medicine* 40 (1966), 407–29

Allen J. Share

Smith, Tony (*b* South Orange, N.J., 23 Sept 1912; *d* New York City, 26 Dec 1980). Architect, painter, and sculptor. He studied at the Art Students League in 1933–36 and worked briefly as an apprentice to Frank Lloyd Wright before pursuing a twenty-year career as an architect and painter. He taught art at New York University from 1946 to 1950 and then at Cooper Union and the Pratt Institute. From 1960 he worked as a sculptor and became an important figure in the development of large-scale minimalist works. From 1962 until his death he taught at Hunter College, which in his honor installed *Tau* (1965–80, welded steel painted black) at the southwest corner of 68th Street and Lexington Avenue.

Nine Sculptures by Tony Smith (Newark, N.J.: Newark Museum, 1970)

Harriet F. Senie

Smith, William, Jr. (*b* New York City, 25 June 1728; *d* Quebec, 3 Dec 1793). Lawyer and historian. After attending Yale College he was admitted to the bar and with William Livingston in 1752 published a digest of colonial laws enacted between 1691 and 1751. A central figure among lawyers, he was an influential contributor to the *Independent Reflector* and the *Occasional Reverberator*. With Livingston and John Morin Scott he published *A Review of the Military Operations* (1758); he became known for *The History of the Province* (1757), the first published history of the province of New York. Appointed chief justice of the province in 1763, he became a member of the provincial council in 1767 and helped to organize the Whig Club. Smith moved to England during the evacuation of the British in 1783; he was later the chief justice of Canada.

Leslie F. S. Upton: *The Loyal Whig: William Smith of New York* (Toronto: University of Toronto Press, 1969)

James E. Mooney

Smith, Willie "the Lion" [William Henry Joseph Bonaparte Bertholoff] (*b* Goshen, N.Y., 25 Nov 1897; *d* New York City, 18 April 1973). Pianist and composer. He grew up in Newark, New Jersey, and began playing the piano at the age of six. In his teens he played professionally in the saloons of New York City and Atlantic City, New Jersey, took part in many "cutting contests" in Harlem, and worked occasionally as a cantor. He recorded for Decca in 1935; among his recordings for Commodore in 1939 was *Echoes of Spring*, a work inspired by a park in New York City. He toured Europe in 1949 and played as a soloist and accompanist and with bands in nightclubs, revues, and theaters across the United States until the end of his career. A pioneer of ragtime, Harlem stride, and jazz and blues piano, Smith was one of the most distinctive figures in the music of the Harlem Renaissance. With George Hoefer he wrote *Music on My Mind: The Memoirs of an American Pianist* (1964).

Kathy J. Ogren

Snook, John Butler (*b* London, 16 July 1815; *d* Brooklyn, 1 Nov 1901). Architect. His most innovative building was the department store of A. T. Stewart at Broadway and Chambers Street (1845–46, with Joseph Trench), the first of its kind in the world. Intended as an elegant palace for the consumer, it had an exterior of marble and plate glass. He also designed hotels, among them the Metropolitan (1850–52), that had elaborate decorations and technically advanced heating and ventilating systems; their lavish interiors inspired the construction of luxury hotels throughout the country. By 1855 he used cast iron for the façade of a building (examples of his cast-iron buildings still stand at 65 Greene Street and 287 Broadway). Well-known buildings by Snook include the Grand Central Depot (1869–71, extensively remodeled 1892, demolished ?1903) at 42nd Street and Park Avenue and the William H. Vanderbilt Houses (1879–82) on 5th Avenue between 51st and 52nd streets.

Mary Beth Betts

Snow [White], **Carmel** (*b* Dublin, 1886; *d* New York City, 7 May 1961). Fashion editor. As an editor for *Vogue* in 1921–32 and *Harper's Bazaar* in 1932–57 she became known for her elegant personal style and her skill at discovering new talent. At *Harper's* she engaged Louise Dahl-Wolfe to experiment with color fashion photography and Munkacsi to take some of the first photographs depicting models in natural settings outside the studio. She also commissioned photographs from Richard Avedon for *Junior Bazaar*, as well as work by artists such as Salvador Dali, Man Ray, Jean Hugo, Bebe Berard, Marcel Vertes, Carl Erickson, and Pavel Tchelitchew. She retired in 1957.

Caroline Rennolds Milbank

Snug Harbor Cultural Center. A center for the performing and visual arts at 1000 Richmond Terrace in Staten Island. It opened in 1976 on a sylvan site of eighty-three acres (thirty-four hectares) formerly occupied by Sailors' Snug Harbor. The site contains twenty-eight historic buildings (dormitories, residences, a chapel, a library, and a music hall) that were constructed between 1831 and 1917 by such prominent architects as Minard Lafever, William Jallade, and the firm of McKim, Mead and White and offer fine examples of Greek Revival, Italianate, Second Empire, and beaux-arts architecture; two of the buildings retain their High Victorian interior decorations. The center houses seventy community arts organizations, including the Staten Island Children's Museum, the Staten Island Botanic Garden, the Staten Island Institute of Arts and Sciences, and the John Noble Collection. The Samuel I. Newhouse Center for Contemporary Art exhibits work by artists from the region and mounts an outdoor sculpture exhibition each summer. Private artists' studios are provided, and musical, dramatic, and dance performances take place throughout the year. The site is listed on the National Register of Historic Places.

Barnett Shepherd

Snyder, Ruth (*b* 1895; *d* Ossining, N.Y., 22 Jan 1928). Murderer. In the hope of collecting a life insurance policy worth $95,000 she tried seven times to kill her husband, Albert Snyder, the art editor of the magazine *Motor Boating*, by methods that included gassing him in his sleep and poisoning his whiskey. She succeeded on 27 February 1927 by hitting her husband with a sash weight, muzzling him with chloroform, and strangling him with picture wire. Both she and her companion, a traveling corset salesman named Henry Judd Gray, confessed to the crime during the police investigation, although each sought to assign most of the blame to the other. The two were executed five minutes apart in the same electric chair at Sing Sing Prison. A photograph of Snyder's electrocution taken surreptitiously and published on the front page of the *Daily News* became legendary in tabloid photojournalism.

John Kobler: *The Trial of Ruth Snyder and Judd Gray* (Garden City, N.Y.: Doubleday, Doran, 1938)

Norris Randolph

soap and toiletries. New York City became a leading manufacturing and distribution center for soaps and toiletry products in the early nineteenth century. As the major Atlantic port and urban center, Manhattan combined ready access to basic and specialized raw materials with a huge consumer market through its rapidly expanding local populace and its shipping connections.

Soap making is a branch of the chemical industry traditionally connected with candle manufacture. During the colonial period a few artisans' shops were established in Manhattan, and soap was made in the home in the rural districts; fine soap was imported from Europe. Since tallow rending and other aspects of the process often produced unpleasant odors, from 1796 the city restricted soap and candle manufacturing to the residential outskirts; workshop production also required substantial space for boiling and presented fire and chemical hazards.

Larger-scale, scientific soap manufacture took root in New York City in the first decade of the nineteenth century, primarily along the lower West Side. In 1806 William Colgate established a small factory on Dutch Street and John Street, and in 1809 David Williams opened a factory on Greenwich Street near Barclay Street that later became known as Enoch Morgan's Sons. Other soap and candle firms of the time included J. C. Hull's Sons (1780); Benjamin T. Babbitt (1836); James Buchan; Johnson, Vroom and Fowler; D. S. and J. Ward; J. D. and W. Lee; Holt and Horn; Patrick Clendenen; John Alsop; C. W. Smith and Company; John Taylor and Sons; W. G. Browning and Company; Lee A. Comstock; John Buchanan; George F. Penrose; John Ramsey; John Kirkman; and John Sexton. By 1845 the introduction of steam power, an expanded knowledge of chemistry, and the discovery of new vegetable and animal oils helped the industry to grow and diversify. One distinct branch that developed was the manufacture of "fancy toilet soaps," an industry that bore some relation to cosmetics. Soaps of this kind were made in the United States from imported oils, perfumes, and coloring agents and competed successfully with similar products from Europe before 1850. Noted makers of fancy soaps at mid century included Thomas Jones, John Lindmark, Levi Beals, John Wyeth, James Mackey, John Ramsey, William White and Company, Robert Reed, John B. Breed, J. M. de Ciphlet, F. F. Gouraud, August Grandjean, and Eugene Roussel. Other specialized products included laundry and shaving soaps and scouring soaps and powders.

In 1847 the firm of Colgate moved its manufacturing operations to Jersey City, New Jersey, where it maintained an important industrial presence (eventually as Colgate–Palmolive) until 1988; it continued to maintain offices on John Street in Manhattan. Despite this departure and others like it, soap factories in New York City continued to increase in size and number to the end of the century. The number of persons employed in the industry in Manhattan grew from 229 in 1840 to 355 in 1855, 679 in 1870, and 1371 in 1900. Eighty to ninety firms were engaged in the soap business in the 1890s, of which about twenty were important manufacturers such as Enoch Morgan's Sons, Benjamin T. Babbitt, James S. Kirk and Company, Charles S. Higgins, and D. S. Brown and Company. Many of their products became nationally known, among them Enoch Morgan's Sapolio soap and two products made by Babbitt: Babbitt's Best Soap and later Bab-O.

After the city was consolidated in 1898 the chemical industries expanded to the outer boroughs and the metropolitan region. Firms in the Regional Planning District accounted for one sixth of all the soap production in the United States in 1900 and for nearly one quarter by 1919. The share of manufacturing in Manhattan however decreased. By 1922 there were 207 soap factories in the region employing 10,231 workers. The largest factories were on the western bank of the Hudson and on Staten Island, where Procter and Gamble built a huge facility at Port Ivory in 1907. Others operated in Brooklyn and Long Island City.

Several trends contributed to the departure of many soap manufacturers from greater New York after the late 1920s. New forms of technology had created additional demands for space and equipment, and the cost of land, labor, energy, and taxes in the region had risen. The industry became concentrated in a few large national and international firms that produced not only soap and toiletries but foods, paper goods, chemicals, cosmetics, and other items. Although there were more than thirty soap manufacturers in the metropolitan region as late as 1956, from that time the number and production of soap firms declined sharply. By 1991 both Colgate–Palmolive and Procter and Gamble had shut down their local operations.

Samuel Mitchell, comp.: *The Case of the Manufacturers of Soap and Candles in the City of New York* (New York: John Buel, 1797)

Leander Bishop: "Colgate & Co.'s Manufactory," *A History of American Manufactures from 1608 to 1860* (Philadelphia: Edward Young, 1868), vol. 3, pp. 163–65

Samuel Colgate: "American Soap Factories," *One Hundred Years of American Commerce*, by Chauncy DePew (New York: D. O. Haynes, 1895), 422–28

George W. Engelhardt: *New York: The Metropolis* (New York: George W. Englehardt, 1902)

Mabel Newcomer: "The Chemical Industry," *Regional Survey*, vol. 1a, *Chemical, Wood, Metal, Tobacco, and Printing Industries* (New York: Regional Plan of New York and Environs, 1927)

Philip N. Schuyler, ed.: *The Hundred Year Book, Being the Story of the Members of the Hundred Year Association of New York* (New York: A. S. Barnes, 1942)

Richard B. Stott: *Workers in the Metropolis* (Ithaca, N.Y.: Cornell University Press, 1990)

Charles L. Sachs

soccer. Soccer has a long history in New York City, especially among its immigrants and college students. In 1873 Columbia University adopted English soccer rules for collegiate play, and the school was a founding member of the first Intercollegiate Soccer Association, formed in 1905. Van Cortlandt Park in the Bronx was an early venue for soccer matches. The United States Soccer Association (formed 1913) staged its first tournament for the U.S. Challenge Cup in Brooklyn between two local teams composed of Irish immigrants. New York City had a team in the first professional soccer league in the United States, the American Soccer League (1923), which during the 1950s broadcast some of its games on television. The formation in 1971 of the New York Cosmos of the North American Soccer League marked the return of professional soccer to New York City; in the same year the league moved its headquarters to Manhattan. The team played its home games at Downing Stadium on Randalls Island and had on its roster the most popular player in American soccer, Randy Horton. It won the league championship in 1972 and in 1975 signed the Brazilian soccer star Pelé, who drew huge crowds and made the Cosmos the most important franchise in American soccer. The team moved to Yankee Stadium in 1976 and then to Giants Stadium at the Meadowlands in New Jersey. Pelé retired in 1977, but the Cosmos continued to dominate the league, qualifying for the playoffs every year between 1975 and 1984. The Cosmos left the league in 1985, and both the team and the league disbanded soon after. Columbia remained a force in intercollegiate soccer: it won several Ivy League championships, and finished fourth in the tournament of the National Collegiate Athletic Association in 1979 and second in 1983. The center of amateur soccer in New York City is the Metropolitan Oval in Maspeth: founded in the 1920s by immigrants from central Europe, later it also became the site of spirited competition between teams from other parts of the world, notably South America.

Chuck Cascio: *Soccer, U.S.A.* (Washington: Robert B. Luce, 1975)

Rohit T. Aggarwala

social clubs. Social clubs are not easily defined, since organizations formed for other purposes often fill a social purpose as well. But in its narrowest sense the term usually refers to a group with a regular meeting place, or clubhouse, that admits new members on the basis of nomination and election by existing members. Although there were political, fraternal, artistic, literary, and athletic groups in New York City during the colonial and early Federal periods, social clubs were not formed until later, and they numbered only three by the late 1830s: the Union Club (1836), which represented the city's oldest families, the Hone Club (1836), and the Kent Club (1838), which was for lawyers. The number increased markedly during the following decades with the formation of the Century Association (1846), the Lotos Club (1870), the Salmagundi Club (1871), and the Lambs (1874). The Knickerbocker Club was formed in 1871 by eighteen members of the Union Club dissatisfied with its new, more liberal admissions policy: they sought to associate with "men of good will and common aspirations," by which they meant members of established Dutch and English families (the founders of the Knickerbocker nevertheless included two Jews: Moses Lazarus and August Belmont). In some cases what motivated the formation of a new club was a political orientation (the Hone Club supported the Whigs between the 1830s and the Civil War, the Manhattan Club the Democrats, and the Union League the Republicans), ethnicity, especially among the city's large German population (who founded the Allemania Club, the German Club, and the Harmonie Club), or a common interest in literature, theater, the arts, or sports such as rowing, sailing, and tennis. Virtually all the clubs modeled themselves after the English gentleman's club and were governed in strikingly similar fashion, with an executive committee and subordinate committees concerned with finance, membership, the house, and the library. By the last quarter of the nineteenth century New York City was second only to London in the number of its clubs (more than a hundred) and club memberships (about fifty thousand). All the members were white men, three quarters were married, and half were bankers or businessmen. A study of club life in 1871 found that half the members descended from only about twenty families and that each man usually held several memberships, perhaps belonging to a university club, a tennis or yachting club, and a literary club. Prominent clubs formed about the turn of the century include the Players (1888), the Montauk Club in Brooklyn (1889), the Metropolitan Club (1891), the Brook (1903), and the Friars Club (1904).

Social clubs in New York City declined in number after the 1920s, as the automobile became increasingly important, members moved to the suburbs, and social patterns changed. Clubs such as the Athenaeum and the New York Club disappeared. By the late twentieth century the social club came to adopt a defensive posture, often fearful of lawsuits over such matters as sexual and ethnic discrimination and challenges to its tax-exempt status. Some clubs sought to avoid publicity at any cost: perhaps the most reticent was the Knickerbocker.

In the decades after the Second World War the term social club took on a new meaning, as immigrants from Cuba, the Dominican Republic, Honduras, and other Latin American countries opened informal clubs, generally unlicensed, that served alcohol and provided musical entertainment.

See also UNIVERSITY CLUBS and WOMEN'S CLUBS.

James E. Mooney

Social Gospel. Christian doctrine seeking to address social ills, also known as social Christianity and Christian socialism. It was developed in response to rapid industrialization during the late nineteenth century and became especially popular in New York City, where laborers were exploited and lived in harsh conditions. Adherents emphasized the doctrine of the kingdom of God and called for the conversion to Christianity of both individuals and social institutions. The many theorists and practitioners of the doctrine included Washington Gladden, Josiah Strong, Richard T. Ely, Charles M. Sheldon, Jane Addams, and Reverdy C. Ransom. The best-known advocate in the city was Walter Rauschenbusch, a pastor of the Second German Baptist Church at the edge of Hell's Kitchen who became a passionate defender of the poor; his book *Christianity and the Social Crisis* (1907) was central to the Social Gospel movement.

Robert T. Handy: *The Social Gospel in America, 1870–1920: Gladden, Ely, Rauschenbusch* (New York: Oxford University Press, 1966)

Paul M. Minus: *Walter Rauschenbusch: American Reformer* (New York: Macmillan, 1988)

Randall Balmer

socialism. New York City became a national center of socialism during the nineteenth century. Between the late 1820s and the 1840s utopian socialism became a tenet of the city's labor movement. Drawing on the ideas of the Welsh reformer Robert Owen, his son Robert Dale Owen, Frances Wright, and Thomas Skidmore, radical workers sought to abolish inheritance, distribute property more equitably, and educate children in state boarding schools. A small group of German immigrants, some of whom such as Wilhelm Weitling had worked with Marx and Engels, introduced Marxist socialism in New York City during the 1840s; after the Civil War they joined with such radical reformers as Victoria Woodhull and Tennessee Claflin to form a branch of the International Workingmen's Association (IWA), which collapsed in 1876 owing largely to German members' strong sympathy for trade unions and discomfort with radical reformers. The Socialist Labor Party, the first socialist party in the United States, was formed in 1877. In the city it appealed to German workers and conducted nearly all its business in German. With the IWA it introduced Marx's ideas to important trade unionists in the city, including Samuel Gompers.

During the 1890s Daniel DeLeon became the leader of the SLP and steered it toward an uncompromising and revolutionary brand of socialism. Tension arose in the party over his dogmatism and his hostility toward trade unions (the leaders of which he condemned as "labor lieutenants of capitalism"). Jewish workers led by Morris Hillquit and Abraham Cahan, editor of the *Jewish Daily Forward*, were especially opposed to DeLeon's policies and joined with trade unionists in 1901 to form the Socialist Party of America (SPA). Soon after, socialism reached a peak of strength in both the city and the rest of the nation. Under Hillquit's leadership the branch of the party in the city stressed immediate reforms and allied itself closely with trade unionism. It built firm ties to the garment workers' unions, which grew and strongly supported Socialist political candidates. Socialism also attracted leading artists and intellectuals, who saw it as an effective challenge to stultifying Victorian conventions and hypocrisies; among those who joined the party were the painter John Sloan, the novelist Theodore Dreiser, the intellectual Max Eastman, the journalists Walter Lippmann and John Reed, and the reformers Florence Kelley, Frances Perkins, and W. E. B. Du Bois. Intellectuals in Greenwich Village published the magazine the *Masses*; the local branch of the Socialist Party of America published the *Call*, a daily newspaper with a large circulation. The party offered adult education at its own school, the Rand School of Social Science. Meyer London was elected to the U.S. House of Representatives in 1914 from the Lower East Side and won reelection in 1916 and 1920. In 1917 voters there and in the Bronx and Brooklyn strongly supported Hillquit in the mayoral election and helped to elect ten Socialists to the state assembly, five to the city's Board of Aldermen, and one to a municipal judgeship.

The party was crippled by its opposition to the country's entrance into the First World War. Members split into factions supporting and opposing the war, and the *Masses* was closed down by the federal government. The party became more divided after the Bolshevik Revolution of 1917 caused some members to abandon socialism for communism; the division was deep and bitter in the city, where Hillquit led socialists opposed to communists. Between 1918 and 1921 Socialist candidates continued to win strong support among Jewish workers. Norman Thomas, the best-known American socialist of the 1920s and 1930s, was a candidate for mayor of New York City in 1925 and 1929 and a member of Mayor Fiorello H. La Guardia's charter revision committee in 1934. Another leading socialist in the city was Max Shachtman (1904–72), editor of the Trotskyist journals the *Militant* and *New International.*

Competition between socialists and communists nearly destroyed the International Ladies' Garment Workers' Union during the 1920s and the Fur and Leather Workers' Union during the 1930s, and by the end of the 1920s socialism seemed a spent force in the city. It revived during the Depression and in 1933 Hillquit won more than 100,000 votes as the mayoral candidate of the SPA. In 1936 a faction that refused to embrace communism formed the Social Democratic Federation (SDF) after splitting off from a faction of the SPA that sought to form a revolutionary front with communists; the SDF launched a journal, the *New Leader.* Socialism became a fringe movement after trade unions and Jewish workers left the SPA to support the New Deal and join the American Labor Party.

After the Second World War those who remained loyal to the SPA devoted themselves to fighting communism, and the journal *Dissent* was launched in 1955 by a small group of intellectuals in the city to preserve socialist ideas, remaining in operation into the 1990s. The emergence of the New Left in the 1960s caused much division among socialists. The League for Industrial Democracy, a group concentrated in the city, helped to form Students for a Democratic Society in 1962. Social Democrats USA, organized in 1972, soon adopted conservative positions on many issues. One of few remaining socialist groups in the city in the mid 1990s was the Democratic Socialists of America, formed in 1982 by Michael Harrington.

David A. Shannon: *The Socialist Party of America: A History* (New York: Macmillan, 1955)

Irving Howe: *World of Our Fathers* (New York: Harcourt Brace Jovanovich, 1975)

Sean Wilentz: *Chants Democratic: New York City and the Rise of the American Working Class, 1790–1850* (New York: Oxford University Press, 1984)

Melvyn Dubofsky

Socialist Labor Party [SLP]. Political party formed in 1877, largely by German-speaking immigrants; it was the first party in the United States to advocate Marxist socialism. The party was especially strong in New York City, where there was a large community of German immigrants. In 1886 it took an active part in Henry George's mayoral campaign. Under the leadership of Daniel DeLeon after 1890 the branch in the city adopted English as its official language. The party split in 1901 after DeLeon alienated many supporters, including German–Americans, Jewish immigrants, and members of trade unions. Ruled with an iron hand by DeLeon until his death in 1914, the party moved increasingly toward the political fringe in the city. It nevertheless remained active into the 1990s, idolizing DeLeon and nominating candidates for local, state, and national office.

Glen Seretan: *Daniel DeLeon: The Odyssey of an American Marxist* (Cambridge: Harvard University Press, 1979)

Melvyn Dubofsky

Socialist Party of America [SPA]. Political party formed in Indianapolis in 1901 that built a large following in New York City among eastern European Jewish workers. The party's most prominent leaders in the city, Morris Hillquit and Meyer London, were engaged as attorneys by the garment workers' unions, which endorsed the party and aggressively sought votes for its candidates. London was elected to the U.S. House of Representatives from the Lower East Side in 1914, 1916, and 1920; Hillquit won more than 22 percent of the vote in the mayoral election of 1917. Largely Jewish districts elected five Socialists to the Board of Aldermen, one to a municipal judgeship, and several to the state assembly. In April 1920 five Socialists from the city were expelled from the state assembly; two were reelected in November but denied their seats after the election, marking the decline of the party's influence. Throughout the 1920s the garment workers' unions continued to endorse the party, which maintained support among Jewish voters but was severely weakened by opposition from conservatives and competition from the Communist Party. The party during the 1930s was reduced to a small faction, as members joined the Democratic and American Labor parties to support the New Deal. It survived in the city largely through the efforts of such leaders as Norman Thomas, Michael Harrington, and Irving Howe and journals such as the *New Leader* and *Dissent.*

David A. Shannon: *The Socialist Party of America: A History* (Chicago: Macmillan, 1955)

Irving Howe: *World of Our Fathers* (New York: Harcourt Brace Jovanovich, 1975)

Charles Leinenweber: "Socialists in the Streets: The New York City Socialist Party in Working-class Neighborhoods, 1908–1918," *Science and Society* 41 (1977), 152–71

Melvyn Dubofsky

Social Science Research Council. An independent association of scholars that conducts interdisciplinary research in the social sciences and on public policy. It was formed in New York City in 1923 by a small group of professors from the University of Chicago and occupied offices in the tower of Grand Central Terminal. In the early 1970s it moved to 605 3rd Avenue at 40th Street. The council has a rotating membership of some three hundred social scientists who are assisted by a professional staff of fifteen. They study such diverse subjects as the urban underclass, the learning process, the Latin American community, international relations, and research methods. The council sponsors workshops, seminars, conferences, and summer training institutes: one series of meetings held in 1982–85 led to the formation of the Committee on New York City, dedicated to scholarly study of the city and its culture, politics, and economy. The committee had about fifteen members, led by Ira Katznelson of the New School for Social Research and John Mollenkopf of the Graduate School at the City University of New York; its work lasted until 1991 and resulted in the publication of four books. In 1989–90 the council worked with the American Council of Learned Societies to restructure its committees and encourage collaboration between scholars in the United States and abroad. A comparative study of New York City, Paris, and Tokyo was being planned in the early 1990s. The board of directors of the council has sixteen members, including scholars representing national associations in the fields of anthropology, economics, history, political science, psychology, sociology, and statistics.

Samuel Z. Klausner and Victor M. Lidz: *The Nationalization of the Social Sciences* (Philadelphia: University of Pennsylvania Press, 1986)

Thomas Bender: *New York Intellect: A History of Intellectual Life in New York City, from 1750 to the Beginnings of Our Own Time* (Baltimore: Johns Hopkins University Press, 1987)

Marjorie Harrison

social work. New York City became a center for the development of professional social work during the nineteenth century. The Association for Improving the Condition of the Poor was formed in 1843, and in 1882 Josephine Shaw Lowell and others formed the Charity Organization Society, a federation of private relief organizations. Under Lowell the society practiced what it called scientific philanthropy: it developed a central listing of relief recipients and a network of "friendly visitors" who investigated and counseled relief applicants. Although the society originally relied on volunteers it increasingly turned to paid caseworkers, who were seen as more reliable and better qualified. Out of the Summer School of Philanthropy (1898), a program to train social workers, evolved the New York School of Social Work (later renamed the Columbia University School of Social Work), the first such school in the nation. From 1891 the society also published the *Charities Review*, which later became the leading social work periodical the *Survey*.

While the Charity Organization Society emphasized the role of casework in social work, settlement houses emphasized the role of social reform. The Lower East Side was the site of the first settlement house in the United States, opened in 1886 and later named University Settlement. In the early twentieth century the Russell Sage Foundation exerted great influence on the field of social work. It sought to promote the new profession of social work and to develop practical applications of social welfare theories. In 1909–28 Mary Richmond wrote case histories for use as teaching guides, organized summer institutes for caseworkers and supervisors, and published the influential books *Social Diagnosis* (1917) and *What Is Social Casework?* (1922), which defined the skills involved in casework and helped to elevate professional standards. The foundation also provided office space for a number of emerging national professional organizations such as the American Association of Social Workers. Francis H. McLean, another employee of the foundation, encouraged cities to form councils of private welfare agencies that could coordinate their activities; in 1925 the Welfare Council was organized as such an agency, partially supplanting the Charity Organization Society, which soon experienced overwhelming competition from public welfare programs.

Both public and private local social agencies were inadequate to face the problems of the Depression, leading the federal government to assume responsibility. Many New Yorkers contributed to the development of federal welfare programs under President Franklin D. Roosevelt, and as the field of social work expanded, many of the leading activists, schools, and professional associations emerged in the city. In 1939 the Charity Organization Society and the Association for Improving the Condition of the Poor merged to form the Community Service Society. Neva Deardorff worked for the Research Bureau of the Welfare Council of Greater New York in 1927–46, demonstrating the value of statistical analysis and sociological data for social work planning. She then helped to form and direct the Health Insurance Plan of Greater New York, a precursor of health maintenance organizations. The American Association of Social Workers was founded in 1922 by Deardorff, David Holbrook, William Hodson, and Dorothy Kahn. In 1920 Holbrook became the head of the American Association for Organizing Family Social Work (based in the city), and in 1925 he joined the National Social Work Council, an organization that provided a forum for other national social work agencies (he remained there for more than twenty years). In 1922 Hodson became the head of the Division of Child Welfare Legislation at the Russell Sage Foundation and later of its Division of Social Legislation; he led the private Welfare Council (1925) and the first state-level public assistance program (1931), and campaigned for federal relief programs, which he also helped to formulate. In 1934 he became the city's commissioner of public welfare. Walter Mott West led the American Association of Social Workers in 1927–42, during which time the organization shaped federal welfare policies; in 1938 Kahn became an assistant to West. As the associate editor from 1930 of the *Survey*, Gertrude Springer called attention to the growing role of the federal government in social welfare. Jane Hoey, Hodson's assistant at the Welfare Council, became the head of the Bureau of Public Assistance of the Social Security Administration in 1935. After the Second World War Kahn directed the Health and Welfare Council (also in New York City), and in 1950–55 she led the Social Welfare Section of the Department of Social Affairs at the United Nations.

Because of the growing importance of the federal government in financing social programs, many national social welfare organizations are now based in Washington, but New York City remains a center for innovation and education in social work. Social work programs are offered at Columbia University (1898), Fordham University (1929), New York University (1955), Hunter College (1958), and Yeshiva University (1959).

Roy Lubove: *The Professional Altruist: The Emergence of Social Work as a Career, 1880–1930* (Cambridge: Harvard University Press, 1965)

Walter I. Trattner: *From Poor Law to Welfare State: A History of Social Welfare in America* (New York: Free Press, 1974; 4th edn 1989)

Judith Ann Trolander: *Professionalism and Social Change: From the Settlement House Movement to Neighborhood Centers, 1886 to the Present* (New York: Columbia University Press, 1987)

Judith Ann Trolander

society. Much more than in Boston, Philadelphia, or Charleston, South Carolina, the upper class in New York City through much of its history was based on status, wealth, and power, and having one of these often led to getting another. The legitimacy and longevity of élite society depended on a delicate balance between on the one hand exclusiveness and isolation, and on the other hand a willingness to defer to the élite on the part of the community at large. Within society a sense of kinship was highly important, traditionally determining the choice of school, camp, dancing class, and college, admission to clubs, membership in charity and cultural boards, invitations to social events, parties, and dinners, and in the end the place of burial. All these distinctions were based originally on success in business and government, the two areas that saw the first changes for the declining old families of the establishment. Later came the disturbance in the careful balance between community leadership and the once-acceptable separation of classes into enclaves.

The group that dominated society in New Amsterdam consisted of old Dutch families. Their sense of aristocracy was based on wealth held in land originally granted by the Dutch West India Company and later by the colonial governments in which the leadership group was powerfully well represented. The manorial system of land ownership along the Hudson River and on Long Island was as close as the northern colonies came to an aristocracy. Another source of early strength among these leaders was wealth earned from mercantile trade, usually wholesale and seldom retail, to which a social stigma was long attached. When the British gained control in 1664 they did not displace the social leaders, whom they joined level for level in business partnerships, church congregations, and marriages. Cadwallader Colden, a colonial governor of New York, described this society as based first on the landed gentry of the large baronial holdings, second on the lawyers, and last on the merchants, but there was a large amount of mixing of these categories in any of the leading families. They held the major royal government offices in the legislative and judicial branches and were close allies of both British- and American-born members of the executive branch. They also controlled land grants, military contracts, and lucrative franchises. Although there were internal competitions for power, as among the Livingston, de Lancey, and other factions, the upper class continued to exercise power no matter which of the contending groups prevailed. The class became a cosmopolitan one of great ethnic variety, with the great Dutch families joined by French Huguenots (the Jays and de Lanceys), English and Scots (the Barclays and Waltons), and Germans (the Beekmans). Together they founded the New York Chamber of Commerce (1768), the Society of New York Hospital, Trinity Church, King's College, and similar institutions.

This group faced difficulties of a massive sort with the coming of the American Revolution, during which the British army occupied the city for nearly all the time between Independence Day in 1776 and Evacuation Day in 1783. When the troops left so did many Loyalists, some belonging to the upper class, for maritime Canada and for England. Many new fortunes were built and new families replaced the departing Loyalists, but they still faced the task of fitting in among the great society families that had remained in New York City or returned there from exile. The absolute social sovereignty of the families of colonial New York City was ended by 1810, when their withdrawal from commerce and government had become apparent and many of the great manorial estates had been broken up. It was about this time, at the beginning of the new nation and the end of the brief tenure of the Federalists, that the old patrician group in its confusion turned toward exclusivity for the first time. Many took this for snobbery, a trait that did not reflect upper-class breeding.

The new patrician society was made up of remnants of the colonial families and of new families from such places as New England. Many members of the new families were merchant bankers, who became active in public affairs because they appreciated the need for close ties between finance and government in the new nation. They often held local political office, first as Federalists and then as Republicans (notably the Clintons, Lewises, and Livingstons). The aristocrats had been superseded by the bourgeoisie of the marketplace, whose standards for admission to the group were more flexible, and the tension between the old families and the new gave vitality to the social life of New York City.

The amalgam of families that led the city supported its existing charities and founded new ones, as the city attracted new residents from the countryside and immigrants from Ireland and Germany. In the years preceding the Civil War society managed to assimilate the new fortunes without changing its accustomed patterns. Social events and other functions were largely the province of men, who looked after their business interests during the day and also established ancillary clubs and hereditary societies. The pace of change at mid century led to a new institution, that of social arbiter: Isaac Brown was the first in a series that came to include Ward McAllister and Harry Lehr.

During the Civil War great fortunes were made by such entrepreneurs as J. P. Morgan, John D. Rockefeller, Jim Fisk, and Jay Gould, and after the war the change in society was dramatic indeed. The old guard was again pushed unceremoniously aside by the new, which advanced with what Louis Auchincloss called "the ineluctable force of a glacier," and the latest old guard sought solace in clubs and in the creation of yet more hereditary societies where family lines were still important. In such clubs willing members of the old guard could meet, dine, and do business with the tough, powerful members of the new élite, people they would never invite into their own homes.

New millionaires who did not have the properly matured credentials and were thus not welcome in more established society were attracted to the idea of the "Four Hundred," a guest-list prepared by McAllister for Mrs. William Astor. (The number of names was in fact 273, said to be the number of guests that could be accommodated in her ballroom.) This inner circle of society included only half a dozen persons with intellectual or artistic interests, and the Four Hundred were rarely involved in cultural gatherings. One member of the group, Mrs. Winthrop Chanler, who had been brought up in Rome in an artistic family and found New York City to be prim and dull, wrote that the Four Hundred "would have fled in a body from a painter, a musician, or a clever Frenchman." The Four Hundred was a group dominated by determined women seeking newspaper publicity for increasingly lavish parties in château-like mansions, and it was avoided by most of the real leaders in business and the community – the Rockefellers, Dodges, Morgans, and Schiffs. But because its membership was continually changing, it did provide an entrée into society for those with good table manners, a little patience, and a great deal of money.

Social events and functions in New York City took place in what newspapers called the "Magic Parallelogram" (between 14th and 59th streets and between 3rd and 6th avenues) during a period called the Gilded Age, after a novel of 1875 by Mark Twain and Charles Dudley Warner. It was Twain who published the joke "In Boston they ask, How much does he know? in Philadelphia, Who were his parents? in New York, How much is he worth?" The period lasted for half a century, during which fashionable society drew the attention of an avid public fed by society writers and gossips. In 1887 this group was given a sort of codification when the *Social Register* appeared with fewer than two thousand New Yorkers listed. In an age of excesses few were as outrageous as the costume ball given by Bradley Martin during the winter of 1896–97, an expensive event described in five pages of agonizing detail in the Hearst newspapers. Criticism of the party for its wasteful ostentation was widespread and fierce, driving the stunned Martins into permanent exile in England. The incident seemed to confirm the remark of Henry Adams that American society was the first to go from barbarism to decadence without passing through civilization.

The Four Hundred was succeeded between the world wars by café society, a vacuous collection of poseurs, playboys, heiresses, and party-givers from Hollywood, Paris, and London. It was the sort of crowd that could appreciate Oscar Wilde's comment about society: that "to be in it is merely a bore, but to be out of it is simply a tragedy." The man who named café society, Maury Henry Biddle Paul, known as Cholly Knickerbocker, was from Philadelphia, where his critics said that he came from the wrong branch of each of the four distinguished families that constituted his name. In 1921 he divided society into two lists, distinguishing café society from the "old guard." Each list had fifty names and only two families were represented in both: the Drexels, with mother in the old guard and son in café society; and the Vanderbilts, with three older ladies including "The Dowager Mrs. Vanderbilt" on the old list and an alcoholic man and a divorced woman on the new. Knickerbocker lived long enough to see the celebrities whom he disdained replace the members of café society whom he had celebrated in his lists and newspaper columns, never realizing that they were all celebrities in the first place and that he had helped make them so.

After the Second World War society in New York City was in tatters. Social secretaries had a difficult time finding eligible escorts for the few remaining assemblies and balls. The survival of society was also threatened by divorce, indifference to cultural and charitable affairs, and the move to the suburbs and beyond. The deferential public whose attention is critical to the existence of a fashionable society abandoned society figures in favor of stars from the worlds of film, television, music, and sports. In his novels Tom Wolfe epitomized a time when the scramble for wealth and power was not only accepted but revered. The new members of the élite held lavish parties in such grand institutions as the Metropolitan Museum of Art, which some now facetiously called "Club Met." Any relation between this group and what used to be thought of as class was purely coincidental.

Dixon Wecter: *The Saga of American Society: A Record of Social Aspiration, 1607–1937* (New York: Charles Scribner's Sons, 1937; repr. 1970)

Frederick Cople Jaher: *The Urban Establishment: Upper Strata in Boston, New York, Charleston, Chicago, and Los Angeles* (Urbana: University of Illinois Press, 1982)

Louis Auchincloss: *The Vanderbilt Era: Profiles of a Gilded Age* (New York: Charles Scribner's Sons, 1989)

James E. Mooney

Society for the Prevention of Crime. Reform organization formed in 1878. In its early years it was led by Howard Crosby and focused on helping the police to arrest gamblers and prostitutes, as well as saloonkeepers who violated the Sunday closing laws. On Crosby's death in 1891 leadership of the society was assumed by Charles H. Parkhurst, pastor of the Madison Square Presbyterian Church, who adopted a more provocative style, touring saloons and brothels in disguise to prove that vice flourished in New York City under police protection. During his tenure the society was widely known as the "Parkhurst society." Detectives employed by it uncovered evidence of widespread protected vice in the city, which led to the appointment of a committee of the state senate to investigate the society's charges of police blackmail and corruption in Tammany Hall; the committee was known as the Lexow Committee, after its chairman, Clarence Lexow of Nyack. The resulting scandal led to the defeat of Tammany Hall and the election of a reform administration in 1894. The society declined in power and influence after Parkhurst resigned as its president in 1908, and it disbanded after the repeal of Prohibition.

Timothy J. Gilfoyle: "The Moral Origins of Political Surveillance: The Preventive Society in New York, 1867–1918," *American Quarterly* 38 (1986), 637–52

Warren Sloat

Society for the Prevention of Cruelty to Children. Children's advocacy organization formed in New York City in December 1874 by Elbridge T(homas) Gerry (1837–1927) and John D. Wright. With Henry Bergh (1811–88) of the American Society for the Prevention of Cruelty to Animals, Gerry prosecuted the adoptive parents of Mary Ellen MacCormack (or Wilson) for having severely beaten her; this was the first case of child abuse brought before the city's courts. The society, also known during its founder's lifetime as the Gerry Society, sought out and rescued abused children and was given law enforcement powers in 1881. It has offices at 161 William Street in Manhattan and 141 Montague Street in Brooklyn.

Alana J. Erickson

Society for the Propagation of the Gospel. Religious organization incorporated by royal charter in 1701 with the aim of settling ministers of the Church of England in America. Because of the multidenominational character of New York City, the city and its environs were an important focus for the society, and missionaries in the area established churches in Manhattan, Queens, Westchester, and Staten Island. The society sought to endow churches, set parish boundaries, provide rectories and glebes (plots of farmland controlled by parishes), and secure public support for the Church of England. Few parishes in the city achieved self-sufficiency during the colonial period, and the society continued to supplement the salaries of the clergy until the American Revolution. In addition to caring for white colonists the society aggressively pursued the conversion of blacks and American Indians. Elias Neau, a missionary from France, operated an innovative school for catechizing slaves in New York City from 1704 until his death in 1722. From 1706 the society supported charity schools in the city to provide rudimentary religious and literary instruction, and in 1754 it was instrumental in founding King's College (later Columbia University), from which the church hoped to obtain a supply of well-educated young men eager to enter the ministry. Throughout the colonial period the society remained controversial; non-Anglicans especially were wary of its missionary program and of its political and social influence. The withdrawal of the Society for the Propagation of the Gospel from the colonies during the revolution was followed by the establishment of the American Episcopal church as an independent entity in 1783.

Frank J. Klingberg: *Anglican Humanitarianism in Colonial New York* (Philadelphia: Church Historical Society, 1940)

Henry Paget Thompson: *Into All Lands: The History of the Society for the Propagation of the Gospel in Foreign Parts, 1701–1950* (London: Society for Promoting Christian Knowledge, 1951)

William Webb Kemp: *The Support of Schools in Colonial New York by the Society for the Propagation of the Gospel in Foreign Parts* (New York: Arno, 1972)

Peter J. Wosh

Society for the Relief of Half-Orphans. Charitable organization formed in 1835 to enable "poor but worthy" widowed parents to work by giving care and training to their children. Parents paid fifty cents a week for these services when they were able. Originally based on 10th Street in Manhattan and run by women, from the early 1950s the group worked closely with the Orphan Asylum Society. It moved in 1867 to larger quarters at 67 West 10th Street and in 1891 to 104th Street. By 1902 male trustees took charge of financial matters while leaving to women the details of daily management. Mrs. Henry Howells in 1914 donated 160 acres (sixty-five hectares) of land in Windham, New York, as a summer home for children. In the mid 1940s the society was restructured and renamed the Windham Society for the Care of Boys.

Phyllis Barr

Society for the Relief of Women and Children. An interdenominational women's association formed in 1797 as the Society for the Relief of Poor Widows with Small Children by Isabella Graham, Elizabeth Seton, and others to assist the growing number of widows made destitute by epidemics and economic depression. During its first year the society aided ninety-eight widows and 223 children and managed a budget of almost $4000. To help widows gain economic security the society employed them in its own sewing and laundering businesses and as teachers in its own schools. It received $15,000 from the city to assist widows during the yellow fever epidemic of 1802. The society remained active into the 1990s.

The Power of Faith: Exemplified in the Life and Writings of the Late Mrs. Isabella Graham, of New York (New York: J. Seymour, 1816)

Isabella Graham: *The Unpublished Letters and Correspondence of Mrs. Isabella Graham, from the Year 1767 to 1814, Exhibiting Her Religious Character in the Different Relations of Life* (New York: J. S. Taylor, 1838)

Page Putnam Miller

Society of the Cincinnati. An exclusive club formed in 1783 in Fishkill, New York, by officers of the Continental Army. Led by George Washington and later Alexander Hamilton, it had a hereditary membership and was often viewed as aristocratic and threatening to American republican government. Alexander McDougall was the first president of the chapter in New York City, which supported the Federalists throughout the early Federal period and was later led by such notable Federalists as the former mayor Richard Varick.

Sidney I. Pomerantz: *New York: an American City, 1783–1803: A Study of Urban Life* (New York: Columbia University Press, 1938; 2nd edn Port Washington, N.Y.: I. J. Friedman, 1965)

Howard Rock

Society of the Friendly Sons of St. Patrick in the City of New York. A charitable and fraternal body formed in 1784 to assist needy Irish immigrants; it is the oldest continuously functioning Irish organization in New York City. In its early years the society had both well-to-do Catholics and Protestants as members and later became predominantly Catholic, although its charitable activities remained ecumenical. Its annual St. Patrick's Day Dinner is an important social event for prominent local residents of Irish descent.

Richard C. Murphy and Lawrence J. Mannion: *The History of the Society of the Friendly Sons of St. Patrick in the City of New York, 1784–1955* (New York: Society of the Friendly Sons of St. Patrick in the City of New York, 1962)

William D. Griffin

Society of Women Engineers [SWE]. Organization formed in 1949–50 by women engineers in New York City, Boston, Philadelphia, and Washington to help women prepare for careers in engineering and to inform the public of the achievements of women engineers. It was incorporated in 1952 and in 1961 became a tenant at the United Engineering Center at 47th Street and 1st Avenue. In 1990 it had fourteen thousand members.

Nancy D. Fitzroy, ed.: *Career Guidance for Women Entering Engineering* (New York: Engineering Foundation / Society of Women Engineers, 1973)

Trudy E. Bell

Advertisement for Blakely's Blizzard Soda

soft drinks. The manufacture of soft drinks in New York City began in 1809, when the chemist Noyes Darling brought soda water to the popular Tontine Coffee House on Wall Street, but flavored soda water did not come to prominence until after the Civil War. Dr. Brown's Cel-Rey (named for its celery flavor) was introduced in 1869; eventually distributed nationwide, it continued to be made into the 1990s. During the 1870s soda fountains drew customers to drugstores and department stores, and such establishments as Hudnut's in the Herald Building were known for their marble soda fountains. Bottled soft drinks became popular in the last quarter of the nineteenth century, and the city became the site of more than a hundred soft drink factories producing such brands as Imperial Inca Cola, John Morgan ginger ale, Golden Key mint sodas, and Centennial root beer. Cream, celery, and coffee sodas were developed and widely sold in the city. The firms of Pepsi-Cola, Seven-Up, and Coca-Cola made and distributed their products in the city from the 1930s, and for a time Canada Dry, Pepsi-Cola, and Coca-Cola had their headquarters there. The city ceased to dominate the industry after several large soft drink companies were formed elsewhere between 1900 and 1950; nonetheless by the mid 1950s the city had 250 soda factories and soft drink sales exceeding $70 million. Many local brands continued to be made, including Manhattan Coffee Soda, Hi-Y-ee, No-Cal, Up-Town, Nifty, and Yoo-Hoo chocolate soda. In 1988 more than 120 million cases of soft drinks were consumed in the city. The American Beverage Corporation achieved success with Soho Natural Soda, and in addition to its own products the Canada Dry Bottling Company in College Point distributed such local brands as Hoffman's, Best Health Natural Soda, Cott, Kirsch, Nedicks, and Dr. Brown's.

John J. Riley: *A History of the American Soft Drink Industry, 1807–1957* (Washington: American Bottlers of Carbonated Beverages, 1958)

James Bradley

SoHo. Neighborhood in lower Manhattan, bounded to the north by Houston Street, to the east by Crosby Street, to the south by Canal Street, and to the west by 6th Avenue; the name stands for "south of Houston." The hilly area contained a path used by Weckquasgeek Indians to travel the length of Manhattan: this later became Broadway. Slaves granted their freedom by the Dutch West India Company in 1644 moved to the area and formed the first settlement of free blacks in Manhattan; there were also some white settlers. The land was used mostly for farming until the end of the eighteenth century. At that time city planners decided to cover the polluted and foul-smelling canal that formed the southern boundary of the neighborhood, using local hills as landfill. The leveled countryside soon became suitable for development, and by 1825 the neighborhood was the most densely populated in Manhattan. Its streets were lined with shops and elegant three- and four-story houses, most built of red brick in the Greek Revival and Federal styles. John Jacob Astor owned much of the land around Canal Street, and the residents were among the wealthiest and most renowned in the city.

Spring Street in SoHo, 1994

The neighborhood became less fashionable about the mid nineteenth century, when many large retail and wholesale firms moved in, including Lord and Taylor, Tiffany, and E. V. Haughwout. Broadway was dominated by expensive hotels, as well as stores built of marble, brownstone, and cast iron; casinos, theaters, music halls, and brothels lined the sidestreets. An influx of businesses caused the population to decline by a quarter between 1860 and 1865, as buildings were demolished to make way for new ones or converted into factories, warehouses, and offices. The neighborhood became known for dry goods, china, glass, silks, satin, lace, ribbons, furs, and tobacco. To glorify their enterprises ambitious businessmen commissioned four- to six-story buildings with elaborate ornamentation. Most of these buildings were made quickly and cheaply from cast iron, which was favored for its strength and versatility and became incorporated into a unique architectural style developed in the neighborhood. Stores and factories (including some that housed sweatshops) had façades in the Victorian Gothic, neo-Grec, Italianate, and Second Empire styles and were carefully painted and decorated with colorful striped awnings. The ground floor often had high windows and a vast interior for displays; upper stories contained offices, storage, and manufacturing areas.

A thriving commercial center until 1890, the neighborhood became depressed after the turn of the century as fashionable businesses moved uptown to 5th Avenue. Local buildings were ill suited to modern industry, and by 1959 the neighborhood was a commercial slum known as "hell's hundred acres." Between 1960 and 1970 artists seeking low rents and space for large works defied zoning laws and converted vacant warehouses into studios, galleries, and living quarters. There was a powerful colony of artists in the neighborhood by 1971, and with other residents they persuaded the city to change the zoning laws governing warehouses. An area of twenty-six blocks was designated a Historic District by the New York City Landmarks Commission in 1973. After it was revitalized in the 1970s and 1980s the neighborhood became the newly fashionable site of boutiques, performance centers, galleries, restaurants, bars, and shops. Many artists who had reclaimed the neighborhood from its former state of neglect found themselves unable to afford the increasing rents brought about by gentrification. SoHo remains one of the most diverse and vibrant neighborhoods in the city. It has many cast-iron buildings, a number of which house small publishing, graphic design, and manufacturing firms; some artists continue to inhabit spacious lofts with high ceilings.

Joyce Gold

Soho News. Alternative weekly newspaper launched by Michael Goldstein in 1973 and published until 1982. Described as the "alternative to alternative papers," it was inspired by an alternative art movement in SoHo in the mid 1970s. The newspaper focused on the arts but also offered news and opinion pieces as well as reviews and listings in a format similar to that of the *Village Voice.* It distinguished itself from other newspapers by remaining politically independent and publishing articles from a range of political perspectives. Between 1978 and 1980 it was owned by the Associated News Group of London, publishers of the *Daily Mail.* The *Soho News* ceased publication after incurring cumulative losses of $6 million.

Tim Page: "Alas, the Soho News Wasn't Cast-iron," *New York Times,* 20 March 1982, §1, p. 27

Amanda Aaron

Sojourner Truth [Isabella] (*b* Hurley, N.Y., *ca* 1797; *d* Battle Creek, Mich., 26 Nov 1883). Abolitionist. Born a slave, she was separated from her parents in 1810 after being sold to a farmer in New Paltz, New York. With a slave named Thomas she had five children including a son, Peter, who was sold to a planter in Alabama despite a state law (1788) prohibiting the sale of slaves out of state. She fled her owner in 1826 and with the help of Quakers undertook a lawsuit that resulted in the return of her son. Freed under state law in 1827, by 1829 she settled with her children in New York City, where she worked as a domestic servant and sometimes attended the Mother African Methodist Episcopal Zion Church at 156 Church Street. She maintained that she took the name Sojourner Truth after hearing a voice in 1843 calling on her to testify against the sins of slavery. She then left the city to travel throughout New England, where she met such noted abolitionists as William Lloyd Garrison, Frederick Douglass, and Wendell Phillips; they invited her to speak at abolitionist gatherings, where she described the experiences of women slaves and the destruction of black families under slavery. The eloquence and religious tone of her speeches became a powerful tool for abolitionists committed to "moral suasion," the policy of at-

Portrait of Sojourner Truth, "I Sell the Shadow to Support the Substance"

tacking slavery by revealing its evils through moral argument. Soon one of the best-known abolitionists in the country, by 1850 she was acquainted with such leaders of the woman suffrage movement as Lucretia Mott and Elizabeth Cady Stanton and spoke at many women's rights conventions, among them the 4th Annual Women's Rights Convention in New York City (1853). She often called on white women to recognize black women as sisters, contending that they had much in common as mothers despite sharp disparities in economic standing. During the Civil War she nursed black troops, worked in a freedmen's community in Arlington, Virginia, and in 1864 was invited to Washington to consult with President Abraham Lincoln about the fate of emancipated blacks; she later unsuccessfully petitioned the U.S. Congress to pass a bill allowing freedmen to claim homesteads on public land in the West.

Jacqueline Bernard: *Journey Toward Freedom: The Story of Sojourner Truth* (New York: W. W. Norton, 1967)
Margaret Washington, ed.: *Narrative of Sojourner Truth* (New York: Vintage, 1993)

Thelma Foote

Soldiers' and Sailors' Monument. A memorial at 89th Street and Riverside Drive in Riverside Park. It stands one hundred feet (thirty meters) tall in the center of an esplanade one hundred feet wide lined with cannons. The first step toward erecting the monument was taken in 1893, when the city established a board of commissioners to propose a means of honoring fallen military heroes. The original proposal was for a monument at Grand Army Plaza at 59th Street and 5th Avenue, but because of objections from the Municipal Art Commission the present site was chosen instead. The cornerstone was laid on 15 December 1900, with Governor Theodore Roosevelt officiating. Work was completed in 1902, although the monument never received its finishing touch: bronze statues intended to sit in five niches in the polished marble interior chamber. In 1976 the monument was declared a municipal landmark.

For illustration see Riverside park.

Kenneth T. Jackson

Solomon R. Guggenheim Museum. Museum of modern art opened in 1939 as the Museum of Non-Objective Painting by the mining tycoon Solomon R. Guggenheim. It began as a collection of works by such modern artists as Wassily Kandinsky, László Moholy-Nagy, Paul Klee, and Amedeo Modigliani amassed between 1929 and 1937 for Guggenheim by the baroness Hilla Rebay von Ehrenwiesen. By 1937 Rebay became the curator of the collection, which was held by the Solomon R. Guggenheim Foundation and placed on public display in 1939 at the Museum of Non-Objective Painting on East 54th Street. Under Rebay's direction the museum became a forum for young artists and exhibited the work of modern artists including Kandinsky and Moholy-Nagy. At her urging Guggenheim commissioned a new building from Frank Lloyd Wright in 1943. A site was acquired on 5th Avenue between 88th and 89th streets and in 1948 the collection was moved temporarily into a townhouse at 1071 5th Avenue. After Guggenheim's death in 1949 his nephew Harry F. Guggenheim became the chairman of the foundation; in 1952 the museum took its current name and Guggenheim replaced Rebay with James Johnson Sweeney, a former curator at the Museum of Modern Art who added sculpture to the collection and documented it more systematically. The new building was Wright's only important commission in the city. Opened in October 1959, it is shaped like a spiral that is narrowest at its base and built entirely of hand-plastered concrete, inside and outside, over a steel frame. Inside the building, around

Solomon R. Guggenheim Museum, interior

Solomon R. Guggenheim Museum, exterior with addition (1992)

a large, central space, a curved ramp leads upward from street level through the height of the building, allowing exhibitions to be mounted in one virtually continuous line; Wright intended for visitors to begin at the top and move downward. Thomas Messer, appointed director in 1960, continued Sweeney's policies and secured the Justin K. Thannhauser Collection, which made the museum's holdings comprehensive and was housed in separate galleries adjacent to the original building and opened in 1972. In 1992 a controversial new ten-story wing opened adjacent to the original building: designed by Gwathmey, Siegel and Associates, it incorporates gallery, storage, and office space. In the same year the museum opened a branch in SoHo, in a building constructed for John Jacob Astor in 1881–82 at 575 Broadway near Prince Street.

Joan M. Lukach: *Hilla Rebay: In Search of the Spirit in Art* (New York: George Braziller, 1983)

Peter L. Donhauser

Soloveitchik, Joseph [Dov] (*b* Pruzhany [now in Belarus], 1903; *d* Brookline, Mass., 8 April 1993). Rabbi and philosopher. The son of a rabbi, he moved to Boston in 1932 with his wife, where he founded the Maimonides School, the first Jewish day school in New England. In 1941 he joined the faculty of Yeshiva University in Manhattan, where he became the preeminent teacher of the Talmud in North America and ordained two thousand rabbis, more than any other seminary teacher in the United States. Orthodox leaders around the world queried him about how to apply Jewish law to modern problems. His annual lectures, which lasted two to five hours, attracted thousands of listeners and were regarded as the major annual academic event for American Orthodoxy.

Kenneth T. Jackson

Sondheim, Stephen (Joshua) (*b* New York City, 22 March 1930). Composer. He began his career on Broadway as the lyricist for *West Side Story* (1957), wrote the lyrics for *Gypsy* (1959) and Richard Rodgers's *Do I Hear a Waltz?* (1965), and wrote both words and music to *A Funny Thing Happened on the Way to the Forum* (1962). In later years he achieved great success with his shows *Company* (1970), *Follies* (1971), *A Little Night Music* (1973), *Sweeney Todd* (1979), *Sunday in the Park with George* (1983), and *Passion* (1994). Sondheim's work is known for its advanced musical idiom (often characterized by more dissonance than is usually heard on Broadway), as well as for its challenging subject matter and literate lyrics.

Sara J. Steen

songs. The first song to feature New York City in its title was probably the "New York Patriotic Song," written by Charles Dibdin and published about 1799. The "Castle Garden March (*ca* 1820) and "New York, Oh What a Charming City" (1831) were other early songs published in sheet music. After the Civil War songs about the city began to appear in larger numbers. Many paid tribute to specific places (notably Broadway and the Bowery), such as "Walking down Broadway" (1868), "The Broadway Opera and the Bowery Crawl" (1871), "Strolling on the Brooklyn Bridge" (1883), and "The Bowery" (1892). In 1894 Charles B. Lawlor and James W. Blake wrote the first enduring song about the city, "The Sidewalks of New York," which portrayed its flourishing Irish population. Many laudatory "anthems" were written in the late nineteenth century and the early twentieth in praise of the city's vitality and diversity, including "In Good Old New York Town" (1899), Victor Herbert's "In Old New York" (1906), "Take Me Back to New York Town" (1907), and the best-known of the time, George M. Cohan's "Give My Regards to Broadway" (1904). By contrast Charles K. Harris's "The City Where Nobody Cares" (1908) and H. Altman's "Die Nyu-Yorker Tiern" (New York tears, 1910) portrayed the city as a cruel place.

In the first half of the twentieth century a number of songs appeared about neighborhoods in New York City, such as "Chinatown, My Chinatown" (1905), "Nestin' Time in Flatbush" (1917), "(I'll Take) Manhattan" (Richard Rodgers and Lorenz Hart, 1925) and Irving Berlin's "Easter Parade" (1933) and "Slumming on Park Avenue" (1937), about the wealthy enclaves of midtown and 5th Avenue. The Yiddish theater and its English-language equivalents offered songs about life in the tenements, notably "Second Hand Rose (from 2nd Avenue)" (1921) and "My Yiddisha Mama" (1925). Broadway and Times Square were featured in the lachrymose "There's a Broken Heart for Every Light on Broadway" (1915) and the exuberant "42nd Street" (1932) and "Lullaby of Broadway" (1935). The neighborhood most often treated in songs of the 1920s and 1930s was Harlem, which like the Bowery and Broadway before it came to symbolize the effervescence of the city. There were quasi-operatic and extended orchestral works such as George Gershwin's *opera scena* "121st Street" (1925) and William Grant Still's ballet "Lenox Avenue" (1937), and also popular songs such as Berlin's "Puttin' on the Ritz" (1929) and "Harlem on My Mind" (1936). The Savoy Ballroom, the best-known dance hall in Harlem, was immortalized in "Stompin' at the Savoy" (1934) and "The Joint Is Jumpin'" (1937). Duke Ellington, a resident of Harlem, wrote the songs "Drop Me Off in Harlem" (1933), "Harlem Speaks" (1935), "Harlem Air Shaft" (1940),

Cover for New York Mud, *sheet music by Will L. Randolph, 1874*

Songs and Compositions Inspired by New York City (selective list)

GENERAL

A Glance at New York (1848), English Burton
A Heart In New York (1981), Benny Gallagher, Graham Lyle
All the Critics Love U in New York (1983), Prince
Another Rainy Day in New York City (1981) [performed by Chicago]
As I Was Walking in New York One Day (*ca* 1836), W. H. Parker
Au Revoir Poland, Hello New York (1964), Albert Hague, Marty Brill
Autumn in New York (1934), Vernon Duke
Boss Tweed (1945), Sigmund Romberg, Dorothy Fields
Boy From New York City (1964), John Taylor
Conquering New York (1955), Leonard Bernstein, Betty Comden, Adolph Green
Croton Water Celebration (1842), George P. Morris, Sidney Pearson
Darlin' of New York (1969), Bill and Patti Jacob
Dawn of a New Day (Song of the New York World's Fair) (1939), George Gershwin, Ira Gershwin
Do the New York (1931), Jack P. Murray, Barry Trivers, Ben Oakland
Down and Out in New York City (1973), Bodie Chandler, Barry de Vorzon
Down in the Depths on the 90th Floor (1936), Cole Porter
Easter Parade (1933), Irving Berlin
Every Street's a Boulevard in Old New York (1953), Jule Styne, Bob Hilliard
Eyes of a New York Woman (1968), Thomas Pynchon, Jeff Ogden
Girls of New York (1925), Seymour Firth, Lee Edwards, R. F. Carroll
Give It Back to the Indians (1939), Richard Rodgers, Lorenz Hart
Hard Times in New York Town (1961), Bob Dylan
Hello New York (1976), Ronnie Britton
(I Like New York in June), How About You (1941), Ralph Freed, Burton Lane
Hudson River (1928), Henry Myers, Henry Sullivan
I Gotta Get Back to New York (1933), Richard Rodgers, Lorenz Hart
I Guess the Lord Must Be in New York City (1969), Harry Nilsson
I Happen to Like New York (1930), Cole Porter
I Hate New York (1983), Hank Williams Jr.
I Have a Friend at Chase Manhattan Bank (1975), Jack Bussins
I Have Grown to Love New York (1943), Vernon Duke, Howard Dietz
I Love a New Yorker (1950), Ralph Blane, Harold Arlen
I Wanna Go to City College (1946), Sammy Fein, George Marion Jr.
I Wouldn't Live in New York City (If They Gave Me the Whole Damn Place) (1970), Buck Owens
I'm Never Going Back to New York City (1983), Bruce Donnelly, Joey Harris
In a Brownstone Mansion (1962), Sol Kaplan, Edward Eliscu
In Gay New York (1896), Hugh Morton, Gustave Kerker
In Good Old New York Town (1899), Paul Dresser
In Old New York (1906), Victor Herbert
Isle de Blackwell (1878), Edward Harrigan, David Braham
It's a Lovely Night on the Hudson River (1937), Richard Lewine, Ted Felter
Jazzhattan Suite 1967 (1967), Oliver Nelson
Just Across from Jersey (1883), Edward Harrigan, David Braham
Knickerbocker Quadrilles (1843) [pubd by Firth and Hall]
Let's Take a Walk around the Block (1934), Harold Arlen, Yip Harburg
Little Old New York (1923), Victor Herbert, Gene Buck
Little Tin Box (1959), Sheldon Harnick, Jerry Bock
Lonely Town (1945), Betty Comden, Adolph Green, Leonard Bernstein
Lonesome in New York (1954), Jerry Herman
Maggie Murphy's Home (1890), Edward Harrigan, David Braham
Minnie the Moocher (1931), Irving Mills, Cab Calloway
Move Over, New York (1964), Walter Marks
My Best Girl's a New Yorker (1895), John Stromberg
My Name's La Guardia (1959), Jerry Bock, Sheldon Harnick
Native New Yorker (1977), Sandy Linzer, Denny Randell
New New York (1930), Arthur Schwartz, Howard Dietz
New York (*ca* 1800), P. Landrin Duport
New York (1925), R. H. Bonnell
New York (1928), George M. Cohan
New York (1943), Nathan Goodman, Irene Shannon
New York (1944), Mario Castelnuovo-Tedesco, Arthur Guiterman
New York (1959), Tommy Wolfe, Fran Landesman
New York, New York (1983), Nina Hagen
New York, New York (1984), Grandmaster Flash and the Furious Five
New York, New York (1945), Leonard Bernstein, Betty Comden, Adolph Green
(Theme from) New York, New York (1980), John Kander, Fred Ebb
New York, Oh What a Charming City (1831), I. A. Gairdner
New York, You've Got Me Dancing (1977) [performed by Andrea True Connection]
New York after Dark (1937), Vernon Duke, Ted Fetter
New York Afternoon (1976), Richie Cole
New York Ain't New York Any More (1925), Billy Rose, Lew Brown
New York Blues (1952), Duke Ellington
New York City (1972), John Lennon
New York City Rhythm (1975), Marty Panzer, Barry Manilow
New York Cliché (1978), Rob Fremont, Doris Willens
New Yorkers (1911), George M. Cohan
New York Forever (1903), Nicholas Biddle, Ben J. Jerome
New York from the Air (1975), Hank Beebe, Bill Heyer
New York Groove (1978), Russ Ballard
New York Hippodrome (1915), John Philip Sousa
New York Isn't Such a Bad Old Town (1912), Jean Schwartz, William Jerome
New York Is So Exciting (1983), Glen Moore
New York Is the Same Old Place (1922), Victor Herbert, B. G. DeSylva
New York Patriotic Song (1799), Mr. Dibdin
New York Profiles (1952), Norman Dello Joio
New York Rhapsody (1931), George Gershwin
New York Serenade (*ca* 1800), Dr. G. K. Jackson
New York Serenade (1928), George Gershwin, Ira Gershwin, P. G. Wodehouse
New York Serenade (1973), Bruce Springsteen
New York Serenading Waltz (*ca* 1800), Peter Weldon
New York's a Lonely Town (1965)
New York '69 (1975), Hank Beebe, Bill Heyer
New York Skyline (1977), Garland Jeffries
New York's My Home (1946), Gordon Jenkins
New York's Not My Home (1976), Jim Croce
New York Society (*ca* 1922)
New York Song (1902), Malcolm Lang
New York State of Mind (1975), Billy Joel
New York Tendaberry (1969), Laura Nyro
New York Town (1896), Gilmore and Leonard
New York Town (1927), Morrie Riskind, Howard Dietz, Henry Souvaine, Jay Gorney
New York Town for Mine Boys (1903), H. H. Niemeyer, Stanley Murphy
Nothing Can Ever Happen in New York (1927), James F. Hanley, Eddie Dowling
N.Y.C. (1977), Martin Chanin, Charles Strouse
Off to See New York (1927), Alfred Nathan, George Oppenheimer

(*continued*)

Songs and Compositions Inspired by New York City (selective list) (*Continued*)

On the Ferry (1922), Emerson Whitmore
On the Hudson (*ca* 1920), Edwin Franko Goldman
One New York (1896), Stafford Waters
Only Right Here in New York City (1975), Hank Beebe, Bill Heyer
Our New York (1939), Sigmund Spaeth
Paddy Duffey's Cart (1881), Edward Harrigan, David Braham
Penthouse Serenade (1931), Will Jason, Val Burton
Riding on the Elevated Railroad (*ca* 1895), Sam Devere
Rockin' Around in N.Y.C. (1980), Marshall Crenshaw
Seeing New York in the Rubber-Neck Hack (1904), Paul West, John W. Bratton
She Is the Belle of New York (1894), Hugh Morton, Gustave Kerker
She Reads the New York Papers Every Day (1902), Paul West, John W. Bratton
Sidewalks of New York (1894), Charles B. Lawlor, James W. Blake
Sophie in New York (1983), Steve Allen
So They Call It New York (1972), Don Pippin, Steve Brown
Sunday in New York (1959), Portia Nelson
Sunday in New York (1963), Carroll Coates, Peter Nero
Sunday Night in New York (1935), Charles Tobias, Charles Newman, Maury Mencher
Take Me Back to New York Town (1907), Andrew B. Sterling, Harry Von Tilzer
Taking in the Town (1890), Edward Harrigan, David Braham
Talkin' New York (1961), Bob Dylan
Tammany (1905), Vincent P. Bryan, Gus Edwards
Tenement Symphony (1941), Sid Kuller, Ray Golden
The Aldermanic Board (1885), Edward Harrigan, David Braham
The Babies on Our Block (1879), Edward Harrigan, David Braham
The Brave Old City of New York (1971), Helen Miller, Eve Merriam
The City Where Nobody Cares (1908), Charles K. Harris
The Daughter of Rosie O'Grady (1918), Monty C. Brice, Walter Donaldson
The East Side and the West Side (1925), J. D. McCarthy
The Great Four Hundred (1890), Edward Harrigan, David Braham
The Great New York Police (1922), George M. Cohan
The Lady Is a Tramp (1937), Richard Rodgers, Oscar Hammerstein
The New York Boy (*ca* 1825)
The New Yorker (*ca* 1920), Edwin Franko Goldman
The New York Fireman (*ca* 1836), A. Yates
The Night Maloney Landed in New York (1889), Joseph Flynn
The Oldest Established (Permanent Floating Crap Game in New York) (1950), Frank Loesser
The Only Living Boy in New York (?1969), Paul Simon
There's a Boat Dat's Leaving for New York (1935), George Gershwin, Ira Gershwin
There's Nothing New in Old New York (1927), Harry Akst, Benny Davis
The Song of New York (1903), Frank Damrosch
The Streets of Old New York (1914), Jeff Branen, Arthur Lange
Thro' the Streets of New York City (1838), C. E. Horn
'Tis My Home, Dear Old New York (Spirit of New York) (1930), Hugh Ross
Typical New Yorkers (1979), Ted Simons, Elinor Guggenheimer
Up on the Hudson Shore (1913), Jean Schwartz, Joseph W. Herbert, Harold Atteridge
Uptown, Downtown (1981), Stephen Sondheim
What New York Swells Are Coming to (*ca* 1871)
When New York Was New York (1937), George M. Cohan
When They Get Through with Reform in New York (*ca* 1900)
When You're Far Away from New York Town (1963), Arthur Schwartz, Howard Dietz
Where Is My Little Old New York (1924), Irving Berlin
Where the Hudson River Flows (1925), Richard Rodgers, Lorenz Hart
You Discover You're in New York (1943), Leo Robin, Harry Warren
You'll Never Be Poor in New York (1971), Jule Styne
You're in New York Now (1973), Matt Dubey, Dean Fuller

STATUE OF LIBERTY

Give Me Your Tired, Your Poor (1949), Irving Berlin
Miss Liberty (1949), Irving Berlin
She Will Be Standing in the Harbor (1943), Carmen Lombardo, John Jacob Loeb
Ten Million Men and a Girl (1942), John Redmond, Jim Cavanaugh, Jack Edwards
The Most Expensive Statue in the World (1949), Irving Berlin

MANHATTAN

A Latin Tune, a Manhattan Moon, and You (1940), Jimmy McHugh, Al Dubin
Love Letter to Manhattan (1950), Harold Rome
(I'll Take) Manhattan (1925), Richard Rodgers, Lorenz Hart
Manhattan Hymn (1923), Christopher Condie
Manhattan Lullaby (1932), Michael H. Cleary, Max Lief, Nathaniel Lief
Manhattan Madness (1931), Irving Berlin
Manhattan Mary (1927), B. G. DeSylva, Lew Brown, Ray Henderson
Manhattan Melodrama (1934), Richard Rodgers, Lorenz Hart
Manhattan Merry Go Round (1936), Pinky Herman, Gustav Haenschen
Manhattan Mood (1942), Harold Adamson, Peter DeRose
Manhattan Rag (*ca* 1929) [performed by Irving Mills and His Hotsy Totsy Gang]
Manhattan Serenade (1928), Louis Alter [lyrics added 1942 by Harold Adamson]
Manhattan Spiritual (1958), Billy Maxted
Manhattan Square Dance (1948), David Rose
Manhattan Transfer (1926), Manning Sherman, Arthur Herzog Jr.
Manhattan Walk (1928), Bert Kalmar, Herbert Stothart, Harry Ruby
May in Manhattan (1960), Tom Romano, Ruth Cleary Patterson
Melody of Manhattan (1976), Ronnie Britton
Monday in Manhattan, Richard Himber, Elliott Grennard
Movie House in Manhattan (1948), Richard Lewine, Arnold B. Horwitt
Oh My! How We Pose (6th Avenue) (*ca* 1884), Edward Harrigan, David Braham
On a Roof in Manhattan (1932), Irving Berlin
Say, Young Man from Manhattan (1930), Vincent Youmans, Clifford Grey
She's a Latin from Manhattan (1935), Richard Rodgers, Lorenz Hart
Take Me Back to Manhattan (1930), Cole Porter
Vineyards of Manhattan (1929), Arthur Schwartz, Agnes Morgan

LOWER MANHATTAN

Ann Street (1921), Charles Ives
Baxter Avenue (1886), Edward Harrigan, David Braham
Belle of 14th Street (*ca* 1871)
Bowery Lass (*ca* 1820)
Bowery Serenade (1942), Eddie DeLange, Johnny Brooks
Castle Garden March (*ca* 1820), E. Riley
Castle Garden Schottische (1852)
Chinatown (1982), Joe Jackson
Chinatown, My Chinatown (1906), William Jerome, Jean Schwartz
Down Where the East River Flows (1930), Vincent Youmans, Harold Adamson, Clifford Grey
I'm Something on Avenue A (1925), George Gershwin
It's a Windy Day on the Battery (1917), Sigmund Romberg, Rida Johnson Young
Minnie the Moocher's Wedding Day (1932), Harold Arlen, Ted Koehler
Moon over Mulberry Street (1935), Raymond B. Egan, Harry Tierney

(*continued*)

Songs and Compositions Inspired by New York City (selective list) (*Continued*)

Mulberry Springs (1886), Edward Harrigan, David Braham
My Pearl's a Bowery Girl (1894), William Jerome, Andrew Mack
Only a Bowery Boy (1894), Charles B. Ward, Gussie L. Davis
Pell Street (1922), Emerson Whitmore
Second Hand Rose (from Second Avenue) (1921), Grant Clarke, James F. Hanley
The Belle of Avenoo A (1895), Safford Waters
The Bowery (1891), Charles B. Hoyt, William Gaunt
The Bowery Bum (1929), Benny Samberg
Wall Street Wail (1930), Duke Ellington

GREENWICH VILLAGE

A Greenwich Village Tragedy (1922), Emerson Whitmore
Belle of Avenue B (*ca* 1922)
Bleecker Street (1961), John Dooley
Bleecker Street (1963), Paul Simon
Bottom End of Bleecker Street (1967), Tom Sankey
Christopher Street (1953), Leonard Bernstein, Betty Comden, Adolph Green
Down at the Village (1928), Ray Perkins, Max Lief, Nathaniel Lief
Down Greenwich Village Way (1922), Albert Von Tilzer, Neville Fleeson
Down in Dear Old Greenwich Village (*ca* 1928)
Greenwich Village (1917), John Murray Anderson, A. Baldwin Sloane, Philip Bartholmae
Greenwich Village (1918), Jerome Kern, P. G. Wodehouse
Greenwich Village Follies (1976), Ronnie Britton
Greenwich Village U.S.A. (1960), Jeanne Bargy, Frank Gehrecke, Herb Cory
Market Day in the Village (1936), Ralph Benatzky, Irving Caesar
On Union Square (1886), Edward Harrigan, David Braham
Positively 4th Street (1965), Bob Dylan
Rose of Washington Square (1920), Ballard MacDonald, James F. Hanley
Second Avenue and 12th Street (1956), Vernon Duke, Ogden Nash
Sullivan Street Flat (1975), Ronnie Britton
Tenth and Greenwich (1971), Melvin Van Peebles
The Sunny Side of Thompson Street (1893), Edward Harrigan, David Braham
Washington Square (1920), Cole Porter
Washington Square (1950), Clay Warnick, Mel Tolkin, Lucille Kallen
Washington Square (1975), Ronnie Britton

MIDTOWN

At the Roxy Music Hall (1938), Lorenz Hart, Richard Rodgers
Belle of Murray Hill (1899), Willis Clark, Maurice Levy
Carnegie Blues (1945), Duke Ellington
Chelsea Hotel (1974), Leonard Cohen
Chelsea Morning (1969), Joni Mitchell
Chimes of St. Patrick's (1922), Emerson Whitmore
Confession to a Park Avenue Mother (I'm in Love with a West Side Girl) (1960), Jerry Herman
Conversation on Park Avenue (1946), Willie "the Lion" Smith
Easter Parade (1933), Irving Berlin
52nd Street (1978), Billy Joel
52nd Street Theme (1948), Thelonious Monk
45th and Broadway (1922), Gene Buck, Dave Stamper
42nd Street (1932), Al Dubin, Harry Warren
42nd Street and Broadway Strut (1922), Albert Von Tilzer and Neville Fleeson
42nd Street Blues (1977), David Langston Smyrl
Hollywood, Park Avenue, and Broadway (1933), Ray Henderson, Lew Brown
L.S.A. All the Way (Lincoln Square Academy March) (1966), Leonard Kirby, Gregory Paul Deutsch
Lullaby of Birdland (1952), George Shearing, George Weiss
Madison Avenue (1979), Ted Simons, Elinor Guggenheimer
Meet Me in Times Square (1940), Gladys Shelley, Irving Gellers
Meet Me under the Maple Tree in Radio City (1942), Frank Turner, Charles Wynn
Memories of Madison Square Garden (1935), Richard Rodgers, Lorenz Hart
Park Avenue's Going to Town (1936), Edgar Fairchild, Milton Pascal
San Juan Hill (1942)
Park Avenue Strut (1929), Phil Baker, Maury Rubens, Moe Jaffe, Harold Atteridge
She Lives on Murray Hill (1882), Edward Harrigan, David Braham
Slumming on Park Avenue (1937), Irving Berlin
Stairway to the Stars (Park Avenue Fantasy) (1935), Mitchell Parrish, Matt Melneck, Frank Signorelli
Tenth Avenue Freeze Out (1975), Bruce Springsteen
The A-1 Belle of Madison Square (*ca* 1871), J. A. Hardwick
The 59th Street Bridge Song (1967), Paul Simon
Times Square (1922), Emerson Whitmore
Times Square (1922), Jerome Kern, Anne Caldwell
Times Square Dance (1940), Sammy Fain, Jack Yellen
Tin Pan Alley (1953), Sammy Fain, Jack Yellen
Uptown Girl (1983), Billy Joel
Way Out West (on West End Avenue) (1937), Richard Rodgers, Lorenz Hart
West End Avenue (1974), Stephen Schwartz
When Love Beckoned on 52nd Street
Yuletide, Park Avenue (1946), Harold Rome

FIFTH AVENUE

Fifth Avenue (1868), William H. Lingard
Fifth Avenue (1901), George V. Hobart, A. B. Sloane
Fifth Avenue (1949), Gordon Jenkins, Tom Adair
Fugitive From Fifth Avenue (1949), Richard Stutz, Nat Hilson
Lady From Fifth Avenue (1937), Walter G. Samuels, Leonard Whitcup, Teddy Powell
Lament on Fifth Avenue (1957), Claire Richardson, Paul Rosner
On Double Fifth Avenue (1927), Abel Baer, Sam Lewis, Joe Young
South Fifth Avenue (1881), Edward Harrigan, David Braham

BROADWAY

A Broadway Musical (1978), Charles Strouse, Lee Adams
A Side Street Off Broadway (1927), Edgar Fairchild, Henry Meyers
Angel of the Great White Way (1937), Elton Box, Desmond Box, Don Pelosi, Paddy Roberts
Belle of the Gay White Way (1909), Charles Shackford
Better Than Broadway (1980), Tom Savage
Boogaloo down Broadway (1967), Jesse James
Broads of Broadway (1926), Gitz Rice, Paul Porter
Broadway (1913), Lew Brown
Broadway (1921), Hank Hawkins, G. E. Johnson
Broadway (1927), B. G. DeSylva, Lew Brown, Ray Henderson
Broadway (1929), Con Conrad, Sidney D. Mitchell, Archie Gottler
Broadway (1930), Percy Weinrich, Harry Clarke
Broadway (1940), Henry Woode, Teddy McRae, Bill Bird
Broadway (1959), Jule Styne, Stephen Sondheim
Broadway (1980), Stephen Lemberg
Broadway, Broadway (1978), Charles Strouse, Lee Adams
Broadway, My Street (1971), John Kander, Fred Ebb
Broadway, New York (1979), Ann Harris
Broadway Baby (1971), Stephen Sondheim
Broadway Baby (1980), Jim Wise, George Harrison, Robin Miller
Broadway Belle (1908), Julian Eltinge, Ted Snyder
Broadway Belles (1919), Arthur J. Jackson, Herbert Spencer
Broadway Blossom (1945), Morton Gould, Betty Comden, Adolph Green

(*continued*)

Songs and Compositions Inspired by New York City (selective list) (*Continued*)

Broadway Blues (1920), Arthur Swanstrom, Carey Morgan
Broadway Caballero (1941), Henry Russell
Broadway Conga (1938), Walter Hirsch, Ernest Lecuona
Broadway Dandy (*ca* 1871)
Broadway Follies (1981), Walter Marks
Broadway Girl (1904), Grace Leonard, Joe Nathan
Broadway Glide (1912), A. Seymour Brown, Bert Grant
Broadway Gypsy (1928), Rob Merwin, Frank Galassi
Broadway Honeymoon (1913), Collin Davis, Joe E. Howard
Broadway Indian Chief (1909), William J. McKenna
Broadway Indians (1923), Gene Buck, Dave Stamper
Broadway Jamboree (1937), Jimmy McHugh
Broadway Lady (1933), Sam H. Stept, Bud Green
Broadway Lights (1939), Enoch Light, Jimmy Eaton, Terry Shand
Broadway Love Song (1949), Jay Gorney, Jean Kerr, Walter Kerr
Broadway Mastery (1927), Jimmy Duffy, Clarence Gaskill
Broadway Melody (1929), Arthur Freed, Nacio Herb Brown
Broadway Moon (1939), Al Koppell, Terry Shand
Broadway of My Heart (1971), Skip Redwine, Larry Frank
Broadway Reverie (1931), Gene Buck, Dave Stamper
Broadway Rhythm (1929), Bob Jaffe, Millard G. Thomas
Broadway Rhythm (1933), Arthur Freed, Nacio Herb Brown
Broadway Rose (1920), Eugene West, Otis Spencer
Broadway's Gone Hawaii (1937), Mack Gordon, Harry Revel
Broadway's Gone Hillbilly (1934), Lew Brown, Jay Gorney
Broadway Sights (1835), N. H. Latham
Broadway Swell and Brooklyn Belle (*ca* 1927), J. D. Kelly
Broadway to Madrid (1926), Morris Hamilton, Grace Henry
Broadway Waltzes (1849), George W. Warren
Don't Blame It on Broadway (1913), Sal Young, Harry Williams, Bert Grant
Forty Five Miles from Broadway (1905), George M. Cohan
From Broadway to Main Street (1923), Harry Archer, Harlan Thompson
Funky Broadway (1966), Arlester Christian
Funky Girl on a Motherless Broadway (1971), Melvin Van Peebles
Girl I Met on Broadway (*ca* 1871), J. Currie
Give My Regards to Broadway (1904), George M. Cohan
Goodbye Broadway, Hello France (1917), Francis Reisner, Benny Davis, Billy Baskette
Hang Up Your Hat on Broadway (1933), Bernard Grossman, Dave Sylvester
Howdy Broadway (1926), Richard Rodgers, Lorenz Hart
I Beg Your Pardon Dear Old Broadway (1911), Irving Berlin
I'm a Vamp from East Broadway (1920), Irving Berlin, Bert Kalmar, Harry Ruby
Indians along Broadway (1920), Benjamin H. Burt
It's Getting Dark on Old Broadway (1922), Louis A. Hirsch, Gene Buck, Dave Stamper
Lullaby for Broadway (1935), Al Dubin, Harry Warren
Milkmaids of Broadway (1930), Alma Sanders, Monte Carlo
Nights on Broadway (1977) [performed by the Bee Gees]
Old Broadway (1906), Joseph E. Howard, Charles K. Harris
On Broadway (1885), Sydney Rosenfeld
On Broadway (1962), Barry Mann, Cynthia Weil, Jerry Lieber, Mike Stoller
On Broadway after Three (1897), Walter De Frece, Edmund Francis
On the Proper Side of Broadway on a Saturday P.M. (1902), Cobb and Edwards
Pearl of Broadway (1927), Jerome Kern, Bert Kalmar, Harry Ruby
Please Don't Monkey with Broadway (1939), Cole Porter
Side Street off Broadway (1927), Henry Meyers, Edgar Fairchild
1617 Broadway (1956), Jerry Bock, George Weiss, Larry Holofcener
Slaves of Broadway (1928), Ray Perkins, Max Lief, Nathaniel Lief
Take Me Back to Broadway (1907), James O'Dea, A. Payson Caldwell
That's Broadway (1944), Gene Herbert, Teddy Hall
The Broadway, Opera, and Bowery Crawl (1871), Philip Stoner, Giuseppe Operti
The Call of Broadway (1927), Maury Rubens, Jack Osterman, Ted Lewis
The Lady from Broadway (1935), Dave Oppenheim, Max Rich
Theme from Mr. Broadway (1964), Dave Brubeck
There's a Broadway Up in Heaven (1935), Edward J. Lambert, Gerald Dolin
There's a Broken Heart for Every Light On Broadway (1915), Howard Johnson, Fred Fisher
Turn Me Loose in Broadway (1952), Vernon Duke, Ogden Nash
Up Broadway (1900), J. Hoyt Toler
Waiting for a Broadway Stage (*ca* 1871)
Walking down Broadway (1870), William Lingrad, Charles E. Pratt
What Would Become of New York Town If Broadway Wasn't There? (1910), Sterling, Costello, Kerry Mills
When a Fella Meets a Flapper on Broadway (1929), Irving Caesar, Philip Charig
Wouldn't You Like to Be on Broadway? (1947), Kurt Weill, Langston Hughes
You Can Have Broadway (1906), George M. Cohan

CENTRAL PARK

Big Back Yard (1945), Sigmund Romberg, Dorothy Fields
Carousel in the Park (1944), Sigmund Romberg, Dorothy Fields
Central Park (*ca* 1920), Edwin Franko Goldman
Central Park 'n' West (1981), Ian Hunter
Central Park on a Sunday Afternoon (1975), Hank Beebe, Bill Heyer
In Central Park (1927), Harold Orlob, Irving Caesar
In the Center of Central Park (1942), Peter Tinturin
Listening to the Music Up in Central Park (1869), George Leyborne
On the Mall (1923), Edwin Franko Goldman
Romanzo di Central Park (1900), Charles Ives
Saturday Night in Central Park (1948), Richard Lewine, Arnold B. Horwitt
Sunday in the Park (1937), Harold Rome
Through Central Park (*ca* 1870), William Lingard
Winter in Central Park (1929), Jerome Kern, Oscar Hammerstein

HARLEM

A Night in Harlem (1962)
Blue Belles of Harlem (1945), Duke Ellington
Bojangles of Harlem (1936), Jerome Kern, Dorothy Fields
Boys from Harlem (1939), Duke Ellington
Come to Harlem (1932), Al Wilson, Charles Weinberg, Ken Macomber
Deep Harlem (1929), Joe Jordan, Homer Tutt, Henry Creamer
Deep in the Heart of Harlem (1964)
Doin' the Uptown Lowdown (1933), Mack Gordon, Harry Revel
Don't Forget 127th Street (1964), Charles Adams, Lee Strouse
Drop Me Off in Harlem (1933), Duke Ellington, Nick Kenny
Echoes of Harlem (1936), Duke Ellington
Everybody's Happy in Jimtown (1928), Fats Waller, Andy Razaf
Formal Night in Harlem (1936), Francis K. Shuman, Johanny Farro, Jules Loman
Happy Heaven of Harlem (1929), Cole Porter
Harlem (1927), Ford Dabney, Jo Trent

(*continued*)

Songs and Compositions Inspired by New York City (selective list) (*Continued*)

Harlem (A Tone Parallel to Harlem) (1952), Duke Ellington
Harlem Air Shaft (1940), Duke Ellington
Harlemania (1930), Richard Rodgers, Lorenz Hart
Harlem Blues (1922), W. C. Handy
Harlem Bolero (1937), Benny Davis, J. Fred Coots
Harlem Congo (1934)
Harlem Dan (1933), Alexander Hill
Harlem Drag (1928), R. Arthur Booker, Walter Bishop
Harlem Flat Blues (1929), Duke Ellington
Harlem Follies (1980), Stephen H. Lemberg
Harlem Holiday (1932), Harold Arlen
Harlem Lullaby (1932), Margot Hillham, Willard Robison
Harlem Mania (1932), Donald Heywood
Harlem Moon (1931), Mann Holiner, Alberta Nichols
Harlem Nocturne (1943), ?Richard R. Rogers, Earle M. Hagan
Harlem on My Mind (1933), Irving Berlin
Harlem on the Ritz (1929)
Harlem River Chanty (1925), Richard Rodgers, Lorenz Hart
Harlem Sandman (1943), Harold Adamson, Jule Styne
Harlem's Goin' to Town (1936), Joseph Elly
Harlem's Poppin' (1940), Maceo Pinkard, William Tracey
Harlem Shuffle (1986), Keith Richards, Mick Jagger
Harlem Speaks (1933), Duke Ellington
Harlem Streets (1972), Micki Grant
Harlem Symphony (1932), James P. Johnson
Harlem Twist (1928), Fud Livingston, Chauncey Morehouse
Harmony in Harlem (1938), Irving Mills, Duke Ellington, Johnny Hodges
Headin' For Harlem (1927), James Hawley, Eddie Dowling
Heart of Harlem (1945)
High Up in Harlem (1939), Jerome Kern, Oscar Hammerstein
Home to Harlem (1933), Ray Henderson, Lew Brown
I Dreamt I Dwelt in Harlem (1941), Robert B. Wright, Jerry Gray, Ben Smith, Leonard B. Ware
I'm Slapping Seventh Avenue with the Sole of My Shoe (1938)
It Was a Sad Night in Harlem (1936), Al Lewis, Helmy Kresa
Jumpin' at the Woodside (1938), Count Basie
Jungle Nights in Harlem (1934)
Old Man Harlem (1933), Hoagy Carmichael, Rudy Vallee
121st Street (1925), George Gershwin
Puttin' on the Ritz (1929), Irving Berlin
Shades of Harlem (1957)
Song of Harlem (1929), Frank Marcus, Bernard Maltin
Spanish Harlem (1960), Jerry Lieber, Phil Spector
Spanish Harlem Incident (1963), Bob Dylan
Stompin' at the Savoy (1934), Edgar Sampson
Sugar Hill Penthouse (1945), Duke Ellington
Take a Trip to Harlem (1930), Eubie Blake, Andy Razaf
Take the "A" Train (1941), Billy Strayhorn
There's a Boy in Harlem (1938), Richard Rodgers, Lorenz Hart
The Spell of Those Harlem Nights (1932), Al Wilson, Charles Weinberg, Ken Macomber
Underneath the Harlem Moon (1932), Mack Gordon, Harry Revel
Uptown (1962), Barry Mann, Cynthia Weil
Uptown Downbeat (1936), Duke Ellington
Uptown Saturday Night (1974), Tom Scott, Morgan Ames
What Harlem Is to Me (1935), Andy Razaf, Russell Wooding, Paul Denniker

BROOKLYN

A Tree Grows in Brooklyn (1944), Moe Jaffe
Born and Bred in Brooklyn (1923), George M. Cohan
Brooklyn (1983), Scott McLarty, Dorothy Chansky
Brooklyn Cantata (1940), George Kleinsinger, Mike Stratton
Brooklyn Dodger Strike (1981), Bob Brush, Martin Chanin
Brooklyn Polka (1944), Zeke Manners
By the Beautiful Sea (1914), Harold R. Atteridge, Harry Carroll
Coney Island (1930), Richard Rodgers, Lorenz Hart
Coney Island, U.S.A. (1964), Jack Lawrence, Stan Freeman
Coney Island Boat (1954), Dorothy Fields, Arthur Schwartz
Coney Island's Shore (*ca* 1871), Johnny Delfield
Danny by My Side (Brooklyn Bridge) (1891), Edward Harrigan, David Braham
Down on Coney Island, W. Warren Bentley
Hail, Brooklyn (*ca* 1920), Edwin Franko Goldman
I'm Gonna Hang My Hat on a Tree in Brooklyn (1944), Dan Shapiro, Milton Pascal, Phil Charig
I've Made My Plans for the Summer (1907), John Philip Sousa
In a Little "Jernt" in Greenpernt (1936), "Gowanus Canal"
Leave Us Go Root for the Dodgers, Rogers (1942), Dan Parker, Bud Green
Manhattan Beach (1893), John Philip Sousa
Miss Euclid Avenue (1961), Jerry Herman
Moon over Brooklyn (1946), Jason Matthews, Terry Shand
Nestin' Time in Flatbush (1917), P. G. Wodehouse, Jerome Kern
No Sleep 'Til Brooklyn (1986), Beastie Boys
Ode on Science (1840), E. C. Embury [dedicated to the Trustees of the Brooklyn Collegiate Institute]
Over the Bridge, George M. Cohan
Strolling on the Brooklyn Bridge (1883), George Cooper, Joseph P. Skelly
Take Me Down to Coney Island (1897), Gustave Kerker, Hugh Morton
The Belles about the Flat Bush (1785)
The Brooklyn Bridge (1947), Jule Styne
The Brooklyn Ferryman (*ca* 1836), W. H. Parker
Two Orphans (Brooklyn Theater Fire) (*ca* 1922), C. A. Fuller

BRONX, QUEENS, STATEN ISLAND

Bronx Express (1922), Creamer and Layton
Christmas in Hollis (1987), Russell Simmons, Daryl McDaniels
Don Jose from Far Rockaway (1952), Harold Rome
I Love the New York Yankees (1981), Paula Lindstrom
On the Banks of the Bronx (1919), William Le Baron, Victor Jacobi
Rockaway Beach (1977) [performed by the Ramones]
The Tremont Avenue Cruisewear Fashion Show (1973), Jerry Livingston, Mark David

SUBWAYS

A Month of Subways (1949), Johnny Mercer, Robert E. Dolan
Don't Sleep in the Subway (1967), Tony Hatch, Jackie Trent
Old Man Subway (1933), Robert Russell Bennett, Owen Murphy, Robert A. Simon
Subway Directions; Ride through the Night (1961), Jule Styne, Betty Comden, Adolph Green
Subway Dream (1971), Helen Miller, Eve Merriam
Subway Rag (1958), Buster Davis, Steven Vinaver
Subway Rider (1980), Micki Grant
Subway Song (1948), Richard Lewine, Arnold B. Horwitt
The Rumble of the Subway (1923), Vincent Youmans, William Carey Duncan, Oscar Hammerstein, Herbert Stothart
The Subway Sun (1928), Ray Perkins, Max Lief, Nathaniel Lief
Third Avenue L (1956), Michael Brown
Up in the Elevated Railway (1954), Sigmund Romberg, Leo Robin

Compiled by Marc Ferris

demand arose for South Asian films on video cassette; these were soon carried by many grocery stores, and appearances by South Asian actors at Madison Square Garden, Colden Center, and Yankee Stadium attracted large crowds. In 1989 the first Global Convention of Overseas Indians was held in the city, drawing Indian leaders from India, Africa, Europe, North America, and the Caribbean.

In 1990 the South Asian population of New York City exceeded a hundred thousand, constituting the largest such community in the United States. In addition to Indians, who remained in the majority, the community included Pakistanis, Bangladeshis, Sri Lankans, and Nepalese. Its members confronted questions about adapting to American life and preserving traditions, especially among generations born in the United States. There was also concern over political participation, violence against Asians, and discrimination.

Maxine P. Fisher: *Indians of New York City: A Study of Immigrants from India* (New Delhi: Heritages, 1980)

Madhulika S. Khandelwal

South Beach. Neighborhood in northeastern Staten Island (1990 pop. 18,000), bounded to the north by the Staten Island Expressway, to the east and south by Lower New York Bay, and to the west by Dongan Hills. It is on the site of Oude Dorp, a Dutch community built in 1661 near the foot of Ocean Avenue. Although no trace of the community remains, reports of the Dutch West India Company mention twelve to fourteen families and a blockhouse. From the 1880s to the 1920s the beach was a major resort, with hotels, beer gardens, bathing pavilions, shooting galleries, ferris wheels, theaters, and dance halls rivaling those of Coney Island. On weekends during the summer as many as 100,000 visitors would travel to the beach by boat and train. By 1891 there were at least twenty-five hotels, including the Pine Grove, set in a park with a scenic railway, a saloon, an eating stand, a pavilion, a beer garden, bathhouses, and a photography studio; nearby was a steam carousel. The Bachmann Hotel had a theater that in 1906 became the Happyland Amusement Park. In 1917 bathing was declared unsafe and the amusement park was destroyed by fire. Long known as an Italian neighborhood, South Beach is characterized by a high rate of homeownership, carefully tended gardens, and well-attended churches, especially the Church of the Holy Rosary on South Lane. In the 1960s a number of blacks and Latin Americans moved into the neighborhood. Important local institutions include the South Beach Psychiatric Center (dedicated in 1973), the largest employer in the area, and the Giuseppe Mazzini Senior Citizen's Center.

Henry G. Steinmeyer: "South Beach: The Resort Era," *Staten Island Historian* 19, no. 3 (July–Sept 1958)

Drew Fetherston: "Steam Carousels and Summers of Fun and Frolic," *Staten Island Advance*, 14 April 1968, §E, p. 4

John E. Hurley: "Glory Days Are Gone," *Staten Island Advance*, 26 June 1989, §B, pp. 1, 2

Howard Weiner

South Bronx. An imprecise term used after 1950 to designate an area of shifting boundaries in the southwestern Bronx. At first applied only to Mott Haven and Melrose, by 1975 it came to include the area along the Cross Bronx Expressway and later Fordham Road as well. The widespread use of the name has done much to obscure the diversity of the neighborhoods making up the South Bronx, which many local residents do not regard as being a neighborhood itself.

South Brooklyn. An obsolete and imprecise term applied to the southern parts of the city of Brooklyn about 1855, and including what are now known as Red Hook, Carroll Gardens, and Park Slope.

South Brooklyn Railway. Freight railway subsidiary of the New York City Transit Authority, operating between 2nd Avenue and Fort Hamilton Parkway in Sunset Park. Brooklyn Rapid Transit inaugurated the line on 13 January 1900 to offer freight services between Bush Terminal and Coney Island. On 28 February 1907 the railway acquired the lease for the tracks on McDonald Avenue from the Brooklyn Heights Railroad, which had in turn acquired the rights in 1899 from the Long Island Rail Road. The line interchanged freight with the Long Island Rail Road and the New Haven Rail Road at Parkville (Avenue I and McDonald Avenue) and with the New York Dock Railway at 2nd Avenue and 37th Street. The cessation of freight interchange at Parkville after Conrail was formed in 1976, along with the poor condition of track along McDonald Avenue, prompted the railway on 1 February 1978 to abandon all track south of Fort Hamilton Parkway.

Jay Bendersky: *Brooklyn's Waterfront Railways* (Uniondale, N.Y.: Meatball, 1988)

John Fink

South Brother Island. An island in the eastern arm of the East River, at the entrance to Long Island Sound. It has an area of seven acres (three hectares) and is part of Queens. The island and its neighbor North Brother Island (about a third of a mile, or half a kilometer, to the east) were called the Gezellen (companions) by the Dutch. South Brother Island was once owned by the brewer Jacob Ruppert, who built a summer home there in 1894 that was destroyed by fire in 1907. The last private owner was a sand company. Now abandoned and densely overgrown, the island is owned by the city, which has put it up for sale.

WPAG

Gerard R. Wolfe

South East Bronx Community Organization [SEBCO]. A group founded in the autumn of 1968 by community leaders in Hunts Point and Longwood North to halt their neighborhood's decline. Their leader was Father Louis R. Gigante, a Roman Catholic priest then assigned to St. Athanasius Church, which is at the center of the redevelopment area. Using a combination of public and private funds, SEBCO has concentrated on the rehabilitation of existing housing, but it has also built more than 250 one- and two-family dwellings as well as many new apartment buildings. By the mid 1990s SEBCO was locally famous for its proven ability to restore once-devastated structures and to bring new vitality to threatened neighborhoods.

Kenneth T. Jackson

Southfield. Former administrative district in southeastern Staten Island, bounded to the north by Arthur Kill Road and Richmond Road, to the east by the Narrows and Lower New York Bay, to the south by the Atlantic Ocean, and to the west by Gifford's Lane; it comprised Stapleton, Clifton, Rosebank, Old Town, South Beach, Dongan Hills, Midland Beach, New Dorp, Oakwood, Richmondtown (the seat), and parts of Great Kills and Eltingville. The area was variously known as South Division and South Quarter; the area encompassing it and Westfield was sometimes called Southside. In 1860 Middletown was formed from a part of the northwestern section along with a bordering part of the town of Castleton. The district was abolished when New York City was consolidated in 1898.

Marjorie Johnson

South Jamaica. Name sometimes applied to an area in southern Queens bounded to the north by Liberty Avenue, to the east by Merrick Boulevard, to the south by the Belt Parkway, and to the west by the Van Wyck Expressway. For most of the nineteenth century the area was covered by vast farms and isolated farmhouses. The Jamaica Racetrack opened in 1894 on a large tract south of Baisley Boulevard and east of New York Boulevard. Several small developments were made after 1900, including Talfourd Lawn, Jamaica Heights, Jamaica Park, and Jamaica Falls. Streets were cut in the 1920s and hundreds of modest one-family houses were built: by the Second World War there was no vacant land. Most of the population was black. The racetrack closed in August 1959 and in December 1963 became the site of Rochdale Village, a complex of 5860 apartments that was the largest middle-income cooperative in the nation. Two smaller apartment complexes are Baisley Park Houses and Cedar Manor Houses. The rest of the housing consists of detached frame houses of two and a half stories each on lots measuring twenty-five by a hundred feet (eight by thirty meters). In the 1980s the neighborhood attracted many immigrants from Jamaica and Guyana, and to a lesser extent from Haiti, Trinidad and Tobago, the Dominican Republic, and Colombia. South Jamaica is the largest black neighborhood in Queens, and one of its most impoverished. Many residents are public employees. York College stands on 160th Street. Baisley Pond (originally a collection pond of the Brooklyn Water Works) and Baisley Park are the most attractive natural features.

Vincent Seyfried

South Ozone Park. Neighborhood in south central Queens, bounded to the north by Rockaway Boulevard, to the east by the Van Wyck Expressway, to the south by the Belt Parkway, and to the west by Aqueduct Racetrack. Until 1908 the area was occupied mostly by truck farms and there were few roads. David P. Leahy, a real-estate agent from Brooklyn, built a development south of Rockaway Turnpike between 131st and 140th streets that he named South Ozone Park in 1909 and promoted so successfully that by 1913 there were almost a hundred houses. Initially sole access to the neighborhood was provided by a trolley on Rockaway Turnpike. Eventually hundreds of detached one-family houses were built along new streets, especially during the 1920s. The neighborhood became largely Italian and Irish. During the 1980s it also attracted many immigrants from Guyana (accounting for almost 30 percent of all recent immigrants), Jamaica (20 percent), Haiti, the Dominican Republic, and Trinidad and Tobago. Many of those who live in South Ozone Park work at Kennedy Airport.

Vincent Seyfried

South Street Seaport. District on the Lower East Side between the Battery and Fulton Street that was the center of the port district from 1815 to 1860. The area was favored by sea captains because it was sheltered from the prevailing westerly winds and from ice that floated down the Hudson River; winds blowing off the shore also facilitated departure from berths there. The original shorefront road was Pearl Street, apparently named for its oyster-shell surface. During the eighteenth century the shoreline was extended with landfill, and a new shorefront road was built (later named Water Street), followed by Front Street and later by South Street in the early nineteenth century. South Street became known worldwide for its proximity to moorings in the harbor: bowsprits and jib booms projected nearly to the buildings across the street that housed the businesses of merchants, ship chandlers, sailmakers, and figurehead carvers, as well as boarding houses, saloons, and brothels. Evangelical organizations attempted to restore respectability and propriety to the often rowdy neighborhood. After 1880 the area began to decline, in part because adequate space to develop facilities was lacking and in part because the water was too shallow to accommodate oceangoing vessels. By the 1930s most of the open piers were covered, as large ships calling at New York City berthed on the West Side of Manhattan and in Hoboken, New Jersey. In 1966 a citizens' group led by Peter Stanford and Norma Stanford formed the Friends of the South Street Maritime Museum. Inspired by the restoration of the waterfront in San Francisco, it gathered a fleet of historic ships and obtained landmark designation for the buildings in the area; the South Street Seaport Museum opened in 1967. In 1973 two blocks were condemned by the city and leased to the museum, and another block was acquired for a state maritime museum that was eventually abandoned.

South Street, ca *1897*

In 1979 development of the South Street Historic District was undertaken by the Rouse Company of Columbia, Maryland, which had rebuilt the historic Quincy Market District in Boston. The project eventually required major investment by the firm, support from the city and the state, the surrender of some properties by the museum, and federal funding in the form of an Urban Development Action Grant. The first section of the district, opened in 1983, consisted of a modern market building on the site of the Fulton markets and two restored blocks of historic buildings; the second, opened in 1985, was a three-story shopping mall pier called Pier 17 built into the East River on the former site of the slip used by the Fulton Fish Market. By the 1990s the South Street Seaport Museum had assembled one of the world's largest collections of historic ships and ship models, as well as fine archaeological holdings (including printing presses, type fonts, and other artifacts), examples of maritime art (oil paintings, prints, clipper cards, and scrimshaw), and historic buildings.

Norman J. Brouwer

South Street, 1878

South Woodhaven. Obsolete name for the neighborhood in Queens now known as AQUEDUCT.

Soyer, Moses (*b* Borisoglebsk, Russia, 25 Dec 1899; *d* New York City, 4 Sept 1974). Painter, twin brother of Raphael Soyer. After emigrating to the United States in 1912 he studied at Cooper Union, the National Academy of Design, the Ferrer Art School, and the Educational Alliance. His first solo exhibition was held in 1929, and during the 1930s he taught at several art schools in New York City and was employed by the Federal Art Project of the Works Progress Administration. Primarily a painter of portraits and figures, he worked in the naturalistic style of his brother but never received as much critical acclaim. Soyer was elected to the National Institute of Arts and Letters in 1966.

Bernard Smith: *Moses Soyer* (New York: ACA Galleries, 1944)

Patricia Hills

Soyer, Raphael (*b* Borisoglebsk, Russia, 25 Dec 1899; *d* New York City, 4 Nov 1987). Painter, twin brother of Moses Soyer. After emigrating to the United States in 1912 he studied at Cooper Union, the National Academy of Design, and the Art Students League. He had his first exhibition in New York City in 1929 and during the Depression taught classes at the John Reed Club, to which he belonged; he also taught at the Art Students League, the New School for Social Research, and the National Academy of Design. In the late 1930s he was a member of the American Artists' Congress. His compassionate, naturalistic paintings of homeless men in the Depression were critically acclaimed, and many were bought by the Metropolitan Museum of Art and the Whitney Museum of American Art, among them *Office Girls* (1936). During the 1950s he was an important member of a group of realists who published the periodical *Reality: A Journal of Artists' Opinions*, which defended realism and figurative painting. He later painted subdued portraits of street people and of his friends, including the poet Allen Ginsberg. A retrospective exhibition of Soyer's work was held in 1967 at the Whitney Museum of American Art. He was elected to the National Institute of Arts and Letters in 1958 and to the American Academy of Arts and Letters in 1969.

Lloyd Goodrich: *Raphael Soyer* (New York: Harry N. Abrams, 1972)

Patricia Hills

SPA. See SOCIALIST PARTY OF AMERICA.

Spanish Harlem. A name commonly used for EL BARRIO.

Spanish-language press. The first Spanish-language newspapers in New York City were published in the late nineteenth century by anticolonialists agitating for Cuban and Puerto Rican independence from Spain. *La Patria* was launched in 1892 by José Martí and other Cuban revolutionaries, and in 1901 the Puerto Rican political leader Luis Muñoz Rivera published the bilingual newspaper *Puerto Rican Herald.* The general-interest newspaper *La Prensa* was published weekly from 1913 and daily from 1918; other important newspapers included the radical *El Grafico* (weekly, 1926–31) and the literary *Revista de Artes y Letras* (monthly, 1933–45). From the late 1940s a large-scale influx to New York City from Puerto Rico and later from the Dominican Republic, Cuba, and other Latin American countries gave rise to several mass-circulation newspapers, including the tabloid newspaper *El Diario* (1948), which in 1963 merged with *La Prensa* to form *El Diario–La Prensa*; this achieved a circulation of more than 100,000. *Noticias del Mundo* was launched as a daily newspaper in 1980. By this time Spanish-language newspapers tended to be published by firms not owned by Latin Americans: *El Diario–La Prensa* was published by Gannett Newspapers from 1981 to 1989, and *Noticias del Mundo* by a branch of the Unification Church.

Virginia Sánchez Korrol: *From Colonia to Community: The History of Puerto Ricans in New York City, 1917–1948* (Westport, Conn.: Greenwood, 1983)

Michael Lapp

Raphael Soyer, The Mission *(ca 1935). Lithograph. Collection of the Whitney Museum of American Art*

sparrows. For information on the species most common in New York City see HOUSE SPARROW.

Spartan Association. Political gang in the Bowery. It was organized in 1840 by the radical Democrat Mike Walsh and was the first gang to become active in local politics. The gang joined with the insurgent "shirtless" Democrats who banded together after a depression and the collapse of the Workingmen's Party and used violent tactics to wrest power from the party's leadership. Its exploits included taking over the nominating conventions of Tammany Hall and invading Whig campaign headquarters.

Michael Walsh: *Sketches of the Speeches and Writings of Michael Walsh, Including His Poems and Correspondence* (New York: T. McSpedon, 1843)

Joshua Brown

speech. The speech of New York City is regarded as distinctive by both phoneticians and nonspecialists. Its characteristics include shifts in vowel quality, devoicing of dentals, with [đ] replaced by [d] and [θ] by [t] (as in the use of "dem" and "dose" for "them" and "those"), use of non-rhotic, linking *r* and intrusive *r*, and transposition of the diphthong [oı] and the sound [r] (as exemplified by the apocryphal pronunciation "Hurt's hoyt" for "Hoyt's hurt").

The speech of New York City became a staple of literature in the mid nineteenth century. In Benjamin A. Baker's play *A Glance at New York* (first staged in 1848) phrases spoken by the character Mose the Bowery B'hoy are written as "Go long wid yer" and "I was a-tryin' to plump one of dem saucy newsboys," and the word "spoil" is given as "spile." In *Maggie: A Girl of the Streets* (1893) Stephen Crane represented the speech of New York City as follows:

> What deh hell, Jimmy.
> Well, it was dis way, Pete, see! I was goin' teh lick dat Riley kid and dey all pitched on me.
> [To another child:] Ah, where deh hell was yeh when I was doin' all deh fightin'? Youse kids make me tired.
> Cheese it, Jimmie, cheese it! Here comes yer fader.

Local speech is rendered similarly in a series of stories written by Edward W. Townsend in the mid 1890s about the character Chimmie Fadden:

> In winter dey dances, an' in summer dey has picnics on dese barges what gits towed up de river, wid mixed ale. Dat's wot makes it social and dat's wot makes it outin'. See? Wot makes it life-savin' is 'cause no gents can pack no gun nor no knife t' de dance, nor t' de outin'.

In *At the Actor's Boarding House* (1905), by Helen Green, the character Clarence the Messenger Boy at one point screams: "Skiddoo! Hully Chee! Jerome's raidin' the place! Youse'll bot be in the papers. Ef youse git outa this town wit' youse healt', youse in luck."

The first trained phonetician to study the speech of New York City was Babbitt (1896), who taught at Columbia College and drew his observations from his students and from New Yorkers heard in the streets. C. K. Thomas, who taught at Cornell University, and Hubbell (1950), a lifelong resident of the city, relied on speech samples elicited in controlled circumstances. For his pivotal study Labov (1966) asked questions of sales clerks in department stores. A number of conclusions may be drawn from the work of these linguists. First, although in the nineteenth century the accent characteristic of New York City was called a "Bowery accent" and in the twentieth it became associated with Brooklyn, in fact it arises from social class and not from a neighborhood, even though in New York City neighborhood and class are closely allied. Most New Yorkers show some trace of the local accent, except for those isolated by their wealth and social status from the rest of the city, but it is most noticeable in those of little education and limited travel. Second, although the speech of New York City is distinctive, some of its elements have been discerned elsewhere. A. J. Liebling remarked on similarities with the common speech of New Orleans, the word "spoil" has been transcribed as "spile" in several other American regions, and it is not known to what extent the speech of New York City before the advent of phonetic transcription and sound recording was heard to differ from the speech of other parts of the country. Third, linguists regard as unprovable and unlikely the common surmise that the speech of New York City is an amalgam of elements from several foreign accents (for example that the devoicing of dentals may be traced to Irish, the slurring together of words to Italian, and the so-called hard [g] to Yiddish).

Like many distinctive local accents the speech of New York City has low prestige in the estimation of those who hear it and those who speak it, and providing speech therapy to New Yorkers to eliminate their local accent has long been a profitable line of work. In the meanwhile the speech traditionally associated with New York City was infrequently heard by the mid 1990s, not because it was being assimilated to a general American accent nor because of speech therapists, but because it was evolving into a new but still distinctive form.

E. H. Babbitt: "The English of the Lower Classes in New York City and Vicinity," *Dialect Notes* 1 (1896), 457–64
Allen F. Hubbell: *The Pronunciation of English in New York City: Consonants and Vowels* (New York: King's Crown, 1950)
Arthur J. Bornstein: "Let's Take Another Look at New York City Speech," *American Speech* 37 (1962), 13–26
William Labov: *The Social Stratification of English in New York City* (Washington: Center for Applied Linguistics, 1966)

George A. Thompson, Jr.

Spellman, Francis (Joseph) (*b* Whitman, Mass., 4 May 1889; *d* New York City, 2 Dec 1967). Cardinal. He graduated from Fordham College in 1911, was ordained a priest of the Archdiocese of Boston on 14 May 1916, and became auxiliary bishop of Boston in 1932. In 1939 he was appointed the sixth archbishop of New York by Pope Pius XII, who was newly elected and a close friend. The appointment surprised many observers who had thought that the post would be given to a New Yorker. During his tenure Spellman showed himself to be a skillful administrator: he modernized and centralized the structure of the archdiocese, refinanced $28 million in debt, formed forty-five new parishes, created a system of diocesan high schools, and spent almost $600 million on expanding Catholic educational and charitable facilities. In 1949 he confronted Eleanor Roosevelt over her opposition to federal aid for parochial schools and accused her of anti-Catholic bigotry. He cultivated strong ties to the Jewish community: in 1945 he inaugurated the annual Alfred E. Smith Dinner (a major event in the political calendar of the city), and maintained a close relationship with its chairman, the Jewish philanthropist Charles H. Silver; he also supported the establishment of the state of Israel. As the Catholic vicar for the armed forces during the Second World War he became the best-known Catholic prelate in the country and was recognized as a symbol of Catholic patriotism. As large numbers of Puerto Ricans and other Latin Americans entered the city, he began an innovative pastoral program that provided them with a large number of Spanish-speaking diocesan priests. On 18 February 1946 Pope Pius named him one of four new American cardinals.

Spellman was a controversial cardinal. To break a strike at Calvary Cemetery in 1949 he employed seminarians as gravediggers and appalled many trade unionists. In the 1950s he was an outspoken critic of communism, and his presence at an address by Senator Joseph R. McCarthy in New York City on 4 April 1953 was widely interpreted as a gesture of support. At the same time he appointed Monsignor Joseph F. Connolly the first coordinator of Spanish Catholic action for the archdiocese in 1953, and sheltered progressive biblical scholars in his seminary from reactionary theological critics. He managed to have the Jesuit John Courtney Murray invited to the Second Vatican Council (1962–65), where Murray helped to win the endorsement of the Declaration on Religious Freedom and *Nostra Aetate*, the conciliatory decree regarding non-Christian religions. In his last years Spellman was often an uncritical proponent of American intervention in Vietnam. A deeply conservative churchman, he came to represent a synthesis of Catholic orthodoxy and American patriotism that had eluded liberal American Catholic leaders of the nineteenth century. He lived in the Archbishop's Residence at 452 Madison Avenue from 1939 until his death.

Robert I. Gannon: *The Cardinal Spellman Story* (Garden City, N.Y.: Doubleday, 1962)

John Cooney: *The American Pope: The Life and Times of Francis Cardinal Spellman* (New York: Times Books, 1984)

Gerald P. Fogarty: "Francis J. Spellman: American and Catholic," *Patterns of Episcopal Leadership*, ed. Gerald P. Fogarty (New York: Macmillan, 1988)

T. J. Shelley

Spence–Chapin Adoption Agency. An agency formed in 1943 by the merger of the Spence and Chapin nurseries for children. The Spence nursery was formed in 1895 by Clara Spence as an organization for crippled and tubercular children and by 1915 evolved into an adoption agency called the Spence Alumnae Society; the Chapin nursery began in 1910 when Alice Chapin and her husband, a pediatrician, first took in abandoned infants. Spence–Chapin was an innovator in using the techniques of social work in the adoption process. It began placing children from racial minority groups in 1946, an effort that led to the formation of the Harlem–Dowling Children's Service in 1969.

Stephen Weinstein

Spencer Estate. Neighborhood in the eastern Bronx. The land once belonged to an estate of 129 acres (fifty-two hectares) owned by Robert Morris, who sold it in 1856 to William Spencer. The original estate extended over parts of what are now Country Club and Pelham Bay Park. Palmer Cove, a small inlet nearby in Eastchester Bay, is widely described in records dating from the American Revolution as a point of reference, a boundary marker, and a place for mooring boats.

John McNamara: *McNamara's Old Bronx* (New York: Bronx County Historical Society, 1989)

Gary D. Hermalyn

Spence School. Private elementary and secondary girls' school opened in 1892 by the educational pioneer Clara Spence as Miss Spence's School for Girls at 6 West 48th Street in Manhattan. The school set high standards and maintained a rigid curriculum that reflected the founder's interest in moral and intellectual development, formal etiquette, and charity (a school society was formed to aid crippled tubercular children), and it rebuffed efforts by parents to influence its policies. The Spence School moved to 22 East 91st Street in 1929 and merged with the Chandor School in 1932.

Richard Schwartz

Sperry, Elmer (Ambrose) (*b* Cortland, N.Y., 12 Oct 1860; *d* Brooklyn, 16 June 1930). Inventor and manufacturer. At the age of twenty he formed the Sperry Electrical Illuminating and Power Company in Chicago, and while living in Brooklyn he formed Sperry Products (precursor of the Sperry Rand Corporation). He was responsible for a number of gyroscope-based inventions, including the Gyrocompass, the Gyrostabilizer, and the Gyro Automatic Pilot. His instrument for finding defective rails improved safety on the New York Central Railroad between New York City and Chicago. Sperry bequeathed $1 million to local branches in Brooklyn and Queens of the YMCA, which sponsored a visit that he made to the Philadelphia Exposition in 1876. He is buried in Green-Wood Cemetery.

"Locating 'Rail Cancer,'" *Literary Digest*, 1 June 1929, p. 20

Obituary, *New York Times*, 17 June 1930, p. 27

Thomas Parke Hughes: *Elmer Sperry: Inventor and Engineer* (Baltimore: Johns Hopkins University Press, 1971)

Val Ginter

Spingarn, Joel E(lias) (*b* New York City, 17 May 1875; *d* New York City, 26 July 1939). Civil rights activist. He attended City College of New York and Columbia University (AB 1895, PhD 1899) and taught comparative literature at Columbia from 1899 until 1911, when he was dismissed after a free-speech conflict with the university's president Nicholas Murray Butler and embarked on a career as an activist and independent scholar (occasionally teaching at the New School for Social Research); he also helped to form the National Association for the Advancement of Colored People (NAACP) in New York City in 1909. In 1911 he purchased the *Amenia Times* in Duchess County, New York, where he maintained a summer estate called Troutbeck. He became chairman of the board of the NAACP in 1913 and in the following year endowed the Spingarn Medal, awarded annually to a prominent black leader; he became president of the NAACP in 1930. In the year after his death leadership of the NAACP passed to his brother Arthur B(arnett) Spingarn (*b* New York City, 28 March 1878; *d* 1 Dec 1971), a lawyer associated with Charles Studin who for thirty years had provided free legal counsel and office space to the association; he remained the head of the association until 1966.

B. Joyce Ross: *J. E. Spingarn and the Rise of the NAACP, 1911–1939* (New York: Atheneum, 1972)

Francis H. Thompson: "Arthur Barnett Spingarn: Advocate for Black Rights," *Historian* 50 (1987), Nov, 54–66

Thea Arnold

Spirit of the Times. Weekly newspaper. Founded by William T. Porter in New York City on 10 December 1831, it was the first comprehensive sporting journal in the United States. The newspaper soon merged with the *Traveller* but was reestablished independently in 1835. Financial troubles compelled Porter to relinquish ownership in 1842, but he remained the editor until 1856. In its first years of publication the newspaper reprinted many articles from British periodicals but increasingly published contributions of sporting news, essays, and fiction from American writers. It celebrated the rich sporting culture of antebellum New York City, focusing on horse racing but also covering other pastimes, among them swimming, rowing, baseball, boxing, cricket, field sports, foot racing, and winter sports. In his editorials Porter wrote tirelessly of the value of recreation and exercise for men, women, and children. With George Wilkes in 1856 he launched *Porter's Spirit of the Times*; on Porter's death in 1858 Wilkes parted with the new editors and founded *Wilkes' Spirit of the Times* on 10 September 1859. *Porter's Spirit of the Times* lasted until late 1859, the *Spirit of the Times* until 1861, *Wilkes' Spirit of the Times* until 1902. The publication of the *Spirit of the Times* marked the emergence of New York City as a national center for sport.

Francis Brinley: *Life of William T. Porter* (New York: D. Appleton, 1860)

Frank Luther Mott: *A History of American Magazines*, vol. 1, *1741–1850* (New York: D. Appleton, 1930), 480–81

Frank Luther Mott: *A History of American Magazines*, vol. 2, *1850–1865* (Cambridge: Harvard University Press, 1938), 204

George B. Kirsch

Spofford Juvenile Center. Detention facility in the Bronx, at 1221 Spofford Avenue in Hunts Point. Designed by the firm of Kahn and Jacobs, it opened in 1957 as the Bronx Youth House for Boys. In its early years the center suffered from such severe problems as drug dealing on the premises, sex offenses, suicides, and assaults, but the situation improved after 1979 because of better case management, the provision of social services after release, improved medical programs, extended school days, and an incentive system that grants extra privileges for good behavior. In the year ending 30 June 1993 there were 4860 persons admitted to secure detention at Spofford, of whom 64 percent were released within ten days.

Val Ginter

sport fishing. The Hudson River estuary and the ocean waters off Sandy Hook became known as superb fishing grounds during colonial times. Such nineteenth-century sportswriters as Henry William Herbert (1807–58) and Genio C. Scott (1809–79) considered New York City ideal for angling, not only because of its proximity to these areas but also because of its tackle shops, supplies of bait at the Fulton Fish Market, and efficient transportation. Anglers in rowboats frequently took striped bass weighing up to fifty pounds (23.7 kilograms) from the shoals and tide rips of Hell Gate. The largest fish ever taken in the waters of Manhattan with rod and reel was a drum weighing more than seventy pounds (31.7 kilograms) pulled from the Harlem River in 1844 near Macomb's Dam. A number of spots in New York Harbor including the waters off Liberty Island and Robbins Reef provided bluefish, striped bass, weakfish, and blackfish (tautog). On summer days scores of boats dotted the Narrows and Gravesend Bay in the pursuit of weakfish. The Kill van Kull and the Arthur Kill were also prime fishing grounds for striped bass and weakfish. Children, the old, and the poor fished off the docks of Manhattan for porgies, flounder, and small striped bass. Only the hardy fished for the sharks measuring up to fourteen feet (4.2 meters) in length that frequented the waters of Manhattan until the late 1890s. The development of steam-powered vessels brought easy access to the rich Atlantic fishing grounds between Long Island and New Jersey. The ocean-fishing steamboat excursion, introduced in 1819, quickly became popular as an inexpensive family outing. Between the 1860s and the 1890s as many as a dozen steamboats from the city and Jersey City, New Jersey, some accommodating as many as three thousand passengers, made scheduled trips to the fishing banks off Sandy Hook and other offshore grounds.

Water pollution and habitat destruction, caused by industrialization and rising population during the late nineteenth century, diminished the aesthetic pleasure of angling and contributed to a decline in the number and variety of fish in the waters off Manhattan. Small ports along the cleaner waters of Sheepshead Bay, Canarsie, Great Kills, and towns in New Jersey around Sandy Hook eventually attracted most of the city's anglers. These areas gained a decisive advantage with the advent of powerboats, which were cheaper to operate, required smaller docking facilities than steamers, and were capable of traveling to local bays, inlets, and even ocean grounds. By the 1920s vessels of this type, some with a capacity of a hundred, dominated charter-boat and party-boat operations in the metropolitan area. After the Second World War such services declined, as a growing number of anglers became able to afford their own boats. Fishing around Manhattan improved somewhat after mid century, owing partly to major efforts at reducing industrial and sewage pollution. In the mid 1990s fine catches of striped bass could be made in the East River near the United Nations, and schools of feeding bluefish occasionally drew charter-boats and party-boats into the harbor.

William Zeisel

sports. Sports in New York City are as dynamic, cosmopolitan, and ever changing as their surroundings. They have helped to shape the economy of the city, its social arrangements, its architecture, and even its politics and have in turn been influenced by them.

1. Colonial Period and Early Nineteenth Century

The Dutch settlers of New Amsterdam indulged their love of physical activity by pursuing a variety of outdoor amusements, including tavern sports, ICE SKATING, and LAWN BOWLING, which from the seventeenth century was played on Bowling Green at the foot of Broadway. The English introduced new sports to the city; the most important was HORSE RACING, which began in 1665 when the first English governor, Richard Nicolls, offered a silver cup for a race to be held each spring and autumn. The growth of sport in the eighteenth century was stimulated by the cosmopolitan nature of the city and the emergence of a wealthy aristocracy. During the American Revolution and its aftermath sporting activities declined, largely because of their association with the colonial aristocracy, gambling, and violations of the Sabbath. A low point for sport was reached in 1802, when thoroughbred horse racing was banned in New York State; harness races were nevertheless held on 3rd Avenue from the early nineteenth century. The return of legalized thoroughbred racing in 1820 marked the beginning of a period of renewed growth in sporting activity, one different from those that preceded it in that the complexity of urban life now made it difficult for New Yorkers to engage in sport informally and spontaneously; instead they relied to an unprecedented degree on voluntary associations and entrepreneurs.

Thoroughbred racing was the first sport to benefit from this trend. In 1821 wealthy New Yorkers formed a jockey club and built the Union Course in Jamaica, and during the next quarter-century New York City and its environs were the national center of the sport: the most important races were held there, attended by the largest crowds and offering the largest purses. The city was the site of five races pitting the best horse from the northern United States against the best from the southern United States. The first of these, held in 1823 between Eclipse and Henry, had several characteristics marking it as an event of more than passing interest: a huge crowd (estimated at fifty thousand but probably smaller), considerable attention from a national press that attached great symbolic importance to the outcome, a large purse, and a large amount of money wagered. The growing popularity of harness racing led to the formation in 1825 of the New York Trotting Club and the building of a racecourse at Centerville on Long Island. After 1845 harness racing overshadowed thoroughbred racing in popularity. By the 1850s there were seven trotting tracks in the metropolitan area, three of which offered races of high quality. There were several reasons for the emergence of harness racing as the leading spectator sport in antebellum New York City, including the outstanding performance of such horses as Lady Suffolk. Of greater importance was the ability of those who controlled the sport to appeal to the growing middle class in the city, which the wealthy traditionalists who controlled thoroughbred racing were unable to do. There were clubs for many other sports as well: for ROWING, CRICKET, racquet sports, gymnastics, yachting, and shooting by 1850, and for twenty-one sports in all by 1870.

The first organized BASEBALL club in the city, the Knickerbockers, was formed in 1845. Other teams followed in the 1850s; there were a dozen in Manhattan and Brooklyn by 1855 and about a hundred several years later. The explosion in the number of clubs led residents of Manhattan and Brooklyn in 1857 to form the National Association of Base Ball Players to clarify and codify the rules of the game. Although the association did not allow ballclubs to pay their players, the Brooklyn Excelsiors paid their star pitcher James Creighton as early as 1860 and other clubs soon followed. Baseball was now being described as the "national pastime" and in the 1860s became a competitive, commercialized, professional spectator sport. Entrepreneurs were quick to capitalize on the desire of the public to attend the contests of leading teams. In 1862 William Cammayer built the first enclosed baseball park, the Union Grounds, at Lee Avenue and Rutledge Street in Brooklyn, and his success led in 1864 to a similar venture, the Capitoline Grounds, at Halsey Street and Marcy, Putnam, and Nostrand avenues; the cost of admission, at first fixed at ten cents, rose to fifty cents by 1870. By 1867 Brooklyn and New York City had three professional teams. Baseball remained exceedingly popular as a participatory sport, but games between the best professional clubs attracted the attention of both spectators and the press.

2. Late Nineteenth Century and Early Twentieth: Sport, Politics, and Society

Interest in participatory and spectator sports in New York City increased dramatically after the Civil War. New Yorkers became acquainted with such sports as TENNIS and formed organizations such as the New York Athletic Club (1868) to promote sports with which they were already familiar. Athletic clubs made it easy for their members to practice a variety of sports, especially track and field. The members generally were affluent white men, and during the 1880s the character of the clubs changed as members were recruited more for their social standing than for their athletic ability: membership in a club became principally a means to proclaim one's like images often enhanced by the use of scrims. Arthur Miller's *Death of a Salesman* (1949) and Williams's *A Streetcar Named Desire* (1947), both designed by Mielziner, are classic examples of this style. Oliver Smith (*b* 1918) bridged the world of theater and dance while carrying poetic realism and fantasy into the musicals of the 1950s. His works included *Brigadoon* (1947) and *My Fair Lady* (1956), both by Alan Jay Lerner and Frederick Loewe, as well as several influential ballets, among them two with choreography by Agnes de Mille, *Rodeo* (1942, music by Aaron Copland) and *Fall River Legend* (1948, music by Morton Gould). The 1950s saw a move away from realism and toward structural and symbolic designs that emphasized theatricality; the stage regained a sense of being a stage rather than a re-creation of another place. Among the first stage designers to move in this direction was Rouben Ter-Arutunian (*b* 1920). Another was Isamu Noguchi, who worked closely with the choreographer Martha Graham from 1935 and developed a sculptural style of stage design. These innovations culminated in the mid 1960s in the work of Ming Cho Lee (*b* 1930), whose designs for the New York Shakespeare Festival at the Delacorte Theater in Central Park and for the New York City Opera made scaffolding, emblematic scenery, textured materials, and collage the basic vocabulary of American design for the next two decades. At the same time Merce Cunningham and other modern and postmodern choreographers engaged as stage designers such visual artists as Robert Rauschenberg, Jasper Johns, and Andy Warhol. In the 1980s work by the artists David Hockney and David Salle and even the architect Frank Gehry appeared on the stages of the Brooklyn Academy of Music and the Metropolitan Opera House. On the other hand the choreographer Twyla Tharp tended to rely on designers who worked principally in the theater, notably Jennifer Tipton (*b* 1937), who shaped modern lighting practice, and Santo Loquasto (*b* 1944), whose costumes influenced fashion design.

Stage design was strongly influenced by avant-garde theater and in particular by theatrical minimalism. Environmental theater, characterized by stage settings that surround the audience, was made popular with the production in 1968 of *Dionysus in 69* by Richard Schechner's Performance Group in a converted garage in SoHo. This iconoclastic approach influenced Eugene Lee's design in 1974 for the Broadway production of *Candide*, by Leonard Bernstein, Hugh Wheeler, and Richard Wilbur. The theater artist Richard Foreman developed idiosyncratic conceptual settings at his loft theater in SoHo in the 1970s as well as for Joseph Papp's revival in 1976 of *The Threepenny Opera*, by Kurt Weill and Bertolt Brecht, at the Vivian Beaumont Theater. At the same time Robert Wilson conceived grandiose settings for such works as Philip Glass's opera *Einstein on the Beach* (1976), which was staged at the Brooklyn Academy of Music and the Metropolitan Opera.

The 1980s saw a trend toward lavish productions with elaborate settings, as in *Cats* (1983) and *Phantom of the Opera* (1988), both British imports by Andrew Lloyd Webber, and *Miss Saigon* (1990), by Claude-Michel Schönberg and Alain Boublil. Tony Walton (*b* 1934) devised more elegant spectacles for such shows as *Grand Hotel* (1989) and *Guys and Dolls* (1992). At the same time a postmodern approach to design emerged in opera and off Broadway, particularly in the work of the designers John Conklin (*b* 1937), George Tsypin (*b* 1954), and Adrianne Lobel (*b* 1955), and also in that of James Clayburgh (*b* 1949) for the avant-garde Wooster Group. The new approach was typified by a multiplicity of incongruous, competing, and conflicting images that made for a historical and stylistic eclecticism. Postmodern designs such as Tsypin's for *Henry IV, Parts 1 and 2* (1992), directed by JoAnne Akalaitis at the Public Theatre, make wide-ranging references to diverse periods of art and architecture, to other productions, and to themselves. Others, such as those of the Wooster Group, "deconstruct" the stage by merging onstage and offstage space, often by using video and sound to separate performer, voice, and image, and by combining simple and technologically advanced elements and objects in an almost random and unfocused way within the performing space.

Mary Clarke and Clement Crisp: *Design for Ballet* (New York: Hawthorn, 1978)

Arnold Aronson: *American Set Design* (New York: Theater Communications Group, 1985)

Orville K. Larson: *Scene Design in the American Theater from 1915 to 1960* (Fayetteville: University of Arkansas Press, 1989)

Arnold Aronson

Stagg Town. Seventeenth-century name for an area also known as LITTLE AFRICA.

stair streets. A number of stair streets were built in hilly areas during the development of New York City. They were given names such as Step Street, Bradley Terrace, and 166th Stair Street. About 90 percent of the city's stair streets are in the Bronx, particularly in Riverdale, along the Grand Concourse ridge, and in Highbridge. Apartment buildings abutting these streets often have entrances from a landing to an upper story.

Gary D. Hermalyn

stamp and coin dealers. Collectors and dealers of stamps and coins frequent New York City from around the world for its conventions, shops, and auctions. Gimbel's in Herald Square was known for its large stamp and coin department as early as the late 1940s. In the mid 1990s the major purveyors of stamps were H. R. Harmer and Company and Robert Siegel; coin dealers included Harmer Rooke, Manfred Tardella and Brooks, and Stack's. The stamp and coin business in the city does about $50 million a year in sales. Important organizations in the city include the Philatelic Foundation (21 East 40th Street) and the American Numismatic Society (Broadway and 156th Street, Audubon Terrace), which maintains a museum and research library.

Rachel Shor

Standard and Poor's. Firm of financial publishers formed by the merger of Poor's Publishing Company and the Standard Statistics Company in 1941. The origins of the firm may be traced to the publications of Henry Varnum Poor (1812–1905), who issued *History of Railroads and Canals of the United States* in 1860 and in 1867 formed a corporation to

Stair street west of Broadway above 231st Street in the Bronx, early 1990s

publish annually a "Manual of the Railroads and Canals of the United States." Poor's *History* was the most valuable financial source of its day and is considered the precursor of financial and investment publications in the United States. Standard Statistics Company was begun in 1913 as Standard Statistics Services by Luther Blake. A subsidiary of McGraw–Hill from 1966, Standard and Poor's rates bonds and commercial promissory notes and issues more than fifty financial publications in printed and electronic form to businesses and to government agencies. Its offices are at 25 Broadway.

Hugh C. Sherwood: *How Corporate and Municipal Debt Is Rated: An Inside Look at Standard and Poor's Rating System* (New York: John Wiley and Sons, 1976)

James D. Norris

Stapleton. Neighborhood in northeastern Staten Island (1991 pop. 50,000), bounded to the north by Grant Street, to the east by Upper New York Bay, to the south by Vanderbilt Avenue, and to the west by St. Paul's Avenue and Van Duzer Street. It consisted at first of farmland; Cornelius Vanderbilt spent his youth on a farm facing the bay on a site now occupied by the Paramount Theatre on Bay Street. In its early years the area was the commercial center of Southfield Township (it became part of the incorporated village of Edgewater in 1866). The Seamen's Retreat, a hospital for sailors entering New York Harbor, was built in 1831 on a site of forty acres (sixteen hectares). In the following year land was acquired from the Vanderbilts and streets were laid out by William J. Staples (1807–83), a merchant and entrepreneur from Manhattan after whom the neighborhood was named, and Minthorne Tompkins (1807–81), a son of Vice President Daniel D. Tompkins. The two established ferry service to Manhattan and advertised their newly created village from 1836. The availability of spring water led several German–American breweries to establish themselves in the area in the nineteenth century: the Bachmann Brewery (1851) and the Bechtel Brewery (1853) merged in 1911 to form the Bachmann–Bechtel Brewing Company, which operated until 1920; the Rubsam and Horrmann Atlantic Brewery Company (1871) was bought by Piels in 1953 and closed in 1963. By 1884 Staten Island Rapid Transit extended its tracks along the waterfront from the foot of Vanderbilt Avenue to Tompkinsville Landing and to ferry facilities in St. George; direct passenger ferry service from Stapleton to Manhattan was discontinued in 1886. The Village Hall (1889) in Tappen Park was designed by Paul Kuhne (1850–1903), a resident of Stapleton. Seamen's Retreat, a hospital for sailors entering New York Harbor, opened in 1831 and later became successively the U.S. Marine Hospital, the U.S. Public Health Service Hospital, and the Bayley Seton Hospital, the largest employer in the area. The waterfront was filled in on the east side of Bay Street. Municipal piers built by New York City in the 1920s were never fully exploited: several were used as the first foreign trade zone in the United States (1937–42), as the New York Port of Embarkation by the U.S. Army and the U.S. Navy (1942–45), and again as a foreign trade zone after the Second World War, but by 1950 only two piers were in use and in the 1970s these were demolished. Stapleton Houses, a housing project sponsored by New York State, opened in 1962, providing 693 subsidized apartments on land formerly belonging to the Seamen's Retreat. A new and controversial home port for the U.S. Navy was constructed and opened in 1990; this closed in 1994.

Among the notable buildings in Stapleton are simple Greek Revival houses from the 1830s at 364 and 390 Van Duzer Street, 60 William Street, and 92 Harrison Street; several historic churches, including St. Paul's Episcopal (1870, Edward Tuckerman Potter), First Presbyterian Church (1887, Josiah C. Cady), Immaculate Conception Church (1908), and Trinity Lutheran Church (1913, Upjohn and Conable); and the Staten Island Savings Bank (1925, Delano and Aldrich). In the 1980s Stapleton attracted a few immigrants from India, Liberia, China, Jamaica, and Trinidad and Tobago, and to a lesser extent the Philippines, Guyana, Korea, and Nigeria. The neighborhood in the mid 1990s was a residential and commercial center inhabited by urban professionals and blue-collar workers, including blacks, Italians, Armenians, and Latin Americans.

Staten Island: A Resource Manual for School and Community (New York: Board of Education of the City of New York, 1964)
"An East Shore Village Revisited: Stapleton, from 1890 to 1920," *Staten Island Historian*, Oct–Dec 1968, pp. 25–36
Harlow McMillen: "Staten Island's Lager Beer Breweries, 1851–1962," *Staten Island Historian*, July–Sept 1969, pp. 15–21

For illustration see Dairying.

Barnett Shepherd

Stapleton Heights. Neighborhood in northeastern Staten Island, near the western boundary of Stapleton along St. Paul's Avenue. It is an area of large houses and lots, and many of the residents have views of the Narrows and the Verrazano Narrows Bridge. Early efforts to restore the area were promoted by the Mud Lane Society (named after the street that later became St. Paul's Avenue). Notable buildings in the neighborhood include 368 St. Paul's Avenue (designed by Paul Kuhne, a resident of Stapleton, for Adolf Baudenhausen of the R&H Brewery) and 387 St. Paul's Avenue, an elaborate Queen Anne house (built for the daughter of George Bechtel, the owner of Bechtel's Brewery).

Barnett Shepherd

Starrett. Firm of general contractors, incorporated in 1922 as Starrett Brothers and later renamed Starrett Brothers and Eken. One of the most successful firms of its kind in the city, it was directed by Paul Starrett (1866–1957) and William A. Starrett (1877–1932), two of five brothers working as builders, often in bitter competition. Although not among the largest contractors in volume of sales, the firm specialized in large buildings and was known for its efficient management and its swiftness in completing projects. In the 1920s it erected many skyscrapers, including the Empire State Building, which was finished forty-five days ahead of schedule and $5 million under budget. It concentrated from the 1930s on such housing complexes as Parkchester in the Bronx (1938–42), Stuyvesant Town (1943), and Peter Cooper Village (1945–47). Andrew J. Eken (1882–1965), a partner, became president in 1938 and was chairman from 1955 to 1961. As developers the Starrett Corporation built Starrett City (1976, Herman J. Jessor) a community for six thousand families in eastern Brooklyn that later became known as Starrett at Spring Creek.

Carol Willis

Starrett at Spring Creek. Housing development in east central Brooklyn (1994 pop. 20,000), lying on a tract of 153 acres (sixty hectares) along Jamaica Bay and bounded to the north by Vandalia and Flatlands avenues, to the east by Schenck Avenue, to the south by the Belt Parkway, and to the west by Louisiana Avenue; it is bisected by Pennsylvania Avenue. Developed by the National Kinney Corporation, it was designed by Herman J. Jessor and known as Twin Pines Village until the Starrett Corporation assumed control and renamed it Starrett City. Construction began in July 1972 on forty-six apartment buildings of as many as twenty stories each, containing a total of nearly six thousand apartments surrounded by ballfields, parks, shopping areas, medical centers, public schools, and religious institutions. In 1975, when the apartments were first rented, 65 percent were reserved for whites and 35 percent for nonwhites. After many complaints the quota system was challenged in 1979. The development took its current name in 1989.

Starrett at Spring Creek is the largest federally funded housing project in the nation. It has its own power plant, a private security force, and a cable television station. It is now recognized as a model integrated community.

"Starrett City with Housing for 25,000 Dedicated in Canarsie Area of Brooklyn," *New York Times*, 14 Oct 1974
"Dispute over Quotas at Starrett City: A Complex Mix of Principles and Politics," *New York Times*, 13 July 1984
"Court's Tip: No Starrett City Quotas," *Daily News*, 7 May 1987
"Starrett City Wins Stay of Bias Ruling," *New York Newsday*, 7 May 1987

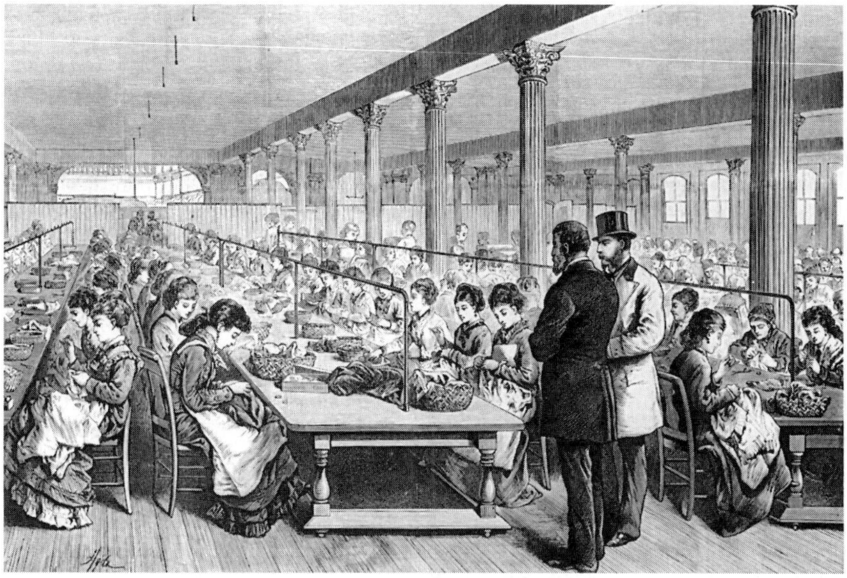

Sewing room at A. T. Stewart's store at Broadway and 10th Street, 1875

nue and 34th Street. His business had gross sales of $50 million in 1865 (primarily from wholesale trade), with domestic and European offices, warehouses, and factories. He avidly collected art and real estate in Manhattan, founded Garden City (Long Island), and maintained ties with the Tweed Ring and the administration of President Ulysses S. Grant. He died childless, and his estate was grossly mismanaged by his attorney Henry Hilton. In 1878 Stewart's body was exhumed and ransomed (it remains unclear whether the body was recovered), and in 1884 the Marble Palace was converted to offices.

Harry E. Resseguie: "A. T. Stewart's Marble Palace, The Cradle of the Department Store," *New York State Historical Society Quarterly* 48 (1964), 131–62
Stephen N. Elias: *Alexander T. Stewart: Forgotten Merchant Prince* (Westport, Conn.: Praeger, 1992)

David B. Sicilia

stickball. Game resembling baseball that developed in the early twentieth century in the streets of New York City. Each neighborhood had its own rules and traditions; many had teams of nine players and used parked cars and "sewers" (manhole covers) as bases. The pitcher threw the ball with one bounce or the batter hit the ball after tossing it in the air. Equipment usually consisted of an old broomstick and a "spaldeen," a pink rubber ball made by the Spalding company. The popularity of stickball declined after the Second World War but revived in the 1960s and 1970s, especially among adults who remembered the game from their childhood. A stickball reunion held in 1968 by residents of East 111th Street in Manhattan to honor the memory of a neighbor became an annual event: sponsored by Budweiser from 1975, it became known as the Budweiser Old Timers Stickball Reunion and drew people from throughout the nation who had grown up in the neighborhood. For a few summers in the mid 1970s three-sewer stickball was featured in a festival of street games sponsored by the parks department to celebrate the sporting heritage of the city. In 1983 and 1984 Spalding sponsored a stickball exhibition on West 60th Street in Manhattan in which baseball stars, celebrities, and members of the Police Athletic League took part. Newman Avenue in Clason Point was renamed Stickball Boulevard in 1987. The United States Stickball League (USSBL), formed by Ronald Babineau in 1984 and based in East Rockaway, Long Island, approves schoolyards and playgrounds in the metropolitan area for play and has about two hundred teams of three to six players each, ranging in age from fifteen to sixty-five. In games played by these teams the pitcher throws a tennis ball to the batter, who stands in front of a strike zone drawn in chalk on a wall; the *Daily News* publishes the standings of the teams. Stickball remains popular among children in the city.

Joseph S. Lieber

Stieglitz, Alfred (*b* Hoboken, N.J., 1 Jan 1864; *d* New York City, 13 July 1946). Photographer. He was educated in New York City before going to Berlin to study engineering, which he soon abandoned for photography. After returning to New York City in 1890 he worked in a photo-engraving business and was an eager amateur photographer. During the next two decades he produced a group of atmospheric street and waterfront scenes, of which one of the best known is *The Hand of Man* (1902). He was active in the Camera Club of New York and became the editor of *Camera Notes.* Soon after, he formed the Photo-Secession, a group of photographers dissatisfied with the dominant styles in photography. Members exhibited their work in "291," a gallery that he directed at 291 5th Avenue. He also published the elegant journal *Camera Work* with the hope of introducing European styles of photography in the United States and encouraging the development of American styles. With Edward Steichen he exhibited and published the work of Picasso, Matisse, and Constantin Brancuși, and eventually promoted the work of a group of American modernists at An Intimate Gallery and An American Place. After 1915 he resumed photography and made portraits of several friends who were artists; these included many images of Georgia O'Keeffe, whom he later married. *Equivalents,* a series of photographs of the land and sky near his summer home on Lake George, New York, and several photographs of skyscrapers taken from his rooms in suite 3003 of the Hotel Shelton (525 Lexington Avenue), attest to his contradictory feelings toward New York City, which he both hated and loved. He lived from 1898 to 1918 at 1111 Madison Avenue, from July 1918 to the end of 1922 at 114 East 59th Street, for ten years beginning in 1924 at the Hotel Shelton, from the autumn of 1936 to October 1942 at 405 East 54th Street, and from October 1942 to the end of his life at 59 East 54th Street.

A. T. Stewart's cast-iron building on Broadway, between 9th and 10th streets

Alfred Stieglitz, The Terminal *(1892), from* Camera Work, *no. 36, 1911. Photogravure. Collection of the Museum of Modern Art. Gift of Georgia O'Keeffe*

Waldo Frank et al., eds.: *America and Alfred Stieglitz: A Collective Portrait* (New York: Doubleday, Doran, 1934; repr. Millerton, N.Y.: Aperture, 1989)

Doris Bry: *Alfred Stieglitz, Photographer* (Boston: Museum of Fine Arts, 1965)

Dorothy Norman: *Alfred Stieglitz: An American Seer* (New York: Random House, 1973)

Sarah Greenough and Juan Hamilton: *Alfred Stieglitz: Photographs and Writings* (Washington: National Gallery of Art, 1983)

See also PHOTOGRAPHY.

Naomi Rosenblum

Stillman, James (*b* Brownsville, Texas, 9 June 1850; *d* New York City, 15 March 1918). Banker. In 1872 he was made a full partner in the cotton brokerage firm of Woodward and Stillman, led by his father, Charles Stillman, at 65 South Street. In 1891 he became the tenth president of National City Bank, a local bank for merchants that he transformed into one of the most important commercial banks in the world. He was advised daily by his lawyer, John W. Sterling, and worked closely with William Rockefeller of Standard Oil; he also helped Jacob Schiff and Edward H. Harriman to reorganize the American railroads. In 1897 he formed a foreign exchange department to serve corporations with overseas operations. At auction in 1899 the bank bought the U.S. Custom House (55 Wall Street), which was remodeled extensively by McKim, Mead and White and became the headquarters of the bank in 1908. With J. P. Morgan and George F. Baker, Stillman helped to stem the panic of 1907. He remained the president of National City Bank until 1909, then served as its chairman until the year of his death.

Anna Robeson Burr: *The Portrait of a Banker: James Stillman, 1850–1918* (New York: Duffield, 1927)

John K. Winkler: *The First Billion: The Stillmans and the National City Bank* (New York: Vanguard, 1934)

Joan L. Silverman

Stimson, Henry L(ewis) (*b* New York City, 21 Sept 1867; *d* Huntington, N.Y., 20 Oct 1950). Secretary of state. He passed the bar in New York State in 1891 and spent his early career in New York City. In 1906 he was appointed U.S. attorney of the Southern District of New York by President Theodore Roosevelt, who supported him when he sought, unsuccessfully, the governorship of New York in 1910. He served from 1911 to 1913 as secretary of war under President William Howard Taft and from 1929 to 1933 as secretary of state under President Herbert Hoover. Although a Republican he was again secretary of war under President Franklin D. Roosevelt from 1940 to 1945. In 1918–27 and 1933–40 Stimson lived and practiced law in New York City.

Godfrey Hodgson: *The Colonel: The Life and Wars of Henry Stimson, 1867–1950* (New York: Alfred A. Knopf, 1990)

See also ESPIONAGE.

Elliot S. Meadows

stock exchanges. For information on the principal stock exchanges in New York City see AMERICAN STOCK EXCHANGE, CONSOLIDATED EXCHANGE, and NEW YORK STOCK EXCHANGE.

Stokes, I(saac) N(ewton) Phelps (*b* New York City, 11 April 1867; *d* Charleston, S.C., 18 Dec 1944). Architect, historian, philanthropist, and housing reformer. He was the eldest of nine children of Helen L. Phelps and Anson Phelps Stokes Sr., whose families had long been involved in charities and reform in New York City. After graduating from Harvard College (1891) he studied architecture and housing design at Columbia University and in Paris from 1894 to 1897. With his friend John Mead Howells (1868–1959) he won a competition in 1897 for the design of the University Settlement House (184 Eldridge Street). The two opened a firm that received commissions nationwide, including a number that survive in New York City: Horace Mann Hall at Teachers College (1901, Broadway and 120th Street), the former building of the Royal Insurance Company (1906, 84 William Street), St. Paul's Chapel (1907, Columbia University), and the Open-Air Pulpit at St. John the Divine (1916, Amsterdam Avenue and 112th Street). After amicably dissolving his partnership with Stokes in 1917 Howells designed several buildings for the Pratt Institute in Brooklyn, the Panhellenic Hotel (1928; 1st Avenue and 49th Street; later the Beekman Tower), and the Daily News Building (with Raymond M. Hood, 1930; 220 East 42nd Street).

Stokes was also known for his work to improve housing for the poor, and as a member of the New York State Tenement House Commission he was the author with Lawrence Veiller of the Tenement House Law of 1901, which dramatically raised the standards for multiple dwellings in New York City. In addition he designed two "model tenements for Negroes," the Tuskegee (1902) and the Hampton (1911), both on the West Side of Manhattan. As a director of the Phelps Stokes Fund he supervised its housing activities and gave advice on the development of publicly subsidized housing programs during the 1920s and 1930s. He was also a pioneer in historic preservation, instrumental in saving the façade of the Bank of the United States on Wall Street (1823; later the Assay Office), which was later installed at the Metropolitan Museum of Art. A collector of prints and maps documenting the city's history, he produced a monumental illustrated reference work in six volumes, *The Iconography of Manhattan Island* (1915–28), which remains an important research tool. For more than twenty years he served on the boards of the Art Commission and the New York Public Library.

Roy Lubove: "I. N. Phelps Stokes: Tenement Architect, Economist, Planner," *Journal of the Society of Architectural Historians* 23 (1964), 75–87

Deborah S. Gardner: "Revisiting I. N. Phelps Stokes' *The Iconography of Manhattan Island, 1498–1909*," *American City History: Modes of Inquiry*, ed. Kathleen Neils Conzen, Michael H. Ebner, Russell Lewis, and Eric H. Monkkonen (Chicago: University of Chicago Press, 1995)

Deborah S. Gardner

a single block in 1935, and by 1939 the population of Harlem approached a million. Neighborhoods throughout the city were also defined as centers of trades (fur, fashion, flowers, art, antiques, meat, books). Along 5th Avenue in the 50s strict zoning ensured that signage remained discreet and all business was conducted indoors. In the 1920s work began on skyscrapers and other tall structures, among them the Empire State Building, the George Washington Bridge, and the Waldorf–Astoria. The high steel frames were usually built by Caughnawagas, formerly known as Christian (or Praying) Mohawks. Construction sites attracted many spectators; the builders of Rockefeller Center were among the first to cut portholes in the fence around the site to accommodate spectators called "sidewalk superintendents." During the construction of the Seagram Building on Park Avenue in 1956 three portholes were cut to accommodate viewers of different heights.

New ethnic enclaves formed after an influx of immigrants during the mid twentieth century. The 30s between Broadway and 6th Avenue became a center of Korean importers, twenty-four-hour grocers, restaurants, and bookstores. East 6th Street was known for its Indian restaurants, usually opened in the first story of a tenement building and decorated with scenes of a garden paradise painted on the front windows. Bodegas opened throughout the city and were known for their bright lights, yellow awnings, and display windows, which often had blue and pink plastic bottles of detergent arranged in a pattern of solid squares. As Chinatown became increasingly congested after 1965, even the smallest spaces along its streets were put to use. Vendors sold congee, tripe, rice noodles, fish balls, tea eggs, pork rinds, and squid from carts along Canal Street; shoe repairers, watchmakers, diviners, and fish sellers worked on the sidewalks; crowds stopped to watch candy makers transform discs of sugar into "dragon's moustaches"; greengrocers worked in trucks trimming vegetables. In Columbus Park elderly men met to practice Tai Chi and play *juk kay*, elderly women to chat and mind young children. Handwritten charms to stop children from crying were sometimes taped to lampposts, and mirrors were mounted over doorways and windows to ward off evil. Small altars with oranges and incense sometimes stood on the ground outside shops, and plastic streamers and potted plants bearing red ribbons with good wishes surrounded the doorways of new shops. During the Chinese New Year teams representing martial-arts clubs wore lion costumes and danced along the streets to bring good luck.

The 1970s and 1980s saw renewed efforts to control street activities. About 1972 the *Guide to the New York City Noise Control Code* described the noise level in the city as "an aural state of siege"; enforcement of this code and others like it was usually selective. In the late 1980s and early 1990s the city cracked down on STREET VENDORS. Those selling used books, especially along Cooper Square, St. Mark's Place, and 2nd Avenue, were protected somewhat by the First Amendment. Street preachers and religious proselytizers gave speeches and solicited funds in the streets, many of them in Times Square because of its bustle around the clock and association with vice. Efforts were also made to discourage sidewalk gambling operations, especially three-card monte and shell games. Some neighborhoods banned clotheslines, satellite dishes, birdbaths, recreational and commercial vehicles, colors of house paint, and certain kinds of mailboxes, awnings, and siding material. Attention also focused on the homeless, who collected redeemable cans and bottles from garbage bins and built shantytowns on vacant lots in the East Village and elsewhere. Residents of devastated neighborhoods transformed vacant lots into small estates, sometimes using rubble to build *casitas*, named for a style of country house in Puerto Rico; these often became meeting places for men displaced from social clubs by rising rents. Parks were also popular with players of "speed" chess, checkers, and backgammon. Many kept up a patter to focus their attention and block out distractions.

Street celebrations are an important element of neighborhood identity. During December in Ozone, a largely Italian section, visitors line up to see Nativity scenes set up in garages and brightly lit holiday displays on front lawns. On Jewish holidays and the Sabbath in Borough Park men relax in shirtsleeves during warm weather and read on the balcony, while women in housecoats, slippers, and kerchiefs socialize on the street. In the late afternoon families stroll along the streets, the women dressed according to the Hasidic custom of *tsnies* (modesty), the men in black kaftans and fur hats. In Williamsburg and other areas notices in Yiddish, Hebrew, and English appear by the hundreds on walls, windows, and lampposts, giving news about fund-raising events, efforts to help families in need, organizational meetings, Purim performances, and sales of holiday goods, as well as admonitions to adhere more strictly to the code of Jewish law. West Indian Carnival is held each Labor Day weekend in Brooklyn. On New Year's Eve crowds gather in Times Square to watch a large lighted ball descend from the top of a building at midnight. The area is also a popular site for demonstrations, as is Union Square. Many parades are held along 5th Avenue; some of the largest are on St. Patrick's Day, Easter, and Columbus Day. For the Halloween parade in Greenwich Village revelers sometimes dress up as buildings (the Empire State and Chrysler buildings are favorites) and even as street corners. Such annual citywide events as the New York City Marathon also draw large crowds.

Much street life in New York City is commercial. Businesses in crowded areas engage "leafers" to thrust advertising fliers into the hands of passers-by. Bicycle messengers wearing helmets and brilliant fluorescent spandex outfits negotiate traffic carrying urgent parcels for typesetters, printers, designers, editors, and photographers in midtown Manhattan. The dark green trucks of private garbage collection companies hurtle along main thoroughfares, often decorated with large stagecoach scenes painted on their sides and polished chrome trim and small colored lights outlining their contours. At street fairs pitchmen demonstrate knives and solvents for sale. Window washers carrying their tools walk the streets looking for work, especially in lower Manhattan during the spring.

Alfred Kazin: *A Walker in the City* (New York: Harcourt, Brace, 1951)

Benjamin Albert Botkin, ed.: *New York City Folklore: Legends, Tall Tales, Anecdotes, Stories, Sagas, Heroes and Characters, Customs, Traditions, and Sayings* (New York: Random House, 1956)

Robert Anthony Orsi: *The Madonna of 115th Street: Faith and Community in Italian Harlem, 1880–1950* (New Haven: Yale University Press, 1985)

Barbara Kirshenblatt-Gimblett: "Ordinary People / Everyday Life: Folk Culture in New York City," *Urban Life: Readings in Urban Anthropology*, ed. George Gmelch and Walter P. Zenner, 2nd edn (Prospect Heights, Ill.: Waveland, 1988), 403–11

Amanda Dargan and Steve Zeitlin: *City Play* (New Brunswick, N.J.: Rutgers University Press, 1990)

Barbara Kirshenblatt-Gimblett

streets. The original configuration of streets in New Amsterdam (1625) at the southern tip of Manhattan closely resembled that of a Dutch medieval city: narrow streets enclosed blocks with solid frontages, and a waterway penetrated the settlement at the Heere Graft (now Broad Street). Originally the shoreline extended only as far west as Greenwich Street and as far east as Pearl Street, but landfill was soon added to create building space. The city had Wall Street as its northern limit until it expanded under English rule in the late seventeenth century. Streets and blocks were developed haphazardly for the next century and a half as public lands and various nearby farms came on the market. The only organizing elements were several roads to agricultural villages and small market towns, such as Heere Straat–Broad Way–Great Georges Road, Kings Way–Great Post Road–Albany Post Road, Kingsbridge Road, Bloomingdale Road, Bowery Lane–Boston Post Road, and Flatbush Road. These roads probably followed Indian and animal trails, which were the easiest routes through the relatively rough topography of the original landscape and over its streams. They were progressively enlarged as the volume of traffic increased and became what are now the city's major transportation corridors.

The municipal government established before the American Revolution became increasingly responsible for urban operations and service, particularly under the charters of Thomas Dongan (1686) and John Montgomerie (1731), but the Common Council was inept at planning, maintaining, and improving streets and sidewalks, which fell into a deplorable state. The city developed in a rectilinear pattern; commercial activities were clustered along the principal streets. Roads were paved gradually, usually through assessments against the owners of abutting property. The first commissioners of streets and roads were named in 1798. The period of improvised expansion of the road network in Manhattan came to an end in 1811 with the adoption of the Commissioners' Plan, also known as the GRID PLAN, which called for streets to be arranged in a strict gridiron formation with fixed block and lot sizes. The width of the east–west cross streets was fixed at sixty feet (eighteen meters) between building lines, that of the roadway in the center at about thirty-four feet (ten meters); the north–south avenues were one hundred feet (thirty meters) wide. These dimensions were set at a time when there was no mechanical street transportation, few people owned horse carriages, and buildings were not expected to reach beyond a height of two or three stories. It was believed that the heaviest traffic would run east and west, and therefore the cross streets were spaced close together. This prediction proved incorrect, and unlike the avenues the cross streets became regarded as suitable for developments of low density and light traffic.

The grid was extended as the city expanded northward, and the natural topography was thoroughly leveled so that valuable land would not be lost. Streets were cut through hills, rocks, and marshes by a large force of laborers who lived in shantytowns that were pushed forward in advance of the work area; the northern end of Manhattan was reached in the early decades of the twentieth century. The rectilinear pattern gave New York City its basic urban image; besides satisfying the original intent of creating convenient building lots for development, the north–south avenues proved capable in most places of accommodating ever growing traffic.

The other boroughs used the same basic grid, developing land in sections without adopting an overall plan: the result frequently was awkward triangular lots, confusing intersections, and patches of unused land. Most small settlements and farms disappeared with the construction of tenements and one-family housing; the larger established centers and the original pattern of their streets remained.

As various modern ideas about town planning took form in the late nineteenth century and the early twentieth, calls to reform the grid pattern were made by some who found it rigid and uninspired. In 1860 a commission was appointed to decide whether to complete the Commissioners' Plan of 1811 above 155th Street. Its duties were taken over in part by the Central Park Commission, which evaluated future patterns for Fort Tryon, Inwood, and their environs and had jurisdiction over the western half of the Bronx, and in part by the newly created park department in 1871. After consolidation the Board of Estimate and Apportionment was given the right to approve street and park plans submitted by the borough presidents. Its chief engineer, Nelson P. Lewis (1902–20), was active in advocating orderly circulation systems and planning in advance of development, in contrast to political officials who thought only in terms of the city's immediate needs. A request to the New York City Improvement Commission (1903) to prepare a comprehensive plan for the city brought no results; the Committee on the City Plan (1914) was the first to conceive the city as part of a region.

The gridiron pattern proved well suited to New York City: when one channel became congested traffic could be diverted to one or more parallel routes, and the grid could accommodate widely differing types of buildings, from private homes to heavy industrial plants, as well as projects like the company town of Steinway (1877), Sunnyside Gardens (1924), and Rockefeller Center (1932). In some parts of New York City curvilinear or diagonal streets and special interior networks were built for sizable developments, including village-like enclaves in the late nineteenth century and such later projects as Forest Hills Gardens (1913), Parkchester (1938), Stuyvesant Town and Peter Cooper Village (1947), Fresh Meadows (1949), Co-op City (1968–70), Roosevelt Island (1974), Starrett City (1976), and Battery Park City (1982). The "superblock," an area with no internal streets to which access is gained from without or underground, is a modification of the grid that found many applications in the city: examples include the campus of Columbia University, the Jacob K. Javits Convention Center, Battery Park City, Rockefeller Center, Lincoln Center, parts of Roosevelt Island, Jamaica Center, and various hospitals, transportation terminals, housing projects, and industrial enclaves.

As the city grew in size and complexity and as traffic loads increased during the second half of the nineteenth century, better streets and highways needed to be developed. The design of Central Park (1857), for example, was characterized by several striking ideas: controlled access, transverse roads beneath the park to carry crosstown traffic, and attention to the aesthetics of movement. Parkways, inspired by the grand boulevards of Paris, were also introduced at this time: built as extensions of the parks system, they had well-delineated lanes divided by strips landscaped with trees, grass, and other plantings, and were intended not for everyday traffic but for strolling and horse carriages, and later for bicycles. Frederick Law Olmsted was one of the leading advocates of PARKWAYS, the most prominent example of which in New York City is Eastern Parkway (1871–74). Others include Western Boulevard (now upper Broadway, 1868–1904), Ocean Parkway (1869–76), Riverside Drive (1872–1902), the Mosholu, Pelham, and Crotona parkways (1884), Park Avenue (1888–1927), the Grand Concourse (1892–1909), and Queens and Northern boulevards (1922). The advent of motor vehicles led to the introduction of a new type of parkway, intended primarily to facilitate the enjoyment of fast motion; the foremost early example in New York City and its environs was the Bronx River Parkway (1913–23).

The Regional Plan of New York and Its Environs (1927–31) provided a comprehensive vision of a modern transportation system: it encompassed an area with a radius of fifty miles (eighty kilometers), reflecting the true size of the metropolis. The principal features of its highway system were a squarish metropolitan loop surrounding the core with principal internal routes (four east–west and four north–south), routes radiating to the periphery, and distant circumferential bypasses. The plan strove to disperse traffic by providing efficient paths between the many important centers of the region. A number of these facilities were later completed, but without achieving the clear order envisioned by the original plan. Between 1924 and 1972 Robert Moses set a standard for motorway construction by building seventeen parkways, fourteen expressways, and one drive in the city and in Nassau, Suffolk, and Westchester counties. He completed parkways on Long Island, the Triborough Bridge (after 1929), and virtually the entire city's highway network, except for the Miller Elevated Highway (popularly known as the West Side Highway), the Harlem River Drive, and the FDR Drive. He also built bridges and parks to which his highways provided the best access.

Although New York City achieved one of the most extensive networks of urban highways in the 1950s, it was among the first cities to limit highway expansion in the 1960s and 1970s, partly out of a concern for air quality. The only major highway projects completed during these years were the Bruckner interchange (1973) and the Staten Island West Shore Expressway (1976), after which no further capital investments in highways were made because of environmental concerns and financial constraints. In the mid 1990s streets and highways in the city were overburdened and inadequately maintained. In addition to rebuilding programs the only active road project was a proposed boulevard and esplanade along the western shore of Manhattan (Route 9A), although there was some discussion of building another crossing of the Hudson River and a northern bypass. At the same time plans were made for automatic toll collection, and proposals were advanced to impose further controls on motor vehicles, such as areawide user charges, extended automobile-free zones, and more restrictive parking policies.

Many highways proposed for New York City generated extensive debate but were never built: these have included the Lower Manhattan Expressway (1940–69), the Richmond Expressway–Parkway (1941–88), the Mid-Manhattan Expressway (1946–69), the Cross-Brooklyn Expressway (1955–69), the Oyster Bay–Rye crossing of Long Island Sound (1967–72), Westway (1972–90), and a number of other extensions and connections.

Robert Moses: *New Parkways in New York City* (New York: Department of Parks, 1937)

"The Urban Pattern," *New York Panorama: A Companion to the WPA Guide to New York City* (New York: Random House, 1938; repr. Pantheon, 1984), 397–422

Robert A. Caro: *The Power Broker: Robert Moses and the Fall of New York* (New York: Alfred A. Knopf, 1974)

Henry Moscow: *The Street Book: An Encyclopedia of Manhattan's Street Names and Their Origins* (New York: Fordham University Press, 1978)

Sigurd Grava: "The Bronx River Parkway: A Case Study in Innovation," *New York Affairs* 7, no.1 (1981), 15–23

David N. Dunlap: *On Broadway: A Journey Uptown over Time* (New York: Rizzoli, 1990)

See also PAVING.

Sigurd Grava

street vendors. Merchants selling their goods in the streets were common in New York City during the colonial period. In the early nineteenth century many immigrants who could not find steady employment resorted to street vending, then often known as peddling: they thus provided other immigrants with goods that were common in their country of origin but scarce in American shops. Shortly after the First World War local retailers in the city expressed strong opposition to what they considered the unfair competition of street vendors, who were able to charge lower prices because they did not pay rent. Some local businesses also considered street vendors an eyesore in a modern and efficient city. The opposition to street vendors prompted the city government to limit the number of vending licenses it would issue and the locations in which vendors could operate. Two kinds of license were established: for the sale of general merchandise and for the sale of food (fresh, processed, or prepared on site). In 1990 the city limited the number of general-merchandise licenses to 853 (not counting licenses automatically granted to military veterans); at the time a waiting list for general-merchandise licenses comprised 710 names. In 1994 Mayor Rudolph W. Giuliani began a controversial initiative to remove unlicensed vendors from 125th Street. Street vendors deal in an astonishing variety of merchandise, including batteries, T-shirts, imitations of designer gold watches, expensive leather briefcases, and baseball cards. They have an uncanny ability to provide needed goods at a moment's notice, such as umbrellas when it rains unexpectedly. Usually street vendors focus on areas with heavy pedestrian traffic, and sometimes several congregate in the same location to form a vendors' market with the unique ambience of an open-air bazaar. In Manhattan there are vendors' markets on Canal Street, 14th Street, and 125th Street. The sale of merchandise without a license is a growing trend, due partly to a surge in the number of immigrants from Latin America, Africa, and the Caribbean for whom informal street vending is a means of subsisting.

John Gaber

Streisand, Barbra [Barbara] **(Joan)** (*b* Brooklyn, 24 April 1942). Singer and actress. She spent her childhood in Brooklyn and began her career singing on local television programs and in such nightclubs as the Bon Soir and the Blue Angel in Manhattan. After signing a contract with Columbia Records she made her début on Broadway in a supporting role in *I Can Get It for You Wholesale* (1962); she became well known in the leading role of *Funny Girl* (1964) and won an Academy Award for her performance in the film version. She later produced, directed, and acted in several motion pictures, including *Yentl* (1983) and *The Prince of Tides* (1991).

David J. Weiner

Striker's Bay [Stryker's Bay]. Section of the former neighborhood of BLOOMINGDALE, bounded to the north by 99th Street, to the east by Central Park West, to the south by 81st Street, and to the west by the Hudson River. It was named for Jacobus Strijker, a magistrate of the Court of New Amsterdam who in 1764 owned a mansion at what is now 96th Street; his descendants lived there for many years. Throughout the nineteenth century the area attracted such renowned residents as Edgar Allan Poe (during summers in the 1840s) and Valentine Mott, a surgeon who owned a house on a parcel of eleven acres (4.5 hectares) covering what is now the area between 93rd and 96th streets. Like other sections of the Upper West Side, Striker's Bay disappeared during a period of rapid growth in the late nineteenth century, when its buildings were razed to make way for new residential development.

Hopper Striker Mott: *The New York of Yesterday* (New York: Knickerbocker, 1908)

James Bradley

Stringfellow, William (*b* Johnstown, R.I., 26 April 1928; *d* Providence, R.I., 2 March 1985). Lawyer. He studied at Harvard University and worked with the East Harlem Protestant Parish, an interdenominational project. An advocate of church-sponsored reform, he wrote *My People Is the Enemy* (1964), which describes his life and work in Harlem and discrimination by the legal system against blacks and the poor. During the Vietnam War he gave sanctuary to Daniel Berrigan, who faced criminal prosecution for having burned draft cards, an action for which he was himself arrested in 1970 (the charges were dismissed by a federal judge). He later became a strong proponent of the ordination of women in the Episcopal church and a defender of James A. Pike, the Episcopal bishop accused of heresy because of his interest in parapsychology and mysticism.

David Meerse

Strivers' Row [King Model Houses]. Group of row houses in Harlem, on West 138th and 139th streets between 7th and 8th avenues in Manhattan. It comprises 130 houses commissioned in 1891 by the developer David H. King Jr. as an example of fine urban housing; the designers were McKim, Mead and White (north side, West 139th Street), Bruce Price and Clarence S. Luce (south side, West 139th Street; north side, West 138th Street), and James Brown Lord (south side, West 138th Street). As blacks moved into Harlem after the First World War the houses became elegant residences for successful black professionals and entertainers, among them the composer W. C. Handy, the comedian Stepin Fetchit, the prizefighter Harry Wills, and the ragtime pianist Eubie Blake.

Sandra Opdycke

Strong, George Templeton (*b* New York City, 26 Jan 1820; *d* New York City, 21 April 1875). Lawyer and diarist. He graduated from Columbia University with high honors in 1838 and soon began to practice law. During the Civil War he was a member of the U.S. Sanitary Commission and helped to form the Union League Club. A trustee of Columbia and a vestryman of Trinity Church, he appreciated music and was president of the Church Music Association and the Philharmonic Society. Strong is best known for his diary, spanning much of the nineteenth century, which provides commentary on the city's musical offerings, politics, and daily life.

James E. Mooney

Strong, Josiah (*b* Naperville, Ill., 19 Jan 1847; *d* New York City, 28 April 1916). Religious leader and reformer. A leader of several reform organizations based in New York City, he encouraged social involvement as a practical expression of social Christianity. With Washington Gladden, Walter Rauschenbusch, and Lyman Abbott he edited the *Kingdom*, the most influential journal of the Social Gospel movement. He wrote five books on social reform, including *Our Country* (1885), a blending of social Christianity and Darwinian theory that sought to expose urban injustices and attribute corruption to wealth. Strong led the American Evangelical Alliance from 1886 to 1898 and the League for Social Service from 1898 to 1904 and also helped to form the Federal Council of Churches in the city in 1908. He lived in Greenwich, Connecticut.

Eileen W. Lindner

Strong, William L(afayette) (*b* Richland County, Ohio, 22 March 1827; *d* New York City, 2 Nov 1900). Mayor. After becoming a millionaire as a merchant and banker he was elected mayor as a reform Republican with the backing of independents and the chamber of commerce, and grudging support from the Republican boss Thomas C. Platt. He took office in 1895 and appointed Theodore Roosevelt police commissioner; his anti-Catholic school reforms, nonpartisan distribution of patronage, and enforcement of Sunday blue laws cost him reelection, and he left office in 1897.

See also BATHHOUSES.

Andrew Wiese

Stroock and Stroock and Lavan. Law firm. It traces its origins to the law practice of M. Warley Platzek (1854–1932), who moved to New York City from South Carolina, established a law office in 1876, and eventually served on the New York State Supreme Court (1907–24). He brought into the firm the brothers Moses Jesse Stroock (1866–1931) and Solomon M. Stroock (1873–1941). Their firm was one of the first largely Jewish law firms to establish an élite reputation. The Stroocks handled commercial matters and trusts and estates, particularly for the leading German Jewish families of New York City, and they were active in numerous civic and Jewish organizations, including the American Jewish Committee, the Jewish Theological Seminary, and the Federation of Jewish Philanthropies of New York. Their corporate clients included many businesses in the tobacco industry and the submarine manufacturer Electric Boat. Peter I. B. Lavan (1898–1988) joined the firm shortly after graduating from Columbia Law School in 1918. In the mid 1990s Stroock and Stroock and Lavan had about 250 lawyers in its offices at 7 Hanover Square.

Jethro K. Lieberman: *Stroock and Stroock and Lavan: An Informal History of the Early Years, 1876 to 1950* (New York: Stroock and Stroock and Lavan, 1987)

Jonathan G. Cedarbaum

Stryker, Francis B(urdett) (*b* Brooklyn, 11 Dec 1811; *d* 14 Jan 1892). Mayor of Brooklyn. A Whig, he served successively as the tax collector, sheriff, and eighth mayor of Brooklyn (1846–48). Later he was county clerk and superintendent of sewers.

Ellen Fletcher

Stuart, Robert Leighton (*b* New York City, 21 July 1806; *d* New York City, 12 Dec 1882). Businessman, philanthropist, and art patron. With his brother Alexander Stuart he formed the sugar-refining firm of R. L. and A. Stuart on Greenwich Street in 1828, which by mid century used innovative steam-based methods to produce more than forty million pounds (eighteen million kilograms) of sugar a year. He was a member of the Century Association (1859) and the Union Club (1863) and a president of the American Museum of Natural History (1872–81). A devout Presbyterian, he was president of Presbyterian Hospital (1880–82) and contributed to the construction of two churches on 5th Avenue. His home at 154 5th Avenue housed an extensive collection of American and European art and a library of fifteen thousand volumes that he bequeathed to the Lenox Library.

Robert L. Stuart: *Catalogue of the Library of Robert L. Stuart* (New York: J. J. Little, 1884)

Paul Spencer Sternberger: "Portrait of a Collector and Patron: Robert Leighton Stuart" (1990) [unpubd, Department of Paintings, Drawings, and Sculpture, New-York Historical Society]

Donna Ann Grossman

Studio 54. Discothèque at 254 West 54th street in Manhattan, opened on 26 April 1977 by Stephen Rubell and Ian Schrager. It attracted a fashionable clientele and was written about ceaselessly by society and gossip columnists. In December 1979 Rubell and Schrager were arrested by federal agents, convicted of tax evasion, and sentenced to three and a half years in prison and fined. After serving a reduced term they sold the club to Mark Fleishman, who reopened it in 1981. Studio 54 closed in 1988.

Marc Ferris

Studio Museum in Harlem. Museum at 144 West 125th Street dedicated solely to the art and artifacts of black America and other cultures of African origin. Incorporated in 1967 as a studio for artists, it began a permanent collection that by 1991 numbered more than ten thousand items, including paintings by Romare Bearden and Jacob Lawrence as well as textiles and photographs. The only black museum accredited by the American Association of Museums and the custodian of the collection of black and Latin American art maintained by New York State, it sponsors exhibitions, lectures, and workshops, and continues to provide studio space for artists. In the early 1990s plans were made for an outdoor sculpture garden.

Betty Kaplan Gubert

Sturges, Jonathan (*b* Southport, Conn., 24 March 1802; *d* New York City, 28 Nov 1874). Merchant, art patron, and philanthropist. After moving to New York City in 1821 he joined the mercantile firm of Luman Reed and in 1836 assumed control of the firm of Reed and Sturges at 125–27 Front Street. Known for his comprehensive collection of American art, he was a patron and honorary member (1837) of the National Academy of Design and a member of the Sketch Club (1840) and helped to form the Century Association (1847), the New-York Gallery of the Fine Arts (1844–58), of which he was president, and the Union League Club (1863), of which he became president in 1864.

Timothy Anglin Burgard

Stuyvesant, Peter [Petrus] (*b* Friesland, 1610; *d* New York City, February 1672). Director general of New Netherland. The son of a minister, he joined the military and was eventually appointed governor of Curaçao before receiving his commission as director general of New Netherland from the States-General. He sailed into New Amsterdam with a fleet of four vessels in 1647 and took up residence in the governor's house in Fort Amsterdam (now the site of the U.S. Custom House). Some of his first ordinances dealt with the sale of intoxicants and religious observance on Sundays; he soon rebuilt the church at Fort Amsterdam, served as a church warden, forbade all religious observances except those of the Reformed church, and sought to prevent Jews from entering the colony. He also outfitted an expedition against the Spanish, who were trespassing in the domain of the West India Company.

In 1651 he bought a farm bounded by what are now 17th Street, the East River, 5th Street, and 4th Avenue. Using his salary of 250 guilders a month he built an elegant home about 1655 called "White Hall" (in his day also called "Stuyvesant's Great House"), at what is now the intersection of Whitehall and State streets; he bought the property in 1658 and made it his official residence. During his tenure he improved relations with English colo-

Peter Stuyvesant, ca *1660 (artist unknown)*

nies, fostered commerce, regulated internal affairs, allowed the formation of municipal government for New Amsterdam, and removed Swedes from the Delaware River. After surrendering to the English in 1664 he withdrew from public affairs and retired to his farm, where he spent the rest of his life at the manor house (now the site of Stuyvesant Street). He was buried beneath the chapel of the house, now the site of St. Mark's Church in the Bowery.

Anna Crouse and Russel Crouse: *Peter Stuyvesant of Old New York* (New York: Random House, 1954)

James E. Mooney

Stuyvesant Heights. Neighborhood in northwestern Brooklyn (1990 pop. 2500), covering twelve blocks in the heart of Bedford–Stuyvesant and bounded to the north by Macon Street, to the east by Stuyvesant Avenue, to the south by Chauncey Street, and to the west by Tompkins Avenue. Most of the brownstones and row houses lining the streets were built in the 1890s. Designated a Historic District in 1971, the area became known for its strong commitment to preservation. Among its many landmarks are the Mount Lebanon Baptist Church and Fulton Park. Stuyvesant Heights is almost entirely residential: its population is middle class and overwhelmingly black, with a large number of immigrants from Guyana, Jamaica, and Barbados.

James Bradley

Stuyvesant High School. Public high school opened in 1904 on East 23rd Street; in 1907 it was destroyed by fire and moved to East 15th Street. Conceived as part of the reform program of the superintendent of schools William H. Maxwell, the school was intended to prepare children of immigrants for careers in science. Between 1909 and 1934 this goal was reaffirmed by its second principal, the physicist Ernst R. von Nardroff. The school admitted only boys until 1969. In September 1992 it moved to a magnificent new building in Battery Park City, constructed at a cost of $150 million. At the time it had about 2700 students, of whom 51 percent were Asian, and about one hundred teachers. The students at Stuyvesant are admitted by special examination and live throughout the city. Each year many are recipients of the Westinghouse Science Talent Award, which is the focus of an informal competition with the Bronx High School of Science. Many renowned scientists and physicians have attended Stuyvesant High School. Its alumni include two recipients of the Nobel Prize (Joshua Lederberg, physiology or medicine, 1958; and Roald Hoffmann, chemistry, 1981), as well as the architectural critic Lewis Mumford, the film actor James Cagney, the jazz pianist Thelonious Monk, and the screenwriter Joseph Mankiewicz.

Stephan F. Brumberg: *Going to America, Going to School: The Jewish Immigrant Public School Encounter* (New York: Praeger, 1986)

Joshua Lederberg

Stuyvesant Square. Neighborhood on the East Side of Manhattan (1990 pop. 7000), bounded to the north by 18th Street, to the east by 1st Avenue, to the south by 14th Street, and to the west by 3rd Avenue. The land was part of Peter Stuyvesant's farm in the late seventeenth century and in 1836 was deeded by Peter Gerard Stuyvesant to the city, which built a park on four acres (1.6 hectares) of land bisected by 2nd Avenue. The area changed markedly during the late nineteenth century, when German, Irish, Jewish, Italian, and Slavic immigrants moved into new brownstones and row houses. Among local religious institutions are St. George's Episcopal Church (1856; for illustration see St. George's Episcopal Church) and the Friends Meeting Houses and Seminary (1860; 15th Street and Rutherford Place), the center of Quakerism in the city. The neighborhood is also the site of Beth Israel Hospital and was formerly that of Stuyvesant High School (from 1904 until the school moved to Battery Park City in 1992). After Stuyvesant Square was designated a Historic District in 1975 it became revitalized.

James Bradley

Stuyvesant Town. Housing project in Manhattan (1990 pop. 20,000), covering eighteen blocks and bounded to the north by 20th Street, to the east by Avenue C, to the south by 14th Street, and to the west by 1st Avenue. It was built in 1943 for $112 million by the Metropolitan Life Insurance Company after the passage of a state law to encourage slum clearance by private firms. Plans were initiated by Robert Moses under the guidance of Mayor Fiorello H. La Guardia. The architects were Irwin Clavan and Gilmore Clarke, who designed thirty-five red-brick buildings of thirteen to fourteen stories each, containing 8756 rent-stabilized apartments; tree-lined walkways complemented the sparse architecture, and a park with a fountain lay at the center of the development. When the first apartments were rented in 1947 there were more than eleven thousand applicants, most of them veterans of the Second World War. All were white, young, and married: single people, unmarried couples, and nonwhites were barred during the tenure of Frederick H. Ecker as chairman of Metropolitan Life from 1936 to 1950. Almost a hundred organizations and individuals protested these restrictions during a hearing of the City Council before the contract to establish Stuyvesant Town was signed. The courts upheld the rental policy until the company changed it voluntarily in August 1950, and in October 1950 three black families moved in. In later years the population became ethnically more diverse, with growing numbers of Dominicans, Puerto Ricans, and Chinese. By 1990 there were almost eight thousand applicants on the waiting list.

B. Kimberly Taylor

Styne, Jule [Stein, Jules] (*b* London, 31 Dec 1905; *d* New York City, 20 Sept 1994). Composer and producer. Educated in the Mid-

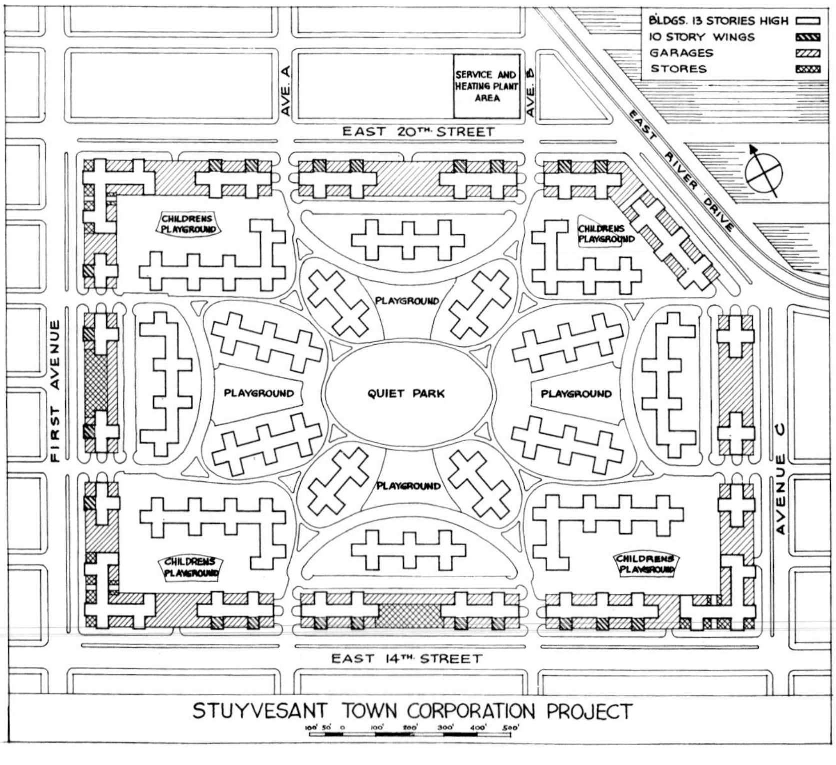

Plan for Stuyvesant Town, ca *1943*

west, he moved to New York City in the mid 1930s. He wrote several successful Broadway shows, including *High Button Shoes* (1947), *Gentlemen Prefer Blondes* (1949), *Gypsy* (1959), and *Funny Girl* (1964), as well as film scores. Among his works inspired by New York City are the show *The Kid from Brooklyn* (1946) and the songs "It Happened in Brooklyn" (1947) and "Ev'ry Street's a Boulevard in Old New York" (1953).

Theodore Taylor: *Jule: The Story of Composer Jule Styne* (New York: Random House, 1979)

Marc Ferris

Subtreasury of the United States. Defunct agency for collecting federal taxes. It was an arm of the subtreasury system (formed in 1846 as part of the independent treasury overseen by the assistant treasurer of the United States) and was responsible for collecting and disbursing two thirds of the nation's revenues; it was also the representative of the U.S. Treasury on Wall Street. From 1862 to 1925 the headquarters were at the Federal Hall National Memorial on the corner of Wall and Nassau streets. Among the well-known heads of the agency were John A. Dix (1798–1879), later governor of New York, John A. Stewart (1822–1926), a banker who formed the U.S. Trust Company, and Thomas C. Acton (*d* 1909), later president of the Bank of New Amsterdam. By the mid 1920s the functions of the subtreasury were taken over by the Federal Reserve Bank of New York.

James Bradley

suburbs. Although New York City is the most densely populated municipality in the United States (1990 density of pop. 23,670 per square mile, or 9143 per square kilometer), universally symbolized by the towering skyline of Manhattan, the city's suburbs are older, larger, and more sprawling than those of any other city in the world. In 1990 the urbanized region comprised not only 7.323 million inhabitants in the city itself but an additional 12.227 million in twenty-five adjacent counties in New York, New Jersey, and Connecticut, for a metropolitan total of 19.55 million.

Brooklyn Heights was the world's first commuter suburb, transformed between 1815 and 1835 from a sleepy rural village into a middle-class bedroom community. Regular steam ferry service to New York City (then consisting only of Manhattan) began in 1814, and in the following year the *Brooklyn Star* predicted that Brooklyn Heights would become "a favorite residence for gentlemen of taste and fortune." Additional ferry lines soon expanded the commuting possibilities, and by 1860 the various ferries across the East River were carrying 100,000 passengers every working day.

Railroads had an even greater impact on suburban growth. Commuter travel in the region by steam railroad began in 1832, and by 1837 the New York and Harlem Railroad offered service to 125th Street. Additions to this same line led to White Plains and central Westchester by 1844. Meanwhile the New York and New Haven Railroad along Long Island Sound reached New Haven, Connecticut, in 1843, and the Harlem River line toward Albany, New York, reached Peekskill in 1849. In the following decade real-estate developments were constructed in Rye, Tarrytown, and New Rochelle. The northbound railroads opened up Westchester County (including what later became the Bronx), largely replacing the steamboats that had run to Yonkers and Peekskill.

At the same time the Long Island Rail Road and the New York and Flushing Railroad enabled former residents of Manhattan to commute from the east. By bringing villages in Queens County within an hour of the business district in the late 1850s, the railroads led an influx into Newtown, Maspeth, and Flushing. On the other side of the Hudson River, Jersey City was the hub of a combined ferry and rail route that enabled commuters to traverse the sixteen miles (twenty-five kilometers) from South Orange, New Jersey, to New York City in less than an hour. Because of this route Llewellyn Park, the world's first picturesque suburb, was developed in the eastern foothills of the Orange Mountains in the decade before the Civil War. Conceived by Llewellyn S. Haskell, a prosperous drug merchant, and planned by Alexander Jackson Davis, the most prolific architect of his generation, the suburb was notable for its use of two features unprecedented in residential development: the curvilinear road and the central open space. The most ambitiously planned suburb of the nineteenth century was Garden City, about twenty miles (thirty kilometers) east of Manhattan in Nassau County. The inspiration of the merchant A. T. Stewart and his long-time architect John Kellum, Garden City was unusual for its large lots and wide streets. Because Stewart chose to rent rather than sell the houses, the community did not prosper until the twentieth century.

By 1900 New York City had more suburbs than any other place in the world, as thousands of businessmen chose opulence over the polyglot ambience of the great city. Every morning hundreds of trains from northern and eastern New Jersey pulled into Hoboken, discharging passengers who then embarked on a ten-minute ferry ride to Manhattan. From southern and eastern Brooklyn and from Nassau County steam locomotives brought passengers to Atlantic Avenue in Brooklyn, where they had easy access to the financial district. Meanwhile Westchester County became the first large suburban area. At the turn of the century the three major passenger railroads running along the Hudson, the Harlem River Valley, and Long Island Sound were carrying 118,000 commuters a day into Grand Central Terminal. The population of Westchester doubled three times in successive twenty-year periods — 1850–70, 1870–90, and 1890–1910 — by the end of which it had 283,000 residents. Most of the development was actively encouraged by the railroads, which developed communities, promoted the advantages of suburban living, and offered frequent, reliable service. Indeed there was more and better commuter service from most of the city's northern suburbs in the late nineteenth century than in the late twentieth.

The suburban shift accelerated after the Second World War, aided by a national mania for the automobile and by federal policies that favored private transportation. By 1970 more than 2200 square miles (5700 square kilometers) had been urbanized, about five times the area urbanized in 1920 even though the population had only doubled. Because suburban residents in the twentieth century rejected annexation by New York City, unlike their predecessors in what became the city's outer boroughs, the metropolitan region became highly fragmented: in 1960 the political scientist Robert C. Wood identified within the region more than fourteen hundred separate suburban governments and taxing authorities.

Employment followed the same path as population. As late as 1920 Manhattan, the Bronx, Brooklyn, Queens, Newark, and Jersey City accounted for about 80 percent of the employment in what was later designated the New York–Northern New Jersey–Long Island Consolidated Metropolitan Statistical Area. Most of the rest was in satellite cities that were well served by rail lines, such as Yonkers and White Plains in Westchester, and Paterson and Passaic in New Jersey. By 1970, however, more than half the employment in the region was outside the old urban core.

Kenneth T. Jackson: *Crabgrass Frontier: The Suburbanization of the United States* (New York: Oxford University Press, 1985)

Kenneth T. Jackson

subways. Serious consideration was given to building a rapid transit system in New York City as early as the 1860s, when the streets of Manhattan were choked with slow-moving traffic. Many proposals were made, most inspired by the first subway in the world, which opened in London in 1863. After delays in construction due to expense, political squabbling, and technological obstacles, the first segment of an experimental elevated line along Greenwich and 9th avenues to 30th Street opened to passengers on 3 July 1868. Its success led elevated lines to be built with private capital and operated under long-term franchises in other parts of Manhattan and in the Bronx and Brooklyn. A pneumatic subway on 312 feet (one hundred meters) of track built illegally under Broadway near City Hall was demonstrated to the public in 1870 but for lack of legislative and financial support was not expanded. In the early 1890s pro-

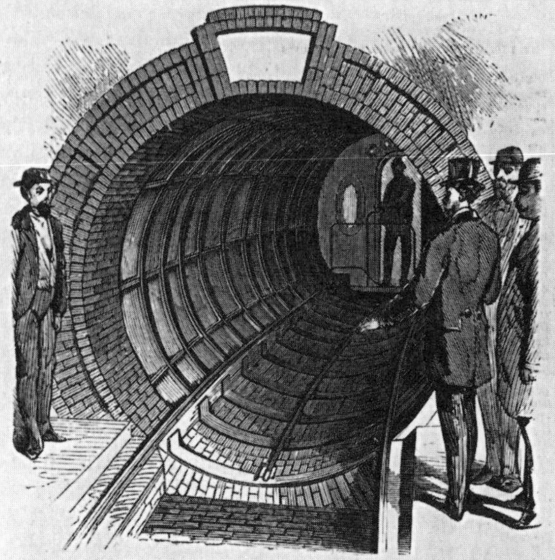

ENTRANCE TO TUNNEL, WITH PASSENGER-CAR COMING IN.

INTERIOR OF THE PASSENGER-CAR.

THE BROADWAY PNEUMATIC TUNNEL.

The series of engravings pertaining to the Pneumatic Railway which we this week present, illustrate the progress of a remarkable work, planned and executed in a remarkable manner. Our great metropolitan thoroughfare has been bored, arched, and a track laid down, by a corps of sappers and miners, who have operated with surprising rapidity and success. They have not only tunneled Broadway, but have done so with the surging throng of humanity, animals and vehicles marching in endless procession directly above their spades. No outward indications of activity below the ground have been exhibited, and, until quite recently, the public has had no knowledge of the matter. The works are hidden by the granite pavement of the street, and but for our engravings, taken from the subterranean structures themselves, it might be difficult to satisfy our readers that we have above stated only the facts.

The Underground Railroad, the highway for rapid city transit, long needed and pressingly demanded by the inhabitants of New York, has at last been commenced, and a short portion has been put in actual operation. We trust it will not be long ere we shall be able to chronicle the full completion of the work from the Battery to the Harlem River. It is evident, from the example now before us, that the construction of an underground railway in this city is not a difficult, nor,

ADVANCING THE SHIELD—INTERIOR OF THE TUNNEL.

necessarily, a tedious operation. Six months or a year's time is quite sufficient, the ways and means being provided, with enterprising men as conductors.

HOW THE TUNNEL CAME TO BE BUILT.

The present tunnel under Broadway has been constructed under the auspices of the Beach Pneumatic Transit Company, a corporation chartered in 1868, with authority to convey letters, parcels and merchandise through tubes not to exceed fifty-four inches mean interior diameter. It was ascertained by the company, after careful investigation, that the cost of laying down two tubes of the above size, constructed together, would be but little more than that of building a single tube. It was also ascertained that the quickest and best method of construction for the two tubes was to bore under the streets, below the water pipes and sewers, and erect a masonry shell or tunnel large enough to inclose both of the fifty-four inch tubes. It is a portion of this outer tunnel that has been erected; and as it proves to be strong enough and large enough for the transit of passengers, it is to be hoped that the company will be compelled by law to omit their intended division walls, and open their tunnel for passenger traffic.

CARRYING CAPACITY OF THE PNEUMATIC RAILROAD.

We have made a little calculation on this point, and find that with two tubes such as that already erected, but perhaps a trifle larger, and with trains

A PROPOSED WAY-STATION FOR THE TUNNEL.

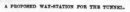

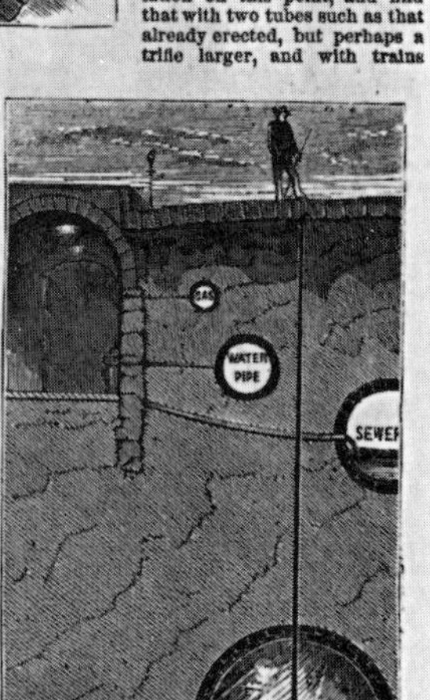

TESTING THE CORRECTNESS OF POSITION AT NIGHT.

NEW YORK CITY.—THE PNEUMATIC TUNNEL IN COURSE OF CONSTRUCTION ON THE LINE OF BROADWAY.

Construction of the pneumatic tunnel under Broadway, from Frank Leslie's Illustrated Newspaper, *19 February 1870*

City Hall Subway Station, ca *1940s*

posals were made for adding rapid transit lines to keep pace with the city's growth. There was widespread interest in building an underground system using new electric motors, but private companies were unwilling to risk investing in such a project.

A plan allowing a subway to be built with city funds was overwhelmingly approved in a referendum in 1894; a public rapid transit board was formed and laid out the route, which ran from a point near City Hall to 42nd Street, then west to Times Square, and then north along Broadway to 96th Street, where the line divided. One branch continued along Broadway to 242nd Street, the other along Lenox Avenue and under the Harlem River to the central Bronx. Bids were solicited in 1900; the contract, awarded for $35 million to the Rapid Transit Subway Construction Company, leased the subway to the contractor for fifty years. The contractor was required to set the fare at five cents, to pay as annual rent the interest on the municipal bonds as well as a sinking fund of 1 percent to amortize the bonds, and to equip and operate the lines at its own expense. In 1902 the Interborough Rapid Transit Company (IRT) was formed to operate the subway and was awarded a second contract, to build a line running south from City Hall under Broadway and the East River to downtown Brooklyn. The first segment opened on 27 October 1904 and was widely praised. The entire system, in operation by 1908, was the first in the world to have four-track service (separate express and local tracks in each direction).

Even before the IRT opened its first line, demands arose to extend routes throughout the metropolitan area, and a bitter struggle ensued over the best way to do so. Trains were badly overcrowded and the rapid transit companies were unwilling to undertake vast expansion. The city hoped to alleviate overcrowding in older neighborhoods and encourage settlement in less congested ones, and members of the Board of Estimate and the state public service commission led by the borough president of Manhattan, George McAneny, met to draw up a plan for building as many lines as possible. On 19 March 1913 they approved the "dual system," under which rapid transit lines controlled by the IRT and the Brooklyn Rapid Transit Company (BRT) were expanded and organized as two networks. The two companies added 123 miles (197 kilometers) of routes and more than doubled the capacity of the rapid transit system at a cost of $302 million, more than had been spent on any other public works project in the country at the time. Each company was granted a lease of forty-nine years to operate its new lines and permitted to charge a five-cent fare. Most track in outlying areas was built on elevated supports to save money.

In 1913 the city's rapid transit system carried 810 million passengers; by 1930, with the addition of the dual-system lines, they carried 2049 million. Under the dual-system plan the original subway line in Manhattan grew to include two north–south lines on the East and West sides joined by a shuttle under 42nd Street. These lines were connected in the Bronx to the Jerome Avenue, White Plains Road, and Pelham lines. In Brooklyn the original subway was connected to the Nostrand Avenue and New Lots lines; and in Queens a line was built to Corona (later extended to Flushing). The BRT was given a lease for a loop under lower Manhattan and a trunk line running under Broadway from lower Manhattan to midtown. Among the lines joined to this trunk were the Astoria line in Queens and the 4th Avenue, Culver, West End, Sea Beach, and Brighton lines to southern Brooklyn. The BRT and the IRT provided joint service on the Astoria line and the Flushing line. The Myrtle Avenue line was improved, the BRT received the right to operate a line along 14th

City Hall Subway Station, ca *1905*

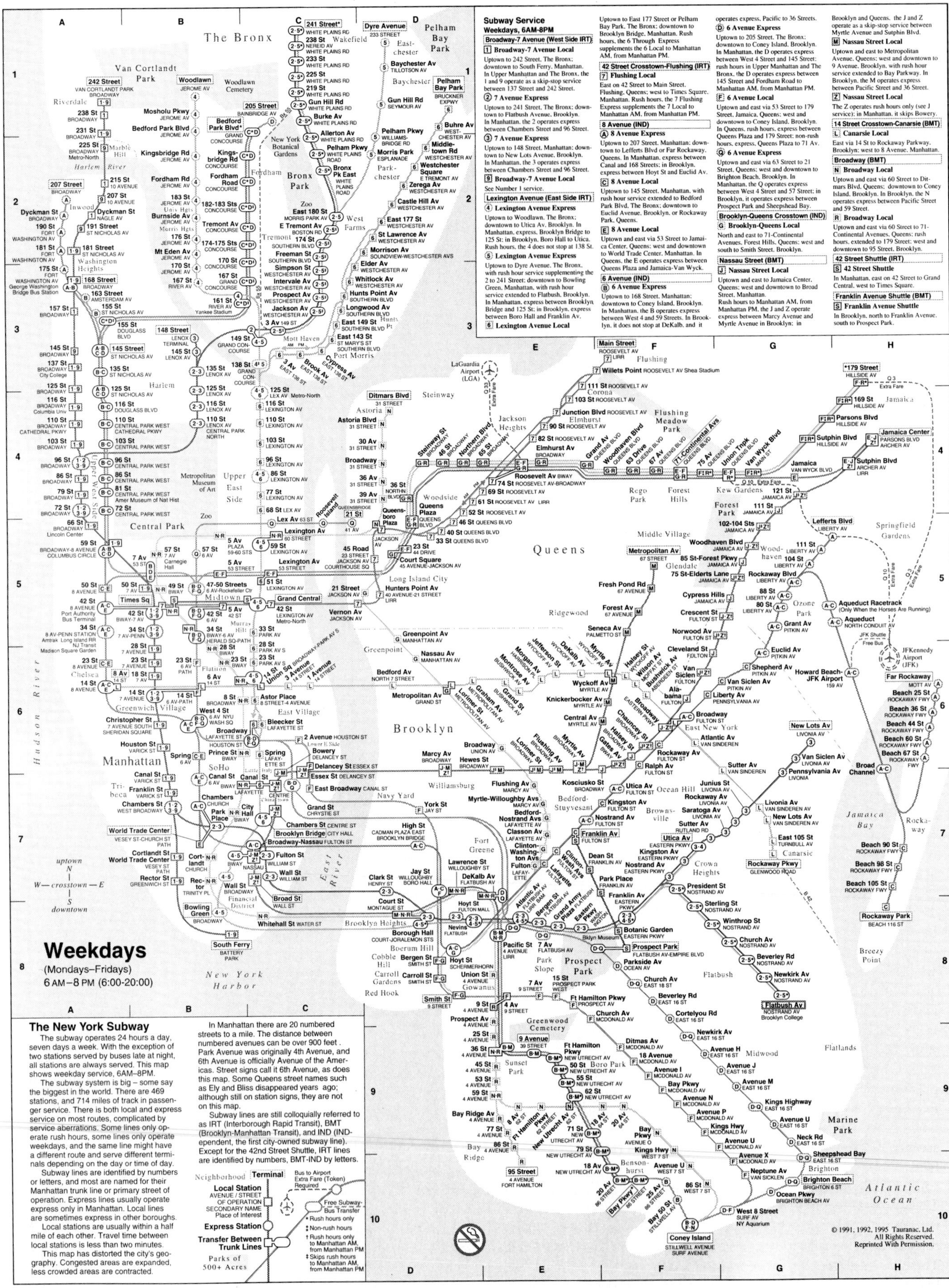

Weekdays

(Mondays–Fridays)
6 AM–8 PM (6:00-20:00)

Subway Service
Weekdays, 6AM-8PM

Broadway-7 Avenue (West Side IRT)

1 Broadway-7 Avenue Local
Uptown to 242 Street, The Bronx; downtown to South Ferry, Manhattan. In Upper Manhattan and The Bronx, the 1 and 9 operate as a skip-stop service between 137 Street and 242 Street.

2 7 Avenue Express
Uptown to 241 Street, The Bronx; downtown to Flatbush Avenue, Brooklyn. In Manhattan, the 2 operates express between Chambers Street and 96 Street.

3 7 Avenue Express
Uptown to 148 Street, Manhattan; downtown to New Lots Avenue, Brooklyn. In Manhattan, the 3 operates express between Chambers Street and 96 Street.

9 Broadway-7 Avenue Local
See Number 1 service.

Lexington Avenue (East Side IRT)

4 Lexington Avenue Express
Uptown to Woodlawn, The Bronx; downtown to Utica Av, Brooklyn. In Manhattan, express, Brooklyn Bridge to 125 St; in Brooklyn, Boro Hall to Utica. Rush hours, the 4 does not stop at 138 St.

5 Lexington Avenue Express
Uptown to Dyre Avenue, The Bronx, with rush hour service supplementing the 2 to 241 Street; downtown to Bowling Green, Manhattan, with rush hour service extended to Flatbush, Brooklyn. In Manhattan, express between Brooklyn Bridge and 125 St; in Brooklyn, express between Boro Hall and Franklin Av.

6 Lexington Avenue Local
Uptown to East 177 Street or Pelham Bay Park, The Bronx; downtown to Brooklyn Bridge, Manhattan. Rush hours, the 6 Through Express supplements the 6 Local to Manhattan AM, from Manhattan PM.

42 Street Crosstown-Flushing (IRT)

7 Flushing Local
East on 42 Street to Main Street, Flushing, Queens; west to Times Square, Manhattan. Rush hours, the 7 Flushing Express supplements the 7 Local to Manhattan AM, from Manhattan PM.

8 Avenue (IND)

A 8 Avenue Express
Uptown to 207 Street, Manhattan; downtown to Lefferts Blvd or Far Rockaway, Queens. In Manhattan, express between Canal and 168 Streets; in Brooklyn, express between Hoyt St and Euclid Av.

C 8 Avenue Local
Uptown to 145 Street, Manhattan, with rush hour service extended to Bedford Park Blvd, The Bronx; downtown to Euclid Avenue, Brooklyn, or Rockaway Park, Queens.

E 8 Avenue Local
Uptown and east via 53 Street to Jamaica Center, Queens; west and downtown to World Trade Center, Manhattan. In Queens, the E operates express between Queens Plaza and Jamaica-Van Wyck.

6 Avenue (IND)

B 6 Avenue Express
Uptown to 168 Street, Manhattan; downtown to Coney Island, Brooklyn. In Manhattan, the B operates express between West 4 and 59 Streets. In Brooklyn, it does not stop at DeKalb, and it operates express, Pacific to 36 Streets.

D 6 Avenue Express
Uptown to 205 Street, The Bronx; downtown to Coney Island, Brooklyn. In Manhattan, the D operates express between West 4 Street and 145 Street; rush hours in Upper Manhattan and The Bronx, the D operates express between 145 Street and Fordham Road to Manhattan AM, from Manhattan PM.

F 6 Avenue Local
Uptown and east via 53 Street to 179 Street, Jamaica, Queens; west and downtown to Coney Island, Brooklyn. In Queens, rush hours, express between Queens Plaza and 179 Street; non-rush hours, express, Queens Plaza to 71 Av.

Q 6 Avenue Express
Uptown and east via 63 Street to 21 Street, Queens; west and downtown to Brighton Beach, Brooklyn. In Manhattan, the Q operates express between West 4 Street and 57 Street; in Brooklyn, it operates express between Prospect Park and Sheepshead Bay.

Brooklyn-Queens Crosstown (IND)

G Brooklyn-Queens Local
North and east to 71-Continental Avenues, Forest Hills, Queens; west and south to Smith Street, Brooklyn.

Nassau Street (BMT)

J Nassau Street Local
Uptown and east to Jamaica Center, Queens; west and downtown to Broad Street, Manhattan.
Rush hours to Manhattan AM, from Manhattan PM, the J and Z operate express between Marcy Avenue and Myrtle Avenue in Brooklyn; in Brooklyn and Queens, the J and Z operate as a skip-stop service between Myrtle Avenue and Sutphin Blvd.

M Nassau Street Local
Uptown and east to Metropolitan Avenue, Queens; west and downtown to 9 Avenue, Brooklyn, with rush hour service extended to Bay Parkway. In Brooklyn, the M operates express between Pacific Street and 36 Street.

Z Nassau Street Local
The Z operates rush hours only (see J service); in Manhattan, it skips Bowery.

14 Street Crosstown-Canarsie (BMT)

L Canarsie Local
East via 14 St to Rockaway Parkway, Brooklyn; west to 8 Avenue, Manhattan.

Broadway (BMT)

N Broadway Local
Uptown and east via 60 Street to Ditmars Blvd, Queens; downtown to Coney Island, Brooklyn. In Brooklyn, the N operates express between Pacific Street and 59 Street.

R Broadway Local
Uptown and east via 60 Street to 71-Continental Avenues, Queens; rush hours, extended to 179 Street; west and downtown to 95 Street, Brooklyn.

42 Street Shuttle (IRT)

S 42 Street Shuttle
In Manhattan, east on 42 Street to Grand Central, west to Times Square.

Franklin Avenue Shuttle (BMT)

S Franklin Avenue Shuttle
In Brooklyn, north to Franklin Avenue, south to Prospect Park.

The New York Subway

The subway operates 24 hours a day, seven days a week. With the exception of two stations served by buses late at night, all stations are always served. This map shows weekday service, 6AM–8PM.

The subway system is big – some say the biggest in the world. There are 469 stations, and 714 miles of track in passenger service. There is both local and express service on most routes, complicated by service aberrations. Some lines only operate rush hours, some lines only operate weekdays, and the same line might have a different route and serve different terminals depending on the day or time of day.

Subway lines are identified by numbers or letters, and most are named for their Manhattan trunk line or primary street of operation. Express lines usually operate express only in Manhattan. Local lines are sometimes express in other boroughs.

Local stations are usually within a half mile of each other. Travel time between local stations is less than two minutes.

This map has distorted the city's geography. Congested areas are expanded, less crowded areas are contracted.

In Manhattan there are 20 numbered streets to a mile. The distance between numbered avenues can be over 900 feet. Park Avenue was originally 4th Avenue, and 6th Avenue is officially Avenue of the Americas. Street signs call it 6th Avenue, as does this map. Some Queens street names such as Ely and Bliss disappeared years ago; although still on station signs, they are not on this map.

Subway lines are still colloquially referred to as IRT (Interborough Rapid Transit), BMT (Brooklyn-Manhattan Transit), and IND (INDependent, the first city-owned subway line). Except for the 42nd Street Shuttle, IRT lines are identified by numbers, BMT-IND by letters.

Street to Canarsie, and the Broadway elevated line was extended to Jamaica. Despite rising construction and operating costs Mayor John F. Hylan refused to allow an increase in fares, leading the BRT to fall into bankruptcy between 1918 and 1923, when it was reorganized as the Brooklyn–Manhattan Transit Corporation (BMT).

During the 1920s additional plans were discussed. Some proposed to extend the IRT and BMT networks and others to build an independent system. In 1925 Hylan, who fiercely opposed the private operators, won approval for the Independent Subway System (IND), which added fifty-nine miles (ninety-four kilometers) of routes that were entirely underground except for a short stretch in Brooklyn. Trunk lines built under 6th and 8th avenues in Manhattan had connections to lower Manhattan and across 53rd Street; feeder lines were built to northern Manhattan and under the Grand Concourse and Queens Boulevard. A line was built to Flatbush, another replaced the old Fulton Street elevated line, and one was also built between Brooklyn and Queens (this was the first in the city that did not cross into Manhattan). The IND, which opened its first line in 1932 and its last in 1940, provided faster, more convenient service than other lines to many areas and encouraged development along Queens Boulevard. Between the world wars there was more development in the areas served by the dual-system and independent system lines than in other parts of the city.

The Transport Workers Union (TWU) successfully fought for salary increases and better working conditions from the 1930s. As the IND lines attracted more passengers the financial problems of the BMT and the IRT intensified. The IRT declared bankruptcy in 1932 and in 1940 the city bought the operating rights, equipment, and some properties from the companies, paying $175 million to the IRT and $161.5 million to the BMT; operation of their networks was assumed by the Board of Transportation, which ran the IND. In 1941 the Dyre Avenue railroad line in the Bronx was incorporated into the subway system. The annual number of subway passengers reached 2050 million in 1947 and steadily declined during the following decades. In 1948 the fare was raised to ten cents. The New York City Transit Authority was formed by the State of New York in 1953 to operate the subway and the public bus system. The fare was raised to fifteen cents on 25 July, requiring the introduction of tokens. By this time sections of the subway, some more than fifty years old, had fallen into disrepair because maintenance and capital renewal were inadequately funded. The Transit Authority used the proceeds from the sale of bonds approved in 1951 to replace subway cars and improve the physical plant. This plan had been approved by the voters largely because they assumed that it called for building a subway along 2nd Avenue. In 1956 the subway system absorbed the Rockaway railroad line in Queens.

Led by Michael J. Quill, the TWU went on strike in 1966 after failing to draw up a new contract with Mayor-elect John V. Lindsay. It eventually won wage settlements and provisions for early retirement that inflated the operating costs of the Transit Authority, and in 1966 the fare was raised to twenty cents to compensate for these costs and for the decreasing number of passengers. The Metropolitan Transportation Authority (MTA) took control of the Transit Authority in 1968 and made plans to build lines to northeastern and southeastern Queens and under 2nd Avenue in Manhattan. Ridership continued to decline as people moved to the suburbs and relied on automobiles, and as employment in the city fell by more than 600,000 between 1969 and 1977, by which time the number of riders was fewer than 1000 million for the first time in many years. The system also lost a large amount of revenue to "fare beaters," who entered stations without paying and sometimes inserted into the turnstiles foreign coins that were the same size as tokens, as well as counterfeit tokens known as slugs (a problem that led to the introduction in 1986 of the "bull's eye" token, which could be counterfeited only with great difficulty). To make up for reduced revenues from fares the Transit Authority required increases in its operating subsidies, which eventually covered more than 40 percent of operating costs. The fare was raised successively to thirty cents (1970), thirty-five cents (1972), fifty cents (1975), and sixty cents (1980).

By the 1980s the subway system had become seriously deteriorated. As crime became more common the perception grew that the subways were unsafe. Passengers were also intimidated by graffiti, panhandling, and homelessness. Richard Ravitch, who became chairman of the MTA in 1979, suspended construction of any additional lines and focused on repairing aging facilities and reversing decay. As a result of innovative financial practices and pressure on the state legislature, the Transit Authority saw its annual capital budget for the subways increased from less than $300 million to more than $1000 million. Between 1982 and 1991 nearly $11,000 million was committed to capital improvements. Under this capital program 4168 subway cars were overhauled, as were track, signals, power systems, maintenance facilities, and stations (often with the assistance of Arts for Transit). By the early 1990s all subway cars were air conditioned. The system also bought 1775 new cars (all with air conditioning and surfaces resistant to graffiti). Under David L. Gunn, president of the Transit Authority, the management of the city's subway and bus system improved. An exhaustive effort to combat graffiti began with the removal from service of the most seriously vandalized cars and the protection of subway yards with barbed wire. During the early 1980s the subways again carried more than 1000 million passengers a year, and the number rose with improvements in service. In addition the Transit Police was expanded and improved, and crime on the subways declined. Although subsidies to the MTA rose so did operating costs; the fare was raised to seventy-five cents in 1981, ninety cents in 1984, $1 in 1986, $1.15 in 1990, and $1.25 in 1992.

Subways remain the most important form of transportation for millions of New Yorkers. In 1989 almost 70 percent of those traveling to the central business district of Manhattan from other parts of the city used subways, and the system continues to run twenty-four hours a day throughout the year. The city's rapid transit system is the most extensive in the world, with 714 miles (1142 kilometers) of track along 244 miles (390 kilometers) of routes; the longest line, the "C," has a length of 32.4 miles (52.1 kilometers). The system is also one of the largest in the number of passengers, fifth in the world in 1990, after Moscow, Tokyo, Paris, and Mexico City. In 1990 there were twenty lines, 469 stations, 3006 turnstiles, and 6089 subway cars in use; the average car traveled 29,948 miles (48,186 kilometers) before breaking down. In the same year 87.9 percent of the city's subways ran on time. Portions of three of the original elevated lines remained, all in Brooklyn (along Myrtle Avenue, Broadway, and Franklin Avenue). In the mid 1990s plans were under way to replace subway tokens with electronic fare cards by 1997.

Brian J. Cudahy: *Under the Sidewalks of New York: The Story of the Greatest Subway System in the World* (Brattleboro, Vt.: Stephen Greene, 1979)

Peter Derrick: "The Dual System of Rapid Transit: The Role of Politics and City Planning in the Second Stage of Subway Construction in New York City, 1902 to 1913" (diss., New York University, 1979)

Clifton Hood: *722 Miles: The Building of the Subways and How They Transformed New York* (New York: Simon and Schuster, 1992)

Peter Derrick

Sudanese. Community leaders estimate that about eight thousand Sudanese live in New York City. The first, Mohammad Eisa, arrived in 1942. Sudanese emigration to the United States after that time was steady and gradual, although the causes varied: from 1978 to 1986 many emigrated in order to study; later, as the Sudanese pound rapidly lost value, the reasons were economic. Most Sudanese New Yorkers drive livery cars and taxicabs. Their livery bases are in Brooklyn, at the intersection of Atlantic and Flatbush avenues, and near the Aquarium. Other Sudanese residential and commercial neighborhoods include Coney Island Avenue, Cortelyou Road, and Avenue C. A few Sudanese also live in upper Manhattan. The first local Sudanese organization, the Sudanese American Organization, was formed by the early immigrants and is mainly social. Another organization, the Sudanese Community in New York and New Jersey, gives legal and medical advice to new immigrants, as well as financial assistance to those in need. Although a small number of Sudanese are Christian or nonreligious, most are Muslim. Sudanese Muslims meet other Arabs primarily at the city's mosques and during the two Muslim holidays Eid al-Fitr, at the end of Ramadan, and Eid al-Adha (commemorating Abraham's attempted sacrifice of Isaac), which are usually celebrated in Prospect Park. After several Sudanese were implicated in alleged plans to bomb tunnels and other sites in New York City, the Sudanese were routinely submitted to extraordinary scrutiny and interrogation at Kennedy Airport.

Paula Hajar

Arbuckle's Sugar Company, 1934

sugar. The first sugar refinery in New York City was opened on Liberty Street in 1730 by Nicholas Bayard. Most raw sugar was imported to the colonies from overseas, and the city was soon a center of sugar refining, largely because of the port and the high local demand for sugar. The industry attracted such prominent families as the Livingstons, the Bayards, the Cuylers, the Roosevelts, the Stewarts, and the Van Cortlandts. The Rhinelander family built a sugar refinery near Rose, Duane, and William streets in 1763, and in 1799 the firm of Edmund Seaman and Company began operating the city's first sugar boiler, on Pine Street. William Havemeyer and Frederick C. Havemeyer, former employees of Seaman, opened the refinery of Wm. and F. C. Havemeyer in 1805 on Vandam Street. In 1857 they helped to form Havemeyer, Townsend and Company on South 3rd Street in Williamsburg, where undeveloped land, a deep-water harbor, and abundant cheap labor soon attracted other refineries. After the sugar industry in the Gulf states was destroyed during the Civil War, sugar refining became concentrated in the city, where the port had become the largest in the country, the transportation system was extensive, and banks were numerous. Sugar refining was the city's most profitable manufacturing industry from 1870 until the First World War: 59 percent of the country's imported raw sugar was processed there in 1872 and 68 percent by 1887. In addition to the firms of the Havemeyers several others in the city were successful, among them Wintjen, Dick and Schumacher (led by William Dick, 1823–1912), Dick and Meyer (1872), DeCastro and Donner in Brooklyn (with two refineries), the Greenpoint Sugar Refining Company, and Brooklyn Sugar Refining.

Because of intense competition refineries in the city tried to fix prices in 1882. Their failure to do so led Henry O. Havemeyer in 1887 to form the Sugar Refineries Company (known as the Sugar Trust) to control the price of sugar and the labor pool. The trust consolidated most of the major refiners in Brooklyn, including Havemeyers and Elder, DeCastro and Donner, Brooklyn Sugar Refining, Dick and Meyer, and Moller, Sierck. After being ruled illegal in 1891 by the state supreme court the trust was reorganized by Havemeyer, who incorporated the American Sugar Refining Company in New Jersey and retained headquarters in the city on Wall Street. In 1900 Havemeyer eliminated the little remaining competition in the region by consolidating the surviving refineries in the city into the National Sugar Refining Company of New Jersey. The American Sugar Refining Company was the most important firm of the Sugar Trust, and the loose network of companies controlled by the Havemeyers dominated the American sugar industry, accounting directly and indirectly for 98 percent of national production by 1907. From that year the American Sugar Company engaged in a protracted legal battle with the federal government over its control of the trust, during which its share of the cane market fell from 53 percent to 32 percent. The struggle ended with a settlement in 1922 that allowed the firm to remain intact but forced it to refrain from unfair business practices, and as competition revived, the firm ceased to dominate the industry.

After the Depression the sugar refining industry declined in the city as alternatives to sugar and modern technology were introduced. Most refineries in the area were closed or destroyed by fire. The National Sugar Refining Company maintained its executive offices on Wall Street and became the American Sugar Company in 1963 after merging with Spreckels Sugar Company. Merged with Domino Sugar in 1966, it was renamed Amstar Corporation in 1970. Its sugar-producing subsidiary, Amstar Sugar, opened headquarters in Rockefeller Center in 1972 and was sold to a British firm in 1988; it opened headquarters at 1251 6th Avenue and in 1990 had more than $1000 million in sales, the highest among sugar companies in the United States. In 1992 the firm changed its name to Domino Sugar Corporation. Amstar in the mid 1990s was one of the five hundred largest companies in the country, maintained offices in the city, and made Domino sugar at the original refinery of Havemeyer and Elders (which by this time extended from South 2nd to South 6th streets along Kent Avenue). The red neon Domino sign is one of the best-known sights on the East River in Brooklyn.

Paul A. Vogt: *The Sugar Refining Industry in the United States* (Philadelphia: University of Pennsylvania Press, 1906)

Alfred S. Eichner: *The Emergence of Oligopoly: Sugar Refining as a Case Study* (Baltimore: Johns Hopkins University Press, 1966)

Harry W. Havemeyer: *Merchants of Williamsburgh: Frederick C. Havemeyer, William Dick, John Mollenhauer, Henry O. Havemeyer* (New York: H. W. Havemeyer, 1989)

James Bradley

Sugar Hill. Neighborhood in Manhattan, lying within Harlem and bounded to the north by 155th Street, to the east by Edgecombe Avenue, to the south by 145th Street, and to the west by St. Nicholas Avenue. Named by 1919 for the "sweet life" of its residents, the neighborhood became known as a wealthy area; it also has a working- and middle-class population. During the first half of the twentieth century many prominent figures lived at 409 Edgecombe Avenue, including the poet and literary critic William Stanley Braithwaite and such leaders of the National Association for the Advancement of Colored People as W. E. B. Du Bois, Walter White, Thurgood Marshall, and Roy Wilkins. In the early 1990s residents and former residents requested that the building be designated a landmark.

Thea Arnold

sugar houses. Many sugar houses, also known as sugar bakeries or refineries, were erected in lower Manhattan during the eighteenth century to alleviate the need for New Yorkers to import all their refined sugar from Europe. The first sugar house was built by Nicholas Bayard in 1730, northeast of Old City Hall between Wall and King streets. The sugar houses were known less for their refining than for their later use by the British as prisons for American soldiers during the American Revolution. Livingston's Sugar House, which stood on Liberty Street, is the only documented prison, but it is likely that other sugar houses were also used as prisons during the war, including Cuyler's on Rose Street, later known as Rhinelander's Sugar House. Livingston's and Rhinelander's sugar houses were similar five-story stone buildings, with small windows and low ceilings, not unlike contemporary prisons. Conditions in Livingston's were notoriously bad, and a large number of Americans died in captivity. Many of these soldiers were buried in the graveyard of Trinity Church nearby.

Chad Ludington

Sullivan, Big Tim [Timothy D(aniel)] (*b* New York City, 23 July 1863; *d* New York City, 13 Aug 1913). Political leader. Born at 125 Greenwich Street, he grew up from the age of four in the poor Irish tenements of the Five Points. As an adult he embarked on careers in politics and business, skillfully using each to support the other. With the backing of Tammany Hall he represented the Bowery in the state assembly (1886–93), the state senate (1893–1902, 1908–12), and the U.S. Congress (1902–6). From 1904 he was an owner of the Sullivan–Considine vaudeville circuit, which included the Dewey Theater on 14th Street and the Gotham Theater on 125th Street and by 1907 was a lucrative national chain of more than forty theaters. He was also a business partner of William Fox and Marcus Loew in the incipient nickelodeon business and made successful investments in entertainments at Coney Island, racetracks (including Metropolitan Racetrack near Jamaica), and athletic clubs. After leaving elective office he remained active in politics: with the young reformer Frances Perkins in 1911 he fought successfully to limit to fifty-four hours a week the amount that women could work in factories in New York State, wrote a number of tenement reform bills as well as the so-called Sullivan Law (1911), the state's first effort at gun control, and was a strong supporter of woman suffrage and organized labor. In 1913 he was declared insane, apparently a victim of tertiary syphilis. He was killed by a train while visiting his brother Patrick in Eastchester; his funeral on the Bowery, which drew as many as 75,000 onlookers, was one of the largest in the city's history.

One of the most powerful and colorful figures in the city at the turn of the century, Sullivan assembled a political machine that ruled the districts of lower Manhattan for twenty-five years. He forged an effective style of urban politics by underpinning the traditional tactics of the machine with his influence in the worlds of commercialized leisure and organized crime. At his huge summer "chowders" he staged theatrical entertainments and amateur athletic contests and gave shoes and food to his constituents; he also offered employment, social services, and legal protection to both ordinary citizens and key figures in the flourishing vice economy of the Lower East Side. His methods were controversial: he used physical intimidation to control votes and was accused by the police lieutenant Thomas Byrnes and the Episcopal bishop Henry Codman Potter of having profited from prostitution and gambling. But even his brutish techniques at the ballot box helped to expand the franchise to the poor, the transient, and the homeless, and his considerable fortune (estimated at $2 million at his death) was based on profits from legitimate entertainment enterprises. Sullivan's unique record of legislative achievement in many ways foreshadowed the future direction of the Democratic Party.

Proceedings of the Legislature of the State of New York on the Life, Character and Public Service of Timothy D. Sullivan (Albany, N.Y.: J. B. Lyon, 1914)

Daniel Czitrom: "Underworlds and Underdogs: Big Tim Sullivan and Metropolitan Politics in New York, 1889–1917," *Journal of American History* 78 (1991), 536–58

Daniel Czitrom

Sullivan, Ed(ward Vincent) (*b* New York City, 28 Sept 1901; *d* New York City, 13 Oct 1974). Television host and journalist. Born in Harlem and brought up in Port Chester, New York, he graduated from high school and worked as a sportswriter for the *Port Chester Daily Item*. During the 1920s he reported for several newspapers, including the *New York Evening Mail*, the *Morning Telegraph*, and the *Leader*, and in 1929 he replaced Walter Winchell as the Broadway columnist for the *New York Evening Graphic*. He also worked as a master of ceremonies for a number of vaudeville shows, radio programs, and benefits. During the Second World War he organized shows in Madison Square Garden for the Army Emergency Relief Fund and the American Red Cross. In 1948 the Columbia Broadcasting System (CBS) made him the host of its weekly television variety program "Toast of the Town," which eventually became "The Ed Sullivan Show." For the next twenty-three years the program made him one of the most powerful people in the entertainment business. An astute judge of talent, he introduced to American television such performers as Humphrey Bogart, Jackie Gleason, Maria Callas, Rudolph Nureyev, and the Beatles. He also featured animal acts, magicians, and oddities. In 1959 he led a variety troupe on a tour of the Soviet Union. Sullivan vigorously supported charities and medical causes and spoke out against bigotry and fraud, and he gave national recognition to such black entertainers as Harry Belafonte and Richard Pryor. In honor of his twentieth year in television CBS in 1967 renamed its studio on Broadway and 53rd Street in his honor. Throughout most of his career he and his wife occupied a suite in Delmonico's Hotel at 59th Street and Park Avenue.

Michael David Harris: *Always on Sunday* (New York: Meredith, 1968)

Robert Sanger Steel

Sullivan and Cromwell. Law firm formed in 1879 by the prominent trial lawyer Algernon Sydney Sullivan (1826–87) and William Nelson Cromwell (1854–1948; Columbia Law School 1876). Sullivan developed the firm's litigation practice while Cromwell focused on corporate matters, providing business and financial counseling to such clients as Henry Villard, John H. Flagler, Edward H. Harriman, and J. P. Morgan. The firm also maintained a trust and estates practice and developed an international clientele: Cromwell represented European bankers and was involved in the development of the Panama Canal, and under the leadership of John Foster Dulles (1926–49) and Arthur H. Dean (1949–72) the international side of the firm was further expanded. In addition to its general corporate and financial work the firm focused on antitrust law, taxation, and especially securities. In the 1970s and 1980s it expanded into mergers and acquisitions. Sullivan and Cromwell in the mid 1990s remained one of the largest and most prestigious law firms in the United States; it had 385 lawyers and represented national and multinational businesses and financial organizations, foreign governments, and various other enterprises.

Arthur H. Dean: *William Nelson Cromwell, 1854–1948: An American Pioneer in Corporation, Comparative and International Law* (New York: Ad Press, 1957)

Marilyn Tobias

Sulzberger, Arthur H(ays) (*b* New York City, 12 Sept 1889; *d* New York City, 11 Dec 1968). Newspaper publisher. He attended Columbia University, served in the U.S. Army, and in 1917 married Iphigene Ochs. In the following year he joined the *New York Times*, owned by his father-in-law, Adolph Simon Ochs, and in 1919 he became a vice-president. He was named publisher on Ochs's death in 1935, and in the same year his wife acquired a controlling interest in the newspaper. With the assistance of the general manager, Julius Ochs Adler (Ochs's nephew), he made important changes, naming Anne O'Hare McCormick foreign affairs columnist, modernizing the printing plants, and adding a crossword puzzle and sections on food and fashion. By making a large commitment of money and staff to covering the Second World War at a time when other newspapers were cutting back on the space they devoted to news, he helped the *Times* to maintain its leadership. He retired in 1961. Sulzberger lived at 5 East 80th Street from 1928 until 1952 and then at 1115 5th Avenue to the end of his life.

B. Kimberly Taylor

Sulzer, William (*b* Elizabeth, N.J., 18 March 1863; *d* New York City, 6 Nov 1941). Governor and legislator. A graduate of Columbia University, he practiced law in New York City before his election to the state assembly as a Democrat in 1888. He became the speaker of the assembly in 1893 and in 1894 was elected to the U.S. House of Representatives from the eleventh congressional district of Manhattan (the East Village). During his seventeen years in office he led several important committees and was considered one of the city's most promising politicians. He was elected governor of New York in 1912 with the support of Tammany Hall but remained independent of it, for which he soon encountered determined opposition: after nine months he was removed from office by the state legislature, on the grounds that records of his campaign contributions and expenditures had been falsified. Only weeks after his impeachment he was again elected to the assembly (as an independent). Until the end of his life Sulzer resided at 118 Washington Place and continued to practice law from his office at 115 Broadway.

James Bradley

Summerville. A disused name for the eastern part of OLD PLACE.

Sun. Daily newspaper launched in 1833 by Benjamin Day. It became the first successful "penny paper" in the United States by means of such innovations as street sales by newsboys, steam-powered printing presses, and abstention from party politics. The newspaper's humorous crime reports on the city's Police Court, by George (Washington) Wisner, its coverage of murder trials, and its exploitation of sensational hoaxes soon gave it the highest daily circulation of any newspaper in New York City. After Day sold the *Sun* to Moses Yale Beach in 1838 it became known for its enterprise in using horse expresses and carrier pigeons in the speedy collection of news. It was the circulation leader of all American daily newspapers until the 1850s. In 1852 Moses Sperry Beach became the editor and sole proprietor of the *Sun*, which he sold in 1868 to a syndicate led by Charles A. Dana. Under Dana the newspaper emphasized human interest reporting, independent but largely Republican conservatism, and concise, lively writing. It was celebrated as a school for journalists, who at the beginning of the twentieth century included Julian Ralph, Arthur Brisbane, Jacob A. Riis, and Will Irwin. The editor Francis P. Church wrote the most famous editorial in American journalism in 1897, in response to a letter from an eight-year-old girl, that read in part as follows:

> Yes, Virginia, there is a Santa Claus. He exists as certainly as love and generosity and devotion exist, and you know that they abound and give to our life its highest beauty and joy. Alas how dreary would the world be if there were no Santa Claus . . . There would be no childlike faith then, no poetry, no romance, to make tolerable this existence. . . . The most real things in the world are those that neither children nor men can see.

The newspaper was purchased in 1916 by the publishing magnate Frank Munsey, who eliminated the morning edition. After Munsey's death in 1925 the newspaper's stock was distributed among its employees. In 1950 the *Sun* was absorbed by the *New York World–Telegram*. From about 1911 until its demise the newspaper was published at 280 Broadway, at the corner of Chambers Street, in a famous building that was the original home of A. T. Stewart's first department store.

Frank M. O'Brien: *The Story of the Sun: New York, 1833–1928* (New York: D. Appleton, 1928)

Frank Luther Mott: *American Journalism: A History of Newspapers in the United States through 260 Years, 1690–1950* (New York: Macmillan, 1941; 3rd edn 1962)

Steven H. Jaffe

Sunday schools. The Sunday school movement was begun about 1781 by Robert Raikes in Gloucester, England. At first the aim was not of providing religious instruction but rather the broader one of bettering poor children's lives, and many churches initially opposed Sunday schools because they considered teaching a desecration of the Sabbath. Raikes's efforts became known in New York City, Boston, and Philadelphia, and in 1792 an evening Sunday school for adults was opened on Mulberry Street in Manhattan by Isabella Graham (1742–1814); blacks and whites were welcome there and at Katy Ferguson's School for the Poor in New York City, which was opened in 1793 for children and adults by Catherine Ferguson (*b* ?1749; *d* 1854), a former slave. Gilbert S. Coutant's Sunday school also began in 1793 in what was then Bowery Village. With her daughter Joanna Graham Bethune and her son-in-law Divie Bethune (1771–1824), Graham opened a school in what is now Chinatown in 1803; in 1814 she and her daughter opened a school in Greenwich Village for women and children of all races. On 24 January 1816 a group of women including Joanna Graham Bethune organized the interdenominational Female Union for the Promotion of Sabbath Schools, later known as the New York Female Sunday-School Union. The New York Sunday-School Union was formed under the direction of Eleazer Lord (1788–1871), the clergyman John M. Mason, and the bishop Richard Varick in February 1816; it merged with the New York Female Sunday-School Union in the late 1820s to form the New York Sunday-School Union.

A number of innovations in the curriculum and organization of Sunday schools were made in the city. Advocates there in 1820 urged the formation of a national society, a proposal that was realized when the American Sunday-School Union was organized in Philadelphia in 1824. Because Sunday school teachers were often untrained volunteers, training was offered by the New York Sunday-School Union, which inspired similar efforts by the national union. The New York Sunday-School Union also produced the first uniform system of lessons, a year-long series of Bible verses accompanied by "Judson's Questions," written by Albert Judson in the city and distributed nationally. The system was adopted by the national union in 1872 and explained in the *American Sunday-School Magazine* by John Hall (1829–98), a clergyman in New York City. The national union promoted the establishment of free public schools so that Sunday schools could concentrate exclusively on religious training. By the 1870s it won the endorsement of churches after demonstrating that Sunday school teachings were based on the Bible. Among its supporters were such prominent New Yorkers as Samuel Bradhurst Schieffelin (1811–1900), Robert Lenox Kennedy (1822–87, president 1873–82), and Morris K. Jesup (president 1896–1908). The New York Sunday-School Union was renamed the New York Sunday School Association in 1876 and had an office at 1 Madison Avenue until 1923; the national union had a branch at 156 5th Avenue until 1958.

The Encyclopedia of Sunday Schools and Religious Education (New York: Thomas Nelson and Sons, 1915)

Edwin Wilbur Rice: *The Sunday-School Movement, 1780–1917, and the American Sunday-School Union, 1817–1917* (Philadelphia: American Sunday-School Union, 1917)

Anne M. Boylan: *Sunday School: The Formation of an*

American Institution, 1790–1880 (New Haven: Yale University Press, 1988)

Alana J. Erickson

Sunnyside (i). Neighborhood in northwestern Queens, lying within Long Island City and bounded to the north by the Sunnyside Yards, to the east by Calvary Cemetery and 51st Street, to the south by the Long Island Expressway, and to the west by Van Dam Street. The area is named for a roadhouse built on Jackson Avenue to accommodate visitors to the Fashion Race Course in Corona during the 1850s and 1860s. South of Jackson Avenue the Fitting, Gosman, Heiser, Lowery, and Van Buren families owned farms that were eventually subdivided in the 1880s and 1890s. A small hamlet was built between Northern and Queens boulevards and became known as Sunnyside. The Pennsylvania Railroad in 1901 adopted a plan to lay out a large railroad yard nearby, connected by tunnels to Manhattan. Most of the land was low-lying and boggy and therefore cheap; from 1902 to 1905 agents of the railroad gradually bought up all the land south of Northern Boulevard between 21st and 43rd streets. The entire area was leveled and the swamps filled in between 1907 and 1908, and the yards opened in November 1910. The remaining land south of Skillman Avenue was dry but uninhabited. The Queensboro Bridge opened in 1909 and from it was built Queens Boulevard, which ran to the center of the borough through Sunnyside, where streets were built along the boulevard. The population grew after the elevated line opened in 1917, and apartment buildings and rows of attached houses were erected in 1921–22. Sunnyside Gardens (1924–29), a complex of attached houses of two and a half stories, with front and rear gardens and a landscaped central court, was one of the nation's first planned communities, hailed for its innovative design by such scholars of urban life as Lewis Mumford (a onetime resident). During the following years the neighborhood became middle class and lower middle class, and largely Irish. In the 1940s and 1950s its large apartments enticed many artists and writers and their families to leave their cramped quarters in lower Manhattan, and the area became known as the "maternity ward of Greenwich Village." Sunnyside during the 1980s attracted immigrants from Korea, Colombia, Romania, and China, though on the whole fewer immigrants than some of the surrounding neighborhoods in northeastern Queens. The Sunnyside Railyards are used by the Long Island Rail Road, Conrail, and Amtrak. The Knickerbocker Laundry nearby is a striking example of art moderne architecture.

Vincent Seyfried

Sunnyside (ii). Neighborhood in northeastern Staten Island (1990 pop. 12,000), bounded to the north by Clove Lakes Park and Silver Lake Park, to the east by Grymes Hill and Fox Hills, and to the west by Castleton Corners. The name is derived from that of a boarding house that stood from 1889 on Clove Road at what is now Richmond Turnpike. Maps from the time of the American Revolution identify houses that may date to 1690. By the 1840s the area had elaborate houses and gardens, including those of the Vanderbilts. Ice harvesting and the pumping of spring water were important activities in the nineteenth century. The Solheim Swedish Home for the Aged was built in the neighborhood in 1909. In the following decades the intersection of Clove Road and Victory Boulevard became busy and congested, in part because of traffic generated by Wagner College and the College of Staten Island. Two large apartment buildings called the Fountains were built (1968), as was a facility of the Health Insurance Plan nearby (1988). The neighborhood was disrupted from the mid 1970s as water mains and sewerage were installed to replace a system of artesian wells and natural drainage. Sunnyside is often cited as an examplar of the change of Staten Island from an area of goat farms, trolleys, marshes, and two-laned roads to one of houses on small plots and busy traffic. Clove Lake Park remains one of the finest open spaces in the city.

Dorothy Valentine Smith: *Staten Island: Gateway to New York* (Philadelphia: Chilton, 1970), 111–21
John E. Hurley: "Lifestyle: Sunnyside," *Staten Island Advance*, 11 Dec 1989, §B, pp. 1–2

Howard Weiner

Sunnyside Gardens. A planned community in northwestern Queens, bounded to the north by 43rd Street and to the south by 51st Street; it covers seventy-seven acres (thirty hectares) and about sixteen blocks. Often called the "garden community," it was built between 1924 and 1929 for low- and middle-income families under the direction of Clarence S. Stein and Henry Wright, who designed it according to ideals of "health, open space, greenery, and idyllic community living for all." One-, two-, and three-family attached brick houses with slate roofs, gables, porches, and garages were constructed around open center-courts with tree-lined pathways and private and communal flower gardens designed by Marjorie Cautley, one of the first women landscape architects in the country. The development lay at a convenient distance from Manhattan and gave many residents their first opportunity to own a home. The Sunnyside Gardens Conservancy was formed in 1981 to restore the neighborhood to its original graciousness. Well-known residents have included the architectural critic Lewis Mumford, the painter Raphael Soyer, the entertainers Rudy Vallee, Perry Como, and Judy Holliday, and the jazz musician Bix Beiderbecke. Sunnyside Gardens has about fifteen hundred houses and a private park and is listed on the National Register of Historic Places.

Patricia A. Doyal

Sunset Hill. Neighborhood in northeastern Staten Island, bounded to the north by West Brighton, to the east by Silver Lake, to the south by Bard Avenue, and to the west by Clove Road. The area was part of West New Brighton until the 1920s, when its streets were laid out in a grid and it was given its present name. The Tyler–Gardiner mansion (*ca* 1840), a landmark, was the home during the Civil War of Julia Gardiner, widow of President John Tyler; according to local reports youths tore town a Confederate flag that she displayed in the yard. The population is upper middle class, the housing consists of one-family houses, and there is shopping on Forest Avenue.

Marjorie Johnson

Sunset Park. Neighborhood in southwestern Brooklyn. Until the 1960s the northern section was considered part of Gowanus and the southern section part of Bay Ridge; the area was renamed in the late 1960s for a local park built by the city in the 1890s. Development began in the 1830s and Green-Wood Cemetery was laid out in 1839 as one of the first rural cemeteries in the nation. Many Irish immigrants settled in the area during the 1840s. Improvements in transport spurred development in a section south of 36th Street, leading to industrial growth. After 1870 brick and brownstone row houses replaced wood houses. Polish, Norwegian, and Finnish immigrants settled in the area during the 1880s and 1890s, followed at the turn of the century by Italians, many of whom worked along the docks. Bush Terminal, a complex of piers, warehouses, and factory lofts, was built by Irving T. Bush in 1890, and industry expanded immensely during the early twentieth century. The Brooklyn Army Terminal was built in 1919. By the 1930s and 1940s several factors contributed to the decline of the neighborhood: the Depression, the cessation of the 3rd Avenue elevated line, and the construction (1941) and widening of the Gowanus Expressway, which separated the industrial sections of the neighborhood from its residential sections. After the Second World War many white residents moved to the suburbs, and many Puerto Ricans moved in and found work on the waterfront and in factories. Decline worsened from the 1950s to the 1970s: corruption in the Federal Housing Administration in the 1950s led to the abandonment of homes, the maritime industry moved to New Jersey, and the Brooklyn Army Terminal was deactivated in the 1970s. With local, state, and federal aid the local economy improved in the 1970s, and the 1980s saw a commercial revival and an influx of immigrants from Latin America, China, and the rest of Asia; many Chinese settled along 8th Avenue, which became known as the third Chinatown of New York City. A large number of new immigrants settled in the neighborhood in the 1980s: one quarter were from China, with roughly an equal number from the Dominican Republic, and smaller numbers from Guyana, Ecuador, India, Vietnam, Colombia, Jordan, and Poland. The Brooklyn Army Terminal reopened as a light industrial center in 1987, and Bush Terminal was converted into an industrial park. Businesses owned by Latin Americans between 35th Street and 60th Street along 5th Avenue include bodegas, restaurants, and stores selling clothing, records, and jewelry.

Ellen Marie Snyder-Grenier

SUNY. See STATE UNIVERSITY OF NEW YORK.

surfing. Surfing in New York City was practiced in 1912 by Duke Kahanamoku of Hawaii, winner of a gold medal in swimming at the Olympic Games, and Joe Ruddy of Rockaway, also the winner of an Olympic medal. Surfing was made popular by the local lifeguard Mickey McManamon in the 1950s, as well as by the singing group the Beach Boys and the film *Endless Summer.* By the mid 1960s surfers could be found throughout the Rockaways. Their favorite spots were 92nd Street (also known as "Chicken Bone Beach"), 111th Street, and 72nd Street, where in 1968 surfers protested a ban on the sport at local beaches. Although the ban was lifted, demands that a beach be designated for surfing went unfulfilled. Among the early surfboard builders was Tony Micheals, who produced surfboards in the back room of his father's garment factory. In the early 1980s Tom Sena of the Rockaway Beach Surf Shop began manufacturing and selling surfing equipment of high quality.

Peter Maguire

Surrogate's Court. Municipal building at 31 Chambers Street in Manhattan. Designed in an eclectic French Renaissance style by John R. Thomas, it was built in 1899–1911 and originally known as the Hall of Records. The granite building houses the city archives in addition to the Surrogate's Court and is an impressive monument to civic virtue. The interior lobby, finished in Siena marble, emulates the foyer of Jean-Louis Garnier's Opéra in Paris; the courtrooms on the fifth floor are finished in English oak and mahogany. In 1963 the building took its current name. The exterior was designated a landmark in 1966, the interior in 1976.

Brooke J. Barr

Survey Associates. Publisher for charitable causes. It began as the National Publication Committee of the Charity Organization Society in 1891. During the same year it launched *Charities Review* (soon renamed *Charities*), a journal that eventually merged with the publications *Commons*, which issued reports about settlement house activities, and *Jewish Charity* to form *Charities and the Commons*; Paul U. Kellogg (1879–1958) became the editor in 1909. Inspired by his work in cataloguing social conditions for the Pittsburgh Survey, he renamed the journal the *Survey* and with his brother Arthur Kellogg (1878–1934) made it and its illustrated companion *Survey Graphic* the most influential publications of their kind. The organization took its current name after becoming independent of the Charity Organization Society in 1912. Survey Associates published reports about housing, recreation, renewal, and industrial conditions in the city before ceasing operations in 1952.

Alana J. Erickson

Sutton, Willie [William Francis, Jr.] (*b* Brooklyn, 30 June 1901; *d* Spring Hill, Fla., 2 Nov 1980). Bank robber. He began robbing banks in 1927 and was soon nicknamed "the actor" because of the elaborate costumes and disguises that he used. He escaped from prison in 1932 and again in 1948. In 1952 he was recognized on a subway in New York City and sentenced to seventeen years in prison for stealing $64,000 from a bank in Queens. He was paroled from the Attica State Correctional Facility in 1967. Sutton was often quoted for having explained that he robbed banks because "that's where the money is." It is estimated that his thefts amounted to $2 million.

Melissa M. Merritt

Sutton Place. Neighborhood on the East Side of Manhattan, lying along York Avenue between 53rd and 59th streets. It is named after Effingham B. Sutton, the entrepreneur who developed the area about 1875. Before the First World War the area was covered by tenements, run-down brownstones, and a brewery. It was perhaps most famous as the home of the gang known widely through films as the Dead End Kids, but after Mrs. William K. Vanderbilt and Anne Morgan moved there in 1920 the neighborhood was gradually transformed into a secluded cluster of expensive private houses and exclusive apartment buildings; its success led to the development of other expensive residential enclaves along the East River at Beekman Place and East End Avenue. The buildings along the east side of the neighborhood are built over the FDR Drive, which runs under the two apartment buildings between 54rd and 56th streets and under a townhouse at 58th Street. Residents from 56th Street to 59th Street have access to landscaped backyards built on the drive by the city as compensation for the loss of access to the river occasioned by the construction of the drive; three vest pocket parks lie between these private yards at the ends of 56th, 57th, and 58th streets.

Owen D. Gutfreund

Swamp. An area in lower Manhattan encompassing Gold, Frankfort, Pearl, Water, and Ferry streets. It became the site of the city's first tanning pits during colonial times and was soon the center of the city's leather industry, which was attracted by the fresh water that flowed into the area from the Collect and by the proximity of the district to the docks along the East River. Although the pond was covered over by 1811, the Swamp remained the site of the city's leather district.

Frank W. Norcross: *A History of the New York Swamp* (New York: Chiswick, 1901)

Lucius F. Ellsworth: *Craft to National Industry in the Nineteenth Century: A Case Study of the Transformation of the New York State Tanning Industry* (New York: Arno, 1975)

Richard C. Wiles

SWE. See SOCIETY OF WOMEN ENGINEERS.

Swedenborgians. The members of the Church of the New Jerusalem (or New Church) are Christians who follow the teachings of the Swedish scientist and mystic Emmanuel Swedenborg (1688–1772); they share his vision of Heaven and Hell and his assertion that a spiritual "last judgment" took place in 1757. After congregations were formed in England, Joseph Russell, an English immigrant, organized a branch in New York City in 1792. Swedenborgianism was avidly promoted in 1795–96 by the Anglican clergyman William Hill, who refused to break with the Anglican church. A group formed in 1805 by Edward Riley, who settled in the city after emigrating from England, met at 16 Chambers Street before moving to larger quarters on James Street in 1807. Among its members were the bookseller James Chesterman and the poet Samuel Woodworth. In 1816 the city's first affiliated Swedenborgian church, the Association of the City of New York for the Dissemination of the Doctrines of the New Jerusalem Church, was formed by twenty-six men including Chesterman, who became the treasurer, and Woodworth, who became the secretary. The church met at the Mount Vernon School on Broadway until 1821, when it bought a large building on Pearl Street. One of the first mystical sects that flourished in the United States, the church attracted many intellectuals during the first half of the nineteenth century, and was closely connected with such movements as mesmerism, transcendentalism, and spiritualism. In 1838 a schism reduced the congregation to a small group that sold the building on Pearl Street and held services at the Lyceum on Broadway near Prince Street.

The church attracted new members after George Bush, a professor of philosophy at New York University, gave lectures throughout the city and became the pastor in 1847. A larger building was erected on three plots of land at 112 East 35th Street, bequeathed to the church by Chesterman; the church was dedicated in 1859 and became highly influential during the next century. Among those who attended were the editor and writer John Bigelow, Henry James (father of the writer), the statesman William H. Seward, and the writer and lecturer Helen Keller. By 1932 the building was enlarged and the church offered Sunday services, a monthly lecture series, and a Sunday school. During the 1950s there were about 160 members and seventy-five students enrolled in the school. By the early 1990s the Church of the New Jerusalem had declined to about thirty-six active members.

Marguerite Beck Block: *The New Church in the New World: A Study of Swedenborgianism* (New York: Henry Holt, 1932)

Robert Ellwood

Swedes. The first known person of Swedish ancestry in New York City was Jonas Bronck, who was born in Copenhagen to Swedish parents and settled in 1639 in what is now the Bronx. Mons Pieterson, a Swede or Swedish-speaking Finn, helped to lay out Harlem, which was cleared in 1661 by a group of settlers that included Swedes. During English rule few Swedes moved to the city and most settled in Manhattan. They numbered about a hundred in 1835, and in 1836 the country's first Scandinavian mutual aid society, Svenska Societen, was formed with twenty-two members. Swedes and other Scandinavians took part in religious services at the Bethel Ship (1845), a German Lutheran church aboard a German ship moored at Pier 11 at the foot of Liberty Street on the Hudson River; the church remained under the leadership of Olof Gustaf Hedstrom (1803–77) for thirty years and received financial assistance from Jenny Lind when she visited New York City in 1850. The first Swedish newspaper in the country, *Skandinaven*, was published from 1851 to 1853 by Anders Gustaf Obom (1812–81), also known as Napoleon Berger. Land shortages and compulsory military service in Sweden at mid century led many Swedes to emigrate. Thousands passed through the city before settling elsewhere in the United States; those who remained were often merchants, carpenters, and longshoremen, among them John Ericsson and a crew that included six other Swedes who built the ironclad warship the *Monitor* at a private yard in Greenpoint.

Between 1860 and 1870 the city's Swedish population rose from about eight hundred to three thousand, and Swedish enclaves developed on the East Side and what is now Cobble Hill in Brooklyn. Gustavus Adolphus Church, the city's first Swedish Lutheran church, opened in 1865 at 155 East 22nd Street. In 1872 the Immanuel Swedish Methodist Episcopal Church was formed on Dean Street near 5th Avenue in Brooklyn by members of the Bethel Ship congregation, and eventually Swedish Congregational and Baptist churches followed. The Swedish-language weekly newspaper *Nordstjernan* (The North Star) began publication in 1872 from offices at 108 Park Row; it later moved to 4 West 22nd Street. The Swedish–American Athletic Society of Brooklyn was organized during the 1880s at 267 6th Avenue and lasted until 1974. Among the Swedish singing groups in Brooklyn were the Lyran Singing Society of Brooklyn (143 West 44th Street) and the Swedish Glee Club (142 Schermerhorn Street), which remained well known into the 1930s. Many Swedes worked on the Brooklyn Bridge and after 1900 in the Brooklyn Navy Yard, where they were supervised by Carl J. Mellin, a Swedish engineer. They formed the American Society of Swedish Engineers (1888), which established the annual John Ericsson Award, and the children of Swedish immigrants often became engineers and building contractors. Women found work as domestic servants. Among the social welfare organizations formed toward the end of the century were the Swedish Aid Society of New York (1891–1906), which had offices in Brooklyn and Manhattan and found employment for twenty thousand Swedes, and the Kallman Home for Children in Brooklyn (1898–1964). Periodicals included the socialist weekly newspaper *Arbetaren* (1896–1928) and the magazine *Valkyrian* (1897–1909).

In 1900 there were 28,320 Swedes in the city, including 14,695 in Brooklyn and 10,936 in Manhattan. Several institutions were opened in the early twentieth century, among them the Scandinavian Young Women's Home (Fridhem) at 149 Portland Avenue in Brooklyn (1902–50), the Swedish Hospital on Rogers Avenue in Brooklyn (24 June 1906, moved to 1350 Bedford Avenue about 1940, closed in 1979), and the Swedish Augustana Home for the Aged (1908–61) at 1680 60th Street in Brooklyn. The Swedish Chamber of Commerce of the USA (1907) set up offices at Rockefeller Center and published the *American Swedish Monthly*; the United Swedish Societies of Greater New York (138 3rd Avenue in Manhattan) was formed in 1911 to promote awareness of Swedish heritage; and the American Scandinavian Foundation (1911; 127 East 73rd Street in Manhattan) included among its founders Emil F. Johnson (1864–1953), a public health inspector who devised a means of controlling the quality of the city's milk supply, and published the *American Scandinavian Review*, a literary quarterly journal. The cartographer Andrew G. Hagstrom (1890–1957) settled in the city in 1909 and opened a mapmaking business in 1916 that soon became widely known.

In 1930 there were 37,200 Swedish immigrants and 24,500 of their children in the city. Most lived in Sunset Park, southern Brooklyn near Hamilton Avenue, and Bay Ridge, some in the northern Bronx, Forest Hills Gardens, and Sunnyside Gardens, and about a quarter in Manhattan. During the following years the number of Swedish immigrants declined as the Swedish economy improved, and few children of immigrants remained in Swedish neighborhoods. In 1980 about three thousand Swedish immigrants lived in the city, which had the country's second-largest concentration of Swedish–Americans, after Chicago. The Swedish Seamen's Church, at 5 East 48th Street, remained in operation into the 1990s. Well-known Swedes in New York City have included the merchant and banker Svante Magnus Svensson (later Swenson; 1816–96), John A. Johnson (1865–1938), who with his sons operated a construction company that built two-family houses and apartment buildings in Bay Ridge, David L. Lindquist (1874–1944), who helped the Otis Elevator Company to develop its first modern elevator, the tenor Jussi Björling (1911–60), who performed regularly at the Metropolitan Opera for twenty-two years, and the actress Greta Garbo, who lived on East 52nd Street until her death.

Alana J. Erickson

swimming. Swimming became a popular recreation in New York City during the nineteenth century, owing largely to the crowded, unsanitary conditions of tenement housing. As early as 1817 two private marine baths were anchored off the Battery. After the Civil War concern about public health and sanitation mounted and municipal funding was set aside for swimming and bathing facilities. Fifteen free-floating baths were installed in the Hudson and East rivers in Manhattan, Brooklyn, and the Bronx between 1890 and 1910, and dozens of public bathhouses were built by 1912. The Coney Island Polar Bear Club was formed in 1903 by the fitness enthusiast Bernarr Macfadden: its members began a long-running tradition of swimming in the ocean on the coldest days of the year. The many accidents suffered by swimmers off the piers led bathhouses to open swimming facilities and offer swimming lessons during the early twentieth century. Indoor pools could be built throughout the city after the Croton Aqueduct was completed in 1842, and the opening of the subways provided access to Coney Island and the Rockaways. Between 1900 and 1925 swimming was refined as a competitive sport, and such organizations as the New York Athletic Club and the New York Women's Swimming Association assembled large swim teams. Some of the first world records were set by swimmers from the city, including Charles M. Daniels (1907), Gertrude Ederle (1922, 1925), Walter Spence (1926), and Eleanor Holm (1932). During the Depression the parks commissioner Robert Moses used money from the Works Progress Administration to build ten public outdoor swimming pools and two public beaches. In 1936 the Astoria Pool in Queens was the site of the swimming and diving trials for the Olympic Games in Berlin. The New York State Marine Amphitheatre, a facility with div-

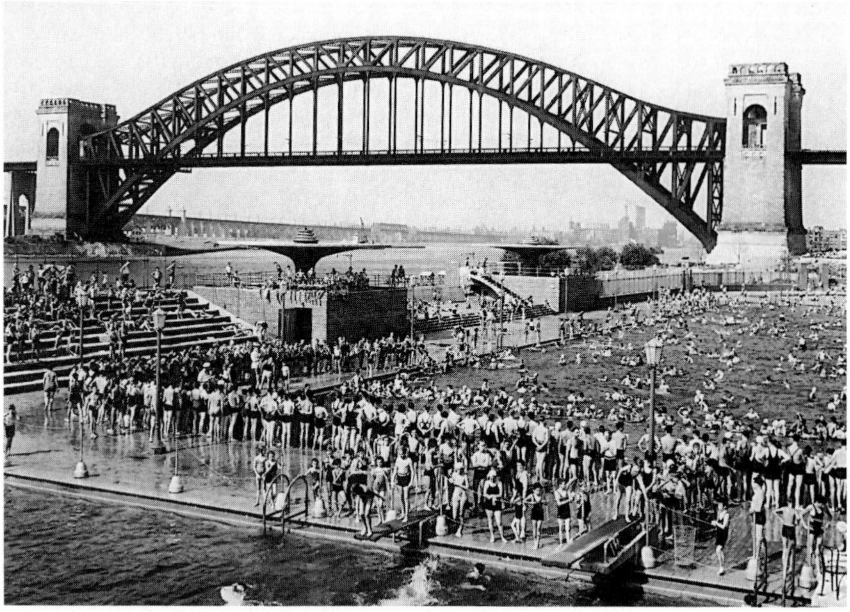

Astoria Pool, ca 1940. Background *Hell Gate Bridge*

ing towers seventy-five feet (twenty-three meters) tall, was built for the World's Fair of 1939–40; it was later renamed the Gertrude Ederle Pool.

A number of long-distance swimmers have swum great distances in the waters of New York City. Byron Sommers in 1927 swam around Manhattan Island, a distance of twenty-eight miles (forty-five kilometers), in eight hours and fifty-six minutes, a record that stood until Diana Nyad completed the swim in seven hours and fifty-seven minutes in 1975. In 1961 Palmer Donnelly became the first person to swim around Staten Island, in twenty-five hours; he repeated his feat in 1979. The swim around Manhattan became a more popular event in the 1980s, and some swimmers completed a double swim around the island (Julie Ridge in 1983) and even a triple swim (Stacy Chanin in 1984). In 1988 Skip Storch set a distance record by swimming 153 miles (246 kilometers) down the Hudson River from Albany, New York, to the Statue of Liberty.

Ann L. Buttenwieser: "Awash in New York: A Chronicle of the City's Floating Baths," *Seaport Magazine* 18 (1984), 12–19

Amanda Aaron

Swinburne Island. A man-made island off the eastern shore of Staten Island. It has an area of two and a half acres (one hectare) and is named for John Swinburne, who oversaw its construction. The island once housed a small hospital that treated arriving immigrants, as well as a crematorium. Now disused, it is part of the Gateway National Recreation Area and is inhabited by colonies of sea birds.

Gerard R. Wolfe

Swingline. Firm of staple and stapler manufacturers, formed in 1925 on the Lower East Side by Jack Linsky as the Parrot Speed Fastener Company. In the late 1920s it began manufacturing staples that were glued together in rows (known as "frozen wire staples"), an innovation at a time when staples were still being inserted into a stapler one at a time or held together with sheet metal. Eventually the firm also introduced the first anti-jam stapler, the Tot 50 automatic stapler, which sold more than 100 million units, and electronic staplers, and became a leader in the cartridge stapling technology used in electronic copiers. In 1991 it became part of Acco USA, a manufacturer of office products and supplies based in Wheeling, Illinois. Swingline is the largest manufacturer of staples and staplers in the world. Its facility in Long Island City is topped with an enormous neon sign that is clearly visible from Shea Stadium.

Rich Scheinin

Swing Street. A popular nickname in the 1930s and 1940s for 52ND STREET between 5th and 6th avenues, the site of many jazz clubs.

Swinton, John (*b* Edinburgh, 12 Dec 1829; *d* Brooklyn, 1901). Labor activist and editor. With only a modest formal education and an apprenticeship as a printer, he emigrated to Canada in 1843 and in 1850 arrived in New York City; there he worked as a printer and briefly attended New York Medical College. By the mid 1850s his participation in the abolitionist movement drew him to Kansas, where in 1857 he joined John Brown's raid at Osawatomie. On returning to New York City he worked successively for the *New York Times* (chief of the editorial staff, 1860–70) and the *Sun* (1870–75; chief editorial writer, 1875–83). During most of this time he lived at 124 East 38th Street. His career as a labor activist began in January 1874, when he witnessed the Tompkins Square Riot, in which unemployed workingmen who had gathered at a peaceful rally were attacked and beaten by the city's police. That autumn he was the unsuccessful mayoral candidate of the Socialist Labor Party, and he became a regular speaker at labor rallies. In October 1883 he began his own weekly labor organ, *John Swinton's Paper*, published at 21 Park Row and widely recognized as the finest publication of its kind. Eschewing all ideological labels and refusing to confine himself to any one movement, Swinton called on the nation's workers to work together for democratically achieved economic and social justice in the face of growing corporate power. His newspaper was particularly influential in Henry George's mayoral campaign of 1886. In 1887 he ceased publishing the newspaper because of financial difficulties and ran for the state senate with the endorsement of the Progressive Labor Party. He rejoined the editorial staff of the *Sun*, where in spite of going blind in 1889 he worked until his death. Swinton's published writings include *John Swinton's Travels* (1880) and *Striking for Life* (1894).

Frank T. Reuter: "John Swinton's Paper," *Labor History* 1 (1960)

Marc Ross: "John Swinton, Journalist and Reformer: The Active Years, 1857–1887" (diss., New York University, 1969)

Sender Garlin: *Three American Radicals* (Boulder, Colo.: Westview, 1991)

Edward O'Donnell

Swope, Herbert Bayard (*b* St. Louis, 5 Jan 1882; *d* New York City, 20 June 1958). Journalist. As a reporter for the *New York World* in 1912 he investigated police corruption and helped to implicate Lieutenant Charles Becker in the murder of the gambler Herman Rosenthal. He became the city editor in 1916, and in the following year filed reports from Germany that won him the first Pulitzer Prize for reporting. As the executive editor of the *World* (1920–29) he developed the feature later known as the "op-ed" page and led sensational crusades against local slumlords and the Ku Klux Klan. Under his direction the *World* was known for its public-spirited liberalism, support of the progressive elements in the Democratic Party, and often dramatic investigative reporting.

Alfred Allen Lewis: *Man of the World: Herbert Bayard Swope: A Charmed Life of Pulitzer Prizes, Poker, and Politics* (New York: Bobbs–Merrill, 1978)

Steven H. Jaffe

Sylvia's. Restaurant at 328 Lenox Avenue in Harlem, between 126th and 127th Streets. Opened on 1 August 1962, it is the most renowned soul-food restaurant in New York City. Over the years it added a second dining room, as well as an outdoor patio that is open during the warmer months.

Kenneth T. Jackson

Syrians and Lebanese. For centuries what are now Syria and Lebanon were part of the same Ottoman province of Greater Syria. At the end of the First World War, after the empire collapsed, the French and the British created separate Lebanese, Syrian, and Palestinian political entities under French and British mandate, thus ending the common history of the Lebanese and Syrians. Immigrants from what became Lebanon nevertheless continued to identify themselves as Syrian into the 1950s.

An influx of emigrants from Greater Syria to New York City began in the 1870s, and perhaps fifteen thousand Syrian-born immigrants and their American-born children lived in the city by 1924, when the U.S. Congress imposed immigration quotas of one hundred persons a year on many countries. Among the reasons often cited for Syrian emigration are economic hardship, inspiration from American missionaries and educators, wanderlust, family competition, and Ottoman conscription. Those who emigrated were mostly Christian villagers from Mount Lebanon, but a large minority were from the cities of Tripoli, Zahle, Aleppo, Damascus, Homs, and Haifa. They first settled around Rector and Washington streets in lower Manhattan, an area that became known as Little Syria. They were displaced in 1940 by the construction of the Brooklyn–Battery Tunnel. At the time Atlantic Avenue in Brooklyn had already been drawing Syrians and their businesses for decades, and a stretch of the avenue from Court Street to the water became the new heart of the community. Later Syrians moved to Park Slope and Bay Ridge, but the heart of the city's Arab community continued to be Atlantic Avenue, the site of old and new Arabic shops and restaurants and of Rashid Sales, the preeminent distribution center for Arabic music and videotapes in the United States.

Many of the early Syrian immigrants began as peddlers and soon accumulated enough capital to establish their own businesses, 383 of which were listed in the Syrian Business Directory of 1908. Most were near Washington Street; included were groceries, import–export firms (which often dealt in Madeira lace and Oriental rugs), and factories producing lingerie, kimonos, and other dry goods. These businesses were largely family run, employed local Syrians, and supplied peddlers and Syrian businesses throughout the nation; the Bardwil, Haddad, Barsa, Tadross, and Trabulsi families were among the most prominent in the business. By the 1920s some "merchant princes" had factories in South America and the Far East. Only a handful of the Syrian dry-goods businesses remained by the 1990s, many third-generation Syrians having abandoned the family firms either to work in other firms or to enter the professions. In the mid 1990s about 40 percent of the members of Salaam Club, the Syrian businessmen's fraternity founded in the early 1940s, worked in the professions.

The early immigrants identified primarily with their religious sects but nonetheless formed many nonsectarian organizations such as the Syrian Ladies Aid Society (1907), the Damascus Masonic Lodge (1908), and the Syrian Young Men's Association (1934), all of which continued to operate into the 1990s. Among the early leaders of the community were the Syrian physician Rizq George Haddad and the philanthropist Salim Malouk (1878–1940), a linen importer who had a shop on 5th Avenue. One beneficiary of Malouk's generosity was al-Rabitah al-Qalamiyya (the Pen League; formed 1920), a group of Syrian émigré writers led by Khalil Gibran and Amin Rihani; its members' experiments with Western literary forms revolutionized Arabic poetry in the Arab world. From the turn of the century until the 1960s the Syrian–Lebanese community in New York City was the largest and most important Arabic-speaking community in the United States, with an economic, literary, and cultural influence that extended throughout the hemisphere and back to the Arab world. Between 1890 and 1940 Syrians in the city published fifty-one Arabic-language periodicals (two thirds of the country's total). The most influential of these was *Al-Hoda* (The Guidance), launched in 1898 by Naoum Mokarzel, who with his brother Salloum Mokarzel counseled the community on assimilation and championed Arab independence abroad. Readership of Arabic-language newspapers declined in the 1930s, primarily because the younger, American-born generation did not learn to read Arabic and because of the freeze on immigration.

The first Syrian immigrants suffered less from overt ethnic prejudice than from American ignorance of the Middle East, for example the beliefs that all Arabs were Muslim and that Syrian churches were not authentically Christian. Syrians responded to prejudice not with protest but by concentrating on acculturation; a rare example of activism was a case brought in 1914, *Dow v. United States* (226 F. 145), which established Syrian eligibility for American citizenship. By the 1940s Syrians were becoming part of the American mainstream, as evidenced by the abandonment of arranged marriages, the employment of women outside the home and outside the family business, and growing aspirations to higher education. A large number were joining American churches or modifying their own Eastern rites, and 80 percent of the third generation of Syrian–Americans in New York City were marrying non-Syrians.

The group was fast becoming invisible. While other groups in the 1970s were advertising their origins, most third-generation Syrians were keeping their ethnicity private, their unusually strong family ties being one of their few distinctions. But Syrian and Lebanese culture continued to be expressed in *haflis*, large parties featuring Arabic dancing and performances by such musicians as the singers Hanan and Kahraman, and by Eddie Kochak, originator of the Ameraba (American Arabic) style of music. Kochak began a long-running career as a featured musician at the Atlantic Antic, an annual street festival on Atlantic Avenue in Brooklyn.

A new influx began when the immigration quotas were lifted in 1965. More likely to be drawn from the professional classes than their turn-of-the-century forerunners and their contemporaries from other Arab countries, the new immigrants settled in such established Syrian neighborhoods as Bay Ridge. By the 1990s the Brooklyn Medical Association had 150 Syrian doctors among its members, many of them recent immigrants. Immigration from Lebanon resumed in earnest after the Lebanese civil war broke out in 1975, and continued until 1990. Many of the immigrants intended to return to Lebanon when peace was restored; others had gone to the United States to stay. They settled in Manhattan (which especially drew young professionals) and Bay Ridge and worked in engineering, computers, and banking, once an important sector of the economy in Beirut. In 1983 the Lebanese immigrant Joe Audi opened a branch of Bank Audi at 5th Avenue and 48th Street. Some Lebanese New Yorkers are linked by active alumni chapters of the American University of Beirut and Beirut University College, and many continue to work toward the reconstruction of Lebanon: a local group called the Friends of Lebanon promotes the study of Lebanese culture, and LEBNET, a computer network formed with the help of a Lebanese student at Columbia University, has two hundred members who use it to discuss the rebuilding of a pluralistic Lebanon.

Although they have reinvigorated Arabic churches and neighborhoods, the new immigrants have had little interaction with the American-born Syrian–Lebanese: contact has been mainly limited to haflis and church. One institution that has bridged the two groups is the St. Nicholas Home for the Aged, a nonsectarian facility opened in 1982 on Ovington Avenue in Bay Ridge by descendants of the first Syrian–Lebanese immigrants. Its board represents the spectrum of religious and national groups among the city's Arabs.

In the 1980s new national organizations such as the American Arab Anti-Discrimination Committee (ADC) began to warn the Syrian–Lebanese about the dangers of anti-Arab racism and the need for grassroots organizing, and a chapter was organized in New York City. Most members of long-established immigrant families left participation and lobbying to newcomers, although even the American-born were roused to anger and found their ethnic consciousness heightened by the Israeli invasion of Lebanon in 1982.

Syrian Jews began arriving in New York City at the beginning of the twentieth century, from Damascus, Homs, and especially Aleppo (Halab). Although they initially settled on the Lower East Side with Jews from Europe, they soon began establishing their own enclaves in Brooklyn, first in Williamsburg, then in suburban Flatbush by the 1930s and Midwood by the 1940s. The Syrian Jews of New York City energetically maintain their own institutions, especially along Ocean Parkway and Kings Highway; these include yeshivas, community centers, residences for the elderly, and synagogues representing Aleppo, Damascus, and Lebanon, as well as Egypt. Like other Syrians they have prospered in the export–import trade, particularly in clothing and electronics. Jews from Syria and Lebanon have much in common linguistically and culturally with other Syrians and Lebanese, but politically they identify with other Jews in the city rather than other Syrians. Particularly among those from Aleppo, marriage outside the group is rare. For this reason Syrian Jews have retained their Arabic culture and values at least as successfully as Syrian Christians and Muslims have. In the mid 1990s the number of Syrian Jews in New York City was estimated at fifteen to thirty thousand.

Prominent Americans of Syrian and Lebanese descent associated with New York City include the opera singer Rosalind Elias, the actor F. Murray Abraham (the first Arab–American to win an Academy Award, 1985), the Broadway stage director A. J. Antoon, the songwriter Paul Jabara, the fashion designers Norma Kamali and Joseph Abboud, the secretary of health and human services Donna Shalala (a former president of Hunter College), and the diplomat Philip Habib. In the mid 1990s there were an estimated sixty thousand New Yorkers of Syrian and Lebanese origin.

Lucius Hopkins Miller: *Our Syrian Population: A Study of the Syrian Communities of Greater New York* (n.p. [?New York]: n.pub., n.d. [?1903])

Philip M. Kayal and Joseph M. Kayal: *The Syrian–Lebanese in America: A Study in Religion and Assimilation* (Boston: Twayne, 1975)

Mary Ann Haick: "The Syrian Lebanese Community of South Ferry, 1900–1977" (thesis, Long Island University, 1979)

Joseph Sutton: *Magic Carpet: Aleppo in Flatbush* (New York: Thayer–Jacoby, 1979)

Alixa Naff: *Becoming American: The Early Arab Immigrant Experience* (Carbondale: Southern Illinois University Press, 1985)

Paula Hajar

Szold, Henrietta (*b* Baltimore, 21 Dec 1860; *d* Jerusalem, 13 Feb 1945). Scholar and political activist. The first woman enrolled at the Jewish Theological Seminary, she worked as an editor and translator in German, English, and Hebrew on such books as Louis Ginzberg's *The Legends of the Jews* (1908–38) and the American Jewish Yearbook. A member of the Federation of American Zionists, she helped to form Hadassah, the first women's Zionist group, in 1912 in New York City, and was its president until 1926. Szold worked as a nurse in Palestine between 1912 and 1926, helped to organize the American Zionist Medical Unit, and directed the Youth Aliyah program from 1933.

Janet Frankston

T

tabloids. Newspapers with pages about half as large as a broadsheet and a large number of illustrations. Tabloid newspapers exerted an important influence on journalism in New York City between the world wars. The prototype for the genre was the *Daily News*, launched in 1919 by Joseph Medill Patterson and Robert McCormick, which had a terse, lively reporting style and coverage that emphasized crime, sex, scandal, sports, and gossip; its circulation reached 400,000 by 1922. The success of the *Daily News* quickly inspired other newspapers to imitate its formula. Among the most prominent were the *Daily Mirror*, published by William Randolph Hearst, and the *New York Evening Graphic*, published by Bernarr Macfadden. By 1926 the three newspapers had captured more than a million and a half readers, only a very few of whom had been won over from the existing daily newspapers: most were poorly educated members of the urban working class, in particular immigrants and their children, who had not been regular newspaper readers at all. The circulation of the *Daily News* reached 1.3 million on weekdays by 1930 and nearly four million on Sundays by 1940, and in 1942 the *New York Post* adopted a tabloid format. Tabloids effectively exploited tensions of class, race, and ethnicity. They had an important influence on advertising and magazines, which freely borrowed such devices as "confession" stories, suggestive headlines, and lurid photographs. Although the critics dismissed them as vulgar and sensational, the tabloids expressed a shrewd awareness of working-class life not found in the more traditional press. The tabloid style remains a central element in print and broadcast journalism, especially in New York City. Three of the four major daily newspapers in the city in the mid 1990s were tabloids: the *Daily News*, the *New York Post*, and *New York Newsday*.

Simon Michael Bessie: *Jazz Journalism: The Story of the Tabloid Newspapers* (New York: E. P. Dutton, 1938)

Daniel Czitrom

Takami, Toyohiko Campbell (*b* Kumamoto, Japan, 1875; *d* Brooklyn, 17 May 1945). Physician. In 1891 he left Yokohama as a "captain's boy" on an English steamship, which he abandoned when it docked in New York City. He worked as a mess-boy at the Brooklyn Navy Yard, studied English and the Bible at a Sunday school in Brooklyn, and with the support of Nancy E. Campbell, an American missionary, attended private preparatory schools in Massachusetts and New Jersey before attending Lafayette College, Brooklyn Polytechnic Institute, Columbia University, and Cornell University Medical College (graduating in 1916). In 1907 he formed the Japanese Mutual Aid Society, serving as its president until 1918. He maintained a private practice near Fort Greene Park, was chief of dermatology at Cumberland Hospital, helped to establish Japanese immigrant organizations, and was the president of the Japanese Association from 1930 until 1933, as well as an active leader in Christian church organizations. In 1909 he married Sona Oguri.

Mitziko Sawada

Takamine, Jokichi (*b* Ishikawa Prefecture, Japan, 1854; *d* New York City, 22 July 1922). Chemist. In 1880 he was sent by the Japanese government to study in England; on his return to Japan he set up the first artificial-fertilizer business and contributed greatly to the development of several other industries. After traveling to the United States several times he assumed a research position at a distillery in Chicago where he shortened the distillation process by introducing an artificial fungus culture. In Clifton, New Jersey, he established the Takamine Research Center, where he perfected a digestive medicine, Taka Diastase, and was the first chemist to extract a hormone (adrenalin) in pure form. He married in 1887 and built an elaborate mansion at 334 Riverside Drive. Takamine was a founding member of the Nippon Club in 1905, a vice-president of the Japan Society in 1907, and a founding member and four-term president of the Japanese Association of New York.

Kiyoshi Karl Kawakami: *Jokichi Takamine: A Record of His American Achievements* (New York: W. E. Ridge, 1928)

Mitziko Sawada

Tallapoosa Point. A name formerly used for a section of the northeastern Bronx lying south of Eastchester Bay in what is now Pelham Bay Park. It was once a privately owned island that in colonial times became attached to the mainland through silting. In the 1890s a German political group, the Tallapoosa Club, leased it as a summer headquarters. Its rocky shores, inclining toward Long Island Sound, made the area a favorite spot for boating and fishing until the 1960s, when it was buried by a refuse dump by New York City. Proposals in the 1970s that the new hill should be used as a ski slope were ignored.

Lloyd Ultan

Tamiris [Becker], **Helen** (*b* New York City, 24 April 1905; *d* New York City, 4 Aug 1966). Dancer, choreographer, and teacher. A pupil of Michel Fokine and Rosina Galli, she formed the School of American Dance in 1930 and Tamiris and Her Group, an all-female company. Her modern dances in the 1930s and 1940s, *Walt Whitman Suite*, *Cycle of Unrest*, and *How Long, Brethren?*, reflected her concern with social issues, and she was an important figure in the Concert Dancers' League, formed to fight the city's "blue laws." She organized the Dance Repertory Theatre (1930–31) and was instrumental in the Federal Theatre Project, sponsored from 1936 to 1939 by the Works Progress Administration, and its offshoot the Federal Dance Project. In 1937 she helped to form the American Dance Association. Between 1943 and 1955 she provided choreography for fourteen musicals, including *Up in Central Park* (as well as its film version), *Annie Get Your Gun*, *Fanny*, and *Plain and Fancy*. With her husband Daniel Nagrin she formed the Tamiris–Nagrin Dance Company in 1960.

Christena L. Schlundt: *Tamiris: A Chronicle of Her Dance Career, 1927–1955* (New York: New York Public Library, 1972)

Norma Adler

Tammany Hall. Political organization formed in 1788 in New York City as the Society of St. Tammany or Columbian Order, in response to the city's more exclusive clubs. Initially most of its members were craftsmen; they adopted Tamanend, a legendary Delaware chief, as their patron and used pseudo-Indian insignia and titles (the lowest ranks were known as braves, the council members as sachems). Meetings were held in a hall on Spruce Street from 1798 to 1812 and in another at Nassau and Frankfort streets from 1812 to 1868.

In the early nineteenth century the society supported Aaron Burr, Martin Van Buren, and such progressive policies as universal male suffrage, lien laws to protect craftsmen, and the abolition of imprisonment for debt. It was soon riddled with graft, scandals, and internal conflicts of which the most notable was a struggle in 1835 between the Locofocos and the conservative old guard. The leaders expanded their political base by helping immigrants to survive, find work, and quickly gain citizenship; the organization also opposed anti-Catholic and nativist movements of the day, thus earning loyalties that endured for generations. During the mid nineteenth century Mayor Fernando Wood furthered his career through the society, as did William M. Tweed (the insigne of his volunteer fire company, a tiger, became the society's symbol). In 1868 the society moved into its "wigwam" on East 14th Street near 3rd Avenue, where it was the host of the Democratic National Convention during the same year.

Tammany Hall did not become a disciplined political machine until it came under the direction of John Kelly (1872–86), the first of ten successive Irish–American bosses; it is said that he found the society a horde and left it an army. He introduced a system of organi-

Tammany Hall decorated for the Democratic National Convention, 4 July 1868. Lithograph printed by W. C. Rodgers for Shannon's Manual, *1868*

zation in which assembly district leaders elected a leader, an unsalaried, extra-legal commander of operations. They also appointed precinct captains whose job it was to help families in their neighborhoods in times of emergency, to find them work, to ease any problems they had with the law, and to make sure that they voted. Although ballot boxes were often stolen on election day, most victories by candidates allied with Tammany Hall were achieved through year-round attention to voters' needs and interests. Because the boss controlled nominations to elective offices, he had the last word in the discretionary appointments made by successful candidates for municipal office and used this power to reward loyal district leaders and supporters and to punish dissenters. Political integration of different ethnic groups varied widely. From mid century Irish men dominated Tammany Hall and virtually monopolized district leaderships, remaining in power despite the changing population of their neighborhoods. Many Jews and Germans were admitted to the Tammany Society and were chosen to be state legislators, congressional representatives, and judges. The growing Italian population was largely ignored, and when the number of black voters in Harlem became significant the neighborhood was subdivided and reallocated to adjacent districts with white majorities. Richard Croker, the boss from 1886 to 1902, retained Kelly's system but delegated decisions about patronage to local leaders more than Kelly had done.

After consolidation in 1898 the primacy of Tammany Hall depended on gaining the cooperation of Democrats in the outer boroughs. Those in Brooklyn opposed the organization until John H. McCooey became the leader of Kings County in 1909. He was a long-time friend of Croker's successor, Charles F. Murphy. One result of their collaboration was the nomination of two mayoral candidates from Brooklyn, William J. Gaynor in 1909 and John F. Hylan in 1921. In state government during these years politicians allied with Tammany Hall sponsored progressive labor laws and opposed Prohibition and censorship. Murphy promised the suffrage leader Carrie Chapman Catt that his organization would do nothing to prevent women from gaining the right to vote; women were later allowed to be district co-leaders but rarely had a voice in decisions. After Murphy's death the leaders decided to replace Mayor Hylan with James J. Walker, a member of Tammany Hall and a state senator. Their efforts were successful owing largely to the support of Edward J. Flynn, the leader in the Bronx, and to an effective campaign against Hylan by Governor Alfred E. Smith; after winning the Democratic primary they swept the November elections.

The machine received money and "kickbacks" from many sources: municipal suppliers, real-estate interests, aspirants for judgeships, and businessmen bidding for transit franchises and pier leases. Legal fees and brokerage commissions were funneled to politically active lawyers and insurance men, and generous campaign contributions were often made by such wealthy families as the Lehmans and the Strauses. Members of the inner circle profited from "honest graft," successful speculations based on confidential information about plans for schools and public works. As George Washington Plunkitt, a sachem who died a millionaire, declared: "I seen my opportunities and I took 'em."

Tammany Hall reached its zenith in 1928. Smith was a powerful and widely respected governor, Walker an extraordinarily popular mayor. George W. Olvany, a college graduate, was the boss, a new building was completed in 1929 on Union Square at 17th Street, and even reformers had few criticisms of Tammany Hall. The organization's fortunes soon changed. Investigations of civic corruption by Samuel Seabury led to Walker's resignation in 1932. John F. Curry, Olvany's successor, sought to block Franklin D. Roosevelt's presi-

Tammany Hall, 14th Street between Irving Place and 3rd Avenue, 1904

dential nomination, allowing Flynn, no longer an ally of Tammany Hall, to become the strongest link between the Democratic White House and the city. In 1933 Mayor John P. O'Brien, the incumbent and a loyalist chosen by Curry, finished last in a three-way mayoral election won by Fiorello H. La Guardia, who led a coalition opposed to Tammany Hall that remained in place for twelve years. Unable to meet mortgage payments, the sachems sold their building to Local 91 of the International Ladies' Garment Workers' Union in 1943. By the time the Democrats recaptured the mayoralty in 1945, Tammany Hall had virtually ceased to exist, although politicians bred in the organization continued to flourish into the 1950s and beyond.

Louis Eisenstein and Elliot Rosenberg: *A Stripe of Tammany's Tiger* (New York: R. Speller, 1966)
Alfred Connable and Edward Silberfarb: *Tigers of Tammany: Nine Men Who Ran New York* (New York: Holt, Rinehart and Winston, 1967)

See also Democratic party.

Frank Vos

Tanenbaum, Marc (*b* Baltimore, 13 Oct 1925; *d* New York City, 3 July 1992). Rabbi. He grew up in Jackson Heights and received his BS from Yeshiva University in 1945. After completing his rabbinical studies at the Jewish Theological Seminary he was ordained in 1950. Known for his efforts to improve relations between Jews and Christians, especially Catholics, he formed ties with Archbishop John O'Connor, the Vatican, and the World Council of Churches in Geneva. Tanenbaum oversaw the international affairs of the Jewish Committee and was a member of presidential commissions on children, the elderly, and the Holocaust. He lived in Manhattan for many years.

Janet Frankston

Tannenbaum, Frank (*b* Galicia, 4 March 1893; *d* New York City, 1 June 1969). Historian. After moving from a farm near Great Barrington, Massachusetts, to New York City in 1906 he joined the Industrial Workers of the World. In 1914 he was imprisoned for almost a year on Blackwell's Island for disturbing the peace by leading homeless men into churches to demand financial assistance and work. Grace Hatch Childs, the wife of the reformer Richard S. Childs, helped pay for his education at Columbia University, from which he graduated in 1921. He received his PhD in economics in 1927 from the Brookings Institution and began teaching at Columbia in 1935, becoming a full professor of Latin American history in 1945. He founded and directed the interdisciplinary University Seminars at Columbia, which grew from five seminars in 1945 to seventy-five in 1990–91. Tannenbaum's published writings on Latin America include *The Mexican Agrarian Revolution* (1928), *Peace by Revolution: Mexico after 1910* (1933), and *Whither Latin America: An Introduction to Its Economic and Social Problems* (1934). He also wrote on crime and prison reform, the labor movement, and race relations, and edited the book *A Community of Scholars: The University Seminars at Columbia* (1965).

L. Paul Jaquith: "The University Seminars at Columbia University: A Living Monument to Frank Tannenbaum" (diss., Teachers College, Columbia University, 1973)
Joseph Maier and Richard W. Weatherhead: *Frank Tannenbaum: A Biographical Essay* (New York: Columbia University, 1974)

See also Unemployment movements.

Bernard Hirschhorn

tap dancing. The origins of tap dancing in New York City may be traced to the Five Points of the 1840s, where the African dances of blacks and the jigs and clog dances of the Irish exerted a reciprocal influence. Early tap dancers included the black minstrel Master Juba (William Henry Lane) and his white rival Master John Diamond, who in 1844 faced each other in a competition at John Tryon's Amphitheater that Lane won. During the last third of the nineteenth century black vaudevillians further refined the tap style, which was more rhythmic and looser than most other dances in vogue at the time.

The successful musical *Shuffle Along* (1921) by Flourney Miller, Aubrey Lyles, Noble Sissle, and Eubie Blake, which opened at Daly's Music Hall on 63rd Street, helped to establish tap dancing on the Broadway stage. In 1923 *Runnin' Wild* (also by Miller and Lyles) opened at the Colonial Theater and featured the Charleston, a fusion of tap and ballroom dancing that became immensely popular. Tap dancing was now important to the success of Broadway revues. The first great exponent of tap dancing was Bill "Bojangles" Robinson. After several years on the vaudeville circuit he performed at clubs in Harlem and then appeared in *Blackbirds of 1928* by Lew Leslie and Will Vodery, in which he performed a "stair dance" for which he became widely known. The first black dancer with widespread appeal among whites, he later danced in other Broadway shows and revues and eventually moved to Hollywood, where he enjoyed a successful film career. Robinson's success inspired many tap dancers during the 1930s, among them Honi Coles, King Rastus Brown, Peg Leg Bates (who tapped on one leg), and such duos as Buck and Bubbles (Ford Lee Washington and John Washington Bubbles), Chuck and Chuckles (Charles Green and James Walker), and Stump and Stumpy (James Cross and Harold Cromer). The brothers Fayard and Harold Nicholas, who regularly performed their acrobatic tap dances at the Cotton Club and the Apollo Theatre during the early 1930s, appeared on Broadway in Florenz Ziegfeld's *Follies* of 1936 and in *Babes in Arms* (1937), by Richard Rodgers and Lorenz Hart.

Although tap remained essentially a black art form there were many important white tap dancers as well, including Fred Astaire, Ruby Keeler, and Gene Kelly. Clarence "Buddy" Bradley taught tap to white students and introduced creative tap choreography. Tap dancers and their students frequented the Hoofers Club, a studio, rehearsal space, and social center that remained open at all hours and was situated at the rear of a pool hall next to the Lafayette Theater at 131st Street and 7th Avenue. The influence of tap was seen in the dance scenes of musicals and films and in such popular dances as the Lindy hop. During the 1940s and early 1950s groups such as the Four Step Brothers remained popular, and tap dancing was incorporated into the routines of such variety performers as Sammy Davis Jr. (1925–90) and the members of the Hines family, who performed as Hines, Hines and Dad (Gregory, Maurice Jr., and Maurice Sr.). Will Gaines and Groundhog Gaines and other performers developed a less refined and more improvisational subgenre known as bebop tap, which was influenced by recent developments in jazz and in turn influenced jazz drumming.

The popularity of tap dancing declined as that of rock-and-roll increased during the 1950s, and as dance critics focused their attention on ballet and modern dance. Interest was eventually renewed, in part by a revival on Broadway in 1969 of Vincent Youmans's musical *No, No, Nanette*, which has several tap dance numbers. In the following years several plays, musicals, and revues included tap dancing, among them *The Wiz* (1975, choreography by Geoffrey Holder), *Bubblin' Brown Sugar* (1976), and *Eubie!* (1978). Innovative dancers such as Jane Goldberg performed at the Brooklyn Academy of Music, and a number of dance schools offered instruction in tap, including the Ned Williams School of Dance, the Professional School of Dance (led by Henry LeTang), the Dance Theatre of Harlem, and the American Ballet Center. In 1975 Jerry Ames formed the first professional ensemble in the United States devoted exclusively to tap, which combined elements of tap with others drawn from jazz and modern dance and even ballet. Other notable groups included the American Tap Dance Orchestra (led by Brenda Bufalino), the Jazz Tap Ensemble (led by Linda Dalley), and Manhattan Tap. During the 1980s and early 1990s tap dancing was featured occasionally at such clubs as Smalls' Paradise, the Red Rooster, Northern Lights, and the Cat Club in Greenwich Village.

Rusty E. Frank: *Tap!: The Greatest Tap Dance Stars and Their Stories* (New York: William Morrow, 1990)

Marc Ferris

Tapia, Carlos (*b* Ponce, Puerto Rico, 27 Dec 1885; *d* New York City, 31 July 1945). Reformer and social activist. A grocer by trade, he worked with other Puerto Rican community activists to form Democratic clubs in Brooklyn between 1900 and 1919. Known as nationality clubs, these offered cultural and athletic programs and social services in addition to dispensing patronage. Tapia was a traditional community leader who believed that by taking part in the electoral process Puerto Ricans in New York City could achieve progress for themselves as well as play a role in deciding the political future of their homeland. Public School 120 in Brooklyn was named for him in 1965.

Virginia Sánchez Korrol

Tappan, Lewis (*b* Northampton, Mass., 23 May 1788; *d* Brooklyn, 21 June 1873). Businessman and abolitionist. He moved to New York City in 1828 to join his brother Arthur (*b* Northampton, 22 May 1786; *d* New Haven, Conn., 23 July 1865), who had moved to the city in 1826 and established the *New York Journal of Commerce* in 1827; the two had a successful partnership as silk jobbers under the name Arthur Tappan and Company from 1828 to 1841. Lewis established the Mercantile Agency, the first commercial credit-rating institution in the United States and a forerunner of Dun and Bradstreet. In the late 1820s the brothers became active in religious and social reform and led movements for stricter observance of the Sabbath and the cessation of mail delivery on Sunday. They also promoted the free church movement and financed a number of bible, tract, Sunday school, mission, and education societies in the antebellum city. Lewis Tappan broke with the American Colonization Society, which sought to repatriate freed slaves to Africa, and with his brother formed the American Anti-Slavery Society (1833), which urged the immediate abolition of slavery. The Tappans' uncompromising resistance to slavery angered many, and in 1834 Lewis Tappan's home at 40 Rose Street was ransacked by an anti-abolitionist mob. The brothers were instrumental in introducing the revivalist Charles G. Finney to the city and built the Broadway Tabernacle for his use in 1836. In 1840 they formed the American and Foreign Anti-Slavery Society, one of the leading abolitionist organizations in the city. After Arthur Tappan's business failed in 1842 the brothers helped to found the anti-slavery American Missionary Society (1846), and by the early 1850s both had retired from business to devote themselves to philanthropy. They resisted the Fugitive Slave Act of 1850 by helping the Underground Railroad to carry slaves to freedom in the North. Lewis Tappan wrote *The Life of Arthur Tappan* (1870).

Bertram Wyatt-Brown: *Lewis Tappan and the Evangelical War against Slavery* (Cleveland: Case Western Reserve University Press, 1969)

Peter J. Wosh

Tarbell, Ida M(inerva) (*b* Erie County, Penn., 5 Nov 1857; *d* Bridgeport, Conn., 6 Jan 1944). Journalist. After graduating from Allegheny College she taught for a few years, traveled, and in 1894 joined the staff of *McClure's*, where she wrote about Napoleon, Washington, and John D. Rockefeller; in the years after 1901 she produced nineteen articles and the book *A History of the Standard Oil Company* (1904), which exposed the firm's ruthless practices and was well received. With several other members of *McClure's* including Lincoln Steffens and Ray Stannard Baker she acquired control of *American Magazine* and for a time wrote about tariff reform. Increasingly mistrustful of politics, she declined an appointment to the tariff commission from President Woodrow Wilson, and in the book *The Business of Being a Woman* (1912) she questioned the causes of woman suffrage and militant feminism. After investigating conditions in factories and Henry Ford's production methods she strongly endorsed the scientific management planner Frederick W. Taylor. She lived at 40 West 9th Street before retiring to Connecticut. Tarbell wrote an autobiography, *All in a Day's Work* (1939).

Kathleen Brady: *Ida Tarbell: Portrait of a Muckraker* (Pittsburgh: University of Pittsburgh Press, 1989)

James E. Mooney

target companies. The first target companies in New York City were formed in the 1830s by volunteer firemen devoted to target practice; the earliest known by name were the Baxter Blues and the Black Joke Volunteers. Unlike the state militia, in which members often served their enlistment of seven years without ever firing their weapons, target companies such as the Pochahontas Guards assembled "the best shooters in the city" for frequent target excursions. Despite casual discipline they were probably at least as effective militarily as militia units of the time. By 1850 it was estimated that the companies had ten thousand members, a large number of whom had volunteered for the Mexican War. Some companies were formed by members of ethnic and political groups — the Asmonean Guard (Jewish), the American Rifles (nativist), and the Meagher Guards (Irish) — and by employees of factories, foundries, and shipyards. Most target companies reportedly were democratic in selecting their officers and enforcing rules, but prosperous members often contributed for uniforms, weapons, and meals, and sometimes their largesse resulted in their being chosen as officers. Like the volunteer fire department, many target companies were closely allied with the Democratic Party and Tammany Hall. The Black Joke Engine Company sponsored the Baxter Blues and the Black Joke Volunteers, who by disobeying orders from the Common Council not to march in a parade for the presidential candidate James K. Polk in 1844 caused the engine company to be temporarily disbanded. Americus Engine Company no. 6 took over the equipment of the Black Joke Volunteers and was led to target practice as the William M. Tweed Guards (named after its foreman, later infamous as Boss Tweed). The *New York Times* observed that almost all politicians in Tammany Hall were leaders of target companies, which they found invaluable as bases of power.

Many companies' target excursions became drunken feasts at which the arms most in use were pocket pistols drawn during quarrels. One of the companies known for its social activity, the Shandley Legion, distributed its prizes by lottery, to the disgust of the few members who were skilled marksmen. Some companies were even named for their love of feasting, among them the Chowder and Epicurean guards; others had frivolous names such as the First Ward Magnetizers and Nobody's Guard.

Political maneuvering led to the only large-scale review of the companies, the Target Parade of 1857. At the height of Mayor Fernando Wood's dispute with the state legislature over control of the city police, the target companies formed two divisions and were led by the fire commissioner Henry Wilson in a parade down Broadway to be reviewed by the mayor; 2700 men took part. Frivolous companies marched alongside units such as the Peterson Guards, who had been invited to West Point to perform for the U.S. Military Academy. A month after the parade supporters of Mayor Wood made an unsuccessful effort to join the companies into a city army.

When the Civil War began in 1861 men of all classes turned to the target companies for instruction. The companies did not enlist as units, but they contributed most of the men for the Fire Zouaves and other regiments such as the Jackson Guard (supported by Tammany Hall) and the Garibaldi Guard. Most New Yorkers expected the war to end quickly, and when it lengthened and turned into a war that would end slavery many Irish workers became resolute Copperheads. President Lincoln's attempt to draft them in July 1863 brought a revolt, and Black Joke Volunteers led an attack on the local conscription office. Entire companies of the volunteer fire department deserted out of sympathy with the rioters, but many others worked to control arson and violence throughout a week of disruption. During the first two days reporters thought they discerned among the rioters a well-organized cadre armed with military rifles. These roughly clad but expert marksmen at one point routed 150 Zouaves reinforced by howitzers, and some believed that they were Confederates smuggled into the city; probably they were members of Irish target companies.

The treachery of the volunteer fire department led to its dissolution in 1865. In the following year a report of the police commissioner recommended that target excursions be outlawed, but the companies still had enough support from Tammany Hall to defeat a bill prohibiting civilian parades under arms. Membership reached its peak soon after the war as companies recruited many former soldiers. An editorial in the *New York Times* reported that "two or three or a half-dozen" companies passed along Newspaper Row every day during several months of 1867. Nearly all had become social clubs, and newspaper descriptions of their parades were no longer respectful: the *Times* alleged that the companies blackmailed saloon keepers, politicians, and employers. A huge "target excursion" provided the cover for opposition to the Orange parade of 1871, which ended in a bloody riot. Discipline broke down among the National Guard defending the marchers; without orders troops fired into the crowd lining the street. The disaster brought efforts to improve discipline and marksmanship in the militia. The National Rifle Association, formed later that year, was intended both to improve the skills of the militia and to put the popularity of target excursions to the service of the National Guard.

Russell S. Gilmore: "New York Target Companies: Informal Military Societies in a Nineteenth-century Metropolis," *Military Collector and Historian* 35, no. 2 (1983), 60–66

Russell S. Gilmore

tattooing. The first mechanized tattoo shop was opened in 1875 at 11 Chatham Square by Samuel F. O'Reilly, who had invented the electric tattoo machine after observing that Thomas Edison's electric engraving pen could be modified to introduce ink into skin with speed and accuracy. The rowdy atmosphere of Chatham Square and the Bowery nurtured O'Reilly and his innovation, and he accepted two apprentices: Charlie Wagner, who took over the tattoo shop on O'Reilly's death in 1908 and went on to develop his own version of the tattoo machine and start a small tattoo supply business; and Ed Smith, who designed dozens of sheets of tattoo designs for the trade. During the first few decades of the twentieth century performers at dime museums on the Bowery visited Wagner's shop regularly. These early "canvas backs" helped to boost the reputation of both Wagner and tattooing, and Chatham Square soon became a world tattoo center, attracting more than a dozen tattooers from as far away as Japan.

Usually operating out of cramped booths in local barber shops, tattooers in Chatham Square decorated the skin of the day laborers who congregated in the area and of those who visited the Bowery in search of amusement. Among the most noted tattooers were Bob Wicks at 9 Chatham Square; Millie Hull at 16 Bowery, the only female tattooer in New York City; and Willie Moskowitz at 12 Bowery, a barber who had learned tattooing from Wagner and was known for his speed. Moskowitz's sons Stanley and Walter inherited his tattoo business and moved with him to 52 Bowery just off Chatham Square. They were the last tattooers to work on the Bowery and among those who were forced to retire from their locations in Coney Island and 48th Street in 1961 when tattooing in New York City was banned.

Michael McCabe

Tavern on the Green. Restaurant in Central Park at West 67th Street. It stands on the site of a sheepfold designed by Jacob Wrey Mould and built in 1870. The restaurant was built by order of the parks commissioner Robert Moses and opened on 20 October 1934; overlooking the gardens of Central Park and filled with stained-glass windows, including one by Louis Comfort Tiffany, it offered a rustic setting that was a rarity in central Manhattan. In the 1950s the designer Raymond Loewy added the Elm Room (later called the Park Room) to the front of the building, and in 1962 Restaurant Associates took over the business from its original manager, Arthur Schleiffer. After the restaurant closed in 1974 the lease was acquired by Warner LeRoy, who undertook extensive renovations: the Crystal Room and the Terrace Room were added, along with fourteen sand-carved mirrors and forty-five chandeliers. The restaurant reopened in 1976 and soon became a popular locale for weddings, opening-night parties, and political fund raisers. During the winter four hundred thousand tiny light bulbs are wrapped around surrounding trees. Tavern on the Green serves an average of two thousand customers a day; it has been a backdrop for several films and marks the finish line of the New York City Marathon.

Nan Lyons and Ivan Lyons: *A Bantam Travel Guide: New York City 1990* (New York: Bantam, 1990)

Marjorie Harrison

taverns. Taverns and similar establishments are discussed in the entry BARS, TAVERNS, AND SALOONS.

taxes. In the early years of New Amsterdam Peter Stuyvesant's government was financed primarily by a tax on liquors. An uncooperative public often stymied other efforts to raise revenue, notably an ill-fated property tax to pay off a debt. Under British rule minor taxes on property in New York City were levied for various municipal functions including public works and relief, a pattern that continued after independence and well into the nineteenth century. The creation of the comptroller's office in 1801 helped facilitate the city's taxing powers.

The city did not pass its first important tax legislation until 1859, when it established a comprehensive system for the assessment and collection of property taxes. There were three commissioners of taxes and assessments, each appointed by the mayor, whose deputies set out every September to appraise property, both real (fixed assets like land and buildings) and personal (financial assets and material items such as jewelry). Citizens were given four months in which to challenge assessments. Once the books were closed the assessments were brought before the Board of Aldermen, which set a rate of taxation according to the city's needs each year: the rate for every $100 in assessed valuation ranged from $0.42 in 1830 to $2.94 in 1875.

The city's system of taxation was widely criticized for being inequitable. Personal property taxes were valued much lower than real-estate taxes (45 percent lower in 1860), even though they were believed to be greater in worth. When William H. Vanderbilt died it was estimated that $40 million of his personal estate was taxable, but he had paid only $500,000 during his lifetime. The city managed to close the differential between personal property and real property rates to 22 percent by 1896, but still only 21,000 of the city's nearly two million inhabitants paid personal property taxes that year. The city's tax commissioner acknowledged in 1891 that his office was able to collect taxes only from "the widows and the orphans," because their personal property was documented in the surrogate's office.

With minor variations the system remained largely intact until the Depression. With the city on the brink of bankruptcy and having to resort to bank loans to pay its debts, it became obvious that the tax system was inadequate: property owners, who supplied more than 80 percent of the city's revenues, simply lacked the means to finance city government on their own. As a result an agreement was reached with the city's financial institutions, known as the "Bankers' Agreement," under which the city committed tax revenues to pay off bank loans and imposed a new tax on utilities to provide unemployment benefits. The agreement was in effect from 1 January 1934 to 31 December 1937 and greatly curtailed the city's taxing and discretionary powers.

Other taxes were adopted during this period as well. In 1934 the city established a business tax of less than 1 percent and a sales tax of 2 percent. The sales tax was intended to be an emergency measure only, but it was eventually raised to 4 percent and remained in place into the 1990s. In the following decades the city added taxes on hotel rooms, parimutuel betting, automobiles, theater tickets, gross payrolls, and other items. An income tax, begun in 1966, applied both to residents and to nonresidents who earned income in the city. Initially those subject to the income tax were required to file a separate tax return with the city, until in 1975 the State of New York began collecting the tax on the city's behalf. With the growth in new taxes the proportion of the city's revenues accounted for by the property tax fell steadily, from 70 percent in the 1950s to 55 percent in the early 1970s.

Major changes in the city's property tax system were made in 1982, when the state passed a law establishing four classes of property for taxation: one-, two-, and three-family houses; apartment buildings (essentially cooperatives and condominiums); utilities; and commercial property. Each class of property had a different ratio of assessed valuation to market value, a formula that worked to the great advantage of homeowners in the outer boroughs. (In the mid 1990s homeowners owned 32.5 percent of the city's property but paid 11.5 percent of its property taxes, while owners of cooperatives and condominiums paid much more.) Property taxes became a contentious political issue during the budget crises of the 1990s, when some observers called for a more equitable system that would generate more revenue.

Like all municipalities in New York State, New York City depends on the legislature for the power to tax. In the mid 1990s the city raised more than $18,000 million a year in taxes, of which 43 percent was derived from property taxes, 19 percent from income taxes, 13 percent from sales taxes, 6 percent from corporate taxes, and 19 percent from other taxes. The city is generally regarded as a highly taxed jurisdiction: in the mid 1990s the income tax rate ranged from 2.51 percent to 4.6 percent, and the hotel tax ranged as high as 21.25 percent, the highest rate in the United States, until it was lowered in September 1994.

Edward D. Durand: *The Finances of New York City* (New York: Macmillan, 1898)

James Bradley

taxicabs. Taxicabs became a popular mode of transport for residents of New York City in 1907, when slow-moving vehicles powered by batteries weighing eight hundred pounds (360 kilograms) that had been in use since 1899 were replaced with gas-powered ones. The new taxicabs were equipped with taximeters to halt widespread fare gouging. As the business grew, drivers became more assertive: five thousand held a strike in November 1907 calling for better wages and the right to unionize. By 1909 there were six major "fleets" employing hundreds of drivers, as well as thousands of independent owner–drivers. In the same year the city government appointed inspectors to monitor taxicabs, and in 1913 it fixed the cost of a taxi ride at fifty cents a mile (thirty cents a kilometer), a figure lower than the prevailing average.

In the early 1920s the taxi business was a largely unregulated one controlled by automobile manufacturers and owners of large fleets: General Motors, the Ford Motor Company, and the Checker Motors Corporation offered easy credit to fleets seeking to purchase automobiles, sometimes set up fleets of their own, and came to wield so much power that they dictated drivers' wages and posed a serious obstacle to their efforts to unionize.

Hansom cab at Union Square and 16th Street, 1896. Alice Austen Collection, Staten Island Historical Society

Large owners sought to drive out small ones by discounting their fares and advocating high bond requirements; reformers accused the city of ignoring corruption and complained of taxicabs that were dangerous, dirty, and uninsured. In response the police department took control of licensing in 1923, on the grounds that taxicabs were often used in burglaries, holdups, and bootlegging; by this time there were sixteen thousand licensed taxicabs in the city. The new licensing requirements were lax, and cab driving remained open to all. The large fleets that controlled the business were increasingly competitive with each other, and rate wars worsened in 1925, with some fleets lowering fares by 50 percent. In the same year the first women became licensed drivers, and the police department gained control over the licensing of taxi drivers through its newly formed Taxicab Commission. Confusion over fares allowed dishonest drivers to bilk their customers, but the real culprits were the automobile manufacturers, who took advantage of the intense competition to unload their surplus vehicles. With fares often about half the maximum allowed by law, the city intensified its efforts to set standard fares and attempted rigorous inspections of the fleets, and it also awarded good-conduct medals to drivers who helped the police to apprehend criminals. In 1930 the Taxicab Commission suggested that owner–drivers be eliminated and that the large fleets be given complete control.

The Depression led to a huge increase in the number of taxi drivers in New York City (75,000 operating nineteen thousand vehicles in 1933) and an upsurge in labor strife. Average weekly pay dropped from $26 in 1929 to $15 in 1933. Loan sharks, racketeers, and corruption plagued the business and its unions and also tainted the government: in 1932 an investigation by the Taxicab Commission revealed that the Checker Cab Company, which owned Parmalee, the largest taxi fleet in New York City, had bribed Mayor James J. Walker, and further inquiries contributed to Walker's resignation. After several years of debate Mayor Fiorello H. La Guardia signed the Haas Act (1937), which established a system of medallions, or official taxicab licenses, available for $10 and limited in number to 13,566. Viewed as a compromise between the owners of large fleets and the independent drivers (each of whom wanted to eliminate the other), the law in fact created a new monopoly, as the owners of medallions became a powerful block intent on limiting access to the trade. For many years most taxi drivers were Jewish, Italian, and Irish immigrants, and except during the Second World War almost all were men. Taxi drivers became a part of the folklore of New York City, regarded as amiable cynics with an encyclopedic knowledge of the city who spoke a colorful argot and were eager to express their opinions on almost any subject. Efforts to unionize drivers in New York City by the International Brotherhood of Teamsters, the Taxi Workers Union, the United Mine Workers, the AFL–CIO, and local unions between 1934 and 1957 met with little success. The organizers had to proceed one garage at a time, which made collective action difficult and subjected the organizers to coercion. Bitter strikes shut down the business in 1934, 1939, 1949, 1956, and 1965, and the fleets retaliated by locking out and dismissing drivers and by calling in replacements. Vehicles were burned and rallies were held in Times Square and on 5th Avenue, and striking drivers blocked avenues, squares, and bridges and confronted their replacements at taxi stands. The strike in 1965 resulted in an election supervised by the National Labor Relations Board in which the Taxi Workers Union, an affiliate of the AFL–CIO led by Harry Van Arsdale, was chosen to represent the city's drivers.

By the 1960s attrition reduced the number of medallion taxicabs in the city to 11,300. Special medallions for veterans of the Second World War were never issued because of political opposition from the unions and independent drivers. In 1967 the city ordered all medallion cabs painted yellow, which further increased the value of a license. By the late 1960s 10 percent of the taxicab drivers in New York City were women. Despite periodic fare increases and union demands for guaranteed wages, pay remained low. Drivers were increasingly the victims of robbery and violent crimes, and bulletproof partitions were installed between the front and back seats of taxicabs in 1967.

The continuing limit on the number of medallions, and an unwillingness by drivers of medallion cabs to serve neighborhoods heavily populated by racial minorities (despite a law requiring them to take orderly passengers anywhere in the city), gave rise to a number of private livery, or "gypsy," services. Unlike medallion cabs the gypsies could offer their services only to passengers who had requested them by telephone, a restriction that nevertheless was often disregarded. Many of the gypsy services operated primarily in black neighborhoods: the largest of these was Black Pearl Livery in Brooklyn. The Taxi and Limousine Commission reported in 1971 that although gypsy drivers earned only about a third of what medallion drivers did, gypsy services were much-needed enterprises in the inner city: they employed nearly thirteen thousand drivers in metropolitan New York, of whom 58 percent were black and 39 percent Puerto Rican.

The trade experienced an influx of black, Middle Eastern, and Latin American drivers in the 1970s, and of Russian Jews, Haitians, and South Asians in the 1990s. A survey by the Taxi and Limousine Commission issued in 1992 found that of applicants for licenses in the preceding year, 42.8 percent were from South Asia, 11.2 percent from Africa, 7.6 percent from the Caribbean, 7 percent from the Middle East, and 6.8 percent from Russia; 10.5 percent were born in the United States. Because many drivers had recently arrived in New York City and did not know its geography, a mandatory orientation program consisting of twenty hours of classroom instruction for new drivers was begun in 1983. In 1979 the fleets won the right to impose a surcharge of fifty cents a ride between 8 p.m. and 6 a.m.; the surcharge was later extended to vehicles not owned by the fleets. Mayor Edward I. Koch's plan to issue special medallions in 1985 that would have permitted drivers to pick up passengers north of 96th Street in Manhattan and in other boroughs was abandoned after city investigators discovered that medallions were missing from the files of the Taxi and Limousine Commission. The cost of medallions rose to $136,000 by 1989; in the same year a survey showed that drivers who leased their taxicabs earned between $21,000 and $31,000 from gratuities and a percentage of their fares (these drivers paid for their own gasoline), that owner–drivers averaged more than $40,000, and that only 30 percent of the city's drivers worked full time. Another survey in 1990 showed that the taxi business was in disarray: fleets were beset by a high turnover of drivers, costly equipment, and competition from radio-equipped limousines, and independent drivers paid as much as $75 a day to lease their vehicles, in addition to the cost of gasoline. Taxi drivers also began to suffer from a perception that they drove too fast and sometimes recklessly. These problems continued into the 1990s, and the drivers' plight was worsened by a rash of armed robberies and murders that cost the lives of forty-one livery drivers and four yellow-cab drivers in 1993 alone. On 26 October 1993 thousands of taxi drivers angered by the slayings snarled traffic in Manhattan by driving slowly in close formation along major avenues.

Taxi driving in New York City has been the subject of several anecdotal memoirs, including *Hacking New York* (1930) by Robert Hazard and *My Flag is Down: Diary of a New York Taxi Driver* (1948) by James Maresca, and figures prominently in Martin Scorsese's film *Taxi Driver* (1976). One well-known former taxi driver is Danny Sullivan, who worked in the city in the early 1970s and won the Indianapolis 500 in 1985.

Charles Vidich: *The New York Cab Driver and His Fare* (Cambridge, Mass.: Shenkman, 1976)

Graham Hodges

taxpayers. One- and two-story buildings that yield sufficient commercial or residential rent to pay real-estate taxes until the landlords can undertake more intensive and more profitable development. After the collapse of the real-estate market in 1929 taxpayers became a common means of "land banking" and kept land productively available to the urban economy, but the term did not come into popular use until after the Depression. One of the best known and most distinctive taxpayers in New York City is Pomander Walk on the Upper West Side of Manhattan, a two-row mews of very small townhouse apartments that extends from 94th Street to 95th Street between Broadway and West End Avenue. Its developer, Thomas Healy, and the architectural firm of King and Campbell obtained the model for its layout from the popular play *Pomander Walk* (1911), which takes place in a mythical suburb of London at the time of George III. Healy had hoped to build a high-rise hotel with six hundred rooms, but by the time construction began in 1921 the hotel project was no longer economically feasible. Much construction during the real-estate expansion of the 1980s took place on sites that had been developed as taxpayers during the Depression.

Elliott Sclar

Taylor, Cecil (Percival) (*b* New York City, 15 March 1933). Pianist. After growing up in Corona he studied at the New England Conservatory, made his début in 1956 at the Five Spot in New York City, and recorded the albums *Jazz Advance* (1956), *Looking Ahead* (1958), and *The New Breed* (1961). At first influenced largely by Thelonious Monk, he soon forged a percussive and often violently atonal style that owed something to the keyboard works of Stravinsky, Bartók, and Stockhausen. His performances and recordings with the drummer Max Roach secured his reputation as the most uncompromising member of the jazz avant-garde. For many years he lived in a loft at 58 West 31st Street.

Marc Ferris

Taylor [Cooney], **Laurette** (*b* New York City, 1 April 1884; *d* New York City, 8 Dec 1946). Actress. In 1912 she achieved success in the play *Bird of Paradise*, as well as in *Peg o' My Heart*, written by her second husband, J. Hartley Manners, who later wrote a number of unsuccessful plays in which she appeared. After his death she became reclusive but then returned to Broadway in 1938 for a revival of Sutton Vanes's *Outward Bound*. Known for her radiance, she won critical acclaim for her profound characterization of Amanda in Tennessee Williams's *The Glass Menagerie* (1945), a role that she continued to play until nearly the end of her life.

Marguerite Courtney: *Laurette* (New York: Atheneum, 1968)

David J. Weiner

Taylor, Moses (*b* New York City, 11 Jan 1806; *d* New York City, 23 May 1882). Industrialist and financier. Born at Broadway and Morris Street, he was the son of John Jacob Astor's business manager. In 1821 he began an apprenticeship to G. G. and S. S. Howland, a leading trader in products from Latin America; he formed his own company at 44 South Street in 1832 for importing Cuban sugar. In 1837 he was made a director of City Bank, which became a treasury for his business empire, as did the Manhattan and Metropolitan insurance companies and Farmers' Loan and Trust. After 1841 he invested aggressively in gas lighting companies in the city, including the Manhattan Gas Light Company, and in 1853 he became a director of the Lackawanna Iron and Coal Company, a producer of rails. He also recognized the importance of anthracite coal to New York City and from 1854 was a director of the Delaware, Lackawanna and Western Railroad, a producer and carrier of coal. During the same year he was made the treasurer of the New York, Newfoundland and London Electric Telegraph Company, which after five attempts linked New York City and London by transatlantic cable (1866). By 1855 the customs duties of Moses Taylor and Company were the second-highest in the nation, after those of A. T. Stewart. Taylor became the president of City Bank in 1856 (remaining until 1882), and as the chairman of the loan committee of the New York Clearing House he gave strong financial support to the Union from 1861 to 1863. By 1865 he controlled the entire gas lighting industry in the city. After the transatlantic cable began operating in 1866 he controlled the American side and became a director of the Western Union Telegraph Company, which had a monopoly on the telegraph industry in the United States. He became a vice-president of Lackawanna Iron and Coal in 1872 and in the 1870s arranged for its conversion to the Bessemer process. At his death he left an estate worth $40 million. Taylor was perhaps the most important businessman in New York City between 1840 and 1880. His varied investments in trade, lighting, communication, and finance were instrumental in making the city a national and international center of business.

Daniel Hodas: *The Business Career of Moses Taylor: Merchant, Finance Capitalist, and Industrialist* (New York: New York University Press, 1976)

See also Citibank.

Joan L. Silverman

Taylor, Paul (*b* Pittsburgh, 29 July 1930). Dancer and choreographer. He moved to New York City in 1952 to study at the Juilliard School, danced with the companies of Merce Cunningham and Pearl Lang, and in 1955 began to perform his own choreography and became a soloist with Martha Graham, for whom he originated the roles of Aegisthus in *Clytemnestra* and Hercules in *Alcestis*. His concert "Seven New Dances" at the 92nd Street YM-YWHA in 1957 became legendary as an exploration of extremes: ordinary movement and stillness, ordinary sounds and quiet. To a degree these concerns continued to color his work. In 1961 he left Graham to devote himself fully to his own company, which performed in New York City and toured consistently into the 1990s. He provided choreography to scores by many modern composers and commissioned designs from several well-known artists. A number of distinguished dancers performed in his company, including Bettie de Jong, Carolyn Adams, Dan Wagoner, Twyla Tharp, and Cliff Keuter. In 1989 he received the Mayor's Award of Honor for Art and Culture and was elected an honorary member of the American Academy and Institute of Arts and Letters. The tension in Taylor's work between light and dark, athleticism and wit, and the lovely and the sinister has created an unusually provocative body of work. One of his most popular and most musical dances is *Aureole* (1962). His published writings include *Private Domain* (1987).

Don McDonagh: *The Complete Guide to Modern Dance* (Garden City, N.Y.: Doubleday, 1976)
Marcia B. Siegel; *The Shapes of Change: Images of American Dance* (Boston: Houghton Mifflin, 1979)

Robert Seder

Teachers College. Graduate school of education, psychology, and health, founded in 1887 at 9 University Place as the New York College for the Training of Teachers by the philanthropist Grace Hoadley Dodge and the philosopher Nicholas Murray Butler. The impetus for the school was the rapid increase in New York City of poor immigrant children, whom it aimed to serve through social services and innovative methods of education. In 1892 it took its present name and received its permanent charter. The need for additional space and a gift of $100,000 from George Vanderbilt prompted the founders in 1894 to move the school to its present location on West 120th Street between Broadway and Amsterdam Avenue, making it the first of many academic institutions to settle in Morningside Heights. Constructed of brick and red sandstone, the four-story building dominated a rocky hilltop otherwise occupied only by farms, squatters, and the Bloomingdale Insane Asylum. Soon after Columbia University moved its campus to the same neighborhood in the mid 1890s Teachers College entered into an academic alliance with it. Their agreement of 1898 provided the college with access to the university's faculty and empowered it to grant degrees in the university's name, while permitting it to retain legal and financial independence. After the turn of the century the college expanded and diversified its curriculum to include emerging fields such as psychology, sociology, health, and nutrition. In the mid 1990s it focused special attention on urban education, research programs, and advanced classroom technology. Teachers College had about four thousand students and three hundred faculty members in 1993. Nearly one thousand students graduate with advanced degrees each year. Among the better-known alumni are Shirley Chisholm, first black woman to serve in the U.S. Congress; Norman Cousins, author and editor of the *Saturday Review*; Patricia A. Graham, dean of the Graduate School of Education at Harvard University; Thomas H. Kean, governor of New Jersey; and the sex therapist Ruth Westheimer. Teachers College Press, established in 1904, is an academic publisher independent of Columbia University Press.

Lawrence Arthur Cremin: *A History of Teachers College* (New York: Columbia University Press, 1954)

Robert Sanger Steel

Teachers Insurance and Annuity Association–College Retirement Equities Fund [TIAA–CREF]. Nonprofit financial institution formed in New York City in 1918 as the Teachers Insurance and Annuity Association by the Carnegie Foundation for the Advancement of Teaching, with an endowment of $1 million from the Carnegie Corporation of New York. It began as a pension and insurance organization that offered life insurance and retirement plans to professors and other employees of colleges and universities. Both employers and employees contribute to the pension, which the employees may take with them from one institution to another. In the 1930s the association began to invest in mortgage loans and became a leader in investing pension assets in mortgages and real estate. The high inflation that followed the Second World War severely eroded the purchasing power of fixed-income investments, and in response the association formed the College Retirement Equities Fund and took its current name. The fund invested in common stocks and offered a variable annuity, a method of managing retirement savings and income that was considered radical at the time but was later adopted by many other companies and pension plans. Group life and disability insurance was added in the 1950s, and eligibility for individual life insurance was extended to public school teachers in 1989. In 1993 TIAA–CREF had more than $125,000 million in assets and was the world's largest pension system and the nation's third-largest insurance company, with more than 1.6 million customers at 5200 colleges, universities, research organizations, and independent schools throughout the nation. Its headquarters are at 730 3rd Avenue. It also owns adjacent office buildings at 750 3rd Avenue and 485 Lexington Avenue, as well as the Seagram Building.

William C. Greenough: *It's My Retirement Money — Take Good Care of It: The TIAA–CREF Story* (Homewood, Ill.: Irwin, 1990)

Carolyn Kopp

teachers' unions. Teachers in New York City first organized in 1913. In 1916 they formed the Teachers' Union, an affiliate of the American Federation of Teachers (AFT). Because teachers were split among many societies the union was not recognized as their bargaining agent but nonetheless effectively defended and advanced their interests. During the early 1930s the union was divided by a struggle between its officers, many of them socialists, and a growing faction led by communists. In 1935 the faction took over and the former leaders left to organize the Teachers' Guild; in 1940 the AFT expelled the Teachers' Union and recognized the Teachers' Guild as the city's local. During the next twenty years the guild grew stronger and more influential but did not represent most teachers, and in 1960 it merged with a large segment of the High School Teachers' Association to form the United Federation of Teachers (UFT) under the direction of Charles Cogen. It held a strike, the first in the history of the school system, on 7 November 1960 for a collective bargaining election promised by the Board of Education; the election was finally held in December 1961 and was won by the UFT, which proved highly effective, conducting strikes in April 1962 and September 1967 that resulted in higher salaries, better working conditions, and a workable grievance procedure.

The UFT made a number of gains under Albert Shanker, who succeeded Cogen as president in 1964 and became a major figure in the local labor movement. Efforts to decentralize the school system led to a major crisis in 1968 when the local school board in the largely black Ocean Hill–Brownsville district ordered the transfer of thirteen teachers and six other school employees, of whom eighteen were white. Despite intense pressure ten of the teachers continued to oppose their involuntary transfer, and this led to a conflict over teachers' contractual rights and community control of schools that culminated in three strikes by the UFT and a citywide political and racial crisis. The final settlement largely upheld the position taken by the UFT, and the teachers were reinstated. Strengthened by its role in the conflict, the UFT also helped to save the city from bankruptcy during its fiscal crisis by urging the trustees of the Teachers' Retirement System to buy bonds of the Municipal Assistance Corporation. Shanker was succeeded by Sandra Feldman in 1986. In the mid 1990s the UFT was the largest local in the country, with more than a hundred thousand members, and served as a model for other unions of teachers and public employees nationwide.

Philip Taft: *United They Teach: The Story of the United Federation of Teachers* (Los Angeles: Nash, 1974)

Irwin Yellowitz

technology. During the seventeenth century commercial activity in New York Harbor encouraged the growth of technology. Shipbuilding employed local blacksmiths and carpenters, who fashioned raw materials into vessels. Wind and water provided the motive power for many other trades that developed near the harbor: millers used waterwheels and windmills to grind grain for bread and for export goods such as beer and flour; sawmills and paper mills also used these sources of power. A system of apprenticeship evolved in the trades that was reminiscent of the medieval European guilds. By the eighteenth century emerging technology in New York City reflected increased wealth. Bricklayers were active as brick became an increasingly common substitute for wood. Engraved silver plates were made by silversmiths; kettles, stills, and maritime instruments by coppersmiths; and ornate goblets and candlesticks by pewterers.

At the same time New Yorkers made plans to build turnpikes and canals to tap the natural resources of the nation's interior and to serve new markets. Transport was seen by many as the most promising area for investment, because unlike commerce or manufacturing it seemed relatively safe and long-lived. Water travel gained in importance during the early nineteenth century: Robert Fulton's boat the *North River Steamboat* marked the beginning of steamboat service with regular trips between Albany (New York) and New York City, and the Erie Canal was completed in 1825, linking Albany to Lake Erie at Buffalo and granting New York City unprecedented access to national markets. Many western cities sought to tie into the canal, while eastern cities sought to compete with New York City by other means: among these were Baltimore, which built a railroad to the Ohio River, and Philadelphia, which set out to establish a connection with Pittsburgh and therefore the Ohio River by canal, turnpike, rail, and inclined plane.

Europeans who emigrated to the United States during the nineteenth century took with them knowledge of technological advances related to textiles, steam engines, daguerreotype photography, railroads, telegraphs, and ocean steamers. By 1840 the American interest in technology was highly visible in New York City: Samuel F. B. Morse made critical contributions to photography and telegraphy at the University of the City of New York (now New York University); John B. Jervis invented a device to improve locomotive cornering. The city's most important role in railroad development was as a source of capital for the extraction and smelting of iron ore, the laying of track, and the manufacture of engines and rolling stock. Railroad promoters made New York City the eastern terminus of the four great antebellum railroad lines.

Much of the groundwork for the city's basic services and utilities was laid during the mid nineteenth century. The Croton Aqueduct, which carried abundant water from outside the city limits to private and public facilities, was constructed in 1837–42. Sewers were dug for storm drainage and waste water, and mains were laid to deliver gas to homes and offices. Paved city streets were continually torn up so that new mains could be laid and new buildings constructed. Of all the technological developments occurring in New York City the farthest-reaching were centrally generated electricity and telephony: businesses in the city provided the money that enabled Thomas Edison and Alexander Graham Bell to capitalize on their inventions. At his laboratory in Menlo Park, New Jersey, Edison developed a high-resistance filament bulb that made electrical lighting economically competitive with gas lighting. In 1882 he placed the first commercial generating station on Pearl Street in the heart of the financial district, offering four months of free service to prospective customers. Edison also worked on the microphone device of the telephone for Western Union, which attempted to patent a telephone on the same day as Bell in 1876. In 1879 the firm contested Bell's patent in court: under a settlement Western Union received $3 million from Bell Telephone to withdraw from telephony and sold to Bell its sets and Edison's patent for the microphone.

During the nineteenth century and the early twentieth New York City was a center of manufacturing, in part because the many southern European immigrants who lived there provided a large supply of labor. Most of the factories were powered by steam engines and built near railroad terminals connected to the waterfront. The city acquired its reputation as a garment center during these years. The early twentieth century also saw many developments in transport as the automobile became popular and Americans began moving to the suburbs. The subway system was a technologically impressive achievement, as were the Lincoln and Holland tunnels and the George Washington Bridge, which made parts of neighboring states more accessible. During the 1960s and later years entrepreneurs in the city financed influential ventures elsewhere and helped to fuel the technological revolution around the country, making substantial investments in the development and manufacture of technologically advanced microelectronic equipment, lasers, computers, and pollution-control equipment.

Robert Greenhalgh Albion: *The Rise of New York Port, 1815–1860* (New York: Charles Scribner's Sons, 1939; repr. 1970)

Matthew Josephson: *Edison: A Biography* (New York: McGraw–Hill, 1959)

Alan I Marcus and Howard P. Segal: *Technology in America: A Brief History* (New York: Harcourt Brace Jovanovich, 1989)

Alan I Marcus

Ted Bates. Advertising agency formed in 1940. It was named for one of its two principals, a former account executive at Benton and Bowles; the other was Rosser Reeves, one of the most influential copywriters in advertising. The agency adopted a strategy formulated by Reeves, the "unique selling proposition," according to which the advertiser makes one strong claim and repeats it for years. It emphasized market research and simple, direct slogans such as "Wonder Bread Helps Build Strong Bodies Twelve Ways." Billings increased more than eightfold between 1945 and 1960. In 1986 the agency was acquired for more than $500 million by the firm Saatchi and Saatchi, which merged it in the following year with its subsidiary Backer and Spielvogel to form Backer Spielvogel Bates Worldwide.

James Playsted Wood: *The Story of Advertising* (New York: Ronald, 1958)

Stephen R. Fox: *The Mirror Makers: A History of American Advertising and Its Creators* (New York: William Morrow, 1984)

Chauncey G. Olinger, Jr.

telegraphy. The telegraph was invented in the 1830s by Samuel F. B. Morse, a professor of art at the University of the City of New York, with the help of Leonard Gale, a fellow professor, and Alfred Vail, a mechanic and former student from Morristown, New Jersey. The first functional line was built in 1844 between Washington and Baltimore by the federal government and operated for a time by the U.S. Post Office. After Congress refused to buy patent rights and establish a permanent postal telegraph system entrepreneurs acquired rights from Morse and his partners to build lines between major American cities. In January 1846 the first sections of a network connecting New York City with Philadelphia, Boston, Buffalo, St. Louis, and New Orleans became operational. The location of the city on the eastern seaboard and its role as the major financial and shipping center in the nation helped to make it the heart of the American telegraph network. Telegraph companies chartered in New York State seeking to consolidate lines and link them to New York City benefited from liberal incorporation laws passed by the state legislature. As a result these companies led the reorganization of the industry during the 1850s, when many small, regional companies were taken over by a few conglomerates such as the Western Union Telegraph Company, which controlled the most important lines west of New York City, and the American Telegraph Company (formed by Cyrus Field, Peter Cooper, and others), which bought enough eastern companies and links to the planned transatlantic cable to dominate the telegraph market in most states on the Atlantic coast. In 1857 representatives from American Telegraph, Western Union, and four other companies met in the city to sign a cartel agreement known as the "treaty of six nations," which carved the market into clearly defined territories. Western Union abrogated the agreement in 1860 when it won a government subsidy to build a transcontinental telegraph; the completion of this system and government subsidies acquired during the Civil War gave Western Union a great competitive advantage, and by 1866 it had almost gained a monopoly by obtaining control of its major competitors, including American Telegraph. About this time it moved its headquarters from Rochester, New York, to the American Telegraph building at 145 Broadway in New York City.

In the decade after the Civil War the city remained the national center for telegraphy.

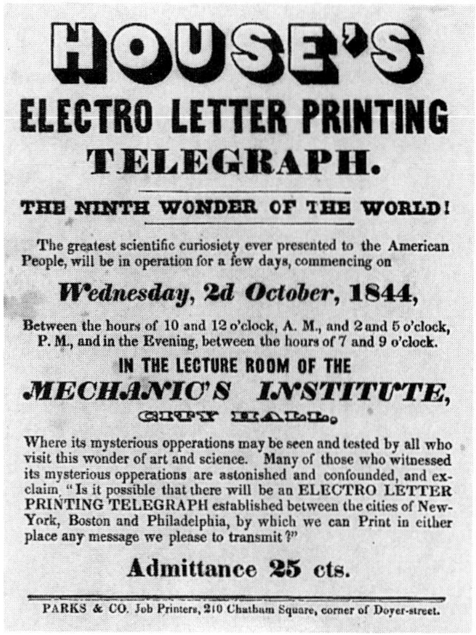

Advertisement for House's Electro Letter Printing Telegraph, 1844

New telegraph companies made their headquarters there, thus gaining access to funds for laying lines and to advanced technology that would reduce their construction costs and make them competitive with the national system operated by Western Union. Many inventors including Thomas Edison settled in the metropolitan area and helped to develop long-distance technology and a distinct urban telegraph industry. The first urban telegraph system, the fire alarm telegraph, was developed in Boston, but in the decade after the Civil War most services and companies evolved in New York City.

The Gold and Stock Telegraph Company installed the first stock tickers at the New York Stock Exchange in 1868 and soon offered market quotations for other exchanges in the city. It also adapted its printing telegraphs to provide communication banks, linkages between courthouses and lawyers' offices, and private lines connecting homes, offices, and factories. Gold and Stock was in competition with several firms; in an effort to control the expansion of its commercial news services outside New York City, Western Union signed an exclusive contract with the Associated Press for the transmission of news and used the local American District Telegraph Companies in major cities and towns to deliver messages. It acquired these local companies in 1901 and combined them into the alarm company that later became known as ADT. The American District Telegraph Companies, the first of which was organized in New York City in 1871, used message boxes connecting homes and businesses with a central station to provide a number of urban telegraph services, including private burglar and fire alarms. Fire and burglar alarms were also an important business of such other firms in the city as the Holmes Burglar Alarm Company, which offered the first major private security service; the Gamewell Fire-Alarm Telegraph Company, which installed most of the municipal fire and police alarm systems in the nation during the rest of the nineteenth century; and American District. Fire and burglar alarm services became separate from telegraphy in the twentieth century.

Western Union continued to dominate the long-distance telegraph industry into the twentieth century even as the telegraph was gradually supplanted by the telephone and the radio. In the decades after the Second World War telegraphy was superseded by other telecommunications and Western Union moved to New Jersey and reduced its operations.

Alvin F. Harlow: *Old Wires and New Waves: The History of the Telegraph, Telephone, and Wireless* (New York: D. Appleton Century, 1936)

Robert Luther Thompson: *Wiring a Continent: The History of the Telegraph Industry in the United States, 1832–1866* (Princeton, N.J.: Princeton University Press, 1947)

William Greer: *A History of Alarm Security* (Washington: National Burglar and Fire Alarm Association, 1979)

Paul B. Israel: *From the Machine Shop to the Industrial Laboratory: Telegraphy and the Changing Context of American Invention, 1830–1920* (Baltimore: Johns Hopkins University Press, 1992)

For a discussion of wireless telegraphy see Radio.

Paul Israel

telephony. The first licenses granted by the American Bell Telephone Company in New York City date from 27 August 1877, and a primitive telephone device was placed on the market soon after. The Metropolitan Telephone and Telegraph Company was formed in 1878, when a central switching office opened in Manhattan, serving 271 subscribers. The only competitor of American Bell in the early years of telephony in New York City was a subsidiary of Western Union; this firm abandoned the field in 1879, and within a year the Metropolitan Telephone and Telegraph Company expanded service beyond Manhattan. New York Telephone was organized in 1896 and absorbed the Bell operations for New York City. Over time American Telephone and Telegraph (AT&T) acquired a controlling interest in New York Telephone, which in 1909 consolidated six regional companies serving New York State, northern New Jersey, and parts of Pennsylvania. In 1927 operations in New Jersey were taken over by New Jersey Bell, and in the same year transatlantic service was established between New York City and London. In 1984 AT&T divested itself of its regional operating companies to comply with the settlement in 1981 of an antitrust suit. New York Telephone then became a subsidiary of NYNEX along with New England Telephone and other, smaller regional subsidiaries. By 1990 New York Telephone employed nearly fifty thousand persons, served

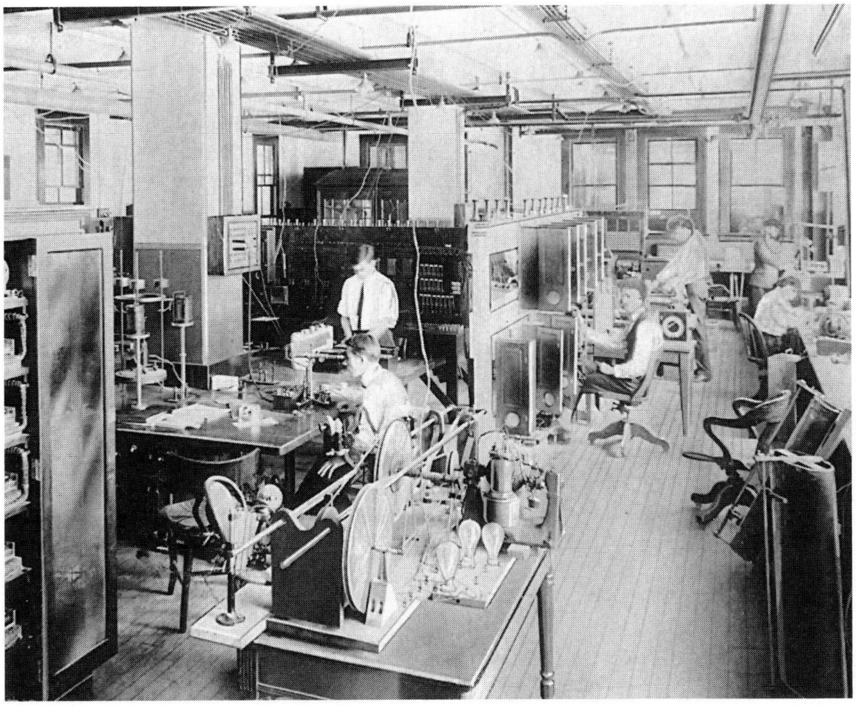

Physical Laboratory of the Western Electric Company, 463 West Street, 1914

9.2 million access lines (connections between the customer and the central switching office, excluding coin and private lines), and handled nearly 106 million telephone calls a day through almost 100 million miles (160 million kilometers) of cable, including calls for new services in data transmission and cellular telephones.

Robert W. Garnet: *The Telephone Enterprise: The Evolution of the Bell System's Horizontal Structure, 1876–1909* (Baltimore: Johns Hopkins University Press, 1985)

See also TECHNOLOGY.

George David Smith

television. Many of the first experiments in broadcasting were conducted in New York City. On 7 April 1927 an image of Herbert Hoover, then the secretary of commerce, was transmitted to Washington from the laboratories of American Telephone and Telegraph on West Street in Manhattan. The first broadcast by the experimental station W2XAB (of the Columbia Broadcasting System, or CBS) on the night of 21 July 1931 included such well-known personalities as Mayor James J. Walker, Kate Smith, and George Gershwin; most other broadcasts consisted of test patterns and cheap, short motion pictures. Another experimental station, W2XBS (of the National Broadcasting Company, or NBC), introduced the first mobile unit in 1937, which it used to broadcast a fire on Wards Island. Scientists continued for most of the 1930s to perfect transmission standards. To ensure that its standard became adopted by the industry, the Radio Corporation of America (RCA), which owned and controlled NBC, began promoting television for the public. Piser's Furniture Store in the Bronx offered some of the first television sets for sale in 1938. RCA broadcast President Franklin D. Roosevelt's opening remarks at the World's Fair of 1939–40, where it also had its own exhibition. On 17 May 1939 the first broadcast of a sporting event was made by NBC of a baseball game between Columbia and Princeton at Baker Field; reception was so poor that according to Leo Durocher (later the manager of the Dodgers and the Giants) the game looked as if it were being played under water. Nonetheless RCA and other manufacturers of television sets hoped for commercial success. At the end of 1941 there were three television stations broadcasting to about five thousand households.

Promotion declined with the entry of the United States into the Second World War, but soon after the war television became a tremendous commercial success. Regular broadcasts began on four networks based in the city: CBS, NBC, Du Mont, and the American Broadcasting Company (ABC). New York City also became the center of network news operations. Affiliation with a network was sought by stations around the country because they could not afford the high costs and risks of making their own programs. Television began with the distinct flavor of New York City. In January 1948 about two thirds of the television sets in the United States were owned by viewers in the metropolitan area, whose affection for Milton Berle and other Jewish comedians dictated the content of network programs; eventually these performers were eclipsed by others considered less identifiably ethnic by viewers from the rest of the country. Several independent stations were formed in New York City, among them WPIX (1948; owned by the *Daily News*), which like other independent stations broadcast mostly sporting events and old motion pictures. During air time that had not been sold for advertising, stations broadcast sessions of the United Nations at Lake Success on Long Island. In 1950–51 WPIX broadcast hearings on channel 11 on organized crime, which were held in Foley Square and led by Senator Estes Kefauver. By then the other

Multiple switchboard of New York Telephone at the Cortlandt Street exchange, from Harper's Weekly, *1891*

Television Shows Set in New York City
(selective list)

Mary Kay and Johnny 1947–50
Tonight on Broadway 1948–49
The Goldbergs 1949–54
Man against Crime 1949–56
That Wonderful Guy 1949–50
I Covered Times Square 1950–51
Penthouse Party 1950–51
The Robbins Nest 1950
I Love Lucy 1951–61
Mr. District Attorney 1951–52
Mr. and Mrs. North 1952–54
Take It from Me 1953–54
The Honeymooners 1954–61
The Thin Man 1957–59
The Ann Southern Show 1958–61
Naked City 1958–63
Car 54, Where Are You? 1961–63
Dick Van Dyke Show 1961–66
The Joey Bishop Show 1961–65
The Nurses 1962–65
Patty Duke Show 1963–66
Man From U.N.C.L.E. 1964–68
The Reporter 1964
Valentine's Day 1964–65
The Trials of O'Brien 1965–66
Family Affair 1966–71
That Girl 1966–71
N.Y.P.D. 1967–69
The Odd Couple 1970–75
All in the Family 1971–83
Kojak 1972–78
Lotsa Luck 1973–74
Shaft 1973–74
Rhoda 1974–78
Baretta 1975–78
Barney Miller 1975–82
The Jeffersons 1975–85
Welcome Back, Kotter 1975–79
Popi 1976
Serpico 1976–77
Fish 1977–78
On Our Own 1977–78
Seventh Avenue 1977
Taxi 1977–81
Diff'rent Strokes 1978–86
13 Queens Boulevard 1979
Flatbush 1979
Bosom Buddies 1980–84
Love, Sidney 1981–83
Nero Wolfe 1981
Nurse 1981–82
Park Place 1981
The Two of Us 1981–82
Cagney and Lacey 1982–89
Cosby 1984–92
Kate and Allie 1984–89
Mama Malone 1984
Mickey Spillane's Mike Hammer 1984–87
Night Court 1984–92
Paper Dolls 1984
The Equalizer 1985–88
Foley Square 1985–86
The Days and Nights of Molly Dodd 1987–88
Melba 1986
Throb 1986–88
Beauty and the Beast 1987–89
Bronx Zoo 1987–88
Law and Order 1990–
Seinfeld 1990–
Brooklyn Bridge 1991

Source: Tim Brooks and Earle Marsh: *The Complete TV Directory to Prime Time News Shows, 1946–Present* (New York: Ballantine, 1988)

Compiled by James Bradley

commercial channels in the city in the powerful very high frequency range were 2 (CBS), 4 (NBC), 5 (Du Mont), 7 (ABC), and 9 (independent). Initially the channels owned by networks were so profitable that they offset losses occasionally incurred in producing and broadcasting programming.

New York City remained the center of television production into the mid 1950s. It benefited in particular from the heavy reliance of early television on live production. At first virtually all programs were live, in part because the major motion picture companies refused to work for television. Broadcasts from other cities were considered impractical because most would not fit into a schedule planned for the eastern time zone. A lack of efficient recording technology meant that elaborate programs could not be repeated for audiences in other zones. In 1953 NBC introduced the "spectacular," an extended live program running as long as two hours. Other live variety shows, dramatic series, and situation comedies such as "The Honeymooners" and "Mr. Peepers" were produced in studios in Manhattan and the Bronx. People who planned careers in television moved to the city; by 1952 there was such demand for studio space that theaters, private dining rooms in hotels, abandoned churches, and car barns were used as stages.

In 1951 CBS began offering the filmed situation comedy "I Love Lucy," which quickly became a success, and by the late 1950s the leading motion picture studios in Hollywood produced series for the networks; these proved popular and were also found to be a valuable source of reruns. Hollywood was conducive to outdoor filming because of its gentle climate and varied terrain and because it had disused motion picture studios, and gradually it displaced New York City as the national center of television. Du Mont ceased operations in 1955; by 1958 most series were filmed in California. In early 1965 all but ten of the ninety-six programs shown by the networks in the evening were produced in Hollywood. Only variety shows continued to be produced in New York City during the 1960s: the longest-lived was "The Ed Sullivan Show," which was shown on Sunday evenings on CBS for more than two decades and found a large audience through the efforts of its host, a columnist for the *Daily News* who was awkward on camera but had an unerring ability to discover talent. In 1954 NBC first broadcast "The Tonight Show," which was shown late on weeknights and employed a format derived from that of the variety program; until 1972 it was produced in New York City, and many of the guests (including some who were unknown) were chosen to appeal to the local audience. Other programs made in the city included locally produced talk shows and several network programs known for their irreverent humor, among them "Saturday Night Live" and "Late Night with David Letterman." The tremendously popular situation comedy "The Cosby Show" was videotaped in the 1980s by NBC in a studio in Queens. Other similar programs were set in the city but made in or near Hollywood.

The city remained the national center of network news programs. The country's leading news program in the 1970s and 1980s, "60 Minutes," was produced in the city, as were the early evening newscasts. Network news producers relied heavily on the *New York Times* in deciding which stories to emphasize: occasionally news "anchors" broadcast their programs from other cities. In the 1980s some network news operations shifted to Washington. The Public Broadcasting System (PBS) was formed by the Broadcasting Act of 1967 and produced most of its programs in the city, including "Sesame Street," its most popular series. Although the act discouraged a centralized programming authority, WNET (Channel 13) became a major provider of programming to the system, including the well-regarded British series "The Forsyte Saga" in the late 1960s; it later produced the arts anthology "Great Performances" and an early-evening news program presented by Robert MacNeil and Jim Lehrer. A fourth commercial network, Fox, began operations in 1986 with WNEW (later WNYW) in New York City as its flagship station.

See also CABLE TELEVISION.

James L. Baughman

Temple Ansche Chesed. Conservative synagogue, opened in 1876 by a traditional German-speaking congregation on 86th Street and 3rd Avenue in Yorkville; it was initially known as Chebra Ansche Chesed. The congregation moved successively to East 112th Street in Harlem (during the 1890s) and to a stately brick temple designed by Edward I. Shire on 114th Street and 7th Avenue (1907), where it flourished under the direction of Jacob Kohn. By the 1920s many Jews had left the neighborhood for the Upper West Side, and after languishing for a number of years the synagogue moved to a new building designed by Edward I. Shire and erected in 1927 at 100th Street and West End Avenue at a cost of $1 million. The facilities there included a sanctuary for a congregation of more than fifteen hundred and a community house containing classrooms, a library, an auditorium, and a social hall. After the Second World War the congregation declined as the surrounding neighborhood changed; it prospered again when the Upper West Side was revitalized during the 1970s.

Jenna Weissman Joselit

Temple Emanu-El. The first Reform congregation in New York City, formed in 1845 as a *cultus verein*, or German literary society, and incorporated as a congregation within ten years. It initially occupied rented rooms and remodeled church buildings on the Lower East Side. By 1868 a synagogue in a Moorish style was erected on 5th Avenue and 43rd Street, where the congregation remained for nearly sixty years. As the neighborhood became increasingly commercial, the congregation moved farther up the East Side, sold its building to the developer Joseph Durst for $7 million, merged with Beth El, another prominent Reform congregation, and moved to 5th Avenue and 65th Street in 1927, where an art deco synagogue designed by Robert D. Kohn, Clarence Stein, Charles Butler, and Bertram Goodhue was built in limestone. One of the largest synagogues in the world, Temple Emanu-El was built with seating for 2500 in its vast sanctuary and ornamented with dazzling stained-glass windows and colorful mosaics in a Viennese Secessionist style. A community house was built on an adjacent site to accommodate a wide range of educational and social activities; several architectural elements from Beth El were incorporated into the design, among them a Tiffany window. Temple Emanu-El remains one of the most prominent Reform congregations in the United States.

Jenna Weissman Joselit

Temple Emanu-El (designed by Leopold Eidlitz), ca 1885

Ten American Painters. A group of impressionist and figurative artists formed in 1898 by Thomas Dewing, Childe Hassam, Willard Leroy Metcalf, Robert Reid, Edward Simmons, John Henry Twachtman, and Julian Alden Weir (all from New York City) and Frank Weston Benson, Joseph Rodefer De Camp, and Edmund Charles Tarbell (all from Boston). When Twachtman died in 1902 William Merritt Chase was elected to take his place. Until 1918 the group held yearly exhibitions in New York City, usually at the Durand–Ruel Gallery or the Montross Gallery.

William H. Gerdts: *American Impressionism* (New York: Abbeville, 1984)

Patricia Hills

Tenderloin. A nightclub district in Manhattan during the 1880s, bounded to the north by 42nd Street, to the east by 5th Avenue, to the south by 24th Street, and to the west by 7th Avenue. The name refers to extortion payments made to the police by legitimate and illegitimate businesses in the area during the heyday of Tammany Hall. Known as Satan's Circus by reformers, the district contained the greatest concentration of saloons, brothels, gambling parlors, dance halls, and "clip joints" in the city. It is now the site of the Empire State Building, the garment district, and Herald Square.

Linda Elsroad

tenements. The construction of multiple-unit residential buildings called tenements began in the mid nineteenth century, providing compact rental housing at $2 to $3 a room a month for poor and working-class immigrants living and working in lower Manhattan. Tenements were inspired by "rookeries," a name applied to warehouses, mansions, churches, and breweries in the fourth ward that were converted in the 1830s so that each floor housed many families in small, cramped, poorly ventilated rooms. The first tenements were built by speculators in response to the growing immigrant population. These were spartan, functional buildings erected on standard lots twenty-five feet (eight meters) wide and one hundred feet (thirty meters) deep: each building had four stories, four apartments to a floor, and dark, unventilated, interior rooms connected like railroad cars (hence the expression "railroad apartment"). Many buildings had no indoor running water, and water could be had only at a single, communal privy in a cellar vault or in the backyard. Often a second tenement known as a "double house" was built in the backyard.

The regulation of construction began about the time of the Civil War, when middle-class citizens began to view the tenements as a social and health menace. In 1867 the state legislature enacted the Tenement House Law to improve living conditions, the first such legislation in the United States. The law defined a tenement house as a multiple dwelling, required landlords to provide a privy and a fire ladder for every twenty tenants, and established the maximum proportion of a lot that could be covered by a building, a minimum area for rear courts, and standards for the open-air ventilation of interiors. But the law encouraged speculators to satisfy only the minimum requirements for ventilation by connecting the front and rear buildings on a lot: the result was buildings that were more than four rooms deep and had interior rooms ventilated only by narrow air shafts or doors fitted with transoms. Throughout this period apartments were designed with a front room, or "parlor," and two inner sleeping chambers barely ten feet (three meters) square, and privies began to be placed in a subterranean vault where the effluvial stench became so powerful that it contributed to concerns about cholera.

By the late 1870s the housing stock contained roughly 21,000 rookeries and railroad apartments. Various municipal reformers and organizations such as the Association for Improving the Condition of the Poor sought to improve the living conditions in these buildings. In 1879 the publication *Plumber and Sanitary Engineer* conducted a competition for the best new design for a tenement. The architect James E. Ware won the contest with the "dumbbell" design, which was intended to raise hygienic standards by providing ventilation and light for interior rooms (see DUMBBELL TENEMENTS). The design was so named because the building resembled a dumbbell when seen from above: between the front and back rooms the exterior walls were indented, creating large air shafts of nearly ten by thirteen feet (three by four meters) between adjacent buildings that extended from the ground to the roof. The tenements had interior toilets with plumbing, vents to guard against sewer gas, two rear bedrooms, each six and a half feet by eight feet (two by two and a quarter meters), a kitchen of seven and a half feet by ten and a half feet (two and a half by three meters), and a living room of eight and a half feet by thirteen feet (two and a half by four meters), for a total area in each apartment of 293 square feet (twenty-seven square meters). The interior rooms were ventilated by horizontal air shafts four feet (one and a half meters) long and a two-foot (sixty-centimeter) indentation formed by the dumbbell. Reformers incorporated these designs into the Tenement House Law of 1879, introducing a

Jacob A. Riis, Elizabeth Street — 44 Water Closets in Yard *(1903)*

clause that forbade the construction of rooms removed from a source of outside air, and that directed the Board of Health to reject plans for buildings that would cover more than 65 percent of a lot.

During the 1880s many real-estate developers were led by continued concern over sewer gas to install sinks and stationary tubs in the hallways, where they could be ventilated by horizontal, "studded" (embedded) shafts, five feet (one and a half meters) long, that were square or octagonal. Soon sanitary regulation and the rising cost of brick construction caused the studded shafts to be replaced by a single shaft, or "light well," two feet (sixty centimeters) square and thirty feet (nine meters) deep. Architects also repositioned stairways and hallways in the indentation of the dumbbell to avoid the layout of a railroad apartment, which had the stairs at the front, and installed extra shafts to ventilate toilets, hallways, and interior rooms. In rough accordance with the law of 1879, builders erected nearly twenty thousand dumbbell tenements in Manhattan and the Bronx between 1880 and 1900; nearly one third of these were in Yorkville and Harlem, and thousands more were on the Lower East Side.

At the end of the nineteenth century five-story tenement houses were designed for twenty families, but these buildings often housed as many as one hundred residents, as well as their boarders. Upwards of two hundred licensed "flophouses" with nearly eighteen thousand bunks lined the Bowery and Oliver, Chatham, and Mulberry streets. Many people lived in basements subject to tidal seepage, and thousands lived in the 2379 rear houses counted in the census of 1897. Apartments with two rooms had no closets: tenants hung their clothing from nails that they tacked into recesses in the walls six inches (fifteen centimeters) deep. Bedrooms had no space for wash basins or bureaus, and kitchens were rarely large enough for people to sit around the four sides of a table. The lack of privacy led families to develop a strict hierarchy, particularly regarding children. Cleanliness was of essential importance: only one third of the city's tenements had running water, and in some blocks it was lacking altogether. Only 306 of the 255,033 persons living on the Lower East Side had bathrooms in their apartments, and most East Siders continued to use a vault privy or one at school even as hallway toilets became standard. In 1893 there were 12,434 persons in the Italian slum of Centre Street, where the typical apartment had two rooms, each housing two persons, and was rented for $4.60 a month. Only 2 percent of all families there had toilets on their floor, and most shared with their neighbors a backyard or vault privy that was "mucked out" by hand (hygienically advanced "school sinks" were ostensibly flushed once a day). Although most working-class families had three rooms (including a dark, inner bedroom), during the 1890s health inspectors found that in dilapidated buildings on Allen, Orchard, and Baxter streets entire families lived in a single room.

The conditions in the tenements prompted to action the reformers Jacob A. Riis, Lillian Wald, Felix Adler, Simon Baruch, and Alfred E. Smith and the many volunteers at settlement houses on the East Side. The Tenement House Committee of the Charity Organization Society, led by Robert De Forest but run by Lawrence Veiller, launched investigations and mounted exhibits that indicted the dumbbell tenement and led to the passage of the Tenement House Law of 1901. Buildings constructed before that date are still referred to as "old law" tenements. The law required that buildings have side courts four feet (one and a third meters) wide and backyards eleven feet (three and a half meters) deep, which meant that a building could cover no more than 72 percent of a standard lot; one room had to have an area of at least 120 square feet (eleven square meters) and none could be smaller than seventy square feet (six and a half square meters), which made the traditional lot size impractical for the development of mass housing. The law also created the Tenement House Department, which administered improvements in upwards of 83,000 "old law" structures and enforced new law standards on buildings under construction on lots forty and fifty feet (twelve and fifteen meters) wide in the outer boroughs.

About the turn of the century a wave of new immigrants arrived in the city, and in response to the heightened demand for housing the department sought to improve the conditions in the old law buildings rather than shut them down. It focused on the 6703 school sinks and toilets in Manhattan and the nearly two thousand in Brooklyn, bringing up to code 331,168 previously undocumented inner rooms and 96,079 rooms with no ventilation. The development of new law buildings and steam-heated apartments in the outer boroughs by the late 1920s decreased the population of the Lower East Side by nearly 250,000, and throughout lower Manhattan landlords boarded up thousands of old law buildings with vacancy rates of 15 to 30 percent. As the housing market moved to the outer boroughs thousands of old structures were removed and major public works projects were executed: 6th and 7th avenues were extended, Allen Street widened, and the notorious stretch of old law tenements between Chrystie and Forsyth streets leveled.

The Multiple Dwellings Law (1929) required that landlords install toilets, fire retardants, and ventilation for inside rooms, and the commissioner of tenement housing Langdon W. Post bolstered the law with radical revisions, notably a six-month limit on the installation of fire retardants and an amendment that expanded the definition of legal ownership to include mortgage holders: as a result landlords and local banks threatened to abandon the 68,000 old law tenements that remained standing in the early 1930s. With the aid of New Deal subsidies for slum clearance Mayor Fiorello H. La Guardia razed nearly 9500 buildings beginning in 1934. The end of the Depression brought a sharp increase in the occupancy of old law buildings, and La Guardia eased the enforcement of the Multiple Dwellings Law. After the Second World War the city's construction coordinator Robert Moses, who believed that the poor should move into public housing, used federal funds granted under Title I of the Housing Act of 1949 to demolish old law buildings on the East Side between the Brooklyn Bridge and 23rd Street and build projects such as the Corlears Hook Houses (1955). Social reformers and architects in the mid 1960s explored various possibilities in tenement renovation. Attempts were made at "gut rehabilitation" of remaining tenements, but the buildings proved difficult to repair and nearly impossible to bring up to code. About 200,000 tenement units remained scattered throughout the city during the mid 1990s, with the largest concentration in lower Manhattan between Houston and Delancey streets and west of Sarah D. Roosevelt Park, a neighborhood of Chinese immigrants adjacent to Chinatown. At 97 Orchard Street the Lower East Side Tenement Museum (opened in 1988) preserves the interior of a typical old law residence.

Robert W. De Forest and Lawrence Veiller, eds.: *The Tenement House Problem* (New York: Macmillan, 1903)

Anthony Jackson: *A Place Called Home: A History of Low-cost Housing in Manhattan* (Cambridge: MIT Press, 1976)

Joel Schwartz

tennis. Tennis was introduced to the United States by Mary Outerbridge, who oversaw the construction of the first lawn court at the Staten Island Cricket and Baseball Club. The growing popularity of the sport led to the formation in New York City on 21 May 1881 of the United States National Lawn Tennis Association (USNLTA), known from 1920 as the United States Lawn Tennis Association (USLTA) and from 1975 as the United States Tennis Association (USTA). The first courts in Manhattan opened in Central Park in 1881. Although primarily for the wealthy, tennis attracted players from all economic and racial groups, and local clubs were organized according to language, ethnicity, and class. Initially the USNLTA had no black clubs or players. The centers for local tennis were the Crescent Athletic Club, bounded by New York Bay, 1st Avenue, 83rd Street, and 85th Street in Bay Ridge, and the West Side Tennis Club in Manhattan, which began as an all-male club on Central Park West in 1892, and moved successively to 238th Street and Broadway (1898), 117th Street and Morningside Drive (1902), and Forest Hills (1914, remaining into the 1990s). The National Indoor Championship was played in the city from 1900 until 1940 and again from 1946 to 1963. In 1902 the Crescent Athletic Club competed for the Davis Cup against players from Great Britain. Robert LeRoy, a student at Columbia University, became the first national intercollegiate champion from the city in 1904.

The West Side Tennis Club was the site of American defenses of the Davis Cup (from 1914), as well as of the national championship from 1915 to 1920 and again from 1924 to 1978, when the championship was first held at Louis Armstrong Stadium in Queens. Much of the growth of the club from the First World War to 1950 was overseen by Julian Myrick, a resident of New York City who was also a president of the USNLTA. Church and club teams were formed by black immigrants from the West Indies, who also helped to establish the Cosmopolitan Tennis Club (at 138th Street and Convent Avenue in Harlem) and the predominantly black American Tennis Association in 1916. Two black players, Gerald Norman and Reginald Weir, competed in several indoor events sponsored by the USNLTA at the Seventh Regiment Armory. The National Public Parks championships began in 1923 and inspired the construction of most of the 550 public courts in the city. In 1938 Don Budge, champion of the USLTA, played against the black champion Jimmy McDaniels in an exhibition at the Cosmopolitan Tennis Club. Althea Gibson received her training at the public courts on 155th Street in Harlem; with the help of Sarah Palfrey, another New Yorker, in 1950 she became the first black member of the West Side Tennis Club, and in 1957 she won Wimbledon and the national championship and became the first black player to be generally recognized as the world champion. Another well-known player of the 1950s from New York City was Dick Savitt. In 1968 the national indoor championship of the USLTA adopted an open format, allowing both amateurs and professionals to compete. Vitas Gerulaitis, a New Yorker who briefly attended Columbia, won major world tournaments during the 1970s; John McEnroe, who grew up in Douglaston, dominated the sport in the 1980s. By the 1990s the U.S. Open was broadcast on television worldwide; the New York Junior Tennis League operated on public courts and schoolyards and was the largest league of its kind in the United States.

Robert Minton: *Forest Hills* (Philadelphia: J. B. Lippincott, 1975)

Arthur Ashe

Tenth Street Studio Building. Building erected in 1857 at 15 10th Street, between 5th and 6th avenues, to house artists' studios, the first such building in the United States or Europe. The address was renumbered 51 West 10th Street in 1866. The building was commissioned by the wealthy businessman James Boorman Johnston and designed by Richard Morris Hunt, the first American architect trained at the École des Beaux-Arts. Its symmetrical plan incorporated a large central exhibition gallery two stories high surrounded by twenty-five studios. In the early years tenants included Frederic E. Church and Albert Bierstadt, both prominent members of the Hudson River School, Winslow Homer (in the 1870s), and William Merritt Chase, who painted cosmopolitan subjects of everyday life as well as landscapes. An annex was added at 55 West 10th Street in 1873. Although a few well-known artists remained into the twentieth century the building became antiquated and was inhabited mostly by illustrators, art teachers, and photographers. It was sold by Johnston's descendants in 1920 and after several changes of ownership was demolished in 1956.

Annette Blaugrund: "The Tenth Street Studio Building: A Roster, 1857–1895," *American Art Journal* 14, no. 2 (spring 1982), 64–71

Annette Blaugrund

terra cotta. Glazed or unglazed ceramic made from clay was used in New York City during the late nineteenth century and the early twentieth to ornament masonry and to make curtain walls. It was introduced in the city in 1853 as a cheaper substitute for cut stone by James Renwick, who engaged a sewer pipe factory to manufacture terra cotta cornices and window surrounds for the Tontine Building, the St. Denis Hotel, and three houses on 9th Street. These projects were successfully completed but met with opposition from stonecutters and masons, who feared that terra cotta would endanger their livelihood and helped to keep it out of the city for many years. The terra cotta industry flourished in other parts of the country, and in 1877 the Chicago Terra Cotta Company supplied unglazed, reddish terra cotta for use on two buildings in New York City: the Braehm Residence (1877, George B. Post) and the Morse Building at 12 Beekman Street (1879, Silliman and Farnsworth). The fireproof qualities of the material were put to use in the Potter Building at 38 Park Row (1883–86, N. G. Starkweather). Its owner, Orlando B. Potter, was committed to fireproof construction after a fire destroyed his previous building on the site. Potter was instrumental in founding the first local terra cotta manufacturer to achieve success, the New York Architectural Terra Cotta Company, in Long Island City in 1886 (offices built in 1892 with terra cotta trim at 42-16 Vernon Boulevard). Another local supplier in the 1890s was B. Kreischer and Sons, a brick-making firm in Charleston, Staten Island. Polychrome glazed terra cotta in blues, whites, yellows, and greens was introduced in 1906 by McKim, Mead and White in the Madison Square Presbyterian Church (Madison Avenue at 24th Street, demolished 1913) but did not become popular for two decades. A wide range of glazes was developed about 1925, including metallic lusters, vivid yellows, and shades of lime green and lavender characteristic of art deco; the McGraw–Hill Building (1931, Hood, Godley and Fouilhoux), at 330 West 42nd Street, was decorated with horizontal bands of blue-green. Other buildings in the city that used terra cotta ornament include the Bayard Building (1898, Louis Sullivan), the Flatiron Building (1901–3, D. H. Burnham), the Alwyn Court Apartments (1909, Harde and Short), the Audubon Theatre and Ballroom (1912, Thomas W. Lamb), the Woolworth Building (1913, Cass Gilbert), 2 Park Avenue (1927, Ely Jacques Kahn), the Pythian Temple at 135 West 70th Street (1927, Lamb), and 235 East 22nd Street (1928, George and Edward Blum). After the International Style was introduced by Henry Russell Hitchcock and Philip Johnson in 1932 in an exhibition at the Museum of Modern Art, architects abandoned the kind of exuberant ornamentation to which terra cotta was suited, and the use of terra cotta diminished during the 1930s.

Virginia Guest Ferriday: *The Last of the Handmade Buildings: Glazed Terra Cotta in Downtown Portland* (Portland, Ore.: Mark Publishing, 1984)

Susan Tunick: *Architectural Terra Cotta: Its Impact on New York* (New York: Lumen, 1986)

Gary F. Kurrutz and Mary Swisher: *Architectural Terra Cotta of Gladding, McBean* (Sausalito, Calif.: Windgate, 1989)

Andrew S. Dolkart and Susan Tunick: *George and Edward Blum: Texture and Design in New York Apartment House Architecture* (New York: Friends of Terra Cotta Press, 1993)

Susan Tunick

terrorism. Because of its size and importance New York City has been an occasional target of terrorists. The Black Tom explosion occurred on 30 July 1916, when barges and railroad cars filled with munitions bound for England and France exploded at the terminal of the Lehigh Valley Railroad on Black Tom Island, west of Ellis Island, killing seven persons. A claims commission ruled in 1939 that the explosion was an act of saboteurs of the Imperial German government. Thirty persons were killed in a terrorist attack on Wall Street on 16 September 1920, when a horse-drawn wagon filled with TNT exploded across from the New York Stock Exchange; Bolshevik terrorists were suspected, but no arrests were ever made. A disgruntled former employee of Consolidated Edison named George P. Metesky terrorized New York City with a series of thirty-three homemade bombs that he planted around the city between 1940 and 1956, and became popularly known as the Mad Bomber. Twenty-three of the bombs detonated before being found, and six caused injuries to a total of fifteen persons. Metesky was arrested at his home in Waterbury, Connecticut, on 18 January 1957, served seventeen years in an asylum for the criminally insane, and was released in 1974. During the 1960s and 1970s a wave of political terrorism swept the United States, and left-wing terrorists attacked several targets in the city. Many were the headquarters of corporations such as Mobil Oil, General Telephone and Electronics, and International Business Machines; other targets were governmental or institutional, including the Federal Office Building and Columbia University. The city's most notable terrorist incident of the 1970s was apparently accidental. On 6 March 1970 an explosion demolished a townhouse at 18 West 11th Street in Greenwich Village, killing three persons, including Theodore Gold, a student at Columbia University. Two women were seen fleeing the explosion, one of whom was Cathlyn Wilkerson, whose father owned the townhouse. Wilkerson and Gold were members of the Weathermen, a violent radical faction of the left-wing group Students for a Democratic Society. Sixty sticks of dynamite and thirty blasting caps were found in the ruins, leading the police to conclude that the building was being used as a bomb factory.

From the 1970s into the mid 1980s several violent attacks were staged on businesses and institutions in the city by advocates of independence for Puerto Rico, in particular by the group Fuerzas Armadas de Liberación Nacional (FALN). In early 1975 the FALN claimed responsibility for a bomb that exploded at Fraunces Tavern and killed four persons, and in 1977 and 1978 the group planted pipe bombs at the headquarters of several major corporations in New York City and at the New York Public Library; it also planted incendiary devices that set off fires at La Guardia, Kennedy, and Newark airports. In 1982 it bombed the lobbies of several financial houses on Wall Street and of the headquarters of the New York Police Department. The FALN is also the main suspect in the unsolved bombing of the Trans World Airlines terminal at La Guardia Airport on 29 December 1975, which killed eleven persons. Other Puerto Rican nationalist groups also attacked targets in New York City: one occupied the Statue of Liberty on 25 October 1977, and another bombed Pennsylvania Station in 1980.

On 28 February 1993 a car bomb exploded in an underground parking garage beneath the World Trade Center, killing five persons. Both towers were closed for several weeks after the explosion. Four Egyptians arrested in connection with the bombing were identified as followers of the Egyptian Muslim cleric Sheik Omar Abdel-Rahman, exiled from Egypt and living in the United States. In late June the Federal Bureau of Investigation arrested eight other Egyptian and Sudanese followers of Abdel-Rahman on charges of plotting to bomb several targets in the city, including the United Nations, the tunnels between Manhattan and New Jersey, and the Javits Federal Office Building, and to assassinate the secretary general of the United Nations, Boutros Boutros-Ghali, President Hosni Mubarak of Egypt, and Senator Alfonse D'Amato. Abdel-Rahman himself was charged as the ringleader of the terrorist group. In 1994 the four main suspects in the bombing of the World Trade Center were convicted on nearly all charges.

Rohit T. Aggarwala

Tesla, Nikola (*b* Smiljan, near Gospic, Croatia, 10 July 1856; *d* New York City, 7 Jan 1943). Physicist, electrical engineer, and inventor. He moved to New York City in 1884 to work for the Edison Machine Works and in the following year joined Westinghouse in Pittsburgh, where he was the leading advocate of alternating current in the debate over its merits relative to direct current. In 1889 he built a laboratory at South 5th Avenue (now La Guardia Place), which he then moved to 46 East Houston Street; there he demonstrated his best-known invention in 1898, a device known as the "Tesla coil" that contributed to the development of broadcasting. Having gained great wealth and prominence from his inventions, Tesla lived at the Waldorf–Astoria, dined at Delmonico's, and was acquainted with John Jacob Astor IV, J. P. Morgan Sr., and Mark Twain, but he died a debt-ridden recluse at the Hotel New Yorker. His

Nikola Tesla demonstrating some of his experiments with high frequency and high voltage electric currents

memoir *My Inventions: The Autobiography of Nikola Tesla* was published posthumously in 1982.

Obituary, *New York Times*, 8 Jan 1943, p. 19
John J. O'Neil: *Prodigal Genius: The Life of Nikola Tesla* (London: Neville Spearman, 1968)
Margaret Cheney: *Tesla, Man Out of Time* (New York: Prentice Hall, 1981)
Stephen S. Hall: "Tesla: A Scientific Saint, Wizard, or Carnival Sideman?," *Smithsonian Magazine*, June 1986, pp. 120–22
Bill Lawren: "The Eccentricity and Inventiveness of an Unappreciated Genius," *Omni*, March 1988, p. 64

Val Ginter

T.G.I. Friday's. Restaurant and bar opened on 15 March 1965 on 1st Avenue in the 60s by Alan Stillman, a perfume and flavor salesman, on the site of a neighborhood bar called the Good Tavern. Generally regarded as the world's first "singles bar," it inspired many imitators in the neighborhood, notably Maxwell's Plum and Mister Laff's. By the time the original location closed in 1994 it had given rise to 294 franchises throughout the world.

Kenneth T. Jackson

Thalia Movie Theater. Movie theater at West 95th Street between Broadway and West End Avenue, occupying the basement of the former Astor Market building (opened in 1915). Originally the site of the Sunken Garden Restaurant, it was converted in 1931 by Raymond Irrera and Ben Schlanger into a theater seating 292 and using many architectural innovations. The long, narrow parabolic reverse floor, dipping in the center and sloping up toward the edges, was invented by Schlanger to provide each seat with the same view of the screen and soon became standard in the construction of movie theaters nationwide. The Thalia offered mainly foreign films initially but added Hollywood films in 1955. Under the direction of Richard Schwartz it became exclusively a revival house by 1977. After years of neglect it closed in 1987, the victim of a struggle for the ownership of the old market building as well as the decline of revival houses. Refurbished by local businessmen for $50,000, the Thalia reopened in 1993, its original architecture and *art moderne* interior intact. In the mid 1990s it remained one of few repertory movie theaters in New York City.

Isabelle Kaplan

Tharp, Twyla (*b* Portland, Ind., 1 July 1941). Dancer and choreographer. A graduate of Barnard College, she danced with the Paul Taylor Dance Company from 1963 until 1965, when she formed her own modern dance company, Twyla Tharp and Dancers. In the 1960s she provided choreography for the postmodern dances *Tank Dive* and *Jam*. Her first ballet was *Deuce Coupe* for the Joffrey Ballet in 1973; for American Ballet Theatre she provided choreography for *Push Comes to Shove* in 1976. Her dances of the 1970s, including *Eight Jelly Rolls* and *Sue's Leg*, are celebrations of vitality, abundance, and complexity; those of the 1980s, such as *The Catherine Wheel* and *Fait Accompli*, are expressions of violence and adult discontentment. She also provided choreography for several films including *Hair* (1979) and *Amadeus* (1984), collaborated with Jerome Robbins on *Brahms/Handel* (1984) for the New York City Ballet, and devised popular dances for Mikhail Baryshnikov, routines for the ice skater John Curry, and dances for the musical *Singin' in the Rain* (1985). She dissolved her own company after her appointment by Baryshnikov in 1987 as an artistic associate of the American Ballet Theatre, which she left in 1989. Her autobiography *Push Comes to Shove* was published in 1992.

Norma Adler

theater. The history of theater in New York City is the history of an inexorable movement up Manhattan Island and toward ever greater centralization and commercialism. From its humble roots as an amateur activity in colonial America, the theater has grown over the centuries into one of the city's most important and recognizable institutions.

1. Colonial Period and Early Republic (1699–1798)

The first record of theater in New York City is a petition to Governor John Nanfan requesting a license to stage plays, filed sometime between 1699 and 1702 by Richard Hunter; there is no record of Hunter's having carried out his plans. During the first half of the eighteenth century theater was confined to infrequent amateur productions presented in makeshift quarters such as the New Theatre (better known as the Theatre in Nassau Street), which opened in 1732 in a house owned by Rip Van Dam, president of the Common Council. The first confirmed professional performance in the city took place there on 5 March 1750, when an English company led by Walter Murray and Thomas Kean mounted a production of *Richard III.* Murray and Kean continued at the Theatre in Nassau Street until July 1751; when they left for Williamsburg, Virginia, the theater was leased to Robert Upton, who had been sent by the theatrical manager William Hallam, of London, to ascertain whether the city could support continued theatrical activity. Although there is no record of Upton's "scouting report," a British troupe billed as the London Company of Comedians and led by William Hallam's brother Lewis arrived in the city in the summer of 1753. When it left for Philadelphia in March 1754 the Theatre in Nassau Street ceased operation.

The company returned to New York City in 1758 under the leadership of David Douglass, who had assumed this position on Hallam's death. In addition to managing the London

Paradise Roof Garden, 7th Avenue and 42nd Street, 1902

John Searle, Interior of the Park Theatre *(1822)*

Company (soon renamed the American Company of Comedians) Douglass embarked on a building campaign that led to the construction of a theater on Cruger's Wharf (1758) and the Theatre in Beekman Street (1761), as well as the Theatre in John Street (1767), which became the best-known playhouse in New York City and remained so until the Park Theatre on Park Row was built in 1797–98. During the American Revolution all professional production ceased and the only theatrical activity in the city was amateur drama presented for the entertainment of British troops. By 1785, when the American Company returned from wartime exile in the West Indies, theater in New York City had survived a major war and more than a century of puritanical opposition. It was on the verge of beginning a period of unprecedented expansion and popularity.

2. Lower Broadway, the Bowery, and the Park (1798–1850)

At the beginning of the nineteenth century the Park Theatre dominated dramatic activity in the city and offered dramatic fare for patrons of all classes. Under the management of William Dunlap (an art critic, playwright, theater historian, and early manager) and then Stephen Price and Edward Simpson, the Park engaged some of the most accomplished actors from England, encouraged American-born actors, and introduced New Yorkers to Italian opera. The Park had no serious competition until 1824, when a theater was erected nearby in the Chatham Gardens on Park Row between Duane and Pearl streets. The building of new and in some cases larger theaters continued (the Bowery Theatre, Vauxhall Garden Theatre, Niblo's Garden and Theatre), and theaters began to concentrate on two of the city's central thoroughfares, Broadway and the Bowery.

The same period saw the beginnings of the "star system" in the American theater, as stage actors from England sought fame in the new country and managers in New York City tried different means of filling their new theaters. The first English star was George Frederick Cooke, engaged by Dunlap in 1810 to stimulate attendance at the Park; he was quickly followed by such well-known performers as Edmund and Charles Kean, Charles Mathews, William Conway, William Charles Macready, and Charles Kemble and his daughter Fanny.

During the 1820s a popular and aggressively democratic theater emerged as the laborer and the recent transplant from rural America began to patronize the theater in larger numbers, seeking not only diversion but confirmation of their aspirations and values. They found both of these in the early melodramas, foreign and American, in "Yankee" plays that appealed specifically to their tastes, in the performances of American-born stars like James

Painters working on scenic backdrops at the Young Brothers and Boss Scenic Studios on West 29th Street, ca *1905*

Hackett, George H. Hill, and Dan Marble, known for their wry humor in Yankee roles, and in the performances of Edwin Forrest and Charlotte Cushman, both renowned for their displays of raw emotional power. The following decades saw the emergence of native-born stars like E. L. Davenport, Lawrence Barrett, Laura Keene, Lester Wallack, John Brougham, Matilda Heron, and E. A. Sothern and theatrical dynasties like those of the Jeffersons, the Drews, the Barrymores, and the Booths.

By the early 1830s popular theaters for working-class audiences complemented those customarily patronized by the *haut monde*. The new theaters furnished the fare demanded by the masses, whom they further accommodated by scaling admission prices to suit their pocketbooks (seventy-five, fifty, and 37½ cents). Theaters like the Park and Burton's remained bastions of the élite, but the Bowery, the National, and the Chatham were claimed by the working classes as their own. Thus while Knickerbocker society quietly appreciated the talents of the Kembles at the Park during the season of 1832–33, the masses flocked to the Bowery in the spring of the same season to see George Gale in the spectacular melodrama *Mazeppa*.

In the 1840s many popular entertainment forms evolved and flourished. MINSTRELSY, descended from the songs and dances performed in the 1830s by Thomas D. "Jim Crow" Rice (1808–60) and other entertainers, attracted New Yorkers in such numbers that it rivaled the legitimate stage. Variety, the rough, raunchy precursor of the more genteel VAUDEVILLE, catered to all-male audiences in museums, saloons, and concert halls. Circuses occupied any vacant lot large enough to hold them; panoramas (giant landscapes or other spectacular scenes painted on canvas) were shown in buildings built especially for their viewing; and dime museums displayed their assorted oddities to thousands each day.

For about the first half of the nineteenth century there was no attempt to centralize the theaters, and consequently they remained scattered throughout the city, settling wherever there was available land and a prospective audience. There were small clusters of theaters at Park Row, on Broadway between City Hall and Houston Street, and on the lower Bowery, while roughly half a dozen theaters were in the regions west of Broadway (including three African theaters, one of which helped to foster the career of Ira Aldridge (1807–67), the first famous black actor in the United States).

3. Lower Broadway and the Bowery to Astor Place (1850–1875)

It was not the legitimate theater but rather one of the popular forms, the minstrel show, that was instrumental in the evolution of the first theater center in New York City. In the 1850s and 1860s a belt of minstrel halls developed along Broadway, extending from Fellow's Opera House at 444 Broadway to a minstrel hall in Hope Chapel just south of Waverly Place. This concentration of theaters was a harbinger of a district that developed around Union Square during the last quarter of the nineteenth century.

Theatrical impresarios in Brooklyn had difficulty competing with their counterparts in Manhattan. The first Brooklyn Academy of Music was not built until 1861, followed by the Park Theatre in 1863 (opposite City Hall on Fulton Street). Frederick and Sarah Conway managed the Park from 1864 until 1871, when they opened the Brooklyn Theatre. Both of their theaters housed repertory companies and presented performances by Sothern, James O'Neill, Kate Claxton, John Gilbert, and Lillian Russell.

By the middle of the nineteenth century trends contributing to the economic centralization of the American theater had already become evident. The success of *Uncle Tom's Cabin*, which ran for more than three hundred performances at the National Theatre in 1853–54, and the ensuing mania for "tom shows" that swept both New York City and the nation, signaled a new preoccupation with long runs in the American theater that persisted to the late twentieth century. Although some managers were at first skeptical about the long run they were quickly persuaded by the success of *The Black Crook*. Based on a melodrama by Charles M. Barras, this show was not only important in the evolution of a new dramatic form, the musical, but ran for 475 performances from 1866 and grossed $1.1 million on an investment of $24,000.

The breakdown of the traditional stock company, which had been the standard producing unit since before the American Revolution, and the advent of the combination company (a company formed for the run of one play and then disbanded) created a need for a completely new industry. Unlike the stock company, which was self-contained and produced scenery, costumes, and properties in its own shops, the combination company was transient, with neither theater nor shop facilities, and was forced to rely on businesses formed specifically to cater to its complex needs. A growing number of actors seeking work created a demand for agents; increased competition among theaters and the consequent demand for better publicity generated a market for the theatrical printer and the bill poster; and the sheer increase in the size of the theatrical community supported many new hotels and restaurants. During the 1870s the coalescence of these enterprises in one area, Union Square, created the first theater district in the city.

4. Union Square (1875–1900)

In the late nineteenth century Union Square was the site of appearances by such leading performers as the Booths, Adelaide Ristori, John McCullough, George L. Fox, Helena Modjeska, Maurice Barrymore, Mary Anderson, Henry Irving, and Ellen Terry. Among the theaters where they performed were the Fourteenth Street Theatre, the Union Square Theatre, and Wallack's Theatre, on Broadway at 13th Street. The area around Union Square was also a center of venues for popular entertainments: the Palace Garden, a pleasure garden on West 14th Street near 6th Avenue; the Hippotheatron, on East 14th Street, which housed equestrian shows and in the 1870s the famous menagerie of P. T. Barnum; a hall on East 14th Street near Irving Place where Dan Bryant's Minstrels appeared; one of the city's largest panoramas, the Battle of Gettysburg, on 4th Avenue between 18th and 19th streets; two of the most popular dime museums in the city, Huber's (on East 14th Street adjacent to Lüchow's) and Bunnell's Museum (on the northwest corner of Broadway and 9th Street); and several small-time variety theaters. The best-known theater in New York City devoted exclusively to popular entertainment was the New Fourteenth Street Theatre of Tony Pastor, which was widely renowned as the birthplace of vaudeville; it was regarded as having the best, most wholesome variety entertainment in the city and the widest array of stars, which included the vaudevillians Russell, May Irwin, Nat Goodwin, the team of Harrigan and Hart, Denman Thompson, Pat Rooney, and Sophie Tucker. Union Square was also the headquarters for grand opera. The Academy of Music, on the corner of East 14th Street and Irving Place, was built expressly for opera (as only three other theaters in the city before it had been).

As Union Square continued to flourish, the Park Theatre in Brooklyn achieved its greatest success under the management of Colonel William E. Sinn (1875–95). When the Brooklyn Theatre was destroyed in 1876 by what was then the worst theater fire in American history (295 lives were lost), Sinn and others improved their shows, and there was a boom in the construction of theaters in Brooklyn in the 1880s and 1890s.

The centrality of Union Square to theatrical life in New York City was virtually ended by 1900, as the city's new legitimate theaters established themselves along the streets around Long Acre Square (now Times Square). The area surrounding Union Square was given over to dime museums, film studios (including the Biograph Studios at 11 East 14th Street), and movie theaters, while 2nd Avenue below 14th Street had become the locus for Yiddish theater in the city. At the same time the theater increasingly underwent structural changes: not only had the stock system been displaced by the combination company and the theater become a thriving, lucrative industry, but the actor–manager in the mold of Brougham, Wallack, William Mitchell, and William Burton had been supplanted by the producer. Businessmen like A. M. Palmer, Marc Klaw, Abraham Erlanger, Charles and Daniel Frohman, and the brothers Sam S., Lee, and J(acob) J. Shubert were astute entrepreneurs with little or no stage experience. A turning point was marked in 1896 when the

Theaters within the Present Boundaries of New York City, by Date of Founding

(List is selective, especially for theaters off Broadway, vaudeville and burlesque houses, and music halls. Each theater is entered under its most important name.)

Corbett Tavern,[1] Broadway and Exchange Place, *ca* 1732
Playhouse on Broadway,[1] Broadway north of Beaver Street, *ca* 1732
New Theatre,[2] 1732–54
Theater on Cruger's Wharf,[3] Cruger's Wharf near Dock and William streets, 1758 to ?1759
Theater in Beekman Street, Beekman (Chapel) Street near Kid Street, 1761–64
Theater in John Street, John Street near Broadway, 1767–97
Rickett's Amphitheatre, Greenwich Street,[4] from 1795
Park Theatre,[5] Park Row, 1798–1848
Theater in Mount Vernon Gardens, Broadway between Leonard and Franklin streets, 1800–3
Grove Theatre,[6] Madison (Bedlow) Street and Catherine Street, 1804–5
Lyceum Theatre, Broadway between Warren and Chambers streets, 1808–9
Broadway Circus, 1812–14
Washington Hall,[7] Broadway and Houston Street, 1812–1945
Anthony Street Theatre, Worth (Anthony) Street near Broadway, 1814–21
Pantheon Mercer Street, between Houston and Prince streets, 1821–22
African Grove Theatre, Church Street between Duane and Anthony streets, from 1821
City Theatre, 15 Warren Street near Broadway, 1822–23
Niblo's Garden Theatre, Broadway and Prince Street, 1822–46
[unnamed African theater], Greene Street and Bleecker Street, 1823
Chatham Garden Theatre, Chatham Street off Pearl Street, 1824–32
Lafayette Theatre, Canal Street between Thompson and Laurens streets, 1825–29
Vauxhall Garden Theatre, Lafayette Place between Broadway and Bowery, 1826–55
Bowery Theatre, 48 Bowery between Bayard and Canal streets, 1826–1929
Richmond Hill Theatre, Varick Street between Charlton and Vandam streets, 1831–49
National Theatre,[8] Church Street between Leonard and Franklin streets, 1833–41
Bowery Amphitheatre,[9] 37–39 Bowery between Bayard and Canal streets, 1833–66
Franklin Theatre, 175 Chatham Street between James and Oliver streets, 1835–54
Broadway Theatre, 410 Broadway at Canal Street, 1837
(Second) City Theatre, Broadway and Ann Street, 1837
Olympic Theatre,[10] 444 Broadway between Howard and Grand streets, 1837–54
Chatham Theatre,[11] Chatham Street between James and Roosevelt streets, 1837–60
Castle Garden Theater, Battery Park, 1839–55
Barnum's American Museum and Lecture Room, Broadway and Ann Street, 1841–65
Apollo Rooms, Broadway between Canal and Walker streets, 1842–51
Palmo's Opera House,[12] 39–41 Chambers Street behind City Hall Park, 1844–76
Astor Place Opera House, Astor Place, 1847–53
Mechanics Hall, 472 Broadway near Grand Street, 1847–57
Broadway Theatre, 326 Broadway, 1847–59
Niblo's Theatre, Broadway and Prince Street, 1849–95
Coliseum, 448 Broadway between Howard and Grand streets, 1850s
Minerva Rooms, Broadway and Grand Street, 1850s
Old Stuyvesant Hall, Broadway between Bleecker and Bond streets, 1850–60
Brougham's Lyceum,[13] Broadway and Broome Street, 1850–69
Tripler Hall,[14] Broadway at Bond Street, 1851–67
Deutsches National Theater, 53 Bowery, 1853
Crystal Palace, Bryant Park, 6th Avenue and 42nd Street, 1853–58
St. Charles Theatre, 17–19 Bowery, 1853–54
Chinese Rooms to Barnum's New American Museum,[15] 539 Broadway between Spring and Prince streets, 1853–68
Fellow's Opera House and Hall of Lyrics, 444 Broadway between Howard and Grand streets, 1854–66
White's Opera House, 49 Bowery, 1854 to ?1870
Academy of Music,[16] East 14th Street between Irving Place and 3rd Avenue, 1854–1926
Kelly and Leon's, 720 Broadway near 12th Street, 1855 to 1860s
Laura Keene's Varieties to Olympic Theatre,[17] Broadway between Houston and Bleecker streets, 1856–80
Buckley's Hall, Broadway between Prince and Houston streets, 1856–81
Atlantic Gardens, 50 Bowery, 1856–1911

(*continued*)

Theaters within the Present Boundaries of New York City, by Date of Founding (*Continued*)

Henry Wood's Marble Hall, 561 Broadway near Houston Street, 1857–59
Hoym's Theatre,[18] Bowery and Spring Street, from 1858
New Bowery Theatre, Bowery between Canal and Hester streets, 1859–66
Irving Hall, Irving Place and 15th Street, 1860–88
Wallack's Theatre, 728 Broadway at 13th Street, 1861–1901
Park Theatre, 383 Fulton Street, Brooklyn, 1863–98
Das Neue Stadt Theatre, 45–47 Bowery, 1864–72
Grand Street Theatre, Grand and Crosby streets, 1865–66
Lucy Rushton's Theatre,[19] Broadway and Waverly Place, 1865–81
Theatre Comique, 514 Broadway between Spring and Broome streets, 1865–84
Fifth Avenue Theatre,[20] southwest corner of 5th Avenue and 24th Street, 1865–1908
Fourteen Street Theatre, West 14th Street between 6th and 7th avenues, 1866–1911
Steinway Hall, 109 East 14th Street, 1866–1925
Daly's Theatre, 1221 Broadway between 29th and 30th streets, 1867–1920
Pike's Opera House,[21] northwest corner of 8th Avenue and 23rd Street, 1868–1960
New York Stadt Theatre,[22] 43 Bowery, 1864–1910
Broadway Athenaeum,[23] 734 Broadway, 1865–1884
Théâtre Français,[24] 14th Street west of 6th Avenue, from 1866
Booth's Theatre, southeast corner of 6th Avenue and 23rd Street, 1869–83
Harlem Music Hall, 3rd Avenue at 130th Street, 1870–85
Koster and Bial's,[25] West 23rd Street between 6th and 7th avenues, 1870–1924
Madison Square Garden,[26] 26th to 27th streets between 5th and Madison avenues, 1870–1925
Union Square Theatre, Broadway and 4th Avenue, 1870–1936
Brooklyn Theatre,[27] Johnson and Washington streets, Brooklyn 1871–90
Neuendorff's Germania Theater, 1872–81
New Park Theatre, 932 Broadway from 21st to 22nd streets, 1873–82
Chickering Hall, 5th Avenue and 18th Street, 1875–1902
San Francisco Music Hall, Broadway and 28th Street, 1875–1907
Eagle Theatre,[28] 6th Avenue between 32nd and 33rd streets, 1875–1909
Third Avenue Theatre,[29] 3rd Avenue between 30th and 31st streets, from 1875
Pendy's Gayety Theatre,[30] 3rd Avenue between 125th and 126th streets, 1877–79
Daly's Fifth Avenue Theatre, northwest corner of Broadway and 28th Street, 1877–1930
Brighton Theatre,[31] 1239 Broadway between 30th and 31st streets, 1878–1915
Das Thalia Theater, 1879–88
Aberle's Theatre,[32] East 8th Street between Broadway and 4th Avenue, 1879–1904
Miner's Bowery Theatre, 169 Bowery, from 1879
Broadway Theatre,[33] southwest corner of Broadway and 41st Street, 1880–1929
Metropolitan Opera Hall, Broadway between 41st and 42nd streets, 1880–1965
Das Star Theater, 1881–83
Miner's Eighth Avenue Theatre, 8th Avenue between 26th and 27th streets, 1881–1902
Tony Pastor's New 14th Street Theatre, East 14th Street between Irving Place and 3rd Avenue, 1881–1928
Oriental Theatre,[34] 104 Bowery, 1882–1898
Wallack's Theatre, northwest corner of Broadway and 30th Street, 1882–1918
Casino Theatre, southeast corner of Broadway and 39th Street, 1882–1930
Temple Theatre,[35] 141 West 23rd Street, 1883 to ?1900
Herald Square Theatre, northeast corner of Broadway and 35th Street, 1883–1914
Metropolitan Opera House, Broadway to 7th Avenue between 39th and 40th streets, 1883–1966
Lyceum Theatre, 4th (Park) Avenue between 23rd and 24th streets, 1885–92
Theatre Comique,[36] 125th Street between 3rd and Lexington avenues, 1885–93
Lyceum Theatre, 4th Avenue between 23rd and 24th streets, 1885–1902
F. F. Proctor's Theatre,[37] Driggs Avenue and South 4th Street, Brooklyn, from 1886
Criterion Theatre, Fulton Street near Grand Street, Brooklyn, 1886–95
Amberg Theatre, 11 Irving Place at 15th Street, 1888–93
Berkley Theatre, 19 West 44th Street, from 1888
Amphion Theatre, Bedford Avenue between South 9th and 10th streets, Brooklyn, 1888–1913
Hyde and Behman's Theatre, Adams Street between Fulton and Myrtle streets, Brooklyn, 1888 to ?1915
Broadway Theatre,[38] southwest corner of Broadway and 41st Street, 1888–1929

(*continued*)

firm of Klaw and Erlanger, which controlled or leased many theaters nationwide, joined forces with the producer Charles Frohman, the booking agent Al(bert) Hayman, and two theater owners from Philadelphia, S. F. Nixon and J. F. Zimmerman, to standardize chaotic booking practices. The result was the Theatrical Syndicate, which soon held a monopoly on American theater production.

5. Times Square (after 1900)

By 1904 it was estimated that the Theatrical Syndicate controlled more than five hundred theaters and had a virtual stranglehold on the American theater, employing a blacklist to keep both the acting profession and independent theater owners in line. Although a few theater professionals were courageous enough to challenge the power of the Theatrical Syndicate (among them Harrison Grey Fiske, Minnie Maddern Fiske, and David Belasco), there were no serious threats to its monopoly until the Shubert brothers early in the twentieth century built a theatrical empire in direct opposition to it. Compared with the Theatrical Syndicate the Shuberts at first appeared to be the benevolent saviors of the American theater, but as they continued to acquire theaters it became apparent that they were creating an organization as powerful and as monopolistic as the Syndicate had been, and that they used similar tactics. After the death in 1905 of Sam S. Shubert in a train wreck his brothers continued to work together; by 1925 they could claim control of the legitimate theater.

The influence of the Shuberts was minimal in Queens, Staten Island, and the Bronx, where professional theater was not standard fare. Repertory companies like the Brooklyn Comedy Company visited the Jamaica Opera House, but entertainment consisted largely of musical evenings, balls, amateur theatrical productions, and lectures. The Bronx Theatre opened in 1908, the first of many vaudeville houses situated on or near East 149th Street, an area known as the Hub.

During these years there was a growing dissatisfaction among actors with their working conditions, particularly with regard to rehearsals, which were unpaid and unlimited; moreover actors often found themselves stranded on the road without sufficient funds to pay for their train fare back to New York City. The theater managers at first refused to redress the actors' grievances, and the phrase "starve the actors out" became their rallying cry. The managers' attitude changed only when the actors went on strike moments before curtain time on 6 August 1919, and a contract between the managers and Actors' Equity was signed on 6 September.

While the economic structure of the professional theater was moving toward a greater degree of centralized control, an upheaval of similar magnitude was taking place in Ameri-

the twentieth century originated there. The first of these, the Neighborhood Playhouse, began in the Henry Street Settlement (well below 42nd Street), was endowed in 1915 by Alice and Irene Lewisohn, and produced not only experimental playscripts (by O'Neill and Shaw, among others) but also avant-garde dance and music. The Washington Square Players, formed in Greenwich Village in 1914 by Philip Moeller, Helen Westley, and Lawrence Langner, had the stated goal of producing "plays of artistic merit." After staging sixty-two one-act plays and six full-length plays the group was disbanded in 1918 and reorganized as the Theatre Guild, which became one of the leading production institutions in New York City, instrumental in introducing Americans to the plays of Shaw, Ibsen, Leonid Andreyev, Maurice Maeterlinck, and August Strindberg, and in producing plays by O'Neill, Saroyan, Sherwood, Rice, and Philip Barry (see §5, above). The Theatre Guild was also one of the first American theater companies to exhibit the style of theater design known as the new stagecraft, which was practiced by Robert Edmond Jones and Lee Simonson. The Provincetown Players were established in 1915 as a playwrights' company presenting the works of Susan Glaspell, Theodore Dreiser, Edna St. Vincent Millay, and Green, but their most notable achievement was their advocacy of O'Neill and their staging of many of his early plays (first in a makeshift theater on a wharf in Provincetown, Massachusetts, later in a small theater at 133 MacDougal Street).

After the furious activity of the teens alternative theater in New York City diminished during the 1920s. One notable exception was the courageous attempt by the actress and director Eva Le Gallienne to establish and maintain a company run on a strict repertory system (1926–31), which entailed a nightly change of bill and a nightly rotation of scenery. During the following decades alternative theater was for the most part confined to the agitprops (propaganda plays) and socially aware dramas of the Group Theatre and other left-wing troupes. One notable black theater, the American Negro Theatre, was formed in the 1940s; like one of its predecessors, the Lafayette Players (formed in 1915 by Anita Bush), it was criticized for imitating Broadway.

The next important phase of alternative theatrical activity in New York City began on 24 April 1952, when Williams's *Summer and Smoke* opened at the Circle in the Square near Sheridan Square, an event widely regarded as marking the beginning of Off Broadway. When the production was reviewed by Brooks Atkinson, drama critic for the *New York Times*, public attention became focused on theater below 42nd Street, and Off Broadway was discovered, legitimated, and made economically viable. The Circle in the Square was the product of a discontent with Broadway not dissimilar from that which prevailed during the teens. The cost of producing on Broadway had grown prohibitive, which meant that fewer new scripts could be staged; the increased conservatism of audiences and backers had severely limited production concepts and all but stifled creativity; and producers were using only experienced actors. In opening the Circle in the Square its founders José Quintero and Theodore Mann were fighting the fiscal, artistic, and political conservatism of mainstream theater.

During the 1950s and early 1960s the commercialism and artistic constraints of Broadway led to the formation of other companies (the Living Theatre of Julian Beck and Judith Malina, the New York Shakespeare Festival of Joseph Papp, the Phoenix Theatre) and individual playhouses (the Sullivan Street Theatre, the Public Theatre, the Theatre de Lys, and the Cherry Lane). In an environment that encouraged experimentation such young, progressive artists as Beck and Malina, Quintero, Geraldine Page, George C. Scott, Peter Falk, Ellis Rabb, Jason Robards, and Dustin Hoffman were allowed to test their talents and ideas; scripts considered too risky for Broadway were staged; and a second hearing was given to some artists who were in danger of being forgotten (such as O'Neill and Williams). It was this nurturing milieu that provided backing and a suitable environment for staging "small" musicals like *The Fantasticks*, which by the early 1990s had already run for decades, and *Little Mary Sunshine*.

The formation in 1967 of the Negro Ensemble Company was a landmark in attempts to forge an autonomous BLACK THEATER. It staged works by such leading black playwrights as Lorraine Hansberry, James Baldwin, LeRoi Jones (later known as Amiri Baraka), Douglas Turner Ward, Ed Bullins, Lonne Elder, and Charles Gordone. The Negro Ensemble Company and other black companies such as AMAS Rep symbolized more than simply an alternative to the production scheme and mainstream values of Broadway: they also enabled blacks to enter the ranks of theatrical producers, dramatically represented black life, and in general promoted the goal articulated by W. E. B. Du Bois, that there should be a theater "about, by, for, and near" black Americans.

In the 1960s political, social, and artistic upheaval created the environment for yet another form of alternative theater, Off Off Broadway. In an era even more turbulent than the teens and the 1930s had been, theatrical radicals rejected the professionally trained actor, the classics, conventional relations between actor and audience, the star system, and even the role of the playwright and the primacy of the script. The Caffe Cino, a small coffeehouse at 31 Cornelia Street, is generally acknowledged as the place where Off Off Broadway began. In 1958 the proprietor, Joe Cino, invited performers and writers to present their work; among those who did were the writers Jean-Claude van Itallie, Lanford Wilson, and Sam Shepard. The Caffe Cino closed when the proprietor took his own life in 1967, but other venues opened and continued to offer a forum for experimental work (Ellen Stewart's La Mama Experimental Theatre Club, the Judson Poets' Theater, Theatre Genesis). In the decades that followed, the rebellion inherent in Off Off Broadway became embodied in the iconoclasm and political activism of the Living Theatre; in experiments by Richard Schechner and the Performance Group with the relation of actor to audience and with the creation of performance "environments"; in the improvisational ensemble work of Joe Chaikin and the Open Theatre; in the use of masks and puppets and the public protests of the Bread and Puppet Theatre; in Allan Kaprow's happenings; and in the high "camp" of Charles Ludlam's Ridiculous Theatrical Company.

Theaters within the Present Boundaries of New York City, by Date of Founding (*Continued*)

101. Used as a movie theater to 1934. Known as the Hollywood to 1936, the Fifty-first Street Theatre to 1949; sold to a church in 1991.
102. Showed films as the RKO Roxy and RKO Center to 1934.
103. Built as meeting hall for the Ancient and Accepted Order of Nobles of the Mystic Shrine 1923.
104. Originally the Theatre de Lys
105. Opened in the 1920s as Billy Rose's Nightclub, later known as the Sheridan Square Playhouse.
106. Originally known as the Priory.
107. Originally the Variety Photoplays movie theater, *ca* 1900.
108. Renovation of the Felt Forum.

Sources: Ruth C. Dimmick: *Our Theatres To-Day and Yesterday* (New York: H. K. Fly, 1913)
Mary C. Henderson: *The City and the Theatre: New York Playhouses from Bowling Green to Times Square* (Clifton, N.J.: James T. White, 1973)
John W. Frick and Carlton Ward, eds.: *Directory of Historic American Theatres* (New York: Greenwood, 1987)
Timothy J. Gilfoyle: *City of Eros: New York City, Prostitution and the Commercialization of Sex, 1790–1920* (New York: W. W. Norton, 1992)

Compiled by Alana J. Erickson

By the 1980s alternative theater in New York City had grown more fragmented, eclectic, and private, encompassing black, Latin American, gay, and lesbian theater, and artists and ensembles as diverse in their ideologies and aesthetics as Robert Wilson, JoAnne Akalaitis, Ethyl Eichelberger, Richard Foreman, Lee Breuer, the Wooster Group, Split Britches, and Michael Kirby's Structuralist Workshop. It was the alternative theater and not Broadway that generated the most influential American playwrights of the 1970s and 1980s. Although their works were routinely produced on Broadway the playwrights Lanford Wilson and August Wilson nevertheless created many of them respectively for the Circle Repertory Theatre and the Yale Repertory Theatre; the premières of David Mamet's plays were generally given off Broadway when they were given in New York City at all; and Shepard, whom many critics consider the most talented playwright of his generation, had his work produced in a prominent theater in New York City (*Operation Sidewinder* at the Vivian Beaumont Theatre in Lincoln Center in 1970), but during the 1970s and 1980s not once in a Broadway theater.

7. The Business of the Theater

A variety of businesses and organizations in New York City help to mount theatrical productions and support the many people who work in the theater.

Labor is by far the major resource used in theatrical production. In the early twentieth century the considerable growth in the number, size, and type of productions and the increasing role of technology led to the formation of theatrical unions and societies to establish contractual guidelines. Theater owners and producers now do business with many such organizations; which ones are involved in a given production will depend on the type of production (play, musical, opera, revue) and on the size and location of the theater. The principal unions and associations include the Dramatists Guild, which represents authors; Actors' Equity Association (which along with six other performers' unions is affiliated with the Associated Actors and Artistes of America), for professional actors and stage managers; the Society of Stage Directors and Choreographers; the United Scenic Artists of America, to which most scenic, costume, and lighting designers belong, along with scenic, mural, display, and diorama artists; Wardrobe Supervisors and Dressers, Local 764; the International Alliance of Theatrical Stage Employees, of which Local 1 in Manhattan represents all carpenters, stagehands, electricians, sound technicians, and property crewmen; Treasurers and Ticket-sellers, Local 751; Porters and Cleaners–Service Employees in Amusement and Cultural Buildings, Local 54; the International Union of Operating Engineers, Local 30, for those who maintain heavy equipment, such as heating and air-conditioning engineers; Ushers and Doormen; the Association of Theatrical Press Agents and Managers; and the American Federation of Musicians, Local 802. In response to difficulties posed by these performers' and technicians' unions after 1910 producers and theater owners formed their own association to represent their interests; this has undergone several reorganizations and changes of name and is now known as the League of American Theaters and Producers. The league is a voluntary body with headquarters in New York City.

Goods and services used in the theater are provided by many businesses in the metropolitan area, including builders and suppliers of scenery, lighting and sound equipment, costumes, and makeup. Traditionally these businesses were situated in and around the theater district, where "walk-in" business accounted for much of their trade, but over the years many moved to the outer boroughs, Long Island, and New Jersey, and some moved farther. This trend was brought about by the rapidly rising cost of real estate and a lack of suitable space in Manhattan. The difficulty of moving goods in and out of midtown was especially troublesome for scenic studios, which deal in large, bulky items: of the thirty-six studios of this kind listed in the *New York Theatrical Sourcebook* for 1990 only six were in Manhattan. Most production suppliers nonetheless chose to remain near Broadway because of the necessity of maintaining a connection with the theater district, no matter how tenuous.

With the growth of the theater in the late nineteenth century came the rise of the theatrical agent and the theatrical manager. Agents advise, represent, and promote performers as well as playwrights, directors, and other creative artists; they arrange bookings in venues ranging from Broadway theaters to small cabarets, negotiate terms and contracts, and mediate disputes. Although some agents operate independently and have only a few clients, large organizations like the William Morris Agency have thousands. Theatrical managers differ from agents in that they often provide their clients with legal and financial guidance.

Theatrical publishing encompasses play publishers and authors' representatives as well as trade and general-interest magazines and newspapers. The acting versions of most plays and the scores of most musicals are published by companies based in New York City. Samuel French and the Dramatists Play Service are the two leading publishing houses for non-musical properties; musicals are controlled by Tams Witmark, Music Theater International, and the Rodgers and Hammerstein Music Library. These companies maintain the sole authority to charge royalty fees and to release plays for production in stock, educational, and amateur theaters throughout the world. All funds collected are apportioned by prior agreement between the publishing houses and their authors.

The first theatrical periodical in the city was the weekly newspaper the *Thespian Mirror*, published for a brief period in 1805. It was followed by hundreds of magazines and newspapers devoted to the theater, including the weekly general-interest newspapers the *New York Clipper* (1853–1924) and the *New York Dramatic Mirror* (1879–1922); the monthly magazine *Theater Arts* (1916–64), which was noted for publishing the complete texts of new plays; *New Theater* (1934–37), the mimeographed monthly organ of the Workers Theaters of U.S.A. and the Workers Dance League; and the *New York Review* (1909–31), a weekly trade newspaper issued by the Shubert Organization as a vehicle to combat the Theatrical Syndicate. Leading periodicals in the mid 1990s included *TDR*, a quarterly journal devoted to performance theory from an anthropological perspective; *American Theater*, a monthly forum for news, features, and opinions; *TCI* and *Lighting Dimensions*, monthly magazines on technical aspects of the theater; and the weekly trade publications *Backstage*, *Show Business*, and *Variety*. The influential publication *Best Plays and Year Book of the Drama in America*, first compiled in 1919 by Burns Mantle (*b* 23 Dec 1873; *d* 9 Feb 1948), contains a detailed overview of every play produced in New York City in the preceding year as well as condensations of ten of the best. Among the most durable figures in theatrical publishing is the artist Al Hirschfeld, who drew his first caricatures for the *New York Times* in 1925 and continued to do so into the 1990s.

The many bookshops in the city devoted to the performing arts have often doubled as informal gathering places for professionals in the theater. This was true in the nineteenth century of such shops as Brentano's Literary Emporium (not strictly a theatrical bookshop although it sold a large number of theater books) and continues to apply at Applause Theater Books, the Theater Arts Bookshop, Theaterbooks, and the city's oldest extant store for theatrical books and periodicals, the Drama Book Shop, which set up shop in 1923 on a card table in the lobby of the ANTA Theater.

8. Acting and Theater Schools

The American Academy of Dramatic Arts, formed in New York City in 1884, was the first school in the United States to provide professional training in acting. Most colleges and universities in the city now have offerings ranging from informal courses to doctoral programs; among the most notable are the Juilliard School, the Graduate School at City University of New York, and the Tisch School of the Arts at New York University. Most acting schools were founded by noted practitioners in the field, including Strasberg (the

Actors Studio), Adler (the Stella Adler Conservatory of Acting), Herbert Berghof and Uta Hagen (HB Studio), and Sanford Meisner (the Neighborhood Playhouse School of the Theater). Certificates in acting are granted by the American Academy of Dramatic Arts, the Circle in the Square Theater School, the National Shakespeare Conservatory, and the American Musical and Dramatic Academy. The Studio of Scene Painting Plus offers certificates in scene painting, costume design, lighting, and set design.

Thomas Allston Brown: *A History of the New York Stage* (New York: Dodd, Mead, 1903)

Alfred L. Bernheim: *The Business of the Theatre: An Economic History of the American Theatre, 1750–1932* (New York: Actors' Equity Association, 1932)

Mary C. Henderson: *The City and the Theatre: New York Playhouses from Bowling Green to Times Square* (Clifton, N.J.: James T. White, 1973)

Stephen Langley: *Theatre Management in America* (New York: Drama Book Publishers, 1974; rev. 1990 as *Theatre Management and Production in America: Commercial, Stock, Resident, College, Community, and Presenting Organizations*)

Mary C. Henderson: *Theater in America* (New York: Harry N. Abrams, 1986)

See also Dance, Musical theater, Performance art, Stage design, Tap dancing, Theater criticism, Tony award, and Yiddish theater.

John W. Frick (§§1–6), Martha S. LoMonaco (§§7–8)

theater architecture. The first of more than a thousand theaters in New York City was perhaps the New Theatre (also known as the Theatre in Nassau Street), built by English colonists about 1732. A theater district took form in 1798 when the Park Theatre was erected across from City Hall Park. Its façade was designed in a neoclassical style by the French-born architect Joseph François Mangin, who later helped to design City Hall. Little survives of the early theaters, but drawings and photographs suggest that their exteriors were designed according to the architectural fashions of the day. The façades of the Chatham Gardens Theatre (1824) and the New York Theatre (1826; later the Bowery Theatre) were built in the Greek Revival style and could easily have been mistaken for those of churches. As the city expanded to the north theaters were built along Broadway, the most fashionable avenue, and became well known. The center of the theater district moved successively to Canal Street, Union Square, Madison Square, and Herald Square; there were also German music halls on the Bowery, theaters for Yiddish productions on 2nd Avenue, theaters and opera houses in Harlem, and a theater district in downtown Brooklyn. Most nineteenth-century theaters were narrow and semicircular; two balconies, one directly above the other, were supported by slender cast-iron columns, and enclosed two-tiered boxes flanked the stage. Theaters with elaborate neoclassical designs were common, such as Haverly's Theatre (1866; later the 14th Street Theatre). Edwin Booth's Theatre (1869) on 23rd Street had a façade in a French style with an enormous mansard roof. Harrigan's Theatre (1890; later the Garrick Theatre) on West 35th Street had a façade in the beaux-arts style.

Proctor's Pleasure Palace, ca *1910*

The theater district moved to Times Square in 1895 when Oscar Hammerstein opened the Olympia theater complex on Broadway at 45th Street, and during the next three decades about eighty-five theaters were built in the blocks between 6th and 8th avenues from 39th Street to Columbus Circle. All were built for impresarios who produced their own shows and sometimes their own plays with companies of actors under contract. These theaters were both auditoriums and business offices, designed to be symbols of the impresarios and their productions. Hammerstein, David Belasco, Daniel Frohman, Winthrop Ames, Henry B. Harris, and Charles Dillingham had theaters built to their specifications and engaged architects who specialized in designing theaters. Commissions were given to many architects, including J. B. McElfatrick and Son, George Keister, Herts and Tallant,

Thomas W. Lamb, V. Hugo Koehler, C. Howard Crane, Carrère and Hastings, Warren and Wetmore, and Harry Creighton Ingalls.

The grand beaux-arts designs popular in the late nineteenth century were used into the early years of the twentieth. The Republic Theatre (Albert E. Westover, 1899; now the Victory Theatre) built for Hammerstein on West 42nd Street is the only remaining theater on Broadway with an interior in the nineteenth-century style; sculpted *putti* look down at the audience from the rim of the ceiling dome. In Frohman's New Lyceum Theatre (1902–3) Herts and Tallant introduced cantilevered balconies to eliminate columns that obscured the view of the stage in the orchestra and the first balcony; they also gave the theater one of the most heavily ornamented façades in the city and an elaborate interior decorated with murals, bronze statues, and unusual lighting fixtures (hundreds of electric bulbs across the ceiling instead of a chandelier). The New Amsterdam Theatre (Herts and Tallant, 1902–3), built for the Theatrical Syndicate of Marc Klaw and Abraham Erlanger, remains the finest *art nouveau* theater in the city. For Dillingham's Globe Theatre (1909–10; now the Lunt–Fontanne Theatre) Carrère and Hastings, the architects of the New York Public Library, designed a monumental, classic beaux-arts façade.

Changes in audiences, entertainment, and technology led to changes in theater design. Second balconies were eliminated as patrons of the cheapest seats abandoned the theater for the movie palace. Interest in "little theater," which consisted of dramatic productions in intimate spaces, led to the restrained neo-Georgian style of Belasco's Stuyvesant Theatre (George Keister, 1906; now the Belasco Theatre) and Ames's Little Theatre on West 44th Street (H. C. Ingalls, 1912; now the Helen Hayes Theatre), both designed to recall the privacy of drawing rooms in Georgian mansions. The Stuyvesant has Tiffany fixtures, a paneled ceiling, and murals by Everett Shinn over the proscenium arch. After the First World War theaters were built for several impresarios, among them Henry Miller, Martin Beck, Irving Berlin, Sam Harris, and the members of the Theatre Guild. Most were built for one of two organizations: the Shuberts, producers who built theaters in Times Square and across the nation for lease to producers or in concert with them, and the Chanins, major developers in the city who built six theaters in three years. Between 1916 and 1927 both organizations gave most of their commissions to Herbert J. Krapp, who was known for designing similar theaters with fine acoustics and sightlines, handsome plasterwork, and minimal ornamentation. He designed simple theaters that often had to fit awkward spaces, such as the Ambassador Theatre (1923), which had an angled entrance. The Plymouth and Broadhurst theaters were intended to be simpler versions of the adjoining Shubert and Booth theaters (Henry B. Herts, 1912): they have inexpensive brick and terra cotta façades and plasterwork in the Adam style. Some of Krapp's simplest façades for the Shuberts are those of the Ritz Theatre (1919–20) and the Imperial Theatre (1923), which were designed to support signboards. For the Chanins he designed the Majestic Theatre, the Royale Theatre, and the Theater Masque (now the Golden Theatre) in 1926–27 in a Spanish–Moorish style executed in simple brickwork with stone trim on the façades.

The Shuberts and the Chanins, both families of immigrants, softened the distinction between the orchestra and the balconies, which was a vestige of class distinction in English theaters; they also replaced separate entryways with a single entrance for all ticket holders, as in the Shuberts' Broadhurst and Plymouth theaters (Krapp, 1917). As the Shuberts strengthened their hold on Broadway theater an area along West 44th and 45th streets between 7th and 8th avenues came to be known informally as "Shubert Alley." The Chanins introduced the "stadium plan" in their 46th Street Theater (Krapp, 1924–25; now the Walter Kerr Theatre), in which the balcony, cantilevered over the lobby rather than the orchestra, merged with the orchestra into an undifferentiated space. Boxes flanking the stage, which had often been reserved for royalty in English theaters, gradually diminished in size and importance: in the Ethel Barrymore Theatre (Krapp, 1928) they were entirely ornamental and contained no seats.

Theaters ceased to be built on Broadway during the Depression, and only five were built in the following half-century (others were built at Columbus Circle and Lincoln Center). The American Place, the Uris Theatre (now the Gershwin Theatre), the Circle in the Square Theatre, and the Minskoff Theatre were built after a zoning resolution was passed to encourage the construction of theaters in new office buildings in Times Square. Despite strong public opposition led by Actors' Equity the Marquis Theatre was built in the Marriott Marquis Hotel on Broadway between 45th and 46th streets, which replaced five theaters (the Folies Bergère, later known as the Fulton Theatre and then as the Helen Hayes Theatre; the Astor Theatre; the Gaiety Theatre; the Bijou Theatre; and the Morosco Theatre). More than forty of the original theater buildings in Times Square were demolished during the late twentieth century. Many of the remaining ones were designated landmarks by the city or the federal government and most were protected by special listing of the New York City Planning Commission.

Randolph Williams Sexton and Ben Franklin Betts, eds.: *American Theatres of Today: Illustrated with Plans, Sections, and Photographs of Exterior and Interior Details* (New York: Architectural Books, 1927–30; repr. Vestal, 1977)

Mary C. Henderson: *The City and the Theatre* (Clifton, N.J.: James T. White, 1973)

See also Movie theaters.

theater criticism. Daily reviews first appeared in New York City when regular theaters opened there in the eighteenth century. Authors writing for the *Daily Advertiser* and the *Gazette of the United States* under the names "Candour" and "Criticus" reviewed plays staged in the John Street Theatre, and by 1796 a circle of daily critics was established in the city. In the beginning of the nineteenth century Washington Irving wrote lively review letters under the name Jonathan Oldstyle for the *Morning Chronicle*, and William Coleman frequently contributed long articles on the theater to the *New York Evening Post*. After 1829 William Leggett carried on Coleman's tradition of providing substantial theater criticism and became the critical champion of Edwin Forrest. In the 1840s plays were reviewed by Edgar Allan Poe for the *Broadway Journal* and the *Evening Mirror* and by Walt Whitman for the *Brooklyn Eagle* (of which he was also the editor). They did not use pseudonyms, unlike many nineteenth-century reviewers including William Winter, who wrote as "Mercutio" for the *Albion* in the early 1860s, and Andrew Carpenter Wheeler, the most influential reviewer just after the Civil War, who wrote for the *New York Weekly Leader* as "Trinculo" and later for the *New York World* and the *Sun* as Nym Crinkle; by the 1870s pseudonyms were rarely used. Winter dominated criticism in the city for several decades, writing under his own name as the drama critic for the *New York Tribune* (where he remained until 1909). Henry James, who was not affiliated with any one newspaper, became well known in 1865–69 and 1874–75 for his writings on European theater. The end of the century saw the rise of a new group of critics receptive to modern drama: J. Ranken Towse of the *New York Post* (1874–1927), James Gibbons Huneker of the *New York Recorder* and later the *New York Advertiser* and the *Sun*, Edward August Dithmar of the *New York Times* (1884–1901), known for his advocacy of the playwright Clyde Fitch, and Alan Dale, perhaps the most influential critic, who wrote for the *Evening World* (1887–95), the *New York Evening Journal* (1897–1915), and the *New York American* (1913–21). Critics sometimes came into conflict with producers eager for good reviews, as James Metcalfe of *Life* did with the Theatrical Syndicate.

The leading critics of the 1920s included such talented writers as Robert Benchley, George Jean Nathan, Gilbert W. Gabriel, John Mason Brown, Stark Young, Heywood Broun, Alexander Woollcott, and Joseph Wood Krutch. Perhaps the best-known was Brooks Atkinson, who began reviewing for the *New York Times* in 1926 and remained there until 1960 (except for a few years in the 1940s); he was the first president of the New York Critics' Circle (formed in 1935). During the same years pressure increased on critics to ensure the commercial success of plays in the city by providing positive reviews. In general they acquiesced, to such an extent that from 1923 to 1950 *Variety* calculated scores based on how often each critic's favorable reviews were followed by success at the box office. The early 1940s were marked by confrontations between on the one hand the producers Jacob and Lee Shubert and on the other Woollcott and Walter Winchell. In an effort to prevent theater managers from denying entry to their productions to reviewers who they thought would be antagonistic, the state legislature passed a bill prohibiting the practice in 1941. The most important critics after the Second World War were Atkinson, Howard Barnes, and later Walter Kerr of the *New York Herald Tribune* and John Chapman of the *Daily News*; others who had considerable influence included Robert Coleman (the *Daily Mirror*), Louis Kronenberger (*PM*), Robert Garland (the *Journal–American*), Richard Watts (the *New York Post*), William Hawkins (the *New York World–Telegram*), and Ward Morehouse (the *Sun*). The ability of critics to make or break a show caused such widespread concern by the late 1940s that the first "paid preview" was offered in 1952 to curtail their power. This financially "opened" the show before the reviews appeared, and allowed time for publicity to work by word of mouth.

Apart from Atkinson reviewers of plays on Broadway paid little attention to the emerging theater of Off Broadway, and consequently there developed in the early 1960s a separate group of critics who specialized in it, among them Jules Novick and Erika Munk of the *Village Voice*. As the number of daily newspapers diminished (only three remained by 1967) the power of each critic increased commensurately. Highly public disputes arose between Howard Taubman of the *New York Times* and David Merrick, and in 1968–69 between Kerr, now at the *Times*, and Joseph Papp. A new generation of Broadway critics became prominent in the 1970s and early 1980s, and many of them remained so into the 1990s: Edwin Wilson of the *Wall Street Journal*, Howard Kissel and Martin Gottfried of *Women's Wear Daily*, Frank Rich of the *New York Times*, Clive Barnes of the *Times* and the *New York Post*, John Beaufort of the *Christian Science Monitor*, and Douglas Watt of the *Daily News*. Reviews on television and radio became more common but lacked the popular influence of those in newspapers. A number of weekly and monthly magazines continued to provide important reviews, among them the *New Yorker* (Edith Oliver, Brendan Gill, and Mimi Kramer), *New York* (John Simon), *Time* (William A. Henry III), *Newsweek* (Jack Kroll), the *Nation*, and the *New Republic*.

Montrose J. Moses and John Mason Brown, eds.: *The American Theatre as Seen by Its Critics, 1752–1934* (New York: Cooper Square, 1967)

Lehman Engel: *The Critics* (New York: Macmillan, 1976)

Marvin Carlson

Theatre Guild. Organization of theater producers. Known initially as the Washington Square Players, it was formed in 1914 by amateurs including the patent lawyer Lawrence Langner (1890–1962), the directors Edward Goodman and Philip Moeller (1880–1958), the actresses Helen Westley (1879–1942) and Ida Rauh, and the bookseller Albert Boni; they sought to present intellectual plays of artistic merit as an alternative to the glossy revues popular on Broadway at the time. The group took its current name in 1918 and in 1920 mounted the American première of George Bernard Shaw's *Heartbreak House*. It moved in 1925 to its own theater at 243 West 52nd Street, designed by Norman Bel Geddes, where it presented plays by Shaw, Robert E. Sherwood, Maxwell Anderson, William Saroyan, and S. N. Behrman; it also presented most of Eugene O'Neill's plays on Broadway, including *Marco Millions* (1927) and *Strange Interlude* (1928), which was so long that a dinner intermission was required after the fifth act. Among the actors and actresses that the guild engaged regularly were Katherine Cornell, Eva Le Gallienne, Judith Anderson, Judy Holliday, and Joseph Schildkraut. It cast Alfred Lunt and Lynn Fontanne in Ferenc Molnar's *The Guardsman* in 1924, and the two later appeared together in eighteen other productions. Sets, lighting, and costumes were designed by Lee Simonson (1888–1967). The guild sold season subscriptions and by the mid 1920s had more than $600,000 in working capital each season. In 1931 it bought the Westport Country Theatre in Connecticut. During the 1920s and 1930s Langner, Westley, Simonson, Moeller, the financier Maurice Wertheim (1886–1950), and Theresa Helburn (1887–1959) made up the board of directors.

Financial pressure during the Depression led the guild to offer more commercial productions, which nonetheless introduced a new level of artistry to Broadway. Such musicals as *Porgy and Bess* (1935) and *Oklahoma!* (1943) were praised for their innovativeness. After 1939 Helburn was the executive director and Langner and his wife, Armina Marshall (1895–1991), were administrators. The guild produced dramatic plays for the "Theatre Guild of the Air" on radio and "The U.S. Steel Hour" on television and also made motion pictures, the best-known being *The Pawnbroker* (1961). Its presentation of *Golda* (1977) on Broadway was extremely successful. The Theatre Guild remained active into the 1990s. Run by Philip Langner from offices at 226 West 47th Street, it operated two theaters in Baltimore and handled subscription series for the Shubert Organization in New York City and elsewhere through a subsidiary, the American Theatre Society.

Norman Nadel: *A Pictorial History of the Theatre Guild* (New York: Crown, 1969)

See also THEATER, §§5, 6.

Alana J. Erickson

Theatrical Syndicate. A trust formed in 1896 by the theater producers Marc Klaw, Abraham Erlanger, and Charles Frohman, the booking agent Al(bert) Hayman, and two theater owners from Philadelphia, S. F. Nixon and J. F. Zimmerman. It was intended to bring order to the chaotic booking practices of the time and by 1903 controlled legitimate theater production throughout the United States. In New York City the syndicate was successfully challenged by only a few independent producers, including David Belasco, Harrison Grey Fiske, and Minnie Maddern Fiske, until its monopoly was broken by the Shubert brothers in 1916.

Don B. Wilmeth

Theosophists. The Theosophical movement, organized to explore ancient wisdom, comparative religion, and science, was founded by the Russian aristocrat Helena Blavatsky (1831–91) and Henry Steel Olcott (1832–1907), a lawyer and journalist in New York City. They met in 1874 in Chittenden, Vermont, at a gathering of Spiritualists. Together they explored the occult and lived among other addresses in an apartment on West 47th Street in Manhattan that became known as the Lamasery, where they sponsored well-attended lectures and parties. They formed the Theosophy Society in September 1875, with Olcott as president and Blavatsky as corresponding secretary. She wrote *Isis Unveiled* (1877) and in 1879 the two moved to India. Theosophy survived in the city, influencing occultism and a number of artists including Nicholas Roerich. The society's branches in the city are the Theosophical Society at 240 East 53rd Street and Theosophy Hall at 347 East 72nd Street. The Roerich Museum is at 107th Street and Riverside Drive in Manhattan.

Bruce F. Campbell: *Ancient Wisdom Revived: A History of the Theosophical Movement* (Berkeley: University of California Press, 1980)

Robert Ellwood

Thomas, Andrew J(ackson) (*b* New York City, 1875; *d* New York City, 25 July 1965). Architect. He distinguished himself by developing the community of Jackson Heights for the Queensboro Corporation and became known as a designer of garden apartments set in full-block, open-court plans. In 1920 he completed the Homewood Garden Apartments for the City and Suburban Homes Company (17th Avenue and 73rd Street,

Brooklyn) and Linden Court. Thomas's later projects included the Dunbar Apartments in central Harlem (1926– 28) for John D. Rockefeller Jr., buildings in Woodside and Astoria for the Metropolitan Life Insurance Company, the Thomas Garden Apartments at 840 Grand Concourse in the Bronx (1928), and the Dunolly Gardens (1939). He wrote *Industrial Housing* (1925).

Marjorie Pearson

Thomas, Franklin A(ugustine) (*b* Brooklyn, 27 May 1934). Lawyer and foundation executive. Educated at Columbia University (BA 1956, LLB 1963), he worked in New York City as a lawyer for the Federal Housing and Home Finance Agency (1963–64), as an assistant U.S. attorney (1964–65), and as an attorney with the police department (1965–67). He was the president and chief executive officer of the Bedford Stuyvesant Restoration Corporation (1967–77). As president of the Ford Foundation (1979–) he focused on domestic poverty, problems of refugees and immigrants, and leadership in state government.

For illustration see BEDFORD STUYVESANT RESTORATION CORPORATION.

Shan Jayakumar

Thomas, Lowell (Jackson) (*b* Woodington, near Greenville, Ohio, 6 April 1892; *d* Pawling, N.Y., 29 Aug 1981). Broadcaster and writer. In 1930 he was made the broadcaster of the first daily network news program on radio by William S. Paley of the Columbia Broadcasting System (CBS), and until 1976 he worked for both CBS and the National Broadcasting Company. He traveled widely and often gave reports at remote locations from which radio broadcasts had never before been made. He was also the narrator of "20th Century–Fox Movietone News," a founder of Capital Cities Communications, and the author of more than fifty books, the best-known of which was *With Lawrence in Arabia* (1924). His broadcasts and much of his other writing were done in collaboration with Prosper Buranelli, a former feature writer for the *New York World*. At the end of his career he was the host of the television series "Lowell Thomas Remembers" for the Public Broadcasting System and of "The Best Years," a daily syndicated radio series about the accomplishments of well-known people in their later years; he also wrote an autobiography, *Good Evening Everybody: From Cripple Creek to Samarkand* (1976). Thomas's was the longest continuous career of any reporter in radio.

Judith Adler Hennessee

Thomas, Norman (Mattoon) (*b* Marion, Ohio, 20 Nov 1884; *d* Huntington, N.Y., 19 Dec 1968). Political leader. He grew up in Marion, where he delivered the local newspaper run by Warren G. Harding. After moving with his family to Lewisburg, Pennsylvania, he attended Bucknell University and then Princeton University, where he graduated in 1905 as the valedictorian of his class. He next moved to New York City and enrolled at Union Theological Seminary, where he was strongly influenced by Henry Sloane Coffin; he became the minister of the East Harlem Presbyterian Church on 116th Street between 2nd and 3rd avenues in 1911 and in 1917 helped to form the National Civil Rights Bureau (later the American Civil Liberties Union). In 1918 he was pressured by church officials and community members to resign his pastorate because he opposed the First World War and belonged to the Socialist Party. After leaving East Harlem he moved with his wife to East 17th Street and entered politics, unsuccessfully seeking election as mayor in 1925 and 1929, state senator in 1926, alderman in 1927, borough president of Manhattan in 1931, and president of the United States in every campaign between 1928 and 1948 (his strongest showing was in 1932, when he received more than 2 percent of all presidential votes cast). A visit to Europe and the Soviet Union in 1937 led him to abandon notions of importing socialism based on the Soviet model, but he remained a committed socialist and peace activist. He formed the Keep America out of War Committee in the city in 1938 but was forced to reassess pacifism by the Spanish Civil War and Nazism; he became an outspoken critic of the internment of Japanese citizens and later protested against nuclear weapons. In 1943 he moved with his family to 20 Gramercy Park. Thomas was at the forefront of American activism during the 1950s and 1960s, protesting McCarthyism and the Korean and Vietnam wars. Toward the end of his life he lived in Cold Spring Harbor, New York, but continued to work in Manhattan and make national speaking tours.

Norman Thomas speaking at a May Day meeting of the Socialist Party, Union Square, 1933. Daily Mirror *photo*

Harry Fleischman: *Norman Thomas* (New York: W. W. Norton, 1969)
W. A. Swanberg: *Norman Thomas: The Last Idealist* (New York: Charles Scribner's Sons, 1976)

Chad Ludington

Thomas, Theodore (Christian Friedrich) (*b* Esens [now in Germany], 11 Oct 1835; *d* Chicago, 4 Jan 1905). Conductor and violinist. He arrived in New York City in 1845 and in 1854 became a violinist with the Philharmonic Society. On 29 April 1859 he made his début as a conductor at the New York Academy of Music, and he then had a distinguished career as the conductor of the Brooklyn Philharmonic Society (1862–91), his own ensemble the Thomas Orchestra (1869–88), and the New York Philharmonic Society (1877–78, 1879–91). He was one of the first orchestral conductors in New York City to popularize German classical music, which he performed at such events as the summer concerts in Central Park (1868–75). After 1885 the American Opera Company experienced financial difficulties and he suffered exhaustion from his competition with the rival conductors Anton Seidl and Frank and Peter Damrosch, and in 1901 he moved to Chicago.

Ezra Schabas: *Theodore Thomas: America's Conductor and Builder of Orchestras* (Champaign: University of Illinois Press, 1989)

Nancy Shear

Thomas Y. Crowell. Firm of book publishers formed in 1876 by Thomas Young Crowell at 744 Broadway. It published little fiction, focusing instead on specially bound gift editions as well as religious and inspirational titles. With its publication in 1886 of Roget's Thesaurus it also developed a strong list of reference books, and in the same year

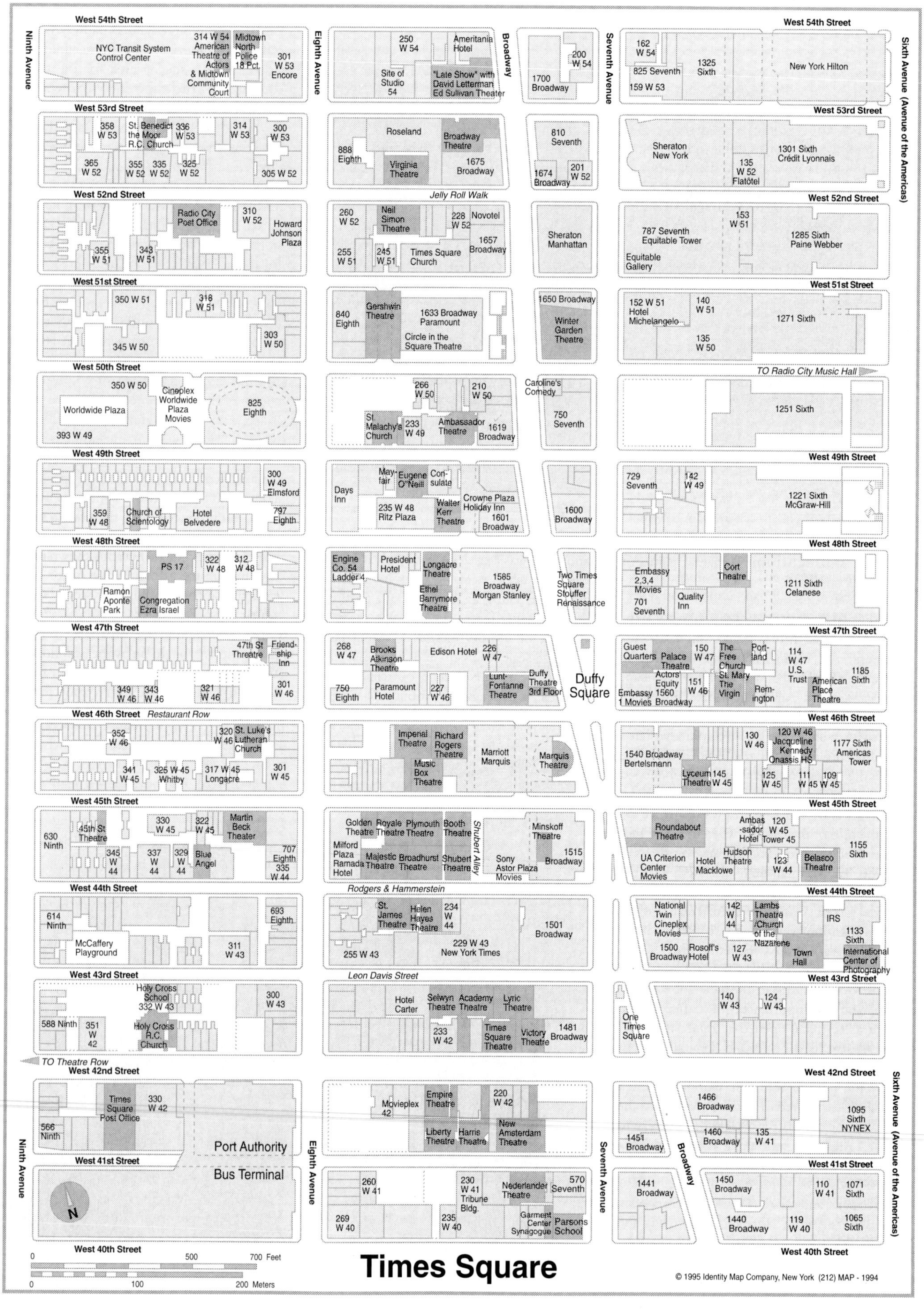
West 54th Street
Ninth Avenue
Eighth Avenue
Broadway
Seventh Avenue
Sixth Avenue (Avenue of the Americas)
NYC Transit System Control Center
314 W 54 American Theatre of Actors & Midtown Community Court
Midtown North Police 18 Pct.
301 W 53 Encore
250 W 54
Ameritania Hotel
Site of Studio 54
"Late Show" with David Letterman Ed Sullivan Theater
200 W 54
1700 Broadway
162 W 54
825 Seventh
159 W 53
1325 Sixth
New York Hilton
West 53rd Street
358 W 53
St. Benedict the Moor R.C. Church
336 W 53
314 W 53
300 W 53
365 W 52
355 W 52
335 W 52
325 W 52
305 W 52
Roseland
Broadway Theatre
888 Eighth
Virginia Theatre
1675 Broadway
810 Seventh
1674 Broadway
201 W 52
Sheraton New York
135 W 52 Flatôtel
1301 Sixth Crédit Lyonnais
West 52nd Street
Jelly Roll Walk
Radio City Post Office
310 W 52
Howard Johnson Plaza
355 W 51
343 W 51
260 W 52
Neil Simon Theatre
228 W 52
Novotel
1657 Broadway
255 W 51
245 W 51
Times Square Church
Sheraton Manhattan
787 Seventh Equitable Tower
153 W 51
Equitable Gallery
1285 Sixth Paine Webber
West 51st Street
350 W 51
318 W 51
345 W 50
303 W 50
840 Eighth
Gershwin Theatre
1633 Broadway Paramount
Circle in the Square Theatre
1650 Broadway
Winter Garden Theatre
152 W 51 Hotel Michelangelo
140 W 51
135 W 50
1271 Sixth
West 50th Street
TO Radio City Music Hall
350 W 50
Worldwide Plaza
Cineplex Worldwide Plaza Movies
825 Eighth
393 W 49
266 W 50
210 W 50
St. Malachy's Church
233 W 49
Ambassador Theatre
1619 Broadway
Caroline's Comedy
750 Seventh
1251 Sixth
West 49th Street
300 W 49 Elmsford
359 W 48
Church of Scientology
Hotel Belvedere
797 Eighth
Days Inn
May-fair
Eugene O'Neill
Con-sulate
235 W 48 Ritz Plaza
Walter Kerr Theatre
Crowne Plaza Holiday Inn
1601 Broadway
1600 Broadway
729 Seventh
142 W 49
1221 Sixth McGraw-Hill
West 48th Street
PS 17
322 W 48
312 W 48
Ramon Aponte Park
Congregation Ezra Israel
Engine Co. 54 Ladder 4
President Hotel
Longacre Theatre
Ethel Barrymore Theatre
1585 Broadway Morgan Stanley
Two Times Square Stouffer Renaissance
Embassy 2,3,4 Movies
701 Seventh
Quality Inn
Cort Theatre
1211 Sixth Celanese
West 47th Street
47th St Threatre
Friend-ship Inn
349 W 46
343 W 46
321 W 46
301 W 46
268 W 47
Brooks Atkinson Theatre
Edison Hotel
226 W 47
750 Eighth
Paramount Hotel
227 W 46
Lunt-Fontanne Theatre
Duffy Theatre 3rd Floor
Duffy Square
Guest Quarters
Palace Theatre
150 W 47
The Free Church St. Mary The Virgin
Port-land
114 W 47 U.S. Trust
1185 Sixth
Actors' Equity 1560 Broadway
151 W 46
Embassy 1 Movies
Rem-ington
American Place Theatre
West 46th Street
Restaurant Row
352 W 46
320 W 46
St. Luke's Lutheran Church
341 W 45
325 W 45 Whitby
317 W 45 Longacre
301 W 45
Imperial Theatre
Richard Rogers Theatre
Music Box Theatre
Marriott Marquis
Marquis Theatre
1540 Broadway Bertelsmann
130 W 46
120 W 46 Jacqueline Kennedy Onassis HS
1177 Sixth Americas Tower
Lyceum Theatre
145 W 45
125 W 45
111 W 45
109 W 45
West 45th Street
630 Ninth
45th St Theatre
330 W 45
322 W 45
Martin Beck Theater
345 W 44
337 W 44
329 W 44
Blue Angel
707 Eighth
335 W 44
Golden Theatre
Royale Theatre
Plymouth Theatre
Booth Theatre
Shubert Alley
Milford Plaza Ramada Hotel
Majestic Theatre
Broadhurst Theatre
Shubert Theatre
Minskoff Theatre
Sony Astor Plaza Movies
1515 Broadway
Roundabout Theatre
Ambas-sador Hotel
120 W 45 Tower 45
1155 Sixth
UA Criterion Center Movies
Hotel Macklowe
Hudson Theatre
123 W 44
Belasco Theatre
West 44th Street
Rodgers & Hammerstein
614 Ninth
McCaffery Playground
693 Eighth
311 W 43
St. James Theatre
Helen Hayes Theatre
234 W 44
255 W 43
229 W 43 New York Times
1501 Broadway
National Twin Cineplex Movies
142 W 44
Lambs Theatre /Church of the Nazarene
IRS
1133 Sixth
1500 Broadway
Rosoff's Hotel
127 W 43
Town Hall
International Center of Photography
West 43rd Street
Leon Davis Street
Holy Cross School 332 W 43
300 W 43
588 Ninth
351 W 42
Holy Cross R.C. Church
Hotel Carter
Selwyn Theatre
Academy Theatre
Lyric Theatre
233 W 42
Times Square Theatre
Victory Theatre
1481 Broadway
One Times Square
140 W 43
124 W 43
TO Theatre Row
West 42nd Street
Times Square Post Office
330 W 42
566 Ninth
Port Authority Bus Terminal
Movieplex 42
Empire Theatre
220 W 42
Liberty Theatre
Harris Theatre
New Amsterdam Theatre
1451 Broadway
1466 Broadway
1095 Sixth NYNEX
1460 Broadway
135 W 41
West 41st Street
260 W 41
269 W 40
230 W 41 Tribune Bldg.
235 W 40
Nederlander Theatre
570 Seventh
Garment Center Synagogue
Parsons School
1441 Broadway
1450 Broadway
110 W 41
1071 Sixth
1440 Broadway
119 W 40
1065 Sixth
N
West 40th Street
0 500 700 Feet
0 100 200 Meters
Times Square
© 1995 Identity Map Company, New York (212) MAP - 1994

area a haven for hustlers (male and female) and other purveyors of erotic entertainment. Attempts during the 1950s to check the growth of disreputable businesses through zoning had little effect. The continuing proliferation of cheap rooming houses, hotels, cafeterias, bars, adult bookstores, peep shows, and arcades was depicted in John Schlesinger's film *Midnight Cowboy* (1968). Efforts during the 1980s and 1990s to redevelop the area met with more success, although many of the erotic businesses only moved west. At the same time the required lighting on new buildings in the area offered a pale reminder of Times Square in its prime.

William R. Taylor, ed.: *Inventing Times Square: Commerce and Culture at the Crossroads of the World, 1880–1939* (New York: Russell Sage Foundation, 1991)

See also THEATER, §5.

William R. Taylor

time standardization. As the commercial and scientific hub of the United States, New York City played a major role in establishing standard time zones. Before 1883 every community ran according to its own local time: in New York City a time ball atop the Western Union building at Broadway and Dey Street descended precisely at noon, and another ball at the Customs House and the South Street Seaport was used by sailors. An early campaign for time standardization was led by William F. Allen, a railroad engineer from New York City who was the head of the American Railway Association, and Frederick A. P. Barnard and J. K. Rees, two prominent scientists at Columbia University who tried to have a national standard time law enacted by the U.S. Congress; Barnard was also instrumental in having meteorological and astronomic observations coordinated to a standard time. Time standardization was first put into effect by railroad engineers, who depended on strict timetables to establish schedules and avoid collisions. Allen edited the *Traveller's Official Guide*, a collection of railway timetables and trade information, and formulated a four-zone plan that was adopted by railroads at noon on Sunday 18 November 1883 without benefit of federal or state law. There was little opposition in New York City, but other parts of the nation objected strenuously to the new time zones.

Michael O'Malley: *Keeping Watch: A History of American Time* (New York: Viking, 1990)

Michael O'Malley

Time Warner. Communications firm formed in 1989 when the publishing firm Time Inc. paid $14,000 million in stock to acquire Warner Communications, a firm engaged in film production, cable television, and book publishing. Formed in 1923 by Henry R. Luce and Briton Hadden, Time Inc. published in addition to the magazine bearing its own name the magazines *Fortune*, *Life*, and *Sports Illustrated*, as well as books under the imprint Time–Life Books from the 1950s. From 1952 it acquired television stations, which earned huge profits in the 1950s and 1960s. In 1970, more than three years after Luce's death, the firm secured a controlling interest in Sterling Communications, which provided cable television service to the southern half of Manhattan. To increase the profitability of Sterling it inaugurated a premium service known as Home Box Office, which for an additional fee allowed subscribers to view recent films and live sporting events; access to a satellite relay system from 1976 made Home Box Office available nationwide, and it became the country's leading cable television service. Time Inc. enlarged its book publishing operations with the acquisition in 1968 of Little, Brown and in 1986 of Scott Foresman. In the 1970s and 1980s the firm successfully launched the magazines *People* and *Money*, but overall magazine publishing declined in significance: in 1988 it accounted for only 40 percent of the company's revenues of $4500 million, compared with 41 percent of revenues for cable television and 20 percent for book publishing. As Time Inc. grew in the 1980s so did the interest of outside investors: the purchase of Warner was intended partly to make the firm more competitive worldwide and partly to stave off an unfriendly takeover. Time Inc. occupied offices at various sites in midtown including the Chrysler Building and Rockefeller Center before moving in 1960 to an office tower that it jointly constructed and owned with Rockefeller Center.

Robert T. Elson: *Time Inc.: The Intimate History of a Publishing Enterprise, 1923–1941* (New York: Atheneum, 1968)

Robert T. Elson: *The World of Time Inc.: The Intimate History of a Publishing Enterprise, 1941–1960* (New York: Atheneum, 1973)

Curtis Prendergast with Geoffrey Colvin: *The World of Time Inc.: The Intimate History of a Changing Enterprise, 1960–1980* (New York: Atheneum, 1986)

James L. Baughman

Tin Pan Alley. Name applied originally to a district in which composers and music publishers were concentrated from the 1890s to the 1950s, and by extension to the style of their music and to the popular music business generally; the term may derive from the tinny sound of the pianos played by song pluggers. In the 1890s the corner of Broadway and 14th Street was the focus of the popular music business. After the eminent publishers M. Witmark and Sons moved uptown in the late 1890s the focus shifted successively to West 28th Street between Broadway and 6th Avenue; in 1903–8 to West 42nd Street, where many large publishers had their offices; in 1911–19 to the vicinity of the Exchange Building at 145 West 45th Street, which housed many smaller publishers; and during the 1920s to an area near 49th Street where the Brill Building was erected in 1931 at 1619 Broadway, although the music district extended as far south as West 42nd Street and as far north as West 56th Street.

Tin Pan Alley changed the way music was produced and marketed. In the early days of music publishing the industry was dispersed across the country; such established firms as Oliver Ditson of Boston and Lee and Walker of Philadelphia issued many kinds of music, which they publicized and distributed with restraint and a lack of imagination; and songwriters of the time, including Stephen Foster, George Root, Will S. Hays, and James Bland, wrote melodies rooted in English and American folk traditions, supported by simple harmonies, and set to lyrics that expressed the values of rural America. In the 1880s there emerged a new group of publishers and songwriters, many of whom were of eastern European and Jewish origin, and the industry changed dramatically after Charles K. Harris's song "After the Ball" (1892) sold nearly five million copies in the 1890s and nearly ten million altogether. New songs were now promoted shrewdly and aggressively— advertised in newspapers and magazines, on the back covers of the sheet music of older songs, and by hired song pluggers who played them on city streets and in theaters, department stores, and retail music shops. Noted singers and unknown organ grinders alike received stipends for publicizing new songs, publishers readily altered pieces to suit the needs of any entertainer, and free copies went to everyone likely to perform the music in public. To advance their music, publishers in Tin Pan Alley also staged musicals and invested in theaters and vaudeville circuits. In the 1920s, when sales of sheet music began to decline, the industry began producing recordings and promoting them on the radio. In the 1930s the advent of motion pictures with sound made possible the filming of musicals and helped bring songs to a wider public.

Through the early years of the twentieth century the best-known songwriters in Tin Pan Alley included Harris, Jean Schwartz ("Bedelia," 1903), George M. Cohan ("Give My Regards to Broadway," 1904), Paul Dresser ("My Gal Sal," 1905), and Harry Von Tilzer ("Wait 'Till the Sun Shines, Nellie," 1905). Between 1910 and 1940 publishers enlisted the talents of a generation of younger composers, including Irving Berlin, Jerome Kern, George Gershwin, Cole Porter, and Richard Rodgers, and lyricists such as Ira Gershwin, Lorenz Hart, and Oscar Hammerstein II. Although they worked in the same idiom as their older colleagues their music was more original and their lyrics more sophisticated. Several black composers made notable contributions to Tin Pan Alley, among them Shelton Brooks ("Some of These Days," 1910), Fats Waller ("Ain't Misbehavin'," 1929), and Duke Ellington ("Do Nothin' Till You Hear from Me," 1943).

During the 1950s and 1960s Tin Pan Alley failed to compete with newly popular styles of music, such as the rock-and-roll of Elvis Presley, the protest folk songs of Peter, Paul and Mary, and country music, and New York City accordingly ceased to dominate the popular music business. Nevertheless the best-known songs of Tin Pan Alley remained in the repertory into the late twentieth century: they inspired films, television productions, and theatrical revivals, and many new songs and Broadway shows drew on their stylistic conventions.

David A. Jasen: *Tin Pan Alley: The Composers, the Songs, the Performers, and Their Times* (New York: Donald I. Fine, 1988)

Nicholas E. Tawa: *The Way to Tin Pan Alley: American Popular Song, 1866–1910* (New York: Schirmer, 1990)

Nicholas E. Tawa

Tipperary Corners. Obsolete name of EGBERTVILLE.

Tishman, David (*b* New York City, 1889; *d* New York City, 18 June 1980). Real-estate developer. With his father, Julius Tishman, he built luxury apartment buildings on the Upper West Side between 1910 and 1920, seventeen similar buildings on the Upper East Side between 1922 and 1929, and several office buildings and lofts in the Garment District. The city's most prominent and successful developer by late 1930, he survived the Depression and built the first postwar office tower in Manhattan (1947, 445 Park Avenue). In 1957 he completed the Tishman Building, a skyscraper at 666 5th Avenue between 52nd and 53rd streets that became the headquarters of his firm, which was taken over during the 1960s by his sons Robert Tishman and Alan Tishman, his nephew John Tishman, and his son-in-law Jerry Speyer.

Marc A. Weiss

TLC Beatrice International Holdings. International holding company based at 9 West 57th Street in New York City, specializing in grocery products and food distribution. Formed in 1987 when Beatrice International was bought for $985 million by Reginald F. Lewis, it is the largest black-owned firm in the United States. In 1990 the firm had five thousand employees and sales of $1500 million. Its operations consist mainly of the former overseas operations of Beatrice Foods, which became a subsidiary of Conagra. Most of the subsidiaries make well-known brands of ice cream, desserts, beverages, and snacks in western Europe; the firm also has interests in Thailand, Puerto Rico, and Canada. After Lewis's death in January 1993 the firm came under the control of his heirs.

Gilbert Tauber

tobacco. Trade in tobacco was begun in New Amsterdam and continued by the merchants of the British colony of New York. During the eighteenth century tobacco was brought north from the Chesapeake River and prepared for export to Europe, becoming the third-most lucrative export crop for the colony, after cotton and flour. The growth in local and regional consumption of snuff and pipe tobacco caused the French Huguenot immigrant Pierre Lorillard to open the first large snuff factory in 1760; its snuff mill was in a rural area now part of the northern Bronx (and the site of the Bronx Botanical Garden), but most snuff mills were in Manhattan, including those of Isaac de Voe and Daniel Snowhill. In the early nineteenth century the firm of G. B. Miller, later known as H. J. Mickle and Sons, was important in increasing the production of chewing tobacco. According to the federal census of 1840 the tobacco business in Manhattan employed more than two hundred workers.

G. H. Boughton, Edict of William the Testy *(1877), depicting protesters smoking on Willem Kieft's doorstep*

By 1846 the city was the principal point of entry for Caribbean cigars, an increasingly valuable import during the first half of the nineteenth century: city directories listed forty-four importers. The production of pipe and chewing tobacco increased slightly in the 1850s, but most of the chewing-tobacco business was moving to the tobacco-growing areas of the South (notably North Carolina), and most snuff manufacturing to Middlesex County, New Jersey. At the same time the growth of the immigrant population increased the consumption of cigars, and it soon became economical to produce cigars domestically. Cigar makers from Cuba, Spain, England, the Netherlands, and Germany worked in a growing number of small shops around Chatham Square, and by the time of the Civil War there were several cigar manufacturers, each with roughly a dozen employees. With the introduction of import duties on foreign tobacco products in 1863 the domestic production of cigars became more profitable, beginning a period of intensely rapid growth in the tobacco business. The expansion of the consumer market and the influx of skilled immigrants from Europe after the Civil War made the city the largest cigar-making center in the United States. In 1870 about 144 million cigars were produced annually in Manhattan (eight times as many as were produced in 1863), and more than 5500 men and women were employed by well over a thousand cigar-making establishments.

Cigar making remained largely a handicraft during the first decade of its expansion, with most of the work done by German-born men with years of experience. During the late 1860s the introduction of the cigar mold enabled workers with much less skill and experience to roll reasonably uniform cigars and to produce more than experienced workers could by hand. There emerged large factories with an intricate division of labor, and by 1881 at least seventeen employers had more than 250 workers each. There were more than fifteen hundred workers in each of the three largest firms: Kerbs and Spiess, Straiton and Storm, and Lichtenstein Brothers. At the same time about seventeen hundred small shops were situated in the city, as well as an indeterminate number of "tenement manufacturers" who rented tenements in which families lived and worked as cigar makers. German immigrants continued to dominate the ranks of cigar makers in the early 1880s and accounted for most of the workers in the large factories, and by the end of the decade there were also many eastern European Jews (most employers in the industry were of German and often Jewish origin until the turn of the century). The pay and status of cigar workers were low until a unionization movement took hold in the late 1870s. After 1880 large factories that produced low-grade cigars expanded while makers of high-quality cigars from Cuban tobacco (known as "clear Havana" cigars) declined. At the time the two largest firms were Ybor y Martinez and De Bary, which each employed about a hundred workers. Both moved out of the city in the early 1880s to concentrate their production near Tampa Bay, Florida, the future seat of clear Havana manufacture in the United States.

During the height of its growth cigar making was concentrated in two sections of Manhattan. Around Chatham Square were many old, small workshops, convenient to the old harbor areas and not far from the immigrant quarters of the Lower East Side. As the industry grew, factories were constructed north of 50th Street in Manhattan, where large numbers of Germans and Bohemians settled. In Brooklyn the industry was smaller and dispersed over a much larger area, with only a few firms employing more than a hundred workers. Although family firms such as Lichtenstein Brothers, Sutro and Newmark, and others were nationally prominent, their owners had little impact on the politics or civic affairs of the city. Only a few families such as the Lorillards remained in the business for more than one generation. At the turn of the century the cigar and tobacco industry was made more productive by the cigar-rolling machine and the suction table (a table with a built-in suction device that pressed down the binder leaf), but the increasing need for space and capital investment made the city an unadvantageous location. Many firms moved to Lancaster County in Pennsylvania or farther south. Some of the cigar manufacturers that remained became part of the American Cigar Company of New York City, a cigar trust formed in 1901 by James B. Duke. Over the next six years the trust was joined by some of the largest firms (including Powell and Smith; Kerbs and Spiess; Wertheim and Schiffer; Hirshorn, Mack and Company; and Straiton and Storm), but it was less successful than trusts in the tobacco trade and in cigarette manufacturing and was dissolved by court order in 1911. By the time of the Second World War few cigars were manufactured in the city, none in major factories.

The decline of cigar making was due largely to the rise of the cigarette industry during the 1880s. Centered in Manhattan and Jersey City, New Jersey, the industry was dominated from the beginning by Duke and the firm of P. Lorillard. By the 1890s cigarette production was mechanized and the work force was ethnically heterogeneous: young women operated cigarette-rolling machines in large factories employing an average of more than five hundred workers. In 1911 six large cigarette factories throughout Manhattan dominated the industry, with a large facility owned by Lorillard in Jersey City overlooking the Hudson. After a merger with among others the firms of Goodwin and Company, Kinney Tobacco, Lorillard, and the Continental Tobacco Company (all in New York City), the newly named Consolidated Tobacco Company of Jersey City dominated the cigarette and "plug" (chewing-tobacco) markets nationwide from 1904 until a court order in 1911 forced the dissolution of the trust into three firms (Lorillard, American Tobacco, and Liggett and Myers).

New York City was the largest metropolitan market for cigarettes and a source of cheap female labor until the 1920s, when more than 30 percent of all North American cigarettes were still manufactured in the metropolitan area. The Depression reduced the size of the region's cigarette industry. By 1963 only about two hundred persons in greater New York were employed in tobacco. The city nevertheless became a center of corporate headquarters for such tobacco conglomerates as Philip Morris, American Brands (successor to the American Tobacco Company), and Lorillard. By the early 1990s there were no longer any tobacco, cigarette-making, or cigar-making facilities in the region.

Report on the Tobacco Industry (Washington: U.S. Bureau of Corporations, 1909)

Dorothee Schneider and Lucy W. Killough: "The Tobacco Products Industry," *Regional Survey of New York and Its Environs* (New York: Committee on Regional Plan of New York and Its Environs, 1924), vol. 1a

William R. Finger: *The Tobacco Industry in Transition: Policies for the 1980s* (Lexington, Mass.: Lexington, 1981)

Dorothee Schneider: "The New York Cigarmakers Strike of 1877," *Labor History* 26 (1985), 325–52

Dorothee Schneider

Tobagonians. Tobagonian immigration is discussed in the entry on TRINIDADIANS AND TOBAGONIANS.

Tobin, Austin J(oseph) (*b* Brooklyn, 25 May 1903; *d* New York City, 8 Feb 1978). Public official. After graduating from Holy Cross College in 1925 he joined the Port of New York Authority in 1927 and earned a law degree from Fordham University in 1928. Appointed executive director of the authority in 1942, he assembled a skilled, politically independent staff and oversaw the development and expansion of three large airports from the 1940s to the 1960s, the establishment of container ports in the 1950s and 1960s, and the construction of the World Trade Center in the 1960s and 1970s. He retired in 1972.

Jameson W. Doig and Erwin C. Hargrove, eds.: *Leadership and Innovation: A Biographical Perspective on Entrepreneurs in Government* (Baltimore: Johns Hopkins University Press, 1987), chap. 5

Jameson W. Doig

Todt Hill. Neighborhood in north central Staten Island, centered at a hill near the intersection of Todt Hill Road and Ocean Terrace that rises 410 feet (125 meters) above sea level and is the highest point on the Atlantic Coast in the United States south of Maine. The area was initially called Yserberg ("iron hill") by Dutch settlers, for the iron in the local serpentine rock, and was eventually renamed for a burial ground at the foot of the hill (now Moravian Cemetery). Large open-pit mines were operated from 1830 to 1885; some were eventually covered by the large golf course of the Richmond County Country Club. In 1928 St. Francis Seminary was built on a lot of forty-four acres (seventeen hectares) north of the golf course. The architect Ernest Flagg built many houses of the native rock, including his own on a side of the hill (now a city landmark). Eventually the golf course and the seminary became part of the Greenbelt, a nature preserve that also includes 140 acres (fifty-seven hectares) to the south covered by Moravian Cemetery and the cemetery of the Vanderbilt family as well as some other private land; the Greenbelt has many marked trails and a study area at High Rock Conservation Center (formerly a Girl Scout camp). Todt Hill is the wealthiest neighborhood on Staten Island and the site of Staten Island Academy, a prestigious private day school. Buttonwood Road is typical of its elegant, tree-lined streets.

Marjorie Johnson

toiletries. The manufacture of toiletries and related products is discussed in the entry SOAP AND TOILETRIES.

tokens. The first token for New York City was issued under Governor Francis Lovelace (1668–73). Struck in bronze and white metal, it depicts on the obverse Cupid and Psyche (a rebus on the name Lovelace) and on the reverse an eagle on a regulated fesse (the crest of the Lovelace arms) within the inscription "New Yorke in America." After independence tokens were issued by the firm of clockmakers Mott in 1789 and by Talbot, Allum and Lee in 1794 and 1795. Several tokens from this period depict buildings in the city: the Theatre at New York token, issued by John Skidmore in London and engraved by Benjamin Jacob, shows an image of the Park Theatre copied from the gatefold in Longworth's Directory of 1797. "Hard times tokens" filled an important gap in the city's circulation after the panic of 1837; tokens were also used during the Civil War and later issued by amusement arcades on Coney Island. The first transportation tokens were customarily used for transfers, as fares were collected with paper tickets. When the dime fare on the subways increased to fifteen cents in 1953 brass tokens were introduced; in later years the design was often altered when fares were increased, to discourage hoarding. About 1990 counterfeit subway tokens made from a plain brass ring around a steel center entered circulation; the counterfeiters were arrested and convicted in 1991, but the counterfeits, popularly known as "people's tokens," continued to circulate.

Wayte Raymond: "Early New York Store Cards," *Coin Collector's Journal* 1 (1934), 66–68, 85–87, 116–17, 136–37, 231–35

George S. Cuhaj: "Medals and Tokens of the New York Subway System," *Numismatist*, vol. 91 (1978), pp. 25–32; vol. 92 (1979), pp. 1887–96

John M. Kleeberg: "The New Yorke in America Token," *Money of Pre-Federal America*, ed. John M. Kleeberg (New York: American Numismatic Society, 1992), 15–57

John M. Kleeberg

Tombs. The name commonly applied to the Manhattan House of Detention for Men at 100 Centre Street in Manhattan, the third prison to occupy the same general site. It is derived from the design for the first building, which was inspired by a photograph of an Egyptian tomb that appeared in a book on the Middle East written by John L. Stephens in 1837. Construction of the prison was made necessary by the city's growing population, the decrepit condition of the Bridewell near City Hall, and the inconvenient location of the penitentiary at Bellevue. The new prison proved inadequate: it had too few cells (two hundred, of which fifty were reserved for women), and because it was built on a swampy landfill near the canal connecting the Hudson and East rivers it soon began to sink; the same happened to a new building constructed in its place in 1902. For decades the prison received widespread attention for its deplorable conditions and became a symbol of much that was wrong in correctional institutions. A renovation of the present structure was completed in 1983. The Tombs is now a modern facility that houses more than four hundred inmates and is one of the most progressive institutions of its kind in the nation. It is connected by a bridge to a new facility on White Street that operates with the same warden and staff. The facilities together operate as a single jail housing more than nine hundred inmates.

Charles Sutton: *The New York Tombs: Its Secrets and its Mysteries*, ed. James B. Mix and Samuel A. Mackeever (New York: United States Publishing, 1874; repr. Montclair, N.J.: Patterson Smith, 1973, with an introd. by Thomas M. McDade)

Joseph P. Viteritti

Tompkins, Daniel D. (*b* Fox Meadow [now Scarsdale], N.Y., 21 June 1774; *d* Staten Island, 11 June 1825). Governor and vice president of the United States. He graduated from Columbia College in 1795, practiced law in New York City, and became associated with Tammany Hall. Elected governor of New York State in 1807 and thrice reelected, he achieved several reforms during his tenure of nearly ten years, notably a commitment by the state to abolish slavery by 1827. During the War of 1812 he resolutely supported President James Madison's policies against legislative opposition, mobilized an unprepared militia, and raised money for the war effort by backing loans with his own credit; he also supervised the ceding of land and construction of forts on the islands of New York Harbor and as the commander of the third military district oversaw the mobilization of the civilian work crews that fortified the city in 1814. His development from the same year of a village called Tompkinsville on Staten Island marked the beginning of the island's integration into greater New York; even while serving as President James Monroe's vice president from 1817 to 1825 he spent much of his time developing this property. His Richmond Turnpike Company built the thoroughfare across the island now known as Victory Boulevard, and it began the first ferry service to Manhattan (with the launching of the steamboat *Nautilus* in 1817) and later the first towing service in the harbor. In 1824 he was the host on Staten Island of the start of the Marquis de Lafayette's triumphant tour of the United States. His last years were marred by ill health and political and financial embarrassment occasioned by his protracted struggle for compensation for his wartime expenditures and unsettled accounts. Tompkins is buried in the churchyard of St. Mark's Church in the Bowery, where a bust was unveiled in 1939. Tompkins Square was named for him in 1833; Tompkins Street was eventually obscured by the FDR Drive.

Ray W. Irwin: *Daniel D. Tompkins: Governor of New York and Vice President of the United States* (New York: New-York Historical Society, 1968)

Mariam Touba

Tompkins Square. Neighborhood on the Lower East Side of Manhattan. It comprises Tompkins Square Park, a public park bounded to the north by 10th Street, to the east by Avenue B, to the south by 7th Street, and to the west by Avenue A, as well as the surrounding area. The square appeared on the map of Manhattan drawn in 1811 after the survey of John Randal Jr. and was designated to remain in perpetuity as public grounds. It was once owned by Daniel D. Tompkins, governor of New York and vice president of the United States under James Monroe, whose estate extended from the East River to what is now 2nd Avenue. The War of 1812 stimulated the growth of foundries and shipyards on the riverfront, and the square became a marketplace for farm produce from Long Island. Workers lived along the avenues; shop owners and British immigrants moved northward along Broadway and 6th Avenue. By 1849 conservative, nativist Whigs inclined toward Temperance opposed Democrats allied with Tammany Hall, immigrants, and workers, and in the same year the square was beset by the violence of the Astor Place Riot. In 1857 demonstrators for public employment paraded from City Hall to the square, and during the depression of 1875 police confronted local residents. Paving was laid in 1866, and trees and grasses were planted soon after. About 1905 Tompkins Square Park was provided with playgrounds, and classes in Americanization were offered for immigrants. Rock concerts were held in the park in the 1960s, and in the following decades nightclubs opened in the neighborhood, young professionals moved in, older residents protested the noise and higher rents, and the homeless built shacks in the southern portion of the park. In August 1988 a curfew was defied as bricks and bottles were thrown at charging mounted police, and the turmoil was reported in detail. The police in the late summer of 1991 cleared the homeless from the park, which was then closed for extensive renovation.

Charles Loring Brace: *The Dangerous Classes of New York* (New York: Wynkoop and Hallenbeck, 1872; repr. National Association of Social Workers, 1973)

Jacob Riis: *How the Other Half Lives* (New York: Charles Scribner's Sons, 1890; repr. Hill and Wang, 1957)

Theodore Dreiser: *The Color of a Great City* (New York: Boni and Liveright, 1923)

Esther Mipaas

Tompkins Square Riot. The name of two riots on the Lower East Side of Manhattan, the first on 13 January 1874 and the second on 6 August 1988; see Riots.

Tompkinsville. Neighborhood in northeastern Staten Island, lying along the eastern shore south of the terminal for the Staten Island Ferry at St. George. The oldest village in eastern Staten Island, it was a landing where early explorers replenished their water supply and was known in colonial times as the Watering Place; a settlement was established there next to the quarantine station in 1815 by Daniel D. Tompkins, who built a dock at the foot of Victory Boulevard and initiated steam ferry service to New York City in 1817. He named several streets after his children: Arietta Street (now Victory Boulevard), Griffin Street, Hannah Street, Sarah Ann Street (now part of Van Duzer Street), and Minthorne Street. A fleet of the U.S. Coast Guard was based there in the early nineteenth century and shared quarters with a regional lighthouse depot. In the mid 1990s the population was Italian, Latin American, and black. The center of the village is a commercial area around Tompkinsville Park, where a statue was placed to honor heroes of the First World War and two smaller markers commemorate Tompkins and the Watering Place.

Barnett Shepherd

tongs. Secret Chinese protective associations that operate legal and illegal enterprises and employ youth gangs to control gambling, drug dealing, and extortion. Wars between tongs took place during periods of rapid ex-

Francis Guy, Tontine Coffee House, New York City *(ca 1797)*

pansion and internal power struggles in Chinatown. From 1910 to 1930 the young "soldiers" of the Hip Sing and On Leung tongs fought in the streets. Gangs sponsored by tongs became strong again in the 1960s when there was an influx of Chinese immigrants. By the 1980s tongs were outnumbered by street gangs, which undertook their own enterprises, expanded into Chinese communities outside Manhattan, and increasingly engaged in violence to assert their authority against other gangs sponsored by tongs. Although such gangs as the Ghost Shadows became known citywide through sensational accounts in the press, their activities were largely confined to Chinese communities.

Betty Lee Sung: *Gangs in New York's Chinatown* (Washington: Department of Health, Education and Welfare, 1977)

Joshua Brown

Tontine Coffee House. Building erected in 1793 at the corner of Wall and Water streets. In 1796 it became the headquarters of the New York Insurance Company, a precursor of the New York Stock Exchange. The twenty-one members of the company's board of directors assigned values to slaves, ships, houses, and effects to form a tontine, a financial arrangement in which each member received a share of profit that increased as the number of participants was reduced by death. The tontine asserted that its actions would "have a tendency to advance the mercantile interest in particular and promote the general welfare of the State." Its first president was Archibald Gracie, whose home on the East River later became the official residence of the mayor.

Anthony Gronowicz

Tony Award. An award presented annually by the American Theater Wing, an educational and service organization of theater professionals, for distinguished achievement on Broadway. It was established in 1947 to honor the actress and director Antoinette "Tony" Perry (*b* 27 June 1888; *d* 28 June 1946), who at the time of her death was the head of the board of directors of the organization. The Tony Award is given to outstanding performers, plays, playwrights, and designers in both dramatic plays and musicals.

Martha S. LoMonaco

Topps Company. Firm of chewing gum and baseball card manufacturers, formed as Topps Chewing Gum in 1938. Its headquarters were initially in Williamsburg before moving in 1946 to Bush Terminal (36th Street). In 1947 the firm introduced Bazooka bubble gum, which became its first important success; major league baseball cards followed in 1951. A factory was in operation at Bush Terminal until 1965. The firm enjoyed tremendous prosperity in the late 1980s, when baseball cards became highly sought-after collector's items. In August 1989 it sponsored a baseball card auction at Hunter College that attracted national attention and yielded more than $1.5 million in receipts. In 1990 the firm's sales exceeded $290 million. The undisputed leader in sports trading cards, Topps issues more than 500 million baseball cards a year as well as cards for other sports and entertainments.

James Bradley

Torres, Edwin (*b* New York City, 7 Jan 1931). Judge and novelist. Born to Puerto Rican parents, he lived as a child at 107th Street and Madison Avenue in Spanish Harlem and graduated from Stuyvesant High School and City College of New York. After serving in the navy overseas he attended Brooklyn Law School, working as a waiter to support himself. In 1958 he became the city's first Puerto Rican assistant district attorney. He worked as a defense attorney from 1961 until 1977, when he became a criminal court judge. In 1975 he published *Carlito's Way*, a novel about a small-time cocaine hustler during the 1940s, 1950s, and 1960s that was one of the first fictional works to deal with Puerto Ricans' experience in the city after the Second World War; it was made into a motion picture, as was *Q&A* (1976), a novel drawn from Torres's experience as a prosecutor and defender. He published a sequel to *Carlito's Way*, *After Hours* (1977), and was appointed to the city supreme court in 1979. Torres has a reputation for toughness on the bench, and once told a defendant that his parole officer had "not been born yet."

Chad Ludington

Toscanini, Arturo (*b* Parma, 25 March 1867; *d* New York City, 16 Jan 1957). Conductor. Named the artistic director of La Scala in 1898, he conducted the world premières of Puccini's *La bohème* (Turin, 1896) and Leoncavallo's *Pagliacci* (Milan, 1892), as well as the Italian premières of works by Richard Strauss and Debussy. He moved to New York City in 1908 to become the artistic director of the Metropolitan Opera, a position he retained until 1915. In 1926 he accepted an invitation to be a guest conductor of the New York Philharmonic, which under his direction became one of the leading orchestras in the world and made its first European tour (1930); he was made associate conductor in 1927 and music director in 1933. During his tenure he became especially well known for his performances of Beethoven, Brahms, Verdi, and

Arturo Toscanini conducting the NBC Symphony Orchestra, ca *1937*

Tony Awards for Best Musical and Best Play

1948	[no award given] / Mister Roberts
1949	Kiss Me Kate / Death of a Salesman
1950	South Pacific / The Cocktail Party
1951	Call Me Madam / The Rose Tattoo
1952	The King and I / The Fourposter
1953	Wonderful Town / The Crucible
1954	Kismet / The Teahouse of the August Moon
1955	The Pajama Game / The Desperate Hours
1956	Damn Yankees / The Diary of Anne Frank
1957	My Fair Lady / Long Day's Journey into Night
1958	The Music Man /The Dark at the Top of the Stairs, Sunrise at Campobello
1959	Redhead / J.B.
1960	The Sound of Music, Fiorello! / The Miracle Worker
1961	Bye, Bye Birdie / Becket
1962	How to Succeed in Business without Really Trying / A Man for All Seasons
1963	A Funny Thing Happened on the Way to the Forum / Who's Afraid of Virginia Woolf?
1964	Hello, Dolly! / Luther
1965	Fiddler on the Roof / The Subject Was Roses
1966	Man of La Mancha / Marat/Sade
1967	Cabaret / The Homecoming
1968	Hallelujah, Baby! /Rosencrantz and Guildenstern Are Dead
1969	1776 / The Great White Hope
1970	Applause / Borstal Boy
1971	Company / Sleuth
1972	Two Gentlemen of Verona / Sticks and Bones
1973	A Little Night Music / That Championship Season
1974	Raisin / The River Niger
1975	The Wiz / Equus, Same Time Next Year
1976	A Chorus Line / Travesties
1977	Annie / The Shadow Box
1978	Ain't Misbehavin' / Da
1979	Sweeney Todd / The Elephant Man
1980	Evita / Children of a Lesser God
1981	42nd Street / Amadeus
1982	Nine / Nicholas Nickleby
1983	Cats / Torch Song Trilogy
1984	La Cage aux Folles / The Real Thing
1985	Big River / Biloxi Blues
1986	The Mystery of Edwin Drood / I'm Not Rappaport
1987	Les Misérables / Fences
1988	The Phantom of the Opera / M. Butterfly
1989	Jerome Robbins's Broadway / The Heidi Chronicles
1990	City of Angels / The Grapes of Wrath
1991	The Will Rogers Follies / Lost in Yonkers
1992	Crazy for You / Dancing at Lughnasa
1993	Kiss of the Spider Woman / Angels in America: Millennium Approaches
1994	Passion / Angels in America: Perestroika

Wagner. He gave his final concert on 29 April 1936. In the following year he was named conductor of the NBC Symphony Orchestra, which was formed expressly for him by David Sarnoff, head of the National Broadcasting Company. The orchestra became known worldwide through its radio broadcasts and its recordings for RCA Victor. Toscanini retired after its last concert, on 4 April 1954 at Carnegie Hall, and spent the rest of his life at his home in Riverdale.

Harvey Sachs: *Toscanini* (Philadelphia: J. B. Lippincott, 1978)

Joseph Horowitz: *Understanding Toscanini: How He Became an American Culture-God and Helped Create a New Audience for Old Music* (New York: Alfred A. Knopf, 1987)

Allen J. Share

Tottenville. Neighborhood in southwestern Staten Island, bounded to the north by the Arthur Kill and Mill Creek, to the south by Raritan Bay, and to the west by the Arthur Kill; it is the most southerly part of New York City and New York State. The land was first inhabited by the Delaware or Lenape Indians, whose burial sites and artifacts were found near Ward's Point. The first European settler was Captain Christopher Billopp, an English naval officer who in 1678 was given twelve hundred acres (486 hectares) by the British government; he built a stone house called Bentley Manor and before 1700 operated a ferry across the Arthur Kill to carry travelers to Philadelphia after they crossed into Staten Island from Manhattan along King's Highway (now Richmond and Amboy roads). Ferry service was continual until Outerbridge Crossing was built in 1927. The local economy was closely linked to that of Amboy (now Perth Amboy), New Jersey. The Totten family owned land in the area during the eighteenth century. Colonel Christopher Billopp, a great-grandson of the first settler, actively supported the British during the American Revolution, and after the war all his land was confiscated. Bentley Manor became known as the Conference House, after an unsuccessful peace conference held there in 1776 between Lord Howe and Benjamin Franklin, John Adams, and Edward Rutledge.

The deep water of the Arthur Kill was well suited to fishing and water transport, and the waterfront flourished in the early nineteenth century as freight and passenger boats docked there on their way to Manhattan. The Staten Island Railroad built a line to the area from St. George in the 1860s. The Atlantic Terra Cotta Company, the primary manufacturer of architectural terra cotta ornaments, built a factory on the Arthur Kill in 1897; it became one of the largest employers on Staten Island and remained in operation until the early 1930s. There were eight boatyards in the neighborhood in 1898 (the best known of which was Brown and Ellis), but after 1900 they declined as steel replaced wood in ship construction. The Nassau Smelting and Refining Company built a plant in 1900 on the Richmond Valley line. In 1915 state officials banned the harvesting of oysters and clams in Raritan Bay because of pollution. The smelting works was bought by Western Electric in 1931; in 1971 it became a metal recycling plant and was renamed the Nassau Recycling Corporation.

In 1990 the population was 94.5 percent white, 4 percent Latin American, 1 percent Asian, and 0.5 percent black. The shopping and business area is on Main Street; many houses in the Federal and Victorian styles remain there and along Amboy Road. Conference House Park lies along the shore and contains two designated landmarks: Conference House and Biddle House. There are seven small marinas serving commercial and sport fishermen.

Marjorie Johnson

Touche Ross. Accounting firm formed on 1 March 1900 at 30 Broad Street as Touche, Nevin by Scottish accountants who merged their operations in order to work in both the United States and Britain. Its first major client was the International Steam Pump Company (later the Worthington Corporation); later clients included the Pillsbury Flour Mills (1913), the Quaker Creamery Company, and the Greyhound Corporation. After the Second World War the firm merged with those of Allen R. Smart and George Bailey to become Touche, Ross, Bailey, and Smart, later taking the name Touche Ross. In 1989 the firm merged with Deloitte, Haskins and Sells to form Deloitte and Touche.

David Grayson Allen and Kathleen McDermott: *Accounting for Success: A History of Price Waterhouse in America, 1890–1990* (Boston: Harvard Business School Press, 1990)

Paul J. Miranti Jr.: *Accountancy Comes of Age: The Development of an American Profession, 1886–1940* (Chapel Hill: University of North Carolina Press, 1990)

Janet Frankston

tour boats. See Excursion boats.

Tourian, Leon Elisee (*b* Üsküdar, Turkey, 1881; *d* New York City, 24 Dec 1933). Archbishop. Born into a prominent Armenian family, he was ordained in 1901 and quickly rose to the rank of bishop (1913). In 1931 he arrived in New York City and became the archbishop of the Armenian Apostolic Diocese of North America. His vocal support of Soviet hegemony over the republic of Armenia was resented by members of the Armenian Revolutionary Federation (known as Dashnags), and during a Christmas Mass he was fatally stabbed at the altar of the Holy Cross Church of Armenia (580 West 187th Street in Manhattan); he was later interred in the church. When nine Dashnags were found guilty of the murder in July 1934, thousands of the party's members left the diocese to form independent parishes.

Harold Takooshian

tourism. Tourists visited New York City in increasing numbers after 1820, when improvements in transportation made travel faster, cheaper, and more comfortable. Journeys through the United States often began in the city, a terminus of major steamship companies. Most tourists first saw the city from the harbor, framed by a number of islands to the east and the Hudson to the north; wharves extended the length of the waterfront, and masts and steeples defined the skyline. By 1850 the city was known for its effervescence and cosmopolitan character. The shopping, entertainment, and jostling crowds on Broadway were noted by many, including Charles Dickens, who visited the city in 1842, and the Scottish publisher William Chambers, who found the hotels on Broadway to be more like palaces than commercial enterprises. The city did little to promote tourism, and guidebooks, pamphlets, and newspapers were among the few sources for planning itineraries. About the turn of the century the Royal Blue Line offered tours of Manhattan and Brooklyn in its nine electric buses; tours of the waterfront were given by sightseeing boats such as the *Halcyon* and the *Tourist*, which sailed from Battery Park. By the mid 1920s viewing the city's skyscrapers was a popular activity. Soon after its completion in 1931 the Empire State Building (often called the "eighth wonder of the world") became a symbol of the city and a destination of most tourists: during the first year a million persons rode the elevator to the top at a cost of a dollar. Transformed by electricity, Broadway at night was considered by Philippe de Rothschild in 1930 and other Europeans as a spectacle unmatched in the world. The city's art galleries, museums, concert halls, and theaters also drew many visitors. In 1935 the city formed the New York Convention and Visitors Bureau to build tourism into a major industry.

By the mid twentieth century tourism was an important part of the city's economy. Sightseeing excursions around Manhattan were introduced in 1945 by the Circle Line, which by 1991 had carried more than 45 million passengers. Mayor John V. Lindsay promoted the city as "fun city" in the 1960s. In 1971 the visitors' bureau under Charles Gillett launched the "Big Apple" promotional campaign, which became one of the most successful ventures of its kind. At the end of the 1980s the city remained the world's most popular city to visit. The Empire State Building alone had about two million visitors a year. Other popular attractions included Central Park (where rides in horse-drawn carriages were especially popular), Dyckman House (the only surviving eighteenth-century farmhouse in Manhattan), the United Nations, McSorley's Old Ale House, the Russian Tea Room, and the Cloisters, the medieval branch of the Metropolitan Museum of Art, which overlooks the Hudson from Fort Tryon Park.

In 1992 there were 3,932,000 overseas travelers landing in New York City, accounting for 22.1 percent of all arrivals in the United States. According to a study issued in December 1994 by the Port Authority of New York and New Jersey, the metropolitan region in 1992 attracted 36.4 million domestic visitors and 6.6 million foreign visitors, who generated about 268,000 jobs in hotels, restaurants, entertainment, recreation, public transportation, and the retail sector and added $20,675 million to the local economy.

Bayrd Still: *Mirror for Gotham: New York as Seen by Contemporaries from Dutch Days to the Present* (New York: New York University Press, 1956)

Mary Dawn Earley, comp.: "A New York Visitors' Book," *New York, N.Y.: An American Heritage Extra*, ed. David G. Lowe (New York: American Heritage, 1968), 134–37

Allen J. Share: "British Travelers and American Cities, 1830–1860: Images and Realities" (diss., University of Toledo, 1973), 97–138

John A. Jakle: *The Tourist: Travel in Twentieth-century North America* (Lincoln: University of Nebraska Press, 1985)

Jan Morris: *Among the Cities* (New York: Oxford University Press, 1985), 259–81

Jan Morris: *Manhattan '45* (New York: Oxford University Press, 1986, 1987)

Tourism's Economic Impact on New York City, 1989 (New York: New York Convention and Visitors Bureau, n.d. [1990])

Allen J. Share

Touro College. Private coeducational institution at 30 West 44th Street in Manhattan, founded by Bernard Lander in 1971. It offers undergraduate programs in liberal arts, general studies, health studies, and Jewish studies; a law school was added in 1980. The college is nonsectarian but requires that students in the liberal arts division earn credits in Hebrew and Jewish studies.

Rachel Sawyer

Toussaint, Pierre (*b* St.-Marc, St.-Domingue [now Haiti], 27 June 1766; *d* New York City, 30 June 1853). Philanthropist and entrepreneur. He was born a slave and moved to New York City in 1787 with the family of his master, the French colonist Jean Bérard du Pithon, who returned to St.-Domingue and died there in 1790. Soon after settling in the city he became a hairdresser to wealthy women and children and with his earnings supported the Bérard family. He was freed on 2 July 1807 and later purchased freedom for his fiancée, Juliette Noël, whom he married on 5 August 1811 at St. Peter's Church (16 Barclay Street). A gentle, generous, and religious man, he gave much financial assistance to Catholic charities, orphanages, white seminarians, priests, and nuns; he also housed many refugees of the revolutions in France and Haiti, welcomed poor blacks to his home, and helped a number of slaves to buy their freedom. He was buried at St. Patrick's Old Cathedral (on Mott Street between Prince and Houston streets) and given eulogies in many newspapers. On the centenary of his death a plaque was laid in his honor at St. Peter's Church. In

Pierre Toussaint, ca 1850. Wet-plate photograph by Nathaniel Fish Moore. Columbiana Collection, Columbia University

1989 the intersection of Barclay and Church streets was designated Pierre Toussaint Square, and in the same year the Archdiocese of New York submitted to the Vatican the canonical documentation necessary for the beatification of Toussaint, a step that could eventually make him the first Haitian to become a Catholic saint.

Hannah Farnham Sawyer Lee: *Memoir of Pierre Toussaint, Born a Slave in St. Domingo* (Boston: Crosby, Nichols, 1854)

Michel S. Laguerre

Advertisement for the New York Consolidated Card Company, 1888

Town Hall. A four-story building at 123 West 43rd Street in Manhattan, housing a concert hall of the same name. Designed in a Georgian Revival style by the firm of McKim, Mead and White, it was built in 1919–21 by the League of Political Education for public meetings, lectures, and concerts. From the outset the hall was a popular forum for debates on a wide range of social and political issues; among those who spoke there were such prominent figures as Booker T. Washington, Theodore Roosevelt, Jane Addams, and Henry James. The concert hall, renowned for its superb acoustics, has been the setting for performances by Richard Strauss, Sergei Rachmaninoff, Dizzy Gillespie, and Joan Sutherland.

Rebecca Read Shanor

Townsend Harris High School. Public high school in Queens, opened in 1906 as a three-year school for boys called Townsend Harris Hall on the campus of City College in Manhattan, with which it was affiliated. It was named for an influential merchant and diplomat who also established the Free Academy (which later became City College). The school offered free tuition to its selectively admitted students, who in early years were frequently immigrants and the sons of immigrants. Notable graduates included the bacteriologist Jonas Salk and the writer Herman Wouk. The school closed in 1942. In 1984 it reopened as a four-year, coeducational school affiliated with Queens College.

Rachel Shor

toys and games. Until the mid nineteenth century the great majority of toys in the United States were imports from Germany. Many of the earliest domestic toymakers were based in New York City, including F. and R. Lockwood (154 Broadway), makers of printed wooden game boards, J. Ruthven and Son (14 John Street), metal, wood, and ivory turners who made whistles, balls, chessmen, and blocks, and Boardman and Hart (6 Burling Slip), pewterers who manufactured miniature utensils and table-settings. After moving to New York City from Rhode Island several members of the Crandall family emerged as the city's most prominent toymakers between 1845 and 1915. The most renowned was Jesse A. Crandall, who in a shop at 73 Fulton Street made wooden hobby horses, sleds, and early bicycles called velocipedes. Other outstanding toymakers were the McLoughlin Brothers, who opened a shop at 24 Beekman Street in 1855 and sold paper dolls and dollhouses, toy books, lithographed wooden toys, board games, and blocks. After the Civil War more elaborate toys helped to free American toymakers from the domination of European imports. The Buckman Manufacturing Company in Brooklyn sold a "Brooklyn toy steam engine," and the Union Manufacturing Company of Brooklyn manufactured cast-iron boats, fire engines, and steam-powered toy factories that included lathes and grindstones. One of the country's largest makers of "clockwork," or windup, toys was R. J. Clay's Automatic Toy Works, which secured patents for a creeping doll and a crying doll. Althof, Bergmann and Company, formed in 1867, advertised 177 tinplate toys and miniatures in its catalogue in 1874. The first department store to open a section devoted to toys was R. H. Macy in 1875. With the growing commercialization of Christmas toy stores rapidly increased in number across the city. Some of the largest included Hinrich's at 29–33 Park Place, Hubbell and Ward at 21st Street and Broadway, E. Ridley and Sons at 309 Grand Street, and F. A. O. Schwarz, which opened a store at 42 East 14th Street in 1880.

To sell their products most nineteenth-century American toymakers relied on catalogues or middlemen. Edward I. Horsman and Company, which manufactured dolls, also imported toys and acted as a wholesale agent for small American makers. George Borgfeldt at 425 Broome Street helped to change the way toys were sold by opening a sample house where manufacturers exhibited their products to retailers. His system was a forerunner of the toy convention, which eventually made New York City the center of the toymaking business and also made the middleman unnecessary. Perhaps the city's most lasting contribution in the field of toymaking was the teddy bear, introduced in 1902 by Morris Michtom, the owner of a cigar and novelty store in Brooklyn who in the following year formed the Ideal Toy and Novelty Company. By 1906 the teddy bear was so popular that Ideal was also a maker of dolls, and through Michtom's nationwide marketing efforts it became the world's largest. The city was also the original location of the Lionel Train Company, a maker of model railroad sets formed in 1903 by Joshua Lionel Cowen (the firm moved to New Haven, Connecticut, in 1910). In 1916 sixty-eight toy companies in the city organized a trade group called the Toy Manufacturers of the USA (now the Toy Manufacturers of America) with headquarters at 200 5th Avenue; in later years the group expanded its headquarters to 1107 Broadway and developed a degree program in toy design at the Fashion Institute of Technology. The city's most successful toy magnate was Louis Marx, an innovator in mass production and mass marketing who formed Marx Toys in 1921 and took advantage of the boycott of German goods occasioned by the First World War to build it into the world's largest toymaker by the late 1920s. In 1972 Marx sold the firm to the Quaker Oats Company for $52 million.

After the Second World War plastic became the most widely used material in toy manufacturing. Many firms in New York City maintained showrooms and corporate headquarters at 200 5th Avenue and other locations but moved their manufacturing elsewhere, sometimes under contract. Among the toymakers that continued to manufacture in the city in the 1950s were Ideal at 184-10 Jamaica Avenue in Hollis, Palmer Plastics at 31 Stone Avenue in Brooklyn, and the Automatic Toy Company at 77 Alaska Street in Staten Island. The number of toy factories in the city declined in the following decades, and those that remained were small. In 1987 there were forty-five plants that made dolls and stuffed toys, with a total employment of fifteen hundred. Among the dollmakers based in the city are the well-known firms of Alexander and Goldberger. Popular toys and games developed in the city include the "action figure" G.I. Joe and the board games Scrabble and Parcheesi.

Marshall McClintock and Inez McClintock: *Toys in America* (Washington: Public Affairs Press, 1961)

Marc Ferris

trade associations. In New York City associations to promote the business interests of various merchants were formed during the earliest days of the colony. Among the first associations were the Society for the Promoting of Arts, Agriculture, and Economy, in the Province of New York (1764) and the Marine Society (1770). The New York Cheap Transportation Association (1873), later renamed the New York Board of Trade and Transportation, rivaled the Chamber of Commerce (1768) in its influence over the development of the city. Most of its members were merchants in wholesale and import commerce who sought to reduce their transportation costs, and they supported congressional investigations of the rate structures used by the railroads in 1904–6. These investigations led to the passage in 1906 of the Hepburn Act, which significantly increased the power of the Interstate Commerce Commission to regulate railroad rates. The Retail Dealers Protective Association was formed by 1899. Other associations of small business included the Neighborhood Cleaners Association, the New York Association of Women Business Owners, the Dairy Council of Metropolitan New York, the Downtown–Lower Manhattan Association, the Boot and Shoe Travelers Association of New York (which sponsored a semiannual trade show that continued into the 1990s), the Box Manufacturers Association of Greater New York, the Business Committee on Midtown Traffic, and the Chinese Merchants Association. By 1990 the New York Board of Trade and Transportation had 580 mostly corporate members, a staff of thirty, and an annual budget of more than $1 million; it represented the interests of business before government bodies, engaged in educational and cultural programs, published a bimonthly magazine, *New York Business Speaks*, and held an annual convention in New York City.

Joseph F. Bradley: *The Role of Trade Associations and Professional Business Societies in America* (University Park: Pennsylvania State University Press, 1965)

Donald R. Stabile

Bronze traffic signal decorated with statue of Mercury, 5th Avenue and 43rd Street, ca *1935*

traffic. The control of traffic and the proper management of street space have long been important issues in New York City. In the eighteenth century carts traveling northward along the road that is now Broadway were required to give way to those traveling southward, and in the nineteenth century the constant stream of vehicles and the wet layer of horse manure in their wake made it necessary to build a pedestrian bridge across Broadway near Fulton Street. Eventually police officers were needed at street intersections to direct competing flows of traffic, and later the officers were aided by mechanical devices known as semaphores. Crude electric traffic signals borrowed from railroad technology gradually took over: the first control tower equipped with one was erected in 1919 at 5th Avenue and 42nd Street, and the last semaphores were eliminated by the 1930s. Parking rules on an extensive scale were implemented before the Second World War: signs were mounted on movable stanchions that could be arranged as needed by the police. Traffic engineering and management became recognized as a profession after the war, largely in response to the rise of the automobile and the shift of freight transport from rail to trucking.

The police department was almost entirely responsible for traffic control until many of its duties were given over to the newly formed Department of Traffic in 1950. Thomas T. Wiley, the commissioner from 1950 to 1961, initiated a number of modern traffic control programs. During his first year in office, parking rules were drafted to facilitate the cleaning of sidestreets (parking was allowed on only one side of the street while the other was being cleaned), and in the following year the first parking meters were installed. To free up streets and generate revenue the city also built garages, the first of which opened in Flushing in 1954. The streets in Manhattan were the first in the city to be marked for one-way traffic, which substantially improved carrying capacity and safety, and in the 1950s and 1960s almost all the avenues were converted for one-way traffic (the last were Madison and 5th avenues in 1966); the program was soon extended to the other boroughs. A traffic con-

Pedestrians weaving between buses, trucks, and automobiles in midtown traffic, 1994

trol unit began in 1960 with a few "meter maids." Wiley's successor Henry A. Barnes (1962–68) was highly effective in gaining support and publicity for the traffic department. Computerized traffic signals that took actual traffic loads into account from minute to minute were introduced in the early 1960s, and the first exclusive bus lanes were designated along Livingston Street in Brooklyn and Victory Boulevard in Staten Island in 1963.

In the 1960s the first national, state, and local laws were passed to clean the air of pollutants produced by internal combustion and diesel engines, including carbon monoxide and ozone (two types of emission for which New York City was soon identified as a "nonattainment" area) and particulates. The State Implementation Plan for air quality was formulated in the early 1970s (not fully implemented as of the mid 1990s), and it became mandatory for developers to write environmental impact statements assuring that their proposed projects would not result in unacceptable levels of congestion and air pollution. In 1969 a consolidated Transportation Administration was formed; this was eventually eliminated and most of its functions were transferred in 1977 to a department of transportation, which in turn assigned responsibility for street operations to its bureaus of traffic and parking violations. Bus lanes were added at the inbound lanes of the Lincoln Tunnel (1970) and the Long Island Expressway (1971); a transitway was implemented on 49th and 50th streets (1979), followed by one along Madison Avenue (1981). Plans to establish pedestrian malls failed on Madison Avenue (1971–73) but succeeded on Nassau Street in lower Manhattan (1969) and Fulton Street in Brooklyn (1984).

By the early 1990s the central districts of New York City were badly congested, and it was estimated conservatively that traffic delays cost the local economy $7000 million a year; queues at the gateways to the city extended for miles every day in the morning hours, and accidents were numerous. The speeds in midtown Manhattan usually ranged on the avenues from twelve to fifteen miles (nineteen to twenty-four kilometers) an hour, and on the cross streets from nine to twelve miles (fourteen to nineteen kilometers) an hour. During the worst periods traffic crawled along at 2.5 miles (four kilometers) an hour areawide. During each work day motor vehicles in New York City covered 52 million vehicle-miles (84 million kilometers) over 6375 miles (more than ten thousand kilometers) of streets and highways; in 1991 more than 758,000 vehicles a day entered Manhattan south of 60th Street.

Unlike most urban areas that have a clearly distinguishable inward flow of traffic in the morning and an outward flow in the late afternoon, central Manhattan fills up in the early morning and remains nearly saturated until the theaters let out late at night. The battle for space is waged among pedestrians, bicyclists, private automobiles, delivery vans, minibuses, taxicabs, commuter vans, trucks, public livery vehicles, buses, emergency vehicles, and limousines. In addition the streets and highways carry a considerable volume of traffic that neither originates nor terminates in the city. Intersections are vulnerable to "gridlock," a term coined in the city to describe the intractable traffic jams caused by vehicles caught in intersections when traffic lights change. Space along curbs in Manhattan is rarely available for parking or standing, off-street facilities are expensive, and many motorists park illegally; in midtown Manhattan not a single on-street space may be used legally by a private motorist during the day. Traffic congestion impedes the movement of firetrucks and ambulances (fire lanes are not always clear of other vehicles), as well as manufacturing and distribution operations. There is also considerable nonmotorized traffic, which is equally affected by congestion: bicycles are used by commuters and messengers, but attempts to create bicycle lanes have met with little success, in part because they reduce the amount of space available to other types of traffic. Walking is frequently the best means in central districts of reaching destinations on time (residents of the city do more walking over long distances than residents of any other American city), but many sidewalks are badly overcrowded and traffic signals are timed for motorists, not pedestrians.

The city's traffic control unit now deploys more than two thousand traffic enforcement agents, who in 1993 wrote about 6.6 million summonses; police officers wrote more than 3.7 million summonses and other uniformed personnel such as fire and sanitation inspectors another one million. The Parking Violations Bureau (PVB) was established under Mayor John V. Lindsay to "decriminalize" parking violations and streamline the collection of fines. These goals were essentially achieved, with much higher returns of revenue, but the bureau also experienced several scandals in the following decades, because of the large amounts of money involved and the need to make various contractual arrangements. The city's Department of Transportation is also responsible for a towing program, under which it removes illegally parked vehicles from critical locations and takes them to six pounds spread throughout the city. In 1992 more than 114,000 automobiles were towed, most of them by far in Manhattan. The fines and costs of retrieving an automobile are high, and scofflaws receive special attention.

The control of traffic is linked to several other functions: filling potholes and repairing cave-ins, removing snow, managing utility excavations, controlling street vendors, monitoring trucks that carry heavy and hazardous cargo, rerouting traffic during parades and emergencies, regulating private vans and jitneys, and maintaining bridges, street and traffic signs, and traffic information systems. The city employs various methods to alleviate traffic congestion, such as marking off loading zones at curbside (as well as red zones for buses), truck routes (of doubtful utility), and boxes in heavily traveled intersections in which motorists may be fined for stopping, as well as applying discretion in ticketing double-parked vehicles. In general the city's efforts do not include efficient land-use planning, the building of more streets and highways, or more than sporadic campaigns to encourage mass transit; most parking garages and lots are now in the outer boroughs. Traffic policy in

New York City is hotly debated. In the view of some it is essential for economic growth that motor vehicles should have unhindered access to establishments in the city. Others favor increased tolls and parking taxes and encouraging travel by bicycle and on foot: the most radical proposal would ban private motor vehicles in Manhattan south of 96th Street.

City Streets: A Report on Policies and Programs (New York: New York Department of Transportation, 1983)

Regional Transportation: Current Conditions and Future Prospects (New York: New Jersey Transportation Coordinating Council and New York Metropolitan Transportation Council, 1989)

Sigurd Grava

Trains Meadow. Former name of JACKSON HEIGHTS. From colonial times the area was mostly lowlands with a few meadows and farms. In 1915 the Board of Estimate abolished Trains Meadow Road and adopted a street grid, making the development of Jackson Heights possible.

Vincent Seyfried

transportation. For discussions of transportation in New York City see the entries AVIATION, BUSES, CABLE CARS, ELEVATED RAILWAYS, FERRIES, HELIPORTS, HORSE-DRAWN VEHICLES, RAILROADS, STREETCARS, SUBWAYS, and TAXICABS.

Transport Workers Union of America [TWU]. Union of transit workers formed in 1934 and based in New York City. Within three years it had thirty thousand members and contracts with the Interborough Rapid Transit Company (IRT), the Brooklyn–Manhattan Transit Corporation (BMT), and the city's major bus and trolley companies. After becoming an affiliate of the Committee for Industrial Organization (CIO) in 1937 it organized transit workers in other cities and airline and railroad workers. In New York City Irish workers initially accounted for half the membership but later declined sharply in number. The union attracted a disproportionately large amount of attention during the 1930s and 1940s, in part because it repeatedly threatened to call a subway strike. Unions of public employees were unusual, and the TWU was unable to win recognition in the Independent Subway System. The union faced a crisis during the city's takeover of the IRT and BMT in 1940, when Mayor Fiorello H. La Guardia refused to engage in collective bargaining or sign union contracts; through strike threats and political maneuvering the TWU forced the city to honor most of the provisions of its contracts with the IRT and the BMT. In the following years it set a precedent for other civil service unions by gradually expanding its role in transit labor relations. In 1941 it shut down most bus lines in Manhattan for twelve days. The union was often at the center of controversy because of its close ties to the Communist Party, its support for the American Labor Party (ALP), and the sharp comments of its president, Michael J. Quill. After winning a bitter factional struggle in 1948 Quill broke with the Communist Party and Communist leaders were expelled from the leadership of the TWU, which left the ALP. The union regained the bargaining rights that it had lost under Mayor La Guardia after lending strong support to Mayors William O'Dwyer and Robert F. Wagner.

After winning a recognition election in 1954 the TWU signed a contract with the New York City Transit Authority, an agency set up in 1953 to run the buses and subways. From this time into the early 1960s the union won only modest wage gains for its members, leading to a week-long strike by subway motormen in December 1957 and the formation of many rival groups. On failing to reach a contract agreement with Mayor-elect John V. Lindsay the TWU called a strike of workers on city-run lines on 1 January 1966. The union was widely criticized for crippling the city, and nine of its leaders were imprisoned, but after twelve days the strike ended on terms highly favorable to the workers. Quill died soon afterward; his successors, such as Matthew Guinan and John E. Lawe, were neither as skillful nor as prominent as he had been. Many members resented the continued domination by Irish workers of Local 100, the main transit unit of the TWU in the city. In 1980 the union called a strike of bus and subway workers that lasted for eleven days. Although still a powerful force in transit, the TWU in the mid 1990s was not as important as it once had been in city politics or in shaping municipal labor relations.

Joshua B. Freeman: *In Transit: The Transport Workers Union in New York City, 1933–1966* (New York: Oxford University Press, 1989)

Joshua B. Freeman

Trans World Airlines [TWA]. International airline, formed in 1928 as Transcontinental Air Transport TWA. An arrangement with the Pennsylvania Railroad enabled it to offer the first transcontinental service by air and rail from greater New York. In 1934 it flew Mayor Fiorello H. La Guardia from Newark Airport in New Jersey to Floyd Bennett Field in Brooklyn to satisfy the implied guarantee of his flight ticket that he would be offered transport into the city. The airline was a steady supporter of the plans to develop what is now La Guardia Airport. It is especially well known for its terminal at Kennedy Airport, designed by Eero Saarinen and completed in 1960. Until the 1980s TWA was the second-largest international carrier in the United States. In 1988 it moved its headquarters from midtown Manhattan to Mount Kisco, New York. In 1994 it moved the headquarters to St. Louis while maintaining large operations at Kennedy and La Guardia airports.

Robert J. Serling: *Howard Hughes' Airline: An Informal History of TWA* (New York: St. Martin's, 1983)

Robert Rummel: *Howard Hughes and TWA* (Washington: Smithsonian Institution Press, 1991)

Paul Barrett

Travelers. Financial services firm at 55 East 65th Street in Manhattan, formed in 1993. Its forerunner was the Primerica Corporation, from which it evolved after a series of mergers with Commercial Credit, Smith Barney, Harris Upham and Company, and Shearson Lehman Brothers. The expansion of the firm was overseen by Gerald Tsai. The Travelers has interests in insurance, securities brokerage, asset management, and consumer lending.

Janet Frankston

Travis. Neighborhood in west central Staten Island (1990 pop. 2000), bounded to the north by Meredith Avenue and Victory Boulevard, to the east by the William T. Davis Wildlife Refuge and Main Creek, to the south by Fresh Kills, and to the west by the Arthur Kill. The area was the site of an Indian village and was renamed many times after being settled by Europeans. Developed as Jersey Wharf and known as New Blazing Star during the Ameri-

Trans World Airlines terminal (designed by Eero Saarinen, 1956–62), John F. Kennedy Airport

can Revolution, it was an important connecting point for ferries to New Jersey. One ferry operated from 1757 by Jacob Fitz Randolph and then for several decades by John Mersereau was a segment of a short route connecting Manhattan and Philadelphia: a road led from the area to the Port Richmond ferry, from which passengers could travel to Manhattan and Bergen Point, New Jersey. In the following decades the area and the local settlement were known variously as Travisville (in the early nineteenth century, after the local property owner Captain Jacob Travis), Long Neck (during the Civil War, because of its peninsular configuration), and Deckertown (after a local family). In 1873 the American Linoleum Company opened a factory and workers' cottages on a tract of three hundred acres (120 hectares) near the docks. Much of the early work force was imported from England, where the process of rolling ground cork and oxidized linseed oil into a floor covering had been developed. Success led to rapid expansion and the area became known as Linoleumville. The firm was an innovator in the development of decorative and inlaid styles of linoleum, surfaces for battleships, railroad cars, and large institutions, and linoleum-making machinery. In the early twentieth century the factory had seven hundred employees, or half the population of Linoleumville. The firm was sold in 1928 and ceased operations in 1931. Residents then voted to rename the village Travis. In later years the relative isolation of the area was disrupted by the building of the West Shore Expressway, of new housing, and of the Teleport, a fiberoptics network and business complex. Important institutions in the neighborhood include the Church of St. Anthony of Padua, which serves a largely Polish and Slavic congregation; a volunteer fire company; and an equestrian group. An Independence Day parade inaugurated in 1911 continued to be held into the 1990s.

Charles L. Sachs: *Made on Staten Island* (New York: Staten Island Historical Society, 1985)
"Travis: A Brief History" (1987) [unpubd, New York Public Library, St. George Branch]
John Hurley: "Travis: A Step Back in Time," *Staten Island Advance*, 10 April 1989

Howard Weiner

Treadwell Farm. Neighborhood on the Upper East Side of Manhattan, bounded to the north by 62nd Street, to the east by 2nd Avenue, to the south by 61st Street, and to the west by 3rd Avenue. The area was once the farmland of Peter Van Zandt and William Beekman and is named for the fur merchant Adam Treadwell, who in 1815 bought Van Zandt's parcel, on which he built his own farm. After his death in 1852 his daughter Elizabeth bought Beekman's parcel. Luxurious brownstones and row houses were erected in the 1860s and 1870s. The neighborhood was designated a Historic District in 1967; among its landmarks is Trinity Baptist Church (1931). Well-known residents have included Walter Lippmann, Tallulah Bankhead, and Eleanor Roosevelt. In the mid 1990s the area was quiet and affluent. The name Treadwell Farm is seldom used.

James Bradley

Tree of Hope. A tree formerly situated at the corner of 131st Street and what is now Adam Clayton Powell Boulevard. It was the site of performances by entertainers who had fallen on hard times and believed that the tree had the power to bring good luck. The tree fell victim to urban renewal and was cut down in the early twentieth century. A second tree on the same site was donated by the entertainer Bill "Bojangles" Robinson, who had a brass plaque embedded in the sidewalk, bearing the inscription "The Original Tree of Hope Beloved by the People of Harlem—You asked for a tree of hope so here it is, Best wishes" along with his signature. The second tree, also cut down, was replaced by an interpretive sculpture of lavender, black, red, and green: a portion of it remains a fixture on the stage of the Apollo Theatre.

Marcella Thum: *Hippocrene U.S.A. Guide to Black America* (New York: Hippocrene, 1991)

Emilyn L. Brown

Tremont. Neighborhood in the west central Bronx, bounded to the north by East 182nd Street and Bronx Park South, to the east by the Bronx River and the Boston Road, to the south by Claremont Park, Mount Eden Avenue, and Mount Eden Parkway, and to the west by the Grand Concourse. It comprehends several smaller neighborhoods, including Claremont, Mount Eden, and Mount Hope. The area was farmland when the New York and Harlem Railroad opened a station in 1841 that soon became the center of a village. The name Upper Morrisania was used until the postmaster, Hiram Tarbox, discovered that it was being confused with that of a neighboring town, Morrisania; in the 1850s he renamed his office Tremont for three hills in the area (Fairmount, Mount Eden, and Mount Hope). Growth hastened after improvements were made to the transit system in the 1890s: a trolley line along Tremont Avenue that served the railroad station in the west, a new subway station to the east in West Farms, and an extension of the 3rd Avenue elevated line running between the two stations. In 1897 the borough hall, designed by George B. Post, opened in Crotona Park at Tremont and Park avenues. One-family frame houses were replaced by apartment buildings and Tremont Avenue became a thriving shopping district. Jews accounted for most of the population; there were also many Italians and Irish who moved from crowded neighborhoods in Manhattan. In 1933 the borough offices were moved to the new Bronx County Building on 161st Street, but other city offices continued to occupy Borough Hall until it was abandoned in 1965; the building was destroyed by fire in 1968. Other city agencies occupied the Bergen Building on Arthur Avenue. In the early 1950s there was strong opposition to plans for the Cross Bronx Expressway, which called for the demolition of homes and the bisecting of the neighborhood. After the expressway was completed in 1955 the population became increasingly black and Latin American. The rate of arson was high in the early 1970s, but at the same time the construction of the innovative scatter-site housing project Twin Parks helped the neighborhood to slowly stabilize. About a third of the immigrants who settled in Tremont in the 1980s were Dominican; there were also many immigrants from Jamaica, Guyana, Honduras, Ecuador, and Guatemala. In the mid 1990s Tremont Avenue remained a thriving local commercial thoroughfare.

Robert Caro: *The Power Broker: Robert Moses and the Fall of New York* (New York: Alfred A. Knopf, 1974)
Lloyd Ultan: *The Beautiful Bronx, 1920–1950* (New Rochelle, N.Y.: Arlington House, 1979)
John McNamara: *McNamara's Old Bronx* (New York: Bronx County Historical Society, 1989)

Lloyd Ultan

Trepša, Norberts (*b* Latvia, 1913; *d* New York City, 1972). Priest and writer. He earned degrees in law, philosophy, theology, and sociology and after the Second World War moved to the United States, where he became known as a community leader and under the pseudonym N. Neiksantis as a writer of novels, poems, and short stories in the Latgalian dialect; he also edited Latvian periodicals abroad, formed the Baltic Appeal to the United Nations (a unit of United Baltic Appeal), and represented the Baltic communities in international forums in New York City during the 1960s.

Vladimir Wertsman

Tresca, Carlo (*b* Sulmona, Italy, 9 March 1879; *d* New York City, 11 Jan 1943). Labor leader and revolutionary. He emigrated from Italy to the United States in 1904 and for more than a decade after his arrival edited several radical newspapers and led striking workers in Italian immigrant communities throughout the East. In 1912–16 he became well known as a labor agitator for the Industrial Workers of the World. He moved his newspaper *L'Avvenire* in 1913 from Steubenville, Ohio, to New York City, where his militant activities and flamboyant personality quickly made him a leader among the city's radicals. He was a key figure in the defense of Sacco and Vanzetti, for whom he mobilized support from 1920 until their execution in 1927. In the early 1920s he attacked the fascist government in Italy in his newspaper *Il Martello*. His arrest and conviction for sending "obscene" matter (a book on birth control) through the mail was engineered by the state department, the Federal Bureau of Investigation, and the postal authorities at the behest of Mussolini's government, and led to his imprisonment for four months in a federal penitentiary in 1925; a protest campaign waged by his friends and political associates in New York City defeated efforts by the government to deport him to Italy. An opponent of Stalinism, he supported the anarchists during the Spanish Civil War (1936–39) and served on the commission led by John Dewey in 1937 that found Trotsky innocent of the conspiracy charges leveled against him by Stalin. From 1941 he fought efforts of communists and prominent former fascists to infiltrate the Mazzini Society and the Italian–American Victory Council, both of which had large followings in New York City.

Tresca was assassinated outside the office of *Il Martello* on 5th Avenue and 15th Street. Although many associates believed that the murder was instigated by the communist Vittorio Vidali or by Generoso Pope, publisher of *Il Progresso*, it is more likely to have been the work of a member of the Mafia named Frank Garofalo, who acted to avenge a personal insult.

Nunzio Pernicone: "Carlo Tresca and the Sacco–Vanzetti Case," *Journal of American History* 66 (1979), 435–47

Dorothy Gallagher: *All the Right Enemies: The Life and Murder of Carlo Tresca* (New Brunswick, N.J.: Rutgers University Press, 1988)

Nunzio Pernicone

Temporary morgue for victims of the Triangle Shirtwaist fire, 1911

Triangle Shirtwaist fire. The worst factory fire in the history of New York City. It occurred on 25 March 1911 in the Asch building at the northwest corner of Washington and Greene streets, where the Triangle Shirtwaist Company occupied the top three of ten floors; five hundred women were employed there, mostly Jewish immigrants between the ages of thirteen and twenty-three. To keep the women at their sewing machines the proprietors had locked the doors leading to the exits. The fire began shortly after 4:30 p.m. in the cutting room on the eighth floor, and fed by thousands of pounds of fabric it spread rapidly. Panicked workers rushed to the stairs, the freight elevator, and the fire escape. Most on the eighth and tenth floors escaped; dozens on the ninth floor died, unable to force open the locked door to the exit. The rear fire escape collapsed, killing many and eliminating an escape route for others still trapped. Some tried to slide down elevator cables but lost their grip; many more, their dresses on fire, jumped to their death from open windows. Pump Engine Company 20 and Ladder Company 20 arrived quickly but were hindered by the bodies of victims who had jumped. The ladders of the fire department extended only to the sixth floor, and life nets broke when workers jumped in groups of three and four. Additional companies were summoned by four more alarms transmitted in rapid succession.

A total of 146 women died in less than fifteen minutes, more than in any other fire in the city except for that aboard the *General Slocum* in 1904. Although there was widespread revulsion and rage over the working conditions that had contributed to the fire, many defended the right of shop owners to resist government safety regulation, and some in government insisted that they were at any rate powerless to impose it. The owners of the company were charged with manslaughter and later acquitted but in 1914 were ordered by a judge to pay damages of $75 each to the families of twenty-three victims who had sued. The Factory Investigating Commission of 1911 gathered testimony, and later that year the city established the Bureau of Fire Investigation under the direction of Robert F. Wagner (i), which gave the fire department additional powers to improve factory safety. The event crystallized support for efforts to organize workers in the garment district and in particular for the International Ladies' Garment Workers' Union. It remains one of the most vivid symbols for the American labor movement of the need for government to ensure a safe workplace.

Leon Stein: *The Triangle Fire* (Philadelphia: J. B. Lippincott, 1962)

Gus Johnson: *The Fire Buff's Handbook of the New York Fire Department, 1900–1975* (New York: Fire Department of New York, 1977)

Donald J. Cannon

Tribeca. Neighborhood in lower Manhattan (1990 pop. 8705), occupying a trapezoidal parcel bounded to the north by Canal Street, to the east by Broadway, to the south by Barclay Street, and to the west by the Hudson River; the name was adopted by real-estate developers in the mid 1970s and stands for "triangle below Canal." Once used as farmland by Dutch settlers, the area was included in a large tract granted in 1705 by Queen Anne to Trinity Church, which built St. John's Chapel on Varick Street in 1807 and several years later laid out St. John's Park on an adjacent lot bounded by what are now Laight Street, Varick Street, Ericsson Place, and Hudson Street; the park could be used only by the wealthy families living in Hudson Square, the surrounding neighborhood of elegant brick houses. A fruit and produce market called Bear Market opened in 1813 at the western edge of the neighborhood along Washington, Vesey, and Fulton streets and became an important wholesale and retail supplier of food to the city. Among the products sold were locally grown fruits and vegetables, wild game, and imported meats, cheeses, and caviar. The neighborhood remained mostly residential until increased shipping and commerce in lower Manhattan attracted businesses in the 1840s and soon made the area a major point of transfer. During the mid nineteenth century the eastern section was the center of the textile and dry-goods industry: five- and six-story buildings with marble, sandstone, and cast-iron façades were built to house stores, factories, and storage facilities. After the Civil War St. John's Park became the site of the freight depot of the New York Central and Hudson River Railroad. The site of the depot is now the exit of the Holland Tunnel.

Bear Market became known as Washington

Market, and the name was eventually applied to the entire neighborhood. During the 1880s warehouses were built to accommodate mercantile exchanges dealing in butter, cheese, and eggs. By 1939 the market stretched from Washington Street to West Street and had a greater volume of business than all the other markets in the city combined. It remained vital until the early 1960s, when fruit and produce markets moved to Hunts Point and city planners approved the Washington Market Urban Renewal Project, leading to the demolition of many old buildings to make way for high-rise housing, office buildings, and educational facilities: among these were Independence Plaza (1975) on Washington Street, a forty-story apartment building for middle-income tenants, the Borough of Manhattan Community College (1980) to the west, and Washington Market Park (1983) to the south. The population increased from 243 in 1970 to 5101 in 1980. Factories and warehouses were converted to residential lofts, many of which became the homes of artists. The Tribeca Film Center at 375 Greenwich Street opened in 1990. Tribeca is a fashionable residential neighborhood with an affluent population. The streets are lined with shops, art galleries, bars, and restaurants.

Joyce Gold

Triborough Bridge. Viaduct structure containing three steel bridges and spanning the waters between Manhattan, the Bronx, and Queens, designed by Othmar H. Ammann and the architect Aymar Embury II. Construction began on 25 October 1929; on the same day the stock market crashed, and construction soon halted when investors were unwilling to purchase municipal bonds. The Triborough Bridge Authority was formed as an alternative source of funds in 1933, and the bridge opened to traffic on 11 July 1936 as the first of several structures built by the authority in New York City. During its first year it carried 9.65 million vehicles and generated $2.72 million in tolls. The most prominent feature is a suspension bridge spanning the East River between Queens and Wards Island that is 2780 feet (848 meters) long, with a height above water of 143 feet (43.6 meters). A lift bridge of 770 feet (235 meters) spans the Harlem River between 125th Street in Manhattan and Randalls Island, and a truss bridge of 1217 feet (371 meters) links Randalls Island to the Bronx.

Rebecca Read Shanor

Triborough Bridge and Tunnel Authority. Municipal agency responsible for financing, constructing, and maintaining bridges and tunnels in New York City. Its origins date to the 1920s, when the city made plans to build a major crossing over the East River at 125th Street in Manhattan. Construction of the Triborough Bridge began at the site on 25 October 1929; on the same day the stock market crashed, construction was soon halted when investors were unwilling to purchase municipal bonds, and in early 1933 Robert Moses, chairman of the New York State Emergency Public Works Commission, initiated state legislation that formed the Triborough Bridge Authority as an alternative source of funds. The authority was structured as an independent public-benefit corporation empowered to sell revenue bonds to the Reconstruction Finance Corporation (RFC) and later the Public Works Administration; once all debts were retired it was to be dismantled and the bridge turned over to the city.

The bridge opened in 1936 and during its first year generated $2.72 million in tolls. Its unexpected success made the authority's bonds attractive in the private market: Moses persuaded the RFC to resell the bonds, which were bought quickly. He then transformed the authority into a permanent, multipurpose agency capable of refinancing its bonds to take on new projects. Once restructured, the authority became a model of fiscal resourcefulness and political independence. It built the Bronx–Whitestone Bridge and the Brooklyn–Battery Tunnel, then took its current name. It also assumed control of the Queens–Midtown Tunnel and acquired or built the New York Coliseum, the Eastside Airline Terminal, several parkway approaches, and five more bridges, including the Verrazano Narrows Bridge (opened in 1964).

The authority's political and fiscal power was curtailed in 1968 when Governor Nelson A. Rockefeller removed Moses as its chairman and merged the authority with the financially troubled regional subway, rail, and bus authorities to form the Metropolitan Transportation Authority (MTA). Eventually its receipts from tolls and other sources came to provide almost 80 percent of the total income of the MTA. During the early 1990s the nine crossings of the Triborough Bridge and Tunnel Authority carried as many as 277 million vehicles a year and generated nearly $640 million in revenues.

Robert G. Smith: *Public Authorities in Urban Areas* (Washington: National Association of Counties Research Foundation, 1969)

Robert A. Caro: *The Power Broker: Robert Moses and the Fall of New York* (New York: Vintage, 1975)

Annmarie Hauck Walsh: *The Public's Business: The Politics and Practices of Government Corporations* (Cambridge: MIT Press, 1978)

David C. Perry

Trilling [née Rubin], **Diana** (*b* New York City, 21 July 1905). Writer. She attended Radcliffe College (BA 1925) and in 1929 married Lionel Trilling. From 1941 to 1949 she was a fiction critic for the *Nation.* Her published writings include *We Must March My Darlings* (1977), *Mrs. Harris: The Death of the Scarsdale Diet Doctor* (1981), and *Beginning the Journey: The Marriage of Diana and Lionel Trilling* (1993). She also edited the uniform edition of her husband's works (1975–80).

Trilling, Lionel (Mordecai) (*b* New York City, 4 July 1905; *d* New York City, 5 Nov 1975). Literary critic. He attended Columbia University (BA 1925, MA 1926, PhD 1938), where he joined the faculty in 1938 and remained for the rest of his career. His first book, a study of Matthew Arnold (1939), marked him as a critical scholar of the first rank, and he soon emerged as a leader of the liberal intellectual community in New York City. Although he disdained the bitter ideological struggles that divided his peers, his criticism nonetheless reflected ideological concerns: his only novel, *The Middle of the Journey* (1947), is a fictionalized account of the retreat from communism by his friend Whittaker Chambers, and in such critical works as *The Liberal Imagination* (1950) he explored the ambiguity of conventional political ideals. Trilling's criticism had a decisive impact on the self-critical, anti-totalitarian liberalism of the 1950s, and as a teacher and mentor he influenced figures as diverse as Norman Podhoretz and Norman Mailer.

Stephen L. Tanner: *Lionel Trilling* (Boston: Twayne, 1988)

Peter Eisenstadt

Trinidadians and Tobagonians. Immigrants from the West Indian nation of Trinidad and Tobago first settled in New York City about 1900, largely for economic reasons. They numbered several thousand in the city by the early 1950s, and most were blacks who lived in Harlem and Bedford–Stuyvesant. Although often skilled, these immigrants were usually denied employment in their trades and consequently did menial and unskilled industrial work outside their neighborhoods. Before the 1930s Trinidadians and Tobagonians formed the Trinidad Benevolent Association and the Tobago Benevolent Society. In the 1930s they also formed the United Mutual Insurance Company, which for decades was the largest black insurance company with headquarters in New York City. Charles Augustin Petioni, a physician, was the best-known leader of the community. Immigration increased markedly with the passage of the Hart–Celler Act in 1965 and continued into the 1990s. The new immigrants included both blacks and East Indians (each group accounts for about 40 percent of the population of Trinidad and Tobago). In the mid 1990s the number of Trinidadian and Tobagonian nationals in New York City was estimated at 150,000. Both blacks and East Indians from Trinidad and Tobago live in the black neighborhoods of Brooklyn, as well as in racially integrated neighborhoods throughout the city: East Indians are especially numerous in Richmond Hill. Most Trinidadians and Tobagonians are unskilled or clerical workers; others work as technicians and managers and in business and the professions. Black Trinidadians have had a noticeable impact on the city's cultural life through the musical genres calypso and soca, and through their participation in the West Indian carnival on Labor Day in Brooklyn, which they were instrumental in creating in the late 1960s. Indo-Trinidadian organizations in the city include the Sanatana Dharma Maha Sabaha of the West Indies.

Ira DeA. Reid: *The Negro Immigrant: His Background, Characteristics, and Social Adjustment, 1899–1939* (New York: Columbia University Press, 1939)

Calvin B. Holder: "The Causes and Composition of West Indian Immigration to New York City, 1900–1952," *Afro-Americans in New York Life and History* 11 (1987)

Veronica Udeogalanya: *A Comparative Analysis of Caribbean Immigrants Admitted into the United States, 1985–1987* (New York: Medgar Evers College, Caribbean Research Center, 1991)

Calvin B. Holder

Trinity Church. Anglican church formed by royal charter from William III on 6 May 1697. During the colonial period and into the nineteenth century the parish encompassed several chapels in Manhattan. The first service was conducted on 13 March 1698 in a new church at Broadway and Wall Street. In 1705 the church was granted by Queen Anne land extending from Christopher Street (north) to Fulton Street (south) that became known as the Queen's Farm. A school for Indians and black slaves was opened in the early eighteenth century, and the parish was instrumental in forming King's College. Chapels were added in the areas now known as midtown Manhattan, Greenwich Village, Harlem, the Lower East Side, and Governors Island. St. Paul's Chapel (1766, Broadway and Fulton Street) became the best-known chapel and in the mid 1990s was the oldest public building in continuous use in Manhattan; a service for George Washington's inauguration was held there on 30 April 1789. A school for freed blacks opened in the late eighteenth century. The church was destroyed by fire in 1776 and replaced by another that was consecrated in 1790 but demolished after structural problems became evident in 1839. This was replaced by a new church in a Gothic Revival style designed by Richard Upjohn.

As industry expanded and the city became more developed the parish adapted to meet the needs of its members. It formed several institutions, including the Trinity Charity School (now the Trinity School), a mission house, a hospital, an infirmary, a home for the elderly (St. Margaret's House), a preschool, the John Heuss Drop-In Center for chronically mentally ill homeless people, the Frederic Fleming House for the homeless elderly, elementary schools, summer camps for city children, and a cemetery and mausoleum at 155th Street. Income from the Queen's Farm enabled the parish to help more than seventeen hundred churches and religious institutions of different denominations worldwide. Trinity later gave about two thirds of the land to the city and to religious institutions of various faiths, including Episcopal, Lutheran, Presbyterian, and Roman Catholic; most of the rest was sold. As the composition of the neighborhood changed, some chapels closed. The chapels of St. Augustine, the Intercession, and St. Luke became independent churches in 1976; St. Cornelius's on Governors Island was given to the federal government in 1987. In the mid 1990s Trinity Parish encompassed Trinity Church, St. Paul's Chapel, and about 6 percent of the Queen's Farm.

Trinity Church and St. Paul's have had many well-known members, including William Kidd, John Jay, and Alexander Hamilton. Among those buried in the churchyard are Francis Lewis, a signer of the Declaration of Independence; Hugh Williamson, a signer of the U.S. Constitution; and Robert Fulton. Clement Clarke Moore, John Jacob Astor, and Alfred Tennyson Dickens (son of the novelist) are buried in Trinity Cemetery at 155th Street.

Morgan Dix: *A History of the Parish of Trinity Church in the City of New York* (New York: G. P. Putnam's Sons [vols. 1–4], Columbia University Press [vol. 5], Rector Churchmen and Vestrymen at the Parish of Trinity Church in the City of New York [vol. 6], Seabury [vol. 7], 1898–1978)

Phyllis Barr

Trinity School. Private, coeducational elementary and secondary school founded by royal charter in 1709 in Manhattan as a charity school, and directed by the headmaster William Huddleston (the first licensed lawyer in the colonies). Classes were held at Trinity Church until 1717; in 1749 the first independent school building was constructed on Rector Street. In later years the school became a private institution along the English model and moved to the Upper West Side of Manhattan, where it now occupies a modern building on West 91st Street. Trinity is the oldest continuously operating educational institution in New York City.

Centuries of Childhood in New York (A Celebration on the Occasion of the 275th Anniversary of Trinity School) (New York: New-York Historical Society / Trinity School, 1984)

Richard Schwartz

Trotsky, Leon [Bronstein, Lev (Davidovich)] (*b* Yanovka [now in Ukraine], 26 Oct 1879; *d* Mexico City, 21 Aug 1940). Revolutionary. After being expelled from France and Spain he settled in New York City with his wife and two sons in January 1917, where they lived for a short time in a three-room apartment at 1522 Vyse Avenue in the Bronx. He was welcomed enthusiastically by the city's Russian expatriates and joined Nikolai Bukharin in producing the newspaper *Novyi Mir* (New world), which was printed in the basement of a building at 77 St. Mark's Place; he was also a popular speaker at gatherings of workers and antiwar activists. Trotsky left the city in March 1917 and made a two-month journey to Russia to join the Bolshevik Revolution.

Kevin Kenny

Trumbull, John (*b* Lebanon, Conn., 6 June 1756; *d* New York City, 10 Nov 1843). Painter. Born to a prominent family, he graduated from Harvard University and fought in the American Revolution before traveling to London to study with the American painter Benjamin West (1738–1820). In 1804 he moved to New York City and became a prominent member of the American Academy of the Fine Arts, serving as its president in 1817–35. Guided by a belief that the fine arts are essential to national welfare, he advocated hanging American portraits and historical paintings beside works by old masters, and generally favored the works of his contemporaries. Although criticized by young artists he was widely regarded for his talent. Commissioned to paint four paintings for the rotunda of the U.S. Capitol, he executed idealized, patriotic scenes and exhibited them in New York City before sending them to Washington. During the 1830s he established at Yale University a gallery of his paintings (still intact), and helped Daniel Wadsworth to build a collection in Hartford, Connecticut, that later became part of the Wadsworth Atheneum. In 1825–37 and 1841–43 Trumbull lived in a boarding house at 256 Broadway.

Irma B. Jaffe: *John Trumbull: Patriot-Artist of the American Revolution* (Boston: New York Graphic Society, 1975)

Helen A. Cooper: *John Trumbull: The Hand and Spirit of a Painter* (New Haven: Yale University Art Gallery, 1982)

Carrie Rebora

Trump, Donald (John) (*b* Queens, 14 June 1946). Real-estate developer. The son of Fred Trump, an important developer and owner of residential housing in the outer boroughs of New York City, he attended the University of Pennsylvania and then entered his family's business. In 1974 he took an option to buy the Penn Central Railroad yards on the Upper West Side and announced plans for what later became known as Trump City, a large proposed development of luxury apartments and mixed-use facilities; in 1976 he received the first tax abatement under the city's new business-incentive program to purchase the distressed Commodore Hotel near Grand Central Station and refurbish it as the Grand Hyatt. In the 1980s he purchased the Plaza Hotel at 59th Street and 5th Avenue. A number of his projects during the 1980s proved controversial. He used tax abatements to finance Trump Tower, a lavish skyscraper on 5th Avenue serving as the organization's headquarters and containing offices, stores, and condominiums, built a number of luxury apartment complexes in midtown Manhattan and on the Upper East Side, including Trump Plaza at 3rd Avenue and 63rd Street, as well as several gambling casinos in Atlantic City, New Jersey, and bought a football team (the New Jersey Generals) and the Eastern Airlines shuttle (which he renamed the Trump Shuttle). Because his investments were highly leveraged, the collapse of the real-estate market in the late 1980s forced him to renegotiate nearly $2000 million in debt and divest himself of various holdings including the air shuttle (bought by US Air). In the 1990s he continued to work on various developments, including a scaled-down version of Trump City that was renamed Riverside South in 1991. In addition to his vast real-estate holdings Trump is known for his flamboyant personality. He is the author of two best-selling autobiographies, *Trump: The Art of the Deal* (1988) and *Trump: Surviving at the Top* (1990).

Marc A. Weiss

"trunk mystery." An incident in 1871 that began when a baggage master discovered a nude female corpse in a trunk measuring three by three by two feet (ninety by ninety by sixty centimeters) at the Hudson River Depot on Saturday 26 August. The body was identified as that of Alice Augusta Bowlsby, a nineteen-year-old unmarried woman from Paterson, New Jersey. An investigation revealed that she had been impregnated by a man named Walter Conklin, who arranged for Jacob Rosenzweig to perform an abortion. After apparently killing Bowlsby unintentionally Rosenzweig sought to conceal the evidence by sending her corpse to Chicago; he was sentenced to seven years in prison, and Conklin took his own life. The case fueled campaigns to outlaw abortion.

James C. Mohr: *Abortion in America: The Origins and Evolution of National Policy, 1800–1900* (New York: Oxford University Press, 1978)

Mary Elizabeth Brown

Truth Teller. Weekly newspaper launched in 1825 by the Catholic priests John Powers and Felix Varela to succeed the *Shamrock* (1810), the first Irish newspaper in New York City. The most influential newspaper of its kind in the country before the 1840s, it provided extensive coverage of Irish nationalist issues and the activities of the Catholic church and had an average circulation of three thousand. Its editors often engaged their Protestant colleagues in heated theological and political debate. The *Truth Teller* declined after the *Freeman's Journal* began publication in 1840; it was absorbed by the *Irish American*, a weekly newspaper, in 1855.

Kevin Kenny

tuberculosis. Although tuberculosis, once known as consumption, or the "white plague," became an unfortunate hazard of life in New York City in colonial days, for most of its history little could be done to combat it. The disease was long thought to be hereditary rather than contagious, and even Robert Koch's discovery in 1882 of the microbe that causes tuberculosis met with some hostility among the local medical community. By 1901 tuberculosis was one of the leading killers of New Yorkers; about twelve thousand new cases occurred that year, and the disease was responsible for about one of every four deaths between the ages of fifteen and sixty-five. By 1904 the number of cases tripled. Privately practicing physicians of the period were hesitant to report their tubercular patients to the health department, for fear of initiating their forcible removal to a sanitarium or quarantine hospital and of losing paying patients in economically difficult times. Despite their reluctance a strong public health campaign was mounted by such local officials as Hermann M. Biggs, T. Mitchell Prudden, William H. Park, and Lawrence Veiller. The city's health department opened the first municipal clinic for tuberculosis in the United States in 1904, and efforts at education, prevention, and isolation helped contribute to the decline of the disease by the late 1930s. Several chemotherapeutic agents that cured tuberculosis were developed between 1944 and 1952.

A further decline was brought about by municipal programs beginning in the 1950s and lasting well into the 1980s that provided daily nursing and medical attention to the city's urban poor and others with tuberculosis. In the mid to late 1980s, however, several events led to a recrudescence of drug-resistant tuberculosis in New York City: diminished resources for public health departments to treat patients with tuberculosis; the tendency of tuberculosis patients to abbreviate their treatment regimen; a wider reservoir of people susceptible to tuberculosis, such as those with human immunodeficiency virus (HIV); and an increase in travel between the United States and countries where tuberculosis and drug-resistant tuberculosis are prevalent. Between 1985 and 1990 the number of cases of tuberculosis in the city increased by 89.1 percent.

C.-E. A. Winslow: *The Life of Hermann Biggs* (Philadelphia: Lea and Febiger, 1929)
John Duffy: *A History of Public Health in New York City* (New York: Russell Sage Foundation, 1968, 1974)
René Dubos and Jean Dubos: *The White Plague: Tuberculosis, Man, and Society* (New Brunswick, N.J.: Rutgers University Press, 1987)

Howard Markel

Tucker, Richard [Ticker, Reuben] (*b* Brooklyn, 28 Aug 1913; *d* Kalamazoo, Mich., 8 Jan 1975). Singer. A tenor noted for his ability to interpret the leading roles of the classical Italian repertory, he was a star at the Metropolitan Opera from the time of his début in January 1945. Although admired for his diction in Italian roles, he retained the cadences of his native Brooklyn when speaking English. He was known for maintaining warm relationships with his fellow singers, except for his brother-in-law Jan Peerce. He died during a concert tour with his friend Robert Merrill. The Richard Tucker Music Foundation aids the careers of American opera singers. In addition to his operatic career Tucker once worked as a cantor.

George A. Thompson, Jr.

Tudor, Antony [Cook, William] (*b* London, 4 April 1908/9; *d* New York City, 19 April 1987). Choreographer. He provided choreography for the Ballet Rambert in London before leaving Britain for New York City in 1939 to join the Ballet Theatre, which had just been formed. For the company's first season in January 1940 he revived three of his earlier ballets: *Jardin aux lilas* (1936), *Dark Elegies* (1937), and *Judgment of Paris* (1938). Although not prolific Tudor gained wide recognition for his explorations of psychological themes, especially in such works as *Pillar of Fire* (1942) and *Romeo and Juliet* (1943).

David Vaughan

Tudor City. Apartment and hotel complex in Manhattan, designed by Fred F. French and H. Douglas Ives and built in 1925–28 at a cost of $25 million. It stands along Tudor City Place east of 2nd Avenue between 40th and 43rd streets, adjacent to the headquarters of the United Nations, and comprises twelve buildings ranging in height from ten to thirty-two stories and containing three thousand apartments and six hundred hotel rooms. The apartment buildings are cooperatively owned and face a private park. Tudor City has long been noted for its architectural elegance, strong sense of community, and quiet; it was declared a Historic District in 1988. In the mid 1990s there were about five thousand residents.

James Bradley

tunnels. Beneath the land and waterways of New York City lie 161 miles (259 kilometers) of tunnel. Of this total subway tunnel accounts for 137 miles (220 kilometers); four vehicular tunnels, two railroad tunnels, and the tunnels of the Port Authority Trans-Hudson Corporation (PATH) account for twenty-four miles (thirty-nine kilometers). Plans for a subaqueous tunnel were first developed in 1807, but the technology necessary to build tunnels through the mud and silt of riverbeds was not perfected until the late 1860s. The first attempt to construct a tunnel under the Hudson River was made in 1874 by Colonel DeWitt C. Haskin, who broke ground in Hoboken, New Jersey, for a tunnel to Morton Street in lower Manhattan. Several financial setbacks caused the project to be abandoned in 1892 after two thousand feet

Tudor City, 1992

(six hundred meters) of tunnel beneath the Hudson had been constructed. In 1902 William Gibbs McAdoo took over the project, formed the New York and New Jersey Railroad (later known as the Hudson and Manhattan Railroad), and completed the tunnel along with one parallel to it, as well as a pair of tunnels between Cortlandt Street in Manhattan and Exchange Place in Jersey City. The tunnels opened in 1908–9 and later became part of the PATH system. Under the East River the piano maker William Steinway began construction in 1892 of the Steinway Tunnels (the oldest surviving tunnels in the city), two trolley tunnels connecting 42nd Street in Manhattan with Queens that opened in 1907 and were converted to accommodate subways in 1915. The tunnels for the first subway line in the city, the Broadway line of Interborough Rapid Transit (IRT), were constructed in 1900–4 through the rocky center of Manhattan from City Hall to the northern tip of Manhattan.

As the city's subway network extended into Brooklyn, Queens, and the Bronx, fourteen tunnels were built under the Harlem River, the East River, and Jamaica Bay. In 1904–10 the Pennsylvania Railroad built two tunnels, a double one beneath the Hudson River and a quadruple one beneath the East River, both running to Pennsylvania Station at 34th Street. The city's first underwater tunnel for motor vehicles was the Holland Tunnel, opened in 1927 and connecting lower Manhattan and New Jersey; its ventilation system became a model for vehicular tunnels worldwide. The Lincoln Tunnel, opened in 1937, connects midtown Manhattan and New Jersey and at first had a single tube, to which parallel tubes were added to the north in 1945 and to the south in 1957. Additional tunnels were built under the East River in 1940 (the Queens–Midtown Tunnel) and 1950 (the Brooklyn–Battery Tunnel). During the 1970s three sections of a tunnel for an eventual subway were built under 2nd Avenue. After being halted for several years the project was being reevaluated in the mid 1990s by the Metropolitan Transportation Authority and the Transit Authority.

Norval White and Elliot Willensky, eds.: *AIA Guide to New York City* (New York: American Institute of Architects, New York Chapter, 1967; 3rd edn San Diego: Harcourt Brace Jovanovich, 1988)

Carl W. Condit: *American Building: Materials and Techniques from the First Colonial Settlements to the Present* (Chicago: University of Chicago Press, 1968)

Rebecca Read Shanor

Tunney, Gene [James Joseph] (*b* New York City, 25 May 1898; *d* Greenwich, Conn., 7 Nov 1978). Boxer. He grew up on Perry Street in Greenwich Village, where he learned to fight in local clubs, and turned professional in 1915. After winning the light heavyweight championship of the American Expeditionary Forces in 1919 he resumed his professional career, briefly holding the American light heavyweight championship in 1922 before losing it to Harry Greb and regaining it in the following year. On 23 September 1926 he defeated Jack Dempsey by decision in Philadelphia for the world heavyweight title, which he successfully defended against Dempsey in the controversial "long count" fight of 22 September 1927 in Chicago, for which he earned $990,000. He retired in 1928 with a record of fifty-five wins, one loss, and one draw, and later became a prominent businessman and civic leader. In addition to his prowess as a fighter, Tunney was known for his wide-ranging interests and deportment outside the ring: he read Shakespeare at training camp, traveled widely, and befriended Shaw and Thornton Wilder. He wrote two autobiographies, *A Man Must Fight* (1932) and *Arms for Living* (1941).

Steven A. Riess

Turks. Turkish-speaking Muslims from the Ottoman Empire settled in New York City from the late eighteenth century and numbered 1401 in 1900. By 1940 the figure had reached 17,663, although most of those counted were probably not ethnic Turks. During these years the city's Turks occupied a low position on the economic ladder. Some settled along Rivington and Forsythe streets in lower Manhattan and supported such clubs as the Turkish Aid Society on Theriot Avenue in Unionport (dominated by Cypriot Turks) and the Turkish Cultural Alliance at 856 Broadway in Williamsburg (mostly Anatolian). After the Second World War many Turkish physicians, scientists, and engineers left for the United States and especially for New York City, where the United Nations became the anchor of the city's Turkish community. In 1977 the Turkish government bought 821 United Nations Plaza at 1st Avenue and 46th Street, which among other organizations houses the Turkish consulate, the Turkish mission to the United Nations, and the Federation of Turkish–American Societies (formed in 1956). The city's Turks eventually became dispersed throughout the five boroughs, with large concentrations in Brighton Beach and in Sunnyside and Richmond Hills in Queens.

Most of the city's seventy thousand to 100,000 ethnic Turks represent the wealthier classes of their home country. Many drive taxicabs, own filling stations and import–export firms, and work in restaurants. Few intend to return to Turkey. The city's Turks take part in many groups, including the Turkish Women's League, the Turkish Cultural Alliance, and the Turkish Music Society of New York. The predominant religion is a secular brand of Islam: Anatolian Turks worship at the Fatih Mosque at 89-11 8th Avenue, Turkestanians at 2302 West 13th Street, and Crimean Turks at 4509 New Utrecht Avenue (all in Brooklyn). For several years Turkish law forbade Turks who took citizenship of another country to inherit property or exercise other property rights in Turkey. These laws were amended in 1985 to allow for dual citizenship, an arrangement that most Turkish–Americans found agreeable. By the early 1990s the city's Turks were beginning to play an increasingly visible role in the city's affairs: the Federation of Turkish–American Societies fought to change the use of the English term Turkey to its Turkish counterpart Türkiye, and the city government designated as Turkish–American Week the week closest to 19 May, the Turkish Youth and Sport Holiday. The most prominent Turkish–American in the city is Ahmet Ertegun, a founder of Atlantic Records and an owner from 1970

Van Cortlandt Mansion, ca *1930*

William Howe; it is now near Broadway and West 242nd Street. Vault Hill nearby holds the family vault, where Augustus Van Cortlandt, the city recorder, hid the municipal records in 1776. The first Croton Aqueduct, built in the 1840s, forms a walkway, as does a remnant of the Putnam Division of the New York Central Railroad (1881–1984). The park's most popular area, the Parade Ground (opened in 1888), was originally used by the National Guard and is now a center for baseball, football, cricket, and hurling. Members of the Van Cortlandt family lived in the mansion continuously until 1889, when they donated the building and surrounding lands to the city as a public park. In 1895 the Van Cortlandt Golf Course became the first municipal golf course in the nation, followed by the Mosholu Golf Course nearby. Playgrounds and a stadium were added in the 1930s and a large swimming pool complex opened in 1970. Despite the intrusion of the Henry Hudson and Mosholu parkways and the Major Deegan Expressway in the 1930s and 1940s, the park still has a bird sanctuary, two nature walkways, a bridle path, the nation's leading cross-country track, picnic areas, and a tree and shrub nursery maintained by the parks department.

Stephen Jenkins: *The Story of the Bronx* (New York: G. P. Putnam's Sons, 1912)

Lloyd Ultan

Van Dam, Rip (*b* Albany, N.Y., *ca* 1660; *d* New York City, 10 June 1749). Merchant and interim governor. After moving to New York City at the age of twenty he became a prominent shipbuilder and trader. He gained notoriety by resisting the restrictions on trade imposed by Governor Richard Coote, earl of Bellomont, against which he and other merchants petitioned the king. From 1693 to 1696 he held a seat on the Board of Aldermen and in 1699 he was elected to the provincial assembly, where he became the leader of the opposition party. Lord Cornbury appointed him in 1702 to the provincial council, of which he eventually became president. He served as interim governor of the colony of New York from 1731 (on the death of Governor John Montgomerie) until his replacement in the following year by the king's appointee William Cosby, with whom he had a bitter dispute after refusing to surrender half the salary he had earned as governor. During legal proceedings in 1733 he was expelled from the provincial council by Cosby, then near death, and while he fought to regain his position the council named as acting governor George Clarke; Van Dam maintained that he was still a member of the council and that his seniority entitled him to the governorship. When armed conflict seemed imminent, orders arrived in 1736 from England naming Clarke the lieutenant governor. Van Dam never held another political office.

Edward T. O'Donnell

Vanderbeeck, Rem Jansen (*b* ?Jever [now in Germany]; *d* ?New Utrecht, New Netherland, Feb 1681). Farmer. He emigrated to America and in 1640 settled in Fort Orange (now Albany), New York. In 1642 he married the daughter of Joris Jansen de Rapalje, the wealthy owner of the Wallabout district of Brooklyn, where he and his family soon settled. His descendants, the Remsens, acquired extensive land holdings and by the late eighteenth century owned nearly all the land from Red Hook Point north to Livingston Street. Among their most prominent members were Henry Remsen, private secretary to John Jay and Thomas Jefferson; another Henry Remsen, president of the Bank of Manhattan Company from 1808 to 1825; Charles Remsen, a director of the Third Avenue Railroad Company and the founder of Remsenburg, New York; and Ira Remsen, a renowned chemist who launched the American Chemical Journal in 1879 and was president of Johns Hopkins University from 1901 to 1914. Remsen Street in Brooklyn Heights is a reminder of the family's prominence.

Margherita Hamm: *Famous Families of New York* (New York: G. P. Putnam's Sons, 1902)
Maude Dillard: *Dutch Houses of Brooklyn* (New York: Richard R. Smith, 1945)

Stephen Weinstein

Vanderbilt, Cornelius (*b* Staten Island, 27 May 1794; *d* New York City, 4 Jan 1877). Entrepreneur, grandfather of William K. Vanderbilt. He attended school in Port Richmond until the age of eleven, when he went to work on his father's lighter in New York Harbor; he later bought a boat and set up a passenger and freight ferry service between Staten Island and Manhattan. During the 1830s he lived on Stone and Madison streets and East Broadway. After assembling a small fleet of vessels that worked around New York City he offered service to Albany, New York, and undercut his competitors. A millionaire by 1846, he built a mansion on Staten Island and a townhouse on Washington Place that became his principal residence. He captured most of the traffic to California during the gold rush by reducing the fare between New York City and San Francisco. At about seventy he merged three inefficient railroad lines operating between the city and points upstate into an efficient line offering dependable service; he then turned to the issue of national transportation and formed one of the largest transportation networks in North America. During the panic of 1873 he paid dividends as usual and issued contracts to build Grand Central Terminal that employed thousands of workers. By the end of his life Vanderbilt had a fortune of more than $100 million, most of which he left to family members; he also gave money to the Church of the Strangers in New York, where a friend was pastor.
See also Aviation and Railroads, §1.

James E. Mooney

Vanderbilt, Gloria (Morgan) (*b* New York City, 20 Feb 1924). Fashion designer, painter, actress, and writer. She was born an heiress to the dynasty founded by her great-great-grandfather, the financier Commodore Cornelius Vanderbilt, and when her father died in 1925 she inherited a trust fund of about $4 million. At the age of ten she became the focus of one of the nation's most notorious child custody cases when her parental aunt, Gertrude Whitney, accused her mother of neglect and sued for custody. After a highly publicized trial during which she was widely referred to as the "poor little rich girl," she was turned over to Whitney. As an adult she embarked on successful careers as a painter, actress, writer, and fashion designer while remaining active as a member of fashionable society. She also attracted considerable attention for her marriages to the Hollywood agent Pasquale di Cocco (1942), the conductor Leopold Stokowski (1945), the film director Sidney Lumet (1956), and the writer Wyatt Cooper (1963).

Barbara Goldsmith: *Little Gloria: Happy at Last* (New York: Alfred A. Knopf, 1980)

Peter Hellman: "Sic Transit Gloria," *New York*, 15 Feb 1993

Robert Sanger Steel

Vanderbilt, William K(issam) (*b* Staten Island, 12 Dec 1849; *d* Paris, 22 July 1920). Industrialist and sportsman, grandson of Cornelius Vanderbilt. With his brothers Cornelius and George he was educated by private tutors and at schools in Switzerland. He later worked for the Hudson River Railroad and by 1877 was a vice-president of the New York Central and Hudson River Railroad; after six years he left to direct other railroads owned by his family. His marriage to Alva Ertskin Smith in 1875 helped him to gain acceptance in élite circles; they were divorced in 1895 and in 1903 he married Anna (Harriman) Sands Rutherfurd. After his brother Cornelius's death in 1899 he left many of his positions in the railroads to manage the family's immense holdings; in 1903 he resigned as executive director of the New York Central and allowed direction of it to pass to the Pennsylvania Railroad, but he retained control through ownership. An avid sportsman, he sailed in the America's Cup race and owned many thoroughbred race horses. Vanderbilt also established the Vanderbilt Clinic, supported the Metropolitan Opera Company and Columbia University, and collected paintings that he bequeathed to the Metropolitan Museum of Art.

Louis Auchincloss: *The Vanderbilt Era: Profiles of a Gilded Age* (New York: Macmillan, 1989)

James E. Mooney

Vanderlip, Frank A(rthur) (*b* Aurora, Ill., 17 Nov 1864; *d* New York City, 29 June 1937). Banker. As an assistant secretary of the treasury from 1897 to 1901 he arranged the Spanish–American War Loan. His work caught the attention of James Stillman, the president of National City Bank, who in 1901 made him its vice-president, a position he retained until he became president in 1909. He helped to plan the Federal Reserve System and in 1911 formed the National City Company, a nationwide bank holding company and securities affiliate of the National City Bank that was not subject to the restrictions of the National Bank Act. His most important achievements were the establishment of branches overseas, beginning in Buenos Aires in 1914, and the acquisition in 1915 of the branches of the International Banking Corporation in the Far East. A volunteer during the First World War, he led the War Savings Certificates Committee from 1917 to 1918. A group led by James A. Stillman (son of James Stillman) and William Rockefeller forced him to resign in 1919. He lived in Scarborough-on-Hudson, New York.

Frank A. Vanderlip with Boyden Sparkes: *From Farm Boy to Financier* (New York: D. Appleton Century, 1935)

Joan L. Silverman

Vanderlyn, John (*b* Kingston, N.Y., 15 Oct 1775; *d* Kingston, 23 Sept 1852). Painter. The grandson of the sign and portrait painter Pieter Vanderlyn (*b ca* 1687; *d* 1778), he became a protégé of Aaron Burr, who introduced him to art patrons in New York City and sent him to Paris for training in 1796. After five years of study he returned to New York City and was commissioned to paint the portraits of many prominent New Yorkers. Edward Livingston made him an envoy for the American Academy of the Fine Arts and sent him to Paris and Rome to paint copies of old masterpieces. After staying abroad much longer than expected he returned with sketches for a grand panorama of the palace and gardens of Versailles. He executed the painting in 1818–19, and it was exhibited for several years in a specially designed rotunda in City Hall Park (it is now held by the Metropolitan Museum of Art). Vanderlyn promoted his paintings of panoramas for the rest of his life and also accepted portrait commissions, although his talents declined in his later years. The Senate House Association in Kingston holds a large collection of his work and papers.

Carrie Rebora

VanDerZee, James (Augustus) (*b* Lenox, Mass., 29 June 1886; *d* Washington, 15 May 1983). Photographer. He acquired an interest in photography while still in his teens and moved in 1905 to New York City, where in 1916 he opened his first photography studio, on 135th Street near Lenox Avenue. During the 1920s he was closely associated with several figures in the Harlem Renaissance and worked as Marcus Garvey's official photographer (1921–24); his portrait studio, consid-

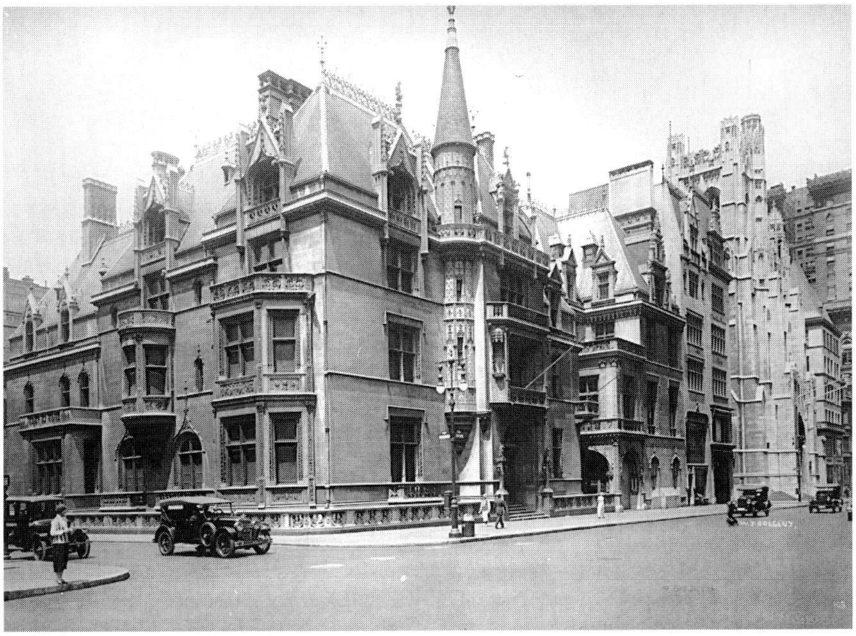

William K. Vanderbilt House (designed by Richard Morris Hunt), 52nd Street and 5th Avenue, 1924

James VanDerZee, Cousin Susan Porter *(ca 1914)*

James VanDerZee, Moorish Jews *(1929)*

ered the most fashionable in Harlem, was moved first to 2069–77 7th Avenue and then to 272 Lenox Avenue. With his second wife, Gaynella (Greenlee) Katz, he also managed a print restoration service. After 1960 the volume of his portrait and restoration commissions declined. He worked from 1967 with the Metropolitan Museum of Art on the exhibition "Harlem on My Mind," which recorded more than sixty years of life in Harlem and to which he became the largest individual contributor; the exhibition opened in January 1969 and brought him international recognition, while at the same time declining business forced him and his wife from the brownstone building that housed their business and their residence. In 1970 the Metropolitan added sixty of his prints to its permanent collection and an institute was formed in his name to promote the work of young minority photographers. He received the first Pierre Toussaint Award from the New York Archdiocese in 1978. From 1979 to the end of his life VanDerZee resumed his career as a portrait photographer and exhibited his work in the United States and abroad.

Reginald McGhee: *The World of James VanDerZee: A Visual Record of Black Americans* (New York: Grove, 1969)

Liliane DeCock and Reginald McGhee: *James VanDerZee* (Dobbs Ferry, N.Y.: Morgan and Morgan, 1973)

Jim Haskins: *James VanDerZee: The Picture-takin' Man* (New York: Dodd, Mead, 1979)

Deborah Willis-Braithwaite: *VanDerZee, Photographer, 1886–1983* (New York: Harry N. Abrams, 1993)

For further illustrations see Baseball and Public health.

Rodger C. Birt

Van Doren, Carl (Clinton) (*b* Hope, Ill., 10 Sept 1884; *d* Torrington, Conn., 18 July 1950). Literary critic, historian, and editor, brother of Mark Van Doren. He attended Columbia University in 1908 to complete work on his PhD and in 1911 accepted a teaching position there in American literature and history. After working briefly as the headmaster of the Brearley School in 1916–18 he was the literary editor of the *Nation* in 1919–22. Van Doren became an influential literary figure in New York City by supporting young, modern writers. His published writings include an authoritative biography of Benjamin Franklin (1938).

Robert Morrow

Van Doren [née Bradford], **Irita** (*b* Birmingham, Ala., 16 March 1891; *d* New York City, 18 Dec 1966). Editor. While earning the PhD at Columbia University she met and married Carl Van Doren in 1912 (they divorced in 1935). In 1919 she joined his editorial staff at the *Nation* and later became the chief assistant to the editor of the *New York Herald Tribune.* After launching a weekly book review supplement (widely considered better written than its counterpart in the *New York Times*) she became literary editor to the newspaper in 1926. She edited the supplement until 1963 and gained an international reputation for her writing.

Robert Morrow

Van Doren, Mark (Albert) (*b* Hope, Ill., 13 June 1894; *d* Torrington, Conn., 10 Dec 1972). Literary critic, brother of Carl Van Doren. After receiving his PhD at Columbia University in 1920 he joined his brother as a member of the faculty in the school's English department until 1959. A gifted and influential professor, he taught several popular courses during a career that lasted thirty-nine years: his students included the poet John Berryman and the theologian Thomas Merton. He wrote fiction and criticism, and received the Pulitzer Prize for his poetry in 1940. Van Doren's published writings include critical studies of John Dryden (1920) and Nathaniel Hawthorne (1949), several books of poetry, novels, and a play, and *Liberal Education* (1943). A teaching award at Columbia is given each year by the students in his honor.

Fred B. Millett: *Contemporary American Authors* (New York: Harcourt, Brace, 1940)

Robert Morrow

Vanity Fair. Name used by four magazines published in New York City. The first appeared from 1859 to 1863 and the second was a glossy publication inspired by such pulp magazines as *Police Gazette.* The third and best-known was published for more than twenty years by Condé Nast, who acquired the rights to the name for $3000, bought out the magazine *Dress* (a competitor of his own fashion magazine *Vogue*), and from 1913 published *Dress and Vanity Fair*; he sought a wide readership by including coverage of fashion, the arts, and sports as well as humorous pieces. His dissatisfaction with the first four issues of the magazine led him to engage Frank Crowninshield, an editor of eclectic tastes who had worked on *Bookman*, *Century*, and *Munsey's.* The magazine, now known by its abbreviated name, published the work of Robert Benchley, Dorothy Parker, Robert E. Sherwood, Donald Ogden Stewart, Clare Boothe, John Peale Bishop, Edna St. Vincent Millay, Edmund Wilson, Gertrude Stein, Aldous Huxley, Noël Coward, Ferenc Molnar, Tristan Tzara, and Colette. It was difficult for *Vanity Fair* to retain its readers during the Depression, and in an effort to broaden its appeal Crowninshield began to publish articles by Walter Lippmann and engaged Jay Franklin and Henry Pringle as members of the editorial staff in 1932. The magazine was nevertheless merged with *Vogue* in 1936. A fourth magazine named *Vanity Fair* was introduced by Condé Nast Publications in March 1983.

American Humor Magazines and Comic Periodicals (Westport, Conn: Greenwood, 1987)

Brenda Wineapple

Van Nest. Neighborhood in the central Bronx, bounded to the north by Park Avenue and the Esplanade, to the east by Bronxdale Avenue, to the south by East Tremont Avenue, and to the west by Bronx River Parkway.

The first European settlers were members of the family of Pieter Pietersen Van Neste, who settled in the area in 1647. A railroad station was built to accommodate visitors to the Morris Park Racecourse. The area remained farmland until the 1870s, when it was divided into seventeen hundred lots for development by the Van Nest Land Improvement Company. Development and a nexus of trolley lines nearby in West Farms led to the construction of one-family frame houses; the streets were named for members of the Van Neste family. The first apartment buildings were constructed in the 1920s. In addition to a large Italian and Irish population, in the 1980s Van Nest and its environs attracted some new immigrants from Jamaica, the Dominican Republic, Guyana, India, and China.

Nicholas DiBrino: *Morris Park Racecourse* (New York: Bronx County Historical Society, 1977)

John McNamara: *McNamara's Old Bronx* (New York: Bronx County Historical Society, 1989)

Gary D. Hermalyn

Van Nostrand, David (*b* New York City, 5 Dec 1811; *d* New York City, 14 June 1886). Publisher. He went to work in publishing at fifteen but left during the panic of 1837. After training as a military engineer he became a bookseller and prospered; he then published a series of volumes on the Civil War, *The Rebellion Record* (1864–68), and launched *Van Nostrand's Electric Engineering Magazine*, which focused on military and technical works. His firm, D. Van Nostrand, eventually became part of Van Nostrand Reinhold.

James E. Mooney

Van Vechten, Carl (*b* Cedar Rapids, Iowa, 17 June 1880; *d* New York City, 21 Dec 1964). Critic and novelist. He graduated from the University of Chicago and worked as a music critic for the *New York Times* and the *New Music Review*; he was also a photographer and became well known for supporting artists of the Harlem Renaissance. After 1920 he abandoned criticism for fiction. An avid collector of books and memorabilia, he donated the James Weldon Johnson Memorial Collection of Negro Arts and Letters to Yale University, the Van Vechten Collection of books and manuscripts to the New York Public Library, and the George Gershwin Collection to Fisk University. Van Vechten's published writings include the novel *Nigger Heaven* (1926), an autobiography (1932), *Fragments from an Unwritten Autobiography* (1955), and *Between Friends* (1961). For many years he lived on Central Park West.

James E. Mooney

Van Wyck, Robert A(nderson) (*b* New York City, 1849; *d* Paris, 13 Nov 1918). Mayor. A graduate of Columbia Law School, he was elected judge of the City Court in 1889 and became its presiding judge. He was nominated for mayor in 1897 by Richard Croker, the leader of Tammany Hall, and prevailed against divided opposition to become the city's first mayor after consolidation. While in office he engaged in questionable practices: he was accused of accepting $500,000 of stock in the American Ice Company but cleared of any wrongdoing by Governor Theodore Roosevelt in 1900. Such scandals became the focus of the election of 1901, in which Van Wyck was defeated by the Republican reformer Seth Low. He lived at 135 East 46th Street.

James E. Mooney

Varela, Felix (*b* Havana, 1788; *d* St. Augustine, Fla., 18 Feb 1853). Religious and political reformer. He taught from 1811 to 1820 at San Carlos Seminary in Spain, where he modernized the curriculum and wrote a number of texts, and was ordained a Roman Catholic priest in 1812. An advocate of republicanism and Cuban independence, he served in the Spanish legislature, the Cortes, until 1823. As a political refugee he moved to New York City in 1824 and continued to promote republicanism and Cuban independence through the newspaper *El Haberno*. He became a diocesan vicar general, wrote articles, edited a number of short-lived Catholic newspapers, published a children's catechistic periodical, and defended Catholicism against nativism. In 1825 he became the pastor of Christ Church, holding services in the basement of the Church of St. Peter until 23 March 1827, when they were moved to Christ Protestant Episcopal Church at 41 Ann Street. Eventually the congregation divided into two branches: Varela became the pastor of one that he named the Church of the Transfiguration, which occupied the former Reformed Scots Presbyterian Church on Chambers and Park streets after a rededication on 31 March 1836. Varela financed the church with his own income and money from family and friends, as most of the congregants were poor residents of the Five Points. In 1850 he moved for reasons of health to St. Augustine, but he continued to aid the parish financially until his death. The parish is now at 23–29 Mott Street.

Helen McCadden and Joseph McCadden: *Father Varela: Torch Bearer from Cuba* (New York: United States Catholic Historical Society, 1969)

Mary Elizabeth Brown

Varèse, Edgar(d Victor Achille Charles) (*b* Paris, 22 Dec 1883; *d* New York City, 6 Nov 1965). Composer. He moved to New York City in December 1915 and formed the International Composers' Guild there in 1921. Many of his major compositions were given their first performances in the city, including *Hyperprism* (1922–23) for winds and percussion, *Ionisation* (1931) for percussion ensemble, *Density 21.5* (1936) for solo flute, and *Nocturnal* for soprano, bass chorus, and small orchestra (1961). After failing in the 1930s to gain a large following for his music, which he termed "organized sound," he turned his attention to early music, in 1943 formed the Greater New York Chorus, which he led until 1947, and taught at Columbia University in 1948. In the 1950s he gained critical recognition for his work with electronic music and in particular for his compositions *Déserts* (1954), for chamber orchestra and tape, and *Poème électronique* (1958), for tape alone. During his last years he lived at 189 Sullivan Street. Varèse's music is often uncompromisingly dissonant and yet accessible because of its colorful instrumentation, which relies heavily on brass and percussion.

Fernand Oullette: *Edgar Varèse* (New York: Orion, 1968)

Barbara L. Tischler

Varian, Isaac L(eggett) (*b* New York City, 25 June 1793; *d* Peekskill, N.Y., 10 Aug 1864). Mayor. An ally of Tammany Hall, he was known for his honest character as an alderman and mayor during the 1830s and early 1840s. A dispute over his selection as the chairman of a meeting of Tammany Hall in the autumn of 1835 led to the formation of the Locofocos, an egalitarian faction of the Democratic Party.

James E. Mooney

Varick, James (*b* Newburgh, N.Y., 1750; *d* New York City, 22 July 1827). Religious leader. A shoemaker and the father of four children, he joined the John Street Methodist Episcopal Church but became disillusioned by the racism of white congregants. After withdrawing in 1796 he helped to form a congregation that became legally established in 1801. He was ordained in 1820 while leading efforts to form the African Methodist Episcopal Zion Church, of which he was elected bishop in 1822 and 1826.

Benjamin F. Wheeler: *The Varick Family* (Mobile, Ala.: n.pub., 1906)

William J. Walls: *The African Methodist Episcopal Zion Church: Reality of the Black Church* (Charlotte, N.C.: A.M.E. Zion Publishing House, 1974)

Dennis C. Dickerson

Varick, Richard (*b* Hackensack, N.J., 25 March 1753; *d* Jersey City, N.J., 30 July 1831). Mayor. He moved to New York City in 1775 and enlisted as a captain in the Continental Army, where he was an aide-de-camp to Benedict Arnold from 1777 to 1780; he later was cleared of complicity in Arnold's treasonous activities and in 1781 became George Washington's secretary. He was the city's recorder from 1784 to 1789, the speaker of the state assembly in 1787–88, and the state attorney general in 1788–89. In 1789 he helped to codify the state's statutes and as a Federalist was appointed mayor by Governor George Clinton. Republicans later criticized his use of marketing and tax-licensing fees, and he was swept out of office in 1801 after a bitter campaign. A street in lower Manhattan is named for him.

Sidney I. Pomerantz: *New York: An American City, 1783–1803: A Study of Urban Life* (New York: Columbia University Press, 1938; 2nd edn Port Washington, N.Y.: I. J. Friedman, 1965)

David William Voorhees

Variety. Weekly publication of the entertainment business, launched in 1905 by Sime Silverman to cover the vaudeville circuit. It later expanded to include coverage of motion pictures, radio, and television. The publication was controlled by Silverman's descendants until 1990, when Gerard A. Byrne became the publisher. In the mid 1990s *Variety* had a circulation of more than thirty thousand and covered entertainment worldwide, including theater, home video, and cable television. It is known for a breezy, jargonistic style of writing and in particular for such memorable headlines as "Wall Street Lays an Egg" (30 October 1929) and "Sticks Nix Hick Pix" (17 July 1935).

Laura Gwinn

varnishes. The manufacture of varnishes and related products is discussed in the entry PAINTS, DYES, AND VARNISHES.

vaudeville. After the Astor Place Riot of 1849 entertainment in New York City was divided along class lines: opera was chiefly for the upper middle and upper classes, minstrel shows and melodramas for the middle class, variety shows in concert saloons for men of the working class and the slumming middle class. Vaudeville was developed by entrepreneurs seeking higher profits from a wider audience. The first vaudeville performer was Tony Pastor, a singer in concert saloons during the Civil War who experimented with different formats into the 1870s. In 1881 he moved his operations to a theater in Tammany Hall (near Union Square in the heart of the theater district), where he reworked old variety shows to preserve their vitality but remove what he called their "cigar-smoking and beer-drinking accompaniment." Soon his audiences ranged from newsboys to middle-class women and leaders of Tammany Hall.

From the 1880s to the 1920s vaudeville was the most popular form of theater in the United States. It attracted performers who worked in other forms of popular entertainment, including variety shows, minstrelsy, melodrama, the street performances of the Bowery, and eventually motion pictures and television; material was adapted for vaudeville from these genres (Pastor was especially influenced by the theater of the Bowery) and music was often provided by musicians from Tin Pan Alley. Managers of vaudeville theaters cultivated audiences that included men and women, native-born and immigrant, from the working class and the middle class, but they excluded blacks. B. F. Keith and E. F. Albee, circus managers from New England, were among the first to plan nationwide tours for which they helped to develop a particularly wholesome form of vaudeville. They opened the first of their many theaters in the city on Union Square in 1893 and in 1900 established a national booking system with headquarters in the city. Despite strikes by performers in a union called the White Rats in 1900 and 1916–17, Keith's office eventually controlled nearly all the most highly sought-after bookings. Times Square became the heart of vaudeville in the city in 1913 after Albee opened the Palace Theatre at 47th Street and 7th Avenue; the theater soon became the center of Keith's operations, which operated a booking office upstairs.

At this time New York City was the national center of vaudeville. Links from the city to transport lines across the country were useful in planning national tours, and many booking agencies made their headquarters in the city, which was often the first stop on the tours. There were vaudeville theaters in virtually every part of the city, ranging from celebrated ones in Times Square, to those catering to an entire borough (the Royal Theatre and the National Theatre in an area known as the Hub in the Bronx), to small theaters in residential neighborhoods (Loew's Avenue B Theatre on the Lower East Side and Fox's Folly Theatre in Williamsburg). A "subway circuit" took shape along subway lines to the outskirts of the city and ran from the Fordham Theatre (owned by Keith) in the Bronx to the Albee Theatre and other points in Brooklyn. Acts by nationally known performers (or their imitators) could tour within the city for weeks. Many performers including Eddie Cantor and Sophie Tucker lived in the city and began their careers singing and dancing on street corners and on the stages of minor theaters. The chances of becoming successful in vaudeville were slim, but performers were attracted by the possibility of achieving national renown and earning high salaries (as much as $2500 a week in 1915). Many who became successful were immigrants and members of the working class.

Mainstream culture was changed immensely by vaudeville, which offered a commercial venue for ethnic cultural forms. Offerings were broad and included such songs as "My Yiddisha Mama" (performed by Tucker) and "Maggie Cline, the Irish Queen." Performances before mixed audiences of songs like "Cyclonic Eva Tanguay" and demonstrations of strength by Eugene Sandow and others helped to break down Victorian notions of propriety. Blacks continued to be excluded from vaudeville theaters and had only stereotyped roles in performances.

With the onset of the Depression and the increasing popularity of sound motion pictures, the Palace became a movie house in 1932 and theatrical vaudeville in New York City ceased. Former vaudeville performers such as Groucho Marx, Fanny Brice, James Cagney, and Eubie Blake adapted their routines to musical theater, radio, film, and television.

Robert W. Snyder: *The Voice of the City: Vaudeville and Popular Culture in New York* (New York: Oxford University Press, 1989)

See also THEATER, §§4–5

Robert W. Snyder

Vaux, Calvert (*b* London, 20 Sept 1824; *d* Brooklyn, 18 Nov 1895). Landscape designer and architect. He moved to the United States in 1850 to work with Andrew Jackson Downing, a collaboration that lasted until Downing's death in 1852. After moving to New York City in 1856 he successfully urged that a competition be held to choose a design for Central Park; the competition was won by his own entry, a collaboration with Frederick Law Olmsted, with whom he also later designed Prospect and Fort Greene parks. After this partnership ended in 1872 Vaux began his own architecture practice. An adherent of reformist ideas current among his contemporaries, he undertook commissions for the Metropolitan Museum of Art and the American Museum of Natural History (with Jacob Wrey Mould; for illustration see AMERICAN MUSEUM OF NATURAL HISTORY), Frederic E. Church's country home, Olana (with Frederic C. Withers, a colleague from Downing's office), the townhouse of Samuel J. Tilden in Gramercy Park, and several lodging houses and industrial schools for the Children's Aid Society. Unwilling to compromise, he was increasingly at odds with the special interests that controlled the parks and unable to adapt to new architectural tastes. Waning commissions and his perceived lack of recognition for Central and Prospect parks disillusioned and embittered him, and he drowned under mysterious circumstances in Gravesend Bay. Vaux's *Villas and Cottages* (1857) shaped an ideal of American domesticity for decades.

Dennis Francis Steadman and Joy M. Kestenbaum: "Calvert Vaux," *Macmillan Encyclopedia of Architects*, vol. 2 (New York: Macmillan, 1982)

Charles E. Beveridge and David Schuyler, eds.: *The Papers of Frederick Law Olmsted*, vol. 3, *Creating Central Park, 1857–1861* (Baltimore: Johns Hopkins University Press, 1983)

Rick Beard

Vega, Bernardo (*b* Cayey, Puerto Rico, 2 Feb 1886; *d* San Juan, June 1965). Cigar maker, political activist, and writer. He gained a political education in the radical world of Puerto Rican cigar makers and moved in 1916 to New York City, where he took part in many leftist and Puerto Rican nationalist organizations. From 1927 to 1931 he edited the weekly Spanish-language newspaper *El Grafico*, and in 1948 he led the Hispanic Division of Henry A. Wallace's presidential campaign. His *Memoirs: A Contribution to the History of the Puerto Rican Community in New York* (1977) is the most comprehensive narrative of Latin American workers' culture in New York City during the first half of the twentieth century. Vega returned to Puerto Rico in the 1950s, where he devoted his energies to the island's independence movement.

Michael Lapp

Veiller, Lawrence (Turnure) (*b* Elizabeth, N.J., 7 Jan 1872; *d* New York City, 30 Aug 1959). Housing reformer. Soon after graduating from City College of New York he became the most important figure in housing reform in the United States. An ardent critic of the dumbbell, or "old law," tenements that were built throughout the city after 1879, he led a campaign for a new tenement code in 1901 requiring that designs include a court, thus providing more light and air to interior rooms than had been delivered formerly by narrow airshafts. As the deputy commissioner of the New York City Tenement House Department (1902–4) and secretary of the Tenement House Committee of Charity Organization, and as an organizer of the National Housing Association (1910) and its first director, he transformed the housing reform movement from a series of local efforts into a national project managed by professionals. In 1921 he played an important role in drafting the Standard Zoning Law of the U.S. Department of Commerce, which with minor modifications was adopted by most communities during the following ten years. Toward the end of his career Veiller was often criticized by younger experts for relying heavily on restrictive legislation rather than public action to ensure the quality of housing.

Roy Lubove: *The Progressives and the Slums: Tenement House Reform in New York City, 1890–1917* (Pittsburgh: University of Pittsburgh Press, 1962)

Stanley Buder

vendors. See STREET VENDORS.

Venuti, Joe [Giuseppe] (*b* Lecco, Italy, 4 April 1898; *d* Seattle, 14 Aug 1978). Violinist. Trained in the classical repertory in Philadelphia, he turned to jazz after forming a partnership with the guitarist Eddie Lang; the two moved to New York City in 1925, played with many well-known bands, and made recordings that became influential in the United States and abroad. After leading a big band from 1935 to 1943 he returned to playing in small groups. His popularity declined until he performed in Newport, Rhode Island, in 1968, an engagement that led to recordings in the 1970s with such musicians as Zoot Sims (*Joe and Zoot*, 1974), and Earl Hines (*Hot Sonatas*, 1975). Venuti is regarded as the most important violinist in the early years of jazz.

James E. Mooney

Vereinigte Deutsche Gewerkschaften. See UNITED GERMAN TRADES.

Verplanck, Gulian C(rommelin) (*b* New York City, 6 Aug 1786; *d* New York City, 18 March 1870). Writer and political leader. Born to a wealthy family from the Hudson Valley, he graduated from Columbia College in 1801. For his role in the commencement riot of 1811 at Columbia he received a stiff fine in mayor's court from De Witt Clinton, provoking him to write a number of satirical pieces on Clinton and his associates under the name Abimelech Coody. As one of the Bucktail Bards he later renewed his attack on Clinton and became well known for writing political pamphlets; he was also a biographer, literary critic, and student of religion, and served in the state assembly (1820–23), the U.S. Congress (1825–33), and the state senate (1838–41). In 1834 he narrowly lost the first direct mayoral election, in which he ran as a Whig. Verplanck helped to form the Century Association and was its president from 1857 until 1864, when he was forced to step down because of his affiliation with the Copperheads.

Evan Cornog

Cartoon from Gulian C. Verplanck's mayoral campaign against Cornelius Van Wyck Lawrence, 1834

Verrazano [Verrazzano], **Giovanni da** (*b* Val di Greve, Italy, *ca* 1485; *d* ?Puerto del Pico, Spain, *ca* 1528). Navigator. On behalf of France he led an expedition to the northeastern coast of North America in 1524; he traveled from Cape Fear to Cape Breton and was the first European known to sail into New York Harbor. The Verrazano Narrows and the bridge across it are named for him.

James E. Mooney

Verrazano Narrows Bridge. Suspension bridge across the Narrows between Staten Island and Brooklyn, opened in November 1964. It is named for the Italian explorer Giovanni da Verrazano, probably the first European to see New York Harbor. A bridge across the Narrows had been proposed for more than eighty years and planned for nearly fifteen when construction began in September 1959. The project was put in motion by Robert Moses, chairman of the Triborough Bridge and Tunnel Authority, who overcame opposition that was particularly intense in Bay Ridge because of the displacement of some eight thousand residents. The bridge was the sixty-sixth in New York City over navigable waterways and the last of eight in the city designed by the Swiss engineer Othmar H. Ammann. Its towers are 623 feet (190 meters) tall and rest on steel and concrete caissons sunk into man-made islands of sand; the anchorages are concrete wedges more than one hundred feet (thirty meters) tall set into the ground at Fort Hamilton in Brooklyn and Fort Wadsworth in Staten Island. The roadway has two levels and is suspended from four steel-wire cables with a diameter of thirty-six inches (ninety-one centimeters). Computers were used to calculate the stresses to which all parts of the bridge would be subjected while the roadbed sections were hoisted into place and anchored to the cables. On its opening day Moses called the bridge a "triumph of simplicity and restraint." In the following years it spurred considerable development on Staten Island. The toll plaza in Staten Island is the starting point for the New York City Marathon (for illustration see RUNNING).

Sharon Reier: *The Bridges of New York* (New York: Quadrant, 1977)

Ellen Fletcher

vest pocket parks. Small parks, often built on vacant lots wedged between buildings. They became popular in New York City during the 1960s, when open space was becoming scarce. Many of the parks were developed with funds from the city, state, and federal governments and were used only until the lots were built on. Often they were built at the

Vest pocket park in midtown Manhattan, 1994

urging of community groups and charitable organizations: examples include the Clinton Community Garden at 48th Street between 9th and 10th avenues and the Dream Street Park at Lexington Avenue and 124th Street, a result of the efforts of the Creative Arts Workshop for Homeless Children. In a few cases private endowments for construction and maintenance gave rise to small parks that endured, such as Paley Park at 53rd Street between 5th and Madison avenues, and Greenacre Park at 51st Street between 2nd and 3rd avenues. Vest pocket parks continue to be enjoyed as sitting areas, community gardens, and playgrounds for neighborhoods that have little open space. The Liz Christie Garden at Houston Street and 2nd Avenue in Manhattan, which dates from the early 1970s, is the oldest operating community garden in the city.

Jonathan Kuhn

Veterans Affairs, U.S. Department of. For a discussion of hospitals maintained by this department and by its predecessor the Veterans Administration see VA MEDICAL CENTERS.

Viacom. Entertainment and communications firm, formed in 1970 by the Columbia Broadcasting System (CBS) to comply with federal regulations preventing networks from owning cable television systems. Over the years the firm acquired such cable systems as Showtime / The Movie Network, Nickelodeon, and MTV, as well as television and radio stations. After a long takeover attempt by the investor Carl Icahn the firm was bought in March 1987 by National Amusements, a chain of movie theaters owned by Sumner Redstone. Viacom in March 1994 acquired Paramount Communications along with one of its most valuable properties, the Madison Square Garden sports and entertainment complex (including the New York Knickerbockers and the New York Rangers), which it then resold in August of the same year for $1100 million. In 1994 Viacom was based at 1515 Broadway in Times Square. Among its subsidiaries are the noted book publishers Macmillan and Simon and Schuster.

James Bradley

Victory Arch. Monument erected in 1918 at the urging of Mayor John F. Hylan to honor the city's war dead. It stood on a site at 5th Avenue and 24th Street formerly occupied by the Dewey Triumphal and Memorial Arch. The architect Thomas Hastings used temporary materials for the memorial, which was modeled after the Arch of Constantine in Rome. Arguments over who was to receive the commission and who was to pay for it doomed completion of the project, and the arch was eventually razed.

Kenneth T. Jackson

Viereck, George Sylvester (*b* Munich, 31 Dec 1884; *d* Holyoke, Mass., 18 March 1962). Essayist and poet. He wrote poetry in German and English and in 1906 graduated from City College as a class poet; for the next nine years he worked for *Current Literature.* Denounced for being an apologist for Germany during the First World War, he worked from 1922 to 1927 for William Randolph Hearst, and continued to produce writing that was widely considered controversial. During the 1930s he defended Hitler, was tried as an unregistered foreign agent, and served a term in a federal penitentiary in Atlanta, during which his son George was killed in the war. He later wrote about these years in *Men into Beasts* (1952).

James E. Mooney

Vietnam Peace Parade Committee. Committee that organized marches in New York City nearly every spring and autumn between 1965 and 1973 to protest the Vietnam War. Its headquarters were at 5 Beekman Street and later at 17 East 17th Street and 156 5th Avenue. Several marches drew hundreds of thousands of participants, including one on 15 April 1967 at which Martin Luther King Jr. spoke. In 1967 the committee sought fifty thousand signatures to force a referendum on ending the war immediately and shifting funds from the military to schools, hospitals, and programs for the poor. It also organized "stop the draft week," a series of protests at the Whitehall Induction Center on 4–8 December.

Jonathan D. Bloom

Viking Press. Firm of book publishers formed in 1925 by Harold K. Guinzburg and George S. Oppenheimer at 30 Irving Place. It developed a reputation for both literary excellence and distinction in design, benefiting especially from the expertise and distinguished list that it acquired by taking over B. W. Huebsch's imprint during its first year. Among the writers whom it published were D. H. Lawrence, John Steinbeck (*The Grapes of Wrath*, 1939), James Joyce (first American edn of *Finnegans Wake*, 1939), Lillian Hellman, Arthur Miller (*Death of a Salesman*, 1949), Rebecca West, Malcolm Cowley, and Saul Bellow. In 1975 the firm was acquired by Penguin Books, which retained Viking as a hardcover imprint. Viking Penguin is at 375 Hudson Street in Manhattan.

Eileen K. Cheng

Village Vanguard. Nightclub. It was opened on Charles Street in 1934 by Max Gordon (1903–89), an immigrant from Lithuania who moved to New York City from Portland, Oregon, in 1926; later the club moved to 178 7th Avenue South (between West 11th Street and Waverly Place), where it occupied a pie-shaped basement space sixty feet (eighteen meters) long. Gordon was admired and respected in musical circles for refusing to follow trends or bow to commercial pressures. In the 1960s, when most clubs ceased to offer jazz because it was unprofitable, the Vanguard became a venue for avant-garde jazz musicians, including Eric Dolphy, John Coltrane, Max Roach, Thelonious Monk, and Charles Mingus. It became one of the most enduring nightclubs in the United States and in addition to jazz offered poetry readings, folk music, blues, and comedy. Performers found its intimate ambience conducive to improvisation; among those who appeared there were Leadbelly, Woody Allen, Pearl Bailey, Wally Cox, Barbra Streisand, Lenny Bruce, the Weavers, and Aretha Franklin. For twenty-five years a big band led by Thad Jones and Mel Lewis performed on Monday nights. Gordon remained the owner of the club until his death.

Max Gordon: *Live at the Village Vanguard* (New York: St. Martin's, 1980)

Kathy J. Ogren

Village Voice. Weekly newspaper launched on 26 October 1955 by the publisher Ed Fancher along with his editor Dan Wolf, the columnist Norman Mailer, and the writer John Wilcox; it occupied offices on University Place in Greenwich Village. Intended as a countercultural response to the "vulgarities of McCarthyism," it covered life in Greenwich Village, reformist politics in New York City, the civil rights and peace movements, and culture, especially Off Broadway theater and the avant-garde. Jules Feiffer joined the staff in 1956 as its first editorial cartoonist. The *Voice* attracted a national readership as an exponent of "new journalism," which eschewed any pretense to journalistic objectivity and emphasized advocacy reporting. In the late 1960s it became an innovative leader in investigative journalism, particularly through the work of Jack Newfield, who revealed corruption among officials in city government and executives; this coverage made the *Voice* an important force in electoral and reform politics. It also offered coverage of the arts, including film reviews by Andrew Sarris, and opinion pieces by such writers as Nat Hentoff. The newspaper was acquired successively by Carter Burden (1970), Clay Felker, publisher of *New York* (1974), Rupert Murdoch (1977), and Leonard Stern (1985, for more than $55 million). In the 1980s it moved its offices to Broadway near Union Square. The *Voice Literary Supplement*, an insert launched in 1981 and published ten times a year, was made available by subscription in 1989. Among those who have contributed to the *Voice* are the writers Alexander Cockburn, Richard Goldstein, Eliot Fremont-Smith, Erika Munk, Ellen Willis, Joe Conason, and James Ridgeway, and the cartoonists Mark Alan Stamaty and Stan Mack. In 1991 the newspaper moved its offices to Cooper Square; its circulation in 1994 was 147,000.

Kevin Michael McAuliffe: *The Great American Newspaper: The Rise and Fall of the "Village Voice"* (New York: Charles Scribner's Sons, 1978)

Marjorie Harrison

Villard, Oswald Garrison (*b* Wiesbaden, Germany, 13 March 1872; *d* New York City, 1 Oct 1949). Newspaper publisher and civil rights advocate. His grandfather was the abolitionist William Lloyd Garrison, founder of the *Liberator*, and his father was Henry Villard, a newspaperman turned railroad owner. In 1881 he bought the *New York Evening Post* and the *Nation*. When his son joined the *Post* in 1897 he resolved to make both newspapers worthy followers of the *Liberator*, and under his leadership in the early twentieth century they became staunch advocates of civil rights. In 1909 he played an important role in forming the National Association for the Advancement of Colored People: he wrote the call for the National Negro Conference held in New York City on 31 May and 1 June, where the plans for a permanent organization were formulated. With Rollo Ogden, editorial page editor of the *Post*, he made the newspaper a progressive, anti-imperialist reformer. During the First World War he was attacked for being insufficiently anti-German. When the war ended he sold the *Post*, which was in debt, and turned his attention to the *Nation*, which he made into a liberal crusader and which he continued to edit until his retirement in 1933. Villard was a member of the Cosmopolitan Club in New York City, an interracial group. A consistent pacifist, in later years he opposed the Second World War. Villard's published writings include *Some Newspapers and Newspaper-Men* (1923), *Prophets True and False* (1928), *Our Military Chaos* (1939), and a biography of John Brown (1943).

James M. McPherson: *The Abolitionist Legacy: From Reconstruction to the NAACP* (Princeton, N.J.: Princeton University Press, 1975), 330

Michael Green

Villard houses. Six brownstone houses built in 1882–83 on property that was purchased by the railroad magnate Henry Villard on Madison Avenue between 50th and 51st streets. The architect Joseph M. Wells of McKim, Mead and White skillfully organized the houses around a central courtyard to create the appearance of an Italian palazzo. Villard reserved the largest house for himself, but his residency was cut short when he declared bankruptcy in 1883 and the house was purchased by Whitelaw Reid. In 1980 the property was sold to Harry B. Helmsley, who preserved some of the interiors as part of the Helmsley Palace Hotel. The northern wing of the courtyard, not part of the hotel, is the home of the Municipal Arts Society, the Parks Council, the Architectural League, and a chapter of the American Institute of Architects.

William C. Shopsin: *The Villard Houses* (New York: Viking, 1980)

Elliott B. Nixon

Vincent Astor Foundation. Charitable organization formed in 1948 by Vincent Astor (*b* 15 Nov 1891; *d* 3 Feb 1959). During his lifetime the foundation annually contributed about $175,000 to such organizations as the Astor Home for Children in Rhinebeck, New York, the New York Public Library, and New York Hospital. His widow, Brooke Astor, became the head of the foundation in 1960. Under her strong leadership the foundation focused exclusively on making donations in New York City in such diverse fields as animal care, botanical gardens, community economic development, health care, homelessness, housing development, historic preservation and church renovation, vocational education, and zoos. Between 1969 and 1985 the foundation's annual giving averaged $7 million and included grants from its principal, which surpassed $100 million in 1972 but was reduced to $20 million by 1985, when the trustees agreed to make grants only from the foundation's income and to focus on projects in literacy and housing. By the end of 1984 grants from the foundation totaled $136 million, including $24 million for education, $23.9 million for museums, $17 million for youth programs, and $10 million for libraries. The foundation authorized grants of $3.2 million in 1991.

Brooke Astor: *Twenty-five Years of Giving in New York: The Vincent Astor Foundation* (New York: Vincent Astor Foundation, 1985)

Kenneth W. Rose

Vinegar Hill (i). Name formerly applied to New Brighton.

Vinegar Hill (ii). Neighborhood in northwestern Brooklyn (1990 pop. 4525), bounded to the north by the East River, to the east by the Brooklyn Navy Yard, to the south by Sands Street, and to the west by Bridge Street; it was once called Irishtown. A large tract of land was bought from the Sands brothers in 1800 by John Jackson, who named part of it Vinegar Hill, after the battle waged in 1798 during the Irish Revolution. Sands Street, the main artery, was adjacent to the mammoth navy yard and in its heyday was lined with bars, gambling dens, and brothels. During the Second World War industries in the neighborhood prospered. The population was working class and lived in nineteenth-century row houses. After the war major industrial firms in the area included Brillo (makers of steel wool) and Boorum and Pease. Vinegar Hill has a small but active population of artists.

Stephen Weinstein

Visiting Nurse Service of New York. Voluntary home care agency. The largest organization of its kind in the United States, it was formed in 1944, when the nursing services of the Henry Street Settlement acquired independent status and moved to 107 East 70th Street. In the early 1990s the service had a budget of more than $200 million and a staff of about a thousand nurses, who made more than two million home visits to more than seventy thousand patients. The service offers acute and long-term care to mothers, children, and AIDS patients, as well as hospice and home health aide care.

Report of the Henry Street Settlement, 1893–1918 (New York: Henry Street Settlement, 1918)

Karen Buhler-Wilkerson

Vitagraph Company. An open-air, rooftop motion picture studio, opened in 1898 by American Vitagraph in the Morse Building at 140 Nassau Street. The film *Burglar on the Roof* was produced at the studio during its first year. In 1900 the company moved its offices to 110–16 Nassau Street and then opened a

Visiting nurse on a rooftop on Hester Street, 1907

glass-enclosed studio in 1906 at 15th Street and Locust Avenue in Flatbush. Under the ownership of J. Stuart Blackton, Albert E. Smith, and William Rock, the facilities expanded rapidly between 1906 and 1915. Warner Brothers purchased American Vitagraph in 1925 and used the studio for many of its Vitaphone short subjects before closing it in 1939; it continued to process film there even after the National Broadcasting Company (NBC) bought the studio in 1952 and began using it for color television broadcasts. Interiors of Elia Kazan's *On the Waterfront* (1954) were shot in the studio. Part of the facility was bought by Yeshiva University in 1962, although NBC continued to use sections of it into the 1990s.

Charles Musser

Vladeck, Baruch Charney [Charney, Baruch] (*b* Dukora, Belarus, 30 Jan 1886; *d* New York City, 30 Oct 1938). Journalist and public official. Well known as a revolutionary orator in Russia, he arrived in the United States in 1908 and settled permanently in New York City in 1916. He worked first as the city editor and from 1918 as the general manager of the *Jewish Daily Forward*. From 1917 to 1921 he served on the Board of Aldermen, representing Williamsburg as a Socialist. He was the host of a weekly radio program that the *Forward* had on WEVD, and led the Jewish Labor Committee from its founding in 1934; in the same year he was appointed to the New York City Housing Authority. In 1937 he was elected as a candidate of the American Labor Party to the City Council, where he led the coalition supporting Mayor Fiorello H. La Guardia. In recognition of his interest in public housing, a housing project on the Lower East Side bears his name.

Daniel Soyer

Vogue. Weekly magazine launched in 1892 by Arthur Turnure and Harry McVickar. Intended for the élite of New York City, it was first edited by Josephine Redding; McVickar left shortly after 1900. The magazine increasingly emphasized fashion, and circulation rose steadily, reaching 25,000 by 1907. During the same year Turnure died and Marie Harrison, his sister-in-law, became the editor. In 1909 the magazine was bought by Condé Nast. Under Edna Woolman Chase from 1914 it became the leading publication in fashion, known for its sleek look; in addition to news about fashion it published innovative art and photography and experimented with new color techniques, types of paper, and methods of reproduction. In 1936 it absorbed Nast's unprofitable magazine *Vanity Fair*, and Frank Crowninshield, a former editor of *Vanity Fair*, joined its staff. Jessica Daves succeeded Chase in 1948, and after Nast's company became part of Advance Publications (led by S. I. Newhouse) Diana Vreeland left *Harper's Bazaar* to take over as the editor in 1962. She herself was succeeded in 1971 by Grace Mirabella, who added features about fashion for working women and saw circulation rise to more than 1.2 million. In 1988 S. I. Newhouse Jr. appointed Anna Wintour as the editor of the magazine; she set out to reach a younger audience.

Edna Woolman Chase and Ilka Chase: *Always in Vogue* (London: Victor Gollancz, 1954)
Caroline Seebohm: *The Man Who Was Vogue: The Life and Times of Condé Nast* (New York: Viking, 1982)

Mary Ellen Zuckerman

Voorhees Technical Institute. Private post-secondary school formed in 1881 as the New York Trade School by the architect Richard T. Auchmuty (1831–93). Specializing at first in the building and mechanical trades, it benefited from the financial support of Auchmuty and J. P. Morgan and from a charter granted by the state legislature in 1892, and by 1900 it was able to expand its offerings to include blacksmithing, tailoring, tinsmithing, gas fitting, printing, and electrical engineering. After the First World War the most popular courses were in automobile mechanics, plumbing and heating, electrical engineering, and sheet metal work. The school moved to 2nd Avenue between 66th and 67th streets in 1930 and added new programs in air conditioning and lithography. Veterans of the Second World War brought enrollment to a peak of 4106 in 1949. In 1961 the school began offering associate degrees and changed its name in honor of the industrialist and trustee Enders M. Voorhees. It moved to 450 West 41st Street in 1963. After discontinuing its apprenticeship program in the following year it was absorbed in 1971 by the New York City Community College of Applied Arts and Sciences, which maintained the campus until 1987 and in the same year gave the name Voorhees Hall to its own engineering technology building at 186 Jay Street in Brooklyn.

Marc Ferris

Vreeland [née Dalziel], **Diana** (*b* Paris, *ca* 1905; *d* New York City, 22 Aug 1989). Fashion editor. From 1936 she wrote a fashion column called "Why Don't You?" for *Harper's Bazaar*, and she was the fashion editor of the magazine in 1937–62. She exerted a profound influence on American fashion as the editor of *Vogue* in 1962–71 and as a consultant to the Costume Institute of the Metropolitan Museum of Art in 1971–89.

Caroline Rennolds Milbank

W

WABC. Radio station. It began broadcasting in October 1921 in Newark, New Jersey, as WJZ under the auspices of Westinghouse, and within a few months opened a studio at the Waldorf–Astoria in Manhattan. In 1924 the station was purchased by the Radio Corporation of America and moved to Aeolian Hall on 42nd Street, where it broadcast news, entertainment, sports, and coverage of political events (including the Democratic National Convention of 1924). When the National Broadcasting Company was formed in 1926 WJZ became the flagship station for its Blue Network. The network was acquired in 1943 by Edward J. Noble, and the station took its current name. When rock-and-roll became popular in the 1960s WABC was an innovator in a brand of programming known as "top forty," characterized by a limited playlist (consisting only of the forty best-selling records), a staff of disc jockeys whom the station heavily advertised as "personalities," frequent contests and promotions, and a policy of broadcasting selections requested by listeners (many of whom were teenagers). It became one of the most influential popular music stations in the United States and by 1968 had captured 25 percent of the radio audience in the metropolitan area, a huge share in a highly competitive market. Perhaps its best-known disc jockey was Bruce Morrow, known as Cousin Brucie. Competition from stations on the FM band inspired a change to an all-talk format in February 1982. In the mid 1990s the most popular programs on WABC were those of the conservative commentators Bob Grant and Rush Limbaugh. The station broadcasts at a frequency of 770 kHz.

Erik Barnouw: *The Tower of Babel: A History of Broadcasting in the United States* (New York: Oxford University Press, 1966)

Murray Burton Levin: *Talk Radio and the American Dream* (Lexington, Mass.: Lexington, 1987)

Bruce Morrow and Laura Baudo: *Cousin Brucie: My Life in Rock 'n Roll Radio* (New York: William Morrow, 1987)

Simon Frith, ed.: *Facing the Music: A Pantheon Guide to Popular Culture* (New York: Pantheon, 1989)

JillEllyn Riley, Rachel Sawyer

WABD-TV. Original name of WNYW-TV.

Wachtell, Lipton, Rosen and Katz. Law firm formed in 1965 by Herbert M. Wachtell (*b* 1932), Martin Lipton (*b* 1931), Leonard M. Rosen (*b* 1930), and George A. Katz (1931–89), all graduates of New York University Law School. In the late 1960s it began specializing in corporate mergers, most often as counsel to companies that were the target of hostile takeovers. Several partners teach at New York University Law School; a former dean of the school, Norman Redlich (*b* 1925), is of counsel. The offices are at 51 West 52nd Street.

Gilbert Tauber

Wadleigh High School. Secondary school opened in 1897 as Girls' High School on East 12th Street, the first public high school for girls in Manhattan. It took its current name in 1900 to honor Lydia F. Wadleigh (*b* ?1818; *d* 1888), the superintendent of Normal College (later Hunter College) and an advocate of public schools for girls. In 1902 Wadleigh High School moved to 114th Street west of 7th Avenue, where it remained until it closed in 1954. The building is now occupied by Wadleigh Junior High School.

Erica Judge

Wagner, Robert F(erdinand) (i) (*b* Nastätten, Germany, 8 June 1877; *d* New York City, 5 May 1953). Senator, father of Robert F. Wagner (ii). He emigrated to the United States and settled in New York City in 1886. His political career began in Yorkville, where he joined the Tammany Society. He won election to the state assembly in 1904 and the state senate in 1908, and was a justice of the New York State Supreme Court from 1918 to 1926. After gaining the support of Tammany Hall he was elected to the U.S. Senate in 1926. In office he became known as a leading spokesman for urban liberalism and the New Deal: he sponsored the National Labor Relations Act of 1935, the Social Security Act of 1935, and the Public Housing Act of 1937.
See also CIVIL SERVICE UNIONS and FACTORY INVESTIGATING COMMISSION.

Chris McNickle

Wagner, Robert F(erdinand) (ii) (*b* New York City, 20 April 1910; *d* New York City, 12 Feb 1991). Mayor, son of Robert F. Wagner (i). He graduated from Yale College, Yale Law School, and Harvard Business School, and was elected to the state assembly (1938–41), resigning to join the Army Air Corps and serve in North Africa during the Second World War. Under Mayor William O'Dwyer he served as tax commissioner (1945–47) and commissioner of housing and buildings (1947–49). He was elected borough president of Manhattan (1950–53) on the Democratic and Liberal lines, and in 1953 he was elected mayor of New York City as a Democrat, winning reelection in 1957 in a landslide after an unsuccessful campaign for the U.S. Senate in 1956 against Jacob K. Javits. In 1961 Democratic officials opposed his reelection after he split with Carmine DeSapio, leader of Tammany Hall, but with support from Herbert H. Lehman, Eleanor Roosevelt, and other reformers he won a decisive victory in the Democratic primary against Arthur Levitt, and then won the general election against his Republican opponent Louis Lefkowitz. His wife, Susan Edwards Wagner, died during his third term, and citing the claims on him of his sons he declined to seek a fourth term. In 1969 he ran for mayor again, narrowly losing the Democratic nomination to Mario Procaccino in a four-way primary.

As mayor Wagner launched the largest municipal public housing program in the nation and authorized city workers to establish unions with formal powers. He prided himself on his commitment to representing the common man, appointed blacks and Puerto Ricans to senior municipal positions, approved local legislation forbidding racial discrimination in housing (1957), and installed the first black Democratic party leader in New York City (J. Raymond Jones, 1964). Critics accused him of indecisiveness; supporters applauded his subtle effectiveness and his unusual ability to forge consensus on controversial issues.

His son, also named Robert F. Wagner (*b* 6 Jan 1944; *d* 15 Nov 1993), was a member of the City Council (1973–77), chairman of the City Planning Commission, deputy mayor, president of the Health and Hospitals Corporation, and president of the Board of Education (1986–89).

Philip Hamburger: *Mayor Watching and Other Pleasures* (New York: Rinehart, 1958)

Michael Ryan: "Back to School," *New York*, 10 Nov 1986

Chris McNickle: *The Be Mayor of New York* (New York: Columbia University Press, 1993)

Chris McNickle

Wagner College. Private four-year liberal arts college in Staten Island, on a wooded campus of eighty-six acres (thirty-five hectares) atop Grymes Hill and overlooking New York Harbor. It was founded in Rochester, New York, as the Rochester Lutheran Proseminary, and was associated with the Evangelical Lutheran Church in America. In 1884 the college was re-founded as Wagner Memorial Lutheran College. Owing in part to the influence of Frederic Sutter, a prominent German Lutheran pastor in Staten Island from 1907 to 1971, it moved in 1918 to the Cunard estate in Staten Island and was rededicated in honor of George Wagner, whose father helped to finance the first campus. In its early years at the new location the college was a six-year German Gymnasium with sixteen students and one professor, which prepared young men for a bilingual German–English ministry. Women were first admitted in 1933. The school was renamed Wagner Lutheran College in 1952 and retained its Lutheran affiliation into the 1990s. In 1959 it took its current name as an indication of its desire to be a small liberal arts college open to the general public. Wagner began recruiting more aggressively in the 1980s and undertook improvements in its computer and athletic fa-

introduced to a circle of writers for the *New Yorker* by his college classmate and brother-in-law S. J. Perelman. His first two novels were *The Dream Life of Balso Snell* (1931) and *Miss Lonelyhearts* (1933), a brilliant satire on moral alienation that sold poorly but is generally regarded as his masterpiece. He left New York City to pursue screenwriting in Hollywood, where he underwent periods of unemployment and poverty. Shortly after the publication of his highly acclaimed novel *The Day of the Locust* (1939) West died in an automobile accident.

Frank Morrow

Westbeth. A complex of thirteen buildings in lower Manhattan, bounded to the north by Bethune Street, to the east by Washington Street, to the south by Bank Street, and to the west by West Street. Designed by Cyrus L. W. Eidlitz and others and built from 1880 to 1900, it was used as a research center by the American Bell Telephone Company, and the vacuum tube, the condenser microphone, and the transistor were all invented there (for illustrations see BELL TELEPHONE LABORATORIES and TELEPHONY). After the firm moved to New Jersey the J. M. Kaplan Fund helped to convert the buildings into artists' housing in 1965; this marked the first conversion of industrial lofts into residential space on a large scale. The inner court as redesigned by Richard Meier and Associates is notable for its stark geometry and semicircular fire egress balconies.

John Voelcker

West Brighton (i). Name by which WEST NEW BRIGHTON is sometimes known.

West Brighton (ii). Neighborhood in southwestern Brooklyn (1990 pop. 16,000), bounded to the north by Neptune Avenue, to the east by Ocean Parkway, to the south by the Atlantic Ocean, and to the west by Stillwell Avenue; south of Surf Avenue stretches a network of narrow walks that were once crammed with restaurants, cheap hotels, carousels, roller coasters, saloons, and amusement stands. The name was most widely used during the late nineteenth century, when the blocks between West 10th and West 16th streets were among the most notorious in the nation and the first houses were built in an area known as the Gut along West 1st, 2nd, and 3rd streets. Blacks who worked at racetracks nearby and Jewish peddlers at the shore settled in the neighborhood. Substandard one- and two-story frame houses remained until the 1950s, when the land was cleared under urban renewal programs and used for more than fifteen apartment buildings of twenty-three stories each, including Trump Village and the Warbasse Houses. The New York Aquarium, built in 1957 at West 8th Street, became an important research center and tourist attraction. The 1980s saw an influx of immigrants from the Soviet Union. The hub of the neighborhood is a shopping center in Trump Village at West 5th Street. Recreational attractions include the ocean, the beach, Seaside Park, which offers summer concerts, and a small part of the amusement district of Coney Island. Much of the population is elderly.

Martha Munzer and Helen Vogel: *Block by Block: Rebuilding City Neighborhoods* (New York: Alfred A. Knopf, 1973)

Stephen Weinstein: "The Nickel Empire: Coney Island and the Creation of Urban Seaside Resorts in the United States" (diss., Columbia University, 1984)

Stephen Weinstein

Westchester Square. Neighborhood in the east central Bronx, centered at an intersection of the same name. English colonists from Connecticut established a village there in 1654 that was the first European settlement in what is now the Bronx. Called Oostdorp (east village) by the Dutch, it was formally acquired in 1664 by Great Britain and renamed West Chester, and the settlers solidified their claims with the Indian treaty of 1692. In the following year an Anglican church was founded that is now known as St. Peter's Episcopal Church. The hamlet became a river port on Westchester Creek, and sea captains and crewmen made up a sizable part of the Anglican and Quaker community. In 1776 the village suffered a weeklong cannonade from British and Hessian forces, but the Continental Army dismantled a bridge over the creek, forcing the enemy to detour to Pell's Point. Fort Schuyler was built on Throgs Neck in the 1840s, and new families, chiefly Irish Catholics, settled in the area as builders, laborers, and stonemasons. During the Civil War rioters invaded the village in 1863 to destroy draft records, unaware that these were safe in Fort Schuyler. The twentieth century brought subway lines, streetcars, and buses to the area, which changed into a busy hub of commerce. The neighborhood remains an important junction, with thriving businesses, banks, shops, churches, schools, and hospitals.

John McNamara: *History in Asphalt: The Origin of Bronx Street and Place Names* (New York: Bronx County Historical Society, 1984)

John McNamara: *McNamara's Old Bronx* (New York: Bronx County Historical Society, 1989)

John McNamara

Westerleigh. Neighborhood in north central Staten Island, bounded to the north by Forest Avenue, to the east by Manor Road, to the south by Watchogue Road, and to the west by Wooley Avenue. It consisted originally of woods and farmland and was first developed in 1887 by the National Prohibition Campground Association, which purchased twenty-five acres (ten hectares) of land and opened Prohibition Park. The University Temple was built in 1891; an auditorium seating four thousand, it attracted such nationally known speakers as William Jennings Bryan before being destroyed by fire in 1903. In 1892 the area took its present name. The Westerleigh Collegiate Institute, a private secondary school, opened in 1895. Many local streets were named for prohibitionists and for states that voted for Prohibition. In the 1890s Westerleigh was a close-knit, upper-class neighborhood with narrow streets and one-family houses, many of which were built during the decade. Well-known residents included Isaac Funk, the editor of the *Funk and Wagnalls Encyclopedia*, the poet Edwin Markham, and the etiquette writer Amy Vanderbilt. The center of the neighborhood is Westerleigh Park; there is no commercial section. Landmarks include Westerleigh Park and its octagonal bandstand (built 1923, renovated 1990), the Immanuel Union Church, and 208 Neal Dow Avenue, a house designed by Ernest Flagg. The Westerleigh Improvement Society (1893) is one of the oldest neighborhood associations in the city.

Barnett Shepherd

Western Electric. Firm of telecommunications equipment manufacturers, incorporated in 1915 in New York City as a wholly owned subsidiary of American Telephone and Telegraph (AT&T). It was a successor to a concern based in Chicago that since 1882 had developed, manufactured, engineered, installed, and maintained telephone equipment and systems for AT&T and its operating companies. The firm was important in enabling AT&T to dominate American telephony and remain technologically advanced. It was also the research arm of the American Bell Telephone Company until the formation of Bell Laboratories in 1925. In 1984 AT&T was divested of its regional operating companies, and the functions of Western Electric were absorbed by the operating companies and various business units of AT&T. The name Western Electric continues to be used by AT&T for products of its network systems.

George David Smith

Western Union. Firm established in 1851 as the New York and Mississippi Valley Printing Telegraph Company, and based during its early years in Rochester, New York. It expanded rapidly by means of agreements with several railroads, which provided rights of way and lines in exchange for trained operators and priority service for railroad messages. Renamed the Western Union Telegraph Company in 1855, the firm soon commanded the most important western routes. During the 1850s liberal incorporation laws passed by the state legislature of New York allowed it to take over many small, regional companies and in doing so to reorganize the industry. With five other companies including the American Telegraph Company it made an agreement in 1857 to divide the market into clearly defined territories; Western Union abrogated the agreement in 1860 by obtaining a government subsidy to build a transcontinental telegraph, which by garnering large government subsidies during the Civil War gave the firm a distinct competitive advantage. By 1866 it had acquired control of its major competitors and moved its headquarters to 145 Broadway in New York City.

After the war the capitalist Jay Gould became the most formidable competitor of Western Union by building his own company that combined telegraph lines from his railroad empire with those of small companies. In 1871 Western Union acquired the Gold and Stock Telegraph Company and operated it as a subsidiary that remained the most important commercial news and market-reporting company to the end of the century. Gould's unrelenting competition allowed him to gain control of Western Union in 1881; his consolidation of the industry reduced opportunities for small telegraph operators and led them to strike in 1883, without success. Western Union entered into exclusive agreements to transmit news for the Associated Press and messages through the national network of American District Telegraph, which it reorganized in 1901 into the alarm company that came to be known in the late twentieth century as ADT. At the same time the near-monopoly in telegraphy achieved by Western Union faced a new challenge from the long-distance telephone network of American Telephone and Telegraph, which briefly acquired control of Western Union in 1909; antitrust action soon led to the separation of the two firms. After the Second World War telegraphy was largely supplanted by other systems, but Western Union continued to be an important telecommunications company until the early 1980s, launching the first communications satellite and establishing one of the first electronic mail services. Later in the decades the firm abandoned most of its communications business and concentrated on financial services, including money transfers (which it began in 1871) and priority message services such as "mailgrams," an overnight mail service introduced in 1970.

Robert Luther Thompson: *Wiring a Continent: The History of the Telegraph Industry in the United States, 1832–1866* (Princeton, N.J.: Princeton University Press, 1947)

Edwin Gabler: *The American Telegrapher: A Social History, 1860–1900* (New Brunswick, N.J.: Rutgers University Press, 1988)

Paul B. Israel: *From the Machine Shop to the Industrial Laboratory: Telegraphy and the Changing Context of American Invention, 1830–1920* (Baltimore: Johns Hopkins University Press, 1992)

See also TECHNOLOGY.

Paul Israel

Westervelt, Jacob Aaron (*b* Tenafly, N.J., 20 Jan 1800; *d* New York City, 21 Feb 1879). Shipbuilder and mayor. For about fifty years he had a shipbuilding firm on the East River that produced about two hundred seagoing vessels. Considered honest but weak during his term as mayor from 1852 to 1854, he introduced reforms and reorganized the police department but was widely criticized for the filthy condition of the streets.

James E. Mooney

West Farms. Neighborhood in the central Bronx, bounded to the north by Bronx Park, to the east by the Bronx River, to the south by Hunts Point, and to the west by Southern Boulevard; some of those who live east of the Bronx River also consider themselves residents of the neighborhood. From about 1812 the area was the site of paint, glass, pottery, and bleaching factories, flour mills, a sawmill, and coal yards, and a large area around it was incorporated as a town in 1846. This was initially named Ten Farms before being renamed for its location west of the village of Westchester. From the Civil War to the 1930s the area was a thriving river port. In 1874 the town was annexed to New York City and became part of the Annexed District, or North Side. After the subway was extended to White Plains Road, apartment buildings were constructed and shops opened; several of these were replaced during a renewal project of the 1960s. In the mid 1990s the population was mostly Latin American, and manufacturing and commerce continued to dominate the neighborhood.

John McNamara: *History in Asphalt: The Origin of Bronx Street and Place Names* (New York: Bronx County Historical Society, 1984)

John McNamara: *McNamara's Old Bronx* (New York: Bronx County Historical Society, 1989)

Gary D. Hermalyn

Westfield. Former administrative district in southwestern Staten Island, bounded to the north by Fresh Kills and Richmond Creek, to the east by Gifford's Lane, to the south by Lower New York Bay, and to the west by the Arthur Kill; towns within its boundaries included Tottenville, Pleasant Plains, Prince's Bay, Woodrow, Kreischerville, Rossville, Greenridge, Annadale, and parts of Eltingville and Great Kills. The district was established after the American Revolution. It was variously called West Division and West Quarter, and the area encompassing it and Southfield was sometimes called Southside. The seat was Richmondtown, in Southfield. The district was dissolved when New York City was consolidated in 1898.

Marjorie Johnson

West Flushing. Original name of CORONA.

Westies. Irish–American gang based in Hell's Kitchen. It was inspired by street gangs of the late nineteenth century and by organized crime and was notorious for violent crimes from the 1960s to the mid 1980s. The extent and coherence of the gang may have been exaggerated by law enforcement officials. Operating mostly from the docks of the West Side, its members successfully engaged in gambling and drug dealing until links with the Mafia led to internal rivalries and assassinations. The Westies disbanded after members were convicted of murder and racketeering.

T. J. English: *The Westies: Inside the Hell's Kitchen Irish Mob* (New York: G. P. Putnam's Sons, 1990)

Joshua Brown

West Jamaica. Original name of DUNTON.

Boston Road in West Farms, November 1898

Westminster Kennel Club. The oldest dog club in New York City and the best-known in the nation. It was formed by a group of sportsmen in 1876 and met in the Westminster Hotel near Union Square until the building was demolished at the turn of the century. Its first dog show was held in 1877 at the Hippodrome (popularly known as Gilmore's Gardens) at 26th Street and Madison Avenue. In 1880 the annual bench show first took place in Madison Square Garden, where it continued to be held with few exceptions; this became the largest annual show of its kind in the United States and the second-oldest continuous annual American sporting event (after the Kentucky Derby). The best-in-show award began in 1907. The club is a nonprofit organization with offices at 51 West 42nd Street.

Joseph S. Lieber

West New Brighton. Neighborhood in north central Staten Island (1980 pop. 32,865), sometimes referred to as West Brighton. The main streets include Richmond Terrace on the waterfront, Castleton Avenue, and Forest Avenue; Broadway and Jewett Avenue run north to south. The area was originally the site of a hunting lodge built in the late seventeenth century by Governor Thomas Dongan on his Manor of Castleton facing the Kill van Kull. The Kruzer–Pelton House, a rambling stone farmhouse at 1262 Richmond Terrace, and the Scott–Edwards House at 752 Delafield Avenue were also built during the colonial period. The first factory was established near Richmond Terrace and Broadway in 1819 by Barrett, Tileson and Company of Maine, reorganized in 1825 as the New-York Dyeing and Printing Establishment for cleaning and dyeing cloth. Factoryville was an early name for the area, and the brick buildings, smokestacks, and pond of the factory were long the principal features. By 1840 a commercial area had developed on Richmond Terrace and Broadway near the factories and the ferry landing at Castleton. Nathan Barrett left the New-York Dyeing and Printing Establishment in 1851 and formed Barrett, Nephews and Company, which opened a factory on Forest Avenue; this merged in 1890 with New-York Dyeing and Printing, and the operations of the new firm were consolidated at Broadway, where operations continued until 1932. A post office opened in 1871 and used the name West New Brighton (after New Brighton, an earlier and wealthier suburb). The C. W. Hunt Company, a manufacturer of heavy coal-handling equipment used in ports worldwide, built a plant in 1872 near Richmond Terrace and Van Street; this became the largest factory on Staten Island before closing during the Depression. Tompkins Department Store opened in 1877 and became the largest retail establishment on Staten Island. Calvary Presbyterian Church was formed in 1894, followed by Church of the Sacred Heart in 1898. Castleton Avenue was extended to Port Richmond in 1911 and became the principal commercial street; the *Staten Island Advance* had its offices at 1267 Castleton Avenue from 1913 to 1960. In 1936 the former estate of the Barrett family was made the site of the Staten Island Zoo. The local YMCA opened on Broadway in the 1950s. West Brighton Plaza, a complex of four hundred apartments subsidized by the federal government, opened in 1962.

The population of West New Brighton in 1980 was largely Italian, Irish, black, and Latin American. In the mid 1990s there were ship repair facilities on the waterfront and a wooded residential area on the southern boundary near the zoo. The West New Brighton Local Development Corporation and the Neighborhood Housing Services have invigorated the community and renovated nineteenth-century houses. Lawrence C. Thompson Park and its swimming pool occupy part of the site once occupied by the factory of New-York Dyeing and Printing.

Staten Island: A Resource Manual for School and Community (New York: Board of Education of the City of New York, 1964)

Dorothy Valentine Smith: "Factoryville," *Staten Island: Gateway to New York* (Philadelphia: Chilton, 1970), 122–28

Charles L. Sachs: *Made on Staten Island: Agriculture, Industry, and Suburban Living in the City* (New York: Staten Island Historical Society, 1988), 34–43, 68–69

Barnett Shepherd

West Side Highway. A popular name variously applied to the highways along the Hudson River in Manhattan. The name was first used for the Miller Elevated Highway (1931–48), an entirely elevated structure along West Street and 12th Avenue that originally extended from Rector Street to 72nd Street. In its early years the highway was noted for its artwork, which included cast-metal reproductions of the seal of New York City, but it suffered from heavy traffic and deferred maintenance. On 15 December 1973 a loaded dump truck plunged through a pothole near the Gansevoort Market, and the highway was closed south of 57th Street on the southbound side and 46th Street on the northbound side. Repairs were delayed as the city and state made plans to build Westway. Most of the elevated structure was demolished in stages from 1976 to 1989; the northernmost segment, between 59th Street to 72nd Street, was repaired and remained in use into the 1990s. The name West Side Highway is also applied to the Henry Hudson Parkway, which runs north from 72nd Street over the Henry Hudson Bridge and through the Bronx to the Westchester county line, where it connects with the Saw Mill River Parkway. It was built in the 1930s as part of Robert Moses's West Side Improvement Project, which included the construction of Riverside Park, and is noted for its graceful curves and riverside views. The section of the Henry Hudson within Manhattan was also closed for a time in the 1970s owing to deterioration from lack of maintenance, but was repaired and restored to use in its entirety.

WPAG

Rohit T. Aggarwala

West Side Tennis Club. Organization formed on 22 April 1892. The thirteen founders rented ground for three tennis courts on Central Park West between 88th and 89th streets. By the end of the first season the membership reached forty-three and two additional courts were built, and in 1897 the club was designated the sponsor of the Metropolitan Matches of the United States National Lawn Tennis Association (USNLTA; later renamed successively the United States Lawn Tennis Association and the United States Tennis Association). In 1902 the club, now with 102 members, moved to Morningside Heights, where it rented eight courts for $20 each from Mrs. John Drexel. The club moved again in 1908 to 238th Street and Broadway, where it rented two city blocks and built twelve grass courts and fifteen clay courts, as well as a two-story shingled clubhouse. In 1911 the club was invited by the USNLTA to stage the matches for the Davis Cup with Great Britain, for which the daily attendance exceeded three thousand. The club then bought ten acres (four hectares) of land in Forest Hills, and after the Davis Cup matches of 1913 were played at the old club the best of the turf was excavated and taken to the new one. In 1915 the new club became the site of the Nationals (now the U.S. Open), which had been held at Newport, Rhode Island, since 1881. The tournament remained at Forest Hills until 1978, except for the years 1921–23 when the men's Nationals were held elsewhere. In 1968 the first "pro-am" tournament in the United States was held at West Side. The club in the 1970s rebuilt the former Singer Bowl in Flushing Meadows: renamed Louis Armstrong Stadium in 1972, this became the centerpiece of the USTA National Tennis Center.

Robert Minton: *Forest Hills: An Illustrated History* (Philadelphia: J. B. Lippincott, 1975)

Eric Wm. Allison

Westway. A controversial building project introduced on 1 April 1972 by political and business leaders in New York City, who proposed to demolish the aging West Side Highway and build in its place a six-lane highway extending from the Battery to 42nd Street (with the portion north of Battery Park City placed underground), an incinerator, a bus depot, and a park; the name of the project was conceived by Deputy Mayor John E. Zuccotti. The plan won the support of such political leaders as

Mayor Abraham D. Beame, Governor Hugh L. Carey, and Nelson A. Rockefeller, leaders of business and labor, and groups such as the Regional Plan Association. Opponents led by Marcy Benstock and the New York Clean Air Campaign argued that the building of Westway would harm air quality and marine life, and that minority groups would receive an insufficient share of the construction work entailed by the project. In the first of many court hearings Judge Thomas P. Griesa of the Federal District Court ruled on 1 April 1982 that the U.S. Army Corps of Engineers had violated environmental requirements, and he ordered federal and state officials not to expend funds on Westway. On 30 March 1989 Governor Mario M. Cuomo, originally a supporter of the project, recommended that commercial development along the planned route be banned. Westway was effectively canceled when federal officials instructed the city and state on 10 August 1990 to repay funds that had been advanced to purchase rights of way.

Paul Ramon Pescatello: "Westway: The Road from New Deal to New Politics" (diss., Cornell University, 1986)

Mark H. Rose

wetlands. Ecosystems that are both terrestrial and aquatic, where the water table is usually at or near the surface and periodic saturation determines soil development, plant life, and animal life. From colonial times wetlands were believed to harbor disease and were thus considered nuisances that needed to be brought under control. This attitude and pressure to develop land around the city led most of the wetlands in the area to be drained, dredged, filled, and built on. From the 1960s scientists demonstrated the importance of wetlands as immensely productive habitats and natural means of flood control and water purification. Over the objections of landowners, federal protection was extended to most American wetlands by the mid 1970s, including most of those remaining in Manhattan, the Bronx, Queens, and Brooklyn. In 1975 the state legislature passed the Freshwater Wetlands Act, requiring the state's Department of Environmental Protection to map wetland sites of more than twelve acres (five hectares) and to prevent any construction injurious to them. In the mid 1990s wetlands on Staten Island remained the center of a struggle over conservation.

Some of the largest tidal wetlands in New York City are those in the Jamaica Bay Wildlife Refuge, a preserve of 9155 acres (3708 hectares) of land and water in the Gateway National Recreation Area known for its salt marshes and shore birds.

Steven D. Garber: *The Urban Naturalist* (New York: John Wiley and Sons, 1987)

Steven D. Garber

WEVD. Radio station. It began broadcasting in October 1927, the call letters chosen in honor of the recently deceased socialist leader Eugene V. Debs. Most of the programming in the early years was in Yiddish and expressed militant advocacy of the labor movement, to such an extent that the Federal Radio Commission sought to take the station off the air. After broadcasting for several years on the AM band it also obtained an FM license, which it relinquished in 1987. In the mid 1990s WEVD broadcast at a frequency of 1050 kHz and its programming was eclectic: programs in Yiddish, Greek, Russian, and French, music of the 1920s and 1930s, and coverage of college and professional sports.

Stephen Weinstein

WFAN. Radio station. It began operations at 1050 kHz on 1 July 1987 as the first station in the world broadcasting sports twenty-four hours a day. In October 1988 it bought the license of WNBC and moved to 660 kHz. The station offers play-by-play coverage of the Mets, Knicks, Jets, Rangers, and the basketball team of St. John's University, special events such as the World Series and the Super Bowl, and several call-in programs.

Jesse Drucker

WGBS. Original name of Wins.

Whalen, Grover A(loysius) (*b* New York City, 2 June 1886; *d* New York City, 20 April 1962). Public official. He oversaw many ticker-tape parades as chairman of the mayor's reception committee (1919–53), and as commissioner of the Department of Plant and Structures he was the principal figure behind the formation in 1924 of the municipal broadcasting system WNYC. Appointed police commissioner by Mayor James J. Walker in December 1928, he served for eighteen months during which he zealously pursued communist organizations. He was president of the corporation that administered the World's Fair of 1939–40 and in 1942 inaugurated the Coty American Fashion Critics' Annual Award for clothing design. Whalen wrote *Mr. New York: The Autobiography of Grover Whalen* (1955).

Kenneth R. Cobb

Wharton [née Jones], **Edith (Newbold)** (*b* New York City, 24 Jan 1862; *d* St.-Brice-sous-forêt, near Paris, 11 Aug 1937). Novelist. Born at 14 West 23rd Street, she was related to the most prominent families in New York City and spent much of her life in Europe and in Newport, Rhode Island; she eventually moved to 28 West 25th Street, where she lived with her husband until 1889, and in 1891 she bought a house at 884 Park Avenue, her last home in New York City. A close friend of Henry James, she wrote about conflicting values of different eras and places. Six of her books are set in the city and treat the metamorphosis of its élite as genteel provincialism cedes to the cosmopolitanism of the Gilded Age: *The Custom of the Country* (1913), *Hudson River Bracketed* (1929), *The Gods Arrive* (1932), *Old New York* (1924), containing four novelettes spanning the years from 1840 to 1880, *The Age of Innocence* (1920), which is set in the 1870s, and *The House of Mirth* (1905), which treats the city of her childhood where people had "always lived well, dressed expensively, and done little else."

See also Literature, §2.

Jeff Finlay

Wheeler [née Thurber], **Candace** (*b* Delhi, N.Y., 24 March 1827; *d* New York City, 5 Aug 1923). Writer and decorator. In 1844 she married Thomas Wheeler, a successful businessman and one of the founders of the National Academy of Design. She became central to the promotion of the decorative arts in the United States, wrote many engaging articles promoting interior and exterior home decorating and gardening, helped to form the Society of Decorative Artists and the Associated Artists, and was both the director of the Women's Building at the World's Columbian Exposition in Chicago in 1893 and the head of the Women's Art Committee. Her principal home was "Nestledown," a house built in 1854 in Hollis that until 1932 stood on the south side of Liberty Avenue between 186th and 187th streets. There she entertained such writers and artists as William Cullen Bryant, James Russell Lowell, Frank R. Stockton, Mark Twain, William Merritt Chase, John Burroughs, Albert Bierstadt, and Eastman Johnson. Wheeler's published writings include *Content in a Garden* (1901), *History of Embroidery in America* (1921), and her autobiography, *Yesterdays in a Busy Life* (1915).

Vincent Seyfried

Whig Party. Political party organized in 1834 that supported tariffs and internal improvements. It drew its support from a broad economic and ethnic spectrum, but was clearly the party of the middle and upper classes. The party elected five mayors between 1837 and 1850, owing much of its success to economic troubles, support from nativists, and divisions within the Democratic Party, its major opponent. The most influential Whig newspaper was the *New York Tribune*, edited by Horace Greeley. By embracing nativism the Whigs ultimately helped to strengthen the Democrats, who developed a broad base of support among immigrants. The Whig Party remained an important force in city politics until it disintegrated in the 1850s.

Evan Cornog

Edith Wharton *by Fernand Paillet, 1890. Miniature on ivory*

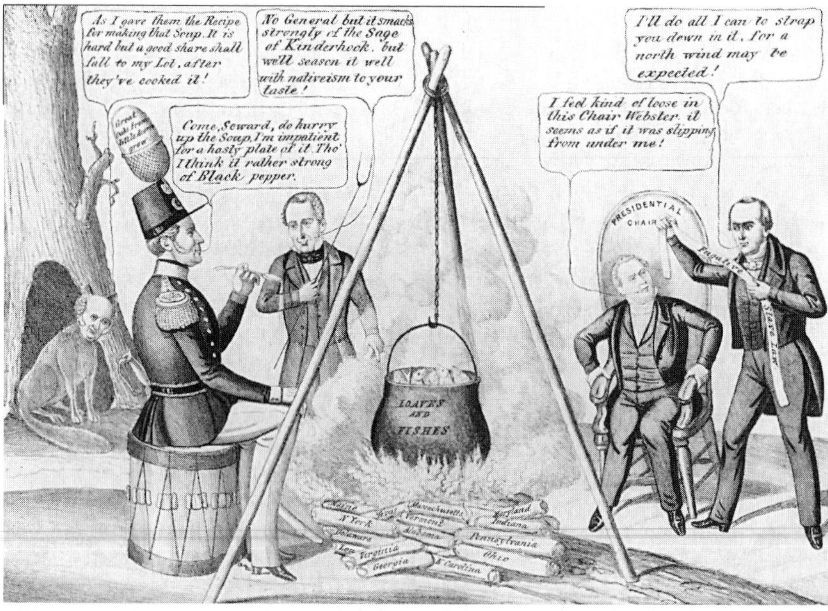

Caricature of Martin Van Buren, Winfield Scott, William H. Seward, Millard Fillmore, and Daniel Webster, 1852

White, Alfred T(redway) (*b* Brooklyn, 28 May 1846; *d* Harriman State Park, Orange County, N.Y., 30 Jan 1921). Housing reformer. As a student at Rensselaer Polytechnic Institute he became interested in building affordable model tenements for workers. After graduating he joined his father in a prosperous importing firm in Brooklyn and traveled frequently to London, where he visited innovative model housing estates. His first housing project, the Tower and Home Buildings, opened in Brooklyn in 1877 at the corner of Baltic and Hicks streets; modeled on houses built by Sir Sidney Waterlow in London and intended for well-paid and "respectable" workers, it had rents that guaranteed investors a return of 5 percent a year. White undertook several other projects that later influenced the work of City and Suburban Homes. He was also a member of several municipal commissions and was associated with a number of campaigns to improve tenements, including one to enforce building codes. As a trustee of the Russell Sage Foundation in 1920 he supported Charles Dyer Norton's efforts to draw up a regional plan, leading to the publication of the *Regional Plan of New York and Its Environs* in 1929 and 1931.

Anthony Jackson: *A Place Called Home: A History of Low Cost Housing* (Cambridge: MIT Press, 1976)

See also LIMITED-DIVIDEND HOUSING.

Stanley Buder

White, Clarence H(udson) (*b* West Carlisle, near Newark, Ohio, 7 April 1871; *d* Mexico City, 8 July 1925). Photographer. He produced some of his finest work in Newark, where he supported himself by working as a grocer's bookkeeper. After moving to New York City in 1906 he became an influential teacher and formed the Clarence H. White School of Photography in 1914; among his pupils were Doris Ullman, Laura Gilpin, Paul Outerbridge, and Anton Bruehl. A leading member of Alfred Stieglitz's Photo Secession, White helped to form the Art Center, an organization for designers, and the Pictorial Photographers of America, a national organization for amateurs.

Bonnie Yochelson

White, E(lwyn) B(rooks) (*b* Mount Vernon, N.Y., 11 July 1899; *d* Brooklin, Maine, 1 Oct 1985). Essayist. As an undergraduate at Cornell University (graduated 1921) he was the editor of the student newspaper. In 1925 was invited to write for the *New Yorker* by its editor, Harold Ross; he wrote the columns "Talk of the Town" (1926–38) and "Notes and Comment" (with James Thurber). After writing the column "One Man's Meat" for *Harper's* from 1938 to 1943 he returned to the *New Yorker* in 1945, where he remained for the next thirty years. In 1959 he helped William Strunk Jr., a professor at Cornell, to revise *The Elements of Style*, a guide to prose writing that became widely used. After retiring he moved to Brooklin. White is best known for his children's stories, especially *Stuart Little* (1945) and *Charlotte's Web* (1952); he also wrote a book about New York City, *Here Is New York* (1949). His wife, Katherine Angell White, was the first fiction editor at the *New Yorker*.

Janet Frankston

White [Weitz], **George** (*b* New York City, 1890; *d* Los Angeles, 10 Oct 1968). Theater producer. Born on the Lower East Side, he began his career as a dancer and appeared in several of Florenz Ziegfeld's *Follies*. In 1919 he produced the jazz revue *Scandals*, which he revived annually throughout the 1920s. Although his shows were less lavish than the *Follies*, they were praised for their distinctive sets, the stylish, revealing costumes worn by their showgirls, and the high quality of their dancers. White also produced *Runnin' Wild* (1923), among other shows.

George A. Thompson, Jr.

White, Stanford (*b* New York City, 9 Nov 1853; *d* New York City, 25 June 1906). Architect. He was born at 110 East 10th Street. In 1878 he traveled to Europe to complete his education, and while abroad he received an invitation to replace William B. Bigelow in the firm of McKim, Mead, and Bigelow as a specialist in drafting and interior design. He returned to the city in 1879 to become a partner in the firm, where he became known as the "master of effects." He admired European antiquities and bought many, which he often incorporated into the interiors of his new buildings. He married in 1884 and during a second trip to Europe gradually abandoned the picturesque aesthetic of H. H. Richardson, a former teacher, and began to formulate a style based on the symmetrical styles of the Italian Renaissance. Named the "free classical" style in 1887, this combined features of several European styles but had no contemporary European equivalent and was White's response to the firm's renewed emphasis on ordered designs under the direction of the principal designer, Joseph M. Wells. Primarily Italian in form, many of White's buildings were made of tawny Roman brick and decorated with terra cotta ornaments. In his free time he also designed book covers, picture frames, and bases for statues and even decorated the city for public celebrations; a temporary arch that he designed for a parade commemorating George Washington's inauguration along 5th Avenue was later rebuilt in stone and set in Washington Square.

At the height of his career in the 1890s White was one of the principal architects of the firm and lived sumptuously, in part from the income that he earned by importing boatloads of antiquities that he sold to clients for their grand homes. He had a studio in the tower of Madison Square Garden and for a time lived in a rented house at 121 East 21st Street and in rooms at 22 West 24th Street. By the mid 1890s he had abandoned the free classical style for the popular styles of the École des Beaux-Arts that adapted the styles of well-known European buildings; he later returned to the free classical style.

Among White's many friends were artists as well as businessmen, and he often returned to the office late after evenings out, producing large quantities of drawings. One of the most prolific architects of the late nineteenth century, he produced many designs, some drawn on table napkins. During the early 1890s he was diagnosed with renal disease and for the rest of his life he visited doctors and sought cures in spas and bottled water. His public and private life became so lavish that he fell deeply in debt. In 1905 he was forced to relinquish his partnership and become a salaried employee. He was quite ill when he was shot and killed on the roof garden of Madison Square Garden by Harry K. Thaw, a wealthy man from Pittsburgh who had long been obsessed with White and suspected him of romantic involvement with his wife, Evelyn Nesbit. After a long, sensational trial Thaw was sent to a mental institution and then allowed to go free. White's reputation was scarred for two generations, his accomplishments played down and his remarkable storehouse of collected treasures thought to be bogus. He was later recognized as a master of creative effects and an important art collector.

Charles C. Baldwin: *Stanford White* (New York: Dodd, Mead, 1931)

Leland M. Roth: *McKim, Mead and White* (New York: Harper and Row, 1983)

Paul R. Baker: *Stanny* (New York: Free Press, 1989)

For illustration see MADISON SQUARE GARDEN.

Mosette G. Broderick

White, Walter (Francis) (*b* Atlanta, 1 July 1893; *d* New York City, 21 March 1955). Writer and civil rights leader. He graduated from Atlanta University in 1916 and in 1918 was appointed the assistant secretary of the National Association for the Advancement of Colored People (NAACP) by James Weldon Johnson, whom he succeeded as its executive secretary in 1931. He expanded the number of branches of the association, increased its membership to more than half a million, and helped to form the NAACP Legal Defense and Educational Fund. Because of his fair skin, blond hair, and blue eyes he was often thought to be white, which helped him to investigate forty-one lynchings and eight race riots. During the Second World War he toured Europe and Japan as a special correspondent for the *New York Post* (1943–45). He played an important role in preparing the NAACP for its victory in the school desegregation case *Brown v. Board of Education* (1954). White wrote two novels and three works of nonfiction, among them *A Man Called White* (1948).

R. L. Harris, Jr.

White and Case. Law firm opened on Nassau Street on 1 May 1901 by Justin White and George Brown Case. Begun with $500 in capital, it soon played a crucial role in forming the Bankers Trust Company. The firm gained many clients through Case's work for the Red Cross; during White's tenure on the Palisades Park Commission he obtained gifts of land from W. Averell Harriman that were important in completing the highway system. It also aided the country's shipbuilding program during the First World War through the efforts of Charles Fey, handled the affiliation of New York Hospital with Cornell University in 1937, represented all underwriters selling bonds issued by the Municipal Assistance Corporation during the city's fiscal crisis in the 1970s, and supervised the takeover of Marathon Oil by U.S. Steel in 1981. In 1989 it had 104 partners, 377 associates, and revenues of more than $144 million. White and Case provides its services pro bono for the Legal Aid Society and the National Association for the Advancement of Colored People. It has offices at 1155 6th Avenue.

George J. Lankevich

White Horse Tavern. Tavern built in 1880 at the corner of Hudson and West 11th streets in Greenwich Village. A certified landmark and one of the few wood-framed buildings remaining in the city, it was a speakeasy throughout Prohibition and a seamen's bar until the late 1940s, when it was frequented by the Welsh poet Dylan Thomas, who stayed at the Chelsea Hotel during his visits to New York City. By the time of his death in 1953 the tavern had become a popular meeting place for young writers and artists, with a room dedicated to Thomas's memory. The tavern figures prominently in Jane Jacobs's influential book *The Death and Life of Great American Cities* (1961).

Ann Charters

Whiteman, Paul (*b* Denver, 28 March 1890; *d* Doylestown, Penn., 29 Dec 1967). Bandleader. After moving to New York City in 1920 he organized a dance band that played at the Palais Royale. He gained popularity through his performances in Florenz Ziegfeld's *Follies* and his recording of *Whispering* (1920), the first disc to sell a million copies. During the 1920s he was the first important figure to incorporate jazz elements into popular music, and he used the nickname the "King of Jazz." At Aeolian Hall on West 42nd Street in 1924 he gave a concert called "An Experiment in Modern Music"; this featured his own arrangements, which incorporated elements of jazz into concert music, along with the first performance of *Rhapsody in Blue* by George Gershwin. He helped to develop the role of the modern arranger by relying on the orchestrations of Ferde Grofé; he also worked with the arranger Bill Challis and performed with the cornetist Bix Beiderbecke, the saxophonist Frank Trumbauer, the bandleaders Tommy and Jimmy Dorsey, the violinist Joe Venuti, the xylophonist Red Norvo, and the singer Bing Crosby, who performed with him between 1926 and 1930 as one of the Rhythm Boys. After his popularity declined in the 1930s he worked in films and radio and in 1943 became the music director of the Blue Network (later the American Broadcasting Company). For many years he owned a farm in New Jersey. Whiteman is best known for introducing an attenuated brand of jazz to a wide audience and for influencing big-band arrangements.

Loren Schoenberg

Whitepot. Name of unknown origin applied until 1910 to REGO PARK and FOREST HILLS GARDENS. In colonial times there were farms owned by the Furman, Springsteen, and Boerum families along what is now Yellowstone Boulevard and Whitepot Road (now 66th Avenue). During the American Revolution British troops were stationed around the Dow Van Duyn house at what is now the intersection of Woodhaven Boulevard and 67th Avenue. The old Whitepot School House stood for years at Woodhaven Boulevard and 66th Avenue. As the area was developed the name Whitepot became disused.

Vincent Seyfried

White Russians [White Ruthenians]. Name sometimes used before 1945 for BELARUSANS.

Whitestone. Neighborhood in north central Queens, bounded to the north by the East River, to the east by Clearview Expressway, to the south by Bayside Avenue and 29th Avenue, and to the west by Whitestone Expressway. The area was settled in 1645. During the American Revolution the British burned the house near 152nd Street and 7th Avenue of the patriot Francis Lewis (later a signer of the Declaration of Independence). In 1838 or 1839 Walt Whitman probably taught in a building on the west side of 11th Avenue between 12th and 13th streets, and the neighborhood was renamed Clintonville in the 1840s for De Witt Clinton. John D. Locke, a manufacturer of tinware and copperware, moved to the area from Brooklyn in 1853 to build a large stamping works; many of his workers moved with him, and by 1860 the population reached eight hundred. A Methodist church was formed in 1850, the first school opened in 1857, and the area was incorporated as a village in April 1869. A number of wealthy New Yorkers built mansions along the East River in the 1880s and 1890s. At the foot of 152nd Street and the foot of Clintonville Street were picnic parks that served steamboat excursion parties from Manhattan and Brooklyn. Stimmel's and Duer's parks had hotels, bars, dancing pavilions, and baseball grounds; crowds were often rowdy and drunken, and the resorts were closed during Prohibition.

Whitestone, 14th Avenue and 150th Street, ca 1941

The Shore Acres Realty Company built a development called Beechhurst at the eastern end of the village in 1906, and in 1909 the trolley was extended to the area, linking it with Flushing and Bayside. During a period of rapid development in the 1920s the southern section was enlarged; streets were laid out and houses built on former farmlands. Railroad service ended during the Depression, but the right of way was used for the Belt Parkway, which was completed in 1938 and provided access to the Bronx–Whitestone Bridge (1939). After the Second World War a large apartment complex was built on the shore between 162nd Street and the Throgs Neck Bridge. Much of Whitestone is upper middle class; the original village and the area south of the parkway are covered by houses and tree-lined streets.

Vincent Seyfried

Whitman, Walt(er) (*b* West Hills, N.Y., 31 May 1819; *d* Camden, N.J., 26 March 1892). Poet. One of nine children in a family of farmers, he taught briefly before turning to journalism. He lived at 41 Tillary Street in Broklyn from 1827 to 1832 and between 1840 and 1845 worked as an editor and printer; he also submitted poems and short stories to such prominent journals as the *Democratic Review*, which published his first poem, "Death in the Schoolroom," in August 1841. In 1842 he left his position as the editor of the *Long Islander* to take charge of the *Aurora*, and within two months he wrote an eloquent commentary on the city's evolving identity. During the same year he lived in a boarding house at 12 Centre Street in Manhattan. He soon returned to Brooklyn, where he spent much of his career and lived at 120 Front Street (1843–44). He became the editor of the *Brooklyn Daily Eagle* in 1846 but resigned in 1847 over his support for the Free Soil Party. From February to May 1848 he visited New Orleans. After returning to Brooklyn he built a house at 106 Myrtle Avenue in 1849 and remained there for three years; he later lived at 142 Skillman Street (1854–55) and 107 Portland Avenue (1859–63). Whitman continued to be associated with the region and lived there briefly in 1870 and 1878. Much of his work is devoted to the city, which he called "the great place . . . the heart, the brain, the focus . . . the no more beyond of the western world." Joyful images suffuse his articles about the city for *Life Illustrated* (1853) and such poems in *Leaves of Grass* (1855) as "A Broadway Pageant," "Give Me the Splendid Silent Sun," "Crossing Brooklyn Ferry," and especially "Manahatta I," a paean to the city's growth.

Joseph J. Rubin and Charles H. Brown: *Walt Whitman of the New York Aurora* (State College: Pennsylvania State University Press, 1950)

Gay Wilson Allen: *The Solitary Singer: A Critical Biography of Walt Whitman* (New York: Macmillan, 1955)

Jeff Finlay

Whitney, Gertrude Vanderbilt (*b* New York City, 9 Jan 1875; *d* New York City, 18 April 1942). Sculptor and arts patron. She confounded traditional expectations to become a sculptor in 1900; her work was in a traditional figurative style but her sympathies were with liberal artists and artistic movements. In 1907 she took a studio at 19 MacDougal Alley and joined the artistic community in Greenwich Village. Her interest in progressive art became known when she

Gertrude Vanderbilt Whitney working on Winged Victory *with her assistant S. F. Bilotti,* ca *1939*

bought four paintings from the historic exhibition of The Eight in 1908, and donated $1000 to the Armory Show in 1913. Between 1914 and 1920 she gained national renown as a sculptor. She leased the townhouse attached to her studio (8 West 8th Street) in 1912 and converted it into the Whitney Studio, an exhibition space that opened in December 1914; in 1918 she established the Whitney Studio Club, a meeting place and gallery for young artists spurned by dealers. After the First World War she received many commissions for public monuments and also had exhibitions of her work in New York City, London, and Paris. The Whitney Studio and the Whitney Studio Club were eventually replaced by the Whitney Studio Galleries (1928–30), which continued to support hundreds of artists through stipends, exhibitions, and purchases of their work. After her collection was rejected by the Metropolitan Museum of Art she founded the Whitney Museum of American Art in 1930 at 8–14 West 8th Street, for which she is best remembered. Examples of Whitney's public sculptures in the city are the Washington Heights War Memorial (1921, Broadway and 168th Street) and *Peter Stuyvesant* (1936, Stuyvesant Square).

B. H. Friedman: *Gertrude Vanderbilt Whitney* (Garden City, N.Y.: Doubleday, 1978)

Janis Conner and Joel Rosenkranz: *Rediscoveries in American Sculpture: Studio Works, 1893–1939* (Austin: University of Texas Press, 1989)

Avis Berman

Whitney, Richard (*b* Beverly, Mass., 1 Aug 1888; *d* Short Hills, N.J., 5 Dec 1974). Financier. The son of a bank president in Boston, he attended Harvard University before taking a seat on the New York Stock Exchange at the age of twenty-three. He became the principal brokerage agent for J. P. Morgan and Company and rose to national prominence during the crash of 1929, when he temporarily stabilized prices by buying stocks for large banks. Elected to the first of four terms as president of the exchange in 1930, he became a symbol of conservative elements who opposed regulatory reform. In 1938 his brokerage firm declared bankruptcy, and investigators discovered that he had embezzled money from a number of customers. He pleaded guilty to embezzlement, served a prison sentence at the state penitentiary in Sing Sing, and never returned to the securities business. The scandal surrounding Whitney had long-lasting effects on Wall Street by inaugurating a period of new leadership and regulatory reform at the New York Stock Exchange.

George Winslow

Whitney, William Collins (*b* Conway, Mass., 5 July 1841; *d* New York City, 2 Feb 1904). Financier. After graduating from Yale University he studied law and opened a practice in New York City, where he had a house at 2 West 57th Street. A Democrat opposed to the Tweed Ring, he supported Grover Cleveland in the presidential election of 1884 and was secretary of the navy from 1885 to 1889. He returned to the city, where he helped to finance utilities and the Metropolitan Street Railway Company. After taking up horse breeding in Lexington (Kentucky) and Saratoga (New York) he won the English Derby and in 1902 published *The Whitney Stud*, a horse-breeding guide. At the end of his life Whitney had ten residences, including a mansion designed by McKim, Mead and White at 5th Avenue and 68th Street.

James E. Mooney

Whitney Museum of American Art. First museum devoted to American art of the twentieth century, founded in 1930 by Gertrude Vanderbilt Whitney. It was preceded by several smaller experimental institutions begun by Whitney to promote living artists neglected by museums and commercial galleries. The Whitney Studio (8 West 8th Street) opened in December 1914 and was run by Juliana Rieser Force (1876–1948), who managed Whitney's activities and shaped her art collection. The Whitney Studio Club, another gathering place and gallery for young artists, opened in 1918 at 147 West 4th Street before moving to 10 West 8th Street in 1923. These institutions were replaced by the Whitney Studio Galleries (1928–30). After her collection of nearly five hundred objects was refused by the Metropolitan Museum of Art in 1929 Whitney established her own museum, with Force as the director; it occupied four townhouses (8–14 West 8th Street) and opened to the public on 18 November 1931. Contemporary and historical works were bought, and biennial and annual invitational exhibitions featured artists from all areas of the country. Hermon More (1887–1968) was appointed director in 1948, and during his tenure the museum moved to 22 West 54th Street. He was succeeded in 1958 by Lloyd Goodrich (1897–1987), who oversaw the construction

Whitney Museum of American Art (designed by Marcel Breuer), ca *1981*

of a gray granite building designed by Marcel Breuer and Hamilton Smith at 945 Madison Avenue, where the museum moved in 1966. Under the direction of John I. H. Baur (1968–74) Jean and Howard Lipman donated about two hundred pieces of sculpture: they became the museum's most important benefactors after the Whitney family. A branch gallery opened at 55 Water Street in 1973 and moved to 33 Maiden Lane in 1988 (later closed); other branches opened in Stamford, Connecticut (1981), at 120 Park Avenue (1983), and at 787 7th Avenue (1986, later closed). Thomas N. Armstrong III (*b* 1932), director from 1974 to 1990, expanded and broadened the permanent collection. The Whitney has the largest and most comprehensive collection of its kind: among its 8500 objects are works by every important American artist active in the twentieth century. It has unrivaled holdings by such artists as Alexander Calder, Edward Hopper, and Reginald Marsh, as well as many examples of Charles Burchfield, Stuart Davis, Jasper Johns, Gaston Lachaise, Georgia O'Keeffe, John Sloan, David Smith, and Frank Stella.

Avis Berman: *Rebels on Eighth Street: Juliana Force and the Whitney Museum of American Art* (New York: Atheneum, 1990)

Avis Berman

wildlife. See FAUNA.

Willets Point. The northwestern point of Fort Totten in northeastern Queens. At one time the name applied to all 150 acres (sixty-one hectares) of the peninsula on which the fort was built. The peninsula was known in the eighteenth century as Thorne's Neck, after its owner Jacob Thorne; the land was acquired in turn by William Wilkens, David Ousterman, Charles Willets (1829), and the federal government (1857). A movement in the U.S. Congress to erect a fort opposite Fort Schuyler in the Bronx that began when the government took title to the property was hastened by the outbreak of the Civil War, and construction began in 1862. But the invention of rifled bores in cannon made stone forts obsolete, and work was abandoned. In 1864–65 Grant Hospital treated members of the Union Army at the fort. At the behest of President William McKinley the fort was renamed in August 1898 to honor Brigadier General Joseph G. Totten (*b* 1838; *d* April 1864), director of the Bureau of Seacoast Defense in the Department of War.

Vincent Seyfried

William A. Read. Forerunner of the investment banking firm DILLON, READ.

William B. May. Firm of real-estate brokers, the oldest in New York State operating continuously under the same name. Formed in 1866, in the following decades it handled the property of such families as the Carnegies, the Fricks, and the Vanderbilts. It was also the first real-estate firm based uptown to open branches in Greenwich Village (1967) and Brooklyn Heights (1983). In the mid 1990s the firm was one of the largest residential and commercial brokerages in New York City.

Kenneth T. Jackson

William Cullen Bryant High School. Secondary school opened in 1889 as Long Island City High School in Smithsonian Hall at Vernon Boulevard and 4th Street in Queens; it was the first public high school in the borough. The school moved in 1890 to the Munson building on Astoria Avenue. In 1904 it merged with Woodside High School, moved to a new building at Academy and Reddee streets, and was renamed in honor of the poet and editor. It offered three courses of study: academic, commercial, and manual training. In 1939 it moved to 48-10 31st Avenue in Long Island City. William Cullen Bryant High School had 3300 students in 1991.

Erica Judge

William Esty Company. Advertising agency formed in 1932 by William Esty (1895–1954), a former employee of the firm of J. Walter Thompson. Its first client was the tobacco manufacturer R. J. Reynolds. From 1934 to 1945 one of its vice-presidents was the early behavioral psychologist John B. Watson. The agency became known in the advertising business for its low profile and for several memorable campaigns and slogans, including those for Noxzema shaving cream ("Take it off, take it all off"), Master Card ("Master the possibilities"), and Minolta cameras ("Only from the mind of Minolta"). In 1982 the agency was bought by Ted Bates and Company in an acquisition unprecedentedly large for the field of advertising. It nevertheless continued to operate autonomously until Ted Bates was acquired in 1986 by the firm of Saatchi and Saatchi, after which Esty lost more than half its clients and laid off much of its staff. In 1988 Saatchi and Saatchi merged Esty with Cambell–Mithun to form Cambell–Mithun–Esty. The new agency handled $892.5 million worth of billings in 1990.

George Winslow

William H. Sadlier. Firm of book publishers formed in 1832 in New York City by the brothers Dennis Sadlier (*d* 1885) and James Sadlier (*d* 1869), who had emigrated from Ireland to the United States earlier that year. The firm specialized in Catholic and educational titles as well as works relating to Ireland. In the mid 1990s William H. Sadlier was one of the oldest publishers in the city.

An American Imprint for 150 Years: The History of William H. Sadlier, Inc. (New York: William H. Sadlier, 1982)

John T. Ridge

William Morrow. Firm of book publishers formed in 1926 by William Morrow at 303 5th Avenue. It attracted many popular authors and soon achieved success by publishing best-sellers such as James Hilton's *Lost Horizon* (1935). During its early years the firm became known for the relative youth of its executives. In 1967 Morrow became a subsidiary of Scott, Foresman and Company, which sold it in 1981 to the Hearst Corporation. Among the notable books published by the firm over the years are *Coming of Age in Samoa* (1928) by Margaret Mead, *The Shoes of the Fisherman* (1963) by Morris West, *The Jewel in the Crown* (1967) by Paul Scott, *The Peter Principle* (1969) by Lawrence J. Peter and Raymund Hull, *Zen and the Art of Motorcycle Maintenance* (1974) by Robert M. Pirsig, *The Cider House Rules* (1985) by John Irving, more then 150 books by Erle Stanley Gardner (including the Perry Mason series), and the children's novels of Beverly Cleary. The current address is 1350 6th Avenue in Manhattan.

Eileen K. Cheng

Williams, Alexander S. (*b* Fairfax, Nova Scotia, 9 July 1839; *d* New York City, 25 March 1917). Police captain. During the 1880s and 1890s he enjoyed good relations with gamblers and procurers and was responsible for the evolution of the Tenderloin. Known as the "clubber" for his harsh justice, he retired with a house on East 10th Street, an estate in Connecticut, and a yacht.

Joseph P. Viteritti

Williams, Bert [Austin, Egbert] (*b* Antigua, 12 Nov 1874; *d* New York City, 4 March 1922). Comedian, singer, and dancer. After his family emigrated to the United States and settled in California he performed in minstrel shows and met his partner, George Walker. Billed as "Two Real Coons," they first performed in New York City in 1896 in the musical *The Gold Bug* and later became renowned in vaudeville. In black theater at the turn of the century they made the cakewalk popular and perfected comic routines in which Williams was the perpetually unfortunate "Jonah Man" and Walker a voluble dandy. They later formed a troupe and presented the musicals *In Dahomey* (1903), *Abyssinia* (1906), and *Bandana Land* (1908). After illness led to Walker's retirement in 1909 Williams performed briefly in vaudeville. In Florenz Ziegfeld's *Follies* he had a role from 1910 and a leading role between 1912 and 1920. An international star who also made recordings and films, he was identified by his mournful signature song "Nobody." Although he was black Williams was forced to perform in blackface so that his appearance would conform to racial stereotypes; he believed that the makeup limited the range of his roles and he became sorrowful and bitter. He spent the end of his life at 2309 7th Avenue.

Ann Charters: *Nobody: The Story of Bert Williams* (New York: Macmillan, 1970)

Robert W. Snyder

Williams, Peter (*b* New York City, 1750; *d* New York City, 1823). Sexton and tobacconist. Born a slave on Beekman Street, he converted to Methodism and in the 1770s became a sexton of the John Street Methodist Church. After being given his freedom by the church he established himself as a tobacconist on Liberty Street. He also helped to establish the Zion Church, a black Methodist congregation at Leonard and Church streets. His son was the prominent Methodist minister Peter Williams Jr.

Williams, Tennessee [Thomas Lanier] (*b* Columbus, Miss., 26 March 1911; *d* New York City, 25 Feb 1983). Playwright. He grew up in Mississippi and St. Louis and after college moved to New York City in the late 1930s. There he lived at the Royalton Hotel, the Hotel Shelton (on 44th Street at the East River), and the West Side YMCA and worked as a waiter at the Beggar Bar in Greenwich Village, an elevator operator in the San Jacinto Hotel (on Madison Avenue), and an usher in the Strand Theatre (on 47th Street and Broadway). His first play to be staged on Broadway was *The Glass Menagerie*, which in 1945 was named the best play of the year by the New York Drama Critics' Circle; the same award was given to his play *A Streetcar Named Desire* (1947), as was the Pulitzer Prize. Later works were also critically successful: *The Rose Tattoo* (1951, Tony Award for best play and playwright), *Cat On A Hot Tin Roof* (1955, New York Drama Critics' Circle award, Pulitzer Prize), and *The Night of the Iguana* (1961, New York Drama Critics' Circle award). From 1948 to the early 1950s he lived at 235 East 58th Street; in his later years he spent periods in New York City at 15 West 72nd Street (1965–68), 145 West 55th Street (mid 1960s), 400 West 43rd Street (for three years from 1978), and the Hotel Élysée, 54–60 East 54th Street (where he died). Williams is second only to Eugene O'Neill as an important and influential American playwright. His lyrical dramas are frequently set in the American South and feature vulnerable yet vibrant characters in search of love, sexual fulfillment, compassion, and dignity in a callous world. His *Memoirs* were published in 1975.

A. J. Devlin: *Conversations with Tennessee Williams* (Jackson: University of Mississippi Press, 1986)

Ronald Hayman: *Tennessee Williams: Everyone Else Is an Audience* (New Haven: Yale University Press, 1993)

Martha S. LoMonaco

Williamsbridge. Neighborhood in the north central Bronx, centered on Gun Hill Road and bounded to the north by East 233rd Street, to the east by Edenwald, to the south by the neighborhood of Pelham Parkway, and to the west by the Bronx River. It was named for a bridge built over the Bronx River in colonial times by John Williams, a local farmer. The area saw several battles and skirmishes during the American Revolution. A route to Manhattan was first provided in 1841 by the New York and Harlem Railroad. After Interborough Rapid Transit extended its subway to White Plains Road the population grew rapidly in the 1920s as Italian, Jewish, and black families moved in. The neighborhood became predominantly black in the 1960s. Almost all the recent immigrants who settled there in the 1980s were blacks from the Caribbean. Most were from Jamaica and many of the rest were from Guyana, the United Kingdom, Antigua–Barbuda, and the Dominican Republic. In the mid 1990s Williamsbridge remained a largely residential area of one-family houses; there was also a low-income development, the Gun Hill Houses.

Lloyd Ultan

Williamsburg(h). Neighborhood in northwestern Brooklyn (1990 pop. 100,000), bounded

Portrait of Peter Williams, ca *1810–15 (artist unknown)*

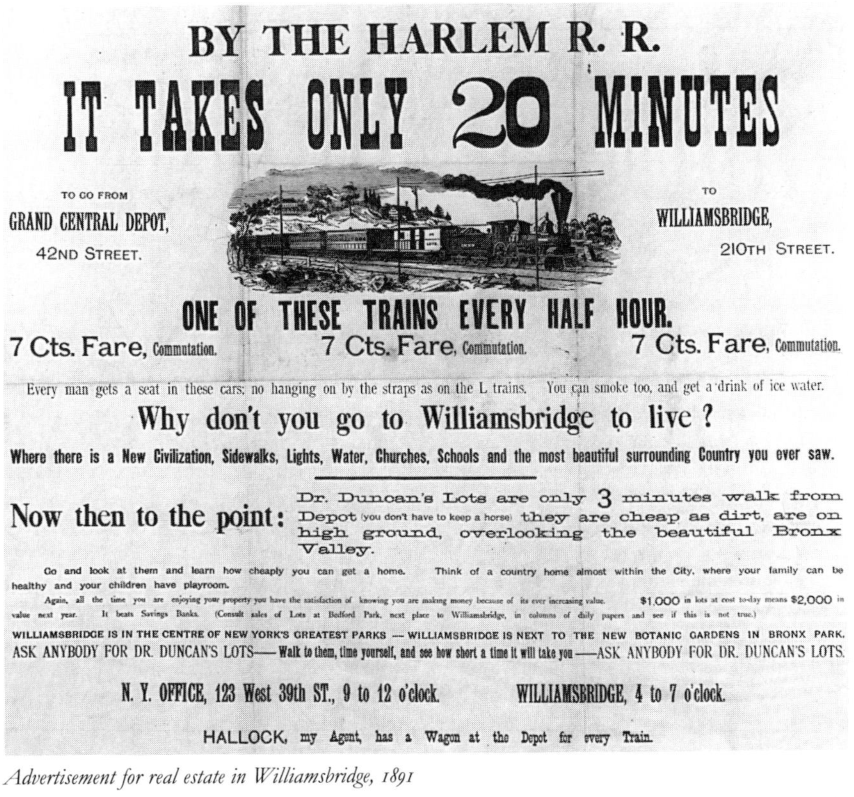

Advertisement for real estate in Williamsbridge, 1891

to the north by 7th Avenue and the Brooklyn–Queens Expressway, to the east by the Queens county line, to the south by Flushing Avenue, and to the west by the East River. Originally part of the Dutch village of Boswijck, the area was chartered in 1660. On marshy land along the East River between what are now South 7th Street and North 1st Street the first European settler, Jean Mesurolle of Picardy, built a farm that according to legend was a favorite boarding place of Captain Kidd. A number of Dutch, French, and Scandinavian farmers and African slaves settled in the area in 1663. A hamlet sometimes known as Cripplebush remained isolated until speculators took interest in land up the East River from the city of Brooklyn. From 1800 Richard M. Woodhull offered ferry service from Corlear's Hook in Manhattan to the foot of what is now North 2nd Street; hoping to develop a town for those working in Manhattan, he bought a parcel of thirteen acres (5.3 hectares) around the ferry landing and named it for Jonathan Williams, the surveyor of the area, but he declared bankruptcy in 1806 after selling only a few lots. Speculation increased after roads were built to replace roundabout tracks used by farmers. In 1818 David Dunham (who became known as the "father of Williamsburgh") opened a steam ferry and lent money to the new development, which was incorporated as the Village of Williamsburgh in 1827 and soon attracted industry; in 1852 it had a population of 31,000 and was incorporated as a city. Later its mayor, Abraham J. Berry, proposed that it be consolidated with Brooklyn; in 1855 his plan was enacted and the final "h" was dropped from the name of the neighborhood (it remains in the name of the Williamsburgh Savings Bank, which has a building designated a landmark on Broadway).

The neighborhood became a fashionable suburb for industrialists and professionals of German, Austrian, and Irish descent. There were hotels, beer gardens, and exclusive clubs; the German section lay along Montrose Avenue and Meserole and Scholes streets. Docks, shipyards, factories, distilleries, taverns, mills, and foundries stood along the waterfront, where some of the largest industrial firms in the nation were built: the Pfizer Pharmaceutical Company (1849), Astral Oil (later Standard Oil), Brooklyn Flint Glass (later Corning Glassware), and the Havemeyers and Elder sugar refinery (later Amstar), once the largest establishment of its kind in the world.

The population grew from 105,000 in 1900 to 260,000 in 1920, a peak for recent years. After the Williamsburg Bridge opened in 1903 thousands of poor and working-class Jews from eastern Europe moved to the neighborhood from the Lower East Side. Lithuanian, Polish, and Russian Orthodox enclaves also developed, as did an Italian one between Bushwick and Union avenues. In July 1903 near North 8th and Havemeyer streets hundreds of Italian residents, many from the village of Nola, held the first annual celebration in the city of a festival called the dancing of the *giglio*. Cold-water flats and six-story tenements replaced brownstones, and by 1917 the neighborhood had the most densely populated blocks in the city. During the early 1930s many businesses in the neighborhood declared bankruptcy and many prosperous residents left. The Jewish community continued to grow, and a large number of Jewish refugees escaping Nazism moved in and formed Hasidic synagogues and schools; there were more than twenty sects from different parts of Europe, including the large Satmar sect from Hungary and Romania, led by its grand rabbi Joel Teitelbaum. Manufacturing, which employed more than a million persons in the city in 1950, attracted many Puerto Ricans during the following decade.

About this time scores of decaying buildings were demolished to make way for enormous public housing projects. In 1957 the construction of the Brooklyn–Queens Expressway bisected the neighborhood and destroyed more than 2200 units of low-income housing. Looting and arson left blocks of abandoned buildings, factories, and warehouses, but some housing was renovated in the 1980s. Although Pfizer and other businesses remained in the neighborhood, in 1990 manufacturing employment had decreased sharply. By this time Puerto Ricans, Dominicans, and other Latin Americans constituted about half the population, with Dominicans alone accounting for more than half the immigrants who settled in the neighborhood during the 1980s. Far smaller numbers arrived from Israel, Poland, Ecuador, and China. The neighborhood was largely overcrowded and poor, and housing remained inadequate; Latin American families often shared cramped apartments, as did Hasidic families.

In the Hasidic district, bounded by Wythe Avenue, Broadway, and Heyward Street and lying along Bedford, Lee, Marcy, and Division avenues, Yiddish remains the primary language and kosher butchers and restaurants abound. Disputes sometimes develop with Latin Americans, and there is occasional violence within the Satmar sect over which followers are the most staunchly traditional. During Simchas Torah thousands of Hasidim dance through the streets with Torah scrolls, clapping and swaying.

Henry Stiles: *The Civil, Political, Professional, and Ecclesiastical History of the County of Kings and the City of Brooklyn, 1683–1884* (New York: W. W. Munsell, 1884)

George Kranzler: *Williamsburg: A Jewish Community in Transition* (New York: Philipp Feldheim, 1961)

Toby Sanchez: "The Williamsburg Neighborhood Profile" (New York: Brooklyn in Touch Information Center, 1990)

For illustrations see GIGLIO and PUBLIC HOUSING.

Judith Berck

Williamsburg Bridge. Steel suspension bridge spanning the East River between Delancey Street on the Lower East Side and Marcy Avenue in Williamsburg. It was designed by Leffert L. Buck and opened in December 1903 as an alternative to the overburdened Brooklyn Bridge. Employed by the commissioner of bridges Gustav Lindenthal during construction in 1902 to improve the aesthetics of the structure, Henry Hornbostel added ornamental detail to the towers and other sections of the bridge and designed the approach in Manhattan. Yet the bridge remained primarily the work of Buck and was

View of Williamsburg Bridge to Manhattan, ca 1903

criticized almost from the moment the plan was unveiled for its graceless form. The second bridge over the East River, it was constructed in seven years (half the time it took to build the Brooklyn Bridge) and was the longest and heaviest suspension bridge in the world and the first suspension bridge with towers made entirely of steel. It is 7308 feet (2229 meters) long, with a main span of sixteen hundred feet (488 meters) suspended from four steel cables, each a foot and a half (half a meter) thick. Steel latticework, called stiffening trusses, extends between the anchorages, giving the bridge great strength (as well as its ungainly appearance). The deck of the bridge supports two subway tracks and four flanking traffic lanes. In the early twentieth century the bridge was seen as a passageway to a new life in Williamsburg by thousands of Jewish immigrants fleeing the slums of the Lower East Side.

Sharon Reier: *The Bridges of New York* (New York: Quadrant, 1977)

Rebecca Read Shanor

Williamsburgh Daily Times. Original name of the BROOKLYN TIMES–UNION.

Williamsburgh Savings Bank. Savings bank in Brooklyn, chartered in 1851 and acquired by the Republic National Bank of New York in 1987. It is best known for its buildings. After occupying rented quarters in Williamsburgh the bank in 1867 bought a site at 175 Broadway and held a competition to design its headquarters. The winning entry, submitted by George B. Post, called for a four-story building of limestone, sandstone, and marble, designed in a Classical Revival style with a monumental arched portico and an ornate cast-iron railing along the sidewalk. Construction began in 1870 and was completed in 1875; additions were made by the firm of Helmle, Hubery and Hudswell in 1905 and by Helmle and Huberty in 1925, among them a dome crowned with an ornate lantern and a delicate weathervane. The bank bought land in 1926 at 1 Hanson Place, behind the Brooklyn Academy of Music and across the street from a terminal of the Long Island Rail Road (now demolished), and engaged the firm of Halsey, McCormick and Helmer to design a skyscraper, which was built between October 1927 and 1 May 1929 and became known as one of the most elegant examples of a modern structure combining Romanesque and Byzantine elements. At 512 feet (156 meters) the tallest structure in Brooklyn, it was built with setbacks at the thirteenth and twenty-sixth stories accented by rounded arches and terra cotta bands. Symbols of thrift were carved into the base in bas relief; a four-faced clock, the largest in the world at the time, and a gilded dome recalling the one at 175 Broadway were also added. The interior was decorated in exquisite detail: polychrome mosaics were installed in the elevator lobby, which was separated from the marble banking room by ornate cast-iron gates; in the banking room the ceiling was built to a height of sixty-three feet (nineteen meters), three windows forty feet (twelve meters) tall were installed overlooking Hanson Place, and a mural of Brooklyn was painted on the rear wall. The city granted landmark status to the building at 175 Broadway in 1966 and to the one at 1 Hanson Place in 1977.

Williamsburgh Savings Bank Tower (designed by Halsey, McCormack and Helmer), 1 Hansen Place, ca *1930*

Barbaralee Diamonstein: *The Landmarks of New York* (New York: Harry N. Abrams, 1988)

Eric Wm. Allison

Williamsburg Trust Company. Commercial bank in Brooklyn. Until 1922 its main branch was a building that is now the HOLY TRINITY CATHEDRAL OF THE UKRAINIAN AUTOCEPHALIC ORTHODOX CHURCH.

William T. Davis Wildlife Refuge. The first wildlife sanctuary in New York City, dedicated in 1929 and occupying 260 acres (105 hectares) of the Greenbelt in New Springville, near the center of Staten Island. The area was once farmland; its artesian wells, connected to the Fresh Kills Creek, supplied the island with water in the 1880s. A preservationist movement led by the National Audubon Society and William Thompson Davis, a naturalist and one of the founders of the Staten Island Institute of Arts and Sciences, prevailed on the city's parks department to take over fifty-two acres (twenty-one hectares) of the area in 1928. Davis paid for a fence to be built around much of the area to halt the hunting of waterfowl and pheasants. In 1955 the area was enlarged to its current size. The refuge harbors a wide range of habitats, as well as tidal marshland, freshwater wetlands, and woodlands.

James Bradley

Willis Avenue Bridge. A bowstring truss swing bridge spanning the Harlem River, connecting 1st Avenue and 125th Street in Manhattan with Willis Avenue and 132nd Street in the Bronx. Intended to relieve traffic on the Third Avenue Bridge and designed by the engineer Thomas C. Clarke (who also designed the Third Avenue Bridge), it opened on 23 August 1901. The bridge measures 3212.5 feet (979 meters) in length, including approaches, and has a clear height of 25.1 feet (7.65 meters).

Rebecca Read Shanor

Willkie, Wendell (Lewis) (*b* Elwood, Ind., 18 Feb 1892; *d* New York City, 8 Oct 1944). Lawyer and presidential candidate. With his wife, Edith, and his son Philip he moved to New York City in 1929 to work for the law firm of Weadcock and Weadcock, general counsel for the public utility holding company the Commonwealth and Southern Corporation, and took up residence in a seven-room apartment at 1010 5th Avenue, near 82nd Street. Named president of the company in 1933, he became a prominent critic of President Franklin D. Roosevelt's policies, particularly regarding public power. He resigned from Commonwealth and Southern in 1940 when he was unexpectedly nominated as the Republican candidate for the presidency. A moderate who rejected some of his party's conservative orthodoxy, he won the nomination in part because of early backing from the *New York Herald Tribune.* Soundly defeated by Roosevelt, he returned to private law practice in 1941 and became a partner of the firm of Willkie, Owen, Otis and Reilly. Willkie remained active in politics and philanthropy in the city during his remaining years. He died at Lenox Hill Hospital.

James Bradley

Willkie Farr and Gallagher. Law firm. Its predecessor, Hornblower and Byrne, was formed on 1 January 1888 with offices at 280 Broadway by William B. Hornblower and James Byrne. Among the first clients was Grant and Ward (the brokerage firm of the former president). Prominent figures associated with the firm in later years included Elihu Root, Felix Franfurter, Lindley M. Garrison (from 1916), former secretary of war, Nathan L. Miller (from 1930), former governor of New York, and Wendell Willkie (from 1941), the Republican presidential nominee in 1940.

The firm underwent more than a dozen changes of name before taking its current name in 1968. In the mid 1990s Willkie Farr had about 260 lawyers and offices at 153 East 53rd Street in Manhattan.

Willowbrook. Neighborhood in south central Staten Island, lying near the Staten Island Expressway. Until development began in the 1960s it was sparsely populated farmland named for the brook that flowed through the area into the Fresh Kill. The main roads are Bradley Avenue and Forest Hill Road; the Center for Basic Research at 1050 Forest Hill Road opened in 1964 and is known worldwide for its research into the causes of mental retardation and other developmental disabilities. For many years the neighborhood was the site of the Willowbrook State School; after it ceased operations the campus was taken over in 1993 by the College of Staten Island.

Barnett Shepherd

Willowbrook State School. School for the mentally disabled in Staten Island, formally known as the Richmond Complex of the Staten Island Developmental Center. It occupied a parcel of 375 acres (151.9 hectares) on Willow Brook Road purchased in 1938 as the intended site of the New York State Department of Mental Hygiene; plans changed with the outbreak of the Second World War, and in 1942 the land became the site of Halloran General Hospital, the nation's largest hospital for wounded solders. Under the control of the Veterans Administration from 1947 to 1951 the hospital admitted mentally retarded and disabled civilians, including infants. In 1952 it was reclaimed by New York State. The hospital often received the most severely retarded children from other state institutions, and its population increased rapidly during the 1950s. By 1963 the facility, designed for 4200 residents, had more than six thousand. The situation caused a public outcry as well as a class-action suit in 1972 against Governor Nelson A. Rockefeller, and on 30 April 1975 Judge Orrin Judd ordered the population to be reduced to 250 and the remaining residents to be transferred to other less restrictive environments, preferably group homes. A legal and bureaucratic struggle ensued that resulted in the closing of Willowbrook. In 1989 the City University of New York acquired the property for use as a campus of the College of Staten Island.

David J. Rothman and Sheila M. Rothman: *The Willowbrook Wars* (New York: Harper and Row, 1984)

Nancy Flood

Wilson, (Harvey) Earl (*b* Rockford, Ohio, 3 May 1907; *d* Yonkers, N.Y., 16 Jan 1987). Columnist. In 1942 he began writing a gossip column about nightlife in New York City called "It Happened Last Night" that appeared six times a week in the *New York Post*; this was carried by about two hundred newspapers by the time he retired in 1983. He was married to Rosemary Lyons, whom he referred to in print as his "BW" (beautiful wife). Wilson specialized in interviews with starlets (illustrated by revealing photographs) and declined to criticize new shows or express political opinions.

Judith Adler Hennessee

Wilson, Edmund (*b* Red Bank, N.J., 8 May 1895; *d* Talcottville, near Rome, N.Y., 12 June 1972). Critic. Highly conscious of his northeastern, upper-class, Protestant background, he graduated from Princeton in 1916 and after his discharge from the army in August 1919 sought a literary career in New York City; he soon moved to West 16th Street, where he remained until 1921. He worked as a freelance for *Vanity Fair* and the *New Republic*, of which he became literary editor. During the 1920s and early 1930s he had several residences: 3 Washington Square North (1921–25), 229 West 13th Street (1925–29; building later renumbered), 224 West 13th Street (from 1929), 314 East 53rd Street (1933–35), 2 Lexington Avenue (early 1940s), and 14 Henderson Place (1944–45). His novel *I Thought of Daisy* (1929) depicted intellectual life in Greenwich Village; he also wrote *Axel's Castle* (1931), an influential study of literary modernism, and *To the Finland Station* (1940), perhaps the finest American treatment of the roots of communism. In his later work, much of which appeared in the *Nation*, he offered his analysis of writers both well-known and obscure. He also wrote treatises on such diverse subjects as the Civil War, the Dead Sea Scrolls, and the purported evils of the income tax. Wilson was married to the writer Mary McCarthy.

Lawson Bowling

Wilson, Elser, Moskowitz, Edelman and Dicker. Law firm formed in 1962. Originally representing Lloyd's of London in the United States, it was initially known for insurance underwriting and quickly became one of the city's most prominent firms. It grew by 88 percent during the 1980s and in 1991 had branches in ten American cities, London, and Tokyo. In the mid 1990s it represented such clients as Alexander and Alexander, the American International Group, and Royal Insurance, and had 350 lawyers. It specializes in malpractice suits and cases dealing with toxic waste. The offices are at 150 West 42nd Street.

George J. Lankevich

Winchell [Winschel], **Walter** (*b* New York City, 7 April 1897; *d* Los Angeles, 20 Feb 1972). Columnist. He worked for a number of newspapers as a drama critic before launching his gossip column "On Broadway" in the *New York Daily Mirror*, in which he carried out personal vendettas against politicians and personages in show business and coined such words as "storked" and "Reno-vated"; the column was eventually syndicated in fifty states and eleven foreign countries, and he also gave weekly radio broadcasts. He lived at 870 7th Avenue during the early 1930s before moving to the St. Moritz Hotel at 50 Central Park South, where he remained for many years. A feud with the entertainer Josephine Baker contributed to the decline of his popularity after 1950. Originally a strong supporter of Franklin D. Roosevelt, Winchell moved increasingly to the political right in his later years. He wrote a memoir, *Winchell Exclusive* (1975).

Neal Gabler: *Winchell: Gossip, Power and the Culture of Celebrity* (New York: Alfred A. Knopf, 1994)

James E. Mooney

Windels, Paul (*b* Brooklyn, 7 Dec 1885; *d* Norwalk, Conn., 15 Dec 1967). Lawyer. Born to an established family of French ancestry, he graduated from Columbia College (1907) and Brooklyn Law School (1909) and served as counsel to the State Bridge and Tunnel Commission (1918–30), corporation counsel of New York City (1934–37), and chairman of the City Traffic Commission (1937–40). He was a zealous reformer, and his policies as corporation counsel saved the city millions of dollars. A Republican leader in Brooklyn, Windels was an important advisor to Fiorello H. La Guardia, whom he provided with essential financial backing and party support. He played a critical role in La Guardia's presidency of the Board of Aldermen (1920) and in his mayoral victories.

Lowell Limpus and Burr W. Leyson: *This Man La Guardia* (New York: E. P. Dutton, 1938)

Thomas Kessner: *Fiorello La Guardia and the Making of Modern New York* (New York: McGraw–Hill, 1989)

Neal C. Garelik

Windham Children's Services. Charitable organization formed in 1947 as the Windham Society for the Care of Boys. In 1949 it merged with Protestant Children's Service, the first agency to provide emergency foster care and to secure placement for black children. Renamed Windham Children's Services, it added an adoption program and a day care center. The organization continued to expand its programs and in the 1950s opened a campus school. In 1969 it merged with the Child Care Center, which operated a tuberculosis prevention program and a group home. Changes in the 1970s effected by the Child Welfare Reform Act, the War on Poverty, and the fiscal crisis in New York City prompted a merger in 1977 with the Graham Home to form Graham–Windham Services to Families and Children.

Phyllis Barr

Windsor Hotel fire. One of the worst hotel fires in the history of New York City. It occurred on the afternoon of 17 March 1899 at the six-story Windsor Hotel on 5th Avenue between 46th and 47th streets, known for many years as one of the most elegant hotels in the city. The fire broke out in one of the sitting rooms in the second story after a guest lit a cigar and then threw the match out the window, igniting a set of lace curtains. Although the fire spread rapidly, many guests were unaware of the danger because the cries of the staff were drowned out by the St. Patrick's Day parade proceeding along 5th Avenue. Spectators eventually noticed the fire and pulled an alarm. Low water pressure hindered firemen's efforts, and many guests jumped from upper-story windows. Within a few hours the hotel was completely destroyed; thirty-three persons were killed and fifty-two injured, and property losses were estimated at $1 million.

Jonathan Aspell

Windsor Terrace. Neighborhood in northwestern Brooklyn (1990 pop. 16,239), bounded to the north by 7th Avenue and Prospect Park Southwest (formerly Coney Island Road), to the east by Prospect Park Southwest, and to the south and west by Green-Wood Cemetery. Once covered by John Vanderbilt's farm, the area was sold to developers in 1849 and became the village of Windsor Terrace in 1851. It remained a small settlement at a crossroads until 1900, when row houses were built throughout the area; many of these were soon occupied by Irish–American workers, and a few continued to be occupied for several decades by descendants of the original owners. The gentrification of Park Slope in the 1980s led to a modest increase in the development of real estate, including several condominiums. The area remained predominantly Irish Catholic, with several neighborhood bars such as Farrell's (opened in 1933) on Prospect Park West.

John J. Gallagher

Winfield. Former neighborhood in northwestern Queens, bounded to the north by Queens Boulevard, to the east by the New York Connecting Rail Road, to the south by Mount Zion Cemetery and Maurice Avenue, and to the west by New Calvary Cemetery; it is considered part of Woodside. A hamlet was built in May 1854 by the developers from Manhattan G. G. Andrews and J. F. Kendall and named after General Winfield Scott, a hero of the Mexican War. The Long Island Rail Road was extended to the area in 1861 and in 1870 Queens Boulevard was laid out, providing a route to Long Island City and Manhattan. The intersection of Shell Road (now 45th Avenue) and Queens Boulevard became the center of the community; there a factory built of brick was used to manufacture Singer sewing machines and later metal coffins before the First World War, when it became the Moisant aircraft factory. The neighborhood lay at the junction of the North Side Division and the Main Line of the Long Island Rail Road and about 1900 became known as Winfield Junction; the railroad station closed in 1929. Most of the housing consisted of small wooden frame houses. The name Winfield became disused after the Second World War.

Vincent Seyfried

Wingate. Neighborhood in north central Brooklyn (1990 pop. 11,000), lying east of Prospect–Lefferts Gardens and south of Crown Heights; it is bounded to the north by Empire Boulevard, to the east by Troy Avenue, to the south by Winthrop Street, and to the west by Nostrand Avenue. The area was known as Pig Town for its many small pig farms until it was renamed for General George Wingate High School, built on Kingston Avenue in 1954. The period between 1920 and the Second World War saw a gradual development of detached and semidetached wooden frame houses, row houses, and walk-up apartment buildings. On Miami, Palm, and Tampa courts during the 1920s an enclave of two-story townhouses was erected: these had their entrances perpendicular to the street, facing each other across interior gardens that formed courtyards. The population consists mostly of descendants of eastern Europeans, Irish, and Caribbean immigrants, and there is an enclave of Orthodox Jews in the northern section. The main commercial areas are on Nostrand Avenue and Empire Boulevard. There are also eight acres (three hectares) of park land: Wingate Playground, Alexander Metz Playground, and All Boys Athletic Field.

Elizabeth Reich Rawson

WINS. Radio station. It began broadcasting in 1924 from Gimbel Brothers Department Store as WGBS and was acquired in the early 1930s by William Randolph Hearst, who gave the station its current name (the new call letters stood for International News Service). In the 1950s the station began playing rock music and attracted popular disc jockeys like Alan Freed, Murray the K, and Cousin Brucie. It became the first station in New York City to broadcast news exclusively in 1965, providing critical information to the city during the power blackout in November of that year. WINS broadcasts at a frequency of 1010 kHz.

JillEllyn Riley

Wise, Stephen S(amuel) (*b* Eger, Hungary, 17 March 1874; *d* New York City, 19 April 1949). Religious and political leader. Known for his skills as a speaker and organizer, he became a leader of the American Zionist movement and helped to form the Free Synagogue in New York City (1907) and the Jewish Institute of Religion (1921); he also directed the American Jewish Congress (1922). He achieved prominence in the city's political circles for his work in municipal reform with his friend John Haynes Holmes, minister of the Church of the Messiah. From 1929 the two mounted a campaign to expose widespread corruption in the government of Mayor James J. Walker; their efforts were vindicated in 1933 by the findings of the Saber Investigatory Commission. During the 1930s Wise's liberal and reformist politics won wide support among the city's Jews. After 1938 he became increasingly preoccupied with the security of European Jewry. Wise is widely considered to have been the country's most influential Jewish leader between the world wars.

Carl H. Voss, ed.: *Stephen S. Wise, Servant of the People* (Philadelphia: Jewish Publication Society of America, 1969)

Melvin I. Urofsky: *A Voice That Spoke for Justice: The Life and Times of Stephen S. Wise* (Albany: State University of New York Press, 1982)

Henry Feingold

WNBC. Radio station, flagship of the radio network of the National Broadcasting Company (NBC). It began broadcasting in 1927, when NBC formed the Red and the Blue networks, and became the most popular station in New York City in the 1930s when it broadcast the radio comedy "Amos 'n' Andy," recorded in Chicago. From 1932 NBC used the same call letters for its television station, which broadcast from atop the Empire State Building. Both the radio and the television station remained in New York City into the 1990s.

Chad Ludington

WNCN. Radio station launched in 1957 at a frequency of 104.3 MHz by the Northeast Concert Network and bought in 1964 by the National Science Network. The station was on the air twenty-four hours a day and broadcast classical music for virtually its entire schedule. It was in serious financial trouble by 1974, when it took the call letters WQIV and abandoned classical music for rock: the new format was introduced in November, when the station played the song "Roll Over, Beethoven." The change prompted the formation of the WNCN Listeners Guild, which pressured the station to revert to its old format and petitioned the Federal Communications Commission (FCC) to threaten revocation of its license. The group prevailed in May 1975 and the station was sold to the GAF Broadcasting Company. In the following years GAF sought to attract more advertisers by appealing to a younger audience. It launched a massive advertising campaign, adopted a breezy announcing style similar to that of rock stations, and severely limited its playlist, which the program director described in 1987 as "eliminating organ music, avant-garde, atonal, aleatoric music, waltzes, virtually all vocal music, [and] all monoraul and historical recordings." In December 1993 the station again changed its format to rock, this time taking the call letters WAQX. By this time the FCC had become far less involved in programming matters, and the change went unchallenged.

Amanda Aaron

WNET. Public television station, the first in New York City. It began operations in late 1962 as WNDT after the chairman of the Federal Communications Commission, Newton N. Minow, used an administrative maneuver in December 1961 to force the sale to educational interests of the commercial station WNTA (channel 13), even though they had been outbid by two commercial parties. The station offered a mix of instructional and cultural programming. Constant financial troubles and bureaucratic in-fighting were only partly relieved by the passage of the Public Broadcasting Act of 1967, which formed the Public Broadcasting System (PBS). The act was intended to discourage the centralized model of programming identified with the commercial networks and establish in its place a system whereby many public stations would develop programming for the entire nation. Owing to its location in New York City, however, WNDT eventually became the principal source of programming. Shortly before taking its current name in 1970 the station arranged for the American distribution of the British series "The Forsyte Saga," the success of which inspired a wave of programming from Britain on PBS. In the early 1970s some 20 percent of all PBS programs originated from WNET. Its series have included "Bill Moyers' Journal," "Sesame Street," "The Great American Dream Machine," "The MacNeil–Lehrer Report," "NET Opera," and "NET Playhouse."

James L. Baughman

WNEW-FM. Radio station. It began broadcasting different material from its counterpart WNEW-AM in 1967, after a ruling in 1965 by the Federal Communications Commission that ended the practice of all-day simultaneous broadcasts by AM and FM stations. In an experiment in 1967 the station employed only women as disk jockeys, and late in the decade it identified itself with the counterculture, as its disc jockeys Scott Muni and Rosco helped the station to develop a "progressive" format that emphasized diverse musical styles, new artists, and longer songs. The station dominated rock radio in New York City in the 1970s and 1980s with a format that combined "classic" and contemporary rock. Owned for many years by Metromedia, it changed hands several times after 1986. WNEW-FM broadcasts at a frequency of 102.7 MHz.

Peter Fornatale and Joshua E. Mills: *Radio in the Television Age* (Woodstock, N.Y.: Overlook, 1980)

JillEllyn Riley

WNEW-TV. Former name of WNYW-TV.

WNYC. Municipal broadcasting system. It includes the noncommercial radio stations WNYC-AM (820 kHz; began broadcasting 17 July 1924) and WNYC-FM (93.9 MHz; 1943) and the noncommercial television station WNYC-TV (channel 31; 1961), and was formed as part of the Department of Plant and Structures at the initiative of its commissioner Grover A. Whalen, originally for emergency communication. WNYC-AM was the first municipally owned noncommercial radio station in the United States. It flourished from 1934 under the administration of Mayor Fiorello H. La Guardia, who gave broadcasts every Sunday that drew a large audience. As managers of the station he appointed Seymour N. Siegel and Morris S. Novick, who developed a unique brand of programming that included classical music, news, and public affairs. Herman Neuman, music director from 1924 to 1969, inaugurated "The Masterwork Hour," which began in 1929 as the first radio program of recorded classical music ever broadcast and continued into the 1990s, and the "American Music Festival," an annual celebration of American music aired between Lincoln's and Washington's birthdays, first presented in 1939. A television production unit set up in 1949 to make short educational films for commercial stations led to the launching of WNYC-TV: its schedule in the following decades came to include documentaries and interviews on local affairs, hearings of city agencies, programs of the Public Broadcasting System, and programs of independent production companies to which the station leased air time. Severe budget cuts in the 1970s led to the formation in 1979 of the WNYC Foundation, which by the early 1990s provided three quarters of the operating budget of the system.

Kenneth R. Cobb

WNYW-TV. Television station, broadcasting on channel 5 in New York City. Granted a license on 2 May 1944 as WABD, it was the first station of what became the Du Mont Television Network. The network was dissolved in 1955 and the call letters became WNEW-TV in 1957. The station was purchased by John W(erner) Kluge along with the radio stations WNEW-AM and WNEW-FM in 1959. As the principal television station of Metromedia, it competed successfully against network-owned stations in the nation's largest television market through innovative "counterprogramming." The station was renamed WNYW after Rupert Murdoch bought the television stations of Metromedia in 1986. From 1953 into the 1990s its studios and offices were in the building originally built for the Central Turn-Verein (1887) at 205 East 67th Street and converted by Du Mont (at a cost of $5 million) into what was the largest facility in television.

Metromedia and the DuMont Legacy: W2XWV, WABD, WNEW-TV (New York: Museum of Broadcasting, n.d.)
Judith Adler Hennessee: "Tabloid TV," *Manhattan, Inc.*, Oct 1986, pp. 151–56
Mary Billard and Patricia O'Toole: "Best Friends at War," *Manhattan, Inc.*, April 1989, pp. 65–72

Val Ginter

Wolfe, Thomas (Clayton) (*b* Asheville, N.C., 3 Oct 1900; *d* Baltimore, 15 Sept 1938). Novelist. After graduating from the University of North Carolina in 1920 he enrolled in George P. Baker's renowned drama class, the 47 Workshop at Harvard University. In 1923 he moved to New York City and took an apartment at 439 West 123rd Street. When he could find no producer interested in his plays he moved to the Albert Hotel at 42 East 11th Street, where he remained until the end of 1926. He taught writing at the Washington Square College of New York University (1924–30), which he later described in several of his novels. On one of his many trips to Europe he began what became his best-known work, *Look Homeward, Angel* (1929), a semi-autobiographical novel based on his youth; he completed the manuscript in a loft at 13 East 8th Street that he shared for a time with the designer Aline Bernstein and prepared the final version, considerably shorter than the original, with the help of the noted editor Maxwell Perkins, his lifelong friend and mentor. After the book was published he gave up teaching to write full time. He lived successively in Manhattan at 263 West 11th Street (October 1927 to June 1928) and 27 West 15th Street (1928–29), in Paris on a Guggenheim Fellowship (where he was unable to write), in Brooklyn at 40 Verandah Place (1931), 111 Columbia Heights (1931), and 5 Montague Terrace (1933), and again in Manhattan at 865 1st Avenue (September 1935 to September 1937) and the Chelsea Hotel (from 1937). During these years he wrote *Of Time and the River* (1935) and *The Story of a Novel* (1936), which describes his own method of writing. Two novels, *The Web and the Rock* (1939) and *You Can't Go Home Again* (1940), as well as a collection of short stories and chapters of an unfinished novel, were published posthumously. Wolfe described New York City as the "ecstatic Northern city."

David Herbert Donald: *Look Homeward: A Life of Thomas Wolfe* (Boston: Little, Brown, 1987)

Anthony Gronowicz

Wolfe, Tom [Thomas Kennerly, Jr.] (*b* Richmond, Va., 2 March 1931). Essayist and novelist. He attended Washington and Lee University (AB 1951) and Yale University (PhD 1957) and came to prominence in the 1960s as a writer for the magazine *New York*, a leader in expanding the scope of journalism to include the subjective interpretation of events. His first book, *The Kandy-kolored Tangerine-flake Streamline Baby* (1965), is an idiosyncratic collection of short pieces that lampoon bourgeois liberalism. In 1987 he published *Bonfire of the Vanities*, a controversial, best-selling novel that explores racial tensions in New York City. Wolfe's style had a profound influence on writers of the 1960s and 1970s, and especially on magazine journalism.

Leslie Gourse

Woman suffrage parade on 5th Avenue, organized by professionals and tradeswomen, 1913

Woman's Journal. Weekly newspaper launched in Boston in 1870 as a voice for women's interests and concerns. It became the official organ of the National American Suffrage Association in 1910 and moved to New York City in 1917. Editors for the newspaper included Mary A. Livermore, Lucy Stone, Henry B. Blackwell, Alice Stone Blackwell, and Virginia Roderick, and the editorial board consisted of such distinguished abolitionists as Julia Ward Howe and William Lloyd Garrison. The *Woman's Journal* ceased publication in 1931.

Sandra Roff

woman suffrage. Although historians tend to characterize American suffragism as middle class, the movement in New York City always had a more complex character. The first New York City Woman Suffrage Association was formed in 1870 by such élite women as the physician Clemence Lozier, the fashionable writer Lillie Devereux Blake, and Charlotte Wilbour, the president of Sorosis, one of the first women's clubs. Suffragists in the city were drawn to the cause of the many wage-earning women there. During a campaign in 1893–94 to have the issue of woman suffrage included at the state constitutional convention, wealthy and well-placed women from the city including Josephine Shaw Lowell, Mary Putnam Jacobi, and Olivia Sage argued before the legislature that upper-class women would provide responsible leadership for the masses of women voters. After this campaign failed, many of these suffragists turned to local politics, especially the exciting mayoral elections at the end of the century, and supported such reform candidates as Seth Low.

The class heterogeneity of the suffrage movement in the city and these experiences with political activism helped to produce a more modern style of activism, which eventually spread through the national suffrage movement. In 1907 Harriot Stanton Blatch formed the Equality League of Self Supporting Women, which recruited wage-earning women and adopted such spectacular tactics as mass parades and outdoor meetings. At Blatch's invitation the English suffragist leader Emmeline Pankhurst visited New York City, where audiences filled Carnegie Hall and Cooper Union to hear her speak. Blatch's style of activism attracted a great deal of publicity. By 1913 the largest suffrage parades in the country were held along 5th Avenue, conducted with military precision and complete with elegant banners and viewing stands for local politicians.

Carrie Chapman Catt, a former president of the National American Woman Suffrage Association, also focused her attention on the movement in New York City, where in 1909 she organized many small societies into the New York City Woman Suffrage Party. She condemned the corruption of urban political machines but used their tactics to organize members of her own party and deploy them in election districts throughout the city (by 1917 there were half a million members). Under intense pressure from suffragists the state legislature in 1913 authorized a referendum in 1915 on whether women should vote in New York State. The city was the center of the campaign; suffragists there had a weekly newspaper that they hawked in the streets, and by November 1915 they reported spending $25,000, holding five thousand outdoor meetings, and reaching 60 percent of the city's voters. The referendum was nonetheless defeated by 85,000 votes in the city and 200,000 statewide. Suffrage activists immediately embarked on a second campaign in which supporters in the city held fewer rallies but spent six times as much money as they had in 1915. Aware of mounting concern over the First World War, organizers presented suffrage as an issue related to women's capacity for national service. More than money and patriotism, political support made the difference. Late in the referendum Tammany Hall let it be known that it would not oppose the suffrage measure. As a result not only did the referendum pass in New York City, where suffrage leaders had assumed the opposition of immigrant voters, but the city accounted for the margin of victory for the whole state. And just as New York City carried the state, New York State carried the country, because its congressional delegation was now obligated to the votes of women as well as men, helping to ensure the passage of the Nineteenth Amendment to the U.S. Constitution in 1920.

Ronald Schaffer: "The New York City Woman Suffrage Party, 1909–1919," *New York History* 43 (1962), 269–87

Elinor Lerner: "Jewish Involvement in the New York City Woman Suffrage Movement," *American Jewish History* 70 (1981), 442–61

Ellen Carol DuBois: "Working Women, Class Relations, and Suffrage Militancy: Harriot Stanton Blatch and the New York Woman Suffrage Movement, 1894–1909," *Journal of American History* 74 (1987), 34–58

See also FEMINISM.

Ellen Carol DuBois

Women's City Club of New York. Voluntary women's association formed in New York City by suffragists in 1915. Its early leaders included Mary Garrett Hay, Katharine Bement Davis, Mary E. Dreier, Belle Moskowitz, Frances Perkins, Eleanor Roosevelt, Genevieve Earle, and Dorothy Kenyon. After women were given the right to vote in New York State in 1917, membership reached several thousand and the club bought a mansion on Park Avenue designed by Stanford White. During the Depression membership fell to about nine hundred and the club began occupying rented space in mid Manhattan. From its earliest days the club sought to educate New Yorkers about local politics, and to influence politics to improve the city. It made the welfare of women and children its chief concern but also worked on issues that affected all citizens, including low-income housing, public education, health care, conditions in the workplace, public transit, charter revision, fiscal responsibility, the judicial system, environmental protection, and civil rights. The club remained active into the 1990s, with offices at 35 East 21st Street and a membership of about eight hundred.

Elisabeth Israels Perry: "Women's Political Choices after Suffrage: The Women's City Club of New York, 1915–present," *New York History* 62 (1990), 417–34

Elisabeth Israels Perry

women's clubs. Some of the first women's clubs in New York City were formed during the antebellum period and the Civil War and were devoted to such causes as temperance, abolitionism, suffrage, and charity and relief. Sorosis, a women's club formed in the city in 1868, became highly influential and inspired many women to undertake social, intellectual, and civic activities in their own clubs throughout the nation. These were in their heyday from the late 1860s until the late 1920s. Members were usually married, middle-class white women who had time for meetings and committee work, but there were groups formed on the basis of shared work experiences, religious convictions, and interests by women of almost every age, class, race, and ethnic background. In 1890 Sorosis invited sixty-three delegates from clubs in seventeen states to form an alliance for mutual aid, which became known as the General Federation of Women's Clubs. Women also formed alumnae associations, patriotic societies, organizations for municipal and legislative reform, neighborhood improvement groups, girls' clubs, networks for workers and professionals, trade unions, suffrage and anti-suffrage organizations, benevolent societies, sororities, groups devoted to such topics as health, music, drama, painting, and conservation, and auxiliaries to men's fraternal organizations, secret societies, and lodges.

Branches of statewide and national organizations have often found strong support in the city, where their local branches contribute a great deal of time and money, provide leadership and ideas, and sponsor regional, national, and international conferences: the elections and resolutions of some have led to changes in government policy, including child labor laws, the creation of juvenile courts, and compulsory schooling. Many national women's organizations have their headquarters in the city. Among those that did in the mid 1990s were Hadassah, the Daughters of Cincinnati, the National Association of Women Artists, the National Council of Jewish Women, the National Council of Women of the United States, the Women's National Republican Club, and the Women's Auxiliary to the American Institute of Mining Engineers. Organizations formerly based in the city include the International Sunshine Society, the International Woman's Peace Society, the American Birth Control League, the Girls' Service League of America, the Lucy Stone League, the Medical Women's National Association, the National Consumers' League, the National Florence Crittenton Mission, and the National Emergency Committee of Near East Relief.

Karen J. Blair: *The Clubwoman as Feminist: True Womanhood Redefined, 1868–1914* (New York: Holmes and Meier, 1980)

Karen J. Blair

Women's Hotel. Original name of the PARK AVENUE HOTEL.

women's hotels. For several decades a number of hotels in New York City offered housing to young women along with rather close supervision. The first women's hotel in the city was built in the 1870s and lasted only two months. The heyday of women's hotels was between 1940 and about 1974, when a directory listed sixteen establishments in Manhattan. Most of the residents were recent graduates of high school or college who had moved to the city to work, attend secretarial or other trade schools, or try breaking into show business. The Barbizon (1927) at Lexington Avenue and 63rd Street was the most exclusive women's hotel and the best-known; fictionalized by Sylvia Plath in her novel *The Bell Jar*, it had a swimming pool, a health club, a library, daily maid service, music studios, and an eighteenth-floor lounge with a terrace. The East End Hotel for Women was similarly élite. Other hotels included the Martha Washington, Webster Apartments, and the Young Women's Towne House.

Many parents agreed to have their daughters live in New York City only on the condition that they remain in the protective surroundings of a women's hotel. The hotels asked prospective residents to give references (the Barbizon required that one be a clergyman) and prescribed strict rules and curfews; men were not allowed on the premises except in designated lounges or semi-private "beau rooms." The length of a woman's stay at a hotel could range from a single day to many years: some residents sought to become engaged to be married and moved out soon after, but others strove to build careers and stayed indefinitely (several of the original residents of the Barbizon remained for more than half a century). In 1973 the New York Commission on Human Rights deemed segregation by sex in public accommodations illegal, although hotels could legally segregate by sex if most of their guests were permanent. By this time women's hotels were already declining in popularity as more women were moving into their own apartments, and although the Barbizon at first fought to remain a single-sex establishment, the management decided to admit men in 1981 after determining that doing so was a financial necessity. Some more modest women's hotels operated by the Salvation Army and the YWCA remained in operation into the 1990s, as did St. Mary's residence and Allerton House for Women (1944).

John A. Kouwenhoven: *Columbia Historical Portrait of New York* (New York: Doubleday, 1953), 348
Nancy Hardin: "Finding a Place to Live If You Are Recently Arrived or Displaced," *Women's Guide to New York* (New York: Workman, 1973), 11–20
"Sic Transit Gloria Barbizon," *Newsweek*, 23 Feb 1981, p. 63

Jacqueline Lalley

Women's House of Detention. Detention center for women awaiting trial, designed in an art deco style by the firm of Sloan and Robertson and built in 1931 at Greenwich Avenue and 10th Street on the former site of the Jefferson Market Prison. It drew strong opposition from the surrounding neighborhood for the shouts of inmates, which could be widely heard, and was demolished in 1973–74 at a time when correctional facilities were placed away from populated areas. The site was later used for the Jefferson Market Greening, a garden tended by volunteers. A courthouse and a clocktower immediately to the north designed by Withers and Vaux was converted into a branch of the New York Public Library.

Nancy Flood

women's magazines. As early as 1794 a magazine for women, the *New York Weekly Magazine*, was published in New York City. Others soon followed, including the *Lady's Weekly Miscellany* (1805–8) and the *Ladies' Literary Cabinet* (1819–22). As the city became a center of dressmaking and pattern manufacturing during the mid nineteenth century, several fashion publications were introduced there, among them Frank Leslie's *Ladies' Gazette of Fashion and Fancy Needlework* (1854–57), *Mme. Demorest's Mirror of Fashion* (1860–65), and *Harper's Bazar* (1867–), which in addition to news about fashion printed pictures and serials. When national magazines supported by advertising became common in the late nineteenth century, the city eclipsed Philadelphia as the largest national center of women's magazine publishing. *Vogue* (1892–), which chronicled the activities and fashions of the city's élite, was bought by Condé Nast in 1909 and under the direction of Edna Woolman Chase became the most important fashion journal. Others that became influential during the first decades of the twentieth century were the *Delineator* (1873–1937), *McCall's* (1876–), *Good Housekeeping* (1885–), the *Woman's Home Companion* (1874–1957; edited by Gertrude Battles Lane, 1911–41), the *Pictorial Review* (1899–1939), and *Ladies' Home Journal* (1883–), which opened offices in the city during the 1920s. Advertising played an important role in the growth of these magazines, especially advertising for products such as clothing and cosmetics that had a strong appeal to female consumers. The 1930s saw the introduction of *Mademoiselle* (1935–) and *Glamour* (1939–) for young women, and the homemaking magazines *Family Circle* (1932–) and *Woman's Day* (1937–). Among the most successful editors at mid century were Lane, Otis Wiese (*McCall's*, 1928–58), Herbert Mayes (*Good Housekeeping*, 1942–58; *McCall's*, 1958–61), and John Mack Carter (*McCall's*, 1961–65; *Ladies' Home Journal*, 1965–74; and *Good Housekeeping*, 1975–).

From the 1960s many magazines sought to address women's changing needs. Under the direction of Helen Gurley Brown from 1965, *Cosmopolitan* (1886–) shifted its focus to advise young women about sexual liberation. *Essence* (1970–) was intended for middle-class black women, and *Ms.* (1972–), edited by Gloria Steinem and published by Patricia Carbine, was one of the first feminist publications with commercial backing and nationwide circulation. By the early 1970s *Good Housekeeping, McCall's, Ladies' Home Journal, Family Circle, Woman's Day, Redbook* (1903–), and *Cosmopolitan* dominated the market, and all were edited in the city. Several magazines were introduced in the late 1980s, including *New York Woman* (1987–). *Lear's* (1988–94), and *Mirabella* (1989–), a fashion magazine for older women launched by Grace Mirabella after she was dismissed as the editor of *Vogue*.

Mary Ellen Zuckerman

Women's Political Union. The name after 1910 of the EQUALITY LEAGUE OF SELF SUPPORTING WOMEN.

Women's Wear Daily. Fashion newspaper. It was established in 1910 by Edmund W. Fairchild and initially covered only trade news; from 1913 its headquarters were at 7 East 12th Street in Greenwich Village. A bureau in Paris was eventually operated by John B. Fairchild, grandson of the founder, who became known for his irreverence toward respected designers. In 1960 he took over and expanded the parent company, Fairchild Publications. Under his direction the *Women's Wear Daily* began to treat a range of topics including film, books, society, and gossip, and became known for enhancing or diminishing the reputations of the famous, for whom it coined the term "beautiful people." Fairchild sponsored some designers and pointedly ignored others. In 1970 he promoted mid-length skirts by ensuring that women wearing skirts of other lengths would not be photographed for the newspaper. Circulation reportedly doubled to 800,000 after he made the newspaper more influential; it remained the only daily publication of the fashion industry and became virtually required reading in not only the garment industry but also social and artistic circles.

Katie Kelly: *The Wonderful World of Women's Wear Daily* (New York: Saturday Review Press, 1972)

Leslie Gourse

Wong Ching Foo (*b ca* 1851; *d* after 1892). Civic leader and newspaperman. He moved to New York City in 1874 and gave a series of provocative lectures in English about Chinese culture and Buddhism. A fluent and captivating speaker, he shocked proper society by criticizing American missionaries for painting false pictures of "the degradation of Chinese, and . . . their bowing to stock and stone" as a means of raising money. He launched a Chinese-language newspaper in New York City in 1882 and another in Chicago in 1892.

New York World, 29 April 1877

Charlie Chin

Wood, Alfred M. (*b* 19 April 1828; *d* ?Germany, 25 Jan 1871). Mayor of Brooklyn. He commanded the 14th Regiment of the New York State Militia and was wounded and captured in 1861 during the First Battle of Bull Run. Eventually discharged, he returned to serve as mayor of Brooklyn in 1864–66.

Henry R. Stiles: *The Civil, Political, Professional and Ecclesiastical History of the County of Kings and the City of Brooklyn, New York from 1683 to 1884* (New York: W. W. Munsell, 1884)

Jerome Mushkat

Wood, Fernando (*b* Philadelphia, 14 Feb 1812; *d* Hot Springs, Ark., 14 Feb 1881). Mayor. During his early career he was a businessman, real-estate speculator, and member of the U.S. Congress (1841–43). As mayor in 1855–57 and 1859–61 he became a prototypical "boss," the model for William M. "Boss" Tweed. While in office he was praised by immigrants and the poor and criticized by members of Tammany Hall, Republicans, and businessmen. He proposed innovative programs to improve the city but few passed, because of his scandalous reputation (he was convicted of defrauding investors during the Gold Rush), dictatorial methods, and reputation for politicizing the police. The state legislature, controlled by Republicans, revised the municipal charter and stripped him of his power in 1857. Scorned by Tammany Hall, he formed his own organization, Mozart Hall, and defended home rule. Before 1861 he was the city's chief defender of slavery in the South, owing to both the city's dependence on the cotton trade and his own racism. He made a notorious suggestion that New York City become a "free city" in 1861 and during the Civil War walked a fine line between loyalty and treason, eventually becoming the city's leading Copperhead. In 1867 he was again elected to the U.S. Congress, where he served to the end of his life.

Jerome Mushkat: *Fernando Wood: A Political Biography* (Kent, Ohio: Kent State University Press, 1990)

See also POLICE.

Jerome Mushkat

Woodhaven. Neighborhood in southwestern Queens, bordering Cypress Hills and bounded to the north by Park Lane South, to the east by 106th and 107th streets, to the south by Atlantic Avenue, and to the west by the Brooklyn line. The area was settled in the eighteenth century and the early nineteenth by members of the Ditmars, Lott, Wyckoff, Suydam, and Snediker families. A racetrack called Union Course was built in 1821 between 78th and 82nd streets south of Jamaica Avenue; races were held there as late as 1868, often between the horses of plantation owners from the South and those of wealthy Northerners. Another track, the Centerville, opened in 1825 east of Woodhaven Boulevard and south of Rockaway Boulevard and was the subject of lithographs produced in the 1850s by Currier and Ives. The area was developed as a workers' village by John R. Pitkin, who moved to Long Island from Connecticut in 1835 to build a manufacturing center in East New York. He abandoned his plan during a depression in 1837 and turned to promoting his village, Woodville, in the 1850s after persuading the railroad in 1850 to build a station. In 1853 he launched a newspaper and the few inhabitants voted to change the name of the village to Woodhaven; a shoe factory opened in 1854.

Development increased after a tinware factory was built in 1863 by Charles Lalance and Florian Grosjean, Frenchmen who improved the process of tin stamping. The factory became immensely successful, eventually covering eleven acres (4.5 hectares). Grosjean, who managed the factory, invited French workers and built company housing. During the 1880s and 1890s the stamping works dominated the village, employing 2100 workers; it also had a feeder steel mill in Harrisburg, Pennsylvania, and branches in Chicago and Boston, and supplied mess kits for the Spanish–American War. Several residential developments were built at the end of the century: Ozone Park (1882–90), Brooklyn Hills (1889), and Forest Parkway (1900). After elevated lines were extended along Liberty Avenue (1915) and Jamaica Avenue (1917) blocks of houses were erected and thousands of Italians and Irish moved to the neighborhood. The red-brick building of the stamping works remained until 1955; in 1984–85 its former clock tower became a bank, and the site of the factory was used for a shopping mall. From 1970 the neighborhood attracted a number of blacks, Latin Americans, and immigrants from Guyana, Jamaica, and China. The character of Woodhaven remains suburban.

Vincent Seyfried

Woodhull, Caleb S. (*b* 26 Feb 1792; *d* 16 July 1866). Mayor. He was elected mayor as a Whig in 1849 against divided Democratic opposition. Among his concerns were designating more public squares and controlling the 750 sites in the city where meat was processed. During the Astor Place Riot his house and the Opera House were targets of vandals.

James E. Mooney

Woodhull [née Claflin], **Victoria** (*b* Homer, Ohio, 23 Sept 1838; *d* Bristol, England, 10 June 1927). Reformer. Born to poverty, she began her career as a spiritualist and in 1868 moved to New York City, where she

Victoria Woodhull

became a leader of the American branch of the INTERNATIONAL WORKINGMEN'S ASSOCIATION and edited a reform newspaper. In 1871 she addressed the U.S. Congress on the issue of woman suffrage. A supporter of "free love" (the doctrine that the state should not interfere with sexual relations), she attacked sexual hypocrisy, most notoriously when in the early 1870s she exposed the adulterous triangle between Henry Ward Beecher, Theodore Tilton, and Elizabeth Beecher. Her actions cost her the acceptance of respectable society, her sanity, and her residence in the United States. She moved to England in 1877.

Ellen Carol DuBois

woodlands. A large part of the metropolitan area was once covered by woodlands, where coniferous and deciduous forests thrived in the rich local soils and coastal temperate climate of the region. Most of the original woodlands were destroyed during the development of New York City. A few trees survived alongside buildings, in parks, and in vacant lots, and in later years species adapted to the harsh city environment were planted for decoration. Much of New York City is classified as an open forest (in that the crowns of trees are not all contiguous), and as an urban forest. A few modified stands of native deciduous forest survive in Inwood, Fort Tryon, Riverside, High Bridge, and Central parks in Manhattan; the New York Botanical Garden and Van Cortlandt and Pelham Bay parks in the Bronx; the Gateway National Recreation Area and Kissena, Cunningham, Forest, and Flushing Meadows–Corona parks in Queens; Prospect Park in Brooklyn; and the William T. Davis Wildlife Refuge and Great Kills, High Rock, Willowbrook, New Springville, and Blue Heron Pond parks in Staten Island. Remnants of native temperate evergreen forest are found in parts of Staten Island. There the dominant species is the needle-leaved pitch pine, which thrives in poor, acidic, sandy soils prone to drought and fire; in the absence of fire such areas generally become oak forests.

Steven D. Garber: *The Urban Naturalist* (New York: John Wiley and Sons, 1987)

Steven D. Garber

Woodlawn. Neighborhood in the north central Bronx, bounded to the north by the city of Yonkers, to the east by the Bronx River Parkway, to the south by Woodlawn Cemetery, and to the west by Van Cortlandt Park. It was settled after the railroad was extended and Woodlawn Cemetery was laid out in 1863. The village was established in 1873 by George Updyke on the former farm of Gilbert Valentine. Also known as Woodlawn Heights, it is a neighborhood mostly of one- and two-family houses with some apartment buildings, and has a predominantly Irish and Italian population.

Gary D. Hermalyn

Woodlawn Cemetery. Nonsectarian cemetery of four hundred acres (160 hectares) in the Bronx, bounded to the north by East 233rd Street, to the east by Webster Avenue, to the south by East 211 Street and Bainbridge Avenue, and to the west by Jerome Avenue. It was laid out in the rural style in 1863 by James C. Sidney about ten miles (sixteen kilometers) from Grand Central Terminal and was easily accessible by railroad up the Bronx River Valley. After the ceremonious burial of Admiral David Farragut in 1870 it became a favorite cemetery among the prominent. Woodlawn accepted reinterments from Manhattan as the island was being built over. During the decades after the Civil War mausoleums for nationally known figures were designed in popular revival styles by such architects as James Renwick, Stanford White, Louis Comfort Tiffany, and John Russell Pope. Many experts regard the cemetery as the most elegant and impressive in the United States.

There are more than 300,000 interments in Woodlawn Cemetery, including those of several important figures. Little space remains for burials, but facilities include new community mausoleums, a crematorium, and columbariums. A railroad station stands across from the main entrance at East 233rd Street and Webster Avenue. Known for its pastoral setting and extraordinary architecture and sculpture, Woodlawn Cemetery also has five of the "great trees" designated by the parks department in 1985, more than any other single place.

Edward F. Bergman: *Woodlawn Remembers: Cemetery of American History* (Utica, N.Y.: North Country, 1988)

Edward F. Bergman

Woodlawn Heights. Alternative name for WOODLAWN.

Woodrow. Neighborhood in south central Staten Island, lying north of the Richmond Parkway. It was a sparsely settled area of woodland and small farms until one-family houses were built in the 1970s. Francis Asbury preached in the area in 1771 and a Methodist church was established there in 1787; the Woodrow United Methodist Church at 1075 Woodrow Road (1842) has white clapboard siding, a Greek Revival portico, an Italianate bell tower, and an adjoining cemetery and parsonage (1850). The main thoroughfares are Woodrow Road and Foster Road.

Barnett Shepherd

Woodruff, Timothy Lester (*b* New Haven, Conn., 4 Aug 1858; *d* New York City, 12 Oct 1913). Businessman and public official. The son of a congressman from Connecticut, he was orphaned at the age of ten, graduated from Yale University, and became a successful businessman by purchasing major interests in a typewriter company and other enterprises. In 1881 he moved to Brooklyn and joined the local Republican club, where he displayed notable political skills and with the support of the state Republican leader Thomas C. Platt became the head of the Republican organization in Brooklyn. He was elected lieutenant governor of New York for three successive terms (1896–1902) and then became chairman of the Republican State Committee. In 1912 Woodruff supported Theodore Roosevelt's Progressive presidential campaign and was the chairman of the Bull Moose County Committee of Brooklyn. He lived for many years at 25 8th Avenue in Brooklyn and was president of the Montauk Club.

Richard Skolnick

Woods, Arthur (*b* Boston, 29 Jan 1870; *d* Washington, 12 May 1942). Police commissioner. A former English teacher at Groton and a protégé of Theodore Roosevelt, he was appointed commissioner in 1914 by the reform mayor John Purroy Mitchel. He was faulted for his zealousness when a state investigation uncovered his indiscriminate use of wiretapping. In 1918 he left the department to become the head of Rockefeller Center.

Joseph P. Viteritti

Woodside. Neighborhood in northwestern Queens, adjoining Long Island City. The area was settled in the late seventeenth century by Joseph Sackett. During the American Revolution a dry ridge known as the Narrow Passage lay near what is now Woodside Avenue and 37th Avenue, and provided a route for troops and couriers; high ground that is now the site of Public School 11 was used by the British as a bivouac area and lookout. Between 1830 and 1860 John Kelly, William Schroeder, and Gustav Sussdorf (all of Charleston, South Carolina) and Louis Windmuller moved to the area and built mansions. The name is derived from a series of articles entitled "Letters from Woodside" written by Kelly's son, the newspaperman John Andrew Kelly. In 1861 the railroad was extended to the area, providing a connection to Manhattan. A village was developed in 1867 by Benjamin W. Hitchcock, who laid out streets and sold lots; his success encouraged other developers during the 1870s and 1880s. The population rose from 1355 in 1875 to 3878 in 1900; many moved to the area after trolley lines were extended in 1895 and a trolley terminal was built (now the Clock Tower Shopping Center). More houses were erected after the extension of the elevated line in 1917, and the last open land disappeared during a period of rapid development in the 1920s. A large number of Irish families moved to the neighborhood from cramped quarters in Manhattan.

After the Second World War some older housing in Woodside was replaced by apartment buildings, notably Big Six Towers on Queens Boulevard and 60th Street, a cooperative housing development sponsored by New York Typographical Union no. 6. The large Irish population was complemented during the 1980s by immigrants from China, Colombia, Korea, and the Dominican Republic, and to a lesser extent from India, Ecuador, the Philippines, Guyana, Peru, and Ireland. The nonprofit organization Woodside on the Move has promoted the revitalization of Roosevelt Avenue, the neighborhood's principal commercial thoroughfare.

Vincent Seyfried

Woodstock. Neighborhood in the southern Bronx, bounded to the north by the Boston Road, to the east by Jackson Avenue, to the south by East 160th Street, and to the west by Cauldwell Avenue. It was populated from the 1860s to the 1920s chiefly by Germans, who formed several political and social clubs and singing societies that became well known (the Woodstock branch of the New York Public Library is one of few buildings remaining from this time). The neighborhood became the site in 1904 of the first public high school in the Bronx, Morris High School. In the mid 1990s the population was mostly black and Latin American.

John McNamara: *McNamara's Old Bronx* (New York: Bronx County Historical Society, 1989)

Gary D. Hermalyn

Woodward, Helen Rosen (*b* New York City, 19 March 1882; *d* New York City, 5 Sept 1969). Advertising executive and writer. She began her career working in the promotion departments of *Woman's Home Companion* and *Pictorial Review* and with the advertising agencies Frank Presbrey Company and Gardner Advertising. One of the first women to become an account executive, she developed advertising for products ranging from soup to mail-order books. In 1924 she left to write a penetrating critique of the industry, *Through Many Windows* (1926). She returned to Madison Avenue in the 1930s and wrote another critical account, *It's an Art* (1938); she also published a popular history of women's magazines, *The Lady Persuaders* (1960).

Mary Ellen Zuckerman

Woollcott, Alexander (Humphreys) (*b* Phalanx, N.J., 19 Jan 1887; *d* New York City, 23 Jan 1943). Theater critic. He began his career as an obituary writer for the *New York Times* (1910) and helped to organize the Algonquin Round Table. As a theater critic for the *New York Herald*, the *Sun*, and the *New York World* (1922–28) he wielded enormous power; his reviews often determined whether a play would succeed or fail. He is considered a pioneer of drama criticism for having freed the critic from the obligation to placate theater owners by reviewing all productions favorably. In his later career he became nationally known through his columns for the *New Yorker* and the radio program "The Town Crier" (on the stations of the Columbia Broadcasting System, 1929–43) for his flamboyance, outspokenness, and intimate although biting style, as well as for his sometimes mawkish enthusiasms. Woollcott lived from 1922 to 1927 at 412 West 47th Street, from to 1927 to 1936 at 450 East 52nd Street, and toward the end of his life at 10 Gracie Square and 2 West 55th Street.

Edwin Hoyt: *Alexander Woollcott: The Man Who Came to Dinner* (New York: Abelard–Schuman, 1944; repr. 1968)

Brenda Wineapple

Woolworth. For information on the chain of retail stores see F. W. WOOLWORTH.

Woolworth, F(rank) W(infield) (*b* Rodman, near Adams, N.Y., 13 April 1852; *d* Glen Cove, N.Y., 8 April 1919). Businessman. After attending a business school in Watertown, New York, he worked in a local grocery. In 1878 he learned of a retail store where each item was priced at five cents, a formula that he copied at his grocery with great success. He then opened a "five-cent store" in Utica, New York, which failed. Convinced that a store with a larger selection of merchandise would succeed, he opened one in Lancaster, Pennsylvania, where some goods were sold for ten cents. This store, the first "five and ten," prospered and he opened many others. In 1886 he moved his headquarters to New York City to be closer to the offices of his suppliers. The firm rented a small office at 104 Chambers Street, and he lived with his family in Brooklyn. In 1896 he opened his first store in New York City, at 17th Street and 6th Avenue. He built a thirty-room mansion in 1901 at 990 5th Avenue, near the homes of many other wealthy merchants. In 1911 he erected the Woolworth Building, the tallest structure in the world, on Broadway and Park Place in lower Manhattan. This neo-Gothic skyscraper was derided as a "cathedral of commerce," but Woolworth took the term as a compliment and began using it himself. At his death there were more than a thousand stores in the Woolworth chain and his personal fortune was estimated at $65 million. He is buried at Woodlawn Cemetery in the Bronx.

James Brough: *The Woolworths* (New York: McGraw–Hill, 1982)

Rohit T. Aggarwala

Woolworth Building. Office building on Broadway at Park Place in Manhattan, across from City Hall Park. It has sixty stories and a height of 792 feet (241 meters), which made it the tallest building in the world from its completion in 1913 until it was surpassed in 1929 by the Chrysler Building. The building was designed by Cass Gilbert, apprenticed many years earlier to the firm of McKim, Mead and White, in a graceful Gothic style intended to emphasize verticality; he described its construction as a masonry and terra cotta covering of a steel frame. Subtle coloring on the upper stories helps to create the impression of shadow on a surface that by necessity is essentially flat. Described at its dedication as a "cathedral of commerce," the building became the model for the skyscrapers that transformed the skyline of New York City after the First World War. It remains one of the world's most distinguished structures.

Frank Winfield Woolworth: *The Master Builders: A Record of the Construction of the World's Highest Commercial Structure* (New York: 1913)
John K. Winkler: *Five and Ten: The Fabulous Life of F. W. Woolworth* (New York: R. M. McBride, 1940)

Woolworth Building, ca 1912–13

Anthony W. Robins: *Designation Report* (New York: Landmarks Preservation Commission, 1983)

Ellen Fletcher

WOR. The call letters of an AM radio, FM radio, and television station in New York City. The AM station (710 kHz), one of the oldest in the United States, began operations in early 1922 in Newark, New Jersey, at Bamberger's department store. At the outset it offered a large amount of music programming, including the first broadcasts of the New York Philharmonic, and it was one of four stations to form the Mutual Broadcasting System in 1934. Among those heard on talk shows over the years were Bernarr Macfadden, H. V. Kaltenborn, Gabriel Heatter, Arlene Francis, and Sherrye Henry, as well as three generations of announcers named John Gambling, hosts of "Rambling with Gamblin" (first broadcast in 1925 and continued into the 1990s). The station also broadcast games of the New York Mets, New York Knicks, New York Rangers, and New York Giants.

WOR-FM (98.7) is best-known for having been one of the first radio stations to adopt a "progressive rock" format in 1966, which proved highly influential although it lasted only until the following year. The station later changed its call letters to WXLO and then WRKS.

WOR-TV (channel 9) began broadcasting on 11 October 1949 from studios on 42nd Street and remained independent of the networks. In the mid 1980s it changed its call letters to WWOR and moved to Secaucus, New Jersey.

Workingman's School. Original name of the ETHICAL CULTURE FIELDSTON SCHOOLS.

Workman Publishing. Firm of book and calendar publishers, formed in 1967 by Peter Workman. It achieved success in its early years with children's and how-to books, "page-a-day" calendars, and cookbooks, and books and miscellaneous items depicting cats drawn by the cartoonist B. Kliban. Among its more successful titles are *The Official Preppy Handbook* (1980) by Lisa Birnbach, which sold 1.5 million copies, and Arlene Eisenberg's *What to Expect When You're Expecting* (1984). The offices are at 708 Broadway.

James E. Mooney

Workmen's Circle [Arbeter Ring]. A fraternal order for Jewish laborers founded on socialist principles as a mutual aid society in 1892 and reorganized as a national order in 1900. For many years beginning about 1912 its headquarters were in the Forward Building at 175 East Broadway. The membership remained centered in New York City, where the order provided material assistance to members, took part in the labor movement, undertook cultural projects, and opened children's schools that offered instruction in the Yiddish language, Jewish history, and socialism. Membership peaked in 1925 at nearly 85,000 and then slowly declined. In the mid 1990s the offices were at 45 East 33rd Street.

Daniel Soyer

Works Progress Administration [Work Projects Administration; WPA]. A federal emergency employment and relief agency established in 1935 by President Franklin D. Roosevelt. Its initial appropriation of $4800 million represented more than half the total federal budget. The agency was closely associated with New York City from its inception and much of its activity was centered there. Its national director, Harry Hopkins, had experience working in a settlement house in Manhattan and with the Association for Improving the Condition of the Poor, and had led the New York State Temporary Emergency Relief Administration and between 1933 and 1935 the Federal Emergency Relief Administration and the Civil Works Administration, both forerunners of the WPA. Moreover New York City was the only city to have a local organization that stood on an equal footing with state organizations: Mayor Fiorello H. La Guardia gained this special treatment for the city because of his influence with Roosevelt and Hopkins, the innovative work relief projects developed by private and public welfare agencies in the city during the Depression, and the city's huge welfare burden (as the home of nearly 7 percent of all Americans on relief in 1935). By 1936 the WPA was spending about $20 million a month in the city, or one seventh of all the funds being spent nationally; from 1935 to 1939 it had a labor force that fluctuated between 100,000 and 245,000, but because of insufficient funding it still could not provide work for all the able-bodied residents of the city who sought it: about 100,000 were on general relief when the agency was at its peak in 1936. The first local director of the WPA was General Hugh Johnson, who served only briefly. During the crucial period 1936–40 the local director was Colonel Brehon B. Somervell of the Army Corps of Engineers. The agency was renamed the Work Projects Administration in 1939.

Two thirds of those employed by the WPA

Performance of the Caravan Theatre of the Federal Theater Project of the Works Progress Administration, Silver Lake, Staten Island, 1930s

in the city worked on construction and engineering projects. The agency was seen by La Guardia as a valuable resource for rebuilding and modernizing his city. In 1937–38 projects sponsored by the agency accounted for 60 percent of all construction under way in the city; among its developments were La Guardia Airport, the portion of the FDR Drive within lower Manhattan and the South Shore Drive in Brooklyn, 255 playgrounds, and seventeen municipal swimming pools. The agency also refurbished Jacob Riis Park, Orchard Beach, and other beaches, developed five thousand acres (two thousand hectares) of new parks, including one at a disused dump and ash heap in Queens that became the site of the World's Fair of 1939–40, repaired two thousand miles (3200 kilometers) of streets and highways, and demolished 5500 decaying structures to make way for public housing projects in Williamsburg, on the Lower East Side (the First Houses), and elsewhere, as well as building and repairing many schools, clinics, hospitals, municipal markets, and police and fire stations.

The remaining third of those employed by the WPA in the city were engaged in white-collar and professional work, which provided city residents with many services not available to them even during the prosperous 1920s: these included adult education classes and day care for preschool children at twenty-eight centers, screening and x-rays for tuberculosis for 400,000 urban residents, and dental services for the poor. Because the city had more actors, artists, musicians, and writers than any other city in the United States it also had the largest program administered by the Federal Arts Project, between 1936 and 1938 accounting for nearly half of the five thousand persons employed by artists' projects nationwide. The Federal Theatre in the city employed more than four thousand actors, dramatists, directors, and stagehands in 1938. It produced classics, new plays, and social documentaries by a troupe called the Living Newspaper; companies affiliated with it produced plays for children, marionette shows, radio plays, and German, black, and Yiddish theater. John Houseman and Rose McClendon, joint directors of the New York Negro Theatre Project, staged an all-black *Macbeth* adapted by Orson Welles, and a Yiddish *King Lear* enjoyed the longest run of any production mounted by the WPA in the city. The Federal Writers Project engaged many writers in the city, of whom some had already been published but had fallen into disfavor (Maxwell Bodenheim and Anzia Yezierska) and others were young and largely unknown (John Cheever and Ralph Ellison). The writings supported by the project ranged from the guidebooks *New York Panorama* (1939) and *New York City Guide* (1939) to Richard Wright's novel *Native Son* (1940). The Federal Art Project supported such painters as Raphael Soyer, Stuart Davis, and Jackson Pollock, as well as sculptors, printmakers, photographers, and teachers. Murals painted under the auspices of the WPA may be seen at the New York Public Library on 5th Avenue and 42nd Street, at Harlem Hospital, and at many municipal buildings. Berenice Abbott took thousands of photographs of the city while attached to the project, some of which appeared in *Changing New York* (1939). Some two thousand musicians in the city belonged to groups sponsored by the Federal Music Project, including a symphony orchestra and jazz, swing, and dance bands; these performed in theaters, on the radio, and in the parks.

In 1938 and 1939 the Un-American Activities Committee and an appropriations subcommittee of the U.S. House of Representatives investigated the Federal Arts Projects, focusing in particular on writers, actors, and artists in the city. Members of the committees charged that the projects were dominated by communists whose works were filled with propaganda for the New Deal and more radical causes. In 1939 the Federal Theatre was eliminated and the other arts projects were drastically curtailed. The WPA ceased operations on 1 February 1943.

In its seven and a half years the WPA in New York City provided income for 700,000 victims of the Depression and their dependents, an amount equal to a quarter of the city's total population of eight million.

Jane D. Matthew: *The Federal Theatre, 1935–1939* (Princeton, N.J.: Princeton University Press, 1967)

Jerre G. Mangione: *The Dream and the Deal: The Federal Writers Project, 1935–1943* (Boston: Little, Brown, 1972)

Francis V. O'Connor, ed.: *The New Deal Art Projects: An Anthology of Memoirs* (Washington: Smithsonian Institution Press, 1972)

Barbara Blumberg: *The New Deal and the Unemployed: The View from New York City* (Lewisburg, Penn.: Bucknell University Press, 1979)

Barbara Blumberg

World Council of Churches. Organization of more than three hundred churches in more than a hundred countries, formed in Amsterdam in August 1948 after years of planning; its members include Anglican, Protestant, Old Catholic, Eastern Orthodox, and Oriental Orthodox churches. The council brings together theologians and church leaders to discuss various issues and promote unity among various Christian groups. The American office is in the Interchurch Center.

Marlin Van Elderen: *Introducing the World Council of Churches* (Geneva: World Council of Churches, 1990)

Thomas E. Bird

World Financial Center. Commercial development built on fourteen acres (5.7 hectares) of landfill in Battery Park City, bounded to the north by Vesey Street, to the east by West Street, to the south by Albany Street, and to the west by the Hudson River. Rights for commercial development in the area were won in a lawsuit by the firm of Olympia and York, which engaged Cesar Pelli as the architect. His design, adapted to a master plan prepared in 1979 by Battery Park City Associates and the firm of Cooper, Eckstut, called for four towers ranging from thirty-three to fifty-one stories in height and containing eight million square feet (743,200 square meters) of space. Ground was broken in December 1981 and construction completed in 1988. Amenities include 220,000 square feet (20,440 square meters) of shops and restaurants clustered around the Plaza, a landscaped park called the Courtyard covering 3.5 acres (1.4 hectares) along the North Cove yacht harbor, and the Winter Garden, a vaulted glass and steel structure 120 feet (thirty-seven meters) high containing a grand marble staircase, a patterned marble floor, and sixteen palm trees forty feet (twelve meters) tall.

Eric Wm. Allison

world's fairs. New York City was the site of world's fairs in 1853–54, 1939–40, and 1964–65. The first held in the city was also the first in the United States: opened on 14 July 1853 at the Crystal Palace on a site now occupied by Bryant Park, it was entitled "Exhibition of the Industry of All Nations" and modeled after the Great Exhibition at the Crystal Palace in London of 1851. More than four thousand displays from the United States and abroad exhibited agricultural and industrial products, sculpture, and paintings. Although paid attendance at the exhibition exceeded one million, the sponsors were left with $300,000 in debt when the exhibition closed on 1 November 1854.

The site of the second fair was Flushing Meadow, also known as the Corona Dumps, a tidal expanse covering 1216 acres (492 hectares) along the Flushing River that for decades had been used as a refuse dump by the firm Brooklyn Ash Removal. Ground was broken on 29 June 1936; to prepare the site the mounds of refuse were leveled and water mains, sewers, and streets were installed. Other projects undertaken in connection with the fair included the Bronx–Whitestone Bridge, the Whitestone Expressway, the Grand Central and Cross Island parkways, the Queens Boulevard line of the Independent subway (extended to Kew Gardens on 31 December 1936), a station of Interborough Rapid Transit at Willets Point Avenue, a station of the Long Island Rail Road, a sewage treatment plant in Bowery Bay, and La Guardia Airport. The fair was overseen by a nonprofit corporation led by Grover A. Whalen, which issued $27,829,500 in bonds due in 1941. These paid 4 percent interest and were backed by receipts from concessions, rents, and admissions (75 cents for adults, 25 cents for children); profits

lished many titles, including *Modern Bride* and *Car and Driver*. Ziff himself was a popular author whose book *The Coming Battle of Germany* (1942) became a best-seller. In the 1980s Ziff–Davis sold many of its existing magazines and entered the business of computer publishing. It became the nation's leader in the field, publishing such magazines as *PC Magazine*, *PC Week*, and *Computer Shopper*. In June 1994 the firm put its assets up for sale; these were purchased in October by the investment firm of Forstmann–Little and Company.

James Bradley

zoning. The impetus for zoning legislation in New York City came from the Fifth Avenue Association, which about 1900 sought to protect the carriage trade and exclude loft buildings and the garment industry; others who favored zoning were residents concerned by the size of skyscrapers such as the Equitable Building (120 Broadway) and reformers who wanted to build a well-planned, healthy city by dividing land according to use, controlling the density and configuration of buildings, and providing for adequate light and air. The state legislature gave the city permission in 1914 to adopt a zoning resolution, and the Board of Estimate responded by establishing the Building Heights and Restrictions Commission, which formulated in its final report on 2 June 1916 a zoning plan that was adopted by the board at the end of the year. The plan allowed for an eventual population of 55 million in the city and outlined modifications of its traditional pattern of development: a system of mapped districts of height, area, and use was to control the rate of development; adequate light and air and proper building density were to be maintained by designing new buildings to fit an imaginary envelope determined by the size of their lots and their location on a block; each district was assigned a maximum streetwall height (the height of a building allowed at the street lot line); building setbacks were made to conform to an "angle of light" plane (later called the sky exposure plane); skyscrapers were allowed by the tower regulation to be of any height as long as they occupied no more than 25 percent of the area of their lots; and yard and building coverage regulations were imposed (specifying the proportion of a lot that could be built up). The guidelines adopted in the city soon became a model for zoning ordinances throughout the nation.

Zoning in the city was changed radically after the Second World War by the *Plan for the Rezoning of New York* (1950), which drew heavily on European modernist principles of town planning and recommended widely spaced skyscrapers set in large blocks resembling parks (superblocks). Its authors intended to limit the population of the city to about eleven or twelve million by imposing a density control called Floor Area Ratio (FAR), under which the size of a lot and its location determined the size and height of the building that could be erected on it. The regulations set forth in the plan were adopted by the city in 1961, superseding those of 1916. Developers were given incentives to build arcades, plazas, and other open spaces accessible to the public under a plan that became known as tower-in-the-park zoning, of which Co-op City in the Bronx and the office towers on the west side of 6th Avenue in midtown Manhattan are examples. Within ten years of its approval by the city this form of zoning had proved highly inflexible and incompatible with the traditional pattern of attached building in the city. The Planning Commission modified the regulations of 1961 by establishing special districts (thirty-five were created by 1990) as well as a system of special permits, which allowed greater flexibility of design for large-scale developments and were increasingly issued for buildings erected in midtown Manhattan in the next twenty years. In keeping with the traditional public concern for daylight in midtown, the Midtown Zoning Regulation of 1982 set a standard for the amount of daylight in new buildings and the public space of the street. The Quality Housing and Contextual Zoning Regulations (1988–90) promoted the construction of housing in keeping with earlier buildings characteristic of the city's older neighborhoods.

Headquarters of Equitable Life Insurance, ca *1915*

Stanislaw J. Makielski Jr.: *The Politics of Zoning: The New York Experience* (New York: Columbia University Press, 1966)

Michael Kwartler

zoos. The Central Park Zoo, the oldest zoo in New York City, began as a menagerie, purportedly opened when the park's workers received a bear and other animals as a gift. By 1864 the menagerie had a separate budget published in the annual report of the parks department, and it was a popular attraction despite the poor condition of its animal cages. It survived proposals by real-estate developers to abolish it or move it to Manhattan Square (now the site of the American Museum of Natural History), to another location in Central Park, or out of Manhattan altogether. Frederick Law Olmsted and Calvert Vaux included zoological grounds in their design of Prospect Park (1866), but the zoo did not open until 1893, when it exhibited sheep, deer, bears, and peafowl.

After a campaign led by the Boone and Crockett Club, the state of New York in 1895 awarded a charter to the New York Zoological Society that empowered it to build a zoological garden. William Hornaday (1844–1937), a well-known zoologist and one of the

Gazelles and hartebeest in an African Plains exhibit at the Bronx Zoo

founders of the National Zoological Park in Washington, became the director of the project in 1896 and selected a site for the new zoo in southern Bronx Park. Plans were drawn up by the architects George Lewis Heins and C. Grant La Farge in 1897, and construction began in the following year. The New York Zoological Park, which became known as the Bronx Zoo, opened in 1899. Its naturalistic, parklike settings were in marked contrast to the small exhibits in Central Park. Among the structures completed within a decade of the opening were the aquatic bird house (1899), the reptile house (1900), the primate house (1902), the lion house (1903), the large bird house (1905), and the elephant house (1908). In 1902 the zoo appointed Reid Blair as the first full-time veterinarian at a zoo in the United States. Hornaday, an authority on the nearly extinct American bison, set aside breeding sanctuaries for the species in the American West. In 1907 the zoo sent fifteen bison to the new Wichita National Bison Reserve in Oklahoma, a project that influenced cooperative wildlife conservation efforts among zoos and nature reserves worldwide. In 1916 it opened an animal hospital, the first of its kind in the United States.

Work relief efforts during the Depression provided for the renovation of zoos in New York City: under the direction of the parks commissioner Robert Moses the old menagerie in Central Park was demolished in 1934 and rebuilt, and in 1935 a new facility was built in Prospect Park to replace the elephant house and other structures. In cooperation with the city's parks department, the Staten Island Zoological Society in 1936 opened the Staten Island Zoo, which became known for its education and breeding programs and its notable collection of reptiles. Early in the tenure of Fairfield Osborn (1887–1969) as president of the New York Zoological Society (1940–68) hidden moats were added to the African Plains exhibit (1941) and a children's zoo (1941) and "farm in the zoo" (1942) were opened. William Conway, who joined the Bronx Zoo in 1956 as an assistant curator of birds, was appointed its director in 1962 and general director in 1966. He believed that zoos should serve as nature refuges and breeding centers for endangered species of wildlife, and developed exhibits that allowed the animals to live in naturalistic replicas of their habitats rather than cages: among his innovations were a new aquatic bird house (1964), the "World of Darkness" (1969), the "World of Birds" (1972), "Wild Asia" (1977), and "Jungle World" (1985). He also designed the Flushing Meadows–Corona Park Zoo, opened by the city in 1968 on the former site of the World's Fair of 1964–65.

In 1980 the parks department prevailed on the New York Zoological Society to remodel the zoos in Central Park, Prospect Park, and Flushing Meadows–Corona Park, which were in disrepair. The Central Park Zoo, closed in 1985, reopened in 1988 as a completely new facility designed by Kevin Roche and John Dinkeloo. The Flushing Meadows–Corona Park Zoo closed in 1988 and reopened after renovation in 1992, now emphasizing the wildlife of North America. The Prospect Park Zoo closed in 1988 and reopened in 1993 as an educationally oriented facility. To lend emphasis to its role in international conservation, the New York Zoological Society in 1993 began using the name the Wildlife Conservation Society; the formal names of the zoos were changed to the Bronx Zoo / Wildlife Conservation Park, the Central Park Zoo Conservation Center, and the Prospect Park Wildlife Conservation Center.

William Bridges: *Gathering of Animals: An Unconventional History of the New York Zoological Society* (New York: Harper and Row, 1974)

Terry Collins and Steven P. Johnson: *Guide to the Archives of the New York Zoological Society* (New York: New York Zoological Society, 1982)

Steven Johnson

Zorach [née Thompson], **Marguerite** (*b* Santa Rosa, Calif., 25 Sept 1887; *d* Brooklyn, 27 June 1968). Painter. After marrying the painter and sculptor William Zorach (1912) she took part in the Armory Show (1913) and the Forum Exhibition of Modern American Painters (1916). Her paintings were influenced by European fauvism and cubism and characterized by bold color, expressive brushwork, and simplified form. She was the director of the Society of Independent Artists (1922–24) and the first president of the New York Society of Women Artists (1925) and was also active as a textile artist.

Roberta K. Tarbell: *Marguerite Zorach: The Early Years, 1908–1920* (Washington: Smithsonian Institution Press for the National Collection of Fine Arts, 1973)

Marilyn Friedman Hoffman: *Marguerite and William Zorach: The Cubist Years, 1915–1918* (Manchester, N.H.: Currier Gallery of Art, 1987)

Carol Lowrey

Zorach, William (*b* Jurbarkas, Lithuania, 28 Feb 1887; *d* Bath, Maine, 15 Nov 1966). Sculptor and painter. After living in Paris, where he was influenced by cubism and fauvism, he moved in 1912 to New York City and settled in Greenwich Village. He and his wife, Marguerite Thompson Zorach, exhibited paintings at the Armory Show in 1913 that were considered wildly modern. In 1917 he took up sculpture, which so fascinated him that he abandoned all painting except watercolors in 1922. Many of his works are large figures of children, animals, lovers, and biblical figures sculpted in granite, marble, onyx, or wood in a primitive style. His *Spirit of the Dance* (1932) was installed at Radio City Music Hall. For several years Zorach lived with his wife and two children at 17 West 9th Street and kept a studio at 2 West 15th Street; from 1939 both home and studio were at 271 Hicks Street in Brooklyn.

Alana J. Erickson

Zoroastrians. Most of the world's Zoroastrians live in Iran or in India (where they are known as Parsis), and those who emigrate are well-educated professionals. In the late nineteenth century a number of Zoroastrian students moved to New York City to study at Columbia University, where in 1895 a professorship in Zoroastrian scriptures was established under A. V. Williams Jackson. Most of the students left the city after their studies, and in 1992 the university discontinued the program. Iranian Zoroastrians established a presence in the city in the 1920s, when the Soroushian family operated a retail carpet business; Philip Lopate's novel *The Rug Merchant* (1987) is loosely based on the family's story. Some Indian Zoroastrians settled in the city after the Immigration Act of 1965 was enacted, and Iranian Zoroastrians increased in number after the Iranian revolution of 1979. Zoroastrians in New York City have not developed lasting religious institutions, but both Parsi and Iranian Zoroastrians from the metropolitan area support the Zoroastrian Association of Greater New York, also known as the Dar-e-Mehr (path of compassion), at New Rochelle in Westchester County. Donated by Arbab Rustam Guiv and others in 1977, this prayer space is used only occasionally on weekends and holidays and does not support an administrative structure or full-time priest. Maintaining the Zoroastrian tradition in New York City is complicated by small numbers, low birthrates, and long prayer services held in the ancient language of Avestan. Another obstacle to the long-term survival of the religion in New York City is that orthodox Zoroastrians reject converts. About two thousand Zoroastrians remained active in New York City and its environs during the mid 1990s.

Marc Ferris

Zukofsky, Louis (*b* New York City, 23 Jan 1904; *d* Port Jefferson, N.Y., 12 May 1978). Poet. Born in poverty on the Lower East Side, he graduated from Columbia University in 1927. During the Depression he worked for the Works Progress Administration at Columbia University, the radio station WNYC, and the New York Arts Project. He later worked as a freelance editor and substitute high school teacher, and taught English at Brooklyn Polytechnic Institute from 1947 until his retirement in 1966. Influenced by Ezra Pound and later by the objectivists, he wrote poetry that was intensely passionate and went unpublished for most of his life. His eight-hundred-page epic *"A,"* which begins with a description of a concert at Carnegie Hall and includes many references to the history and life of New York City, took fifty years to complete. Zukofsky lived at 135 Willow Street in Brooklyn, spent some time at 77 7th Avenue, and moved to Long Island in 1972.

Marc Ferris

NOTES ON THE CONTRIBUTORS

Amanda Aaron, who lives and works in New York City, has a bachelor's degree in history from Columbia College and a master's degree in cinema studies from New York University.

Susan Aaronson is a professorial lecturer in international business at the American University and a doctoral candidate in history at Johns Hopkins University.

Elaine Abelson (PhD New York University) is an associate professor of history and the coordinator of the Urban Studies Program at the New School for Social Research, Eugene Lang College, and the author of *When Ladies Go A-Thieving: Middle-Class Shoplifters in the Victorian Department Store* (1989). Her latest book project is *Gender and Homelessness in the Great Depression*, a study of female poverty in New York City and Chicago.

Alan David Aberbach (BA Rutgers, PhD University of Florida) is an associate professor at Simon Fraser University.

Joan Acocella (PhD Rutgers) is a dance critic, the editor of *Andre Levinson on Dance: Writings from Paris in the Twenties* (1991), and the author of *Mark Morris* (1993).

Arthur G. Adams, founding president of the Hudson River Maritime Center in Kingston, New York, is the author of *The Hudson through the Years* (1983), *The Hudson: A Guidebook to the River* (1981), and *Railroad Ferries of the Hudson* (with Raymond J. Baxter, 1987), and the editor of *The Hudson River in Literature: An Anthology* (1988).

Melvin L. Adelman (PhD University of Illinois 1980) teaches at Ohio State University, where his specialty is the history of American sports.

Norma Adler (BA UCLA, MFA Smith College, MPhil New York University) is an editor at *Playbill*, *Theatre Design and Technology*, and *New York Theatre Critics' Reviews*, and has written for *New York Native*, *Dance Research Journal*, *Women and Performance*, the *Drama Review*, and *Theater Week*.

Emery E. Adoradio (AB in history, University of California, Berkeley; MA in history, New York University) has been an assistant district attorney in New York County since 1987, and is now assigned to the prosecution of cases involving corruption in the criminal justice system.

Rohit T. Aggarwala (BA in history, Columbia University, 1993) is a native of New York City and a special assistant at the Federal Railroad Administration in Washington.

Irving Lewis Allen is a professor of sociology at the University of Connecticut, Storrs, and the author of *New York in Slang: Popular Speech about City Life, 1850 to the Present Suburban Age* (1992).

Jane Allen is a program officer at the IRI Research Institute in Stamford, Connecticut.

Eric Wm. Allison (BA Columbia College 1994) is a resident of Brooklyn.

Rabbi Marc D. Angel (PhD Yeshiva University) is the rabbi of Congregation Shearith Israel, the historic Spanish and Portuguese Synagogue of New York City; the president of the Rabbinical Council of America; and the founder and chairman of the board of Sephardic House. His books include *The Rhythms of Jewish Living: A Sephardic Approach* (1986) and *The Orphaned Adult: Confronting the Death of a Parent* (1987).

Thea Arnold is a doctoral candidate at the State University of New York, Binghamton. Her dissertation is provisionally entitled "'To Get at the Truth, One Must Read Both Sides': Mary White Ovington and the Race Question, 1909–1947."

Arnold Aronson (PhD New York University) is a professor of theater at Hunter College and the author of *American Set Design* (1989) and *The History and Theory of Environmental Scenography* (1981).

Marc H. Aronson is an editor for Harper Collins and a doctoral student at New York University completing a dissertation on William Crary Brownell and publishing at the end of the nineteenth century.

Arthur Ashe (BS UCLA) won the U.S. Open Tennis Championship at Forest Hills in 1968 and was the author of *A Hard Road to Glory: A History of the African American Athlete* (1988).

Arten Ashjian (master's degree in theology, Harvard Divinity School) is an instructor of Armenian Church History and Liturgics at St. Nersess Armenian Seminary in New Rochelle, New York.

Jean Ashton (PhD Columbia University) is a librarian in the rare book and manuscript division at Columbia and the author of *Harriet Beecher Stowe: A Reference Guide* (1977). She was the curator of the exhibition "P. T. Barnum: Merchant of Delight" at the New-York Historical Society.

Jonathan Aspell (BA Columbia College) is attending the University of Buenos Aires.

John C. Aubry is the archivist of the College Board.

Simon Baatz (PhD University of Pennsylvania) is a senior historian at the Wistar Institute of Anatomy and Biology and the author of *Knowledge, Culture, and Science in the Metropolis* (1990).

Ellen D. Baer (Registered Nurse, PhD, Fellowship in the American Association of Nurses) is an associate professor at the School of Nursing of the University of Pennsylvania and the associate director of its Center for the Study of the History of Nursing.

David A. Balcom is the director of development for the Lawyers' Committee for Civil Rights under Law in Washington. He is completing a doctorate in American history at the Graduate School and University Center, City University of New York, and is writing a book on philanthropy in the civil rights movement.

Andrea Balis is an adjunct instructor in history at Hunter College.

Randall Balmer (PhD Princeton University) is an associate professor of religion at Barnard College and the author of *A Perfect Babel of Confusion: Dutch Religion and English Culture in the Middle Colonies* (1989).

Sally Banes (PhD New York University) is a member of the faculty at the University of Wisconsin and the author of *Terpischore in Sneakers: Post-Modern Dance* (1979) and *Democracy's Body: Judson Dance Theater 1962–1964* (1980).

Rudolf Baranik, a painter born in Lithuania, studied at the Art Institute of Chicago, at the Art Students League, and in Paris, was active in the antiwar movement in the 1960s, and teaches at the Art Students League and at Pratt Institute, where he is a professor emeritus.

Barbara Barker is an associate professor and the head of the dance program at the University of Minnesota. She is the author of *Ballet or Balleyhoo?* (1984) and the editor of *Bolossy Kiralfy: An Autobiography* (1988).

Brooke J. Barr is a PhD candidate in American studies at Yale University who is writing a history of the New York City Landmarks Preservation Commission.

Phyllis Barr (BA in English Literature and journalism, Adelphi University, 1964; MA and MPhil in history and certificate in archival management, New York University) is a certified archivist, records manager, and historian. For fourteen years she was the director of archives of the Parish of Trinity Church in New York City.

Paul Barrett (PhD University of Illinois, Chicago) is an associate professor of history at the Illinois Institute of Technology in Chicago and the author of *The Automobile and Urban Transit: Public Policy in Chicago, 1900–1930* (1983).

James L. Baughman is a professor at the school of journalism and mass communication of the University of Wisconsin, Madison.

Marcia Bayne-Smith is an assistant professor of health education at Queens College. Her research focuses on health issues of women and minority populations.

Thomas D. Beal is working on his dissertation, under the direction of Eric E. Lampard, in the history department of the State University of New York, Stony Brook.

Rick Beard is the executive director of the Atlanta History Center.

Elizabeth Beirne (PhD Fordham University) is an editor and writer and a professor of philosophy at the College of Mount St. Vincent.

Trudy E. Bell (AM New York University), senior editor since 1983 of *Spectrum* (magazine of the Institute of Electrical and Electronics Engineers), was an editor at *Scientific American* and a senior editor at *Omni.* She is also an avid touring bicyclist.

Martha S. Bendix, a graduate of Allegheny College, has worked as the public relations director for the Newark Museum in New Jersey and as an editor, feature writer, and columnist for the *Staten Island Advance.*

Gerald Benjamin, the principal research advisor to the New York City Charter Revision Commission (1987–89), is a professor of political science at the State University of New York, College at New Paltz, and the director of the Governors Project at the Rockefeller Institute of Government, State University of New York, in Albany.

Judith Berck is a freelance writer whose articles have appeared in the *New York Times* and the *Washington Post.* She is the author of *Children in Crisis* (1994).

Ira Berger is a magazine editor by profession, the curator of a book and oral history collection on jazz, and a writer of articles on jazz.

Edward F. Bergman is a professor of geography at Lehman College and the author of *A Geography of the New York Metropolitan Region* (1975) and *Woodlawn Remembers: Cemetery of American History* (1988).

Edward A. Berlin (PhD in musicology) is one of the foremost scholars of ragtime and the author of *Ragtime: A Musical and Cultural History* (1980), *Reflections and Research on Ragtime* (1987), and *King of Ragtime: Scott Joplin and His Era* (1994).

Avis Berman (MA Rutgers) is an arts writer and critic and the author of *Rebels on Eighth Street: Juliana Force and the Whitney Museum of American Art* (1990).

Greta Berman (PhD Columbia University) is a professor of art history at the Juilliard School and the author of *The Lost Years: Mural Painting in New York City under the Works Progress Administration's Federal Art Project, 1935–1943* (1975) and of many articles in art journals.

Iver Bernstein, a professor of history at Washington University in St. Louis, is the author of *The New York City Draft Riots: Their Significance for American Society and Politics in the Age of the Civil War* (1990) and of many essays and reviews on nineteenth-century American history.

Selma Berrol (PhD City University of New York) is a professor of history at Baruch College and the author of *Immigrants at School: New York City, 1898–1914* (1967) and *Getting Down to Business: Baruch College in the City of New York* (1989).

Mary Beth Betts (MPhil Graduate School and University Center, City University of New York) is an associate curator of architectural collections at the New-York Historical Society.

Craig D. Bida (BA Yale University 1988) is an urban planner for the New York City Department of Housing Preservation and Development as well as a writer on urban and rural issues, focusing on man's impact on the natural world.

Eugenie Ladner Birch (American Institute of Certified Planners) is a professor of urban planning at Hunter College and a member of the New York City Planning Commission.

Thomas E. Bird is a professor of Slavic and eastern European studies at Queens College and the assistant historian of the St. Nicholas Society of the City of New York.

Rodger C. Birt (PhD) is an associate professor of humanities at San Francisco State University.

Elizabeth Blackmar is an associate professor of history at Columbia University.

Karen J. Blair is an associate professor of history at Central Washington University and the author of *The Clubwoman as Feminist: True Womanhood Redefined, 1868–1914* (1980).

Annette Blaugrund was the Andrew W. Mellon senior curator and the director of institutional planning at the New-York Historical Society.

Jack Blicksilver is a professor of economics, emeritus, at Georgia State University and the author of *Defenders and Defense of Big Business in the United States, 1880–1900* (1985) and of three monographs on home service life insurance.

Alexander Bloom is an associate professor of American history at Wheaton College and the author of *Prodigal Sons: The New York Intellectuals and Their World* (1986).

Jonathan D. Bloom is a historian and the executive director of the Workers Defense League.

Barbara Blumberg (PhD Columbia University) is an associate professor of history at Pace University and the author of *The New Deal and the Unemployed: The View from New York City* (1979) and *Celebrating the Immigrant: An Administrative History of the Statue of Liberty National Monument* (1985).

Stuart M. Blumin (PhD University of Pennsylvania) is a professor of American history at Cornell University, the author of several books including *The Emergence of the Middle Class: Social Experience in the American City, 1760–1900* (1989), and the editor of *George G. Foster: New York by Gas-Light, and Other Urban Sketches* (1990).

Michele H. Bogart is an associate professor of art history at the State University of New York, Stony Brook.

Patricia U. Bonomi (PhD Columbia University) is a professor of history at New York University and the author of *A Factious People: Politics and Society in Colonial New York* (1971) and *Under the Cope of Heaven: Religion, Society, and Politics in Colonial America* (1986).

Lawson Bowling (PhD Columbia University) teaches history, American studies, and education at Manhattanville College.

Mary B. Bowling (Master of Library Science, Columbia University) is a curator of manuscripts at the New York Public Library.

James Bradley is a freelance journalist and writer based in Brooklyn.

James D. Bratt is a professor of history at Calvin College and a scholar of American religion.

Frank O. Braynard, a retired engineer, is the curator of the American Merchant Marine Museum in Kings Point, New York, and the author of many books on maritime history, including *S.S. Savannah* (1963) and *The Elegant Steam Ship* (1988), and was a consultant to *Great Liners* (1978).

Charles Brecher is the director of research at the Citizens Budget Committee.

Richard Briffault is a professor of law at Columbia University.

Mosette G. Broderick teaches at New York University and writes about nineteenth-century American architecture.

Norman J. Brouwer is a marine historian, curator of ships at the South Street Seaport Museum, and the author of the *International Register of Historic Ships* (1985).

Emilyn L. Brown (BA in education) has worked as a historical researcher for the African Burial Ground Project since 1992 and as a freelance writer, her most recent work including a compilation of African–American historical resources of the Municipal Archives of New York City.

Joshua Brown is the art director of the American Social History Project at Hunter College.

Mary Elizabeth Brown teaches the history of the United States at Kutztown University. For her doctorate (Columbia University 1987) she wrote a dissertation on Italian Catholic parishes in the city and Archidiocese of New York from 1880 to 1950.

Stuart Bruchey is the Allan Nevins Professor Emeritus of American Economic History at Columbia University.

Stephan F. Brumberg (EdD Harvard University) is a professor of education at Brooklyn College and the university director of teacher education and international education in the Office of Academic Affairs at the City University of New York.

Roy S. Bryce-Laporte is the John D. and Catherine T. MacArthur Professor of Sociology at Colgate University. He has conducted extensive research on migratory patterns of Africans in the diaspora.

Peter G. Buckley is an assistant professor on the faculty of humanities and social sciences at Cooper Union.

Stanley Buder (PhD University of Chicago) is a professor of history at Baruch College and at the Graduate School and University Center, City University of New York. He is the author of *Visionaries and Planners: The Garden City Movement and the Modern Community*

(1990) and *Pullman: An Experiment in Industrial Order and Community Planning* (1967).

Karen Buhler-Wilkerson (Registered Nurse, PhD, Fellowship in the American Association of Nurses) is an associate professor of community health nursing at the School of Nursing of the University of Pennsylvania and the associate director of its Center for the Study of the History of Nursing.

John Bull, field associate for the American Museum of Natural History, is the author of *Birds of the New York Area* (1964), *Birds of New York State* (1974), and the *Macmillan Field Guide to the Birds of North America: Eastern Region* (1985).

Timothy Anglin Burgard was the assistant curator of paintings, drawings, and sculpture at the New-York Historical Society and an author of *Mr. Luman Reed's Picture Gallery: A Pioneer Collection of American Art* (1990).

Clarissa L. Bushman (BA Harvard College, MBA Columbia University) is a former professional dancer and investment banker.

Inea Bushnaq is the editor and translator of *Arab Folktales* (1986).

Ann L. Buttenwieser (PhD Columbia University) is an adjunct associate professor of urban planning at Columbia, a vice-president of the New York City Public Development Corporation, and the author of *Manhattan Water-Bound: Planning and Developing Manhattan's Waterfront from the Seventeenth Century to the Present* (1987).

Bernadette G. Callery (MA University of Chicago) is the research librarian of the New York Botanical Garden.

Kerry Candaele (MA University of California, Santa Barbara) is a doctoral student in history at Columbia University.

Donald J. Cannon (PhD Fordham University), professor of history at St. Peter's College, is the editor of *Heritage of Flames: The Illustrated History of Early American Firefighting* (1977) and an honorary deputy chief of the Fire Department of New York.

Marvin Carlson is the Sidney E. Cohn Professor of Theatre Studies at the Graduate School and University Center, City University of New York.

Betty Boyd Caroli is a professor of history at Kingsborough Community College.

Marion R. Casey is a PhD candidate in history at New York University and the president of the New York Irish History Roundtable.

S. D. R. Cashman is a freelance writer and a consultant to the Ford Foundation. He is the author of several books on American history, a subject that he has taught at the University of Manchester in England, at New York University, and at Adelphi University, where he was also a dean.

Graciela M. Castex (EdD Columbia University 1990) is an assistant professor of social work at Lehman College.

Jonathan G. Cedarbaum (AB Harvard University; MPhil in history, Yale University) is a third-year student at Yale Law School.

Mario A. Charles is a faculty member of the library staff at Baruch College.

Ann Charters (PhD Columbia University) is a professor of English at the University of Connecticut and the author of several books on Jack Kerouac and the beat writers.

George Chauncey Jr. is an assistant professor of U.S. history at the University of Chicago and the author of *Gay New York: Gender, Urban Culture, and the Makings of the Gay Male World, 1890–1940* (1994).

Gladys Chen was born in New York City and studied political science and biology at Columbia College (BA 1995).

Eileen K. Cheng is a graduate student in history at Yale University.

Barbara A. Chernow (PhD Columbia University) is an associate editor of the Syrett edition of *The Papers of Alexander Hamilton* (1961–81), the author of *Robert Morris: Land Speculator, 1790–1801*, and an editor of the thirteenth edition of *The Reader's Adviser* (1986), the second edition of *The Concise Columbia Encyclopedia* (1989), and the fifth edition of *The Columbia Encyclopedia* (1993).

William David "Charlie" Chin is a former community education director at the New York Chinatown History Project, Center for Community Studies.

James Ciment is writing a dissertation entitled "In the Light of Failure: Bankruptcy, Insolvency, and Financial Failure in New York City, 1790–1860" at the Graduate School and University Center, City University of New York.

Lawrence A. Clayton (PhD Tulane University) is a professor of history at the University of Alabama and the author of *Grace: W. R. Grace & Co.: The Formative Years, 1850–1930* (1985).

Kenneth R. Cobb is the director of the New York City Municipal Archives.

Peter A. Coclanis (PhD Columbia University) is an associate professor of history at the University of North Carolina, Chapel Hill, and the author of *The Shadow of a Dream: Economic Life and Death in the South Carolina Low Country, 1670–1920* (1989).

Gerald Leonard Cohen (PhD Columbia University) is a professor of foreign languages at the University of Missouri, Rolla, who specializes in etymology.

Barbara Cohen-Stratyner (PhD New York University) is the editor of *Performing Arts Resources* and the author of the *Biographical Dictionary of Dance* (1982).

Theresa Collins holds degrees from New York University. She is a research associate of the Thomas A. Edison Papers and is writing a biography of Otto H. Kahn.

John J. Concannon is a journalist (retired from *Newsweek*), author, and editor. He is the national historian and national press officer for the Ancient Order of Hibernians in America, and an author and compiler of *The Irish Directory* (1983) and *The Irish–American Who's Who* (1984).

Robert P. Cook is a resource management specialist at Gateway National Recreation Area in Brooklyn.

Terry A. Cooney (PhD State University of New York, Stony Brook) is a professor of history and associate academic dean at the University of Puget Sound, and the author of *The Rise of the New York Intellectuals: Partisan Review and Its Circle* (1986).

Cynthia Copeland (BA in government and public administration, John Jay College of Criminal Justice) is a public educator with the Office of Public Education and Interpretation of the African Burial Ground and a founder of *ZuZu*, a multi-cultural children's newspaper published in New York City.

Michael R. Corbett, an architectural historian in Berkeley, California, worked for the New York City Landmarks Preservation Commission in 1988–90.

Francesco Cordasco (PhD New York University) is a professor of education at Montclair State College and the author of *Medical Education in the United States* (1980), *American Medical Imprints* (1984), and *Medical Publishing in 19th Century America* (1990).

Steven H. Corey (MPhil New York University) is a doctoral candidate in American history at New York University who is writing his dissertation on the history of solid-waste management in New York City. He is an adjunct instructor of history at the University of Rhode Island, has taught at Yeshiva University, and is a research curator at the New York Public Library for an exhibition on the history of garbage, sanitation, and public health in New York City from 1850 to the present.

Evan Cornog is a graduate student in American history at Columbia University and was press secretary to Mayor Edward I. Koch in 1982–83.

William S. Cottam (PhD University of Utah) is the director of the Latter-Day Saints' Institute of Religion and a former bishop of the church in New York City.

Edward Countryman (PhD Cornell University) is a reader in American History at the University of Warwick, England, and the author of *A People in Revolution: The American Revolution and Political Society in New York, 1760–1790* (1981) and *The American Revolution* (1985).

Robert Emmett Curran is an associate professor of history at Georgetown University. His latest work is the *Bicentennial History of Georgetown University* (1993).

Mary E. Curry, a business historian, received her master's and doctoral degrees in history from the American University. She has worked for the National Portrait Gallery in Washington, the Winthrop Group in Cambridge, Massachusetts, Wells Fargo Investigative Services of New York, and the Investigative Group, an international fact-finding firm. She is the author of *Creating an American Institution: The Merchandising Genius of J. C. Penney* (1993).

Daniel Czitrom is in the department of history at Mount Holyoke College.

Phyllis Dain (Doctor of Library Science, Columbia University), professor of library service at Columbia, is the author of *The New York Public Library: A History of Its Founding and Early Years* (1972) and of various articles on library history, and the editor with John Y. Cole of *Libraries and Scholarly Communication in the United States: The Historical Dimension* (1990).

Douglas Henry Daniels, professor of black studies at the University of California, Santa Barbara, is the author of *Pioneer Urbanites: A Social and Cultural History of Black San Francisco* (1980).

Mimi Gisolfi D'Aponte (PhD City University of New York) is a professor of speech and theater at Baruch College and the Graduate School and University Center, City University of New York, and the author of *Teatro religioso e rituale della Penisola Sorrentina e la Costiera Amalfitana* (1984).

Amanda Dargan (PhD in folklore, University of Pennsylvania) is a folklorist for a folk arts center at the Bank Street College of Education and the author with Steve Zeitlin of *City Play* (1990).

Colin J. Davis (PhD State University of New York, Binghamton) is an assistant professor at the University of Alabama, Birmingham. He has completed a manuscript on the national rail strike of 1922 and is now engaged in a comparative study of the dock strikes in London and New York City of 1948.

Thomas J. Davis (PhD Columbia University, JD University of Buffalo) is a professor of history and African–American studies at the State University of New York, Buffalo. He is the author of *A Rumor of Revolt: The Great Negro Plot in Colonial New York* (1985) and (with Michael Conniff) *Africans in the Americas: A History of the Black Diaspora* (1994). He is also the editor of *The New York Conspiracy* (1971).

Harriet Davis-Kram is an adjunct instructor at a number of colleges in greater New York and a doctoral candidate at the Graduate School and University Center, City University of New York.

Gloria Deák is the author of *American Views: Prospects and Vistas* (1976), *Picturing America, 1497–1899* (1988), and *William James Bennett, Master of the Aquatint View* (1988).

James Deaville teaches music criticism at McMaster University (Hamilton, Ontario), is an editor of the journal *Criticus Musicus*, and has contributed articles and dictionary entries about music criticism to various publications.

GraceAnne A. DeCandido is the executive editor of *School Library Journal* and a freelance writer, editor, and critic.

Gerald F. De Jong (PhD University of Wisconsin) is a professor emeritus of history at the University of South Dakota and the author of *The Dutch in America, 1609–1974* (1975) and *The Dutch Reformed Church in the American Colonies* (1978).

Ormonde de Kay, a freelance writer and former articles editor of *Horizon*, is the author of two books of world history, three biographies of famous Americans for young readers, and many historical and biographical articles in various magazines.

Jane DeLuca (MS, Registered Nurse) is a clinical nurse specialist at Long Island College Hospital in Brooklyn.

Peter Derrick (PhD New York University) is an assistant director in the Capital Program Management Department of the Metropolitan Transportation Authority in New York City. He also teaches urban history at the School of General Studies of Fordham University.

Samuel Devons is a professor of physics at Columbia University.

Dennis C. Dickerson (PhD Washington University) is a professor of history at Williams College, historiographer of the African Methodist Episcopal Church, and the author of *Out of the Crucible: Black Steelworkers in Western Pennsylvania, 1875–1980* (1986).

Michael N. Dobkowski is a professor of religious studies at Hobart and William Smith Colleges.

Jameson W. Doig is a professor of politics and public affairs at the Woodrow Wilson School and the department of politics at Princeton University. He has written on transportation, urban development, and criminal justice, with particular reference to New York City.

Andrew S. Dolkart is an architectural historian specializing in the architecture and development of New York City and an adjunct associate professor at the Columbia University School of Architecture. He has written extensively on architecture in the city and been the curator of several exhibitions on the subject.

Peter L. Donhauser is an assistant museum educator at the Metropolitan Museum of Art and a PhD candidate in the history of architecture at the Institute of Fine Arts at New York University.

George Dorris (PhD Northwestern University) is an editor of *Dance Chronicle* and an associate professor of English at York College.

Susan J. Douglas (PhD Brown University) is an associate professor of media and American studies at Hampshire College and the author of *Inventing American Broadcasting* (1987).

Patricia A. Doyal (BA Queens College, MA Queens College, MS Syracuse University) is an assistant professor at Baruch College and a former library director for the Institute of Public Administration in New York City.

Joe Doyle (MA in history, New York University, 1986) is a columnist for *Seaport Magazine* and the editor of *Work History News.*

Matthew Drennan is a professor in the department of city and regional planning at Cornell University. He has published many articles about the economy of New York City and the fiscal condition of the city and state.

Jesse Drucker (BA Columbia College) is a reporter at the *New York Observer.*

James O. Drummond is a teacher of social studies at Westfield Senior High School in New Jersey.

Melvyn Dubofsky (PhD University of Rochester) is a professor of history and sociology at the State University of New York, Binghamton, and the author of *We Shall Be All: A History of the Industrial Workers of the World* (1969) and *John L. Lewis: A Biography* (1977).

Ellen Carol DuBois is a professor of history at UCLA and the author of *Feminism and Suffrage: The Emergence of an Independent Women's Movement in America, 1848–1869* (1977).

James Duplacey (BA University of New Brunswick) is the managing editor of the *NHL Guide and Record Book* and the author of *Toronto Maple Leafs: Images of Glory* (1990) and *The Stanley Cup: 100 Years of Hockey* (1992).

Seymour Durst (BA University of Southern California) is a real-estate investor in New York City, an author of *Your Future in Real Estate* (1960) and *Holdouts!* (1984), and the founder of the Old York Library.

Martin Ebon worked for the U.S. Office of War Information during the Second World War, for the Foreign Policy Association, and for the Voice of America. He is the author of more than seventy books, ranging from *World Communism Today* (1948) to *KGB: Death and Rebirth* (1994).

Brenda Edmands has written a medical supply catalogue, and advertising and jacket copy for several scholarly books. She left a career in publishing to pursue an MFA in creative writing at Colorado State University.

Susan Edmiston, a native New Yorker now living in Berkeley, California, is a freelance writer and the author (with Linda Cirino) of *Literary New York: A History and Guide* (1976).

Edward A. Eigen is a doctoral candidate in the history, theory, and criticism program of the department of architecture at the Massachusetts Institute of Technology. He is John Ockman's collaborator on *Architecture Culture, 1943–1968* (1993).

Fred Eisenstadt has studied architecture and works in the management of a computer network for the City of New York.

Peter Eisenstadt was a managing editor of the *Encyclopedia of New York City* and of the *Encyclopedia of African American Culture and History* (forthcoming).

Nan Ellin is the author of *Postmodern Urbanism* (1995).

David Maldwyn Ellis (PhD Cornell University) is an emeritus professor of history at Hamilton College and the author of *New York: State and City* (1979).

Robert Ellwood is a professor of religion at UCLA and writes on new religious movements.

Linda Elsroad (MA Columbia University) was a student services administrator for the Bank Street College of Education from 1982 to 1991.

Michael Emery is the author with his father, Edwin Emery, of *The Press and America* (7th edn 1992; 8th edn forthcoming), an editor with Ted Curtis Smythe of *Readings in Mass Communication* (11th edn 1994), and a free-lance correspondent for the *Village Voice*, the *Los Angeles Times*, and other publications.

Stephen D. Engle (PhD Florida State University), assistant professor of history at Florida Atlantic University, is the author of *Thunder in the Hills: Military Operations in Jefferson County, West Virginia, during the American Civil War* (1989) and *Yankee Dutchman* (1993).

Alana J. Erickson received the PhD in American history from Columbia University.

Robert Ernst (PhD Columbia University), professor emeritus of history at Adelphi University, is the author of *Rufus King: American Federalist* (1968) and *Weakness Is a Crime: The Life of Bernarr Macfadden* (1991).

Alice Fahs (PhD New York University 1993) teaches at the University of California, Irvine, and specializes in American intellectual and cultural history.

Henry Feingold (PhD in history, New York University, 1966) is a professor of history at Baruch College and the Graduate School and University Center, City University of New York. He is the author of *The Politics of Rescue: The Roosevelt Administration and the Holocaust, 1938–1945* (1970) and the general editor of "The Jewish People in America," a five-volume series published by Johns Hopkins University Press.

Marc Ferris (MA in history, University of Massachusetts, Amherst) has taught history at City College of New York and Pace University. He is the author of "The Workingmen's Party of Hampshire County, 1811–1835," *Historical Journal of Massachusetts* (winter 1990), and "To Share the Blessings of Allah: Immigrant Muslim Communities in New York City," *Muslim Communities in North America*, ed. Yvonne Haddad and Jane Smith (1994).

Corinne T. Field is a doctoral candidate in history at Columbia University. Her interests focus on women and work in nineteenth-century New York City.

Peter Field is a doctoral candidate at Columbia University and an adjunct lecturer in history at City College of New York.

Albert Figone (PhD), a professor of health and physical education at Humboldt State University in California, has been an educator for thirty-one years.

John (Johann) Fink, a native of Brooklyn and a long-time subway aficionado, is a historian specializing in railroads and central European topics.

Anita Finkel is the editor and publisher of the *New Dance Review* and an editor at *Collier's Encyclopedia.*

Jeff Finlay is a doctoral student in American civilization at New York University, where he also teaches.

Ellen Fletcher is a writer and interpretive planner with a particular interest in the history of New York Harbor. She is the author of *South Street: A Photographic Guide to New York's Historic Seaport* (1977) and other books about historic places and architecture in New York City.

Richard W. Flint (MA Cooperstown Graduate Programs, State University of New York) is the assistant director of the Maryland Historical Society and a past president of the Circus Historical Society.

Nancy Flood (BA Columbia College 1989) is a former resident of Staten Island and a free-lance writer.

Martha Foley is an archivist, was the associate producer of the documentary *Rebel Girl* (1993), about Elizabeth Gurley Flynn, and is the curator of the Elizabeth Gurley Flynn Collection at the Tamiment Collection, New York University.

James D. Folts is an archivist at the New York State Archives and Records Administration in Albany.

Nancy Foner, professor of anthropology at the State University of New York, Purchase, has done research in rural Jamaica as well as among Jamaicans in New York City and London. Her books include *Status and Power in Rural Jamaica* (1973), *Jamaica Farewell: Jamaican Migrants in London* (1978), and *New Immigrants in New York* (1987).

Thelma Foote is an assistant professor of history at the University of California, Irvine.

Stanford M. Forrester is a native of Staten Island. He has studied Spanish literature and worked for an academic press in Connecticut.

Ella M. Foshay is the author of *Mr. Luman Reed's Picture Gallery: A Pioneer Collection of American Art* (1990) and *Reflections of Nature: Flowers in American Art* (1984).

Gino Francesconi established the first archive at Carnegie Hall in 1986 and opened the Rose Museum at Carnegie Hall in 1991.

Luis H. Francia is a poet, critic, and journalist who writes on politics and the arts for publications such as the *Village Voice*, the *Daily News*, *A. Magazine*, and *Special Edition Press.* He is the author of *The Arctic Archipelago and Other Poems* (1992) and the editor of *Brown River, White Ocean: An Anthology of 20th Century Philippine Literature in English* (1993).

Janet Frankston graduated from Columbia College with a degree in history in 1995.

Steve Fraser is a vice-president and executive editor of Basic Books and an editor of *The Rise and Fall of the New Deal Order, 1930–1980* (1989).

John W. Freeman, associate editor of *Opera News*, is the author of *The Metropolitan Opera Stories of the Great Operas* (1984) and a co-author of *The Golden Horseshoe* (1965) and *Toscanini* (1987).

Joshua B. Freeman, associate professor of history at Columbia University, has written extensively on the history of workers and unions.

Alice Cooney Frelinghuysen is a curator in the department of decorative arts at the Metropolitan Museum of Art. She is the author of *American Porcelain, 1770–1920* (1989) and a co-author of *In Pursuit of Beauty: Americans and the Aesthetic Movement* (1986), *Splendid Legacy: The Havemeyer Collection* (1993), and *Herter Brothers: Furniture and Interiors for a Gilded Age* (1994).

John W. Frick, assistant professor of theatre history and dramatic literature at the University of Virginia, is the author of *New York's First Theatrical Center: The Rialto at Union Square* (1985) and an editor of *The Directory of Historic American Theatres* (1987).

Robert Friedel (PhD Johns Hopkins University) is an associate professor of history at the University of Maryland, College Park, and the author of *Pioneer Plastic: The Making and Selling of Celluloid* (1983) and *A Material World* (1988).

Walter Friedman is a graduate student in history at Columbia University and was a deputy managing editor of the *Encyclopedia of New York City.*

Erik J. Friis (BS, MA) was for many years the editor and director of publications of the American–Scandinavian Foundation. He is now the publisher of the *Scandinavian–American Bulletin* and the book series "Library of Nordic Literature." He has translated twenty books from Norwegian, Swedish, and Danish and has been decorated by all five Scandinavian governments.

William Lee Frost is a trustee of the Collegiate School and president of the Lucius N. Littauer Foundation.

John Gaber received his PhD in urban planning from Columbia University in 1993 and is now a visiting assistant professor in the department of community and regional planning at the University of Nebraska. He has published articles on ethnographic research methods and ethnic enterprises.

Edmund Gaither is at the Museum of the National Center for Afro-American Artists in Boston.

John J. Gallagher is a writer, historian, and lecturer in Brooklyn and the author of *The Battle of Brooklyn, 1776* (1995).

Wendy Gamber teaches history at Indiana University.

Steven D. Garber (PhD in ecology, Rutgers) has taught biology at Rutgers, Cornell University, and the City University of New York and worked as a biologist at the American Museum of Natural History, the National Park Service, the Peabody Museum of Natural History and the Medical School at Yale University, and the New York City Department of Parks and Recreation. He is the author of *The Urban Naturalist* (1987) and more than two hundred scientific articles.

Deborah S. Gardner (PhD Columbia University), an urban historian, was the first managing editor of the *Encyclopedia of New York City.* She has written about the history of the New York Stock Exchange, low-income housing in New York City, and the city's architectural and social history and is writing a biography of Isaac Newton Phelps Stokes.

Neal C. Garelik wrote an honor's thesis at Columbia University on the New York City Board of Estimate and now owns and operates a security firm in New York City.

Bradford Garnett is a real-estate consultant in New York City who considers himself fortunate for being able to admire the city's architecture while making his business rounds.

Margot Gayle is a preservationist and writer long identified with the preservation of cast-iron architecture. She is the author of *Cast Iron Architecture in New York* (1974) and a co-author of *Metals in America's Historic Buildings* (1980) and *Guide to Manhattan's Outdoor Sculpture* (1988).

Rosalie Genevro is the executive director of the Architectural League of New York.

Eugenia Georges (PhD Columbia University) is an assistant professor of anthropology at Rice University and the author of *The Making of a Transnational Community: Migration, Development and Cultural Change in the Dominican Republic* (1990).

Donald F. M. Gerardi, born in Connecticut and educated at Wesleyan, Harvard, and Columbia universities, lives in Greenwich Village and is a professor of history and religious studies at Brooklyn College.

Marvin E. Gettleman attended public schools in New York City, graduated from City College of New York in 1957, and took graduate degrees at Johns Hopkins University (PhD 1972). He is a professor of history at Polytechnic University and the editor of *Science and Society.*

Robert J. Gibbons studied economic history at Yale University (PhD 1972) and is a vice-president of the American Institute for Chartered Property Casualty Underwriters, the educational institution that administers the professional designation for property-casualty insurance.

Ann C. Gibson is a former assistant archivist at Chase Manhattan Bank.

Timothy J. Gilfoyle (PhD Columbia University) is an assistant professor of history at Loyola University of Chicago and the author of *City of Eros: New York City, Prostitution and the Commercialization of Sex, 1790–1920* (1992).

Juliana F. Gilheany (PhD New York University) is an adjunct assistant professor of history at Fordham University.

Paul A. Gilje (PhD Brown University) is an associate professor of history at the University of Oklahoma and the author of *The Road to Mobocracy: Popular Disorder in New York City, 1763–1834* (1987).

Russell S. Gilmore (doctorate in American history, University of Wisconsin) is the director of the Harbor Defense Museum in Fort Hamilton, the author of *Guarding America's Front Door: Harbor Forts in the Defense of New York City* (1983), and a fellow of the Company of Military Historians.

Val Ginter, owner of Ginter–Gotham Urban History and the author of *Manhattan Trivia: The Ultimate Challenge* (1985), is a member of the Society of Architectural Historians and the National Trust for Historic Preservation Forum.

Lisa Gitelman works at the Thomas A. Edison Papers.

James Glass (JD) is a former president of the Marshall Chess Club in New York City.

Joyce Gold (MA New York University) is a tour guide, a member of the faculty of the New School for Social Research and New York University, and the author of two guidebooks to lower Manhattan, *From Windmills to the World Trade Center: A Walking Guide to Lower Manhattan History* (1982) and *From Trout Stream to Bohemia: A Walking Guide to Greenwich Village History* (1988).

Joanne Abel Goldman is an assistant professor of history at the University of Northern Iowa.

Eric A. Goldstein is an author of *The New York Environment Book* (1990) and a senior attorney with the Natural Resources Defense Council.

Robert I. Goler (MA Case Western Reserve University) is the curator of decorative and industrial arts at the Chicago Historical Society, the author of *Capital City: New York after the Revolution* (1987), and the editor of *Federal New York: A Symposium* (1990).

David L. González is a reporter at the *New York Times.*

Evelyn Gonzalez teaches at William Paterson College and is completing a PhD dissertation at Columbia University on the growth and change of neighborhoods in the South Bronx.

Lynn D. Gordon is an associate professor of education and history at the University of Rochester.

Elliott J. Gorn (PhD in American studies, Yale University, 1983) is an associate professor of history and the director of American studies at Miami University of Ohio, and the author of *The Manly Art: Bare Knuckle Prize Fighting in America* (1986).

Brenda Dixon Gottschild, associate professor in the dance department at Temple University, writes and lectures extensively on Afrocentric and postmodern performance, modern dance traditions, and performance history and aesthetics. She is the Philadelphia correspondent for *Dancemagazine*, an author of *The History of Dance in Art and Education* (3rd edn, 1991), the author of the final chapter of *Black Dance from 1619 to Today* (2nd edn, 1994), and a consultant to the Dance Project for WNET in New York City.

Leslie Gourse is a freelance writer on culture for newspapers and magazines. She has written one novel, three books on jazz, and three books about New York City, including *The Best Guided Walking Tours of New York City* (1989).

Chandler B. Grannis is a former editor-in-chief of *Publishers Weekly*, to which he is now a contributing editor.

Martha W. Grannis is a freelance copy editor.

James Grant, editor of *Grant's Interest Rate Observer*, is the author of *Bernard Baruch: The Adventures of a Wall Street Legend* (1983).

Sigurd Grava is a professor at Columbia University, the director of its urban planning program, and a vice-president and the technical director of planning for Parsons Brinckerhoff. He has been a consultant to the United Nations, the City of New York, and the city of Riga, Latvia.

Barbara Grcevic (JD Brooklyn Law School) is the principal court attorney to Acting Justice Robert S. Kreindler in the Supreme Court of Kings County and a former president of the Brooklyn Women's Bar Association.

Ashbel Green is a native of New York City who holds two degrees from Columbia University. He has been an editor for a publishing house in New York City for more than thirty years.

Michael Green is a doctoral candidate in American history at Columbia University, where he is working on a dissertation on the ideology of the Republican Party during the Civil War.

William Green (PhD Columbia University), professor of English at Queens College, is the author of many books and articles on theater and drama.

Brian Greenberg (PhD Princeton University) has taught at the University of Delaware and is now at Monmouth College.

Cheryl Greenberg (PhD Columbia University) is an assistant professor at Trinity College and the author of *"Or Does It Explode?": Black Harlem in the Great Depression* (1991).

Larry A. Greene (PhD Columbia University 1979) was the head of the history department at Seton Hall University and is now director of the multicultural program at Seton Hall. He is the author of articles published in the *Encyclopedia of American Economic History: Studies of the Principal Movements and Ideas* (1980), the *Dictionary of American Biography*, and the periodicals *Afro-Americans in New York Life and History* and *Rutgers Library Journal.*

William D. Griffin (PhD Columbia University) is a professor of history at St. John's University and the author of *A Portrait of the Irish in America* (1981) and *The Book of Irish Americans* (1990).

Gerald N. Grob is the Henry E. Sigerist Professor of the History of Medicine at Rutgers, the State University of New Jersey. An elected member of the Institute of Medicine at the National Academy of Sciences, he is the author of half a dozen books and many articles dealing with the history of the care and treatment of the mentally ill in America and the evolution of psychiatry.

Nancy Groce is an ethnomusicologist and historian and the senior program officer at the New York Council for the Humanities.

Carol Groneman is a professor of history at John Jay College of Criminal Justice.

Anthony Gronowicz, assistant professor of history at Pennsylvania State University, Hazelton, has written several articles on the political culture of New York City, as well as the forthcoming book *Democratic Republicanism and Labor: The Politics of Class and Race in New York City, 1626–1863*.

Donna Ann Grossman is a graduate student in art history at Columbia University.

Robert S. Grumet works for the National Park Service in Pennsylvania and is the author of *Native American Place Names in New York City* (1981).

Betty Kaplan Gubert is the retired head of general research and reference at the Schomburg Center for Research in Black Culture of the New York Public Library. She is the editor of *Early Black Bibliographies, 1863–1918* (1982), a co-editor of *Nine Decades of Scholarship* (1986), and the compiler of *Invisible Wings: An Annotated Bibliography of Blacks in Aviation, 1916–1993* (1994).

Allen C. Guelzo (PhD University of Pennsylvania) is the Grace F. Kea Associate Professor of American History at Eastern College.

Jeffrey S. Gurock is the Libby M. Klaperman Professor of Jewish History at Yeshiva University.

Owen D. Gutfreund (MA and MPhil Columbia University) is a doctoral candidate in American history at Columbia University.

Laura Gwinn (BA Boston College, MFA Columbia University) is a freelance writer and public relations professional.

Mona Hadler is an associate professor at Brooklyn College and the Graduate School and University Center, City University of New York. She has published on twentieth-century European and American art, especially abstract expressionism.

Paula Hajar (BA Radcliffe College) is a doctoral candidate at the Harvard Graduate School of Education, an educator, and a long-time researcher on the Arab–American community of New York City.

David C. Hammack is an associate professor of history at Case Western Reserve University and the author of *Power and Society: Greater New York at the Turn of the Century* (1982).

Ian Hancock is the representative to the United Nations and UNICEF of the International Romani Union, and a professor of linguistics, English, and eastern European studies at the University of Texas, Austin.

Eleanor Hannah is a PhD candidate in American history at the University of Chicago. She is writing a dissertation on the growth of the National Guard in Illinois.

R. L. Harris, Jr. (PhD Northwestern University), is an associate professor of Afro-American History at the Africana Studies and Research Center of Cornell University and the author of *Teaching Afro-American History* (1985).

Marjorie Harrison is a graduate student at Columbia University.

C. Lowell Harriss is a professor emeritus of economics at Columbia University, a senior advisor to the Academy of Political Science, and the president of the Robert Schalkenbach Foundation.

Gabriel Haslip-Viera teaches in the department of Latin American and Hispanic Caribbean Studies at City College of New York and is an editor of *Latinos in New York: Communities in Transition* (1994).

Constantine G. Hatzidimitriou (PhD Columbia University) teaches modern Greek language and culture at La Guardia Community College and has published articles on Byzantine and modern Greek history in scholarly journals.

William J. Hausman (PhD University of Illinois) is a professor of economics at the College of William and Mary.

Pamela W. Hawkes (MS in historic preservation, Columbia University; MArch University of California, Berkeley) is an architect with Ann Beha Associates in Boston.

Barbara Haws (MA New York University) is the archivist and historian for the New York Philharmonic.

Mary Hedge received her undergraduate degree from the University of Warwick, England, and an MA in Latin American studies from Georgetown University, and is a graduate of the program in archival management at New York University. She is the corporate historian and archivist for American Express.

Anthony Heilbut is the author of *The Gospel Sound: Good News and Bad Times* (1971), *Exiled in Paradise: German Refugee Artists and Intellectuals in America from the 1930's to the Present* (1983), and *Thomas Mann: A Biography* (1985).

Stephen Heller is the senior art director of the *New York Times*, editor of the *AIGA Journal of Graphic Design*, and the author or editor of more than twenty books.

Clara J. Hemphill is an editorial writer for *New York Newsday* specializing in welfare and poverty.

Floyd M. Henderson (PhD University of Kansas), professor of geography and planning at the State University of New York, Albany, has had a long-time professional interest in the geographical aspects of the cultural landscape.

Judith Adler Hennessee is an author and journalist who writes for several national magazines. She is the former media columnist for *Manhattan, Inc.*

Gary D. Hermalyn received his doctorate from Columbia University and is the executive director of the Bronx County Historical Society. He is the author of *Morris High School and the Creation of the New York City Public High School System* (1993), a co-author of *The Bronx in the Innocent Years, 1890–1925* (1985) and *Landmarks of the Bronx* (1989), and the editor of the book series "Bicentennial of the United States Constitution" and the *Bronx County Historical Society Journal*.

Michele Herman (MFA Columbia University) is a freelance writer specializing in subjects relating to New York City. She contributes regularly to *Metropolis*, *American Heritage*, and other publications.

Thomas M. Hilbink, a graduate of Columbia College, was the director of the WKCR Oral History Project in 1991–93 and the archivist for the American Civil Liberties Union. He has received two awards for his thesis on the Lawyers Constitutional Defense Committee.

E. G. Hill is a professor of drama and oratory, emeritus, at Dartmouth College.

Robert Hillenbrand was the head track coach at Northern Highlands Regional High School in Allendale, New Jersey, from 1979 to 1989. He has completed fifteen marathons, four in New York City.

Patricia Hills (BA Stanford University, MA Hunter College, PhD Institute of Fine Arts, New York University) teaches American art history at Boston University. She has taught at York College, the Graduate School and University Center, City University of New York, Columbia University, and the Institute of Fine Arts, New York University. Her books and articles focus on painters from New York City, including Eastman Johnson, John Sloan, Stuart Davis, Alice Neel, Jacob Lawrence, and Philip Evergood.

Lee R. Hiltzik (PhD in history, State University of New York, Stony Brook, 1993) is an archivist at the Rockefeller University Archives.

Bernard Hirschhorn (PhD Columbia University) is the chairman of the social studies department at Fiorello La Guardia High School of Music and Art and the Performing Arts, editor of the urban history issue of the *Magazine of History* (1990), and the author of a number of articles on Richard S. Childs and a forthcoming biography of Childs.

Graham Hodges (PhD New York University) is an associate professor of history at Colgate University and the author of *New York City Cartmen, 1676–1850* (1986).

Calvin B. Holder (PhD) is an associate professor of history at the College of Staten Island.

Joel Honig is a contributor to the *Dictionary of American Biography*, the *Dictionary of American History*, and the annual supplement to the *Book of Knowledge*.

Clifton Hood is an assistant professor of history at Hobart and William Smith Colleges and the author of *722 Miles: The Building of the Subways and How They Transformed New York* (1993).

Kim Hopper (PhD Columbia University) is a research scientist at the Nathan S. Kline Institute for Psychiatric Research, a founder of the Coalition for the Homeless, and the author of *A Bed for the Night: Homeless Men in New York City* (forthcoming).

Joseph A. Horrigan is the curator and director of research information for the Pro Football Hall of Fame and the author of *The Official Pro Football Hall of Fame Answer Book* (1993).

Raymond D. Horton (BA Grinnell College, JD Harvard University, PhD in political science, Columbia University) is a professor of business at Columbia University and president of the Citizens Budget Commission. He is the author with Charles Brecher of *Power Failure: New York City Politics and Policy since 1960* (1993).

Elizabeth Hovey (PhD Columbia University) teaches at La Guardia Community College. Her dissertation was entitled "Stamping Out Smut: The Enforcement of Obscenity Laws, 1872–1936."

Anne H. Hoy (MA New York University) is an author and editor of works on photography and art history, curator at the International Center of Photography, and managing editor of the *Art Bulletin*, the quarterly journal of the College Art Association.

Lee Hudson (PhD University of Texas) was the liaison to the lesbian and gay community in the Office of the Mayor of New York City from 1983 to 1990, and the executive assistant to the director of housing for the State of New York.

Deborah Huisken, American by birth, is a freelance writer living in London. She is the editor and publisher of *Hoppin'*, an international newsletter devoted to the Lindy hop.

Kathleen Hulser (MA New York University) is an urban historian who also writes about the performing arts. Her video documentaries include *f u cn rd this*, a look at social mobility through subway advertising, and *It Takes a Tough Ad Agency to Make a Tender Chicken*, about the industrial folklore of chicken.

Leon Hurwitz (PhD Syracuse University) is a professor of political science and an associate dean at the College of Arts and Sciences of Cleveland State University.

Yarema Hutsaliuk studied military history at Columbia University and is the public affairs officer for the 369th Regiment of the New York National Guard and the 15th Regiment, New York Guard.

Gordon Hyatt (Bachelor of Fine Arts), a documentary film producer, was president of the Associates of the Art Commission from 1986 to 1988.

Paul Israel (PhD Rutgers), an assistant editor with the Thomas A. Edison Papers, is the author of *Edison's Electric Light: Biography of an Invention* (1986) and *From Machine Shop to Industrial Laboratory: Telegraphy and the Changing Context of American Invention, 1830–1920* (1992). He is beginning work on a new biography of Thomas Edison.

Maurice Isserman teaches American history at Hamilton College. He is the author of *Which Side Were You on?: The American Communist Party during the Second World War* (1982) and *If I Had A Hammer. . . : The Death of the Old Left and the Birth of the New Left* (1987) and a co-author of *Dorothy Healey Remembers: A Life in the American Communist Party* (1990).

Mark A. Izeman, an author of *The New York Environment Book* (1990), is a project attorney with the Natural Resources Defense Council.

Ira Jacknis (PhD University of Chicago) is an anthropologist specializing in American Indian art and the history of anthropology.

Kenneth T. Jackson is the Jacques Barzun Professor of History and the Social Sciences at Columbia University and the editor of this encyclopedia.

Steven H. Jaffe (PhD Harvard University), lecturer at Harvard University, is the author of *Unmasking the City: Privacy, Publicity, and the Rise of the Newspaper Reporter in New York, 1800–1850* (forthcoming).

David James is the author of *To Free the Cinema: Jonas Mekas and the New York Underground* (1992) and *Allegories of Cinema: American Film in the Sixties* (1989).

Shan Jayakumar is a writer born in India, brought up in the United States, and educated at Columbia and Cambridge universities.

David R. Johnson, professor of history at the University of Texas, San Antonio, is the author of "A Sinful Business: The Origins of Gambling Syndicates in the United States, 1840–1887," *Police and Society*, ed. David H. Bayley (1977).

Marjorie Johnson is a research aide at the Staten Island Historical Society and a co-author of *The Swaim–Tysen Family of Staten Island, New York, New Jersey, and Southern States* (1984).

Peter J. Johnson has an advanced degree in American history from Syracuse University and has been employed by the Rockefeller family for nearly twenty years. He is a co-author of *The Rockefeller Century* (1988) and *The Rockefeller Conscience: An American Family in Public and Private* (1991).

Steven Johnson is a supervising archivist and librarian for the New York Zoological Society.

Susanna Jones is at Columbia University.

Jenna Weissman Joselit (PhD in history, Columbia University) teaches American religious history at Princeton University. She is the author of *The Wonders of America: Reinventing Jewish Culture, 1880–1950* (1994), *Our Gang: Jewish Crime and the New York Jewish Community, 1900–1940* (1983), and *New York's Jewish Jews: The Orthodox Community of the Interwar Years* (1990) and the editor with Susan Braunstein of *Getting Comfortable in New York: The American Jewish Home, 1880–1950* (1990). She is currently writing a book on religion and fashion.

Michael Joseph is a former rare books librarian at the New-York Historical Society, where he helped to develop a research collection of early children's books and engraved woodblocks.

Jacob Judd (PhD New York University), professor of history and chairman of the history department at Lehman College, is the editor of the *Van Cortlandt Family Papers*.

Erica Judge (BA University of Virginia) is a native of New York City who now works for the U.S. Foreign Service.

Matthew Kachur is a doctoral candidate in urban history at the Graduate School and University Center, City University of New York.

Seth Kamil is a doctoral candidate in American urban and ethnic history at Columbia University and the founder of Big Onion Walking Tours.

Nathan Kantrowitz is the director of demographic studies, social planning, and education at the New York City Planning Department.

Howard Kaplan is a regular contributor to the *Daily News* and magazines.

Isabelle Kaplan works at the New York Association for New Americans.

James S. Kaplan is a lawyer who has extensively studied the political and economic history of New York City. He leads walking tours of its neighborhoods for the 92nd Street YM-YWHA and other groups and is an author of *New Yorkwalks* (1992).

Edward Kasinec is the chief of the Slavic and Baltic Division, New York Public Library. Since 1969 he has published and edited more than two hundred books, articles, reviews, review essays, and catalogues.

Philip Kasinitz teaches sociology at Hunter College.

Esther Katz (PhD New York University), adjunct assistant professor of history and research associate at New York University, is the editor and director of the Margaret Sanger Papers Project.

Montana Katz (PhD) is the author of *Get Smart!: A Woman's Guide To Equality on Campus* (1988).

Peter Keepnews (BA Grinnell College) writes about jazz for the *New York Times* and other publications. He is the author of *Monk's Dream: The Life and Music of Thelonious Monk* (forthcoming).

James M. Keller (MPhil Yale University), a musicologist and journalist, writes about music for the *New Yorker*, the *Piano Quarterly*, *Opera News*, *Musical America*, and other publications.

Mollie Keller (PhD New York University) is an independent historian who has worked as a researcher, writer, archivist, planner, and curator for clients ranging from the U.S. Customs Service to local historical societies. She is currently the archivist for the City of Bridgeport, Connecticut.

Kevin Kenny, a native of Dublin, received his BA and MA in modern history from the University of Edinburgh and his MA and PhD in

American history from Columbia University. He is an assistant professor of history at the University of Texas, Austin.

Barry Kernfeld, an independent scholar, is the editor of *The New Grove Dictionary of Jazz* (1988) and *The Blackwell Guide to Recorded Jazz* (1991), the author of *What to Listen for in Jazz* (1995), and a contributor to *The New Harvard Dictionary of Music* (1986) and *American National Biography*.

K. Austin Kerr is a professor of history and the series editor for "Historical Perspectives on Business Enterprise" at Ohio State University.

Thomas Kessner is a professor of history at the Graduate School and University Center, City University of New York, and the author of *Fiorello H. La Guardia and the Making of Modern New York* (1989) and *The Golden Door: Italian and Jewish Immigrant Mobility in New York City, 1880–1915* (1977).

Joy M. Kestenbaum (Sarah Lawrence College, BA and MA New York University Institute of Fine Arts) teaches at the school of architecture and fine arts of the New York Institute of Technology.

Edward F. Keuchel (PhD Cornell University), professor of history at Florida State University, is an author of *American Economic History: From Abundance to Constraint* (1989).

Madhulika S. Khandelwal is a professor of Asian–American studies and a research associate at the Asian–American Center of Queens College.

Cynthia A. Kierner (PhD University of Virginia), assistant professor of history at the University of North Carolina, Charlotte, is the author of *Traders and Gentlefolk: The Livingstons of New York, 1675–1790* (1992).

Ilsoo Kim, who emigrated to the United States from Korea in 1970, teaches at Mercy College and is the author of *New Urban Immigrants: The Korean Community in New York* (1981).

David J. S. King is a graduate student at Johns Hopkins University.

Vitaut Kipel was born in Minsk, Belarus, and received degrees in geology from the University of Louvain and in librarianship from Rutgers. He has worked for more than twenty-five years at the New York Public Library in various capacities, including that of acting chief of the Science and Technology Division.

George B. Kirsch (PhD Columbia University), professor of history at Manhattan College, is the author of *The Creation of American Team Sports: Baseball and Cricket, 1838–72* (1989), and *Jeremy Belknap: A Biography* (1982).

Barbara Kirshenblatt-Gimblett (PhD Indiana University) is a professor of performance studies at the Tisch School of the Arts, New York University, head of the board of City Lore: New York Center for Urban Folk Culture, and the author with Lucjan Dobroszycki of *Image before My Eyes: A Photographic History of Jewish Life in Poland, 1864–1939* (1977).

Benjamin J. Klebaner, professor of economics at City College, is a former associate editor of the *Journal of Money, Credit and Banking* (1975–79) and regional economist, Second National Bank Region, of the Office of the Comptroller of the Currency (1966–82).

John M. Kleeberg, a native New Yorker, attended Stuyvesant High School, Yale University (BA), and Oxford University (DPhil in modern history). Since 1990 he has been the curator of modern coins and currency at the American Numismatic Society in New York City.

Amie Klempnauer received her MA from Union Theological Seminary. Her thesis was entitled "A Perfectly Normal Place: Eco-justice and the Church in Fernald, Ohio."

Margaret M. Knapp (PhD City University of New York) is an associate professor of theater at Arizona State University and the author of many articles and reviews on American theater history and American musical theater.

Richard Kobliner, a researcher, consultant, writer, and teacher, is affiliated with several professional organizations of American historians and with the Association of Teacher Educators and the National Council for Social Studies.

Gerard Thomas Koeppel is an editor and producer of network radio news programming and is writing a book on the history of the water supply in New York City. He is a graduate of Riverdale Country School and Wesleyan University and lives in New York City.

Carolyn Kopp (MA UCLA) is the archivist of Teachers Insurance and Annuity Association–College Retirement Equities Fund.

Anne E. Kornblut (BA in American history, Columbia College) is on the editorial staff of the *Daily News*.

Virginia Sánchez Korrol (PhD in history, State University of New York, Stony Brook, 1981) is a professor and head of the department of Puerto Rican studies at Brooklyn College and co-director of its Center of Latino Studies, and the founding president of the Puerto Rican Studies Association.

Hadassa Kosak (PhD City University of New York) teaches history at Yeshiva University.

William C. Kostlevy is a PhD candidate at the University of Notre Dame, a lecturer in history at Transylvania University, and a bibliographer for the Wesleyan–Holiness Study Project at Asbury Theological Seminary.

Frances Kraljic is a professor of history at Kingsborough Community College and the author of *Croatian Migration to and from the United States, 1900–1914* (1978).

Elizabeth J. Kramer is a graduate of Yale University.

Walter Donald Kring was the minister of the Unitarian Church of All Souls in New York City from 1955 to 1978 and is now minister emeritus.

Carol Krinsky (PhD New York University) is a professor of fine arts at New York University and the director of its urban design studies program. She is the author of *Rockefeller Center* (1987), *Synagogues of Europe: Architecture, History, Meaning* (1985), and *Gordon Bunshaft of Skidmore, Owings & Merrill* (1988).

Jeffrey A. Kroessler (PhD City University of New York 1981) has taught at Queens College, Adelphi University, and Long Island University. In addition to his dissertation, "Building Queens: The Urbanization of New York's Largest Borough," he is the author of *Historic Preservation in Queens* (1990) and *A Guide to Historical Map Resources for Greater New York* (1988).

Jonathan Kuhn (MA in art history, Columbia University) is the curator of monuments and historian for the New York City Department of Parks and Recreation. He is the author of many articles and publications on parks history, art, and urban design, including *Historic Houses in New York City Parks* (1989; rev. and enlarged 1993).

Michael Kwartler, an architect and urban designer, is the director of the Environmental Simulation Center at the New School for Social Research and a fellow of the American Institute of Architects.

Chibu Lagman, a native of the Philippines, has conducted research on the Filipino community in New York City.

Michel S. Laguerre is a professor of social anthropology in the department of African–American studies at the University of California, Berkeley. He is a member of the editorial board of *Migration World*, an advisory editor of *American Anthropologist*, and the author of several books including *Voodoo and Politics in Haiti* (1989), *Urban Poverty in the Caribbean* (1990), and *American Odyssey: Haitians in New York City* (1989).

Mark Laiosa is a former orchestra manager of the Bronx Symphony Orchestra and an arts producer at WBAI.

Jacqueline Lalley is a writer and editor and the assistant director of publications for the Family Resource Coalition in Chicago.

Sarah Bradford Landau (PhD Institute of Fine Arts, New York University) is an associate professor of fine arts at New York University, the author of *Edward T. and William A. Potter: American Victorian Architects* (1979) and *P. B. Wight: Architect, Contractor, and Critic, 1838–1925* (1981), and a member of the New York City Landmarks Preservation Commission.

George J. Lankevich received his graduate degrees from Columbia University and is a professor of history at Bronx Community College. He has written or edited more than twenty books of history and is now preparing a series of books on international cooperation in the twentieth century.

Michael Lapp is an assistant professor of history at the College of New Rochelle. He is completing a book about Puerto Ricans in New York City in the 1940s and 1950s.

Margaret Latimer, who received her doctorate

Cooke, Jay, 284
Cooke, Marvel, 339
Cooke, Sam, 475
Coolidge, Calvin, 318, *489*, 567, 836, 938, 999, 1126
Coolidge, Elizabeth Sprague, 75
Cooney, Joan Ganz, 214
Cooper, Alexander, 40, 88, 89
Cooper, Eleanor, 665
Cooper, L. Gordon, *1183*
Cooper, James (circus owner), 226
Cooper, James Fenimore (novelist), 127, 159, 318, 352, 590, 640, 681, 713
Cooper, Kent, 60
Cooper, Leon, 146
Cooper, Myles, 33, 259
Cooper, Paula, 58
Cooper, Sarah, 542
Cooper, Wyatt, 1223
Coote, Richard, earl of Bellomont, 360, 478, 636, 1222
Copley, John Singleton, 559
Coppo, Ernest, 224
Coppola, Francis Ford, 406
Copra, Joyce, 337
Coralli, Jean, 312
Corbin, Abel R., 414
Corbitt, Ted, 1029
Corcoran, John, 283
Corea, Chick, 319
Corelli, Franco, 938
Corio, Ann, 169
Cornell, Charles G., *268*
Cornell, J. B., 91, 187
Cornell, Richard, 391, 686
Cornell, Thomas, 142, 239
Cornell, W. W., 91, 187
Cornish, Philip Bell, 2
Corree, Joseph, 308
Corridan, John M., 693, 1279
Corrigan, Douglas "Wrong Way," *1181*, 1183
Corrigan, E. Gerald, 395
Corsaro, Frank, 5, 98
Corsi, Edward, 605, *740*
Corso, Gregory, 93
Corson, Mrs. Celmington, *1181*
Cort, John, 61
Cortelyou, George B., 674
Cortines, Ramon C., *122*, 960
Cortissoz, Royal, 47, 57
Cortlandt, V. J., 71
Cosby, William, 196, 294, 478, *479*, 680, 939, 1052, 1222
Cosgrave, Jessica Garetson, 407
Cosgrave, William T., *1181*
Coste, Dieudonne, *1181*
Costello, Lou, 169
Costello, Maurice, 637
Coster, Charles, 627
Costinescu, Gheorghe, 147
Cotheal, Alexander Isaac, 25
Cotten, Elizabeth, 1012
Cotter, Kitty, 665
Cotton, John, 577
Cotton, Joseph P., 176
Coudert, Frederic R. (congressman), *484*, 986
Coudert, Frédéric René (lawyer), 288
Coulter, Art, 843
Coup, William, 78
Cournand, André F., 260
Cousins, Norman, 1044, 1156
Cousteau, Jacques, 360
Coutant, Gilbert S., 1142
Covello, Dallice, 665
Covert, James, *481*
Coward, Noël, 14, 74, 354, 563
Cowdery, Mae v., 664
Cowdrey, Peter A., 285
Cowell, Henry, 242, 270, 574, 793, 808
Cowen, Joshua Lionel, 1194
Cowles, Charles, 59
Cowles, Henry B., *480*
Cowles, John, Jr., 528
Cox, Ainslee, 73
Cox, James, *489*
Cox, Kenyon, 57, 781, 1285
Cox, Palmer, 1036
Cox, Samuel S., *481*
Cox, Wally, 1228
Coxe, Daniel, 439
Cozzens, William B., *735*
Craig, Charles L., *270*
Craig, Edward Gordon, 1109
Craigee, Mary E., 160
Crain, Thomas T. C., 1056
Cram, Ralph Adams, 189, 473, 537
Crandall, Jesse A., 1194
Crane, C. Howard, 778, 1177
Crane, Hart, 155, 682, 683
Crane, Ichabod, 168
Crane, Jonathan, 576
Cravath, Paul D., 296
Craven, Alfred W., 377
Crawford, Bruce, 758
Crawford, Cheryl, 5, 246, 512, 632, 1126
Crawford, Freddie, 835
Crawford, Jennie L., 287
Crawford, John J., 1118
Creamer, Thomas, *481*
Creeley, Robert, 684
Creighton, James, 1103
Crèvecoeur, Hector St. John de, 2, 191
Crimmins, Lily Lalor, 299
Crimp, Douglas, 58
Crisona, James J., *130*
Crittenberger, Willis D., *1182*
Croce, Arlene, 314
Crocheron, Henry, *480*
Crocheron, Jacob, *480*
Crolius, Clarkson, 200, 1026
Crolius, Clarkson, Jr., 200
Crolius, John, 200
Crolius, William, 200
Cromer, Harold, 1151
Cromwell, William Nelson, 1141
Cronkite, Walter, 257
Crooke, Philip S., *481*
Crooke, Mrs. Philip S., 762
Crooke, Robert L., 762
Crookes, John, *812*
Cropsey, James C., *912*
Cropsey, Jasper F., *572*, 799
Crosby, Bing, 244, 530, 800, 975, 1260
Crosby, Fanny, 834
Crosby, Howard, 1086
Cross, James, 1151
Croswell, Harry, 809
Crouch, George, 301
Crouse, Russel, 1172
Crowell, F. Elisabeth, 760
Crowell, Thomas Young, 1179
Crowninshield, Frank, 272, 714, 781, 1224, 1230
Crum, Jason, 782
Cruz, Celia, 422
Cugat, Xavier, 707
Culbertson, Judi, 514
Cullen, Thomas H., *483*
Culver, Andrew R., 303, 946
Cumming, Thomas W., *481*
Cummings, Amos J., *482*
Cummings, Angela, 1183
Cummings, Thomas Sier, 588
Cummins, George David, 993
Cummins, Maria Susanna, 918
Cunard, Edward, 1115
Cunard, Samuel, 303
Cunningham, Arthur, *270*
Cunningham, John P., 246
Cunningham, William, 608
Curley, Edward W., *483*
Curran, Henry H., *129*, *738*
Curran, Joseph, 728
Currier, Nathaniel, 304
Curry, Daniel, 548
Curry, John (ice skater), 1165
Curtis, Cyrus H. K., 8, 839
Curtis, Edward, *480*
Curtis, Glenn, 493
Curtis, King, 1012
Curtis, Tony, 575
Curtis, William B., 825
Curtius, Alexander, 909
Custis, Nellie, 239
Cuthbert, R. L., 59
Cutler, Timothy, 625
Cutting, Francis B., *481*
Cutting, R. Fulton, 228, 473
Cutting, William, 397
Cuyler, Cornelius, 445
Czolgosz, Leon, 37

Da Costa, Charles M., 659
da Cunha, George, 280
Daddy Kane, 986
Dafora, Asadata, 312, 421
Daggett, Ezra, 178
Daille, Pierre, 574
Dake, Arthur, 212, 732
Dakin, James, 1216
Dale, Alan, 1177
Dale, Harry H., *483*
Daley, Charles, 947
Daley, Linda, 1151
Dali, Salvador, 1038, 1081
Dalley, Elizabeth, 437
Dallis, Nick, 185
Dalrymple, Jean, 228
Daly, Augustin, 1109
Daly, Charles P., 291
Daly, John (television host), 21
D'Agostino, Nicolas, 307
D'Agostino, Nicolas, Jr., 307
D'Agostino, Pasquale (Patsy), 307
Damas, Thomas L., 240
D'Amato, Alfonse, 1164
d'Amboise, Jacques, 72, 391
Damrosch, Clara, 724
Damrosch, Peter, 1179
Dancer, Earl, 1246
Dane, Maxwell, 320
Daniel, Clifton, 847
Danielian, Leon, 313
Daniels, Charles M., 1145
Daniels, George Henry, 1207
Dannay, Frederic, 919
Dante, Nicholas, 1109
Danto, Arthur, 58
Daphnis, Nassos, 782
Darbouze, Rollin, 517
d'Arcangelo, Allan, 782
Darling, William A., *481*, *736*
Darrin, Bobby, 146, 1012
Dasch, George, 383

Dattner, Richard, 49
Daugherty, Harry, 1123, 1215
Davenport, E. L., 1167
Daves, Jessica, 1230
David, Hal, 1012
Davidson, Bruce, 338, 901
Davidson, Irwin, *484*
Davidson, Jo, 164, 1055
Davidson, Joan K., 623
Davidson, Robert, 938
David-Weill, Michel, 660
Davies, Arthur B., 55, 366, 630
Davies, Henry, 285
Davies, Marion, 404, 405, 975, 1241
D'Avignon, Francis, 135, 376
Davis, Benjamin O., Sr., 525
Davis, Cornelius, 9
Davis, Douglas, 58
Davis, Eddie "Lockjaw," 764
Davis, Gary, 1012
Davis, Katharine Bement, 1269
Davis, Larry, 645
Davis, Leon J., 688
Davis, Ossie, 40
Davis, Peter, 337
Davis, Rebecca Harding, 590
Davis, Richard R., 755
Davis, Ruth, 475
Davis, Sadie Warren, 36
Davis, Sammy, Jr., 1151
Davis, Thomas J., 549
Davis, William E., Jr. (architect), 49
Davis, William Thompson (naturalist), 1266
Davison, Henry P., 74, 627
Davitt, Michael, 603
Dawson, Catherin Amy, 909
Day, Henry, 694
Day, John, 82, 831, 837
Dayton, J. Wilson, 90
Dean, Arthur H., 1141
Dean, Bashford, 1248
Dean, James, 632
Dean, Laura, 623
Dean, William F., *1182*
de Antonio, Emile, 337
Deardorff, Neva, 1084
de Armas, Raul, 1073
de Basil, Wassily, 313
Debevoise, Eli Whitney, 322
DeBevoise, Henry S., *690*
de Blois, Natalie, 48
Debs, Eugene V., 277, 408, *489*, 1257, 1285
DeBusschere, Dave, 835
De Camp, Joseph Rodefer, 1161
Decasse, Louis François, 200
de Ciphlet, J. M., 1081
Decter, Midge, 909
Decter, Moshe, 22
de Casali, Giovanni Francesco Secchi, 660
de Casseres, Benjamin, 57
Decker, John W., 1107
Decker, Levi, 108
Decker, Mary, 763
Decker, Thomas W., 309
DeCoppet, Edward J., 179
DeCormier, Robert, 219
de Dampiere, Jacques, *1181*
Dee, Joey, 1012
de Feriet, Jenika, 440
de Filippis, Daisy Cocco, 340
DeForeest, Henry, *811*, 939
DeForest, Hendricus, 574
DeForest, Isaac, 574
de Forrest, Jean, 440
de Francisci, Anthony, 1211
de Galard-Terraube, Geneviève, *1182*
De Gasperi, Alcide, *1181*, *1182*
de Gaulle, Charles, *1181*, *1182*
Degnon, Michael J., 594, 611
de Golyer, Everett, 19
De Graff, Robert, 126
de Hirsch, Maurice, 78
Dehon, Theodore, 457
Deitch, Gene, 395
DeJesus, Carlos, 337
de Jong, Bettie, 1156
de Kay, Charles, 57
De Koven, Reginald, 790
de la Boissiere, Tanguy, *812*
de Laboulaye, Édouard, 1119
Delafield, Francis, 324
Delafield, John, 848
Delafield, Joseph, 402
Delafond, John, *812*
Delamar, Joseph R., 467
Delamarre, Jacques, 40
De La Montanya, James, *480*
de Lancey, Oliver, 31, 33, 698
de Lancey, Susannah, 2
Delaney, James J., *484*
Delaney, John J., *483*
Delano, Franklin H., 511, 554
Delano, Warren, 853
Delano, William Adams, 148, 640
Delanoy, Peter, 203, 662, *744*
Delaplaine, Isaac C., *481*
DeLarverie, Storme, 665
Delavall, Thomas, *744*
Del Duca, Robert, 337
Dell, Floyd, 590, 667, 734
Della Vos, Victor, 943
Delli Carri, Joseph, 147
Del Monaco, Mario, 758
de Los Angeles, Victoria, 758
Delsarte, François, 312
De Luca, Giuseppe, 757
DeLury, John J., 24, 1210
De Maria, Walter, 1055
De Meyer, Nicholas, 360, *744*
DeMille, Cecil B., 404
Demo, Antonio, 222
de Montebello, Philippe, 757
Demorest, Williams Jennings, 326
Denby, Edwin, 314
Denham, Sergei, 313
Denise, Nicholas, 87
Dennett, Mary Ware, 388
Denning, William, *480*
Dennis, Donna, 1056
Denniston, David, *812*
Denoyelles, Pierre, *480*
Dent, Thomas C., 844
Denton, Frederick W., 551
De Palma, Brian, 406
De Peyster, Johannes, *744*
De Reimer, Isaac, *744*
de Reszke, Édouard, 757
de Reszke, Jean, 757
de Reus, Manuel de Gerrit, 112
DeRham, H. C., 240
De Rivera, Belle, 826
De Ronde, Lambertus, 726
Dervall, William, *744*
Deskey, Donald, 322, 975
Desobry, Jacques, 629
Destine, Jean-Léon, 313, 422
Destinn, Emmy, 757
DeSylva, Buddy, 465, 791
Deutsch, Albert, 750
Deutsch, Bernard S., *230*
Devi, Ratan, 312
Devine, William J., *912*
Devlin, Daniel, 599
Devoe, F. W., 329
de Voe, Isaac, 1188
De Vries, David Pietersen, 1112
Dewey, Charles Melville, 210
Dewey, George, 331, *1181*
Dewing, Thomas W., 781, 1161
De Witt, Simeon, 510
Dey, Frederick Marmaduke Van Rensselaer, 919
De Zayas, Marius, 57, 1065
d'Harnoncourt, René, 785
Diaghilev, Serge, 72, 312, 317
Diamond, David, 243
Diamond, Jack "Legs," 944
Diamond, Master John, 1151
Diamond, Neil, 1012
Diat, Louis, 423
Diaz, Armando V., *1181*
Diaz, Emilio Cabral, 28
Dibdin, Charles, 1090
di Cesnola, Luigi Palma, 756
Dick, William, 1140
Dickens, Alfred Tennyson, 1201
Dickey, Bill, 850
Dickinson, Clarence, 137
Dickinson, John, 32
Dickson, William Kennedy Laurie, 403
Dickstein, Samuel, *483*
di Cocco, Pasquale, 1223
Diddley, Bo, 40
Didion, Joan, 843
Diem, Ngo Dinh, *1182*
Dieterich, George, 71
Dietz, Howard, 791
Diggs, J. Daniel, 114
Dilks, Thomas, 73
Dillingham, Charles, 1176
Dilvelis, Callinikos, 355
DiMaggio, Joe, 84, 145, 850, 1069
DiMaio, Dominick, 746
Dimov, Osip (Joseph Perlman), 1282
DiMucci, Dion, 1012
d'Indy, Vincent, 925
Dine, Jim, 436
Dinkeloo, John, 425, 757, 1289
Di Prima, Diane, 93, 684
Dircksen, Cornelis, 156
Dirks, Rudloph, 184
Disney, Walt, 704
Di Stefano, Giuseppe, 758
Dithmar, Edward August, 1177
Ditmars, Abraham D., *690*
Ditmarse, Johannes, 335
Ditmas, Charles A., 335
Ditmas, Henry Suydam, 335
Ditmas, John, 335
Ditson, Oliver, 1184
di Verdura, Fulco, 618
Dix, Dorothea, 749
Dix, John A. (governor), 277, 783, 1135
Dix, John (mayoral candidate), *736*
Dix, Richard, 342
Dixey, John, 289
Dixon, Rod, *1028*
diZerega, Augustus, 401
Dobzhansky, Theodosius, 110
Dockstader, Lew, 764
Dodd, Frank, 338
Dodd, Jonathan, 338

Dodd, Moses Woodruff, 338
Dodd, Walter, 903
Dodds, Thomas, 789
Dodge, Charles F., 617
Dodge, Cleveland H., 52, 1008
Dodge, David Low, 31
Dodge, Edwin, 699
Dodge, Samuel W., 1008
Dodge, William E., 144, 339, *481*, 1008
Dodworth, Allen, 73, 315
Dodworth, George, 315
Dodworth, Harvey, 73
D'Oench, Albert F., 513
Doherty, Joseph, 603
Dohrenwend, Bruce, 750
Doggett, John, Jr., 230
Dolan, Jay P., 514
Dole, Vincent, 345
Dollinger, Isidore, *484*
Domingo, Plácido, 758, 827
Domino, Fats, 1012
Donaldson, William, 341
Donegan, Horace William Baden, *380*, 381
Donnelly, Palmer, 1146
Donovan, Bernard E., *122*
Donovan, Eddie, 835
Donovan, Jerome F., *483*
Dooling, Peter J., *483*
Doolittle, Issac, 78
Doran, George H., 125
Doran, Katy, 665
Doremus, Robert P., 179
Dorfman, Daniel, 1235
Dorgan, Tad, 1123
Dorlan, Sidney, 1026
Dorland, John M., 332
Dorman, John J., *411*
Dorn, Francis, *484*
Doubleday, Abner, 429
Doubleday, Frank Nelson, 125, 342, 345
Doughty, Charles, 637
Douglas, Bob, 86
Douglas, George, 342
Douglas, Stephen, *486–87*, 1049
Douglas, William H. (congressman), *482*
Douglas, William O. (jurist), 436
Douglas, William P. (yachtsman), 342
Douglass, Benjamin, 348
Douglass, David (actor), 1165
Douglass, David Bates (architect), 509
Douglass, Frederick, 10, 113, 343, 1027, 1088
Douglass, Sarah M., 9
Dove, Ulysses, 12
Dow, Charles, 342, 1234
Dow, Olivia, 255
Dowd, Michael, 766
Dowd, William, *736*
Dowdy, James H., 525
Dowling, Frank L., *129*, *230*
Downes, Olin, 793
Downey, Robert, 406
Downing, David L., 73
Doyle, Alexander, 1053
Doyle, Joseph, 155
Doyle, Ned, 320
Draper, Dorothy, 593
Draper, John William, 823, 848
Draper, Theodore, 843
Drayton, Ronnie, 1013
Drennan, Thomas J., *411*
Dresser, Paul, 1187
Drew, Elizabeth, 830
Drew, Robert, 337
Drexel, Francis M., 345
Drexel, Mrs. John, 1256
Dreyfus, René, 68
Dreyfuss, Henry, 74, 1207, 1276
Driggs, Edmund H., *482*
Driscol, Dennis, *812*
Drissel, J. A. H., 98
Drumgoole, John C., 777, 908
Dryden, John (insurance executive), 671
Dryfoos, Orvil, 847
Duane, Tom, 456
Du Bois, Gualtherus, 993
Duboy, Paul E. M., *1009*, 1053
Dubuffet, Jean, 1056
Dudley, Edward R., *129*
Dudley, Jane, 313
Dudley, Pendleton, 955
du Fais, John, 1210
Duffy, Ben, 88
Dugro, Anton, 464
Dugro, P. Henry, *482*, 607
Dukakis, Michael S., *491*, 622
Duke, James B., 21, 1189
Duke, Vernon, 465, 1096
Dulon, Rudolph, 1069
Dun, Robert Graham, 348
Duncan, Robert, 684
Duncan, William, 230
Dundy, Elmer, 273, 545
Dunham, David, 1265
Dunlap, George T., 125, 511
Dunlap, Robert, 532
Dunn, Edward, 261
Dunn, Judith, 314
Dunn, L. C., 110
Dunn, Robert, 314
Dunning, John R., 260
Dunning, William, 590
Dunphy, Edward J., *482*
Dunphy, Mary Ambrose, 251
Dunton, Frederick W., 350
Dunwell, Charles T., *482*
Dupee, F. W., 591, 684
du Pithon, Jean Bérard, 1193
du Pont, Pierre S., 376
Dupree, Cornell, 1012
Durand, J. N. L., 159
Durand, John, 57
Durang, John, 311
Durant, Charles, 68, 188
Durant, William, 284
Durante, Jimmy, 224, 282, 697, 1022
Durell, William, 213
Durocher, Leo, 156, 831, 1159
Durr, Louis, 787
Durrie, George Henry, 305
Durst, Joseph, 1161
Duryea, Christian, 351
Duse, Eleanora, 1170
Dutra, Eurico Gaspar, *1182*
Dutton, Edward Payson, 125, 379
Duvalier, François, 517
Duvalier, Jean-Claude, 517
Duÿcking, Everett, 469
Dwan, Allan, 405
Dwight, Theodore, 252, 259, 657, 835
Dwyer, Big Bill, 559
Dwyer, Mike, 558
Dwyer, Philip, 558
Dyckman, Jan, 353
Dyckman, William, 353
Dyre, William, *744*
Dyson, John S., 379

Eagleton, J. Joseph, 1008
Eames, Emma, 757
Eames, Ray Kaiser, 354
Earhart, Amelia, 1, 1181
Earle, Morris, 769
Earle, Pliny, 119
Eastlake, Charles, 162
Eastman, George, 717
Eato, E. V. C., 823
Eaton, Dorman B., 952
Eayres, Ellen Knowles, 521
Ebb, Fred, 663, 1096
Ebbets, Charles, 358, 906
Eberle, Abastenia St. Leger, 1054
Eberson, John, 689, 778
Ebert, Carl, 109
Eckener, Hugo, *1181*
Eckert, Wallace J., 271
Eckford, Henry, 209, 1067
Eckhoff, Anthony, *481*
Eckstine, Billy, 467
Eckstut, Stanton, 88
Edbrooke, Willoughby J., 393
Eddy, Arthur Jerome, 57
Eddy, Thomas, 119, 215, 749, 1045
Edel, Deborah, 665
Edelman, Gerald, 1051
Edelman, Harold, 1036
Edelman, Judith, 48
Edelstadt, David, 1283
Edelstein, M. Michael, *484*
Eden, John H., 363
Edgerton, Giles, 57
Edison, Harry "Sweets," 85
Edmonds, Harry, 594
Edson, Franklin, *736*, *744*, 840
Edward Albert, prince of Wales, *1181*
Edwards, Douglas, 257
Egan, Charles, 843
Egbert, Joseph, *480*
Egleston, Thomas, 1050
Egli, Konrad, 423
Ehret, George, 136, 423, 464, *639*, 853
Eichelberger, Ethel, 1175
Eiffel, Gustave, 1119
Einstein, Albert, 594, 1221
Einstein, Edwin, *481*, *736*
Einstein, Izzy, 942
Eisa, Mohammad, 1139
Eisenberg, Arlene, 1274
Eisenman, Peter, 48
Eisfeld, Theodore, 838
Eisner, Will, 184, 395
Eken, Andrew J., 1111
Elder, Lonne, 1174
Elder, Ruth, *1181*
Eldert, Garret, 520
Eldredge, Niles, 461
Elias, Rosalind, 42, 1147
Eliot, Charles William, 250
Eliot, T. S., 686
Elizabeth, queen of Belgium, *1181*
Elizabeth II, queen of Great Britain, *1182*
Ellet, Thomas Harlan, 930–31
Ellington, Ruth, 371
Elliot, Andrew, 694
Elliot, Samuel MacKenzie, 687
Elliott, Donald H., 233
Elliott, John L., 61, 209, 1060
Elliott, Philip, 413
Elliott, Ramblin' Jack, 422
Ellis, David Maldwyn, 549
Ellis, Havelock, 542, 664
Ellis, Jabex, 1183
Ellis, Samuel, 372, 1253

Ellison, John, 686
Ellison, Thomas, 686
Ellsberg, Daniel, 131
Ellsler, Fanny, 312
Elman, Mischa, 38, 577
Ely, Charles, 576
Ely, Nathan C., *268*
Ely, Richard, 109, 1082
Embury, Aymar, 48, 1200, 1209, 1276
Embury, Philip, 536, 598, 753
Emerson, Ralph Waldo, 272, 375, 532, 660
Emerson, William, 375
Emmet, Elizabeth, *443*
Emmet, J. K., 791
Emmet, Thomas Addis, Jr., 710
Endicott, Francis, 376
Endicott, George, 376
Endicott, Sarah, 376
Endicott, William, 376
Engel, Eliot, 106, *484*
Engel, Martin, 947
Engel, Morris, 902
Engelsman, Bernhard, 321
England, Marshall, 525
Englis, John, 1067
English, Thomas Dunn, 909
Eno, Amos, 402
Enoch, Kurt, 126, 806
Enright, Richard E., *912*
Enriquez, Carlos, 803
Epstein, Barbara, 592, 684, 843
Epstein, Jason, 126, 592, 684
Erhardt, Joel B., *736*
Erickson, Carl, 1081
Erkins, Henri, 784
Erlanger, Abraham, 1069, 1168, 1169, 1177, 1178
Ernst, Max, 594, 776, 843
Errol, Leon, 169
Erskine, Carl, 156
Ertegun, Ahmet, 1012, 1203–4
Ertegun, Nesuhi, 1012
Erving, Julius, 86
Ervis, Charlie, *372*
Espenscheid, Nicholas, 532
Espinosa, Andres, *1028*
Esposito, Phil, 843
Estern, Neil, 497, 1055
Esteves, Sandra Maria, 963
Esty, William, 1262
Eszterhas, Joe, 1017
Ettinger, E. P., 125
Ettinger, William L., *122*
Ettor, Joseph, 588
Evangelides, Christodoulos M. L., 503
Evans, Bill, 246, 319
Evans, Gil, 319, 615
Evans, Harry C., 934
Evans, Herschel, 85
Evans, Larry, 212, 732
Evans, Marcellus H., *483*
Evans, Margaret, 436
Everdell, William, *268*
Everett, Edward, 385, 836
Everett, Thomas H., 130, 559
Evers, John, 435
Eversley, Frederick, 351
Evertsen, Cornelis, 352
Ewbank, Weeb, 834, 1253
Ewing, Maurice, 461
Ewing, Patrick, 835

Fagan, Garth, 314, 316
Fairbanks, Douglas, 14
Fairbanks, Douglas, Sr., 1241
Fairbridge, Rhodes, 461
Fairchild, Benjamin, *482*
Fairchild, Edmund W., 387, 1271
Fairchild, John B., 1271
Faisal, Daoud Ahmed, 793
Falckner, Justus, 700
Falk, Peter, 1174
Fancher, Ed, 17
Farah, empress of Iran, *1182*
Farber, Barry, *742*
Farber, Viola, 304
Farbstein, Leonard, *484*
Farkas, George, 13
Farkas, Mary, 165
Farley, Michael F., *483*
Farley, Samuel, *811*
Farley, Thomas, 1057
Farmer, A. D., 940
Farmer, Frances, 512
Farmer, James, 115, 1276
Farnham, Paulding, 1183
Farragut, David G., 391, 1272
Farrakhan, Louis, 794
Farrar, John, 126, 391
Farrell, Frank, 850
Farrell, James T., 210, 591, 924
Farrow, Mia, 14
Fassett, J. S., 1046
Faulkner, William, 806, 924, 985
Fay, James H., *484*
Fay, Larry, 514
Fay, Leslie, 453
Fay, William, 322
Faye, Joey, 169
Fearing, Kenneth, 804
Fedde, Elizabeth, 700, 855
Feelings, Tom, 844
Feemster, Robert, 1235
Feerick, John, 237
Fein, Benjamin "Dopey Benny," 452
Feininger, Andreas, 901, 1071
Feinman, Diane Stettin, 6
Feinstein, Henry, 24
Feld, Eliot, 20, 395
Feldman, Morton, 304
Feldman, Ronald, 58
Feldman, Sandra, 1157
Feliciano, Lydia, 521
Felker, Clay, 387, 822, 1229
Fellows, John R., *482*
Felt, Abraham, 396
Fenno, John, 809, *812*
Ferber, Herbert, 1055
Ferguson, Frank W., 473
Ferguson, John, *744*
Ferguson, Katy, 113, 1142
Ferkauf, Eugene, 366
Fern, Fanny, 836, 1096
Fernandez, Joseph A., *122*, 123
Fernbach, Henry, 47, 199
Ferrer, Fernando, *129*, 145
Ferrer, Francisco, 37
Ferris, Charles G., *480*
Ferro, Vanessa, 665
Fesco, Michael, 316
Fetchit, Stepin, 1032
Fey, Charles, 1259
Field, Anne, 1096
Field, Marshall, 327
Field, Marshall, III, 909
Field, Thomas F., *735*
Fields, Joseph, 1172
Fields, Lew, 188, 1250, *1250*
Fierman, Harold L., 631
Figueroa, Sotero, 962
Fillmore, Charles W., 114
Fillmore, Millard, *486*, *1258*
Finch, William, 407
Finck, Henry T., 792–93
Fine, Jean, 1059
Fine, Sidney A., *484*
Finger, Bill, 184
Finkelstein, Louis, 620
Finletter, Thomas, 662
Finley, Karen, 197
Finn, David, 1027
Finney, Lydia Andrews, 715
Fino, Paul A., *484*
Firpo, Luis, 134, 326, 1004
Fischer, Israel F., *482*
Fischer, R. M., 89
Fischler, Steven, 337
Fish, Elizabeth Sackett, 413
Fish, Hamilton, 413, *480*, 999, 1053
Fish, Jonathan, 413
Fisher, Bud, 184, *184*
Fisher, John, 469
Fisher, Joseph, 238
Fisher, Richard, 469
Fisher, Rudolph, 114, 683
Fisher, Stanley, 93
Fisher, Zachary, 595
Fisk, Jonathan, *480*
Fiske, Haley, 672
Fiske, Harrison Grey, 414, 1169, 1178
Fiske, Josiah M., 1218
Fiske, Robert B., 320
Fitch, Ashbel P., *482*
Fitch, Clyde, 1170, 1177
Fitch, Emory, 407
Fitch, Ezra H., 1
Fitch, James Marston, 49, 546
Fitzgerald, Ella, 614, 1022, 1250
Fitzgerald, Frank T., *482*
Fitzgerald, John J. (congressman), *482*
Fitz Gerald, John J. (reporter), 107
Fitzgerald, Maurice A., *130*
Fitzgibbon, Irene, 192, *434*, 830
Fitzmaurice, James A., *1181*
Fitzpatrick, James M., *483*
Fitzsimmons, Bob, 283
Flagg, George W., 992
Flagg, Jacob Bradley, 907
Flagg, James Montgomery, 942
Flagg, Louise, 202
Flagler, Henry Morrison, 932
Flagler, John H., 1141
Flagstad, Kirsten, 758
Flake, Floyd H., 10, *484*
Flammer, John A., 416, 1127
Flanagan, Dennis, 1051
Flanagan, Hallie, 1171
Flanner, Janet, 665, 830
Flato, Paul, 618
Flavin, David, 186
Fleischman, Doris E., 105
Fleischman, Mark, 1033
Fleischmann, Charles, 418
Fleischmann, Maximilian, 418
Fleischmann, Raoul H., 418, 1023
Fleming, Ian, 806
Fleming, Tom, *1028*
Fleming, Walter, 437
Fletcher, Alice, 1096
Fletcher, Benjamin, 142, 360, 478, 937
Fletcher, Isaac, 466
Floda, Liviu, 1018
Flom, Joseph, 660, 1073

Florence, Billy, 437
Florio, Caryl, 240
Flower, Roswell P., 419
Floyd, Charles A., *480*
Floyd, John G., *481*
Floyd, William, *480*
Flynn, Joseph V., *483*
Foch, Ferdinand, *1181*
Foelker, Otto G., *482*
Foley, Thomas F., 421
Folwell, Arthur Hamilton, 961
Fonda, Henry, 406, 699
Fontaine, V., 832
Fontanne, Lynn, 14, 700, 1178
Forbes, John Murray, 223
Force, Juliana Rieser, 1261
Ford, Edsel, 425
Ford, George, 993
Ford, Gerald R., *491*, 638, 779
Ford, Henry, 425, 731, 1152
Ford, Henry, II, 425
Ford, John, 124, 781
Ford, Whitey, 850
Foreman, Richard, 1110, 1175
Forest, Gerardo, 962
Forgione, Larry, 1000
Forman, Milos, 406
Fornes, Charles V., *230*, *482*
Forster, George H., *268*
Forti, Simone, 314
Fortunoff, Clara, 433
Fortunoff, Max, 433
Fosdick, Raymond B., 1015
Foster, Christopher, 14, 1022
Foster, George W., 46
Foster, Richard, 625, 849
Foster, Rube, 83–84
Foster, Thomas, 14, 1022
Foster, William Dewey (architect), 931
Foster, William Z. (communist leader), 591
Foutz, Dave, *85*
Fowle, Bruce S., 435
Fowler, Frank, 781
Fowler, Lorenzo, 902
Fowler, Orson Squire, 902
Fox, Billy, 653
Fox, George (religious leader), 436
Fox, John, *471*
Fox, Robert, 435
Fox, Sheldon, 641
Fox, Thomas, 321
Fox, William (film producer), 66, 94, 404, 405, 778, 1141
Fox, William Henry (museum director), 159
France, Anatole, 1109
Francher, Ed, 1229
Francis, Arlene, 53, 407, 1274
Francis, Charles, 941
Francis, Samuel, 986
Francis, William, 311
Francisco, Jan, 112
Francisquy, M., 311
Francius, George B., *483*
François, André, 210
Frank, John, 550
Frank, Leo, 731
Frank, Robert, 93, 406
Frankel, Lee, 672
Frankel, Max, 847
Frankfurter, Felix, 229, 282, 432, 436, 543, 807, 1265
Frankl, Paul T., 322
Franklin, Aretha, 1013, 1228
Franklin, Benjamin, 64, 108, 159, 275, 667, 904, 1192
Franklin, Frederick, 313
Franklin, George, 176
Franklin, Jay, 1224
Franklin, Morris, *268*, *735*
Franklin, William, 33
Franks, David C. (publisher), 230
Franzen, Ulrich, 44
Frasier, James Early, 1276
Frazee, John, 1053
Frazier, Joe, 134, 837
Frazier, Walt, 835
Frederic, Harold, 352
Frederick, Christine, 8
Frederick, J. George, 8
Frederika, queen of Greece, *1182*
Freed, Alan, 975, 1012, 1267
Freed, James Ingo, 49, 57, 607
Freedlander, Joseph H., 785
Freedman, Bonnie, 337
Freedman, Doris C., 1056
Freeman, Buck, 86
Freeman, Joseph, 17, 591, 686
Freeman, Joshua, 549
Freeman, Pliny, 836
Frémont, Jessie, 439
Fremont-Smith, Eliot, 1229
Fremstad, Olive, 757
French, Philip, *744*
Freneau, Philip, 680, *812*
Freni, Mirella, 758
Freska, Friedrich, 1109
Freud, Sigmund, 140
Friebus, Florida, 662
Fried, Elaine, 323
Fried, George, *1181*
Fried, Michael, 58
Friedan, Betty, 137, 396
Friedberg, Carl, 628
Friedberg, M. Paul, 89, 170
Friedlander, Lee, 338
Friedlander, Leo, 1276
Friedman, Meryl, 665
Friedman, Stanley, 326, 917
Friendly, Fred W., 257, 784
Friendly, Henry, 1073
Fries, Catherine, 1047
Fries, Gladys, 529
Friml, Rudolf, 520, 791, 1171
Frink, John, 694
Frisell, Bill, 1013
Frith, Fred, 1013
Frohman, Charles, 1168, 1169, 1178
Frohman, Daniel, 404, 1168, 1176
Frondizi, Arturo, *1182*
Frost, Aaron V., 111
Frost, Joel, *480*
Frost, Robert, 682
Fry, William Henry, 240, 792
Fuchs, Klaus, 383, 1022
Fueter, Daniel Christian, 1070
Fugard, Athol, 116
Fulani, Lenora, 806
Fuller, Blair, 684
Fuller, Charles, 388
Fuller, Loie, 312, 314
Fuller, Meta Warrick, 527
Fuller, R. Buckminster, 420
Funk, Isaac Kauffman, 680
Furer, Howard B., 549
Furey, Jim, 85
Furillo, Carl, 156
Furman, Gabriel, 635
Furness, Frank, 575
Furtwängler, Wilhelm, 838
Fussell, Jacob, 309

Gabel, Hortense, 796
Gabel, Max, 1282
Gabriel, Gilbert W., 1177
Gadd, May, 421
Gadski, Joanna, 757
Gaeta, Anthony R., *130*
Gage, Charles, 447
Gager, C. Stuart, 131
Gagosian, Larry, 59
Gailis, Janis, 656
Gaines, Groundhog, 1151
Gaines, Will (dancer), 1151
Gaines, William M. (magazine publisher), 184, 710
Gaither, H. Rowan, 425
Galamian, Ivan, 53
Galamison, Milton, 114
Galas, Diamanda, 12
Gale, George, 1167
Gale, Leonard, 774, 1158
Gallatin, Frederick, 1120
Gallatin, Harry, 835
Gallaudet, Thomas, 321
Gallegos, Romulo, *1182*
Galli, Rosina, 312, 1149
Gallo, Joey, 510, 685
Gallup, George, 8, 1285
Galvin, John, *268*
Gambling, John, 1274
Gambold, Hector, 769
Ganly, James V., *483*
Gano, John, 75
Gans, John H., 512
Garabedian, Edna, 53
Garcia, Anthony Portuguis, 112
Garcia, Carlos P., *1182*
Garcia, Elie, 516
Garcia, Jerry, 10013
Garcia, Jose, 337
García, Manuel, 239, 792
Garcia, Robert, 145, *484*, 917
Garcia, Salvador, *1028*
Gard, Louise, 209
Garden, Nancy, 665
Gardie, Mme, 311–12
Gardiner, Julia, 1143
Gardner, Alexander, 135
Gardner, Erle Stanley, 1262
Garelik, Sanford D., *230*, 495
Garfield, James A., *487*, *810*
Garfield, John, 512, 1171
Garfunkel, Art, 1071, 1096
Garland, Judy, 181, 310
Garland, Red, 319
Garland, Robert, 1178
Garmey, Stephen, 549
Garnier, Jean-Louis, 1143
Garofalo, Frank, 1199
Garrett, Charles, 549
Garrett, Paul, 955
Garrison, Jimmy, 257
Garrison, Lindley M., 1265
Garrison, William Lloyd (abolitionist), 19, 424, 1088, 1229, 1269
Garrison, William Phillips (editor), 798
Gartner, Mike, 843
Gary, Sidney Howard, 687
Gasser, Herbert S., 1051
Gatti-Casazza, Giulio, 109, 757, 758

Gatty, Harold, *1181*
Gautier, Andrew, 445
Gauvreau, Emile, 830
Gavagan, Joseph A., *483*
Gawtry, Harrison E., 674
Gay, John, 168, 790
Gaye, Marvin, 40
Gedda, Nicolai, 758
Geddes, Robert, 849
Geer, Seth, 255, *735*
Gehry, Frank, 1110
Geisel, Theodor Seuss, 214
Gelb, Arthur, 847
Gelb, John, 790
Gelber, Jack, 684
Gellis, Isaac, 367, 642
Genet, Henry W., *268*
Genet, Jean, 116
Genin, John, 532
Genovese, Eugene, 916
Genovese, Kitty, 635
Genovese, Vito, 856, 1220
Gentry, Gary, 837
George, Henry, Jr. (congressman), *483*
George, prince of Greece, 355
Gerosa, Lawrence E., *270*, *740–41*
Gerritsen, Wolfert, 465
Gerry, Elbridge T., 1086
Gerts, Benjamin, 465
Gerts, Ida, 465
Gerulaitis, Vitas, 684, 1163
Gettler, Alexander O., 853
Getty, Ann, 512
Gever, Martha, 58
Giacomin, Ed, 843
Gibbons, James, 193
Gibbs, Frederick S., *736*
Gibbs, George, 987
Gibbs, Joan, 665
Gibbs, Josiah Willard, 904
Gibbs, Oliver, 1216
Gibbs, William Francis, 1215
Gibbs, Wolcott, 823, 830
Gibran, Khalil, 1147
Gibson, Billy, 664
Gibson, Josh, 1280
Gibson, Robert W., 1036
Giddins, Gary, 793
Gideonse, Harry D., 155
Gifford, Daniel, 503
Gifford, Frank, 831, 1105
Gifford, Robert Swain, 941
Gifford, Sanford Robinson, 572
Gigante, Louis, 569, 688, 917, 1098
Gigli, Beniamino, 757
Gilbert, Bradford L., 1074
Gilbert, Charles Kendall, *380*
Gilbert, Jacob H., *484*
Gilbert, John, 1167
Gilbert, Rod, 843
Gilbert, Ronnie, 1250
Gilbert and George (artists), 436
Gildersleeve, Virginia C., 77
Gilhooley, Ed, 917
Gill, Brendan, 48, 830, 1178
Gill, Charles, 671
Gillam, Bernard, 183
Gillett, Charles, 107, 1193
Gilliland, John L., 469
Gilman, Lawrence, 793
Gilman, Robbins, 1217
Gilmartin, Gregory, 549
Gilmore, Margallo, 14
Gilpin, Charles, 115
Gilpin, Laura, 1258
Gilpin, William, 572
Gilsey, Peter, 187, 468
Gimbel, Adam, 327, 468, 1038
Gimbel, Bernard, 468, 1038
Gingrich, Arnold, 683
Ginsbern, Horace, 954
Ginzberg, Louis, 1148
Ginzberg, Ralph, 924
Giorno, John, 1239
Giovanni, Nikki, 684
Giroux, Robert, 391
Gish, Dorothy, *404*, 917
Gittings, Barbara, 665
Gladden, Washington, 1082, 1132
Gladstone, Barbara, 59
Gladwin, Walter, 114
Glanz, Aaron, 470
Glaser, Milton, 501, 822
Glasgow, Ellen, 682
Glashow, Sheldon, 146
Glaspell, Susan, 948, 1174
Gleason, Teddy, 693
Glenn, John (astronaut), 419, *1182*, 1183
Glenn, John (philanthropist), 1029
Glick, Deborah, 456, 665
Glintenkamp, Henry, 60
Glover, John, 144
Gluck, Alma, 577
Glucksman, Lewis L., 662
Glueck, Grace, 58
Godowsky, Leopold, 901
Godwin, Parke, 839, 964
Goelet, Otto, 366
Goerk, Casimir, 717
Goethals, Goerge W., 323, 471
Goetschius, Percy, 628
Goetz, Bernhard, 645
Goffin, Gerry, 1012
Golan, Sion, 1281
Gold, Ben, 594
Gold, Herb, 683
Gold, Ted, 807, 1164
Goldberg, Jacob, 1058
Goldberg, Jane, 1151
Goldberger, Paul, 48, 1216
Golden, Howard, *129*
Golden, John, 90
Goldenburg, Samuel, 1282
Goldenson, Leonard, 21
Goldenweiser, Alexander, 39, 101
Goldfadn, Avrom, 1282
Goldfogle, Henry M., *482*, 621
Goldhammer, Albert, 18, 46
Goldin, Harrison J., *270*, *743*
Goldin, Nan, 338
Goldkette, Jean, 97, 341
Goldman, Edward, 73
Goldman, Edwin Franko, 73
Goldman, Henry, 903
Goldman, Marcus, 472
Goldmark, Pauline, 944
Goldmark, Peter C., Jr., 925, 1015
Goldmark, Rubin, 282, 628
Goldstein, Al, 924
Goldstein, Bertha, 1282
Goldstein, Harry, 182
Goldstein, Herbert S., 523
Goldstein, Jennie, 1282
Goldstein, Jonah J., *739*
Goldstein, Michael, 1088
Goldstein, Richard, 1229
Goldstone, Harmon, 546, 1216
Goldstone, Lafayette, 5
Goldstone, Platt, 546
Goldwater, Barry, *490*
Goldwyn, Samuel, 178, 404
Golomb, David, 385
Golomb, Jacob, 385
Golub, Leon, 59
Golway, Terry, 838
Gómez, Alexis, 340
Gómez, Estéban, 386, 571
Gomez, Jewelle, 665
Gompers, Clara, 917
Gonzales, Thomas A., 746, 853
Gonzalez, Julio, 521, 1080
Gooch, William Tyson, 550
Good, John, 1021
Goodell, Charles E., 277
Gooden, Dwight, 837
Goodman, Edward, 1178
Goodman, Edwin, 104
Goodman, George J. W., 254
Goodman, Marian, 58
Goodman, Paul, 37, 592
Goodman, Percival, 1055
Goodman, Roy M., 208, *742*, 999
Goodrich, A. T., 513
Goodrich, Lloyd, 57, 1261–62
Goodwin, C. T., 71
Goodwin, John Daly, 220
Goodwin, Nat, 1168
Goodwin, Philip L., 785
Goodyear, Charles, Jr., 1068
Gordon, David, 314, 315
Gordon, Dexter, 616
Gordon, George P., 940
Gordon, Jacob, 6, 1282, 1283
Gordon, Louis E., *1181*
Gordon, Max, 1228
Gordon, Waxey, 134
Gordone, Charles, 116, 1174
Gorham, Jabez, 474
Gorham, Nathaniel, 276
Gorman, Miki, *1028*
Gorme, Eydie, 499
Gotbaum, Betsy, 833
Gotbaum, Victor, 24, 25, 649
Gotfried, Martin, 1178
Gotshal, Sylvan, 1252
Gottlieb, Leo (basketball player), 835
Gottlieb, Leo (lawyer), 244
Gottlieb, Robert, 830
Gottman, Jean, 748
Gottschalk, Louis Moreau, 238, 240, 510
Goulart, João, *1182*
Gould, Elgin R. L., 177, 567
Gould, Elliott, 103
Gould, Joe, 804
Gould, Milton S., 1064
Gould, Stephen Jay, 461, 843, 1278
Goulden, Joseph A., *482*
Gouraud, F. F., 1081
Gouverneur, Nicholas, 360
Gouverneur, Samuel, 767, 938
Govern, S. K., 302
Gowon, William, 128
Grace, J. Peter, 1277
Grace, princess of Monaco, 1233
Graetz, F., 961
Grafulla, Claudius, 73
Graham, Augustus, 159
Graham, Bill (promoter), 403, 1013
Graham, Billy (evangelist), 997, 1001, 1247

Graham, Ernest R., 381, 1074
Graham, Frank, 1106
Graham, Isabella, 1052, 1086, 1142
Graham, James, 285, 445
Graham, John (artist), 323, 843
Graham, John H. (congressman), *482*
Graham, Patricia A., 1156
Gram, Hans Burch, 554
Grandjean, August, 1081
Grange, Red, 424, 1104
Grann, Phyllis, 127
Grant, Bob, 1231
Grant, Cary, 1242
Grant, Edward, 611
Grant, Jane, 14, 829, 1023
Grant, Julia Dent, 500, 501
Grant, Micki, 116
Grau, Maurice, 757
Graubard, Moritz, 621
Gray, Dorothy, 286
Gray, Henry Judd, 1081
Gray, Jesse, 114
Gray, Neil, *268*
Greatorex, Henry W., 503
Greaves, William, 337
Greb, Harry, 1203
Green, Bill, 1070
Green, Charles, 1151
Green, Dallas, 837
Green, Elizabeth, 1048
Green, Freddie, 85
Green, Helen, 1101
Green, J. Wilson, *268*
Green, Mark, 949
Green, Paul, 512, 1170, 1174
Green, Richard R., *122*
Green, S. William, *484*
Green, Stewart, 1252
Green, William, 19
Greenberg, Alan C., 92
Greenberg, Ann, 61
Greenberg, Clement, 58, 261, 843, 992
Greenberg, Hank, 773
Greene, Adolphus, 1010
Greene, Balcomb, 782
Greene, Belle da Costa, 905
Greene, Francis V., *912*, 985
Greene, Gael, 231, 822
Greene, Nathaniel, 428
Greenglass, David, 1022
Greenleaf, Thomas, *811*, *812*, 1006
Greenwich, Ellie, 1012
Greer, David Hummell, *380*, 381
Greer, Sonny, *372*
Gregorian, Vartan, 841
Gregory, David, 20
Gregory, Dick, 358
Gregory, Isaac M., 628
Grein, Richard F., *380*, 381
Gresser, Lawrence, *129*, 277
Grierson, John, 336
Griesa, Thomas P., 1257
Griffin, Anthony J., *483*
Griffin, Cyrus, 276
Griffin, Daniel J., *483*
Griffin, Percy, 228
Griffith, D. W., 110, 468
Griffith, Edward, 445
Griffith, Emile, 134
Griffith, Robert E., 939
Griffith, Vincent, 154
Griffiths, Paul, 793
Grimes, Burleigh, 155
Grimes, Claire, 602
Grimes, Patrick, 602
Grimes, William Henry, 1235
Grimké, Angelina Weld, 540, 664
Grimm, Peter, 227
Grinnell, George Bird, 800, 1050
Grinnell, Henry, 510, 511
Grinnell, Joseph, 414, 510
Grinnell, Moses Hicks, *480*, 510, 511, 677
Grissom, Virgil I., *1183*
Griswold, Denny, 955
Griswold, Frank, 436
Griswold, Glenn, 955
Grofé, Ferde, 1259
Grolier, Jean, 511
Gronchi, Giovanni, *1182*
Groninger, Homer M., 839
Gronouski, John, 914
Grooms, Red, 436
Gropper, William, 624
Grosjean, Florian, 1271
Gross, Calvin E., *122*
Gross, Chaim, 365, 1055
Gross, Elliot M., 496, 746, 747
Gross, Magnus, 464
Gross, Sam, 802
Grosset, Alexander, 125, 511
Grossman, Sid, 338, 902
Grosz, George, 92
Grout, Edward M., *129*, *270*
Grover, Jan, 58
Grumet, Jacob, *411*
Grunfeld, Ernie, 835
Grymes, Suzette, 512
Guare, John, 843
Guerin, Richie, 835
Guernsey, R. S., 548
Guggenheim, Daniel, 68
Guggenheim, Harry F., 1089
Guggenheim, Peggy, 58, 513, 843, 914, 1024
Guggenheim, Solomon, 513
Guggenheimer, Elinor, 233
Guggenheimer, Randolph, *230*
Guider, Joseph A., *129*
Guidry, Ron, 850
Guinan, Matthew, 1197
Guinzberg, Harold K., 126, 1228
Gul, Roman, 856
Gulick, James, 410–11
Gunn, David, 496, 1139
Gunter, A. C., 664
Gunther, C. Godfrey, *736*, *744*
Gustavus Adolphus, crown prince of Sweden, *1181*
Guston, Philip, 782, 843
Gutfreund, John, 1039
Guthrie, Edwin, 5
Guthrie, Tyrone, 109
Guthrie, William D., 659
Gutiérrez, Franklin, 340
Gutterman, William, 568
Gutwasser, Johann Ernst, 463, 700
Gutzkow, Karl, 6
Guy, Buddy, 1013
Guy, Edna, 312
Guy, Francis, *1191*
Guyon, James, Jr., *480*
Guzman, Pablo, 1285

Haas, Richard, 17, 782
Haberman, François Xavier, *32*
Habib, Philip, 42, 1147
Hackett, Buddy, 103
Hackett, Frances, 1008
Hackett, Frank Sutcliff, 1008
Hackett, James, 404, 925, 1166–67
Hackett, John, 292
Hadden, Briton, 698, 1184, 1187
Haden, Charles, 249
Haffen, Louis F., *129*
Hagel, Hansel Mieth, 901
Hagel, Otto, 901
Hagen, Uta, 1176
Haggard, Edith, 680
Hagstrom, Andrew G., 1145
Haig, Robert, 260
Haight, Edward, *481*
Ha il, Muhammad, 1281
Haire, Mary Vincent, 1072
Hakmoun, Hassan, 771
Haldeman, George W., *1181*
Hale, David, 810
Hale, Ethel, 1129
Hale, Lorraine E., 517
Hale, Mother (Clara M.), 517
Hale, Nathan, 96, 382
Hale, Oliver, 1129
Hale, Ruth, 14
Hall, Carl, 475
Hall, Gus, 270
Hall, John, 1142
Hall, Leonard, *484*
Hall, Murray, 664
Hall, Otis T., *268*
Hallam, Lewis, 311, 1165
Hallam, William, 1165
Halleck, Dee Dee, 337
Halley, Rudolph, *230*, *740*
Hallidie, A. S., 174
Hallock, Gerard, 627, 810
Halpern, Seymour, *484*
Halsband, Frances, 48
Halsey, Stephen A., 63
Halsey, William F., Jr., *1181*
Halsman, Philippe, 901
Halstead, William, 1020
Halverson, Richard F., *122*
Hamid, Sufi Abdul, 114
Hamill, Pete, 822
Hamilton, Alexander (grandson of the statesman), 640
Hamilton, Andrew, 294, 939
Hamilton, Grant, 628, 961
Hamilton, Theodore L., *912*
Hamilton, Thomas, 714
Hamilton, William, 9, 823
Hamlet, James, 3
Hamlisch, Marvin, 1109
Hammel, Louis, 520
Hammer, Alvin, 261, 550
Hammer, Armand, 773
Hammer, Borgny, 855
Hammerstein, Arthur, 96, 364
Hammett, Dashiell, 538, 617, 683, 919
Hammid, Alexander, 328
Hammond, Abijah, 1070
Hammond, Joe "the Destroyer," 86
Hammond, John Henry, 181
Hampton, Mabel, 665
Hampton, Mark, 323
Hanbury, Harry A., *482*
Hancock, Herbie, 319
Hancock, John, 276
Hancock, Winfield, *487*
Handler, Milton, 631
Handwerker, Nathan, 423, 798
Handy, Robert T., 1212
Hanford, Phebe, 1096
Hanlon, Ned, 155
Hannagan, Stephen, 955

Hannan, John H., 1068
Hapgood, Norman, 621
Harcourt, Alfred, 125, 521
Harden, Jon B., 338
Harding, George Edward, 550
Harding, Warren G., 1, *489*, 531
Hardwick, Toby, *372*
Hardy, Charles, *479*
Hare, David, 843
Harison, Richard, 1215
Harkavy, Alexander, 1283
Harkness, Anna M., 268
Harkness, Edward S., 268, 936–37
Harkness, Harry S., 67
Harkness, Mary S., 268
Harkness, Rebekah, 523, 623
Harlan, John Marshall, 331, 836
Harmer, H. R., 1110
Harmon, Arthur Loomis, 564, 1074
Harmon, William Elmer, 526
Harmsworth, Alfred Charles William, Viscount Northcliffe, 307
Harney, Ben, 976
Harney, George E., 64
Harnick, Sheldon, 792, 939, 1173
Harootian, Khoren Der, 53
Harper, Conrad K., 62, 660
Harper, Fletcher, 528
Harper, John, 528
Harper, Joseph Wesley, 528
Harrar, J. George, 1015
Harrelson, Bud, 837
Harrigan, Edward, 529, 599, 791, 1109
Harriman, Florence "Daisy" Jaffray (Mrs. J. Borden), 255
Harriman, Mary, 529
Harrington, Donald, 1212
Harris, Charles K., 1090, 1187
Harris, Henry B., 1176
Harris, Julie, 632, *1247*
Harris, Sam, 105, 1177
Harrison, Abe, 302
Harrison, Benjamin, *487–88*, 774, 992
Harrison, Beverly Wildung, 1212
Harrison, Francis B., *482*
Harrison, George, 395
Harrison, John T., 374
Harrison, Marie, 1230
Harrison, William Henry, *486*
Harrisson, C., *812*
Harrisson, John, *812*
Harrisson, Margaret, *812*
Harry, Deborah, 195
Harsen, Jacob, 530, 1216
Hart, Eli, 1007, 1209
Hart, Francis, 329
Hart, Margie, 169
Hart, Moss, 6
Hart, Tony, 529, 599, 791
Hartigan, Grace, 843
Hartley, Hal, 406
Hartley, Robert M., 61, 309, 933, 952
Harvey, Charles, 368
Harvey, George U., *129*
Harvey, James B., 217
Harway, G. W., 90
Haskell, Llewellyn S., 1135
Haskell, Reuben L., *483*
Haskin, DeWitt C., 1202
Haskin, John B., *481*
Haskins, Charles Waldo, 4, 325, 532
Hassan II, king of Morocco, *1183*
Hassard, John, 792
Hastings, Thomas, 240, 442, 1008, 1054
Haswell, Charles H., *268*
Hatch, Edward P., 694
Hatch, Grace Pauline, 214
Hatch, Stephen, 468, 784
Hatcher, Elizabeth, 1047
Hatfield, R. G., 1237
Hathorne, George, 290
Hatzikiris (confectioner), 503
Haughwout, E. V., 455
Hauptmann, Bruno Richard, 678
Hausmann, Charles I., 994
Havell, Robert, Jr., 66
Havemeyer, Frederick C., 1140
Havemeyer, Louisine, 756
Havens, Jonathan N., *480*
Haviland, Paul, 57
Hawaweeny, Raphael, 355
Hawes, Elizabeth, 392
Hawking, Connie, 86
Hawkins, Coleman, 524, 539, 615
Hawkins, Edler, 938
Hawkins, William, 1178
Haws, J. H. Hobart, *481*
Hawthorne, Julian, 919
Hawthorne, Nathaniel, 640, 654
Hay, Deborah, 314
Hay, Mary Garrett, 1269
Hayden, Melissa, 72
Hayden, Tom, 592
Haydn, Hiram, 126, 683
Hayes, Albert, 844
Hayes, Alfred, 395
Hayes, Carlton, 260
Hayes, James, *268*
Hayes, John F., *129*
Hayes, Nicholas J., *411*
Hayes, Ralph, 829
Hayes, Robert, 553
Hayes, Rutherford B., 385, *487*, 798, 1058, 1061, 1215
Hayford, Casely, 664
Hayhanen, Reino, 1
Hayman, Al, 1169, 1178
Haynes, Elizabeth Ross, 534
Haynes, Tod, 406
Haynes, William, 924
Hays, James S., 631
Hays, Lee, 422, 1250
Hays, Will S., 1184
Hayter, Stanley William, 942
Haywood, Big Bill, 588, 590
Hazard, Ebenezer, 276
Hazard, Robert, 1155
Hazzard, Eli, 437
Hazzard, Marguerite, 76
Hazzard, Shirley, 684
Head, Edith, 392
Heade, Martin Johnson, 572
Headley, Joel T., 548
Heald, Henry T., 425, 849
Healy, James C., *484*
Healy, Thomas, 916, 1155
Heap, Jane, 686
Hearn, George Arnold, 56, 281, 282
Hearn, George Arnold, Jr., 535
Hearst, George, 784
Hearst, William Randolph, Jr., 834
Hearst, Mrs. William Randolph, Jr., 612
Heath, William, 517
Heathcote, Caleb, 445, *744*
Heatter, Gabriel, 1274
Hecht, Ben, 771, 909
Hecker, John, *736*
Heckscher, August (philanthropist), 198
Heckscher, August (parks commissioner), 199
Hedman, Axel, 154
Hedstrom, Olof Gustaf, 1144
Heezen, Bruce, 461
Heffernan, James J., *484*
Hegeman, John, 672
Heide, Henry, 274, 423
Heifetz, Jascha, 14
Height, Dorothy I., 802
Heilbroner, Robert, 808
Heinck, Heinrich, 383
Heine-Haimovitch, Sara, 6
Heinrich, Anthony Philip, 240
Heins, George Lewis, 54, 536, 1289
Heinsheimer, Alfred M., 830
Heinze, Frederick, 284
Heise, William, 403
Heisman, John W., 343
Heiss, Carol, *1182*
Heizer, Michael, 1055
Helburn, Theresa, 1178
Held, Anna, 1287
Heller, Louis B., *484*
Hellerman, Fred, 1250
Helmle, Frank J., 282
Helmuth, William Tod, 554
Helpern, Milton, 746
Hely Laboratories, 15
Hemingway, Ernest, 17, 254, 432, 909
Hemstreet, Charles, 548
Henahan, Donal, 793
Henderson, David, 844
Henderson, Ray, 791
Henderson, William James, 792, 793
Hendricks, Henry, 620
Hendricks, Thomas, 671
Hendrix, Jimi, 403, 1013
Hendrix, Joseph C., *482*
Henle, James, 126
Henna, Julio J., 962
Hennessy, W. J., 57
Henning, Carol, 1121
Hennisart, Martha, 920
Henrich, Tommy, 850
Henriksen, Anneken, 855
Henry, John T., *268*
Henry, Joseph, 904
Henry, Sherrye, 1274
Henry, William A., III, 1178
Henschel, Georg, 628
Henson, Matthew A., 349
Hentoff, Nat, 1229
Hepburn, A. Barton, 208
Herbert, Henry William, 1102
Herbert, John, 432
Herbert, Therese, 541
Herman, Jerry, 1173
Herman, Mary Ann, 421
Herman, Michael, 421
Herman, Woody, 403
Hermann, Jane, 20
Hernandez, Keith, 837
Herne, James A., 1170
Hernton, Calvin C., 844
Hernton, Mildred, 844
Heron, Matilda, 1167
Herrick, Anson, *481*
Herrington, John S., 522
Herschel, John, 768
Herscu, George, 73
Hersey, John, 683, 830
Hershey, Milton S., 274
Herskovits, Melville, 39
Herter, Christian, 541

Herter, Ernst, 1054
Herter, Gustave, 541
Herts, Henry Beaumont, 541
Hertz, Rosie, 947
Herz, Henri, 240
Hess, Elizabeth, 58
Hess, Jacob, *912*
Hess, Leon, 19, 1106, 1253
Hess, Rudolf, 830
Hess, Tom, 58
Hester, James, 849
Hesterberg, Henry, *129*
Heuss, Theodor, *1182*
Hevesi, Alan G., 70, *270*
Hewes, Henry, *743*
Hewitt, Eleanor, 281
Hewitt, James, 239
Hewitt, Sarah, 281
Hextall, Bryan, 843
Heye, George Gustav, 785
Heywood, Donald, 1246
Hicks, Elias, 965
Hicks, Frederick C., *483*
Hicks, Henry (mayoral candidate), *736*
Hicks, Henry W. (businessman), 836
Hicks, Jacob Middagh, 157
Hicks, John, 14, 157
Hicks, Stephen, 14
Hicks, Thomas, 90, 342, 686
Hicks, Whitehead, *744*
Higbie, Abraham, 1107
Higgins, A. Foster, 625
Higgins, Marguerite, 832
Higgins, Norman, *1028*
Highet, Gilbert, 260
Hilbok, Albert, 321
Hildebrand, Wilhelm, 1242
Hill, Abram, 116
Hill, Edward Burlingame, 1180
Hill, Frederick, 1036
Hill, George H. (actor), 1167
Hill, George Washington (businessman), 21
Hill, Harry, 80, 119, 133, 315, 947
Hill, James, 284, 529, 644, 845, 1047
Hill, Jerome, 38
Hill, John (engraver), 543
Hill, John (publisher), 707
Hill, John Henry (painter), 543
Hill, John W. (businessman), 543
Hill, Marjorie, 665
Hill, Stanley, 25
Hill, Ureli Corelli, 838
Hill, William, 1144
Hilton, Henry, 1124
Hilton, James, 1262
Himes, Chester, 919–20
Hindemith, Paul, 474
Hines, Earl, 1022, 1227
Hines, Gregory, 1151
Hines, Ike, 976
Hines, Maurice, Jr., 1151
Hines, Maurice, Sr., 1151
Hinsdale, Elizur B., 419
Hinton, Milt, 176
Hirons, Frederick C., 94
Hirsch, Charles S., 746
Hirschbein, Peretz, 1282, 1283
Hirschfeld, Nina, 545
Hirschfield, Leo, 274, 423
Hirschman, Ethel, 1129
Hirschman, Oliver, 1129
Hiss, Alger, 201, 295, 670, 704
Hitchcock, Benjamin W., 1273
Hitchcock, Henry Russell, 322, 624, 1164
Hobart, George V., 397
Hobson, Charles, 337
Hobson, Thayer, 127
Hochstim, Max, 947
Hockney, David, 1110
Hocq, Robert, 183
Hodges, Edward, 240
Hodges, Gil, 84, 156, 837
Hodges, Johnny, 371
Hodgson, Edwin, 321
Hodson, William, 1084
Hoe, Richard M., 144, 940, 1003
Hoey, Jane, 1084
Hoffman, Abbie, 37, 807
Hoffman, Charles Fenno, 352
Hoffman, Eugene Augustus, 458
Hoffman, Gertrude, 312,
Hoffman, Irwin, 147
Hoffman, John T., 282, 549, *736*, *744*
Hoffman, Josiah Ogden, *480*
Hoffman, Paul G., 425
Hoffman, Rob, 802
Hoffmann, Roald, 1134
Hofmann, Hans, 644
Hogan, Ben, *1182*
Hogan, Ernest, 115
Hogan, John V. L., 1277
Hogan, Michael J., *483*
Hogart, Burne, 1048
Hoiby, Lee, 827
Hokinson, Helen, 830
Holbrook, David, 1084
Holder, Geoffrey, 1151
Hollaender, Victor, 1109
Holland, Clifford M., 550
Holland, Edward, *744*
Holland, Fred, 314
Holland, Henry, 570
Holland, John Phillip, 603
Holland, Josiah Gilbert, 200
Holland, Michael P., Jr., 550
Holland, Michael P., Sr., 550
Hollander, John, 4
Holley, Alexander Lyman, 1243
Hollis, Roy, 307
Holly, Flora May, 680
Holm, Eleanor, 1022, 1145
Holmes, John Clellon, 93
Holmes, Oliver Wendell, 3, 37, 101, 179, 1126
Holmes, Violet, 1016
Holt, Edith, 675
Holt, Elizabeth, *811*
Holt, Henry (publisher), 125, 680
Holt, Henry (dancer), 311
Holt, John, 32, 809, *811*, 940
Holt, Winifred, 675
Holtzman, Elizabeth, 195, *270*, 335, *484*, 796
Holtzman, Lester, *484*
Holtzman, Red, 835
Homaira, queen of Afghanistan, *1183*
Homans, Sheppard, 671
Homer, Louise, 757
Homer, Sidney, 1039
Hones, John, 65
Hooghlandt, Francis, 360
Hooker, John Lee, 353
Hooks, Benjamin L., 800
Hooper, Chauncey, 525
Hooper, Franklin W., 159
Hooper, Lloyd P., 645
Hoover, J. Edgar, 164, 383
Hope, Bob, 102, 800
Hopkins, Arthur, 1109
Hopkins, Claude, 1022
Hopkins, George F., *812*
Hopkins, Mark, 541
Hopkinson, Francis, 239
Hopwood, Avery, 1170
Hora, Michael, 1214
Horkheimer, Max, 589
Hornaday, William, 1288–89
Hornblower, William B., 1265
Hornbostel, Henry, 538, 970, 1265
Horne, Marilyn, 758
Horner, Samuel, *811*
Horowitz, Gedale B., 1039
Horowitz, Israel, 212
Horsman, Edward I., 1194
Horst, Louis, 312
Horton, J. M., 309
Horton, Lester, 12
Horton, Randy, 1082
Horton, Raymond, 227
Hostos, Eugenio María de, 655, 962
Hotovitsky, Alexander, 355
Hottelet, Richard C., 257
Houghton, Amory, 469
Houghton, G. H., 224
Houk, Ralph, 850
Houphouët-Boigny, Félix, *1182*
Housman, A. A., 80
Houston, Cisco, 422
Houston-Jones, Ishmael, 314
Hovhaness, Alan, 53
Hoving, Thomas (parks commissioner), 199
Hoving, Thomas P. F. (philanthropist), 757
Hoving, Walter, 1183
Howard, Daniel D., 604
Howard, Ebenezer, 109
Howard, Elston, 1105
Howard, Frank, 837
Howard, George, 512
Howard, Harry, 411
Howard, John Tasker, 244
Howard, May, 169
Howard, Oliver Otis, 158
Howard, Roy W., 850
Howard, Sidney, 1170
Howard, William J., 569
Howe, Elias, 451, 510, 1062, 1071
Howe, George, 666
Howe, James R., *482*
Howe, Julia Ward, 853, 1269
Howe, Marie Jenney, 542
Howe, Richard, 33, 275, 493, 1193
Howe, Will D. (publisher), 521
Howe, William F. (lawyer), 659, 717
Howe, William (general), 33, 430, 697, 759, 1221
Howe, William Wirt (writer), 918
Howell, Harry, 843
Howell, Jim Lee, 690
Howells, John M., 47, 48, 307, 555, 1125
Howells, Mrs. Henry, 1086
Howland, John, 735
Hoyt, Charles M., 131
Hoyt, Mark, 1068
Hubbell, Allen F., 1101
Hubbell, Carl, 84, 831
Hubert, Philip, 280, 415
Hudde, Andries, 417
Huddleston, William, 1201
Hudlin, Warrington, 337
Hudson, Lee, 665
Huebner, Clarence R., *1182*
Huebsch, Ben W., 126, 1228
Huenefeld, Baron von, *1181*
Huff, Sam, 831, 1105
Huggins, Miller, 850, 1280

Huggins, Nathan Irvin, 514
Hughes, Allen, 314
Hughes, Benjamin, H., 9
Hughes, Howard, 69, 174, 419, *1181*, 1183
Hughes, Jasper W., 1070
Hughes, John (humorist), 802
Hughes, Patrick, 210
Hughes, Robert (art critic), 58
Hughes, Robert Ball (sculptor), 1053
Hugo, Jean, 1081
Hulbert, G. Murray, *230*, *483*
Hulett, William C., 239, 311
Hull, Helen, 540, 542
Hull, Millie, 1153
Hull, Raymond, 1262
Hull, William, 514
Hume, William, 238
Humes, Helen, 85
Hummel, Abe, 659, 717
Hummel, Henry, 617
Humphrey, Hubert H., *490*
Humphrey, James (Republican congressman), *481*
Humphrey, James Morgan (Democratic congressman), *481*
Humphreys, Solon, 769
Huncke, Herbert, 468
Hung-Chang, Li, 217
Hunt, C. W., 1256
Hunt, Freeman, 25
Hunt, John, 531
Hunt, Nelson Bunker, 284, 949
Hunt, Richard Howland, 694
Hunt, W. Herbert, 284, 949
Hunt, Walter, 1062
Hunt, William Morris, 440
Hunt, Wilson G., *735*
Hunter, Bobby, 86
Hunter, Catfish, 850
Hunter, Evan, 919
Hunter, George, 576
Hunter, James, 225
Hunter, Joel D., 309
Hunter, John W., *149*, *471*
Hunter, Joyce, 665
Hunter, Richard, 1165
Hunter, Robert (colonial governor), 360, 478, *479*, 939, 1052
Hunter, Robert (reformer), 933, 1060, 1232
Hunter, Thomas, 251, 575, 576
Hunter, William, 189
Huntington, Abel, *480*
Huntington, Archer Milton, 66, 545, 576, 788, 856
Huntington, Charles Pratt, 66, 545–46
Huntington, Collis P., 144, 545
Huntington, James Otis Sargent, 381
Hurd, Richard M., 989
Hurley, Dennis M., *482*
Hurst, Fannie, 563, 682
Hurt, Mississippi John, 1012
Hurtin, William, Jr., *812*
Hurwitz, Leo, 337
Hurwitz, Moshe Ish-HaLevi, 1282
Hussein, Ibrahim, *1028*
Hussein, king of Jordan, 1
Huston, John, 337
Huston, Tillinghast l'Hommedieu "Cap," 850, 1280
Huston, Walter, 177
Hutcheson, Ernest, 628
Hutchings, Edward, 445
Hutchins, John, 247
Hutchins, Waldo, *481*
Hutchinson, William (colonist), 577
Hutchinson, WIlliam (inventor), 676
Hutin, Francisque, 168, 312
Hutton, Timothy, 496
Hutton, William, 1242
Hutzler, Morton, 1039
Huxtable, Ada Louise, 48
Hwang, David Henry, 843
Hyde, Henry Baldwin, 381, 671
Hyde, James (insurance executive), 672
Hyde, James H. (jeweler), 111
Hyde, James T. (cat fancier), 194
Hyer, Jacob, 133
Hyer, Tom, 133
Hyman, Leon, 147
Hynes, Charles J., *411*
Hynes, Elizabeth, 98

Ibsen, Henrik, 414, 1170, 1172, 1174
Icahn, Carl, 1228
Iceland, Reuben, 1283
Ickes, Harold, 413
Ide, Lemuel, 379
Ignatoff, David, 1283
Ikangaa, Juma, *1028*
Illava, Karl, 575
Illions, M. C., 182
Indiana, Robert, 942
Ingalls, Albert G., 1051
Ingalls, Harry Creighton, 1177
Ingalls, Laura, 419
Inge, William, 246, 1172
Ingersoll, Ralph, 908
Ingersoll, Raymond V., *129*
Inglis, Charles, 380, 1052
Ingoldsby, Richard, *478*, *479*, 663
Innes, Frederick, 73
Inness, George, 941
Innis, Roy, 525
Irish, Ned, 86, 712, 835, 1105
Irrera, Raymond, 1165
Irvin, Monte, 1105
Irvin, Rea, 830
Irving, Henry, 1167
Irving, John, 1262
Irving, William, 713
Irwin, Elisabeth, 75, 686
Irwin, May, 1168
Irwin, Will, 846
Isaacs, Samuel, 620
Isacson, Leo, 30, *484*
Isley, Alex, 501
Ison, Big Joe, 449
Isozaki, Arata, 159
Israels, Henry, 775
Ito, Michio, 312
Ives, Burl, 422
Ives, Elam, Jr., 240
Ives, H. Douglas, 40, 1202
Ives, Irving M., 185
Ives, James Merritt, 305
Ives, Levi Silliman, 705
Iving, William, *480*

Jabara, Paul, 1147
Jackson, A. V. Williams, 1289
Jackson, Andrew, 135, 326, 646
Jackson, David S., *268*, *480*
Jackson, Dolores, 665
Jackson, James L., 187
Jackson, Jesse, 492, 622, 1064
Jackson, John, 1229
Jackson, Jumpin' Jackie, 86
Jackson, Mahalia, 475, 1064
Jackson, Mark, 835
Jackson, Michael, 976
Jackson, Peter, 282
Jackson, Reggie, 145, 850
Jackson, Ron, 86
Jackson, T. R., 1074
Jackson, Thomas ("Stonewall"), 429, 1240
Jackson, Thomas B., *480*
Jacob, Benjamin, 1189
Jacob, Ken, 406
Jacobs, Bernard, 1069
Jacobs, Jacob, 1282
Jacobs, Jane, 48, 233, 1259
Jacobs, Jim, 1173
Jacobs, Lewis, 337
Jacobs, Mike, 134
Jacobson, Anita, 697
Jacques, Moses, *735*
Jahn, Friedrich Ludwig, 1204
Jakobi, Paula, 542
Jakobson, Roman, 808
Jallade, William, 1081
James, Arthur Curtis, 220
James, C. L. R., 17
James, Edwin L., 847
James, Harry, 474
James, Henry (father of the writer), 1144
James, Skip, 1012
James, Thomas, 32
Janáček, Leoš, 827
Jani, Robert, 975
Janis, Sidney, 58, 59
Jansen, Johannes, *744*
Jansen, William (ferryman), 397
Jansen, William (schools superintendent), *122*
Jarmulowsky, Sender, 367, 614
Jarmusch, Jim, 406
Jarves, James Jackson, 57
Jarvis, Nathaniel, Jr., *268*
Jastrow, Robert, 471
Jay, John, Jr., 380, 787, 1215
Jay, John C., 1032
Jay, Karla, 665
Jay, Peter, 574
Jay, Sarah Livingston, 614
Jay, William, 380, 469
Jean Louis (fashion designer), 180
Jeffers, Robinson, 683
Jefferson, Joseph, 851
Jeffries, Jim, 133, 273, 283
Jeffries, Leonard, 229
Jelliffe, Smith Ely, 750
Jennings, Oliver G., 415
Jennings, Peter, 22, 177
Jenrette, Richard H., 341, 382, 673
Jeritza, Maria, 757
Jeroloman, John, *268*
Jerome, Jennie, 247
Jessor, Herman J., 677, 1111
Jessup, Maria De Witt, 618
Jeter, Claude, 475
Jett, Joan, 195
Jewell, Edward Alden, 476, 1024
Jimirro, James P., 802
Joans, Ted, 93
Joffre, Joseph J. C., *1181*
Jogues, Isaac, 191, 700
Johansson, Ingemar, 134
John, Gwen, 973
John Paul II, 193, *1183*
Johnson, Albert, 1109
Johnson, Alfred W., *1181*
Johnson, Andrew, 659, 846, 987–88
Johnson, Billy, 115
Johnson, Bunk, 615
Johnson, Davey, 837
Johnson, Edward (assemblyman), 113

Johnson, Edward (opera director), 313, 758
Johnson, Emil, 1145
Johnson, F. Ross, 1010
Johnson, Georgia Douglas, 664
Johnson, Harriet, 75
Johnson, Henry Lincoln (army corporal), 525
Johnson, Henry W. (businessman), 625
Johnson, Herbert, 455
Johnson, Howard, 837
Johnson, Hugh, 1274
Johnson, Ivan "Ching," 842
Johnson, J. Rosamond, 115
Johnson, Jere, 774
Johnson, Jeremiah, *149*
Johnson, Jeromus, *480*
Johnson, John (mayor), *744*
Johnson, John A. (builder), 1145
Johnson, John H. (activist), 114
Johnson, Joseph (fire commissioner), *411*
Johnson, Joseph (writer), 844
Johnson, Joyce, 93
Johnson, Lyndon B., 115, 373, *490*, 633, 679, 695, 779, 934, 1030, 1276
Johnson, Malvin Gray, 114, 526
Johnson, Margaret, *214*
Johnson, Nunnally, 156
Johnson, Pete, 626
Johnson, Sargent, 527
Johnson, William F. (preacher), 158
Johnson, William M. (dairy farmer), 309
Johnston, Francis Benjamin, 901
Johnston, James Boorman, 1163
Johnston, Jill, 315, 665
Johnston, John B. (congressman), *483*
Johnston, John Taylor (railroad executive), 755
Joline, Adrian, 632
Jonas, Alexander, 830
Jonas, Ralph, 693
Jones, Alfred, 941
Jones, Bill T., 12, 314, *523*
Jones, Bobby, 1181
Jones, Charles F., 1003
Jones, Clarence E., 36
Jones, Cleon, 837
Jones, Edward, 342, 1234
Jones, Elvin, 257
Jones, George, 846, 987
Jones, Grace, 523
Jones, Hettie, 93
Jones, Isaac, 210
Jones, James (writer), 684
Jones, James Earl (actor), 116
Jones, Jennifer, 1016
Jones, Jo, 85
Jones, John (banker), 210
Jones, John (tavern owner), 985
Jones, John Price (public relations executive), 955
Jones, LeRoi, 37, 93, 116, 592, 684, 844, 986, 1174
Jones, Morgan, *268*, *471*
Jones, Pamela, 549
Jones, Paul, 395
Jones, Philly Joe, 319
Jones, Rebecca Colford, 670
Jones, Robert Edmond, 948, 1109, 1174
Jones, Steve, *1028*
Jones, Thad, 1228
Jones, Thomas (soap maker), 1081
Jones, Thomas, Jr. (insurance executive), 671
Jones, Thomas R. (judge), *95*
Jones, Walter Restored, 65
Jones, Walter Restored, Jr., 625
Jonnes, Jill, 549
Joplin, Janis, 403
Joralemon, Teunis, 157
Joseffy, Rafael, 241
Joseph, Jacob, 621, 642
Joseph, Lazarus, *270*
Josephson, Matthew, 682, 683
Josman, Martin, 219
Jovanovich, Peter, 522
Jovanovich, William, 126, 521
Jowitt, Deborah, 315
Joyce, James, 682, 686, 924, 973
Joyner-Kersee, Jackie, 763
Juba, Master (William Henry Lane), 1151
Judd, Bertha Grimmell, 76
Judd, Orrin, 1256
Judson, Albert, 1142
Judson, Edward S. (religious leader), 76, 628
Judson, Edward Zane Carroll (writer), 522, 918
Juet, Robert, 571
Juilliard, August D., 628
Juilliard, Frederick A., 628
Juliana, queen of the Netherlands, *1182*
Jullien (conductor), 241

Kael, Pauline, 830
Kafka, Barbara, 231
Kahan, Richard, 1219
Kahanamoku, Duke, 1143
Kahn, Dorothy, 1084
Kahn, Gus, 698
Kahn, Louis, 1055
Kahn, Marci, 665
Kahn, Michael, 628
Kaiser, Amy, 219
Kaiser, Georg, 1170
Kalich, Bertha, 1282
Kalikow, Peter, 228, 840
Kallen, Horace, 583, 590, 808
Kalm, Peter, 352, 378
Kalmanovich, H., 1282
Kaltenmeier, John, 573
Kamali, Norma, 42, 393, 453, 1147, 1243
Kander, John, 663, 1096
Kane, Bob, 184
Kane, Patrick, 917
Kanin, Garson, 550
Kanoui, Joseph, 183
Kaplan, Aaron, 163
Kaprow, Allan, 521, 1174
Karlin, Sheldon, *1028*
Karloff, Boris, 310
Kashdan, Issac, 212
Kashkarov, Yuri, 856
Kaslow, Berta, 680
Kassal, Bentley, 285
Kasson, John F., 514
Katz, Gaynella, 1224
Katz, George A., 1231
Katzman, Allen, 358
Katznelson, Ira, 1084
Kaufman, Boris, 406
Kauser, Alice, 680
Kavanagh, Dudley, 108, 109
Kaye, Benjamin, 631
Kaye, Danny, 163
Kaye, Nora, 313
Kaye, Sammy, 1030
Kean, Charles, 851
Kean, Edmund, 1166
Kean, Thomas (actor), 168, 311, 1165
Kean, Thomas H. (governor), 1156
Keating, Charles, 631
Kebbon, Eric, 930
Keefe, Tim, 831
Keeler, Ruby, 514, 1151
Keene, Christopher, 827
Keene, Laura, 131, 1167
Kefauver, Estes, 288, 654, 1159
Keilin, Eugene J., 781
Keister, George, 413, 1176, 1177
Keith, B. F., 778, 1226
Keller, Charlie, 499, 850
Keller, Julius, 423
Kellerman, Annette, 545
Kelley, Florence, 472
Kellogg, Arthur, 1144
Kellogg, Paul U., 1144
Kelly, Bruce, 1127
Kelly, Edmond, 473
Kelly, Edna F., *484*
Kelly, Ellsworth, 186, 942
Kelly, Eugene, 1038
Kelly, Frank, 601
Kelly, Gene, 1151
Kelly, James, *268*
Kelly, John Andrew (newspaperman), 1273
Kelly, Paul, 357, 415
Kelly, Raymond, *912*
Kemble, Charles, 1166
Kemble, Fanny, 1166
Kemble, Gouverneur, *480*
Kempton, Murray, 684, 838
Kendall, J. F., 1267
Kendall, William Mitchell, 66, 781, 930, 1074
Kennedy, Adrienne, 116
Kennedy, Archibald, 725, 1052
Kennedy, Florynce, 659
Kennedy, James C., 1118
Kennedy, John F., *490*, 778, 938, *1182*
Kennedy, John M., 61, 201, 827, 1053
Kennedy, Martin J., *483*
Kennedy, Robert (Confederate army captain), 1240
Kennedy, Robert Lenox (Sunday school advocate), 1142
Kennedy, Stephen P., *912*
Kennelly, Brian L., 543
Kenney, Doug, 802
Kensett, Thomas W., 178
Kent, Blackie, 664
Kent, Bubbles, 664
Kenyon, Dorothy, 659, 1269
Keogh, Eugene J., *484*
Keppel, Frederick P., 180
Keppler, Joseph, 961
Kermoyan, Michael, 53
Kerner, Otto, 679
Kerr, Walter, 1178
Kerrigan, James E., *481*
Kertész, André, 901
Kesselring, Joseph, 1172
Kessler, David, 1282
Kessner, Thomas, 549
Keteltas, William, 635, *812*
Kettering, Charles F., 749
Keuter, Cliff, 1156
Key, Francis Barton, 1069
Khan, Liaquat Ali, *1182*
Khrushchev, Nikita, 529, 564
Kidd, Michael, 313
Kieft, Willem, 27, 148, 351
Kiernan, Patrick, *268*
Kierstade, Hans, 43
Kilgore, Bernard, 1235
Kimball, Florence Page, 938
Kimmelman, Michael, 58
Kindred, John J., *483*
King, Albert, 86
King, B. B., 1013
King, Bernard, 835
King, Carole, 1012

King, Charles, 259
King, David H., 708, 1032
King, Gamaliel, 45, 154, 633
King, James G., 262
King, John A., *480*, 610
King, Joseph, 637
King, Kenneth, 314
King, Martin Luther, Jr., 70, 115, 525, 542, 1030, 1228, 1241
King, Moses, 513
King, W. A., 240
Kingman, Eliab, 810
Kingsbury, John A., 953
Kingsley, Darwin, 672, 836
Kingsley, Sidney, 320, 1109
Kingsley, William C., 154
Kinkaid, Thomas C., *1182*
Kinoy, Arthur, 659
Kinsella, Thomas, *481*
Kiok, Susan, 782
Kip, Jacob, 360, 638
Kipling, Rudyard, 295, 1036
Kipnis, Alexander, 242
Kirby, Jack, 184
Kirby, Michael, 1175
Kirby, William F., 1235
Kirchheimer, Otto, 589
Kirchner, Leon, 827
Kirchwey, George W., 944
Kirchwey, Freda, 799
Kirk, Grayson, 260, 1007
Kirk, Thomas, *812*
Kirk, William P., *268*
Kirkland, Bryant, 402
Kirkland, Gelsey, 20
Kirkland, Lane, 24
Kirkman, John, 1081
Kirkwood, James, 843, 1109
Kirshner, Don, 1012
Kirsten, Dorothy, 758
Kissel, Howard, 1178
Kissel, John, *483*
Kisselgoff, Anna, 315
Kisseloff, Jeff, 549
Kitson, Henry Hudson, 576
Kiviat, Abel, 1028–29
Klaw, Marc, 1069, 1168, 1169, 1177, 1178
Kleban, Edward, 1109
Klein, Arthur G., *484*
Klein, Murray, 1287
Kleinbaum, Sharon, 666
Kleine, George, 336
Kliban, B., 1274
Kline, Herbert, 337
Klopfer, Donald S., 126, 985
Kluge, John W., 754
Knapp, Whitman, 640
Kneisel, Franz, 628
Knight, James, 903
Knight, Marie, 475
Knoll, Michael Christian, 700
Knopf, Alfred A., 13, 125
Knopf, Alfred A. (Pat), 126
Knopf, Blanche, 13
Knorr, Nathan, 617
Knowings, Hermann "Helicopter," 86
Knowles, John H., 1015
Knowlton, Donald, 543
Knowlton, Winthrop, 528
Knox, Charles, 532, 599
Knox, Edward M., 532
Knox, Henry, 276
Koblentz, Edna, 608
Kobrin, Leon, 1283
Koch, Robert, 949, 1202
Kochak, Eddie, 1147
Kodjian, Mihran, 53
Kodjian, Varoujian, 53
Koehl, Hermann, *1181*
Koehler, V. Hugo, 1177
Koenig, Frederick, 917
Koenig, Fritz, 1056
Koenig, Samuel, 621
Kogel, Marcus, 146
Kohlmann, Anthony, 191
Kohn, Eugene, 641
Kohn, Jacob, 1161
Kohn, Robert D., 1120, 1161, 1276
Kohut, Rebekah, 288
Kolff, Cornelious G., 375, 1069
Kollock, Shepard, *811*
Komp, Albert, 641
Konitz, Lee, 319
Konner, Joan, 258
Konovsky, Kristo, 167
Koosman, Jerry, 837
Kootz, Samuel, 92, 843
Kopkind, Andrew, 843
Koplik, Henry, 309
Koplowitz, Ralph, 835
Koppel, Ted, 22
Kopple, Barbara, 337
Kornfeld, Lawrence, 628
Kortwright, Elizabeth, 766
Kościuszko, Tadeusz, 642
Kosloff, Theodore, 312
Kossalko, Jozef, 1078
Kostelanetz, André, 839
Kosugi, Takehisa, 304
Kotchever, Eva, 455
Kotzky, Alex, 185
Koufax, Sandy, 103
Kouros, Yannis, 1028
Koussevitzky, Serge, 80
Kouwenhoven, John Atlee, 514, 549
Kouzel, Al, 395
Koyré, Alexandre, 808
Kozloff, Max, 58
Krackowizer, Ernst, 663
Krackowizer, Marie, 123
Kramer, Hilton, 58, 592, 838, 1178
Krassner, Paul, 17
Kraus, H. P., 106
Krauss, Rosalind, 58
Krauss, Ruth, 1059
Krehbiel, Henry, 792, 793
Kreischer, Balthazar, 111, 202
Kresevich, Joseph, 1122
Kressyn, Miriam, 1283
Kriendler, Jack, 1000, 1207
Krim, Seymour, 93
Kring, Walter Donald, 1212
Kristal, Holly, 195
Kristiansen, Ingrid, *1028*
Kristol, Irving, 592
Krock, Arthur, 847
Kroeber, Alfred, 39
Kroll, Jack, 1178
Kronenberger, Louis, 1178
Kross, Anna M., 365
Krupa, Gene, 474
Krutch, Joseph Wood, 1177
Krygier, Marcin, 909
Krzyzanowski, Wladimir, 909–10, 914
Kubelka, Peter, 39
Kuchar, George, 406
Kuchar, Mike, 406
Kucsik, Nina, *1028*
Kuhn, Edmund, 403
Kuhn, Fritz, 295, 462
Kuhn, Walt, 55
Kuhne, Paul, 1111
Kunc-Milanov, Zinka, 300
Kunitz, Stanley, 4
Kuniyoshi, Yasuo, 782
Kunz, George Frederick, 1183
Kunze, John Christopher, 701
Kupferberg, Tuli, 93, 684
Kupferman, Theodore R., *484*
Kuraoka, Nobuyoshi, 423
Kurka, Robert, 827
Kurzman, Harvey, 710
Kusch, Polykarp, 260, 904
Kuspit, Donald, 58

Labasse, Claude, 312
Labov, William, 1101
Laboyteaux, Gabriel, 574
Lachaise, Gaston, 1262
Lachman, Charles, 1001
Lack, John, 779
Ladd, Kate Macy, 627
Ladnier, Tommy, 1080
Laemmle, Carl, 404, 925
La Farge, Christopher Grant, 537
Laffan, William Mackay, 1184
LaFollette, Robert, *489*
LaFreniere, Oliver B., 177
Lahey, James W., 403
Lahr, Bert, 1022
Laidlie, Archibald, 726, 993, 1052
Laight, Henry, 1249
Laight, William, 1249
Laing, Edgar, 187
Laing, Hugh, 313
Lalance, Charles, 1271
Lalique, René, 540
Lama, Alfred A., 765
Lamar, E. B., 303
Lamb, Alexander, 183
Lamb, Charles R., 331
Lamb, Horace, 660
Lamb, John, 33
Lamb, Joseph F., 976
Lamb, Martha, 548
Lamb, Willis E., 260, 904
Lambert, Edward A., *149*
Lambert, William, 9, 753
Lamberti, Ralph J., *130*
Lambertse, Thomas, 94
La Meri (dancer), 421
Lamm, Norman, 1281
Lamont, Aeneas, *811*
Lamont, Florence, 653
Lampell, Millard, 422
Lancaster, Burt, 332
Lancaster, Frederick J., 98, 363
Lancaster, Joseph, 9, 956
Lancaster, Mark, 304
Lancefield, Rebecca, 1016
Landau, Zisha, 1283
Landon, Alfred, *489*
Landrey, John T., 1035
Landsowne, Helen, 629
Lane, Charles, 406
Laney, Lucy, 528
Lan-fang, Mei, 1170
Lang, Dorothea, 902
Lang, Eddie, 1227
Lang, Eugene M., 384
Lang, Harold, 313
Lang, Hermann, 383

Lang, John L., 302
Lang, Paul Henry, 793
Lang, Pearl, 1156
Langdell, Christopher Columbus, 658
Langdon, Olivia, 1204
Langner, Lawrence, 1174, 1178
Langner, Philip, 1178
Langtree, Samuel, 640
Langtry, Lillie, 632
Lanin, Sam, 1022
Lankevich, George J., 549
Lannuier, Charles-Honoré, 322, 445
Lansburgh, G. Albert, 778
Lantry, Francis J., *411*
Lantz, Walter, 704
Lanzetta, James J., *483*, 650
Lapine, James, 843
Lardner, Ring, 6, 522, 771, 1107
LaRouche, Lyndon, Jr., 607, 806
Larsen, Don, 84
Larsen, Kay, 58
Larsen, Nella, 683
Lasker, Albert, 424, 654, 694
Lasker, Emmanuel, 211, 212
Laski, Harold, 376, 799
Lassalle, Ferdinand, 596
Lasser, David, 1210
Laswell, Bill, 1013
Lateiner, Joseph, 1282
Latham, Gray, 403
Latham, Henry J., *484*
Latham, Otway, 403
Latham, Woodville, 403
Lathen, Emma, 920
Lathrop, George, 655
Latimer, John, 919
Latis, Mary Jane, 920
Latto, Thomas, 1053
Lauder, Leonard, 656
Lauder, Ronald, 656, *743*
Laughlin, Ledlie, 223
Laurence, John, *480*
Laurens, Henry, 440
Laurent, Robert, 1054
Laurents, Arthur, 792
Lauriano, Tony, 423
Lausner, Bertha, 680
Laval, Pierre, *1181*
Lavan, Peter I. B., 1033
Laviera, Tato, 963
Law, Charles B., *482*
Lawe, John E., 1197
Lawlor, Charles B., 1090
Lawrence, A. R., *736*
Lawrence, Cornelius W., *480*, *735*, 736, *744*
Lawrence, D. H., 686
Lawrence, F. N., 90
Lawrence, Gertrude, 228
Lawrence, Jacob, 58, 1033
Lawrence, John (mayor), *744*
Lawrence, John W. (congressman), *480*
Lawrence, Lawrence Shubert, Jr., 1069
Lawrence, Richard Hoe, *476*
Lawrence, William, 90, 1127
Lawrie, Lee, 1015
Lawson, Ernest, 366
Lawson, James, 680
Lawson, John D. (congressman), *481*
Lawson, John Howard (playwright), 512, 1170
Lawson, Thomas, 672, 779
Lazard, Alexandre, 660
Lazard, Élie, 660
Lazard, Simon, 660
Lazarus, Fred, 327
Lazarus, Moses, 640, 1082
Lazarus, Ralph, 327
Leach, Wilford, 652
Leacock, Eleanor Burke, 916
Leacock, Richard, 337
Leadbelly, 422, 524, 1228, 1250
Leahy, David P., 1099
Leary, Howard R., *912*
Leavis, F. R., 909
Leavitt, G. Howland, 90
Leavitt, Joshua, 587
Leavitt, Michael B., 168
Lebedev, Aaron, 1282
LeBoeuf, Randall, 660
LeBoutillier, John, *484*
LeBoutillier, Philip, 105
Lebow, Fred, 1028
LeClerq, Tanaquil, 72
Le Corbusier, 462, 1073
LeCoze, Gilbert, 1000
Lederer, George W., 791
Lederer, William, 1278
Lederle, Ernest J., 309
Lederman, Leon, 905, 1051
Ledwith, Thomas A., *736*
Lee, Ang, 406
Lee, Arthur, 276
Lee, Canada, 40, 116
Lee, Charles, 33
Lee, Eugene, 1110
Lee, Frederick R., *268*
Lee, Gideon, *480*, *744*, 1068
Lee, Gypsy Rose, 169
Lee, James (athlete), 1026
Lee, James (editor), 628
Lee, James (merchant), 1053
Lee, Kirby, 185
Lee, Mabel, 76
Lee, Manfred B., 919
Lee, Mary Ann, 312
Lee, Ming Cho, 1110
Lee, Richard Henry, 276
Lee, Robert E., 429, 1240
Lee, Stan, 185
Lee, T. D., 218, 260, 905
Lee, Tom, 838
Lee, Thomas R., *268*
Lee, Tsung-Dao, 1051
Lee, Warren I., *483*
Leech, Margaret, 14
Lees, Edith, 542, 664
Leetch, Brian, 843
LeFevre, William Maynard, 223
Leffers, Beverly, 746
Lefferts, John, 94, *480*
Lefferts, Lefffert, 94
Lefferts, Peter, 661
Leffingwell, Russell, 627
Lefkowitz, Louis, 492, *740–41*, 1231
Lefrak, Samuel, 661
Léger, Fernand, 440
Leggett, Samuel, 673
Leggett, William, 839, 1177
Lehman, Emmanuel, 662
Lehman, Henry, 662
Lehman, Mayer, 662
Lehman, Philip, 662
Lehman, Robert, 662, 757
Lehmann, Lilli, 757
Lehmann, Lotte, 242
Lehr, Harry, 62, 1085
Lehrer, Jim, 1160
Lehrman, Lewis, 304
Leibowitz, Samuel, 659
Leiby, Adrian, 660
Leigh, Douglas, 59
Leigh, George, 1096
Leinsdorf, Erich, 242
Leipzig, Arthur, 902
Leipziger, Henry, 365
Leitsch, Dick, 455
Leivick, H. (Leivick Halpern), 1282, 1283
Lelyveld, Joseph, 847
Lemlich, Clara, 849
Lemus, José Maria, *1182*
L'Enfant, Pierre, 231, 250, 276, 510
Lenox, James, 575, 663, 668, 787, 840, 937, 1053
Lent, James, *480*
Lent, Lewis B., 226
Leonard, Moses G., *480*
Leone, Celestine, 717
Leone, Gene, 717
Leone, Gerolamo, 717
Leone, Luisa, 717
Leone, Sebastian, *129*, 1107
Lerner, Alan Jay, 13, 792, 1110, 1172
LeRoux, Bartholomew, 574, 1070
LeRoux, Charles, 1070
LeRoux, John, 1070
LeRoy, Herman, 89
LeRoy, Robert, 1163
LeRoy, Warner, 735, 1153
Leslie, Alfred, 93
Leslie, Lew, 1151
L'Espérance, Élise, 953
Lessler, Montague, *482*
LeTang, Henry, 1151
Leupp, Charles M., 1068
Levane, Fuzzy, 835
Leventhal, Albert Rice, 126, 214
Levertov, Denise, 59
Levi, F., 94
Levi, Julian C., 662
Levin, Jennifer Dawn, 936
Levin, Kim, 58
Levine, David, 185, 843
Levine, James, 758
Levine, Suzanne Braun, 258
Levinthal, Israel H., 158
Leviss, Sidney, *130*
Lévi-Strauss, Claude, 39, 440, 808
Levitt, Arthur, 492, *740*
Levitt, Helen, 337, 901
Levy, Abigail, 436
Levy, Benjamin, 1039
Levy, Gustave L., 472
Levy, Irving, 110
Levy, Jefferson M., *482*
Levy, Julien, 58, 475, 843
Levy, Leon, 261, 828
Levy, Lionel, 261, 828
Levy, Marvin David, 758
Levy, Maurice, 287
Levy, Morris, 110
Levy, Moses, 436
Levy, Samuel, *129*
Lewis, Anthony, 847
Lewis, Bobby, 512
Lewis, Carl, 763
Lewis, Francis, 1253, 1260
Lewis, George (clarinetist), 615
Lewis, George W. (real-estate developer), 716
Lewis, John (jazz pianist), 319
Lewis, John L. (labor leader), 24, 276, 543
Lewis, Martin, 942
Lewis, Meade "Lux," 626
Lewis, Mel, 1228
Lewis, Morgan, 1253

Lewis, Nelson P., 377, 1131
Lewis, Norman, 843
Lewis, Reginald F., 1188
Lewis, Robert, 5, 632
Lewis, Samuel, *268*
Lewis, Sinclair, 6, 682, 1172
Lewis, William, *811*
Lewis, Wyndham, 686
Lewisohn, Adolph, 228, 241, 620, 666, 1213
Lewisohn, Alice, 666, 804, 1174
Lewisohn, Irene, 666, 804, 1174
Lewisohn, Julius, 666
Lexow, Charles K., 661
Lexow, Clarence, 292, 617, 667, 947, 1086
Leyda, Jay, 337
Leyeles, A. (Aaron Glanz), 1283
Leyendecker, John Christian, 942
Leypoldt, Frederick W., 125, 540, 961
Lhévinne, Josef, 628
Lhévinne, Rosina, 628
Libby, James S., *735*
Libin, Z., 1282
Libsohn, Sol, 338
Lie, Trygve, 1214
Lieb, Fred, 850
Lieber, Jerry, 1012
Lieberman, Nancy, 86
Liebmann, Samuel, 1001
Liebovitz, Annie, 1017
Lilienthal, Samuel, 554
Lillie, Beatrice, 1022
Limbaugh, Rush, 1231
Linares, Guillermo, 597, 1242
Lind, Jenny, 8, 78, 88, 188, 241, 604, 1144
Lindbergh, Charles A., 1, 68, 707, 1181
Lindemann, Leo, 679
Lindmark, John, 1081
Lindquist, David L., 1145
Lindsay, Ben, 381
Lindsay, George H. (congressman 1901–13), *482*
Lindsay, George W. (congressman 1923–35), *483*
Lindsay, Howard, 1172
Lindsay, Samuel McCune, 944
Linker, Kate, 58
Linowitz, Sol, 288
Linsky, Jack, 1146
Linton, Ralph, 39
Lipchitz, Jacques, 1055
Lipman, Howard, 1262
Lipman, Jean, 1262
Lipmann, Fritz, 1016
Lippard, George, 918
Lippard, Lucy R., 58, 60
Lippincott, Richard, 33
Lipscomb, Jim, 337
Lipset, Seymour Martin, 591
Lipton, Marty, 660, 1231
Lipton, Thomas, 1233
Liptzin, Keni, 1282
Liquori, Marty, 763
Liston, Sonny, 134
Lit, Jacob, 327
Lit, Samuel, 327
Litchfield, Electus B., 120, 679
Litscho, Daniel, 909
Little, Ella, 716
Little, Joseph J., *482*
Little Anthony, 112
Little Manuel, 112
Little Richard, 1012
Littleton, Martin W., *129*, *483*
Littlewood, George, 1028
Liveright, Horace, 124, 125
Livermore, Mary A., 1269
Livingston, Chancellor, 2
Livingston, John, 726
Livingston, Maria, 346
Livingston, Walter, 276
Livingstone, David, 101
LL Cool J, 986
Lloyd, Clinton, 1010
Lloyd, Emily, 1043
Lloyd, John Henry, 84
Lloyd, Richard, 1013
Lloyd George, David, *1181*
Lloyd Webber, Andrew, 792, 1110, 1173
Lobeck, Armand, 461
Lobel, Adrianne, 1110
Lobis, Joan, 665
Locke, John D., 1260
Locke, Richard Adams, 768
Lockwood, Charles, 549
Lockwood, Sarah M., 548
Lodwick, Charles, 445, *744*
Loeb, Betty, 540
Loeb, James, 628
Loeb, Janice, 337
Loeb, Louis, 62
Loeb, Morris, 211
Loeb, Solomon, 644
Loeb, Theresa, 1047
Loew, Marcus, 652, 689, 778, 1141
Loewe, Frederick, 792, 1110, 1173
Loft, George W., *483*
Loft, William, 274
Logan, Andy, 830
Logan, Thomas Francis, 694
Loguen, Jermain, 10
Lomax, Alan, 422
Lomax, Bess, 422
Lomax, John A., 422
Lombardi, G., 1000
Lombardy, William, 212
Long, George, 625
Long, John Luther, 98
Long, Lois, 830
Longfellow, Henry Wadsworth, 101, 391, 713, 909, 964
Longstreet, Stephen, 549
Longworth, David, 230
Longworth, Thomas, 230
Looff, Charles I. D., 182
Lookstein, Joseph H., 275, 985
Loomis, Silas L., 308
Loos, Anita, 1030
Loosely, Charles, *811*
Lopate, Philip, 1289
Loquasto, Santo, 1110
Lord, Daniel (lawyer, father of Daniel DeForest Lord), 694
Lord, Daniel DeForest (lawyer, son of Daniel Lord), 694
Lord, Daniel M. (advertising executive), 694
Lord, Eleazer, 1142
Lord, Frederick W., *480*
Lord, James Brown, 1032
Lord, John T., 694
Lord, Samuel, 694
Lorde, Audre, 665
Lore, Ludwig, 830
Lorentz, Pare, 337
Lorenz, William, 694
Lorillard, Jacob, 99, 401
Lorillard, Pierre, 908, 1188
Loroupe, Tegla, *1028*
Lossing, Benson J., 548
Loudon, Samuel, 598, *811*, 940
Loudon, Samuel, Jr., *812*
Loughlin, James, 126
Loughlin, John D., 251, 1035
Louis, Joe, 134, 524, 564
Louis-Dreyfus, Robert, 1032
Louise, crown princess of Sweden, *1181*
Love, Barbara, 665
Lovecraft, H. P., 992
Lovelace, Thomas, 360
Lovell, James A., *1183*
Loveman, Amy, 101
Low, Daniel, 429
Low, Juliette Gordon, 468
Low, Philip B., *482*
Low, Will H., 781
Lowe, Sandra, 665
Lowell, Amy, 682
Lowell, Guy, 290
Lowell, James Russell, 713, 964, 1257
Lowerre, Benjamin, 15
Lowery, Robert O., *411*
Lowey, Nita M., *484*
Lowie, Robert, 39
Lowson, Denys C. F., *1182*
Lozier, Clemence, 1269
Lozowick, Louis, 58, 624, 931, 942
Lucas, Sam, 115
Luce, Clarence S., 1032
Luciano, Felipe, 1285
Luckman, Sid, 424
Luddy, Joshua, 33
Ludendorff, Ehrich, 1241
Ludlam, Charles, 1005, 1174
Luening, Otto, 243
Lufkin, Dan, 341
Lumsden, Lynne A., 338
Lunceford, Jimmie, 40, 288
Lundborg, Florence, 942
Lunden, Blue, 665
Lundy, Irving, 700
Lundy, James J., *130*
Lurting, Robert, *744*
Lusk, Clayton R., 985
Luyck, Eagidius, 360
Lybrand, William, 281
Lyle, Sparky, 850
Lyles, Aubrey, 115, 312, 1151
Lyman, Richard, 1015
Lyman, Susan E., 549
Lynch, James, 102
Lynch, John A., *130*
Lynch, Patrick, 602
Lynch, Walter A., *484*
Lyne, James, 939
Lynes, George Platt, 900
Lyon, Danny, 338
Lyons, Jacques Judah, 620
Lyons, Rosemary, 1266

Mabie, Hamilton Wright, 835
Mabley, Jackie "Moms," 524
McAlmon, Robert, 686
McAlpine, William, 1242
McAndrew, Jim, 837
Macapagal, Diosdado, *1183*
MacArthur, Charles, 14
McAuley, Jerry, *1000*, 1001
Macauley, Rose, 683
McAvor, Clifford T., *740*
McBain, Ed, 919
McBean, Thomas, 1037
McBride, Mary Margaret, 542
McBride, Patricia, 72
McBurney, William, 1020
McCabe, James D., Jr., 514, 563

McCall, Edward E., *737*, 764
McCall, H. Carl, 36
McCall, James, 703
McCall, John, 672, 673, 836
McCann, Harrison, 703
McCarthy, Eugene J., 696, 1121
McCarthy, James, 765
McCarthy, Joe, 850
McCarthy, John H., *482*
McCarthy, Michael, 1073
McCarty, Maclyn, 110
McCartney, Paul, 663
McCausland, Elizabeth, 57, 901, 902
Macchiarola, Frank J., *122*
Maccioni, Sirio, 423
MacCrate, John, *483*
McCreery, James, 327
McClellan, George B. (general), *487*
McClellan, John, 224
McClelland, Nancy, 593
McClendon, Rose, 115, 1275
McClintic, Guthrie, 283
McClure, J. S., 125
McClure, Michael, 684
McColgan, Liz, *1028*
MacColl, Christina I., 220, 1060
McConnell, David, 69, 286
McCook, Anson G., *481*
McCormack, Charles J., *130*
MacCormack (Wilson), Mary Ellen, 1086
McCormick, Anne O'Hare, 847, 1142
McCormick, Daniel, 598
McCormick, Kenneth D., 126
McCormick, Richard C., *482*
McCormick, Robert, 1147
MacCormick, Thomas J., 127
MacCoun, Townsend, *719*
MacCracken, Henry Mitchell, 162, 518, 848
McCraw, Harold W., Jr., 127
McCreery, James, 187
McCullers, Carson, 246, 683
McCulloch, Hugh, 671
McCullough, David W., 549
McCullough, John, 1167
McCunn, John, 292
McCurdy, Richard, 672, 795
McCutcheon, Wallace, 110
McDaniels, Jimmy, 1163
McDarrah, Fred, 93
MacDermott, Galt, 843
McDermott, John 1028
MacDonald, Alexander, 1052
MacDonald, Allan, 1232
Macdonald, Dwight, 17, 37, 591, 683, 686, 763, 830
Macdonald, James, 119
MacDonald, Ramsay, *1181*
Macdonald-Wright, Stanton, 103
McDonough, William J., 395
MacDougal, Edward A., 607
McDowall, John R., 715, 947
McElfatrick, J. B., 1176
McElligott, John J., *411*
McEvers, James, 598
McEvilley, Thomas, 58
MacFarland, W. W., 56
M'Farlane, Monteith, *812*
McGhee, Brownie, 1012
McGiffert, Arthur Cushman, 1212
McGinnity, Joe, 831
McGlynn, Thomas, 223
Macgonigle, H. Van Buren, 1054
McGovern, George S., *491*
McGowan, Kenneth, 948
McGowan, Patrick, *230*
McGrath, Christopher C., *484*
McGrath, Diane, *743*
MacGrath, Leueen, 631, 925
McGraw, James H., 707
McGuire, Dick, 835
McGuire, Robert J., *912*
MacInnes, Helen, 1053
McIntosh, Millicent Cary, 77
McIntyre, Dianne, 314
McIntyre, O. O., 834
Mack, Connie, 831, *1182*
Mack, Stan, 185, 1229
McKay, Claude, 114, 526, 611, 682, 683
McKay, Douglas I., *912*
MacKay, Malcolm, 228
McKay, Robert B., 228
McKayle, Donald, 12, 313
McKee, Elizabeth, 680
McKelway, Clair, 156
McKenna, James, 601
McKeon, John, *480*
Mackey, James, 1081
McKiniry, Richard F., *483*
McKinley, Ray, 342
McKinley, William, 37, *488*, 501, 628, 659, 784, 1240, 1262, 1281
McKinsey, James O., 709
McKissick, Floyd, 36
MacLaine, Shirley, 976
McLaren, Malcolm, 1013
McLaughlin, George V., *912*
McLaughlin, John, 319, 616
McLaurin, Dunbar, 438
Maclay, William B., *480*
M'Lean, A., 394, *812*
McLean, Francis H., 1084
M'Lean, J., 394, *811*, *812*
McLeary, Kindred, 931
McLennan, Donald R., 732
McLeod, Colin, 110
McLeod, Donald, 1052
McLeod, Dorothy, 475
McLoughlin, Charles, 709
McLoughlin, Edmund, 709
McLoughlin, Hugh, 152
McLoughlin, James G., 709
McLoughlin, John, 709
McMahon, Gregory, *484*
McManamon, Mickey, 1143
McManus, George, 184
McMaster, James A., 439
McMein, Neysa, 14
Macmillan, Alexander, 579
McMillen, Eleanor, 593
McMillen, Loring, 1118
MacNeil, Hermon A., *31*, 576, 1243
MacNeil, Robert, 177, 1160
MacNeven, James, 599
Macomb, Robert, 710
MacPhail, Larry, 156
McQueen, Robert, 752
MacRae, Cameron, 660
MacRae, Elmer, 55
Macrae, John, 379
Macrae, John (Jack), III, 379
Macready, William Charles, 428, 1007, 1166
McSorley, John, 710
McSpedon, Thomas, *268*
McTeigue, Walter P., 618
McVickar, Harry, 1230
McVickar, John, 598
Macy, George, 126
Macy, Rowland H., 327, 1001
Madden, Owney, 134, 288
Maddow, Ben, 337
Madison, James, 245, 325, 326, 616, 711, 1190
Madonia, Benedetto, 79
Madonna, 523
Maestro, Johnny, 1012
Maeterlinck, Maurice, 1174
Magill, Andrew, 413
Maglie, Sal, 831
Magloire, Paul Eugène, *1182*
Magner, Thomas F., *482*
Magnus, Charles, 941
Maher, John P., *483*
Mahler, Gustav, 181, 241, 838
Mahoney, J. Daniel, 277
Mahoney, Jeremiah T., *739*
Mahoney, Peter P., *482*
Maiman, Theodore, 1051
Maioglio, Sebastiano, 1000
Major, Clarence, 844
Makarios (archbishop), *1182*
Makarova, Natalia, 20
Makemie, Francis, 598, 937
Malcolm, Janet, 830
Malibran, Maria, 241
Malina, Judith, 591, 687, 1174
Maling, Arthur, 920
Malone, Dudley, 1216
Maloney, Carolyn B., *484*, 1070
Malouk, Salim, 1147
Mamet, David, 1175
Man, Albon, Jr., 635
Man, Albon P., 635, 1004
Man, Aldrick, 635
Mandela, Nelson, *1183*
Maney, Richard, 955
Manges, Horace, 1252
Manigault, Earl "the Goat," 86
Mani-Leyb, 1283
Maniscalco, Albert V., *130*
Mankiewicz, Herman, 14
Mankiewicz, Joseph, 1134
Mann, Barry, 1012
Mann, Daniel, 110
Mann, Theodore, 225, 1174
Mann, Thomas, 686, 806
Manners, J. Hartley, 1155
Mannes, Clara Damrosch, 1060
Mannes, David, 241, 724, 1060
Mannes, Leopold, 901
Manning, Harry, *1182*
Manning, John, 1020
Manning, Mary, 1020
Mansfield, Helen Josephine "Josie," 414
Manteo, Aggrippino, 725
Manteo, Miguel, 725
Mantle, Burns, 1175
Mantle, Mickey, 84, 145, 850
Manton, Thomas J., *484*
Manzano, Sonia, *214*
Mapelson, James H., 4, 757
Mapes, James J., 339
Mappa, Adam, 940
Mara, Wellington, 698, 831
Marble, Dan, 1167
Marbury, Elisabeth, 664, 680
Marchais, Jacques, 608
Marconi, Guglielmo, 973, *974*
Marcos, Ferdinand, 403
Marcotte, Leon, 322, 1061
Marcus, Greil, 1017
Marcus, Herbert, 327
Marcus, James, 1046
Marcus, Joseph, 75
Marcuse, Herbert, 37, 589

Marcuse, Maxwell F., 649
Maresca, James, 1155
Maretzek, Max, 241, 908
Margiotta, Joseph, 295
Margolis, Moses Z., 985
Marie, queen of Romania, *1181*
Marín, Francisco Gonzálo, 962
Marin, John, 155, 942
Marinelli, Al, 605
Mariotta, John, 1251
Maris, Roger, 145, 850
Maritain, Jacques, 808
Mark, Herman F., 916
Markel, Lester, 847
Markham, Pigmeat, 524
Markova, Alicia, 313
Marks, Marcus A., *129*
Marks, Matthew, 59
Marlin, George J., *743*
Marlowe, Julia, 1096
Marmor, Kalman, 1283
Marquand, Isaac, 111
Marquand, John, Jr., 684
Marquand, John P., 683
Marquand, Rube, 831
Marsalis, Wynton, 615, 616, 628
Marsh, Helen M., 98
Marsh, Henry W., 732
Marshall, Armina, 1178
Marshall, Ernset, 321
Marshall, Frank J., 212, 732
Marshall, John, 465, 687
Marshall, Kenneth, 525
Marshall, Susan, 314
Marsteller, Bill, 169
Martello, Romualdo, 466
Martha, crown princess of Norway, *1181*
Martin, Billy, 850
Martin, Bradley, 1085
Martin, Dean, 442
Martin, E. S., 1129
Martin, John, 20, 314, 421, 574
Martin, Thomas, 98
Martin, Townsend, 1253
Martin, William R., 1009
Martinelli, Giovanni, 757
Martinex, Hugo, 495
Martins, Peter, 72, 391, 826, 1010
Martin the Armenian, 52
Martiny, Charles, 331
Martyn, Thomas, 714, 821
Marx, Karl, 595
Marx, Louis, 1194
Masaryk, Tomáš, 1078
Maslow, Sophie, 313, 497
Mason, Daniel Gregory, 242
Mason, John (merchant), 210
Mason, John (minister), 1052, 1142
Mason, John Mitchell (minister), 1052
Mason, Lowell, 240
Mason, Max, 1015
Mason, Mrs. R. Osgood, 526
Masquerier, Lewis, 595
Massee, May, 125, 214
Massengale, John, 549
Massey, Raymond, 631
Massey, William, 189
Masson, Jeffrey, 830
Masteroff, Joe, 663
Masui, Yasuo, 47
Masur, Harold Q., 919
Masur, Kurt, 838, 839
Mateos, Adolfo López, *1182*
Mather, Frank Jewett, Jr., 57
Mathews, Charles, 1166
Mathews, Cornelius, 713, 918
Mathews, David, 177
Mathews, Gustav, 1005
Mathews, James M., 848
Mathewson, Douglas, *129*
Mathewson, Rufus, 260
Matias, Bienvenida, 337
Matisse, Henri, 1120, 1250
Matta (Roberto Matta Echaurren), 843
Matthews, David, *744*
Matthews, John, 1058
Matthiessen, Peter, 684
Maugham, W. Somerset, 74, 686, 1170
Maurice, James, *481*, 777
Maurin, Peter, 17, 192, 320, 533
Maverick, Peter, 350
Maxwell, Robert, 127, 308, 522, 709, 820
May, George O., 939
May, Gladys, 664
May, Mitchell, *482*
Maycock, George A., 716
Mayer, Ferdinand, 941
Mayer, Harold C., 92
Mayer, Louis B., 1069
Mayes, Herbert, 1270
Maynard, Don, 834
Maynard, George W., 791
Mayr, Ernst, 31, 110
Mays, Willie, 84, 831, 1105
Maysles, Albert, 337
Maysles, David, 337
Maywood, Augusta, 312
Mazet, Robert, 947, 1046
Mazur, Jay, 594
Mazursky, Paul, 406
Mazzini, Giuseppe, 451
Mead, Edward S., 338
Mead, Henry, 200
Mead, Marcia, 46
Mead, William Rutherford, 708
Meade, Edwin, *481*
Meadows, Audrey, *470*
Mecke, John A., 202
Mecklowitz, Bernard, *122*
Mecom, John, *811*
Mednis, Edmar, 732
Meehan, Patrick, 602
Meeks, J., 322
Meeks, J. W., 322
Megapolensis, Johannes, 995
Mehdi, M. T., 598
Mehrlust, Jacob, 618
Mehta, Zubin, 758, 838, 839
Meier, Joachim, 748
Meier, Richard, 49, 1207
Meigs, Henry, *268*, *480*
Meisner, Sanford, 512, 804, 1176
Mejia, Paul, 391
Mekas, Jonas, 38, 337, 406, 685
Melba, Nellie, 757
Melchior, Lauritz, 38, 242, 757, 758
Melish, John, 308
Mellin, Carl J., 1145
Mellins, Thomas, 549
Mellish, David B., *481*
Mellon, Paul, 38
Meloney, Marie Mattingly, 324
Melyn, Cornelis, 1112
Meminger, Dean, 835
Mencken, H. L., 682, 683
Mencken, Helen, 664
Mendels, Emmanuel S., Jr., 35
Mendelsohn, Walter, 945
Mengelberg, Willem, 838
Menken, Adah Isaacs, 168
Mennin, Peter, 243, 628
Menotti, Gian Carlo, 827
Menuhin, Yehudi, 80
Menut, Alexander, *812*
Menzies, Robert Gordon, *1182*
Mergenthaler, Ottmar, 848
Merkle, "Bonehead" Fred, 83, 831
Merrell, Ike, 1243
Merrett, William, *744*
Merrifield, R. Bruce, 1051
Merrill, Bradford, 1281
Merrill, Charles E., 752
Merrill, John Ogden, 1073
Merrill, Robert, 103, 758, 1202
Merriman, Truman A., *482*
Merritt, Kim, *1028*
Mersereau, John, 806, 1198
Mersereau, William, 546
Merwin, W. S., 4
Merz, Charles, 847
Messer, Thomas, 1090
Messier, Mark, 843
Messinger, Ruth, *129*
Mestrovic, Ivan, 299–300, 1055
Mesurolle, Jean, 1264
Metcalf, Willard Leroy, 1161
Metcalfe, Henry B., *481*
Metcalfe, James, 1177
Metesky, George P., 711, 1164
Methfessel, Anion, 1118
Metz, Herman A., *270*, *483*
Metzger, Juan, 309, 423
Meyer, Adolf, 750
Meyer, André, 660
Meyer, George C., 426
Meyer, H. C., 917
Meyer, Helen, 125
Meyer, Henry (landowner), 435
Meyer, Henry A. (grocer), 416
Meyers, Sidney, 337
Michaux, Lewis H., 128, 802
Micheals, Tony, 1143
Micheaux, Oscar, 405
Michelson, A. A., 904
Michelson, Annette, 58
Michtom, Morris, 1194
Mickle, H. J., 1188
Middagh, John, 157
Middleton, Peter, 1052
Mielziner, Jo, 1109, 1110
Mies van der Rohe, Ludwig, 48, 168, 1057, 1075
Mihaesco, Eugen, 1018
Mihalesco, Mikhel, 1282
Milanov, Zinka, 758
Milbank, Jeremiah, 128, 178, 761
Milborne, Jacob, 663, 992
Miles, Bill, 337
Miles, Edith, 255
Miles, George Carpenter, 856
Miley, Bubber, 371, *372*
Milgram, Lillian, 1046
Milhau, John, 187
Milhaud, Darius, 994
Milken, Michael R., 345
Millard, J. W., 13, 572
Millay, Edna St. Vincent, 682, 1174
Miller, Adeline, 947
Miller, Alice Duer, 14
Miller, Charles R., 846, 847
Miller, Cyrus C., *129*
Miller, David, 807
Miller, Dorothy, 1121

Olcott, Henry Steel, 1178
Olcott, J. Van Vechten, *482*
Oldenburg, Richard E., 785
O'Leary, Denis, *483*
O'Leary, James A., *483*
O'Leary, Jean, 665
Olgin, Moses J., 770, 1283
Oliva, L. Jay, 849
Oliver, Daniel C., *483*
Oliver, Edith, 1178
Oliver, Frank, *483*
Olmsted, Frederick Law, Jr., 46, 427, 431, 989
Olmsted, John Charles, 559
Olshan, Kenneth, 1252
Olshanetsky, Alexander, 1282
O'Mahony, John, 603
O'Malley, John, 189
O'Malley, Matthew V., *483*
O'Malley, Walter, 156, 1005, 1105
Onckelbag, Gerrit, 1070, *1070*
Onderdonk, Benjamin Treadwell, 380
Ondieki, Lisa, *1029*
O'Neal, Frederick, 116
O'Neill, Hugh, 599
O'Neill, James, 404, 1167
O'Neill, John, 603
O'Neill, Kevin, 165
O'Neill, Ralph, 68
Ono, Yoko, 663, 772
Oort, Sarah Bradley Cox, 636
Opatoshu, Joseph, 1283
Oppenheim, James, 1061
Oppenheimer, George S., 126, 1228
Opper, Frederick Burr, 184, 961
Oram, James, *812*
O'Reilly, Daniel, *481*
O'Reilly, Samuel F., 1153
Orgen, Jacob "Little Orgen," 452
Orkin, Ruth, 338
Orlovsky, Peter, 93
O'Rourke, P. J., 802, 1017
Orozco, José Clemente, 782
Orton, Lawrence, 232
Orwell, George, 261
O'Ryan, John F., *912*
Osborn, Alex, 88
Osborne, Danvers, *479*
Osganian, Khachadur, 52
Osgood, Samuel, 226, 276
O'Shea, William J., *122*
O'Sullivan, Timothy, 135
Oswald, Eleazar, *811*
Otis, Elisha Graves, 370
O'Toole, Donald L., *484*
Ottendorfer, Anna, 663
Ottendorfer, Oswald, 329, 464, 513, 663, 830, 1208
Ottinger, Richard, 277
Ottley, James Henry, 703
Ousterman, David, 1262
Outerbridge, Eugenius, 825
Outerbridge, Mary, 1163
Owen, Mickey, 84
Owen, Robert, 64, 1083
Owen, Robert Dale, 16, 64, 378, 385, 590, 1083
Owens, Craig, 58
Owens, Major R., *484*
Owings, Nathaniel, 1073
Oysher, Moyshe, 1282

Pach, Alexander, 321
Pach, Walter, 55, 59
Pacino, Al, 5
Packard, Silas, 4
Padmore, George, 347
Padon, Andrew J., 437
Padrino (religious leader), 1043–44
Page, Alfred R., 292
Page, Arthur, 955
Page, Walter (jazz musician), 85
Page, Walter (publisher), 125
Pahlavi, Mohammad Reza, 597, *1182*
Paillet, Fernand, *1258*
Palfrey, Sarah, 1163
Palm, Charles, 829
Palma, Joseph A., *130*
Palmer, A. M., 1168
Palmer, Benjamin, 142, 231
Palmer, Elihu, 64
Palmer, Fanny, 305, 941
Palmer, John, 391
Palmer, Lowell M., 280, 1108
Palmer, Stuart, 919
Palmer, Volney B., 7
Panelius, Emil, 408
Panfil, Wanda, *1028*
Panizza, Ettore, 757
Panken, Jacob, *738*
Pankhurst, Emmeline, 1269
Parcells, Bill, 831
Paret, Benny, 134
Parish, Daniel, Jr., 856
Park, Brad, 843
Park, Chung Hee, *1183*
Park, William H., 334, 1202
Parker, Alice, 219
Parker, Alton B., *488*
Parker, Horatio, 241, 606
Parker, James, 713, *811*, 939, 940
Parker, Louis N., 916
Parker, Pat, 665
Parkhurst, Helen, 310
Parkman, Francis, 640
Parks, Rosa, 573
Parmentier, Andrew, 559
Parnell, Charles Stewart, 603
Parr, Albert E., 31
Parrish, Stephen, 941
Parsons, Betty, 58, 843
Parsons, Calvert, Jr., 130
Parsons, Charles, 376, 941
Parsons, David, 395
Parsons, Frank Alvah, 593
Parsons, Herbert, *482*
Parsons, Louella, 834
Parsons, M. B., 783
Parsons, Reuben, 694
Parsons, Samuel Bowne, 559, 637, 1010
Parsons, Willard, 441
Parton, Sara, 836, 1096
Partridge, John N., *912*
Pasatieri, Thomas, 827
Pásztory, Ditta, 80
Pataki, George E., 934
Paterson, Basil, 626
Patrick, Albert F., 1003
Patrick, Lester, 842
Patrick, Lynn, 843
Patten, Bernard M., *129*
Patten, Thomas G., *483*
Patten, William Gilbert, 734
Patterson, Eleanor "Cissy," 307
Patterson, Ellmore, 266
Patterson, Floyd, 134
Patterson, Frederick Douglass, 1214
Patterson, John, *811*
Patterson, William, 426
Patti, Adelina, 241, 851
Paul, Maury ("Cholly Knickerbocker"), 834, 1000, 1086
Paul, Thomas, 112
Paulding, William I., 1220
Paul I, king of Greece, *1182*
Paullin, Ethel, 223
Paullin, Telford, 223
Paul VI, 193
Paur, Emil, 838
Pavlov, Ivan, 1247
Paxton, Steve, 314
Payne, Oliver H., 747
Payson, Joan Whitney, 837
Peabody, Charles A., 795
Peabody, George, 627
Pearl, Jack, 169, 975
Pearson, Drew, 307
Peartree, William, *744*
Peary, Robert E., 25
Pease, Lewis M., 415
Peck, Jared V., *481*
Peck, William J., *268*
Pederson, William, 641
Peet, Harvey Pringle, 321
Pegler, Westbrook, 850, 852, 1106
Pegram, George B., 260, 904
Peirce, Charles, 388
Peiss, Kathy, 514
Pekarsky, Mel, 782
Pelé, 1082, 1106
Pelham, George F., 40, 45, 281
Pelissier, Victor, 239
Pell, Alfred S., 671, 795
Pell, F. Livinston, 282
Pell, Herbert C., *483*
Pell, Thomas, 80, 142, 354
Pelli, Cesar, 89, 170, 785, 789, 1075, 1275
Pelton, Guy R., *481*
Pemberton, Murdock, 14
Pendergast, W. A., *270*
Pène du Bois, Guy, 59, 874
Penelope, Julia, 665
Penfield, William, 942
Penn, Irving, 900
Pennebaker, D. A., 337
Penney, James Cash, 616
Penniman, John, 376
Penrose, George F., 1081
Penzias, Arno, 161
Pépin, Victor, 225
Pepush, Johann, 790
Perelman, Ronald O., 703, 1001
Peretti, Elsa, 1183
Perez, Richie, 1285
Periconi, Joseph, *129*
Perit, Pelatiah, 474
Perkins, Ephraim, 308
Perkins, Evelina Ball, 1248
Perkins, George (banker), 627, 1248
Perkins, George W. (insurance executive), 672, 836, 1008
Perlman, Itzhak, 155, 628
Perlman, Nathan D., *483*
Perlmutter, Sholem, 1282
Perona, John, 374
Perot, H. Ross, *491*
Perreault, John, 58
Perrin, Alain-Dominique, 183
Perry, Antoinette "Tony," *1191*
Perry, Caroline, 100
Perry, Clarence Arthur, 993
Perry, Isaac G., 54

Perry, Matthew C., 159, 559
Perry, Nick, 612
Perry, Roland H., 331
Perry, Ronald, 316
Pershing, John J., *1181*
Peslinger, Jack, 495
Peter, Lawrence J., 1262
Peters, Augustus W., *129*
Peters, Harry, 305
Peters, Paul, 115
Peters, Roberta, 499
Peterson, Andrew N., *483*
Peterson, John, 9
Petioni, Charles Augustin, 1200
Petiot, Ferdinand "Pete," 423
Petipa, Jean, 312
Petipa, Marius, 312
Petlin, Irving, 59
Petrie, George H., 1284
Petry, George, *690*
Petterson, Alicia, 838
Pettingill, S. M., 7
Petto, Tomasso, 79
Peyser, Theodore A., *483*
Pfeffer, Jeff, 155
Pfeifer, Joseph L., *483*
Pfeiffer, Carl, 907
Pfyfe, John C., 907
Pheiffer, William T., *484*
Phelan, Michael, 108
Phelps, Anson G., 131
Phelps, Helen L., 1125
Phelps, Robert, 512
Phelps Stokes, Anson, Sr., 1125
Phelps Stokes, James Graham, 1060, 1126, 1232
Pherentinos, Paisos, 355
Philips, William E., *912*
Philipse, Eva, 1221
Philipp, Julius, 1039
Philipp, Oscar, 1039
Phillips, David Graham, 497
Phillips, Flip, 707
Phillips, John M., 277
Phillips, Jonas N., *268*
Phillips, Warren, 1235
Phillips, Wendell, 1088
Phillips, William, 591, 683
Phoenix, J. Phillips, *480*, *735*
Phumiphon Adundet, king of Thailand, *1182*
Piaf, Edith, 181
Picasso, Pablo, 1056
Picasso, Paloma, 1183
Piccirilli, Attilio, 261, 1054
Pickens, William, *800*
Pickford, Mary, 177, 925
Picon, Molly, 1282
Piel, Gerard, 1051
Pierce, Franklin, 100, *486*, 1053
Pierce, George, 942
Pierce, Louise, 1016
Pierce, Nathaniel, *268*
Pieret, Pierre, 574
Pierpont, Hezekiah, 156
Pierre, Charles, 905
Pierrepont, Edwards, 1215
Pierrepont, William Constable, 906
Pierson, Jeremiah H., *480*
Pieterson, Mons, 1144
Pike, James Albert, 381, 1032
Pike, Samuel, 209
Pilcher, Lewis G., 54
Pileggi, Nicholas, 822
Pillsbury, Parker, 1001
Pilmoor, Joseph, 753
Pilsudski, Joseph, 856
Pinckney, Benjamin F., *268*
Pinckney, Charles T., *268*
Pincus-Witten, Robert, 58
Pinhorne, William, 360
Pinski, David, 1282
Pink, Louis H., 568
Pinkerton, Robert, 329
Pinza, Ezio, 38
Pipa, Arshi, 12
Pippig, Uta, *1028*
Pirandello, Luigi, 1170
Piro, Frank "Killer Joe," 316
Piron, A. J., 1022
Pirsig, Robert M., 1262
Pirsson, William, 9
Piscator, Erwin, 97, 687, 808
Pitino, Rick, 835
Pitkin, John R., 357, 1271
Pitts, Zasu, 563
Pius XII, 192, 1101
Pizzolato, Orlando, *1028*
Placide, Alexandre, 311
Plant, Morton F., 183
Plath, Sylvia, 1270
Platt, Caroline, 75
Platt, Charles A., 45, 46
Platt, George, 322
Platzek, M. Warley, 1033
Plaza Lasso, Galo, *1182*
Pleasant, Richard, 20
Pleshette, Suzanne, 407
Plimpton, Francis T. P., 322
Plimpton, George, 684
Plunz, Richard, 549
Podell, Bertram L., *484*
Poitier, Sidney, 40
Poli, Gianni, *1028*
Polisi, Joseph, 628
Polk, Frank L., 320
Polk, James K., 91, *486*, 1152
Polk, Ralph L., 230
Pollack, Ben, 474
Pollard, Calvin, 154
Pollard, George Mort, 280, 563
Polshek, James Stewart, 89
Pomare, Eleo, 314
Pomeroy, A. D., 769
Pomus, Doc, 1012
Pond, Theron, 286
Poné, Gundars, 656
Pons, Lily, 38, 757
Ponselle, Rosa, 242, 757
Poor, Alfred Easton, 954–55
Poor, Henry Varnum, 1110
Pope, John Russell, 1020, 1272
Pope, Virginia, 392
Porter, Andrew, 793
Porter, Fairfield, 58
Porter, Rufus, 1051
Porter, Seton, 965
Porter, Susan, *1223*
Post, Jotham, Jr., *480*
Post, Langdon W., 413, 1163
Post, Wiley, 1181
Post, William, 329
Potamkin, Harry, 405
Potenziani, Ludovico Spado, *1181*
Potter, Clare, 392
Potter, Clarkson N., *481*
Potter, Horatio, 178, *380*, 381
Potter, Orlando B., 1164
Potter, Pauline, 180
Pottier, Auguste, 541, 932
Potts, David M., *4884*
Poulsen, Neil, 187
Pound, Ezra, 686, 973, 1044
Pounds, Lewis H., *129*, 335, *738*
Powell, Betty, 665
Powell, C. B., 36
Powell, William (actor), 563
Powell, William (schoolmaster), 99
Powell, William P. (abolitionist),
Power, James, 936
Power, John, 191
Power, Tyrone, 599
Powers, Ann, 793
Powers, Francis Gary, 1
Powers, John, 1202
Praa, Peter, 505
Prall, Anning S., *483*
Pratt, Babe, 843
Pratt, Carroll, 931
Pratt, John, 936
Pratt, Frederic, 728
Pratt, Parley P., 771
Pratt, Zadock, 308
Preer, Andrew, 288
Prendergast, Maurice, 366
Presley, Elvis, 364, 1238
Pressman, Barney, 78
Pressman, Fred, 78
Pressman, Lee, 276
Presetes de Albuquerque, Julio, *1181*
Price, Ned, 920
Price, Stephen, 1166
Price, Uvedale, 572
Price, William, 1215
Prieti, Pedro, 963
Prime, Samuel Irenaeus, 838
Primus, Pearl, 12, 313, 422
Prince, John D., 260
Prince, Samuel, 322
Prince, William, 968
Pringle, Henry, 1224
Procaccino, Mario, *270*, 492, 679, *741*, 1231
Prokofiev, Sergei, 181
Proskauer, Joseph, 945
Proskauer, Mrs. Joseph, 619
Prosser, Seward, 74
Provost, David, *744*
Prud'homme, J. F. E., 941
Pryor, Richard, 1141
Puente, Tito, 422
Pugsley, Cornelius A., *482*
Pujo, Arsène, 70, 596, 627, 769
Purdee, Bernard, 1012
Purdy, Elijah F., *268*
Purdy, Stephen, *812*
Purdy, Stephen, Jr., *812*
Purroy, Henry D., *268*
Pursh, Frederick, 559
Purvitis, Vilhelms, 656
Putnam, Frederic, 39
Putnam, George Haven, 125, 494
Putnam, George Palmer, 125, 127, 494, 625, 681
Putnam, Israel, 156, 493
Putnam, J. Pickering, 722
Pyle, Charles, 242, 1104

Quack, Roosevelt, 1077
Quayle, Frank J., *411*
Quayle, John F., *483*
Queen, Frank, 828
Quennell, Nicholas, 89

Temple, Shirley, 1011
Tennent, John van Brugh, 1052
Ter-Arutunian, Rouben, 53, 1110
Terreforte, Juan de Mata, 962
Terrell, Mary Church, 528
Terry, Bill, 831
Terry, Clark, 318
Terry, Ellen, 1167
Terry, Paul, 704
Terry, Sonny, 1012
Terry, Walter, 314
Tese, Vincent, 1219
Tetley, Glen, 316
Thacher, Thomas (lawyer), 1071
Thacher, Thomas Day (reformer), 208
Thackrey, Theodore O., 839
Tharp, Marie, 461
Tharpe, Rosetta, 475
Thatcher, Harvey D., 309
Thaw, Harry K., 617, 1259
Thayer, Abbott, 799
Thayer, Scofield, 682
Thebaud, Augustus J., 425
Theobald, John J., *122*
Theodorovich, John, 1208
Thomas, Ambrose L., 694
Thomas, Andrew, 676, 677
Thomas, Augustus, 1170
Thomas, Brooks, 528
Thomas, C. K., 1101
Thomas, Charles, 1026
Thomas, Clara Fargo, 96
Thomas, Dylan, 210, 1259
Thomas, Griffith, 64
Thomas, John R., 46, 754, 1143
Thomas, Joseph G., 96
Thomas, Linda Lee, 925
Thomas, Piri, 963
Thomas, Robert D., 1253
Thomas, S. B., 71, 423
Thomas, William, 94
Thomashevsky, Bessie, 1282
Thomashevsky, Boris, 365, 1282
Thompkins, Erastus O., 111
Thompson, Benjamin, 904
Thompson, Clara, 750
Thompson, Denman, 1168
Thompson, Edward, *411*
Thompson, Frank, 302
Thompson, Frederick, 273, 545
Thompson, George, 636
Thompson, Hank, 1105
Thompson, Henry C., 94
Thompson, Hunter S., 1017
Thompson, James Walter, 629
Thompson, John (banker), 208, 694
Thompson, John C. (builder), 500
Thompson, Jonathan, 1237
Thompson, Joseph P., 141, 587
Thompson, Louise, 516
Thompson, Lydia, 168
Thompson, Margaret, 856
Thompson, Vance, 685
Thomson, Bobby, 84, 831, 1053
Thong, Walter, 445
Thorburn, Grant, 1052
Thoreau, Henry David, 272, 375, 964
Thorne, Jacob, 1262
Thorne, Joel, 68
Throckmorton, John, 142, 1180
Thurber, Jeanette, 241, 353
Thurman, Wallace, 526, 527, 683, 686
Thutmose III, 244
Tibbett, Lawrence, 757
Tidyman, Ernset, 920
Tiebout, Cornelius, 941
Tiebout, John, *812*
Tienhoven, Cornelius Van, 43
Tiffany, Charles L., 1183
Tiffany, H. D., 436
Tikhon (bishop), 355
Tilden, Marmaduke, 650
Tillich, Paul, 248, 997, 1212
Tillman, Sarah A., 158
Tilton, John, Jr., 762
Tilton, Theodore, 96, 587, 1272
Tilyou, George C., 273
Timbers, William, 1073
Tio, Lola Rodríguez de, 962
Tipton, Jennifer, 1110
Tisch, Laurence, 258, 689
Tisch, Preston, 689, 827
Tittle, Y. A., 831
Titus, Erastus, 71
Titus, Melle, 659
Tobias, Tobi, 315
Tobin, Mary Jane, 1005
Todd, Charles B., 548
Todd, Laurie, 1052
Todd, Robert, 239
Todd, Roberto, 962
Tokatyan, Armand, 53
Toklas, Alice B., 542, 664
Toller, Ernst, 1170
Tollner, Eugene, 447
Tolman, William Howe, 514
Tomlinson, Mel, 316
Tompkins, Caleb, *480*
Tompkins, Minthorne, 1111
Tone, Franchot, 512, 1171
Tonry, Richard J., *484*
Toohey, John Peter, 14
Toomer, Jean, 114, 526, 683
Topping, Dan, 424, 850
Torborg, Jeff, 837
Torre, Joe, 837
Torre, Susana, 48
Torrence, Ridgely, 115, 526
Torrens, James H., *484*
Torres, Felipe, 917
Torrey, John, 130
Torrio, Johnny "the Brain," 415, 944
Toscanini, Wanda, 557
Totten, Joseph G., 431, 1262
Touré, Sékou, *1182*
Tourian, Ghevont, 52
Town, Ithiel, 44, 318, 393, 1216
Towne, Charles A., *482*
Townes, Charles H., 260, 1051
Towns, Charles B., 345
Towns, Edolphus, *484*
Townsend, Adina, 947
Townsend, Charles H., 824
Townsend, Dwight, *481*
Townsend, Edward W., 1101
Townsend, George, *480*
Townsend, Robert, 382
Townshend, Henry, 965
Towse, J. Ranken, 1177
Tracy, Benjamin, *737*
Tracy, Spencer, 540
Trager, James, 549
Trainor, George, 714
Traubel, Helen, 758
Travers, William R., 558, 825
Travis, Jacob, 1198
Treadwell, Adam, 1198
Treadwell, E., 71
Tredwell, Thomas, *480*
Treigle, Norman, 827
Trench, Joseph, 1081
Trent, Harrison, 828
Trent, William J., Jr., 1214
Trièrge, Pauline, 440
Trippe, Juan, 68
Tristano, Lennie, 615
Trnina, Milka, 300
Trotter, Jonathan, *149*, *268*
Trow, John F., 230
Troyanos, Tatiana, 758
Trujillo, Rafael, 340
Truman, Harry, S., 80, 104, 276, 331, 386, *490*, 504
Trumbauer, Frankie, 97, 1260
Trumbauer, Horace, 46
Trumbull, Jonathan, 391
Trump, Fred, 1201
Truscott, Alan F., 137
Trusty, Shep, 302
Tryon, John, 1151
Tryon, William, 33, 431, *479*
Tsai, Gerald, 1197
Tsuno, Keiko, 337
Tsypin, George, 1110
Tubman, Harriet, 10
Tubman, William V. S., *1182*
Tucci, Oscar, 325
Tucker, Ed "Snakehips," 288
Tucker, Sophie, 522, 622, 1168, 1226
Tucker, Willie, 473
Tuckey, William, 239
Tudor, David, 304
Tudor, Frederic, 579
Tugwell, Rexford, 232, 233, 260, 543
Tune, Tommy, 792
Tunnell, Emlen, 831
Turini, Giovanni, 1054
Turk, Robert, 704
Turner, C. Y., 781
Turner, Charles H., *482*
Turner, George Kibbe, 779
Turner, Henry C., 1204
Turner, J. M. W., 221
Turner, Jessie Franklin, 392
Turner, Peter, 1035
Turnure, Arthur, 1230
Tuthill, William B., 181
Tucker, Marcia, 58
Tuckerman, Arthur, 756
Tuckerman, Henry T., 57
Tumbridge, William, 1034
Turnbull, Julia, 312
Turner, Big Joe, 1012
Turner, Charles Yardley, 1044
Turner, Kylo, 475
Twachtman, John Henry, 1161
Tweed, Harrison, 62, 292, 661
Twichell, Harmony, 606
Twombly, Cy, 186
Tyler, John, 1143
Tyner, McCoy, 257
Tyson, Jacob, *480*
Tyson, Mike, 134, 163

Ullman, Bernard, 241
Ullman, Doris, 1258
Ulmer, Edgar G., 405
Ulmer, James Blood, 1013
Unanue, Don Prudencio, 494
Underhill, John (commander), 27
Underhill, John Q. (congressman), *482*
Underhill, Walter, *480*
Underwood, Horace, 937

Unwin, Raymond, 993
Updike, John, 684, 830
Updyke, George, 1272
Uppington, George, 230
Upton, Robert, 311, 1165
Urban, Joseph, 199, 322, 758, 1109
Uris, Harris H., 1036
Uris, Percy, 1036
Uris, Ruth, 757
Ury, John, 191
Usher, George, 1058
Ussachevsky, Vladimir, 243

Vaccaro, John, 1005
Vail, Alfred, 774, 1158
Vail, Ira, 68
Vail, Thomas, 1067
Vaillande, Suzanne, 311
Vails, Nelson, 107
Valaitis, Jonas, 684
Valenstein, Larry, 510
Valentín, Gilberto Gerena, 963
Valentina (fashion designer), 392
Valentine, Gilbert, 1272
Valentine, Isaac, 1220
Valentino, Rudolph, 63, 563
Valk, William W., *481*
Valli, Frankie, 1012
Vallone, Peter, 606
Valusek, Andrew J., 1078
van Alen, William, 47, 221
Van Amburgh, Isaac, 225
Vanbiesbrouck, John, 843
Van Brugh, Johannes, 360
Van Buren, Martin, 162, 245, 325, *486*, 688, 1149
Van Buren, W. H., 1216
Vance, Cyrus, 659, 1071
Vance, Samuel B. H., *268*, *744*
van Corlear, Jacob, 417
Van Cortlandt, Augustus, 1222
Van Cortlandt, Frederick, 1221
Van Cortlandt, Jacobus, *744*, 1221
Van Cortlandt, Oloff, 360, 1221
van Courtlandt, John, 210
van Couwenhoven, Wolfert Gerritsen, 417
Van Dam, José, 758
Vanderbilt, Amy, 1254
Vanderbilt, Consuelo, 1066
Vanderbilt, George, 1156
Vanderbilt, Jacob, 512, 520
van der Bilt, Jan Arentzen, 855
Vanderbilt, John, 1267
Vanderbilt, Mrs. William K., 1144
Vanderbilt, William H., 196, 806, 1153
Vander Burch, Cornelius, 1070
van der Donck, Adriaen, 142
Vandergaw, John, *429*
Vanderpoel, J. H., 1285
Vanderveer, Abraham, *480*
Van Dusen, Henry P., 1212
Van Dyck, Peter, 1070
Van Dyke, Willard, 337
Van Etten, Nathan B., 146
Van Fleet, James A., *1182*
Van Houten, Isaac B., *480*
van Huyven, Cornelius, 360
Van Kleek, John R., 473
van Itallie, Jean-Claude, 1174
Van Loon, Henrik, 683
VanName, Calvin, *130*
Van Neste, Pieter Pietersen, 1225
Van Nuyse, Johannes, 761
van Remunde, Johan, 764
Van Rensselaer, Mariana Griswold, 47, 57
Van Ronk, Dave, 422, 1012
van Salee, Anthony Jansen, 821
Van Schaick, George, 672
Van Schaick, Myndert, *735*, 848
Van Schaick, William, 457
Van Slyke, Louisa, 531
Van Steenwyck, Cornelius, *744*
Van Sweeten, Ouzeel, 445
van Twiller, Wouter, 148, 417, 493, 1020, 1237
Van Voorhis, Daniel, 1070
Van Werckhoven, Cornelis, 285, 822
Van Wyck, Theodorus, 825
Van Wyck, William, *268*
Van Zandt, Peter, 1198
Van Zandt, Wynant, 342
Varnay, Astrid, 758
Vaughan, Sarah, 626
Vazquez, Viveca, 314
Veblen, Thorstein, 253, 808
Vedeer, William, *481*
Veeber, Agaate, 384
Vehslage, John H. G., *482*
Velazquez, Nydia M., *484*
Vélez, Ramón, 963
Venturi, Robert, 49
Verdon, Gwen, 433
Verhulst, William, 764, 1207
Verlaine, Tom, 10013
Vernam, Remington, 60
Vernon, Raymond, 993
Vertes, Marcel, 1081
Vesey, William, 380
Vida, Ginny, 665
Vidal, Gore, 379
Vidali, Vittorio, 1199
Videla, Gabriel Gonzalez, *1182*
Viele, Egbert L., *482*, 1208–9
Villard, Henry, 839, 1034, 1141, 1229
Villela, Edward, 72
Villiers, Alan J., *1182*
Vincent, George E., 1015
Vinchevsky, Morris, 1283
Viollet-le-Duc, Eugène, 1025
Vivian, Charles S., 437
Vlasto, Solon, 503
Vodery, Will, 1151
Vogelsang, Peter, 823
Voight, Herman, 104
Volcker, Paul, 395
Volk, Lester D., *483*
Volpe, Edmond, 251
Volpe, Joseph, 758
Volunbrun, Jeanne Mathusine Droibillan, 516
von Brieson, Arthur, 661
von der Capellan toe Ryssel, Baron, 1112
von Grona, Eugene, 313
Von Magonigle, Harold, 261
von Nardoff, Ernst R., 1134
von Pirquet, Clemens, 1046
von Sternberg, Josef, 333
Von Tilzer, Harry, 83, 1187
Voorhees, Enders M., 1230
Voorhees, Stephen A., 1276
Vorse, Mary Heaton, 667
Vose, John D., 918

Wachtell, Herbert M., 1231
Waddell, Alexander, 471
Waddell, Robert Ross, 598
Waddington, Joshua, 519, 1030
Wade, John E., *122*
Wade, William, *268*
Wadleigh, Lydia F., 1231
Wadsworth, Daniel, 19, 1201
Wadsworth, James S., 433
Wagner, Albert, 961
Wagner, Charlie, 1153
Wagner, Emilie, 241
Wagner, George, 1231
Wagner, Robin, 1109
Wagner, Susan Edwards, 1231
Wagoner, Dan, 1156
Waikihuri, Douglas, *1028*
Wainwright, Jonathan Mayhew, 380, *1181*
Wait, William, 117, 834
Waitz, Grete, *1028*, 1106
Wake, Ransom F., 9
Wakeman, Abram, *481*
Walbridge, Hiram, *481*
Walcott, Brenda, 844
Walcott, Derek, 116
Wald, D. Everett, 282
Wald, George, 161
Waldo, George E., *482*
Waldo, Rhinelander, *411*, *912*
Waldon, Alton R., Jr., *484*
Wales, James Albert, 628
Wales, Marguerite, 540
Wales, Salem H., *736*
Walker, A'lelia, 527, 664, 1233
Walker, Frank, 1080
Walker, George, 115, 1262
Walker, James (dancer), 1151
Walker, John Brisben, 287
Walker, Kate, 676
Walker, Lillian, 637
Walker, Stanley, 832
Walker, William, *481*
Walkmieser, Alice, 844
Wall, William (congressman), *481*
Wall, William Guy (artist), 941
Wallace, DeWitt, 714, 989
Wallace, George C., *490*
Wallace, Henry A., 30, 276, *490*, 1226
Wallace, Hugh, 598
Wallace, Lew, 671
Wallace, Lila Acheson, 714, 989
Wallace, Michele, 58
Wallace, William C., *482*
Wallach, Eli, 632
Wallack, Lester, 131, 850, 1167, 1168
Wallander, Arthur W., *912*
Walling, William English, 799
Wallis, Brian, 58
Wallstein, Leonard M., 746
Walsh, Daniel, 752
Walsh, James J., *482*
Walsh, Lawrence E., 320
Walsh, Michael, *481*
Walsh, Patrick J., *411*
Walsh, Raoul, 404
Walsh, Richard, 126
Walter, Bruno, 105, 242, 838, 839
Walter, Eugene, 1109, 1170
Walter, Thomas U., 28
Walters, Alexander, 10, 528
Walters, Barbara, 22
Walters, Robert, *744*
Walton, Lester A., 824
Walton, Tony, 1110
Wanamaker, John, 19, 327, 1235
Wanamaker, Rodman, 762
Wang, Wayne, 406
Ward, Aaron, *480*
Ward, Arch, 1106
Ward, Artemus, 128
Ward, Bartholomew, 1237
Ward, Benjamin, *912*

Ward, Caleb T., 109, 1236
Ward, Douglas Turner, 804, 1174
Ward, Elijah, *481*
Ward, Harry F., 269
Ward, Jasper, 1237
Ward, John M., 82, *85*
Ward, Jonathan, *480*
Ward, Nathaniel, 261
Ward, Robert (baseball owner), 83
Ward, Robert (composer), 827
Ward, Samuel (banker and art patron), 249, 262
Ward, Samuel Ringgold (abolitionist minister), 9
Ward, Theodore, 116
Ward, William Greene (Civil War general), 512, 1115
Ward, William L. (congressman), *482*
Wardwell, Allen, 320
Ware, Henry, 1212
Ware, WIlliam (clergyman), 1212
Ware, William R. (architect), 46, 575
Warner, Charles Dudley, 1085
Warner, Rawleigh, 765
Warren, Charlotte, 2
Warren, Joseph A., *912*
Warren, Leonard, 758
Warren, Peter, 2, 506
Warren, Robert Penn, 684
Warren, Whitney, 498, 850
Wartels, Nat, 126
Washburn, Edward A., 381
Washington, Booker T., 38, 347, 432, 453, 528, 802, 823, 1194
Washington, Ernestine B., 475
Washington, F. D., 475
Washington, Robert, 49
Wasserman, Lew, 744–45
Waterlow, Sidney, 1258
Waterman, Frank D., *738*
Waters, Edward, 657
Waters, Muddy, 1012
Watkins, Ann, 680
Watson, Doc, 1012
Watson, Forbes, 57
Watson, Henry C., 792
Watson, James (judge), 626
Watson, James J., Sr. (businessman), 593
Watson, James Sibley, Jr. (magazine publisher), 682
Watson, "Sliding Billy," 169
Watson, Thomas J., 137, 270
Watt, Douglas, 1178
Watt, James, 1053
Watts, André, 4
Watts, John, *480*
Watts, Richard, 1178
Waumetompack (Indian chief), 27
Wayburn, Ned, 62, 1253
Wayland, Levi, *812*
Webb, Alexander Russell, 793
Webb, Clifton, 342
Webb, David, 618
Webb, Del, 850
Webb, Eckford, 1067
Webb, George James, 240
Webb, Isaac, 1067
Webb, James Watson, 803, 810, 846, 987
Webb, Thomas, 753
Webb, William H., 1067
Weber, Jake, 835
Weber, Joe, 1250
Weber, Lawrence, 169
Webern, Anton, 243
Webster, Charles (filmmaker), 403
Webster, Charles (publisher), *811*
Webster, Daniel, 135
Webster, Margaret, 109, 758
Wechsler, James A., 839, 909, 1047
Wechsler, Joseph, 3
Wed-Neuwiebl, Maximillian zu, 787
Weed, Thurlow, 504, 769, 803, 846, 987
Weeks, Ezra, 494
Weeks, James, 1251
Weicker, Theodore, 1108
Weidenfeld, George, 512
Weidman, Charles, 312, 496, 574, 677, 808, 1033
Weil, Claudia, 337
Weil, Frank, 1252
Weill, Alexandre, 660
Weiman, Adolf A., 781
Weinbaum, Mark, 855
Weinberg, Harry, 170, 402
Weinberg, Morris, 1284
Weinberg, Sidney J., 472
Weinberg, Steven, 146
Weiner, Dan, 338, 902
Weiner, Leo, 1022
Weinman, Adolph A., 428, *428*
Weinreich, Uriel, 1283
Weir, Julian Alden, 532, 799, 1161, 1184
Weir, Reginald, 1163
Weisgall, Hugo, 827
Weiss, Adolph, 242
Weiss, Ted, *484*, 575
Weisz, Charles C., 367
Weitenkampf, Frank, 548
Welch, Evelyn, 288
Welch, John F., 457
Welch, Mickey, 831
Welch, Priscilla, *1028*
Welch, William H., 952
Welitsch, Ljuba, 758
Weller, Royal H., *483*
Wells, Dicky, 85
Wells, George, 281
Wells, James N., 209
Wells, John, 175, 1053
Wells, Joseph M., 1229
Wells, Mary, 1252
Wells, Joseph M., 1259
Wells, Samuel Roberts, 902
Wells, Thomas, 281
Welsh, Freddy, 664
Wendehack, Clifford, 473
Wendell, Evertt, Jr., 445
Wendell, Jacob, 445
Wendover, Peter H., *480*
Wenner, Jann, 1017
Wenzel, Edward, *1113*
Wersing, Martin, 61
Wertheim, Maurice, 1178
Wertheimer, David, 456
Wesendonck, Hugo, 513, 671
Wesendonck, Otto, 513
Wesley, John, 753
West, Benjamin, 148, 324, 1201
West, Herbert, 828
West, James, 225
West, Morris, 1262
West, Thomas, 26
West, Walter Mott, 1084
West, William, 595
Westbrook, Peter, 397
Westenburg, Richard, 219
Westervelt, Aaron, 1067
Westervelt, Daniel, 1067
Westheimer, Ruth, 1156
Westley, Helen, 1174, 1178
Weston, Edward, 902
Weston, Theodore, 756
Westover, Albert E., 1177
Westrum, Wes, 837
Wexler, Jerry, 1012
Weybright, Victor, 126, 806
Weyl, Walter, 807
Weyman, William, *811*, 940
Whaites, Archibald, 789
Wheat, Zach, 155, 156
Wheeler, Andrew Carpenter, 1177
Wheeler, Hugh, 1110
Wheeler, John, *481*
Wheeler, Thomas, 1257
Whelan, Charles, 191
Whistler, James McNeill, 941
White, Charlie, 764
White, Campbell, *480*
White, David, 316
White, Horace, 839
White, James, 439
White, John, 439
White, Justin, 1259
White, Mrs. Stanford, 708
White, Norval, 514
White, Pearl, 90, 405
White, Percival, 56
White, S. B., 693
White, Sampson, 272
White, Sara, 344
White, Steven V., *482*
White, Theodore H., 254
White, Wilbert Webster, 846
White, William (religious leader), 457
White, William Allen (journalist), 682
Whitefield, George, 1001
Whitehead, Robert, 632
Whitehead, Wilbur F., 137
Whiting, James R., *268*, *736*
Whitman, Charles, 94
Whitney, Daniel D., *149*
Whitney, Dorothy, 1126
Whitney, John Hay, 832
Whitney, Payne, 747
Whitney, Thomas R., *481*
Whiton, Augustus Sherrill, 843
Whittier, John Greenleaf, 640
Whittredge, Worthington, 755
Wickenden, William, 75
Wicker, Tom, 847
Wickersham, George W., 175
Wickes, Eliphalet, *480*
Wickes, Thomas, 342
Wickham, William H., *736*, *744*
Wics, Bob, 1153
Wiedoeft, Rudy, 1220
Wiegart, Robert, 782
Wien, Lawrence, 539
Wiese, Otis, 1270
Wiggin, Albert H., 208
Wight, P. B., 799
Wigman, Mary, 313, 551
Wilbour, Charlotte, 1269
Wilbur, Richard, 4, 1110
Wilcox, John, 1229
Wilcox, Preston, 525
Wilde, Kathryn, 48
Wilde, Oscar, 666, 1044
Wilde, Willie, 666
Wilder, Thornton, 74, 1109
Wilentz, Elias, 93, 128, 366
Wilentz, Ted, 93, 366
Wiley, Charles, 625, 681
Wiley, John, 125, 494, 625, 681
Wiley, Major, 625
Wiley, Thomas T., 1195

Wiley, W. Bradford, II, 625
Wiley, William H., 625
Wilgus, William J., 498, 983
Wilhousky, P. J., 219
Wilerson, David, 1001
Wilkens, William, 1262
Wilkerson, Catherine, 1164
Wilkes, George, 1102
Wilkes, Hamilton, 1032
Wilkins, Barron, 976
Wilkins, Roy, 36, 137, 800, 1141
Will, George F., 802
Willard, Jess, 1004
Willard, Xerxes A., 308
Willensky, Elliot, 514
Willet, Thomas (landowner), 65
Willets, Charles, 1262
Willett, Thomas (mayor), 735, *744*
Willett, Marinus, 183, *744*
Willett, William, *482*
William of Orange, 662
Williams, A. V., *268*
Williams, Barney, 599
Williams, Clara, 637
Williams, Clarence, 1080
Williams, Cootie, 371, 935
Williams, David, 1081
Williams, Elizabeth Sprague, 254
Williams, George, 302
Williams, Henry L., 918
Williams, Jabez, 1067
Williams, John (bishop), 458
Williams, John (farmer), 1263
Williams, John Mason (publisher), *812*
Williams, Jonathan, 88, 188, 189, 493, 1265
Williams, Lavinia, 313
Williams, Leighton, 76
Williams, Marion, 475
Williams, Percy, 104
Williams, Peter, Jr. (minister), 1037, 1263
Williams, Smokey Joe, 84
Williams, Theodore Chickering, 1212
Williams, Tony, 319
Williams, William Carlos, 682, 686
Williamson, Hugh, 1201
Williamson, Samuel, 714
Willis, Benjamin, *481*
Willis, Ellen, 1229
Willis, Nathaniel Parker, 713
Wills, Harry, 1032
Wilpon, Fred, 837
Wilson, August, 116, 1175
Wilson, Ebenezer, 445, *744*
Wilson, Edmund Beecher (scientist), 110, 823
Wilson, Edwin, 1178
Wilson, Francis H., *482*
Wilson, Frank E., *482*
Wilson, Frederick, 726
Wilson, Gahan, 802
Wilson, Harry, 961
Wilson, Henry, 1152
Wilson, John Louis, 46, 954
Wilson, Joseph, 179
Wilson, Lanford, 652, 1174, 1175
Wilson, Martha, 436
Wilson, Robert (performance artist), 469, 1110, 1175
Wilson, Robert A. (bookseller), 93
Wilson, Teddy, 474, 550, 615
Wilson, Woodrow, 1, 80, *488–89*, 565, 601, 703, 764, 836, 944, 1020, 1241
Wilton, Joseph, 1053
Wiman, Erastus, 837, 1034, 1114
Winans, R. Foster, 1235
Wind, Herbert Warren, 1107
Winder, Samuel, 445
Windmuller, Louis, 1273
Winfield, Hemsley, 312
Wingate, George Wood, 802
Winham, Aldridge, Jr., 226
Winn, A. C., 650
Winogrand, Garry, 338
Winstanley, William, 941
Winston, Harry, 618
Winter, Charles Allen, *734*
Winter, Johnny, 1013
Winter, William, 1177
Winters, Shelley, 808
Winthrop, Francis Bayard, 638
Wintour, Anna, 1230
Wise, Jonah B., 199
Wismer, Harry, 834
Wisner, George, 846
Wissler, Clark, 39
Witham, Charles, 1109
Withers, Frederick Clarke, 616, 1020, 1226
Wittkower, Rudolf, 627
Wodehouse, P. G., 634, 791
Wodiska, Julius, 618
Wojciechowicz, Alex, 424
Wolf, Daniel, 17, 1229
Wolfe, George C., 843
Wolfe, Gerard R., 514, 1233
Wolfe, Paul (conductor), 147
Wolfe, Paul Austin (pastor), 137
Wolff, Abraham, 630, 644
Wolff, Addie, 630
Wolff, Christian, 304
Wolff, Helen, 126, 521
Wolff, Kurt, 126, 521
Wolff, Lester L., *484*
Wolpe, Stefan, 242
Woltmann, Frederick, 850
Wonder, Stevie, 40
Wood, Ben D., 270
Wood, Benjamin, *481*
Wood, Charles, 1070
Wood, Edith Elmer, 567
Wood, John J., *480*
Wood, Joseph, 614
Wood, Robert C., 1135
Wood, Ruby Ross, 593
Wood, Samuel, 127, 213, 834
Wood, Silas, 476, *480*
Wood, William, 159
Woodford, Stewart L., *481*
Woodhull, Abraham, 382
Woodhull, Albert, 836
Woodhull, Richard M., 1265
Woodman, Raymond H., 413
Woodruff, Thomas, *480*
Woods, Love B., 564
Woodside, Lyndon, 220
Woodworth, Samuel, 713, 1144
Woolman, John, 437
Woolsey, John M., 726
Workman, Peter, 1274
Worsley, Gump, 843
Worth, Thomas, 941
Worth, William J., 711
Wouk, Herman, 1194
Wright, Benjamin, 618
Wright, C. Anderson, 645
Wright, Carol von Pressentin, 514
Wright, Frances, 16, 64, 378, 385, 810, 1083
Wright, Frank Lloyd, 49, 789, 1080, 1089, 1090
Wright, Harold L., 381
Wright, Harry, 82
Wright, Henry (architect), 46, 109, 676, 990, 1143
Wright, Henry J. (editor), 471
Wright, Isaac, 226
Wright, John (colonial landowner), 689
Wright, John D. (reformer), 1086
Wright, Louis T., 525
Wright, Russel, 322
Wright, Timothy, 475
Wright, Wilbur, 493
Wright, Willard Huntington, 57, 919
Wriston, Walter B., 227, 266, 1013
Wu, Chei-shiung, 905
Wundt, Wilhelm, 949
Wurf, Jerry, 24
Wurman, R. S., 514
Wyatt, Jane, 512
Wyckoff, Pieter Claesen, 1278
Wyckoff, William F., 543
Wyeth, John, 1081
Wylie, Andrew, 680
Wylie, Elinor, 101
Wylie, Ida, 542

Yablokoff, Herman, 1282
Yakovlev, Anatoly, 383
Yale, Frankie, 415
Yamaoka, George, 613
Yamasaki, Minoru, 49, 1056, 1075, 1276
Yanovsky, Saul, 438
Yang, C. N., 218
Yard, Raymond C., 618
Yardley, Herbert O., 382–83
Yates, Peter, 110
Yeats, John Butler, 973
Yeats, William Butler, 601, 686
Yehoash (Solomon Bloomgarten), 1283
Yergan, Max, 114
Yerkes, Charles T., 345
Yezierska, Anzia, 1275
Yordan, Philip, 116
York, Bernard J., *912*
Yoshimura, Junzo, 614
Youmans, Edward L., 317
Youmans, Vincent, 1151, 1171
Young, Brigham, 771
Young, Charles P., 407
Young, John B. (jeweler), 1183
Young, John Orr (advertising executive), 1285
Young, John W. (astronaut), *1183*
Young, La Monte, 243
Young, Owen D., 988
Young, Richard, *483*
Young, Stark, 246, 1177
Young, Whitney, 802
Younger, Ruth, 381
Youskevitch, Igor, 313
Youtz, Philip, 159

Zaborowski, Olbracht, 909
Zaimi, Nemnie, 12
Zale, Tony, 502
Zangwill, Israel, 583, 1233
Zausner, Philip, 167
Zawinul, Joe, 319, 616
Zeferetti, Leo C., *484*
Zelenko, Herbert, *484*
Zenger, Catherine, 127
Zetlin, Mark, 856
Ziegler, Henry, 1121
Ziegler, William, 716, 774, 1057
Ziff, William B., 1287–88
Zimmerman, J. F., 1169, 1178
Zimmermann, Bernd Alois, 827
Zimmermann, Marie, 1070

Zivic, Fritzie, 712
Zolatrevsky, Isidore, 1282
Zollar, Jawole Willa Jo, 314
Zorn, John, 243, 1013
Zotti, Frank, 299
Zuccotti, John E., 912, 1256
Zuckerman, Mortimer B., 177, 261, 308, 820
Zuille, John J., 823
Zukertort, Johannes, 212
Zukor, Adolph, 404, 925
Zunser, Eliakum, 1283
Zwillenberg, Joseph, 366